PETERSON'S® GRADUATE & PROFESSIONAL PROGRAMS

AN OVERVIEW

2019

PETERSON'S®

PETERSON'S®

About Peterson's®

Peterson's® has been your trusted educational publisher for over 50 years. It's a milestone we're quite proud of, as we continue to offer the most accurate, dependable, high-quality educational content in the field, providing you with everything you need to succeed. No matter where you are on your academic or professional path, you can rely on Peterson's for its books, online information, expert test-prep tools, the most up-to-date education exploration data, and the highest quality career success resources—everything you need to achieve your education goals. For our complete line of products, visit **www.petersons.com**.

For more information about Peterson's range of educational products, contact Peterson's, 8740 Lucent Blvd., Suite 400 Highlands Ranch, CO 80129, or find us online at **www.petersons.com.**

ISSN 1093-8443
ISBN: 978-0-7689-4228-6

Printed in the United States of America

10 9 8 7 6 5 4 3 2 1 20 19 18

Fifty-third Edition

CONTENTS

A Note from the Peterson's Editors

The six volumes of Peterson's *Graduate and Professional Programs*, the only annually updated reference work of its kind, provide wide-ranging information on the graduate and professional programs offered by accredited colleges and universities in the United States, U.S. territories, and Canada and by those institutions outside the United States that are accredited by U.S. accrediting bodies. More than 44,000 individual academic and professional programs at nearly 2,300 institutions are listed. Peterson's *Graduate and Professional Programs* have been used for more than fifty years by prospective graduate and professional students, placement counselors, faculty advisers, and all others interested in postbaccalaureate education.

Graduate & Professional Programs: An Overview contains information on institutions as a whole, while the other books in the series are devoted to specific academic and professional fields:

- ***Graduate Programs in the Biological/Biomedical Sciences & Health-Related Medical Professions***
- ***Graduate Programs in Business, Education, Information Studies, Law & Social Work***
- ***Graduate Programs in Engineering & Applied Sciences***
- ***Graduate Programs in the Humanities, Arts & Social Sciences***
- ***Graduate Programs in the Physical Sciences, Mathematics, Agricultural Sciences, the Environment & Natural Resources***

The books may be used individually or as a set. For example, if you have chosen a field of study but do not know what institution you want to attend or if you have a college or university in mind but have not chosen an academic field of study, it is best to begin with the Overview guide.

Graduate & Professional Programs: An Overview presents several directories to help you identify programs of study that might interest you; you can then research those programs further in the other books in the series by using the Directory of Graduate and Professional Programs by Field, which lists 500 fields and gives the names of those institutions that offer graduate degree programs in each.

For geographical or financial reasons, you may be interested in attending a particular institution and will want to know what it has to offer. You should turn to the Directory of Institutions and Their Offerings, which lists the degree programs available at each institution. As in the Directory of Graduate and Professional Programs by Field, the level of degrees offered is also indicated.

All books in the series include advice on graduate education, including topics such as admissions tests, financial aid, and accreditation. **The Graduate Adviser** includes two essays and information about accreditation. The first essay, "The Admissions Process," discusses general admission requirements, admission tests, factors to consider when selecting a graduate school or program, when and how to apply, and how admission decisions are made. Special information for international students and tips for minority students are also included. The second essay, "Financial Support," is an overview of the broad range of support available at the graduate level. Fellowships, scholarships, and grants; assistantships and internships; federal and private loan programs, as well as Federal Work-Study; and the GI bill are detailed. This essay concludes with advice on applying for need-based financial aid. "Accreditation and Accrediting Agencies" gives information on accreditation and its purpose and lists institutional accrediting agencies first and then specialized accrediting agencies relevant to each volume's specific fields of study.

With information on more than 40,000 graduate programs in more than 500 disciplines, Peterson's *Graduate and Professional Programs* give you all the information you need about the programs that are of interest to you in three formats: **Profiles** (capsule summaries of basic information), **Displays** (information that an institution or program wants to emphasize), and **Close-Ups** (written by administrators, with more expansive information than the **Profiles**, emphasizing different aspects of the programs). By using these various formats of program information, coupled with **Appendixes** and **Indexes** covering directories and subject areas for all six books, you will find that these guides provide the most comprehensive, accurate, and up-to-date graduate study information available.

Peterson's publishes a full line of resources with information you need to guide you through the graduate admissions process. Peterson's publications can be found at college libraries and career centers and your local bookstore or library—or visit us on the Web at www.petersons.com.

Colleges and universities will be pleased to know that Peterson's helped you in your selection. Admissions staff members are more than happy to answer questions, address specific problems, and help in any way they can. The editors at Peterson's wish you great success in your graduate program search!

THE GRADUATE ADVISER

The Admissions Process

Generalizations about graduate admissions practices are not always helpful because each institution has its own set of guidelines and procedures. Nevertheless, some broad statements can be made about the admissions process that may help you plan your strategy.

Factors Involved in Selecting a Graduate School or Program

Selecting a graduate school and a specific program of study is a complex matter. Quality of the faculty; program and course offerings; the nature, size, and location of the institution; admission requirements; cost; and the availability of financial assistance are among the many factors that affect one's choice of institution. Other considerations are job placement and achievements of the program's graduates and the institution's resources, such as libraries, laboratories, and computer facilities. If you are to make the best possible choice, you need to learn as much as you can about the schools and programs you are considering before you apply.

The following steps may help you narrow your choices.

- Talk to alumni of the programs or institutions you are considering to get their impressions of how well they were prepared for work in their fields of study.
- Remember that graduate school requirements change, so be sure to get the most up-to-date information possible.
- Talk to department faculty members and the graduate adviser at your undergraduate institution. They often have information about programs of study at other institutions.
- Visit the websites of the graduate schools in which you are interested to request a graduate catalog. Contact the department chair in your chosen field of study for additional information about the department and the field.
- Visit as many campuses as possible. Call ahead for an appointment with the graduate adviser in your field of interest and be sure to check out the facilities and talk to students.

General Requirements

Graduate schools and departments have requirements that applicants for admission must meet. Typically, these requirements include undergraduate transcripts (which provide information about undergraduate grade point average and course work applied toward a major), admission test scores, and letters of recommendation. Most graduate programs also ask for an essay or personal statement that describes your personal reasons for seeking graduate study. In some fields, such as art and music, portfolios or auditions may be required in addition to other evidence of talent. Some institutions require that the applicant have an undergraduate degree in the same subject as the intended graduate major.

Most institutions evaluate each applicant on the basis of the applicant's total record, and the weight accorded any given factor varies widely from institution to institution and from program to program.

The Application Process

You should begin the application process at least one year before you expect to begin your graduate study. Find out the application deadline for each institution (many are provided in the **Profile** section of this guide). Go to the institution's website and find out if you can apply online. If not, request a paper application form. Fill out this form thoroughly and neatly. Assume that the school needs all the information it is requesting and that the admissions officer will be sensitive to the neatness and overall quality of what you submit. Do not supply more information than the school requires.

The institution may ask at least one question that will require a three- or four-paragraph answer. Compose your response on the assumption that the admissions officer is interested in both what you think and how you express yourself. Keep your statement brief and to the point, but, at the same time, include all pertinent information about your past experiences and your educational goals. Individual statements vary greatly in style and content, which helps admissions officers differentiate among applicants. Many graduate departments give considerable weight to the statement in making their admissions decisions, so be sure to take the time to prepare a thoughtful and concise statement.

If recommendations are a part of the admissions requirements, carefully choose the individuals you ask to write them. It is generally best to ask current or former professors to write the recommendations, provided they are able to attest to your intellectual ability and motivation for doing the work required of a graduate student. It is advisable to provide stamped, preaddressed envelopes to people being asked to submit recommendations on your behalf.

Completed applications, including references, transcripts, and admission test scores, should be received at the institution by the specified date.

Be advised that institutions do not usually make admissions decisions until all materials have been received. Enclose a self-addressed postcard with your application, requesting confirmation of receipt. Allow at least ten days for the return of the postcard before making further inquiries.

If you plan to apply for financial support, it is imperative that you file your application early.

ADMISSION TESTS

The major testing program used in graduate admissions is the Graduate Record Examinations (GRE®) testing program, sponsored by the GRE Board and administered by Educational Testing Service, Princeton, New Jersey.

The Graduate Record Examinations testing program consists of a General Test and six Subject Tests. The General Test measures critical thinking, verbal reasoning, quantitative reasoning, and analytical writing skills. It is offered as an Internet-based test (iBT) in the United States, Canada, and many other countries.

The GRE® revised General Test's questions were designed to reflect the kind of thinking that students need to do in graduate or business school and demonstrate that students are indeed ready for graduate-level work.

- **Verbal Reasoning**—Measures ability to analyze and evaluate written material and synthesize information obtained from it, analyze relationships among component parts of sentences, and recognize relationships among words and concepts.
- **Quantitative Reasoning**—Measures problem-solving ability, focusing on basic concepts of arithmetic, algebra, geometry, and data analysis.
- **Analytical Writing**—Measures critical thinking and analytical writing skills, specifically the ability to articulate and support complex ideas clearly and effectively.

The computer-delivered GRE® revised General Test is offered year-round at Prometric™ test centers and on specific dates at testing locations outside of the Prometric test center network. Appointments are scheduled on a first-come, first-served basis. The GRE® revised General Test is also offered as a paper-based test three times a year in areas where computer-based testing is not available.

You can take the computer-delivered GRE® revised General Test once every twenty-one days, up to five times within any continuous rolling twelve-month period (365 days)—even if you canceled your scores on a previously taken test. You may take the paper-based GRE® revised General Test as often as it is offered.

Three scores are reported on the revised General Test:

1. A **Verbal Reasoning score** is reported on a 130–170 score scale, in 1-point increments.
2. A **Quantitative Reasoning score** is reported on a 130–170 score scale, in 1-point increments.
3. An **Analytical Writing score** is reported on a 0–6 score level, in half-point increments.

The GRE® Subject Tests measure achievement and assume undergraduate majors or extensive background in the following six disciplines:

- Biology
- Chemistry
- Literature in English
- Mathematics
- Physics
- Psychology

The Subject Tests are available three times per year as paper-based administrations around the world. Testing time is approximately 2 hours and 50 minutes. You can obtain more information about the GRE® by visiting the ETS website at **www.ets.org** or consulting the *GRE® Information Bulletin.* The *Bulletin* can be obtained at many undergraduate colleges. You can also download it from the ETS website or obtain it by contacting Graduate Record Examinations, Educational Testing Service, P.O. Box 6000, Princeton, NJ 08541-6000; phone: 609-771-7670 or 866-473-4373.

If you expect to apply for admission to a program that requires any of the GRE® tests, you should select a test date well in advance of the application deadline. Scores on the computer-based General Test are reported within ten to fifteen days; scores on the paper-based Subject Tests are reported within six weeks.

Another testing program, the Miller Analogies Test® (MAT®), is administered at more than 500 Controlled Testing Centers in the United States, Canada, and other countries. The MAT® computer-based test is now available. Testing time is 60 minutes. The test consists of 120 partial analogies. You can obtain the *Candidate Information Booklet,* which contains a list of test centers and instructions for taking the test, from **www.milleranalogies.com** or by calling 800-328-5999 (toll-free).

Check the specific requirements of the programs to which you are applying.

How Admission Decisions Are Made

The program you apply to is directly involved in the admissions process. Although the final decision is usually made by the graduate dean (or an associate) or the faculty admissions committee, recommendations from faculty members in your intended field are important. At some institutions, an interview is incorporated into the decision process.

A Special Note for International Students

In addition to the steps already described, there are some special considerations for international students who intend to apply for graduate study in the United States. All graduate schools require an indication of competence in English. The purpose of the Test of English as a Foreign Language (TOEFL®) is to evaluate the English proficiency of people who are nonnative speakers of English and want to study at colleges and universities where English is the language of instruction. The TOEFL® is administered by Educational Testing Service (ETS) under the general direction of a policy board established by the College Board and the Graduate Record Examinations Board.

The TOEFL iBT® assesses four basic language skills: listening, reading, writing, and speaking. The Internet-based test is administered at secure, official test centers. The testing time is approximately 4 hours.

The TOEFL® is also offered in a paper-based format in areas of the world where internet-based testing is not available. In 2017, ETS launched a revised TOEFL® paper-based Test, that more closely aligned to the TOEFL iBT® test. This revised paper-based test consists of three sections—listening, reading, and writing. The testing time is approximately 3 hours.

You can obtain more information for both versions of the TOEFL® by visiting the ETS website at **www.ets.org/toefl**. Information can also be obtained by contacting TOEFL® Services, Educational Testing Service, P.O. Box 6151, Princeton, NJ 08541-6151. Phone: 609-771-7100 or 877-863-3546 (toll free).

International students should apply especially early because of the number of steps required to complete the admissions process. Furthermore, many United States graduate schools have a limited number of spaces for international students, and many more students apply than the schools can accommodate.

International students may find financial assistance from institutions very limited. The U.S. government requires international applicants to submit a certification of support, which is a statement attesting to the applicant's financial resources. In addition, international students *must* have health insurance coverage.

Tips for Minority Students

Indicators of a university's values in terms of diversity are found both in its recruitment programs and its resources directed to student success. Important questions: Does the institution vigorously recruit minorities for its graduate programs? Is there funding available to help with the costs associated with visiting the school? Are minorities represented in the institution's brochures or website or on their faculty rolls? What campus-based resources or services (including assistance in locating housing or career counseling and placement) are available? Is funding available to members of underrepresented groups?

At the program level, it is particularly important for minority students to investigate the "climate" of a program under consideration. How many minority students are enrolled and how many have graduated? What opportunities are there to work with diverse faculty and mentors whose research interests match yours? How are conflicts resolved or concerns addressed? How interested are faculty in building strong and supportive relations with students? "Climate" concerns should be addressed by posing questions to various individuals, including faculty members, current students, and alumni.

Information is also available through various organizations, such as the Hispanic Association of Colleges & Universities (HACU), and publications such as *Diverse Issues in Higher Education* and *Hispanic Outlook* magazine. There are also books devoted to this topic, such as *The Multicultural Student's Guide to Colleges* by Robert Mitchell.

Financial Support

The range of financial support at the graduate level is very broad. The following descriptions will give you a general idea of what you might expect and what will be expected of you as a financial support recipient.

Fellowships, Scholarships, and Grants

These are usually outright awards of a few hundred to many thousands of dollars with no service to the institution required in return. Fellowships and scholarships are usually awarded on the basis of merit and are highly competitive. Grants are made on the basis of financial need or special talent in a field of study. Many fellowships, scholarships, and grants not only cover tuition, fees, and supplies but also include stipends for living expenses with allowances for dependents. However, the terms of each should be examined because some do not permit recipients to supplement their income with outside work. Fellowships, scholarships, and grants may vary in the number of years for which they are awarded.

In addition to the availability of these funds at the university or program level, many excellent fellowship programs are available at the national level and may be applied for before and during enrollment in a graduate program. A listing of many of these programs can be found at the Council of Graduate Schools' website, **https://cgsnet.org/**. There is a wealth of information in the "Programs" and "Awards" sections.

Assistantships and Internships

Many graduate students receive financial support through assistantships, particularly involving teaching or research duties. It is important to recognize that such appointments should not be viewed simply as employment relationships but rather should constitute an integral and important part of a student's graduate education. As such, the appointments should be accompanied by strong faculty mentoring and increasingly responsible apprenticeship experiences. The specific nature of these appointments in a given program should be considered in selecting that graduate program.

TEACHING ASSISTANTSHIPS

These usually provide a salary and full or partial tuition remission and may also provide health benefits. Unlike fellowships, scholarships, and grants, which require no service to the institution, teaching assistantships require recipients to provide the institution with a specific amount of undergraduate teaching, ideally related to the student's field of study. Some teaching assistants are limited to grading papers, compiling bibliographies, taking notes, or monitoring laboratories. At some graduate schools, teaching assistants must carry lighter course loads than regular full-time students.

RESEARCH ASSISTANTSHIPS

These are very similar to teaching assistantships in the manner in which financial assistance is provided. The difference is that recipients are given basic research assignments in their disciplines rather than teaching responsibilities. The work required is normally related to the student's field of study; in most instances, the assistantship supports the student's thesis or dissertation research.

ADMINISTRATIVE INTERNSHIPS

These are similar to assistantships in application of financial assistance funds, but the student is given an assignment on a part-time basis, usually as a special assistant with one of the university's administrative offices. The assignment may not necessarily be directly related to the recipient's discipline.

RESIDENCE HALL AND COUNSELING ASSISTANTSHIPS

These assistantships are frequently assigned to graduate students in psychology, counseling, and social work, but they may be offered to students in other disciplines, especially if the student has worked in this capacity during his or her undergraduate years. Duties can vary from being available in a dean's office for a specific number of hours for consultation with undergraduates to living in campus residences and being responsible for both counseling and administrative tasks or advising student activity groups. Residence hall assistantships often include a room and board allowance and, in some cases, tuition assistance and stipends. Contact the Housing and Student Life Office for more information.

Health Insurance

The availability and affordability of health insurance is an important issue and one that should be considered in an applicant's choice of institution and program. While often included with assistantships and fellowships, this is not always the case and, even if provided, the benefits may be limited. It is important to note that the U.S. government requires international students to have health insurance.

The GI Bill

This provides financial assistance for students who are veterans of the United States armed forces. If you are a veteran, contact your local Veterans Administration office to determine your eligibility and to get full details about benefits. There are a number of programs that offer educational benefits to current military enlistees. Some states have tuition assistance programs for members of the National Guard. Contact the VA office at the college for more information.

Federal Work-Study Program (FWS)

Employment is another way some students finance their graduate studies. The federally funded Federal Work-Study Program provides eligible students with employment opportunities, usually in public and private nonprofit organizations. Federal funds pay up to 75 percent of the wages, with the remainder paid by the employing agency. FWS is available to graduate students who demonstrate financial need. Not all schools have these funds, and some only award them to undergraduates. Each school sets its application deadline and workstudy earnings limits. Wages vary and are related to the type of work done. You must file the Free Application for Federal Student Aid (FAFSA) to be eligible for this program.

Loans

Many graduate students borrow to finance their graduate programs when other sources of assistance (which do not have to be repaid) prove insufficient. You should always read and understand the terms of any loan program before submitting your application.

FEDERAL DIRECT LOANS

Federal Direct Loans. The Federal Direct Loan Program offers a variable-fixed interest rate loan to graduate students with the Department of Education acting as the lender. Students receive a new rate with each new loan, but that rate is fixed for the life of the loan. Beginning with loans made on or after July 1, 2013, the interest rate for loans made each July 1st to June 30th period are determined based on the last 10-year Treasury note auction prior to June 1st of that year, plus an added percentage. The interest rate can be no higher than 9.5%.

Beginning July 1, 2012, the Federal Direct Loan for graduate students is an unsubsidized loan. Under the *unsubsidized* program, the grad borrower pays the interest on the loan from the day proceeds are issued and is responsible for paying interest during all periods. If the borrower chooses not to pay the interest while in school, or during the grace periods, deferment, or forbearance, the interest accrues and will be capitalized.

Graduate students may borrow up to $20,500 per year through the Direct Loan Program, up to a cumulative maximum of $138,500, including undergraduate borrowing. No more than $65,500 of the $138,500 can be from subsidized loans, including loans the grad borrower may have received for periods of enrollment that began before July 1, 2012, or for prior undergraduate borrowing. You may borrow up to the cost of attendance at the school in which you are enrolled or will attend, minus estimated financial assistance from other federal, state, and private sources, up to a maximum of $20,500. Grad borrowers who reach the aggregate loan limit over the course of their education cannot receive additional loans; however, if they repay some of their loans to bring the outstanding balance below the aggregate limit, they could be eligible to borrow again, up to that limit.

Under the *subsidized* Federal Direct Loan Program, repayment begins six months after your last date of enrollment on at least a half-time basis. Under the *unsubsidized* program, repayment of interest begins within thirty days from disbursement of the loan proceeds, and repayment of the principal begins six months after your last enrollment on at least a half-time basis. Some borrowers may choose to defer interest payments while they are in school. The accrued interest is added to the loan balance when the borrower begins repayment. There are several repayment options.

Federal Perkins Loans. The Federal Perkins Loan is available to students demonstrating financial need and is administered directly by the school. Not all schools have these funds, and some may award them to undergraduates only. Eligibility is determined from the information you provide on the FAFSA. The school will notify you of your eligibility.

Eligible graduate students may borrow up to $8,000 per year, up to a maximum of $60,000, including undergraduate borrowing (even if your previous Perkins Loans have been repaid). The interest rate for Federal Perkins Loans is 5 percent, and no interest accrues while you remain in school at least half-time. Students who are attending less than half-time need to check with their school to determine the length of their grace period. There are no guarantee, loan, or disbursement fees. Repayment begins nine months after your last date of enrollment on at least a half-time basis and may extend over a maximum of ten years with no prepayment penalty.

Federal Direct Graduate PLUS Loans. Effective July 1, 2006, graduate and professional students are eligible for Graduate PLUS loans. This program allows students to borrow up to the cost of attendance, less any other aid received. These loans have a fixed interest rate (7.6% for loans first disbursed on or after July 1, 2018, and before July 1, 2019) and interest begins to accrue at the time of disbursement. Beginning with loans made on or after July 1, 2013, the interest rate for loans made each July 1st to June 30th period are determined based on the last 10-year Treasury note auction prior to June 1st of that year. The interest rate can be no higher than 10.5%. The PLUS loans do involve a credit check; a PLUS borrower may obtain a loan with a cosigner if his or her credit is not good enough. Grad PLUS loans may be deferred while a student is in school and for the six months following a drop below half-time enrollment. For more information, you should contact a representative in your college's financial aid office.

Deferring Your Federal Loan Repayments. If you borrowed under the Federal Direct Loan Program, Federal Direct PLUS Loan Program, or the Federal Perkins Loan Program for previous undergraduate or graduate study, your payments may be deferred when you return to graduate school, depending on when you borrowed and under which program.

There are other deferment options available if you are temporarily unable to repay your loan. Information about these deferments is provided at your entrance and exit interviews. If you believe you are eligible for a deferment of your loan payments, you must contact your lender or loan servicer to request a deferment. The deferment must be filed prior to the time your payment is due, and it must be re-filed when it expires if you remain eligible for deferment at that time.

SUPPLEMENTAL (PRIVATE) LOANS

Many lending institutions offer supplemental loan programs and other financing plans, such as the ones described here, to students seeking additional assistance in meeting their education expenses. Some loan programs target all types of graduate students; others are designed specifically for business, law, or medical students. In addition, you can use private loans not specifically designed for education to help finance your graduate degree.

If you are considering borrowing through a supplemental or private loan program, you should carefully consider the terms and be sure to read the fine print. Check with the program sponsor for the most current terms that will be applicable to the amounts you intend to borrow for graduate study. Most supplemental loan programs for graduate study offer unsubsidized, credit-based loans. In general, a credit-ready borrower is one who has a satisfactory credit history or no credit history at all. A creditworthy borrower generally must pass a credit test to be eligible to borrow or act as a cosigner for the loan funds.

Many supplemental loan programs have minimum and maximum annual loan limits. Some offer amounts equal to the cost of attendance minus any other aid you will receive for graduate study. If you are planning to borrow for several years of graduate study, consider whether there is a cumulative or aggregate limit on the amount you may borrow. Often this cumulative or aggregate limit will include any amounts you borrowed and have not repaid for undergraduate or previous graduate study.

The combination of the annual interest rate, loan fees, and the repayment terms you choose will determine how much you will repay over time. Compare these features in combination before you decide which loan program to use. Some loans offer interest rates that are adjusted monthly, quarterly, or annually. Some offer interest rates that are lower during the in-school, grace, and deferment periods and then increase when you begin repayment. Some programs include a loan origination fee, which is usually deducted from the principal amount you receive when the loan is disbursed and must be repaid along with the interest and other principal when you graduate, withdraw from school, or drop below half-time study. Sometimes the loan fees are reduced if you borrow with a qualified cosigner. Some programs allow you to defer interest and/or principal payments while you are enrolled in graduate school. Many programs allow you to capitalize your interest payments; the interest due on your loan is added to the outstanding balance of your loan, so you don't have to repay immediately, but this increases the amount you owe. Other programs allow you to pay the interest as you go, which reduces the amount you later have to repay. The private loan market is very competitive, and your financial aid office can help you evaluate these programs.

Applying for Need-Based Financial Aid

Schools that award federal and institutional financial assistance based on need will require you to complete the FAFSA and, in some cases, an institutional financial aid application.

If you are applying for federal student assistance, you **must** complete the FAFSA. A service of the U.S. Department of Education, the FAFSA is free to all applicants. Most applicants apply online at **www.fafsa.ed.gov**. Paper applications are available at the financial aid office of your local college.

After your FAFSA information has been processed, you will receive a Student Aid Report (SAR). If you provided an e-mail address on the FAFSA, this will be sent to you electronically; otherwise, it will be mailed to your home address.

Follow the instructions on the SAR if you need to correct information reported on your original application. If your situation changes after you file your FAFSA, contact your financial aid officer to discuss amending your information. You can also appeal your financial aid award if you have extenuating circumstances.

If you would like more information on federal student financial aid, visit the FAFSA website or download the most recent version of *Do You Need Money for College* at www.studentaid.ed.gov/sa/sites/default/files/2018-19-do-you-need-money.pdf. This guide is also available in Spanish.

The U.S. Department of Education also has a toll-free number for questions concerning federal student aid programs. The number is 1-800-4-FED AID (1-800-433-3243). If you are hearing impaired, call toll-free, 1-800-730-8913.

Summary

Remember that these are generalized statements about financial assistance at the graduate level. Because each institution allots its aid differently, you should communicate directly with the school and the specific department of interest to you. It is not unusual, for example, to find that an endowment vested within a specific department supports one or more fellowships. You may fit its requirements and specifications precisely.

Accreditation and Accrediting Agencies

Colleges and universities in the United States, and their individual academic and professional programs, are accredited by nongovernmental agencies concerned with monitoring the quality of education in this country. Agencies with both regional and national jurisdictions grant accreditation to institutions as a whole, while specialized bodies acting on a nationwide basis—often national professional associations—grant accreditation to departments and programs in specific fields.

Institutional and specialized accrediting agencies share the same basic concerns: the purpose an academic unit—whether university or program—has set for itself and how well it fulfills that purpose, the adequacy of its financial and other resources, the quality of its academic offerings, and the level of services it provides. Agencies that grant institutional accreditation take a broader view, of course, and examine university-wide or college-wide services with which a specialized agency may not concern itself.

Both types of agencies follow the same general procedures when considering an application for accreditation. The academic unit prepares a self-evaluation, focusing on the concerns mentioned above and usually including an assessment of both its strengths and weaknesses; a team of representatives of the accrediting body reviews this evaluation, visits the campus, and makes its own report; and finally, the accrediting body makes a decision on the application. Often, even when accreditation is granted, the agency makes a recommendation regarding how the institution or program can improve. All institutions and programs are also reviewed every few years to determine whether they continue to meet established standards; if they do not, they may lose their accreditation.

Accrediting agencies themselves are reviewed and evaluated periodically by the U.S. Department of Education and the Council for Higher Education Accreditation (CHEA). Recognized agencies adhere to certain standards and practices, and their authority in matters of accreditation is widely accepted in the educational community.

This does not mean, however, that accreditation is a simple matter, either for schools wishing to become accredited or for students deciding where to apply. Indeed, in certain fields the very meaning and methods of accreditation are the subject of a good deal of debate. For their part, those applying to graduate school should be aware of the safeguards provided by regional accreditation, especially in terms of degree acceptance and institutional longevity. Beyond this, applicants should understand the role that specialized accreditation plays in their field, as this varies considerably from one discipline to another. In certain professional fields, it is necessary to have graduated from a program that is accredited in order to be eligible for a license to practice, and in some fields the federal government also makes this a hiring requirement. In other disciplines, however, accreditation is not as essential, and there can be excellent programs that are not accredited. In fact, some programs choose not to seek accreditation, although most do.

Institutions and programs that present themselves for accreditation are sometimes granted the status of candidate for accreditation, or what is known as "preaccreditation." This may happen, for example, when an academic unit is too new to have met all the requirements for accreditation. Such status signifies initial recognition and indicates that the school or program in question is working to fulfill all requirements; it does not, however, guarantee that accreditation will be granted.

Institutional Accrediting Agencies—Regional

MIDDLE STATES COMMISSION ON HIGHER EDUCATION

Accredits institutions in Delaware, District of Columbia, Maryland, New Jersey, New York, Pennsylvania, Puerto Rico, and the Virgin Islands.

Dr. Elizabeth Sibolski, President
Middle States Commission on Higher Education
3624 Market Street, Second Floor West
Philadelphia, Pennsylvania 19104
Phone: 267-284-5000
Fax: 215-662-5501
E-mail: info@msche.org
Website: www.msche.org

NEW ENGLAND ASSOCIATION OF SCHOOLS AND COLLEGES

Accredits institutions in Connecticut, Maine, Massachusetts, New Hampshire, Rhode Island, and Vermont.

Dr. Barbara E. Brittingham, President/Director
Commission on Institutions of Higher Education
3 Burlington Woods Drive, Suite 100
Burlington, Massachusetts 01803-4531
Phone: 855-886-3272 or 781-425-7714
Fax: 781-425-1001
E-mail: cihe@neasc.org
Website: https://cihe.neasc.org

THE HIGHER LEARNING COMMISSION

Accredits institutions in Arizona, Arkansas, Colorado, Illinois, Indiana, Iowa, Kansas, Michigan, Minnesota, Missouri, Nebraska, New Mexico, North Dakota, Ohio, Oklahoma, South Dakota, West Virginia, Wisconsin, and Wyoming.

Dr. Barbara Gellman-Danley, President
The Higher Learning Commission
230 South LaSalle Street, Suite 7-500
Chicago, Illinois 60604-1413
Phone: 800-621-7440 or 312-263-0456
Fax: 312-263-7462
E-mail: info@hlcommission.org
Website: www.hlcommission.org

NORTHWEST COMMISSION ON COLLEGES AND UNIVERSITIES

Accredits institutions in Alaska, Idaho, Montana, Nevada, Oregon, Utah, and Washington.

Dr. Sandra E. Elman, President
8060 165th Avenue, NE, Suite 100
Redmond, Washington 98052
Phone: 425-558-4224
Fax: 425-376-0596
E-mail: selman@nwccu.org
Website: www.nwccu.org

SOUTHERN ASSOCIATION OF COLLEGES AND SCHOOLS

Accredits institutions in Alabama, Florida, Georgia, Kentucky, Louisiana, Mississippi, North Carolina, South Carolina, Tennessee, Texas, and Virginia.

Dr. Belle S. Wheelan, President
Commission on Colleges
1866 Southern Lane
Decatur, Georgia 30033-4097
Phone: 404-679-4500 Ext. 4504
Fax: 404-679-4558
E-mail: questions@sacscoc.org
Website: www.sacscoc.org

WESTERN ASSOCIATION OF SCHOOLS AND COLLEGES

Accredits institutions in California, Guam, and Hawaii.

Jamienne S. Studley, President
WASC Senior College and University Commission
985 Atlantic Avenue, Suite 100
Alameda, California 94501
Phone: 510-748-9001
Fax: 510-748-9797
E-mail: wasc@wscuc.org
Website: https://www.wscuc.org/

Institutional Accrediting Agencies—Other

ACCREDITING COUNCIL FOR INDEPENDENT COLLEGES AND SCHOOLS
Michelle Edwards, President
750 First Street NE, Suite 980
Washington, DC 20002-4223
Phone: 202-336-6780
Fax: 202-842-2593
E-mail: info@acics.org
Website: www.acics.org

DISTANCE EDUCATION ACCREDITING COMMISSION (DEAC)
Leah Matthews, Executive Director
1101 17th Street NW, Suite 808
Washington, DC 20036-4704
Phone: 202-234-5100
Fax: 202-332-1386
E-mail: info@deac.org
Website: www.deac.org

Specialized Accrediting Agencies

ACUPUNCTURE AND ORIENTAL MEDICINE
Mark S. McKenzie, LAc MsOM DiplOM, Executive Director
Accreditation Commission for Acupuncture and Oriental Medicine
8941 Aztec Drive, Suite 2
Eden Prairie, Minnesota 55347
Phone: 952-212-2434
Fax: 301-313-0912
E-mail: info@acaom.org
Website: www.acaom.org

ALLIED HEALTH
Kathleen Megivern, Executive Director
Commission on Accreditation of Allied Health Education Programs (CAAHEP)
25400 US Hwy 19 North, Suite 158
Clearwater, Florida 33763
Phone: 727-210-2350
Fax: 727-210-2354
E-mail: mail@caahep.org
Website: www.caahep.org

ART AND DESIGN
Karen P. Moynahan, Executive Director
National Association of Schools of Art and Design (NASAD)
Commission on Accreditation
11250 Roger Bacon Drive, Suite 21
Reston, Virginia 20190-5248
Phone: 703-437-0700
Fax: 703-437-6312
E-mail: info@arts-accredit.org
Website: http://nasad.arts-accredit.org

ATHLETIC TRAINING EDUCATION
Pamela Hansen, CAATE Director of Accreditation
Commission on Accreditation of Athletic Training Education (CAATE)
6850 Austin Center Blvd., Suite 100
Austin, Texas 78731-3184
Phone: 512-733-9700
E-mail: pamela@caate.net
Website: www.caate.net

AUDIOLOGY EDUCATION
Meggan Olek, Director
Accreditation Commission for Audiology Education (ACAE)
11480 Commerce Park Drive, Suite 220
Reston, Virginia 20191
Phone: 202-986-9500
Fax: 202-986-9550
E-mail: info@acaeaccred.org
Website: https://acaeaccred.org/

AVIATION
Dr. Gary J. Northam, President
Aviation Accreditation Board International (AABI)
3410 Skyway Drive
Auburn, Alabama 36830
Phone: 334-844-2431
Fax: 334-844-2432
E-mail: gary.northam@auburn.edu
Website: www.aabi.aero

BUSINESS
Stephanie Bryant, Executive Vice President and Chief Accreditation Officer
AACSB International—The Association to Advance Collegiate Schools of Business
777 South Harbour Island Boulevard, Suite 750
Tampa, Florida 33602
Phone: 813-769-6500
Fax: 813-769-6559
E-mail: stephanie.bryant@aacsb.edu
Website: www.aacsb.edu

BUSINESS EDUCATION
Dr. Phyllis Okrepkie, President
International Assembly for Collegiate Business Education (IACBE)
11374 Strang Line Road
Lenexa, Kansas 66215
Phone: 913-631-3009
Fax: 913-631-9154
E-mail: iacbe@iacbe.org
Website: www.iacbe.org

CHIROPRACTIC
Dr. Craig S. Little, President
Council on Chiropractic Education (CCE)
Commission on Accreditation
8049 North 85th Way
Scottsdale, Arizona 85258-4321
Phone: 480-443-8877 or 888-443-3506
Fax: 480-483-7333
E-mail: cce@cce-usa.org
Website: www.cce-usa.org

CLINICAL LABORATORY SCIENCES
Dianne M. Cearlock, Ph.D., Chief Executive Officer
National Accrediting Agency for Clinical Laboratory Sciences
5600 North River Road, Suite 720
Rosemont, Illinois 60018-5119
Phone: 773-714-8880 or 847-939-3597
Fax: 773-714-8886
E-mail: info@naacls.org
Website: www.naacls.org

CLINICAL PASTORAL EDUCATION
Trace Haythorn, Ph.D., Executive Director/CEO
Association for Clinical Pastoral Education, Inc.
One West Court Square, Suite 325
Decatur, Georgia 30030-2576
Phone: 678-363-6226
Fax: 404-320-0849
E-mail: acpe@acpe.edu
Website: www.acpe.edu

DANCE
Karen P. Moynahan, Executive Director
National Association of Schools of Dance (NASD)
Commission on Accreditation
11250 Roger Bacon Drive, Suite 21
Reston, Virginia 20190-5248
Phone: 703-437-0700
Fax: 703-437-6312
E-mail: info@arts-accredit.org
Website: http://nasd.arts-accredit.org

DENTISTRY
Dr. Kathleen T. O'Loughlin, Executive Director
Commission on Dental Accreditation
American Dental Association
211 East Chicago Avenue
Chicago, Illinois 60611
Phone: 312-440-2500
E-mail: accreditation@ada.org
Website: www.ada.org

DIETETICS AND NUTRITION
Mary B. Gregoire, Ph.D., Executive Director; RD, FADA, FAND
Academy of Nutrition and Dietetics
Accreditation Council for Education in Nutrition and Dietetics (ACEND)
120 South Riverside Plaza
Chicago, Illinois 60606-6995
Phone: 800-877-1600 or 312-899-0040
E-mail: acend@eatright.org
Website: www.eatright.org/cade

EDUCATION PREPARATION
Christopher Koch, President
Council for the Accreditation of Educator Preparation (CAEP)
1140 19th Street NW, Suite 400
Washington, DC 20036
Phone: 202-223-0077
Fax: 202-296-6620
E-mail: caep@caepnet.org
Website: www.caepnet.org

ENGINEERING
Michael Milligan, Ph.D., PE, Executive Director
Accreditation Board for Engineering and Technology, Inc. (ABET)
415 North Charles Street
Baltimore, Maryland 21201
Phone: 410-347-7700
E-mail: accreditation@abet.org
Website: www.abet.org

FORENSIC SCIENCES
Nancy J. Jackson, Director of Development and Accreditation
American Academy of Forensic Sciences (AAFS)
Forensic Science Education Program Accreditation Commission (FEPAC)
410 North 21st Street
Colorado Springs, Colorado 80904
Phone: 719-636-1100
Fax: 719-636-1993
E-mail: njackson@aafs.org
Website: www.fepac-edu.org

FORESTRY
Carol L. Redelsheimer
Director of Science and Education
Society of American Foresters
10100 Laureate Way
Bethesda, Maryland 20814-2198
Phone: 301-897-8720 or 866-897-8720
Fax: 301-897-3690
E-mail: membership@safnet.org
Website: www.eforester.com

HEALTHCARE MANAGEMENT
Commission on Accreditation of Healthcare Management Education (CAHME)
Anthony Stanowski, President and CEO
6110 Executive Boulevard, Suite 614
Rockville, Maryland 20852
Phone: 301-298-1820
E-mail: info@cahme.org
Website: www.cahme.org

HEALTH INFORMATICS AND HEALTH MANAGEMENT
Angela Kennedy, EdD, MBA, RHIA, Chief Executive Officer
Commission on Accreditation for Health Informatics and Information Management Education (CAHIIM)
233 North Michigan Avenue, 21st Floor
Chicago, Illinois 60601-5800
Phone: 312-233-1134
Fax: 312-233-1948
E-mail: info@cahiim.org
Website: www.cahiim.org

HUMAN SERVICE EDUCATION
Dr. Elaine Green, President
Council for Standards in Human Service Education (CSHSE)
3337 Duke Street
Alexandria, Virginia 22314
Phone: 571-257-3959
E-mail: info@cshse.org
Website: www.cshse.org

INTERIOR DESIGN
Holly Mattson, Executive Director
Council for Interior Design Accreditation
206 Grandview Avenue, Suite 350
Grand Rapids, Michigan 49503-4014
Phone: 616-458-0400
Fax: 616-458-0460
E-mail: info@accredit-id.org
Website: www.accredit-id.org

JOURNALISM AND MASS COMMUNICATIONS
Patricia Thompson, Executive Director
Accrediting Council on Education in Journalism and Mass Communications (ACEJMC)
201 Bishop Hall
P.O. Box 1848
University, MS 38677-1848
Phone: 662-915-5504
E-mail: pthomps1@olemiss.edu
Website: www.acejmc.org

LANDSCAPE ARCHITECTURE
Nancy Somerville, Executive Vice President, CEO
American Society of Landscape Architects (ASLA)
636 Eye Street, NW
Washington, DC 20001-3736
Phone: 202-898-2444
Fax: 202-898-1185
E-mail: info@asla.org
Website: www.asla.org

LAW
Barry Currier, Managing Director of Accreditation & Legal Education
American Bar Association
321 North Clark Street, 21st Floor
Chicago, Illinois 60654
Phone: 312-988-6738
Fax: 312-988-5681
E-mail: legaled@americanbar.org
Website: https://www.americanbar.org/groups/legal_education/accreditation.html

LIBRARY
Karen O'Brien, Director
Office for Accreditation
American Library Association
50 East Huron Street
Chicago, Illinois 60611-2795
Phone: 800-545-2433, ext. 2432 or 312-280-2432
Fax: 312-280-2433
E-mail: accred@ala.org
Website: http://www.ala.org/aboutala/offices/accreditation/

MARRIAGE AND FAMILY THERAPY
Tanya A. Tamarkin, Director of Educational Affairs
Commission on Accreditation for Marriage and Family Therapy Education (COAMFTE)
American Association for Marriage and Family Therapy
112 South Alfred Street
Alexandria, Virginia 22314-3061
Phone: 703-838-9808
Fax: 703-838-9805
E-mail: coa@aamft.org
Website: www.aamft.org

MEDICAL ILLUSTRATION
Kathleen Megivern, Executive Director
Commission on Accreditation of Allied Health Education Programs (CAAHEP)
25400 US Highway 19 North, Suite 158
Clearwater, Florida 33756
Phone: 727-210-2350
Fax: 727-210-2354
E-mail: mail@caahep.org
Website: www.caahep.org

MEDICINE
Liaison Committee on Medical Education (LCME)
Robert B. Hash, M.D., LCME Secretary
American Medical Association
Council on Medical Education
330 North Wabash Avenue, Suite 39300
Chicago, Illinois 60611-5885
Phone: 312-464-4933
E-mail: lcme@aamc.org
Website: www.ama-assn.org

Liaison Committee on Medical Education (LCME)
Heather Lent, M.A., Director
Accreditation Services
Association of American Medical Colleges
655 K Street, NW
Washington, DC 20001-2399
Phone: 202-828-0596
E-mail: lcme@aamc.org
Website: www.lcme.org

MUSIC
Karen P. Moynahan, Executive Director
National Association of Schools of Music (NASM)
Commission on Accreditation
11250 Roger Bacon Drive, Suite 21
Reston, Virginia 20190-5248
Phone: 703-437-0700
Fax: 703-437-6312
E-mail: info@arts-accredit.org
Website: http://nasm.arts-accredit.org/

NATUROPATHIC MEDICINE
Daniel Seitz, J.D., Ed.D., Executive Director
Council on Naturopathic Medical Education
P.O. Box 178
Great Barrington, Massachusetts 01230
Phone: 413-528-8877
E-mail: https://cnme.org/contact-us/
Website: www.cnme.org

NURSE ANESTHESIA
Francis R.Gerbasi, Ph.D., CRNA, COA Executive Director
Council on Accreditation of Nurse Anesthesia Educational Programs (CoA-NAEP)
American Association of Nurse Anesthetists
222 South Prospect Avenue
Park Ridge, Illinois 60068-4001
Phone: 847-655-1160
Fax: 847-692-7137
E-mail: accreditation@coa.us.com
Website: http://www.coacrna.org

NURSE EDUCATION
Jennifer L. Butlin, Executive Director
Commission on Collegiate Nursing Education (CCNE)
One Dupont Circle, NW, Suite 530
Washington, DC 20036-1120
Phone: 202-887-6791
Fax: 202-887-8476
E-mail: jbutlin@aacn.nche.edu
Website: www.aacn.nche.edu/accreditation

Marsal P. Stoll, Chief Executive Officer
Accreditation Commission for Education in Nursing (ACEN)
3343 Peachtree Road, NE, Suite 850
Atlanta, Georgia 30326
Phone: 404-975-5000
Fax: 404-975-5020
E-mail: mstoll@acenursing.org
Website: www.acenursing.org

NURSE MIDWIFERY
Heather L. Maurer, M.A., Executive Director
Accreditation Commission for Midwifery Education (ACME)
American College of Nurse-Midwives
8403 Colesville Road, Suite 1550
Silver Spring, Maryland 20910
Phone: 240-485-1800
Fax: 240-485-1818
E-mail: info@acnm.org
Website: www.midwife.org/Program-Accreditation

NURSE PRACTITIONER
Gay Johnson, CEO
National Association of Nurse Practitioners in Women's Health
Council on Accreditation
505 C Street, NE
Washington, DC 20002
Phone: 202-543-9693 Ext. 1
Fax: 202-543-9858
E-mail: info@npwh.org
Website: www.npwh.org

NURSING
Marsal P. Stoll, Chief Executive Director
Accreditation Commission for Education in Nursing (ACEN)
3343 Peachtree Road, NE, Suite 850
Atlanta, Georgia 30326
Phone: 404-975-5000
Fax: 404-975-5020
E-mail: info@acenursing.org
Website: www.acenursing.org

OCCUPATIONAL THERAPY
Heather Stagliano, DHSc, OTR/L, Executive Director
The American Occupational Therapy Association, Inc.
4720 Montgomery Lane, Suite 200
Bethesda, Maryland 20814-3449
Phone: 301-652-6611 Ext. 2682
TDD: 800-377-8555
Fax: 240-762-5150
E-mail: accred@aota.org
Website: www.aoteonline.org

OPTOMETRY
Joyce L. Urbeck, Administrative Director
Accreditation Council on Optometric Education (ACOE)
American Optometric Association
243 North Lindbergh Boulevard
St. Louis, Missouri 63141-7881
Phone: 314-991-4100, Ext. 4246
Fax: 314-991-4101
E-mail: accredit@aoa.org
Website: www.theacoe.org

OSTEOPATHIC MEDICINE
Director, Department of Accreditation
Commission on Osteopathic College Accreditation (COCA)
American Osteopathic Association
142 East Ontario Street
Chicago, Illinois 60611
Phone: 312-202-8048
Fax: 312-202-8202
E-mail: predoc@osteopathic.org
Website: www.aoacoca.org

PHARMACY
Peter H. Vlasses, PharmD, Executive Director
Accreditation Council for Pharmacy Education
135 South LaSalle Street, Suite 4100
Chicago, Illinois 60603-4810
Phone: 312-664-3575
Fax: 312-664-4652
E-mail: csinfo@acpe-accredit.org
Website: www.acpe-accredit.org

PHYSICAL THERAPY
Sandra Wise, Senior Director
Commission on Accreditation in Physical Therapy Education (CAPTE)
American Physical Therapy Association (APTA)
1111 North Fairfax Street
Alexandria, Virginia 22314-1488
Phone: 703-706-3245
Fax: 703-706-3387
E-mail: accreditation@apta.org
Website: www.capteonline.org

PHYSICIAN ASSISTANT STUDIES
Sharon L. Luke, Executive Director
Accredittion Review Commission on Education for the Physician Assistant, Inc. (ARC-PA)
12000 Findley Road, Suite 275
Johns Creek, Georgia 30097
Phone: 770-476-1224
Fax: 770-476-1738
E-mail: arc-pa@arc-pa.org
Website: www.arc-pa.org

PLANNING
Jesmarie Soto Johnson, Executive Director
American Institute of Certified Planners/Association of Collegiate Schools of Planning/American Planning Association
Planning Accreditation Board (PAB)
2334 West Lawrence Avenue, Suite 209
Chicago, Illinois 60625
Phone: 773-334-7200
E-mail: smerits@planningaccreditationboard.org
Website: www.planningaccreditationboard.org

PODIATRIC MEDICINE
Heather Stagliano, OTR/L, DHSc, Executive Director
Council on Podiatric Medical Education (CPME)
American Podiatric Medical Association (APMA)
9312 Old Georgetown Road
Bethesda, Maryland 20814-1621
Phone: 301-581-9200
Fax: 301-571-4903
Website: www.cpme.org

PSYCHOLOGY AND COUNSELING
Jacqueline Remondet, Associate Executive Director, CEO of the Accrediting Unit,
Office of Program Consultation and Accreditation
American Psychological Association
750 First Street, NE
Washington, DC 20002-4202
Phone: 202-336-5979 or 800-374-2721
TDD/TTY: 202-336-6123
Fax: 202-336-5978
E-mail: apaaccred@apa.org
Website: www.apa.org/ed/accreditation

Kelly Coker, Executive Director
Council for Accreditation of Counseling and Related Educational Programs (CACREP)
1001 North Fairfax Street, Suite 510
Alexandria, Virginia 22314
Phone: 703-535-5990
Fax: 703-739-6209
E-mail: cacrep@cacrep.org
Website: www.cacrep.org

Richard M. McFall, Executive Director
Psychological Clinical Science Accreditation System (PCSAS)
1101 East Tenth Street
IU Psychology Building
Bloomington, Indiana 47405-7007
Phone: 812-856-2570
Fax: 812-322-5545
E-mail: rmmcfall@pcsas.org
Website: www.pcsas.org

PUBLIC HEALTH
Laura Rasar King, M.PH., MCHES, Executive Director
Council on Education for Public Health
1010 Wayne Avenue, Suite 220
Silver Spring, Maryland 20910
Phone: 202-789-1050
Fax: 202-789-1895
E-mail: Lking@ceph.org
Website: www.ceph.org

PUBLIC POLICY, AFFAIRS AND ADMINISTRATION
Crystal Calarusse, Chief Accreditation Officer
Commission on Peer Review and Accreditation
Network of Schools of Public Policy, Affairs, and Administration (NASPAA-COPRA)
1029 Vermont Avenue, NW, Suite 1100
Washington, DC 20005
Phone: 202-628-8965
Fax: 202-626-4978
E-mail: copra@naspaa.org
Website: accreditation.naspaa.org

RADIOLOGIC TECHNOLOGY
Leslie Winter, Chief Executive Officer Joint Review Committee on Education in Radiologic Technology (JRCERT)
20 North Wacker Drive, Suite 2850
Chicago, Illinois 60606-3182
Phone: 312-704-5300
Fax: 312-704-5304
E-mail: mail@jrcert.org
Website: www.jrcert.org

REHABILITATION EDUCATION
Frank Lane, Ph.D., Executive Director
Council for Accreditation of Counseling and Related Educational Programs (CACREP)
1001 North Fairfax Street, Suite 510
Alexandria, Virginia 22314
Phone: 703-535-5990
Fax: 703-739-6209
E-mail: cacrep@cacrep.org
Website: www.cacrep.org

RESPIRATORY CARE
Thomas Smalling, Executive Director
Commission on Accreditation for Respiratory Care (CoARC)
1248 Harwood Road
Bedford, Texas 76021-4244
Phone: 817-283-2835
Fax: 817-354-8519
E-mail: tom@coarc.com
Website: www.coarc.com

SOCIAL WORK
Dr. Stacey Borasky, Director of Accreditation
Office of Social Work Accreditation
Council on Social Work Education
1701 Duke Street, Suite 200
Alexandria, Virginia 22314
Phone: 703-683-8080
Fax: 703-519-2078
E-mail: info@cswe.org
Website: www.cswe.org

SPEECH-LANGUAGE PATHOLOGY AND AUDIOLOGY
Kimberlee Moore, Accreditation Executive Director
American Speech-Language-Hearing Association
Council on Academic Accreditation in Audiology and Speech-Language Pathology
2200 Research Boulevard #310
Rockville, Maryland 20850-3289
Phone: 301-296-5700
Fax: 301-296-8750
E-mail: accreditation@asha.org
Website: http://caa.asha.org

TEACHER EDUCATION
Christopher A. Koch, President
National Council for Accreditation of Teacher Education (NCATE)
Teacher Education Accreditation Council (TEAC)
1140 19th Street, Suite 400
Washington, DC 20036
Phone: 202-223-0077
Fax: 202-296-6620
E-mail: caep@caepnet.org
Website: www.ncate.org

TECHNOLOGY
Michale S. McComis, Ed.D., Executive Director
Accrediting Commission of Career Schools and Colleges
2101 Wilson Boulevard, Suite 302
Arlington, Virginia 22201
Phone: 703-247-4212
Fax: 703-247-4533
E-mail: mccomis@accsc.org
Website: www.accsc.org

TECHNOLOGY, MANAGEMENT, AND APPLIED ENGINEERING
Kelly Schild, Director of Accreditation
The Association of Technology, Management, and Applied Engineering (ATMAE)
275 N. York Street, Suite 401
Elmhurst, Illinois 60126
Phone: 630-433-4514
Fax: 630-563-9181
E-mail: Kelly@atmae.org
Website: www.atmae.org

THEATER
Karen P. Moynahan, Executive Director
National Association of Schools of Theatre Commission on Accreditation
11250 Roger Bacon Drive, Suite 21
Reston, Virginia 20190
Phone: 703-437-0700
Fax: 703-437-6312
E-mail: info@arts-accredit.org
Website: http://nast.arts-accredit.org/

THEOLOGY
Dr. Bernard Fryshman, Executive VP
Emeritus and Interim Executive Director
Association of Advanced Rabbinical and Talmudic Schools (AARTS)
Accreditation Commission
11 Broadway, Suite 405
New York, New York 10004
Phone: 212-363-1991
Fax: 212-533-5335
E-mail: k.sharfman.aarts@gmail.com

Frank Yamada, Executive Director
Association of Theological Schools in the United States and Canada (ATS)
Commission on Accrediting
10 Summit Park Drive
Pittsburgh, Pennsylvania 15275
Phone: 412-788-6505
Fax: 412-788-6510
E-mail: ats@ats.edu
Website: www.ats.edu

Dr. Timothy Eaton, President
Transnational Association of Christian Colleges and Schools (TRACS)
Accreditation Commission
15935 Forest Road
Forest, Virginia 24551
Phone: 434-525-9539
Fax: 434-525-9538
E-mail: info@tracs.org
Website: www.tracs.org

VETERINARY MEDICINE
Dr. Karen Brandt, Director of Education and Research
American Veterinary Medical Association (AVMA)
Council on Education
1931 North Meacham Road, Suite 100
Schaumburg, Illinois 60173-4360
Phone: 847-925-8070 Ext. 6674
Fax: 847-285-5732
E-mail: info@avma.org
Website: www.avma.org

How to Use These Guides

As you identify the particular programs and institutions that interest you, you can use both the ***Graduate & Professional Programs: An Overview*** volume and the specialized volumes in the series to obtain detailed information.

- ***Graduate Programs in the Biological/Biomedical Sciences & Health-Related Professions***
- ***Graduate Programs in Business, Education, Information Studies, Law & Social Work***
- ***Graduate Programs in Engineering & Applied Sciences***
- ***Graduate Programs the Humanities, Arts & Social Sciences***
- ***Graduate Programs in the Physical Sciences, Mathematics, Agricultural Sciences, the Environment & Natural Resources***

Each of the specialized volumes in the series is divided into sections that contain one or more directories devoted to programs in a particular field. If you do not find a directory devoted to your field of interest in a specific volume, consult "Directories and Subject Areas" (located at the end of each volume). After you have identified the correct volume, consult the "Directories and Subject Areas in This Book" index, which shows (as does the more general directory) what directories cover subjects not specifically named in a directory or section title.

Each of the specialized volumes in the series has a number of general directories. These directories have entries for the largest unit at an institution granting graduate degrees in that field. For example, the general Engineering and Applied Sciences directory in the ***Graduate Programs in Engineering & Applied Sciences*** volume consists of **Profiles** for colleges, schools, and departments of engineering and applied sciences.

General directories are followed by other directories, or sections, that give more detailed information about programs in particular areas of the general field that has been covered. The general Engineering and Applied Sciences directory, in the previous example, is followed by nineteen sections with directories in specific areas of engineering, such as Chemical Engineering, Industrial/Management Engineering, and Mechanical Engineering.

Because of the broad nature of many fields, any system of organization is bound to involve a certain amount of overlap. Environmental studies, for example, is a field whose various aspects are studied in several types of departments and schools. Readers interested in such studies will find information on relevant programs in the ***Graduate Programs in the Biological/Biomedical Sciences & Health-Related Professions*** volume under Ecology and Environmental Biology and Environmental and Occupational Health; in the ***Graduate Programs in the Physical Sciences, Mathematics, Agricultural Sciences, the Environment & Natural Resources*** volume under Environmental Management and Policy and Natural Resources; and in the ***Graduate Programs in Engineering & Applied Sciences*** volume under Energy Management and Policy and Environmental Engineering. To help you find all of the programs of interest to you, the introduction to each section within the specialized volumes includes, if applicable, a paragraph suggesting other sections and directories with information on related areas of study.

Directory of Institutions and Their Offerings

This directory lists institutions in alphabetical order and includes beneath each name the academic fields in which each institution offers graduate programs. The degree level in each field is also indicated, provided that the institution has supplied that information in response to Peterson's Annual Survey of Graduate and Professional Institutions.

An M indicates that a master's degree program is offered; a D indicates that a doctoral degree program is offered; an O signifies that other advanced degrees (e.g., certificates or specialist degrees) are offered; and an * (asterisk) indicates that a **Close-Up** and/or **Display** is located in this volume. See the index, "Close-Ups and Displays," for the specific page number.

Profiles of Academic and Professional Programs in the Specialized Volumes

Each section of **Profiles** has a table of contents that lists the Program Directories, **Displays**, and **Close-Ups.** Program Directories consist of the **Profiles** of programs in the relevant fields, with **Displays** following if programs have chosen to include them. **Close-Ups,** which are more individualized statements, are also listed for those graduate schools or programs that have chosen to submit them.

The **Profiles** found in the 500 directories in the specialized volumes provide basic data about the graduate units in capsule form for quick reference. To make these directories as useful as possible, **Profiles** are generally listed for an institution's smallest academic unit within a subject area. In other words, if an institution has a College of Liberal Arts that administers many related programs, the **Profile** for the individual program (e.g., Program in History), not the entire College, appears in the directory.

There are some programs that do not fit into any current directory and are not given individual **Profiles**. The directory structure is reviewed annually in order to keep this number to a minimum and to accommodate major trends in graduate education.

The following outline describes the **Profile** information found in the guides and explains how best to use that information. Any item that does not apply to or was not provided by a graduate unit is omitted from its listing. The format of the **Profiles** is constant, making it easy to compare one institution with another and one program with another.

A ★ graphic next to the school's name indicates the institution has additional detailed information in a "Premium Profile" on Petersons.com. After reading their information here, you can learn more about the school by visiting www.petersons.com and searching for that particular college or university's graduate program.

Identifying Information. The institution's name, in boldface type, is followed by a complete listing of the administrative structure for that field of study. (For example, University of Akron, Buchtel College of Arts and Sciences, Department of Theoretical and Applied Mathematics, Program in Mathematics.) The last unit listed is the one to which all information in the **Profile** pertains. The institution's city, state, and ZIP code follow.

Offerings. Each field of study offered by the unit is listed with all postbaccalaureate degrees awarded. Degrees that are not preceded by a specific concentration are awarded in the general field listed in the unit name. Frequently, fields of study are broken down into subspecializations, and those appear following the degrees awarded; for example, "Offerings in secondary education (M.Ed.), including English education, mathematics education, science education." Students enrolled in the M.Ed. program would be able to specialize in any of the three fields mentioned.

Professional Accreditation. Some **Profiles** indicate whether a program is professionally accredited. Because it is possible for a program to receive or lose professional accreditation at any time, students entering fields in which accreditation is important to a career should verify the status of programs by contacting either the chairperson or the appropriate accrediting association.

Jointly Offered Degrees. Explanatory statements concerning programs that are offered in cooperation with other institutions are included in the list of degrees offered. This occurs most commonly on a regional basis (for example, two state universities offering a cooperative Ph.D. in special education) or where the specialized nature of the institutions encourages joint efforts (a J.D./M.B.A. offered by a law school at an institution with no formal business programs and an institution with a business school but lacking a law school). Only programs that are truly cooperative are listed; those involving only limited course work at another institution are not. Interested students should contact the heads of such units for further information.

Program Availability. This may include the following: part-time, evening/weekend, online only, 100% online, blended/hybrid learning, and/or minimal on-campus study. When information regarding the availability of part-time or evening/weekend study appears in the **Profile**, it means that students are able to earn a degree exclusively through such study. Blended/hybrid learning describes those courses in which some traditional in-class time has been replaced by online learning activities. Hybrid courses take advantage of the best features of both face-to-face and online learning.

Faculty. Figures on the number of faculty members actively involved with graduate students through teaching or research are separated into full- and part-time as well as men and women whenever the information has been supplied.

Students. Figures for the number of students enrolled in graduate and professional programs pertain to the semester of highest enrollment from the 2017–18 academic year. These figures are broken down into full- and part-time and men and women whenever the data have been supplied. Information on the number of matriculated students enrolled in the unit who are members of a minority group or are international students appears here. The average age of the matriculated students is followed by the number of applicants, the percentage accepted, and the number enrolled for fall 2017.

Degrees Awarded. The number of degrees awarded in the calendar year is listed. Many doctoral programs offer a terminal master's degree if students leave the program after completing only part of the requirements for a doctoral degree; that is indicated here. All degrees are classified into one of four types: master's, doctoral, first professional, and other advanced degrees. A unit may award one or several degrees at a given level; however, the data are only collected by type and may therefore represent several different degree programs.

Degree Requirements. The information in this section is also broken down by type of degree, and all information for a degree level pertains to all degrees of that type unless otherwise specified. Degree requirements are collected in a simplified form to provide some very basic information on the nature of the program and on foreign language, thesis or dissertation, comprehensive exam, and registration requirements. Many units also provide a short list of additional requirements, such as fieldwork or an internship. For complete information on graduation requirements, contact the graduate school or program directly.

Entrance Requirements. Entrance requirements are broken down into the four degree levels of master's, doctoral, first professional, and other advanced degrees. Within each level, information may be provided in two basic categories: entrance exams and other requirements. The entrance exams are identified by the standard acronyms used by the testing agencies, unless they are not well known. Other entrance requirements are quite varied, but they often contain an undergraduate or graduate grade point average (GPA). Unless otherwise stated, the GPA is calculated on a 4.0 scale and is listed as a minimum required for admission. Additional exam requirements/recommendations for international students may be listed here. Application deadlines for domestic and international students, the application fee, and whether electronic applications are accepted may be listed here. Note that the deadline should be used for reference only; these dates are subject to change, and students interested in applying should always contact the graduate unit directly about application procedures and deadlines.

Expenses. The typical cost of study for the 2018–2019 academic year (2017–18 if 2018–19 figures were not available) is given in two basic categories: tuition and fees. Cost of study may be quite complex at a graduate institution. There are often sliding scales for part-time study, a different cost for first-year students, and other variables that make it impossible to completely cover the cost of study for each graduate program. To provide the most usable information, figures are given for full-time study for a full year where available and for part-time study in terms of a per-unit rate (per credit, per semester hour, etc.). Occasionally, variances may be noted in tuition and fees for reasons such as the type of program, whether courses are taken during the day or evening, whether courses are at the master's or doctoral level, or other institution-specific reasons. Respondents were also given the opportunity to provide more specific and detailed tuition and fees information at the unit level. When provided, this information will appear in place of any typical costs entered elsewhere on the university-level survey. Expenses are usually subject to change; for exact costs at any given time, contact your chosen schools and programs directly. Keep in mind that the tuition of Canadian institutions is usually given in Canadian dollars.

Financial Support. This section contains data on the number of awards administered by the institution and given to graduate students during the 2017–18 academic year. The first figure given represents the total number of students receiving financial support enrolled in that unit. If the unit has provided information on graduate appointments, these are broken down into three major categories: fellowships give money to graduate students to cover the cost of study and living expenses and are not based on a work obligation or research commitment, research assistantships provide stipends to graduate students for assistance in a formal research project with a faculty member, and teaching assistantships provide stipends to graduate students for teaching or for assisting faculty members in teaching undergraduate classes. Within each category, figures are given for the total number of awards, the average yearly amount per award, and whether full or partial tuition reimbursements are awarded. In addition to graduate appointments, the availability of several other financial aid sources is covered in this section. Tuition waivers are routinely part of a graduate appointment, but units sometimes waive part or all of a student's tuition even if a graduate appointment is not available. Federal Work Study is made available to students who demonstrate need and meet the federal guidelines; this form of aid normally includes 10 or more hours of work per week in an office of the institution. Institutionally sponsored loans are low-interest loans available to graduate students to cover both educational and living expenses. Career-related internships or fieldwork offer money to students who are participating in a formal off-campus research project or practicum. Grants, scholarships, traineeships, unspecified assistantships, and other awards may also be noted. The availability of financial support to part-time students is also indicated here.

Some programs list the financial aid application deadline and the forms that need to be completed for students to be eligible for financial awards. There are two forms: FAFSA, the Free Application for Federal Student Aid, which is required for federal aid, and the CSS PROFILE®.

Faculty Research. Each unit has the opportunity to list several keyword phrases describing the current research involving faculty members and graduate students. Space limitations prevent the unit from listing complete information on all research programs. The total expenditure for funded research from the previous academic year may also be included.

Unit Head and Application Contact. The head of the graduate program for each unit may be listed with academic title, phone and fax numbers, and e-mail address. In addition to the unit head's contact information, many graduate programs also list a separate contact for application and admission information, followed by the graduate school, program, or department's website. If no unit head or application contact is given, you should contact the overall institution for information on graduate admissions.

Displays and Close-Ups

The **Displays** and **Close-Ups** are supplementary insertions submitted by deans, chairs, and other administrators who wish to offer an additional, more individualized statement to readers. A number of graduate school and program administrators have attached a **Display** ad near the **Profile** listing. Here you will find information that an institution or program wants to emphasize. The **Close-Ups** are by their very nature more expansive and flexible than the **Profiles**, and the administrators who have written them may emphasize different aspects of their programs. All of the **Close-Ups** are organized in the same way (with the exception of a few that describe research and training opportunities instead of degree programs), and in each one you will find information on the same basic topics, such as programs of study, research facilities, tuition and fees, financial aid, and application procedures. If an institution or program has submitted a **Close-Up**, a boldface cross-reference appears below its **Profile**. As with the **Displays**, all of the **Close-Ups** in the guides have been submitted by choice; the absence of a **Display** or **Close-Up** does not reflect any type of editorial judgment on the part of Peterson's, and their presence in the guides should not be taken as an indication of status, quality, or approval. Statements regarding a university's objectives and accomplishments are a reflection of its own beliefs and are not the opinions of the Peterson's editors.

Appendixes

This section contains two appendixes. The first, "Institutional Changes Since the 2018 Edition," lists institutions that have closed, merged, or changed their name or status since the last edition of the guides. The second, "Abbreviations Used in the Guides," gives abbreviations of degree names, along with what those abbreviations stand for. These appendixes are identical in all six volumes of ***Peterson's Graduate and Professional Programs***.

Indexes

There are three indexes presented here. The first index, "Close-Ups and Displays," gives page references for all programs that have chosen to place **Close-Ups** and **Displays** in this volume. It is arranged alphabetically by institution; within institutions, the arrangement is alphabetical by subject area. It is not an index to all programs in the book's directories of **Profiles**; readers must refer to the directories themselves for **Profile** information on programs that have not submitted the additional, more individualized statements. The second index, "Directories and Subject Areas in Other Books in This Series", gives book references for the directories in the specialized volumes and also includes cross-references for subject area names not used in the directory structure, for example, "Computing Technology (see Computer Science)." The third index, "Directories and Subject Areas in This Book," gives page references for the directories in this volume and cross-references for subject area names not used in this volume's directory structure.

Data Collection Procedures

The information published in the directories and Profiles of all the books is collected through Peterson's Annual Survey of Graduate and Professional Institutions. The survey is sent each spring to nearly 2,300 institutions offering postbaccalaureate degree programs, including accredited institutions in the United States, U.S. territories, and Canada and those institutions outside the United States that are accredited by U.S. accrediting bodies. Deans and other administrators complete these surveys, providing information on programs in the 500 academic and professional fields covered in the guides as well as overall institutional information. While every effort has been made to ensure the accuracy and completeness of the data, information is sometimes unavailable or changes occur after publication deadlines. All usable information received in time for publication has been included. The omission of any particular item from a directory or Profile signifies either that the item is not applicable to the institution or program or that information was not available. Profiles of programs scheduled to begin during the 2018–19 academic year cannot, obviously, include statistics on enrollment or, in many cases, the number of faculty members. If no usable data were submitted by an institution, its name, address, and program name appear in order to indicate the availability of graduate work.

Criteria for Inclusion in This Guide

To be included in this guide, an institution must have full accreditation or be a candidate for accreditation (preaccreditation) status by an institutional or specialized accrediting body recognized by the U.S. Department of Education or the Council for Higher Education Accreditation (CHEA). Institutional accrediting bodies, which review each institution as a whole, include the six regional associations of schools and colleges (Middle States, New England, North Central, Northwest, Southern, and Western), each of which is responsible for a specified portion of the United States and its territories. Other institutional accrediting bodies are national in scope and accredit specific kinds of institutions (e.g., Bible colleges, independent colleges, and rabbinical and Talmudic schools). Program registration by the New York State Board of Regents is considered to be the equivalent of institutional accreditation, since the board requires that all programs offered by an institution meet its standards before recognition is granted. A Canadian institution must be chartered and authorized to grant degrees by the provincial government, affiliated with a chartered institution, or accredited by a recognized U.S. accrediting body. This guide also includes institutions outside the United States that are accredited by these U.S. accrediting bodies. There are recognized specialized or professional accrediting bodies in more than fifty different fields, each of which is authorized to accredit institutions or specific programs in its particular field. For specialized institutions that offer programs in one field only, we designate this to be the equivalent of institutional accreditation. A full explanation of the accrediting process and complete information on recognized institutional (regional and national) and specialized accrediting bodies can be found online at **www.chea.org** or at **www.ed.gov/admins/finaid/accred/index.html.**

NOTICE: Certain portions of or information contained in this book have been submitted and paid for by the educational institution identified, and such institutions take full responsibility for the accuracy, timeliness, completeness and functionality of such contents. Such portions or information include (i) each display ad that comprises a half page of information covering a single educational institution or program and (ii) each two-page description or Close-Up of a graduate school or program that appear in the different sections of this guide. The "Close-Ups and Displays" are listed in various sections throughout the book.

DIRECTORY OF GRADUATE AND PROFESSIONAL PROGRAMS BY FIELD

ACCOUNTING

Abilene Christian University	M
Adelphi University	M
Adrian College	M
Alabama State University	M
Albany State University	M
Albertus Magnus College	M
Alfred University	M
American Business & Technology University	M
American InterContinental University Online	M
American International College	M,D,O
American Public University System	M,D
American University	M,O
American University of Sharjah	M,D
Anderson University (IN)	M,D
Andrews University	M
Angelo State University	M
Appalachian State University	M
Argosy University, Atlanta	M,D
Argosy University, Chicago	M,D
Argosy University, Hawai'i	M,D,O
Argosy University, Los Angeles	M,D
Argosy University, Northern Virginia	M,D,O
Argosy University, Orange County	M,D,O
Argosy University, Phoenix	M,D
Argosy University, Seattle	M,D
Argosy University, Tampa	M,D
Argosy University, Twin Cities	M,D
Arizona State University at the Tempe campus	M,D
Arkansas State University	M
Ashland University	M
Assumption College	M,O
Auburn University	M*
Auburn University at Montgomery	M
Augustana University	M
Aurora University	M
Averett University	M
Avila University	M
Azusa Pacific University	M*
Babson College	M,O
Baker College Center for Graduate Studies–Online	M,D
Baldwin Wallace University	M
Ball State University	M
Barry University	M
Baruch College of the City University of New York	M,D*
Bayamón Central University	M
Baylor University	M
Bay Path University	M
Belmont University	M
Benedictine University	M
Bentley University	M,D
Binghamton University, State University of New York	M
Bloomfield College	M
Bloomsburg University of Pennsylvania	M
Bluffton University	M
Bob Jones University	M,D,O
Boise State University	M
Boston College	M
Bowling Green State University	M
Bradley University	M
Brandman University	M
Brenau University	M
Bridgewater State University	M
Brock University	M
Brooklyn College of the City University of New York	M
Bryant University	M
Butler University	M
Cabrini University	M,D
Cairn University	M,O
Caldwell University	M
California Baptist University	M
California Polytechnic State University, San Luis Obispo	M*
California State Polytechnic University, Pomona	M
California State University, East Bay	M
California State University, Fullerton	M
California State University, Los Angeles	M
California State University, Sacramento	M
California State University, San Bernardino	M
California Western School of Law	M,D
Calvin College	M
Canisius College	M
Capella University	M,D
Carnegie Mellon University	D
Case Western Reserve University	M,D*
The Catholic University of America	M
Centenary University	M
Central Connecticut State University	M
Central Michigan University	M,O
Chaminade University of Honolulu	M
Chapman University	M*
Charleston Southern University	M
Chatham University	M
Christian Brothers University	M,O
City University of Seattle	M,O
Clarion University of Pennsylvania	M
Clark Atlanta University	M
Clark University	M
Clayton State University	M
Clemson University	M
Cleveland State University	M
Coastal Carolina University	M,O
The College at Brockport, State University of New York	M,O
College of Charleston	M
The College of Saint Rose	M
College of Staten Island of the City University of New York	M
The College of William and Mary	M*
Colorado State University	M
Colorado State University–Global Campus	M
Colorado Technical University Aurora	M
Colorado Technical University Colorado Springs	M,D
Columbia College (MO)	M
Columbia University	M,D*
Cornell University	M,D
Creighton University	M,D
Culver-Stockton College	M
Daemen College	M
Dallas Baptist University	M
Davenport University	M
Delaware Valley University	M
Delta State University	M
DePaul University	M,D
DeSales University	M
DeVry University–Folsom Campus	M
Dominican College	M
Dominican University	M
Drake University	M
Drexel University	M,D,O*
Duke University	D*
Duquesne University	M
East Carolina University	M
Eastern Connecticut State University	M
Eastern Illinois University	M
Eastern Michigan University	M
Eastern Washington University	M
East Tennessee State University	M
Edgewood College	M
Elms College	M,O
Emory University	M,D
Emporia State University	M
Everglades University	M
Fairfield University	M,O
Fairleigh Dickinson University, Florham Campus	M
Fairleigh Dickinson University, Metropolitan Campus	M,O
Fitchburg State University	M
Florida Agricultural and Mechanical University	M
Florida Atlantic University	M
Florida Gulf Coast University	M
Florida International University	M
Florida National University	M
Florida Southern College	M
Florida State University	M,D
Fontbonne University	M
Fordham University	M,D
Franklin University	M
Freed-Hardeman University	M
Friends University	M
George Fox University	M,D
George Mason University	M
The George Washington University	M
Georgia College & State University	M
Georgia Southern University	M
Georgia State University	M
Golden Gate University	M,D,O
Gonzaga University	M
Governors State University	M
The Graduate Center, City University of New York	D
Grand Canyon University	M
Grand Valley State University	M
Harvard University	D*
HEC Montreal	M,D,O
Hendrix College	M
Herzing University Online	M
Hodges University	M
Hofstra University	M,O
Holy Family University	M
Hood College	M,O*
Howard University	M
Hunter College of the City University of New York	M
IGlobal University	M
Illinois State University	M
Indiana Tech	M
Indiana University Kokomo	M,O
Indiana University Northwest	M,O
Indiana University–Purdue University Indianapolis	M
Indiana University South Bend	M,O
Indiana Wesleyan University	M,O
Instituto Tecnologico de Santo Domingo	M,O
Inter American University of Puerto Rico, Aguadilla Campus	M
Inter American University of Puerto Rico, Arecibo Campus	M
Inter American University of Puerto Rico, Barranquitas Campus	M
Inter American University of Puerto Rico, Metropolitan Campus	M
Inter American University of Puerto Rico, Ponce Campus	M
Inter American University of Puerto Rico, San Germán Campus	M,D
Iona College	M,O
Iowa State University of Science and Technology	M
Ithaca College	M
Jackson State University	M
Jacksonville University	M*
James Madison University	M
John Carroll University	M
Johnson & Wales University	M
Juniata College	M
Kansas State University	M
Kean University	M
Keiser University	M
Kennesaw State University	M
Kent State University	M,D
Keystone College	M
King University	M
Lakeland University	M
Lamar University	M
La Roche College	M
La Salle University	M,O
La Sierra University	M,O
Lehigh University	M
Lehman College of the City University of New York	M
Lenoir-Rhyne University	M
Lewis University	M
Liberty University	M,D
Lincoln University (MO)	M
Lindenwood University	M
Lipscomb University	M,O
Long Island University–LIU Brooklyn	M,O
Long Island University–LIU Post	M
Louisiana State University and Agricultural & Mechanical College	M,D
Louisiana Tech University	M,D
Loyola Marymount University	M
Loyola University Chicago	M
Maharishi University of Management	M,D
Manhattanville College	M,O
Marquette University	M
Marshall University	M
Maryville University of Saint Louis	M,O
McGill University	M,D,O
Mercer University	M
Mercy College	M
Mercyhurst University	M,O
Merrimack College	M
Metropolitan State University of Denver	M
Miami University	M
Michigan State University	M,D
Michigan Technological University	M
Middle Tennessee State University	M
Millennia Atlantic University	M
Millsaps College	M
Minnesota State University Mankato	M
Minnesota State University Moorhead	M
Misericordia University	M
Mississippi College	M,O
Mississippi State University	M
Missouri State University	M
Missouri Western State University	M
Molloy College	M,O
Monmouth University	M,O*
Monroe College	M
Montana State University	M
Montclair State University	M,O
Moravian College	M
Morgan State University	M,D
Mount Aloysius College	M
Murray State University	M
National American University (TX)	M,D
National University	M,O
Neumann University	M
New England College	M
New Jersey City University	M,O
New Mexico State University	M
New York University	M,D*
Niagara University	M
North Carolina Agricultural and Technical State University	M
North Carolina State University	M
North Dakota State University	M*
Northeastern Illinois University	M
Northeastern State University	M
Northeastern University	M
Northern Illinois University	M
Northern Kentucky University	M,O
Northwest Christian University	M
Northwestern University	M,D
Nova Southeastern University	M*
Oakland University	M,O
Ohio Christian University	M
Ohio Dominican University	M
Ohio Northern University	M
The Ohio State University	M
Oklahoma Christian University	M
Oklahoma State University	M,D
Old Dominion University	M
Oral Roberts University	M
Oregon State University	M,D
Our Lady of the Lake University	M
Pace University	M,O
Pacific Lutheran University	M
Pacific States University	M,O
Penn State Erie, The Behrend College	M
Penn State Harrisburg	M,O
Penn State University Park	M,D*
Pepperdine University	M
Pittsburg State University	M
Plymouth State University	M
Polytechnic University of Puerto Rico, Miami Campus	M
Polytechnic University of Puerto Rico, Orlando Campus	M
Pontifical Catholic University of Puerto Rico	M,O
Post University	M
Prairie View A&M University	M
Providence College	M
Purdue University Northwest	M
Queens College of the City University of New York	M
Quinnipiac University	M
Ramapo College of New Jersey	M
Regent University	M,D,O
Regis University	M,O
Rhode Island College	M,O
Rhodes College	M
Rider University	M,O
Robert Morris University Illinois	M
Rochester Institute of Technology	M
Rockhurst University	M,O
Rocky Mountain College	M
Roosevelt University	M
Rutgers University–Newark	M,D
Sacred Heart University	M,O
St. Ambrose University	M
St. Bonaventure University	M
St. Edward's University	M
St. Francis College	M
St. John's University (NY)	M
St. Joseph's College, Long Island Campus	M
St. Joseph's College, New York	M
Saint Joseph's College of Maine	M
Saint Joseph's University	M,O*
Saint Leo University	M,D
Saint Louis University	M*
Saint Mary's College of California	M
Saint Mary's University of Minnesota	M
Saint Peter's University	M
St. Thomas University	M,O
Samford University	M
Sam Houston State University	M
San Diego State University	M
San Francisco State University	M
San Jose State University	M
Seattle University	M
Seton Hall University	M,O
Seton Hill University	M
Shorter University	M
Siena College	M
Slippery Rock University of Pennsylvania	M
Southeast Missouri State University	M
Southern Adventist University	M
Southern Illinois University Carbondale	M,D
Southern Illinois University Edwardsville	M
Southern Methodist University	M
Southern New Hampshire University	M,D,O
Southern Oregon University	M,O
Southern Utah University	M
Southwestern Adventist University	M
State University of New York at New Paltz	M
State University of New York College at Geneseo	M
State University of New York College at Old Westbury	M
State University of New York Polytechnic Institute	M
Stephen F. Austin State University	M
Stetson University	M
Stony Brook University, State University of New York	M,O
Stratford University (VA)	M,D
Strayer University	M
Suffolk University	M,O
Syracuse University	M*
Tabor College	M
Tarleton State University	M
Temple University	M,D*
Tennessee Technological University	M
Tennessee Wesleyan University	M
Texas A&M International University	M
Texas A&M University	M
Texas A&M University–Central Texas	M,O
Texas A&M University–Commerce	M
Texas A&M University–Corpus Christi	M
Texas A&M University–San Antonio	M
Texas A&M University–Texarkana	M
Texas Christian University	M
Texas Lutheran University	M
Texas State University	M
Texas Tech University	M,D
Texas Woman's University	M
Thomas Edison State University	M
Towson University	M
Trinity University	M
Troy University	M
Truman State University	M
Tulane University	M,D
Union University	M
Universidad del Este	M
Universidad del Turabo	M
Universidad Metropolitana	M
Université de Sherbrooke	M
Université du Québec à Montréal	M,O
Université du Québec à Trois-Rivières	M
Université du Québec en Outaouais	M,O
Université Laval	M,O
University at Buffalo, the State University of New York	M,D
The University of Akron	M
The University of Alabama	M,D
The University of Alabama at Birmingham	M
The University of Alabama in Huntsville	M,O
University of Alberta	D
The University of Arizona	M
University of Arkansas	M
University of Baltimore	M,O
University of Bridgeport	M
The University of British Columbia	D
University of California, Berkeley	D,O
University of California, Davis	M
University of California, Irvine	M
University of California, Los Angeles	M,D*
University of California, Riverside	M,D
University of Central Arkansas	M
University of Central Florida	M

University of Central Missouri	M,D,O
University of Charleston	M
University of Chicago	M,O
University of Cincinnati	M,D
University of Colorado Denver	M
University of Connecticut	M,D*
University of Dallas	M,D
University of Dayton	M
University of Delaware	M*
University of Denver	M
University of Detroit Mercy	M,O
The University of Findlay	M,D
University of Florida	M,D
University of Georgia	M
University of Hartford	M,O
University of Hawaii at Manoa	M,D
University of Houston	M,D
University of Houston–Clear Lake	M
University of Houston–Downtown	M
University of Houston–Victoria	M
University of Idaho	M
University of Illinois at Chicago	M
University of Illinois at Springfield	M
University of Illinois at Urbana–Champaign	M,D
The University of Iowa	M,D*
University of Kansas	M
University of Kentucky	M
University of La Verne	M
University of Lethbridge	M,D
University of Louisiana at Lafayette	M
University of Louisville	M
The University of Manchester	M
University of Mary Hardin-Baylor	M
University of Maryland University College	M
University of Massachusetts Amherst	M,D*
University of Massachusetts Boston	M
University of Massachusetts Dartmouth	M,O
University of Memphis	M,D
University of Michigan	M,D*
University of Michigan–Dearborn	M
University of Michigan–Flint	M,O
University of Minnesota, Twin Cities Campus	M,D
University of Mississippi	M,D
University of Missouri	M,D,O
University of Missouri–Kansas City	M,D
University of Missouri–St. Louis	M,D,O
University of Montana	M
University of Nebraska at Kearney	M
University of Nebraska at Omaha	M
University of Nebraska–Lincoln	M,D
University of Nevada, Las Vegas	M,O
University of Nevada, Reno	M
University of New Hampshire	M
University of New Haven	M,O*
University of New Mexico	M
University of New Orleans	M
University of North Alabama	M
The University of North Carolina at Chapel Hill	M,D
The University of North Carolina at Charlotte	M
The University of North Carolina at Greensboro	M,O
The University of North Carolina Wilmington	M
University of Northern Colorado	M
University of Northern Iowa	M
University of North Florida	M
University of North Texas	M,D,O
University of North Texas at Dallas	M
University of Notre Dame	M
University of Oklahoma	M,D*
University of Oregon	M,D
University of Pennsylvania	M,D*
University of Phoenix–Bay Area Campus	M,D
University of Phoenix–Central Valley Campus	M
University of Phoenix–Dallas Campus	M
University of Phoenix–Hawaii Campus	M
University of Phoenix–Houston Campus	M
University of Phoenix–Las Vegas Campus	M
University of Phoenix–Online Campus	M,O
University of Phoenix–Phoenix Campus	M,O
University of Phoenix–Sacramento Valley Campus	M
University of Phoenix–San Antonio Campus	M
University of Phoenix–San Diego Campus	M
University of Pittsburgh	M,D*
University of Puerto Rico–Río Piedras	M,D
University of Rhode Island	M*
University of Rochester	M,D*
University of St. Thomas (TX)	M
University of St. Thomas (MN)	M
University of San Diego	M
University of Saskatchewan	M
The University of Scranton	M
University of South Africa	M,D
University of South Alabama	M
University of South Carolina	M
University of South Dakota	M
University of Southern California	M*
University of Southern Indiana	M
University of Southern Maine	M
University of Southern Mississippi	M
University of South Florida	M,D*
The University of Tampa	M,O
The University of Tennessee	M,D
The University of Tennessee at Chattanooga	M
The University of Texas at Arlington	M,D
The University of Texas at Austin	M,D
The University of Texas at Dallas	M
The University of Texas at El Paso	M
The University of Texas at San Antonio	M,D
The University of Texas at Tyler	M
The University of Texas of the Permian Basin	M
The University of Texas Rio Grande Valley	M
University of the Cumberlands	M
University of the Sacred Heart	M,O
The University of Toledo	M
The University of Tulsa	M
University of Utah	M,D
University of Vermont	M
University of Virginia	M
University of Washington	M,D
University of Washington, Tacoma	M
University of Waterloo	M,D
University of West Florida	M
University of West Georgia	M
University of Wisconsin–Madison	M,D
University of Wisconsin–Whitewater	M
University of Wyoming	M
Upper Iowa University	M
Ursuline College	M
Utah State University	M
Utah Valley University	M
Utica College	M
Valdosta State University	M
Vanderbilt University	M*
Villanova University	M
Virginia Commonwealth University	M
Virginia International University	M,O
Virginia Polytechnic Institute and State University	M,D
Wagner College	M
Wake Forest University	M
Walden University	M,D,O
Walsh College of Accountancy and Business Administration	M
Warner University	M
Washburn University	M
Washington & Jefferson College	M,O
Washington State University	M
Washington University in St. Louis	M
Wayland Baptist University	M,D
Wayne State University	M,D,O
Webber International University	M
Weber State University	M
Webster University	M
Western Carolina University	M
Western Connecticut State University	M
Western Governors University	M
Western Illinois University	M
Western Michigan University	M
Western New England University	M
Westfield State University	M
Westminster College (UT)	M,O
West Texas A&M University	M
West Virginia University	M,D,O
Wheeling Jesuit University	M
Wichita State University	M
Wilfrid Laurier University	M,D
Wilkes University	M
Wilmington University	M,D
Wilson College	M
Wingate University	M
Worcester State University	M
Wright State University	M
Xavier University	M*
Yale University	D
Yeshiva University	M
York College of Pennsylvania	M
York University	M,D
Youngstown State University	M

ACOUSTICS

Naval Postgraduate School	M,D
Penn State University Park	M,D*
Rensselaer Polytechnic Institute	D
The University of Kansas	M,D,O

ACTUARIAL SCIENCE

Ball State University	M
Boston University	M*
California State University, East Bay	M
Central Connecticut State University	M,O
Columbia University	M*
Florida State University	M,D
Georgia State University	M
Governors State University	M
Lock Haven University of Pennsylvania	M
Maryville University of Saint Louis	M
Middle Tennessee State University	M
The Ohio State University	M,D
Oregon State University	M,D
Roosevelt University	M
St. John's University (NY)	M
Simon Fraser University	M,D
Temple University	M*
Université du Québec à Montréal	O
University of Illinois at Urbana–Champaign	M,D
The University of Iowa	M,D*
The University of Manchester	M,D
University of Nebraska–Lincoln	M
The University of Texas at Austin	M,D
The University of Texas at Dallas	M,D
University of Waterloo	M,D
University of Wisconsin–Madison	D
University of Wisconsin–Milwaukee	M,D*

ACUPUNCTURE AND ORIENTAL MEDICINE

Academy for Five Element Acupuncture	M
Academy of Chinese Culture and Health Sciences	M
Acupuncture & Integrative Medicine College, Berkeley	M
Acupuncture and Massage College	M
American Academy of Acupuncture and Oriental Medicine	M,D
American College of Acupuncture and Oriental Medicine	M
AOMA Graduate School of Integrative Medicine	M,D
Arizona School of Acupuncture and Oriental Medicine	M
Atlantic Institute of Oriental Medicine	M,D
Bastyr University	M,D
California Institute of Integral Studies	M,D
Canadian Memorial Chiropractic College	O
Colorado School of Traditional Chinese Medicine	M
Dongguk University Los Angeles	M
Dragon Rises College of Oriental Medicine	M
East West College of Natural Medicine	M
Emperor's College of Traditional Oriental Medicine	M,D
Five Branches University	M,D
Florida College of Integrative Medicine	M
Institute of Clinical Acupuncture and Oriental Medicine	M
Institute of Taoist Education and Acupuncture	M
Maryland University of Integrative Health	M,D,O
MCPHS University	M
Midwest College of Oriental Medicine	M,O
National University of Health Sciences	M,D
National University of Natural Medicine	M,D
New York Chiropractic College	M*
New York College of Health Professions	M
New York College of Traditional Chinese Medicine	M
Northwestern Health Sciences University	M
Oregon College of Oriental Medicine	M,D
Pacific College of Oriental Medicine	M,D
Pacific College of Oriental Medicine–Chicago	M
Pacific College of Oriental Medicine-New York	M
Phoenix Institute of Herbal Medicine & Acupuncture	M
Seattle Institute of Oriental Medicine	M
South Baylo University	M
Southern California University of Health Sciences	M,D
Southwest Acupuncture College	M
Swedish Institute, College of Health Sciences	M
Texas Health and Science University	M,D
Tri-State College of Acupuncture	M,O
University of Bridgeport	M
University of East-West Medicine	M,D
WON Institute of Graduate Studies	M,O
World Medicine Institute	M
Yo San University of Traditional Chinese Medicine	M

ACUTE CARE/CRITICAL CARE NURSING

Augusta University	D
Barry University	M,O
Case Western Reserve University	M*
The College of New Rochelle	M,O
Columbia University	M,O*
Drexel University	M*
Duke University	M,D,O*
Elms College	M,D
Georgetown University	M,D
Goldfarb School of Nursing at Barnes-Jewish College	M
Grand Canyon University	M,D,O
Indiana University–Purdue University Indianapolis	M
Inter American University of Puerto Rico, Arecibo Campus	M
Inter American University of Puerto Rico, Barranquitas Campus	M
Marquette University	M,D,O
Maryville University of Saint Louis	M,D
Moravian College	M
Mount Carmel College of Nursing	M,D
New York University	M,D,O*
Northeastern University	M,D,O
Point Loma Nazarene University	M
Purdue University Northwest	M
San Francisco State University	M,O
Southern Adventist University	M,D
Tennessee Technological University	D
Texas Tech University Health Sciences Center	M,D,O
Texas Woman's University	M,D
Universidad de Iberoamerica	M,D
The University of Alabama in Huntsville	M,D,O
University of Central Florida	M,D,O
University of Cincinnati	M,D
University of Guelph	M,D,O
University of Illinois at Chicago	M,O
University of Miami	M,D*
The University of North Carolina at Charlotte	M,D,O
University of Northern Colorado	M,D
University of Pennsylvania	M*
University of Pittsburgh	M,D*
University of Puerto Rico–Medical Sciences Campus	M
University of Rhode Island	M,D,O*
University of Rochester	M,D*
University of South Africa	M,D
University of South Carolina	M,O
University of South Florida	M,D,O*
The University of Texas Health Science Center at San Antonio	M,D,O
University of Virginia	M,D
Vanderbilt University	M,D,O*
Wayne State University	M,D
Winona State University	M,D,O
Wright State University	M

ADDICTIONS/SUBSTANCE ABUSE COUNSELING

Adler Graduate School	M
Adler University	O
Alliant International University–Los Angeles	M
Antioch University New England	M
Argosy University, Hawai`i	O
Arkansas State University	M,O
Assumption College	O
Bay Path University	M
Cambridge College	M,O
Capella University	M,D
The College of New Jersey	M,O
College of St. Joseph	M
The College of William and Mary	M,D*
Coppin State University	M
East Carolina University	M,D,O
Fairfield University	M,O
The George Washington University	M
Governors State University	M
Hazelden Betty Ford Graduate School of Addiction Studies	M,O
Hofstra University	M,O
Houston Baptist University	M
Indiana University Northwest	M,O
Indiana University South Bend	M,O
Indiana Wesleyan University	M
Johnson & Wales University	M
Kean University	M
Lenoir-Rhyne University	M
Lewis & Clark College	M
Liberty University	M,D,O
Loma Linda University	M,D,O
Long Island University–Hudson	M,O
Maryville University of Saint Louis	M
Monmouth University	M,O*
Montclair State University	O
Northern Vermont University–Johnson	M
Northwest Nazarene University	M
Nova Southeastern University	M,D,O*
Oral Roberts University	M,D
Pace University	M,D
Palm Beach Atlantic University	M
Plymouth State University	M
Post University	M
Regent University	M,D,O
Rider University	M,O
Saint Mary's University of Minnesota	M,O
Salve Regina University	M,O
Stephens College	M,O
Stony Brook University, State University of New York	M,O
Syracuse University	M,O*
Texas Tech University Health Sciences Center	M
United States International University–Africa	M
Universidad Central del Caribe	M
University of California, Berkeley	O
University of Central Oklahoma	M
University of Cincinnati	M,D,O
University of Detroit Mercy	M,D,O
University of Illinois at Springfield	M,O
University of Lethbridge	M,D
University of Louisville	M,D,O
University of Nevada, Las Vegas	M,D,O
University of New Hampshire	M,O
The University of North Carolina at Charlotte	M,D,O
University of Oklahoma	M*

*M—masters degree; D—doctorate; O—other advanced degree; *—Close-Up and/or Display*

University of South Dakota	M
University of Southern Maine	M,O
University of South Florida	M,D*
The University of Tennessee at Martin	M
Viterbo University	M
Walden University	M,D
Washburn University	M
Waynesburg University	M,D
Winona State University	M,O

ADULT EDUCATION

Alverno College	M
Antioch University Seattle	M
Argosy University, Chicago	M,D,O
Argosy University, Hawai'i	M,D
Argosy University, Phoenix	M,D,O
Argosy University, Seattle	M,D
Athabasca University	M,O
Auburn University	M,D,O*
Aurora University	M,D
Ball State University	M,D
Buffalo State College, State University of New York	M,O
California Baptist University	M
Capella University	M,D
Carroll University	M
Chicago State University	M
Cleveland State University	M,D,O
Colorado State University	M,D
Concordia University (Canada)	M,O
Coppin State University	M
Cornell University	M,D
Dallas Theological Seminary	M,D,O
Delaware State University	M
DePaul University	M
East Carolina University	M,O
Eastern Washington University	M
Edgewood College	M,D,O
Florida Agricultural and Mechanical University	M,D
Florida Atlantic University	M,D,O
Florida International University	M,D,O
The George Washington University	O
Georgia Southern University–Armstrong Campus	M,O
Grand Valley State University	M
Indiana University of Pennsylvania	M
Instituto Tecnologico de Santo Domingo	M,O
Kansas State University	M,D,O
Lesley University	M,D,O
Marshall University	M
Memorial University of Newfoundland	M,D,O
Merrimack College	M,O
Michigan State University	M,D,O
Montana State University	M,D,O
Morehead State University	M,O
Mount Saint Vincent University	M
National Louis University	M,D,O
North Carolina Agricultural and Technical State University	M
North Carolina State University	M,D
Northern Illinois University	M,D
Northwestern Oklahoma State University	M
Northwestern State University of Louisiana	M
Oregon State University	M,D
Penn State Harrisburg	M,D,O
Penn State University Park	M,D,O*
Plymouth State University	D
Point Park University	M,D
Regent University	M,D,O
St. Francis Xavier University	M
Saint Joseph's College of Maine	M
San Francisco State University	M
Seattle University	M,O
Southern Arkansas University–Magnolia	M
State University of New York Empire State College	M
Teachers College, Columbia University	M,D
Texas A&M University–Kingsville	M
Texas A&M University–Texarkana	M
Texas State University	M,D
Trident University International	M,D
Troy University	M
Universidad del Este	M
Universidad Metropolitana	M
University of Alberta	M,D,O
University of Arkansas	M,D
University of Arkansas at Little Rock	M
The University of British Columbia	M,D
University of Calgary	M,D
University of Central Arkansas	M,O
University of Central Oklahoma	M
University of Colorado Denver	M
University of Connecticut	M,O*
University of Georgia	D,O
University of Houston–Victoria	M,O
University of Manitoba	M
University of Memphis	M,D,O
University of Minnesota, Twin Cities Campus	M,D,O
University of Missouri	M,D,O
University of Missouri–St. Louis	M,O
University of Nebraska–Lincoln	M,D,O
The University of North Carolina at Greensboro	M,D,O
University of North Florida	M
University of Oklahoma	M,D*
University of Phoenix–Bay Area Campus	M,D,O
University of Phoenix–Online Campus	M,O
University of Phoenix–Phoenix Campus	M
University of Phoenix–Sacramento Valley Campus	M,O
University of Regina	M
University of South Africa	M,D
University of South Dakota	M,D,O
University of Southern Maine	M,O
University of South Florida	M,D,O*
The University of Tennessee	M,D
University of the District of Columbia	O
The University of West Alabama	M
University of Wisconsin–Milwaukee	M,D,O*
University of Wisconsin–Platteville	M
Virginia Commonwealth University	M
Walden University	M,D,O
Western Kentucky University	M,D,O
Western Washington University	M
Widener University	M,D

ADULT NURSING

Adelphi University	M
Allen College	M,D
Azusa Pacific University	M,D*
Bloomsburg University of Pennsylvania	M,D
Boston College	M,D
California Baptist University	M
Clarkson College	M,O
College of Staten Island of the City University of New York	M,D,O
Columbia University	M,O*
Creighton University	M,D,O
Daemen College	M,D,O
Duke University	M,D,O*
Eastern Michigan University	M,O
Emory University	M
Felician University	M,O
Florida International University	M,D
Florida Southern College	M
George Mason University	M,D,O
The George Washington University	M,D,O
Georgia Southern University–Armstrong Campus	M,O
Georgia State University	M,D,O
Gwynedd Mercy University	M,D
Hunter College of the City University of New York	M
Indiana University–Purdue University Fort Wayne	M,O
Jacksonville University	M,D,O*
Kent State University	M,D
La Salle University	M,D,O
Lehman College of the City University of New York	M
Lewis University	M,D
Loma Linda University	M
Long Island University–LIU Brooklyn	M,O
Loyola University Chicago	M,D,O
Madonna University	M
Marian University (WI)	M
Marquette University	M,D,O
Maryville University of Saint Louis	M,D
Medical University of South Carolina	M,D
Monmouth University	M,D,O*
Mount Carmel College of Nursing	M,D
Mount Saint Mary College	M,O
Neumann University	M,O
New York University	M,D,O*
North Park University	M
Nova Southeastern University	M,D*
Old Dominion University	M,D
Purdue University Northwest	M
Quinnipiac University	D
Research College of Nursing	M
Rush University	D,O
Rutgers University–Newark	M,D,O
St. Catherine University	M,D
St. Joseph's College, Long Island Campus	M
St. Joseph's College, New York	M
Saint Mary's College	D
Saint Peter's University	M,D,O
Seattle Pacific University	M,O
Seton Hall University	M,D
Shenandoah University	M,D,O
Southern Adventist University	M,D
South University	M
Spalding University	M,D,O
Stony Brook University, State University of New York	M,D,O
Temple University	D*
Texas Christian University	M,O
Texas Woman's University	M,D
Troy University	M,D
Universidad del Turabo	M,O
University at Buffalo, the State University of New York	M,D,O
The University of Alabama at Birmingham	M,D
University of Central Arkansas	M,O
University of Cincinnati	M,D
University of Colorado Colorado Springs	M,D
University of Colorado Denver	M,D
University of Delaware	M,O*
University of Hawaii at Manoa	M,D,O
University of Illinois at Chicago	M,O
The University of Kansas	M,D,O
University of Massachusetts Amherst	M,D*
University of Massachusetts Medical School	M,D,O
University of Miami	M,D*
University of Missouri	M,D,O
University of Missouri–Kansas City	M,D
University of Missouri–St. Louis	D,O
The University of North Carolina at Chapel Hill	M,D,O
The University of North Carolina at Greensboro	M,D,O
University of Pennsylvania	M*
University of Puerto Rico–Medical Sciences Campus	M
University of Rhode Island	M,D,O*
University of Rochester	M,D*
University of San Diego	M,D
University of South Carolina	M
University of Southern Maine	M,D,O
University of South Florida	M,D,O*
The University of Tampa	M
The University of Texas at Austin	M,D
The University of Texas Rio Grande Valley	M,O
University of Wisconsin–Eau Claire	M,D
University of Wisconsin–Madison	D
University of Wisconsin–Oshkosh	M
Ursuline College	M,D
Vanderbilt University	M,D,O*
Villanova University	M,D,O
Virginia Commonwealth University	M,D,O
Walden University	M,D,O
Walsh University	M,D
Wayne State University	M,D
Western Connecticut State University	M,D
William Paterson University of New Jersey	M,D,O
Wilmington University	M,D
Winona State University	M,D,O
Wright State University	M

ADVERTISING AND PUBLIC RELATIONS

Academy of Art University	M
Arcadia University	M
Ball State University	M
Boston University	M*
California Baptist University	M
Central Connecticut State University	M,O
Clarion University of Pennsylvania	O
Colorado State University	M,D
DePaul University	M
Georgetown University	M
Hofstra University	M
Iona College	M,O
Kansas State University	M
Kent State University	M
La Salle University	M,O
Lasell College	M,O
La Sierra University	M
Liberty University	M,D
Lindenwood University	M
Marquette University	M,O
Marshall University	M,O
Michigan State University	M,D
Mississippi College	M
Monmouth University	M,O*
Montana State University Billings	M
Montclair State University	M
Murray State University	M
New York University	M*
Northern Kentucky University	M,O
Quinnipiac University	M
Rowan University	M
San Diego State University	M
Savannah College of Art and Design	M
Seton Hall University	M
Southeastern Louisiana University	M
Southern Illinois University Edwardsville	M
Southern Methodist University	M
Southern New Hampshire University	M,D,O
Suffolk University	M
Syracuse University	M*
Universidad Autonoma de Guadalajara	M,D
Université Laval	O
University of Colorado Boulder	M,D
University of Florida	M,D
University of Houston	M
University of Illinois at Urbana–Champaign	M
University of Maryland, College Park	M,D
University of Miami	M,D*
University of Nebraska–Lincoln	M,D
University of North Texas	M,D,O
University of Saint Mary	M
University of Southern California	M*
The University of Tennessee	M,D
The University of Texas at Austin	M,D
University of the Sacred Heart	M
University of Wisconsin–Stevens Point	M
Virginia Commonwealth University	M
Virginia International University	M,O
Wayne State University	M,D,O
Webster University	M
Western New England University	M
William Woods University	M,D,O

AEROSPACE/AERONAUTICAL ENGINEERING

Air Force Institute of Technology	M,D
Arizona State University at the Tempe campus	M,D
Auburn University	M,D*
California Institute of Technology	M,D,O
California Polytechnic State University, San Luis Obispo	M*
California State Polytechnic University, Pomona	M
Carleton University	M,D
Case Western Reserve University	M,D*
The Citadel, The Military College of South Carolina	M,O
Concordia University (Canada)	M
Cornell University	M,D
École Polytechnique de Montréal	M,D,O
Embry-Riddle Aeronautical University–Daytona	M,D
Embry-Riddle Aeronautical University–Worldwide	M
Florida Institute of Technology	M,D
The George Washington University	M,D,O
Georgia Institute of Technology	M,D
Illinois Institute of Technology	M,D
Inter American University of Puerto Rico, Bayamón Campus	M
Iowa State University of Science and Technology	M,D
Johns Hopkins University	M*
Massachusetts Institute of Technology	M,D,O
McGill University	M,D
Middle Tennessee State University	M
Mississippi State University	M,D
Missouri University of Science and Technology	M,D
Naval Postgraduate School	M,D,O
New Mexico State University	M,D
North Carolina State University	M,D
The Ohio State University	M,D
Old Dominion University	M,D
Penn State University Park	M,D*
Princeton University	M,D
Purdue University	M,D
Rensselaer Polytechnic Institute	M,D
Rutgers University–New Brunswick	M,D
San Diego State University	M,D
San Jose State University	M
Stanford University	M,D,O
Stevens Institute of Technology	M,O
Syracuse University	M,D*
Texas A&M University	M,D
Université Laval	M
University at Buffalo, the State University of New York	M,D
The University of Alabama	M,D
The University of Alabama in Huntsville	M,D
The University of Arizona	M,D
University of California, Davis	M,D,O
University of California, Irvine	M,D
University of California, Los Angeles	M,D*
University of California, San Diego	M,D*
University of Central Florida	M
University of Central Missouri	M,D,O
University of Cincinnati	M,D
University of Colorado Boulder	M,D
University of Colorado Colorado Springs	M,D
University of Dayton	M,D
University of Florida	M,D
University of Illinois at Urbana–Champaign	M,D
The University of Kansas	M,D
The University of Manchester	M,D
University of Maryland, College Park	M,D
University of Miami	M,D*
University of Michigan	M,D*
University of Minnesota, Twin Cities Campus	M,D
University of Missouri	M,D
University of Nevada, Las Vegas	M,D,O
University of Notre Dame	M,D
University of Oklahoma	M,D*
University of Ottawa	M,D
University of Puerto Rico–Mayagüez	M,D
University of Southern California	M,D,O*
The University of Tennessee	M,D
The University of Texas at Arlington	M,D
The University of Texas at Austin	M,D
University of Toronto	M,D
University of Virginia	M,D
University of Washington	M,D
Utah State University	M,D
Virginia Polytechnic Institute and State University	M,D,O
Washington University in St. Louis	M,D
Webster University	M,D,O
Western Michigan University	M,D
West Virginia University	M,D
Wichita State University	M,D
Worcester Polytechnic Institute	M,D
Wright State University	M

AFRICAN-AMERICAN STUDIES

Boston University	M*
Carnegie Mellon University	D
Clark Atlanta University	M,D
Columbia University	M,D*
Cornell University	M,D
Eastern Michigan University	O
Georgia State University	M
Harvard University	D*
Indiana University Bloomington	M,D
Michigan State University	M,D
Morgan State University	M,D
North Carolina Agricultural and Technical State University	M
Northwestern University	D
Oblate School of Theology	M,D,O
The Ohio State University	M,D
Rutgers University–New Brunswick	D
Syracuse University	M*
Temple University	M,D*
Trinity Lutheran Seminary	M

University at Albany, State University of New York	M
University of California, Berkeley	D
University of California, Los Angeles	M*
University of California, Santa Barbara	D
The University of Kansas	M,O
University of Louisville	M
University of Massachusetts Amherst	M,D*
University of Memphis	M,D,O
University of Wisconsin–Madison	M
Wayne State University	M,D,O
Yale University	D

AFRICAN STUDIES

Arizona State University at the Tempe campus	M,D,O
California State University, Long Beach	M
Carnegie Mellon University	D
Claremont Graduate University	M,D,O
College of Staten Island of the City University of New York	M
Columbia University	M,D*
Cornell University	M,D
Florida International University	M
Harvard University	D*
Howard University	M,D
Indiana University Bloomington	M
Lehigh University	M,O
Michigan State University	M,D
New York University	M,D,O*
Northwestern University	O
The Ohio State University	M,D
Ohio University	M
Rice University	D
Rutgers University–New Brunswick	D
Stony Brook University, State University of New York	M,O
Syracuse University	M*
University at Albany, State University of New York	M
The University of Arizona	M,D,O
University of California, Los Angeles	M*
University of Illinois at Urbana–Champaign	M
The University of Kansas	M,O
University of Louisville	M
University of Michigan	M*
The University of North Carolina at Charlotte	O
University of Pennsylvania	M,D*
University of Pittsburgh	O*
University of South Florida	M,D,O*
The University of Texas at Austin	M,D
University of Wisconsin–Madison	M,D
University of Wisconsin–Milwaukee	D*
Yale University	M

AGRICULTURAL ECONOMICS AND AGRIBUSINESS

Alcorn State University	M
American University of Beirut	M
Arizona State University at the Tempe campus	D
Auburn University	M*
Colorado State University	M,D
Cornell University	M,D
Delaware Valley University	M
Illinois State University	M
Instituto Centroamericano de Administración de Empresas	M
Iowa State University of Science and Technology	M,D
Kansas State University	M,D
Louisiana State University and Agricultural & Mechanical College	M,D
McGill University	M
Michigan State University	M,D
Mississippi State University	M
New Mexico State University	M,D
North Carolina Agricultural and Technical State University	M
North Carolina State University	M
North Dakota State University	M*
Northwest Missouri State University	M
The Ohio State University	M,D
Oklahoma State University	M,D
Penn State University Park	M,D,O*
Purdue University	M,D
Rutgers University–New Brunswick	M
South Carolina State University	M
Southern Illinois University Carbondale	M
Texas A&M University	M,D
Texas A&M University–Kingsville	M,D
Texas Tech University	M,D
Tropical Agriculture Research and Higher Education Center	M,D
Tuskegee University	M
Universidad del Este	M
Université Laval	M
University of Alberta	M,D
The University of Arizona	M
University of Arkansas	M
The University of British Columbia	M
University of California, Berkeley	D
University of California, Davis	M,D
University of California, Santa Barbara	M,D
University of Connecticut	M,D*
University of Delaware	M*
University of Florida	M,D
University of Georgia	M,D
University of Guelph	M,D
University of Idaho	M
University of Illinois at Urbana–Champaign	M,D
University of Kentucky	M,D
University of Maine	M
University of Manitoba	M,D
University of Maryland, College Park	M,D
University of Massachusetts Amherst	M,D*
University of Missouri	M,D
University of Nebraska–Lincoln	M,D
University of Nevada, Reno	M,D
University of Puerto Rico–Mayagüez	M
University of Saskatchewan	M,D,O
The University of Tennessee at Martin	M
University of Vermont	M
University of Wisconsin–Madison	M,D
University of Wyoming	M
Utah State University	M,D
Virginia Polytechnic Institute and State University	M,D
Washington State University	M,D,O
West Texas A&M University	M

AGRICULTURAL EDUCATION

Alcorn State University	M,O
Arkansas State University	M,O
California Polytechnic State University, San Luis Obispo	M*
California State University, Chico	M
Clemson University	M,D
Colorado State University	M
Cornell University	M,D
Eastern Kentucky University	M
Iowa State University of Science and Technology	M,D
Ithaca College	M
Kansas State University	M
Louisiana State University and Agricultural & Mechanical College	M,D
Mississippi State University	M,D
Montana State University	M
Murray State University	M,O
New Mexico State University	M
North Carolina Agricultural and Technical State University	M
North Carolina State University	M,O
North Dakota State University	M*
Northwest Missouri State University	M
The Ohio State University	M
Oklahoma State University	M,D
Oregon State University	M,D
Penn State University Park	M,D,O*
Purdue University	M,D,O
Saint Leo University	M
South Dakota State University	M
State University of New York at Oswego	M
Stephen F. Austin State University	M
Tennessee State University	M,D
Texas A&M University	M,D
Texas State University	M
Texas Tech University	M,D
The University of Arizona	M,O
University of Arkansas	M
University of Connecticut	M,D*
University of Delaware	M*
University of Florida	M,D
University of Illinois at Urbana–Champaign	M
University of Missouri	M,D,O
University of Nebraska–Lincoln	M
University of Puerto Rico–Mayagüez	M
The University of Tennessee	M
University of Wisconsin–River Falls	M
Utah State University	M
West Virginia University	M,D

AGRICULTURAL ENGINEERING

Cornell University	M,D
Dalhousie University	M,D
Illinois Institute of Technology	M
Instituto Tecnológico y de Estudios Superiores de Monterrey, Campus Monterrey	M,D
Iowa State University of Science and Technology	M,D
Kansas State University	M,D
Louisiana State University and Agricultural & Mechanical College	M,D
McGill University	M,D
New York University	M,D*
North Carolina State University	M,D,O
The Ohio State University	M,D
Oklahoma State University	M,D
Oregon State University	M,D
Penn State University Park	M,D*
Purdue University	M,D
South Dakota State University	M,D
Texas A&M University	M,D
Université Laval	M
The University of Arizona	M,D
University of Arkansas	M,D
University of Florida	M,D,O
University of Illinois at Urbana–Champaign	M,D
University of Kentucky	M,D
University of Missouri	M,D
University of Nebraska–Lincoln	M,D
The University of Tennessee	M
University of Wisconsin–Madison	M,D
Virginia Polytechnic Institute and State University	M,D
Washington State University	M,D

AGRICULTURAL SCIENCES—GENERAL

Alabama Agricultural and Mechanical University	M,D
Alcorn State University	M
Angelo State University	M
Arkansas State University	M,O
Auburn University	M,D*
Brigham Young University	M,D
California Polytechnic State University, San Luis Obispo	M*
California State Polytechnic University, Pomona	M
California State University, Chico	M
Clemson University	M,D
Colorado State University	M,D
Dalhousie University	M
Illinois State University	M
Instituto Tecnológico y de Estudios Superiores de Monterrey, Campus Monterrey	M,D
Iowa State University of Science and Technology	M,D
Kansas State University	M,D,O
Louisiana State University and Agricultural & Mechanical College	M,D
Louisiana Tech University	M,D,O
McGill University	M,D,O
McNeese State University	M
Michigan State University	M,D
Mississippi State University	M,D
Missouri State University	M
Montana State University	M,D
Morehead State University	M
Murray State University	M,O
New Mexico State University	M,D
North Carolina Agricultural and Technical State University	M
North Carolina State University	M,D,O
North Dakota State University	M,D*
Northwest Missouri State University	M
The Ohio State University	M,D
Oklahoma State University	M,D
Penn State University Park	M,D,O*
Prairie View A&M University	M
Purdue University	M,D
Sam Houston State University	M
South Dakota State University	M,D
Southern Arkansas University–Magnolia	M
Southern Illinois University Carbondale	M
Southern University and Agricultural and Mechanical College	M
Tarleton State University	M
Tennessee State University	M,D
Tennessee Technological University	D
Texas A&M University	M,D
Texas A&M University–Commerce	M
Texas A&M University–Kingsville	M,D
Texas Tech University	M,D
Tropical Agriculture Research and Higher Education Center	M,D
Universidad Nacional Pedro Henríquez Ureña	M
Université Laval	M,D,O
University of Alberta	M,D
The University of Arizona	M,D,O
University of Arkansas	M,D
The University of British Columbia	M,D
University of California, Davis	M
University of Connecticut	M,D*
University of Delaware	M,D*
University of Florida	M,D,O
University of Georgia	M,D
University of Guelph	M,D,O
University of Hawaii at Manoa	M,D
University of Illinois at Urbana–Champaign	M
The University of Iowa	M,D,O*
University of Kentucky	M,D
University of Lethbridge	M,D
University of Maine	M,D,O
University of Manitoba	M,D
University of Maryland, College Park	M,D
University of Maryland Eastern Shore	M,D
University of Minnesota, Twin Cities Campus	M,D
University of Missouri	M,D
University of Nebraska–Lincoln	M,D
University of Nevada, Reno	M,D
University of New Hampshire	M,D
University of Puerto Rico–Mayagüez	M
University of Saskatchewan	M,D,O
University of South Africa	M,D
The University of Tennessee	M,D
The University of Tennessee at Martin	M
The University of Texas Rio Grande Valley	M
University of Vermont	M,D,O
University of Wisconsin–Madison	M,D
University of Wisconsin–River Falls	M
University of Wyoming	M,D
Utah State University	M,D
Virginia Polytechnic Institute and State University	M,D,O
Western Kentucky University	M
West Texas A&M University	M,D
West Virginia University	M,D

AGRONOMY AND SOIL SCIENCES

Alabama Agricultural and Mechanical University	M,D
Alcorn State University	M
Auburn University	M,D*
Colorado State University	M,D
Cornell University	M,D
Dalhousie University	M
Iowa State University of Science and Technology	M,D
Kansas State University	M,D,O
McGill University	M,D
Michigan State University	M,D
Mississippi State University	M,D
North Carolina Agricultural and Technical State University	M
North Carolina State University	M,D
North Dakota State University	M,D*
The Ohio State University	M,D
Oklahoma State University	M,D
Oregon State University	M,D
Penn State University Park	M,D*
Purdue University	M,D
South Dakota State University	M,D
Southern Illinois University Carbondale	M
Tennessee State University	M,D
Texas A&M University	M,D
Texas A&M University–Kingsville	M
Texas Tech University	M,D
Tuskegee University	M
Université Laval	M,D
University of Alberta	M,D
The University of Arizona	M,D,O
University of Arkansas	M,D
The University of British Columbia	M,D
University of California, Davis	M,D
University of California, Riverside	M,D
University of Connecticut	M,D*
University of Delaware	M,D*
University of Florida	M,D
University of Georgia	M,D
University of Guelph	M,D
University of Illinois at Urbana–Champaign	M,D
University of Kentucky	M,D
University of Manitoba	M,D
University of Minnesota, Twin Cities Campus	M,D
University of Nebraska–Lincoln	M,D
University of Puerto Rico–Mayagüez	M
University of Saskatchewan	M,D,O
University of Vermont	M,D,O
University of Wisconsin–Madison	M,D
University of Wyoming	M,D
Utah State University	M,D
Virginia Polytechnic Institute and State University	M,D
Washington State University	M,D,O
West Virginia University	M,D

ALLIED HEALTH—GENERAL

Alabama State University	M,D
American College of Healthcare Sciences	M,O
Andrews University	M
Athabasca University	M,O
A.T. Still University	M,D,O
Augusta University	D
Baylor University	M,D
Belmont University	M,D
Bennington College	O
Boston University	M,D*
Brock University	M,O
Canisius College	M,O
Cleveland State University	M
Concordia University, St. Paul	M,D
Creighton University	M,D
Dominican College	M,D
Drexel University	M,D,O*
Duquesne University	M,D,O
East Carolina University	M,D,O
Eastern Kentucky University	M
East Tennessee State University	M
Emory University	M,D
Ferris State University	M
Florida Agricultural and Mechanical University	M,D
Florida Gulf Coast University	M,D
Georgia Southern University	M,D,O
Georgia State University	M
Grand Valley State University	M,D
Hampton University	M
Harding University	M,D
Howard University	M,D
Idaho State University	M,D,O
Ithaca College	M,D
Jacksonville University	M,D*
Loma Linda University	M,D
Long Island University–LIU Post	M,O
Marymount University	M,D,O
Maryville University of Saint Louis	M,D,O
Medical University of South Carolina	M,D
Mercy College	M,D
Midwestern University, Glendale Campus	M,D

*M—masters degree; D—doctorate; O—other advanced degree; *—Close-Up and/or Display*

Minnesota State University Mankato	M,D,O
Misericordia University	M,D
Moravian College	M
New Jersey City University	M
Northeastern University	M,D,O
Northern Arizona University	M,D,O
Northern Kentucky University	M
Nova Southeastern University	M,D*
Oakland University	M,D,O
The Ohio State University	M
Old Dominion University	M,D
Oregon State University	M,D
Purdue University	M,D
Quinnipiac University	M
Regis University	M,D,O
Rosalind Franklin University of Medicine and Science	M,D,O
Rutgers University–Newark	M,D,O
Saint Louis University	M,D,O*
Sam Houston State University	M
Seton Hall University	D
Shenandoah University	M,D,O
South Carolina State University	M
Southwestern Oklahoma State University	M
Temple University	M,D*
Tennessee State University	M,D,O
Texas Christian University	M,D,O
Texas State University	M,D
Texas Woman's University	M,D
Towson University	M
University at Buffalo, the State University of New York	M,D,O
The University of Alabama at Birmingham	M,D,O
University of Detroit Mercy	M,D,O
University of Florida	M,D,O
University of Illinois at Chicago	M,D,O
The University of Kansas	M,D,O
University of Kentucky	M,D
University of Maryland, Baltimore	M
University of Massachusetts Lowell	M,D
University of Memphis	M,O
University of Mississippi Medical Center	M
University of Nebraska Medical Center	M,D,O
University of Nevada, Las Vegas	M,D,O
University of New Mexico	M,D,O
The University of North Carolina at Chapel Hill	M,D
University of Northern Iowa	M,D
University of North Florida	M,D,O
University of Oklahoma Health Sciences Center	M,D,O
University of Phoenix–Las Vegas Campus	M
University of Puerto Rico–Medical Sciences Campus	M,D,O
University of South Alabama	M,D
University of South Dakota	M,D,O
The University of Tennessee Health Science Center	M,D
The University of Texas at El Paso	D
The University of Texas Medical Branch	M,D
University of Vermont	M,D,O
University of Wisconsin–Milwaukee	M,D,O*
Virginia Commonwealth University	D
Western University of Health Sciences	M,D
Wichita State University	M,D

ALLOPATHIC MEDICINE

Albany Medical College	D
Albert Einstein College of Medicine	D
American University of Beirut	M,D
Augusta University	D
Baylor College of Medicine	D
Boston University	D*
Brown University	D
California Northstate University	D
Case Western Reserve University	D*
Charles R. Drew University of Medicine and Science	D
Columbia University	M,D*
Creighton University	D
Dalhousie University	M,D
Dartmouth College	D*
Drexel University	D*
Duke University	D*
East Carolina University	D
Eastern Virginia Medical School	D
East Tennessee State University	D
Emory University	D
Florida International University	M,D
Florida State University	D
Geisinger Commonwealth School of Medicine	D
Georgetown University	D
The George Washington University	D
Harvard University	D*
Hofstra University	D
Howard University	D
Icahn School of Medicine at Mount Sinai	D
Indiana University–Purdue University Indianapolis	M,D
Instituto Tecnologico de Santo Domingo	M,D
Johns Hopkins University	D*
Loma Linda University	M,D
Louisiana State University Health Sciences Center	M,D
Louisiana State University Health Sciences Center at Shreveport	D
Marshall University	D
Mayo Clinic School of Medicine	D
McGill University	M,D
Medical College of Wisconsin	D
Medical University of South Carolina	D
Meharry Medical College	D
Mercer University	M,D
Michigan State University	D
Morehouse School of Medicine	D
New York Medical College	D
New York University	M,D*
Northeast Ohio Medical University	D
Northwestern University	
Nova Southeastern University	D*
The Ohio State University	D
Oregon Health & Science University	D
Penn State Hershey Medical Center	M,D
Ponce Health Sciences University	D
Pontificia Universidad Catolica Madre y Maestra	D
Queen's University at Kingston	D
Quinnipiac University	D
Rosalind Franklin University of Medicine and Science	D
Rowan University	D
Rush University	D
Rutgers University–Newark	D
Rutgers University–New Brunswick	D
Saint Louis University	D*
San Juan Bautista School of Medicine	M,D
Seton Hall University	D
Stanford University	D
State University of New York Downstate Medical Center	M,D
State University of New York Upstate Medical University	D
Stony Brook University, State University of New York	D
Temple University	D*
Texas A&M University	M,D
Texas Tech University Health Sciences Center	D
Texas Tech University Health Sciences Center El Paso	D
Thomas Jefferson University	D
Tufts University	D*
Tulane University	D
Uniformed Services University of the Health Sciences	M,D*
Universidad Autonoma de Guadalajara	D
Universidad Central del Caribe	M,D
Universidad Central del Este	D
Universidad de Ciencias Medicas	M,D,O
Universidad de Iberoamerica	M,D
Universidad Iberoamericana	D
Universidad Nacional Pedro Henriquez Urena	D
Université de Montréal	D
Université de Sherbrooke	D
Université Laval	D,O
University at Buffalo, the State University of New York	D
The University of Alabama at Birmingham	D
The University of Arizona	M,D
University of Arkansas for Medical Sciences	D
The University of British Columbia	M,D
University of Calgary	D
University of California, Berkeley	
University of California, Davis	D
University of California, Irvine	D
University of California, Los Angeles	D*
University of California, Riverside	D
University of California, San Diego	D*
University of California, San Francisco	D
University of Central Florida	M,D
University of Chicago	D
University of Cincinnati	D
University of Colorado Denver	D
University of Connecticut Health Center	D
University of Florida	D
University of Hawaii at Manoa	D
University of Illinois at Chicago	D
The University of Iowa	D*
The University of Kansas	D
University of Kentucky	D
University of Louisville	D
University of Lynchburg	D
University of Manitoba	M
University of Maryland, Baltimore	D
University of Massachusetts Medical School	D
University of Miami	D*
University of Michigan	D*
University of Minnesota, Duluth	D
University of Minnesota, Twin Cities Campus	M,D
University of Mississippi Medical Center	D
University of Missouri	D
University of Missouri–Kansas City	M,D
University of Nebraska Medical Center	D,O
University of Nevada, Reno	D
University of New Mexico	D
The University of North Carolina at Chapel Hill	D
University of Oklahoma Health Sciences Center	D
University of Ottawa	M,D
University of Pennsylvania	D*
University of Pittsburgh	D*
University of Puerto Rico–Medical Sciences Campus	D
University of Rochester	D*
University of Saskatchewan	D
University of South Alabama	D
University of South Carolina	D
University of South Dakota	D,O
University of Southern California	D*
University of South Florida	M,D*
The University of Tennessee Health Science Center	D
The University of Texas at Austin	D
The University of Texas Health Science Center at Houston	D
The University of Texas Health Science Center at San Antonio	M,D
The University of Texas Medical Branch	D
The University of Texas Rio Grande Valley	D
The University of Texas Southwestern Medical Center	D
University of Toronto	M,D
University of Utah	D
University of Vermont	M,D,O
University of Virginia	M,D
University of Washington	D
The University of Western Ontario	M,D
University of Wisconsin–Madison	D
Vanderbilt University	M,D*
Virginia Commonwealth University	D
Wake Forest University	D
Washington State University	M,D
Washington University in St. Louis	D
Wayne State University	D
West Virginia University	M,D
Wright State University	D
Yale University	D

AMERICAN INDIAN/NATIVE AMERICAN STUDIES

Central Michigan University	M
Montana State University	M
Navajo Technical University	M
Northeastern State University	M
Northern Arizona University	O
Trent University	M,D
The University of Arizona	M,D
University of California, Davis	M,D
University of California, Los Angeles	M*
The University of Kansas	M,O
University of Lethbridge	M,D
University of Manitoba	M
University of New Mexico	M,D
University of Oklahoma	M*
University of South Dakota	M,D,O
The University of Tulsa	M,D,O

AMERICAN STUDIES

American Public University System	M,D
American University	M,D,O
Appalachian State University	M
Baylor University	M
Boston University	D*
Bowling Green State University	M,D
Brown University	M,D
California State University, Fullerton	M
The Catholic University of America	M,D
Central Michigan University	M,O
Claremont Graduate University	M,D,O
Clark University	D
The College at Brockport, State University of New York	M
College of Staten Island of the City University of New York	M
The College of William and Mary	M,D*
The Colorado College	M
Columbia University	M,D*
Cornell University	M,D
Drew University	M,D,O
East Carolina University	M
Emory & Henry College	M,D
Fairfield University	M
Florida State University	M,D
Georgetown University	M,D
The George Washington University	M,D
Georgia Southern University–Armstrong Campus	M
Harvard University	D*
Indiana University–Purdue University Indianapolis	M,D
Inter American University of Puerto Rico, Metropolitan Campus	M,D
James Madison University	M
Kennesaw State University	M
Lake Forest College	M
La Salle University	M,O
Lehigh University	M,D,O
Michigan State University	M,D
Monmouth University	M*
New Mexico Highlands University	M
New York University	M,D*
Northwestern Oklahoma State University	M
Northwestern University	M
Penn State Harrisburg	M,D,O
Pepperdine University	M
Portland State University	M
Providence College	M
Purdue University	M,D
Regent University	M
Rice University	D
Rutgers University–Newark	M,D
Saint Louis University	M,D*
Salisbury University	M
Stockton University	M,O
Texas Christian University	M,D
Trinity College (United States)	M
Universidad de las Américas Puebla	M
University at Buffalo, the State University of New York	M,D
The University of Alabama	M
University of Colorado Denver	M
University of Dallas	M
University of Delaware	M*
University of Hawaii at Manoa	M,D,O
The University of Iowa	M,D*
The University of Kansas	M,D
University of Louisiana at Lafayette	M,D
University of Maryland, College Park	M,D
University of Massachusetts Amherst	M,D*
University of Massachusetts Boston	M
University of Michigan	M,D*
University of Michigan–Flint	M
University of Minnesota, Twin Cities Campus	D
University of Missouri–St. Louis	M,D
University of New Mexico	M,D
University of Southern California	D*
University of Southern Maine	M,O
University of South Florida	M,D*
The University of Texas at Austin	M,D
University of Utah	M,D
University of West Florida	M
University of Wisconsin–Madison	M,D
University of Wyoming	M
Utah State University	M
Washington State University	M,D
Wilfrid Laurier University	M,D
Yale University	D

ANALYTICAL CHEMISTRY

Auburn University	M,D*
Binghamton University, State University of New York	M,D
Brigham Young University	M,D
California State University, Los Angeles	M
Cornell University	D
Eastern New Mexico University	M
Florida State University	M,D
Georgetown University	D
The George Washington University	M,D
Georgia State University	M,D
Governors State University	M
Howard University	M,D
Illinois Institute of Technology	M,D
Indiana University Bloomington	M,D
Iowa State University of Science and Technology	M,D
Laurentian University	M
Marquette University	M,D
McMaster University	M,D
Old Dominion University	M,D
Oregon State University	M,D
Purdue University	M,D
Rutgers University–Newark	M,D
Seton Hall University	M,D
Southern University and Agricultural and Mechanical College	M
Stevens Institute of Technology	M,D,O
University of Calgary	M,D
University of Cincinnati	M,D
University of Georgia	M,D
University of Louisville	M,D
The University of Manchester	M,D
University of Maryland, College Park	M,D
University of Massachusetts Lowell	M,D
University of Memphis	M,D
University of Michigan	M,D*
University of Missouri	D
University of Missouri–Kansas City	M,D
University of Montana	M,D
University of Nebraska–Lincoln	M,D
University of Oklahoma	M,D*
University of Regina	M,D
The University of Tennessee	M,D
The University of Texas at Austin	D
The University of Toledo	M,D
Vanderbilt University	M,D*
Virginia Commonwealth University	M,D
Wake Forest University	M,D
Wayne State University	M,D
Youngstown State University	M

ANATOMY

Albert Einstein College of Medicine	D
Augusta University	D
Barry University	M
Boston University	M,D*
Case Western Reserve University	M*
Columbia University	M,D*
Creighton University	M
Dalhousie University	M,D
Des Moines University	M
Duke University	D*
D'Youville College	M
East Tennessee State University	D
Howard University	M,D
Indiana University–Purdue University Indianapolis	M,D
Johns Hopkins University	D*
Liberty University	M,D
Loma Linda University	D
Louisiana State University Health Sciences Center	D
Louisiana State University Health Sciences Center at Shreveport	M,D
McGill University	M,D
New York Academy of Art	M
New York Chiropractic College	M*
The Ohio State University	M,D
Palmer College of Chiropractic	M
Penn State Hershey Medical Center	M,D
Purdue University	M,D
Queen's University at Kingston	M,D
Rosalind Franklin University of Medicine and Science	D
Rush University	M,D
Saint Louis University	M,D*
State University of New York Upstate Medical University	M,D

Stony Brook University, State University of New York	D
Universidad Central del Caribe	M,D
Universidad de Ciencias Medicas	M,D,O
Université Laval	O
University at Buffalo, the State University of New York	M,D
University of California, Irvine	M,D
University of California, Los Angeles	M,D*
University of Chicago	D
University of Colorado Denver	M,D
University of Connecticut Health Center	D
University of Guelph	M,D
University of Illinois at Chicago	M
The University of Iowa	D*
The University of Kansas	M,D
University of Kentucky	D
University of Louisville	M,D
University of Manitoba	M,D
University of Mississippi Medical Center	M,D
University of Missouri	M,D
University of Nebraska Medical Center	M,D
University of North Texas Health Science Center at Fort Worth	M,D
University of Prince Edward Island	M,D
University of Puerto Rico–Medical Sciences Campus	M,D
University of Rochester	D*
University of Saskatchewan	M,D
University of South Florida	M,D*
The University of Tennessee	M,D
University of Utah	D
The University of Western Ontario	M,D
Virginia Commonwealth University	M
Wake Forest University	D
Wayne State University	M,D,O
Wright State University	M
Youngstown State University	M

ANESTHESIOLOGIST ASSISTANT STUDIES

Case Western Reserve University	M*
Emory University	M
Nova Southeastern University	M,D*
Quinnipiac University	M
South University (GA)	M
Université Laval	O
University of Colorado Denver	M
University of Guelph	M,D,O

ANIMAL BEHAVIOR

Arizona State University at the Tempe campus	M,D
Bucknell University	M
Cornell University	D
Emory University	D
Hunter College of the City University of New York	M,O
Illinois State University	M,D
University of California, Davis	D
University of Massachusetts Amherst	M,D*
University of Minnesota, Twin Cities Campus	M,D
University of Montana	M,D,O
The University of Tennessee	M,D
The University of Texas at Austin	D
University of Washington	M,D

ANIMAL SCIENCES

Alcorn State University	M
American University of Beirut	M
Auburn University	M,D*
Bergin University of Canine Studies	M
Boise State University	M,D
Brigham Young University	M,D
California State University, Fresno	M
Clemson University	M,D
Colorado State University	M,D
Cornell University	M,D
Dalhousie University	M,D
Fort Valley State University	M
Iowa State University of Science and Technology	M,D
Kansas State University	M,D
Louisiana State University and Agricultural & Mechanical College	M,D
McGill University	M,D
Michigan State University	M,D
Mississippi State University	M,D
Missouri Western State University	M
Montana State University	M,D
New Mexico State University	M,D
North Carolina Agricultural and Technical State University	M
North Carolina State University	M,D
North Dakota State University	M,D*
The Ohio State University	M,D
Oklahoma State University	M,D
Oregon State University	M
Penn State University Park	M,D*
Purdue University	M,D
Rutgers University–New Brunswick	M,D
South Dakota State University	M,D
Southern Illinois University Carbondale	M
Sul Ross State University	M
Texas A&M University	M,D
Texas A&M University–Kingsville	M
Texas Tech University	M,D
Tufts University	M*
Tuskegee University	M
Universidad Nacional Pedro Henriquez Urena	M
Université Laval	M,D
The University of Arizona	M,D
University of Arkansas	M,D
The University of British Columbia	M,D
University of California, Davis	M,D
University of Connecticut	M,D*
University of Delaware	M,D*
University of Florida	M,D
University of Georgia	M,D
University of Guelph	M,D
University of Hawaii at Manoa	M
University of Idaho	M,D
University of Illinois at Urbana–Champaign	M,D
University of Kentucky	M,D
University of Manitoba	M,D
University of Maryland, College Park	M,D
University of Massachusetts Amherst	M,D*
University of Minnesota, Twin Cities Campus	M,D
University of Missouri	M,D
University of Nebraska–Lincoln	M,D
University of Nevada, Reno	M
University of New Hampshire	M,D
University of Puerto Rico–Mayagüez	M
University of Rhode Island	M,D*
University of Saskatchewan	M,D
The University of Tennessee	M,D
University of Vermont	M,D
University of Wisconsin–Madison	M,D
University of Wyoming	M,D
Utah State University	M,D
Virginia Polytechnic Institute and State University	M,D
Washington State University	M,D
West Texas A&M University	M
West Virginia University	M,D

ANTHROPOLOGY

American University	M,D,O
American University of Beirut	M,D
Arizona State University at the Tempe campus	M,D,O
Ball State University	M,O
Binghamton University, State University of New York	M,D
Biola University	M,D,O
Boise State University	M
Boston University	M,D*
Brandeis University	M,D
Brigham Young University	M
Brown University	M,D
California State University, Bakersfield	M
California State University, Chico	M
California State University, East Bay	M
California State University, Fullerton	M
California State University, Long Beach	M
California State University, Los Angeles	M
California State University, Northridge	M
California State University, Sacramento	M
Canisius College	M
Carleton University	M
Case Western Reserve University	M,D*
The Catholic University of America	M
Central European University	M,D
Central Washington University	M
Clemson University	M
The College of William and Mary	M,D*
Colorado State University	M,D
Columbia University	M,D*
Concordia University (Canada)	M,D
Cornell University	D
Creighton University	M
Dalhousie University	M,D
East Carolina University	M
Eastern New Mexico University	M
Edinboro University of Pennsylvania	M
Emory University	D
Florida Atlantic University	M
George Mason University	M,D
The George Washington University	M,D
Georgia State University	M
The Graduate Center, City University of New York	D
Harvard University	M,D*
Humboldt State University	M
Hunter College of the City University of New York	M
Idaho State University	M
Indiana University Bloomington	M,D
Iowa State University of Science and Technology	M
Johns Hopkins University	D*
Kent State University	M
Louisiana State University and Agricultural & Mechanical College	M,D
McGill University	M,D
McMaster University	M,D
Memorial University of Newfoundland	M,D
Mercyhurst University	M
Michigan State University	M,D
Minnesota State University Mankato	M
Mississippi State University	M
Monmouth University	M*
New Mexico Highlands University	M
New Mexico State University	M,O
The New School	M,D
New York University	M,D*
North Carolina State University	M
North Dakota State University	M*
Northern Arizona University	M
Northern Illinois University	M
Northwestern University	D
The Ohio State University	M,D
Oregon State University	M
Penn State University Park	M,D*
Portland State University	M,D,O
Princeton University	D
Purdue University	M,D
Rice University	M,D
Rutgers University–New Brunswick	M,D
San Diego State University	M
San Francisco State University	M
San Jose State University	M
Simon Fraser University	M,D
Sonoma State University	M
Southern Illinois University Carbondale	M,D
Southern Methodist University	M,D
Stanford University	M,D
Stony Brook University, State University of New York	M,D
Syracuse University	M,D*
Teachers College, Columbia University	M,D
Temple University	D*
Texas A&M University	M,D
Texas State University	M
Texas Tech University	M
Trent University	M
Tulane University	D
Universidad de las Américas Puebla	M
Université de Montréal	M,D
Université Laval	M,D
University at Albany, State University of New York	M,D
University at Buffalo, the State University of New York	M,D
The University of Alabama	M,D
The University of Alabama at Birmingham	M
University of Alaska Anchorage	M
University of Alaska Fairbanks	M,D
University of Alberta	M,D
The University of Arizona	M,D,O
University of Arkansas	M,D
The University of British Columbia	M,D
University of Calgary	M,D
University of California, Berkeley	D
University of California, Davis	M,D
University of California, Irvine	M,D
University of California, Los Angeles	M,D*
University of California, Riverside	M,D
University of California, San Diego	D*
University of California, San Francisco	D
University of California, Santa Barbara	M,D
University of California, Santa Cruz	D*
University of Central Florida	M
University of Chicago	D
University of Cincinnati	M
University of Colorado Boulder	M,D
University of Colorado Denver	M
University of Connecticut	M,D*
University of Denver	M
University of Florida	M,D
University of Georgia	M,D
University of Guelph	M,D
University of Hawaii at Manoa	M,D
University of Houston	M
University of Idaho	M
University of Illinois at Chicago	M,D
University of Illinois at Urbana–Champaign	M,D
University of Indianapolis	M
The University of Iowa	M,D*
The University of Kansas	M,D
University of Kentucky	M,D
University of Lethbridge	M,D
University of Louisville	M
University of Maine	D
The University of Manchester	M,D
University of Manitoba	M,D
University of Maryland, College Park	M
University of Massachusetts Amherst	M,D*
University of Memphis	M
University of Michigan	D*
University of Minnesota, Duluth	M
University of Minnesota, Twin Cities Campus	M,D
University of Mississippi	M,D
University of Missouri	M,D
University of Montana	M,D
University of Nebraska–Lincoln	M
University of Nevada, Las Vegas	M,D
University of Nevada, Reno	M,D
University of New Brunswick Fredericton	M
University of New Mexico	M,D
The University of North Carolina at Chapel Hill	M,D
The University of North Carolina at Charlotte	M
University of North Georgia	M
University of North Texas	M,D,O
University of Oklahoma	M,D*
University of Oregon	M,D
University of Ottawa	M
University of Pennsylvania	M,D*
University of Pittsburgh	M,D*
University of Regina	M
University of Rhode Island	M*
University of Saskatchewan	M
University of South Africa	M,D
University of South Carolina	M,D
University of Southern Mississippi	M
University of South Florida	M,D,O*
The University of Tennessee	M,D
The University of Texas at Arlington	M
The University of Texas at Austin	M,D
The University of Texas at El Paso	M,O
The University of Texas at San Antonio	M,D
University of Toronto	M,D
The University of Tulsa	M,D
University of Utah	M,D
University of Victoria	M
University of Virginia	M,D
University of Washington	M,D
University of Waterloo	M
The University of Western Ontario	M,D
University of West Florida	M
University of Wisconsin–Madison	D
University of Wisconsin–Milwaukee	M,D,O*
University of Wyoming	M,D
Utah State University	M,D
Vanderbilt University	M,D*
Washington State University	M,D
Washington University in St. Louis	D
Wayne State University	M,D
Western Kentucky University	M
Western Michigan University	M
Western Washington University	M
Wichita State University	M
Yale University	M,D
York University	M,D

APPLIED ARTS AND DESIGN—GENERAL

Academy of Art University	M
Alfred University	M
Arizona State University at the Tempe campus	M,D
The Art Institute of Dallas, a branch of Miami International University of Art & Design	M
Bowling Green State University	M
California College of the Arts	M
California Institute of the Arts	M,O
California State University, Fresno	M
California State University, Fullerton	M
California State University, Los Angeles	M
Carnegie Mellon University	M,D
College for Creative Studies	M
Concordia University (Canada)	M,O
Drexel University	M,D*
Emily Carr University of Art + Design	M
Fashion Institute of Technology	M
Ferris State University	M
Florida Atlantic University	M
Howard University	M
Illinois Institute of Technology	M,D
Indiana University Bloomington	M
Iowa State University of Science and Technology	M,D
Louisiana State University and Agricultural & Mechanical College	M
Maryland Institute College of Art	M
Massachusetts College of Art and Design	M,O
Miami International University of Art & Design	M
Millersville University of Pennsylvania	M
Minneapolis College of Art and Design	M
New England Institute of Technology	M
The New School	M
New York Institute of Technology	M
New York University	M*
North Carolina State University	M,D
Northeastern University	M
NSCAD University	M
Oklahoma State University	M,D
Pacific Northwest College of Art	M
Pratt Institute	M,O*
Purdue University	M,D
Rhode Island School of Design	M
Rutgers University–New Brunswick	M
San Diego State University	M
San Francisco State University	M
Savannah College of Art and Design	M
School of the Art Institute of Chicago	M
School of Visual Arts (NY)	M
Southern Illinois University Carbondale	M
Stanford University	M,D,O
Stephen F. Austin State University	M
Suffolk University	M
Syracuse University	M*
Texas State University	M
University of Alberta	M
University of Baltimore	M
University of Bridgeport	M
University of California, Berkeley	O
University of California, Los Angeles	M*
University of Central Oklahoma	M
University of Cincinnati	M

*M—masters degree; D—doctorate; O—other advanced degree; *—Close-Up and/or Display*

University of Connecticut	M*
University of Delaware	M*
University of Illinois at Chicago	M
University of Illinois at Urbana–Champaign	M,D
The University of Kansas	M
University of Kentucky	M
University of Louisville	M,D
University of Michigan	M,D*
University of Minnesota, Twin Cities Campus	M,D,O
University of North Texas	M,D,O
University of Notre Dame	M
University of Oklahoma	M,D*
University of Oregon	M
The University of Texas at Austin	M
The University of Tulsa	M
University of Washington	M
University of Wisconsin–Madison	M,D
University of Wisconsin–Milwaukee	M*
Western Carolina University	M
Western Michigan University	M
Yale University	M
York University	M

APPLIED BEHAVIOR ANALYSIS

Antioch University New England	M,O
Arcadia University	M
Arizona State University at the Tempe campus	M,D
Assumption College	M,O
Aurora University	M,D
Ball State University	M
Baylor University	M,D,O
Bay Path University	M
Cairn University	M,O
Caldwell University	M,D,O
California State University, Fresno	M,O
California State University, Sacramento	M
California State University, Stanislaus	M
Capella University	M
The Chicago School of Professional Psychology	M,D
The Chicago School of Professional Psychology at Downtown Los Angeles	M,D
College of Saint Elizabeth	M,O
Drake University	M,D,O
Drexel University	M,D*
Elms College	M,O
Endicott College	M,D,O
Fairfield University	M,O
Florida Institute of Technology	M,D
Florida International University	M,D
Florida State University	M
Georgian Court University	M,O
Hofstra University	M,D,O
James Madison University	M
Johns Hopkins University	O*
Lindenwood University	M,D,O
Lipscomb University	M,D,O
Long Island University–LIU Brooklyn	M,O
Long Island University–LIU Post	M,O
Long Island University–Riverhead	M,O
McNeese State University	M,O
Mercyhurst University	M
Missouri State University	M,O
Monmouth University	M,D,O*
Montana State University Billings	M
National University	M,O
Niagara University	M,D,O
Northeastern University	M,D,O
Northern Michigan University	M
Northern Vermont University–Johnson	M
Oakland University	M,O
Oklahoma City University	M
Oklahoma State University	M,D,O
Penn State Harrisburg	M,D,O
Philadelphia College of Osteopathic Medicine	M,D,O*
Queens College of the City University of New York	M
Regis College (MA)	M,D,O
Rollins College	M
Rowan University	M,O
Sage Graduate School	M,O
St. Cloud State University	M
Saint Louis University	M,D*
Saint Peter's University	M,D,O
Salve Regina University	M,O
Shenandoah University	M
Simmons College	M,D,O
Teachers College, Columbia University	M,D,O
Temple University	M,D,O*
Tennessee Technological University	D
University of California, Riverside	M,D,O
The University of Kansas	M,D,O
University of Louisville	M,D,O
University of Massachusetts Dartmouth	M,O
University of Memphis	M,D,O
University of Michigan–Dearborn	M
University of Nebraska at Omaha	M,D,O
University of Nebraska Medical Center	M,D
The University of North Carolina Wilmington	M,D
University of North Florida	M
University of North Texas	M,D,O
University of Oklahoma	M,D*
University of Pittsburgh	M,D*
University of San Francisco	M
University of Southern Maine	M,O
University of South Florida	M,D*
The University of Texas at San Antonio	M,O
University of Utah	M,D
University of West Florida	M
Wayne State University	M,D,O
Western New England University	M,D
Westfield State University	M
Wright State University	M
Youngstown State University	M

APPLIED ECONOMICS

Auburn University	M,D*
Auburn University at Montgomery	M
Brandeis University	M
Bryant University	M,O
Buffalo State College, State University of New York	M
Clemson University	M,D
Cornell University	M,D
DePaul University	M,D
East Carolina University	M
Florida State University	M,D
Georgia Southern University	M,O
HEC Montreal	M,D
Johns Hopkins University	M*
Mills College	M
New York University	M,D,O*
North Carolina Agricultural and Technical State University	M
Ohio University	M
Oregon State University	M,D
St. Cloud State University	M
Southern Methodist University	M,D
Southern New Hampshire University	M,D,O
Texas Tech University	M,D
Thomas Jefferson University	M,D,O
The University of Arizona	M
University of California, Los Angeles	M*
University of California, Santa Cruz	M*
University of Cincinnati	M
University of Georgia	M,D
University of Houston	M,D
University of Illinois at Urbana–Champaign	M,D
University of Massachusetts Boston	M
University of Michigan	M*
University of Minnesota, Twin Cities Campus	M,D
University of Nevada, Las Vegas	M,O
University of Nevada, Reno	M,D
University of New Brunswick Fredericton	M
The University of North Carolina at Charlotte	M,O
The University of North Carolina at Greensboro	M
University of North Dakota	M
University of Oklahoma	M,D*
University of Pennsylvania	D*
University of Regina	M
University of Vermont	M
University of Wisconsin–Madison	M,D
University of Wyoming	M
Utah State University	M,D
Virginia Polytechnic Institute and State University	M,D
Washington & Jefferson College	M,O
Western Kentucky University	M
Western Michigan University	M,D
Wright State University	M

APPLIED MATHEMATICS

Air Force Institute of Technology	M,D
Arizona State University at the Tempe campus	M,D,O
Auburn University	M,D*
Bowie State University	M
Brown University	M,D
California Baptist University	M
California Institute of Technology	M,D
California State Polytechnic University, Pomona	M
California State University, Fullerton	M
California State University, Long Beach	M,D
California State University, Los Angeles	M
California State University, Northridge	M
Case Western Reserve University	M,D*
Central European University	M,D
Claremont Graduate University	M,D
The College of William and Mary	M,D*
Colorado School of Mines	M,D
Columbia University	M,D*
Cornell University	M,D
Dalhousie University	M,D
Delaware State University	M,D
DePaul University	M,D
École Polytechnique de Montréal	M,D,O
Elizabeth City State University	M
Florida Atlantic University	M,D
Florida Institute of Technology	M,D
Florida State University	M,D
The George Washington University	M,D,O
Hampton University	M
Harvard University	M,D*
Howard University	M,D
Hunter College of the City University of New York	M
Illinois Institute of Technology	M,D
Indiana University Bloomington	M,D
Indiana University of Pennsylvania	M
Indiana University–Purdue University Fort Wayne	M,O
Indiana University–Purdue University Indianapolis	M,D
Indiana University South Bend	M,O
Inter American University of Puerto Rico, San Germán Campus	M
Iowa State University of Science and Technology	M,D
Jackson State University	M
Johns Hopkins University	M,D,O*
Kent State University	M,D
Lehigh University	M,D
Long Island University–LIU Post	M,O
Manhattan College	M
McGill University	M,D
Michigan State University	M,D
Michigan Technological University	M,D
Missouri University of Science and Technology	M,D
Montclair State University	M
Naval Postgraduate School	M,D
New Jersey Institute of Technology	M,D,O
New Mexico Institute of Mining and Technology	M,D
North Carolina Agricultural and Technical State University	M
North Carolina State University	M,D
North Dakota State University	M,D*
Northeastern Illinois University	M
Northeastern University	M,D
Northwestern University	M,D
Oakland University	M,D
Oklahoma State University	M,D
Old Dominion University	M,D
Oregon State University	M,D
Princeton University	D
Queens College of the City University of New York	M
Rensselaer Polytechnic Institute	M
Rice University	M,D
Rochester Institute of Technology	M
Rutgers University–Camden	M
Rutgers University–New Brunswick	M,D
St. John's University (NY)	M
San Diego State University	M
Santa Clara University	M,D,O
Simon Fraser University	M,D
Southern Illinois University Edwardsville	M
Southern Methodist University	M,D
Stevens Institute of Technology	M
Stony Brook University, State University of New York	M,D,O
Temple University	M,D*
Texas Christian University	M,D
Texas State University	M
Towson University	M
The University of Akron	M
The University of Alabama	M,D
The University of Alabama at Birmingham	D
The University of Alabama in Huntsville	M,D
University of Alberta	M,D,O
The University of Arizona	M,D
University of Arkansas at Little Rock	M,O
University of California, Berkeley	M,D
University of California, Davis	M,D
University of California, Irvine	M,D
University of California, Merced	M,D
University of California, San Diego	M,D*
University of California, Santa Barbara	M,D
University of California, Santa Cruz	M,D*
University of Central Arkansas	M
University of Central Missouri	M,D,O
University of Central Oklahoma	M
University of Cincinnati	M,D
University of Colorado Boulder	M,D
University of Colorado Colorado Springs	M
University of Colorado Denver	M,D
University of Connecticut	M*
University of Dayton	M
University of Delaware	M,D*
University of Georgia	M,D
University of Guelph	M,D
University of Houston	M,D
University of Illinois at Urbana–Champaign	M,D
The University of Iowa	D*
The University of Kansas	M,D,O
University of Kentucky	M,D
University of Louisville	M,D
The University of Manchester	M,D
University of Maryland, Baltimore County	M,D
University of Maryland, College Park	M,D
University of Massachusetts Amherst	M,D*
University of Memphis	M,D
University of Michigan–Dearborn	M
University of Minnesota, Duluth	M
University of Missouri	M,D
University of New Hampshire	M,D,O
The University of North Carolina at Charlotte	M,D
University of Northern Iowa	M
University of Notre Dame	M,D
University of Pennsylvania	D*
University of Pittsburgh	M,D*
University of Puerto Rico–Mayagüez	M
University of Rhode Island	M,D*
University of Southern California	M,D*
University of South Florida	M,D*
The University of Tennessee	M,D
The University of Tennessee at Chattanooga	M
The University of Texas at Arlington	M,D
The University of Texas at Austin	M,D
The University of Texas at Dallas	M,D
The University of Texas at San Antonio	M
The University of Toledo	M,D
The University of Tulsa	M
University of Washington	M,D
University of Waterloo	M,D
The University of Western Ontario	M,D
University of Wisconsin–Milwaukee	M,D*
University of Wisconsin–Stout	M
Utah State University	M,D
Virginia Commonwealth University	M
Washington State University	M,D
Wayne State University	M,D
West Chester University of Pennsylvania	M,O
Western Michigan University	M,D
Wichita State University	M,D
Worcester Polytechnic Institute	M,D,O
Wright State University	M
Yale University	M,D
York University	M,D
Youngstown State University	M

APPLIED PHYSICS

Air Force Institute of Technology	M,D
Binghamton University, State University of New York	M,D
California Institute of Technology	M,D
Carnegie Mellon University	M,D
Christopher Newport University	M
The College of William and Mary	M,D*
Colorado School of Mines	M,D
Columbia University	M,D*
Cornell University	M,D
East Carolina University	M,D
George Mason University	M,D
Georgia Southern University	M
Harvard University	M,D*
Idaho State University	M,D
Illinois Institute of Technology	M,D
Iowa State University of Science and Technology	M,D
Johns Hopkins University	M,O*
Laurentian University	M
Louisiana Tech University	M,D,O
Michigan Technological University	M,D
Naval Postgraduate School	M,D,O
New Jersey Institute of Technology	M,D,O
New York University	M*
Northern Arizona University	M,D
Northwestern University	D
Rice University	M,D
Rutgers University–Newark	M,D
Southern Illinois University Carbondale	M,D
Stanford University	M,D
Texas A&M University	M,D
Towson University	M
University of Arkansas	M,D
University of California, San Diego	M,D*
University of Massachusetts Boston	M
University of Michigan	D*
University of Missouri–St. Louis	M,D
The University of North Carolina at Charlotte	M,D
University of South Florida	M,D*
The University of Texas at Austin	M,D
University of Washington	M,D
Virginia Commonwealth University	M
Yale University	M,D

APPLIED PSYCHOLOGY

Adler University	M
Antioch University New England	M,D,O
Arizona State University at the Tempe campus	M
Athabasca University	M,O
Boston College	M,D
California State University, Chico	M
The Catholic University of America	M,D
Central Michigan University	M,D
The Chicago School of Professional Psychology: Online	M,O
Clayton State University	M
Clemson University	M,D
DEREE - The American College of Greece	M
Eastern Washington University	M
Fairfield University	M,O
Fordham University	M,O
Francis Marion University	M,O
The George Washington University	D
Laurentian University	M
Liberty University	M,D,O
London Metropolitan University	M,D
Loras College	M
Lynn University	M
Mississippi State University	M,D
New York University	M,D,O*
Oklahoma State University	M,D,O
Old Dominion University	D
Penn State Erie, The Behrend College	M
Penn State Harrisburg	M,D,O
Rutgers University–New Brunswick	M,D
Sacred Heart University	M
Saint Mary's University (Canada)	M,D
Tarleton State University	M
Teachers College, Columbia University	M,D
University of Arkansas at Little Rock	M
University of Baltimore	M
University of Calgary	M,D
University of Guelph	M,D
University of Maryland, Baltimore County	D

University of Pennsylvania	M*
University of Pittsburgh	M,D*
University of Regina	M,D
University of South Carolina Aiken	M
The University of Tennessee	M,D
The University of Texas at El Paso	M,O
The University of Texas of the Permian Basin	M
University of West Florida	M
University of Windsor	M,D
University of Wisconsin–Stout	M
Walden University	M,D,O
William James College	M,D,O

APPLIED SCIENCE AND TECHNOLOGY

The College of William and Mary	M,D*
Colorado State University–Pueblo	M
Harvard University	M,O*
Kansas State University	M,O
Louisiana State University and Agricultural & Mechanical College	M
Missouri State University	M,O
Naval Postgraduate School	M,D
Saint Mary's University (Canada)	M
Southeastern Louisiana University	M
Thomas Edison State University	M,O
University of Arkansas at Little Rock	M,D
University of California, Berkeley	D
University of California, Davis	M,D
University of Colorado Denver	M
University of Mississippi	M,D

APPLIED SOCIAL RESEARCH

American University	M,O
California State University, Dominguez Hills	M
Concordia University Irvine	M*
Florida State University	M,D
Hunter College of the City University of New York	M
Laurentian University	M
Loma Linda University	M,D
The New School	M,D
New York University	M*
Portland State University	M,D
Queens College of the City University of New York	M

APPLIED STATISTICS

American University	M,O
Bay Path University	M
Bowling Green State University	M
Brigham Young University	M
California State University, East Bay	M
California State University, Long Beach	M
Clemson University	M,D
Cleveland State University	M
Colorado School of Mines	M,D
Cornell University	M,D
DePaul University	M,D
Florida State University	M,D
Fordham University	M,D
Indiana University Bloomington	M,D
Indiana University–Purdue University Fort Wayne	M,O
Indiana University–Purdue University Indianapolis	M,D
Instituto Tecnológico y de Estudios Superiores de Monterrey, Campus Monterrey	M,D
Kennesaw State University	M
Louisiana State University and Agricultural & Mechanical College	M
Loyola University Chicago	M
McMaster University	M
Michigan State University	M,D
Minnesota State University Mankato	M
New Jersey Institute of Technology	M,D,O
New Mexico State University	M,D,O
New York University	M*
Northern Arizona University	M,O
Oakland University	M
Penn State University Park	M,D*
Portland State University	M,D,O
Rochester Institute of Technology	M,O
Rutgers University–New Brunswick	M,D
Southern Methodist University	M,D
Stevens Institute of Technology	O
Syracuse University	M*
Teachers College, Columbia University	M,D
The University of Alabama	M,D
University of Arkansas at Little Rock	M,O
University of California, Santa Barbara	M,D
University of Chicago	M
University of Colorado Denver	M,D
University of Guelph	M,D
University of Illinois at Urbana–Champaign	M,D
The University of Kansas	M,D,O
University of Memphis	M,D
University of Michigan	M,D*
The University of North Carolina Wilmington	M,O
University of Northern Colorado	M,D
University of Notre Dame	M,D
University of Pittsburgh	M,D*
University of South Carolina	M,D,O
The University of Tennessee at Chattanooga	M
The University of Texas at San Antonio	M,D
University of the Incarnate Word	M
Villanova University	M
Virginia Polytechnic Institute and State University	M,D
West Chester University of Pennsylvania	M,O
Western Illinois University	M
Worcester Polytechnic Institute	M,D,O
Wright State University	M

AQUACULTURE

American University of Beirut	M
Auburn University	M,D*
Dalhousie University	M
Kentucky State University	M
Memorial University of Newfoundland	M
Oregon State University	M,D
Purdue University	M,D
Texas A&M University–Corpus Christi	M
University of Arkansas at Pine Bluff	M,D
University of Florida	M,D
University of Guelph	M
University of Rhode Island	M,D*

ARCHAEOLOGY

American University of Beirut	M,D
Arizona State University at the Tempe campus	M,D,O
Boston University	M,D*
Brown University	D
Bryn Mawr College	M,D
California State University, Northridge	M
California State University, San Bernardino	M
Columbia University	M,D*
Cornell University	M,D
Florida State University	M,D
Gordon-Conwell Theological Seminary	M,D
The Graduate Center, City University of New York	D
Harvard University	M,D*
Illinois State University	M
Indiana University Bloomington	M,D
Indiana University of Pennsylvania	M
Johns Hopkins University	D*
Massachusetts Institute of Technology	M,D,O
Memorial University of Newfoundland	M,D
Mercyhurst University	M
Michigan Technological University	M,D
New York University	M,D*
Princeton University	D
Rice University	M,D
St. Cloud State University	M,O
San Francisco State University	M
Simon Fraser University	M,D
Southern Methodist University	M,D
Stanford University	M,D
Trinity International University	M,D,O
Universidad de las Américas Puebla	M
Université Laval	M,D
University of Alberta	M,D
The University of British Columbia	M
University of Calgary	M
University of California, Berkeley	M,D
University of California, Los Angeles	M,D*
University of Chicago	D
University of Colorado Denver	M
University of Denver	M
University of Lethbridge	M,D
The University of Manchester	D
University of Massachusetts Boston	M
University of Memphis	M,D,O
University of Michigan	M,D*
University of Minnesota, Twin Cities Campus	M,D
University of Nebraska–Lincoln	M,D
University of New Mexico	M,D
The University of North Carolina at Chapel Hill	M,D
University of Oklahoma	M,D*
University of Pennsylvania	M,D*
University of Rhode Island	M*
University of Saskatchewan	M,D
University of South Africa	M,D
University of South Florida	M,D,O*
The University of Tennessee	M,D
The University of Texas at Austin	M,D
University of West Florida	M
University of Wisconsin–Madison	D
Washington State University	M,D
Washington University in St. Louis	M,D
Wheaton College	M,D
Yale University	M,D

ARCHITECTURAL ENGINEERING

California Polytechnic State University, San Luis Obispo	M*
California State University, Fullerton	M
Carnegie Mellon University	M,D
Drexel University	M,D*
Illinois Institute of Technology	M,D
Kansas State University	M
Lawrence Technological University	M,D
Milwaukee School of Engineering	M
Penn State University Park	M,D*
University of California, San Diego	M*
University of Colorado Boulder	M,D
University of Detroit Mercy	M
The University of Kansas	M
University of Louisiana at Lafayette	M
University of Massachusetts Amherst	M,D*
University of Miami	M,D*
University of Nebraska–Lincoln	M,D
The University of Texas at Austin	M

ARCHITECTURAL HISTORY

Arizona State University at the Tempe campus	D
Cornell University	M,D
The Graduate Center, City University of New York	D
Harvard University	D*
Massachusetts Institute of Technology	M,D
New York University	M*
Roger Williams University	M,O
Savannah College of Art and Design	M
University of California, Berkeley	M,D
University of Colorado Denver	D
University of Pittsburgh	M,D*
The University of Texas at Austin	M,D
University of Virginia	M,D

ARCHITECTURE

Academy of Art University	M
Andrews University	M
Arizona State University at the Tempe campus	M,D
Athabasca University	M,O
Auburn University	M*
Ball State University	M
Boston Architectural College	M
California Baptist University	M
California College of the Arts	M
California Polytechnic State University, San Luis Obispo	M*
California State Polytechnic University, Pomona	M
Carleton University	M
Carnegie Mellon University	M,D
The Catholic University of America	M,O
City College of the City University of New York	M
Clemson University	M,D,O
Columbia University	M,D*
Cooper Union for the Advancement of Science and Art	M
Cornell University	M,D
Cranbrook Academy of Art	M
Dalhousie University	M
Ferris State University	M
Florida Agricultural and Mechanical University	M
Florida International University	M
Florida State University	M
Georgia Institute of Technology	M,D
Harvard University	M,D*
Illinois Institute of Technology	M,D
Instituto Tecnológico y de Estudios Superiores de Monterrey, Campus Estado de México	M,D
Instituto Tecnológico y de Estudios Superiores de Monterrey, Campus Irapuato	M,D
Iowa State University of Science and Technology	M
Judson University	M
Kansas State University	M
Kennesaw State University	M
Kent State University	M
Lawrence Technological University	M,O
London Metropolitan University	M,D
Louisiana State University and Agricultural & Mechanical College	M
Louisiana Tech University	M,D,O
Marywood University	M
Massachusetts College of Art and Design	M
Massachusetts Institute of Technology	M,D
McGill University	M,D,O
Miami University	M
Montana State University	M
Morgan State University	M
New Jersey Institute of Technology	M,D
The New School	M
NewSchool of Architecture and Design	M
New York Institute of Technology	M
North Carolina State University	M
North Dakota State University	M*
Northeastern University	M
The Ohio State University	M,D
Penn State University Park	M,D*
Pontificia Universidad Catolica Madre y Maestra	M
Portland State University	M
Prairie View A&M University	M
Pratt Institute	M*
Princeton University	M,D
Rensselaer Polytechnic Institute	M
Rhode Island School of Design	M
Rice University	M,D
Rochester Institute of Technology	M
Roger Williams University	M,O
Savannah College of Art and Design	M
School of Architecture at Taliesin	M
School of the Art Institute of Chicago	M
Southern California Institute of Architecture	M*
Southern Illinois University Carbondale	M
Syracuse University	M*
Temple University	M*
Texas A&M University	M,D
Texas Tech University	M,D
Thomas Jefferson University	M
Tulane University	M
Universidad Autonoma de Guadalajara	M,D
Universidad Nacional Pedro Henriquez Urena	M
Université Laval	M
University at Buffalo, the State University of New York	M
The University of Arizona	M
The University of British Columbia	M
University of Calgary	M,D
University of California, Berkeley	M,D
University of California, Los Angeles	M,D*
University of Cincinnati	M
University of Colorado Denver	M
University of Florida	M,D
University of Hartford	M
University of Hawaii at Manoa	D
University of Houston	M
University of Idaho	M
University of Illinois at Chicago	M
University of Illinois at Urbana–Champaign	M,D
The University of Kansas	M,D,O
University of Kentucky	M
The University of Manchester	M,D
University of Manitoba	M
University of Maryland, College Park	M
University of Massachusetts Amherst	M*
University of Memphis	M
University of Miami	M*
University of Michigan	M*
University of Minnesota, Twin Cities Campus	M
University of Nebraska–Lincoln	M,D
University of Nevada, Las Vegas	M,O
University of New Mexico	M,D
The University of North Carolina at Charlotte	M
The University of North Carolina at Greensboro	M,O
University of Notre Dame	M
University of Oklahoma	M,D*
University of Oregon	M
University of Pennsylvania	M,D,O*
University of Puerto Rico–Río Piedras	M
University of Southern California	M,D*
University of South Florida	M*
The University of Tennessee	M
The University of Texas at Arlington	M
The University of Texas at Austin	M
The University of Texas at San Antonio	M
University of the District of Columbia	M
University of Toronto	M
University of Utah	M
University of Virginia	M
University of Washington	M,D,O
University of Waterloo	M
University of Wisconsin–Milwaukee	M,D,O*
Washington State University	M
Washington University in St. Louis	M
Wentworth Institute of Technology	M
Woodbury University	M
Yale University	M,D

ARCHIVES/ARCHIVAL ADMINISTRATION

Claremont Graduate University	M,D,O
Clayton State University	M
Columbia University	M*
Drexel University	M*
East Tennessee State University	M,O
Middle Tennessee State University	M,D,O
Montclair State University	M
New York University	M,D,O*
Queens College of the City University of New York	M,O
The University of British Columbia	M,D
University of California, Los Angeles	M,D,O*
University of California, Riverside	M,D
University of Manitoba	M,D
University of Massachusetts Boston	M
University of Oklahoma	M,D,O*
University of Rochester	M*
University of South Carolina	M,O
Wayne State University	M,O

ART/FINE ARTS

Academy of Art University	M
Adelphi University	M
Alfred University	M,D
Anna Maria College	M,O
Arizona State University at the Tempe campus	M,D
ArtCenter College of Design	M
Azusa Pacific University	M*
Ball State University	M
Bard College	M
Barry University	M
Bob Jones University	M,D,O
Boise State University	M
Boston University	M*
Bowling Green State University	M
Bradley University	M
Brandeis University	O
Brigham Young University	M
Brooklyn College of the City University of New York	M
Butler University	M
California College of the Arts	M

*M—masters degree; D—doctorate; O—other advanced degree; *—Close-Up and/or Display*

California Institute of the Arts	M,O
California State University, Chico	M
California State University, Fresno	M
California State University, Fullerton	M
California State University, Long Beach	M
California State University, Los Angeles	M
California State University, Northridge	M
California State University, Sacramento	M
California State University, San Bernardino	M
Carlow University	M
Carnegie Mellon University	M
Central Washington University	M
Christie's Education	O
City College of the City University of New York	M
Claremont Graduate University	M
Clemson University	M
The College at Brockport, State University of New York	M
College for Creative Studies	M
Colorado State University	M
Columbia College Chicago	M
Columbia University	M,D*
Columbus College of Art & Design	M
Concordia University (Canada)	M
Cornell University	M
Cranbrook Academy of Art	M
Drew University	M,D,O
Duke University	M,D*
East Carolina University	M
Eastern Illinois University	M
Eastern Michigan University	M
East Tennessee State University	M
Edinboro University of Pennsylvania	M
Emily Carr University of Art + Design	M
Fairleigh Dickinson University, Metropolitan Campus	M
Ferris State University	M
Florida Atlantic University	M
Florida International University	M,O
Florida State University	M
Fontbonne University	M
Fort Hays State University	M
Full Sail University	M
George Mason University	M
The George Washington University	M,O
Georgia Southern University	M
Georgia State University	M
Hollins University	M
Hood College	M,O*
Houston Baptist University	M
Howard University	M
Hunter College of the City University of New York	M
Idaho State University	M
Illinois State University	M
Indiana State University	M
Indiana University Bloomington	M
Indiana University of Pennsylvania	M
Indiana University–Purdue University Indianapolis	M
Institute for Doctoral Studies in the Visual Arts	D
Inter American University of Puerto Rico, San Germán Campus	M
Iowa State University of Science and Technology	M
Ithaca College	M
Jacksonville University	M*
James Madison University	M
John F. Kennedy University	M
Kansas State University	M
Kent State University	M
Laguna College of Art & Design	M
Lake Forest College	M
Lee University	M,O
Lehman College of the City University of New York	M
Lesley University	M,D,O
Liberty University	M
Long Island University–LIU Post	M
Louisiana State University and Agricultural & Mechanical College	M
Louisiana Tech University	M,D,O
Loyola Marymount University	M
Maine College of Art	M
Maryland Institute College of Art	M,O
Marywood University	M
Massachusetts College of Art and Design	M,O
Miami University	M
Michigan State University	M
Millersville University of Pennsylvania	M
Mills College	M
Minneapolis College of Art and Design	M,O
Minnesota State University Mankato	M
Mississippi College	M
Missouri State University	M
Montana State University	M
Montclair State University	M
Moore College of Art & Design	M
Morehead State University	M
New Hampshire Institute of Art	M
New Jersey City University	M
New Mexico State University	M
The New School	M
New York Academy of Art	M
New York Institute of Technology	M
New York Studio School of Drawing, Painting and Sculpture	M,O*
New York University	M,D,O*
Norfolk State University	M
Northeastern University	M
Northern Illinois University	M
Northern Vermont University–Johnson	M
Northwestern State University of Louisiana	M
Northwestern University	M
Nova Southeastern University	M,D,O*
NSCAD University	M
The Ohio State University	M
Ohio University	M
Oregon College of Art and Craft	M
Otis College of Art and Design	M
Pacific Northwest College of Art	M
Paris College of Art	M
Penn State University Park	M,D,O*
Pennsylvania Academy of the Fine Arts	M,O
Pensacola Christian College	M,D,O
Pontifical Catholic University of Puerto Rico	M
Portland State University	M
Pratt Institute	M*
Prescott College	M
Purchase College, State University of New York	M
Purdue University	M,D
Queens College of the City University of New York	M
Radford University	M
Rensselaer Polytechnic Institute	D
Rhode Island College	M
Rhode Island School of Design	M
Rochester Institute of Technology	M
Rutgers University–New Brunswick	M
San Diego State University	M
San Francisco Art Institute	M,O
San Francisco State University	M
Savannah College of Art and Design	M
School of the Art Institute of Chicago	M
School of Visual Arts (NY)	M
Sotheby's Institute of Art–London	M
Sotheby's Institute of Art–New York	M
Southern Illinois University Carbondale	M
Southern Illinois University Edwardsville	M
Southern Methodist University	M
Southwest University of Visual Arts	M
Spring Hill College	M,O
Stanford University	M,D
State University of New York at New Paltz	M
State University of New York at Oswego	M
Stephen F. Austin State University	M
Stony Brook University, State University of New York	M
Sul Ross State University	M
Syracuse University	M*
Temple University	M*
Texas A&M University	M
Texas A&M University–Commerce	M,D,O
Texas A&M University–Corpus Christi	M
Texas Christian University	M
Texas Southern University	M
Texas Tech University	M,D
Texas Woman's University	M
Thomas Jefferson University	M
Tiffin University	M
Towson University	M
Tufts University	M,O*
Tulane University	M
United Theological Seminary of the Twin Cities	M,D,O
Universidad del Turabo	M
Université du Québec à Chicoutimi	M
Université du Québec à Montréal	M
Université Laval	M
University at Albany, State University of New York	M
University at Buffalo, the State University of New York	M
The University of Alabama	M
University of Alaska Fairbanks	M
University of Alberta	M
The University of Arizona	M
University of Arkansas	M
University of Arkansas at Little Rock	M
The University of British Columbia	M,D
University of Calgary	M
University of California, Berkeley	M,O
University of California, Davis	M
University of California, Irvine	M,D
University of California, Los Angeles	M*
University of California, Riverside	M
University of California, San Diego	M,D*
University of California, Santa Barbara	M
University of California, Santa Cruz	M,D*
University of Central Florida	M
University of Chicago	M
University of Cincinnati	M
University of Colorado Boulder	M
University of Colorado Denver	M,O
University of Dallas	M
University of Dayton	M
University of Delaware	M*
University of Denver	M
University of Florida	M,D
University of Georgia	M,D
University of Guam	M
University of Guelph	M
University of Hartford	M
University of Hawaii at Manoa	M
University of Houston	M
University of Idaho	M
University of Illinois at Chicago	M,D
University of Illinois at Urbana–Champaign	M
University of Indianapolis	M
The University of Iowa	M*
The University of Kansas	M,D
University of Kentucky	M
University of Lethbridge	M,D
University of Maine	M
The University of Manchester	M,D
University of Maryland, College Park	M
University of Massachusetts Amherst	M*
University of Massachusetts Dartmouth	M,O
University of Memphis	M,O
University of Miami	M*
University of Michigan	M*
University of Michigan–Flint	M
University of Minnesota, Duluth	M
University of Minnesota, Twin Cities Campus	M
University of Mississippi	M,D
University of Missouri	M
University of Missouri–Kansas City	M,D
University of Montana	M
University of Nebraska at Omaha	M
University of Nebraska–Lincoln	M
University of Nevada, Las Vegas	M
University of Nevada, Reno	M
University of New Mexico	M
University of New Orleans	M
The University of North Carolina at Chapel Hill	M
The University of North Carolina at Greensboro	M
University of North Dakota	M
University of Northern Colorado	M
University of Northern Iowa	M
University of North Texas	M,D,O
University of Notre Dame	M
University of Oklahoma	M*
University of Oregon	M
University of Pennsylvania	M,O*
University of Regina	M
University of Rochester	D*
University of Saint Francis (IN)	M
University of Saskatchewan	M
The University of Scranton	M
University of South Alabama	M
University of South Carolina	M
University of South Dakota	M
University of Southern California	M,D,O*
University of South Florida	M*
The University of Tennessee	M
The University of Texas at Arlington	M
The University of Texas at Austin	M
The University of Texas at El Paso	M
The University of Texas at San Antonio	M
The University of Texas at Tyler	M
The University of Texas Rio Grande Valley	M
The University of the Arts	M
The University of Tulsa	M
University of Utah	M
University of Victoria	M
University of Washington	M
University of Waterloo	M
University of Windsor	M
University of Wisconsin–Madison	M
University of Wisconsin–River Falls	M
University of Wisconsin–Stout	M
University of Wisconsin–Superior	M
Utah State University	M
Vermont College of Fine Arts	M
Virginia Commonwealth University	M,D
Warren Wilson College	M
Washington State University	M
Washington University in St. Louis	M
Wayne State University	M
Webster University	M
Western Carolina University	M
Western Connecticut State University	M
West Texas A&M University	M
West Virginia University	M,D
Wichita State University	M
Wilson College	M
Winthrop University	M
Yale University	M
York University	M,D

ART EDUCATION

Academy of Art University	M
Adelphi University	M
Alabama Agricultural and Mechanical University	M
American University of Puerto Rico	M
Arcadia University	M,D,O
Arizona State University at the Tempe campus	M,D
Art Academy of Cincinnati	M
Avila University	M,O
Boston University	M*
Bowling Green State University	M
Bridgewater State University	M
Brigham Young University	M
Brooklyn College of the City University of New York	M
Buffalo State College, State University of New York	M
California State University, Long Beach	M
California State University, Los Angeles	M
California State University, Northridge	M
Carthage College	M,O
Case Western Reserve University	M*
Central Connecticut State University	M,O
Chatham University	M
Cleveland State University	M
The College of New Rochelle	M
The Colorado College	M
Colorado State University–Pueblo	M
Columbus State University	M
Concordia University (United States)	M,D
Concordia University (Canada)	M,D
Concordia University Wisconsin	M
Converse College	M
Delaware State University	M
East Carolina University	M
Eastern Illinois University	M
Eastern Kentucky University	M
Eastern Michigan University	M
Edinboro University of Pennsylvania	M
Ferris State University	M
Fitchburg State University	M,O
Florida International University	M,D,O
Florida State University	M,D
Fontbonne University	M
Framingham State University	M
George Mason University	M
The George Washington University	M
Georgia State University	M
Harding University	M,O
Harvard University	M*
Hofstra University	M,D,O
Indiana University Bloomington	M,D,O
James Madison University	M
Kean University	M
Kennesaw State University	M
Kent State University	M
Kutztown University of Pennsylvania	M
Lake Forest College	M
Lesley University	M,D,O
Long Island University–LIU Post	M,D,O
Manhattanville College	M,O
Mansfield University of Pennsylvania	M
Maryland Institute College of Art	M
Marywood University	M
Massachusetts College of Art and Design	M,O
McNeese State University	O
Miami University	M
Millersville University of Pennsylvania	M
Minnesota State University Mankato	M
Mississippi College	M,D,O
Montclair State University	M
Moore College of Art & Design	M
Morehead State University	M
Nazareth College of Rochester	M
New Hampshire Institute of Art	M
New Jersey City University	M
New York University	M,O*
The Ohio State University	M,D
Penn State University Park	M,D,O*
Piedmont College	M,D,O
Plymouth State University	M
Pratt Institute	M,O*
Purdue University	M,D,O
Queens College of the City University of New York	M,O
Rhode Island College	M
Rhode Island School of Design	M
Rochester Institute of Technology	M
Rocky Mountain College of Art + Design	M
Saint Michael's College	M,O
Salem College	M
Salem State University	M
School of the Art Institute of Chicago	M
School of Visual Arts (NY)	M
School of Visual Arts (NY)	M
Simon Fraser University	M,D
Southern Connecticut State University	M
Southwestern Oklahoma State University	M
Spalding University	M
State University of New York at New Paltz	M
State University of New York at Oswego	M
Sul Ross State University	M
Syracuse University	M*
Teachers College, Columbia University	M,D,O
Temple University	M*
Texas Tech University	M
Texas Woman's University	M
Towson University	M,O
Tufts University	M,D,O*
The University of Akron	M
The University of Alabama at Birmingham	M
The University of Arizona	M,D
University of Arkansas at Little Rock	M
The University of British Columbia	M,D
University of Central Florida	M
University of Cincinnati	M

University of Denver	M,O
University of Florida	M,D
University of Illinois at Urbana–Champaign	M,D
University of Indianapolis	M
The University of Iowa	M,D*
The University of Kansas	M
University of Kentucky	M
University of Louisville	M,D,O
University of Maryland, Baltimore County	M
University of Massachusetts Amherst	M*
University of Massachusetts Dartmouth	M
University of Minnesota, Twin Cities Campus	M
University of Missouri	M,D,O
University of Montana	M
University of Nebraska at Kearney	M
University of New Mexico	M
The University of North Carolina at Charlotte	M,D,O
The University of North Carolina at Pembroke	M
University of Northern Colorado	M
University of Northern Iowa	M
University of North Texas	M,D,O
University of Rio Grande	M
University of St. Francis (IL)	M,D,O
University of South Alabama	M,D
University of South Carolina	M,D
University of South Dakota	M
The University of Tennessee	M,D,O
The University of Texas at Austin	M
The University of Texas at El Paso	M
The University of the Arts	M
The University of Toledo	M,D,O
The University of Tulsa	M
University of Utah	M
University of Victoria	M,D
University of Wisconsin–Milwaukee	M,D,O*
University of Wisconsin–Superior	M
Vermont College of Fine Arts	M
Virginia Commonwealth University	M,D
Wayne State University	M,D,O
Western Kentucky University	M
Western Michigan University	M
West Virginia University	M,D
William Carey University	M,O
Winthrop University	M

ART HISTORY

Academy of Art University	M
American University	M
American University of Beirut	M,D
Arizona State University at the Tempe campus	M,D
Bard Graduate Center	M,D*
Binghamton University, State University of New York	M,D
Boston University	M,D,O*
Bowling Green State University	M
Brooklyn College of the City University of New York	M
Brown University	D
Bryn Mawr College	M,D
California State University, Chico	M
California State University, Fullerton	M
California State University, Los Angeles	M
California State University, Northridge	M
Caribbean University	M,D
Carleton University	M
Case Western Reserve University	M,D*
Christie's Education	M
City College of the City University of New York	M
Cleveland State University	M
Colorado State University	M
Columbia College Chicago	M
Columbia University	M,D*
Concordia University (Canada)	M,D
Cornell University	D
Dominican University of California	M
Duke University	M,D*
Emory University	D
Fashion Institute of Technology	M
Florida State University	M,D
George Mason University	M
The George Washington University	M
Georgia State University	M
The Graduate Center, City University of New York	D
Graduate Theological Union	M,D,O
Harvard University	D*
Howard University	M
Hunter College of the City University of New York	M
Illinois State University	M
Indiana University Bloomington	M,D
James Madison University	M
Johns Hopkins University	M,D*
Kent State University	M
Lancaster Theological Seminary	M,D,O
Lindenwood University	M
Louisiana State University and Agricultural & Mechanical College	M
Massachusetts Institute of Technology	M,D
McGill University	M,D
Montana State University	M
New Mexico State University	M
New York University	M,D*
Northwestern University	D
The Ohio State University	M,D
Ohio University	M
Oklahoma State University	M
Penn State University Park	M,D*
Pratt Institute	M*
Purchase College, State University of New York	M
Queens College of the City University of New York	M
Rice University	D
Richmond, The American International University in London	M
Roger Williams University	M,O
Rutgers University–New Brunswick	M,D,O
San Diego State University	M
San Francisco Art Institute	M
San Jose State University	M
Savannah College of Art and Design	M
School of the Art Institute of Chicago	M
School of Visual Arts (NY)	M
Southern Methodist University	M,D
Stony Brook University, State University of New York	M,D
Sul Ross State University	M
Syracuse University	M*
Temple University	M,D*
Texas Christian University	M
Texas Tech University	M
Texas Woman's University	M
Towson University	M
Tufts University	M*
Tulane University	M
Université de Montréal	M,D
Université du Québec à Montréal	M,D
Université Laval	M,D
University at Buffalo, the State University of New York	M,D
The University of Alabama	M
The University of Alabama at Birmingham	M
University of Alberta	M
The University of Arizona	M,D
University of Arkansas at Little Rock	M
The University of British Columbia	M,D
University of California, Berkeley	D
University of California, Davis	M
University of California, Los Angeles	M,D*
University of California, Riverside	M,D
University of California, San Diego	M,D*
University of California, Santa Barbara	D
University of Chicago	M,D
University of Cincinnati	M
University of Colorado Boulder	M
University of Delaware	M,D*
University of Denver	M
University of Florida	M,D
University of Georgia	M,D
University of Hawaii at Manoa	M
University of Houston	M
University of Illinois at Chicago	M,D
University of Illinois at Urbana–Champaign	M,D
The University of Iowa	M,D*
The University of Kansas	M,D
University of Kentucky	M
University of Louisville	M,D
The University of Manchester	D
University of Maryland, College Park	M,D
University of Massachusetts Amherst	M*
University of Massachusetts Dartmouth	M
University of Memphis	M,O
University of Miami	M*
University of Michigan	M,D*
University of Minnesota, Twin Cities Campus	M,D
University of Montana	M
University of Nebraska–Lincoln	M
University of New Mexico	M,D
The University of North Carolina at Chapel Hill	M,D
University of Northern Colorado	M
University of North Texas	M,D,O
University of Notre Dame	M
University of Oklahoma	M,D*
University of Oregon	M,D*
University of Pennsylvania	M,D*
University of Pittsburgh	M,D*
University of Rochester	D*
University of St. Thomas (MN)	M,O
University of South Africa	M,D
University of South Carolina	M,D
University of Southern California	M,D,O*
University of South Florida	M*
The University of Texas at Austin	M,D
The University of Texas at Dallas	M,D
The University of Texas at San Antonio	M
The University of Texas at Tyler	M
University of Toronto	M,D
The University of Tulsa	M
University of Utah	M
University of Victoria	M,D
University of Virginia	M,D
University of Washington	M,D
University of Wisconsin–Madison	M,D
University of Wisconsin–Milwaukee	M*
University of Wisconsin–Superior	M
Virginia Commonwealth University	M,D
Washington University in St. Louis	M,D
Wayne State University	M
Webster University	M
West Virginia University	M,D
Williams College	M
Yale University	D
York University	M,D

ARTIFICIAL INTELLIGENCE/ROBOTICS

The American University in Cairo	M,D,O
Brandeis University	M
California State University, Northridge	M
Carnegie Mellon University	M,D
College of Staten Island of the City University of New York	M
The College of William and Mary	M,D*
Cornell University	M,D
Georgia Institute of Technology	D
Illinois Institute of Technology	M,D
Indiana University Bloomington	D
Instituto Tecnológico y de Estudios Superiores de Monterrey, Campus Monterrey	M,D
Johns Hopkins University	M*
Lawrence Technological University	M,O
New York University	M*
Northwestern University	M
Oregon State University	M,D
Portland State University	M,D,O
South Dakota School of Mines and Technology	M
Stevens Institute of Technology	M,D,O
Temple University	M,D*
Tufts University	M,D*
University of California, Riverside	M,D
University of California, San Diego	M,D*
University of Georgia	M
University of Michigan	M,D*
University of Nebraska at Omaha	M,O
University of Pennsylvania	M*
University of Pittsburgh	M,D*
University of Rochester	M,D*
University of Southern California	M,D*
Villanova University	M,O
Worcester Polytechnic Institute	M,D

ARTS ADMINISTRATION

American University	M,O
Arizona State University at the Tempe campus	M,D
Baruch College of the City University of New York	M*
Boston University	M,O*
Brooklyn College of the City University of New York	M
Carnegie Mellon University	M
Christie's Education	M,O
Claremont Graduate University	M
The College at Brockport, State University of New York	M,O
College of Charleston	O
Colorado State University	M
Daemen College	M
Drexel University	M*
Eastern Michigan University	M
Fashion Institute of Technology	M
Florida State University	M,D
George Mason University	M
Goucher College	M
HEC Montreal	O
Indiana University Bloomington	M
Kutztown University of Pennsylvania	M
Le Moyne College	M
London Metropolitan University	M,D
Montclair State University	M
Moore College of Art & Design	M
New York University	M*
Northwestern University	M
The Ohio State University	M
Pratt Institute	M*
Purchase College, State University of New York	M
Rhode Island College	M
Rocky Mountain College of Art + Design	M
Roosevelt University	M,O
Rowan University	M
Ryerson University	M
St. Thomas University	M
Savannah College of Art and Design	M
School of the Art Institute of Chicago	M
Seattle University	M
Sotheby's Institute of Art–London	M
Sotheby's Institute of Art–New York	M
Southern Methodist University	M
Southern Utah University	M
Teachers College, Columbia University	M,D,O
Temple University	M,D*
Universidad del Turabo	M
University at Buffalo, the State University of New York	M
The University of Akron	M
University of Cincinnati	M,D
University of Kentucky	M
The University of Manchester	D
University of Michigan–Flint	M
University of New Orleans	M
The University of North Carolina at Charlotte	M,O
University of Southern California	M*
University of Wisconsin–Madison	M
Valparaiso University	M
Winthrop University	M

ARTS JOURNALISM

Academy of Art University	M
School of the Art Institute of Chicago	M
Syracuse University	M*

ART THERAPY

Adler Graduate School	M
Adler University	M,D
Albertus Magnus College	M
Athabasca University	M,O
Caldwell University	M,O
California Institute of Integral Studies	M,D
California State University, Los Angeles	M
Cedar Crest College	M
The College of New Rochelle	M
Concordia University (Canada)	M
Drexel University	M,O*
Eastern Virginia Medical School	M
Edinboro University of Pennsylvania	M,O
Emporia State University	M
Florida State University	M,D
The George Washington University	M,O
Georgia College & State University	M
Goddard College	M
Hofstra University	M,O
Indiana University–Purdue University Indianapolis	M
Lesley University	M,D,O
Long Island University–LIU Post	M
Marywood University	M,O
Mount Mary University	M,D
Naropa University	M
Nazareth College of Rochester	M
New York University	M*
Notre Dame de Namur University	M,D
Ottawa University	M
Phillips Graduate University	M
Pratt Institute	M*
Prescott College	M
Saint Mary-of-the-Woods College	M,O
School of the Art Institute of Chicago	M
School of Visual Arts (NY)	M
Seton Hill University	M
Southern Illinois University Edwardsville	M
Southwestern College (NM)	M
Springfield College	M,O
University of Louisville	M,D
University of Maryland, College Park	M,D,O
University of Wisconsin–Superior	M
Ursuline College	M

ASIAN-AMERICAN STUDIES

Binghamton University, State University of New York	M,O
California State University, Long Beach	M
San Francisco State University	M
Stony Brook University, State University of New York	M
University of California, Los Angeles	M*

ASIAN LANGUAGES

Cornell University	M,D
Harvard University	M,D*
Indiana University Bloomington	M,D
The Ohio State University	M,D
St. John's College (NM)	M
Stanford University	M,D
University of California, Berkeley	M,D
University of California, Irvine	M,D
University of California, Los Angeles	M,D*
University of California, Santa Barbara	M,D
University of Chicago	D
University of Hawaii at Manoa	M,D
University of Illinois at Urbana–Champaign	M,D
The University of Iowa	M*
The University of Kansas	M,O
University of Michigan	D*
University of Minnesota, Twin Cities Campus	D
University of Oregon	M,D
University of Southern California	M,D*
The University of Texas at Austin	M,D
University of Washington	M,D
University of Wisconsin–Madison	M,D
Washington University in St. Louis	M,D
Yale University	D

ASIAN STUDIES

American University	O
Binghamton University, State University of New York	M,O
Brown University	D
California Institute of Integral Studies	M,D,O
California State University, Long Beach	M
College of Staten Island of the City University of New York	M
Columbia University	M,D,O*
Cornell University	M,D
Dallas Baptist University	M
Duke University	M,O*
Florida International University	M
Florida State University	M
Georgetown University	M

*M—masters degree; D—doctorate; O—other advanced degree; *—Close-Up and/or Display*

The George Washington University M
Harvard University M,D*
Indiana University Bloomington M,D
Johns Hopkins University M,D,O*
Maharishi University of Management M,D
McGill University M,D
New York University M,D*
The Ohio State University M
Ohio University M
Princeton University D
Rutgers University–New Brunswick M,D
St. John's College (NM) M
St. John's University (NY) M
San Diego State University M
Seton Hall University M
Stanford University M
Stony Brook University, State University of New York M
United Theological Seminary of the Twin Cities M,D,O
University of Alberta M
The University of Arizona M,D
University of Bridgeport M
The University of British Columbia M,D
University of California, Berkeley M,D
University of California, Los Angeles M,D*
University of California, Riverside M
University of California, Santa Barbara M,D
University of Chicago M,D
University of Colorado Boulder M,D
University of Hawaii at Manoa O
University of Illinois at Urbana–Champaign M,D
The University of Iowa M*
The University of Kansas M,O
The University of Manchester D
University of Michigan M,D,O*
University of Minnesota, Twin Cities Campus D
University of Oregon M
University of Pennsylvania M,D*
University of Pittsburgh M,O*
University of San Francisco M
University of Southern California M,D*
The University of Texas at Austin M,D
University of Toronto M,D
University of Utah M
University of Victoria M
University of Virginia M
University of Washington M,D
University of Wisconsin–Madison M,D
Washington University in St. Louis M,D
Yale University M

ASTRONOMY

Boston University M,D*
Brigham Young University M,D
California Institute of Technology D
Case Western Reserve University M,D*
Columbia University M,D*
Cornell University D
Dartmouth College D*
George Mason University M,D
Georgia State University D
Harvard University D*
Hunter College of the City University of New York M,D
Indiana University Bloomington M,D
Johns Hopkins University D*
Louisiana State University and Agricultural & Mechanical College M,D
Michigan State University M,D
Minnesota State University Mankato M
New Mexico State University M,D
Northwestern University D
The Ohio State University M,D
Ohio University M,D
Penn State University Park M,D*
Princeton University D
Rensselaer Polytechnic Institute M
Rice University M,D
Rutgers University–New Brunswick M,D
Saint Mary's University (Canada) M,D
San Diego State University M
San Francisco State University M
Stony Brook University, State University of New York D
Texas A&M University M,D
Texas Tech University M,D
Université de Moncton M
The University of Alabama M,D
The University of Alabama in Huntsville M,D
The University of Arizona D
The University of British Columbia M,D
University of Calgary M,D
University of California, Los Angeles M,D*
University of California, Santa Cruz D*
University of Chicago D
University of Delaware M,D*
University of Florida M,D
University of Hawaii at Manoa M,D
University of Illinois at Urbana–Champaign M,D
The University of Iowa M*
The University of Kansas M,D
University of Kentucky M,D
The University of Manchester M,D
University of Maryland, College Park M,D
University of Massachusetts Amherst M,D*
University of Michigan D*
University of Missouri M,D
University of Nebraska–Lincoln M,D
University of Nevada, Las Vegas M,D
The University of North Carolina at Chapel Hill M,D
University of Rochester D*
University of South Carolina M,D
The University of Texas at Austin M,D
University of Toronto M,D
University of Victoria M,D
University of Virginia M,D
University of Washington M,D
The University of Western Ontario M,D
University of Wisconsin–Madison D
Vanderbilt University M,D*
Wesleyan University M
West Chester University of Pennsylvania M,O
Yale University M,D
York University M,D

ASTROPHYSICS

Air Force Institute of Technology M,D
Arizona State University at the Tempe campus M,D
Cornell University D
Harvard University D*
Indiana University Bloomington M,D
Iowa State University of Science and Technology M,D
Louisiana State University and Agricultural & Mechanical College M,D
McMaster University D
Michigan State University M,D
New Mexico Institute of Mining and Technology M,D
New Mexico State University M,D
Penn State University Park M,D*
Princeton University D
Rochester Institute of Technology M,D
Texas Christian University M,D
Tufts University M,D*
University of Alaska Fairbanks M,D
University of Alberta M,D
University of California, Berkeley D
University of California, Los Angeles M,D*
University of California, Santa Cruz D*
University of Chicago D
University of Colorado Boulder M,D
The University of Manchester M,D
University of Michigan D*
University of Minnesota, Twin Cities Campus M,D
University of Missouri–St. Louis M,D
The University of North Carolina at Chapel Hill M,D
University of North Dakota M,D
The University of Toledo M,D
University of Toronto M,D
University of Victoria M,D
Yale University M,D

ATHLETIC TRAINING AND SPORTS MEDICINE

Adrian College M
A.T. Still University M,D,O
Azusa Pacific University M*
Barry University M
Baylor University M,D
Bellarmine University M,D
Bloomsburg University of Pennsylvania M
Boston University M,D*
Bridgewater College M
Brigham Young University M,D
California Baptist University M
California State University, Long Beach M
California University of Pennsylvania M
Chapman University M*
The College of St. Scholastica M
Drake University M,D
Eastern Michigan University M,O
East Stroudsburg University of Pennsylvania M
Florida International University M
Franklin College M
Gannon University M
George Mason University M,O
Georgia Southern University–Armstrong Campus M,O
Georgia State University M
Grand View University M,O
High Point University M,D
Idaho State University M
Indiana State University M,D
Indiana University Bloomington M,D
Inter American University of Puerto Rico, Metropolitan Campus M
Kent State University M,D
Lebanon Valley College M
Lenoir-Rhyne University M
Life University M
Lock Haven University of Pennsylvania M
London Metropolitan University M,D
Long Island University–LIU Brooklyn M,D,O
Manchester University M
Marshall University M
Mercer University M,D
Merrimack College M
Missouri State University M
Montana State University Billings M
Moravian College M,D
North Dakota State University M,D*
Ohio University M
Old Dominion University M
Oregon State University M
Pacific University M,D
Plymouth State University M
Saint Louis University M,D*
Salisbury University M
Samford University M,D
San Jose State University M
Seton Hall University M
Shenandoah University M,D,O
South Dakota State University M,D
Spalding University M
Springfield College M
Stephen F. Austin State University M
Tarleton State University M
Temple University M,D*
Texas A&M University M
Texas State University M
Texas Tech University Health Sciences Center M
Thomas Jefferson University M
Trinity International University M
Universidad del Turabo M
University of Arkansas M
University of Central Oklahoma M
University of Evansville M
The University of Findlay M,D
University of Florida M,D
University of Idaho M,D
The University of Iowa M,D*
University of Kentucky M,D
University of Lynchburg M
University of Miami M,D*
University of Nebraska at Omaha M,D
The University of North Carolina at Chapel Hill M
The University of North Carolina at Greensboro M,D
University of Northern Iowa M
University of North Georgia M
University of Pittsburgh M*
University of St. Augustine for Health Sciences M
University of South Florida M,D*
The University of Tennessee M,D
The University of Tennessee at Chattanooga M
The University of Texas at Arlington M,D
The University of Toledo M,D
University of Wisconsin–La Crosse M
University of Wisconsin–Milwaukee M,D*
Wayne State University M,D
Weber State University M
West Chester University of Pennsylvania M,O
Western Michigan University M
West Virginia University M,D
West Virginia Wesleyan College M
Xavier University M*

ATMOSPHERIC SCIENCES

Bard College M,O
Carnegie Mellon University D
City College of the City University of New York M
The College of William and Mary M,D*
Colorado State University M,D
Columbia University M,D*
Cornell University M,D
Florida State University M,D
George Mason University D
Georgia Institute of Technology M,D
Hampton University M,D
Howard University M,D
Jackson State University M,D
Massachusetts Institute of Technology M,D
McGill University M,D
Michigan Technological University M,D,O
Millersville University of Pennsylvania M
Mississippi State University M,D
New Mexico Institute of Mining and Technology M,D
North Carolina State University M,D
Northern Arizona University M,D,O
The Ohio State University M,D
Oregon State University M,D
Princeton University D
Purdue University M,D
Rutgers University–New Brunswick M,D
South Dakota School of Mines and Technology M,D
Stevens Institute of Technology M,D,O
Stony Brook University, State University of New York M,D
Texas Tech University M,D
Université du Québec à Montréal M,D,O
University at Albany, State University of New York M,D
The University of Alabama in Huntsville M,D
University of Alaska Fairbanks M,D
The University of Arizona M,D
The University of British Columbia M,D
University of California, Davis M,D
University of California, Los Angeles M,D*
University of Chicago D
University of Colorado Boulder M,D
University of Guelph M,D
University of Houston M,D
University of Illinois at Urbana–Champaign M,D
The University of Kansas M,D,O
The University of Manchester M,D
University of Maryland, Baltimore County M,D
University of Michigan M,D*
University of Nevada, Reno M,D
University of North Dakota M,D
University of Utah M,D
University of Washington M,D
University of Wisconsin–Madison M,D
University of Wisconsin–Milwaukee M,D*
University of Wyoming M,D
Yale University D

AUTOMOTIVE ENGINEERING

Clemson University M,D,O
College for Creative Studies M
Lawrence Technological University M,D
Michigan Technological University M,D,O
Minnesota State University Mankato M
University of Michigan M,D*
University of Michigan–Dearborn M,D
The University of Tennessee at Chattanooga M
University of Wisconsin–Madison M,D
Wayne State University M,O

AVIATION

Embry-Riddle Aeronautical University–Prescott M
Everglades University M
Florida Institute of Technology M,D
Lewis University M
National Test Pilot School M
Oklahoma State University M,D,O
Southeastern Oklahoma State University M
University of North Dakota M
The University of Tennessee M

AVIATION MANAGEMENT

Arizona State University at the Tempe campus M
Delta State University M
Embry-Riddle Aeronautical University–Worldwide M
Florida Institute of Technology M
Lewis University M
Lynn University M
Middle Tennessee State University M
National American University (TX) M,D
Purdue University M
Southeastern Oklahoma State University M
Vaughn College of Aeronautics and Technology M

BACTERIOLOGY

Illinois State University M,D
The University of Iowa M,D*
University of Prince Edward Island M,D
University of Wisconsin–Madison M

BIOCHEMICAL ENGINEERING

Brown University M,D
Cornell University M,D
Drexel University M*
Lehigh University M,D
Rutgers University–New Brunswick M,D
University of California, Irvine M,D
University of Georgia M
The University of Iowa M,D*
The University of Manchester M,D
University of Maryland, Baltimore County M,D,O
The University of Western Ontario M,D
Villanova University M,O

BIOCHEMISTRY

Albert Einstein College of Medicine D
American University of Beirut M,D
Arizona State University at the Tempe campus M,D
Auburn University M,D*
Augusta University D
Baylor College of Medicine D
Baylor University M,D
Boston College M,D
Boston University M,D*
Bradley University M
Brandeis University M,D
Brigham Young University M,D
Brown University M,D
California Institute of Technology M,D
California Polytechnic State University, San Luis Obispo M*
California State University, East Bay M
California State University, Long Beach M
California State University, Los Angeles M
California State University, Northridge M
California State University, Sacramento M
Carnegie Mellon University M,D
Case Western Reserve University M,D*
City College of the City University of New York M,D
Clark University D
Colorado State University M,D
Colorado State University–Pueblo M
Columbia University M,D*
Cornell University M,D
Dalhousie University M,D
Dartmouth College M,D*
Drexel University M,D*
Duke University D*
Eastern New Mexico University M
East Tennessee State University D
Emory University D
Florida Institute of Technology M
Florida State University M,D
George Mason University M,D
Georgetown University M,D

The George Washington University	D
Georgia State University	M,D
The Graduate Center, City University of New York	D
Harvard University	D*
Howard University	M,D
Hunter College of the City University of New York	M,D
Illinois Institute of Technology	M,D
Illinois State University	M,D
Indiana University Bloomington	M,D
Indiana University–Purdue University Indianapolis	M,D
Irell & Manella Graduate School of Biological Sciences	D*
Johns Hopkins University	M,D*
Kansas State University	M,D
Kennesaw State University	M
Laurentian University	M
Lehigh University	M,D
Loma Linda University	M,D
Louisiana State University and Agricultural & Mechanical College	M,D
Louisiana State University Health Sciences Center at Shreveport	M,D
Loyola University Chicago	M,D
Massachusetts Institute of Technology	D
Mayo Clinic Graduate School of Biomedical Sciences	M,D
McGill University	M,D
McMaster University	M,D
Medical College of Wisconsin	D
Medical University of South Carolina	M,D
Meharry Medical College	D
Memorial University of Newfoundland	M,D
Miami University	M,D
Michigan State University	M,D
Michigan Technological University	M,D,O
Mississippi College	M
Mississippi State University	M,D
Montana State University	M,D
Montclair State University	M
Mount Allison University	M
New York Medical College	M,D
North Carolina State University	D
North Dakota State University	M,D*
Northern Illinois University	M,D
Northwestern University	D
The Ohio State University	M,D
Ohio University	M,D
Oklahoma State University	M,D
Old Dominion University	M,D
Oregon Health & Science University	M,D
Oregon State University	M,D
Pace University	M
Penn State Hershey Medical Center	M,D
Penn State University Park	M,D*
Purdue University	M,D
Queen's University at Kingston	M,D
Rensselaer Polytechnic Institute	M,D
Rice University	M,D
Rosalind Franklin University of Medicine and Science	D
Rush University	M,D
Rutgers University–Newark	M,D
Rutgers University–New Brunswick	M,D
Saint Louis University	D*
San Diego State University	M,D
San Francisco State University	M
Seton Hall University	M,D
Simon Fraser University	M,D,O
Sonoma State University	M
Southern Illinois University Carbondale	M,D
Southern University and Agricultural and Mechanical College	M
Stanford University	D
State University of New York College of Environmental Science and Forestry	M,D
State University of New York Upstate Medical University	M,D
Stevens Institute of Technology	M,D,O
Stony Brook University, State University of New York	M,D
Texas A&M University	M,D
Texas Christian University	M,D
Texas State University	M
Thomas Jefferson University	D
Tufts University	D*
Tulane University	M
Universidad Central del Caribe	M,D
Université de Moncton	M
Université de Montréal	M,D,O
Université de Sherbrooke	M,D
Université Laval	M,D,O
University at Buffalo, the State University of New York	M,D
The University of Alabama at Birmingham	D
University of Alaska Fairbanks	M,D
University of Alberta	M,D
The University of Arizona	M,D
University of Arkansas for Medical Sciences	M,D,O
The University of British Columbia	M,D
University of Calgary	M,D
University of California, Berkeley	D
University of California, Davis	M,D
University of California, Irvine	M,D
University of California, Los Angeles	M,D*
University of California, Merced	M,D
University of California, Riverside	M,D
University of California, San Diego	M,D*
University of California, San Francisco	D
University of California, Santa Barbara	D
University of California, Santa Cruz	M,D*
University of Cincinnati	M,D
University of Colorado Boulder	M,D
University of Colorado Denver	D
University of Connecticut Health Center	D
University of Dayton	M
University of Delaware	M,D*
University of Florida	D
University of Georgia	M,D
University of Guelph	M,D
University of Houston	M,D
University of Idaho	M,D
University of Illinois at Chicago	D
University of Illinois at Urbana–Champaign	M,D
The University of Iowa	M,D*
The University of Kansas	D
University of Kentucky	D
University of Lethbridge	M,D
University of Louisville	M,D
The University of Manchester	M,D
University of Manitoba	M,D
University of Maryland, Baltimore	M,D
University of Maryland, College Park	M,D
University of Massachusetts Amherst	M,D*
University of Massachusetts Dartmouth	M,D
University of Massachusetts Lowell	M,D
University of Massachusetts Medical School	M,D
University of Miami	D*
University of Michigan	M,D*
University of Minnesota, Duluth	M,D
University of Minnesota, Twin Cities Campus	D
University of Mississippi Medical Center	D
University of Missouri	M,D
University of Missouri–Kansas City	D
University of Missouri–St. Louis	M,D
University of Montana	D
University of Nebraska–Lincoln	M,D
University of Nebraska Medical Center	M
University of Nevada, Las Vegas	M,D
University of Nevada, Reno	M,D
University of New Hampshire	M,D
University of New Mexico	M,D
The University of North Carolina at Chapel Hill	M,D
The University of North Carolina at Greensboro	M
University of North Texas	M,D,O
University of North Texas Health Science Center at Fort Worth	M,D
University of Notre Dame	M,D
University of Oklahoma	M,D*
University of Oklahoma Health Sciences Center	M,D
University of Oregon	M,D
University of Ottawa	M,D
University of Pennsylvania	D*
University of Puerto Rico–Medical Sciences Campus	M,D
University of Regina	M,D
University of Rhode Island	M,D*
University of Rochester	D*
University of Saint Joseph	M
University of Saskatchewan	M,D
The University of Scranton	M
University of South Carolina	M,D
University of Southern California	M*
University of Southern Mississippi	M,D
The University of Tennessee	M,D
The University of Texas at Austin	D
The University of Texas at Dallas	M,D
The University of Texas at El Paso	M,D
The University of Texas Health Science Center at Houston	M,D
The University of Texas Health Science Center at San Antonio	M,D
The University of Texas Medical Branch	D
The University of Texas Southwestern Medical Center	D
University of the Sciences	M,D
The University of Toledo	M,D
University of Toronto	M,D
The University of Tulsa	M,D
University of Utah	M,D
University of Vermont	M,D
University of Victoria	M,D
University of Virginia	D
University of Washington	D
University of Waterloo	M,D
The University of Western Ontario	M,D
University of Windsor	M,D
University of Wisconsin–Madison	M,D
University of Wisconsin–Milwaukee	M,D*
Utah State University	M,D
Vanderbilt University	M,D*
Virginia Commonwealth University	M,D
Virginia Polytechnic Institute and State University	M,D
Wake Forest University	D
Washington State University	M,D
Washington University in St. Louis	D
Wayne State University	M,D,O
Weill Cornell Medicine	M,D
Wesleyan University	D
West Virginia University	M,D
Worcester Polytechnic Institute	M,D
Wright State University	M
Yale University	D
Youngstown State University	M

BIOENGINEERING

Alfred University	M,D
Baylor College of Medicine	D
California Institute of Technology	M,D
Carnegie Mellon University	M,D
Clemson University	M,D,O
Colorado School of Mines	M,D
Colorado State University	M,D
Cornell University	M,D
Dalhousie University	M,D
Florida Atlantic University	M,D
George Mason University	D
Georgia Institute of Technology	M,D
Harvard University	M,D*
Illinois Institute of Technology	M,D
Johns Hopkins University	M,D*
Kansas State University	M,D
Lehigh University	M,D
Louisiana State University and Agricultural & Mechanical College	M,D
Massachusetts Institute of Technology	M,D
McGill University	M,D
Mississippi State University	M,D
New York Institute of Technology	M
North Carolina Agricultural and Technical State University	M
North Carolina State University	M,D,O
Northeastern University	M,D,O
Northern Arizona University	M,D
Northwestern University	D
The Ohio State University	M,D
Oklahoma State University	M,D
Oregon State University	M,D
Penn State University Park	M,D*
Princeton University	M,D
Rice University	M,D
Santa Clara University	M,D,O
South Dakota School of Mines and Technology	D
Stanford University	M,D
Syracuse University	M,D*
Temple University	M,D*
Texas A&M University	M,D
Texas Tech University	M
Tufts University	M,D,O*
University at Buffalo, the State University of New York	M,D,O
University of Arkansas	M
The University of British Columbia	M,D
University of California, Berkeley	M,D
University of California, Davis	M,D
University of California, Los Angeles	M,D*
University of California, Merced	M,D
University of California, Riverside	M,D
University of California, San Diego	M,D*
University of California, San Francisco	D
University of California, Santa Barbara	M,D
University of Chicago	D
University of Colorado Denver	M,D
University of Dayton	M
University of Denver	M,D
University of Florida	M,D,O
University of Guelph	M,D
University of Hawaii at Manoa	M
University of Idaho	M,D
University of Illinois at Chicago	M,D
University of Illinois at Urbana–Champaign	M,D
The University of Kansas	M,D
University of Louisville	M,D
University of Maryland, College Park	M,D
University of Michigan–Dearborn	M
University of Missouri	M,D
University of Nebraska–Lincoln	M,D
University of Notre Dame	M,D
University of Ottawa	M,D
University of Pennsylvania	M,D*
University of Pittsburgh	M,D*
University of Puerto Rico–Mayagüez	M,D
University of Saskatchewan	M,D
The University of Texas at Arlington	M,D
The University of Toledo	M,D
University of Utah	M,D
University of Vermont	D
University of Washington	M,D
Utah State University	M,D
Virginia Polytechnic Institute and State University	M,D
Washington State University	M,D
Wilkes University	M

BIOETHICS

Albany Medical College	M,D,O
Case Western Reserve University	M*
Clarkson University	M,O
Cleveland State University	M,O
Columbia University	M*
Creighton University	M
Duke University	M*
Duquesne University	M,D,O
Emory University	M
Hofstra University	M,D,O
Icahn School of Medicine at Mount Sinai	M
Indiana University–Purdue University Indianapolis	M,D,O
Instituto Tecnologico de Santo Domingo	M,O
Johns Hopkins University	M,D*
Kansas City University of Medicine and Biosciences	M
Loma Linda University	M,O
Loyola Marymount University	M
Loyola University Chicago	M,D,O
McGill University	M,D,O
Medical College of Wisconsin	M,O
New York University	M*
Northeast Ohio Medical University	M,D,O
Saint Louis University	D,O*
Stony Brook University, State University of New York	
Trinity International University	M,D
Université de Montréal	M,D,O
University of Louisville	M,D
University of Mary	M
University of Pennsylvania	M*
University of Pittsburgh	M*
University of South Dakota	D,O
University of South Florida	O*
The University of Tennessee	M,D
University of Toronto	M,D
University of Washington	M
Washington State University	M,D,O
Washington University in St. Louis	M

BIOINFORMATICS

Arizona State University at the Tempe campus	M,D
Boston University	M,D*
Brandeis University	M
California State University Channel Islands	M
California State University, Dominguez Hills	M
Clemson University	M,D,O
Dalhousie University	M,D
Duke University	D,O*
Emory University	M,D
George Mason University	M,D,O
Georgetown University	M,O
Georgia Institute of Technology	M,D
Georgia State University	M,D
Grand Valley State University	M
Hood College	M,O*
Hunter College of the City University of New York	M
Indiana University Bloomington	M,D,O
Indiana University–Purdue University Indianapolis	M,D
Iowa State University of Science and Technology	M,D
Johns Hopkins University	M*
Lawrence Technological University	M,O
Lewis University	M
Marquette University	M,D
Massachusetts Institute of Technology	M,D
McGill University	M,D
Morgan State University	M
New Jersey Institute of Technology	M,D,O
New Mexico State University	M,D
New York University	M*
North Carolina State University	M,D
North Dakota State University	M,D*
Northeastern University	M,D
Nova Southeastern University	M,D,O*
Oregon Health & Science University	M,D,O
Oregon State University	D
Penn State Hershey Medical Center	
Rice University	M,D
Rochester Institute of Technology	M
Rowan University	M
Rutgers University–Newark	M,D
Saint Louis University	M*
San Jose State University	M
Simon Fraser University	M,D,O
State University of New York at Oswego	M
Stevens Institute of Technology	M,D,O
Stony Brook University, State University of New York	M,D,O
Tufts University	M,D*
Université de Montréal	M,D
University at Buffalo, the State University of New York	M,D
The University of Alabama at Birmingham	D
University of Arkansas at Little Rock	M,D
University of Arkansas for Medical Sciences	M,D,O
The University of British Columbia	M,D
University of California, Los Angeles	M,D*
University of California, Riverside	D
University of California, San Diego	D*
University of California, San Francisco	D
University of California, Santa Cruz	M,D*
University of Chicago	M
University of Cincinnati	D,O
University of Colorado Denver	D
University of Georgia	M,D
University of Idaho	M,D
University of Illinois at Chicago	M,D
University of Illinois at Urbana–Champaign	M,D,O
The University of Iowa	M,D,O*

*M—masters degree; D—doctorate; O—other advanced degree; *—Close-Up and/or Display*

University of Louisville	M,D
University of Maine	M,D
The University of Manchester	M,D
University of Maryland, College Park	D
University of Massachusetts Medical School	M,D
University of Memphis	M,D
University of Michigan	M,D*
University of Minnesota Rochester	M,D
University of Missouri	M
University of Missouri–Kansas City	M,D,O
University of Nebraska at Omaha	M,D
University of Nebraska–Lincoln	M,D
University of Nebraska Medical Center	M,D
The University of North Carolina at Chapel Hill	D
The University of North Carolina at Charlotte	M,D,O
University of Pittsburgh	M,D,O*
University of Southern California	D*
University of South Florida	M,D,O*
The University of Tennessee at Chattanooga	M,O
The University of Texas at El Paso	M,D
The University of Texas Health Science Center at Houston	M,D,O
The University of Texas Medical Branch	D
University of the Sciences	M
The University of Toledo	M,O
University of Utah	M,D,O
University of Washington	M,D
University of Wisconsin–Madison	M,D
Vanderbilt University	M,D*
Virginia Polytechnic Institute and State University	M,D
Wayne State University	M,D
Wesleyan University	D
Worcester Polytechnic Institute	M,D
Yale University	D

BIOLOGICAL AND BIOMEDICAL SCIENCES—GENERAL

Acadia University	M
Adelphi University	M
Alabama Agricultural and Mechanical University	M,D
Alabama State University	M,D
Albert Einstein College of Medicine	D
Alcorn State University	M
American Museum of Natural History–Richard Gilder Graduate School	D
American University	M
American University of Beirut	M,D
Andrews University	M
Angelo State University	M
Appalachian State University	M
Arizona State University at the Tempe campus	M,D
Arkansas State University	M,O
A.T. Still University	M,D
Auburn University	M,D*
Austin Peay State University	M
Ball State University	M,D
Barry University	M
Baylor College of Medicine	M,D
Baylor University	M,D
Bemidji State University	M
Binghamton University, State University of New York	M,D
Bloomsburg University of Pennsylvania	M
Boise State University	M,D
Boston College	D
Boston University	M,D*
Bowling Green State University	M,D
Bradley University	M
Brandeis University	M,D,O
Brigham Young University	M,D
Brock University	M,D
Brooklyn College of the City University of New York	M
Brown University	M,D
Bucknell University	M
Buffalo State College, State University of New York	M
Cabrini University	M,D
California Institute of Technology	D
California Polytechnic State University, San Luis Obispo	M*
California State Polytechnic University, Pomona	M
California State University, Bakersfield	M
California State University, Chico	M
California State University, Dominguez Hills	M
California State University, East Bay	M
California State University, Fresno	M
California State University, Fullerton	M
California State University, Long Beach	M
California State University, Los Angeles	M
California State University, Northridge	M
California State University, Sacramento	M
California State University, San Bernardino	M
California State University, San Marcos	M
Carleton University	M,D
Carnegie Mellon University	M,D
Case Western Reserve University	M,D*
The Catholic University of America	M,D
Cedars-Sinai Medical Center	M,D
Central Connecticut State University	M,D
Central Michigan University	M
Central Washington University	M
Chatham University	M
Chicago State University	M
The Citadel, The Military College of South Carolina	M,O
City College of the City University of New York	M,D
Clark Atlanta University	M,D
Clarkson University	M
Clark University	M,D
Clayton State University	M
Clemson University	M,D
Cleveland State University	M,D
Cold Spring Harbor Laboratory	D
The College at Brockport, State University of New York	M,O
College of Staten Island of the City University of New York	M
The College of William and Mary	M*
Colorado State University	M,D
Colorado State University–Pueblo	M
Columbia University	M,D,O*
Columbus State University	M
Concordia University (Canada)	M,D,O
Cornell University	D
Creighton University	M,D
Dalhousie University	M,D
Dartmouth College	D*
Delaware State University	M
Delta State University	M
DePaul University	M,D
Des Moines University	M
Dominican University of California	M
Drew University	M,D,O
Drexel University	M,D,O*
Duke University	M,D*
Duquesne University	D
East Carolina University	M
Eastern Illinois University	M
Eastern Kentucky University	M
Eastern Mennonite University	M
Eastern Michigan University	M
Eastern New Mexico University	M
Eastern Virginia Medical School	M,D
Eastern Washington University	M
East Stroudsburg University of Pennsylvania	M
East Tennessee State University	M,D
Elizabeth City State University	M
Elms College	M
Emory University	D
Emporia State University	M
Fairleigh Dickinson University, Florham Campus	M
Fairleigh Dickinson University, Metropolitan Campus	M
Fisk University	M
Fitchburg State University	M
Florida Atlantic University	M,D
Florida Institute of Technology	M,D
Florida International University	M,D
Florida State University	M,D
Fordham University	M,D,O
Fort Hays State University	M
Frostburg State University	M
Geisinger Commonwealth School of Medicine	M
George Mason University	M,D,O
Georgetown University	M,D
The George Washington University	M,D
Georgia College & State University	M
Georgia Institute of Technology	M,D
Georgia Southern University	M,D
Georgia State University	M,D
Gerstner Sloan Kettering Graduate School of Biomedical Sciences	D*
Goucher College	O
The Graduate Center, City University of New York	D
Grand Valley State University	M
Hampton University	M
Harvard University	M,D,O*
Hofstra University	M
Hood College	M*
Howard University	M,D
Humboldt State University	M
Hunter College of the City University of New York	M,D
Icahn School of Medicine at Mount Sinai	M,D
Idaho State University	M,D
Illinois Institute of Technology	M,D
Illinois State University	M,D
Indiana State University	M,D
Indiana University Bloomington	M,D
Indiana University of Pennsylvania	M
Indiana University–Purdue University Fort Wayne	M
Indiana University–Purdue University Indianapolis	M,D
Inter American University of Puerto Rico, Barranquitas Campus	M
Iowa State University of Science and Technology	M,D
Irell & Manella Graduate School of Biological Sciences	D*
Jackson State University	M
Jacksonville State University	M
James Madison University	M
John Carroll University	M
Johns Hopkins University	M,D*
Kansas City University of Medicine and Biosciences	M
Kansas State University	M,D
Keck Graduate Institute	M,D,O
Kennesaw State University	M
Kent State University	M,D
Kutztown University of Pennsylvania	M,D
Lake Erie College of Osteopathic Medicine	M,D,O
Lakehead University	M
Lamar University	M
Laurentian University	M,D
Lee University	M,O
Lehigh University	M,D
Lehman College of the City University of New York	M
Liberty University	M,D
London Metropolitan University	M,D
Long Island University–LIU Brooklyn	M,D,O
Long Island University–LIU Post	M,O
Louisiana State University and Agricultural & Mechanical College	M,D
Louisiana State University Health Sciences Center	D
Louisiana State University Health Sciences Center at Shreveport	M
Louisiana State University in Shreveport	M
Louisiana Tech University	M,D,O
Loyola University Chicago	M,D
Loyola University Chicago	M,D
Manhattanville College	M,O
Marquette University	M,D
Marshall University	M,D
Massachusetts Institute of Technology	M,D
McGill University	M,D
McMaster University	M,D
Medical College of Wisconsin	M,D,O
Medical University of South Carolina	M,D
Meharry Medical College	D
Memorial University of Newfoundland	M,D,O
Miami University	M,D
Michigan State University	M,D
Michigan Technological University	M,D
Middle Tennessee State University	M
Midwestern State University	M
Midwestern University, Downers Grove Campus	M
Midwestern University, Glendale Campus	M
Mills College	O
Minnesota State University Mankato	M
Mississippi College	M
Mississippi State University	M,D
Missouri State University	M
Missouri University of Science and Technology	M
Missouri Western State University	M
Montana State University	M,D
Montclair State University	M
Morehead State University	M
Morehouse School of Medicine	M,D
Morgan State University	M,D
Mount Allison University	M
Murray State University	M
National University	M,O
New Jersey Institute of Technology	M,D,O
New Mexico Institute of Mining and Technology	M,D
New Mexico State University	M,D
New York Medical College	M,D
New York University	M,D,O*
North Carolina Agricultural and Technical State University	M
North Carolina Central University	M
North Carolina State University	M,D,O
North Dakota State University	M,D*
Northeastern Illinois University	M
Northeastern University	M,D
Northern Arizona University	M,D
Northern Illinois University	M,D
Northern Michigan University	M
Northwestern University	D
Northwest Missouri State University	M,O
Nova Southeastern University	M,D*
Oakland University	M,D,O
Occidental College	M
The Ohio State University	M,D
Ohio University	M,D
Oklahoma State University	M,D
Oklahoma State University Center for Health Sciences	M,D
Old Dominion University	M,D
Oregon Health & Science University	M,D,O
Oregon State University	M,D
Pace University	M,O
Penn State Hershey Medical Center	M,D
Penn State University Park	M,D*
Philadelphia College of Osteopathic Medicine	M*
Pittsburg State University	M
Point Loma Nazarene University	M
Ponce Health Sciences University	D
Pontifical Catholic University of Puerto Rico	M
Portland State University	M,D
Purdue University	M,D
Purdue University Northwest	M
Queens College of the City University of New York	M,O
Queen's University at Kingston	M,D
Quinnipiac University	M
Regis University	M
Rensselaer Polytechnic Institute	M,D
Rhode Island College	M,O
Rochester Institute of Technology	M
The Rockefeller University	M,D*
Rocky Vista University	M
Rosalind Franklin University of Medicine and Science	M,D
Rowan University	M
Rutgers University–Camden	M
Rutgers University–Newark	M,D,O
Rutgers University–New Brunswick	M,D
St. Cloud State University	M
Saint Francis University	M
St. Francis Xavier University	M
St. John Fisher College	M
St. John's University (NY)	M,D
Saint Joseph's University	M*
Saint Louis University	M,D*
Salisbury University	M
Sam Houston State University	M
San Diego State University	M,D
Sanford Burnham Prebys Medical Discovery Institute	D
San Francisco State University	M
San Jose State University	M
The Scripps Research Institute	D
Seton Hall University	M,D
Shippensburg University of Pennsylvania	M
Simon Fraser University	M,D,O
Smith College	M
Sonoma State University	M
South Carolina State University	M
South Dakota State University	M,D
Southeastern Louisiana University	M
Southeast Missouri State University	M
Southern Connecticut State University	M
Southern Illinois University Carbondale	M,D
Southern Illinois University Edwardsville	M
Southern Methodist University	M,D
Southern University and Agricultural and Mechanical College	M
Stanford University	M,D
State University of New York at Fredonia	M,O
State University of New York College at Oneonta	M
State University of New York Downstate Medical Center	M,D
State University of New York Upstate Medical University	M,D
Stephen F. Austin State University	M
Stevenson University	M
Stony Brook University, State University of New York	M,D,O
Sul Ross State University	M
Syracuse University	M,D*
Tarleton State University	M
Teachers College, Columbia University	M,D
Temple University	M,D*
Tennessee State University	D
Tennessee Technological University	M,D
Texas A&M International University	M
Texas A&M University	M,D,O
Texas A&M University–Commerce	M,O
Texas A&M University–Corpus Christi	M,D
Texas A&M University–Kingsville	M
Texas Christian University	M
Texas Southern University	M
Texas State University	M
Texas Tech University	M,D
Texas Tech University Health Sciences Center	M,D
Texas Tech University Health Sciences Center El Paso	M
Texas Woman's University	M,D
Thomas Jefferson University	M,D,O
Towson University	M
Trent University	M,D
Troy University	M,O
Truett McConnell University	M
Truman State University	M
Tufts University	M,D,O*
Tulane University	M,D
Tuskegee University	M,D
Uniformed Services University of the Health Sciences	M,D*
Universidad Central del Caribe	M,D
Universidad de Ciencias Medicas	M,D,O
Université de Moncton	M
Université de Montréal	M,D
Université de Sherbrooke	M,D,O
Université du Québec à Montréal	M,D
Université du Québec en Abitibi-Témiscamingue	M,D
Université du Québec, Institut National de la Recherche Scientifique	M,D
Université Laval	M,D,O
University at Albany, State University of New York	M,D
University at Buffalo, the State University of New York	M,D
The University of Akron	M,D
The University of Alabama	M,D
The University of Alabama at Birmingham	M,D
The University of Alabama in Huntsville	M,D
University of Alaska Anchorage	M
University of Alaska Fairbanks	M,D,O
University of Alberta	M,D
The University of Arizona	M,D
University of Arkansas	M,D
University of Arkansas at Little Rock	M
University of Arkansas for Medical Sciences	M,D,O
University of Calgary	M,D
University of California, Berkeley	D
University of California, Irvine	M,D
University of California, Los Angeles	M,D*

University of California, Merced	M,D
University of California, Riverside	M,D
University of California, San Diego	M,D*
University of California, San Francisco	D
University of Central Arkansas	M
University of Central Florida	M,D
University of Central Missouri	M,D,O
University of Central Oklahoma	M
University of Chicago	D
University of Cincinnati	M,D,O
University of Colorado Denver	M,D
University of Connecticut Health Center	D
University of Dayton	M,D
University of Delaware	M,D*
University of Denver	M,D
University of Florida	M,D
University of Georgia	D
University of Guam	M
University of Guelph	M,D
University of Hartford	M
University of Hawaii at Manoa	M,D
University of Holy Cross	M,D
University of Houston	M,D
University of Houston–Clear Lake	M
University of Houston–Victoria	M
University of Idaho	M,D
University of Illinois at Chicago	M,D
University of Illinois at Springfield	M
University of Illinois at Urbana–Champaign	M,D
University of Indianapolis	M
The University of Iowa	M,D*
The University of Kansas	D
University of Kentucky	M,D
University of Lethbridge	M,D
University of Louisiana at Lafayette	M,D
University of Louisiana at Monroe	M
University of Louisville	M,D
University of Maine	M,D
The University of Manchester	M,D
University of Manitoba	M,D,O
University of Maryland, Baltimore	M,D,O
University of Maryland, Baltimore County	M,D
University of Maryland, College Park	M,D
University of Massachusetts Amherst	M,D*
University of Massachusetts Boston	M,D
University of Massachusetts Dartmouth	M,D
University of Massachusetts Lowell	M
University of Massachusetts Medical School	M,D
University of Memphis	M,D
University of Miami	M,D*
University of Michigan	M,D*
University of Michigan–Flint	M
University of Minnesota, Duluth	M,D
University of Minnesota, Twin Cities Campus	M
University of Mississippi	M,D
University of Mississippi Medical Center	M,D
University of Missouri	M,D
University of Missouri–Kansas City	M,D
University of Missouri–St. Louis	M,D,O
University of Montana	M,D
University of Nebraska at Kearney	M
University of Nebraska at Omaha	M,O
University of Nebraska–Lincoln	M,D
University of Nebraska Medical Center	M,D
University of Nevada, Las Vegas	M,D
University of Nevada, Reno	M
University of New Brunswick Fredericton	M,D
University of New Brunswick Saint John	M,D
University of New England	M
University of New Hampshire	M,D
University of New Mexico	M,D
University of New Orleans	M
The University of North Carolina at Chapel Hill	M,D
The University of North Carolina at Charlotte	M,D
The University of North Carolina at Greensboro	M
The University of North Carolina Wilmington	M,D
University of North Dakota	M,D
University of Northern Colorado	M
University of Northern Iowa	M
University of North Florida	M
University of North Texas	M,D,O
University of North Texas Health Science Center at Fort Worth	M,D
University of Notre Dame	M,D
University of Oklahoma	D*
University of Oklahoma Health Sciences Center	M,D
University of Oregon	M,D
University of Ottawa	M,D
University of Pennsylvania	M,D*
University of Pittsburgh	M,D*
University of Prince Edward Island	M,D
University of Puerto Rico–Mayagüez	M
University of Puerto Rico–Medical Sciences Campus	M,D
University of Puerto Rico–Río Piedras	M,D
University of Regina	M,D
University of Rhode Island	M,D*
University of Rochester	M,D*
University of Saint Joseph	M
University of San Francisco	M
University of Saskatchewan	M,D
University of South Alabama	M,D
University of South Carolina	M,D,O
University of South Dakota	M,D
University of Southern California	M,D,O*
University of Southern Maine	M
University of Southern Mississippi	M,D
University of South Florida	M,D*
The University of Tennessee	M,D
The University of Tennessee Health Science Center	M,D
The University of Tennessee–Oak Ridge National Laboratory	M,D
The University of Texas at Arlington	M,D
The University of Texas at Austin	M,D
The University of Texas at Dallas	M,D
The University of Texas at El Paso	M,D
The University of Texas at San Antonio	M,D
The University of Texas at Tyler	M
The University of Texas Health Science Center at Houston	M,D
The University of Texas Health Science Center at San Antonio	D
The University of Texas Medical Branch	M,D
The University of Texas of the Permian Basin	M
The University of Texas Rio Grande Valley	M
The University of Texas Southwestern Medical Center	M,D
University of the Incarnate Word	M
University of the Pacific	M
The University of Toledo	M,D,O
The University of Tulsa	M,D
University of Utah	M,D,O
University of Vermont	M,D
University of Victoria	M,D
University of Virginia	M,D
University of Washington	M,D
University of Waterloo	M,D
The University of Western Ontario	M,D
University of West Florida	M
University of West Georgia	M,O
University of Windsor	M,D
University of Wisconsin–La Crosse	M
University of Wisconsin–Madison	
University of Wisconsin–Milwaukee	M,D*
University of Wisconsin–Oshkosh	M
Utah State University	M,D
Vanderbilt University	M,D*
Villanova University	M
Virginia Commonwealth University	M,D,O
Virginia Polytechnic Institute and State University	M,D
Virginia State University	M
Wake Forest University	M,D
Walla Walla University	M
Washington State University	M,D
Washington University in St. Louis	D
Wayne State University	M,D
Weill Cornell Medicine	M,D
Wesleyan University	D
West Chester University of Pennsylvania	M,O
Western Carolina University	M
Western Illinois University	M,O
Western Kentucky University	M
Western Michigan University	M,D,O
Western University of Health Sciences	M
Western Washington University	M
West Liberty University	M
West Texas A&M University	M
West Virginia University	M,D
Wichita State University	M
Wilfrid Laurier University	M
William Paterson University of New Jersey	M,D,O
Winthrop University	M
Worcester Polytechnic Institute	M,D
Wright State University	M,D
Yale University	D
York University	M,D
Youngstown State University	M

BIOLOGICAL ANTHROPOLOGY

Duke University	D*
Kent State University	M,D
Mercyhurst University	M

BIOMATHEMATICS

The College of William and Mary	M,D*
North Carolina State University	M,D
University of California, Los Angeles	M,D*

BIOMEDICAL ENGINEERING

American University of Beirut	M,D
American University of Sharjah	M,D
Arizona State University at the Tempe campus	M,D
Baylor College of Medicine	D
Baylor University	M,D
Binghamton University, State University of New York	M,D
Boston University	M,D*
Brown University	M,D
California Polytechnic State University, San Luis Obispo	M*
Carleton University	M
Carnegie Mellon University	M,D
Case Western Reserve University	M,D*
The Catholic University of America	M,D
City College of the City University of New York	M,D
Clemson University	M,D,O
Cleveland State University	D
Colorado State University	M,D
Columbia University	M,D*
Cornell University	M,D
Dalhousie University	M,D
Dartmouth College	M,D*
Drexel University	M,D*
Duke University	M,D*
East Carolina University	M
École Polytechnique de Montréal	M,D,O
Florida Agricultural and Mechanical University	M,D
Florida Institute of Technology	M,D
Florida International University	M,D
Florida State University	M,D
The George Washington University	M,D
Georgia Institute of Technology	D
Harvard University	D*
Illinois Institute of Technology	M,D
Indiana University–Purdue University Indianapolis	M,D
Johns Hopkins University	M,D,O*
Lawrence Technological University	M,D
Louisiana Tech University	M,D,O
Marquette University	M,D
Massachusetts Institute of Technology	M,D
Mayo Clinic Graduate School of Biomedical Sciences	M,D
McGill University	M,D
Mercer University	M
Michigan Technological University	M,D
Mississippi State University	M,D
New Jersey Institute of Technology	M,D
New York University	M,D*
North Carolina State University	M,D
Northwestern University	M,D
The Ohio State University	M,D
Ohio University	M
Old Dominion University	M,D
Oregon Health & Science University	M,D
Purdue University	M,D
Rensselaer Polytechnic Institute	M,D
Rice University	M,D
Rose-Hulman Institute of Technology	M
Rutgers University–Newark	O
Rutgers University–New Brunswick	M,D
St. Cloud State University	M,O
Saint Louis University	M,D*
San Jose State University	M
South Dakota School of Mines and Technology	M,D
Southern Illinois University Carbondale	M
Stanford University	M,D,O
State University of New York Downstate Medical Center	M,D
Stevens Institute of Technology	M,D,O
Stony Brook University, State University of New York	M,D,O
Tennessee State University	M,D
Texas A&M University	M,D
Tufts University	M,D*
Tulane University	M,D
Université de Montréal	M,D,O
University at Buffalo, the State University of New York	M,D
The University of Akron	M,D
The University of Alabama at Birmingham	M,D
University of Alberta	M,D
The University of Arizona	M,D
University of Arkansas	M
University of Bridgeport	M
The University of British Columbia	M,D
University of Calgary	M,D
University of California, Davis	M,D
University of California, Irvine	M,D
University of California, Los Angeles	M,D*
University of Central Oklahoma	M
University of Cincinnati	M,D
University of Connecticut	M,D*
University of Florida	M,D,O
University of Houston	D
The University of Iowa	M,D*
University of Kentucky	M,D
University of Maine	M,D
University of Massachusetts Boston	D
University of Massachusetts Dartmouth	D
University of Memphis	M,D
University of Miami	M,D*
University of Michigan	M,D*
University of Minnesota, Twin Cities Campus	M,D
University of Nebraska–Lincoln	M,D
University of Nevada, Las Vegas	M,D,O
University of Nevada, Reno	M,D
University of New Haven	M*
University of New Mexico	M,D
The University of North Carolina at Chapel Hill	M,D
University of North Texas	M,D,O
University of Oklahoma	M,D*
University of Ottawa	M
University of Portland	M
University of Rhode Island	M,D*
University of Rochester	M,D*
University of Saskatchewan	M,D
University of Southern California	M,D*
University of South Florida	M,D,O*
The University of Tennessee	M,D
The University of Tennessee Health Science Center	M,D
The University of Texas at Austin	M,D
The University of Texas at Dallas	M,D
The University of Texas at El Paso	M,D,O
The University of Texas at San Antonio	M,D
The University of Texas Health Science Center at San Antonio	M,D
The University of Texas Southwestern Medical Center	M,D
The University of Toledo	D
University of Toronto	M,D
University of Vermont	M
University of Virginia	M,D
University of Wisconsin–Madison	M,D
University of Wisconsin–Milwaukee	M,D*
Vanderbilt University	M,D*
Virginia Commonwealth University	M,D
Virginia Polytechnic Institute and State University	M,D
Wake Forest University	M,D
Washington University in St. Louis	M,D
Wayne State University	M,D,O
Wichita State University	M
Widener University	M
Worcester Polytechnic Institute	M,D,O
Wright State University	M
Yale University	M,D

BIOMETRY

Cornell University	M,D
San Diego State University	M
University of Wisconsin–Madison	M

BIOPHYSICS

Albert Einstein College of Medicine	D
Baylor College of Medicine	D
Boston University	M,D*
Brandeis University	M,D
California Institute of Technology	D
Carnegie Mellon University	M,D
Case Western Reserve University	M,D*
Columbia University	M,D*
Cornell University	D
Dalhousie University	M,D
East Carolina University	M,D
Emory University	D
Harvard University	D*
Howard University	D
Illinois State University	M,D
Iowa State University of Science and Technology	M,D
Johns Hopkins University	D*
Northwestern University	D
The Ohio State University	M,D
Oregon State University	M,D
Purdue University	M,D
Rensselaer Polytechnic Institute	M,D
Rosalind Franklin University of Medicine and Science	M,D
Stanford University	D
Stony Brook University, State University of New York	D
Texas Christian University	M,D
Université de Sherbrooke	M,D
Université du Québec à Trois-Rivières	M,D
University at Buffalo, the State University of New York	M,D
University of California, Berkeley	D
University of California, Davis	M,D
University of California, Irvine	D
University of California, San Diego	M,D*
University of California, San Francisco	D
University of California, Santa Barbara	D
University of Chicago	D
University of Cincinnati	D
University of Colorado Denver	M
University of Connecticut	M,D*
University of Guelph	M,D
University of Illinois at Chicago	M,D
University of Illinois at Urbana–Champaign	M,D
The University of Iowa	M,D*
The University of Kansas	D
The University of Manchester	M,D
University of Maryland, College Park	D
University of Miami	D*
University of Michigan	D*
University of Minnesota, Duluth	M,D
University of Minnesota, Twin Cities Campus	M,D
University of Mississippi Medical Center	D
University of Missouri–Kansas City	D
The University of North Carolina at Chapel Hill	M,D
University of Regina	M,D
University of Rochester	D*
University of Southern California	M,D*
The University of Texas Medical Branch	D
University of Toronto	M,D
University of Virginia	M,D
University of Washington	D

*M—masters degree; D—doctorate; O—other advanced degree; *—Close-Up and/or Display*

The University of Western Ontario	M,D
University of Wisconsin–Madison	D
Vanderbilt University	M,D*
Washington State University	M,D
Weill Cornell Medicine	M,D
Yale University	D

BIOPSYCHOLOGY

American University	M,D,O
Argosy University, Atlanta	M,D,O
Argosy University, Twin Cities	M,D,O
Binghamton University, State University of New York	D
Boston University	M*
Carnegie Mellon University	D
Cornell University	D
Drexel University	M,D*
Duke University	D*
Florida State University	M,D
The Graduate Center, City University of New York	D
Harvard University	D*
Howard University	M,D
Liberty University	M,D
Louisiana State University and Agricultural & Mechanical College	M,D
Memorial University of Newfoundland	M,D
Northwestern University	D
Oregon Health & Science University	D
Palo Alto University	D
Penn State University Park	M,D*
Philadelphia College of Osteopathic Medicine	M,D,O*
Rutgers University–Newark	D
Rutgers University–New Brunswick	D
The University of British Columbia	M,D
University of Connecticut	M,D*
University of Michigan	D*
University of Minnesota, Twin Cities Campus	D
University of Nebraska–Lincoln	M,D
The University of North Carolina at Chapel Hill	D
University of Oklahoma Health Sciences Center	M,D
University of Oregon	M,D
The University of Texas at Austin	D
University of Windsor	M,D
University of Wisconsin–Madison	D
Wayne State University	M,D,O

BIOSTATISTICS

American University	M,O
American University of Beirut	M,D
Boston University	M,D*
Brown University	M,D
California State University, East Bay	M
Case Western Reserve University	M,D*
Columbia University	M,D*
Dartmouth College	M,D*
Drexel University	M,D,O*
Duke University	M*
East Tennessee State University	M,D,O
Emory University	M,D
Florida International University	M,D
Florida State University	M,D
George Mason University	M,D,O
Georgetown University	M,O
The George Washington University	M,D
Georgia Southern University	M,D
Georgia State University	M,D
Grand Valley State University	M
Harvard University	M,D*
Indiana University Bloomington	M,D
Indiana University–Purdue University Indianapolis	M,D,O
Iowa State University of Science and Technology	M,D
Johns Hopkins University	M,D*
Kent State University	M,D
Loma Linda University	M,D
Louisiana State University Health Sciences Center	M,D
McGill University	M,D,O
Medical College of Wisconsin	D
Medical University of South Carolina	M,D
Middle Tennessee State University	M
Monroe College	M
New Jersey Institute of Technology	M,D,O
New York Medical College	M,D,O
New York University	D*
Northwestern University	D
The Ohio State University	M,D
Old Dominion University	M,D
Oregon State University	M,D
Penn State Hershey Medical Center	D
Rice University	M,D
Rutgers University–New Brunswick	M,D,O
San Diego State University	M,D
Southern Methodist University	M,D
Stanford University	M,D
Texas A&M University	M,D
Tufts University	M,D,O*
Tulane University	M,D
University at Albany, State University of New York	M,D
University at Buffalo, the State University of New York	M,D
The University of Alabama at Birmingham	M,D
University of Alberta	M,D,O
The University of Arizona	M,D
University of Arkansas for Medical Sciences	M,D,O
University of California, Berkeley	M,D
University of California, Davis	M,D
University of California, Los Angeles	M,D*
University of California, San Diego	D*
University of Cincinnati	M,D
University of Colorado Denver	M,D
University of Florida	M,D,O
University of Illinois at Chicago	M,D
The University of Iowa	M,D,O*
The University of Kansas	M,D,O
University of Kentucky	D
University of Louisville	M,D
University of Maryland, Baltimore	M,D
University of Maryland, Baltimore County	M,D
University of Maryland, College Park	M,D
University of Massachusetts Amherst	M,D*
University of Memphis	M,D
University of Michigan	M,D*
University of Minnesota, Twin Cities Campus	M,D
University of Nebraska Medical Center	D
The University of North Carolina at Chapel Hill	M,D
University of North Texas Health Science Center at Fort Worth	M,D,O
University of Oklahoma Health Sciences Center	M,D
University of Pennsylvania	M,D*
University of Pittsburgh	M,D*
University of Puerto Rico–Medical Sciences Campus	M
University of Rochester	M*
University of South Carolina	M,D
University of Southern California	M,D*
University of Southern Mississippi	M
University of South Florida	M,D,O*
The University of Texas Health Science Center at Houston	M,D,O
The University of Toledo	M,O
University of Toronto	M,D
University of Utah	M,D
University of Vermont	M
University of Washington	M,D
University of Waterloo	M,D
The University of Western Ontario	M,D
University of Wisconsin–Milwaukee	M,D,O*
Virginia Commonwealth University	M,D
Washington University in St. Louis	M,D,O
West Virginia University	M,D
Yale University	M,D

BIOSYSTEMS ENGINEERING

Auburn University	M,D*
Clemson University	M,D
Michigan State University	M,D
South Dakota State University	M,D
The University of Arizona	M,D
University of Manitoba	M,D
University of Minnesota, Twin Cities Campus	M,D
The University of Tennessee	M,D

BIOTECHNOLOGY

Adelphi University	M
American University	M
The American University in Cairo	M,D,O
Arizona State University at the Tempe campus	M,D
Arkansas State University	M,O
Azusa Pacific University	M*
Brandeis University	M
Brigham Young University	M,D
Brock University	M,D
Brown University	M,D
California State University Channel Islands	M
California State University, Fullerton	M
California State University, San Marcos	M
Carnegie Mellon University	M
The Catholic University of America	M,D
Claflin University	M
Clarkson University	D
College of Staten Island of the City University of New York	M
Columbia University	M,D*
Concordia University (Canada)	M,D,O
Cornell University	M,D
Duquesne University	M
East Carolina University	M
Eastern Virginia Medical School	M
Florida Institute of Technology	M,D
The George Washington University	M,D,O
Harvard University	M,O*
Hood College	M*
Howard University	M,D
Husson University	M
Illinois State University	M
Indiana University Bloomington	M,D
Instituto Tecnológico y de Estudios Superiores de Monterrey, Campus Monterrey	M,D
Inter American University of Puerto Rico, Barranquitas Campus	M
Inter American University of Puerto Rico, Bayamón Campus	M
Johns Hopkins University	M*
Kean University	M
Marywood University	M
McGill University	M,D,O
Michigan Technological University	M,D
Middle Tennessee State University	M
Mount St. Mary's University (MD)	M
New Mexico State University	M,D
New York University	M*
North Carolina State University	M
Northeastern University	M,D
Northwestern University	M,D
Oregon State University	M,D
Penn State University Park	M,D*
Pontifical John Paul II Institute for Studies on Marriage and Family	M,D,O
Purdue University	D
Purdue University Northwest	M
Regis College (MA)	M
Roosevelt University	M
St. John's University (NY)	M
San Francisco State University	M
San Jose State University	M
Simon Fraser University	M,D,O
Southeastern Oklahoma State University	M
Stephen F. Austin State University	M
Temple University	M,D*
Tennessee State University	M,D
Texas Tech University	M,D
Texas Tech University Health Sciences Center	M
Thomas Jefferson University	M
Tufts University	M,D,O*
Universidad de las Américas Puebla	M
University at Buffalo, the State University of New York	M
The University of Alabama at Birmingham	M
The University of Alabama in Huntsville	M,D
University of Alberta	M,D
University of Calgary	M
University of California, Irvine	M
University of Central Florida	M,D
University of Delaware	M,D*
University of Guelph	M,D
University of Houston–Clear Lake	M
The University of Kansas	M
The University of Manchester	M,D
University of Maryland, Baltimore County	M,O
University of Maryland University College	M,O
University of Massachusetts Amherst	M,D*
University of Massachusetts Boston	M,D
University of Massachusetts Dartmouth	D
University of Minnesota, Twin Cities Campus	M
University of Missouri–St. Louis	M,D
University of Nevada, Reno	M
University of North Texas Health Science Center at Fort Worth	M,D
University of Pennsylvania	M*
University of Rhode Island	M,D*
University of San Francisco	M
University of Saskatchewan	M
University of Southern California	M*
University of South Florida	M,D,O*
The University of Texas at Dallas	M,D
The University of Texas at San Antonio	M,D
University of the Sciences	M
University of Toronto	M
University of Utah	M
University of Washington	D
University of Wyoming	D
Virginia Polytechnic Institute and State University	M,D
West Virginia State University	M
William Paterson University of New Jersey	M,D,O
Worcester Polytechnic Institute	M,D
Worcester State University	M
Yeshiva University	M

BOTANY

Auburn University	M,D*
Central Washington University	M
Claremont Graduate University	M,D
Colorado State University	M,D
Dalhousie University	M
Emporia State University	M
Illinois State University	M,D
Kent State University	M,D
North Carolina State University	M,D
North Dakota State University	M,D*
Oklahoma State University	M,D
Oregon State University	M,D
Purdue University	M,D
The University of British Columbia	M,D
University of California, Riverside	M,D
University of Connecticut	M,D*
University of Florida	M,D
University of Guelph	M,D
University of Hawaii at Manoa	M,D
University of Maine	M,D
University of Manitoba	M,D
The University of North Carolina at Chapel Hill	M,D
University of Wisconsin–Madison	M,D
University of Wisconsin–Oshkosh	M
University of Wyoming	M,D

BROADCAST JOURNALISM

The American University in Cairo	M,O
Northwestern University	M
Quinnipiac University	M
Syracuse University	M*
University of Maryland, College Park	M,D
University of Miami	M,D*
University of the Sacred Heart	M,O

BUILDING SCIENCE

Arizona State University at the Tempe campus	M,D
Carnegie Mellon University	M,D
Georgia Institute of Technology	M,D
Pontificia Universidad Catolica Madre y Maestra	M
University of California, Berkeley	M,D

BUSINESS ADMINISTRATION AND MANAGEMENT—GENERAL

Abilene Christian University	M
Adams State University	M
Adelphi University	M
Alabama Agricultural and Mechanical University	M
Alabama State University	M
Alaska Pacific University	M
Albany State University	M
Albertus Magnus College	M
Alcorn State University	M
Alfred University	M
Alliant International University–Los Angeles	D
Alliant International University–San Diego	M
Alvernia University	M
Alverno College	M
Amberton University	M
American Business & Technology University	M
American College Dublin	M
The American College of Financial Services	M
American College of Thessaloniki	M,O
American Graduate University	M,O
American InterContinental University Houston	M
American InterContinental University Online	M
American International College	M,D,O
American Jewish University	M
American National University	M
American Public University System	M,D
American Sentinel University	M
American University	M,O
American University in Bulgaria	M
The American University in Cairo	M,O
The American University in Dubai	M
American University of Armenia	M
American University of Beirut	M
The American University of Paris	M
American University of Sharjah	M,D
Anaheim University	M,D,O
Anderson University (IN)	M,D
Anderson University (SC)	M
Angelo State University	M
Anna Maria College	M,O
Antioch University Los Angeles	M
Antioch University New England	M
Antioch University Santa Barbara	M
Apollos University	M,D
Appalachian State University	M
Aquinas College (MI)	M
Arcadia University	M
Argosy University, Atlanta	M,D
Argosy University, Chicago	M,D
Argosy University, Hawai'i	M,D,O
Argosy University, Los Angeles	M,D
Argosy University, Northern Virginia	M,D,O
Argosy University, Orange County	M,D,O
Argosy University, Phoenix	M,D
Argosy University, Seattle	M,D
Argosy University, Tampa	M,D
Argosy University, Twin Cities	M,D
Arizona State University at the Tempe campus	M,D
Arkansas State University	M
Arkansas Tech University	M
Ashland University	M
Ashworth College	M
Aspen University	M,O
Assumption College	M,O
Athabasca University	M,D,O
Atlantis University	M,D
Auburn University	M,D*
Auburn University at Montgomery	M
Augsburg University	M
Augusta University	M
Aurora University	M
Austin Peay State University	M
Averett University	M
Avila University	M
Azusa Pacific University	M*
Babson College	M,O
Baker College Center for Graduate Studies–Online	M,D
Baker University	M
Bakke Graduate University	M,D
Baldwin Wallace University	M
Ball State University	M,O
Barry University	M,O
Baruch College of the City University of New York	M,D,O*
Bayamón Central University	M
Baylor University	M
Belhaven University (MS)	M
Bellarmine University	M
Bellevue University	M,D
Belmont University	M
Benedictine College	M
Benedictine University	M,D
Bentley University	M,D,O
Berkeley College–Woodland Park Campus	M
Berry College	M
Bethel College	M
Bethel University (MN)	M,D,O
Bethel University (TN)	M
Binghamton University, State University of New York	M,D
Biola University	M
Black Hills State University	M
Bloomsburg University of Pennsylvania	M,O
Bluffton University	M
Bob Jones University	M,D,O
Boise State University	M

Boston College	M
Boston University	M,D*
Bowie State University	M
Bowling Green State University	M
Bradley University	M
Brandeis University	M
Brandman University	M
Brenau University	M
Brescia University	M
Bridgewater State University	M
Briercrest Seminary	M
Brigham Young University	M
Broadview University–West Jordan	M
Brock University	M
Brooklyn College of the City University of New York	M
Bryan College	M
Bryant University	M
Bryan University	M
Butler University	M
Cairn University	M,O
Caldwell University	M
California Baptist University	M
California Coast University	M
California Institute of Advanced Management	M
California Intercontinental University	M,D
California International Business University	M,D
California Lutheran University	M,O
California Miramar University	M
California Polytechnic State University, San Luis Obispo	M*
California State Polytechnic University, Pomona	M
California State University, Bakersfield	M
California State University Channel Islands	M
California State University, Chico	M
California State University, Dominguez Hills	M
California State University, East Bay	M
California State University, Fresno	M
California State University, Fullerton	M
California State University, Long Beach	M
California State University, Los Angeles	M,O
California State University, Monterey Bay	M
California State University, Northridge	M
California State University, Sacramento	M
California State University, San Bernardino	M
California State University, San Marcos	M
California State University, Stanislaus	M
California University of Management and Sciences	M,D
California University of Pennsylvania	M
Cambridge College	M
Cameron University	M
Campbellsville University	M,D
Campbell University	M
Canisius College	M
Cape Breton University	M
Capella University	M,D
Capital University	M
Capitol Technology University	M
Cardinal Stritch University	M
Carleton University	M,D
Carlos Albizu University, Miami Campus	M,D
Carlow University	M
Carnegie Mellon University	M,D
Carroll University	M
Carson-Newman University	M
Case Western Reserve University	M,D*
The Catholic University of America	M
Cedar Crest College	M
Cedarville University	M,D
Centenary College of Louisiana	M
Centenary University	M
Central Connecticut State University	M
Central European University	M,D
Central Michigan University	M,O
Chadron State College	M
Chaminade University of Honolulu	M
Champlain College	M
Chapman University	M*
Charleston Southern University	M
Charter College	M
Chatham University	M
Christian Brothers University	M,O
The Citadel, The Military College of South Carolina	M
City College of the City University of New York	M
City University of Seattle	M,O
Claflin University	M
Claremont Graduate University	M,D,O
Clarion University of Pennsylvania	M
Clark Atlanta University	M
Clarke University	M
Clarkson University	O
Clark University	M
Clayton State University	M
Cleary University	M,O
Clemson University	M,D
Cleveland State University	M,D
Coastal Carolina University	M,O
Coker College	M
College of Charleston	M
College of Saint Elizabeth	M
College of St. Joseph	M
The College of Saint Rose	M
The College of St. Scholastica	M,O
College of Staten Island of the City University of New York	M
The College of William and Mary	M*
Colorado Christian University	M
Colorado Mesa University	M
Colorado State University	M
Colorado State University–Global Campus	M
Colorado State University–Pueblo	M
Colorado Technical University Aurora	M
Colorado Technical University Colorado Springs	M,D
Columbia College (MO)	M
Columbia College Chicago	M
Columbia Southern University	M,D
Columbia University	M,D*
Columbus State University	M,O
Concordia University (United States)	M
Concordia University (Canada)	M,D,O
Concordia University Chicago	M
Concordia University Irvine	M*
Concordia University, St. Paul	M
Concordia University Wisconsin	M
Copenhagen Business School	M,D
Corban University	M
Cornell University	M,D
Cornerstone University	M,O
Creighton University	M,D
Culver-Stockton College	M
Cumberland University	M
Curry College	M,O
Daemen College	M
Dakota State University	M,D,O
Dalhousie University	M,O
Dallas Baptist University	M,D
Dartmouth College	M*
Davenport University	M
Defiance College	M
Delaware State University	M
Delaware Valley University	M
Delta State University	M
DePaul University	M,D
DeSales University	M
DeVry College of New York–Midtown Manhattan Campus	M
DeVry University–Alpharetta Campus	M
DeVry University–Arlington Campus	M
DeVry University–Charlotte Campus	M
DeVry University–Chesapeake Campus	M
DeVry University–Chicago Campus	M
DeVry University–Chicago Loop Campus	M
DeVry University–Cincinnati Campus	M
DeVry University–Columbus Campus	M
DeVry University–Decatur Campus	M
DeVry University–Folsom Campus	M
DeVry University–Fremont Campus	M
DeVry University–Ft. Washington Campus	M
DeVry University–Henderson Campus	M
DeVry University–Irving Campus	M
DeVry University–Jacksonville Campus	M
DeVry University–Long Beach Campus	M
DeVry University–Miramar Campus	M
DeVry University–Morrisville Campus	M
DeVry University–Nashville Campus	M
DeVry University–North Brunswick Campus	M
DeVry University Online	M
DeVry University–Orlando Campus	M
DeVry University–Phoenix Campus	M
DeVry University–Pomona Campus	M
DeVry University–San Diego Campus	M,O
DeVry University–Seven Hills Campus	M,O
DeVry University–Tinley Park Campus	M
Doane University	M
Dominican College	M
Dominican University	M
Dominican University of California	M
Drake University	M
Drexel University	M,D,O*
Drury University	M
Duke University	M,D,O*
Duquesne University	M
D'Youville College	M
East Carolina University	M,D,O
Eastern Illinois University	M
Eastern Kentucky University	M
Eastern Mennonite University	M
Eastern Michigan University	M,O
Eastern Nazarene College	M
Eastern New Mexico University	M
Eastern Oregon University	M
Eastern University	M,D,O
Eastern Washington University	M
East Tennessee State University	M,O
East Texas Baptist University	M
Edgewood College	M
Elmhurst College	M
Elms College	M,O
Elon University	M
Embry-Riddle Aeronautical University–Daytona	M
Embry-Riddle Aeronautical University–Worldwide	M
Emmanuel College (United States)	M,O
Emory University	M,D
Emporia State University	M
Endicott College	M
ESSEC Business School	M,D
Everglades University	M
Excelsior College	M,O
Fairfield University	M,O
Fairleigh Dickinson University, Florham Campus	M,O
Fairleigh Dickinson University, Metropolitan Campus	M,O
Fairmont State University	M
Fashion Institute of Technology	M
Faulkner University	M
Fayetteville State University	M
Felician University	M,D
Ferris State University	M
Fisher College	M
Fitchburg State University	M
Florida Agricultural and Mechanical University	M
Florida Atlantic University	M
Florida Gulf Coast University	M
Florida Institute of Technology	M,D
Florida Memorial University	M
Florida National University	M
Florida Southern College	M
Florida State University	M,D
Fontbonne University	M
Fordham University	M,D
Fort Hays State University	M
Framingham State University	M
Franciscan University of Steubenville	M
Francis Marion University	M
Franklin Pierce University	M,D,O
Franklin University	M
Freed-Hardeman University	M
Fresno Pacific University	M
Frostburg State University	M
Full Sail University	M
Gannon University	M
Gardner-Webb University	M
Geneva College	M
George Fox University	M,D
George Mason University	M
Georgetown University	M
The George Washington University	M,D,O
Georgia College & State University	M
Georgia Institute of Technology	M,D
Georgian Court University	M,O
Georgia Southern University	M
Georgia Southern University–Armstrong Campus	M,O
Georgia Southwestern State University	M
Georgia State University	M,D
Goddard College	M
Golden Gate University	M,D,O
Goldey-Beacom College	M
Gonzaga University	M
Governors State University	M
The Graduate Center, City University of New York	D
Grand Canyon University	M,D
Grand Valley State University	M
Granite State College	M
Grantham University	M,O
Green Mountain College	M
Gwynedd Mercy University	M
Hallmark University	M
Hamline University	M,D
Hampton University	M,D
Harding University	M
Hardin-Simmons University	M
Harvard University	M,D,O*
Hawai`i Pacific University	M
HEC Montreal	M,D,O
Heidelberg University	M
Henderson State University	M
Herzing University Online	M
High Point University	M,D
Hodges University	M
Hofstra University	M,O
Holy Family University	M
Holy Names University	M
Hood College	M,O*
Houston Baptist University	M,D
Howard Payne University	M
Howard University	M
Hult International Business School (United States)	M
Humboldt State University	M
Huntington University	M,D
Husson University	M
Idaho State University	M,O
IGlobal University	M
Illinois Institute of Technology	M,D
Illinois State University	M
IMCA–International Management Centres Association	M
Independence University	M
Indiana State University	M
Indiana Tech	M
Indiana University Bloomington	M,D
Indiana University Kokomo	M,O
Indiana University Northwest	M,O
Indiana University of Pennsylvania	M
Indiana University–Purdue University Fort Wayne	M
Indiana University–Purdue University Indianapolis	M
Indiana University South Bend	M,O
Indiana University Southeast	M
Indiana Wesleyan University	M,O
Instituto Centroamericano de Administración de Empresas	M
Instituto Tecnologico de Santo Domingo	M,O
Instituto Tecnológico y de Estudios Superiores de Monterrey, Campus Central de Veracruz	M
Instituto Tecnológico y de Estudios Superiores de Monterrey, Campus Ciudad de México	M,D
Instituto Tecnológico y de Estudios Superiores de Monterrey, Campus Ciudad Juárez	M
Instituto Tecnológico y de Estudios Superiores de Monterrey, Campus Ciudad Obregón	M
Instituto Tecnológico y de Estudios Superiores de Monterrey, Campus Cuernavaca	M
Instituto Tecnológico y de Estudios Superiores de Monterrey, Campus Estado de México	M,D
Instituto Tecnológico y de Estudios Superiores de Monterrey, Campus Guadalajara	M
Instituto Tecnológico y de Estudios Superiores de Monterrey, Campus Irapuato	M,D
Instituto Tecnológico y de Estudios Superiores de Monterrey, Campus Laguna	M
Instituto Tecnológico y de Estudios Superiores de Monterrey, Campus León	M
Instituto Tecnológico y de Estudios Superiores de Monterrey, Campus Monterrey	M,D
Instituto Tecnológico y de Estudios Superiores de Monterrey, Campus Querétaro	M
Instituto Tecnológico y de Estudios Superiores de Monterrey, Campus Sonora Norte	M
Instituto Tecnológico y de Estudios Superiores de Monterrey, Campus Toluca	M
Inter American University of Puerto Rico, Aguadilla Campus	M
Inter American University of Puerto Rico, Arecibo Campus	M
Inter American University of Puerto Rico, Barranquitas Campus	M
Inter American University of Puerto Rico, Fajardo Campus	M
Inter American University of Puerto Rico, Guayama Campus	M
Inter American University of Puerto Rico, Metropolitan Campus	M
Inter American University of Puerto Rico, San Germán Campus	M,D
International Technological University	M,D
International University in Geneva	M,D
The International University of Monaco	M
Iona College	M,O
Iowa State University of Science and Technology	M
Ithaca College	M
Jackson State University	M,D
Jacksonville State University	M
Jacksonville University	M,D*
James Madison University	M
John Brown University	M
John Carroll University	M
John F. Kennedy University	M
Johns Hopkins University	M,O*
Johnson & Wales University	M
Judson University	M
Kansas State University	M,O
Kansas Wesleyan University	M
Kean University	M
Keiser University	M,D
Kennesaw State University	M,D
Kent State University	M
Kent State University at Stark	M
Kentucky State University	M
Kettering University	M
Keuka College	M
Keystone College	M
King University	M
Kutztown University of Pennsylvania	M
Lake Erie College	M
Lake Forest Graduate School of Management	M
Lakeland University	M
Lamar University	M
La Salle University	M,O
Lasell College	M,O
La Sierra University	M,O
Laurentian University	M
Lawrence Technological University	M,D,O
Lebanese American University	M
Lebanon Valley College	M
Lee University	M
Lehigh University	M
Le Moyne College	M
Lenoir-Rhyne University	M

*M—masters degree; D—doctorate; O—other advanced degree; *—Close-Up and/or Display*

LeTourneau University	M
Lewis University	
Liberty University	M,D
LIM College	M
Limestone College	M
Lincoln Memorial University	M
Lincoln University (CA)	M,D
Lincoln University (MO)	M
Lindenwood University	M,O
Lindenwood University–Belleville	M
Lipscomb University	M,O
Long Island University–LIU Brooklyn	M,O
Long Island University–LIU Post	M
Longwood University	M
Louisiana State University and Agricultural & Mechanical College	M,D
Louisiana State University in Shreveport	M
Louisiana Tech University	M,D,O
Lourdes University	M
Loyola Marymount University	M
Loyola University Chicago	M,O
Loyola University Maryland	M
Loyola University New Orleans	M
Lynn University	M
Maastricht School of Management	M,D
Madonna University	M
Maharishi University of Management	M,D
Malone University	M
Manhattan College	M
Marconi International University	M,D
Marian University (WI)	M
Marist College	M,O
Marlboro College	M
Marquette University	M,O
Marshall University	M,O
Maryland Institute College of Art	M
Marymount California University	M
Marymount University	M,O
Maryville University of Saint Louis	M,O
Marywood University	M
Massachusetts College of Liberal Arts	M,O
Massachusetts Institute of Technology	M,D
McGill University	M,D,O
McKendree University	M
McMaster University	M,D
McNeese State University	M
Medaille College	M
Melbourne Business School	M,D,O
Memorial University of Newfoundland	M
Mercer University	M
Mercer University	M
Mercy College	M
Meredith College	M
Merrimack College	M
Messiah College	M,O
Methodist University	M
Metropolitan College of New York	M
Metropolitan State University	M,D,O
Miami University	M
Michigan State University	M,D
Michigan Technological University	M
Mid-America Christian University	M
MidAmerica Nazarene University	M
Middle Tennessee State University	M
Midway University	M
Midwestern State University	M
Millennia Atlantic University	M
Milligan College	M,O
Millikin University	M
Millsaps College	M
Mills College	M
Milwaukee School of Engineering	M
Minnesota State University Mankato	M
Minnesota State University Moorhead	M
Minot State University	M
Misericordia University	M
Mississippi College	M,O
Mississippi State University	M,D
Missouri Baptist University	M,O
Missouri Southern State University	M
Missouri State University	M
Missouri University of Science and Technology	M
Missouri Western State University	M
Molloy College	M,O
Monmouth University	M,O*
Monroe College	M
Montclair State University	M,O
Moravian College	M
Morehead State University	M
Morgan State University	M,D
Mount Aloysius College	M
Mount Marty College	M
Mount Mary University	M
Mount Mercy University	M
Mount St. Joseph University	M
Mount Saint Mary College	M
Mount Saint Mary's University (CA)	M,D,O
Mount St. Mary's University (MD)	M
Mount Vernon Nazarene University	M
Murray State University	M
National American University (TX)	M,D
National Louis University	M
National University	M,O
National University College	M
Naval Postgraduate School	M
Nazareth College of Rochester	M
Neumann University	M
New Charter University	M
New England College	M
New Jersey City University	M,O
New Jersey Institute of Technology	M,D,O
Newman University	M
New Mexico Highlands University	M
New Mexico State University	M,D
New York Institute of Technology	M
New York Medical College	M,D,O
New York University	M,D,O*
Niagara University	M
Nicholls State University	M
Nichols College	M
North Carolina Agricultural and Technical State University	M
North Carolina Central University	M
North Carolina State University	M
North Central College	M
Northcentral University	M,D,O
North Dakota State University	M*
Northeastern Illinois University	M
Northeastern State University	M
Northeastern University	M,D,O
Northern Arizona University	M,O
Northern Illinois University	M
Northern Kentucky University	M,O
Northern Michigan University	M
North Park University	M
Northwest Christian University	M
Northwestern Polytechnic University	M,D
Northwestern University	M,D
Northwest Missouri State University	M
Northwest Nazarene University	M
Northwest University	M
Northwood University, Michigan Campus	M
Norwich University	M
Notre Dame de Namur University	M
Notre Dame of Maryland University	M
Nova Southeastern University	M*
Nyack College	M
Oakland City University	M
Oakland University	M,O
Oglala Lakota College	M
Ohio Christian University	M
Ohio Dominican University	M
The Ohio State University	M,D
Ohio University	M
Oklahoma Baptist University	M
Oklahoma Christian University	M
Oklahoma City University	M
Oklahoma State University	M,D
Old Dominion University	M,D
Olivet Nazarene University	M
Open University	M
Oral Roberts University	M
Oregon State University	M,D
Ottawa University	M
Otterbein University	M
Our Lady of the Lake University	M
Pace University	M,D,O
Pacific Lutheran University	M
Pacific States University	M,O
Pacific University	M
Palm Beach Atlantic University	M
Park University	M,O
Penn State Erie, The Behrend College	M
Penn State Great Valley	M,O
Penn State Harrisburg	M,O
Penn State University Park	M,D*
Pensacola Christian College	M,D,O
Pepperdine University	M
Pfeiffer University	M
Phillips Theological Seminary	M,D
Piedmont College	M
Pittsburg State University	M
Plymouth State University	M
Point Loma Nazarene University	M
Point Park University	M
Point University	M
Polytechnic University of Puerto Rico	M
Polytechnic University of Puerto Rico, Miami Campus	M
Polytechnic University of Puerto Rico, Orlando Campus	M
Pontifical Catholic University of Puerto Rico	M,D,O
Pontificia Universidad Catolica Madre y Maestra	M
Portland State University	M,D,O
Post University	M
Prairie View A&M University	M
Presidio Graduate School (CA)	M,O
Providence College	M
Purdue University	M,D
Purdue University Global	M
Purdue University Northwest	M
Queen's University at Kingston	M
Queens University of Charlotte	M
Quincy University	M
Quinnipiac University	M
Radford University	M
Ramapo College of New Jersey	M
Regent's University London	M
Regent University	M,D,O
Reinhardt University	M
Rensselaer at Hartford	M
Rensselaer Polytechnic Institute	M,D
Rice University	M
Rider University	M
Rivier University	M
Robert Morris University	M
Robert Morris University Illinois	M
Roberts Wesleyan College	M
Rochester Institute of Technology	M
Rockford University	M
Rockhurst University	M,O
Rogers State University	M
Roger Williams University	M
Rollins College	M
Roosevelt University	M
Roseman University of Health Sciences	M,O
Rosemont College	M
Rowan University	M,O
Royal Military College of Canada	M
Rutgers University–Camden	M
Rutgers University–Newark	M,D
Ryerson University	M
Sacred Heart University	M,O
Sage Graduate School	M
Saginaw Valley State University	M
St. Ambrose University	M,D
St. Bonaventure University	M
St. Catherine University	M
Saint Francis University	M
St. John Fisher College	M
St. John's University (NY)	M
St. Joseph's College, Long Island Campus	M
St. Joseph's College, New York	M
Saint Joseph's College of Maine	M
Saint Joseph's University	M,O*
Saint Leo University	M,D
Saint Louis University	M*
Saint Martin's University	M
Saint Mary's College of California	M
Saint Mary's University (Canada)	M,D
St. Mary's University (United States)	M
Saint Mary's University of Minnesota	M,D
St. Norbert College	M
Saint Peter's University	M
St. Thomas Aquinas College	M
St. Thomas University	M,O
Saint Vincent College	M
Saint Xavier University	M,O
Salem International University	M
Salem State University	M
Salisbury University	M
Salve Regina University	M,O
Samford University	M
Sam Houston State University	M
San Diego State University	M
San Francisco State University	M
San Ignacio University	M
San Jose State University	M
Santa Clara University	M
Savannah State University	M
Schiller International University (United States)	M
Schiller International University (Germany)	M
Schiller International University	M
Schiller International University (Spain)	M
Schreiner University	M
Seattle Pacific University	M
Seattle University	M,O
Seton Hall University	M,O
Seton Hill University	M
Shenandoah University	M,O
Shippensburg University of Pennsylvania	M,D,O
Shorter University	M
Siena College	M
Silver Lake College of the Holy Family	M
Simmons College	M
Simon Fraser University	M,D,O
SIT Graduate Institute	M
Slippery Rock University of Pennsylvania	M
Sonoma State University	M
South Carolina State University	M
Southeastern Louisiana University	M
Southeastern Oklahoma State University	M
Southeastern University (FL)	M,D
Southeast Missouri State University	M
Southern Adventist University	M
Southern Arkansas University–Magnolia	M
Southern Connecticut State University	M
Southern Illinois University Carbondale	M,D
Southern Illinois University Edwardsville	M
Southern Methodist University	M
Southern Nazarene University	M
Southern New Hampshire University	M,D,O
Southern Oregon University	M,O
Southern University and Agricultural and Mechanical College	M
Southern Utah University	M
Southern Wesleyan University	M
South University	M
South University	M
South University	M
South University (TX)	M
South University (SC)	M
South University (GA)	M
South University (AL)	M
South University	M
Southwest Baptist University	M
Southwestern Adventist University	M
Southwestern College (KS)	M
Southwestern College (KS)	M
Southwestern Oklahoma State University	M
Southwest Minnesota State University	M
Southwest University	M
Spring Arbor University	M
Springfield College	M
Spring Hill College	M
Stanford University	M,D
State University of New York at New Paltz	M
State University of New York at Oswego	M
State University of New York College at Geneseo	M
State University of New York College at Old Westbury	M
State University of New York Empire State College	M
State University of New York Polytechnic Institute	M
Stephen F. Austin State University	M
Stetson University	M
Stevens Institute of Technology	M,O
Stockton University	M
Stony Brook University, State University of New York	M,O
Stratford University (VA)	M,D
Strayer University	M
Suffolk University	M
Sullivan University	M,D
Sul Ross State University	M
Syracuse University	M,D*
Tabor College	M
Tarleton State University	M
Temple University	M,D*
Tennessee State University	M
Tennessee Technological University	M
Tennessee Wesleyan University	M
Texas A&M International University	M,D
Texas A&M University	M
Texas A&M University–Central Texas	M,O
Texas A&M University–Commerce	M
Texas A&M University–Corpus Christi	M
Texas A&M University–Kingsville	M
Texas A&M University–San Antonio	M
Texas A&M University–Texarkana	M
Texas Christian University	M
Texas Health and Science University	M,D
Texas Southern University	M
Texas State University	M
Texas Tech University	M,D
Texas Wesleyan University	M
Texas Woman's University	M
Thomas College	M
Thomas Edison State University	M
Thomas Jefferson University	M
Thomas More College	M
Thomas University	M
Thompson Rivers University	M
Tiffin University	M
Trevecca Nazarene University	M
Trident University International	M,D
Trine University	M
Trinity International University	M,D,O
Trinity University	M
Trinity Washington University	M
Trinity Western University	M
Troy University	M
Truett McConnell University	M
Tulane University	M,D
Tusculum College	M
Union University	M
United States International University–Africa	M
Universidad Autonoma de Guadalajara	M,D
Universidad de las Americas, A.C.	M
Universidad de las Américas Puebla	M
Universidad del Este	M
Universidad del Turabo	M,D
Universidad Iberoamericana	M,D
Universidad Metropolitana	M
Université de Moncton	M
Université de Sherbrooke	M,D,O
Université du Québec à Chicoutimi	M
Université du Québec à Montréal	M,D,O
Université du Québec à Rimouski	M,O
Université du Québec à Trois-Rivières	M,D
Université du Québec en Abitibi-Témiscamingue	M
Université Laval	M,D,O
University at Albany, State University of New York	M
University at Buffalo, the State University of New York	M,D
The University of Akron	M
The University of Alabama	M,D
The University of Alabama at Birmingham	M
The University of Alabama in Huntsville	M,O
University of Alaska Anchorage	M
University of Alaska Fairbanks	M
University of Alberta	M,D
University of Antelope Valley	M
The University of Arizona	M,D,O
University of Arkansas	M,D
University of Arkansas at Little Rock	M,O
University of Baltimore	M,O
University of Bridgeport	M
The University of British Columbia	M,D
University of Calgary	M,D
University of California, Berkeley	M,D,O
University of California, Davis	M
University of California, Irvine	M,D
University of California, Los Angeles	M,D*
University of California, Riverside	M,D
University of California, San Diego	M,D*
University of Central Arkansas	M
University of Central Florida	M,D,O

University of Central Missouri	M,D,O
University of Charleston	M
University of Chicago	M,D,O
University of Cincinnati	M,D
University of Colorado Boulder	M,D
University of Colorado Colorado Springs	M
University of Colorado Denver	M
University of Connecticut	M,D*
University of Dallas	M,D
University of Dayton	M
University of Delaware	M,D*
University of Denver	M
University of Detroit Mercy	M,O
University of Dubuque	M
The University of Findlay	M,D
University of Florida	M,D
University of Georgia	M
University of Guam	M
University of Guelph	M,D
University of Hartford	M
University of Hawaii at Manoa	M
University of Holy Cross	M,D
University of Houston	M,D
University of Houston–Clear Lake	M
University of Houston–Downtown	M
University of Houston–Victoria	M
University of Idaho	M
University of Illinois at Chicago	M,D
University of Illinois at Springfield	M
University of Illinois at Urbana–Champaign	M,D
University of Indianapolis	M,O
The University of Iowa	M,D*
The University of Kansas	M,D
University of Kentucky	M,D
University of La Verne	M,D,O
University of Lethbridge	M,D
University of Louisiana at Lafayette	M
University of Louisiana at Monroe	M,O
University of Louisville	M
University of Lynchburg	M
University of Maine	M,O
University of Management and Technology	M,D,O
The University of Manchester	M
University of Manitoba	M,D
University of Mary	M
University of Mary Hardin-Baylor	M
University of Maryland, College Park	M,D
University of Maryland University College	M,D,O
University of Mary Washington	M
University of Massachusetts Amherst	M,D*
University of Massachusetts Boston	M
University of Massachusetts Dartmouth	M,O
University of Massachusetts Lowell	M,D
University of Memphis	M,D
University of Miami	M,D*
University of Michigan	M,D*
University of Michigan–Dearborn	M
University of Michigan–Flint	M,O
University of Minnesota, Duluth	M
University of Minnesota Rochester	M,D
University of Minnesota, Twin Cities Campus	M,D
University of Mississippi	M,D
University of Missouri	M,D
University of Missouri–Kansas City	M,D
University of Missouri–St. Louis	M,D,O
University of Mobile	M
University of Montana	M
University of Montevallo	M
University of Mount Olive	M
University of Nebraska at Kearney	M
University of Nebraska at Omaha	M,O
University of Nebraska–Lincoln	M,D
University of Nevada, Las Vegas	M,O
University of Nevada, Reno	M
University of New Brunswick Fredericton	M
University of New Brunswick Saint John	M
University of New Hampshire	M,O
University of New Haven	M*
University of New Mexico	M
University of New Orleans	M
University of North Alabama	M
The University of North Carolina at Chapel Hill	M,D
The University of North Carolina at Charlotte	M,D,O
The University of North Carolina at Greensboro	M,O
The University of North Carolina at Pembroke	M
The University of North Carolina Wilmington	M
University of North Dakota	M
University of Northern Colorado	M
University of Northern Iowa	M
University of North Florida	M
University of North Georgia	M
University of North Texas	M,D,O
University of North Texas at Dallas	M
University of Northwestern Ohio	M
University of Northwestern–St. Paul	M
University of Notre Dame	M
University of Oklahoma	M,D*
University of Oregon	M,D
University of Ottawa	M
University of Pennsylvania	M,D*
University of Phoenix–Bay Area Campus	M,D
University of Phoenix–Central Valley Campus	M
University of Phoenix–Dallas Campus	M
University of Phoenix–Hawaii Campus	M
University of Phoenix–Houston Campus	M
University of Phoenix–Las Vegas Campus	M
University of Phoenix–Online Campus	M,D,O
University of Phoenix–Phoenix Campus	M,O
University of Phoenix–Sacramento Valley Campus	M
University of Phoenix–San Antonio Campus	M
University of Phoenix–San Diego Campus	M
University of Pikeville	M
University of Pittsburgh	M,D*
University of Portland	M
University of Puerto Rico–Mayagüez	M
University of Puerto Rico–Río Piedras	M,D
University of Redlands	M
University of Regina	M,O
University of Rhode Island	M,D*
University of Richmond	M
University of Rochester	M,D*
University of Saint Francis (IN)	M
University of Saint Joseph	M
University of Saint Mary	M
University of St. Thomas (TX)	M
University of St. Thomas (MN)	M
University of San Diego	M
University of San Francisco	M
University of Saskatchewan	M
The University of Scranton	M
University of Sioux Falls	M
University of South Africa	M,D
University of South Alabama	M,D
University of South Carolina	M,D
University of South Carolina Aiken	M
University of South Dakota	M,O
University of Southern California	M,D*
University of Southern Indiana	M
University of Southern Maine	M,O
University of Southern Mississippi	M
University of South Florida	M*
University of South Florida, St. Petersburg	M
University of South Florida Sarasota-Manatee	M
The University of Tampa	M,O
The University of Tennessee	M,D
The University of Tennessee at Chattanooga	M
The University of Tennessee at Martin	M
The University of Texas at Austin	M,D
The University of Texas at Dallas	M,D
The University of Texas at El Paso	M,D,O
The University of Texas at San Antonio	M,D,O
The University of Texas at Tyler	M
The University of Texas of the Permian Basin	M
The University of Texas Rio Grande Valley	M,D
University of the Cumberlands	M
University of the District of Columbia	M
University of the Incarnate Word	M,D
University of the Pacific	M
University of the People	M
University of the Potomac	M
University of the Sacred Heart	M,O
University of the Southwest	M
University of the Virgin Islands	M
University of the West	M
The University of Toledo	M
University of Toronto	M,D
The University of Tulsa	M
University of Utah	M,D,O
University of Vermont	M
University of Victoria	M
University of Virginia	M,D,O
University of Washington	M,D
University of Washington, Bothell	M
University of Washington, Tacoma	M
University of Waterloo	M
The University of West Alabama	M
The University of Western Ontario	M,D
University of West Florida	M
University of West Georgia	M
University of Windsor	M
University of Wisconsin–Eau Claire	M
University of Wisconsin–Green Bay	M
University of Wisconsin–Madison	M
University of Wisconsin–Milwaukee	M,D,O*
University of Wisconsin–Oshkosh	M
University of Wisconsin–Parkside	M
University of Wisconsin–River Falls	M
University of Wisconsin–Whitewater	M
University of Wyoming	M
Upper Iowa University	M
Urbana University–A Branch Campus of Franklin University	M
Ursuline College	M
Utah State University	M
Utah Valley University	M
Valdosta State University	M
Valparaiso University	M,O
Vancouver Island University	M
Vanderbilt University	M*
Villanova University	M
Virginia Commonwealth University	M,D
Virginia International University	M,O
Virginia Polytechnic Institute and State University	M,D
Virginia Wesleyan University	M
Viterbo University	M
Wagner College	M
Wake Forest University	M
Walden University	M,D,O
Walsh College of Accountancy and Business Administration	M
Walsh University	M
Warner University	M
Washburn University	M
Washington Adventist University	M
Washington State University	M,D
Washington University in St. Louis	M,D
Wayland Baptist University	M,D
Waynesburg University	M,D
Wayne State College	M
Wayne State University	M,D,O
Webber International University	M
Weber State University	M,O
Webster University	M,D,O
Wesleyan College	M
Wesley College	M
West Chester University of Pennsylvania	M,O
Western Carolina University	M
Western Connecticut State University	M
Western Governors University	M
Western Illinois University	M,O
Western Kentucky University	M
Western Michigan University	M
Western New England University	M
Western New Mexico University	M
Western Washington University	M
Westminster College (UT)	M,O
West Texas A&M University	M
West Virginia University	M,D,O
West Virginia Wesleyan College	M
Wheeling Jesuit University	M
Whitworth University	M
WHU - Otto Beisheim School of Management	M
Wichita State University	M
Widener University	M
Wilfrid Laurier University	M,D
Wilkes University	M
Willamette University	M
William Carey University	M
William Paterson University of New Jersey	M,O
William Woods University	M,D,O
Wilmington University	M,D
Wilson College	M
Wingate University	M
Winston-Salem State University	M
Winthrop University	M
Woodbury University	M
Worcester Polytechnic Institute	M,D,O
Worcester State University	M
Wright State University	M
Xavier University	M*
Yale University	M,D
Yeshiva University	M
York College of Pennsylvania	M
York University	M,D
Youngstown State University	M,O

BUSINESS ANALYTICS

Abilene Christian University	M
American Public University System	M,D
Ashland University	M
Babson College	M,O
Baldwin Wallace University	M
Bentley University	M,O
Boston University	M*
Bryant University	M
California Polytechnic State University, San Luis Obispo	M*
California State University, Fullerton	M
California University of Pennsylvania	M
Case Western Reserve University	M*
Central European University	M,D
Clark University	M
Cleary University	M,O
Clemson University	M
The College of Saint Rose	M
The College of William and Mary	M*
Creighton University	M,D
Dakota State University	M,D,O
DePaul University	M,D
Duke University	M*
Fairfield University	M,O
The George Washington University	M,O
Golden Gate University	M,D,O
Grand Canyon University	M
HEC Montreal	M
Hult International Business School (United States)	M
Iowa State University of Science and Technology	M
Johns Hopkins University	M*
La Salle University	M,O
Lenoir-Rhyne University	M
Lewis University	M
Loyola University Chicago	M,O
Merrimack College	M
Metropolitan State University	M,D,O
Michigan State University	M
Moravian College	M
National University	M,O
Northwestern University	M,D
Northwest Missouri State University	M
Nova Southeastern University	M*
Point Park University	M
Regent University	M,D,O
Rensselaer Polytechnic Institute	M
Robert Morris University Illinois	M
Rockhurst University	M,O
St. John's University (NY)	M
Saint Joseph's University	M*
Saint Mary's College of California	M
Santa Clara University	M
Shippensburg University of Pennsylvania	M,D,O
Southern Illinois University Edwardsville	M
Southern Methodist University	M
Southern New Hampshire University	M,D,O
Stevens Institute of Technology	M,O
Syracuse University	M*
Texas A&M University–Commerce	M
Texas Woman's University	M
Thomas Jefferson University	M
Tulane University	M,D
University at Albany, State University of New York	M
University at Buffalo, the State University of New York	M,D
The University of Alabama in Huntsville	M,O
The University of British Columbia	M
University of California, Davis	M
University of California, Los Angeles	M,D*
University of California, San Diego	M,D*
University of Central Oklahoma	M
University of Cincinnati	M,D
University of Connecticut	M,D*
University of Dallas	M,D
The University of Iowa	M*
The University of Manchester	M
University of Massachusetts Boston	M
The University of North Carolina at Charlotte	M,D,O
University of Notre Dame	M
University of Oklahoma	M,O*
University of Pittsburgh	D*
University of South Dakota	M,O
The University of Tampa	M,O
The University of Tulsa	M
University of Wisconsin–Milwaukee	M,O*
Virginia Polytechnic Institute and State University	M,D
Wake Forest University	M
Walsh College of Accountancy and Business Administration	M
West Chester University of Pennsylvania	M,O
West Virginia University	M,D,O
William Paterson University of New Jersey	M,O
York University	M,D

BUSINESS EDUCATION

Alabama Agricultural and Mechanical University	M,O
Arkansas State University	O
Ball State University	M,O
Bloomsburg University of Pennsylvania	M
Bowling Green State University	M
Buffalo State College, State University of New York	M
Canisius College	M,O
Capella University	D
Chadron State College	M,O
Clemson University	M,D
Colorado Christian University	M
East Carolina University	M,O
Eastern Kentucky University	M
Florida Agricultural and Mechanical University	M
Hofstra University	M,D,O
Indiana University of Pennsylvania	M
Inter American University of Puerto Rico, Metropolitan Campus	M
Inter American University of Puerto Rico, San Germán Campus	M
Johnson & Wales University	M
Lehman College of the City University of New York	M
Lock Haven University of Pennsylvania	M
Louisiana State University and Agricultural & Mechanical College	M,D
Manhattanville College	M,O
Maryville University of Saint Louis	M,O
Middle Tennessee State University	M
Milwaukee School of Engineering	M
Mississippi College	M,D,O
Morehead State University	M,O
New York University	M,O*
North Carolina Agricultural and Technical State University	M
North Carolina State University	M
Nova Southeastern University	M*

*M—masters degree; D—doctorate; O—other advanced degree; *—Close-Up and/or Display*

Old Dominion University	M,D
Pepperdine University	M
Pontifical Catholic University of Puerto Rico	M,D
Regis University	M,O
Robert Morris University	M,D,O
Salve Regina University	M,O
South Carolina State University	M
Spalding University	M
State University of New York at Oswego	M
Temple University	M*
Thomas College	M
University of Delaware	M,D*
University of Georgia	M,D,O
University of Missouri	M,D,O
The University of North Carolina at Charlotte	D
University of South Carolina	M,D
University of the Cumberlands	M,D,O
The University of Toledo	M,D,O
University of West Georgia	M,D,O
University of Wisconsin–Whitewater	M
Utah State University	D
Washington State University	M,D
Wayne State College	M
West Chester University of Pennsylvania	M,O

CANADIAN STUDIES

Carleton University	M,D
Queen's University at Kingston	M,D
Saint Mary's University (Canada)	M,O
Trent University	M,D
Université de Saint-Boniface	M
Université de Sherbrooke	M,D
Université du Québec à Chicoutimi	M
University at Buffalo, the State University of New York	M,D
University of Lethbridge	M,D
University of Manitoba	M
University of Ottawa	D
University of Regina	M,D
University of Saskatchewan	M,D
Wilfrid Laurier University	M,D

CANCER BIOLOGY/ONCOLOGY

Augusta University	D
Baylor College of Medicine	D
Case Western Reserve University	D*
Duke University	D*
Emory University	D
Gerstner Sloan Kettering Graduate School of Biomedical Sciences	D*
Grand Valley State University	M
Irell & Manella Graduate School of Biological Sciences	D*
McMaster University	M,D
Medical University of South Carolina	D
Meharry Medical College	D
Memorial University of Newfoundland	M,D
New York University	M,D*
Oregon Health & Science University	D
Purdue University	D
Queen's University at Kingston	M,D
Rutgers University–Newark	D,O
Rutgers University–New Brunswick	M,D
Saint Francis University	M
Thomas Jefferson University	D
Tufts University	D*
Université Laval	O
University at Buffalo, the State University of New York	M
The University of Alabama at Birmingham	D
University of Alberta	M,D
The University of Arizona	D
University of Calgary	M,D
University of Chicago	D
University of Cincinnati	D
University of Colorado Denver	D
University of Delaware	M,D*
The University of Kansas	M,D
The University of Manchester	M,D
University of Manitoba	M
University of Maryland, Baltimore	D
University of Massachusetts Medical School	M,D
University of Miami	D*
University of Michigan	M,D*
University of Minnesota, Twin Cities Campus	D
University of Nebraska Medical Center	D
University of North Texas Health Science Center at Fort Worth	M,D
University of Pennsylvania	D*
University of Regina	M,D
University of Southern California	D*
University of South Florida	M,D*
The University of Texas Health Science Center at Houston	M,D
The University of Texas Southwestern Medical Center	D
University of the District of Columbia	M
The University of Toledo	M,D
University of Utah	M,D
University of Wisconsin–La Crosse	M
University of Wisconsin–Madison	D
Wake Forest University	D
Wayne State University	M,D,O
West Virginia University	M,D

CARDIOVASCULAR SCIENCES

Albany Medical College	M,D
Augusta University	D
Baylor College of Medicine	D
Johns Hopkins University	M,D*
Marquette University	M
McMaster University	M,D
Medical University of South Carolina	D
Memorial University of Newfoundland	M,D
Midwestern University, Glendale Campus	M
Milwaukee School of Engineering	M
Queen's University at Kingston	M,D
Quinnipiac University	M
Université Laval	O
University of Calgary	M,D
University of Guelph	M,D,O
University of Mary	M
University of South Dakota	M,D
University of South Florida	O*
The University of Toledo	M,D

CELL BIOLOGY

Albany College of Pharmacy and Health Sciences	M
Albany Medical College	M,D
Albert Einstein College of Medicine	D
American University of Beirut	M,D
Appalachian State University	M
Arizona State University at the Tempe campus	M,D
Auburn University	M,D*
Augusta University	D
Baylor College of Medicine	D
Boston University	M,D*
Brandeis University	M,D
Brown University	M,D
California Institute of Technology	D
California State University, Sacramento	M
Carnegie Mellon University	M,D
Case Western Reserve University	D*
The Catholic University of America	M,D
Columbia University	M,D*
Cornell University	D
Dartmouth College	D*
Drexel University	M,D*
Duke University	D,O*
Emory University	D
Emporia State University	M
Florida Institute of Technology	M,D
Florida State University	M,D
Georgia State University	M,D
Grand Valley State University	M
Harvard University	D*
Illinois Institute of Technology	M,D
Illinois State University	M,D
Indiana State University	M,D
Indiana University Bloomington	M,D
Indiana University–Purdue University Indianapolis	M,D
Iowa State University of Science and Technology	M,D
Irell & Manella Graduate School of Biological Sciences	D*
Johns Hopkins University	D*
Kent State University	M,D
Lehigh University	M,D
Liberty University	M,D
Louisiana State University Health Sciences Center	D
Louisiana State University Health Sciences Center at Shreveport	M,D
Loyola University Chicago	M,D
Marquette University	M,D
Massachusetts Institute of Technology	D
McGill University	M,D
McMaster University	M,D
Medical University of South Carolina	D
Michigan State University	M,D
Missouri State University	M
New York Medical College	M,D
New York University	D*
North Carolina State University	M,D
North Dakota State University	D*
Northeastern Illinois University	M
Northwestern University	D
The Ohio State University	M,D
Ohio University	M,D
Oregon Health & Science University	D
Oregon State University	M,D
Penn State Hershey Medical Center	D
Penn State University Park	M,D*
Purdue University	M,D
Queen's University at Kingston	M,D
Quinnipiac University	M
Rice University	M,D
Rosalind Franklin University of Medicine and Science	D
Rush University	M,D
Rutgers University–Newark	D
Rutgers University–New Brunswick	M,D
San Diego State University	M,D
San Francisco State University	M
Southern Methodist University	M,D
State University of New York Downstate Medical Center	D
State University of New York Upstate Medical University	M,D
Stony Brook University, State University of New York	M,D
Texas Tech University Health Sciences Center	M,D
Thomas Jefferson University	M,D
Tufts University	D*
Tulane University	M,D
Uniformed Services University of the Health Sciences	M,D*
Universidad Central del Caribe	M,D
Université de Montréal	M,D
Université de Sherbrooke	M,D
Université Laval	M,D
University at Buffalo, the State University of New York	M,D
The University of Alabama at Birmingham	D
University of Alberta	M,D
The University of Arizona	D
University of Arkansas	M,D
The University of British Columbia	M,D
University of California, Berkeley	D
University of California, Davis	M,D
University of California, Irvine	M,D
University of California, Los Angeles	M,D*
University of California, Riverside	M,D
University of California, San Francisco	D
University of California, Santa Barbara	M,D
University of California, Santa Cruz	M,D*
University of Chicago	D
University of Cincinnati	D
University of Colorado Boulder	M,D
University of Colorado Denver	M,D
University of Connecticut	M,D*
University of Connecticut Health Center	D
University of Delaware	M,D*
University of Denver	M,D
University of Florida	M,D
University of Georgia	M,D
University of Guelph	M,D
University of Illinois at Chicago	M,D
University of Illinois at Urbana–Champaign	D
The University of Iowa	M,D*
The University of Kansas	M,D
The University of Manchester	M,D
University of Maryland, Baltimore	M,D
University of Maryland, Baltimore County	D
University of Maryland, College Park	M,D
University of Massachusetts Amherst	M,D*
University of Miami	D*
University of Michigan	M,D*
University of Minnesota, Twin Cities Campus	M,D
University of Missouri–Kansas City	D
University of Montana	D
University of Nebraska Medical Center	M,D
University of Nevada, Reno	M,D
University of New Haven	M*
University of New Mexico	M,D
The University of North Carolina at Chapel Hill	M,D
University of Notre Dame	M,D
University of Oklahoma Health Sciences Center	M,D
University of Ottawa	M,D
University of Pennsylvania	D*
University of Pittsburgh	D*
University of Puerto Rico–Río Piedras	M,D
University of Rhode Island	M,D*
University of Saskatchewan	M,D
University of South Carolina	M,D
University of South Dakota	M,D
University of Southern California	M,D*
University of South Florida	M,D*
The University of Texas at Austin	D
The University of Texas at Dallas	M,D
The University of Texas at San Antonio	M,D
The University of Texas Health Science Center at Houston	M,D
The University of Texas Health Science Center at San Antonio	M,D
The University of Texas Medical Branch	M,D
The University of Texas Southwestern Medical Center	D
University of the Sciences	M
University of Toronto	M,D
University of Vermont	D
University of Virginia	D
University of Washington	D
The University of Western Ontario	M,D
University of Wisconsin–La Crosse	M
University of Wisconsin–Madison	D
University of Wisconsin–Milwaukee	M,D*
University of Wyoming	D
Vanderbilt University	M,D*
Washington University in St. Louis	D
Wayne State University	M,D,O
Weill Cornell Medicine	M,D
Wesleyan University	D
Yale University	D

CELTIC LANGUAGES

Harvard University	D*

CERAMIC SCIENCES AND ENGINEERING

Alfred University	M,D
Missouri University of Science and Technology	M,D

CHEMICAL ENGINEERING

American University of Sharjah	M,D
Arizona State University at the Tempe campus	M,D
Auburn University	M,D*
Brigham Young University	M,D
Brown University	M,D
Bucknell University	M
California Institute of Technology	M,D
Carnegie Mellon University	M,D
Case Western Reserve University	M,D*
City College of the City University of New York	M,D
Clarkson University	M,D
Clemson University	M,D
Cleveland State University	M,D
Colorado School of Mines	M,D
Colorado State University	M,D
Columbia University	M,D*
Cooper Union for the Advancement of Science and Art	M
Cornell University	M,D
Dalhousie University	M,D
Dartmouth College	M,D*
Drexel University	M,D*
École Polytechnique de Montréal	M,D,O
Fairleigh Dickinson University, Florham Campus	M,O
Florida Agricultural and Mechanical University	M,D
Florida Institute of Technology	M,D
Florida State University	M,D
Georgia Institute of Technology	M,D
Howard University	M
Illinois Institute of Technology	M,D
Instituto Tecnológico y de Estudios Superiores de Monterrey, Campus Monterrey	M,D
Iowa State University of Science and Technology	M,D
Johns Hopkins University	M,D*
Kansas State University	M,D,O
Lamar University	M,D
Lehigh University	M,D
Louisiana State University and Agricultural & Mechanical College	M,D
Manhattan College	M
Massachusetts Institute of Technology	M,D
McGill University	M,D
McMaster University	M,D
McNeese State University	M
Miami University	M
Michigan State University	M,D
Michigan Technological University	M,D
Mississippi State University	M,D
Missouri University of Science and Technology	M,D
Montana State University	M,D
New Jersey Institute of Technology	M,D
New Mexico State University	M,D
New York University	M,D*
North Carolina Agricultural and Technical State University	M
North Carolina State University	M,D
Northeastern University	M,D,O
Northwestern University	M,D
The Ohio State University	M,D
Ohio University	M,D
Oklahoma State University	M,D
Oregon State University	M,D
Penn State University Park	M,D*
Princeton University	M,D
Purdue University	M,D
Queen's University at Kingston	M,D
Rensselaer Polytechnic Institute	M,D
Rice University	M,D
Rose-Hulman Institute of Technology	M
Rowan University	M
Royal Military College of Canada	M,D
Rutgers University–New Brunswick	M,D
San Jose State University	M
South Dakota School of Mines and Technology	M,D
Stanford University	M,D
Stevens Institute of Technology	M,D,O
Syracuse University	M,D*
Tennessee Technological University	M
Texas A&M University	M,D
Texas A&M University–Kingsville	M
Texas Tech University	M,D
Tufts University	M,D*
Tulane University	M,D
Universidad de las Américas Puebla	M
Université de Sherbrooke	M,D
Université Laval	M,D
University at Buffalo, the State University of New York	M,D,O
The University of Akron	M,D
The University of Alabama	M,D
The University of Alabama in Huntsville	M,D
University of Alberta	M,D
The University of Arizona	M,D
University of Arkansas	M,D
The University of British Columbia	M,D
University of Calgary	M,D
University of California, Berkeley	M,D
University of California, Davis	M,D
University of California, Irvine	M,D
University of California, Los Angeles	M,D*
University of California, Riverside	M,D
University of California, San Diego	M,D*
University of California, Santa Barbara	M,D
University of Cincinnati	M,D
University of Colorado Boulder	M,D
University of Connecticut	M,D*
University of Dayton	M

University of Delaware	M,D*
University of Florida	M,D,O
University of Houston	M,D
University of Idaho	M,D
University of Illinois at Chicago	M,D
University of Illinois at Urbana–Champaign	M,D
The University of Iowa	M,D*
The University of Kansas	M,D,O
University of Kentucky	M,D
University of Louisiana at Lafayette	M
University of Louisville	M,D
University of Maine	M,D
The University of Manchester	M,D
University of Maryland, Baltimore County	M,D
University of Maryland, College Park	M,D
University of Massachusetts Amherst	M,D*
University of Massachusetts Lowell	M,D
University of Michigan	M,D,O*
University of Minnesota, Twin Cities Campus	M,D
University of Mississippi	M,D
University of Missouri	M,D
University of Nebraska–Lincoln	M,D
University of Nevada, Reno	M,D
University of New Brunswick Fredericton	M,D
University of New Hampshire	M,D
University of New Mexico	M,D
University of North Dakota	M,D
University of Notre Dame	M,D
University of Oklahoma	M,D*
University of Ottawa	M,D
University of Pennsylvania	M,D*
University of Pittsburgh	M,D*
University of Puerto Rico–Mayagüez	M,D
University of Rhode Island	M,D,O*
University of Rochester	M,D*
University of Saskatchewan	M,D
University of South Africa	M
University of South Alabama	M
University of South Carolina	M,D
University of Southern California	M,D,O*
University of South Florida	M,D,O*
The University of Tennessee	M,D
The University of Tennessee at Chattanooga	M
The University of Texas at Austin	M,D
The University of Toledo	M,D
University of Toronto	M,D
The University of Tulsa	M,D
University of Utah	M,D
University of Virginia	M,D
University of Washington	M,D
University of Waterloo	M,D
The University of Western Ontario	M,D
University of Wisconsin–Madison	D
University of Wyoming	M,D
Vanderbilt University	M,D*
Villanova University	M,O
Virginia Polytechnic Institute and State University	M,D
Washington State University	M,D
Washington University in St. Louis	M,D
Wayne State University	M,D,O
Western Michigan University	M,D
West Virginia University	M,D
Widener University	M
Worcester Polytechnic Institute	M,D
Yale University	M,D

CHEMICAL PHYSICS

Columbia University	M,D*
Cornell University	D
Harvard University	D*
Kent State University	M,D
Lewis University	M
Marquette University	M,D
McMaster University	M,D
Michigan State University	M,D
The Ohio State University	M,D
Tufts University	M,D*
University of Illinois at Urbana–Champaign	M,D
University of Louisville	M,D
University of Maryland, College Park	M,D
University of Minnesota, Twin Cities Campus	M,D
University of Nevada, Reno	D
The University of Tennessee	M,D
University of Utah	M,D
Virginia Commonwealth University	M,D
Wesleyan University	D

CHEMISTRY

Acadia University	M
American University	M
The American University in Cairo	M,D,O
American University of Beirut	M,D
Arizona State University at the Tempe campus	M,D
Arkansas State University	M,O
Auburn University	M,D*
Ball State University	M,D
Baylor University	M,D
Binghamton University, State University of New York	M,D
Boise State University	M
Boston College	M,D
Boston University	M,D*
Bowling Green State University	M,D
Bradley University	M
Brandeis University	M,D
Brigham Young University	M,D
Brock University	M,D
Brooklyn College of the City University of New York	M,D
Brown University	D
Bryn Mawr College	M,D
Bucknell University	M
Buffalo State College, State University of New York	M
Cabrini University	M,D
California Institute of Technology	M,D
California Polytechnic State University, San Luis Obispo	M*
California State Polytechnic University, Pomona	M
California State University, East Bay	M
California State University, Fresno	M
California State University, Fullerton	M
California State University, Long Beach	M
California State University, Los Angeles	M
California State University, Northridge	M
California State University, Sacramento	M
Carleton University	M,D
Carnegie Mellon University	D
Case Western Reserve University	M,D*
Central Michigan University	M
Central Washington University	M
City College of the City University of New York	M,D
Clark Atlanta University	M,D
Clarkson University	M,D
Clark University	D
Clemson University	M,D
Cleveland State University	M,D
The College at Brockport, State University of New York	M,O
The College of William and Mary	M*
Colorado School of Mines	M,D
Colorado State University	M,D
Colorado State University–Pueblo	M
Columbia University	M,D*
Columbus State University	M,O
Concordia University (Canada)	M,D
Cornell University	D
Dalhousie University	M,D
Dartmouth College	M,D*
Delaware State University	M,D
DePaul University	M,D
Drew University	M,D,O
Drexel University	M,D*
Duke University	D*
Duquesne University	D
East Carolina University	M
Eastern Illinois University	M
Eastern Kentucky University	M
Eastern Michigan University	M
Eastern New Mexico University	M
East Tennessee State University	M
Emory University	D
Fairleigh Dickinson University, Florham Campus	M
Fairleigh Dickinson University, Metropolitan Campus	M
Fisk University	M
Florida Agricultural and Mechanical University	M
Florida Atlantic University	M,D
Florida Institute of Technology	M,D
Florida International University	M,D
Florida State University	M,D
Furman University	M
George Mason University	M,D
Georgetown University	D
The George Washington University	M,D
Georgia Institute of Technology	M,D
Georgia State University	M,D
The Graduate Center, City University of New York	D
Hampton University	M
Harvard University	D*
Howard University	M,D
Hunter College of the City University of New York	D
Idaho State University	M
Illinois Institute of Technology	M,D
Illinois State University	M
Indiana University Bloomington	M,D
Indiana University of Pennsylvania	M
Indiana University–Purdue University Indianapolis	M,D
Instituto Tecnológico y de Estudios Superiores de Monterrey, Campus Monterrey	M,D
Iowa State University of Science and Technology	M,D
Jackson State University	M,D
Johns Hopkins University	M,D*
Kansas State University	M,D
Kennesaw State University	M
Kent State University	M,D
Lakehead University	M
Lamar University	M
Laurentian University	M
Lehigh University	M,D
Lewis University	M
Long Island University–LIU Brooklyn	M,D,O
Louisiana State University and Agricultural & Mechanical College	M,D
Louisiana Tech University	M,D,O
Loyola University Chicago	M,D
Manhattanville College	M,O
Marquette University	M,D
Marshall University	M
Massachusetts Institute of Technology	D
McGill University	M,D
McMaster University	M,D
McNeese State University	M
MCPHS University	M,D
Memorial University of Newfoundland	M,D
Miami University	M,D
Michigan State University	M,D
Michigan Technological University	M,D
Middle Tennessee State University	M
Mississippi College	M
Mississippi State University	M,D
Missouri State University	M
Missouri University of Science and Technology	M,D
Missouri Western State University	M
Montana State University	M,D
Montclair State University	M
Morgan State University	M
Mount Allison University	M
Murray State University	M
New Jersey Institute of Technology	M,D,O
New Mexico Highlands University	M
New Mexico Institute of Mining and Technology	M,D
New Mexico State University	M,D
New York University	M,D,O*
North Carolina Agricultural and Technical State University	M,D
North Carolina Central University	M
North Carolina State University	M,D
North Dakota State University	M,D*
Northeastern Illinois University	M
Northeastern University	M,D
Northern Arizona University	M
Northern Illinois University	M,D
Northwestern University	D
Oakland University	M,D
The Ohio State University	M,D
Oklahoma State University	M,D
Old Dominion University	M,D
Oregon State University	M,D
Pace University	M,O
Penn State University Park	M,D*
Pittsburg State University	M
Pontifical Catholic University of Puerto Rico	M
Portland State University	M,D
Prairie View A&M University	M
Princeton University	M,D
Purdue University	M,D
Queens College of the City University of New York	M
Queen's University at Kingston	M,D
Rensselaer Polytechnic Institute	M,D
Rice University	M,D
Rochester Institute of Technology	M
Roosevelt University	M
Royal Military College of Canada	M,D
Rutgers University–Camden	M
Rutgers University–Newark	M,D
Rutgers University–New Brunswick	M,D
Sacred Heart University	M
St. Francis Xavier University	M
St. John Fisher College	M
St. John's University (NY)	M
Saint Louis University	M,D*
Sam Houston State University	M
San Diego State University	M,D
San Francisco State University	M
San Jose State University	M
The Scripps Research Institute	D
Seton Hall University	M,D
Simon Fraser University	M,D
Smith College	M
South Dakota State University	M,D
Southeast Missouri State University	M
Southern Connecticut State University	M
Southern Illinois University Carbondale	M,D
Southern Illinois University Edwardsville	M
Southern Methodist University	M,D
Southern University and Agricultural and Mechanical College	M
Stanford University	D
State University of New York at New Paltz	M,O
State University of New York at Oswego	M
State University of New York College of Environmental Science and Forestry	M,D
Stephen F. Austin State University	M
Stevens Institute of Technology	M,D,O
Stevenson University	M
Stony Brook University, State University of New York	M,D
Syracuse University	M,D*
Teachers College, Columbia University	M,D
Temple University	M,D*
Tennessee State University	M
Tennessee Technological University	M,D
Texas A&M University	M,D
Texas A&M University–Commerce	M,O
Texas A&M University–Corpus Christi	M,D
Texas A&M University–Kingsville	M
Texas Christian University	M,D
Texas Southern University	M
Texas State University	M
Texas Tech University	M,D
Texas Woman's University	M
Trent University	M
Tufts University	M,D*
Tulane University	M,D
Tuskegee University	M
Universidad del Turabo	M,D
Université de Moncton	M
Université de Montréal	M,D
Université de Sherbrooke	M,D,O
Université du Québec à Montréal	M,D
Université du Québec à Trois-Rivières	M
Université Laval	M,D
University at Albany, State University of New York	M,D
University at Buffalo, the State University of New York	M,D
The University of Akron	M,D
The University of Alabama	M,D
The University of Alabama at Birmingham	M,D
The University of Alabama in Huntsville	M,D
University of Alaska Fairbanks	M,D
University of Alberta	M,D
The University of Arizona	M,D
University of Arkansas	M,D
University of Arkansas at Little Rock	M
The University of British Columbia	M,D
University of Calgary	M,D
University of California, Berkeley	D
University of California, Davis	M,D
University of California, Irvine	M,D
University of California, Los Angeles	M,D*
University of California, Merced	M,D
University of California, Riverside	M,D
University of California, San Diego	M,D*
University of California, San Francisco	D
University of California, Santa Barbara	M,D
University of California, Santa Cruz	M,D*
University of Central Florida	M,D,O
University of Chicago	D
University of Cincinnati	M,D
University of Colorado Boulder	M,D
University of Colorado Denver	M
University of Connecticut	M,D*
University of Dayton	M
University of Delaware	M,D*
University of Denver	M,D
University of Detroit Mercy	M,D
University of Florida	M,D
University of Georgia	M,D
University of Guelph	M,D
University of Hawaii at Manoa	M,D
University of Houston	M,D
University of Houston–Clear Lake	M
University of Idaho	M,D
University of Illinois at Chicago	M,D
University of Illinois at Urbana–Champaign	M,D
The University of Iowa	D*
The University of Kansas	M,D
University of Kentucky	M,D
University of Lethbridge	M,D
University of Louisville	M,D
University of Maine	M,D
The University of Manchester	M,D
University of Manitoba	M,D
University of Maryland, Baltimore County	M,D,O
University of Maryland, College Park	M,D
University of Maryland Eastern Shore	M,D
University of Massachusetts Amherst	M,D*
University of Massachusetts Boston	M,D
University of Massachusetts Dartmouth	M,D
University of Massachusetts Lowell	M,D
University of Memphis	M,D
University of Miami	M,D*
University of Michigan	M,D*
University of Minnesota, Duluth	M
University of Minnesota, Twin Cities Campus	M,D
University of Mississippi	M,D
University of Missouri	D
University of Missouri–Kansas City	M,D
University of Missouri–St. Louis	M,D
University of Montana	M,D
University of Nebraska–Lincoln	M,D
University of Nevada, Las Vegas	M,D
University of Nevada, Reno	M,D
University of New Brunswick Fredericton	M,D
University of New Hampshire	M,D
University of New Mexico	M,D
University of New Orleans	M,D
The University of North Carolina at Chapel Hill	M,D
The University of North Carolina at Charlotte	M,D
The University of North Carolina at Greensboro	M
The University of North Carolina Wilmington	M

*M—masters degree; D—doctorate; O—other advanced degree; *—Close-Up and/or Display*

University of North Dakota	M,D
University of Northern Colorado	M,D
University of North Texas	M,D,O
University of Notre Dame	M,D
University of Oklahoma	M,D*
University of Oregon	M,D
University of Ottawa	M,D
University of Pennsylvania	M,D*
University of Pittsburgh	M,D*
University of Prince Edward Island	M,D
University of Puerto Rico–Mayagüez	M,D
University of Puerto Rico–Río Piedras	M,D
University of Regina	M,D
University of Rhode Island	M,D*
University of Rochester	D*
University of Saint Joseph	M
University of San Francisco	M
University of Saskatchewan	M,D
The University of Scranton	M
University of South Alabama	M
University of South Carolina	M,D
University of South Dakota	M,D
University of Southern California	D*
University of Southern Mississippi	M,D
University of South Florida	M,D*
The University of Tennessee	M,D
The University of Texas at Arlington	M,D
The University of Texas at Austin	D
The University of Texas at Dallas	M,D
The University of Texas at El Paso	M,D
The University of Texas at San Antonio	M,D
The University of Texas Rio Grande Valley	M
University of the Sciences	M,D
The University of Toledo	M,D
University of Toronto	M,D
The University of Tulsa	M,D
University of Utah	M,D
University of Vermont	M,D
University of Victoria	M,D
University of Virginia	M,D
University of Washington	M,D
University of Waterloo	M,D
The University of Western Ontario	M,D
University of Windsor	M,D
University of Wisconsin–Madison	M,D
University of Wisconsin–Milwaukee	M,D*
University of Wyoming	M,D
Utah State University	M,D
Vanderbilt University	M,D*
Villanova University	M
Virginia Commonwealth University	M,D
Virginia Polytechnic Institute and State University	M,D
Wake Forest University	M,D
Washington State University	M,D
Washington University in St. Louis	D
Wayne State University	M,D
Wesleyan University	D
West Chester University of Pennsylvania	O
Western Carolina University	M
Western Illinois University	M
Western Kentucky University	M
Western Michigan University	M,D,O
Western Washington University	M
West Texas A&M University	M
West Virginia University	M,D
Wichita State University	M,D
Wilfrid Laurier University	M
Worcester Polytechnic Institute	M,D
Wright State University	M
Yale University	D
York University	M,D
Youngstown State University	M

CHILD AND FAMILY STUDIES

Alabama Agricultural and Mechanical University	M
Amberton University	M
Arizona State University at the Tempe campus	M,D
Asbury University	M
Assumption College	M,O
Auburn University	M,D*
Bank Street College of Education	M
Brandeis University	M,D
Brigham Young University	M,D
Brock University	M
California State University, East Bay	M
California State University, Los Angeles	M
California State University, San Marcos	M
Capella University	M
Central Michigan University	M,O
Central Washington University	M
Colorado State University	M,D
Concordia University (Canada)	M
Concordia University Wisconsin	M
Cornell University	M,D
Dallas Theological Seminary	M,D,O
East Carolina University	M,D
Eastern University	D
Fairfield University	M,O
Florida State University	M,D
Iowa State University of Science and Technology	M,D
Kansas State University	M,D,O
Kean University	M
Kent State University	M
Liberty University	M,D,O
Loma Linda University	M,D,O
London Metropolitan University	M,D
Miami University	M
Michigan State University	M,D
Mississippi State University	M,D
Missouri State University	M
Montclair State University	M,D,O
Mount Saint Vincent University	M
North Carolina Agricultural and Technical State University	M
North Dakota State University	M,D,O*
Northern Illinois University	M
The Ohio State University	M,D
Ohio University	M
Oklahoma State University	M,D
Oregon State University	M,D
Oxford Graduate School	M,D
Penn State University Park	M,D*
Purdue University	M,D
Purdue University Northwest	M
Queens College of the City University of New York	M,O
Roberts Wesleyan College	M
St. Cloud State University	M
San Diego State University	M
South Carolina State University	M
Spring Arbor University	M
State University of New York at Oswego	M
Syracuse University	M,D*
Texas State University	M
Texas Tech University	M,D
Texas Woman's University	M,D
Towson University	M,O
Tufts University	M,D*
The University of Akron	M
The University of Alabama	M
The University of Arizona	M,D,O
University of Central Oklahoma	M
University of Colorado Denver	M,D
University of Connecticut	M,D*
University of Delaware	M,D*
University of Denver	M,D,O
University of Georgia	M
University of Guelph	M,D
University of Illinois at Springfield	M,O
University of Kentucky	M,D
University of La Verne	M
University of Maryland, College Park	M,D
University of Massachusetts Amherst	M,D,O*
University of Minnesota, Twin Cities Campus	M,D
University of Missouri	M,D
University of Montana	M,D,O
University of Nebraska–Lincoln	M,D
University of Nevada, Reno	M
University of New Hampshire	M,O
University of New Mexico	M,D
University of North Alabama	M
The University of North Carolina at Charlotte	M,D,O
The University of North Carolina at Greensboro	M,D
University of North Texas	M,D,O
University of Rhode Island	M*
University of Southern California	M,D*
University of Southern Mississippi	M
University of South Florida	M,D,O*
The University of Tennessee	M,D
The University of Tennessee at Martin	M
The University of Texas at Austin	M,D
The University of Texas at Dallas	M,D
University of Utah	M
University of Victoria	M,D
University of Wisconsin–Madison	M,D
Utah State University	M,D
Vanderbilt University	M*
Walden University	M,D
Washington University in St. Louis	M,D

CHILD DEVELOPMENT

California State University, Los Angeles	M
California State University, Sacramento	M,D,O
California State University, San Bernardino	M
Chaminade University of Honolulu	M
East Carolina University	M,D
Erikson Institute	M
Fielding Graduate University	M,D,O
Kansas State University	M,D,O
Lee University	M
Michigan State University	M,D
Montclair State University	M,O
Mount Saint Mary College	M,O
North Carolina Agricultural and Technical State University	M
North Dakota State University	M*
Ohio University	M
Purdue University	M,D
Purdue University Northwest	M
Rutgers University–Camden	M,D
San Diego State University	M
San Jose State University	M,D
Sarah Lawrence College	M
Texas Woman's University	M,D
Tufts University	M,D*
The University of Akron	M
University of California, Davis	M
University of Florida	M
University of La Verne	M
University of Minnesota, Twin Cities Campus	M,D
University of Nebraska–Lincoln	M,D
The University of North Carolina at Charlotte	M,D,O
The University of Tennessee at Martin	M
The University of Texas at Austin	M,D
The University of West Alabama	M,O
University of Wyoming	M
Whittier College	M

CHINESE

Arizona State University at the Tempe campus	M,D
Brandeis University	M
DePaul University	M
Harvard University	D*
Hofstra University	M,D,O
Hunter College of the City University of New York	M
Indiana University Bloomington	M,D
Middlebury College	M
New York University	M,D,O*
The Ohio State University	M,D
Saginaw Valley State University	M
San Francisco State University	M
Stanford University	M,D
University of Alberta	M
University of California, Berkeley	D
University of California, Irvine	M,D
University of Colorado Boulder	M,D
University of Delaware	M*
University of Hawaii at Manoa	M,D,O
The University of Iowa	M*
The University of Manchester	D
University of Massachusetts Amherst	M*
University of Oregon	M,D
University of Pittsburgh	M*
University of Washington	M,D
University of Wisconsin–Madison	M,D
Washington University in St. Louis	M,D

CHIROPRACTIC

Canadian Memorial Chiropractic College	D,O
Cleveland University–Kansas City	D
D'Youville College	D
Institut Franco-Européen de Chiropraxie	D
Life Chiropractic College West	D
Life University	D
Logan University	D
National University of Health Sciences	M,D
New York Chiropractic College	D*
Northwestern Health Sciences University	D
Palmer College of Chiropractic	D
Parker University	D
Sherman College of Chiropractic	D
Southern California University of Health Sciences	D
Texas Chiropractic College	D
Université du Québec à Trois-Rivières	D
University of Bridgeport	D
University of Western States	D

CIVIL ENGINEERING

American University of Beirut	M,D
American University of Sharjah	M,D
Arizona State University at the Tempe campus	M,D
Auburn University	M,D*
Boise State University	M
Bradley University	M
Brigham Young University	M,D
Bucknell University	M
California Baptist University	M
California Institute of Technology	M,D,O
California Polytechnic State University, San Luis Obispo	M*
California State Polytechnic University, Pomona	M
California State University, Fresno	M
California State University, Fullerton	M
California State University, Long Beach	M
California State University, Los Angeles	M
California State University, Northridge	M
California State University, Sacramento	M
Carleton University	M,D
Carnegie Mellon University	M,D
Case Western Reserve University	M,D*
The Catholic University of America	M,D,O
The Citadel, The Military College of South Carolina	M,O
City College of the City University of New York	M,D
Clarkson University	M,D
Clemson University	M,D
Cleveland State University	M,D
Colorado School of Mines	M,D
Colorado State University	M,D
Columbia University	M,D*
Concordia University (Canada)	M,D,O
Cooper Union for the Advancement of Science and Art	M
Cornell University	M,D
Dalhousie University	M,D
Drexel University	M,D*
Duke University	M,D*
École Polytechnique de Montréal	M,D,O
Embry-Riddle Aeronautical University–Daytona	M
Florida Agricultural and Mechanical University	M,D
Florida Atlantic University	M
Florida Institute of Technology	M,D
Florida International University	M,D
Florida State University	M,D
George Mason University	M,D
The George Washington University	M,D,O
Georgia Institute of Technology	M,D
Georgia Southern University	M
Howard University	M
Idaho State University	M
Illinois Institute of Technology	M,D
Indiana University–Purdue University Fort Wayne	M
Instituto Tecnológico y de Estudios Superiores de Monterrey, Campus Monterrey	M,D
Iowa State University of Science and Technology	M,D
Jackson State University	M,D
Johns Hopkins University	M,D,O*
Kansas State University	M,D
Kennesaw State University	M
Lawrence Technological University	M,D
Lehigh University	M,D
Louisiana State University and Agricultural & Mechanical College	M,D
Loyola Marymount University	M
Manhattan College	M
Marquette University	M,D,O
Massachusetts Institute of Technology	M,D,O
McGill University	M,D
McMaster University	M,D
McNeese State University	M
Memorial University of Newfoundland	M,D
Merrimack College	M
Michigan State University	M,D
Michigan Technological University	M,D
Milwaukee School of Engineering	M
Mississippi State University	M,D
Missouri University of Science and Technology	M,D
Montana State University	M,D
Morgan State University	M,D,O
New Mexico State University	M,D
New York University	M,D*
North Carolina Agricultural and Technical State University	M
North Carolina State University	M,D
North Dakota State University	M,D*
Northeastern University	M,D,O
Northern Arizona University	M
Northwestern University	M,D
Norwich University	M
The Ohio State University	M,D
Ohio University	M,D
Oklahoma State University	M,D
Old Dominion University	M,D
Oregon State University	M,D
Penn State Harrisburg	M,O
Penn State University Park	M,D*
Polytechnic University of Puerto Rico	M
Portland State University	M,D,O
Princeton University	M,D
Purdue University	M,D
Queen's University at Kingston	M,D
Rensselaer Polytechnic Institute	M,D
Rice University	M,D
Rose-Hulman Institute of Technology	M
Rowan University	M
Royal Military College of Canada	M,D
Rutgers University–New Brunswick	M,D
Saint Martin's University	M
San Diego State University	M
San Jose State University	M
Santa Clara University	M,D,O
South Carolina State University	M
South Dakota School of Mines and Technology	M,D
South Dakota State University	M
Southern Illinois University Carbondale	M,D
Southern Illinois University Edwardsville	M
Southern Methodist University	M,D
Stanford University	M,D,O
Stevens Institute of Technology	M,D,O
Stony Brook University, State University of New York	M,D,O
Syracuse University	M,D*
Temple University	M,D,O*
Tennessee State University	M,D
Tennessee Technological University	M
Texas A&M University	M,D
Texas A&M University–Kingsville	M
Texas State University	M
Texas Tech University	M,D
Tufts University	M,D*
United States Merchant Marine Academy	M
Université de Moncton	M
Université de Sherbrooke	M,D
Université Laval	M,D,O
University at Buffalo, the State University of New York	M,D
The University of Akron	M,D
The University of Alabama	M,D
The University of Alabama at Birmingham	M,D
The University of Alabama in Huntsville	M,D
University of Alaska Fairbanks	M,D,O
University of Alberta	M,D
University of Arkansas	M,D
The University of British Columbia	M,D
University of Calgary	M,D
University of California, Berkeley	M,D
University of California, Davis	M,D,O
University of California, Irvine	M,D
University of California, Los Angeles	M,D*
University of Central Florida	M,D,O
University of Cincinnati	M,D
University of Colorado Boulder	M,D
University of Colorado Denver	M,D
University of Connecticut	M,D*

University of Dayton	M
University of Delaware	M,D*
University of Detroit Mercy	M,D
University of Florida	M,D
University of Hawaii at Manoa	M,D
University of Houston	M,D
University of Idaho	M,D
University of Illinois at Chicago	M,D
University of Illinois at Urbana–Champaign	M,D
The University of Iowa	M,D*
The University of Kansas	M,D
University of Kentucky	M,D
University of Louisiana at Lafayette	M
University of Louisville	M,D
University of Maine	M,D
The University of Manchester	M,D
University of Manitoba	M,D
University of Maryland, College Park	M,D
University of Massachusetts Amherst	M,D*
University of Massachusetts Dartmouth	M
University of Massachusetts Lowell	M,D
University of Memphis	M,D,O
University of Miami	M,D*
University of Michigan	M,D,O*
University of Minnesota, Twin Cities Campus	M,D,O
University of Mississippi	M,D
University of Missouri	M,D
University of Missouri–Kansas City	M,D,O
University of Nebraska–Lincoln	M,D
University of Nevada, Las Vegas	M,D
University of Nevada, Reno	M,D
University of New Brunswick Fredericton	M,D
University of New Hampshire	M,D
University of New Haven	M*
University of New Mexico	M,D
University of New Orleans	M
The University of North Carolina at Charlotte	M,D
University of North Dakota	M,D
University of North Florida	M
University of Notre Dame	M,D
University of Oklahoma	M,D*
University of Ottawa	M,D
University of Pittsburgh	M,D*
University of Portland	M
University of Puerto Rico–Mayagüez	M,D
University of Rhode Island	M,D*
University of Saskatchewan	M,D
University of South Alabama	M
University of South Carolina	M,D
University of Southern California	M,D,O*
University of South Florida	M,D,O*
The University of Tennessee	M,D
The University of Tennessee at Chattanooga	M
The University of Texas at Arlington	M,D
The University of Texas at Austin	M,D
The University of Texas at El Paso	M,D,O
The University of Texas at San Antonio	M,D
The University of Texas at Tyler	M
The University of Toledo	M,D
University of Toronto	M,D
University of Utah	M,D
University of Vermont	M,D
University of Virginia	M,D
University of Washington	M,D
University of Waterloo	M,D
The University of Western Ontario	M,D
University of Windsor	M,D
University of Wisconsin–Madison	M
University of Wisconsin–Milwaukee	M,D*
University of Wyoming	M,D
Utah State University	M,D,O
Vanderbilt University	M,D*
Villanova University	M
Virginia Polytechnic Institute and State University	M,D,O
Washington State University	M,D
Wayne State University	M,D
Wentworth Institute of Technology	M
Western Michigan University	M
Western New England University	M
West Virginia University	M,D
Widener University	M
Worcester Polytechnic Institute	M,D,O
Youngstown State University	M

CLASSICS

Asbury University	M
Bethel Seminary	M,D,O
Boston College	M
Boston University	M,D*
Brandeis University	M
Brigham Young University	M
Brock University	M
Brown University	M,D
Bryn Mawr College	M,D
The Catholic University of America	M,D,O
Columbia University	M,D*
Cornell University	D
Dalhousie University	M,D
Duke University	D*
Duquesne University	M
Florida State University	M,D
Fordham University	M,D
The Graduate Center, City University of New York	M,D
Harvard University	D*
Heritage Christian University	M
Hunter College of the City University of New York	M
Indiana University Bloomington	M,D
Johns Hopkins University	D*
Knox Theological Seminary	M
Manhattanville College	M,O
McMaster University	M,D
Memorial University of Newfoundland	M
New York University	M,D,O*
The Ohio State University	M,D
Princeton University	D
Queen's University at Kingston	M
Rutgers University–New Brunswick	M,D
San Francisco State University	M
Stanford University	M,D
Tufts University	M*
Tulane University	M
Université de Montréal	M
University at Buffalo, the State University of New York	M,D,O
University of Alberta	M,D
The University of Arizona	M
The University of British Columbia	M,D
University of Calgary	M,D
University of California, Berkeley	M,D
University of California, Irvine	M,D
University of California, Los Angeles	M,D*
University of California, Riverside	D
University of California, Santa Barbara	M,D
University of Chicago	M,D
University of Cincinnati	M,D
University of Colorado Boulder	M,D
University of Dallas	M
University of Florida	M,D
University of Georgia	M
University of Illinois at Urbana–Champaign	M,D
The University of Iowa	M,D*
The University of Kansas	M
University of Kentucky	M
The University of Manchester	D
University of Manitoba	M
University of Maryland, College Park	M
University of Massachusetts Amherst	M*
University of Massachusetts Boston	M
University of Michigan	M,D,O*
University of Minnesota, Twin Cities Campus	M,D
University of Nebraska–Lincoln	M
University of New Brunswick Fredericton	M
The University of North Carolina at Chapel Hill	M,D
The University of North Carolina at Greensboro	M
University of Oregon	M
University of Ottawa	M,D
University of Pennsylvania	M,D*
University of South Africa	M,D
University of Southern California	M,D*
The University of Texas at Austin	M,D
University of Toronto	M,D
University of Vermont	M,O
University of Victoria	M,D
University of Virginia	M,D
University of Washington	M,D
The University of Western Ontario	M
University of Wisconsin–Madison	M,D
University of Wisconsin–Milwaukee	M,O*
Vanderbilt University	M*
Villanova University	M
Washington University in St. Louis	M,D
Yale University	M,D

CLINICAL LABORATORY SCIENCES/ MEDICAL TECHNOLOGY

Albany College of Pharmacy and Health Sciences	M
Austin Peay State University	M
Baylor College of Medicine	M,D
The Catholic University of America	M,D
The College of William and Mary	M,D*
Dominican University of California	M
Duke University	M*
Fairleigh Dickinson University, Metropolitan Campus	M
Inter American University of Puerto Rico, Metropolitan Campus	M
Lipscomb University	M
Mayo Clinic Graduate School of Biomedical Sciences	M,D
Medical College of Wisconsin	M
Michigan State University	M
Milwaukee School of Engineering	M
Northern Michigan University	M
Northwestern University	M
Pontifical Catholic University of Puerto Rico	O
Rush University	M
Rutgers University–Newark	M
Rutgers University–New Brunswick	M
State University of New York Upstate Medical University	M
Tarleton State University	M
Thomas Jefferson University	M
Tufts University	M,D,O*
Universidad de las Américas Puebla	M
Université de Sherbrooke	M,D
University at Buffalo, the State University of New York	M
The University of Alabama at Birmingham	M,D
University of Alberta	M,D
University of California, San Diego	M,D*
University of Colorado Denver	M,D
University of Florida	M,D
University of Maryland, Baltimore	M
University of Massachusetts Lowell	M
University of Minnesota, Twin Cities Campus	M
University of Nebraska Medical Center	M,O
University of New Mexico	M,O
University of North Dakota	M,D
University of Pennsylvania	M*
University of Pittsburgh	D*
University of Puerto Rico–Medical Sciences Campus	M,O
University of Rhode Island	M,D*
University of Southern Mississippi	M
The University of Tennessee Health Science Center	M,D
The University of Texas at Austin	M,D
The University of Texas Health Science Center at San Antonio	D
The University of Texas Medical Branch	M,D
The University of Texas Rio Grande Valley	M
University of Utah	M
University of Vermont	M,D,O
University of Washington	M
Virginia Commonwealth University	M,D

CLINICAL PSYCHOLOGY

Abilene Christian University	M
Acadia University	M
Adams State University	M,D
Adelphi University	D
Adler Graduate School	M
Adler University	M,D
Alabama Agricultural and Mechanical University	M,O
Alliant International University–Fresno	D
Alliant International University–Los Angeles	D
Alliant International University–Sacramento	D
Alliant International University–San Diego	M,D
Alliant International University–San Francisco	M,D,O
American International College	M,D,O
American University	M,D,O
American University of Beirut	M,D
Andrews University	M
Antioch University Los Angeles	M
Antioch University New England	M,D
Antioch University Santa Barbara	M,D
Antioch University Seattle	M,D
Appalachian State University	M
Argosy University, Atlanta	M,D,O
Argosy University, Chicago	M,D
Argosy University, Hawai`i	M,D,O
Argosy University, Los Angeles	M,D
Argosy University, Northern Virginia	M,D
Argosy University, Orange County	M,D
Argosy University, Phoenix	M,D
Argosy University, Seattle	M,D,O
Argosy University, Tampa	M,D
Argosy University, Twin Cities	M,D,O
Arizona State University at the Tempe campus	M,D
Arkansas State University	M,O
Ashland Theological Seminary	M,D
Auburn University at Montgomery	M,O
Augusta University	M,O
Austin Peay State University	M
Azusa Pacific University	D*
Ball State University	M,D
Barry University	M,O
Baylor University	D
Bay Path University	M
Benedictine University	M
Bethel Seminary	M,D,O
Binghamton University, State University of New York	D
Biola University	D
Bowling Green State University	M,D
Bradley University	M
Brigham Young University	D
Butler University	M,O
California Institute of Integral Studies	M,D
California Lutheran University	M,D
California State University, Dominguez Hills	M
California State University, Fullerton	M
California State University, Northridge	M
California State University, San Bernardino	M
California University of Pennsylvania	M
Capella University	M,D
Cardinal Stritch University	M
Carlos Albizu University	M,D
Carlos Albizu University, Miami Campus	M,D
Case Western Reserve University	D*
The Catholic University of America	M,D
Central Michigan University	D
Chestnut Hill College	M,D,O
The Chicago School of Professional Psychology	M,D
The Chicago School of Professional Psychology at Downtown Los Angeles	M,D
The Chicago School of Professional Psychology at Irvine	D
The Chicago School of Professional Psychology: Online	M
Chicago State University	M
City College of the City University of New York	M,D
Clark University	D
Clayton State University	M
Clemson University	M,D,O
College of St. Joseph	M
College of Staten Island of the City University of New York	M
Columbus State University	M,D,O
Concordia University (Canada)	D,O
Dalhousie University	M,D
DePaul University	M,D
Divine Mercy University	M,D
Drexel University	D*
Duke University	D*
Duquesne University	M,D,O
East Carolina University	M,D,O
East Central University	M
Eastern Illinois University	M,O
Eastern Kentucky University	M,O
Eastern Michigan University	M,D
Eastern Virginia Medical School	D
Eastern Washington University	M
East Tennessee State University	M,D
Edinboro University of Pennsylvania	M,O
Emory University	D
Emporia State University	M
Evangel University	M
Fairfield University	M,O
Fairleigh Dickinson University, Florham Campus	M
Fairleigh Dickinson University, Metropolitan Campus	M,D
Fielding Graduate University	M,D,O
Fisk University	M
Florida Gulf Coast University	M
Florida Institute of Technology	D
Florida International University	M,D,O
Florida State University	D
Fordham University	D
Franciscan University of Steubenville	M
Francis Marion University	M,O
Fuller Theological Seminary	M,D,O
Gallaudet University	M,D,O
Gannon University	M
Geneva College	M
George Fox University	M,D,O
George Mason University	M,D,O
The George Washington University	M,D
Georgian Court University	M,O
Georgia Southern University	M,D
Georgia State University	D
Goddard College	M
Grace College	M
The Graduate Center, City University of New York	D
Hawai`i Pacific University	M
Heidelberg University	M
Hodges University	M
Hofstra University	M,D
Hood College	M*
Howard University	M,D
Husson University	M
Idaho State University	D
Illinois Institute of Technology	M,D
Illinois State University	M,D,O
Immaculata University	M,D,O
Indiana State University	M,D,O
Indiana University of Pennsylvania	M,D
Indiana University–Purdue University Indianapolis	M,D
Indiana University South Bend	M,O
Jackson State University	M,D
James Madison University	D
John Brown University	M,O
Johns Hopkins University	M,D*
Johnson & Wales University	M
Johnson University	M,D,O
Judson University	M
Kean University	M,D
Kent State University	M,D
Kutztown University of Pennsylvania	M
LaGrange College	M
Lakehead University	M,D
Lamar University	M
La Salle University	M,D
Lenoir-Rhyne University	M
Lesley University	M,D,O
Lewis University	M
Liberty University	M,D,O
Lipscomb University	M,O
Lock Haven University of Pennsylvania	M
Loma Linda University	D
London Metropolitan University	M,D
Long Island University–Brentwood Campus	M,O
Long Island University–LIU Brooklyn	M,D,O
Long Island University–LIU Post	M,D,O
Louisiana State University and Agricultural & Mechanical College	M,D
Louisiana Tech University	M,D,O
Loyola University Chicago	M,D,O
Loyola University Maryland	M,D,O
Loyola University New Orleans	M

*M—masters degree; D—doctorate; O—other advanced degree; *—Close-Up and/or Display*

Madonna University	M
Marquette University	M,D
Marshall University	M,D,O
Marymount University	M
Marywood University	M,D
McGill University	M,D
McKendree University	M
Medaille College	M,D
Memorial University of Newfoundland	M,D
Mercer University	M,D
Merrimack College	M,O
Messiah College	M,O
Michigan School of Professional Psychology	M,D
MidAmerica Nazarene University	M
Middle Tennessee State University	M,O
Midwestern State University	M
Midwestern University, Downers Grove Campus	D
Midwestern University, Glendale Campus	D
Millersville University of Pennsylvania	M
Milligan College	M,O
Minnesota State University Mankato	M,D
Mississippi State University	M,D,O
Missouri State University	M,O
Molloy College	M
Montclair State University	M
Morehead State University	M
Mount Mary University	M,O
Murray State University	M,O
National University	M,O
Neumann University	M,D,O
New Mexico Highlands University	M
The New School	M,D
Nicholls State University	M,O
Norfolk State University	M
North Carolina Central University	M
North Dakota State University	M,D*
Northern Kentucky University	M
Northern State University	M
Northwestern State University of Louisiana	M
Northwestern University	D
Northwest Nazarene University	M
Notre Dame de Namur University	M
Nova Southeastern University	M,D,O*
The Ohio State University	D
Ohio University	D
Oklahoma State University	M,D
Old Dominion University	D
Oregon State University	M,D
Pace University	M,D
Pacifica Graduate Institute	M,D
Pacific University	M,D
Palo Alto University	M,D
Penn State Erie, The Behrend College	M
Penn State Harrisburg	M,D,O
Pepperdine University	M,D
Philadelphia College of Osteopathic Medicine	M,D,O*
Pillar College	M
Pittsburg State University	M
Plymouth State University	O
Point Loma Nazarene University	M
Point Park University	M,D
Ponce Health Sciences University	D
Pontifical Catholic University of Puerto Rico	D
Pontificia Universidad Catolica Madre y Maestra	M
Post University	M
Prairie View A&M University	M,D
Purdue University	D
Queen's University at Kingston	M,D
Quincy University	M
Radford University	M
Regent University	M,D,O
Richmont Graduate University	M
Rider University	M,O
Rivier University	M
Roberts Wesleyan College	M,D
Roger Williams University	M
Roosevelt University	M
Rosalind Franklin University of Medicine and Science	M,D
Rowan University	M,O
Rutgers University–New Brunswick	M,D
St. John's University (NY)	M,D,O
Saint Louis University	M,D*
Saint Michael's College	M
Sam Houston State University	M,D,O
San Diego State University	M,D
San Francisco State University	M,O
San Jose State University	M
Saybrook University	M
Seattle Pacific University	D
Seminary of the Southwest	M,O
Shippensburg University of Pennsylvania	M,D
Siena Heights University	M,O
Slippery Rock University of Pennsylvania	M
Sofia University	M,D
Sonoma State University	M
Southeastern Oklahoma State University	M
Southern Illinois University Carbondale	M,D
Southern Illinois University Edwardsville	M
Southern Methodist University	D
Southern New Hampshire University	M
Spalding University	M,D
Springfield College	M,D,O
State University of New York at New Paltz	M,O
State University of New York at Plattsburgh	M,O
Stephens College	M,O
Stony Brook University, State University of New York	D
Suffolk University	M,D,O
Syracuse University	M,D*
Teachers College, Columbia University	M,D
Texas A&M University	M,D
Texas A&M University–Central Texas	M,O
Texas A&M University–Corpus Christi	M
Texas A&M University–San Antonio	M
Texas State University	M
Texas Tech University	M,D
Texas Tech University Health Sciences Center	M
Trinity Washington University	M
Uniformed Services University of the Health Sciences	D*
Union College (KY)	M
Union Institute & University	M
Universidad de Iberoamerica	M,D
Université Laval	D
University at Albany, State University of New York	M,D
The University of Akron	M
The University of Alabama	D
The University of Alabama at Birmingham	M,D
University of Alaska Anchorage	M,D
University of Alaska Fairbanks	D
University of Bridgeport	M
The University of British Columbia	M,D
University of Calgary	M,D
University of California, San Diego	D*
University of California, Santa Barbara	M,D,O
University of Central Florida	M,D
University of Cincinnati	D
University of Colorado Denver	M,D
University of Connecticut	M,D*
University of Dallas	M
University of Dayton	M,O
University of Delaware	D*
University of Denver	M,D,O
University of Detroit Mercy	M,D,O
University of Florida	M,D
University of Guelph	M,D
University of Hartford	M,D
University of Hawaii at Manoa	M,D,O
University of Houston	M,D
University of Houston–Clear Lake	M
University of Indianapolis	M,D
The University of Kansas	M,D
University of La Verne	D
University of Louisiana at Monroe	M
University of Louisville	D
University of Lynchburg	M
The University of Manchester	M,D
University of Manitoba	M,D
University of Mary Hardin-Baylor	M
University of Maryland, Baltimore County	M,D
University of Maryland, College Park	M,D
University of Massachusetts Amherst	M,D*
University of Massachusetts Boston	D
University of Massachusetts Dartmouth	M,O
University of Memphis	M,D,O
University of Miami	M,D*
University of Michigan	D*
University of Michigan–Dearborn	M
University of Minnesota, Twin Cities Campus	D
University of Missouri–St. Louis	M,D,O
University of Montana	M,D,O
University of Nebraska–Lincoln	M,D
University of Nevada, Las Vegas	M,D,O
University of Nevada, Reno	D
University of New Brunswick Saint John	M,D
University of New Mexico	D
University of North Alabama	M
The University of North Carolina at Chapel Hill	D
The University of North Carolina at Greensboro	M,D
The University of North Carolina Wilmington	M,D
University of North Dakota	M,D
University of Northern Colorado	M
University of North Texas	M,D,O
University of North Texas at Dallas	M
University of Oklahoma	M,O*
University of Oregon	D
University of Phoenix–Phoenix Campus	M
University of Pittsburgh	M,D*
University of Puerto Rico–Río Piedras	M,D
University of Regina	M,D
University of Rhode Island	M,D*
University of Rochester	D*
University of Saint Francis (IN)	M,O
University of Saint Joseph	M
University of San Francisco	D
The University of Scranton	M
University of South Africa	M,D
University of South Alabama	M,D,O
University of South Carolina	M,D
University of South Carolina Aiken	M
University of South Dakota	M,D
University of Southern California	M,D*
University of South Florida	D*
The University of Tennessee	M,D
The University of Texas at Austin	D
The University of Texas at El Paso	M,D
The University of Texas at Tyler	M
The University of Texas of the Permian Basin	M
The University of Texas Rio Grande Valley	M
The University of Texas Southwestern Medical Center	D
University of the Cumberlands	D
The University of Toledo	M,D
The University of Tulsa	M,D
University of Utah	M,D,O
University of Vermont	M,D
University of Victoria	M,D
University of Virginia	D
University of Washington	M,D
The University of West Alabama	M
University of Windsor	M,D
University of Wisconsin–Madison	D
University of Wisconsin–Parkside	M
University of Wisconsin–Stout	M
Utah State University	M,D
Valparaiso University	M
Vanguard University of Southern California	M
Virginia Commonwealth University	D
Virginia State University	M,D
Walden University	M,D,O
Washburn University	M
Washington State University	M,D
Waynesburg University	M,D
Wayne State University	M,D
West Chester University of Pennsylvania	M,D,O
Western Connecticut State University	M
Western Illinois University	M,O
Western Kentucky University	M,O
Western Michigan University	M,D
Westminster College (PA)	M
West Virginia University	M,D
Wheaton College	M,D
Wichita State University	D
Widener University	D
William James College	M,D,O
William Paterson University of New Jersey	M,D,O
Wilmington University	M
Winona State University	M,O
Wisconsin School of Professional Psychology	M,D
The Wright Institute	D
Wright State University	D
Xavier University	M,D*
Yale University	D
Yeshiva University	D

CLINICAL RESEARCH

Albert Einstein College of Medicine	D
American University of Beirut	M,D
American University of Health Sciences	M
Augusta University	M
Boston University	M*
Case Western Reserve University	M,D*
Clemson University	M,D,O
Duke University	M*
Eastern Michigan University	M,O
Emory University	M
Fordham University	M
Icahn School of Medicine at Mount Sinai	M,D
Johns Hopkins University	M,D*
Loyola University Chicago	M
Medical College of Wisconsin	
Medical University of South Carolina	M
Memorial University of Newfoundland	M
Morehouse School of Medicine	M
National University of Natural Medicine	M
New York University	M*
Northwestern University	M,O
Oregon Health & Science University	M,O
Palmer College of Chiropractic	M
Stanford University	M,D
Thomas Jefferson University	M,O
Trident University International	M,D,O
University of California, Berkeley	O
University of California, Davis	M
University of California, Los Angeles	M*
University of California, San Diego	M*
University of Colorado Denver	M,D
University of Connecticut Health Center	M
University of Florida	M,D,O
The University of Iowa	M,D*
The University of Kansas	M
University of Kentucky	M
University of Maryland, Baltimore	M,D,O
University of Massachusetts Medical School	M,D
University of Michigan	M*
University of Minnesota, Twin Cities Campus	M
The University of North Carolina at Chapel Hill	M,D
The University of North Carolina Wilmington	M,D,O
University of Pittsburgh	M,O*
University of Puerto Rico–Medical Sciences Campus	M,O
University of Rochester	M*
University of Southern California	M,D,O*
University of South Florida	M,D,O*
The University of Texas Health Science Center at San Antonio	M
University of Virginia	M
University of Washington	M,D
University of Wisconsin–Madison	M,D
Walden University	M,D,O
Washington University in St. Louis	M

CLOTHING AND TEXTILES

Alabama Agricultural and Mechanical University	M
Auburn University	M,D*
Central Michigan University	M,O
Cornell University	M,D
Drexel University	M*
Eastern Michigan University	M
Fashion Institute of Technology	M
Georgia State University	M
Iowa State University of Science and Technology	M,D
Kansas State University	M,D
LIM College	M
Mississippi State University	M,D
New Mexico State University	M
The New School	M
North Carolina State University	D
Oklahoma State University	M,D
Rutgers University–Newark	M
Savannah College of Art and Design	M
Thomas Jefferson University	M
The University of Akron	M
The University of Alabama	M
University of Alberta	M,D
University of California, Davis	M
University of Delaware	M*
University of Georgia	M,D
The University of Manchester	M,D
University of Minnesota, Twin Cities Campus	M,D,O
University of Missouri	M,D
University of Nebraska–Lincoln	M,D
University of Rhode Island	M,O*
The University of Tennessee	M,D
University of the Incarnate Word	M
Washington State University	M
Wayne State University	M

COGNITIVE SCIENCES

American University	M,D,O
Arizona State University at the Tempe campus	M,D
Ball State University	M
Binghamton University, State University of New York	D
Brandeis University	M,D
Brigham Young University	D
Brown University	M,D
Carleton University	D
Carnegie Mellon University	D
Case Western Reserve University	M*
Central European University	D
Claremont Graduate University	M,D,O
Cornell University	D
Dartmouth College	D*
Duke University	D*
Emory University	D
Florida International University	M,D
Florida State University	D
George Mason University	M,D,O
The George Washington University	D
Georgia State University	D
The Graduate Center, City University of New York	D
Grand Canyon University	D
Harvard University	M,D*
Illinois State University	M,D,O
Indiana University Bloomington	D
Iowa State University of Science and Technology	M,D
Johns Hopkins University	M,D*
Louisiana State University and Agricultural & Mechanical College	M,D
Massachusetts Institute of Technology	D
Michigan Technological University	M,D,O
Mississippi State University	M,D
The New School	M,D
New York University	M,D,O*
North Dakota State University	M,D*
Northwestern University	D
The Ohio State University	D
Oregon State University	M,D
Purdue University	D
Queen's University at Kingston	M,D
Rensselaer Polytechnic Institute	D
Rice University	M,D
Rochester Institute of Technology	O
Rutgers University–Newark	D
Rutgers University–New Brunswick	D
Stony Brook University, State University of New York	D
Syracuse University	D*
Texas Christian University	M,D
Tufts University	M,D*
University at Albany, State University of New York	M,D
The University of British Columbia	M,D
University of California, Merced	M,D
University of California, San Diego	D*
University of California, Santa Barbara	M,D
University of Central Florida	D
University of Connecticut	M,D*
University of Delaware	M,D*
University of Guelph	M,D
The University of Kansas	M,D
University of Louisiana at Lafayette	D
University of Louisville	D

University of Maryland, Baltimore County	D
University of Maryland, College Park	D
University of Massachusetts Amherst	M,D*
University of Massachusetts Boston	M
University of Michigan	D*
University of Minnesota, Twin Cities Campus	D
University of Nebraska–Lincoln	M,D,O
University of Nevada, Reno	M,D
University of New Mexico	D
The University of North Carolina at Chapel Hill	D
The University of North Carolina at Charlotte	M,D,O
The University of North Carolina at Greensboro	M,D
University of Notre Dame	D
University of Oregon	M,D
University of Rochester	D*
University of Southern California	M,D*
University of South Florida	D*
The University of Texas at Dallas	M,D
University of Washington	M,D
University of Wisconsin–Madison	D
Wayne State University	M,D
Wilfrid Laurier University	M,D
Yale University	D

COMMUNICATION—GENERAL

Abilene Christian University	M
American University	M,D
The American University in Cairo	M,D,O
The American University of Paris	M
Andrews University	M
Angelo State University	M
Arizona State University at the Tempe campus	M,D
Arkansas State University	M,O
Ashland University	M
Auburn University	M,O*
Austin Peay State University	M
Ball State University	M,O
Barry University	M,O
Baylor University	M
Bellarmine University	M
Boise State University	M
Boston University	M*
Bowling Green State University	M,D
Brigham Young University	M
Bryant University	M,O
Cabrini University	M,D
California Baptist University	M
California State University, Chico	M
California State University, East Bay	M
California State University, Fresno	M
California State University, Fullerton	M
California State University, Long Beach	M
California State University, Los Angeles	M
California State University, Northridge	M
California State University, Sacramento	M
California State University, San Bernardino	M
Carleton University	M,D
Carnegie Mellon University	M,D
Central Connecticut State University	M,O
Central Michigan University	M
Chapman University	M*
Chatham University	M
Clarion University of Pennsylvania	M
Clarks Summit University	M,D
Clark University	M
Clemson University	M
Cleveland State University	M,D,O
The College at Brockport, State University of New York	M
The College of New Rochelle	M,O
Columbia College Chicago	M
Columbia University	M,D*
Concordia University (Canada)	M,D,O
Cornell University	M,D
Dallas Baptist University	M
DePaul University	M
DEREE - The American College of Greece	M
Drake University	M
Drexel University	M*
Drury University	M
Duquesne University	M,D
Eastern Illinois University	M
Eastern Michigan University	M
Eastern New Mexico University	M
Eastern University	M,O
Eastern Washington University	M
East Tennessee State University	M,O
Edinboro University of Pennsylvania	M
Fairfield University	M
Fairleigh Dickinson University, Metropolitan Campus	M
Fitchburg State University	M,O
Florida Atlantic University	M,O
Florida Institute of Technology	M
Florida International University	M
Florida State University	M,D
Fordham University	M,D
Fort Hays State University	M
George Mason University	M,D,O
Georgetown University	M
The George Washington University	M
Georgia State University	M,D
Governors State University	M
Grand Valley State University	M
Harvard University	M,O*
Hawai`i Pacific University	M
Howard University	M,D
Idaho State University	M
Illinois Institute of Technology	M,D
Illinois State University	M
Indiana State University	M
Indiana University of Pennsylvania	D
Indiana University–Purdue University Fort Wayne	M
Indiana University–Purdue University Indianapolis	M,D
Indiana University South Bend	M,D
Instituto Tecnologico de Santo Domingo	M,O
Instituto Tecnológico y de Estudios Superiores de Monterrey, Campus Ciudad Obregón	M
Instituto Tecnológico y de Estudios Superiores de Monterrey, Campus Monterrey	M,D
International University in Geneva	M,D
James Madison University	M
Johns Hopkins University	M,O*
Kansas State University	M,D,O
Kean University	M
Kennesaw State University	M
Kent State University	M
La Salle University	M,O
Lasell College	M,O
La Sierra University	M
Lawrence Technological University	M,O
Liberty University	M
Lindenwood University	M,O
Lindenwood University–Belleville	M
Louisiana State University and Agricultural & Mechanical College	M,D
Loyola Marymount University	M
Loyola University Chicago	M
Lynn University	M,O
Marist College	M
Marquette University	M,O
Marshall University	M
Marywood University	M
McGill University	M,D
Michigan State University	M,D
Minnesota State University Mankato	M,O
Mississippi College	M
Mississippi State University	M,D
Missouri State University	M,O
Monmouth University	M,O*
Montana State University Billings	M
Moore College of Art & Design	M
Morehead State University	M
New Mexico State University	M
New York Institute of Technology	M
New York University	M,D*
Norfolk State University	M
North Carolina State University	M
North Dakota State University	M,D*
Northeastern State University	M
Northern Arizona University	M,O
Northern Illinois University	M
Northern Kentucky University	M,O
Northwestern University	M,D
Notre Dame of Maryland University	M
The Ohio State University	M,D
Ohio University	M,D
Old Dominion University	M,O
Pace University	M
Penn State Harrisburg	M,D,O
Penn State University Park	M,D*
Pepperdine University	M
Pittsburg State University	M
Point Park University	M
Purdue University	M,D
Purdue University Northwest	M
Queen's University at Kingston	M,D
Queens University of Charlotte	M
Quinnipiac University	M
Regent University	M,D
Rochester Institute of Technology	M
Roosevelt University	M
Rutgers University–New Brunswick	D
Sacred Heart University	M
Saginaw Valley State University	M
Saint Louis University	M*
St. Mary's University (United States)	M
St. Thomas University	M,D,O
Sam Houston State University	M
San Diego State University	M
San Jose State University	M
Seton Hall University	M
Shippensburg University of Pennsylvania	M
Simmons College	M
Simon Fraser University	M,D
South Dakota State University	M
Southeastern Louisiana University	M
Southern Illinois University Carbondale	M,D
Southern Utah University	M
Spring Arbor University	M
Stanford University	M,D
State University of New York at Oswego	M
Stephen F. Austin State University	M
Stevens Institute of Technology	M,D,O
Stevenson University	M
Syracuse University	M,D*
Tarleton State University	M
Teachers College, Columbia University	M,D
Temple University	M,D*
Texas A&M University	M,D
Texas A&M University–Corpus Christi	M
Texas Christian University	M
Texas Southern University	M
Texas State University	M
Texas Tech University	M
Tiffin University	M
Towson University	M
Trinity Washington University	M
Troy University	M
Université de Montréal	M,D
Université du Québec à Montréal	M,D
Université du Québec à Trois-Rivières	M,O
University at Albany, State University of New York	M,D
University at Buffalo, the State University of New York	M,D
The University of Akron	M
The University of Alabama	M,D
The University of Alabama at Birmingham	M
University of Alaska Fairbanks	M
University of Alberta	M
The University of Arizona	M,D
University of Arkansas	M
University of Bridgeport	M
University of Calgary	M,D
University of California, Davis	M
University of California, San Diego	D*
University of California, Santa Barbara	D
University of California, Santa Cruz	O*
University of Central Florida	M,O
University of Central Missouri	M,D,O
University of Cincinnati	M
University of Colorado Boulder	M,D
University of Colorado Colorado Springs	M
University of Colorado Denver	M
University of Connecticut	M*
University of Dayton	M
University of Delaware	M*
University of Denver	M,D,O
University of Dubuque	M
University of Florida	M,D
University of Georgia	M,D
University of Hartford	M
University of Hawaii at Manoa	M,O
University of Houston	M
University of Illinois at Chicago	M,D
University of Illinois at Springfield	M
University of Illinois at Urbana–Champaign	M,D
The University of Iowa	M,D*
The University of Kansas	M,D,O
University of Kentucky	M,D
University of Louisiana at Lafayette	M
University of Louisiana at Monroe	M
University of Louisville	M
University of Maine	M,D
University of Maryland, Baltimore County	M
University of Maryland, College Park	M,D
University of Massachusetts Amherst	M,D*
University of Memphis	M,D
University of Miami	M,D*
University of Michigan	D*
University of Michigan–Flint	M
University of Minnesota, Twin Cities Campus	M,D,O
University of Missouri	M,D
University of Missouri–St. Louis	M
University of Montana	M
University of Nebraska at Omaha	M,O
University of Nebraska–Lincoln	M,D
University of Nevada, Las Vegas	M
University of New Mexico	M,D
The University of North Carolina at Chapel Hill	M,D,O
The University of North Carolina at Charlotte	M
The University of North Carolina at Greensboro	M
University of North Dakota	D
University of Northern Colorado	M
University of Northern Iowa	M
University of North Texas	M,D,O
University of Oklahoma	M,D,O*
University of Oregon	M,D
University of Ottawa	M
University of Pennsylvania	D*
University of Pittsburgh	M,D*
University of Portland	M
University of Puerto Rico–Río Piedras	M
University of Rhode Island	M*
University of San Francisco	M
University of South Africa	M,D
University of South Alabama	M
University of South Dakota	M
University of Southern California	M,D*
University of Southern Indiana	M
University of South Florida	M,D*
The University of Tennessee	M,D
The University of Tennessee at Martin	M
The University of Texas at Arlington	M
The University of Texas at Austin	M,D
The University of Texas at Dallas	M,D
The University of Texas at El Paso	M
The University of Texas at San Antonio	M
The University of Texas at Tyler	M
The University of Texas Rio Grande Valley	M
University of the Incarnate Word	M,D
University of the Pacific	M
University of the Sacred Heart	M,O
The University of Toledo	O
University of Utah	M,D
University of Washington	M,D
University of West Florida	M
University of Windsor	M
University of Wisconsin–Madison	M,D
University of Wisconsin–Milwaukee	M,D,O*
University of Wisconsin–Stevens Point	M
University of Wisconsin–Superior	M
University of Wisconsin–Whitewater	M
University of Wyoming	M
Utah State University	M
Valparaiso University	M,O
Villanova University	M
Virginia Commonwealth University	D
Virginia Polytechnic Institute and State University	M,D,O
Wake Forest University	M
Walden University	M,D,O
Walla Walla University	M
Washington State University	M,D
Wayne State College	M
Wayne State University	M,D,O
Weber State University	M
Webster University	M,O
West Chester University of Pennsylvania	M
Western Illinois University	M
Western Kentucky University	M,O
Western Michigan University	M
Western New England University	M
Westminster College (UT)	M
West Texas A&M University	M
West Virginia University	M,D
Wichita State University	M
Wilfrid Laurier University	M
York University	M,D

COMMUNICATION DISORDERS

Abilene Christian University	M
Adelphi University	M,D
Alabama Agricultural and Mechanical University	M
Andrews University	M
Appalachian State University	M
Arizona State University at the Tempe campus	M,D
Arkansas State University	M,O
A.T. Still University	M,D,O
Auburn University	M,D*
Baldwin Wallace University	M
Ball State University	M,D
Barry University	M
Baylor University	M
Biola University	M,O
Bloomsburg University of Pennsylvania	M,D
Boston University	M,D*
Bowling Green State University	M,D
Bridgewater State University	M
Brigham Young University	M
Brooklyn College of the City University of New York	M,D
Buffalo State College, State University of New York	M
California Baptist University	M
California State University, Chico	M
California State University, East Bay	M
California State University, Fresno	M
California State University, Fullerton	M
California State University, Long Beach	M
California State University, Los Angeles	M
California State University, Northridge	M
California State University, Sacramento	M
California State University, San Marcos	M
California University of Pennsylvania	M
Canisius College	M,O
Carlos Albizu University	M,D
Carlos Albizu University, Miami Campus	M,D
Case Western Reserve University	M,D*
Central Michigan University	M,D
Chapman University	M*
Clarion University of Pennsylvania	M
Cleveland State University	M
The College of Saint Rose	M
Dalhousie University	M
Duquesne University	M,D
East Carolina University	M,D
Eastern Illinois University	M
Eastern Kentucky University	M
Eastern Michigan University	M
Eastern New Mexico University	M
Eastern Washington University	M
East Stroudsburg University of Pennsylvania	M
East Tennessee State University	M,D

*M—masters degree; D—doctorate; O—other advanced degree; *—Close-Up and/or Display*

Edinboro University of Pennsylvania	M
Elmhurst College	M
Emerson College	M
Florida Atlantic University	M
Florida International University	M
Florida State University	M,D
Fontbonne University	M
Fort Hays State University	M
Gallaudet University	M,D,O
The George Washington University	M
Georgia Southern University–Armstrong Campus	M
Georgia State University	M,D
Governors State University	M
The Graduate Center, City University of New York	D
Grand Valley State University	M
Hampton University	M
Harding University	M
Hofstra University	M,D,O
Howard University	M,D
Hunter College of the City University of New York	M
Idaho State University	M,D
Illinois State University	M
Indiana State University	M,D,O
Indiana University Bloomington	M,D
Indiana University of Pennsylvania	M
Iona College	M
Ithaca College	M
Jackson State University	M
Jacksonville University	M*
James Madison University	M,D
Kansas State University	M,D,O
Kean University	M,D
Kent State University	M,D,O
Lamar University	M,D
La Salle University	M
Lebanon Valley College	M
Lehman College of the City University of New York	M
Lewis & Clark College	M
Lindenwood University	M,D,O
Loma Linda University	M,D
Long Island University–LIU Brooklyn	M,D,O
Long Island University–LIU Post	M,D,O
Longwood University	M
Louisiana State University and Agricultural & Mechanical College	M,D
Louisiana State University Health Sciences Center	M,D
Louisiana Tech University	M,D,O
Loyola University Maryland	M
Marquette University	M,O
Marshall University	M
Maryville University of Saint Louis	M
Marywood University	M
Massachusetts Institute of Technology	M,D
McGill University	M,D
Mercy College	M
MGH Institute of Health Professions	M,O
Miami University	M
Michigan State University	M,D
Midwestern University, Glendale Campus	M
Minnesota State University Mankato	M
Minnesota State University Moorhead	M,D,O
Minot State University	M
Misericordia University	M
Mississippi University for Women	M,D,O
Missouri State University	M,D
Molloy College	M
Monmouth University	M,D,O*
Montclair State University	M,D
Murray State University	M,O
Nazareth College of Rochester	M
New Mexico State University	M,D,O
New York Medical College	M,D,O
New York University	M,D*
North Carolina Central University	M
Northeastern State University	M
Northeastern University	M,D,O
Northern Arizona University	M
Northern Illinois University	M,D
Northwestern University	M,D
Nova Southeastern University	M,D*
The Ohio State University	M,D
Ohio University	M,D
Oklahoma State University	M
Old Dominion University	M
Our Lady of the Lake University	M
Pacific University	M,D
Penn State University Park	M,D,O*
Portland State University	M
Purdue University	M,D
Queens College of the City University of New York	M,O
Radford University	M
Rockhurst University	M
Rocky Mountain University of Health Professions	D
Rush University	M,D
Sacred Heart University	M
St. Ambrose University	M
St. Cloud State University	M
St. John's University (NY)	M,D
Saint Joseph's University	M,D,O*
Saint Louis University	M*
Saint Mary's College	M
Saint Xavier University	M
Salus University	M,D,O
Samford University	M,D
San Diego State University	M,D
San Francisco State University	M
San Jose State University	M,D
Seton Hall University	M
South Carolina State University	M
Southeastern Louisiana University	M
Southeast Missouri State University	M
Southern Connecticut State University	M
Southern Illinois University Carbondale	M
Southern Illinois University Edwardsville	M
Southern University and Agricultural and Mechanical College	M
State University of New York at Fredonia	M,O
State University of New York at New Paltz	M
State University of New York at Plattsburgh	M
State University of New York College at Cortland	M
Stephen F. Austin State University	M
Stockton University	M
Syracuse University	M,D*
Teachers College, Columbia University	M,D,O
Temple University	M,D*
Tennessee State University	M
Texas A&M University–Kingsville	M
Texas Christian University	M
Texas State University	M
Texas Tech University Health Sciences Center	M,D
Texas Woman's University	M,D
Touro College	M,D
Towson University	M,D
Truman State University	M
Universidad del Turabo	M
Université de Montréal	M,O
Université Laval	M
University at Buffalo, the State University of New York	M,D
The University of Akron	M,D
The University of Alabama	M,D
University of Alberta	M,D
The University of Arizona	M,D,O
University of Arkansas	M
University of Arkansas for Medical Sciences	M,D
The University of British Columbia	M,D
University of California, San Diego	D*
University of Central Arkansas	M,D
University of Central Florida	M,D,O
University of Central Missouri	M,D,O
University of Central Oklahoma	M
University of Cincinnati	M,D
University of Colorado Boulder	M,D
University of Connecticut	M,D*
University of Delaware	M*
University of Florida	M,D
University of Georgia	M,D,O
University of Hawaii at Manoa	M
University of Houston	M
University of Illinois at Urbana–Champaign	M,D
The University of Iowa	M,D*
The University of Kansas	M,D
University of Kentucky	M
University of Louisiana at Lafayette	M,D
University of Louisiana at Monroe	M
University of Louisville	M,D
University of Maine	M
The University of Manchester	M,D
University of Maryland, College Park	M,D
University of Massachusetts Amherst	M,D*
University of Memphis	M,D
University of Minnesota, Duluth	M
University of Minnesota, Twin Cities Campus	M,D
University of Mississippi	M,D
University of Missouri	M,D
University of Montana	M,O
University of Montevallo	M
University of Nebraska at Kearney	M
University of Nebraska at Omaha	M
University of Nebraska–Lincoln	M,D
University of Nevada, Reno	M,D
University of New Hampshire	M
University of New Mexico	M
The University of North Carolina at Chapel Hill	M,D
The University of North Carolina at Greensboro	M,D
University of North Dakota	M
University of Northern Colorado	M,D
University of Northern Iowa	M
University of North Florida	M
University of North Texas	M,D,O
University of Oklahoma Health Sciences Center	M,D,O
University of Oregon	M,D
University of Ottawa	M
University of Pittsburgh	M,D*
University of Puerto Rico–Medical Sciences Campus	M,D
University of Redlands	M
University of Rhode Island	M*
University of South Alabama	M,D
University of South Carolina	M,D
University of South Dakota	M,D
University of Southern Mississippi	M,D
University of South Florida	M,D,O*
The University of Tennessee	M,D,O
The University of Tennessee Health Science Center	M,D
The University of Texas at Austin	M,D
The University of Texas at Dallas	M,D
The University of Texas at El Paso	M
The University of Texas Health Science Center at San Antonio	M,D
The University of Texas Rio Grande Valley	M
University of the District of Columbia	M
University of the Pacific	M,D
The University of Toledo	M,D,O
University of Toronto	M,D
The University of Tulsa	M
University of Utah	M,D
University of Vermont	M
University of Virginia	M,D
University of Washington	M,D
The University of Western Ontario	M
University of West Georgia	M,D,O
University of Wisconsin–Eau Claire	M
University of Wisconsin–Madison	M,D
University of Wisconsin–Milwaukee	M*
University of Wisconsin–River Falls	M
University of Wisconsin–Stevens Point	M,D
University of Wisconsin–Whitewater	M
University of Wyoming	M
Utah State University	M,D,O
Valdosta State University	M,D,O
Vanderbilt University	M,D*
Washington State University	M
Washington University in St. Louis	M,D
Wayne State University	M,D
Webster University	M
West Chester University of Pennsylvania	M
Western Carolina University	M
Western Illinois University	M
Western Kentucky University	M
Western Michigan University	M,D
Western Washington University	M
West Texas A&M University	M
West Virginia University	M,D
Wichita State University	M,D
William Paterson University of New Jersey	M,D,O
Worcester State University	M
Yeshiva University	M

COMMUNITY COLLEGE EDUCATION

Argosy University, Chicago	M,D,O
Argosy University, Los Angeles	M,D
Argosy University, Northern Virginia	M,D,O
Argosy University, Orange County	M,D
Argosy University, Phoenix	M,D,O
Argosy University, Seattle	M,D
Argosy University, Tampa	M,D,O
Arkansas State University	M,D,O
California State University, San Bernardino	M
California State University, Stanislaus	D
Central Michigan University	M,D,O
Drew University	M,D,O
East Carolina University	M,D,O
Eastern Michigan University	M,D,O
Elizabeth City State University	M
Ferris State University	D
Lenoir-Rhyne University	M
Marymount University	M,O
Mississippi State University	M,D,O
Morgan State University	D
National American University (TX)	M,D
North Carolina State University	M,D
Northern Arizona University	M,D,O
Old Dominion University	M,D
University of Arkansas at Little Rock	M,D
University of Central Florida	M,O
University of Memphis	M,D,O
University of Northern Iowa	M
University of South Florida	M,D,O*
Wingate University	M,D,O

COMMUNITY HEALTH

Adelphi University	M,O
Adler University	M
American University of Beirut	M,D
Arizona State University at the Tempe campus	M,D,O
Baylor University	M,D
Bloomsburg University of Pennsylvania	M,D
Boston University	M,D*
Brooklyn College of the City University of New York	M
Brown University	M,D
Canisius College	M,O
Clark University	M
The College at Brockport, State University of New York	M
Columbia University	M,D*
Daemen College	M
Dalhousie University	M
Eastern Kentucky University	M
East Tennessee State University	M,D,O
George Mason University	M,O
The George Washington University	M,D
Georgia Southern University	M,D
Icahn School of Medicine at Mount Sinai	M,D
Idaho State University	O
Independence University	M
Indiana University Bloomington	M,D
Indiana University–Purdue University Indianapolis	M,D,O
Johns Hopkins University	M,D*
Long Island University–LIU Brooklyn	M,D,O
Louisiana State University Health Sciences Center	M,D
McGill University	M,D,O
Medical College of Wisconsin	D
Memorial University of Newfoundland	M,D,O
Midwestern State University	M,O
Minnesota State University Mankato	M,O
Monroe College	M
New Jersey City University	M
New York University	M,D*
North Dakota State University	M*
Old Dominion University	M
Quinnipiac University	D
Saint Louis University	M*
San Francisco State University	M
Southern Illinois University Carbondale	M
State University of New York College at Cortland	M
State University of New York College at Potsdam	M
State University of New York Downstate Medical Center	M
Stony Brook University, State University of New York	M,D,O
Suffolk University	M
Teachers College, Columbia University	M,D,O
Texas A&M University	M,D
Tulane University	M,D
Universidad de Ciencias Medicas	M,D,O
Université de Montréal	M,D,O
Université Laval	M,D,O
University at Buffalo, the State University of New York	M,D,O
The University of Alabama	M
The University of Alabama at Birmingham	M
University of Alberta	M,D
University of Arkansas	M,D
University of Calgary	M,D
University of California, Los Angeles	M,D*
University of Colorado Denver	M,D,O
University of Illinois at Chicago	M,D
University of Illinois at Springfield	M,O
University of Illinois at Urbana–Champaign	M,D
The University of Iowa	M,D*
The University of Kansas	M,D,O
University of Louisville	M
University of Manitoba	M,D,O
University of Massachusetts Amherst	M,D*
University of Miami	D*
University of Minnesota, Twin Cities Campus	M
University of Missouri	M,D
University of Montana	M
University of Nevada, Las Vegas	M,D,O
University of New Mexico	M
The University of North Carolina at Charlotte	M,D,O
The University of North Carolina at Greensboro	M,D
University of Northern British Columbia	M,D,O
University of Northern Colorado	M
University of Northern Iowa	M
University of North Florida	M,O
University of Ottawa	D,O
University of Phoenix–Central Valley Campus	M
University of Phoenix–Hawaii Campus	M
University of Pittsburgh	M,D,O*
University of Saskatchewan	M,D
University of South Florida	M,D,O*
The University of Tennessee	M,D
The University of Texas Health Science Center at Houston	M,D,O
University of Toronto	M,D
University of Vermont	M
University of Virginia	M,D
University of Washington	M,D
University of Wisconsin–La Crosse	M
University of Wisconsin–Milwaukee	D*
University of Wyoming	M,D
Virginia State University	M,D
Walden University	M,D,O
Washington State University	M,D,O
William James College	M,D,O

COMMUNITY HEALTH NURSING

Allen College	M,D
American University of Beirut	M
Binghamton University, State University of New York	M,D,O
Hampton University	M,D
Hunter College of the City University of New York	M
Husson University	M,O
Independence University	M
Johns Hopkins University	*
Kean University	M
La Salle University	M,D,O
Louisiana State University Health Sciences Center	M,D,O
Oregon Health & Science University	M,O
Rush University	D
San Francisco State University	M,O
University of Hartford	M
University of Hawaii at Manoa	M,D,O
University of Illinois at Chicago	M,O
The University of Kansas	M,D,O
University of Maryland, Baltimore	M,D,O
University of Massachusetts Amherst	M,D*
University of Massachusetts Dartmouth	M,D
University of North Dakota	M,D,O
University of Puerto Rico–Medical Sciences Campus	M

University of South Carolina M
The University of Texas at Austin M,D
The University of Texas Health Science Center at San Antonio M,D,O
The University of Toledo M,O
University of Washington, Tacoma M
Wayne State University M,D
Worcester State University M

COMPARATIVE AND INTERDISCIPLINARY ARTS

Brigham Young University M
Florida Atlantic University D
Goddard College M
John F. Kennedy University M
Ohio University D
Simon Fraser University M

COMPARATIVE LITERATURE

American University M
The American University in Cairo M,O
Arizona State University at the Tempe campus M,D,O
Binghamton University, State University of New York M,D
Brigham Young University M
Brock University M
Brown University D
California State University, Northridge M
Carleton University D
Carnegie Mellon University M,D
Case Western Reserve University M*
Claremont Graduate University M,D
Columbia University M,D*
Cornell University D
Dartmouth College M*
Duke University D*
East Carolina University M,D,O
Emory University D,O
Fairleigh Dickinson University, Metropolitan Campus M
Florida Atlantic University M
Georgetown University M,D
The Graduate Center, City University of New York M,D
Harrison Middleton University M,D
Harvard University D*
Hunter College of the City University of New York M
Indiana University Bloomington M,D
Johns Hopkins University D*
Louisiana State University and Agricultural & Mechanical College M,D
New York University M,D*
Northwestern University M,D
Penn State University Park M,D*
Princeton University D
Purdue University M,D
Rutgers University–New Brunswick M,D
San Francisco State University M
Stanford University D
Stony Brook University, State University of New York M,D,O
Université de Montréal M,D
Université de Sherbrooke M,D
Université du Québec à Chicoutimi M
Université du Québec à Montréal M,D
Université du Québec à Rimouski M,D
Université du Québec à Trois-Rivières M
Université Laval M,D
University at Buffalo, the State University of New York M,D
University of Arkansas M,D
University of California, Berkeley D
University of California, Davis D
University of California, Irvine M,D
University of California, Los Angeles M,D*
University of California, Riverside M,D
University of California, Santa Barbara D
University of California, Santa Cruz M,D*
University of Chicago M,D
University of Dallas D
University of Georgia M,D
University of Guelph D
University of Houston M
University of Illinois at Urbana–Champaign M,D
University of Maryland, College Park M,D
University of Massachusetts Amherst M,D*
University of Memphis M,D,O
University of Michigan D*
University of Minnesota, Twin Cities Campus D
University of Nebraska–Lincoln M,D
University of New Mexico M,D
University of Notre Dame D
University of Oregon M,D
University of Pennsylvania M,D*
University of Puerto Rico–Río Piedras M
University of Rochester M*
University of South Carolina M,D
University of Southern California D*
University of South Florida O*
The University of Texas at Austin M,D
The University of Texas at Dallas M,D
University of Toronto M,D
University of Utah M,D
University of Washington M,D
The University of Western Ontario M,D
University of Wisconsin–Madison M,D
University of Wisconsin–Milwaukee M,O*
Washington University in St. Louis M,D
Western Kentucky University M
Yale University D

COMPUTATIONAL BIOLOGY

Albert Einstein College of Medicine D
Baylor College of Medicine D
Carnegie Mellon University M,D
Claremont Graduate University M,D
The College of William and Mary M,D*
Cornell University D
Duke University D,O*
George Mason University M,D,O
Harvard University M*
Iowa State University of Science and Technology M,D
Lewis University M
Massachusetts Institute of Technology D
New York University D*
Oregon Health & Science University M,D,O
Oregon State University M,D
Princeton University D
Rutgers University–Camden M,D
Rutgers University–Newark M
Rutgers University–New Brunswick D
Saint Louis University M*
University of California, Irvine D
University of Colorado Denver M,D
University of Idaho M,D
University of Illinois at Urbana–Champaign M,D
The University of Iowa M,D,O*
The University of Kansas D
University of Maryland, College Park D
University of Massachusetts Medical School M,D
University of Minnesota Rochester M,D
The University of North Carolina at Chapel Hill D
University of Pennsylvania D*
University of Pittsburgh D*
University of Rochester D*
University of Southern California D*
University of South Florida M,D*
The University of Texas Medical Branch D
University of Wyoming D
Washington University in St. Louis D
Wayne State University M,D
Weill Cornell Medicine D
Worcester Polytechnic Institute M,D
Yale University D

COMPUTATIONAL SCIENCES

American University of Beirut M,D
California Institute of Technology M,D
Chapman University M,D*
Claremont Graduate University M,D
The College of William and Mary M*
Cornell University M,D
Duke University M,D*
Emory University D
Florida State University M,D
Georgia Institute of Technology M,D
Hampton University M
Harvard University M,D*
Marquette University M,D
Massachusetts Institute of Technology M
McGill University M,D
Memorial University of Newfoundland M
Michigan Technological University M,D,O
Middle Tennessee State University D
Morgan State University M,D
North Carolina Agricultural and Technical State University M
The Ohio State University M,D
Oregon State University M,D
Princeton University D
Purdue University D
Rice University M,D
St. John's University (NY) M
Sam Houston State University M,D
San Diego State University M,D
San Jose State University M
Simon Fraser University M,D
South Dakota State University M,D
Southern Illinois University Edwardsville M
Southern Methodist University M,D
Stanford University M,D
Stockton University M
Texas A&M University–Commerce M,O
University at Buffalo, the State University of New York D,O
The University of Alabama at Birmingham D
University of Alaska Fairbanks M,D
University of California, San Diego M,D*
University of California, Santa Barbara M,D
University of Central Oklahoma M
University of Chicago M
University of Colorado Denver M,D
The University of Iowa D*
University of Lethbridge M,D
University of Manitoba M
University of Massachusetts Boston D
University of Memphis M
University of Michigan–Dearborn M
University of Minnesota, Duluth M
University of Minnesota, Twin Cities Campus M,D
University of Notre Dame M,D
University of Pennsylvania M,D*
University of Pittsburgh M,D,O*
University of Puerto Rico–Mayagüez M
University of Southern Mississippi M,D
The University of Tennessee at Chattanooga D
The University of Texas at Austin M,D
University of Utah M
University of Washington M,D
Valparaiso University M
Western Kentucky University M
Western Michigan University M,D

COMPUTER AND INFORMATION SYSTEMS SECURITY

American InterContinental University Online M
American Public University System M,D
Auburn University at Montgomery M
Augusta University M
Austin Peay State University M
Bay Path University M
Benedictine University M
Boston University M,D,O*
Brandeis University M
California State University, San Bernardino M
California State University, San Marcos M
California University of Pennsylvania M
Capella University M,D
Capitol Technology University M,D
Cardinal Stritch University M
Carlow University M,O
Carnegie Mellon University M
Central Michigan University O
Champlain College M
City University of Seattle M,O
Claremont Graduate University M,D,O
College of Saint Elizabeth M,O
College of Staten Island of the City University of New York M
Colorado Christian University M
Colorado Technical University Aurora M
Colorado Technical University Colorado Springs M,D
Columbus State University M,O
Concordia University (Canada) M,D,O
Concordia University, Nebraska M
Concordia University of Edmonton M
Concordia University, St. Paul M
Davenport University M
DePaul University M,D
DeSales University M,O
Drury University O
East Carolina University M,D,O
Eastern Illinois University M
Eastern Michigan University O
EC-Council University M
Embry-Riddle Aeronautical University–Daytona M
Embry-Riddle Aeronautical University–Worldwide M
Endicott College M,O
Excelsior College M,O
Fairfield University M,O
Ferris State University M
Florida Institute of Technology M
Florida International University M,D
Florida State University M,D
Fordham University M
George Mason University M
The George Washington University M,D,O
Georgia Institute of Technology M
Georgia Southern University–Armstrong Campus M,O
Hampton University M
Harrisburg University of Science and Technology M
Hofstra University M
Hood College M,O*
Illinois Institute of Technology M,D
Indiana University Bloomington M,D
Indiana University–Purdue University Indianapolis M,D,O
Inter American University of Puerto Rico, Guayama Campus M
Iona College M,O
James Madison University M
Johns Hopkins University M,O*
Johnson & Wales University M
Keiser University M
Kennesaw State University M,O
Kent State University M
Lawrence Technological University M,D,O
Lewis University M
Liberty University M,D
Lindenwood University M,O
Lipscomb University M,O
London Metropolitan University M,D
Long Island University–Riverhead M,O
Louisiana Tech University M,D
Marymount University M,D,O
Maryville University of Saint Louis M,O
Marywood University M
Mercy College M
Mercyhurst University M
Metropolitan State University M,D,O
Michigan Technological University M,D
Middle Georgia State University M
Missouri Western State University M
National University M
Naval Postgraduate School M,D
New Jersey City University M,D,O
New Jersey Institute of Technology M,D,O
New York Institute of Technology M
New York University M*
Niagara University M
Northcentral University M,D,O
Northeastern University M,D,O
Northern Kentucky University M,O
Northwestern University M
Norwich University M
Nova Southeastern University M,D*
Our Lady of the Lake University M
Pace University M,D,O
Penn State Great Valley M,O
Portland State University M,D,O
Purdue University M
Purdue University Global M
Regent University M
Regis University M,O
Robert Morris University M,D
Robert Morris University Illinois M
Rochester Institute of Technology M,O
Roger Williams University M
Rowan University O
Sacred Heart University M
St. Cloud State University M
Saint Leo University M,D
St. Mary's University (United States) M,O
Saint Mary's University of Minnesota M
Salem International University M
Salve Regina University M,O
Sam Houston State University M,D
San Jose State University M
The SANS Technology Institute M
Seattle Pacific University M
Shippensburg University of Pennsylvania M,O
Southern Arkansas University–Magnolia M
Southern New Hampshire University M
Southern Utah University M
State University of New York Polytechnic Institute M
Stevens Institute of Technology M,D,O
Stevenson University M
Stratford University (VA) M,D
Strayer University M
Syracuse University M,O*
Temple University M,D*
Thomas Edison State University M,O
Trident University International M,D
Tuskegee University M
Universidad del Este M
Université de Sherbrooke M
University at Albany, State University of New York M,D,O
University of Advancing Technology M
The University of Alabama at Birmingham M
The University of Alabama in Huntsville M,D,O
University of Colorado Colorado Springs M,D
University of Dallas M,D
University of Dayton M
University of Denver M,D
University of Detroit Mercy M,D,O
University of Houston M
University of Louisville M,D,O
University of Maryland, Baltimore County M,O
University of Maryland University College M,O
University of Michigan–Dearborn D
University of Minnesota, Twin Cities Campus M
University of Missouri–St. Louis M,D,O
University of Nebraska at Omaha M,D,O
University of Nevada, Las Vegas M,D,O
University of New Hampshire M,O
University of New Haven M*
University of New Mexico M
The University of North Carolina at Charlotte M,D,O
University of Rhode Island M,D,O*
University of San Diego M
University of Southern California M,D*
University of South Florida M,D*
The University of Tampa M
The University of Texas at Austin M,D
The University of Texas at El Paso M,D,O
The University of Texas at San Antonio M,D,O
The University of Texas at Tyler M
The University of Tulsa M,D
University of Utah M,O
University of Washington M,D
University of West Florida M
University of Wisconsin–Madison M
Utah Valley University O
Utica College M
Valparaiso University M
Vanderbilt University M*
Virginia International University M,O
Virginia Polytechnic Institute and State University M,O
Walden University M,D,O
Walsh College of Accountancy and Business Administration M
Webster University M
West Chester University of Pennsylvania M,O

*M—masters degree; D—doctorate; O—other advanced degree; *—Close-Up and/or Display*

Western Governors University	M
West Virginia University	M,D,O
Wilmington University	M

COMPUTER ART AND DESIGN

Academy of Art University	M
Alfred University	M
ArtCenter College of Design	M
Bowling Green State University	M
California College of the Arts	M
Carnegie Mellon University	M
Chatham University	M
City College of the City University of New York	M
Claremont Graduate University	M
Concordia University (Canada)	M,O
Cornell University	M,D
DePaul University	M,D
DigiPen Institute of Technology	M
Drexel University	M,D*
East Tennessee State University	M
Emily Carr University of Art + Design	M
Full Sail University	M
Georgia Institute of Technology	M,D
Georgian Court University	M,O
Goucher College	M
Indiana University–Purdue University Indianapolis	M
International Technological University	M
Lindenwood University–Belleville	M
Lynn University	M,O
Michigan State University	M
Minneapolis College of Art and Design	O
New Mexico Highlands University	M
The New School	M
New York Institute of Technology	M
North Carolina Agricultural and Technical State University	M
North Carolina State University	D
Northern Vermont University–Johnson	M
The Ohio State University	M
Old Dominion University	M
Purchase College, State University of New York	M
Purdue University	M,D
Rensselaer Polytechnic Institute	D
Rhode Island School of Design	M
Rochester Institute of Technology	M
Savannah College of Art and Design	M
School of Visual Arts (NY)	M
Stevens Institute of Technology	M,D,O
Syracuse University	M*
Texas State University	M
Universidad Autonoma de Guadalajara	M,D
Universidad de las Américas Puebla	M
University of Alaska Fairbanks	M
University of California, Santa Cruz	M,D*
University of Central Arkansas	M
University of Central Florida	M
University of Denver	M
University of Florida	M,D
University of Maryland, Baltimore County	M
University of Montana	M
University of Pennsylvania	M,D*
University of Rhode Island	M*
University of Southern California	M*
University of South Florida, St. Petersburg	M
University of Victoria	M
Virginia International University	M,O

COMPUTER EDUCATION

Arcadia University	M,D,O
Ball State University	M,D,O
Eastern Washington University	M
Florida Institute of Technology	M
Illinois Institute of Technology	M,D
Kent State University	M,D
Lesley University	M,D,O
Mississippi College	M,D,O
Ohio University	M,D
Stony Brook University, State University of New York	M
Teachers College, Columbia University	M,D
Thomas College	M
University of Bridgeport	M,D,O
University of Illinois at Chicago	D
University of Phoenix–Central Valley Campus	M
University of Phoenix–Online Campus	M,O
University of Phoenix–San Diego Campus	M

COMPUTER ENGINEERING

Air Force Institute of Technology	M,D
American University of Beirut	M,D
American University of Sharjah	M,D
Arizona State University at the Tempe campus	M,D
Atlantis University	M
Auburn University	M,D*
Baylor University	M,D
Boise State University	M,D
Boston University	M,D,O*
Brigham Young University	M,D
Brown University	M,D
Bucknell University	M
California State University, Chico	M
California State University, Fresno	M
California State University, Fullerton	M
California State University, Long Beach	M
Carnegie Mellon University	M,D
Case Western Reserve University	M,D*
The Citadel, The Military College of South Carolina	M,O
Clarkson University	M,D
Clemson University	M,D
Colorado Technical University Aurora	M
Colorado Technical University Colorado Springs	M
Columbia University	M,D*
Concordia University (Canada)	M,D
Cornell University	M,D
Dalhousie University	M,D
Dartmouth College	M,D*
Drexel University	M*
Duke University	M,D*
East Carolina University	M,D,O
École Polytechnique de Montréal	M,D,O
Fairfield University	M,O
Fairleigh Dickinson University, Metropolitan Campus	M
Florida Atlantic University	M,D
Florida Institute of Technology	M,D
Florida International University	M,D
George Mason University	M,D,O
The George Washington University	M,D,O
Georgia Institute of Technology	M,D
Grand Valley State University	M
Illinois Institute of Technology	M,D
Indiana State University	M
Indiana University–Purdue University Fort Wayne	M
Indiana University–Purdue University Indianapolis	M,D
Instituto Tecnológico y de Estudios Superiores de Monterrey, Campus Chihuahua	M,O
International Technological University	M
Iowa State University of Science and Technology	M,D
Johns Hopkins University	M,D,O*
Kansas State University	M,D
Lakehead University	M
Lawrence Technological University	M,D
Lehigh University	M,D
Louisiana State University and Agricultural & Mechanical College	M,D
Manhattan College	M
Marquette University	M,D,O
Marshall University	M
Massachusetts Institute of Technology	M,D,O
McGill University	M,D
Memorial University of Newfoundland	M,D
Mercer University	M
Miami University	M
Michigan Technological University	M,D,O
Mississippi State University	M,D
Missouri University of Science and Technology	M,D
Montana State University	M,D
Naval Postgraduate School	M,D,O
New Jersey Institute of Technology	M,D
New Mexico State University	M,D,O
New York Institute of Technology	M
New York University	M*
Norfolk State University	M
North Carolina Agricultural and Technical State University	M,D
North Carolina State University	M,D
Northeastern University	M,D,O
Northern Arizona University	M,D
Northwestern Polytechnic University	M,D
Northwestern University	M,D
Oakland University	M,D
The Ohio State University	M,D
Oklahoma Christian University	M
Oklahoma State University	M,D
Old Dominion University	M,D
Oregon Health & Science University	M,D
Oregon State University	M,D
Penn State University Park	M,D*
Polytechnic University of Puerto Rico	M
Portland State University	M,D
Purdue University	M,D
Purdue University Northwest	M
Queen's University at Kingston	M,D
Rensselaer at Hartford	M
Rensselaer Polytechnic Institute	M,D
Rice University	M,D
Rochester Institute of Technology	M
Rose-Hulman Institute of Technology	M
Royal Military College of Canada	M,D
Rutgers University–New Brunswick	M,D
St. Mary's University (United States)	M
San Jose State University	M
Santa Clara University	M,D,O
Southern Illinois University Carbondale	M,D
Southern Methodist University	M,D
Stevens Institute of Technology	M,D,O
Stony Brook University, State University of New York	M,D
Syracuse University	M,D*
Tennessee State University	M,D
Texas A&M University	M,D
Universidad del Turabo	M
The University of Akron	M,D
The University of Alabama	M,D
The University of Alabama at Birmingham	M,D
The University of Alabama in Huntsville	M,D
University of Alberta	M,D
The University of Arizona	M,D
University of Arkansas	M,D
University of Bridgeport	M,D
The University of British Columbia	M,D
University of Calgary	M,D
University of California, Davis	M,D
University of California, Los Angeles	M,D*
University of California, Riverside	M
University of California, San Diego	M,D*
University of California, Santa Barbara	M,D
University of California, Santa Cruz	M,D*
University of Central Florida	M,D
University of Cincinnati	M,D
University of Colorado Boulder	M,D
University of Dayton	M,D
University of Delaware	M,D*
University of Denver	M,D
University of Detroit Mercy	M,D
University of Florida	M,D
University of Houston–Clear Lake	M
University of Illinois at Chicago	M,D
University of Illinois at Urbana–Champaign	M,D
The University of Iowa	M,D*
The University of Kansas	M
University of Louisiana at Lafayette	M,D
University of Louisville	M,D,O
University of Maine	M,D
University of Manitoba	M,D
University of Maryland, Baltimore County	M,D
University of Maryland, College Park	M,D
University of Massachusetts Amherst	M,D*
University of Massachusetts Dartmouth	M,D,O
University of Massachusetts Lowell	M,D
University of Memphis	M,D,O
University of Miami	M,D*
University of Michigan	M,D*
University of Michigan–Dearborn	M,D
University of Minnesota, Duluth	M
University of Minnesota, Twin Cities Campus	M,D
University of Missouri–Kansas City	M,D,O
University of Nebraska–Lincoln	M,D
University of Nevada, Las Vegas	M,D
University of Nevada, Reno	M,D
University of New Brunswick Fredericton	M,D
University of New Haven	M*
University of New Mexico	M,D
The University of North Carolina at Charlotte	M,D
University of North Texas	M,D,O
University of Notre Dame	M,D
University of Oklahoma	M,D*
University of Ottawa	M,D
University of Pittsburgh	M,D*
University of Puerto Rico–Mayagüez	M,D
University of Regina	M,D
University of Rhode Island	M,D*
University of Rochester	M,D*
University of San Diego	M
University of South Alabama	M
University of South Carolina	M,D
University of Southern California	M,D,O*
University of South Florida	M,D*
The University of Tennessee	M,D
The University of Texas at Arlington	M,D
The University of Texas at Austin	M,D
The University of Texas at Dallas	M,D
The University of Texas at San Antonio	M,D
University of Toronto	M,D
University of Utah	M,D
University of Victoria	M,D
University of Virginia	M,D
University of Washington, Bothell	M
University of Washington, Tacoma	M
University of Waterloo	M,D
The University of Western Ontario	M,D
University of Wisconsin–Milwaukee	M,D*
Villanova University	M,O
Virginia Polytechnic Institute and State University	M,D,O
Washington State University	M,D
Washington University in St. Louis	M,D
Wayne State University	M,D
Weber State University	M
Western Michigan University	M,D
West Virginia University	M,D
Wichita State University	M,D
Worcester Polytechnic Institute	M,D,O
Wright State University	M,D
Youngstown State University	M

COMPUTER SCIENCE

Acadia University	M
Air Force Institute of Technology	M,D
Alabama Agricultural and Mechanical University	M
Alcorn State University	M
American Sentinel University	M
The American University in Cairo	M,D,O
American University of Armenia	M
American University of Beirut	M,D
Appalachian State University	M
Arizona State University at the Tempe campus	M,D
Arkansas State University	M
Auburn University	M,D*
Ball State University	M
Baylor University	M,D
Binghamton University, State University of New York	M,D
Boise State University	M,O
Boston University	M,D,O*
Bowie State University	M,D
Bowling Green State University	M
Bradley University	M
Brandeis University	M,D
Bridgewater State University	M
Brigham Young University	M,D
Brock University	M
Brooklyn College of the City University of New York	M,O
Brown University	M,D
California Institute of Technology	M,D
California Polytechnic State University, San Luis Obispo	M*
California State Polytechnic University, Pomona	M
California State University Channel Islands	M
California State University, Chico	M
California State University, Dominguez Hills	M
California State University, East Bay	M
California State University, Fresno	M
California State University, Fullerton	M
California State University, Long Beach	M
California State University, Los Angeles	M
California State University, Northridge	M
California State University, Sacramento	M
California State University, San Bernardino	M
California State University, San Marcos	M
Capitol Technology University	M
Carleton University	M,D
Carnegie Mellon University	M,D
Case Western Reserve University	M,D*
The Catholic University of America	M,D
Central Connecticut State University	M,O
Central Michigan University	M
Chicago State University	M
Christopher Newport University	M
City College of the City University of New York	M,D
City University of Seattle	M,O
Clark Atlanta University	M
Clarkson University	M,D
Clemson University	M,D
Coastal Carolina University	M,D,O
College of Charleston	M
The College of Saint Rose	M,O
College of Staten Island of the City University of New York	M
The College of William and Mary	M,D*
Colorado School of Mines	M,D
Colorado State University	M,D
Colorado Technical University Aurora	M
Colorado Technical University Colorado Springs	M,D
Columbia University	M,D*
Columbus State University	M,O
Concordia University (Canada)	M,D,O
Concordia University, Nebraska	M
Cornell University	M,D
Dakota State University	M,D,O
Dalhousie University	M,D
Dartmouth College	M,D*
DePaul University	M,D
DigiPen Institute of Technology	M
Drexel University	M,D,O*
Duke University	M,D*
East Carolina University	M,D,O
Eastern Illinois University	M
Eastern Michigan University	M,O
Eastern Washington University	M
East Stroudsburg University of Pennsylvania	M
East Tennessee State University	M,O
École Polytechnique de Montréal	M,D,O
Elizabeth City State University	M
Emory University	M,D
Fairleigh Dickinson University, Florham Campus	M
Fairleigh Dickinson University, Metropolitan Campus	M
Fitchburg State University	M
Florida Atlantic University	M,D
Florida Institute of Technology	M,D
Florida International University	M,D
Florida State University	M,D
Fontbonne University	M
Fordham University	M
Franklin University	M
Frostburg State University	M
Gannon University	M
George Mason University	M,D,O
Georgetown University	M,D
The George Washington University	M,D,O
Georgia Institute of Technology	M,D
Georgia Southern University	M
Georgia Southern University–Armstrong Campus	M
Georgia Southwestern State University	M,O
Georgia State University	M,D
Governors State University	M
The Graduate Center, City University of New York	D

Grand Valley State University	M
Hampton University	M
Harvard University	M,D*
Hood College	M,O*
Howard University	M
Illinois Institute of Technology	M,D
Indiana State University	M
Indiana University Bloomington	M,D,O
Indiana University–Purdue University Fort Wayne	M
Indiana University–Purdue University Indianapolis	M,D,O
Indiana University South Bend	M,O
Instituto Tecnológico y de Estudios Superiores de Monterrey, Campus Central de Veracruz	M
Instituto Tecnológico y de Estudios Superiores de Monterrey, Campus Ciudad de México	M,D
Instituto Tecnológico y de Estudios Superiores de Monterrey, Campus Cuernavaca	M,D
Instituto Tecnológico y de Estudios Superiores de Monterrey, Campus Estado de México	M,D
Instituto Tecnológico y de Estudios Superiores de Monterrey, Campus Irapuato	M,D
Instituto Tecnológico y de Estudios Superiores de Monterrey, Campus Monterrey	M,D
Inter American University of Puerto Rico, Fajardo Campus	M
Inter American University of Puerto Rico, Guayama Campus	M
Inter American University of Puerto Rico, Metropolitan Campus	M
Iona College	M
Iowa State University of Science and Technology	M,D
Jackson State University	M
Jacksonville State University	M
James Madison University	M
Johns Hopkins University	M,D,O*
Kansas State University	M,D
Kennesaw State University	M
Kent State University	M,D
Kentucky State University	M
Kutztown University of Pennsylvania	M
Lakehead University	M
Lamar University	M
La Salle University	M,O
Lawrence Technological University	M,O
Lebanese American University	M
Lehigh University	M,D
Lehman College of the City University of New York	M
Lewis University	M
Long Island University–LIU Brooklyn	M,O
Louisiana State University and Agricultural & Mechanical College	M,D
Louisiana State University in Shreveport	M
Louisiana Tech University	M,D,O
Loyola University Chicago	M
Maharishi University of Management	M
Marist College	M,O
Marquette University	M,D
Marshall University	M
Massachusetts Institute of Technology	M,D,O
McGill University	M,D
McMaster University	M,D
McNeese State University	M
Memorial University of Newfoundland	M,D
Merrimack College	M
Michigan State University	M,D
Michigan Technological University	M,D
Middle Tennessee State University	M,D
Midwestern State University	M
Mills College	M,O
Minnesota State University Mankato	M,O
Mississippi College	M
Mississippi State University	M,D
Missouri State University	M
Missouri University of Science and Technology	M,D
Monmouth University	M*
Monroe College	M
Montana State University	M,D
Montclair State University	M,O
Morgan State University	M
Murray State University	M
National University	M
Naval Postgraduate School	M,D,O
New Jersey Institute of Technology	M,D,O
New Mexico Highlands University	M
New Mexico Institute of Mining and Technology	M,D
New Mexico State University	M,D
New York Institute of Technology	M
New York University	M,D*
Norfolk State University	M
North Carolina Agricultural and Technical State University	M
North Carolina State University	M,D
North Central College	M
Northcentral University	M,D,O
Northeastern Illinois University	M
Northeastern University	M,D
Northern Arizona University	M,D
Northern Illinois University	M
Northern Kentucky University	M,O
Northwestern Polytechnic University	M,D
Northwestern University	M,D
Northwest Missouri State University	M
Notre Dame College (OH)	M,O
Nova Southeastern University	M,D*
Oakland University	M,D
The Ohio State University	M,D
Ohio University	M,D
Oklahoma Christian University	M
Oklahoma City University	M
Oklahoma State University	M,D
Old Dominion University	M,D
Oregon Health & Science University	M,D
Oregon State University	M,D
Pace University	M,D,O
Pacific States University	M
Penn State Harrisburg	M,O
Penn State University Park	M,D*
Polytechnic University of Puerto Rico	M
Portland State University	M,D,O
Prairie View A&M University	M,D
Princeton University	M,D
Purdue University	M,D
Purdue University Northwest	M
Queens College of the City University of New York	M
Queen's University at Kingston	M,D
Regis University	M,O
Rensselaer at Hartford	M
Rensselaer Polytechnic Institute	M,D
Rice University	M,D
Rivier University	M
Rochester Institute of Technology	M,D
Roosevelt University	M
Rowan University	M
Royal Military College of Canada	M
Rutgers University–Camden	M
Rutgers University–New Brunswick	M,D
Sacred Heart University	M
St. Cloud State University	M,O
St. Francis Xavier University	M
Saint Joseph's University	M,O*
Saint Louis University	M*
St. Mary's University (United States)	M
Saint Xavier University	M
Sam Houston State University	M,D
San Diego State University	M
San Francisco State University	M
San Jose State University	M
Santa Clara University	M,D,O
Seattle University	M
Shippensburg University of Pennsylvania	M,O
Simon Fraser University	M,D
Sofia University	M,D
Southern Arkansas University–Magnolia	M
Southern Connecticut State University	M
Southern Illinois University Carbondale	M,D
Southern Illinois University Edwardsville	M
Southern Methodist University	M,D
Southern Oregon University	M
Southern University and Agricultural and Mechanical College	M
Stanford University	M,D
State University of New York at New Paltz	M
State University of New York Polytechnic Institute	M
Stephen F. Austin State University	M
Stevens Institute of Technology	M,D,O
Stony Brook University, State University of New York	M,D,O
Stratford University (VA)	M,D
Syracuse University	M*
Télé-université	M,D
Temple University	M,D*
Tennessee Technological University	M
Texas A&M University	M,D
Texas A&M University–Corpus Christi	M
Texas A&M University–Kingsville	M
Texas Southern University	M
Texas State University	M,D
Texas Tech University	M,D
Towson University	M
Toyota Technological Institute at Chicago	D
Trent University	M
Troy University	M
Tufts University	M,D,O*
Universidad Autonoma de Guadalajara	M,D
Universidad de las Américas Puebla	M,D
Université de Moncton	M,O
Université de Montréal	M,D
Université du Québec à Trois-Rivières	M
Université du Québec en Outaouais	M,D,O
Université Laval	M,D
University at Albany, State University of New York	M,D
University at Buffalo, the State University of New York	M,D,O
University of Advancing Technology	M
The University of Akron	M
The University of Alabama	M,D
The University of Alabama at Birmingham	M,D
The University of Alabama in Huntsville	M,D,O
University of Alaska Fairbanks	M
University of Alberta	M,D
The University of Arizona	M,D
University of Arkansas	M,D
University of Arkansas at Little Rock	M,D
University of Bridgeport	M,D
The University of British Columbia	M,D
University of Calgary	M,D
University of California, Berkeley	M,D
University of California, Davis	M,D
University of California, Irvine	M,D
University of California, Los Angeles	M,D*
University of California, Merced	M,D
University of California, Riverside	M,D
University of California, San Diego	M,D*
University of California, Santa Barbara	M,D
University of California, Santa Cruz	M,D*
University of Central Arkansas	M
University of Central Florida	M,D
University of Central Missouri	M,D,O
University of Central Oklahoma	M
University of Chicago	M,D
University of Cincinnati	M,D
University of Colorado Boulder	M,D
University of Colorado Colorado Springs	M,D
University of Colorado Denver	M,D
University of Connecticut	M,D*
University of Dayton	M
University of Delaware	M,D*
University of Denver	M,D
University of Detroit Mercy	M,D,O
University of Florida	M,D
University of Georgia	M,D
University of Guelph	M,D
University of Hawaii at Manoa	M,D,O
University of Houston	M,D
University of Houston–Clear Lake	M
University of Houston–Victoria	M
University of Idaho	M,D
University of Illinois at Chicago	M,D
University of Illinois at Springfield	M
University of Illinois at Urbana–Champaign	M,D
The University of Iowa	M,D*
The University of Kansas	M,D
University of Kentucky	M,D
University of Lethbridge	M,D
University of Louisville	M,D,O
University of Maine	M,D,O
University of Management and Technology	M,O
The University of Manchester	M,D
University of Manitoba	M,D
University of Maryland, Baltimore County	M,D
University of Maryland, College Park	M,D
University of Maryland Eastern Shore	M
University of Massachusetts Amherst	M,D*
University of Massachusetts Boston	M,D
University of Massachusetts Dartmouth	M,O
University of Massachusetts Lowell	M,D
University of Memphis	M,D
University of Miami	M,D*
University of Michigan	M,D*
University of Michigan–Dearborn	D
University of Michigan–Flint	M
University of Minnesota, Duluth	M
University of Minnesota, Twin Cities Campus	M,D
University of Mississippi	M,D
University of Missouri–Kansas City	M,D,O
University of Missouri–St. Louis	M,D
University of Montana	M
University of Nebraska at Omaha	M,O
University of Nebraska–Lincoln	M,D
University of Nevada, Las Vegas	M,D
University of Nevada, Reno	M,D
University of New Brunswick Fredericton	M,D
University of New Hampshire	M,D
University of New Haven	M,O*
University of New Mexico	M,D
University of New Orleans	M,D
The University of North Carolina at Chapel Hill	M,D
The University of North Carolina at Charlotte	M,D
The University of North Carolina at Greensboro	M
The University of North Carolina Wilmington	M
University of North Dakota	M
University of Northern British Columbia	M,D,O
University of North Florida	M
University of North Texas	M,D,O
University of Notre Dame	M,D
University of Oklahoma	M,D*
University of Oregon	M,D
University of Ottawa	M,D
University of Pennsylvania	M,D*
University of Pittsburgh	M,D*
University of Portland	M
University of Puerto Rico–Mayagüez	M,D
University of Regina	M,D
University of Rhode Island	M,D,O*
University of Rochester	M,D*
University of San Francisco	M
University of Saskatchewan	M,D
University of South Alabama	M,D
University of South Carolina	M,D
University of South Dakota	M
University of Southern California	M,D*
University of Southern Maine	M,O
University of Southern Mississippi	M,D
University of South Florida	M,D*
The University of Tennessee	M,D
The University of Tennessee at Chattanooga	M,O
The University of Texas at Arlington	M,D
The University of Texas at Austin	M,D
The University of Texas at Dallas	M,D
The University of Texas at El Paso	M,D,O
The University of Texas at San Antonio	M,D
The University of Texas at Tyler	M
The University of Texas of the Permian Basin	M
The University of Texas Rio Grande Valley	M
University of the District of Columbia	M
The University of Toledo	M,D
University of Toronto	M,D
The University of Tulsa	M,D
University of Utah	M,D
University of Vermont	M,D
University of Victoria	M,D
University of Virginia	M,D
University of Waterloo	M,D
The University of Western Ontario	M,D
University of West Florida	M
University of West Georgia	M,O
University of Windsor	M,D
University of Wisconsin–Madison	M,D
University of Wisconsin–Milwaukee	M,D*
University of Wisconsin–Parkside	M
University of Wisconsin–Platteville	M
University of Wyoming	M,D
Utah State University	M,D
Vanderbilt University	M,D*
Villanova University	M,O
Virginia Commonwealth University	M,D
Virginia International University	M,O
Virginia Polytechnic Institute and State University	M,D,O
Virginia State University	M
Wake Forest University	M
Washington State University	M,D
Washington University in St. Louis	M,D
Wayne State University	M,D
Webster University	M
Wentworth Institute of Technology	M
Wesleyan University	M,D
West Chester University of Pennsylvania	M,O
Western Illinois University	M
Western Kentucky University	M
Western Michigan University	M,D
Western Washington University	M
West Virginia University	M,D
Wichita State University	M,D
Winston-Salem State University	M
Worcester Polytechnic Institute	M,D,O
Wright State University	M,D
Yale University	M,D
York University	M,D
Youngstown State University	M

CONDENSED MATTER PHYSICS

Iowa State University of Science and Technology	M,D
Memorial University of Newfoundland	M,D
Rutgers University–New Brunswick	M,D
University of Alberta	M,D
The University of Manchester	M,D
University of Victoria	M,D

CONFLICT RESOLUTION AND MEDIATION/PEACE STUDIES

Abilene Christian University	M,O
American Public University System	M,D
American University	M,D,O
The American University of Paris	M
Anabaptist Mennonite Biblical Seminary	M,O
Arcadia University	M
Bethany Theological Seminary	M,O
Bethel University (TN)	M
Brandeis University	M,D
California State University, Dominguez Hills	M
California University of Pennsylvania	M
Cambridge College	M
Carleton University	M,O
Champlain College	M
Colgate Rochester Crozer Divinity School	M,D,O
Colorado Technical University Aurora	M
Colorado Technical University Colorado Springs	M,D
Columbia University	M*
Cornell University	M,D
Creighton University	M,D,O
Dallas Baptist University	M
Drew University	M,D,O
Eastern Mennonite University	M,O

*M—masters degree; D—doctorate; O—other advanced degree; *—Close-Up and/or Display*

Excelsior College	M,O
Fresno Pacific University	M,O
George Mason University	M,D,O
Georgetown University	M
Henley-Putnam School of Strategic Security	M
Kansas State University	M,D,O
Kennesaw State University	M,D
Kent State University	M,D
Lesley University	M,D,O
Lipscomb University	M,O
London Metropolitan University	M,D
Middlebury Institute of International Studies at Monterey	M
Montclair State University	M,O
Naval Postgraduate School	M,D
New York University	M*
Norwich University	M
Nova Southeastern University	M,D,O*
Old Dominion University	M,D
Pepperdine University	M
Portland State University	M
Regent University	M,D
Royal Roads University	M,O
Saint Mary's College of California	M
St. Mary's University (United States)	M,O
Saint Paul University	M
Salisbury University	M
Salve Regina University	M,D
SIT Graduate Institute	M
Southern Methodist University	M,O
Syracuse University	O*
Trident University International	M,D
United States International University–Africa	M
United Theological Seminary of the Twin Cities	M,D,O
Universidad del Turabo	M
Université de Sherbrooke	M,D,O
University of Arkansas at Little Rock	O
University of Baltimore	M
University of Bridgeport	M
University of Denver	M
University of Hawaii at Manoa	M,O
The University of Manchester	D
University of Massachusetts Amherst	M,D*
University of Massachusetts Boston	M,O
University of Massachusetts Lowell	M
University of Missouri	M,D
University of New Brunswick Fredericton	M
University of New Haven	M,O*
The University of North Carolina at Greensboro	M,O
The University of North Carolina Wilmington	M
University of Notre Dame	M,D
University of Phoenix–Online Campus	M,O
University of San Diego	M
University of the Sacred Heart	M
University of Victoria	M,D
University of Wisconsin–Milwaukee	M,D,O*
Walden University	M,D,O
Wayne State University	M,D,O
Wilfrid Laurier University	D
Willamette University	M,D
Yeshiva University	M,D

CONSERVATION BIOLOGY

Antioch University New England	M
Arizona State University at the Tempe campus	M,D
California State University, Sacramento	M
California State University, Stanislaus	M
Central Michigan University	M
Colorado State University	M,D
Columbia University	M,D*
Cornell University	M,D
Florida Institute of Technology	M
Fordham University	M,D,O
Frostburg State University	M
Illinois State University	M,D
North Dakota State University	M,D*
Oregon State University	M,D
State University of New York College of Environmental Science and Forestry	M,D
Texas State University	M
Tropical Agriculture Research and Higher Education Center	M,D
University of Alberta	M,D
University of Central Florida	M,D
University of Hawaii at Hilo	M*
University of Illinois at Urbana–Champaign	M,D
University of Maryland, College Park	M
University of Minnesota, Twin Cities Campus	M,D
University of Nevada, Reno	D
University of New Hampshire	M
The University of West Alabama	M
University of Wisconsin–Madison	M
University of Wisconsin–Stout	M

CONSTRUCTION ENGINEERING

The American University in Cairo	M,D,O
Arizona State University at the Tempe campus	M,D
Auburn University	M*
Bradley University	M
Clemson University	M,D
Colorado School of Mines	M,D
Columbia University	M,D*
Concordia University (Canada)	M,D,O
George Mason University	M,D
Illinois Institute of Technology	M,D
Iowa State University of Science and Technology	M,D
Lawrence Technological University	M,D
Marquette University	M,D,O
Massachusetts Institute of Technology	M,D,O
Montana State University	M,D
Ohio University	M,D
Oregon State University	M,D
Pittsburg State University	M
Stanford University	M,D,O
Stevens Institute of Technology	M,O
Texas Tech University	M,D
The University of Alabama	M,D
The University of Alabama at Birmingham	M
University of Alberta	M,D
University of Michigan	M,D,O*
University of Missouri–Kansas City	M,D,O
University of New Brunswick Fredericton	M,D
University of Puerto Rico–Mayagüez	M,D
University of Southern Mississippi	M
University of Virginia	D
University of Washington	M,D
University of Wisconsin–Madison	M
Wentworth Institute of Technology	M

CONSTRUCTION MANAGEMENT

The American University in Dubai	M
Arizona State University at the Tempe campus	M,D
Brigham Young University	M
California Baptist University	M
California State University, Chico	M
California State University, East Bay	M
California State University, Northridge	M
Carnegie Mellon University	M,D
Central Connecticut State University	M,O
Clemson University	M,D
Colorado State University	M
Columbia University	M,D*
Drexel University	M*
East Carolina University	M,O
Eastern Michigan University	M,O
Farmingdale State College	M
Florida International University	M
Georgia Southern University	M
Illinois Institute of Technology	M,D
Indiana University–Purdue University Fort Wayne	M
Instituto Tecnologico de Santo Domingo	M,O
Kennesaw State University	M
Louisiana State University and Agricultural & Mechanical College	M,D
Manhattan College	M
Marquette University	M,D,O
Michigan State University	M,D
Missouri State University	M
New England Institute of Technology	M
NewSchool of Architecture and Design	M
New York University	M*
North Carolina Agricultural and Technical State University	M
Norwich University	M
Pittsburg State University	M,O
Polytechnic University of Puerto Rico, Miami Campus	M
Polytechnic University of Puerto Rico, Orlando Campus	M
Purdue University	M
South Dakota School of Mines and Technology	M
Stevens Institute of Technology	M,O
Texas A&M University	M
Thomas Jefferson University	M
Universidad de las Américas Puebla	M
The University of Alabama at Birmingham	M
University of Alaska Fairbanks	M,D,O
University of Arkansas at Little Rock	M
University of California, Berkeley	O
University of Denver	M
University of Florida	M,D
University of Houston	M
The University of Kansas	M
University of Nevada, Las Vegas	M,O
University of New Mexico	M,D
The University of North Carolina at Charlotte	M,O
University of North Florida	M
University of Oklahoma	M,D,O*
University of Southern California	M,D,O*
The University of Tennessee at Chattanooga	M,O
The University of Texas at Arlington	M,D
The University of Texas at El Paso	M,D,O
University of Washington	M
University of Wisconsin–Stout	M
Wentworth Institute of Technology	M
Western Carolina University	M
Worcester Polytechnic Institute	M,D,O

CONSUMER ECONOMICS

Colorado State University	M
Cornell University	M,D
Kansas State University	M,D,O
North Carolina Agricultural and Technical State University	M
North Dakota State University	M,O*
Ohio University	M
Oklahoma State University	M,D
Purdue University	M,D
South Dakota State University	M
State University of New York at Oswego	M
Texas Tech University	M,D
Université Laval	O
The University of Alabama	M
University of Guelph	M
University of Idaho	M
University of Illinois at Urbana–Champaign	M,D
University of Missouri	D
University of Nebraska–Lincoln	M,D
University of South Carolina	M
The University of Tennessee	M,D
University of Wisconsin–Madison	M,D
University of Wyoming	M
Utah State University	M

CORPORATE AND ORGANIZATIONAL COMMUNICATION

American University	M
Ashland University	M
Austin Peay State University	M
Barry University	M,O
Baruch College of the City University of New York	M*
Bellevue University	M
Boston University	M*
Bowie State University	M,O
Bryant University	M,O
California State University, San Bernardino	M
Canisius College	M
Carnegie Mellon University	M
City College of the City University of New York	M
Columbia University	M*
Concordia University, St. Paul	M
Concordia University Wisconsin	M
Cornell University	M,D
Dallas Baptist University	M
DePaul University	M
Drexel University	M*
East Carolina University	M,D,O
Eastern Michigan University	M,O
Fairleigh Dickinson University, Florham Campus	M
Florida State University	M,D
Franklin University	M
Georgia Southern University–Armstrong Campus	M,O
HEC Montreal	O
High Point University	M,D
Howard University	M,D
Illinois Institute of Technology	M
Iowa State University of Science and Technology	M,D
La Salle University	M,O
Lasell College	M,O
Loyola University Chicago	M
Manhattanville College	M,O
Marist College	M
Minnesota State University Mankato	M,O
Mississippi College	M
Monmouth University	M,O*
Montclair State University	M
Murray State University	M
New Mexico State University	M,D
New York University	M*
Northeastern University	M
Northwestern University	M,D
Ohio University	M,D
Radford University	M
Regent University	M,D
Regis College (MA)	M
Rider University	M
Roosevelt University	M
Rowan University	O
St. Bonaventure University	M
Seton Hall University	M
Southern Illinois University Edwardsville	M
Spalding University	M
State University of New York at Oswego	M
Stevens Institute of Technology	O
Suffolk University	M
Temple University	M,D*
Texas Christian University	M
Towson University	M
Troy University	M
Universidad Autonoma de Guadalajara	M,D
Universidad Iberoamericana	M,D
Université de Sherbrooke	M
University of Alaska Fairbanks	M
University of Central Florida	M,O
University of Colorado Denver	M
University of Illinois at Urbana–Champaign	M
University of Nebraska–Lincoln	M,D
University of Oklahoma	M,D*
University of Portland	M
University of Southern California	M*
University of South Florida	M,O*
University of Wisconsin–Stevens Point	M
University of Wisconsin–Whitewater	M
Washington State University	M,D
Webster University	M
Western Kentucky University	M,O
West Virginia University	M,O

COUNSELING PSYCHOLOGY

Abilene Christian University	M
Adelphi University	M
Adler Graduate School	M
Adler University	M
Alabama Agricultural and Mechanical University	M,O
Alaska Pacific University	M
Alfred University	M,D,O
Amberton University	M
American International College	M,D
Amridge University	M,D
Andrews University	M,D
Anna Maria College	M
Antioch University New England	M
Appalachian State University	M
Arcadia University	M
Argosy University, Chicago	D
Argosy University, Hawai'i	D
Argosy University, Los Angeles	M,D
Argosy University, Northern Virginia	M,D
Argosy University, Orange County	M,D
Argosy University, Phoenix	M
Argosy University, Seattle	M,D
Argosy University, Tampa	M,D
Arizona State University at the Tempe campus	D
Assumption College	M,O
Athabasca University	M,O
Austin Peay State University	M
Avila University	M
Ball State University	M,D
Baruch College of the City University of New York	M*
Bastyr University	M,O
Becker College	M
Bethel University (MN)	M,D,O
Boston College	M,D
Boston Graduate School of Psychoanalysis	M
Boston University	M*
Bowie State University	M
Bradley University	M
Brandman University	M
Brigham Young University	M,D,O
Brooklyn College of the City University of New York	M,D,O
Caldwell University	M,O
California Baptist University	M
California Institute of Integral Studies	M,D
California State University, Bakersfield	M
California State University, Fresno	M
California State University, San Bernardino	M
California State University, Stanislaus	M
California University of Pennsylvania	M
Cambridge College	M,O
Capella University	M
Carlos Albizu University, Miami Campus	M,D
Carlow University	M,D,O
Centenary University	M
Central Michigan University	M,D,O
Central Washington University	M
Chaminade University of Honolulu	M
Chatham University	M,D
Chestnut Hill College	M,O
City University of Seattle	M
Cleveland State University	M,D,O
The College at Brockport, State University of New York	M,O
The College of New Rochelle	M,O
College of Saint Elizabeth	M,D
College of St. Joseph	M
The College of Saint Rose	M,O
College of Staten Island of the City University of New York	M,O
Colorado Christian University	M
Concordia University Chicago	M
Delaware Valley University	M
DePaul University	M,D
Dominican University of California	M
Duquesne University	M,D,O
Eastern Nazarene College	M
Eastern University	M,O
Eastern Washington University	M
East Texas Baptist University	M
Edinboro University of Pennsylvania	M,O
Emporia State University	M
Evangel University	M
Fairfield University	M,O
Fairleigh Dickinson University, Florham Campus	M
Felician University	M,D
Fitchburg State University	M
Florida International University	M,D,O
Fordham University	M,D
Fort Valley State University	M
Framingham State University	M
Franciscan University of Steubenville	M
Francis Marion University	M,O
Frostburg State University	M
Gallaudet University	M,D,O
Gannon University	M
Gardner-Webb University	M
Geneva College	M
George Fox University	M,O
Georgian Court University	M,O
Georgia Southern University	M
Georgia State University	M,O
Governors State University	M
Hardin-Simmons University	M
Heidelberg University	M
Henderson State University	M,O
Hodges University	M
Hofstra University	M,O
Holy Family University	M
Holy Names University	M
Houston Baptist University	M
Howard University	D
Humboldt State University	M

Husson University	M
Idaho State University	M,D,O
Illinois State University	M,D,O
Immaculata University	M,D,O
Indiana University Northwest	M,O
Indiana University South Bend	M,O
Indiana Wesleyan University	M
Instituto Tecnologico de Santo Domingo	M,O
Inter American University of Puerto Rico, Aguadilla Campus	M
Inter American University of Puerto Rico, Metropolitan Campus	M,D
Inter American University of Puerto Rico, San Germán Campus	M,D
Iona College	M,O
Iowa State University of Science and Technology	M,D
Jacksonville University	M*
James Madison University	D
John Brown University	M,O
John Carroll University	M,O
John F. Kennedy University	M
Johns Hopkins University	M,O*
Kean University	M
Kent State University	M
Kutztown University of Pennsylvania	M
Lamar University	M
Lancaster Bible College	M,D
La Salle University	M
Lee University	M
Lehigh University	M,D,O
Lenoir-Rhyne University	M
Lesley University	M,D,O
LeTourneau University	M
Lewis & Clark College	M
Lewis University	M
Liberty University	M,D,O
Lindenwood University	M,D,O
Lindsey Wilson College	M,D
Lipscomb University	M,O
Lock Haven University of Pennsylvania	M
London Metropolitan University	M,D
Long Island University–Brentwood Campus	M,O
Long Island University–Hudson	M,O
Long Island University–LIU Brooklyn	M,O
Long Island University–LIU Post	M,D,O
Louisiana Tech University	M,D,O
Loyola Marymount University	M
Loyola University Chicago	M,D,O
Loyola University Maryland	M,D,O
Lynn University	M
Manhattan College	M,O
Marian University (IN)	M
Marist College	M,O
Marquette University	M,D
Marymount University	M
Marywood University	M
McGill University	M,D,O
McKendree University	M
McNeese State University	M,O
Medaille College	M,O
Mercy College	M,O
Messiah College	M,O
Mid-America Christian University	M
Middle Tennessee State University	M
Midwestern State University	M
Minnesota State University Mankato	M,D
Mississippi College	M,O
Missouri State University	M
Monmouth University	M,O*
Montana State University Billings	M
Moody Theological Seminary–Michigan	M,O
Morehead State University	M,O
Mount Mary University	M,O
Mount Saint Mary's University (CA)	M,D,O
Naropa University	M
National University	M,O
New England College	M
New Mexico Highlands University	M
New Mexico State University	M,D,O
New York University	M,D,O*
Niagara University	M,D,O
North Dakota State University	M,D*
Northeastern University	M,D,O
Northern Arizona University	M,D,O
Northern Kentucky University	M
Northern State University	M
Northwest Christian University	M
Northwestern Oklahoma State University	M
Northwest University	M,D
Nova Southeastern University	M,D,O*
Nyack College	M
Oakland University	M,D,O
Old Dominion University	M,D,O
Ottawa University	M
Our Lady of the Lake University	D
Pace University	M,D
Pacifica Graduate Institute	M,D
Palm Beach Atlantic University	M
Palo Alto University	M
Philadelphia College of Osteopathic Medicine	M,D,O*
Phoenix Seminary	M,D,O
Prescott College	M
Providence University College & Theological Seminary	M,D,O
Purdue University Northwest	M
Queens College of the City University of New York	M,O
Radford University	D
Regent University	M,D,O
Regis College (MA)	M,D,O
Rhode Island College	M,O
Rivier University	M,D,O
Robert Morris University	M,D,O
Rosemont College	M
Rutgers University–New Brunswick	M
Sage Graduate School	M
St. Bonaventure University	M,O
St. Edward's University	M
St. John Fisher College	M
St. John's University (NY)	M,O
Saint Martin's University	M
St. Mary's University (United States)	M
Saint Mary's University of Minnesota	M,D,O
Saint Paul University	M
St. Thomas University	M
Salem State University	M,O
Salve Regina University	M,O
Santa Clara University	M,O
Saybrook University	M
The Seattle School of Theology and Psychology	M
Seton Hall University	M,D
Siena Heights University	M,O
Simpson University	M
Slippery Rock University of Pennsylvania	M
Sofia University	M,D
Sonoma State University	M
Southeastern Oklahoma State University	M
Southeastern University (FL)	M
Southeast Missouri State University	M,O
Southern Adventist University	M
Southern California Seminary	M,D
Southern Illinois University Carbondale	M,D
Southern Nazarene University	M
Southern Oregon University	M
South University	M
South University	M
South University (TX)	M
South University (SC)	M
South University (GA)	M
South University (AL)	M
South University	M
Southwestern Assemblies of God University	M
Southwestern College (NM)	M,O
Spring Arbor University	M
Springfield College	M,D,O
State University of New York at New Paltz	M,O
State University of New York at Oswego	M
State University of New York at Plattsburgh	M,O
State University of New York College at Old Westbury	M
Stetson University	M
Suffolk University	M,D,O
Tarleton State University	M
Teachers College, Columbia University	M,D
Temple University	M,D,O*
Tennessee State University	M
Texas A&M International University	M
Texas A&M University	M,D
Texas A&M University–Texarkana	M
Texas Tech University	M,D
Texas Woman's University	M,D,O
Touro College	M,D
Towson University	M
Trinity Christian College	M
Trinity International University	M,D,O
Trinity International University Florida	M
Trinity Washington University	M
Trinity Western University	M
Truett McConnell University	M
Union College (KY)	M
United States International University–Africa	M
Universidad del Turabo	M,D,O
Universidad Metropolitana	M
University at Albany, State University of New York	M,D,O
University at Buffalo, the State University of New York	M,D,O
The University of Akron	M,D
University of Alberta	M,D
The University of Arizona	M
University of Baltimore	M
University of Bridgeport	M
The University of British Columbia	M,D,O
University of Calgary	M,D
University of California, Berkeley	O
University of California, Santa Barbara	M,D,O
University of Central Arkansas	M
University of Central Missouri	M,D,O
University of Central Oklahoma	M
University of Colorado Denver	M
University of Connecticut	M,D*
University of Dayton	M,O
University of Denver	M,D,O
University of Florida	M,D
University of Hawaii at Hilo	M*
University of Houston	M,D
University of Houston–Victoria	M
University of Indianapolis	M,D
The University of Iowa	M,D,O*
The University of Kansas	M,D
University of Kentucky	M,D,O
University of Lethbridge	M,D
University of Louisiana at Monroe	M
University of Louisville	M,D
University of Lynchburg	M
The University of Manchester	M,D
University of Mary Hardin-Baylor	M
University of Maryland, College Park	M,D,O
University of Massachusetts Boston	M,D
University of Memphis	M,D
University of Miami	D*
University of Minnesota, Twin Cities Campus	D
University of Missouri	M,D,O
University of Missouri–Kansas City	M,D,O
University of Montana	M,D,O
University of Nebraska at Kearney	M,O
University of Nebraska–Lincoln	M,D,O
University of Nevada, Las Vegas	M,D,O
The University of North Carolina at Greensboro	M,D,O
The University of North Carolina at Pembroke	M
University of North Dakota	M,D
University of Northern Colorado	D
University of Northern Iowa	M
University of North Florida	M
University of North Georgia	M
University of North Texas	M,D,O
University of Notre Dame	D
University of Oklahoma	M*
University of Oregon	M,D
University of Pennsylvania	M*
University of Phoenix–Las Vegas Campus	M
University of Phoenix–Phoenix Campus	M
University of Providence	M
University of Puget Sound	M
University of Rhode Island	M*
University of Saint Francis (IN)	M,O
University of Saint Joseph	M
University of Saint Mary	M
University of St. Thomas (MN)	M,D
University of San Diego	M
University of San Francisco	M
The University of Scranton	M
University of South Africa	M,D
University of South Alabama	M,D,O
University of South Dakota	M,D,O
University of Southern Maine	M,O
University of South Florida	M,D,O*
The University of Tennessee	M,D
The University of Texas at Austin	M,D
The University of Texas at Tyler	M
University of the Cumberlands	M
University of the District of Columbia	M
University of the Southwest	M
University of Utah	M,D,O
University of Vermont	M
University of Victoria	M,D
The University of Western Ontario	M
University of West Florida	M
University of Wisconsin–Madison	D
University of Wisconsin–Milwaukee	M,D,O*
University of Wisconsin–Stout	M
Utah State University	M,D
Virginia Commonwealth University	M,D
Viterbo University	M
Walden University	M,D,O
Walsh University	M
Washington Adventist University	M
Washington State University	M
Wayland Baptist University	M
Waynesburg University	M,D
Wayne State University	M,D,O
Webster University	M
Western Kentucky University	M
Western Michigan University	M,D
Western Washington University	M
Westfield State University	M
Westminster College (UT)	M
West Virginia University	M,D
Wheaton College	M,D
William Carey University	M
William James College	M,D,O
William Paterson University of New Jersey	M,D,O
Wilmington University	M
Winebrenner Theological Seminary	M,D
The Wright Institute	M
Xavier University	M*
Yeshiva University	M
Youngstown State University	M

COUNSELOR EDUCATION

Acadia University	M
Adams State University	M,D
Adler Graduate School	M
Adler University	D
Alabama Agricultural and Mechanical University	M,O
Alabama State University	M,D,O
Albany State University	M,O
Alcorn State University	M,O
Alfred University	M,D,O
Alliant International University–San Francisco	M
Amberton University	M
American International College	M,D,O
Amridge University	M,D
Angelo State University	M
Antioch University Seattle	M,D
Appalachian State University	M
Argosy University, Atlanta	M,D,O
Argosy University, Chicago	D
Argosy University, Northern Virginia	M,D
Argosy University, Tampa	M,D,O
Arizona State University at the Tempe campus	M
Arkansas State University	M,O
Arkansas Tech University	M,D,O
Ashland Theological Seminary	M,D
Athabasca University	M,O
Auburn University at Montgomery	M,O
Augusta University	M,O
Austin Peay State University	M,O
Azusa Pacific University	M*
Ball State University	M,D
Barry University	M,D,O
Bayamón Central University	M,O
Becker College	M
Bellevue University	M
Bloomsburg University of Pennsylvania	M
Bob Jones University	M,D,O
Boise State University	M,O
Bowie State University	M
Bowling Green State University	M
Bradley University	M
Brandman University	M,D
Brandon University	M,O
Bridgewater State University	M,O
Brooklyn College of the City University of New York	M
Buena Vista University	M
Butler University	M,O
Caldwell University	M,O
California Baptist University	M
California Lutheran University	M,D
California State University, Bakersfield	M
California State University, Dominguez Hills	M
California State University, East Bay	M
California State University, Fresno	M
California State University, Fullerton	M
California State University, Long Beach	M,D
California State University, Los Angeles	M,D
California State University, Northridge	M
California State University, Sacramento	M,D,O
California State University, San Bernardino	M
California State University, Stanislaus	M
California University of Pennsylvania	M
Cambridge College	M,O
Campbell University	M
Canisius College	M
Capella University	M,D
Carson-Newman University	M
Carthage College	M,O
Central Connecticut State University	M,O
Central Methodist University	M
Central Michigan University	M
Chadron State College	M,O
Chapman University	M,D,O*
Chicago State University	M
The Citadel, The Military College of South Carolina	M,O
City University of Seattle	M,O
Clark Atlanta University	M
Clarks Summit University	M
Clemson University	M,D,O
Cleveland State University	M,D,O
The College at Brockport, State University of New York	M,O
The College of New Jersey	M
College of St. Joseph	M
The College of Saint Rose	M,O
The College of William and Mary	M,D*
Colorado State University	M
Columbia International University	M,D,O
Columbus State University	M,D,O
Concordia University Chicago	M,D,O
Concordia University Irvine	M*
Concordia University Wisconsin	M
Creighton University	M
Dallas Baptist University	M
Delta State University	M,D,O
DePaul University	M,D
Doane University	M
Drake University	M,D,O
Duquesne University	M,D,O
East Carolina University	M,D,O
Eastern Illinois University	M
Eastern Kentucky University	M
Eastern Mennonite University	M
Eastern Michigan University	M,O
Eastern New Mexico University	M
Eastern Washington University	M
East Tennessee State University	M
Edinboro University of Pennsylvania	M,O
Emporia State University	M
Evangel University	M
Fairfield University	M,O
Faulkner University	M
Fitchburg State University	M,O
Florida Agricultural and Mechanical University	M,D
Florida Atlantic University	M,D
Florida International University	M,D,O
Fordham University	M,D
Fort Hays State University	M
Fort Valley State University	M,O
Freed-Hardeman University	M,O

*M—masters degree; D—doctorate; O—other advanced degree; *—Close-Up and/or Display*

Fresno Pacific University	M
Frostburg State University	M
Gallaudet University	M,D,O
Geneva College	M
George Fox University	M,O
George Mason University	M
The George Washington University	M,D,O
Georgian Court University	M,O
Georgia Southern University	M
Georgia State University	M,O
Grambling State University	M,D,O
Gwynedd Mercy University	M,D
Hampton University	M,D,O
Harding University	M,O
Hardin-Simmons University	M
Henderson State University	M,O
Heritage University	M
Hofstra University	M,O
Houston Baptist University	M,D
Howard University	M
Hunter College of the City University of New York	M
Husson University	M
Idaho State University	M,D,O
Indiana State University	M,D,O
Indiana University Bloomington	M,D,O
Indiana University of Pennsylvania	M
Indiana University–Purdue University Fort Wayne	M,O
Indiana University–Purdue University Indianapolis	M,O
Indiana University South Bend	M,O
Indiana University Southeast	M
Indiana Wesleyan University	M
Inter American University of Puerto Rico, Arecibo Campus	M
Inter American University of Puerto Rico, Metropolitan Campus	M,D
Inter American University of Puerto Rico, San Germán Campus	M,D
Iowa State University of Science and Technology	M,D
Jackson State University	M
Jacksonville State University	M
John Brown University	M,O
John Carroll University	M,O
Johns Hopkins University	M,O*
Johnson University	M,D,O
Kansas State University	M,D,O
Kean University	M
Keene State College	M,O
Kent State University	M,D,O
Kutztown University of Pennsylvania	M
Lakeland University	M
Lamar University	M
Lancaster Bible College	M,D
La Sierra University	M,O
Lee University	M
Lehigh University	M,D,O
Lehman College of the City University of New York	M
Lenoir-Rhyne University	M
Lewis University	M
Liberty University	M,D,O
Lincoln Memorial University	M,D,O
Lincoln University (MO)	M
Lindenwood University–Belleville	M
Lindsey Wilson College	M,D
Loma Linda University	M,D,O
Long Island University–Brentwood Campus	M,O
Long Island University–Hudson	M,O
Long Island University–LIU Brooklyn	M,O
Longwood University	M
Louisiana State University and Agricultural & Mechanical College	M,D,O
Louisiana State University in Shreveport	M
Loyola Marymount University	M
Loyola University Chicago	M,O
Loyola University Maryland	M,O
Malone University	M
Manhattan College	M,O
Marian University (IN)	M
Marquette University	M,D
Marshall University	M
Marymount University	M
Marywood University	M
McDaniel College	M
McNeese State University	M
Mercer University	M,D
Mercy College	M,O
Messiah College	M,O
Michigan State University	M,D,O
Middle Tennessee State University	M
Midwestern State University	M
Milligan College	M,O
Minnesota State University Mankato	M,D
Minnesota State University Moorhead	M,D,O
Mississippi College	M,O
Mississippi State University	M,D,O
Missouri Baptist University	M,O
Missouri State University	M
Montana State University Billings	M
Montana State University–Northern	M
Montclair State University	M,D
Morehead State University	M,D
Mount Mary University	M,D
Murray State University	M,D,O
Naropa University	M
National Louis University	M,D,O
National University	M,O
New Jersey City University	M
New Mexico Highlands University	M
New Mexico State University	M,D,O
New York Institute of Technology	M,O
New York University	M,D,O*
Niagara University	M,O
Nicholls State University	M,O
North Carolina Agricultural and Technical State University	M
North Carolina Central University	M
North Carolina State University	M,D
North Dakota State University	M,D*
Northeastern Illinois University	M
Northern Arizona University	M,D,O
Northern Illinois University	M,D
Northern Kentucky University	M
Northern State University	M
Northern Vermont University–Johnson	M
Northern Vermont University–Lyndon	M
Northwest Christian University	M
Northwestern Oklahoma State University	M
Northwestern State University of Louisiana	M,O
Northwest Nazarene University	M
Nova Southeastern University	M,D,O*
Nyack College	M
Ohio University	M,D
Oklahoma City University	M
Old Dominion University	M,D,O
Oregon State University	M,D
Ottawa University	M
Our Lady of the Lake University	M
Palm Beach Atlantic University	M
Penn State University Park	M,D,O*
Phillips Graduate University	M
Pittsburg State University	M
Plymouth State University	M
Point Loma Nazarene University	M
Pontifical Catholic University of Puerto Rico	M
Prairie View A&M University	M,D
Prescott College	M,D
Providence College	M
Purdue University	M,D,O
Purdue University Northwest	M
Queens College of the City University of New York	M,O
Quincy University	M
Radford University	M
Regent University	M,D,O
Regis University	M,D,O
Rhode Island College	M,O
Richmont Graduate University	M
Rider University	M,O
Rivier University	M,D,O
Roberts Wesleyan College	M,D
Rollins College	M
Rosemont College	M
Rowan University	M
Rutgers University–New Brunswick	M
Sage Graduate School	M,O
St. Bonaventure University	M,O
St. Cloud State University	M
St. John's University (NY)	M,O
St. Lawrence University	M,O
Saint Mary's College of California	M,O
St. Mary's University (United States)	D
Saint Peter's University	M,O
St. Thomas University	M,O
Saint Xavier University	M
Salem College	M
Salem State University	M
Sam Houston State University	M,D
San Diego State University	M
San Jose State University	M,D
Santa Clara University	M,O
Seattle Pacific University	M,D,O
Seattle University	M,D
Seton Hall University	M,D
Shippensburg University of Pennsylvania	M,D
Simon Fraser University	M
Slippery Rock University of Pennsylvania	M
South Carolina State University	M
South Dakota State University	M
Southeastern Louisiana University	M
Southeastern Oklahoma State University	M
Southeastern University (FL)	M
Southeast Missouri State University	M,O
Southern Adventist University	M
Southern Arkansas University–Magnolia	M
Southern Connecticut State University	M,O
Southern Methodist University	M,O
Southern University and Agricultural and Mechanical College	M
Southwestern Oklahoma State University	M
Spalding University	M
Springfield College	M,D,O
State University of New York at New Paltz	M,O
State University of New York at Plattsburgh	M,O
State University of New York College at Oneonta	M,O
Stephen F. Austin State University	M
Stephens College	M,O
Stetson University	M
Suffolk University	M,D,O
Sul Ross State University	M
Syracuse University	M,D*
Texas A&M International University	M
Texas A&M University–Central Texas	M,O
Texas A&M University–Commerce	M,D,O
Texas A&M University–Corpus Christi	M,D
Texas A&M University–Kingsville	M
Texas A&M University–San Antonio	M
Texas Christian University	M,D
Texas Southern University	M,D
Texas State University	M
Texas Tech University	M,D
Texas Woman's University	M,D
Trevecca Nazarene University	M,D
Trinity Washington University	M
Troy University	M,O
Universidad del Turabo	M
Université de Moncton	M
Université Laval	M,D
University at Buffalo, the State University of New York	M,D,O
The University of Akron	M,D
The University of Alabama	M,D,O
The University of Alabama at Birmingham	M
University of Alaska Fairbanks	M,O
University of Alberta	M,D
The University of Arizona	M
University of Arkansas	M,D
University of Arkansas at Little Rock	M
University of Central Arkansas	M
University of Central Florida	M,D,O
University of Central Missouri	M,D,O
University of Central Oklahoma	M
University of Cincinnati	M,D,O
University of Colorado Colorado Springs	M,D
University of Colorado Denver	M
University of Connecticut	M,D*
University of Dayton	M,O
University of Florida	M,D,O
University of Georgia	M,D,O
University of Guam	M
University of Hartford	M,O
University of Holy Cross	M,D
University of Houston–Clear Lake	M
University of Houston–Victoria	M,O
University of Idaho	M,O
University of Illinois at Urbana–Champaign	M,D,O
The University of Iowa	M,D*
University of La Verne	M,D,O
University of Lethbridge	M,D
University of Louisiana at Lafayette	M
University of Louisiana at Monroe	M
University of Louisville	M,D
University of Lynchburg	M
University of Manitoba	M
University of Mary Hardin-Baylor	M
University of Maryland, College Park	M,D,O
University of Maryland Eastern Shore	M
University of Massachusetts Amherst	M,D,O*
University of Massachusetts Boston	M
University of Memphis	M,D
University of Miami	M,O*
University of Minnesota, Twin Cities Campus	M
University of Mississippi	M,D,O
University of Missouri–Kansas City	M,D,O
University of Missouri–St. Louis	D
University of Montana	M,D,O
University of Montevallo	M
University of Nebraska at Kearney	M,O
University of Nebraska at Omaha	M
University of Nevada, Las Vegas	M,D,O
University of Nevada, Reno	M,D,O
University of New Mexico	M,D
University of New Orleans	M,D
University of North Alabama	M
The University of North Carolina at Chapel Hill	M
The University of North Carolina at Charlotte	M,D,O
The University of North Carolina at Greensboro	M,D,O
The University of North Carolina at Pembroke	M
University of Northern Colorado	M,D
University of Northern Iowa	M
University of North Florida	M,D
University of North Texas	M,D,O
University of North Texas at Dallas	M
University of Pennsylvania	M*
University of Phoenix–Las Vegas Campus	M
University of Phoenix–Phoenix Campus	M
University of Puerto Rico–Río Piedras	M,D
University of Puget Sound	M
University of Rochester	M,D*
University of Saint Francis (IN)	M,O
University of Saint Joseph	M
University of St. Thomas (TX)	M,D
University of San Diego	M
University of San Francisco	M
The University of Scranton	M
University of South Africa	M,D
University of South Alabama	M,D,O
University of South Carolina	D,O
University of South Dakota	M,D,O
University of Southern California	M*
University of Southern Maine	M,O
University of South Florida	M,D,O*
The University of Tennessee	M,D,O
The University of Tennessee at Chattanooga	M,D,O
The University of Tennessee at Martin	M
The University of Texas at Austin	M,D
The University of Texas at El Paso	M
The University of Texas at San Antonio	M,D
The University of Texas of the Permian Basin	M
The University of Texas Rio Grande Valley	M
University of the Cumberlands	M,D,O
University of the Southwest	M
The University of Toledo	M,D,O
University of Utah	M,D,O
University of Vermont	M
University of Victoria	M,D
University of Virginia	M,D,O
The University of West Alabama	M,O
University of West Georgia	M,D,O
University of Wisconsin–Madison	M
University of Wisconsin–Oshkosh	M
University of Wisconsin–River Falls	M,O
University of Wisconsin–Superior	M
University of Wyoming	M,D
Utah State University	M,D
Valdosta State University	M,O
Vanderbilt University	M*
Villanova University	M
Virginia Commonwealth University	M,D
Virginia Polytechnic Institute and State University	M,D,O
Virginia State University	M
Wake Forest University	M
Walden University	M,D
Walsh University	M
Waynesburg University	M,D
Wayne State College	M
Wayne State University	M,D,O
West Chester University of Pennsylvania	M,O
Western Connecticut State University	M
Western Illinois University	M
Western Kentucky University	M
Western Michigan University	M,D
Western Washington University	M
Westfield State University	M
Westminster College (PA)	M
West Texas A&M University	M
West Virginia University	M,D
Whitworth University	M
Wichita State University	M,D,O
Widener University	M,D
William Paterson University of New Jersey	M,O
Wilmington University	M,D
Winona State University	M,O
Winthrop University	M
Wright State University	M
Xavier University	M*
Xavier University of Louisiana	M
Youngstown State University	M

CRIMINAL JUSTICE AND CRIMINOLOGY

Adler University	M
Adrian College	M
Albany State University	M
Albertus Magnus College	M
Alliant International University–San Francisco	M
American Public University System	M,D
American University	M,D
American University of Puerto Rico	M
Anderson University (SC)	M
Angelo State University	M
Anna Maria College	M
Arizona State University at the Tempe campus	M,D,O
Arkansas State University	M,O
Ashworth College	M
Auburn University at Montgomery	M
Ball State University	M,O
Bellevue University	M
Boise State University	M
Boston University	M*
Bowling Green State University	M
Bridgewater State University	M
Buffalo State College, State University of New York	M
Cabrini University	M,D
California Coast University	M
California State University, Fresno	M
California State University, Long Beach	M
California State University, Los Angeles	M
California State University, Sacramento	M
California State University, San Bernardino	M
California State University, Stanislaus	M
California University of Pennsylvania	M
Calumet College of Saint Joseph	M
Capella University	M,D
Cardinal Stritch University	M
Caribbean University	M,D
Carnegie Mellon University	M
The Catholic University of America	M
Central Connecticut State University	M
Chaminade University of Honolulu	M
Charleston Southern University	M
Chicago State University	M
Clark Atlanta University	M
Clayton State University	M
Clemson University	M
Coker College	M

College of Saint Elizabeth	M,O
Colorado State University–Global Campus	M
Colorado Technical University Aurora	M
Colorado Technical University Colorado Springs	M
Columbia College (MO)	M
Columbia College (SC)	M
Columbia Southern University	M
Columbus State University	M
Coppin State University	M
Curry College	M
Dallas Baptist University	M
Delta State University	M
DeSales University	M,O
East Carolina University	M,O
East Central University	M
Eastern Kentucky University	M
Eastern Michigan University	M
East Tennessee State University	M,O
Excelsior College	M,O
Fairleigh Dickinson University, Metropolitan Campus	M
Fairmont State University	M
Faulkner University	M
Fayetteville State University	M
Ferris State University	M
Florida Agricultural and Mechanical University	M
Florida Atlantic University	M
Florida Gulf Coast University	M
Florida International University	M,D
Florida State University	M,D
Gannon University	M
George Mason University	M,D
The George Washington University	M,O
Georgia College & State University	M
Georgian Court University	M,O
Georgia Southern University–Armstrong Campus	M,O
Georgia State University	M,D,O
Governors State University	M
The Graduate Center, City University of New York	D
Grambling State University	M
Grand Valley State University	M
Hilbert College	M
Holy Family University	M
Howard Payne University	M
Husson University	M
Illinois State University	M
Indiana State University	M
Indiana University Bloomington	M,D
Indiana University Northwest	M,O
Indiana University of Pennsylvania	M,D
Indiana University–Purdue University Indianapolis	M,O
Inter American University of Puerto Rico, Aguadilla Campus	M
Inter American University of Puerto Rico, Barranquitas Campus	M
Inter American University of Puerto Rico, Metropolitan Campus	M
Inter American University of Puerto Rico, Ponce Campus	M
Iona College	M,O
Jackson State University	M
Jacksonville State University	M
John Jay College of Criminal Justice of the City University of New York	M,D
Johnson & Wales University	M
Kean University	M
Keiser University	M
Kennesaw State University	M
Kent State University	M,D
Keuka College	M
Lamar University	M
Lasell College	M,O
Lewis University	M
Liberty University	M,D,O
Lincoln University (MO)	M
Lindenwood University	M,O
Lindenwood University–Belleville	M
Loma Linda University	M,D
London Metropolitan University	M,D
Long Island University–Brentwood Campus	M,O
Long Island University–LIU Post	M,O
Loyola University Chicago	M
Loyola University New Orleans	M
Lynn University	M
Madonna University	M
Marshall University	M
Marywood University	M
McNeese State University	M
Mercer University	M,D
Mercyhurst University	M,O
Merrimack College	M,O
Methodist University	M
Metropolitan State University	M
Michigan State University	M,D
Middle Tennessee State University	M
Midwestern State University	M,O
Minnesota State University Mankato	M
Mississippi College	M,O
Mississippi Valley State University	M
Missouri Southern State University	M
Missouri State University	M,O
Molloy College	M
Monmouth University	M,O*
Monroe College	M
Morehead State University	M
Mount Mercy University	M
National American University (TX)	M,D
National University	M
New Charter University	M
New Jersey City University	M,D,O
New Mexico State University	M
Niagara University	M
Norfolk State University	M
North Carolina Central University	M
North Dakota State University	M,D*
Northeastern State University	M
Northeastern University	M,D
Northern Arizona University	M,O
Norwich University	M
Nova Southeastern University	M,D,O*
Oklahoma City University	M
Old Dominion University	M,D
Penn State Harrisburg	M,D,O
Penn State University Park	M,D*
Point Park University	M
Pontifical Catholic University of Puerto Rico	M
Pontificia Universidad Catolica Madre y Maestra	M
Portland State University	M
Purdue University Global	M
Radford University	M,O
Regent University	M,D,O
Regis University	M,O
Robert Morris University Illinois	M
Rochester Institute of Technology	M
Roger Williams University	M
Rowan University	M
Rutgers University–Camden	M
Rutgers University–Newark	M,D
Sacred Heart University	M
St. Ambrose University	M
St. Cloud State University	M
St. John's University (NY)	M
Saint Joseph's University	M,O*
Saint Leo University	M
Saint Louis University	M*
Saint Mary's University (Canada)	M
St. Mary's University (United States)	M
Saint Peter's University	M
St. Thomas University	M,O
Salem State University	M
Salve Regina University	M,O
Sam Houston State University	M,D
San Diego State University	M
San Francisco State University	M
San Jose State University	M
Seattle University	M,O
Shippensburg University of Pennsylvania	M
Simon Fraser University	M,D
Simpson College	M
Slippery Rock University of Pennsylvania	M
Southeast Missouri State University	M
Southern Illinois University Carbondale	M,D
Southern New Hampshire University	M
Southern University and Agricultural and Mechanical College	M
Southern University at New Orleans	M
South University	M
South University (SC)	M
South University (GA)	M
South University (AL)	M
South University	M
Southwestern College (KS)	M
Southwest University	M
Stockton University	M
Suffolk University	M
Sul Ross State University	M
Tarleton State University	M
Temple University	M,D*
Tennessee State University	M
Texas A&M International University	M
Texas A&M University–Central Texas	M,O
Texas A&M University–Commerce	M,D,O
Texas A&M University–Kingsville	M
Texas Christian University	M
Texas Southern University	M,D
Texas State University	M,D
Tiffin University	M
Trident University International	M,D
Trine University	M
Troy University	M
Universidad del Este	M
Universidad del Turabo	M
Université de Montréal	M,D
University at Albany, State University of New York	M,D
The University of Alabama	M
The University of Alabama at Birmingham	M
University of Alaska Fairbanks	M
University of Alberta	M,D
University of Antelope Valley	M
University of Arkansas at Little Rock	M,D
University of Baltimore	M
University of California, Irvine	M,D
University of Central Florida	M,D,O
University of Central Missouri	M,D,O
University of Central Oklahoma	M
University of Cincinnati	M,D
University of Colorado Colorado Springs	M
University of Colorado Denver	M,D
University of Delaware	M,D*
University of Denver	M,O
University of Detroit Mercy	M,D,O
University of Florida	M,D
University of Guelph	M,D
University of Houston–Clear Lake	M
University of Houston–Downtown	M
University of Illinois at Chicago	M,D
University of Louisiana at Monroe	M
University of Louisville	M,D
University of Lynchburg	M
University of Management and Technology	M,O
The University of Manchester	M,D
University of Maryland, College Park	M,D
University of Maryland Eastern Shore	M
University of Massachusetts Lowell	M
University of Memphis	M
University of Michigan–Dearborn	M
University of Michigan–Flint	M
University of Minnesota, Duluth	M
University of Mississippi	M,D
University of Missouri–Kansas City	M
University of Missouri–St. Louis	M,D
University of Montana	M
University of Nebraska at Omaha	M,D,O
University of Nevada, Las Vegas	M,D
University of Nevada, Reno	M,D
University of New Haven	M,D,O*
University of North Alabama	M
The University of North Carolina at Charlotte	M
The University of North Carolina at Greensboro	M
The University of North Carolina at Pembroke	M
The University of North Carolina Wilmington	M
University of North Dakota	D
University of Northern Colorado	M
University of North Florida	M
University of North Georgia	M
University of North Texas	M,D,O
University of North Texas at Dallas	M
University of Oklahoma	M,O*
University of Ottawa	M,D
University of Pennsylvania	M,D*
University of Phoenix–Bay Area Campus	M
University of Phoenix–Dallas Campus	M
University of Phoenix–Online Campus	M
University of Phoenix–Phoenix Campus	M
University of Phoenix–San Antonio Campus	M
University of Pittsburgh	M*
University of Providence	M
University of Regina	M
University of San Diego	M
University of South Africa	M,D
University of South Carolina	M,D
University of South Dakota	M
University of Southern Mississippi	M,D
University of South Florida	M,D,O*
University of South Florida Sarasota-Manatee	M
The University of Tampa	M
The University of Tennessee	M,D
The University of Tennessee at Chattanooga	M
The University of Texas at Arlington	M
The University of Texas at Dallas	M,D
The University of Texas at San Antonio	M
The University of Texas at Tyler	M
The University of Texas of the Permian Basin	M
The University of Texas Rio Grande Valley	M
University of the Fraser Valley	M
The University of Toledo	M,O
University of Toronto	M,D
University of West Florida	M
University of West Georgia	M,D,O
University of Windsor	M,D
University of Wisconsin–Milwaukee	M,O*
University of Wisconsin–Platteville	M
Urbana University–A Branch Campus of Franklin University	M
Utica College	M
Virginia Commonwealth University	M,O
Virginia State University	M
Walden University	M,D,O
Waldorf University	M
Washburn University	M
Washington State University	M,D
Wayland Baptist University	M
Waynesburg University	M,D
Wayne State University	M
Webber International University	M
Webster University	M,D,O
West Chester University of Pennsylvania	M
Western Illinois University	M,O
Western Kentucky University	M
Western Oregon University	M
Westfield State University	M
West Texas A&M University	M
West Virginia State University	M
Wichita State University	M
Widener University	M
Wilfrid Laurier University	M
Wilmington University	M
Wright State University	M
Xavier University	M*
Youngstown State University	M

CULTURAL ANTHROPOLOGY

Brandeis University	M,D
California Institute of Integral Studies	M,D,O
Concordia University (Canada)	M,D
Cornell University	D
Duke University	D*
The Graduate Center, City University of New York	D
Memorial University of Newfoundland	M,D
North Carolina State University	M
Rice University	M,D
San Francisco State University	M
Southern Illinois University Edwardsville	M
Southern Methodist University	M,D
University of California, Santa Barbara	M,D
University of California, Santa Cruz	D*
University of Denver	M
University of Michigan	D*
The University of Tennessee	M,D
University of Wisconsin–Madison	D
Washington State University	M,D

CULTURAL STUDIES

American University	M,D,O
The American University of Paris	M
Appalachian State University	M
Arizona State University at the Tempe campus	M,D
Assemblies of God Theological Seminary	M,D
Athabasca University	M,O
Biola University	M,D,O
Boston University	M*
Brock University	M
Carnegie Mellon University	D
Central Michigan University	M
Chapman University	M,D,O*
Charlotte Christian College and Theological Seminary	M,D
Claremont Graduate University	M,D,O
Columbia International University	M,D,O
Concordia University Irvine	M*
Cornell University	M,D
Drew University	M,D,O
Eastern Michigan University	O
Florida State University	M,D
Gardner-Webb University	M,D
George Fox University	M,D,O
George Mason University	D
Georgia State University	M,O
Goucher College	M
Grace Theological Seminary	M,D,O
Graduate Theological Union	M,D,O
Johnson University	M,D,O
Lincoln Christian University	M
Maranatha Baptist University	M
McMaster University	M,D
Michigan Technological University	M,D
Nazarene Theological Seminary	M,D,O
New Mexico State University	M,D,O
New York University	M,D,O*
North Central College	M
Northern Kentucky University	M,O
Northwest University	M
Old Dominion University	M,D,O
Pacific Northwest College of Art	M
Plymouth State University	M
Regent University	M,D
St. Francis Xavier University	M
San Francisco State University	M
School of Visual Arts (NY)	M
Simmons College	M
Simon Fraser University	D
Southern Illinois University Carbondale	M
Stanford University	M,D
Stony Brook University, State University of New York	M,D,O
Taylor College and Seminary	M,O
Texas A&M University	M
Texas A&M University–Kingsville	M
Texas Tech University	M,D
Trent University	D
Trinity College (United States)	M
Union Institute & University	M,D
Union University	M
University of Alaska Fairbanks	M
University of Arkansas	M,D
University of California, Davis	M,D
University of California, Irvine	D
University of California, Riverside	D
University of California, Santa Barbara	M,D
University of Dayton	M
University of Denver	M,O
University of Hawaii at Hilo	M,D*
University of Hawaii at Manoa	O
University of Houston	M
University of Houston–Clear Lake	M
The University of Kansas	M,D
University of Louisiana at Lafayette	M,D
University of Louisville	M,D
The University of Manchester	M,D
University of Massachusetts Boston	M
University of Minnesota, Twin Cities Campus	D
University of Montana	M,D,O

*M—masters degree; D—doctorate; O—other advanced degree; *—Close-Up and/or Display*

University of New Mexico	M,D
University of North Carolina at Asheville	M,O
The University of North Carolina at Charlotte	M,O
University of Oklahoma	M,D*
University of Pittsburgh	O*
University of Southern California	D*
University of Southern Indiana	M
University of Southern Maine	M,O
The University of Texas at Austin	M,D
The University of Texas at San Antonio	M,D
University of the Sacred Heart	M
University of Utah	M,D
University of Washington, Bothell	M
Washington State University	M,D
Wayne State University	M,D
West Chester University of Pennsylvania	M,O
Wheaton College	M,O
Wilfrid Laurier University	M
Wilson College	M

CURRICULUM AND INSTRUCTION

Acadia University	M
Adams State University	M
American College of Education	M
American InterContinental University Online	M
Andrews University	M,D,O
Angelo State University	M
Appalachian State University	M
Arcadia University	M,D,O
Arizona State University at the Tempe campus	M
Arlington Baptist University	M
Auburn University	M,D,O*
Augusta University	M,O
Aurora University	M,D
Austin Peay State University	M,O
Averett University	M
Azusa Pacific University	M*
Ball State University	M,D
Barry University	D,O
Baylor University	M,D
Bay Path University	M
Benedictine University	M
Berry College	M,O
Biola University	M,O
Black Hills State University	M
Bloomsburg University of Pennsylvania	M,O
Bluffton University	M
Bob Jones University	M,D,O
Boise State University	M,D,O
Boston College	M,D,O
Bowling Green State University	M
Bradley University	M
Brandman University	M,D
Brandon University	M,O
Brescia University	M
Buena Vista University	M
Cabrini University	M,D
Caldwell University	M,D,O
California Baptist University	M
California Coast University	M,D
California State Polytechnic University, Pomona	M
California State University, Chico	M
California State University, Fresno	M
California State University, Los Angeles	M
California State University, Northridge	M
California State University, Sacramento	M,D,O
California State University, Stanislaus	M
Calvary University	M
Calvin College	M
Cambridge College	M,D,O
Capella University	M,D
Caribbean University	M,D
Carlow University	M
Carson-Newman University	M
Castleton University	M
Central Michigan University	M,D,O
Central Washington University	M
Chapman University	M,D,O*
City University of Seattle	M,O
Clarion University of Pennsylvania	M
Clark Atlanta University	M
Clarks Summit University	M
Clemson University	M,D,O
Coker College	M
The College at Brockport, State University of New York	M
The College of Idaho	M
The College of Saint Rose	M,O
The College of William and Mary	M,D*
Colorado Christian University	M
Columbia International University	M,D,O
Columbus State University	M,D,O
Concordia University (United States)	M,D
Concordia University Ann Arbor	M
Concordia University Chicago	M
Concordia University Irvine	M*
Concordia University, St. Paul	M,D,O
Coppin State University	M
Cornell University	M,D
Dakota Wesleyan University	M
Dallas Baptist University	M
Delaware State University	M
Delaware Valley University	M
DePaul University	M,D
DeVry University–Folsom Campus	M
Doane University	M,D,O
Drexel University	M,D*
Drury University	M
Duquesne University	M,O
East Carolina University	M,O
Eastern Illinois University	M
Eastern Kentucky University	M
Eastern Mennonite University	M
Eastern Michigan University	M,O
Eastern New Mexico University	M
Eastern Washington University	M
East Tennessee State University	M,O
Emporia State University	M
Evangel University	M,D
Fairleigh Dickinson University, Metropolitan Campus	M,O
Faulkner University	M
Ferris State University	M
Fitchburg State University	M
Florida Atlantic University	M,D,O
Florida Gulf Coast University	M
Florida International University	M,D,O
Florida State University	M,D,O
Fontbonne University	M
Fordham University	M,O
Framingham State University	M
Franciscan University of Steubenville	M
Franklin Pierce University	M,D,O
Freed-Hardeman University	M,O
Fresno Pacific University	M
Frostburg State University	M,D
Furman University	M,O
Gannon University	M,O
Gardner-Webb University	M,D,O
George Mason University	M
The George Washington University	M,D,O
Georgia College & State University	M
Georgia Southern University	M,D
Georgia Southern University–Armstrong Campus	M,O
Georgia State University	M,D
Graceland University (IA)	M
Grambling State University	M,D,O
Grand Canyon University	M,D,O
Grand Valley State University	M
Harvard University	M*
Henderson State University	M,O
Hood College	M,O*
Houston Baptist University	M
Illinois State University	M,D
Indiana State University	M,D
Indiana University Bloomington	M,D,O
Indiana University of Pennsylvania	D
Indiana University–Purdue University Indianapolis	M,O
Inter American University of Puerto Rico, Arecibo Campus	M
Inter American University of Puerto Rico, Barranquitas Campus	M
Inter American University of Puerto Rico, Metropolitan Campus	M,D
Inter American University of Puerto Rico, San Germán Campus	D
Iowa State University of Science and Technology	M,D
John Brown University	M
Kansas State University	M,D,O
Kean University	M
Keene State College	M,O
Kennesaw State University	O
Kent State University	M,D,O
Kent State University at Stark	M
Kutztown University of Pennsylvania	M,D
LaGrange College	M,O
Lasell College	M,O
La Sierra University	M,D,O
Lee University	M,O
Lehigh University	M,D,O
Lesley University	M,D,O
LeTourneau University	M
Lewis & Clark College	M
Lewis University	M
Liberty University	M,D,O
Lincoln Memorial University	M,D,O
Louisiana State University in Shreveport	M,D
Louisiana Tech University	M,D,O
Lourdes University	M
Loyola University Chicago	M,D
Loyola University Maryland	M
Malone University	M
Marian University (WI)	M,D
Marquette University	M,D,O
Martin Luther College	M
Marygrove College	M,O
Marymount University	M
Massachusetts College of Liberal Arts	M,O
McDaniel College	M
McGill University	M,D,O
McKendree University	M,D,O
McNeese State University	M
Medaille College	M
Memorial University of Newfoundland	M,D,O
Mercer University	M,D,O
Mercer University	M,D,O
Merrimack College	M,O
Messiah College	M
Michigan State University	M,D,O
Middle Tennessee State University	M,O
Midwestern State University	M
Minnesota State University Moorhead	M,D,O
Misericordia University	M,D
Mississippi College	M,D,O
Mississippi State University	M,D,O
Mississippi University for Women	M
Montana State University	M,D,O
Montana State University Billings	M
Montclair State University	M
Moravian College	M
Morehead State University	M,O
Mount Saint Vincent University	M
National Louis University	M,D,O
Newman University	M
New Mexico Highlands University	M
New Mexico State University	M,D,O
Nicholls State University	M
North Carolina State University	M,D
Northern Arizona University	M,D
Northern Illinois University	M,D
Northern Michigan University	M
Northern State University	M
Northern Vermont University–Johnson	M
Northern Vermont University–Lyndon	M
Northwestern Oklahoma State University	M
Northwestern State University of Louisiana	M,D
Northwest Nazarene University	M,D,O
Notre Dame de Namur University	M
Oakland City University	M,D
Ohio Dominican University	M
Ohio University	M,D
Ohio Valley University	M
Oklahoma State University	M,D
Old Dominion University	M,D
Olivet Nazarene University	M
Oral Roberts University	M,D
Ottawa University	M
Our Lady of the Lake University	M
Pacific Lutheran University	M
Park University	M,O
Penn State Harrisburg	M,D,O
Penn State University Park	M,D,O*
Penn State York	M,O
Pensacola Christian College	M,D,O
Peru State College	M
Piedmont College	M,D,O
Piedmont International University	M,D
Plymouth State University	D
Point Park University	M,D
Pontifical Catholic University of Puerto Rico	M,D
Post University	M
Prairie View A&M University	M
Purdue University	M,D,O
Quincy University	M
Randolph College	M
Regent University	M,D,O
Regis University	M,O
Rivier University	M,D,O
St. Catherine University	M
St. Francis Xavier University	M
St. John's University (NY)	D
Saint Joseph's University	M,D,O*
Saint Louis University	M,D*
Saint Vincent College	M
Saint Xavier University	M
Salem International University	M
Salisbury University	M
Sam Houston State University	M,D
San Diego State University	M
San Jose State University	M,D
Shawnee State University	M
Shaw University	M
Shepherd University (WV)	M
Shippensburg University of Pennsylvania	M
Simon Fraser University	M,D
Simpson University	M
Sitting Bull College	M
Sonoma State University	M,O
South Dakota State University	M
Southeastern Louisiana University	M
Southeastern University (FL)	M,D
Southern Arkansas University–Magnolia	M
Southern Illinois University Carbondale	M,D
Southern Illinois University Edwardsville	M
Southern New Hampshire University	M,D,O
Southwestern Adventist University	M
Southwestern Assemblies of God University	M
Southwestern College (KS)	M,D
Stanford University	M
State University of New York at Fredonia	M
State University of New York at Oswego	M
State University of New York at Plattsburgh	M
State University of New York College at Potsdam	M
Syracuse University	M,D,O*
Tarleton State University	M
Teachers College, Columbia University	M,D
Tennessee State University	M,D
Tennessee Technological University	M,O
Texas A&M International University	M
Texas A&M University	M,D
Texas A&M University–Central Texas	M,O
Texas A&M University–Commerce	M,D,O
Texas A&M University–Corpus Christi	M,D
Texas A&M University–Texarkana	M
Texas Christian University	M,D
Texas Southern University	M,D
Texas Tech University	M,D
Texas Woman's University	M,D
Trevecca Nazarene University	M,O
Trinity Baptist College	M
Trinity Washington University	M
Tusculum College	M
Universidad Adventista de las Antillas	M
Universidad del Turabo	M,D
Universidad Metropolitana	M
Université de Montréal	M,D,O
Université Laval	M,D
University at Albany, State University of New York	M,D,O
University at Buffalo, the State University of New York	M,D,O
The University of Akron	M
The University of Alabama at Birmingham	O
University of Arkansas	M,D,O
University of Arkansas at Little Rock	M
The University of British Columbia	M,D
University of Calgary	M,D
University of California, Davis	M,D
University of California, San Diego	M,D*
University of Central Arkansas	M,O
University of Central Florida	M,D,O
University of Cincinnati	M,D
University of Colorado Boulder	M,D
University of Colorado Colorado Springs	M,D
University of Connecticut	M,D*
University of Delaware	M,D,O*
University of Denver	M,D,O
University of Detroit Mercy	M,D,O
University of Florida	M,D,O
University of Hawaii at Manoa	M,D
University of Houston	M,D
University of Houston–Clear Lake	M
University of Houston–Downtown	M
University of Houston–Victoria	M,O
University of Idaho	M,O
University of Illinois at Chicago	M,D
University of Illinois at Urbana–Champaign	M,D,O
University of Indianapolis	M
University of Jamestown	M
The University of Kansas	M,D
University of Kentucky	M,D
University of Louisiana at Lafayette	M
University of Louisiana at Monroe	M,D
University of Louisville	M,D,O
University of Lynchburg	M
University of Manitoba	M
University of Mary	M,D
University of Mary Hardin-Baylor	M,D
University of Maryland, College Park	M,D,O
University of Massachusetts Lowell	M
University of Memphis	M,D,O
University of Michigan–Dearborn	D,O
University of Michigan–Flint	M,D,O
University of Minnesota, Twin Cities Campus	M,D
University of Missouri	M,D,O
University of Missouri–Kansas City	M,D,O
University of Missouri–St. Louis	M
University of Montana	M,D
University of Nebraska at Kearney	M
University of Nebraska–Lincoln	M,D,O
University of Nevada, Las Vegas	M,D,O
University of Nevada, Reno	D
University of New England	M,D,O
University of New Hampshire	D,O
The University of North Carolina at Chapel Hill	M,D
The University of North Carolina at Charlotte	M,D,O
The University of North Carolina at Greensboro	M,D,O
The University of North Carolina Wilmington	M,D
University of Northern Colorado	M,D
University of Northern Iowa	D
University of North Georgia	M
University of North Texas	M,D,O
University of North Texas at Dallas	M
University of Oklahoma	M,D*
University of Oregon	M,D
University of Phoenix–Central Valley Campus	M
University of Phoenix–Dallas Campus	M
University of Phoenix–Hawaii Campus	M
University of Phoenix–Houston Campus	M
University of Phoenix–Las Vegas Campus	M
University of Phoenix–Online Campus	M,D,O
University of Phoenix–Phoenix Campus	M
University of Phoenix–Sacramento Valley Campus	M,O
University of Phoenix–San Antonio Campus	M
University of Phoenix–San Diego Campus	M
University of Puerto Rico–Río Piedras	M,D
University of Regina	M
University of Rochester	M,D*
University of St. Francis (IL)	M,D,O
University of Saint Joseph	M
University of St. Thomas (TX)	M,D
University of San Diego	M
University of San Francisco	M,D
University of Saskatchewan	M,D,O
The University of Scranton	M
University of South Africa	M,D
University of South Carolina	D
University of South Dakota	M,D,O
University of Southern Mississippi	M,D

University of South Florida Sarasota-Manatee	M
The University of Tampa	M
The University of Tennessee	M,D,O
The University of Tennessee at Martin	M
The University of Texas at Arlington	M
The University of Texas at Austin	M,D
The University of Texas at El Paso	M,D
The University of Texas at San Antonio	M,D
The University of Texas Rio Grande Valley	M,D
University of the Pacific	M,D,O
University of the Southwest	M
The University of Toledo	M,D,O
University of Vermont	M
University of Victoria	M,D
University of Virginia	M,D,O
University of Washington	M,D
The University of Western Ontario	M
University of West Florida	M,O
University of Wisconsin–Madison	M,D
University of Wisconsin–Milwaukee	M,D,O*
University of Wisconsin–Oshkosh	M
University of Wisconsin–Superior	M
University of Wyoming	M,D
Utah State University	D
Vanguard University of Southern California	M
Virginia Commonwealth University	D
Virginia Polytechnic Institute and State University	M,D,O
Virginia Union University	M
Walden University	M,D,O
Walla Walla University	M
Warner University	M
Washburn University	M
Washington State University	M,D
Waynesburg University	M,D
Wayne State College	M
Wayne State University	M,D,O
Weber State University	M
Western Connecticut State University	M
Western Illinois University	M
Western New England University	M
West Texas A&M University	M
West Virginia University	M,D
Wichita State University	M
William Woods University	M,D,O
Wisconsin Lutheran College	M
Worcester State University	M,O
Wright State University	O
Xavier University of Louisiana	M
Youngstown State University	M

DANCE

Arizona State University at the Tempe campus	M
Bennington College	M
California Institute of the Arts	M,O
California State University, Long Beach	M
Case Western Reserve University	M*
The College at Brockport, State University of New York	M
Eastern Michigan University	M
Florida State University	M
The George Washington University	M,O
Hollins University	M
Jacksonville University	M*
Mills College	M
New Mexico State University	M,D,O
New York University	M,D,O*
Northern Illinois University	M
The Ohio State University	M,D
Saint Mary's College of California	M
Sam Houston State University	M
Sarah Lawrence College	M
Smith College	M
Temple University	M,D*
Texas Woman's University	M,D
Tulane University	M
Université du Québec à Montréal	M
University at Buffalo, the State University of New York	M,D
The University of Arizona	M
University of California, Irvine	M
University of California, Los Angeles	M,D*
University of California, Riverside	M
University of California, San Diego	M,D*
University of Colorado Boulder	M,D
University of Hawaii at Manoa	M,D
University of Illinois at Urbana–Champaign	M
The University of Iowa	M*
University of Maryland, Baltimore County	M
University of Maryland, College Park	M
University of Michigan	M*
University of New Mexico	M
The University of North Carolina at Greensboro	M
University of Oklahoma	M*
University of Oregon	M
The University of Texas at Austin	M,D
University of Utah	M,O
University of Washington	M
Washington University in St. Louis	M
Wayne State University	M,D,O
Wilson College	M
York University	M,D

DATA SCIENCE/DATA ANALYTICS

American University	M,O
Austin Peay State University	M
Azusa Pacific University	M*
Boston University	M,O*
Brandman University	M
Central European University	D
Claremont Graduate University	M,D,O
Clarion University of Pennsylvania	M
College of Saint Elizabeth	M
College of Staten Island of the City University of New York	M,O
Colorado Technical University Aurora	M
Colorado Technical University Colorado Springs	M,D
Columbia University	M*
DePaul University	M,D
DeSales University	M,O
Elmhurst College	M
Emerson College	M
Fairfield University	M,O
Ferris State University	M
Fitchburg State University	M
Florida International University	M,D
Fordham University	M
George Mason University	M,D,O
Grand Canyon University	D
Grand Valley State University	M
HEC Montreal	D
IGlobal University	M
Illinois Institute of Technology	M,D
Indiana University Bloomington	M,O
Indiana University–Purdue University Indianapolis	M,D,O
Johnson & Wales University	M
Kansas State University	M,O
Kennesaw State University	M,D,O
Lawrence Technological University	M,O
Lewis University	M
Lipscomb University	M,O
London Metropolitan University	M,D
Manhattan College	M
Maryville University of Saint Louis	M
Merrimack College	M
Metropolitan State University	M,D,O
Michigan Technological University	M,D,O
Montclair State University	O
National University	M
New College of Florida	M
New Jersey Institute of Technology	M,D,O
The New School	M
New York University	M*
Northcentral University	M,D,O
Northeastern University	M,D
Northwestern University	M
Ohio Dominican University	M
Oregon State University	M
Penn State Great Valley	M,O
Queens College of the City University of New York	M
Radford University	M
Regis University	M,O
Robert Morris University	M,D
Rochester Institute of Technology	O
Rockhurst University	M,O
St. John's University (NY)	M
Saint Leo University	M,D
Saint Mary's College	M
Saint Mary's University of Minnesota	M
Saint Peter's University	M
Seattle Pacific University	M
Slippery Rock University of Pennsylvania	M
Southern Arkansas University–Magnolia	M
Southern Methodist University	M,D
Southern New Hampshire University	M,D,O
Stevens Institute of Technology	M,D,O
Stockton University	M
Suffolk University	M
Syracuse University	M,O*
Texas Tech University	M,D
Tufts University	M,D*
University at Buffalo, the State University of New York	M,D
The University of Arizona	M
University of California, Berkeley	M
University of California, San Diego	M*
University of Colorado Denver	M
University of Denver	M,D
University of Houston–Downtown	M
University of Illinois at Springfield	M
University of Louisville	M,D,O
University of Maryland, Baltimore County	M
University of Maryland University College	M,O
University of Massachusetts Dartmouth	M
University of Michigan	M,D,O*
University of Michigan–Dearborn	M,D
University of Minnesota, Twin Cities Campus	M
University of Mississippi	M,D
University of Nebraska at Omaha	M,D,O
University of Nevada, Las Vegas	M,O
The University of North Carolina Wilmington	M
University of Oklahoma	M*
University of Pennsylvania	M*
University of Pittsburgh	M,D,O*
University of Rochester	M*
University of St. Thomas (MN)	M,O
University of San Francisco	M
University of Southern Indiana	M
University of South Florida	M,D,O*
The University of Tennessee	D
The University of Texas at Dallas	M,D
The University of Texas Health Science Center at Houston	M,D,O
University of Vermont	M,D
University of Virginia	M
University of Washington	M,D
University of West Florida	M
University of Wisconsin–La Crosse	M
Virginia International University	M,O
Walsh College of Accountancy and Business Administration	M
Washington University in St. Louis	M
Wayne State University	M,D,O
Western Governors University	M
Worcester Polytechnic Institute	M,D,O
Yeshiva University	M

DECORATIVE ARTS

Bard Graduate Center	M,D*
Sotheby's Institute of Art–London	M
Sotheby's Institute of Art–New York	M

DEMOGRAPHY AND POPULATION STUDIES

Bowling Green State University	M,D
Cornell University	M,D
Florida State University	M
Harvard University	M,D*
Johns Hopkins University	M,D*
Miami University	M,D
New York University	M,D*
Princeton University	D,O
Université de Montréal	M,D
Université du Québec, Institut National de la Recherche Scientifique	M,D,O
University at Albany, State University of New York	M,D,O
University of Alberta	M,D
University of California, Berkeley	M,D
University of California, Irvine	M
University of Colorado Denver	D
University of Guelph	M,D
University of Hawaii at Manoa	O
University of Pennsylvania	M,D*
University of Puerto Rico–Medical Sciences Campus	M
The University of Texas at San Antonio	D
The University of Texas Medical Branch	D
University of Wisconsin–Madison	M,D

DENTAL HYGIENE

Eastern Washington University	M
Idaho State University	M
Missouri Southern State University	M
The Ohio State University	M,D
Old Dominion University	M
Texas A&M University	M,D,O
Texas Woman's University	M,D
Université de Montréal	O
University of Alberta	O
University of Bridgeport	M
University of Michigan	M*
University of Missouri–Kansas City	M,D,O
University of New Mexico	M
The University of North Carolina at Chapel Hill	M,D
West Virginia University	M,D

DENTISTRY

A.T. Still University	M,D,O
Augusta University	D
Boston University	M,D,O*
Case Western Reserve University	D*
Columbia University	D*
Creighton University	D
East Carolina University	D
Harvard University	M,D,O*
Howard University	D,O
Idaho State University	O
Indiana University–Purdue University Indianapolis	M,D,O
Jacksonville University	M,O*
Loma Linda University	M,D,O
Louisiana State University Health Sciences Center	D
Marquette University	D
McGill University	M,D,O
Medical University of South Carolina	D
Meharry Medical College	D
Midwestern University, Downers Grove Campus	D
Midwestern University, Glendale Campus	D
New York University	D*
Nova Southeastern University	M,D*
The Ohio State University	M,D
Oregon Health & Science University	D,O
Roseman University of Health Sciences	M,D,O
Rutgers University–Newark	M,D,O
Saint Louis University	M*
Southern Illinois University Edwardsville	D
Stony Brook University, State University of New York	D,O
Temple University	D*
Texas A&M University	M,D,O
Tufts University	D*
Universidad Central del Este	D
Universidad Iberoamericana	M,D
Universidad Nacional Pedro Henriquez Urena	D
Université Laval	D
University at Buffalo, the State University of New York	D
The University of Alabama at Birmingham	D
University of Alberta	D
The University of British Columbia	D
University of California, Los Angeles	D,O*
University of California, San Francisco	D
University of Colorado Denver	D,O
University of Connecticut Health Center	D,O
University of Detroit Mercy	M,D,O
University of Florida	D,O
University of Illinois at Chicago	D
The University of Iowa	M,D,O*
University of Kentucky	D
University of Louisville	M,D
The University of Manchester	M,D
University of Manitoba	D
University of Maryland, Baltimore	D,O
University of Michigan	D*
University of Minnesota, Twin Cities Campus	D
University of Mississippi Medical Center	M,D
University of Missouri–Kansas City	M,D,O
University of Nebraska Medical Center	M,D,O
University of Nevada, Las Vegas	M,D,O
University of New England	D
The University of North Carolina at Chapel Hill	D
University of Oklahoma Health Sciences Center	D,O
University of Pennsylvania	D*
University of Pittsburgh	M,D,O*
University of Puerto Rico–Medical Sciences Campus	D
University of Saskatchewan	D
University of Southern California	D*
The University of Tennessee Health Science Center	D
The University of Texas Health Science Center at Houston	M,D
The University of Texas Health Science Center at San Antonio	M,D,O
University of the Pacific	M,D,O
University of Toronto	D
University of Utah	D
University of Washington	M,D,O
The University of Western Ontario	D
Virginia Commonwealth University	M,D
Western University of Health Sciences	D
West Virginia University	M,D

DEVELOPMENTAL BIOLOGY

Albert Einstein College of Medicine	D
Baylor College of Medicine	D
Brigham Young University	M,D
California Institute of Technology	D
California State University, Sacramento	M
Carnegie Mellon University	M,D
Columbia University	M,D*
Cornell University	D
Duke University	O*
Emory University	D
Illinois State University	M,D
Iowa State University of Science and Technology	M,D
Irell & Manella Graduate School of Biological Sciences	D*
Johns Hopkins University	D*
Louisiana State University Health Sciences Center	D
Marquette University	M,D
Massachusetts Institute of Technology	D
Medical University of South Carolina	D
New York University	M,D*
Northwestern University	D
The Ohio State University	M,D
Oregon Health & Science University	D
Penn State Hershey Medical Center	D
Purdue University	M,D
Rutgers University–Newark	D,O
Rutgers University–New Brunswick	M,D
San Francisco State University	M
Stanford University	M,D
Stony Brook University, State University of New York	M,D
Thomas Jefferson University	M
Tufts University	D*
The University of Alabama at Birmingham	D
The University of British Columbia	M,D
University of California, Davis	M,D
University of California, Irvine	M,D
University of California, Los Angeles	M,D*
University of California, Riverside	M,D
University of California, San Francisco	D
University of California, Santa Barbara	M,D

*M—masters degree; D—doctorate; O—other advanced degree; *—Close-Up and/or Display*

University of California, Santa Cruz	M,D*
University of Chicago	D
University of Cincinnati	D
University of Colorado Boulder	M,D
University of Colorado Denver	M,D
University of Connecticut	M,D*
University of Connecticut Health Center	D
University of Delaware	M,D*
University of Hawaii at Manoa	M,D
University of Illinois at Urbana–Champaign	D
The University of Kansas	D
The University of Manchester	M,D
University of Massachusetts Amherst	D*
University of Miami	D*
University of Michigan	M,D*
University of Minnesota, Twin Cities Campus	M,D
University of Montana	D
The University of North Carolina at Chapel Hill	M,D
University of Pennsylvania	D*
University of Pittsburgh	D*
University of South Carolina	M,D
University of Southern California	D*
The University of Texas Southwestern Medical Center	D
Vanderbilt University	M,D*
Washington University in St. Louis	D
Wesleyan University	D
West Virginia University	M,D
Yale University	D

DEVELOPMENTAL EDUCATION

East Tennessee State University	M,O
Ferris State University	M
Grambling State University	M,D,O
Instituto Tecnológico y de Estudios Superiores de Monterrey, Campus Ciudad Obregón	M
National Louis University	M,D,O
North Carolina State University	M,D,O
Penn State Harrisburg	M,D,O
Rutgers University–New Brunswick	M
Sam Houston State University	M,D
Texas State University	M,D
The University of Iowa	M,D*
Walden University	M,D,O

DEVELOPMENTAL PSYCHOLOGY

Andrews University	M,D
Arizona State University at the Tempe campus	M,D
Azusa Pacific University	M*
Bay Path University	M
Boston College	M,D
Boston Graduate School of Psychoanalysis	O
Bowling Green State University	M,D
Brandeis University	M,D
Capella University	M
Carnegie Mellon University	D
Chatham University	M,D
Claremont Graduate University	M,D,O
Clark University	D
Clayton State University	M
Cornell University	M,D
Delaware Valley University	M
Duke University	D*
Emory University	D
Erikson Institute	M,O
Fielding Graduate University	M,D,O
Florida International University	M,D
Florida State University	D
Fordham University	D
George Mason University	M,D,O
Georgia State University	D
The Graduate Center, City University of New York	D
Harvard University	D*
Howard University	M,D
Humboldt State University	M
Illinois State University	M,D,O
Indiana University Bloomington	D
La Salle University	M,D
Liberty University	M,D,O
Louisiana State University and Agricultural & Mechanical College	M,D
Loyola University Chicago	M,D
McGill University	M,D,O
New York University	M,D*
North Carolina State University	D
North Dakota State University	D*
The Ohio State University	D
Pace University	M,D
Pontificia Universidad Catolica Madre y Maestra	M
Queen's University at Kingston	M,D
Regis University	M,D,O
San Francisco State University	M,O
Teachers College, Columbia University	M,D
Texas Christian University	M,D
Université de Montréal	M,D
The University of Alabama at Birmingham	M,D
The University of British Columbia	M,D
University of Connecticut	M,D*
University of Denver	D
University of Houston	M,D
University of Illinois at Chicago	M,D
The University of Kansas	M,D
University of Louisville	D
The University of Manchester	M,D
University of Maryland, Baltimore County	D
University of Maryland, College Park	M,D
University of Massachusetts Amherst	M,D*
University of Miami	M,D*
University of Michigan	D*
University of Montana	M,D,O
University of Nebraska–Lincoln	M,D,O
University of New Mexico	D
The University of North Carolina at Chapel Hill	D
The University of North Carolina at Greensboro	M,D
University of Notre Dame	D
University of Oregon	M,D
University of Pittsburgh	M,D*
University of Rochester	D*
University of Southern California	M,D*
The University of Texas at Austin	D
University of Utah	D
University of Vermont	D
University of Victoria	M,D
University of Washington	M,D
University of Wisconsin–Madison	D
University of Wisconsin–Milwaukee	M,D,O*
Viterbo University	M
Washington University in St. Louis	D
Wilfrid Laurier University	M,D
Yale University	D

DISABILITY STUDIES

Brandeis University	D
Brock University	M,O
California Baptist University	M
Chapman University	M,D,O*
Montclair State University	M,O
Syracuse University	O*
University of Hawaii at Manoa	O
University of Illinois at Chicago	M,D
University of Manitoba	M
University of Northern British Columbia	M,D,O
University of Pittsburgh	O*
Utah State University	M,D,O
York University	M,D

DISTANCE EDUCATION DEVELOPMENT

Athabasca University	M,D,O
Barry University	O
Boise State University	M,D,O
Brandeis University	M
California Baptist University	M
Capella University	M,D
Carlow University	M,O
Clemson University	M,D,O
Coastal Carolina University	M,O
College of Saint Elizabeth	M,O
Colorado Christian University	M
Dallas Baptist University	M
East Carolina University	M,O
Eastern Michigan University	M,O
Emporia State University	M,O
Endicott College	M
The George Washington University	O
Kansas State University	M,D,O
Keiser University	M
Lenoir-Rhyne University	M
Lesley University	M,D,O
Millersville University of Pennsylvania	M
National University	M,O
New Mexico State University	O
Nova Southeastern University	M,D,O*
Post University	M
Regent University	M,D,O
Télé-université	M,D
Thomas Edison State University	M,O
University at Buffalo, the State University of New York	M,D,O
University of Colorado Denver	M
University of Illinois at Springfield	M,O
University of Maryland, Baltimore County	M,O
University of Maryland University College	M
University of Nevada, Las Vegas	M,D,O
University of South Florida	O*
Virginia Polytechnic Institute and State University	M,O
Walden University	M,D,O
Waynesburg University	M,D
Wayne State University	M,D,O
Western Illinois University	M,O
Wilkes University	M,D

EARLY CHILDHOOD EDUCATION

Alabama Agricultural and Mechanical University	M,D,O
Alabama State University	M,O
Albany State University	M,O
Albright College	M
American International College	M,D,O
Anna Maria College	M,O
Antioch University New England	M
Arcadia University	M,D,O
Arkansas State University	M,D,O
Auburn University at Montgomery	M,O
Avila University	M,O
Bank Street College of Education	M
Barry University	M,D,O
Bayamón Central University	M,O
Berry College	M
Binghamton University, State University of New York	M
Biola University	M,O
Bloomsburg University of Pennsylvania	M
Boise State University	M
Boston College	M
Brandman University	M,D
Brenau University	M,O
Bridgewater State University	M
Brooklyn College of the City University of New York	M,O
Buffalo State College, State University of New York	M
Cabrini University	M,D
California State University, Dominguez Hills	M
California State University, East Bay	M
California State University, Fresno	M
California State University, Northridge	M
California State University, Sacramento	M,D,O
California University of Pennsylvania	M
Cambridge College	M,D,O
Canisius College	M
Capella University	M
Caribbean University	M,D
Carlow University	M,O
Carroll University	M
The Catholic University of America	M,O
Central Connecticut State University	M,O
Central Michigan University	M,O
Chaminade University of Honolulu	M
Champlain College	M
Chatham University	M
Chestnut Hill College	M
Chicago State University	M
The Citadel, The Military College of South Carolina	M,O
City College of the City University of New York	M
Clarion University of Pennsylvania	M
Clarkson University	M
Clemson University	M,D,O
Cleveland State University	M
The College at Brockport, State University of New York	M
College of Charleston	M
The College of New Jersey	M
The College of New Rochelle	M
College of Saint Elizabeth	M,O
The College of Saint Rose	M,O
College of Staten Island of the City University of New York	M
Colorado Christian University	M
Columbia International University	M,D,O
Columbus State University	M,O
Concordia University (United States)	M,D
Concordia University Chicago	M,D
Concordia University, Nebraska	M
Concordia University, St. Paul	M,D,O
Concordia University Wisconsin	M
Daemen College	M
Dallas Baptist University	M,D
DePaul University	M,D
Dominican University	M
Duquesne University	M
East Carolina University	M,D
Eastern Connecticut State University	M
Eastern Illinois University	M
Eastern Michigan University	M
Eastern Nazarene College	M,O
Eastern New Mexico University	M
Eastern University	M,O
Eastern Washington University	M
East Stroudsburg University of Pennsylvania	M
East Tennessee State University	M,D,O
Edinboro University of Pennsylvania	M,O
Elms College	M,O
Emporia State University	M
Endicott College	M
Erikson Institute	M,D
Fairleigh Dickinson University, Florham Campus	M,O
Fairleigh Dickinson University, Metropolitan Campus	M
Fielding Graduate University	M,D,O
Fitchburg State University	M
Five Towns College	M,D
Florida Atlantic University	M,D,O
Florida International University	M,D,O
Florida State University	M,D,O
Fontbonne University	M
Fordham University	M,O
Framingham State University	M
Furman University	M,O
Gallaudet University	M,D,O
Gateway Seminary	M,D,O
George Mason University	M
The George Washington University	M
Georgia College & State University	M
Georgia Southern University	M,O
Georgia Southern University–Armstrong Campus	M,O
Georgia Southwestern State University	M,O
Georgia State University	M,D,O
Gordon College	M,O
Governors State University	M
Grand Canyon University	M,D,O
Grand Valley State University	M
Hampton University	M
Harding University	M,O
Hebrew College	M,O
Henderson State University	M,O
Hofstra University	M,D,O
Holy Family University	M
Hunter College of the City University of New York	M,D,O
Indiana University–Purdue University Indianapolis	M,O
Inter American University of Puerto Rico, Guayama Campus	M
Iona College	M
Jackson State University	M,D,O
Jacksonville State University	M
James Madison University	M
Johns Hopkins University	M*
Jose Maria Vargas University	M
Kansas State University	M,D,O
Kean University	M
Kennesaw State University	M
Kent State University	M,D,O
Keuka College	M
Keystone College	M
Lander University	M
La Salle University	M,O
Lee University	M,O
Lehigh University	M,D,O
Lehman College of the City University of New York	M
Le Moyne College	M,O
Lesley University	M,D,O
Lewis University	M
Lincoln University (PA)	M
London Metropolitan University	M,D
Long Island University–Brentwood Campus	M,O
Long Island University–Hudson	M,O
Long Island University–LIU Brooklyn	M,O
Long Island University–LIU Post	M,D,O
Long Island University–Riverhead	M,O
Louisiana Tech University	M,D,O
Loyola University Maryland	M,O
Lynn University	M,D
Manhattan College	M,O
Manhattanville College	M,O
Martin Luther College	M
Marygrove College	M,O
Maryville University of Saint Louis	M,D
Marywood University	M
McNeese State University	O
Mercer University	M,D,O
Mercer University	M,D,O
Mercy College	M
Merrimack College	M,O
Middle Tennessee State University	M,O
Millersville University of Pennsylvania	M
Milligan College	M,D,O
Mills College	M
Mississippi State University	M,D,O
Missouri Southern State University	M
Missouri State University	M
Missouri Western State University	M,O
Molloy College	M,O
Monmouth University	M,D,O*
Mount St. Joseph University	M,O
Murray State University	M,O
National Louis University	M,D,O
Nazareth College of Rochester	M
New Jersey City University	M
New Mexico State University	M,D,O
New York Institute of Technology	M
New York University	M*
Niagara University	M,O
Norfolk State University	M
North Carolina Agricultural and Technical State University	M
Northeastern Illinois University	M
Northeastern State University	M
Northern Arizona University	M,D,O
Northern Illinois University	M
Northwestern College	M,O
Northwestern State University of Louisiana	M
Northwest Missouri State University	M,D,O
Oakland University	M,D,O
Oklahoma City University	M
Old Dominion University	M,D
Ottawa University	M
Pace University	M,O
Pacific Oaks College	M
Pacific University	M
Piedmont College	M,D,O
Pontificia Universidad Catolica Madre y Maestra	M
Prescott College	M,D
Queens College of the City University of New York	M,O
Radford University	M
Regent University	M,D,O
Reinhardt University	M
Rhode Island College	M
Rider University	M
Rivier University	M,D,O
Roberts Wesleyan College	M
Rockford University	M
Roosevelt University	M
Rutgers University–New Brunswick	M,D
Saginaw Valley State University	M
St. Ambrose University	M
St. Bonaventure University	M
St. Catherine University	M
St. John's University (NY)	M,D,O
St. Joseph's College, Long Island Campus	M
Saint Joseph's University	M,D,O*
Saint Mary's College of California	M
Saint Xavier University	M
Salem State University	M
San Francisco State University	M,D,O
San Ignacio University	M
Shaw University	M
Shenandoah University	M,D,O
Shippensburg University of Pennsylvania	M
Siena Heights University	M,O
Sonoma State University	M,O
South Carolina State University	M
Southern New Hampshire University	M,D,O
Southern Oregon University	M
Southwestern College (KS)	M,D

Southwestern Oklahoma State University	M
Southwest Minnesota State University	M
Springfield College	M,O
Spring Hill College	M
State University of New York at Fredonia	M
State University of New York at New Paltz	M
State University of New York at Oswego	M
State University of New York at Plattsburgh	O
State University of New York College at Cortland	M
State University of New York College at Potsdam	M
Stephen F. Austin State University	M
Syracuse University	M*
Teachers College, Columbia University	M,D
Teachers College of San Joaquin	M
Tennessee Technological University	M,O
Texas A&M University–Commerce	M,D,O
Texas A&M University–Corpus Christi	M,D
Texas A&M University–Kingsville	M
Texas A&M University–San Antonio	M
Texas State University	M
Texas Woman's University	M,D
Theological University of the Caribbean	M,D
Towson University	M,O
Trident University International	M
Trinity Washington University	M
Troy University	M,O
Universidad del Turabo	M
University at Buffalo, the State University of New York	M,D,O
The University of Alabama at Birmingham	M,D
University of Alaska Anchorage	M,O
University of Arkansas	M
University of Bridgeport	M,D,O
University of Central Florida	D
University of Central Missouri	M,D,O
University of Central Oklahoma	M
University of Colorado Denver	M,D
University of Dayton	M
University of Denver	M,D,O
University of Florida	M,D,O
University of Hartford	M
University of Hawaii at Manoa	M
University of Houston–Clear Lake	M
University of Illinois at Chicago	M,D
The University of Kansas	M,D,O
University of Kentucky	M,D
University of Louisiana at Lafayette	M
University of Louisville	M,D,O
University of Maine	M,D,O
University of Maine at Farmington	M
University of Maryland, Baltimore County	M
University of Massachusetts Amherst	M,D,O*
University of Massachusetts Boston	D
University of Memphis	M,D,O
University of Miami	M,O*
University of Michigan–Dearborn	M
University of Michigan–Flint	M,D,O
University of Minnesota, Twin Cities Campus	M,D,O
University of Mississippi	M,D,O
University of Missouri	M,D,O
University of Missouri–St. Louis	M
University of Montana	M,D
University of Nebraska at Kearney	M
University of Nebraska–Lincoln	M,D
University of Nevada, Las Vegas	M,D,O
University of New England	M,D,O
University of New Hampshire	M
University of New Mexico	D
The University of North Carolina at Chapel Hill	M,D
The University of North Carolina at Charlotte	M,D,O
The University of North Carolina at Greensboro	M,D,O
The University of North Carolina Wilmington	M
University of North Dakota	M
University of Northern Iowa	M
University of North Georgia	M
University of North Texas	M,D,O
University of Oklahoma	M,D*
University of Phoenix–Bay Area Campus	M,D,O
University of Phoenix–Online Campus	M,O
University of Phoenix–Phoenix Campus	M
University of Pittsburgh	M*
University of Puerto Rico–Río Piedras	M
University of South Alabama	M,D
University of South Carolina	M,D
University of South Carolina Upstate	M
University of South Dakota	M,D,O
University of South Florida	M,D,O*
The University of Tennessee	M,D,O
The University of Texas at Austin	M,D
The University of Texas at San Antonio	M,D
The University of Texas at Tyler	M
The University of Texas of the Permian Basin	M
The University of Texas Rio Grande Valley	M
University of the District of Columbia	M
University of the Sacred Heart	M,O
University of the Southwest	M
The University of Toledo	M,D,O
University of Utah	M,D
University of Vermont	M
University of Victoria	M,D
University of Virginia	M,D
The University of West Alabama	M,O
University of West Georgia	M,D,O
University of Wisconsin–Milwaukee	M*
University of Wisconsin–Oshkosh	M
Upper Iowa University	M
Ursuline College	M
Virginia Commonwealth University	M
Viterbo University	M,O
Wagner College	M
Walden University	M,D,O
Wayne State College	M
Wayne State University	M,D,O
Webster University	M,O
Wesleyan College	M
West Chester University of Pennsylvania	M,O
Western Kentucky University	M,O
Western Oregon University	M
Westfield State University	M
Westminster College (PA)	M
West Virginia University	M,D
Wichita State University	M
Widener University	M,D
William Paterson University of New Jersey	M,O
Worcester State University	M,O
Xavier University	M*
Youngstown State University	M

EAST EUROPEAN AND RUSSIAN STUDIES

Boston College	M
Brown University	M,D
Carleton University	M,O
Columbia University	M,D*
Cornell University	M,D
Florida State University	M
Georgetown University	M
The George Washington University	M
Harvard University	M*
Indiana University Bloomington	M,O
The Ohio State University	M,D
Stanford University	M
University of Alberta	M,D
The University of British Columbia	M,D
University of Colorado Boulder	M
University of Illinois at Chicago	M,D
University of Illinois at Urbana–Champaign	M
The University of Kansas	M,O
The University of Manchester	D
University of Michigan	M,O*
The University of North Carolina at Chapel Hill	M
University of Pittsburgh	O*
University of Saskatchewan	M
The University of Texas at Austin	M
University of Toronto	M
University of Washington	M
Yale University	M,D

ECOLOGY

Baylor University	D
Brown University	D
California Institute of Integral Studies	M,D,O
California State University, Stanislaus	M
Central Washington University	M
Columbia University	M,D*
Cornell University	M,D
Dalhousie University	M
Dartmouth College	D*
Duke University	D,O*
Eastern Kentucky University	M
Emory University	D
Florida Institute of Technology	M,D
Florida State University	M,D
Frostburg State University	M
George Mason University	M,D
Illinois State University	M,D
Indiana State University	M,D
Indiana University Bloomington	M,D,O
Inter American University of Puerto Rico, Bayamón Campus	M
Iowa State University of Science and Technology	M,D
Kent State University	M,D
Laurentian University	M,D
Lesley University	M,D,O
Marquette University	M,D
Michigan State University	D
Michigan Technological University	M,D
Montana State University	M,D
Montclair State University	M
Naropa University	M
Northeastern Illinois University	M
The Ohio State University	M,D
Ohio University	M,D
Oklahoma State University	M,D
Old Dominion University	D
Oregon State University	M,D
Penn State University Park	M,D*
Princeton University	D
Purdue University	M,D
Rice University	M,D
Rutgers University–New Brunswick	M,D
San Diego State University	M,D
San Francisco State University	M
San Jose State University	M
Stanford University	M,D
State University of New York College of Environmental Science and Forestry	M,D
Stony Brook University, State University of New York	M,D
Tulane University	M,D
Universidad Nacional Pedro Henriquez Urena	M
University at Buffalo, the State University of New York	M,D,O
University of Alberta	M,D
The University of Arizona	M,D
University of California, Davis	M,D
University of California, Irvine	M,D
University of California, Los Angeles	M,D*
University of California, Santa Barbara	M,D
University of California, Santa Cruz	M,D*
University of Chicago	D
University of Colorado Boulder	M,D
University of Colorado Denver	M
University of Connecticut	M,D*
University of Delaware	M,D*
University of Denver	M,D
University of Florida	M,D,O
University of Georgia	M,D
University of Guelph	M,D
University of Illinois at Urbana–Champaign	M,D
The University of Kansas	M,D
The University of Manchester	M,D
University of Manitoba	M,D
University of Maryland, College Park	M,D
University of Michigan	M,D*
University of Minnesota, Twin Cities Campus	M,D
University of Missouri	M,D
University of Montana	M,D
University of Nevada, Reno	D
University of New Haven	M*
The University of North Carolina at Chapel Hill	M,D
University of Notre Dame	M,D
University of Oklahoma	M,D*
University of Oregon	M,D
University of Pittsburgh	D*
University of Puerto Rico–Río Piedras	M,D
University of Rhode Island	M,D*
University of Rochester	M,D*
University of South Carolina	M,D
University of South Florida	M,D*
The University of Tennessee	M,D
The University of Texas at Austin	D
The University of Texas at San Antonio	M
The University of Toledo	M,D
University of Toronto	M,D
University of Washington	M,D
University of Wisconsin–Madison	M
University of Wyoming	M,D
Utah State University	M,D
Washington University in St. Louis	D
Wesleyan University	D
Western Illinois University	D
Yale University	D

ECONOMIC DEVELOPMENT

Albany State University	M
The American University in Cairo	M,O
Ball State University	M,O
Boston University	M*
The Catholic University of America	M
Claremont Graduate University	M,D,O
Cleveland State University	M,O
Concordia University (Canada)	O
Cornell University	M,D
East Carolina University	M,O
East Tennessee State University	M,O
Fordham University	M,O
Georgetown University	D
Georgia Institute of Technology	M,D
Georgia State University	M,D,O
Indiana University Bloomington	M,D,O
Johnson & Wales University	M
Murray State University	M
New Mexico State University	M,D,O
Northeastern University	M
Southern New Hampshire University	M,D,O
State University of New York Empire State College	M
Thomas Edison State University	M
Troy University	M
Université de Sherbrooke	D
University at Buffalo, the State University of New York	M,D,O
University of Central Arkansas	M,O
University of Colorado Denver	M
University of Houston–Victoria	M
University of Massachusetts Lowell	M,O
University of New Hampshire	M
University of North Alabama	M
The University of North Carolina at Greensboro	M,D,O
University of Oklahoma	M,D*
University of Pennsylvania	M,O*
University of Puerto Rico–Río Piedras	M
University of Southern California	M,D*
University of Southern Mississippi	M
University of Waterloo	M
Vanderbilt University	M,D*
Wayne State University	M,D,O
Western Illinois University	M
Williams College	M
Yale University	M

ECONOMICS

Albany State University	M
American University	M,D,O
The American University in Cairo	M,O
American University of Armenia	M
American University of Beirut	M,D
Andrews University	M
Arizona State University at the Tempe campus	D
Assumption College	M,O
Auburn University	M,D*
Auburn University at Montgomery	M
Bard College	M
Baruch College of the City University of New York	M*
Baylor University	M
Binghamton University, State University of New York	M,D
Boise State University	M
Boston College	D
Boston University	M*
Bowling Green State University	M
Brandeis University	M,D
Brock University	M
Brooklyn College of the City University of New York	M
Brown University	D
Buffalo State College, State University of New York	M
California Polytechnic State University, San Luis Obispo	M*
California State Polytechnic University, Pomona	M
California State University, East Bay	M
California State University, Fullerton	M
California State University, Long Beach	M
California State University, Los Angeles	M
California University of Management and Sciences	M,D
Campbellsville University	M,D
Carleton University	M,D
Carnegie Mellon University	D
Central European University	M,D
Central Michigan University	M
City College of the City University of New York	M
Claremont Graduate University	M,D,O
Clark Atlanta University	M
Clark University	D
Clemson University	M,D
Cleveland State University	M,O
Colorado State University	M,D
Columbia University	M,D*
Concordia University (Canada)	M,D,O
Copenhagen Business School	M,D
Cornell University	M,D
Dalhousie University	M,D
DePaul University	M,D
Drexel University	M,D,O*
Duke University	M,D*
Eastern Illinois University	M
Eastern Michigan University	M,O
Emory University	D
Florida Atlantic University	M
Florida International University	M,D
Florida State University	M,D
Fordham University	M,D,O
George Mason University	M,D
Georgetown University	D
The George Washington University	M,D
Georgia Institute of Technology	M,D
Georgia State University	M,D
The Graduate Center, City University of New York	D
Harvard University	D*
Howard University	M,D
Hunter College of the City University of New York	M
Illinois State University	M
Indiana University Bloomington	M,D
Indiana University–Purdue University Indianapolis	M
Instituto Tecnologico de Santo Domingo	M,O
Instituto Tecnológico y de Estudios Superiores de Monterrey, Campus Ciudad de México	M,D
Iowa State University of Science and Technology	M,D
Johns Hopkins University	D*
Kansas State University	M,D
Kent State University	M
Lakehead University	M
Lee University	M,O
Lehigh University	M,D
Louisiana State University and Agricultural & Mechanical College	M,D
Loyola University Chicago	M
Marquette University	M,O
Massachusetts Institute of Technology	M,D
McGill University	M,D
McMaster University	M,D
Memorial University of Newfoundland	M
Miami University	M

*M—masters degree; D—doctorate; O—other advanced degree; *—Close-Up and/or Display*

Michigan State University	M,D
Middle Tennessee State University	M,D
Mississippi State University	M,D
Morgan State University	M
Murray State University	M
New Mexico State University	M,D,O
The New School	M,D
New York University	M,D,O*
North Carolina State University	M,D
Northeastern University	M,D
Northern Illinois University	M,D
Northwestern University	D
Oakland University	M,O
The Ohio State University	M,D
Ohio University	M
Oklahoma State University	M,D
Old Dominion University	M
Pace University	O
Penn State University Park	M,D*
Pepperdine University	M
Peru State College	M
Portland State University	M,D,O
Princeton University	D,O
Purdue University	D
Regent University	M,D,O
Regis University	M,O
Rice University	M,D
Roosevelt University	M
Rutgers University–Newark	M,D
Rutgers University–New Brunswick	M,D
St. Cloud State University	M
San Diego State University	M
San Francisco State University	M
San Jose State University	M
Simon Fraser University	M,D
South Dakota State University	M
Southern Illinois University Carbondale	M,D
Southern Illinois University Edwardsville	M
Southern Methodist University	M,D
Southern New Hampshire University	M,D,O
Stanford University	D
State University of New York College of Environmental Science and Forestry	M,D
Stony Brook University, State University of New York	M,D
Syracuse University	M,D*
Teachers College, Columbia University	M,D
Temple University	M,D*
Texas A&M University	M,D
Texas Tech University	M,D
Troy University	M
Tufts University	M,D*
Tulane University	M,D
Universidad de las Américas Puebla	M
Université de Moncton	M
Université de Montréal	M,D,O
Université de Sherbrooke	M,D
Université du Québec à Montréal	M,D
Université Laval	M,D
University at Albany, State University of New York	M,D,O
University at Buffalo, the State University of New York	M,D,O
The University of Akron	M
The University of Alabama	M,D
University of Alaska Fairbanks	M
University of Alberta	M,D
The University of Arizona	M,D
University of Arkansas	M,D
The University of British Columbia	M,D
University of Calgary	M,D
University of California, Berkeley	D
University of California, Davis	M,D
University of California, Irvine	M,D
University of California, Los Angeles	D*
University of California, Riverside	M,D
University of California, San Diego	D*
University of California, Santa Barbara	M,D
University of California, Santa Cruz	D*
University of Chicago	M,D,O
University of Cincinnati	D
University of Colorado Boulder	M,D
University of Colorado Denver	M
University of Connecticut	M,D*
University of Delaware	M,D*
University of Denver	M
University of Detroit Mercy	M,D,O
University of Florida	M,D
University of Georgia	M,D
University of Guelph	M,D
University of Hawaii at Manoa	M,D
University of Houston	M,D
University of Illinois at Chicago	M,D
University of Illinois at Urbana–Champaign	M,D
The University of Iowa	D*
The University of Kansas	M,D
University of Kentucky	M,D
University of Lethbridge	M,D
University of Maine	M
University of Manitoba	M,D
University of Maryland, Baltimore County	M,D
University of Maryland, College Park	M,D
University of Massachusetts Amherst	M,D*
University of Massachusetts Lowell	M,O
University of Memphis	M,D
University of Michigan	M,D*
University of Minnesota, Twin Cities Campus	M,D
University of Mississippi	M,D
University of Missouri	M,D
University of Missouri–Kansas City	M,D
University of Missouri–St. Louis	M
University of Montana	M
University of Nebraska at Omaha	M
University of Nebraska–Lincoln	M,D
University of Nevada, Las Vegas	M
University of Nevada, Reno	M
University of New Brunswick Fredericton	M
University of New Hampshire	M,D
University of New Mexico	M,D
University of New Orleans	D
The University of North Carolina at Chapel Hill	M,D
The University of North Carolina at Charlotte	M,O
The University of North Carolina at Greensboro	D
University of North Florida	M
University of North Texas	M,D,O
University of Notre Dame	M,D
University of Oklahoma	M,D*
University of Oregon	M,D
University of Ottawa	M,D
University of Pennsylvania	M,D*
University of Pittsburgh	M,D*
University of Puerto Rico–Río Piedras	M
University of Regina	M,D,O
University of Rhode Island	M,D*
University of Rochester	D*
University of San Francisco	M
University of Saskatchewan	M,O
University of South Africa	M,D
University of South Carolina	M,D
University of Southern California	M,D*
University of Southern Mississippi	M
University of South Florida	M,D*
The University of Tennessee	M,D
The University of Texas at Arlington	M
The University of Texas at Austin	M,D
The University of Texas at Dallas	M,D
The University of Texas at El Paso	M
The University of Texas at San Antonio	M
The University of Toledo	M,D,O
University of Toronto	M,D
University of Utah	M,D
University of Vermont	M,D,O
University of Victoria	M,D
University of Virginia	M,D
University of Washington	D
University of Waterloo	M,D
The University of Western Ontario	M,D
University of Windsor	M
University of Wisconsin–Madison	D
University of Wisconsin–Milwaukee	M,D*
University of Wyoming	M,D
Utah State University	M,D
Vanderbilt University	M,D*
Virginia Commonwealth University	M
Virginia Polytechnic Institute and State University	M,D
Virginia State University	M
Washington State University	M,D,O
Washington University in St. Louis	D
Wayne State University	M,D
Western Illinois University	M
Western Michigan University	M,D
West Texas A&M University	M
West Virginia University	M,D,O
Wichita State University	M
Wilfrid Laurier University	M,D
Wright State University	M
Yale University	M,D
Yeshiva University	M
York University	M,D
Youngstown State University	M

EDUCATION—GENERAL

Abilene Christian University	M,O
Acacia University	M
Acadia University	M,D
Adams State University	M
Adelphi University	M,D,O
Alabama Agricultural and Mechanical University	M,D,O
Alabama State University	M,D,O
Alaska Pacific University	M
Albany State University	M,O
Albertus Magnus College	M
Albright College	M
Alcorn State University	M,O
Alfred University	M
Alliant International University–Los Angeles	M,O
Alliant International University–Sacramento	M,O
Alliant International University–San Diego	M,O
Alliant International University–San Francisco	M,O
Alvernia University	M
Alverno College	M
American College of Education	M
American InterContinental University Online	M
American International College	M,D
American Jewish University	M
American University	M,O
The American University in Cairo	M
The American University in Dubai	M
American University of Beirut	M,D
American University of Puerto Rico	M
Anderson University (IN)	M
Anderson University (SC)	M
Andrews University	M,D,O
Anna Maria College	M,O
Antioch University Los Angeles	M
Antioch University New England	M,O
Antioch University Santa Barbara	M
Antioch University Seattle	M
Aquinas College (MI)	M
Aquinas College (TN)	M
Arcadia University	M,D,O
Argosy University, Atlanta	M,D,O
Argosy University, Chicago	M,D,O
Argosy University, Hawai'i	M,D
Argosy University, Los Angeles	M,D
Argosy University, Northern Virginia	M,D,O
Argosy University, Orange County	M,D
Argosy University, Phoenix	M,D,O
Argosy University, Seattle	M,D
Argosy University, Tampa	M,D,O
Argosy University, Twin Cities	M,D,O
Arizona State University at the Tempe campus	M,D,O
Arkansas State University	M,D,O
Arkansas Tech University	M,D,O
Arlington Baptist University	M
Ashland University	M,D
Athabasca University	M,D,O
Auburn University	M,D,O*
Auburn University at Montgomery	M,O
Augsburg University	M
Augustana University	M
Augusta University	M,D,O
Aurora University	M,D
Austin College	M
Austin Peay State University	M,O
Averett University	M
Avila University	M,O
Azusa Pacific University	M,D*
Baker University	M,D
Baldwin Wallace University	M
Ball State University	M,D,O
Bank Street College of Education	M
Bard College	M
Barry University	M,D,O
Bayamón Central University	M,O
Baylor University	M,D,O
Belhaven University (MS)	M,D,O
Bellarmine University	M,D,O
Bemidji State University	M
Benedictine College	M
Benedictine University	M
Berry College	M,O
Bethany College	M
Bethel College	M
Bethel University (MN)	M,D,O
Binghamton University, State University of New York	M,D,O
Biola University	M,O
Bishop's University	M,O
Bloomsburg University of Pennsylvania	M,O
Bluefield College	M
Bluffton University	M
Boise State University	M,D,O
Boston College	M,D,O
Boston University	M,D,O*
Bowie State University	M
Bradley University	M,D,O
Brandman University	M,D
Brandon University	M,O
Brenau University	M,O
Bridgewater State University	M,O
Brigham Young University	M,D,O
Brock University	M,D
Brooklyn College of the City University of New York	M,O
Brown University	M
Bucknell University	M
Buena Vista University	M
Butler University	M,O
Cairn University	M,O
Caldwell University	M,D,O
California Baptist University	M
California Coast University	M,D
California Lutheran University	M,D
California Polytechnic State University, San Luis Obispo	M*
California State University, Bakersfield	M,D
California State University, Dominguez Hills	M
California State University, East Bay	M
California State University, Fresno	M,D
California State University, Long Beach	M,D
California State University, Los Angeles	M,D,O
California State University, Monterey Bay	M
California State University, Northridge	M,D
California State University, Sacramento	M,D,O
California State University, San Bernardino	M
California State University, San Marcos	M,D
California State University, Stanislaus	M,D
California University of Pennsylvania	M,D
Calvary University	M
Calvin College	M
Cambridge College	M,D,O
Cameron University	M
Campbellsville University	M
Campbell University	M
Canisius College	M,O
Capella University	M,D
Cardinal Stritch University	M,D
Caribbean University	M,D
Carlow University	M,O
Carroll University	M
Carson-Newman University	M
Carthage College	M,O
Castleton University	M,O
The Catholic University of America	M,O
Cedar Crest College	M
Centenary College of Louisiana	M
Centenary University	M,D
Central Methodist University	M
Central Michigan University	M,D,O
Central Washington University	M
Chadron State College	M,O
Chaminade University of Honolulu	M
Chapman University	M,D,O*
Charleston Southern University	M
Chatham University	M
Chestnut Hill College	M
Cheyney University of Pennsylvania	M,O
Chicago State University	M,D
Chowan University	M
Christian Brothers University	M
Christopher Newport University	M
The Citadel, The Military College of South Carolina	M,O
City College of the City University of New York	M,O
City University of Seattle	M,O
Claremont Graduate University	M,D,O
Clarion University of Pennsylvania	M
Clark Atlanta University	M,D,O
Clarke University	M
Clarkson University	M
Clark University	M,D
Clayton State University	M
Clemson University	M,D,O
Cleveland State University	M,D,O
Coastal Carolina University	M,O
The College at Brockport, State University of New York	M,O
College of Charleston	M,O
The College of Idaho	M
College of Mount Saint Vincent	M,O
The College of New Jersey	M,O
The College of New Rochelle	M,O
College of Saint Elizabeth	M,O
College of St. Joseph	M
College of Saint Mary	M
The College of Saint Rose	M,O
The College of St. Scholastica	M,O
College of Staten Island of the City University of New York	M,O
The College of William and Mary	M,D,O*
Colorado Christian University	M
The Colorado College	M
Colorado Mesa University	M,O
Colorado State University	M,D
Colorado State University–Global Campus	M
Colorado State University–Pueblo	M
Columbia College (MO)	M
Columbia College (SC)	M
Columbia International University	M,D,O
Columbus State University	M,D,O
Concordia College	M
Concordia University (United States)	M,D
Concordia University (Canada)	M,D,O
Concordia University Chicago	M,D
Concordia University Irvine	M*
Concordia University, Nebraska	M
Concordia University, St. Paul	M,D,O
Concordia University Texas	M
Concordia University Wisconsin	M
Concord University	M
Coppin State University	M
Corban University	M
Cornell University	M,O
Cornerstone University	M
Covenant College	M
Crandall University	M
Creighton University	M
Cumberland University	M
Curry College	M,O
Daemen College	M
Dakota State University	M
Dakota Wesleyan University	M
Dallas Baptist University	M
Defiance College	M
Delaware State University	M,D
Delta State University	M,D,O
DePaul University	M,D
DeSales University	M,O
Doane University	M,D,O
Dominican College	M
Dominican University	M
Dominican University of California	M
Dordt College	M
Drake University	M,D,O
Drew University	M,D,O
Drexel University	M,D*
Drury University	M
Duke University	M*
Duquesne University	M,D,O
D'Youville College	M,D
Earlham College	M
East Carolina University	M,D,O
East Central University	M
Eastern Connecticut State University	M
Eastern Illinois University	M,O
Eastern Kentucky University	M
Eastern Mennonite University	M
Eastern Michigan University	M,D,O
Eastern Nazarene College	M,O
Eastern New Mexico University	M
Eastern Oregon University	M
Eastern Washington University	M
East Stroudsburg University of Pennsylvania	M,D
East Tennessee State University	M,D,O
East Texas Baptist University	M
Edgewood College	M,D,O
Elizabeth City State University	M

Elms College	M,O
Elon University	M
Embry-Riddle Aeronautical University–Worldwide	M
Emmanuel College (United States)	M,O
Emory & Henry College	M,D
Emory University	M,D
Emporia State University	M
Evangel University	M
The Evergreen State College	M
Fairfield University	M,O
Fairleigh Dickinson University, Florham Campus	M,O
Fairleigh Dickinson University, Metropolitan Campus	M,O
Fairmont State University	M
Faulkner University	M
Felician University	M,O
Ferris State University	M
Fielding Graduate University	M,D
Florida Agricultural and Mechanical University	M,D
Florida Atlantic University	M,D,O
Florida Gulf Coast University	M
Florida Institute of Technology	M
Florida Memorial University	M
Florida Southern College	M,D
Florida State University	M,D,O
Fontbonne University	M
Fordham University	M,D,O
Fort Hays State University	M,O
Franciscan University of Steubenville	M
Francis Marion University	M
Freed-Hardeman University	M,O
Fresno Pacific University	M,O
Frostburg State University	M,D
Furman University	M,O
Gallaudet University	M,D,O
Gannon University	M,O
Gardner-Webb University	M,D,O
Geneva College	M
George Fox University	M,D,O
George Mason University	M,D,O
Georgetown College	M
The George Washington University	M,D,O
Georgia College & State University	M,O
Georgian Court University	M,O
Georgia Southern University	M,D,O
Georgia Southern University–Armstrong Campus	M,O
Georgia Southwestern State University	M,O
Georgia State University	M,D,O
Goddard College	M
Gonzaga University	M,D
Gordon College	M,O
Goucher College	M,O
Governors State University	M
Graceland University (IA)	M
Grambling State University	M,D,O
Grand Canyon University	M,D,O
Grand Valley State University	M
Gratz College	M
Greensboro College	M
Greenville University	M
Gwynedd Mercy University	M,D
Hamline University	M,D
Hampton University	M,D,O
Hannibal-LaGrange University	M
Harding University	M,O
Hardin-Simmons University	M,D
Harrison Middleton University	M,D
Harvard University	M,D*
Hastings College	M
Hebrew College	M,O
Hebrew Union College–Jewish Institute of Religion (NY)	M
Heidelberg University	M
Henderson State University	M,O
Heritage University	M
Hofstra University	M,D,O
Hollins University	M
Holy Family University	M,D
Holy Names University	M,O
Hood College	M,O*
Hope International University	M
Houston Baptist University	M,D
Howard University	M,D,O
Humboldt State University	M
Hunter College of the City University of New York	M,D,O
Idaho State University	M,D,O
Illinois College	M
Illinois State University	M,D,O
Indiana State University	M,D,O
Indiana University Bloomington	M,D,O
Indiana University East	M
Indiana University Northwest	M,O
Indiana University of Pennsylvania	M,D,O
Indiana University–Purdue University Fort Wayne	M,O
Indiana University–Purdue University Indianapolis	M,O
Indiana University South Bend	M,O
Indiana University Southeast	M
Institute for Christian Studies	M,D
Instituto Tecnologico de Santo Domingo	M,O
Instituto Tecnológico y de Estudios Superiores de Monterrey, Campus Central de Veracruz	M
Instituto Tecnológico y de Estudios Superiores de Monterrey, Campus Ciudad de México	M,D
Instituto Tecnológico y de Estudios Superiores de Monterrey, Campus Ciudad Juárez	M
Instituto Tecnológico y de Estudios Superiores de Monterrey, Campus Ciudad Obregón	M
Instituto Tecnológico y de Estudios Superiores de Monterrey, Campus Estado de México	M,D
Instituto Tecnológico y de Estudios Superiores de Monterrey, Campus Irapuato	M,D
Instituto Tecnológico y de Estudios Superiores de Monterrey, Campus Sonora Norte	M
Inter American University of Puerto Rico, Arecibo Campus	M
Inter American University of Puerto Rico, Barranquitas Campus	M
Inter American University of Puerto Rico, Metropolitan Campus	M,D
International Baptist College and Seminary	M
Iona College	M
Iowa State University of Science and Technology	M,D
Jackson State University	M,D,O
Jacksonville State University	M,O
John Brown University	M
John Carroll University	M
John F. Kennedy University	M
Johns Hopkins University	M,D,O*
Johnson & Wales University	M
Johnson University	M,D,O
Kansas State University	M,D,O
Kean University	M
Keene State College	M,O
Keiser University	M
Kennesaw State University	M,D,O
Kent State University	M,D,O
Kent State University at Stark	M
King's College	M
Kutztown University of Pennsylvania	M,D
LaGrange College	M,O
Lake Erie College	M
Lake Forest College	M
Lakehead University	M,D
Lakeland University	M
Lamar University	M,D,O
Lander University	M
Langston University	M
La Salle University	M,O
Lasell College	M,O
La Sierra University	M,D,O
Lee University	M,O
Lehigh University	M,D,O
Lehman College of the City University of New York	M
Le Moyne College	M,O
Lenoir-Rhyne University	M
Lesley University	M,D,O
Lewis University	M,D
Liberty University	M,D,O
Lincoln Memorial University	M,D,O
Lindenwood University	M,D,O
Lindenwood University–Belleville	M
Lipscomb University	M,D,O
Lock Haven University of Pennsylvania	M
London Metropolitan University	M,D
Long Island University–LIU Brooklyn	M,O
Long Island University–LIU Post	M,D,O
Longwood University	M
Louisiana College	M
Louisiana State University and Agricultural & Mechanical College	M,D,O
Louisiana State University in Shreveport	M,D
Louisiana Tech University	M,D,O
Loyola Marymount University	M,D
Loyola University Chicago	M,D,O
Loyola University Maryland	M,O
Loyola University New Orleans	M
Lynn University	M,D
Madonna University	M
Malone University	M
Manhattan College	M,O
Manhattanville College	M,D,O
Mansfield University of Pennsylvania	M
Maranatha Baptist University	M
Marian University (IN)	M
Marian University (WI)	M,D
Marist College	M,O
Marquette University	M,D,O
Marshall University	M,D,O
Martin Luther College	M
Mary Baldwin University	M
Marymount University	M
Maryville University of Saint Louis	M,D
Marywood University	M
Massachusetts College of Liberal Arts	M,O
McGill University	M,D,O
McKendree University	M,D,O
McNeese State University	O
McPherson College	M
Medaille College	M
Memorial University of Newfoundland	M,D,O
Mercer University	M,D,O
Mercer University	M,D,O
Mercy College	M,O
Meredith College	M,O
Merrimack College	M,O
Metropolitan State University of Denver	M
Miami University	M,D,O
Michigan State University	M,D,O
MidAmerica Nazarene University	M
Middle Tennessee State University	M,D,O
Midway University	M
Midwestern State University	M
Millersville University of Pennsylvania	M,D,O
Milligan College	M,D,O
Mills College	M,D,O
Minnesota State University Mankato	M,D,O
Minnesota State University Moorhead	M,D,O
Misericordia University	M
Mississippi College	M,D,O
Mississippi State University	M,D,O
Mississippi University for Women	M
Mississippi Valley State University	M
Missouri Baptist University	M,O
Missouri Southern State University	M
Molloy College	M,O
Monmouth University	M,D,O*
Montana State University	M,D,O
Montana State University Billings	M,O
Montana State University–Northern	M
Montclair State University	M,D,O
Moravian College	M
Morehead State University	M,O
Morgan State University	M,D
Morningside College	M
Mount Mary University	M
Mount Mercy University	M
Mount St. Joseph University	M,O
Mount Saint Mary College	M,O
Mount Saint Mary's University (CA)	M,D,O
Mount St. Mary's University (MD)	M
Mount Saint Vincent University	M
Mount Vernon Nazarene University	M
Multnomah University	M
Murray State University	M,D,O
Muskingum University	M
National Louis University	M,D,O
National University	M,O
Nazareth College of Rochester	M
Neumann University	M
New England College	M,D
New Jersey City University	M,D
Newman University	M
New Mexico Highlands University	M
New Mexico State University	M,D,O
New York Institute of Technology	M,O
New York University	M,D,O*
Niagara University	M,O
Nicholls State University	M
Nipissing University	M,O
Norfolk State University	M
North Carolina Agricultural and Technical State University	M
North Carolina Central University	M
North Carolina State University	M,D,O
North Central College	M
Northcentral University	M,D,O
North Dakota State University	M,D,O*
Northeastern Illinois University	M
Northeastern State University	M
Northern Arizona University	M,D,O
Northern Illinois University	M,D,O
Northern Kentucky University	M,D,O
Northern Michigan University	M
Northern State University	M
Northern Vermont University–Johnson	M
Northern Vermont University–Lyndon	M
North Greenville University	M,D
North Park University	M
Northwest Christian University	M
Northwestern College	M,O
Northwestern Oklahoma State University	M
Northwestern State University of Louisiana	M,O
Northwestern University	M,D
Northwest Missouri State University	M,D,O
Northwest Nazarene University	M,D,O
Northwest University	M
Notre Dame de Namur University	M
Notre Dame of Maryland University	M
Nova Southeastern University	M,D,O*
Oakland City University	M,D
Oakland University	M,D,O
Ohio Dominican University	M
The Ohio State University	M,D,O
The Ohio State University at Mansfield	M
The Ohio State University at Marion	M
The Ohio State University at Newark	M
Ohio University	M,D
Ohio Valley University	M
Oklahoma State University	M,D,O
Old Dominion University	M,D,O
Olivet Nazarene University	M,D
Open University	M
Oral Roberts University	M,D
Oregon State University	M,D
Oregon State University–Cascades	M
Ottawa University	M
Otterbein University	M
Pace University	M,O
Pacific Lutheran University	M
Pacific Oaks College	M
Pacific Union College	M
Pacific University	M
Palm Beach Atlantic University	M
Park University	M,O
Penn State Harrisburg	M,D,O
Penn State University Park	M,D,O*
Penn State York	M,O
Peru State College	M
Piedmont College	M,D,O
Pittsburg State University	M,O
Plymouth State University	O
Point Loma Nazarene University	M
Point Park University	M,D
Pontifical Catholic University of Puerto Rico	M,D
Portland State University	M,D
Post University	M
Prairie View A&M University	M,D
Prescott College	M,D
Purdue University	M,D,O
Purdue University Global	M
Purdue University Northwest	M
Queens College of the City University of New York	M,O
Queen's University at Kingston	M,D
Queens University of Charlotte	M
Quincy University	M
Quinnipiac University	M,O
Randolph College	M
Regent University	M,D,O
Regis College (MA)	M,D
Regis University	M
Reinhardt University	M
Relay Graduate School of Education	M
Rhode Island College	D
Rice University	M
Rider University	M,O
Rivier University	M,D,O
Robert Morris University	M,D,O
Roberts Wesleyan College	M
Rockford University	M
Rockhurst University	M
Roger Williams University	M,O
Rollins College	M
Roosevelt University	M
Rosemont College	M
Rowan University	M,D,O
Rutgers University–New Brunswick	M,D
Sacred Heart University	M,O
Sage Graduate School	M,D,O
Saginaw Valley State University	M,O
St. Ambrose University	M
St. Bonaventure University	M,O
St. Catherine University	M,O
St. Cloud State University	M,D,O
St. Edward's University	M,O
Saint Francis University	M
St. Francis Xavier University	M
St. John Fisher College	M,D,O
St. John's University (NY)	M,D,O
St. Joseph's College, New York	M
Saint Joseph's College of Maine	M
Saint Joseph's University	M,D,O*
St. Lawrence University	M,O
Saint Leo University	M,O
Saint Louis University	M,D*
Saint Martin's University	M
Saint Mary's College of California	M,D,O
St. Mary's College of Maryland	M
St. Mary's University (United States)	M
Saint Mary's University of Minnesota	M,O
Saint Michael's College	M,O
Saint Peter's University	M,D,O
St. Thomas Aquinas College	M,O
St. Thomas University	M,D,O
Saint Vincent College	M
Saint Xavier University	M
Salem College	M
Salem International University	M
Samford University	M,D,O
Sam Houston State University	M,D
San Diego Christian College	M
San Diego State University	M,D
San Francisco State University	M,D,O
San Ignacio University	M
San Jose State University	M,D
Santa Clara University	M,O
Sarah Lawrence College	M
Schreiner University	M,O
Seattle Pacific University	D
Seattle University	M,D,O
Seton Hall University	M,D,O
Shawnee State University	M
Shenandoah University	M,D,O
Shippensburg University of Pennsylvania	M,D
Siena Heights University	M,O
Sierra Nevada College	M
Silver Lake College of the Holy Family	M
Simmons College	M,D,O
Simon Fraser University	M,D,O
Simpson College	M
Simpson University	M
Sinte Gleska University	M
Slippery Rock University of Pennsylvania	M,D
Smith College	M
Sonoma State University	M,O
South Carolina State University	M
South Dakota State University	M,D
Southeastern Louisiana University	M,D
Southeastern Oklahoma State University	M
Southeastern University (FL)	M,D
Southern Adventist University	M
Southern Arkansas University–Magnolia	M
Southern Connecticut State University	M,D,O

*M—masters degree; D—doctorate; O—other advanced degree; *—Close-Up and/or Display*

Southern Illinois University Carbondale	M,D
Southern Illinois University Edwardsville	M,D,O
Southern Methodist University	M,D
Southern New Hampshire University	M,D,O
Southern Oregon University	M
Southern University and Agricultural and Mechanical College	M,D
Southern Utah University	M,O
Southern Wesleyan University	M
Southwest Baptist University	M,O
Southwestern Adventist University	M
Southwestern Assemblies of God University	M
Southwestern College (KS)	M,D
Southwestern Oklahoma State University	M
Southwest Minnesota State University	M
Spalding University	M,D
Spring Arbor University	M
Springfield College	M,O
Spring Hill College	M
Stanford University	M,D
State University of New York at Fredonia	M
State University of New York at New Paltz	M,O
State University of New York at Oswego	M,O
State University of New York College at Cortland	M,O
State University of New York College at Geneseo	M
State University of New York College at Old Westbury	M
State University of New York College at Oneonta	M,O
State University of New York Empire State College	M
Stephen F. Austin State University	M,D
Stetson University	M
Stevenson University	M
Stockton University	M
Strayer University	M
Sul Ross State University	M,O
Sweet Briar College	M
Syracuse University	M,D,O*
Taft University System	M
Tarleton State University	M,D,O
Teachers College, Columbia University	M,D
Teachers College of San Joaquin	M
Temple University	M,D,O*
Tennessee State University	M,D,O
Tennessee Technological University	M,D,O
Texas A&M International University	M
Texas A&M University	M,D
Texas A&M University–Commerce	M,D,O
Texas A&M University–Corpus Christi	M,D
Texas A&M University–Kingsville	M,D,O
Texas A&M University–San Antonio	M
Texas A&M University–Texarkana	M
Texas Christian University	M,D
Texas Southern University	M,D
Texas State University	M,D,O
Texas Tech University	M,D
Texas Wesleyan University	M,D
Texas Woman's University	M,D,O
Thomas More College	M
Thomas University	M
Thompson Rivers University	M
Tiffin University	M
Touro College	M
Touro University California	M,D
Towson University	M
Trevecca Nazarene University	M,O
Trident University International	M,D
Trinity International University	M
Trinity University	M
Trinity Washington University	M
Troy University	M,O
Truman State University	M
Tufts University	M,D,O*
Tusculum College	M
Union College (KY)	M
Union Institute & University	D
Union University	M,D,O
Universidad Autonoma de Guadalajara	M,D
Universidad de las Americas, A.C.	M
Universidad de las Américas Puebla	M
Universidad del Turabo	M,D
Universidad Metropolitana	M
Université de Moncton	M
Université de Montréal	M,D,O
Université de Saint-Boniface	M
Université de Sherbrooke	M,O
Université du Québec à Chicoutimi	M,D
Université du Québec à Montréal	M,D,O
Université du Québec à Rimouski	M,D,O
Université du Québec à Trois-Rivières	M,D
Université du Québec en Abitibi-Témiscamingue	M,D,O
Université du Québec en Outaouais	M,D,O
Université Laval	M,D,O
Université Sainte-Anne	M
University at Albany, State University of New York	M,D,O
University at Buffalo, the State University of New York	M,D,O
The University of Akron	M
The University of Alabama at Birmingham	M,D,O
The University of Alabama in Huntsville	M,O
University of Alaska Anchorage	M,O
University of Alaska Fairbanks	M,O
University of Alaska Southeast	M
The University of Arizona	M,D,O
University of Arkansas	M,D,O
University of Arkansas at Little Rock	M,D,O
University of Arkansas at Monticello	M
University of Arkansas at Pine Bluff	M
University of Bridgeport	M,D,O
The University of British Columbia	M,D,O
University of California, Berkeley	M,D,O
University of California, Davis	M,D
University of California, Irvine	M,D
University of California, Los Angeles	M,D*
University of California, Riverside	M,D,O
University of California, San Diego	M,D*
University of California, Santa Barbara	M,D,O
University of California, Santa Cruz	M,D*
University of Central Arkansas	M,O
University of Central Missouri	M,D,O
University of Central Oklahoma	M
University of Cincinnati	M,D,O
University of Colorado Boulder	M,D
University of Colorado Colorado Springs	M,D
University of Colorado Denver	M,D,O
University of Connecticut	M,D*
University of Delaware	M,D,O*
University of Denver	M,D,O
The University of Findlay	M,D
University of Florida	M,D,O
University of Georgia	M,D,O
University of Guam	M
University of Hartford	M,D,O
University of Hawaii at Hilo	M*
University of Hawaii at Manoa	M,D,O
University of Holy Cross	M,D
University of Houston	M,D
University of Houston–Clear Lake	M,D
University of Houston–Victoria	M,O
University of Idaho	M,D,O
University of Illinois at Chicago	M,D
University of Illinois at Springfield	M,O
University of Illinois at Urbana–Champaign	M,D,O
University of Indianapolis	M
The University of Iowa	M,D,O*
University of Jamestown	M
The University of Kansas	M,D,O
University of Kentucky	M,D,O
University of La Verne	M,O
University of Lethbridge	M,D
University of Louisiana at Lafayette	M,D
University of Louisiana at Monroe	M,D
University of Louisville	M,D,O
University of Maine	M,D,O
University of Maine at Farmington	M
The University of Manchester	M,D
University of Manitoba	M,D
University of Mary	M,D
University of Mary Hardin-Baylor	M,D
University of Maryland, Baltimore County	M,O
University of Maryland, College Park	M,D,O
University of Maryland Eastern Shore	M
University of Maryland University College	M
University of Mary Washington	M
University of Massachusetts Amherst	M,D,O*
University of Massachusetts Boston	M,D,O
University of Massachusetts Dartmouth	M,D,O
University of Massachusetts Lowell	M
University of Memphis	M,D,O
University of Miami	M,D,O*
University of Michigan	M,D*
University of Michigan–Dearborn	M
University of Michigan–Flint	M,D,O
University of Minnesota, Duluth	M,D
University of Minnesota, Twin Cities Campus	M,D,O
University of Mississippi	M,D,O
University of Missouri	M,D,O
University of Missouri–Kansas City	M,D,O
University of Missouri–St. Louis	M,D,O
University of Mobile	M
University of Montana	M,D,O
University of Montevallo	M,O
University of Nebraska at Kearney	M,O
University of Nebraska at Omaha	M,D,O
University of Nevada, Las Vegas	M,D,O
University of Nevada, Reno	M,D,O
University of New Brunswick Fredericton	M,D
University of New England	M,D,O
University of New Hampshire	M,D,O
University of New Mexico	M,D,O
University of North Alabama	M,O
The University of North Carolina at Chapel Hill	M,D
The University of North Carolina at Charlotte	M,D,O
The University of North Carolina at Greensboro	M,D,O
The University of North Carolina at Pembroke	M
The University of North Carolina Wilmington	M,D
University of North Dakota	M,D,O
University of Northern British Columbia	M,D,O
University of Northern Colorado	M,D,O
University of Northern Iowa	M,D,O
University of North Florida	M,D
University of North Georgia	M
University of North Texas	M,D,O
University of Northwestern–St. Paul	M
University of Notre Dame	M
University of Oklahoma	M,D,O*
University of Oregon	M,D
University of Ottawa	M,D,O
University of Pennsylvania	M,D,O*
University of Phoenix–Bay Area Campus	M,D,O
University of Phoenix–Central Valley Campus	M
University of Phoenix–Dallas Campus	M
University of Phoenix–Hawaii Campus	M
University of Phoenix–Houston Campus	M
University of Phoenix–Las Vegas Campus	M
University of Phoenix–Online Campus	M,O
University of Phoenix–Phoenix Campus	M
University of Phoenix–Sacramento Valley Campus	M,O
University of Phoenix–San Diego Campus	M
University of Pikeville	M
University of Pittsburgh	M,D*
University of Portland	M,D
University of Prince Edward Island	M,D
University of Puerto Rico–Río Piedras	M,D
University of Puget Sound	M
University of Redlands	M,D,O
University of Regina	M,D,O
University of Rhode Island	M,D*
University of Rio Grande	M
University of Rochester	M,D*
University of St. Francis (IL)	M,D,O
University of Saint Francis (IN)	M
University of Saint Joseph	M
University of Saint Mary	M
University of St. Thomas (MN)	M,D,O
University of St. Thomas (TX)	M,D
University of San Diego	M,D,O
University of San Francisco	M,D
University of Saskatchewan	M,D,O
The University of Scranton	M
University of Sioux Falls	M,O
University of South Africa	M,D
University of South Alabama	M,D,O
University of South Carolina	M,D,O
University of South Carolina Upstate	M
University of South Dakota	M,D,O
University of Southern California	M,D*
University of Southern Indiana	M,D
University of Southern Maine	M,D,O
University of Southern Mississippi	M,D,O
University of South Florida	M,D,O*
University of South Florida, St. Petersburg	M
The University of Tampa	M
The University of Tennessee	M,D,O
The University of Tennessee at Chattanooga	M,D,O
The University of Tennessee at Martin	M
The University of Texas at Arlington	M,D
The University of Texas at Austin	M,D
The University of Texas at El Paso	M,D
The University of Texas of the Permian Basin	M
The University of Texas Rio Grande Valley	M,D
University of the Cumberlands	M,D,O
University of the Incarnate Word	M,D
University of the Pacific	M,D,O
University of the Sacred Heart	M,O
University of the Southwest	M
University of the Virgin Islands	M,D,O
The University of Toledo	M,D,O
University of Toronto	M,D
The University of Tulsa	M
University of Utah	M,D,O
University of Vermont	M,D
University of Victoria	M,D
University of Virginia	M,D,O
University of Washington	M,D
University of Washington, Bothell	M
University of Washington, Tacoma	M
The University of West Alabama	M,O
The University of Western Ontario	M
University of West Georgia	M,D,O
University of Windsor	M,D
University of Wisconsin–Eau Claire	M
University of Wisconsin–Green Bay	M
University of Wisconsin–La Crosse	M,O
University of Wisconsin–Madison	M,D,O
University of Wisconsin–Milwaukee	M,D,O*
University of Wisconsin–Oshkosh	M
University of Wisconsin–Platteville	M
University of Wisconsin–River Falls	M
University of Wisconsin–Stevens Point	M,D
University of Wisconsin–Stout	M,D,O
University of Wisconsin–Superior	M
University of Wisconsin–Whitewater	M,O
Upper Iowa University	M
Urbana University–A Branch Campus of Franklin University	M
Utah State University	M,D,O
Utah Valley University	M
Utica College	M,O
Valley City State University	M
Valparaiso University	M,O
Vanderbilt University	M,D*
Vanguard University of Southern California	M
Villanova University	M
Virginia Commonwealth University	M,D,O
Virginia International University	M
Virginia Polytechnic Institute and State University	M,O
Virginia State University	M,D
Virginia Union University	M
Virginia Wesleyan University	M
Viterbo University	M,O
Wagner College	M
Wake Forest University	M
Walden University	M,D,O
Walla Walla University	M
Walsh University	M
Warner Pacific University	M
Warner University	M
Washburn University	M
Washington State University	M,D
Washington University in St. Louis	M,D
Wayland Baptist University	M
Wayne State College	M,O
Wayne State University	M,D,O
Weber State University	M
Webster University	M,O
Wesleyan College	M
Wesley College	M
West Chester University of Pennsylvania	M,D,O
Western Carolina University	M
Western Connecticut State University	M,D
Western Governors University	M,O
Western Illinois University	M,D,O
Western Michigan University	M,D,O
Western New Mexico University	M
Western Oregon University	M
Western State Colorado University	M
Western Washington University	M
Westfield State University	M
West Liberty University	M
Westminster College (UT)	M
West Texas A&M University	M
West Virginia University	M,D
West Virginia Wesleyan College	M
Wheaton College	M
Whittier College	M
Whitworth University	M
Wichita State University	M,D,O
Widener University	M,D
Wilkes University	M,D
William Carey University	M,O
William Jessup University	M
William Jewell College	M
William Paterson University of New Jersey	M,O
Williams Baptist College	M
Wilmington College	M
Wilmington University	M,D
Wilson College	M
Wingate University	M,D,O
Winona State University	O
Winston-Salem State University	M
Winthrop University	M
Wittenberg University	M
Worcester State University	M,O
Wright State University	M,O
Xavier University	M,D*
Xavier University of Louisiana	M
York College of Pennsylvania	M
York University	M,D
Youngstown State University	M,D

EDUCATIONAL LEADERSHIP AND ADMINISTRATION

Abilene Christian University	M,D,O
Acacia University	M
Acadia University	M
Adams State University	M
Alabama State University	M,D,O
Albany State University	M,O
Alliant International University–San Diego	M,D,O
Alliant International University–San Francisco	M,D,O
Alverno College	M
American College of Education	M
American InterContinental University Online	M
American International College	M,D
American Public University System	M,D
The American University in Cairo	M
American University of Beirut	M,D
Anderson University (SC)	M
Andrews University	M,D,O
Angelo State University	M
Antioch University New England	M,O
Appalachian State University	M,O
Arcadia University	M,D,O
Argosy University, Atlanta	M,D,O

Argosy University, Chicago	M,D,O
Argosy University, Hawai`i	M,D
Argosy University, Los Angeles	M,D
Argosy University, Northern Virginia	M,D,O
Argosy University, Orange County	M,D
Argosy University, Phoenix	M,D,O
Argosy University, Seattle	M,D
Argosy University, Tampa	M,D,O
Argosy University, Twin Cities	M,D,O
Arizona State University at the Tempe campus	M,D
Arkansas State University	M,D,O
Arkansas Tech University	M,D,O
Arlington Baptist University	M
Asbury University	M
Ashland University	M
Auburn University	M,D,O*
Auburn University at Montgomery	M,O
Augusta University	M,O
Aurora University	M,D
Austin Peay State University	M,O
Averett University	M
Azusa Pacific University	M,D*
Baldwin Wallace University	M
Ball State University	M,D,O
Bank Street College of Education	M
Barry University	M,D,O
Baruch College of the City University of New York	M,O*
Bayamón Central University	M,O
Baylor University	M,O
Bay Path University	M
Belhaven University (MS)	M,D,O
Bellarmine University	M,D,O
Benedictine College	M
Benedictine University	M,D
Berry College	O
Bethel University (MN)	M,D,O
Bethel University (TN)	M
Binghamton University, State University of New York	M,D,O
Bloomsburg University of Pennsylvania	M
Bluffton University	M
Bob Jones University	M,D,O
Boise State University	M,D,O
Boston College	M,D,O
Bowie State University	M,D
Bowling Green State University	M,D,O
Bradley University	M
Brandeis University	M,O
Brandman University	M,D
Brandon University	M,O
Bridgewater State University	M,O
Brigham Young University	M,D
Brooklyn College of the City University of New York	M
Buffalo State College, State University of New York	O
Butler University	M,O
Cabrini University	M,D
Cairn University	M,O
Caldwell University	M,D,O
California Baptist University	M
California Coast University	M,D
California Lutheran University	M,D
California State Polytechnic University, Pomona	D
California State University, Bakersfield	M,D
California State University, East Bay	M,D
California State University, Fresno	M,D
California State University, Fullerton	M,D
California State University, Long Beach	M,D
California State University, Northridge	M,D
California State University, Sacramento	M,D,O
California State University, San Bernardino	M,D
California State University, San Marcos	M,D
California State University, Stanislaus	M,D
California University of Pennsylvania	M,D
Calumet College of Saint Joseph	M
Calvary University	M
Cambridge College	M,D,O
Cameron University	M
Campbellsville University	M
Campbell University	M
Canisius College	M,O
Capella University	M,D
Cardinal Stritch University	M,D
Caribbean University	M,D
Carroll University	M
Carson-Newman University	M
Carthage College	M,O
Castleton University	M,O
The Catholic University of America	M,O
Centenary University	M,D
Central Connecticut State University	M,D,O
Central Michigan University	M,D,O
Central Washington University	M
Chadron State College	M,O
Chaminade University of Honolulu	M
Chapman University	M,D,O*
Charleston Southern University	M
Chestnut Hill College	M
Cheyney University of Pennsylvania	M,O
Chicago State University	M,D
Christian Brothers University	M
The Citadel, The Military College of South Carolina	M,O
City College of the City University of New York	M,O
City University of Seattle	M,D,O
Claremont Graduate University	M,D,O
Clark Atlanta University	M,D,O
Clarke University	M
Clarks Summit University	M
Clemson University	M,D,O
Cleveland State University	M,D,O
Coastal Carolina University	M,O
The College at Brockport, State University of New York	M,O
The College of New Jersey	M,O
The College of New Rochelle	M,O
College of Saint Elizabeth	M,D,O
College of Saint Mary	M
The College of Saint Rose	M,O
College of Staten Island of the City University of New York	O
The College of William and Mary	M,D*
Colorado Mesa University	M,O
Colorado State University	M,D
Colorado State University–Global Campus	M
Columbia College (MO)	M
Columbia College (SC)	M
Columbia International University	M,D,O
Columbus State University	M,D,O
Concordia University (United States)	M,D
Concordia University Ann Arbor	M
Concordia University Chicago	M,D,O
Concordia University Irvine	M*
Concordia University, Nebraska	M
Concordia University, St. Paul	M,D,O
Concordia University Wisconsin	M
Concord University	M
Converse College	M,O
Creighton University	M,D
Dakota Wesleyan University	M
Dallas Baptist University	M,D
Dallas Theological Seminary	M,D,O
Delaware State University	M,D
Delaware Valley University	M
Delta State University	M,D,O
DePaul University	M,D
DeVry University–Folsom Campus	M
Doane University	M,D,O
Drake University	M,D,O
Drexel University	M,D*
Drury University	M
Duquesne University	M,D,O
D'Youville College	M,D
East Carolina University	M,D,O
Eastern Illinois University	M,O
Eastern Kentucky University	M
Eastern Michigan University	M,D,O
Eastern Nazarene College	M,O
Eastern New Mexico University	M
Eastern University	M,D,O
Eastern Washington University	M
East Tennessee State University	M,D,O
Edgewood College	M,D,O
Edinboro University of Pennsylvania	M
Elizabeth City State University	M
Elmhurst College	M
Emporia State University	M
Endicott College	M,D
Evangel University	M,D
Fairleigh Dickinson University, Florham Campus	M
Fairleigh Dickinson University, Metropolitan Campus	M
Fayetteville State University	M,D
Felician University	M,O
Ferris State University	M,D
Fitchburg State University	M,O
Florida Agricultural and Mechanical University	M,D
Florida Atlantic University	M,D,O
Florida Gulf Coast University	M
Florida International University	M,D,O
Florida Southern College	M,D
Florida State University	M,D,O
Fordham University	M,D,O
Fort Hays State University	M,O
Fort Lewis College	M,O
Framingham State University	M
Franciscan University of Steubenville	M
Freed-Hardeman University	M,O
Fresno Pacific University	M
Frostburg State University	M,D
Furman University	M,O
Gannon University	D,O
Gardner-Webb University	M,D,O
Gateway Seminary	M,D,O
Geneva College	M
George Fox University	M,D,O
George Mason University	M,O
The George Washington University	M,D,O
Georgia College & State University	M,O
Georgian Court University	M,O
Georgia Southern University	M,D,O
Georgia State University	M,D,O
Gonzaga University	M,D
Gordon College	M,O
Goucher College	M,O
Governors State University	M,D
Graceland University (IA)	M
Grambling State University	M,D,O
Grand Canyon University	M,D,O
Grand Valley State University	M,O
Grand View University	M,O
Gratz College	M,D
Gwynedd Mercy University	M,D
Hampton University	M,D
Harding University	M,O
Hardin-Simmons University	D
Harvard University	M,D*
Hawai`i Pacific University	M
Henderson State University	M,O
Heritage University	M
High Point University	M,D
High Tech High Graduate School of Education	M
Hofstra University	M,D,O
Holy Family University	M,D
Hood College	M,O*
Hope International University	M
Houston Baptist University	M,D
Howard Payne University	M
Howard University	M,D,O
Hunter College of the City University of New York	D,O
Husson University	M,O
Huston-Tillotson University	M
Idaho State University	M,D,O
Illinois State University	M,D
Immaculata University	M,D,O
Indiana State University	M,D,O
Indiana University Bloomington	M,D,O
Indiana University Northwest	M,O
Indiana University of Pennsylvania	D,O
Indiana University–Purdue University Fort Wayne	M,O
Indiana University–Purdue University Indianapolis	M,O
Indiana University South Bend	M,O
Indiana Wesleyan University	M,O
Instituto Tecnologico de Santo Domingo	M,O
Instituto Tecnológico y de Estudios Superiores de Monterrey, Campus Central de Veracruz	M
Instituto Tecnológico y de Estudios Superiores de Monterrey, Campus Ciudad Juárez	M
Instituto Tecnológico y de Estudios Superiores de Monterrey, Campus Estado de México	M,D
Instituto Tecnológico y de Estudios Superiores de Monterrey, Campus Irapuato	M,D
Inter American University of Puerto Rico, Aguadilla Campus	M
Inter American University of Puerto Rico, Arecibo Campus	M
Inter American University of Puerto Rico, Barranquitas Campus	M
Inter American University of Puerto Rico, Fajardo Campus	M
Inter American University of Puerto Rico, Metropolitan Campus	M,D
Iona College	M
Iowa State University of Science and Technology	M,D
Jackson State University	M,D,O
Jacksonville State University	M,O
Jacksonville University	M*
James Madison University	M
Johns Hopkins University	M,D,O*
Johnson & Wales University	D
Kansas State University	M,D,O
Kean University	M,D
Keene State College	M,O
Keiser University	M,D,O
Kennesaw State University	M,D,O
Kent State University	M,D,O
Keystone College	M
Kutztown University of Pennsylvania	M
Lamar University	M,D
La Salle University	M,D
Lasell College	M,O
La Sierra University	M,D,O
Lee University	M,O
Lehigh University	M,D,O
Le Moyne College	M,O
Lenoir-Rhyne University	M
Lesley University	M,D,O
LeTourneau University	M
Lewis & Clark College	M,D,O
Lewis University	M,D
Liberty University	M,D,O
Lincoln Memorial University	M,D,O
Lincoln University (PA)	M
Lindenwood University	M,D,O
Lindenwood University–Belleville	M
Lindsey Wilson College	M
Lipscomb University	M,D,O
Lock Haven University of Pennsylvania	M
Long Island University–Brentwood Campus	M,O
Long Island University–Hudson	M,O
Long Island University–LIU Brooklyn	M,O
Long Island University–LIU Post	M,D,O
Loras College	M
Louisiana State University and Agricultural & Mechanical College	M,D,O
Louisiana State University in Shreveport	M,D
Louisiana Tech University	M,D,O
Lourdes University	M
Loyola Marymount University	M,D
Loyola University Chicago	M,D,O
Loyola University Maryland	M,O
Lynn University	M,D
Madonna University	M
Malone University	M
Manhattan College	M,O
Manhattanville College	M,D,O
Marconi International University	M,D
Marian University (WI)	M,D
Marquette University	M,D,O
Marshall University	M
Martin Luther College	M
Marygrove College	M,O
Maryville University of Saint Louis	M,D
Marywood University	M,D
Massachusetts College of Liberal Arts	M,O
McDaniel College	M
McGill University	M,D,O
McKendree University	M,D,O
McNeese State University	M,O
Memorial University of Newfoundland	M,D,O
Mercer University	M,D,O
Mercer University	M,D,O
Mercy College	M,O
Mercyhurst University	M,O
Merrimack College	M,O
Miami University	M,D
Michigan State University	M,D,O
Middle Tennessee State University	M,O
Midwestern State University	M
Millersville University of Pennsylvania	M,D
Milligan College	M,D,O
Mills College	
Minnesota State University Mankato	M
Minnesota State University Moorhead	M,D,O
Mississippi College	M,D,O
Mississippi State University	M,D,O
Mississippi University for Women	M
Missouri Baptist University	M,O
Missouri State University	M,O
Monmouth University	M,D,O*
Montana State University	M,D,O
Montclair State University	M,D
Morehead State University	M,O
Morgan State University	M,D
Mount Holyoke College	M
Mount Mercy University	M
Murray State University	M,D,O
National American University (TX)	M,D
National Louis University	M,D,O
National University	M,O
Neumann University	M,D
New England College	M,D
New Jersey City University	M
Newman University	M
New Mexico Highlands University	M
New Mexico State University	M,D
New York Institute of Technology	O
New York University	M,D,O*
Niagara University	M,D,O
Nicholls State University	M
Norfolk State University	M
North American University	M
North Carolina Agricultural and Technical State University	M
North Carolina Central University	M
North Carolina State University	M,D
North Central College	M
North Dakota State University	M,O*
Northeastern Illinois University	M
Northeastern State University	M
Northeastern University	M
Northern Arizona University	M,D,O
Northern Illinois University	M,D,O
Northern Kentucky University	M,D,O
Northern Michigan University	M
Northern State University	M
Northwestern College	M,O
Northwestern Oklahoma State University	M
Northwestern State University of Louisiana	M,O
Northwestern University	M
Northwest Missouri State University	M,D,O
Northwest Nazarene University	M,D,O
Notre Dame de Namur University	M
Notre Dame of Maryland University	M,D
Oakland City University	M,D
Oakland University	M,D,O
Oglala Lakota College	M
Ohio Dominican University	M
The Ohio State University	M,D,O
Ohio University	M,D
Oklahoma State University	M,D
Old Dominion University	M,D,O
Olivet Nazarene University	M
Oral Roberts University	M,D
Oregon State University	M,D
Ottawa University	M
Park University	M,O
Penn State University Park	M,D,O*
Pensacola Christian College	M,D,O
Pepperdine University	M,D
Piedmont International University	M,D
Pittsburg State University	M,O
Plymouth State University	M,D,O
Point Loma Nazarene University	M
Point Park University	M,D
Pontifical Catholic University of Puerto Rico	D
Post University	M
Prairie View A&M University	M,D
Prescott College	M,D
Providence College	M
Purdue University	M,D,O
Purdue University Global	M
Purdue University Northwest	M
Queens College of the City University of New York	M,O
Queens University of Charlotte	M
Quincy University	M
Quinnipiac University	M,O
Radford University	M
Ramapo College of New Jersey	M
Regent University	M,D,O

*M—masters degree; D—doctorate; O—other advanced degree; *—Close-Up and/or Display*

Regis College (MA)	M,D
Regis University	M,O
Rhode Island College	M,O
Rivier University	M,D,O
Robert Morris University	M,D,O
Robert Morris University Illinois	M
Rocky Mountain College	M
Roosevelt University	M
Rowan University	M,D,O
Rutgers University–Camden	M
Rutgers University–New Brunswick	M,D
Sacred Heart University	O
Sage Graduate School	D
Saginaw Valley State University	M,O
St. Ambrose University	M
St. Bonaventure University	M,O
St. Cloud State University	M,D
Saint Francis University	M
St. Francis Xavier University	M
St. John Fisher College	M,D
St. John's University (NY)	M,D,O
St. Joseph's College, Long Island Campus	M
St. Joseph's College, New York	M
Saint Joseph's College of Maine	M
Saint Joseph's University	M,D,O*
St. Lawrence University	M,O
Saint Leo University	M,O
Saint Louis University	M,D,O*
Saint Mary's College of California	M,D,O
St. Mary's University (United States)	M
Saint Mary's University of Minnesota	M,D,O
Saint Michael's College	M,O
Saint Peter's University	M,D
St. Thomas Aquinas College	M,O
St. Thomas University	M,D,O
Saint Vincent College	M
Saint Xavier University	M
Salem International University	M
Salem State University	M
Salisbury University	M
Salve Regina University	O
Samford University	M,D,O
Sam Houston State University	M,D
San Diego State University	M
San Francisco State University	M,D,O
San Ignacio University	M
San Jose State University	M,D
Santa Clara University	M,O
Schreiner University	M,O
Seattle Pacific University	M,D,O
Seattle University	M,D,O
Seton Hall University	D,O
Shasta Bible College	M
Shenandoah University	M,D,O
Shippensburg University of Pennsylvania	M,D
Siena Heights University	M,O
Sierra Nevada College	M
Silver Lake College of the Holy Family	M
Simon Fraser University	M,D
Simpson University	M
SIT Graduate Institute	M
Slippery Rock University of Pennsylvania	M,D
Soka University of America	M*
Sonoma State University	M,O
South Carolina State University	D,O
South Dakota State University	M
Southeastern Louisiana University	M,D
Southeastern Oklahoma State University	M
Southeastern University (FL)	M,D
Southeast Missouri State University	M,D,O
Southern Adventist University	M
Southern Arkansas University–Magnolia	M
Southern Connecticut State University	M,D,O
Southern Illinois University Carbondale	M,D
Southern Illinois University Edwardsville	M,D,O
Southern New Hampshire University	M,D,O
Southern Oregon University	M
Southern University and Agricultural and Mechanical College	M
Southwest Baptist University	M,O
Southwestern Adventist University	M
Southwestern Assemblies of God University	M
Southwestern College (KS)	M,D
Southwestern Oklahoma State University	M
Southwest Minnesota State University	M
Spalding University	M,D
Springfield College	M,D,O
Stanford University	M
State University of New York at New Paltz	M,O
State University of New York at Oswego	O
State University of New York at Plattsburgh	O
State University of New York College at Cortland	O
Stephen F. Austin State University	M,D
Stetson University	M
Stevenson University	M
Stony Brook University, State University of New York	M,O
Suffolk University	M,O
Sul Ross State University	M
Syracuse University	M,D,O*
Tarleton State University	M,D,O
Teachers College, Columbia University	M,D
Teachers College of San Joaquin	M
Temple University	M,D*
Tennessee Technological University	M,O
Texas A&M International University	M
Texas A&M University	M,D
Texas A&M University–Central Texas	M,O
Texas A&M University–Commerce	M,D,O
Texas A&M University–Corpus Christi	M,D
Texas A&M University–Kingsville	M,D
Texas A&M University–San Antonio	M
Texas A&M University–Texarkana	M
Texas Christian University	M,D
Texas Southern University	M,D
Texas State University	M,D
Texas Tech University	M,D
Texas Woman's University	M,D
Thomas Edison State University	M,O
Thomas More College	M
Tiffin University	M
Touro College	M
Towson University	M,O
Trevecca Nazarene University	M,D,O
Trident University International	M,D
Trinity Baptist College	M
Trinity University	M
Trinity Washington University	M
Trinity Western University	M,O
Troy University	M,O
Union College (KY)	M
Union University	M,D,O
Universidad Adventista de las Antillas	M
Universidad del Turabo	M,D
Universidad Iberoamericana	M,D
Universidad Metropolitana	M
Université de Moncton	M
Université de Montréal	M,D,O
Université de Sherbrooke	M
Université du Québec à Trois-Rivières	O
Université Laval	M,D,O
University at Albany, State University of New York	M,D,O
University at Buffalo, the State University of New York	M,D,O
The University of Akron	M,O
The University of Alabama	M,D,O
The University of Alabama at Birmingham	M,D,O
University of Alaska Anchorage	M,O
University of Alaska Southeast	M
University of Alberta	M,D,O
The University of Arizona	M,D,O
University of Arkansas	M,D,O
University of Arkansas at Little Rock	M,D,O
University of Arkansas at Monticello	M
University of Bridgeport	M,D,O
The University of British Columbia	M,D
University of Calgary	M,D
University of California, Berkeley	M,D
University of California, Irvine	M,D
University of California, Los Angeles	D*
University of California, Riverside	M,D,O
University of California, San Diego	M,D*
University of Central Arkansas	M,D,O
University of Central Florida	M,D,O
University of Central Missouri	M,D,O
University of Central Oklahoma	M
University of Cincinnati	M,D,O
University of Colorado Colorado Springs	M,D
University of Colorado Denver	M,D,O
University of Connecticut	M*
University of Dayton	M,D,O
University of Delaware	M,D,O*
University of Denver	M,D,O
University of Detroit Mercy	M,D,O
The University of Findlay	M,D
University of Florida	M,D,O
University of Georgia	D,O
University of Guam	M
University of Hartford	D,O
University of Hawaii at Manoa	M,D
University of Holy Cross	M,D
University of Houston	M,D
University of Houston–Clear Lake	M,D
University of Houston–Victoria	M,O
University of Idaho	M,O
University of Illinois at Chicago	M,D
University of Illinois at Springfield	M,O
University of Illinois at Urbana–Champaign	M,D,O
University of Indianapolis	M
The University of Iowa	M,D,O*
The University of Kansas	M,D
University of Kentucky	M,D,O
University of La Verne	M,D,O
University of Lethbridge	M,D
University of Louisiana at Lafayette	M,D
University of Louisville	M,D,O
University of Lynchburg	M,D
University of Maine	M,D,O
University of Maine at Farmington	M
University of Manitoba	M
University of Mary	M,D
University of Mary Hardin-Baylor	M,D
University of Maryland, College Park	M,D,O
University of Maryland Eastern Shore	D
University of Massachusetts Amherst	M,D,O*
University of Massachusetts Boston	M,D,O
University of Massachusetts Dartmouth	D
University of Memphis	M,D,O
University of Michigan–Dearborn	M,D,O
University of Michigan–Flint	M,D,O
University of Minnesota, Twin Cities Campus	M,D
University of Mississippi	M,D,O
University of Missouri	M,D,O
University of Missouri–Kansas City	M,D,O
University of Missouri–St. Louis	D
University of Mobile	M
University of Montana	M,D,O
University of Montevallo	M,O
University of Mount Union	M
University of Nebraska at Kearney	M,O
University of Nebraska at Omaha	M,D,O
University of Nebraska–Lincoln	M,D,O
University of Nevada, Las Vegas	M,D,O
University of Nevada, Reno	M,D,O
University of New England	M,D,O
University of New Hampshire	M,O
University of New Mexico	M,D,O
University of New Orleans	M,D
University of North Alabama	M,O
The University of North Carolina at Chapel Hill	M,D
The University of North Carolina at Charlotte	M,D,O
The University of North Carolina at Greensboro	M,D,O
The University of North Carolina at Pembroke	M
The University of North Carolina Wilmington	M,D
University of North Dakota	M,D,O
University of Northern Colorado	M,D,O
University of Northern Iowa	M,D
University of North Florida	M,D
University of North Georgia	D,O
University of North Texas	M,D,O
University of North Texas at Dallas	M
University of Oklahoma	M,D*
University of Oregon	M,D
University of Pennsylvania	M,D*
University of Phoenix–Bay Area Campus	M,D,O
University of Phoenix–Hawaii Campus	M
University of Phoenix–Las Vegas Campus	M
University of Phoenix–Online Campus	M,D,O
University of Phoenix–Phoenix Campus	M
University of Pikeville	M
University of Pittsburgh	M,D*
University of Portland	M,D
University of Prince Edward Island	M,D
University of Puerto Rico–Río Piedras	M,D
University of Regina	M
University of Rio Grande	M
University of Rochester	M,D*
University of St. Francis (IL)	M,D,O
University of St. Thomas (MN)	M,D,O
University of St. Thomas (TX)	M,D
University of San Diego	M,D,O
University of San Francisco	M,D
University of Saskatchewan	M,D,O
The University of Scranton	M
University of Sioux Falls	M,O
University of South Africa	M,D
University of South Alabama	M,D
University of South Carolina	M,D,O
University of South Dakota	M,D,O
University of Southern California	D*
University of Southern Indiana	M,D
University of Southern Maine	M,O
University of Southern Mississippi	M,D,O
University of South Florida	M,D,O*
University of South Florida, St. Petersburg	M
University of South Florida Sarasota-Manatee	M
The University of Tampa	M
The University of Tennessee	M,D,O
The University of Tennessee at Chattanooga	M,D,O
The University of Tennessee at Martin	M
The University of Texas at Arlington	M,D
The University of Texas at Austin	M,D
The University of Texas at El Paso	M,D
The University of Texas at San Antonio	M,D
The University of Texas at Tyler	M
The University of Texas of the Permian Basin	M
The University of Texas Rio Grande Valley	M,D
University of the Cumberlands	M,D,O
University of the Pacific	M,D,O
University of the Southwest	M
University of the Virgin Islands	M,D,O
The University of Toledo	M,D,O
University of Utah	M,D
University of Vermont	M,D
University of Victoria	M,D
University of Virginia	M,D,O
University of Washington	M,D
University of Washington, Bothell	M
University of Washington, Tacoma	M
The University of West Alabama	M,O
University of West Florida	M,D
University of West Georgia	M,D,O
University of Wisconsin–Madison	M,D,O
University of Wisconsin–Milwaukee	M,D,O*
University of Wisconsin–Oshkosh	M
University of Wisconsin–Stevens Point	M,D
University of Wisconsin–Superior	M,O
University of Wisconsin–Whitewater	M
University of Wyoming	M,D,O
Upper Iowa University	M
Ursuline College	M
Utah Valley University	M
Valdosta State University	M,D,O
Valparaiso University	M,O
Vanderbilt University	M,D*
Vanguard University of Southern California	M
Villanova University	M
Virginia Commonwealth University	M,D
Virginia Polytechnic Institute and State University	M,D,O
Virginia State University	M,D
Virginia Theological Seminary	M,D
Viterbo University	M,O
Walden University	M,D,O
Waldorf University	M
Walla Walla University	M
Washburn University	M
Washington State University	M,D
Wayland Baptist University	M
Waynesburg University	M,D
Wayne State College	M,O
Wayne State University	M,D,O
West Chester University of Pennsylvania	M,D,O
Western Connecticut State University	D
Western Governors University	M,O
Western Illinois University	M,D,O
Western Kentucky University	M,D,O
Western Michigan University	M,D,O
Western New Mexico University	M
Western State Colorado University	M
Western Washington University	M
West Liberty University	M
Westminster College (PA)	M
West Texas A&M University	M
West Virginia University	M,D
Wheeling Jesuit University	M
Whittier College	M
Whitworth University	M
Wichita State University	M,D,O
Widener University	M,D
Wilkes University	M,D
William Paterson University of New Jersey	M,O
William Woods University	M,D,O
Wilmington University	M,D
Wingate University	M,D,O
Winona State University	M,O
Winthrop University	M
Wisconsin Lutheran College	M
Worcester State University	M
Wright State University	O
Xavier University	M,D*
Xavier University of Louisiana	M
Yeshiva University	M,D,O
York College of Pennsylvania	M
Youngstown State University	M,D

EDUCATIONAL MEASUREMENT AND EVALUATION

American InterContinental University Online	M
American University	M,O
Arizona State University at the Tempe campus	D
Ball State University	M,D,O
Boston College	M,D
Brandeis University	O
Brigham Young University	D
Cambridge College	M,D,O
Claremont Graduate University	M,D,O
Clemson University	M,D,O
College of Saint Mary	M
Duquesne University	M
Eastern Michigan University	M,O
Florida State University	M,D,O
Georgetown University	M
Georgia Southern University	M,D,O
Georgia State University	M,D
Houston Baptist University	M,D
Indiana University Bloomington	M,D,O
Iowa State University of Science and Technology	M,D
James Madison University	M,D
Kent State University	M,D
Louisiana State University and Agricultural & Mechanical College	M,D,O
Loyola University Chicago	M,D,O
McNeese State University	M,O
Michigan State University	M,D,O
Missouri State University	O
Missouri Western State University	M,O
Montclair State University	O
New Mexico State University	M,D,O
North Carolina State University	D
Ohio University	M,D
Old Dominion University	D
Rutgers University–New Brunswick	M
Seton Hall University	M,D,O
Southern Connecticut State University	M,D,O

Southwestern Oklahoma State University	M
Sul Ross State University	M,O
Syracuse University	M,D,O*
Teachers College, Columbia University	M,D
Teachers College of San Joaquin	M
Tennessee Technological University	D
Texas A&M University–San Antonio	M
Université Laval	M,D,O
The University of Akron	M,O
University of Arkansas	M,D
The University of British Columbia	M,D,O
University of Calgary	M,D
University of California, Riverside	M,D,O
University of Colorado Boulder	D
University of Colorado Denver	M,D
University of Denver	M,D,O
University of Florida	M,D,O
University of Illinois at Chicago	M,D
The University of Iowa	M,D,O*
The University of Kansas	M,D
University of Kentucky	M,D
University of Louisville	M,D
University of Maryland, College Park	M,D
University of Massachusetts Amherst	M,D,O*
University of Memphis	M,D
University of Miami	M,D*
University of Michigan–Dearborn	M
University of Minnesota, Twin Cities Campus	M,D
University of Missouri–St. Louis	M,O
University of Nebraska–Lincoln	M,D,O
The University of North Carolina at Chapel Hill	M,D
The University of North Carolina at Greensboro	D
University of Northern Colorado	M,D
University of Northern Iowa	M
University of North Texas	M,D,O
University of Pennsylvania	M,D*
University of Pittsburgh	M,D*
University of Puerto Rico–Río Piedras	M
University of St. Thomas (TX)	M,D
University of South Carolina	M,D
University of Southern Mississippi	M,D,O
University of South Florida	O*
The University of Tennessee	M,D,O
The University of Texas at El Paso	M
The University of Texas at San Antonio	M,O
The University of Toledo	M,D,O
University of Victoria	M,D
University of Virginia	M,D,O
University of Washington	M,D
University of Wisconsin–Milwaukee	M,D,O*
Utah State University	M,D
Virginia Commonwealth University	D
Virginia Polytechnic Institute and State University	M,D,O
Walden University	M,D,O
Washington University in St. Louis	D
Wayland Baptist University	M
Wayne State University	M,D,O
Western Michigan University	M,D,O
West Texas A&M University	M
Wilkes University	M,D

EDUCATIONAL MEDIA/INSTRUCTIONAL TECHNOLOGY

Adelphi University	M
Alabama Agricultural and Mechanical University	M,O
Alabama State University	M,D,O
Alverno College	M
American College of Education	M
American InterContinental University Online	M
American University	M,O
Antioch University New England	M,O
Appalachian State University	M,O
Arcadia University	M,D,O
Argosy University, Atlanta	M,D,O
Argosy University, Orange County	M,D
Argosy University, Phoenix	M,D,O
Argosy University, Seattle	M,D
Argosy University, Twin Cities	M,D,O
Arizona State University at the Tempe campus	M,O
Arkansas Tech University	M,D,O
Auburn University	M,D,O*
Auburn University at Montgomery	M,O
Augustana University	M
Augusta University	D
Aurora University	M,D
Avila University	M
Azusa Pacific University	M*
Baldwin Wallace University	M
Ball State University	M,D
Barry University	M,D,O
Bay Path University	M
Bellevue University	M
Bloomsburg University of Pennsylvania	M,O
Boise State University	M,D,O
Bowling Green State University	M
Brandman University	M,D
Bridgewater State University	M
Brigham Young University	M,D
Buffalo State College, State University of New York	M
California Baptist University	M
California State University, East Bay	M
California State University, Fullerton	M
California State University, Northridge	M
California State University, Sacramento	M,D,O
California State University, Stanislaus	M
Cambridge College	M,D,O
Canisius College	M,O
Capella University	M,D
Caribbean University	M,D
Central Michigan University	M,D,O
Chestnut Hill College	M,O
Clarion University of Pennsylvania	M
Cleveland State University	D
Coastal Carolina University	M,O
Coker College	M
College of Mount Saint Vincent	M,O
The College of William and Mary	M,D*
Colorado Christian University	M
Colorado State University–Pueblo	M
Concordia University (United States)	M,D
Concordia University (Canada)	M,O
Concordia University Chicago	M
Concordia University Irvine	M*
Concordia University, St. Paul	M,D,O
Dakota State University	M
Dallas Baptist University	M
Delaware Valley University	M
DeSales University	M,O
DeVry University–Folsom Campus	M
Drexel University	M,D*
Drury University	M
Duquesne University	M,D,O
East Carolina University	M,O
Eastern Connecticut State University	M
Eastern Michigan University	M,O
Eastern New Mexico University	M
East Stroudsburg University of Pennsylvania	M
East Tennessee State University	M,O
Emporia State University	M,O
Fairfield University	M,O
Fairleigh Dickinson University, Florham Campus	M,O
Fairleigh Dickinson University, Metropolitan Campus	M,O
Fairmont State University	M
Florida Atlantic University	M
Florida Institute of Technology	M
Florida International University	M,D,O
Florida State University	M,D,O
Fontbonne University	M
Fort Hays State University	M
Framingham State University	M
Franklin University	M
Fresno Pacific University	M
Frostburg State University	M,D
Full Sail University	M
George Fox University	M,O
George Mason University	M
The George Washington University	M,O
Georgia College & State University	M
Georgian Court University	M,O
Georgia Southern University	M,O
Georgia State University	M,D,O
Goucher College	M,O
Graceland University (IA)	M
Grambling State University	M,D,O
Grand Canyon University	M,D,O
Grand Valley State University	M
Harrisburg University of Science and Technology	M
Harvard University	M,O*
Hofstra University	M,D,O
Houston Baptist University	M,D
Idaho State University	M,D
Indiana State University	M,D
Indiana University Bloomington	M,D
Indiana University of Pennsylvania	M,D
Indiana University South Bend	M,O
Instituto Tecnológico y de Estudios Superiores de Monterrey, Campus Central de Veracruz	M
Instituto Tecnológico y de Estudios Superiores de Monterrey, Campus Ciudad de México	M,D
Instituto Tecnológico y de Estudios Superiores de Monterrey, Campus Ciudad Juárez	M,D
Instituto Tecnológico y de Estudios Superiores de Monterrey, Campus Estado de México	M,D
Instituto Tecnológico y de Estudios Superiores de Monterrey, Campus Irapuato	M,D
Inter American University of Puerto Rico, Metropolitan Campus	M
Iowa State University of Science and Technology	M,D
Jacksonville State University	M
James Madison University	M
Johns Hopkins University	M*
Johnson University	M,D,O
Kansas State University	M,D,O
Keiser University	D,O
Kennesaw State University	M,D,O
Kent State University	M,D
Kutztown University of Pennsylvania	M
Lamar University	M,D
La Salle University	M,O
Lawrence Technological University	M,O
Lehigh University	M,D
Lenoir-Rhyne University	M
Lesley University	M,D,O
Lewis University	M
Lindenwood University	M,D,O
Lipscomb University	M,D,O
Long Island University–LIU Post	M,D,O
Longwood University	M
Louisiana State University and Agricultural & Mechanical College	M,D,O
Loyola University Maryland	M
Manhattan College	M
Marconi International University	M,D
Marian University (WI)	M,D
Marlboro College	M,O
Martin Luther College	M
Marygrove College	M,O
Massachusetts College of Liberal Arts	M,O
McDaniel College	M
McNeese State University	M,O
Memorial University of Newfoundland	M,D,O
Michigan State University	M,D,O
MidAmerica Nazarene University	M
Middle Tennessee State University	M,O
Midwestern State University	M
Misericordia University	M
Mississippi State University	M,D,O
Missouri Southern State University	M
Missouri State University	M
Molloy College	M,O
Montana State University Billings	M
Morehead State University	M,O
Murray State University	M,D,O
National Louis University	M,D,O
National University	M,O
Nazareth College of Rochester	M
New Jersey City University	M,D
New York Institute of Technology	M,O
New York University	M,D,O*
North Carolina Agricultural and Technical State University	M
North Carolina Central University	M
North Carolina State University	M,D
Northeastern State University	M
Northern Arizona University	M,O
Northern Illinois University	M,D
Northern State University	M
Northwestern State University of Louisiana	M,O
Northwestern University	M,D
Northwest Missouri State University	M
Nova Southeastern University	M,D,O*
Ohio University	M,D
Old Dominion University	M,D,O
Ottawa University	M
Pace University	M,O
Penn State University Park	M,D,O*
Pepperdine University	M,D
Piedmont College	M,D,O
Pittsburg State University	M
Post University	M
Purdue University	M,D,O
Purdue University Global	M
Purdue University Northwest	M
Quinnipiac University	M
Ramapo College of New Jersey	M
Regent University	M,D,O
Rockford University	M
Rowan University	M,O
Saginaw Valley State University	M
St. Cloud State University	M,O
St. John Fisher College	M
Saint Leo University	M,O
Saint Mary's University of Minnesota	M,D
St. Thomas University	M,D,O
Saint Vincent College	M
Saint Xavier University	M
Salem State University	M
Samford University	M,D,O
San Diego State University	M,D
San Francisco State University	M
Seattle Pacific University	M
Seton Hall University	M
Seton Hill University	M
Simon Fraser University	M,D
Slippery Rock University of Pennsylvania	M,D
Southern Illinois University Edwardsville	M,O
Southern New Hampshire University	M,D,O
Southern University and Agricultural and Mechanical College	M
Stanford University	M
State University of New York College at Potsdam	M
State University of New York Empire State College	M
Stockton University	M
Stony Brook University, State University of New York	M,O
Strayer University	M
Syracuse University	M,O*
Tarleton State University	M
Teachers College, Columbia University	M,D
Tennessee Technological University	M,O
Texas A&M University	M,D
Texas A&M University–Commerce	M,D,O
Texas A&M University–Corpus Christi	M,D
Texas A&M University–Kingsville	M
Texas A&M University–Texarkana	M
Texas State University	M
Texas Tech University	M,D
Thomas Edison State University	M,O
Tiffin University	M
Touro College	M
Towson University	M
Trevecca Nazarene University	M
Trident University International	M,D
Université Laval	M,D
University at Albany, State University of New York	M,D,O
University at Buffalo, the State University of New York	M,D,O
The University of Akron	M
University of Alaska Southeast	M
University of Alberta	M,D
University of Arkansas	M
University of Arkansas at Little Rock	M
University of Central Arkansas	M
University of Central Florida	M,D,O
University of Central Missouri	M,D,O
University of Central Oklahoma	M
University of Colorado Denver	M
University of Connecticut	M,D*
University of Dayton	M
The University of Findlay	M,D
University of Georgia	M,D,O
University of Hartford	M
University of Hawaii at Manoa	M,D
University of Houston–Clear Lake	M
University of Houston–Victoria	M,O
University of Illinois at Springfield	M,O
The University of Kansas	M,D
University of Kentucky	M,D
University of Louisiana at Lafayette	M
University of Maine	M,D,O
University of Maine at Farmington	M
University of Maryland, Baltimore County	M,O
University of Maryland, College Park	M,D,O
University of Maryland University College	M
University of Massachusetts Amherst	M,D,O*
University of Massachusetts Boston	M,O
University of Memphis	M,D,O
University of Michigan–Dearborn	M
University of Michigan–Flint	M,D,O
University of Minnesota, Twin Cities Campus	M,D,O
University of Missouri	D
University of Nebraska at Kearney	M
University of Nevada, Las Vegas	M,D,O
University of New Hampshire	M,O
University of New Mexico	M,D,O
The University of North Carolina at Charlotte	M,D,O
The University of North Carolina at Greensboro	M,D,O
The University of North Carolina Wilmington	M
University of North Dakota	M
University of Northern Iowa	M
University of North Florida	M,D
University of Oklahoma	M,D,O*
University of Pennsylvania	M*
University of Phoenix–Online Campus	D,O
University of Saint Joseph	M
University of San Francisco	M,D
University of Sioux Falls	M,O
University of South Africa	M,D
University of South Alabama	M,D,O
University of South Carolina	M
University of South Carolina Aiken	M
University of South Dakota	M
University of Southern Mississippi	M,D
University of South Florida	O*
University of Tampa	M
The University of Tennessee	M,D,O
The University of Texas at Austin	M,D
The University of Texas at San Antonio	M,D
The University of Texas Rio Grande Valley	M,D
University of the Sacred Heart	M
The University of Toledo	M,D,O
University of Utah	M,D,O
University of Virginia	M,D,O
University of Washington	M,D
The University of West Alabama	M,O
University of West Florida	M,D
University of West Georgia	M,D,O
University of Wisconsin–Milwaukee	M,O*
University of Wyoming	M,D
Utah State University	M,D,O
Utah Valley University	M
Valley City State University	M
Virginia Commonwealth University	M
Virginia Polytechnic Institute and State University	M,O
Walden University	M,D,O
Warner University	M
Wayland Baptist University	M
Waynesburg University	M,D
Wayne State University	M,D,O
Webster University	M,O
West Chester University of Pennsylvania	M,O
Western Connecticut State University	M
Western Governors University	M,O
Western Illinois University	M,O
Western Kentucky University	M,O

*M—masters degree; D—doctorate; O—other advanced degree; *—Close-Up and/or Display*

Western Michigan University	M,D,O
Western Oregon University	M
West Texas A&M University	M
West Virginia University	M,D
Widener University	M,D
Wilkes University	M,D
William Paterson University of New Jersey	M,O
William Woods University	M,D,O
Wilmington University	M,D
Wilson College	M
Wisconsin Lutheran College	M
Worcester Polytechnic Institute	M,D
York College of Pennsylvania	M
Youngstown State University	M

EDUCATIONAL POLICY

Alabama State University	M,D,O
American University of Beirut	M,D
Arizona State University at the Tempe campus	D
Ball State University	D
Brigham Young University	M,D
California State University, Sacramento	M,D,O
Cleveland State University	D
The College of William and Mary	M,D*
Cornell University	M,D
Eastern Michigan University	M
Florida State University	M,D,O
The George Washington University	M,D,O
Georgia State University	M,D,O
Harvard University	M*
Howard University	M,D
Illinois State University	M,D
Indiana University Bloomington	M,D,O
Johns Hopkins University	D*
Loyola University Chicago	M,D
Marquette University	M,D,O
Michigan State University	D
New York University	M,D*
Niagara University	M,D,O
Northwest Missouri State University	M,D,O
The Ohio State University	M,D,O
Oregon State University	M,D
Penn State University Park	M,D,O*
Rutgers University–Camden	M
Rutgers University–New Brunswick	D
Stanford University	M
Teachers College, Columbia University	M,D
University at Albany, State University of New York	M,D,O
University of Alberta	M,D,O
University of Arkansas	D
The University of British Columbia	M,D
University of California, Riverside	M,D,O
University of Colorado Boulder	M,D
University of Colorado Denver	M,D,O
University of Denver	M,D,O
University of Florida	M,D,O
University of Georgia	D,O
University of Hawaii at Manoa	D
University of Illinois at Chicago	M,D
University of Illinois at Urbana–Champaign	M,D,O
The University of Iowa	M,D,O*
The University of Kansas	M,D
University of Kentucky	M,D
University of Maryland, Baltimore County	M,D
University of Massachusetts Amherst	M,D,O*
University of Massachusetts Boston	D
University of Massachusetts Dartmouth	M,D,O
University of Minnesota, Twin Cities Campus	M,D
University of Missouri–St. Louis	D
University of Mobile	M
The University of North Carolina Wilmington	M
University of Northern Colorado	M,D,O
University of Pennsylvania	M,D*
University of Pittsburgh	D*
University of Rochester	M,D*
University of Southern California	D*
The University of Texas at Arlington	M,D
University of Utah	M,D
University of Vermont	D
University of Virginia	D
University of Washington	M,D
The University of Western Ontario	M
University of Wisconsin–Madison	M,D,O
University of Wisconsin–Milwaukee	M,O*
Vanderbilt University	M,D*
Virginia Polytechnic Institute and State University	M,D,O
Wayne State University	M,D,O
West Chester University of Pennsylvania	M,D,O

EDUCATIONAL PSYCHOLOGY

Alliant International University–Irvine	M,D,O
Alliant International University–Los Angeles	M,D,O
Alliant International University–San Diego	M,D,O
Alliant International University–San Francisco	M,D,O
American International College	M,D,O
Andrews University	M,D
Ball State University	M,D
Baylor University	M,D,O
Boston College	M,D
Brigham Young University	M,D
California Coast University	M,D
California State University, Long Beach	M,D
California State University, Northridge	M
Capella University	M,D
Chapman University	M,D,O*
Clark Atlanta University	M
The College of Saint Rose	M,O
Eastern Michigan University	M,O
Edinboro University of Pennsylvania	M,O
Florida State University	M,D,O
Fordham University	M,D
George Mason University	M,D
Georgia State University	M,D
The Graduate Center, City University of New York	D
Harvard University	M*
Holy Names University	M,O
Howard University	D
Immaculata University	M,D,O
Indiana University Bloomington	M,D,O
Indiana University of Pennsylvania	M,O
Instituto Tecnologico de Santo Domingo	M,O
John Carroll University	M,O
Kent State University	M,D
La Sierra University	M,O
McGill University	M,D,O
Memorial University of Newfoundland	M,D,O
Miami University	M,O
Michigan School of Professional Psychology	M,D
Michigan State University	M,D,O
Mississippi State University	M,D,O
Mount Saint Vincent University	M
National Louis University	M,D,O
New York University	M,D*
Northern Arizona University	M,D,O
Northern Illinois University	M,D,O
Oklahoma State University	M,D,O
Old Dominion University	D
Penn State University Park	M,D,O*
Philadelphia College of Osteopathic Medicine	M,D,O*
Pontifical Catholic University of Puerto Rico	M
Purdue University	M,D,O
Regent University	M,D,O
Rutgers University–New Brunswick	M,D
Simon Fraser University	M,D
Southern Illinois University Carbondale	M,D
State University of New York College at Oneonta	M,O
Teachers College, Columbia University	M,D,O
Temple University	M,D,O*
Tennessee Technological University	M,O
Texas A&M University	M,D
Texas A&M University–Central Texas	M,O
Texas A&M University–Commerce	M,D,O
Texas Tech University	M,D
Universidad de Iberoamerica	M,D
Université de Moncton	M
Université de Montréal	M,D,O
Université du Québec à Trois-Rivières	M,D
Université du Québec en Outaouais	M
Université Laval	M,D
University at Buffalo, the State University of New York	M,D,O
University of Alberta	M,D
The University of Arizona	M,D,O
University of California, Davis	M,D
University of California, Riverside	M,D,O
University of Colorado Boulder	M,D
University of Connecticut	M,D,O*
University of Georgia	O
University of Hawaii at Manoa	M,D
University of Houston	M,D
University of Illinois at Chicago	M,D
University of Illinois at Urbana–Champaign	M,D,O
The University of Iowa	M,D,O*
The University of Kansas	M,D
University of Kentucky	M,D,O
University of Louisville	M,D
The University of Manchester	M,D
University of Manitoba	M
University of Memphis	M,D
University of Minnesota, Twin Cities Campus	M,D,O
University of Missouri	M,D,O
University of Missouri–St. Louis	D
University of Nebraska–Lincoln	M,D,O
University of Nevada, Reno	M,D,O
University of New Mexico	M,D
The University of North Carolina at Chapel Hill	M,D
University of Northern Colorado	M,D
University of Northern Iowa	M
University of North Texas	M,D,O
University of Oklahoma	M,D*
University of Regina	M
University of Saskatchewan	M,D,O
University of South Africa	M,D
University of South Carolina	M,D
University of South Dakota	M,D,O
University of Southern California	D*
University of Southern Maine	M,O
University of South Florida	M,D,O*
The University of Tennessee	M,D,O
The University of Texas at Austin	M,D
The University of Texas at El Paso	M
The University of Texas at San Antonio	M,O
The University of Texas Rio Grande Valley	M
University of the Pacific	M,D,O
The University of Toledo	M,D,O
University of Utah	M,D,O
University of Victoria	M,D
University of Virginia	M,D,O
University of Washington	M,D
The University of Western Ontario	M
University of Wisconsin–Madison	M,D
University of Wisconsin–Milwaukee	M,D,O*
Virginia Commonwealth University	D
Walden University	M,D,O
Washington State University	M,D
Wayne State University	M,D,O
Webster University	M,O
West Virginia University	M,D
Wichita State University	M,D,O
Widener University	M,D

EDUCATION OF STUDENTS WITH SEVERE/MULTIPLE DISABILITIES

Cleveland State University	M
Georgia State University	M
Hunter College of the City University of New York	M
Norfolk State University	M
Syracuse University	M*
Teachers College, Columbia University	M,D,O
University of Illinois at Urbana–Champaign	M,D,O
West Liberty University	M

EDUCATION OF THE GIFTED

Arkansas State University	M,D,O
Ball State University	M,D,O
Barry University	M,D,O
Canisius College	M,O
Carlos Albizu University, Miami Campus	M,D
Carthage College	M,O
The College of New Rochelle	O
The College of William and Mary	M*
Colorado Mesa University	M,O
Converse College	M
Eastern New Mexico University	M
Elon University	M
Emporia State University	M
Florida Gulf Coast University	M
George Mason University	M
Grand Canyon University	M,D,O
Hardin-Simmons University	M
Hofstra University	M,D,O
James Madison University	M
Johns Hopkins University	M,O*
Kent State University	M,D,O
Liberty University	M,D,O
Lindenwood University	M,D,O
Lynn University	M,D
McNeese State University	M
Meredith College	M,O
Millersville University of Pennsylvania	M
Mississippi University for Women	M
Morehead State University	M,O
Northeastern Illinois University	M
Pacific University	M
Purdue University	M,D,O
Regent University	M,D,O
St. Bonaventure University	M,O
St. John's University (NY)	D,O
Saint Leo University	M,O
Saint Mary's University of Minnesota	M,O
St. Thomas University	M,D,O
Samford University	M,D,O
Southeastern University (FL)	M,D
Southern Arkansas University–Magnolia	M
Southern Methodist University	M,D
Teachers College, Columbia University	M,D
Tennessee Technological University	D
University at Buffalo, the State University of New York	M,D,O
The University of Alabama	M,D,O
University of Arkansas at Little Rock	M,O
University of Central Arkansas	M,O
University of Connecticut	O*
University of Louisiana at Lafayette	M
University of Minnesota, Twin Cities Campus	M,D,O
University of Nebraska at Kearney	M
The University of North Carolina at Charlotte	M,D,O
University of Northern Colorado	M,D
University of North Texas	M,D,O
University of Southern Maine	M,O
The University of Toledo	M,D,O
University of Virginia	M,D,O
Viterbo University	M,O
Western Washington University	M
West Virginia University	M,D
Whitworth University	M
Wichita State University	M
William Carey University	M,O
Wilmington University	M,D
Youngstown State University	M

ELECTRICAL ENGINEERING

Air Force Institute of Technology	M,D
Alfred University	M,D
The American University in Cairo	M,D,O
American University of Beirut	M,D
American University of Sharjah	M,D
Arizona State University at the Tempe campus	M,D,O
Arkansas Tech University	M
Auburn University	M,D*
Baylor University	M,D
Binghamton University, State University of New York	M,D
Boise State University	M,D
Boston University	M,D*
Bradley University	M
Brigham Young University	M,D
Brown University	M,D
Bucknell University	M
California Institute of Technology	M,D,O
California Polytechnic State University, San Luis Obispo	M*
California State Polytechnic University, Pomona	M
California State University, Chico	M
California State University, Fresno	M
California State University, Fullerton	M
California State University, Long Beach	M
California State University, Los Angeles	M
California State University, Northridge	M
California State University, Sacramento	M
Capitol Technology University	M
Carleton University	M,D
Carnegie Mellon University	M,D
Case Western Reserve University	M,D*
The Catholic University of America	M,D
The Citadel, The Military College of South Carolina	M,O
City College of the City University of New York	M,D
Clarkson University	M,D
Clemson University	M,D
Cleveland State University	M,D
Colorado School of Mines	M,D
Colorado State University	M,D
Colorado Technical University Aurora	M
Colorado Technical University Colorado Springs	M
Columbia University	M,D*
Concordia University (Canada)	M,D
Cooper Union for the Advancement of Science and Art	M
Cornell University	M,D
Dalhousie University	M,D
Dartmouth College	M,D*
Drexel University	M*
Duke University	M,D*
École Polytechnique de Montréal	M,D,O
Embry-Riddle Aeronautical University–Daytona	M
Fairfield University	M,O
Fairleigh Dickinson University, Metropolitan Campus	M
Farmingdale State College	M
Florida Agricultural and Mechanical University	M,D
Florida Atlantic University	M,D
Florida Institute of Technology	M,D
Florida International University	M,D
Florida State University	M,D
Gannon University	M
George Mason University	M,D,O
The George Washington University	M,D,O
Georgia Institute of Technology	M,D
Georgia Southern University	M
Grand Valley State University	M
Harvard University	M,D*
Howard University	M,D
Illinois Institute of Technology	M,D
Indiana University–Purdue University Fort Wayne	M
Indiana University–Purdue University Indianapolis	M,D
Instituto Tecnológico y de Estudios Superiores de Monterrey, Campus Chihuahua	M,O
Instituto Tecnológico y de Estudios Superiores de Monterrey, Campus Monterrey	M,D
Inter American University of Puerto Rico, Bayamón Campus	M
International Technological University	M,D
Iowa State University of Science and Technology	M,D
Johns Hopkins University	M,D,O*
Kansas State University	M,D
Kennesaw State University	M
Kettering University	M
Lakehead University	M
Lamar University	M,D
Lawrence Technological University	M,D
Lehigh University	M,D
Louisiana State University and Agricultural & Mechanical College	M,D
Loyola Marymount University	M
Manhattan College	M
Marquette University	M,D,O
Marshall University	M
Massachusetts Institute of Technology	M,D,O
McGill University	M,D
McMaster University	M,D
McNeese State University	M
Memorial University of Newfoundland	M,D
Mercer University	M
Miami University	M
Michigan State University	M,D
Michigan Technological University	M,D,O
Mississippi State University	M,D
Missouri University of Science and Technology	M,D
Montana State University	M,D

Montana Tech of The University of Montana M
Morgan State University M,D,O
National University M
Naval Postgraduate School M,D,O
New Jersey Institute of Technology M,D
New Mexico Institute of Mining and Technology M
New Mexico State University M,D,O
New York Institute of Technology M
New York University M,D*
Norfolk State University M
North Carolina Agricultural and Technical State University M,D
North Carolina State University M,D
Northeastern University M,D,O
Northern Arizona University M,D
Northern Illinois University M
Northwestern Polytechnic University M,D
Northwestern University M,D
Oakland University M,D
The Ohio State University M,D
Ohio University M,D
Oklahoma Christian University M
Oklahoma State University M,D
Old Dominion University M,D
Oregon Health & Science University M,D
Oregon State University M,D
Penn State Harrisburg M,O
Penn State University Park M,D*
Pittsburg State University M
Polytechnic University of Puerto Rico M
Portland State University M,D
Prairie View A&M University M,D
Princeton University M,D
Purdue University M,D
Purdue University Northwest M
Queen's University at Kingston M,D
Rensselaer at Hartford M
Rensselaer Polytechnic Institute M,D
Rice University M,D
Rochester Institute of Technology M
Rose-Hulman Institute of Technology M
Rowan University M
Royal Military College of Canada M,D
Rutgers University–New Brunswick M,D
St. Cloud State University M
St. Mary's University (United States) M
San Diego State University M
San Francisco State University M
San Jose State University M
Santa Clara University M,D,O
South Dakota School of Mines and Technology M
South Dakota State University M,D
Southern Illinois University Carbondale M,D
Southern Illinois University Edwardsville M
Southern Methodist University M,D
Stanford University M,D
State University of New York at New Paltz M
Stevens Institute of Technology M,D,O
Stony Brook University, State University of New York M,D
Syracuse University M,D*
Temple University M,D*
Tennessee State University M,D
Tennessee Technological University M
Texas A&M University M,D
Texas A&M University–Kingsville M
Texas State University M
Texas Tech University M,D
Tufts University M,D,O*
Tuskegee University M
Universidad de las Américas Puebla M
Universidad del Turabo M
Université de Moncton M
Université de Sherbrooke M,D
Université du Québec à Trois-Rivières M,D
Université Laval M,D
University at Buffalo, the State University of New York M,D
The University of Akron M,D
The University of Alabama M,D
The University of Alabama at Birmingham M,D
The University of Alabama in Huntsville M,D
University of Alaska Fairbanks M
University of Alberta M,D
The University of Arizona M,D
University of Arkansas M,D
University of Bridgeport M
The University of British Columbia M,D
University of Calgary M,D
University of California, Berkeley M,D
University of California, Davis M,D
University of California, Irvine M,D
University of California, Los Angeles M,D*
University of California, Merced M,D
University of California, Riverside M,D
University of California, San Diego M,D*
University of California, Santa Barbara M,D
University of California, Santa Cruz M,D*
University of Central Florida M,D
University of Central Oklahoma M
University of Cincinnati M,D
University of Colorado Boulder M,D
University of Colorado Colorado Springs M,D
University of Colorado Denver M,D
University of Connecticut M,D*
University of Dayton M,D
University of Delaware M,D*
University of Denver M,D
University of Detroit Mercy M,D
University of Florida M,D
University of Hawaii at Manoa M,D
University of Houston M,D
University of Idaho M,D
University of Illinois at Chicago M,D
University of Illinois at Urbana–Champaign M,D
The University of Iowa M,D*
The University of Kansas M,D
University of Kentucky M,D
University of Louisville M,D
University of Maine M,D
The University of Manchester M,D
University of Manitoba M,D
University of Maryland, Baltimore County M,D
University of Maryland, College Park M,D
University of Massachusetts Amherst M,D*
University of Massachusetts Dartmouth M,D,O
University of Massachusetts Lowell M,D
University of Memphis M,D,O
University of Miami M,D*
University of Michigan M,D*
University of Michigan–Dearborn M,D
University of Minnesota, Duluth M
University of Minnesota, Twin Cities Campus M,D
University of Mississippi M,D
University of Missouri–Kansas City M,D,O
University of Nebraska–Lincoln M,D
University of Nevada, Las Vegas M,D
University of Nevada, Reno M,D
University of New Brunswick Fredericton M,D
University of New Hampshire M,D,O
University of New Haven M*
University of New Mexico M,D
University of New Orleans M
The University of North Carolina at Charlotte M,D
University of North Dakota M,D
University of North Florida M
University of North Texas M,D,O
University of Notre Dame M,D
University of Oklahoma M,D*
University of Ottawa M,D
University of Pennsylvania M,D*
University of Pittsburgh M,D*
University of Portland M
University of Puerto Rico–Mayagüez M,D
University of Rhode Island M,D*
University of Rochester M,D*
University of St. Thomas (MN) M,O
University of Saskatchewan M,D,O
University of South Alabama M
University of South Carolina M,D
University of Southern California M,D,O*
University of South Florida M,D*
The University of Tennessee M,D
The University of Tennessee at Chattanooga M
The University of Texas at Arlington M,D
The University of Texas at Austin M,D
The University of Texas at Dallas M,D
The University of Texas at San Antonio M,D
The University of Texas at Tyler M
The University of Texas Rio Grande Valley M
University of the District of Columbia M
The University of Toledo M,D
University of Toronto M,D
The University of Tulsa M,D
University of Utah M,D
University of Vermont M,D
University of Victoria M,D
University of Virginia M,D
University of Washington M,D
University of Waterloo M,D
The University of Western Ontario M,D
University of Windsor M,D
University of Wisconsin–Madison M,D
University of Wisconsin–Milwaukee M,D*
University of Wyoming M,D
Utah State University M,D
Vanderbilt University M,D*
Villanova University M,O
Virginia Polytechnic Institute and State University M,D,O
Washington State University M,D
Wayne State University M,D
Western Michigan University M,D
Western New England University M
West Virginia University M,D
Wichita State University M,D
Widener University M
Wilkes University M
Worcester Polytechnic Institute M,D,O
Wright State University M
Yale University M,D
Youngstown State University M

ELECTRONIC COMMERCE

California State University, Fullerton M
Claremont Graduate University M,D,O
Dalhousie University M,D
DePaul University M,D
Eastern Michigan University M,O
Fairleigh Dickinson University, Metropolitan Campus M
Florida Institute of Technology M,D
Fordham University M,D
HEC Montreal M,O
Instituto Tecnológico y de Estudios Superiores de Monterrey, Campus Central de Veracruz M
Instituto Tecnológico y de Estudios Superiores de Monterrey, Campus Ciudad Juárez M
Instituto Tecnológico y de Estudios Superiores de Monterrey, Campus Estado de México M,D
Instituto Tecnológico y de Estudios Superiores de Monterrey, Campus Irapuato M,D
Lewis University M
Northwestern University M
Pace University O
Stevens Institute of Technology M,O
Towson University M,O
Universidad del Este M
Université de Montréal M,D
Université de Sherbrooke M
Université Laval M,O
University at Buffalo, the State University of New York M,D,O
University of New Brunswick Saint John M
University of North Florida M
University of Ottawa M,D,O
University of Phoenix–Dallas Campus M
University of Phoenix–Houston Campus M
University of Phoenix–San Antonio Campus M

ELECTRONIC MATERIALS

Colorado School of Mines M,D
Princeton University D
University of Arkansas M,D
University of Memphis M,O
Wayne State University M

ELEMENTARY EDUCATION

Acacia University M
Adelphi University M
Alabama Agricultural and Mechanical University M,D,O
Alabama State University M,D,O
Alaska Pacific University M
Albright College M
Alcorn State University M,O
American International College M,D,O
American University of Beirut M,D
American University of Puerto Rico M
Anderson University (SC) M
Andrews University M,D,O
Anna Maria College M,O
Antioch University New England M,O
Appalachian State University M,O
Aquinas College (TN) M
Arcadia University M,D,O
Argosy University, Atlanta M,D,O
Argosy University, Chicago M,D,O
Argosy University, Hawai`i M,D
Argosy University, Los Angeles M,D
Argosy University, Northern Virginia M,D,O
Argosy University, Orange County M,D,O
Argosy University, Phoenix M,D,O
Argosy University, Seattle M,D
Argosy University, Tampa M,D,O
Argosy University, Twin Cities M,D,O
Arizona State University at the Tempe campus M
Arkansas State University M,D,O
Arkansas Tech University M,D,O
Auburn University at Montgomery M,O
Augusta University M,O
Austin Peay State University M,O
Avila University M,O
Ball State University M,D,O
Bank Street College of Education M
Barry University M,D,O
Barton College M
Bayamón Central University M,O
Bellarmine University M,D,O
Benedictine University M
Bethel University (MN) M,D,O
Blue Mountain College M
Bob Jones University M,D,O
Boston College M
Bowie State University M
Brandeis University M,O
Brandman University M,D
Bridgewater State University M
Brooklyn College of the City University of New York M,O
Brown University M
Buffalo State College, State University of New York M
Cabrini University M,D
California Lutheran University M,D
California State University, Fullerton M
California State University, Long Beach M
California State University, Los Angeles M
California State University, Northridge M
California State University, Sacramento M,D,O
California State University, Stanislaus M
California University of Pennsylvania M
Calvary University M
Cambridge College M,D,O
Campbell University M
Canisius College M,O
Capella University M,D
Caribbean University M,D
Carroll University M
Carson-Newman University M
Catawba College M
Centenary College of Louisiana M
Central Connecticut State University M,O
Central Michigan University M,D,O
Chadron State College M,O
Chaminade University of Honolulu M
Chapman University M,D,O*
Charleston Southern University M
Chatham University M
Chestnut Hill College M
Cheyney University of Pennsylvania M
Chicago State University M
City University of Seattle M,O
Clemson University M,D,O
College of Charleston M
The College of New Jersey M
The College of New Rochelle M
College of Saint Elizabeth M,O
College of St. Joseph M
College of Staten Island of the City University of New York M
The College of William and Mary M*
Colorado Christian University M
The Colorado College M
Columbia College (SC) M
Columbia International University M,D,O
Concordia University (United States) M,D
Concordia University Chicago M
Concordia University, Nebraska M
Converse College M
Creighton University M
Curry College M,O
Dallas Baptist University M
Delta State University M,D,O
DePaul University M,D
Dominican College M
Dominican University M
Drew University M,D,O
Drury University M
Duquesne University M
D'Youville College M,D
East Carolina University M,O
Eastern Connecticut State University M
Eastern Illinois University M
Eastern Kentucky University M
Eastern Nazarene College M,O
Eastern New Mexico University M
Eastern Oregon University M
Eastern University M,O
Eastern Washington University M
East Stroudsburg University of Pennsylvania M
East Tennessee State University M,O
Elizabeth City State University M
Elms College M,O
Elon University M
Emporia State University M
Endicott College M
Fairfield University M,O
Faulkner University M
Fayetteville State University M
Fitchburg State University M
Florida Agricultural and Mechanical University M
Florida Atlantic University M
Florida Gulf Coast University M
Florida Institute of Technology M
Florida International University M,D,O
Florida Memorial University M
Florida State University M,D,O
Fontbonne University M
Fordham University M,O
Framingham State University M
Franklin Pierce University M,D,O
Frostburg State University M,D
Gallaudet University M,D,O
George Mason University M
The George Washington University M
Georgia State University M,D,O
Gonzaga University M,D
Gordon College M,O
Goucher College M,O
Grand Canyon University M,D,O
Grand Valley State University M
Greensboro College M
Greenville University M
Harding University M,O
Hawai`i Pacific University M
High Point University M,D
Hofstra University M,D,O
Holy Family University M
Hood College M,O*
Hope International University M
Houston Baptist University M
Howard University M
Hunter College of the City University of New York M
Huntington University M,D
Idaho State University M
Indiana University Bloomington M,D,O
Indiana University Northwest M,O

M—masters degree; D—doctorate; O—other advanced degree; *—Close-Up and/or Display

Indiana University–Purdue University Fort Wayne	M
Indiana University South Bend	M,O
Indiana University Southeast	M
Inter American University of Puerto Rico, Aguadilla Campus	M
Inter American University of Puerto Rico, Arecibo Campus	M
Inter American University of Puerto Rico, Barranquitas Campus	M
Inter American University of Puerto Rico, Guayama Campus	M
Inter American University of Puerto Rico, Metropolitan Campus	M
Inter American University of Puerto Rico, Ponce Campus	M
Inter American University of Puerto Rico, San Germán Campus	M
Iowa State University of Science and Technology	M,D
Ithaca College	M
Jackson State University	M,D,O
Jacksonville State University	M
James Madison University	M
Johns Hopkins University	M*
Johnson & Wales University	M
Kansas State University	M,D,O
Keuka College	M
Kutztown University of Pennsylvania	M
Lake Forest College	M
Lancaster Bible College	M,D
Langston University	M
Lasell College	M,O
Lee University	M,O
Lehigh University	M,D
Lehman College of the City University of New York	M
Le Moyne College	M,O
Lesley University	M,D,O
Lewis & Clark College	M
Lewis University	M
Liberty University	M,D,O
Lincoln University (MO)	M
Lock Haven University of Pennsylvania	M
Long Island University–Brentwood Campus	M,O
Long Island University–Hudson	M,O
Long Island University–Riverhead	M,O
Longwood University	M
Louisiana State University and Agricultural & Mechanical College	M,D,O
Louisiana Tech University	M,D,O
Loyola Marymount University	M
Loyola University Chicago	M
Loyola University Maryland	M,O
Manhattan College	M,O
Manhattanville College	M,O
Mansfield University of Pennsylvania	M
Marquette University	M,D,O
Mars Hill University	M
Mary Baldwin University	M
Marygrove College	M,O
Marymount University	M
Maryville University of Saint Louis	M,D
Marywood University	M
McDaniel College	M,O
McNeese State University	M,O
Medaille College	M
Mercy College	M
Meredith College	M,O
Merrimack College	M,O
Metropolitan College of New York	M
Metropolitan State University of Denver	M
Middle Tennessee State University	M,O
Milligan College	M,D,O
Minot State University	M
Mississippi College	M,D,O
Mississippi State University	M,D,O
Missouri State University	M,O
Monmouth University	M,D,O*
Montana State University Billings	M,O
Morehead State University	M,O
Morgan State University	M
Mount Saint Vincent University	M
Murray State University	M,O
National Louis University	M,D,O
Nazareth College of Rochester	M
Neumann University	M
New Jersey City University	M
New York Institute of Technology	M
New York University	M*
Niagara University	M,O
Nicholls State University	M
North Carolina Agricultural and Technical State University	M
North Carolina State University	M
Northeastern Illinois University	M
Northeastern University	M
Northern Arizona University	M,D
Northern Illinois University	M
Northwest Christian University	M
Northwestern Oklahoma State University	M
Northwestern State University of Louisiana	M,O
Northwestern University	M
Northwest Missouri State University	M,D,O
Nyack College	M
Oakland City University	M,D
Oakland University	M,O
Oklahoma City University	M
Old Dominion University	M,O
Olivet Nazarene University	M
Oregon State University	M
Ottawa University	M
Pace University	M,O
Pacific Union College	M
Pacific University	M
Pfeiffer University	M
Point Park University	M,D
Prescott College	M,D
Providence College	M
Purdue University	M,D,O
Queens College of the City University of New York	M,O
Queens University of Charlotte	M
Quinnipiac University	M
Regent University	M,D,O
Regis College (MA)	M,D
Regis University	M,O
Rhode Island College	M
Rider University	M
Rivier University	M,D,O
Rockford University	M
Rollins College	M
Roosevelt University	M
Rosemont College	M
Rutgers University–New Brunswick	M,D
Sage Graduate School	M
St. John Fisher College	M,O
St. John's University (NY)	M
Saint Joseph's University	M,D,O*
Saint Mary's University of Minnesota	M
Saint Peter's University	M,O
St. Thomas Aquinas College	M,O
St. Thomas University	M,D,O
Saint Xavier University	M
Salem College	M
Salem State University	M
Samford University	M,D,O
San Diego State University	M
San Francisco State University	M
San Jose State University	M,D
Seton Hill University	M
Shenandoah University	M,D,O
Shippensburg University of Pennsylvania	M
Siena Heights University	M,O
Sierra Nevada College	M
Simmons College	M,D,O
Sinte Gleska University	M
Slippery Rock University of Pennsylvania	M
Smith College	M
South Carolina State University	M
Southeastern Louisiana University	M
Southeastern University (FL)	M,D
Southeast Missouri State University	M,D,O
Southern Connecticut State University	M,O
Southern New Hampshire University	M,D,O
Southern Oregon University	M
Southern University and Agricultural and Mechanical College	M
Southwestern College (KS)	M,D
Southwestern Oklahoma State University	M
Spalding University	M
Springfield College	M,O
Spring Hill College	M
Stanford University	M
State University of New York at New Paltz	M
State University of New York at Oswego	M
State University of New York at Plattsburgh	M,O
State University of New York College at Oneonta	M
State University of New York College at Potsdam	M
Stephen F. Austin State University	M
Sul Ross State University	M
Tarleton State University	M
Teachers College, Columbia University	M,D
Tennessee State University	M,D
Tennessee Technological University	M,O
Texas A&M University–Commerce	M,D,O
Texas A&M University–Corpus Christi	M
Texas State University	M
Texas Tech University	M,D
Towson University	M
Trevecca Nazarene University	M,O
Trinity Washington University	M
Troy University	M,O
Tufts University	M,D*
Union College (KY)	M
Universidad del Este	M
Universidad Metropolitana	M
Université de Sherbrooke	M,O
University at Buffalo, the State University of New York	M,D,O
The University of Akron	M
The University of Alabama	M,D,O
The University of Alabama at Birmingham	M
University of Alaska Southeast	M
University of Alberta	M,D
The University of Arizona	M,D
University of Arkansas at Pine Bluff	M
University of Bridgeport	M,D,O
University of California, Irvine	M,D
University of Central Florida	M,D
University of Central Missouri	M,D,O
University of Central Oklahoma	M
University of Colorado Denver	M
University of Connecticut	M,D*
University of Dayton	M
University of Florida	M,D,O
University of Hartford	M
University of Illinois at Chicago	M,D
University of Indianapolis	M
The University of Iowa	M,D*
University of Kentucky	M,D
University of La Verne	M,D,O
University of Louisiana at Monroe	M
University of Louisville	M,D,O
University of Mary Hardin-Baylor	M,D
University of Maryland, Baltimore County	M
University of Mary Washington	M
University of Massachusetts Amherst	M,D,O*
University of Memphis	M,D,O
University of Minnesota, Twin Cities Campus	M
University of Mississippi	M,D,O
University of Missouri	M,D,O
University of Missouri–St. Louis	M
University of Montevallo	M
University of Nebraska at Kearney	M
University of Nebraska at Omaha	M
University of Nevada, Las Vegas	M,D,O
University of Nevada, Reno	M
University of New Hampshire	M,O
University of New Mexico	M
University of North Alabama	M,O
The University of North Carolina at Charlotte	M,O
The University of North Carolina at Greensboro	D
The University of North Carolina at Pembroke	M
The University of North Carolina Wilmington	M
University of North Dakota	M
University of Northern Colorado	M
University of Northern Iowa	M
University of North Florida	M
University of Oklahoma	M,D*
University of Pennsylvania	M*
University of Phoenix–Bay Area Campus	M,D,O
University of Phoenix–Central Valley Campus	M
University of Phoenix–Hawaii Campus	M
University of Phoenix–Las Vegas Campus	M
University of Phoenix–Online Campus	M,O
University of Phoenix–Phoenix Campus	M
University of Phoenix–Sacramento Valley Campus	M,O
University of Phoenix–San Diego Campus	M
University of Pittsburgh	M*
University of Puget Sound	M
University of St. Francis (IL)	M,D,O
University of Saint Joseph	M
University of Saint Mary	M
University of St. Thomas (TX)	M,D
University of South Alabama	M,D
University of South Carolina	M,D
University of South Carolina Upstate	M
University of South Dakota	M
University of Southern Indiana	M
University of Southern Mississippi	M,D
University of South Florida	M,D,O*
University of South Florida, St. Petersburg	M
University of South Florida Sarasota-Manatee	M
The University of Tennessee	M,D,O
The University of Tennessee at Chattanooga	M,D,O
The University of Tennessee at Martin	M
The University of Texas Rio Grande Valley	M,D
University of the Cumberlands	M,D,O
University of the District of Columbia	M
The University of Toledo	M,D,O
University of Utah	M,D,O
University of Vermont	M
University of Virginia	M,D,O
University of Washington, Tacoma	M
The University of West Alabama	M,O
University of West Florida	M
University of Wisconsin–Milwaukee	M*
University of Wisconsin–River Falls	M
University of Wisconsin–Stevens Point	M
Utah State University	M
Utah Valley University	M
Valdosta State University	M
Valley City State University	M
Valparaiso University	M,O
Vanderbilt University	M*
Virginia Commonwealth University	M
Wagner College	M
Walden University	M,D,O
Warner University	M
Washington State University	M,D
Washington University in St. Louis	M
Wayland Baptist University	M
Wayne State College	M
Wayne State University	M,D,O
Webster University	M,O
Western Governors University	M,O
Western Kentucky University	M,O
Western New Mexico University	M
Western Washington University	M
Westfield State University	M
West Virginia University	M,D
Wheaton College	M
Whittier College	M
Whitworth University	M
Widener University	M,D
William Carey University	M,O
William Paterson University of New Jersey	M,O
Wilmington University	M,D
Wilson College	M
Wingate University	M,D,O
Worcester State University	M,O
Wright State University	M
Xavier University	M*

EMERGENCY MANAGEMENT

Adelphi University	O
Adler University	M
Anna Maria College	M,O
Arizona State University at the Tempe campus	M,D
Arkansas State University	M,O
Arkansas Tech University	M
Auburn University at Montgomery	M
Ball State University	M,O
Benedictine University	M
Boston University	M*
California State University, Long Beach	M
California State University Maritime Academy	M
Capella University	M,D
Columbia Southern University	M
Drexel University	M*
Endicott College	M,O
Excelsior College	M
Florida Institute of Technology	M,D
Florida International University	M
Fordham University	M
Georgetown University	M,D
The George Washington University	M,D,O
Georgia State University	M,D,O
Grand Canyon University	M
Indiana University–Purdue University Indianapolis	M,O
Jacksonville State University	M,D
Lander University	M
Lasell College	M,O
Liberty University	M,D,O
London Metropolitan University	M,D
Massachusetts Maritime Academy	M
Metropolitan College of New York	M
Millersville University of Pennsylvania	M
National University	M
New Jersey Institute of Technology	M,D,O
New York Medical College	M,D,O
Norwich University	M
Nova Southeastern University	M,D,O*
Oklahoma State University	M,D
Pace University	M
Park University	M,O
Post University	M
Regent University	M
Royal Roads University	M,O
Rutgers University–New Brunswick	M,D,O
Saint Leo University	M
Saint Louis University	M*
San Diego State University	M,D
Sul Ross State University	M
Syracuse University	O*
Thomas Jefferson University	M
Trident University International	M,D,O
Trine University	M
Tulane University	M,D
Université de Montréal	O
University at Albany, State University of New York	M,D,O
University of Alaska Fairbanks	M
University of Central Florida	M,O
University of Chicago	M
University of Colorado Denver	M,D
University of Delaware	M,D*
University of Denver	M,O
University of Florida	M
University of Hawaii at Manoa	O
University of Illinois at Springfield	M,O
University of Maryland, Baltimore County	M,D,O
University of Nebraska Medical Center	M
University of Nevada, Las Vegas	M,D,O
University of New Haven	M,O*
The University of North Carolina at Charlotte	M,O
The University of North Carolina at Pembroke	M
University of North Texas	M,D,O
University of South Florida	O*
The University of Texas Rio Grande Valley	M
The University of Toledo	M,O
Upper Iowa University	M
Virginia Commonwealth University	M,O
Walden University	M,D,O
Waldorf University	M
Wheaton College	M
York University	M

EMERGENCY MEDICAL SERVICES

Baylor University	D
Creighton University	M
Drexel University	M*
San Diego State University	M,D
Université Laval	O
University of Guelph	M,D,O

ENERGY AND POWER ENGINEERING

Appalachian State University	M
Arizona State University at the Tempe campus	M,D
Carnegie Mellon University	M,D
The Catholic University of America	M,D
Clarkson University	M
Cornell University	M,D
Dartmouth College	M,D*
Florida State University	M,D
Georgia Southern University	M

Instituto Tecnologico de Santo Domingo	M,D,O
Inter American University of Puerto Rico, Bayamón Campus	M
Kansas State University	M,D
Lawrence Technological University	M,D
Lehigh University	M
New Jersey Institute of Technology	M,D
New York Institute of Technology	O
North Carolina Agricultural and Technical State University	M,D
Northeastern University	M,D,O
San Francisco State University	M
Santa Clara University	M,D,O
Southern Illinois University Carbondale	D
Stanford University	M,D,O
Texas A&M University–Kingsville	D
Texas Tech University	M,D
Universidad Autonoma de Guadalajara	M,D
University at Buffalo, the State University of New York	M,D
University of Alberta	M,D
The University of British Columbia	M
University of Calgary	M,D
University of Colorado Colorado Springs	M,D
University of Illinois at Urbana–Champaign	M,D
The University of Iowa	M,D*
University of Massachusetts Lowell	M,D
University of Memphis	M,D,O
University of Michigan	M,D*
University of Michigan–Dearborn	M
The University of North Carolina at Charlotte	M,O
University of North Texas	M,D,O
University of Puerto Rico–Mayagüez	M,D
University of Rochester	M*
The University of Tennessee	D
The University of Tennessee at Chattanooga	M,O
The University of Texas at El Paso	M,D,O
Washington State University	M,D
Wayne State University	M,O
West Virginia University	M,D
Worcester Polytechnic Institute	M,D,O

ENERGY MANAGEMENT AND POLICY

American College Dublin	M
American University of Armenia	M
Boston University	M,D*
Clarkson University	M,O
Colorado School of Mines	M,D
Colorado State University	M
Duke University	M,O*
Eastern Illinois University	M
Franklin Pierce University	M,D,O
Indiana University Bloomington	M,D,O
Instituto Tecnologico de Santo Domingo	M,D,O
Johns Hopkins University	M,O*
Kansas State University	M,D
Michigan Technological University	M,D
New York Institute of Technology	O
Norwich University	M
Oklahoma Baptist University	M
Oklahoma City University	M
Portland State University	M,D,O
Rice University	M,D
Samford University	M
SIT Graduate Institute	M
Stony Brook University, State University of New York	M
Tulane University	M,D
Université du Québec, Institut National de la Recherche Scientifique	M,D
University of Calgary	M,D
University of California, Berkeley	M,D
University of California, San Diego	M*
University of Colorado Denver	M
University of Delaware	M,D*
University of Illinois at Urbana–Champaign	M
University of Mary	M
University of Phoenix–Bay Area Campus	M,D
University of Phoenix–Online Campus	M,O
University of Phoenix–Phoenix Campus	M,O
University of Pittsburgh	M*
University of San Francisco	M
The University of Texas at Tyler	M
The University of Tulsa	M
Vermont Law School	M
Waynesburg University	M,D

ENGINEERING AND APPLIED SCIENCES—GENERAL

Air Force Institute of Technology	M,D
Alabama Agricultural and Mechanical University	M,D
Alfred University	M,D
The American University in Cairo	M,D,O
American University of Beirut	M,D
Arizona State University at the Tempe campus	M,D
Arkansas State University	M
Arkansas Tech University	M
Atlantis University	M
Auburn University	M,D,O*
Austin Peay State University	M
Binghamton University, State University of New York	M,D
Boise State University	M,D,O
Boston University	M,D*
Bradley University	M
Brigham Young University	M,D
Brown University	M,D
Bucknell University	M
California Institute of Technology	M,D,O
California Polytechnic State University, San Luis Obispo	M*
California State University, Chico	M
California State University, East Bay	M
California State University, Fresno	M
California State University, Fullerton	M
California State University, Los Angeles	M
California State University, Northridge	M
California State University, Sacramento	M
Carleton University	M,D
Case Western Reserve University	M,D*
The Catholic University of America	M,D,O
Central Connecticut State University	M
Central Michigan University	M
Christian Brothers University	M
The Citadel, The Military College of South Carolina	M,O
City College of the City University of New York	M,D
Clarkson University	M,D,O
Clemson University	M,D,O
Cleveland State University	M,D
Colorado School of Mines	M,D,O
Colorado State University	M,D
Colorado State University–Pueblo	M
Columbia University	M,D*
Concordia University (Canada)	M,D,O
Cooper Union for the Advancement of Science and Art	M
Cornell University	M,D
Dalhousie University	M,D
Dartmouth College	M,D*
Drexel University	M,D,O*
Duke University	M*
Eastern Illinois University	M,O
Eastern Michigan University	M
École Polytechnique de Montréal	M,D,O
Fairfield University	M,O
Fairleigh Dickinson University, Metropolitan Campus	M
Florida Agricultural and Mechanical University	M,D
Florida Atlantic University	M,D
Florida Institute of Technology	M,D
Florida International University	M,D
Florida State University	M,D
George Mason University	M,D,O
The George Washington University	M,D,O
Georgia Institute of Technology	M,D
Georgia Southern University	M,O
Gonzaga University	M,O
Grand Valley State University	M
Grantham University	M
Harvard University	M,D*
Hofstra University	M
Howard University	M,D
Idaho State University	M,D,O
Illinois Institute of Technology	M,D
Indiana State University	M
Indiana University–Purdue University Fort Wayne	M,O
Instituto Tecnologico de Santo Domingo	M,O
Instituto Tecnológico y de Estudios Superiores de Monterrey, Campus Ciudad Obregón	M
Instituto Tecnológico y de Estudios Superiores de Monterrey, Campus Monterrey	M,D
James Madison University	M
Johns Hopkins University	M,D,O*
Kansas State University	M,D,O
Kennesaw State University	M
Lakehead University	M
Lamar University	M,D
Laurentian University	M,D
Lawrence Technological University	M,D
Lehigh University	M,D,O
LeTourneau University	M
Louisiana State University and Agricultural & Mechanical College	M,D
Louisiana Tech University	M,D,O
Manhattan College	M
Marquette University	M,D,O
Marshall University	M,O
Massachusetts Institute of Technology	M,D,O
McGill University	M,D,O
McMaster University	M,D
McNeese State University	M
Memorial University of Newfoundland	M,D
Mercer University	M
Merrimack College	M
Miami University	M
Michigan State University	M,D
Michigan Technological University	M,D,O
Milwaukee School of Engineering	M
Mississippi State University	M,D
Missouri Western State University	M
Montana State University	M,D
Montana Tech of The University of Montana	M
Morgan State University	M,D,O
National University	M
New Jersey Institute of Technology	M,D
New Mexico State University	M,D,O
New York Institute of Technology	M,O
New York University	M,D,O*
North Carolina Agricultural and Technical State University	M,D
North Carolina State University	M,D
Northeastern University	M,D,O
Northern Arizona University	M,D,O
Northern Illinois University	M
Northwestern Polytechnic University	M,D
Northwestern University	M,D,O
Oakland University	M,D,O
The Ohio State University	M,D
Ohio University	M,D
Oklahoma Christian University	M
Oklahoma State University	M,D
Old Dominion University	M,D
Open University	M
Oregon State University	M,D
Penn State Great Valley	M,O
Penn State Harrisburg	M,O
Penn State University Park	M,D*
Pontificia Universidad Catolica Madre y Maestra	M
Portland State University	M,D,O
Prairie View A&M University	M,D
Princeton University	M,D
Purdue University	M,D,O
Purdue University Northwest	M
Queen's University at Kingston	M,D
Rensselaer at Hartford	M
Rensselaer Polytechnic Institute	M,D
Rice University	M,D
Robert Morris University	M
Rochester Institute of Technology	M,D,O
Rose-Hulman Institute of Technology	M
Rowan University	M
Royal Military College of Canada	M,D
Saginaw Valley State University	M
St. Cloud State University	M,O
San Diego State University	M,D
San Francisco State University	M
San Jose State University	M
Santa Clara University	M,D,O
Seattle University	M
Simon Fraser University	M,D
South Dakota School of Mines and Technology	M,D
South Dakota State University	M,D
Southern Illinois University Carbondale	M,D
Southern Illinois University Edwardsville	M
Southern Methodist University	M,D
Southern University and Agricultural and Mechanical College	M
Stanford University	M,D,O
Stevens Institute of Technology	M,D,O
Stony Brook University, State University of New York	M,D,O
Syracuse University	M,D,O*
Temple University	D*
Tennessee State University	M,D
Tennessee Technological University	M,D
Texas A&M University–Kingsville	M,D
Texas State University	M
Texas Tech University	M,D
Tufts University	M,D*
Tuskegee University	M,D
Universidad de las Américas Puebla	M,D
Universidad del Turabo	M
Université de Moncton	M
Université de Sherbrooke	M,D,O
Université du Québec à Chicoutimi	M,D
Université du Québec à Rimouski	M
Université du Québec, École de technologie supérieure	M,D,O
Université du Québec en Abitibi-Témiscamingue	M,O
Université Laval	M,D,O
University at Albany, State University of New York	M,D,O
University at Buffalo, the State University of New York	M,D,O
The University of Akron	M,D
The University of Alabama	M,D
The University of Alabama at Birmingham	D
The University of Alabama in Huntsville	M,D
University of Alaska Fairbanks	D
The University of Arizona	M,D,O
University of Arkansas	M,D
University of Bridgeport	M,D
The University of British Columbia	M,D
University of Calgary	M,D
University of California, Berkeley	M,D,O
University of California, Davis	M,D,O
University of California, Irvine	M,D
University of California, Los Angeles	M,D*
University of California, Merced	M,D
University of California, Santa Barbara	M,D
University of California, Santa Cruz	M,D*
University of Central Florida	M,D,O
University of Central Oklahoma	M
University of Cincinnati	M,D
University of Colorado Boulder	M,D
University of Colorado Colorado Springs	M,D
University of Colorado Denver	M,D
University of Connecticut	M,D*
University of Delaware	M,D*
University of Denver	M,D
University of Detroit Mercy	M,D
University of Florida	M,D,O
University of Guelph	M,D
University of Hartford	M
University of Hawaii at Manoa	M,D
University of Houston	M,D
University of Idaho	M,D
University of Illinois at Chicago	M,D
University of Illinois at Urbana–Champaign	M,D
The University of Iowa	M,D*
The University of Kansas	M,D,O
University of Kentucky	M,D
University of Louisville	M,D,O
University of Maine	M,D
University of Manitoba	M,D
University of Maryland, Baltimore County	M,D,O
University of Maryland, College Park	M
University of Massachusetts Amherst	M,D*
University of Massachusetts Dartmouth	D
University of Massachusetts Lowell	M,D
University of Memphis	M,D,O
University of Miami	M,D*
University of Michigan	M,D,O*
University of Michigan–Dearborn	M,D
University of Minnesota, Twin Cities Campus	M,D,O
University of Mississippi	M,D
University of Missouri	M,D,O
University of Missouri–Kansas City	M,D,O
University of Nebraska–Lincoln	M,D
University of Nevada, Las Vegas	M,D,O
University of Nevada, Reno	M,D
University of New Brunswick Fredericton	M,D,O
University of New Haven	M,O*
University of New Mexico	M,D
University of New Orleans	M,D
The University of North Carolina at Charlotte	M,D,O
University of North Dakota	D
University of North Texas	M,D,O
University of Notre Dame	M,D
University of Oklahoma	M,D*
University of Ottawa	M,D,O
University of Pennsylvania	M,D*
University of Pittsburgh	M,D*
University of Portland	M
University of Puerto Rico–Mayagüez	M,D
University of Regina	M,D
University of Rhode Island	M,D,O*
University of Rochester	M,D*
University of St. Thomas (MN)	M,O
University of Saskatchewan	M,D,O
University of South Africa	M
University of South Alabama	M,D
University of South Carolina	M,D
University of Southern California	M,D,O*
University of Southern Indiana	M,D
University of South Florida	M,D,O*
The University of Tennessee	M,D
The University of Texas at Arlington	M,D
The University of Texas at Austin	M,D
The University of Texas at Dallas	M,D
The University of Texas at San Antonio	M,D
University of the District of Columbia	M
University of the Pacific	M
The University of Toledo	M
University of Toronto	M,D
The University of Tulsa	M,D
University of Utah	M,D
University of Vermont	M,D
University of Victoria	M,D
University of Virginia	M,D
University of Washington	M,D,O
University of Waterloo	M,D
The University of Western Ontario	M,D
University of Windsor	M,D
University of Wisconsin–Madison	M,D
University of Wisconsin–Milwaukee	M,D*
University of Wisconsin–Platteville	M
University of Wyoming	M,D
Utah State University	M,D,O
Vanderbilt University	M,D*
Villanova University	M,D,O
Virginia Commonwealth University	M,D
Virginia Polytechnic Institute and State University	M,D
Washington State University	M,D,O
Washington University in St. Louis	M,D
Wayne State University	M,D,O
Western Michigan University	M,D
Western New England University	M,D
West Texas A&M University	M
West Virginia University	M,D
Wichita State University	M,D
Widener University	M
Wilkes University	M
Worcester Polytechnic Institute	M,D,O
Wright State University	M,D
Yale University	M,D
Youngstown State University	M

*M—masters degree; D—doctorate; O—other advanced degree; *—Close-Up and/or Display*

ENGINEERING DESIGN

Harvard University	M,D*
Northwestern University	M
Ohio Dominican University	M
Penn State University Park	M*
Rochester Institute of Technology	M
San Diego State University	M,D
Stanford University	M
Stevens Institute of Technology	M
The University of Alabama at Birmingham	M
University of Michigan	M,D*
Worcester Polytechnic Institute	M,D,O

ENGINEERING MANAGEMENT

Air Force Institute of Technology	M
American University of Beirut	M,D
American University of Sharjah	M,D
Arkansas State University	M
California State Polytechnic University, Pomona	M
California State University, East Bay	M
California State University, Long Beach	M,D
California State University Maritime Academy	M
California State University, Northridge	M
Case Western Reserve University	M*
The Catholic University of America	M,O
Central Michigan University	M,O
The Citadel, The Military College of South Carolina	M,O
Clarkson University	M
Colorado School of Mines	M,D
Cornell University	M,D
Dallas Baptist University	M
Dartmouth College	M*
Drexel University	M,O*
Duke University	M*
Eastern Michigan University	M
Embry-Riddle Aeronautical University–Worldwide	M
Florida Institute of Technology	M,D
Florida International University	M
Gannon University	M
The George Washington University	M,D,O
Georgia Southern University	M
Indiana Tech	M
Instituto Tecnológico y de Estudios Superiores de Monterrey, Campus Chihuahua	M,O
International Technological University	M
Johns Hopkins University	M*
Kansas State University	M,D
Kennesaw State University	M
Kettering University	M
Lamar University	M,D
Lawrence Technological University	M,D
Lehigh University	M,D,O
LeTourneau University	M
Long Island University–LIU Post	M
Louisiana Tech University	M,D,O
Loyola Marymount University	M
Marquette University	M,D,O
Marshall University	M
Massachusetts Institute of Technology	M
McNeese State University	M
Mercer University	M
Merrimack College	M
Middle Tennessee State University	M
Milwaukee School of Engineering	M
Missouri University of Science and Technology	M,D
National University	M
Naval Postgraduate School	M,D,O
New England Institute of Technology	M
New Jersey Institute of Technology	M,D
New Mexico Institute of Mining and Technology	M
Northeastern University	M,D,O
Northwestern University	M
Oakland University	M,D,O
Oklahoma Christian University	M
Old Dominion University	D
Oregon State University	M,D
Penn State Great Valley	M,O
Penn State Harrisburg	M,O
Point Park University	M
Polytechnic University of Puerto Rico	M
Polytechnic University of Puerto Rico, Orlando Campus	M
Portland State University	M,D,O
Robert Morris University	M
Rochester Institute of Technology	M
Rose-Hulman Institute of Technology	M
Saint Martin's University	M
St. Mary's University (United States)	M
San Jose State University	M
Santa Clara University	M,D,O
South Dakota School of Mines and Technology	M
Southern Illinois University Carbondale	M
Southern Methodist University	M,D
Southern New Hampshire University	M,D,O
Stanford University	M,D
Stevens Institute of Technology	M,D,O
Syracuse University	M*
Tarleton State University	M
Temple University	M,O*
Texas A&M University	M,D
Texas Tech University	M,D
Trine University	M
Tufts University	M*
Université de Sherbrooke	M,O
University at Buffalo, the State University of New York	M,D,O
The University of Alabama at Birmingham	M
University of Alberta	M,D
The University of Arizona	M,D,O
University of California, Berkeley	M,D
University of California, Irvine	M
University of Colorado Boulder	M
University of Colorado Colorado Springs	M,D
University of Dayton	M
University of Denver	M,D
University of Detroit Mercy	M,D
The University of Kansas	M,O
University of Louisville	M,D,O
University of Management and Technology	M
The University of Manchester	M,D
University of Maryland, Baltimore County	M,O
University of Michigan–Dearborn	M
University of Minnesota, Duluth	M
University of Missouri–Kansas City	M,D,O
University of Nebraska–Lincoln	M,D
University of New Brunswick Fredericton	M
University of New Haven	M,O*
University of New Orleans	M
The University of North Carolina at Charlotte	M,O
University of Ottawa	M,O
University of Puerto Rico–Mayagüez	M,D
University of Regina	M,O
University of St. Thomas (MN)	M,O
University of Southern California	M,D,O*
University of Southern Indiana	M
University of South Florida	M,D*
The University of Tennessee	M,D
The University of Tennessee at Chattanooga	M,O
The University of Texas at Arlington	M
The University of Texas at Tyler	M
The University of Texas Rio Grande Valley	M
University of Vermont	M
University of Waterloo	M,D
Valparaiso University	M,O
Virginia Polytechnic Institute and State University	M,O
Washington State University	M,O
Wayne State University	M,D,O
Western Michigan University	M,D
Western New England University	M,D
Wichita State University	M,D
Widener University	M
Wilkes University	M

ENGINEERING PHYSICS

Air Force Institute of Technology	M,D
Cornell University	M,D
École Polytechnique de Montréal	M,D,O
Embry-Riddle Aeronautical University–Daytona	M,D
George Mason University	M,D
Louisiana Tech University	M,D,O
McMaster University	M,D
Rensselaer Polytechnic Institute	M,D
Stanford University	M,D
University of California, San Diego	M,D*
University of Central Oklahoma	M
University of Oklahoma	M,D*
University of Saskatchewan	M,D
The University of Tulsa	M,D
University of Virginia	M,D
University of Wisconsin–Madison	M,D
Yale University	M,D

ENGLISH

Abilene Christian University	M
Acadia University	M
The American University in Cairo	M,O
American University of Beirut	M,D
Andrews University	M
Angelo State University	M
Appalachian State University	M
Arcadia University	M
Arizona State University at the Tempe campus	M,D,O
Arkansas State University	M,O
Arkansas Tech University	M
Asbury University	M
Auburn University	M,D,O*
Austin Peay State University	M
Azusa Pacific University	M*
Ball State University	M,D
Bard College	M
Baylor University	M,D
Bemidji State University	M
Binghamton University, State University of New York	M,D
Bob Jones University	M,D,O
Boston College	M,D
Boston University	M,D*
Bowie State University	M
Bowling Green State University	M,D
Bradley University	M
Brandeis University	M,D
Bridgewater State University	M
Brigham Young University	M
Brock University	M
Brooklyn College of the City University of New York	M
Brown University	M,D
Bucknell University	M
Buffalo State College, State University of New York	M
Butler University	M
Cabrini University	M,D
California Baptist University	M
California Polytechnic State University, San Luis Obispo	M*
California State Polytechnic University, Pomona	M
California State University, Bakersfield	M
California State University, Chico	M
California State University, Dominguez Hills	M,O
California State University, East Bay	M
California State University, Fresno	M
California State University, Fullerton	M
California State University, Long Beach	M
California State University, Los Angeles	M,O
California State University, Northridge	M
California State University, Sacramento	M
California State University, San Bernardino	M
California State University, San Marcos	M
California State University, Stanislaus	M,O
Carleton University	M,D
Carnegie Mellon University	M,D
Case Western Reserve University	M,D*
The Catholic University of America	M,D,O
Central Connecticut State University	M,O
Central Michigan University	M
Central Washington University	M
Chapman University	M*
Chicago State University	M
The Citadel, The Military College of South Carolina	M
City College of the City University of New York	M
Claremont Graduate University	M,D
Clark Atlanta University	M,D
Clarks Summit University	M
Clark University	M
Cleveland State University	M
The College at Brockport, State University of New York	M,O
College of Charleston	M
The College of New Jersey	M
College of Staten Island of the City University of New York	M
The College of William and Mary	M*
Colorado State University	M
Columbia College Chicago	M
Columbia University	M,D*
Concordia University (Canada)	M,D
Converse College	M
Cornell University	M,D
Creighton University	M
Dalhousie University	M,D
DePaul University	M
Drew University	M,D,O
Duke University	D*
Duquesne University	M,D
East Carolina University	M,D,O
Eastern Illinois University	M
Eastern Kentucky University	M
Eastern Michigan University	M
Eastern New Mexico University	M
Eastern Washington University	M
East Tennessee State University	M,O
Emory University	D,O
Emporia State University	M
Fairleigh Dickinson University, Metropolitan Campus	M
Fitchburg State University	M,O
Florida Atlantic University	M
Florida Gulf Coast University	M
Florida International University	M
Florida State University	M,D
Fordham University	M,D
Fort Hays State University	M
Framingham State University	M
Gannon University	M
Gardner-Webb University	M
George Mason University	M,D,O
Georgetown University	M
The George Washington University	M,D
Georgia College & State University	M
Georgia Southern University	M
Georgia State University	M,D
Governors State University	M
The Graduate Center, City University of New York	D
Grambling State University	M,D,O
Grand Valley State University	M
Hardin-Simmons University	M
Harvard University	M,D,O*
Heritage University	M
Hofstra University	M
Hollins University	M,O
Houston Baptist University	M,D
Howard University	M,D
Humboldt State University	M
Idaho State University	M,D,O
Illinois State University	M,D,O
Indiana State University	M
Indiana University Bloomington	M,D
Indiana University of Pennsylvania	M,D
Indiana University–Purdue University Fort Wayne	M,O
Indiana University–Purdue University Indianapolis	M,O
Indiana University South Bend	M,O
Inter American University of Puerto Rico, Metropolitan Campus	M
Iona College	M
Iowa State University of Science and Technology	M,D
Jackson State University	M
Jacksonville State University	M
James Madison University	M
John Carroll University	M
Johns Hopkins University	M,D*
Kansas State University	M,O
Kent State University	M,D
Kutztown University of Pennsylvania	M
Lakehead University	M
Lamar University	M
La Salle University	M,O
La Sierra University	M
Lee University	M,O
Lehigh University	M,D
Lehman College of the City University of New York	M
Liberty University	M
Lipscomb University	M,D,O
Long Island University–LIU Brooklyn	M,D,O
Long Island University–LIU Post	M,O
Louisiana State University and Agricultural & Mechanical College	M,D
Louisiana Tech University	M,D,O
Loyola Marymount University	M
Loyola University Chicago	M,D
Manhattan College	M,O
Manhattanville College	M,O
Marquette University	M,D
Marshall University	M,O
Mary Baldwin University	M
Marymount University	M,O
McGill University	M,D
McMaster University	M,D
McNeese State University	M
Memorial University of Newfoundland	M,D
Mercy College	M
Miami University	M,D
Michigan State University	M,D
Middlebury College	M
Middle Tennessee State University	M,D
Midwestern State University	M,D
Millersville University of Pennsylvania	M,O
Mills College	M,O
Minnesota State University Mankato	M,O
Mississippi College	M
Mississippi State University	M
Missouri State University	M,O
Monmouth University	M*
Montana State University	M
Montclair State University	M
Morehead State University	M
Morgan State University	M,D
Mount Mary University	M
Mount Saint Mary's University (CA)	M,D,O
Murray State University	M,D,O
National University	M,O
New Mexico Highlands University	M
New Mexico State University	M,D
New York University	M,D*
North Carolina Agricultural and Technical State University	M
North Carolina Central University	M
North Carolina State University	M
North Dakota State University	M,D*
Northeastern Illinois University	M
Northeastern State University	M
Northeastern University	M,D
Northern Arizona University	M,D,O
Northern Illinois University	M,O
Northern Kentucky University	M,O
Northern Michigan University	M,O
Northwestern State University of Louisiana	M
Northwestern University	M,D
Northwest Missouri State University	M,O
Oakland University	M
Ohio Dominican University	M
The Ohio State University	M,D
Ohio University	M,D
Oklahoma State University	M,D
Old Dominion University	M,D
Oregon State University	M
Our Lady of the Lake University	M
Pace University	M,O
Penn State University Park	M,D*
Pittsburg State University	M
Portland State University	M
Princeton University	D
Purdue University	M,D
Purdue University Northwest	M
Queens College of the City University of New York	M
Queen's University at Kingston	M,D
Radford University	M
Rhode Island College	M,O
Rice University	M,D
Rivier University	M
Rutgers University–Camden	M
Rutgers University–Newark	M
Rutgers University–New Brunswick	D
St. Cloud State University	M
St. John's University (NY)	M,D
Saint Louis University	M,D*
Saint Louis University–Madrid Campus	M
St. Mary's University (United States)	M
Salem State University	M
Salisbury University	M
Sam Houston State University	M
San Diego State University	M
San Francisco State University	M,O
San Jose State University	M

Seton Hall University	M
Simmons College	M
Simon Fraser University	M,D
Slippery Rock University of Pennsylvania	M
Sonoma State University	M
South Carolina State University	M
South Dakota State University	M
Southeastern Louisiana University	M
Southeast Missouri State University	M
Southern Connecticut State University	M
Southern Illinois University Carbondale	M,D
Southern Illinois University Edwardsville	M,O
Southern Methodist University	M,D
Southern New Hampshire University	M
Spring Hill College	M,O
Stanford University	M,D
State University of New York at Fredonia	M,O
State University of New York at New Paltz	M
State University of New York at Oswego	M
State University of New York College at Cortland	M
Stephen F. Austin State University	M
Stony Brook University, State University of New York	M,D,O
Sul Ross State University	M
Syracuse University	M,D*
Tarleton State University	M
Temple University	M,D*
Tennessee Technological University	M
Texas A&M International University	M
Texas A&M University	M,D
Texas A&M University–Commerce	M,D,O
Texas A&M University–Corpus Christi	M
Texas A&M University–Kingsville	M
Texas A&M University–San Antonio	M
Texas A&M University–Texarkana	M
Texas Christian University	M,D
Texas Southern University	M
Texas State University	M
Texas Tech University	M,D
Texas Woman's University	M,D
Tiffin University	M
Trinity College (United States)	M
Trinity Western University	M
Truman State University	M
Tufts University	M,D*
Tulane University	M
Universidad de las Américas Puebla	M
Université de Montréal	M,D
Université Laval	M,D
University at Albany, State University of New York	M,D
University at Buffalo, the State University of New York	M,D,O
The University of Akron	M
The University of Alabama	M,D
The University of Alabama at Birmingham	M
The University of Alabama in Huntsville	M,O
University of Alaska Anchorage	M
University of Alaska Fairbanks	M
University of Alberta	M,D
The University of Arizona	M,D
University of Arkansas	M,D
The University of British Columbia	M,D
University of Calgary	M,D
University of California, Berkeley	D
University of California, Davis	M,D
University of California, Irvine	M,D
University of California, Los Angeles	M,D*
University of California, Riverside	M,D
University of California, San Diego	M,D*
University of California, Santa Barbara	D
University of California, Santa Cruz	M,D*
University of Central Arkansas	M
University of Central Florida	M,D,O
University of Central Missouri	M,D,O
University of Central Oklahoma	M
University of Chicago	M,D
University of Cincinnati	M,D
University of Colorado Boulder	M,D
University of Colorado Denver	M
University of Connecticut	M,D*
University of Dallas	M,D
University of Dayton	M
University of Delaware	M,D*
University of Denver	M,D
University of Florida	M,D
University of Georgia	M,D
University of Guam	M
University of Guelph	M
University of Hawaii at Manoa	M,D
University of Houston–Clear Lake	M
University of Houston–Downtown	M
University of Illinois at Chicago	M,D
University of Illinois at Springfield	M,O
University of Illinois at Urbana–Champaign	M,D
University of Indianapolis	M
The University of Iowa	M,D*
The University of Kansas	M,D
University of Kentucky	M,D
University of La Verne	M,O
University of Lethbridge	M,D
University of Louisiana at Lafayette	M,D
University of Louisiana at Monroe	M
University of Louisville	M,D
University of Maine	M
The University of Manchester	D
University of Manitoba	M,D
University of Maryland, Baltimore County	M
University of Maryland, College Park	M,D
University of Massachusetts Amherst	M,D*
University of Massachusetts Boston	M
University of Memphis	M,D,O
University of Miami	M,D*
University of Michigan	M,D,O*
University of Michigan–Flint	M
University of Minnesota, Duluth	M
University of Minnesota, Twin Cities Campus	M,D
University of Mississippi	M,D
University of Missouri	M,D
University of Missouri–Kansas City	M,D
University of Missouri–St. Louis	M
University of Montana	M
University of Montevallo	M
University of Nebraska at Kearney	M
University of Nebraska at Omaha	M,O
University of Nebraska–Lincoln	M,D
University of Nevada, Las Vegas	M,D
University of Nevada, Reno	M,D
University of New Brunswick Fredericton	M,D
University of New Hampshire	M,D
University of New Mexico	M,D
University of New Orleans	M
University of North Alabama	M
The University of North Carolina at Chapel Hill	M,D
The University of North Carolina at Charlotte	M,O
The University of North Carolina at Greensboro	M,D
The University of North Carolina Wilmington	M
University of North Dakota	M,D
University of Northern Colorado	M,D
University of Northern Iowa	M
University of North Florida	M
University of North Texas	M,D,O
University of Notre Dame	M,D
University of Oklahoma	M,D*
University of Oregon	M,D
University of Ottawa	M,D
University of Pennsylvania	M,D*
University of Pittsburgh	M,D*
University of Puerto Rico–Mayagüez	M
University of Puerto Rico–Río Piedras	M,D
University of Regina	M,D
University of Rhode Island	M,D*
University of Rochester	M,D*
University of St. Thomas (MN)	M,O
University of Saskatchewan	M,D
University of South Africa	M,D
University of South Alabama	M
University of South Carolina	M,D
University of South Dakota	M,D
University of Southern California	M,D*
University of Southern Indiana	M
University of Southern Mississippi	M,D
University of South Florida	M,D,O*
The University of Tennessee	M,D
The University of Tennessee at Chattanooga	M
The University of Texas at Arlington	M,D
The University of Texas at Austin	M,D
The University of Texas at El Paso	M,D,O
The University of Texas at San Antonio	M,D
The University of Texas at Tyler	M
The University of Texas of the Permian Basin	M
The University of Texas Rio Grande Valley	M
The University of the South	M
The University of Toledo	M,O
University of Toronto	M,D
The University of Tulsa	M,D
University of Utah	M,D
University of Vermont	M
University of Victoria	M,D
University of Virginia	M,D
University of Washington	M,D
University of Waterloo	M,D
The University of Western Ontario	M,D
University of West Florida	M
University of West Georgia	M,O
University of Windsor	M
University of Wisconsin–Eau Claire	M
University of Wisconsin–Madison	M,D
University of Wisconsin–Milwaukee	M,D*
University of Wisconsin–Oshkosh	M
University of Wyoming	M
Utah State University	M
Valdosta State University	M
Valparaiso University	M
Vanderbilt University	M,D*
Villanova University	M
Virginia Commonwealth University	M
Virginia Polytechnic Institute and State University	M,D,O
Wake Forest University	M
Washington State University	M,D
Washington University in St. Louis	M,D
Wayne State University	M,D
Weber State University	M
West Chester University of Pennsylvania	M,O
Western Carolina University	M,O
Western Connecticut State University	M
Western Illinois University	M,O
Western Kentucky University	M
Western Michigan University	M,D
Western Washington University	M
Westfield State University	M
West Texas A&M University	M
West Virginia University	M,D
Wichita State University	M
Wilfrid Laurier University	M,D
William Paterson University of New Jersey	M,D,O
Wilson College	M
Winona State University	M
Winthrop University	M
Wright State University	M
Xavier University	M*
Yale University	M,D
York University	M,D
Youngstown State University	M

ENGLISH AS A SECOND LANGUAGE

Acacia University	M
Adelphi University	M,O
Albright College	M
Alliant International University–San Diego	M,D,O
Alliant International University–San Francisco	M,O
American College of Education	M
American University	M,O
The American University in Cairo	M,O
American University of Armenia	M
American University of Beirut	M,D
American University of Sharjah	M,D
Anaheim University	M,D,O
Andrews University	M,D,O
Angelo State University	M
Arizona State University at the Tempe campus	M,D,O
Arkansas Tech University	M
Asbury University	M
Aurora University	M,D
Avila University	M,O
Azusa Pacific University	M*
Ball State University	M
Barry University	M,D,O
Binghamton University, State University of New York	M
Biola University	M,D,O
Bishop's University	M,O
Boise State University	M
Boricua College	M
Brigham Young University	M
Brock University	M
Brown University	M,D
Buena Vista University	M
Cabrini University	M,D
California Baptist University	M
California State University, Dominguez Hills	M,O
California State University, East Bay	M
California State University, Fresno	M
California State University, Long Beach	M,O
California State University, Sacramento	M
California State University, Stanislaus	M,O
Cambridge College	M,D,O
Canisius College	M,O
Carlos Albizu University, Miami Campus	M,D
Carson-Newman University	M
Central Connecticut State University	M,O
Central Michigan University	M
Central Washington University	M
City College of the City University of New York	M
Clarkson University	M
Cleveland State University	M
Coastal Carolina University	M,O
College of Charleston	O
College of Mount Saint Vincent	M,O
The College of New Jersey	M,O
The College of New Rochelle	M,O
College of Saint Elizabeth	M,O
College of Saint Mary	M
College of Staten Island of the City University of New York	M,O
The College of William and Mary	M*
Colorado Mesa University	M,O
Columbia International University	M,D,O
Columbus State University	O
Concordia University (United States)	M,D
Concordia University (Canada)	M,O
Cornerstone University	M,O
Dallas Baptist University	M
DeSales University	M,O
Dominican University	M
Duquesne University	M
East Carolina University	M,D,O
Eastern Michigan University	M,O
Eastern Nazarene College	M,O
Eastern New Mexico University	M
Eastern University	M,O
Eastern Washington University	M
East Tennessee State University	M,O
Elms College	M,O
Emporia State University	M,O
Erikson Institute	M,O
Fairfield University	M,O
Florida Atlantic University	M,D,O
Florida Gulf Coast University	M
Florida International University	M,D,O
Florida State University	M,D,O
Fordham University	M,O
Framingham State University	M,O
Fresno Pacific University	M,O
Furman University	M,O
Gannon University	O
George Fox University	M,O
George Mason University	M
Gonzaga University	M
Gordon College	M,O
Grand Canyon University	M,D,O
Grand Valley State University	M
Greensboro College	M
Hamline University	M,D
Harding University	M,O
Hawai`i Pacific University	M
Henderson State University	M,O
Heritage University	M
Hofstra University	M,D,O
Holy Family University	M
Houston Baptist University	M,D
Humboldt State University	M
Hunter College of the City University of New York	M
Huntington University	M,D
Idaho State University	M,D,O
Immaculata University	M
Indiana State University	M,D,O
Indiana University Bloomington	M,D
Indiana University of Pennsylvania	M,D
Indiana University–Purdue University Fort Wayne	M,O
Indiana University–Purdue University Indianapolis	M,O
Inter American University of Puerto Rico, Arecibo Campus	M
Inter American University of Puerto Rico, Barranquitas Campus	M
Inter American University of Puerto Rico, Metropolitan Campus	M
Inter American University of Puerto Rico, Ponce Campus	M
Inter American University of Puerto Rico, San Germán Campus	M
Iowa State University of Science and Technology	M
James Madison University	M
Kansas State University	M,D,O
Kean University	M
Kennesaw State University	M
Kent State University	M,D
Langston University	M
La Salle University	M,O
Lasell College	M,O
Lee University	M,O
Lehman College of the City University of New York	M
Le Moyne College	M,O
Lesley University	M,D,O
Lewis University	M
Lindenwood University	M,D,O
Long Island University–Hudson	M,O
Long Island University–LIU Brooklyn	M,O
Long Island University–LIU Post	M,D,O
Long Island University–Riverhead	M,O
Madonna University	M
Manhattanville College	M,O
Marlboro College	M
McDaniel College	M
Mercy College	M,O
Meredith College	M,O
Merrimack College	M,O
Messiah College	M
Michigan State University	M,D
MidAmerica Nazarene University	M
Middlebury Institute of International Studies at Monterey	M
Middle Tennessee State University	M,O
Millersville University of Pennsylvania	M
Minnesota State University Mankato	M,O
Minnesota State University Moorhead	M
Mississippi College	M
Missouri State University	M,O
Missouri Western State University	M,O
Molloy College	M,O
Monmouth University	M,D,O*
Montclair State University	M,O
Mount Saint Vincent University	M
Multnomah University	M
Murray State University	M,D,O
Nazareth College of Rochester	M
New Jersey City University	M
Newman University	M
New Mexico State University	M,D,O
The New School	M
New York University	M,D,O*
Niagara University	M,O
Northeastern Illinois University	M
Northern Arizona University	M,D,O
Northern Michigan University	M,O
Northwest Christian University	M

*M—masters degree; D—doctorate; O—other advanced degree; *—Close-Up and/or Display*

Northwest Missouri State University M,D,O
Notre Dame of Maryland University M
Nyack College M
Oakland University M,O
Ohio Dominican University M
Oklahoma City University M
Old Dominion University M
Pacific University M
Penn State Harrisburg M,D,O
Penn State University Park M,D*
Penn State York M,O
Pittsburg State University M,O
Pontifical Catholic University of Puerto Rico M
Portland State University M,O
Post University M
Providence University College & Theological Seminary M,D,O
Queens College of the City University of New York M,O
Quincy University M
Regent University M,D,O
Rhode Island College M
Rider University M
Rowan University O
Rutgers University–New Brunswick M,D
St. John's University (NY) M,O
Saint Michael's College M,O
St. Thomas University M,D,O
Saint Xavier University M
Salem College M
Salem State University M
Salisbury University M
San Diego State University M,O
San Francisco State University M
San Jose State University M
Seattle Pacific University M
Seattle University M,O
Simon Fraser University M
SIT Graduate Institute M
Slippery Rock University of Pennsylvania M
Southeastern University (FL) M,D
Southeast Missouri State University M
Southern Connecticut State University M
Southern Illinois University Carbondale M
Southern Illinois University Edwardsville M,O
Southern Methodist University M,D
Southern New Hampshire University M,D,O
Southwest Minnesota State University M
State University of New York at Fredonia M
State University of New York at New Paltz M,O
State University of New York College at Cortland M
Stony Brook University, State University of New York M
Syracuse University M,O*
Taylor College and Seminary M,O
Teachers College, Columbia University M,D,O
Temple University M*
Tennessee Technological University M
Texas A&M University–Commerce M,D,O
Texas A&M University–Kingsville M,D
Touro College M
Trevecca Nazarene University M,O
Trinity Western University M
Troy University M
Universidad del Este M
Universidad del Turabo M
University at Buffalo, the State University of New York M,D,O
The University of Alabama M,D
The University of Alabama at Birmingham M,O
The University of Alabama in Huntsville M,O
University of Alberta M,D
The University of Arizona M,D
University of Arkansas at Little Rock M
The University of British Columbia M,D
University of California, Berkeley O
University of California, Los Angeles M,D,O*
University of California, Riverside M,D,O
University of Central Florida M,D,O
University of Central Missouri M,D,O
University of Central Oklahoma M
University of Cincinnati M,D
University of Colorado Colorado Springs M,D
University of Dayton M
University of Delaware M,D,O*
The University of Findlay M,D
University of Florida M,D,O
University of Guam M
University of Hawaii at Manoa M,D,O
University of Illinois at Chicago M,D
University of Illinois at Springfield M,O
University of Illinois at Urbana–Champaign M,D
The University of Iowa M,D*
University of Louisiana at Lafayette M,D
University of Manitoba M
University of Maryland, Baltimore County M,O
University of Maryland, College Park M,D,O
University of Massachusetts Amherst M,D,O*
University of Massachusetts Dartmouth M,D,O
University of Memphis M,D,O
University of Minnesota, Twin Cities Campus M,D,O
University of Missouri–St. Louis M
University of Nebraska at Kearney M
University of Nebraska at Omaha M,O
University of Nevada, Las Vegas M,D,O
University of Nevada, Reno M
University of New Mexico M,D
The University of North Carolina at Chapel Hill M
The University of North Carolina at Charlotte M,D,O
The University of North Carolina at Greensboro M,D,O
The University of North Carolina Wilmington M
University of Northern Colorado M,D
University of Northern Iowa M
University of North Florida M
University of North Texas M,D,O
University of Pennsylvania M*
University of Phoenix–Online Campus M,O
University of Phoenix–San Diego Campus M
University of Pittsburgh D,O*
University of Portland M,D
University of Puerto Rico–Río Piedras M
University of St. Francis (IL) M,D,O
University of Saint Joseph M
University of St. Thomas (TX) M,D
University of San Diego M
University of South Africa M,D
University of South Carolina M,D,O
University of South Dakota M
University of Southern California M*
University of Southern Indiana M
University of Southern Maine M,O
University of South Florida M,D,O*
The University of Tennessee M,D,O
The University of Texas at Arlington M
The University of Texas at El Paso M,O
The University of Texas at San Antonio M,D,O
The University of Texas of the Permian Basin M
The University of Texas Rio Grande Valley M
University of the Southwest M
The University of Toledo M,D,O
University of Washington M,D
University of Wisconsin–Madison M,D
University of Wisconsin–Milwaukee M,D,O*
University of Wisconsin–River Falls M
Upper Iowa University M
Utah Valley University M
Valley City State University M
Valparaiso University M,O
Virginia International University M
Walden University M,D,O
Washington State University M,D
Wayland Baptist University M
Wayne State College M
Wayne State University M,D,O
Webster University M,O
West Chester University of Pennsylvania M,O
Western Carolina University M,O
Western Illinois University M,O
Western Kentucky University M
Western New Mexico University M
Wheaton College M,O
Wilkes University M,D
William Paterson University of New Jersey M,D,O
Wilmington University M,D
Winona State University M
Worcester State University M,O

ENGLISH EDUCATION

Alabama Agricultural and Mechanical University M,O
Alabama State University M,O
Albany State University M
Andrews University M,D,O
Anna Maria College M,O
Appalachian State University M
Arcadia University M,D,O
Arkansas State University M,O
Arkansas Tech University M
Binghamton University, State University of New York M
Bloomsburg University of Pennsylvania M
Bob Jones University M,D,O
Boise State University M
Brooklyn College of the City University of New York M
Brown University M
Buffalo State College, State University of New York M
California Baptist University M
California State University, Northridge M
Campbellsville University M
Caribbean University M,D
Carthage College M,O
Central Connecticut State University M,O
Chadron State College M,O
Chatham University M
The Citadel, The Military College of South Carolina M,O
City College of the City University of New York M,O
Clayton State University M
The College at Brockport, State University of New York M,O
College of St. Joseph M
College of Staten Island of the City University of New York M
The Colorado College M
Columbus State University M,O
Converse College M
Delta State University M
Duquesne University M
East Carolina University M,D,O
Eastern Kentucky University M
Eastern Michigan University M
Eastern University M,O
Elms College M,O
Fitchburg State University M,O
Florida Agricultural and Mechanical University M
Florida Gulf Coast University M
Florida International University M,D,O
Florida State University M,D,O
Gardner-Webb University M
George Mason University M,D,O
Georgia Southern University M
Georgia Southwestern State University M,O
Georgia State University M,D
Grand Valley State University M
Hampton University M
Harding University M,O
Hofstra University M,D,O
Houston Baptist University M
Hunter College of the City University of New York M
Indiana University of Pennsylvania M,D
Indiana University–Purdue University Fort Wayne M,O
Iona College M
Ithaca College M
Jackson State University M
Kansas State University M,D,O
Kennesaw State University M
Kent State University M,D
Kutztown University of Pennsylvania M,D
Lake Forest College M
Lehman College of the City University of New York M
Le Moyne College M,O
Lewis University M
Lincoln Memorial University M,D,O
Lipscomb University M,D,O
London Metropolitan University M,D
Manhattanville College M,O
Marymount University M,O
Millersville University of Pennsylvania M
Mississippi College M,D,O
Missouri State University M,O
Molloy College M,O
Montclair State University M,O
Morehead State University M,O
Murray State University M,D,O
National Louis University M,D,O
New Mexico State University M,D
New York Institute of Technology M
New York University M,D,O*
North Carolina Agricultural and Technical State University M
North Carolina State University M
Northeastern Illinois University M
Northwest Missouri State University M,O
Oregon State University M
Plymouth State University M
Purdue University M,D,O
Queens College of the City University of New York M,O
Quinnipiac University M
Rhode Island College M
Rowan University O
Rutgers University–New Brunswick M
St. John Fisher College M
San Francisco State University M,O
Simon Fraser University M,D
Slippery Rock University of Pennsylvania M
Smith College M
South Carolina State University M
Southeastern Louisiana University M
Southern Illinois University Edwardsville M,O
Southwestern Oklahoma State University M
State University of New York at Fredonia M,O
State University of New York at New Paltz M,O
State University of New York at Plattsburgh M
State University of New York College at Cortland M
State University of New York College at Geneseo M
State University of New York College at Old Westbury M
State University of New York College at Potsdam M
Stony Brook University, State University of New York M,D,O
Syracuse University M*
Teachers College, Columbia University M,D,O
Temple University M*
Texas Woman's University M,D
Trinity Washington University M
University at Buffalo, the State University of New York M,D,O
The University of Akron M
The University of Alabama in Huntsville M,O
The University of Arizona M,D
University of Arkansas at Pine Bluff M
University of Central Florida M
University of Colorado Denver M
University of Connecticut M,D*
University of Florida M,D,O
University of Georgia M,D
University of Illinois at Springfield M,O
University of Indianapolis M
The University of Iowa M,D*
University of Manitoba M
University of Maryland, Baltimore County M
University of Michigan D*
University of Minnesota, Twin Cities Campus M
University of Missouri M,D,O
University of Montana M
University of New Mexico M,D
The University of North Carolina at Chapel Hill M
The University of North Carolina at Greensboro M,D
The University of North Carolina at Pembroke M
University of Northern Colorado M,D
University of Northern Iowa M
University of North Georgia M
University of Oklahoma M,D*
University of Pennsylvania M,D*
University of Phoenix–Online Campus M,O
University of Pittsburgh M,D*
University of Puerto Rico–Mayagüez M
University of St. Francis (IL) M,D,O
University of South Carolina M,D
University of Southern Mississippi M,D
University of South Florida, St. Petersburg M
University of South Florida Sarasota-Manatee M
The University of Tennessee M,D,O
The University of Texas at El Paso M,D,O
University of the District of Columbia M
University of the Sacred Heart M,O
The University of Toledo M,D,O
The University of Tulsa M
University of Victoria M,D
University of Virginia M,D,O
University of Washington M,D
The University of West Alabama M
University of Wisconsin–La Crosse M,O
University of Wisconsin–Milwaukee M,D*
University of Wisconsin–Stevens Point M
Valdosta State University M
Valley City State University M
Vanderbilt University M*
Wagner College M
Wayland Baptist University M
Wayne State College M
Wayne State University M,D,O
West Chester University of Pennsylvania M,O
Western Governors University M,O
Western Kentucky University M
Western Michigan University M,D
Western New England University M
West Virginia University M,D
Widener University M,D
William Carey University M,O
William Jessup University M
Worcester State University M

ENTERTAINMENT MANAGEMENT

Berklee College of Music M
California Intercontinental University M
California State University, Northridge M,O
Carnegie Mellon University M
Columbia College Chicago M
Full Sail University M
Hofstra University M,O
Manhattanville College M,O
Point Park University M
Southern New Hampshire University M,D,O
Syracuse University M*
Universidad Autonoma de Guadalajara M,D
University of Colorado Denver M
University of Dallas M,D
University of Massachusetts Amherst *
University of South Carolina M
Valparaiso University M

ENTOMOLOGY

Auburn University M,D*
Clemson University M,D
Colorado State University M,D
Cornell University M,D
Illinois State University M,D
Iowa State University of Science and Technology M,D
Kansas State University M,D
Louisiana State University and Agricultural & Mechanical College M,D
McGill University M,D
Michigan State University M,D
New Mexico State University M
North Carolina State University M,D
North Dakota State University M,D*
The Ohio State University M,D
Oklahoma State University M,D
Penn State University Park M,D*
Purdue University M,D

Rutgers University–New Brunswick	M,D
Simon Fraser University	M,D,O
State University of New York College of Environmental Science and Forestry	M,D
Texas A&M University	M,D
The University of Arizona	M,D
University of Arkansas	M,D
University of California, Davis	M,D
University of California, Riverside	M,D
University of Delaware	M,D*
University of Georgia	M,D
University of Guelph	M,D
University of Hawaii at Manoa	M,D
University of Idaho	M,D
University of Illinois at Urbana–Champaign	M,D
University of Kentucky	M,D
University of Maine	M,D
University of Manitoba	M,D
University of Maryland, College Park	M,D
University of Minnesota, Twin Cities Campus	M,D
University of Nebraska–Lincoln	M,D
The University of Tennessee	M,D
University of Vermont	M,D,O
University of Wisconsin–Madison	M,D
University of Wyoming	M,D
Virginia Polytechnic Institute and State University	M,D
Washington State University	M,D
West Virginia University	M,D

ENTREPRENEURSHIP

American College of Thessaloniki	M,O
American University	M,D,O
Anaheim University	M,D,O
Arizona State University at the Tempe campus	M,D
Ashland University	M
Azusa Pacific University	M*
Babson College	M,O
Bakke Graduate University	M,D
Baruch College of the City University of New York	M,D*
Baylor University	D
Bay Path University	M
Benedictine University	M
Brandeis University	M
Brandman University	M
Brigham Young University	M
Butler University	M
Cairn University	M,O
California Institute of Advanced Management	M
California Intercontinental University	M,D
California Lutheran University	M,O
California State University, San Bernardino	M
California University of Pennsylvania	M
Cambridge College	M
Cameron University	M
Capella University	M,D
Carlos Albizu University, Miami Campus	M,D
Carnegie Mellon University	D
City Vision University	M
Clarion University of Pennsylvania	M
Clemson University	M,D
Cogswell Polytechnical College	M
Columbia University	M*
Dallas Baptist University	M
Dartmouth College	D*
Delaware Valley University	M
DePaul University	M,D
Drexel University	M*
Duke University	M,O*
Eastern Michigan University	M,O
East Tennessee State University	M,O
Elms College	M,O
Embry-Riddle Aeronautical University–Worldwide	M
Emory University	M
Everglades University	M
Fairleigh Dickinson University, Florham Campus	M,O
Fairleigh Dickinson University, Metropolitan Campus	M,O
Felician University	M,D
Florida Atlantic University	M
Florida Institute of Technology	M
Fordham University	M,D
Georgia State University	M,D
Golden Gate University	M,D,O
Grand Canyon University	M
Harrisburg University of Science and Technology	M
HEC Montreal	M,O
Hult International Business School (United States)	M
IGlobal University	M
Illinois Institute of Technology	M
Indiana University–Purdue University Indianapolis	M
International University in Geneva	M,D
The International University of Monaco	M
James Madison University	M
Kansas State University	M,O
Lamar University	M
Lehigh University	M
Lenoir-Rhyne University	M
Lindenwood University	M
Loyola University Chicago	M
Lynn University	M
Manhattanville College	M
Marlboro College	M
Marquette University	M,O
McGill University	M,D,O
Mercer University	M
Mercyhurst University	M,O
Meredith College	M
Monroe College	M
New York University	M*
North Carolina State University	M
Northeastern University	M
Northwestern University	M,D
Nova Southeastern University	M*
Oakland University	M,O
Oklahoma State University	M,D
Old Dominion University	M,O
Oral Roberts University	M
Pace University	M
Penn State Great Valley	M,O
Penn State University Park	M*
Peru State College	M
Point Loma Nazarene University	M
Pontificia Universidad Catolica Madre y Maestra	M
Purchase College, State University of New York	M
Purdue University Global	M
Queen's University at Kingston	M
Regent University	M,D,O
Rensselaer Polytechnic Institute	M
Rochester Institute of Technology	M
Rockhurst University	M,O
Rollins College	M
Salve Regina University	M
Samford University	M
San Diego State University	M
San Francisco State University	M
Seton Hall University	M,O
Seton Hill University	M
SIT Graduate Institute	M
South Carolina State University	M
Southeastern University (FL)	M,D
Southeast Missouri State University	M
Southern Methodist University	M
Southern New Hampshire University	M,D,O
South University (GA)	M
Stevens Institute of Technology	M,O
Stony Brook University, State University of New York	M,O
Suffolk University	M
Syracuse University	M*
Temple University	M,D*
Texas A&M University	M
Tufts University	M*
Tulane University	M,D
United States International University–Africa	M
Université Laval	M,O
University at Albany, State University of New York	M
The University of Alabama in Huntsville	M,O
University of Arkansas at Little Rock	O
University of Baltimore	M
University of Bridgeport	M
University of California, Davis	M
University of California, Merced	M,D
University of Central Florida	M,O
University of Chicago	M,O
University of Colorado Denver	M
University of Delaware	M,D*
University of Florida	M,D,O
University of Hawaii at Manoa	M,O
University of Houston–Victoria	M
University of Louisiana at Lafayette	M
University of Louisville	M,D
The University of Manchester	M
University of Massachusetts Amherst	M,D*
University of Massachusetts Lowell	M,D
University of Minnesota, Twin Cities Campus	D
University of New Brunswick Fredericton	M
University of New Mexico	M
University of Notre Dame	M
University of Oklahoma	M,D*
University of Pennsylvania	M*
University of Pikeville	M
University of Portland	M
University of Rhode Island	M,D,O*
University of Rochester	M*
University of San Francisco	M
University of Sioux Falls	M
University of Southern California	M*
University of South Florida	M,O*
The University of Tampa	M,O
The University of Texas at Austin	M,D
The University of Texas at Dallas	M,D
University of Washington	M,D
University of Waterloo	M
The University of Western Ontario	M,D
University of Wisconsin–Milwaukee	M,D,O*
Ursuline College	M
Virginia International University	M,O
Walden University	M,D,O
Washington University in St. Louis	M
Wayne State University	M,D,O
Western Carolina University	M
Wichita State University	M
Wilkes University	M
Wingate University	M

ENVIRONMENTAL AND OCCUPATIONAL HEALTH

American University of Beirut	M,D
Augusta University	M
Boise State University	M,O
Boston University	M,D*
California State University, Fullerton	M
California State University, Northridge	M
Capella University	M,D
Clemson University	M,D
Colorado State University	M,D
Columbia Southern University	M
Columbia University	M,D*
Duke University	O*
East Carolina University	M,D,O
Eastern Kentucky University	M
East Tennessee State University	M,D,O
Embry-Riddle Aeronautical University–Worldwide	M
Emory University	M,D
Florida International University	M,D
Fort Valley State University	M
Gannon University	M
The George Washington University	D
Georgia Southern University	M,D,O
Harvard University	M,D*
Indiana State University	M
Indiana University Bloomington	M,D
Indiana University of Pennsylvania	M,D
Indiana University–Purdue University Indianapolis	M,D,O
Johns Hopkins University	M,D*
Kent State University	M,D
Lehigh University	M,O
Lewis University	M
Loma Linda University	M
Louisiana State University Health Sciences Center	M,D
McGill University	M,D,O
Meharry Medical College	M
Mercer University	M,D
Mississippi Valley State University	M
Murray State University	M
New York Medical College	M,D,O
New York University	M,D*
North Carolina Agricultural and Technical State University	M
Oakland University	M
Oregon State University	M,D
Purdue University	M,D
Rochester Institute of Technology	M
Rutgers University–New Brunswick	M,D,O
San Diego State University	M,D
Southeastern Oklahoma State University	M
Syracuse University	O*
Temple University	M,D*
Texas A&M University	M,D
Towson University	D
Trident University International	M,D,O
Tufts University	M,D*
Tulane University	M,D
Uniformed Services University of the Health Sciences	M,D*
Universidad Autonoma de Guadalajara	M,D
Universidad de Ciencias Medicas	M,D,O
Université de Montréal	M
Université du Québec à Montréal	O
Université Laval	O
University at Albany, State University of New York	M,D
The University of Alabama at Birmingham	M,D
University of Alberta	M,D
University of Arkansas for Medical Sciences	M,D,O
University of California, Berkeley	M,D
University of California, Irvine	M,D
University of California, Los Angeles	M,D*
University of Central Missouri	M,D,O
University of Cincinnati	M,D
University of Colorado Denver	M
University of Connecticut	O*
University of Florida	M,D,O
University of Georgia	M,D
University of Illinois at Chicago	M,D
University of Illinois at Springfield	M,O
The University of Iowa	M,D,O*
University of Maryland, College Park	M
University of Massachusetts Amherst	M,D*
University of Memphis	M,D
University of Miami	M*
University of Michigan	M,D*
University of Minnesota, Twin Cities Campus	M,D,O
University of Nebraska Medical Center	D
University of Nevada, Reno	M,D
University of New Haven	M*
The University of North Carolina at Chapel Hill	M,D
University of Oklahoma Health Sciences Center	M,D
University of Pennsylvania	M*
University of Pittsburgh	M,D*
University of Puerto Rico–Medical Sciences Campus	M,D
University of Saint Francis (IN)	M
University of South Alabama	M
University of South Carolina	M,D
University of Southern California	M*
University of South Florida	M,D,O*
The University of Texas at Tyler	M
The University of Texas Health Science Center at Houston	M,D,O
University of the Sacred Heart	M
The University of Toledo	M,D,O
University of Toronto	M,D
University of Vermont	M,O
University of Washington	M,D
University of Wisconsin–Milwaukee	M,D,O*
University of Wisconsin–Whitewater	M
West Virginia University	M,D
Yale University	M,D

ENVIRONMENTAL BIOLOGY

Baylor University	M,D
Chatham University	M
Dalhousie University	M
Dartmouth College	D*
Emporia State University	M
Georgia State University	M,D
Governors State University	M
Hampton University	M
Hood College	M,O*
Massachusetts Institute of Technology	M,D,O
Missouri University of Science and Technology	M
Morgan State University	D
Nicholls State University	M
Ohio University	M,D
Oregon State University	M,D
Regis University	M
Rutgers University–New Brunswick	M,D
State University of New York College of Environmental Science and Forestry	M,D
Universidad del Turabo	M,D
University of Alberta	M,D
University of California, Santa Cruz	M,D*
University of Guelph	M,D
University of Louisiana at Lafayette	M,D
University of Louisville	M,D
The University of Manchester	M,D
University of Massachusetts Amherst	M,D*
University of Southern California	M,D*
University of South Florida	M,D*
University of Wisconsin–Madison	M,D
Washington University in St. Louis	D
Youngstown State University	M

ENVIRONMENTAL DESIGN

Arizona State University at the Tempe campus	D
ArtCenter College of Design	M
Columbia University	M*
Cornell University	M
Kansas State University	D
Kent State University	M
Michigan State University	M,D
San Diego State University	M
Texas Tech University	M,D
Université de Montréal	M,D,O
University of Calgary	M,D
University of California, Berkeley	M,D
University of California, Irvine	D
University of Georgia	M
The University of Manchester	M,D
Virginia Polytechnic Institute and State University	M,D
Yale University	M,D

ENVIRONMENTAL EDUCATION

Alaska Pacific University	M
Antioch University New England	M
Arcadia University	M,D,O
Ball State University	M,O
Brooklyn College of the City University of New York	M
Chatham University	M
Concordia University (United States)	M,D
Concordia University Wisconsin	M
Florida Atlantic University	M
Florida Institute of Technology	M
Goshen College	M
Hamline University	M,D
Instituto Tecnologico de Santo Domingo	M,D,O
Montclair State University	M
New York University	M*
Oregon State University	M,D
Prescott College	M,D
Royal Roads University	M,O
Slippery Rock University of Pennsylvania	M
Southern Connecticut State University	M,O
Southern Oregon University	M
State University of New York College at Cortland	M
Université du Québec à Montréal	M,D,O
University of Florida	M,D,O
University of South Africa	M,D
University of Victoria	M,D
Western Washington University	M

ENVIRONMENTAL ENGINEERING

Air Force Institute of Technology	M
The American University in Cairo	M,D,O
Arizona State University at the Tempe campus	M,D
California Institute of Technology	M,D

*M—masters degree; D—doctorate; O—other advanced degree; *—Close-Up and/or Display*

California Polytechnic State University, San Luis Obispo	M*
California State University, Fullerton	M
Carleton University	M,D
Carnegie Mellon University	M,D
The Catholic University of America	M,D
Clarkson University	M,D
Clemson University	M,D
Cleveland State University	M,D
Colorado School of Mines	M,D
Columbia University	M,D*
Concordia University (Canada)	M,D,O
Cornell University	M,D
Dalhousie University	M,D
Drexel University	M,D*
Duke University	M,D*
École Polytechnique de Montréal	M,D,O
Florida Atlantic University	M
Florida International University	M,D
Florida State University	M,D
Gannon University	M
The George Washington University	M,D,O
Georgia Institute of Technology	M
Harvard University	M,D*
Idaho State University	M
Illinois Institute of Technology	M,D
Instituto Tecnologico de Santo Domingo	M,O
Instituto Tecnológico y de Estudios Superiores de Monterrey, Campus Ciudad de México	M,D
Instituto Tecnológico y de Estudios Superiores de Monterrey, Campus Monterrey	M,D
Iowa State University of Science and Technology	M,D
Jackson State University	M,D
Johns Hopkins University	M,D,O*
Kansas State University	M,D
Kennesaw State University	M
Lakehead University	M
Lamar University	M,D
Lehigh University	M,D
Louisiana State University and Agricultural & Mechanical College	M,D
Manhattan College	M
Marquette University	M,D,O
Marshall University	M
Massachusetts Institute of Technology	M,D,O
McGill University	M,D
Memorial University of Newfoundland	M
Mercer University	M
Michigan State University	M,D
Michigan Technological University	M,D,O
Missouri University of Science and Technology	M,D
Montana State University	M,D
Montana Tech of The University of Montana	M
New Jersey Institute of Technology	M,D
New Mexico Institute of Mining and Technology	M
New Mexico State University	M,D
New York Institute of Technology	M
New York University	M*
North Dakota State University	M,D*
Northeastern University	M,D,O
Northwestern University	M,D
Norwich University	M
Ohio University	M,D
Oklahoma State University	M,D
Old Dominion University	M,D
Oregon Health & Science University	M,D
Oregon State University	M,D
Penn State Harrisburg	M,O
Penn State University Park	M,D*
Polytechnic University of Puerto Rico, Miami Campus	M
Polytechnic University of Puerto Rico, Orlando Campus	M
Portland State University	M,D
Princeton University	M,D
Purdue University	M,D
Rensselaer Polytechnic Institute	M,D
Rice University	M,D
Rose-Hulman Institute of Technology	M
Royal Military College of Canada	M,D
Rutgers University–New Brunswick	M,D
Southern Illinois University Carbondale	D
Southern Illinois University Edwardsville	M
Southern Methodist University	M,D
Stanford University	M,D,O
State University of New York College of Environmental Science and Forestry	M,D
Stevens Institute of Technology	M,D,O
Syracuse University	M*
Temple University	M,D,O*
Tennessee State University	M,D
Texas A&M University–Kingsville	M,D
Texas Tech University	M,D
Tufts University	M,D*
Universidad Central del Este	M
Universidad Nacional Pedro Henriquez Urena	M
Université de Sherbrooke	M
Université Laval	M,D
University at Buffalo, the State University of New York	M,D
The University of Alabama	M,D
The University of Alabama in Huntsville	M,D
University of Alaska Fairbanks	M,D,O
University of Alberta	M,D
The University of Arizona	M,D
University of Arkansas	M,D
University of Calgary	M,D
University of California, Berkeley	M,D
University of California, Davis	M,D,O
University of California, Irvine	M,D
University of California, Los Angeles	M,D*
University of California, Merced	M,D
University of California, Riverside	M,D
University of Central Florida	M,D
University of Cincinnati	M,D
University of Colorado Boulder	M,D
University of Colorado Denver	M,D
University of Connecticut	M,D*
University of Dayton	M
University of Delaware	M,D*
University of Detroit Mercy	M,D
University of Florida	M,D,O
University of Georgia	M
University of Guelph	M,D
University of Hawaii at Manoa	M,D
University of Illinois at Urbana–Champaign	M,D
The University of Iowa	M,D*
The University of Kansas	M,D
The University of Manchester	M,D
University of Maryland, Baltimore County	M,D
University of Maryland, College Park	M,D
University of Massachusetts Amherst	M,D*
University of Massachusetts Lowell	M,D
University of Memphis	M,D,O
University of Michigan	M,D,O*
University of Mississippi	M,D
University of Missouri	M,D
University of Nebraska–Lincoln	M,D
University of Nevada, Las Vegas	M,D
University of New Brunswick Fredericton	M,D
University of New Hampshire	M,D
University of New Haven	M*
The University of North Carolina at Chapel Hill	M,D
The University of North Carolina at Charlotte	M,D
University of North Dakota	M,D
University of Notre Dame	M,D
University of Oklahoma	M,D*
University of Pittsburgh	M,D*
University of Puerto Rico–Mayagüez	M,D
University of Regina	M,D
University of Rhode Island	M,D*
University of South Alabama	M
University of Southern California	M,D,O*
University of South Florida	M,D*
The University of Tennessee	M
The University of Texas at Austin	M,D
The University of Texas at El Paso	M,D,O
The University of Texas at San Antonio	M,D
The University of Texas at Tyler	M
University of Utah	M,D
University of Vermont	M,D
University of Washington	M,D
University of Waterloo	M,D
The University of Western Ontario	M,D
University of Windsor	M,D
University of Wisconsin–Madison	M
University of Wyoming	M
Utah State University	M,D,O
Vanderbilt University	M,D*
Villanova University	M,O
Virginia Polytechnic Institute and State University	M,O
Washington State University	M,D
Washington University in St. Louis	M,D
Worcester Polytechnic Institute	M,D,O
Yale University	M,D
Youngstown State University	M

ENVIRONMENTAL LAW

Chapman University	M,D*
Florida State University	M,D
Georgetown University	M,D
Golden Gate University	M,D
Lehigh University	M,O
Lewis & Clark College	M,D
Montclair State University	O
Pace University	M,D
St. Mary's University (United States)	M
Stanford University	M,D
University at Buffalo, the State University of New York	M,D
University of Calgary	M,O
University of Colorado Denver	M,D
University of Florida	M,D
University of Houston	M,D
University of Pittsburgh	M*
The University of Tulsa	M,D,O
Vermont Law School	M
Western Michigan University Thomas M. Cooley Law School	M,D

ENVIRONMENTAL MANAGEMENT AND POLICY

Adelphi University	M
Air Force Institute of Technology	M
American Public University System	M,D
American University	M,D,O
American University of Beirut	M,D
Antioch University New England	M,D
Arizona State University at the Tempe campus	M
Ball State University	M,O
Bard College	M,O
Baylor University	M,D
Bemidji State University	M
Binghamton University, State University of New York	M,D
California State University, Fullerton	M
Central European University	M,D
Central Washington University	M
The Citadel, The Military College of South Carolina	M,O
Clarkson University	M
Clark University	M
Clemson University	M,D
Cleveland State University	M,O
College of the Atlantic	M
Colorado State University	M,D
Columbia University	M*
Columbus State University	M
Concordia University (Canada)	M,D,O
Cornell University	M,D
Dalhousie University	M
Drexel University	M*
Duke University	D*
Duquesne University	M,O
The Evergreen State College	M
Florida Gulf Coast University	M
Florida Institute of Technology	M
Florida International University	M,D
George Mason University	M,D
The George Washington University	M
Georgia Institute of Technology	M,D
Georgia State University	M,D,O
Green Mountain College	M
Hardin-Simmons University	M
Harvard University	M,O*
Humboldt State University	M
Idaho State University	M
Illinois Institute of Technology	M
Indiana University Bloomington	M,D,O
Indiana University Northwest	M,O
Indiana University of Pennsylvania	M
Instituto Tecnologico de Santo Domingo	M,D,O
Instituto Tecnológico y de Estudios Superiores de Monterrey, Campus Estado de México	M,D
Instituto Tecnológico y de Estudios Superiores de Monterrey, Campus Irapuato	M,D
Inter American University of Puerto Rico, Metropolitan Campus	M
James Madison University	M
Johns Hopkins University	M,O*
Kentucky State University	M
Lake Forest College	M
Lamar University	M,D
Lehigh University	M,O
Long Island University–LIU Post	M,O
Louisiana State University and Agricultural & Mechanical College	M,D
McGill University	M,D
Michigan Technological University	M,D
Middlebury Institute of International Studies at Monterey	M
Millersville University of Pennsylvania	M
Missouri State University	M,O
Montclair State University	M,D
Morehead State University	M
New Jersey Institute of Technology	M,D,O
The New School	M
New York Institute of Technology	O
New York University	M*
Northeastern Illinois University	M,O
Northeastern University	M,D
Northern Arizona University	M,D,O
The Ohio State University	M,D
Ohio University	M,O
Oregon State University	M,D
Pace University	M
Penn State University Park	M*
Point Park University	M
Polytechnic University of Puerto Rico	M
Polytechnic University of Puerto Rico, Miami Campus	M
Polytechnic University of Puerto Rico, Orlando Campus	M
Portland State University	M,D,O
Prescott College	M
Purdue University	M,D
Rice University	M
Royal Roads University	M,O
St. Edward's University	M
Samford University	M
San Francisco State University	M
San Jose State University	M
Shippensburg University of Pennsylvania	M
Simon Fraser University	M,D,O
SIT Graduate Institute	M
Slippery Rock University of Pennsylvania	M
Southeast Missouri State University	M
Southern Illinois University Carbondale	M,D
Southern Illinois University Edwardsville	M
Southern New Hampshire University	M,D,O
State University of New York College of Environmental Science and Forestry	M,D
Stony Brook University, State University of New York	M,O
Tennessee Technological University	M
Texas Southern University	M,D
Texas Tech University	M,D
Thomas Edison State University	M
Towson University	M
Trent University	M,D
Tropical Agriculture Research and Higher Education Center	M,D
Troy University	M
Tufts University	M,D,O*
Universidad Autonoma de Guadalajara	M,D
Universidad del Turabo	M,D
Universidad Metropolitana	M
Université de Montréal	O
Université du Québec à Chicoutimi	M
Université du Québec, Institut National de la Recherche Scientifique	M,D
Université Laval	M,D,O
University of Alaska Fairbanks	M
University of Alberta	M,D
The University of Arizona	M,D
The University of British Columbia	M,D
University of Calgary	M,D,O
University of California, Berkeley	M,D,O
University of California, San Diego	M*
University of California, Santa Barbara	M,D
University of California, Santa Cruz	D*
University of Central Missouri	M,D,O
University of Chicago	M
University of Colorado Boulder	M,D
University of Colorado Denver	M,D,O
University of Dayton	M,D
University of Delaware	M,D*
University of Denver	M,O
The University of Findlay	M,D
University of Guelph	M,D
University of Hawaii at Manoa	M,D,O
University of Houston–Clear Lake	M
University of Illinois at Springfield	M
University of Maine	D
The University of Manchester	M,D
University of Maryland, Baltimore County	M,D
University of Maryland Eastern Shore	M,D
University of Maryland University College	M
University of Massachusetts Amherst	M,D*
University of Massachusetts Dartmouth	M,O
University of Michigan	M,D*
University of Minnesota, Twin Cities Campus	M,D
University of Montana	M
University of Nevada, Reno	M
University of New Brunswick Fredericton	M,D
University of New Hampshire	M
University of New Haven	M*
University of New Mexico	M
The University of North Carolina Wilmington	M
University of Northern British Columbia	M,D,O
University of Oregon	M,D
University of Pennsylvania	M*
University of Puerto Rico–Río Piedras	M
University of Rhode Island	M,D*
University of South Africa	M,D
University of South Alabama	M,D
University of South Carolina	M
University of South Florida	M,D,O*
University of South Florida, St. Petersburg	M
The University of Tennessee	M,D
The University of Texas at Austin	M
University of Washington	M,D
University of Waterloo	M,D
University of Wisconsin–Green Bay	M
Utah State University	M,D
Vanderbilt University	M,D*
Vermont Law School	M
Virginia Commonwealth University	M
Virginia Polytechnic Institute and State University	M,D,O
Webster University	M
Wesley College	M
Western State Colorado University	M
Wilfrid Laurier University	M,D
Wilmington University	M,D
Yale University	M,D
York University	M,D
Youngstown State University	M,O

ENVIRONMENTAL SCIENCES

Adelphi University	M
Alaska Pacific University	M
American University	M,O
American University of Beirut	M,D
Antioch University New England	M,D
Arizona State University at the Tempe campus	M,D,O
Arkansas State University	M,D
Ball State University	D
Baylor University	D
Boston University	M,D*
Brigham Young University	M,D
California Institute of Technology	M,D
California State Polytechnic University, Pomona	M
California State University, Chico	M
California State University, East Bay	M
California State University, Northridge	M
California State University, San Bernardino	M
Carnegie Mellon University	D
Christopher Newport University	M
Clarkson University	M,D
Clark University	M
Clemson University	M,D
Cleveland State University	M,D

The College at Brockport, State University of New York	M
College of Charleston	M
College of Staten Island of the City University of New York	M
The College of William and Mary	M,D*
Colorado School of Mines	M,D*
Columbia University	M,D*
Columbus State University	M,O
Cornell University	M,D
Dalhousie University	M
DePaul University	M,D
Drexel University	M,D*
Duke University	M,D*
Duquesne University	M,O
Florida Agricultural and Mechanical University	M,D
Florida Gulf Coast University	M
Florida Institute of Technology	M,D
Florida State University	M,D
Gannon University	M
George Mason University	M,D
Georgia Southern University	M,O
The Graduate Center, City University of New York	D
Harvard University	M,D*
Howard University	M,D
Humboldt State University	M
Idaho State University	M,O
Indiana University Bloomington	M,D,O
Instituto Tecnologico de Santo Domingo	M,D,O
Instituto Tecnológico y de Estudios Superiores de Monterrey, Campus Ciudad de México	M,D
Inter American University of Puerto Rico, San Germán Campus	M
Iowa State University of Science and Technology	M,D
Jackson State University	M
Johns Hopkins University	M,O*
Kansas State University	M,D,O
Laurentian University	M,D
Lehigh University	M,D
Lincoln University (MO)	M
Louisiana State University and Agricultural & Mechanical College	M,D
Loyola Marymount University	M
Marshall University	M
Massachusetts Institute of Technology	M,D,O
McNeese State University	M
Memorial University of Newfoundland	M,D
Mercer University	M
Miami University	M
Michigan State University	M,D
Minnesota State University Mankato	M
Montana State University	M,D
Montclair State University	M
Murray State University	M,O
New Jersey Institute of Technology	M,D,O
New Mexico State University	M,D
New York University	M*
North Carolina Agricultural and Technical State University	M
North Carolina Central University	M
North Dakota State University	M,D*
Northeastern University	M,D
Northern Arizona University	M,D,O
Oakland University	M,D
The Ohio State University	M,D
Oklahoma State University	M,D,O
Old Dominion University	M,D
Oregon Health & Science University	M,D
Oregon State University	M,D
Pace University	M
Penn State Harrisburg	M,O
Penn State University Park	M*
Pontifical Catholic University of Puerto Rico	M
Portland State University	M,D,O
Queens College of the City University of New York	M
Rice University	M,D
Rochester Institute of Technology	M,D
Royal Military College of Canada	M,D
Rutgers University–Newark	M,D
Rutgers University–New Brunswick	M,D
Sitting Bull College	M
South Dakota School of Mines and Technology	D
Southeast Missouri State University	M
Southern Connecticut State University	M,O
Southern Illinois University Carbondale	D
Southern Illinois University Edwardsville	M
Southern University and Agricultural and Mechanical College	M
Stanford University	M,D,O
State University of New York College of Environmental Science and Forestry	M,D
Stephen F. Austin State University	M
Stockton University	M
Tarleton State University	M
Tennessee Technological University	M,D
Texas A&M University–Commerce	M,O
Texas A&M University–Corpus Christi	M
Texas Christian University	M
Texas Tech University	M,D
Thompson Rivers University	M
Towson University	M,O
Tuskegee University	M
Universidad del Turabo	M,D
Universidad Nacional Pedro Henriquez Urena	M
Université de Sherbrooke	M,O
Université du Québec à Montréal	M,D,O
Université du Québec à Trois-Rivières	M,D
Université du Québec en Abitibi-Témiscamingue	M,D
Université Laval	M,D
University at Buffalo, the State University of New York	M,D
University of Alberta	M,D
The University of Arizona	M,D,O
University of California, Berkeley	M,D
University of California, Davis	M,D
University of California, Los Angeles	M,D*
University of California, Riverside	M
University of California, Santa Barbara	M,D
University of Chicago	M
University of Cincinnati	M,D
University of Colorado Colorado Springs	M
University of Colorado Denver	M
University of Guam	M
University of Guelph	M,D
University of Hawaii at Hilo	M*
University of Houston–Clear Lake	M
University of Idaho	M,D
University of Illinois at Springfield	M
University of Illinois at Urbana–Champaign	M,D
The University of Kansas	M,D
University of Lethbridge	M,D
University of Louisiana at Lafayette	M
The University of Manchester	M,D
University of Manitoba	M,D
University of Maryland, Baltimore	M,D
University of Maryland, Baltimore County	M,D
University of Maryland, College Park	M,D
University of Maryland Eastern Shore	M,D
University of Massachusetts Boston	M,D
University of Massachusetts Lowell	M,D
University of Michigan	M,D*
University of Michigan–Dearborn	M
University of Montana	M
University of Nevada, Las Vegas	M,D,O
University of Nevada, Reno	M,D
University of New Haven	M*
University of New Orleans	M,D
The University of North Carolina at Chapel Hill	M,D
The University of North Carolina Wilmington	M
University of North Texas	M,D,O
University of Oklahoma	M,D*
University of Pennsylvania	M,D*
University of Pittsburgh	M,D*
University of Prince Edward Island	M,D
University of Puerto Rico–Mayagüez	M,D
University of Puerto Rico–Río Piedras	M,D
University of Rhode Island	M,D*
University of San Diego	M
University of Saskatchewan	M
University of South Africa	M,D
University of South Florida	M,D*
University of South Florida, St. Petersburg	M
The University of Tennessee at Chattanooga	M
The University of Texas at Arlington	M,D
The University of Texas at El Paso	M,D
The University of Texas at San Antonio	M,D
The University of Texas Rio Grande Valley	M
University of the Virgin Islands	M
The University of Toledo	M,D
University of Toronto	M,D
University of Utah	M
University of Vermont	M
University of Virginia	M,D
University of Waterloo	M,D
The University of Western Ontario	M,D
University of West Florida	M
University of Windsor	M,D
University of Wisconsin–Green Bay	M
University of Wisconsin–Madison	M
University of Wisconsin–Milwaukee	M,D*
Vanderbilt University	M*
Virginia Polytechnic Institute and State University	M,O
Washington State University	M,D
Wesleyan University	M
Western Illinois University	D
Western Washington University	M
West Texas A&M University	M
Wichita State University	M
Wilfrid Laurier University	M,D
Wright State University	D
Yale University	M,D

EPIDEMIOLOGY

American University of Beirut	M,D
Boston University	M,D*
Brown University	M,D
California State University, Northridge	M
Capella University	D
Case Western Reserve University	D*
Colorado State University	M,D
Columbia University	M,D*
Daemen College	M
Dalhousie University	M
Dartmouth College	M,D*
Drexel University	M,D,O*
East Tennessee State University	M,D,O
Emory University	M,D
Florida International University	M,D
George Mason University	M,O
Georgetown University	M,O
The George Washington University	M
Georgia Southern University	M,D
Harvard University	M,D*
Indiana University Bloomington	M,D
Indiana University–Purdue University Indianapolis	M,D,O
Johns Hopkins University	M,D*
Kent State University	M,D
Liberty University	M,D
Loma Linda University	M,D
Louisiana State University Health Sciences Center	M,D
McGill University	M,D,O
Medical University of South Carolina	M,D
Memorial University of Newfoundland	M,D,O
Michigan State University	M,D
Monroe College	M
New York Medical College	M,D,O
New York University	M,D*
North Carolina State University	M,D
Northwestern University	D
Oregon State University	M,D
Ponce Health Sciences University	M,D
Purdue University	M,D
Queen's University at Kingston	M,D
Rutgers University–Newark	M,O
Rutgers University–New Brunswick	M,D,O
San Diego State University	M,D
Stanford University	M,D
Temple University	M,D*
Texas A&M University	M,D
Tufts University	M,D,O*
Tulane University	M,D
Université Laval	M,D
University at Albany, State University of New York	M,D
University at Buffalo, the State University of New York	M,D
The University of Alabama at Birmingham	M,D
University of Alberta	M,D
The University of Arizona	M,D
University of Arkansas for Medical Sciences	M,D,O
University of California, Berkeley	M,D
University of California, Davis	M,D
University of California, Irvine	M,D
University of California, Los Angeles	M,D*
University of California, San Diego	D*
University of Cincinnati	M,D
University of Colorado Denver	M,D
University of Florida	M,D,O
University of Guelph	M,D
University of Hawaii at Manoa	D
University of Illinois at Chicago	M,D
University of Illinois at Springfield	M,O
The University of Iowa	M,D*
The University of Kansas	M
University of Kentucky	D
University of Louisville	M,D
University of Maryland, Baltimore	M,D,O
University of Maryland, Baltimore County	M,D,O
University of Maryland, College Park	M,D
University of Massachusetts Amherst	M,D*
University of Memphis	M,D
University of Miami	M,D*
University of Michigan	M,D*
University of Minnesota, Twin Cities Campus	M,D
University of Nebraska Medical Center	D
University of New Mexico	M
The University of North Carolina at Chapel Hill	M,D
University of North Texas Health Science Center at Fort Worth	M,D,O
University of Oklahoma Health Sciences Center	M,D
University of Ottawa	M
University of Pennsylvania	M*
University of Pittsburgh	M,D*
University of Prince Edward Island	M,D
University of Puerto Rico–Medical Sciences Campus	M
University of Rochester	D*
University of Saskatchewan	M,D
University of South Carolina	M,D
University of Southern California	M,D*
University of Southern Mississippi	M
University of South Florida	M,D,O*
The University of Tennessee Health Science Center	M,D
The University of Texas Health Science Center at Houston	M,D,O
The University of Toledo	M,O
University of Toronto	M,D
University of Vermont	M,O
University of Washington	M,D
The University of Western Ontario	M,D
University of Wisconsin–Madison	M,D
University of Wisconsin–Milwaukee	M,D,O*
Walden University	M,D,O
Washington University in St. Louis	M,D
Weill Cornell Medicine	M
West Virginia University	M,D
Yale University	M,D

ERGONOMICS AND HUMAN FACTORS

Arizona State University at the Tempe campus	M
Bentley University	M
California State University, Long Beach	M
The Catholic University of America	M,D
Clemson University	M,D
Cornell University	M
Embry-Riddle Aeronautical University–Daytona	M,D
Florida Institute of Technology	M,D
Georgia Institute of Technology	M,D
Harvard University	M,D*
Indiana University Bloomington	M,D
Michigan Technological University	M,D,O
Mississippi State University	M,D
New York University	M,D*
North Carolina State University	D
Old Dominion University	D
Purdue University	M,D
San Jose State University	M
Tufts University	M,D*
Université de Montréal	O
Université du Québec à Montréal	O
The University of Alabama	M
University of Cincinnati	M,D
The University of Iowa	M,D,O*
University of Miami	M*
University of Wisconsin–Madison	M,D
University of Wisconsin–Milwaukee	M*
Wright State University	M,D

ETHICS

American University	M,D,O
Anabaptist Mennonite Biblical Seminary	M,O
Arizona State University at the Tempe campus	M,D
Azusa Pacific University	M*
Boston University	M,D*
Chicago Theological Seminary	M,D
Claremont Graduate University	M,D
Claremont Lincoln University	M
Claremont School of Theology	M,D
Columbia University	M*
Duke University	M,O*
Emory University	M,D
Fordham University	M,O
Freed-Hardeman University	M
George Mason University	M
Georgetown University	M,D
Graduate Theological Union	M,D,O
John Brown University	M
Lancaster Theological Seminary	M,D,O
Lebanon Valley College	M
Lee University	M
Loyola University Chicago	M
Lutheran Theological Seminary Saskatoon	M,D
Marquette University	M,D
New England College of Business and Finance	M
Northwestern University	M
Oregon State University	M
Phillips Theological Seminary	M,D
Pontifical John Paul II Institute for Studies on Marriage and Family	M,D,O
Santa Clara University	M,D,O
Schreiner University	M
Southeastern Baptist Theological Seminary	M,D
Spring Hill College	M,O
Stevens Institute of Technology	M,O
Suffolk University	M,O
Texas State University	M
Université de Sherbrooke	M,D,O
Université du Québec à Chicoutimi	O
Université du Québec à Rimouski	M,O
Université Laval	O
University of Chicago	D
University of Detroit Mercy	M,O
University of Maryland, Baltimore	O
The University of North Carolina at Charlotte	M,O
University of North Florida	M,O
University of Pennsylvania	M,D*
University of St. Thomas (MN)	M,D
University of South Africa	M,D
The University of Tennessee at Chattanooga	M,O
Valparaiso University	M,O
Viterbo University	M,O
West Chester University of Pennsylvania	M,O
Xavier University	M*

ETHNIC STUDIES

Colorado State University	M
Cornell University	M,D
DePaul University	M
Minnesota State University Mankato	M
Northern Arizona University	O

*M—masters degree; D—doctorate; O—other advanced degree; *—Close-Up and/or Display*

San Francisco State University	M
United Theological Seminary of the Twin Cities	M,D,O
Université Laval	M,D
The University of British Columbia	M
University of California, Berkeley	D
University of California, Riverside	D
University of California, San Diego	D*
University of Colorado Boulder	D
University of Colorado Denver	M,O
University of New Mexico	M,D

EVOLUTIONARY BIOLOGY

Arizona State University at the Tempe campus	M,D
Brown University	D
Columbia University	M,D*
Cornell University	D
Dartmouth College	D*
Emory University	D
Florida State University	M,D
Harvard University	D*
Illinois State University	M,D
Indiana State University	M,D
Indiana University Bloomington	M,D
Iowa State University of Science and Technology	M,D
Johns Hopkins University	D*
Michigan State University	D
Montclair State University	M
The Ohio State University	M,D
Ohio University	M,D
Oklahoma State University	M,D
Princeton University	D
Purdue University	M,D
Rice University	M,D
Rutgers University–New Brunswick	M,D
Stony Brook University, State University of New York	M,D
Tulane University	M,D
University at Buffalo, the State University of New York	M,D,O
University of Alberta	M,D
The University of Arizona	M,D
University of California, Davis	D
University of California, Irvine	M,D
University of California, Los Angeles	M,D*
University of California, Riverside	M,D
University of California, Santa Barbara	M,D
University of California, Santa Cruz	M,D*
University of Chicago	D
University of Colorado Boulder	M,D
University of Delaware	M,D*
University of Denver	M,D
University of Guelph	M,D
University of Illinois at Urbana–Champaign	M,D
The University of Iowa	M,D*
The University of Kansas	M,D
University of Louisiana at Lafayette	M,D
The University of Manchester	M,D
University of Maryland, College Park	M,D
University of Massachusetts Amherst	M,D*
University of Miami	M,D*
University of Michigan	M,D*
University of Minnesota, Twin Cities Campus	M,D
University of Missouri	M,D
University of Nevada, Reno	D
University of New Hampshire	D
The University of North Carolina at Chapel Hill	M,D
University of Notre Dame	M,D
University of Oklahoma	M,D*
University of Oregon	M,D
University of Pittsburgh	D*
University of Puerto Rico–Río Piedras	M,D
University of Rhode Island	M,D*
University of South Carolina	M,D
University of Southern California	D*
University of South Florida	M,D*
The University of Tennessee	M,D
The University of Texas at Austin	D
University of Toronto	M,D
Washington University in St. Louis	D
Wesleyan University	D
Yale University	D

EXERCISE AND SPORTS SCIENCE

Adams State University	M
American International College	M,D,O
Appalachian State University	M
Arizona State University at the Tempe campus	M,D
Arkansas State University	M,O
Ashland University	M
Auburn University	M,D,O*
Auburn University at Montgomery	M,O
Austin Peay State University	M
Ball State University	M,D
Barry University	M
Baylor University	M,D
Benedictine University	M
Bloomsburg University of Pennsylvania	M
Brigham Young University	M,D
Brooklyn College of the City University of New York	M
California Baptist University	M
California State University, Fresno	M
California State University, Long Beach	M
California State University, Sacramento	M
California University of Pennsylvania	M
Carroll University	M
Central Connecticut State University	M,O
Central Michigan University	M,D
The Citadel, The Military College of South Carolina	M,O
The College of St. Scholastica	M
Colorado State University	M,D
Columbus State University	M
Concordia University (Canada)	M
Concordia University Chicago	M
Concordia University, St. Paul	M,D
Delaware State University	M
Delta State University	M
East Carolina University	M,D,O
Eastern Illinois University	M
Eastern Kentucky University	M
Eastern Michigan University	M
Eastern New Mexico University	M
Eastern Washington University	M
East Tennessee State University	M,D
Fairmont State University	M
Florida Atlantic University	M
Florida State University	M,D
Gannon University	M
Gardner-Webb University	M
George Mason University	M,O
The George Washington University	M
Georgia College & State University	M
Georgia Southern University–Armstrong Campus	M,O
Georgia State University	M
Hofstra University	M,O
Howard University	M
Indiana University Bloomington	M,D
Indiana University of Pennsylvania	M
Inter American University of Puerto Rico, Metropolitan Campus	M
Iowa State University of Science and Technology	M
Ithaca College	M
James Madison University	M
Kean University	M
Kennesaw State University	M
Kent State University	M,D
Lakehead University	M
Liberty University	M,D
Life University	M
Lipscomb University	M
Logan University	M,D
Long Island University–LIU Brooklyn	M,D,O
Manhattanville College	M,O
Marshall University	M
Marywood University	M
McNeese State University	M
Memorial University of Newfoundland	M
Merrimack College	M
Miami University	M
Middle Tennessee State University	M,D
Midwestern State University	M
Mississippi State University	M,D
Montclair State University	M,O
Morehead State University	M
New Mexico Highlands University	M
North Dakota State University	M,D*
Northeastern Illinois University	M
Northeastern University	M,D,O
Northern Michigan University	M
Northwest Missouri State University	M
Oakland University	M,D,O
Ohio University	M,D
Old Dominion University	M
Pittsburg State University	M
Point Loma Nazarene University	M
Purdue University	M,D
Queens College of the City University of New York	M,O
Queen's University at Kingston	M,D
Rowan University	M
Sacred Heart University	M
St. Ambrose University	M
Saint Mary's College of California	M
San Diego State University	M
San Jose State University	M
Smith College	M
Sonoma State University	M
South Dakota State University	M,D
Southeast Missouri State University	M
Southern Connecticut State University	M
Southern Illinois University Edwardsville	M
Southern Utah University	M
Springfield College	M,D,O
Syracuse University	M*
Tennessee State University	M
Texas A&M University–Commerce	M,D,O
Texas Tech University	M
Texas Woman's University	M,D
United States Sports Academy	M
University at Buffalo, the State University of New York	M,D,O
The University of Akron	M
The University of Alabama	M,D
University of Alberta	M,D
University of Arkansas at Little Rock	M
University of California, Davis	M
University of Central Florida	M,D
University of Central Oklahoma	M
University of Connecticut	M,D*
University of Dayton	M
University of Florida	M,D
University of Houston	M,D
University of Houston–Clear Lake	M
University of Idaho	M,D
The University of Iowa	M,D*
The University of Kansas	M,D
University of Kentucky	M,D
University of Lethbridge	M,D
University of Louisiana at Monroe	M
University of Louisville	M,D,O
University of Maine	M,D,O
University of Mary	M
University of Mary Hardin-Baylor	M
University of Massachusetts Boston	M,D
University of Memphis	M,O
University of Miami	M,D*
University of Minnesota, Twin Cities Campus	M,D
University of Mississippi	M,D
University of Montana	M
University of Nebraska at Kearney	M
University of Nebraska at Omaha	M,D
University of Nebraska–Lincoln	M,D
University of Nevada, Las Vegas	M,D
University of New Brunswick Fredericton	M
University of New Mexico	D
University of North Alabama	M
The University of North Carolina at Chapel Hill	M
The University of North Carolina at Pembroke	M
University of Northern Colorado	M,D
University of North Florida	M,D
University of Oklahoma	M,D*
University of Pittsburgh	M,D*
University of Puerto Rico–Mayagüez	M
University of Puerto Rico–Río Piedras	M
University of Rhode Island	M*
University of South Alabama	M
University of South Carolina	M,D
University of South Dakota	M
The University of Tampa	M
The University of Tennessee	M,D,O
The University of Texas at Arlington	M,D
The University of Texas at Austin	M,D
The University of Texas Rio Grande Valley	M
University of the Pacific	M
The University of Toledo	M,D
University of West Florida	M
University of Wisconsin–La Crosse	M
University of Wisconsin–Milwaukee	M,D*
University of Wyoming	M
Valdosta State University	M
Virginia Commonwealth University	M
Virginia Polytechnic Institute and State University	M,D
Wake Forest University	M
Washington State University	M
Wayne State College	M
Wayne State University	M,D
West Chester University of Pennsylvania	M,O
Western Michigan University	M
Western Washington University	M
West Texas A&M University	M
West Virginia University	M,D
Wichita State University	M
William Paterson University of New Jersey	M,D,O

EXPERIMENTAL PSYCHOLOGY

Azusa Pacific University	M*
Bowling Green State University	M,D
Brooklyn College of the City University of New York	M,D
California State University, Fresno	M,O
California State University, Northridge	M
Case Western Reserve University	D*
The Catholic University of America	M,D
Central Michigan University	M,D
Central Washington University	M
Cornell University	D
Duke University	D*
Eastern Washington University	M
East Tennessee State University	D
Fairleigh Dickinson University, Metropolitan Campus	M,O
The Graduate Center, City University of New York	D
Harvard University	D*
Howard University	M,D
Idaho State University	D
Iona College	M,O
James Madison University	M
Kent State University	M,D
Lakehead University	M,D
Laurentian University	M
McGill University	M,D
McNeese State University	M,O
Memorial University of Newfoundland	M,D
Middle Tennessee State University	M,O
Missouri State University	M,O
Morehead State University	M
Murray State University	M,O
North Carolina State University	D
Nova Southeastern University	M,D,O*
Ohio University	D
Radford University	M
Rivier University	M
Rochester Institute of Technology	M
Saint Louis University	M,D*
San Jose State University	M
Seton Hall University	M
Southern Illinois University Carbondale	M,D
Texas A&M University–Central Texas	M,O
Texas Christian University	M,D
Texas Tech University	M,D
Towson University	M
The University of Alabama	D
University of Central Oklahoma	M
University of Cincinnati	D
University of Connecticut	M,D*
University of Hartford	M
University of Idaho	M,D
University of Louisville	D
University of Maryland, College Park	M,D
University of Massachusetts Dartmouth	M,O
University of Memphis	M,D,O
University of Mississippi	M,D
University of Montana	M,D,O
University of New Brunswick Saint John	M,D
University of Regina	M,D
University of South Carolina	M,D
The University of Tennessee	M,D
The University of Tennessee at Chattanooga	M
The University of Texas at Arlington	M,D
The University of Texas at El Paso	M,D
The University of Texas of the Permian Basin	M
The University of Texas Rio Grande Valley	M
The University of Toledo	M,D
University of Vermont	D
University of Victoria	M,D
The University of West Alabama	M
University of West Florida	M
University of Wisconsin–Oshkosh	M
Washington State University	M,D
Western Illinois University	M,O
Western Kentucky University	M,O
Western Washington University	M

FACILITIES MANAGEMENT

Cornell University	M
Indiana University–Purdue University Fort Wayne	M
Liberty University	M,D
Maastricht School of Management	M,D
Massachusetts Maritime Academy	M
Pratt Institute	M*
Université Laval	M,O
University of California, Berkeley	O
University of New Haven	M,O*
The University of North Carolina at Charlotte	M,O
Wentworth Institute of Technology	M

FAMILY AND CONSUMER SCIENCES-GENERAL

Alabama Agricultural and Mechanical University	M
Ball State University	M
California State University, Northridge	M
Central Michigan University	M,O
Central Washington University	M
Clemson University	D,O
Florida State University	M,D
Fontbonne University	M
Hofstra University	M,D,O
Illinois State University	M
Iowa State University of Science and Technology	M
Kansas State University	M,D,O
Lamar University	M
Louisiana State University and Agricultural & Mechanical College	M,D
New Mexico State University	M
North Dakota State University	M*
The Ohio State University	M,D
Oklahoma State University	M,D
Queens College of the City University of New York	M,O
Sam Houston State University	M
San Francisco State University	M
South Carolina State University	M
South Dakota State University	M
Stephen F. Austin State University	M
Tennessee State University	M,D
Texas A&M University–Kingsville	M
Texas Southern University	M
Texas State University	M
Tufts University	M,D*
The University of Alabama	M,D
University of Alberta	M,D
The University of Arizona	D
University of Arkansas	M
University of Central Arkansas	M
University of Central Oklahoma	M
University of Colorado Denver	M,D
University of Florida	M
University of Georgia	M,D
University of Houston	M
University of Maryland, College Park	M,D
University of Missouri	M,D,O
University of Nebraska–Lincoln	M,D
University of Puerto Rico–Río Piedras	M
University of South Africa	M,D
The University of Tennessee	D
The University of Tennessee at Martin	M
The University of Texas at Austin	M,D
University of Wisconsin–Madison	M,D
University of Wisconsin–Stevens Point	O

Utah State University	M,D
Western Michigan University	M

FAMILY NURSE PRACTITIONER STUDIES

Albany State University	M
Allen College	M,D
Alvernia University	M,D,O
Alverno College	M,D
American International College	M,D,O
Anderson University (SC)	M,D
Angelo State University	M
Arizona State University at the Tempe campus	M,D,O
Ashland University	D
Auburn University at Montgomery	M
Augsburg University	M,D
Augusta University	D
Austin Peay State University	M
Azusa Pacific University	M,D*
Ball State University	M,D,O
Barry University	M,O
Baylor University	M,D
Bellarmine University	M,D
Bellin College	M
Binghamton University, State University of New York	M,D,O
Bloomsburg University of Pennsylvania	M,D
Bowie State University	M
Bradley University	M,D,O
Brenau University	M
Brigham Young University	M
California Baptist University	M
California State University, Bakersfield	M
California State University, San Marcos	M
Carlow University	M,O
Carson-Newman University	M
Case Western Reserve University	M*
Cedarville University	M,D
Clarion University of Pennsylvania	M
Clarke University	D
Clarkson College	M,O
Clayton State University	M
Clemson University	M,D,O
College of Mount Saint Vincent	M,O
The College of New Rochelle	M,O
Colorado Mesa University	M,D,O
Columbia University	M,O*
Columbus State University	M
Concordia University Wisconsin	M,D
Coppin State University	M,O
Cox College	M
Creighton University	M,D,O
Delta State University	M,D
DePaul University	M,D
DeSales University	M,D,O
Dominican College	M,D
Drexel University	M*
Duke University	M,D,O*
Duquesne University	M,O
D'Youville College	M,D,O
Eastern Kentucky University	M
East Tennessee State University	M,D,O
Edinboro University of Pennsylvania	M,D
Elms College	M,D
Emory University	M
Endicott College	M,O
Fairfield University	M,D
Felician University	M,O
Florida National University	M
Florida Southern College	M
Florida State University	D,O
Franciscan Missionaries of Our Lady University	M
Francis Marion University	M
Fresno Pacific University	M
Frontier Nursing University	M,D,O*
Gannon University	M,O
Gardner-Webb University	M,D
George Mason University	M,D,O
Georgetown University	M,D
The George Washington University	M,D,O
Georgia Southern University	M
Georgia Southern University–Armstrong Campus	M,O
Georgia Southwestern State University	M,O
Georgia State University	M,D,O
Goshen College	M
Graceland University (IA)	M,D,O
Grambling State University	M,O
Grand Canyon University	M,D,O
Gwynedd Mercy University	M,D
Hampton University	M,D
Hardin-Simmons University	M
Hofstra University	M,O
Holy Names University	M
Howard University	M
Hunter College of the City University of New York	D
Husson University	M,O
Illinois State University	M,D,O
Indiana State University	M,D
Indiana University Kokomo	M
Indiana University–Purdue University Fort Wayne	M,O
Indiana University–Purdue University Indianapolis	M
Indiana University South Bend	M
Jacksonville University	M*
James Madison University	M,D
Johns Hopkins University	D*
Keiser University	M
Kent State University	M,D
King University	M,D
La Salle University	M,D,O
Le Moyne College	M,O
Lewis University	M,D
Liberty University	M,D
Lincoln Memorial University	M
Long Island University–Brentwood Campus	M,O
Long Island University–LIU Brooklyn	M,O
Long Island University–LIU Post	M,O
Louisiana State University Health Sciences Center	M,D,O
Loyola University Chicago	M,D,O
Loyola University New Orleans	M,D
Malone University	M
Marian University (IN)	M,D
Marquette University	M,D,O
Marymount University	M,D,O
Maryville University of Saint Louis	M,D
McGill University	M,D,O
McMurry University	M
McNeese State University	M
Medical University of South Carolina	M,D
Mercer University	M,D,O
Middle Tennessee State University	M,O
Midwestern State University	M
Millersville University of Pennsylvania	M,O
Millikin University	M,D
Minnesota State University Mankato	M,D
Missouri State University	M,D
Molloy College	M,D,O
Monmouth University	M,D,O*
Montana State University	M,D,O
Morningside College	M
Mount Carmel College of Nursing	M,D
Mount Saint Mary College	M,O
Murray State University	D
National University	M,O
New Mexico State University	M,D,O
New York University	M,D,O*
Nicholls State University	M
Northeastern University	M,D,O
Northern Arizona University	M,D,O
Nova Southeastern University	M,D*
Oakland University	M,O
Ohio University	M,D
Old Dominion University	M
Olivet Nazarene University	M
Oregon Health & Science University	M
Otterbein University	M,D,O
Pace University	M,D,O
Pacific Lutheran University	D
Palm Beach Atlantic University	M,D
Point Loma Nazarene University	M
Purdue University	M,D,O
Purdue University Northwest	M
Queen's University at Kingston	M,D,O
Quinnipiac University	D
Ramapo College of New Jersey	M
Regis College (MA)	M,D,O
Research College of Nursing	M
Rivier University	M,D
Rocky Mountain University of Health Professions	D
Rush University	D
Rutgers University–Camden	D
Rutgers University–Newark	M,D,O
Sacred Heart University	M,D,O
Sage Graduate School	M
Saginaw Valley State University	M,D
Saint Francis Medical Center College of Nursing	M,D,O
Saint Joseph's College of Maine	M,O
Saint Mary's College	D
Salisbury University	D
Samford University	M,D
Samuel Merritt University	M,D,O
San Francisco State University	M,O
San Jose State University	M,O
Seattle Pacific University	M,O
Shenandoah University	M,D,O
Simmons College	M,D,O
Sonoma State University	M
Southern Adventist University	M,D
Southern Connecticut State University	M,D
Southern Illinois University Edwardsville	M,D,O
Southern University and Agricultural and Mechanical College	M,D,O
South University	M
South University	M
South University	M
Spalding University	M,D,O
State University of New York Downstate Medical Center	M,O
State University of New York Polytechnic Institute	M,O
State University of New York Upstate Medical University	M,O
Stony Brook University, State University of New York	M,D,O
Temple University	D*
Tennessee State University	M,O
Tennessee Technological University	M,D
Texas A&M International University	M
Texas A&M University	M
Texas A&M University–Corpus Christi	M,D
Texas Christian University	D
Texas State University	M
Texas Tech University Health Sciences Center	M,D,O
Texas Woman's University	M,D
Troy University	M,D
Tusculum College	M
Uniformed Services University of the Health Sciences	M,D*
Union University	M,D,O
United States University	M
Universidad del Turabo	M,O
University at Buffalo, the State University of New York	M,D,O
The University of Alabama at Birmingham	M,D
The University of Alabama in Huntsville	M,D,O
The University of Arizona	M,D,O
University of Central Arkansas	M,O
University of Central Florida	M,D,O
University of Colorado Denver	M,D
University of Delaware	M,O*
University of Detroit Mercy	M,D,O
University of Hawaii at Manoa	M,D,O
University of Houston	M
University of Illinois at Chicago	M,O
University of Indianapolis	M,D
University of Louisiana at Lafayette	M,D
University of Louisville	M,D
University of Maine	M,O
University of Mary	M,D
University of Mary Hardin-Baylor	M,D,O
University of Maryland, Baltimore	M,D,O
University of Massachusetts Amherst	M,D*
University of Massachusetts Lowell	M
University of Massachusetts Medical School	M,D,O
University of Memphis	M,O
University of Miami	M,D*
University of Michigan–Flint	M,D,O
University of Minnesota, Twin Cities Campus	M,D
University of Missouri	M,D,O
University of Missouri–Kansas City	M,D
University of Missouri–St. Louis	D,O
University of Nevada, Las Vegas	M,D,O
University of New Hampshire	M,D,O
The University of North Carolina at Chapel Hill	M,D,O
The University of North Carolina at Charlotte	M,D,O
The University of North Carolina Wilmington	M,D,O
University of North Dakota	M,D,O
University of Northern Colorado	M,D
University of North Florida	M,D,O
University of North Georgia	M,O
University of Pennsylvania	M,O*
University of Phoenix–Hawaii Campus	M
University of Phoenix–Online Campus	M,O
University of Phoenix–Phoenix Campus	M,O
University of Phoenix–Sacramento Valley Campus	M
University of Pittsburgh	M,D*
University of Portland	M,D
University of Puerto Rico–Medical Sciences Campus	M
University of Rhode Island	M,D,O*
University of Rochester	M,D*
University of St. Francis (IL)	M,D,O
University of Saint Francis (IN)	M,D,O
University of Saint Joseph	M,D
University of San Diego	M,D
The University of Scranton	M,D,O
University of South Carolina	M
University of Southern Indiana	M,D,O
University of Southern Maine	M,D,O
University of South Florida	M,D,O*
The University of Tampa	M
The University of Tennessee at Chattanooga	M,D,O
The University of Tennessee Health Science Center	D,O
The University of Texas at Arlington	M,D
The University of Texas at Austin	M,D
The University of Texas at El Paso	M,D,O
The University of Texas at Tyler	M,D
The University of Texas Health Science Center at San Antonio	M,D,O
The University of Texas Rio Grande Valley	M,O
The University of Toledo	M,O
The University of Tulsa	D
University of Victoria	M,D
University of Wisconsin–Eau Claire	M,D
University of Wisconsin–Milwaukee	M,D,O*
University of Wisconsin–Oshkosh	M
Ursuline College	M,D
Valdosta State University	M
Vanderbilt University	M,D,O*
Villanova University	M,D,O
Virginia Commonwealth University	M
Wagner College	M,D,O
Walden University	M,D,O
Washington State University	M,D,O
West Coast University	M,D
Westminster College (UT)	M
West Texas A&M University	M
West Virginia Wesleyan College	M,O
Wilmington University	M,D
Winona State University	M,D,O
Winston-Salem State University	M,D
Wright State University	M

FILM, TELEVISION, AND VIDEO PRODUCTION

Academy of Art University	M
American Film Institute Conservatory	M
American University	M
Arizona State University at the Tempe campus	M
ArtCenter College of Design	M
Azusa Pacific University	M*
Bard College	M
Bob Jones University	M,D,O
Boston University	M*
Bowling Green State University	M,D
Brigham Young University	M
Brooklyn College of the City University of New York	M
California College of the Arts	M
California Institute of the Arts	M,O
California State University, Fullerton	M
California State University, Northridge	M
Carleton University	M
Carnegie Mellon University	M
Central Michigan University	M
Chapman University	M*
Chatham University	M
Columbia College Chicago	M
Columbia University	M*
Concordia University (Canada)	M,D
DePaul University	M,D
Drexel University	M*
Florida Atlantic University	M,O
Florida State University	M
Georgia State University	M,D
Governors State University	M
Hollins University	M
Howard University	M
Johns Hopkins University	M*
Lake Forest College	M
Lindenwood University	M
Lipscomb University	M
Loyola Marymount University	M
Maryland Institute College of Art	M
Massachusetts College of Art and Design	M,O
Miami International University of Art & Design	M
Minneapolis College of Art and Design	M
Missouri State University	M,O
Montana State University	M
Mount Saint Mary's University (CA)	M,D,O
National University	M
New York Film Academy	M
New York University	M*
Northwestern University	M,D
Ohio University	M
Quinnipiac University	M
Regent University	M,D
Rochester Institute of Technology	M
Sacred Heart University	M
St. Thomas University	M
San Diego State University	M
San Francisco State University	M
Savannah College of Art and Design	M
School of the Art Institute of Chicago	M
School of Visual Arts (NY)	M
Stanford University	M,D
Stevens Institute of Technology	M
Stony Brook University, State University of New York	M
Syracuse University	M*
Temple University	M*
Universidad Autonoma de Guadalajara	M,D
The University of British Columbia	M
University of California, Los Angeles	M,D*
University of California, Santa Barbara	D
University of Central Arkansas	M
University of Central Florida	M
University of Colorado Boulder	M
The University of Iowa	M*
University of Memphis	M,D
University of Miami	M,D*
University of Mississippi	M,D
University of Montana	M
University of Nevada, Las Vegas	M,O
University of New Orleans	M
The University of North Carolina at Greensboro	M
University of North Carolina School of the Arts	M
University of North Texas	M,D,O
University of Regina	M
University of Rhode Island	M,D*
University of Southern California	M*
The University of Texas at Arlington	M
The University of Texas at Austin	M,D
University of the Sacred Heart	M,O
University of Utah	M
University of Victoria	M
Vermont College of Fine Arts	M
Virginia Commonwealth University	M,D
Watkins College of Art, Design, & Film	M
Western State Colorado University	M
York University	M,D

FILM, TELEVISION, AND VIDEO THEORY AND CRITICISM

Brooklyn College of the City University of New York	M
California College of the Arts	M
Central Michigan University	M

*M—masters degree; D—doctorate; O—other advanced degree; *—Close-Up and/or Display*

Claremont Graduate University	M,D
College of Staten Island of the City University of New York	M
Columbia University	M*
Concordia University (Canada)	M,D
DePaul University	M
Emory University	M,D,O
Hollins University	M
National University	M,O
New York University	M,D*
Ohio University	M
San Francisco State University	M
Savannah College of Art and Design	M
Texas A&M University–Commerce	M,D,O
Tiffin University	M
Université de Montréal	M,D
Université Laval	M,D
University at Buffalo, the State University of New York	M,D,O
The University of Arizona	M
The University of British Columbia	M
University of California, Berkeley	D
University of California, Santa Cruz	D*
University of Chicago	D
The University of Iowa	M,D*
The University of Kansas	M,D
University of Miami	M,D*
University of Michigan	D,O*
University of Oklahoma	M,D*
University of Pittsburgh	M,D,O*
University of Southern California	M,D*
University of South Florida	M*
University of Toronto	M,D
University of Wisconsin–Madison	M,D
University of Wisconsin–Milwaukee	M,D*
Walla Walla University	M
Wayne State University	M,D
Wilfrid Laurier University	M,D
Yale University	D

FINANCE AND BANKING

Abilene Christian University	M
Adelphi University	M
American Business & Technology University	M
The American College of Financial Services	M
American College of Thessaloniki	M,O
American InterContinental University Online	M
American University	M,O
The American University in Cairo	M,O
The American University in Dubai	M
American University of Beirut	M,D
Andrews University	M
Argosy University, Atlanta	M,D
Argosy University, Chicago	M,D
Argosy University, Hawai`i	M,D,O
Argosy University, Los Angeles	M,D
Argosy University, Northern Virginia	M,D,O
Argosy University, Orange County	M,D,O
Argosy University, Phoenix	M,D
Argosy University, Seattle	M,D
Argosy University, Tampa	M,D
Argosy University, Twin Cities	M,D
Arizona State University at the Tempe campus	M,D
Ashland University	M
Aspen University	M,O
Assumption College	M,O
Auburn University	M*
Avila University	M
Azusa Pacific University	M*
Babson College	M,O
Baker College Center for Graduate Studies–Online	M,D
Barry University	O
Baruch College of the City University of New York	M,D*
Bayamón Central University	M
Bellevue University	M,D
Benedictine University	M
Bentley University	M
Binghamton University, State University of New York	D
Bluffton University	M
Boston College	M,D
Boston University	M*
Brandeis University	M,D
Brandman University	M
Bridgewater State University	M
Brigham Young University	M
Brooklyn College of the City University of New York	M
Bryant University	M
Butler University	M
California College of the Arts	M
California Intercontinental University	M,D
California Lutheran University	M,O
California State University, East Bay	M
California State University, Fullerton	M
California State University, Los Angeles	M
California State University, San Bernardino	M
Capella University	M,D
Carnegie Mellon University	D
Case Western Reserve University	M*
Central European University	M,D
Central Michigan University	M
Charleston Southern University	M
City University of Seattle	M,O
Clarion University of Pennsylvania	M
Clark University	M
Cleary University	M,O
College for Financial Planning	M
The College of Saint Rose	O
Colorado State University	M
Colorado State University–Global Campus	M
Colorado Technical University Aurora	M
Colorado Technical University Colorado Springs	M,D
Columbia Southern University	M
Columbia University	M,D*
Concordia University (Canada)	M,D,O
Concordia University Wisconsin	M
Cornell University	D
Creighton University	M,D
Culver-Stockton College	M
Curry College	M,O
Dalhousie University	M
Dallas Baptist University	M
Davenport University	M
Delaware Valley University	M
DePaul University	M,D
DeSales University	M
DeVry University–Folsom Campus	M
Drew University	M,D,O
Drexel University	M,D,O*
Duke University	M,D,O*
Duquesne University	M
Eastern Michigan University	M,O
Elms College	M,O
Embry-Riddle Aeronautical University–Daytona	M
Embry-Riddle Aeronautical University–Worldwide	M
Emory University	M,D
Fairfield University	M,O
Fairleigh Dickinson University, Florham Campus	M,O
Fairleigh Dickinson University, Metropolitan Campus	M,O
Florida Agricultural and Mechanical University	M
Florida International University	M
Florida National University	M
Florida State University	M,D
Fordham University	M,D
Gannon University	M
Geneva College	M
George Fox University	M,D
Georgetown University	M,D
The George Washington University	M,D
Georgia State University	M,D,O
Golden Gate University	M,D,O
Goldey-Beacom College	M
Gordon College	M
The Graduate Center, City University of New York	D
Grand Canyon University	M
Hawai`i Pacific University	M
HEC Montreal	M,D,O
Hofstra University	M,O
Holy Family University	M
Holy Names University	M
Hood College	M,O*
Howard University	M
Hult International Business School (United States)	M
IGlobal University	M
Illinois Institute of Technology	M,D
Indiana University Bloomington	M,D,O
Indiana University–Purdue University Indianapolis	M
Indiana University South Bend	M,O
Indiana University Southeast	M
Instituto Centroamericano de Administración de Empresas	M
Instituto Tecnologico de Santo Domingo	M,O
Instituto Tecnológico y de Estudios Superiores de Monterrey, Campus Central de Veracruz	M
Instituto Tecnológico y de Estudios Superiores de Monterrey, Campus Ciudad de México	M,D
Instituto Tecnológico y de Estudios Superiores de Monterrey, Campus Ciudad Obregón	M
Instituto Tecnológico y de Estudios Superiores de Monterrey, Campus Cuernavaca	M
Instituto Tecnológico y de Estudios Superiores de Monterrey, Campus Estado de México	M,D
Instituto Tecnológico y de Estudios Superiores de Monterrey, Campus Guadalajara	M
Instituto Tecnológico y de Estudios Superiores de Monterrey, Campus Irapuato	M,D
Instituto Tecnológico y de Estudios Superiores de Monterrey, Campus Monterrey	M
Inter American University of Puerto Rico, Aguadilla Campus	M
Inter American University of Puerto Rico, Arecibo Campus	M
Inter American University of Puerto Rico, Metropolitan Campus	M
Inter American University of Puerto Rico, Ponce Campus	M
Inter American University of Puerto Rico, San Germán Campus	M,D
The International University of Monaco	M
Iona College	M,O
Iowa State University of Science and Technology	M
Jacksonville University	M*
Johns Hopkins University	M,D,O*
Johnson & Wales University	M
Kansas State University	M,D,O
Kent State University	D
King University	M
Lake Forest Graduate School of Management	M
Lakeland University	M
La Salle University	M,O
La Sierra University	M,O
Lawrence Technological University	M,D,O
Lehigh University	M
Lewis University	M
Liberty University	M,D
Lincoln University (CA)	M,D
Lincoln University (PA)	M
Lindenwood University	M
Lipscomb University	M,O
Long Island University–LIU Post	M
Louisiana State University and Agricultural & Mechanical College	M,D
Louisiana Tech University	M,D
Loyola University Chicago	M
Loyola University Maryland	M
Manhattanville College	M,O
Marquette University	M,O
Maryville University of Saint Louis	M,O
Marywood University	M
McGill University	M,D,O
Metropolitan College of New York	M
Michigan State University	M,D
Minnesota State University Moorhead	M
Mississippi College	M,O
Mississippi State University	M,D
Molloy College	M,O
Monmouth University	M,O*
Monroe College	M
Mount Saint Mary College	M
Murray State University	M
Naval Postgraduate School	M
New Charter University	M
New England College of Business and Finance	M
New Jersey City University	M,O
Newman University	M
New Mexico State University	M,O
The New School	M,D
New York Institute of Technology	M
New York University	M,D*
Niagara University	M
North Central College	M
Northeastern State University	M
Northeastern University	M
Northern State University	M
North Greenville University	M,D
Northwestern University	M,D
Norwich University	M
Notre Dame de Namur University	M
Nova Southeastern University	M*
Oakland University	M,O
Ohio Christian University	M
Ohio Dominican University	M
The Ohio State University	M
Ohio University	M
Oklahoma Christian University	M
Oklahoma State University	M,D
Old Dominion University	D
Oral Roberts University	M
Oregon State University	M,D
Ottawa University	M
Our Lady of the Lake University	M
Pace University	M,D,O
Pacific Lutheran University	M
Pacific States University	M,O
Pacific University	M
Park University	M,O
Penn State Great Valley	M,O
Penn State Harrisburg	M,D,O
Pepperdine University	M
Polytechnic University of Puerto Rico, Miami Campus	M
Polytechnic University of Puerto Rico, Orlando Campus	M
Pontifical Catholic University of Puerto Rico	M
Pontificia Universidad Catolica Madre y Maestra	M
Portland State University	M
Post University	M
Princeton University	M
Providence College	M
Purdue University	M
Purdue University Global	M
Queens College of the City University of New York	M
Queen's University at Kingston	M
Quinnipiac University	M
Regent's University London	M
Regent University	M,D,O
Regis University	M,O
Rhode Island College	M,O
Rider University	M
Robert Morris University Illinois	M
Rochester Institute of Technology	M
Rockhurst University	M,O
Rollins College	M
Rutgers University–Newark	M,D
Sacred Heart University	M,D,O
St. John's University (NY)	M
Saint Joseph's University	M,O*
Saint Louis University	M*
Saint Mary's College of California	M
Saint Peter's University	M
St. Thomas Aquinas College	M
Saint Xavier University	M,O
Samford University	M
Sam Houston State University	M
San Diego State University	M
San Francisco State University	M
Santa Clara University	M
Schiller International University (United States)	M
Seattle University	M,O
Seton Hall University	M,O
Shippensburg University of Pennsylvania	M,D,O
Simon Fraser University	M,D,O
Slippery Rock University of Pennsylvania	M
Southeast Missouri State University	M
Southern Adventist University	M
Southern Illinois University Edwardsville	M
Southern Methodist University	M
Southern New Hampshire University	M,D,O
Southwestern Adventist University	M
State University of New York Polytechnic Institute	M
Stevens Institute of Technology	M,O
Stony Brook University, State University of New York	M,O
Strayer University	M
Suffolk University	M
Syracuse University	M,D*
Télé-université	M,D
Temple University	M,D*
Tennessee Technological University	M
Texas A&M International University	M
Texas A&M University	M
Texas A&M University–Commerce	M
Texas A&M University–Corpus Christi	M
Texas Tech University	M,D
Thomas Edison State University	M
Tiffin University	M
Trident University International	M,D
Troy University	M
Tulane University	M,D
United States International University–Africa	M
Universidad Central del Este	M
Universidad de las Americas, A.C.	M
Universidad de las Américas Puebla	M
Universidad Metropolitana	M
Université de Sherbrooke	M
Université du Québec à Montréal	O
Université du Québec à Trois-Rivières	O
Université du Québec en Outaouais	M,O
Université Laval	M,O
University at Albany, State University of New York	M,D,O
University at Buffalo, the State University of New York	M,D
The University of Akron	M
The University of Alabama	M,D
The University of Alabama at Birmingham	M
The University of Alabama in Huntsville	M,O
University of Alaska Fairbanks	M
University of Alberta	M,D
The University of Arizona	M
University of Baltimore	M
University of Bridgeport	M
The University of British Columbia	D
University of California, Berkeley	D,O
University of California, Davis	M
University of California, Los Angeles	M,D*
University of California, Riverside	M,D
University of California, San Diego	M,D*
University of California, Santa Barbara	M,D
University of California, Santa Cruz	M*
University of Central Missouri	M,D,O
University of Chicago	M,O
University of Cincinnati	M,D
University of Colorado Denver	M
University of Connecticut	M,D,O*
University of Dallas	M,D
University of Dayton	M
University of Delaware	M*
University of Denver	M
University of Detroit Mercy	M,D,O
University of Florida	M,D,O
University of Hawaii at Manoa	M,D
University of Houston	M
University of Houston–Clear Lake	M
University of Houston–Downtown	M
University of Houston–Victoria	M
University of Illinois at Chicago	M
University of Illinois at Urbana–Champaign	M,D
The University of Iowa	M,D*
The University of Kansas	M,D
University of La Verne	M
University of Lethbridge	M,D
University of Louisiana at Lafayette	M
University of Maine	M
The University of Manchester	M
University of Maryland University College	M
University of Massachusetts Amherst	M,D*
University of Massachusetts Boston	M
University of Massachusetts Dartmouth	M,O
University of Memphis	M,D
University of Michigan–Dearborn	M
University of Michigan–Flint	M,O
University of Minnesota, Twin Cities Campus	M,D
University of Mississippi	M,D
University of Missouri	M,D

University of Missouri–Kansas City	M,D
University of Nebraska–Lincoln	M,D
University of Nevada, Reno	M
University of New Haven	M,O*
University of New Mexico	M
University of New Orleans	M
University of North Alabama	M
The University of North Carolina at Chapel Hill	D
The University of North Carolina at Charlotte	M,O
The University of North Carolina at Greensboro	M,O
University of North Florida	M
University of North Texas	M,D,O
University of Notre Dame	M
University of Oklahoma	M,D*
University of Oregon	D
University of Ottawa	D,O
University of Pennsylvania	M,D*
University of Pittsburgh	M,D*
University of Portland	M
University of Puerto Rico–Mayagüez	M
University of Puerto Rico–Río Piedras	M,D
University of Rhode Island	M,D*
University of Rochester	M,D*
University of Saint Mary	M
University of St. Thomas (TX)	M
University of San Diego	M
University of San Francisco	M
University of Saskatchewan	M
The University of Scranton	M
University of Southern Maine	M
University of South Florida	M,D*
The University of Tampa	M,O
The University of Tennessee	M,D
The University of Tennessee at Martin	M
The University of Texas at Arlington	M,D
The University of Texas at Austin	M,D
The University of Texas at Dallas	M
The University of Texas at San Antonio	M,D
The University of Texas Rio Grande Valley	M,D
University of the West	M
The University of Toledo	M
University of Toronto	M
The University of Tulsa	M
University of Utah	M,D
University of Virginia	M
University of Washington, Tacoma	M
University of Waterloo	M,D
The University of West Alabama	M
The University of Western Ontario	M,D
University of Wisconsin–Madison	M,D
University of Wisconsin–Whitewater	M
University of Wyoming	M
Upper Iowa University	M
Ursuline College	M
Utah State University	M
Valparaiso University	M,O
Vancouver Island University	M
Vanderbilt University	M*
Villanova University	M
Virginia Commonwealth University	M
Virginia International University	M,O
Virginia Polytechnic Institute and State University	M,D
Wagner College	M
Walden University	M,D,O
Walsh College of Accountancy and Business Administration	M
Washington University in St. Louis	M,D
Waynesburg University	M,D
Wayne State University	M,D,O
Webster University	M
Western Michigan University Thomas M. Cooley Law School	M,D
West Texas A&M University	M
West Virginia University	M,D,O
Wilfrid Laurier University	M,D
Wilkes University	M
Wilmington University	M,D
Wingate University	M
Xavier University	M*
Yale University	D
York College of Pennsylvania	M
York University	M,D
Youngstown State University	M

FINANCIAL ENGINEERING

Baruch College of the City University of New York	M*
Claremont Graduate University	M
Columbia University	M,D*
HEC Montreal	M,D
The International University of Monaco	M
New York University	M*
North Carolina State University	M
Princeton University	M,D
Rensselaer Polytechnic Institute	M
Stevens Institute of Technology	M,D,O
Temple University	M*
University of California, Berkeley	M
University of California, Los Angeles	M,D*
University of Illinois at Urbana–Champaign	M

FIRE PROTECTION ENGINEERING

Oklahoma State University	M,D
University of Maryland, College Park	M
University of New Haven	M,O*
The University of North Carolina at Charlotte	M,O
Worcester Polytechnic Institute	M,D,O

FISH, GAME, AND WILDLIFE MANAGEMENT

Arkansas Tech University	M
Auburn University	M,D*
Brigham Young University	M,D
Central Washington University	M
Clemson University	M,D
Colorado State University	M,D
Cornell University	M,D
Frostburg State University	M
Humboldt State University	M
Iowa State University of Science and Technology	M,D
Louisiana State University and Agricultural & Mechanical College	M,D
McGill University	M,D
Memorial University of Newfoundland	M,O
Michigan State University	M,D
Mississippi State University	M,D
Montana State University	M,D
New Mexico State University	M
North Carolina State University	M,D
The Ohio State University	M,D
Oregon State University	M,D
Penn State University Park	M,D*
Purdue University	M,D
Simon Fraser University	M,D,O
South Dakota State University	M,D
State University of New York College of Environmental Science and Forestry	M,D
Sul Ross State University	M
Tarleton State University	M
Tennessee Technological University	M
Texas A&M University	M,D
Texas A&M University–Kingsville	M,D
Texas State University	M
Texas Tech University	M,D
Université du Québec à Rimouski	M,D,O
University of Alaska Fairbanks	M,D,O
University of Arkansas at Pine Bluff	M,D
University of Delaware	M,D*
University of Florida	M,D,O
University of Maine	M,D
University of Maryland Eastern Shore	M,D
University of Massachusetts Amherst	M,D*
University of Miami	M,D*
University of Montana	M,D
University of New Hampshire	M
University of North Dakota	M,D
University of Rhode Island	M,D*
The University of Tennessee	M
University of Washington	M,D
University of Wisconsin–Madison	M,D
Utah State University	M,D
Virginia Polytechnic Institute and State University	M,D
West Virginia University	M,D

FOLKLORE

The George Washington University	M,D
Indiana University Bloomington	M,D
Memorial University of Newfoundland	M,D
Penn State Harrisburg	M,D,O
University of Alberta	M,D
University of California, Berkeley	M
University of Louisiana at Lafayette	M,D
The University of North Carolina at Chapel Hill	M
University of Oregon	M
The University of Texas at Austin	M,D
University of Wisconsin–Madison	M,D
Utah State University	M

FOOD SCIENCE AND TECHNOLOGY

Alabama Agricultural and Mechanical University	M,D
American University of Beirut	M
Auburn University	M,D,O*
Boston University	M*
Brigham Young University	M
California Polytechnic State University, San Luis Obispo	M*
Chapman University	M*
Colorado State University	M,D
Cornell University	M,D
Dalhousie University	M,D
Drexel University	M*
Florida State University	M,D
Illinois Institute of Technology	M
Iowa State University of Science and Technology	M,D
Kansas State University	M,D
London Metropolitan University	M,D
Louisiana State University and Agricultural & Mechanical College	M,D
McGill University	M,D
Memorial University of Newfoundland	M,D
Michigan State University	M,D
Mississippi State University	M,D
New Mexico State University	M
New York University	M,D*
North Carolina State University	M,D
North Dakota State University	M,D*
The Ohio State University	M,D
Oklahoma State University	M,D
Oregon State University	M,D
Penn State University Park	M,D*
Portland State University	M,D,O
Purdue University	M,D
Rutgers University–New Brunswick	M,D
Texas A&M University	M,D
Texas Tech University	M,D
Texas Woman's University	M,D
Tuskegee University	M
Universidad de las Américas Puebla	M
Université de Moncton	M
Université Laval	M,D
University at Buffalo, the State University of New York	M,D,O
University of Arkansas	M,D
The University of British Columbia	M,D
University of California, Davis	M,D
University of Delaware	M,D*
University of Florida	M,D
University of Georgia	M,D
University of Guelph	M,D
University of Hawaii at Manoa	M
University of Idaho	M,D
University of Illinois at Urbana–Champaign	M,D
University of Kentucky	M,D
University of Manitoba	M,D
University of Maryland, College Park	M,D
University of Maryland Eastern Shore	M,D
University of Massachusetts Amherst	M,D*
University of Minnesota, Twin Cities Campus	M,D
University of Mississippi	M,D
University of Missouri	M,D
University of Nebraska–Lincoln	M,D
University of Puerto Rico–Mayagüez	M
University of Rhode Island	M,D*
University of Saskatchewan	M,D
University of Southern California	M,D,O*
University of Southern Mississippi	M
The University of Tennessee	M,D
The University of Tennessee at Martin	M
University of Vermont	M,D
University of Wisconsin–Madison	M,D
University of Wisconsin–Stout	M
University of Wyoming	M
Utah State University	M,D
Washington State University	M,D
Wayne State University	M,D,O
West Virginia University	M,D

FOREIGN LANGUAGES EDUCATION

Andrews University	M,D,O
Appalachian State University	M
Arizona State University at the Tempe campus	M,D
Augusta University	M,O
Binghamton University, State University of New York	M
Brandeis University	M
Brigham Young University	M
Brooklyn College of the City University of New York	M
California State University, Sacramento	M
Caribbean University	M,D
Central Connecticut State University	M,O
Cleveland State University	M
College of Charleston	M
The College of William and Mary	M*
The Colorado College	M
Colorado State University–Pueblo	M
Columbia University	M,D*
Concordia College	M
Cornell University	M,D
Delaware State University	M
DePaul University	M,D
Duquesne University	M
Eastern Michigan University	M,O
Eastern University	M,O
Elms College	M,O
Florida International University	M,D,O
Florida State University	M,D,O
George Mason University	M
The George Washington University	M
Georgia Southern University	M
Georgia State University	M,O
Harding University	M,O
Hofstra University	M,D,O
Hunter College of the City University of New York	M
Indiana State University	M,D,O
Indiana University Bloomington	M,D
Indiana University of Pennsylvania	M
Indiana University–Purdue University Indianapolis	M,O
Inter American University of Puerto Rico, Arecibo Campus	M
Inter American University of Puerto Rico, Barranquitas Campus	M
Inter American University of Puerto Rico, Metropolitan Campus	M
Iona College	M
James Madison University	M
Kean University	M
Lamar University	M
Le Moyne College	M,O
Lewis University	M
London Metropolitan University	M,D
Manhattanville College	M,O
Marquette University	M
McGill University	M,D,O
Michigan State University	D
Middlebury Institute of International Studies at Monterey	M
Middle Tennessee State University	M
Minnesota State University Mankato	M
Mississippi State University	M
Molloy College	M,O
Morehead State University	M
New Mexico State University	M,D,O
New York University	M,D,O*
Northern Arizona University	M
Pace University	M,O
Portland State University	M
Purdue University	M,D,O
Queens College of the City University of New York	M,O
Quinnipiac University	M
Rhode Island College	M
Rider University	M
Rivier University	M
Rutgers University–New Brunswick	M,D
Saginaw Valley State University	M
St. John Fisher College	M
Saint Xavier University	M
Shippensburg University of Pennsylvania	M
Southern Connecticut State University	M
Southern Oregon University	M
Spalding University	M
State University of New York at Plattsburgh	M
State University of New York College at Old Westbury	M
Stony Brook University, State University of New York	M,O
Texas A&M International University	M
Texas A&M University–Kingsville	M
Universidad del Este	M
Université du Québec en Outaouais	O
University at Buffalo, the State University of New York	M,D,O
University of Arkansas at Little Rock	M
University of California, Irvine	M,D
University of Central Florida	M,O
University of Connecticut	M,D*
University of Dayton	M
University of Delaware	M*
University of Florida	M,D
University of Hawaii at Hilo	M,D*
University of Hawaii at Manoa	M,D,O
University of Illinois at Chicago	M,D
University of Illinois at Urbana–Champaign	M,D
University of Indianapolis	M
The University of Iowa	M,D*
University of Kentucky	M
University of Maine	M
University of Maryland, Baltimore County	M
University of Maryland, College Park	D
University of Massachusetts Amherst	M*
University of Michigan	M,D*
University of Minnesota, Twin Cities Campus	M
University of Mississippi	M,D
University of Missouri	M,D,O
University of Nebraska at Kearney	M
University of Nebraska at Omaha	M
University of Nevada, Reno	M
The University of North Carolina at Chapel Hill	M
The University of North Carolina at Charlotte	M,D,O
The University of North Carolina at Greensboro	M,D,O
University of Northern Colorado	M,D
University of Northern Iowa	M
University of Oklahoma	M,D*
University of Pittsburgh	M,D*
University of Puerto Rico–Río Piedras	M,D
University of South Carolina	M,D
University of Southern Mississippi	M
University of South Florida	O*
The University of Tennessee	M,D,O
University of the Sacred Heart	M,O
The University of Toledo	M,D,O
University of Vermont	M,O
University of Victoria	M
University of Virginia	M,D,O
University of Wisconsin–Milwaukee	M,O*
Vanderbilt University	M,D*
Wagner College	M
Washington State University	M
Wayne State University	M,D,O
West Chester University of Pennsylvania	M,O
Western Kentucky University	M
Worcester State University	M

FORENSIC NURSING

Aspen University	M
Duquesne University	M,O
Fitchburg State University	M,O
Monmouth University	M,D,O*
Texas A&M University	M

*M—masters degree; D—doctorate; O—other advanced degree; *—Close-Up and/or Display*

FORENSIC PSYCHOLOGY

Adler University	M
Alliant International University–Fresno	D
Alliant International University–Irvine	D
Alliant International University–Los Angeles	D
Alliant International University–Sacramento	D
Alliant International University–San Diego	D
Alliant International University–San Francisco	M,D
American International College	M,D,O
Argosy University, Atlanta	M,D,O
Argosy University, Chicago	D
Argosy University, Hawai'i	M
Argosy University, Los Angeles	M,D
Argosy University, Northern Virginia	M,D
Argosy University, Orange County	M
Argosy University, Phoenix	M
Argosy University, Twin Cities	M,D,O
California Baptist University	M
Castleton University	M
The Chicago School of Professional Psychology	M,D
The Chicago School of Professional Psychology at Downtown Los Angeles	D
The Chicago School of Professional Psychology at Irvine	D
The Chicago School of Professional Psychology: Online	M,O
Drexel University	D*
Fairleigh Dickinson University, Metropolitan Campus	M
The George Washington University	O
Holy Names University	M
Immaculata University	M,D,O
John Jay College of Criminal Justice of the City University of New York	M,D
Kean University	M
Liberty University	M
London Metropolitan University	M,D
Marymount University	M
Montclair State University	O
Nova Southeastern University	M,D,O*
Pontificia Universidad Catolica Madre y Maestra	M
Post University	M
Prairie View A&M University	M,D
Roger Williams University	M
Sage Graduate School	M,O
Tiffin University	M
Universidad de Iberoamerica	M,D
Universidad del Turabo	M,D,O
University of Central Oklahoma	M
University of Denver	M,D,O
University of Houston–Victoria	M
University of Louisiana at Monroe	M
University of New Haven	M,O*
University of North Dakota	M,D
Walden University	M,D,O
Westfield State University	M
William James College	M,D

FORENSIC SCIENCES

Alabama State University	M
Alliant International University–Irvine	D
Arcadia University	M
Bay Path University	M
Boston University	M*
Carlow University	M
Cedar Crest College	M
Champlain College	M
DeSales University	M,O
Duquesne University	M
Emporia State University	M,O
Florida Gulf Coast University	M
Florida International University	M,D
George Mason University	M
The George Washington University	M,O
Georgia State University	M,O
Golden Gate University	M,O
Indiana University–Purdue University Indianapolis	M,O
Iona College	M
James Madison University	M
John Jay College of Criminal Justice of the City University of New York	M,D
La Salle University	M,O
Long Island University–LIU Brooklyn	M,D,O
Marshall University	M,O
McGill University	M,D,O
Mercyhurst University	M
Michigan State University	M,D
Middle Georgia State University	M
Missouri Western State University	M,O
National University	M,O
Nebraska Wesleyan University	M
Niagara University	M
Oklahoma State University Center for Health Sciences	M
Pace University	M
Penn State University Park	M*
Philadelphia College of Osteopathic Medicine	M*
St. Joseph's College, Long Island Campus	M
St. Joseph's College, New York	M
Saint Leo University	M
Salve Regina University	M,O
Sam Houston State University	M,D
Seattle University	M,O
Stevenson University	M
Stratford University (VA)	M,D
Syracuse University	M,O*
Texas Tech University	M
Towson University	M
Universidad del Turabo	M
University at Albany, State University of New York	M
The University of Alabama at Birmingham	M
University of California, Davis	M
University of Central Florida	M,D
University of Central Oklahoma	M
University of Charleston	M
University of Colorado Denver	M
University of Detroit Mercy	M,O
University of Florida	M,O
University of Houston–Victoria	M
University of Illinois at Chicago	M
University of Maryland, Baltimore	M
University of New Haven	M,O*
University of North Texas Health Science Center at Fort Worth	M,D
University of Rhode Island	M,D,O*
University of St. Francis (IL)	M,O
University of Southern Mississippi	M,D
University of South Florida	M,D,O*
Virginia Commonwealth University	M
Webster University	M
West Virginia University	M,D

FORESTRY

Auburn University	M,D*
California Polytechnic State University, San Luis Obispo	M*
Clemson University	M,D
Cornell University	M,D
Harvard University	M*
Humboldt State University	M
Iowa State University of Science and Technology	M,D
Lakehead University	M,D
Louisiana State University and Agricultural & Mechanical College	M,D
McGill University	M,D
Michigan State University	M,D
Michigan Technological University	M,D
Mississippi State University	M,D
North Carolina State University	M,D
Northern Arizona University	M,D
The Ohio State University	M,D
Oklahoma State University	M,D
Oregon State University	M,D
Penn State University Park	M,D*
Purdue University	M,D
Southern Illinois University Carbondale	M
Southern University and Agricultural and Mechanical College	M
State University of New York College of Environmental Science and Forestry	M,D
Stephen F. Austin State University	M,D
Texas A&M University	M,D
Tropical Agriculture Research and Higher Education Center	M,D
Université du Québec en Abitibi-Témiscamingue	M,D
Université Laval	M,D
University of Alberta	M,D
The University of Arizona	M,D
University of Arkansas at Monticello	M
The University of British Columbia	M,D
University of California, Berkeley	M,D
University of Florida	M,D
University of Georgia	M,D
University of Kentucky	M
University of Maine	M,D
University of Massachusetts Amherst	M,D*
University of Minnesota, Twin Cities Campus	M,D
University of Montana	M,D
University of New Brunswick Fredericton	M,D
University of New Hampshire	M
The University of Tennessee	M
University of Toronto	M,D
University of Vermont	M,D,O
University of Washington	M,D
University of Wisconsin–Madison	M,D
Utah State University	M,D
Virginia Polytechnic Institute and State University	M,D
West Virginia University	M,D
Yale University	M,D

FOUNDATIONS AND PHILOSOPHY OF EDUCATION

Antioch University New England	M,O
Arkansas State University	M,D,O
Ball State University	D
Bank Street College of Education	M
Binghamton University, State University of New York	D
Brigham Young University	M,D
Chicago State University	M
Columbia University	M,D*
Curry College	M,O
DePaul University	M,D
Duquesne University	M
Eastern Michigan University	M
Eastern Washington University	M
Fairfield University	M,O
Fairleigh Dickinson University, Metropolitan Campus	M
Florida State University	M,D,O
Georgia State University	M,D
Harvard University	M,O*
Indiana University Bloomington	M,D,O
Iowa State University of Science and Technology	M,D
Kent State University	M,D
Marquette University	M,D,O
McGill University	M,D,O
Mount Saint Vincent University	M
New York University	M,D*
Northern Arizona University	M,D,O
Northern Illinois University	M,D,O
Northern Vermont University–Johnson	M
Penn State University Park	M,D,O*
Purdue University	M,D,O
Rutgers University–New Brunswick	M,D
Saint Louis University	M,D*
Simon Fraser University	M,D
Southern Illinois University Edwardsville	M
Spring Hill College	M
Syracuse University	M,D,O*
Teachers College, Columbia University	M,D,O
University at Buffalo, the State University of New York	M,D,O
The University of British Columbia	M,D
University of California, Riverside	M,D,O
University of Central Oklahoma	M
University of Cincinnati	M,D
University of Hawaii at Manoa	M,D
University of Houston	M,D
University of Houston–Clear Lake	M
The University of Iowa	M,D,O*
University of Manitoba	M
University of Maryland, College Park	M,D,O
University of Minnesota, Twin Cities Campus	M,D
University of New Mexico	M,D
University of Pennsylvania	M,D*
University of Pittsburgh	M,D*
University of Rochester	D*
University of Saskatchewan	M,D,O
University of South Africa	M,D
University of South Carolina	D
The University of Tennessee	M,D,O
The University of Texas of the Permian Basin	M
The University of Toledo	M,D,O
University of Utah	M,D
University of Victoria	M,D
University of Washington	M,D
University of Wisconsin–Milwaukee	M,D,O*
Wayne State University	M,D,O
West Chester University of Pennsylvania	M,O
Western Illinois University	M,O
Widener University	M,D
William Paterson University of New Jersey	M,D,O

FRENCH

American University	M,O
Arizona State University at the Tempe campus	M
Asbury University	M
Binghamton University, State University of New York	M
Boston College	M
Bowling Green State University	M
Brigham Young University	M
Brooklyn College of the City University of New York	M
Brown University	D
California State University, Long Beach	M
California State University, Los Angeles	M
Carleton University	M
Case Western Reserve University	M*
Central Connecticut State University	M,O
Colorado State University	M
Columbia University	M,D*
Concordia University (Canada)	M,O
Cornell University	D
Dalhousie University	M,D
DePaul University	M
Drew University	M,D,O
Duke University	D*
Emory University	D
Florida Atlantic University	M
Florida State University	M,D
George Mason University	M
Georgia State University	M,O
The Graduate Center, City University of New York	D
Harvard University	M,D*
Hofstra University	M,D,O
Howard University	M
Hunter College of the City University of New York	M
Illinois State University	M
Indiana University Bloomington	M,D
Johns Hopkins University	M,D*
Kansas State University	M
Kent State University	M,D
Lake Forest College	M
Louisiana State University and Agricultural & Mechanical College	M,D
Manhattanville College	M,O
McGill University	M,D
McMaster University	M
Memorial University of Newfoundland	M
Miami University	M
Michigan State University	M,D
Middlebury College	M,D
Middle Tennessee State University	M
Millersville University of Pennsylvania	M
Minnesota State University Mankato	M
Montclair State University	M
New York University	M,D,O*
North Carolina State University	M
Northern Illinois University	M
Northwestern University	D,O
The Ohio State University	M,D
Ohio University	M
Penn State University Park	M,D*
Portland State University	M
Princeton University	D
Purdue University	M,D
Queens College of the City University of New York	M
Queen's University at Kingston	M,D
Rutgers University–New Brunswick	M,D
St. John Fisher College	M
Saint Louis University	M*
San Francisco State University	M
Simon Fraser University	M
Southern Oregon University	M
Stanford University	M,D
State University of New York at New Paltz	M,O
State University of New York College at Geneseo	M
Stony Brook University, State University of New York	M
Syracuse University	M*
Tufts University	M*
Tulane University	M,D
Université de Moncton	M,D
Université de Montréal	M,D
Université de Sherbrooke	M,D
Université du Québec à Chicoutimi	O
University at Buffalo, the State University of New York	M,D,O
The University of Alabama	M,D
University of Alberta	M,D
The University of Arizona	M
University of Arkansas	M
The University of British Columbia	M,D
University of Calgary	M,D
University of California, Berkeley	D
University of California, Davis	D
University of California, Irvine	M,D
University of California, Los Angeles	M,D*
University of California, Santa Barbara	D
University of Chicago	D
University of Cincinnati	M,D
University of Colorado Boulder	M,D
University of Delaware	M*
University of Florida	M,D
University of Georgia	M,D
University of Guelph	M
University of Hawaii at Manoa	M
University of Illinois at Chicago	M
University of Illinois at Urbana–Champaign	M,D
The University of Iowa	M,D*
The University of Kansas	M,D
University of Lethbridge	M,D
University of Louisiana at Lafayette	M,D
University of Louisville	M,O
University of Maine	M
The University of Manchester	D
University of Manitoba	M,D
University of Maryland, College Park	M,D
University of Massachusetts Amherst	M*
University of Memphis	M
University of Miami	D*
University of Michigan	D*
University of Minnesota, Twin Cities Campus	M,D
University of Missouri	M,D
University of Missouri–Kansas City	M
University of Montana	M
University of Nebraska–Lincoln	M,D
University of Nevada, Reno	M
University of New Mexico	M,D
The University of North Carolina at Chapel Hill	M,D
The University of North Carolina at Greensboro	M
University of North Texas	M,D,O
University of Notre Dame	M
University of Oklahoma	M,D*
University of Oregon	M
University of Ottawa	M,D
University of Pennsylvania	M,D*
University of Pittsburgh	M,D*
University of Regina	M
University of Saskatchewan	M
University of South Africa	M,D
University of South Carolina	M,D
University of South Florida	M,D*
The University of Tennessee	M,D
The University of Texas at Arlington	M
The University of Texas at Austin	M,D
The University of Toledo	M
University of Toronto	M,D
University of Utah	M,D
University of Victoria	M
University of Virginia	M,D
University of Washington	M,D
University of Waterloo	M,D
The University of Western Ontario	M,D
University of Wisconsin–Madison	M,D,O
University of Wisconsin–Milwaukee	M,O*
University of Wyoming	M
Vanderbilt University	M,D*
Washington University in St. Louis	D
Wayne State University	M,D

West Chester University of Pennsylvania	M,O
Western Kentucky University	M
Yale University	M,D
York University	M,D

GAME DESIGN AND DEVELOPMENT

Academy of Art University	M
Concordia University (Canada)	M,D,O
DePaul University	M,D
Full Sail University	M
Iona College	M
Long Island University–LIU Post	M
Michigan State University	M
New York University	M*
Rochester Institute of Technology	M
Sacred Heart University	M
Savannah College of Art and Design	M
University of Advancing Technology	M
University of California, Santa Cruz	M,D*
University of Central Florida	M
The University of North Carolina at Charlotte	M,O
University of Pennsylvania	M,D*
University of Southern California	M,D*
University of Utah	M
Virginia International University	M,O
Worcester Polytechnic Institute	M

GENDER STUDIES

Adler University	M
American University	M,D,O
The American University in Cairo	M,O
Arizona State University at the Tempe campus	M,D,O
Brandeis University	M,D
Carnegie Mellon University	D
Central European University	M,D
Central Michigan University	M
The College of New Jersey	O
Cornell University	M,D
Delta State University	M
DePaul University	M
Dominican University of California	M
Eastern Michigan University	M,O
George Mason University	M
The George Washington University	O
Georgia State University	M,O
Indiana University Bloomington	D
Indiana University Northwest	M,O
Instituto Tecnologico de Santo Domingo	M,O
Kansas State University	O
Memorial University of Newfoundland	M,D
Middle Tennessee State University	O
Minnesota State University Mankato	M
Murray State University	M,D,O
New York University	M*
Northern Arizona University	O
Northwestern University	O
The Ohio State University	M,D
Old Dominion University	M,O
Oregon State University	M,D
Queen's University at Kingston	M,D
Rutgers University–New Brunswick	M,D
Saint Mary's University (Canada)	M
San Diego State University	O
Simmons College	M
Simon Fraser University	M,D
Stony Brook University, State University of New York	O
Texas Woman's University	M,D
University at Albany, State University of New York	M
University at Buffalo, the State University of New York	M,D
The University of Arizona	M,D,O
The University of British Columbia	M,D
University of California, Los Angeles	M,D*
University of Chicago	M
University of Colorado Denver	M,O
University of Florida	M,O
University of Lethbridge	M,D
University of Memphis	O
University of Michigan–Flint	M
The University of North Carolina at Charlotte	M,D,O
The University of North Carolina at Greensboro	M,O
University of Northern British Columbia	M,D,O
University of Northern Iowa	M
University of Oklahoma	O*
University of Rhode Island	M,D,O*
University of Saskatchewan	M,D
University of South Florida	M,O*
The University of Toledo	O
University of Toronto	M,D
University of Wisconsin–Milwaukee	M,O*
Wayne State University	M,D,O
Wilfrid Laurier University	M
York University	M,D

GENETIC COUNSELING

Arcadia University	M
Augustana University	M
Baylor College of Medicine	M
Bay Path University	M
Boston University	M*
Brandeis University	M
California State University, Stanislaus	M
Case Western Reserve University	M,D*
Emory University	M
Icahn School of Medicine at Mount Sinai	M,D
Johns Hopkins University	M,D*
Long Island University–LIU Post	M,O
McGill University	M,D
Northwestern University	M
Sarah Lawrence College	M
Thomas Jefferson University	M
Université de Montréal	O
The University of Alabama at Birmingham	M
University of Arkansas for Medical Sciences	M,D
The University of British Columbia	M
University of California, Irvine	M
University of Cincinnati	M
University of Colorado Denver	M
University of Manitoba	M,D
University of Maryland, Baltimore	M
University of Michigan	M,D*
University of Minnesota, Twin Cities Campus	M,D
The University of North Carolina at Greensboro	M
University of Oklahoma Health Sciences Center	M
University of Pittsburgh	M,D,O*
University of South Carolina	M
The University of Texas Health Science Center at Houston	M,D
University of Toronto	M,D
University of Wisconsin–Madison	M,D
Wayne State University	M,D,O

GENETICS

Albert Einstein College of Medicine	D
Baylor College of Medicine	D
Boston University	D*
Brandeis University	M,D
California Institute of Technology	D
Carnegie Mellon University	M,D
Clemson University	M,D,O
Columbia University	M,D*
Cornell University	D
Dartmouth College	D*
Drexel University	M,D*
Duke University	D*
Emory University	D
Harvard University	M,D*
Illinois State University	M,D
Indiana University Bloomington	M,D
Iowa State University of Science and Technology	M,D
Irell & Manella Graduate School of Biological Sciences	D*
Johns Hopkins University	M,D*
Kansas State University	M,D
Kent State University	M,D
Marquette University	M,D
Massachusetts Institute of Technology	D
Mayo Clinic Graduate School of Biomedical Sciences	D
McMaster University	M,D
Medical University of South Carolina	D
Michigan State University	M,D
Mississippi State University	M,D
New York University	M,D*
North Carolina State University	M,D
The Ohio State University	M,D
Oregon Health & Science University	D
Oregon State University	M,D
Purdue University	M,D
Rutgers University–New Brunswick	M,D
Stanford University	D
Stony Brook University, State University of New York	D
Thomas Jefferson University	D
Tufts University	D*
Université de Montréal	O
Université du Québec à Chicoutimi	M
University at Buffalo, the State University of New York	M,D
The University of Alabama at Birmingham	D
University of Alberta	M,D
The University of Arizona	M,D
The University of British Columbia	M,D
University of Calgary	M,D
University of California, Davis	M,D
University of California, Irvine	D
University of California, Riverside	D
University of California, San Francisco	D
University of Chicago	D
University of Colorado Denver	D
University of Connecticut	M,D*
University of Connecticut Health Center	D
University of Delaware	M,D*
University of Florida	D
University of Georgia	M,D
University of Hawaii at Manoa	M,D
University of Illinois at Chicago	D
The University of Iowa	M,D*
The University of Manchester	M,D
University of Massachusetts Amherst	M,D*
University of Miami	M,D*
University of Minnesota, Twin Cities Campus	M,D
University of Nebraska Medical Center	M,D
University of New Hampshire	M,D
University of New Mexico	M,D
The University of North Carolina at Chapel Hill	M,D
University of North Dakota	M,D
University of North Texas Health Science Center at Fort Worth	M,D
University of Notre Dame	M,D
University of Oregon	M,D
University of Pennsylvania	D*
University of Puerto Rico–Río Piedras	M,D
University of Rochester	M,D*
The University of Tennessee	M,D
The University of Texas Health Science Center at Houston	M,D
The University of Texas MD Anderson Cancer Center	M
The University of Texas Southwestern Medical Center	D
University of Washington	M,D,O
University of Wisconsin–Madison	M,D
University of Wyoming	D
Van Andel Institute Graduate School	D
Virginia Polytechnic Institute and State University	M,D
Washington State University	M,D
Washington University in St. Louis	M,D
Wesleyan University	D
West Virginia University	M,D
Yale University	D

GENOMIC SCIENCES

Albert Einstein College of Medicine	D
Augusta University	D
Black Hills State University	M
Boston University	D*
Case Western Reserve University	M,D*
Concordia University (Canada)	M,D,O
Cornell University	D
Duke University	D*
Manchester University	M
Massachusetts Institute of Technology	M,D
New York University	D*
North Carolina State University	M,D
North Dakota State University	M,D*
Oregon State University	M,D
Penn State Hershey Medical Center	
Purdue University	D
Thomas Jefferson University	D
University at Buffalo, the State University of New York	M,D
The University of Alabama at Birmingham	D
University of California, Riverside	D
University of California, San Francisco	D
University of Chicago	D
University of Cincinnati	M,D
University of Colorado Denver	D
University of Connecticut	M,D*
University of Georgia	M,D
University of Maryland, Baltimore	M,D
University of Maryland, College Park	D
University of Pennsylvania	D*
University of Rochester	D*
University of Southern California	D*
The University of Tennessee	M,D
The University of Tennessee–Oak Ridge National Laboratory	M,D
The University of Texas Health Science Center at Houston	M,D,O
The University of Toledo	M,O
University of Washington	D
Wake Forest University	D
Washington University in St. Louis	M
Wayne State University	M,D,O
Wesleyan University	D
Yale University	D

GEOCHEMISTRY

California Institute of Technology	M,D
Colorado School of Mines	M,D
Cornell University	M,D
Georgia State University	M,D
Indiana University Bloomington	M,D
Massachusetts Institute of Technology	M,D
McMaster University	M,D
Missouri University of Science and Technology	M,D
Montana Tech of The University of Montana	M
New Mexico Institute of Mining and Technology	M,D
Ohio University	M
Oregon State University	M,D
University of California, Los Angeles	M,D*
University of Hawaii at Manoa	M,D
The University of Manchester	M,D
University of Nevada, Reno	M,D
Yale University	D

GEODETIC SCIENCES

The Ohio State University	M,D
Université Laval	M,D
University of New Brunswick Fredericton	M,D

GEOGRAPHIC INFORMATION SYSTEMS

Acadia University	M
Appalachian State University	M
Arizona State University at the Tempe campus	M,D,O
Auburn University at Montgomery	M
Ball State University	M,O
Boston University	M,D*
Central Michigan University	M
Chicago State University	M
Claremont Graduate University	M,D,O
Clark University	M
Cleveland State University	M,O
The College of William and Mary	M,D*
East Carolina University	M,O
Eastern Illinois University	M
Eastern Michigan University	M,O
East Tennessee State University	M,O
Elizabeth City State University	M
Elmhurst College	M
Florida State University	M,D
George Mason University	M,D,O
Georgia Institute of Technology	M,D
Georgia State University	O
Hood College	M,O*
Hunter College of the City University of New York	M,O
Idaho State University	M,O
Indiana University of Pennsylvania	M,O
Indiana University–Purdue University Indianapolis	M,O
Johns Hopkins University	M,O*
Kansas State University	M,D,O
Kent State University	M,D
Michigan Technological University	M
Millersville University of Pennsylvania	M
Montclair State University	O
Naval Postgraduate School	M,D,O
North Carolina Central University	M
North Carolina State University	M,D
Northeastern Illinois University	M,O
Northeastern University	M
Northern Arizona University	M,O
Northern Kentucky University	M,O
Northwest Missouri State University	M,O
Oregon State University	M
Saint Mary's University of Minnesota	M,O
Salisbury University	M
Sam Houston State University	M,O
San Francisco State University	M
State University of New York College of Environmental Science and Forestry	M,D
Stony Brook University, State University of New York	O
Temple University	M,D,O*
Texas A&M University–Corpus Christi	M,D
Texas State University	M,D
Université du Québec à Montréal	O
Université Laval	M,O
University at Albany, State University of New York	M,O
University at Buffalo, the State University of New York	M,D
The University of Alabama	M,D
University of Alaska Fairbanks	M
The University of Arizona	M,D,O
University of Central Arkansas	M,O
University of Central Florida	M,O
University of Colorado Denver	M,D
University of Denver	M,D,O
University of Florida	M,D,O
The University of Iowa	M,D,O*
The University of Kansas	M,D,O
University of Lethbridge	M,D
University of Maryland, Baltimore County	M,O
University of Memphis	M,D,O
University of Minnesota, Twin Cities Campus	M,D
University of Missouri	M,O
University of Nebraska at Omaha	M,O
University of New Hampshire	O
University of New Haven	M*
University of North Alabama	M
The University of North Carolina at Charlotte	M,D
The University of North Carolina at Greensboro	M,D,O
The University of North Carolina Wilmington	M,O
University of North Dakota	M
University of North Texas Health Science Center at Fort Worth	M,D,O
University of Pennsylvania	M,D,O*
University of Pittsburgh	M,D*
University of Redlands	M
University of Southern California	M,O*
University of South Florida	M,D,O*
The University of Texas at Dallas	M,D
The University of Toledo	M,D,O
University of Utah	M,D
University of West Florida	M
University of West Georgia	M,O
University of Wisconsin–Madison	M,D,O
University of Wisconsin–Milwaukee	M,D,O*
Virginia Commonwealth University	O
West Chester University of Pennsylvania	M,O
Western Illinois University	M,O
Western Michigan University	M,O

GEOGRAPHY

Appalachian State University	M
Arizona State University at the Tempe campus	M,D,O
Auburn University	M*
Ball State University	M,O
Binghamton University, State University of New York	M
Brock University	M

*M—masters degree; D—doctorate; O—other advanced degree; *—Close-Up and/or Display*

California State University, East Bay	M
California State University, Fullerton	M
California State University, Long Beach	M
California State University, Los Angeles	M
California State University, Northridge	M
Carleton University	M,D
Central Connecticut State University	M
Central Washington University	M
Clark University	D
Concordia University (Canada)	M,D,O
East Carolina University	M,O
East Stroudsburg University of Pennsylvania	M
Florida State University	M,D
Fort Hays State University	M
George Mason University	M,D,O
The George Washington University	M,O
Georgia State University	M,D
Hunter College of the City University of New York	M,O
Indiana University Bloomington	D
Indiana University of Pennsylvania	M
Kansas State University	M,D,O
Kent State University	M,D
Louisiana State University and Agricultural & Mechanical College	M,D
Marshall University	M,O
McGill University	M,D
McMaster University	M,D
Memorial University of Newfoundland	M,D
Miami University	M
Michigan State University	M,D
Minnesota State University Mankato	M
Mississippi State University	M,D
Missouri State University	M,O
New Mexico State University	M
Northeastern Illinois University	M,O
Northern Arizona University	M,O
Northern Illinois University	M,D
The Ohio State University	M,D
Ohio University	M
Oklahoma State University	M,D
Oregon State University	M,D
Penn State University Park	M,D*
Portland State University	M,D
Queen's University at Kingston	M,D
Rutgers University–New Brunswick	M,D
St. Cloud State University	M,O
Salem State University	M
San Diego State University	M,D
San Francisco State University	M
San Jose State University	M
Shippensburg University of Pennsylvania	M
Simon Fraser University	M,D
South Dakota State University	M
Southern Illinois University Carbondale	M,D
Southern Illinois University Edwardsville	M
Syracuse University	M,D*
Temple University	M,D,O*
Texas A&M University	M,D
Texas State University	M,D
Texas Tech University	M,D
Thomas Jefferson University	M
Towson University	M
Trent University	M,D
Université de Montréal	M,D,O
Université de Sherbrooke	M,D
Université du Québec à Montréal	M
Université Laval	M,D
University at Albany, State University of New York	M,O
University at Buffalo, the State University of New York	M,D
The University of Alabama	M,D
The University of Arizona	M,D,O
University of Arkansas	M
The University of British Columbia	M,D
University of Calgary	M,D
University of California, Berkeley	D
University of California, Davis	M,D
University of California, Los Angeles	M,D*
University of California, Santa Barbara	M,D
University of Cincinnati	M,D
University of Colorado Boulder	M,D
University of Colorado Colorado Springs	M
University of Connecticut	M,D*
University of Delaware	M,D*
University of Denver	M,D
University of Florida	M,D
University of Georgia	M,D
University of Guelph	M,D
University of Hawaii at Manoa	M,D,O
University of Idaho	M,D
University of Illinois at Chicago	M
University of Illinois at Urbana–Champaign	M,D
The University of Iowa	M,D,O*
The University of Kansas	M,D,O
University of Kentucky	M,D
University of Lethbridge	M,D
University of Louisville	M
The University of Manchester	M,D
University of Manitoba	M,D
University of Maryland, Baltimore County	M,D
University of Maryland, College Park	M,D
University of Massachusetts Amherst	M*
University of Memphis	M,D,O
University of Miami	M*
University of Minnesota, Twin Cities Campus	M,D
University of Missouri	M,O
University of Montana	M
University of Nebraska at Omaha	M,O
University of Nebraska–Lincoln	M,D
University of Nevada, Reno	M,D
University of New Mexico	M
The University of North Carolina at Chapel Hill	M,D
The University of North Carolina at Charlotte	M,D
The University of North Carolina at Greensboro	M,D,O
University of North Dakota	M
University of Northern Iowa	M
University of North Texas	M,D,O
University of Oklahoma	M,D*
University of Oregon	M,D
University of Ottawa	M,D
University of Prince Edward Island	M
University of Regina	M,D
University of Saskatchewan	M,D
University of South Africa	M,D
University of South Carolina	M,D
University of Southern California	M,O*
University of Southern Mississippi	M,D
University of South Florida	O*
The University of Tennessee	M,D
The University of Texas at Austin	M,D
The University of Texas at Dallas	M,D
The University of Toledo	M,D,O
University of Toronto	M,D
University of Utah	M,D
University of Victoria	M,D
University of Washington	M,D
University of Waterloo	M,D
The University of Western Ontario	M,D
University of Wisconsin–Madison	M,D,O
University of Wisconsin–Milwaukee	M,D*
University of Wyoming	M
Utah State University	M,D
Virginia Polytechnic Institute and State University	M,D
West Chester University of Pennsylvania	M,O
Western Illinois University	M,O
Western Michigan University	M,D,O
Western Washington University	M
West Virginia University	M,D
Wilfrid Laurier University	M,D
York University	M,D

GEOLOGICAL ENGINEERING

Arizona State University at the Tempe campus	M,D
Colorado School of Mines	M,D
Missouri University of Science and Technology	M,D
Montana Tech of The University of Montana	M
New Mexico Institute of Mining and Technology	M
New Mexico State University	M,D
South Dakota School of Mines and Technology	M,D
The University of Akron	M
University of Alaska Fairbanks	M
The University of Arizona	M,D,O
The University of British Columbia	M,D
University of Hawaii at Manoa	M,D
University of Idaho	M,D
University of Minnesota, Twin Cities Campus	M,D,O
University of Mississippi	M,D
University of Nevada, Reno	M,D
University of North Dakota	M,D
University of Oklahoma	M,D*
University of Saskatchewan	M,D
University of Utah	M,D
University of Wisconsin–Madison	M,D

GEOLOGY

Acadia University	M
American University of Beirut	M,D
Arizona State University at the Tempe campus	M,D
Auburn University	M*
Ball State University	M,D
Binghamton University, State University of New York	M,D
Boston College	M
Bowling Green State University	M
Brigham Young University	M
Brooklyn College of the City University of New York	M,D
California Institute of Technology	M,D
California State Polytechnic University, Pomona	M
California State University, Bakersfield	M
California State University, Chico	M
California State University, East Bay	M
California State University, Fresno	M
California State University, Fullerton	M
California State University, Long Beach	M
California State University, Los Angeles	M
California State University, Northridge	M
Case Western Reserve University	M,D*
Central Washington University	M
City College of the City University of New York	M
Colorado School of Mines	M,D
Cornell University	M,D
Duke University	M,D*
East Carolina University	M,O
Eastern Kentucky University	M,D
Florida Atlantic University	M,D
Florida State University	M,D
Fort Hays State University	M
Georgia State University	M
Humboldt State University	M
Idaho State University	M,O
Indiana University Bloomington	M,D
Indiana University–Purdue University Indianapolis	M,D
Iowa State University of Science and Technology	M,D
Kansas State University	M
Kent State University	M,D
Lakehead University	M
Laurentian University	M,D
Lehigh University	M,D
Louisiana State University and Agricultural & Mechanical College	M,D
Massachusetts Institute of Technology	M,D
McMaster University	M,D
Memorial University of Newfoundland	M,D
Miami University	M,D
Mississippi State University	M,D
Missouri State University	M,O
Missouri University of Science and Technology	M,D
Montana Tech of The University of Montana	M
New Mexico Institute of Mining and Technology	M,D
New Mexico State University	M
Northern Arizona University	M,D,O
Northern Illinois University	M,D
Northwestern University	D
The Ohio State University	M,D
Ohio University	M
Oklahoma State University	M,D
Oregon State University	M,D
Portland State University	M,D,O
Queens College of the City University of New York	M
Queen's University at Kingston	M,D
Rensselaer Polytechnic Institute	M,D
Rutgers University–Newark	M
Rutgers University–New Brunswick	M,D
St. Francis Xavier University	M
San Diego State University	M
San Jose State University	M
South Dakota School of Mines and Technology	M,D
Southern Illinois University Carbondale	M,D
Southern Methodist University	M,D
Stephen F. Austin State University	M
Sul Ross State University	M
Syracuse University	M,D*
Temple University	M,D*
Texas A&M University	M,D
Texas Christian University	M
Université du Québec à Montréal	M,D,O
Université Laval	M,D
University at Buffalo, the State University of New York	M,D
The University of Akron	M
The University of Alabama	M,D
University of Arkansas	M
The University of British Columbia	M,D
University of Calgary	M,D
University of California, Berkeley	M,D
University of California, Davis	M,D
University of California, Los Angeles	M,D*
University of California, Riverside	M,D
University of Cincinnati	M,D
University of Colorado Boulder	M,D
University of Connecticut	M,D*
University of Delaware	M,D*
University of Florida	M,D
University of Georgia	M,D
University of Hawaii at Manoa	M,D
University of Houston	M,D
University of Idaho	M,D
University of Illinois at Chicago	M,D
University of Illinois at Urbana–Champaign	M,D
The University of Kansas	M,D
University of Kentucky	M,D
University of Maine	M,O
University of Manitoba	M,D
University of Maryland, College Park	M,D
University of Memphis	M,D,O
University of Minnesota, Duluth	M,D
University of Minnesota, Twin Cities Campus	M,D
University of Mississippi	M,D
University of Missouri	M,D
University of Montana	M,D
University of Nevada, Reno	M,D
University of New Brunswick Fredericton	M,D
University of New Hampshire	M
The University of North Carolina at Chapel Hill	M,D
University of North Dakota	M,D
University of Oklahoma	M,D*
University of Oregon	M,D
University of Pittsburgh	M,D*
University of Puerto Rico–Mayagüez	M
University of Regina	M,D
University of Rochester	M,D*
University of Saskatchewan	M,D,O
University of South Carolina	M,D
University of Southern Mississippi	M,D
University of South Florida	M,D,O*
The University of Tennessee	M,D
The University of Texas at Arlington	M,D
The University of Texas at Austin	M,D
The University of Texas at El Paso	M,D
The University of Texas at San Antonio	M
The University of Texas of the Permian Basin	M
The University of Toledo	M,D
University of Toronto	M,D
University of Utah	M,D
University of Vermont	M
University of Washington	M,D
The University of Western Ontario	M,D
University of Wisconsin–Madison	M,D
University of Wisconsin–Milwaukee	M,D*
University of Wyoming	M,D
Utah State University	M
Vanderbilt University	M*
Washington State University	M,D
Wayne State University	M
Western Kentucky University	M
Western Washington University	M
West Virginia University	M,D
Wichita State University	M
Wright State University	O
Yale University	D

GEOPHYSICS

Boston College	M
Bowling Green State University	M
California Institute of Technology	M,D
Colorado School of Mines	M,D
Cornell University	M,D
Florida State University	D
Idaho State University	M,O
Indiana University Bloomington	M,D
Louisiana State University and Agricultural & Mechanical College	M,D
Massachusetts Institute of Technology	M,D
Memorial University of Newfoundland	M,D
Michigan Technological University	M,D
Missouri University of Science and Technology	M,D
New Mexico Institute of Mining and Technology	M,D
Oregon State University	M,D
Rice University	M
Saint Louis University	M,D*
Southern Methodist University	M,D
Stanford University	M,D
Texas A&M University	M,D
University of Alaska Fairbanks	M
University of Alberta	M,D
The University of British Columbia	M,D
University of Calgary	M,D
University of California, Berkeley	M,D
University of California, Los Angeles	M,D*
University of California, San Diego	M,D*
University of Chicago	D
University of Colorado Boulder	M,D
University of Hawaii at Manoa	M,D
University of Houston	M,D
University of Manitoba	M,D
University of Memphis	M,D,O
University of Miami	M,D*
University of Minnesota, Twin Cities Campus	M,D
University of Nevada, Reno	M,D
University of Oklahoma	M,D*
University of Rhode Island	M,D*
The University of Texas at El Paso	M,D
The University of Tulsa	M,D
University of Utah	M,D
University of Washington	M,D
The University of Western Ontario	M,D
University of Wisconsin–Madison	M,D
University of Wyoming	M,D
Wright State University	M
Yale University	D

GEOSCIENCES

Arizona State University at the Tempe campus	M,D
Ball State University	M
Baylor University	M,D
Boston University	M,D*
Brock University	M
Brooklyn College of the City University of New York	M
Brown University	D
California State University, Chico	M
California State University, San Bernardino	M
Carleton University	M,D
Case Western Reserve University	M,D*
City College of the City University of New York	M
Colorado State University	M,D
Columbia University	M,D*
Cornell University	M,D
Dalhousie University	M,D
Dartmouth College	M,D*
Duke University	M,D*
Eastern Michigan University	M,O
East Tennessee State University	M,O
Emporia State University	M,O
Florida Atlantic University	M,D
Florida Institute of Technology	M
Florida International University	M,D
Florida State University	M,D
Fort Hays State University	M

George Mason University	M,D,O
Georgia Institute of Technology	M,D
Georgia State University	M,D,O
The Graduate Center, City University of New York	D
Harvard University	M,D*
Hunter College of the City University of New York	M
Idaho State University	M,O
Indiana University Bloomington	M,D
Indiana University–Purdue University Indianapolis	M,D
Iowa State University of Science and Technology	M,D
Jackson State University	M,D
Johns Hopkins University	M,D*
Lehigh University	M,D
Long Island University–LIU Post	M,O
Manhattanville College	M,O
Massachusetts Institute of Technology	M,D
McGill University	M,D
McMaster University	M,D
Memorial University of Newfoundland	M,D
Michigan State University	M,D
Middle Tennessee State University	O
Mississippi State University	M,D
Missouri State University	M,O
Montana State University	M,D
Montana Tech of The University of Montana	M
Montclair State University	M
Murray State University	M,O
New Mexico Institute of Mining and Technology	M,D
North Carolina Central University	M
North Carolina State University	M,D
Northwestern University	D
The Ohio State University	M,D
Pace University	M,O
Penn State University Park	M,D*
Princeton University	D
Purdue University	M,D
Queens College of the City University of New York	M
Rice University	M,D
St. Francis Xavier University	M
Saint Louis University	M,D*
St. Thomas University	M,D,O
San Francisco State University	M
Simon Fraser University	M,D
South Dakota State University	D
Southern Illinois University Carbondale	M,D
Stanford University	M,D,O
State University of New York at New Paltz	M,O
Stony Brook University, State University of New York	M,D
Teachers College, Columbia University	M,D
Temple University	M,D*
Tennessee Technological University	D
Texas Tech University	M,D
Université du Québec à Chicoutimi	M
Université du Québec à Montréal	M,D,O
Université du Québec, Institut National de la Recherche Scientifique	M,D
Université Laval	M,D
University at Buffalo, the State University of New York	M,D
The University of Akron	M
The University of Alabama	M,D
The University of Alabama in Huntsville	M,D
University of Alberta	M,D
The University of Arizona	M,D
University of Arkansas at Little Rock	O
University of Calgary	M,D
University of California, Irvine	M,D
University of California, Los Angeles	M,D*
University of California, San Diego	M,D*
University of California, Santa Barbara	M,D
University of California, Santa Cruz	M,D*
University of Chicago	D
University of Florida	M,D
University of Illinois at Chicago	M,D
University of Illinois at Urbana–Champaign	M,D
The University of Iowa	M,D*
University of Louisiana at Lafayette	M
University of Lynchburg	M
University of Maine	M,D
The University of Manchester	M,D
University of Massachusetts Amherst	M,D*
University of Michigan	M,D*
University of Missouri–Kansas City	M,D
University of Montana	M,D
University of Nebraska–Lincoln	M,D
University of Nevada, Las Vegas	M,D
University of New Hampshire	M
University of New Haven	M*
University of New Mexico	M,D
University of New Orleans	M,D
The University of North Carolina at Charlotte	M,D
The University of North Carolina Wilmington	M,O
University of North Dakota	M,D
University of Northern Colorado	M
University of Northern Iowa	M
University of Notre Dame	M,D
University of Ottawa	M,D
University of Pennsylvania	M,D*
University of Rhode Island	M,D,O*
University of Rochester	M,D*
University of South Carolina	M,D
University of Southern California	M,D*
University of South Florida	M,D*
The University of Texas at Austin	M,D
The University of Texas at Dallas	M,D
The University of Texas Rio Grande Valley	M
The University of Tulsa	M,D
University of Victoria	M,D
University of Waterloo	M,D
The University of Western Ontario	M,D
University of Windsor	M,D
Virginia Polytechnic Institute and State University	M,D
Washington University in St. Louis	D
Wesleyan University	M
West Chester University of Pennsylvania	M,O
Western Connecticut State University	M
Western Kentucky University	M
Western Michigan University	M,D,O
Yale University	D
York University	M,D

GEOTECHNICAL ENGINEERING

The Citadel, The Military College of South Carolina	M,O
Clemson University	M,D
Cornell University	M,D
Drexel University	M,D*
École Polytechnique de Montréal	M,D,O
Illinois Institute of Technology	M,D
Iowa State University of Science and Technology	M,D
Kansas State University	M,D
Kennesaw State University	M
Louisiana State University and Agricultural & Mechanical College	M,D
Massachusetts Institute of Technology	M,D,O
McGill University	M,D
Northwestern University	M,D
Norwich University	M
Ohio University	M,D
Old Dominion University	M
Oregon State University	M,D
Penn State University Park	M,D*
Southern Illinois University Edwardsville	M
Southern Methodist University	M,D
Stanford University	M,D,O
Tufts University	M,D*
University of Alberta	M,D
University of Calgary	M,D
University of California, Berkeley	M,D
University of Central Florida	M,D,O
University of Colorado Denver	M,D
University of Dayton	M
University of Delaware	M,D*
University of Massachusetts Amherst	M,D*
University of Memphis	M,D,O
University of New Brunswick Fredericton	M,D
University of Puerto Rico–Mayagüez	M,D
University of Rhode Island	M,D*
University of Southern California	M,D,O*
University of South Florida	M,D*
The University of Texas at Austin	M,D
University of Washington	M,D
University of Wisconsin–Madison	M

GERMAN

Arizona State University at the Tempe campus	M
Bowling Green State University	M
Brown University	D
California State University, Long Beach	M
Central Connecticut State University	M,O
Columbia University	M,D*
Cornell University	M,D
Dalhousie University	M
DePaul University	M
Duke University	D*
Florida State University	M
Georgetown University	M,D
Georgia State University	O
Harvard University	D*
Hofstra University	M,D,O
Illinois State University	M
Indiana University Bloomington	M,D
Johns Hopkins University	M,D*
Kansas State University	M
Kent State University	M,D
McGill University	M,D
Memorial University of Newfoundland	M
Michigan State University	M,D
Middlebury College	M,D
Middle Tennessee State University	M
Millersville University of Pennsylvania	M
New York University	M,D*
Northwestern University	D
The Ohio State University	M,D
Penn State University Park	M,D*
Portland State University	M
Princeton University	D
Purdue University	M,D
Queen's University at Kingston	M,D
Rutgers University–New Brunswick	M,D
San Francisco State University	M
Stanford University	M,D
Tufts University	M*
Université de Montréal	M
University at Buffalo, the State University of New York	M,D,O
The University of Alabama	M,D
University of Alberta	M,D
The University of Arizona	M,D
University of Arkansas	M
The University of British Columbia	M,D
University of Calgary	M,D
University of California, Berkeley	D
University of California, Davis	M,D
University of California, Irvine	M,D
University of California, Los Angeles	M,D*
University of Chicago	M,D
University of Cincinnati	M,D
University of Colorado Boulder	M
University of Delaware	M*
University of Florida	M,D
University of Georgia	M
University of Illinois at Chicago	M,D
University of Illinois at Urbana–Champaign	M,D
University of Kentucky	M
University of Lethbridge	M,D
The University of Manchester	D
University of Manitoba	M
University of Maryland, College Park	M,D
University of Massachusetts Amherst	M,D*
University of Michigan	M,D,O*
University of Minnesota, Twin Cities Campus	M,D
University of Missouri	M
University of Montana	M
University of Nebraska–Lincoln	M,D
University of Nevada, Reno	M
University of New Mexico	M,D
The University of North Carolina at Chapel Hill	D
University of Oklahoma	M*
University of Oregon	M,D
University of Pennsylvania	M,D*
University of Saskatchewan	M
University of South Africa	M,D
University of South Carolina	M,D
The University of Tennessee	M,D
The University of Texas at Austin	M,D
The University of Toledo	M
University of Toronto	M,D
University of Vermont	M
University of Victoria	M
University of Virginia	M
University of Washington	M,D
University of Waterloo	M,D
University of Wisconsin–Madison	M,D
University of Wisconsin–Milwaukee	M,O*
University of Wyoming	M
Vanderbilt University	M,D*
Washington University in St. Louis	D
Wayne State University	M,D
West Chester University of Pennsylvania	M,O
Western Kentucky University	M
Yale University	D

GERONTOLOGICAL NURSING

Allen College	M,D
Alvernia University	M,D,O
American University of Beirut	M
Arizona State University at the Tempe campus	M,D,O
Augusta University	D
Azusa Pacific University	M,D*
Ball State University	M,D,O
Binghamton University, State University of New York	M,D,O
Boise State University	M,D,O
Boston College	M,D
California State University, Stanislaus	M
Capella University	M
Caribbean University	M,D
Case Western Reserve University	M*
Clemson University	M,D,O
College of Staten Island of the City University of New York	M,D,O
Columbia University	M,O*
Creighton University	M,D,O
Duke University	M,D,O*
East Tennessee State University	M,D,O
Elms College	M,D
Fairleigh Dickinson University, Florham Campus	M
Felician University	M,O
Florida Southern College	M
George Mason University	M,D,O
Georgia Southern University–Armstrong Campus	M,O
Goldfarb School of Nursing at Barnes-Jewish College	M
Graceland University (IA)	M,D,O
Gwynedd Mercy University	M,D
Hofstra University	M
Hunter College of the City University of New York	M,D
Independence University	M
Indiana University–Purdue University Fort Wayne	M,O
Indiana University–Purdue University Indianapolis	M
Jacksonville University	M,D,O*
James Madison University	M,D
Johns Hopkins University	D*
Kent State University	M,D
Keuka College	M
La Salle University	M,D,O
Lehman College of the City University of New York	M
Loma Linda University	M
Louisiana State University Health Sciences Center	M,D,O
Marquette University	M,D,O
Maryville University of Saint Louis	M,D
Medical University of South Carolina	M,D
Mercer University	M,D,O
MGH Institute of Health Professions	M,D,O
Middle Georgia State University	M
Molloy College	M,D,O
Monmouth University	M,D,O*
Morningside College	M
Mount Carmel College of Nursing	M,D
Neumann University	M,D
New York University	M,D,O*
Northeastern University	M,D,O
Nova Southeastern University	M,D*
Oakland University	M,O
Old Dominion University	M,D
Oregon Health & Science University	M
Point Loma Nazarene University	M
Purdue University	M,D,O
Research College of Nursing	M
Rush University	D,O
Rutgers University–Camden	D
Sage Graduate School	M,O
St. Catherine University	M,D
Saint Francis Medical Center College of Nursing	M,D,O
St. Joseph's College, Long Island Campus	M
St. Joseph's College, New York	M
Saint Mary's College	D
Salem State University	M
Seattle Pacific University	M,O
Seton Hall University	M,O
Shenandoah University	M,D,O
Southern Adventist University	M,D
Southern University and Agricultural and Mechanical College	M,D,O
Stony Brook University, State University of New York	M,D,O
Tennessee Technological University	D
Texas Christian University	M,O
Texas Tech University Health Sciences Center	M,D,O
Texas Woman's University	M,D
Uniformed Services University of the Health Sciences	M,D*
University at Buffalo, the State University of New York	M,D,O
The University of Alabama at Birmingham	M,D
The University of Alabama in Huntsville	M,D,O
University of Central Florida	M,D,O
University of Cincinnati	M,D
University of Colorado Colorado Springs	M,D
University of Connecticut	O*
University of Delaware	M,O*
University of Illinois at Chicago	M,D,O
The University of Kansas	M,D,O
University of Louisville	M,D
University of Maryland, Baltimore	M,D,O
University of Massachusetts Amherst	M,D*
University of Massachusetts Lowell	M
University of Massachusetts Medical School	M,D,O
University of Minnesota, Twin Cities Campus	M,D
University of Missouri	M,D,O
University of Missouri–Kansas City	M,D
University of Missouri–St. Louis	D,O
The University of North Carolina at Chapel Hill	M,D,O
The University of North Carolina at Charlotte	M,D,O
The University of North Carolina at Greensboro	M,D,O
University of North Dakota	M,D,O
University of Pennsylvania	M*
University of Phoenix–Bay Area Campus	M,D
University of Phoenix–Phoenix Campus	M,O
University of Pittsburgh	M,D*
University of Puerto Rico–Medical Sciences Campus	M
University of Rhode Island	M,D,O*
University of Rochester	M,D*
University of San Diego	M,D
University of Southern Maine	M,D,O
University of South Florida	M,D,O*
The University of Tennessee at Chattanooga	M,D,O
The University of Tennessee Health Science Center	D,O
The University of Texas at Austin	M,D

*M—masters degree; D—doctorate; O—other advanced degree; *—Close-Up and/or Display*

The University of Texas Health Science Center at San Antonio	M,D,O
The University of Tulsa	D
University of Utah	M,O
University of Wisconsin–Eau Claire	M,D
University of Wisconsin–Madison	D
Ursuline College	M,D
Valdosta State University	M
Vanderbilt University	M,D,O*
Villanova University	M,D,O
Walden University	M,D,O
Wayne State University	M,D
West Chester University of Pennsylvania	M,D,O
Western Connecticut State University	M,D
William Paterson University of New Jersey	M,D,O
Wilmington University	M,D
Winona State University	M,D,O
Wright State University	M
York College of Pennsylvania	M

GERONTOLOGY

Adelphi University	M,O
Alliant International University–Los Angeles	M
Arizona State University at the Tempe campus	M,D,O
Arkansas State University	M,D,O
California State University, Fullerton	M
California State University, Long Beach	M
Capella University	M
Central Michigan University	M,O
The College at Brockport, State University of New York	M,O
Concordia University Chicago	M
DeSales University	M,D,O
Duke University	M,D,O*
East Carolina University	M,O
Eastern Illinois University	M
Eastern Michigan University	O
East Tennessee State University	M,D,O
Georgia State University	M,O
Kansas State University	M,D
Kent State University	M,D
Lakehead University	M,D
La Salle University	M,D,O
Loma Linda University	M,D
Long Island University–LIU Brooklyn	M,O
Long Island University–LIU Post	M,O
Marywood University	M
McDaniel College	M,O
Mercer University	M,D
Miami University	M,D
Middle Tennessee State University	O
Minnesota State University Mankato	M
Morehead State University	M
Mount Saint Vincent University	M
North Dakota State University	D,O*
Northeastern Illinois University	M
Oregon Health & Science University	M,O
Sage Graduate School	M
San Diego State University	M
San Francisco State University	M
Simon Fraser University	M,D
Temple University	D*
Texas Christian University	D
Texas State University	M
Texas Tech University	M,D
Université de Sherbrooke	M
Université Laval	O
The University of Akron	D
University of Arkansas at Little Rock	O
University of Central Missouri	M,D,O
University of Central Oklahoma	M
University of Georgia	O
University of Illinois at Springfield	M,O
University of Indianapolis	M,D,O
The University of Kansas	D
University of Kentucky	D,O
University of La Verne	M,O
University of Louisiana at Monroe	M,O
University of Louisville	M,D,O
University of Maryland, Baltimore	M,D
University of Maryland, Baltimore County	M,D
University of Massachusetts Boston	M,D,O
University of Michigan–Flint	M,D,O
University of Nebraska at Omaha	M,D,O
University of Nebraska–Lincoln	M,D
The University of North Carolina at Charlotte	M,D,O
The University of North Carolina at Greensboro	M,O
The University of North Carolina Wilmington	M
University of Northern Colorado	M,D
University of North Texas	M,D,O
University of Phoenix–Central Valley Campus	M
University of Phoenix–Hawaii Campus	M
University of Puerto Rico–Medical Sciences Campus	M,O
University of Regina	M
University of South Carolina	O
University of Southern California	M,D,O*
University of Southern Indiana	M,D,O
University of South Florida	M,D,O*
The University of Tennessee	M
The University of Toledo	M,O
University of Utah	M,O
University of Wisconsin–Milwaukee	M,D,O*
Virginia Commonwealth University	M,D
Walden University	M,D
Washington University in St. Louis	M,D
Wayne State University	M,D,O
Webster University	M
West Chester University of Pennsylvania	M,O
Wichita State University	M
Youngstown State University	M

GRAPHIC DESIGN

Academy of Art University	M
ArtCenter College of Design	M
Atlantic University College	M
Bob Jones University	M,D,O
Boston University	M*
Bowling Green State University	M
Bradley University	M
California College of the Arts	M
California Institute of the Arts	M,O
California State University, Fullerton	M
California State University, Los Angeles	M
Central Connecticut State University	M
Central Washington University	M
City College of the City University of New York	M
East Carolina University	M
Florida Atlantic University	M
Full Sail University	M
George Mason University	M
Georgia Southern University	M
Georgia State University	M
Illinois State University	M
Indiana State University	M
Indiana University–Purdue University Indianapolis	M
Inter American University of Puerto Rico, San Germán Campus	M
Iowa State University of Science and Technology	M
Kent State University	M
Liberty University	M
Louisiana State University and Agricultural & Mechanical College	M
Louisiana Tech University	M,D,O
Lynn University	M,O
Maryland Institute College of Art	M
Marywood University	M
Minneapolis College of Art and Design	M,O
Morehead State University	M
New York Institute of Technology	M
North Carolina Agricultural and Technical State University	M
North Carolina State University	M
Ohio University	M
Oklahoma State University	M
Otis College of Art and Design	M
Pensacola Christian College	M,D,O
Pittsburg State University	M,O
Pratt Institute	M*
Rhode Island School of Design	M
Rochester Institute of Technology	M
San Diego State University	M
Savannah College of Art and Design	M
School of the Art Institute of Chicago	M
School of Visual Arts (NY)	M
State University of New York at Oswego	M
Suffolk University	M
Temple University	M*
Texas State University	M
Texas Woman's University	M
Université Laval	M
University of Baltimore	D
University of Cincinnati	M
University of Guam	M
University of Illinois at Chicago	M
University of Illinois at Urbana–Champaign	M
University of Memphis	M,O
University of Miami	M*
University of Minnesota, Duluth	M
University of Notre Dame	M
University of Pennsylvania	M,O*
University of South Dakota	M
The University of Tennessee	M
University of Utah	M
Vermont College of Fine Arts	M
Wayne State University	M
West Virginia University	M,D
Yale University	M

HAZARDOUS MATERIALS MANAGEMENT

Humboldt State University	M
Marquette University	M,D,O
New Mexico Institute of Mining and Technology	M
Rutgers University–New Brunswick	M,D
University of Colorado Denver	M
The University of Manchester	M,D
University of New Haven	M*
University of South Carolina	M,D
University of Southern California	M,D,O*

HEALTH COMMUNICATION

Arkansas State University	M,O
Boston University	M*
Chatham University	M
The College of New Jersey	M
Cornell University	M,D
DePaul University	M
East Carolina University	M,O
Fontbonne University	M
Gannon University	M
The George Washington University	M,D
Indiana University–Purdue University Indianapolis	M,D
Johns Hopkins University	M,D*
Kansas State University	M
Lasell College	M,O
Marquette University	M,O
Michigan State University	M
Ohio University	M,D
Rider University	M
Southeastern Louisiana University	M
Southern Illinois University Edwardsville	M
State University of New York at Oswego	M
Stony Brook University, State University of New York	M,O
Tufts University	M,D,O*
University of Florida	M,D,O
University of Houston	M
University of Missouri	M,D
The University of North Carolina at Chapel Hill	M,D,O
University of Oklahoma	M,D*
University of St. Thomas (MN)	M
University of Southern California	M,D*
Wayne State University	M,D,O

HEALTH EDUCATION

Adelphi University	M,O
Alabama State University	M
Albany State University	M,O
Alcorn State University	M,O
Allen College	M,D
American University	M,O
Arcadia University	M
Arizona State University at the Tempe campus	D
Arkansas State University	M,D,O
Auburn University	M,D,O*
Austin Peay State University	M
Baldwin Wallace University	M
Baylor University	M,D
Benedictine University	M
Boston University	M*
Brandeis University	D
California Baptist University	M
California State University, Long Beach	M
California State University, Northridge	M,O
California State University, San Marcos	M
Cambridge College	M,D,O
Central Washington University	M
Clark University	M
Cleveland State University	M
Cleveland University–Kansas City	M
The College at Brockport, State University of New York	M
College of Saint Mary	D
Colorado State University–Pueblo	M
Columbus State University	M
Concordia University (United States)	M,D
Concordia University Wisconsin	M,D
Daemen College	M
Dalhousie University	M
Delta State University	M
Drew University	M,D,O
East Carolina University	M
Eastern Kentucky University	M
Eastern Michigan University	M,O
Eastern University	M,O
East Stroudsburg University of Pennsylvania	M
Emory University	M,D
Excelsior College	M
Fairfield University	M,D
Florida State University	M,D
Fort Hays State University	M
Georgia College & State University	M
Georgia Southern University	M,D
Georgia State University	M
Harding University	M,O
Hofstra University	M,D,O
Howard University	M
Idaho State University	M
Illinois State University	M
Indiana State University	M,D
Indiana University Bloomington	M,D
Indiana University of Pennsylvania	M
Indiana University–Purdue University Indianapolis	M,D
Inter American University of Puerto Rico, Metropolitan Campus	M
Inter American University of Puerto Rico, San Germán Campus	M
Ithaca College	M
Jackson State University	M
James Madison University	M
John F. Kennedy University	M
Johns Hopkins University	M,D*
Kansas State University	M,D
Keiser University	M
Kent State University	M,D
Lake Erie College of Osteopathic Medicine	M,D,O
Lehman College of the City University of New York	M
Lock Haven University of Pennsylvania	M
Logan University	M,D
Loma Linda University	M,D
Longwood University	M
Marshall University	M
Marymount University	M
Marywood University	D
Massachusetts College of Liberal Arts	M,O
McNeese State University	O
Meredith College	M,O
Merrimack College	M
Middle Tennessee State University	M
Minnesota State University Mankato	M,O
Mississippi University for Women	M,D,O
Montana State University	M
Montclair State University	M
Morehead State University	M
New Jersey City University	M
New Mexico Highlands University	M
New York Medical College	M,D,O
Nicholls State University	M
North Carolina Agricultural and Technical State University	M
Northeastern State University	M
Northwestern State University of Louisiana	M
Northwest Missouri State University	M
Nova Southeastern University	M,D,O*
Oklahoma State University	M,D,O
Old Dominion University	M,D
Penn State Harrisburg	M,D,O
Pennsylvania College of Health Sciences	M
Pittsburg State University	M
Plymouth State University	M
Prairie View A&M University	M
Purdue University	M,D
Rhode Island College	M,O
Rosalind Franklin University of Medicine and Science	M
Rutgers University–Newark	M,D
Rutgers University–New Brunswick	M,D,O
Sage Graduate School	M
Saint Francis University	M
Saint Joseph's College of Maine	M
San Francisco State University	M
Shenandoah University	M,D,O
Simmons College	M,D,O
Southeastern Louisiana University	M
Southern Connecticut State University	M
Southern Illinois University Carbondale	M,D
Southern Illinois University Edwardsville	M,D,O
State University of New York College at Cortland	M
Stony Brook University, State University of New York	M,O
Teachers College, Columbia University	M,D,O
Tennessee Technological University	M
Texas A&M University	M,D
Texas A&M University–Kingsville	M
Texas Southern University	M
Texas State University	M
Texas Woman's University	M,D
Thomas Jefferson University	M,D,O
Trident University International	M,D,O
Union College (KY)	M
The University of Alabama	M,D
The University of Alabama at Birmingham	D
University of Arkansas	M,D
University of Arkansas at Little Rock	M,D
University of Arkansas for Medical Sciences	M,D,O
University of Central Arkansas	M
University of Cincinnati	M,D
University of Colorado Denver	M,D
University of Florida	M,D,O
University of Georgia	M,D
University of Houston	M,D
University of Illinois at Chicago	M
University of Illinois at Springfield	M,O
The University of Kansas	M,D,O
University of Louisville	M,D,O
University of Maryland, College Park	M,D
University of Massachusetts Amherst	M,D*
University of Michigan	M,D*
University of Michigan–Flint	M
University of Missouri	M,D,O
University of Missouri–Kansas City	M,D
University of Montana	M
University of Nebraska at Omaha	M,D
University of New Mexico	M
The University of North Carolina at Pembroke	M
University of Northern Colorado	M
University of Northern Iowa	M
University of Oklahoma Health Sciences Center	D
University of Phoenix–Online Campus	M,O
University of Pittsburgh	M,D*
University of Puerto Rico–Medical Sciences Campus	M
University of Rhode Island	M*
University of St. Augustine for Health Sciences	M,D
University of South Africa	M,D
University of South Alabama	M
University of South Carolina	M,D,O
University of Southern California	M*
University of South Florida	M,D*
The University of Tennessee	M
The University of Texas at Austin	M,D
The University of Texas at San Antonio	M
The University of Texas at Tyler	M
The University of Toledo	M,D,O
University of Utah	M,D
University of Waterloo	M,D
University of Wisconsin–La Crosse	M
University of Wyoming	M
Utah State University	M,D
Virginia State University	M,D
Walden University	M,D,O

Washburn University	M
Wayne State University	M,D,O
Western Illinois University	M
Western Michigan University	D,O
Western Oregon University	M
Western University of Health Sciences	M
Widener University	M,D
Worcester State University	M
Wright State University	M

HEALTH INFORMATICS

Adelphi University	M,O
American Public University System	M,D
American Sentinel University	M
Arkansas Tech University	M
Augusta University	M
Barry University	O
Belmont University	D
Benedictine University	M
Boston University	M,O*
Brandeis University	M
Brooklyn College of the City University of New York	M,O
Canisius College	M,O
Capella University	M
Chatham University	M
Claremont Graduate University	M,D,O
Clarkson University	M
The College of St. Scholastica	M,O
Colorado Mesa University	M,D,O
Dakota State University	M,D,O
Dartmouth College	M,D*
DePaul University	M,D
DeSales University	M,O
Duke University	M*
East Carolina University	M,O
Emory University	M,D
Excelsior College	M
George Mason University	M,D,O
Georgia Southwestern State University	M,O
Georgia State University	M,D,O
Grand Canyon University	M,D,O
Hofstra University	M,O
Indiana University Bloomington	M,D
Indiana University–Purdue University Indianapolis	M,D
Jacksonville University	M*
Johns Hopkins University	M,D,O*
Kennesaw State University	M,O
Kent State University	M
Liberty University	M,D
Lipscomb University	M,D
Logan University	M,D
Louisiana Tech University	M,D,O
Marshall University	M
Marymount University	M,O
Mercer University	M,D
Middle Georgia State University	M
Midwestern State University	M,O
Millennia Atlantic University	M
Montana Tech of The University of Montana	O
National University	M,O
Northeastern University	M,D
Northern Kentucky University	M,O
Northwestern University	M,D
Nova Southeastern University	M,D,O*
Oregon Health & Science University	M,D,O
Regis University	M,O
Roberts Wesleyan College	M
Rochester Institute of Technology	M
Sacred Heart University	M
St. Catherine University	M
St. Joseph's College, Long Island Campus	M
St. Joseph's College, New York	M
Saint Joseph's University	M*
Samford University	M
Slippery Rock University of Pennsylvania	M
Southern Illinois University Edwardsville	M
Southern New Hampshire University	M,D,O
State University of New York at Oswego	M
Stephens College	M,O
Stevens Institute of Technology	M,D,O
Stony Brook University, State University of New York	M,D,O
Temple University	M,D*
Texas State University	M
Trident University International	M,D,O
The University of Alabama at Birmingham	M
University of Central Florida	M,O
University of Cincinnati	M
University of Colorado Denver	M
The University of Findlay	M,D
University of Illinois at Chicago	M,O
University of Illinois at Urbana–Champaign	M,D,O
The University of Iowa	M,D,O*
The University of Kansas	M,O
University of Lynchburg	O
University of Maryland, Baltimore County	M
University of Maryland University College	M
University of Michigan	M,D*
University of Michigan–Dearborn	M
University of Michigan–Flint	M
University of Minnesota, Twin Cities Campus	M,D
University of New England	M,D,O
The University of North Carolina at Charlotte	M,O
University of Phoenix–Online Campus	M,O
University of Pittsburgh	M*
University of Puerto Rico–Medical Sciences Campus	M
University of St. Augustine for Health Sciences	M
University of San Diego	M,D
University of San Francisco	M
University of South Carolina Upstate	M
University of South Florida	M,D,O*
The University of Tennessee Health Science Center	M,D
The University of Texas Health Science Center at Houston	M,D,O
University of Toronto	M
University of Victoria	M
University of Virginia	M
University of Washington	M,D
University of Waterloo	M,D
University of Wisconsin–Milwaukee	M,D*
Virginia International University	M,O
Walden University	M,D,O
Weill Cornell Medicine	M

HEALTH LAW

Boston University	M,D*
Case Western Reserve University	M,D*
DePaul University	M,D
Drexel University	M,D*
Florida State University	M,D
Georgetown University	M,D
Hofstra University	M,D,O
Indiana University–Purdue University Indianapolis	M,D,O
Loyola University Chicago	M,D,O
Nova Southeastern University	M,D*
St. Mary's University (United States)	M
Seattle University	M,D
Seton Hall University	M,D
Southern Illinois University Carbondale	M
Suffolk University	M,D
Université de Sherbrooke	M,D,O
University of California, San Francisco	M
University of Houston	M,D
The University of Manchester	M,D
University of Pittsburgh	M*
The University of Tulsa	M,D,O
Widener University	M,D

HEALTH PHYSICS/RADIOLOGICAL HEALTH

East Carolina University	M,D
Georgetown University	M
Georgia Institute of Technology	M,D
Idaho State University	M,D
Illinois Institute of Technology	M,D
McMaster University	M,D
Midwestern State University	M
Northwestern State University of Louisiana	M
Oregon State University	M,D
Purdue University	M,D
Quinnipiac University	M
Rutgers University–Newark	M
San Diego State University	M
Thomas Jefferson University	M
Université Laval	O
University of Alberta	M,D
University of Arkansas for Medical Sciences	M,D
University of Cincinnati	M
University of Kentucky	M
University of Massachusetts Lowell	M
University of Michigan	M,D,O*
University of Missouri	M
University of Nevada, Las Vegas	M,D,O
University of Oklahoma Health Sciences Center	M,D
University of Toronto	M,D
Vanderbilt University	M,D*
Virginia Commonwealth University	D
Weber State University	M

HEALTH PROMOTION

American College of Healthcare Sciences	M,O
American University	M
American University of Beirut	M,D
Arizona State University at the Tempe campus	M,D
Ball State University	M
Benedictine University	M
Boise State University	M,O
Bridgewater State University	M
Brigham Young University	M,D
California Baptist University	M
California State University, Fresno	M
California State University, Fullerton	M
Claremont Graduate University	M,D
Cleveland University–Kansas City	M
Concord University	M
Creighton University	M
East Carolina University	M
Eastern Kentucky University	M
Eastern Michigan University	M,O
Emory University	M
Fairmont State University	M
Florida Atlantic University	M
Florida International University	M,D
George Mason University	M,O
Georgetown University	M,D
Georgia College & State University	M
Goddard College	M
Harvard University	M,D*
Immaculata University	M
Independence University	M
Indiana University Bloomington	M,D
Instituto Tecnologico de Santo Domingo	M,O
Kent State University	M,D
Lehman College of the City University of New York	M
Liberty University	M,D,O
Lindenwood University	M
Lock Haven University of Pennsylvania	M
Manhattanville College	M,O
Maryland University of Integrative Health	M,O
Marymount University	M
McNeese State University	M
Merrimack College	M
Mount St. Joseph University	M,O
National University	M,O
Nebraska Methodist College	M
New York University	M,D,O*
Old Dominion University	M
Oregon State University	M,D
Plymouth State University	M,O
Portland State University	M,D
Rosalind Franklin University of Medicine and Science	M
Rowan University	M
San Diego State University	M,D
Simmons College	M,D,O
Sonoma State University	M
Southern Methodist University	M,D
Springfield College	M,D,O
Stony Brook University, State University of New York	M,O
Tennessee Technological University	M
Texas A&M University	M,D
Tulane University	M
Union Institute & University	M
Universidad del Turabo	M
The University of Alabama	M,D
The University of Alabama at Birmingham	D
University of Alberta	M,O
University of Arkansas	M,D
University of Arkansas for Medical Sciences	M,D,O
University of Central Oklahoma	M
University of Chicago	M,D
University of Cincinnati	M,D
University of Delaware	M*
University of Georgia	M,D
The University of Kansas	M,D,O
University of Kentucky	M,D
University of Lynchburg	M
University of Massachusetts Lowell	D
University of Memphis	M,O
University of Michigan	M,D*
University of Mississippi	M,D
University of Nebraska–Lincoln	M,D
University of Nebraska Medical Center	D
University of North Alabama	M
The University of North Carolina at Chapel Hill	M
University of Northern Iowa	M
University of Oklahoma	M,D*
University of Oklahoma Health Sciences Center	M,D
University of Puerto Rico–Medical Sciences Campus	O
University of South Carolina	M,D,O
University of Southern California	M*
The University of Tennessee	M
The University of Texas Health Science Center at Houston	M,D,O
The University of Toledo	M,D,O
University of Toronto	M,D
University of Utah	M,D
University of Vermont	M
University of West Florida	M
University of Wisconsin–Milwaukee	M,D,O*
University of Wisconsin–Parkside	M
University of Wisconsin–Stevens Point	M,O
University of Wyoming	M
Utah State University	M,D
Walden University	M,D,O
Wilfrid Laurier University	M
Wright State University	M

HEALTH PSYCHOLOGY

Adler University	M
Alliant International University–Los Angeles	D
Appalachian State University	M
Argosy University, Atlanta	M,D,O
Argosy University, Chicago	D
Argosy University, Northern Virginia	M,D
Argosy University, Twin Cities	M,D,O
Bastyr University	M,O
California Institute of Integral Studies	M,D
California State University, Dominguez Hills	M
Central Michigan University	M,D
Chatham University	M,D
Claremont Graduate University	M,D,O
Drexel University	D*
Duke University	D*
East Carolina University	M,D,O
Georgian Court University	M,O
John F. Kennedy University	M
La Salle University	M,D
Lesley University	M,D,O
North Dakota State University	M,D*
Northern Kentucky University	M,O
Oklahoma State University	M,D,O
Oregon State University	M,D
Penn State Harrisburg	M,D,O
Prescott College	M
Rhode Island College	M,O
Rutgers University–New Brunswick	D
San Diego State University	M,D
Saybrook University	M,D
Southwestern College (NM)	O
Stony Brook University, State University of New York	D
United States International University–Africa	M
The University of Alabama at Birmingham	M,D
The University of British Columbia	M,D
University of Colorado Denver	D
University of Florida	M,D
University of Michigan–Dearborn	M
University of New Mexico	D
The University of North Carolina at Chapel Hill	M,D
The University of North Carolina at Charlotte	M,D,O
University of Pittsburgh	D*
The University of Texas at Arlington	M,D
University of the Sciences	M
Virginia Commonwealth University	D
Virginia State University	M,D
Viterbo University	M
Walden University	M,D,O
Yeshiva University	D

HEALTH SERVICES MANAGEMENT AND HOSPITAL ADMINISTRATION

Abilene Christian University	M
Adelphi University	M
Adventist University of Health Sciences	M
Alaska Pacific University	M
Albany State University	M
Albertus Magnus College	M
American InterContinental University Online	M
American Sentinel University	M
American University	M,O
American University of Beirut	M,D
Anderson University (SC)	M
Antioch University Midwest	M
Aquinas Institute of Theology	M,D,O
Argosy University, Atlanta	M,D
Argosy University, Chicago	M,D
Argosy University, Hawai'i	M,D,O
Argosy University, Los Angeles	M,D
Argosy University, Northern Virginia	M,D,O
Argosy University, Orange County	M,D,O
Argosy University, Phoenix	M,D
Argosy University, Seattle	M,D
Argosy University, Tampa	M,D
Argosy University, Twin Cities	M,D
Arizona State University at the Tempe campus	M,D
Arkansas State University	M,D,O
Ashland University	M
Ashworth College	M
Assumption College	M,O
Atlantis University	M
A.T. Still University	M,D,O
Avila University	M
Baker College Center for Graduate Studies–Online	M,D
Baldwin Wallace University	M
Barry University	M,O
Baruch College of the City University of New York	M*
Baylor University	M
Belhaven University (MS)	M
Bellevue University	M
Belmont University	M
Benedictine University	M
Binghamton University, State University of New York	M,D
Bluffton University	M
Boston University	M,D*
Bradley University	M,D,O
Brandeis University	M
Brandman University	M
Brenau University	M
Brigham Young University	M
Broadview University–West Jordan	M
Brooklyn College of the City University of New York	M
Bryan College	M
California Baptist University	M
California Coast University	M
California Intercontinental University	M,D
California State University, Bakersfield	M
California State University, Chico	M
California State University, East Bay	M
California State University, Fresno	M
California State University, Long Beach	M
California State University, Los Angeles	M,O
California State University, Northridge	M
California State University, San Bernardino	M
California University of Pennsylvania	M

*M—masters degree; D—doctorate; O—other advanced degree; *—Close-Up and/or Display*

Cambridge College	M
Capella University	M,D
Cardinal Stritch University	M
Carlow University	M
Carnegie Mellon University	M
Case Western Reserve University	M*
The Catholic University of America	M
Cedarville University	M,D
Central Michigan University	M,D,O
Champlain College	M
The Chicago School of Professional Psychology: Online	M
Clarion University of Pennsylvania	M
Clarkson University	M,O
Cleary University	M,O
Cleveland State University	M
The College at Brockport, State University of New York	M,O
College of Saint Elizabeth	M
College of Staten Island of the City University of New York	M
Colorado State University–Global Campus	M
Columbia Southern University	M
Columbia University	M*
Columbus State University	M
Concordia University Irvine	M*
Concordia University, St. Paul	M
Concordia University Wisconsin	M,D
Copenhagen Business School	M,D
Cornell University	M,D
Creighton University	M
Daemen College	M
Dalhousie University	M,D
Dallas Baptist University	M
Dartmouth College	M,D*
Davenport University	M
Delta State University	M,D
DeSales University	M
Des Moines University	M
Dominican College	M
Drew University	M,D,O
Duke University	M,O*
Duquesne University	M,D
D'Youville College	M,D,O
East Carolina University	M,O
Eastern Kentucky University	M
Eastern Mennonite University	M
Eastern Michigan University	M,O
Eastern University	M
East Tennessee State University	M,D,O
Elmhurst College	M
Elms College	M,O
Emory University	M,D
Excelsior College	M,O
Fairleigh Dickinson University, Florham Campus	M
Fairleigh Dickinson University, Metropolitan Campus	M
Felician University	M
Ferris State University	M
Florida Atlantic University	M
Florida Institute of Technology	M
Florida International University	M,D
Florida National University	M
Fordham University	M,D
Framingham State University	M
Franciscan Missionaries of Our Lady University	M,D
Francis Marion University	M
Franklin Pierce University	M,D,O
Friends University	M
George Mason University	M,D,O
The George Washington University	M,D,O
Georgia Institute of Technology	M
Georgia Southern University	M,D
Georgia Southern University–Armstrong Campus	M
Georgia State University	M,D,O
Goldey-Beacom College	M
Governors State University	M
Grambling State University	M
Grand Canyon University	M,D,O
Grand Valley State University	M
Grantham University	M
Gwynedd Mercy University	M
Harvard University	M,D*
Herzing University Online	M
Hilbert College	M
Hodges University	M
Hofstra University	M,O
Holy Family University	M
Husson University	M
IGlobal University	M
Independence University	M
Indiana Tech	M
Indiana University Bloomington	M,D
Indiana University Kokomo	M,O
Indiana University Northwest	M,O
Indiana University of Pennsylvania	M,D
Indiana University–Purdue University Indianapolis	M,D,O
Indiana University South Bend	M,O
Indiana Wesleyan University	M,O
Institute of Public Administration	M,O
Iona College	M,O
Johns Hopkins University	M,D*
Kean University	M
Keiser University	M
Kennesaw State University	M
Kent State University	M,D
King's College	M
King University	M
Lake Erie College	M
Lake Forest Graduate School of Management	M
Lakeland University	M
Lamar University	M
Lasell College	M,O
Lawrence Technological University	M,D,O
Lebanon Valley College	M
Lehigh University	M,O
Lenoir-Rhyne University	M
LeTourneau University	M
Lewis University	M
Lindenwood University	M,O
Lindenwood University–Belleville	M
Lipscomb University	M,O
Lock Haven University of Pennsylvania	M
Loma Linda University	M
London Metropolitan University	M,D
Long Island University–Brentwood Campus	M,O
Long Island University–Hudson	M,O
Long Island University–LIU Brooklyn	M,O
Long Island University–LIU Post	M,O
Louisiana State University Health Sciences Center	M,D
Louisiana State University in Shreveport	M
Loyola University Chicago	M
Madonna University	M
Marshall University	M
Marymount University	M
Maryville University of Saint Louis	M,O
Marywood University	M
McGill University	M,D,O
MCPHS University	M
Medical University of South Carolina	M,D
Meharry Medical College	M
Mercy College	M
Mercy College of Ohio	M
Midwestern State University	M,O
Milligan College	M,O
Milwaukee School of Engineering	M
Minnesota State University Moorhead	M,O
Misericordia University	M
Mississippi College	M
Missouri State University	M
Molloy College	M,D,O
Monroe College	M
Montana State University Billings	M
Moravian College	M
Mount Aloysius College	M
Mount St. Joseph University	D
Mount Saint Mary College	M
Mount Saint Mary's University (CA)	M,D,O
Mount St. Mary's University (MD)	M
National American University (TX)	M,D
National University	M,O
Nebraska Methodist College	M
New Charter University	M
New England College	M
New Jersey City University	M
New Jersey Institute of Technology	M,D
New York Medical College	M,D,O
New York University	M,D,O*
Niagara University	M
Northeast Ohio Medical University	M,D,O
Northwestern University	M,D
Ohio Christian University	M
Ohio Dominican University	M
The Ohio State University	M,D
Ohio University	M
Oklahoma Christian University	M
Oklahoma State University Center for Health Sciences	M
Oregon Health & Science University	M,O
Oregon State University	M,D
Our Lady of the Lake University	M
Pace University	M
Pacific University	M
Park University	M,O
Penn State Great Valley	M,O
Penn State Harrisburg	M,D,O
Penn State University Park	M,D*
Pennsylvania College of Health Sciences	M
Pfeiffer University	M
Philadelphia College of Osteopathic Medicine	M,D,O*
Point Loma Nazarene University	M
Point Park University	M
Portland State University	M,D,O
Post University	M
Purdue University Global	M,O
Queen's University at Kingston	M,D
Quinnipiac University	M
Regent University	M,D,O
Regis College (MA)	M,D,O
Regis University	M,D,O
Rhode Island College	M
Rice University	M
Robert Morris University Illinois	M
Roberts Wesleyan College	M
Rochester Institute of Technology	M,O
Rockhurst University	M,O
Roger Williams University	M
Rosalind Franklin University of Medicine and Science	M,O
Rush University	M,D
Rutgers University–Camden	M,O
Rutgers University–Newark	M,D,O
Rutgers University–New Brunswick	M,D,O
Sage Graduate School	M
Saginaw Valley State University	M
St. Ambrose University	M,D
St. Catherine University	M
St. Joseph's College, Long Island Campus	M
St. Joseph's College, New York	M
Saint Joseph's College of Maine	M
Saint Joseph's University	M,O*
Saint Leo University	M,D
Saint Louis University	M,D*
Saint Mary-of-the-Woods College	M
Saint Mary's University of Minnesota	M
St. Norbert College	M
Saint Peter's University	M
St. Thomas University	M,O
Saint Xavier University	M,O
Salve Regina University	M,O
Samford University	M
San Diego State University	M,D
San Francisco State University	M
Seton Hall University	M,D
Seton Hill University	M
Shenandoah University	M,D,O
Shippensburg University of Pennsylvania	M,D,O
Siena Heights University	M,O
Simmons College	M
South Carolina State University	M
Southeastern University (FL)	M,D
Southern Adventist University	M
Southern Illinois University Carbondale	M
Southern Nazarene University	M
Southern New Hampshire University	M,D,O
South University	M
South University (SC)	M
South University (GA)	M
South University (AL)	M
South University	M
Southwest Baptist University	M
Stevenson University	M
Stony Brook University, State University of New York	M,D,O
Stratford University (VA)	M,D
Strayer University	M
Suffolk University	M
Syracuse University	O*
Temple University	M*
Texas A&M University	M,D
Texas A&M University–Corpus Christi	M,D
Texas Christian University	M,O
Texas Health and Science University	M,D
Texas Southern University	M
Texas State University	M
Texas Tech University	M,D
Texas Tech University Health Sciences Center	M
Texas Woman's University	M
Thomas Jefferson University	M,D,O
Tiffin University	M
Towson University	M,O
Trevecca Nazarene University	M
Trident University International	M,D,O
Trinity University	M
Trinity Western University	M,O
Troy University	M
Tufts University	M,D,O*
Tulane University	M,D
Uniformed Services University of the Health Sciences	M,D*
Union Institute & University	M
Universidad de Ciencias Medicas	M,D,O
Universidad de Iberoamerica	M,D
Université de Montréal	M,O
University at Albany, State University of New York	M,D,O
University at Buffalo, the State University of New York	M,D
The University of Akron	M
The University of Alabama at Birmingham	M,D
The University of Alabama in Huntsville	M,D,O
University of Alaska Anchorage	M,D
University of Alberta	M,D
University of Arkansas for Medical Sciences	M,D,O
University of Arkansas–Fort Smith	M
University of Baltimore	M
The University of British Columbia	M,D
University of California, Berkeley	D
University of California, Irvine	M
University of California, Los Angeles	M,D*
University of California, San Diego	M*
University of Central Florida	M,O
University of Chicago	M,O
University of Colorado Denver	M
University of Connecticut	M,D*
University of Dallas	M,D
University of Denver	M,O
University of Detroit Mercy	M,D,O
University of Evansville	M
The University of Findlay	M,D
University of Florida	M,D
University of Holy Cross	M,D
University of Houston–Clear Lake	M
University of Illinois at Chicago	M,D
University of Illinois at Urbana–Champaign	M,D
The University of Iowa	M,D*
The University of Kansas	M,D
University of Kentucky	M
University of La Verne	M,D,O
University of Louisville	M
University of Management and Technology	M
University of Mary	M
University of Maryland, Baltimore County	M,D,O
University of Maryland, College Park	M,D
University of Maryland University College	M
University of Massachusetts Amherst	M,D*
University of Massachusetts Dartmouth	M
University of Memphis	M,D
University of Michigan	M,D*
University of Michigan–Flint	M,O
University of Minnesota, Twin Cities Campus	M,D
University of Missouri	M,D
University of Nebraska Medical Center	M,D
University of Nevada, Las Vegas	M
University of New England	M,D,O
University of New Haven	M,O*
University of New Mexico	M
University of New Orleans	M
University of North Alabama	M
The University of North Carolina at Chapel Hill	M,D
The University of North Carolina at Charlotte	M,D,O
The University of North Carolina at Pembroke	M
University of Northern Colorado	M
University of North Texas	M,D,O
University of North Texas Health Science Center at Fort Worth	M,D,O
University of Oklahoma	M,O*
University of Oklahoma Health Sciences Center	M,D
University of Ottawa	M
University of Pennsylvania	M,D*
University of Phoenix–Bay Area Campus	M,D
University of Phoenix–Central Valley Campus	M
University of Phoenix–Hawaii Campus	M
University of Phoenix–Houston Campus	M
University of Phoenix–Online Campus	M,D,O
University of Phoenix–Phoenix Campus	M,O
University of Phoenix–Sacramento Valley Campus	M
University of Phoenix–San Antonio Campus	M
University of Pikeville	M
University of Pittsburgh	M,D,O*
University of Portland	M
University of Puerto Rico–Medical Sciences Campus	M
University of Regina	M,D,O
University of Rhode Island	M,D,O*
University of Rochester	M,D*
University of St. Augustine for Health Sciences	M
University of Saint Francis (IN)	M
University of Saint Mary	M
University of St. Thomas (MN)	M
University of San Francisco	M
University of Saskatchewan	M
The University of Scranton	M
University of Sioux Falls	M
University of South Africa	M,D
University of South Carolina	M,D
University of South Dakota	M,D
University of Southern California	M,O*
University of Southern Indiana	M
University of Southern Maine	M
University of Southern Mississippi	M
University of South Florida	M,D,O*
The University of Tennessee	M
The University of Texas at Arlington	M
The University of Texas at Dallas	M,D
The University of Texas at El Paso	M,D,O
The University of Texas at Tyler	M
The University of Texas Health Science Center at Houston	M,D,O
The University of Texas Rio Grande Valley	M
University of the Incarnate Word	M,D
University of the Sciences	M,D
The University of Toledo	M,O
University of Toronto	M
University of Utah	M,D
University of Vermont	M,O
University of Virginia	M
University of Washington	M,D
The University of Western Ontario	M,D
University of West Florida	M
University of West Georgia	M,D,O
University of Wisconsin–Milwaukee	M,D*
University of Wisconsin–Oshkosh	M
University of Wyoming	M,D
Ursuline College	M
Utica College	M
Valdosta State University	M
Valparaiso University	M
Vanderbilt University	M*
Villanova University	M
Virginia Commonwealth University	M,D
Virginia International University	M,O
Viterbo University	M
Walden University	M,D,O
Walsh University	M
Washington Adventist University	M
Washington State University	M
Wayland Baptist University	M,D
Waynesburg University	M,D
Wayne State University	M,D
Weber State University	M
Webster University	M,D,O
West Chester University of Pennsylvania	M,O
West Coast University	M,D
Western Carolina University	M
Western Connecticut State University	M
Western Governors University	M
Western Kentucky University	M

Western Michigan University M,D,O
Widener University M
Wilkes University M
William Woods University M,D,O
Wilmington University M,D
Wilson College M
Wingate University M
Winston-Salem State University M
Worcester State University M
Xavier University M*
Yale University M,D
York College of Pennsylvania M
Youngstown State University M

HEALTH SERVICES RESEARCH

Albany College of Pharmacy and Health Sciences M,D
American University of Beirut M,D
Boston University M,D*
Brown University D
Clarkson University M
Dartmouth College M,D*
Emory University M,D
Florida Agricultural and Mechanical University M,D
George Mason University M,D,O
The George Washington University M,D,O
Lakehead University M
McMaster University M,D
Northwestern University D
Old Dominion University D
Penn State Hershey Medical Center M
Stanford University M,D
Texas A&M University M,D
Thomas Jefferson University M,D,O
The University of Alabama at Birmingham M,D
University of Alberta M,D
University of Arkansas for Medical Sciences M,D,O
University of Cincinnati M
University of Colorado Denver M,D
University of Florida M,D
University of Illinois at Chicago M,D
University of La Verne M
University of Maryland, Baltimore M,D
University of Massachusetts Medical School M,D
University of Minnesota, Twin Cities Campus M,D
University of Nebraska Medical Center M,D
University of New Brunswick Fredericton M
The University of North Carolina at Charlotte D
University of North Texas Health Science Center at Fort Worth M,D,O
University of Ottawa D,O
University of Pennsylvania M*
University of Pittsburgh M*
University of Puerto Rico–Medical Sciences Campus M
University of Rochester D*
University of Southern California D*
The University of Tennessee Health Science Center M,D
University of Utah M,D
University of Virginia M
University of Washington M,D
Virginia Commonwealth University D
Wake Forest University M
Washington University in St. Louis M,O
Wayne State University M,D
Weill Cornell Medicine M

HIGHER EDUCATION

Abilene Christian University M
Alliant International University–San Diego M,D,O
Alliant International University–San Francisco M,D,O
Andrews University M,D,O
Angelo State University M
Appalachian State University M,O
Argosy University, Atlanta M,D,O
Argosy University, Chicago M,D,O
Argosy University, Hawai`i M,D
Argosy University, Los Angeles M,D
Argosy University, Northern Virginia M,D,O
Argosy University, Orange County M,D
Argosy University, Phoenix M,D,O
Argosy University, Seattle M,D
Argosy University, Tampa M,D,O
Argosy University, Twin Cities M,D,O
Arizona State University at the Tempe campus M
Auburn University M,D,O*
Azusa Pacific University M,D*
Ball State University M,D
Barry University M,D
Baruch College of the City University of New York M*
Bay Path University M
Bellarmine University M,D,O
Benedictine University D
Boston College M,D
Bowling Green State University D
California Baptist University M
California Lutheran University M,D
California State University, Long Beach M,D
California State University, Sacramento M,D,O
Capella University M,D
Cardinal Stritch University M,D
Central Michigan University M,D,O
Central Washington University M
Chicago State University M,D
Claremont Graduate University M,D,O
Clemson University M,D,O
Cleveland State University D
College of Saint Elizabeth M,D,O
The College of Saint Rose M,O
Colorado State University M,D
Columbia College (SC) M
Columbus State University M,D,O
Concordia University (United States) M,D
Dallas Baptist University M,D
Delta State University D
DePaul University M,D
DeVry University–Folsom Campus M
Drexel University M,D*
East Carolina University M,D
Eastern Kentucky University M
Eastern Michigan University M,D,O
Fitchburg State University M,O
Florida Atlantic University M,D,O
Florida International University M,D,O
Florida State University M,D,O
Geneva College M
George Mason University M,D,O
The George Washington University M,D,O
Georgia Southern University M,D
Grambling State University M,D,O
Grand Valley State University M
Hardin-Simmons University D
Hofstra University M,D,O
Houston Baptist University M,D
Illinois State University M,D
Indiana State University M,D,O
Indiana University Bloomington M,D,O
Indiana University of Pennsylvania M
Indiana Wesleyan University M
Inter American University of Puerto Rico, Metropolitan Campus M
Iowa State University of Science and Technology M,D
Jackson State University M,D,O
James Madison University M
Johnson University M,D,O
Kent State University M,D,O
Lee University M,O
Lewis University M
Lincoln Memorial University M,D,O
Lincoln University (MO) M
London Metropolitan University M,D
Louisiana State University and Agricultural & Mechanical College M,D,O
Louisiana Tech University M,D,O
Loyola Marymount University M
Loyola University Chicago M,D
Maryville University of Saint Louis M,D
Marywood University M,D
McKendree University M,D,O
Mercer University M,D,O
Mercer University M,D,O
Mercyhurst University M,O
Merrimack College M,O
Messiah College M
Michigan State University M,D,O
Minnesota State University Mankato M
Mississippi College M,D,O
Mississippi State University M,D,O
Missouri State University M
Montana State University M,D,O
Morehead State University M,O
Morgan State University M,D
National American University (TX) M,D
National University M,O
New England College M,D
New Mexico State University M,D
New York University M,D*
North Carolina State University M,D
North Dakota State University O*
Northeastern University M,D
Northern Arizona University M,D,O
Northern Illinois University M,D
Northwest Missouri State University M,D,O
Oakland University M,D,O
Ohio University M,D
Oklahoma State University M,D
Old Dominion University M,D,O
Oral Roberts University M,D
Oregon State University M,D
Penn State University Park M,D,O*
Phillips Theological Seminary M,D
Plymouth State University D,O
Purdue University M,D,O
Purdue University Global M
Regent University M,D,O
Regis College (MA) M,D
Rider University M
Robert Morris University M,D,O
Robert Morris University Illinois M
Rowan University M
St. Cloud State University D
Saint Louis University M,D,O*
Saint Peter's University M,D
Salem State University M
Sam Houston State University M,D
San Diego State University M
Seton Hall University D
Shippensburg University of Pennsylvania M
Siena Heights University M,O
Southeast Missouri State University M,D,O
Southern Arkansas University–Magnolia M
Southern Illinois University Carbondale M
Southern Illinois University Edwardsville M
Southern New Hampshire University M,D,O
Southwestern College (KS) M,D
Springfield College M,D,O
Stony Brook University, State University of New York M,O
Syracuse University M,D*
Taylor University M
Teachers College, Columbia University M,D
Texas A&M University–Commerce M,D,O
Texas Southern University M,D
Texas State University M
Texas Tech University M,D
Tiffin University M
Trident University International M,D
Union University M,D,O
Universidad Central del Este M
Université de Sherbrooke M,O
University at Albany, State University of New York M,D,O
University at Buffalo, the State University of New York M,D,O
The University of Akron M
The University of Alabama M,D
The University of Arizona M,D
University of Arkansas M,D,O
University of Arkansas at Little Rock M,D
The University of British Columbia M,D
University of California, Riverside M,D,O
University of Central Florida M,D,O
University of Connecticut M*
University of Delaware M,D,O*
University of Denver M,D,O
University of Florida M,D,O
University of Georgia M,D
University of Houston M,D
University of Houston–Victoria M,O
University of Illinois at Springfield M,O
The University of Iowa M,D*
The University of Kansas M,D
University of Kentucky M,D
University of La Verne M
University of Louisville M,D,O
University of Lynchburg M
University of Maine M,D,O
University of Manitoba M
University of Mary Hardin-Baylor M,D
University of Massachusetts Amherst M,D,O*
University of Massachusetts Boston D
University of Memphis M,D,O
University of Miami M,D,O*
University of Minnesota, Twin Cities Campus M,D
University of Mississippi M,D,O
University of Missouri M,D,O
University of Missouri–Kansas City M,D,O
University of Missouri–St. Louis M,O
University of Nevada, Las Vegas M,D,O
University of New Hampshire O
University of New Mexico O
University of New Orleans M,D
University of North Alabama M
The University of North Carolina at Greensboro D
The University of North Carolina Wilmington M,D
University of Northern Colorado M,D
University of Northern Iowa M
University of North Georgia D
University of North Texas M,D,O
University of Oklahoma M,D*
University of Pennsylvania M,D*
University of Phoenix–Bay Area Campus M,D,O
University of Phoenix–Online Campus D,O
University of Pittsburgh M,D*
University of Puerto Rico–Mayagüez M
University of Rochester M,D*
University of St. Thomas (MN) M,O
University of San Diego M,D,O
University of South Carolina M
University of South Dakota M,D,O
University of Southern California D*
University of Southern Maine M,O
University of Southern Mississippi M,D,O
University of South Florida M,D,O*
The University of Texas at Arlington M,D
The University of Texas at San Antonio M,D
The University of Toledo M,D,O
University of Utah M,D
University of Vermont M
University of Virginia M,D,O
University of Washington M,D
The University of West Alabama M
University of Wisconsin–La Crosse M,D
University of Wisconsin–Madison M,D,O
University of Wisconsin–Milwaukee M,O*
Upper Iowa University M,O
Vanderbilt University M,D*
Wagner College M
Walden University M,D,O
Walsh University M
Wayland Baptist University M
West Chester University of Pennsylvania M,O
Western Illinois University M
Western Kentucky University M
Western Michigan University M,D
Western Washington University M
West Virginia University M,D
William Paterson University of New Jersey M,O
Wilmington University M,D

HISPANIC AND LATIN AMERICAN LANGUAGES

Boston University M,D*
Brigham Young University M
California State University, San Marcos M
Cornell University D
The Graduate Center, City University of New York D
Indiana University Bloomington M,D
Indiana University of Pennsylvania M
Michigan State University M,D
Queens College of the City University of New York M
Stony Brook University, State University of New York M,D
Université de Montréal M,D
University of California, Berkeley D
University of California, Los Angeles D*
University of California, Santa Barbara M,D
University of Colorado Boulder M,D
University of Illinois at Chicago M,D
University of Massachusetts Amherst M,D*
University of Minnesota, Twin Cities Campus M,D
The University of North Carolina at Greensboro M,O
The University of Texas at Austin M,D
University of Washington M

HISPANIC STUDIES

Brown University D
California State University, Los Angeles M
California State University, Northridge M
California State University, San Marcos M
The Catholic University of America M,D
The Citadel, The Military College of South Carolina O
Columbia University M,D*
La Salle University M,O
Louisiana State University and Agricultural & Mechanical College M
McGill University M,D
Michigan State University M,D
Oregon State University M
Pontifical Catholic University of Puerto Rico M,O
Queen's University at Kingston M
St. Thomas University M,O
San Jose State University M
Texas A&M University–Kingsville D
University of Alberta M,D
The University of British Columbia M,D
University of California, Riverside M,D
University of California, Santa Barbara M,D
University of Houston M,D
University of Illinois at Chicago M,D
University of Kentucky M,D
University of Nevada, Las Vegas M,O
The University of North Carolina at Greensboro M,O
The University of North Carolina Wilmington M,O
University of Puerto Rico–Mayagüez M
University of Puerto Rico–Río Piedras M,D
The University of Texas at Austin M
University of Victoria M
Villanova University M

HISTORIC PRESERVATION

The American University of Rome M
Arkansas State University M,D
Ball State University M
Boston Architectural College M
Boston University M*
Buffalo State College, State University of New York M,O
Clemson University M,O
Cleveland State University M,O
College of Charleston M
Columbia University M,D,O*
Cornell University M,D
Delaware State University M
Eastern Michigan University M,O
The George Washington University M,O
Georgia State University M,D
Goucher College M
Morgan State University M,D
New York University *
Penn State Harrisburg M,D,O
Plymouth State University M,O
Pratt Institute M*
Roger Williams University M,O
Rutgers University–New Brunswick M,D,O
St. Cloud State University M,O
Savannah College of Art and Design M
School of the Art Institute of Chicago M
Southeast Missouri State University M,O
Universidad Nacional Pedro Henriquez Urena M
University at Buffalo, the State University of New York M,D,O

*M—masters degree; D—doctorate; O—other advanced degree; *—Close-Up and/or Display*

University of California, Los Angeles	M*
University of Colorado Denver	M
University of Delaware	M,D*
University of Florida	M,D
University of Georgia	M
University of Hawaii at Manoa	O
The University of Kansas	M,D,O
University of Kentucky	M
University of Maryland, College Park	M,O
University of Massachusetts Amherst	M*
University of New Mexico	O
University of North Alabama	M
The University of North Carolina at Greensboro	M,O
University of Oregon	M
University of Pennsylvania	M,O*
University of Rochester	M*
University of South Carolina	M,O
The University of Texas at Austin	M
University of Vermont	M
University of Washington	O
Ursuline College	M

HISTORY

Adams State University	M
Alabama State University	M
American Public University System	M,D
American University	M,D
American University of Beirut	M,D
Appalachian State University	M
Arizona State University at the Tempe campus	M,D,O
Arkansas State University	M,O
Arkansas Tech University	M
Ashland University	M
Auburn University	M,D,O*
Ball State University	M
Bard College	M
Baylor University	M,D
Binghamton University, State University of New York	M,D
Bob Jones University	M,D,O
Boise State University	M
Boston College	M,D
Boston University	M,D*
Bowling Green State University	M,D
Brandeis University	M,D
Brock University	M
Brooklyn College of the City University of New York	M
Brown University	M,D
Buffalo State College, State University of New York	M
Butler University	M
Cabrini University	M,D
California Polytechnic State University, San Luis Obispo	M*
California State Polytechnic University, Pomona	M
California State University, Bakersfield	M
California State University, Chico	M
California State University, East Bay	M
California State University, Fresno	M
California State University, Fullerton	M
California State University, Long Beach	M
California State University, Los Angeles	M
California State University, Northridge	M
California State University, San Marcos	M
California State University, Stanislaus	M
Carleton University	M,D
Carnegie Mellon University	D
Case Western Reserve University	M,D*
The Catholic University of America	M,D
Central Connecticut State University	M,O
Central European University	M,D
Central Michigan University	M,O
Central Washington University	M
Centro de Estudios Avanzados de Puerto Rico y el Caribe	M,D
Chicago State University	M
The Citadel, The Military College of South Carolina	M,O
City College of the City University of New York	M
Claremont Graduate University	M,D,O
Clark University	D
Clayton State University	M
Clemson University	M
Cleveland State University	M
The College at Brockport, State University of New York	M
College of Charleston	M
College of Staten Island of the City University of New York	M
The College of William and Mary	M,D*
Colorado State University	M
Columbia University	M,D*
Columbus State University	M,O
Concordia University (Canada)	M,D
Converse College	M
Cornell University	M,D
Dalhousie University	M,D
DePaul University	M
Dominican University of California	M
Drew University	M,D,O
Duke University	M,D*
Duquesne University	M
East Carolina University	M
Eastern Illinois University	M
Eastern Kentucky University	M
Eastern Michigan University	M
Eastern Washington University	M
East Stroudsburg University of Pennsylvania	M
East Tennessee State University	M,O
Edinboro University of Pennsylvania	M
Emory & Henry College	M,D
Emory University	D
Emporia State University	M
Fairleigh Dickinson University, Metropolitan Campus	M
Fitchburg State University	M
Florida Agricultural and Mechanical University	M
Florida Atlantic University	M
Florida Gulf Coast University	M
Florida International University	M,D
Florida State University	M,D
Fordham University	M,D
Fort Hays State University	M
George Mason University	M,D,O
Georgetown University	M,D
The George Washington University	M,D
Georgia Southern University	M,O
Georgia Southern University–Armstrong Campus	M
Georgia State University	M,D
The Graduate Center, City University of New York	D
Hardin-Simmons University	M
Harvard University	D*
Howard University	M,D
Hunter College of the City University of New York	M
Idaho State University	M
Illinois State University	M
Indiana State University	M
Indiana University Bloomington	M,D
Indiana University of Pennsylvania	M
Indiana University–Purdue University Indianapolis	M
Inter American University of Puerto Rico, Barranquitas Campus	M
Inter American University of Puerto Rico, Metropolitan Campus	M,D
Iona College	M
Iowa State University of Science and Technology	M,D
Jackson State University	M
Jacksonville State University	M
James Madison University	M
Johns Hopkins University	D*
Kansas State University	M,D
Kent State University	M,D
Lake Forest College	M
Lakehead University	M
Lamar University	M
La Salle University	M,O
Laurentian University	M
Lee University	M,O
Lehigh University	M,D
Lehman College of the City University of New York	M
Liberty University	M
Lincoln University (MO)	M
Long Island University–LIU Post	M,O
Louisiana State University and Agricultural & Mechanical College	M,D
Louisiana Tech University	M,D,O
Loyola University Chicago	M,D
Marquette University	M,D
Marshall University	M,O
McGill University	M,D
McMaster University	M,D
Memorial University of Newfoundland	M,D
Miami University	M
Michigan State University	M,D
Middle Tennessee State University	M
Midwestern State University	M
Millersville University of Pennsylvania	M
Minnesota State University Mankato	M
Mississippi College	M,O
Mississippi State University	M,O
Missouri State University	M,O
Monmouth University	M*
Montana State University	M,D
Morgan State University	M,D
Murray State University	M
Nebraska Wesleyan University	M
New Jersey Institute of Technology	M,D,O
New Mexico Highlands University	M
New Mexico State University	M
The New School	M,D
New York University	M,D,O*
North Carolina Central University	M
North Carolina State University	M
North Dakota State University	M,D*
Northeastern Illinois University	M
Northeastern University	M,D
Northern Arizona University	M
Northern Illinois University	M,D
Northwestern University	M,D
Norwich University	M
Oakland University	M
The Ohio State University	M,D
Ohio University	M,D
Oklahoma State University	M,D
Old Dominion University	M
Open University	M
Penn State University Park	M,D*
Pittsburg State University	M
Pontifical Catholic University of Puerto Rico	M
Portland State University	M
Princeton University	D
Providence College	M
Purdue University	M,D
Purdue University Northwest	M
Queens College of the City University of New York	M
Rhode Island College	M
Rice University	M,D
Roosevelt University	M
Rowan University	M,O
Rutgers University–Camden	M
Rutgers University–Newark	M
Rutgers University–New Brunswick	D
St. Cloud State University	M
St. John's University (NY)	M,D
Saint Louis University	M,D*
Saint Mary's University (Canada)	M
Salem State University	M
Salisbury University	M
Sam Houston State University	M
San Diego State University	M
San Francisco State University	M
San Jose State University	M
Sarah Lawrence College	M
Seton Hall University	M
Shippensburg University of Pennsylvania	M
Simmons College	M
Simon Fraser University	M,D
Slippery Rock University of Pennsylvania	M
Smith College	M
Sonoma State University	M
Southeastern Louisiana University	M
Southeast Missouri State University	M,O
Southern Connecticut State University	M
Southern Illinois University Carbondale	M,D
Southern Illinois University Edwardsville	M
Southern Methodist University	M,D
Southern New Hampshire University	M
Southern University and Agricultural and Mechanical College	M
Southwestern Assemblies of God University	M
Stanford University	M,D
State University of New York at Oswego	M
State University of New York College at Cortland	M
Stephen F. Austin State University	M
Stony Brook University, State University of New York	M,D
Sul Ross State University	M
Syracuse University	M,D*
Tarleton State University	M
Temple University	M,D*
Texas A&M International University	M
Texas A&M University	M,D
Texas A&M University–Central Texas	M,O
Texas A&M University–Commerce	M,D,O
Texas A&M University–Corpus Christi	M
Texas Christian University	M,D
Texas Southern University	M
Texas State University	M
Texas Tech University	M,D
Texas Woman's University	M
Trinity Western University	M
Troy University	M
Tufts University	M,D*
Tulane University	M,D
Union Institute & University	M
Université de Moncton	M
Université de Montréal	M,D
Université de Sherbrooke	M
Université du Québec à Montréal	M,D
Université Laval	M,D
University at Albany, State University of New York	M,D,O
University at Buffalo, the State University of New York	M,D,O
The University of Akron	M,D
The University of Alabama	M,D
The University of Alabama at Birmingham	M
The University of Alabama in Huntsville	M
University of Alaska Fairbanks	M
University of Alberta	M,D
The University of Arizona	M,D,O
University of Arkansas	M,D
The University of British Columbia	M,D
University of Calgary	M,D
University of California, Berkeley	M,D
University of California, Davis	M,D
University of California, Irvine	M,D
University of California, Los Angeles	M,D*
University of California, Riverside	M,D
University of California, San Diego	M,D*
University of California, Santa Barbara	D
University of California, Santa Cruz	M,D*
University of Central Arkansas	M
University of Central Florida	M
University of Central Missouri	M,D,O
University of Central Oklahoma	M
University of Chicago	D
University of Cincinnati	M,D
University of Colorado Boulder	M,D
University of Colorado Colorado Springs	M
University of Colorado Denver	M
University of Connecticut	M,D*
University of Delaware	M,D*
University of Denver	M,O
University of Florida	M,D
University of Georgia	M,D
University of Guelph	M,D
University of Hawaii at Manoa	M,D
University of Houston	M,D
University of Houston–Clear Lake	M
University of Idaho	M,D
University of Illinois at Chicago	M,D
University of Illinois at Springfield	M
University of Illinois at Urbana–Champaign	M,D
University of Indianapolis	M
The University of Iowa	M,D*
The University of Kansas	M,D
University of Kentucky	M,D
University of Louisiana at Lafayette	M,D
University of Louisiana at Monroe	M
University of Louisville	M,O
University of Maine	M,D
The University of Manchester	D
University of Manitoba	M,D
University of Maryland, Baltimore County	M
University of Maryland, College Park	M,D
University of Massachusetts Amherst	M,D*
University of Massachusetts Boston	M
University of Memphis	M,D
University of Miami	M,D*
University of Michigan	D,O*
University of Minnesota, Twin Cities Campus	M,D
University of Mississippi	M,D
University of Missouri	M,D
University of Missouri–Kansas City	M,D
University of Missouri–St. Louis	M,O
University of Montana	M,D
University of Nebraska at Kearney	M
University of Nebraska at Omaha	M
University of Nebraska–Lincoln	M,D
University of Nevada, Las Vegas	M,D
University of Nevada, Reno	M,D
University of New Brunswick Fredericton	M,D
University of New Hampshire	M,D
University of New Mexico	M,D
University of New Orleans	M
University of North Alabama	M
The University of North Carolina at Chapel Hill	M,D
The University of North Carolina at Charlotte	M
The University of North Carolina at Greensboro	M,D,O
The University of North Carolina Wilmington	M
University of North Dakota	M,D
University of Northern British Columbia	M,D,O
University of Northern Colorado	M
University of Northern Iowa	M
University of North Florida	M
University of North Georgia	M
University of North Texas	M,D,O
University of Notre Dame	M,D
University of Oklahoma	M,D*
University of Oregon	M,D
University of Ottawa	M,D
University of Pennsylvania	M,D*
University of Pittsburgh	M,D*
University of Puerto Rico–Río Piedras	M,D
University of Regina	M
University of Rhode Island	M*
University of Rochester	M,D*
University of Saskatchewan	M,D
University of South Africa	M,D
University of South Alabama	M
University of South Carolina	M,D,O
University of South Dakota	M
University of Southern California	D*
University of Southern Mississippi	M,D
University of South Florida	M,D*
The University of Tennessee	M,D
The University of Texas at Arlington	M,D
The University of Texas at Austin	M,D
The University of Texas at Dallas	M,D
The University of Texas at El Paso	M,D
The University of Texas at San Antonio	M
The University of Texas at Tyler	M
The University of Texas of the Permian Basin	M
The University of Texas Rio Grande Valley	M
The University of Toledo	M,D
University of Toronto	M,D
The University of Tulsa	M
University of Utah	M,D
University of Vermont	M
University of Victoria	M,D
University of Virginia	M,D
University of Washington	M,D
University of Waterloo	M,D
The University of West Alabama	M
The University of Western Ontario	M,D
University of West Florida	M
University of West Georgia	M,O
University of Windsor	M
The University of Winnipeg	M
University of Wisconsin–Eau Claire	M
University of Wisconsin–Madison	M,D
University of Wisconsin–Milwaukee	M,D*
University of Wyoming	M
Utah State University	M
Vanderbilt University	M,D*

- Villanova University M
- Virginia Commonwealth University M
- Washington State University M,D
- Washington University in St. Louis D
- Wayland Baptist University M
- Wayne State University M,D,O
- West Chester University of Pennsylvania M
- Western Carolina University M
- Western Connecticut State University M
- Western Illinois University M
- Western Kentucky University M
- Western Michigan University M,D
- Western Washington University M
- West Texas A&M University M
- West Virginia University M,D
- Wichita State University M
- Wilfrid Laurier University M,D
- William Paterson University of New Jersey M,D,O
- Winthrop University M
- Worcester State University M
- Wright State University M
- Yale University M,D
- York University M,D
- Youngstown State University M

HISTORY OF MEDICINE
- The College at Brockport, State University of New York M,O
- McGill University M,D
- Rutgers University–New Brunswick D
- The University of Manchester M,D
- University of Minnesota, Twin Cities Campus M,D
- Yale University M,D

HISTORY OF SCIENCE AND TECHNOLOGY
- Arizona State University at the Tempe campus M,D
- Brown University D
- Carnegie Mellon University D
- Cornell University M,D
- Drexel University M*
- Georgia Institute of Technology M,D
- Harvard University M,D*
- Indiana University Bloomington M,D
- Johns Hopkins University M,D*
- Massachusetts Institute of Technology D
- Oregon State University M,D
- Princeton University D
- Rensselaer Polytechnic Institute M,D
- Rutgers University–New Brunswick D
- University of California, Berkeley D
- University of California, San Diego D*
- University of California, San Francisco M,D
- University of Delaware M,D*
- The University of Manchester M,D
- University of Minnesota, Twin Cities Campus M,D
- University of Notre Dame M,D
- University of Oklahoma M,D*
- University of Pennsylvania M,D*
- University of Pittsburgh D*
- University of Toronto M,D
- University of Wisconsin–Madison M,D
- Yale University M,D

HIV/AIDS NURSING
- University of Delaware M,O*

HOLOCAUST AND GENOCIDE STUDIES
- Chapman University M*
- Clark University D
- College of Saint Elizabeth M,O
- Gratz College M,D
- Kean University M
- Stockton University M
- Texas A&M University–Commerce M,D,O
- West Chester University of Pennsylvania M,O

HOME ECONOMICS EDUCATION
- Alabama Agricultural and Mechanical University M,O
- Central Washington University M
- Eastern Kentucky University M
- Louisiana State University and Agricultural & Mechanical College M,D
- Montana State University M
- Purdue University M,D,O
- South Carolina State University M
- Texas Tech University M,D
- The University of British Columbia M,D
- University of Nebraska–Lincoln M,D
- Utah State University M
- Wayne State College M

HOMELAND SECURITY
- Angelo State University M
- Arizona State University at the Tempe campus M,D
- Auburn University at Montgomery M
- Aurora University M
- Ball State University M,O
- Capella University M
- The Citadel, The Military College of South Carolina M,O
- Columbus State University M
- Drexel University M*
- Endicott College M,O
- Excelsior College M
- Fairleigh Dickinson University, Metropolitan Campus M
- Georgian Court University M,O
- Henley-Putnam School of Strategic Security M
- Indiana University–Purdue University Indianapolis M,O
- Johns Hopkins University M,O*
- Keiser University M
- Lasell College M,O
- Liberty University M
- London Metropolitan University M,D
- Long Island University–Riverhead M,O
- Missouri State University M,O
- Monmouth University M,O*
- National Defense University M,O
- The National Graduate School of Quality Management M,D
- National University M
- Naval Postgraduate School M,D
- Nichols College M
- Northeastern University M,D
- Northwestern State University of Louisiana M
- Notre Dame College (OH) M,O
- Pace University M
- Penn State Harrisburg M,D,O
- Post University M
- Regent University M
- Rider University M
- St. John's University (NY) M
- St. Mary's University (United States) M,O
- Salve Regina University M,O
- Sam Houston State University M
- Southern Illinois University Carbondale M
- Texas A&M University M,O
- Texas A&M University–Commerce M,D,O
- Thomas Edison State University M
- Tiffin University M
- Towson University M,O
- Tulane University M
- University at Albany, State University of New York M,D,O
- University of Alaska Fairbanks M
- University of Central Florida M,O
- University of Colorado Denver M,D
- University of Denver M,D,O
- University of Illinois at Springfield M,O
- University of Management and Technology M
- University of Oklahoma Health Sciences Center M
- University of Phoenix–Online Campus M
- University of Phoenix–Phoenix Campus M
- University of Southern California M,O*
- University of the District of Columbia M
- Upper Iowa University M
- Virginia Commonwealth University M,O
- Walden University M,D,O
- Wayland Baptist University M
- Western Kentucky University M
- Western Michigan University Thomas M. Cooley Law School M,D
- Wilmington University M,D

HORTICULTURE
- Auburn University M,D*
- Colorado State University M,D
- Cornell University M,D
- Dalhousie University M
- Iowa State University of Science and Technology M,D
- Kansas State University M,D
- Michigan State University M,D
- Mississippi State University M,D
- New Mexico State University M,D
- North Carolina State University M,D,O
- North Dakota State University M,D*
- The Ohio State University M,D
- Oklahoma State University M,D
- Oregon State University M,D
- Penn State University Park M,D*
- Purdue University M,D
- Rutgers University–New Brunswick M,D
- Texas A&M University M,D
- Texas A&M University–Kingsville M,D
- Texas Tech University M,D
- Universidad Nacional Pedro Henriquez Urena M
- University of Arkansas M
- University of California, Davis M
- University of Delaware M*
- University of Florida M,D
- University of Georgia M,D
- University of Guelph M,D
- University of Hawaii at Manoa M,D
- University of Maine M,D,O
- University of Manitoba M,D
- University of Maryland, College Park M,D
- University of Nebraska–Lincoln M,D
- University of Puerto Rico–Mayagüez M
- University of South Africa M,D
- University of Vermont M,D,O
- University of Washington M,D
- University of Wisconsin–Madison M,D
- Utah State University M,D
- Virginia Polytechnic Institute and State University M,D
- Washington State University M,D
- West Virginia University M,D

HOSPICE NURSING
- Central Connecticut State University M
- Madonna University M

HOSPITALITY MANAGEMENT
- Alabama Agricultural and Mechanical University M
- American International College M,D,O
- Boston University M*
- California State Polytechnic University, Pomona M
- California State University, Northridge M,O
- Cornell University M,D
- DePaul University M,D
- Drexel University M*
- East Carolina University M,O
- Eastern Michigan University O
- Ecole Hôtelière de Lausanne M
- ESSEC Business School M,D
- Fairleigh Dickinson University, Florham Campus M
- Fairleigh Dickinson University, Metropolitan Campus M
- Florida International University M
- Georgetown University M,D
- The George Washington University M,O
- Glion Institute of Higher Education M
- Husson University M
- IGlobal University M
- Johnson & Wales University M
- Kansas State University M,D
- Kent State University M
- Lasell College M,O
- Les Roches International School of Hotel Management M
- Lynn University M
- Michigan State University M
- Monroe College M
- Morgan State University M
- New York University M,D*
- Oklahoma State University M,D
- Penn State University Park M,D*
- Pontificia Universidad Catolica Madre y Maestra M
- Purdue University M,D
- Rochester Institute of Technology M
- Roosevelt University M
- San Francisco State University M
- San Ignacio University M
- Schiller International University (United States) M
- South University (GA) M
- Stratford University (MD) M
- Strayer University M
- Syracuse University M,O*
- Temple University M,D*
- Texas Tech University M,D
- Thomas Edison State University M
- The University of Alabama M
- University of Central Florida M,D,O
- University of Delaware M*
- The University of Findlay M,D
- University of Guelph M
- University of Houston M
- University of Kentucky M
- University of Louisiana at Lafayette M
- University of Massachusetts Amherst M,D*
- University of Memphis M,O
- University of Mississippi M,D
- University of Missouri M,D
- University of Nevada, Las Vegas M,D
- University of New Orleans M
- University of North Texas M,D,O
- University of South Carolina M
- University of South Florida Sarasota-Manatee M
- The University of Tennessee M
- University of the Pacific M
- Virginia International University M,O

HUMAN-COMPUTER INTERACTION
- Brandeis University M
- Carnegie Mellon University M,D
- Cornell University M,D
- Dalhousie University M,D
- DePaul University M,D
- Florida Institute of Technology M
- Georgia Institute of Technology M
- Harrisburg University of Science and Technology M
- Indiana University Bloomington M,D
- Indiana University–Purdue University Indianapolis M,D
- Iowa State University of Science and Technology M,D
- Rochester Institute of Technology M
- State University of New York at Oswego M
- Tufts University O*
- University of Baltimore M
- University of Illinois at Urbana–Champaign M,D,O
- University of Rochester M,D*
- University of Washington M,D,O

HUMAN DEVELOPMENT
- Alabama Agricultural and Mechanical University M
- Argosy University, Chicago D
- Arizona State University at the Tempe campus M,D
- Auburn University M,D*
- Ball State University M,D,O
- Bradley University M
- Brigham Young University M,D
- Brock University M,D
- California State University, Fresno M,D
- Central Michigan University M,O
- Claremont Graduate University M,D,O
- Colorado State University M,D
- Cornell University M,D
- Duke University D*
- Eastern Illinois University M
- Erikson Institute M,O
- Fielding Graduate University M,D,O
- Florida State University M,D
- Georgetown University M,D
- The George Washington University M
- Georgia State University M,D,O
- Harvard University M*
- Hofstra University M,D,O
- Hood College M,O*
- Iowa State University of Science and Technology M,D
- Kansas State University M,D,O
- Kent State University M,D
- Laurentian University M
- Lindsey Wilson College M,D
- Marywood University D
- Mississippi State University M,D
- Montana State University M
- Murray State University M,D,O
- National Louis University M,D,O
- New York University M,D,O*
- Northern Arizona University O
- Northwestern University D
- The Ohio State University M,D
- Oregon State University M,D
- Pacific Oaks College M
- Penn State University Park M,D*
- Purdue University M,D
- St. Lawrence University M,O
- Saint Mary's University of Minnesota M
- Syracuse University M,D*
- Texas A&M University–Corpus Christi M,D
- Texas Tech University M,D
- Tufts University M,D*
- The University of Alabama M
- The University of Arizona M,D,O
- The University of British Columbia M,D,O
- University of California, Berkeley M,D
- University of California, Davis D
- University of Central Oklahoma M
- University of Chicago D
- University of Colorado Denver M,D
- University of Connecticut M,D*
- University of Dayton M,O
- University of Delaware M,D*
- University of Guelph M,D
- University of Illinois at Chicago M,D
- University of Illinois at Springfield M
- University of Illinois at Urbana–Champaign M,D
- University of Maine M,D,O
- University of Maryland, College Park M,D
- University of Missouri M,D
- University of Nebraska–Lincoln M,D,O
- University of Nevada, Reno M
- University of New Mexico M,D
- The University of North Carolina at Greensboro M,D
- University of North Texas M,D,O
- University of Pennsylvania M,D*
- University of Rhode Island M*
- University of Rochester M,D*
- University of St. Thomas (MN) D
- University of South Africa M,D
- University of South Dakota M,D,O
- The University of Texas at Austin M,D
- University of Utah M
- University of Victoria M,D
- University of Washington M,D
- University of Wisconsin–Madison M,D
- University of Wisconsin–Stevens Point M,O
- Utah State University M,D
- Vanderbilt University M*
- Washington State University D

HUMAN GENETICS
- Baylor College of Medicine D
- Case Western Reserve University M,D*
- Emory University M
- Louisiana State University Health Sciences Center D
- McGill University M,D
- Memorial University of Newfoundland M,D
- Sarah Lawrence College M
- Thomas Jefferson University M
- Tulane University M
- University of California, Los Angeles M,D*
- University of Chicago D
- University of Manitoba M,D
- University of Maryland, Baltimore M,D
- University of Michigan M,D*
- University of Pennsylvania M*
- University of Pittsburgh M,D,O*
- University of Utah M,D
- Vanderbilt University D*
- Virginia Commonwealth University M,D
- Washington University in St. Louis D

*M—masters degree; D—doctorate; O—other advanced degree; *—Close-Up and/or Display*

HUMANITIES

Adams State University	M
The American University in Cairo	M,O
Antioch University New England	M
Arcadia University	M
Brandeis University	M
Brigham Young University	M
California Institute of Integral Studies	M,D,O
California State University, Dominguez Hills	M
Central Michigan University	M
Claremont Graduate University	M,D,O
The Colorado College	M
Colorado School of Mines	O
Concordia University (Canada)	D
Dominican University of California	M
Duke University	M*
Faulkner University	M,D
Georgetown University	M,D
Harrison Middleton University	M,D
Hofstra University	M,D,O
Hollins University	M
Hood College	M*
Illinois Institute of Technology	M,D
Instituto Tecnologico de Santo Domingo	M,O
Instituto Tecnológico y de Estudios Superiores de Monterrey, Campus Central de Veracruz	M
Instituto Tecnológico y de Estudios Superiores de Monterrey, Campus Ciudad de México	M,D
Instituto Tecnológico y de Estudios Superiores de Monterrey, Campus Ciudad Juárez	M
Instituto Tecnológico y de Estudios Superiores de Monterrey, Campus Estado de México	M,D
Instituto Tecnológico y de Estudios Superiores de Monterrey, Campus Irapuato	M,D
John Carroll University	M
Laurentian University	M
Loyola University Chicago	M
Marshall University	M,O
Memorial University of Newfoundland	M
Mount Saint Mary's University (CA)	M,D,O
New York University	M,O*
Northeast Ohio Medical University	M,D,O
Nova Southeastern University	M,D,O*
Old Dominion University	M,O
Penn State Harrisburg	M,D,O
Pepperdine University	M
Prescott College	M
Roosevelt University	M
St. Edward's University	M,O
Salve Regina University	M,D
Sam Houston State University	M,D,O
San Francisco State University	M
Simon Fraser University	M
Tiffin University	M
Towson University	M
Trinity Western University	M
Union Institute & University	D
United Theological Seminary of the Twin Cities	M,D,O
University at Buffalo, the State University of New York	M
University of California, Merced	M,D
University of California, Santa Cruz	D*
University of Chicago	M
University of Colorado Denver	M,O
University of Dallas	M
University of Houston–Clear Lake	M
University of Louisville	M,D
University of South Florida	M*
The University of Texas at Dallas	M,D
The University of Texas Medical Branch	M,D
University of Utah	M
Virginia Polytechnic Institute and State University	M,D,O
Wayland Baptist University	M
Wilson College	M
Wright State University	M
York University	M,D

HUMAN RESOURCES DEVELOPMENT

Abilene Christian University	M
Amberton University	M
Antioch University Los Angeles	M
Barry University	M,D
Bowie State University	M
California State University, Sacramento	M
Claremont Graduate University	M,D,O
Clemson University	M,D,O
The College of New Rochelle	M,O
Drexel University	M,D*
Florida International University	M,D,O
The George Washington University	M,D,O
Grantham University	M,O
HEC Montreal	O
Illinois Institute of Technology	M,D
Indiana State University	M
Indiana Tech	M
Indiana University of Pennsylvania	M
Inter American University of Puerto Rico, Metropolitan Campus	M
Inter American University of Puerto Rico, San Germán Campus	M,D
Iowa State University of Science and Technology	M,D
John F. Kennedy University	M,O
Kentucky State University	M,D
La Salle University	M,O
Lawrence Technological University	M,O
Lincoln Memorial University	M,D,O
Louisiana State University and Agricultural & Mechanical College	M,D
Marquette University	M
McDaniel College	M
Midwestern State University	M
Mississippi State University	M,D,O
Moravian College	M
National Louis University	M
New York University	M*
North Carolina State University	M
Northeastern Illinois University	M
Ottawa University	M
Penn State Great Valley	M,O
Penn State University Park	M*
Pittsburg State University	M
Regent University	M,D,O
Rochester Institute of Technology	M
Rockhurst University	M,O
Rollins College	M
Roosevelt University	M
South Dakota State University	M
Texas A&M University	M,D
Towson University	M
Tusculum College	M
Universidad Central del Este	M
Universidad Iberoamericana	M,D
University of Arkansas	M,D,O
University of Bridgeport	M
University of Houston	M
University of Louisville	M,D,O
University of Minnesota, Twin Cities Campus	M,D,O
University of Nebraska at Omaha	M,D,O
University of Regina	M
The University of Scranton	M
University of South Africa	M,D
University of South Florida	O*
The University of Tennessee	M
The University of Texas at Tyler	M,D
University of Wisconsin–Stout	M
Villanova University	M
Virginia Commonwealth University	M
Waldorf University	M
Webster University	M,D,O
Western Seminary	M
William Woods University	M,D,O
Xavier University	M,D*

HUMAN RESOURCES MANAGEMENT

Abilene Christian University	M
Adelphi University	M,O
Albany State University	M
Albertus Magnus College	M
Amberton University	M
American InterContinental University Online	M
American University	M,O
American University of Beirut	M
Anderson University (SC)	M
Ashland University	M
Ashworth College	M
Assumption College	M,O
Averett University	M
Avila University	M
Baker College Center for Graduate Studies–Online	M,D
Baldwin Wallace University	M
Barry University	O
Baruch College of the City University of New York	M,D*
Belhaven University (MS)	M
Bellevue University	M,D
Benedictine University	M
Brandman University	M
Brigham Young University	M
Bryan College	M
Buffalo State College, State University of New York	M,O
California Coast University	M
California Intercontinental University	M,D
California State University, East Bay	M
California State University, Sacramento	M
Capella University	M,D
Caribbean University	M,D
Carlow University	M
The Catholic University of America	M
Central Michigan University	M,O
Charleston Southern University	M
City University of Seattle	M,O
Claremont Graduate University	M
Clarkson University	O
Clayton State University	M
Cleveland State University	M
College of Saint Elizabeth	M
Colorado State University–Global Campus	M
Colorado Technical University Aurora	M
Colorado Technical University Colorado Springs	M,D
Columbia College (MO)	M
Columbia Southern University	M
Columbia University	M*
Columbus State University	M,O
Concordia University, St. Paul	M
Concordia University Wisconsin	M
Cornell University	M,D
Dallas Baptist University	M
Davenport University	M
Delaware Valley University	M
DePaul University	M,D
DeSales University	M
DeVry University–Folsom Campus	M
East Central University	M
Eastern Michigan University	M,O
Embry-Riddle Aeronautical University–Daytona	M
Embry-Riddle Aeronautical University–Worldwide	M
Emmanuel College (United States)	M,O
Everglades University	M
Excelsior College	M,O
Fairleigh Dickinson University, Florham Campus	M
Fairleigh Dickinson University, Metropolitan Campus	M,O
Fitchburg State University	M,D
Florida Institute of Technology	M,D
Florida International University	M,D
Florida State University	M,D
Framingham State University	M
Franklin Pierce University	M,D,O
Gannon University	M
George Fox University	M,D
George Mason University	M
Georgetown University	M,D
The George Washington University	M,O
Georgia State University	M,D
Golden Gate University	M,D,O
Goldey-Beacom College	M
Grambling State University	M
Grand Canyon University	M
Grantham University	M,O
Hawai`i Pacific University	M
HEC Montreal	M,D,O
Herzing University Online	M
Hofstra University	M,O
Holy Family University	M
Hood College	M,O*
Houston Baptist University	M
Howard University	M
Idaho State University	M,D
IGlobal University	M
Indiana Tech	M
Indiana University South Bend	M,O
Indiana Wesleyan University	M,O
Instituto Tecnologico de Santo Domingo	M,O
Instituto Tecnológico y de Estudios Superiores de Monterrey, Campus Cuernavaca	M
Inter American University of Puerto Rico, Aguadilla Campus	M
Inter American University of Puerto Rico, Arecibo Campus	M
Inter American University of Puerto Rico, Barranquitas Campus	M
Inter American University of Puerto Rico, Bayamón Campus	M
Inter American University of Puerto Rico, Fajardo Campus	M
Inter American University of Puerto Rico, Metropolitan Campus	M
Inter American University of Puerto Rico, Ponce Campus	M
Inter American University of Puerto Rico, San Germán Campus	M,D
Iona College	M,O
James Madison University	M
Johnson & Wales University	M
King University	M
La Roche College	M,O
La Salle University	M,O
Lasell College	M,O
La Sierra University	M,O
Lebanon Valley College	M
Lewis University	M
Lincoln University (CA)	M,D
Lincoln University (PA)	M
Lindenwood University	M,O
Lindenwood University–Belleville	M
London Metropolitan University	M,D
Long Island University–LIU Brooklyn	M,O
Loyola University Chicago	M
Lynn University	M
Manhattanville College	M,O
Marquette University	M,O
Marshall University	M
Marygrove College	M,O
Marymount University	O
Maryville University of Saint Louis	M,O
McKendree University	M
McMaster University	M,D
Mercy College	M
Mercyhurst University	M,O
Meredith College	M
Michigan State University	M,D
Middle Tennessee State University	M
Millennia Atlantic University	M
Misericordia University	M
Monmouth University	M,O*
Monroe College	M
Moravian College	M
Mount Mercy University	M
Murray State University	M
National American University (TX)	M,D
National Louis University	M
National University	M,O
Nazareth College of Rochester	M
New Mexico Highlands University	M
New York Institute of Technology	M,O
New York University	M*
Niagara University	M
North Carolina Agricultural and Technical State University	M
North Central College	M
North Greenville University	M,D
Northwestern University	M,D
Northwest Missouri State University	M
Norwich University	M
Notre Dame de Namur University	M
Nova Southeastern University	M*
Oakland University	M,O
Ohio Christian University	M
The Ohio State University	M,D
Oklahoma Christian University	M
Ottawa University	M
Pace University	M
Penn State Great Valley	M,O
Penn State Harrisburg	M,D,O
Penn State University Park	M*
Pepperdine University	M
Polytechnic University of Puerto Rico, Miami Campus	M
Polytechnic University of Puerto Rico, Orlando Campus	M
Pontifical Catholic University of Puerto Rico	M,O
Pontificia Universidad Catolica Madre y Maestra	M
Portland State University	M,D,O
Purdue University	M,D
Purdue University Global	M
Regent's University London	M
Regent University	M,D,O
Regis University	M,O
Robert Morris University	M
Robert Morris University Illinois	M
Rollins College	M
Roosevelt University	M
Rutgers University–Newark	M,D
Rutgers University–New Brunswick	M,D
Sacred Heart University	M,O
St. Ambrose University	M,D
Saint Francis University	M
St. Joseph's College, Long Island Campus	M
St. Joseph's College, New York	M
Saint Joseph's University	M*
Saint Leo University	M,D
Saint Mary's University of Minnesota	M
Saint Peter's University	M
St. Thomas University	M,O
Salve Regina University	M,O
San Diego State University	M
San Ignacio University	M
Savannah State University	M
Seattle Pacific University	M
Southern New Hampshire University	M,D,O
State University of New York Polytechnic Institute	M
Stevens Institute of Technology	M
Stony Brook University, State University of New York	M,O
Strayer University	M
Tarleton State University	M
Temple University	M*
Tennessee State University	M,D
Tennessee Technological University	M
Texas A&M University	M
Texas A&M University–Central Texas	M,O
Texas State University	M
Texas Woman's University	M
Thomas College	M
Thomas Edison State University	M
Tiffin University	M
Towson University	M
Trident University International	M,D
Trinity International University	M,D
Trinity Washington University	M
Troy University	M
United States International University–Africa	M
Universidad del Este	M
Universidad del Turabo	M
Universidad Metropolitana	M
University at Albany, State University of New York	M,D,O
University at Buffalo, the State University of New York	M,D,O
The University of Alabama in Huntsville	M,O
University of Bridgeport	M
University of California, Berkeley	O
University of Cincinnati	M
University of Colorado Denver	M
University of Connecticut	M,D*
University of Dallas	M,D
University of Denver	M,O
University of Florida	M,D
University of Hawaii at Manoa	M
University of Houston–Clear Lake	M
University of Houston–Downtown	M
University of Illinois at Urbana–Champaign	M,D,O
The University of Kansas	M,D
University of La Verne	M,O
University of Lethbridge	M,D
University of Louisiana at Lafayette	M
University of Louisville	M,D,O
The University of Manchester	M
University of Mary	M
University of Memphis	M,O
University of Minnesota, Twin Cities Campus	M
University of Missouri–St. Louis	M,D,O
University of Nebraska at Kearney	M
University of New Haven	M,O*
University of New Mexico	M
University of Northern Colorado	M
University of North Florida	M
University of North Texas	M,D,O
University of North Texas at Dallas	M
University of Oklahoma	M,O*
University of Phoenix–Bay Area Campus	M,D
University of Phoenix–Central Valley Campus	M
University of Phoenix–Dallas Campus	M
University of Phoenix–Hawaii Campus	M
University of Phoenix–Houston Campus	M

University of Phoenix–Las Vegas Campus	M
University of Phoenix–Online Campus	M,O
University of Phoenix–Phoenix Campus	M,O
University of Phoenix–Sacramento Valley Campus	M
University of Phoenix–San Antonio Campus	M
University of Phoenix–San Diego Campus	M
University of Pittsburgh	M,D*
University of Puerto Rico–Mayagüez	M
University of Puerto Rico–Río Piedras	M,D
University of Regina	M,O
University of Rhode Island	M,O*
University of Saint Mary	M
University of South Carolina	M
University of South Dakota	M
University of Southern Indiana	M
University of South Florida	M*
The University of Texas at Arlington	M
University of the Sacred Heart	M
University of Toronto	M,D
University of Wisconsin–Madison	M,D
University of Wisconsin–Milwaukee	M,O*
University of Wisconsin–Platteville	M
Upper Iowa University	M
Utah State University	M
Virginia Commonwealth University	M
Virginia International University	M,O
Walden University	M,D,O
Walsh College of Accountancy and Business Administration	M
Warner University	M
Wayland Baptist University	M,D
Waynesburg University	M,D
Wayne State University	M,D
Webster University	M,D,O
West Chester University of Pennsylvania	M,O
Wilfrid Laurier University	M,D
Wilkes University	M
Wilmington University	M,D
York University	M,D

HUMAN SERVICES

Abilene Christian University	M,O
Albertus Magnus College	M
Amridge University	M,D
Bellevue University	M
Boricua College	M
Brandeis University	M
California State University, Sacramento	M
Capella University	M,D
Carlos Albizu University, Miami Campus	M,D
Chestnut Hill College	M,O
Concordia University Chicago	M
Coppin State University	M
Eastern Illinois University	M
Eastern Michigan University	O
East Tennessee State University	M
Ferris State University	M
Georgia State University	M,O
Governors State University	M,D
Judson University	M
Kansas State University	M,D,O
Kent State University	M,D,O
Lehigh University	M,D,O
Lenoir-Rhyne University	M
Liberty University	M,D,O
Lincoln University (PA)	M
Lock Haven University of Pennsylvania	M
Louisiana Tech University	M,D,O
McDaniel College	M
Mercer University	M,D
Minnesota State University Mankato	M
Murray State University	M,D,O
National Louis University	M,D,O
National University	M,O
New England College	M
Northeastern University	M
Pontifical Catholic University of Puerto Rico	M,D
Post University	M
Purdue University Northwest	M
Regent University	M,D,O
Roberts Wesleyan College	M
Rosemont College	M
St. Joseph's College, Long Island Campus	M
St. Joseph's College, New York	M
Saint Leo University	M
South Carolina State University	M
Southeastern University (FL)	M
Springfield College	M
Texas Southern University	M
Thomas University	M
Universidad del Turabo	M
Université de Montréal	D
University of Baltimore	M
University of Bridgeport	M
University of Central Missouri	M,D,O
University of Colorado Colorado Springs	M,D
University of Idaho	M,O
University of Illinois at Springfield	M,O
University of Illinois at Urbana–Champaign	M,D
University of Maryland, Baltimore County	M,D
University of Massachusetts Boston	M
University of Nebraska at Kearney	M
University of Northern Iowa	M
University of North Georgia	M
University of Northwestern–St. Paul	M
University of Oklahoma	M,O*
University of Providence	M
Upper Iowa University	M
Walden University	M,D
Warner Pacific University	M
Washburn University	M
Webster University	M
Western Michigan University	D,O
West Virginia University	M,D
Wichita State University	M
Wilmington University	M
Winona State University	M,O
Youngstown State University	M

HYDRAULICS

Drexel University	M,D*
École Polytechnique de Montréal	M,D,O
McGill University	M,D
Old Dominion University	M
University of Colorado Denver	M,D

HYDROGEOLOGY

Clemson University	M,D
East Carolina University	M,O
Illinois State University	O
Indiana University Bloomington	M,D
Montana Tech of The University of Montana	M
Oregon State University	M,D
University of Hawaii at Manoa	M,D
University of Nevada, Reno	M,D
University of South Florida	O*

HYDROLOGY

California State University, Bakersfield	M
Colorado School of Mines	M,D
Cornell University	M,D
Drexel University	M,D*
Idaho State University	M,O
Illinois State University	O
Massachusetts Institute of Technology	M,D,O
New Mexico Institute of Mining and Technology	M,D
New Mexico State University	M,D
Oregon State University	M,D
Portland State University	M,D,O
Stanford University	M,D,O
Stevens Institute of Technology	M,D,O
Temple University	M,O*
Université du Québec, Institut National de la Recherche Scientifique	M,D
The University of Arizona	D,O
University of Calgary	M,D
University of California, Davis	M,D
University of Colorado Denver	M,D
University of Florida	M,D
University of Minnesota, Twin Cities Campus	M,D
University of Mississippi	M,D
University of Nevada, Reno	M,D
University of New Brunswick Fredericton	M,D
University of New Hampshire	M
University of Rhode Island	M,D,O*
University of Southern Mississippi	M,D
University of Washington	M,D

ILLUSTRATION

Academy of Art University	M
Bob Jones University	M,D,O
California College of the Arts	M
California State University, Fullerton	M
East Carolina University	M
Fashion Institute of Technology	M
Hollins University	M,O
Kent State University	M
Maryland Institute College of Art	M
Marywood University	M
Mills College	M,O
Minneapolis College of Art and Design	M
Savannah College of Art and Design	M
School of Visual Arts (NY)	M
Syracuse University	M*
Western Connecticut State University	M

IMMUNOLOGY

Albany Medical College	M,D
Albert Einstein College of Medicine	D
American University of Beirut	M,D
Baylor College of Medicine	D
Boston University	D*
California Institute of Technology	D
Case Western Reserve University	D*
Colorado State University	M,D
Creighton University	M,D
Dalhousie University	M,D
Dartmouth College	D*
Drexel University	M,D*
Duke University	D*
Emory University	D
Georgetown University	M,D
The George Washington University	D
Hood College	M*
Illinois State University	M,D
Indiana University–Purdue University Indianapolis	M,D
Iowa State University of Science and Technology	M,D
Irell & Manella Graduate School of Biological Sciences	D*
Johns Hopkins University	M,D*
London Metropolitan University	M,D
Louisiana State University Health Sciences Center	D
Louisiana State University Health Sciences Center at Shreveport	M,D
Loyola University Chicago	M,D
Massachusetts Institute of Technology	D
Mayo Clinic Graduate School of Biomedical Sciences	D
McGill University	M,D
McMaster University	M,D
Medical University of South Carolina	M,D
Meharry Medical College	D
Memorial University of Newfoundland	M,D
Montana State University	M,D
New York Medical College	M,D
New York University	M,D*
Old Dominion University	M
Oregon Health & Science University	D
Oregon State University	M,D
Penn State Hershey Medical Center	M,D
Purdue University	M,D
Queen's University at Kingston	M,D
Rosalind Franklin University of Medicine and Science	D
Rush University	M,D
Rutgers University–Newark	D
Rutgers University–New Brunswick	M,D
Saint Louis University	D*
Stanford University	D
State University of New York Upstate Medical University	M,D
Stony Brook University, State University of New York	M,D
Thomas Jefferson University	D
Tufts University	D*
Tulane University	M
Uniformed Services University of the Health Sciences	D*
Universidad Central del Caribe	M,D
Université de Montréal	M,D
Université de Sherbrooke	M,D
Université du Québec, Institut National de la Recherche Scientifique	M,D
Université Laval	M,D
University at Buffalo, the State University of New York	M,D
The University of Alabama at Birmingham	D
University of Alberta	M,D
The University of Arizona	D
University of Arkansas for Medical Sciences	M,D,O
The University of British Columbia	M,D
University of Calgary	M,D
University of California, Berkeley	D
University of California, Davis	M,D
University of California, Los Angeles	M,D*
University of Chicago	D
University of Cincinnati	M,D
University of Colorado Denver	D
University of Connecticut Health Center	D
University of Florida	D
University of Guelph	M,D,O
University of Illinois at Chicago	D
The University of Iowa	M,D*
University of Kentucky	D
University of Louisville	M,D
The University of Manchester	M,D
University of Manitoba	M,D
University of Maryland, Baltimore	D
University of Massachusetts Medical School	M,D
University of Miami	D*
University of Michigan	M,D*
University of Minnesota, Duluth	M,D
University of Minnesota, Twin Cities Campus	D
University of Missouri	D
University of Montana	D
University of Nebraska Medical Center	M,D
The University of North Carolina at Chapel Hill	M,D
University of North Texas Health Science Center at Fort Worth	M,D
University of Oklahoma Health Sciences Center	M,D
University of Ottawa	M,D
University of Pennsylvania	D*
University of Pittsburgh	D*
University of Prince Edward Island	M,D
University of Rochester	M,D*
University of Saskatchewan	M,D
University of South Dakota	M,D
University of Southern California	M*
University of Southern Maine	M
University of South Florida	M,D*
The University of Texas Health Science Center at Houston	M,D
The University of Texas Health Science Center at San Antonio	M,D
The University of Texas Medical Branch	M,D
The University of Texas Southwestern Medical Center	D
The University of Toledo	M,D
University of Toronto	M,D
University of Washington	D
The University of Western Ontario	M,D
Vanderbilt University	M,D*
Virginia Commonwealth University	M,D
Wake Forest University	D
Washington State University	M,D
Washington University in St. Louis	D
Wayne State University	M,D,O
Weill Cornell Medicine	M,D
West Virginia University	M,D
Wright State University	M
Yale University	D

INDUSTRIAL/MANAGEMENT ENGINEERING

American University of Armenia	M
Arizona State University at the Tempe campus	M,D
Auburn University	M,D,O*
Binghamton University, State University of New York	M,D
Bradley University	M
Buffalo State College, State University of New York	M
California Polytechnic State University, San Luis Obispo	M*
California State University, Fresno	M
California State University, Northridge	M
Clemson University	M,D
Colorado State University–Pueblo	M
Columbia University	M,D*
Concordia University (Canada)	M,D,O
Cornell University	M,D
Dalhousie University	M,D
Eastern Kentucky University	M
École Polytechnique de Montréal	M,D,O
Florida Agricultural and Mechanical University	M,D
Florida State University	M,D
Georgia Institute of Technology	M,D
Illinois State University	M
Indiana University–Purdue University Fort Wayne	M
Instituto Tecnologico de Santo Domingo	M,O
Instituto Tecnológico y de Estudios Superiores de Monterrey, Campus Chihuahua	M,O
Instituto Tecnológico y de Estudios Superiores de Monterrey, Campus Ciudad de México	M,D
Instituto Tecnológico y de Estudios Superiores de Monterrey, Campus Laguna	M
Instituto Tecnológico y de Estudios Superiores de Monterrey, Campus Monterrey	M,D
Iowa State University of Science and Technology	M,D
Kansas State University	M,D
Lamar University	M,D
Lawrence Technological University	M,D
Lehigh University	M,D,O
Mississippi State University	M,D
Montana State University	M,D
Montana Tech of The University of Montana	M
Morehead State University	M
Morgan State University	M,D,O
New Jersey Institute of Technology	M,D,O
New Mexico State University	M,D,O
New York University	M*
North Carolina Agricultural and Technical State University	M,D
North Carolina State University	M,D
North Dakota State University	M,D*
Northeastern University	M,D,O
Northern Illinois University	M
Northwestern University	M,D
The Ohio State University	M,D
Ohio University	M,D
Oklahoma State University	M,D
Oregon State University	M,D
Penn State University Park	M,D*
Purdue University	M,D
Rensselaer Polytechnic Institute	M,D
Rochester Institute of Technology	M
Rutgers University–New Brunswick	M,D
St. Mary's University (United States)	M
San Jose State University	M
South Dakota State University	M
Southern Illinois University Edwardsville	M
Stanford University	M,D
Texas A&M University	M,D
Texas A&M University–Kingsville	M
Texas Southern University	M
Texas State University	M
Texas Tech University	M,D
Universidad de las Américas Puebla	M
Université de Moncton	M
Université du Québec à Trois-Rivières	M,O
Université Laval	O
University at Buffalo, the State University of New York	M,D,O
The University of Alabama in Huntsville	M,D
The University of Arizona	M,D,O
University of Arkansas	M,D
University of California, Berkeley	M,D
University of Central Florida	M,D,O
University of Cincinnati	M,D

*M—masters degree; D—doctorate; O—other advanced degree; *—Close-Up and/or Display*

University of Florida	M,D,O
University of Houston	M,D
University of Illinois at Chicago	M,D
University of Illinois at Urbana–Champaign	M,D
The University of Iowa	M,D*
University of Louisville	M,D,O
University of Manitoba	M,D
University of Massachusetts Amherst	M,D*
University of Massachusetts Dartmouth	M,O
University of Massachusetts Lowell	D
University of Miami	M,D*
University of Michigan	M,D*
University of Michigan–Dearborn	M,D
University of Minnesota, Twin Cities Campus	M,D
University of Missouri	M,D
University of Nebraska–Lincoln	M,D
University of New Haven	M,O*
University of Oklahoma	M,D*
University of Pittsburgh	M,D*
University of Puerto Rico–Mayagüez	M
University of Regina	M,D
University of Rhode Island	M,D*
University of Southern California	M,D,O*
University of South Florida	M,D,O*
The University of Tennessee	M,D
The University of Texas at Arlington	M,D
The University of Texas at Austin	M,D
The University of Toledo	M,D
University of Toronto	M,D
University of Washington	M,D
University of Windsor	M,D
University of Wisconsin–Madison	M,D
University of Wisconsin–Milwaukee	M,D*
University of Wisconsin–Stout	M
Virginia Polytechnic Institute and State University	M,O
Wayne State University	M,D,O
Western Carolina University	M
Western Michigan University	M,D
Western New England University	M
West Virginia University	M,D
Wichita State University	M,D
Wright State University	M
Youngstown State University	M

INDUSTRIAL AND LABOR RELATIONS

Baruch College of the City University of New York	M*
Carnegie Mellon University	D
Cleveland State University	M
Cornell University	M,D
Georgetown University	D
Georgia State University	M,D
Indiana University of Pennsylvania	M
Inter American University of Puerto Rico, Metropolitan Campus	M,D
McMaster University	M
Memorial University of Newfoundland	M
Michigan State University	M,D
New York Institute of Technology	M,O
The Ohio State University	M,D
Penn State University Park	M*
Queen's University at Kingston	M
Rutgers University–New Brunswick	M,D
State University of New York Empire State College	M
Temple University	M,O*
Université de Montréal	M,D,O
Université du Québec à Trois-Rivières	O
Université du Québec en Outaouais	M,D,O
Université Laval	M,D
University of Alberta	D
University of California, Berkeley	D
University of Cincinnati	M
University of Illinois at Urbana–Champaign	M,D
The University of Manchester	M
University of Massachusetts Amherst	M*
University of Minnesota, Twin Cities Campus	M
University of Rhode Island	M,O*
University of Toronto	M,D
University of Wisconsin–Milwaukee	M,O*
Wayne State University	M,D
West Virginia University	M,D,O

INDUSTRIAL AND MANUFACTURING MANAGEMENT

American InterContinental University Online	M
Baruch College of the City University of New York	M,D*
Bluffton University	M
California State University, East Bay	M
Carnegie Mellon University	M,D
Case Western Reserve University	M,D*
Cedarville University	M
Central Connecticut State University	M,O
Central Michigan University	M
Colorado Technical University Aurora	M
Colorado Technical University Colorado Springs	M,D
Duke University	M,D,O*
East Carolina University	M,D,O
Embry-Riddle Aeronautical University–Worldwide	M
Emory University	M
Everglades University	M
Georgetown University	D
Harvard University	D*
HEC Montreal	M
Illinois Institute of Technology	M
Instituto Tecnologico de Santo Domingo	M,O
Instituto Tecnológico y de Estudios Superiores de Monterrey, Campus Estado de México	M,D
Instituto Tecnológico y de Estudios Superiores de Monterrey, Campus Irapuato	M,D
Inter American University of Puerto Rico, Metropolitan Campus	M
Inter American University of Puerto Rico, San Germán Campus	M,D
Lawrence Technological University	M,D
Marquette University	M,O
McGill University	M,D,O
Milligan College	M,O
Milwaukee School of Engineering	M
Mississippi State University	M,D
Northern Illinois University	M
Northwestern University	M,D
Oakland University	M,O
Penn State Erie, The Behrend College	M
Polytechnic University of Puerto Rico	M
Polytechnic University of Puerto Rico, Miami Campus	M
Polytechnic University of Puerto Rico, Orlando Campus	M
Regis University	M,O
Rochester Institute of Technology	M
San Francisco State University	M
Southern New Hampshire University	M,D,O
Stevens Institute of Technology	M
Texas A&M University–Kingsville	M
Universidad de las Américas Puebla	M
The University of Alabama	M,D
University of Arkansas	M,D
University of Bridgeport	M
University of Central Missouri	M,D,O
University of Chicago	M,O
University of Cincinnati	D
The University of Manchester	M,D
University of Michigan–Flint	M,O
University of New Haven	M,O*
The University of North Carolina at Charlotte	M,D,O
University of North Texas	M,D,O
University of Pittsburgh	M*
University of Portland	M
University of Puerto Rico–Mayagüez	M
University of Puerto Rico–Río Piedras	M,D
University of Rochester	D*
University of Southern Indiana	M
The University of Tennessee	M,D
The University of Texas at Austin	M,D
The University of Texas at Dallas	M,D
The University of Texas at Tyler	M
University of Utah	M,D,O
Wayne State University	M,D
Wilkes University	M,D

INDUSTRIAL AND ORGANIZATIONAL PSYCHOLOGY

Adler University	M,D
Alliant International University–Fresno	M,D
Alliant International University–Los Angeles	M,D
Alliant International University–San Diego	M,D
Alliant International University–San Francisco	M,D
American InterContinental University Online	M
Angelo State University	M
Anna Maria College	M
Argosy University, Atlanta	M,D,O
Argosy University, Chicago	M,D
Argosy University, Phoenix	M
Argosy University, Tampa	M,D
Argosy University, Twin Cities	M,D,O
Austin Peay State University	M
Azusa Pacific University	M*
Baruch College of the City University of New York	M,D*
Bayamón Central University	M
Bowling Green State University	M,D
Brooklyn College of the City University of New York	M,D
California State University, Long Beach	M
California State University, Sacramento	M
California State University, San Bernardino	M
Capella University	M,D
Carlos Albizu University	M,D
Carlos Albizu University, Miami Campus	M,D
Central Michigan University	M,D
Chatham University	M,D
The Chicago School of Professional Psychology	M,D
The Chicago School of Professional Psychology at Downtown Los Angeles	M
The Chicago School of Professional Psychology: Online	M,D,O
Claremont Graduate University	M,D,O
Clemson University	M,D
East Carolina University	M,D,O
Eastern Kentucky University	M,O
Elmhurst College	M
Emporia State University	M
Fairleigh Dickinson University, Florham Campus	M
Florida Institute of Technology	M,D
Florida International University	M,D
George Mason University	M,D,O
The Graduate Center, City University of New York	D
Grand Canyon University	D
Hofstra University	M,D
Illinois Institute of Technology	M,D
Illinois State University	M,D,O
Indiana University–Purdue University Indianapolis	M,D
Inter American University of Puerto Rico, Metropolitan Campus	M,D
Iona College	M,O
John F. Kennedy University	M,O
Kean University	M
Keiser University	M,D
Lamar University	M
La Salle University	M
Liberty University	M,D,O
London Metropolitan University	M,D
Louisiana Tech University	M,D,O
Lynn University	M
Meredith College	M
Middle Tennessee State University	M,O
Minnesota State University Mankato	M,D
Missouri State University	M,O
Missouri University of Science and Technology	M
Montclair State University	M
New York University	M,D,O*
North Carolina State University	D
Northern Kentucky University	M,O
Ohio University	D
Old Dominion University	D
Philadelphia College of Osteopathic Medicine	M,D,O*
Pontifical Catholic University of Puerto Rico	D
Purdue University	D
Radford University	M
Rice University	M,D
Roosevelt University	M,D
Sacred Heart University	M
St. Cloud State University	M
Saint Louis University	M,D*
Saint Mary's University (Canada)	M,D
St. Mary's University (United States)	M
San Diego State University	M,D
San Francisco State University	M,O
San Jose State University	M
Seattle Pacific University	M,D
South Dakota State University	M
Southeastern Louisiana University	M
Southern Illinois University Edwardsville	M
Springfield College	M,D,O
Teachers College, Columbia University	M,D
Texas A&M University	M,D
Thomas Edison State University	M,O
Touro College	M,D
University at Albany, State University of New York	M,D
The University of Akron	M,D
The University of Alabama in Huntsville	M
University of Central Florida	M,D
University of Connecticut	M,D*
University of Detroit Mercy	M,D,O
University of Guelph	M,D
University of Houston	M,D
The University of Manchester	M
University of Maryland, Baltimore County	M
University of Maryland, College Park	M,D
University of Minnesota, Twin Cities Campus	D
University of Nebraska at Omaha	M,D,O
University of New Haven	M,O*
The University of North Carolina at Charlotte	M,D,O
University of Oklahoma	M,D*
University of Phoenix–Online Campus	M,D,O
University of Puerto Rico–Río Piedras	M,D
University of South Africa	M,D
University of South Florida	D*
The University of Tennessee	D
The University of Tennessee at Chattanooga	M
The University of Texas at Arlington	M,D
University of the Incarnate Word	M,D
The University of Tulsa	M,D
University of West Florida	M
University of Wisconsin–Oshkosh	M
Valdosta State University	M,O
Walden University	M,D,O
Wayne State University	M,D
West Chester University of Pennsylvania	M,D,O
Western Kentucky University	M,O
Western Michigan University	M,D
William James College	M,D,O
Wright State University	M,D
Xavier University	M,D*

INDUSTRIAL DESIGN

Academy of Art University	M
ArtCenter College of Design	M
Auburn University	M*
California College of the Arts	M
Carleton University	M
Florida State University	M
Georgia Institute of Technology	M
Iowa State University of Science and Technology	M
The New School	M
North Carolina State University	M
The Ohio State University	M
Pratt Institute	M*
Purdue University	M,D
Rhode Island School of Design	M
Rochester Institute of Technology	M
Savannah College of Art and Design	M
Thomas Jefferson University	M
University of Cincinnati	M
University of Detroit Mercy	M,D
University of Illinois at Urbana–Champaign	M
University of Notre Dame	M
The University of the Arts	M
University of Washington	M
Wayne State University	M

INDUSTRIAL HYGIENE

California State University, Northridge	M
Eastern Kentucky University	M
Montana Tech of The University of Montana	M
New York Medical College	M,D,O
Old Dominion University	M
The University of Alabama at Birmingham	M,D
University of Central Missouri	M,D,O
University of Cincinnati	M,D
The University of Iowa	M,D,O*
University of Michigan	M,D*
University of Minnesota, Twin Cities Campus	M,D
University of Puerto Rico–Medical Sciences Campus	M
University of South Carolina	M,D
The University of Toledo	M,D,O
University of Wisconsin–Stout	M
West Virginia University	M,D

INFECTIOUS DISEASES

Georgetown University	M,D
The George Washington University	M,D,O
Johns Hopkins University	M,D*
Loyola University Chicago	M,D,O
Montana State University	M,D
North Carolina State University	M,D
North Dakota State University	M*
Rutgers University–Newark	D,O
Thomas Jefferson University	O
Tufts University	M,D*
Uniformed Services University of the Health Sciences	D*
Université Laval	O
The University of British Columbia	M,D
University of Calgary	M,D
University of California, Berkeley	M,D
University of Georgia	D
University of Guelph	M,D,O
University of Manitoba	M,D
University of Minnesota, Twin Cities Campus	M,D
University of Nebraska Medical Center	M,D
University of Pittsburgh	M,D*
University of South Florida	M,D*
The University of Texas Health Science Center at Houston	M,D
Washington State University	M,D
Yale University	D

INFORMATION SCIENCE

Alcorn State University	M
American InterContinental University Atlanta	M
American InterContinental University Online	M
American University of Armenia	M
Arizona State University at the Tempe campus	M
Arkansas Tech University	M
Aspen University	M,O
Auburn University at Montgomery	M
Ball State University	M,O
Barry University	M
Bellevue University	M
Bentley University	M
Bradley University	M
Brigham Young University	M
Brooklyn College of the City University of New York	M,O
California State University, Fullerton	M
Capitol Technology University	M
Carleton University	M,D
Carnegie Mellon University	M,D
Case Western Reserve University	M,D*
The Citadel, The Military College of South Carolina	M
Claremont Graduate University	M,D,O
Clarion University of Pennsylvania	M,O
Clark Atlanta University	M
Clark University	M
The College of Saint Rose	M,O
Cornell University	D
Dakota State University	M,D,O
DePaul University	M,D
Drexel University	M,D,O*
East Tennessee State University	M,O
Florida Institute of Technology	M
Florida International University	M,D
Gannon University	M
George Mason University	M,D,O
Georgia Southern University–Armstrong Campus	M
Georgia State University	M,D,O
Grand Valley State University	M
Hardin-Simmons University	M
Harvard University	M,D,O*

Hood College	M,O*
Indiana University Bloomington	M,D,O
Indiana University–Purdue University Fort Wayne	M
Indiana University–Purdue University Indianapolis	M
Instituto Tecnologico de Santo Domingo	M,O
Instituto Tecnológico y de Estudios Superiores de Monterrey, Campus Cuernavaca	M,D
Instituto Tecnológico y de Estudios Superiores de Monterrey, Campus Estado de México	M,D
Instituto Tecnológico y de Estudios Superiores de Monterrey, Campus Irapuato	M,D
Instituto Tecnológico y de Estudios Superiores de Monterrey, Campus Monterrey	M,D
Instituto Tecnológico y de Estudios Superiores de Monterrey, Campus Sonora Norte	M
Iowa State University of Science and Technology	M
Kennesaw State University	M,O
Kent State University	M
Lawrence Technological University	M,D,O
Lehigh University	M
Loyola University Chicago	M
Marshall University	M
Maryville University of Saint Louis	M,O
Massachusetts Institute of Technology	M,D,O
Minnesota State University Mankato	M,O
Missouri University of Science and Technology	M
Monroe College	M
Naval Postgraduate School	M,D,O
New Jersey Institute of Technology	M,D,O
Northern Kentucky University	M,O
Northwestern University	M
Nova Southeastern University	M,D*
Oklahoma State University	M,D
Old Dominion University	D
Pace University	M,D,O
Penn State Great Valley	M,O
Penn State University Park	M,D*
Regis University	M,O
Rensselaer at Hartford	M
Rensselaer Polytechnic Institute	M
Robert Morris University	M,D
Rochester Institute of Technology	M,D
Rutgers University–New Brunswick	M
Sacred Heart University	M
St. John's University (NY)	
St. Mary's University (United States)	M
Sam Houston State University	M,D
Shippensburg University of Pennsylvania	M,O
Simmons College	M,D,O
Southern Methodist University	M,D
State University of New York Polytechnic Institute	M
Stevens Institute of Technology	M,O
Strayer University	M
Syracuse University	M,D*
Temple University	M,D*
Texas Woman's University	M
Thomas Edison State University	M,O
Towson University	M,D,O
Trevecca Nazarene University	M,O
Université de Sherbrooke	M,D
University at Albany, State University of New York	M,D
The University of Alabama at Birmingham	M,D
University of Arkansas at Little Rock	M,D,O
University of California, Irvine	M,D
University of California, Merced	M,D
University of Central Missouri	M,D,O
University of Cincinnati	M,O
University of Colorado Boulder	D
University of Colorado Denver	M,D
University of Delaware	M,D*
University of Denver	M,O
University of Florida	M,D
University of Hawaii at Manoa	M,D
University of Houston	M,D
University of Houston–Clear Lake	M
University of Illinois at Urbana–Champaign	M,D,O
The University of Iowa	M,D,O*
University of Kentucky	M
University of Maine	M,D,O
University of Maryland, Baltimore County	M,D
University of Maryland University College	M
University of Michigan	M,D*
University of Michigan–Dearborn	M,D
University of Michigan–Flint	M
University of Nebraska at Omaha	M,D,O
University of Nebraska–Lincoln	M,D
University of New Mexico	M
University of North Alabama	M
The University of North Carolina at Charlotte	M,O
University of North Texas	M,D,O
University of Oregon	M,D
University of Ottawa	M,O
University of Pennsylvania	M,D*
University of Pittsburgh	M,D,O*
University of Puerto Rico–Mayagüez	M,D
University of Puerto Rico–Río Piedras	M,O
University of St. Thomas (MN)	M,O
University of South Africa	M,D
University of South Carolina Upstate	M
University of Southern Mississippi	M,O
University of South Florida	M*
The University of Tennessee	M,D
The University of Texas at El Paso	M,D,O
The University of Texas at San Antonio	M,D,O
University of the Sacred Heart	O
University of Washington	M,D
University of Waterloo	M,D
University of Wisconsin–Parkside	M
University of Wisconsin–Stout	M
Western Governors University	M
Youngstown State University	M

INFORMATION STUDIES

The Catholic University of America	M,O
Central Connecticut State University	M
Columbia University	M*
Cornell University	D
Dalhousie University	M
Dominican University	M,D,O
Florida State University	M,D,O
Lock Haven University of Pennsylvania	M
Louisiana State University and Agricultural & Mechanical College	M
Mansfield University of Pennsylvania	M
McGill University	M,D,O
Metropolitan State University	M,D,O
Missouri Western State University	M
Monmouth University	M*
North Carolina Central University	M
Pratt Institute	M,O*
Queens College of the City University of New York	M,O
Queen's University at Kingston	M,D
Rutgers University–New Brunswick	M,D
St. Catherine University	M
St. John's University (NY)	M,O
Southern Connecticut State University	M,O
Syracuse University	M*
Universidad del Turabo	M
Université de Montréal	M,D
University at Buffalo, the State University of New York	M,O
The University of Alabama	M,D
University of Alberta	M
The University of Arizona	M,D
The University of British Columbia	M,D
University of California, Berkeley	M,D
University of California, Los Angeles	M,D,O*
University of Hawaii at Manoa	M,O
University of Illinois at Urbana–Champaign	M,D,O
The University of Iowa	M,D*
University of Maryland, College Park	M,D
University of Michigan	M,D*
University of Missouri	D
The University of North Carolina at Chapel Hill	M,D,O
The University of North Carolina at Greensboro	M
University of Oklahoma	M,D,O*
University of Puerto Rico–Río Piedras	M,O
University of Rhode Island	M*
University of South Carolina	M,D,O
University of South Florida	M,O*
The University of Texas at Austin	M,D
University of Toronto	M,D
The University of Western Ontario	M,D
University of Wisconsin–Madison	M,D
University of Wisconsin–Milwaukee	M,D,O*
Valdosta State University	M
Wayne State University	M,O

INORGANIC CHEMISTRY

Auburn University	M,D*
Binghamton University, State University of New York	M,D
Boston College	M,D
Brandeis University	M,D
Cornell University	D
Florida State University	M,D
Georgetown University	D
The George Washington University	M,D
Harvard University	D*
Howard University	M,D
Illinois Institute of Technology	M,D
Indiana University Bloomington	M,D
Iowa State University of Science and Technology	M,D
Marquette University	M,D
Massachusetts Institute of Technology	D
McMaster University	M,D
Old Dominion University	M,D
Purdue University	M,D
Rice University	M,D
Rutgers University–Newark	M,D
Rutgers University–New Brunswick	M,D
Seton Hall University	M,D
Southern University and Agricultural and Mechanical College	M
University of Calgary	M,D
University of Cincinnati	M,D
University of Louisville	M,D
The University of Manchester	M,D
University of Maryland, College Park	M,D
University of Massachusetts Lowell	M,D
University of Memphis	M,D
University of Miami	M,D*
University of Michigan	M,D*
University of Missouri–Kansas City	M,D
University of Montana	M,D
University of Nebraska–Lincoln	M,D
University of Notre Dame	M,D
University of Oklahoma	M,D*
University of Regina	M,D
University of Rochester	D*
The University of Tennessee	M,D
The University of Texas at Austin	D
The University of Toledo	M,D
Vanderbilt University	M,D*
Virginia Commonwealth University	M,D
Wake Forest University	M,D
Wesleyan University	D
Yale University	D
Youngstown State University	M

INSURANCE

California State University, Fullerton	M
Florida State University	M,D
Georgia State University	M,D,O
Olivet College	M
Pontificia Universidad Catolica Madre y Maestra	M
St. John's University (NY)	M
Temple University	D*
University of Colorado Denver	M
University of Florida	M,D,O
University of Pennsylvania	M,D*
University of Wisconsin–Madison	M,D
Western Michigan University Thomas M. Cooley Law School	M,D

INTELLECTUAL PROPERTY LAW

Case Western Reserve University	M,D*
DePaul University	M,D
Drexel University	M,D*
Fordham University	M,D
Golden Gate University	M,D
Hofstra University	M,D,O
Indiana University–Purdue University Indianapolis	M,D,O
Michigan State University College of Law	M,D
Montclair State University	M,O
Santa Clara University	M,D,O
Suffolk University	M,D
Texas A&M University	M,D
University of Baltimore	M,D
University of Houston	M,D
University of New Hampshire	M,D,O
University of Pittsburgh	M*
University of San Francisco	M
University of Washington	M,D
Western Michigan University Thomas M. Cooley Law School	M,D
Yeshiva University	M,D

INTERDISCIPLINARY STUDIES

Alaska Pacific University	M
Amberton University	M
Antioch University New England	M
Arizona State University at the Tempe campus	M
Athabasca University	M,O
Baylor University	D
Boise State University	M
Bowling Green State University	M,D
Buffalo State College, State University of New York	M
California Institute of Integral Studies	M,D,O
California State University, Bakersfield	M
California State University, East Bay	M
California State University, San Bernardino	M
California State University, Stanislaus	M
Cambridge College	M,D,O
Campbell University	M
Central Washington University	M
The Citadel, The Military College of South Carolina	M,O
Clarkson University	M,D
Colorado State University	M,D
Concordia University (Canada)	M,D
Dalhousie University	D
Dallas Baptist University	M
DePaul University	M
Eastern Washington University	M
Emory University	D
Fitchburg State University	O
Florida Gulf Coast University	M
Florida Institute of Technology	M
Fresno Pacific University	M
Frostburg State University	M,D
George Mason University	M
Georgetown University	M,D
Goddard College	M
Grand Rapids Theological Seminary of Cornerstone University	M
Harrison Middleton University	M,D
Hiram College	M
Hollins University	M
Hood College	M,O*
Indiana University Southeast	M,O
Iowa State University of Science and Technology	M
Kansas State University	M,O
Lehigh University	M,D
Lesley University	M,D,O
Long Island University–LIU Post	M,D,O
Marquette University	D
Marywood University	D
Massachusetts College of Art and Design	M,O
Michigan Technological University	M,D,O
Mills College	M,O
Minnesota State University Mankato	M
Montana State University Billings	M
Montana Tech of The University of Montana	M
Murray State University	M,O
New Mexico State University	M,D
New York Institute of Technology	M,O
New York University	M*
Niagara University	M
Northeastern University	M,D,O
Nova Southeastern University	M,D,O*
The Ohio State University	M,D
Oregon State University	M
Regent University	M,D,O
Rensselaer Polytechnic Institute	M,D
Rochester Institute of Technology	M
Rosalind Franklin University of Medicine and Science	D
Rutgers University–New Brunswick	D
San Diego State University	M
Sonoma State University	M
Southern Illinois University Edwardsville	M
Southern Oregon University	M
Southern Utah University	M
State University of New York at Fredonia	M,O
Stephen F. Austin State University	M
Teachers College, Columbia University	M,D
Texas A&M University–Texarkana	M
Texas State University	M
Texas Tech University	M,D
Trinity Western University	M
Tufts University	D*
Tulane University	D
Union Institute & University	D
University at Buffalo, the State University of New York	M
The University of Alabama	D
University of Alaska Fairbanks	M,D
The University of Arizona	M,D
University of Arkansas at Little Rock	M
University of California, Santa Barbara	D
University of California, Santa Cruz	M,D*
University of Central Florida	M,O
University of Central Oklahoma	M
University of Cincinnati	D
University of Colorado Colorado Springs	M
University of Dayton	M
University of Florida	M,D
University of Houston–Victoria	M
University of Idaho	M
University of Illinois at Chicago	D
University of Illinois at Springfield	M
University of Illinois at Urbana–Champaign	D
The University of Kansas	D
University of Louisville	M,D
University of Maine	M,D
University of Manitoba	M,D
University of Massachusetts Medical School	M,D
University of Memphis	M,D,O
University of Minnesota, Twin Cities Campus	D
University of Missouri–Kansas City	D
University of Montana	M,D
University of New Brunswick Fredericton	M,D
University of North Alabama	M
The University of North Carolina at Charlotte	M,D,O
University of Northern British Columbia	M,D,O
University of North Texas	M,D,O
University of Oklahoma	M,D*
University of Oregon	M
University of Ottawa	D,O
University of Pittsburgh	D*
University of Regina	M
University of South Dakota	M
University of South Florida	M,D*
The University of Tennessee at Martin	M
The University of Texas at Dallas	M
The University of Texas at El Paso	M
The University of Texas at San Antonio	M,D
The University of Texas at Tyler	M
The University of Texas Health Science Center at San Antonio	D
The University of Texas Rio Grande Valley	M
University of Vermont	M

*M—masters degree; D—doctorate; O—other advanced degree; *—Close-Up and/or Display*

University of Virginia M,D
University of Washington, Tacoma M
The University of Western Ontario M,D
Virginia Commonwealth University M
Virginia Polytechnic Institute and State University M,D
Virginia State University M
Walden University M,D,O
Washington State University D
Western Kentucky University M,O
Western New Mexico University M
West Texas A&M University M
Worcester Polytechnic Institute M,D,O
York University M

INTERIOR DESIGN

Academy of Art University M
Ball State University M
Boston Architectural College M
Brenau University M
California State Polytechnic University, Pomona M
Chatham University M
Cornell University M
Drexel University M*
Eastern Michigan University M
Endicott College M
Florida International University M,O
Florida State University M
The George Washington University M
Georgia State University M
Interior Designers Institute M
Iowa State University of Science and Technology M
Kansas State University M
Lawrence Technological University M,O
Marymount University M
Marywood University M
Miami University M
Michigan State University M,D
Moore College of Art & Design M
The New School M
New York School of Interior Design M
The Ohio State University M
Paris College of Art M
Pontificia Universidad Catolica Madre y Maestra M
Pratt Institute M*
Purdue University M,D
Queens University of Charlotte M
Rhode Island School of Design M
San Diego State University M
Savannah College of Art and Design M
School of the Art Institute of Chicago M
Suffolk University M
Texas Tech University M,D
Thomas Jefferson University M
University of California, Berkeley O
University of Cincinnati M
University of Florida M,D
University of Georgia M,D
University of Kentucky M
University of Manitoba M
University of Massachusetts Amherst M*
University of Minnesota, Twin Cities Campus M,D,O
University of Nebraska–Lincoln M,D
The University of North Carolina at Greensboro M,O
University of North Texas M,D,O
University of Oklahoma M,O*
University of Oregon M
The University of Tennessee at Chattanooga M
The University of Texas at Austin M
Virginia Commonwealth University M,D
Washington State University M
Wayne State University M

INTERNATIONAL AFFAIRS

American Graduate School in Paris M,D
American Public University System M,D
American University M,D,O
The American University in Cairo M,O
American University of Armenia M
American University of Beirut M,D
The American University of Paris M
Anabaptist Mennonite Biblical Seminary M,O
Arcadia University M
Baruch College of the City University of New York M*
Baylor University M,D
Boston University M*
Brandeis University M
Brigham Young University M
Brock University M
Brooklyn College of the City University of New York M
Carleton University M,D
The Catholic University of America M,D
Central Connecticut State University M
Central European University M,D
Central Michigan University M,O
Chapman University M*
City College of the City University of New York M
Claremont Graduate University M,D
Cleveland State University M
Columbia University M,D*
Concordia University Irvine M*
Cornell University D
Dallas Baptist University M
DePaul University M
East Carolina University M,O
Eastern University M
Embry-Riddle Aeronautical University–Worldwide M
Fairleigh Dickinson University, Metropolitan Campus M
Florida International University M,D
Florida State University M
Fordham University M,O
George Mason University M,D
Georgetown University M,D
The George Washington University M,D
Georgia Institute of Technology M
Harvard University D*
Indiana University Bloomington M
Indiana University South Bend M,O
Instituto Tecnologico de Santo Domingo M,O
Instituto Tecnológico y de Estudios Superiores de Monterrey, Campus Ciudad Obregón M
International University in Geneva M,D
Johns Hopkins University M,D,O*
Kennesaw State University M
Lebanese American University M
Lesley University M,D,O
Liberty University M,D
Lipscomb University M,O
London Metropolitan University M,D
Marquette University M,D
McMaster University M,D
Middlebury Institute of International Studies at Monterey M
Middle Tennessee State University M
Missouri State University M
Morgan State University M
New England College M
The New School M
New York University M,D*
North Carolina State University M
Northeastern University M,D
Northwestern University M,D,O
Norwich University M
Ohio University M
Oklahoma State University M,D,O
Old Dominion University M,D
Penn State University Park M*
Pepperdine University M,D
Pepperdine University M,D
Pontificia Universidad Catolica Madre y Maestra M
Portland State University M
Princeton University M,D
Queen's University at Kingston M,D
Regent's University London M
Regent University M
Richmond, The American International University in London M
Rutgers University–Camden M
Rutgers University–Newark M,D
Rutgers University–New Brunswick M,D
St. Mary's University (United States) M,O
Salve Regina University M,O
San Francisco State University M
Schiller International University M
Seton Hall University M,O
Simon Fraser University M
SIT Graduate Institute M
Syracuse University M*
Teachers College, Columbia University M,D,O
Texas A&M University M,O
Texas State University M
Troy University M
Tufts University M,D*
United States International University–Africa M
Universidad de las Americas, A.C. M
Universidad Nacional Pedro Henriquez Urena M
Université de Montréal M,O
Université Laval M,D
University of Bridgeport M
The University of British Columbia M
University of California, Berkeley M
University of California, San Diego M,D*
University of California, Santa Barbara M,D
University of California, Santa Cruz D*
University of Chicago M
University of Colorado Denver M,O
University of Connecticut M*
University of Delaware M,D*
University of Denver M,D,O
University of Florida M
University of Georgia M,D
University of Hawaii at Manoa O
University of Indianapolis M
The University of Kansas M
University of Kentucky M
University of Maine M
The University of Manchester D
University of Massachusetts Boston M
University of Miami M,D*
University of Michigan–Flint M
The University of North Carolina at Chapel Hill M
University of Northern British Columbia M,D,O
University of North Georgia M
University of North Texas M,D,O
University of Notre Dame M
University of Oklahoma M*
University of Oregon M
University of Pennsylvania M*
University of Pittsburgh M,D,O*
University of San Diego M
University of San Francisco M
University of South Carolina M,D
University of Southern California M,D*
University of South Florida O*
University of the Pacific M,D
University of Toronto M
University of Utah M,D
University of Virginia M,D
University of Washington M,D
University of Waterloo M,D
University of Wyoming M
Virginia International University M
Virginia Polytechnic Institute and State University M,D
Walden University M,D,O
Webster University M
Western Michigan University M,D
Wilfrid Laurier University M,D
Yale University M
York University M

INTERNATIONAL AND COMPARATIVE EDUCATION

The American University in Cairo M
Andrews University M
Boston College M
Bowling Green State University M
California Baptist University M
California State University, Dominguez Hills M
The College of New Jersey M,O
Drexel University M,D*
East Carolina University M,O
Florida International University M,D,O
Florida State University M,D,O
Gallaudet University M,D,O
The George Washington University M,D,O
Harvard University M*
Indiana University Bloomington M,D,O
Louisiana State University and Agricultural & Mechanical College M,D
Loyola University Chicago M,D
Middlebury Institute of International Studies at Monterey M
Morehead State University M,O
New York University M,D,O*
St. John's University (NY) D
SIT Graduate Institute M
Stanford University M,D
Teachers College, Columbia University M,D
University at Albany, State University of New York M,D,O
University of Bridgeport M,D,O
University of Massachusetts Amherst M,D,O*
University of Minnesota, Twin Cities Campus M,D
University of Pennsylvania M*
University of Pittsburgh M,D*
University of San Francisco M,D
University of South Africa M,D
University of Wisconsin–Madison M,D,O
Vanderbilt University M,D*
Walden University M,D,O
Wilkes University M,D

INTERNATIONAL BUSINESS

Abilene Christian University M
Amberton University M
American Business & Technology University M
American College Dublin M
American InterContinental University Atlanta M
American InterContinental University Online M
The American University in Dubai M
The American University of Paris M
Anaheim University M,D,O
Argosy University, Atlanta M,D
Argosy University, Chicago M,D
Argosy University, Hawai`i M,D,O
Argosy University, Los Angeles M,D
Argosy University, Northern Virginia M,D,O
Argosy University, Orange County M,D,O
Argosy University, Phoenix M,D
Argosy University, Seattle M,D
Argosy University, Tampa M,D
Argosy University, Twin Cities M,D
Arizona State University at the Tempe campus M,D
Ashland University M
Ashworth College M
Assumption College M,O
Avila University M
Azusa Pacific University M*
Baldwin Wallace University M
Barry University O
Baruch College of the City University of New York M,D*
Benedictine University M
Boston University M*
Brandeis University M,D
Brandman University M
Brooklyn College of the City University of New York M
Bryant University M
Butler University M
California Intercontinental University M,D
California Lutheran University M,O
California State University, Fullerton M
California State University, Los Angeles M
California State University, San Bernardino M
California University of Management and Sciences M,D
Canisius College M
Central European University M,D
Central Michigan University M,O
Christian Brothers University M,O
City University of Seattle M,O
Clarkson University O
Clayton State University M
Colorado State University–Global Campus M
Columbia University M*
Concordia University Wisconsin M
Copenhagen Business School M,D
Daemen College M
Dallas Baptist University M
Delaware Valley University M
DePaul University M,D
Duke University M,O*
D'Youville College M
Eastern Michigan University M,O
Embry-Riddle Aeronautical University–Worldwide M
Emory University M
ESSEC Business School M,D
Fairleigh Dickinson University, Florham Campus M,O
Fairleigh Dickinson University, Metropolitan Campus M
Florida Atlantic University M
Florida International University M,D
Florida State University M
Franklin University Switzerland M
George Mason University M,O
Georgetown University M,D
The George Washington University M,D
Georgia Institute of Technology M
Georgia State University M
Golden Gate University M,D,O
Goldey-Beacom College M
Hallmark University M
Harding University M
Hawai`i Pacific University M
HEC Montreal M,D
Hofstra University M,O
Hope International University M
Houston Baptist University M
Howard University M
Hult International Business School (United States) M
IGlobal University M
Indiana Tech D
Instituto Tecnologico de Santo Domingo M,O
Instituto Tecnológico y de Estudios Superiores de Monterrey, Campus Central de Veracruz M
Instituto Tecnológico y de Estudios Superiores de Monterrey, Campus Chihuahua M,O
Instituto Tecnológico y de Estudios Superiores de Monterrey, Campus Ciudad de México M,D
Instituto Tecnológico y de Estudios Superiores de Monterrey, Campus Cuernavaca M
Instituto Tecnológico y de Estudios Superiores de Monterrey, Campus Irapuato M,D
Instituto Tecnológico y de Estudios Superiores de Monterrey, Campus Monterrey M
Inter American University of Puerto Rico, Metropolitan Campus M,D
Inter American University of Puerto Rico, San Germán Campus M,D
International University in Geneva M,D
The International University of Monaco M
Iona College M,O
John Brown University M
Kean University M
Keiser University M,D
Lake Forest Graduate School of Management M
La Salle University M,O
Lenoir-Rhyne University M
Lewis University M
Liberty University M,D
Lincoln University (CA) M,D
Lindenwood University M
Long Island University–LIU Post M
Loyola University Chicago M
Lynn University M
Madonna University M
Maine Maritime Academy M
Manhattanville College M,O
Marconi International University M,D
Marquette University M,O
McGill University M,D,O
McKendree University M
Milwaukee School of Engineering M
National American University (TX) M,D
National University M,D
Newman University M
New Mexico Highlands University M
New York University M,D*
Niagara University M
Northeastern University M
Northern Arizona University M
Northwestern University M,D
Northwest University M
Norwich University M
Nova Southeastern University M*
Oakland University M,O
Oklahoma Christian University M
Oklahoma State University M,D
Old Dominion University M
Oral Roberts University M
Pace University M,O
Pacific States University M,O
Park University M,O
Pepperdine University M
Pittsburg State University M
Point Park University M
Polytechnic University of Puerto Rico M
Polytechnic University of Puerto Rico, Miami Campus M
Polytechnic University of Puerto Rico, Orlando Campus M
Pontifical Catholic University of Puerto Rico M
Pontificia Universidad Catolica Madre y Maestra M
Portland State University M
Providence College M

Purdue University	M
Purdue University Global	M
Regent's University London	M
Rochester Institute of Technology	M
Rockhurst University	M,O
Rollins College	M
Rutgers University–Newark	D
St. John's University (NY)	M
Saint Joseph's University	M,O*
Saint Leo University	M,D
Saint Louis University	M,D*
Saint Peter's University	M
St. Thomas University	M,O
Salem International University	M
San Francisco State University	M
San Ignacio University	M
Schiller International University (United States)	M
Schiller International University (Germany)	M
Schiller International University	M
Schiller International University (Spain)	M
Seton Hall University	M,O
SIT Graduate Institute	M
Southeastern University (FL)	M,D
Southern New Hampshire University	M,D,O
Southern Oregon University	M,O
State University of New York Empire State College	M
Stevens Institute of Technology	M
Suffolk University	M
Temple University	M,D*
Tennessee Technological University	M
Texas A&M International University	M,D
Texas A&M University–Corpus Christi	M
Thomas Edison State University	M
Tiffin University	M
Trident University International	M,D
Trinity Western University	M
Tufts University	M,D*
Tulane University	M,D
United States International University–Africa	M
Universidad Autonoma de Guadalajara	M,D
Universidad Metropolitana	M
Université de Sherbrooke	M
Université du Québec, École nationale d'administration publique	M,O
Université Laval	M,O
University at Buffalo, the State University of New York	M,D
The University of Akron	M
University of Alberta	M
University of Baltimore	M
University of Bridgeport	M
University of California, Berkeley	O
University of California, San Diego	M*
University of Chicago	M,O
University of Colorado Denver	M,D
University of Dallas	M,D
University of Florida	M,D
University of Hawaii at Manoa	M,D
University of Houston–Downtown	M
University of Houston–Victoria	M
University of Kentucky	M
University of La Verne	M
University of Lethbridge	M,D
University of Louisiana at Lafayette	M
University of Louisville	M
The University of Manchester	M
University of Mary Hardin-Baylor	M
University of Massachusetts Boston	M
University of Michigan–Flint	M,O
University of New Brunswick Saint John	M
University of New Haven	M*
University of New Mexico	M
University of North Alabama	M
The University of North Carolina Wilmington	M
University of North Florida	M
University of Oklahoma	M,D*
University of Pennsylvania	M*
University of Phoenix–Bay Area Campus	M,D
University of Phoenix–Central Valley Campus	M
University of Phoenix–Dallas Campus	M
University of Phoenix–Hawaii Campus	M
University of Phoenix–Houston Campus	M
University of Phoenix–Las Vegas Campus	M
University of Phoenix–Online Campus	M,O
University of Phoenix–Phoenix Campus	M,O
University of Phoenix–Sacramento Valley Campus	M
University of Phoenix–San Antonio Campus	M
University of Phoenix–San Diego Campus	M
University of Pittsburgh	O*
University of Puerto Rico–Río Piedras	M,D
University of Regina	M,O
University of St. Thomas (TX)	M
University of San Diego	M
University of San Francisco	M
University of Saskatchewan	M,D
The University of Scranton	M
University of South Carolina	M
The University of Tampa	M,O
The University of Texas at Dallas	M,D
The University of Texas at El Paso	M,D,O
University of the West	M
The University of Toledo	M
University of Virginia	M,O
University of Washington	M,D,O
The University of Western Ontario	M,D
University of Wisconsin–Oshkosh	M
Vancouver Island University	M
Villanova University	M
Virginia International University	M,O
Viterbo University	M
Walden University	M,D,O
Walsh College of Accountancy and Business Administration	M
Warner University	M
Wayland Baptist University	M,D
Webber International University	M
Webster University	M
Wilkes University	M
Xavier University	M*
York University	M,D

INTERNATIONAL DEVELOPMENT

American University	M,D,O
Andrews University	M
Athabasca University	M,O
Clark University	M
The College of William and Mary	M*
Dalhousie University	M
Duke University	M*
Eastern University	M
Fordham University	M,O
Georgetown University	M
The George Washington University	M,D
Harvard University	M*
Hope International University	M
Indiana University Bloomington	M,D,O
Johns Hopkins University	M,D,O*
Marymount California University	M
McGill University	M,D,O
Middlebury Institute of International Studies at Monterey	M
Norwich University	M
Ohio University	M
Old Dominion University	M,D
Rutgers University–Camden	M
Saint Mary's University (Canada)	M,O
St. Mary's University (United States)	M,O
Saint Mary's University of Minnesota	M
Tufts University	M*
Tulane University	M,D
University of California, San Diego	M*
University of Denver	M,D,O
University of Florida	M,D,O
University of Guelph	M,D
University of Hawaii at Manoa	M,D,O
The University of Manchester	M,D
University of Massachusetts Boston	M,D
University of Minnesota, Twin Cities Campus	M
University of New Brunswick Fredericton	M
University of New Mexico	M,D
University of Ottawa	M
University of Pittsburgh	M,D*
University of San Francisco	M
University of Southern Mississippi	M,D
Walden University	M,D,O

INTERNATIONAL ECONOMICS

American University	M,D,O
Baruch College of the City University of New York	M*
Bryant University	M
Claremont Graduate University	M,D,O
Cleveland State University	M
Fordham University	M,D,O
Johns Hopkins University	M,D,O*
The New School	M,D
Pace University	O
University of California, San Diego	M*
University of New Mexico	M,D
Valparaiso University	M
Wayne State University	M,D
Wichita State University	M
Wilfrid Laurier University	M
Yale University	M

INTERNATIONAL HEALTH

Arizona State University at the Tempe campus	M,D,O
A.T. Still University	M,D,O
Boston University	M,D*
Brandeis University	M,D
Cedarville University	M,D
Central Michigan University	M,D,O
Clark University	M
Clemson University	M,D,O
The College of New Jersey	M
Duke University	M*
East Tennessee State University	M,D,O
Emory University	M
Endicott College	M,O
George Mason University	M,O
Georgetown University	M,D
The George Washington University	M,D
Harvard University	M,D*
Indiana University–Purdue University Indianapolis	M,D,O
Johns Hopkins University	M,D*
Liberty University	M,D
Loma Linda University	M
Medical University of South Carolina	M
National University of Natural Medicine	M
New York Institute of Technology	O
New York Medical College	M,D,O
New York University	M,D*
Northwestern University	M
Oregon State University	M,D
Park University	M,O
St. Catherine University	M
San Diego State University	M,D
Seton Hall University	M,O
Simon Fraser University	M,D,O
Syracuse University	M*
Trident University International	M,D,O
Tulane University	M,D
Uniformed Services University of the Health Sciences	M,D*
University of Alberta	M,D
University of California, Riverside	M,D
University of California, San Diego	D*
University of Colorado Denver	M
University of Denver	M,D,O
University of Florida	M,D
University of Maryland, Baltimore	M,D,O
University of Michigan	M,D*
University of Minnesota, Twin Cities Campus	M,D
University of Northern Colorado	M
University of North Texas Health Science Center at Fort Worth	M,D,O
University of Pennsylvania	M*
University of Pittsburgh	M,D,O*
University of Southern California	M,O*
University of South Florida	M,D,O*
The University of Toledo	M,O
University of Vermont	M,O
University of Washington	M,D
Walden University	M,D,O
Washington University in St. Louis	M,D
William James College	M,D,O
Yale University	M,D

INTERNATIONAL TRADE POLICY

Baruch College of the City University of New York	M*
The George Washington University	M
Middlebury Institute of International Studies at Monterey	M
Valparaiso University	M

INTERNET AND INTERACTIVE MULTIMEDIA

Academy of Art University	M
Alfred University	M
Ball State University	M
Boston University	M,O*
Brandeis University	M
Brooklyn College of the City University of New York	M
California State University, East Bay	M
Champlain College	M
College of Saint Elizabeth	M
Concordia University (Canada)	M,D,O
DePaul University	M,D
Elon University	M
Excelsior College	M,O
Fairfield University	M,O
Full Sail University	M
Georgetown University	M
Georgia Institute of Technology	M,D
Ithaca College	M
Kutztown University of Pennsylvania	M
Liberty University	M
Lindenwood University	M
Lindenwood University–Belleville	M
Lindsey Wilson College	M
London Metropolitan University	M,D
Long Island University–LIU Post	M
Louisiana State University and Agricultural & Mechanical College	M
Lynn University	M,O
Minneapolis College of Art and Design	M
Mount Mary University	M
National University	M
New Mexico Highlands University	M
The New School	M
New York University	M*
Northeastern University	M
Northwestern University	M
The Ohio State University	M
Ohio University	M
Pace University	M,D,O
Pratt Institute	M*
Quinnipiac University	M
Robert Morris University	M,D
Rochester Institute of Technology	O
Rocky Mountain College of Art + Design	M
Sam Houston State University	M
San Diego State University	M
Savannah College of Art and Design	M
School of Visual Arts (NY)	M
Southern New Hampshire University	M,D,O
State University of New York at Oswego	M
Stevens Institute of Technology	M,D,O
Tennessee Technological University	M
Texas Woman's University	M
Thomas Jefferson University	M
Touro College	M
Towson University	M,O
Universidad Autonoma de Guadalajara	M,D
University of Advancing Technology	M
The University of British Columbia	M
University of California, Santa Cruz	M,D*
University of Chicago	M
University of Colorado Boulder	D
University of Miami	M*
University of Montana	M
University of North Texas	M,D,O
University of Pennsylvania	M,O*
University of Southern California	M,D,O*
University of South Florida	M,O*
The University of Texas at Dallas	M,D
University of the Sacred Heart	M,O
University of Utah	M,D
Virginia Polytechnic Institute and State University	M,D
Walla Walla University	M
Webster University	M
Wilmington University	M
Worcester Polytechnic Institute	M

INTERNET ENGINEERING

Hofstra University	M
New Jersey Institute of Technology	M,D
Wilmington University	M

INVESTMENT MANAGEMENT

Alaska Pacific University	M,O
Creighton University	M,D
Fordham University	M,D
The George Washington University	M,D
Hofstra University	M,O
Johns Hopkins University	M,O*
Lincoln University (CA)	M,D
Loyola University Maryland	M
Lynn University	M
Manhattanville College	M,O
Marywood University	M
New York University	M*
Pace University	M,O
Regent University	M,D,O
Sacred Heart University	M,D,O
Saint Mary's College of California	M
Southern New Hampshire University	M,D,O
Temple University	M,O*
University of Houston–Downtown	M
University of Notre Dame	M
University of Wisconsin–Madison	D
University of Wisconsin–Milwaukee	M,O*
Walsh College of Accountancy and Business Administration	M

ITALIAN

Binghamton University, State University of New York	M
Boston College	M
Brown University	D
Central Connecticut State University	M,O
Columbia University	M,D*
Cornell University	D
DePaul University	M
Drew University	M,D,O
Duke University	D*
Florida State University	M
The Graduate Center, City University of New York	M,D
Harvard University	M,D*
Hofstra University	M,D,O
Hunter College of the City University of New York	M
Indiana University Bloomington	M,D
Johns Hopkins University	M,D*
Manhattanville College	M,O
McGill University	M,D
Middlebury College	M,D
New York University	M,D,O*
Northwestern University	D,O
The Ohio State University	M,D
Queens College of the City University of New York	M
Rutgers University–New Brunswick	M,D
San Francisco State University	M
Stanford University	M,D
Stony Brook University, State University of New York	M
University of Alberta	M,D
University of California, Berkeley	D
University of California, Los Angeles	M,D*
University of Chicago	D
University of Georgia	M,D
University of Illinois at Urbana–Champaign	M,D
University of Massachusetts Amherst	M*
University of Michigan	D*
The University of North Carolina at Chapel Hill	M,D
University of Notre Dame	M
University of Oregon	M
University of Pennsylvania	M,D*
University of Pittsburgh	M,D*
University of South Africa	M,D
The University of Tennessee	D
The University of Texas at Austin	M,D
University of Toronto	M,D
University of Victoria	M
University of Washington	M,D
University of Wisconsin–Madison	M,D
Wayne State University	M,D
Yale University	D

*M—masters degree; D—doctorate; O—other advanced degree; *—Close-Up and/or Display*

JAPANESE

Arizona State University at the Tempe campus	M
Columbia University	M,D*
DePaul University	M
Harvard University	D*
Indiana University Bloomington	M,D
Kent State University	M,D
New York University	M,D,O*
The Ohio State University	M,D
Portland State University	M
Purdue University	M,D
San Francisco State University	M
Stanford University	M,D
University of Alberta	M
University of California, Berkeley	D
University of California, Irvine	M,D
University of Colorado Boulder	M,D
University of Hawaii at Manoa	M,D,O
The University of Manchester	D
University of Massachusetts Amherst	M*
University of Oregon	M,D
University of Pittsburgh	M*
University of Washington	M,D
University of Wisconsin–Madison	M,D
Washington University in St. Louis	M,D

JEWISH STUDIES

Academy for Jewish Religion California	M
American Jewish University	M
Biola University	M,D,O
Brandeis University	M,D
Brooklyn College of the City University of New York	M
Central Yeshiva Tomchei Tmimim-Lubavitch	M
Columbia University	M,D*
Concordia University (Canada)	M
Cornell University	M,D
Criswell College	M
Dallas Theological Seminary	M,D,O
Graduate Theological Union	M,D,O
Gratz College	M,O
Harvard University	M,D*
Hebrew College	M,O
Hebrew Union College–Jewish Institute of Religion (NY)	M
Indiana University Bloomington	M,D
The Jewish Theological Seminary	M,D
McGill University	M
New York University	M,D,O*
Reconstructionist Rabbinical College	M,D,O
Rice University	D
Rutgers University–New Brunswick	M,O
Seton Hall University	M,O
Southern Evangelical Seminary	M,D,O
Spertus Institute for Jewish Learning and Leadership	M,D
Telshe Yeshiva–Chicago	O
Touro College	M
Towson University	M,O
University of California, San Diego	M,D*
University of Connecticut	M*
University of Florida	M,D
University of Maryland, College Park	M
University of Michigan	M,D,O*
University of St. Michael's College	M,D,O
University of Wisconsin–Madison	M,D
Washington University in St. Louis	M
Yeshiva University	M,D

JOURNALISM

American University	M
The American University in Cairo	M,O
Arizona State University at the Tempe campus	M,D
Arkansas State University	M
Arkansas Tech University	M
Ball State University	M
Baylor University	M
Bob Jones University	M,D,O
Boston University	M*
California State University, Northridge	M
Carleton University	M,D
Clarion University of Pennsylvania	M
Columbia University	M,D*
Concordia University (Canada)	M,O
CUNY Graduate School of Journalism	M
DePaul University	M
Florida Agricultural and Mechanical University	M
Florida International University	M
Full Sail University	M
Georgetown University	M,D
Harvard University	M,O*
Hofstra University	M
Iowa State University of Science and Technology	M
Kansas State University	M
Kent State University	M
Lindenwood University	M
Marquette University	M,O
Marshall University	M,O
Michigan State University	M
Murray State University	M
National University	M
New York University	M,D,O*
Northeastern University	M
Northwestern University	M
Ohio University	M,D
Point Park University	M
Quinnipiac University	M
Regent University	M,D
Sacred Heart University	M
School of the Art Institute of Chicago	M
South Dakota State University	M
Southeastern Louisiana University	M
Stony Brook University, State University of New York	M,O
Syracuse University	M*
Temple University	M*
Université Laval	O
The University of Alabama	M
The University of Arizona	M
University of Arkansas	M
The University of British Columbia	M
University of California, Berkeley	M
University of Colorado Boulder	M,D
University of Florida	M,D
University of Georgia	M,D
University of Illinois at Springfield	M
University of Illinois at Urbana–Champaign	M
The University of Iowa	M,D*
The University of Kansas	M,D
University of King's College	M
University of Maryland, College Park	M,D
University of Memphis	M,O
University of Miami	M,D*
University of Mississippi	M
University of Missouri	M,D
University of Montana	M
University of Nebraska–Lincoln	M
University of Nevada, Las Vegas	M
University of Nevada, Reno	M
The University of North Carolina at Chapel Hill	M,D,O
University of North Texas	M,D,O
University of Oklahoma	M,D*
University of Oregon	M,D
University of Puerto Rico–Río Piedras	M
University of Regina	M
University of South Carolina	M,D
University of Southern California	M*
University of South Florida	M,O*
University of South Florida, St. Petersburg	M
The University of Tennessee	M,D
The University of Texas at Austin	M,D
The University of Western Ontario	M
University of Wisconsin–Madison	M,D
Virginia Commonwealth University	M
Wayne State University	M,D,O
West Virginia University	M,O

KINESIOLOGY AND MOVEMENT STUDIES

Alabama Agricultural and Mechanical University	M
A.T. Still University	M,D,O
Azusa Pacific University	M*
Ball State University	M,D,O
Barry University	M
Baylor University	M,D
Boise State University	M
Bowling Green State University	M
Brooklyn College of the City University of New York	M
California State Polytechnic University, Pomona	M
California State University, Chico	M
California State University, Fresno	M
California State University, Long Beach	M
California State University, Los Angeles	M,O
California State University, Northridge	M
California State University, San Marcos	M
Canisius College	M
Columbia University	M,D*
Dalhousie University	M
Dallas Baptist University	M
East Carolina University	M,D,O
Eastern Illinois University	M
Eastern Michigan University	M
East Tennessee State University	M,D
East Texas Baptist University	M
Fresno Pacific University	M
Georgia College & State University	M
Georgia Southern University	M
Georgia State University	D
Hardin-Simmons University	M
Houston Baptist University	M
Humboldt State University	M
Indiana University Bloomington	M,D
Indiana University–Purdue University Indianapolis	M,O
Inter American University of Puerto Rico, San Germán Campus	M
Iowa State University of Science and Technology	M,D
Jacksonville University	M*
James Madison University	M
Kansas State University	M,D
Lakehead University	M
Lamar University	M
Louisiana State University and Agricultural & Mechanical College	M,D
Louisiana Tech University	M,D,O
McDaniel College	M
McGill University	M,D,O
McMaster University	M,D
Memorial University of Newfoundland	M
Michigan State University	M,D
Michigan Technological University	M,D
Mississippi College	M
Mississippi State University	M,D
Missouri State University	M
New Mexico State University	D
New York University	M,D,O*
Northeastern State University	M
Northwestern University	D
The Ohio State University	M,D
Old Dominion University	M,D
Oregon State University	M,D
Penn State University Park	M,D,O*
Point Loma Nazarene University	M
Prairie View A&M University	M
Purdue University	M,D
Saint Mary's College of California	M
Sam Houston State University	M
San Diego State University	M
San Francisco State University	M
San Jose State University	M
Sarah Lawrence College	M
Simon Fraser University	M,D
Sonoma State University	M
Southeastern Louisiana University	M
Southeastern University (FL)	M,D
Southern Arkansas University–Magnolia	M
Southern Illinois University Carbondale	M
Southern Illinois University Edwardsville	M
Southwestern Oklahoma State University	M
Stephen F. Austin State University	M
Syracuse University	M,D,O*
Tarleton State University	M
Teachers College, Columbia University	M,D
Temple University	M,D*
Tennessee Technological University	M
Texas A&M University	M,D
Texas A&M University–Commerce	M,D,O
Texas A&M University–Corpus Christi	M,D
Texas A&M University–Kingsville	M
Texas A&M University–San Antonio	M
Texas Christian University	M
Texas Tech University	M
Texas Woman's University	M,D
Université de Montréal	M,D,O
Université de Sherbrooke	M,O
Université du Québec à Montréal	M
Université Laval	M,D
The University of Alabama	M,D
University of Arkansas	M,D
The University of British Columbia	M,D
University of Calgary	M,D
University of Central Arkansas	M
University of Central Missouri	M,D,O
University of Colorado Boulder	M,D
University of Delaware	M,D*
University of Florida	M,D
University of Georgia	M,D
University of Hawaii at Manoa	M,D
University of Houston	M,D
University of Idaho	M,D
University of Illinois at Chicago	M,D
University of Illinois at Urbana–Champaign	M,D
University of Kentucky	M,D
University of Lethbridge	M,D
University of Maine	M,D,O
University of Manitoba	M
University of Mary	M
University of Maryland, College Park	M,D
University of Massachusetts Amherst	M,D*
University of Michigan	M,D*
University of Minnesota, Twin Cities Campus	M,D
University of Mississippi	M,D
University of Nebraska at Omaha	M,D
University of Nevada, Las Vegas	M,D
University of New Hampshire	M,O
University of North Alabama	M
The University of North Carolina at Chapel Hill	D
The University of North Carolina at Charlotte	M
The University of North Carolina at Greensboro	M,D
University of North Dakota	M
University of Northern Iowa	M
University of North Georgia	M
University of North Texas	M,D,O
University of Ottawa	M
University of Puerto Rico–Mayagüez	M
University of Regina	M,D
University of Saskatchewan	M,D,O
University of South Alabama	M
University of South Dakota	M
University of Southern California	M,D*
The University of Tennessee	M,D
The University of Texas at Arlington	M,D
The University of Texas at Austin	M,D
The University of Texas at El Paso	M
The University of Texas at San Antonio	M
The University of Texas at Tyler	M
The University of Texas of the Permian Basin	M
The University of Texas Rio Grande Valley	M
University of the Incarnate Word	M,D
University of Toronto	M,D
The University of Tulsa	M
University of Utah	M,D
University of Victoria	M
University of Virginia	M,D
University of Waterloo	M,D
The University of Western Ontario	M,D
University of Windsor	M
University of Wisconsin–Madison	M,D
University of Wisconsin–Milwaukee	M,D*
University of Wyoming	M
Utah State University	M,D
Washington University in St. Louis	D
Wayne State University	M,D
West Chester University of Pennsylvania	M,O
Western Illinois University	M
Wilfrid Laurier University	M
York University	M,D

LANDSCAPE ARCHITECTURE

Academy of Art University	M
Arizona State University at the Tempe campus	M,D
Auburn University	M*
Ball State University	M
Boston Architectural College	M
California State Polytechnic University, Pomona	M
City College of the City University of New York	M
Clemson University	M,D,O
Colorado State University	M,D
Columbia University	M*
The Conway School	M
Cornell University	M
Florida Agricultural and Mechanical University	M
Florida International University	M
Harvard University	M,D*
Illinois Institute of Technology	M,D
Iowa State University of Science and Technology	M
Kansas State University	M
Kent State University	M
Louisiana State University and Agricultural & Mechanical College	M
Mississippi State University	M
Morgan State University	M
North Carolina State University	M
North Dakota State University	M*
The Ohio State University	M,D
Oklahoma State University	M,D
Penn State University Park	M,D*
Polytechnic University of Puerto Rico	M
Pontificia Universidad Catolica Madre y Maestra	M
Rhode Island School of Design	M
State University of New York College of Environmental Science and Forestry	M
Temple University	M*
Texas A&M University	M,D
Texas Tech University	M
The University of Arizona	M
The University of British Columbia	M
University of Calgary	M,D
University of California, Berkeley	M,D,O
University of Colorado Denver	M
University of Florida	M,D
University of Georgia	M
University of Guelph	M
University of Illinois at Urbana–Champaign	M,D
The University of Manchester	M,D
University of Manitoba	M
University of Maryland, College Park	M
University of Massachusetts Amherst	M*
University of Michigan	M*
University of Minnesota, Twin Cities Campus	M
University of New Mexico	M
University of Oklahoma	M*
University of Oregon	M,D
University of Pennsylvania	M,O*
The University of Tennessee	M
The University of Texas at Arlington	M
The University of Texas at Austin	M
University of Toronto	M
University of Virginia	M
University of Washington	M
University of Wisconsin–Madison	M,D
Utah State University	M
Virginia Polytechnic Institute and State University	M,D
Washington State University	M
West Virginia University	M,D

LATIN AMERICAN STUDIES

American University	M,O
Boricua College	M
Boston University	M*
Brown University	M,D
California State University, Los Angeles	M
Centro de Estudios Avanzados de Puerto Rico y el Caribe	M,D
College of Staten Island of the City University of New York	M
Columbia University	M,D*
Cornell University	M,D
Duke University	M,D*
Florida International University	M
Georgetown University	M
The George Washington University	M
Georgia State University	M,O
Indiana University Bloomington	M
La Salle University	M,O
Michigan State University	D
New York University	M,O*
Northeastern Illinois University	M
The Ohio State University	M
Ohio University	M
San Diego State University	M

Simon Fraser University M,O
Texas Christian University M,D
Tulane University M,D
University at Albany, State University of New York M,D,O
The University of Arizona M
University of California, Los Angeles M*
University of California, San Diego M*
University of California, Santa Barbara M
University of Chicago M
University of Connecticut M*
University of Florida M,O
University of Illinois at Chicago M
University of Illinois at Urbana–Champaign M
The University of Kansas M,O
University of Louisiana at Lafayette M
The University of Manchester D
University of Massachusetts Dartmouth M,D
University of Miami M*
University of New Mexico M,D
The University of North Carolina at Chapel Hill M,D,O
The University of North Carolina at Charlotte M,D,O
University of Notre Dame M
University of Pittsburgh O*
University of Southern California D*
University of South Florida M,D,O*
The University of Texas at Austin M
The University of Texas at Dallas M,D
University of Utah M
University of Wisconsin–Madison M,D
University of Wisconsin–Milwaukee M,O*
Vanderbilt University M*
Yale University D

LAW

Abraham Lincoln University School of Law D
Albany Law School M,D
Alliant International University–San Francisco D
American University M,D
The American University in Cairo M,O
American University of Armenia M
The American University of Paris M
Appalachian School of Law D
Arizona State University at the Tempe campus M,D
Arizona Summit Law School D
Atlanta's John Marshall Law School M,D
Ave Maria School of Law D
Barry University D
Baylor University D
Belmont University D
Boston College D
Boston University M,D*
Brigham Young University M,D
Brooklyn Law School M,D
California Western School of Law M,D
Campbell University D
Capital University M,D
Case Western Reserve University M,D*
The Catholic University of America M,D
Central European University M,D
Champlain College M
Chapman University M,D*
Charleston School of Law D
City University of New York School of Law D
Cleveland State University M,D,O
The College of William and Mary M,D*
Columbia University M,D*
Concordia University (United States) D
Concord Law School D
Cornell University M,D
Creighton University M,D,O
Dalhousie University M,D
DePaul University M,D
Drake University M,D
Drexel University M,D*
Duke University M,D*
Dunlap-Stone University M
Duquesne University M,D
Elon University D
Emory University M,D,O
Empire College M,D
Faulkner University D
Florida Agricultural and Mechanical University D
Florida Coastal School of Law D
Florida International University M,D
Florida State University M,D
Fordham University M,D
Friends University M
George Mason University M,D
Georgetown University M,D
The George Washington University M,D
Georgia State University D
Golden Gate University M,D
Gonzaga University D
Harvard University M,D*
Hofstra University M,D,O
Howard University M,D
Humphreys University D
Illinois Institute of Technology M,D
Indiana University Bloomington M,D,O
Indiana University–Purdue University Indianapolis M,D,O
Instituto Tecnológico y de Estudios Superiores de Monterrey, Campus Ciudad de México O
Inter American University of Puerto Rico School of Law D
John F. Kennedy University D
The John Marshall Law School M,D
The Judge Advocate General's School, U.S. Army M
Lewis & Clark College M,D
Liberty University M
Lincoln Memorial University D
London Metropolitan University M,D
Louisiana State University and Agricultural & Mechanical College M,D
Loyola Marymount University M,D
Loyola University Chicago M,D,O
Loyola University New Orleans M,D
Marquette University D
Massachusetts School of Law at Andover D
McGill University M,D,O
Mercer University D
Michigan State University College of Law M,D
Mississippi College D,O
Mitchell Hamline School of Law M,D
Montclair State University M,O
New England Law–Boston M,D
New York Law School M,D
New York University M,D,O*
North Carolina Central University D
Northeastern University M,D
Northern Illinois University D
Northern Kentucky University D
Northwestern University M,D
Nova Southeastern University M,D*
Ohio Northern University M,D
The Ohio State University M,D
Oklahoma City University M,D
Pace University M,D
Penn State University–Dickinson Law M,D
Penn State University Park M,D*
Pepperdine University M,D
Pontifical Catholic University of Puerto Rico D
Pontificia Universidad Catolica Madre y Maestra M
Purdue University Global M
Queen's University at Kingston M,D
Quinnipiac University M,D
Regent University M,D
Roger Williams University M,D
Rutgers University–Camden D
Rutgers University–Newark D
St. John's University (NY) D
Saint Joseph's University M,O*
Saint Louis University M,D*
St. Mary's University (United States) M,D
St. Thomas University M,D
Samford University M,D
San Joaquin College of Law D
The Santa Barbara and Ventura Colleges of Law–Santa Barbara M,D
The Santa Barbara and Ventura Colleges of Law–Ventura M,D
Santa Clara University M,D,O
Savannah Law School D
Seattle University M,D
Seton Hall University M,D
Southern Illinois University Carbondale M,D
Southern Methodist University M,D
Southern University and Agricultural and Mechanical College D
South Texas College of Law Houston D
Southwestern Law School M,D*
Stanford University M,D
Stetson University M,D
Suffolk University M,D
Syracuse University M,D*
Taft University System M,D
Temple University M,D,O*
Texas A&M University M,D
Texas Southern University D
Texas Tech University M,D
Thomas Jefferson School of Law D
Touro College M,D
Trinity International University M,D
Tufts University M,D*
Tulane University M,D
Universidad Autonoma de Guadalajara M,D
Universidad Central del Este D
Universidad Iberoamericana M,D
Université de Montréal M,D,O
Université de Sherbrooke M,D,O
Université du Québec à Montréal O
Université Laval M,D,O
University at Buffalo, the State University of New York M,D
The University of Akron M,D
The University of Alabama M,D
University of Alberta M,D
The University of Arizona M,D
University of Arkansas M,D
University of Arkansas at Little Rock D
University of Baltimore M,D
The University of British Columbia M,D
University of Calgary M,D,O
University of California, Berkeley M,D
University of California, Davis M,D
University of California, Hastings College of the Law M,D
University of California, Irvine D
University of California, Los Angeles M,D*
University of Chicago M,D
University of Cincinnati M,D
University of Colorado Boulder D
University of Connecticut D*
University of Dayton M,D
University of Denver M,D,O
University of Detroit Mercy D
University of Florida M,D
University of Georgia M,D
University of Hawaii at Manoa M,D,O
University of Houston M,D
University of Idaho M,D
University of Illinois at Urbana–Champaign M,D
The University of Iowa M,D*
The University of Kansas D
University of Kentucky D
University of La Verne D
University of Louisville D
University of Maine D
The University of Manchester M,D
University of Manitoba M
University of Maryland, Baltimore M,D
University of Maryland, College Park
University of Massachusetts Dartmouth D
University of Memphis D
University of Miami M,D*
University of Michigan M,D*
University of Minnesota, Twin Cities Campus M,D
University of Mississippi M,D
University of Missouri M,D
University of Missouri–Kansas City M,D
University of Montana D
University of Nebraska–Lincoln M,D
University of Nevada, Las Vegas M,D
University of New Hampshire M,D,O
University of New Mexico D
University of North Alabama M
The University of North Carolina at Chapel Hill M,D
University of North Dakota D
University of North Texas at Dallas D
University of Notre Dame M,D
University of Oklahoma M,D*
University of Oregon M,D
University of Ottawa M,D
University of Pennsylvania M,D*
University of Pittsburgh M*
University of Puerto Rico–Río Piedras M,D
University of Richmond D
University of St. Thomas (MN) M,D
University of San Diego M,D,O
University of San Francisco D
University of Saskatchewan M,D
University of South Africa M,D
University of South Carolina D
University of South Dakota D
University of Southern California M,D*
The University of Tennessee D
The University of Texas at Austin M,D
The University of Texas at Dallas M,D
University of the District of Columbia M,D
University of the Pacific M,D
The University of Toledo M,D,O
University of Toronto M,D
The University of Tulsa M,D,O
University of Utah M,D
University of Victoria M,D
University of Virginia M,D
University of Washington M,D
The University of Western Ontario M,D,O
University of Wisconsin–Madison M,D
University of Wyoming D
Valparaiso University M,D
Vanderbilt University M,D*
Vermont Law School D
Villanova University D
Wake Forest University M,D
Walden University M,D,O
Washburn University M,D
Washington and Lee University D
Washington University in St. Louis M,D
Wayne State University M,D
Western Michigan University Thomas M. Cooley Law School M,D
Western New England University M,D
Western State College of Law at Argosy University D
West Virginia University M,D
Widener University M,D
Willamette University M,D
Yale University M,D
Yeshiva University M,D
York University M,D

LEGAL AND JUSTICE STUDIES

Arizona State University at the Tempe campus M,D,O
Auburn University at Montgomery M
Binghamton University, State University of New York M,D
Brock University M
California University of Pennsylvania M
Campbellsville University M
Capital University M
Carleton University M,O
Case Western Reserve University M,D*
The Catholic University of America M,D,O
Central European University M,D
Columbia University M,D*
The George Washington University M,D,O
Georgian Court University M,O
Golden Gate University M,D
Governors State University M
Harrison Middleton University M,D
Harvard University D*
Hodges University M
Hofstra University M,D,O
Illinois Institute of Technology M,D
Indiana University South Bend M,O
John Jay College of Criminal Justice of the City University of New York M,D
Liberty University M
Loyola University Chicago M,O
Marlboro College M
Marygrove College M,O
Michigan State University College of Law M,D
Mississippi College M,O
Montclair State University O
National Paralegal College M
National University M
New York University M,D*
Northeastern University M,D
Nova Southeastern University M,D*
Pace University M,D
Prairie View A&M University M,D
Prescott College M
Purdue University Global M,O
Queen's University at Kingston M,D
Regent University M,D
Rhode Island College M
Royal Roads University M,O
Rutgers University–New Brunswick M,D
St. John's University (NY) M
Saint Leo University M
St. Mary's University (United States) M
San Francisco State University M
San Jose State University M
The Santa Barbara and Ventura Colleges of Law–Santa Barbara M,D
The Santa Barbara and Ventura Colleges of Law–Ventura M,D
Simon Fraser University M,D
Southern Illinois University Carbondale M
Southern New Hampshire University M,D,O
Stanford University M,D
Taft University System M,D
Temple University M,D*
Texas State University M
Texas Tech University M,D
Touro College M,D
Trident University International M,D,O
Universidad Autonoma de Guadalajara M,D
Université Laval O
University at Buffalo, the State University of New York M,D
University of Baltimore M
University of Calgary M,O
University of California, Berkeley D
University of Charleston M
University of Denver M,O
University of Illinois at Springfield M
University of Massachusetts Lowell M
University of Montana M
University of Nebraska–Lincoln M
University of Nevada, Reno M,D
University of New Hampshire M,D,O
University of Pennsylvania M,D*
University of Pittsburgh M*
University of San Diego M,D,O
University of South Florida O*
University of the District of Columbia M,D
University of the Sacred Heart M
University of Washington M,D
University of Windsor M
Vermont Law School M
Washburn University M,D
Weber State University M
Webster University M,O
Western Michigan University Thomas M. Cooley Law School M,D
West Virginia University M,D
Wilfrid Laurier University D

LEISURE STUDIES

Bowling Green State University M
California State University, Long Beach M
Dalhousie University M
East Carolina University M,O
Howard University M
Indiana University Bloomington M,D
Penn State University Park M,D*
Prescott College M
San Francisco State University M
Southeast Missouri State University M
Southern Connecticut State University M
Texas State University M
Universidad Metropolitana M
Université du Québec à Trois-Rivières M,O
University of Illinois at Urbana–Champaign M,D
The University of Iowa M,D*
University of Nebraska at Kearney M
The University of Tennessee M,D
The University of Toledo M,D
University of Utah M,D

*M—masters degree; D—doctorate; O—other advanced degree; *—Close-Up and/or Display*

University of Victoria	M
University of Waterloo	M,D
University of West Florida	M

LIBERAL STUDIES

Abilene Christian University	M
Alaska Pacific University	M
Albertus Magnus College	M
Alvernia University	M
Arizona State University at the Tempe campus	M
Arkansas Tech University	M
Auburn University at Montgomery	M
Baker University	M
Barry University	M
Binghamton University, State University of New York	M
Brooklyn College of the City University of New York	M
Cardinal Stritch University	M
Clayton State University	M
Coastal Carolina University	M
The College at Brockport, State University of New York	M
College of Staten Island of the City University of New York	M
The Colorado College	M
Colorado State University	M
Concordia University Chicago	M
Converse College	M
Dallas Baptist University	M
Dartmouth College	M*
Delta State University	M
DePaul University	M
Dominican University of California	M
Drew University	M,D,O
Duke University	M*
Eastern Washington University	M
East Tennessee State University	M,O
Excelsior College	M
Florida International University	M
Fort Hays State University	M
Georgetown University	M,D
The Graduate Center, City University of New York	M
Hampton University	M,D,O
Harvard University	M,O*
Hawai`i Pacific University	M
Henderson State University	M
Hollins University	M
Houston Baptist University	M
Indiana University Northwest	M,O
Indiana University–Purdue University Indianapolis	M,D,O
Indiana University South Bend	M,O
Jacksonville State University	M
Johns Hopkins University	M,O*
Kean University	M
Kent State University	M
Lake Forest College	M
Louisiana State University and Agricultural & Mechanical College	M
Louisiana State University in Shreveport	M
Madonna University	M
McDaniel College	M,O
Metropolitan State University	M
Mississippi College	M
The New School	M
North Carolina State University	M
North Central College	M
Northern Arizona University	M
Northern Kentucky University	M
Northwestern University	M
Notre Dame of Maryland University	M
Oakland University	M
Queens College of the City University of New York	M
Reed College	M
Rice University	M
Rollins College	M
Rutgers University–Camden	M
St. Edward's University	M,O
St. John's College (MD)	M
St. John's College (NM)	M
St. John's University (NY)	M
St. Norbert College	M
San Diego State University	M
San Francisco State University	M
Simon Fraser University	M
Southern Methodist University	M,D
Spring Hill College	M,O
State University of New York College at Old Westbury	M
State University of New York Empire State College	M
Stony Brook University, State University of New York	M,O
Texas A&M University–Central Texas	M,O
Texas Christian University	M
Thomas Edison State University	M,O
Towson University	M
Tulane University	M
University at Albany, State University of New York	M
University of Central Oklahoma	M
University of Chicago	M
University of Delaware	M*
University of Detroit Mercy	M,D,O
University of Memphis	M,O
University of Miami	M*
University of Michigan–Flint	M
University of Minnesota, Duluth	M
University of New Hampshire	M
University of North Carolina at Asheville	M,O
The University of North Carolina at Charlotte	M,D,O
The University of North Carolina at Greensboro	M
The University of North Carolina Wilmington	M
University of Pennsylvania	M*
University of St. Thomas (TX)	M
University of Southern Indiana	M
University of South Florida	M,D*
University of South Florida, St. Petersburg	M
University of South Florida Sarasota-Manatee	M
The University of Texas at El Paso	M
University of the Virgin Islands	M
The University of Toledo	M
University of Wisconsin–Milwaukee	M*
Ursuline College	M
Vanderbilt University	M*
Villanova University	M
Virginia Polytechnic Institute and State University	M,O
Wake Forest University	M
Washburn University	M
Wesleyan University	M,O
Western Illinois University	M
Wichita State University	M
Winthrop University	M

LIBRARY SCIENCE

Appalachian State University	M,O
The Catholic University of America	M,O
Chicago State University	M
Clarion University of Pennsylvania	M,O
Dalhousie University	M
Drexel University	M,D,O*
East Carolina University	M,O
Eastern Kentucky University	M
East Tennessee State University	M,O
Emporia State University	M,D,O
Florida State University	M,D,O
Indiana University Bloomington	M,D,O
Indiana University–Purdue University Indianapolis	M,O
Instituto Tecnológico y de Estudios Superiores de Monterrey, Campus Irapuato	M,D
Inter American University of Puerto Rico, Barranquitas Campus	M
Inter American University of Puerto Rico, San Germán Campus	M
Kent State University	M
Kutztown University of Pennsylvania	M
Long Island University–Brentwood Campus	M,O
Long Island University–LIU Post	M,D,O
Louisiana State University and Agricultural & Mechanical College	M
Mansfield University of Pennsylvania	M
McDaniel College	M
McGill University	M,D,O
McNeese State University	O
North Carolina Central University	M
Old Dominion University	M,O
Olivet Nazarene University	M
Pratt Institute	M,O*
Queens College of the City University of New York	M,O
Rowan University	M,D,O
Rutgers University–New Brunswick	D
St. Catherine University	M
St. John's University (NY)	M,O
Sam Houston State University	M
San Jose State University	M
Simmons College	M,D,O
Southern Arkansas University–Magnolia	M
Southern Connecticut State University	M,O
Syracuse University	M*
Tennessee Technological University	M,O
Texas A&M University–Commerce	M,D,O
Texas Woman's University	M
Trevecca Nazarene University	M,O
Universidad del Turabo	M
Université de Montréal	M,D
University at Buffalo, the State University of New York	M,O
The University of Alabama	M,D
University of Alberta	M
The University of Arizona	M,D
The University of British Columbia	M,D
University of California, Los Angeles	M,D,O*
University of Central Arkansas	M
University of Central Missouri	M,D,O
University of Central Oklahoma	M
University of Denver	M,D,O
University of Hawaii at Manoa	M,O
University of Houston–Clear Lake	M
University of Illinois at Urbana–Champaign	M,D,O
The University of Iowa	M,D*
University of Kentucky	M
University of Maryland, College Park	
University of Missouri	D
University of Nebraska at Kearney	M
The University of North Carolina at Chapel Hill	M,D,O
The University of North Carolina at Greensboro	M
University of Oklahoma	M,D,O*
University of Pittsburgh	M,D*
University of Puerto Rico–Río Piedras	M,O
University of Rhode Island	M*
University of South Carolina	M,D,O
University of Southern Mississippi	M,O
University of South Florida	M*
University of Washington	M,D
The University of Western Ontario	M,D
University of Wisconsin–Eau Claire	M
University of Wisconsin–Madison	M,D
University of Wisconsin–Milwaukee	M,D,O*
Valdosta State University	M
Valley City State University	M
Wayne State University	M,O

LIGHTING DESIGN

The New School	M
New York School of Interior Design	M
Rensselaer Polytechnic Institute	M,D
University of Washington	M,D,O

LIMNOLOGY

Baylor University	M,D
Cornell University	D
Oregon State University	M,D
University of Alaska Fairbanks	M,D
University of Florida	M,D

LINGUISTICS

Arizona State University at the Tempe campus	M,D,O
Ball State University	M
Biola University	M,D,O
Boston College	M
Boston University	M,D*
Brandeis University	M
Brigham Young University	M
Brown University	M,D
California State University, Fresno	M
California State University, Fullerton	M
California State University, Long Beach	M,O
California State University, Northridge	M
Carleton University	M
Carnegie Mellon University	M,D
Case Western Reserve University	M*
Concordia University (Canada)	M,O
Cornell University	M,D
East Carolina University	M,D,O
Eastern Michigan University	M
Florida Atlantic University	M
Florida International University	M
Gallaudet University	M,D,O
George Mason University	M,D,O
Georgetown University	M,D
Georgia State University	M,D
The Graduate Center, City University of New York	M,D
Graduate Institute of Applied Linguistics	M,O
Grand Valley State University	M
Harvard University	D*
Hofstra University	M,D,O
Indiana State University	M,D,O
Indiana University Bloomington	M,D
Instituto Tecnologico de Santo Domingo	M,O
Iowa State University of Science and Technology	M,D
Kent State University	M,D
Massachusetts Institute of Technology	D
McGill University	M,D
Memorial University of Newfoundland	M,D
Michigan State University	M,D
Montclair State University	M,O
New York University	M,D*
Northeastern Illinois University	M
Northern Arizona University	M,D,O
Northwestern University	D
Oakland University	M,O
The Ohio State University	M,D
Ohio University	M
Old Dominion University	M
Penn State University Park	M,D*
Purdue University	M,D
Queens College of the City University of New York	M,O
Rice University	M,D
Rutgers University–New Brunswick	D
San Diego State University	M,O
San Francisco State University	M
San Jose State University	M
Simon Fraser University	M,D
Southern Illinois University Carbondale	M
Stanford University	M,D
Stony Brook University, State University of New York	M,D
Syracuse University	M*
Teachers College, Columbia University	M,D,O
Texas A&M University–Commerce	M,D,O
Trinity Western University	M
Universidad de las Américas Puebla	M
Université de Montréal	M,D,O
Université de Sherbrooke	M,D
Université du Québec à Chicoutimi	M
Université du Québec à Montréal	M,D
Université Laval	M,D
University at Buffalo, the State University of New York	M,D
University of Alaska Fairbanks	M
University of Alberta	M,D
The University of Arizona	M,D
The University of British Columbia	M,D
University of Calgary	M,D
University of California, Berkeley	D
University of California, Davis	M,D
University of California, Los Angeles	M,D*
University of California, San Diego	D*
University of California, Santa Barbara	M,D
University of California, Santa Cruz	M,D*
University of Chicago	M,D
University of Colorado Boulder	M,D
University of Colorado Denver	M
University of Connecticut	M,D*
University of Delaware	M,D*
The University of Findlay	M,D
University of Florida	M,D,O
University of Georgia	M,D
University of Hawaii at Manoa	M,D
University of Houston	M,D
University of Illinois at Chicago	M
University of Illinois at Urbana–Champaign	M,D
The University of Iowa	M,D*
The University of Kansas	M,D
University of Louisville	M,D
The University of Manchester	D
University of Manitoba	M,D
University of Maryland, Baltimore County	M
University of Maryland, College Park	M,D
University of Massachusetts Amherst	M,D*
University of Massachusetts Boston	M,D
University of Memphis	M,D,O
University of Michigan	D*
University of Minnesota, Twin Cities Campus	M,D
University of Montana	M,D
University of New Hampshire	M,D
University of New Mexico	M,D
The University of North Carolina at Chapel Hill	M
The University of North Carolina at Charlotte	M,O
University of North Dakota	M
University of North Texas	M,D,O
University of Oregon	M,D
University of Ottawa	M,D
University of Pennsylvania	M,D*
University of Pittsburgh	M,D*
University of Puerto Rico–Río Piedras	M,D
University of Regina	M
University of Rochester	M*
University of South Africa	M,D
University of South Carolina	M,D,O
University of Southern California	M,D*
University of South Florida	M,D*
The University of Tennessee	D
The University of Texas at Arlington	M,D
The University of Texas at Austin	M,D
The University of Texas at El Paso	M,O
University of Toronto	M,D
University of Utah	M,D
University of Victoria	M,D
University of Virginia	M
University of Washington	M,D
University of Wisconsin–Madison	M,D
University of Wisconsin–Milwaukee	M,D,O*
Virginia International University	M
Wayne State University	M
Wesley Biblical Seminary	M
Yale University	D
York University	M,D

LOGISTICS

Air Force Institute of Technology	M,D
Albany State University	M
American Public University System	M,D
Athens State University	M
Benedictine University	M
Case Western Reserve University	M,D*
Central Connecticut State University	M,O
Central Michigan University	M,O
Colorado Technical University Colorado Springs	M,D
Copenhagen Business School	M,D
East Carolina University	M,D,O
Embry-Riddle Aeronautical University–Worldwide	M
Florida Institute of Technology	M,D
Friends University	M
George Mason University	M
Georgia College & State University	M
Georgia Institute of Technology	M
Georgia Southern University	D
HEC Montreal	M
Maryville University of Saint Louis	M,O
Massachusetts Institute of Technology	M
Michigan State University	M,D
Naval Postgraduate School	M
North Dakota State University	M,D*
Norwich University	M
The Ohio State University	M
Polytechnic University of Puerto Rico, Miami Campus	M
Pontifical Catholic University of Puerto Rico	O
Pontificia Universidad Catolica Madre y Maestra	M
Purdue University Global	M
Rutgers University–Newark	M
Shippensburg University of Pennsylvania	M,D,O
Stevens Institute of Technology	O
Trident University International	M,D
Universidad del Turabo	M
University at Buffalo, the State University of New York	M,D

The University of Alabama in Huntsville	M,O
University of Alaska Anchorage	M
University of Dallas	M,D
University of Houston	M
The University of Kansas	M,D
University of Louisville	M,D,O
University of Missouri–St. Louis	M,D,O
The University of North Carolina at Charlotte	M,O
University of North Florida	M
University of North Texas	M,D,O
University of South Africa	M,D
The University of Tennessee	M,D
The University of Tennessee at Chattanooga	M,O
The University of Texas at Arlington	M
University of Washington	O
Virginia International University	M,O
Wright State University	M

MANAGEMENT INFORMATION SYSTEMS

Adelphi University	M
Air Force Institute of Technology	M
American Business & Technology University	M
American InterContinental University Atlanta	M
American Sentinel University	M
American University	M,D,O
American University of Armenia	M
Argosy University, Atlanta	M,D
Argosy University, Chicago	M,D
Argosy University, Hawai`i	M,D,O
Argosy University, Los Angeles	M,D
Argosy University, Northern Virginia	M,D,O
Argosy University, Orange County	M,D,O
Argosy University, Phoenix	M,D
Argosy University, Seattle	M,D
Argosy University, Tampa	M,D
Argosy University, Twin Cities	M,D
Arizona State University at the Tempe campus	M,D
Arkansas State University	O
Ashland University	M
Aspen University	M,O
Auburn University at Montgomery	M
Avila University	M
Baker College Center for Graduate Studies–Online	M,D
Ball State University	M,O
Barry University	O
Baruch College of the City University of New York	M,D*
Baylor University	M,D
Bay Path University	M
Bellevue University	M
Benedictine University	M
Binghamton University, State University of New York	D
Boston University	M,O*
Bowie State University	M,O
Brandeis University	M
Broadview University–West Jordan	M
California Intercontinental University	M,D
California Lutheran University	M,O
California State Polytechnic University, Pomona	M
California State University, Fullerton	M
California State University, Los Angeles	M
California State University, Monterey Bay	M
California State University, San Bernardino	M
California University of Management and Sciences	M,D
Capella University	M,D
Capitol Technology University	M
Carnegie Mellon University	M,D
The Catholic University of America	M,O
Central Michigan University	M,O
Central Penn College	M
Charleston Southern University	M
City College of the City University of New York	M,D
City University of Seattle	M,O
Claremont Graduate University	M,D,O
Clark University	M
Clemson University	M,D
Cleveland State University	D
Coastal Carolina University	M,D,O
College of Charleston	M
The College of St. Scholastica	M,O
Colorado State University	M
Colorado State University–Global Campus	M
Concordia University Wisconsin	M
Copenhagen Business School	M,D
Daemen College	M
Dakota State University	M,D,O
Dalhousie University	M
Dallas Baptist University	M
DePaul University	M,D
DeSales University	M,O
DeVry University–Folsom Campus	M
Dominican University	M,D,O
Drexel University	M,D,O*
Duquesne University	M
East Carolina University	M,D,O
Eastern Michigan University	M,O
Elmhurst College	M
Embry-Riddle Aeronautical University–Worldwide	M
Emory University	M,D
Endicott College	M
Fairfield University	M,O
Fairleigh Dickinson University, Metropolitan Campus	M,O
Ferris State University	M
Florida Agricultural and Mechanical University	M
Florida Atlantic University	M
Florida Gulf Coast University	M
Florida Institute of Technology	M,D
Florida International University	M,D
Florida State University	M,D,O
Fordham University	M,D
Franklin Pierce University	M,D,O
Friends University	M
George Mason University	M
The George Washington University	M,D
Georgia College & State University	M
Georgia Institute of Technology	M
Georgia Southern University	M,O
Georgia Southwestern State University	M,O
Georgia State University	M,D,O
Golden Gate University	M,D,O
Goldey-Beacom College	M
Governors State University	M
The Graduate Center, City University of New York	D
Grand Valley State University	M
Grantham University	M,O
Harrisburg University of Science and Technology	M
Hawai`i Pacific University	M
HEC Montreal	M,O
Hodges University	M
Hofstra University	M,O
Holy Family University	M
Hood College	M,O*
Howard University	M
Idaho State University	M,O
IGlobal University	M
Illinois Institute of Technology	M,D
Illinois State University	M
Indiana University Bloomington	M,D,O
Indiana University Northwest	M,O
Instituto Tecnológico y de Estudios Superiores de Monterrey, Campus Central de Veracruz	M
Instituto Tecnológico y de Estudios Superiores de Monterrey, Campus Ciudad de México	M,D
Instituto Tecnológico y de Estudios Superiores de Monterrey, Campus Ciudad Juárez	M
Instituto Tecnológico y de Estudios Superiores de Monterrey, Campus Ciudad Obregón	M
Instituto Tecnológico y de Estudios Superiores de Monterrey, Campus Estado de México	M,D
Instituto Tecnológico y de Estudios Superiores de Monterrey, Campus Irapuato	M,D
Instituto Tecnológico y de Estudios Superiores de Monterrey, Campus Laguna	M
Inter American University of Puerto Rico, Aguadilla Campus	M
Inter American University of Puerto Rico, Fajardo Campus	M
Inter American University of Puerto Rico, Metropolitan Campus	M
Inter American University of Puerto Rico, San Germán Campus	M,D
Iona College	M,O
Iowa State University of Science and Technology	M,D
James Madison University	M
Johns Hopkins University	M,O*
Johnson & Wales University	M
Kean University	M
Keiser University	M
Kent State University	D
Lake Erie College	M
Le Moyne College	M
Lenoir-Rhyne University	M
Lewis University	M
Liberty University	M,D
Lincoln University (CA)	M,D
Lincoln University (MO)	M
Lindenwood University	M,O
Lipscomb University	M,O
London Metropolitan University	M,D
Long Island University–LIU Post	M
Louisiana State University and Agricultural & Mechanical College	M,D
Louisiana Tech University	M,D
Loyola University Chicago	M
Loyola University Maryland	M
Marist College	M,O
Marquette University	M,O
Marymount University	M,O
Marywood University	M
McGill University	M,D,O
McMaster University	D
Metropolitan State University	M,D,O
Michigan State University	M,D
Middle Georgia State University	M
Middle Tennessee State University	M
Minot State University	M
Mississippi State University	M,D
Morehead State University	M
Morgan State University	D
Murray State University	M
National American University (TX)	M,D
National University	M,O
Naval Postgraduate School	M,D,O
New England Institute of Technology	M
New Jersey Institute of Technology	M,D,O
Newman University	M
New Mexico State University	M
New York University	M,D*
North Carolina Agricultural and Technical State University	M
Northeastern University	M,D,O
Northern Illinois University	M
Northwestern University	M
Northwest Missouri State University	M
Nova Southeastern University	M,D*
Oakland University	M,D,O
The Ohio State University	M,D
Oklahoma State University	M,D
Old Dominion University	M,D
Our Lady of the Lake University	M
Pace University	M,D,O
Pacific States University	M,O
Park University	M,O
Penn State Harrisburg	M,O
Penn State University Park	M,D*
Point Park University	M
Polytechnic University of Puerto Rico	M
Pontifical Catholic University of Puerto Rico	M,O
Prairie View A&M University	M,D
Purdue University	M
Purdue University Global	M
Radford University	M
Regent's University London	M
Regis University	M,O
Rivier University	M
Robert Morris University	M,D
Robert Morris University Illinois	M
Rochester Institute of Technology	O
Rose-Hulman Institute of Technology	M
Rutgers University–Newark	M,D
St. John's University (NY)	M
Saint Peter's University	M
San Diego State University	M
San Francisco State University	M
Santa Clara University	M
Schiller International University (United States)	M
Schiller International University (Germany)	M
Seattle Pacific University	M
Shippensburg University of Pennsylvania	M,D,O
Southeastern Oklahoma State University	M
Southern Illinois University Edwardsville	M
Southern Methodist University	M
Southern New Hampshire University	M,D,O
Southern University at New Orleans	M
South University	M
South University	M
South University (TX)	M
South University (AL)	M
South University	M
Stevens Institute of Technology	M,D,O
Stony Brook University, State University of New York	M,D,O
Stratford University (VA)	M,D
Strayer University	M
Suffolk University	M
Syracuse University	M,D,O*
Tarleton State University	M
Temple University	M,D*
Tennessee Technological University	M
Texas A&M International University	M,D
Texas A&M University	M
Texas A&M University–Central Texas	M,O
Texas Southern University	M
Texas State University	M
Texas Tech University	M,D
Touro College	M
Trident University International	M,D,O
Trine University	M
Troy University	M
Tulane University	M
Tuskegee University	M
United States International University–Africa	M
Universidad del Este	M
Universidad del Turabo	D
Universidad Metropolitana	M
Université de Sherbrooke	M,O
Université du Québec à Montréal	M
Université Laval	M,O
University at Albany, State University of New York	M,D,O
University at Buffalo, the State University of New York	M,D,O
The University of Akron	M
The University of Alabama at Birmingham	M
The University of Alabama in Huntsville	M,O
The University of Arizona	M,O
University of Arkansas	M
University of Arkansas at Little Rock	M,O
University of Baltimore	M,O
University of Bridgeport	M
The University of British Columbia	D
University of California, Berkeley	M,D,O
University of California, Santa Cruz	D*
University of Central Missouri	M,D,O
University of Cincinnati	M,D
University of Colorado Denver	M,D
University of Connecticut	M,D*
University of Dallas	M,D
University of Delaware	M,D*
University of Detroit Mercy	M,D,O
University of Florida	M,D,O
University of Hawaii at Manoa	M,D,O
University of Houston–Clear Lake	M
University of Houston–Victoria	M
University of Illinois at Chicago	M,D
University of Illinois at Springfield	M
University of Illinois at Urbana–Champaign	M,D,O
The University of Kansas	M
University of La Verne	M
University of Lethbridge	M,D
University of Management and Technology	M,O
University of Mary Hardin-Baylor	M
University of Massachusetts Boston	M
University of Memphis	M,D,O
University of Michigan–Dearborn	M
University of Michigan–Flint	M,O
University of Minnesota, Twin Cities Campus	M,D
University of Mississippi	M,D
University of Missouri–St. Louis	M,D,O
University of Nebraska at Kearney	M
University of Nebraska at Omaha	M,D,O
University of Nebraska–Lincoln	M
University of Nevada, Las Vegas	M,O
University of Nevada, Reno	M
University of New Hampshire	M,O
University of New Mexico	M
University of North Alabama	M
The University of North Carolina at Chapel Hill	D
The University of North Carolina at Charlotte	M,D,O
The University of North Carolina at Greensboro	M,D,O
The University of North Carolina Wilmington	M
University of North Florida	M
University of North Texas	M,D,O
University of Oklahoma	M,D,O*
University of Oregon	M
University of Pennsylvania	M,D*
University of Phoenix–Bay Area Campus	M,D
University of Phoenix–Central Valley Campus	M
University of Phoenix–Dallas Campus	M
University of Phoenix–Hawaii Campus	M
University of Phoenix–Houston Campus	M
University of Phoenix–Las Vegas Campus	M
University of Phoenix–Online Campus	M
University of Phoenix–Sacramento Valley Campus	M
University of Phoenix–San Antonio Campus	M
University of Phoenix–San Diego Campus	M
University of Pittsburgh	M,D*
University of Redlands	M
University of Rochester	M,D*
University of San Francisco	M
The University of Scranton	M
University of South Africa	M
University of South Alabama	M,D
University of South Florida	M,D,O*
The University of Tampa	M,O
The University of Texas at Arlington	M,D
The University of Texas at Austin	M,D
The University of Texas at Dallas	M
The University of Texas Rio Grande Valley	M
University of the Sacred Heart	M
University of the West	M
University of Utah	M,D,O
University of Washington	M,D
University of Wisconsin–Madison	D
Utah State University	M
Valparaiso University	M
Virginia Commonwealth University	M
Virginia International University	M,O
Virginia Polytechnic Institute and State University	M,D,O
Walden University	M,D,O
Walsh College of Accountancy and Business Administration	M
Wayland Baptist University	M,D
Wayne State University	M,D,O
Webster University	M,D,O
West Chester University of Pennsylvania	M,O
Western Governors University	M
Wichita State University	M
Wilmington University	M,D
Winston-Salem State University	M
Worcester Polytechnic Institute	M,D,O
Wright State University	M

MANAGEMENT OF TECHNOLOGY

Air Force Institute of Technology	M,D
Arizona State University at the Tempe campus	M
Athabasca University	M,D,O
Atlantis University	M
Boston University	M*

*M—masters degree; D—doctorate; O—other advanced degree; *—Close-Up and/or Display*

California Lutheran University M,O
California State University, Los Angeles M
Cambridge College M
Campbellsville University M,D
Capella University M,D
Carleton University M
The Catholic University of America M,O
Central Connecticut State University M,O
Central European University M,D
Champlain College M
City University of Seattle M,O
Colorado School of Mines M,D
Colorado Technical University Aurora M
Colorado Technical University Colorado Springs M,D
Columbia University M*
Dallas Baptist University M
Duke University M,O*
East Carolina University M,D,O
Eastern Michigan University D
École Polytechnique de Montréal M,D,O
Embry-Riddle Aeronautical University–Worldwide M
Excelsior College M,O
Fairfield University M,O
Fairleigh Dickinson University, Florham Campus M,O
Farmingdale State College M
Florida Institute of Technology M,D
George Mason University M
Georgetown University M,D
The George Washington University M,D
Golden Gate University M,D,O
Grand Canyon University M
Harrisburg University of Science and Technology M
Harvard University D*
Herzing University Online M
Illinois State University M
Indiana State University M,D
Indiana University–Purdue University Indianapolis M
Instituto Centroamericano de Administración de Empresas M
Instituto Tecnológico y de Estudios Superiores de Monterrey, Campus Cuernavaca M,D
Instituto Tecnológico y de Estudios Superiores de Monterrey, Campus Irapuato M,D
Iona College M,O
Johns Hopkins University M,O*
Kansas State University M
Keiser University M
Kennesaw State University M
La Salle University M,O
Lewis University M
Liberty University M,D
Lipscomb University M,O
London Metropolitan University M,D
Louisiana Tech University M,D,O
Marist College M,O
Marquette University M,O
Marshall University M,O
Mercer University M
National University M
New Jersey Institute of Technology M,D,O
New York University M,D*
North Carolina Agricultural and Technical State University M
North Carolina State University D
Northern Kentucky University M
Pacific States University M,O
Pittsburg State University M,O
Polytechnic University of Puerto Rico M
Polytechnic University of Puerto Rico, Orlando Campus M
Portland State University M,D
Purdue University M,D
Rutgers University–Newark D
Ryerson University M
St. Ambrose University M
Seton Hall University M,O
Simon Fraser University M,D,O
South Dakota School of Mines and Technology M
Southeast Missouri State University M
State University of New York Polytechnic Institute M
Stevens Institute of Technology M,D,O
Stevenson University M
Stony Brook University, State University of New York M
Stratford University (VA) M,D
Texas A&M University M
Texas A&M University–Commerce M,O
Texas State University M
Towson University M,O
University of Advancing Technology M
The University of Alabama in Huntsville M,O
University of Bridgeport M,D
University of California, Los Angeles M,D*
University of California, Santa Barbara M
University of California, Santa Cruz D*
University of Central Missouri M,D,O
University of Colorado Denver M
University of Dallas M,D
University of Delaware M*
University of Illinois at Urbana–Champaign M,D
University of Maryland, Baltimore County M
University of Massachusetts Dartmouth M
University of Miami M,D*
University of Minnesota, Twin Cities Campus M
University of New Mexico M
University of Phoenix–Bay Area Campus M,D
University of Phoenix–Central Valley Campus M
University of Phoenix–Dallas Campus M
University of Phoenix–Hawaii Campus M
University of Phoenix–Houston Campus M
University of Phoenix–Las Vegas Campus M
University of Phoenix–Online Campus M,O
University of Phoenix–Phoenix Campus M,O
University of Phoenix–Sacramento Valley Campus M
University of Phoenix–San Antonio Campus M
University of Phoenix–San Diego Campus M
University of Portland M
University of St. Thomas (MN) M,O
University of South Florida O*
The University of Texas at Dallas M
The University of Texas at San Antonio M,D,O
University of Toronto M
University of Virginia M
University of Washington M,D
University of Waterloo M,D
University of Wisconsin–Madison M
University of Wisconsin–Milwaukee M,O*
Walsh College of Accountancy and Business Administration M
Washington State University M,O
Webster University M,D,O
Wentworth Institute of Technology M
Western Kentucky University M
Wilfrid Laurier University M,D

MANAGEMENT STRATEGY AND POLICY

Amberton University M
Antioch University Santa Barbara M
Arizona State University at the Tempe campus M,D
Bay Path University M
Black Hills State University M
Boston University M,O*
Brandeis University M
California Miramar University M
California State University, East Bay M
Capella University M,D
Claremont Graduate University M,D,O
Cleary University M,O
College of Staten Island of the City University of New York M
Davenport University M
Defiance College M
DePaul University M,D
Drexel University M,D,O*
Duke University M,D,O*
East Tennessee State University M
Fisher College M
Florida State University M,D
Freed-Hardeman University M
Friends University M
The George Washington University M,D,O
Georgia State University M,D
Grantham University M,O
Gwynedd Mercy University M
Harrisburg University of Science and Technology M
Harvard University D*
HEC Montreal M
Hofstra University M,O
James Madison University D
Lawrence Technological University M,D,O
Lenoir-Rhyne University M
LeTourneau University M
Lipscomb University M,O
Manhattanville College M,O
McGill University M,D,O
Mercyhurst University M,O
Messiah College M,O
Michigan State University M,D
Middle Tennessee State University M
Mount Mercy University M
Neumann University M
New England College M
The New School M,O
New York University M,D*
Niagara University M
North Central College M
Northwestern University M,D
Norwich University M
Nova Southeastern University M*
Oakland City University M
Ohio Dominican University M
Oklahoma Wesleyan University M
Pace University M
Pontificia Universidad Catolica Madre y Maestra M
Regent University M,D,O
Regis University M,O
Roberts Wesleyan College M
Rockhurst University M,O
St. John's University (NY) M
Saint Mary-of-the-Woods College M
Salve Regina University M,O
Southeastern University (FL) M,D
Southern Methodist University M
Stevens Institute of Technology M
Stockton University M
Suffolk University M
Temple University D*
Tennessee State University M,D
Tennessee Technological University M
Thomas Jefferson University M,D
Tufts University O*
Tulane University M,D
United States International University–Africa M
Universidad del Este M
The University of Arizona M,D
The University of British Columbia D
University of Calgary M,D
University of California, Davis M
University of California, Los Angeles M,D*
University of Charleston M
University of Chicago M,O
University of Colorado Denver M
University of Dallas M,D
University of Detroit Mercy M,O
University of Illinois at Urbana–Champaign M,D,O
The University of Kansas M,D
University of Lethbridge M,D
The University of Manchester M
University of Massachusetts Amherst M,D*
University of Memphis M,O
University of Minnesota, Twin Cities Campus D
University of New Haven M*
University of New Mexico M
The University of North Carolina at Chapel Hill D
University of North Texas M,D,O
University of North Texas at Dallas M
University of Pittsburgh M,D*
University of Rhode Island M,D,O*
University of Rochester M*
University of South Florida M,D,O*
The University of Texas at Dallas M
University of Utah M,D,O
University of Virginia M,O
The University of Western Ontario M,D
University of Wisconsin–Madison M,D
University of Wisconsin–Milwaukee M,D,O*
Valparaiso University M,O
Vanderbilt University M*
Villanova University M
Walsh College of Accountancy and Business Administration M
Wayne State University M,D,O
Western Governors University M
Xavier University M*

MANUFACTURING ENGINEERING

American University of Armenia M
Arizona State University at the Tempe campus M
Boston University M,D*
Bradley University M
Brigham Young University M
California State University, Northridge M
The Citadel, The Military College of South Carolina M,O
Cornell University M,D
Eastern Kentucky University M
East Tennessee State University M
Florida State University M,D
Georgia Southern University M,O
Grand Valley State University M
Illinois Institute of Technology M,D
Instituto Tecnológico y de Estudios Superiores de Monterrey, Campus Monterrey M,D
Kansas State University M,D
Kettering University M
Lawrence Technological University M,D
Massachusetts Institute of Technology M,D,O
Michigan State University M,D
Minnesota State University Mankato M
Missouri University of Science and Technology M,D
New Jersey Institute of Technology M,D
New York University M*
North Carolina State University M
North Dakota State University M,D*
Oregon Institute of Technology M
Oregon State University M,D
Pittsburg State University M
Polytechnic University of Puerto Rico M
Rochester Institute of Technology M
Southern Methodist University M,D
Stevens Institute of Technology M
Tennessee State University M,D
Texas A&M University M
Texas State University M
Tufts University O*
Universidad Autonoma de Guadalajara M,D
Universidad de las Américas Puebla M
University at Buffalo, the State University of New York M,D,O
University of Calgary M,D
University of California, Irvine M,D
University of California, Los Angeles M*
The University of Iowa M,D*
University of Kentucky M
University of Manitoba M,D
University of Maryland, College Park M,D
University of Michigan M,D*
University of Michigan–Dearborn M
University of Missouri M,D
University of Nebraska–Lincoln M,D
University of New Mexico M
University of Puerto Rico–Mayagüez M,D
University of St. Thomas (MN) M,O
University of Southern California M,D,O*
The University of Texas at San Antonio M,D
The University of Texas Rio Grande Valley M
University of Toronto M
University of Windsor M,D
University of Wisconsin–Madison M
University of Wisconsin–Milwaukee M,D*
University of Wisconsin–Stout M
Villanova University M,O
Wayne State University M,D,O
Western Illinois University M
Western Michigan University M
Western New England University M
Wichita State University M,D
Worcester Polytechnic Institute M,D

MARINE AFFAIRS

Dalhousie University M
Louisiana State University and Agricultural & Mechanical College M,D
Memorial University of Newfoundland M,D,O
Oregon State University M
Stevens Institute of Technology M
Stony Brook University, State University of New York M
Université du Québec à Rimouski M,O
University of Delaware M,D*
University of Massachusetts Dartmouth M,D
University of Miami M*
University of Rhode Island M,D*
University of Washington M,O

MARINE BIOLOGY

College of Charleston M
Florida Institute of Technology M,D
Montclair State University M
Nicholls State University M
Northeastern University M,D
Nova Southeastern University M,D*
Princeton University D
Rutgers University–New Brunswick M,D
San Francisco State University M
Texas A&M University M,D
Texas A&M University–Corpus Christi M,D
Texas State University M,D
University of Alaska Fairbanks M,D
University of California, Santa Barbara M,D
University of Guam M
University of Hawaii at Hilo M*
University of Hawaii at Manoa M,D
University of Massachusetts Dartmouth M,D
University of Miami M,D*
University of New Hampshire M,D
The University of North Carolina Wilmington M,D
University of Oregon M,D
University of Rhode Island M,D*
University of Southern California M,D*
Western Illinois University M,O
Woods Hole Oceanographic Institution D

MARINE GEOLOGY

Cornell University M,D
Massachusetts Institute of Technology M,D
University of Delaware M,D*
University of Hawaii at Manoa M,D
University of Miami M,D*
University of Rhode Island M,D*
University of Washington M,D
Woods Hole Oceanographic Institution D

MARINE SCIENCES

California State University, East Bay M
California State University, Fresno M
California State University, Monterey Bay M
Coastal Carolina University M,D,O
College of Charleston M
The College of William and Mary M,D*
Cornell University M,D
Duke University M,D*
Florida Institute of Technology M,D
Florida State University M,D
Hawai`i Pacific University M
Instituto Tecnologico de Santo Domingo M,D,O
Jacksonville University M*
Medical University of South Carolina D
Memorial University of Newfoundland M,O
North Carolina State University M,D
Oregon State University M
San Francisco State University M
San Jose State University M
Savannah State University M
Southern Connecticut State University M,O
Stony Brook University, State University of New York M,D
Texas A&M University M

Texas A&M University–Corpus Christi — M,D
University of Alaska Fairbanks — M,D
The University of British Columbia — M,D
University of California, San Diego — M*
University of California, Santa Barbara — M,D
University of California, Santa Cruz — M,D*
University of Delaware — M,D*
University of Florida — M,D
University of Georgia — M,D
University of Hawaii at Manoa — O
University of Maine — M,D
University of Maryland, Baltimore — M,D
University of Maryland, Baltimore County — M,D
University of Maryland, College Park — M,D
University of Maryland Eastern Shore — M,D
University of Massachusetts Amherst — M,D*
University of Massachusetts Boston — M,D
University of Massachusetts Dartmouth — M,D
University of Miami — M,D*
University of New England — M
The University of North Carolina at Chapel Hill — M,D
The University of North Carolina Wilmington — M,D,O
University of Puerto Rico–Mayagüez — M,D
University of Rhode Island — M,D*
University of South Alabama — M,D
University of South Carolina — M,D
University of Southern California — M,D*
University of Southern Mississippi — M,D
University of South Florida — M,D*
The University of Texas at Austin — M,D
University of the Virgin Islands — M
University of Wisconsin–La Crosse — M
University of Wisconsin–Madison — M,D
Western Washington University — M

MARKETING

Abilene Christian University — M
Adelphi University — M
American Business & Technology University — M
American College of Thessaloniki — M,O
American InterContinental University Online — M
American University — M
The American University in Dubai — M
Anderson University (SC) — M
Aquinas College (MI) — M
Argosy University, Atlanta — M,D
Argosy University, Chicago — M,D
Argosy University, Hawai`i — M,D,O
Argosy University, Los Angeles — M,D
Argosy University, Northern Virginia — M,D,O
Argosy University, Orange County — M,D,O
Argosy University, Phoenix — M,D
Argosy University, Seattle — M,D
Argosy University, Tampa — M,D
Argosy University, Twin Cities — M,D
Arizona State University at the Tempe campus — M,D
Ashworth College — M
Assumption College — M,O
Averett University — M
Avila University — M
Azusa Pacific University — M*
Baker College Center for Graduate Studies–Online — M,D
Barry University — O
Baruch College of the City University of New York — M,D*
Bayamón Central University — M
Benedictine University — M
Bentley University — M
Binghamton University, State University of New York — D
Brandeis University — M
Brandman University — M
Brigham Young University — M
Bryan College — M
Butler University — M
California Coast University — M
California Intercontinental University — M,D
California Lutheran University — M,O
California State University, East Bay — M
California State University, Los Angeles — M
California State University, San Bernardino — M
Capella University — M,D
Cardinal Stritch University — M
Carnegie Mellon University — D
Central Michigan University — M,O
City College of the City University of New York — M
City University of Seattle — M,O
Clark University — M
Clemson University — M
Cleveland State University — D
Colorado Technical University Aurora — M
Colorado Technical University Colorado Springs — M,D
Columbia Southern University — M
Columbia University — M,D*
Concordia University (Canada) — M,D,O
Concordia University Wisconsin — M
Cornell University — D
Daemen College — M
Dallas Baptist University — M
DePaul University — M,D
DEREE - The American College of Greece — M
DeSales University — M
Drexel University — M,D,O*
Duke University — M,D,O*
Duquesne University — M
Eastern Michigan University — M,O
East Tennessee State University — M,O
Emory University — M,D
Fairfield University — M,O
Fairleigh Dickinson University, Florham Campus — M,O
Fairleigh Dickinson University, Metropolitan Campus — M,O
Fashion Institute of Technology — M
Florida Agricultural and Mechanical University — M
Florida International University — M
Florida National University — M
Florida State University — M,D
Fordham University — M,D
Franklin University — M
Full Sail University — M
Gannon University — M
Geneva College — M
George Fox University — M,D
The George Washington University — M,D
Georgia State University — M,D
Golden Gate University — M,D,O
Goldey-Beacom College — M
Grand Canyon University — M,D
Harvard University — D*
Hawai`i Pacific University — M
HEC Montreal — M,D
Herzing University Online — M
Hofstra University — M,O
Holy Names University — M
Hood College — M,O*
Hope International University — M
Howard University — M
Hult International Business School (United States) — M
Illinois Institute of Technology — M
Indiana Tech — M
Indiana University–Purdue University Indianapolis — M
Indiana University South Bend — M,O
Instituto Tecnologico de Santo Domingo — M,O
Instituto Tecnológico y de Estudios Superiores de Monterrey, Campus Central de Veracruz — M
Instituto Tecnológico y de Estudios Superiores de Monterrey, Campus Ciudad Obregón — M
Instituto Tecnológico y de Estudios Superiores de Monterrey, Campus Cuernavaca — M
Instituto Tecnológico y de Estudios Superiores de Monterrey, Campus Estado de México — M,D
Instituto Tecnológico y de Estudios Superiores de Monterrey, Campus Monterrey — M
Inter American University of Puerto Rico, Aguadilla Campus — M
Inter American University of Puerto Rico, Fajardo Campus — M
Inter American University of Puerto Rico, Guayama Campus — M
Inter American University of Puerto Rico, Metropolitan Campus — M
Inter American University of Puerto Rico, Ponce Campus — M
Inter American University of Puerto Rico, San Germán Campus — M,D
International University in Geneva — M,D
The International University of Monaco — M
Iona College — M,O
Jacksonville University — M*
Johns Hopkins University — M*
Kansas State University — M,O
Keiser University — M,D
Kent State University — D
King University — M
Lake Forest Graduate School of Management — M
La Salle University — M,O
Lasell College — M,O
La Sierra University — M,O
Lawrence Technological University — M,D,O
Lewis University — M
Liberty University — M,D
LIM College — M
Lindenwood University — M,O
Long Island University–LIU Post — M
Louisiana Tech University — M,D
Loyola University Chicago — M
Loyola University Maryland — M
Lynn University — M
Manhattanville College — M,O
Marist College — M
Marquette University — M,O
Maryville University of Saint Louis — M,O
McGill University — M,D,O
Melbourne Business School — M,D,O
Michigan State University — M,D
Milwaukee School of Engineering — M
Mississippi State University — D
Molloy College — M,O
Monmouth University — M,O*
Monroe College — M
Morgan State University — D
Murray State University — M
National American University (TX) — M,D
National University — M,O
National University College — M
New England College — M
New Jersey City University — M
New Mexico State University — D
New York Institute of Technology — M
New York University — M,D*
Niagara University — M
Northwestern University — M,D
Northwest Missouri State University — M
Notre Dame de Namur University — M
Nova Southeastern University — M*
Oakland University — M,O
Ohio Christian University — M
Oklahoma Christian University — M
Oklahoma State University — M,D
Old Dominion University — M,D
Oral Roberts University — M
Ottawa University — M
Pace University — M,D,O
Polytechnic University of Puerto Rico, Miami Campus — M
Pontifical Catholic University of Puerto Rico — M
Pontificia Universidad Catolica Madre y Maestra — M
Post University — M
Providence College — M
Purdue University Global — M
Queen's University at Kingston — M
Regent's University London — M
Regent University — M,D,O
Regis University — M,O
Roberts Wesleyan College — M
Roosevelt University — M
Rowan University — O
Rutgers University–Newark — D
Sacred Heart University — M,O
St. Bonaventure University — M
St. Catherine University — M
St. John's University (NY) — M
Saint Joseph's University — M,O*
Saint Leo University — M,D
Saint Peter's University — M
St. Thomas Aquinas College — M
Saint Xavier University — M,O
Samford University — M
San Diego State University — M
San Francisco State University — M
San Ignacio University — M
Seton Hall University — M,O
Slippery Rock University of Pennsylvania — M
Southeastern Louisiana University — M
Southern Adventist University — M
Southern Methodist University — M
Southern New Hampshire University — M,D,O
Southwest Minnesota State University — M
State University of New York Polytechnic Institute — M
Stephen F. Austin State University — M
Stevens Institute of Technology — M,O
Stony Brook University, State University of New York — M,O
Strayer University — M
Suffolk University — M
Syracuse University — M*
Tarleton State University — M
Temple University — M,D*
Texas A&M University — M
Texas A&M University–Commerce — M
Texas Tech University — M,D
Thomas Jefferson University — M
Tiffin University — M
Trident University International — M,D
United States International University–Africa — M
Universidad del Turabo — M
Universidad Iberoamericana — M,D
Universidad Metropolitana — M
Université de Sherbrooke — M
Université Laval — M,O
University at Albany, State University of New York — M
University at Buffalo, the State University of New York — M,D
The University of Akron — M
The University of Alabama — M,D
The University of Alabama at Birmingham — M
The University of Alabama in Huntsville — M,O
University of Alberta — D
The University of Arizona — M,D
University of Baltimore — M
University of Bridgeport — M
The University of British Columbia — D
University of California, Berkeley — D,O
University of California, Davis — M
University of California, Los Angeles — M,D*
University of Central Missouri — M,D,O
University of Chicago — M,O
University of Cincinnati — M,D
University of Colorado Denver — M
University of Connecticut — M,D*
University of Dallas — M,D
University of Dayton — M
University of Denver — M
University of Florida — M,D
University of Hawaii at Manoa — M,D
University of Houston — D
University of Houston–Victoria — M
The University of Iowa — M,D*
The University of Kansas — M,D
University of La Verne — M
University of Lethbridge — M,D
The University of Manchester — M
University of Massachusetts Amherst — M,D*
University of Memphis — M,D
University of Michigan–Flint — M,O
University of Minnesota, Twin Cities Campus — M,D
University of Mississippi — M,D
University of Missouri–St. Louis — M,D,O
University of Nebraska at Kearney — M
University of Nebraska–Lincoln — M,D
University of New Brunswick Fredericton — M,D
University of New Haven — M*
University of New Mexico — M
The University of North Carolina at Chapel Hill — D
The University of North Carolina at Greensboro — M,D
University of North Texas — M,D,O
University of Notre Dame — M
University of Oklahoma — M,D*
University of Oregon — D
University of Pennsylvania — M,D*
University of Phoenix–Bay Area Campus — M,D
University of Phoenix–Central Valley Campus — M
University of Phoenix–Dallas Campus — M
University of Phoenix–Hawaii Campus — M
University of Phoenix–Houston Campus — M
University of Phoenix–Las Vegas Campus — M
University of Phoenix–Online Campus — M,O
University of Phoenix–Phoenix Campus — M,O
University of Phoenix–Sacramento Valley Campus — M
University of Phoenix–San Antonio Campus — M
University of Phoenix–San Diego Campus — M
University of Pittsburgh — M,D*
University of Portland — M
University of Puerto Rico–Río Piedras — M,D
University of Rhode Island — M,D*
University of Rochester — M,D*
University of Saint Mary — M
University of San Francisco — M
University of Saskatchewan — M
The University of Scranton — M
University of Sioux Falls — M
University of South Africa — M,D
University of South Alabama — M,D
University of South Dakota — M,O
University of South Florida — M,D*
The University of Tampa — M,O
The University of Tennessee — M,D
The University of Texas at Arlington — M
The University of Texas at Austin — M,D
The University of Texas at Dallas — M
The University of Texas at San Antonio — M,D
The University of Texas at Tyler — M
The University of Texas Rio Grande Valley — M,D
University of the Cumberlands — M,D,O
University of the Sacred Heart — M
The University of Toledo — M
University of Utah — M,D
University of Virginia — M
The University of Western Ontario — M,D
University of Wisconsin–Madison — D
University of Wisconsin–Whitewater — M
Ursuline College — M
Vancouver Island University — M
Vanderbilt University — M*
Villanova University — M
Virginia International University — M,O
Virginia Polytechnic Institute and State University — M,D
Wagner College — M
Walden University — M,D,O
Walsh College of Accountancy and Business Administration — M
Walsh University — M
Webster University — M,D,O
West Virginia University — M,D,O
Wilfrid Laurier University — M,D
William Woods University — M,D,O
Wilmington University — M,D
Wingate University — M
Worcester Polytechnic Institute — M,D,O
Worcester State University — M
Xavier University — M*
Yale University — D
Yeshiva University — M
York College of Pennsylvania — M
Youngstown State University — M

MARKETING RESEARCH

Baldwin Wallace University — M
Hofstra University — M,O
Instituto Tecnológico y de Estudios Superiores de Monterrey, Campus Irapuato — M,D
Marquette University — M
Michigan State University — M,D

*M—masters degree; D—doctorate; O—other advanced degree; *—Close-Up and/or Display*

Pacific Lutheran University	M
Saint Leo University	M,D
Southern Illinois University Edwardsville	M
Towson University	M,O
Universidad Autonoma de Guadalajara	M,D
Universidad de las Americas, A.C.	M
University of Missouri–St. Louis	M,D,O
University of Rochester	M*
The University of Texas at Arlington	M
University of Wisconsin–Madison	M

MARRIAGE AND FAMILY THERAPY

Abilene Christian University	M
Adler Graduate School	M
Adler University	M,D,O
Alliant International University–Irvine	M,D
Alliant International University–Los Angeles	M,D
Alliant International University–Sacramento	M,D
Alliant International University–San Diego	M,D
Amberton University	M
Amridge University	M,D
Antioch University New England	M,D,O
Antioch University Seattle	M,D
Appalachian State University	M
Arcadia University	M
Argosy University, Atlanta	M,D,O
Argosy University, Chicago	D
Argosy University, Hawai'i	M
Argosy University, Los Angeles	M,D
Argosy University, Northern Virginia	M,D
Argosy University, Orange County	M,D
Argosy University, Tampa	M,D
Argosy University, Twin Cities	M,D,O
Arizona State University at the Tempe campus	M,D
Azusa Pacific University	D*
Barry University	M,O
Bayamón Central University	M,O
Bethel Seminary	M,D,O
Brandman University	M
Briercrest Seminary	M
Brigham Young University	M,D
California Lutheran University	M,D
California State University, Chico	M
California State University, Dominguez Hills	M
California State University, East Bay	M
California State University, Fresno	M
California State University, Long Beach	M,D
California State University, Northridge	M
Cambridge College	M,O
Campbellsville University	M
Capella University	M
Carlos Albizu University, Miami Campus	M,D
Central Connecticut State University	M,O
Chaminade University of Honolulu	M
Chapman University	M*
Chatham University	M,D
Chestnut Hill College	M,D,O
The Chicago School of Professional Psychology at Downtown Los Angeles	M,D
The Chicago School of Professional Psychology at Irvine	M,D
Christian Theological Seminary	M,D
The College of New Jersey	O
The College of New Rochelle	M
The College of William and Mary	M,D*
Colorado State University	M,D
Converse College	M
Denver Seminary	M,D,O
Dominican University of California	M
Drexel University	M,D*
Duquesne University	M,D,O
East Carolina University	M,D
Eastern Nazarene College	M
Eastern University	D
East Tennessee State University	M
Evangelical Seminary	M
Fairfield University	M,O
Fielding Graduate University	M
Florida State University	M,D
Fresno Pacific University	M
Friends University	M
Fuller Theological Seminary	M,D,O
Geneva College	M
George Fox University	M,O
Gonzaga University	M,D
Hampton University	M
Hardin-Simmons University	M
Hofstra University	M,O
Hope International University	M
Houston Baptist University	M
Idaho State University	M,D,O
Indiana University–Purdue University Fort Wayne	M,O
Indiana University South Bend	M,O
Indiana Wesleyan University	M
Instituto Tecnologico de Santo Domingo	M,O
Iona College	M
Jacksonville University	M*
John Brown University	M,O
Kansas State University	M,D,O
Kean University	M
Kutztown University of Pennsylvania	M
Lancaster Bible College	M,D
La Salle University	M
Lee University	M
LeTourneau University	M
Lewis & Clark College	M
Liberty University	M,D,O
Lipscomb University	M,O
Loma Linda University	M,D,O
Long Island University–Hudson	M,O
Long Island University–LIU Brooklyn	M,O
Loyola Marymount University	M
Loyola University New Orleans	M
Manhattan College	M
Maryville University of Saint Louis	M
Medaille College	M,D
Mercy College	M,O
Messiah College	M,O
Michigan State University	M,D
Mid-America Christian University	M
MidAmerica Nazarene University	M
Mississippi College	M,O
Mount Mercy University	M
National University	M,O
Northcentral University	M,D,O
Northeastern Illinois University	M
Northern Kentucky University	M,O
Northwestern University	M
Northwest Nazarene University	M
Notre Dame de Namur University	M
Nova Southeastern University	M,D,O*
Nyack College	M
Oklahoma Baptist University	M
Oral Roberts University	M,D
Ottawa University	M
Our Lady of the Lake University	M
Pacific Lutheran University	M
Pacific Oaks College	M
Palm Beach Atlantic University	M
Palo Alto University	M
Pepperdine University	M,D
Phillips Graduate University	M
Pillar College	M
Plymouth State University	M
Point Loma Nazarene University	M
Pontifical John Paul II Institute for Studies on Marriage and Family	M,D,O
Purdue University	M,D
Purdue University Northwest	M
Reformed Theological Seminary–Jackson Campus	M,D,O
Regent University	M,D,O
Regis University	M,D,O
Richmont Graduate University	M
St. Cloud State University	M
Saint Mary's College of California	M,O
Saint Mary's University of Minnesota	M
Saint Paul University	M
St. Thomas University	M,O
San Francisco State University	M
Saybrook University	M,D
Seattle Pacific University	M,O
Seattle University	M
Seton Hall University	M
Seton Hill University	M
Sioux Falls Seminary	M
Southeastern University (FL)	M
Southern California Seminary	M,D
Southern Nazarene University	M
Stetson University	M
Syracuse University	M,D*
Texas A&M University–Central Texas	M,O
Texas A&M University–San Antonio	M
Texas State University	M
Texas Tech University	M,D
Texas Woman's University	M,D
Thomas Jefferson University	M
Trevecca Nazarene University	M,D
Universidad de las Americas, A.C.	M
The University of Akron	M
The University of Alabama	M
University of Central Florida	M,O
University of Central Oklahoma	M
University of Colorado Denver	M
University of Denver	M,D,O
University of Florida	M,D,O
University of Guelph	M,D
University of Holy Cross	M,D
University of Houston–Clear Lake	M
The University of Iowa	M,D*
University of La Verne	M
University of Louisiana at Monroe	M,D
University of Louisville	M,D,O
University of Mary Hardin-Baylor	M
University of Maryland, College Park	M,D
University of Massachusetts Boston	M
University of Miami	M,O*
University of Minnesota, Twin Cities Campus	M,D
University of Mobile	M
University of Nebraska–Lincoln	M,D
University of Nevada, Las Vegas	M
University of New Hampshire	M,O
The University of North Carolina at Greensboro	M,D,O
University of Oregon	M,D
University of Phoenix–Bay Area Campus	M
University of Phoenix–Central Valley Campus	M
University of Phoenix–Las Vegas Campus	M
University of Phoenix–Phoenix Campus	M
University of Rhode Island	M*
University of Rochester	M*
University of Saint Joseph	M
University of San Diego	M
University of San Francisco	M
University of Southern California	M*
University of South Florida	M,D,O*
The University of Texas at Tyler	M
The University of West Alabama	M
The University of Winnipeg	M,O
University of Wisconsin–Stout	M
Utah State University	M,D
Valdosta State University	M,O
Walden University	M,D
Western Kentucky University	M
Western Seminary–Sacramento Campus	M
Western Seminary–San Jose Campus	M,O
Wheaton College	M,D

MASS COMMUNICATION

American University	M,D,O
The American University in Cairo	M,O
Arizona State University at the Tempe campus	M,D
Arkansas State University	M
Boston University	M*
Brigham Young University	M
Bryant University	M,O
California State University, Fullerton	M
California State University, Northridge	M
Clarion University of Pennsylvania	M
Drexel University	M*
Florida International University	M
Fordham University	M
The George Washington University	M,O
Georgia State University	M,D
Grambling State University	M
Howard University	M,D
Iona College	M,O
Iowa State University of Science and Technology	M
Kansas State University	M
Kent State University	M
Lindenwood University	M
Louisiana State University and Agricultural & Mechanical College	M,D
Lynn University	M,O
Marquette University	M,O
Middle Tennessee State University	M
Murray State University	M
North Dakota State University	M,D*
Oklahoma State University	M
Penn State University Park	M,D*
Point Park University	M
St. Cloud State University	M
St. John's University (NY)	M
San Jose State University	M
Southern Illinois University Carbondale	M,D
Southern Illinois University Edwardsville	M
Southern University and Agricultural and Mechanical College	M
Stephen F. Austin State University	M
Syracuse University	M,D*
Texas Christian University	M
Texas State University	M
Texas Tech University	M,D
Université Laval	M,D
The University of Alabama	D
University of Arkansas at Little Rock	M
University of Colorado Boulder	M,D
University of Denver	M
University of Florida	M,D
University of Georgia	M,D
University of Houston	M
The University of Iowa	M,D*
University of Minnesota, Twin Cities Campus	M,D
University of Nebraska–Lincoln	M
University of Oklahoma	M,D*
University of Puerto Rico–Río Piedras	M
University of South Florida	M,O*
University of Wisconsin–Madison	M,D
University of Wisconsin–Superior	M
University of Wisconsin–Whitewater	M
Virginia Commonwealth University	M

MATERIALS ENGINEERING

Alabama Agricultural and Mechanical University	M
Arizona State University at the Tempe campus	M,D
Auburn University	M,D*
Binghamton University, State University of New York	M,D
Boise State University	M,D
Boston University	M,D*
California State University, Northridge	M
Carleton University	M,D
Carnegie Mellon University	M,D
Case Western Reserve University	M,D*
The Catholic University of America	M
Clarkson University	D
Clemson University	M,D
The College of William and Mary	M,D*
Colorado School of Mines	M,D
Columbia University	M,D*
Cornell University	M,D
Dalhousie University	M,D
Dartmouth College	M,D*
Drexel University	M,D*
Duke University	M*
Florida International University	M,D
Florida State University	M,D
Georgia Institute of Technology	M,D
Illinois Institute of Technology	M,D
Instituto Tecnológico y de Estudios Superiores de Monterrey, Campus Estado de México	M,D
Iowa State University of Science and Technology	M,D
Johns Hopkins University	M,D*
Lehigh University	M,D
Massachusetts Institute of Technology	M,D,O
McGill University	M,D,O
McMaster University	M,D
Michigan State University	M,D
Michigan Technological University	M,D
Missouri University of Science and Technology	M,D
New Jersey Institute of Technology	M,D,O
New Mexico Institute of Mining and Technology	M,D
North Carolina State University	M,D
Northwestern University	M,D,O
The Ohio State University	M,D
Oklahoma State University	M,D
Penn State University Park	M,D*
Portland State University	M,D
Purdue University	M,D
Rensselaer Polytechnic Institute	M,D
Rochester Institute of Technology	M
Rutgers University–New Brunswick	M,D
San Jose State University	M
South Dakota School of Mines and Technology	M,D
Stanford University	M,D,O
Stevens Institute of Technology	M,D
Stony Brook University, State University of New York	M,D
Texas A&M University	M,D
Texas State University	D
Tuskegee University	D
The University of Alabama	M,D
The University of Alabama at Birmingham	M,D
University of Alberta	M,D
The University of Arizona	M,D
The University of British Columbia	M,D
University of California, Berkeley	M,D
University of California, Davis	M,D
University of California, Irvine	M,D
University of California, Los Angeles	M,D*
University of California, Riverside	M
University of California, Santa Barbara	M,D
University of Central Florida	M,D
University of Cincinnati	M,D
University of Colorado Boulder	M,D
University of Connecticut	M*
University of Dayton	M,D
University of Delaware	M,D*
University of Denver	M,D
University of Florida	M,D
University of Illinois at Chicago	M,D
University of Illinois at Urbana–Champaign	M,D
The University of Iowa	M,D*
University of Kentucky	M,D
University of Maryland, College Park	M,D
University of Michigan	M,D*
University of Minnesota, Twin Cities Campus	M,D
University of Nebraska–Lincoln	M,D
University of Nevada, Las Vegas	M,D,O
University of Nevada, Reno	M,D
University of New Hampshire	M,D
University of Pennsylvania	M,D*
University of Puerto Rico–Mayagüez	M,D
University of Southern California	M,D,O*
University of South Florida	M,D,O*
The University of Tennessee	M,D
The University of Texas at Arlington	M,D
The University of Texas at Austin	M,D
The University of Texas at Dallas	M,D
The University of Texas at El Paso	M,D
The University of Texas at San Antonio	M,D
University of Toronto	M,D
University of Utah	M,D
University of Washington	M,D
The University of Western Ontario	M,D
University of Windsor	M,D
University of Wisconsin–Madison	M,D
University of Wisconsin–Milwaukee	M,D*
Washington State University	M,D
West Virginia University	M,D
Worcester Polytechnic Institute	M,D
Wright State University	M

MATERIALS SCIENCES

Air Force Institute of Technology	M,D
Alabama Agricultural and Mechanical University	M,D
Alfred University	M,D
Arizona State University at the Tempe campus	M,D
Binghamton University, State University of New York	M,D
Boston University	M,D*
Brown University	M,D
California Institute of Technology	M,D
Carnegie Mellon University	M,D
Case Western Reserve University	M,D*
The Catholic University of America	M
Central Michigan University	D
Clarkson University	D
Clemson University	M,D

The College of William and Mary	M,D*
Colorado School of Mines	M,D
Colorado State University	M,D
Columbia University	M,D*
Cornell University	M,D
Dartmouth College	M,D*
Duke University	M,D*
Florida International University	M,D
Florida State University	M,D
Georgetown University	D
The George Washington University	M,D
Harvard University	M,D*
Illinois Institute of Technology	M,D
Indiana University Bloomington	M,D
Instituto Tecnológico y de Estudios Superiores de Monterrey, Campus Estado de México	M,D
Iowa State University of Science and Technology	M,D
Jackson State University	M,D
Johns Hopkins University	M,D*
Lehigh University	M,D
Louisiana Tech University	M,D,O
Massachusetts Institute of Technology	M,D,O
McMaster University	M,D
Michigan State University	M,D
Missouri State University	M
Missouri University of Science and Technology	M,D
Montana Tech of The University of Montana	D
New Jersey Institute of Technology	M,D,O
Norfolk State University	M
North Carolina State University	M,D
North Dakota State University	M,D*
Northwestern University	M,D,O
The Ohio State University	M,D
Oklahoma State University	M,D
Oregon State University	M,D
Penn State University Park	M,D*
Princeton University	D
Rice University	M,D
Rochester Institute of Technology	M
Royal Military College of Canada	M,D
Rutgers University–New Brunswick	M,D
School of the Art Institute of Chicago	M
South Dakota School of Mines and Technology	M,D
Stanford University	M,D,O
State University of New York College of Environmental Science and Forestry	M,D,O
Stevens Institute of Technology	M,D
Stony Brook University, State University of New York	M,D
Texas A&M University	M,D
Texas State University	M,D
Trent University	M
Université du Québec, Institut National de la Recherche Scientifique	M,D
University at Buffalo, the State University of New York	M,D
The University of Alabama	D
The University of Alabama in Huntsville	M,D
The University of Arizona	M,D
University of Calgary	M,D
University of California, Berkeley	M,D
University of California, Davis	M,D
University of California, Irvine	M,D
University of California, Los Angeles	M,D*
University of California, Riverside	M
University of California, San Diego	M,D*
University of California, Santa Barbara	M,D
University of Central Florida	M,D
University of Cincinnati	M,D
University of Colorado Boulder	M,D
University of Connecticut	M,D*
University of Delaware	M,D*
University of Denver	M,D
University of Florida	M,D
University of Idaho	M,D
University of Illinois at Urbana–Champaign	M,D
University of Kentucky	M,D
The University of Manchester	M,D
University of Maryland, College Park	M,D
University of Michigan	M,D*
University of Minnesota, Twin Cities Campus	M,D
University of Mississippi Medical Center	M,D
University of Nebraska–Lincoln	M,D
University of New Brunswick Fredericton	M,D
University of New Hampshire	M,D
University of Pennsylvania	M,D*
University of Pittsburgh	M,D*
University of Puerto Rico–Mayagüez	M,D
University of Rochester	M,D*
University of Southern California	M,D,O*
University of South Florida	M,D,O*
The University of Tennessee	M,D
The University of Texas at Arlington	M,D
The University of Texas at Austin	M,D
The University of Texas at Dallas	M,D
The University of Texas at El Paso	M,D
The University of Toledo	M,D
University of Toronto	M,D
University of Utah	M,D
University of Vermont	M,D
University of Virginia	M,D
University of Washington	M,D
Vanderbilt University	M,D*
Washington State University	M,D
Washington University in St. Louis	M,D
Wayne State University	M,D,O
West Virginia University	M,D
William Paterson University of New Jersey	M,D,O
Worcester Polytechnic Institute	M,D
Wright State University	M

MATERNAL AND CHILD/NEONATAL NURSING

Baylor University	M,D
Boston College	M,D
Case Western Reserve University	M*
Creighton University	M,D,O
Duke University	M,D,O*
Hardin-Simmons University	M
Lehman College of the City University of New York	M
Louisiana State University Health Sciences Center	M,D,O
Medical University of South Carolina	M,D
Northeastern University	M,D,O
Old Dominion University	M,D
Regis University	M,D,O
Rush University	D,O
Saint Francis Medical Center College of Nursing	M,D,O
Stony Brook University, State University of New York	M,D,O
University of Alberta	D
University of Cincinnati	M,D
University of Connecticut	O*
University of Delaware	M,O*
University of Illinois at Chicago	M,O
University of Indianapolis	M,D
University of Louisville	M,D
University of Maryland, Baltimore	M,D,O
University of Missouri–Kansas City	M,D
University of Pennsylvania	M*
University of Pittsburgh	M,D*
University of Puerto Rico–Medical Sciences Campus	M
University of Rochester	M,D*
University of South Africa	M,D
The University of Texas at Austin	M,D
Vanderbilt University	M,D,O*
Wayne State University	M,D
Wright State University	M

MATERNAL AND CHILD HEALTH

Bank Street College of Education	M
Bastyr University	M,O
Columbia University	M,D*
East Carolina University	M,D,O
Instituto Tecnologico de Santo Domingo	M,O
Oakland University	D,O
Troy University	M,D
The University of Alabama at Birmingham	M,D
University of California, Davis	M
University of Manitoba	M
University of Maryland, College Park	M,D
University of Minnesota, Twin Cities Campus	M
The University of North Carolina at Chapel Hill	M,D
University of Puerto Rico–Medical Sciences Campus	M
University of South Florida	O*
The University of Texas Health Science Center at Houston	M,D,O
University of Washington	M,D

MATHEMATICAL AND COMPUTATIONAL FINANCE

Austin Peay State University	M
Boston University	M,D*
Carnegie Mellon University	M,D
DePaul University	M,D
Florida State University	M,D
The George Washington University	M,D,O
Georgia Institute of Technology	M
Illinois Institute of Technology	M,D
Johns Hopkins University	M,D,O*
New Jersey Institute of Technology	M,D,O
New York University	M,D*
North Carolina State University	M
Oregon State University	M,D
Rice University	M,D
Rochester Institute of Technology	M
Université de Montréal	M,D,O
University of Alberta	M,D,O
University of California, Santa Barbara	M,D
University of Chicago	M
University of Connecticut	M*
University of Dayton	M
The University of Manchester	M,D
University of Miami	M,D*
The University of North Carolina at Charlotte	M,O
University of Notre Dame	M,D
University of Southern California	M,D*
University of Toronto	M

MATHEMATICAL PHYSICS

Indiana University Bloomington	M,D
New Mexico Institute of Mining and Technology	M,D
University of Alberta	M,D,O
University of Colorado Boulder	M,D

MATHEMATICS

Acadia University	M
Alabama State University	M
American University	M,O
American University of Beirut	M,D
American University of Sharjah	M,D
Appalachian State University	M
Arizona State University at the Tempe campus	M,D,O
Arkansas State University	M
Auburn University	M,D*
Augustana University	M
Aurora University	M
Ball State University	M
Baylor University	M,D
Bemidji State University	M
Binghamton University, State University of New York	M,D
Boise State University	M
Boston College	D
Boston University	M,D*
Bowling Green State University	M,D
Brandeis University	M,D
Brigham Young University	M,D
Brock University	M
Brooklyn College of the City University of New York	M
Brown University	D
Bryn Mawr College	M,D
Bucknell University	M
Cabrini University	M,D
California Institute of Technology	D
California Polytechnic State University, San Luis Obispo	M*
California State Polytechnic University, Pomona	M
California State University Channel Islands	M
California State University, East Bay	M
California State University, Fresno	M
California State University, Fullerton	M
California State University, Long Beach	M
California State University, Los Angeles	M
California State University, Northridge	M
California State University, Sacramento	M
California State University, San Bernardino	M
California State University, San Marcos	M
Carleton University	M,D
Carlow University	M
Carnegie Mellon University	M,D
Case Western Reserve University	M,D*
Central Connecticut State University	M,O
Central European University	M,D
Central Michigan University	M,D
Chicago State University	M
City College of the City University of New York	M
Claremont Graduate University	M,D
Clark Atlanta University	M
Clarkson University	M,D
Clemson University	M,D
Cleveland State University	M
The College at Brockport, State University of New York	M,O
College of Charleston	M
The College of William and Mary	M*
Colorado State University	M,D
Columbia University	M,D*
Columbus State University	M,O
Concordia University (Canada)	M,D
Cornell University	D
Dalhousie University	M,D
Dartmouth College	M,D*
Delaware State University	M,D
DePaul University	M,D
Drew University	M,D,O
Drexel University	M,D*
Duke University	D*
Duquesne University	M
East Carolina University	M
Eastern Illinois University	M
Eastern Kentucky University	M
Eastern Michigan University	M
East Tennessee State University	M,O
Elizabeth City State University	M
Emory University	M,D
Emporia State University	M
Fairfield University	M
Fairleigh Dickinson University, Metropolitan Campus	M
Florida Atlantic University	M,D
Florida Gulf Coast University	M
Florida International University	M
Florida State University	M,D
George Mason University	M,D
Georgetown University	M
The George Washington University	M,D,O
Georgia Institute of Technology	M,D
Georgia Southern University	M
Georgia State University	M,D
Governors State University	M
The Graduate Center, City University of New York	D
Hardin-Simmons University	M
Harvard University	D*
Hofstra University	M,D,O
Houston Baptist University	M,D
Howard University	M,D
Hunter College of the City University of New York	M
Idaho State University	M,D
Illinois State University	M
Indiana State University	M
Indiana University Bloomington	M,D
Indiana University of Pennsylvania	M
Indiana University–Purdue University Fort Wayne	M,O
Indiana University–Purdue University Indianapolis	M,D
Instituto Tecnologico de Santo Domingo	M,D,O
Iowa State University of Science and Technology	M,D
Jackson State University	M
Jacksonville State University	M
Jacksonville University	M*
John Carroll University	M
Johns Hopkins University	D*
Kansas State University	M,D,O
Kent State University	M,D
Kutztown University of Pennsylvania	M,D
Lakehead University	M
Lamar University	M
Lee University	M,O
Lehigh University	M,D
Lehman College of the City University of New York	M
Louisiana State University and Agricultural & Mechanical College	M,D
Louisiana Tech University	M,D,O
Loyola University Chicago	M
Manhattan College	M,O
Manhattanville College	M,O
Marquette University	M,D
Marshall University	M
Marygrove College	M,O
Massachusetts Institute of Technology	D
McGill University	M,D
McMaster University	M,D
McNeese State University	M
Memorial University of Newfoundland	M,D
Mercer University	M,D,O
Miami University	M
Michigan State University	M,D
Michigan Technological University	M,D
Middle Tennessee State University	M
Minnesota State University Mankato	M
Mississippi College	M
Mississippi State University	M,D
Missouri State University	M
Missouri University of Science and Technology	M,D
Montana State University	M,D
Montclair State University	M
Morgan State University	M,D
Murray State University	M
New Jersey Institute of Technology	M,D,O
New Mexico Institute of Mining and Technology	M,D
New Mexico State University	M,D
New York University	M,D*
North Carolina Agricultural and Technical State University	M
North Carolina Central University	M
North Carolina State University	M,D
North Dakota State University	M,D*
Northeastern Illinois University	M
Northeastern University	M,D
Northern Arizona University	M,O
Northern Illinois University	M,D
Northwestern University	D
Northwest Missouri State University	M,O
Oakland University	M
The Ohio State University	M,D
Ohio University	M,D
Oklahoma State University	M,D
Old Dominion University	M,D
Oregon State University	M,D
Pace University	M,O
Penn State University Park	M,D*
Pepperdine University	M,D
Pittsburg State University	M
Portland State University	M,D,O
Princeton University	D
Purdue University	M,D
Purdue University Northwest	M
Queens College of the City University of New York	M
Queen's University at Kingston	M,D
Regent University	M,D,O
Rensselaer Polytechnic Institute	M,D
Rhode Island College	M,O
Rice University	D
Rivier University	M
Rochester Institute of Technology	M,D,O
Roosevelt University	M
Rowan University	M
Royal Military College of Canada	M
Rutgers University–Camden	M
Rutgers University–Newark	D
Rutgers University–New Brunswick	M,D
St. John's University (NY)	M
Saint Joseph's University	M,O*
Saint Louis University	M,D*
Salem State University	M
Sam Houston State University	M
San Diego State University	M,D
San Francisco State University	M
San Jose State University	M
Simon Fraser University	M,D
Smith College	O
South Carolina State University	M
South Dakota State University	M,D
Southeast Missouri State University	M

*M—masters degree; D—doctorate; O—other advanced degree; *—Close-Up and/or Display*

Southern Connecticut State University	M
Southern Illinois University Carbondale	M,D
Southern Illinois University Edwardsville	M
Southern Methodist University	M,D
Southern University and Agricultural and Mechanical College	M
Stanford University	M,D
State University of New York College at Cortland	M
State University of New York College at Potsdam	M
Stephen F. Austin State University	M
Stevens Institute of Technology	M,D
Stony Brook University, State University of New York	M,D
Syracuse University	M,D*
Tarleton State University	M
Temple University	M,D*
Tennessee State University	M,D
Tennessee Technological University	M
Texas A&M International University	M
Texas A&M University	M,D
Texas A&M University–Central Texas	M,O
Texas A&M University–Commerce	M,O
Texas A&M University–Corpus Christi	M
Texas A&M University–Kingsville	M
Texas Christian University	M,D
Texas Southern University	M
Texas State University	M
Texas Tech University	M,D
Texas Woman's University	M
Tufts University	M,D*
Tulane University	M,D
Université de Moncton	M
Université de Montréal	M,D,O
Université de Sherbrooke	M,D
Université du Québec à Montréal	M,D
Université du Québec à Trois-Rivières	M
Université Laval	M,D
University at Albany, State University of New York	M,D
University at Buffalo, the State University of New York	M,D
The University of Akron	M
The University of Alabama	M,D
The University of Alabama at Birmingham	M
The University of Alabama in Huntsville	M,D
University of Alaska Fairbanks	M,D,O
University of Alberta	M,D,O
The University of Arizona	M,D
University of Arkansas	M,D
University of Arkansas at Little Rock	M,O
The University of British Columbia	M,D
University of Calgary	M,D
University of California, Berkeley	M,D
University of California, Davis	M,D
University of California, Irvine	M,D
University of California, Los Angeles	M,D*
University of California, Riverside	M,D
University of California, San Diego	M,D*
University of California, Santa Barbara	M,D
University of California, Santa Cruz	M,D*
University of Central Arkansas	M
University of Central Florida	M,D,O
University of Central Missouri	M,D,O
University of Central Oklahoma	M
University of Chicago	D
University of Cincinnati	M,D
University of Colorado Boulder	M,D
University of Colorado Colorado Springs	D
University of Colorado Denver	M,D
University of Delaware	M,D*
University of Denver	M,D
The University of Findlay	M,D
University of Florida	M,D
University of Georgia	M,D
University of Guelph	M,D
University of Hawaii at Manoa	M,D
University of Houston	M,D
University of Houston–Clear Lake	M
University of Idaho	M,D
University of Illinois at Chicago	M,D
University of Illinois at Urbana–Champaign	M,D
The University of Iowa	M,D*
The University of Kansas	M,D,O
University of Kentucky	M,D
University of Lethbridge	M,D
University of Louisiana at Lafayette	M,D
University of Louisville	M,D
University of Lynchburg	M
University of Maine	M
The University of Manchester	M,D
University of Manitoba	M,D
University of Maryland, College Park	M,D
University of Massachusetts Amherst	M,D*
University of Massachusetts Lowell	D
University of Memphis	M,D,O
University of Miami	M,D*
University of Michigan	M,D*
University of Michigan–Flint	M
University of Minnesota, Twin Cities Campus	M,D,O
University of Mississippi	M,D
University of Missouri	M,D
University of Missouri–Kansas City	M,D
University of Missouri–St. Louis	M,D
University of Montana	M,D
University of Nebraska at Omaha	M
University of Nebraska–Lincoln	M,D
University of Nevada, Las Vegas	M,D
University of Nevada, Reno	M
University of New Brunswick Fredericton	M,D
University of New Hampshire	M,D,O
University of New Mexico	M,D
University of New Orleans	M
The University of North Carolina at Chapel Hill	M,D
The University of North Carolina at Charlotte	M,D,O
The University of North Carolina at Greensboro	M,D
The University of North Carolina Wilmington	M,O
University of North Dakota	M
University of Northern British Columbia	M,D,O
University of Northern Colorado	M,D
University of Northern Iowa	M
University of North Florida	M
University of North Texas	M,D,O
University of Notre Dame	M,D
University of Oklahoma	M,D*
University of Oregon	M,D
University of Ottawa	M,D
University of Pennsylvania	M,D*
University of Pittsburgh	M,D*
University of Puerto Rico–Mayagüez	M
University of Puerto Rico–Río Piedras	M,D
University of Regina	M,D
University of Rhode Island	M,D*
University of Rochester	D*
University of San Diego	M
University of Saskatchewan	M,D
University of South Alabama	M
University of South Carolina	M,D
University of South Dakota	M
University of Southern California	M,D*
University of Southern Mississippi	M,D
University of South Florida	M,D,O*
The University of Tennessee	M,D
The University of Tennessee at Chattanooga	M
The University of Texas at Arlington	M,D
The University of Texas at Austin	M,D
The University of Texas at Dallas	M,D
The University of Texas at El Paso	M
The University of Texas at San Antonio	M
The University of Texas at Tyler	M
The University of Texas Rio Grande Valley	M
University of the Incarnate Word	M
University of the Virgin Islands	M
The University of Toledo	M,D
University of Toronto	M,D
The University of Tulsa	M,D
University of Utah	M,D
University of Vermont	M,D
University of Victoria	M,D
University of Virginia	M,D
University of Washington	M,D
University of Waterloo	M,D
The University of Western Ontario	M,D
University of West Florida	M
University of West Georgia	M,O
University of Windsor	M,D
University of Wisconsin–Madison	D
University of Wisconsin–Milwaukee	M,D*
University of Wyoming	M,D
Utah State University	M,D
Vanderbilt University	M,D*
Villanova University	M
Virginia Commonwealth University	M
Virginia Polytechnic Institute and State University	M,D
Virginia State University	M
Wake Forest University	M
Washington State University	M,D
Washington University in St. Louis	M,D
Wayne State University	M,D,O
Wesleyan University	M,D
West Chester University of Pennsylvania	M,O
Western Connecticut State University	M
Western Illinois University	M
Western Kentucky University	M
Western Michigan University	M,D
Western Washington University	M
West Texas A&M University	M
West Virginia University	M,D
Wichita State University	M,D
Wilfrid Laurier University	M
Wilkes University	M
Worcester Polytechnic Institute	M,D,O
Wright State University	M
Yale University	M,D
Yeshiva University	M
York University	M,D
Youngstown State University	M

MATHEMATICS EDUCATION

Adams State University	M
Alabama Agricultural and Mechanical University	M,O
Alabama State University	M,O
American University of Beirut	M,D
Appalachian State University	M
Arcadia University	M,D,O
Arizona State University at the Tempe campus	M,D,O
Arkansas State University	M
Asbury University	M
Aurora University	M
Austin Peay State University	M
Ball State University	M
Bank Street College of Education	M
Bard College	M
Bemidji State University	M
Binghamton University, State University of New York	M
Bloomsburg University of Pennsylvania	M
Bob Jones University	M,D,O
Boise State University	M
Bowling Green State University	M,D
Bridgewater State University	M
Brigham Young University	M
Brooklyn College of the City University of New York	M
Buffalo State College, State University of New York	M
California State University, Bakersfield	M
California State University, Chico	M
California State University, East Bay	M
California State University, Fresno	M
California State University, Fullerton	M
California State University, Long Beach	M
California State University, Northridge	M
California State University, San Bernardino	M
California University of Pennsylvania	M
Cambridge College	M,D,O
Caribbean University	M,D
Central Michigan University	M,D
Chatham University	M
The Citadel, The Military College of South Carolina	M,O
City College of the City University of New York	M,O
Clarion University of Pennsylvania	M
Clark Atlanta University	M
Clayton State University	M
Clemson University	M,D,O
Cleveland State University	M
The College at Brockport, State University of New York	M,O
College of Charleston	M
College of Staten Island of the City University of New York	M
The College of William and Mary	M*
The Colorado College	M
Columbus State University	M,O
Concordia University (United States)	M,D
Concordia University (Canada)	M,D
Converse College	M
Cornell University	M,D
Delaware State University	M
DePaul University	M,D
Drake University	M,D,O
Duquesne University	M
East Carolina University	M,O
Eastern Illinois University	M
Eastern Kentucky University	M
Eastern University	M,O
Elizabeth City State University	M
Fitchburg State University	M
Florida Agricultural and Mechanical University	M
Florida Gulf Coast University	M
Florida Institute of Technology	M,D,O
Florida International University	M,D,O
Florida State University	M,D,O
Framingham State University	M
Fresno Pacific University	M
George Mason University	M
The George Washington University	M
Georgia Southwestern State University	M,O
Georgia State University	M,D,O
Gordon College	M,O
Grambling State University	M,D,O
Hampton University	M
Harding University	M,O
Harvard University	M,O*
High Point University	M,D
Hofstra University	M,D,O
Hood College	M,O*
Hunter College of the City University of New York	M
Idaho State University	M,D
Illinois Institute of Technology	M,D
Illinois State University	M,D
Indiana University Bloomington	M,D,O
Indiana University of Pennsylvania	M
Indiana University–Purdue University Fort Wayne	M,O
Indiana University–Purdue University Indianapolis	M,D
Instituto Tecnológico y de Estudios Superiores de Monterrey, Campus Ciudad Obregón	M
Inter American University of Puerto Rico, Arecibo Campus	M
Inter American University of Puerto Rico, Metropolitan Campus	M
Inter American University of Puerto Rico, Ponce Campus	M
Inter American University of Puerto Rico, San Germán Campus	M
Iona College	M
Iowa State University of Science and Technology	M,D
Jackson State University	M
James Madison University	M
Kennesaw State University	M
Kent State University	M,D
Lake Forest College	M
Lebanon Valley College	M,O
Lee University	M,O
Lehman College of the City University of New York	M
Lesley University	M,D,O
Lewis University	M
Liberty University	M,D,O
Longwood University	M
Loyola Marymount University	M
Manhattanville College	M,O
Marquette University	M,D
McDaniel College	M,O
McNeese State University	O
Miami University	M
Michigan State University	M,D
Middle Tennessee State University	M,D
Millersville University of Pennsylvania	M
Minnesota State University Mankato	M
Minot State University	M
Mississippi College	M,D,O
Missouri State University	M
Missouri University of Science and Technology	M,D
Molloy College	M,O
Montana State University	M,D
Montclair State University	M,D,O
Morehead State University	M
Morgan State University	M,D
Mount Holyoke College	M
Murray State University	M
National Louis University	M,D,O
National University	M,O
New Jersey City University	M
New York Institute of Technology	M,O
New York University	M*
North Carolina State University	M,D
North Dakota State University	D*
Northeastern Illinois University	M
Northeastern State University	M
Northern Arizona University	M,O
Northwest Missouri State University	M,D,O
The Ohio State University	M,D
Oregon State University	M,D
Plymouth State University	M
Portland State University	M,D,O
Providence College	M
Purdue University	M,D,O
Purdue University Global	M
Purdue University Northwest	M
Queens College of the City University of New York	M,O
Quinnipiac University	M
Radford University	M
Rhode Island College	M
Rowan University	M,O
Rutgers University–Camden	M
Rutgers University–New Brunswick	M,D
St. John Fisher College	M
St. John's University (NY)	D
St. Joseph's College, Long Island Campus	M
Saint Peter's University	M,D,O
Salem State University	M
Salisbury University	M
San Diego State University	M,D
San Francisco State University	M,O
San Jose State University	M
Seattle Pacific University	M
Shippensburg University of Pennsylvania	M
Simon Fraser University	M,D
Slippery Rock University of Pennsylvania	M
Smith College	M
South Carolina State University	M
Southeastern Oklahoma State University	M
Southern Illinois University Edwardsville	M
Southern University and Agricultural and Mechanical College	D
Southwestern Oklahoma State University	M
Southwest Minnesota State University	M
State University of New York at Fredonia	M,O
State University of New York at Plattsburgh	M
State University of New York College at Cortland	M
State University of New York College at Old Westbury	M
State University of New York College at Potsdam	M
Stephen F. Austin State University	M
Stevenson University	M
Stony Brook University, State University of New York	M,O
Syracuse University	M,D*
Teachers College, Columbia University	M,D
Teachers College of San Joaquin	M
Temple University	M*
Tennessee Technological University	M,O
Texas Christian University	M
Texas State University	M,D
Texas Woman's University	M
Touro College	M
Towson University	M
Tufts University	M,D*
Universidad Autonoma de Guadalajara	M,D

University at Buffalo, the State University of New York	M,D,O
The University of Akron	M
The University of Alabama in Huntsville	M,D,O
University of Alaska Southeast	M
The University of Arizona	M
University of Arkansas	M
University of Arkansas at Pine Bluff	M
The University of British Columbia	M,D
University of California, Berkeley	M,D
University of California, San Diego	D*
University of Central Arkansas	M
University of Central Florida	M,D,O
University of Cincinnati	M,D
University of Colorado Denver	M,D
University of Connecticut	M,D*
University of Dayton	M
University of Detroit Mercy	M,D
University of Florida	M,D,O
University of Georgia	M,D,O
University of Illinois at Chicago	M,D
University of Illinois at Urbana–Champaign	M,D
University of Indianapolis	M
The University of Iowa	M,D*
University of Louisiana at Lafayette	M
University of Maryland, Baltimore County	M
University of Massachusetts Dartmouth	M,D,O
University of Memphis	M,D
University of Miami	D*
University of Minnesota, Twin Cities Campus	M,D,O
University of Mississippi	M,D,O
University of Missouri	M,D,O
University of Montana	M,D
University of Nebraska at Kearney	M
University of Nevada, Reno	M
University of New Hampshire	M,D,O
The University of North Carolina at Chapel Hill	M
The University of North Carolina at Greensboro	M,D,O
The University of North Carolina at Pembroke	M
University of Northern Colorado	M,D
University of Northern Iowa	M
University of North Georgia	M
University of Oklahoma	M,D*
University of Phoenix–Online Campus	M,O
University of Pittsburgh	M,D*
University of Puerto Rico–Mayagüez	M
University of Puerto Rico–Río Piedras	M,D
University of St. Francis (IL)	M,D,O
University of South Africa	M,D
University of South Carolina	M,D
University of South Dakota	M
University of Southern Indiana	M
University of South Florida, St. Petersburg	M
The University of Tennessee	M,D,O
The University of Tennessee at Chattanooga	M
The University of Texas at Arlington	M,D
The University of Texas at Dallas	M
The University of Texas at San Antonio	M
University of the District of Columbia	M
University of the Incarnate Word	M
University of the Sacred Heart	M,O
University of the Virgin Islands	M
The University of Toledo	M,D,O
The University of Tulsa	M
University of Utah	M,D
University of Victoria	M,D
University of Virginia	M,D,O
University of Washington	M,D
University of Washington, Tacoma	M
The University of West Alabama	M
University of Wisconsin–Milwaukee	M,D,O*
University of Wisconsin–Oshkosh	M
University of Wisconsin–River Falls	M
University of Wyoming	M,D
Utah Valley University	M
Virginia State University	M
Wagner College	M
Walden University	M,D,O
Washington State University	M,D
Wayne State College	M
Wayne State University	M,D,O
Webster University	M,O
West Chester University of Pennsylvania	M,O
Western Governors University	M,O
Western Michigan University	M,D
Western New England University	M
Western Oregon University	M
Westfield State University	M
Widener University	M,D
William Jessup University	M
Wright State University	D
Youngstown State University	M

MECHANICAL ENGINEERING

Alfred University	M,D
The American University in Cairo	M,D,O
American University of Beirut	M,D
American University of Sharjah	M,D
Arizona State University at the Tempe campus	M,D
Arkansas Tech University	M
Auburn University	M,D*
Baylor University	M,D
Binghamton University, State University of New York	M,D
Boise State University	M
Boston University	M,D*
Bradley University	M
Brigham Young University	M,D
Brown University	M,D
Bucknell University	M
California Baptist University	M
California Institute of Technology	M,D,O
California Polytechnic State University, San Luis Obispo	M*
California State Polytechnic University, Pomona	M
California State University, Fresno	M
California State University, Fullerton	M
California State University, Long Beach	M,D
California State University, Los Angeles	M
California State University, Northridge	M
California State University, Sacramento	M
Carleton University	M,D
Carnegie Mellon University	M,D
Case Western Reserve University	M,D*
The Catholic University of America	M,D
The Citadel, The Military College of South Carolina	M,O
City College of the City University of New York	M,D
Clarkson University	M,D
Clemson University	M,D
Cleveland State University	M,D
Colorado School of Mines	M,D
Colorado State University	M,D
Columbia University	M,D*
Concordia University (Canada)	M,D,O
Cooper Union for the Advancement of Science and Art	M
Cornell University	M,D
Dalhousie University	M,D
Dartmouth College	M,D*
Drexel University	M,D*
Duke University	M,D*
École Polytechnique de Montréal	M,D,O
Embry-Riddle Aeronautical University–Daytona	M,D
Fairfield University	M,O
Farmingdale State College	M
Florida Agricultural and Mechanical University	M,D
Florida Atlantic University	M,D
Florida Institute of Technology	M,D
Florida International University	M,D
Florida State University	M,D
Gannon University	M
The George Washington University	M,D,O
Georgia Institute of Technology	M,D
Georgia Southern University	M
Grand Valley State University	M
Harvard University	M,D*
Howard University	M,D
Idaho State University	M
Illinois Institute of Technology	M,D
Indiana University–Purdue University Fort Wayne	M
Indiana University–Purdue University Indianapolis	M,D
Instituto Tecnológico y de Estudios Superiores de Monterrey, Campus Chihuahua	M,O
Instituto Tecnológico y de Estudios Superiores de Monterrey, Campus Monterrey	M,D
Inter American University of Puerto Rico, Bayamón Campus	M
Iowa State University of Science and Technology	M,D
Johns Hopkins University	M,D,O*
Kansas State University	M,D
Kennesaw State University	M
Kettering University	M
Lamar University	M,D
Lawrence Technological University	M,D
Lehigh University	M,D
Louisiana State University and Agricultural & Mechanical College	M,D
Loyola Marymount University	M
Manhattan College	M
Marquette University	M,D,O
Marshall University	M
Massachusetts Institute of Technology	M,D,O
McGill University	M,D
McMaster University	M,D
McNeese State University	M
Memorial University of Newfoundland	M,D
Mercer University	M
Merrimack College	M
Miami University	M
Michigan State University	M,D
Michigan Technological University	M,D,O
Mississippi State University	M,D
Missouri University of Science and Technology	M,D
Montana State University	M,D
Naval Postgraduate School	M,D,O
New Jersey Institute of Technology	M,D
New Mexico Institute of Mining and Technology	M
New Mexico State University	M,D
New York Institute of Technology	M
New York University	M,D*
North Carolina Agricultural and Technical State University	M,D
North Carolina State University	M,D
North Dakota State University	M,D*
Northeastern University	M,D,O
Northern Arizona University	M,D
Northern Illinois University	M
Northwestern University	M,D
Oakland University	M,D
The Ohio State University	M,D
Ohio University	M
Oklahoma Christian University	M
Oklahoma State University	M,D
Old Dominion University	M,D
Oregon State University	M,D
Penn State Harrisburg	M,O
Penn State University Park	M,D*
Pittsburg State University	M
Polytechnic University of Puerto Rico	M
Portland State University	M,D,O
Princeton University	M,D
Purdue University	M,D,O
Purdue University Northwest	M
Queen's University at Kingston	M,D
Rensselaer at Hartford	M
Rensselaer Polytechnic Institute	M,D
Rice University	M,D
Rochester Institute of Technology	M
Rose-Hulman Institute of Technology	M
Rowan University	M
Royal Military College of Canada	M,D
Rutgers University–New Brunswick	M,D
Saint Martin's University	M
San Diego State University	M,D
San Jose State University	M
Santa Clara University	M,D,O
Simon Fraser University	M,D
South Carolina State University	M
South Dakota School of Mines and Technology	M,D
South Dakota State University	M,D
Southern Illinois University Carbondale	M,D
Southern Illinois University Edwardsville	M
Southern Methodist University	M,D
Stanford University	M,D,O
Stevens Institute of Technology	M,D,O
Stony Brook University, State University of New York	M,D
Syracuse University	M,D*
Temple University	M,D*
Tennessee State University	M,D
Tennessee Technological University	M
Texas A&M University	M,D
Texas A&M University–Kingsville	M
Texas State University	M
Texas Tech University	M,D
Tufts University	M,D*
Tuskegee University	M
Universidad del Turabo	M
Université de Moncton	M
Université de Sherbrooke	M,D
Université Laval	M,D
University at Buffalo, the State University of New York	M,D
The University of Akron	M,D
The University of Alabama	M,D
The University of Alabama at Birmingham	M
The University of Alabama in Huntsville	M,D
University of Alaska Fairbanks	M
University of Alberta	M,D
The University of Arizona	M,D
University of Arkansas	M,D
University of Bridgeport	M
The University of British Columbia	M,D
University of Calgary	M,D
University of California, Berkeley	M,D
University of California, Davis	M,D,O
University of California, Irvine	M,D
University of California, Los Angeles	M,D*
University of California, Merced	M,D
University of California, Riverside	M,D
University of California, San Diego	M,D*
University of California, Santa Barbara	M,D
University of Central Florida	M,D
University of Central Oklahoma	M
University of Cincinnati	M,D
University of Colorado Boulder	M,D
University of Colorado Colorado Springs	M,D
University of Colorado Denver	M
University of Connecticut	M,D*
University of Dayton	M,D
University of Delaware	M,D*
University of Denver	M,D
University of Detroit Mercy	M,D
University of Florida	M,D
University of Hawaii at Manoa	M,D
University of Houston	M,D
University of Idaho	M,D
University of Illinois at Chicago	M,D
University of Illinois at Urbana–Champaign	M,D
The University of Iowa	M,D*
The University of Kansas	M,D
University of Kentucky	M,D
University of Louisiana at Lafayette	M
University of Louisville	M,D
University of Maine	M,D
The University of Manchester	M,D
University of Manitoba	M,D
University of Maryland, Baltimore County	M,D
University of Maryland, College Park	M,D
University of Massachusetts Amherst	M,D*
University of Massachusetts Dartmouth	M,O
University of Massachusetts Lowell	M,D
University of Memphis	M,D,O
University of Miami	M,D*
University of Michigan	M,D*
University of Michigan–Dearborn	M,D
University of Michigan–Flint	M
University of Minnesota, Twin Cities Campus	M,D
University of Mississippi	M,D
University of Missouri	M,D
University of Missouri–Kansas City	M,D,O
University of Nebraska–Lincoln	M,D
University of Nevada, Las Vegas	M,D,O
University of Nevada, Reno	M,D
University of New Brunswick Fredericton	M,D
University of New Hampshire	M,D
University of New Haven	M*
University of New Mexico	M,D
University of New Orleans	M
The University of North Carolina at Charlotte	M,D
University of North Dakota	M,D
University of North Florida	M
University of North Texas	M,D,O
University of Notre Dame	M,D
University of Oklahoma	M,D*
University of Ottawa	M,D
University of Pennsylvania	M,D*
University of Pittsburgh	M,D*
University of Portland	M
University of Puerto Rico–Mayagüez	M,D
University of Rochester	M,D*
University of St. Thomas (MN)	M,O
University of Saskatchewan	M,D
University of South Alabama	M
University of South Carolina	M,D
University of Southern California	M,D,O*
University of South Florida	M,D*
The University of Tennessee	M,D
The University of Tennessee at Chattanooga	M
The University of Texas at Arlington	M,D
The University of Texas at Austin	M,D
The University of Texas at Dallas	M,D
The University of Texas at San Antonio	M,D
The University of Texas at Tyler	M
The University of Texas Rio Grande Valley	M
The University of Toledo	M,D
University of Toronto	M,D
The University of Tulsa	M,D
University of Utah	M,D
University of Vermont	M,D
University of Victoria	M,D
University of Virginia	M,D
University of Washington	M,D
University of Waterloo	M,D
The University of Western Ontario	M,D
University of Windsor	M,D
University of Wisconsin–Madison	M,D
University of Wisconsin–Milwaukee	M,D*
University of Wyoming	M,D
Utah State University	M,D
Vanderbilt University	M,D*
Villanova University	M,O
Virginia Commonwealth University	M,D
Washington State University	M,D
Washington University in St. Louis	M,D
Wayne State University	M,D
Western Michigan University	M,D
Western New England University	M
West Virginia University	M,D
Wichita State University	M,D
Widener University	M
Wilkes University	M
Worcester Polytechnic Institute	M,D,O
Wright State University	M
Yale University	M,D
Youngstown State University	M

MECHANICS

Brown University	M,D
California Institute of Technology	M,D
Carnegie Mellon University	M,D
Columbia University	M,D*
Cornell University	M,D
Drexel University	M,D*
École Polytechnique de Montréal	M,D,O
Georgia Institute of Technology	M
Iowa State University of Science and Technology	M,D
Johns Hopkins University	M*
Lehigh University	M,D
Louisiana State University and Agricultural & Mechanical College	M,D
McGill University	M,D
Michigan State University	M,D

*M—masters degree; D—doctorate; O—other advanced degree; *—Close-Up and/or Display*

Michigan Technological University M,D,O
Montana State University M,D
New Mexico Institute of Mining and Technology M
Northwestern University M,D
Ohio University M,D
Penn State University Park M,D*
Rutgers University–New Brunswick M,D
San Diego State University M,D
Southern Illinois University Carbondale M
Stanford University M,D,O
The University of Alabama M,D
University of Calgary M,D
University of California, Berkeley M,D
University of California, Merced M,D
University of California, San Diego M,D*
University of Cincinnati M,D
University of Colorado Denver M
University of Dayton M
University of Illinois at Urbana–Champaign M,D
University of Maryland, Baltimore County O
University of Maryland, College Park M,D
University of Massachusetts Amherst M,D*
University of Minnesota, Twin Cities Campus M,D
University of Nebraska–Lincoln M,D
University of New Brunswick Fredericton M,D
University of Pennsylvania M,D*
University of Southern California M,D,O*
The University of Texas at Austin M,D
University of Washington M,D
University of Wisconsin–Madison M,D
University of Wisconsin–Milwaukee M,D*

MEDIA STUDIES

Adler University M
American University M,D
American University of Beirut M,D
Angelo State University M
Arizona State University at the Tempe campus M,D
Arkansas State University M
Austin Peay State University M
Bob Jones University M,D,O
Boston University M,D*
Bowling Green State University M,D
Brooklyn College of the City University of New York M
Carnegie Mellon University M
Central Michigan University M
Champlain College M
City College of the City University of New York M
Claremont Graduate University M,D,O
Clarion University of Pennsylvania M
College of Staten Island of the City University of New York M
Colorado State University M,D
Columbia University M*
Concordia University (Canada) M,D,O
Cornell University M,D
Dallas Theological Seminary M,D,O
DePaul University M
Drexel University M*
Duke University M*
Fairleigh Dickinson University, Metropolitan Campus M
Fielding Graduate University M,D,O
Florida Atlantic University M,O
Florida State University M,D
Fordham University M,D
Full Sail University M
Georgetown University M,D
Georgia State University M,D
Howard University M,D
Hunter College of the City University of New York M
Indiana State University M
Indiana University Bloomington M,D
Indiana University of Pennsylvania D
International University in Geneva M,D
Johns Hopkins University M*
Kent State University M
La Salle University M,O
Lindenwood University M,O
Lindenwood University–Belleville M
Long Island University–LIU Brooklyn M,D,O
Louisiana State University and Agricultural & Mechanical College M,D
Loyola University Maryland M
Lynn University M,O
Massachusetts College of Art and Design M,O
Massachusetts Institute of Technology M,D
Metropolitan College of New York M
Michigan State University M,D
Missouri Western State University M,O
Monmouth University M,O*
New Mexico Highlands University M
The New School M,O
New York University M,D*
Norfolk State University M
Northern Kentucky University M,O
Northwestern University M,D
Ohio University M,D
Old Dominion University M,O
Pace University M,D
Paris College of Art M
Penn State University Park M,D*
Pepperdine University M
Point Park University M
Pratt Institute M*
Purchase College, State University of New York M
Queens College of the City University of New York M
Rhode Island School of Design M
Rochester Institute of Technology M
Rowan University O
Saginaw Valley State University M
San Diego State University M
San Francisco State University M
San Jose State University M
Savannah College of Art and Design M
Southern Illinois University Carbondale M,D
Southern Illinois University Edwardsville O
Stevens Institute of Technology M
Syracuse University M*
Temple University M*
Texas Tech University M,D
Trinity College (United States) M
University at Buffalo, the State University of New York M,D,O
University of Bridgeport M
University of California, Los Angeles M,D*
University of California, Santa Barbara M,D
University of Chicago M,D
University of Colorado Boulder M,D
University of Colorado Denver M
University of Denver M
University of Illinois at Urbana–Champaign M,D
The University of Iowa M,D*
The University of Kansas M,D
University of Lethbridge M,D
University of Maryland, College Park M,D
University of Massachusetts Dartmouth M
University of Michigan M*
University of Nevada, Las Vegas M
The University of North Carolina at Chapel Hill M,D,O
The University of North Carolina at Greensboro M
University of Oklahoma M,D*
University of Oregon M,D
University of South Carolina M
University of Southern California M,D*
University of South Florida M*
University of South Florida, St. Petersburg M
The University of Tennessee M,D
The University of Texas at Austin M,D
The University of Western Ontario M,D
University of Wisconsin–Madison M,D
University of Wisconsin–Milwaukee M,D*
University of Wisconsin–Stevens Point M
Valparaiso University M,O
Virginia Commonwealth University M,D
Virginia State University M
Wagner College M
Wayne State University M,D,O
Webster University M
West Virginia State University M
West Virginia University M,O
Wilfrid Laurier University M

MEDICAL/SURGICAL NURSING

Case Western Reserve University M*
Daemen College M,D,O
Eastern Virginia Medical School M
Inter American University of Puerto Rico, Arecibo Campus M
Inter American University of Puerto Rico, Barranquitas Campus M
Pontifical Catholic University of Puerto Rico M
Saint Francis Medical Center College of Nursing M,D,O
State University of New York Downstate Medical Center M,O
Universidad Adventista de las Antillas M
University of South Africa M,D
University of South Carolina M
Ursuline College M,D

MEDICAL ILLUSTRATION

Augusta University M
Johns Hopkins University M*
Rochester Institute of Technology M
University of Illinois at Chicago M

MEDICAL IMAGING

Boston University M*
Cedars-Sinai Medical Center M,D
Illinois Institute of Technology M,D
Medical University of South Carolina D
National University of Health Sciences M,D
New York University D*
Oregon State University M,D
Rutgers University–Newark M
University of California, San Francisco M
University of Cincinnati M,D
University of Guelph M,D,O
University of Southern California M,D*
University of Wisconsin–Milwaukee D*
Wayne State University M,D,O

MEDICAL INFORMATICS

Arizona State University at the Tempe campus M,D
Brandeis University M
Columbia University M,D,O*
Dalhousie University M,D
Excelsior College M
Grand Valley State University M
Johns Hopkins University M,D,O*
Michigan Technological University M
Middle Tennessee State University M
Northwestern University M,D
Nova Southeastern University M,D,O*
Oregon Health & Science University M,D,O
Regis University M,O
Rutgers University–Newark M,D,O
Stanford University M,D
University at Buffalo, the State University of New York M,D
The University of Arizona M,D,O
University of California, Davis M
University of Colorado Denver M,D
University of Illinois at Urbana–Champaign M,D,O
The University of Kansas M,D,O
University of Phoenix–Phoenix Campus M,O
University of Washington M,D
University of Wisconsin–Milwaukee M*

MEDICAL MICROBIOLOGY

The Citadel, The Military College of South Carolina M,O
Creighton University M,D
HEC Montreal D
Idaho State University M,D
Rutgers University–New Brunswick M,D
Université du Québec, Institut National de la Recherche Scientifique M,D
University of Alberta M,D
University of Hawaii at Manoa M,D
University of Manitoba M,D
University of Minnesota, Duluth M,D
University of Southern California D*
University of South Florida M,D*
University of Wisconsin–La Crosse M
University of Wisconsin–Madison D

MEDICAL PHYSICS

The College of William and Mary M,D*
Columbia University M,D*
Creighton University M
Duke University M,D*
East Carolina University M,D
Hampton University M,D
Harvard University D*
Hofstra University M
Indiana University Bloomington M,D
Louisiana State University and Agricultural & Mechanical College M,D
Massachusetts Institute of Technology M,D
McGill University M,D
McMaster University M,D
Oakland University M,D
Oregon State University M,D
Purdue University M,D
Rush University M,D
Southern Illinois University Carbondale M
Stony Brook University, State University of New York M,D
University at Buffalo, the State University of New York M,D
University of Alberta M,D
The University of Arizona M
University of California, Los Angeles M,D*
University of Chicago D
University of Cincinnati M
University of Florida M,D,O
University of Kentucky M
University of Minnesota, Twin Cities Campus M,D
University of Oklahoma Health Sciences Center M,D
University of Pennsylvania M,D*
University of Rhode Island M,D*
University of South Florida M,D*
The University of Texas Health Science Center at Houston M,D
The University of Texas Health Science Center at San Antonio D
The University of Toledo M,D
University of Utah M,D
University of Victoria M,D
University of Wisconsin–Madison M,D
Virginia Commonwealth University M,D
Wayne State University M,D,O

MEDICINAL AND PHARMACEUTICAL CHEMISTRY

Duquesne University M,D
Florida Agricultural and Mechanical University M,D
Idaho State University M,D
Medical University of South Carolina D
New Jersey Institute of Technology M,D,O
Purdue University D
Rutgers University–New Brunswick M,D
Temple University M,D*
University at Buffalo, the State University of New York M,D
University of California, Irvine D
University of California, San Francisco D
University of Connecticut M,D*
University of Florida M,D
University of Illinois at Chicago M,D
The University of Iowa M,D*
The University of Kansas M,D
University of Michigan D*
University of Minnesota, Twin Cities Campus M,D
University of Mississippi M,D
University of Montana M,D
University of Rhode Island M,D*
The University of Texas at Austin M,D
University of the Sciences M,D
The University of Toledo M,D
University of Utah M,D
University of Washington D
Virginia Commonwealth University M,D
Wayne State University M,D

MEDIEVAL AND RENAISSANCE STUDIES

Arizona State University at the Tempe campus M,D,O
The Catholic University of America M,D,O
Central European University M,D
Columbia University M,D*
Cornell University M,D
Fordham University M,O
Georgetown University M,D
Harvard University D*
Indiana University Bloomington M,D
Loyola University Chicago M,D
Rutgers University–New Brunswick D
Southern Methodist University M
University of California, Santa Barbara M,D
University of Chicago D
University of Connecticut M,D*
University of Guelph D
University of Minnesota, Twin Cities Campus M,D
University of Notre Dame M,D
University of Pittsburgh O*
University of Toronto M,D
Yale University M,D

METALLURGICAL ENGINEERING AND METALLURGY

Colorado School of Mines M,D
Michigan Technological University M,D
Missouri University of Science and Technology M,D
Montana Tech of The University of Montana M
The Ohio State University M,D
Université Laval M,D
The University of Alabama M,D
University of Connecticut M*
The University of Manchester M,D
University of Nebraska–Lincoln M,D
University of Nevada, Reno M,D
University of Utah M,D

METEOROLOGY

Ball State University M,O
Florida Institute of Technology M
Florida State University M,D
Iowa State University of Science and Technology M,D
McGill University M,D
Millersville University of Pennsylvania M
Mississippi State University M,D
Naval Postgraduate School M,D
North Carolina State University M,D
Northern Arizona University M,D,O
Penn State University Park M,D*
Saint Louis University M,D*
San Jose State University M
SIT Graduate Institute M
Texas A&M University M,D
Université du Québec à Montréal M,D,O
University of California, San Diego M*
University of Hawaii at Manoa M,D
University of Maryland, College Park M,D
University of Miami M,D*
University of Oklahoma M,D*
Utah State University M,D
Yale University D

MICROBIOLOGY

Alabama State University M,D
Albany Medical College M,D
Albert Einstein College of Medicine D
American University of Beirut M,D
Arizona State University at the Tempe campus M,D
Baylor College of Medicine D
Boston University D*
Brandeis University M,D
Brigham Young University M,D
California State University, Long Beach M
Case Western Reserve University D*
The Catholic University of America M,D
Central Washington University M
Clemson University M,D
Colorado State University M,D
Columbia University M,D*
Cornell University D
Dalhousie University M,D
Dartmouth College D*
Drexel University M,D*
Duke University D*
East Tennessee State University M,D
Emory University D
Emporia State University M
Georgetown University M,D
The George Washington University M,D,O
Georgia State University M,D
Harvard University D*
Hood College M*
Howard University D
Idaho State University M,D

Illinois Institute of Technology M,D
Illinois State University M,D
Indiana University Bloomington M,D
Indiana University–Purdue University Indianapolis M,D
Inter American University of Puerto Rico, Metropolitan Campus M
Iowa State University of Science and Technology M,D
Johns Hopkins University M,D*
Loma Linda University M,D
Louisiana State University Health Sciences Center D
Louisiana State University Health Sciences Center at Shreveport M,D
Loyola University Chicago M,D
Marquette University M,D
Massachusetts Institute of Technology D
McGill University M,D
Medical University of South Carolina M,D
Meharry Medical College D
Miami University M,D
Michigan State University M,D
Montana State University M,D
New York Medical College M,D
New York University M,D*
North Carolina State University M,D
North Dakota State University M,D*
The Ohio State University M,D
Ohio University M,D
Oklahoma State University M,D
Old Dominion University M
Oregon Health & Science University D
Oregon State University M,D
Purdue University M,D
Queen's University at Kingston M,D
Rosalind Franklin University of Medicine and Science D
Rush University M,D
Rutgers University–Newark D
Rutgers University–New Brunswick M,D
Saint Louis University D*
San Diego State University M
San Francisco State University M
Seton Hall University M,D
South Dakota State University M,D
Southern Illinois University Carbondale M,D
Southwestern Oklahoma State University M
Stanford University D
State University of New York Upstate Medical University M,D
Stony Brook University, State University of New York D
Texas A&M University M,D
Texas Tech University M,D
Thomas Jefferson University M,D
Tufts University D*
Tulane University M
Universidad Central del Caribe M,D
Université de Montréal M,D
Université de Sherbrooke M,D
Université du Québec, Institut National de la Recherche Scientifique M,D
Université Laval M,D
University at Buffalo, the State University of New York M,D
The University of Alabama at Birmingham D
University of Alberta M,D
The University of Arizona D
University of Arkansas for Medical Sciences M,D,O
The University of British Columbia M,D
University of Calgary M,D
University of California, Berkeley D
University of California, Davis M,D
University of California, Irvine M,D
University of California, Los Angeles M,D*
University of California, Riverside M,D
University of Chicago D
University of Cincinnati M,D
University of Colorado Denver D
University of Connecticut M,D*
University of Delaware M,D*
University of Florida M,D
University of Georgia M,D
University of Guelph M,D
University of Hawaii at Manoa M,D
University of Idaho M,D
University of Illinois at Chicago D
University of Illinois at Urbana–Champaign M,D
The University of Iowa M,D*
The University of Kansas M,D
University of Kentucky D
University of Louisville M,D
University of Maine M,D
The University of Manchester M,D
University of Manitoba M,D
University of Maryland, Baltimore D
University of Massachusetts Amherst M,D*
University of Massachusetts Medical School M,D
University of Miami D*
University of Michigan M,D*
University of Minnesota, Twin Cities Campus D
University of Mississippi Medical Center D
University of Missouri D
University of Montana D
University of New Hampshire M,D
University of New Mexico M,D
The University of North Carolina at Chapel Hill M,D
University of North Texas Health Science Center at Fort Worth M,D
University of Oklahoma M,D*
University of Oklahoma Health Sciences Center M,D
University of Ottawa M,D
University of Pennsylvania D*
University of Pittsburgh M,D*
University of Puerto Rico–Medical Sciences Campus M,D
University of Rhode Island M,D*
University of Rochester M,D*
University of Saskatchewan M,D
University of South Dakota M,D
University of Southern California M*
University of South Florida M,D*
The University of Tennessee M,D
The University of Texas at Austin D
The University of Texas Health Science Center at Houston M,D
The University of Texas Health Science Center at San Antonio M,D
The University of Texas Medical Branch M,D
The University of Texas Southwestern Medical Center D
University of Victoria M,D
University of Virginia D
University of Washington D
The University of Western Ontario M,D
University of Wisconsin–La Crosse M
University of Wisconsin–Madison D
University of Wisconsin–Milwaukee M,D*
University of Wisconsin–Oshkosh M
University of Wyoming D
Vanderbilt University M,D*
Virginia Commonwealth University M,D
Wagner College M
Wake Forest University D
Washington University in St. Louis D
Wayne State University M,D,O
Wright State University M
Yale University D
Youngstown State University M

MIDDLE SCHOOL EDUCATION

Alaska Pacific University M
Albany State University M,O
American International College M,D,O
Appalachian State University M
Arkansas State University M,D,O
Augusta University M,O
Avila University M,O
Ball State University M,O
Bellarmine University M,D,O
Berry College M
Bloomsburg University of Pennsylvania M
Brenau University M,O
Brooklyn College of the City University of New York M,O
Cabrini University M,D
California Lutheran University M,D
California State University, Bakersfield M
Campbell University M
Canisius College M
Capella University M,D
Chestnut Hill College M
Chicago State University M
The Citadel, The Military College of South Carolina M,O
City College of the City University of New York M,O
Clarkson University M
Clemson University M,D,O
The College at Brockport, State University of New York M
College of Mount Saint Vincent M,O
College of Saint Elizabeth M,O
The College of Saint Rose M,O
College of Staten Island of the City University of New York M
Columbus State University M,O
Converse College M
Daemen College M
DePaul University M,D
Drury University M
Duquesne University M
East Carolina University M
Eastern Illinois University M
Eastern Michigan University M
Eastern Nazarene College M,O
Eastern University M,O
East Tennessee State University M,O
Edinboro University of Pennsylvania M
Emory University M,D
Fayetteville State University M
Fitchburg State University M
Florida Gulf Coast University M
Fontbonne University M
Georgia College & State University M
Georgia Southern University M,O
Georgia Southwestern State University M,O
Georgia State University M,D
Gordon College M,O
Goucher College M,O
Grand Valley State University M
Hampton University M
Hebrew College M,O
Henderson State University M,O
Hofstra University M,D,O
Hood College M,O*
Houston Baptist University M
Huntington University M,D
James Madison University M
Kansas State University M,D,O
Kennesaw State University D,O
Kent State University M
Kutztown University of Pennsylvania M,D
LaGrange College M,O
La Salle University M,O
Lee University M,O
Le Moyne College M,O
Lesley University M,D,O
Lewis University M
Liberty University M,D,O
Lincoln University (MO) M
Long Island University–Hudson M,O
Long Island University–LIU Post M,D,O
Longwood University M
Louisiana Tech University M,D,O
Lynn University M,D
Manhattanville College M,O
Mary Baldwin University M
Marygrove College M,O
Maryville University of Saint Louis M,D
McNeese State University O
Mercer University M,D,O
Mercy College M,O
Merrimack College M,O
Middle Tennessee State University M,O
Milligan College M,D,O
Minot State University M
Mississippi State University M,D,O
Morehead State University M,O
Mount St. Joseph University M,O
Mount Saint Mary College M,O
Mount Saint Vincent University M
Murray State University M,D,O
National Louis University M,D,O
Nazareth College of Rochester M
New York Institute of Technology M
New York University M,D,O*
Niagara University M,O
Nicholls State University M
North Carolina State University M
Northwestern State University of Louisiana M
Northwest Missouri State University M,D,O
Ohio University M,D
Old Dominion University M,O
Pacific University M
Piedmont College M,D,O
Point Park University M,D
Portland State University M,D,O
Queens College of the City University of New York M,O
Roberts Wesleyan College M
Roger Williams University M,O
Rowan University O
St. Bonaventure University M
St. John Fisher College M
Saint Joseph's University M,D,O*
Saint Peter's University M,O
St. Thomas Aquinas College M,O
Salem College M
Salem State University M
Salisbury University M
Seton Hill University M
Shenandoah University M,D,O
Shippensburg University of Pennsylvania M
Smith College M
Southeast Missouri State University M
Spalding University M
State University of New York at Fredonia M,O
State University of New York at Oswego M
State University of New York College at Potsdam M
Temple University M*
Tennessee Technological University M
Theological University of the Caribbean M,D
Tufts University M,D*
Union College (KY) M
University of Arkansas M,D,O
University of Arkansas at Little Rock M
University of Bridgeport M,D,O
University of Central Florida M
University of Dayton M
University of Kentucky M,D
University of Louisville M,D,O
University of Massachusetts Dartmouth M,D,O
University of Missouri–St. Louis M
The University of North Carolina at Charlotte M,D,O
The University of North Carolina at Greensboro M,D,O
The University of North Carolina Wilmington M
University of Northern Iowa M
University of North Georgia M
University of Phoenix–Online Campus M,O
University of South Florida, St. Petersburg M
University of the Cumberlands M,D,O
University of the District of Columbia M
The University of Toledo M,D,O
University of Vermont M
University of Washington, Bothell M
University of West Florida M
University of Wisconsin–Milwaukee M*
Ursuline College M
Wagner College M
Webster University M,O
Western Kentucky University M,O
Wichita State University M
Widener University M,D
Wilkes University M,D
William Paterson University of New Jersey M,O
Winston-Salem State University M
Worcester State University M,O
Youngstown State University M

MILITARY AND DEFENSE STUDIES

Adler University M
American Public University System M,D
Austin Peay State University M
Bellevue University M
The Citadel, The Military College of South Carolina M,O
East Carolina University M
Embry-Riddle Aeronautical University–Prescott M
The George Washington University M
Hawai`i Pacific University M
Henley-Putnam School of Strategic Security M
The Institute of World Politics M,O
Johns Hopkins University M*
The Judge Advocate General's School, U.S. Army M
Liberty University M,D
London Metropolitan University M,D
Missouri State University M,O
National Defense University M
National Intelligence University M
Naval Postgraduate School M,D
Norwich University M
Royal Military College of Canada M,D
School of Advanced Air and Space Studies M
United States Army Command and General Staff College M
University of Calgary M,D
University of Colorado Denver M,D
University of Pittsburgh M*

MINERAL/MINING ENGINEERING

Colorado School of Mines M,D
Dalhousie University M,D
Laurentian University M,D
McGill University M,D,O
Missouri University of Science and Technology M,D
Montana Tech of The University of Montana M
New Mexico Institute of Mining and Technology M
Penn State University Park M,D*
Queen's University at Kingston M,D
South Dakota School of Mines and Technology M
Southern Illinois University Carbondale M,D
Université du Québec en Abitibi-Témiscamingue M,O
Université Laval M,D
University of Alaska Fairbanks M
University of Alberta M,D
The University of Arizona M,D,O
The University of British Columbia M,D
University of Kentucky M,D
University of Nevada, Reno M
The University of Texas at Austin M
University of Utah M,D
West Virginia University M,D

MINERAL ECONOMICS

Colorado School of Mines M,D
Michigan Technological University M
The University of Texas at Austin M

MINERALOGY

Cornell University M,D
Indiana University Bloomington M,D
Université du Québec à Chicoutimi D
Université du Québec à Montréal M,D,O
The University of Texas at Dallas M,D

MISSIONS AND MISSIOLOGY

Abilene Christian University M
Acadia University M,D
Anderson University (IN) M,D
Asbury Theological Seminary M,D,O
Assemblies of God Theological Seminary M,D
Bethel Seminary M,D,O
Biblical Theological Seminary M,D,O
Biola University M,D,O
Boston University M,D*
Briercrest Seminary M
Calvin Theological Seminary M,D
Catholic Theological Union M,D,O
Cedarville University M,D
Central Baptist Theological Seminary M,O
Clarks Summit University M,D
Columbia International University M,D,O
Dallas Baptist University M
Dallas Theological Seminary M,D,O
Eastern University M
Ecclesia College M
Evangelical Seminary M
Fresno Pacific University M

*M—masters degree; D—doctorate; O—other advanced degree; *—Close-Up and/or Display*

Fuller Theological Seminary	M,D,O
Gardner-Webb University	M,D
Global University	M,D
Gordon-Conwell Theological Seminary	M,D
Grace Mission University	M,D
Grace Theological Seminary	M,D,O
Hope International University	M
Liberty University	M,D
Luther Seminary	M,D
Mid-America Baptist Theological Seminary	M,D
Milligan College	M,D,O
Northern Seminary	M,D
Northwest Nazarene University	M
Northwest University	M
Nyack College	M,D
Oral Roberts University	M,D
Phillips Theological Seminary	M,D
Providence University College & Theological Seminary	M,D,O
Reformed Theological Seminary–Jackson Campus	M,D,O
Regent University	M,D
Rochester College	M
Saint Paul University	M
Simpson University	M
Southeastern Baptist Theological Seminary	M,D
Southern Adventist University	M
The Southern Baptist Theological Seminary	M,D
Southern Evangelical Seminary	M,D,O
Southwestern Assemblies of God University	M
Southwestern Baptist Theological Seminary	M,D
Southwestern Christian University	M
Taylor College and Seminary	M,O
Theological University of the Caribbean	M,D
Trinity Bible College and Graduate School	M
Trinity International University	M,D,O
Trinity Lutheran Seminary	M
Trinity School for Ministry	M,D,O
Tyndale University College & Seminary	M,O
University of South Africa	M,D
Villanova University	M
Wesley Biblical Seminary	M
Westminster Theological Seminary	M,D,O
Wheaton College	M
Whitworth University	M

MODELING AND SIMULATION

Arizona State University at the Tempe campus	M,D
Carnegie Mellon University	M,D
Columbus State University	M,O
Naval Postgraduate School	M,D
Old Dominion University	M,D
Portland State University	M,D,O
Rochester Institute of Technology	D
Stevens Institute of Technology	M,D,O
Trent University	M,D
Université Laval	M,O
University at Buffalo, the State University of New York	M,D
The University of Alabama in Huntsville	M,D,O
University of California, San Diego	M,D*
University of Central Florida	M,D,O
The University of Manchester	M,D
University of Pittsburgh	M,D*
University of Southern California	M,D*
Worcester Polytechnic Institute	M,D,O

MOLECULAR BIOLOGY

Albany College of Pharmacy and Health Sciences	M
Albany Medical College	M,D
Albert Einstein College of Medicine	D
American University of Beirut	M,D
Appalachian State University	M
Arizona State University at the Tempe campus	M,D
Arkansas State University	M,D
Auburn University	M,D*
Baylor College of Medicine	D
Boise State University	M,D
Boston University	M,D*
Brandeis University	M,D
Brigham Young University	M,D
Brown University	M,D
California Institute of Technology	D
California State University, Sacramento	M
Carnegie Mellon University	M,D
Case Western Reserve University	D*
Central Connecticut State University	M,O
Clemson University	D
Columbia University	D*
Cornell University	M,D
Dartmouth College	D*
Drexel University	M,D*
Duke University	D,O*
East Carolina University	M
Emory University	D
Florida Institute of Technology	M,D
Florida State University	M,D
Georgetown University	M,D
Georgia State University	M,D
Grand Valley State University	M
Harvard University	D*
Hood College	M*
Howard University	M,D
Illinois Institute of Technology	M,D
Illinois State University	M,D
Indiana State University	M,D
Indiana University Bloomington	M,D
Indiana University–Purdue University Indianapolis	M,D
Inter American University of Puerto Rico, Metropolitan Campus	M
Iowa State University of Science and Technology	M,D
Irell & Manella Graduate School of Biological Sciences	D*
Johns Hopkins University	M,D*
Kent State University	M,D
Lehigh University	M,D
Lipscomb University	M
Louisiana State University Health Sciences Center at Shreveport	M,D
Louisiana Tech University	M,D,O
Loyola University Chicago	M,D
Marquette University	M,D
Massachusetts Institute of Technology	M,D,O
Mayo Clinic Graduate School of Biomedical Sciences	M,D
McMaster University	M,D
Medical University of South Carolina	M,D
Michigan State University	M,D
Michigan Technological University	M,D,O
Middle Tennessee State University	D
Mississippi State University	M,D
Missouri State University	M
Montclair State University	M,O
New Mexico State University	M,D
New York Medical College	M,D
New York University	M,D*
North Dakota State University	D*
Northeastern Illinois University	M
Northwestern University	D
The Ohio State University	M,D
Ohio University	D
Oklahoma State University	M,D
Oregon Health & Science University	M,D
Oregon State University	M,D
Pace University	M
Penn State University Park	M,D*
Princeton University	D
Purdue University	M,D
Queen's University at Kingston	M,D
Quinnipiac University	M
Rosalind Franklin University of Medicine and Science	D
Rutgers University–Newark	M,D
Rutgers University–New Brunswick	M,D
Sacred Heart University	M
Saint Louis University	D*
San Diego State University	M,D
San Francisco State University	M
San Jose State University	M
Seton Hall University	M,D
Simon Fraser University	M,D,O
Southern Illinois University Carbondale	M,D
Southern Methodist University	M,D
State University of New York Downstate Medical Center	D
State University of New York Upstate Medical University	M,D
Stony Brook University, State University of New York	M,D
Texas Woman's University	M,D
Tufts University	D*
Tulane University	M,D
Uniformed Services University of the Health Sciences	M,D*
Universidad Central del Caribe	M,D
Université de Montréal	M,D
Université Laval	M,D
University at Buffalo, the State University of New York	D
The University of Alabama at Birmingham	D
University of Alberta	M,D
The University of Arizona	D
University of Arkansas	M,D
University of Arkansas for Medical Sciences	M,D,O
The University of British Columbia	M,D
University of Calgary	M,D
University of California, Berkeley	D
University of California, Davis	M,D
University of California, Irvine	M,D
University of California, Los Angeles	M,D*
University of California, Riverside	M,D
University of California, San Francisco	D
University of California, Santa Barbara	M,D
University of California, Santa Cruz	M,D*
University of Chicago	D
University of Cincinnati	M,D
University of Colorado Boulder	M,D
University of Colorado Denver	D
University of Connecticut	M,D*
University of Connecticut Health Center	D
University of Delaware	M,D*
University of Denver	M,D
University of Florida	M,D
University of Georgia	M,D
University of Guelph	M,D
University of Hawaii at Manoa	M,D
University of Illinois at Chicago	D
The University of Iowa	D*
The University of Kansas	D
University of Lethbridge	M,D
University of Maine	M,D
The University of Manchester	M,D
University of Maryland, Baltimore	M,D
University of Maryland, Baltimore County	M,D
University of Maryland, College Park	D
University of Miami	D*
University of Michigan	M,D*
University of Minnesota, Duluth	M,D
University of Minnesota, Twin Cities Campus	M,D
University of Missouri–Kansas City	D
University of Montana	D
University of Nebraska Medical Center	M
University of Nevada, Reno	M,D
University of New Haven	M*
University of New Mexico	M,D
The University of North Carolina at Chapel Hill	M,D
University of North Texas	M,D,O
University of Notre Dame	M,D
University of Oklahoma Health Sciences Center	M,D
University of Oregon	M,D
University of Ottawa	M,D
University of Pennsylvania	D*
University of Pittsburgh	D*
University of Puerto Rico–Río Piedras	M,D
University of Rhode Island	M,D*
University of Rochester	M,D*
University of South Carolina	M,D
University of South Dakota	M,D
University of Southern California	M,D*
University of Southern Maine	M
University of South Florida	M,D*
The University of Texas at Austin	D
The University of Texas at Dallas	M,D
The University of Texas at San Antonio	M,D
University of Utah	D
University of Vermont	D
University of Washington	D
University of Wisconsin–La Crosse	M
University of Wisconsin–Madison	D
University of Wisconsin–Milwaukee	M,D*
University of Wisconsin–Parkside	M
University of Wyoming	M,D
Vanderbilt University	M,D*
Virginia Commonwealth University	M,D
Washington University in St. Louis	D
Wayne State University	M,D,O
Weill Cornell Medicine	M,D
Wesleyan University	D
West Virginia University	M,D
Wright State University	M
Yale University	D
Youngstown State University	M

MOLECULAR BIOPHYSICS

Baylor College of Medicine	D
California Institute of Technology	M,D
Carnegie Mellon University	D
Duke University	O*
Florida State University	D
Illinois Institute of Technology	M,D
Johns Hopkins University	D*
Rutgers University–New Brunswick	D
University at Buffalo, the State University of New York	M,D
University of Arkansas for Medical Sciences	M,D,O
University of Chicago	D
University of Massachusetts Amherst	D*
University of Pennsylvania	D*
University of Pittsburgh	D*
The University of Texas Medical Branch	D
The University of Texas Southwestern Medical Center	D
Washington University in St. Louis	D
Wesleyan University	D
Yale University	D

MOLECULAR GENETICS

Albert Einstein College of Medicine	D
Duke University	D*
Emory University	D
Georgia State University	M,D
Harvard University	D*
Illinois State University	M,D
Indiana University–Purdue University Indianapolis	M,D
Iowa State University of Science and Technology	M,D
Michigan State University	M,D
New York University	M,D*
Northern Michigan University	M
The Ohio State University	M,D
Oklahoma State University	M,D
Penn State Hershey Medical Center	M,D
Rutgers University–Newark	D
Rutgers University–New Brunswick	M,D
Stony Brook University, State University of New York	D
University of Calgary	M,D
University of California, Irvine	M,D
University of California, Los Angeles	M,D*
University of Cincinnati	M,D
University of Colorado Denver	D
University of Florida	M
University of Guelph	M,D
University of Illinois at Chicago	D
University of Louisville	M,D
The University of Manchester	M,D
University of Maryland, College Park	M,D
University of Nebraska Medical Center	M,D
University of Pittsburgh	D*
University of Rhode Island	M,D*
University of Toronto	M,D
University of Virginia	D
Van Andel Institute Graduate School	D
Virginia Commonwealth University	M,D
Wake Forest University	D
Washington University in St. Louis	D
Wayne State University	M,D,O

MOLECULAR MEDICINE

Augusta University	D
Baylor College of Medicine	D
Boston University	D*
Case Western Reserve University	D*
Cleveland State University	M,D
Dartmouth College	*
Drexel University	M*
Elmezzi Graduate School of Molecular Medicine	D
The George Washington University	D
Hofstra University	D
Johns Hopkins University	D*
Liberty University	M,D
Oregon Health & Science University	M,D
Penn State Hershey Medical Center	D
Queen's University at Kingston	M,D
Rutgers University–Newark	D
Tufts University	D*
The University of Alabama at Birmingham	D
The University of Arizona	M,D
University of Cincinnati	D
University of Maryland, Baltimore	D
University of Nebraska Medical Center	D
University of South Florida	M,D*
The University of Texas Health Science Center at San Antonio	M,D
Wake Forest University	M,D
Wayne State University	M,D,O
Yale University	D

MOLECULAR PATHOGENESIS

Dartmouth College	D*
Emory University	D
North Dakota State University	M,D*
Washington University in St. Louis	D

MOLECULAR PATHOLOGY

Rutgers University–Newark	D
Texas Tech University Health Sciences Center	M
University of Michigan	D*
University of Pittsburgh	D*
University of Wisconsin–Madison	D

MOLECULAR PHARMACOLOGY

Albert Einstein College of Medicine	D
Brown University	M,D
Harvard University	D*
Loyola University Chicago	M,D
Mayo Clinic Graduate School of Biomedical Sciences	M,D
Medical University of South Carolina	M,D
New York University	D*
Purdue University	D
Rosalind Franklin University of Medicine and Science	M,D
Rutgers University–New Brunswick	M,D
Thomas Jefferson University	D
University at Buffalo, the State University of New York	D
University of Massachusetts Medical School	M,D
University of Nevada, Reno	D
University of Pittsburgh	D*
University of Southern California	M,D*
University of South Florida	M,D*

MOLECULAR PHYSIOLOGY

Baylor College of Medicine	D
Loyola University Chicago	M,D
Rutgers University–New Brunswick	M,D
Stony Brook University, State University of New York	D
University of California, Los Angeles	D*
University of Illinois at Urbana–Champaign	M,D
The University of North Carolina at Chapel Hill	D
University of Pittsburgh	D*
University of Virginia	M,D
Vanderbilt University	M,D*
Yale University	D

MOLECULAR TOXICOLOGY

Massachusetts Institute of Technology	D
New York University	M,D*
North Carolina State University	M,D
Oregon State University	M,D
Penn State Hershey Medical Center	D
University of California, Berkeley	D
University of California, Los Angeles	D*
University of Cincinnati	M,D

MULTILINGUAL AND MULTICULTURAL EDUCATION

Alliant International University–San Francisco	M,O
American College of Education	M
Bank Street College of Education	M
Boise State University	M

Brooklyn College of the City University of New York	M
Brown University	M,D
Buffalo State College, State University of New York	M
California State University, Fullerton	M
California State University, Northridge	M
California State University, Sacramento	M,D,O
California State University, Stanislaus	M
Chicago State University	M
City College of the City University of New York	M
The College at Brockport, State University of New York	M,O
College of Mount Saint Vincent	M,O
The College of New Rochelle	M,O
College of Staten Island of the City University of New York	O
The College of William and Mary	M*
Columbia International University	M,D,O
Dallas Baptist University	M
DePaul University	M,D
Eastern New Mexico University	M
Eastern University	M,O
Fairfield University	M,O
Fairleigh Dickinson University, Metropolitan Campus	M
Florida Atlantic University	M,D,O
Florida International University	M,D,O
Gallaudet University	M,D,O
George Mason University	M
The George Washington University	M,D,O
Georgia Southern University	D
Graduate Institute of Applied Linguistics	M,O
Heritage University	M
Hofstra University	M,D,O
Houston Baptist University	M,D
Howard University	M,D
Hunter College of the City University of New York	M
Immaculata University	M
Indiana State University	M,D,O
Indiana University Bloomington	M,D
James Madison University	M
Kean University	M
Langston University	M
La Salle University	M,O
Lehman College of the City University of New York	M
Long Island University–Hudson	M,O
Long Island University–LIU Brooklyn	M,O
Loyola Marymount University	M
Manhattan College	M,O
Manhattanville College	M,O
Molloy College	M,O
Mount St. Joseph University	M,O
New Jersey City University	M
New Mexico State University	M,D,O
New York University	M,D,O*
Northern Arizona University	M,O
Queens College of the City University of New York	M,O
Quincy University	M
Rider University	M
Rutgers University–New Brunswick	M,D
St. John's University (NY)	M,O
Saint Mary's University of Minnesota	M,O
San Diego State University	M,D
Southern Connecticut State University	M
Southern Methodist University	M,D
State University of New York at New Paltz	M,O
State University of New York College at Geneseo	M
Sul Ross State University	M
Teachers College, Columbia University	M,D,O
Texas A&M University	M,D
Texas A&M University–Kingsville	M,D
Texas A&M University–San Antonio	M
Texas Southern University	M,D
Texas State University	M
Texas Tech University	M,D
University at Buffalo, the State University of New York	M,D,O
University of Alaska Fairbanks	M
University of Alberta	M
University of Calgary	M,D
University of California, Riverside	M,D,O
University of California, San Diego	M,D*
University of Colorado Boulder	M,D
University of Colorado Denver	M
University of Connecticut	M,D*
University of Delaware	M,D,O*
University of Houston–Clear Lake	M
University of Maryland, Baltimore County	M,D
University of Massachusetts Amherst	M,D,O*
University of Miami	D*
University of Minnesota, Twin Cities Campus	M,D,O
University of New Mexico	M,D
The University of North Carolina at Greensboro	M,D,O
University of Northern Colorado	M,D
University of Pennsylvania	M*
University of St. Thomas (TX)	M,D
University of San Francisco	M,D
University of Southern California	D*
The University of Tennessee	M,D,O
The University of Texas at Austin	M,D
The University of Texas at El Paso	M,D,O
The University of Texas at San Antonio	M,D
The University of Texas Rio Grande Valley	M
University of the Southwest	M
University of Washington	M,D
University of Wisconsin–Milwaukee	M,D,O*
Utah State University	M
Vanderbilt University	M,D*
Walden University	M,D,O
Wayne State University	M,D,O
Western New Mexico University	M
Western Oregon University	M
William Paterson University of New Jersey	M,D,O
Winona State University	O
Xavier University	M*

MUSEUM EDUCATION

Bank Street College of Education	M
Eastern Michigan University	O
The George Washington University	M
Tufts University	M,D*
The University of the Arts	M

MUSEUM STUDIES

American Museum of Natural History–Richard Gilder Graduate School	D
Arizona State University at the Tempe campus	M,D,O
Bard College	M
Baylor University	M
Boston University	M,D,O*
California College of the Arts	M
California State University, Chico	M
California State University, Fullerton	M
Caribbean University	M,D
Case Western Reserve University	M*
Christie's Education	M
City College of the City University of New York	M
Claremont Graduate University	M,D,O
Cleveland State University	M
Columbia University	M,D*
Eastern Michigan University	M,O
Fashion Institute of Technology	M
Florida International University	M,O
Florida State University	M,D
The George Washington University	M,D,O
Harvard University	M,O*
Indiana University–Purdue University Indianapolis	M,O
John F. Kennedy University	M,O
Johns Hopkins University	M,O*
Long Island University–LIU Post	M
Marist College	M
Maryland Institute College of Art	M
Morgan State University	M,D
New Mexico State University	M,O
The New School	M
New York University	M,O*
Penn State Harrisburg	M,D,O
St. John's University (NY)	M
San Francisco Art Institute	M
San Francisco State University	M
Seton Hall University	M
Southern Illinois University Edwardsville	O
Southern University at New Orleans	M
State University of New York College at Oneonta	M
Syracuse University	M*
Texas Tech University	M,D
Trinity College (United States)	M
Tufts University	M,D,O*
Université de Montréal	M
Université du Québec à Montréal	M
Université Laval	O
University at Buffalo, the State University of New York	M,D
The University of British Columbia	M,D
University of Central Oklahoma	M
University of Colorado Boulder	M
University of Denver	M
University of Florida	M,D
University of Hawaii at Manoa	O
University of Illinois at Chicago	M,D
The University of Kansas	M,O
University of Louisville	M,D
The University of Manchester	D
University of Memphis	M,O
University of Michigan–Flint	M
University of Missouri–St. Louis	M,O
University of New Hampshire	M,D
The University of North Carolina at Greensboro	M,D,O
University of North Texas	M,D,O
University of Oklahoma	M,O*
University of St. Thomas (MN)	M,O
University of San Francisco	M
University of South Carolina	M,O
University of South Florida	O*
The University of the Arts	M
University of Toronto	M
The University of Tulsa	M
University of Washington	M
University of West Georgia	M,O
University of Wisconsin–Milwaukee	M,D,O*
Virginia Commonwealth University	M,D
Wayne State University	M,D,O
Western Illinois University	M,O

MUSIC

Academy of Art University	M
American University	M,O
Andrews University	M
Appalachian State University	M
Aquinas Institute of Theology	M,D,O
Arizona State University at the Tempe campus	M,D
Arkansas State University	M,O
Austin Peay State University	M
Azusa Pacific University	M*
Ball State University	M,D,O
The Baptist College of Florida	M
Bard College	M,O
Baylor University	M,D
Bennington College	M,D
Berklee College of Music	M,O
Bethesda University	M
Binghamton University, State University of New York	M
Bob Jones University	M,D,O
Boise State University	M
Boston University	M,D,O*
Bowling Green State University	M,D
Brandeis University	M,D
Brandon University	M
Brigham Young University	M
Brooklyn College of the City University of New York	M
Brown University	D
Butler University	M
California Baptist University	M
California Institute of the Arts	M,O
California State University, East Bay	M
California State University, Fresno	M
California State University, Fullerton	M
California State University, Long Beach	M
California State University, Los Angeles	M
California State University, Northridge	M
California State University, Sacramento	M
Campbellsville University	M
Capital University	M
Carleton University	M
Carnegie Mellon University	M
Case Western Reserve University	M,D*
The Catholic University of America	M,D,O
Central Michigan University	M
Central Washington University	M
Claremont Graduate University	M,D
Cleveland Institute of Music	M,D,O
Cleveland State University	M
The Colburn School Conservatory of Music	M,O
Colorado State University	M
Columbia College Chicago	M
Columbia University	M,D*
Columbus State University	M,O
Concordia University (Canada)	O
Concordia University Chicago	M
Concordia University Wisconsin	M
Conservatorio de Musica de Puerto Rico	O
Converse College	M
Cornell University	M,D
Curtis Institute of Music	M
Dalhousie University	M
Dartmouth College	M*
DePaul University	M,O
Dominican University of California	M
Duke University	D*
Duquesne University	M,O
East Carolina University	M,O
Eastern Illinois University	M
Eastern Kentucky University	M
Eastern Michigan University	M
Eastern University	M,O
Eastern Washington University	M
Emory University	M
Emporia State University	M
Five Towns College	M,D
Florida Atlantic University	M
Florida International University	M
Florida State University	M,D
Fuller Theological Seminary	M,D,O
Garrett-Evangelical Theological Seminary	M,D
George Mason University	M,D
Georgia Institute of Technology	M,D
Georgia Southern University	M
Georgia State University	M,D,O
The Graduate Center, City University of New York	D
Hardin-Simmons University	M
Harvard University	M,D*
Hebrew College	M,O
Hebrew Union College–Jewish Institute of Religion (NY)	M
Hollins University	M
Holy Names University	M,O
Hope International University	M
Houghton College	M
Houston Baptist University	M,D
Howard University	M
Hunter College of the City University of New York	M
Illinois State University	M
Indiana State University	M
Indiana University Bloomington	M,D,O
Indiana University of Pennsylvania	M
Indiana University–Purdue University Indianapolis	M,D
Indiana University South Bend	M,D
Inter American University of Puerto Rico, San Germán Campus	M
Ithaca College	M
Jacksonville State University	M
James Madison University	M,D
The Jewish Theological Seminary	M
Johns Hopkins University	M,D,O*
The Juilliard School	M,D,O
Kansas State University	M
Kent State University	M,D
Lamar University	M
Lee University	M
Liberty University	M,D
Long Island University–LIU Post	M
Louisiana State University and Agricultural & Mechanical College	M,D
Loyola University New Orleans	M
Lynn University	M,O
Manhattan School of Music	M,D,O
Mansfield University of Pennsylvania	M
Marshall University	M
McGill University	M,D
Memorial University of Newfoundland	M,D
Mercer University	M
Messiah College	M
Miami University	M
Michigan State University	M,D
Middle Tennessee State University	M
Midwestern Baptist Theological Seminary	M,D,O
Mills College	M
Minnesota State University Mankato	M
Mississippi College	M
Missouri State University	M
Montclair State University	M,O
Morehead State University	M
Morgan State University	M
Murray State University	M
Nazareth College of Rochester	M
New England Conservatory of Music	M,D,O
New Jersey City University	M
New Mexico State University	M
New Orleans Baptist Theological Seminary	M,D
The New School	M,O
New York University	M,D,O*
Norfolk State University	M
North Carolina Central University	M
North Dakota State University	M,D*
Northeastern Illinois University	M
Northern Arizona University	M,O
Northern Illinois University	M,O
North Park University	M
Northwestern State University of Louisiana	M
Northwestern University	M,D
Oakland University	M,D
Oberlin College	M,O
The Ohio State University	M,D
Ohio University	M,O
Oklahoma City University	M
Oklahoma State University	M
Old Dominion University	M
Open University	M
Park University	M,O
Penn State University Park	M,D,O*
Pensacola Christian College	M,D,O
Phillips Theological Seminary	M,D
Pittsburg State University	M
Point Park University	M
Portland State University	M
Pratt Institute	M*
Princeton University	D
Purchase College, State University of New York	M
Queens College of the City University of New York	M,O
Radford University	M
Rice University	M,D
Rider University	M
Roosevelt University	M,O
Rowan University	M
Rutgers University–Newark	M
Rutgers University–New Brunswick	M,D,O
Saint John's University (MN)	M
Salem College	M
Samford University	M
Sam Houston State University	M
San Diego State University	M
San Francisco Conservatory of Music	M,O
San Francisco State University	M
San Jose State University	M
Savannah College of Art and Design	M
School of the Art Institute of Chicago	M
Shenandoah University	M,D,O
Silver Lake College of the Holy Family	M
Southeastern Baptist Theological Seminary	M,D
Southeastern Louisiana University	M
Southern Illinois University Carbondale	M
Southern Illinois University Edwardsville	M
Southern Methodist University	M,D
Southern Oregon University	M
Southern Utah University	M
Southwestern Baptist Theological Seminary	M,D
Southwestern Oklahoma State University	M

*M—masters degree; D—doctorate; O—other advanced degree; *—Close-Up and/or Display*

Stanford University	M,D
State University of New York at Fredonia	M
State University of New York at New Paltz	M
State University of New York College at Potsdam	M
Stephen F. Austin State University	M
Stony Brook University, State University of New York	M,D
Syracuse University	M*
Temple University	M,D*
Texas A&M University	M
Texas A&M University–Commerce	M,D,O
Texas A&M University–Kingsville	M
Texas Christian University	M,D
Texas Southern University	M
Texas State University	M
Texas Tech University	M,D
Texas Woman's University	M
Towson University	M
Trinity College (Canada)	M,D,O
Trinity Lutheran Seminary	M
Truman State University	M
Tufts University	M*
Tulane University	M
Université de Montréal	M,D,O
Université Laval	M,D
University at Buffalo, the State University of New York	M,D,O
The University of Akron	M
The University of Alabama	M,D
University of Alaska Fairbanks	M
University of Alberta	M,D
The University of Arizona	M,D
University of Arkansas	M
The University of British Columbia	M,D
University of Calgary	M,D
University of California, Berkeley	D
University of California, Davis	M,D
University of California, Irvine	M
University of California, Los Angeles	M,D*
University of California, Riverside	M,D
University of California, San Diego	M,D*
University of California, Santa Barbara	M,D
University of California, Santa Cruz	M,D*
University of Central Arkansas	M,O
University of Central Florida	M
University of Central Missouri	M,D,O
University of Central Oklahoma	M
University of Chicago	M,D
University of Cincinnati	M,D,O
University of Colorado Boulder	M,D
University of Colorado Denver	M
University of Connecticut	M,D*
University of Delaware	M*
University of Denver	M,O
University of Florida	M,D
University of Georgia	M,D
University of Hartford	M,D,O
University of Hawaii at Manoa	M,D
University of Houston	M,D
University of Idaho	M
University of Illinois at Urbana–Champaign	M,D
The University of Iowa	M,D*
The University of Kansas	M,D
University of Kentucky	M,D
University of Lethbridge	M,D
University of Louisiana at Lafayette	M
University of Louisville	M
University of Maine	M
The University of Manchester	D
University of Manitoba	M
University of Maryland, Baltimore County	O
University of Maryland, College Park	M,D
University of Massachusetts Amherst	M,D*
University of Massachusetts Lowell	M
University of Memphis	M,D
University of Miami	M,D,O*
University of Michigan	M,D,O*
University of Michigan–Flint	M
University of Minnesota, Duluth	M
University of Minnesota, Twin Cities Campus	M,D
University of Mississippi	M,D
University of Missouri	M,O
University of Missouri–Kansas City	M,D
University of Montana	M
University of Nebraska at Omaha	M
University of Nebraska–Lincoln	M,D
University of Nevada, Las Vegas	M,D,O
University of Nevada, Reno	M
University of New Hampshire	M
University of New Mexico	M
University of New Orleans	M
The University of North Carolina at Chapel Hill	M,D
The University of North Carolina at Charlotte	O
The University of North Carolina at Greensboro	M,D
University of North Carolina School of the Arts	M,O
University of North Dakota	M,D
University of Northern Colorado	M,D
University of Northern Iowa	M
University of North Texas	M,D,O
University of Oklahoma	M,D,O*
University of Oregon	M,D
University of Ottawa	M,O
University of Pennsylvania	M,D*
University of Pittsburgh	M,D*
University of Redlands	M
University of Regina	M
University of Rhode Island	M*
University of Rochester	M,D*
University of St. Thomas (MN)	M,D
University of St. Thomas (TX)	M
University of Saskatchewan	M
University of South Africa	M,D
University of South Alabama	M
University of South Carolina	M,D,O
University of South Dakota	M
University of Southern California	M,D,O*
University of Southern Maine	M
University of Southern Mississippi	M,D
University of South Florida	M,D*
The University of Tennessee	M
The University of Tennessee at Chattanooga	M
The University of Texas at Arlington	M
The University of Texas at Austin	M,D
The University of Texas at El Paso	M
The University of Texas at San Antonio	M
The University of Texas Rio Grande Valley	M
The University of the Arts	M
University of the Pacific	M
The University of Toledo	M,O
University of Toronto	M,D
University of Utah	M,D
University of Valley Forge	M
University of Victoria	M,D
University of Virginia	M,D
University of Washington	M,D
The University of Western Ontario	M,D
University of West Georgia	M,O
University of Wisconsin–Madison	M,D
University of Wyoming	M
Utah State University	M
Vermont College of Fine Arts	M
Virginia Commonwealth University	M
Washington State University	M
Washington University in St. Louis	M,D
Wayne State University	M,O
Webster University	M
Wesleyan University	M,D
West Chester University of Pennsylvania	M,O
Western Illinois University	M
Western Michigan University	M,O
Western Oregon University	M
Western Washington University	M
West Texas A&M University	M
West Virginia University	M,D
Wichita State University	M
William Paterson University of New Jersey	M
Winthrop University	M
World Mission University	M,D
Yale University	M,D,O
York University	M,D
Youngstown State University	M

MUSIC EDUCATION

Acadia University	M
Adams State University	M
Alabama Agricultural and Mechanical University	M
Alabama State University	M,O
Anderson University (SC)	M
Arcadia University	M,D,O
Arizona State University at the Tempe campus	M,D
Arkansas State University	M,O
Augusta University	M,O
Austin Peay State University	M
Azusa Pacific University	M*
Ball State University	M,D,O
Bob Jones University	M,D,O
Boise State University	M
Boston University	M,D*
Bowling Green State University	M,D
Brandon University	M
Brigham Young University	M
Brooklyn College of the City University of New York	M
Butler University	M
California Baptist University	M
California State University, Fresno	M
California State University, Fullerton	M
California State University, Los Angeles	M
California State University, Northridge	M
Campbellsville University	M
Capital University	M
Carnegie Mellon University	M
Case Western Reserve University	M,D*
The Catholic University of America	M,D,O
Central Connecticut State University	M,O
Central Methodist University	M
Central Michigan University	M
Central Washington University	M
Cleveland State University	M
College of Charleston	M
The Colorado College	M
Colorado State University–Pueblo	M
Columbus State University	M,O
Conservatorio de Musica de Puerto Rico	M
Converse College	M
DePaul University	M,O
Duquesne University	M,O
East Carolina University	M,O
Eastern Illinois University	M
Eastern Kentucky University	M
Eastern Washington University	M
Five Towns College	M,D
Florida International University	M
George Mason University	M
Georgia College & State University	M
Georgia Southern University	M
Georgia State University	M,D,O
Gordon College	M
Hampton University	M
Hardin-Simmons University	M
Hebrew College	M,O
Heidelberg University	M
Hofstra University	M,D,O
Holy Names University	M,O
Howard University	M
Hunter College of the City University of New York	M
Idaho State University	M
Indiana State University	M
Indiana University of Pennsylvania	M
Inter American University of Puerto Rico, Metropolitan Campus	M
Inter American University of Puerto Rico, San Germán Campus	M
Ithaca College	M
Jackson State University	M
James Madison University	M
Kent State University	M,D
Lake Forest College	M
Lebanon Valley College	M
Lee University	M
Lehman College of the City University of New York	M
Liberty University	M,D
Long Island University–LIU Post	M,D,O
Louisiana State University and Agricultural & Mechanical College	M,D
Loyola University Maryland	M,O
Manhattanville College	M,O
Marywood University	M
McGill University	M,D
McKendree University	M,D,O
McNeese State University	O
Miami University	M
Michigan State University	M,D
Minnesota State University Mankato	M
Mississippi College	M
Montclair State University	M
Morehead State University	M
Murray State University	M
Nazareth College of Rochester	M
New Jersey City University	M
New Mexico State University	M
New York University	M,D,O*
Norfolk State University	M
North Dakota State University	M,D*
Northeastern Illinois University	M
Northern State University	M
Northwestern University	M,D
Oakland University	M,D
Ohio University	M,O
Oklahoma State University	M
Old Dominion University	M
Oregon State University	M
Penn State University Park	M,D,O*
Piedmont College	M,D,O
Pittsburg State University	M
Plymouth State University	M
Queens College of the City University of New York	M,O
Rhode Island College	M
Rider University	M
Rutgers University–New Brunswick	M,D,O
Saint Xavier University	M
Samford University	M
San Diego State University	M
San Francisco Conservatory of Music	M,O
San Francisco State University	M
San Jose State University	M
Shenandoah University	M,D,O
Southern Illinois University Edwardsville	M,O
Southern Methodist University	M
Southwestern Oklahoma State University	M
State University of New York at Fredonia	M
State University of New York College at Potsdam	M
Syracuse University	M*
Tarleton State University	M
Teachers College, Columbia University	M,D,O
Temple University	M,D*
Tennessee Technological University	M
Texas A&M University–Commerce	M,D,O
Texas A&M University–Kingsville	M
Texas Christian University	M,D
Texas State University	M
Texas Tech University	M,D
Texas Woman's University	M
Towson University	M
Union College (KY)	M
Université Laval	M,D
University at Buffalo, the State University of New York	M,D,O
The University of Akron	M
The University of Alabama	M,D,O
The University of Arizona	M,D
University of Bridgeport	M,D,O
The University of British Columbia	M,D
University of Central Arkansas	M,O
University of Central Oklahoma	M
University of Cincinnati	M
University of Colorado Boulder	M,D
University of Connecticut	M,D*
University of Dayton	M
University of Delaware	M*
University of Denver	M,O
University of Florida	M,D
University of Georgia	M,D
University of Hartford	M,D,O
University of Houston	M,D
University of Illinois at Urbana–Champaign	M,D
The University of Iowa	M,D*
The University of Kansas	M,D
University of Kentucky	M,D
University of Louisiana at Lafayette	M
University of Louisville	M,D,O
University of Maryland, Baltimore County	M
University of Maryland, College Park	M,D
University of Massachusetts Amherst	M,D*
University of Massachusetts Lowell	M
University of Memphis	M,D
University of Miami	M,D,O*
University of Michigan	M,D,O*
University of Minnesota, Duluth	M
University of Missouri	M,D,O
University of Missouri–Kansas City	M,D
University of Nebraska at Kearney	M
University of Nebraska–Lincoln	M,D
University of New Mexico	M
The University of North Carolina at Chapel Hill	M
The University of North Carolina at Greensboro	M,D
University of North Dakota	M,D
University of Northern Colorado	M,D
University of Northern Iowa	M
University of North Texas	M,D,O
University of Oklahoma	M,D,O*
University of Oregon	M,D
University of Ottawa	M,O
University of Rhode Island	M*
University of Rochester	M,D*
University of St. Thomas (MN)	M,D
University of South Alabama	M
University of South Carolina	M,D,O
University of South Dakota	M
University of Southern California	M,D,O*
University of Southern Maine	M
University of Southern Mississippi	M,D
University of South Florida	M,D*
The University of Tennessee	M
The University of Tennessee at Chattanooga	M
The University of Texas at Arlington	M
The University of Texas at Austin	M,D
The University of Texas at El Paso	M
The University of the Arts	M
University of the Pacific	M
The University of Toledo	M,O
University of Toronto	M,D
University of Utah	M,D
University of Victoria	M,D
University of Washington	M,D
University of West Georgia	M,O
University of Wisconsin–Madison	M,D
University of Wisconsin–Stevens Point	M
University of Wyoming	M
Utah State University	M
VanderCook College of Music	M
Virginia Commonwealth University	M
Wayne State College	M
Wayne State University	M,O
Webster University	M
West Chester University of Pennsylvania	M,O
Western Connecticut State University	M
Western Kentucky University	M
Western Michigan University	M,O
West Virginia University	M,D
Wichita State University	M
Winthrop University	M
Wright State University	M
Youngstown State University	M

NANOTECHNOLOGY

The American University in Cairo	M,D,O
Arizona State University at the Tempe campus	M,D
Carnegie Mellon University	D
The College of William and Mary	M,D*
Cornell University	M,D
Indiana University of Pennsylvania	M
Johns Hopkins University	M*
Louisiana Tech University	M,D,O
Michigan Technological University	M,D,O
North Dakota State University	M,D*
South Dakota School of Mines and Technology	D
State University of New York Polytechnic Institute	M,D
Stevens Institute of Technology	D
University at Buffalo, the State University of New York	M,D,O
University of Alberta	M,D
University of California, Riverside	M
University of California, San Diego	M,D*
University of Central Florida	M
University of New Mexico	M,D
University of Pennsylvania	M*
University of South Florida	M,D*
University of Washington	M,D
Virginia Commonwealth University	M,D

NATIONAL SECURITY

American Public University System	M,D
American University	M,D,O
Angelo State University	M
Bellevue University	M

California State University, San Bernardino	M
The Citadel, The Military College of South Carolina	M,O
Daniel Morgan Graduate School of National Security	M
George Mason University	M,D,O
The George Washington University	M,D
Henley-Putnam School of Strategic Security	D
The Institute of World Politics	M,O
Kansas State University	M,D
National Defense University	M
Naval Postgraduate School	M,D,O
Naval War College	M
New Jersey City University	M,D,O
Regent University	M,D
Texas A&M University	M,O
Trinity Washington University	M
University of Central Florida	M,D,O
University of Nebraska at Omaha	M,O
University of New Haven	M,O*
Virginia Polytechnic Institute and State University	M,O
Western Michigan University Thomas M. Cooley Law School	M,D

NATURAL RESOURCES

American University	M,D,O
Auburn University	M,D*
Ball State University	M,O
Boise State University	M,D,O
California Polytechnic State University, San Luis Obispo	M*
Central Washington University	M
Colorado State University	M,D
Cornell University	M,D
Dalhousie University	M
Delaware State University	M
Duke University	M,D*
Florida International University	M,D
Humboldt State University	M
Indiana University–Purdue University Indianapolis	M,D,O
Instituto Tecnologico de Santo Domingo	M,D,O
Iowa State University of Science and Technology	M,D
Kansas State University	M,D
Laurentian University	M,D
Louisiana State University and Agricultural & Mechanical College	M,D
McGill University	M,D
Michigan State University	M,D
Montana State University	M
New Mexico Highlands University	M
North Carolina State University	M,D
North Dakota State University	M,D*
Northeastern State University	M
The Ohio State University	M,D
Oklahoma State University	M,D
Oregon State University	M
Purdue University	M,D
State University of New York College of Environmental Science and Forestry	M,D
Sul Ross State University	M
Tarleton State University	M
Texas A&M University	M,D
Texas Tech University	M,D
Unity College	M
Universidad Metropolitana	M
Universidad Nacional Pedro Henriquez Urena	M
Université du Québec à Montréal	M,D,O
Université du Québec en Abitibi-Témiscamingue	M,D
University of Alaska Fairbanks	M,D
University of Alberta	M,D
The University of Arizona	M,D
University of Arkansas at Monticello	M
The University of British Columbia	M,D
University of California, Berkeley	M,D
University of Connecticut	M,D*
University of Delaware	M*
University of Florida	M,D
University of Georgia	M,D
University of Guelph	M,D
University of Hawaii at Manoa	M,D
University of Idaho	M,D
University of Illinois at Urbana–Champaign	M,D
University of Louisiana at Lafayette	M
The University of Manchester	M,D
University of Manitoba	M,D
University of Maryland, College Park	M,D
University of Michigan	M,D*
University of Minnesota, Twin Cities Campus	M,D
University of Montana	M,D
University of Nebraska–Lincoln	M,D
University of New Brunswick Saint John	M
University of New Hampshire	M,D
University of New Mexico	M,D
University of Northern British Columbia	M,D,O
University of Rhode Island	M,D*
University of San Francisco	M
University of South Africa	M,D
The University of Texas at Austin	M
University of Vermont	M,D,O
University of Washington	M,D
University of Wisconsin–Madison	M,D
University of Wisconsin–Stevens Point	M
University of Wyoming	M,D
Utah State University	M
Virginia Polytechnic Institute and State University	M,D,O
Washington State University	M,D
West Virginia University	M,D

NATUROPATHIC MEDICINE

Bastyr University	D,O
Canadian College of Naturopathic Medicine	O
Maryland University of Integrative Health	D
National University of Natural Medicine	M,D
Southwest College of Naturopathic Medicine and Health Sciences	D
Universidad del Turabo	D
University of Bridgeport	D

NEAR AND MIDDLE EASTERN LANGUAGES

The American University in Cairo	M,O
American University of Beirut	M,D
Bethel Seminary	M,D,O
Brandeis University	M,D
California University of Pennsylvania	M
The Catholic University of America	M,D
DePaul University	M
Georgetown University	M,O
Harvard University	M,D*
Hebrew Union College–Jewish Institute of Religion (NY)	D
Hofstra University	M,D,O
Houston Baptist University	M
Indiana University Bloomington	M,D
Johns Hopkins University	D*
Kent State University	M,D
London Metropolitan University	M,D
Middlebury College	M
The Ohio State University	M,D
Oral Roberts University	M,D
University of California, Los Angeles	M,D*
University of Chicago	D
University of Michigan	M,D*
University of South Africa	M,D
The University of Texas at Austin	M,D
University of Utah	M,D
University of Wisconsin–Madison	M,D
Wayne State University	M,D
Yale University	M,D

NEAR AND MIDDLE EASTERN STUDIES

The American University in Cairo	M,O
American University of Beirut	M,D
The American University of Paris	M
Brandeis University	M,D
Brown University	D
California State University, Long Beach	M
The Catholic University of America	M,D,O
College of Staten Island of the City University of New York	M
Columbia University	M,D*
Cornell University	M,D
George Mason University	M,O
Georgetown University	M,O
The George Washington University	M
Harvard University	M,D*
Johns Hopkins University	D*
McGill University	M,D,O
New York University	M,D,O*
Princeton University	M,D
Rice University	D
Southern Evangelical Seminary	M,D,O
Southwestern Baptist Theological Seminary	M,D
The University of Arizona	M,D,O
University of California, Berkeley	M,D
University of California, Los Angeles	M,D*
University of Chicago	M,D
University of Illinois at Urbana–Champaign	M
The University of Kansas	M,O
The University of Manchester	D
University of Memphis	M,D
University of Michigan	M,D*
University of Pennsylvania	M,D*
University of South Africa	M,D
The University of Texas at Austin	M,D
University of Toronto	M,D
University of Utah	M,D
University of Virginia	M
University of Washington	M,D
University of Waterloo	M
University of Wisconsin–Madison	M,D
Washington University in St. Louis	M
Wayne State University	M,D
Yale University	M,D

NEUROBIOLOGY

Boston University	M,D*
Brandeis University	M,D
California Institute of Technology	D
Carnegie Mellon University	M,D
Columbia University	D*
Cornell University	D
Dalhousie University	M,D
Duke University	D*
Georgia State University	M,D
Harvard University	D*
Illinois State University	M,D
Indiana University–Purdue University Indianapolis	D
Louisiana State University Health Sciences Center	D
Massachusetts Institute of Technology	D
New York University	M,D*
Northwestern University	M,D
Penn State Hershey Medical Center	D
Purdue University	M,D
Queen's University at Kingston	M,D
Université Laval	M,D
University of Arkansas for Medical Sciences	M,D,O
University of California, Irvine	M,D
University of California, Los Angeles	M,D*
University of Chicago	D
University of Connecticut	M,D*
The University of Iowa	M,D*
University of Kentucky	D
University of Louisville	M,D
The University of Manchester	M,D
University of Maryland, Baltimore	D
University of Minnesota, Twin Cities Campus	M,D
The University of North Carolina at Chapel Hill	D
University of Oklahoma	M,D*
University of Rochester	D*
University of Southern California	D*
The University of Texas at Austin	D
The University of Texas at San Antonio	M,D
University of Utah	D
University of Washington	D
Virginia Commonwealth University	M
Wake Forest University	D
Wesleyan University	D
Yale University	D

NEUROSCIENCE

Albany Medical College	M,D
Albert Einstein College of Medicine	D
Alliant International University–San Diego	M,D,O
American University	M,D,O
American University of Beirut	M,D
Argosy University, Chicago	D
Argosy University, Phoenix	M,D
Argosy University, Tampa	M,D
Arizona State University at the Tempe campus	M,D
Augusta University	D
Ball State University	M,D,O
Baylor College of Medicine	D
Boston University	D*
Brandeis University	M,D
Brigham Young University	M,D
Brock University	M,D
Brown University	D
California Institute of Technology	M,D
Carleton University	M,D
Carnegie Mellon University	D
Case Western Reserve University	D*
Central Michigan University	M,D
College of Staten Island of the City University of New York	M
The College of William and Mary	M,D*
Dalhousie University	M,D
Dartmouth College	D*
Delaware State University	M,D
Drexel University	M,D*
Duke University	D,O*
Emory University	D
Fielding Graduate University	O
Florida Atlantic University	D
Florida International University	M,D
Florida State University	M,D
Gallaudet University	M,D,O
George Mason University	M,D,O
Georgetown University	D
Georgia State University	D
The Graduate Center, City University of New York	D
Harvard University	D*
Icahn School of Medicine at Mount Sinai	M,D
Illinois State University	M,D
Immaculata University	M,D,O
Indiana University Bloomington	D
Iowa State University of Science and Technology	M,D
Irell & Manella Graduate School of Biological Sciences	D*
Johns Hopkins University	D*
Kent State University	M,D
Louisiana State University Health Sciences Center	D
Loyola University Chicago	M,D
Marquette University	M,D
Massachusetts Institute of Technology	D
Mayo Clinic Graduate School of Biomedical Sciences	M,D
McGill University	M,D
McMaster University	M,D
Medical College of Wisconsin	D
Medical University of South Carolina	M,D
Meharry Medical College	D
Memorial University of Newfoundland	M,D
Michigan State University	M,D
Montana State University	M,D
New York University	D*
Northwestern University	D
The Ohio State University	D
Ohio University	M,D
Oregon Health & Science University	D
Penn State Hershey Medical Center	M,D
Princeton University	D
Purdue University	D
Queens College of the City University of New York	M
Queen's University at Kingston	M,D
Rosalind Franklin University of Medicine and Science	D
Rush University	M,D
Rutgers University–Newark	D
Rutgers University–New Brunswick	M,D
Seton Hall University	M,D
State University of New York Downstate Medical Center	D
State University of New York Upstate Medical University	D
Stony Brook University, State University of New York	M,D
Syracuse University	M,D*
Teachers College, Columbia University	M,D
Texas Christian University	M,D
Thomas Jefferson University	D
Tufts University	M,D*
Tulane University	M,D
Uniformed Services University of the Health Sciences	D*
Universidad de Iberoamerica	M,D
Université de Montréal	M,D
University at Albany, State University of New York	M,D
University at Buffalo, the State University of New York	M,D
The University of Alabama at Birmingham	M,D
University of Alaska Fairbanks	M,D
University of Alberta	M,D
The University of Arizona	D
The University of British Columbia	M,D
University of Calgary	M,D
University of California, Berkeley	D
University of California, Davis	D
University of California, Irvine	D
University of California, Los Angeles	D*
University of California, Riverside	D
University of California, San Diego	M,D*
University of California, San Francisco	D
University of California, Santa Barbara	D
University of Chicago	D
University of Cincinnati	D
University of Colorado Denver	D
University of Connecticut	M,D*
University of Connecticut Health Center	D
University of Delaware	D*
University of Florida	D
University of Georgia	D
University of Guelph	M,D,O
University of Hartford	M
University of Illinois at Chicago	M,D
University of Illinois at Urbana–Champaign	D
The University of Iowa	D*
The University of Kansas	M,D
University of Lethbridge	M,D
The University of Manchester	M,D
University of Maryland, Baltimore	D
University of Maryland, Baltimore County	D
University of Maryland, College Park	M,D
University of Massachusetts Amherst	M,D*
University of Massachusetts Medical School	M,D
University of Miami	M,D*
University of Michigan	D*
University of Michigan–Flint	D,O
University of Minnesota, Twin Cities Campus	M,D
University of Mississippi Medical Center	D
University of Missouri–St. Louis	M,D,O
University of Montana	M,D
University of Nebraska Medical Center	D
University of New Mexico	M,D
The University of North Carolina at Chapel Hill	D
University of North Texas Health Science Center at Fort Worth	M,D
University of Oklahoma Health Sciences Center	M,D
University of Oregon	M,D
University of Pennsylvania	D*
University of Pittsburgh	D*
University of Puerto Rico–Río Piedras	M,D
University of Rochester	D*
University of South Dakota	M,D
University of Southern California	M,D*
University of South Florida	M,D,O*
The University of Texas at Austin	D
The University of Texas at Dallas	M,D
The University of Texas Health Science Center at Houston	M,D
The University of Texas Health Science Center at San Antonio	D
The University of Texas Medical Branch	D
The University of Texas Southwestern Medical Center	D
The University of Toledo	M,D
University of Utah	D

*M—masters degree; D—doctorate; O—other advanced degree; *—Close-Up and/or Display*

University of Vermont	D
University of Virginia	D
University of Washington	M,D
The University of Western Ontario	M,D
University of Wisconsin–Madison	D
Virginia Commonwealth University	M,D,O
Wake Forest University	D
Washington State University	M,D
Washington University in St. Louis	D
Wayne State University	M,D,O
Weill Cornell Medicine	M,D
Wilfrid Laurier University	M,D
Wright State University	M
Yale University	D

NONPROFIT MANAGEMENT

Abilene Christian University	M
Adler University	M
American Jewish University	M
American University	M,D,O
Antioch University Santa Barbara	M
Arizona State University at the Tempe campus	M,D,O
Assumption College	M,O
Avila University	M
Baruch College of the City University of New York	M*
Bay Path University	M
Bradley University	M
Brandeis University	M
Brigham Young University	M
Cairn University	M,O
California Baptist University	M
California State University, Northridge	O
Capella University	D
Carlos Albizu University, Miami Campus	M,D
Case Western Reserve University	M,D,O*
Central Michigan University	M,O
Chaminade University of Honolulu	M
Cleveland State University	M,O
The College at Brockport, State University of New York	M,O
Columbia University	M*
Corban University	M
Daemen College	M
Dallas Baptist University	M
DePaul University	M
Drury University	M
Eastern Mennonite University	M
Eastern Michigan University	M,O
Eastern University	D,O
East Tennessee State University	M,O
Fairleigh Dickinson University, Metropolitan Campus	M,O
Florida Atlantic University	M,D
Fordham University	M,D
Geneva College	M
The George Washington University	M,O
Georgian Court University	M,O
Georgia Southern University	O
Georgia State University	M,D,O
Grand Valley State University	M
Gratz College	M
Hamline University	M,D
Hebrew Union College–Jewish Institute of Religion (NY)	M
Hope International University	M
Indiana University Bloomington	M,D,O
Indiana University Northwest	M,O
Indiana University of Pennsylvania	D
Indiana University–Purdue University Indianapolis	M,O
Indiana University South Bend	M,O
Iona College	M,O
James Madison University	M,D
John Carroll University	M
Johns Hopkins University	M,O*
Johnson & Wales University	M
Johnson University	M,D,O
Kean University	M
La Salle University	M
Lawrence Technological University	M,D,O
Lewis University	M
Liberty University	M
Lindenwood University	M
Lipscomb University	M,O
Long Island University–LIU Brooklyn	M,O
Long Island University–LIU Post	M,O
Louisiana State University in Shreveport	M
Marymount University	M,O
Mercer University	M,D
Minnesota State University Mankato	M,O
Mount Aloysius College	M
Murray State University	M,O
New England College	M
The New School	M
New York University	M,D,O*
North Carolina State University	M,D,O
Northeastern University	M,D
Northern Kentucky University	M,O
North Park University	M
Norwich University	M
Notre Dame of Maryland University	M
Oakland University	M,O
Oklahoma Christian University	M
Oklahoma State University	M,D,O
Oral Roberts University	M
Our Lady of the Lake University	M
Pace University	M
Park University	M,O
Penn State Harrisburg	M,D,O
Portland State University	M,D,O
Post University	M
Regent University	M,D,O
Regis University	M,O
Rockhurst University	M,O
Saint Mary-of-the-Woods College	M
Salve Regina University	M,O
San Francisco State University	M
Seton Hall University	M,O
Simmons College	M
Southern New Hampshire University	M,D,O
Suffolk University	M
Texas A&M University	M,O
Thomas Edison State University	M
Tiffin University	M
Trinity Washington University	M
Trinity Western University	M,O
Tufts University	O*
University at Albany, State University of New York	M,D,O
University of Arkansas at Little Rock	O
University of California, San Diego	M*
University of Central Florida	M,O
University of Central Oklahoma	M,O
University of Colorado Denver	M,D
University of Connecticut	M,O*
University of Florida	M,O
University of Georgia	M,D,O
University of Houston–Downtown	M
University of La Verne	M,D
University of Louisville	M,D
University of Lynchburg	M
University of Maryland, Baltimore County	M,O
University of Memphis	M,O
University of Michigan–Flint	M
University of Missouri	M,D,O
University of Missouri–St. Louis	M,O
University of Nevada, Las Vegas	M,D,O
University of New Haven	M,O*
The University of North Carolina at Charlotte	M,O
The University of North Carolina at Greensboro	M,O
University of Northern Iowa	M
University of North Florida	M,O
University of North Texas	M,D,O
University of Notre Dame	M
University of Oklahoma	M,O*
University of Oregon	M,O
University of Pennsylvania	M,O*
University of Pittsburgh	M*
University of Portland	M
University of San Diego	M,D,O
University of San Francisco	M
University of Southern California	M,O*
University of Southern Indiana	M
University of South Florida	O*
The University of Tampa	M,O
The University of Tennessee at Chattanooga	M,O
The University of Texas at Dallas	M,D
University of the Sacred Heart	M
University of the West	M
The University of Toledo	M,O
University of West Georgia	M,D,O
University of Wisconsin–Milwaukee	M,D,O*
Upper Iowa University	M
Villanova University	M,O
Virginia Commonwealth University	O
Virginia Polytechnic Institute and State University	M,O
Walden University	M,D,O
Warner Pacific University	M
Wayne State University	M,D
Webster University	M,D,O
West Chester University of Pennsylvania	M,O
Western Michigan University	M,D,O
Westfield State University	M
Worcester State University	M

NORTHERN STUDIES

University of Alaska Fairbanks	M
University of Manitoba	M

NUCLEAR ENGINEERING

Air Force Institute of Technology	M,D
Arizona State University at the Tempe campus	M,D,O
Colorado School of Mines	M,D
École Polytechnique de Montréal	M,D,O
Georgia Institute of Technology	M,D
Idaho State University	M,D
Kansas State University	M,D
Massachusetts Institute of Technology	M,D,O
McMaster University	M,D
Missouri University of Science and Technology	M,D
North Carolina State University	M,D
The Ohio State University	M,D
Oregon State University	M,D
Penn State University Park	M,D*
Purdue University	M,D
Rensselaer Polytechnic Institute	M,D
Royal Military College of Canada	M,D
Stevens Institute of Technology	M,D,O
Texas A&M University	M,D
University of California, Berkeley	M,D
University of Cincinnati	M,D
University of Florida	M,D
University of Idaho	M,D
University of Illinois at Urbana–Champaign	M,D
The University of Manchester	M,D
University of Maryland, College Park	M,D
University of Massachusetts Lowell	M,D
University of Michigan	M,D,O*
University of Nevada, Las Vegas	M,D,O
University of New Mexico	M,D
University of South Carolina	M,D
The University of Tennessee	M,D
University of Utah	M,D
University of Wisconsin–Madison	M,D
Virginia Commonwealth University	M,D
Worcester Polytechnic Institute	M,D,O

NURSE ANESTHESIA

Adventist University of Health Sciences	M
Albany Medical College	M
Arkansas State University	M,D,O
Augusta University	D
Barry University	M
Baylor College of Medicine	D
Bloomsburg University of Pennsylvania	M,D
Boston College	M,D
Bryan College of Health Sciences	M
California State University, Fullerton	M,D
Case Western Reserve University	M*
Columbia University	M,O*
DeSales University	M,D,O
Drexel University	M*
Duke University	M,D,O*
Fairfield University	M,D
Florida Gulf Coast University	M
Florida International University	M,D
Franciscan Missionaries of Our Lady University	D
Gannon University	M,O
Georgetown University	M,D
Goldfarb School of Nursing at Barnes-Jewish College	M
Inter American University of Puerto Rico, Arecibo Campus	M
La Roche College	M,D
La Salle University	M,D,O
Lincoln Memorial University	M
Louisiana State University Health Sciences Center	M,D,O
Lourdes University	M
Marian University (IN)	M,D
Marshall University	D
Mayo Clinic School of Health Sciences	D
Medical University of South Carolina	M
Middle Tennessee School of Anesthesia	M,D
Midwestern University, Glendale Campus	M
Millikin University	M,D
Missouri State University	D
Mount Marty College	M
Murray State University	D
National University	M,O
Newman University	M
Oakland University	M,O
Old Dominion University	D
Oregon Health & Science University	M
Otterbein University	M,D,O
Quinnipiac University	D
Rosalind Franklin University of Medicine and Science	D
Rush University	D,O
Rutgers University–Newark	M,D,O
Saint Mary's University of Minnesota	M
Saint Vincent College	M,D
Samford University	M,D
Samuel Merritt University	M,D,O
Southern Illinois University Edwardsville	D
State University of New York Downstate Medical Center	M
Texas Christian University	D
Texas Wesleyan University	M,D
Uniformed Services University of the Health Sciences	M,D*
Union University	M,D,O
University at Buffalo, the State University of New York	M,D,O
The University of Alabama at Birmingham	M,D
University of Cincinnati	M,D
University of Detroit Mercy	M,D,O
The University of Kansas	D
University of Maryland, Baltimore	M,D,O
University of Miami	M,D*
University of Michigan–Flint	D
University of Minnesota, Twin Cities Campus	M,D
University of New England	M,D
The University of North Carolina at Charlotte	M,D,O
The University of North Carolina at Greensboro	M,D,O
University of North Dakota	M,D,O
University of North Florida	M,D,O
University of Pennsylvania	M*
University of Pittsburgh	D*
University of Saint Francis (IN)	M,D,O
The University of Scranton	M,D,O
University of South Carolina	M
University of Southern California	D*
University of South Florida	M,D,O*
The University of Tennessee at Chattanooga	M,D,O
University of Wisconsin–La Crosse	M
Villanova University	M,D,O
Virginia Commonwealth University	M,D
Wake Forest University	M
Wayne State University	M,D,O
Webster University	D
Westminster College (UT)	M
Wolford College	M,D
York College of Pennsylvania	M

NURSE MIDWIFERY

Bastyr University	M,O
Baylor University	M,D
Bethel University (MN)	M,D,O
Case Western Reserve University	M*
Columbia University	M*
DeSales University	M,D,O
Emory University	M
Frontier Nursing University	M,D,O*
Georgetown University	M,D
James Madison University	M,D
Marquette University	M,D,O
Midwives College of Utah	M
National College of Midwifery	M,D
New York University	M,D,O*
Oregon Health & Science University	M
Shenandoah University	M,D,O
State University of New York Downstate Medical Center	M,O
Stony Brook University, State University of New York	M,D,O
Thomas Jefferson University	M
University of Cincinnati	M,D
University of Colorado Denver	M,D
University of Illinois at Chicago	M,O
University of Indianapolis	M,D
The University of Kansas	M,D,O
The University of Manchester	M,D
University of Miami	M,D*
University of Minnesota, Twin Cities Campus	M,D
University of Pennsylvania	M*
University of Pittsburgh	D*
University of Puerto Rico–Medical Sciences Campus	M,O
University of South Africa	M,D
Vanderbilt University	M,D,O*
Wayne State University	M,D
West Virginia Wesleyan College	M,O

NURSING—GENERAL

Abilene Christian University	D
Adelphi University	D
Albany State University	M
Alcorn State University	M
Allen College	M,D
Alvernia University	M,D,O
Alverno College	M,D
American Public University System	M,D
American Sentinel University	M
American University of Beirut	M
Anderson University (SC)	M,D
Andrews University	M,D
Angelo State University	M
Arizona State University at the Tempe campus	M,D,O
Arkansas State University	M,D,O
Arkansas Tech University	M
Ashland University	D
Aspen University	M
Athabasca University	M,O
Auburn University	M*
Auburn University at Montgomery	M
Augsburg University	M,D
Augusta University	D
Austin Peay State University	M
Azusa Pacific University	M,D*
Ball State University	M,D,O
Barry University	M,D,O
Baylor University	M,D
Bellarmine University	M,D
Bellin College	M
Belmont University	M,D
Benedictine University	M
Bethel College	M
Binghamton University, State University of New York	M,D,O
Blessing-Rieman College of Nursing & Health Sciences	M
Bloomsburg University of Pennsylvania	M,D
Boise State University	M,D,O
Boston College	M,D
Bowie State University	M
Bradley University	M,D,O
Brandman University	D
Briar Cliff University	M,D,O
Brigham Young University	M
Brookline College	M
California Baptist University	M,D
California State University, Bakersfield	M
California State University, Chico	M
California State University, Dominguez Hills	M
California State University, Fresno	M,D
California State University, Fullerton	M,D
California State University, Long Beach	M,D,O
California State University, Los Angeles	M,O
California State University, Sacramento	M
California State University, San Bernardino	M
California State University, San Marcos	M
California State University, Stanislaus	M
California University of Pennsylvania	M
Capella University	M,D
Capital University	M
Cardinal Stritch University	M
Carlow University	D
Carson-Newman University	M
Case Western Reserve University	M,D*
The Catholic University of America	M,D,O
Cedar Crest College	M
Central Connecticut State University	M
Central Methodist University	M
Chatham University	M,D
Chicago State University	M
Clarion University of Pennsylvania	M,D
Clarke University	D
Clarkson College	M,O
Clayton State University	M

Clemson University	M,D,O
Cleveland State University	M,D
College of Mount Saint Vincent	M,O
The College of New Jersey	M,O
The College of New Rochelle	M,O
College of Saint Elizabeth	M
College of Saint Mary	M
The College of St. Scholastica	M,O
College of Staten Island of the City University of New York	D
Colorado Mesa University	M,D,O
Colorado State University–Pueblo	M
Columbia College of Nursing	M
Columbia University	M,D,O*
Columbus State University	M
Concordia University Irvine	M*
Concordia University Wisconsin	M,D
Coppin State University	M,O
Cox College	M
Creighton University	M,D,O
Curry College	M
Daemen College	M,D,O
Dalhousie University	M,D
Delaware State University	M
Delta State University	M,D
DePaul University	M,D
DeSales University	M,D,O
Drexel University	M,D*
Duke University	D*
Duquesne University	M,D,O
D'Youville College	M,D,O
East Carolina University	M,D
Eastern Kentucky University	M
Eastern Mennonite University	M,D
Eastern New Mexico University	M
East Tennessee State University	M,D,O
Edgewood College	M,D
Edinboro University of Pennsylvania	M,D
EDP University of Puerto Rico–San Sebastian	M
Elmhurst College	M
Elms College	M,D
Emmanuel College (United States)	M,O
Emory University	M,D
Endicott College	M,O
Excelsior College	M
Fairfield University	M,D
Fairleigh Dickinson University, Florham Campus	M
Fairleigh Dickinson University, Metropolitan Campus	M,D,O
Felician University	M,D,O
Ferris State University	M
Florida Agricultural and Mechanical University	M,D
Florida Atlantic University	M,D,O
Florida International University	M,D
Florida National University	M
Florida Southern College	M,D
Florida State University	D,O
Fort Hays State University	M
Framingham State University	M
Franciscan Missionaries of Our Lady University	M,D
Franciscan University of Steubenville	M
Francis Marion University	M
Fresno Pacific University	M
Frontier Nursing University	M,D,O*
Frostburg State University	M
Gannon University	D
Gardner-Webb University	M,D
George Mason University	M,D,O
Georgetown University	M,D
The George Washington University	M,D,O
Georgia College & State University	M,D,O
Georgia Southern University	D
Georgia Southern University–Armstrong Campus	M,O
Georgia Southwestern State University	M,O
Georgia State University	M,D,O
Goldfarb School of Nursing at Barnes-Jewish College	M
Gonzaga University	M,D
Goshen College	M
Governors State University	M
Graceland University (IA)	M,D,O
The Graduate Center, City University of New York	D
Grambling State University	M,O
Grand Canyon University	M,D,O
Grand Valley State University	M,D
Grantham University	M
Gwynedd Mercy University	M,D
Hampton University	M,D
Hardin-Simmons University	M
Hawai`i Pacific University	M,D
Herzing University Online	M
Hofstra University	M
Holy Family University	M
Holy Names University	M,O
Howard University	M
Hunter College of the City University of New York	M,D,O
Husson University	M,O
Idaho State University	M,D
Illinois State University	M,D,O
Immaculata University	M
Independence University	M
Indiana State University	M,D
Indiana University East	M
Indiana University Kokomo	M
Indiana University of Pennsylvania	D
Indiana University–Purdue University Fort Wayne	M,O
Indiana University–Purdue University Indianapolis	M,D
Indiana University South Bend	M
Indiana Wesleyan University	M
Inter American University of Puerto Rico, Arecibo Campus	M
Inter American University of Puerto Rico, Barranquitas Campus	M
Jacksonville State University	M
Jacksonville University	M,D*
James Madison University	M,D
Jefferson College of Health Sciences	M
Johns Hopkins University	M,D,O*
Kean University	M
Keiser University	M
Kennesaw State University	M,D
Kent State University	M,D
Kentucky State University	M,D
Keuka College	M
King University	M,D
Lamar University	M
Lander University	M
La Roche College	M
La Salle University	M,D,O
Laurentian University	M
Lehman College of the City University of New York	M
Le Moyne College	M,O
Lenoir-Rhyne University	M
Lewis University	M,D
Liberty University	M,D
Lincoln Memorial University	M
Lindenwood University	M
Loma Linda University	D
Long Island University–LIU Brooklyn	M,O
Louisiana State University Health Sciences Center	M,D,O
Loyola University Chicago	M,D,O
Loyola University New Orleans	M,D
Madonna University	M
Malone University	M
Mansfield University of Pennsylvania	M
Marian University (IN)	M,D
Marian University (WI)	M
Marquette University	M,D,O
Marshall University	M,O
Marymount University	M,D,O
Maryville University of Saint Louis	M,D
McGill University	M,D,O
McKendree University	M
McMaster University	M,D
McMurry University	M
McNeese State University	M,O
MCPHS University	M
Medical University of South Carolina	D
Memorial University of Newfoundland	M,D
Mercer University	M,D,O
Mercy College	M
Mercy College of Ohio	M
Metropolitan State University	M,D
MGH Institute of Health Professions	M,D,O
Miami Regional University	M
Michigan State University	M,D
MidAmerica Nazarene University	M
Middle Tennessee State University	M,O
Midwestern State University	M
Millersville University of Pennsylvania	D
Millikin University	M,D
Minnesota State University Mankato	M,D
Minnesota State University Moorhead	M,O
Misericordia University	M,D
Mississippi University for Women	M,D,O
Missouri Southern State University	M,D
Missouri State University	M,D
Missouri Western State University	M,O
Molloy College	M,D,O
Monmouth University	M,D,O*
Montana State University	M,D,O
Moravian College	M
Morgan State University	M,D
Morningside College	M
Mount Carmel College of Nursing	M,D
Mount Marty College	M
Mount Mercy University	M
Mount St. Joseph University	M,D
Mount Saint Mary College	M,O
Mount Saint Mary's University (CA)	M,D,O
Murray State University	D
Nebraska Methodist College	M
Nebraska Wesleyan University	M
Neumann University	M,O
New Mexico State University	M,D,O
New York University	M,D,O*
Nicholls State University	M
North Dakota State University	D*
Northeastern University	M,D,O
Northern Arizona University	M,D,O
Northern Illinois University	M,D
Northern Kentucky University	M,D,O
Northern Michigan University	D
North Park University	M
Northwestern State University of Louisiana	M
Norwich University	M
Nova Southeastern University	M,D*
Oakland University	M,D,O
The Ohio State University	M,D
Ohio University	M,D
Oklahoma Baptist University	M
Oklahoma City University	M,D
Old Dominion University	D
Olivet Nazarene University	M
Oregon Health & Science University	M,D,O
Otterbein University	M,D,O
Pace University	M,D,O
Pacific Lutheran University	M,D
Palm Beach Atlantic University	M,D
Penn State University Park	M,D*
Pensacola Christian College	M,D,O
Pittsburg State University	M,D
Point Loma Nazarene University	M,D,O
Pontifical Catholic University of Puerto Rico	M
Prairie View A&M University	M,D
Purdue University	M,D,O
Purdue University Global	M
Purdue University Northwest	M
Queen's University at Kingston	M,D,O
Queens University of Charlotte	M
Quinnipiac University	D
Radford University	D
Ramapo College of New Jersey	M
Regis College (MA)	M,D,O
Research College of Nursing	M
Resurrection University	M
Rhode Island College	M,D
Rivier University	M,D
Robert Morris University	M,D
Roberts Wesleyan College	M
Rowan University	M
Rush University	D
Rutgers University–Camden	D
Rutgers University–Newark	M,D,O
Sacred Heart University	M,D,O
Sage Graduate School	M,D,O
Saginaw Valley State University	M
Saint Anthony College of Nursing	M
St. Catherine University	M,D
Saint Francis Medical Center College of Nursing	M,D,O
Saint Francis University	M
St. John Fisher College	M,D,O
St. Joseph's College, Long Island Campus	M
St. Joseph's College, New York	M
Saint Joseph's College of Maine	M,O
Saint Louis University	M,D,O*
Saint Mary-of-the-Woods College	M
Saint Mary's College	D
Saint Peter's University	M,D,O
Saint Xavier University	M,O
Salem State University	M
Salisbury University	M,D
Salve Regina University	D
Samford University	M,D
Samuel Merritt University	M,D,O
San Diego State University	M
San Francisco State University	M,O
San Jose State University	M
Seattle Pacific University	M,O
Seattle University	D
Seton Hall University	M,D
Shenandoah University	M,D,O
Simmons College	M,D,O
Sonoma State University	M
South Dakota State University	M,D
Southeastern Louisiana University	M,D
Southeast Missouri State University	M
Southern Adventist University	M,D
Southern Connecticut State University	M,D
Southern Illinois University Edwardsville	M,D,O
Southern Nazarene University	M
Southern New Hampshire University	M,O
Southern University and Agricultural and Mechanical College	M,D,O
South University	M
South University	M
South University	M
South University (SC)	M
South University (GA)	M
South University (AL)	M
South University	M
Spalding University	M,D,O
Spring Arbor University	M
Spring Hill College	M,O
Stanbridge University	M
State University of New York College of Technology at Delhi	M
State University of New York Downstate Medical Center	M,O
State University of New York Upstate Medical University	M,O
Stevenson University	M
Stockton University	M
Stony Brook University, State University of New York	M,D,O
Tarleton State University	M
Temple University	D*
Tennessee State University	M,O
Tennessee Technological University	M,D
Texas A&M International University	M
Texas A&M University	M
Texas A&M University–Corpus Christi	M,D
Texas Christian University	M,D,O
Texas Tech University Health Sciences Center	M,D,O
Texas Tech University Health Sciences Center El Paso	M
Texas Woman's University	M,D
Thomas Edison State University	M,D
Thomas Jefferson University	M,D
Thomas University	M
Towson University	O
Trinity Western University	M
Troy University	M,D
Tusculum College	M
Uniformed Services University of the Health Sciences	M,D*
Union University	M,D,O
Universidad Metropolitana	M,O
Université de Montréal	M,D,O
Université du Québec à Rimouski	M,O
Université du Québec à Trois-Rivières	M,O
Université du Québec en Outaouais	M,O
Université Laval	M,D,O
University at Buffalo, the State University of New York	M,D,O
The University of Akron	M,D
The University of Alabama	M,D
The University of Alabama at Birmingham	M,D
The University of Alabama in Huntsville	M,D,O
University of Alberta	M,D
The University of Arizona	M,D,O
University of Arkansas	M
University of Arkansas for Medical Sciences	D
The University of British Columbia	M,D
University of Calgary	M,D,O
University of California, Irvine	M
University of California, Los Angeles	M,D*
University of California, San Francisco	M,D
University of Central Arkansas	M,O
University of Central Florida	M,D,O
University of Central Missouri	M,D,O
University of Central Oklahoma	M
University of Cincinnati	M,D
University of Colorado Colorado Springs	M,D
University of Colorado Denver	M,D
University of Connecticut	D,O*
University of Delaware	M,O*
University of Detroit Mercy	M,D,O
University of Florida	M,D
University of Hartford	M
University of Hawaii at Hilo	D*
University of Hawaii at Manoa	M,D,O
University of Houston	M
University of Illinois at Chicago	M,D,O
University of Indianapolis	M,D
The University of Iowa	M,D*
The University of Kansas	M,D,O
University of Kentucky	D
University of Lethbridge	M,D
University of Louisiana at Lafayette	M,D
University of Louisville	M,D
University of Maine	M,O
The University of Manchester	M,D
University of Manitoba	M
University of Mary	M,D
University of Mary Hardin-Baylor	M,D,O
University of Maryland, Baltimore	M,D,O
University of Massachusetts Amherst	M,D*
University of Massachusetts Boston	M,D
University of Massachusetts Dartmouth	M,D
University of Massachusetts Lowell	M,D
University of Massachusetts Medical School	M,D,O
University of Memphis	M,O
University of Miami	M,D*
University of Michigan	M,D,O*
University of Michigan–Flint	M,D,O
University of Minnesota, Twin Cities Campus	M,D
University of Mississippi Medical Center	M,D
University of Missouri	M,D,O
University of Missouri–Kansas City	M,D
University of Missouri–St. Louis	D,O
University of Mobile	M,D
University of Mount Olive	M
University of Nebraska Medical Center	D
University of Nevada, Las Vegas	M,D,O
University of Nevada, Reno	M,D
University of New Brunswick Fredericton	M
University of New Hampshire	M,D,O
University of New Mexico	M,D
University of North Alabama	M
The University of North Carolina at Chapel Hill	M,D,O
The University of North Carolina at Charlotte	M,D,O
The University of North Carolina at Greensboro	M,D,O
The University of North Carolina at Pembroke	M
The University of North Carolina Wilmington	M,D,O
University of North Dakota	M,D,O
University of Northern Colorado	M,D
University of North Florida	M,D,O
University of Oklahoma Health Sciences Center	M
University of Ottawa	M,D,O
University of Pennsylvania	M,D,O*
University of Phoenix–Bay Area Campus	M,D
University of Phoenix–Central Valley Campus	M
University of Phoenix–Hawaii Campus	M
University of Phoenix–Houston Campus	M

*M—masters degree; D—doctorate; O—other advanced degree; *—Close-Up and/or Display*

University of Phoenix–Online Campus	M,D,O
University of Phoenix–Phoenix Campus	M,O
University of Phoenix–Sacramento Valley Campus	M
University of Phoenix–San Antonio Campus	M
University of Phoenix–San Diego Campus	M
University of Pittsburgh	D*
University of Portland	M,D
University of Puerto Rico–Medical Sciences Campus	M
University of Regina	M,D
University of Rhode Island	M,D,O*
University of Rochester	M,D*
University of St. Augustine for Health Sciences	M,D
University of St. Francis (IL)	M,D,O
University of Saint Francis (IN)	M,D,O
University of Saint Joseph	M,D
University of Saint Mary	M
University of San Diego	M,D
University of San Francisco	D
University of Saskatchewan	M
The University of Scranton	M,D,O
University of South Alabama	M,D,O
University of South Carolina	M,O
University of Southern Indiana	M,D,O
University of Southern Maine	M,D,O
University of Southern Mississippi	M,D,O
University of South Florida	M,D,O*
The University of Tampa	M
The University of Tennessee	M,D
The University of Tennessee at Chattanooga	M,D,O
The University of Tennessee Health Science Center	M,D,O
The University of Texas at Arlington	M,D
The University of Texas at Austin	M,D
The University of Texas at El Paso	M,D,O
The University of Texas at Tyler	M,D
The University of Texas Health Science Center at Houston	M,D
The University of Texas Health Science Center at San Antonio	M,D,O
The University of Texas Medical Branch	M,D
The University of Texas Rio Grande Valley	M,O
University of the Incarnate Word	M,D
The University of Toledo	M,D,O
University of Toronto	M,D
The University of Tulsa	D
University of Utah	M,D
University of Vermont	M,D,O
University of Victoria	M,D
University of Virginia	M,D
University of Washington	M,D,O
University of Washington, Bothell	M
University of Washington, Tacoma	M
The University of Western Ontario	M,D
University of West Florida	M
University of West Georgia	M,D,O
University of Windsor	M
University of Wisconsin–Eau Claire	M,D
University of Wisconsin–Madison	D
University of Wisconsin–Milwaukee	M,D,O*
University of Wisconsin–Oshkosh	M
University of Wyoming	M
Urbana University–A Branch Campus of Franklin University	M
Ursuline College	M,D
Utah Valley University	M
Valdosta State University	M
Valparaiso University	M,D,O
Vanderbilt University	M,D,O*
Vanguard University of Southern California	M
Villanova University	M,D,O
Virginia Commonwealth University	M,D,O
Viterbo University	D
Wagner College	M,D,O
Walden University	M,D,O
Walsh University	M,D
Washburn University	M,D,O
Washington Adventist University	M
Washington State University	M,D,O
Waynesburg University	M,D
Wayne State University	M,D
Weber State University	M
Webster University	M
Wesley College	M
West Chester University of Pennsylvania	M,D,O
West Coast University	M,D
Western Carolina University	M,D,O
Western Connecticut State University	M,D
Western Kentucky University	M
Western Michigan University	M
Western University of Health Sciences	M,D
Westminster College (UT)	M
West Texas A&M University	M
West Virginia University	M,D,O
West Virginia Wesleyan College	M,O
Wheeling Jesuit University	M
Wichita State University	M,D
Widener University	M,D,O
Wilkes University	M,D
William Carey University	M
William Paterson University of New Jersey	M,D,O
Wilmington University	M,D
Wilson College	M
Winona State University	M,D,O
Winston-Salem State University	M,D
Wright State University	M
Xavier University	M,D,O*
Yale University	M,D,O
York College of Pennsylvania	M
York University	M
Youngstown State University	M

NURSING AND HEALTHCARE ADMINISTRATION

Abilene Christian University	D
Adelphi University	M,O
Allen College	M,D
Alvernia University	M,D,O
American International College	M,D,O
American University of Beirut	M
Anderson University (SC)	M,D
Arizona State University at the Tempe campus	M,D,O
Aspen University	M
Athabasca University	M,O
Augusta University	M,D
Austin Peay State University	M
Azusa Pacific University	M,D*
Barry University	M,D,O
Bellarmine University	M,D
Blessing-Rieman College of Nursing & Health Sciences	M
Bloomsburg University of Pennsylvania	M,D
Bowie State University	M
Bradley University	M,D,O
Brenau University	M
Brookline College	M
California Baptist University	M
California State University, Fullerton	M,D
California State University, San Marcos	M
California University of Pennsylvania	M
Capella University	M
Capital University	M
Carlow University	M
Cedar Crest College	M
Central Methodist University	M
Chatham University	M,D
Clarke University	D
Clarkson College	M,O
Clarkson University	M,O
College of Mount Saint Vincent	M,O
The College of New Rochelle	M,O
Columbus State University	M
Cox College	M
Creighton University	M,D,O
Daemen College	M,D,O
DeSales University	M,D,O
Drexel University	M*
Duke University	M,D,O*
Eastern Mennonite University	M,D
Eastern Michigan University	M,O
East Tennessee State University	M,D,O
Elms College	M,D
Emmanuel College (United States)	M,O
Emory University	M
Endicott College	M,O
Excelsior College	M
Fairfield University	M,D
Felician University	M,D,O
Ferris State University	M
Florida Agricultural and Mechanical University	M,D
Florida Atlantic University	M,D,O
Florida National University	M
Florida Southern College	M
Framingham State University	M
Franklin Pierce University	M,D,O
Frostburg State University	M
Gannon University	M
The George Washington University	M,D,O
Georgia Southwestern State University	M,O
Georgia State University	M,D,O
Goldfarb School of Nursing at Barnes-Jewish College	M
Grand Valley State University	M,D
Grand View University	M,O
Grantham University	M
Hampton University	M,D
Herzing University Online	M
Hofstra University	M,D,O
Holy Family University	M,D
Holy Names University	M,O
Immaculata University	M
Independence University	M
Indiana State University	M,D
Indiana University Kokomo	M
Indiana University of Pennsylvania	M
Indiana University–Purdue University Fort Wayne	M,O
Indiana University–Purdue University Indianapolis	M,D
Indiana Wesleyan University	M
Jacksonville University	M*
James Madison University	M,D
Jefferson College of Health Sciences	M
Johns Hopkins University	M,D*
Kean University	M,D
Kennesaw State University	M
Kent State University	M,D
King University	M,D
Lamar University	M
La Roche College	M
La Salle University	M,D,O
Le Moyne College	M,O
Lenoir-Rhyne University	M
Lewis University	M,D
Liberty University	M,D
Loma Linda University	M
Louisiana State University Health Sciences Center	M,D,O
Lourdes University	M
Loyola University Chicago	M,D,O
Madonna University	M
Marquette University	M,D,O
McKendree University	M
Medical University of South Carolina	M
Mercer University	M,D
Mercy College	M
Metropolitan State University	M,D
Miami Regional University	M
MidAmerica Nazarene University	M
Middle Tennessee State University	M
Milwaukee School of Engineering	M
Missouri Western State University	M,O
Monmouth University	M,D,O*
Montana State University	M,D,O
Moravian College	M
Mount Carmel College of Nursing	M,D
Mount Mary University	M
Mount Mercy University	M
Mount St. Joseph University	M
Mount Saint Mary College	M,O
National American University (TX)	M,D
National University	M,O
Nebraska Methodist College	M
New Mexico State University	M,D,O
New York University	M,O*
Nicholls State University	M
Northeastern State University	M
Northeastern University	M,D,O
North Park University	M
Northwest Nazarene University	M
Norwich University	M
Ohio University	M,D
Oklahoma Wesleyan University	M
Old Dominion University	M,D
Oregon Health & Science University	M
Otterbein University	M,D,O
Pace University	M,D,O
Palm Beach Atlantic University	M,D
Pennsylvania College of Health Sciences	M
Purdue University Global	M
Purdue University Northwest	M
Queens University of Charlotte	M
Quinnipiac University	D
Ramapo College of New Jersey	M
Regis University	M,D,O
Research College of Nursing	M
Rivier University	M,D
Roberts Wesleyan College	M
Rush University	M
Sacred Heart University	M,D,O
Saint Francis Medical Center College of Nursing	M,D,O
Saint Francis University	M
Saint Joseph's College of Maine	M,O
Saint Peter's University	M,D,O
Salem State University	M
Salisbury University	M,D
Samford University	M,D
Samuel Merritt University	M,D,O
San Francisco State University	M,O
Seattle Pacific University	M,O
Seton Hall University	M,D
Shenandoah University	M,D,O
Southern Illinois University Edwardsville	M,O
Southern Nazarene University	M
Southern New Hampshire University	M,O
Southern University and Agricultural and Mechanical College	M,D,O
Spalding University	M,D,O
Spring Hill College	M,O
State University of New York College of Technology at Delhi	M
Stevenson University	M
Stony Brook University, State University of New York	M,D,O
Tarleton State University	M
Teachers College, Columbia University	M,D
Tennessee Technological University	M,D
Texas A&M University	M,D
Texas A&M University–Corpus Christi	M,D
Texas Christian University	M,D,O
Texas Tech University Health Sciences Center	M,D,O
Texas Woman's University	M,D
Thomas Edison State University	M
Union University	M,D,O
Universidad Metropolitana	M,O
University at Buffalo, the State University of New York	M,D,O
The University of Alabama at Birmingham	M,D
University of Central Arkansas	M,O
University of Cincinnati	M,D
University of Colorado Denver	M,D
University of Delaware	M,O*
University of Hawaii at Manoa	M,D,O
University of Houston	M
University of Illinois at Chicago	M,O
University of Indianapolis	M,D
University of Louisiana at Lafayette	M
University of Louisville	M,D
University of Mary	M,D
University of Maryland, Baltimore	M,D,O
University of Massachusetts Amherst	M,D*
University of Massachusetts Medical School	M,D,O
University of Memphis	M,O
University of Minnesota, Twin Cities Campus	M,D
University of Missouri	M,D,O
University of Missouri–Kansas City	M,D
University of Mobile	M,D
The University of North Carolina at Chapel Hill	M,D,O
The University of North Carolina at Charlotte	M,D,O
The University of North Carolina at Greensboro	M,D,O
The University of North Carolina at Pembroke	M
University of Pennsylvania	M,D*
University of Phoenix–Bay Area Campus	M,D
University of Pittsburgh	M,D*
University of Rochester	M,D*
University of St. Augustine for Health Sciences	M
University of St. Francis (IL)	M,D,O
University of Saint Mary	M
University of San Diego	M,D
The University of Scranton	M,D,O
University of South Alabama	M,D,O
University of South Carolina	M
University of Southern Indiana	M,D,O
University of Southern Maine	M,D,O
The University of Texas at Arlington	M,D
The University of Texas at Austin	M,D
The University of Texas at El Paso	M,D,O
The University of Texas at Tyler	M,D
The University of Texas Health Science Center at San Antonio	M,D,O
The University of Texas Rio Grande Valley	M,O
The University of Toledo	M,O
University of Victoria	M,D
University of Virginia	M,D
University of Washington, Tacoma	M
University of Wisconsin–Eau Claire	M,D
University of Wisconsin–Green Bay	M
Vanderbilt University	M,D,O*
Virginia Commonwealth University	M,D,O
Walden University	M,D,O
Walsh University	M,D
Washburn University	M,D,O
Washington Adventist University	M
Waynesburg University	M,D
Weber State University	M
Western Governors University	M
Western University of Health Sciences	M
West Virginia Wesleyan College	M,O
Wilmington University	M,D
Wilson College	M
Winona State University	M,D,O
Wright State University	M

NURSING EDUCATION

Abilene Christian University	D
Adelphi University	M,O
Albany State University	M
Allen College	M,D
Alvernia University	M,D,O
American International College	M,D,O
Anderson University (SC)	M,D
Angelo State University	M
Arizona State University at the Tempe campus	M,D,O
Aspen University	M
Auburn University	M*
Auburn University at Montgomery	M
Austin Peay State University	M
Azusa Pacific University	M,D*
Ball State University	M,D,O
Barry University	M,O
Bellarmine University	M,D
Bellin College	M
Bethel University (MN)	M,D,O
Blessing-Rieman College of Nursing & Health Sciences	M
Bowie State University	M
Bradley University	M,D,O
Brenau University	M
California Baptist University	M
California State University, Fullerton	M,D
California State University, San Marcos	M
California State University, Stanislaus	M
California University of Pennsylvania	M
Capella University	M,D
Carlow University	M
Carson-Newman University	M
Case Western Reserve University	M*
Cedar Crest College	M
Cedarville University	M,D
Central Methodist University	M
Chatham University	M,D
Clarkson College	M,O
Cleveland State University	D
College of Mount Saint Vincent	M,O
The College of New Rochelle	M,O
Colorado Mesa University	M,D,O
Columbus State University	M
Cox College	M
Daemen College	M,D,O
Delta State University	M,D
DeSales University	M,D,O
Drexel University	M*
Duke University	M,D,O*
Duquesne University	M,O
Eastern Michigan University	M,O
East Tennessee State University	M,D,O
Edinboro University of Pennsylvania	M,D
Elms College	M,D
Emmanuel College (United States)	M,O
Endicott College	M,O
Excelsior College	M
Felician University	M,O
Ferris State University	M
Florida Gulf Coast University	M
Florida National University	M
Florida Southern College	M

Framingham State University	M
Francis Marion University	M
Franklin Pierce University	M,D,O
Frostburg State University	M
George Mason University	M,D,O
Georgetown University	M,D
The George Washington University	M,D,O
Georgia Southern University	O
Georgia Southwestern State University	M,O
Graceland University (IA)	M,D,O
Grand Canyon University	M,D,O
Grand Valley State University	M,D
Grand View University	M,O
Grantham University	M
Gwynedd Mercy University	M,D
Hampton University	M,D
Hardin-Simmons University	M
Herzing University Online	M
Holy Family University	M
Howard University	M
Immaculata University	M
Indiana State University	M,D
Indiana University Kokomo	M
Indiana University of Pennsylvania	M
Indiana University–Purdue University Fort Wayne	M,O
Indiana University–Purdue University Indianapolis	M
Indiana Wesleyan University	M
Jacksonville University	M*
Jefferson College of Health Sciences	M
Johns Hopkins University	O*
Kennesaw State University	M
Kent State University	M,D
Keuka College	M
King University	M,D
Lamar University	M
La Roche College	M
La Salle University	M,D,O
Le Moyne College	M,O
Lenoir-Rhyne University	M
Lewis University	M,D
Liberty University	M,D
Loma Linda University	M
Long Island University–LIU Brooklyn	M,O
Long Island University–LIU Post	M,O
Louisiana State University Health Sciences Center	M,D,O
Lourdes University	M
Marian University (IN)	M,D
Marian University (WI)	M
McKendree University	M
McMurry University	M
McNeese State University	M
Medical University of South Carolina	M
Mercy College	M
Messiah College	M
Metropolitan State University	M,D
MGH Institute of Health Professions	M,D,O
Miami Regional University	M
MidAmerica Nazarene University	M
Middle Tennessee State University	M
Midwestern State University	M
Millersville University of Pennsylvania	M,O
Millikin University	M,D
Minnesota State University Mankato	M,D
Missouri State University	M,D
Missouri Western State University	M,O
Molloy College	M,D,O
Monmouth University	M,D,O*
Montana State University	M,D,O
Moravian College	M
Mount Carmel College of Nursing	M,D
Mount Mercy University	M
Mount St. Joseph University	M
Mount Saint Mary College	M,O
National American University (TX)	M,D
Nebraska Methodist College	M
New York University	M,O*
Nicholls State University	M
Northeastern State University	M
Norwich University	M
Nova Southeastern University	M,D*
Ohio University	M,D
Oklahoma Baptist University	M
Oklahoma City University	M,D
Oklahoma Wesleyan University	M
Old Dominion University	M,D
Oregon Health & Science University	M,O
Otterbein University	M,D,O
Pennsylvania College of Health Sciences	M
Pittsburg State University	M,D
Purdue University Global	M
Queens University of Charlotte	M
Ramapo College of New Jersey	M
Regis College (MA)	M,D,O
Regis University	M,D,O
Rivier University	M,D
Roberts Wesleyan College	M
Sacred Heart University	M,D,O
Sage Graduate School	D
St. Catherine University	M,D
Saint Francis Medical Center College of Nursing	M,D,O
Saint Francis University	M
St. Joseph's College, Long Island Campus	M
St. Joseph's College, New York	M
Saint Joseph's College of Maine	M,O
Salem State University	M
Salisbury University	M
Seattle Pacific University	M,O
Seton Hall University	M,D
Shenandoah University	M,D,O
Southern Adventist University	M,D
Southern Connecticut State University	M,D
Southern Illinois University Edwardsville	M,O
Southern Nazarene University	M
Southern New Hampshire University	M,O
Southern University and Agricultural and Mechanical College	M,D,O
South University	M
South University (GA)	M
Spalding University	M,D,O
State University of New York College of Technology at Delhi	M
State University of New York Empire State College	M
State University of New York Polytechnic Institute	M,O
Stevenson University	M
Stony Brook University, State University of New York	M,O
Tarleton State University	M
Teachers College, Columbia University	M,D,O
Tennessee Technological University	M
Texas A&M University	M
Texas A&M University–Corpus Christi	M,D
Texas Christian University	M,O
Texas Tech University Health Sciences Center	M,D,O
Texas Woman's University	M,D
Thomas Edison State University	M
Towson University	O
Union University	M,D,O
The University of Alabama in Huntsville	M,D,O
University of Central Arkansas	M,O
University of Central Florida	M,D,O
University of Detroit Mercy	M,D,O
University of Hartford	M
University of Houston	M
University of Indianapolis	M,D
University of Louisiana at Lafayette	M,D
University of Louisville	M,D
University of Maine	M,O
University of Mary	M,D
University of Mary Hardin-Baylor	M,D,O
University of Maryland, Baltimore	M,D,O
University of Massachusetts Medical School	M,D,O
University of Memphis	M,O
University of Missouri–Kansas City	M,D
University of Mobile	M,D
University of Nevada, Las Vegas	M,D,O
University of New Brunswick Fredericton	M
The University of North Carolina at Chapel Hill	M,D,O
The University of North Carolina at Charlotte	M,D,O
The University of North Carolina at Greensboro	M,D,O
The University of North Carolina at Pembroke	M
The University of North Carolina Wilmington	M,D,O
University of North Dakota	M,D,O
University of Northern Colorado	M,D
University of North Georgia	M
University of Phoenix–Bay Area Campus	M,D
University of Phoenix–Hawaii Campus	M
University of Phoenix–Online Campus	M,O
University of Phoenix–Phoenix Campus	M,O
University of Phoenix–Sacramento Valley Campus	M
University of Phoenix–San Diego Campus	M
University of Portland	M,D
University of Rhode Island	M,D,O*
University of Rochester	M,D*
University of St. Augustine for Health Sciences	M
University of St. Francis (IL)	M,D,O
University of Saint Joseph	M,D
University of Saint Mary	M
University of South Alabama	M,D,O
University of Southern Indiana	M,D,O
University of Southern Maine	M,D,O
University of South Florida	M,D,O*
The University of Tennessee at Chattanooga	M,D,O
The University of Texas at Arlington	M,D
The University of Texas at Austin	M,D
The University of Texas at El Paso	M,D,O
The University of Texas at Tyler	M,D
The University of Texas Health Science Center at San Antonio	M,D,O
The University of Texas Rio Grande Valley	M,O
The University of Toledo	M,D,O
University of Victoria	M,D
University of Washington, Tacoma	M
University of West Georgia	M,D,O
University of Wisconsin–Eau Claire	M,D
Ursuline College	M,D
Valparaiso University	M,D,O
Villanova University	M,D,O
Virginia Commonwealth University	M,D,O
Wagner College	M,D,O
Walden University	M,D,O
Walsh University	M,D
Washington Adventist University	M
Waynesburg University	M,D
Weber State University	M
Webster University	M
West Chester University of Pennsylvania	M,D,O
Western Connecticut State University	D
Western Governors University	M
West Virginia Wesleyan College	M,O
William Paterson University of New Jersey	M,D,O
Wilson College	M
Winona State University	M,D,O
Winston-Salem State University	M,D
Worcester State University	M

NURSING INFORMATICS

Allen College	M,D
Aspen University	M
Austin Peay State University	M
Columbus State University	M
Duke University	M,D,O*
Excelsior College	M
Ferris State University	M
Georgia Southwestern State University	M,O
Georgia State University	M,D,O
Grantham University	M
Holy Names University	M,O
Jacksonville University	M*
Le Moyne College	M,O
Liberty University	M,D
National American University (TX)	M,D
National University	M,O
New York University	M,O*
Nova Southeastern University	M,D*
Roberts Wesleyan College	M
Rutgers University–Newark	M
Samford University	M,D
Seattle Pacific University	M,O
Thomas Edison State University	M
Troy University	M,D
The University of Alabama at Birmingham	M,D
University of Maryland, Baltimore	M,D,O
University of Minnesota, Twin Cities Campus	M,D
The University of North Carolina at Chapel Hill	M,D,O
University of Phoenix–Bay Area Campus	M,D
University of Phoenix–Phoenix Campus	M,O
University of Pittsburgh	M,D*
University of St. Augustine for Health Sciences	M
Vanderbilt University	M,D,O*
Walden University	M,D,O
Waynesburg University	M,D
Western Governors University	M

NUTRITION

Abilene Christian University	M,O
Adelphi University	M,D,O
Alabama Agricultural and Mechanical University	M
American College of Healthcare Sciences	M,O
American University	M,O
American University of Beirut	M,D
Andrews University	M,O
Appalachian State University	M
Arizona State University at the Tempe campus	M,D
Auburn University	M,D,O*
Ball State University	M
Bastyr University	M,D
Baylor University	M,D
Benedictine University	M
Boston University	M,D*
Bradley University	M
Brigham Young University	M
Brooklyn College of the City University of New York	M
California Polytechnic State University, San Luis Obispo	M*
California State University, Chico	M
California State University, Long Beach	M
California State University, Los Angeles	M,O
California University of Pennsylvania	M
Canisius College	M,O
Case Western Reserve University	M,D*
Cedar Crest College	O
Central Michigan University	M,D,O
Central Washington University	M
Chapman University	M*
College of Saint Elizabeth	M,O
Colorado State University	M,D
Columbia University	M,D*
Cornell University	M,D
D'Youville College	M
East Carolina University	M
Eastern Illinois University	M
Eastern Kentucky University	M
Eastern Michigan University	M
East Tennessee State University	M
Emory University	M,D
Florida International University	M,D
Florida State University	M,D
Framingham State University	M
Franciscan Missionaries of Our Lady University	M,D
George Mason University	M,O
Georgia Southern University	O
Georgia State University	M
Grand Valley State University	M
Harvard University	D*
Howard University	M,D
Hunter College of the City University of New York	M
Huntington University of Health Sciences	M,D
Immaculata University	M
Indiana University Bloomington	M,D
Indiana University of Pennsylvania	M
Indiana University–Purdue University Indianapolis	M,D
Instituto Tecnologico de Santo Domingo	M,O
Iowa State University of Science and Technology	M,D
James Madison University	M
Johns Hopkins University	M,D*
Kansas State University	M,D
Kent State University	M
Lehman College of the City University of New York	M
Liberty University	M,D
Life University	M
Lipscomb University	M
Logan University	M,D
Loma Linda University	M,D
London Metropolitan University	M,D
Long Island University–LIU Post	M,O
Louisiana State University and Agricultural & Mechanical College	M,D
Louisiana Tech University	M,D,O
Loyola University Chicago	M,D,O
Marshall University	M,O
Maryland University of Integrative Health	M,D,O
Marywood University	M,O
McGill University	M,D,O
McMaster University	M,D
McNeese State University	M
Meredith College	M,O
Michigan State University	M,D
Mississippi State University	M,D
Missouri State University	M,D,O
Montclair State University	M,O
Mount Mary University	M
Mount Saint Vincent University	M
Murray State University	M,O
National University of Natural Medicine	M
New York Chiropractic College	M*
New York Institute of Technology	M
New York University	M,D*
North Carolina Agricultural and Technical State University	M
North Carolina State University	M,D
North Dakota State University	M,D*
Northeastern University	M
Northern Illinois University	M
Northwestern Health Sciences University	M
Nova Southeastern University	M,D,O*
The Ohio State University	M,D
Ohio University	M
Oklahoma State University	M,D
Oregon Health & Science University	M,O
Oregon State University	M,D
Penn State University Park	M,D*
Purdue University	M,D
Queens College of the City University of New York	M,O
Rosalind Franklin University of Medicine and Science	M
Rush University	M
Rutgers University–Newark	M,D,O
Rutgers University–New Brunswick	M,D
Sacred Heart University	M
Sage Graduate School	M,O
Saint Louis University	M*
Samford University	M
Sam Houston State University	M
San Diego State University	M
San Jose State University	M
Saybrook University	M,D,O
Simmons College	M,D,O
South Carolina State University	M
South Dakota State University	M,D
Southern Illinois University Carbondale	M
State University of New York College at Oneonta	M
Stony Brook University, State University of New York	M,O
Syracuse University	M,D*
Teachers College, Columbia University	M,D,O
Texas A&M University	M,D
Texas State University	M
Texas Tech University	M,D
Texas Woman's University	M,D
Tufts University	M,D,O*
Tuskegee University	M
Université de Moncton	M
Université de Montréal	M,D,O
Université Laval	M,D
University at Buffalo, the State University of New York	M,D,O
The University of Alabama	M
The University of Alabama at Birmingham	M,D
The University of Arizona	M,D
University of Arkansas for Medical Sciences	M,D,O
University of Bridgeport	M
The University of British Columbia	M,D
University of California, Berkeley	M,D
University of California, Davis	M,D
University of Central Arkansas	M

*M—masters degree; D—doctorate; O—other advanced degree; *—Close-Up and/or Display*

University of Central Oklahoma	M
University of Chicago	D
University of Cincinnati	M
University of Connecticut	M,D*
University of Delaware	M*
University of Florida	M,D
University of Georgia	M,D
University of Guelph	M,D
University of Hawaii at Manoa	M,D
University of Houston	M,D
University of Illinois at Chicago	M,D
University of Illinois at Urbana–Champaign	M,D
The University of Kansas	M,D,O
University of Kentucky	M,D
University of Manitoba	M,D
University of Maryland, College Park	M,D
University of Massachusetts Amherst	M,D*
University of Memphis	M,O
University of Miami	M*
University of Michigan	M,D*
University of Minnesota, Twin Cities Campus	M,D
University of Mississippi	M,D
University of Missouri	M,D
University of Nebraska–Lincoln	M,D
University of Nebraska Medical Center	O
University of Nevada, Las Vegas	M,D
University of Nevada, Reno	M
University of New England	M,D,O
University of New Hampshire	M,D
University of New Haven	M,O*
University of New Mexico	M
The University of North Carolina at Chapel Hill	M,D
The University of North Carolina at Greensboro	M,D
University of North Florida	M
University of Oklahoma Health Sciences Center	M
University of Pittsburgh	M*
University of Puerto Rico–Medical Sciences Campus	M,D,O
University of Puerto Rico–Río Piedras	M
University of Rhode Island	M*
University of Saint Joseph	M
University of Southern Mississippi	M
University of South Florida	M,D,O*
The University of Tampa	M
The University of Tennessee	M
The University of Tennessee at Martin	M
The University of Texas at Austin	M,D
The University of Texas Rio Grande Valley	M
The University of Texas Southwestern Medical Center	M
University of the District of Columbia	M
University of the Incarnate Word	M
The University of Toledo	M,O
University of Toronto	M,D
University of Utah	M,D
University of Vermont	M
University of Washington	M,D
University of Wisconsin–Madison	M,D
University of Wisconsin–Milwaukee	M,D*
University of Wisconsin–Stevens Point	M
University of Wisconsin–Stout	M
University of Wyoming	M
Utah State University	M,D
Virginia Polytechnic Institute and State University	M,D
Washington State University	M
Wayne State University	M,D,O
West Chester University of Pennsylvania	M
West Virginia University	M,D
Winthrop University	M,O

OCCUPATIONAL HEALTH NURSING

Rutgers University–Newark	M,D,O
University of Cincinnati	M,D
University of Illinois at Chicago	M,O
University of Minnesota, Twin Cities Campus	M,D
The University of North Carolina at Chapel Hill	M
University of South Florida	M,D,O*
University of the Sacred Heart	M

OCCUPATIONAL THERAPY

Abilene Christian University	M
Adventist University of Health Sciences	M
Alabama State University	M
Allen College	M,D
Alvernia University	M
American International College	M,D,O
Arkansas State University	D
A.T. Still University	M,D,O
Augusta University	M
Barry University	M
Bay Path University	M,D
Belmont University	M,D
Boston University	D*
Brenau University	M
Cabarrus College of Health Sciences	M
California State University, Dominguez Hills	M
Carroll University	M
Chatham University	M,D
Chicago State University	M
Clarkson University	M
Cleveland State University	M
College of Saint Mary	M
The College of St. Scholastica	M
Colorado State University	M,D
Columbia University	M,D*
Concordia University Wisconsin	M
Creighton University	D
Dalhousie University	M
Dominican College	M
Dominican University of California	M
Drake University	M,D
Duquesne University	M,D
D'Youville College	M
East Carolina University	M,D,O
Eastern Kentucky University	M
Eastern Michigan University	M
Eastern Washington University	M
Elizabethtown College	M
Elmhurst College	M
Emory & Henry College	M,D
Florida Agricultural and Mechanical University	M
Florida Gulf Coast University	M
Florida International University	M
Gannon University	M,D
Governors State University	M
Grand Valley State University	M
Hofstra University	M,O
Howard University	M,D
Huntington University	M,D
Idaho State University	M
Indiana State University	M,D
Indiana University–Purdue University Indianapolis	M,D
Ithaca College	M
Jacksonville University	D*
James Madison University	M
Jefferson College of Health Sciences	M
Johnson & Wales University	D
Kean University	M
Keiser University	M
Keuka College	M
Le Moyne College	M
Lenoir-Rhyne University	M
Loma Linda University	M,D
Long Island University–LIU Brooklyn	M,D,O
Louisiana State University Health Sciences Center	M
Mary Baldwin University	D
Maryville University of Saint Louis	M
McMaster University	M
Medical University of South Carolina	M
Mercy College	M
MGH Institute of Health Professions	D
Midwestern University, Downers Grove Campus	M
Midwestern University, Glendale Campus	M
Milligan College	M
Misericordia University	M,D
Missouri State University	M
Mount Mary University	M,D
New England Institute of Technology	M
New York Institute of Technology	M
New York University	M,D*
Northeastern State University	M
Northern Arizona University	D
Nova Southeastern University	M,D*
The Ohio State University	M
Pacific University	D
Queen's University at Kingston	M,D
Radford University	M
Regis College (MA)	M,D,O
Regis University	M,D,O
Rochester Institute of Technology	M
Rockhurst University	M
Rocky Mountain University of Health Professions	D
Rush University	D
Sacred Heart University	M
Sage Graduate School	M
Saginaw Valley State University	M
St. Ambrose University	D
St. Catherine University	M,D
Saint Francis University	M
Saint Louis University	M*
Salem State University	M
Salus University	M,O
Samuel Merritt University	D
San Jose State University	M
Seton Hall University	M
Shawnee State University	M
Sonoma State University	M
South University	D
Spalding University	M
Springfield College	M
Stanbridge University	M
State University of New York Downstate Medical Center	M
Stockton University	M
Stony Brook University, State University of New York	M,D,O
Temple University	M,D*
Tennessee State University	M
Texas Tech University Health Sciences Center	M
Texas Woman's University	M,D
Thomas Jefferson University	M,D
Touro College	M,D
Towson University	M
Tufts University	M,D,O*
Tuskegee University	M
Université de Montréal	O
University at Buffalo, the State University of New York	M
The University of Alabama at Birmingham	M,O
University of Alberta	M,D
The University of British Columbia	M
University of Central Arkansas	M
The University of Findlay	M,D
University of Florida	M
University of Illinois at Chicago	M,D
University of Indianapolis	M,D
The University of Kansas	M,D
University of Louisiana at Monroe	M
University of Manitoba	M,D
University of Mary	M
University of Minnesota Rochester	M,D
University of Mississippi Medical Center	M
University of Missouri	M
University of New England	M,D
University of New Hampshire	M,O
University of New Mexico	M
The University of North Carolina at Chapel Hill	M,D
University of North Dakota	M
University of Oklahoma Health Sciences Center	M
University of Pittsburgh	M,D*
University of Puerto Rico–Medical Sciences Campus	M
University of Puget Sound	M,D
University of St. Augustine for Health Sciences	M,D
The University of Scranton	M
University of South Alabama	M
University of South Dakota	M,D
University of Southern California	M,D*
University of Southern Indiana	M
University of Southern Maine	M
The University of Tennessee at Chattanooga	D
The University of Tennessee Health Science Center	M,D
The University of Texas at El Paso	M
The University of Texas Health Science Center at San Antonio	M,D
The University of Texas Medical Branch	M
The University of Texas Rio Grande Valley	M
University of the Sciences	M,D
The University of Toledo	M,D
University of Toronto	M
University of Utah	M,D
University of Washington	M,D
The University of Western Ontario	M
University of Wisconsin–La Crosse	M
University of Wisconsin–Madison	M,D
University of Wisconsin–Milwaukee	M*
Utica College	M
Virginia Commonwealth University	M,D
Washington University in St. Louis	M,D
Wayne State University	M
West Coast University	M,D
Western Michigan University	M
Western New England University	D
Western New Mexico University	M
West Virginia University	M,D
Winston-Salem State University	M
Worcester State University	M
Xavier University	M*

OCEAN ENGINEERING

Florida Atlantic University	M,D
Florida Institute of Technology	M,D
Massachusetts Institute of Technology	M,D,O
Memorial University of Newfoundland	M,D
Oregon State University	M,D
Princeton University	D
Stevens Institute of Technology	M,D
University of California, San Diego	M,D*
University of Delaware	M,D*
University of Florida	M,D
University of Hawaii at Manoa	M,D
University of Michigan	M,D,O*
University of New Hampshire	M,D,O
University of Rhode Island	M,D*
Virginia Polytechnic Institute and State University	M,O
Woods Hole Oceanographic Institution	D

OCEANOGRAPHY

Cornell University	D
Dalhousie University	M,D
Florida Institute of Technology	M,D
Florida State University	M,D
Louisiana State University and Agricultural & Mechanical College	M,D
Massachusetts Institute of Technology	M,D,O
McGill University	M,D
Memorial University of Newfoundland	M,D
Naval Postgraduate School	M,D
North Carolina State University	M,D
Nova Southeastern University	M,D*
Old Dominion University	M,D
Oregon State University	M,D
Princeton University	D
Rutgers University–New Brunswick	M,D
Texas A&M University	M,D
Université du Québec à Rimouski	M,D
Université Laval	D
University of Alaska Fairbanks	M,D
The University of British Columbia	M,D
University of California, Los Angeles	M,D*
University of California, San Diego	M,D*
University of Colorado Boulder	M,D
University of Delaware	M,D*
University of Hawaii at Manoa	M,D
University of Maryland, College Park	M,D
University of Miami	M,D*
University of New Hampshire	M,D,O
University of Rhode Island	M,D*
University of San Diego	M
University of Southern California	M,D*
University of South Florida	M,D*
The University of Texas Rio Grande Valley	M
University of Victoria	M,D
University of Washington	M,D
University of Wisconsin–Madison	M,D
Woods Hole Oceanographic Institution	D
Yale University	D

ONCOLOGY NURSING

Gwynedd Mercy University	M,D
Universidad Metropolitana	M,O
University of Delaware	M,O*
University of South Florida	M,D,O*

OPERATIONS RESEARCH

Air Force Institute of Technology	M,D
Bowling Green State University	M
Capella University	M
Carnegie Mellon University	D
Case Western Reserve University	M,D*
Claremont Graduate University	M,D
The College of William and Mary	M*
Colorado School of Mines	M,D
Columbia University	M,D*
Cornell University	M,D
École Polytechnique de Montréal	M,D,O
Florida Institute of Technology	M,D
George Mason University	M,D,O
Georgia Institute of Technology	M,D
Georgia State University	M,D
HEC Montreal	O
Idaho State University	M
Indiana University–Purdue University Fort Wayne	M,O
Iowa State University of Science and Technology	M,D
Johns Hopkins University	M,D*
Kansas State University	M,D
Massachusetts Institute of Technology	M,D
Mississippi State University	M,D
Naval Postgraduate School	M,D
New Mexico Institute of Mining and Technology	M,D
North Carolina State University	M,D
Northeastern University	M,D,O
The Ohio State University	M
Princeton University	M,D
Rutgers University–New Brunswick	D
Simon Fraser University	M,D
Southern Illinois University Edwardsville	M
Southern Methodist University	M,D
The University of Alabama in Huntsville	M,D
University of Arkansas	M,D
University of California, Berkeley	M,D
University of Colorado Denver	M,D
University of Delaware	M*
University of Illinois at Chicago	M,D
The University of Iowa	M,D*
University of Massachusetts Amherst	M,D*
University of Michigan	M,D*
The University of North Carolina at Chapel Hill	M,D
University of Southern California	M,D,O*
The University of Texas at Austin	M,D
University of Waterloo	M,D

OPTICAL SCIENCES

Air Force Institute of Technology	M,D
Alabama Agricultural and Mechanical University	M,D
The College of William and Mary	M,D*
Delaware State University	M,D
Duke University	M*
École Polytechnique de Montréal	M,D,O
Norfolk State University	M
North Carolina Agricultural and Technical State University	M,D
The Ohio State University	M,D
Rochester Institute of Technology	M,D
Rose-Hulman Institute of Technology	M
The University of Alabama in Huntsville	M,D
The University of Arizona	M,D,O
University of Central Florida	M,D
University of Dayton	M,D
University of New Mexico	M,D
The University of North Carolina at Charlotte	M,D
University of Rochester	M,D*

OPTOMETRY

Ferris State University	D
Illinois College of Optometry	D
Indiana University Bloomington	M,D
Inter American University of Puerto Rico School of Optometry	D
Marshall B. Ketchum University	M,D
MCPHS University	D
Midwestern University, Downers Grove Campus	D
Midwestern University, Glendale Campus	D
New England College of Optometry	M,D
Northeastern State University	D
Nova Southeastern University	M,D*
The Ohio State University	M,D

Pacific University	M,D
Salus University	D
Southern College of Optometry	D
State University of New York College of Optometry	D
Université de Montréal	D
The University of Alabama at Birmingham	D
University of California, Berkeley	D,O
University of Houston	D
The University of Manchester	M,D
University of Missouri–St. Louis	D
University of Pikeville	D
University of the Incarnate Word	D
University of Waterloo	M,D
Western University of Health Sciences	D

ORAL AND DENTAL SCIENCES

American University of Beirut	M,D
A.T. Still University	M,D,O
Augusta University	M,D
Boston University	M,D*
Case Western Reserve University	M,O*
Columbia University	M,D,O*
Dalhousie University	
Harvard University	M,D,O*
Howard University	D,O
Idaho State University	O
Jacksonville University	M,O*
Loma Linda University	M,O
Marquette University	M,O
McGill University	M,D,O
Metropolitan State University	M,D
New York University	M,D,O*
The Ohio State University	M,D
Oregon Health & Science University	M,D,O
Rutgers University–Newark	M,D,O
Saint Louis University	M*
Seton Hill University	M,O
Stony Brook University, State University of New York	M,D,O
Temple University	M,O*
Texas A&M University	M,D,O
Tufts University	M,O*
Université de Montréal	M,O
Université Laval	M,O
University at Buffalo, the State University of New York	M,D,O
The University of Alabama at Birmingham	M
University of Alberta	M,D
The University of British Columbia	M,D
University of California, Los Angeles	M,D*
University of California, San Francisco	M,D
University of Colorado Denver	D,O
University of Connecticut Health Center	M
University of Detroit Mercy	M,D,O
University of Florida	M,D,O
University of Illinois at Chicago	M,D
The University of Iowa	M,D,O*
University of Kentucky	M
University of Louisville	M,D
The University of Manchester	M,D
University of Manitoba	M,D
University of Maryland, Baltimore	M,D,O
University of Michigan	M,D*
University of Minnesota, Twin Cities Campus	M,D,O
University of Mississippi Medical Center	M,D
University of Missouri–Kansas City	M,D,O
University of Nebraska Medical Center	M,D
University of Nevada, Las Vegas	M,D,O
The University of North Carolina at Chapel Hill	M,D
University of Oklahoma Health Sciences Center	M
University of Pittsburgh	M,D,O*
University of Puerto Rico–Medical Sciences Campus	O
University of Rochester	M*
University of Southern California	M,D,O*
The University of Tennessee Health Science Center	M,D
The University of Toledo	M
University of Toronto	M,D
University of Washington	M,D,O
The University of Western Ontario	M
West Virginia University	M,D

ORGANIC CHEMISTRY

Auburn University	M,D*
Boston College	M,D
Brandeis University	M,D
Cleveland State University	M,D
Cornell University	D
Eastern New Mexico University	M
Florida State University	M,D
Georgetown University	D
The George Washington University	M,D
Georgia State University	M,D
Harvard University	D*
Howard University	M,D
Indiana University Bloomington	M,D
Instituto Tecnológico y de Estudios Superiores de Monterrey, Campus Monterrey	M,D
Iowa State University of Science and Technology	M,D
Laurentian University	M
Marquette University	M,D
Massachusetts Institute of Technology	M,D,O
McMaster University	M,D
Old Dominion University	M,D
Purdue University	M,D
Rice University	M,D
Rutgers University–Newark	M,D
Rutgers University–New Brunswick	M,D
Seton Hall University	M,D
Southern University and Agricultural and Mechanical College	M
State University of New York College of Environmental Science and Forestry	M,D
University of Calgary	M,D
University of Cincinnati	M,D
University of Louisville	M,D
The University of Manchester	M,D
University of Maryland, College Park	M,D
University of Massachusetts Lowell	M,D
University of Memphis	M,D
University of Miami	M,D*
University of Michigan	M,D*
University of Missouri–Kansas City	M,D
University of Montana	M,D
University of Nebraska–Lincoln	M,D
University of Notre Dame	M,D
University of Oklahoma	M,D*
University of Regina	M,D
University of Rochester	D*
The University of Tennessee	M,D
The University of Texas at Austin	D
The University of Toledo	M,D
Vanderbilt University	M,D*
Virginia Commonwealth University	M,D
Wake Forest University	M,D
Wesleyan University	D
Yale University	D
Youngstown State University	M

ORGANIZATIONAL BEHAVIOR

Argosy University, Chicago	D
Arizona State University at the Tempe campus	M,D
A.T. Still University	M,D,O
Baruch College of the City University of New York	M,D*
Benedictine University	M,D
Boston College	D
Brooklyn College of the City University of New York	M,D
California State University, East Bay	M
Carnegie Mellon University	D
Case Western Reserve University	M,D*
Clemson University	M,D
Cornell University	M,D
Drexel University	M,D,O*
Fairleigh Dickinson University, Florham Campus	M,O
Florida Institute of Technology	M
Florida State University	M,D
The Graduate Center, City University of New York	D
Hampton University	M
Harvard University	D*
International Institute for Restorative Practices	M,O
John Jay College of Criminal Justice of the City University of New York	M,D
Lake Forest Graduate School of Management	M
New York University	M,D*
Northwestern University	M
Phillips Graduate University	D
Purdue University	D
Saybrook University	M,D
Suffolk University	M
Universidad de las Americas, A.C.	M
Université de Sherbrooke	M
University at Albany, State University of New York	M,D,O
The University of British Columbia	D
University of California, Berkeley	D
University of California, Davis	M
University of Chicago	M,O
University of Hartford	M
University of Hawaii at Manoa	M
The University of Kansas	M,D
University of New Mexico	M
The University of North Carolina at Chapel Hill	D
University of North Texas at Dallas	M
University of Oklahoma	M,O*
University of Pittsburgh	M,D*
The University of Texas at Austin	M
University of Utah	M,D
Wayne State University	M,D
Wilfrid Laurier University	M,D

ORGANIZATIONAL MANAGEMENT

Albertus Magnus College	M
Alvernia University	D
The American College of Financial Services	M
American University	M,D,O
Anderson University (SC)	M
Antioch University Los Angeles	M
Apollos University	M,D
Aquinas College (MI)	M
Argosy University, Chicago	D
Argosy University, Hawai`i	D
Argosy University, Los Angeles	M,D
Argosy University, Northern Virginia	M,D,O
Argosy University, Orange County	D
Argosy University, Seattle	M,D
Argosy University, Tampa	M,D
Argosy University, Twin Cities	M,D
Athabasca University	M,O
Atlantic University	M,O
Auburn University at Montgomery	M
Augsburg University	M
Austin Peay State University	M
Avila University	M
Azusa Pacific University	M*
Baker University	M
Bellevue University	M
Benedictine University	M,D
Bethel University (MN)	M,D,O
Binghamton University, State University of New York	D
Boise State University	M,O
Boston College	D
Boston University	M*
Bowling Green State University	M
Brandman University	M
Brenau University	M
Briercrest Seminary	M
Cabrini University	M,D
Cairn University	M,O
California Baptist University	M
California Coast University	M,D
California College of the Arts	M
California Intercontinental University	M,D
California State University, Fullerton	M
Calvary University	M
Capella University	M,D
Carlos Albizu University, Miami Campus	M,D
Carlow University	M,D,O
Carson-Newman University	M
Central Penn College	M
Charleston Southern University	M
Charter Oak State College	M
The Chicago School of Professional Psychology	M,D
City University of Seattle	M,O
Clarks Summit University	M,D
College of Saint Elizabeth	M
College of Saint Mary	M
The College of Saint Rose	O
Colorado State University–Global Campus	M
Columbia College (SC)	M
Columbia Southern University	M
Columbus State University	M,O
Concordia College–New York	M
Concordia University (Canada)	M,O
Concordia University Ann Arbor	M
Concordia University, St. Paul	M
Concordia University Wisconsin	M
Crandall University	M
Creighton University	M
Dallas Baptist University	M,D
Drury University	M
Duke University	M,D,O*
Duquesne University	M
Eastern Connecticut State University	M
Eastern Mennonite University	M
Eastern Michigan University	M,O
Eastern University	M,D,O
Embry-Riddle Aeronautical University–Worldwide	M
Emory & Henry College	M,D
Emory University	M,D
Endicott College	M
Evangel University	M
Excelsior College	M
Fairleigh Dickinson University, Florham Campus	M,O
Fielding Graduate University	O
Florida Institute of Technology	M
Gannon University	D
Gardner-Webb University	M,D,O
Geneva College	M
George Fox University	M,D
George Mason University	M
The George Washington University	M,O
Georgia State University	M,D
Gonzaga University	M,D
Graceland University (IA)	M,D,O
Grand Canyon University	M,D
Grand View University	M,O
Granite State College	M
Harding University	M
Hawai`i Pacific University	M
HEC Montreal	M
Hood College	M,D,O*
Huntington University	M,D
Husson University	M
Immaculata University	M
Indiana Tech	M
Indiana University Bloomington	M,D,O
Indiana University–Purdue University Fort Wayne	M,O
Indiana University–Purdue University Indianapolis	M,O
Indiana Wesleyan University	M,D,O
Instituto Tecnologico de Santo Domingo	M,O
Jacksonville University	M*
James Madison University	D
John F. Kennedy University	M,O
Johns Hopkins University	M*
Johnson & Wales University	M
Judson University	M
Keiser University	M
LaGrange College	M
Lenoir-Rhyne University	M
Lewis University	M
Lincoln Christian University	M
Lipscomb University	M,O
Lourdes University	M
Loyola University New Orleans	M
Malone University	M
Manhattan College	M
Manhattanville College	M,O
Mansfield University of Pennsylvania	M
Maranatha Baptist University	M
Marian University (WI)	M
Marlboro College	M
Medaille College	M
Mercer University	M,D
Mercy College	M
Mercyhurst University	M,O
Messiah College	M,O
Mid-America Christian University	M
Midway University	M
Misericordia University	M
Mount St. Joseph University	M
National University	M,O
Neumann University	M
New Jersey City University	M
Newman University	M
The New School	M,O
New York University	M,D*
Nichols College	M
Northern Arizona University	M
Northern Kentucky University	M
Northwestern University	M,D
Northwest University	M
Norwich University	M
Nyack College	M
Oakland City University	M,D
Oakland University	M,D,O
Ohio Christian University	M
Oklahoma Christian University	M
Olivet Nazarene University	M
Our Lady of the Lake University	M,D
Oxford Graduate School	M,D
Palm Beach Atlantic University	M
Peirce College	M
Penn State University Park	M,D*
Pepperdine University	M,D
Peru State College	M
Pfeiffer University	M
Point Loma Nazarene University	M
Point Park University	M
Purdue University Global	M
Queens University of Charlotte	M
Quinnipiac University	M
Regent University	M,D,O
Regis University	M,O
Rider University	M
Robert Morris University	M,D
Rochester Institute of Technology	O
Roosevelt University	M
Rutgers University–Newark	D
Sage Graduate School	M
St. Ambrose University	M
St. Catherine University	M
St. Edward's University	M
St. Joseph's College, Long Island Campus	M
St. Joseph's College, New York	M
Saint Mary-of-the-Woods College	M
Saint Mary's College of California	M
Saint Mary's University of Minnesota	M
Salve Regina University	M,O
San Diego Christian College	M
Saybrook University	M,D
Seattle University	M,O
Shippensburg University of Pennsylvania	M
Siena Heights University	M,O
Simpson University	M
SIT Graduate Institute	M
Southeastern University (FL)	M,D
Southern Arkansas University–Magnolia	M
Southern New Hampshire University	M,D,O
South University	M
South University (SC)	M
South University (GA)	M
Southwest University	M
Springfield College	M
Stockton University	D
Syracuse University	O*
Thomas Edison State University	M
Trevecca Nazarene University	M,D
Trine University	M
Trinity Washington University	M
Trinity Western University	M,O
Tufts University	M*
Union Institute & University	M
United States International University–Africa	M
Université Laval	M,O
University of Alberta	D
The University of Arizona	M,D
University of Central Arkansas	D
University of Charleston	D
University of Cincinnati	M
University of Colorado Boulder	
University of Dallas	M,D
University of Denver	M,O
University of Guelph	M
University of Hawaii at Manoa	M,D
The University of Kansas	M,D,O
University of La Verne	M,D,O
University of Maryland Eastern Shore	D
University of Massachusetts Amherst	M,D*
University of Michigan–Flint	M,O
University of Missouri	M,D,O
University of Nebraska at Omaha	M
University of New Haven	M,O*
University of New Mexico	M
University of Northwestern–St. Paul	M
University of Oklahoma	M,O*

*M—masters degree; D—doctorate; O—other advanced degree; *—Close-Up and/or Display*

University of Pennsylvania	M,O*
University of Phoenix–Bay Area Campus	M,D
University of Phoenix–Online Campus	D,O
University of Portland	M,D
University of Regina	M,O
University of Saint Francis (IN)	M
University of St. Thomas (MN)	D
University of San Francisco	M
University of South Dakota	M
University of Southern California	M*
The University of Texas at San Antonio	D
The University of Texas at Tyler	M
University of the Incarnate Word	M,D
University of Wisconsin–Platteville	M
Upper Iowa University	M
Vanderbilt University	M,D*
Viterbo University	M,O
Walden University	M,D,O
Waldorf University	M
Warner Pacific University	M
Washington University in St. Louis	M
Wayland Baptist University	M,D
Waynesburg University	M,D
Wayne State College	M
Wayne State University	M,D
Western New England University	M
West Liberty University	M
Wheeling Jesuit University	M
Wilfrid Laurier University	M,D
Wilkes University	M
William Penn University	M
Williamson College	M
Wilmington University	M,D
Winona State University	M,D,O
Woodbury University	M
Worcester Polytechnic Institute	M,D,O
Worcester State University	M
Yale University	D

OSTEOPATHIC MEDICINE

Alabama College of Osteopathic Medicine	D
A.T. Still University	M,D
Campbell University	D
Des Moines University	D
Edward Via College of Osteopathic Medicine–Carolinas Campus	D
Edward Via College of Osteopathic Medicine–Virginia Campus	D
Georgia Campus–Philadelphia College of Osteopathic Medicine	D*
Kansas City University of Medicine and Biosciences	D
Lake Erie College of Osteopathic Medicine	M,D,O
Liberty University	D
Lincoln Memorial University	D
Marian University (IN)	M,D
Michigan State University	D
Midwestern University, Downers Grove Campus	D
Midwestern University, Glendale Campus	D
New York Institute of Technology	O
Nova Southeastern University	M,D,O*
Ohio University	D
Oklahoma State University Center for Health Sciences	D
Pacific Northwest University of Health Sciences	D
Philadelphia College of Osteopathic Medicine	D*
Rocky Vista University	D
Rowan University	D
Touro University California	M,D
University of New England	D
University of North Texas Health Science Center at Fort Worth	D
University of Pikeville	D
University of the Incarnate Word	M,D
Western University of Health Sciences	D
West Virginia School of Osteopathic Medicine	D
William Carey University	D

PACIFIC AREA/PACIFIC RIM STUDIES

The University of British Columbia	M
University of Guam	M
University of Hawaii at Manoa	M,O
University of San Francisco	M
University of Victoria	M

PALEONTOLOGY

Cornell University	M,D
Duke University	D*
East Tennessee State University	M,O
South Dakota School of Mines and Technology	M,D
University of Chicago	D
The University of Manchester	M,D
Yale University	D

PAPER AND PULP ENGINEERING

Georgia Institute of Technology	M,D
North Carolina State University	M,D
State University of New York College of Environmental Science and Forestry	M,D,O
The University of Manchester	M,D
University of Minnesota, Twin Cities Campus	M,D
Western Michigan University	M,D

PARASITOLOGY

Illinois State University	M,D
Louisiana State University Health Sciences Center	D
McGill University	M,D,O
Oregon State University	M,D
Tulane University	M,D,O
University of Notre Dame	M,D
University of Prince Edward Island	M,D

PASTORAL MINISTRY AND COUNSELING

Abilene Christian University	M,D
Acadia University	M,D
Ambrose University	M,O
American Baptist Seminary of the West	M
Amridge University	M,D
Anabaptist Mennonite Biblical Seminary	M,O
Anderson University (SC)	M,D
Andrews University	M,D,O
Appalachian Bible College	M
Aquinas Institute of Theology	M,D,O
Asbury Theological Seminary	M,D,O
Ashland Theological Seminary	M,D
Assemblies of God Theological Seminary	M,D
Atlantic School of Theology	M,O
Atlantic University	O
Austin Presbyterian Theological Seminary	M,D
Ave Maria University	M,D
Azusa Pacific University	M*
Bakke Graduate University	M,D
Baptist Bible College	M
The Baptist College of Florida	M
Baptist Theological Seminary at Richmond	M,D,O
Barry University	M,D
Bethany Global University	M
Bethany Theological Seminary	M,O
Bethel College	M
Bethel Seminary	M,D,O
Biblical Theological Seminary	M,D,O
Biola University	M,D,O
Bob Jones University	M,D,O
Boston College	M,D,O
Boston University	M,D*
Briercrest Seminary	M
Brite Divinity School	M,D,O
Bryan College	M
Cairn University	M
California Baptist University	M
Calvary University	M
Calvin Theological Seminary	M,D
Campbell University	M,D
Canadian Southern Baptist Seminary	M
Cardinal Stritch University	M
Carolina Christian College	M
Catholic Theological Union	M,D,O
The Catholic University of America	M,D,O
Cedarville University	M,D
Chaminade University of Honolulu	M
Charlotte Christian College and Theological Seminary	M,D
Chicago Theological Seminary	M,D
Christian Theological Seminary	M,D
Christ the King Seminary	M
Cincinnati Christian University	M
City Vision University	M
Claremont Lincoln University	M
Claremont School of Theology	M,D
Clarks Summit University	M,D
College of Saint Elizabeth	M,O
Columbia International University	M,D,O
Concordia University, Nebraska	M
Corban University	M,D,O
Covenant Theological Seminary	M,D,O
Criswell College	M
Dallas Baptist University	M,D
Dallas Theological Seminary	M,D,O
Denver Seminary	M,D,O
Earlham School of Religion	M
Eastern Mennonite University	M,O
Ecumenical Theological Seminary	D
Emory University	M,D
Evangelical Seminary	M
Fairfield University	M,O
Faith Baptist Bible College and Theological Seminary	M
Faulkner University	M,D
Fordham University	M,D,O
Freed-Hardeman University	M
Fresno Pacific University	M
Fuller Theological Seminary	M,D,O
Gannon University	M,O
Gardner-Webb University	M,D
Garrett-Evangelical Theological Seminary	M,D
Gateway Seminary	M,D,O
General Theological Seminary	M,D,O
Geneva College	M
George Fox University	M,D,O
Global University	M,D
Gordon-Conwell Theological Seminary	M,D
Grace Theological Seminary	M,D,O
Grand Canyon University	D
Grand Rapids Theological Seminary of Cornerstone University	M
Greenville University	M
Hampton University	M,D,O
Harding School of Theology	M,D
Harding University	M
Hardin-Simmons University	M,D
Hartford Seminary	M,D,O
Heritage Christian University	M
Holmes Institute	M
Holy Names University	M
Houston Baptist University	M
Houston Graduate School of Theology	M,D
Howard Payne University	M
Huntington University	M,D
Huntsville Bible College	M
Iliff School of Theology	M,D
Indiana Wesleyan University	M
Inter American University of Puerto Rico, Metropolitan Campus	D
Interdenominational Theological Center	M,D
International Baptist College and Seminary	M,D
Johnson University	M,D,O
Johnson University Florida	M
Judson University	M
The King's University	M,D,O
Kingswood University	M
Knox Theological Seminary	D
Lancaster Bible College	M,D,O
La Sierra University	M
Lee University	M
Liberty University	M,D,O
Lincoln Christian Seminary	M,D
Lincoln Christian University	M
Lipscomb University	M,D
Loras College	M
Louisiana College	M
Loyola Marymount University	M
Loyola University Chicago	M,O
Lutheran School of Theology at Chicago	M,D
Lutheran Theological Seminary Saskatoon	M,D
Luther Rice College & Seminary	M,D
Luther Seminary	M,D
Madonna University	M
Maple Springs Baptist Bible College and Seminary	M,D,O
Maranatha Baptist University	M,D
Martin University	M
Marymount University	M
The Master's University	M,D
McCormick Theological Seminary	M,D,O
McMaster University	M,D,O
Meadville Lombard Theological School	M,D
Mercer University	M,D
Mesivta Torah Vodaath Rabbinical Seminary	O
Mid-America Baptist Theological Seminary	M,D
Mid-America Christian University	M
Midwestern Baptist Theological Seminary	M,D,O
Milligan College	M,D,O
Missouri Baptist University	M,O
Moody Bible Institute	M,O
Mount Marty College	M
Mount St. Joseph University	M,O
Nashotah House Theological Seminary	M,D,O
Neumann University	M,D,O
New Brunswick Theological Seminary	M,D
New Orleans Baptist Theological Seminary	M,D
Northern Seminary	M,D
North Greenville University	M,D
North Park Theological Seminary	M,O
Northwest Nazarene University	M
Northwest University	M
Nyack College	M,D
Oakland City University	M,D
Oakwood University	M
Oblate School of Theology	M,D,O
Ohio Christian University	M
Olivet Nazarene University	M
Oral Roberts University	M,D
Ottawa University	M
Pacific Rim Christian University	M
Pentecostal Theological Seminary	M,D
Pepperdine University	M
Phillips Theological Seminary	D
Phoenix Seminary	M,D,O
Piedmont International University	M,D
Pittsburgh Theological Seminary	M,D
Point Loma Nazarene University	M
Point University	M
Providence University College & Theological Seminary	M,D,O
Randall University	M
Reformed Theological Seminary–Charlotte Campus	M,D
Reformed Theological Seminary–Jackson Campus	M,D,O
Reformed Theological Seminary–Orlando Campus	M,D,O
Regent University	M,D,O
Regis College (Canada)	M,D,O
Richmont Graduate University	M,O
Sacred Heart Major Seminary	M
St. Ambrose University	M
St. Augustine's Seminary of Toronto	M,O
St. Bernard's School of Theology and Ministry	M,O
St. Catherine University	M,O
St. John's Seminary (CA)	M
Saint John's University (MN)	M
Saint Joseph's College of Maine	M
St. Joseph's Seminary	M
Saint Paul University	M,D,O
Saints Cyril and Methodius Seminary	M
St. Stephen's College	M,D
St. Thomas University	M,D,O
Saint Vincent Seminary	M
Santa Clara University	M
Seattle University	M
Selma University	M
Seminary of the Southwest	M,O
Seton Hall University	M,O
Shasta Bible College	M
Shepherds Theological Seminary	M
Shiloh University	M,D
Simpson University	M
Sioux Falls Seminary	M
Southeastern University (FL)	M,D
The Southern Baptist Theological Seminary	M,D
Southern Evangelical Seminary	M,D,O
Southern Methodist University	M,D
Southern Wesleyan University	M
South University (GA)	D
Southwestern Assemblies of God University	M
Southwestern Baptist Theological Seminary	M,D,O
Southwestern Christian University	M
Spring Arbor University	M
Spring Hill College	M,O
SUM Bible College & Theological Seminary	M
Theological University of the Caribbean	M,D
Trevecca Nazarene University	M
Trinity Bible College and Graduate School	M
Trinity College (Canada)	M,D,O
Trinity International University	M,D,O
Trinity Lutheran Seminary	M
Trinity School for Ministry	M,D,O
Trinity Western University	M,D
Tyndale University College & Seminary	M,O
Union University	M,D
United Lutheran Seminary	M,D
United Lutheran Seminary	M,D,O
United Theological Seminary	M,D
United Theological Seminary of the Twin Cities	M,D,O
University of Chicago	M
University of Dallas	M
University of Dayton	M,D
University of Fort Lauderdale	M
University of Northwestern–St. Paul	M
University of Portland	M
University of Saint Mary of the Lake–Mundelein Seminary	M,D
University of St. Michael's College	M,D,O
University of St. Thomas (MN)	M
University of St. Thomas (TX)	M
University of South Africa	M,D
University of the Incarnate Word	M
Ursuline College	M
Virginia Beach Theological Seminary	M
Virginia University of Lynchburg	M,D
Viterbo University	M,O
Walla Walla University	M
Walsh University	M
Wayland Baptist University	M
Welch College	M
Wesley Biblical Seminary	M
Western Seminary	M,D,O
Western Seminary–Sacramento Campus	M,O
Western Seminary–San Jose Campus	M,O
Western Theological Seminary	M,D,O
Westminster Theological Seminary	M,D,O
Whitworth University	M
Wilfrid Laurier University	M,D,O
World Mission University	M,D
Xavier University	M*
Xavier University of Louisiana	M

PATHOBIOLOGY

Brown University	M,D
Columbia University	M,D*
Drexel University	M,D*
Johns Hopkins University	D*
Kansas State University	M,D
Medical University of South Carolina	D
Michigan State University	M,D
Penn State University Park	M,D*
Purdue University	M,D
The University of Alabama at Birmingham	D
University of Cincinnati	D
University of Connecticut	M,D*
University of Illinois at Urbana–Champaign	M,D
University of Missouri	M,D
University of Toronto	M,D
University of Washington	D
University of Wyoming	M
Wake Forest University	M,D

PATHOLOGY

Albert Einstein College of Medicine	D
Boston University	M,D*
Case Western Reserve University	M,D*
Colorado State University	M,D
Columbia University	M,D*
Dalhousie University	M,D
Duke University	M,D*
Harvard University	D*
Indiana University–Purdue University Indianapolis	M,D
Iowa State University of Science and Technology	M,D
Johns Hopkins University	D*
Loma Linda University	D
McGill University	M,D
Medical University of South Carolina	M,D
Michigan State University	M,D
New York Medical College	M,D
North Carolina State University	M,D
North Dakota State University	M,D*
Purdue University	M,D
Queen's University at Kingston	M,D
Quinnipiac University	M
Rosalind Franklin University of Medicine and Science	M
Rutgers University–Newark	D
Saint Louis University	D*
Stony Brook University, State University of New York	M,D
Tufts University	M,D*
Université de Montréal	M,D
Université Laval	O

University at Buffalo, the State University of New York	M,D
University of Alberta	M,D
The University of British Columbia	M,D
University of Calgary	M,D
University of California, Davis	M,D
University of California, Irvine	D
University of California, Los Angeles	M,D*
University of Cincinnati	D
University of Georgia	M,D
University of Guelph	M,D,O
The University of Iowa	M*
The University of Kansas	M,D
University of Manitoba	M
University of Maryland, Baltimore	M
University of Michigan	D*
University of Mississippi Medical Center	D
University of Missouri	M,D
University of Nebraska Medical Center	M,D
University of New Mexico	M,D
The University of North Carolina at Chapel Hill	D
University of Oklahoma Health Sciences Center	D
University of Pittsburgh	D*
University of Prince Edward Island	M,D
University of Rochester	D*
University of Saskatchewan	M,D
University of Southern California	M*
University of South Florida	M,D*
The University of Tennessee Health Science Center	M,D
The University of Texas Medical Branch	D
The University of Toledo	M,O
University of Utah	M,D
University of Vermont	M
University of Virginia	D
University of Washington	D
The University of Western Ontario	M,D
University of Wisconsin–Madison	D
Vanderbilt University	D*
Wayne State University	M,D,O
West Virginia University	M,D
Yale University	M,D

PEDIATRIC NURSING

Augusta University	D
Azusa Pacific University	M,D*
Boston College	M,D
Caribbean University	M,D
Case Western Reserve University	M*
Columbia University	M,O*
Creighton University	M,D,O
Drexel University	M*
Duke University	M,D,O*
East Tennessee State University	M,D,O
Emory University	M
Florida International University	M,D
Georgia State University	M,D,O
Gwynedd Mercy University	M,D
Indiana University–Purdue University Indianapolis	M
Johns Hopkins University	D,O*
Kent State University	M,D
King University	M,D
Lehman College of the City University of New York	M
Loma Linda University	M
Marquette University	M,D,O
Maryville University of Saint Louis	M,D
MGH Institute of Health Professions	M,D,O
Molloy College	M,D,O
New York University	M,D,O*
Northeastern University	M,D,O
Old Dominion University	M,D
Oregon Health & Science University	M
Point Loma Nazarene University	M
Purdue University	M,D,O
Queen's University at Kingston	M,D,O
Rush University	D,O
St. Catherine University	M,D
San Francisco State University	M,O
Seton Hall University	M,D
Spalding University	M,D,O
Stony Brook University, State University of New York	M,D,O
Texas Christian University	M,D,O
Texas Tech University Health Sciences Center	M,D,O
Texas Woman's University	M,D
The University of Alabama at Birmingham	M,D
University of Cincinnati	M,D
University of Colorado Denver	M,D
University of Delaware	M,O*
University of Illinois at Chicago	M,O
University of Maryland, Baltimore	M,D,O
University of Michigan	M,D,O*
University of Minnesota, Twin Cities Campus	M,D
University of Missouri	M,D,O
University of Missouri–Kansas City	M,D
University of Missouri–St. Louis	D,O
The University of North Carolina at Chapel Hill	M,D,O
University of Pennsylvania	M*
University of Pittsburgh	M,D*
University of Puerto Rico–Medical Sciences Campus	M
University of Rochester	M,D*
University of San Diego	M,D
University of South Carolina	M
University of South Florida	M,D,O*
The University of Tennessee Health Science Center	D,O
The University of Texas at Austin	M,D
The University of Texas Health Science Center at San Antonio	M,D,O
The University of Toledo	M,O
University of Wisconsin–Madison	D
Vanderbilt University	M,D,O*
Villanova University	M,D,O
Virginia Commonwealth University	M,D,O
Wayne State University	M,D,O
Wright State University	M

PERFUSION

Milwaukee School of Engineering	M
Quinnipiac University	M
Rush University	M
The University of Arizona	M,D
University of Nebraska Medical Center	M

PETROLEUM ENGINEERING

Colorado School of Mines	M,D
Louisiana State University and Agricultural & Mechanical College	M,D
Missouri University of Science and Technology	M,D
Montana Tech of The University of Montana	M
New Mexico Institute of Mining and Technology	M,D
Texas A&M University	M,D
Texas A&M University–Kingsville	M
Texas Tech University	M,D
University of Alaska Fairbanks	M
University of Alberta	M,D
University of Calgary	M,D
University of Houston	M,D
The University of Kansas	M,D,O
University of Louisiana at Lafayette	M
University of Oklahoma	M,D,O*
University of Pittsburgh	M,D*
University of Regina	M,D
University of Southern California	M,D,O*
The University of Texas at Austin	M,D
The University of Tulsa	M,D
University of Utah	M,D
University of Wyoming	M,D
West Virginia University	M,D

PHARMACEUTICAL ADMINISTRATION

Belmont University	D
Columbia University	M*
Duquesne University	M
Fairleigh Dickinson University, Metropolitan Campus	M,O
Florida Agricultural and Mechanical University	M,D
Idaho State University	M,D
New Jersey Institute of Technology	M,D
Northeast Ohio Medical University	M,D,O
The Ohio State University	M,D
Purdue University	M,D,O
Rutgers University–Newark	M
St. John's University (NY)	M
San Diego State University	M
Temple University	M*
University of Florida	M,D
University of Georgia	D
University of Houston	M,D
University of Illinois at Chicago	M,D
University of Maryland, Baltimore	M,D
University of Michigan	D*
University of Minnesota, Twin Cities Campus	M,D
University of Mississippi	M,D
The University of North Carolina at Chapel Hill	M,D
University of Pittsburgh	M*
University of Southern California	M*
University of the Sciences	M
The University of Toledo	M
University of Utah	M,D
University of Wisconsin–Madison	M,D
Virginia Commonwealth University	M,D

PHARMACEUTICAL ENGINEERING

New Jersey Institute of Technology	M,D
University of Michigan	M,D*

PHARMACEUTICAL SCIENCES

Albany College of Pharmacy and Health Sciences	M,D
Auburn University	M,D*
Boston University	D*
Butler University	M,D
Campbell University	M,D
Chapman University	M,D*
Creighton University	M,D
Drexel University	M*
Duquesne University	M,D
East Tennessee State University	D
Florida Agricultural and Mechanical University	M,D
Idaho State University	M,D
Irell & Manella Graduate School of Biological Sciences	D*
Johns Hopkins University	M*
Long Island University–Hudson	M,O
Long Island University–LIU Brooklyn	M,D
MCPHS University	M,D
Memorial University of Newfoundland	M,D
Mercer University	D
Northeastern University	M,D,O
Northeast Ohio Medical University	M,D,O
Oregon State University	M,D
Purdue University	M,D
Queen's University at Kingston	M,D
Rowan University	M
Rush University	M,D
Rutgers University–New Brunswick	M,D
St. John's University (NY)	M,D
South Dakota State University	M,D
Stevens Institute of Technology	M,O
Temple University	M,D*
Texas Southern University	M,D
Texas Tech University Health Sciences Center	M,D
Université de Montréal	M,D,O
Université Laval	M,D,O
University at Buffalo, the State University of New York	M,D
University of Alberta	M,D
The University of Arizona	M,D
The University of British Columbia	M,D
University of California, Irvine	D
University of California, San Francisco	D
University of Cincinnati	M,D
University of Colorado Denver	D
University of Connecticut	M,D*
University of Florida	M,D
University of Georgia	M,D
University of Hawaii at Hilo	D*
University of Houston	M,D
University of Illinois at Chicago	M,D
The University of Iowa	M,D*
University of Kentucky	M,D
The University of Manchester	M,D
University of Manitoba	M,D
University of Maryland, Baltimore	D
University of Maryland Eastern Shore	M,D
University of Michigan	D*
University of Minnesota, Twin Cities Campus	M,D
University of Mississippi	M,D
University of Montana	M,D
University of Nebraska Medical Center	M,D
University of New Mexico	M,D
The University of North Carolina at Chapel Hill	M,D
University of North Texas Health Science Center at Fort Worth	M,D
University of Oklahoma Health Sciences Center	M,D
University of Pittsburgh	M,D*
University of Puerto Rico–Medical Sciences Campus	M,D
University of Rhode Island	M,D*
University of Saskatchewan	M,D
University of South Carolina	M,D
University of Southern California	M,D,O*
University of South Florida	M,D*
The University of Tennessee Health Science Center	M,D
The University of Texas at Austin	M,D
University of the Pacific	M,D
University of the Sciences	M,D
The University of Toledo	M
University of Toronto	M,D
University of Utah	M,D
University of Washington	M,D
University of Wisconsin–Madison	M,D
Virginia Commonwealth University	M,D
Wayne State University	M,D
Western University of Health Sciences	M
West Virginia University	D
York College of the City University of New York	M

PHARMACOLOGY

Albany College of Pharmacy and Health Sciences	M,D
Albany Medical College	M,D
Alliant International University–San Francisco	M
American University of Beirut	M,D
Argosy University, Hawai`i	M,O
Augusta University	D
Baylor College of Medicine	D
Boston University	M,D*
Case Western Reserve University	D*
The Chicago School of Professional Psychology: Online	M
Columbia University	M,D*
Creighton University	M,D
Dalhousie University	M,D
Drexel University	M,D*
Duke University	D*
Duquesne University	M,D
East Carolina University	D
East Tennessee State University	D
Emory University	D
Fairleigh Dickinson University, Florham Campus	M,O
Florida Agricultural and Mechanical University	M,D
Georgetown University	M,D
Howard University	M,D
Husson University	M,D
Idaho State University	M,D
Indiana University–Purdue University Indianapolis	M,D
Johns Hopkins University	D*
Kent State University	M,D
Loma Linda University	D
London Metropolitan University	M,D
Long Island University–LIU Brooklyn	M,D
Louisiana State University Health Sciences Center	D
Louisiana State University Health Sciences Center at Shreveport	M,D
McGill University	M,D
McMaster University	M,D
MCPHS University	M,D
Medical College of Wisconsin	D
Meharry Medical College	D
Michigan State University	M,D
Montclair State University	M
New Jersey Institute of Technology	M,D
New York Medical College	M,D
North Carolina State University	M,D
Northeastern University	M,D,O
The Ohio State University	M,D
Oregon Health & Science University	D
Purdue University	M,D
Queen's University at Kingston	M,D
Rush University	M,D
Rutgers University–Newark	D
Saint Louis University	D*
Southern Illinois University Carbondale	M,D
State University of New York Upstate Medical University	D
Stony Brook University, State University of New York	M,D
Thomas Jefferson University	M
Tulane University	M
Universidad Central del Caribe	M,D
Université de Montréal	M,D
Université de Sherbrooke	M,D
University at Buffalo, the State University of New York	M,D
University of Alberta	M,D
The University of Arizona	M,D
University of Arkansas for Medical Sciences	M,D,O
The University of British Columbia	M,D
University of California, Davis	M,D
University of California, Los Angeles	M,D*
University of California, San Francisco	D
University of Cincinnati	D
University of Colorado Denver	D
University of Connecticut	M,D*
University of Florida	M,D
University of Georgia	M,D
University of Guelph	M,D
University of Hawaii at Hilo	M*
University of Houston	M,D
University of Illinois at Chicago	D
The University of Iowa	M,D*
The University of Kansas	M,D
University of Kentucky	D
University of Louisville	M,D
The University of Manchester	M,D
University of Manitoba	M,D
University of Maryland, Baltimore	M,D
University of Miami	D*
University of Michigan	M,D*
University of Minnesota, Duluth	M,D
University of Minnesota, Twin Cities Campus	M,D
University of Mississippi	M,D
University of Mississippi Medical Center	D
University of Missouri	M,D
University of Nebraska Medical Center	D
The University of North Carolina at Chapel Hill	D
University of North Texas Health Science Center at Fort Worth	M,D
University of Pennsylvania	D*
University of Prince Edward Island	M,D
University of Puerto Rico–Medical Sciences Campus	M,D
University of Rhode Island	M,D*
University of Rochester	M,D*
University of Saskatchewan	M,D
University of South Dakota	M,D
The University of Tennessee Health Science Center	M,D
The University of Texas at Austin	M,D
The University of Texas Health Science Center at Houston	M,D
The University of Texas Health Science Center at San Antonio	D
The University of Texas Medical Branch	M,D
University of the Sciences	M,D
The University of Toledo	M,D
University of Toronto	M,D
University of Utah	D
University of Vermont	M,D
University of Virginia	D
University of Washington	D
University of Wisconsin–Madison	D
Vanderbilt University	D*
Virginia Commonwealth University	M,D,O
Wake Forest University	D
Wayne State University	M,D,O
Weill Cornell Medicine	M,D
Wright State University	M
Yale University	D

PHARMACY

Albany College of Pharmacy and Health Sciences	M,D
Appalachian College of Pharmacy	D
Auburn University	D*
Belmont University	D
Binghamton University, State University of New York	D

*M—masters degree; D—doctorate; O—other advanced degree; *—Close-Up and/or Display*

Butler University	M,D
California Health Sciences University	D
California Northstate University	D
Campbell University	M,D
Cedarville University	M,D
Chapman University	M,D*
Chicago State University	D
Concordia University Wisconsin	M,D
Creighton University	D
Drake University	M,D
Duquesne University	D
D'Youville College	D
East Tennessee State University	D
Fairleigh Dickinson University, Florham Campus	D
Ferris State University	D
Florida Agricultural and Mechanical University	D
Georgia Campus–Philadelphia College of Osteopathic Medicine	D*
Harding University	D
High Point University	M,D
Howard University	D
Husson University	M,D
Idaho State University	M,D
Keck Graduate Institute	D
Lake Erie College of Osteopathic Medicine	M,D,O
Lebanese American University	D
Lipscomb University	M,D
Loma Linda University	D
Long Island University–Hudson	M,O
Long Island University–LIU Brooklyn	M,D
Manchester University	D
Marshall B. Ketchum University	M,D
Marshall University	D
MCPHS University	D
Medical College of Wisconsin	D
Medical University of South Carolina	D
Mercer University	D
Midwestern University, Downers Grove Campus	D
Midwestern University, Glendale Campus	D
North Dakota State University	M,D*
Northeastern University	M,D,O
Northeast Ohio Medical University	D
Notre Dame of Maryland University	D
Nova Southeastern University	M,D*
Ohio Northern University	D
The Ohio State University	M,D
Oregon State University	D
Pacific University	D
Palm Beach Atlantic University	D
Presbyterian College	D
Purdue University	D
Regis University	M,D,O
Roosevelt University	D
Rosalind Franklin University of Medicine and Science	D
Roseman University of Health Sciences	D
Rutgers University–New Brunswick	M,D
St. John Fisher College	D
St. John's University (NY)	M,D
St. Louis College of Pharmacy	D
Samford University	D
Shenandoah University	D
South College	D
South Dakota State University	D
Southern Illinois University Edwardsville	D
South University (SC)	D
South University (GA)	
Southwestern Oklahoma State University	D
Stony Brook University, State University of New York	D
Sullivan University	D
Temple University	M,D*
Texas A&M University	D
Texas Southern University	D
Thomas Jefferson University	D
Touro University California	M,D
Union University	D
Universidad de Ciencias Medicas	M,D,O
University at Buffalo, the State University of New York	D
University of Alberta	M,D
The University of Arizona	D
University of Arkansas for Medical Sciences	M,D
The University of British Columbia	M,D
University of California, San Diego	D*
University of California, San Francisco	D
University of Charleston	D
University of Cincinnati	D
University of Colorado Denver	D
University of Connecticut	D*
The University of Findlay	M,D
University of Florida	M,D
University of Georgia	M,D,O
University of Hawaii at Hilo	D*
University of Houston	M,D
University of Illinois at Chicago	D
The University of Iowa	M,D*
The University of Kansas	M,D
University of Kentucky	D
University of Louisiana at Monroe	D
The University of Manchester	M,D
University of Maryland, Baltimore	M,D
University of Michigan	D*
University of Minnesota, Duluth	M,D
University of Minnesota, Twin Cities Campus	D
University of Mississippi	M,D
University of Missouri–Kansas City	D
University of Montana	M,D
University of Nebraska Medical Center	D
University of New England	D
University of New Mexico	D
The University of North Carolina at Chapel Hill	M,D
University of Oklahoma Health Sciences Center	D
University of Pittsburgh	D*
University of Puerto Rico–Medical Sciences Campus	M,D
University of Rhode Island	D*
University of Saint Joseph	D
University of South Carolina	D
University of Southern California	D*
University of South Florida	M,D,O*
The University of Tennessee Health Science Center	M,D
The University of Texas at Austin	D
The University of Texas at Tyler	D
University of the Incarnate Word	D
University of the Pacific	D
University of the Sciences	D
The University of Toledo	M,D
University of Utah	D
University of Washington	M,D
University of Wisconsin–Madison	D
University of Wyoming	M,D
Virginia Commonwealth University	D
Washington State University	M,D
Wayne State University	D
West Coast University	M,D
Western New England University	D
Western University of Health Sciences	D
West Virginia University	D
Wilkes University	D
Wingate University	D
Xavier University of Louisiana	D

PHILANTHROPIC STUDIES

Indiana University–Purdue University Indianapolis	M,D
Saint Mary's University of Minnesota	M

PHILOSOPHY

Acadia University	M
American University	M
The American University in Cairo	M,O
American University of Beirut	M,D
Arizona State University at the Tempe campus	M,D,O
Baylor University	M,D
Binghamton University, State University of New York	M,D
Boston College	M,D
Boston University	M,D*
Bowling Green State University	M,D
Brandeis University	M
Brock University	M
Brown University	D
California Institute of Integral Studies	M,D,O
California State University, Long Beach	M
California State University, Los Angeles	M,O
Carleton University	M
Carnegie Mellon University	M,D
The Catholic University of America	M,D,O
Central European University	M,D
Claremont Graduate University	M,D
Cleveland State University	M,O
Collège Dominicain de Philosophie et de Théologie	M,D
Colorado State University	M
Columbia University	M,D*
Concordia University (Canada)	M
Cornell University	D
Dalhousie University	M,D
Dallas Theological Seminary	M,D,O
Delta State University	M
Dominican School of Philosophy and Theology	M,O
Dominican University of California	M
Duke University	D*
Duquesne University	M,D
Eastern Michigan University	M
Emory University	D,O
Florida State University	M,D
Fordham University	M,D
Franciscan University of Steubenville	M
George Mason University	M
Georgetown University	M,D
The George Washington University	M
Georgia State University	M
Gonzaga University	M
The Graduate Center, City University of New York	M,D
Harrison Middleton University	M,D
Harvard University	M,D*
Houston Baptist University	M
Howard University	M
Indiana University Bloomington	M,D
Indiana University–Purdue University Indianapolis	M,O
Institute for Christian Studies	M,D
Institute for Doctoral Studies in the Visual Arts	D
Johns Hopkins University	M,D*
Kent State University	M
Lake Forest College	M
Lincoln Christian University	M
Louisiana State University and Agricultural & Mechanical College	M
Loyola Marymount University	M
Loyola University Chicago	M,D
Marquette University	M,D
Massachusetts Institute of Technology	D
McGill University	M,D
McMaster University	M,D
Memorial University of Newfoundland	M,D
Miami University	M
Michigan State University	M,D
Midwestern State University	M,D
Mount St. Mary's University (MD)	M
The New School	M,D
New York University	M,D*
Northern Illinois University	M
Northwestern University	D
The Ohio State University	M,D
Ohio University	M
Oklahoma State University	M
Old Dominion University	M,O
Open University	M
Penn State University Park	M,D*
Princeton University	D
Purdue University	M,D
Queen's University at Kingston	M,D
Regis College (Canada)	M,D,O
Rice University	M,D
Roosevelt University	M
Rutgers University–New Brunswick	D
Saint Charles Borromeo Seminary, Overbrook	M
Saint Louis University	M,D*
Saint Mary's University (Canada)	M
San Diego State University	M
San Francisco State University	M
San Jose State University	M
Simon Fraser University	M,D
Southeastern Baptist Theological Seminary	M,D
The Southern Baptist Theological Seminary	M,D
Southern Evangelical Seminary	M,D,O
Southern Illinois University Carbondale	M,D
Stanford University	M,D
Stony Brook University, State University of New York	M,D,O
Syracuse University	M,D*
Teachers College, Columbia University	M,D,O
Temple University	M,D*
Texas A&M University	M,D
Texas State University	M
Texas Tech University	M
Trinity Western University	M
Tufts University	M*
Tulane University	M,D
Universidad Autonoma de Guadalajara	M,D
Université de Montréal	M,D
Université de Sherbrooke	M,D,O
Université du Québec à Montréal	M,D
Université du Québec à Trois-Rivières	M,D
Université Laval	M,D
University at Albany, State University of New York	M,D
University at Buffalo, the State University of New York	M,D
University of Alberta	M,D
The University of Arizona	M,D
University of Arkansas	M,D
The University of British Columbia	M,D
University of Calgary	M,D
University of California, Berkeley	D
University of California, Davis	M,D
University of California, Irvine	M,D
University of California, Los Angeles	M,D*
University of California, Riverside	M,D
University of California, San Diego	D*
University of California, Santa Barbara	D
University of California, Santa Cruz	M,D*
University of Chicago	M,D
University of Cincinnati	M,D
University of Colorado Boulder	M,D
University of Connecticut	M,D*
University of Dallas	M,D
University of Florida	M,D
University of Georgia	M,D
University of Guelph	M,D
University of Hawaii at Manoa	M,D
University of Houston	M
University of Idaho	M,D
University of Illinois at Chicago	M,D
University of Illinois at Urbana–Champaign	M,D
The University of Iowa	D*
The University of Kansas	M,D
University of Kentucky	M,D
University of Lethbridge	M,D
University of Louisville	M,D
The University of Manchester	M,D
University of Manitoba	M
University of Maryland, College Park	M,D
University of Massachusetts Amherst	M,D*
University of Memphis	M,D
University of Miami	M,D*
University of Michigan	M,D*
University of Minnesota, Twin Cities Campus	M,D
University of Mississippi	M,D
University of Missouri	M,D
University of Missouri–St. Louis	M
University of Montana	M
University of Nebraska–Lincoln	M,D
University of Nevada, Reno	M
University of New Mexico	M,D
The University of North Carolina at Chapel Hill	M,D
The University of North Carolina at Charlotte	M,O
University of North Florida	M,O
University of North Georgia	M
University of North Texas	M,D,O
University of Notre Dame	D
University of Oklahoma	M,D*
University of Oregon	M,D
University of Ottawa	M,D
University of Pennsylvania	M,D*
University of Pittsburgh	D*
University of Puerto Rico–Río Piedras	M
University of Regina	M
University of Rochester	D*
University of St. Thomas (TX)	M,D
University of Saskatchewan	M
University of South Africa	M,D
University of South Carolina	M,D
University of Southern California	M,D*
University of South Florida	M,D*
The University of Tennessee	M,D
The University of Texas at Austin	D
The University of Texas at El Paso	M
The University of Texas at San Antonio	M
The University of Toledo	M
University of Toronto	M,D
University of Utah	M,D
University of Victoria	M
University of Virginia	M,D
University of Washington	M,D
University of Waterloo	M,D
The University of Western Ontario	M,D
University of Windsor	M
University of Wisconsin–Madison	M,D
University of Wisconsin–Milwaukee	M*
University of Wyoming	M
Vanderbilt University	M,D*
Villanova University	D
Washington University in St. Louis	D
Wayne State University	M,D
West Chester University of Pennsylvania	M,O
Western Michigan University	M
Wilfrid Laurier University	M
Yale University	D
York University	M,D

PHOTOGRAPHY

Academy of Art University	M
Ball State University	M
Bard College	M
Barry University	M
Bradley University	M
Brooklyn College of the City University of New York	M
California Institute of the Arts	M,O
California State University, Fullerton	M
California State University, Los Angeles	M
Central Washington University	M
Claremont Graduate University	M
Columbia College Chicago	M
Cornell University	M,D
Cranbrook Academy of Art	M
East Carolina University	M
Ferris State University	M
The George Washington University	M,O
Georgia State University	M,D
Governors State University	M
Howard University	M
Illinois State University	M
Indiana State University	M
Indiana University–Purdue University Indianapolis	M
Inter American University of Puerto Rico, San Germán Campus	M
Ithaca College	M
James Madison University	M
Kent State University	M
Lesley University	M
Louisiana State University and Agricultural & Mechanical College	M
Louisiana Tech University	M,D,O
Maryland Institute College of Art	M
Marywood University	M
Massachusetts College of Art and Design	M,O
Mills College	M
Minneapolis College of Art and Design	M
New Hampshire Institute of Art	M
The New School	M
New York Film Academy	M
Northern Vermont University–Johnson	M
Ohio University	M
Oklahoma City University	M
Otis College of Art and Design	M
Paris College of Art	M
Purdue University	M,D
Rhode Island School of Design	M
Rochester Institute of Technology	M
San Jose State University	M
Savannah College of Art and Design	M
School of the Art Institute of Chicago	M
School of Visual Arts (NY)	M
Southwest University of Visual Arts	M
Syracuse University	M*
Temple University	M*
Texas Woman's University	M

The University of Alabama	M
University of Alaska Fairbanks	M
University of Colorado Boulder	M
University of Illinois at Urbana–Champaign	M
University of Memphis	M,O
University of Miami	M*
University of Montana	M
University of New Mexico	M,D
University of Notre Dame	M,D
University of Oklahoma	M,D*
University of Rochester	M*
University of South Dakota	M
University of Southern California	M*
The University of Tennessee	M
University of Utah	M
University of Victoria	M
University of Washington	M
Virginia Commonwealth University	M,D
Wayne State University	M
West Virginia University	M,D
Wichita State University	M
Yale University	M

PHOTONICS

Duke University	M*
Johns Hopkins University	M,O*
Lehigh University	M,D
Oklahoma State University	M,D
Princeton University	D
Queens College of the City University of New York	M
Stevens Institute of Technology	M,D,O
The University of Alabama in Huntsville	M,D
University of Arkansas	M,D
University of California, San Diego	M,D*
University of California, Santa Barbara	M,D
University of Central Florida	M,D
University of Dayton	M,D
University of New Mexico	M,D

PHYSICAL CHEMISTRY

Auburn University	M,D*
Binghamton University, State University of New York	M,D
Boston College	M,D
Brandeis University	M,D
Cleveland State University	M,D
Cornell University	D
Dartmouth College	M,D*
Eastern New Mexico University	M
Florida State University	M,D
The George Washington University	M,D
Georgia State University	M,D
Harvard University	D*
Howard University	M,D
Indiana University Bloomington	M,D
Iowa State University of Science and Technology	M,D
Laurentian University	M
Marquette University	M,D
Massachusetts Institute of Technology	D
McMaster University	M,D
Old Dominion University	M,D
Purdue University	M,D
Rice University	M,D
Rutgers University–Newark	M,D
Rutgers University–New Brunswick	M,D
Seton Hall University	M,D
Southern University and Agricultural and Mechanical College	M
University of Calgary	M,D
University of Cincinnati	M,D
University of Louisville	M,D
The University of Manchester	M,D
University of Maryland, College Park	M,D
University of Memphis	M,D
University of Miami	M,D*
University of Michigan	M,D*
University of Missouri–Kansas City	M,D
University of Montana	M,D
University of Nebraska–Lincoln	M,D
University of Notre Dame	M,D
University of Oklahoma	M,D*
University of Puerto Rico–Mayagüez	M,D
University of Rochester	D*
University of Southern California	D*
The University of Tennessee	M,D
The University of Texas at Austin	D
The University of Toledo	M,D
Vanderbilt University	M,D*
Virginia Commonwealth University	M,D
Wake Forest University	M,D
Yale University	D
Youngstown State University	M

PHYSICAL EDUCATION

Adams State University	M
Adelphi University	M,O
Alabama Agricultural and Mechanical University	M
Alabama State University	M
Albany State University	M,O
Alcorn State University	M,O
American University of Puerto Rico	M
Arizona State University at the Tempe campus	M
Arkansas State University	M,O
Auburn University	M,D,O*
Auburn University at Montgomery	M,O
Avila University	M,O
Ball State University	M
Baylor University	M,D
Bridgewater State University	M
Brooklyn College of the City University of New York	M
California Baptist University	M
California State University, East Bay	M
California State University, Fullerton	M
California State University, Long Beach	M
California State University, Los Angeles	M,O
California State University, Sacramento	M
California State University, Stanislaus	M
Campbell University	M
Canisius College	M
Caribbean University	M,D
Central Connecticut State University	M,O
Central Washington University	M
Chicago State University	M
The Citadel, The Military College of South Carolina	M,O
Cleveland State University	M
The College at Brockport, State University of New York	M,O
Colorado State University–Pueblo	M
Columbus State University	M
Concordia University (United States)	M,D
Concordia University Irvine	M*
Delta State University	M
DePaul University	M,D
East Carolina University	M,D,O
Eastern Kentucky University	M
Eastern Michigan University	M
Eastern New Mexico University	M
Eastern University	M,O
Eastern Washington University	M
East Stroudsburg University of Pennsylvania	M
Emporia State University	M
Florida Agricultural and Mechanical University	M
Florida International University	M,D,O
Fort Hays State University	M
Gardner-Webb University	M
George Mason University	M
Georgia College & State University	M
Georgia Southern University–Armstrong Campus	M,O
Georgia State University	M,D
Goucher College	M,O
Henderson State University	M
Hofstra University	M,D,O
Howard University	M
Idaho State University	M
Illinois State University	M
Indiana State University	M,D
Indiana University Bloomington	M,D
Indiana University of Pennsylvania	M
Indiana University–Purdue University Indianapolis	M,O
Inter American University of Puerto Rico, Metropolitan Campus	M
Inter American University of Puerto Rico, San Germán Campus	M
Ithaca College	M
Jackson State University	M
Jacksonville State University	M,O
James Madison University	M
Longwood University	M
Massachusetts College of Liberal Arts	M,O
McGill University	M,D,O
McNeese State University	O
Memorial University of Newfoundland	M
Meredith College	M,O
Middle Tennessee State University	M
Millersville University of Pennsylvania	M,O
Minnesota State University Mankato	M
Mississippi State University	M,D
Missouri State University	M
Montclair State University	M
Morehead State University	M
North Carolina Agricultural and Technical State University	M
North Carolina Central University	M
Northern Illinois University	M
Northwest Missouri State University	M
The Ohio State University	M,D
Ohio University	M
Old Dominion University	M,D
Pittsburg State University	M
Purdue University	M,D
Queens College of the City University of New York	M,O
Rhode Island College	M,O
Salem State University	M
Shenandoah University	M,D,O
Slippery Rock University of Pennsylvania	M
Southern Connecticut State University	M
Southern Illinois University Carbondale	M
Southern Illinois University Edwardsville	M
Springfield College	M,D,O
State University of New York College at Cortland	M
Stony Brook University, State University of New York	M,O
Sul Ross State University	M
Teachers College, Columbia University	M,D
Temple University	M,D*
Tennessee State University	M
Tennessee Technological University	M
Texas Southern University	M
Texas State University	M
Texas Woman's University	M,D
Union College (KY)	M
United States Sports Academy	M
Universidad del Turabo	M
Universidad Metropolitana	M
Université de Montréal	M,D,O
Université de Sherbrooke	M,O
Université du Québec à Trois-Rivières	M
The University of Akron	M
The University of Alabama	M,D
University of Alberta	M,D
University of Arkansas	M
The University of British Columbia	M,D
University of Dayton	M
University of Florida	M,D
University of Georgia	M,D
University of Houston	M,D
University of Idaho	M,D
University of Indianapolis	M
The University of Kansas	M,D
University of Kentucky	M,D
University of Louisville	M,D,O
University of Maine	M,D,O
University of Manitoba	M
University of Mary	M
University of Memphis	M,O
University of Montana	M
University of Nebraska at Kearney	M
University of New Brunswick Fredericton	M
University of New Hampshire	M,O
University of New Mexico	D
University of North Alabama	M
The University of North Carolina at Chapel Hill	M
The University of North Carolina at Pembroke	M
University of Northern Colorado	M,D
University of Northern Iowa	M
University of North Georgia	M
University of Rhode Island	M*
University of Rio Grande	M
University of South Alabama	M
University of South Carolina	M,D
University of Southern Mississippi	M,D
The University of Tennessee at Chattanooga	M
The University of Tennessee at Martin	M
The University of Texas at Austin	M,D
The University of Toledo	M
University of Toronto	M,D
University of Victoria	M
University of Virginia	M,D
University of Washington	M,D
The University of West Alabama	M
University of West Florida	M,D
University of Wisconsin–La Crosse	M
University of Wyoming	M
Utah State University	M,D
Wayne State College	M
Wayne State University	M,D
West Chester University of Pennsylvania	M,O
Western Kentucky University	M
Western Michigan University	M
Western Washington University	M
Westfield State University	M
West Liberty University	M
West Virginia University	M,D
Wilfrid Laurier University	M
William Woods University	M,D,O
Winthrop University	M

PHYSICAL THERAPY

Adventist University of Health Sciences	D
Alabama State University	D
American International College	M,D,O
Andrews University	D
Angelo State University	D
Arcadia University	D
Arkansas State University	D
A.T. Still University	M,D,O
Augusta University	D
Azusa Pacific University	D*
Baylor University	D
Bellarmine University	M,D
Belmont University	M,D
Boston University	M,D*
Bradley University	D
California State University, Fresno	D
California State University, Long Beach	D
California State University, Northridge	M
California State University, Sacramento	D
Campbell University	M,D
Carroll University	D
Central Michigan University	M,D
Chapman University	D*
Chatham University	D
Clarke University	D
Clarkson University	D
Cleveland State University	D
The College of St. Scholastica	D
College of Staten Island of the City University of New York	D
Columbia University	D*
Concordia University, St. Paul	M,D
Concordia University Wisconsin	D
Creighton University	D
Daemen College	D,O
Dalhousie University	M
Des Moines University	D
Dominican College	M,D
Drexel University	M,D,O*
Duke University	D*
Duquesne University	M,D
D'Youville College	D,O
East Carolina University	D
Eastern Washington University	D
East Tennessee State University	D
Elon University	D
Emory & Henry College	M,D
Emory University	D
Florida Agricultural and Mechanical University	D
Florida Gulf Coast University	D
Florida International University	D
Franciscan Missionaries of Our Lady University	M,D
Franklin Pierce University	M,D,O
Gannon University	D
George Fox University	D
The George Washington University	D
Georgia Campus–Philadelphia College of Osteopathic Medicine	D*
Georgia Southern University–Armstrong Campus	D
Georgia State University	D
Governors State University	D
Grand Valley State University	D
Hampton University	D
Harding University	D
Hardin-Simmons University	D
High Point University	M,D
Howard University	M,D
Hunter College of the City University of New York	D
Husson University	D
Idaho State University	D
Indiana State University	M,D
Indiana University–Purdue University Indianapolis	M,D
Ithaca College	D
Kean University	D
Langston University	D
Lebanon Valley College	D
Loma Linda University	M,D
Long Island University–LIU Brooklyn	M,D,O
Louisiana State University Health Sciences Center	D
Marist College	D
Marquette University	D
Marshall University	D
Marymount University	D
Maryville University of Saint Louis	D
Mayo Clinic School of Health Sciences	D
McMaster University	M
MCPHS University	D
Medical University of South Carolina	D
Mercer University	M,D
Mercy College	D
MGH Institute of Health Professions	M,D,O
Midwestern University, Downers Grove Campus	D
Midwestern University, Glendale Campus	D
Misericordia University	D
Missouri State University	D
Mount St. Joseph University	D
Mount Saint Mary's University (CA)	M,D,O
Nazareth College of Rochester	D
Neumann University	D
New York Institute of Technology	D
New York Medical College	M,D,O
New York University	M,D,O*
Northern Arizona University	D
Northern Illinois University	D
Northwestern University	D
Nova Southeastern University	M,D*
Oakland University	D,O
The Ohio State University	D
Ohio University	D
Old Dominion University	D
Pacific University	M,D
Queen's University at Kingston	M,D
Radford University	D
Regis University	M,D,O
Rockhurst University	D
Rocky Mountain University of Health Professions	D
Rosalind Franklin University of Medicine and Science	M,D
Rush University	M
Rutgers University–Camden	D
Rutgers University–Newark	D
Sacred Heart University	D
Sage Graduate School	D
St. Ambrose University	D
St. Catherine University	D
Saint Francis University	D
Saint Louis University	M,D*
Samford University	M,D
Samuel Merritt University	D
San Diego State University	D
San Francisco State University	D
Seton Hall University	D
Shenandoah University	M,D,O
Simmons College	M,D,O
Slippery Rock University of Pennsylvania	D
Sonoma State University	M

*M—masters degree; D—doctorate; O—other advanced degree; *—Close-Up and/or Display*

Southwest Baptist University	D
Springfield College	D
State University of New York Upstate Medical University	D
Stockton University	D
Stony Brook University, State University of New York	M,D,O
Temple University	D*
Tennessee State University	D
Texas State University	D
Texas Tech University Health Sciences Center	D
Texas Woman's University	D
Thomas Jefferson University	D
Touro College	M,D
Trine University	D
University at Buffalo, the State University of New York	D
The University of Alabama at Birmingham	D
University of Alberta	M,D
The University of British Columbia	M
University of California, San Francisco	D
University of Central Arkansas	D
University of Central Florida	D
University of Cincinnati	D
University of Colorado Denver	D
University of Connecticut	D*
University of Dayton	D
University of Delaware	D*
University of Evansville	D
The University of Findlay	M,D
University of Florida	D
University of Hartford	M,D
University of Illinois at Chicago	M,D
University of Indianapolis	M,D
The University of Iowa	M,D*
University of Jamestown	D
The University of Kansas	D
University of Kentucky	D
University of Lynchburg	D
University of Manitoba	M,D
University of Mary	D
University of Mary Hardin-Baylor	D
University of Maryland, Baltimore	D
University of Maryland Eastern Shore	D
University of Massachusetts Lowell	D
University of Miami	D*
University of Michigan–Flint	D,O
University of Minnesota, Twin Cities Campus	M,D
University of Mississippi Medical Center	M
University of Missouri	D
University of Montana	D
University of Mount Union	D
University of Nebraska Medical Center	D
University of Nevada, Las Vegas	D
University of New England	M,D
University of New Mexico	D
The University of North Carolina at Chapel Hill	D
University of North Dakota	D
University of North Florida	M,D
University of North Georgia	D
University of North Texas Health Science Center at Fort Worth	M,D
University of Oklahoma Health Sciences Center	M
University of Pittsburgh	M,D*
University of Puerto Rico–Medical Sciences Campus	M
University of Puget Sound	D
University of Rhode Island	D*
University of St. Augustine for Health Sciences	D
University of Saint Mary	D
The University of Scranton	D
University of South Alabama	D
University of South Dakota	D
University of Southern California	M,D*
University of South Florida	D*
The University of Tennessee at Chattanooga	D
The University of Tennessee Health Science Center	M,D
The University of Texas at El Paso	D
The University of Texas Health Science Center at San Antonio	M,D
The University of Texas Medical Branch	M,D
The University of Texas Southwestern Medical Center	D
University of the Incarnate Word	D
University of the Pacific	M,D
University of the Sciences	D
The University of Toledo	M,D
University of Toronto	M
University of Utah	D
University of Vermont	D
University of Washington	M,D
The University of Western Ontario	M,O
University of Wisconsin–La Crosse	D
University of Wisconsin–Madison	D
University of Wisconsin–Milwaukee	M,D*
Utica College	D
Virginia Commonwealth University	M,D
Walsh University	D
Washington University in St. Louis	D
Wayne State University	D
West Coast University	M,D
Western Carolina University	D
Western Kentucky University	D
Western University of Health Sciences	D
West Virginia University	M,D
Wheeling Jesuit University	D
Wichita State University	D
Widener University	M,D
Wingate University	D
Winston-Salem State University	D
Youngstown State University	D

PHYSICIAN ASSISTANT STUDIES

Adventist University of Health Sciences	M
Albany Medical College	M
Alderson Broaddus University	M
Arcadia University	M
A.T. Still University	M,D,O
Augsburg University	M
Augusta University	M
Baldwin Wallace University	M
Barry University	M
Baylor College of Medicine	M
Bay Path University	M
Bethel University (MN)	M,D,O
Bethel University (TN)	M
Boston University	M*
Bryant University	M
Butler University	M,D
California Baptist University	M
Campbell University	M,D
Carroll University	M
Case Western Reserve University	M*
Central Michigan University	M,D
Chapman University	M*
Chatham University	M
Christian Brothers University	M
Clarkson University	M
Cleveland State University	M
Daemen College	M
Des Moines University	M
Drexel University	M*
Duke University	M*
Duquesne University	M,D
D'Youville College	M
East Carolina University	M
Eastern Michigan University	M
Eastern Virginia Medical School	M
Elon University	M
Emory & Henry College	M,D
Emory University	M
Florida Gulf Coast University	M
Florida International University	M,D
Franciscan Missionaries of Our Lady University	M,D
Francis Marion University	M
Franklin Pierce University	M,D,O
Gannon University	M
Gardner-Webb University	M
The George Washington University	M
Grand Valley State University	M
Harding University	M
Hardin-Simmons University	M,D
High Point University	M,D
Hofstra University	M
Howard University	M,D
Idaho State University	M
Indiana State University	M,D
James Madison University	M
Jefferson College of Health Sciences	M
Johnson & Wales University	M
Keiser University	M
Kettering College	M
King's College	M
Le Moyne College	M
Lenoir-Rhyne University	M
Lock Haven University of Pennsylvania	M
Loma Linda University	M
Long Island University–LIU Brooklyn	M,D,O
Louisiana State University Health Sciences Center	M
Marietta College	M
Marquette University	M
Marywood University	M
MCPHS University	M
Medical University of South Carolina	M
Mercer University	M,D
Mercy College	M
Mercyhurst University	M
Methodist University	M
MGH Institute of Health Professions	M
Midwestern University, Downers Grove Campus	M
Midwestern University, Glendale Campus	M
Milligan College	M
Missouri State University	M
Monmouth University	M,D,O*
New York Institute of Technology	M
Northern Arizona University	M
Nova Southeastern University	M,D*
Ohio Dominican University	M
Oregon Health & Science University	M
Pace University	M
Pacific University	M
Philadelphia College of Osteopathic Medicine	M*
Quinnipiac University	M
Rocky Mountain College	M
Rocky Mountain University of Health Professions	M
Rocky Vista University	M
Rosalind Franklin University of Medicine and Science	M
Rush University	M
Rutgers University–Newark	M
Sacred Heart University	M
St. Ambrose University	M
St. Catherine University	M
Saint Francis University	M
Saint Louis University	M*
Salus University	M
Samuel Merritt University	M
Seton Hall University	M
Seton Hill University	M
Shenandoah University	M,D,O
Slippery Rock University of Pennsylvania	M
South College	M
Southern Illinois University Carbondale	M
South University	M
South University (GA)	M
Springfield College	M
Stephens College	M,O
Stony Brook University, State University of New York	M,D,O
Texas Tech University Health Sciences Center	M
Thomas Jefferson University	M
Touro College	M,D
Towson University	M
Trevecca Nazarene University	M
Trine University	M
Tufts University	M,D,O*
Union College (NE)	M
The University of Alabama at Birmingham	M
University of Arkansas for Medical Sciences	M,D
University of Bridgeport	M
University of Charleston	M
University of Colorado Denver	M
University of Dayton	M
University of Detroit Mercy	M,D,O
The University of Findlay	M,D
University of Florida	M
The University of Iowa	M*
University of Kentucky	M
University of Lynchburg	M
University of Mount Union	M
University of Nebraska Medical Center	M
University of New England	M,D
University of New Mexico	M
University of North Dakota	M
University of North Texas Health Science Center at Fort Worth	M,D
University of Oklahoma Health Sciences Center	M
University of Pittsburgh	M,D*
University of St. Francis (IL)	M,O
University of Saint Francis (IN)	M
University of South Alabama	M
University of South Dakota	M
University of Southern California	M*
The University of Tennessee Health Science Center	M,D
The University of Texas Health Science Center at San Antonio	M,D
The University of Texas Medical Branch	M
The University of Texas Rio Grande Valley	M
The University of Texas Southwestern Medical Center	M
University of the Cumberlands	M
The University of Toledo	M
University of Utah	M
University of Wisconsin–La Crosse	M
University of Wisconsin–Madison	M
Valparaiso University	M,D,O
Wayne State University	M
Weill Cornell Medicine	M
Western Michigan University	M
Western University of Health Sciences	M
Westfield State University	M
West Liberty University	M
Wichita State University	M
Wingate University	M
Yale University	M
York College of the City University of New York	M

PHYSICS

Alabama Agricultural and Mechanical University	M,D
The American University in Cairo	M,D,O
American University of Beirut	M,D
Arizona State University at the Tempe campus	M,D
Auburn University	M,D*
Ball State University	M
Baylor University	M,D
Binghamton University, State University of New York	M,D
Boston College	M,D
Boston University	D*
Bowling Green State University	M
Brandeis University	M,D
Brigham Young University	M,D
Brock University	M
Brooklyn College of the City University of New York	M
Brown University	M,D
Bryn Mawr College	M,D
California Institute of Technology	D
California State University, Fresno	M
California State University, Fullerton	M
California State University, Long Beach	M
California State University, Los Angeles	M
California State University, Northridge	M
Carleton University	M,D
Carnegie Mellon University	M,D
Case Western Reserve University	M,D*
The Catholic University of America	M,D
Central Michigan University	M,D
Christopher Newport University	M
City College of the City University of New York	M,D
Clark Atlanta University	M
Clarkson University	M,D
Clark University	D
Clemson University	M,D
Cleveland State University	M
The College of William and Mary	M,D*
Colorado School of Mines	M,D
Colorado State University	M,D
Columbia University	M,D*
Concordia University (Canada)	M,D
Cornell University	M,D
Creighton University	M
Dalhousie University	M,D
Dartmouth College	D*
Delaware State University	M,D
DePaul University	M,D
Drexel University	M,D*
Duke University	D*
East Carolina University	M,D
Eastern Michigan University	M
Emory University	D
Fisk University	M
Florida Agricultural and Mechanical University	M,D
Florida Atlantic University	M,D
Florida Institute of Technology	M,D
Florida International University	M,D
Florida State University	M,D
George Mason University	M,D
The George Washington University	M,D
Georgia Institute of Technology	M,D
Georgia State University	M,D
The Graduate Center, City University of New York	D
Hampton University	M,D
Harvard University	D*
Howard University	M,D
Hunter College of the City University of New York	M,D
Idaho State University	M,D
Illinois Institute of Technology	M,D
Indiana University Bloomington	M,D
Indiana University of Pennsylvania	M
Indiana University–Purdue University Indianapolis	M,D
Iowa State University of Science and Technology	M,D
Jackson State University	M,D
Johns Hopkins University	M,D*
Kansas State University	M,D
Kent State University	M,D
Lakehead University	M
Lehigh University	M,D
Lewis University	M
Louisiana State University and Agricultural & Mechanical College	M,D
Manhattanville College	M,O
Marshall University	M
Massachusetts Institute of Technology	M,D
McGill University	M,D
McMaster University	D
Memorial University of Newfoundland	M,D
Miami University	M
Michigan State University	M,D
Michigan Technological University	M,D
Minnesota State University Mankato	M
Mississippi State University	M,D
Missouri State University	M
Missouri University of Science and Technology	M,D
Montana State University	M,D
Naval Postgraduate School	M,D
New Mexico Institute of Mining and Technology	M,D
New Mexico State University	M,D
New York University	M,D,O*
North Carolina Agricultural and Technical State University	M
North Carolina Central University	M
North Carolina State University	M,D
North Dakota State University	M,D*
Northeastern University	M,D
Northern Arizona University	M,D
Northern Illinois University	M,D
Northwestern University	D
Oakland University	M,D
The Ohio State University	M,D
Ohio University	M,D
Oklahoma State University	M,D
Old Dominion University	M,D
Oregon State University	M,D
Pace University	M,O
Penn State University Park	M,D*
Pittsburg State University	M
Portland State University	M,D
Princeton University	D
Purdue University	M,D
Queens College of the City University of New York	M
Queen's University at Kingston	M,D
Rensselaer Polytechnic Institute	M,D
Rice University	M,D
Royal Military College of Canada	M
Rutgers University–New Brunswick	M,D
St. John Fisher College	M
San Diego State University	M
San Francisco State University	M
San Jose State University	M
Simon Fraser University	M,D
South Dakota School of Mines and Technology	M,D
South Dakota State University	M
Southern Illinois University Carbondale	M,D
Southern Methodist University	M,D
Southern University and Agricultural and Mechanical College	M
Stanford University	D
State University of New York College at Cortland	M
Stephen F. Austin State University	M

Stevens Institute of Technology	M,D,O
Stony Brook University, State University of New York	M,D
Syracuse University	M,D*
Teachers College, Columbia University	M,D
Temple University	M,D*
Texas A&M University	M,D
Texas A&M University–Commerce	M,O
Texas Christian University	M,D
Texas State University	M
Texas Tech University	M,D
Trent University	M
Tufts University	M,D*
Tulane University	M,D
Université de Moncton	M
Université de Montréal	M,D
Université de Sherbrooke	M,D
Université du Québec à Trois-Rivières	M,D
Université Laval	M,D
University at Albany, State University of New York	M,D
University at Buffalo, the State University of New York	M,D
The University of Akron	M
The University of Alabama	M,D
The University of Alabama at Birmingham	M,D
The University of Alabama in Huntsville	M,D
University of Alaska Fairbanks	M,D
University of Alberta	M,D
The University of Arizona	M,D
University of Arkansas	M,D
The University of British Columbia	M,D
University of Calgary	M,D
University of California, Berkeley	D
University of California, Davis	M,D
University of California, Irvine	M,D
University of California, Los Angeles	M,D*
University of California, Merced	M,D
University of California, Riverside	M,D
University of California, San Diego	M,D*
University of California, Santa Barbara	D
University of California, Santa Cruz	M,D*
University of Central Florida	M,D
University of Central Oklahoma	M
University of Chicago	M,D
University of Cincinnati	M,D
University of Colorado Boulder	M,D
University of Colorado Colorado Springs	D
University of Connecticut	M,D*
University of Delaware	M,D*
University of Denver	M,D
University of Florida	M,D
University of Georgia	M,D
University of Guelph	M,D
University of Hawaii at Manoa	M,D
University of Houston	M,D
University of Houston–Clear Lake	M
University of Idaho	M,D
University of Illinois at Chicago	M,D
University of Illinois at Urbana–Champaign	M,D
The University of Iowa	M,D*
The University of Kansas	M,D
University of Kentucky	M,D
University of Lethbridge	M,D
University of Louisiana at Lafayette	M
University of Louisville	M,D
University of Maine	M,D
The University of Manchester	M,D
University of Manitoba	M,D
University of Maryland, Baltimore County	M,D
University of Maryland, College Park	M,D
University of Massachusetts Amherst	M,D*
University of Massachusetts Dartmouth	M
University of Massachusetts Lowell	M,D
University of Memphis	M
University of Miami	M,D*
University of Michigan	D*
University of Minnesota, Duluth	M
University of Minnesota, Twin Cities Campus	M,D
University of Mississippi	M,D
University of Missouri	M,D
University of Missouri–Kansas City	M,D
University of Missouri–St. Louis	M,D
University of Nebraska–Lincoln	M,D
University of Nevada, Las Vegas	M,D
University of Nevada, Reno	M,D
University of New Brunswick Fredericton	M,D
University of New Hampshire	M,D
University of New Mexico	M,D
University of New Orleans	M,D
The University of North Carolina at Chapel Hill	M,D
University of North Dakota	M,D
University of Northern Iowa	M
University of Notre Dame	M,D
University of Oklahoma	M,D*
University of Oregon	M,D
University of Ottawa	M,D
University of Pennsylvania	M,D*
University of Pittsburgh	M,D*
University of Puerto Rico–Mayagüez	M
University of Puerto Rico–Río Piedras	M,D
University of Regina	M,D
University of Rhode Island	M,D*
University of Rochester	D*
University of Saskatchewan	M,D
University of South Carolina	M,D
University of South Dakota	M,D
University of Southern California	M,D*
University of Southern Mississippi	M,D
University of South Florida	M,D*
The University of Tennessee	M,D
The University of Texas at Arlington	M,D
The University of Texas at Austin	M,D
The University of Texas at Dallas	M,D
The University of Texas at El Paso	M
The University of Texas at San Antonio	M,D
The University of Texas Rio Grande Valley	M
The University of Toledo	M,D
University of Toronto	M,D
The University of Tulsa	M,D
University of Utah	M,D
University of Vermont	M
University of Victoria	M,D
University of Virginia	M,D
University of Washington	M,D
University of Waterloo	M,D
The University of Western Ontario	M,D
University of Windsor	M,D
University of Wisconsin–Madison	M,D
University of Wisconsin–Milwaukee	M,D*
Utah State University	M,D
Vanderbilt University	M,D*
Virginia Commonwealth University	M
Virginia Polytechnic Institute and State University	M,D
Wake Forest University	M,D
Washington State University	M,D
Washington University in St. Louis	D
Wayne State University	M,D
Wesleyan University	D
Western Illinois University	M
Western Kentucky University	M
Western Michigan University	M,D,O
West Virginia University	M,D
Wichita State University	M,D
Worcester Polytechnic Institute	M,D
Wright State University	M
Yale University	D
York University	M,D

PHYSIOLOGY

Albert Einstein College of Medicine	D
American College of Healthcare Sciences	M,O
American University of Beirut	M,D
Augusta University	D
Ball State University	M
Baylor University	M,D
Boston University	M,D*
Brigham Young University	M,D
Brown University	M,D
Case Western Reserve University	M,D*
Central Washington University	M
Columbia University	M,D*
Cornell University	M,D
Dalhousie University	M,D
Eastern Michigan University	M
East Tennessee State University	D
Georgetown University	M,D
Georgia Institute of Technology	M,D
Georgia State University	M,D
Gonzaga University	M,D
Howard University	D
Illinois State University	M,D
Indiana State University	M,D
James Madison University	M
Johns Hopkins University	D*
Kansas State University	M,D
Kent State University	M,D
Loma Linda University	D
Louisiana State University Health Sciences Center	D
Louisiana State University Health Sciences Center at Shreveport	M,D
Loyola University Chicago	M,D
Maharishi University of Management	D
Marquette University	M,D
Mayo Clinic Graduate School of Biomedical Sciences	M,D
McGill University	M,D
McMaster University	M,D
Medical College of Wisconsin	D
Michigan State University	M,D
Montclair State University	M
New York Medical College	M,D
New York University	D*
North Carolina State University	M,D
Northwestern University	M
Ohio University	M,D
Oregon Health & Science University	D
Oregon State University	M,D
Penn State University Park	M,D*
Purdue University	M,D
Queen's University at Kingston	M,D
Rocky Mountain University of Health Professions	D
Rosalind Franklin University of Medicine and Science	M,D
Rush University	D
Rutgers University–Newark	D
Rutgers University–New Brunswick	M,D
Saint Louis University	D*
Salisbury University	M
San Francisco State University	M
San Jose State University	M
Southern Illinois University Carbondale	M,D
Southern Methodist University	M,D
Stanford University	D
State University of New York Upstate Medical University	M,D
Stony Brook University, State University of New York	D
Teachers College, Columbia University	M,D
Tulane University	M
Universidad Central del Caribe	M,D
Université de Montréal	M,D
Université de Sherbrooke	M,D
Université Laval	M,D
University at Buffalo, the State University of New York	M,D
University of Alberta	M,D
The University of Arizona	M,D
University of Arkansas for Medical Sciences	M,D,O
University of Calgary	M,D
University of California, Berkeley	M,D
University of California, Davis	M,D
University of California, Irvine	D
University of California, Los Angeles	M,D*
University of Central Florida	M
University of Colorado Boulder	M,D
University of Connecticut	M,D*
University of Delaware	M,D*
University of Florida	M,D
University of Georgia	M,D
University of Guelph	M,D
University of Hawaii at Manoa	M,D
University of Illinois at Chicago	M,D
University of Illinois at Urbana–Champaign	M,D
The University of Iowa	M,D*
The University of Kansas	D
University of Kentucky	D
University of Louisville	M,D
The University of Manchester	M,D
University of Manitoba	M,D
University of Massachusetts Amherst	M,D*
University of Miami	D*
University of Michigan	M,D*
University of Minnesota, Duluth	M,D
University of Minnesota, Twin Cities Campus	D
University of Mississippi Medical Center	D
University of Missouri	M,D
University of Nebraska Medical Center	D
University of Nevada, Reno	D
University of New Mexico	M,D
University of North Texas Health Science Center at Fort Worth	M,D
University of Notre Dame	M,D
University of Oklahoma Health Sciences Center	M,D
University of Oregon	M,D
University of Pennsylvania	D*
University of Prince Edward Island	M,D
University of Puerto Rico–Medical Sciences Campus	M,D
University of Rochester	M,D*
University of Saskatchewan	M,D
University of South Dakota	M,D
University of Southern California	M*
University of South Florida	M,D*
The University of Tennessee	M,D
The University of Texas Medical Branch	M,D
University of Toronto	M,D
University of Utah	M,D
University of Virginia	D
University of Washington	D
The University of Western Ontario	M,D
University of Wisconsin–La Crosse	M
University of Wisconsin–Madison	M,D
University of Wyoming	M,D
Virginia Commonwealth University	M,D
Wake Forest University	D
Wayne State University	M,D,O
Weill Cornell Medicine	M,D
Western Michigan University	M
Wright State University	M
Yale University	D
Youngstown State University	M

PLANETARY AND SPACE SCIENCES

Air Force Institute of Technology	M,D
Alabama Agricultural and Mechanical University	M,D
Arizona State University at the Tempe campus	M,D
California Institute of Technology	M,D
Cornell University	D
Florida Institute of Technology	M,D
Hampton University	M,D
Harvard University	M,D*
Johns Hopkins University	M,D*
Massachusetts Institute of Technology	M,D
McGill University	M,D
St. Thomas University	M,D,O
The University of Arizona	M,D
University of Arkansas	M,D
University of California, Los Angeles	M,D*
University of California, Santa Cruz	M,D*
University of Chicago	D
University of Hawaii at Manoa	M,D
University of Houston	M,D
University of Michigan	M,D*
University of New Mexico	M,D
University of North Dakota	M
Washington University in St. Louis	D
Western Connecticut State University	M
Yale University	M,D
York University	M,D

PLANT BIOLOGY

Arizona State University at the Tempe campus	M,D
Clemson University	M,D
Cornell University	M,D
Illinois State University	M,D
Indiana University Bloomington	M,D
Iowa State University of Science and Technology	M,D
Michigan State University	M,D
New York University	M,D*
North Carolina State University	M,D
Northwestern University	M,D
Ohio University	M,D
Oklahoma State University	M,D
Penn State University Park	M,D*
Rutgers University–New Brunswick	M,D
Southern Illinois University Carbondale	M,D
Université Laval	M,D
University of Alberta	M,D
University of California, Berkeley	D
University of California, Davis	M,D
University of California, Riverside	M,D
University of Florida	M,D
University of Georgia	M,D
University of Illinois at Urbana–Champaign	M,D
University of Maryland, College Park	M,D
University of Massachusetts Amherst	M,D*
University of Minnesota, Twin Cities Campus	M,D
University of Oklahoma	M,D*
The University of Texas at Austin	M,D
University of Vermont	M,D
Washington University in St. Louis	D
Yale University	D

PLANT MOLECULAR BIOLOGY

Cornell University	M,D
Illinois State University	M,D
Oregon State University	D
Rutgers University–New Brunswick	M,D
University of California, Riverside	M,D
University of Florida	M,D
University of Massachusetts Amherst	M,D*

PLANT PATHOLOGY

Auburn University	M,D*
Colorado State University	M,D
Cornell University	M,D
Dalhousie University	M
Iowa State University of Science and Technology	M,D
Kansas State University	M,D
Louisiana State University and Agricultural & Mechanical College	M,D
Michigan State University	M,D
Montana State University	M,D
New Mexico State University	M
North Carolina State University	M,D
North Dakota State University	M,D*
The Ohio State University	M,D
Oklahoma State University	M,D
Oregon State University	M,D
Penn State University Park	M,D*
Purdue University	M,D
Rutgers University–New Brunswick	M,D
State University of New York College of Environmental Science and Forestry	M,D
Texas A&M University	M,D
The University of Arizona	M,D
University of Arkansas	M
University of California, Davis	M,D
University of California, Riverside	M,D
University of Florida	M,D
University of Georgia	M,D
University of Guelph	M,D
University of Hawaii at Manoa	M,D
University of Idaho	M,D
University of Kentucky	M,D
University of Maine	M,D
University of Minnesota, Twin Cities Campus	M,D
The University of Tennessee	M,D
University of Vermont	M,D,O
University of Wisconsin–Madison	M,D
Virginia Polytechnic Institute and State University	M,D
Washington State University	M,D
West Virginia University	M,D

PLANT PHYSIOLOGY

Cornell University	M,D
Dalhousie University	M

*M—masters degree; D—doctorate; O—other advanced degree; *—Close-Up and/or Display*

Oregon State University	M,D
Purdue University	M,D
University of Manitoba	M,D
University of Massachusetts Amherst	M,D*
The University of Tennessee	M,D
Virginia Polytechnic Institute and State University	M,D

PLANT SCIENCES

Alabama Agricultural and Mechanical University	M,D
American University of Beirut	M
Brigham Young University	M,D
California State University, Fresno	M
Colorado State University	M,D
Cornell University	M,D
Delaware State University	M
Illinois State University	M,D
Iowa State University of Science and Technology	M,D
Kansas State University	M,D,O
Lehman College of the City University of New York	D
McGill University	M,D,O
Michigan State University	M,D
Mississippi State University	M,D
Missouri State University	M
Montana State University	M,D
New Mexico State University	M
North Carolina Agricultural and Technical State University	M
North Dakota State University	M,D*
The Ohio State University	D
Oklahoma State University	M,D
Penn State University Park	M,D*
Purdue University	D
South Dakota State University	M,D
Southern Illinois University Carbondale	M
State University of New York College of Environmental Science and Forestry	M,D
Tennessee State University	M,D
Texas A&M University–Kingsville	M
Texas Tech University	M,D
Tuskegee University	M
The University of Arizona	M,D
University of Arkansas	D
The University of British Columbia	M,D
University of California, Riverside	M,D
University of Connecticut	M,D*
University of Delaware	M,D*
University of Florida	D
University of Georgia	M,D
University of Hawaii at Manoa	M,D
University of Idaho	M,D
University of Kentucky	M,D
The University of Manchester	M,D
University of Manitoba	M,D
University of Massachusetts Amherst	M,D*
University of Minnesota, Twin Cities Campus	M,D
University of Saskatchewan	M,D
The University of Tennessee	M
University of Vermont	M,D,O
University of Wisconsin–Madison	M,D
Utah State University	M,D
West Texas A&M University	M
West Virginia University	M,D

PLASMA PHYSICS

Princeton University	D
University of Colorado Boulder	M,D

PODIATRIC MEDICINE

Barry University	D
Des Moines University	D
Kent State University	D
Midwestern University, Glendale Campus	D
New York College of Podiatric Medicine	D
Rosalind Franklin University of Medicine and Science	D
Samuel Merritt University	D
Temple University	D*
Western University of Health Sciences	D

POLITICAL SCIENCE

Acadia University	M
American Public University System	M,D
American University	M,D,O
American University of Armenia	M
American University of Beirut	M,D
Appalachian State University	M
Arizona State University at the Tempe campus	M,D
Arkansas State University	M,O
Ashland University	M
Auburn University	M,D,O*
Auburn University at Montgomery	M,D
Ball State University	M
Baylor University	M,D
Binghamton University, State University of New York	M,D
Boise State University	M
Boston College	M,D
Boston University	D*
Brandeis University	M,D
Brigham Young University	M
Brock University	M
Brooklyn College of the City University of New York	M
Brown University	D
California Polytechnic State University, San Luis Obispo	M*
California State University, Chico	M
California State University, Fullerton	M
California State University, Long Beach	M
California State University, Los Angeles	M
California State University, Northridge	M
California State University, Sacramento	M
Carleton University	M,D
Case Western Reserve University	M,D*
The Catholic University of America	M,D
Central European University	M,D
Central Michigan University	M,O
The Citadel, The Military College of South Carolina	M
Claremont Graduate University	M,D
Clark Atlanta University	M,D
Colorado State University	M,D
Columbia University	M,D*
Columbus State University	M
Concordia University (Canada)	M,D
Converse College	M
Cornell University	D
Dalhousie University	M,D
Dominican University of California	M
Duke University	M,D*
East Carolina University	M,O
Eastern Illinois University	M
Eastern Kentucky University	M
East Stroudsburg University of Pennsylvania	M
Edinboro University of Pennsylvania	M
Emory University	D
Fairleigh Dickinson University, Metropolitan Campus	M
Florida Agricultural and Mechanical University	M
Florida Atlantic University	M
Florida International University	M,D
Florida State University	M,D
Fordham University	M
George Mason University	M,D
Georgetown University	M,D
The George Washington University	M,D
Georgia State University	M,D
Governors State University	M
The Graduate Center, City University of New York	M,D
Grambling State University	M,D
Harvard University	M,D*
Hillsdale College	M,D
Howard University	M,D
Idaho State University	M,D
Illinois State University	M
Indiana University Bloomington	M,D
Indiana University–Purdue University Indianapolis	M
Institute for Christian Studies	M,D
The Institute of World Politics	M,O
Iowa State University of Science and Technology	M
Jackson State University	M
Jacksonville State University	M
James Madison University	M
Johns Hopkins University	M,D,O*
Kansas State University	M
Kent State University	M,D
Lamar University	M
Lehigh University	M
Liberty University	M
Long Island University–LIU Brooklyn	M,D,O
Long Island University–LIU Post	M,O
Louisiana State University and Agricultural & Mechanical College	M,D
Loyola University Chicago	M,D
Marquette University	M
Marshall University	M
Massachusetts Institute of Technology	M,D
McGill University	M,D
McMaster University	M,D
Memorial University of Newfoundland	M
Miami University	M
Michigan State University	M,D
Middle Tennessee State University	M
Midwestern State University	M
Mississippi College	M,O
Mississippi State University	M,D
Missouri State University	M,O
Montclair State University	M,O
Murray State University	M
New Mexico Highlands University	M
New Mexico State University	M
The New School	M,D
New York University	M,D*
Northeastern Illinois University	M
Northeastern University	M,D
Northern Arizona University	M,D,O
Northern Illinois University	M,D
Northwestern University	D
The Ohio State University	D
Ohio University	M
Oklahoma State University	M,D
Penn State University Park	M,D*
Pepperdine University	M
Portland State University	M
Princeton University	D
Purdue University	M,D
Purdue University Global	M,O
Queen's University at Kingston	M,D
Regent University	M
Rice University	D
Rutgers University–Newark	M
Rutgers University–New Brunswick	M,D
St. John's University (NY)	M,O
Saint Louis University	M*
Sam Houston State University	M
San Diego State University	M
San Francisco State University	M
Simon Fraser University	M,D
Sonoma State University	M
Southern Connecticut State University	M
Southern Illinois University Carbondale	M,D
Southern New Hampshire University	M
Southern University and Agricultural and Mechanical College	M
Stanford University	M,D
Stony Brook University, State University of New York	M,D
Suffolk University	M,O
Sul Ross State University	M
Syracuse University	M,D,O*
Tarleton State University	M
Teachers College, Columbia University	M,D
Temple University	M,D*
Texas A&M International University	M
Texas A&M University	M,D
Texas A&M University–Central Texas	M,O
Texas A&M University–Commerce	M,D,O
Texas State University	M
Texas Tech University	M,D
Texas Woman's University	M
Tulane University	D
Universidad Nacional Pedro Henriquez Urena	M
Université de Montréal	M,D
Université du Québec à Montréal	M,D
Université Laval	M,D
University at Albany, State University of New York	M,D
University at Buffalo, the State University of New York	M,D
The University of Akron	M
The University of Alabama	M,D
University of Alberta	M,D
The University of Arizona	M,D
University of Arkansas	M
The University of British Columbia	M,D
University of Calgary	M,D
University of California, Berkeley	D
University of California, Davis	M,D
University of California, Irvine	D
University of California, Los Angeles	M,D*
University of California, Riverside	M,D
University of California, San Diego	M,D*
University of California, Santa Barbara	M,D
University of California, Santa Cruz	D*
University of Central Florida	M,D,O
University of Central Oklahoma	M
University of Chicago	D
University of Cincinnati	M,D
University of Colorado Boulder	M,D
University of Colorado Denver	M,D
University of Connecticut	M,D*
University of Dallas	M,D
University of Delaware	M,D*
University of Florida	M,D,O
University of Georgia	M,D
University of Guelph	M
University of Hawaii at Manoa	M,D
University of Houston	M,D
University of Idaho	M,D
University of Illinois at Chicago	M,D
University of Illinois at Springfield	M
University of Illinois at Urbana–Champaign	M,D
The University of Iowa	D*
The University of Kansas	M,D
University of Kentucky	M,D
University of Lethbridge	M,D
University of Louisville	M
The University of Manchester	M,D
University of Manitoba	M
University of Maryland, College Park	D
University of Massachusetts Amherst	M,D*
University of Memphis	M
University of Miami	M*
University of Michigan	D*
University of Michigan–Flint	M
University of Minnesota, Twin Cities Campus	D
University of Mississippi	M,D
University of Missouri	M,D,O
University of Missouri–Kansas City	M
University of Missouri–St. Louis	M,D
University of Montana	M
University of Nebraska at Omaha	M,O
University of Nebraska–Lincoln	M,D,O
University of Nevada, Las Vegas	M,D
University of Nevada, Reno	M,D
University of New Brunswick Fredericton	M
University of New Hampshire	M,O
University of New Mexico	M,D
University of New Orleans	M,D
University of North Alabama	M
The University of North Carolina at Chapel Hill	M,D,O
The University of North Carolina at Greensboro	M,O
University of Northern British Columbia	M,D,O
University of North Texas	M,D,O
University of Notre Dame	D
University of Oklahoma	M,D*
University of Oregon	M,D
University of Ottawa	M,D
University of Pennsylvania	M,D,O*
University of Pittsburgh	M,D*
University of Regina	M
University of Rhode Island	M*
University of Rochester	D*
University of Saskatchewan	M
University of South Africa	M,D
University of South Carolina	M,D
University of Southern California	M,D*
University of Southern Mississippi	M,D
University of South Florida	M,D,O*
The University of Tennessee	M,D
The University of Texas at Arlington	M
The University of Texas at Austin	M,D
The University of Texas at Dallas	M,D
The University of Texas at El Paso	M
The University of Texas at San Antonio	M
The University of Texas at Tyler	M
The University of Texas of the Permian Basin	M
The University of Toledo	M,O
University of Toronto	M,D
University of Utah	M,D
University of Victoria	M,D
University of Virginia	M,D
University of Washington	M,D
University of Waterloo	M,D
The University of Western Ontario	M,D
University of West Florida	M
University of Windsor	M
University of Wisconsin–Madison	D
University of Wisconsin–Milwaukee	M,D*
University of Wyoming	M
Utah State University	M
Vanderbilt University	M,D*
Villanova University	M
Virginia Commonwealth University	M,D,O
Virginia Polytechnic Institute and State University	M,O
Walden University	M,D,O
Washington State University	M,D,O
Washington University in St. Louis	D
Wayne State University	M,D
Western Illinois University	M
Western Kentucky University	M
Western Michigan University	M,D
Western Washington University	M
West Virginia University	M,D
Wilfrid Laurier University	M,D
Yale University	D
York University	M,D

POLYMER SCIENCE AND ENGINEERING

Auburn University	M,D*
California Polytechnic State University, San Luis Obispo	M*
Carnegie Mellon University	M,D
Case Western Reserve University	M,D*
The College of William and Mary	M,D*
Cornell University	M,D
DePaul University	M,D
Eastern Michigan University	M,O
Lehigh University	M,D
North Carolina State University	D
North Dakota State University	M,D*
Pittsburg State University	M
Stevens Institute of Technology	M,D,O
The University of Akron	M,D
University of Connecticut	M,D*
The University of Manchester	M,D
University of Massachusetts Amherst	M,D*
University of Massachusetts Lowell	M,D
University of Missouri–Kansas City	M,D
University of Southern Mississippi	M,D
Wayne State University	M,D,O

PORTUGUESE

Brigham Young University	M
Emory University	D,O
Harvard University	M,D*
Indiana University Bloomington	M,D
Michigan State University	M,D
New York University	M,D*
Northwestern University	D
The Ohio State University	M,D
Princeton University	D
Tulane University	M,D
University of California, Los Angeles	M*
University of California, Santa Barbara	M,D
University of Georgia	M,D
University of Illinois at Urbana–Champaign	M,D
The University of Manchester	D
University of Maryland, College Park	M,D
University of Massachusetts Amherst	M,D*
University of Massachusetts Dartmouth	M,D
University of Minnesota, Twin Cities Campus	M,D
University of New Mexico	M,D
The University of North Carolina at Chapel Hill	M,D
University of South Africa	M,D
The University of Tennessee	D
The University of Texas at Austin	M,D
University of Toronto	M,D
University of Washington	M
University of Wisconsin–Madison	M,D

University of Wisconsin–Milwaukee	M*
Vanderbilt University	M,D*
Yale University	D

PROJECT MANAGEMENT

Albertus Magnus College	M
Amberton University	M
American Business & Technology University	M
American InterContinental University Online	M
American University	M,O
Ashland University	M
Aspen University	M,O
Athabasca University	M,D,O
Avila University	M
Bellevue University	M
Boston University	M,O*
Brandeis University	M
Brenau University	M
California Intercontinental University	M,D
Capella University	M,D
Carlow University	M
The Catholic University of America	M,O
Christian Brothers University	M,O
The Citadel, The Military College of South Carolina	M,O
City University of Seattle	M,O
Colorado Christian University	M
Colorado State University–Global Campus	M
Colorado Technical University Aurora	M
Colorado Technical University Colorado Springs	M,D
Dallas Baptist University	M
DeSales University	M,O
DeVry University–Folsom Campus	M
Drexel University	M*
Elmhurst College	M
Embry-Riddle Aeronautical University–Worldwide	M
Everglades University	M
Ferris State University	M
Florida Institute of Technology	M,D
Geneva College	M
George Mason University	M,D
The George Washington University	M,D,O
Golden Gate University	M,D,O
Grand Canyon University	M
Granite State College	M
Grantham University	M,O
Harrisburg University of Science and Technology	M
Herzing University Online	M
Hult International Business School (United States)	M
IGlobal University	M
Iona College	M,O
King University	M
Lakeland University	M
Lasell College	M,O
Lawrence Technological University	M,D,O
Lebanon Valley College	M
Lehigh University	M
Lewis University	M
Liberty University	M,D
Lindenwood University	M,O
Marlboro College	M
Marymount University	M,O
Maryville University of Saint Louis	M,O
Meredith College	M
Metropolitan State University	M,D,O
Mississippi State University	M,D
Missouri State University	M
Montana Tech of The University of Montana	M
Morgan State University	M
Mount Aloysius College	M
National American University (TX)	M,D
New England College	M
New York University	M*
Northeastern University	M
Northwestern University	M
Northwest University	M
Norwich University	M
Oklahoma Christian University	M
Pacific States University	M,O
Point Loma Nazarene University	M
Polytechnic University of Puerto Rico, Miami Campus	M
Post University	M
Purdue University Global	M
Queen's University at Kingston	M
Regis University	M,O
Robert Morris University	M,D
Rochester Institute of Technology	O
Saint Leo University	M,D
Saint Mary's University of Minnesota	M,O
Saint Xavier University	M,O
Sam Houston State University	M
Southern Illinois University Edwardsville	M
Southern New Hampshire University	M,D,O
Stevens Institute of Technology	M,O
Stevenson University	M
Thomas Edison State University	M
Trident University International	M,D
Universidad del Turabo	M
Universidad Nacional Pedro Henriquez Urena	M
Université du Québec à Chicoutimi	M
Université du Québec à Montréal	M,O
Université du Québec à Rimouski	M,O
Université du Québec en Abitibi-Témiscamingue	M,O
Université du Québec en Outaouais	M,O
The University of Alabama in Huntsville	M,O
University of Calgary	M,D
University of California, Berkeley	O
University of Connecticut	M,D*
University of Dallas	M,D
University of Denver	M,O
University of Houston	M
University of Houston–Downtown	M
The University of Kansas	M
University of Louisiana at Lafayette	M
University of Management and Technology	M,D,O
The University of Manchester	M
University of Mary	M
University of Michigan–Dearborn	M
University of Nebraska at Omaha	M,D,O
University of North Alabama	M
University of Oklahoma	M,O*
University of Ottawa	M,O
University of Phoenix–Bay Area Campus	M,D
University of Phoenix–Online Campus	M,O
University of Phoenix–Phoenix Campus	M,O
University of Regina	M,O
The University of Tennessee at Chattanooga	M,O
The University of Texas at Dallas	M,D
University of Wisconsin–Platteville	M
University of Wisconsin–Stout	M
Virginia International University	M,O
Viterbo University	M
Walden University	M,D,O
Walsh College of Accountancy and Business Administration	M
Wayland Baptist University	M,D
Western Carolina University	M,O
Wilmington University	M
Wingate University	M

PSYCHIATRIC NURSING

Allen College	M,D
Alverno College	M,D
American University of Beirut	M
Anderson University (SC)	M,D
Arizona State University at the Tempe campus	M,D,O
Augusta University	D
Azusa Pacific University	M,D*
Binghamton University, State University of New York	M,D,O
Boston College	M,D
California State University, San Marcos	M
Case Western Reserve University	M*
Clarke University	D
Columbia University	M,O*
Creighton University	M,D,O
Drexel University	M*
East Tennessee State University	M,D,O
Fairfield University	M,D
Fairleigh Dickinson University, Florham Campus	M
Florida International University	M,D
Florida State University	D,O
Frontier Nursing University	M,D,O*
George Mason University	M,D,O
Georgia Southern University	M
Georgia State University	M,D,O
Hofstra University	M
Hunter College of the City University of New York	M,D,O
Husson University	M,O
Jacksonville University	M*
James Madison University	M,D
Johns Hopkins University	O*
Kent State University	M,D
Lincoln Memorial University	M
McNeese State University	M,O
MGH Institute of Health Professions	M,D,O
Midwestern State University	M
Molloy College	M,D,O
Monmouth University	M,D,O*
Montana State University	M,D,O
National University	M,O
New Mexico State University	M,D,O
New York University	M,D,O*
Nicholls State University	M
Northeastern University	M,D,O
Nova Southeastern University	M,D*
Oregon Health & Science University	M
Pontifical Catholic University of Puerto Rico	M
Rivier University	M,D
Rush University	D
Sage Graduate School	M,O
Saint Francis Medical Center College of Nursing	M,D,O
Shenandoah University	M,D,O
Southern Adventist University	M,D
Southern Arkansas University–Magnolia	M
Stony Brook University, State University of New York	M,D,O
Tennessee Technological University	D
Uniformed Services University of the Health Sciences	M,D*
University at Buffalo, the State University of New York	M,D,O
The University of Alabama at Birmingham	M,D
University of Colorado Denver	M,D
University of Delaware	M,O*
The University of Kansas	M,D,O
University of Louisville	M,D
University of Maryland, Baltimore	M,D,O
University of Michigan–Flint	M,D,O
University of Minnesota, Twin Cities Campus	M,D
University of Missouri	M,D,O
University of Missouri–St. Louis	D,O
University of New Hampshire	M,D,O
The University of North Carolina at Chapel Hill	M,D,O
University of North Dakota	M,D,O
University of Pennsylvania	M*
University of Pittsburgh	M,D*
University of Puerto Rico–Medical Sciences Campus	M
University of Rochester	M,D*
University of St. Francis (IL)	M,D,O
University of Saint Joseph	M,D
University of San Diego	M,D
University of South Carolina	M,O
University of Southern Indiana	M,D,O
University of Southern Maine	M,D,O
The University of Tennessee Health Science Center	D,O
The University of Texas at Austin	M,D
The University of Texas Health Science Center at San Antonio	M,D,O
The University of Texas Rio Grande Valley	M,O
University of Virginia	M,D
University of Wisconsin–Madison	D
Valdosta State University	M
Vanderbilt University	M,D,O*
Virginia Commonwealth University	M,D,O
Washington State University	M,D,O
Wayne State University	M,D
West Virginia Wesleyan College	M,O
Wright State University	M

PSYCHOANALYSIS AND PSYCHOTHERAPY

Adler Graduate School	M
Argosy University, Chicago	D
Atlantic University	O
Boston Graduate School of Psychoanalysis	M,D,O
Immaculata University	M,D,O
Naropa University	M
The New School	M,D
New York University	M,D,O*
Prescott College	M
University of Manitoba	M

PSYCHOLOGY—GENERAL

Abilene Christian University	M
Acadia University	M
Adelphi University	M
Alabama Agricultural and Mechanical University	M,O
Alliant International University–Fresno	M,D
Alliant International University–Los Angeles	M,D
Alliant International University–Sacramento	M,D
Alliant International University–San Diego	M,D
Alliant International University–San Francisco	M,D,O
American International College	M,D,O
American University	M,D,O
The American University in Cairo	M,O
American University of Beirut	M,D
Andrews University	M,D,O
Angelo State University	M
Antioch University Los Angeles	M
Appalachian State University	M
Arcadia University	M,D,O
Argosy University, Atlanta	M,D,O
Argosy University, Chicago	M,D
Argosy University, Hawai`i	M,D,O
Argosy University, Los Angeles	M,D
Argosy University, Northern Virginia	M,D
Argosy University, Orange County	M,D
Argosy University, Phoenix	M,D
Argosy University, Seattle	M,D,O
Argosy University, Tampa	M,D
Argosy University, Twin Cities	M,D,O
Arizona State University at the Tempe campus	M,D
Arkansas Tech University	M
Auburn University	M,D*
Auburn University at Montgomery	M
Augusta University	M
Austin Peay State University	M
Avila University	M
Azusa Pacific University	M*
Ball State University	M
Barry University	M,O
Baylor University	M,D
Binghamton University, State University of New York	D
Biola University	D
Boston College	D
Boston Graduate School of Psychoanalysis	M
Boston University	M,D*
Bowling Green State University	M,D
Brandeis University	M,D
Brandman University	M
Brenau University	M
Bridgewater State University	M
Brigham Young University	D
Brock University	M,D
Brooklyn College of the City University of New York	M,D
Brown University	M,D
Bucknell University	M
California Coast University	M
California Institute of Integral Studies	M,D,O
California Lutheran University	M,D
California Polytechnic State University, San Luis Obispo	M*
California State Polytechnic University, Pomona	M
California State University, Chico	M
California State University, Dominguez Hills	M
California State University, Fresno	M,O
California State University, Fullerton	M
California State University, Long Beach	M
California State University, Los Angeles	M
California State University, Northridge	M
California State University, Sacramento	M
California State University, San Bernardino	M
California State University, San Marcos	M
California State University, Stanislaus	M
Cambridge College	M,O
Cameron University	M
Capella University	M,D
Cardinal Stritch University	M
Carleton University	M,D
Carlos Albizu University	M,D
Carlos Albizu University, Miami Campus	M,D
Carlow University	M
Carnegie Mellon University	D
Case Western Reserve University	M,D*
Castleton University	M
The Catholic University of America	M,D
Central Connecticut State University	M
Central Michigan University	M,D,O
Central Washington University	M,O
Chestnut Hill College	M,D,O
The Chicago School of Professional Psychology	M,D
The Chicago School of Professional Psychology at Irvine	D
The Chicago School of Professional Psychology: Online	M,D
The Citadel, The Military College of South Carolina	M,O
City College of the City University of New York	M,D
Claremont Graduate University	M,D,O
Clayton State University	M
Cleveland State University	M,D,O
The College at Brockport, State University of New York	M
College of Saint Elizabeth	M,D
College of St. Joseph	M
The College of William and Mary	M*
Colorado State University	M,D
Columbia University	M,D*
Concordia University (Canada)	M
Concordia University Chicago	M
Cornell University	D
Dalhousie University	M,D
Dartmouth College	D*
DePaul University	M,D
Divine Mercy University	M
Drexel University	M,D*
Duke University	D*
Duquesne University	D
East Central University	M
Eastern Illinois University	M,O
Eastern Kentucky University	M,O
Eastern Michigan University	M,D
Eastern Washington University	M,O
East Tennessee State University	D
Elizabeth City State University	M
Emory University	D
Emporia State University	M
Fairleigh Dickinson University, Florham Campus	M,O
Fairleigh Dickinson University, Metropolitan Campus	M,D,O
Fayetteville State University	M
Fielding Graduate University	M,D,O
Fisk University	M
Fitchburg State University	O
Florida Agricultural and Mechanical University	M
Florida Atlantic University	M
Florida Institute of Technology	M,D
Florida International University	M,D
Florida State University	M,D
Fordham University	M,D
Fort Hays State University	M,O
Francis Marion University	M,O
Frostburg State University	M
Gardner-Webb University	M
Geneva College	M
George Mason University	M,D,O
Georgetown University	D
The George Washington University	M,D,O
Georgia Institute of Technology	M,D
Georgia Southern University	M,D
Georgia State University	D
Goddard College	M
Golden Gate University	M,D,O

*M—masters degree; D—doctorate; O—other advanced degree; *—Close-Up and/or Display*

Governors State University	M
The Graduate Center, City University of New York	D
Grand Canyon University	D
Hampton University	M
Hardin-Simmons University	M
Harvard University	D*
Hofstra University	M,D
Hood College	M,O*
Houston Baptist University	M
Howard University	M,D
Humboldt State University	M
Hunter College of the City University of New York	M,O
Idaho State University	D
Illinois Institute of Technology	M,D
Illinois State University	M,D,O
Immaculata University	M,D,O
Indiana State University	M,D
Indiana Tech	M
Indiana University Bloomington	D
Indiana University of Pennsylvania	M,D
Indiana University–Purdue University Indianapolis	M,D
Inter American University of Puerto Rico, Metropolitan Campus	M,D
Inter American University of Puerto Rico, San Germán Campus	M,D
Iona College	M,O
Iowa State University of Science and Technology	M,D
Jackson State University	D
Jacksonville State University	M
James Madison University	M
John F. Kennedy University	M,D,O
Johns Hopkins University	D*
Kansas State University	M,D
Kean University	M
Keiser University	M,D
Kent State University	M,D
Kentucky State University	M
Lakehead University	M,D
Lamar University	M
La Salle University	M,D
Laurentian University	M
Lehigh University	M,D
Lesley University	M,D,O
LeTourneau University	M
Liberty University	M,D,O
Lipscomb University	M,O
Loma Linda University	D
Long Island University–LIU Brooklyn	M,D,O
Long Island University–LIU Post	M,O
Louisiana State University and Agricultural & Mechanical College	M,D
Loyola University Maryland	M,D,O
Lynn University	M
Madonna University	M
Mansfield University of Pennsylvania	M
Marietta College	M
Marist College	M,O
Marquette University	D
Marshall University	M,D,O
Martin University	M
Marywood University	M
McGill University	M,D
McMaster University	M,D
McNeese State University	M,O
Medaille College	M,D
Memorial University of Newfoundland	M,D
Mercy College	M
Meredith College	M
Miami University	M,D
Michigan School of Professional Psychology	M,D
Michigan State University	M,D
Middle Tennessee State University	M,O
Millersville University of Pennsylvania	M
Minnesota State University Mankato	M,D
Mississippi State University	M,D
Missouri State University	M,O
Monmouth University	M,O*
Montana State University	M
Montana State University Billings	M
Montclair State University	M
Morehead State University	M
Morgan State University	M,D
Murray State University	M,O
Naropa University	M
National Louis University	M,D,O
New Mexico Highlands University	M
New Mexico State University	M,D
The New School	M,D
New York Medical College	M,D,O
New York University	M,D,O*
Norfolk State University	M,D
North Carolina Central University	M
North Carolina State University	D
Northcentral University	M,D,O
North Dakota State University	M,D*
Northeastern State University	M
Northeastern University	M,D
Northern Arizona University	M
Northern Illinois University	M,D
Northern Michigan University	M
Northwestern State University of Louisiana	M
Northwestern University	D
Northwest University	M,D
Nova Southeastern University	M,D,O*
The Ohio State University	D
Ohio University	D
Oklahoma State University	M,D
Old Dominion University	M,D
Oregon State University	M,D
Our Lady of the Lake University	M
Pace University	M
Pacifica Graduate Institute	M,D
Pacific University	M,D
Palo Alto University	M,D
Penn State Harrisburg	M,D,O
Penn State University Park	M,D*
Pepperdine University	M,D
Philadelphia College of Osteopathic Medicine	M,D,O*
Phillips Graduate University	M
Pittsburg State University	M
Pontifical Catholic University of Puerto Rico	M,D
Pontificia Universidad Catolica Madre y Maestra	M
Portland State University	M,D,O
Princeton University	D
Purdue University	D
Queens College of the City University of New York	M
Queen's University at Kingston	M,D
Radford University	M
Rhode Island College	M,O
Rice University	M,D
Rivier University	M
Roberts Wesleyan College	M,D
Rochester Institute of Technology	M,O
Roosevelt University	M,D
Rosalind Franklin University of Medicine and Science	M,D
Rowan University	M,O
Rutgers University–Camden	M
Rutgers University–Newark	D
Rutgers University–New Brunswick	D
Sage Graduate School	M,O
St. Cloud State University	M,D
St. John's University (NY)	M
Saint Joseph's University	M,O*
Saint Louis University	M,D*
Saint Mary's University (Canada)	M,D
Salem State University	M,O
Sam Houston State University	M,D,O
San Diego State University	M,D
San Francisco State University	M,O
San Jose State University	M
Saybrook University	M,D
The Seattle School of Theology and Psychology	M
Seattle University	M
Seton Hall University	M,D
Shippensburg University of Pennsylvania	M
Simon Fraser University	M,D
Sofia University	M,D
Southeastern Baptist Theological Seminary	M,D
Southeastern Louisiana University	M
Southern Adventist University	M
Southern California Seminary	M,D
Southern Connecticut State University	M
Southern Illinois University Carbondale	M,D
Southern Illinois University Edwardsville	M,O
Southern Methodist University	D
Southern Nazarene University	M
Southern New Hampshire University	M
Southern Oregon University	M
Southern University and Agricultural and Mechanical College	M
Southwestern College (NM)	O
Spalding University	M,D
Stanford University	D
State University of New York at New Paltz	M,O
State University of New York at Plattsburgh	M,O
Stephen F. Austin State University	M
Stony Brook University, State University of New York	M,D
Suffolk University	M,D,O
Sul Ross State University	M
Syracuse University	D*
Teachers College, Columbia University	M,D
Temple University	M,D*
Tennessee State University	M
Texas A&M International University	M
Texas A&M University	M,D
Texas A&M University–Commerce	M,D,O
Texas A&M University–Corpus Christi	M
Texas A&M University–Kingsville	M
Texas A&M University–Texarkana	M
Texas Christian University	M,D
Texas Southern University	M
Texas State University	M
Texas Tech University	M,D
Texas Woman's University	M,D,O
Tiffin University	M
Towson University	M
Tufts University	M,D*
Tulane University	M,D
Uniformed Services University of the Health Sciences	D*
Union College (KY)	M
Universidad de las Americas, A.C.	M
Universidad de las Américas Puebla	M
Université de Montréal	M,D
Université de Sherbrooke	M
Université du Québec à Montréal	D
Université du Québec à Trois-Rivières	D,O
Université Laval	D
University at Albany, State University of New York	M,D
University at Buffalo, the State University of New York	M,D
The University of Akron	M,D
The University of Alabama	D
The University of Alabama at Birmingham	M,D
The University of Alabama in Huntsville	M
University of Alaska Anchorage	M,D
University of Alaska Fairbanks	D
University of Alberta	M,D
The University of Arizona	M,D
University of Arkansas	M,D
University of Arkansas at Little Rock	M
The University of British Columbia	M,D
University of Calgary	M,D
University of California, Berkeley	D
University of California, Davis	D
University of California, Irvine	D
University of California, Los Angeles	M,D*
University of California, Merced	M,D
University of California, Riverside	D
University of California, San Diego	D*
University of California, Santa Barbara	D
University of California, Santa Cruz	D*
University of Central Arkansas	M,D,O
University of Central Florida	M,D
University of Central Missouri	M,D,O
University of Central Oklahoma	M
University of Chicago	D
University of Cincinnati	D
University of Colorado Boulder	M,D
University of Colorado Colorado Springs	M,D
University of Connecticut	M,D*
University of Dallas	M
University of Dayton	M
University of Delaware	D*
University of Denver	M,D,O
University of Florida	M,D
University of Georgia	D
University of Guelph	M,D
University of Hartford	M,D
University of Hawaii at Manoa	M,D,O
University of Houston	M,D
University of Houston–Clear Lake	M
University of Houston–Victoria	M
University of Idaho	M,D
University of Illinois at Chicago	M,D
University of Illinois at Urbana–Champaign	M,D
University of Indianapolis	M,D
The University of Iowa	M,D,O*
The University of Kansas	M,D,O
University of Kentucky	M,D
University of La Verne	M,D
University of Lethbridge	M,D
University of Louisiana at Lafayette	M
University of Louisiana at Monroe	M
University of Louisville	D
University of Maine	M,D
The University of Manchester	M,D
University of Manitoba	M,D
University of Maryland, Baltimore County	M,D
University of Maryland, College Park	M,D
University of Massachusetts Amherst	M,D*
University of Massachusetts Dartmouth	M,O
University of Massachusetts Lowell	M
University of Memphis	M,D,O
University of Miami	M,D*
University of Michigan	D,O*
University of Minnesota, Twin Cities Campus	D
University of Missouri	M,D,O
University of Missouri–Kansas City	M,D
University of Missouri–St. Louis	M,D,O
University of Montana	M,D,O
University of Nebraska at Omaha	M,D,O
University of Nebraska–Lincoln	M,D
University of Nevada, Las Vegas	M,D,O
University of Nevada, Reno	M,D
University of New Brunswick Fredericton	M,D
University of New Brunswick Saint John	M,D
University of New Hampshire	D
University of New Mexico	D
University of New Orleans	M,D
The University of North Carolina at Chapel Hill	D
The University of North Carolina at Charlotte	M,D,O
The University of North Carolina at Greensboro	M,D
The University of North Carolina Wilmington	M,D
University of North Dakota	M,D
University of Northern British Columbia	M,D,O
University of Northern Iowa	M
University of North Florida	M
University of North Texas	M,D,O
University of Notre Dame	D
University of Oklahoma	M,D,O*
University of Oregon	M,D
University of Ottawa	D
University of Pennsylvania	D*
University of Philosophical Research	M
University of Phoenix–Online Campus	M,O
University of Phoenix–Phoenix Campus	M
University of Pittsburgh	D*
University of Puerto Rico–Río Piedras	M,D
University of Regina	M,D
University of Rhode Island	M,D*
University of Rochester	D*
University of Saint Mary	M
University of Saskatchewan	M,D
University of South Africa	M,D
University of South Alabama	M
University of South Carolina	M,D
University of South Dakota	M,D
University of Southern California	M,D*
University of Southern Mississippi	M,D
University of South Florida	D*
University of South Florida, St. Petersburg	M
The University of Tennessee	M,D
The University of Tennessee at Chattanooga	M
The University of Texas at Arlington	M,D
The University of Texas at Austin	D
The University of Texas at Dallas	M,D
The University of Texas at El Paso	M,D
The University of Texas at San Antonio	M,D
The University of Texas at Tyler	M
The University of Texas of the Permian Basin	M
The University of Texas Rio Grande Valley	M
University of the Pacific	M
University of the Rockies	M,D
University of the West	M
The University of Toledo	M,D
University of Toronto	M,D
The University of Tulsa	M,D
University of Utah	D
University of Vermont	D
University of Victoria	M,D
University of Virginia	M,D
University of Washington	M,D
University of Waterloo	M,D
The University of Western Ontario	M,D
University of West Florida	M
University of West Georgia	M,D,O
University of Windsor	M,D
University of Wisconsin–Eau Claire	M,O
University of Wisconsin–La Crosse	M,O
University of Wisconsin–Madison	D
University of Wisconsin–Milwaukee	M,D*
University of Wisconsin–Oshkosh	M
University of Wisconsin–Whitewater	M,O
University of Wyoming	M,D
Utah State University	M,D
Valdosta State University	M,O
Vanderbilt University	D*
Villanova University	M
Virginia Polytechnic Institute and State University	M,D
Virginia State University	M,D
Wake Forest University	M
Walden University	M,D,O
Washburn University	M
Washington State University	M,D
Washington University in St. Louis	D
Wayne State University	M,D
Webster University	M
West Chester University of Pennsylvania	M,D,O
Western Carolina University	M
Western Illinois University	M,O
Western Kentucky University	M,O
Western Michigan University	M,D
Western Washington University	M
Westfield State University	M
West Texas A&M University	M
West Virginia University	M,D
Wheaton College	M,D
Wichita State University	D
Widener University	
Wilfrid Laurier University	M,D
William Carey University	M
William James College	M,D,O
Winthrop University	M,O
Wisconsin School of Professional Psychology	M,D
The Wright Institute	D
Wright State University	M,D
Xavier University	M,D*
Yale University	D
Yeshiva University	M,D
York University	M,D
Youngstown State University	M

PUBLIC ADMINISTRATION

Adams State University	M
Adler University	M
Albany State University	M
Alfred University	M
American University	M,D,O
The American University in Cairo	M,O
American University of Beirut	M,D
Anabaptist Mennonite Biblical Seminary	M,O
Anna Maria College	M
Appalachian State University	M
Argosy University, Chicago	M,D
Argosy University, Los Angeles	M,D
Argosy University, Northern Virginia	M,D,O

Argosy University, Orange County	M,D,O
Argosy University, Phoenix	M,D
Argosy University, Seattle	M,D
Argosy University, Tampa	M,D
Argosy University, Twin Cities	M,D
Arizona State University at the Tempe campus	M,D
Arkansas State University	M,O
Auburn University	M,D,O*
Auburn University at Montgomery	M,D
Ball State University	M,O
Barry University	M
Baruch College of the City University of New York	M*
Baylor University	M,D
Belhaven University (MS)	M
Bellevue University	M
Binghamton University, State University of New York	M
Boise State University	M,D,O
Bowie State University	M
Bowling Green State University	M
Brandman University	M
Bridgewater State University	M
Brigham Young University	M
California Baptist University	M
California State Polytechnic University, Pomona	M
California State University, Bakersfield	M
California State University, Chico	M
California State University, Dominguez Hills	M
California State University, East Bay	M
California State University, Fresno	M
California State University, Fullerton	M
California State University, Long Beach	M,O
California State University, Los Angeles	M
California State University, Northridge	M,O
California State University, Sacramento	M
California State University, San Bernardino	M
California State University, Stanislaus	M
Capella University	M,D
Carleton University	M,D
Carnegie Mellon University	M
Central European University	M,D
Central Michigan University	M,O
Cheyney University of Pennsylvania	M
City College of the City University of New York	M,D
Clark Atlanta University	M
Clark University	M,O
Clemson University	M,D,O
Cleveland State University	M,D,O
The College at Brockport, State University of New York	M,O
College of Charleston	M
The College of New Rochelle	M
College of Saint Elizabeth	M,O
Columbia University	M*
Columbus State University	M
Concordia University (Canada)	M,D
Concordia University Wisconsin	M
Copenhagen Business School	M,D
Cumberland University	M
Dalhousie University	M,O
DePaul University	M
DeVry University–Folsom Campus	M
Drake University	M
East Carolina University	M,O
Eastern Kentucky University	M
Eastern Michigan University	M,O
Eastern University	D,O
Eastern Washington University	M
East Stroudsburg University of Pennsylvania	M
East Tennessee State University	M,O
The Evergreen State College	M
Excelsior College	M
Fairfield University	M
Fairleigh Dickinson University, Florham Campus	M
Fairleigh Dickinson University, Metropolitan Campus	M,O
Florida Agricultural and Mechanical University	M
Florida Atlantic University	M,D
Florida Gulf Coast University	M
Florida Institute of Technology	M,D
Florida International University	M,D
Florida National University	M
Florida State University	M,D,O
Framingham State University	M
Gallaudet University	M,D,O
Gannon University	M
George Mason University	M
The George Washington University	M,D
Georgia College & State University	M
Georgia Southern University	M
Georgia State University	M,D,O
Golden Gate University	M,D,O
Governors State University	M
Grambling State University	M
Grand Valley State University	M
Hamline University	M,D
Harvard University	M*
Hawai`i Pacific University	M
Hilbert College	M
Hood College	M,O*
Howard University	M
Idaho State University	M
IGlobal University	M
Illinois Institute of Technology	M
Indiana State University	M
Indiana University Bloomington	M,D,O
Indiana University Kokomo	M,O
Indiana University Northwest	M,O
Indiana University–Purdue University Indianapolis	M,O
Indiana University South Bend	M,O
Institute of Public Administration	M,O
Instituto Tecnológico y de Estudios Superiores de Monterrey, Campus Ciudad Juárez	M
International University in Geneva	M,D
Iowa State University of Science and Technology	M
Jackson State University	M,D
James Madison University	M
John Jay College of Criminal Justice of the City University of New York	M
Johns Hopkins University	M,O*
Kansas State University	M
Kean University	M
Kennesaw State University	M
Kent State University	M,D
Kentucky State University	M,D
Kutztown University of Pennsylvania	M
Lamar University	M
Liberty University	M,D
Lincoln University (MO)	M
Lindenwood University	M
Lipscomb University	M
London Metropolitan University	M,D
Long Island University–Hudson	M,O
Long Island University–LIU Brooklyn	M,O
Long Island University–LIU Post	M,O
Louisiana State University and Agricultural & Mechanical College	M,D
Marist College	M
Marshall University	M
Marywood University	M
McMaster University	M,D
Metropolitan College of New York	M
Mid-America Christian University	M
Middlebury Institute of International Studies at Monterey	M
Minnesota State University Mankato	M
Mississippi State University	M,D
Missouri State University	M,O
Montana State University	M
Morehead State University	M
National University	M
New Charter University	M
New Mexico State University	M
New York University	M,D,O*
North Carolina Central University	M
North Carolina State University	M,D
Northeastern University	M,D
Northern Arizona University	M,D,O
Northern Illinois University	M
Northern Kentucky University	M,O
Northwestern University	M
Norwich University	M
Notre Dame de Namur University	M
Nova Southeastern University	M*
Oakland University	M,O
The Ohio State University	M,D
Ohio University	M,O
Old Dominion University	M
Pace University	M
Park University	M,O
Penn State Harrisburg	M,D,O
Pontifical Catholic University of Puerto Rico	M
Portland State University	M,D,O
Post University	M
Regent University	M
Reinhardt University	M
Rhode Island College	M
Roger Williams University	M
Rutgers University–Camden	M
Rutgers University–Newark	M,D
Sacred Heart University	M
Saginaw Valley State University	M
St. John's University (NY)	M,O
St. Mary's University (United States)	M,O
Saint Mary's University of Minnesota	M
Saint Peter's University	M
St. Thomas University	M,O
Sam Houston State University	M
San Diego State University	M
San Francisco State University	M
San Jose State University	M
Savannah State University	M
Seattle University	M
Seton Hall University	M,O
Shippensburg University of Pennsylvania	M
Sonoma State University	M
Southeast Missouri State University	M
Southern Arkansas University–Magnolia	M
Southern Illinois University Carbondale	M
Southern Illinois University Edwardsville	M
Southern New Hampshire University	M,D,O
Southern University and Agricultural and Mechanical College	M
Southern Utah University	M
South University (GA)	M
South University (AL)	M
South University	M
Stephen F. Austin State University	M
Strayer University	M
Suffolk University	M
Syracuse University	M,D*
Tarleton State University	M
Tennessee State University	M,D
Texas A&M International University	M
Texas A&M University	M,O
Texas A&M University–Corpus Christi	M
Texas Southern University	M
Texas State University	M
Texas Tech University	M,D
Thomas Edison State University	M
Trident University International	M,D
Troy University	M
Tufts University	O*
Université de Moncton	M
Université de Sherbrooke	M
Université du Québec à Montréal	M
Université du Québec, École nationale d'administration publique	D,O
University at Albany, State University of New York	M,D,O
The University of Akron	M
The University of Alabama	M,D
The University of Alabama at Birmingham	M
University of Alaska Anchorage	M
University of Alaska Southeast	M
The University of Arizona	M,D,O
University of Arkansas	M
University of Arkansas at Little Rock	M
University of Baltimore	M,D
University of Central Florida	M,O
University of Central Oklahoma	M
University of Colorado Colorado Springs	M
University of Colorado Denver	M,D
University of Connecticut	M*
University of Dayton	M
University of Delaware	M*
University of Evansville	M
The University of Findlay	M,D
University of Georgia	M,D
University of Guam	M
University of Guelph	M
University of Hawaii at Manoa	M,O
University of Houston	M,D
University of Idaho	M,D
University of Illinois at Chicago	M,D
University of Illinois at Springfield	M,D,O
The University of Kansas	M,D,O
University of Kentucky	M,D,O
University of La Verne	M,D
University of Louisiana at Monroe	M
University of Louisville	M,D
University of Management and Technology	M,O
University of Manitoba	M
University of Maryland, College Park	M
University of Massachusetts Amherst	M*
University of Massachusetts Boston	M
University of Massachusetts Dartmouth	M,O
University of Memphis	M,O
University of Michigan–Dearborn	M
University of Michigan–Flint	M
University of Missouri	M,D,O
University of Missouri–Kansas City	M,D
University of Missouri–St. Louis	M,D,O
University of Montana	M
University of Nebraska at Omaha	M,D,O
University of Nevada, Las Vegas	M,D,O
University of Nevada, Reno	M
University of New Brunswick Fredericton	M
University of New Hampshire	M,O
University of New Haven	M,O*
University of New Mexico	M
University of New Orleans	M
The University of North Carolina at Chapel Hill	M
The University of North Carolina at Charlotte	M,O
The University of North Carolina at Pembroke	M
The University of North Carolina Wilmington	M
University of North Dakota	M
University of North Florida	M,O
University of North Georgia	M
University of North Texas	M,D,O
University of North Texas at Dallas	M
University of Oklahoma	M*
University of Oregon	M
University of Ottawa	D,O
University of Pennsylvania	M,O*
University of Phoenix–Bay Area Campus	M,D
University of Phoenix–Central Valley Campus	M
University of Phoenix–Dallas Campus	M
University of Phoenix–Hawaii Campus	M
University of Phoenix–Houston Campus	M
University of Phoenix–Las Vegas Campus	M
University of Phoenix–Online Campus	M,O
University of Phoenix–Phoenix Campus	M
University of Phoenix–Sacramento Valley Campus	M
University of Phoenix–San Antonio Campus	M
University of Phoenix–San Diego Campus	M
University of Pittsburgh	M,D*
University of Puerto Rico–Río Piedras	M
University of Regina	M,D,O
University of Rhode Island	M*
University of St. Thomas (TX)	M
University of San Francisco	M
University of South Africa	M,D
University of South Alabama	M
University of South Carolina	M
University of Southern California	M,O*
University of Southern Indiana	M
University of South Florida	O*
The University of Tennessee	M
The University of Tennessee at Chattanooga	M,O
The University of Texas at Arlington	M
The University of Texas at Austin	M,D
The University of Texas at Dallas	M,D
The University of Texas at San Antonio	M
The University of Texas at Tyler	M
The University of Texas Rio Grande Valley	M
University of the District of Columbia	M
The University of Toledo	M,O
University of Utah	M,D
University of Vermont	M
University of Victoria	M,D
University of Washington	M,D
University of West Florida	M
University of West Georgia	M,D,O
The University of Winnipeg	M
University of Wisconsin–Milwaukee	M*
University of Wisconsin–Oshkosh	M
University of Wyoming	M
Upper Iowa University	M
Valdosta State University	M,D
Villanova University	M,O
Virginia Commonwealth University	M
Virginia International University	M
Virginia Polytechnic Institute and State University	M,D
Walden University	M,D,O
Waldorf University	M
Washington Adventist University	M
Wayne State University	M,D
Webster University	M,D,O
West Chester University of Pennsylvania	M,O
Western Kentucky University	M
Western Michigan University	M,D,O
Westfield State University	M
West Virginia University	M,D
Wichita State University	M
Widener University	M
Wilmington University	M,D
Wright State University	M
York University	M

PUBLIC AFFAIRS

Arizona State University at the Tempe campus	M,D
Binghamton University, State University of New York	D
Cleveland State University	D
Concordia University (Canada)	O
Cornell University	M
Drake University	M
Florida International University	M,D
George Mason University	M
The George Washington University	M,O
Indiana University Bloomington	M,D,O
Indiana University Northwest	M,O
Indiana University of Pennsylvania	M
Indiana University–Purdue University Indianapolis	M,O
Indiana University South Bend	M,O
The Institute of World Politics	M,O
Jackson State University	M,D
McMaster University	M,D
Merrimack College	M,O
Metropolitan College of New York	M
New Mexico Highlands University	M
Notre Dame de Namur University	M
The Ohio State University	M,D
Park University	M,O
Penn State Harrisburg	M,D,O
Portland State University	M,D,O
Princeton University	M,D,O
Syracuse University	*
Texas A&M University	M,O
The University of Alabama in Huntsville	M
University of Arkansas at Little Rock	M,O
University of Baltimore	M,D
University of California, Berkeley	M
University of California, Los Angeles	M,D*
University of Central Florida	D
University of Colorado Colorado Springs	M
University of Colorado Denver	M,D
University of Florida	M,D,O
University of Louisville	M,D

*M—masters degree; D—doctorate; O—other advanced degree; *—Close-Up and/or Display*

University of Minnesota, Twin Cities Campus	M,D
University of Missouri	M,D,O
University of Missouri–Kansas City	M,D
University of Nevada, Las Vegas	M,D,O
The University of North Carolina at Greensboro	M,O
University of San Francisco	M
University of Saskatchewan	M,D
University of South Florida	O*
The University of Texas at Austin	M,D
The University of Texas Rio Grande Valley	M
University of Washington	M,D
University of Waterloo	M
University of Wisconsin–Madison	M
Virginia Commonwealth University	M,D,O
Virginia Polytechnic Institute and State University	M,D
Washington State University	M,D,O
West Chester University of Pennsylvania	M,O
Western Carolina University	M
Western Michigan University	M,D,O
York University	M

PUBLIC HEALTH—GENERAL

Adelphi University	M
Allen College	M,D
American University of Armenia	M
American University of Beirut	M,D
Andrews University	M,O
Arcadia University	M
Argosy University, Atlanta	M
Argosy University, Chicago	M
Argosy University, Hawai`i	M
Argosy University, Los Angeles	M
Argosy University, Northern Virginia	M
Argosy University, Orange County	M
Argosy University, Phoenix	M
Argosy University, Seattle	M
Argosy University, Tampa	M
Argosy University, Twin Cities	M
Arizona State University at the Tempe campus	M,D,O
A.T. Still University	M,D,O
Augusta University	M
Austin Peay State University	M
Azusa Pacific University	M*
Baldwin Wallace University	M
Barry University	
Belmont University	D
Benedictine University	M
Boise State University	M,D,O
Boston University	M,D*
Bowling Green State University	M
Brigham Young University	M
Brooklyn College of the City University of New York	M
Brown University	M
California Baptist University	M
California State University, Fresno	M
California State University, Fullerton	M
California State University, Long Beach	M
California State University, Northridge	M
California State University, San Bernardino	M
California State University, San Marcos	M
Case Western Reserve University	M*
Charles R. Drew University of Medicine and Science	M
Chicago State University	M
Claremont Graduate University	M,D
Clemson University	M,D,O
Cleveland State University	M
The College at Brockport, State University of New York	M
The College of New Jersey	M
College of Saint Elizabeth	M
Columbia University	M,D*
Creighton University	M
Daemen College	M
Dartmouth College	M*
Davenport University	M
DePaul University	M
Des Moines University	M
Drexel University	M,D,O*
East Carolina University	M,D,O
Eastern Virginia Medical School	M
Eastern Washington University	M
East Stroudsburg University of Pennsylvania	M
East Tennessee State University	M,D,O
Elmhurst College	M
Emory University	M,D
Everglades University	M
Excelsior College	M
Ferris State University	M
Florida Agricultural and Mechanical University	M,D
Florida International University	M,D
Florida State University	M
Fort Valley State University	M
George Mason University	M,O
Georgetown University	M,D
The George Washington University	M,D
Georgia Southern University	M,D
Georgia Southern University–Armstrong Campus	M
Georgia State University	M,D,O
Grand Canyon University	M,D,O
Grand Valley State University	M
Harvard University	M,D*
Hawai`i Pacific University	M
Hofstra University	M,O
Howard University	M
Hunter College of the City University of New York	M
Icahn School of Medicine at Mount Sinai	M,D
Idaho State University	M
Independence University	M
Indiana University Bloomington	M,D
Indiana University–Purdue University Indianapolis	M,D,O
Jackson State University	M,D
Johns Hopkins University	M,D*
Kansas State University	M,D,O
Kent State University	M,D
Lamar University	M
La Salle University	M
Laurentian University	D
Lenoir-Rhyne University	M
Liberty University	M,D
Loma Linda University	M,D
London Metropolitan University	M,D
Long Island University–LIU Brooklyn	M,D,O
Louisiana State University Health Sciences Center	M,D
Louisiana State University in Shreveport	M
Loyola University Chicago	M,O
Marshall University	M
Medical College of Wisconsin	M,D,O
Meharry Medical College	M
Mercer University	M,D
Michigan State University	M
MidAmerica Nazarene University	M
Mississippi University for Women	M,D,O
Missouri State University	M
Monroe College	M
Montclair State University	M
Morehouse School of Medicine	M
National University	M,O
New England Institute of Technology	M
New Mexico State University	M,O
New York Medical College	M,D,O
New York University	M,D*
North Dakota State University	M*
Northeast Ohio Medical University	M,D,O
Northern Illinois University	M
Northwestern University	M
Nova Southeastern University	M,D,O*
The Ohio State University	M,D
Ohio University	M
Old Dominion University	M
Oregon State University	M,D
Penn State Hershey Medical Center	M,D
Philadelphia College of Osteopathic Medicine	M,D,O*
Ponce Health Sciences University	M,D
Portland State University	M,D
Purdue University	M,D
Queen's University at Kingston	M,D
Rivier University	M,D
Rollins College	M
Rutgers University–Camden	M,O
Rutgers University–Newark	M,O
Rutgers University–New Brunswick	M,D
Sacred Heart University	M
St. Ambrose University	M
St. Catherine University	M
St. John's University (NY)	M
Saint Louis University	M,D*
Salus University	M
Samford University	M
San Diego State University	M,D
San Francisco State University	M
San Jose State University	M
San Juan Bautista School of Medicine	M,D
Sarah Lawrence College	M
Shenandoah University	M,D,O
Simmons College	M
Simon Fraser University	M,D,O
Slippery Rock University of Pennsylvania	M
Southern Connecticut State University	M
State University of New York Downstate Medical Center	M
Stony Brook University, State University of New York	M,O
Tarleton State University	M
Temple University	M,D*
Tennessee State University	M
Texas A&M University	M,D,O
Thomas Edison State University	M
Thomas Jefferson University	M,O
Touro University California	M,D
Trident University International	M,D,O
Trinity Washington University	M
Tufts University	M,D,O*
Tulane University	M,D
Uniformed Services University of the Health Sciences	M,D*
Université de Montréal	M,D,O
University at Albany, State University of New York	M,D
University at Buffalo, the State University of New York	M,D
The University of Alabama at Birmingham	M,D
University of Alaska Anchorage	M
University of Alberta	M,D
The University of Arizona	M,D
University of Arkansas for Medical Sciences	M,D,O
The University of British Columbia	M,D
University of California, Berkeley	M,D
University of California, Irvine	M,D
University of California, Los Angeles	M,D*
University of California, San Diego	D*
University of Cincinnati	M,D
University of Colorado Denver	M,D
University of Connecticut Health Center	M
University of Florida	M,D,O
University of Georgia	D
University of Hawaii at Manoa	M,D,O
University of Illinois at Chicago	M,D
University of Illinois at Springfield	M,O
University of Illinois at Urbana–Champaign	M,D
University of Indianapolis	M
The University of Iowa	M,D,O*
The University of Kansas	M
University of Kentucky	M,D
University of La Verne	M
University of Louisville	M,D
University of Lynchburg	M
The University of Manchester	M,D
University of Maryland, College Park	M,D
University of Massachusetts Amherst	M,D*
University of Memphis	M,D
University of Miami	M,D*
University of Michigan	M,D*
University of Michigan–Flint	M
University of Minnesota, Twin Cities Campus	M,D,O
University of Montana	M,O
University of Nebraska Medical Center	M
University of Nevada, Las Vegas	M,D,O
University of Nevada, Reno	M,D
University of New England	M,D,O
University of New Hampshire	M,O
University of New Mexico	M
The University of North Carolina at Chapel Hill	M,D
The University of North Carolina at Charlotte	M,D,O
University of North Dakota	M
University of Northern Colorado	M
University of North Florida	M,O
University of North Texas Health Science Center at Fort Worth	M,D,O
University of Oklahoma Health Sciences Center	M,D
University of Ottawa	D
University of Pennsylvania	M*
University of Pittsburgh	M,D,O*
University of Rochester	M*
University of Saint Joseph	M
University of San Francisco	M
University of South Africa	M,D
University of South Carolina	M
University of South Dakota	M
University of Southern California	M*
University of Southern Maine	M,O
University of Southern Mississippi	M,D
University of South Florida	M,D,O*
The University of Tennessee	M
The University of Texas at El Paso	M,O
The University of Texas Health Science Center at Houston	M,D,O
The University of Texas Medical Branch	M
University of the Sciences	M
The University of Toledo	M,D,O
University of Toronto	M,D
University of Utah	M,D
University of Vermont	M,O
University of Virginia	M,D
University of Washington	M
University of Waterloo	M,D
University of West Florida	M
University of Wisconsin–La Crosse	M
University of Wisconsin–Madison	M
University of Wisconsin–Milwaukee	M,D,O*
Utah State University	M,D
Valparaiso University	M,D,O
Vanderbilt University	M*
Virginia Polytechnic Institute and State University	M,D
Walden University	M,D,O
Washington University in St. Louis	M,D
Wayne State University	M,D,O
West Chester University of Pennsylvania	M,O
Western Illinois University	M
Western Kentucky University	M
Westminster College (UT)	M
West Virginia University	M,D
Wright State University	M
Yale University	M,D

PUBLIC HISTORY

Arizona State University at the Tempe campus	M,D,O
California State University, East Bay	M
California State University, Sacramento	M,D
The College at Brockport, State University of New York	M
College of Staten Island of the City University of New York	O
Colorado State University	M
Drew University	M,D,O
Duquesne University	M
East Carolina University	M
Florida State University	M,D
Georgia Southern University	M,O
Georgia Southern University–Armstrong Campus	M
Georgia State University	M,D
Indiana University of Pennsylvania	M
Indiana University–Purdue University Indianapolis	M
James Madison University	M
La Salle University	M,O
Lehigh University	M,D
Loyola University Chicago	M,D
Middle Tennessee State University	D
New York University	M,D,O*
North Carolina State University	M
Northern Kentucky University	M
Rutgers University–Camden	M
St. John's University (NY)	M,D
Shippensburg University of Pennsylvania	M
Sonoma State University	M
Southeast Missouri State University	M,O
Texas A&M University–Commerce	M,D,O
University at Albany, State University of New York	M,D,O
University at Buffalo, the State University of New York	M,D,O
University of Arkansas at Little Rock	M
University of California, Santa Barbara	D
University of Colorado Denver	M
University of Illinois at Springfield	M
University of Louisiana at Lafayette	M
University of Louisville	M,O
University of Maryland, Baltimore County	M,D
University of North Alabama	M
University of Northern Iowa	M
University of South Carolina	M,O
The University of Texas at Austin	M,D
University of West Florida	M
University of West Georgia	M,O
Wayne State University	M,D,O

PUBLIC POLICY

Adler University	M
Albany State University	M
American Public University System	M,D
American University	M,D,O
The American University in Cairo	M,O
American University of Beirut	M,D
The American University of Paris	M
Arizona State University at the Tempe campus	M,D
Auburn University at Montgomery	M,D
Aurora University	M
Baruch College of the City University of New York	M*
Baylor University	M,D
Boise State University	M,D,O
Brandeis University	M
Brock University	M
Brooklyn College of the City University of New York	M
Brown University	M
California Lutheran University	M,O
California State University, East Bay	M
California State University, Long Beach	M,O
California State University, Sacramento	M
Carleton University	M,D
Carnegie Mellon University	M,D
The Catholic University of America	M
Central European University	M,D
Claremont Graduate University	M,D,O
Clemson University	D,O
The College of William and Mary	M*
Columbia University	M*
Concordia University (Canada)	M,D
Cornell University	M,D
DePaul University	M
Duke University	M,D*
Eastern Michigan University	M,O
Excelsior College	M,O
Florida State University	M,D,O
Frederick S. Pardee RAND Graduate School	D
George Mason University	M,D
Georgetown University	M,D
The George Washington University	M,D
Georgia Institute of Technology	M,D
Georgia State University	M,D,O
Harvard University	M,D*
Indiana University Bloomington	M,D,O
Indiana University Kokomo	M,O
Indiana University–Purdue University Fort Wayne	M,O
The Institute of World Politics	M,O
Jackson State University	M,D
Jacksonville University	M*
John Jay College of Criminal Justice of the City University of New York	M,D
Johns Hopkins University	M,D*
Liberty University	M
Lincoln University (MO)	M
Lipscomb University	M
London Metropolitan University	M,D
Loyola University Chicago	M
McMaster University	M,D
Mills College	M
Mississippi State University	M,D
Morehead State University	M
National Louis University	M,D,O
New England College	M,D
The New School	M,D
New York University	M*
Northeastern University	M,D,O
Northwestern University	M,D
Norwich University	M
The Ohio State University	M,D
Oregon State University	M,D
Pepperdine University	M
Portland State University	M,D,O
Princeton University	M,D
Queen's University at Kingston	M

- Regent University M
- Rochester Institute of Technology M
- Rutgers University–Camden M
- Rutgers University–Newark M,D,O
- Rutgers University–New Brunswick M,D
- San Francisco State University M
- Seton Hall University M,O
- Simmons College M
- Simon Fraser University M
- Southern University and Agricultural and Mechanical College D
- State University of New York Empire State College M
- Stony Brook University, State University of New York M
- Suffolk University M,O
- Trinity College (United States) M
- Tufts University M,D*
- Union Institute & University M,D
- Universidad Autonoma de Guadalajara M,D
- Universidad del Este M
- Université de Montréal O
- University at Albany, State University of New York M,D,O
- The University of Arizona M,D,O
- University of Arkansas D
- The University of British Columbia M
- University of Calgary M
- University of California, Berkeley M,D
- University of California, Los Angeles M*
- University of California, Riverside M,D
- University of California, San Diego M*
- University of Chicago M,D
- University of Delaware M,D*
- University of Denver M
- University of Georgia M,D
- University of Guelph M
- University of Hawaii at Manoa O
- University of Houston M
- University of Kentucky M,D,O
- University of Louisville M,D
- University of Maryland, Baltimore County M,D,O
- University of Maryland, College Park M,D
- University of Massachusetts Amherst M*
- University of Massachusetts Boston M,D
- University of Massachusetts Dartmouth M,O
- University of Memphis M,O
- University of Michigan M,D*
- University of Minnesota, Twin Cities Campus M,D
- University of Missouri M,D,O
- University of Missouri–St. Louis M,D,O
- University of Nebraska–Lincoln M,D,O
- University of Nevada, Las Vegas M,D,O
- University of New Brunswick Fredericton M
- University of New Hampshire M
- The University of North Carolina at Chapel Hill D
- The University of North Carolina at Charlotte M,D,O
- University of Northern Iowa M
- University of Oklahoma M*
- University of Pennsylvania M,D*
- University of Pittsburgh M,D*
- University of Puerto Rico–Río Piedras M
- University of Regina M,D,O
- University of Rhode Island M*
- University of St. Thomas (TX) M
- University of Saskatchewan M,D
- University of Southern California M,D,O*
- University of Southern Maine M
- The University of Texas at Arlington M,D
- The University of Texas at Austin M,D
- The University of Texas at Dallas M,D
- The University of Texas Rio Grande Valley M
- University of the Pacific M,D
- University of Utah M
- University of Virginia M
- University of Washington M,D
- University of Washington, Bothell M
- Vanderbilt University D*
- Virginia Commonwealth University D
- Virginia Polytechnic Institute and State University M,D
- Walden University M,D,O
- Wayne State University M,D,O
- Wilfrid Laurier University M
- William Paterson University of New Jersey M,D,O
- York University M

PUBLISHING

- Arizona State University at the Tempe campus M,D,O
- Brown University M,D
- Carnegie Mellon University M
- DePaul University M
- Emerson College M
- The George Washington University M
- New York University M*
- Northwestern University M
- Pace University M,O
- Rosemont College M
- Rowan University O
- Sam Houston State University M
- Simon Fraser University M
- University of Baltimore M
- University of Houston–Victoria M
- University of St. Thomas (MN) M,O
- Vermont College of Fine Arts M

QUALITY MANAGEMENT

- California Intercontinental University M,D
- California State University, Dominguez Hills M
- Calumet College of Saint Joseph M
- Eastern Michigan University M,O
- Florida Institute of Technology M,D
- Hofstra University M,O
- Instituto Tecnologico de Santo Domingo M,O
- Instituto Tecnológico y de Estudios Superiores de Monterrey, Campus Ciudad de México M,D
- Instituto Tecnológico y de Estudios Superiores de Monterrey, Campus Ciudad Juárez M
- Instituto Tecnológico y de Estudios Superiores de Monterrey, Campus Estado de México M,D
- Instituto Tecnológico y de Estudios Superiores de Monterrey, Campus Irapuato M,D
- Madonna University M
- Mount Mercy University M
- The National Graduate School of Quality Management M,D
- Northwestern University M
- Penn State Erie, The Behrend College M
- Regis College (MA) M
- Rutgers University–New Brunswick M,D
- Southern New Hampshire University M,D,O
- Stevens Institute of Technology M,O
- Stevenson University M
- Trident University International M,D,O
- Universidad de las Americas, A.C. M
- Universidad del Turabo M
- The University of Alabama M
- University of Central Florida M,D,O
- University of Massachusetts Boston M,O
- The University of Tennessee at Chattanooga M,O
- The University of Texas at Tyler M
- University of Wisconsin–Stout M

QUANTITATIVE ANALYSIS

- Baruch College of the City University of New York M*
- Columbia University M,D*
- Drexel University M,D,O*
- Duke University M,D,O*
- Fordham University M,D
- Harvard University M,D*
- Hofstra University M,O
- Instituto Tecnologico de Santo Domingo M,O
- Lehigh University M
- Rutgers University–Newark M,O
- San Francisco State University M
- Southern New Hampshire University M,D,O
- Stockton University M
- University at Buffalo, the State University of New York M,D
- The University of Alabama at Birmingham M,D
- The University of British Columbia M,D
- University of California, Santa Barbara M,D
- University of Connecticut M,O*
- University of Florida M,D,O
- The University of Iowa M,D,O*
- University of Maryland, College Park M,D
- University of Michigan M,D*
- University of Minnesota, Twin Cities Campus M,D,O
- University of New Hampshire M,O
- University of New Mexico D
- University of North Texas M,D,O
- University of Oregon M
- University of Puerto Rico–Río Piedras M,D
- University of South Africa M,D
- University of Southern California M,D*
- The University of Texas at Arlington M,D
- The University of Texas at Austin M,D
- The University of Texas Health Science Center at Houston M,D
- Vanderbilt University M*
- Virginia Polytechnic Institute and State University M,O

RADIATION BIOLOGY

- Georgetown University M
- Université de Sherbrooke M,D
- The University of Iowa M*
- University of Oklahoma Health Sciences Center M,D

RANGE SCIENCE

- Kansas State University M,D,O
- Montana State University M,D
- New Mexico State University M,D
- Oregon State University M,D
- Sul Ross State University M
- Texas A&M University–Kingsville M
- The University of Arizona M,D
- University of California, Berkeley M
- University of Wyoming M,D
- Utah State University M,D

READING EDUCATION

- Abilene Christian University M
- Adelphi University M
- Alabama Agricultural and Mechanical University M,D,O
- Alabama State University M,O
- Alfred University M
- Alverno College M
- American International College M,D,O
- Appalachian State University M
- Arcadia University M,D,O
- Arkansas State University M,D,O
- Asbury University M
- Augustana University M
- Aurora University M,D
- Austin Peay State University M,O
- Avila University M,O
- Baldwin Wallace University M
- Ball State University M,D,O
- Bank Street College of Education M
- Barry University M,D,O
- Belhaven University (MS) M,D,O
- Bellarmine University M,D,O
- Benedictine University M
- Berry College M
- Binghamton University, State University of New York M
- Bloomsburg University of Pennsylvania M
- Blue Mountain College M
- Bluffton University M
- Boise State University M
- Boston College M,O
- Bowie State University M
- Bowling Green State University M,O
- Bridgewater State University M,O
- Buffalo State College, State University of New York M
- Cabrini University M,D
- Caldwell University M,D,O
- California Baptist University M
- California State Polytechnic University, Pomona M
- California State University, East Bay M
- California State University, Fresno M
- California State University, Fullerton M
- California State University, Northridge M
- California State University, Sacramento M,D,O
- California State University, San Marcos M,D
- California State University, Stanislaus M
- California University of Pennsylvania M
- Canisius College M,O
- Capella University M,D
- Cardinal Stritch University M,D
- Carthage College M,O
- Castleton University M,O
- Centenary University M,D
- Central Connecticut State University M,O
- Central Michigan University M,D,O
- Central Washington University M
- Chestnut Hill College M
- Chicago State University M
- The Citadel, The Military College of South Carolina M,O
- City College of the City University of New York M
- City University of Seattle M,O
- Clarion University of Pennsylvania M
- Clemson University M,D,O
- Coastal Carolina University M,O
- Coker College M
- The College at Brockport, State University of New York M
- The College of New Jersey M,O
- The College of New Rochelle M
- College of St. Joseph M
- The College of Saint Rose M,O
- The College of William and Mary M*
- Concordia University (United States) M,D
- Concordia University Chicago M
- Concordia University, Nebraska M
- Concordia University, St. Paul M,D,O
- Concordia University Wisconsin M
- Concord University M
- Converse College O
- Coppin State University M
- Crandall University M
- Curry College M,O
- Dallas Baptist University M
- Delaware State University M
- DePaul University M,D
- Dominican University M
- Drake University M,D,O
- Drury University M
- Duquesne University M
- East Carolina University M
- Eastern Mennonite University M
- Eastern Michigan University M,O
- Eastern Nazarene College M,O
- Eastern New Mexico University M
- Eastern University M,O
- Eastern Washington University M
- East Stroudsburg University of Pennsylvania M
- East Tennessee State University M,O
- Edinboro University of Pennsylvania M,O
- Elms College M,O
- Emory & Henry College M,D
- Emporia State University M
- Endicott College M
- Evangel University M
- Fairleigh Dickinson University, Florham Campus M,O
- Fairleigh Dickinson University, Metropolitan Campus M,O
- Fairmont State University M
- Fitchburg State University O
- Florida Atlantic University M
- Florida Gulf Coast University M
- Florida International University M,D,O
- Florida Memorial University M
- Florida State University M,D,O
- Fontbonne University M
- Framingham State University M
- Fresno Pacific University M,O
- Frostburg State University M,D
- Furman University M,O
- Gannon University M,O
- George Fox University M,O
- George Mason University M
- Georgetown College M
- Georgia Southern University M,O
- Georgia Southern University–Armstrong Campus M,O
- Georgia State University M,D
- Gordon College M,O
- Goucher College M,O
- Governors State University M
- Graceland University (IA) M
- Grambling State University M,D,O
- Grand Canyon University M,D,O
- Grand Valley State University M
- Hamline University M,D
- Hannibal-LaGrange University M
- Harding University M,O
- Hardin-Simmons University M
- Harvard University M*
- Heritage University M
- Hofstra University M,D,O
- Holy Family University M
- Hood College M,O*
- Houston Baptist University M,D
- Idaho State University M
- Illinois State University M
- Indiana University Bloomington M,D,O
- Indiana University of Pennsylvania M,O
- Indiana University–Purdue University Indianapolis M,O
- Jackson State University M,D,O
- Jacksonville State University M
- James Madison University M
- Johns Hopkins University M*
- Judson University M
- Kansas State University M,D,O
- Kennesaw State University M
- Kent State University M
- Kutztown University of Pennsylvania M
- La Salle University M,O
- Lehman College of the City University of New York M
- Le Moyne College M,O
- Lesley University M,D,O
- Lewis University M
- Liberty University M,D,O
- Lipscomb University M,D,O
- Long Island University–Brentwood Campus M,O
- Long Island University–Hudson M,O
- Long Island University–LIU Post M,D,O
- Long Island University–Riverhead M,O
- Longwood University M
- Lourdes University M
- Loyola Marymount University M
- Loyola University Maryland M
- Madonna University M
- Manhattanville College M,O
- Marquette University M,D,O
- Marshall University M
- Marygrove College M,O
- Maryville University of Saint Louis M,D
- Marywood University M
- Massachusetts College of Liberal Arts M,O
- McDaniel College M
- McKendree University M,D,O
- McNeese State University M
- Medaille College M
- Mercy College M,O
- Meredith College M,O
- MGH Institute of Health Professions M,O
- Michigan State University M
- MidAmerica Nazarene University M
- Middle Tennessee State University M,D
- Midwestern State University M
- Millersville University of Pennsylvania M
- Misericordia University M
- Mississippi State University M,D,O
- Mississippi University for Women M
- Missouri State University M
- Monmouth University M,D,O*
- Montana State University Billings M
- Montclair State University M
- Morehead State University M,O
- Mount Mercy University M
- Mount St. Joseph University M,O
- Mount Saint Mary College M,O
- Mount Saint Vincent University M
- National Louis University M,D,O
- Nazareth College of Rochester M
- Newman University M
- New Mexico State University M,D,O
- New York University M*
- Niagara University M

*M—masters degree; D—doctorate; O—other advanced degree; *—Close-Up and/or Display*

North Carolina Agricultural and Technical State University	M
Northeastern Illinois University	M
Northeastern State University	M
Northern Michigan University	M
Northern Vermont University–Lyndon	M
Northwestern Oklahoma State University	M
Northwestern State University of Louisiana	M,O
Northwest Missouri State University	M,D,O
Notre Dame College (OH)	M,O
Oakland University	M,D,O
Ohio University	M,D
Old Dominion University	M,D
Olivet Nazarene University	M
Pace University	M,O
Park University	M,O
Penn State Harrisburg	M,D,O
Providence College	M
Purdue University	M,D,O
Purdue University Global	M
Queens College of the City University of New York	M,O
Queens University of Charlotte	M
Quincy University	M
Radford University	M
Regent University	M,D,O
Regis University	M,O
Rhode Island College	M
Rivier University	M,D,O
Robert Morris University	M,D,O
Roberts Wesleyan College	M
Rockford University	M
Roger Williams University	M,O
Roosevelt University	M
Rowan University	M,O
Rutgers University–New Brunswick	M,D
Sacred Heart University	O
Sage Graduate School	M
Saginaw Valley State University	M
St. Bonaventure University	M
Saint Francis University	M
St. John Fisher College	M
St. John's University (NY)	M,D,O
St. Joseph's College, Long Island Campus	M
St. Joseph's College, New York	M
Saint Joseph's University	M,D,O*
Saint Leo University	M,O
Saint Mary's University of Minnesota	M,O
Saint Michael's College	M,O
Saint Peter's University	M,O
St. Thomas Aquinas College	M,O
St. Thomas University	M,D,O
Saint Xavier University	M
Salem College	M
Salem State University	M
Salisbury University	M,D
Sam Houston State University	M,D
San Diego State University	M
San Francisco State University	M,O
Seattle Pacific University	M
Shenandoah University	M,D,O
Shippensburg University of Pennsylvania	M
Siena Heights University	M,O
Simmons College	M,D,O
Simon Fraser University	D
Slippery Rock University of Pennsylvania	M
Sonoma State University	M,O
Southeastern Louisiana University	M
Southeastern Oklahoma State University	M
Southeastern University (FL)	M,D
Southern Adventist University	M
Southern Connecticut State University	M,O
Southern Illinois University Edwardsville	M,O
Southern Methodist University	M,D
Southern New Hampshire University	M,D,O
Southern Oregon University	M
Southwestern Adventist University	M
Southwest Minnesota State University	M
Spring Arbor University	M
State University of New York at Fredonia	M
State University of New York at New Paltz	M
State University of New York at Oswego	M
State University of New York at Plattsburgh	M
State University of New York College at Cortland	M
State University of New York College at Geneseo	M
State University of New York College at Oneonta	M
State University of New York College at Potsdam	M
Sul Ross State University	M,O
Syracuse University	M,D*
Teachers College, Columbia University	M,D,O
Tennessee Technological University	M,D,O
Texas A&M University–Commerce	M,D,O
Texas A&M University–Corpus Christi	M,D
Texas A&M University–Kingsville	M
Texas A&M University–San Antonio	M
Texas Christian University	M
Texas State University	M
Texas Tech University	M,D
Texas Woman's University	M,D,O
Touro College	M
Towson University	M,O
Trident University International	M
Trinity Washington University	M
Union College (KY)	M
University at Albany, State University of New York	M,D,O
University at Buffalo, the State University of New York	M,D,O
The University of Akron	M
The University of Alabama at Birmingham	M
The University of Alabama in Huntsville	M,O
University of Alaska Southeast	M
The University of Arizona	M,D,O
University of Arkansas at Little Rock	M,D,O
University of Bridgeport	M,D,O
The University of British Columbia	M,D
University of Central Arkansas	M
University of Central Florida	M,D,O
University of Central Missouri	M,D,O
University of Central Oklahoma	M
University of Cincinnati	M,D
University of Colorado Denver	M
University of Connecticut	M,D*
University of Dayton	M
The University of Findlay	M,D
University of Florida	M,D,O
University of Georgia	M,D
University of Guam	M
University of Houston–Clear Lake	M
University of Houston–Victoria	M,O
University of Kentucky	M,D
University of La Verne	M,O
University of Lynchburg	M
University of Maine	M,D,O
University of Mary	M,D
University of Maryland, College Park	M,D,O
University of Massachusetts Amherst	M,D,O*
University of Memphis	M,D,O
University of Miami	D*
University of Michigan–Flint	M,D,O
University of Minnesota, Twin Cities Campus	M,D,O
University of Mississippi	M,D,O
University of Missouri	M,D,O
University of Missouri–Kansas City	M,D,O
University of Missouri–St. Louis	M
University of Nebraska at Kearney	M
University of Nevada, Reno	M,D
University of New England	M,D,O
University of New Mexico	M,D
The University of North Carolina at Chapel Hill	M,D
The University of North Carolina at Charlotte	M,O
The University of North Carolina at Greensboro	M,D,O
The University of North Carolina at Pembroke	M
The University of North Carolina Wilmington	M
University of North Dakota	M
University of Northern Colorado	M
University of Northern Iowa	M
University of North Florida	M
University of Oklahoma	M,D*
University of Oklahoma Health Sciences Center	M,D,O
University of Pennsylvania	M*
University of Phoenix–Online Campus	M,O
University of Phoenix–Phoenix Campus	M
University of Pittsburgh	M,D*
University of Portland	M,D
University of Rhode Island	M,D*
University of St. Francis (IL)	M,D,O
University of Saint Joseph	M
University of St. Thomas (TX)	M,D
University of San Diego	M
University of San Francisco	M,D
The University of Scranton	M
University of Sioux Falls	M,O
University of South Alabama	M,D
University of South Carolina	M,D
University of South Dakota	M
University of Southern Maine	M,O
University of South Florida	M,D,O*
University of South Florida, St. Petersburg	M
The University of Tennessee	M,D,O
The University of Texas at Arlington	M
The University of Texas at Austin	M,D
The University of Texas at El Paso	M,D
The University of Texas at San Antonio	M,D
The University of Texas at Tyler	M
The University of Texas of the Permian Basin	M
The University of Texas Rio Grande Valley	M
University of the Cumberlands	M,D,O
University of Utah	M,D,O
University of Victoria	M,D
University of Virginia	M,D
University of Washington	M,D
University of West Florida	M
University of West Georgia	M,D,O
University of Wisconsin–Eau Claire	M
University of Wisconsin–La Crosse	M,O
University of Wisconsin–Milwaukee	M*
University of Wisconsin–Oshkosh	M
University of Wisconsin–River Falls	M
University of Wisconsin–Stevens Point	M
University of Wisconsin–Superior	M
Upper Iowa University	M
Utah Valley University	M
Vanderbilt University	M*
Virginia Commonwealth University	M,O
Viterbo University	M,O
Walden University	M,D,O
Walla Walla University	M
Walsh University	M
Washburn University	M
Washington State University	M,D
Wayne State University	M,D,O
Webster University	M,O
West Chester University of Pennsylvania	M,O
Western Connecticut State University	M
Western Illinois University	M
Western Kentucky University	M,O
Western Michigan University	M,D
Western New Mexico University	M
Western State Colorado University	M
Westfield State University	M
West Liberty University	M
Westminster College (PA)	M
West Texas A&M University	M
West Virginia University	M,D
Widener University	M,D
Wilkes University	M,D
William Paterson University of New Jersey	M,O
Wilmington College	M
Wilmington University	M,D
Worcester State University	M,O
Xavier University	M*
York College of Pennsylvania	M
Youngstown State University	M

REAL ESTATE

American University	M,O
Arizona State University at the Tempe campus	M,D
Auburn University	M*
Baruch College of the City University of New York	M*
Brandeis University	M
California State University, Sacramento	M
Clemson University	M
Cleveland State University	M,O
Columbia University	M*
Cornell University	M
DePaul University	M,D
Drexel University	M*
Emory University	M
Florida International University	M
Georgetown University	M,D
The George Washington University	O
Georgia State University	M,D,O
Instituto Centroamericano de Administración de Empresas	M
Johns Hopkins University	M*
Longwood University	M
Marquette University	M
Massachusetts Institute of Technology	M
Monmouth University	M,O*
New York University	M*
Northwestern University	M,D
Pacific States University	M,O
Pontificia Universidad Catolica Madre y Maestra	M
Portland State University	M,D,O
Pratt Institute	M*
Roosevelt University	M
Rutgers University–Newark	M
Southern Methodist University	M
Syracuse University	M*
Texas A&M University	M
Thomas Jefferson University	M
Universidad Iberoamericana	M,D
University at Buffalo, the State University of New York	M,D,O
University of California, Berkeley	D
University of Central Florida	M
University of Denver	M
University of Florida	M,D,O
University of Hawaii at Manoa	M
University of Illinois at Chicago	M
University of Maryland, College Park	M
University of Memphis	M,D
University of Miami	M,D*
The University of North Carolina at Charlotte	M,O
University of Pennsylvania	M,D*
University of San Diego	M
University of South Africa	M,D
University of Southern California	M*
University of South Florida	M,D*
The University of Texas at Arlington	M,D
The University of Texas at Dallas	M
University of Utah	M
University of Wisconsin–Madison	M,D
Villanova University	M
Virginia Commonwealth University	O

RECREATION AND PARK MANAGEMENT

Acadia University	M
Bowling Green State University	M
California State University, Chico	M
California State University, East Bay	M
California State University, Long Beach	M
California State University, Northridge	M,O
California State University, Sacramento	M
Central Michigan University	M,O
Clemson University	M,D,O
Colorado State University	M,D
Delta State University	M
East Carolina University	M,O
Eastern Kentucky University	M
Eastern Washington University	M
Florida International University	M,D,O
Frostburg State University	M
Hardin-Simmons University	M
Indiana State University	M,D
Indiana University Bloomington	M,D
Iona College	M,O
Kent State University	M
Lasell College	M,O
Lehman College of the City University of New York	M
Loyola Marymount University	M
Michigan State University	M,D
Middle Tennessee State University	M
Naropa University	M
New England College	M
North Carolina Central University	M
North Carolina State University	M,D
Northern Arizona University	M,O
Northwest Missouri State University	M
Ohio University	M
Penn State University Park	M,D*
Purdue University	M,D
San Francisco State University	M
Slippery Rock University of Pennsylvania	M
South Dakota State University	M,D
Southern Connecticut State University	M
Southern Illinois University Carbondale	M
Southern University and Agricultural and Mechanical College	M
Southwestern Oklahoma State University	M
Springfield College	M
State University of New York College at Cortland	M
Temple University	M,D*
Texas A&M University	M,D
Texas State University	M
United States Sports Academy	M
Universidad Metropolitana	M
University of Alberta	M,D
University of Arkansas	M,D
University of Florida	M,D
The University of Iowa	M,D*
University of Louisiana at Monroe	M
University of Manitoba	M
University of Mississippi	M,D
University of Montana	M,D
University of Nebraska at Kearney	M
University of New Brunswick Fredericton	M
University of New Hampshire	M
The University of North Carolina at Greensboro	M
University of Rhode Island	M*
The University of Tennessee	M,D
The University of Toledo	M,D
University of Utah	M,D
University of Waterloo	M,D
University of Wisconsin–La Crosse	M
University of Wisconsin–Milwaukee	M*
Utah State University	M,D
Virginia Commonwealth University	M
Western Illinois University	M
Western Kentucky University	M
West Virginia University	M,D

REHABILITATION COUNSELING

Adler University	M
Alabama Agricultural and Mechanical University	M,O
Alabama State University	M,O
Arkansas State University	M,O
Assumption College	M,O
Ball State University	M,D
Barry University	M,O
Bayamón Central University	M,O
California State University, Fresno	M
California State University, Los Angeles	M,D
California State University, San Bernardino	M
Cambridge College	M,O
Central Connecticut State University	M,O
Coppin State University	M
East Carolina University	M,D,O
East Central University	M
Edinboro University of Pennsylvania	M,O
Emporia State University	M
Florida International University	M,D,O
Fort Valley State University	M
The George Washington University	M
Georgia State University	M
Hofstra University	M,O
Hunter College of the City University of New York	M
Illinois Institute of Technology	M,D
Kent State University	M
Langston University	M
Louisiana State University Health Sciences Center	M

Maryville University of Saint Louis	M
Mercer University	M,D
Michigan State University	M,D,O
Minnesota State University Mankato	M
Mississippi State University	M,D,O
Montana State University Billings	M
Mount Mary University	M,O
Northeastern Illinois University	M
Ohio University	M,D
Pontifical Catholic University of Puerto Rico	M
Rutgers University–Newark	M,D
St. Bonaventure University	M,O
Salve Regina University	M,O
San Diego State University	M
South Carolina State University	M
Southern University and Agricultural and Mechanical College	M
Springfield College	M
Texas Tech University Health Sciences Center	M
Thomas University	M
University at Buffalo, the State University of New York	M,D,O
The University of Arizona	M,D
University of Arkansas	M,D
University of Arkansas at Little Rock	M,O
University of Idaho	M,O
The University of Iowa	M,D*
University of Kentucky	M,D
University of Maryland, College Park	M,D,O
University of Maryland Eastern Shore	M
University of Massachusetts Boston	M,D
University of Memphis	M,D
The University of North Carolina at Chapel Hill	M
University of Northern Colorado	M,D
University of North Texas	M,D,O
University of Pittsburgh	M,D*
University of Puerto Rico–Río Piedras	M
The University of Scranton	M
University of South Carolina	M,O
University of Southern Maine	M,O
University of South Florida	M,D,O*
The University of Tennessee	M,D
The University of Texas at Austin	M,D
The University of Texas at El Paso	M
The University of Texas Rio Grande Valley	M,D
The University of Texas Southwestern Medical Center	M
University of the District of Columbia	M
University of Wisconsin–Madison	M,D
University of Wisconsin–Stout	M
Utah State University	M
Virginia Commonwealth University	M
Wayne State University	M,D,O
Western Michigan University	M
Western Oregon University	M
Western Washington University	M
West Virginia University	M,D
Wilberforce University	M
Winston-Salem State University	M
Wright State University	M

REHABILITATION SCIENCES

Alabama State University	M
Augusta University	D
Boston University	M,D*
Central Michigan University	M,D
Clarion University of Pennsylvania	M
Concordia University Wisconsin	M
Duquesne University	M,D
East Carolina University	M,D,O
East Stroudsburg University of Pennsylvania	M
George Mason University	D,O
Indiana University–Purdue University Indianapolis	M,D
Jackson State University	M
Lasell College	M
Logan University	M,D
Loma Linda University	M,D
Marquette University	M,D
McGill University	M,D,O
McMaster University	M,D
Medical University of South Carolina	D
New York University	M,D*
Northwestern University	D
The Ohio State University	D
Old Dominion University	D
Queen's University at Kingston	M,D
Salus University	M,O
Stony Brook University, State University of New York	M,D,O
Temple University	M,D*
Texas Tech University Health Sciences Center	D
Université de Montréal	O
University at Buffalo, the State University of New York	O
The University of Alabama at Birmingham	D
University of Alberta	D
The University of British Columbia	M,D
University of Colorado Denver	D
University of Florida	D
University of Illinois at Urbana–Champaign	M,D
The University of Iowa	M,D*
The University of Kansas	M,D
University of Kentucky	D
University of Manitoba	M,D
University of Maryland, Baltimore	D
University of Maryland Eastern Shore	M
University of Northern Colorado	M,D
University of North Texas Health Science Center at Fort Worth	M,D
University of Oklahoma Health Sciences Center	M
University of Ottawa	M
University of Pittsburgh	M,D*
University of South Carolina	M,O
University of South Florida	D*
The University of Texas Medical Branch	D
University of Toronto	M,D
The University of Tulsa	M
University of Utah	D
University of Vermont	D
University of Washington	M,D
University of Wisconsin–La Crosse	M
University of Wisconsin–Milwaukee	D*
Virginia Commonwealth University	D
Washington University in St. Louis	D
Western Michigan University	M

RELIABILITY ENGINEERING

Arizona State University at the Tempe campus	M
University of Maryland, College Park	M,D
The University of Tennessee	M,D

RELIGION

Abilene Christian University	M
Ambrose University	M,O
The American University of Rome	M
Amridge University	M,D
Arizona State University at the Tempe campus	M,D,O
Athens State University	M
The Baptist College of Florida	M
Baptist Theological Seminary at Richmond	M,D,O
Baylor University	M,D
Bethany Theological Seminary	M,O
Bethel Seminary	M,D,O
Bethesda University	M
Beulah Heights University	M
Biola University	M,D,O
Bob Jones University	M,D,O
Boston University	M,D*
Briercrest Seminary	M
Brown University	D
Bryn Athyn College of the New Church	M
Cairn University	M
California Institute of Integral Studies	M,D,O
California State University, Long Beach	M
Calvin Theological Seminary	M,D
Canadian Southern Baptist Seminary	M
Cardinal Stritch University	M
The Catholic University of America	M,D,O
Charlotte Christian College and Theological Seminary	M,D
Chicago Theological Seminary	M,D
Christian Brothers University	M
Christian Theological Seminary	M,D
Cincinnati Christian University	M
Claremont Graduate University	M,D
Claremont Lincoln University	M
Claremont School of Theology	M,D
Clarks Summit University	M,D
Columbia University	M,D*
Concordia University (Canada)	M,D
Concordia University Chicago	M,D
Concordia University Irvine	M*
Concordia University of Edmonton	M
Cornell University	M,D
Dallas Baptist University	M
Dallas Theological Seminary	M,D,O
Delta State University	M
Denver Seminary	M,D,O
Dominican University of California	M
Drew University	M,D,O
Duke University	M,D*
Earlham School of Religion	M
Eastern Mennonite University	M,O
East Texas Baptist University	M
Elms College	M
Emory University	D
Faith Baptist Bible College and Theological Seminary	M
Florida International University	M
Florida State University	M,D
Fordham University	M,D,O
General Theological Seminary	M,D,O
George Mason University	M
Georgetown University	M,D
The George Washington University	M
Georgia State University	M
Gordon-Conwell Theological Seminary	M,D
Grace College of Divinity	M
Graceland University (IA)	M
Graduate Theological Union	M,D,O
Grand Rapids Theological Seminary of Cornerstone University	M
Hardin-Simmons University	M
Harrison Middleton University	M,D
Hartford Seminary	M,D,O
Harvard University	D*
Heritage Christian University	M
Hope International University	M
Iliff School of Theology	M,D
Indiana University Bloomington	M,D
The Jewish Theological Seminary	M,D
John Carroll University	M
Kentucky Christian University	M
Knox Theological Seminary	M
Lancaster Theological Seminary	M,D,O
La Sierra University	M
Lee University	M
Liberty University	M,D
Lincoln Christian University	M
Loma Linda University	M
Louisville Presbyterian Theological Seminary	M,D
Lutheran Theological Seminary Saskatoon	M,D
Luther Rice College & Seminary	M,D
Maranatha Baptist University	M
McGill University	M,D
McMaster University	M,D
Memorial University of Newfoundland	M
Milligan College	M,D,O
Missouri State University	M,O
Moody Theological Seminary–Michigan	M,O
Mount St. Joseph University	M,O
Mount Saint Mary's University (CA)	M,D,O
Naropa University	M
Nashotah House Theological Seminary	M,D,O
New Saint Andrews College	M,O
New York University	M,O*
Northern Seminary	M,D
Northwestern University	M,D
Northwest Nazarene University	M
Nyack College	M
Oblate School of Theology	M,D,O
Olivet Nazarene University	M
Oxford Graduate School	M,D
Pacific School of Religion	M,D,O
Pepperdine University	M
Princeton Theological Seminary	M,D
Princeton University	D
Queen's University at Kingston	M
Reformed Theological Seminary–Charlotte Campus	M,D
Reformed Theological Seminary–Houston Campus	M
Reformed Theological Seminary–Jackson Campus	M,D,O
Reformed Theological Seminary–Washington D.C.	M
Regent University	M,D
Rice University	D
The Robert E. Webber Institute for Worship Studies	M,D
Rutgers University–New Brunswick	M,O
Saint John's Seminary (MA)	M
St. Joseph's Seminary	M
Saint Mary's University (Canada)	M
Salve Regina University	M,D
Santa Clara University	M,D,O
Seattle Pacific University	M,O
The Seattle School of Theology and Psychology	M
Selma University	M
Seminary of the Southwest	M,O
Seton Hall University	M,O
Sioux Falls Seminary	M
Southern Adventist University	M
The Southern Baptist Theological Seminary	M,D
Southern California Seminary	M,D
Southern Evangelical Seminary	M,D,O
Southern Methodist University	M,D
Southwestern Assemblies of God University	M
Stanford University	D
SUM Bible College & Theological Seminary	M
Syracuse University	M,D*
Temple University	M,D*
Trevecca Nazarene University	M
Trinity Baptist College	M
Trinity International University Florida	M,O
Trinity School for Ministry	M,D,O
Union University	M,D
United Lutheran Seminary	M,D
United Lutheran Seminary	M,D,O
United Theological Seminary of the Twin Cities	M,D,O
Université de Montréal	M,D,O
Université de Sherbrooke	M,D,O
Université du Québec à Montréal	M,D
Université Laval	M,D
The University of British Columbia	M,D
University of Calgary	M,D
University of California, Berkeley	D
University of California, Riverside	M,D
University of California, Santa Barbara	M,D
University of Chicago	M,D
University of Colorado Boulder	M
University of Denver	M,D,O
University of Florida	M,D
University of Georgia	M
University of Hawaii at Manoa	M
University of Illinois at Urbana–Champaign	M
The University of Iowa	M,D*
The University of Kansas	M,O
University of Lethbridge	M,D
The University of Manchester	D
University of Manitoba	M,D
University of Michigan	M,D*
University of Minnesota, Twin Cities Campus	M,D
University of Missouri	M
The University of North Carolina at Chapel Hill	M,D
The University of North Carolina at Charlotte	M
University of Notre Dame	M
University of Ottawa	M,D
University of Pennsylvania	D*
University of Regina	M
University of St. Thomas (MN)	M
University of St. Thomas (TX)	M
University of Saskatchewan	M
University of South Africa	M,D
University of South Carolina	M
University of South Florida	M,D*
The University of Tennessee	M,D
University of the Cumberlands	M,D
University of the West	M
University of Toronto	M,D
University of Valley Forge	M
University of Virginia	M,D
University of Washington	M,D
University of Waterloo	D
The University of Winnipeg	M
Vancouver School of Theology	M,O
Vanderbilt University	M,D*
Vanguard University of Southern California	M
Virginia University of Lynchburg	M,D
Wake Forest University	M
Walla Walla University	M
Washington Adventist University	M
Washington University in St. Louis	M
Wayland Baptist University	M
Wesley Biblical Seminary	M
Western Michigan University	M,O
Western Seminary	M,O
Westminster Seminary California	M
Westminster Theological Seminary	M,D,O
Wilfrid Laurier University	M,D
WON Institute of Graduate Studies	M
Wycliffe College	M,D,O
Yale University	D
Yeshiva Derech Chaim	D

RELIGIOUS EDUCATION

Andrews University	M,D,O
Asbury Theological Seminary	M,D,O
Baptist Theological Seminary at Richmond	M,D,O
Biola University	M,D,O
Boston College	M,D,O
Boston University	M,D*
Brandeis University	M
Brigham Young University	M
Calvary University	M
Calvin Theological Seminary	M,D
Carolina Christian College	M
Claremont School of Theology	M,D
Clarks Summit University	M,D
Columbia International University	M,D,O
Concordia University Chicago	M
Concordia University, Nebraska	M
Dallas Baptist University	M
Dallas Theological Seminary	M,D,O
Felician University	M,O
Fordham University	M,D,O
Gardner-Webb University	M,D
Garrett-Evangelical Theological Seminary	M,D
Global University	M,D
Gratz College	M,D
Hebrew College	M,O
Hebrew Union College–Jewish Institute of Religion (NY)	M
Houston Baptist University	M,D
Inter American University of Puerto Rico, Metropolitan Campus	D
Interdenominational Theological Center	M,D
The Jewish Theological Seminary	M,D
Lancaster Theological Seminary	M,D,O
La Sierra University	M
Liberty University	M,D
Lincoln Christian Seminary	M,D
Loyola University Chicago	M,O
Maple Springs Baptist Bible College and Seminary	M,D,O
Midwestern Baptist Theological Seminary	M,D,O
Milligan College	M,D,O
Moody Theological Seminary–Michigan	M,O
Newman Theological College	M,O
New Orleans Baptist Theological Seminary	M,D
Oral Roberts University	M,D
Palm Beach Atlantic University	M
Pfeiffer University	M
Phillips Theological Seminary	M,D
Pontifical Catholic University of Puerto Rico	M
Providence University College & Theological Seminary	M,D,O
Reformed Theological Seminary–Jackson Campus	M,D,O
Regent University	M,D,O
Rochester College	M
St. Augustine's Seminary of Toronto	M,O
Saint Mary's University of Minnesota	M
Saints Cyril and Methodius Seminary	M
Selma University	M
Shasta Bible College	M
Southeastern Baptist Theological Seminary	M,D

*M—masters degree; D—doctorate; O—other advanced degree; *—Close-Up and/or Display*

Southern Adventist University	M
Southern Evangelical Seminary	M,D,O
Southwestern Assemblies of God University	M
Southwestern Baptist Theological Seminary	M,D
Trinity International University	M,D,O
Trinity Lutheran Seminary	M
Unification Theological Seminary	M,D
Union Presbyterian Seminary	M,D
University of Detroit Mercy	M,D,O
University of St. Michael's College	M,D,O
University of St. Thomas (TX)	M,D
University of St. Thomas (MN)	M
University of San Francisco	M,D
Vancouver School of Theology	M,O
Vanguard University of Southern California	M
Walsh University	M
Wesley Biblical Seminary	M
Wheaton College	M
Xavier University	M*
Yeshiva University	M,D,O

REPRODUCTIVE BIOLOGY

Eastern Virginia Medical School	M
Queen's University at Kingston	M,D
Rutgers University–New Brunswick	M,D
Tufts University	M,D*
The University of British Columbia	M,D
University of Hawaii at Manoa	M,D
University of Saskatchewan	M,D
University of Wyoming	M,D

RHETORIC

Abilene Christian University	M
Arizona State University at the Tempe campus	M,D,O
Ball State University	M,D
Bob Jones University	M,D,O
Boise State University	M
Bowling Green State University	M,D
Brigham Young University	M
California State University, Dominguez Hills	M,O
California State University, Fresno	M
California State University, Northridge	M
California State University, Stanislaus	M,O
Carnegie Mellon University	M,D
The Catholic University of America	M,D,O
Clemson University	M,D
Colorado State University	M
DePaul University	M
Duquesne University	M,D
East Carolina University	M,D,O
Eastern Washington University	M
Florida State University	M,D
George Mason University	M,D,O
Georgia State University	M,D
Indiana University Bloomington	M,D
Iowa State University of Science and Technology	M,D
James Madison University	M
Kent State University	M,D
Michigan State University	M,D
Michigan Technological University	M,D
Missouri Western State University	M,O
Monmouth University	M*
New Mexico Highlands University	M
New Mexico State University	M,D
North Carolina State University	D
North Dakota State University	M,D*
Northern Arizona University	M,D,O
Northern Kentucky University	M,O
Northwestern University	M,D
Ohio University	M,D
Old Dominion University	M
Oregon State University	M
Rensselaer Polytechnic Institute	M,D
Rowan University	O
St. Cloud State University	M
San Diego State University	M
Southern Illinois University Carbondale	M,D
Syracuse University	M,D*
Texas Christian University	M,D
Texas State University	M
Texas Tech University	M,D
Texas Woman's University	M,D
The University of Alabama	M,D
The University of Alabama at Birmingham	M
The University of Arizona	M,D
University of Arkansas at Little Rock	M
University of California, Berkeley	D
University of Central Oklahoma	M
University of Dayton	M
University of Denver	M,D
The University of Findlay	M,D
University of Houston–Downtown	M
The University of Iowa	M,D*
University of Louisiana at Lafayette	M,D
University of Louisville	M,D
University of Massachusetts Amherst	M,D*
University of Michigan–Flint	M
University of Nebraska–Lincoln	M,D
University of North Alabama	M
The University of North Carolina at Greensboro	M,D
University of Oklahoma	M,D*
University of Southern California	D*
University of South Florida	M,D*
The University of Tennessee at Chattanooga	M
The University of Texas at El Paso	M,D,O
University of Utah	M,D
University of Wisconsin–Madison	M,D
University of Wisconsin–Milwaukee	M,D,O*
Wayne State University	M,D
Western Carolina University	M,O

RISK MANAGEMENT

Boston University	M*
Brandeis University	M
California State University, Fullerton	M
Concordia University Wisconsin	M
DePaul University	M,D
Florida State University	M,D
Georgia State University	M,D,O
Husson University	M
Iona College	M,O
Johns Hopkins University	M*
Loyola University Chicago	M
Metropolitan College of New York	M
New York University	M*
Ohio Dominican University	M
Pace University	M
Queens College of the City University of New York	M
St. John's University (NY)	M
Saint Peter's University	M
Temple University	D*
University of Colorado Denver	M
University of Connecticut	M,D*
University of Michigan	M,D*
University of Pennsylvania	M,D*
University of Saint Mary	M
The University of Texas at Austin	M,D
The University of Tulsa	M
University of Wisconsin–Madison	M,D
Yeshiva University	M

ROMANCE LANGUAGES

Boston University	M,D*
Columbia University	M,D*
Cornell University	M,D
Hunter College of the City University of New York	M
Johns Hopkins University	M,D*
Michigan State University	M,D
New York University	M,D*
Northern Illinois University	M
Queens College of the City University of New York	M
San Diego State University	M
Stony Brook University, State University of New York	M
Texas Tech University	M,D
University at Buffalo, the State University of New York	M,D
The University of Alabama	M,D
University of California, Berkeley	D
University of Chicago	M,D
University of Cincinnati	M,D
University of Illinois at Urbana–Champaign	D
University of Miami	D*
University of Missouri	M,D
University of Missouri–Kansas City	M
University of New Orleans	M
The University of North Carolina at Chapel Hill	M,D
University of Notre Dame	M
University of Oregon	M,D
University of Pennsylvania	M,D*
University of South Africa	M,D
The University of Texas at Austin	M,D
Washington University in St. Louis	D
Wayne State University	M,D

RURAL PLANNING AND STUDIES

Brandon University	M,O
Dalhousie University	M
East Carolina University	M,O
Iowa State University of Science and Technology	D
Université Laval	O
University of Alaska Fairbanks	M
University of Guelph	M,D
University of Montana	M
University of Wyoming	M

RURAL SOCIOLOGY

Cornell University	M,D
Iowa State University of Science and Technology	M,D
The Ohio State University	M,D
Penn State University Park	M,D,O*
University of Alberta	M,D
University of Missouri	M,D
University of Montana	M
University of Puerto Rico–Mayagüez	M
University of Wisconsin–Madison	M,D

RUSSIAN

American University	M,O
Boston College	M
Brown University	M,D
Columbia University	M,D*
Harvard University	D*
Hofstra University	M,D,O
Kent State University	M,D
McGill University	M,D
Middlebury College	M,D
New York University	M*
Penn State University Park	M,D*
Princeton University	D
The University of Arizona	M
University of California, Berkeley	D
University of Missouri	M
University of Oregon	M
University of South Africa	M,D
The University of Tennessee	D
University of Washington	M,D
University of Waterloo	M,D
Yale University	D

SAFETY ENGINEERING

Embry-Riddle Aeronautical University–Prescott	M
Florida Institute of Technology	M
Indiana University Bloomington	M,D
Murray State University	M
New Jersey Institute of Technology	M,D
Rochester Institute of Technology	M
University of Minnesota, Duluth	M
University of Southern California	M,D,O*
West Virginia University	M,D

SCANDINAVIAN LANGUAGES

Cornell University	M,D
Harvard University	D*
University of California, Berkeley	D
University of California, Los Angeles	M*
University of Massachusetts Amherst	M,D*
University of Minnesota, Twin Cities Campus	M,D
University of Washington	M,D
University of Wisconsin–Madison	M,D

SCHOOL NURSING

California State University, Fullerton	M,D
Cambridge College	M,D,O
Eastern Mennonite University	M,D
Eastern University	M,O
La Salle University	M,D,O
Lewis University	M,D
Monmouth University	M,D,O*
Rowan University	M,D,O
Seton Hall University	M,D
University of Illinois at Chicago	M,O
West Chester University of Pennsylvania	M,D,O
William Paterson University of New Jersey	M,D,O
Wright State University	M

SCHOOL PSYCHOLOGY

Abilene Christian University	O
Adelphi University	M
Adler University	M
Alabama Agricultural and Mechanical University	M,O
Alfred University	M,D,O
Alliant International University–Irvine	M,D,O
Alliant International University–Los Angeles	M,D,O
Alliant International University–San Diego	M,D,O
Alliant International University–San Francisco	M,D,O
American University of Beirut	M,D
Andrews University	M,O
Appalachian State University	M
Argosy University, Hawai`i	M
Argosy University, Phoenix	M,D
Arkansas State University	M,O
Assumption College	M,O
Auburn University at Montgomery	M,O
Augusta University	M,O
Azusa Pacific University	M,D*
Ball State University	M,D,O
Barry University	M,O
Baylor University	M,D,O
Brigham Young University	M,D,O
Brooklyn College of the City University of New York	M,O
Caldwell University	M,O
California Baptist University	M
California State University, Chico	M
California State University, Dominguez Hills	M
California State University, Fresno	M,O
California State University, Los Angeles	M,D
California State University, Northridge	M
California State University, Sacramento	M,D,O
California University of Pennsylvania	M
Cambridge College	M,O
Campbellsville University	M
Canisius College	M
Capella University	M,D
Central Connecticut State University	M,O
Central Michigan University	D,O
Central Washington University	O
Chaminade University of Honolulu	M
Chapman University	M,D,O*
The Chicago School of Professional Psychology	D,O
The Chicago School of Professional Psychology at Washington DC	O
The Citadel, The Military College of South Carolina	M,O
The College of New Rochelle	M
College of Saint Elizabeth	M,D
College of St. Joseph	M
The College of Saint Rose	M,O
The College of William and Mary	M,O*
Creighton University	M
DePaul University	M,D
Doane University	M,D,O
Duquesne University	M,D
Eastern Illinois University	M,O
Eastern Kentucky University	M,O
Eastern University	M,O
Eastern Washington University	O
East Tennessee State University	M
Edinboro University of Pennsylvania	M,O
Emporia State University	M,O
Evangel University	M
Fairfield University	M,O
Fairleigh Dickinson University, Metropolitan Campus	M,D
Florida Gulf Coast University	M
Florida International University	M,D,O
Florida State University	M,D,O
Fordham University	M,D
Fort Hays State University	O
Francis Marion University	M,O
Fresno Pacific University	M
Gallaudet University	M,D,O
Gardner-Webb University	M
George Fox University	M,O
Georgian Court University	M,O
Georgia Southern University	M,O
Georgia State University	M,D,O
Grand Valley State University	M,O
Heidelberg University	M
Hofstra University	M,D
Hood College	M*
Houston Baptist University	M
Howard University	M,D
Humboldt State University	M
Husson University	M
Idaho State University	M,D,O
Illinois State University	D,O
Immaculata University	M,D,O
Indiana State University	M,D,O
Indiana University Bloomington	M,D,O
Indiana University of Pennsylvania	D,O
Indiana University South Bend	M,O
Inter American University of Puerto Rico, Metropolitan Campus	M,D
Inter American University of Puerto Rico, San Germán Campus	M,D
Iona College	M,O
Jackson State University	M
James Madison University	M,D,O
Kean University	D,O
Keene State College	M,O
Kent State University	M,D,O
La Sierra University	M,O
Lehigh University	D,O
Lesley University	M,D,O
LeTourneau University	M
Lewis & Clark College	M,O
Liberty University	M,D,O
Lindenwood University	M,D,O
Lipscomb University	M,D,O
Long Island University–Hudson	M,O
Long Island University–LIU Post	M,D,O
Louisiana State University and Agricultural & Mechanical College	M,D
Louisiana State University in Shreveport	O
Loyola Marymount University	M
Loyola University Chicago	D,O
Marist College	M,O
Marshall University	O
McGill University	M,D,O
McNeese State University	M,O
Mercer University	M,O
Mercy College	M
Merrimack College	M,O
Michigan State University	M,D,O
MidAmerica Nazarene University	M
Middle Tennessee State University	M,O
Millersville University of Pennsylvania	M
Minnesota State University Mankato	M,D
Minnesota State University Moorhead	M,O
Minot State University	O
Mississippi State University	M,D,O
Monmouth University	M,D,O*
Montana State University	M,D,O
Mount Saint Vincent University	M
Murray State University	M,D,O
National Louis University	M,D,O
National University	M,O
New Mexico State University	M,D,O
Niagara University	M
Nicholls State University	M,O
North Carolina State University	D
North Dakota State University	M,D*
Northeastern University	M,D,O
Northern Arizona University	M,D,O
Northern Vermont University–Johnson	M
Northwest Nazarene University	M
Nova Southeastern University	M,D,O*
Old Dominion University	M,D,O
Oregon State University	M,D
Oregon State University–Cascades	M
Ottawa University	M
Our Lady of the Lake University	M
Pace University	M,D
Penn State University Park	M,D,O*
Philadelphia College of Osteopathic Medicine	M,D,O*
Phillips Graduate University	M
Pittsburg State University	O
Plymouth State University	O
Purdue University Northwest	M
Queens College of the City University of New York	M,O
Quincy University	M
Radford University	O
Rhode Island College	M,O
Rider University	O
Roberts Wesleyan College	M,D
Rochester Institute of Technology	M,O
Roosevelt University	M
Rowan University	M,O
Rutgers University–New Brunswick	M,D
St. John's University (NY)	M,D

Saint Mary's College of California	M,O
Sam Houston State University	M,D,O
San Diego State University	M
San Francisco State University	M,O
Seattle University	M,O
Seton Hall University	M
Slippery Rock University of Pennsylvania	M
Sonoma State University	M
Southern Connecticut State University	M,O
Southern Illinois University Edwardsville	O
Southwestern Oklahoma State University	M
State University of New York at Plattsburgh	M,O
Stephen F. Austin State University	M
Syracuse University	M,D,O*
Teachers College, Columbia University	M,D,O
Temple University	M,D,O*
Texas A&M University	M,D
Texas A&M University–Central Texas	M,O
Texas State University	O
Texas Woman's University	M,D,O
Towson University	M
Trinity University	M
Tufts University	M,O*
Union College (KY)	M
The University of Akron	M
University of Alberta	M,D
The University of Arizona	D,O
The University of British Columbia	M,D,O
University of Calgary	M,D
University of California, Riverside	M,D,O
University of California, Santa Barbara	M,D,O
University of Central Arkansas	M,D,O
University of Central Florida	O
University of Central Oklahoma	M
University of Cincinnati	D,O
University of Colorado Denver	M
University of Dayton	M,O
University of Delaware	M,D,O*
University of Denver	M,D,O
University of Detroit Mercy	M,D,O
University of Florida	M,D,O
University of Hartford	M
University of Houston–Clear Lake	M
University of Houston–Victoria	M
The University of Iowa	M,D,O*
The University of Kansas	D,O
University of Kentucky	M,D,O
University of La Verne	M,O
University of Louisville	M,D
University of Lynchburg	M
University of Manitoba	M,D
University of Maryland, College Park	M,D,O
University of Massachusetts Amherst	M,D,O*
University of Massachusetts Boston	M,D
University of Memphis	M,D,O
University of Minnesota, Twin Cities Campus	M,D,O
University of Missouri	M,D,O
University of Missouri–St. Louis	M,O
University of Montana	M,D,O
University of Nebraska at Kearney	M,O
University of Nebraska at Omaha	M,D,O
University of Nebraska–Lincoln	M,D,O
The University of North Carolina at Chapel Hill	M,D
The University of North Carolina at Greensboro	M,D,O
University of Northern Colorado	O
University of Northern Iowa	M,O
University of Oklahoma	M*
University of Oregon	M,D
University of Phoenix–Las Vegas Campus	M
University of Rhode Island	M,D*
University of San Diego	M
University of South Carolina	D
University of South Dakota	M,D,O
University of Southern Maine	M,D
University of South Florida	M,D,O*
The University of Tennessee	M,D,O
The University of Tennessee at Chattanooga	M,D,O
The University of Texas at Austin	M,D
The University of Texas at San Antonio	M,O
The University of Texas at Tyler	M
The University of Texas Rio Grande Valley	M
University of the Pacific	M,D,O
University of the Virgin Islands	M,D,O
The University of Toledo	M,D,O
University of Utah	M,D,O
University of Vermont	M
University of Virginia	M,D
University of Washington	M,D
University of Wisconsin–Eau Claire	M,O
University of Wisconsin–La Crosse	M,O
University of Wisconsin–Milwaukee	M,D,O*
University of Wisconsin–River Falls	M,O
University of Wisconsin–Stout	M,O
University of Wisconsin–Superior	M
University of Wisconsin–Whitewater	M,O
Utah State University	M,D
Valparaiso University	M,O
Wayne State University	M,D,O
Western Illinois University	M,O
Western Kentucky University	M,O
Wichita State University	M,D,O
William James College	M,D,O
Worcester State University	M,O
Yeshiva University	D
Youngstown State University	M

SCIENCE EDUCATION

Adams State University	M
Alabama Agricultural and Mechanical University	M,O
Alabama State University	M,O
Alverno College	M
American University of Beirut	M,D
American University of Puerto Rico	M
Andrews University	M,D,O
Antioch University New England	M
Appalachian State University	M
Arcadia University	M,D,O
Arkansas State University	M,O
Asbury University	M
Athabasca University	M,O
Augustana University	M
Aurora University	M
Austin Peay State University	M
Bard College	M
Benedictine University	M
Binghamton University, State University of New York	M
Biola University	M,O
Bloomsburg University of Pennsylvania	M
Blue Mountain College	M
Boston College	M,D
Bowling Green State University	M
Bridgewater State University	M
Brigham Young University	M,D
Brooklyn College of the City University of New York	M
Brown University	M
Buffalo State College, State University of New York	M
California Baptist University	M
California State University, Bakersfield	M
California State University, Long Beach	M
California State University, Northridge	M
California University of Pennsylvania	M
Cambridge College	M,D,O
Campbellsville University	M
Caribbean University	M,D
Carlow University	M
Carthage College	M,O
Catawba College	M
Central Connecticut State University	M,O
Central Michigan University	M
Chatham University	M
The Citadel, The Military College of South Carolina	M,O
City College of the City University of New York	M
Clarion University of Pennsylvania	M
Clark Atlanta University	M
Clemson University	D,O
Cleveland State University	M
The College at Brockport, State University of New York	M,O
College of Charleston	M
The College of William and Mary	M*
The Colorado College	M
Columbia University	M,D,O*
Columbus State University	M,O
Concordia University (United States)	M,D
Converse College	M
Delaware State University	M,D
DePaul University	M,D
Drake University	M,D,O
Duquesne University	M
East Carolina University	M,O
Eastern Kentucky University	M
Eastern Michigan University	M,O
Eastern University	M,O
Elizabeth City State University	M
Elms College	M,O
Fairleigh Dickinson University, Metropolitan Campus	M
Fitchburg State University	M
Florida Agricultural and Mechanical University	M
Florida Atlantic University	M,D
Florida Gulf Coast University	M
Florida Institute of Technology	M,D,O
Florida International University	M,D,O
Florida State University	M,D,O
Fresno Pacific University	M
George Mason University	M
The George Washington University	M
Georgia State University	M,D
Grambling State University	M,D,O
Grand Canyon University	M,D,O
Hamline University	M,D
Hampton University	M
Hardin-Simmons University	M,D
Harrison Middleton University	M,D
Heritage University	M
Hofstra University	M,D,O
Hood College	M,O*
Houston Baptist University	M,D
Hunter College of the City University of New York	M
Illinois Institute of Technology	M,D
Indiana State University	M,D
Indiana University Bloomington	M,D,O
Instituto Tecnológico y de Estudios Superiores de Monterrey, Campus Monterrey	M,D
Inter American University of Puerto Rico, Arecibo Campus	M
Inter American University of Puerto Rico, Metropolitan Campus	M
Inter American University of Puerto Rico, Ponce Campus	M
Inter American University of Puerto Rico, San Germán Campus	M
Iona College	M
Iowa State University of Science and Technology	M
Jackson State University	M,D
Kennesaw State University	M
Lake Forest College	M
Laurentian University	O
Lawrence Technological University	M,O
Lebanon Valley College	M,O
Lehman College of the City University of New York	M
Lesley University	M,D,O
Lewis University	M
Manhattanville College	M,O
McDaniel College	M,O
McNeese State University	O
Mercer University	M,D,O
Michigan State University	M,D
Michigan Technological University	M,D,O
Middle Tennessee State University	M,D
Millersville University of Pennsylvania	M,D
Minnesota State University Mankato	M
Minot State University	M
Mississippi College	M,D,O
Missouri State University	M,O
Molloy College	M,O
Montclair State University	M
Morehead State University	M
Morgan State University	M,D
National Louis University	M,D,O
New Mexico Institute of Mining and Technology	M
New York Institute of Technology	M,O
New York University	M,D,O*
North Carolina Agricultural and Technical State University	M
North Carolina State University	M,D
North Dakota State University	D*
Northeastern Illinois University	M
Northeastern State University	M
Northern Arizona University	M
Northern Michigan University	M
Northern Vermont University–Lyndon	M
Northwest Missouri State University	M,O
Oregon State University	M,D
Our Lady of the Lake University	M
Pacific University	M
Pepperdine University	M,D
Portland State University	M,D,O
Purdue University	M,D,O
Purdue University Global	M
Purdue University Northwest	M
Queens College of the City University of New York	M,O
Quinnipiac University	M
Regent University	M,D,O
Rice University	M,D
Rowan University	M,O
Rutgers University–New Brunswick	M,D
St. John Fisher College	M
St. John's University (NY)	D
Saint Xavier University	M
Salem State University	M
San Diego State University	M,D
Seattle Pacific University	M
Shippensburg University of Pennsylvania	M
Slippery Rock University of Pennsylvania	M
Smith College	M
South Carolina State University	M
Southern Connecticut State University	M,O
Southern University and Agricultural and Mechanical College	D
Southwestern Oklahoma State University	M
State University of New York at New Paltz	M,O
State University of New York at Plattsburgh	M
State University of New York College at Cortland	M
State University of New York College at Old Westbury	M
State University of New York College at Potsdam	M
Stevenson University	M
Stony Brook University, State University of New York	M,D,O
Syracuse University	M,D*
Teachers College, Columbia University	M,D
Teachers College of San Joaquin	M
Temple University	M*
Tennessee Technological University	M,O
Texas A&M University–Kingsville	M
Texas Christian University	M,D
Texas Tech University	M,D
Tufts University	M,D*
Universidad Nacional Pedro Henriquez Urena	M
University at Buffalo, the State University of New York	M,D,O
The University of Akron	M
The University of Alabama in Huntsville	M,D,O
University of Arkansas at Pine Bluff	M
The University of British Columbia	M,D
University of California, Berkeley	M,D
University of California, San Diego	D*
University of Central Florida	M,D,O
University of Chicago	D
University of Colorado Denver	M,D
University of Connecticut	M,D*
The University of Findlay	M
University of Florida	M,D,O
University of Georgia	M,D,O
University of Illinois at Chicago	D
University of Illinois at Urbana–Champaign	M,D
University of Indianapolis	M
The University of Iowa	M,D*
University of Lynchburg	M
University of Maryland, Baltimore County	M
University of Massachusetts Amherst	M,D,O*
University of Massachusetts Dartmouth	M,D,O
University of Memphis	M,D,O
University of Miami	D*
University of Michigan–Dearborn	M
University of Minnesota, Twin Cities Campus	M
University of Missouri	M,D,O
University of Nebraska at Kearney	M
University of Nebraska at Omaha	M,O
University of New Hampshire	M,D
University of New Mexico	O
The University of North Carolina at Chapel Hill	M
The University of North Carolina at Greensboro	M,D,O
The University of North Carolina at Pembroke	M
University of Northern Colorado	M,D
University of Northern Iowa	M
University of North Georgia	M
University of Oklahoma	M,D*
University of Pennsylvania	M,O*
University of Phoenix–Online Campus	M,O
University of Pittsburgh	M,D*
University of Puerto Rico–Río Piedras	M,D
University of St. Francis (IL)	M,D,O
University of San Diego	M
University of South Africa	M,D
University of South Alabama	M,D
University of South Carolina	M,D
University of South Dakota	M
University of South Florida, St. Petersburg	M
The University of Tennessee	M,D,O
The University of Texas at Arlington	M
The University of Texas at Dallas	M
The University of Toledo	M,D,O
The University of Tulsa	M
University of Utah	M,D
University of Vermont	M,D
University of Victoria	M,D
University of Virginia	M,D,O
University of Washington	M,D
University of Washington, Tacoma	M
The University of West Alabama	M
University of Wisconsin–Milwaukee	M*
University of Wisconsin–River Falls	M
University of Wisconsin–Stevens Point	M
University of Wyoming	M
Vanderbilt University	M,D*
Wagner College	M
Walden University	M,D,O
Warner University	M
Wayland Baptist University	M
Wayne State College	M
Wayne State University	M,D,O
West Chester University of Pennsylvania	M,O
Western Governors University	M,O
Western Michigan University	M,D,O
Western Oregon University	M
Western Washington University	M
Westfield State University	M
Widener University	M,D
Wisconsin Lutheran College	M
Wright State University	M,D
Youngstown State University	M

SECONDARY EDUCATION

Acacia University	M
Adelphi University	M
Alabama Agricultural and Mechanical University	M,O
Alabama State University	M,O
Alcorn State University	M,O
American International College	M,D,O
American Public University System	M,D
Andrews University	M,D,O
Aquinas College (TN)	M
Arcadia University	M,D,O
Argosy University, Atlanta	M,D,O
Argosy University, Chicago	M,D,O

*M—masters degree; D—doctorate; O—other advanced degree; *—Close-Up and/or Display*

Argosy University, Hawai`i	M,D
Argosy University, Los Angeles	M,D
Argosy University, Northern Virginia	M,D,O
Argosy University, Orange County	M,D
Argosy University, Phoenix	M,D,O
Argosy University, Seattle	M,D
Argosy University, Tampa	M,D,O
Argosy University, Twin Cities	M,D,O
Arizona State University at the Tempe campus	M
Auburn University at Montgomery	M,O
Augusta University	M,O
Austin Peay State University	M,O
Avila University	M,O
Ball State University	M
Bard College	M
Bellarmine University	M,D,O
Benedictine University	M
Berry College	M
Bethel University (MN)	M,D,O
Binghamton University, State University of New York	M
Blue Mountain College	M
Bob Jones University	M,D,O
Boston College	M
Bowie State University	M
Brandeis University	M,O
Brandman University	M,D
Brenau University	M,O
Bridgewater State University	M
Brooklyn College of the City University of New York	M
Brown University	M
Cabrini University	M,D
California State University, Bakersfield	M
California State University, Fullerton	M
California State University, Long Beach	M
California State University, Northridge	M
California State University, Stanislaus	M
California University of Pennsylvania	M
Campbell University	M
Canisius College	M,O
Carroll University	M
Carson-Newman University	M
The Catholic University of America	M,O
Centenary College of Louisiana	M
Central Connecticut State University	M,O
Central Michigan University	M,D,O
Chadron State College	M,O
Chaminade University of Honolulu	M
Chapman University	M,D,O*
Chatham University	M
Chestnut Hill College	M
Chicago State University	M
The Citadel, The Military College of South Carolina	M,O
City College of the City University of New York	M,O
Clarkson University	M
Clemson University	M,D,O
Colgate University	M
The College of New Jersey	M
College of St. Joseph	M
The College of Saint Rose	M,O
College of Staten Island of the City University of New York	M
The College of William and Mary	M*
The Colorado College	M
Columbus State University	M,O
Concordia University (United States)	M,D
Concordia University Chicago	M
Concordia University, Nebraska	M
Converse College	M
Cornell University	M,D
Creighton University	M
Dakota Wesleyan University	M
Dallas Baptist University	M
Delta State University	M,D,O
DePaul University	M,D
DeSales University	M,O
Dominican University	M
Drew University	M,D,O
Drury University	M
Duquesne University	M
D'Youville College	M,D
Eastern Connecticut State University	M
Eastern Illinois University	M
Eastern Kentucky University	M
Eastern Michigan University	M
Eastern Nazarene College	M,O
Eastern New Mexico University	M
Eastern Oregon University	M
Eastern University	M,O
East Stroudsburg University of Pennsylvania	M,D
East Tennessee State University	M,O
Edinboro University of Pennsylvania	M
Elms College	M,O
Emory University	M,D
Endicott College	M
Evangel University	M
Fairfield University	M,O
Fayetteville State University	M
Florida Agricultural and Mechanical University	M
Florida Atlantic University	M
Fontbonne University	M
Frostburg State University	M,D
Gallaudet University	M,D,O
George Mason University	M
The George Washington University	M
Georgia College & State University	M
Georgia Southern University	M,O
Georgia Southern University–Armstrong Campus	M,O
Georgia State University	M,D
Gonzaga University	M,D
Gordon College	M,O
Goucher College	M,O
Grand Canyon University	M,D,O
Grand Valley State University	M
Greenville University	M
Harding University	M,O
Hawai`i Pacific University	M
High Point University	M,D
Hofstra University	M,D,O
Hood College	M,O*
Hope International University	M
Howard University	M
Hunter College of the City University of New York	M
Idaho State University	M
Immaculata University	M,D,O
Indiana University Bloomington	M,D,O
Indiana University Northwest	M,O
Indiana University–Purdue University Fort Wayne	M
Indiana University South Bend	M,O
Indiana University Southeast	M
Instituto Tecnologico de Santo Domingo	M,O
Ithaca College	M
Jacksonville State University	M
James Madison University	M
John Brown University	M
Johns Hopkins University	M*
Johnson & Wales University	M
Kennesaw State University	M,D,O
Kent State University	M,D
Keuka College	M
Kutztown University of Pennsylvania	M,D
LaGrange College	M,O
Lake Forest College	M
Lancaster Bible College	M,D
La Salle University	M,O
Lee University	M,O
Le Moyne College	M,O
Lenoir-Rhyne University	M
Lesley University	M,D,O
Lewis & Clark College	M
Lewis University	M
Liberty University	M,D,O
Lincoln University (MO)	M
Long Island University–LIU Post	M,D,O
Louisiana State University and Agricultural & Mechanical College	M,D,O
Louisiana Tech University	M,D,O
Loyola Marymount University	M
Loyola University Chicago	M
Loyola University Maryland	M
Loyola University New Orleans	M
Manhattanville College	M,O
Mansfield University of Pennsylvania	M
Marquette University	M,D,O
Marymount University	M
Maryville University of Saint Louis	M,D
Marywood University	M
McDaniel College	M,O
McNeese State University	M,O
Medaille College	M
Mercer University	M,D,O
Mercer University	M,D,O
Mercy College	M,O
Mercyhurst University	M,O
Merrimack College	M,O
Middle Tennessee State University	M,O
Milligan College	M,D,O
Mississippi College	M,D,O
Mississippi State University	M,D,O
Missouri State University	M,O
Monmouth University	M,D,O*
Montana State University Billings	M
Morehead State University	M,O
Mount St. Joseph University	M,O
Murray State University	M,D,O
National Louis University	M,D,O
Neumann University	M
New Jersey City University	M
New York Institute of Technology	M
New York University	M,D,O*
Niagara University	M,O
Nicholls State University	M
Norfolk State University	M
North Carolina Agricultural and Technical State University	M
North Carolina State University	M
Northeastern Illinois University	M
Northern Arizona University	M,D,O
Northwest Christian University	M
Northwestern Oklahoma State University	M
Northwestern State University of Louisiana	M,O
Northwestern University	M
Oakland City University	M,D
Oakland University	M,O
Ohio University	M,D
Old Dominion University	M
Olivet Nazarene University	M
Pacific Union College	M
Pacific University	M
Piedmont College	M,D,O
Pittsburg State University	M,O
Point Park University	M,D
Prescott College	M,D
Providence College	M
Purdue University Global	M
Queens College of the City University of New York	M,O
Quinnipiac University	M
Regis University	M,O
Rhode Island College	M
Rider University	M
Roberts Wesleyan College	M
Rochester Institute of Technology	M
Rockford University	M
Roosevelt University	M
St. Bonaventure University	M
St. John's University (NY)	M
Saint Joseph's University	M,D,O*
Saint Mary's University of Minnesota	M
Saint Peter's University	M,O
St. Thomas Aquinas College	M,O
Saint Xavier University	M
Salem College	M
Salem State University	M
Salisbury University	M
Samford University	M,D,O
San Diego State University	M
San Francisco State University	M,O
Seattle Pacific University	M
Shenandoah University	M,D,O
Siena Heights University	M,O
Sierra Nevada College	M
Simpson College	M
Slippery Rock University of Pennsylvania	M
Smith College	M
South Carolina State University	M
Southeast Missouri State University	M,D,O
Southern Oregon University	M
Southern University and Agricultural and Mechanical College	M
Southwestern Assemblies of God University	M
Southwestern Oklahoma State University	M
Spalding University	M
Springfield College	M,O
Spring Hill College	M
Stanford University	M
State University of New York at Fredonia	M
State University of New York at New Paltz	M
State University of New York at Oswego	M
State University of New York at Plattsburgh	M
State University of New York College at Cortland	M
State University of New York College at Geneseo	M
State University of New York College at Potsdam	M
Stephen F. Austin State University	M,D
Sul Ross State University	M
Tarleton State University	M
Teachers College, Columbia University	M,D
Temple University	M*
Tennessee Technological University	M,O
Texas A&M University–Commerce	M,D,O
Texas A&M University–Corpus Christi	M
Texas Southern University	M,D
Texas State University	M
Texas Tech University	M,D
Towson University	M
Trevecca Nazarene University	M,O
Trinity Washington University	M
Troy University	M
Tufts University	M,D*
Union College (KY)	M
Universidad Metropolitana	M
The University of Akron	M
The University of Alabama	M,D,O
The University of Alabama at Birmingham	M
The University of Alabama in Huntsville	M,O
University of Alaska Southeast	M
University of Alberta	M,D
The University of Arizona	M,D
University of Arkansas	M,O
University of Arkansas at Little Rock	M
University of Arkansas at Pine Bluff	M
University of Bridgeport	M,D,O
University of California, Irvine	M,D
University of Central Oklahoma	M
University of Colorado Denver	M
University of Connecticut	M,D*
University of Dayton	M
University of Guam	M
University of Illinois at Chicago	M,D
University of Indianapolis	M
The University of Iowa	M,D*
University of Kentucky	M,D
University of La Verne	M,D,O
University of Louisiana at Monroe	M
University of Louisville	M,D,O
University of Mary Hardin-Baylor	M,D
University of Maryland, College Park	M,D,O
University of Massachusetts Amherst	M,D,O*
University of Massachusetts Dartmouth	M,D,O
University of Memphis	M,D,O
University of Michigan–Flint	M,D,O
University of Mississippi	M,D,O
University of Missouri–St. Louis	M
University of Montevallo	M
University of Nebraska at Kearney	M
University of Nebraska at Omaha	M,O
University of Nevada, Las Vegas	M,D,O
University of Nevada, Reno	M
University of New Hampshire	M,O
University of New Mexico	M
University of North Alabama	M
The University of North Carolina at Chapel Hill	M
The University of North Carolina at Charlotte	M,D,O
The University of North Carolina Wilmington	M
University of Northern Iowa	M
University of North Florida	M
University of North Georgia	M
University of Pennsylvania	M*
University of Phoenix–Bay Area Campus	M,D,O
University of Phoenix–Central Valley Campus	M
University of Phoenix–Hawaii Campus	M
University of Phoenix–Online Campus	M,O
University of Phoenix–Phoenix Campus	M
University of Phoenix–Sacramento Valley Campus	M,O
University of Phoenix–San Diego Campus	M
University of Pittsburgh	M,D*
University of Puget Sound	M
University of St. Francis (IL)	M,D,O
University of Saint Francis (IN)	M
University of Saint Joseph	M
University of St. Thomas (TX)	M,D
The University of Scranton	M
University of South Alabama	M,D
University of South Carolina	M,D
University of South Dakota	M
University of Southern Indiana	M
University of Southern Mississippi	M,D
University of South Florida	O*
The University of Tennessee	M,D,O
The University of Tennessee at Chattanooga	M,D,O
The University of Tennessee at Martin	M
The University of Texas Rio Grande Valley	M,D
University of the Cumberlands	M,D,O
University of the District of Columbia	M
University of the Virgin Islands	M
The University of Toledo	M,D,O
University of Utah	M,D
University of Vermont	M
University of Washington, Bothell	M
The University of West Alabama	M
University of West Florida	M
University of West Georgia	M,D,O
University of Wisconsin–Eau Claire	M
University of Wisconsin–Milwaukee	M,D*
University of Wisconsin–Stevens Point	M
Ursuline College	M
Utah State University	M
Valparaiso University	M,O
Vanderbilt University	M*
Virginia Wesleyan University	M
Wagner College	M
Wake Forest University	M
Washington State University	M,D
Washington University in St. Louis	M
Wayland Baptist University	M
Wayne State University	M,D,O
Webster University	M,O
Western Kentucky University	M,O
Western New Mexico University	M
Western Oregon University	M
Western Washington University	M
Westfield State University	M
West Virginia University	M,D
Wheaton College	M
Whittier College	M
Whitworth University	M
Wichita State University	M
William Carey University	M,O
William Paterson University of New Jersey	M,O
Wilmington University	M,D
Wilson College	M
Winthrop University	M
Worcester State University	M,O
Wright State University	M
Xavier University	M*
Youngstown State University	M

SLAVIC LANGUAGES

Brown University	M,D
Columbia University	M,D*
Cornell University	M,D
Duke University	M,O*
Florida State University	M
Harvard University	D*
Indiana University Bloomington	M,D
New York University	M*
Northwestern University	D
The Ohio State University	M,D
Princeton University	D
Stanford University	D
University of Alberta	M,D
University of California, Berkeley	D
University of California, Los Angeles	M,D*
University of Chicago	M
University of Illinois at Chicago	M,D
University of Illinois at Urbana–Champaign	M,D
The University of Kansas	M,D
University of Manitoba	M
University of Michigan	M,D*
The University of North Carolina at Chapel Hill	D
University of Pittsburgh	M,D*
University of Southern California	M,D*
The University of Texas at Austin	M,D
University of Toronto	M,D

University of Virginia	M,D
University of Washington	M,D
University of Wisconsin–Madison	M,D
Yale University	D

SOCIAL PSYCHOLOGY

Adler University	M
Alliant International University–Los Angeles	D
Alvernia University	M
Alverno College	M
Andrews University	M
Argosy University, Atlanta	M,D,O
Argosy University, Chicago	M,D
Argosy University, Northern Virginia	M,D
Arizona State University at the Tempe campus	M,D
Ball State University	M
Becker College	M
Bowling Green State University	M,D
Brandeis University	M,D
Brock University	M,D
Brooklyn College of the City University of New York	M,D
California Institute of Integral Studies	M,D
California State University, East Bay	M
California State University, Fullerton	M
Canisius College	M
Carnegie Mellon University	D
Claremont Graduate University	M,D,O
Clark University	D
College of St. Joseph	M
Cornell University	M,D
Delaware Valley University	M
Florida Agricultural and Mechanical University	M
Florida State University	D
Future Generations University	M
The George Washington University	D
Georgia State University	D
The Graduate Center, City University of New York	D
Harvard University	D*
Hofstra University	M,D
Howard University	M,D
Humboldt State University	M
Husson University	M
Indiana University Bloomington	D
Indiana University of Pennsylvania	M
Indiana University–Purdue University Indianapolis	M,D
Indiana Wesleyan University	M
Iowa State University of Science and Technology	M,D
Lesley University	M,D,O
Loyola University Chicago	M,O
Marquette University	M,D
Martin University	M
Marymount California University	M
Missouri Valley College	M
Mount Aloysius College	M
The New School	M,D
New York University	M,D,O*
Norfolk State University	M
North Carolina State University	M
North Dakota State University	M,D*
Northwestern University	D
The Ohio State University	D
Oregon State University–Cascades	M
Penn State Harrisburg	M,D,O
Queen's University at Kingston	M,D
Rutgers University–Newark	D
Rutgers University–New Brunswick	D
Sacred Heart University	M
Sage Graduate School	M
St. Bonaventure University	M,O
Saint Martin's University	M
San Francisco State University	M,O
Southwestern College (NM)	O
Stony Brook University, State University of New York	D
Syracuse University	D*
Teachers College, Columbia University	M,D
Temple University	M,D,O*
Texas Christian University	M,D
Thomas Jefferson University	M
Thomas University	M
Université du Québec à Rimouski	M
Université Laval	D
University at Albany, State University of New York	M,D
University of Alaska Anchorage	M,D
University of Alaska Fairbanks	M,D,O
University of Bridgeport	M
The University of British Columbia	M,D
University of Central Arkansas	M
University of Connecticut	M,D*
University of Delaware	D*
University of Denver	D
University of Guelph	M,D
University of Hawaii at Manoa	M,D,O
University of Houston	M,D
The University of Kansas	M,D
University of Maryland, Baltimore County	M,D
University of Maryland, College Park	M,D
University of Massachusetts Amherst	M,D*
University of Massachusetts Lowell	M
University of Michigan	D*
University of Minnesota, Twin Cities Campus	D
University of Missouri–Kansas City	M,D
University of Nebraska–Lincoln	M,D
University of Nevada, Reno	D
University of New Haven	M,O*
The University of North Carolina at Chapel Hill	D
The University of North Carolina at Greensboro	M,D
University of Oregon	M,D
University of Phoenix–Phoenix Campus	M
University of Pittsburgh	D*
University of Puerto Rico–Río Piedras	M,D
University of Rochester	M,D*
University of South Carolina	M,D
University of Southern California	M,D*
The University of Tennessee at Chattanooga	M,D,O
The University of Tennessee at Martin	M
University of Utah	D
University of Vermont	D
University of Victoria	M,D
University of Washington	M,D
University of Windsor	M,D
University of Wisconsin–Madison	D
University of Wisconsin–Superior	M
Walden University	M,D,O
Wayne State University	M,D,O
Western Illinois University	M,O
Wichita State University	D
Wilfrid Laurier University	M,D
Yale University	D

SOCIAL SCIENCES

Assumption College	O
Augusta University	M
California Institute of Technology	M,D
California State University, Chico	M
California State University, San Bernardino	M
Campbellsville University	M
Carnegie Mellon University	D
The Citadel, The Military College of South Carolina	M
Colorado School of Mines	O
Columbia University	M,D*
East Carolina University	M,D,O
Eastern Michigan University	M
Elms College	M,O
Evangel University	M
Florida Agricultural and Mechanical University	M
Graduate Theological Union	M,D,O
Harrison Middleton University	M,D
Hollins University	M
Humboldt State University	M
Indiana University Bloomington	M,D,O
Indiana University–Purdue University Indianapolis	M,D,O
Massachusetts Institute of Technology	D
Mississippi College	M,O
Montclair State University	M
The New School	M,D
New York University	M,D*
Nova Southeastern University	M,D,O*
The Ohio State University	M,D
Ohio University	M
Oregon State University	M,D
Southern University and Agricultural and Mechanical College	M
Syracuse University	M,D*
Texas A&M International University	M
Towson University	M
Troy University	M
University at Buffalo, the State University of New York	M
University of California, Merced	M,D
University of California, Santa Barbara	D
University of California, Santa Cruz	D*
University of Chicago	M,D
University of Florida	M,D,O
University of Illinois at Springfield	M,O
The University of Manchester	M,D
University of Maryland, Baltimore County	D
University of Memphis	M,D
University of Michigan	D*
University of Michigan–Flint	M
University of Northern Iowa	M
University of Regina	M
University of South Florida Sarasota-Manatee	M
The University of Texas at Tyler	M
University of the Virgin Islands	M
University of Toronto	M,D
University of Washington	M,D
Wilfrid Laurier University	M
Worcester Polytechnic Institute	M,D,O
Yale University	M,D

SOCIAL SCIENCES EDUCATION

Alabama Agricultural and Mechanical University	M,O
Alabama State University	M,O
Andrews University	M,D,O
Appalachian State University	M
Arkansas State University	M,D,O
Asbury University	M
Binghamton University, State University of New York	M
Bloomsburg University of Pennsylvania	M
Bob Jones University	M,D,O
Bridgewater State University	M
Brooklyn College of the City University of New York	M
Brown University	M
Buffalo State College, State University of New York	M
California State University, East Bay	M
California State University, Fresno	M
Caribbean University	M,D
Carthage College	M,O
Chadron State College	M,O
Chatham University	M
The Citadel, The Military College of South Carolina	M,O
City College of the City University of New York	M,O
The College at Brockport, State University of New York	M,O
College of St. Joseph	M
The Colorado College	M
Columbus State University	M,O
Concordia University (United States)	M,D
Converse College	M
Delta State University	M
Duquesne University	M
East Carolina University	M
Eastern Kentucky University	M
Eastern University	M,O
Fayetteville State University	M
Fitchburg State University	M
Florida Agricultural and Mechanical University	M
Florida Gulf Coast University	M
Florida International University	M,D,O
Florida State University	M,D,O
George Mason University	M
Georgia State University	M,D
Grambling State University	M
Harding University	M,O
Hofstra University	M,D,O
Hunter College of the City University of New York	M
Indiana University Bloomington	M,D,O
Instituto Tecnologico de Santo Domingo	M,O
Inter American University of Puerto Rico, Arecibo Campus	M
Inter American University of Puerto Rico, Metropolitan Campus	M
Inter American University of Puerto Rico, Ponce Campus	M
Iona College	M
Johns Hopkins University	M*
Kent State University	M,D
Kutztown University of Pennsylvania	M,D
Lake Forest College	M
La Salle University	M,O
Lebanon Valley College	M,O
Lee University	M,O
Lehman College of the City University of New York	M
Le Moyne College	M,O
Lewis University	M
Long Island University–LIU Brooklyn	M,D,O
Manhattanville College	M,O
Michigan State University	M,D
Minnesota State University Mankato	M
Mississippi College	M,D,O
Missouri State University	M,O
Molloy College	M,O
Morehead State University	M,O
New York Institute of Technology	M
New York University	M,D,O*
North Carolina State University	M
Northeastern Illinois University	M
Northwest Missouri State University	M,O
Oregon State University	M,D
Pace University	M,O
Plymouth State University	M
Portland State University	M
Purdue University	M,D,O
Queens College of the City University of New York	M,O
Quinnipiac University	M
Rhode Island College	M
Rivier University	M
Rutgers University–New Brunswick	M,D
St. John Fisher College	M
Slippery Rock University of Pennsylvania	M
Smith College	M
South Carolina State University	M
Southwestern Oklahoma State University	M
State University of New York at New Paltz	M,O
State University of New York at Plattsburgh	M
State University of New York College at Geneseo	M
State University of New York College at Old Westbury	M
State University of New York College at Potsdam	M
Stony Brook University, State University of New York	M,O
Syracuse University	M*
Teachers College, Columbia University	M,D,O
Temple University	M*
Texas Tech University	M,D
Trinity Washington University	M
University at Buffalo, the State University of New York	M,D,O
The University of Akron	M
The University of Alabama in Huntsville	M,O
University of Arkansas at Pine Bluff	M
The University of British Columbia	M,D
University of California, Santa Cruz	M*
University of Central Florida	M,D
University of Connecticut	M,D*
University of Florida	M,D,O
University of Illinois at Chicago	D
University of Indianapolis	M
The University of Iowa	M,D*
University of Maine	M,D,O
University of Maryland, Baltimore County	M
University of Minnesota, Twin Cities Campus	M
University of Missouri	M,D,O
University of Missouri–St. Louis	M,O
The University of North Carolina at Chapel Hill	M
The University of North Carolina at Greensboro	M,D,O
The University of North Carolina at Pembroke	M
University of North Georgia	M
University of Oklahoma	M,D*
University of Pittsburgh	M,D*
University of Puerto Rico–Río Piedras	M,D
University of St. Francis (IL)	M,D,O
University of South Carolina	M,D
University of South Florida	M,D,O*
The University of Tennessee	M,D,O
University of the District of Columbia	M
The University of Toledo	M,D,O
The University of Tulsa	M
University of Victoria	M,D
University of Virginia	M,D,O
University of Washington	M,D
The University of West Alabama	M
University of Wisconsin–Milwaukee	M*
University of Wisconsin–River Falls	M
University of Wisconsin–Stevens Point	M
Virginia Polytechnic Institute and State University	M,D,O
Wagner College	M
Wayland Baptist University	M
Wayne State College	M
Wayne State University	M,D,O
Western Oregon University	M
Westfield State University	M
Widener University	M,D
William Carey University	M,O
Worcester State University	M

SOCIAL WORK

Abilene Christian University	M
Adelphi University	M,D
Alabama Agricultural and Mechanical University	M,O
Alabama State University	M
Albany State University	M
American Jewish University	M
Andrews University	M
Anna Maria College	M
Appalachian State University	M
Arizona State University at the Tempe campus	M,D,O
Arkansas State University	M,O
Asbury University	M
Augsburg University	M
Aurora University	M,D
Austin Peay State University	M
Azusa Pacific University	M*
Barry University	M,D
Baylor University	M,D
Binghamton University, State University of New York	M
Boise State University	M
Boston College	M,D
Boston University	M,D*
Brandman University	M
Brescia University	M
Bridgewater State University	M
Brigham Young University	M
Bryn Mawr College	M,D
California Baptist University	M
California State University, Bakersfield	M
California State University, Chico	M
California State University, Dominguez Hills	M
California State University, East Bay	M
California State University, Fresno	M
California State University, Fullerton	M
California State University, Long Beach	M
California State University, Los Angeles	M
California State University, Monterey Bay	M
California State University, Northridge	M,O
California State University, Sacramento	M

*M—masters degree; D—doctorate; O—other advanced degree; *—Close-Up and/or Display*

California State University, San Bernardino	M
California State University, San Marcos	M
California State University, Stanislaus	M
California University of Pennsylvania	M
Campbellsville University	M
Capella University	D
Carleton University	M
Carlow University	M
Case Western Reserve University	M,D*
The Catholic University of America	M,D
Chicago State University	M
Clark Atlanta University	M,D
Clarke University	M
Cleveland State University	M
The College at Brockport, State University of New York	M,O
The College of Saint Rose	M
The College of St. Scholastica	M
College of Staten Island of the City University of New York	M
Colorado State University	M,D
Columbia University	M,D*
Concord University	M
Cornell University	M,D
Daemen College	M
Dalhousie University	M
Delaware State University	M
DePaul University	M
Dominican University	M
East Carolina University	M,O
Eastern Michigan University	M
Eastern Washington University	M
East Tennessee State University	M
Edinboro University of Pennsylvania	M
Fayetteville State University	M
Ferris State University	M
Florida Agricultural and Mechanical University	M
Florida Atlantic University	M,D
Florida Gulf Coast University	M
Florida International University	M,D
Florida State University	M,D
Fordham University	M,D
Gallaudet University	M,D,O
George Fox University	M
George Mason University	M
Georgia State University	M,O
Governors State University	M
The Graduate Center, City University of New York	D
Grambling State University	M
Grand Valley State University	M
Gratz College	M,O
Hawai`i Pacific University	M
Howard University	M,D
Humboldt State University	M
Hunter College of the City University of New York	M
Illinois State University	M
Indiana State University	M
Indiana University East	M
Indiana University Northwest	M
Indiana University–Purdue University Indianapolis	M,D,O
Indiana University South Bend	M
Institute for Clinical Social Work	D
Inter American University of Puerto Rico, Metropolitan Campus	M
Jackson State University	M,D
Johnson C. Smith University	M
Kean University	M
Kennesaw State University	M
Keuka College	M
Kutztown University of Pennsylvania	M,D
Lakehead University	M
Laurentian University	M
Lewis University	M
Loma Linda University	M,D
London Metropolitan University	M,D
Long Island University–Brentwood Campus	M,O
Long Island University–LIU Brooklyn	M,D,O
Long Island University–LIU Post	M,O
Louisiana State University and Agricultural & Mechanical College	M,D
Loyola University Chicago	M,D,O
Marshall University	M
Marywood University	M,D
McGill University	M,D,O
McMaster University	M
Memorial University of Newfoundland	M,D
Metropolitan State University of Denver	M
Michigan State University	M,D
Middle Tennessee State University	M
Millersville University of Pennsylvania	M,D
Minnesota State University Mankato	M
Missouri State University	M
Monmouth University	M,O*
Morgan State University	M
Nazareth College of Rochester	M
Newman University	M
New Mexico Highlands University	M
New Mexico State University	M
New York University	M,D*
Norfolk State University	M,D
North Carolina Agricultural and Technical State University	M
North Carolina State University	M
Northern Kentucky University	M
Northwest Nazarene University	M
Nyack College	M
The Ohio State University	M,D
The Ohio State University at Lima	M
The Ohio State University at Mansfield	M
The Ohio State University at Newark	M
Ohio University	M
Our Lady of the Lake University	M
Pacific University	M
Park University	M,O
Phillips Theological Seminary	M,D
Pontifical Catholic University of Puerto Rico	M
Portland State University	M,D
Quinnipiac University	M
Radford University	M
Ramapo College of New Jersey	M
Rhode Island College	M
Roberts Wesleyan College	M
Rutgers University–New Brunswick	M,D
Sacred Heart University	M
Saginaw Valley State University	M
St. Ambrose University	M
St. Catherine University	M,D
Saint Leo University	M
Saint Louis University	M,D*
Salem State University	M
Salisbury University	M
Samford University	M
San Diego State University	M
San Francisco State University	M
San Jose State University	M
Savannah State University	M
Seattle University	M
Seton Hall University	M
Shippensburg University of Pennsylvania	M
Simmons College	M,D,O
Smith College	M,D
Southeastern University (FL)	M
Southern Adventist University	M
Southern Connecticut State University	M
Southern Illinois University Carbondale	M
Southern Illinois University Edwardsville	M
Southern University at New Orleans	M
Spalding University	M
Springfield College	M,O
Stephen F. Austin State University	M
Stockton University	M
Stony Brook University, State University of New York	M,D
Syracuse University	M*
Tarleton State University	M
Temple University	M*
Tennessee State University	M,D
Texas A&M University–Commerce	M,D,O
Texas Christian University	M
Texas State University	M
Texas Tech University	M
Thompson Rivers University	M
Touro College	M
Troy University	M
Tulane University	M,D
Union University	M
Universidad del Este	M
Université de Moncton	M
Université de Montréal	O
Université de Sherbrooke	M
Université du Québec à Montréal	M
Université du Québec en Abitibi-Témiscamingue	M
Université du Québec en Outaouais	M
Université Laval	M,D
University at Albany, State University of New York	M,D
University at Buffalo, the State University of New York	M,D
The University of Akron	M
The University of Alabama	M,D
University of Alaska Anchorage	M,O
University of Arkansas	M
University of Arkansas at Little Rock	M
The University of British Columbia	M,D
University of Calgary	M,D,O
University of California, Berkeley	M,D
University of California, Los Angeles	M,D*
University of Central Florida	M,O
University of Chicago	M,D
University of Cincinnati	M
University of Connecticut	M,D*
University of Denver	M,D,O
University of Georgia	M,D,O
University of Guam	M
University of Hawaii at Manoa	M,D
University of Houston	M,D
University of Houston–Downtown	M
University of Illinois at Chicago	M,D,O
University of Illinois at Urbana–Champaign	M,D
The University of Iowa	M,D*
The University of Kansas	M,D
University of Kentucky	M,D
University of Louisville	M,D,O
University of Maine	M,O
The University of Manchester	M,D
University of Manitoba	M,D
University of Maryland, Baltimore	M,D
University of Maryland, College Park	
University of Memphis	M
University of Michigan	M*
University of Minnesota, Duluth	M
University of Minnesota, Twin Cities Campus	M,D
University of Mississippi	M,D
University of Missouri–Kansas City	M
University of Missouri–St. Louis	M
University of Montana	M
University of Nebraska at Omaha	M
University of Nevada, Las Vegas	M
University of Nevada, Reno	M
University of New England	M,D,O
University of New Hampshire	M,O
The University of North Carolina at Chapel Hill	M,D
The University of North Carolina at Charlotte	M
The University of North Carolina at Greensboro	M
The University of North Carolina at Pembroke	M
The University of North Carolina Wilmington	M
University of North Dakota	M
University of Northern British Columbia	M,D,O
University of Northern Iowa	M
University of Oklahoma	M*
University of Ottawa	M
University of Pennsylvania	M,D*
University of Pittsburgh	M,D,O*
University of Puerto Rico–Río Piedras	M,D
University of Regina	M,D
University of St. Francis (IL)	M,O
University of St. Thomas (MN)	M,D
University of South Africa	M,D
University of South Carolina	M,D
University of South Dakota	M,D
University of Southern California	M,D*
University of Southern Indiana	M
University of Southern Maine	M
University of Southern Mississippi	M
University of South Florida	M,D,O*
University of South Florida Sarasota-Manatee	M
The University of Tennessee	M,D
The University of Tennessee at Chattanooga	M
The University of Texas at Arlington	M,D
The University of Texas at Austin	M,D
The University of Texas at El Paso	M
The University of Texas at San Antonio	M
The University of Texas Rio Grande Valley	M
University of the Fraser Valley	M
The University of Toledo	M,O
University of Toronto	M,D
University of Utah	M,D
University of Vermont	M
University of Victoria	M
University of Washington	M,D
University of Washington, Tacoma	M
University of West Florida	M
University of Windsor	M
University of Wisconsin–Green Bay	M
University of Wisconsin–Madison	M,D
University of Wisconsin–Milwaukee	M,D,O*
University of Wisconsin–Oshkosh	M
University of Wyoming	M
Utah State University	M,D
Valdosta State University	M
Virginia Commonwealth University	M,D
Walden University	M,D
Walla Walla University	M
Washburn University	M
Washington University in St. Louis	M,D
Wayne State University	M,D,O
West Chester University of Pennsylvania	M,O
Western Carolina University	M
Western Illinois University	M
Western Kentucky University	M
Western Michigan University	M
Western New Mexico University	M
Westfield State University	M
West Texas A&M University	M
West Virginia University	M
Wichita State University	M
Widener University	M,D
Wilfrid Laurier University	M,D
Winthrop University	M
Yeshiva University	M,D
York University	M,D

SOCIOLOGY

Acadia University	M
American University	M,O
American University of Beirut	M,D
Angelo State University	M
Arizona State University at the Tempe campus	M,D
Arkansas State University	M,O
Arkansas Tech University	M
Auburn University	M*
Ball State University	M
Baylor University	M,D
Binghamton University, State University of New York	M,D
Boston College	M,D
Boston University	M,D*
Bowling Green State University	M,D
Brandeis University	M,D
Brigham Young University	M
Brock University	M
Brooklyn College of the City University of New York	M,D
Brown University	M,D
California State University, Bakersfield	M
California State University, Dominguez Hills	M
California State University, Fullerton	M
California State University, Los Angeles	M
California State University, Northridge	M
California State University, Sacramento	M
California State University, San Marcos	M
Carleton University	M,D
Case Western Reserve University	M,D*
The Catholic University of America	M
Central European University	M,D
City College of the City University of New York	M
Clark Atlanta University	M
Clemson University	M
Colorado State University	M,D
Columbia University	M,D*
Concordia University (Canada)	M,D
Cornell University	M,D
Dalhousie University	M,D
DePaul University	M
Duke University	M,D*
East Carolina University	M
Eastern Michigan University	M
East Tennessee State University	M
Emory University	D
Fayetteville State University	M
Florida Atlantic University	M
Florida International University	M,D
Florida State University	M,D
George Mason University	M,D
The George Washington University	M
Georgia Southern University	M
Georgia State University	M,D
The Graduate Center, City University of New York	D
Harvard University	D*
Howard University	M,D
Humboldt State University	M
Hunter College of the City University of New York	M
Idaho State University	M
Illinois State University	M
Indiana University Bloomington	M,D
Indiana University of Pennsylvania	M*
Indiana University–Purdue University Indianapolis	M
Iowa State University of Science and Technology	M,D
Jackson State University	M
Johns Hopkins University	D*
Kansas State University	M,D
Kent State University	M,D
Lakehead University	M
Laurentian University	M
Lehigh University	M
Lincoln University (MO)	M
Louisiana State University and Agricultural & Mechanical College	M,D
Loyola University Chicago	M,D
Marshall University	M
McGill University	M,D,O
McMaster University	M,D
Memorial University of Newfoundland	M,D
Michigan State University	M,D
Middle Tennessee State University	M
Minnesota State University Mankato	M
Mississippi State University	M,D
Morehead State University	M
Morgan State University	M
Murray State University	M
New Mexico Highlands University	M
New Mexico State University	M
The New School	M,D
New York University	M,D*
North Carolina State University	M,D
North Dakota State University	M*
Northeastern University	M,D
Northern Arizona University	M
Northern Illinois University	M
Northwestern University	M,D
The Ohio State University	D
Ohio University	M
Oklahoma City University	M
Oklahoma State University	M,D
Old Dominion University	M
Our Lady of the Lake University	M
Oxford Graduate School	M,D
Penn State University Park	M,D*
Portland State University	M,D,O
Prairie View A&M University	M
Princeton University	D,O
Purdue University	M,D
Queens College of the City University of New York	M
Queen's University at Kingston	M,D
Rice University	D
Roosevelt University	M
Rutgers University–New Brunswick	M,D
St. John's University (NY)	M
Sam Houston State University	M
San Diego State University	M
San Jose State University	M
Shippensburg University of Pennsylvania	M
Simon Fraser University	M,D
South Dakota State University	M,D
Southeastern Louisiana University	M
Southern Connecticut State University	M
Southern Illinois University Carbondale	M,D
Southern Illinois University Edwardsville	M
Stanford University	D

Stony Brook University, State University of New York	M,D
Syracuse University	M,D*
Teachers College, Columbia University	M,D
Temple University	M,D*
Texas A&M International University	M
Texas A&M University	M,D
Texas A&M University–Commerce	M,D,O
Texas A&M University–Kingsville	M
Texas Southern University	M
Texas State University	M
Texas Tech University	M
Texas Woman's University	M,D
Tulane University	M
Université de Montréal	M,D
Université du Québec à Montréal	M,D
Université Laval	M,D
University at Albany, State University of New York	M,D,O
University at Buffalo, the State University of New York	M,D
The University of Akron	M,D
The University of Alabama at Birmingham	D
University of Alberta	M,D
The University of Arizona	M,D
University of Arkansas	M
The University of British Columbia	M,D
University of Calgary	M,D
University of California, Berkeley	D
University of California, Davis	M,D
University of California, Irvine	D
University of California, Los Angeles	M,D*
University of California, Merced	M,D
University of California, Riverside	M,D
University of California, San Diego	D*
University of California, San Francisco	D
University of California, Santa Barbara	D
University of California, Santa Cruz	D*
University of Central Florida	M,D
University of Central Missouri	M,D,O
University of Central Oklahoma	M
University of Chicago	D
University of Cincinnati	M,D
University of Colorado Boulder	D
University of Colorado Colorado Springs	M
University of Colorado Denver	M,O
University of Connecticut	M,D*
University of Delaware	M,D*
University of Florida	M,D
University of Georgia	M,D
University of Guelph	M,D
University of Hawaii at Manoa	M,D
University of Houston	M
University of Houston–Clear Lake	M
University of Illinois at Chicago	M,D
University of Illinois at Urbana–Champaign	M,D
University of Indianapolis	M
The University of Iowa	M,D*
The University of Kansas	D
University of Kentucky	M,D
University of Lethbridge	M,D
University of Louisiana at Lafayette	M,D
University of Louisville	M,D
The University of Manchester	M,D
University of Manitoba	M,D
University of Maryland, Baltimore County	M
University of Maryland, College Park	M,D
University of Massachusetts Amherst	M,D*
University of Massachusetts Boston	M,D
University of Massachusetts Lowell	M,O
University of Memphis	M
University of Miami	M,D*
University of Michigan	D*
University of Minnesota, Duluth	M
University of Minnesota, Twin Cities Campus	M,D
University of Missouri	M,D
University of Missouri–Kansas City	M
University of Montana	M
University of Nebraska at Omaha	M
University of Nebraska–Lincoln	M,D
University of Nevada, Las Vegas	M,D
University of Nevada, Reno	M
University of New Brunswick Fredericton	M,D
University of New Hampshire	M,D
University of New Mexico	M,D
University of New Orleans	M
The University of North Carolina at Chapel Hill	M,D
The University of North Carolina at Charlotte	M
The University of North Carolina at Greensboro	M
The University of North Carolina Wilmington	M
University of North Dakota	M
University of Northern Colorado	M
University of North Texas	M,D,O
University of Notre Dame	D
University of Oklahoma	M,D*
University of Oregon	M,D
University of Ottawa	M
University of Pennsylvania	M,D*
University of Pittsburgh	M,D*
University of Puerto Rico–Río Piedras	M
University of Regina	M
University of Saskatchewan	M,D
University of South Africa	M,D
University of South Alabama	M
University of South Carolina	M,D
University of Southern California	D*
University of South Florida	M,D*
The University of Tennessee	M,D
The University of Texas at Arlington	M
The University of Texas at Austin	M,D
The University of Texas at El Paso	M,O
The University of Texas at San Antonio	M
The University of Texas at Tyler	M
The University of Texas Rio Grande Valley	M
The University of Toledo	M,D
University of Toronto	M,D
University of Utah	M,D
University of Victoria	M,D
University of Virginia	M,D
University of Washington	M,D
University of Waterloo	M,D
The University of Western Ontario	M,D
University of West Georgia	M,D,O
University of Windsor	M,D
University of Wisconsin–Madison	M,D
University of Wisconsin–Milwaukee	M,D*
University of Wyoming	M,D
Utah State University	M,D
Vanderbilt University	M,D*
Virginia Commonwealth University	M
Washington State University	M,D
Wayne State University	M,D
Western Illinois University	M
Western Kentucky University	M
Western Michigan University	M,D
West Virginia University	M,D
Wichita State University	M
Wilfrid Laurier University	M,D
William Paterson University of New Jersey	M,D,O
Yale University	D
York University	M,D

SOFTWARE ENGINEERING

Arizona State University at the Tempe campus	M,D
Auburn University	M,D*
Boston University	M,O*
Bowling Green State University	M
Brandeis University	M
California Baptist University	M
California State University, Fullerton	M
California State University, Northridge	M
California State University, Sacramento	M
Carnegie Mellon University	M,D
Carroll University	M
Cleveland State University	M,D
College of Staten Island of the City University of New York	M
Colorado Technical University Aurora	M
Colorado Technical University Colorado Springs	M,D
Concordia University (Canada)	M,D,O
DePaul University	M,D
Drexel University	M,D,O*
East Carolina University	M
Embry-Riddle Aeronautical University–Daytona	M
Fairfield University	M,O
Florida Agricultural and Mechanical University	M
Florida Institute of Technology	M,D
Gannon University	M
Grand Valley State University	M
Harrisburg University of Science and Technology	M
Illinois Institute of Technology	M,D
Indiana University–Purdue University Indianapolis	M,D,O
Instituto Tecnologico de Santo Domingo	M,O
International Technological University	M
Jacksonville State University	M
Kennesaw State University	M,O
Lewis University	M
Lipscomb University	M,O
Loyola University Chicago	M
Marist College	M,O
Marymount University	M,O
McMaster University	M,D
Mercer University	M
Monmouth University	M,O*
Naval Postgraduate School	M,D
New Jersey Institute of Technology	M,D,O
New York University	O*
North Dakota State University	M,D,O*
Northern Kentucky University	M,O
Northwestern University	M
Oakland University	M,D
Oklahoma Christian University	M
Pace University	M,D,O
Penn State Great Valley	M,O
Regis University	M,O
Rochester Institute of Technology	M
Rose-Hulman Institute of Technology	M
Royal Military College of Canada	M,D
Saint Louis University	M*
St. Mary's University (United States)	M,O
San Jose State University	M
Santa Clara University	M,D,O
Shippensburg University of Pennsylvania	M,O
Southern Methodist University	M,D
Stevens Institute of Technology	M,O
Stony Brook University, State University of New York	M,D,O
Stratford University (VA)	M,D
Strayer University	M
Texas State University	M
Texas Tech University	M,D
Université Laval	O
The University of Alabama in Huntsville	M,D,O
University of Calgary	M,D
University of Colorado Colorado Springs	M,D
University of Connecticut	M,D*
University of Detroit Mercy	M,D
University of Houston–Clear Lake	M
University of Management and Technology	M,O
University of Massachusetts Dartmouth	M,O
University of Michigan–Dearborn	M,D
University of Minnesota, Twin Cities Campus	M
University of Missouri–Kansas City	M,D,O
University of Nebraska at Omaha	M,O
University of New Haven	M,O*
University of North Florida	M
University of Regina	M,D
University of St. Thomas (MN)	M,O
The University of Scranton	M
University of South Carolina	M,D
University of Southern California	M,D*
University of Southern Maine	M,O
The University of Texas at Arlington	M,D
The University of Texas at Dallas	M,D
The University of Texas at El Paso	M,D,O
University of Utah	M,D,O
University of Washington, Bothell	M
University of Washington, Tacoma	M
University of Waterloo	M,D
University of West Florida	M
University of Wisconsin–La Crosse	M
Vermont Technical College	M
Virginia International University	M,O
Virginia Polytechnic Institute and State University	M,O
West Virginia University	M,D

SPANISH

American University	M,O
Arizona State University at the Tempe campus	M,D
Asbury University	M
Auburn University	M*
Bard College	M
Baylor University	M
Binghamton University, State University of New York	M
Boston College	M
Bowling Green State University	M
Brigham Young University	M
Brooklyn College of the City University of New York	M
California State University, Bakersfield	M
California State University, Fresno	M
California State University, Fullerton	M
California State University, Long Beach	M
California State University, Los Angeles	M
California State University, Northridge	M
California State University, San Bernardino	M
California State University, San Marcos	M
The Catholic University of America	M,D
Central Connecticut State University	M,O
Central Michigan University	M
City College of the City University of New York	M
Cleveland State University	M
Columbia University	M,D*
Cornell University	D
DePaul University	M
Duke University	D*
Eastern University	M,O
Emory University	D,O
Florida Atlantic University	M
Florida International University	M,D
Florida State University	M,D
George Mason University	M
Georgetown University	M,D
Georgia Southern University	M
Georgia State University	M,O
Harvard University	M,D*
Hofstra University	M,D,O
Houston Baptist University	M
Howard University	M
Hunter College of the City University of New York	M
Illinois State University	M
Indiana State University	M,D,O
Indiana University Bloomington	M,D
Inter American University of Puerto Rico, Metropolitan Campus	M
Inter American University of Puerto Rico, Ponce Campus	M
Iona College	M
Johns Hopkins University	M,D*
Kansas State University	M
Kent State University	M,D
Lake Forest College	M
Lamar University	M
Lee University	M,O
Lehman College of the City University of New York	M
Loyola University Chicago	M
Manhattanville College	M,O
Marquette University	M
Michigan State University	M,D
Middlebury College	M,D
Middle Tennessee State University	M
Millersville University of Pennsylvania	M
Minnesota State University Mankato	M
Montclair State University	M
New Mexico State University	M,D,O
New York University	M,D,O*
North Carolina State University	M
Northern Arizona University	M
Northern Illinois University	M
Northwestern University	D
The Ohio State University	M,D
Ohio University	M
Penn State University Park	M,D*
Pontifical Catholic University of Puerto Rico	M,O
Portland State University	M
Princeton University	D
Purdue University	M,D
Queens College of the City University of New York	M
Queen's University at Kingston	M
Rutgers University–New Brunswick	M,D
St. John's University (NY)	M
Saint Louis University	M*
Saint Louis University–Madrid Campus	M
Saint Xavier University	M
Salem State University	M
Sam Houston State University	M
San Diego State University	M
San Francisco State University	M
San Jose State University	M
Southern Oregon University	M
Stanford University	M,D
State University of New York at New Paltz	M,O
State University of New York College at Geneseo	M
Syracuse University	M*
Temple University	M,D*
Texas A&M University	M,D
Texas A&M University–Commerce	M,D,O
Texas A&M University–Kingsville	M
Texas State University	M
Texas Tech University	M,D
Tulane University	M,D
Universidad Autonoma de Guadalajara	M,D
Université de Montréal	M
Université Laval	M,D
University at Albany, State University of New York	M,D
University at Buffalo, the State University of New York	M,D,O
The University of Akron	M
The University of Alabama	M,D
The University of Arizona	M,D
University of Arkansas	M
University of Calgary	M,D
University of California, Berkeley	D
University of California, Davis	M,D
University of California, Irvine	M,D
University of California, Los Angeles	M*
University of California, Riverside	M,D
University of California, Santa Barbara	M,D
University of Central Arkansas	M
University of Central Florida	M
University of Chicago	D
University of Cincinnati	M,D
University of Colorado Boulder	M,D
University of Colorado Denver	M
University of Delaware	M*
University of Florida	M,D
University of Georgia	M,D
University of Hawaii at Manoa	M
University of Houston	M,D
University of Illinois at Chicago	M,D
University of Illinois at Urbana–Champaign	M,D
The University of Iowa	M,D*
The University of Kansas	M,D
University of Lethbridge	M,D
University of Louisville	M,O
The University of Manchester	D
University of Maryland, College Park	M,D
University of Massachusetts Amherst	M,D*
University of Memphis	M
University of Miami	M,D*
University of Michigan	D*

*M—masters degree; D—doctorate; O—other advanced degree; *—Close-Up and/or Display*

University of Minnesota, Twin Cities Campus	M,D
University of Missouri–Kansas City	M
University of Montana	M
University of Nebraska–Lincoln	M,D
University of Nevada, Reno	M
University of New Hampshire	M,O
University of New Mexico	M,D
The University of North Carolina at Chapel Hill	M,D
The University of North Carolina at Charlotte	M,O
The University of North Carolina at Greensboro	M,O
The University of North Carolina Wilmington	M,O
University of Northern Iowa	M
University of North Texas	M,D,O
University of Notre Dame	M
University of Oklahoma	M,D*
University of Oregon	M
University of Ottawa	M,D
University of Pennsylvania	M,D*
University of Pittsburgh	D*
University of Rhode Island	M*
University of South Africa	M,D
University of South Carolina	M,D
University of Southern California	D*
University of Southern Mississippi	M
University of South Florida	M,D*
The University of Tennessee	M,D
The University of Texas at Arlington	M
The University of Texas at Austin	M,D
The University of Texas at El Paso	M,O
The University of Texas at San Antonio	M
The University of Texas of the Permian Basin	M
The University of Texas Rio Grande Valley	M
The University of Toledo	M
University of Toronto	M,D
University of Utah	M,D
University of Virginia	M,D
University of Washington	M
The University of Western Ontario	M,D
University of Wisconsin–Madison	M,D
University of Wisconsin–Milwaukee	M,O*
University of Wyoming	M
Vanderbilt University	M,D*
Washington University in St. Louis	D
Wayne State University	M,D
West Chester University of Pennsylvania	M,O
Western Kentucky University	M
Western Michigan University	M,D
Wichita State University	M
Worcester State University	M
Yale University	D

SPECIAL EDUCATION

Acacia University	M
Acadia University	M
Adelphi University	M,O
Alabama Agricultural and Mechanical University	M,D,O
Alabama State University	M,O
Albany State University	M,O
Albright College	M
Alcorn State University	M,O
Alliant International University–San Francisco	M,O
Alverno College	M
American International College	M,D,O
American University of Puerto Rico	M
Andrews University	M
Antioch University New England	M,O
Appalachian State University	M
Arcadia University	M,D,O
Arizona State University at the Tempe campus	M,O
Arkansas State University	M,D,O
Arkansas Tech University	M,D,O
Asbury University	M
Assumption College	M,O
Auburn University	M,D*
Auburn University at Montgomery	M,O
Augustana University	M
Augusta University	M,O
Aurora University	M,D
Averett University	M
Avila University	M,O
Azusa Pacific University	M*
Baldwin Wallace University	M
Ball State University	M,D,O
Bank Street College of Education	M
Barry University	M,D,O
Bayamón Central University	M,O
Baylor University	M,D,O
Bay Path University	M
Bemidji State University	M
Benedictine University	M
Bethel University (MN)	M,D,O
Binghamton University, State University of New York	M
Biola University	M,O
Bloomsburg University of Pennsylvania	M,O
Bluffton University	M
Bob Jones University	M,D,O
Boise State University	M
Boston College	M,O
Bowie State University	M
Bowling Green State University	M
Brandman University	M,D
Brandon University	M,O
Brenau University	M,O
Bridgewater State University	M
Brigham Young University	M,D,O
Brooklyn College of the City University of New York	M,O
Buffalo State College, State University of New York	M
Cabrini University	M,D
Caldwell University	M,D,O
California Baptist University	M
California Lutheran University	M,D
California State University, Bakersfield	M
California State University, Chico	M
California State University, Dominguez Hills	M
California State University, East Bay	M
California State University, Fresno	M
California State University, Fullerton	M
California State University, Long Beach	M,D
California State University, Los Angeles	M,D
California State University, Northridge	M
California State University, Sacramento	M,D,O
California State University, San Marcos	M,D
California State University, Stanislaus	M
California University of Pennsylvania	M
Cambridge College	M,D,O
Campbellsville University	M
Canisius College	M,O
Capella University	M,D
Cardinal Stritch University	M,D
Caribbean University	M,D
Carlos Albizu University, Miami Campus	M,D
Carlow University	M,O
Castleton University	M,O
The Catholic University of America	M,O
Centenary University	M,D
Central Connecticut State University	M,O
Central Michigan University	M,O
Chaminade University of Honolulu	M
Chapman University	M,D,O*
Chatham University	M
Chestnut Hill College	M,O
Cheyney University of Pennsylvania	M
Chicago State University	M
City College of the City University of New York	M,O
City University of Seattle	M,O
Claremont Graduate University	M,D,O
Clarion University of Pennsylvania	M
Clark Atlanta University	M
Clemson University	M,D,O
Cleveland State University	M
Coastal Carolina University	M,O
College of Charleston	M
The College of New Jersey	M,O
The College of New Rochelle	M
College of Saint Elizabeth	M,O
College of St. Joseph	M
The College of Saint Rose	M,O
College of Staten Island of the City University of New York	M,O
The College of William and Mary	M*
Colorado Christian University	M
Colorado Mesa University	M,O
Colorado State University–Pueblo	M
Columbus State University	M,O
Concordia College–New York	M
Concordia University, St. Paul	M,D,O
Concordia University Wisconsin	M
Concord University	M
Converse College	M
Coppin State University	M
Curry College	M,O
Daemen College	M
Dallas Baptist University	M
Delaware State University	M
Delta State University	M
DePaul University	M,D
DeSales University	M,O
Dominican College	M
Dominican University	M
Dominican University of California	M
Drake University	M,D,O
Drew University	M,D,O
Drexel University	M,D*
Drury University	M
Duquesne University	M,D
D'Youville College	M,D
East Carolina University	M,O
Eastern Illinois University	M
Eastern Kentucky University	M
Eastern Mennonite University	M
Eastern Michigan University	M,O
Eastern Nazarene College	M,O
Eastern New Mexico University	M
Eastern University	M,O
East Stroudsburg University of Pennsylvania	M
East Tennessee State University	M,O
Edgewood College	M,D,O
Edinboro University of Pennsylvania	M,O
Elmhurst College	M
Elms College	M,O
Elon University	M
Emmanuel College (United States)	M,O
Emporia State University	M
Endicott College	M,D,O
Fairfield University	M,O
Fairleigh Dickinson University, Metropolitan Campus	M
Fairmont State University	M
Ferris State University	M
Fitchburg State University	M
Flagler College	M
Florida Atlantic University	M,D
Florida Gulf Coast University	M
Florida International University	M,D,O
Florida Memorial University	M
Florida State University	M,D,O
Fontbonne University	M
Fordham University	M,O
Fort Hays State University	M
Framingham State University	M
Francis Marion University	M
Franklin Pierce University	M,D,O
Freed-Hardeman University	M,O
Fresno Pacific University	M
Frostburg State University	M
Furman University	M,O
Gallaudet University	M,D,O
George Fox University	M,O
George Mason University	M,O
Georgetown College	M
The George Washington University	M,D,O
Georgia College & State University	M,O
Georgian Court University	M,O
Georgia Southern University	M,O
Georgia Southern University–Armstrong Campus	M,O
Georgia Southwestern State University	M,O
Georgia State University	M,D
Gonzaga University	M,D
Gordon College	M,O
Goucher College	M,O
Governors State University	M
Graceland University (IA)	M
Grambling State University	M
Grand Canyon University	M,D,O
Grand Valley State University	M
Greensboro College	M
Gwynedd Mercy University	M,D
Harding University	M,O
Hebrew College	M,O
Henderson State University	M,O
Heritage University	M
High Point University	M,D
Hofstra University	M,D,O
Holy Family University	M
Holy Names University	M,O
Hood College	M,O*
Houston Baptist University	M,D
Howard University	M
Hunter College of the City University of New York	M
Idaho State University	M
Illinois State University	M,D,O
Immaculata University	M,D,O
Indiana University Bloomington	M,D,O
Indiana University of Pennsylvania	M
Indiana University–Purdue University Fort Wayne	M,O
Indiana University–Purdue University Indianapolis	M,O
Indiana University South Bend	M,O
Inter American University of Puerto Rico, Barranquitas Campus	M
Inter American University of Puerto Rico, Fajardo Campus	M
Inter American University of Puerto Rico, Metropolitan Campus	M
Inter American University of Puerto Rico, San Germán Campus	M
Iona College	M
Iowa State University of Science and Technology	M,D
Jackson State University	M,D
Jacksonville State University	M
James Madison University	M
Johns Hopkins University	M,O*
Johnson & Wales University	M
Kansas State University	M,D,O
Kean University	M
Keene State College	M,O
Kennesaw State University	M,D,O
Kent State University	M,D,O
Kentucky State University	M,D
Lamar University	M,D
Lancaster Bible College	M,D
La Salle University	M,O
Lasell College	M,O
Lee University	M,O
Lehigh University	M,D
Lehman College of the City University of New York	M
Le Moyne College	M,O
Lesley University	M,D,O
Lewis & Clark College	M
Lewis University	M
Liberty University	M,D,O
Lincoln University (PA)	M
Lipscomb University	M,D,O
London Metropolitan University	M,D
Long Island University–Brentwood Campus	M,O
Long Island University–Hudson	M,O
Long Island University–LIU Brooklyn	M,O
Long Island University–LIU Post	M,D,O
Long Island University–Riverhead	M,O
Longwood University	M
Loras College	M
Louisiana Tech University	M,D,O
Loyola Marymount University	M
Loyola University Chicago	M
Lynn University	M,D
Madonna University	M
Malone University	M
Manhattan College	M,O
Manhattanville College	M,O
Mansfield University of Pennsylvania	M
Marian University (WI)	M,D
Marshall University	M
Martin Luther College	M
Marygrove College	M,O
Marymount University	M
Marywood University	M
Massachusetts College of Liberal Arts	M,O
McDaniel College	M
McKendree University	M,D,O
McNeese State University	M,O
Medaille College	M
Mercyhurst University	M
Meredith College	M,O
Merrimack College	M,O
Messiah College	M
Metropolitan College of New York	M
Metropolitan State University of Denver	M
Michigan State University	M,D,O
Middle Tennessee State University	M
Midwestern State University	M
Millersville University of Pennsylvania	M
Milligan College	M,D,O
Minnesota State University Mankato	M,O
Minnesota State University Moorhead	M,D,O
Minot State University	M
Misericordia University	M
Mississippi College	M,D,O
Mississippi State University	M,D,O
Missouri State University	M
Missouri Western State University	M,O
Molloy College	M,O
Monmouth University	M,D,O*
Montana State University Billings	M
Montclair State University	M
Morehead State University	M,O
Morningside College	M
Mount Mercy University	M
Mount St. Joseph University	M,O
Mount Saint Mary College	M,O
Mount Saint Vincent University	M
Murray State University	M,O
National Louis University	M,D,O
National University	M,O
National University College	M
Neumann University	M
New England College	M,D
New Jersey City University	M
New Mexico Highlands University	M
New Mexico State University	M,D,O
New York University	M*
Niagara University	M,O
Norfolk State University	M
North Carolina Central University	M
North Carolina State University	M
Northeastern Illinois University	M
Northeastern State University	M
Northeastern University	M
Northern Arizona University	M,O
Northern Illinois University	M
Northern Kentucky University	M,O
Northern Michigan University	M
Northern Vermont University–Johnson	M
Northern Vermont University–Lyndon	M
Northwest Christian University	M
Northwestern State University of Louisiana	M,O
Northwest Missouri State University	M,D,O
Northwest Nazarene University	M,D,O
Notre Dame College (OH)	M,O
Notre Dame de Namur University	M
Nyack College	M
Oakland University	M,O
The Ohio State University	D
Ohio University	M,D
Old Dominion University	M,D
Ottawa University	M
Pace University	M,O
Pacific Oaks College	M
Pacific University	M
Penn State University Park	M,D,O*
Piedmont College	M,D,O
Pittsburg State University	M,O
Point Loma Nazarene University	M
Point Park University	M,D
Prescott College	M,D
Providence College	M
Purdue University	M,D,O
Purdue University Global	M
Purdue University Northwest	M
Queens College of the City University of New York	M,O
Radford University	M,O
Ramapo College of New Jersey	M
Randolph College	M
Regent University	M,D,O
Regis College (MA)	M,D
Regis University	M,O
Rhode Island College	M,O
Rider University	M,O
Rivier University	M,D,O
Robert Morris University	M,D,O
Roberts Wesleyan College	M
Rochester Institute of Technology	M
Rockford University	M
Roosevelt University	M
Rowan University	M,O
Rutgers University–New Brunswick	M,D
Sage Graduate School	M
Saginaw Valley State University	M
St. Bonaventure University	M,O
St. Cloud State University	M,O
St. John Fisher College	M,O
St. John's University (NY)	M,O
St. Joseph's College, Long Island Campus	M
St. Joseph's College, New York	M

Saint Joseph's University	M,D,O*
Saint Louis University	M,D*
Saint Mary's College of California	M
Saint Mary's University of Minnesota	M,O
Saint Michael's College	M,O
Saint Peter's University	M,O
St. Thomas Aquinas College	M,O
St. Thomas University	M,D,O
Saint Vincent College	M
Saint Xavier University	M
Salem College	M
Salem State University	M
Salus University	M,O
Samford University	M,D,O
Sam Houston State University	M,D
San Diego State University	M
San Francisco State University	M,D,O
San Ignacio University	M
Seattle University	M,O
Seton Hall University	M
Seton Hill University	M
Shenandoah University	M,D,O
Shippensburg University of Pennsylvania	M,D
Siena Heights University	M,O
Simmons College	M,D,O
Slippery Rock University of Pennsylvania	M,D
Sonoma State University	M,O
South Carolina State University	M
Southeastern Louisiana University	M
Southeast Missouri State University	M
Southern Connecticut State University	M
Southern Illinois University Carbondale	M,D
Southern Illinois University Edwardsville	M,O
Southern Methodist University	M,D
Southern New Hampshire University	M,D,O
Southern Oregon University	M
Southern University and Agricultural and Mechanical College	M,D
Southwestern College (KS)	M,D
Southwestern Oklahoma State University	M
Southwest Minnesota State University	M
Spalding University	M
Spring Arbor University	M
Springfield College	M,O
State University of New York at New Paltz	M
State University of New York at Oswego	M
State University of New York at Plattsburgh	M
State University of New York College at Cortland	M
State University of New York College at Oneonta	M,O
State University of New York College at Potsdam	M
Stephen F. Austin State University	M
Syracuse University	M,D*
Tarleton State University	M
Teachers College, Columbia University	M,D,O
Teachers College of San Joaquin	M
Tennessee State University	M,D
Tennessee Technological University	M,O
Texas A&M International University	M
Texas A&M University	M,D
Texas A&M University–Commerce	M,D,O
Texas A&M University–Corpus Christi	M
Texas A&M University–Kingsville	M
Texas A&M University–San Antonio	M
Texas A&M University–Texarkana	M
Texas Christian University	M
Texas State University	M
Texas Tech University	M,D
Texas Woman's University	M,D
Touro College	M
Towson University	M,O
Trevecca Nazarene University	M,O
Trinity Baptist College	M
Trinity Christian College	M
Trinity Washington University	M
Tusculum College	M
Union College (KY)	M
Universidad del Este	M
Universidad del Turabo	M
Universidad Iberoamericana	M,D
Universidad Metropolitana	M
Université de Sherbrooke	M,O
University at Buffalo, the State University of New York	M,D,O
The University of Akron	M
The University of Alabama	M,D,O
The University of Alabama at Birmingham	M
The University of Alabama in Huntsville	M,O
University of Alaska Anchorage	M,O
University of Alaska Fairbanks	M
University of Alaska Southeast	M
University of Alberta	M,D
The University of Arizona	M,D
University of Arkansas	M
University of Arkansas at Little Rock	M,O
The University of British Columbia	M,D,O
University of California, Berkeley	M,D
University of California, Los Angeles	D*
University of California, Riverside	M,D,O
University of Central Arkansas	M,O
University of Central Florida	M,O
University of Central Missouri	M,D,O
University of Central Oklahoma	M
University of Cincinnati	M,D
University of Colorado Colorado Springs	M,D
University of Colorado Denver	M,D
University of Denver	M,D,O
University of Detroit Mercy	M,D,O
University of Florida	M,D,O
University of Georgia	M,D,O
University of Guam	M
University of Hawaii at Manoa	M,D
University of Houston	M,D
University of Houston–Victoria	M,O
University of Idaho	M,O
University of Illinois at Chicago	M,D
University of Illinois at Urbana–Champaign	M,D,O
The University of Iowa	M,D*
The University of Kansas	M,D,O
University of Kentucky	M,D
University of La Verne	M,D,O
University of Louisiana at Lafayette	M
University of Louisiana at Monroe	M
University of Louisville	M,D,O
University of Lynchburg	M
University of Maine	M,D,O
University of Manitoba	M
University of Mary	M,D
University of Maryland Eastern Shore	M
University of Massachusetts Amherst	M,D,O*
University of Massachusetts Boston	M
University of Massachusetts Dartmouth	M,O
University of Memphis	M,D,O
University of Miami	M,D,O*
University of Michigan–Dearborn	M
University of Minnesota, Twin Cities Campus	M,D
University of Mississippi	M,D,O
University of Missouri	D
University of Missouri–Kansas City	M,D,O
University of Missouri–St. Louis	M
University of Nebraska at Kearney	M,O
University of Nebraska at Omaha	M
University of Nebraska–Lincoln	M,D,O
University of Nevada, Las Vegas	M,D,O
University of Nevada, Reno	M,D
University of New Hampshire	M,O
University of New Mexico	M,D,O
University of North Alabama	M
The University of North Carolina at Charlotte	M,D,O
The University of North Carolina at Greensboro	M,D,O
The University of North Carolina Wilmington	M
University of North Dakota	M
University of Northern Colorado	M,D
University of Northern Iowa	M
University of North Florida	M
University of North Texas	M,D,O
University of Oklahoma	M,D*
University of Oklahoma Health Sciences Center	M,D,O
University of Oregon	M,D
University of Phoenix–Bay Area Campus	M,D,O
University of Phoenix–Hawaii Campus	M
University of Phoenix–Online Campus	M,O
University of Phoenix–Phoenix Campus	M
University of Pittsburgh	M,D*
University of Portland	M,D
University of Puerto Rico–Medical Sciences Campus	O
University of Puerto Rico–Río Piedras	M
University of Rhode Island	M,D*
University of Rio Grande	M
University of St. Francis (IL)	M,D,O
University of Saint Francis (IN)	M
University of Saint Joseph	M,O
University of Saint Mary	M
University of St. Thomas (MN)	M,O
University of St. Thomas (TX)	M,D
University of San Diego	M
University of San Francisco	M,D
University of Saskatchewan	M,D,O
The University of Scranton	M
University of South Alabama	M,D
University of South Carolina	M,D
University of South Carolina Upstate	M
University of South Dakota	M,D,O
University of Southern Maine	M,O
University of Southern Mississippi	M,D
University of South Florida	O*
The University of Tennessee	M,D,O
The University of Tennessee at Chattanooga	M,D,O
The University of Tennessee at Martin	M
The University of Texas at Austin	M,D
The University of Texas at El Paso	M
The University of Texas at San Antonio	M,D
The University of Texas at Tyler	M
The University of Texas Health Science Center at San Antonio	M,D
The University of Texas of the Permian Basin	M
The University of Texas Rio Grande Valley	M
University of the Cumberlands	M,D,O
University of the Pacific	M,D,O
University of the Southwest	M
The University of Toledo	M,D,O
University of Utah	M,D
University of Vermont	M
University of Victoria	M,D
University of Virginia	M,D,O
University of Washington	M,D
University of Washington, Tacoma	M
The University of West Alabama	M,O
The University of Western Ontario	M
University of West Florida	M
University of West Georgia	M,D,O
University of Wisconsin–Eau Claire	M
University of Wisconsin–La Crosse	M,O
University of Wisconsin–Madison	M,D
University of Wisconsin–Milwaukee	M,D,O*
University of Wisconsin–Oshkosh	M
University of Wisconsin–Stevens Point	M
University of Wisconsin–Superior	M
University of Wisconsin–Whitewater	M,O
University of Wyoming	M,D,O
Ursuline College	M
Utah State University	M,D,O
Valdosta State University	M,D,O
Vanderbilt University	M,D*
Virginia Commonwealth University	M,D
Viterbo University	M,O
Wagner College	M
Walden University	M,D,O
Walla Walla University	M
Washburn University	M
Washington State University	M,D
Washington University in St. Louis	M,D
Wayland Baptist University	M
Waynesburg University	M,D
Wayne State College	M
Wayne State University	M,D,O
Webster University	M,O
West Chester University of Pennsylvania	M,O
Western Connecticut State University	M
Western Governors University	M,O
Western Illinois University	M
Western Kentucky University	M,O
Western Michigan University	M,D
Western New Mexico University	M
Western Oregon University	M
Westfield State University	M
West Liberty University	M
Westminster College (PA)	M
West Virginia University	M,D
Whitworth University	M
Wichita State University	M
Widener University	M,D
Wilkes University	M,D
William Carey University	M,O
William Paterson University of New Jersey	M,O
Wilmington College	M
Wilmington University	M,D
Wilson College	M
Winona State University	M
Winston-Salem State University	M
Winthrop University	M
Worcester State University	M,O
Wright State University	M
Xavier University	M*
Youngstown State University	M

SPEECH AND INTERPERSONAL COMMUNICATION

Ball State University	M
Bob Jones University	M,D,O
Brooklyn College of the City University of New York	M,D
California State University, Fullerton	M
California State University, Northridge	M
Colorado State University	M,D
Georgia State University	M,D
Marquette University	M,D
New York University	M,D*
North Dakota State University	M,D*
Northeastern Illinois University	M
Northwestern University	M,D
Ohio University	M,D
Old Dominion University	M
Portland State University	M,O
Rensselaer Polytechnic Institute	M,D
San Francisco State University	M
Seton Hall University	M
Southern Illinois University Carbondale	M,D
Southern Illinois University Edwardsville	M
Texas Christian University	M
The University of Alabama	M
University of Arkansas at Little Rock	M
University of California, Santa Barbara	D
University of Denver	M,D
University of Hawaii at Manoa	M
University of Houston	M
The University of Iowa	M,D*
University of Maryland, College Park	M,D
University of Nebraska–Lincoln	M,D
University of Nevada, Reno	M
University of South Carolina	M,D
University of Southern Mississippi	M,D
The University of Tennessee	M,D
University of Wisconsin–Madison	M,D
University of Wisconsin–Stevens Point	M
University of Wisconsin–Superior	M
Wake Forest University	M
Washington University in St. Louis	M,D

SPORT PSYCHOLOGY

Adams State University	M
Adler University	M
Argosy University, Atlanta	M,D,O
Argosy University, Orange County	M
Argosy University, Phoenix	M,D
A.T. Still University	M,D,O
Ball State University	M
Barry University	M
California State University, Fresno	M
California State University, Long Beach	M
California University of Pennsylvania	M
Capella University	M
Chatham University	M,D
Florida State University	M,D,O
John F. Kennedy University	M
Lock Haven University of Pennsylvania	M
Purdue University	M,D
Queen's University at Kingston	M,D
Seton Hall University	M
Southern Illinois University Edwardsville	M
Springfield College	M,D,O
University of Denver	M,D,O
University of Rhode Island	M*
The University of Texas at Austin	M,D
West Virginia University	M,D

SPORTS AND ENTERTAINMENT LAW

Arizona State University at the Tempe campus	M,D
Chapman University	M,D*
Drexel University	M,D*
London Metropolitan University	M,D
New York University	M*
Pepperdine University	M
Southwestern Law School	M,D*
University of Miami	M,D*
University of New Hampshire	M,D,O

SPORTS MANAGEMENT

Adams State University	M
Adelphi University	M
American Public University System	M,D
American University	M,O
Angelo State University	M
Arkansas State University	M,O
Ashland University	M
Auburn University at Montgomery	M,O
Augustana University	M
Austin Peay State University	M
Azusa Pacific University	M*
Ball State University	M
Barry University	M
Belhaven University (MS)	M
Boise State University	M
Bowling Green State University	M
Brooklyn College of the City University of New York	M
Bryan College	M
Butler University	M,O
California Baptist University	M
California State University, Fresno	M
California State University, Long Beach	M
California University of Management and Sciences	M,D
California University of Pennsylvania	M
Campbellsville University	M
Canisius College	M
Cardinal Stritch University	M
Central Michigan University	M,O
Central Washington University	M
The Citadel, The Military College of South Carolina	M,O
Clayton State University	M
Clemson University	M,D,O
Coastal Carolina University	M,D,O
Coker College	M
The College at Brockport, State University of New York	M,O
Columbia University	M*
Concordia University Irvine	M*
Concordia University, St. Paul	M,D
Dallas Baptist University	M
Drexel University	M*
Duquesne University	M
East Carolina University	M,D,O
Eastern Kentucky University	M
Eastern Michigan University	M
Eastern New Mexico University	M
Eastern Washington University	M

*M—masters degree; D—doctorate; O—other advanced degree; *—Close-Up and/or Display*

East Stroudsburg University of Pennsylvania	M
East Tennessee State University	M,D
Endicott College	M
Fairleigh Dickinson University, Florham Campus	M
Fairleigh Dickinson University, Metropolitan Campus	M
Florida Agricultural and Mechanical University	M
Florida Atlantic University	M
Florida International University	M,D,O
Florida State University	M,D
Franklin Pierce University	M,D,O
George Mason University	M,O
Georgetown University	M,D
The George Washington University	M,O
Georgia Southern University	M
Georgia State University	M
Gonzaga University	M,D
Grambling State University	M
Grand Canyon University	M
Grand View University	M,O
Hampton University	M
Hardin-Simmons University	M
Henderson State University	M
Hofstra University	M,O
Houston Baptist University	M
Howard Payne University	M
Howard University	M
Husson University	M
Idaho State University	M
Indiana State University	M,D
Indiana University Bloomington	M,D
Indiana University of Pennsylvania	M
Iona College	M,O
Ithaca College	M
Jackson State University	M
Jacksonville University	M*
Johnson & Wales University	M
Kansas Wesleyan University	M
Kennesaw State University	M
Kent State University	M
Keystone College	M
Lasell College	M,O
Lewis University	M
Liberty University	M,D,O
Lindenwood University	M
Lock Haven University of Pennsylvania	M
Lynn University	M
Manhattanville College	M,O
Marquette University	M,O
Marshall University	M
Maryville University of Saint Louis	M,O
Mercyhurst University	M,O
Messiah College	M
Midwestern State University	M
Millersville University of Pennsylvania	M,O
Misericordia University	M
Mississippi State University	M,D
Missouri State University	M,O
Missouri Western State University	M
Montclair State University	M
Morehead State University	M
Mount St. Mary's University (MD)	M
Neumann University	M
New England College	M
New Mexico Highlands University	M
North Carolina State University	M,D
Northeastern University	M
Northern State University	M
Northwestern University	M
Ohio Dominican University	M
Ohio University	M
Old Dominion University	M
Pittsburg State University	M
Point Loma Nazarene University	M
Point Park University	M
Purdue University	M,D
Robert Morris University Illinois	M
St. John's University (NY)	M
Saint Mary's College of California	M
St. Thomas University	M,O
Sam Houston State University	M
San Diego State University	M
San Jose State University	M
Seattle University	M
Seton Hall University	M,O
Sonoma State University	M
Southeastern University (FL)	M,D
Southeast Missouri State University	M
Southern Methodist University	M,D
Southern Nazarene University	M
Southern New Hampshire University	M,D,O
Springfield College	M,D,O
State University of New York College at Cortland	M
Syracuse University	M*
Temple University	M,D*
Tennessee State University	M
Tennessee Technological University	M
Texas A&M University	M,D
Texas Tech University	M
Texas Woman's University	M,D
Tiffin University	M
Troy University	M,D
United States Sports Academy	M,D
The University of Alabama	M
University of Alberta	M
University of Arkansas	M,D
University of Arkansas at Little Rock	M
University of Central Florida	M
University of Cincinnati	M
University of Colorado Denver	M
University of Connecticut	M*
University of Dallas	M,D
University of Florida	M,D
University of Idaho	M,D
University of Indianapolis	M
The University of Iowa	M,D*
The University of Kansas	M,D
University of Louisiana at Monroe	M
University of Louisville	M,D,O
University of Mary	M
University of Mary Hardin-Baylor	M
University of Massachusetts Amherst	M,D*
University of Miami	M*
University of Michigan	M,D*
University of Minnesota, Twin Cities Campus	M,D
University of Nebraska at Kearney	M
University of New Brunswick Fredericton	M
University of New Haven	M,O*
University of New Mexico	D
The University of North Carolina at Chapel Hill	M
The University of North Carolina at Pembroke	M
University of Northern Colorado	M,D
University of Northern Iowa	M
University of North Florida	M,D
University of Oregon	M
University of San Francisco	M
University of South Alabama	M
University of South Carolina	M
University of Southern Indiana	M
University of South Florida	M,D*
The University of Tennessee	M,D
University of the Incarnate Word	M,D
University of the Southwest	M
University of Wisconsin–Parkside	M
Upper Iowa University	M
Valparaiso University	M
Waldorf University	M
Washington State University	M,D
Wayland Baptist University	M
Wayne State College	M
Wayne State University	M,D
Webber International University	M
West Chester University of Pennsylvania	M,O
Western Illinois University	M
Western Kentucky University	M
Western Michigan University	M
Western New England University	M
West Liberty University	M
West Texas A&M University	M
West Virginia University	M,D
Wichita State University	M
Wingate University	M
Winona State University	M,O
Xavier University	M*

STATISTICS

Acadia University	M
American University	M,O
Arizona State University at the Tempe campus	M,D,O
Auburn University	M,D*
Ball State University	M
Baruch College of the City University of New York	M*
Baylor University	M,D
Binghamton University, State University of New York	M,D
Bowling Green State University	M,D
Brigham Young University	M
Brock University	M
California State University, East Bay	M
Carnegie Mellon University	M,D
Central Connecticut State University	M,O
Claremont Graduate University	M,D
Clemson University	M,D
Colorado State University	M,D
Columbia University	M,D*
Concordia University (Canada)	M,D
Cornell University	M,D
Dalhousie University	M,D
Duke University	M,D*
East Carolina University	M
Florida Atlantic University	M,D
Florida International University	M
Florida State University	M,D
George Mason University	M,D,O
Georgetown University	M
The George Washington University	M,D,O
Georgia Institute of Technology	M
Georgia State University	M,D
Hampton University	M
Harvard University	M,D*
Hunter College of the City University of New York	M
Indiana University Bloomington	M,D
Indiana University–Purdue University Indianapolis	M,D
Iowa State University of Science and Technology	M,D
Jackson State University	M
Johns Hopkins University	M,D*
Kansas State University	M,D,O
Lehigh University	M,D
Louisiana State University and Agricultural & Mechanical College	M
Loyola University Chicago	M
McGill University	M,D,O
McMaster University	M
McNeese State University	M
Memorial University of Newfoundland	M,D
Miami University	M
Michigan State University	M,D
Michigan Technological University	M,D
Minnesota State University Mankato	M
Mississippi State University	M,D
Missouri University of Science and Technology	M,D
Montana State University	M,D
Montclair State University	M
Murray State University	M
New Jersey Institute of Technology	M,D,O
New Mexico Institute of Mining and Technology	M,D
New York University	M,D*
North Carolina State University	M,D
North Dakota State University	M,D*
Northern Arizona University	M,O
Northern Illinois University	M
Northwestern University	M,D
Oakland University	O
The Ohio State University	M,D
Oklahoma State University	M,D
Old Dominion University	M,D
Oregon State University	M,D
Penn State University Park	M,D*
Portland State University	M,D,O
Purdue University	M,D
Queen's University at Kingston	M,D
Rice University	M,D
Rochester Institute of Technology	O
Rutgers University–New Brunswick	M,D
St. John's University (NY)	M
Sam Houston State University	M
San Diego State University	M
San Jose State University	M
Simon Fraser University	M,D
South Dakota State University	M,D
Southern Illinois University Edwardsville	M
Southern Methodist University	M,D
Stanford University	M,D
Stephen F. Austin State University	M
Stevens Institute of Technology	M,O
Stony Brook University, State University of New York	M,D,O
Temple University	M,D*
Texas A&M University	M,D
Texas A&M University–Kingsville	M
Texas Tech University	M,D
Université de Montréal	M,D,O
Université Laval	M
The University of Akron	M
University of Alaska Fairbanks	M,D,O
University of Alberta	M,D,O
The University of Arizona	M,D
University of Arkansas	M
The University of British Columbia	M,D
University of Calgary	M,D
University of California, Berkeley	M,D
University of California, Davis	M,D
University of California, Irvine	M,D
University of California, Los Angeles	M,D*
University of California, Riverside	M
University of California, San Diego	M,D*
University of California, Santa Barbara	M,D
University of California, Santa Cruz	M,D*
University of Central Florida	M,O
University of Central Oklahoma	M
University of Chicago	M,D,O
University of Cincinnati	M,D
University of Colorado Denver	M,D
University of Connecticut	M,D*
University of Delaware	M*
University of Florida	M,D
University of Georgia	M,D
University of Guelph	M,D
University of Houston–Clear Lake	M
University of Idaho	M
University of Illinois at Chicago	M,D
University of Illinois at Urbana–Champaign	M,D
The University of Iowa	M,D,O*
The University of Kansas	M,D,O
University of Kentucky	M,D
The University of Manchester	M,D
University of Manitoba	M,D
University of Maryland, Baltimore County	M,D
University of Maryland, College Park	M,D
University of Massachusetts Amherst	M,D*
University of Memphis	M,D
University of Michigan	M,D,O*
University of Minnesota, Twin Cities Campus	M,D
University of Missouri	M,D
University of Missouri–Kansas City	M,D
University of Nebraska–Lincoln	M,D
University of New Brunswick Fredericton	M,D
University of New Mexico	M,D
The University of North Carolina at Chapel Hill	M,D
The University of North Carolina Wilmington	M,O
University of North Florida	M
University of Notre Dame	M,D
University of Ottawa	M,D
University of Pennsylvania	M,D*
University of Pittsburgh	M,D*
University of Regina	M,D
University of Rhode Island	M,D,O*
University of Rochester	M,D*
University of Saskatchewan	M,D
University of South Africa	M,D
University of South Carolina	M,D,O
University of Southern California	M,D*
University of Southern Maine	M,O
University of South Florida	M,D*
The University of Tennessee	M,D
The University of Texas at Austin	M,D
The University of Texas at Dallas	M,D
The University of Texas at El Paso	M
The University of Texas at San Antonio	M,D
The University of Toledo	M,D
University of Toronto	M,D
University of Utah	M,D,O
University of Vermont	M
University of Victoria	M,D
University of Virginia	M,D
University of Washington	M,D
University of Waterloo	M,D
The University of Western Ontario	M,D
University of Windsor	M,D
University of Wisconsin–Madison	M,D
University of Wisconsin–Milwaukee	M,D*
University of Wyoming	M,D
Utah State University	M,D
Virginia Polytechnic Institute and State University	M,D
Washington University in St. Louis	M,D
Wayne State University	M,D
Western Michigan University	M,D,O
West Virginia University	M,D
Yale University	M,D
York University	M,D
Youngstown State University	M

STRUCTURAL BIOLOGY

Albert Einstein College of Medicine	D
Baylor College of Medicine	D
Carnegie Mellon University	M,D
Columbia University	D*
Duke University	O*
Florida State University	D
Illinois State University	M,D
Iowa State University of Science and Technology	M,D
Massachusetts Institute of Technology	D
Michigan State University	D
New York University	D*
Northwestern University	D
Stanford University	D
Stony Brook University, State University of New York	D
Tufts University	D*
Tulane University	M,D
University at Buffalo, the State University of New York	M,D
The University of Alabama at Birmingham	D
University of Connecticut	M,D*
The University of Manchester	M,D
University of Minnesota, Twin Cities Campus	D
University of Oklahoma	M,D*
University of Pittsburgh	D*
University of Rochester	D*
The University of Texas Health Science Center at San Antonio	M,D
The University of Texas Medical Branch	D
University of Washington	D
Weill Cornell Medicine	M,D

STRUCTURAL ENGINEERING

California State University, Northridge	M
The Citadel, The Military College of South Carolina	M,O
Clemson University	M,D
Cornell University	M,D
Drexel University	M,D*
École Polytechnique de Montréal	M,D,O
Illinois Institute of Technology	M,D
Instituto Tecnologico de Santo Domingo	M,O
Iowa State University of Science and Technology	M,D
Kansas State University	M,D
Kennesaw State University	M
Louisiana State University and Agricultural & Mechanical College	M,D
Marquette University	M,D,O
Massachusetts Institute of Technology	M,D,O
McGill University	M,D
Northwestern University	M,D
Norwich University	M
Ohio University	M,D
Old Dominion University	M
Oregon State University	M,D
Penn State Harrisburg	M,O
Pontificia Universidad Catolica Madre y Maestra	M
Southern Illinois University Edwardsville	M
Southern Methodist University	M,D
Stanford University	M,D,O
Stevens Institute of Technology	M,D,O
Tufts University	M,D*
University at Buffalo, the State University of New York	M,D
The University of Alabama at Birmingham	M
University of Alberta	M,D
University of Calgary	M,D
University of California, Berkeley	M,D
University of California, San Diego	M,D*
University of Central Florida	M,D,O
University of Colorado Denver	M,D
University of Dayton	M
University of Delaware	M,D*
The University of Manchester	M,D
University of Massachusetts Amherst	M,D*
University of Memphis	M,D,O

University of Michigan	M,D,O*
University of New Brunswick Fredericton	M,D
University of Puerto Rico–Mayagüez	M,D
University of South Florida	M,D*
The University of Texas at Tyler	M
University of Washington	M,D
University of Wisconsin–Madison	M

STUDENT AFFAIRS

Adler University	M
Alfred University	M
Alliant International University–Los Angeles	M,D,O
Alliant International University–San Diego	M,D,O
Appalachian State University	M
Arkansas State University	M,O
Arkansas Tech University	M,D,O
Binghamton University, State University of New York	M
Bloomsburg University of Pennsylvania	M
Bob Jones University	M,D,O
Bowling Green State University	M
Bucknell University	M
Buffalo State College, State University of New York	M
California State University, Bakersfield	M
California State University, Fresno	M
California State University, Long Beach	M,D
Canisius College	M,O
Cardinal Stritch University	M,D
Carlow University	M
Central Michigan University	M,D,O
The Citadel, The Military College of South Carolina	M,O
Claremont Graduate University	M,D,O
Clemson University	M,D,O
The College of Saint Rose	M
Colorado State University	M,D
Dallas Baptist University	M
DePaul University	M,D
Eastern Illinois University	M
Eastern Michigan University	M,D,O
Fresno Pacific University	M,O
George Mason University	M,O
The George Washington University	M,D,O
Grambling State University	M,D,O
Hampton University	M,D,O
Illinois State University	M
Indiana State University	M,D,O
Indiana University Bloomington	M,D,O
Indiana University of Pennsylvania	M
Iowa State University of Science and Technology	M,D
Kansas State University	M,D,O
Kent State University	M
Lewis & Clark College	M,D,O
Lewis University	M
Manhattan College	M,O
Marquette University	M,D,O
Merrimack College	M,O
Messiah College	M
Miami University	M,D
Minnesota State University Mankato	M,D
Mississippi State University	M,D,O
Missouri State University	M
Monmouth University	M,D,O*
Morgan State University	M,D
New York University	M,D*
Northern Arizona University	M,D,O
Northwestern State University of Louisiana	M
Nova Southeastern University	M,D,O*
Ohio University	M,D
Oregon State University	M
Providence University College & Theological Seminary	M,D,O
Purdue University Global	M
Quincy University	M
Regent University	M,D,O
Rutgers University–New Brunswick	M
St. Cloud State University	M
St. Edward's University	M
Saint Louis University	M,D,O*
Seton Hall University	M
Shippensburg University of Pennsylvania	M,D
Slippery Rock University of Pennsylvania	M
Southern Arkansas University–Magnolia	M
Southern Illinois University Edwardsville	M
Springfield College	M,D,O
State University of New York at Plattsburgh	M,O
Syracuse University	M*
Texas State University	M
University of Arkansas at Little Rock	M,D
University of Bridgeport	M
University of Central Arkansas	M
University of Central Florida	M,O
University of Central Missouri	M,D,O
University of Central Oklahoma	M
University of Dayton	M,O
University of Florida	M,D,O
University of Georgia	M,D,O
The University of Iowa	M,D*
University of La Verne	M
University of Louisville	M,D
University of Maryland, College Park	M,D,O
University of Minnesota, Twin Cities Campus	M
University of Nebraska at Kearney	M,O
University of Northern Colorado	M,D
University of Northern Iowa	M
University of Oklahoma	M,D*
University of Rhode Island	M*
University of Rochester	M*
University of St. Thomas (MN)	M,D,O
University of South Carolina	M
University of Southern California	M*
University of Southern Mississippi	M,D,O
University of South Florida	M,D,O*
The University of Tennessee	M
The University of Tennessee at Martin	M
University of the Cumberlands	M,D,O
University of Utah	M,D
University of Virginia	M,D,O
The University of West Alabama	M
University of West Florida	M
University of Wisconsin–La Crosse	M,D
University of Wyoming	M,D
Virginia Commonwealth University	M
Walsh University	M
West Chester University of Pennsylvania	M,O
Western Illinois University	M
Western Kentucky University	M
William James College	M,D,O

SUPPLY CHAIN MANAGEMENT

Abilene Christian University	M
Adelphi University	M
Albany State University	M
American Graduate University	M,O
Anderson University (SC)	M
Arizona State University at the Tempe campus	M,D
Ashland University	M
Athens State University	M
Binghamton University, State University of New York	D
Boston University	M*
Brigham Young University	M
Bryant University	M
California Polytechnic State University, San Luis Obispo	M*
California State University, East Bay	M
California State University, San Bernardino	M
Capella University	M,D
Case Western Reserve University	M,D*
Central Connecticut State University	M,O
Clarkson University	O
Clayton State University	M
Clemson University	M,D
Concordia University (Canada)	M,D,O
Delaware Valley University	M
DePaul University	M,D
DeSales University	M
Duquesne University	M
Eastern Michigan University	M,O
Elmhurst College	M
Embry-Riddle Aeronautical University–Worldwide	M
Fairleigh Dickinson University, Florham Campus	M
Ferris State University	M
Florida Institute of Technology	M,D
Fontbonne University	M
Friends University	M
Georgia Southern University	D
Golden Gate University	M,D,O
HEC Montreal	M,O
Howard University	M
Indiana University–Purdue University Indianapolis	M
Johnson & Wales University	M
Lindenwood University	M
Loyola University Chicago	M,O
Maine Maritime Academy	M
Marquette University	M,O
Maryville University of Saint Louis	M,O
Metropolitan State University	M,D,O
Michigan State University	M,D
Moravian College	M
Naval Postgraduate School	M
New York Institute of Technology	M
Niagara University	M
North Carolina Agricultural and Technical State University	M
North Carolina State University	M
Norwich University	M
Nova Southeastern University	M*
Old Dominion University	M
Penn State Harrisburg	M,O
Polytechnic University of Puerto Rico, Miami Campus	M
Portland State University	M
Purdue University Global	M
Quinnipiac University	M
Rensselaer Polytechnic Institute	M
Rutgers University–Newark	D
Saint Leo University	M,D
St. Norbert College	M
Santa Clara University	M
Seton Hall University	M,O
Shippensburg University of Pennsylvania	M,D,O
Southern Arkansas University–Magnolia	M
Southern New Hampshire University	M,D,O
Strayer University	M
Suffolk University	M
Syracuse University	M*
Towson University	M,O
University at Buffalo, the State University of New York	M,D
The University of Akron	M
The University of Alabama in Huntsville	M,O
University of Dallas	M,D
University of Florida	M,D,O
University of Houston	M
University of Houston–Downtown	M
The University of Kansas	M,D
University of La Verne	M
University of Louisville	M,D,O
The University of Manchester	M
University of Memphis	M,D
University of Michigan	M,D*
University of Michigan–Dearborn	M
University of Minnesota, Twin Cities Campus	M,D
University of Missouri–St. Louis	M,D,O
The University of North Carolina at Charlotte	M,O
The University of North Carolina at Greensboro	M,D,O
University of North Texas	M,D,O
University of Oklahoma	M,D*
University of Pittsburgh	M*
University of Rhode Island	M,D*
University of San Diego	M,O
University of South Dakota	M,O
University of Southern California	M,D,O*
The University of Tennessee at Chattanooga	M,O
The University of Texas at Austin	M,D
The University of Texas at Dallas	M
University of Washington	M,D
University of Wisconsin–Madison	M
University of Wisconsin–Platteville	M
University of Wisconsin–Stout	M
Walden University	M,D,O
Washington University in St. Louis	M,D
Western Illinois University	M,O
Wichita State University	M
Wilfrid Laurier University	M,D
Worcester Polytechnic Institute	M,D,O
Wright State University	M

SURVEYING SCIENCE AND ENGINEERING

University of New Brunswick Fredericton	M,D

SURVEY METHODOLOGY

University of Maryland, College Park	M,D
University of Michigan	M,D,O*
University of Nebraska–Lincoln	M,D

SUSTAINABILITY MANAGEMENT

Adler University	M
American University	M
Anaheim University	M,D,O
Antioch University New England	M
Aquinas College (MI)	M
Argosy University, Chicago	M,D
Argosy University, Hawai`i	M,D,O
Argosy University, Los Angeles	M,D
Argosy University, Northern Virginia	M,D,O
Argosy University, Orange County	M,D,O
Argosy University, Phoenix	M,D
Argosy University, Seattle	M,D
Argosy University, Tampa	M,D
Argosy University, Twin Cities	M,D
Bard College	M,O
Baruch College of the City University of New York	M,D*
Bluffton University	M
Case Western Reserve University	D*
Chatham University	M
City University of Seattle	M,O
Clark University	M
Colorado State University	M
Columbia University	M*
DePaul University	M,D
Duquesne University	M
Edgewood College	M
Fairleigh Dickinson University, Florham Campus	O
Franklin Pierce University	M,D,O
Goddard College	M
Illinois Institute of Technology	M
Indiana University Bloomington	M,D,O
James Madison University	M
Maastricht School of Management	M,D
Maharishi University of Management	M,D
Michigan Technological University	M,D,O
Naropa University	M
National University	M
The New School	M
Oklahoma State University	M,D,O
Oregon State University	M,D
Penn State Great Valley	M,O
Presidio Graduate School (CA)	M,O
Rochester Institute of Technology	M,D
Royal Roads University	M,O
San Francisco State University	M
Seattle Pacific University	M
SIT Graduate Institute	M
Southeastern Louisiana University	M
Southern New Hampshire University	M,D,O
South University (GA)	M
State University of New York College of Environmental Science and Forestry	M,D,O
Syracuse University	O*
The University of British Columbia	M,D
University of California, Berkeley	O
University of California, Merced	M,D
University of Colorado Denver	M
University of Louisville	M,D
University of New Hampshire	M,O
University of Portland	M
University of Saint Francis (IN)	M
University of Saskatchewan	M
University of Southern Maine	M
University of South Florida	M,O*
University of Vermont	M
University of Wisconsin–Green Bay	M
University of Wisconsin–Parkside	M
University of Wisconsin–Stout	M
University of Wisconsin–Superior	M

SUSTAINABLE DEVELOPMENT

American University	M,D,O
The American University in Cairo	M,D,O
Antioch University Los Angeles	M
Antioch University New England	M,O
Arizona State University at the Tempe campus	M,D,O
Baruch College of the City University of New York	M*
Binghamton University, State University of New York	M
Boston Architectural College	M
Brandeis University	M
California State University, Stanislaus	M
Carnegie Mellon University	M,D
The Catholic University of America	M,O
City College of the City University of New York	M
Clarkson University	M,D
Clark University	M
Cleveland State University	M,O
Colorado State University	M,O
Columbia University	M,D*
Cornell University	M,D
Dartmouth College	D*
DePaul University	M
Eastern Illinois University	M
Eastern Michigan University	M,O
Emory University	M
Future Generations University	M
Hawai`i Pacific University	M
HEC Montreal	O
Hofstra University	M
Hunter College of the City University of New York	M,O
Instituto Centroamericano de Administración de Empresas	M
Instituto Tecnologico de Santo Domingo	M,O
Iowa State University of Science and Technology	M,D
Johnson & Wales University	M
Judson University	M
Lehigh University	M,O
Lenoir-Rhyne University	M
Lesley University	M,D,O
Lipscomb University	M,O
Long Island University–LIU Post	M,O
Manhattanville College	M,O
Minneapolis College of Art and Design	M,O
Mississippi State University	M,D
Montclair State University	M
New Jersey Institute of Technology	M,D,O
New York School of Interior Design	M
New York University	M*
Northern Arizona University	M
Penn State University Park	M*
Pratt Institute	M*
Rochester Institute of Technology	M,D
St. Edward's University	M
Savannah College of Art and Design	M
Saybrook University	M,D
SIT Graduate Institute	M
Southern Illinois University Edwardsville	M
Southern Methodist University	M,D
Stanford University	M,D,O
State University of New York College of Environmental Science and Forestry	M,D,O
Temple University	M,O*
Texas A&M University–Kingsville	D
Texas State University	M
Texas Tech University	M,D
Thomas Jefferson University	M
Unity College	M
University at Buffalo, the State University of New York	M,D
The University of Alabama at Birmingham	M
University of Alaska Fairbanks	M,D
The University of British Columbia	M
University of Calgary	M,D
University of California, Berkeley	M,O
University of California, Santa Barbara	M,D
University of Colorado Denver	M,D
University of Florida	M,O
University of Georgia	M,D
University of Hawaii at Manoa	M,D,O
University of Houston	M
The University of Iowa	M,D*
University of Maryland, College Park	M
University of Massachusetts Amherst	M*

*M—masters degree; D—doctorate; O—other advanced degree; *—Close-Up and/or Display*

University of Michigan	M,D*
University of New Brunswick Fredericton	M
University of North Carolina at Asheville	M,O
University of Notre Dame	M
University of Oklahoma	M,D*
University of South Dakota	M,D
University of Southern California	M,D,O*
University of South Florida	M,O*
The University of Texas at Austin	M
The University of Texas Rio Grande Valley	M
University of Vermont	M
University of Washington	M,D
The University of Western Ontario	M,D
University of Wisconsin–Madison	M
University of Wisconsin–Stevens Point	D
Walden University	M,D,O
West Chester University of Pennsylvania	M,O
Xavier University	M*

SYSTEMS BIOLOGY

Albert Einstein College of Medicine	D
George Mason University	M,D,O
The George Washington University	D
Harvard University	D*
Massachusetts Institute of Technology	D
Michigan State University	D
Northwestern University	D
Oregon State University	M,D
Purdue University	D
Rutgers University–New Brunswick	D
Stanford University	D
University of California, Irvine	D
University of California, Merced	M,D
University of California, San Diego	D*
University of Chicago	D
University of Cincinnati	D
University of Colorado Denver	M,D
University of Pittsburgh	D*
University of Toronto	M,D
Virginia Commonwealth University	D
Washington University in St. Louis	D
Weill Cornell Medicine	M,D

SYSTEMS ENGINEERING

Air Force Institute of Technology	M,D
Arizona State University at the Tempe campus	M
Auburn University	M,D,O*
Boston University	M,D*
California Institute of Technology	M,D
California State Polytechnic University, Pomona	M
California State University, Fullerton	M
California State University, Northridge	M
Carleton University	M,D
Carnegie Mellon University	M
Case Western Reserve University	M,D*
The Catholic University of America	M,O
The Citadel, The Military College of South Carolina	M,O
Clarkson University	M
Colorado State University	M,D
Colorado State University–Pueblo	M
Colorado Technical University Aurora	M
Colorado Technical University Colorado Springs	M
Concordia University (Canada)	M,D,O
Cornell University	M,D
Dartmouth College	M,D*
Embry-Riddle Aeronautical University–Daytona	M
Embry-Riddle Aeronautical University–Worldwide	M
Florida Institute of Technology	M,D
George Mason University	M,D,O
Georgetown University	M,D
The George Washington University	M,D,O
Georgia Institute of Technology	M,D
Georgia Southern University	M
Harrisburg University of Science and Technology	M
Indiana University Bloomington	D
Indiana University–Purdue University Fort Wayne	M
Instituto Tecnológico y de Estudios Superiores de Monterrey, Campus Chihuahua	M,O
Instituto Tecnológico y de Estudios Superiores de Monterrey, Campus Monterrey	M,D
Iowa State University of Science and Technology	M
Johns Hopkins University	M,O*
Kennesaw State University	M
Lehigh University	M,D,O
Loyola Marymount University	M
Massachusetts Institute of Technology	M,D
Mississippi State University	M,D
Missouri University of Science and Technology	M,D
Naval Postgraduate School	M,D,O
New Mexico Institute of Mining and Technology	M
New Mexico State University	M,D,O
North Carolina Agricultural and Technical State University	M,D
Northeastern University	M,D,O
Oakland University	M,D,O
The Ohio State University	M,D
Ohio University	M
Old Dominion University	M,D
Oregon State University	M,D
Penn State Great Valley	M,O
Regis University	M,O
Rensselaer Polytechnic Institute	M,D
Rochester Institute of Technology	M,D
Rose-Hulman Institute of Technology	M
Rutgers University–New Brunswick	M,D
San Jose State University	M
Simon Fraser University	M,D
Southern Methodist University	M,D
Stevens Institute of Technology	M,D,O
Stony Brook University, State University of New York	M
Tennessee State University	M,D
Texas A&M University–Kingsville	D
Texas Tech University	M,D
The University of Alabama in Huntsville	M,D
University of Alberta	M,D
The University of Arizona	M,D,O
University of Arkansas at Little Rock	M,D,O
University of California, Merced	M,D
University of Central Florida	M,D,O
University of Colorado Colorado Springs	M,D
University of Florida	M,D,O
University of Houston–Clear Lake	M
University of Illinois at Urbana–Champaign	M,D
University of Louisiana at Lafayette	M,D
University of Maryland, Baltimore County	M,O
University of Maryland, College Park	M
University of Massachusetts Dartmouth	M,O
University of Michigan	M,D*
University of Michigan–Dearborn	M,D
University of Nebraska at Omaha	M,O
University of New Mexico	M,D
The University of North Carolina at Charlotte	M,D,O
University of Pennsylvania	M,D*
University of Regina	M,D
University of Rhode Island	M,D*
University of St. Thomas (MN)	M,O
University of South Alabama	D
University of Southern California	M,D,O*
University of South Florida	O*
The University of Texas at Arlington	M
The University of Texas at Dallas	M,D
The University of Texas Rio Grande Valley	M
University of Utah	M,O
University of Virginia	M,D
University of Washington	M,D
University of Waterloo	M,D
University of Wisconsin–Madison	M,D
Virginia Polytechnic Institute and State University	M,O
Wayne State University	M,D,O
Worcester Polytechnic Institute	M,D,O

SYSTEMS SCIENCE

Arizona State University at the Tempe campus	M,D
Binghamton University, State University of New York	M,D
Carleton University	M,D
Claremont Graduate University	M,D,O
Eastern Illinois University	M,O
Fairleigh Dickinson University, Metropolitan Campus	M
Harrisburg University of Science and Technology	M
Hood College	M*
Louisiana State University and Agricultural & Mechanical College	M,D
Louisiana State University in Shreveport	M
Miami University	M
New Jersey Institute of Technology	M,D,O
Oakland University	M,D
Portland State University	M,D,O
Rensselaer at Hartford	M
Stevens Institute of Technology	M,D,O
Strayer University	M
Universidad Autonoma de Guadalajara	M,D
University of Michigan	M,D*
University of Ottawa	M,D,O
Worcester Polytechnic Institute	M,D,O

TAXATION

American International College	M,D,O
American University	M,O
Appalachian State University	M
Baruch College of the City University of New York	M*
Bentley University	M
Boise State University	M
Bryant University	M
California Miramar University	M
California Polytechnic State University, San Luis Obispo	M*
California State University, Fullerton	M
California State University, Northridge	M,O
Capital University	M
Chapman University	M,D*
DePaul University	M,D
Fairfield University	M,O
Fairleigh Dickinson University, Florham Campus	M,O
Fairleigh Dickinson University, Metropolitan Campus	M
Florida Gulf Coast University	M
Florida State University	M,D
Fordham University	M,D
Georgetown University	M,D
Georgia State University	M
Golden Gate University	M,D,O
Goldey-Beacom College	M
Gonzaga University	M
Grand Valley State University	M
HEC Montreal	M,O
Hofstra University	M,O
Illinois Institute of Technology	M,D
Instituto Tecnologico de Santo Domingo	M,O
James Madison University	M
Liberty University	M,D
Lipscomb University	M,O
Long Island University–LIU Brooklyn	M,O
Long Island University–LIU Post	M
Loyola University Chicago	M,D,O
Metropolitan State University of Denver	M
Michigan State University	M,D
Mississippi State University	M
National Paralegal College	M
New York University	M,D,O*
Northeastern University	M
Northern Illinois University	M
Northern Kentucky University	M,O
Northwestern University	M,D
Pace University	M
Robert Morris University	M
St. John's University (NY)	M
St. Thomas University	M,D
San Jose State University	M
Seton Hall University	O
Southern Illinois University Edwardsville	M
Southern Methodist University	M,D
Southern New Hampshire University	M,D,O
State University of New York College at Old Westbury	M
Strayer University	M
Suffolk University	M,O
Taft University System	M,D
Temple University	M,D*
Texas Christian University	M
Texas Tech University	M,D
Thomas Jefferson University	M
Université de Montréal	M,D,O
Université de Sherbrooke	M,O
The University of Akron	M
The University of Alabama	M,D
The University of Alabama in Huntsville	M
University of Baltimore	M,D
The University of British Columbia	M,D
University of Cincinnati	M
University of Colorado Denver	M
University of Denver	M
University of Florida	M,D
University of Hartford	M,O
University of Hawaii at Manoa	M
University of Houston	M,D
University of Miami	M,D*
University of Michigan	M,D*
University of Minnesota, Twin Cities Campus	M
University of Mississippi	M,D
University of Missouri	M,D,O
University of New Haven	M,O*
University of New Mexico	M
University of New Orleans	M
University of Notre Dame	M
University of San Diego	M,D,O
University of Southern California	M*
University of South Florida	M,D*
The University of Texas at Arlington	M,D
University of the Sacred Heart	M
University of Washington	M,D
University of Waterloo	M,D
University of Wisconsin–Madison	M
University of Wisconsin–Milwaukee	M,O*
Villanova University	M
Wake Forest University	M
Walsh College of Accountancy and Business Administration	M
Wayne State University	M,D,O
Weber State University	M
Western Michigan University Thomas M. Cooley Law School	M,D
Wichita State University	M
Widener University	M
Yeshiva University	M

TECHNICAL COMMUNICATION

Auburn University	M,D,O*
Boise State University	M
Bowling Green State University	M,D
Drexel University	M*
East Carolina University	M,D,O
Eastern Michigan University	M,O
Eastern Washington University	M
Harvard University	M*
Indiana University–Purdue University Indianapolis	M
Lawrence Technological University	M,O
Minnesota State University Mankato	M,O
Missouri University of Science and Technology	M
Missouri Western State University	M,O
Montana Tech of The University of Montana	M
New Jersey Institute of Technology	M,D,O
North Carolina State University	M
Northeastern University	M
Texas State University	M
University of Houston–Downtown	M
University of Nebraska at Omaha	M,O
University of South Florida	O*
University of Wisconsin–Stout	M

TECHNICAL WRITING

Carnegie Mellon University	M
Drexel University	M*
Illinois Institute of Technology	M,D
James Madison University	M
Johns Hopkins University	M,O*
Laurentian University	O
Louisiana Tech University	M,D,O
Massachusetts Institute of Technology	M
Metropolitan State University	M
Texas Tech University	M,D
The University of Alabama in Huntsville	M,O
University of Arkansas at Little Rock	M
University of North Alabama	M
The University of North Carolina at Charlotte	M,O
The University of North Carolina at Greensboro	M,D,O
University of the Sciences	M,O
University of Waterloo	M,D
Western Carolina University	M,O

TECHNOLOGY AND PUBLIC POLICY

Arizona State University at the Tempe campus	M
Carnegie Mellon University	M,D
Eastern Michigan University	M
The George Washington University	M,O
Massachusetts Institute of Technology	M,D
Rensselaer Polytechnic Institute	M,D
Rochester Institute of Technology	M
Stony Brook University, State University of New York	D
University of Minnesota, Twin Cities Campus	M
University of South Africa	M,D
The University of Texas at Austin	M

TELECOMMUNICATIONS

Ball State University	M
Boston University	M,O*
California Miramar University	M
Claremont Graduate University	M,D,O
Drexel University	M*
Fairfield University	M,O
Florida International University	M,D
Franklin Pierce University	M,D,O
The George Washington University	M,D,O
Illinois Institute of Technology	M,D
Instituto Tecnologico de Santo Domingo	M,O
Michigan State University	M
New Jersey Institute of Technology	M,D
Northeastern University	M,D,O
Ohio University	M
Pace University	M,D,O
Rochester Institute of Technology	M
Saint Mary's University of Minnesota	M
Southern Methodist University	M,D
Stevens Institute of Technology	M,D,O
Stony Brook University, State University of New York	M,D,O
Stratford University (VA)	M,D
Universidad del Turabo	M
Université du Québec, Institut National de la Recherche Scientifique	M,D
University of Alberta	M,D
University of Arkansas	M,D
University of California, San Diego	M,D*
University of Colorado Boulder	M
University of Florida	M,D
University of Hawaii at Manoa	O
University of Houston	M
University of Maryland, College Park	M
University of Massachusetts Dartmouth	M,D,O
University of Mississippi	M,D
University of Missouri–Kansas City	M,D,O
The University of North Carolina at Chapel Hill	M,D,O
University of Oklahoma	M*
University of Southern California	M,D,O*
The University of Texas at Dallas	M,D

TELECOMMUNICATIONS MANAGEMENT

Alaska Pacific University	M
Boston University	M,O*
California Miramar University	M
Capitol Technology University	M
Carnegie Mellon University	M
Concordia University (Canada)	M,D,O
East Carolina University	M,D,O
Instituto Tecnológico y de Estudios Superiores de Monterrey, Campus Ciudad de México	M
Instituto Tecnológico y de Estudios Superiores de Monterrey, Campus Ciudad Obregón	M
Instituto Tecnológico y de Estudios Superiores de Monterrey, Campus Estado de México	M,D
Instituto Tecnológico y de Estudios Superiores de Monterrey, Campus Irapuato	M,D
Murray State University	M
Oklahoma State University	M,D,O
San Diego State University	M
Stevens Institute of Technology	M,D,O
Strayer University	M

University of Colorado Boulder	M
University of South Africa	M,D
University of Wisconsin–Stout	M

TEXTILE DESIGN

Academy of Art University	M
Arizona State University at the Tempe campus	M,D
California State University, Los Angeles	M
Concordia University (Canada)	M
Cornell University	M,D
Cranbrook Academy of Art	M
Drexel University	M*
East Carolina University	M
Illinois State University	M
Kent State University	M
Massachusetts College of Art and Design	M,O
The New School	M
Paris College of Art	M
Rhode Island School of Design	M
Savannah College of Art and Design	M
School of the Art Institute of Chicago	M,O
Temple University	M*
Thomas Jefferson University	M
University of California, Davis	M
University of Cincinnati	M
The University of Kansas	M
The University of Manchester	M,D
University of Minnesota, Twin Cities Campus	M,D,O
The University of North Carolina at Greensboro	M,D
University of North Texas	M,D,O
Wayne State University	M

TEXTILE SCIENCES AND ENGINEERING

Cornell University	M,D
North Carolina State University	M,D
Thomas Jefferson University	M,D
The University of Texas at Austin	M

THANATOLOGY

Brooklyn College of the City University of New York	M
The College of New Rochelle	M,O
Hood College	M,O*
Marian University (WI)	M
Southwestern College (NM)	M,O
University of Maryland, Baltimore	O
Washington & Jefferson College	M,O

THEATER

Academy of Art University	M
American Conservatory Theater	M,O
Arcadia University	M,D,O
Arizona State University at the Tempe campus	M,D
Baylor University	M
Berklee College of Music	M,O
Binghamton University, State University of New York	M
Bob Jones University	M,D,O
Boston University	M,O*
Bowling Green State University	M,D
Brandeis University	M
Brigham Young University	M
Brooklyn College of the City University of New York	M
Brown University	M,D
California Institute of the Arts	M,O
California State University, Fullerton	M
California State University, Long Beach	M
California State University, Los Angeles	M
California State University, Northridge	M
Carnegie Mellon University	M
Case Western Reserve University	M*
The Catholic University of America	M,O
Central Washington University	M
Columbia University	M,D*
Columbus State University	M
Cornell University	D
Dell'Arte International School of Physical Theatre	M
DePaul University	M
Eastern Michigan University	M
Florida Atlantic University	M
Florida State University	M,D
Fontbonne University	M
Fordham University	M
George Mason University	M
The George Washington University	M,O
The Graduate Center, City University of New York	D
Hollins University	M,O
Hunter College of the City University of New York	M
Idaho State University	M
Illinois State University	M
Indiana University Bloomington	M,D
The Juilliard School	M,D,O
Kansas State University	M
Kent State University	M
Long Island University–LIU Post	M
Louisiana State University and Agricultural & Mechanical College	M,D
Mary Baldwin University	M
Miami University	M
Michigan State University	M
Minnesota State University Mankato	M
Missouri State University	M
Montclair State University	M
Naropa University	M
The New School	M
New York University	M,D,O*
Northern Illinois University	M
Northern Michigan University	M,O
Northwestern University	M,D
The Ohio State University	M,D
Ohio University	M
Oklahoma State University	M
Pace University	M
Penn State University Park	M*
Pensacola Christian College	M,D,O
Point Park University	M
Portland State University	M
Purdue University	M
Regent University	M,D
Roosevelt University	M
Rowan University	M
Rutgers University–New Brunswick	M
San Diego State University	M
San Francisco State University	M
Sarah Lawrence College	M
Savannah College of Art and Design	M
Smith College	M
Southern Illinois University Carbondale	M,D
Southern Methodist University	M
Southern Oregon University	M
Stanford University	D
Stony Brook University, State University of New York	M
Temple University	M*
Texas A&M University–Commerce	M,D,O
Texas State University	M
Texas Tech University	M
Texas Woman's University	M
Towson University	M
Tufts University	M,D*
Tulane University	M
Université de Sherbrooke	M,D
Université Laval	M,D
University at Buffalo, the State University of New York	M,D
The University of Akron	M
The University of Alabama	M
University of Alberta	M
The University of Arizona	M
University of Arkansas	M
The University of British Columbia	M,D
University of Calgary	M
University of California, Berkeley	D
University of California, Davis	M,D
University of California, Irvine	M,D
University of California, Los Angeles	M,D*
University of California, San Diego	M,D*
University of California, Santa Barbara	M,D
University of California, Santa Cruz	O*
University of Central Florida	M
University of Central Missouri	M,D,O
University of Chicago	M
University of Cincinnati	M,D
University of Colorado Boulder	M,D
University of Connecticut	M*
University of Delaware	M*
University of Florida	M
University of Georgia	M,D
University of Guelph	M,D
University of Hawaii at Manoa	M,D
University of Houston	M
University of Idaho	M
University of Illinois at Urbana–Champaign	M,D
The University of Iowa	M*
The University of Kansas	M,D
University of Lethbridge	M,D
University of Louisville	M
The University of Manchester	D
University of Maryland, Baltimore County	M
University of Maryland, College Park	M,D
University of Massachusetts Amherst	M*
University of Memphis	M
University of Minnesota, Twin Cities Campus	M,D
University of Missouri	M,D
University of Missouri–Kansas City	M
University of Montana	M
University of Nebraska–Lincoln	M
University of Nevada, Las Vegas	M
University of New Mexico	M
University of New Orleans	M
The University of North Carolina at Chapel Hill	M
The University of North Carolina at Charlotte	M,D,O
The University of North Carolina at Greensboro	M
University of North Carolina School of the Arts	M
University of Oregon	M,D
University of Ottawa	M
University of Pittsburgh	M,D*
University of Portland	M
University of San Diego	M
University of Saskatchewan	M
University of South Carolina	M,D
University of South Dakota	M
University of Southern California	M*
University of Southern Mississippi	M
The University of Tennessee	M
The University of Texas at Austin	M,D
University of the Cumberlands	M,D,O
University of Toronto	M,D
University of Victoria	M
University of Virginia	M
University of Washington	M,D
University of Wisconsin–Madison	M,D
University of Wisconsin–Superior	M
Utah State University	M
Villanova University	M
Virginia Commonwealth University	M
Washington University in St. Louis	M
Wayne State University	M
Western Illinois University	M
West Virginia University	M,D
Yale University	M,D,O
York University	M,D

THEOLOGY

Abilene Christian University	M
Acadia University	M,D
Ambrose University	M,O
American Baptist Seminary of the West	M
American Jewish University	M
Amridge University	M,D
Anabaptist Mennonite Biblical Seminary	M,O
Anderson University (IN)	M,D
Andrews University	M,D,O
Apex School of Theology	M,D
Aquinas Institute of Theology	M,D,O
Arlington Baptist University	M
Asbury Theological Seminary	M,D,O
Ashland Theological Seminary	M,D
Assemblies of God Theological Seminary	M,D
The Athenaeum of Ohio	M,O
Atlantic School of Theology	M,O
Austin Graduate School of Theology	M
Austin Presbyterian Theological Seminary	M,D
Ave Maria University	M,D
Azusa Pacific University	M,D*
Bakke Graduate University	M,D
Baptist Bible College	M
The Baptist College of Florida	M
Baptist Missionary Association Theological Seminary	M
Baptist Theological Seminary at Richmond	M,D,O
Barclay College	M
Barry University	M,D
Baylor University	M,D
Bethany Theological Seminary	M,O
Bethel College	M
Bethel Seminary	M,D,O
Bethesda University	M
Beth HaMedrash Shaarei Yosher Institute	
Beth Hatalmud Rabbinical College	
Bethlehem College & Seminary	M
Beth Medrash Govoha	
Bethune-Cookman University	M
Bexley Seabury Seminary	M,D,O
Biblical Theological Seminary	M,D,O
Biola University	M,D,O
Bob Jones University	M,D,O
Boston College	M,D,O
Boston University	M,D*
Briercrest Seminary	M
Brite Divinity School	M,D,O
Bryn Athyn College of the New Church	M
Byzantine Catholic Seminary of Saints Cyril and Methodius	M
Cairn University	M
California Lutheran University	M,D,O
Calvary University	M
Calvin Theological Seminary	M,D
Campbellsville University	M
Campbell University	M,D
Canadian Southern Baptist Seminary	M
Carey Theological College	M,D
Carson-Newman University	M
Catholic Distance University	M
Catholic Theological Union	M,D,O
The Catholic University of America	M,D,O
Central Baptist Theological Seminary	M,O
Central Yeshiva Tomchei Tmimim-Lubavitch	M
Chaminade University of Honolulu	M
Charlotte Christian College and Theological Seminary	M,D
Chicago Theological Seminary	M,D
Christendom College	M
Christian Theological Seminary	M,D
Christ the King Seminary	M
Church Divinity School of the Pacific	M,D,O
Cincinnati Christian University	M
Claremont Graduate University	M,D
Claremont School of Theology	M,D
Clarks Summit University	M,D
Colgate Rochester Crozer Divinity School	M,D,O
Collège Dominicain de Philosophie et de Théologie	M,D,O
College of Emmanuel and St. Chad	M,D,O
College of Saint Elizabeth	M,O
Columbia International University	M,D,O
Columbia Theological Seminary	M,D
Concordia Lutheran Seminary	M,O
Concordia Seminary	M,D,O
Concordia Theological Seminary	M,D
Concordia University (Canada)	M
Concordia University Irvine	M*
Concordia University of Edmonton	M
Corban University	M,D,O
Covenant Theological Seminary	M,D,O
Creighton University	M
Criswell College	M
Crown College	M
Dallas Baptist University	M
Dallas Theological Seminary	M,D,O
Denver Seminary	M,D,O
Dominican House of Studies, Pontifical Faculty of the Immaculate Conception	M,D,O
Dominican School of Philosophy and Theology	M,O
Drew University	M,D,O
Duke University	M,D*
Duquesne University	M,D
Earlham School of Religion	M
Eastern Mennonite University	M,O
Eastern University	M
Ecumenical Theological Seminary	M
Eden Theological Seminary	M,D
Emory University	M,D
Erskine Theological Seminary	M,D
Evangelical Seminary	M
Evangelical Seminary of Puerto Rico	M,D
Faith Baptist Bible College and Theological Seminary	M
Faith International University	M,D
Faith Theological Seminary	M,D
Faulkner University	M,D
Fordham University	M,D
Franciscan School of Theology	M
Franciscan University of Steubenville	M
Freed-Hardeman University	M
Fresno Pacific University	M
Fuller Theological Seminary	M,D,O
Gannon University	M,O
Gardner-Webb University	M,D
Garrett-Evangelical Theological Seminary	M,D
Gateway Seminary	M,D,O
General Theological Seminary	M,D,O
George Fox University	M,D,O
Georgetown University	D
Georgian Court University	M,O
Global University	M,D
Gonzaga University	M
Gordon-Conwell Theological Seminary	M,D
Graceland University (IA)	M
Grace School of Theology	M
Grace Theological Seminary	M,D,O
Graduate Theological Union	M,D,O
Grand Rapids Theological Seminary of Cornerstone University	M
Harding School of Theology	M,D
Hardin-Simmons University	M
Hartford Seminary	M,D,O
Harvard University	M*
Hebrew College	M
Hebrew Union College–Jewish Institute of Religion (NY)	M,D
Heritage College and Seminary	M,O
Holy Apostles College and Seminary	M,O
Holy Cross Greek Orthodox School of Theology	M
Hood Theological Seminary	M,D
Houston Baptist University	M
Houston Graduate School of Theology	M,D
Howard Payne University	M
Howard University	M,D
Iliff School of Theology	M,D
Indiana Wesleyan University	M
Institute for Christian Studies	M,D
Inter American University of Puerto Rico, Metropolitan Campus	D
Interdenominational Theological Center	M,D
International Baptist College and Seminary	M
The Jewish Theological Seminary	M,D,O
John Carroll University	M
John Paul the Great Catholic University	M
Johnson University	M,D,O
Kehilath Yakov Rabbinical Seminary	
Kenrick-Glennon Seminary	M
Kentucky Christian University	M
The King's University	M,D,O
Kingswood University	M
Knox College	M,D
Knox Theological Seminary	M
Lakeland University	M
Lancaster Bible College	M,D,O
Lancaster Theological Seminary	M,D,O
Lee University	M
Lenoir-Rhyne University	M
Lexington Theological Seminary	M,D
Liberty University	M,D,O
Lincoln Christian Seminary	M,D
Lincoln Christian University	M
Lipscomb University	M,D
Logos Evangelical Seminary	M,D,O
Loras College	M
Louisiana College	M
Louisville Presbyterian Theological Seminary	M,D
Lourdes University	M
Loyola Marymount University	M
Loyola University Chicago	M,D,O
Loyola University Chicago	M,D,O
Loyola University Maryland	M
Loyola University New Orleans	M,O
Lubbock Christian University	M
Lutheran School of Theology at Chicago	M,D
Lutheran Theological Seminary Saskatoon	M,D
Luther Rice College & Seminary	M,D
Luther Seminary	M,D

*M—masters degree; D—doctorate; O—other advanced degree; *—Close-Up and/or Display*

Machzikei Hadath Rabbinical College	O
Madonna University	M
Malone University	M
Maple Springs Baptist Bible College and Seminary	M,D,O
Maranatha Baptist University	M
Marquette University	M,D
The Master's University	M,D
McCormick Theological Seminary	M,D,O
McGill University	M,D
McMaster University	M,D,O
Meadville Lombard Theological School	M,D
Memphis Theological Seminary	M,D
Mercer University	M,D
Merrimack College	M,O
Mesivta of Eastern Parkway–Yeshiva Zichron Meilech	
Mesivta Torah Vodaath Rabbinical Seminary	O
Mesivtha Tifereth Jerusalem of America	
Methodist Theological School in Ohio	M,D
Mid-America Baptist Theological Seminary	M,D
Mid-America Baptist Theological Seminary Northeast Branch	M
Mid-America Reformed Seminary	M
Midwestern Baptist Theological Seminary	M,D,O
Milligan College	M,D,O
Mirrer Yeshiva Central Institute	
Moody Bible Institute	M,O
Moody Theological Seminary–Michigan	M,O
Moravian Theological Seminary	M,O
Mount Angel Seminary	M
Mount St. Joseph University	M,O
Mount St. Mary's University (MD)	M
Mount Vernon Nazarene University	M
Multnomah University	M,D
Naropa University	M
Nashotah House Theological Seminary	M,D,O
Nazarene Theological Seminary	M,D,O
Ner Israel Rabbinical College	M,D,O
Ner Israel Yeshiva College of Toronto	
New Brunswick Theological Seminary	M,D
Newman Theological College	M
Newman University	M
New Orleans Baptist Theological Seminary	M,D
New Saint Andrews College	M,O
New York Theological Seminary	M,D
Northeastern Seminary at Roberts Wesleyan College	M,D
Northern Seminary	M,D
North Park Theological Seminary	M,D
Northwest Nazarene University	M
Northwest University	M
Notre Dame Seminary	M
Nyack College	M,D
Oakland City University	M,D
Oblate School of Theology	M,D,O
Ohio Christian University	M
Ohio Dominican University	M
Ohr Hameir Theological Seminary	
Oklahoma Christian University	M
Oklahoma Wesleyan University	M
Olivet Nazarene University	M
Oral Roberts University	M,D
Pacific School of Religion	M,D,O
Palm Beach Atlantic University	M
Payne Theological Seminary	M
Pentecostal Theological Seminary	M,D
Pfeiffer University	M
Phillips Theological Seminary	M,D
Phoenix Seminary	M,D,O
Piedmont International University	M,D
Pittsburgh Theological Seminary	M,D
Point Loma Nazarene University	M
Pontifical Catholic University of Puerto Rico	M
Pontifical College Josephinum	M
Pontifical John Paul II Institute for Studies on Marriage and Family	M,D,O
Pope St. John XXIII National Seminary	M
Princeton Theological Seminary	M,D
Providence College	M
Providence University College & Theological Seminary	M,D,O
Queen's University at Kingston	M,O
Rabbinical Academy Mesivta Rabbi Chaim Berlin	O
Rabbinical College Beth Shraga	
Rabbinical College Bobover Yeshiva B'nei Zion	O
Rabbinical College of Long Island	
Rabbinical Seminary of America	
Reconstructionist Rabbinical College	M,D,O
Reformed Episcopal Seminary	M
Reformed Presbyterian Theological Seminary	M,D
Reformed Theological Seminary–Atlanta Campus	M,D,O
Reformed Theological Seminary–Charlotte Campus	M,D
Reformed Theological Seminary–Dallas Campus	M
Reformed Theological Seminary–Jackson Campus	M,D,O
Reformed Theological Seminary–Orlando Campus	M,D,O
Reformed Theological Seminary–Washington D.C.	M
Regent College	M,O
Regent University	M,D
Regis College (Canada)	M,D,O
Sacred Heart Major Seminary	M
Sacred Heart Seminary and School of Theology	M,O
St. Andrew's College	M,D,O
St. Andrew's College in Winnipeg	M
St. Augustine's Seminary of Toronto	M,O
St. Bernard's School of Theology and Ministry	M,O
St. Catherine University	M,O
Saint Charles Borromeo Seminary, Overbrook	M
St. John's Seminary (CA)	M
Saint John's Seminary (MA)	M
Saint John's University (MN)	M
St. John's University (NY)	M
St. Joseph's Seminary	M
Saint Leo University	M,O
Saint Louis University	M,D*
Saint Mary Seminary and Graduate School of Theology	M,D
St. Mary's Seminary and University	M,D,O
Saint Mary's University (Canada)	M
St. Mary's University (United States)	M
Saint Meinrad School of Theology	M
St. Norbert College	M
St. Patrick's Seminary & University	M,O
Saint Paul School of Theology	M,D
Saint Paul University	M,D,O
St. Peter's Seminary	M
Saints Cyril and Methodius Seminary	M
St. Stephen's College	M,D
St. Thomas University	M,D,O
St. Tikhon's Orthodox Theological Seminary	M
St. Vincent de Paul Regional Seminary	M
Saint Vincent Seminary	M
St. Vladimir's Orthodox Theological Seminary	M,D
Samford University	M,D
San Francisco Theological Seminary	M,D
Santa Clara University	M,D,O
Seattle Pacific University	M,O
The Seattle School of Theology and Psychology	M
Seattle University	M,D,O
Seminary of the Southwest	M,O
Seton Hall University	M,O
Shaw University	M
Shepherds Theological Seminary	M
Shiloh University	M,D
Sh'or Yoshuv Rabbinical College	
Sioux Falls Seminary	M,D,O
Southeastern Baptist Theological Seminary	M,D
Southeastern University (FL)	M,D
Southern Adventist University	M
The Southern Baptist Theological Seminary	M,D
Southern California Seminary	M,D
Southern Evangelical Seminary	M,D,O
Southern Methodist University	M,D
South Florida Bible College and Theological Seminary	M
Southwestern Assemblies of God University	M
Southwestern Baptist Theological Seminary	M,D
Spring Arbor University	M
Spring Hill College	M,O
Starr King School for the Ministry	M
SUM Bible College & Theological Seminary	M
Talmudic University	M
Taylor College and Seminary	M,O
Toronto School of Theology	M,D
Trinity Bible College and Graduate School	M
Trinity College (Canada)	M,D,O
Trinity International University	M,D,O
Trinity Lutheran Seminary	M
Trinity School for Ministry	M,D,O
Trinity Western University	M,D
Tri-State Bible College	M
Truett McConnell University	M
Tyndale University College & Seminary	M,O
Unification Theological Seminary	M,D
Union Theological Seminary in the City of New York	M,D
United Lutheran Seminary	M,D
United Lutheran Seminary	M,D,O
United Talmudical Seminary	
United Theological Seminary	M,D
United Theological Seminary of the Twin Cities	M,D,O
Université de Montréal	M,D,O
Université de Sherbrooke	M,D,O
Université du Québec à Chicoutimi	M,D
Université Laval	M,D
University of Chicago	D
University of Dallas	M
University of Dayton	M,D
University of Denver	D,O
University of Dubuque	M,D
University of Holy Cross	M,D
The University of Manchester	D
University of Northwestern–St. Paul	M
University of Notre Dame	M,D
University of Philosophical Research	M
University of Saint Mary of the Lake–Mundelein Seminary	M,D
University of St. Michael's College	M,D,O
University of St. Thomas (MN)	M
University of St. Thomas (TX)	M
The University of Scranton	M
University of South Africa	M,D
The University of the South	M,D
University of the West	M
University of Valley Forge	M
The University of Winnipeg	M,O
Urshan Graduate School of Theology	M
Ursuline College	M
Vancouver School of Theology	M,O
Vanderbilt University	M*
Vanguard University of Southern California	M
Victoria University	M,D,O
Villanova University	M,D
Virginia Baptist College	M
Virginia Beach Theological Seminary	M
Virginia Theological Seminary	M,D
Virginia Union University	M,D
Walsh University	M
Wartburg Theological Seminary	M
Wayland Baptist University	M
Welch College	M
Wesley Biblical Seminary	M
Wesley Theological Seminary	M,D
Western Seminary	M,O
Western Seminary–Sacramento Campus	M,O
Western Seminary–San Jose Campus	M,O
Western Theological Seminary	M,D,O
Westminster Seminary California	M
Westminster Theological Seminary	M,D,O
Wheaton College	M,D
Whitworth University	M
Wilfrid Laurier University	M,D,O
Winebrenner Theological Seminary	M,D
World Mission University	M,D
Wycliffe College	M,D,O
Xavier University	M*
Xavier University of Louisiana	M
Yale University	M
Yeshiva Beth Moshe	O
Yeshiva Karlin Stolin	O
Yeshiva of Nitra Rabbinical College	O
Yeshiva Shaar Hatorah Talmudic Research Institute	
Yeshivath Zichron Moshe	O

THEORETICAL CHEMISTRY

Carnegie Mellon University	D
Cornell University	D
Georgetown University	D
Laurentian University	M
University of Calgary	M,D
The University of Manchester	M,D
University of Regina	M,D
The University of Tennessee	M,D
Vanderbilt University	M,D*
Wesleyan University	D
Yale University	D

THEORETICAL PHYSICS

American University of Beirut	M,D
Cornell University	M,D
Delaware State University	D
Emory University	D
Harvard University	D*
Rutgers University–New Brunswick	M,D
The University of Manchester	M,D
University of Victoria	M,D

THERAPIES—DANCE, DRAMA, AND MUSIC

Antioch University New England	M,O
Antioch University Seattle	M
Appalachian State University	M
Arizona State University at the Tempe campus	M,D
California Institute of Integral Studies	M,D
Concordia University (Canada)	M
Drexel University	M,O*
East Carolina University	M,O
Florida State University	M,D
Georgia College & State University	M
Immaculata University	M
Indiana University–Purdue University Indianapolis	M,D
Lesley University	M,D,O
Loyola University New Orleans	M
Maryville University of Saint Louis	M
Michigan State University	M,D
Molloy College	M
Montclair State University	M,O
Naropa University	M
Nazareth College of Rochester	M
New York University	M*
Ohio University	M,O
Pratt Institute	M*
Saint Mary-of-the-Woods College	M
Shenandoah University	M,D,O
Slippery Rock University of Pennsylvania	M
State University of New York at New Paltz	M
Temple University	M,D*
Texas Woman's University	M
The University of Kansas	M,D
University of Kentucky	M,D
University of Miami	M,D,O*
University of Missouri–Kansas City	M,D
University of the Pacific	M
Western Michigan University	M,O
Wilfrid Laurier University	M

TOXICOLOGY

Clemson University	M,D
Columbia University	M,D*
Cornell University	M,D
Duke University	O*
Florida Agricultural and Mechanical University	M,D
The George Washington University	M,O
Indiana University Bloomington	M,D,O
Indiana University–Purdue University Indianapolis	M,D
Iowa State University of Science and Technology	M,D
Long Island University–LIU Brooklyn	M,D
Louisiana State University and Agricultural & Mechanical College	M,D
Massachusetts Institute of Technology	M,D
Medical College of Wisconsin	D
Medical University of South Carolina	D
Michigan State University	M,D
New York University	M,D*
North Carolina State University	M,D
Oklahoma State University Center for Health Sciences	M
Oregon State University	M,D
Purdue University	M,D
Queen's University at Kingston	M,D
Rutgers University–New Brunswick	M,D
St. John's University (NY)	M
San Diego State University	M,D
Simon Fraser University	M,D,O
Texas Southern University	M,D
Texas Tech University	M,D
Thomas Jefferson University	M
Université de Montréal	O
University at Albany, State University of New York	M,D
University at Buffalo, the State University of New York	M,D
The University of Alabama at Birmingham	M,D
University of Arkansas for Medical Sciences	M,D,O
University of California, Davis	M,D
University of California, Irvine	M,D
University of California, Los Angeles	D*
University of California, Riverside	M,D
University of California, Santa Cruz	M,D*
University of Colorado Denver	D
University of Connecticut	M,D*
University of Florida	M,D,O
University of Guelph	M,D
University of Illinois at Chicago	M,D
The University of Iowa	M,D*
The University of Kansas	M,D
University of Kentucky	M,D
University of Louisiana at Monroe	D
University of Louisville	M,D
The University of Manchester	M,D
University of Maryland, Baltimore	M,D
University of Maryland Eastern Shore	M,D
University of Michigan	M,D*
University of Minnesota, Duluth	M,D
University of Minnesota, Twin Cities Campus	M,D
University of Mississippi	M,D
University of Mississippi Medical Center	D
University of Montana	M,D
University of Nebraska–Lincoln	M,D
University of Nebraska Medical Center	D
University of New Mexico	M,D
The University of North Carolina at Chapel Hill	M,D
University of Prince Edward Island	M,D
University of Puerto Rico–Medical Sciences Campus	M,D
University of Rhode Island	M,D*
University of Rochester	D*
University of Saskatchewan	M,D,O
University of South Alabama	M
University of Southern California	M,D*
University of South Florida	O*
The University of Texas at Austin	M,D
The University of Texas Health Science Center at San Antonio	M
The University of Texas Medical Branch	M,D
University of the Sciences	M,D
University of Utah	D
University of Washington	M,D
University of Wisconsin–Madison	M,D
Utah State University	M,D
Virginia Commonwealth University	M,D,O
Wayne State University	M,D
Wright State University	M

TRANSCULTURAL NURSING

Augsburg University	M,D
Rutgers University–Newark	M,D,O

TRANSLATIONAL BIOLOGY

Baylor College of Medicine	D
Boston University	D*
Cedars-Sinai Medical Center	M,D
Rutgers University–New Brunswick	M
University of California, Irvine	M
The University of Iowa	M,D*
University of Massachusetts Medical School	M,D
The University of Texas at San Antonio	D

The University of Texas Medical Branch	M,D

TRANSLATION AND INTERPRETATION

American University of Sharjah	M,D
Arizona State University at the Tempe campus	M,D,O
Babel University Professional School of Translation	M
Binghamton University, State University of New York	D,O
Columbia University	M,D*
Concordia University (Canada)	M,O
East Tennessee State University	M,O
Gallaudet University	M,D,O
Georgia State University	O
Kent State University	M,D
La Salle University	M,O
London Metropolitan University	M,D
Middlebury Institute of International Studies at Monterey	M
Mills College	M,O
Montclair State University	O
New York University	M*
Rochester Institute of Technology	M
Rutgers University–New Brunswick	M,D
Texas A&M International University	M
Universidad Autonoma de Guadalajara	M,D
Université de Montréal	M,D,O
Université Laval	M,D,O
University of California, Santa Barbara	M,D
University of Delaware	M*
University of Denver	M,O
University of Illinois at Urbana–Champaign	M
The University of Manchester	D
University of Nevada, Las Vegas	M,O
University of Northern Colorado	M
University of North Florida	M
University of Ottawa	M,D
University of Puerto Rico–Río Piedras	M,O
University of Rochester	M,O*
The University of Texas Rio Grande Valley	M
University of Wisconsin–Milwaukee	M,O*
Wesley Biblical Seminary	M
York University	M

TRANSPERSONAL AND HUMANISTIC PSYCHOLOGY

Atlantic University	M
California Institute of Integral Studies	M,D,O
John F. Kennedy University	M
Michigan School of Professional Psychology	M,D
Saybrook University	M,D
Seattle University	M
Sofia University	M,D

TRANSPORTATION AND HIGHWAY ENGINEERING

Arizona State University at the Tempe campus	M,D,O
ArtCenter College of Design	M
The Catholic University of America	M,D,O
The Citadel, The Military College of South Carolina	M,O
Clemson University	M,D
College for Creative Studies	M
Cornell University	M,D
École Polytechnique de Montréal	M,D,O
George Mason University	M,D
Illinois Institute of Technology	M,D
Iowa State University of Science and Technology	M,D
Kansas State University	M,D
Kennesaw State University	M
Louisiana State University and Agricultural & Mechanical College	M,D
Marquette University	M,D,O
Marshall University	M
Massachusetts Institute of Technology	M,D,O
Morgan State University	M,D
New Jersey Institute of Technology	M,D,O
New York University	M,D*
North Dakota State University	D*
Northwestern University	M,D
Ohio University	M,D
Old Dominion University	M
Oregon State University	M,D
Rensselaer Polytechnic Institute	M,D
South Carolina State University	M
Southern Illinois University Edwardsville	M
Southern Methodist University	M,D
Stevens Institute of Technology	M,D,O
Texas Southern University	M
University of Arkansas	M,D
University of Calgary	M,D
University of California, Berkeley	M,D
University of California, Davis	M,D
University of California, Irvine	M,D
University of Central Florida	M,D,O
University of Colorado Denver	M,D
University of Dayton	M
University of Delaware	M,D*
The University of Iowa	M,D*
University of Massachusetts Amherst	M,D*
University of Memphis	M,D,O
University of Nevada, Las Vegas	M,D,O
University of New Brunswick Fredericton	M,D
University of Puerto Rico–Mayagüez	M,D
University of Southern California	M,D,O*
University of South Florida	M,D,O*
The University of Texas at Tyler	M,D
University of Washington	M,D
University of Wisconsin–Madison	M
Virginia Polytechnic Institute and State University	M,O
Wentworth Institute of Technology	M

TRANSPORTATION MANAGEMENT

American Public University System	M,D
California State University Maritime Academy	M
Florida Institute of Technology	M,D
George Mason University	M
Instituto Tecnologico de Santo Domingo	M,O
Iowa State University of Science and Technology	M
Maine Maritime Academy	M
McGill University	M,D
Naval Postgraduate School	M
New Jersey Institute of Technology	M,D
New York University	M*
North Dakota State University	M,D*
Pontifical Catholic University of Puerto Rico	O
San Jose State University	M
State University of New York Maritime College	M
Temple University	M,O*
Texas A&M University	M
Texas Southern University	M
University at Buffalo, the State University of New York	M
The University of British Columbia	D
University of California, Davis	M,D
University of California, Santa Barbara	M,D
University of Hawaii at Manoa	M,D,O
University of New Orleans	M
The University of Tennessee	M,D
University of Washington	O

TRAVEL AND TOURISM

Arizona State University at the Tempe campus	M,D,O
Boston University	M*
California State University, Chico	M
California State University, East Bay	M
California State University, Fullerton	M
California State University, Northridge	M
Clemson University	M,D,O
Colorado State University	M,D
The George Washington University	M,O
IGlobal University	M
Indiana University Bloomington	M,D
Johnson & Wales University	M
Kent State University	M
Lasell College	M,O
Liberty University	M,D,O
New Mexico State University	M
New York University	M*
North Carolina State University	M,D
Penn State University Park	M,D*
Pontificia Universidad Catolica Madre y Maestra	M
Purdue University	M,D
Rochester Institute of Technology	M
Royal Roads University	M,O
San Francisco State University	M
San Ignacio University	M
Savannah College of Art and Design	M
Schiller International University (United States)	M
Strayer University	M
Syracuse University	M*
Temple University	M,D*
Tropical Agriculture Research and Higher Education Center	M,D
Université du Québec à Trois-Rivières	M,O
University of Central Florida	M,D,O
University of Florida	M,D
University of Hawaii at Manoa	M
University of Idaho	M
University of Massachusetts Amherst	M,D*
University of Minnesota, Twin Cities Campus	M,D
University of New Orleans	M
University of North Texas	M,D,O
University of South Africa	M,D
University of South Carolina	M,D
University of South Florida	M,O*
The University of Tennessee	M,D
Western Illinois University	M
West Virginia University	M,D

URBAN AND REGIONAL PLANNING

Alabama Agricultural and Mechanical University	M
American University of Beirut	M,D
American University of Sharjah	M,D
Andrews University	M
Arizona State University at the Tempe campus	M,D,O
Auburn University	M*
Ball State University	M,O
Boston University	M*
California Polytechnic State University, San Luis Obispo	M*
California State Polytechnic University, Pomona	M
The Catholic University of America	M,O
Clark University	M
Cleveland State University	M,O
College of Charleston	O
Columbia University	M,D*
Concordia University (Canada)	O
Cornell University	M,D
Dalhousie University	M
Delta State University	M
East Carolina University	M,O
Eastern Kentucky University	M
Eastern Michigan University	M,O
Eastern University	M
East Tennessee State University	M,O
Florida Atlantic University	M
Florida State University	M,D
Future Generations University	M
Georgetown University	M,D
Georgia Institute of Technology	M,D
Georgia State University	M,D,O
Harvard University	M,D*
Hunter College of the City University of New York	M
Indiana University of Pennsylvania	M
Iowa State University of Science and Technology	M
Jackson State University	M,D
Kansas State University	M
Lesley University	M,D,O
Massachusetts Institute of Technology	M,D
McGill University	M,D
Michigan State University	M,D
Minnesota State University Mankato	M,O
Missouri State University	M,O
Morgan State University	M,D
New York University	M*
North Dakota State University	M*
Northern Arizona University	M,O
Northwest University	M,D
The Ohio State University	M,D
Pratt Institute	M*
Queen's University at Kingston	M
Roger Williams University	M,O
Rutgers University–New Brunswick	M,D
St. Francis Xavier University	M
Saint Louis University	M*
San Diego State University	M
Savannah State University	M
Southeastern University (FL)	M
Southern California Institute of Architecture	M*
State University of New York College of Environmental Science and Forestry	M,D
Syracuse University	O*
Temple University	M,O*
Texas A&M University	M,D
Texas Southern University	M,D
Thomas Edison State University	M
Thomas Jefferson University	M
Tufts University	M*
Université de Montréal	M,D,O
Université du Québec à Rimouski	M,D,O
Université du Québec en Outaouais	M
Université Laval	M,D
University at Albany, State University of New York	M,O
University at Buffalo, the State University of New York	M,D,O
The University of Arizona	M
The University of British Columbia	M,D
University of California, Berkeley	M,D
University of California, Davis	M
University of California, Irvine	M,D
University of California, Los Angeles	M,D*
University of Central Arkansas	M,O
University of Central Florida	M,O
University of Central Oklahoma	M,O
University of Cincinnati	M
University of Colorado Denver	M,D
University of Detroit Mercy	M
University of Florida	M,D
University of Hawaii at Manoa	M,D,O
University of Idaho	M
University of Illinois at Chicago	M,D
University of Illinois at Urbana–Champaign	M,D
The University of Iowa	M*
The University of Kansas	M
University of Louisville	M,D
University of Manitoba	M
University of Maryland, College Park	M,D
University of Massachusetts Amherst	M,D*
University of Massachusetts Boston	M
University of Massachusetts Lowell	M,O
University of Memphis	M
University of Michigan	M,D*
University of Minnesota, Twin Cities Campus	M,D
University of Nebraska–Lincoln	M,D
University of New Brunswick Fredericton	M
University of New Mexico	M
University of New Orleans	M
The University of North Carolina at Chapel Hill	M,D
The University of North Carolina at Charlotte	M,O
University of Oklahoma	M,D*
University of Oregon	M
University of Pennsylvania	M,D,O*
University of Pittsburgh	M*
University of Puerto Rico–Río Piedras	M
University of Southern California	M,D,O*
University of Southern Maine	M,O
University of South Florida	O*
The University of Texas at Arlington	D
The University of Texas at Austin	M,D
The University of Texas at San Antonio	M
The University of Toledo	M,D,O
University of Toronto	M,D
University of Utah	M,D
University of Virginia	M
University of Washington	M,D
University of Waterloo	M,D
University of West Georgia	M,D,O
University of Wisconsin–Madison	M,D
University of Wisconsin–Milwaukee	M*
Utah State University	M,D
Vanderbilt University	M*
Virginia Commonwealth University	M
Virginia Polytechnic Institute and State University	M,D
Wayne State University	M,O
West Chester University of Pennsylvania	M,O

URBAN DESIGN

American University of Beirut	M,D
Arizona State University at the Tempe campus	M,D
Ball State University	M
Carnegie Mellon University	M,D
City College of the City University of New York	M
Cornell University	M,D
DePaul University	M
Drexel University	M*
Georgia Institute of Technology	M,D
Harvard University	M*
Hofstra University	M
Judson University	M
Kent State University	M
Lawrence Technological University	M,O
London Metropolitan University	M,D
The New School	M
New York Institute of Technology	M
Pratt Institute	M*
Rice University	M,D
Savannah College of Art and Design	M
Southern California Institute of Architecture	M*
State University of New York College of Environmental Science and Forestry	M
University at Buffalo, the State University of New York	M,D,O
The University of British Columbia	M,D
University of California, Berkeley	M,D
University of California, Los Angeles	M,D*
University of Colorado Denver	M
University of Houston	M
The University of Kansas	M,D,O
University of Miami	M*
University of Michigan	M*
The University of North Carolina at Charlotte	M
University of Pennsylvania	M,D,O*
University of South Florida	M*
The University of Texas at Austin	M
University of Toronto	M,D
University of Utah	M,D
University of Washington	M,D,O
Washington University in St. Louis	M

URBAN EDUCATION

Alvernia University	M
Bakke Graduate University	M,D
Brown University	M
Cardinal Stritch University	M,D
Cheyney University of Pennsylvania	M
Claremont Graduate University	M,D,O
Cleveland State University	D
College of Mount Saint Vincent	M,O
Eastern Michigan University	M,O
Emmanuel College (United States)	M,O
Florida International University	M,D,O
Georgia State University	M,D,O
The Graduate Center, City University of New York	D
Grand View University	M,O
Holy Names University	M,O
Johns Hopkins University	O*
Langston University	M
Long Island University–LIU Brooklyn	M,O
Loyola Marymount University	M,O
Manhattanville College	M,O
Morgan State University	D
New Jersey City University	M
Norfolk State University	M
Northeastern Illinois University	M
Providence College	M
Teachers College, Columbia University	M,D
Temple University	M*
University of Chicago	M
University of Houston–Downtown	M
University of Illinois at Chicago	M,D
University of Massachusetts Boston	D
University of Memphis	M,D,O
University of Michigan–Dearborn	M,D
University of Nebraska at Omaha	M,O
University of Pennsylvania	M*
University of San Francisco	M
University of Southern California	D*

*M—masters degree; D—doctorate; O—other advanced degree; *—Close-Up and/or Display*

University of Wisconsin–Milwaukee	M,D,O*
Vanderbilt University	M*
Virginia Commonwealth University	D

URBAN STUDIES

Arizona State University at the Tempe campus	M,D,O
Azusa Pacific University	M*
Boston University	M*
Brooklyn College of the City University of New York	M
Cleveland State University	M,D,O
Columbus State University	M
Concordia University (Canada)	M,D,O
Fordham University	M
Fresno Pacific University	M
Hunter College of the City University of New York	M
Indiana University Northwest	M,O
Le Moyne College	M,O
Long Island University–LIU Brooklyn	M,D,O
Loyola University Chicago	M
Massachusetts Institute of Technology	M,D
Minnesota State University Mankato	M,O
Moody Bible Institute	M,O
New Jersey City University	M
New Jersey Institute of Technology	M,D
New York University	M*
Norfolk State University	M
North Dakota State University	M,D*
Northeastern University	M
Queens College of the City University of New York	M
Rutgers University–Newark	M,D
Savannah State University	M
Simon Fraser University	M,O
Temple University	M,D,O*
Tufts University	M*
Université du Québec à Montréal	M,D
Université du Québec, École nationale d'administration publique	M
Université du Québec, Institut National de la Recherche Scientifique	M,D,O
University at Albany, State University of New York	M,D,O
University of California, Irvine	M,D
University of Delaware	M,D*
University of Lethbridge	M,D
University of Louisville	M,D
University of Maryland, Baltimore County	M,D
University of New Orleans	M,D
University of San Francisco	M
University of Wisconsin–Milwaukee	M,D*
Virginia Polytechnic Institute and State University	M,D
Wayne State University	M,D,O

VETERINARY MEDICINE

Auburn University	D*
Colorado State University	D
Cornell University	D
Iowa State University of Science and Technology	M
Kansas State University	D
Louisiana State University and Agricultural & Mechanical College	D
Michigan State University	D
Mississippi State University	D
North Carolina State University	M,D
Oklahoma State University	D
Oregon State University	D
Purdue University	D
Texas A&M University	M,D
Tufts University	M,D*
Tuskegee University	M,D
Université de Montréal	D
University of California, Davis	D
University of Florida	D
University of Georgia	M,D
University of Guelph	M,D,O
University of Illinois at Urbana–Champaign	D
University of Maryland, College Park	D
University of Minnesota, Twin Cities Campus	D
University of Missouri	M,D
University of Pennsylvania	D*
University of Prince Edward Island	D
University of Saskatchewan	M,D
The University of Tennessee	D
University of Wisconsin–Madison	M,D
Virginia Polytechnic Institute and State University	M,D
Washington State University	D
Western University of Health Sciences	D

VETERINARY SCIENCES

Clemson University	M,D
Colorado State University	M,D
Drexel University	M*
Iowa State University of Science and Technology	M,D
Kansas State University	M,O
Louisiana State University and Agricultural & Mechanical College	M,D
Michigan State University	M,D
Mississippi State University	M,D
North Carolina State University	M,D
The Ohio State University	M,D
Oklahoma State University	M,D
Penn State Hershey Medical Center	M
Purdue University	M,D
South Dakota State University	M,D
Texas A&M University	M,D
Tuskegee University	M,D
Université de Montréal	M,O
University of California, Davis	M,O
University of Florida	M,D,O
University of Guelph	M,D,O
University of Idaho	M,D
University of Illinois at Urbana–Champaign	M,D
University of Kentucky	M,D
University of Maryland, College Park	M,D
University of Minnesota, Twin Cities Campus	M,D
University of Missouri	M
University of Nebraska–Lincoln	M,D
University of Prince Edward Island	M,D
University of Saskatchewan	M,D
University of Vermont	M,D
University of Washington	M
University of Wisconsin–Madison	M,D
Utah State University	M,D
Virginia Polytechnic Institute and State University	M,D
Washington State University	M,D

VIROLOGY

Baylor College of Medicine	D
Case Western Reserve University	D*
Mayo Clinic Graduate School of Biomedical Sciences	D
McMaster University	M,D
Oregon State University	M,D
Penn State Hershey Medical Center	M,D
Purdue University	M,D
Rush University	M,D
Rutgers University–New Brunswick	M,D
Université de Montréal	D
Université du Québec, Institut National de la Recherche Scientifique	M,D
The University of Iowa	M,D*
University of Minnesota, Twin Cities Campus	D
University of Pennsylvania	D*
University of Prince Edward Island	M,D
Yale University	D

VISION SCIENCES

Eastern Virginia Medical School	O
Marshall B. Ketchum University	M,D
New England College of Optometry	M,D
Pacific University	M,D
Salus University	M,D
State University of New York College of Optometry	D
Université de Montréal	M,O
The University of Alabama at Birmingham	M,D
University of Alberta	M,D
University of California, Berkeley	M,D
University of Guelph	M,D,O
University of Houston	M,D
The University of Manchester	M,D
University of Massachusetts Boston	M
University of Pittsburgh	M,D*
University of Waterloo	M,D

VITICULTURE AND ENOLOGY

California State University, Fresno	M
University of California, Davis	M,D

VOCATIONAL AND TECHNICAL EDUCATION

Alcorn State University	M,O
Appalachian State University	M
Athens State University	M
Bowling Green State University	M
Buffalo State College, State University of New York	M
California Baptist University	M
California University of Pennsylvania	M
Capella University	D
Central Connecticut State University	M
Central Washington University	M
Chicago State University	M
Clarion University of Pennsylvania	M
Clarkson University	M
Concordia University (United States)	M,O
East Carolina University	M,O
Eastern Kentucky University	M
Eastern New Mexico University	M
Fitchburg State University	M
Florida Agricultural and Mechanical University	M
The George Washington University	O
Indiana State University	M
Indiana University of Pennsylvania	M
Inter American University of Puerto Rico, Metropolitan Campus	M
Iowa State University of Science and Technology	M,D
Jackson State University	M,D
James Madison University	M
Kent State University	M
Louisiana State University and Agricultural & Mechanical College	M,D
Middle Tennessee State University	M
Millersville University of Pennsylvania	M
Mississippi State University	M,D,O
Montana State University	M,D,O
Morehead State University	M
Murray State University	M,O
North Carolina Agricultural and Technical State University	M
Northern Arizona University	M,O
Old Dominion University	M,D
Penn State University Park	M,D,O*
Pittsburg State University	M,O
Purdue University	M,D,O
South Carolina State University	M
Southern Illinois University Carbondale	M,D
State University of New York at Oswego	M
Temple University	M*
Texas State University	M
University of Arkansas	M,D,O
The University of British Columbia	M,D
University of Central Florida	M,D,O
University of Central Missouri	M,D,O
University of Georgia	M,D,O
University of Idaho	M,O
University of Maryland Eastern Shore	M
University of Minnesota, Twin Cities Campus	M,D,O
University of Missouri	M,D,O
University of Nebraska–Lincoln	M,D,O
University of New England	M,D,O
University of Northern Iowa	M,D
University of North Texas	M,D,O
University of Phoenix–Phoenix Campus	M
University of South Africa	M,D
University of South Florida	M,D,O*
The University of Toledo	M,D,O
University of Victoria	M,D
University of Wisconsin–Stout	M,D,O
Utah State University	D
Valley City State University	M
Virginia Polytechnic Institute and State University	M,D,O
Washington State University	M,D
Wayne State College	M
Western Michigan University	M
Westfield State University	M
Wilmington University	M,D

WATER RESOURCES

Albany State University	M
California State University, Monterey Bay	M
Colorado State University	M,D
Cornell University	M,D
Dalhousie University	M
Humboldt State University	M
Marquette University	M,D,O
Michigan Technological University	M,D,O
Missouri University of Science and Technology	M,D
Montclair State University	O
New Mexico State University	M,D
Old Dominion University	M
Oregon State University	M,D
Rutgers University–New Brunswick	M,D
State University of New York College of Environmental Science and Forestry	M,D
Tropical Agriculture Research and Higher Education Center	M,D
The University of Arizona	M,D,O
The University of British Columbia	M
University of Calgary	M,D
University of California, Riverside	M,D
University of Colorado Denver	M,D
University of Florida	M,D
University of Idaho	M,D
The University of Iowa	M,D*
University of Maine	M,D
University of Massachusetts Amherst	M,D*
University of Minnesota, Twin Cities Campus	M,D
University of Nevada, Las Vegas	M
University of New Brunswick Fredericton	M,D
University of New Hampshire	M
University of New Mexico	M
University of Southern California	M,D,O*
University of the District of Columbia	M
University of the Pacific	M,D
University of Wisconsin–Madison	M
University of Wisconsin–Milwaukee	M,D*
University of Wyoming	M,D
Utah State University	M,D

WATER RESOURCES ENGINEERING

American University of Beirut	M,D
Carnegie Mellon University	M,D
Clemson University	M,D
Cornell University	M,D
Indiana University Bloomington	M,D,O
Kansas State University	M,D
Kennesaw State University	M
Lawrence Technological University	M,D
Louisiana State University and Agricultural & Mechanical College	M,D
Marquette University	M,D,O
McGill University	M,D
New Mexico Institute of Mining and Technology	M
Ohio University	M,D
Oregon State University	M,D
State University of New York College of Environmental Science and Forestry	M,D
Stevens Institute of Technology	M,D,O
Tufts University	M,D*
University at Buffalo, the State University of New York	M,D
University of Alberta	M,D
University of California, Berkeley	M,D
University of Central Florida	M,D,O
University of Dayton	M
University of Delaware	M,D*
University of Guelph	M,D
University of Idaho	M,D
The University of Iowa	M,D*
University of Massachusetts Amherst	M,D*
University of Memphis	M,D,O
University of New Haven	M*
University of Oklahoma	M,D*
University of South Florida	M,D,O*
The University of Texas at Austin	M,D
The University of Texas at Tyler	M
University of Wisconsin–Madison	M
Villanova University	M,O

WESTERN EUROPEAN STUDIES

American University	M,D,O
Boston College	M,D
Brown University	M,D
Carleton University	M,O
The Catholic University of America	M,D
Central Michigan University	M,O
Claremont Graduate University	M,D,O
College of Staten Island of the City University of New York	M
Columbia University	M,D*
Cornell University	M,D
Dallas Baptist University	M
Drew University	M,D,O
East Carolina University	M
Georgetown University	M
The George Washington University	M
Georgia Southern University–Armstrong Campus	M
Indiana University Bloomington	M
Indiana University–Purdue University Indianapolis	M
La Salle University	M,O
Monmouth University	M*
New York University	M*
San Diego State University	M
University of Colorado Denver	M
University of Connecticut	M*
University of Guelph	M
University of Illinois at Urbana–Champaign	M
University of Louisiana at Lafayette	M
University of Nevada, Reno	D
University of Pittsburgh	O*
University of South Florida	M,D*
University of Virginia	M

WOMEN'S HEALTH NURSING

Boston College	M,D
California State University, Fullerton	M,D
Carlow University	M,O
Case Western Reserve University	M*
Drexel University	M*
Duke University	M,D,O*
East Tennessee State University	M,D,O
Emory University	M
Frontier Nursing University	M,D,O*
Georgia State University	M,D,O
Loyola University Chicago	M,D,O
MGH Institute of Health Professions	M,D,O
Queen's University at Kingston	M,D,O
Rutgers University–Newark	M,D,O
San Francisco State University	M,O
Stony Brook University, State University of New York	M,D,O
Tennessee Technological University	D
Texas Woman's University	M,D
Uniformed Services University of the Health Sciences	M,D*
The University of Alabama at Birmingham	M,D
University of Cincinnati	M,D
University of Colorado Denver	M,D
University of Delaware	M,O*
University of Illinois at Chicago	M,O
University of Indianapolis	M,D
University of Louisville	M,D
University of Minnesota, Twin Cities Campus	M,D
University of Missouri–Kansas City	M,D
University of Missouri–St. Louis	D,O
University of Pennsylvania	M*
University of South Carolina	M
Vanderbilt University	M,D,O*
Virginia Commonwealth University	M,D,O
Wayne State University	M,D

WOMEN'S STUDIES

American University	O
The American University in Cairo	M,O
Benedictine University	M
Brandeis University	M,D
California Institute of Integral Studies	M,D,O
Carnegie Mellon University	D
Chatham University	M
Claremont Graduate University	M,D
Cornell University	M,D
DePaul University	M
Eastern Michigan University	M,O
Emory University	D,O
Florida Atlantic University	M
George Mason University	M
The George Washington University	M,O
Georgia State University	M,O
Grace Theological Seminary	M,D,O
Inter American University of Puerto Rico, Metropolitan Campus	M
The Jewish Theological Seminary	M,D
Kansas State University	O
Lakehead University	M,D
Lesley University	M,D,O
London Metropolitan University	M,D
Middle Tennessee State University	O

Minnesota State University Mankato	M
Mount Saint Vincent University	M
Northern Arizona University	O
The Ohio State University	M,D
Old Dominion University	M
Oregon State University	M,D
Queen's University at Kingston	M,D
Reconstructionist Rabbinical College	M,D,O
Rutgers University–New Brunswick	M,D
Saint Mary's University (Canada)	M
San Diego State University	M
San Francisco State University	M
Sarah Lawrence College	M
Simon Fraser University	M,D
Smith College	O
Southeastern Baptist Theological Seminary	M,D
Southern Connecticut State University	M
Stony Brook University, State University of New York	O
Texas Woman's University	M,D
Towson University	M,O
United Theological Seminary of the Twin Cities	M,D,O
Université Laval	O
University at Albany, State University of New York	M
The University of Alabama	M
The University of Arizona	M,D,O
University of California, Santa Barbara	M,D
University of Cincinnati	M,O
University of Colorado Denver	M,O
University of Florida	M,O
University of Georgia	O
University of Hawaii at Manoa	O
The University of Iowa	O*
University of Lethbridge	M,D
University of Louisville	M,O
University of Maryland, College Park	M,D
University of Michigan	D,O*
University of Minnesota, Twin Cities Campus	D
University of New Hampshire	O
The University of North Carolina at Charlotte	M,D,O
The University of North Carolina at Greensboro	M,D,O
University of Northern Iowa	M
University of Oklahoma	O*
University of Ottawa	M
University of Pittsburgh	O*
University of Regina	M
University of Rhode Island	O*
University of Saskatchewan	M,D
University of South Carolina	O
University of South Florida	M*
The University of Toledo	O
University of Toronto	M,D
University of Washington	D
University of Wisconsin–Madison	M,D
University of Wisconsin–Milwaukee	M,O*
Wayne State University	M,D,O
Western Seminary	M
Western Seminary–Sacramento Campus	O
Western Seminary–San Jose Campus	M,O
Wilson College	M
York University	M,D

WRITING

Abilene Christian University	M
Academy of Art University	M
Adelphi University	M
Albertus Magnus College	M
American College Dublin	M
American University	M
Antioch University Santa Barbara	M
Arcadia University	M
Arizona State University at the Tempe campus	M,D
Asbury University	M
Ashland University	M
Auburn University at Montgomery	M
Ball State University	M,D
Bard College	M
Bay Path University	M
Bennington College	M
Binghamton University, State University of New York	M,D
Boston University	M*
Bowling Green State University	M,D
Brigham Young University	M
Brooklyn College of the City University of New York	M
Brown University	M,D
Butler University	M
California College of the Arts	M
California Institute of Integral Studies	M,D,O
California Institute of the Arts	M,O
California State University, Fresno	M
California State University, Long Beach	M
California State University, Northridge	M
California State University, Sacramento	M
California State University, San Bernardino	M
California State University, San Marcos	M
California State University, Stanislaus	M,O
Carlow University	M
Carnegie Mellon University	M
Cedar Crest College	M
Central Michigan University	M
Central Washington University	M
Chapman University	M*
Chatham University	M
Chicago State University	M
City College of the City University of New York	M
Claremont Graduate University	M,D
Clemson University	M,D
Cleveland State University	M
Coastal Carolina University	M
The College at Brockport, State University of New York	M,O
College of Charleston	M
Colorado State University	M
Columbia College Chicago	M
Columbia University	M*
Concordia University (Canada)	M
Converse College	M
Cornell University	M,D
Creighton University	M
DePaul University	M
Dominican University of California	M
Drew University	M,D,O
East Carolina University	M,D,O
Eastern Kentucky University	M
Eastern Michigan University	M,O
Emerson College	M
Fairfield University	M
Fairleigh Dickinson University, Florham Campus	M
Fitchburg State University	M
Florida International University	M
Florida State University	M,D
Full Sail University	M
George Mason University	M
Georgia College & State University	M
Georgia Southern University–Armstrong Campus	M,O
Georgia State University	M,D
Goddard College	M
Goucher College	M
Hamline University	M
Hofstra University	M
Hollins University	M,O
Holy Names University	M
Hunter College of the City University of New York	M
Illinois State University	O
Indiana State University	M
Indiana University Bloomington	M,D
Indiana University–Purdue University Indianapolis	M,O
Indiana University South Bend	M,O
Institute of American Indian Arts	M
Iowa State University of Science and Technology	M,D
Ithaca College	M
James Madison University	M
Johns Hopkins University	M,O*
Kean University	M
Kennesaw State University	M
Kent State University	M,D
Lake Forest College	M
La Sierra University	M
Lenoir-Rhyne University	M
Lesley University	M,D,O
Lindenwood University	M,O
Lipscomb University	M
London Metropolitan University	M,D
Long Island University–LIU Brooklyn	M,D,O
Louisiana State University and Agricultural & Mechanical College	M,D
Loyola Marymount University	M
Maharishi University of Management	M
Manhattanville College	M
Massachusetts Institute of Technology	M
McDaniel College	M,O
McNeese State University	M
Michigan State University	M,D
Millersville University of Pennsylvania	M,O
Mills College	M,O
Minnesota State University Mankato	M,O
Missouri State University	M,O
Missouri Western State University	M,O
Monmouth University	M*
Montclair State University	O
Mount Mary University	M
Mount Saint Mary's University (CA)	M,D,O
Murray State University	M,D,O
Naropa University	M
National Louis University	M,D,O
National University	M,O
New England College	M
New Hampshire Institute of Art	M
New Mexico Highlands University	M
New Mexico State University	M,D
New Saint Andrews College	M,O
The New School	M
New York University	M*
North Carolina State University	M
North Dakota State University	M,D*
Northern Arizona University	M,D,O
Northern Kentucky University	M,O
Northern Michigan University	M,O
Northwestern University	M
Oklahoma City University	M
Oklahoma State University	M,D
Old Dominion University	M
Oregon State University	M
Otis College of Art and Design	M
Our Lady of the Lake University	M
Pacific Lutheran University	M
Pacific University	M
Park University	M,O
Pepperdine University	M
Pittsburg State University	M
Portland State University	M
Pratt Institute	M*
Purdue University	M,D
Queens College of the City University of New York	M
Queens University of Charlotte	M
Randolph College	M
Regent University	M,D
Regis University	M,O
Reinhardt University	M
Rhode Island College	M,O
Rivier University	M
Roosevelt University	M
Rosemont College	M
Rowan University	M,O
Rutgers University–Camden	M
Rutgers University–Newark	M
Rutgers University–New Brunswick	M
St. Cloud State University	M
St. Joseph's College, New York	M
Saint Joseph's University	M*
Saint Leo University	M
Saint Mary's College of California	M
Salve Regina University	M
Sam Houston State University	M
San Diego State University	M
San Francisco State University	M
San Jose State University	M
Sarah Lawrence College	M
Savannah College of Art and Design	M
School of the Art Institute of Chicago	M,O
School of Visual Arts (NY)	M
Seattle Pacific University	M
Seton Hill University	M
Shenandoah University	M,D,O
Simmons College	M,D,O
Sonoma State University	M
Southeastern Louisiana University	M
Southern Illinois University Carbondale	M
Southern Illinois University Edwardsville	M
Southern New Hampshire University	M
Spalding University	M
State University of New York at Fredonia	M,O
Stephens College	M,O
Stetson University	M
Stony Brook University, State University of New York	M,O
Syracuse University	M,D*
Temple University	M,D*
Texas A&M University–Commerce	M,D,O
Texas State University	M
Tiffin University	M
Towson University	M
Trinity College (United States)	M
Union Institute & University	M
The University of Akron	M
The University of Alabama	M,D
The University of Alabama at Birmingham	M
University of Alaska Anchorage	M
University of Alaska Fairbanks	M
The University of Arizona	M
University of Arkansas	M
University of Arkansas at Little Rock	M
University of Baltimore	M
The University of British Columbia	M,D
University of California, Berkeley	O
University of California, Davis	M,D
University of California, Irvine	M
University of California, Riverside	M
University of California, San Diego	M,D*
University of California, Santa Barbara	D
University of California, Santa Cruz	M*
University of Central Arkansas	M
University of Central Florida	M,D,O
University of Central Oklahoma	M
University of Chicago	M
University of Colorado Boulder	M,D
University of Colorado Denver	M
University of Dayton	M
University of Denver	M,D,O
The University of Findlay	M,D
University of Florida	M,D
University of Houston	M,D
University of Houston–Victoria	M
University of Idaho	M
University of Illinois at Urbana–Champaign	M,D
The University of Iowa	M,D*
The University of Kansas	M,D
University of King's College	M
University of Louisiana at Lafayette	M,D
University of Louisville	M,D
The University of Manchester	D
University of Maryland, College Park	M,D
University of Massachusetts Amherst	M,D*
University of Massachusetts Boston	M
University of Massachusetts Dartmouth	M,O
University of Memphis	M,D,O
University of Miami	M,D*
University of Michigan	M*
University of Michigan–Flint	M
University of Mississippi	M,D
University of Missouri–St. Louis	M
University of Montana	M
University of Nebraska at Kearney	M
University of Nebraska at Omaha	M,O
University of Nebraska–Lincoln	M,D
University of Nevada, Las Vegas	M,D,O
University of New Hampshire	M,D
University of New Mexico	M
University of New Orleans	M
University of North Alabama	M
The University of North Carolina at Charlotte	M,O
The University of North Carolina at Greensboro	M
The University of North Carolina Wilmington	M
University of Northern Iowa	M
University of North Florida	M
University of North Texas	M,D,O
University of Notre Dame	M
University of Oklahoma	M,D*
University of Oregon	M
University of Pittsburgh	M,D*
University of Regina	M,D
University of Rhode Island	M,D*
University of St. Thomas (MN)	M,O
University of San Francisco	M
University of South Alabama	M
University of South Carolina	M,D
University of Southern California	M,D*
University of Southern Maine	M
University of Southern Mississippi	M,D
University of South Florida	M,D,O*
The University of Tampa	M
The University of Tennessee at Chattanooga	M
The University of Texas at Austin	M,D
The University of Texas at El Paso	M,D,O
The University of Texas Rio Grande Valley	M
University of the Sacred Heart	M,O
The University of the South	M
The University of Toledo	M,O
University of Toronto	M,D
University of Utah	M,D
University of Victoria	M
University of Virginia	M
University of Washington	M
University of Washington, Bothell	M
University of West Florida	M
University of Windsor	M
University of Wisconsin–Eau Claire	M
University of Wisconsin– Madison	M,D
University of Wisconsin– Milwaukee	M,D*
University of Wyoming	M
Utah State University	M
Vanderbilt University	M*
Vermont College of Fine Arts	M
Virginia Commonwealth University	M
Virginia Polytechnic Institute and State University	M,D,O
Warren Wilson College	M
Washington & Jefferson College	M,O
Washington University in St. Louis	M
Wayne State University	M,D
Wesleyan University	M,O
West Chester University of Pennsylvania	M,O
Western Carolina University	M,O
Western Connecticut State University	M
Western Kentucky University	M
Western Michigan University	M,D
Western New England University	M
Western State Colorado University	M
Westminster College (UT)	M
West Virginia University	M,D
West Virginia Wesleyan College	M
Wichita State University	M
Wilkes University	M
William Paterson University of New Jersey	M,D,O
Yale University	M,D,O

ZOOLOGY

Auburn University	M,D*
Canisius College	M
Colorado State University	M,D
Emporia State University	M
Illinois State University	M,D
Indiana University Bloomington	M,D
Michigan State University	M,D
North Carolina State University	M,D
North Dakota State University	M,D*
Southern Illinois University Carbondale	M,D
Texas Tech University	M,D
Uniformed Services University of the Health Sciences	M,D*
The University of British Columbia	M,D
University of California, Davis	M
University of Chicago	D
University of Florida	M,D
University of Guelph	M,D
University of Hawaii at Manoa	M,D
University of Illinois at Urbana–Champaign	M,D
University of Maine	M,D
University of Manitoba	M,D
University of Montana	M,D
University of North Dakota	M,D
University of Wisconsin–Madison	M,D
University of Wisconsin–Oshkosh	M
University of Wyoming	M,D
Western Illinois University	M,O
West Liberty University	M

*M—masters degree; D—doctorate; O—other advanced degree; *—Close-Up and/or Display*

DIRECTORY OF INSTITUTIONS AND THEIR OFFERINGS

ABILENE CHRISTIAN UNIVERSITY
Accounting M
Business Administration and Management—General M
Business Analytics M
Clinical Psychology M
Communication Disorders M
Communication—General M
Conflict Resolution and Mediation/Peace Studies M,O
Counseling Psychology M
Education—General M,O
Educational Leadership and Administration M,D,O
English M
Finance and Banking M
Health Services Management and Hospital Administration M
Higher Education M
Human Resources Development M
Human Resources Management M
Human Services M,O
International Business M
Liberal Studies M
Marketing M
Marriage and Family Therapy M
Missions and Missiology M
Nonprofit Management M
Nursing and Healthcare Administration D
Nursing Education D
Nursing—General D
Nutrition M,O
Occupational Therapy M
Pastoral Ministry and Counseling M,D
Psychology—General M
Reading Education M
Religion M
Rhetoric M
School Psychology O
Social Work M
Supply Chain Management M
Theology M
Writing M

ABRAHAM LINCOLN UNIVERSITY SCHOOL OF LAW
Law D

ACACIA UNIVERSITY
Education—General M
Educational Leadership and Administration M
Elementary Education M
English as a Second Language M
Secondary Education M
Special Education M

ACADEMY FOR FIVE ELEMENT ACUPUNCTURE
Acupuncture and Oriental Medicine M

ACADEMY FOR JEWISH RELIGION CALIFORNIA
Jewish Studies M

ACADEMY OF ART UNIVERSITY
Advertising and Public Relations M
Applied Arts and Design—General M
Architecture M
Art Education M
Art History M
Art/Fine Arts M
Arts Journalism M
Computer Art and Design M
Film, Television, and Video Production M
Game Design and Development M
Graphic Design M
Illustration M
Industrial Design M
Interior Design M
Internet and Interactive Multimedia M
Landscape Architecture M
Music M
Photography M
Textile Design M
Theater M
Writing M

ACADEMY OF CHINESE CULTURE AND HEALTH SCIENCES
Acupuncture and Oriental Medicine M

ACADIA UNIVERSITY
Biological and Biomedical Sciences—General M
Chemistry M
Clinical Psychology M
Computer Science M
Counselor Education M
Curriculum and Instruction M
Education—General M,D
Educational Leadership and Administration M
English M
Geographic Information Systems M
Geology M
Mathematics M
Missions and Missiology M,D
Music Education M
Pastoral Ministry and Counseling M,D
Philosophy M
Political Science M
Psychology—General M
Recreation and Park Management M
Sociology M
Special Education M
Statistics M
Theology M,D

ACUPUNCTURE & INTEGRATIVE MEDICINE COLLEGE, BERKELEY
Acupuncture and Oriental Medicine M

ACUPUNCTURE AND MASSAGE COLLEGE
Acupuncture and Oriental Medicine M

ADAMS STATE UNIVERSITY
Business Administration and Management—General M
Clinical Psychology M,D
Counselor Education M,D
Curriculum and Instruction M
Education—General M
Educational Leadership and Administration M
Exercise and Sports Science M
History M
Humanities M
Mathematics Education M
Music Education M
Physical Education M
Public Administration M
Science Education M
Sport Psychology M
Sports Management M

ADELPHI UNIVERSITY
Accounting M
Adult Nursing M
Art Education M
Art/Fine Arts M
Biological and Biomedical Sciences—General M
Biotechnology M
Business Administration and Management—General M
Clinical Psychology D
Communication Disorders M,D
Community Health M,O
Counseling Psychology M
Education—General M,D,O
Educational Media/Instructional Technology M
Elementary Education M
Emergency Management O
English as a Second Language M,O
Environmental Management and Policy M
Environmental Sciences M
Finance and Banking M
Gerontology M,O
Health Education M,O
Health Informatics M,O
Health Services Management and Hospital Administration M
Human Resources Management M,O
Management Information Systems M
Marketing M
Nursing and Healthcare Administration M,O
Nursing Education M,O
Nursing—General D
Nutrition M,D,O
Physical Education M,O
Psychology—General M
Public Health—General M
Reading Education M
School Psychology M
Secondary Education M
Social Work M,D
Special Education M,O
Sports Management M
Supply Chain Management M
Writing M

ADLER GRADUATE SCHOOL
Addictions/Substance Abuse Counseling M
Art Therapy M
Clinical Psychology M
Counseling Psychology M
Counselor Education M
Marriage and Family Therapy M
Psychoanalysis and Psychotherapy M

ADLER UNIVERSITY
Addictions/Substance Abuse Counseling O
Applied Psychology M
Art Therapy M,D
Clinical Psychology M,D
Community Health M
Counseling Psychology M
Counselor Education D
Criminal Justice and Criminology M
Emergency Management M
Forensic Psychology M
Gender Studies M
Health Psychology M
Industrial and Organizational Psychology M,D
Marriage and Family Therapy M,D,O
Media Studies M
Military and Defense Studies M
Nonprofit Management M
Public Administration M
Public Policy M
Rehabilitation Counseling M
School Psychology M
Social Psychology M
Sport Psychology M
Student Affairs M
Sustainability Management M

ADRIAN COLLEGE
Accounting M
Athletic Training and Sports Medicine M
Criminal Justice and Criminology M

ADVENTIST UNIVERSITY OF HEALTH SCIENCES
Health Services Management and Hospital Administration M
Nurse Anesthesia M
Occupational Therapy M
Physical Therapy D
Physician Assistant Studies M

AIR FORCE INSTITUTE OF TECHNOLOGY
Aerospace/Aeronautical Engineering M,D
Applied Mathematics M,D
Applied Physics M,D
Astrophysics M,D
Computer Engineering M,D
Computer Science M,D
Electrical Engineering M,D
Engineering and Applied Sciences—General M,D
Engineering Management M
Engineering Physics M,D
Environmental Engineering M
Environmental Management and Policy M
Logistics M,D
Management Information Systems M
Management of Technology M,D
Materials Sciences M,D
Nuclear Engineering M,D
Operations Research M,D
Optical Sciences M,D
Planetary and Space Sciences M,D
Systems Engineering M,D

ALABAMA AGRICULTURAL AND MECHANICAL UNIVERSITY
Agricultural Sciences—General M,D
Agronomy and Soil Sciences M,D
Art Education M
Biological and Biomedical Sciences—General M,D
Business Administration and Management—General M
Business Education M,O
Child and Family Studies M
Clinical Psychology M,O
Clothing and Textiles M
Communication Disorders M
Computer Science M
Counseling Psychology M,O
Counselor Education M,O
Early Childhood Education M,D,O
Education—General M,D,O
Educational Media/Instructional Technology M,O
Elementary Education M,D,O
Engineering and Applied Sciences—General M,D
English Education M,O
Family and Consumer Sciences-General M
Food Science and Technology M,D
Home Economics Education M,O
Hospitality Management M
Human Development M
Kinesiology and Movement Studies M
Materials Engineering M
Materials Sciences M,D
Mathematics Education M,O
Music Education M
Nutrition M
Optical Sciences M,D
Physical Education M
Physics M,D
Planetary and Space Sciences M,D
Plant Sciences M,D
Psychology—General M,O
Reading Education M,D,O
Rehabilitation Counseling M,O
School Psychology M,O
Science Education M,O
Secondary Education M,O
Social Sciences Education M,O
Social Work M,O
Special Education M,D,O
Urban and Regional Planning M

ALABAMA COLLEGE OF OSTEOPATHIC MEDICINE
Osteopathic Medicine D

ALABAMA STATE UNIVERSITY
Accounting M
Allied Health—General M,D
Biological and Biomedical Sciences—General M,D
Business Administration and Management—General M
Counselor Education M,D,O
Early Childhood Education M,O
Education—General M,D,O
Educational Leadership and Administration M,D,O
Educational Media/Instructional Technology M,D,O
Educational Policy M,D,O
Elementary Education M,O
English Education M,O
Forensic Sciences M
Health Education M
History M
Mathematics Education M,O
Mathematics M
Microbiology M,D
Music Education M,O
Occupational Therapy M
Physical Education M
Physical Therapy D
Reading Education M,O
Rehabilitation Counseling M
Rehabilitation Sciences M
Science Education M,O
Secondary Education M,O
Social Sciences Education M,O
Social Work M
Special Education M,O

ALASKA PACIFIC UNIVERSITY
Business Administration and Management—General M
Counseling Psychology M
Education—General M
Elementary Education M
Environmental Education M
Environmental Sciences M
Health Services Management and Hospital Administration M
Interdisciplinary Studies M
Investment Management M,O
Liberal Studies M
Middle School Education M
Telecommunications Management M

ALBANY COLLEGE OF PHARMACY AND HEALTH SCIENCES
Cell Biology M
Clinical Laboratory Sciences/Medical Technology M
Health Services Research M,D
Molecular Biology M
Pharmaceutical Sciences M,D
Pharmacology M,D
Pharmacy M,D

ALBANY LAW SCHOOL
Law M,D

ALBANY MEDICAL COLLEGE
Allopathic Medicine D
Bioethics M,D,O
Cardiovascular Sciences M,D
Cell Biology M,D
Immunology M,D
Microbiology M,D
Molecular Biology M,D
Neuroscience M,D
Nurse Anesthesia M
Pharmacology M,D
Physician Assistant Studies M

ALBANY STATE UNIVERSITY
Accounting M
Business Administration and Management—General M
Counselor Education M,O
Criminal Justice and Criminology M
Early Childhood Education M,O
Economic Development M
Economics M
Education—General M,O
Educational Leadership and Administration M,O
English Education M
Family Nurse Practitioner Studies M
Health Education M,O
Health Services Management and Hospital Administration M
Human Resources Management M
Logistics M
Middle School Education M,O
Nursing Education M
Nursing—General M
Physical Education M,O
Public Administration M
Public Policy M
Social Work M
Special Education M,O
Supply Chain Management M
Water Resources M

ALBERT EINSTEIN COLLEGE OF MEDICINE
Allopathic Medicine D
Anatomy D
Biochemistry D
Biological and Biomedical Sciences—General D
Biophysics D
Cell Biology D
Clinical Research D
Computational Biology D
Developmental Biology D
Genetics D
Genomic Sciences D
Immunology D
Microbiology D
Molecular Biology D
Molecular Genetics D
Molecular Pharmacology D
Neuroscience D
Pathology D
Physiology D
Structural Biology D
Systems Biology D

ALBERTUS MAGNUS COLLEGE
Accounting M
Art Therapy M
Business Administration and Management—General M
Criminal Justice and Criminology M
Education—General M
Health Services Management and Hospital Administration M
Human Resources Management M
Human Services M
Liberal Studies M
Organizational Management M
Project Management M
Writing M

ALBRIGHT COLLEGE
Early Childhood Education M
Education—General M
Elementary Education M
English as a Second Language M
Special Education M

ALCORN STATE UNIVERSITY
Agricultural Economics and Agribusiness M
Agricultural Education M,O
Agricultural Sciences—General M
Agronomy and Soil Sciences M
Animal Sciences M
Biological and Biomedical Sciences—General M
Business Administration and Management—General M
Computer Science M
Counselor Education M,O
Education—General M,O
Elementary Education M,O
Health Education M,O
Information Science M
Nursing—General M
Physical Education M,O
Secondary Education M,O
Special Education M,O
Vocational and Technical Education M,O

ALDERSON BROADDUS UNIVERSITY
Physician Assistant Studies M

ALFRED UNIVERSITY
Accounting M
Applied Arts and Design—General M
Art/Fine Arts M,D
Bioengineering M,D
Business Administration and Management—General M
Ceramic Sciences and Engineering M,D
Computer Art and Design M
Counseling Psychology M,D,O
Counselor Education M,D,O
Education—General M
Electrical Engineering M,D
Engineering and Applied Sciences—General M,D
Internet and Interactive Multimedia M
Materials Sciences M,D
Mechanical Engineering M,D
Public Administration M
Reading Education M
School Psychology M,D,O
Student Affairs M

ALLEN COLLEGE
Adult Nursing M,D
Community Health Nursing M,D
Family Nurse Practitioner Studies M,D
Gerontological Nursing M,D
Health Education M,D
Nursing and Healthcare Administration M,D
Nursing Education M,D
Nursing Informatics M,D
Nursing—General M,D
Occupational Therapy M,D
Psychiatric Nursing M,D
Public Health—General M,D

ALLIANT INTERNATIONAL UNIVERSITY–FRESNO
Clinical Psychology D
Forensic Psychology D
Industrial and Organizational Psychology M,D
Psychology—General M,D

ALLIANT INTERNATIONAL UNIVERSITY–IRVINE
Educational Psychology M,D,O
Forensic Psychology D
Forensic Sciences D
Marriage and Family Therapy M,D
School Psychology M,D,O

ALLIANT INTERNATIONAL UNIVERSITY–LOS ANGELES
Addictions/Substance Abuse Counseling M
Business Administration and Management—General D
Clinical Psychology D
Education—General M,D
Educational Psychology M,D,O
Forensic Psychology D
Gerontology M
Health Psychology D
Industrial and Organizational Psychology M,D
Marriage and Family Therapy M,D
Psychology—General M,D
School Psychology M,D,O
Social Psychology D
Student Affairs M,D,O

ALLIANT INTERNATIONAL UNIVERSITY–SACRAMENTO
Clinical Psychology D
Education—General M,O
Forensic Psychology D
Marriage and Family Therapy M,D
Psychology—General M,D

ALLIANT INTERNATIONAL UNIVERSITY–SAN DIEGO
Business Administration and Management—General M
Clinical Psychology M,D
Education—General M,O
Educational Leadership and Administration M,D,O
Educational Psychology M,D,O
English as a Second Language M,D,O
Forensic Psychology D
Higher Education M,D,O
Industrial and Organizational Psychology M,D
Marriage and Family Therapy M,D
Neuroscience M,D,O
Psychology—General M,D
School Psychology M,D,O
Student Affairs M,D,O

ALLIANT INTERNATIONAL UNIVERSITY–SAN FRANCISCO
Clinical Psychology M,D,O
Counselor Education M
Criminal Justice and Criminology M
Education—General M,O
Educational Leadership and Administration M,D,O
Educational Psychology M,D,O
English as a Second Language M,O
Forensic Psychology M,D
Higher Education M,D,O
Industrial and Organizational Psychology M,D
Law D
Multilingual and Multicultural Education M,O
Pharmacology M
Psychology—General M,D,O
School Psychology M,D,O
Special Education M,O

ALVERNIA UNIVERSITY
Business Administration and Management—General M
Education—General M
Family Nurse Practitioner Studies M,D,O
Gerontological Nursing M,D,O
Liberal Studies M
Nursing and Healthcare Administration M,D,O
Nursing Education M,D,O
Nursing—General M,D,O
Occupational Therapy M
Organizational Management D
Social Psychology M
Urban Education M

ALVERNO COLLEGE
Adult Education M
Business Administration and Management—General M
Education—General M
Educational Leadership and Administration M
Educational Media/Instructional Technology M
Family Nurse Practitioner Studies M,D
Nursing—General M,D
Psychiatric Nursing M,D
Reading Education M
Science Education M
Social Psychology M
Special Education M

AMBERTON UNIVERSITY
Business Administration and Management—General M
Child and Family Studies M
Counseling Psychology M
Counselor Education M
Human Resources Development M
Human Resources Management M
Interdisciplinary Studies M
International Business M
Management Strategy and Policy M
Marriage and Family Therapy M
Project Management M

AMBROSE UNIVERSITY
Pastoral Ministry and Counseling M,O
Religion M,O
Theology M,O

AMERICAN ACADEMY OF ACUPUNCTURE AND ORIENTAL MEDICINE
Acupuncture and Oriental Medicine M,D

AMERICAN BAPTIST SEMINARY OF THE WEST
Pastoral Ministry and Counseling M
Theology M

AMERICAN BUSINESS & TECHNOLOGY UNIVERSITY
Accounting M
Business Administration and Management—General M
Finance and Banking M
International Business M
Management Information Systems M
Marketing M
Project Management M

AMERICAN COLLEGE DUBLIN
Business Administration and Management—General M
Energy Management and Policy M
International Business M
Writing M

AMERICAN COLLEGE OF ACUPUNCTURE AND ORIENTAL MEDICINE
Acupuncture and Oriental Medicine M

AMERICAN COLLEGE OF EDUCATION
Curriculum and Instruction M
Education—General M
Educational Leadership and Administration M
Educational Media/Instructional Technology M
English as a Second Language M
Multilingual and Multicultural Education M

THE AMERICAN COLLEGE OF FINANCIAL SERVICES
Business Administration and Management—General M
Finance and Banking M
Organizational Management M

AMERICAN COLLEGE OF HEALTHCARE SCIENCES
Allied Health—General M,O
Health Promotion M,O
Nutrition M,O
Physiology M,O

AMERICAN COLLEGE OF THESSALONIKI
Business Administration and Management—General M,O
Entrepreneurship M,O
Finance and Banking M,O
Marketing M,O

AMERICAN CONSERVATORY THEATER
Theater M,O

AMERICAN FILM INSTITUTE CONSERVATORY
Film, Television, and Video Production M

AMERICAN GRADUATE SCHOOL IN PARIS
International Affairs M,D

AMERICAN GRADUATE UNIVERSITY
Business Administration and Management—General M,O
Supply Chain Management M,O

AMERICAN INTERCONTINENTAL UNIVERSITY ATLANTA
Information Science M
International Business M
Management Information Systems M

AMERICAN INTERCONTINENTAL UNIVERSITY HOUSTON
Business Administration and Management—General M

AMERICAN INTERCONTINENTAL UNIVERSITY ONLINE
Accounting M
Business Administration and Management—General M
Computer and Information Systems Security M
Curriculum and Instruction M
Education—General M
Educational Leadership and Administration M
Educational Measurement and Evaluation M
Educational Media/Instructional Technology M
Finance and Banking M
Health Services Management and Hospital Administration M
Human Resources Management M
Industrial and Manufacturing Management M
Industrial and Organizational Psychology M
Information Science M
International Business M
Marketing M
Project Management M

AMERICAN INTERNATIONAL COLLEGE
Accounting M,D,O
Business Administration and Management—General M,D,O
Clinical Psychology M,D,O
Counseling Psychology M,D
Counselor Education M,D,O
Early Childhood Education M,D,O
Education—General M,D
Educational Leadership and Administration M,D
Educational Psychology M,D,O
Elementary Education M,D,O
Exercise and Sports Science M,D,O
Family Nurse Practitioner Studies M,D,O
Forensic Psychology M,D,O
Hospitality Management M,D,O
Middle School Education M,D,O
Nursing and Healthcare Administration M,D,O
Nursing Education M,D,O
Occupational Therapy M,D,O
Physical Therapy M,D,O
Psychology—General M,D,O
Reading Education M,D,O
Secondary Education M,D,O
Special Education M,D,O
Taxation M,D,O

AMERICAN JEWISH UNIVERSITY
Business Administration and Management—General M
Education—General M
Jewish Studies M
Nonprofit Management M
Social Work M
Theology M

AMERICAN MUSEUM OF NATURAL HISTORY–RICHARD GILDER GRADUATE SCHOOL
Biological and Biomedical Sciences—General D
Museum Studies D

AMERICAN NATIONAL UNIVERSITY
Business Administration and Management—General M

AMERICAN PUBLIC UNIVERSITY SYSTEM
Accounting M,D
American Studies M,D
Business Administration and Management—General M,D
Business Analytics M,D
Computer and Information Systems Security M,D
Conflict Resolution and Mediation/Peace Studies M,D
Criminal Justice and Criminology M,D
Educational Leadership and Administration M,D
Environmental Management and Policy M,D
Health Informatics M,D
History M,D
International Affairs M,D
Logistics M,D
Military and Defense Studies M,D
National Security M,D
Nursing—General M,D
Political Science M,D
Public Policy M,D
Secondary Education M,D
Sports Management M,D
Transportation Management M,D

AMERICAN SENTINEL UNIVERSITY
Business Administration and Management—General M
Computer Science M
Health Informatics M
Health Services Management and Hospital Administration M
Management Information Systems M
Nursing—General M

AMERICAN UNIVERSITY
Accounting M,O
American Studies M,D,O
Anthropology M,D,O
Applied Social Research M,O
Applied Statistics M,O
Art History M
Arts Administration M,O
Asian Studies O
Biological and Biomedical Sciences—General M
Biopsychology M,D,O
Biostatistics M,O
Biotechnology M
Business Administration and Management—General M,O
Chemistry M
Clinical Psychology M,D,O
Cognitive Sciences M,D,O
Communication—General M,D
Comparative Literature M
Conflict Resolution and Mediation/Peace Studies M,D,O
Corporate and Organizational Communication M
Criminal Justice and Criminology M,D
Cultural Studies M,D,O
Data Science/Data Analytics M,O
Economics M,D,O
Education—General M,D
Educational Measurement and Evaluation M,O
Educational Media/Instructional Technology M,O
English as a Second Language M,O
Entrepreneurship M,D,O
Environmental Management and Policy M,D,O
Environmental Sciences M,O
Ethics M,D,O
Film, Television, and Video Production M
Finance and Banking M,O
French M,O
Gender Studies M,D,O
Health Education M,O
Health Promotion M
Health Services Management and Hospital Administration M,O
History M,D
Human Resources Management M,O
International Affairs M,D,O
International Development M,D,O
International Economics M,D,O
Journalism M
Latin American Studies M,D
Law M,D
Management Information Systems M,D,O
Marketing M
Mass Communication M,D,O
Mathematics M,D,O
Media Studies M,D
Music M,O
National Security M,D,O
Natural Resources M,D,O
Neuroscience M,D,O
Nonprofit Management M,D,O
Nutrition M,O
Organizational Management M,D,O
Philosophy M
Political Science M,D,O
Project Management M,O

*M—masters degree; D—doctorate; O—other advanced degree; *—Close-Up and/or Display*

Psychology—General M,D,O
Public Administration M,D,O
Public Policy M,D,O
Real Estate M,O
Russian M,O
Sociology M,O
Spanish M,O
Sports Management M,O
Statistics M,O
Sustainability Management M
Sustainable Development M,D,O
Taxation M,O
Western European Studies M,D,O
Women's Studies O
Writing M

AMERICAN UNIVERSITY IN BULGARIA
Business Administration and Management—General M

THE AMERICAN UNIVERSITY IN CAIRO
Artificial Intelligence/Robotics M,D,O
Biotechnology M,D,O
Broadcast Journalism M,O
Business Administration and Management—General M,O
Chemistry M,D,O
Communication—General M,D,O
Comparative Literature M,O
Computer Science M,D,O
Construction Engineering M,D,O
Economic Development M,O
Economics M,O
Education—General M
Educational Leadership and Administration M
Electrical Engineering M,D,O
Engineering and Applied Sciences—General M,D,O
English as a Second Language M,O
English M,O
Environmental Engineering M,D,O
Finance and Banking M,O
Gender Studies M,O
Humanities M,O
International Affairs M,O
International and Comparative Education M
Journalism M,O
Law M,O
Mass Communication M,O
Mechanical Engineering M,D,O
Nanotechnology M,D,O
Near and Middle Eastern Languages M,O
Near and Middle Eastern Studies M,O
Philosophy M,O
Physics M,D,O
Psychology—General M,O
Public Administration M,O
Public Policy M,O
Sustainable Development M,D,O
Women's Studies M,O

THE AMERICAN UNIVERSITY IN DUBAI
Business Administration and Management—General M
Construction Management M
Education—General M
Finance and Banking M
International Business M
Marketing M

AMERICAN UNIVERSITY OF ARMENIA
Business Administration and Management—General M
Computer Science M
Economics M
Energy Management and Policy M
English as a Second Language M
Industrial/Management Engineering M
Information Science M
International Affairs M
Law M
Management Information Systems M
Manufacturing Engineering M
Political Science M
Public Health—General M

AMERICAN UNIVERSITY OF BEIRUT
Agricultural Economics and Agribusiness M
Allopathic Medicine M,D
Animal Sciences M
Anthropology M,D
Aquaculture M
Archaeology M,D
Art History M,D
Biochemistry M,D
Biological and Biomedical Sciences—General M,D
Biomedical Engineering M,D
Biostatistics M,D
Business Administration and Management—General M
Cell Biology M,D
Chemistry M,D
Civil Engineering M,D
Clinical Psychology M,D
Clinical Research M,D
Community Health Nursing M
Community Health M,D
Computational Sciences M,D
Computer Engineering M,D
Computer Science M,D
Economics M,D
Education—General M,D
Educational Leadership and Administration M,D
Educational Policy M,D
Electrical Engineering M,D
Elementary Education M,D
Engineering and Applied Sciences—General M,D
Engineering Management M,D
English as a Second Language M,D
English M,D
Environmental and Occupational Health M,D
Environmental Management and Policy M,D
Environmental Sciences M,D
Epidemiology M,D
Finance and Banking M,D
Food Science and Technology M
Geology M,D
Gerontological Nursing M
Health Promotion M,D
Health Services Management and Hospital Administration M,D
Health Services Research M,D
History M,D
Human Resources Management M,D
Immunology M,D
International Affairs M,D
Mathematics Education M,D
Mathematics M,D
Mechanical Engineering M,D
Media Studies M,D
Microbiology M,D
Molecular Biology M,D
Near and Middle Eastern Languages M,D
Near and Middle Eastern Studies M,D
Neuroscience M,D
Nursing and Healthcare Administration M
Nursing—General M
Nutrition M
Oral and Dental Sciences M,D
Pharmacology M,D
Philosophy M,D
Physics M,D
Physiology M,D
Plant Sciences M
Political Science M,D
Psychiatric Nursing M
Psychology—General M,D
Public Administration M,D
Public Health—General M,D
Public Policy M,D
School Psychology M,D
Science Education M,D
Sociology M,D
Theoretical Physics M,D
Urban and Regional Planning M,D
Urban Design M,D
Water Resources Engineering M,D

AMERICAN UNIVERSITY OF HEALTH SCIENCES
Clinical Research M

THE AMERICAN UNIVERSITY OF PARIS
Business Administration and Management—General M
Communication—General M
Conflict Resolution and Mediation/Peace Studies M
Cultural Studies M
International Affairs M
International Business M
Law M
Near and Middle Eastern Studies M
Public Policy M

AMERICAN UNIVERSITY OF PUERTO RICO
Art Education M
Criminal Justice and Criminology M
Education—General M
Elementary Education M
Physical Education M
Science Education M
Special Education M

THE AMERICAN UNIVERSITY OF ROME
Historic Preservation M
Religion M

AMERICAN UNIVERSITY OF SHARJAH
Accounting M,D
Biomedical Engineering M,D
Business Administration and Management—General M,D
Chemical Engineering M,D
Civil Engineering M,D
Computer Engineering M,D
Electrical Engineering M,D
Engineering Management M,D
English as a Second Language M,D
Mathematics M,D
Mechanical Engineering M,D
Translation and Interpretation M,D
Urban and Regional Planning M,D

AMRIDGE UNIVERSITY
Counseling Psychology M,D
Counselor Education M,D
Human Services M,D
Marriage and Family Therapy M,D
Pastoral Ministry and Counseling M,D
Religion M,D
Theology M,D

ANABAPTIST MENNONITE BIBLICAL SEMINARY
Conflict Resolution and Mediation/Peace Studies M,O
Ethics M,O
International Affairs M,O
Pastoral Ministry and Counseling M,O
Public Administration M,O
Theology M,O

ANAHEIM UNIVERSITY
Business Administration and Management—General M,D,O
English as a Second Language M,D,O
Entrepreneurship M,D,O
International Business M,D,O
Sustainability Management M,D,O

ANDERSON UNIVERSITY (IN)
Accounting M,D
Business Administration and Management—General M,D
Education—General M
Missions and Missiology M,D
Theology M,D

ANDERSON UNIVERSITY (SC)
Business Administration and Management—General M
Criminal Justice and Criminology M
Education—General M
Educational Leadership and Administration M
Elementary Education M
Family Nurse Practitioner Studies M,D
Health Services Management and Hospital Administration M
Human Resources Management M
Marketing M
Music Education M
Nursing and Healthcare Administration M,D
Nursing Education M,D
Nursing—General M,D
Organizational Management M
Pastoral Ministry and Counseling M,D
Psychiatric Nursing M,D
Supply Chain Management M

ANDREWS UNIVERSITY
Accounting M
Allied Health—General M
Architecture M
Biological and Biomedical Sciences—General M
Clinical Psychology M
Communication Disorders M
Communication—General M
Counseling Psychology M,D
Curriculum and Instruction M,D,O
Developmental Psychology M,D
Economics M
Education—General M,D,O
Educational Leadership and Administration M,D,O
Educational Psychology M,D
Elementary Education M,D,O
English as a Second Language M,D,O
English Education M,D,O
English M
Finance and Banking M
Foreign Languages Education M,D,O
Higher Education M,D,O
International and Comparative Education M
International Development M
Music M
Nursing—General M,D
Nutrition M,O
Pastoral Ministry and Counseling M,D,O
Physical Therapy D
Psychology—General M,D,O
Public Health—General M,O
Religious Education M,D,O
School Psychology M,O
Science Education M,D,O
Secondary Education M,D,O
Social Psychology M
Social Sciences Education M,D,O
Social Work M
Special Education M
Theology M,D,O
Urban and Regional Planning M

ANGELO STATE UNIVERSITY
Accounting M
Agricultural Sciences—General M
Biological and Biomedical Sciences—General M
Business Administration and Management—General M
Communication—General M
Counselor Education M
Criminal Justice and Criminology M
Curriculum and Instruction M
Educational Leadership and Administration M
English as a Second Language M
English M
Family Nurse Practitioner Studies M
Higher Education M
Homeland Security M
Industrial and Organizational Psychology M
Media Studies M
National Security M
Nursing Education M
Nursing—General M
Physical Therapy D
Psychology—General M
Sociology M
Sports Management M

ANNA MARIA COLLEGE
Art/Fine Arts M,O
Business Administration and Management—General M,O
Counseling Psychology M
Criminal Justice and Criminology M
Early Childhood Education M,O
Education—General M,O
Elementary Education M,O
Emergency Management M,O
English Education M,O
Industrial and Organizational Psychology M
Public Administration M
Social Work M

ANTIOCH UNIVERSITY LOS ANGELES
Business Administration and Management—General M
Clinical Psychology M
Education—General M
Human Resources Development M
Organizational Management M
Psychology—General M
Sustainable Development M

ANTIOCH UNIVERSITY MIDWEST
Health Services Management and Hospital Administration M

ANTIOCH UNIVERSITY NEW ENGLAND
Addictions/Substance Abuse Counseling M
Applied Behavior Analysis M,O
Applied Psychology M,D,O
Business Administration and Management—General M
Clinical Psychology M,D
Conservation Biology M
Counseling Psychology M
Early Childhood Education M
Education—General M,O
Educational Leadership and Administration M,O
Educational Media/Instructional Technology M,O
Elementary Education M,O
Environmental Education M
Environmental Management and Policy M,D
Environmental Sciences M,D
Foundations and Philosophy of Education M,O
Humanities M
Interdisciplinary Studies M
Marriage and Family Therapy M,D,O
Science Education M
Special Education M,O
Sustainability Management M
Sustainable Development M,O
Therapies—Dance, Drama, and Music M,O

ANTIOCH UNIVERSITY SANTA BARBARA
Business Administration and Management—General M
Clinical Psychology M,D
Education—General M
Management Strategy and Policy M
Nonprofit Management M
Writing M

ANTIOCH UNIVERSITY SEATTLE
Adult Education M
Clinical Psychology M,D
Counselor Education M,D
Education—General M
Marriage and Family Therapy M,D
Therapies—Dance, Drama, and Music M

AOMA GRADUATE SCHOOL OF INTEGRATIVE MEDICINE
Acupuncture and Oriental Medicine M,D

APEX SCHOOL OF THEOLOGY
Theology M,D

APOLLOS UNIVERSITY
Business Administration and Management—General M,D
Organizational Management M,D

APPALACHIAN BIBLE COLLEGE
Pastoral Ministry and Counseling M

APPALACHIAN COLLEGE OF PHARMACY
Pharmacy D

APPALACHIAN SCHOOL OF LAW
Law D

APPALACHIAN STATE UNIVERSITY
Accounting M
American Studies M
Biological and Biomedical Sciences—General M
Business Administration and Management—General M
Cell Biology M
Clinical Psychology M
Communication Disorders M
Computer Science M
Counseling Psychology M
Counselor Education M
Cultural Studies M
Curriculum and Instruction M
Educational Leadership and Administration M,O
Educational Media/Instructional Technology M,O
Elementary Education M
Energy and Power Engineering M
English Education M
English M
Exercise and Sports Science M
Foreign Languages Education M
Geographic Information Systems M
Geography M
Health Psychology M
Higher Education M,O
History M
Library Science M,O
Marriage and Family Therapy M
Mathematics Education M
Mathematics M
Middle School Education M
Molecular Biology M
Music M
Nutrition M
Political Science M
Psychology—General M
Public Administration M
Reading Education M
School Psychology M

Science Education	M
Social Sciences Education	M
Social Work	M
Special Education	M
Student Affairs	M
Taxation	M
Therapies—Dance, Drama, and Music	M
Vocational and Technical Education	M

AQUINAS COLLEGE (MI)

Business Administration and Management—General	M
Education—General	M
Marketing	M
Organizational Management	M
Sustainability Management	M

AQUINAS COLLEGE (TN)

Education—General	M
Elementary Education	M
Secondary Education	M

AQUINAS INSTITUTE OF THEOLOGY

Health Services Management and Hospital Administration	M,D,O
Music	M,D,O
Pastoral Ministry and Counseling	M,D,O
Theology	M,D,O

ARCADIA UNIVERSITY

Advertising and Public Relations	M
Applied Behavior Analysis	M
Art Education	M,D,O
Business Administration and Management—General	M
Computer Education	M,D,O
Conflict Resolution and Mediation/Peace Studies	M
Counseling Psychology	M
Curriculum and Instruction	M,D,O
Early Childhood Education	M,D,O
Education—General	M,D,O
Educational Leadership and Administration	M,D,O
Educational Media/Instructional Technology	M,D,O
Elementary Education	M,D,O
English Education	M,D,O
English	M
Environmental Education	M,D,O
Forensic Sciences	M
Genetic Counseling	M
Health Education	M
Humanities	M
International Affairs	M
Marriage and Family Therapy	M
Mathematics Education	M,D,O
Music Education	M,D,O
Physical Therapy	D
Physician Assistant Studies	M
Psychology—General	M,D,O
Public Health—General	M
Reading Education	M,D,O
Science Education	M,D,O
Secondary Education	M,D,O
Special Education	M,D,O
Theater	M,D,O
Writing	M

ARGOSY UNIVERSITY, ATLANTA

Accounting	M,D
Biopsychology	M,D,O
Business Administration and Management—General	M,D
Clinical Psychology	M,D,O
Counselor Education	M,D,O
Education—General	M,D,O
Educational Leadership and Administration	M,D,O
Educational Media/Instructional Technology	M,D,O
Elementary Education	M,D,O
Finance and Banking	M,D
Forensic Psychology	M,D,O
Health Psychology	M,D,O
Health Services Management and Hospital Administration	M,D
Higher Education	M,D,O
Industrial and Organizational Psychology	M,D,O
International Business	M,D
Management Information Systems	M,D
Marketing	M,D
Marriage and Family Therapy	M,D,O
Psychology—General	M,D,O
Public Health—General	M
Secondary Education	M,D,O
Social Psychology	M,D,O
Sport Psychology	M,D,O

ARGOSY UNIVERSITY, CHICAGO

Accounting	M,D
Adult Education	M,D,O
Business Administration and Management—General	M,D
Clinical Psychology	M,D
Community College Education	M,D,O
Counseling Psychology	D
Counselor Education	D
Education—General	M,D,O
Educational Leadership and Administration	M,D,O
Elementary Education	M,D,O
Finance and Banking	M,D
Forensic Psychology	D
Health Psychology	D
Health Services Management and Hospital Administration	M,D
Higher Education	M,D,O
Human Development	D
Industrial and Organizational Psychology	M,D
International Business	M,D
Management Information Systems	M,D
Marketing	M,D
Marriage and Family Therapy	D
Neuroscience	D
Organizational Behavior	D
Organizational Management	D
Psychoanalysis and Psychotherapy	D
Psychology—General	M,D
Public Administration	M,D
Public Health—General	M
Secondary Education	M,D,O
Social Psychology	M,D
Sustainability Management	M,D

ARGOSY UNIVERSITY, HAWAI'I

Accounting	M,D,O
Addictions/Substance Abuse Counseling	O
Adult Education	M,D
Business Administration and Management—General	M,D,O
Clinical Psychology	M,D,O
Counseling Psychology	D
Education—General	M,D
Educational Leadership and Administration	M,D
Elementary Education	M,D
Finance and Banking	M,D,O
Forensic Psychology	M
Health Services Management and Hospital Administration	M,D,O
Higher Education	M,D
International Business	M,D,O
Management Information Systems	M,D,O
Marketing	M,D,O
Marriage and Family Therapy	M
Organizational Management	D
Pharmacology	M,O
Psychology—General	M,D,O
Public Health—General	M
School Psychology	M
Secondary Education	M,D
Sustainability Management	M,D,O

ARGOSY UNIVERSITY, LOS ANGELES

Accounting	M,D
Business Administration and Management—General	M,D
Clinical Psychology	M,D
Community College Education	M,D
Counseling Psychology	M,D
Education—General	M,D
Educational Leadership and Administration	M,D
Elementary Education	M,D
Finance and Banking	M,D
Forensic Psychology	M,D
Health Services Management and Hospital Administration	M,D
Higher Education	M,D
International Business	M,D
Management Information Systems	M,D
Marketing	M,D
Marriage and Family Therapy	M,D
Organizational Management	M,D
Psychology—General	M,D
Public Administration	M,D
Public Health—General	M
Secondary Education	M,D
Sustainability Management	M,D

ARGOSY UNIVERSITY, NORTHERN VIRGINIA

Accounting	M,D,O
Business Administration and Management—General	M,D,O
Clinical Psychology	M,D
Community College Education	M,D,O
Counseling Psychology	M,D
Counselor Education	M,D,O
Education—General	M,D,O
Educational Leadership and Administration	M,D,O
Elementary Education	M,D,O
Finance and Banking	M,D,O
Forensic Psychology	M,D
Health Psychology	M,D
Health Services Management and Hospital Administration	M,D,O
Higher Education	M,D,O
International Business	M,D,O
Management Information Systems	M,D,O
Marketing	M,D,O
Marriage and Family Therapy	M,D
Organizational Management	M,D,O
Psychology—General	M,D,O
Public Administration	M,D,O
Public Health—General	M
Secondary Education	M,D,O
Social Psychology	M,D
Sustainability Management	M,D,O

ARGOSY UNIVERSITY, ORANGE COUNTY

Accounting	M,D,O
Business Administration and Management—General	M,D,O
Clinical Psychology	M,D
Community College Education	M,D
Counseling Psychology	M,D
Education—General	M,D
Educational Leadership and Administration	M,D
Educational Media/Instructional Technology	M,D
Elementary Education	M,D
Finance and Banking	M,D,O
Forensic Psychology	M
Health Services Management and Hospital Administration	M,D,O
Higher Education	M,D
International Business	M,D,O
Management Information Systems	M,D,O
Marketing	M,D,O
Marriage and Family Therapy	M,D
Organizational Management	D
Psychology—General	M,D
Public Administration	M,D,O
Public Health—General	M,D
Secondary Education	M,D
Sport Psychology	M
Sustainability Management	M,D,O

ARGOSY UNIVERSITY, PHOENIX

Accounting	M,D
Adult Education	M,D,O
Business Administration and Management—General	M,D
Clinical Psychology	M,D
Community College Education	M,D,O
Counseling Psychology	M
Education—General	M,D,O
Educational Leadership and Administration	M,D,O
Educational Media/Instructional Technology	M,D,O
Elementary Education	M,D,O
Finance and Banking	M,D
Forensic Psychology	M
Health Services Management and Hospital Administration	M,D
Higher Education	M,D,O
Industrial and Organizational Psychology	M
International Business	M,D
Management Information Systems	M,D
Marketing	M,D
Neuroscience	M,D
Psychology—General	M,D
Public Administration	M,D
Public Health—General	M
School Psychology	M,D
Secondary Education	M,D,O
Sport Psychology	M,D
Sustainability Management	M,D

ARGOSY UNIVERSITY, SEATTLE

Accounting	M,D
Adult Education	M,D
Business Administration and Management—General	M,D
Clinical Psychology	M,D,O
Community College Education	M,D
Counseling Psychology	M,D
Education—General	M,D
Educational Leadership and Administration	M,D
Educational Media/Instructional Technology	M,D
Elementary Education	M,D
Finance and Banking	M,D
Health Services Management and Hospital Administration	M,D
Higher Education	M,D
International Business	M,D
Management Information Systems	M,D
Marketing	M,D
Organizational Management	M,D
Psychology—General	M,D,O
Public Administration	M,D
Public Health—General	M
Secondary Education	M,D
Sustainability Management	M,D

ARGOSY UNIVERSITY, TAMPA

Accounting	M,D
Business Administration and Management—General	M,D
Clinical Psychology	M,D
Community College Education	M,D,O
Counseling Psychology	M,D
Counselor Education	M,D,O
Education—General	M,D,O
Educational Leadership and Administration	M,D,O
Elementary Education	M,D,O
Finance and Banking	M,D
Health Services Management and Hospital Administration	M,D
Higher Education	M,D,O
Industrial and Organizational Psychology	M,D
International Business	M,D
Management Information Systems	M,D
Marketing	M,D
Marriage and Family Therapy	M,D
Neuroscience	M,D
Organizational Management	M,D
Psychology—General	M,D
Public Administration	M,D
Public Health—General	M
Secondary Education	M,D,O
Sustainability Management	M,D

ARGOSY UNIVERSITY, TWIN CITIES

Accounting	M,D
Biopsychology	M,D,O
Business Administration and Management—General	M,D
Clinical Psychology	M,D,O
Education—General	M,D,O
Educational Leadership and Administration	M,D,O
Educational Media/Instructional Technology	M,D,O
Elementary Education	M,D,O
Finance and Banking	M,D,O
Forensic Psychology	M,D,O
Health Psychology	M,D,O
Health Services Management and Hospital Administration	M,D
Higher Education	M,D,O
Industrial and Organizational Psychology	M,D,O
International Business	M,D
Management Information Systems	M,D
Marketing	M,D
Marriage and Family Therapy	M,D,O
Organizational Management	M,D
Psychology—General	M,D,O
Public Administration	M,D
Public Health—General	M
Secondary Education	M,D,O
Sustainability Management	M,D

ARIZONA SCHOOL OF ACUPUNCTURE AND ORIENTAL MEDICINE

Acupuncture and Oriental Medicine	M

ARIZONA STATE UNIVERSITY AT THE TEMPE CAMPUS

Accounting	M,D
Aerospace/Aeronautical Engineering	M,D
African Studies	M,D,O
Agricultural Economics and Agribusiness	D
Animal Behavior	M,D
Anthropology	M,D,O
Applied Arts and Design—General	M,D
Applied Behavior Analysis	M,D
Applied Mathematics	M,D,O
Applied Psychology	M
Archaeology	M,D,O
Architectural History	D
Architecture	M,D
Art Education	M,D
Art History	M,D
Art/Fine Arts	M,D
Arts Administration	M,D
Astrophysics	M,D
Aviation Management	M
Biochemistry	M,D
Bioinformatics	M,D
Biological and Biomedical Sciences—General	M,D
Biomedical Engineering	M,D
Biotechnology	M,D
Building Science	M,D
Business Administration and Management—General	M,D
Cell Biology	M,D
Chemical Engineering	M,D
Chemistry	M,D
Child and Family Studies	M,D
Chinese	M,D
Civil Engineering	M,D
Clinical Psychology	M,D
Cognitive Sciences	M,D
Communication Disorders	M,D
Communication—General	M,D
Community Health	M,D,O
Comparative Literature	M,D,O
Computer Engineering	M,D
Computer Science	M,D
Conservation Biology	M,D
Construction Engineering	M,D
Construction Management	M,D
Counseling Psychology	D
Counselor Education	M
Criminal Justice and Criminology	M,D,O
Cultural Studies	M,D
Curriculum and Instruction	M
Dance	M
Developmental Psychology	M,D
Economics	D
Education—General	M,D,O
Educational Leadership and Administration	M,D
Educational Measurement and Evaluation	D
Educational Media/Instructional Technology	M,O
Educational Policy	D
Electrical Engineering	M,D,O
Elementary Education	M
Emergency Management	M,D
Energy and Power Engineering	M,D
Engineering and Applied Sciences—General	M,D
English as a Second Language	M,D,O
English	M,D,O
Entrepreneurship	M,D
Environmental Design	D
Environmental Engineering	M,D
Environmental Management and Policy	M
Environmental Sciences	M,D,O
Ergonomics and Human Factors	M
Ethics	M,D
Evolutionary Biology	M,D
Exercise and Sports Science	M,D
Family Nurse Practitioner Studies	M,D,O
Film, Television, and Video Production	M
Finance and Banking	M,D
Foreign Languages Education	M,D
French	M
Gender Studies	M,D,O
Geographic Information Systems	M,D,O
Geography	M,D,O
Geological Engineering	M,D
Geology	M,D
Geosciences	M,D
German	M
Gerontological Nursing	M,D,O
Gerontology	M,D,O
Health Education	D
Health Promotion	M,D

*M—masters degree; D—doctorate; O—other advanced degree; *—Close-Up and/or Display*

Health Services Management and Hospital Administration M,D
Higher Education M,D
History of Science and Technology M,D
History M,D,O
Homeland Security M,D
Human Development M,D
Industrial/Management Engineering M,D
Information Science M
Interdisciplinary Studies M
International Business M,D
International Health M,D,O
Japanese M
Journalism M,D
Landscape Architecture M,D
Law M,D
Legal and Justice Studies M,D,O
Liberal Studies M
Linguistics M,D,O
Management Information Systems M,D
Management of Technology M
Management Strategy and Policy M,D
Manufacturing Engineering M
Marketing M,D
Marriage and Family Therapy M,D
Mass Communication M,D
Materials Engineering M,D
Materials Sciences M,D
Mathematics Education M,D,O
Mathematics M,D,O
Mechanical Engineering M,D
Media Studies M,D
Medical Informatics M,D
Medieval and Renaissance Studies M,D,O
Microbiology M,D
Modeling and Simulation M,D
Molecular Biology M,D
Museum Studies M,D,O
Music Education M,D
Music M,D
Nanotechnology M,D
Neuroscience M,D
Nonprofit Management M,D,O
Nuclear Engineering M,D,O
Nursing and Healthcare Administration M,D,O
Nursing Education M,D,O
Nursing—General M,D,O
Nutrition M,D
Organizational Behavior M,D
Philosophy M,D,O
Physical Education M
Physics M,D
Planetary and Space Sciences M,D
Plant Biology M,D
Political Science M,D
Psychiatric Nursing M,D,O
Psychology—General M,D
Public Administration M,D
Public Affairs M,D
Public Health—General M,D,O
Public History M,D,O
Public Policy M,D
Publishing M,D,O
Real Estate M,D
Reliability Engineering M
Religion M,D,O
Rhetoric M,D,O
Secondary Education M
Social Psychology M,D
Social Work M,D,O
Sociology M,D
Software Engineering M,D
Spanish M,D
Special Education M,O
Sports and Entertainment Law M
Statistics M,D,O
Supply Chain Management M,D
Sustainable Development M,D,O
Systems Engineering M
Systems Science M,D
Technology and Public Policy M
Textile Design M,D
Theater M,D
Therapies—Dance, Drama, and Music M,D
Translation and Interpretation M,D,O
Transportation and Highway Engineering M,D,O
Travel and Tourism M,D,O
Urban and Regional Planning M,D,O
Urban Design M,D
Urban Studies M,D,O
Writing M,D

ARIZONA SUMMIT LAW SCHOOL
Law D

ARKANSAS STATE UNIVERSITY
Accounting M
Addictions/Substance Abuse Counseling M,O
Agricultural Education M,O
Agricultural Sciences—General M,O
Biological and Biomedical Sciences—General M,O
Biotechnology M,O
Business Administration and Management—General M
Business Education O
Chemistry M,O
Clinical Psychology M,O
Communication Disorders M,O
Communication—General M,O
Community College Education M,D,O
Computer Science M
Counselor Education M,O
Criminal Justice and Criminology M,O
Early Childhood Education M,D,O
Education of the Gifted M,D,O
Education—General M,D,O
Educational Leadership and Administration M,D,O
Elementary Education M,D,O
Emergency Management M,O
Engineering and Applied Sciences—General M
Engineering Management M
English Education M,O
English M,O
Environmental Sciences M,D
Exercise and Sports Science M,O
Foundations and Philosophy of Education M,D,O
Gerontology M,D,O
Health Communication M,O
Health Education M,D,O
Health Services Management and Hospital Administration M,D,O
Historic Preservation M,D
History M,O
Journalism M
Management Information Systems O
Mass Communication M
Mathematics Education M
Mathematics M
Media Studies M
Middle School Education M,D,O
Molecular Biology M,D
Music Education M,O
Music M,O
Nurse Anesthesia M,D,O
Nursing—General M,D,O
Occupational Therapy D
Physical Education M,O
Physical Therapy D
Political Science M,O
Public Administration M,O
Reading Education M,D,O
Rehabilitation Counseling M,O
School Psychology M,O
Science Education M,O
Social Sciences Education M,D,O
Social Work M,O
Sociology M,O
Special Education M,D,O
Sports Management M,O
Student Affairs M

ARKANSAS TECH UNIVERSITY
Business Administration and Management—General M
Counselor Education M,D,O
Education—General M,D,O
Educational Leadership and Administration M,D,O
Educational Media/Instructional Technology M,D,O
Electrical Engineering M
Elementary Education M,D,O
Emergency Management M
Engineering and Applied Sciences—General M
English as a Second Language M
English Education M
English M
Fish, Game, and Wildlife Management M
Health Informatics M
History M
Information Science M
Journalism M
Liberal Studies M
Mechanical Engineering M
Nursing—General M
Psychology—General M
Sociology M
Special Education M,D,O
Student Affairs M,D,O

ARLINGTON BAPTIST UNIVERSITY
Curriculum and Instruction M
Education—General M
Educational Leadership and Administration M
Theology M

ART ACADEMY OF CINCINNATI
Art Education M

ARTCENTER COLLEGE OF DESIGN
Art/Fine Arts M
Computer Art and Design M
Environmental Design M
Film, Television, and Video Production M
Graphic Design M
Industrial Design M
Transportation and Highway Engineering M

THE ART INSTITUTE OF DALLAS, A BRANCH OF MIAMI INTERNATIONAL UNIVERSITY OF ART & DESIGN
Applied Arts and Design—General M

ASBURY THEOLOGICAL SEMINARY
Missions and Missiology M,D,O
Pastoral Ministry and Counseling M,D,O
Religious Education M,D,O
Theology M,D,O

ASBURY UNIVERSITY
Child and Family Studies M
Classics M
Educational Leadership and Administration M
English as a Second Language M
English M
French M
Mathematics Education M
Reading Education M
Science Education M
Social Sciences Education M
Social Work M
Spanish M
Special Education M
Writing M

ASHLAND THEOLOGICAL SEMINARY
Clinical Psychology M,D
Counselor Education M,D
Pastoral Ministry and Counseling M,D
Theology M,D

ASHLAND UNIVERSITY
Accounting M
Business Administration and Management—General M
Business Analytics M
Communication—General M
Corporate and Organizational Communication M
Education—General M,D
Educational Leadership and Administration M,D
Entrepreneurship M
Exercise and Sports Science M
Family Nurse Practitioner Studies D
Finance and Banking M
Health Services Management and Hospital Administration M
History M
Human Resources Management M
International Business M
Management Information Systems M
Nursing—General D
Political Science M
Project Management M
Sports Management M
Supply Chain Management M
Writing M

ASHWORTH COLLEGE
Business Administration and Management—General M
Criminal Justice and Criminology M
Health Services Management and Hospital Administration M
Human Resources Management M
International Business M
Marketing M

ASPEN UNIVERSITY
Business Administration and Management—General M,O
Finance and Banking M,O
Forensic Nursing M
Information Science M,O
Management Information Systems M,O
Nursing and Healthcare Administration M
Nursing Education M
Nursing Informatics M
Nursing—General M
Project Management M,O

ASSEMBLIES OF GOD THEOLOGICAL SEMINARY
Cultural Studies M,D
Missions and Missiology M,D
Pastoral Ministry and Counseling M,D
Theology M,D

ASSUMPTION COLLEGE
Accounting M,O
Addictions/Substance Abuse Counseling O
Applied Behavior Analysis M,O
Business Administration and Management—General M,O
Child and Family Studies M,O
Counseling Psychology M,O
Economics M,O
Finance and Banking M,O
Health Services Management and Hospital Administration M,O
Human Resources Management M,O
International Business M,O
Marketing M,O
Nonprofit Management M,O
Rehabilitation Counseling M,O
School Psychology M,O
Social Sciences O
Special Education M,O

ATHABASCA UNIVERSITY
Adult Education M,O
Allied Health—General M,O
Applied Psychology M,O
Architecture M,O
Art Therapy M,O
Business Administration and Management—General M,D,O
Counseling Psychology M,O
Counselor Education M,O
Cultural Studies M,O
Distance Education Development M,D,O
Education—General M,D,O
Interdisciplinary Studies M,O
International Development M,O
Management of Technology M,D,O
Nursing and Healthcare Administration M,O
Nursing—General M,O
Organizational Management M,O
Project Management M,D,O
Science Education M,O

THE ATHENAEUM OF OHIO
Theology M,O

ATHENS STATE UNIVERSITY
Logistics M
Religion M
Supply Chain Management M
Vocational and Technical Education M

ATLANTA'S JOHN MARSHALL LAW SCHOOL
Law M,D

ATLANTIC INSTITUTE OF ORIENTAL MEDICINE
Acupuncture and Oriental Medicine M,D

ATLANTIC SCHOOL OF THEOLOGY
Pastoral Ministry and Counseling M,O
Theology M,O

ATLANTIC UNIVERSITY
Organizational Management M,O
Pastoral Ministry and Counseling O
Psychoanalysis and Psychotherapy O
Transpersonal and Humanistic Psychology M

ATLANTIC UNIVERSITY COLLEGE
Graphic Design M

ATLANTIS UNIVERSITY
Business Administration and Management—General M,D
Computer Engineering M
Engineering and Applied Sciences—General M
Health Services Management and Hospital Administration M
Management of Technology M

A.T. STILL UNIVERSITY
Allied Health—General M,D,O
Athletic Training and Sports Medicine M,D,O
Biological and Biomedical Sciences—General M,D
Communication Disorders M,D,O
Dentistry M,D,O
Health Services Management and Hospital Administration M,D,O
International Health M,D,O
Kinesiology and Movement Studies M,D,O
Occupational Therapy M,D,O
Oral and Dental Sciences M,D,O
Organizational Behavior M,D,O
Osteopathic Medicine M,D
Physical Therapy M,D,O
Physician Assistant Studies M,D,O
Public Health—General M,D,O
Sport Psychology M,D,O

AUBURN UNIVERSITY
Accounting M
Adult Education M,D,O
Aerospace/Aeronautical Engineering M,D
Agricultural Economics and Agribusiness M
Agricultural Sciences—General M,D
Agronomy and Soil Sciences M,D
Analytical Chemistry M,D
Animal Sciences M,D
Applied Economics M,D
Applied Mathematics M,D
Aquaculture M,D
Architecture M
Biochemistry M,D
Biological and Biomedical Sciences—General M,D
Biosystems Engineering M,D
Botany M,D
Business Administration and Management—General M,D
Cell Biology M,D
Chemical Engineering M,D
Chemistry M,D
Child and Family Studies M,D
Civil Engineering M,D
Clothing and Textiles M,D
Communication Disorders M,D
Communication—General M,D
Computer Engineering M,D
Computer Science M,D
Construction Engineering M
Curriculum and Instruction M,D,O
Economics M,D
Education—General M,D,O
Educational Leadership and Administration M,D,O
Educational Media/Instructional Technology M,D,O
Electrical Engineering M,D
Engineering and Applied Sciences—General M,D,O
English M,D,O*
Entomology M,D
Exercise and Sports Science M,D,O
Finance and Banking M
Fish, Game, and Wildlife Management M,D
Food Science and Technology M,D,O
Forestry M,D
Geography M
Geology M
Health Education M,D,O
Higher Education M,D,O
History M,D,O
Horticulture M,D
Human Development M,D
Industrial Design M
Industrial/Management Engineering M,D,O
Inorganic Chemistry M,D
Landscape Architecture M,D
Materials Engineering M,D
Mathematics M,D
Mechanical Engineering M,D
Molecular Biology M,D
Natural Resources M,D
Nursing Education M
Nursing—General M
Nutrition M,D,O
Organic Chemistry M,D
Pharmaceutical Sciences M,D
Pharmacy D
Physical Chemistry M,D

Physical Education	M,D,O
Physics	M,D
Plant Pathology	M,D
Political Science	M,D,O
Polymer Science and Engineering	M,D
Psychology—General	M,D
Public Administration	M,D,O
Real Estate	M
Sociology	M
Software Engineering	M,D
Spanish	M
Special Education	M,D
Statistics	M,D
Systems Engineering	M,D,O
Technical Communication	M,D,O
Urban and Regional Planning	M
Veterinary Medicine	D
Zoology	M,D

AUBURN UNIVERSITY AT MONTGOMERY

Accounting	M
Applied Economics	M
Business Administration and Management—General	M
Clinical Psychology	M,O
Computer and Information Systems Security	M
Counselor Education	M,O
Criminal Justice and Criminology	M
Early Childhood Education	M,O
Economics	M
Education—General	M,O
Educational Leadership and Administration	M,O
Educational Media/Instructional Technology	M,O
Elementary Education	M,O
Emergency Management	M
Exercise and Sports Science	M,O
Family Nurse Practitioner Studies	M
Geographic Information Systems	M
Homeland Security	M
Information Science	M
Legal and Justice Studies	M
Liberal Studies	M
Management Information Systems	M
Nursing Education	M
Nursing—General	M
Organizational Management	M
Physical Education	M,O
Political Science	M,D
Psychology—General	M,O
Public Administration	M,D
Public Policy	M,D
School Psychology	M,O
Secondary Education	M,O
Special Education	M,O
Sports Management	M,O
Writing	M

AUGSBURG UNIVERSITY

Business Administration and Management—General	M
Education—General	M
Family Nurse Practitioner Studies	M,D
Nursing—General	M,D
Organizational Management	M
Physician Assistant Studies	M
Social Work	M
Transcultural Nursing	M,D

AUGUSTANA UNIVERSITY

Accounting	M
Education—General	M
Educational Media/Instructional Technology	M
Genetic Counseling	M
Mathematics	M
Reading Education	M
Science Education	M
Special Education	M
Sports Management	M

AUGUSTA UNIVERSITY

Acute Care/Critical Care Nursing	D
Allied Health—General	D
Allopathic Medicine	D
Anatomy	D
Biochemistry	D
Business Administration and Management—General	M
Cancer Biology/Oncology	D
Cardiovascular Sciences	D
Cell Biology	D
Clinical Psychology	M,O
Clinical Research	M
Computer and Information Systems Security	M
Counselor Education	M,O
Curriculum and Instruction	M,O
Dentistry	D
Education—General	M,D,O
Educational Leadership and Administration	M,O
Educational Media/Instructional Technology	D
Elementary Education	M,O
Environmental and Occupational Health	M
Family Nurse Practitioner Studies	D
Foreign Languages Education	M,O
Genomic Sciences	D
Gerontological Nursing	D
Health Informatics	M
Medical Illustration	M
Middle School Education	M,O
Molecular Medicine	D
Music Education	M,O
Neuroscience	D
Nurse Anesthesia	D
Nursing and Healthcare Administration	M,D
Nursing—General	D
Occupational Therapy	M
Oral and Dental Sciences	M,D
Pediatric Nursing	D
Pharmacology	D
Physical Therapy	D
Physician Assistant Studies	M
Physiology	D
Psychiatric Nursing	D
Psychology—General	M
Public Health—General	M
Rehabilitation Sciences	D
School Psychology	M,O
Secondary Education	M,O
Social Sciences	M
Special Education	M,O

AURORA UNIVERSITY

Accounting	M
Adult Education	M,D
Applied Behavior Analysis	M,D
Business Administration and Management—General	M
Curriculum and Instruction	M,D
Education—General	M,D
Educational Leadership and Administration	M,D
Educational Media/Instructional Technology	M,D
English as a Second Language	M,D
Homeland Security	M
Mathematics Education	M
Mathematics	M
Public Policy	M
Reading Education	M,D
Science Education	M
Social Work	M,D
Special Education	M,D

AUSTIN COLLEGE

Education—General	M

AUSTIN GRADUATE SCHOOL OF THEOLOGY

Theology	M

AUSTIN PEAY STATE UNIVERSITY

Biological and Biomedical Sciences—General	M
Business Administration and Management—General	M
Clinical Laboratory Sciences/Medical Technology	M
Clinical Psychology	M
Communication—General	M
Computer and Information Systems Security	M
Corporate and Organizational Communication	M
Counseling Psychology	M
Counselor Education	M,O
Curriculum and Instruction	M,O
Data Science/Data Analytics	M
Education—General	M,O
Educational Leadership and Administration	M,O
Elementary Education	M,O
Engineering and Applied Sciences—General	M
English	M
Exercise and Sports Science	M
Family Nurse Practitioner Studies	M
Health Education	M
Industrial and Organizational Psychology	M
Mathematical and Computational Finance	M
Mathematics Education	M
Media Studies	M
Military and Defense Studies	M
Music Education	M
Music	M
Nursing and Healthcare Administration	M
Nursing Education	M
Nursing Informatics	M
Nursing—General	M
Organizational Management	M
Psychology—General	M
Public Health—General	M
Reading Education	M,O
Science Education	M
Secondary Education	M,O
Social Work	M
Sports Management	M

AUSTIN PRESBYTERIAN THEOLOGICAL SEMINARY

Pastoral Ministry and Counseling	M,D
Theology	M,D

AVE MARIA SCHOOL OF LAW

Law	D

AVE MARIA UNIVERSITY

Pastoral Ministry and Counseling	M,D
Theology	M,D

AVERETT UNIVERSITY

Accounting	M
Business Administration and Management—General	M
Curriculum and Instruction	M
Education—General	M
Educational Leadership and Administration	M
Human Resources Management	M
Marketing	M
Special Education	M

AVILA UNIVERSITY

Accounting	M
Art Education	M,O
Business Administration and Management—General	M
Counseling Psychology	M
Early Childhood Education	M,O
Education—General	M,O
Educational Media/Instructional Technology	M
Elementary Education	M,O
English as a Second Language	M,O
Finance and Banking	M
Health Services Management and Hospital Administration	M
Human Resources Management	M
International Business	M
Management Information Systems	M
Marketing	M
Middle School Education	M,O
Nonprofit Management	M
Organizational Management	M
Physical Education	M,O
Project Management	M
Psychology—General	M
Reading Education	M,O
Secondary Education	M,O
Special Education	M,O

AZUSA PACIFIC UNIVERSITY

Accounting	M
Adult Nursing	M,D
Art/Fine Arts	M
Athletic Training and Sports Medicine	M
Biotechnology	M*
Business Administration and Management—General	M
Clinical Psychology	D
Counselor Education	M
Curriculum and Instruction	M
Data Science/Data Analytics	M
Developmental Psychology	M
Education—General	M,D
Educational Leadership and Administration	M,D
Educational Media/Instructional Technology	M
English as a Second Language	M
English	M
Entrepreneurship	M
Ethics	M
Experimental Psychology	M
Family Nurse Practitioner Studies	M,D
Film, Television, and Video Production	M
Finance and Banking	M
Gerontological Nursing	M,D
Higher Education	M,D
Industrial and Organizational Psychology	M
International Business	M
Kinesiology and Movement Studies	M
Marketing	M
Marriage and Family Therapy	D
Music Education	M
Music	M
Nursing and Healthcare Administration	M,D
Nursing Education	M,D
Nursing—General	M,D
Organizational Management	M
Pastoral Ministry and Counseling	M
Pediatric Nursing	M,D
Physical Therapy	D
Psychiatric Nursing	M,D
Psychology—General	M
Public Health—General	M
School Psychology	M,D
Social Work	M
Special Education	M
Sports Management	M
Theology	M,D
Urban Studies	M

BABEL UNIVERSITY PROFESSIONAL SCHOOL OF TRANSLATION

Translation and Interpretation	M

BABSON COLLEGE

Accounting	M,O
Business Administration and Management—General	M,O
Business Analytics	M,O
Entrepreneurship	M,O
Finance and Banking	M,O

BAKER COLLEGE CENTER FOR GRADUATE STUDIES–ONLINE

Accounting	M,D
Business Administration and Management—General	M,D
Finance and Banking	M,D
Health Services Management and Hospital Administration	M,D
Human Resources Management	M,D
Management Information Systems	M,D
Marketing	M,D

BAKER UNIVERSITY

Business Administration and Management—General	M
Education—General	M,D
Liberal Studies	M
Organizational Management	M

BAKKE GRADUATE UNIVERSITY

Business Administration and Management—General	M,D
Entrepreneurship	M,D
Pastoral Ministry and Counseling	M,D
Theology	M,D
Urban Education	M,D

BALDWIN WALLACE UNIVERSITY

Accounting	M
Business Administration and Management—General	M
Business Analytics	M
Communication Disorders	M
Education—General	M
Educational Leadership and Administration	M
Educational Media/Instructional Technology	M
Health Education	M
Health Services Management and Hospital Administration	M
Human Resources Management	M
International Business	M
Marketing Research	M
Physician Assistant Studies	M
Public Health—General	M
Reading Education	M
Special Education	M

BALL STATE UNIVERSITY

Accounting	M
Actuarial Science	M
Adult Education	M,D
Advertising and Public Relations	M
Anthropology	M,O
Applied Behavior Analysis	M
Architecture	M
Art/Fine Arts	M
Biological and Biomedical Sciences—General	M,D
Business Administration and Management—General	M,O
Business Education	M,O
Chemistry	M,D
Clinical Psychology	M,D
Cognitive Sciences	M,D
Communication Disorders	M,D
Communication—General	M,D
Computer Education	M,D,O
Computer Science	M
Counseling Psychology	M,D
Counselor Education	M,D
Criminal Justice and Criminology	M,O
Curriculum and Instruction	M,D
Economic Development	M,O
Education of the Gifted	M,D,O
Education—General	M,D,O
Educational Leadership and Administration	M,D,O
Educational Measurement and Evaluation	M,D,O
Educational Media/Instructional Technology	M,D
Educational Policy	D
Educational Psychology	M,D
Elementary Education	M,D,O
Emergency Management	M,O
English as a Second Language	M
English	M,D
Environmental Education	M,O
Environmental Management and Policy	M,O
Environmental Sciences	D
Exercise and Sports Science	M,D
Family and Consumer Sciences-General	M
Family Nurse Practitioner Studies	M,D,O
Foundations and Philosophy of Education	D
Geographic Information Systems	M,O
Geography	M,O
Geology	M,D
Geosciences	M,D
Gerontological Nursing	M,D,O
Health Promotion	M
Higher Education	M,D
Historic Preservation	M,O
History	M
Homeland Security	M,O
Human Development	M,D,O
Information Science	M,O
Interior Design	M
Internet and Interactive Multimedia	M
Journalism	M
Kinesiology and Movement Studies	M,D,O
Landscape Architecture	M
Linguistics	M,D
Management Information Systems	M,O
Mathematics Education	M
Mathematics	M
Meteorology	M,O
Middle School Education	M,O
Music Education	M,D,O
Music	M,D,O
Natural Resources	M,O
Neuroscience	M,D,O
Nursing Education	M,D,O
Nursing—General	M,D,O
Nutrition	M
Photography	M
Physical Education	M
Physics	M
Physiology	M
Political Science	M
Psychology—General	M
Public Administration	M,O
Reading Education	M,D,O
Rehabilitation Counseling	M,O
Rhetoric	M,D
School Psychology	M,D,O
Secondary Education	M
Social Psychology	M
Sociology	M
Special Education	M,D,O
Speech and Interpersonal Communication	M
Sport Psychology	M

*M—masters degree; D—doctorate; O—other advanced degree; *—Close-Up and/or Display*

Sports Management	M
Statistics	M
Telecommunications	M
Urban and Regional Planning	M,O
Urban Design	M
Writing	M,D

BANK STREET COLLEGE OF EDUCATION

Child and Family Studies	M
Early Childhood Education	M
Education—General	M
Educational Leadership and Administration	M
Elementary Education	M
Foundations and Philosophy of Education	M
Maternal and Child Health	M
Mathematics Education	M
Multilingual and Multicultural Education	M
Museum Education	M
Reading Education	M
Special Education	M

BAPTIST BIBLE COLLEGE

Pastoral Ministry and Counseling	M
Theology	M

THE BAPTIST COLLEGE OF FLORIDA

Music	M
Pastoral Ministry and Counseling	M
Religion	M
Theology	M

BAPTIST MISSIONARY ASSOCIATION THEOLOGICAL SEMINARY

Theology	M

BAPTIST THEOLOGICAL SEMINARY AT RICHMOND

Pastoral Ministry and Counseling	M,D,O
Religion	M,D,O
Religious Education	M,D,O
Theology	M,D,O

BARCLAY COLLEGE

Theology	M

BARD COLLEGE

Art/Fine Arts	M
Atmospheric Sciences	M,O
Economics	M
Education—General	M
English	M
Environmental Management and Policy	M,O
Film, Television, and Video Production	M
History	M
Mathematics Education	M
Museum Studies	M
Music	M,O
Photography	M
Science Education	M
Secondary Education	M
Spanish	M
Sustainability Management	M,O
Writing	M

BARD GRADUATE CENTER

Art History	M,D*
Decorative Arts	M,D

BARRY UNIVERSITY

Accounting	M
Acute Care/Critical Care Nursing	M,O
Anatomy	M
Art/Fine Arts	M
Athletic Training and Sports Medicine	M
Biological and Biomedical Sciences—General	M
Business Administration and Management—General	M,O
Clinical Psychology	M,O
Communication Disorders	M
Communication—General	M,O
Corporate and Organizational Communication	M,O
Counselor Education	M,D,O
Curriculum and Instruction	D,O
Distance Education Development	O
Early Childhood Education	M,D,O
Education of the Gifted	M,D,O
Education—General	M,D,O
Educational Leadership and Administration	M,D,O
Educational Media/Instructional Technology	M,D,O
Elementary Education	M,D,O
English as a Second Language	M,D,O
Exercise and Sports Science	M
Family Nurse Practitioner Studies	M,O
Finance and Banking	O
Health Informatics	O
Health Services Management and Hospital Administration	M,O
Higher Education	M,D
Human Resources Development	M,D
Human Resources Management	O
Information Science	M
International Business	O
Kinesiology and Movement Studies	M
Law	D
Liberal Studies	M
Management Information Systems	O
Marketing	O
Marriage and Family Therapy	M,O
Nurse Anesthesia	M
Nursing and Healthcare Administration	M,D,O
Nursing Education	M,O
Nursing—General	M,D,O
Occupational Therapy	M
Pastoral Ministry and Counseling	M,D
Photography	M
Physician Assistant Studies	M
Podiatric Medicine	D
Psychology—General	M,O
Public Administration	M
Public Health—General	M
Reading Education	M,D,O
Rehabilitation Counseling	M,O
School Psychology	M,O
Social Work	M,D
Special Education	M,D,O
Sport Psychology	M
Sports Management	M
Theology	M,D

BARTON COLLEGE

Elementary Education	M

BARUCH COLLEGE OF THE CITY UNIVERSITY OF NEW YORK

Accounting	M,D
Arts Administration	M
Business Administration and Management—General	M,D,O
Corporate and Organizational Communication	M
Counseling Psychology	M
Economics	M
Educational Leadership and Administration	M,O
Entrepreneurship	M,D
Finance and Banking	M,D
Financial Engineering	M
Health Services Management and Hospital Administration	M
Higher Education	M
Human Resources Management	M,D
Industrial and Labor Relations	M
Industrial and Manufacturing Management	M,D
Industrial and Organizational Psychology	M,D
International Affairs	M*
International Business	M,D
International Economics	M
International Trade Policy	M
Management Information Systems	M,D
Marketing	M,D
Nonprofit Management	M
Organizational Behavior	M,D
Public Administration	M
Public Policy	M
Quantitative Analysis	M
Real Estate	M
Statistics	M
Sustainability Management	M,D
Sustainable Development	M
Taxation	M

BASTYR UNIVERSITY

Acupuncture and Oriental Medicine	M,D
Counseling Psychology	M,O
Health Psychology	M,O
Maternal and Child Health	M,O
Naturopathic Medicine	D,O
Nurse Midwifery	M,O
Nutrition	M,O

BAYAMÓN CENTRAL UNIVERSITY

Accounting	M
Business Administration and Management—General	M
Counselor Education	M,O
Early Childhood Education	M,O
Education—General	M,O
Educational Leadership and Administration	M,O
Elementary Education	M,O
Finance and Banking	M
Industrial and Organizational Psychology	M
Marketing	M
Marriage and Family Therapy	M,O
Rehabilitation Counseling	M,O
Special Education	M,O

BAYLOR COLLEGE OF MEDICINE

Allopathic Medicine	D
Biochemistry	D
Bioengineering	D
Biological and Biomedical Sciences—General	M,D
Biomedical Engineering	D
Biophysics	D
Cancer Biology/Oncology	D
Cardiovascular Sciences	D
Cell Biology	D
Clinical Laboratory Sciences/Medical Technology	M,D
Computational Biology	D
Developmental Biology	D
Genetic Counseling	M
Genetics	D
Human Genetics	D
Immunology	D
Microbiology	D
Molecular Biology	D
Molecular Biophysics	D
Molecular Medicine	D
Molecular Physiology	D
Neuroscience	D
Nurse Anesthesia	D
Pharmacology	D
Physician Assistant Studies	M
Structural Biology	D
Translational Biology	D
Virology	D

BAYLOR UNIVERSITY

Accounting	M
Allied Health—General	M,D
American Studies	M
Applied Behavior Analysis	M,D,O
Athletic Training and Sports Medicine	M,D
Biochemistry	M,D
Biological and Biomedical Sciences—General	M,D
Biomedical Engineering	M,D
Business Administration and Management—General	M
Chemistry	M,D
Clinical Psychology	D
Communication Disorders	M
Communication—General	M
Community Health	M,D
Computer Engineering	M,D
Computer Science	M,D
Curriculum and Instruction	M,D
Ecology	D
Economics	M
Education—General	M,D,O
Educational Leadership and Administration	M,O
Educational Psychology	M,D,O
Electrical Engineering	M,D
Emergency Medical Services	D
English	M,D
Entrepreneurship	D
Environmental Biology	M,D
Environmental Management and Policy	M,D
Environmental Sciences	D
Exercise and Sports Science	M,D
Family Nurse Practitioner Studies	M,D
Geosciences	M,D
Health Education	M,D
Health Services Management and Hospital Administration	M
History	M,D
Interdisciplinary Studies	D
International Affairs	M,D
Journalism	M
Kinesiology and Movement Studies	M,D
Law	D
Limnology	M,D
Management Information Systems	M,D
Maternal and Child/Neonatal Nursing	M,D
Mathematics	M,D
Mechanical Engineering	M,D
Museum Studies	M
Music	M,D
Nurse Midwifery	M,D
Nursing—General	M,D
Nutrition	M,D
Philosophy	M,D
Physical Education	M,D
Physical Therapy	D
Physics	M,D
Physiology	M,D
Political Science	M,D
Psychology—General	M,D
Public Administration	M,D
Public Policy	M,D
Religion	M,D
School Psychology	M,D,O
Social Work	M,D
Sociology	M,D
Spanish	M
Special Education	M,D,O
Statistics	M,D
Theater	M
Theology	M,D

BAY PATH UNIVERSITY

Accounting	M
Addictions/Substance Abuse Counseling	M
Applied Behavior Analysis	M
Applied Statistics	M
Clinical Psychology	M
Computer and Information Systems Security	M
Curriculum and Instruction	M
Developmental Psychology	M
Educational Leadership and Administration	M
Educational Media/Instructional Technology	M
Entrepreneurship	M
Forensic Sciences	M
Genetic Counseling	M
Higher Education	M
Management Information Systems	M
Management Strategy and Policy	M
Nonprofit Management	M
Occupational Therapy	M,D
Physician Assistant Studies	M
Special Education	M
Writing	M

BECKER COLLEGE

Counseling Psychology	M
Counselor Education	M
Social Psychology	M

BELHAVEN UNIVERSITY (MS)

Business Administration and Management—General	M
Education—General	M,D,O
Educational Leadership and Administration	M,D,O
Health Services Management and Hospital Administration	M
Human Resources Management	M
Public Administration	M
Reading Education	M,D,O
Sports Management	M

BELLARMINE UNIVERSITY

Athletic Training and Sports Medicine	M,D
Business Administration and Management—General	M
Communication—General	M
Education—General	M,D,O
Educational Leadership and Administration	M,D,O
Elementary Education	M,D,O
Family Nurse Practitioner Studies	M,D
Higher Education	M,D,O
Middle School Education	M,D,O
Nursing and Healthcare Administration	M,D
Nursing Education	M,D
Nursing—General	M,D
Physical Therapy	M,D
Reading Education	M,D,O
Secondary Education	M,D,O

BELLEVUE UNIVERSITY

Business Administration and Management—General	M,D
Corporate and Organizational Communication	M
Counselor Education	M
Criminal Justice and Criminology	M
Educational Media/Instructional Technology	M
Finance and Banking	M,D
Health Services Management and Hospital Administration	M
Human Resources Management	M,D
Human Services	M
Information Science	M
Management Information Systems	M
Military and Defense Studies	M
National Security	M
Organizational Management	M
Project Management	M
Public Administration	M

BELLIN COLLEGE

Family Nurse Practitioner Studies	M
Nursing Education	M
Nursing—General	M

BELMONT UNIVERSITY

Accounting	M
Allied Health—General	M,D
Business Administration and Management—General	M
Health Informatics	D
Health Services Management and Hospital Administration	M
Law	D
Nursing—General	M,D
Occupational Therapy	M,D
Pharmaceutical Administration	D
Pharmacy	D
Physical Therapy	M,D
Public Health—General	D

BEMIDJI STATE UNIVERSITY

Biological and Biomedical Sciences—General	M
Education—General	M
English	M
Environmental Management and Policy	M
Mathematics Education	M
Mathematics	M
Special Education	M

BENEDICTINE COLLEGE

Business Administration and Management—General	M
Education—General	M
Educational Leadership and Administration	M

BENEDICTINE UNIVERSITY

Accounting	M
Business Administration and Management—General	M,D
Clinical Psychology	M
Computer and Information Systems Security	M
Curriculum and Instruction	M
Education—General	M
Educational Leadership and Administration	M,D
Elementary Education	M
Emergency Management	M
Entrepreneurship	M
Exercise and Sports Science	M
Finance and Banking	M
Health Education	M
Health Informatics	M
Health Promotion	M
Health Services Management and Hospital Administration	M
Higher Education	D
Human Resources Management	M
International Business	M
Logistics	M
Management Information Systems	M
Marketing	M
Nursing—General	M
Nutrition	M
Organizational Behavior	M,D
Organizational Management	M,D
Public Health—General	M
Reading Education	M
Science Education	M
Secondary Education	M
Special Education	M
Women's Studies	M

BENNINGTON COLLEGE

Allied Health—General	O
Dance	M
Music	M
Writing	M

BENTLEY UNIVERSITY

Accounting	M,D
Business Administration and Management—General	M,D,O
Business Analytics	M,O
Ergonomics and Human Factors	M
Finance and Banking	M
Information Science	M
Marketing	M
Taxation	M

BERGIN UNIVERSITY OF CANINE STUDIES

Animal Sciences	M

BERKELEY COLLEGE–WOODLAND PARK CAMPUS

Business Administration and Management—General	M

BERKLEE COLLEGE OF MUSIC

Entertainment Management	M
Music	M,O
Theater	M,O

BERRY COLLEGE

Business Administration and Management—General	M
Curriculum and Instruction	M,O
Early Childhood Education	M
Education—General	M,O
Educational Leadership and Administration	O
Middle School Education	M
Reading Education	M
Secondary Education	M

BETHANY COLLEGE

Education—General	M

BETHANY GLOBAL UNIVERSITY

Pastoral Ministry and Counseling	M

BETHANY THEOLOGICAL SEMINARY

Conflict Resolution and Mediation/Peace Studies	M,O
Pastoral Ministry and Counseling	M,O
Religion	M,O
Theology	M,O

BETHEL COLLEGE

Business Administration and Management—General	M
Education—General	M
Nursing—General	M
Pastoral Ministry and Counseling	M
Theology	M

BETHEL SEMINARY

Classics	M,D,O
Clinical Psychology	M,D,O
Marriage and Family Therapy	M,D,O
Missions and Missiology	M,D,O
Near and Middle Eastern Languages	M,D,O
Pastoral Ministry and Counseling	M,D,O
Religion	M,D,O
Theology	M,D,O

BETHEL UNIVERSITY (MN)

Business Administration and Management—General	M,D,O
Counseling Psychology	M,D,O
Education—General	M,D,O
Educational Leadership and Administration	M,D,O
Elementary Education	M,D,O
Nurse Midwifery	M,D,O
Nursing Education	M,D,O
Organizational Management	M,D,O
Physician Assistant Studies	M,D,O
Secondary Education	M,D,O
Special Education	M,D,O

BETHEL UNIVERSITY (TN)

Business Administration and Management—General	M
Conflict Resolution and Mediation/Peace Studies	M
Educational Leadership and Administration	M
Physician Assistant Studies	M

BETHESDA UNIVERSITY

Music	M
Religion	M
Theology	M

BETH HAMEDRASH SHAAREI YOSHER INSTITUTE

Theology	

BETH HATALMUD RABBINICAL COLLEGE

Theology	

BETHLEHEM COLLEGE & SEMINARY

Theology	M

BETH MEDRASH GOVOHA

Theology	

BETHUNE-COOKMAN UNIVERSITY

Theology	M

BEULAH HEIGHTS UNIVERSITY

Religion	M

BEXLEY SEABURY SEMINARY

Theology	M,D,O

BIBLICAL THEOLOGICAL SEMINARY

Missions and Missiology	M,D,O
Pastoral Ministry and Counseling	M,D,O
Theology	M,D,O

BINGHAMTON UNIVERSITY, STATE UNIVERSITY OF NEW YORK

Accounting	M
Analytical Chemistry	M,D
Anthropology	M,D
Applied Physics	M,D
Art History	M,D
Asian Studies	M,O
Asian-American Studies	M,O
Biological and Biomedical Sciences—General	M,D
Biomedical Engineering	M,D
Biopsychology	D
Business Administration and Management—General	M,D
Chemistry	M,D
Clinical Psychology	D
Cognitive Sciences	D
Community Health Nursing	M,D,O
Comparative Literature	M,D
Computer Science	M,D
Early Childhood Education	M,D
Economics	M,D
Education—General	M,D,O
Educational Leadership and Administration	M,D,O
Electrical Engineering	M,D
Engineering and Applied Sciences—General	M,D
English as a Second Language	M
English Education	M
English	M,D
Environmental Management and Policy	M,D
Family Nurse Practitioner Studies	M,D,O
Finance and Banking	D
Foreign Languages Education	M
Foundations and Philosophy of Education	D
French	M,D
Geography	M
Geology	M,D
Gerontological Nursing	M,D,O
Health Services Management and Hospital Administration	M,D
History	M,D
Industrial/Management Engineering	M,D
Inorganic Chemistry	M,D
Italian	M
Legal and Justice Studies	M,D
Liberal Studies	M
Management Information Systems	D
Marketing	D
Materials Engineering	M,D
Materials Sciences	M,D
Mathematics Education	M
Mathematics	M,D
Mechanical Engineering	M,D
Music	M
Nursing—General	M,D,O
Organizational Management	D
Pharmacy	D
Philosophy	M,D
Physical Chemistry	M,D
Physics	M,D
Political Science	M,D
Psychiatric Nursing	M,D,O
Psychology—General	D
Public Administration	M,D
Public Affairs	D
Reading Education	M
Science Education	M
Secondary Education	M
Social Sciences Education	M
Social Work	M
Sociology	M,D
Spanish	M
Special Education	M
Statistics	M,D
Student Affairs	M
Supply Chain Management	D
Sustainable Development	M,D
Systems Science	M,D
Theater	M
Translation and Interpretation	D,O
Writing	M,D

BIOLA UNIVERSITY

Anthropology	M,D,O
Business Administration and Management—General	M
Clinical Psychology	D
Communication Disorders	M,O
Cultural Studies	M,D,O
Curriculum and Instruction	M,O
Early Childhood Education	M,O
Education—General	M,O
English as a Second Language	M,D,O
Jewish Studies	M,D,O
Linguistics	M,D,O
Missions and Missiology	M,D,O
Pastoral Ministry and Counseling	M,D,O
Psychology—General	D
Religion	M,D,O
Religious Education	M,D,O
Science Education	M,O
Special Education	M,O
Theology	M,D,O

BISHOP'S UNIVERSITY

Education—General	M,O
English as a Second Language	M,O

BLACK HILLS STATE UNIVERSITY

Business Administration and Management—General	M
Curriculum and Instruction	M
Genomic Sciences	M
Management Strategy and Policy	M

BLESSING-RIEMAN COLLEGE OF NURSING & HEALTH SCIENCES

Nursing and Healthcare Administration	M
Nursing Education	M
Nursing—General	M

BLOOMFIELD COLLEGE

Accounting	M

BLOOMSBURG UNIVERSITY OF PENNSYLVANIA

Accounting	M
Adult Nursing	M,D
Athletic Training and Sports Medicine	M
Biological and Biomedical Sciences—General	M
Business Administration and Management—General	M,O
Business Education	M
Communication Disorders	M,D
Community Health	M
Counselor Education	M
Curriculum and Instruction	M,O
Early Childhood Education	M
Education—General	M,O
Educational Leadership and Administration	M
Educational Media/Instructional Technology	M,O
English Education	M
Exercise and Sports Science	M
Family Nurse Practitioner Studies	M,D
Mathematics Education	M
Middle School Education	M
Nurse Anesthesia	M,D
Nursing and Healthcare Administration	M,D
Nursing—General	M,D
Reading Education	M
Science Education	M
Social Sciences Education	M
Special Education	M,O
Student Affairs	M

BLUEFIELD COLLEGE

Education—General	M

BLUE MOUNTAIN COLLEGE

Elementary Education	M
Reading Education	M
Science Education	M
Secondary Education	M

BLUFFTON UNIVERSITY

Accounting	M
Business Administration and Management—General	M
Curriculum and Instruction	M
Education—General	M
Educational Leadership and Administration	M
Finance and Banking	M
Health Services Management and Hospital Administration	M
Industrial and Manufacturing Management	M
Reading Education	M
Special Education	M
Sustainability Management	M

BOB JONES UNIVERSITY

Accounting	M,D,O
Art/Fine Arts	M,D,O
Business Administration and Management—General	M,D,O
Counselor Education	M,D,O
Curriculum and Instruction	M,D,O
Educational Leadership and Administration	M,D,O
Elementary Education	M,D,O
English Education	M,D,O
English	M,D,O
Film, Television, and Video Production	M,D,O
Graphic Design	M,D,O
History	M,D,O
Illustration	M,D,O
Journalism	M,D,O
Mathematics Education	M,D,O
Media Studies	M,D,O
Music Education	M,D,O
Music	M,D,O
Pastoral Ministry and Counseling	M,D,O
Religion	M,D,O
Rhetoric	M,D,O
Secondary Education	M,D,O
Social Sciences Education	M,D,O
Special Education	M,D,O
Speech and Interpersonal Communication	M,D,O
Student Affairs	M,D,O
Theater	M,D,O
Theology	M,D,O

BOISE STATE UNIVERSITY

Accounting	M
Animal Sciences	M,D
Anthropology	M
Art/Fine Arts	M
Biological and Biomedical Sciences—General	M,D
Business Administration and Management—General	M
Chemistry	M
Civil Engineering	M
Communication—General	M
Computer Engineering	M,D
Computer Science	M,D
Counselor Education	M
Criminal Justice and Criminology	M
Curriculum and Instruction	M,D,O
Distance Education Development	M,D,O
Early Childhood Education	M,D,O
Economics	M
Education—General	M,D,O
Educational Leadership and Administration	M,D,O
Educational Media/Instructional Technology	M,D,O
Electrical Engineering	M,D
Engineering and Applied Sciences—General	M,D,O
English as a Second Language	M
English Education	M
Environmental and Occupational Health	M,O
Gerontological Nursing	M,D,O
Health Promotion	M,O
History	M
Interdisciplinary Studies	M
Kinesiology and Movement Studies	M
Materials Engineering	M,D
Mathematics Education	M
Mathematics	M
Mechanical Engineering	M
Molecular Biology	M,D
Multilingual and Multicultural Education	M
Music Education	M
Music	M
Natural Resources	M,D,O
Nursing—General	M,D,O
Organizational Management	M,O
Political Science	M
Public Administration	M,D,O
Public Health—General	M,D,O
Public Policy	M,D,O
Reading Education	M
Rhetoric	M
Social Work	M
Special Education	M
Sports Management	M
Taxation	M
Technical Communication	M

BORICUA COLLEGE

English as a Second Language	M
Human Services	M
Latin American Studies	M

BOSTON ARCHITECTURAL COLLEGE

Architecture	M
Historic Preservation	M
Interior Design	M
Landscape Architecture	M
Sustainable Development	M

BOSTON COLLEGE

Accounting	M
Adult Nursing	M,D
Applied Psychology	M,D
Biochemistry	M,D
Biological and Biomedical Sciences—General	D
Business Administration and Management—General	M
Chemistry	M,D
Classics	M
Counseling Psychology	M,D
Curriculum and Instruction	M,D,O
Developmental Psychology	M,D
Early Childhood Education	M
East European and Russian Studies	M
Economics	D
Education—General	M,D,O
Educational Leadership and Administration	M,D,O
Educational Measurement and Evaluation	M,D
Educational Psychology	M,D
Elementary Education	M
English	M,D
Finance and Banking	M,D
French	M
Geology	M
Geophysics	M
Gerontological Nursing	M,D
Higher Education	M,D
History	M,D
Inorganic Chemistry	M,D
International and Comparative Education	M
Italian	M
Law	D
Linguistics	M
Maternal and Child/Neonatal Nursing	M,D
Mathematics	D
Nurse Anesthesia	M,D
Nursing—General	M,D
Organic Chemistry	M,D
Organizational Behavior	D
Organizational Management	D
Pastoral Ministry and Counseling	M,D,O
Pediatric Nursing	M,D
Philosophy	M,D
Physical Chemistry	M,D
Physics	M,D
Political Science	M,D
Psychiatric Nursing	M,D
Psychology—General	D
Reading Education	M,D
Religious Education	M,D,O
Russian	M
Science Education	M,D
Secondary Education	M
Social Work	M,D
Sociology	M,D
Spanish	M
Special Education	M,O
Theology	M,D,O
Western European Studies	M
Women's Health Nursing	M,D

BOSTON GRADUATE SCHOOL OF PSYCHOANALYSIS

Counseling Psychology	M
Developmental Psychology	O
Psychoanalysis and Psychotherapy	M,D,O
Psychology—General	M

BOSTON UNIVERSITY

Actuarial Science	M
Advertising and Public Relations	M
African-American Studies	M
Allied Health—General	M,D

*M—masters degree; D—doctorate; O—other advanced degree; *—Close-Up and/or Display*

Allopathic Medicine	D
American Studies	D
Anatomy	M,D
Anthropology	M,D
Archaeology	M,D
Art Education	M
Art History	M,D,O
Art/Fine Arts	M
Arts Administration	M,O
Astronomy	M,D
Athletic Training and Sports Medicine	M,D
Biochemistry	M,D
Bioinformatics	M,D
Biological and Biomedical Sciences—General	M,D
Biomedical Engineering	M,D
Biophysics	M,D
Biopsychology	M
Biostatistics	M,D
Business Administration and Management—General	M,D
Business Analytics	M
Cell Biology	M,D
Chemistry	M,D
Classics	M,D
Clinical Research	M
Communication Disorders	M,D
Communication—General	M
Community Health	M,D
Computer and Information Systems Security	M,D,O
Computer Engineering	M,D,O
Computer Science	M,D,O
Corporate and Organizational Communication	M
Counseling Psychology	M
Criminal Justice and Criminology	M
Cultural Studies	M
Data Science/Data Analytics	M,O
Dentistry	M,D,O
Economic Development	M
Economics	M
Education—General	M,D,O
Electrical Engineering	M,D
Emergency Management	M
Energy Management and Policy	M,D
Engineering and Applied Sciences—General	M,D
English	M,D
Environmental and Occupational Health	M,D
Environmental Sciences	M,D
Epidemiology	M,D
Ethics	M,D
Film, Television, and Video Production	M
Finance and Banking	M
Food Science and Technology	M
Forensic Sciences	M
Genetic Counseling	M
Genetics	D
Genomic Sciences	D
Geographic Information Systems	M,D
Geosciences	M,D
Graphic Design	M
Health Communication	M
Health Education	M
Health Informatics	M,O
Health Law	M,O
Health Services Management and Hospital Administration	M,D
Health Services Research	M,D
Hispanic and Latin American Languages	M,D
Historic Preservation	M
History	M,D
Hospitality Management	M
Immunology	D
International Affairs	M*
International Business	M
International Health	M,D
Internet and Interactive Multimedia	M,O
Journalism	M
Latin American Studies	M
Law	M,D
Linguistics	M,D
Management Information Systems	M,O
Management of Technology	M
Management Strategy and Policy	M,O
Manufacturing Engineering	M,D
Mass Communication	M
Materials Engineering	M,D
Materials Sciences	M,D
Mathematical and Computational Finance	M,D
Mathematics	M,D
Mechanical Engineering	M,D
Media Studies	M,D
Medical Imaging	M
Microbiology	D
Missions and Missiology	M,D
Molecular Biology	M,D
Molecular Medicine	D
Museum Studies	M,D,O
Music Education	M,D
Music	M,D,O
Neurobiology	M,D
Neuroscience	D
Nutrition	M,D
Occupational Therapy	D
Oral and Dental Sciences	M,D
Organizational Management	M
Pastoral Ministry and Counseling	M,D
Pathology	M,D
Pharmaceutical Sciences	D
Pharmacology	M,D
Philosophy	M,D
Physical Therapy	M,D
Physician Assistant Studies	M
Physics	D
Physiology	M,D
Political Science	D
Project Management	M,O
Psychology—General	M,D
Public Health—General	M,D
Rehabilitation Sciences	M,D
Religion	M,D
Religious Education	M,D
Risk Management	M
Romance Languages	M,D
Social Work	M,D
Sociology	M,D
Software Engineering	M,O
Supply Chain Management	M
Systems Engineering	M,D
Telecommunications Management	M,O
Telecommunications	M,O
Theater	M,O
Theology	M,D
Translational Biology	D
Travel and Tourism	M
Urban and Regional Planning	M
Urban Studies	M
Writing	M

BOWIE STATE UNIVERSITY

Applied Mathematics	M
Business Administration and Management—General	M
Computer Science	M,D
Corporate and Organizational Communication	M,O
Counseling Psychology	M
Counselor Education	M
Education—General	M
Educational Leadership and Administration	M,D
Elementary Education	M
English	M
Family Nurse Practitioner Studies	M
Human Resources Development	M
Management Information Systems	M,O
Nursing and Healthcare Administration	M
Nursing Education	M
Nursing—General	M
Public Administration	M
Reading Education	M
Secondary Education	M
Special Education	M

BOWLING GREEN STATE UNIVERSITY

Accounting	M
American Studies	M,D
Applied Arts and Design—General	M
Applied Statistics	M
Art Education	M
Art History	M
Art/Fine Arts	M
Biological and Biomedical Sciences—General	M,D
Business Administration and Management—General	M
Business Education	M
Chemistry	M,D
Clinical Psychology	M,D
Communication Disorders	M,D
Communication—General	M,D
Computer Art and Design	M
Computer Science	M
Counselor Education	M
Criminal Justice and Criminology	M
Curriculum and Instruction	M
Demography and Population Studies	M,D
Developmental Psychology	M,D
Economics	M
Educational Leadership and Administration	M,D,O
Educational Media/Instructional Technology	M
English	M,D
Experimental Psychology	M,D
Film, Television, and Video Production	M,D
French	M
Geology	M
Geophysics	M
German	M
Graphic Design	M
Higher Education	D
History	M,D
Industrial and Organizational Psychology	M,D
Interdisciplinary Studies	M,D
International and Comparative Education	M
Kinesiology and Movement Studies	M
Leisure Studies	M
Mathematics Education	M,D
Mathematics	M,D
Media Studies	M,D
Music Education	M,D
Music	M,D
Operations Research	M
Organizational Management	M
Philosophy	M,D
Physics	M
Psychology—General	M,D
Public Administration	M
Public Health—General	M
Reading Education	M,O
Recreation and Park Management	M
Rhetoric	M,D
Science Education	M
Social Psychology	M,D
Sociology	M,D
Software Engineering	M
Spanish	M
Special Education	M
Sports Management	M
Statistics	M,D
Student Affairs	M
Technical Communication	M,D
Theater	M,D
Vocational and Technical Education	M
Writing	M,D

BRADLEY UNIVERSITY

Accounting	M
Art/Fine Arts	M
Biochemistry	M
Biological and Biomedical Sciences—General	M
Business Administration and Management—General	M
Chemistry	M
Civil Engineering	M
Clinical Psychology	M
Computer Science	M
Construction Engineering	M
Counseling Psychology	M
Counselor Education	M
Curriculum and Instruction	M
Education—General	M,D,O
Educational Leadership and Administration	M
Electrical Engineering	M
Engineering and Applied Sciences—General	M
English	M
Family Nurse Practitioner Studies	M,D,O
Graphic Design	M
Health Services Management and Hospital Administration	M,D,O
Human Development	M
Industrial/Management Engineering	M
Information Science	M
Manufacturing Engineering	M
Mechanical Engineering	M
Nonprofit Management	M
Nursing and Healthcare Administration	M,D,O
Nursing Education	M,D,O
Nursing—General	M,D,O
Nutrition	M
Photography	M
Physical Therapy	D

BRANDEIS UNIVERSITY

Anthropology	M,D
Applied Economics	M
Art/Fine Arts	O
Artificial Intelligence/Robotics	M
Biochemistry	M,D
Bioinformatics	M
Biological and Biomedical Sciences—General	M,D,O
Biophysics	M,D
Biotechnology	M
Business Administration and Management—General	M
Cell Biology	M,D
Chemistry	M,D
Child and Family Studies	M,D
Chinese	M
Classics	M
Cognitive Sciences	M,D
Computer and Information Systems Security	M
Computer Science	M,D
Conflict Resolution and Mediation/Peace Studies	M,D
Cultural Anthropology	M,D
Developmental Psychology	M,D
Disability Studies	D
Distance Education Development	M
Economics	M,D
Educational Leadership and Administration	M,O
Educational Measurement and Evaluation	O
Elementary Education	M,O
English	M,D
Entrepreneurship	M
Finance and Banking	M,D
Foreign Languages Education	M
Gender Studies	M,D
Genetic Counseling	M
Genetics	M,D
Health Education	D
Health Informatics	M
Health Services Management and Hospital Administration	M
History	M,D
Human Services	M
Human-Computer Interaction	M
Humanities	M
Inorganic Chemistry	M,D
International Affairs	M
International Business	M,D
International Health	M,D
Internet and Interactive Multimedia	M
Jewish Studies	M,D
Linguistics	M
Management Information Systems	M
Management Strategy and Policy	M
Marketing	M
Mathematics	M,D
Medical Informatics	M
Microbiology	M,D
Molecular Biology	M,D
Music	M,D
Near and Middle Eastern Languages	M,D
Near and Middle Eastern Studies	M,D
Neurobiology	M,D
Neuroscience	M,D
Nonprofit Management	M
Organic Chemistry	M,D
Philosophy	M
Physical Chemistry	M,D
Physics	M,D
Political Science	M,D
Project Management	M
Psychology—General	M,D
Public Policy	M
Real Estate	M
Religious Education	M,O
Risk Management	M
Secondary Education	M,O
Social Psychology	M,D
Sociology	M,D
Software Engineering	M
Sustainable Development	M
Theater	M
Women's Studies	M,D

BRANDMAN UNIVERSITY

Accounting	M
Business Administration and Management—General	M
Counseling Psychology	M
Counselor Education	M,D
Curriculum and Instruction	M,D
Data Science/Data Analytics	M
Early Childhood Education	M,D
Education—General	M,D
Educational Leadership and Administration	M,D
Educational Media/Instructional Technology	M,D
Elementary Education	M,D
Entrepreneurship	M
Finance and Banking	M
Health Services Management and Hospital Administration	M
Human Resources Management	M
International Business	M
Marketing	M
Marriage and Family Therapy	M
Nursing—General	D
Organizational Management	M
Psychology—General	M
Public Administration	M
Secondary Education	M,D
Social Work	M
Special Education	M,D

BRANDON UNIVERSITY

Counselor Education	M,O
Curriculum and Instruction	M,O
Education—General	M,O
Educational Leadership and Administration	M,O
Music Education	M
Music	M
Rural Planning and Studies	M,O
Special Education	M,O

BRENAU UNIVERSITY

Accounting	M
Business Administration and Management—General	M
Early Childhood Education	M,O
Education—General	M,O
Family Nurse Practitioner Studies	M
Health Services Management and Hospital Administration	M
Interior Design	M
Middle School Education	M,O
Nursing and Healthcare Administration	M
Nursing Education	M
Occupational Therapy	M
Organizational Management	M
Project Management	M
Psychology—General	M
Secondary Education	M,O
Special Education	M,O

BRESCIA UNIVERSITY

Business Administration and Management—General	M
Curriculum and Instruction	M
Social Work	M

BRIAR CLIFF UNIVERSITY

Nursing—General	M,D,O

BRIDGEWATER COLLEGE

Athletic Training and Sports Medicine	M

BRIDGEWATER STATE UNIVERSITY

Accounting	M
Art Education	M
Business Administration and Management—General	M
Communication Disorders	M
Computer Science	M
Counselor Education	M,O
Criminal Justice and Criminology	M
Early Childhood Education	M
Education—General	M,O
Educational Leadership and Administration	M,O
Educational Media/Instructional Technology	M
Elementary Education	M
English	M
Finance and Banking	M
Health Promotion	M
Mathematics Education	M
Physical Education	M
Psychology—General	M
Public Administration	M
Reading Education	M,O
Science Education	M
Secondary Education	M
Social Sciences Education	M
Social Work	M
Special Education	M

BRIERCREST SEMINARY

Business Administration and Management—General	M
Marriage and Family Therapy	M
Missions and Missiology	M
Organizational Management	M
Pastoral Ministry and Counseling	M
Religion	M
Theology	M

BRIGHAM YOUNG UNIVERSITY
Agricultural Sciences—General M,D
Analytical Chemistry M,D
Animal Sciences M,D
Anthropology M
Applied Statistics M
Art Education M
Art/Fine Arts M
Astronomy M,D
Athletic Training and Sports Medicine M,D
Biochemistry M,D
Biological and Biomedical Sciences—General M,D
Biotechnology M,D
Business Administration and Management—General M
Chemical Engineering M,D
Chemistry M,D
Child and Family Studies M,D
Civil Engineering M,D
Classics M
Clinical Psychology D
Cognitive Sciences D
Communication Disorders M
Communication—General M
Comparative and Interdisciplinary Arts M
Comparative Literature M
Computer Engineering M,D
Computer Science M,D
Construction Management M
Counseling Psychology M,D,O
Developmental Biology M,D
Education—General M,D,O
Educational Leadership and Administration M,D
Educational Measurement and Evaluation D
Educational Media/Instructional Technology M,D
Educational Policy M,D
Educational Psychology M,D
Electrical Engineering M,D
Engineering and Applied Sciences—General M,D
English as a Second Language M
English M
Entrepreneurship M
Environmental Sciences M,D
Exercise and Sports Science M,D
Family Nurse Practitioner Studies M
Film, Television, and Video Production M
Finance and Banking M
Fish, Game, and Wildlife Management M,D
Food Science and Technology M
Foreign Languages Education M
Foundations and Philosophy of Education M,D
French M
Geology M
Health Promotion M,D
Health Services Management and Hospital Administration M
Hispanic and Latin American Languages M
Human Development M,D
Human Resources Management M
Humanities M
Information Science M
International Affairs M
Law M,D
Linguistics M
Manufacturing Engineering M
Marketing M
Marriage and Family Therapy M,D
Mass Communication M
Mathematics Education M
Mathematics M,D
Mechanical Engineering M,D
Microbiology M,D
Molecular Biology M,D
Music Education M
Music M
Neuroscience M,D
Nonprofit Management M
Nursing—General M
Nutrition M
Physics M,D
Physiology M,D
Plant Sciences M,D
Political Science M
Portuguese M
Psychology—General D
Public Administration M
Public Health—General M
Religious Education M
Rhetoric M
School Psychology M,D,O
Science Education M,D
Social Work M
Sociology M,D
Spanish M
Special Education M,D,O
Statistics M
Supply Chain Management M
Theater M
Writing M

BRITE DIVINITY SCHOOL
Pastoral Ministry and Counseling M,D,O
Theology M,D,O

BROADVIEW UNIVERSITY–WEST JORDAN
Business Administration and Management—General M
Health Services Management and Hospital Administration M
Management Information Systems M

BROCK UNIVERSITY
Accounting M
Allied Health—General M,D
Biological and Biomedical Sciences—General M,D
Biotechnology M,D
Business Administration and Management—General M
Chemistry M,D
Child and Family Studies M
Classics M
Comparative Literature M
Computer Science M
Cultural Studies M
Disability Studies M,O
Economics M
Education—General M,D
English as a Second Language M
English M
Geography M
Geosciences M
History M
Human Development M,D
International Affairs M
Legal and Justice Studies M
Mathematics M
Neuroscience M,D
Philosophy M
Physics M
Political Science M
Psychology—General M,D
Public Policy M
Social Psychology M,D
Sociology M
Statistics M

BROOKLINE COLLEGE
Nursing and Healthcare Administration M
Nursing—General M

BROOKLYN COLLEGE OF THE CITY UNIVERSITY OF NEW YORK
Accounting M
Art Education M
Art History M
Art/Fine Arts M
Arts Administration M
Biological and Biomedical Sciences—General M
Business Administration and Management—General M
Chemistry M,D
Communication Disorders M,D
Community Health M
Computer Science M,O
Counseling Psychology M,D,O
Counselor Education M
Early Childhood Education M,O
Economics M
Education—General M,O
Educational Leadership and Administration M
Elementary Education M,O
English Education M
English M
Environmental Education M
Exercise and Sports Science M
Experimental Psychology M,D
Film, Television, and Video Production M
Film, Television, and Video Theory and Criticism M
Finance and Banking M
Foreign Languages Education M
French M
Geology M,D
Geosciences M
Health Informatics M,O
Health Services Management and Hospital Administration M
History M
Industrial and Organizational Psychology M,D
Information Science M,O
International Affairs M
International Business M
Internet and Interactive Multimedia M
Jewish Studies M
Kinesiology and Movement Studies M
Liberal Studies M
Mathematics Education M
Mathematics M
Media Studies M
Middle School Education M,O
Multilingual and Multicultural Education M
Music Education M
Music M
Nutrition M
Organizational Behavior M,D
Photography M
Physical Education M
Physics M
Political Science M
Psychology—General M,D
Public Health—General M
Public Policy M
School Psychology M,O
Science Education M
Secondary Education M
Social Psychology M,D
Social Sciences Education M
Sociology M,D
Spanish M
Special Education M,O
Speech and Interpersonal Communication M,D
Sports Management M
Thanatology M
Theater M
Urban Studies M
Writing M

BROOKLYN LAW SCHOOL
Law M,D

BROWN UNIVERSITY
Allopathic Medicine D
American Studies M,D
Anthropology M,D
Applied Mathematics M,D
Archaeology D
Art History D
Asian Studies D
Biochemical Engineering M,D
Biochemistry M,D
Biological and Biomedical Sciences—General M,D
Biomedical Engineering M,D
Biostatistics M,D
Biotechnology M,D
Cell Biology M,D
Chemical Engineering M,D
Chemistry D
Classics M,D
Cognitive Sciences M,D
Community Health M,D
Comparative Literature D
Computer Engineering M,D
Computer Science M,D
East European and Russian Studies M,D
Ecology D
Economics D
Education—General M
Electrical Engineering M,D
Elementary Education M
Engineering and Applied Sciences—General M,D
English as a Second Language M,D
English Education M
English M,D
Epidemiology M,D
Evolutionary Biology D
French D
Geosciences D
German D
Health Services Research D
Hispanic Studies D
History of Science and Technology D
History M,D
Italian D
Latin American Studies M,D
Linguistics M,D
Materials Sciences M,D
Mathematics D
Mechanical Engineering M,D
Mechanics M,D
Molecular Biology M,D
Molecular Pharmacology M,D
Multilingual and Multicultural Education M,D
Music D
Near and Middle Eastern Studies D
Neuroscience D
Pathobiology M,D
Philosophy D
Physics M,D
Physiology M,D
Political Science D
Psychology—General M,D
Public Health—General M
Public Policy M
Publishing M,D
Religion D
Russian M,D
Science Education M
Secondary Education M
Slavic Languages M,D
Social Sciences Education M
Sociology M,D
Theater M,D
Urban Education M
Western European Studies M,D
Writing M,D

BRYAN COLLEGE
Business Administration and Management—General M
Health Services Management and Hospital Administration M
Human Resources Management M
Marketing M
Pastoral Ministry and Counseling M
Sports Management M

BRYAN COLLEGE OF HEALTH SCIENCES
Nurse Anesthesia M

BRYANT UNIVERSITY
Accounting M
Applied Economics M,O
Business Administration and Management—General M
Business Analytics M
Communication—General M,O
Corporate and Organizational Communication M,O
Finance and Banking M
International Business M
International Economics M
Mass Communication M,O
Physician Assistant Studies M
Supply Chain Management M
Taxation M

BRYAN UNIVERSITY
Business Administration and Management—General M

BRYN ATHYN COLLEGE OF THE NEW CHURCH
Religion M
Theology M

BRYN MAWR COLLEGE
Archaeology M,D
Art History M,D
Chemistry M,D
Classics M,D
Mathematics M,D
Physics M,D
Social Work M,D

BUCKNELL UNIVERSITY
Animal Behavior M
Biological and Biomedical Sciences—General M
Chemical Engineering M
Chemistry M
Civil Engineering M
Computer Engineering M
Education—General M
Electrical Engineering M
Engineering and Applied Sciences—General M
English M
Mathematics M
Mechanical Engineering M
Psychology—General M
Student Affairs M

BUENA VISTA UNIVERSITY
Counselor Education M
Curriculum and Instruction M
Education—General M
English as a Second Language M

BUFFALO STATE COLLEGE, STATE UNIVERSITY OF NEW YORK
Adult Education M,O
Applied Economics M
Art Education M
Biological and Biomedical Sciences—General M
Business Education M
Chemistry M
Communication Disorders M
Criminal Justice and Criminology M
Early Childhood Education M
Economics M
Educational Leadership and Administration O
Educational Media/Instructional Technology M
Elementary Education M
English Education M
English M
Historic Preservation M,O
History M
Human Resources Management M,O
Industrial/Management Engineering M
Interdisciplinary Studies M
Mathematics Education M
Multilingual and Multicultural Education M
Reading Education M
Science Education M
Social Sciences Education M
Special Education M
Student Affairs M
Vocational and Technical Education M

BUTLER UNIVERSITY
Accounting M
Art/Fine Arts M
Business Administration and Management—General M
Clinical Psychology M,O
Counselor Education M,O
Education—General M,O
Educational Leadership and Administration M,O
English M
Entrepreneurship M
Finance and Banking M
History M
International Business M
Marketing M
Music Education M
Music M
Pharmaceutical Sciences M,D
Pharmacy M,D
Physician Assistant Studies M,D
Sports Management M,O
Writing M

BYZANTINE CATHOLIC SEMINARY OF SAINTS CYRIL AND METHODIUS
Theology M

CABARRUS COLLEGE OF HEALTH SCIENCES
Occupational Therapy M

CABRINI UNIVERSITY
Accounting M,D
Biological and Biomedical Sciences—General M,D
Chemistry M,D
Communication—General M,D
Criminal Justice and Criminology M,D
Curriculum and Instruction M,D
Early Childhood Education M,D
Educational Leadership and Administration M,D
Elementary Education M,D
English as a Second Language M,D

*M—masters degree; D—doctorate; O—other advanced degree; *—Close-Up and/or Display*

English M,D
History M,D
Mathematics M,D
Middle School Education M,D
Organizational Management M,D
Reading Education M,D
Secondary Education M,D
Special Education M,D

CAIRN UNIVERSITY
Accounting M,O
Applied Behavior Analysis M,O
Business Administration and Management—General M,O
Education—General M,O
Educational Leadership and Administration M,O
Entrepreneurship M,O
Nonprofit Management M,O
Organizational Management M,O
Pastoral Ministry and Counseling M
Religion M
Theology M

CALDWELL UNIVERSITY
Accounting M
Applied Behavior Analysis M,D,O
Art Therapy M,O
Business Administration and Management—General M
Counseling Psychology M,O
Counselor Education M,O
Curriculum and Instruction M,D,O
Education—General M,D,O
Educational Leadership and Administration M,D,O
Reading Education M,D,O
School Psychology M,O
Special Education M,D,O

CALIFORNIA BAPTIST UNIVERSITY
Accounting M
Adult Education M
Adult Nursing M
Advertising and Public Relations M
Applied Mathematics M
Architecture M
Athletic Training and Sports Medicine M
Business Administration and Management—General M
Civil Engineering M
Communication Disorders M
Communication—General M
Construction Management M
Counseling Psychology M
Counselor Education M
Curriculum and Instruction M
Disability Studies M
Distance Education Development M
Education—General M
Educational Leadership and Administration M
Educational Media/Instructional Technology M
English as a Second Language M
English Education M
English M
Exercise and Sports Science M
Family Nurse Practitioner Studies M
Forensic Psychology M
Health Education M
Health Promotion M
Health Services Management and Hospital Administration M
Higher Education M
International and Comparative Education M
Mechanical Engineering M
Music Education M
Music M
Nonprofit Management M
Nursing and Healthcare Administration M
Nursing Education M
Nursing—General M,D
Organizational Management M
Pastoral Ministry and Counseling M
Physical Education M
Physician Assistant Studies M
Public Administration M
Public Health—General M
Reading Education M
School Psychology M
Science Education M
Social Work M
Software Engineering M
Special Education M
Sports Management M
Vocational and Technical Education M

CALIFORNIA COAST UNIVERSITY
Business Administration and Management—General M
Criminal Justice and Criminology M
Curriculum and Instruction M,D
Education—General M,D
Educational Leadership and Administration M,D
Educational Psychology M,D
Health Services Management and Hospital Administration M
Human Resources Management M
Marketing M
Organizational Management M,D
Psychology—General M

CALIFORNIA COLLEGE OF THE ARTS
Applied Arts and Design—General M
Architecture M
Art/Fine Arts M
Computer Art and Design M
Film, Television, and Video Production M
Film, Television, and Video Theory and Criticism M
Finance and Banking M
Graphic Design M
Illustration M
Industrial Design M
Museum Studies M
Organizational Management M
Writing M

CALIFORNIA HEALTH SCIENCES UNIVERSITY
Pharmacy D

CALIFORNIA INSTITUTE OF ADVANCED MANAGEMENT
Business Administration and Management—General M
Entrepreneurship M

CALIFORNIA INSTITUTE OF INTEGRAL STUDIES
Acupuncture and Oriental Medicine M,D
Art Therapy M,D
Asian Studies M,D,O
Clinical Psychology M,D
Counseling Psychology M,D
Cultural Anthropology M,D,O
Ecology M,D,O
Health Psychology M,D
Humanities M,D,O
Interdisciplinary Studies M,D,O
Philosophy M,D,O
Psychology—General M,D,O
Religion M,D,O
Social Psychology M,D
Therapies—Dance, Drama, and Music M,D
Transpersonal and Humanistic Psychology M,D,O
Women's Studies M,D,O
Writing M,D,O

CALIFORNIA INSTITUTE OF TECHNOLOGY
Aerospace/Aeronautical Engineering M,D,O
Applied Mathematics M,D
Applied Physics M,D
Astronomy D
Biochemistry M,D
Bioengineering M,D
Biological and Biomedical Sciences—General D
Biophysics D
Cell Biology D
Chemical Engineering M,D
Chemistry M,D
Civil Engineering M,D,O
Computational Sciences M,D
Computer Science M,D
Developmental Biology D
Electrical Engineering M,D,O
Engineering and Applied Sciences—General M,D,O
Environmental Engineering M,D
Environmental Sciences M,D
Genetics D
Geochemistry M,D
Geology M,D
Geophysics M,D
Immunology D
Materials Sciences M,D
Mathematics D
Mechanical Engineering M,D,O
Mechanics M,D
Molecular Biology D
Molecular Biophysics M,D
Neurobiology D
Neuroscience M,D
Physics D
Planetary and Space Sciences M,D
Social Sciences M,D
Systems Engineering M,D

CALIFORNIA INSTITUTE OF THE ARTS
Applied Arts and Design—General M,O
Art/Fine Arts M,O
Dance M,O
Film, Television, and Video Production M,O
Graphic Design M,O
Music M,O
Photography M,O
Theater M,O
Writing M,O

CALIFORNIA INTERCONTINENTAL UNIVERSITY
Business Administration and Management—General M,D
Entertainment Management M
Entrepreneurship M,D
Finance and Banking M,D
Health Services Management and Hospital Administration M,D
Human Resources Management M,D
International Business M,D
Management Information Systems M,D
Marketing M,D
Organizational Management M,D
Project Management M,D
Quality Management M,D

CALIFORNIA INTERNATIONAL BUSINESS UNIVERSITY
Business Administration and Management—General M,D

CALIFORNIA LUTHERAN UNIVERSITY
Business Administration and Management—General M,O
Clinical Psychology M,D
Counselor Education M,D
Education—General M,D
Educational Leadership and Administration M,D
Elementary Education M,D
Entrepreneurship M,O
Finance and Banking M,O
Higher Education M,D
International Business M,O
Management Information Systems M,O
Management of Technology M,O
Marketing M,O
Marriage and Family Therapy M,D
Middle School Education M,D
Psychology—General M,D
Public Policy M,O
Special Education M,D
Theology M,D,O

CALIFORNIA MIRAMAR UNIVERSITY
Business Administration and Management—General M
Management Strategy and Policy M
Taxation M
Telecommunications Management M
Telecommunications M

CALIFORNIA NORTHSTATE UNIVERSITY
Allopathic Medicine D
Pharmacy D

CALIFORNIA POLYTECHNIC STATE UNIVERSITY, SAN LUIS OBISPO
Accounting M
Aerospace/Aeronautical Engineering M
Agricultural Education M
Agricultural Sciences—General M
Architectural Engineering M
Architecture M
Biochemistry M
Biological and Biomedical Sciences—General M*
Biomedical Engineering M
Business Administration and Management—General M
Business Analytics M
Chemistry M
Civil Engineering M
Computer Science M
Economics M
Education—General M
Electrical Engineering M
Engineering and Applied Sciences—General M
English M
Environmental Engineering M
Food Science and Technology M
Forestry M
History M
Industrial/Management Engineering M
Mathematics M
Mechanical Engineering M
Natural Resources M
Nutrition M*
Political Science M
Polymer Science and Engineering M
Psychology—General M
Supply Chain Management M
Taxation M
Urban and Regional Planning M*

CALIFORNIA STATE POLYTECHNIC UNIVERSITY, POMONA
Accounting M
Aerospace/Aeronautical Engineering M
Agricultural Sciences—General M
Applied Mathematics M
Architecture M
Biological and Biomedical Sciences—General M
Business Administration and Management—General M
Chemistry M
Civil Engineering M
Computer Science M
Curriculum and Instruction M
Economics M
Educational Leadership and Administration D
Electrical Engineering M
Engineering Management M
English M
Environmental Sciences M
Geology M
History M
Hospitality Management M
Interior Design M
Kinesiology and Movement Studies M
Landscape Architecture M
Management Information Systems M
Mathematics M
Mechanical Engineering M
Psychology—General M
Public Administration M
Reading Education M
Systems Engineering M
Urban and Regional Planning M

CALIFORNIA STATE UNIVERSITY, BAKERSFIELD
Anthropology M
Biological and Biomedical Sciences—General M
Business Administration and Management—General M
Counseling Psychology M
Counselor Education M
Education—General M,D
Educational Leadership and Administration M,D
English M
Family Nurse Practitioner Studies M
Geology M
Health Services Management and Hospital Administration M
History M
Hydrology M
Interdisciplinary Studies M
Mathematics Education M
Middle School Education M
Nursing—General M
Public Administration M
Science Education M
Secondary Education M
Social Work M
Sociology M
Spanish M
Special Education M
Student Affairs M

CALIFORNIA STATE UNIVERSITY CHANNEL ISLANDS
Bioinformatics M
Biotechnology M
Business Administration and Management—General M
Computer Science M
Mathematics M

CALIFORNIA STATE UNIVERSITY, CHICO
Agricultural Education M
Agricultural Sciences—General M
Anthropology M
Applied Psychology M
Art History M
Art/Fine Arts M
Biological and Biomedical Sciences—General M
Business Administration and Management—General M
Communication Disorders M
Communication—General M
Computer Engineering M
Computer Science M
Construction Management M
Curriculum and Instruction M
Electrical Engineering M
Engineering and Applied Sciences—General M
English M
Environmental Sciences M
Geology M
Geosciences M
Health Services Management and Hospital Administration M
History M
Kinesiology and Movement Studies M
Marriage and Family Therapy M
Mathematics Education M
Museum Studies M
Nursing—General M
Nutrition M
Political Science M
Psychology—General M
Public Administration M
Recreation and Park Management M
School Psychology M
Social Sciences M
Social Work M
Special Education M
Travel and Tourism M

CALIFORNIA STATE UNIVERSITY, DOMINGUEZ HILLS
Applied Social Research M
Bioinformatics M
Biological and Biomedical Sciences—General M
Business Administration and Management—General M
Clinical Psychology M
Computer Science M
Conflict Resolution and Mediation/Peace Studies M
Counselor Education M
Early Childhood Education M
Education—General M
English as a Second Language M,O
English M,O
Health Psychology M
Humanities M
International and Comparative Education M
Marriage and Family Therapy M
Nursing—General M
Occupational Therapy M
Psychology—General M
Public Administration M
Quality Management M
Rhetoric M,O
School Psychology M
Social Work M
Sociology M
Special Education M

CALIFORNIA STATE UNIVERSITY, EAST BAY
Accounting M
Actuarial Science M
Anthropology M
Applied Statistics M
Biochemistry M
Biological and Biomedical Sciences—General M
Biostatistics M
Business Administration and Management—General M
Chemistry M
Child and Family Studies M
Communication Disorders M
Communication—General M

Computer Science	M
Construction Management	M
Counselor Education	M
Early Childhood Education	M
Economics	M
Education—General	M
Educational Leadership and Administration	M,D
Educational Media/Instructional Technology	M
Engineering and Applied Sciences—General	M
Engineering Management	M
English as a Second Language	M
English	M
Environmental Sciences	M
Finance and Banking	M
Geography	M
Geology	M
Health Services Management and Hospital Administration	M
History	M
Human Resources Management	M
Industrial and Manufacturing Management	M
Interdisciplinary Studies	M
Internet and Interactive Multimedia	M
Management Strategy and Policy	M
Marine Sciences	M
Marketing	M
Marriage and Family Therapy	M
Mathematics Education	M
Mathematics	M
Music	M
Organizational Behavior	M
Physical Education	M
Public Administration	M
Public History	M
Public Policy	M
Reading Education	M
Recreation and Park Management	M
Social Psychology	M
Social Sciences Education	M
Social Work	M
Special Education	M
Statistics	M
Supply Chain Management	M
Travel and Tourism	M

CALIFORNIA STATE UNIVERSITY, FRESNO

Animal Sciences	M
Applied Arts and Design—General	M
Applied Behavior Analysis	M,O
Art/Fine Arts	M
Biological and Biomedical Sciences—General	M
Business Administration and Management—General	M
Chemistry	M
Civil Engineering	M
Communication Disorders	M
Communication—General	M
Computer Engineering	M
Computer Science	M
Counseling Psychology	M
Counselor Education	M
Criminal Justice and Criminology	M
Curriculum and Instruction	M
Early Childhood Education	M
Education—General	M,D
Educational Leadership and Administration	M,D
Electrical Engineering	M
Engineering and Applied Sciences—General	M
English as a Second Language	M
English	M
Exercise and Sports Science	M
Experimental Psychology	M,O
Geology	M
Health Promotion	M
Health Services Management and Hospital Administration	M
History	M
Human Development	M,D
Industrial/Management Engineering	M
Kinesiology and Movement Studies	M
Linguistics	M
Marine Sciences	M
Marriage and Family Therapy	M
Mathematics Education	M
Mathematics	M
Mechanical Engineering	M
Music Education	M
Music	M
Nursing—General	M,D
Physical Therapy	D
Physics	M
Plant Sciences	M
Psychology—General	M,O
Public Administration	M
Public Health—General	M
Reading Education	M
Rehabilitation Counseling	M
Rhetoric	M
School Psychology	M,O
Social Sciences Education	M
Social Work	M
Spanish	M
Special Education	M
Sport Psychology	M
Sports Management	M
Student Affairs	M
Viticulture and Enology	M
Writing	M

CALIFORNIA STATE UNIVERSITY, FULLERTON

Accounting	M
American Studies	M
Anthropology	M
Applied Arts and Design—General	M
Applied Mathematics	M
Architectural Engineering	M
Art History	M
Art/Fine Arts	M
Biological and Biomedical Sciences—General	M
Biotechnology	M
Business Administration and Management—General	M
Business Analytics	M
Chemistry	M
Civil Engineering	M
Clinical Psychology	M
Communication Disorders	M
Communication—General	M
Computer Engineering	M
Computer Science	M
Counselor Education	M
Economics	M
Educational Leadership and Administration	M,D
Educational Media/Instructional Technology	M
Electrical Engineering	M
Electronic Commerce	M
Elementary Education	M
Engineering and Applied Sciences—General	M
English	M
Environmental and Occupational Health	M
Environmental Engineering	M
Environmental Management and Policy	M
Film, Television, and Video Production	M
Finance and Banking	M
Geography	M
Geology	M
Gerontology	M
Graphic Design	M
Health Promotion	M
History	M
Illustration	M
Information Science	M
Insurance	M
International Business	M
Linguistics	M
Management Information Systems	M
Mass Communication	M
Mathematics Education	M
Mathematics	M
Mechanical Engineering	M
Multilingual and Multicultural Education	M
Museum Studies	M
Music Education	M
Music	M
Nurse Anesthesia	M,D
Nursing and Healthcare Administration	M,D
Nursing Education	M,D
Nursing—General	M,D
Organizational Management	M
Photography	M
Physical Education	M
Physics	M
Political Science	M
Psychology—General	M
Public Administration	M
Public Health—General	M
Reading Education	M
Risk Management	M
School Nursing	M,D
Secondary Education	M
Social Psychology	M
Social Work	M
Sociology	M
Software Engineering	M
Spanish	M
Special Education	M
Speech and Interpersonal Communication	M
Systems Engineering	M
Taxation	M
Theater	M
Travel and Tourism	M
Women's Health Nursing	M,D

CALIFORNIA STATE UNIVERSITY, LONG BEACH

African Studies	M
Anthropology	M
Applied Mathematics	M,D
Applied Statistics	M
Art Education	M
Art/Fine Arts	M
Asian Studies	M
Asian-American Studies	M
Athletic Training and Sports Medicine	M
Biochemistry	M
Biological and Biomedical Sciences—General	M
Business Administration and Management—General	M
Chemistry	M
Civil Engineering	M
Communication Disorders	M
Communication—General	M
Computer Engineering	M
Computer Science	M
Counselor Education	M,D
Criminal Justice and Criminology	M
Dance	M
Economics	M
Education—General	M,D
Educational Leadership and Administration	M,D
Educational Psychology	M,D
Electrical Engineering	M
Elementary Education	M
Emergency Management	M
Engineering Management	M,D
English as a Second Language	M,O
English	M
Ergonomics and Human Factors	M
Exercise and Sports Science	M
French	M
Geography	M
Geology	M
German	M
Gerontology	M
Health Education	M
Health Services Management and Hospital Administration	M
Higher Education	M,D
History	M
Industrial and Organizational Psychology	M
Kinesiology and Movement Studies	M
Leisure Studies	M
Linguistics	M,O
Marriage and Family Therapy	M,D
Mathematics Education	M
Mathematics	M
Mechanical Engineering	M,D
Microbiology	M
Music	M
Near and Middle Eastern Studies	M
Nursing—General	M,D,O
Nutrition	M
Philosophy	M
Physical Education	M
Physical Therapy	D
Physics	M
Political Science	M
Psychology—General	M
Public Administration	M,O
Public Health—General	M
Public Policy	M,O
Recreation and Park Management	M
Religion	M
Science Education	M
Secondary Education	M
Social Work	M
Spanish	M
Special Education	M,D
Sport Psychology	M
Sports Management	M
Student Affairs	M,D
Theater	M
Writing	M

CALIFORNIA STATE UNIVERSITY, LOS ANGELES

Accounting	M
Analytical Chemistry	M
Anthropology	M
Applied Arts and Design—General	M
Applied Mathematics	M
Art Education	M
Art History	M
Art Therapy	M
Art/Fine Arts	M
Biochemistry	M
Biological and Biomedical Sciences—General	M
Business Administration and Management—General	M,O
Chemistry	M
Child and Family Studies	M
Child Development	M
Civil Engineering	M
Communication Disorders	M
Communication—General	M
Computer Science	M
Counselor Education	M,D
Criminal Justice and Criminology	M
Curriculum and Instruction	M
Economics	M
Education—General	M,D,O
Electrical Engineering	M
Elementary Education	M
Engineering and Applied Sciences—General	M
English	M,O
Finance and Banking	M
French	M
Geography	M
Geology	M
Graphic Design	M
Health Services Management and Hospital Administration	M,O
Hispanic Studies	M
History	M
International Business	M
Kinesiology and Movement Studies	M,O
Latin American Studies	M
Management Information Systems	M
Management of Technology	M
Marketing	M
Mathematics	M
Mechanical Engineering	M
Music Education	M
Music	M
Nursing—General	M,O
Nutrition	M,O
Philosophy	M,O
Photography	M
Physical Education	M,O
Physics	M
Political Science	M
Psychology—General	M
Public Administration	M
Rehabilitation Counseling	M,D
School Psychology	M,D
Social Work	M
Sociology	M
Spanish	M
Special Education	M,D
Textile Design	M
Theater	M

CALIFORNIA STATE UNIVERSITY MARITIME ACADEMY

Emergency Management	M
Engineering Management	M
Transportation Management	M

CALIFORNIA STATE UNIVERSITY, MONTEREY BAY

Business Administration and Management—General	M
Education—General	M
Management Information Systems	M
Marine Sciences	M
Social Work	M
Water Resources	M

CALIFORNIA STATE UNIVERSITY, NORTHRIDGE

Anthropology	M
Applied Mathematics	M
Archaeology	M
Art Education	M
Art History	M
Art/Fine Arts	M
Artificial Intelligence/Robotics	M
Biochemistry	M
Biological and Biomedical Sciences—General	M
Business Administration and Management—General	M
Chemistry	M
Civil Engineering	M
Clinical Psychology	M
Communication Disorders	M
Communication—General	M
Comparative Literature	M
Computer Science	M
Construction Management	M
Counselor Education	M
Curriculum and Instruction	M
Early Childhood Education	M
Education—General	M,D
Educational Leadership and Administration	M,D
Educational Media/Instructional Technology	M
Educational Psychology	M
Electrical Engineering	M
Elementary Education	M
Engineering and Applied Sciences—General	M
Engineering Management	M
English Education	M
English	M
Entertainment Management	M,O
Environmental and Occupational Health	M
Environmental Sciences	M
Epidemiology	M
Experimental Psychology	M
Family and Consumer Sciences-General	M
Film, Television, and Video Production	M
Geography	M
Geology	M
Health Education	M,O
Health Services Management and Hospital Administration	M
Hispanic Studies	M
History	M
Hospitality Management	M,O
Industrial Hygiene	M
Industrial/Management Engineering	M
Journalism	M
Kinesiology and Movement Studies	M
Linguistics	M
Manufacturing Engineering	M
Marriage and Family Therapy	M
Mass Communication	M
Materials Engineering	M
Mathematics Education	M
Mathematics	M
Mechanical Engineering	M
Multilingual and Multicultural Education	M
Music Education	M
Music	M
Nonprofit Management	O
Physical Therapy	M
Physics	M
Political Science	M
Psychology—General	M
Public Administration	M,O
Public Health—General	M
Reading Education	M
Recreation and Park Management	M,O
Rhetoric	M
School Psychology	M
Science Education	M
Secondary Education	M
Social Work	M,O
Sociology	M
Software Engineering	M
Spanish	M
Special Education	M
Speech and Interpersonal Communication	M
Structural Engineering	M

*M—masters degree; D—doctorate; O—other advanced degree; *—Close-Up and/or Display*

Systems Engineering M
Taxation M,O
Theater M
Travel and Tourism M
Writing M

CALIFORNIA STATE UNIVERSITY, SACRAMENTO
Accounting M
Anthropology M
Applied Behavior Analysis M
Art/Fine Arts M
Biochemistry M
Biological and Biomedical Sciences—General M
Business Administration and Management—General M
Cell Biology M
Chemistry M
Child Development M,D,O
Civil Engineering M
Communication Disorders M
Communication—General M
Computer Science M
Conservation Biology M
Counselor Education M,D,O
Criminal Justice and Criminology M
Curriculum and Instruction M,D,O
Developmental Biology M
Early Childhood Education M,D,O
Education—General M,D,O
Educational Leadership and Administration M,D,O
Educational Media/Instructional Technology M,D,O
Educational Policy M,D,O
Electrical Engineering M
Elementary Education M,D,O
Engineering and Applied Sciences—General M
English as a Second Language M
English M
Exercise and Sports Science M
Foreign Languages Education M
Higher Education M,D,O
Human Resources Development M
Human Resources Management M
Human Services M
Industrial and Organizational Psychology M
Mathematics M
Mechanical Engineering M
Molecular Biology M
Multilingual and Multicultural Education M,D,O
Music M
Nursing—General M
Physical Education M
Physical Therapy D
Political Science M
Psychology—General M
Public Administration M
Public History M,D
Public Policy M
Reading Education M,D,O
Real Estate M
Recreation and Park Management M
School Psychology M,D,O
Social Work M
Sociology M
Software Engineering M
Special Education M,D,O
Writing M

CALIFORNIA STATE UNIVERSITY, SAN BERNARDINO
Accounting M
Archaeology M
Art/Fine Arts M
Biological and Biomedical Sciences—General M
Business Administration and Management—General M
Child Development M
Clinical Psychology M
Communication—General M
Community College Education M
Computer and Information Systems Security M
Computer Science M
Corporate and Organizational Communication M
Counseling Psychology M
Counselor Education M
Criminal Justice and Criminology M
Education—General M
Educational Leadership and Administration M,D
English M
Entrepreneurship M
Environmental Sciences M
Finance and Banking M
Geosciences M
Health Services Management and Hospital Administration M
Industrial and Organizational Psychology M
Interdisciplinary Studies M
International Business M
Management Information Systems M
Marketing M
Mathematics Education M
Mathematics M
National Security M
Nursing—General M
Psychology—General M
Public Administration M
Public Health—General M
Rehabilitation Counseling M
Social Sciences M
Social Work M
Spanish M
Supply Chain Management M
Writing M

CALIFORNIA STATE UNIVERSITY, SAN MARCOS
Biological and Biomedical Sciences—General M
Biotechnology M
Business Administration and Management—General M
Child and Family Studies M
Communication Disorders M
Computer and Information Systems Security M
Computer Science M
Education—General M,D
Educational Leadership and Administration M,D
English M
Family Nurse Practitioner Studies M
Health Education M
Hispanic and Latin American Languages M
Hispanic Studies M
History M
Kinesiology and Movement Studies M
Mathematics M
Nursing and Healthcare Administration M
Nursing Education M
Nursing—General M
Psychiatric Nursing M
Psychology—General M
Public Health—General M
Reading Education M,D
Social Work M
Sociology M
Spanish M
Special Education M,D
Writing M

CALIFORNIA STATE UNIVERSITY, STANISLAUS
Applied Behavior Analysis M
Business Administration and Management—General M
Community College Education D
Conservation Biology M
Counseling Psychology M
Counselor Education M
Criminal Justice and Criminology M
Curriculum and Instruction M
Ecology M
Education—General M,D
Educational Leadership and Administration M,D
Educational Media/Instructional Technology M
Elementary Education M
English as a Second Language M,O
English M
Genetic Counseling M
Gerontological Nursing M
History M
Interdisciplinary Studies M
Multilingual and Multicultural Education M
Nursing Education M
Nursing—General M
Physical Education M
Psychology—General M
Public Administration M
Reading Education M
Rhetoric M,O
Secondary Education M
Social Work M
Special Education M
Sustainable Development M
Writing M,O

CALIFORNIA UNIVERSITY OF MANAGEMENT AND SCIENCES
Business Administration and Management—General M,D
Economics M,D
International Business M,D
Management Information Systems M,D
Sports Management M,D

CALIFORNIA UNIVERSITY OF PENNSYLVANIA
Athletic Training and Sports Medicine M
Business Administration and Management—General M
Business Analytics M
Clinical Psychology M
Communication Disorders M
Computer and Information Systems Security M
Conflict Resolution and Mediation/Peace Studies M
Counseling Psychology M
Counselor Education M
Criminal Justice and Criminology M
Early Childhood Education M
Education—General M,D
Educational Leadership and Administration M,D
Elementary Education M
Entrepreneurship M
Exercise and Sports Science M
Health Services Management and Hospital Administration M
Legal and Justice Studies M
Mathematics Education M
Near and Middle Eastern Languages M
Nursing and Healthcare Administration M
Nursing Education M
Nursing—General M
Nutrition M
Reading Education M
School Psychology M
Science Education M
Secondary Education M
Social Work M
Special Education M

Sport Psychology M
Sports Management M
Vocational and Technical Education M

CALIFORNIA WESTERN SCHOOL OF LAW
Accounting M,D
Law M,D

CALUMET COLLEGE OF SAINT JOSEPH
Criminal Justice and Criminology M
Educational Leadership and Administration M
Quality Management M

CALVARY UNIVERSITY
Curriculum and Instruction M
Education—General M
Educational Leadership and Administration M
Elementary Education M
Organizational Management M
Pastoral Ministry and Counseling M
Religious Education M
Theology M

CALVIN COLLEGE
Accounting M
Curriculum and Instruction M
Education—General M

CALVIN THEOLOGICAL SEMINARY
Missions and Missiology M,D
Pastoral Ministry and Counseling M,D
Religion M,D
Religious Education M,D
Theology M,D

CAMBRIDGE COLLEGE
Addictions/Substance Abuse Counseling M,O
Business Administration and Management—General M
Conflict Resolution and Mediation/Peace Studies M
Counseling Psychology M,O
Counselor Education M,O
Curriculum and Instruction M,D,O
Early Childhood Education M,D,O
Education—General M,D,O
Educational Leadership and Administration M,D,O
Educational Measurement and Evaluation M,D,O
Educational Media/Instructional Technology M,D,O
Elementary Education M,D,O
English as a Second Language M,D,O
Entrepreneurship M
Health Education M,D,O
Health Services Management and Hospital Administration M
Interdisciplinary Studies M,D,O
Management of Technology M
Marriage and Family Therapy M,O
Mathematics Education M,D,O
Psychology—General M,O
Rehabilitation Counseling M,O
School Nursing M,D,O
School Psychology M,O
Science Education M,D,O
Special Education M,D,O

CAMERON UNIVERSITY
Business Administration and Management—General M
Education—General M
Educational Leadership and Administration M
Entrepreneurship M
Psychology—General M

CAMPBELLSVILLE UNIVERSITY
Business Administration and Management—General M,D
Economics M,D
Education—General M
Educational Leadership and Administration M
English Education M
Legal and Justice Studies M
Management of Technology M,D
Marriage and Family Therapy M
Music Education M
Music M
School Psychology M
Science Education M
Social Sciences M
Social Work M
Special Education M
Sports Management M
Theology M

CAMPBELL UNIVERSITY
Business Administration and Management—General M
Counselor Education M
Education—General M
Educational Leadership and Administration M
Elementary Education M
Interdisciplinary Studies M
Law D
Middle School Education M
Osteopathic Medicine D
Pastoral Ministry and Counseling M,D
Pharmaceutical Sciences M,D
Pharmacy M,D
Physical Education M
Physical Therapy M,D
Physician Assistant Studies M,D
Secondary Education M
Theology M,D

CANADIAN COLLEGE OF NATUROPATHIC MEDICINE
Naturopathic Medicine O

CANADIAN MEMORIAL CHIROPRACTIC COLLEGE
Acupuncture and Oriental Medicine O
Chiropractic D,O

CANADIAN SOUTHERN BAPTIST SEMINARY
Pastoral Ministry and Counseling M
Religion M
Theology M

CANISIUS COLLEGE
Accounting M
Allied Health—General M,O
Anthropology M
Business Administration and Management—General M
Business Education M,O
Communication Disorders M,O
Community Health M,O
Corporate and Organizational Communication M
Counselor Education M,O
Early Childhood Education M
Education of the Gifted M,O
Education—General M,O
Educational Leadership and Administration M,O
Educational Media/Instructional Technology M,O
Elementary Education M,O
English as a Second Language M,O
Health Informatics M,O
International Business M
Kinesiology and Movement Studies M
Middle School Education M
Nutrition M,O
Physical Education M
Reading Education M,O
School Psychology M
Secondary Education M,O
Social Psychology M
Special Education M,O
Sports Management M
Student Affairs M,O
Zoology M

CAPE BRETON UNIVERSITY
Business Administration and Management—General M

CAPELLA UNIVERSITY
Accounting M,D
Addictions/Substance Abuse Counseling M,D
Adult Education M,D
Applied Behavior Analysis M
Business Administration and Management—General M,D
Business Education D
Child and Family Studies M
Clinical Psychology M,D
Computer and Information Systems Security M
Counseling Psychology M
Counselor Education M,D
Criminal Justice and Criminology M,D
Curriculum and Instruction M,D
Developmental Psychology M,D
Distance Education Development M,D
Early Childhood Education M,D
Education—General M,D
Educational Leadership and Administration M,D
Educational Media/Instructional Technology M,D
Educational Psychology M,D
Elementary Education M,D
Emergency Management M,D
Entrepreneurship M,D
Environmental and Occupational Health M,D
Epidemiology D
Finance and Banking M,D
Gerontological Nursing M
Gerontology M
Health Informatics M
Health Services Management and Hospital Administration M,D
Higher Education M,D
Homeland Security M,D
Human Resources Management M,D
Human Services M,D
Industrial and Organizational Psychology M,D
Management Information Systems M,D
Management of Technology M,D
Management Strategy and Policy M,D
Marketing M,D
Marriage and Family Therapy M
Middle School Education M,D
Nonprofit Management D
Nursing and Healthcare Administration M
Nursing Education M
Nursing—General M,D
Operations Research M
Organizational Management M,D
Project Management M,D
Psychology—General M,D
Public Administration M,D
Reading Education M,D
School Psychology M,D
Social Work D
Special Education M,D
Sport Psychology M
Supply Chain Management M,D
Vocational and Technical Education D

CAPITAL UNIVERSITY
Business Administration and Management—General M
Law M,D
Legal and Justice Studies M
Music Education M

Music M
Nursing and Healthcare Administration M
Nursing—General M
Taxation M

CAPITOL TECHNOLOGY UNIVERSITY
Business Administration and Management—General M
Computer and Information Systems Security M
Computer Science M
Electrical Engineering M
Information Science M
Management Information Systems M
Telecommunications Management M

CARDINAL STRITCH UNIVERSITY
Business Administration and Management—General M
Clinical Psychology M
Computer and Information Systems Security M
Criminal Justice and Criminology M
Education—General M,D
Educational Leadership and Administration M,D
Health Services Management and Hospital Administration M
Higher Education M,D
Liberal Studies M
Marketing M
Nursing—General M
Pastoral Ministry and Counseling M
Psychology—General M
Reading Education M,D
Religion M
Special Education M
Sports Management M
Student Affairs M,D
Urban Education M,D

CAREY THEOLOGICAL COLLEGE
Theology M,D

CARIBBEAN UNIVERSITY
Art History M,D
Criminal Justice and Criminology M,D
Curriculum and Instruction M,D
Early Childhood Education M,D
Education—General M,D
Educational Leadership and Administration M,D
Educational Media/Instructional Technology M,D
Elementary Education M,D
English Education M,D
Foreign Languages Education M,D
Gerontological Nursing M,D
Human Resources Management M,D
Mathematics Education M,D
Museum Studies M,D
Pediatric Nursing M,D
Physical Education M,D
Science Education M,D
Social Sciences Education M,D
Special Education M,D

CARLETON UNIVERSITY
Aerospace/Aeronautical Engineering M,D
Anthropology M
Architecture M
Art History M
Biological and Biomedical Sciences—General M,D
Biomedical Engineering M
Business Administration and Management—General M,D
Canadian Studies M,D
Chemistry M,D
Civil Engineering M,D
Cognitive Sciences D
Communication—General M,D
Comparative Literature D
Computer Science M,D
Conflict Resolution and Mediation/Peace Studies M,O
East European and Russian Studies M,O
Economics M,D
Electrical Engineering M,D
Engineering and Applied Sciences—General M,D
English M,D
Environmental Engineering M,D
Film, Television, and Video Production M
French M
Geography M,D
Geosciences M,D
History M,D
Industrial Design M
Information Science M,D
International Affairs M,D
Journalism M,D
Legal and Justice Studies M,O
Linguistics M
Management of Technology M
Materials Engineering M,D
Mathematics M,D
Mechanical Engineering M,D
Music M
Neuroscience M,D
Philosophy M
Physics M,D
Political Science M,D
Psychology—General M,D
Public Administration M,D
Public Policy M,D
Social Work M
Sociology M,D
Systems Engineering M,D
Systems Science M,D
Western European Studies M,O

CARLOS ALBIZU UNIVERSITY
Clinical Psychology M,D
Communication Disorders M,D
Industrial and Organizational Psychology M,D
Psychology—General M,D

CARLOS ALBIZU UNIVERSITY, MIAMI CAMPUS
Business Administration and Management—General M,D
Clinical Psychology M,D
Communication Disorders M,D
Counseling Psychology M,D
Education of the Gifted M,D
English as a Second Language M,D
Entrepreneurship M,D
Human Services M,D
Industrial and Organizational Psychology M,D
Marriage and Family Therapy M,D
Nonprofit Management M,D
Organizational Management M,D
Psychology—General M,D
Special Education M,D

CARLOW UNIVERSITY
Art/Fine Arts M
Business Administration and Management—General M
Computer and Information Systems Security M,O
Counseling Psychology M,D,O
Curriculum and Instruction M
Distance Education Development M,O
Early Childhood Education M,O
Education—General M,O
Family Nurse Practitioner Studies M,O
Forensic Sciences M
Health Services Management and Hospital Administration M
Human Resources Management M
Mathematics M
Nursing and Healthcare Administration M
Nursing Education M
Nursing—General D
Organizational Management M,D,O
Project Management M
Psychology—General M
Science Education M
Social Work M
Special Education M,O
Student Affairs M
Women's Health Nursing M,O
Writing M

CARNEGIE MELLON UNIVERSITY
Accounting D
African Studies D
African-American Studies D
Applied Arts and Design—General M,D
Applied Physics M,D
Architectural Engineering M,D
Architecture M,D
Art/Fine Arts M
Artificial Intelligence/Robotics M,D
Arts Administration M
Atmospheric Sciences D
Biochemistry M,D
Bioengineering M,D
Biological and Biomedical Sciences—General M,D
Biomedical Engineering M,D
Biophysics M,D
Biopsychology D
Biotechnology M
Building Science M,D
Business Administration and Management—General M,D
Cell Biology M,D
Chemical Engineering M,D
Chemistry D
Civil Engineering M,D
Cognitive Sciences D
Communication—General M,D
Comparative Literature M,D
Computational Biology M,D
Computer and Information Systems Security M
Computer Art and Design M
Computer Engineering M,D
Computer Science M,D
Construction Management M,D
Corporate and Organizational Communication M
Criminal Justice and Criminology M
Cultural Studies D
Developmental Biology M,D
Developmental Psychology D
Economics D
Electrical Engineering M,D
Energy and Power Engineering M,D
English M,D
Entertainment Management M
Entrepreneurship D
Environmental Engineering M,D
Environmental Sciences D
Film, Television, and Video Production M
Finance and Banking D
Gender Studies D
Genetics M,D
Health Services Management and Hospital Administration M
History of Science and Technology D
History D
Human-Computer Interaction M,D
Industrial and Labor Relations D
Industrial and Manufacturing Management M,D
Information Science M,D
Linguistics M,D
Management Information Systems M,D
Marketing D
Materials Engineering M,D
Materials Sciences M,D
Mathematical and Computational Finance M,D
Mathematics M,D
Mechanical Engineering M,D
Mechanics M,D
Media Studies M
Modeling and Simulation M,D
Molecular Biology M,D
Molecular Biophysics D
Music Education M
Music M
Nanotechnology D
Neurobiology M,D
Neuroscience D
Operations Research D
Organizational Behavior D
Philosophy M,D
Physics M,D
Polymer Science and Engineering M
Psychology—General D
Public Administration M
Public Policy M,D
Publishing M
Rhetoric M,D
Social Psychology D
Social Sciences D
Software Engineering M,D
Statistics M,D
Structural Biology M,D
Sustainable Development M,D
Systems Engineering M
Technical Writing M
Technology and Public Policy M,D
Telecommunications Management M
Theater M
Theoretical Chemistry D
Urban Design M
Water Resources Engineering M,D
Women's Studies D
Writing M

CAROLINA CHRISTIAN COLLEGE
Pastoral Ministry and Counseling M
Religious Education M

CARROLL UNIVERSITY
Adult Education M
Business Administration and Management—General M
Early Childhood Education M
Education—General M
Educational Leadership and Administration M
Elementary Education M
Exercise and Sports Science M
Occupational Therapy M
Physical Therapy D
Physician Assistant Studies M
Secondary Education M
Software Engineering M

CARSON-NEWMAN UNIVERSITY
Business Administration and Management—General M
Counselor Education M
Curriculum and Instruction M
Education—General M
Educational Leadership and Administration M
Elementary Education M
English as a Second Language M
Family Nurse Practitioner Studies M
Nursing Education M
Nursing—General M
Organizational Management M
Secondary Education M
Theology M

CARTHAGE COLLEGE
Art Education M,O
Counselor Education M,O
Education of the Gifted M,O
Education—General M,O
Educational Leadership and Administration M,O
English Education M,O
Reading Education M,O
Science Education M,O
Social Sciences Education M,O

CASE WESTERN RESERVE UNIVERSITY
Accounting M,D
Acute Care/Critical Care Nursing M
Aerospace/Aeronautical Engineering M,D
Allopathic Medicine D
Anatomy M
Anesthesiologist Assistant Studies M
Anthropology M,D
Applied Mathematics M,D
Art Education M
Art History M,D
Astronomy M,D
Biochemistry M,D
Bioethics M
Biological and Biomedical Sciences—General M,D
Biomedical Engineering M,D*
Biophysics M,D
Biostatistics M,D
Business Administration and Management—General M,D
Business Analytics M
Cancer Biology/Oncology D
Cell Biology D
Chemical Engineering M,D
Chemistry M,D
Civil Engineering M,D
Clinical Psychology D
Clinical Research M,D
Cognitive Sciences M
Communication Disorders M,D
Comparative Literature M
Computer Engineering M,D
Computer Science M,D
Dance M
Dentistry D
Electrical Engineering M,D
Engineering and Applied Sciences—General M,D
Engineering Management M
English M,D
Epidemiology D
Experimental Psychology D
Family Nurse Practitioner Studies M
Finance and Banking M
French M
Genetic Counseling M,D
Genomic Sciences M,D
Geology M,D
Geosciences M,D
Gerontological Nursing M
Health Law M,D
Health Services Management and Hospital Administration M
History M,D
Human Genetics M,D
Immunology D
Industrial and Manufacturing Management M,D
Information Science M,D
Intellectual Property Law M,D
Law M,D
Legal and Justice Studies M,D
Linguistics M
Logistics M,D
Materials Engineering M,D
Materials Sciences M,D
Maternal and Child/Neonatal Nursing M
Mathematics M,D
Mechanical Engineering M,D
Medical/Surgical Nursing M
Microbiology D
Molecular Biology D
Molecular Medicine D
Museum Studies M
Music Education M,D
Music M,D
Neuroscience D
Nonprofit Management M,D,O
Nurse Anesthesia M
Nurse Midwifery M
Nursing Education M
Nursing—General M,D
Nutrition M,D
Operations Research M,D
Oral and Dental Sciences M,O
Organizational Behavior M,D
Pathology M,D
Pediatric Nursing M
Pharmacology D
Physician Assistant Studies M
Physics M,D
Physiology M,D
Political Science M,D
Polymer Science and Engineering M,D
Psychiatric Nursing M
Psychology—General M,D
Public Health—General M
Social Work M,D
Sociology M,D
Supply Chain Management M,D
Sustainability Management D
Systems Engineering M,D
Theater M
Virology D
Women's Health Nursing M

CASTLETON UNIVERSITY
Curriculum and Instruction M
Education—General M,O
Educational Leadership and Administration M,O
Forensic Psychology M
Psychology—General M
Reading Education M,O
Special Education M,O

CATAWBA COLLEGE
Elementary Education M
Science Education M

CATHOLIC DISTANCE UNIVERSITY
Theology M

CATHOLIC THEOLOGICAL UNION
Missions and Missiology M,D,O
Pastoral Ministry and Counseling M,D,O
Theology M,D,O

THE CATHOLIC UNIVERSITY OF AMERICA
Accounting M
American Studies M,D
Anthropology M
Applied Psychology M,D
Architecture M,O
Biological and Biomedical Sciences—General M,D

*M—masters degree; D—doctorate; O—other advanced degree; *—Close-Up and/or Display*

Biomedical Engineering	M,D
Biotechnology	M,D
Business Administration and Management—General	M
Cell Biology	M,D
Civil Engineering	M,D,O
Classics	M,D,O
Clinical Laboratory Sciences/Medical Technology	M,D
Clinical Psychology	M,D
Computer Science	M,D
Criminal Justice and Criminology	M
Early Childhood Education	M,O
Economic Development	M
Education—General	M,O
Educational Leadership and Administration	M,O
Electrical Engineering	M,D
Energy and Power Engineering	M,D
Engineering and Applied Sciences—General	M,D,O
Engineering Management	M,O
English	M,D,O
Environmental Engineering	M,D
Ergonomics and Human Factors	M,D
Experimental Psychology	M,D
Health Services Management and Hospital Administration	M
Hispanic Studies	M,D
History	M,D
Human Resources Management	M
Information Studies	M,O
International Affairs	M,D
Law	M,D
Legal and Justice Studies	M,D,O
Library Science	M,O
Management Information Systems	M,O
Management of Technology	M,O
Materials Engineering	M
Materials Sciences	M
Mechanical Engineering	M,D
Medieval and Renaissance Studies	M,D,O
Microbiology	M,D
Music Education	M,D,O
Music	M,D,O
Near and Middle Eastern Languages	M,D
Near and Middle Eastern Studies	M,D,O
Nursing—General	M,D,O
Pastoral Ministry and Counseling	M,D,O
Philosophy	M,D,O
Physics	M,D
Political Science	M,D
Project Management	M,O
Psychology—General	M,D
Public Policy	M
Religion	M,D,O
Rhetoric	M,D,O
Secondary Education	M,O
Social Work	M,D
Sociology	M
Spanish	M,D
Special Education	M,O
Sustainable Development	M,O
Systems Engineering	M,O
Theater	M,O
Theology	M,D,O
Transportation and Highway Engineering	M,D,O
Urban and Regional Planning	M,O
Western European Studies	M,D

CEDAR CREST COLLEGE

Art Therapy	M
Business Administration and Management—General	M
Education—General	M
Forensic Sciences	M
Nursing and Healthcare Administration	M
Nursing Education	M
Nursing—General	M
Nutrition	O
Writing	M

CEDARS-SINAI MEDICAL CENTER

Biological and Biomedical Sciences—General	M,D
Medical Imaging	M,D
Translational Biology	M,D

CEDARVILLE UNIVERSITY

Business Administration and Management—General	M,D
Family Nurse Practitioner Studies	M,D
Health Services Management and Hospital Administration	M,D
Industrial and Manufacturing Management	M,D
International Health	M,D
Missions and Missiology	M,D
Nursing Education	M,D
Pastoral Ministry and Counseling	M,D
Pharmacy	M,D

CENTENARY COLLEGE OF LOUISIANA

Business Administration and Management—General	M
Education—General	M
Elementary Education	M
Secondary Education	M

CENTENARY UNIVERSITY

Accounting	M
Business Administration and Management—General	M
Counseling Psychology	M
Education—General	M,D
Educational Leadership and Administration	M,D
Reading Education	M,D
Special Education	M,D

CENTRAL BAPTIST THEOLOGICAL SEMINARY

Missions and Missiology	M,O
Theology	M,O

CENTRAL CONNECTICUT STATE UNIVERSITY

Accounting	M
Actuarial Science	M,O
Advertising and Public Relations	M,O
Art Education	M,O
Biological and Biomedical Sciences—General	M,D
Business Administration and Management—General	M
Communication—General	M,O
Computer Science	M,O
Construction Management	M,O
Counselor Education	M,O
Criminal Justice and Criminology	M
Early Childhood Education	M,O
Educational Leadership and Administration	M,D,O
Elementary Education	M,O
Engineering and Applied Sciences—General	M
English as a Second Language	M,O
English Education	M,O
English	M,O
Exercise and Sports Science	M,O
Foreign Languages Education	M,O
French	M,O
Geography	M
German	M,O
Graphic Design	M
History	M,O
Hospice Nursing	M
Industrial and Manufacturing Management	M,O
Information Studies	M
International Affairs	M
Italian	M,O
Logistics	M,O
Management of Technology	M,O
Marriage and Family Therapy	M,O
Mathematics	M,O
Molecular Biology	M,O
Music Education	M,O
Nursing—General	M
Physical Education	M,O
Psychology—General	M
Reading Education	M,O
Rehabilitation Counseling	M,O
School Psychology	M,O
Science Education	M,O
Secondary Education	M,O
Spanish	M,O
Special Education	M,O
Statistics	M,O
Supply Chain Management	M,O
Vocational and Technical Education	M

CENTRAL EUROPEAN UNIVERSITY

Anthropology	M,D
Applied Mathematics	M,D
Business Administration and Management—General	M,D
Business Analytics	M,D
Cognitive Sciences	D
Data Science/Data Analytics	D
Economics	M,D
Environmental Management and Policy	M,D
Finance and Banking	M,D
Gender Studies	M,D
History	M,D
International Affairs	M,D
International Business	M,D
Law	M,D
Legal and Justice Studies	M,D
Management of Technology	M,D
Mathematics	M,D
Medieval and Renaissance Studies	M,D
Philosophy	M,D
Political Science	M,D
Public Administration	M,D
Public Policy	M,D
Sociology	M,D

CENTRAL METHODIST UNIVERSITY

Counselor Education	M
Education—General	M
Music Education	M
Nursing and Healthcare Administration	M
Nursing Education	M
Nursing—General	M

CENTRAL MICHIGAN UNIVERSITY

Accounting	M,O
American Indian/Native American Studies	M
American Studies	M,O
Applied Psychology	M,D
Biological and Biomedical Sciences—General	M
Business Administration and Management—General	M,O
Chemistry	M
Child and Family Studies	M,O
Clinical Psychology	D
Clothing and Textiles	M,O
Communication Disorders	M,D
Communication—General	M
Community College Education	M,D,O
Computer and Information Systems Security	O
Computer Science	M
Conservation Biology	M
Counseling Psychology	M,D,O
Counselor Education	M
Cultural Studies	M
Curriculum and Instruction	M,D,O
Early Childhood Education	M,O
Economics	M
Education—General	M,D,O
Educational Leadership and Administration	M,D,O
Educational Media/Instructional Technology	M,D,O
Elementary Education	M,D,O
Engineering and Applied Sciences—General	M
Engineering Management	M,O
English as a Second Language	M,O
English	M
Exercise and Sports Science	M,D
Experimental Psychology	M,D
Family and Consumer Sciences-General	M,O
Film, Television, and Video Production	M
Film, Television, and Video Theory and Criticism	M
Finance and Banking	M
Gender Studies	M
Geographic Information Systems	M
Gerontology	M,O
Health Psychology	M,D
Health Services Management and Hospital Administration	M,D,O
Higher Education	M,D,O
History	M,O
Human Development	M,O
Human Resources Management	M,O
Humanities	M
Industrial and Manufacturing Management	M
Industrial and Organizational Psychology	M,D
International Affairs	M,O
International Business	M,O
International Health	M,D,O
Logistics	M,O
Management Information Systems	M,O
Marketing	M,O
Materials Sciences	D
Mathematics Education	M,D
Mathematics	M,D
Media Studies	M
Music Education	M
Music	M
Neuroscience	M,D
Nonprofit Management	M,O
Nutrition	M,D,O
Physical Therapy	M,D
Physician Assistant Studies	M,D
Physics	M,D
Political Science	M,O
Psychology—General	M,D,O
Public Administration	M,O
Reading Education	M,D,O
Recreation and Park Management	M,O
Rehabilitation Sciences	M,D
School Psychology	D,O
Science Education	M
Secondary Education	M,D,O
Spanish	M
Special Education	M,O
Sports Management	M,O
Student Affairs	M,D,O
Western European Studies	M,O
Writing	M

CENTRAL PENN COLLEGE

Management Information Systems	M
Organizational Management	M

CENTRAL WASHINGTON UNIVERSITY

Anthropology	M
Art/Fine Arts	M
Biological and Biomedical Sciences—General	M
Botany	M
Chemistry	M
Child and Family Studies	M
Counseling Psychology	M
Curriculum and Instruction	M
Ecology	M
Education—General	M
Educational Leadership and Administration	M
English as a Second Language	M
English	M
Environmental Management and Policy	M
Experimental Psychology	M
Family and Consumer Sciences-General	M
Fish, Game, and Wildlife Management	M
Geography	M
Geology	M
Graphic Design	M
Health Education	M
Higher Education	M
History	M
Home Economics Education	M
Interdisciplinary Studies	M
Microbiology	M
Music Education	M
Music	M
Natural Resources	M
Nutrition	M
Photography	M
Physical Education	M
Physiology	M
Psychology—General	M,O
Reading Education	M
School Psychology	O
Sports Management	M
Theater	M
Vocational and Technical Education	M
Writing	M

CENTRAL YESHIVA TOMCHEI TMIMIM-LUBAVITCH

Jewish Studies	M
Theology	M

CENTRO DE ESTUDIOS AVANZADOS DE PUERTO RICO Y EL CARIBE

History	M,D
Latin American Studies	M,D

CHADRON STATE COLLEGE

Business Administration and Management—General	M
Business Education	M,O
Counselor Education	M,O
Education—General	M,O
Educational Leadership and Administration	M,O
Elementary Education	M,O
English Education	M,O
Secondary Education	M,O
Social Sciences Education	M,O

CHAMINADE UNIVERSITY OF HONOLULU

Accounting	M
Business Administration and Management—General	M
Child Development	M
Counseling Psychology	M
Criminal Justice and Criminology	M
Early Childhood Education	M
Education—General	M
Educational Leadership and Administration	M
Elementary Education	M
Marriage and Family Therapy	M
Nonprofit Management	M
Pastoral Ministry and Counseling	M
School Psychology	M
Secondary Education	M
Special Education	M
Theology	M

CHAMPLAIN COLLEGE

Business Administration and Management—General	M
Computer and Information Systems Security	M
Conflict Resolution and Mediation/Peace Studies	M
Early Childhood Education	M
Forensic Sciences	M
Health Services Management and Hospital Administration	M
Internet and Interactive Multimedia	M
Law	M
Management of Technology	M
Media Studies	M

CHAPMAN UNIVERSITY

Accounting	M
Athletic Training and Sports Medicine	M
Business Administration and Management—General	M
Communication Disorders	M
Communication—General	M
Computational Sciences	M,D*
Counselor Education	M,D,O
Cultural Studies	M,D,O
Curriculum and Instruction	M,D,O
Disability Studies	M,D,O
Education—General	M,D,O
Educational Leadership and Administration	M,D,O
Educational Psychology	M,D,O
Elementary Education	M,D,O
English	M
Environmental Law	M,D
Film, Television, and Video Production	M
Food Science and Technology	M*
Holocaust and Genocide Studies	M
International Affairs	M
Law	M,D
Marriage and Family Therapy	M
Nutrition	M
Pharmaceutical Sciences	M,D
Pharmacy	M,D
Physical Therapy	D
Physician Assistant Studies	M
School Psychology	M,D,O
Secondary Education	M,D,O
Special Education	M,D,O
Sports and Entertainment Law	M,D
Taxation	M,D
Writing	M

CHARLES R. DREW UNIVERSITY OF MEDICINE AND SCIENCE

Allopathic Medicine	D
Public Health—General	M

CHARLESTON SCHOOL OF LAW

Law	D

CHARLESTON SOUTHERN UNIVERSITY

Accounting	M
Business Administration and Management—General	M
Criminal Justice and Criminology	M
Education—General	M
Educational Leadership and Administration	M
Elementary Education	M
Finance and Banking	M
Human Resources Management	M
Management Information Systems	M
Organizational Management	M

CHARLOTTE CHRISTIAN COLLEGE AND THEOLOGICAL SEMINARY

Cultural Studies	M,D
Pastoral Ministry and Counseling	M,D
Religion	M,D
Theology	M,D

CHARTER COLLEGE
Business Administration and Management—General M

CHARTER OAK STATE COLLEGE
Organizational Management M

CHATHAM UNIVERSITY
Accounting M
Art Education M
Biological and Biomedical Sciences—General M
Business Administration and Management—General M
Communication—General M
Computer Art and Design M
Counseling Psychology M,D
Developmental Psychology M,D
Early Childhood Education M
Education—General M
Elementary Education M
English Education M
Environmental Biology M
Environmental Education M
Film, Television, and Video Production M
Health Communication M
Health Informatics M
Health Psychology M,D
Industrial and Organizational Psychology M,D
Interior Design M
Marriage and Family Therapy M,D
Mathematics Education M
Nursing and Healthcare Administration M,D
Nursing Education M,D
Nursing—General M,D
Occupational Therapy M,D
Physical Therapy D
Physician Assistant Studies M
Science Education M
Secondary Education M
Social Sciences Education M
Special Education M
Sport Psychology M,D
Sustainability Management M
Women's Studies M
Writing M

CHESTNUT HILL COLLEGE
Clinical Psychology M,D,O
Counseling Psychology M,O
Early Childhood Education M
Education—General M
Educational Leadership and Administration M
Educational Media/Instructional Technology M,O
Elementary Education M,O
Human Services M,O
Marriage and Family Therapy M,D,O
Middle School Education M
Psychology—General M,D,O
Reading Education M
Secondary Education M
Special Education M,O

CHEYNEY UNIVERSITY OF PENNSYLVANIA
Education—General M,O
Educational Leadership and Administration M,O
Elementary Education M
Public Administration M
Special Education M
Urban Education M

THE CHICAGO SCHOOL OF PROFESSIONAL PSYCHOLOGY
Applied Behavior Analysis M,D
Clinical Psychology M,D
Forensic Psychology M,D
Industrial and Organizational Psychology M,D
Organizational Management M,D
Psychology—General M,D
School Psychology D,O

THE CHICAGO SCHOOL OF PROFESSIONAL PSYCHOLOGY AT DOWNTOWN LOS ANGELES
Applied Behavior Analysis M,D
Clinical Psychology M,D
Forensic Psychology D
Industrial and Organizational Psychology M
Marriage and Family Therapy M,D

THE CHICAGO SCHOOL OF PROFESSIONAL PSYCHOLOGY AT IRVINE
Clinical Psychology D
Forensic Psychology D
Marriage and Family Therapy M,D
Psychology—General D

THE CHICAGO SCHOOL OF PROFESSIONAL PSYCHOLOGY AT WASHINGTON DC
School Psychology O

THE CHICAGO SCHOOL OF PROFESSIONAL PSYCHOLOGY: ONLINE
Applied Psychology M,O
Clinical Psychology M
Forensic Psychology M,O
Health Services Management and Hospital Administration M
Industrial and Organizational Psychology M,D,O
Pharmacology M
Psychology—General M,D

CHICAGO STATE UNIVERSITY
Adult Education M
Biological and Biomedical Sciences—General M
Clinical Psychology M
Computer Science M
Counselor Education M
Criminal Justice and Criminology M
Early Childhood Education M
Education—General M,D
Educational Leadership and Administration M,D
Elementary Education M
English M
Foundations and Philosophy of Education M
Geographic Information Systems M
Higher Education M,D
History M
Library Science M
Mathematics M
Middle School Education M
Multilingual and Multicultural Education M
Nursing—General M
Occupational Therapy M
Pharmacy D
Physical Education M
Public Health—General M
Reading Education M
Secondary Education M
Social Work M
Special Education M
Vocational and Technical Education M
Writing M

CHICAGO THEOLOGICAL SEMINARY
Ethics M,D
Pastoral Ministry and Counseling M,D
Religion M,D
Theology M,D

CHOWAN UNIVERSITY
Education—General M

CHRISTENDOM COLLEGE
Theology M

CHRISTIAN BROTHERS UNIVERSITY
Accounting M,O
Business Administration and Management—General M,O
Education—General M
Educational Leadership and Administration M
Engineering and Applied Sciences—General M
International Business M,O
Physician Assistant Studies M
Project Management M,O
Religion M

CHRISTIAN THEOLOGICAL SEMINARY
Marriage and Family Therapy M,D
Pastoral Ministry and Counseling M,D
Religion M,D
Theology M,D

CHRISTIE'S EDUCATION
Art History M
Art/Fine Arts O
Arts Administration M,O
Museum Studies M

CHRISTOPHER NEWPORT UNIVERSITY
Applied Physics M
Computer Science M
Education—General M
Environmental Sciences M
Physics M

CHRIST THE KING SEMINARY
Pastoral Ministry and Counseling M
Theology M

CHURCH DIVINITY SCHOOL OF THE PACIFIC
Theology M,D,O

CINCINNATI CHRISTIAN UNIVERSITY
Pastoral Ministry and Counseling M
Religion M
Theology M

THE CITADEL, THE MILITARY COLLEGE OF SOUTH CAROLINA
Aerospace/Aeronautical Engineering M,O
Biological and Biomedical Sciences—General M,O
Business Administration and Management—General M
Civil Engineering M,O
Computer Engineering M,O
Counselor Education M,O
Early Childhood Education M,O
Education—General M,O
Educational Leadership and Administration M,O
Electrical Engineering M,O
Engineering and Applied Sciences—General M,O
Engineering Management M,O
English Education M,O
English M
Environmental Management and Policy M,O
Exercise and Sports Science M,O
Geotechnical Engineering M,O
Hispanic Studies O
History M,O
Homeland Security M,O
Information Science M
Interdisciplinary Studies M,O
Manufacturing Engineering M,O
Mathematics Education M,O
Mechanical Engineering M,O
Medical Microbiology M,O
Middle School Education M,O
Military and Defense Studies M,O
National Security M,O
Physical Education M,O
Political Science M
Project Management M,O
Psychology—General M,O
Reading Education M,O
School Psychology M,O
Science Education M,O
Secondary Education M,O
Social Sciences Education M,O
Social Sciences M
Sports Management M,O
Structural Engineering M,O
Student Affairs M,O
Systems Engineering M,O
Transportation and Highway Engineering M,O

CITY COLLEGE OF THE CITY UNIVERSITY OF NEW YORK
Architecture M
Art History M
Art/Fine Arts M
Atmospheric Sciences M
Biochemistry M,D
Biological and Biomedical Sciences—General M,D
Biomedical Engineering M,D
Business Administration and Management—General M
Chemical Engineering M,D
Chemistry M,D
Civil Engineering M,D
Clinical Psychology M,D
Computer Art and Design M
Computer Science M,D
Corporate and Organizational Communication M
Early Childhood Education M
Economics M
Education—General M,O
Educational Leadership and Administration M,O
Electrical Engineering M,D
Engineering and Applied Sciences—General M,D
English as a Second Language M
English Education M,O
English M
Geology M
Geosciences M
Graphic Design M
History M
International Affairs M
Landscape Architecture M
Management Information Systems M,D
Marketing M
Mathematics Education M,O
Mathematics M
Mechanical Engineering M,D
Media Studies M
Middle School Education M,O
Multilingual and Multicultural Education M
Museum Studies M
Physics M,D
Psychology—General M,D
Public Administration M,D
Reading Education M
Science Education M
Secondary Education M,O
Social Sciences Education M,O
Sociology M
Spanish M
Special Education M,O
Sustainable Development M
Urban Design M
Writing M

CITY UNIVERSITY OF NEW YORK SCHOOL OF LAW
Law D

CITY UNIVERSITY OF SEATTLE
Accounting M,O
Business Administration and Management—General M,O
Computer and Information Systems Security M,O
Computer Science M,O
Counseling Psychology M
Counselor Education M,O
Curriculum and Instruction M,O
Education—General M,O
Educational Leadership and Administration M,D,O
Elementary Education M,O
Finance and Banking M,O
Human Resources Management M,O
International Business M,O
Management Information Systems M,O
Management of Technology M,O
Marketing M,O
Organizational Management M,O
Project Management M,O
Reading Education M,O
Special Education M,O
Sustainability Management M,O

CITY VISION UNIVERSITY
Entrepreneurship M
Pastoral Ministry and Counseling M

CLAFLIN UNIVERSITY
Biotechnology M
Business Administration and Management—General M

CLAREMONT GRADUATE UNIVERSITY
African Studies M,D,O
American Studies M,D,O
Applied Mathematics M,D
Archives/Archival Administration M,D,O
Art/Fine Arts M
Arts Administration M
Botany M,D
Business Administration and Management—General M,D,O
Cognitive Sciences M,D,O
Comparative Literature M,D
Computational Biology M,D
Computational Sciences M,D
Computer and Information Systems Security M,D,O
Computer Art and Design M
Cultural Studies M,D,O
Data Science/Data Analytics M,D,O
Developmental Psychology M,D,O
Economic Development M,D,O
Economics M,D,O
Education—General M,D,O
Educational Leadership and Administration M,D,O
Educational Measurement and Evaluation M,D,O
Electronic Commerce M,D,O
English M,D
Ethics M,D
Film, Television, and Video Theory and Criticism M,D
Financial Engineering M
Geographic Information Systems M,D,O
Health Informatics M,D,O
Health Promotion M,D
Health Psychology M,D,O
Higher Education M,D,O
History M,D,O
Human Development M,D,O
Human Resources Development M,D,O
Human Resources Management M
Humanities M,D,O
Industrial and Organizational Psychology M,D,O
Information Science M,D,O
International Affairs M,D
International Economics M,D,O
Management Information Systems M,D,O
Management Strategy and Policy M,D,O
Mathematics M,D
Media Studies M,D,O
Museum Studies M,D,O
Music M,D
Operations Research M,D
Philosophy M,D
Photography M
Political Science M,D
Psychology—General M,D,O
Public Health—General M,D
Public Policy M,D,O
Religion M,D
Social Psychology M,D,O
Special Education M,D,O
Statistics M,D
Student Affairs M,D,O
Systems Science M,D,O
Telecommunications M,D,O
Theology M,D
Urban Education M,D,O
Western European Studies M,D,O
Women's Studies M,D
Writing M,D

CLAREMONT LINCOLN UNIVERSITY
Ethics M
Pastoral Ministry and Counseling M
Religion M

CLAREMONT SCHOOL OF THEOLOGY
Ethics M,D
Pastoral Ministry and Counseling M,D
Religion M,D
Religious Education M,D
Theology M,D

CLARION UNIVERSITY OF PENNSYLVANIA
Accounting M
Advertising and Public Relations O
Business Administration and Management—General M
Communication Disorders M
Communication—General M
Curriculum and Instruction M
Data Science/Data Analytics M
Early Childhood Education M
Education—General M
Educational Media/Instructional Technology M
Entrepreneurship M
Family Nurse Practitioner Studies M
Finance and Banking M
Health Services Management and Hospital Administration M
Information Science M
Journalism M
Library Science M,O
Mass Communication M
Mathematics Education M
Media Studies M
Nursing—General M,D
Reading Education M
Rehabilitation Sciences M
Science Education M
Special Education M
Vocational and Technical Education M

*M—masters degree; D—doctorate; O—other advanced degree; *—Close-Up and/or Display*

CLARK ATLANTA UNIVERSITY

Program	Degree	(column headings added; not printed)
Accounting	M	
African-American Studies	M,D	
Biological and Biomedical Sciences—General	M,D	
Business Administration and Management—General	M	
Chemistry	M,D	
Computer Science	M	
Counselor Education	M	
Criminal Justice and Criminology	M	
Curriculum and Instruction	M	
Economics	M	
Education—General	M,D,O	
Educational Leadership and Administration	M,D,O	
Educational Psychology	M	
English	M,D	
Information Science	M	
Mathematics Education	M	
Mathematics	M	
Physics	M	
Political Science	M,D	
Public Administration	M	
Science Education	M	
Social Work	M,D	
Sociology	M	
Special Education	M	

CLARKE UNIVERSITY

Business Administration and Management—General	M
Education—General	M
Educational Leadership and Administration	M
Family Nurse Practitioner Studies	D
Nursing and Healthcare Administration	D
Nursing—General	D
Physical Therapy	D
Psychiatric Nursing	D
Social Work	M

CLARKSON COLLEGE

Adult Nursing	M,O
Family Nurse Practitioner Studies	M,O
Nursing and Healthcare Administration	M,O
Nursing Education	M,O
Nursing—General	M,O

CLARKSON UNIVERSITY

Bioethics	M,O
Biological and Biomedical Sciences—General	M
Biotechnology	D
Business Administration and Management—General	O
Chemical Engineering	M,D
Chemistry	M,D
Civil Engineering	M,D
Computer Engineering	M,D
Computer Science	M,D
Early Childhood Education	M
Education—General	M
Electrical Engineering	M,D
Energy and Power Engineering	M
Energy Management and Policy	M,O
Engineering and Applied Sciences—General	M,D,O
Engineering Management	M
English as a Second Language	M
Environmental Engineering	M,D
Environmental Management and Policy	M
Environmental Sciences	M,D
Health Informatics	M
Health Services Management and Hospital Administration	M,O
Health Services Research	M
Human Resources Management	O
Interdisciplinary Studies	M,D
International Business	O
Materials Engineering	D
Materials Sciences	D
Mathematics	M,D
Mechanical Engineering	M,D
Middle School Education	M
Nursing and Healthcare Administration	M,O
Occupational Therapy	M
Physical Therapy	D
Physician Assistant Studies	M
Physics	M,D
Secondary Education	M
Supply Chain Management	O
Sustainable Development	M,D
Systems Engineering	M
Vocational and Technical Education	M

CLARKS SUMMIT UNIVERSITY

Communication—General	M,D
Counselor Education	M
Curriculum and Instruction	M
Educational Leadership and Administration	M
English	M
Missions and Missiology	M,D
Organizational Management	M,D
Pastoral Ministry and Counseling	M,D
Religion	M,D
Religious Education	M,D
Theology	M,D

CLARK UNIVERSITY

Accounting	M
American Studies	D
Biochemistry	D
Biological and Biomedical Sciences—General	M,D
Business Administration and Management—General	M
Business Analytics	M
Chemistry	D
Clinical Psychology	D
Communication—General	M
Community Health	M
Developmental Psychology	D
Economics	D
Education—General	M,D
English	M
Environmental Management and Policy	M
Environmental Sciences	M
Finance and Banking	M
Geographic Information Systems	M
Geography	D
Health Education	M
History	D
Holocaust and Genocide Studies	D
Information Science	M
International Development	M
International Health	M
Management Information Systems	M
Marketing	M
Physics	D
Public Administration	M,O
Social Psychology	D
Sustainability Management	M
Sustainable Development	M
Urban and Regional Planning	M

CLAYTON STATE UNIVERSITY

Accounting	M
Applied Psychology	M
Archives/Archival Administration	M
Biological and Biomedical Sciences—General	M
Business Administration and Management—General	M
Clinical Psychology	M
Criminal Justice and Criminology	M
Developmental Psychology	M
Education—General	M
English Education	M
Family Nurse Practitioner Studies	M
History	M
Human Resources Management	M
International Business	M
Liberal Studies	M
Mathematics Education	M
Nursing—General	M
Psychology—General	M
Sports Management	M
Supply Chain Management	M

CLEARY UNIVERSITY

Business Administration and Management—General	M,O
Business Analytics	M,O
Finance and Banking	M,O
Health Services Management and Hospital Administration	M,O
Management Strategy and Policy	M,O

CLEMSON UNIVERSITY

Accounting	M
Agricultural Education	M,D
Agricultural Sciences—General	M,D
Animal Sciences	M,D
Anthropology	M
Applied Economics	M,D
Applied Psychology	M,D
Applied Statistics	M,D
Architecture	M,D,O
Art/Fine Arts	M
Automotive Engineering	M,D,O
Bioengineering	M,D,O
Bioinformatics	M,D,O
Biological and Biomedical Sciences—General	M,D
Biomedical Engineering	M,D,O
Biosystems Engineering	M,D
Business Administration and Management—General	M,D
Business Analytics	M
Business Education	M,D
Chemical Engineering	M,D
Chemistry	M,D
Civil Engineering	M,D
Clinical Psychology	M,D,O
Clinical Research	M,D,O
Communication—General	M
Computer Engineering	M,D
Computer Science	M,D
Construction Engineering	M,D
Construction Management	M,D
Counselor Education	M,D,O
Criminal Justice and Criminology	M
Curriculum and Instruction	M,D,O
Distance Education Development	M,D,O
Early Childhood Education	M,D,O
Economics	M,D
Education—General	M,D,O
Educational Leadership and Administration	M,D,O
Educational Measurement and Evaluation	M,D,O
Electrical Engineering	M,D
Elementary Education	M,D,O
Engineering and Applied Sciences—General	M,D,O
Entomology	M,D
Entrepreneurship	M,D
Environmental and Occupational Health	M,D
Environmental Engineering	M,D
Environmental Management and Policy	M,D
Environmental Sciences	M,D
Ergonomics and Human Factors	M,D
Family and Consumer Sciences-General	D,O
Family Nurse Practitioner Studies	M,D,O
Fish, Game, and Wildlife Management	M,D
Forestry	M,D
Genetics	M,D,O
Geotechnical Engineering	M,D
Gerontological Nursing	M,D,O
Higher Education	M,D,O
Historic Preservation	M,O
History	M
Human Resources Development	M,D,O
Hydrogeology	M,D
Industrial and Organizational Psychology	M,D
Industrial/Management Engineering	M,D
International Health	M,D,O
Landscape Architecture	M,D,O
Management Information Systems	M,D,O
Marketing	M,D
Materials Engineering	M,D
Materials Sciences	M,D
Mathematics Education	M,D,O
Mathematics	M,D
Mechanical Engineering	M,D
Microbiology	M,D
Middle School Education	M,D,O
Molecular Biology	D
Nursing—General	M,D,O
Organizational Behavior	M,D
Physics	M,D
Plant Biology	M,D
Public Administration	M,D,O
Public Health—General	M,D,O
Public Policy	D,O
Reading Education	M,D,O
Real Estate	M
Recreation and Park Management	M,D,O
Rhetoric	M,D
Science Education	D,O
Secondary Education	M,D,O
Sociology	M
Special Education	M,D,O
Sports Management	M,D,O
Statistics	M,D
Structural Engineering	M,D
Student Affairs	M,D,O
Supply Chain Management	M,D
Toxicology	M,D
Transportation and Highway Engineering	M,D
Travel and Tourism	M,D,O
Veterinary Sciences	M,D
Water Resources Engineering	M,D
Writing	M,D

CLEVELAND INSTITUTE OF MUSIC

Music	M,D,O

CLEVELAND STATE UNIVERSITY

Accounting	M
Adult Education	M,D,O
Allied Health—General	M
Applied Statistics	M
Art Education	M
Art History	M
Bioethics	M,O
Biological and Biomedical Sciences—General	M,D
Biomedical Engineering	D
Business Administration and Management—General	M,D
Chemical Engineering	M,D
Chemistry	M,D
Civil Engineering	M,D
Communication Disorders	M
Communication—General	M,D,O
Counseling Psychology	M,D,O
Counselor Education	M,D,O
Early Childhood Education	M
Economic Development	M,O
Economics	M,O
Education of Students with Severe/Multiple Disabilities	M
Education—General	M,D,O
Educational Leadership and Administration	M,D,O
Educational Media/Instructional Technology	D
Educational Policy	D
Electrical Engineering	M,D
Engineering and Applied Sciences—General	M,D
English as a Second Language	M
English	M
Environmental Engineering	M,D
Environmental Management and Policy	M,O
Environmental Sciences	M,D
Foreign Languages Education	M
Geographic Information Systems	M,O
Health Education	M
Health Services Management and Hospital Administration	M
Higher Education	D
Historic Preservation	M,O
History	M
Human Resources Management	M
Industrial and Labor Relations	M
International Affairs	M
International Economics	M
Law	M,D,O
Management Information Systems	D
Marketing	D
Mathematics Education	M
Mathematics	M
Mechanical Engineering	M,D
Molecular Medicine	M,D
Museum Studies	M
Music Education	M
Music	M
Nonprofit Management	M,O
Nursing Education	D
Nursing—General	M,D
Occupational Therapy	M
Organic Chemistry	M,D
Philosophy	M,O
Physical Chemistry	M,D
Physical Education	M
Physical Therapy	D
Physician Assistant Studies	M
Physics	M
Psychology—General	M,D,O
Public Administration	M,D,O
Public Affairs	D
Public Health—General	M
Real Estate	M,O
Science Education	M
Social Work	M
Software Engineering	M,D
Spanish	M
Special Education	M
Sustainable Development	M,O
Urban and Regional Planning	M,O
Urban Education	D
Urban Studies	M,D,O
Writing	M

CLEVELAND UNIVERSITY–KANSAS CITY

Chiropractic	D
Health Education	M
Health Promotion	M

COASTAL CAROLINA UNIVERSITY

Accounting	M,O
Business Administration and Management—General	M,O
Computer Science	M,D,O
Distance Education Development	M,O
Education—General	M,O
Educational Leadership and Administration	M,O
Educational Media/Instructional Technology	M,O
English as a Second Language	M,O
Liberal Studies	M
Management Information Systems	M,D,O
Marine Sciences	M,D,O
Reading Education	M,O
Special Education	M,O
Sports Management	M,D,O
Writing	M

COGSWELL POLYTECHNICAL COLLEGE

Entrepreneurship	M

COKER COLLEGE

Business Administration and Management—General	M
Criminal Justice and Criminology	M
Curriculum and Instruction	M
Educational Media/Instructional Technology	M
Reading Education	M
Sports Management	M

THE COLBURN SCHOOL CONSERVATORY OF MUSIC

Music	M,O

COLD SPRING HARBOR LABORATORY

Biological and Biomedical Sciences—General	D

COLGATE ROCHESTER CROZER DIVINITY SCHOOL

Conflict Resolution and Mediation/Peace Studies	M,D,O
Theology	M,D,O

COLGATE UNIVERSITY

Secondary Education	M

THE COLLEGE AT BROCKPORT, STATE UNIVERSITY OF NEW YORK

Accounting	M,O
American Studies	M
Art/Fine Arts	M
Arts Administration	M,O
Biological and Biomedical Sciences—General	M,O
Chemistry	M,O
Communication—General	M
Community Health	M
Counseling Psychology	M,O
Counselor Education	M,O
Curriculum and Instruction	M
Dance	M
Early Childhood Education	M,O
Education—General	M,O
Educational Leadership and Administration	M,O
English Education	M,O
English	M,O
Environmental Sciences	M
Gerontology	M,O
Health Education	M
Health Services Management and Hospital Administration	M,O
History of Medicine	M,O
History	M,O
Liberal Studies	M,O
Mathematics Education	M,O
Mathematics	M,O
Middle School Education	M
Multilingual and Multicultural Education	M,O
Nonprofit Management	M,O
Physical Education	M,O
Psychology—General	M
Public Administration	M,O
Public Health—General	M
Public History	M
Reading Education	M
Science Education	M,O
Social Sciences Education	M,O
Social Work	M,O
Sports Management	M,O
Writing	M,O

COLLÈGE DOMINICAIN DE PHILOSOPHIE ET DE THÉOLOGIE

Philosophy	M,D
Theology	M,D,O

COLLEGE FOR CREATIVE STUDIES
- Applied Arts and Design—General M
- Art/Fine Arts M
- Automotive Engineering M
- Transportation and Highway Engineering M

COLLEGE FOR FINANCIAL PLANNING
- Finance and Banking M

COLLEGE OF CHARLESTON
- Accounting M
- Arts Administration O
- Business Administration and Management—General M
- Computer Science M
- Early Childhood Education M
- Education—General M,O
- Elementary Education M
- English as a Second Language O
- English M
- Environmental Sciences M
- Foreign Languages Education M
- Historic Preservation M
- History M
- Management Information Systems M
- Marine Biology M
- Marine Sciences M
- Mathematics Education M
- Mathematics M
- Music Education M
- Public Administration M
- Science Education M
- Special Education M
- Urban and Regional Planning O
- Writing M

COLLEGE OF EMMANUEL AND ST. CHAD
- Theology M,D,O

THE COLLEGE OF IDAHO
- Curriculum and Instruction M
- Education—General M

COLLEGE OF MOUNT SAINT VINCENT
- Education—General M,O
- Educational Media/Instructional Technology M,O
- English as a Second Language M,O
- Family Nurse Practitioner Studies M,O
- Middle School Education M,O
- Multilingual and Multicultural Education M,O
- Nursing and Healthcare Administration M,O
- Nursing Education M,O
- Nursing—General M,O
- Urban Education M,O

THE COLLEGE OF NEW JERSEY
- Addictions/Substance Abuse Counseling M,O
- Counselor Education M
- Early Childhood Education M
- Education—General M,O
- Educational Leadership and Administration M,O
- Elementary Education M
- English as a Second Language M,O
- English M
- Gender Studies O
- Health Communication M
- International and Comparative Education M,O
- International Health M
- Marriage and Family Therapy O
- Nursing—General M,O
- Public Health—General M
- Reading Education M
- Secondary Education M
- Special Education M,O

THE COLLEGE OF NEW ROCHELLE
- Acute Care/Critical Care Nursing M,O
- Art Education M
- Art Therapy M
- Communication—General M,O
- Counseling Psychology M,O
- Early Childhood Education M,O
- Education of the Gifted O
- Education—General M,O
- Educational Leadership and Administration M,O
- Elementary Education M
- English as a Second Language M,O
- Family Nurse Practitioner Studies M,O
- Human Resources Development M,O
- Marriage and Family Therapy M
- Multilingual and Multicultural Education M,O
- Nursing and Healthcare Administration M,O
- Nursing Education M,O
- Nursing—General M,O
- Public Administration M
- Reading Education M
- School Psychology M
- Special Education M
- Thanatology M,O

COLLEGE OF SAINT ELIZABETH
- Applied Behavior Analysis M,O
- Business Administration and Management—General M
- Computer and Information Systems Security M,O
- Counseling Psychology M,D
- Criminal Justice and Criminology M,O
- Data Science/Data Analytics M
- Distance Education Development M,O
- Early Childhood Education M,O
- Education—General M,O
- Educational Leadership and Administration M,D,O
- Elementary Education M,O
- English as a Second Language M,O
- Health Services Management and Hospital Administration M
- Higher Education M,D,O
- Holocaust and Genocide Studies M,O
- Human Resources Management M
- Internet and Interactive Multimedia M
- Middle School Education M,O
- Nursing—General M,O
- Nutrition M,O
- Organizational Management M
- Pastoral Ministry and Counseling M,O
- Psychology—General M,D
- Public Administration M,O
- Public Health—General M
- School Psychology M,D
- Special Education M,O
- Theology M,O

COLLEGE OF ST. JOSEPH
- Addictions/Substance Abuse Counseling M
- Business Administration and Management—General M
- Clinical Psychology M
- Counseling Psychology M
- Counselor Education M
- Education—General M
- Elementary Education M
- English Education M
- Psychology—General M
- Reading Education M
- School Psychology M
- Secondary Education M
- Social Psychology M
- Social Sciences Education M
- Special Education M

COLLEGE OF SAINT MARY
- Education—General M
- Educational Leadership and Administration M
- Educational Measurement and Evaluation M
- English as a Second Language M
- Health Education D
- Nursing—General M
- Occupational Therapy M
- Organizational Management M

THE COLLEGE OF SAINT ROSE
- Accounting M
- Business Administration and Management—General M
- Business Analytics M
- Communication Disorders M
- Computer Science M,O
- Counseling Psychology M,O
- Counselor Education M,O
- Curriculum and Instruction M,O
- Early Childhood Education M,O
- Education—General M,O
- Educational Leadership and Administration M,O
- Educational Psychology M,O
- Finance and Banking O
- Higher Education M,O
- Information Science M,O
- Middle School Education M,O
- Organizational Management O
- Reading Education M,O
- School Psychology M,O
- Secondary Education M,O
- Social Work M
- Special Education M,O
- Student Affairs M

THE COLLEGE OF ST. SCHOLASTICA
- Athletic Training and Sports Medicine M
- Business Administration and Management—General M,O
- Education—General M,O
- Exercise and Sports Science M
- Health Informatics M,O
- Management Information Systems M,O
- Nursing—General M,O
- Occupational Therapy M
- Physical Therapy D
- Social Work M

COLLEGE OF STATEN ISLAND OF THE CITY UNIVERSITY OF NEW YORK
- Accounting M
- Adult Nursing M,D,O
- African Studies M
- American Studies M
- Artificial Intelligence/Robotics M
- Asian Studies M
- Biological and Biomedical Sciences—General M
- Biotechnology M
- Business Administration and Management—General M
- Clinical Psychology M
- Computer and Information Systems Security M
- Computer Science M
- Counseling Psychology M,O
- Data Science/Data Analytics M,O
- Early Childhood Education M
- Education—General M,O
- Educational Leadership and Administration O
- Elementary Education M
- English as a Second Language M,O
- English Education M
- English M
- Environmental Sciences M
- Film, Television, and Video Theory and Criticism M
- Gerontological Nursing M,D,O
- Health Services Management and Hospital Administration M
- History M
- Latin American Studies M
- Liberal Studies M
- Management Strategy and Policy M
- Mathematics Education M
- Media Studies M
- Middle School Education M
- Multilingual and Multicultural Education O
- Near and Middle Eastern Studies M
- Neuroscience M
- Nursing—General D
- Physical Therapy D
- Public History O
- Secondary Education M
- Social Work M
- Software Engineering M
- Special Education M,O
- Western European Studies M

COLLEGE OF THE ATLANTIC
- Environmental Management and Policy M

THE COLLEGE OF WILLIAM AND MARY
- Accounting M
- Addictions/Substance Abuse Counseling M,D
- American Studies M,D
- Anthropology M,D
- Applied Mathematics M,D
- Applied Physics M,D
- Applied Science and Technology M,D
- Artificial Intelligence/Robotics M,D
- Atmospheric Sciences M,D
- Biological and Biomedical Sciences—General M
- Biomathematics M,D
- Business Administration and Management—General M
- Business Analytics M
- Chemistry M
- Clinical Laboratory Sciences/Medical Technology M,D
- Computational Biology M,D
- Computational Sciences M,D
- Computer Science M,D
- Counselor Education M,D
- Curriculum and Instruction M,D
- Education of the Gifted M
- Education—General M,D,O*
- Educational Leadership and Administration M,D
- Educational Media/Instructional Technology M,D
- Educational Policy M,D
- Elementary Education M
- English as a Second Language M
- English M
- Environmental Sciences M,D
- Foreign Languages Education M
- Geographic Information Systems M,D
- History M,D
- International Development M
- Law M,D
- Marine Sciences M,D
- Marriage and Family Therapy M,D
- Materials Engineering M,D
- Materials Sciences M,D
- Mathematics Education M
- Mathematics M
- Medical Physics M,D
- Multilingual and Multicultural Education M
- Nanotechnology M,D
- Neuroscience M,D
- Operations Research M
- Optical Sciences M,D
- Physics M,D
- Polymer Science and Engineering M,D
- Psychology—General M
- Public Policy M
- Reading Education M
- School Psychology M,O
- Science Education M
- Secondary Education M
- Special Education M

COLORADO CHRISTIAN UNIVERSITY
- Business Administration and Management—General M
- Business Education M
- Computer and Information Systems Security M
- Counseling Psychology M
- Curriculum and Instruction M
- Distance Education Development M
- Early Childhood Education M
- Education—General M
- Educational Media/Instructional Technology M
- Elementary Education M
- Project Management M
- Special Education M

THE COLORADO COLLEGE
- American Studies M
- Art Education M
- Education—General M
- Elementary Education M
- English Education M
- Foreign Languages Education M
- Humanities M
- Liberal Studies M
- Mathematics Education M
- Music Education M
- Science Education M
- Secondary Education M
- Social Sciences Education M

COLORADO MESA UNIVERSITY
- Business Administration and Management—General M
- Education of the Gifted M,O
- Education—General M,O
- Educational Leadership and Administration M,O
- English as a Second Language M,O
- Family Nurse Practitioner Studies M,D,O
- Health Informatics M,D,O
- Nursing Education M,D,O
- Nursing—General M,D,O
- Special Education M,O

COLORADO SCHOOL OF MINES
- Applied Mathematics M,D
- Applied Physics M,D
- Applied Statistics M,D
- Bioengineering M,D
- Chemical Engineering M,D
- Chemistry M,D
- Civil Engineering M,D
- Computer Science M,D
- Construction Engineering M,D
- Electrical Engineering M,D
- Electronic Materials M,D
- Energy Management and Policy M,D
- Engineering and Applied Sciences—General M,D,O
- Engineering Management M,D
- Environmental Engineering M,D
- Environmental Sciences M,D
- Geochemistry M,D
- Geological Engineering M,D
- Geology M,D
- Geophysics M,D
- Humanities O
- Hydrology M,D
- Management of Technology M,D
- Materials Engineering M,D
- Materials Sciences M,D
- Mechanical Engineering M,D
- Metallurgical Engineering and Metallurgy M,D
- Mineral Economics M,D
- Mineral/Mining Engineering M,D
- Nuclear Engineering M,D
- Operations Research M,D
- Petroleum Engineering M,D
- Physics M,D
- Social Sciences O

COLORADO SCHOOL OF TRADITIONAL CHINESE MEDICINE
- Acupuncture and Oriental Medicine M

COLORADO STATE UNIVERSITY
- Accounting M
- Adult Education M,D
- Advertising and Public Relations M,D
- Agricultural Economics and Agribusiness M,D
- Agricultural Education M
- Agricultural Sciences—General M,D
- Agronomy and Soil Sciences M,D
- Animal Sciences M,D
- Anthropology M,D
- Art History M
- Art/Fine Arts M
- Arts Administration M
- Atmospheric Sciences M,D
- Biochemistry M,D
- Bioengineering M,D
- Biological and Biomedical Sciences—General M,D
- Biomedical Engineering M,D
- Botany M,D
- Business Administration and Management—General M
- Chemical Engineering M,D
- Chemistry M,D
- Child and Family Studies M,D
- Civil Engineering M,D
- Computer Science M,D
- Conservation Biology M,D
- Construction Management M
- Consumer Economics M
- Counselor Education M,D
- Economics M,D
- Education—General M,D
- Educational Leadership and Administration M,D
- Electrical Engineering M,D
- Energy Management and Policy M
- Engineering and Applied Sciences—General M,D
- English M
- Entomology M,D
- Environmental and Occupational Health M,D
- Environmental Management and Policy M,D
- Epidemiology M,D
- Ethnic Studies M
- Exercise and Sports Science M,D
- Finance and Banking M
- Fish, Game, and Wildlife Management M,D
- Food Science and Technology M,D
- French M
- Geosciences M,D

*M—masters degree; D—doctorate; O—other advanced degree; *—Close-Up and/or Display*

Higher Education	M,D
History	M
Horticulture	M,D
Human Development	M,D
Immunology	M,D
Interdisciplinary Studies	M,D
Landscape Architecture	M,D
Liberal Studies	M
Management Information Systems	M
Marriage and Family Therapy	M,D
Materials Sciences	M,D
Mathematics	M,D
Mechanical Engineering	M,D
Media Studies	M,D
Microbiology	M,D
Music	M
Natural Resources	M,D
Nutrition	M,D
Occupational Therapy	M,D
Pathology	M,D
Philosophy	M
Physics	M,D
Plant Pathology	M,D
Plant Sciences	M,D
Political Science	M,D
Psychology—General	M,D
Public History	M
Recreation and Park Management	M,D
Rhetoric	M
Social Work	M,D
Sociology	M,D
Speech and Interpersonal Communication	M,D
Statistics	M,D
Student Affairs	M,D
Sustainability Management	M
Sustainable Development	M,O
Systems Engineering	M,D
Travel and Tourism	M,D
Veterinary Medicine	D
Veterinary Sciences	M,D
Water Resources	M,D
Writing	M
Zoology	M,D

COLORADO STATE UNIVERSITY–GLOBAL CAMPUS

Accounting	M
Business Administration and Management—General	M
Criminal Justice and Criminology	M
Education—General	M
Educational Leadership and Administration	M
Finance and Banking	M
Health Services Management and Hospital Administration	M
Human Resources Management	M
International Business	M
Management Information Systems	M
Organizational Management	M
Project Management	M

COLORADO STATE UNIVERSITY–PUEBLO

Applied Science and Technology	M
Art Education	M
Biochemistry	M
Biological and Biomedical Sciences—General	M
Business Administration and Management—General	M
Chemistry	M
Education—General	M
Educational Media/Instructional Technology	M
Engineering and Applied Sciences—General	M
Foreign Languages Education	M
Health Education	M
Industrial/Management Engineering	M
Music Education	M
Nursing—General	M
Physical Education	M
Special Education	M
Systems Engineering	M

COLORADO TECHNICAL UNIVERSITY AURORA

Accounting	M
Business Administration and Management—General	M
Computer and Information Systems Security	M
Computer Engineering	M
Computer Science	M
Conflict Resolution and Mediation/Peace Studies	M
Criminal Justice and Criminology	M
Data Science/Data Analytics	M
Electrical Engineering	M
Finance and Banking	M
Human Resources Management	M
Industrial and Manufacturing Management	M
Management of Technology	M
Marketing	M
Project Management	M
Software Engineering	M
Systems Engineering	M

COLORADO TECHNICAL UNIVERSITY COLORADO SPRINGS

Accounting	M,D
Business Administration and Management—General	M,D
Computer and Information Systems Security	M,D
Computer Engineering	M
Computer Science	M,D
Conflict Resolution and Mediation/Peace Studies	M,D
Criminal Justice and Criminology	M
Data Science/Data Analytics	M,D
Electrical Engineering	M
Finance and Banking	M,D
Human Resources Management	M,D
Industrial and Manufacturing Management	M,D
Logistics	M,D
Management of Technology	M,D
Marketing	M,D
Project Management	M,D
Software Engineering	M,D
Systems Engineering	M

COLUMBIA COLLEGE (MO)

Accounting	M
Business Administration and Management—General	M
Criminal Justice and Criminology	M
Education—General	M
Educational Leadership and Administration	M
Human Resources Management	M

COLUMBIA COLLEGE (SC)

Criminal Justice and Criminology	M
Education—General	M
Educational Leadership and Administration	M
Elementary Education	M
Higher Education	M
Organizational Management	M

COLUMBIA COLLEGE CHICAGO

Art History	M
Art/Fine Arts	M
Business Administration and Management—General	M
Communication—General	M
English	M
Entertainment Management	M
Film, Television, and Video Production	M
Music	M
Photography	M
Writing	M

COLUMBIA COLLEGE OF NURSING

Nursing—General	M

COLUMBIA INTERNATIONAL UNIVERSITY

Counselor Education	M,D,O
Cultural Studies	M,D,O
Curriculum and Instruction	M,D,O
Early Childhood Education	M,D,O
Education—General	M,D,O
Educational Leadership and Administration	M,D,O
Elementary Education	M,D,O
English as a Second Language	M,D,O
Missions and Missiology	M,D,O
Multilingual and Multicultural Education	M,D,O
Pastoral Ministry and Counseling	M,D,O
Religious Education	M,D,O
Theology	M,D,O

COLUMBIA SOUTHERN UNIVERSITY

Business Administration and Management—General	M,D
Criminal Justice and Criminology	M
Emergency Management	M
Environmental and Occupational Health	M
Finance and Banking	M
Health Services Management and Hospital Administration	M
Human Resources Management	M
Marketing	M
Organizational Management	M

COLUMBIA THEOLOGICAL SEMINARY

Theology	M,D

COLUMBIA UNIVERSITY

Accounting	M,D
Actuarial Science	M
Acute Care/Critical Care Nursing	M,O
Adult Nursing	M,O
African Studies	M,D
African-American Studies	M,D
Allopathic Medicine	M,D
American Studies	M,D
Anatomy	M,D
Anthropology	M,D
Applied Mathematics	M,D
Applied Physics	M,D
Archaeology	M,D
Architecture	M,D
Archives/Archival Administration	M
Art History	M,D
Art/Fine Arts	M,D*
Asian Studies	M,D,O
Astronomy	M,D
Atmospheric Sciences	M,D
Biochemistry	M,D
Bioethics	M
Biological and Biomedical Sciences—General	M,D,O*
Biomedical Engineering	M,D
Biophysics	M,D
Biostatistics	M,D
Biotechnology	M,D
Business Administration and Management—General	M,D
Cell Biology	M,D
Chemical Engineering	M,D
Chemical Physics	M,D
Chemistry	M,D
Civil Engineering	M,D
Classics	M,D
Communication—General	M,D
Community Health	M,D
Comparative Literature	M,D
Computer Engineering	M,D
Computer Science	M,D
Conflict Resolution and Mediation/Peace Studies	M
Conservation Biology	M,D
Construction Engineering	M,D
Construction Management	M,D
Corporate and Organizational Communication	M
Data Science/Data Analytics	M
Dentistry	D
Developmental Biology	M,D
East European and Russian Studies	M,D
Ecology	M,D
Economics	M,D
Electrical Engineering	M,D
Engineering and Applied Sciences—General	M,D
English	M,D
Entrepreneurship	M
Environmental and Occupational Health	M,D
Environmental Design	M
Environmental Engineering	M,D
Environmental Management and Policy	M
Environmental Sciences	M,D
Epidemiology	M,D
Ethics	M
Evolutionary Biology	M,D
Family Nurse Practitioner Studies	M,O
Film, Television, and Video Production	M
Film, Television, and Video Theory and Criticism	M
Finance and Banking	M,D
Financial Engineering	M,D
Foreign Languages Education	M,D
Foundations and Philosophy of Education	M,D
French	M,D
Genetics	M,D
Geosciences	M,D
German	M,D
Gerontological Nursing	M,O
Health Services Management and Hospital Administration	M
Hispanic Studies	M,D
Historic Preservation	M,D,O
History	M,D
Human Resources Management	M
Industrial/Management Engineering	M,D
Information Studies	M
International Affairs	M,D
International Business	M
Italian	M,D
Japanese	M,D
Jewish Studies	M,D
Journalism	M,D
Kinesiology and Movement Studies	M,D
Landscape Architecture	M
Latin American Studies	M,D
Law	M,D
Legal and Justice Studies	M,D
Management of Technology	M
Marketing	M,D
Materials Engineering	M,D
Materials Sciences	M,D
Maternal and Child Health	M,D
Mathematics	M,D
Mechanical Engineering	M,D*
Mechanics	M,D
Media Studies	M
Medical Informatics	M,D,O
Medical Physics	M,D
Medieval and Renaissance Studies	M,D
Microbiology	M,D
Molecular Biology	D
Museum Studies	M,D
Music	M,D
Near and Middle Eastern Studies	M,D
Neurobiology	D
Nonprofit Management	M
Nurse Anesthesia	M,O
Nurse Midwifery	M
Nursing—General	M,D,O
Nutrition	M,D
Occupational Therapy	M,D
Operations Research	M,D
Oral and Dental Sciences	M,D,O
Pathobiology	M,D
Pathology	M,D
Pediatric Nursing	M,O
Pharmaceutical Administration	M
Pharmacology	M,D
Philosophy	M,D
Physical Therapy	D
Physics	M,D
Physiology	M,D
Political Science	M,D
Psychiatric Nursing	M,O
Psychology—General	M,D
Public Administration	M
Public Health—General	M,D
Public Policy	M
Quantitative Analysis	M,D
Real Estate	M
Religion	M,D
Romance Languages	M,D
Russian	M,D
Science Education	M,D,O
Slavic Languages	M,D
Social Sciences	M,D
Social Work	M,D
Sociology	M,D
Spanish	M,D
Sports Management	M
Statistics	M,D
Structural Biology	D
Sustainability Management	M
Sustainable Development	M,D
Theater	M,D
Toxicology	M,D
Translation and Interpretation	M,D
Urban and Regional Planning	M,D
Western European Studies	M,D
Writing	M

COLUMBUS COLLEGE OF ART & DESIGN

Art/Fine Arts	M

COLUMBUS STATE UNIVERSITY

Art Education	M
Biological and Biomedical Sciences—General	M
Business Administration and Management—General	M,O
Chemistry	M,O
Clinical Psychology	M,D,O
Computer and Information Systems Security	M,O
Computer Science	M,O
Counselor Education	M,D,O
Criminal Justice and Criminology	M
Curriculum and Instruction	M,D,O
Early Childhood Education	M,O
Education—General	M,D,O
Educational Leadership and Administration	M,D,O
English as a Second Language	O
English Education	M,O
Environmental Management and Policy	M
Environmental Sciences	M,O
Exercise and Sports Science	M
Family Nurse Practitioner Studies	M
Health Education	M
Health Services Management and Hospital Administration	M
Higher Education	M,D,O
History	M,O
Homeland Security	M
Human Resources Management	M,O
Mathematics Education	M,O
Mathematics	M,O
Middle School Education	M,O
Modeling and Simulation	M,O
Music Education	M,O
Music	M,O
Nursing and Healthcare Administration	M
Nursing Education	M
Nursing Informatics	M
Nursing—General	M
Organizational Management	M,O
Physical Education	M
Political Science	M
Public Administration	M
Science Education	M,O
Secondary Education	M,O
Social Sciences Education	M,O
Special Education	M,O
Theater	M
Urban Studies	M

CONCORDIA COLLEGE

Education—General	M
Foreign Languages Education	M

CONCORDIA COLLEGE–NEW YORK

Organizational Management	M
Special Education	M

CONCORDIA LUTHERAN SEMINARY

Theology	M,O

CONCORDIA SEMINARY

Theology	M,D,O

CONCORDIA THEOLOGICAL SEMINARY

Theology	M,D

CONCORDIA UNIVERSITY (CANADA)

Adult Education	M,O
Aerospace/Aeronautical Engineering	M
Anthropology	M,D
Applied Arts and Design—General	M,O
Art Education	M,D
Art History	M,D
Art Therapy	M
Art/Fine Arts	M
Biological and Biomedical Sciences—General	M,D,O
Biotechnology	M,D,O
Business Administration and Management—General	M,D,O
Chemistry	M,D
Child and Family Studies	M
Civil Engineering	M,D,O
Clinical Psychology	D,O
Communication—General	M,D,O
Computer and Information Systems Security	M,D,O
Computer Art and Design	M,O
Computer Engineering	M,D
Computer Science	M,D,O
Construction Engineering	M,D,O
Cultural Anthropology	M,D
Economic Development	O
Economics	M,D,O
Education—General	M,O
Educational Media/Instructional Technology	M,O
Electrical Engineering	M,D
Engineering and Applied Sciences—General	M,D,O
English as a Second Language	M,O
English	M,D
Environmental Engineering	M,D,O
Environmental Management and Policy	M,D,O
Exercise and Sports Science	M
Film, Television, and Video Production	M,D
Film, Television, and Video Theory and Criticism	M,D
Finance and Banking	M,D,O
French	M,O

Game Design and Development	M,D,O
Genomic Sciences	M,D,O
Geography	M,D,O
History	M,D
Humanities	D
Industrial/Management Engineering	M,D,O
Interdisciplinary Studies	M,D
Internet and Interactive Multimedia	M,D,O
Jewish Studies	M
Journalism	M,O
Linguistics	M,O
Marketing	M,D,O
Mathematics Education	M,D
Mathematics	M,D
Mechanical Engineering	M,D,O
Media Studies	M,D,O
Music	O
Organizational Management	M,O
Philosophy	M
Physics	M,D
Political Science	M,D
Psychology—General	M
Public Administration	M,D
Public Affairs	O
Public Policy	M,D
Religion	M,D
Sociology	M,D
Software Engineering	M,D,O
Statistics	M,D
Supply Chain Management	M,D,O
Systems Engineering	M,D,O
Telecommunications Management	M,D,O
Textile Design	M
Theology	M
Therapies—Dance, Drama, and Music	M
Translation and Interpretation	M,O
Urban and Regional Planning	O
Urban Studies	M,D,O
Writing	M

CONCORDIA UNIVERSITY (UNITED STATES)

Art Education	M,D
Business Administration and Management—General	M
Curriculum and Instruction	M,D
Early Childhood Education	M,D
Education—General	M,D
Educational Leadership and Administration	M,D
Educational Media/Instructional Technology	M,D
Elementary Education	M,D
English as a Second Language	M,D
Environmental Education	M,D
Health Education	M,D
Higher Education	M,D
Law	D
Mathematics Education	M,D
Physical Education	M,D
Reading Education	M,D
Science Education	M,D
Secondary Education	M,D
Social Sciences Education	M,D
Vocational and Technical Education	M,D

CONCORDIA UNIVERSITY ANN ARBOR

Curriculum and Instruction	M
Educational Leadership and Administration	M
Organizational Management	M

CONCORDIA UNIVERSITY CHICAGO

Business Administration and Management—General	M
Counseling Psychology	M
Counselor Education	M,O
Curriculum and Instruction	M
Early Childhood Education	M,D
Education—General	M
Educational Leadership and Administration	M,D,O
Educational Media/Instructional Technology	M
Elementary Education	M
Exercise and Sports Science	M
Gerontology	M
Human Services	M
Liberal Studies	M
Music	M
Psychology—General	M
Reading Education	M
Religion	M
Religious Education	M
Secondary Education	M

CONCORDIA UNIVERSITY IRVINE

Applied Social Research	M
Business Administration and Management—General	M
Counselor Education	M
Cultural Studies	M
Curriculum and Instruction	M
Education—General	M
Educational Leadership and Administration	M
Educational Media/Instructional Technology	M
Health Services Management and Hospital Administration	M
International Affairs	M*
Nursing—General	M
Physical Education	M
Religion	M
Sports Management	M
Theology	M

CONCORDIA UNIVERSITY, NEBRASKA

Computer and Information Systems Security	M
Computer Science	M
Early Childhood Education	M
Education—General	M
Educational Leadership and Administration	M
Elementary Education	M
Pastoral Ministry and Counseling	M
Reading Education	M
Religious Education	M
Secondary Education	M

CONCORDIA UNIVERSITY OF EDMONTON

Computer and Information Systems Security	M
Religion	M
Theology	M

CONCORDIA UNIVERSITY, ST. PAUL

Allied Health—General	M,D
Business Administration and Management—General	M
Computer and Information Systems Security	M
Corporate and Organizational Communication	M
Curriculum and Instruction	M,D,O
Early Childhood Education	M,D,O
Education—General	M,D,O
Educational Leadership and Administration	M,D,O
Educational Media/Instructional Technology	M,D,O
Exercise and Sports Science	M,D
Health Services Management and Hospital Administration	M
Human Resources Management	M
Organizational Management	M
Physical Therapy	M,D
Reading Education	M,D,O
Special Education	M,D,O
Sports Management	M,D

CONCORDIA UNIVERSITY TEXAS

Education—General	M

CONCORDIA UNIVERSITY WISCONSIN

Art Education	M
Business Administration and Management—General	M
Child and Family Studies	M
Corporate and Organizational Communication	M
Counselor Education	M
Early Childhood Education	M
Education—General	M
Educational Leadership and Administration	M
Environmental Education	M
Family Nurse Practitioner Studies	M,D
Finance and Banking	M
Health Education	M,D
Health Services Management and Hospital Administration	M
Human Resources Management	M
International Business	M
Management Information Systems	M
Marketing	M
Music	M
Nursing—General	M,D
Occupational Therapy	M
Organizational Management	M
Pharmacy	M,D
Physical Therapy	D
Public Administration	M
Reading Education	M
Rehabilitation Sciences	M
Risk Management	M
Special Education	M

CONCORD LAW SCHOOL

Law	D

CONCORD UNIVERSITY

Education—General	M
Educational Leadership and Administration	M
Health Promotion	M
Reading Education	M
Social Work	M
Special Education	M

CONSERVATORIO DE MUSICA DE PUERTO RICO

Music Education	M
Music	O

CONVERSE COLLEGE

Art Education	M
Education of the Gifted	M
Educational Leadership and Administration	M,O
Elementary Education	M
English Education	M
English	M
History	M
Liberal Studies	M
Marriage and Family Therapy	M
Mathematics Education	M
Middle School Education	M
Music Education	M
Music	M
Political Science	M
Reading Education	O
Science Education	M
Secondary Education	M
Social Sciences Education	M
Special Education	M
Writing	M

THE CONWAY SCHOOL

Landscape Architecture	M

COOPER UNION FOR THE ADVANCEMENT OF SCIENCE AND ART

Architecture	M
Chemical Engineering	M
Civil Engineering	M
Electrical Engineering	M
Engineering and Applied Sciences—General	M
Mechanical Engineering	M

COPENHAGEN BUSINESS SCHOOL

Business Administration and Management—General	M,D
Economics	M,D
Health Services Management and Hospital Administration	M,D
International Business	M,D
Logistics	M,D
Management Information Systems	M,D
Public Administration	M,D

COPPIN STATE UNIVERSITY

Addictions/Substance Abuse Counseling	M
Adult Education	M
Criminal Justice and Criminology	M
Curriculum and Instruction	M
Education—General	M
Family Nurse Practitioner Studies	M,O
Human Services	M
Nursing—General	M,O
Reading Education	M
Rehabilitation Counseling	M
Special Education	M

CORBAN UNIVERSITY

Business Administration and Management—General	M
Education—General	M
Nonprofit Management	M
Pastoral Ministry and Counseling	M,D,O
Theology	M,D,O

CORNELL UNIVERSITY

Accounting	M,D
Adult Education	M,D
Aerospace/Aeronautical Engineering	M,D
African Studies	M,D
African-American Studies	M,D
Agricultural Economics and Agribusiness	M,D
Agricultural Education	M,D
Agricultural Engineering	M,D
Agronomy and Soil Sciences	M,D
American Studies	M,D
Analytical Chemistry	D
Animal Behavior	D
Animal Sciences	M,D
Anthropology	D
Applied Economics	M,D
Applied Mathematics	M,D
Applied Physics	M,D
Applied Statistics	M,D
Archaeology	M,D
Architectural History	M,D
Architecture	M,D
Art History	D
Art/Fine Arts	M
Artificial Intelligence/Robotics	M,D
Asian Languages	M,D
Asian Studies	M,D
Astronomy	D
Astrophysics	D
Atmospheric Sciences	M,D
Biochemical Engineering	M,D
Biochemistry	M,D
Bioengineering	M,D
Biological and Biomedical Sciences—General	D
Biomedical Engineering	M,D
Biometry	M,D
Biophysics	D
Biopsychology	D
Biotechnology	M,D
Business Administration and Management—General	M,D
Cell Biology	D
Chemical Engineering	M,D
Chemical Physics	D
Chemistry	D
Child and Family Studies	M,D
Civil Engineering	M,D
Classics	D
Clothing and Textiles	M,D
Cognitive Sciences	D
Communication—General	M,D
Comparative Literature	D
Computational Biology	D
Computational Sciences	M,D
Computer Art and Design	M,D
Computer Engineering	M,D
Computer Science	M,D
Conflict Resolution and Mediation/Peace Studies	M,D
Conservation Biology	M,D
Consumer Economics	M,D
Corporate and Organizational Communication	M,D
Cultural Anthropology	D
Cultural Studies	M,D
Curriculum and Instruction	M,D
Demography and Population Studies	M,D
Developmental Biology	D
Developmental Psychology	M,D
East European and Russian Studies	M,D
Ecology	M,D
Economic Development	M,D
Economics	M,D
Education—General	M,D
Educational Policy	M,D
Electrical Engineering	M,D
Energy and Power Engineering	M,D
Engineering and Applied Sciences—General	M,D
Engineering Management	M,D
Engineering Physics	M,D
English	M,D
Entomology	M,D
Environmental Design	M
Environmental Engineering	M,D
Environmental Management and Policy	M,D
Environmental Sciences	M,D
Ergonomics and Human Factors	M
Ethnic Studies	M,D
Evolutionary Biology	D
Experimental Psychology	D
Facilities Management	M
Finance and Banking	D
Fish, Game, and Wildlife Management	M,D
Food Science and Technology	M,D
Foreign Languages Education	M,D
Forestry	M,D
French	D
Gender Studies	M,D
Genetics	D
Genomic Sciences	D
Geochemistry	M,D
Geology	M,D
Geophysics	M,D
Geosciences	M,D
Geotechnical Engineering	M,D
German	M,D
Health Communication	M,D
Health Services Management and Hospital Administration	M,D
Hispanic and Latin American Languages	D
Historic Preservation	M,D
History of Science and Technology	M,D
History	M,D
Horticulture	M,D
Hospitality Management	M,D
Human Development	M,D
Human Resources Management	M,D
Human-Computer Interaction	M,D
Hydrology	M,D
Industrial and Labor Relations	M,D
Industrial/Management Engineering	M,D
Information Science	D
Information Studies	D
Inorganic Chemistry	D
Interior Design	M
International Affairs	D
Italian	D
Jewish Studies	M,D
Landscape Architecture	M
Latin American Studies	M,D
Law	M,D
Limnology	D
Linguistics	M,D
Manufacturing Engineering	M,D
Marine Geology	M,D
Marine Sciences	M,D
Marketing	D
Materials Engineering	M,D
Materials Sciences	M,D
Mathematics Education	M,D
Mathematics	D
Mechanical Engineering	M,D
Mechanics	M,D
Media Studies	M,D
Medieval and Renaissance Studies	M,D
Microbiology	D
Mineralogy	M,D
Molecular Biology	M,D
Music	M,D
Nanotechnology	M,D
Natural Resources	M,D
Near and Middle Eastern Studies	M,D
Neurobiology	D
Nutrition	M,D
Oceanography	D
Operations Research	M,D
Organic Chemistry	D
Organizational Behavior	M,D
Paleontology	M,D
Philosophy	D
Photography	M,D
Physical Chemistry	D
Physics	M,D
Physiology	M,D
Planetary and Space Sciences	D
Plant Biology	M,D
Plant Molecular Biology	M,D
Plant Pathology	M,D
Plant Physiology	M,D
Plant Sciences	M,D
Political Science	D
Polymer Science and Engineering	M,D
Psychology—General	D
Public Affairs	M
Public Policy	M,D
Real Estate	M
Religion	M,D
Romance Languages	M,D
Rural Sociology	M,D
Scandinavian Languages	M,D
Secondary Education	M,D
Slavic Languages	M,D
Social Psychology	M,D
Social Work	M,D

*M—masters degree; D—doctorate; O—other advanced degree; *—Close-Up and/or Display*

Sociology M,D
Spanish D
Statistics M,D
Structural Engineering M,D
Sustainable Development M,D
Systems Engineering M,D
Textile Design M,D
Textile Sciences and Engineering M,D
Theater D
Theoretical Chemistry D
Theoretical Physics M,D
Toxicology M,D
Transportation and Highway Engineering M,D
Urban and Regional Planning M,D
Urban Design M,D
Veterinary Medicine D
Water Resources Engineering M,D
Water Resources M,D
Western European Studies M,D
Women's Studies M,D
Writing M,D

CORNERSTONE UNIVERSITY
Business Administration and Management—General M,O
Education—General M,O
English as a Second Language M,O

COVENANT COLLEGE
Education—General M

COVENANT THEOLOGICAL SEMINARY
Pastoral Ministry and Counseling M,D,O
Theology M,D,O

COX COLLEGE
Family Nurse Practitioner Studies M
Nursing and Healthcare Administration M
Nursing Education M
Nursing—General M

CRANBROOK ACADEMY OF ART
Architecture M
Art/Fine Arts M
Photography M
Textile Design M

CRANDALL UNIVERSITY
Education—General M
Organizational Management M
Reading Education M

CREIGHTON UNIVERSITY
Accounting M,D
Adult Nursing M,D,O
Allied Health—General M,D
Allopathic Medicine D
Anatomy M
Anthropology M
Bioethics M
Biological and Biomedical Sciences—General M,D
Business Administration and Management—General M,D
Business Analytics M,D
Conflict Resolution and Mediation/Peace Studies M,D,O
Counselor Education M
Dentistry D
Education—General M
Educational Leadership and Administration M,D
Elementary Education M
Emergency Medical Services M
English M
Family Nurse Practitioner Studies M,D,O
Finance and Banking M,D
Gerontological Nursing M,D,O
Health Promotion M
Health Services Management and Hospital Administration M
Immunology M,D
Investment Management M,D
Law M,D,O
Maternal and Child/Neonatal Nursing M,D,O
Medical Microbiology M,D
Medical Physics M
Nursing and Healthcare Administration M,D,O
Nursing—General M,D,O
Occupational Therapy D
Organizational Management M
Pediatric Nursing M,D,O
Pharmaceutical Sciences M
Pharmacology M,D
Pharmacy D
Physical Therapy D
Physics M
Psychiatric Nursing M,D,O
Public Health—General M
School Psychology M
Secondary Education M
Theology M
Writing M

CRISWELL COLLEGE
Jewish Studies M
Pastoral Ministry and Counseling M
Theology M

CROWN COLLEGE
Theology M

CULVER-STOCKTON COLLEGE
Accounting M
Business Administration and Management—General M
Finance and Banking M

CUMBERLAND UNIVERSITY
Business Administration and Management—General M
Education—General M
Public Administration M

CUNY GRADUATE SCHOOL OF JOURNALISM
Journalism M

CURRY COLLEGE
Business Administration and Management—General M,O
Criminal Justice and Criminology M
Education—General M,O
Elementary Education M,O
Finance and Banking M,O
Foundations and Philosophy of Education M,O
Nursing—General M
Reading Education M,O
Special Education M,O

CURTIS INSTITUTE OF MUSIC
Music M

DAEMEN COLLEGE
Accounting M
Adult Nursing M,D,O
Arts Administration M
Business Administration and Management—General M
Community Health M
Early Childhood Education M
Education—General M
Epidemiology M
Health Education M
Health Services Management and Hospital Administration M
International Business M
Management Information Systems M
Marketing M
Medical/Surgical Nursing M,D,O
Middle School Education M
Nonprofit Management M
Nursing and Healthcare Administration M,D,O
Nursing Education M,D,O
Nursing—General M,D,O
Physical Therapy D,O
Physician Assistant Studies M
Public Health—General M
Social Work M
Special Education M

DAKOTA STATE UNIVERSITY
Business Administration and Management—General M,D,O
Business Analytics M,D,O
Computer Science M,D,O
Education—General M
Educational Media/Instructional Technology M
Health Informatics M,D,O
Information Science M,D,O
Management Information Systems M,D,O

DAKOTA WESLEYAN UNIVERSITY
Curriculum and Instruction M
Education—General M
Educational Leadership and Administration M
Secondary Education M

DALHOUSIE UNIVERSITY
Agricultural Engineering M,D
Agricultural Sciences—General M
Agronomy and Soil Sciences M
Allopathic Medicine M,D
Anatomy M,D
Animal Sciences M
Anthropology M,D
Applied Mathematics M,D
Aquaculture M
Architecture M
Biochemistry M,D
Bioengineering M,D
Bioinformatics M,D
Biological and Biomedical Sciences—General M,D
Biomedical Engineering M,D
Biophysics M,D
Botany M,D
Business Administration and Management—General M,O
Chemical Engineering M,D
Chemistry M,D
Civil Engineering M,D
Classics M,D
Clinical Psychology M,D
Communication Disorders M
Community Health M
Computer Engineering M,D
Computer Science M,D
Ecology M,D
Economics M,D
Electrical Engineering M,D
Electronic Commerce M,D
Engineering and Applied Sciences—General M,D
English M,D
Environmental Biology M
Environmental Engineering M,D
Environmental Management and Policy M
Environmental Sciences M
Epidemiology M
Finance and Banking M
Food Science and Technology M,D
French M,D
Geosciences M,D
German M
Health Education M
Health Services Management and Hospital Administration M,D
History M,D
Horticulture M
Human-Computer Interaction M
Immunology M,D
Industrial/Management Engineering M,D
Information Studies M
Interdisciplinary Studies D
International Development M
Kinesiology and Movement Studies M
Law M,D
Leisure Studies M
Library Science M
Management Information Systems M
Marine Affairs M
Materials Engineering M,D
Mathematics M,D
Mechanical Engineering M,D
Medical Informatics M,D
Microbiology M,D
Mineral/Mining Engineering M,D
Music M
Natural Resources M
Neurobiology M,D
Neuroscience M,D
Nursing—General M,D
Occupational Therapy M
Oceanography M,D
Oral and Dental Sciences M
Pathology M,D
Pharmacology M,D
Philosophy M,D
Physical Therapy M
Physics M,D
Physiology M,D
Plant Pathology M
Plant Physiology M
Political Science M,D
Psychology—General M,D
Public Administration M,O
Rural Planning and Studies M
Social Work M
Sociology M,D
Statistics M,D
Urban and Regional Planning M
Water Resources M

DALLAS BAPTIST UNIVERSITY
Accounting M
Asian Studies M
Business Administration and Management—General M,D
Communication—General M
Conflict Resolution and Mediation/Peace Studies M
Corporate and Organizational Communication M
Counselor Education M
Criminal Justice and Criminology M
Curriculum and Instruction M
Distance Education Development M
Early Childhood Education M,D
Education—General M
Educational Leadership and Administration M,D
Educational Media/Instructional Technology M
Elementary Education M
Engineering Management M
English as a Second Language M
Entrepreneurship M
Finance and Banking M
Health Services Management and Hospital Administration M
Higher Education M,D
Human Resources Management M
Interdisciplinary Studies M
International Affairs M
International Business M
Kinesiology and Movement Studies M
Liberal Studies M
Management Information Systems M
Management of Technology M
Marketing M
Missions and Missiology M
Multilingual and Multicultural Education M
Nonprofit Management M
Organizational Management M,D
Pastoral Ministry and Counseling M,D
Project Management M
Reading Education M
Religion M
Religious Education M
Secondary Education M
Special Education M
Sports Management M
Student Affairs M
Theology M
Western European Studies M

DALLAS THEOLOGICAL SEMINARY
Adult Education M,D,O
Child and Family Studies M,D,O
Educational Leadership and Administration M,D,O
Jewish Studies M,D,O
Media Studies M,D,O
Missions and Missiology M,D,O
Pastoral Ministry and Counseling M,D,O
Philosophy M,D,O
Religion M,D,O
Religious Education M,D,O
Theology M,D,O

DANIEL MORGAN GRADUATE SCHOOL OF NATIONAL SECURITY
National Security M

DARTMOUTH COLLEGE
Allopathic Medicine D
Astronomy D
Biochemistry M,D
Biological and Biomedical Sciences—General D
Biomedical Engineering M,D
Biostatistics M,D
Business Administration and Management—General M

Cell Biology D
Chemical Engineering M,D
Chemistry M,D
Cognitive Sciences D
Comparative Literature M
Computer Engineering M,D
Computer Science M,D
Ecology D
Electrical Engineering M,D
Energy and Power Engineering M,D
Engineering and Applied Sciences—General M,D
Engineering Management M
Entrepreneurship D
Environmental Biology D
Epidemiology M,D
Evolutionary Biology D
Genetics D
Geosciences M,D
Health Informatics M,D
Health Services Management and Hospital Administration M,D
Health Services Research M,D
Immunology D
Liberal Studies M*
Materials Engineering M,D
Materials Sciences M,D
Mathematics M,D
Mechanical Engineering M,D
Microbiology D
Molecular Biology D
Molecular Medicine
Molecular Pathogenesis D
Music M
Neuroscience D
Physical Chemistry M,D
Physics D
Psychology—General D
Public Health—General M
Sustainable Development D
Systems Engineering M,D

DAVENPORT UNIVERSITY
Accounting M
Business Administration and Management—General M
Computer and Information Systems Security M
Finance and Banking M
Health Services Management and Hospital Administration M
Human Resources Management M
Management Strategy and Policy M
Public Health—General M

DEFIANCE COLLEGE
Business Administration and Management—General M
Education—General M
Management Strategy and Policy M

DELAWARE STATE UNIVERSITY
Adult Education M
Applied Mathematics M,D
Art Education M
Biological and Biomedical Sciences—General M
Business Administration and Management—General M
Chemistry M,D
Curriculum and Instruction M
Education—General M,D
Educational Leadership and Administration M,D
Exercise and Sports Science M
Foreign Languages Education M
Historic Preservation M
Mathematics Education M
Mathematics M
Natural Resources M
Neuroscience M,D
Nursing—General M
Optical Sciences M,D
Physics M,D
Plant Sciences M
Reading Education M
Science Education M,D
Social Work M
Special Education M
Theoretical Physics D

DELAWARE VALLEY UNIVERSITY
Accounting M
Agricultural Economics and Agribusiness M
Business Administration and Management—General M
Counseling Psychology M
Curriculum and Instruction M
Developmental Psychology M
Educational Leadership and Administration M
Educational Media/Instructional Technology M
Entrepreneurship M
Finance and Banking M
Human Resources Management M
International Business M
Social Psychology M
Supply Chain Management M

DELL'ARTE INTERNATIONAL SCHOOL OF PHYSICAL THEATRE
Theater M

DELTA STATE UNIVERSITY
Accounting M
Aviation Management M
Biological and Biomedical Sciences—General M
Business Administration and Management—General M
Counselor Education M,D,O
Criminal Justice and Criminology M
Education—General M,D,O

Educational Leadership and Administration	M,D,O
Elementary Education	M,D,O
English Education	M
Exercise and Sports Science	M
Family Nurse Practitioner Studies	M,D
Gender Studies	M
Health Education	M
Health Services Management and Hospital Administration	M,D
Higher Education	D
Liberal Studies	M
Nursing Education	M,D
Nursing—General	M,D
Philosophy	M
Physical Education	M
Recreation and Park Management	M
Religion	M
Secondary Education	M,D,O
Social Sciences Education	M
Special Education	M
Urban and Regional Planning	M

DENVER SEMINARY

Marriage and Family Therapy	M,D,O
Pastoral Ministry and Counseling	M,D,O
Religion	M,D,O
Theology	M,D,O

DEPAUL UNIVERSITY

Accounting	M,D
Adult Education	M
Advertising and Public Relations	M
Applied Economics	M,D
Applied Mathematics	M,D
Applied Statistics	M,D
Biological and Biomedical Sciences—General	M,D
Business Administration and Management—General	M,D
Business Analytics	M,D
Chemistry	M,D
Chinese	M
Clinical Psychology	M,D
Communication—General	M
Computer and Information Systems Security	M,D
Computer Art and Design	M,D
Computer Science	M,D
Corporate and Organizational Communication	M
Counseling Psychology	M,D
Counselor Education	M,D
Curriculum and Instruction	M,D
Data Science/Data Analytics	M,D
Early Childhood Education	M,D
Economics	M,D
Education—General	M,D
Educational Leadership and Administration	M,D
Electronic Commerce	M,D
Elementary Education	M,D
English	M
Entrepreneurship	M,D
Environmental Sciences	M,D
Ethnic Studies	M
Family Nurse Practitioner Studies	M,D
Film, Television, and Video Production	M,D
Film, Television, and Video Theory and Criticism	M
Finance and Banking	M,D
Foreign Languages Education	M,D
Foundations and Philosophy of Education	M,D
French	M
Game Design and Development	M,D
Gender Studies	M
German	M
Health Communication	M
Health Informatics	M,D
Health Law	M,D
Higher Education	M,D
History	M
Hospitality Management	M,D
Human Resources Management	M,D
Human-Computer Interaction	M,D
Information Science	M,D
Intellectual Property Law	M,D
Interdisciplinary Studies	M
International Affairs	M
International Business	M,D
Internet and Interactive Multimedia	M,D
Italian	M
Japanese	M
Journalism	M
Law	M,D
Liberal Studies	M
Management Information Systems	M,D
Management Strategy and Policy	M,D
Marketing	M,D
Mathematical and Computational Finance	M,D
Mathematics Education	M,D
Mathematics	M,D
Media Studies	M
Middle School Education	M,D
Multilingual and Multicultural Education	M,D
Music Education	M,O
Music	M,O
Near and Middle Eastern Languages	M
Nonprofit Management	M
Nursing—General	M,D
Physical Education	M,D
Physics	M,D
Polymer Science and Engineering	M,D
Psychology—General	M,D
Public Administration	M
Public Health—General	M
Public Policy	M
Publishing	M
Reading Education	M,D
Real Estate	M,D
Rhetoric	M
Risk Management	M,D
School Psychology	M,D
Science Education	M,D
Secondary Education	M,D
Social Work	M
Sociology	M
Software Engineering	M,D
Spanish	M
Special Education	M,D
Student Affairs	M,D
Supply Chain Management	M,D
Sustainability Management	M,D
Sustainable Development	M
Taxation	M,D
Theater	M
Urban Design	M
Women's Studies	M
Writing	M

DEREE - THE AMERICAN COLLEGE OF GREECE

Applied Psychology	M
Communication—General	M
Marketing	M

DESALES UNIVERSITY

Accounting	M
Business Administration and Management—General	M
Computer and Information Systems Security	M,O
Criminal Justice and Criminology	M,O
Data Science/Data Analytics	M,O
Education—General	M,O
Educational Media/Instructional Technology	M,O
English as a Second Language	M,O
Family Nurse Practitioner Studies	M,D,O
Finance and Banking	M
Forensic Sciences	M,O
Gerontology	M,D,O
Health Informatics	M,O
Health Services Management and Hospital Administration	M
Human Resources Management	M
Management Information Systems	M,O
Marketing	M
Nurse Anesthesia	M,D,O
Nurse Midwifery	M,D,O
Nursing and Healthcare Administration	M,D,O
Nursing Education	M,D,O
Nursing—General	M,D,O
Project Management	M,O
Secondary Education	M,O
Special Education	M,O
Supply Chain Management	M

DES MOINES UNIVERSITY

Anatomy	M
Biological and Biomedical Sciences—General	M
Health Services Management and Hospital Administration	M
Osteopathic Medicine	D
Physical Therapy	D
Physician Assistant Studies	M
Podiatric Medicine	D
Public Health—General	M

DEVRY COLLEGE OF NEW YORK–MIDTOWN MANHATTAN CAMPUS

Business Administration and Management—General	M

DEVRY UNIVERSITY–ALPHARETTA CAMPUS

Business Administration and Management—General	M

DEVRY UNIVERSITY–ARLINGTON CAMPUS

Business Administration and Management—General	M

DEVRY UNIVERSITY–CHARLOTTE CAMPUS

Business Administration and Management—General	M

DEVRY UNIVERSITY–CHESAPEAKE CAMPUS

Business Administration and Management—General	M

DEVRY UNIVERSITY–CHICAGO CAMPUS

Business Administration and Management—General	M

DEVRY UNIVERSITY–CHICAGO LOOP CAMPUS

Business Administration and Management—General	M

DEVRY UNIVERSITY–CINCINNATI CAMPUS

Business Administration and Management—General	M

DEVRY UNIVERSITY–COLUMBUS CAMPUS

Business Administration and Management—General	M

DEVRY UNIVERSITY–DECATUR CAMPUS

Business Administration and Management—General	M

DEVRY UNIVERSITY–FOLSOM CAMPUS

Accounting	M
Business Administration and Management—General	M
Curriculum and Instruction	M
Educational Leadership and Administration	M
Educational Media/Instructional Technology	M
Finance and Banking	M
Higher Education	M
Human Resources Management	M
Management Information Systems	M
Project Management	M
Public Administration	M

DEVRY UNIVERSITY–FREMONT CAMPUS

Business Administration and Management—General	M

DEVRY UNIVERSITY–FT. WASHINGTON CAMPUS

Business Administration and Management—General	M

DEVRY UNIVERSITY–HENDERSON CAMPUS

Business Administration and Management—General	M

DEVRY UNIVERSITY–IRVING CAMPUS

Business Administration and Management—General	M

DEVRY UNIVERSITY–JACKSONVILLE CAMPUS

Business Administration and Management—General	M

DEVRY UNIVERSITY–LONG BEACH CAMPUS

Business Administration and Management—General	M

DEVRY UNIVERSITY–MIRAMAR CAMPUS

Business Administration and Management—General	M

DEVRY UNIVERSITY–MORRISVILLE CAMPUS

Business Administration and Management—General	M

DEVRY UNIVERSITY–NASHVILLE CAMPUS

Business Administration and Management—General	M

DEVRY UNIVERSITY–NORTH BRUNSWICK CAMPUS

Business Administration and Management—General	M

DEVRY UNIVERSITY ONLINE

Business Administration and Management—General	M

DEVRY UNIVERSITY–ORLANDO CAMPUS

Business Administration and Management—General	M

DEVRY UNIVERSITY–PHOENIX CAMPUS

Business Administration and Management—General	M

DEVRY UNIVERSITY–POMONA CAMPUS

Business Administration and Management—General	M

DEVRY UNIVERSITY–SAN DIEGO CAMPUS

Business Administration and Management—General	M,O

DEVRY UNIVERSITY–SEVEN HILLS CAMPUS

Business Administration and Management—General	M,O

DEVRY UNIVERSITY–TINLEY PARK CAMPUS

Business Administration and Management—General	M

DIGIPEN INSTITUTE OF TECHNOLOGY

Computer Art and Design	M
Computer Science	M

DIVINE MERCY UNIVERSITY

Clinical Psychology	M,D
Psychology—General	M

DOANE UNIVERSITY

Business Administration and Management—General	M
Counselor Education	M
Curriculum and Instruction	M,D,O
Education—General	M,D,O
Educational Leadership and Administration	M,D,O
School Psychology	M,D,O

DOMINICAN COLLEGE

Accounting	M
Allied Health—General	M,D
Business Administration and Management—General	M
Education—General	M
Elementary Education	M
Family Nurse Practitioner Studies	M,D
Health Services Management and Hospital Administration	M
Occupational Therapy	M
Physical Therapy	M,D
Special Education	M

DOMINICAN HOUSE OF STUDIES, PONTIFICAL FACULTY OF THE IMMACULATE CONCEPTION

Theology	M,D,O

DOMINICAN SCHOOL OF PHILOSOPHY AND THEOLOGY

Philosophy	M,O
Theology	M,O

DOMINICAN UNIVERSITY

Accounting	M
Business Administration and Management—General	M
Early Childhood Education	M
Education—General	M
Elementary Education	M
English as a Second Language	M
Information Studies	M,D,O
Management Information Systems	M,D,O
Reading Education	M
Secondary Education	M
Social Work	M
Special Education	M

DOMINICAN UNIVERSITY OF CALIFORNIA

Art History	M
Biological and Biomedical Sciences—General	M
Business Administration and Management—General	M
Clinical Laboratory Sciences/Medical Technology	M
Counseling Psychology	M
Education—General	M
Gender Studies	M
History	M
Humanities	M
Liberal Studies	M
Marriage and Family Therapy	M
Music	M
Occupational Therapy	M
Philosophy	M
Political Science	M
Religion	M
Special Education	M
Writing	M

DONGGUK UNIVERSITY LOS ANGELES

Acupuncture and Oriental Medicine	M

DORDT COLLEGE

Education—General	M

DRAGON RISES COLLEGE OF ORIENTAL MEDICINE

Acupuncture and Oriental Medicine	M

DRAKE UNIVERSITY

Accounting	M
Applied Behavior Analysis	M,D,O
Athletic Training and Sports Medicine	M,D
Business Administration and Management—General	M
Communication—General	M
Counselor Education	M,D,O
Education—General	M,D,O
Educational Leadership and Administration	M,D,O
Law	M,D
Mathematics Education	M,D,O
Occupational Therapy	M,D
Pharmacy	M,D
Public Administration	M
Public Affairs	M
Reading Education	M,D,O
Science Education	M,D,O
Special Education	M,D,O

DREW UNIVERSITY

American Studies	M,D,O
Art/Fine Arts	M,D,O
Biological and Biomedical Sciences—General	M,D,O
Chemistry	M,D,O
Community College Education	M,D,O
Conflict Resolution and Mediation/Peace Studies	M,D,O
Cultural Studies	M,D,O
Education—General	M,D,O
Elementary Education	M,D,O
English	M,D,O
Finance and Banking	M,D,O
French	M,D,O
Health Education	M,D,O
Health Services Management and Hospital Administration	M,D,O
History	M,D,O
Italian	M,D,O
Liberal Studies	M,D,O
Mathematics	M,D,O
Public History	M,D,O
Religion	M,D,O
Secondary Education	M,D,O
Special Education	M,D,O
Theology	M,D,O
Western European Studies	M,D,O
Writing	M,D,O

DREXEL UNIVERSITY

Accounting	M,D,O
Acute Care/Critical Care Nursing	M
Allied Health—General	M,D,O
Allopathic Medicine	D

*M—masters degree; D—doctorate; O—other advanced degree; *—Close-Up and/or Display*

Applied Arts and Design—General M,D
Applied Behavior Analysis M,D
Architectural Engineering M,D
Archives/Archival Administration M
Art Therapy M,O
Arts Administration M
Biochemical Engineering M
Biochemistry M,D
Biological and Biomedical Sciences—General M,D,O
Biomedical Engineering M,D
Biopsychology M,D
Biostatistics M,D,O
Business Administration and Management—General M,D,O
Cell Biology M,D
Chemical Engineering M,D
Chemistry M,D
Civil Engineering M,D
Clinical Psychology D
Clothing and Textiles M
Communication—General M
Computer Art and Design M,D
Computer Engineering M
Computer Science M,D,O*
Construction Management M
Corporate and Organizational Communication M
Curriculum and Instruction M,D
Economics M,D,O
Education—General M,D*
Educational Leadership and Administration M,D
Educational Media/Instructional Technology M,D
Electrical Engineering M
Emergency Management M
Emergency Medical Services M
Engineering and Applied Sciences—General M,D,O
Engineering Management M,O
Entrepreneurship M
Environmental Engineering M,D
Environmental Management and Policy M
Environmental Sciences M,D
Epidemiology M,D,O
Family Nurse Practitioner Studies M
Film, Television, and Video Production M
Finance and Banking M,D,O
Food Science and Technology M
Forensic Psychology D
Genetics M,D
Geotechnical Engineering M,D
Health Law M,D
Health Psychology D
Higher Education M,D
History of Science and Technology M
Homeland Security M
Hospitality Management M
Human Resources Development M,D
Hydraulics M,D
Hydrology M,D
Immunology M,D
Information Science M,D,O
Intellectual Property Law M,D
Interior Design M
International and Comparative Education M,D
Law M,D
Library Science M,D,O
Management Information Systems M,D,O
Management Strategy and Policy M,D,O
Marketing M,D,O
Marriage and Family Therapy M,D
Mass Communication M
Materials Engineering M,D
Mathematics M,D
Mechanical Engineering M,D
Mechanics M,D
Media Studies M
Microbiology M,D
Molecular Biology M,D
Molecular Medicine M
Neuroscience M,D
Nurse Anesthesia M
Nursing and Healthcare Administration M
Nursing Education M
Nursing—General M,D
Organizational Behavior M,D,O
Pathobiology M,D
Pediatric Nursing M
Pharmaceutical Sciences M
Pharmacology M,D
Physical Therapy M,D,O
Physician Assistant Studies M
Physics M,D
Project Management M
Psychiatric Nursing M
Psychology—General M,D
Public Health—General M,D,O
Quantitative Analysis M,D,O
Real Estate M
Software Engineering M,D,O
Special Education M,D
Sports and Entertainment Law M,D
Sports Management M
Structural Engineering M,D
Technical Communication M
Technical Writing M
Telecommunications M
Textile Design M
Therapies—Dance, Drama, and Music M,O
Urban Design M
Veterinary Sciences M
Women's Health Nursing M

DRURY UNIVERSITY

Business Administration and Management—General M
Communication—General M
Computer and Information Systems Security O
Curriculum and Instruction M
Education—General M
Educational Leadership and Administration M
Educational Media/Instructional Technology M
Elementary Education M
Middle School Education M
Nonprofit Management M
Organizational Management M
Reading Education M
Secondary Education M
Special Education M

DUKE UNIVERSITY

Accounting D
Acute Care/Critical Care Nursing M,D,O
Adult Nursing M,D,O
Allopathic Medicine D
Anatomy D
Art History M,D
Art/Fine Arts M,D
Asian Studies M,O
Biochemistry D
Bioethics M
Bioinformatics D,O
Biological and Biomedical Sciences—General M,D
Biological Anthropology D
Biomedical Engineering M,D
Biopsychology D
Biostatistics M
Business Administration and Management—General M,D,O
Business Analytics M
Cancer Biology/Oncology D
Cell Biology D,O
Chemistry D
Civil Engineering M,D
Classics D
Clinical Laboratory Sciences/Medical Technology M
Clinical Psychology D
Clinical Research M
Cognitive Sciences D
Comparative Literature D
Computational Biology D,O
Computational Sciences M,D
Computer Engineering M,D
Computer Science M,D
Cultural Anthropology D
Developmental Biology O
Developmental Psychology D
Ecology D,O
Economics M,D
Education—General M
Electrical Engineering M,D*
Energy Management and Policy M,O
Engineering and Applied Sciences—General M
Engineering Management M
English D
Entrepreneurship M,O
Environmental and Occupational Health O
Environmental Engineering M,D
Environmental Management and Policy D
Environmental Sciences M,D
Ethics M,O
Experimental Psychology D
Family Nurse Practitioner Studies M,D,O
Finance and Banking M,D,O
French D
Genetics D
Genomic Sciences D
Geology M,D
Geosciences M,D
German D
Gerontological Nursing M,D,O
Gerontology M,D,O
Health Informatics M
Health Psychology D
Health Services Management and Hospital Administration M,O
History M,D
Human Development D
Humanities M
Immunology D
Industrial and Manufacturing Management M,D,O
International Business M,O
International Development M
International Health M
Italian D
Latin American Studies M,D
Law M,D
Liberal Studies M
Management of Technology M,D
Management Strategy and Policy M,D,O
Marine Sciences M,D
Marketing M,D,O
Materials Engineering M,D
Materials Sciences M,D
Maternal and Child/Neonatal Nursing M,D,O
Mathematics D
Mechanical Engineering M,D
Media Studies M
Medical Physics M,D
Microbiology D
Molecular Biology D,O
Molecular Biophysics O
Molecular Genetics D
Music D
Natural Resources M,D
Neurobiology D
Neuroscience D,O
Nurse Anesthesia M,D,O
Nursing and Healthcare Administration M,D,O
Nursing Education M,D,O
Nursing Informatics M,D,O
Nursing—General D
Optical Sciences M
Organizational Management M,D,O
Paleontology D
Pathology M,D
Pediatric Nursing M,D,O
Pharmacology D
Philosophy D
Photonics M
Physical Therapy D
Physician Assistant Studies M
Physics D
Political Science M,D
Psychology—General D
Public Policy M,D
Quantitative Analysis M,D,O
Religion M,D
Slavic Languages M,O
Sociology M,D
Spanish D
Statistics M,D
Structural Biology O
Theology M,D
Toxicology O
Women's Health Nursing M,D,O

DUNLAP-STONE UNIVERSITY

Law M

DUQUESNE UNIVERSITY

Accounting M
Allied Health—General M,D,O
Bioethics M,D,O
Biological and Biomedical Sciences—General D
Biotechnology M
Business Administration and Management—General M
Chemistry D
Classics M
Clinical Psychology M,D,O
Communication Disorders M,D
Communication—General M,D
Counseling Psychology M,D,O
Counselor Education M,D,O
Curriculum and Instruction M,O
Early Childhood Education M
Education—General M,D,O
Educational Leadership and Administration M,D,O
Educational Measurement and Evaluation M
Educational Media/Instructional Technology M,D,O
Elementary Education M
English as a Second Language M
English Education M
English M,D
Environmental Management and Policy M,O
Environmental Sciences M,O
Family Nurse Practitioner Studies M,O
Finance and Banking M
Foreign Languages Education M
Forensic Nursing M,O
Forensic Sciences M
Foundations and Philosophy of Education M
Health Services Management and Hospital Administration M,D
History M
Law M,D
Management Information Systems M
Marketing M
Marriage and Family Therapy M,D,O
Mathematics Education M
Mathematics M
Medicinal and Pharmaceutical Chemistry M,D
Middle School Education M
Music Education M,O
Music M,O
Nursing Education M,D,O
Nursing—General M,D,O
Occupational Therapy M,D
Organizational Management M
Pharmaceutical Administration M,D
Pharmaceutical Sciences M,D
Pharmacology M,D
Pharmacy D
Philosophy M,D
Physical Therapy M,D
Physician Assistant Studies M,D
Psychology—General D
Public History M
Reading Education M
Rehabilitation Sciences M,D
Rhetoric M,D
School Psychology M,D
Science Education M
Secondary Education M
Social Sciences Education M
Special Education M,D
Sports Management M
Supply Chain Management M
Sustainability Management M
Theology M,D

D'YOUVILLE COLLEGE

Anatomy M
Business Administration and Management—General M
Chiropractic D
Education—General M,D
Educational Leadership and Administration M,D
Elementary Education M,D
Family Nurse Practitioner Studies M,D,O
Health Services Management and Hospital Administration M,D,O
International Business M
Nursing—General M,D,O
Nutrition M
Occupational Therapy M
Pharmacy D
Physical Therapy D,O
Physician Assistant Studies M
Secondary Education M,D
Special Education M,D

EARLHAM COLLEGE

Education—General M

EARLHAM SCHOOL OF RELIGION

Pastoral Ministry and Counseling M
Religion M
Theology M

EAST CAROLINA UNIVERSITY

Accounting M
Addictions/Substance Abuse Counseling M,D,O
Adult Education M,O
Allied Health—General M,D,O
Allopathic Medicine D
American Studies M
Anthropology M
Applied Economics M
Applied Physics M,D
Art Education M
Art/Fine Arts M
Biological and Biomedical Sciences—General M
Biomedical Engineering M
Biophysics M,D
Biotechnology M
Business Administration and Management—General M,D,O
Business Education M,O
Chemistry M
Child and Family Studies M,D
Child Development M,D
Clinical Psychology M,D,O
Communication Disorders M,D
Community College Education M,D,O
Comparative Literature M,D,O
Computer and Information Systems Security M,D,O
Computer Engineering M,D,O
Computer Science M,D,O
Construction Management M,O
Corporate and Organizational Communication M,D,O
Counselor Education M,D,O
Criminal Justice and Criminology M,O
Curriculum and Instruction M,O
Dentistry D
Distance Education Development M,O
Early Childhood Education M,D
Economic Development M,O
Education—General M,D,O
Educational Leadership and Administration M,D,O
Educational Media/Instructional Technology M,O
Elementary Education M,O
English as a Second Language M,D,O
English Education M,D,O
English M,D,O
Environmental and Occupational Health M,D,O
Exercise and Sports Science M,D,O
Geographic Information Systems M,O
Geography M,O
Geology M,O
Gerontology M,O
Graphic Design M
Health Communication M,O
Health Education M
Health Informatics M,O
Health Physics/Radiological Health M,D
Health Promotion M
Health Psychology M,D,O
Health Services Management and Hospital Administration M,O
Higher Education M,O
History M
Hospitality Management M,O
Hydrogeology M,O
Illustration M
Industrial and Manufacturing Management M,D,O
Industrial and Organizational Psychology M,D,O
International Affairs M,O
International and Comparative Education M,O
Kinesiology and Movement Studies M,D,O
Leisure Studies M,O
Library Science M,O
Linguistics M,D,O
Logistics M,D,O
Management Information Systems M,D,O
Management of Technology M,D,O
Marriage and Family Therapy M,D
Maternal and Child Health M,D,O
Mathematics Education M,O
Mathematics M
Medical Physics M,D
Middle School Education M
Military and Defense Studies M
Molecular Biology M
Music Education M,O
Music M,O
Nursing—General M,D
Nutrition M
Occupational Therapy M,D,O
Pharmacology D
Photography M
Physical Education M,D,O
Physical Therapy D
Physician Assistant Studies M
Physics M,D

Political Science	M,O
Public Administration	M,O
Public Health—General	M,D,O
Public History	M
Reading Education	M
Recreation and Park Management	M,O
Rehabilitation Counseling	M,D,O
Rehabilitation Sciences	M,D,O
Rhetoric	M,D,O
Rural Planning and Studies	M,O
Science Education	M,O
Social Sciences Education	M
Social Sciences	M,D,O
Social Work	M,O
Sociology	M
Software Engineering	M
Special Education	M,O
Sports Management	M,D,O
Statistics	M
Technical Communication	M,D,O
Telecommunications Management	M,D,O
Textile Design	M
Therapies—Dance, Drama, and Music	M,O
Urban and Regional Planning	M,O
Vocational and Technical Education	M,O
Western European Studies	M
Writing	M,D,O

EAST CENTRAL UNIVERSITY

Clinical Psychology	M
Criminal Justice and Criminology	M
Education—General	M
Human Resources Management	M
Psychology—General	M
Rehabilitation Counseling	M

EASTERN CONNECTICUT STATE UNIVERSITY

Accounting	M
Early Childhood Education	M
Education—General	M
Educational Media/Instructional Technology	M
Elementary Education	M
Organizational Management	M
Secondary Education	M

EASTERN ILLINOIS UNIVERSITY

Accounting	M
Art Education	M
Art/Fine Arts	M
Biological and Biomedical Sciences—General	M
Business Administration and Management—General	M
Chemistry	M
Clinical Psychology	M,O
Communication Disorders	M
Communication—General	M
Computer and Information Systems Security	M
Computer Science	M
Counselor Education	M
Curriculum and Instruction	M
Early Childhood Education	M
Economics	M
Education—General	M,O
Educational Leadership and Administration	M,O
Elementary Education	M
Energy Management and Policy	M
Engineering and Applied Sciences—General	M,O
English	M
Exercise and Sports Science	M
Geographic Information Systems	M
Gerontology	M
History	M
Human Development	M
Human Services	M
Kinesiology and Movement Studies	M
Mathematics Education	M
Mathematics	M
Middle School Education	M
Music Education	M
Music	M
Nutrition	M
Political Science	M
Psychology—General	M,O
School Psychology	M,O
Secondary Education	M
Special Education	M
Student Affairs	M
Sustainable Development	M
Systems Science	M,O

EASTERN KENTUCKY UNIVERSITY

Agricultural Education	M
Allied Health—General	M
Art Education	M
Biological and Biomedical Sciences—General	M
Business Administration and Management—General	M
Business Education	M
Chemistry	M
Clinical Psychology	M,O
Communication Disorders	M
Community Health	M
Counselor Education	M
Criminal Justice and Criminology	M
Curriculum and Instruction	M
Ecology	M
Education—General	M
Educational Leadership and Administration	M
Elementary Education	M
English Education	M
English	M
Environmental and Occupational Health	M
Exercise and Sports Science	M
Family Nurse Practitioner Studies	M
Geology	M,D
Health Education	M
Health Promotion	M
Health Services Management and Hospital Administration	M
Higher Education	M
History	M
Home Economics Education	M
Industrial and Organizational Psychology	M,O
Industrial Hygiene	M
Industrial/Management Engineering	M
Library Science	M
Manufacturing Engineering	M
Mathematics Education	M
Mathematics	M
Music Education	M
Music	M
Nursing—General	M
Nutrition	M
Occupational Therapy	M
Physical Education	M
Political Science	M
Psychology—General	M,O
Public Administration	M
Recreation and Park Management	M
School Psychology	M,O
Science Education	M
Secondary Education	M
Social Sciences Education	M
Special Education	M
Sports Management	M
Urban and Regional Planning	M
Vocational and Technical Education	M
Writing	M

EASTERN MENNONITE UNIVERSITY

Biological and Biomedical Sciences—General	M
Business Administration and Management—General	M
Conflict Resolution and Mediation/Peace Studies	M,O
Counselor Education	M
Curriculum and Instruction	M
Education—General	M
Health Services Management and Hospital Administration	M
Nonprofit Management	M
Nursing and Healthcare Administration	M,D
Nursing—General	M,D
Organizational Management	M
Pastoral Ministry and Counseling	M,O
Reading Education	M
Religion	M,O
School Nursing	M,D
Special Education	M
Theology	M,O

EASTERN MICHIGAN UNIVERSITY

Accounting	M
Adult Nursing	M,O
African-American Studies	O
Art Education	M
Art/Fine Arts	M
Arts Administration	M
Athletic Training and Sports Medicine	M,O
Biological and Biomedical Sciences—General	M
Business Administration and Management—General	M,O
Chemistry	M
Clinical Psychology	M,D
Clinical Research	M,O
Clothing and Textiles	M
Communication Disorders	M
Communication—General	M
Community College Education	M,D,O
Computer and Information Systems Security	O
Computer Science	M,O
Construction Management	M,O
Corporate and Organizational Communication	M,O
Counselor Education	M,O
Criminal Justice and Criminology	M
Cultural Studies	O
Curriculum and Instruction	M,O
Dance	M
Distance Education Development	M,O
Early Childhood Education	M
Economics	M,O
Education—General	M,D,O
Educational Leadership and Administration	M,D,O
Educational Measurement and Evaluation	M,O
Educational Media/Instructional Technology	M,O
Educational Policy	M
Educational Psychology	M,O
Electronic Commerce	M,O
Engineering and Applied Sciences—General	M
Engineering Management	M
English as a Second Language	M,O
English Education	M
English	M
Entrepreneurship	M,O
Exercise and Sports Science	M
Finance and Banking	M,O
Foreign Languages Education	M,O
Foundations and Philosophy of Education	M
Gender Studies	M,O
Geographic Information Systems	M,O
Geosciences	M,O
Gerontology	O
Health Education	M,O
Health Promotion	M,O
Health Services Management and Hospital Administration	M,O
Higher Education	M,D,O
Historic Preservation	M,O
History	M
Hospitality Management	O
Human Resources Management	M,O
Human Services	O
Interior Design	M
International Business	M,O
Kinesiology and Movement Studies	M
Linguistics	M
Management Information Systems	M,O
Management of Technology	D
Marketing	M,O
Mathematics	M
Middle School Education	M
Museum Education	O
Museum Studies	M,O
Music	M
Nonprofit Management	M,O
Nursing and Healthcare Administration	M,O
Nursing Education	M,O
Nutrition	M
Occupational Therapy	M
Organizational Management	M,O
Philosophy	M
Physical Education	M
Physician Assistant Studies	M
Physics	M
Physiology	M
Polymer Science and Engineering	M,O
Psychology—General	M,D
Public Administration	M,O
Public Policy	M,O
Quality Management	M,O
Reading Education	M,O
Science Education	M,O
Secondary Education	M
Social Sciences	M
Social Work	M
Sociology	M
Special Education	M,O
Sports Management	M
Student Affairs	M,D,O
Supply Chain Management	M,O
Sustainable Development	M,O
Technical Communication	M,O
Technology and Public Policy	M
Theater	M
Urban and Regional Planning	M,O
Urban Education	M,O
Women's Studies	M,O
Writing	M,O

EASTERN NAZARENE COLLEGE

Business Administration and Management—General	M
Counseling Psychology	M
Early Childhood Education	M,O
Education—General	M,O
Educational Leadership and Administration	M,O
Elementary Education	M,O
English as a Second Language	M,O
Marriage and Family Therapy	M
Middle School Education	M,O
Reading Education	M,O
Secondary Education	M,O
Special Education	M,O

EASTERN NEW MEXICO UNIVERSITY

Analytical Chemistry	M
Anthropology	M
Biochemistry	M
Biological and Biomedical Sciences—General	M
Business Administration and Management—General	M
Chemistry	M
Communication Disorders	M
Communication—General	M
Counselor Education	M
Curriculum and Instruction	M
Early Childhood Education	M
Education of the Gifted	M
Education—General	M
Educational Leadership and Administration	M
Educational Media/Instructional Technology	M
Elementary Education	M
English as a Second Language	M
English	M
Exercise and Sports Science	M
Multilingual and Multicultural Education	M
Nursing—General	M
Organic Chemistry	M
Physical Chemistry	M
Physical Education	M
Reading Education	M
Secondary Education	M
Special Education	M
Sports Management	M
Vocational and Technical Education	M

EASTERN OREGON UNIVERSITY

Business Administration and Management—General	M
Education—General	M
Elementary Education	M
Secondary Education	M

EASTERN UNIVERSITY

Business Administration and Management—General	M,D,O
Child and Family Studies	D
Communication—General	M,O
Counseling Psychology	M,O
Early Childhood Education	M,O
Educational Leadership and Administration	M,D,O
Elementary Education	M,O
English as a Second Language	M,O
English Education	M,O
Foreign Languages Education	M,O
Health Education	M,O
Health Services Management and Hospital Administration	M
International Affairs	M
International Development	M
Marriage and Family Therapy	D
Mathematics Education	M,O
Middle School Education	M,O
Missions and Missiology	M
Multilingual and Multicultural Education	M,O
Music	M,O
Nonprofit Management	D,O
Organizational Management	M,D,O
Physical Education	M,O
Public Administration	D,O
Reading Education	M,O
School Nursing	M,O
School Psychology	M,O
Science Education	M,O
Secondary Education	M,O
Social Sciences Education	M,O
Spanish	M,O
Special Education	M,O
Theology	M
Urban and Regional Planning	M

EASTERN VIRGINIA MEDICAL SCHOOL

Allopathic Medicine	D
Art Therapy	M
Biological and Biomedical Sciences—General	M,D
Biotechnology	M
Clinical Psychology	D
Medical/Surgical Nursing	M
Physician Assistant Studies	M
Public Health—General	M
Reproductive Biology	M
Vision Sciences	O

EASTERN WASHINGTON UNIVERSITY

Accounting	M
Adult Education	M
Applied Psychology	M
Biological and Biomedical Sciences—General	M
Business Administration and Management—General	M
Clinical Psychology	M
Communication Disorders	M
Communication—General	M
Computer Education	M
Computer Science	M
Counseling Psychology	M
Counselor Education	M
Curriculum and Instruction	M
Dental Hygiene	M
Early Childhood Education	M
Education—General	M
Educational Leadership and Administration	M
Elementary Education	M
English as a Second Language	M
English	M
Exercise and Sports Science	M
Experimental Psychology	M
Foundations and Philosophy of Education	M
History	M
Interdisciplinary Studies	M
Liberal Studies	M
Music Education	M
Music	M
Occupational Therapy	M
Physical Education	M
Physical Therapy	D
Psychology—General	M,O
Public Administration	M
Public Health—General	M
Reading Education	M
Recreation and Park Management	M
Rhetoric	M
School Psychology	O
Social Work	M
Sports Management	M
Technical Communication	M

EAST STROUDSBURG UNIVERSITY OF PENNSYLVANIA

Athletic Training and Sports Medicine	M
Biological and Biomedical Sciences—General	M
Communication Disorders	M
Computer Science	M
Early Childhood Education	M
Education—General	M,D
Educational Media/Instructional Technology	M
Elementary Education	M
Geography	M
Health Education	M
History	M
Physical Education	M
Political Science	M
Public Administration	M
Public Health—General	M
Reading Education	M
Rehabilitation Sciences	M

*M—masters degree; D—doctorate; O—other advanced degree; *—Close-Up and/or Display*

Secondary Education	M,D
Special Education	M
Sports Management	M

EAST TENNESSEE STATE UNIVERSITY

Accounting	M
Allied Health—General	M
Allopathic Medicine	D
Anatomy	D
Archives/Archival Administration	M,O
Art/Fine Arts	M
Biochemistry	D
Biological and Biomedical Sciences—General	M,D
Biostatistics	M,D,O
Business Administration and Management—General	M,O
Chemistry	M
Clinical Psychology	M,D
Communication Disorders	M,D
Communication—General	M,O
Community Health	M,D,O
Computer Art and Design	M
Computer Science	M,O
Counselor Education	M
Criminal Justice and Criminology	M,O
Curriculum and Instruction	M,O
Developmental Education	M,O
Early Childhood Education	M,D,O
Economic Development	M,O
Education—General	M,D,O
Educational Leadership and Administration	M,D,O
Educational Media/Instructional Technology	M,O
Elementary Education	M,O
English as a Second Language	M,O
English	M,O
Entrepreneurship	M,O
Environmental and Occupational Health	M,D,O
Epidemiology	M,D,O
Exercise and Sports Science	M,D
Experimental Psychology	D
Family Nurse Practitioner Studies	M,D,O
Geographic Information Systems	M,O
Geosciences	M,O
Gerontological Nursing	M,D,O
Gerontology	M,D,O
Health Services Management and Hospital Administration	M,D,O
History	M,O
Human Services	M
Information Science	M,O
International Health	M,D,O
Kinesiology and Movement Studies	M,D
Liberal Studies	M,O
Library Science	M,O
Management Strategy and Policy	M,O
Manufacturing Engineering	M
Marketing	M,O
Marriage and Family Therapy	M
Mathematics	M,O
Microbiology	M,D
Middle School Education	M,O
Nonprofit Management	M,O
Nursing and Healthcare Administration	M,D,O
Nursing Education	M,D,O
Nursing—General	M,D,O
Nutrition	M
Paleontology	M,O
Pediatric Nursing	M,D,O
Pharmaceutical Sciences	D
Pharmacology	D
Pharmacy	D
Physical Therapy	D
Physiology	D
Psychiatric Nursing	M,D,O
Psychology—General	D
Public Administration	M,O
Public Health—General	M,D,O
Reading Education	M,O
School Psychology	M
Secondary Education	M,O
Social Work	M
Sociology	M
Special Education	M,O
Sports Management	M,D
Translation and Interpretation	M,O
Urban and Regional Planning	M,O
Women's Health Nursing	M,D,O

EAST TEXAS BAPTIST UNIVERSITY

Business Administration and Management—General	M
Counseling Psychology	M
Education—General	M
Kinesiology and Movement Studies	M
Religion	M

EAST WEST COLLEGE OF NATURAL MEDICINE

Acupuncture and Oriental Medicine	M

ECCLESIA COLLEGE

Missions and Missiology	M

EC-COUNCIL UNIVERSITY

Computer and Information Systems Security	M

ECOLE HÔTELIÈRE DE LAUSANNE

Hospitality Management	M

ÉCOLE POLYTECHNIQUE DE MONTRÉAL

Aerospace/Aeronautical Engineering	M,D,O
Applied Mathematics	M,D,O
Biomedical Engineering	M,D,O
Chemical Engineering	M,D,O
Civil Engineering	M,D,O
Computer Engineering	M,D,O
Computer Science	M,D,O
Electrical Engineering	M,D,O
Engineering and Applied Sciences—General	M,D,O
Engineering Physics	M,D,O
Environmental Engineering	M,D,O
Geotechnical Engineering	M,D,O
Hydraulics	M,D,O
Industrial/Management Engineering	M,D,O
Management of Technology	M,D,O
Mechanical Engineering	M,D,O
Mechanics	M,D,O
Nuclear Engineering	M,D,O
Operations Research	M,D,O
Optical Sciences	M,D,O
Structural Engineering	M,D,O
Transportation and Highway Engineering	M,D,O

ECUMENICAL THEOLOGICAL SEMINARY

Pastoral Ministry and Counseling	D
Theology	M

EDEN THEOLOGICAL SEMINARY

Theology	M,D

EDGEWOOD COLLEGE

Accounting	M
Adult Education	M,D,O
Business Administration and Management—General	M
Education—General	M,D,O
Educational Leadership and Administration	M,D,O
Nursing—General	M,D
Special Education	M,D,O
Sustainability Management	M

EDINBORO UNIVERSITY OF PENNSYLVANIA

Anthropology	M
Art Education	M
Art Therapy	M,O
Art/Fine Arts	M
Clinical Psychology	M,O
Communication Disorders	M
Communication—General	M
Counseling Psychology	M,O
Counselor Education	M,O
Early Childhood Education	M,O
Educational Leadership and Administration	M
Educational Psychology	M,O
Family Nurse Practitioner Studies	M,D
History	M
Middle School Education	M
Nursing Education	M,D
Nursing—General	M,D
Political Science	M
Reading Education	M,O
Rehabilitation Counseling	M,O
School Psychology	M,O
Secondary Education	M
Social Work	M
Special Education	M,O

EDP UNIVERSITY OF PUERTO RICO–SAN SEBASTIAN

Nursing—General	M

EDWARD VIA COLLEGE OF OSTEOPATHIC MEDICINE–CAROLINAS CAMPUS

Osteopathic Medicine	D

EDWARD VIA COLLEGE OF OSTEOPATHIC MEDICINE–VIRGINIA CAMPUS

Osteopathic Medicine	D

ELIZABETH CITY STATE UNIVERSITY

Applied Mathematics	M
Biological and Biomedical Sciences—General	M
Community College Education	M
Computer Science	M
Education—General	M
Educational Leadership and Administration	M
Elementary Education	M
Geographic Information Systems	M
Mathematics Education	M
Mathematics	M
Psychology—General	M
Science Education	M

ELIZABETHTOWN COLLEGE

Occupational Therapy	M

ELMEZZI GRADUATE SCHOOL OF MOLECULAR MEDICINE

Molecular Medicine	D

ELMHURST COLLEGE

Business Administration and Management—General	M
Communication Disorders	M
Data Science/Data Analytics	M
Educational Leadership and Administration	M
Geographic Information Systems	M
Health Services Management and Hospital Administration	M
Industrial and Organizational Psychology	M
Management Information Systems	M
Nursing—General	M
Occupational Therapy	M
Project Management	M
Public Health—General	M
Special Education	M
Supply Chain Management	M

ELMS COLLEGE

Accounting	M,O
Acute Care/Critical Care Nursing	M,D
Applied Behavior Analysis	M,O
Biological and Biomedical Sciences—General	M
Business Administration and Management—General	M,O
Early Childhood Education	M,O
Education—General	M,O
Elementary Education	M,O
English as a Second Language	M,O
English Education	M,O
Entrepreneurship	M,O
Family Nurse Practitioner Studies	M,D
Finance and Banking	M,O
Foreign Languages Education	M,O
Gerontological Nursing	M,D
Health Services Management and Hospital Administration	M,O
Nursing and Healthcare Administration	M,D
Nursing Education	M,D
Nursing—General	M,D
Reading Education	M,O
Religion	M
Science Education	M,O
Secondary Education	M,O
Social Sciences	M,O
Special Education	M,O

ELON UNIVERSITY

Business Administration and Management—General	M
Education of the Gifted	M
Education—General	M
Elementary Education	M
Internet and Interactive Multimedia	M
Law	D
Physical Therapy	D
Physician Assistant Studies	M
Special Education	M

EMBRY-RIDDLE AERONAUTICAL UNIVERSITY–DAYTONA

Aerospace/Aeronautical Engineering	M,D
Business Administration and Management—General	M
Civil Engineering	M
Computer and Information Systems Security	M
Electrical Engineering	M
Engineering Physics	M,D
Ergonomics and Human Factors	M,D
Finance and Banking	M
Human Resources Management	M
Mechanical Engineering	M,D
Software Engineering	M
Systems Engineering	M

EMBRY-RIDDLE AERONAUTICAL UNIVERSITY–PRESCOTT

Aviation	M
Military and Defense Studies	M
Safety Engineering	M

EMBRY-RIDDLE AERONAUTICAL UNIVERSITY–WORLDWIDE

Aerospace/Aeronautical Engineering	M
Aviation Management	M
Business Administration and Management—General	M
Computer and Information Systems Security	M
Education—General	M
Engineering Management	M
Entrepreneurship	M
Environmental and Occupational Health	M
Finance and Banking	M
Human Resources Management	M
Industrial and Manufacturing Management	M
International Affairs	M
International Business	M
Logistics	M
Management Information Systems	M
Management of Technology	M
Organizational Management	M
Project Management	M
Supply Chain Management	M
Systems Engineering	M

EMERSON COLLEGE

Communication Disorders	M
Data Science/Data Analytics	M
Publishing	M
Writing	M

EMILY CARR UNIVERSITY OF ART + DESIGN

Applied Arts and Design—General	M
Art/Fine Arts	M
Computer Art and Design	M

EMMANUEL COLLEGE (UNITED STATES)

Business Administration and Management—General	M,O
Education—General	M,O
Human Resources Management	M,O
Nursing and Healthcare Administration	M,O
Nursing Education	M,O
Nursing—General	M,O
Special Education	M,O
Urban Education	M,O

EMORY & HENRY COLLEGE

American Studies	M,D
Education—General	M,D
History	M,D
Occupational Therapy	M,D
Organizational Management	M,D
Physical Therapy	M,D
Physician Assistant Studies	M,D
Reading Education	M,D

EMORY UNIVERSITY

Accounting	M,D
Adult Nursing	M
Allied Health—General	M,D
Allopathic Medicine	D
Anesthesiologist Assistant Studies	M
Animal Behavior	D
Anthropology	D
Art History	D
Biochemistry	D
Bioethics	M
Bioinformatics	M,D
Biological and Biomedical Sciences—General	D
Biophysics	D
Biostatistics	M,D
Business Administration and Management—General	M,D
Cancer Biology/Oncology	D
Cell Biology	D
Chemistry	D
Clinical Psychology	D
Clinical Research	M
Cognitive Sciences	D
Comparative Literature	D,O
Computational Sciences	D
Computer Science	M,D
Developmental Biology	D
Developmental Psychology	D
Ecology	D
Economics	D
Education—General	M,D
English	D,O
Entrepreneurship	M
Environmental and Occupational Health	M,D
Epidemiology	M,D
Ethics	M,D
Evolutionary Biology	D
Family Nurse Practitioner Studies	M
Film, Television, and Video Theory and Criticism	M,D,O
Finance and Banking	M,D
French	D
Genetic Counseling	M
Genetics	D
Health Education	M,D
Health Informatics	M,D
Health Promotion	M
Health Services Management and Hospital Administration	M,D
Health Services Research	M,D
History	D
Human Genetics	M
Immunology	D
Industrial and Manufacturing Management	M
Interdisciplinary Studies	D
International Business	M
International Health	M
Law	M,D,O
Management Information Systems	M,D
Marketing	M,D
Mathematics	M,D
Microbiology	D
Middle School Education	M,D
Molecular Biology	D
Molecular Genetics	D
Molecular Pathogenesis	D
Music	M
Neuroscience	D
Nurse Midwifery	M
Nursing and Healthcare Administration	M
Nursing—General	M,D
Nutrition	M,D
Organizational Management	M,D
Pastoral Ministry and Counseling	M,D
Pediatric Nursing	M
Pharmacology	D
Philosophy	D,O
Physical Therapy	D
Physician Assistant Studies	M
Physics	D
Political Science	D
Portuguese	D,O
Psychology—General	D
Public Health—General	M,D
Real Estate	M
Religion	D
Secondary Education	M,D
Sociology	D
Spanish	D,O
Sustainable Development	M
Theology	M,D
Theoretical Physics	D
Women's Health Nursing	M
Women's Studies	D,O

EMPEROR'S COLLEGE OF TRADITIONAL ORIENTAL MEDICINE

Acupuncture and Oriental Medicine	M,D

EMPIRE COLLEGE

Law	M,D

EMPORIA STATE UNIVERSITY

Accounting	M
Art Therapy	M
Biological and Biomedical Sciences—General	M
Botany	M
Business Administration and Management—General	M
Cell Biology	M
Clinical Psychology	M
Counseling Psychology	M
Counselor Education	M
Curriculum and Instruction	M
Distance Education Development	M,O
Early Childhood Education	M
Education of the Gifted	M

Education—General	M
Educational Leadership and Administration	M
Educational Media/Instructional Technology	M,O
Elementary Education	M
English as a Second Language	M,O
English	M
Environmental Biology	M
Forensic Sciences	M,O
Geosciences	M,O
History	M
Industrial and Organizational Psychology	M
Library Science	M,D,O
Mathematics	M
Microbiology	M
Music	M
Physical Education	M
Psychology—General	M
Reading Education	M
Rehabilitation Counseling	M
School Psychology	M,O
Special Education	M
Zoology	M

ENDICOTT COLLEGE

Applied Behavior Analysis	M,D,O
Business Administration and Management—General	M
Computer and Information Systems Security	M,O
Distance Education Development	M
Early Childhood Education	M
Educational Leadership and Administration	M,D
Elementary Education	M
Emergency Management	M,O
Family Nurse Practitioner Studies	M,O
Homeland Security	M,O
Interior Design	M
International Health	M,O
Management Information Systems	M
Nursing and Healthcare Administration	M,O
Nursing Education	M,O
Nursing—General	M,O
Organizational Management	M
Reading Education	M
Secondary Education	M
Special Education	M,D,O
Sports Management	M

ERIKSON INSTITUTE

Child Development	M
Developmental Psychology	M,O
Early Childhood Education	M,O
English as a Second Language	M,O
Human Development	M,O

ERSKINE THEOLOGICAL SEMINARY

Theology	M,D

ESSEC BUSINESS SCHOOL

Business Administration and Management—General	M,D
Hospitality Management	M,D
International Business	M,D

EVANGELICAL SEMINARY

Marriage and Family Therapy	M
Missions and Missiology	M
Pastoral Ministry and Counseling	M
Theology	M

EVANGELICAL SEMINARY OF PUERTO RICO

Theology	M,D

EVANGEL UNIVERSITY

Clinical Psychology	M
Counseling Psychology	M
Counselor Education	M
Curriculum and Instruction	M,D
Education—General	M
Educational Leadership and Administration	M,D
Organizational Management	M
Reading Education	M
School Psychology	M
Secondary Education	M
Social Sciences	M

EVERGLADES UNIVERSITY

Accounting	M
Aviation	M
Business Administration and Management—General	M
Entrepreneurship	M
Human Resources Management	M
Industrial and Manufacturing Management	M
Project Management	M
Public Health—General	M

THE EVERGREEN STATE COLLEGE

Education—General	M
Environmental Management and Policy	M
Public Administration	M

EXCELSIOR COLLEGE

Business Administration and Management—General	M,O
Computer and Information Systems Security	M,O
Conflict Resolution and Mediation/Peace Studies	M,O
Criminal Justice and Criminology	M,O
Emergency Management	M
Health Education	M
Health Informatics	M
Health Services Management and Hospital Administration	M,O
Homeland Security	M
Human Resources Management	M,O
Internet and Interactive Multimedia	M,O
Liberal Studies	M
Management of Technology	M,O
Medical Informatics	M
Nursing and Healthcare Administration	M
Nursing Education	M
Nursing Informatics	M
Nursing—General	M
Organizational Management	M
Public Administration	M
Public Health—General	M
Public Policy	M,O

FAIRFIELD UNIVERSITY

Accounting	M,O
Addictions/Substance Abuse Counseling	M,O
American Studies	M
Applied Behavior Analysis	M,O
Applied Psychology	M,O
Business Administration and Management—General	M,O
Business Analytics	M,O
Child and Family Studies	M,O
Clinical Psychology	M,O
Communication—General	M
Computer and Information Systems Security	M,O
Computer Engineering	M,O
Counseling Psychology	M,O
Counselor Education	M,O
Data Science/Data Analytics	M,O
Education—General	M,O
Educational Media/Instructional Technology	M,O
Electrical Engineering	M,O
Elementary Education	M,O
Engineering and Applied Sciences—General	M,O
English as a Second Language	M,O
Family Nurse Practitioner Studies	M,D
Finance and Banking	M,O
Foundations and Philosophy of Education	M,O
Health Education	M,D
Internet and Interactive Multimedia	M,O
Management Information Systems	M,O
Management of Technology	M,O
Marketing	M,O
Marriage and Family Therapy	M,O
Mathematics	M
Mechanical Engineering	M,O
Multilingual and Multicultural Education	M,O
Nurse Anesthesia	M,D
Nursing and Healthcare Administration	M,D
Nursing—General	M,D
Pastoral Ministry and Counseling	M,O
Psychiatric Nursing	M,D
Public Administration	M
School Psychology	M,O
Secondary Education	M,O
Software Engineering	M,O
Special Education	M,O
Taxation	M,O
Telecommunications	M,O
Writing	M

FAIRLEIGH DICKINSON UNIVERSITY, FLORHAM CAMPUS

Accounting	M
Biological and Biomedical Sciences—General	M
Business Administration and Management—General	M,O
Chemical Engineering	M,O
Chemistry	M
Clinical Psychology	M
Computer Science	M
Corporate and Organizational Communication	M
Counseling Psychology	M
Early Childhood Education	M,O
Education—General	M,O
Educational Leadership and Administration	M
Educational Media/Instructional Technology	M,O
Entrepreneurship	M,O
Finance and Banking	M,O
Gerontological Nursing	M
Health Services Management and Hospital Administration	M
Hospitality Management	M
Human Resources Management	M
Industrial and Organizational Psychology	M
International Business	M,O
Management of Technology	M,O
Marketing	M,O
Nursing—General	M
Organizational Behavior	M,O
Organizational Management	M,O
Pharmacology	M,O
Pharmacy	D
Psychiatric Nursing	M
Psychology—General	M,O
Public Administration	M
Reading Education	M,O
Sports Management	M
Supply Chain Management	M
Sustainability Management	O
Taxation	M,O
Writing	M

FAIRLEIGH DICKINSON UNIVERSITY, METROPOLITAN CAMPUS

Accounting	M,O
Art/Fine Arts	M
Biological and Biomedical Sciences—General	M
Business Administration and Management—General	M,O
Chemistry	M
Clinical Laboratory Sciences/Medical Technology	M
Clinical Psychology	M,D
Communication—General	M
Comparative Literature	M
Computer Engineering	M
Computer Science	M
Criminal Justice and Criminology	M
Curriculum and Instruction	M,O
Early Childhood Education	M
Education—General	M,O
Educational Leadership and Administration	M
Educational Media/Instructional Technology	M,O
Electrical Engineering	M
Electronic Commerce	M
Engineering and Applied Sciences—General	M
English	M
Entrepreneurship	M,O
Experimental Psychology	M,O
Finance and Banking	M,O
Forensic Psychology	M
Foundations and Philosophy of Education	M
Health Services Management and Hospital Administration	M
History	M
Homeland Security	M
Hospitality Management	M
Human Resources Management	M,O
International Affairs	M
International Business	M
Management Information Systems	M,O
Marketing	M,O
Mathematics	M
Media Studies	M
Multilingual and Multicultural Education	M
Nonprofit Management	M,O
Nursing—General	M,D,O
Pharmaceutical Administration	M,O
Political Science	M
Psychology—General	M,D,O
Public Administration	M,O
Reading Education	M,O
School Psychology	M,D
Science Education	M
Special Education	M
Sports Management	M
Systems Science	M
Taxation	M

FAIRMONT STATE UNIVERSITY

Business Administration and Management—General	M
Criminal Justice and Criminology	M
Education—General	M
Educational Media/Instructional Technology	M
Exercise and Sports Science	M
Health Promotion	M
Reading Education	M
Special Education	M

FAITH BAPTIST BIBLE COLLEGE AND THEOLOGICAL SEMINARY

Pastoral Ministry and Counseling	M
Religion	M
Theology	M

FAITH INTERNATIONAL UNIVERSITY

Theology	M,D

FAITH THEOLOGICAL SEMINARY

Theology	M,D

FARMINGDALE STATE COLLEGE

Construction Management	M
Electrical Engineering	M
Management of Technology	M
Mechanical Engineering	M

FASHION INSTITUTE OF TECHNOLOGY

Applied Arts and Design—General	M
Art History	M
Arts Administration	M
Business Administration and Management—General	M
Clothing and Textiles	M
Illustration	M
Marketing	M
Museum Studies	M

FAULKNER UNIVERSITY

Business Administration and Management—General	M
Counselor Education	M
Criminal Justice and Criminology	M
Curriculum and Instruction	M
Education—General	M
Elementary Education	M
Humanities	M,D
Law	D
Pastoral Ministry and Counseling	M,D
Theology	M,D

FAYETTEVILLE STATE UNIVERSITY

Business Administration and Management—General	M
Criminal Justice and Criminology	M
Educational Leadership and Administration	M,D
Elementary Education	M
Middle School Education	M
Psychology—General	M
Secondary Education	M
Social Sciences Education	M
Social Work	M
Sociology	M

FELICIAN UNIVERSITY

Adult Nursing	M,O
Business Administration and Management—General	M,D
Counseling Psychology	M,D
Education—General	M,O
Educational Leadership and Administration	M,O
Entrepreneurship	M,D
Family Nurse Practitioner Studies	M,O
Gerontological Nursing	M,O
Health Services Management and Hospital Administration	M
Nursing and Healthcare Administration	M,D,O
Nursing Education	M,O
Nursing—General	M,D,O
Religious Education	M,O

FERRIS STATE UNIVERSITY

Allied Health—General	M
Applied Arts and Design—General	M
Architecture	M
Art Education	M
Art/Fine Arts	M
Business Administration and Management—General	M
Community College Education	D
Computer and Information Systems Security	M
Criminal Justice and Criminology	M
Curriculum and Instruction	M
Data Science/Data Analytics	M
Developmental Education	M
Education—General	M
Educational Leadership and Administration	M,D
Health Services Management and Hospital Administration	M
Human Services	M
Management Information Systems	M
Nursing and Healthcare Administration	M
Nursing Education	M
Nursing Informatics	M
Nursing—General	M
Optometry	D
Pharmacy	D
Photography	M
Project Management	M
Public Health—General	M
Social Work	M
Special Education	M
Supply Chain Management	M

FIELDING GRADUATE UNIVERSITY

Child Development	M,D,O
Clinical Psychology	M,D,O
Developmental Psychology	M,D,O
Early Childhood Education	M,D,O
Education—General	M,D
Human Development	M,D,O
Marriage and Family Therapy	M
Media Studies	M,D,O
Neuroscience	O
Organizational Management	O
Psychology—General	M,D,O

FISHER COLLEGE

Business Administration and Management—General	M
Management Strategy and Policy	M

FISK UNIVERSITY

Biological and Biomedical Sciences—General	M
Chemistry	M
Clinical Psychology	M
Physics	M
Psychology—General	M

FITCHBURG STATE UNIVERSITY

Accounting	M
Art Education	M,O
Biological and Biomedical Sciences—General	M
Business Administration and Management—General	M
Communication—General	M,O
Computer Science	M
Counseling Psychology	M
Counselor Education	M,O
Curriculum and Instruction	M
Data Science/Data Analytics	M
Early Childhood Education	M
Educational Leadership and Administration	M,O
Elementary Education	M
English Education	M,O
English	M,O
Forensic Nursing	M,O
Higher Education	M,O
History	M
Human Resources Management	M
Interdisciplinary Studies	O
Mathematics Education	M
Middle School Education	M
Psychology—General	O
Reading Education	O
Science Education	M
Social Sciences Education	M
Special Education	M

*M—masters degree; D—doctorate; O—other advanced degree; *—Close-Up and/or Display*

Vocational and Technical Education	M
Writing	M

FIVE BRANCHES UNIVERSITY

Acupuncture and Oriental Medicine	M,D

FIVE TOWNS COLLEGE

Early Childhood Education	M,D
Music Education	M,D
Music	M,D

FLAGLER COLLEGE

Special Education	M

FLORIDA AGRICULTURAL AND MECHANICAL UNIVERSITY

Accounting	M
Adult Education	M,D
Allied Health—General	M,D
Architecture	M
Biomedical Engineering	M,D
Business Administration and Management—General	M
Business Education	M
Chemical Engineering	M,D
Chemistry	M
Civil Engineering	M,D
Counselor Education	M,D
Criminal Justice and Criminology	M
Education—General	M,D
Educational Leadership and Administration	M,D
Electrical Engineering	M,D
Elementary Education	M
Engineering and Applied Sciences—General	M,D
English Education	M
Environmental Sciences	M,D
Finance and Banking	M
Health Services Research	M,D
History	M
Industrial/Management Engineering	M,D
Journalism	M
Landscape Architecture	M
Law	D
Management Information Systems	M
Marketing	M
Mathematics Education	M
Mechanical Engineering	M,D
Medicinal and Pharmaceutical Chemistry	M,D
Nursing and Healthcare Administration	M,D
Nursing—General	M,D
Occupational Therapy	M
Pharmaceutical Administration	M,D
Pharmaceutical Sciences	M,D
Pharmacology	M,D
Pharmacy	D
Physical Education	M
Physical Therapy	D
Physics	M
Political Science	M
Psychology—General	M
Public Administration	M
Public Health—General	M,D
Science Education	M
Secondary Education	M
Social Psychology	M
Social Sciences Education	M
Social Sciences	M
Social Work	M
Software Engineering	M
Sports Management	M
Toxicology	M,D
Vocational and Technical Education	M

FLORIDA ATLANTIC UNIVERSITY

Accounting	M
Adult Education	M,D,O
Anthropology	M
Applied Arts and Design—General	M
Applied Mathematics	M
Art/Fine Arts	M
Bioengineering	M,D
Biological and Biomedical Sciences—General	M,D
Business Administration and Management—General	M
Chemistry	M,D
Civil Engineering	M
Communication Disorders	M
Communication—General	M,O
Comparative and Interdisciplinary Arts	D
Comparative Literature	M
Computer Engineering	M,D
Computer Science	M,D
Counselor Education	M,D
Criminal Justice and Criminology	M
Curriculum and Instruction	M,D,O
Early Childhood Education	M,D,O
Economics	M
Education—General	M,D,O
Educational Leadership and Administration	M,D,O
Educational Media/Instructional Technology	M
Electrical Engineering	M,D
Elementary Education	M
Engineering and Applied Sciences—General	M,D
English as a Second Language	M,D,O
English	M
Entrepreneurship	M
Environmental Education	M
Environmental Engineering	M
Exercise and Sports Science	M
Film, Television, and Video Production	M,O
French	M
Geology	M,D
Geosciences	M,D
Graphic Design	M
Health Promotion	M
Health Services Management and Hospital Administration	M
Higher Education	M,D,O
History	M
International Business	M
Linguistics	M
Management Information Systems	M
Mathematics	M,D
Mechanical Engineering	M,D
Media Studies	M,O
Multilingual and Multicultural Education	M,D,O
Music	M
Neuroscience	D
Nonprofit Management	M,D
Nursing and Healthcare Administration	M,D,O
Nursing—General	M,D,O
Ocean Engineering	M,D
Physics	M,D
Political Science	M
Psychology—General	M,D
Public Administration	M,D
Reading Education	M
Science Education	M,D
Secondary Education	M
Social Work	M,D
Sociology	M
Spanish	M
Special Education	M,D
Sports Management	M
Statistics	M,D
Theater	M
Urban and Regional Planning	M
Women's Studies	M

FLORIDA COASTAL SCHOOL OF LAW

Law	D

FLORIDA COLLEGE OF INTEGRATIVE MEDICINE

Acupuncture and Oriental Medicine	M

FLORIDA GULF COAST UNIVERSITY

Accounting	M
Allied Health—General	M,D
Business Administration and Management—General	M
Clinical Psychology	M
Criminal Justice and Criminology	M
Curriculum and Instruction	M
Education of the Gifted	M
Education—General	M
Educational Leadership and Administration	M
Elementary Education	M
English as a Second Language	M
English Education	M
English	M
Environmental Management and Policy	M
Environmental Sciences	M
Forensic Sciences	M
History	M
Interdisciplinary Studies	M
Management Information Systems	M
Mathematics Education	M
Mathematics	M
Middle School Education	M
Nurse Anesthesia	M
Nursing Education	M
Occupational Therapy	M
Physical Therapy	D
Physician Assistant Studies	M
Public Administration	M
Reading Education	M
School Psychology	M
Science Education	M
Social Sciences Education	M
Social Work	M
Special Education	M
Taxation	M

FLORIDA INSTITUTE OF TECHNOLOGY

Aerospace/Aeronautical Engineering	M,D
Applied Behavior Analysis	M,D
Applied Mathematics	M,D
Aviation Management	M
Aviation	M,D
Biochemistry	M
Biological and Biomedical Sciences—General	M,D
Biomedical Engineering	M,D
Biotechnology	M,D
Business Administration and Management—General	M,D
Cell Biology	M,D
Chemical Engineering	M,D
Chemistry	M,D
Civil Engineering	M,D
Clinical Psychology	D
Communication—General	M
Computer and Information Systems Security	M
Computer Education	M
Computer Engineering	M,D
Computer Science	M,D
Conservation Biology	M
Ecology	M,D
Education—General	M
Educational Media/Instructional Technology	M
Electrical Engineering	M,D
Electronic Commerce	M,D
Elementary Education	M
Emergency Management	M,D
Engineering and Applied Sciences—General	M,D
Engineering Management	M,D
Entrepreneurship	M
Environmental Education	M
Environmental Management and Policy	M
Environmental Sciences	M,D
Ergonomics and Human Factors	M,D
Geosciences	M
Health Services Management and Hospital Administration	M
Human Resources Management	M,D
Human-Computer Interaction	M
Industrial and Organizational Psychology	M,D
Information Science	M
Interdisciplinary Studies	M
Logistics	M,D
Management Information Systems	M,D
Management of Technology	M,D
Marine Biology	M,D
Marine Sciences	M,D
Mathematics Education	M,D,O
Mechanical Engineering	M,D
Meteorology	M
Molecular Biology	M,D
Ocean Engineering	M,D
Oceanography	M,D
Operations Research	M,D
Organizational Behavior	M,D
Organizational Management	M
Physics	M,D
Planetary and Space Sciences	M,D
Project Management	M,D
Psychology—General	M,D
Public Administration	M,D
Quality Management	M,D
Safety Engineering	M
Science Education	M,D,O
Software Engineering	M,D
Supply Chain Management	M,D
Systems Engineering	M,D
Transportation Management	M,D

FLORIDA INTERNATIONAL UNIVERSITY

Accounting	M
Adult Education	M,D,O
Adult Nursing	M,D
African Studies	M
Allopathic Medicine	M,D
Applied Behavior Analysis	M,D
Architecture	M
Art Education	M,D,O
Art/Fine Arts	M,O
Asian Studies	M
Athletic Training and Sports Medicine	M
Biological and Biomedical Sciences—General	M,D
Biomedical Engineering	M,D
Biostatistics	M,D
Chemistry	M,D
Civil Engineering	M,D
Clinical Psychology	M,D,O
Cognitive Sciences	M,D
Communication Disorders	M
Communication—General	M
Computer and Information Systems Security	M,D
Computer Engineering	M,D
Computer Science	M,D
Construction Management	M
Counseling Psychology	M,D,O
Counselor Education	M,D,O
Criminal Justice and Criminology	M,D
Curriculum and Instruction	M,D,O
Data Science/Data Analytics	M,D
Developmental Psychology	M,D
Early Childhood Education	M,D,O
Economics	M,D
Educational Leadership and Administration	M,D,O
Educational Media/Instructional Technology	M,D,O
Electrical Engineering	M,D
Elementary Education	M,D,O
Emergency Management	M
Engineering and Applied Sciences—General	M,D
Engineering Management	M
English as a Second Language	M,D,O
English Education	M,D,O
English	M
Environmental and Occupational Health	M,D
Environmental Engineering	M,D
Environmental Management and Policy	M,D
Epidemiology	M,D
Finance and Banking	M
Foreign Languages Education	M,D,O
Forensic Sciences	M,D
Geosciences	M,D
Health Promotion	M,D
Health Services Management and Hospital Administration	M,D
Higher Education	M,D,O
History	M,D
Hospitality Management	M,D
Human Resources Development	M,D,O
Human Resources Management	M,D
Industrial and Organizational Psychology	M,D
Information Science	M,D
Interior Design	M
International Affairs	M,D
International and Comparative Education	M,D,O
International Business	M,D
Journalism	M
Landscape Architecture	M
Latin American Studies	M
Law	M,D
Liberal Studies	M
Linguistics	M
Management Information Systems	M,D
Marketing	M
Mass Communication	M
Materials Engineering	M,D
Materials Sciences	M,D
Mathematics Education	M,D,O
Mathematics	M,D
Mechanical Engineering	M,D
Multilingual and Multicultural Education	M,D,O
Museum Studies	M,O
Music Education	M
Music	M
Natural Resources	M,D
Neuroscience	M,D
Nurse Anesthesia	M,D
Nursing—General	M,D
Nutrition	M,D
Occupational Therapy	M
Pediatric Nursing	M,D
Physical Education	M,D,O
Physical Therapy	D
Physician Assistant Studies	M,D
Physics	M,D
Political Science	M,D
Psychiatric Nursing	M,D
Psychology—General	M,D
Public Administration	M,D
Public Affairs	M,D
Public Health—General	M,D
Reading Education	M,D,O
Real Estate	M
Recreation and Park Management	M,D,O
Rehabilitation Counseling	M,D,O
Religion	M
School Psychology	M,D,O
Science Education	M,D,O
Social Sciences Education	M,D,O
Social Work	M,D
Sociology	M,D
Spanish	M,D
Special Education	M,D,O
Sports Management	M,D,O
Statistics	M
Telecommunications	M
Urban Education	M,D,O
Writing	M

FLORIDA MEMORIAL UNIVERSITY

Business Administration and Management—General	M
Education—General	M
Elementary Education	M
Reading Education	M
Special Education	M

FLORIDA NATIONAL UNIVERSITY

Accounting	M
Business Administration and Management—General	M
Family Nurse Practitioner Studies	M
Finance and Banking	M
Health Services Management and Hospital Administration	M
Marketing	M
Nursing and Healthcare Administration	M
Nursing Education	M
Nursing—General	M
Public Administration	M

FLORIDA SOUTHERN COLLEGE

Accounting	M
Adult Nursing	M
Business Administration and Management—General	M
Education—General	M
Educational Leadership and Administration	M,D
Family Nurse Practitioner Studies	M
Gerontological Nursing	M
Nursing and Healthcare Administration	M
Nursing Education	M
Nursing—General	M

FLORIDA STATE UNIVERSITY

Accounting	M,D
Actuarial Science	M
Allopathic Medicine	D
American Studies	M
Analytical Chemistry	M,D
Applied Behavior Analysis	M
Applied Economics	M,D
Applied Mathematics	M,D
Applied Social Research	M,D
Applied Statistics	M,D
Archaeology	M,D
Architecture	M
Art Education	M,D
Art History	M,D
Art Therapy	M,D
Art/Fine Arts	M
Arts Administration	M,D
Asian Studies	M
Atmospheric Sciences	M,D
Biochemistry	M,D
Biological and Biomedical Sciences—General	M,D
Biomedical Engineering	M,D
Biopsychology	M,D
Biostatistics	M,D
Business Administration and Management—General	M,D
Cell Biology	M,D
Chemical Engineering	M,D
Chemistry	M,D
Child and Family Studies	M,D
Civil Engineering	M,D
Classics	M,D
Clinical Psychology	D
Cognitive Sciences	D
Communication Disorders	M,D
Communication—General	M,D
Computational Sciences	M,D
Computer and Information Systems Security	M,D
Computer Science	M,D

Corporate and Organizational Communication	M,D
Criminal Justice and Criminology	M,D
Cultural Studies	M,D
Curriculum and Instruction	M,D,O
Dance	M
Demography and Population Studies	M
Developmental Psychology	D
Early Childhood Education	M,D,O
East European and Russian Studies	M
Ecology	M,D
Economics	M,D
Education—General	M,D,O
Educational Leadership and Administration	M,D,O
Educational Measurement and Evaluation	M,D,O
Educational Media/Instructional Technology	M,D,O
Educational Policy	M,D,O
Educational Psychology	M,D,O
Electrical Engineering	M,D
Elementary Education	M,D,O
Energy and Power Engineering	M,D
Engineering and Applied Sciences—General	M,D
English as a Second Language	M,D,O
English Education	M,D,O
English	M,D
Environmental Engineering	M,D
Environmental Law	M,D
Environmental Sciences	M,D
Evolutionary Biology	M,D
Exercise and Sports Science	M,D
Family and Consumer Sciences-General	M,D
Family Nurse Practitioner Studies	D,O
Film, Television, and Video Production	M
Finance and Banking	M,D
Food Science and Technology	M,D
Foreign Languages Education	M,D,O
Foundations and Philosophy of Education	M,D,O
French	M,D
Geographic Information Systems	M,D
Geography	M,D
Geology	M,D
Geophysics	D
Geosciences	M,D
German	M
Health Education	M,D
Health Law	M,D
Higher Education	M,D,O
History	M,D
Human Development	M,D
Human Resources Management	M,D
Industrial Design	M
Industrial/Management Engineering	M,D
Information Studies	M,D,O
Inorganic Chemistry	M,D
Insurance	M,D
Interior Design	M
International Affairs	M
International and Comparative Education	M,D,O
International Business	M
Italian	M
Law	M,D
Library Science	M,D,O
Management Information Systems	M,D,O
Management Strategy and Policy	M,D
Manufacturing Engineering	M,D
Marine Sciences	M,D
Marketing	M,D
Marriage and Family Therapy	M,D
Materials Engineering	M,D
Materials Sciences	M,D
Mathematical and Computational Finance	M,D
Mathematics Education	M,D,O
Mathematics	M,D
Mechanical Engineering	M,D
Media Studies	M,D
Meteorology	M,D
Molecular Biology	M,D
Molecular Biophysics	D
Museum Studies	M,D
Music	M,D
Neuroscience	M,D
Nursing—General	D,O
Nutrition	M,D
Oceanography	M,D
Organic Chemistry	M,D
Organizational Behavior	M,D
Philosophy	M,D
Physical Chemistry	M,D
Physics	M,D
Political Science	M,D
Psychiatric Nursing	D,O
Psychology—General	M,D
Public Administration	M,D,O
Public Health—General	M
Public History	M,D
Public Policy	M,D,O
Reading Education	M,D,O
Religion	M,D
Rhetoric	M,D
Risk Management	M,D
School Psychology	M,D,O
Science Education	M,D,O
Slavic Languages	M
Social Psychology	D
Social Sciences Education	M,D,O
Social Work	M,D
Sociology	M,D
Spanish	M,D
Special Education	M,D,O
Sport Psychology	M,D,O
Sports Management	M,D
Statistics	M,D
Structural Biology	D
Taxation	M,D
Theater	M,D
Therapies—Dance, Drama, and Music	M,D
Urban and Regional Planning	M,D
Writing	M,D

FONTBONNE UNIVERSITY

Accounting	M
Art Education	M
Art/Fine Arts	M
Business Administration and Management—General	M
Communication Disorders	M
Computer Science	M
Curriculum and Instruction	M
Early Childhood Education	M
Education—General	M
Educational Media/Instructional Technology	M
Elementary Education	M
Family and Consumer Sciences-General	M
Health Communication	M
Middle School Education	M
Reading Education	M
Secondary Education	M
Special Education	M
Supply Chain Management	M
Theater	M

FORDHAM UNIVERSITY

Accounting	M,D
Applied Psychology	M,D
Applied Statistics	M,D
Biological and Biomedical Sciences—General	M,D,O
Business Administration and Management—General	M,D
Classics	M,D
Clinical Psychology	D
Clinical Research	M
Communication—General	M,D
Computer and Information Systems Security	M
Computer Science	M
Conservation Biology	M,D,O
Counseling Psychology	M,D
Counselor Education	M,D
Curriculum and Instruction	M,O
Data Science/Data Analytics	M
Developmental Psychology	D
Early Childhood Education	M,O
Economic Development	M,O
Economics	M,D,O
Education—General	M,D,O
Educational Leadership and Administration	M,D,O
Educational Psychology	M,D
Electronic Commerce	M,D
Elementary Education	M,O
Emergency Management	M
English as a Second Language	M,O
English	M,D
Entrepreneurship	M,D
Ethics	M,D
Finance and Banking	M,D
Health Services Management and Hospital Administration	M,D
History	M,D
Intellectual Property Law	M,D
International Affairs	M,O
International Development	M,O
International Economics	M,D,O
Investment Management	M,D
Law	M,D
Management Information Systems	M,D
Marketing	M,D
Mass Communication	M
Media Studies	M,D
Medieval and Renaissance Studies	M,O
Nonprofit Management	M,D
Pastoral Ministry and Counseling	M,D,O
Philosophy	M,D
Political Science	M,D
Psychology—General	M,D
Quantitative Analysis	M,D
Religion	M,D,O
Religious Education	M,D,O
School Psychology	M,D,O
Social Work	M,D
Special Education	M,O
Taxation	M,D
Theater	M
Theology	M,D
Urban Studies	M

FORT HAYS STATE UNIVERSITY

Art/Fine Arts	M
Biological and Biomedical Sciences—General	M
Business Administration and Management—General	M
Communication Disorders	M
Communication—General	M
Counselor Education	M
Education—General	M,O
Educational Leadership and Administration	M,O
Educational Media/Instructional Technology	M
English	M
Geography	M
Geology	M
Geosciences	M
Health Education	M
History	M
Liberal Studies	M
Nursing—General	M
Physical Education	M
Psychology—General	M,O
School Psychology	O
Special Education	M

FORT LEWIS COLLEGE

Educational Leadership and Administration	M,O

FORT VALLEY STATE UNIVERSITY

Animal Sciences	M
Counseling Psychology	M
Counselor Education	M,O
Environmental and Occupational Health	M
Public Health—General	M
Rehabilitation Counseling	M

FRAMINGHAM STATE UNIVERSITY

Art Education	M
Business Administration and Management—General	M
Counseling Psychology	M
Curriculum and Instruction	M
Early Childhood Education	M
Educational Leadership and Administration	M
Educational Media/Instructional Technology	M
Elementary Education	M
English as a Second Language	M,O
English	M
Health Services Management and Hospital Administration	M
Human Resources Management	M
Mathematics Education	M
Nursing and Healthcare Administration	M
Nursing Education	M
Nursing—General	M
Nutrition	M
Public Administration	M
Reading Education	M
Special Education	M

FRANCISCAN MISSIONARIES OF OUR LADY UNIVERSITY

Family Nurse Practitioner Studies	M
Health Services Management and Hospital Administration	M,D
Nurse Anesthesia	D
Nursing—General	M,D
Nutrition	M,D
Physical Therapy	M,D
Physician Assistant Studies	M,D

FRANCISCAN SCHOOL OF THEOLOGY

Theology	M

FRANCISCAN UNIVERSITY OF STEUBENVILLE

Business Administration and Management—General	M
Clinical Psychology	M
Counseling Psychology	M
Curriculum and Instruction	M
Education—General	M
Educational Leadership and Administration	M
Nursing—General	M
Philosophy	M
Theology	M

FRANCIS MARION UNIVERSITY

Applied Psychology	M,O
Business Administration and Management—General	M
Clinical Psychology	M,O
Counseling Psychology	M,O
Education—General	M
Family Nurse Practitioner Studies	M
Health Services Management and Hospital Administration	M
Nursing Education	M
Nursing—General	M
Physician Assistant Studies	M
Psychology—General	M,O
School Psychology	M,O
Special Education	M

FRANKLIN COLLEGE

Athletic Training and Sports Medicine	M

FRANKLIN PIERCE UNIVERSITY

Business Administration and Management—General	M,D,O
Curriculum and Instruction	M,D,O
Elementary Education	M,D,O
Energy Management and Policy	M,D,O
Health Services Management and Hospital Administration	M,D,O
Human Resources Management	M,D,O
Management Information Systems	M,D,O
Nursing and Healthcare Administration	M,D,O
Nursing Education	M,D,O
Physical Therapy	M,D,O
Physician Assistant Studies	M,D,O
Special Education	M,D,O
Sports Management	M,D,O
Sustainability Management	M,D,O
Telecommunications	M,D,O

FRANKLIN UNIVERSITY

Accounting	M
Business Administration and Management—General	M
Computer Science	M
Corporate and Organizational Communication	M
Educational Media/Instructional Technology	M
Marketing	M

FRANKLIN UNIVERSITY SWITZERLAND

International Business	M

FREDERICK S. PARDEE RAND GRADUATE SCHOOL

Public Policy	D

FREED-HARDEMAN UNIVERSITY

Accounting	M
Business Administration and Management—General	M
Counselor Education	M,O
Curriculum and Instruction	M,O
Education—General	M,O
Educational Leadership and Administration	M,O
Ethics	M
Management Strategy and Policy	M
Pastoral Ministry and Counseling	M
Special Education	M,O
Theology	M

FRESNO PACIFIC UNIVERSITY

Business Administration and Management—General	M
Conflict Resolution and Mediation/Peace Studies	M,O
Counselor Education	M
Curriculum and Instruction	M
Education—General	M,O
Educational Leadership and Administration	M
Educational Media/Instructional Technology	M
English as a Second Language	M,O
Family Nurse Practitioner Studies	M
Interdisciplinary Studies	M
Kinesiology and Movement Studies	M
Marriage and Family Therapy	M
Mathematics Education	M
Missions and Missiology	M
Nursing—General	M
Pastoral Ministry and Counseling	M
Reading Education	M,O
School Psychology	M
Science Education	M
Special Education	M
Student Affairs	M,O
Theology	M
Urban Studies	M

FRIENDS UNIVERSITY

Accounting	M
Health Services Management and Hospital Administration	M
Law	M
Logistics	M
Management Information Systems	M
Management Strategy and Policy	M
Marriage and Family Therapy	M
Supply Chain Management	M

FRONTIER NURSING UNIVERSITY

Family Nurse Practitioner Studies	M,D,O
Nurse Midwifery	M,D,O
Nursing—General	M,D,O*
Psychiatric Nursing	M,D,O
Women's Health Nursing	M,D,O

FROSTBURG STATE UNIVERSITY

Biological and Biomedical Sciences—General	M
Business Administration and Management—General	M
Computer Science	M
Conservation Biology	M
Counseling Psychology	M
Counselor Education	M
Curriculum and Instruction	M,D
Ecology	M
Education—General	M,D
Educational Leadership and Administration	M,D
Educational Media/Instructional Technology	M,D
Elementary Education	M,D
Fish, Game, and Wildlife Management	M
Interdisciplinary Studies	M,D
Nursing and Healthcare Administration	M
Nursing Education	M
Nursing—General	M
Psychology—General	M
Reading Education	M,D
Recreation and Park Management	M
Secondary Education	M,D
Special Education	M

FULLER THEOLOGICAL SEMINARY

Clinical Psychology	M,D,O
Marriage and Family Therapy	M,D,O
Missions and Missiology	M,D,O
Music	M,D,O
Pastoral Ministry and Counseling	M,D,O
Theology	M,D,O

FULL SAIL UNIVERSITY

Art/Fine Arts	M
Business Administration and Management—General	M
Computer Art and Design	M
Educational Media/Instructional Technology	M
Entertainment Management	M
Game Design and Development	M
Graphic Design	M
Internet and Interactive Multimedia	M

*M—masters degree; D—doctorate; O—other advanced degree; *—Close-Up and/or Display*

Journalism	M
Marketing	M
Media Studies	M
Writing	M

FURMAN UNIVERSITY

Chemistry	M
Curriculum and Instruction	M,O
Early Childhood Education	M,O
Education—General	M,O
Educational Leadership and Administration	M,O
English as a Second Language	M,O
Reading Education	M,O
Special Education	M,O

FUTURE GENERATIONS UNIVERSITY

Social Psychology	M
Sustainable Development	M
Urban and Regional Planning	M

GALLAUDET UNIVERSITY

Clinical Psychology	M,D,O
Communication Disorders	M,D,O
Counseling Psychology	M,D,O
Counselor Education	M,D,O
Early Childhood Education	M,D,O
Education—General	M,D,O
Elementary Education	M,D,O
International and Comparative Education	M,D,O
Linguistics	M,D,O
Multilingual and Multicultural Education	M,D,O
Neuroscience	M,D,O
Public Administration	M,D,O
School Psychology	M,D,O
Secondary Education	M,D,O
Social Work	M,D,O
Special Education	M,D,O
Translation and Interpretation	M,D,O

GANNON UNIVERSITY

Athletic Training and Sports Medicine	M
Business Administration and Management—General	M
Clinical Psychology	M
Computer Science	M
Counseling Psychology	M
Criminal Justice and Criminology	M
Curriculum and Instruction	M,O
Education—General	M,O
Educational Leadership and Administration	D,O
Electrical Engineering	M
Engineering Management	M
English as a Second Language	O
English	M
Environmental and Occupational Health	M
Environmental Engineering	M
Environmental Sciences	M
Exercise and Sports Science	M
Family Nurse Practitioner Studies	M,O
Finance and Banking	M
Health Communication	M
Human Resources Management	M
Information Science	M
Marketing	M
Mechanical Engineering	M
Nurse Anesthesia	M,O
Nursing and Healthcare Administration	M
Nursing—General	D
Occupational Therapy	M,D
Organizational Management	D
Pastoral Ministry and Counseling	M,O
Physical Therapy	D
Physician Assistant Studies	M
Public Administration	M
Reading Education	M,O
Software Engineering	M
Theology	M,O

GARDNER-WEBB UNIVERSITY

Business Administration and Management—General	M
Counseling Psychology	M
Cultural Studies	M,D
Curriculum and Instruction	M,D,O
Education—General	M,D,O
Educational Leadership and Administration	M,D,O
English Education	M
English	M
Exercise and Sports Science	M
Family Nurse Practitioner Studies	M,D
Missions and Missiology	M,D
Nursing—General	M,D
Organizational Management	M,D,O
Pastoral Ministry and Counseling	M,D
Physical Education	M
Physician Assistant Studies	M
Psychology—General	M
Religious Education	M,D
School Psychology	M
Theology	M,D

GARRETT-EVANGELICAL THEOLOGICAL SEMINARY

Music	M,D
Pastoral Ministry and Counseling	M,D
Religious Education	M,D
Theology	M,D

GATEWAY SEMINARY

Early Childhood Education	M,D,O
Educational Leadership and Administration	M,D,O
Pastoral Ministry and Counseling	M,D,O
Theology	M,D,O

GEISINGER COMMONWEALTH SCHOOL OF MEDICINE

Allopathic Medicine	D
Biological and Biomedical Sciences—General	M

GENERAL THEOLOGICAL SEMINARY

Pastoral Ministry and Counseling	M,D,O
Religion	M,D,O
Theology	M,D,O

GENEVA COLLEGE

Business Administration and Management—General	M
Clinical Psychology	M
Counseling Psychology	M
Counselor Education	M
Education—General	M
Educational Leadership and Administration	M
Finance and Banking	M
Higher Education	M
Marketing	M
Marriage and Family Therapy	M
Nonprofit Management	M
Organizational Management	M
Pastoral Ministry and Counseling	M
Project Management	M
Psychology—General	M

GEORGE FOX UNIVERSITY

Accounting	M,D
Business Administration and Management—General	M,D
Clinical Psychology	M,D,O
Counseling Psychology	M,D,O
Counselor Education	M,O
Cultural Studies	M,D,O
Education—General	M,D,O
Educational Leadership and Administration	M,D,O
Educational Media/Instructional Technology	M,O
English as a Second Language	M,O
Finance and Banking	M,D
Human Resources Management	M,D
Marketing	M,D
Marriage and Family Therapy	M,O
Organizational Management	M,D
Pastoral Ministry and Counseling	M,D,O
Physical Therapy	D
Reading Education	M,O
School Psychology	M,O
Social Work	M
Special Education	M,O
Theology	M,D,O

GEORGE MASON UNIVERSITY

Accounting	M
Adult Nursing	M,D,O
Anthropology	M,D
Applied Physics	M,D
Art Education	M
Art History	M
Art/Fine Arts	M
Arts Administration	M
Astronomy	M,D
Athletic Training and Sports Medicine	M,O
Atmospheric Sciences	D
Biochemistry	M,D
Bioengineering	D
Bioinformatics	M,D,O
Biological and Biomedical Sciences—General	M,D,O
Biostatistics	M,D,O
Business Administration and Management—General	M
Chemistry	M,D
Civil Engineering	M,D
Clinical Psychology	M,D,O
Cognitive Sciences	M,D,O
Communication—General	M,D,O
Community Health	M,O
Computational Biology	M,D,O
Computer and Information Systems Security	M
Computer Engineering	M,D,O
Computer Science	M,D,O
Conflict Resolution and Mediation/Peace Studies	M,D,O
Construction Engineering	M,D
Counselor Education	M
Criminal Justice and Criminology	M,D
Cultural Studies	D
Curriculum and Instruction	M
Data Science/Data Analytics	M,D,O
Developmental Psychology	M,D,O
Early Childhood Education	M
Ecology	M,D
Economics	M,D
Education of the Gifted	M
Education—General	M,D,O
Educational Leadership and Administration	M,O
Educational Media/Instructional Technology	M
Educational Psychology	M,O
Electrical Engineering	M,D,O
Elementary Education	M
Engineering and Applied Sciences—General	M,D,O
Engineering Physics	M
English as a Second Language	M
English Education	M,D,O
English	M,D,O
Environmental Management and Policy	M,D
Environmental Sciences	M,D
Epidemiology	M,O
Ethics	M
Exercise and Sports Science	M,O
Family Nurse Practitioner Studies	M,D,O
Foreign Languages Education	M
Forensic Sciences	M
French	M
Gender Studies	M
Geographic Information Systems	M,D,O
Geography	M,D,O
Geosciences	M,D,O
Gerontological Nursing	M,D,O
Graphic Design	M
Health Informatics	M,D,O
Health Promotion	M,O
Health Services Management and Hospital Administration	M,D,O
Health Services Research	M,D,O
Higher Education	M,D,O
History	M,D,O
Human Resources Management	M
Industrial and Organizational Psychology	M,D,O
Information Science	M,D,O
Interdisciplinary Studies	M
International Affairs	M
International Business	M,O
International Health	M,O
Law	M,D
Linguistics	M,D,O
Logistics	M
Management Information Systems	M
Management of Technology	M
Mathematics Education	M
Mathematics	M,D
Multilingual and Multicultural Education	M
Music Education	M
Music	M,D
National Security	M,D,O
Near and Middle Eastern Studies	M,O
Neuroscience	M,D,O
Nursing Education	M,D,O
Nursing—General	M,D,O
Nutrition	M,O
Operations Research	M,D,O
Organizational Management	M
Philosophy	M
Physical Education	M
Physics	M,D
Political Science	M,D
Project Management	M,D
Psychiatric Nursing	M,D,O
Psychology—General	M,D,O
Public Administration	M
Public Affairs	M
Public Health—General	M,O
Public Policy	M,D
Reading Education	M
Rehabilitation Sciences	D,O
Religion	M
Rhetoric	M,D,O
Science Education	M
Secondary Education	M
Social Sciences Education	M
Social Work	M
Sociology	M,D
Spanish	M
Special Education	M,O
Sports Management	M,O
Statistics	M,D,O
Student Affairs	M,O
Systems Biology	M,D,O
Systems Engineering	M,D,O
Theater	M
Transportation and Highway Engineering	M,D
Transportation Management	M
Women's Studies	M
Writing	M

GEORGETOWN COLLEGE

Education—General	M
Reading Education	M
Special Education	M

GEORGETOWN UNIVERSITY

Acute Care/Critical Care Nursing	M,D
Advertising and Public Relations	M
Allopathic Medicine	D
American Studies	M,D
Analytical Chemistry	D
Asian Studies	M
Biochemistry	M,D
Bioinformatics	M,O
Biological and Biomedical Sciences—General	M,D
Biostatistics	M,O
Business Administration and Management—General	M
Chemistry	D
Communication—General	M
Comparative Literature	M,D
Computer Science	M,D
Conflict Resolution and Mediation/Peace Studies	M
East European and Russian Studies	M
Economic Development	D
Economics	D
Educational Measurement and Evaluation	M
Emergency Management	M,D
English	M
Environmental Law	M,D
Epidemiology	M,D
Ethics	M,D
Family Nurse Practitioner Studies	M,D
Finance and Banking	M,D
German	M,D
Health Law	M,D
Health Physics/Radiological Health	M
Health Promotion	M,D
History	M,D
Hospitality Management	M,D
Human Development	M,D
Human Resources Management	M,D
Humanities	M,D
Immunology	M,D
Industrial and Labor Relations	D
Industrial and Manufacturing Management	D
Infectious Diseases	M,D
Inorganic Chemistry	D
Interdisciplinary Studies	M,D
International Affairs	M,D
International Business	M,D
International Development	M
International Health	M,D
Internet and Interactive Multimedia	M
Journalism	M,D
Latin American Studies	M
Law	M,D
Liberal Studies	M,D
Linguistics	M,D
Management of Technology	M,D
Materials Sciences	D
Mathematics	M
Media Studies	M,D
Medieval and Renaissance Studies	M,D
Microbiology	M,D
Molecular Biology	M,D
Near and Middle Eastern Languages	M,O
Near and Middle Eastern Studies	M,O
Neuroscience	D
Nurse Anesthesia	M,D
Nurse Midwifery	M,D
Nursing Education	M,D
Nursing—General	M,D
Organic Chemistry	D
Pharmacology	M,D
Philosophy	M,D
Physiology	M,D
Political Science	M,D
Psychology—General	D
Public Health—General	M,D
Public Policy	M,D
Radiation Biology	M
Real Estate	M,D
Religion	M,D
Spanish	M,D
Sports Management	M,D
Statistics	M
Systems Engineering	M,D
Taxation	M,D
Theology	D
Theoretical Chemistry	D
Urban and Regional Planning	M,D
Western European Studies	M

THE GEORGE WASHINGTON UNIVERSITY

Accounting	M
Addictions/Substance Abuse Counseling	M
Adult Education	O
Adult Nursing	M,D,O
Aerospace/Aeronautical Engineering	M,D,O
Allopathic Medicine	D
American Studies	M,D
Analytical Chemistry	M,D
Anthropology	M,D
Applied Mathematics	M,D,O
Applied Psychology	D
Art Education	M
Art History	M
Art Therapy	M,O
Art/Fine Arts	M,O
Asian Studies	M
Biochemistry	D
Biological and Biomedical Sciences—General	M,D
Biomedical Engineering	M,D
Biostatistics	M,D
Biotechnology	M,D,O
Business Administration and Management—General	M,D,O
Business Analytics	M,O
Chemistry	M,D
Civil Engineering	M,D,O
Clinical Psychology	M,D
Cognitive Sciences	D
Communication Disorders	M
Communication—General	M
Community Health	M,D
Computer and Information Systems Security	M,D,O
Computer Engineering	M,D,O
Computer Science	M,D,O
Counselor Education	M,D,O
Criminal Justice and Criminology	M,O
Curriculum and Instruction	M,D,O
Dance	M,O
Distance Education Development	O
Early Childhood Education	M
East European and Russian Studies	M
Economics	M,D
Education—General	M,D,O
Educational Leadership and Administration	M,D,O
Educational Media/Instructional Technology	M,O
Educational Policy	M,D,O
Electrical Engineering	M,D,O
Elementary Education	M
Emergency Management	M,D,O
Engineering and Applied Sciences—General	M,D,O
Engineering Management	M,D,O
English	M,D
Environmental and Occupational Health	D
Environmental Engineering	M,D,O
Environmental Management and Policy	M
Epidemiology	M
Exercise and Sports Science	M
Family Nurse Practitioner Studies	M,D,O
Finance and Banking	M,D
Folklore	M,D
Foreign Languages Education	M
Forensic Psychology	O
Forensic Sciences	M,O
Gender Studies	O
Geography	M,O
Health Communication	M,D

Health Services Management and Hospital Administration	M,D,O
Health Services Research	M,D,O
Higher Education	M,D,O
Historic Preservation	M,D
History	M,D
Hospitality Management	M,O
Human Development	M
Human Resources Development	M,D,O
Human Resources Management	M,O
Immunology	D
Infectious Diseases	M,D,O
Inorganic Chemistry	M,D
Interior Design	M
International Affairs	M,D
International and Comparative Education	M,D,O
International Business	M,D
International Development	M,D
International Health	M
International Trade Policy	M,D
Investment Management	M,D
Latin American Studies	M
Law	M,D
Legal and Justice Studies	M,D,O
Management Information Systems	M,D
Management of Technology	M,D
Management Strategy and Policy	M,D,O
Marketing	M,D
Mass Communication	M,O
Materials Sciences	M,D
Mathematical and Computational Finance	M,D,O
Mathematics Education	M
Mathematics	M,D,O
Mechanical Engineering	M,D,O
Microbiology	M,D,O
Military and Defense Studies	M
Molecular Medicine	D
Multilingual and Multicultural Education	M,D,O
Museum Education	M
Museum Studies	M,D,O
National Security	M,D
Near and Middle Eastern Studies	M
Nonprofit Management	M,O
Nursing and Healthcare Administration	M,D,O
Nursing Education	M,D,O
Nursing—General	M,D,O
Organic Chemistry	M,D
Organizational Management	M,O
Philosophy	M
Photography	M,O
Physical Chemistry	M,D
Physical Therapy	D
Physician Assistant Studies	M
Physics	M,D
Political Science	M,D
Project Management	M,D,O
Psychology—General	M,D,O
Public Administration	M,D
Public Affairs	M,D
Public Health—General	M,D
Public Policy	M,D
Publishing	M
Real Estate	O
Rehabilitation Counseling	M
Religion	M
Science Education	M
Secondary Education	M
Social Psychology	D
Sociology	M
Special Education	M,D,O
Sports Management	M,O
Statistics	M,D,O
Student Affairs	M,D,O
Systems Biology	D
Systems Engineering	M,D,O
Technology and Public Policy	M,D
Telecommunications	M,D,O
Theater	M,O
Toxicology	M,O
Travel and Tourism	M,O
Vocational and Technical Education	O
Western European Studies	M
Women's Studies	M,O

GEORGIA CAMPUS–PHILADELPHIA COLLEGE OF OSTEOPATHIC MEDICINE

Osteopathic Medicine	D
Pharmacy	D*
Physical Therapy	D*

GEORGIA COLLEGE & STATE UNIVERSITY

Accounting	M
Art Therapy	M
Biological and Biomedical Sciences—General	M
Business Administration and Management—General	M
Criminal Justice and Criminology	M
Curriculum and Instruction	M
Early Childhood Education	M
Education—General	M,O
Educational Leadership and Administration	M,O
Educational Media/Instructional Technology	M
English	M
Exercise and Sports Science	M
Health Education	M
Health Promotion	M
Kinesiology and Movement Studies	M
Logistics	M
Management Information Systems	M
Middle School Education	M
Music Education	M
Nursing—General	M,D,O
Physical Education	M
Public Administration	M
Secondary Education	M
Special Education	M,O
Therapies—Dance, Drama, and Music	M
Writing	M

GEORGIA INSTITUTE OF TECHNOLOGY

Aerospace/Aeronautical Engineering	M,D
Architecture	M,D
Artificial Intelligence/Robotics	D
Atmospheric Sciences	M,D
Bioengineering	M,D
Bioinformatics	M,D
Biological and Biomedical Sciences—General	M,D
Biomedical Engineering	D
Building Science	M,D
Business Administration and Management—General	M,D
Chemical Engineering	M,D
Chemistry	M,D
Civil Engineering	M,D
Computational Sciences	M,D
Computer and Information Systems Security	M
Computer Art and Design	M,D
Computer Engineering	M,D
Computer Science	M,D
Economic Development	M,D
Economics	M,D
Electrical Engineering	M,D
Engineering and Applied Sciences—General	M,D
Environmental Engineering	M,D
Environmental Management and Policy	M,D
Ergonomics and Human Factors	M,D
Geographic Information Systems	M,D
Geosciences	M,D
Health Physics/Radiological Health	M,D
Health Services Management and Hospital Administration	M
History of Science and Technology	M,D
Human-Computer Interaction	M
Industrial Design	M
Industrial/Management Engineering	M,D
International Affairs	M
International Business	M
Internet and Interactive Multimedia	M,D
Logistics	M
Management Information Systems	M
Materials Engineering	M,D
Mathematical and Computational Finance	M
Mathematics	M,D
Mechanical Engineering	M,D
Mechanics	M
Music	M,D
Nuclear Engineering	M,D
Operations Research	M,D
Paper and Pulp Engineering	M,D
Physics	M,D
Physiology	M,D
Psychology—General	M,D
Public Policy	M,D
Statistics	M
Systems Engineering	M
Urban and Regional Planning	M,D
Urban Design	M

GEORGIAN COURT UNIVERSITY

Applied Behavior Analysis	M,O
Business Administration and Management—General	M,O
Clinical Psychology	M,O
Computer Art and Design	M,O
Counseling Psychology	M,O
Counselor Education	M,O
Criminal Justice and Criminology	M,O
Education—General	M,O
Educational Leadership and Administration	M,O
Educational Media/Instructional Technology	M,O
Health Psychology	M,O
Homeland Security	M,O
Legal and Justice Studies	M,O
Nonprofit Management	M,O
School Psychology	M,O
Special Education	M,O
Theology	M,O

GEORGIA SOUTHERN UNIVERSITY

Accounting	M
Allied Health—General	M,D,O
Applied Economics	M,O
Applied Physics	M
Art/Fine Arts	M
Biological and Biomedical Sciences—General	M
Biostatistics	M,D
Business Administration and Management—General	M
Civil Engineering	M
Clinical Psychology	M,D
Community Health	M,D
Computer Science	M
Construction Management	M
Counseling Psychology	M
Counselor Education	M
Curriculum and Instruction	M,D
Early Childhood Education	M,D
Education—General	M,D,O
Educational Leadership and Administration	M,D,O
Educational Measurement and Evaluation	M,D,O
Educational Media/Instructional Technology	M,O
Electrical Engineering	M
Energy and Power Engineering	M
Engineering and Applied Sciences—General	M,O
Engineering Management	M
English Education	M
English	M
Environmental and Occupational Health	M,D,O
Environmental Sciences	M,O
Epidemiology	M,D
Family Nurse Practitioner Studies	M,D
Foreign Languages Education	M
Graphic Design	M
Health Education	M,D
Health Services Management and Hospital Administration	M,D
Higher Education	M,D
History	M,O
Kinesiology and Movement Studies	M
Logistics	D
Management Information Systems	M,O
Manufacturing Engineering	M,O
Mathematics	M
Mechanical Engineering	M
Middle School Education	M,O
Multilingual and Multicultural Education	D
Music Education	M
Music	M
Nonprofit Management	O
Nursing Education	O
Nursing—General	D
Nutrition	O
Psychiatric Nursing	M
Psychology—General	M,D
Public Administration	M
Public Health—General	M,D
Public History	M,O
Reading Education	M,O
School Psychology	M,O
Secondary Education	M,O
Sociology	M
Spanish	M
Special Education	M,O
Sports Management	M
Supply Chain Management	D
Systems Engineering	M

GEORGIA SOUTHERN UNIVERSITY–ARMSTRONG CAMPUS

Adult Education	M,O
Adult Nursing	M,O
American Studies	M
Athletic Training and Sports Medicine	M,O
Business Administration and Management—General	M,O
Communication Disorders	M
Computer and Information Systems Security	M,O
Computer Science	M
Corporate and Organizational Communication	M,O
Criminal Justice and Criminology	M,O
Curriculum and Instruction	M,O
Early Childhood Education	M,O
Education—General	M,O
Exercise and Sports Science	M,O
Family Nurse Practitioner Studies	M,O
Gerontological Nursing	M,O
Health Services Management and Hospital Administration	M
History	M
Information Science	M
Nursing—General	M,O
Physical Education	M,O
Physical Therapy	M,O
Public Health—General	M
Public History	M
Reading Education	M,O
Secondary Education	M,O
Special Education	M,O
Western European Studies	M
Writing	M,O

GEORGIA SOUTHWESTERN STATE UNIVERSITY

Business Administration and Management—General	M
Computer Science	M,O
Early Childhood Education	M,O
Education—General	M,O
English Education	M,O
Family Nurse Practitioner Studies	M,O
Health Informatics	M,O
Management Information Systems	M,O
Mathematics Education	M,O
Middle School Education	M,O
Nursing and Healthcare Administration	M,O
Nursing Education	M,O
Nursing Informatics	M,O
Nursing—General	M,O
Special Education	M,O

GEORGIA STATE UNIVERSITY

Accounting	M
Actuarial Science	M
Adult Nursing	M,D,O
African-American Studies	M
Allied Health—General	M
Analytical Chemistry	M,D
Anthropology	M
Art Education	M
Art History	M
Art/Fine Arts	M
Astronomy	D
Athletic Training and Sports Medicine	M
Biochemistry	M,D
Bioinformatics	M,D
Biological and Biomedical Sciences—General	M,D
Biostatistics	M,D
Business Administration and Management—General	M,D
Cell Biology	M,D
Chemistry	M,D
Clinical Psychology	D
Clothing and Textiles	M
Cognitive Sciences	D
Communication Disorders	M,D
Communication—General	M,D
Computer Science	M,D
Counseling Psychology	M,O
Counselor Education	M,O
Criminal Justice and Criminology	M,D,O
Cultural Studies	M,D
Curriculum and Instruction	M,D
Developmental Psychology	D
Early Childhood Education	M,D,O
Economic Development	M,D,O
Economics	M,D
Education of Students with Severe/Multiple Disabilities	M
Education—General	M,D,O
Educational Leadership and Administration	M,D,O
Educational Measurement and Evaluation	M,D
Educational Media/Instructional Technology	M,D,O
Educational Policy	M,D,O
Educational Psychology	M,D
Elementary Education	M,D,O
Emergency Management	M,D,O
English Education	M,D
English	M,D
Entrepreneurship	M,D
Environmental Biology	M,D
Environmental Management and Policy	M,D,O
Exercise and Sports Science	M
Family Nurse Practitioner Studies	M,D,O
Film, Television, and Video Production	M,D
Finance and Banking	M,D,O
Foreign Languages Education	M,O
Forensic Sciences	M,O
Foundations and Philosophy of Education	M,D
French	M,O
Gender Studies	M,O
Geochemistry	M,D
Geographic Information Systems	O
Geography	M,D
Geology	M
Geosciences	M,D,O
German	O
Gerontology	M,O
Graphic Design	M
Health Education	M
Health Informatics	M,D,O
Health Services Management and Hospital Administration	M,D,O
Historic Preservation	M,D
History	M,D
Human Development	M,D,O
Human Resources Management	M,D
Human Services	M,O
Industrial and Labor Relations	M,D
Information Science	M,D,O
Insurance	M,D,O
Interior Design	M
International Business	M
Kinesiology and Movement Studies	D
Latin American Studies	M,O
Law	D
Linguistics	M,D
Management Information Systems	M,D,O
Management Strategy and Policy	M,D
Marketing	M,D
Mass Communication	M,D
Mathematics Education	M,D,O
Mathematics	M,D
Media Studies	M,D
Microbiology	M,D
Middle School Education	M,D
Molecular Biology	M,D
Molecular Genetics	M,D
Music Education	M,D,O
Music	M,D,O
Neurobiology	M,D
Neuroscience	D
Nonprofit Management	M,D,O
Nursing and Healthcare Administration	M,D,O
Nursing Informatics	M,D,O
Nursing—General	M,D,O
Nutrition	M
Operations Research	M,D
Organic Chemistry	M,D
Organizational Management	M,D
Pediatric Nursing	M,D,O
Philosophy	M
Photography	M,D
Physical Chemistry	M,D
Physical Education	M
Physical Therapy	D
Physics	M,D
Physiology	M,D
Political Science	M,D
Psychiatric Nursing	M,D,O
Psychology—General	D
Public Administration	M,D,O
Public Health—General	M,D,O
Public History	M,D
Public Policy	M,D,O

*M—masters degree; D—doctorate; O—other advanced degree; *—Close-Up and/or Display*

Reading Education	M,D
Real Estate	M,D,O
Rehabilitation Counseling	M
Religion	M
Rhetoric	M,D
Risk Management	M,D,O
School Psychology	M,D,O
Science Education	M,D
Secondary Education	M,D
Social Psychology	D
Social Sciences Education	M,D
Social Work	M,D
Sociology	M,D
Spanish	M,O
Special Education	M,D
Speech and Interpersonal Communication	M,D
Sports Management	M
Statistics	M,D
Taxation	M
Translation and Interpretation	O
Urban and Regional Planning	M,D,O
Urban Education	M,D,O
Women's Health Nursing	M,D,O
Women's Studies	M,O
Writing	M,D

GERSTNER SLOAN KETTERING GRADUATE SCHOOL OF BIOMEDICAL SCIENCES

Biological and Biomedical Sciences—General	D
Cancer Biology/Oncology	D*

GLION INSTITUTE OF HIGHER EDUCATION

Hospitality Management	M

GLOBAL UNIVERSITY

Missions and Missiology	M,D
Pastoral Ministry and Counseling	M,D
Religious Education	M,D
Theology	M,D

GODDARD COLLEGE

Art Therapy	M
Business Administration and Management—General	M
Clinical Psychology	M
Comparative and Interdisciplinary Arts	M
Education—General	M
Health Promotion	M
Interdisciplinary Studies	M
Psychology—General	M
Sustainability Management	M
Writing	M

GOLDEN GATE UNIVERSITY

Accounting	M,D,O
Business Administration and Management—General	M,D,O
Business Analytics	M,D,O
Entrepreneurship	M,D,O
Environmental Law	M,D
Finance and Banking	M,D,O
Forensic Sciences	M,O
Human Resources Management	M,D,O
Intellectual Property Law	M,D
International Business	M,D,O
Law	M,D
Legal and Justice Studies	M,D
Management Information Systems	M,D,O
Management of Technology	M,D,O
Marketing	M,D,O
Project Management	M,D,O
Psychology—General	M,D,O
Public Administration	M,D,O
Supply Chain Management	M,D,O
Taxation	M,D,O

GOLDEY-BEACOM COLLEGE

Business Administration and Management—General	M
Finance and Banking	M
Health Services Management and Hospital Administration	M
Human Resources Management	M
International Business	M
Management Information Systems	M
Marketing	M
Taxation	M

GOLDFARB SCHOOL OF NURSING AT BARNES-JEWISH COLLEGE

Acute Care/Critical Care Nursing	M
Gerontological Nursing	M
Nurse Anesthesia	M
Nursing and Healthcare Administration	M
Nursing—General	M

GONZAGA UNIVERSITY

Accounting	M
Business Administration and Management—General	M
Education—General	M,D
Educational Leadership and Administration	M,D
Elementary Education	M,D
Engineering and Applied Sciences—General	M,O
English as a Second Language	M
Law	D
Marriage and Family Therapy	M,D
Nursing—General	M,D
Organizational Management	M,D
Philosophy	M
Physiology	M,D
Secondary Education	M,D
Special Education	M,D
Sports Management	M,D
Taxation	M
Theology	M

GORDON COLLEGE

Early Childhood Education	M,O
Education—General	M,O
Educational Leadership and Administration	M,O
Elementary Education	M,O
English as a Second Language	M,O
Finance and Banking	M
Mathematics Education	M,O
Middle School Education	M,O
Music Education	M
Reading Education	M,O
Secondary Education	M,O
Special Education	M,O

GORDON-CONWELL THEOLOGICAL SEMINARY

Archaeology	M,D
Missions and Missiology	M,D
Pastoral Ministry and Counseling	M,D
Religion	M,D
Theology	M,D

GOSHEN COLLEGE

Environmental Education	M
Family Nurse Practitioner Studies	M
Nursing—General	M

GOUCHER COLLEGE

Arts Administration	M
Biological and Biomedical Sciences—General	O
Computer Art and Design	M
Cultural Studies	M
Education—General	M,O
Educational Leadership and Administration	M,O
Educational Media/Instructional Technology	M,O
Elementary Education	M,O
Historic Preservation	M
Middle School Education	M,O
Physical Education	M,O
Reading Education	M,O
Secondary Education	M,O
Special Education	M,O
Writing	M

GOVERNORS STATE UNIVERSITY

Accounting	M
Actuarial Science	M
Addictions/Substance Abuse Counseling	M
Analytical Chemistry	M
Business Administration and Management—General	M
Communication Disorders	M
Communication—General	M
Computer Science	M
Counseling Psychology	M
Criminal Justice and Criminology	M
Early Childhood Education	M
Education—General	M
Educational Leadership and Administration	M,D
English	M
Environmental Biology	M
Film, Television, and Video Production	M
Health Services Management and Hospital Administration	M
Human Services	M,D
Legal and Justice Studies	M
Management Information Systems	M
Mathematics	M
Nursing—General	M
Occupational Therapy	M
Photography	M
Physical Therapy	D
Political Science	M
Psychology—General	M
Public Administration	M
Reading Education	M
Social Work	M
Special Education	M

GRACE COLLEGE

Clinical Psychology	M

GRACE COLLEGE OF DIVINITY

Religion	M

GRACELAND UNIVERSITY (IA)

Curriculum and Instruction	M
Education—General	M
Educational Leadership and Administration	M
Educational Media/Instructional Technology	M
Family Nurse Practitioner Studies	M,D,O
Gerontological Nursing	M,D,O
Nursing Education	M,D,O
Nursing—General	M,D,O
Organizational Management	M,D,O
Reading Education	M
Religion	M
Special Education	M
Theology	M

GRACE MISSION UNIVERSITY

Missions and Missiology	M,D

GRACE SCHOOL OF THEOLOGY

Theology	M

GRACE THEOLOGICAL SEMINARY

Cultural Studies	M,D,O
Missions and Missiology	M,D,O
Pastoral Ministry and Counseling	M,D,O
Theology	M,D,O
Women's Studies	M,D,O

THE GRADUATE CENTER, CITY UNIVERSITY OF NEW YORK

Accounting	D
Anthropology	D
Archaeology	D
Architectural History	D
Art History	D
Biochemistry	D
Biological and Biomedical Sciences—General	D
Biopsychology	D
Business Administration and Management—General	D
Chemistry	D
Classics	M,D
Clinical Psychology	D
Cognitive Sciences	D
Communication Disorders	D
Comparative Literature	M,D
Computer Science	D
Criminal Justice and Criminology	D
Cultural Anthropology	D
Developmental Psychology	D
Economics	D
Educational Psychology	D
English	D
Environmental Sciences	D
Experimental Psychology	D
Finance and Banking	D
French	D
Geosciences	D
Hispanic and Latin American Languages	D
History	D
Industrial and Organizational Psychology	D
Italian	M,D
Liberal Studies	M
Linguistics	M,D
Management Information Systems	D
Mathematics	D
Music	D
Neuroscience	D
Nursing—General	D
Organizational Behavior	D
Philosophy	M,D
Physics	D
Political Science	M,D
Psychology—General	D
Social Psychology	D
Social Work	D
Sociology	D
Theater	D
Urban Education	D

GRADUATE INSTITUTE OF APPLIED LINGUISTICS

Linguistics	M,O
Multilingual and Multicultural Education	M,O

GRADUATE THEOLOGICAL UNION

Art History	M,D,O
Cultural Studies	M,D,O
Ethics	M,D,O
Jewish Studies	M,D,O
Religion	M,D,O
Social Sciences	M,D,O
Theology	M,D,O

GRAMBLING STATE UNIVERSITY

Counselor Education	M,D,O
Criminal Justice and Criminology	M
Curriculum and Instruction	M,D,O
Developmental Education	M,D,O
Education—General	M,D,O
Educational Leadership and Administration	M,D,O
Educational Media/Instructional Technology	M,D,O
English	M,D,O
Family Nurse Practitioner Studies	M,O
Health Services Management and Hospital Administration	M
Higher Education	M,D,O
Human Resources Management	M
Mass Communication	M
Mathematics Education	M,D,O
Nursing—General	M,O
Political Science	M
Public Administration	M
Reading Education	M,D,O
Science Education	M,D,O
Social Sciences Education	M
Social Work	M
Special Education	M
Sports Management	M
Student Affairs	M,D,O

GRAND CANYON UNIVERSITY

Accounting	M
Acute Care/Critical Care Nursing	M,D,O
Business Administration and Management—General	M,D
Business Analytics	M
Cognitive Sciences	D
Curriculum and Instruction	M,D,O
Data Science/Data Analytics	D
Early Childhood Education	M,D,O
Education of the Gifted	M,D,O
Education—General	M,D,O
Educational Leadership and Administration	M,D,O
Educational Media/Instructional Technology	M,D,O
Elementary Education	M,D,O
Emergency Management	M
English as a Second Language	M,D,O
Entrepreneurship	M
Family Nurse Practitioner Studies	M,D,O
Finance and Banking	M
Health Informatics	M,D,O
Health Services Management and Hospital Administration	M,D,O
Human Resources Management	M
Industrial and Organizational Psychology	D
Management of Technology	M
Marketing	M,D
Nursing Education	M,D,O
Nursing—General	M,D,O
Organizational Management	M,D
Pastoral Ministry and Counseling	D
Project Management	M
Psychology—General	D
Public Health—General	M,D,O
Reading Education	M,D,O
Science Education	M,D,O
Secondary Education	M,D,O
Special Education	M,D,O
Sports Management	M

GRAND RAPIDS THEOLOGICAL SEMINARY OF CORNERSTONE UNIVERSITY

Interdisciplinary Studies	M
Pastoral Ministry and Counseling	M
Religion	M
Theology	M

GRAND VALLEY STATE UNIVERSITY

Accounting	M
Adult Education	M
Allied Health—General	M,D
Bioinformatics	M
Biological and Biomedical Sciences—General	M
Biostatistics	M
Business Administration and Management—General	M
Cancer Biology/Oncology	M
Cell Biology	M
Communication Disorders	M
Communication—General	M
Computer Engineering	M
Computer Science	M
Criminal Justice and Criminology	M
Curriculum and Instruction	M
Data Science/Data Analytics	M
Early Childhood Education	M
Education—General	M
Educational Leadership and Administration	M,O
Educational Media/Instructional Technology	M
Electrical Engineering	M
Elementary Education	M
Engineering and Applied Sciences—General	M
English as a Second Language	M
English Education	M
English	M
Health Services Management and Hospital Administration	M
Higher Education	M
Information Science	M
Linguistics	M
Management Information Systems	M
Manufacturing Engineering	M
Mechanical Engineering	M
Medical Informatics	M
Middle School Education	M
Molecular Biology	M
Nonprofit Management	M
Nursing and Healthcare Administration	M,D
Nursing Education	M,D
Nursing—General	M,D
Nutrition	M
Occupational Therapy	M
Physical Therapy	D
Physician Assistant Studies	M
Public Administration	M
Public Health—General	M
Reading Education	M
School Psychology	M,O
Secondary Education	M
Social Work	M
Software Engineering	M
Special Education	M
Taxation	M

GRAND VIEW UNIVERSITY

Athletic Training and Sports Medicine	M,O
Educational Leadership and Administration	M,O
Nursing and Healthcare Administration	M,O
Nursing Education	M,O
Organizational Management	M,O
Sports Management	M,O
Urban Education	M,O

GRANITE STATE COLLEGE

Business Administration and Management—General	M
Organizational Management	M
Project Management	M

GRANTHAM UNIVERSITY

Business Administration and Management—General	M,O
Engineering and Applied Sciences—General	M
Health Services Management and Hospital Administration	M
Human Resources Development	M,O
Human Resources Management	M,O
Management Information Systems	M,O
Management Strategy and Policy	M,O
Nursing and Healthcare Administration	M
Nursing Education	M
Nursing Informatics	M
Nursing—General	M
Project Management	M,O

GRATZ COLLEGE

Education—General	M
Educational Leadership and Administration	M,D
Holocaust and Genocide Studies	M,D
Jewish Studies	M,D
Nonprofit Management	M
Religious Education	M,D
Social Work	M,D

GREEN MOUNTAIN COLLEGE
- Business Administration and Management—General M
- Environmental Management and Policy M

GREENSBORO COLLEGE
- Education—General M
- Elementary Education M
- English as a Second Language M
- Special Education M

GREENVILLE UNIVERSITY
- Education—General M
- Elementary Education M
- Pastoral Ministry and Counseling M
- Secondary Education M

GWYNEDD MERCY UNIVERSITY
- Adult Nursing M,D
- Business Administration and Management—General M
- Counselor Education M,D
- Education—General M,D
- Educational Leadership and Administration M,D
- Family Nurse Practitioner Studies M,D
- Gerontological Nursing M,D
- Health Services Management and Hospital Administration M
- Management Strategy and Policy M
- Nursing Education M,D
- Nursing—General M,D
- Oncology Nursing M,D
- Pediatric Nursing M,D
- Special Education M,D

HALLMARK UNIVERSITY
- Business Administration and Management—General M
- International Business M

HAMLINE UNIVERSITY
- Business Administration and Management—General M,D
- Education—General M,D
- English as a Second Language M,D
- Environmental Education M,D
- Nonprofit Management M,D
- Public Administration M,D
- Reading Education M,D
- Science Education M,D
- Writing M

HAMPTON UNIVERSITY
- Allied Health—General M
- Applied Mathematics M
- Atmospheric Sciences M,D
- Biological and Biomedical Sciences—General M
- Business Administration and Management—General M,D
- Chemistry M
- Communication Disorders M
- Community Health Nursing M
- Computational Sciences M
- Computer and Information Systems Security M
- Computer Science M
- Counselor Education M,D,O
- Early Childhood Education M
- Education—General M,D,O
- Educational Leadership and Administration M,D
- English Education M
- Environmental Biology M
- Family Nurse Practitioner Studies M,D
- Liberal Studies M,D,O
- Marriage and Family Therapy M
- Mathematics Education M
- Medical Physics M,D
- Middle School Education M
- Music Education M
- Nursing and Healthcare Administration M,D
- Nursing Education M,D
- Nursing—General M,D
- Organizational Behavior M
- Pastoral Ministry and Counseling M,D,O
- Physical Therapy D
- Physics M,D
- Planetary and Space Sciences M,D
- Psychology—General M
- Science Education M
- Sports Management M
- Statistics M
- Student Affairs M,D,O

HANNIBAL-LAGRANGE UNIVERSITY
- Education—General M
- Reading Education M

HARDING SCHOOL OF THEOLOGY
- Pastoral Ministry and Counseling M,D
- Theology M,D

HARDING UNIVERSITY
- Allied Health—General M,D
- Art Education M,O
- Business Administration and Management—General M
- Communication Disorders M
- Counselor Education M,O
- Early Childhood Education M,O
- Education—General M,O
- Educational Leadership and Administration M,O
- Elementary Education M,O
- English as a Second Language M,O
- English Education M,O
- Foreign Languages Education M,O
- Health Education M,O
- International Business M
- Mathematics Education M,O
- Organizational Management M
- Pastoral Ministry and Counseling M
- Pharmacy D
- Physical Therapy D
- Physician Assistant Studies M
- Reading Education M,O
- Secondary Education M,O
- Social Sciences Education M,O
- Special Education M,O

HARDIN-SIMMONS UNIVERSITY
- Business Administration and Management—General M
- Counseling Psychology M
- Counselor Education M
- Education of the Gifted M
- Education—General M,D
- Educational Leadership and Administration D
- English M
- Environmental Management and Policy M
- Family Nurse Practitioner Studies M
- Higher Education D
- History M
- Information Science M
- Kinesiology and Movement Studies M
- Marriage and Family Therapy M
- Maternal and Child/Neonatal Nursing M
- Mathematics M
- Music Education M
- Music M
- Nursing Education M
- Nursing—General M
- Pastoral Ministry and Counseling M,D
- Physical Therapy D
- Physician Assistant Studies M,D
- Psychology—General M
- Reading Education M
- Recreation and Park Management M
- Religion M
- Science Education M,D
- Sports Management M
- Theology M

HARRISBURG UNIVERSITY OF SCIENCE AND TECHNOLOGY
- Computer and Information Systems Security M
- Educational Media/Instructional Technology M
- Entrepreneurship M
- Human-Computer Interaction M
- Management Information Systems M
- Management of Technology M
- Management Strategy and Policy M
- Project Management M
- Software Engineering M
- Systems Engineering M
- Systems Science M

HARRISON MIDDLETON UNIVERSITY
- Comparative Literature M,D
- Education—General M,D
- Humanities M,D
- Interdisciplinary Studies M,D
- Legal and Justice Studies M,D
- Philosophy M,D
- Religion M,D
- Science Education M,D
- Social Sciences M,D

HARTFORD SEMINARY
- Pastoral Ministry and Counseling M,D,O
- Religion M,D,O
- Theology M,D,O

HARVARD UNIVERSITY
- Accounting D
- African Studies D
- African-American Studies D
- Allopathic Medicine D
- American Studies D
- Anthropology M,D
- Applied Mathematics M,D
- Applied Physics M,D
- Applied Science and Technology M,O
- Archaeology M,D
- Architectural History D
- Architecture M,D
- Art Education M
- Art History D
- Asian Languages M,D
- Asian Studies M,D
- Astronomy D
- Astrophysics D
- Biochemistry D
- Bioengineering M,D
- Biological and Biomedical Sciences—General M,D,O
- Biomedical Engineering D
- Biophysics D*
- Biopsychology D
- Biostatistics M,D
- Biotechnology M,O
- Business Administration and Management—General M,D,O
- Cell Biology D
- Celtic Languages D
- Chemical Physics D
- Chemistry D
- Chinese D
- Classics D
- Cognitive Sciences M,D
- Communication—General M,O
- Comparative Literature D
- Computational Biology M,D
- Computational Sciences M,D
- Computer Science M,D
- Curriculum and Instruction M
- Demography and Population Studies M,D
- Dentistry M,D,O
- Developmental Psychology D
- East European and Russian Studies M
- Economics D
- Education—General M,D
- Educational Leadership and Administration M,D
- Educational Media/Instructional Technology M,O
- Educational Policy M
- Educational Psychology M
- Electrical Engineering M,D
- Engineering and Applied Sciences—General M,D
- Engineering Design M,D
- English M,D,O
- Environmental and Occupational Health M,D
- Environmental Engineering M,D
- Environmental Management and Policy M,O
- Environmental Sciences M,D
- Epidemiology M,D
- Ergonomics and Human Factors M,D
- Evolutionary Biology D
- Experimental Psychology D
- Forestry M
- Foundations and Philosophy of Education M,O
- French M,D
- Genetics M,D
- Geosciences M,D
- German D
- Health Promotion M,D
- Health Services Management and Hospital Administration M,D
- History of Science and Technology M,D
- History D
- Human Development M
- Industrial and Manufacturing Management D
- Information Science M,D,O
- Inorganic Chemistry D
- International Affairs D
- International and Comparative Education M
- International Development M
- International Health M,D
- Italian M,D
- Japanese D
- Jewish Studies M,D
- Journalism M,O
- Landscape Architecture M,D
- Law M,D
- Legal and Justice Studies D
- Liberal Studies M,O
- Linguistics D
- Management of Technology D
- Management Strategy and Policy D
- Marketing D
- Materials Sciences M,D
- Mathematics Education M,O
- Mathematics D
- Mechanical Engineering M,D
- Medical Physics D
- Medieval and Renaissance Studies D
- Microbiology D
- Molecular Biology D
- Molecular Genetics D
- Molecular Pharmacology D
- Museum Studies M,O
- Music M,D
- Near and Middle Eastern Languages M,D
- Near and Middle Eastern Studies M,D
- Neurobiology D
- Neuroscience D
- Nutrition D
- Oral and Dental Sciences M,D,O
- Organic Chemistry D
- Organizational Behavior D
- Pathology D
- Philosophy M,D
- Physical Chemistry D
- Physics D
- Planetary and Space Sciences M,D
- Political Science M,D
- Portuguese M,D
- Psychology—General D
- Public Administration M,D
- Public Health—General M,D*
- Public Policy M,D
- Quantitative Analysis M,D
- Reading Education M
- Religion D
- Russian D
- Scandinavian Languages D
- Slavic Languages D
- Social Psychology D
- Sociology D
- Spanish M,D
- Statistics M,D
- Systems Biology D
- Technical Communication M
- Theology M
- Theoretical Physics D
- Urban and Regional Planning M,D
- Urban Design M

HASTINGS COLLEGE
- Education—General M

HAWAI'I PACIFIC UNIVERSITY
- Business Administration and Management—General M
- Clinical Psychology M
- Communication—General M
- Educational Leadership and Administration M
- Elementary Education M
- English as a Second Language M
- Finance and Banking M
- Human Resources Management M
- International Business M
- Liberal Studies M
- Management Information Systems M
- Marine Sciences M
- Marketing M
- Military and Defense Studies M
- Nursing—General M,D
- Organizational Management M
- Public Administration M
- Public Health—General M
- Secondary Education M
- Social Work M
- Sustainable Development M

HAZELDEN BETTY FORD GRADUATE SCHOOL OF ADDICTION STUDIES
- Addictions/Substance Abuse Counseling M,O

HEBREW COLLEGE
- Early Childhood Education M,O
- Education—General M,O
- Jewish Studies M,O
- Middle School Education M,O
- Music Education M,O
- Music M,O
- Religious Education M,O
- Special Education M,O
- Theology M

HEBREW UNION COLLEGE–JEWISH INSTITUTE OF RELIGION (NY)
- Education—General M
- Jewish Studies M
- Music M
- Near and Middle Eastern Languages D
- Nonprofit Management M
- Religious Education M
- Theology M,D

HEC MONTREAL
- Accounting M,D,O
- Applied Economics M,D
- Arts Administration O
- Business Administration and Management—General M,D,O
- Business Analytics M
- Corporate and Organizational Communication O
- Data Science/Data Analytics D
- Electronic Commerce M,O
- Entrepreneurship M,O
- Finance and Banking M,D,O
- Financial Engineering M,D
- Human Resources Development O
- Human Resources Management M,D,O
- Industrial and Manufacturing Management M
- International Business M,D
- Logistics M,O
- Management Information Systems M,O
- Management Strategy and Policy M,O
- Marketing M,D
- Medical Microbiology D
- Operations Research O
- Organizational Management M
- Supply Chain Management M,O
- Sustainable Development O
- Taxation M,O

HEIDELBERG UNIVERSITY
- Business Administration and Management—General M
- Clinical Psychology M
- Counseling Psychology M
- Education—General M
- Music Education M
- School Psychology M

HENDERSON STATE UNIVERSITY
- Business Administration and Management—General M
- Counseling Psychology M,O
- Counselor Education M,O
- Curriculum and Instruction M,O
- Early Childhood Education M,O
- Education—General M,O
- Educational Leadership and Administration M,O
- English as a Second Language M,O
- Liberal Studies M
- Middle School Education M,O
- Physical Education M
- Special Education M,O
- Sports Management M

HENDRIX COLLEGE
- Accounting M

HENLEY-PUTNAM SCHOOL OF STRATEGIC SECURITY
- Conflict Resolution and Mediation/Peace Studies M
- Homeland Security M
- Military and Defense Studies M
- National Security D

HERITAGE CHRISTIAN UNIVERSITY
- Classics M
- Pastoral Ministry and Counseling M
- Religion M

HERITAGE COLLEGE AND SEMINARY
- Theology M,O

HERITAGE UNIVERSITY
- Counselor Education M
- Education—General M

*M—masters degree; D—doctorate; O—other advanced degree; *—Close-Up and/or Display*

Educational Leadership and Administration M
English as a Second Language M
English M
Multilingual and Multicultural Education M
Reading Education M
Science Education M
Special Education M

HERZING UNIVERSITY ONLINE
Accounting M
Business Administration and Management—General M
Health Services Management and Hospital Administration M
Human Resources Management M
Management of Technology M
Marketing M
Nursing and Healthcare Administration M
Nursing Education M
Nursing—General M
Project Management M

HIGH POINT UNIVERSITY
Athletic Training and Sports Medicine M,D
Business Administration and Management—General M,D
Corporate and Organizational Communication M,D
Educational Leadership and Administration M,D
Elementary Education M,D
Mathematics Education M,D
Pharmacy M,D
Physical Therapy M,D
Physician Assistant Studies M,D
Secondary Education M,D
Special Education M,D

HIGH TECH HIGH GRADUATE SCHOOL OF EDUCATION
Educational Leadership and Administration M

HILBERT COLLEGE
Criminal Justice and Criminology M
Health Services Management and Hospital Administration M
Public Administration M

HILLSDALE COLLEGE
Political Science M,D

HIRAM COLLEGE
Interdisciplinary Studies M

HODGES UNIVERSITY
Accounting M
Business Administration and Management—General M
Clinical Psychology M
Counseling Psychology M
Health Services Management and Hospital Administration M
Legal and Justice Studies M
Management Information Systems M

HOFSTRA UNIVERSITY
Accounting M,O
Addictions/Substance Abuse Counseling M,O
Advertising and Public Relations M
Allopathic Medicine D
Applied Behavior Analysis M,D,O
Art Education M,D,O
Art Therapy M,O
Bioethics M,D,O
Biological and Biomedical Sciences—General M
Business Administration and Management—General M,O
Business Education M,D,O
Chinese M,D,O
Clinical Psychology M,D
Communication Disorders M,D,O
Computer and Information Systems Security M
Counseling Psychology M,O
Counselor Education M,O
Early Childhood Education M,D,O
Education of the Gifted M,D,O
Education—General M,D,O
Educational Leadership and Administration M,D,O
Educational Media/Instructional Technology M,D,O
Elementary Education M,D,O
Engineering and Applied Sciences—General M
English as a Second Language M,D,O
English Education M,D,O
English M
Entertainment Management M,O
Exercise and Sports Science M,O
Family and Consumer Sciences-General M,D,O
Family Nurse Practitioner Studies M,O
Finance and Banking M,O
Foreign Languages Education M,D,O
French M,D,O
German M,D,O
Gerontological Nursing M
Health Education M,D,O
Health Informatics M,D,O
Health Law M,D,O
Health Services Management and Hospital Administration M,O
Higher Education M,D,O
Human Development M,D,O
Human Resources Management M,O
Humanities M,D,O
Industrial and Organizational Psychology M,D
Intellectual Property Law M,D,O
International Business M,O
Internet Engineering M
Investment Management M,O
Italian M,D,O
Journalism M,O
Law M,D,O
Legal and Justice Studies M,D,O
Linguistics M,D,O
Management Information Systems M,O
Management Strategy and Policy M,O
Marketing Research M,O
Marketing M,O
Marriage and Family Therapy M,O
Mathematics Education M,D,O
Mathematics M,D,O
Medical Physics M
Middle School Education M,D,O
Molecular Medicine D
Multilingual and Multicultural Education M,D,O
Music Education M,D,O
Near and Middle Eastern Languages M,D,O
Nursing and Healthcare Administration M,D,O
Nursing—General M
Occupational Therapy M,D
Physical Education M,D,O
Physician Assistant Studies M
Psychiatric Nursing M
Psychology—General M,D
Public Health—General M,O
Quality Management M,O
Quantitative Analysis M,O
Reading Education M,D,O
Rehabilitation Counseling M,O
Russian M,D,O
School Psychology M,D
Science Education M,D,O
Secondary Education M,D,O
Social Psychology M,D
Social Sciences Education M,D,O
Spanish M,D,O
Special Education M,D,O
Sports Management M,O
Sustainable Development M
Taxation M,O
Urban Design M
Writing M

HOLLINS UNIVERSITY
Art/Fine Arts M
Dance M
Education—General M
English M,O
Film, Television, and Video Production M
Film, Television, and Video Theory and Criticism M
Humanities M
Illustration M,O
Interdisciplinary Studies M
Liberal Studies M
Music M
Social Sciences M
Theater M,O
Writing M,O

HOLMES INSTITUTE
Pastoral Ministry and Counseling M

HOLY APOSTLES COLLEGE AND SEMINARY
Theology M,O

HOLY CROSS GREEK ORTHODOX SCHOOL OF THEOLOGY
Theology M

HOLY FAMILY UNIVERSITY
Accounting M
Business Administration and Management—General M
Counseling Psychology M
Criminal Justice and Criminology M
Early Childhood Education M
Education—General M,D
Educational Leadership and Administration M,D
Elementary Education M
English as a Second Language M
Finance and Banking M
Health Services Management and Hospital Administration M
Human Resources Management M
Management Information Systems M
Nursing and Healthcare Administration M
Nursing Education M
Nursing—General M
Reading Education M
Special Education M

HOLY NAMES UNIVERSITY
Business Administration and Management—General M
Counseling Psychology M
Education—General M,O
Educational Psychology M,O
Family Nurse Practitioner Studies M,O
Finance and Banking M
Forensic Psychology M
Marketing M
Music Education M,O
Music M,O
Nursing and Healthcare Administration M,O
Nursing Informatics M,O
Nursing—General M,O
Pastoral Ministry and Counseling M,O
Special Education M,O
Urban Education M,O
Writing M

HOOD COLLEGE
Accounting M,O
Art/Fine Arts M,O
Bioinformatics M,O
Biological and Biomedical Sciences—General M
Biotechnology M
Business Administration and Management—General M,O
Clinical Psychology M
Computer and Information Systems Security M,O
Computer Science M,O
Curriculum and Instruction M,O
Education—General M,O
Educational Leadership and Administration M,O
Elementary Education M,O
Environmental Biology M,O
Finance and Banking M,O
Geographic Information Systems M,O
Human Development M,O
Human Resources Management M,O
Humanities M
Immunology M
Information Science M,O
Interdisciplinary Studies M,O
Management Information Systems M,O
Marketing M,O
Mathematics Education M
Microbiology M,O
Middle School Education M,O
Molecular Biology M
Organizational Management M,D,O
Psychology—General M,O
Public Administration M,O
Reading Education M,O
School Psychology M
Science Education M,O
Secondary Education M,O
Special Education M,O
Systems Science M
Thanatology M,O

HOOD THEOLOGICAL SEMINARY
Theology M,D

HOPE INTERNATIONAL UNIVERSITY
Education—General M
Educational Leadership and Administration M
Elementary Education M
International Business M
International Development M
Marketing M
Marriage and Family Therapy M
Missions and Missiology M
Music M
Nonprofit Management M
Religion M
Secondary Education M

HOUGHTON COLLEGE
Music M

HOUSTON BAPTIST UNIVERSITY
Addictions/Substance Abuse Counseling M
Art/Fine Arts M
Business Administration and Management—General M,D
Counseling Psychology M,D
Counselor Education M,D
Curriculum and Instruction M,D
Education—General M,D
Educational Leadership and Administration M,D
Educational Measurement and Evaluation M,D
Educational Media/Instructional Technology M,D
Elementary Education M
English as a Second Language M,D
English Education M
English M,D
Higher Education M,D
Human Resources Management M
International Business M
Kinesiology and Movement Studies M
Liberal Studies M
Marriage and Family Therapy M
Mathematics M,D
Middle School Education M
Multilingual and Multicultural Education M,D
Music M
Near and Middle Eastern Languages M,D
Pastoral Ministry and Counseling M
Philosophy M
Psychology—General M
Reading Education M,D
Religious Education M,D
School Psychology M
Science Education M,D
Spanish M
Special Education M,D
Sports Management M
Theology M

HOUSTON GRADUATE SCHOOL OF THEOLOGY
Pastoral Ministry and Counseling M,D
Theology M,D

HOWARD PAYNE UNIVERSITY
Business Administration and Management—General M
Criminal Justice and Criminology M
Educational Leadership and Administration M
Pastoral Ministry and Counseling M
Sports Management M
Theology M

HOWARD UNIVERSITY
Accounting M
African Studies M,D
Allied Health—General M,D
Allopathic Medicine D
Analytical Chemistry M,D
Anatomy M,D
Applied Arts and Design—General M
Applied Mathematics M,D
Art History M
Art/Fine Arts M
Atmospheric Sciences M,D
Biochemistry M,D
Biological and Biomedical Sciences—General M,D
Biophysics D
Biopsychology M,D
Biotechnology M,D
Business Administration and Management—General M
Chemical Engineering M
Chemistry M,D
Civil Engineering M
Clinical Psychology M,D
Communication Disorders M,D
Communication—General M,D
Computer Science M
Corporate and Organizational Communication M,D
Counseling Psychology D
Counselor Education M,D
Dentistry D,O
Developmental Psychology M,D
Economics M,D
Education—General M,D,O
Educational Leadership and Administration M,D,O
Educational Policy M,D,O
Educational Psychology D
Electrical Engineering M,D
Elementary Education M
Engineering and Applied Sciences—General M,D
English M,D
Environmental Sciences M,D
Exercise and Sports Science M
Experimental Psychology M,D
Family Nurse Practitioner Studies M
Film, Television, and Video Production M
Finance and Banking M
French M
Health Education M
History M,D
Human Resources Management M
Inorganic Chemistry M,D
International Business M
Law M,D
Leisure Studies M
Management Information Systems M
Marketing M
Mass Communication M,D
Mathematics M,D
Mechanical Engineering M,D
Media Studies M,D
Microbiology D
Molecular Biology M,D
Multilingual and Multicultural Education M,D
Music Education M
Music M
Nursing Education M
Nursing—General M
Nutrition M,D
Occupational Therapy M
Oral and Dental Sciences D,O
Organic Chemistry M,D
Pharmacology M,D
Pharmacy D
Philosophy M
Photography M
Physical Chemistry M,D
Physical Education M
Physical Therapy M,D
Physician Assistant Studies M,D
Physics M,D
Physiology D
Political Science M,D
Psychology—General M,D
Public Administration M
Public Health—General M
School Psychology M,D
Secondary Education M
Social Psychology M,D
Social Work M,D
Sociology M,D
Spanish M
Special Education M
Sports Management M
Supply Chain Management M
Theology M,D

HULT INTERNATIONAL BUSINESS SCHOOL (UNITED STATES)
Business Administration and Management—General M
Business Analytics M
Entrepreneurship M
Finance and Banking M
International Business M
Marketing M
Project Management M

HUMBOLDT STATE UNIVERSITY
Anthropology M
Biological and Biomedical Sciences—General M
Business Administration and Management—General M
Counseling Psychology M
Developmental Psychology M
Education—General M
English as a Second Language M
English M
Environmental Management and Policy M
Environmental Sciences M
Fish, Game, and Wildlife Management M

Forestry	M
Geology	M
Hazardous Materials Management	M
Kinesiology and Movement Studies	M
Natural Resources	M
Psychology—General	M
School Psychology	M
Social Psychology	M
Social Sciences	M
Social Work	M
Sociology	M
Water Resources	M

HUMPHREYS UNIVERSITY

Law	D

HUNTER COLLEGE OF THE CITY UNIVERSITY OF NEW YORK

Accounting	M
Adult Nursing	M
Animal Behavior	M,O
Anthropology	M
Applied Mathematics	M
Applied Social Research	M
Art History	M
Art/Fine Arts	M
Astronomy	M,D
Biochemistry	M,D
Bioinformatics	M
Biological and Biomedical Sciences—General	M,D
Chemistry	D
Chinese	M
Classics	M
Communication Disorders	M
Community Health Nursing	M
Comparative Literature	M
Counselor Education	M
Early Childhood Education	M,D,O
Economics	M
Education of Students with Severe/Multiple Disabilities	M
Education—General	M,D,O
Educational Leadership and Administration	D,O
Elementary Education	M
English as a Second Language	M
English Education	M
Family Nurse Practitioner Studies	D
Foreign Languages Education	M
French	M
Geographic Information Systems	M,O
Geography	M,O
Geosciences	M
Gerontological Nursing	M,D
History	M
Italian	M
Mathematics Education	M
Mathematics	M
Media Studies	M
Multilingual and Multicultural Education	M
Music Education	M
Music	M
Nursing—General	M,D,O
Nutrition	M
Physical Therapy	D
Physics	M,D
Psychiatric Nursing	M,D,O
Psychology—General	M,O
Public Health—General	M
Rehabilitation Counseling	M
Romance Languages	M
Science Education	M
Secondary Education	M
Social Sciences Education	M
Social Work	M
Sociology	M
Spanish	M
Special Education	M
Statistics	M
Sustainable Development	M,O
Theater	M
Urban and Regional Planning	M
Urban Studies	M
Writing	M

HUNTINGTON UNIVERSITY

Business Administration and Management—General	M,D
Elementary Education	M,D
English as a Second Language	M,D
Middle School Education	M,D
Occupational Therapy	M,D
Organizational Management	M,D
Pastoral Ministry and Counseling	M,D

HUNTINGTON UNIVERSITY OF HEALTH SCIENCES

Nutrition	M,D

HUNTSVILLE BIBLE COLLEGE

Pastoral Ministry and Counseling	M

HUSSON UNIVERSITY

Biotechnology	M
Business Administration and Management—General	M
Clinical Psychology	M
Community Health Nursing	M,O
Counseling Psychology	M
Counselor Education	M
Criminal Justice and Criminology	M
Educational Leadership and Administration	M,O
Family Nurse Practitioner Studies	M,O
Health Services Management and Hospital Administration	M
Hospitality Management	M
Nursing—General	M,O
Organizational Management	M
Pharmacology	M,D
Pharmacy	M,D
Physical Therapy	D
Psychiatric Nursing	M,O
Risk Management	M
School Psychology	M
Social Psychology	M
Sports Management	M

HUSTON-TILLOTSON UNIVERSITY

Educational Leadership and Administration	M

ICAHN SCHOOL OF MEDICINE AT MOUNT SINAI

Allopathic Medicine	D
Bioethics	M
Biological and Biomedical Sciences—General	M,D
Clinical Research	M,D
Community Health	M,D
Genetic Counseling	M,D
Neuroscience	M,D
Public Health—General	M,D

IDAHO STATE UNIVERSITY

Allied Health—General	M,D,O
Anthropology	M
Applied Physics	M,D
Art/Fine Arts	M
Athletic Training and Sports Medicine	M
Biological and Biomedical Sciences—General	M,D
Business Administration and Management—General	M,O
Chemistry	M
Civil Engineering	M
Clinical Psychology	D
Communication Disorders	M,D
Communication—General	M
Community Health	O
Counseling Psychology	M,D,O
Counselor Education	M,D,O
Dental Hygiene	M
Dentistry	O
Education—General	M,D,O
Educational Leadership and Administration	M,D,O
Educational Media/Instructional Technology	M,D
Elementary Education	M
Engineering and Applied Sciences—General	M,D,O
English as a Second Language	M,D,O
English	M,D,O
Environmental Engineering	M
Environmental Management and Policy	M
Environmental Sciences	M,O
Experimental Psychology	D
Geographic Information Systems	M,O
Geology	M,O
Geophysics	M,O
Geosciences	M,O
Health Education	M
Health Physics/Radiological Health	M,D
History	M
Human Resources Management	M,O
Hydrology	M,O
Management Information Systems	M,O
Marriage and Family Therapy	M,D,O
Mathematics Education	M,D
Mathematics	M,D
Mechanical Engineering	M
Medical Microbiology	M,D
Medicinal and Pharmaceutical Chemistry	M,D
Microbiology	M,D
Music Education	M
Nuclear Engineering	M,D
Nursing—General	M,D
Occupational Therapy	M
Operations Research	M
Oral and Dental Sciences	O
Pharmaceutical Administration	M,D
Pharmaceutical Sciences	M,D
Pharmacology	M,D
Pharmacy	M,D
Physical Education	M
Physical Therapy	D
Physician Assistant Studies	M
Physics	M,D
Political Science	M,D
Psychology—General	D
Public Administration	M
Public Health—General	M
Reading Education	M
School Psychology	M,D,O
Secondary Education	M
Sociology	M
Special Education	M
Sports Management	M
Theater	M

IGLOBAL UNIVERSITY

Accounting	M
Business Administration and Management—General	M
Data Science/Data Analytics	M
Entrepreneurship	M
Finance and Banking	M
Health Services Management and Hospital Administration	M
Hospitality Management	M
Human Resources Management	M
International Business	M
Management Information Systems	M
Project Management	M
Public Administration	M
Travel and Tourism	M

ILIFF SCHOOL OF THEOLOGY

Pastoral Ministry and Counseling	M,D
Religion	M,D
Theology	M,D

ILLINOIS COLLEGE

Education—General	M

ILLINOIS COLLEGE OF OPTOMETRY

Optometry	D

ILLINOIS INSTITUTE OF TECHNOLOGY

Aerospace/Aeronautical Engineering	M,D
Agricultural Engineering	M
Analytical Chemistry	M,D
Applied Arts and Design—General	M,D
Applied Mathematics	M,D
Applied Physics	M,D
Architectural Engineering	M,D
Architecture	M,D
Artificial Intelligence/Robotics	M,D
Biochemistry	M,D
Bioengineering	M,D
Biological and Biomedical Sciences—General	M,D
Biomedical Engineering	M,D
Business Administration and Management—General	M,D
Cell Biology	M,D
Chemical Engineering	M,D
Chemistry	M,D
Civil Engineering	M,D
Clinical Psychology	M,D
Communication—General	M,D
Computer and Information Systems Security	M,D
Computer Education	M,D
Computer Engineering	M,D
Computer Science	M,D
Construction Engineering	M,D
Construction Management	M,D
Corporate and Organizational Communication	M
Data Science/Data Analytics	M,D
Electrical Engineering	M,D
Engineering and Applied Sciences—General	M,D
Entrepreneurship	M
Environmental Engineering	M,D
Environmental Management and Policy	M
Finance and Banking	M,D
Food Science and Technology	M
Geotechnical Engineering	M,D
Health Physics/Radiological Health	M,D
Human Resources Development	M,D
Humanities	M,D
Industrial and Manufacturing Management	M
Industrial and Organizational Psychology	M,D
Inorganic Chemistry	M,D
Landscape Architecture	M,D
Law	M,D
Legal and Justice Studies	M,D
Management Information Systems	M,D
Manufacturing Engineering	M,D
Marketing	M
Materials Engineering	M,D
Materials Sciences	M,D
Mathematical and Computational Finance	M,D
Mathematics Education	M,D
Mechanical Engineering	M,D
Medical Imaging	M,D
Microbiology	M,D
Molecular Biology	M,D
Molecular Biophysics	M,D
Physics	M,D
Psychology—General	M,D
Public Administration	M
Rehabilitation Counseling	M,D
Science Education	M,D
Software Engineering	M,D
Structural Engineering	M,D
Sustainability Management	M
Taxation	M,D
Technical Writing	M,D
Telecommunications	M,D
Transportation and Highway Engineering	M,D

ILLINOIS STATE UNIVERSITY

Accounting	M
Agricultural Economics and Agribusiness	M
Agricultural Sciences—General	M
Animal Behavior	M,D
Archaeology	M
Art History	M
Art/Fine Arts	M
Bacteriology	M,D
Biochemistry	M,D
Biological and Biomedical Sciences—General	M,D
Biophysics	M,D
Biotechnology	M
Botany	M,D
Business Administration and Management—General	M
Cell Biology	M,D
Chemistry	M
Clinical Psychology	M,D,O
Cognitive Sciences	M,D,O
Communication Disorders	M
Communication—General	M
Conservation Biology	M,D
Counseling Psychology	M,D,O
Criminal Justice and Criminology	M
Curriculum and Instruction	M,D
Developmental Biology	M,D
Developmental Psychology	M,D,O
Ecology	M,D
Economics	M
Education—General	M,D,O
Educational Leadership and Administration	M,D
Educational Policy	M,D
English	M,D,O
Entomology	M,D
Evolutionary Biology	M,D
Family and Consumer Sciences-General	M
Family Nurse Practitioner Studies	M,D,O
French	M
Genetics	M,D
German	M
Graphic Design	M
Health Education	M
Higher Education	M,D
History	M
Hydrogeology	O
Hydrology	O
Immunology	M,D
Industrial and Organizational Psychology	M,D,O
Industrial/Management Engineering	M
Management Information Systems	M
Management of Technology	M
Mathematics Education	M,D
Mathematics	M
Microbiology	M,D
Molecular Biology	M,D
Molecular Genetics	M,D
Music	M
Neurobiology	M,D
Neuroscience	M,D
Nursing—General	M,D,O
Parasitology	M,D
Photography	M
Physical Education	M
Physiology	M,D
Plant Biology	M,D
Plant Molecular Biology	M,D
Plant Sciences	M,D
Political Science	M
Psychology—General	M,D,O
Reading Education	M
School Psychology	D,O
Social Work	M
Sociology	M
Spanish	M
Special Education	M,D,O
Structural Biology	M,D
Student Affairs	M
Textile Design	M
Theater	M
Writing	O
Zoology	M,D

IMCA–INTERNATIONAL MANAGEMENT CENTRES ASSOCIATION

Business Administration and Management—General	M

IMMACULATA UNIVERSITY

Clinical Psychology	M,D,O
Counseling Psychology	M,D,O
Educational Leadership and Administration	M,D,O
Educational Psychology	M,D,O
English as a Second Language	M
Forensic Psychology	M,D,O
Health Promotion	M
Multilingual and Multicultural Education	M
Neuroscience	M,D,O
Nursing and Healthcare Administration	M
Nursing Education	M
Nursing—General	M
Nutrition	M
Organizational Management	M
Psychoanalysis and Psychotherapy	M,D,O
Psychology—General	M,D,O
School Psychology	M,D,O
Secondary Education	M,D,O
Special Education	M,D,O
Therapies—Dance, Drama, and Music	M

INDEPENDENCE UNIVERSITY

Business Administration and Management—General	M
Community Health Nursing	M
Community Health	M
Gerontological Nursing	M
Health Promotion	M
Health Services Management and Hospital Administration	M
Nursing and Healthcare Administration	M
Nursing—General	M
Public Health—General	M

INDIANA STATE UNIVERSITY

Art/Fine Arts	M
Athletic Training and Sports Medicine	M,D
Biological and Biomedical Sciences—General	M,D
Business Administration and Management—General	M
Cell Biology	M,D
Clinical Psychology	M,D,O
Communication Disorders	M,D,O
Communication—General	M
Computer Engineering	M
Computer Science	M

*M—masters degree; D—doctorate; O—other advanced degree; *—Close-Up and/or Display*

Counselor Education	M,D,O
Criminal Justice and Criminology	M
Curriculum and Instruction	M,D
Ecology	M,D
Education—General	M,D,O
Educational Leadership and Administration	M,D,O
Educational Media/Instructional Technology	M,D
Engineering and Applied Sciences—General	M
English as a Second Language	M,D,O
English	M
Environmental and Occupational Health	M
Evolutionary Biology	M,D
Family Nurse Practitioner Studies	M,D
Foreign Languages Education	M,D,O
Graphic Design	M
Health Education	M,D
Higher Education	M,D,O
History	M
Human Resources Development	M
Linguistics	M,D,O
Management of Technology	M,D
Mathematics	M
Media Studies	M
Molecular Biology	M,D
Multilingual and Multicultural Education	M,D,O
Music Education	M
Music	M
Nursing and Healthcare Administration	M,D
Nursing Education	M,D
Nursing—General	M,D
Occupational Therapy	M,D
Photography	M
Physical Education	M,D
Physical Therapy	M,D
Physician Assistant Studies	M,D
Physiology	M,D
Psychology—General	M,D
Public Administration	M
Recreation and Park Management	M,D
School Psychology	M,D,O
Science Education	M,D
Social Work	M
Spanish	M,D,O
Sports Management	M,D
Student Affairs	M,D,O
Vocational and Technical Education	M
Writing	M

INDIANA TECH

Accounting	M
Business Administration and Management—General	M
Engineering Management	M
Health Services Management and Hospital Administration	M
Human Resources Development	M
Human Resources Management	M
International Business	D
Marketing	M
Organizational Management	M
Psychology—General	M

INDIANA UNIVERSITY BLOOMINGTON

African Studies	M
African-American Studies	M,D
Analytical Chemistry	M,D
Anthropology	M,D
Applied Arts and Design—General	M
Applied Mathematics	M,D
Applied Statistics	M,D
Archaeology	M,D
Art Education	M,D,O
Art History	M,D
Art/Fine Arts	M
Artificial Intelligence/Robotics	D
Arts Administration	M
Asian Languages	M,D
Asian Studies	M,D
Astronomy	M,D
Astrophysics	M,D
Athletic Training and Sports Medicine	M,D
Biochemistry	M,D
Bioinformatics	M,D,O
Biological and Biomedical Sciences—General	M,D
Biostatistics	M,D
Biotechnology	M,D
Business Administration and Management—General	M,D
Cell Biology	M,D
Chemistry	M,D
Chinese	M,D
Classics	M,D
Cognitive Sciences	D
Communication Disorders	M,D
Community Health	M,D
Comparative Literature	M,D
Computer and Information Systems Security	M,D
Computer Science	M,D,O
Counselor Education	M,D,O
Criminal Justice and Criminology	M,D
Curriculum and Instruction	M,D,O
Data Science/Data Analytics	M,O
Developmental Psychology	D
East European and Russian Studies	M,O
Ecology	M,D,O
Economic Development	M,D,O
Economics	M,D
Education—General	M,D,O
Educational Leadership and Administration	M,D,O
Educational Measurement and Evaluation	M,D,O
Educational Media/Instructional Technology	M,D
Educational Policy	M,D,O
Educational Psychology	M,D,O
Elementary Education	M,D,O
Energy Management and Policy	M,D,O
English as a Second Language	M,D
English	M,D
Environmental and Occupational Health	M,D
Environmental Management and Policy	M,D,O
Environmental Sciences	M,D,O
Epidemiology	M,D
Ergonomics and Human Factors	M,D
Evolutionary Biology	M,D
Exercise and Sports Science	M,D
Finance and Banking	M,D,O
Folklore	M,D
Foreign Languages Education	M,D
Foundations and Philosophy of Education	M,D,O
French	M,D
Gender Studies	D
Genetics	M,D
Geochemistry	M,D
Geography	D
Geology	M,D
Geophysics	M,D
Geosciences	M,D
German	M,D
Health Education	M,D
Health Informatics	M,D
Health Promotion	M,D
Health Services Management and Hospital Administration	M,D
Higher Education	M,D,O
Hispanic and Latin American Languages	M,D
History of Science and Technology	M,D
History	M,D
Human-Computer Interaction	M,D
Hydrogeology	M,D
Information Science	M,D,O
Inorganic Chemistry	M,D
International Affairs	M
International and Comparative Education	M,D,O
International Development	M,D,O
Italian	M,D
Japanese	M,D
Jewish Studies	M
Kinesiology and Movement Studies	M,D
Latin American Studies	M
Law	M,D,O
Leisure Studies	M,D
Library Science	M,D,O
Linguistics	M,D
Management Information Systems	M,D,O
Materials Sciences	M,D
Mathematical Physics	M,D
Mathematics Education	M,D,O
Mathematics	M,D
Media Studies	M,D
Medical Physics	M,D
Medieval and Renaissance Studies	M,D
Microbiology	M,D
Mineralogy	M,D
Molecular Biology	M,D
Multilingual and Multicultural Education	M,D
Music	M,D,O
Near and Middle Eastern Languages	M,D
Neuroscience	D
Nonprofit Management	M,D,O
Nutrition	M,D
Optometry	M,D
Organic Chemistry	M,D
Organizational Management	M,D,O
Philosophy	M,D
Physical Chemistry	M,D
Physical Education	M,D
Physics	M,D
Plant Biology	M,D
Political Science	M,D
Portuguese	M,D
Psychology—General	D
Public Administration	M,D,O
Public Affairs	M,D,O
Public Health—General	M,D
Public Policy	M,D,O
Reading Education	M,D,O
Recreation and Park Management	M,D
Religion	M,D
Rhetoric	M,D
Safety Engineering	M,D
School Psychology	M,D,O
Science Education	M,D,O
Secondary Education	M,D,O
Slavic Languages	M,D
Social Psychology	D
Social Sciences Education	M,D,O
Social Sciences	M,D,O
Sociology	M,D
Spanish	M,D
Special Education	M,D,O
Sports Management	M,D
Statistics	M,D
Student Affairs	M,D,O
Sustainability Management	M,D,O
Systems Engineering	D
Theater	M,D
Toxicology	M,D,O
Travel and Tourism	M,D
Water Resources Engineering	M,D,O
Western European Studies	M
Writing	M,D
Zoology	M,D

INDIANA UNIVERSITY EAST

Education—General	M
Nursing—General	M
Social Work	M

INDIANA UNIVERSITY KOKOMO

Accounting	M,O
Business Administration and Management—General	M,O
Family Nurse Practitioner Studies	M
Health Services Management and Hospital Administration	M,O
Nursing and Healthcare Administration	M
Nursing Education	M
Nursing—General	M
Public Administration	M,O
Public Policy	M,O

INDIANA UNIVERSITY NORTHWEST

Accounting	M,O
Addictions/Substance Abuse Counseling	M,O
Business Administration and Management—General	M,O
Counseling Psychology	M,O
Criminal Justice and Criminology	M,O
Education—General	M,O
Educational Leadership and Administration	M,O
Elementary Education	M,O
Environmental Management and Policy	M,O
Gender Studies	M,O
Health Services Management and Hospital Administration	M,O
Liberal Studies	M,O
Management Information Systems	M,O
Nonprofit Management	M,O
Public Administration	M,O
Public Affairs	M,O
Secondary Education	M,O
Social Work	M
Urban Studies	M,O

INDIANA UNIVERSITY OF PENNSYLVANIA

Adult Education	M
Applied Mathematics	M
Archaeology	M
Art/Fine Arts	M
Biological and Biomedical Sciences—General	M
Business Administration and Management—General	M
Business Education	M
Chemistry	M
Clinical Psychology	M,D
Communication Disorders	M
Communication—General	D
Counselor Education	M
Criminal Justice and Criminology	M,D
Curriculum and Instruction	D
Education—General	M,D,O
Educational Leadership and Administration	D,O
Educational Media/Instructional Technology	M,D
Educational Psychology	M,O
English as a Second Language	M,D
English Education	M,D
English	M,D
Environmental and Occupational Health	M,D
Environmental Management and Policy	M
Exercise and Sports Science	M
Foreign Languages Education	M
Geographic Information Systems	M,O
Geography	M
Health Education	M
Health Services Management and Hospital Administration	M,D
Higher Education	M
Hispanic and Latin American Languages	M
History	M
Human Resources Development	M
Industrial and Labor Relations	M
Mathematics Education	M
Mathematics	M
Media Studies	D
Music Education	M
Music	M
Nanotechnology	M
Nonprofit Management	D
Nursing and Healthcare Administration	M
Nursing Education	M
Nursing—General	D
Nutrition	M
Physical Education	M
Physics	M
Psychology—General	M,D
Public Affairs	M
Public History	M
Reading Education	M,O
School Psychology	D,O
Social Psychology	M
Sociology	M
Special Education	M
Sports Management	M
Student Affairs	M
Urban and Regional Planning	M
Vocational and Technical Education	M

INDIANA UNIVERSITY–PURDUE UNIVERSITY FORT WAYNE

Adult Nursing	M,O
Applied Mathematics	M,O
Applied Statistics	M,O
Biological and Biomedical Sciences—General	M
Business Administration and Management—General	M
Civil Engineering	M
Communication—General	M
Computer Engineering	M
Computer Science	M
Construction Management	M
Counselor Education	M,O
Education—General	M,O
Educational Leadership and Administration	M,O
Electrical Engineering	M
Elementary Education	M
Engineering and Applied Sciences—General	M,O
English as a Second Language	M,O
English Education	M,O
English	M,O
Facilities Management	M
Family Nurse Practitioner Studies	M,O
Gerontological Nursing	M,O
Industrial/Management Engineering	M
Information Science	M
Marriage and Family Therapy	M,O
Mathematics Education	M,O
Mathematics	M,O
Mechanical Engineering	M
Nursing and Healthcare Administration	M,O
Nursing Education	M,O
Nursing—General	M,O
Operations Research	M,O
Organizational Management	M,O
Public Policy	M,O
Secondary Education	M
Special Education	M,O
Systems Engineering	M

INDIANA UNIVERSITY–PURDUE UNIVERSITY INDIANAPOLIS

Accounting	M
Acute Care/Critical Care Nursing	M
Allopathic Medicine	M,D
American Studies	M,D
Anatomy	M,D
Applied Mathematics	M,D
Applied Statistics	M,D
Art Therapy	M
Art/Fine Arts	M
Biochemistry	M,D
Bioethics	M,D,O
Bioinformatics	M,D
Biological and Biomedical Sciences—General	M,D
Biomedical Engineering	M,D
Biostatistics	M,D,O
Business Administration and Management—General	M
Cell Biology	M,D
Chemistry	M,D
Clinical Psychology	M,D
Communication—General	M,D
Community Health	M,D,O
Computer and Information Systems Security	M,D,O
Computer Art and Design	M
Computer Engineering	M,D
Computer Science	M,D,O
Counselor Education	M,O
Criminal Justice and Criminology	M,O
Curriculum and Instruction	M,O
Data Science/Data Analytics	M,D,O
Dentistry	M,D,O
Early Childhood Education	M,O
Economics	M
Education—General	M,O
Educational Leadership and Administration	M,O
Electrical Engineering	M,D
Emergency Management	M,O
English as a Second Language	M,O
English	M,O
Entrepreneurship	M
Environmental and Occupational Health	M,D,O
Epidemiology	M,D,O
Family Nurse Practitioner Studies	M
Finance and Banking	M
Foreign Languages Education	M,O
Forensic Sciences	M
Geographic Information Systems	M,O
Geology	M,D
Geosciences	M,D
Gerontological Nursing	M
Graphic Design	M
Health Communication	M,O
Health Education	M,D
Health Informatics	M,D
Health Law	M,D,O
Health Services Management and Hospital Administration	M,D,O
History	M
Homeland Security	M,O
Human-Computer Interaction	M,D
Immunology	M,D
Industrial and Organizational Psychology	M,D
Information Science	M
Intellectual Property Law	M,D,O
International Health	M,D,O
Kinesiology and Movement Studies	M,O
Law	M,D,O
Liberal Studies	M,D,O
Library Science	M,O
Management of Technology	M
Marketing	M
Mathematics Education	M,D
Mathematics	M,D
Mechanical Engineering	M,D
Microbiology	M,D
Molecular Biology	M,D
Molecular Genetics	M,D
Museum Studies	M,O
Music	M,D
Natural Resources	M,D,O
Neurobiology	D
Nonprofit Management	M,O
Nursing and Healthcare Administration	M,D
Nursing Education	M
Nursing—General	M,D
Nutrition	M,D

- Occupational Therapy M,D
- Organizational Management M,O
- Pathology M,D
- Pediatric Nursing M
- Pharmacology M,D
- Philanthropic Studies M,D
- Philosophy M,D
- Photography M
- Physical Education M,O
- Physical Therapy M,D
- Physics M,D
- Political Science M
- Psychology—General M,D
- Public Administration M,D
- Public Affairs M,O
- Public Health—General M,D,O
- Public History M
- Reading Education M,O
- Rehabilitation Sciences M,D
- Social Psychology M,D
- Social Sciences M,D,O
- Social Work M,D,O
- Sociology M
- Software Engineering M,D,O
- Special Education M,O
- Statistics M,D
- Supply Chain Management M
- Technical Communication M
- Therapies—Dance, Drama, and Music M,D
- Toxicology M,D
- Western European Studies M
- Writing M,O

INDIANA UNIVERSITY SOUTH BEND
- Accounting M,O
- Addictions/Substance Abuse Counseling M,O
- Applied Mathematics M,O
- Business Administration and Management—General M,O
- Clinical Psychology M,D
- Communication—General M,D
- Computer Science M,O
- Counseling Psychology M,O
- Counselor Education M,O
- Education—General M,O
- Educational Leadership and Administration M,O
- Educational Media/Instructional Technology M,O
- Elementary Education M,O
- English M,O
- Family Nurse Practitioner Studies M
- Finance and Banking M,O
- Health Services Management and Hospital Administration M,O
- Human Resources Management M,O
- International Affairs M,O
- Legal and Justice Studies M,O
- Liberal Studies M,O
- Marketing M,O
- Marriage and Family Therapy M,O
- Music M,D
- Nonprofit Management M,O
- Nursing—General M
- Public Administration M,O
- Public Affairs M,O
- School Psychology M,O
- Secondary Education M,O
- Social Work M
- Special Education M,O
- Writing M,O

INDIANA UNIVERSITY SOUTHEAST
- Business Administration and Management—General M
- Counselor Education M
- Education—General M
- Elementary Education M
- Finance and Banking M
- Interdisciplinary Studies M,O
- Secondary Education M

INDIANA WESLEYAN UNIVERSITY
- Accounting M,O
- Addictions/Substance Abuse Counseling M
- Business Administration and Management—General M,O
- Counseling Psychology M,O
- Counselor Education M,O
- Educational Leadership and Administration M,O
- Health Services Management and Hospital Administration M,O
- Higher Education M
- Human Resources Management M,O
- Marriage and Family Therapy M
- Nursing and Healthcare Administration M
- Nursing Education M
- Nursing—General M
- Organizational Management M,D,O
- Pastoral Ministry and Counseling M
- Social Psychology M
- Theology M

INSTITUTE FOR CHRISTIAN STUDIES
- Education—General M,D
- Philosophy M,D
- Political Science M,D
- Theology M,D

INSTITUTE FOR CLINICAL SOCIAL WORK
- Social Work D

INSTITUTE FOR DOCTORAL STUDIES IN THE VISUAL ARTS
- Art/Fine Arts D
- Philosophy D

INSTITUTE OF AMERICAN INDIAN ARTS
- Writing M

INSTITUTE OF CLINICAL ACUPUNCTURE AND ORIENTAL MEDICINE
- Acupuncture and Oriental Medicine M

INSTITUTE OF PUBLIC ADMINISTRATION
- Health Services Management and Hospital Administration M,O
- Public Administration M,O

INSTITUTE OF TAOIST EDUCATION AND ACUPUNCTURE
- Acupuncture and Oriental Medicine M

THE INSTITUTE OF WORLD POLITICS
- Military and Defense Studies M,O
- National Security M,O
- Political Science M,O
- Public Affairs M,O
- Public Policy M,O

INSTITUT FRANCO-EUROPÉEN DE CHIROPRAXIE
- Chiropractic D

INSTITUTO CENTROAMERICANO DE ADMINISTRACIÓN DE EMPRESAS
- Agricultural Economics and Agribusiness M
- Business Administration and Management—General M
- Finance and Banking M
- Management of Technology M
- Real Estate M
- Sustainable Development M

INSTITUTO TECNOLOGICO DE SANTO DOMINGO
- Accounting M,O
- Adult Education M,O
- Allopathic Medicine M,D
- Bioethics M,O
- Business Administration and Management—General M,O
- Communication—General M,O
- Construction Management M,O
- Counseling Psychology M,O
- Economics M,O
- Education—General M,O
- Educational Leadership and Administration M,O
- Educational Psychology M,O
- Energy and Power Engineering M,D,O
- Energy Management and Policy M,D,O
- Engineering and Applied Sciences—General M,O
- Environmental Education M,D,O
- Environmental Engineering M,O
- Environmental Management and Policy M,D,O
- Environmental Sciences M,D,O
- Finance and Banking M,O
- Gender Studies M,O
- Health Promotion M,O
- Human Resources Management M,O
- Humanities M,O
- Industrial and Manufacturing Management M,O
- Industrial/Management Engineering M,O
- Information Science M,O
- International Affairs M,O
- International Business M,O
- Linguistics M,O
- Marine Sciences M,D,O
- Marketing M,O
- Marriage and Family Therapy M,O
- Maternal and Child Health M,O
- Mathematics M,D,O
- Natural Resources M,D,O
- Nutrition M,O
- Organizational Management M,O
- Quality Management M,O
- Quantitative Analysis M,O
- Secondary Education M,O
- Social Sciences Education M,O
- Software Engineering M,O
- Structural Engineering M,O
- Sustainable Development M,O
- Taxation M,O
- Telecommunications M,O
- Transportation Management M,O

INSTITUTO TECNOLÓGICO Y DE ESTUDIOS SUPERIORES DE MONTERREY, CAMPUS CENTRAL DE VERACRUZ
- Business Administration and Management—General M
- Computer Science M
- Education—General M
- Educational Leadership and Administration M
- Educational Media/Instructional Technology M
- Electronic Commerce M
- Finance and Banking M
- Humanities M
- International Business M
- Management Information Systems M
- Marketing M

INSTITUTO TECNOLÓGICO Y DE ESTUDIOS SUPERIORES DE MONTERREY, CAMPUS CHIHUAHUA
- Computer Engineering M,O
- Electrical Engineering M,O
- Engineering Management M,O
- Industrial/Management Engineering M,O
- International Business M,O
- Mechanical Engineering M,O
- Systems Engineering M,O

INSTITUTO TECNOLÓGICO Y DE ESTUDIOS SUPERIORES DE MONTERREY, CAMPUS CIUDAD DE MÉXICO
- Business Administration and Management—General M,D
- Computer Science M,D
- Economics M,D
- Education—General M,D
- Educational Media/Instructional Technology M,D
- Environmental Engineering M,D
- Environmental Sciences M,D
- Finance and Banking M,D
- Humanities M,D
- Industrial/Management Engineering M,D
- International Business M,D
- Law O
- Management Information Systems M,D
- Quality Management M,D
- Telecommunications Management M

INSTITUTO TECNOLÓGICO Y DE ESTUDIOS SUPERIORES DE MONTERREY, CAMPUS CIUDAD JUÁREZ
- Business Administration and Management—General M
- Education—General M
- Educational Leadership and Administration M
- Educational Media/Instructional Technology M,D
- Electronic Commerce M
- Humanities M
- Management Information Systems M
- Public Administration M
- Quality Management M

INSTITUTO TECNOLÓGICO Y DE ESTUDIOS SUPERIORES DE MONTERREY, CAMPUS CIUDAD OBREGÓN
- Business Administration and Management—General M
- Communication—General M
- Developmental Education M
- Education—General M
- Engineering and Applied Sciences—General M
- Finance and Banking M
- International Affairs M
- Management Information Systems M
- Marketing M
- Mathematics Education M
- Telecommunications Management M

INSTITUTO TECNOLÓGICO Y DE ESTUDIOS SUPERIORES DE MONTERREY, CAMPUS CUERNAVACA
- Business Administration and Management—General M
- Computer Science M,D
- Finance and Banking M
- Human Resources Management M
- Information Science M,D
- International Business M
- Management of Technology M,D
- Marketing M

INSTITUTO TECNOLÓGICO Y DE ESTUDIOS SUPERIORES DE MONTERREY, CAMPUS ESTADO DE MÉXICO
- Architecture M,D
- Business Administration and Management—General M,D
- Computer Science M,D
- Education—General M,D
- Educational Leadership and Administration M,D
- Educational Media/Instructional Technology M,D
- Electronic Commerce M,D
- Environmental Management and Policy M,D
- Finance and Banking M,D
- Humanities M,D
- Industrial and Manufacturing Management M,D
- Information Science M,D
- Management Information Systems M,D
- Marketing M,D
- Materials Engineering M,D
- Materials Sciences M,D
- Quality Management M,D
- Telecommunications Management M,D

INSTITUTO TECNOLÓGICO Y DE ESTUDIOS SUPERIORES DE MONTERREY, CAMPUS GUADALAJARA
- Business Administration and Management—General M
- Finance and Banking M

INSTITUTO TECNOLÓGICO Y DE ESTUDIOS SUPERIORES DE MONTERREY, CAMPUS IRAPUATO
- Architecture M,D
- Business Administration and Management—General M,D
- Computer Science M,D
- Education—General M,D
- Educational Leadership and Administration M,D
- Educational Media/Instructional Technology M,D
- Electronic Commerce M,D
- Environmental Management and Policy M,D
- Finance and Banking M,D
- Humanities M,D
- Industrial and Manufacturing Management M,D
- Information Science M,D
- International Business M,D
- Library Science M,D
- Management Information Systems M,D
- Management of Technology M,D
- Marketing Research M,D
- Quality Management M,D
- Telecommunications Management M,D

INSTITUTO TECNOLÓGICO Y DE ESTUDIOS SUPERIORES DE MONTERREY, CAMPUS LAGUNA
- Business Administration and Management—General M
- Industrial/Management Engineering M
- Management Information Systems M

INSTITUTO TECNOLÓGICO Y DE ESTUDIOS SUPERIORES DE MONTERREY, CAMPUS LEÓN
- Business Administration and Management—General M

INSTITUTO TECNOLÓGICO Y DE ESTUDIOS SUPERIORES DE MONTERREY, CAMPUS MONTERREY
- Agricultural Engineering M,D
- Agricultural Sciences—General M,D
- Applied Statistics M,D
- Artificial Intelligence/Robotics M,D
- Biotechnology M,D
- Business Administration and Management—General M,D
- Chemical Engineering M,D
- Chemistry M,D
- Civil Engineering M,D
- Communication—General M,D
- Computer Science M,D
- Electrical Engineering M,D
- Engineering and Applied Sciences—General M,D
- Environmental Engineering M,D
- Finance and Banking M
- Industrial/Management Engineering M,D
- Information Science M,D
- International Business M
- Manufacturing Engineering M,D
- Marketing M
- Mechanical Engineering M,D
- Organic Chemistry M,D
- Science Education M,D
- Systems Engineering M,D

INSTITUTO TECNOLÓGICO Y DE ESTUDIOS SUPERIORES DE MONTERREY, CAMPUS QUERÉTARO
- Business Administration and Management—General M

INSTITUTO TECNOLÓGICO Y DE ESTUDIOS SUPERIORES DE MONTERREY, CAMPUS SONORA NORTE
- Business Administration and Management—General M
- Education—General M
- Information Science M

INSTITUTO TECNOLÓGICO Y DE ESTUDIOS SUPERIORES DE MONTERREY, CAMPUS TOLUCA
- Business Administration and Management—General M

INTER AMERICAN UNIVERSITY OF PUERTO RICO, AGUADILLA CAMPUS
- Accounting M
- Business Administration and Management—General M
- Counseling Psychology M
- Criminal Justice and Criminology M
- Educational Leadership and Administration M
- Elementary Education M
- Finance and Banking M
- Human Resources Management M
- Management Information Systems M
- Marketing M

INTER AMERICAN UNIVERSITY OF PUERTO RICO, ARECIBO CAMPUS
- Accounting M
- Acute Care/Critical Care Nursing M
- Business Administration and Management—General M
- Counselor Education M
- Curriculum and Instruction M
- Education—General M
- Educational Leadership and Administration M
- Elementary Education M
- English as a Second Language M
- Finance and Banking M
- Foreign Languages Education M
- Human Resources Management M

*M—masters degree; D—doctorate; O—other advanced degree; *—Close-Up and/or Display*

- Mathematics Education M
- Medical/Surgical Nursing M
- Nurse Anesthesia M
- Nursing—General M
- Science Education M
- Social Sciences Education M

INTER AMERICAN UNIVERSITY OF PUERTO RICO, BARRANQUITAS CAMPUS
- Accounting M
- Acute Care/Critical Care Nursing M
- Biological and Biomedical Sciences—General M
- Biotechnology M
- Business Administration and Management—General M
- Criminal Justice and Criminology M
- Curriculum and Instruction M
- Education—General M
- Educational Leadership and Administration M
- Elementary Education M
- English as a Second Language M
- Foreign Languages Education M
- History M
- Human Resources Management M
- Library Science M
- Medical/Surgical Nursing M
- Nursing—General M
- Special Education M

INTER AMERICAN UNIVERSITY OF PUERTO RICO, BAYAMÓN CAMPUS
- Aerospace/Aeronautical Engineering M
- Biotechnology M
- Ecology M
- Electrical Engineering M
- Energy and Power Engineering M
- Human Resources Management M
- Mechanical Engineering M

INTER AMERICAN UNIVERSITY OF PUERTO RICO, FAJARDO CAMPUS
- Business Administration and Management—General M
- Computer Science M
- Educational Leadership and Administration M
- Human Resources Management M
- Management Information Systems M
- Marketing M
- Special Education M

INTER AMERICAN UNIVERSITY OF PUERTO RICO, GUAYAMA CAMPUS
- Business Administration and Management—General M
- Computer and Information Systems Security M
- Computer Science M
- Early Childhood Education M
- Elementary Education M
- Marketing M

INTER AMERICAN UNIVERSITY OF PUERTO RICO, METROPOLITAN CAMPUS
- Accounting M
- American Studies M,D
- Athletic Training and Sports Medicine M
- Business Administration and Management—General M
- Business Education M
- Clinical Laboratory Sciences/Medical Technology M
- Computer Science M
- Counseling Psychology M,D
- Counselor Education M,D
- Criminal Justice and Criminology M
- Curriculum and Instruction M,D
- Education—General M,D
- Educational Leadership and Administration M,D
- Educational Media/Instructional Technology M
- Elementary Education M
- English as a Second Language M
- English M
- Environmental Management and Policy M
- Exercise and Sports Science M
- Finance and Banking M
- Foreign Languages Education M
- Health Education M
- Higher Education M
- History M,D
- Human Resources Development M
- Human Resources Management M
- Industrial and Labor Relations M,D
- Industrial and Manufacturing Management M
- Industrial and Organizational Psychology M,D
- International Business M,D
- Management Information Systems M
- Marketing M
- Mathematics Education M
- Microbiology M
- Molecular Biology M
- Music Education M
- Pastoral Ministry and Counseling D
- Physical Education M
- Psychology—General M,D
- Religious Education D
- School Psychology M,D
- Science Education M
- Social Sciences Education M
- Social Work M
- Spanish M
- Special Education M
- Theology D

- Vocational and Technical Education M
- Women's Studies M

INTER AMERICAN UNIVERSITY OF PUERTO RICO, PONCE CAMPUS
- Accounting M
- Criminal Justice and Criminology M
- Elementary Education M
- English as a Second Language M
- Finance and Banking M
- Human Resources Management M
- Marketing M
- Mathematics Education M
- Science Education M
- Social Sciences Education M
- Spanish M

INTER AMERICAN UNIVERSITY OF PUERTO RICO, SAN GERMÁN CAMPUS
- Accounting M,D
- Applied Mathematics M
- Art/Fine Arts M
- Business Administration and Management—General M,D
- Business Education M
- Counseling Psychology M,D
- Counselor Education M,D
- Curriculum and Instruction D
- Elementary Education M
- English as a Second Language M
- Environmental Sciences M
- Finance and Banking M,D
- Graphic Design M
- Health Education M
- Human Resources Development M,D
- Human Resources Management M,D
- Industrial and Manufacturing Management M,D
- International Business M,D
- Kinesiology and Movement Studies M
- Library Science M
- Management Information Systems M,D
- Marketing M,D
- Mathematics Education M
- Music Education M
- Music M
- Photography M
- Physical Education M
- Psychology—General M,D
- School Psychology M,D
- Science Education M
- Special Education M

INTER AMERICAN UNIVERSITY OF PUERTO RICO SCHOOL OF LAW
- Law D

INTER AMERICAN UNIVERSITY OF PUERTO RICO SCHOOL OF OPTOMETRY
- Optometry D

INTERDENOMINATIONAL THEOLOGICAL CENTER
- Pastoral Ministry and Counseling M,D
- Religious Education M,D
- Theology M,D

INTERIOR DESIGNERS INSTITUTE
- Interior Design M

INTERNATIONAL BAPTIST COLLEGE AND SEMINARY
- Education—General M
- Pastoral Ministry and Counseling M,D
- Theology M

INTERNATIONAL INSTITUTE FOR RESTORATIVE PRACTICES
- Organizational Behavior M,O

INTERNATIONAL TECHNOLOGICAL UNIVERSITY
- Business Administration and Management—General M,D
- Computer Art and Design M
- Computer Engineering M
- Electrical Engineering M,D
- Engineering Management M
- Software Engineering M

INTERNATIONAL UNIVERSITY IN GENEVA
- Business Administration and Management—General M,D
- Communication—General M,D
- Entrepreneurship M,D
- International Affairs M,D
- International Business M,D
- Marketing M,D
- Media Studies M,D
- Public Administration M,D

THE INTERNATIONAL UNIVERSITY OF MONACO
- Business Administration and Management—General M
- Entrepreneurship M
- Finance and Banking M
- Financial Engineering M
- International Business M
- Marketing M

IONA COLLEGE
- Accounting M,O
- Advertising and Public Relations M,O
- Business Administration and Management—General M,O
- Communication Disorders M
- Computer and Information Systems Security M,O
- Computer Science M
- Counseling Psychology M,O
- Criminal Justice and Criminology M,O
- Early Childhood Education M
- Education—General M

- Educational Leadership and Administration M
- English Education M
- English M
- Experimental Psychology M,O
- Finance and Banking M,O
- Foreign Languages Education M
- Forensic Sciences M,O
- Game Design and Development M
- Health Services Management and Hospital Administration M,O
- History M
- Human Resources Management M,O
- Industrial and Organizational Psychology M,O
- International Business M,O
- Management Information Systems M,O
- Management of Technology M,O
- Marketing M,O
- Marriage and Family Therapy M
- Mass Communication M,O
- Mathematics Education M
- Nonprofit Management M,O
- Project Management M,O
- Psychology—General M,O
- Recreation and Park Management M,O
- Risk Management M,O
- School Psychology M,O
- Science Education M
- Social Sciences Education M
- Spanish M
- Special Education M
- Sports Management M,O

IOWA STATE UNIVERSITY OF SCIENCE AND TECHNOLOGY
- Accounting M
- Aerospace/Aeronautical Engineering M,D
- Agricultural Economics and Agribusiness M,D
- Agricultural Education M,D
- Agricultural Engineering M,D
- Agricultural Sciences—General M,D
- Agronomy and Soil Sciences M,D
- Analytical Chemistry M,D
- Animal Sciences M,D
- Anthropology M
- Applied Arts and Design—General M,D
- Applied Mathematics M,D
- Applied Physics M,D
- Architecture M
- Art/Fine Arts M
- Astrophysics M,D
- Bioinformatics M,D
- Biological and Biomedical Sciences—General M,D
- Biophysics M,D
- Biostatistics M,D
- Business Administration and Management—General M
- Business Analytics M
- Cell Biology M,D
- Chemical Engineering M,D
- Chemistry M,D
- Child and Family Studies M,D
- Civil Engineering M,D
- Clothing and Textiles M,D
- Cognitive Sciences M,D
- Computational Biology M,D
- Computer Engineering M,D
- Computer Science M,D
- Condensed Matter Physics M,D
- Construction Engineering M,D
- Corporate and Organizational Communication M,D
- Counseling Psychology M,D
- Counselor Education M,D
- Curriculum and Instruction M,D
- Developmental Biology M,D
- Ecology M,D
- Economics M,D
- Education—General M,D
- Educational Leadership and Administration M,D
- Educational Measurement and Evaluation M,D
- Educational Media/Instructional Technology M,D
- Electrical Engineering M,D
- Elementary Education M,D
- English as a Second Language M
- English M,D
- Entomology M,D
- Environmental Engineering M,D
- Environmental Sciences M,D
- Evolutionary Biology M,D
- Exercise and Sports Science M
- Family and Consumer Sciences-General M
- Finance and Banking M
- Fish, Game, and Wildlife Management M,D
- Food Science and Technology M,D
- Forestry M,D
- Foundations and Philosophy of Education M,D
- Genetics M,D
- Geology M,D
- Geosciences M,D
- Geotechnical Engineering M,D
- Graphic Design M
- Higher Education M,D
- History M,D
- Horticulture M,D
- Human Development M,D
- Human Resources Development M,D
- Human-Computer Interaction M,D
- Immunology M,D
- Industrial Design M

- Industrial/Management Engineering M,D
- Information Science M
- Inorganic Chemistry M,D
- Interdisciplinary Studies M
- Interior Design M
- Journalism M
- Kinesiology and Movement Studies M,D
- Landscape Architecture M
- Linguistics M
- Management Information Systems M,D
- Mass Communication M,D
- Materials Engineering M,D
- Materials Sciences M,D
- Mathematics Education M,D
- Mathematics M,D
- Mechanical Engineering M,D
- Mechanics M,D
- Meteorology M,D
- Microbiology M,D
- Molecular Biology M,D
- Molecular Genetics M,D
- Natural Resources M,D
- Neuroscience M,D
- Nutrition M,D
- Operations Research M,D
- Organic Chemistry M,D
- Pathology M,D
- Physical Chemistry M,D
- Physics M,D
- Plant Biology M,D
- Plant Pathology M,D
- Plant Sciences M,D
- Political Science M
- Psychology—General M,D
- Public Administration M
- Rhetoric M,D
- Rural Planning and Studies D
- Rural Sociology M,D
- Science Education M
- Social Psychology M,D
- Sociology M,D
- Special Education M,D
- Statistics M,D
- Structural Biology M,D
- Structural Engineering M,D
- Student Affairs M,D
- Sustainable Development M,D
- Systems Engineering M
- Toxicology M,D
- Transportation and Highway Engineering M,D
- Transportation Management M
- Urban and Regional Planning M
- Veterinary Medicine M
- Veterinary Sciences M,D
- Vocational and Technical Education M,D
- Writing M,D

IRELL & MANELLA GRADUATE SCHOOL OF BIOLOGICAL SCIENCES
- Biochemistry D
- Biological and Biomedical Sciences—General D*
- Cancer Biology/Oncology D
- Cell Biology D
- Developmental Biology D
- Genetics D
- Immunology D
- Molecular Biology D
- Neuroscience D
- Pharmaceutical Sciences D

ITHACA COLLEGE
- Accounting M
- Agricultural Education M
- Allied Health—General M,D
- Art/Fine Arts M
- Business Administration and Management—General M
- Communication Disorders M
- Elementary Education M
- English Education M
- Exercise and Sports Science M
- Health Education M
- Internet and Interactive Multimedia M
- Music Education M
- Music M
- Occupational Therapy M
- Photography M
- Physical Education M
- Physical Therapy D
- Secondary Education M
- Sports Management M
- Writing M

JACKSON STATE UNIVERSITY
- Accounting M
- Applied Mathematics M
- Atmospheric Sciences M,D
- Biological and Biomedical Sciences—General M
- Business Administration and Management—General M,D
- Chemistry M,D
- Civil Engineering M,D
- Clinical Psychology M,D
- Communication Disorders M
- Computer Science M
- Counselor Education M
- Criminal Justice and Criminology M
- Early Childhood Education M,D,O
- Education—General M,D,O
- Educational Leadership and Administration M,D,O
- Elementary Education M,D,O
- English Education M
- English M
- Environmental Engineering M
- Environmental Sciences M
- Geosciences M,D
- Health Education M
- Higher Education M,D,O
- History M

Materials Sciences M,D
Mathematics Education M
Mathematics M
Music Education M
Physical Education M
Physics M,D
Political Science M
Psychology—General D
Public Administration M,D
Public Affairs M,D
Public Health—General M,D
Public Policy M,D
Reading Education M,D,O
Rehabilitation Sciences M
School Psychology M
Science Education M,D
Social Work M,D
Sociology M
Special Education M,O
Sports Management M
Statistics M
Urban and Regional Planning M,D
Vocational and Technical Education M,D

JACKSONVILLE STATE UNIVERSITY

Biological and Biomedical Sciences—General M
Business Administration and Management—General M
Computer Science M
Counselor Education M
Criminal Justice and Criminology M
Early Childhood Education M
Education—General M,O
Educational Leadership and Administration M,O
Educational Media/Instructional Technology M
Elementary Education M
Emergency Management M,D
English M
History M
Liberal Studies M
Mathematics M
Music M
Nursing—General M
Physical Education M,O
Political Science M
Psychology—General M
Reading Education M
Secondary Education M
Software Engineering M
Special Education M

JACKSONVILLE UNIVERSITY

Accounting M
Adult Nursing M,D,O
Allied Health—General M,D
Art/Fine Arts M
Business Administration and Management—General M,D*
Communication Disorders M
Counseling Psychology M
Dance M
Dentistry M,O
Educational Leadership and Administration M
Family Nurse Practitioner Studies M
Finance and Banking M
Gerontological Nursing M,D,O
Health Informatics M
Kinesiology and Movement Studies M
Marine Sciences M
Marketing M
Marriage and Family Therapy M
Mathematics M
Nursing and Healthcare Administration M
Nursing Education M
Nursing Informatics M
Nursing—General M,D
Occupational Therapy D
Oral and Dental Sciences M,O
Organizational Management M
Psychiatric Nursing M
Public Policy M
Sports Management M

JAMES MADISON UNIVERSITY

Accounting M
American Studies M
Applied Behavior Analysis M
Art Education M
Art History M
Art/Fine Arts M
Biological and Biomedical Sciences—General M
Business Administration and Management—General M
Clinical Psychology D
Communication Disorders M,D
Communication—General M
Computer and Information Systems Security M
Computer Science M
Counseling Psychology D
Early Childhood Education M
Education of the Gifted M
Educational Leadership and Administration M
Educational Measurement and Evaluation M,D
Educational Media/Instructional Technology M
Elementary Education M
Engineering and Applied Sciences—General M
English as a Second Language M
English M
Entrepreneurship M
Environmental Management and Policy M
Exercise and Sports Science M
Experimental Psychology M
Family Nurse Practitioner Studies M,D
Foreign Languages Education M
Forensic Sciences M
Gerontological Nursing M,D
Health Education M
Higher Education M
History M
Human Resources Management M
Kinesiology and Movement Studies M
Management Information Systems M
Management Strategy and Policy D
Mathematics Education M
Middle School Education M
Multilingual and Multicultural Education M
Music Education M
Music M,D
Nonprofit Management M,D
Nurse Midwifery M,D
Nursing and Healthcare Administration M,D
Nursing—General M,D
Nutrition M
Occupational Therapy M
Organizational Management D
Photography M
Physical Education M
Physician Assistant Studies M
Physiology M
Political Science M
Psychiatric Nursing M,D
Psychology—General M
Public Administration M
Public History M
Reading Education M
Rhetoric M
School Psychology M,D,O
Secondary Education M
Special Education M
Sustainability Management M
Taxation M
Technical Writing M
Vocational and Technical Education M
Writing M

JEFFERSON COLLEGE OF HEALTH SCIENCES

Nursing and Healthcare Administration M
Nursing Education M
Nursing—General M
Occupational Therapy M
Physician Assistant Studies M

THE JEWISH THEOLOGICAL SEMINARY

Jewish Studies M,D
Music M
Religion M,D
Religious Education M,D
Theology M,D,O
Women's Studies M,D

JOHN BROWN UNIVERSITY

Business Administration and Management—General M
Clinical Psychology M,O
Counseling Psychology M,O
Counselor Education M,O
Curriculum and Instruction M
Education—General M
Ethics M
International Business M
Marriage and Family Therapy M,O
Secondary Education M

JOHN CARROLL UNIVERSITY

Accounting M
Biological and Biomedical Sciences—General M
Business Administration and Management—General M
Counseling Psychology M,O
Counselor Education M,O
Education—General M
Educational Psychology M,O
English M
Humanities M
Mathematics M
Nonprofit Management M
Religion M
Theology M

JOHN F. KENNEDY UNIVERSITY

Art/Fine Arts M
Business Administration and Management—General M,O
Comparative and Interdisciplinary Arts M
Counseling Psychology M
Education—General M
Health Education M
Health Psychology M
Human Resources Development M,O
Industrial and Organizational Psychology M,O
Law D
Museum Studies M,O
Organizational Management M,O
Psychology—General M,D,O
Sport Psychology M
Transpersonal and Humanistic Psychology M

JOHN JAY COLLEGE OF CRIMINAL JUSTICE OF THE CITY UNIVERSITY OF NEW YORK

Criminal Justice and Criminology M,D
Forensic Psychology M,D
Forensic Sciences M,D
Legal and Justice Studies M,D
Organizational Behavior M,D
Public Administration M
Public Policy M,D

THE JOHN MARSHALL LAW SCHOOL

Law M,D

JOHN PAUL THE GREAT CATHOLIC UNIVERSITY

Theology M

JOHNS HOPKINS UNIVERSITY

Aerospace/Aeronautical Engineering M
Allopathic Medicine D
Anatomy D
Anthropology D
Applied Behavior Analysis O
Applied Economics M
Applied Mathematics M,D,O
Applied Physics M,O
Archaeology D
Art History M,D
Artificial Intelligence/Robotics M
Asian Studies M,D,O
Astronomy D
Biochemistry M,D
Bioengineering M,D
Bioethics M,D
Bioinformatics M
Biological and Biomedical Sciences—General M,D
Biomedical Engineering M,D,O
Biophysics D
Biostatistics M,D
Biotechnology M
Business Administration and Management—General M,O
Business Analytics M
Cardiovascular Sciences M,D
Cell Biology D
Chemical Engineering M,D
Chemistry M,D
Civil Engineering M,D,O
Classics D
Clinical Psychology M,D
Clinical Research M,D
Cognitive Sciences M,D
Communication—General M,O
Community Health Nursing
Community Health M,D
Comparative Literature D
Computer and Information Systems Security M,O
Computer Engineering M,D,O
Computer Science M,D,O
Counseling Psychology M,O
Counselor Education M,O
Demography and Population Studies M,D
Developmental Biology D
Early Childhood Education M
Economics D
Education of the Gifted M,O
Education—General M,D,O
Educational Leadership and Administration M,D,O
Educational Media/Instructional Technology M
Educational Policy D
Electrical Engineering M,D,O
Elementary Education M
Energy Management and Policy M,O
Engineering and Applied Sciences—General M,D,O
Engineering Management M
English M,D
Environmental and Occupational Health M,D
Environmental Engineering M,D,O
Environmental Management and Policy M,O
Environmental Sciences M,O
Epidemiology M,D
Evolutionary Biology D
Family Nurse Practitioner Studies D
Film, Television, and Video Production M
Finance and Banking M,D,O
French M,D
Genetic Counseling M,D
Genetics M,D
Geographic Information Systems M,O
Geosciences M,D
German M,D
Gerontological Nursing D
Health Communication M,D
Health Education M,D
Health Informatics M,D,O
Health Services Management and Hospital Administration M,D
History of Science and Technology M,D
History D
Homeland Security M,O
Immunology M,D
Infectious Diseases M,D
International Affairs M,D,O
International Development M,D,O
International Economics M,D,O
International Health M,D
Investment Management M,O
Italian M,D
Liberal Studies M,O
Management Information Systems M,O
Management of Technology M,O
Marketing M
Materials Engineering M,D
Materials Sciences M,D
Mathematical and Computational Finance M,D,O
Mathematics D
Mechanical Engineering M,D,O
Mechanics M
Media Studies M
Medical Illustration M
Medical Informatics M,D,O
Microbiology M,D
Military and Defense Studies M
Molecular Biology M,D
Molecular Biophysics D
Molecular Medicine D
Museum Studies M,O
Music M,D,O
Nanotechnology M
Near and Middle Eastern Languages D
Near and Middle Eastern Studies D
Neuroscience D
Nonprofit Management M,O
Nursing and Healthcare Administration M,D
Nursing Education O
Nursing—General M,D,O*
Nutrition M,D
Operations Research M,D
Organizational Management M
Pathobiology D
Pathology D
Pediatric Nursing D,O
Pharmaceutical Sciences M
Pharmacology D
Philosophy M,D
Photonics M,O
Physics M,D
Physiology D
Planetary and Space Sciences M,D
Political Science M,D,O
Psychiatric Nursing O
Psychology—General D
Public Administration M,O
Public Health—General M,D
Public Policy M,D
Reading Education M
Real Estate M
Risk Management M
Romance Languages M,D
Secondary Education M
Social Sciences Education M
Sociology D
Spanish M,D
Special Education M,O
Statistics M,D
Systems Engineering M,O
Technical Writing M,O
Urban Education O
Writing M,O

JOHNSON & WALES UNIVERSITY

Accounting M
Addictions/Substance Abuse Counseling M
Business Administration and Management—General M
Business Education M
Clinical Psychology M
Computer and Information Systems Security M
Criminal Justice and Criminology M
Data Science/Data Analytics M
Economic Development M
Education—General M
Educational Leadership and Administration D
Elementary Education M
Finance and Banking M
Hospitality Management M
Human Resources Management M
Management Information Systems M
Nonprofit Management M
Occupational Therapy D
Organizational Management M
Physician Assistant Studies M
Secondary Education M
Special Education M
Sports Management M
Supply Chain Management M
Sustainable Development M
Travel and Tourism M

JOHNSON C. SMITH UNIVERSITY

Social Work M

JOHNSON UNIVERSITY

Clinical Psychology M,D,O
Counselor Education M,D,O
Cultural Studies M,D,O
Education—General M,D,O
Educational Media/Instructional Technology M,D,O
Higher Education M,D,O
Nonprofit Management M,D,O
Pastoral Ministry and Counseling M,D,O
Theology M,D,O

JOHNSON UNIVERSITY FLORIDA

Pastoral Ministry and Counseling M

JOSE MARIA VARGAS UNIVERSITY

Early Childhood Education M

THE JUDGE ADVOCATE GENERAL'S SCHOOL, U.S. ARMY

Law M
Military and Defense Studies M

JUDSON UNIVERSITY

Architecture M
Business Administration and Management—General M
Clinical Psychology M
Human Services M
Organizational Management M
Pastoral Ministry and Counseling M
Reading Education M,D
Sustainable Development M
Urban Design M

*M—masters degree; D—doctorate; O—other advanced degree; *—Close-Up and/or Display*

THE JUILLIARD SCHOOL

Music	M,D,O
Theater	M,D,O

JUNIATA COLLEGE

Accounting	M

KANSAS CITY UNIVERSITY OF MEDICINE AND BIOSCIENCES

Bioethics	M
Biological and Biomedical Sciences—General	M
Osteopathic Medicine	D

KANSAS STATE UNIVERSITY

Accounting	M
Adult Education	M,D,O
Advertising and Public Relations	M
Agricultural Economics and Agribusiness	M,D
Agricultural Education	M
Agricultural Engineering	M,D
Agricultural Sciences—General	M,D,O
Agronomy and Soil Sciences	M,D,O
Animal Sciences	M,D
Applied Science and Technology	M,O
Architectural Engineering	M
Architecture	M
Art/Fine Arts	M
Biochemistry	M,D
Bioengineering	M,D
Biological and Biomedical Sciences—General	M,D
Business Administration and Management—General	M,O
Chemical Engineering	M,D,O
Chemistry	M,D
Child and Family Studies	M,D,O
Child Development	M,D,O
Civil Engineering	M,D
Clothing and Textiles	M,D
Communication Disorders	M,D,O
Communication—General	M,D,O
Computer Engineering	M,D
Computer Science	M,D
Conflict Resolution and Mediation/Peace Studies	M,D,O
Consumer Economics	M,D,O
Counselor Education	M,D,O
Curriculum and Instruction	M,D,O
Data Science/Data Analytics	M,O
Distance Education Development	M,D,O
Early Childhood Education	M,D,O
Economics	M,D
Education—General	M,D,O
Educational Leadership and Administration	M,D,O
Educational Media/Instructional Technology	M,D,O
Electrical Engineering	M,D,O
Elementary Education	M,D,O
Energy and Power Engineering	M,D
Energy Management and Policy	M,D
Engineering and Applied Sciences—General	M,D,O
Engineering Management	M,D
English as a Second Language	M,D,O
English Education	M,D,O
English	M,D
Entomology	M,D
Entrepreneurship	M,D
Environmental Design	D
Environmental Engineering	M,D,O
Environmental Sciences	M,D,O
Family and Consumer Sciences-General	M,D,O
Finance and Banking	M,D,O
Food Science and Technology	M,D
French	M
Gender Studies	O
Genetics	M,D,O
Geographic Information Systems	M,D,O
Geography	M,D,O
Geology	M
Geotechnical Engineering	M,D
German	M
Gerontology	M,O
Health Communication	M
Health Education	M,D
History	M,D
Horticulture	M,D
Hospitality Management	M,D
Human Development	M,D,O
Human Services	M,D,O
Industrial/Management Engineering	M,D
Interdisciplinary Studies	M,D
Interior Design	M
Journalism	M
Kinesiology and Movement Studies	M,D
Landscape Architecture	M
Management of Technology	M,D
Manufacturing Engineering	M,D
Marketing	M,O
Marriage and Family Therapy	M,D,O
Mass Communication	M
Mathematics	M,D,O
Mechanical Engineering	M,D
Middle School Education	M,D,O
Music	M
National Security	M,D
Natural Resources	M,D
Nuclear Engineering	M,D
Nutrition	M,D
Operations Research	M,D
Pathobiology	M,D
Physics	M,D
Physiology	M,D
Plant Pathology	M,D
Plant Sciences	M,D,O
Political Science	M
Psychology—General	M,D
Public Administration	M
Public Health—General	M,D,O
Range Science	M,D,O
Reading Education	M,D,O
Sociology	M,D
Spanish	M
Special Education	M,D,O
Statistics	M,D,O
Structural Engineering	M,D
Student Affairs	M,D,O
Theater	M
Transportation and Highway Engineering	M,D
Urban and Regional Planning	M
Veterinary Medicine	D
Veterinary Sciences	M,O
Water Resources Engineering	M,D
Women's Studies	O

KANSAS WESLEYAN UNIVERSITY

Business Administration and Management—General	M
Sports Management	M

KEAN UNIVERSITY

Accounting	M
Addictions/Substance Abuse Counseling	M
Art Education	M
Biotechnology	M
Business Administration and Management—General	M
Child and Family Studies	M
Clinical Psychology	M,D
Communication Disorders	M,D
Communication—General	M
Community Health Nursing	M
Counseling Psychology	M
Counselor Education	M
Criminal Justice and Criminology	M
Curriculum and Instruction	M
Early Childhood Education	M
Education—General	M
Educational Leadership and Administration	M,D
English as a Second Language	M
Exercise and Sports Science	M
Foreign Languages Education	M
Forensic Psychology	M
Health Services Management and Hospital Administration	M
Holocaust and Genocide Studies	M
Industrial and Organizational Psychology	M
International Business	M
Liberal Studies	M
Management Information Systems	M
Marriage and Family Therapy	M
Multilingual and Multicultural Education	M
Nonprofit Management	M
Nursing and Healthcare Administration	M,D
Nursing—General	M
Occupational Therapy	M
Physical Therapy	D
Psychology—General	M
Public Administration	M
School Psychology	D,O
Social Work	M
Special Education	M
Writing	M

KECK GRADUATE INSTITUTE

Biological and Biomedical Sciences—General	M,D,O
Pharmacy	D

KEENE STATE COLLEGE

Counselor Education	M,O
Curriculum and Instruction	M,O
Education—General	M,O
Educational Leadership and Administration	M,O
School Psychology	M,O
Special Education	M,O

KEHILATH YAKOV RABBINICAL SEMINARY

Theology	

KEISER UNIVERSITY

Accounting	M
Business Administration and Management—General	M,D
Computer and Information Systems Security	M
Criminal Justice and Criminology	M
Distance Education Development	M
Education—General	M
Educational Leadership and Administration	M,D,O
Educational Media/Instructional Technology	D,O
Family Nurse Practitioner Studies	M
Health Education	M
Health Services Management and Hospital Administration	M
Homeland Security	M
Industrial and Organizational Psychology	M,D
International Business	M,D
Management Information Systems	M
Management of Technology	M
Marketing	M,D
Nursing—General	M
Occupational Therapy	M
Organizational Management	M
Physician Assistant Studies	M
Psychology—General	M,D

KENNESAW STATE UNIVERSITY

Accounting	M
American Studies	M
Applied Statistics	M
Architecture	M
Art Education	M
Biochemistry	M
Biological and Biomedical Sciences—General	M
Business Administration and Management—General	M,D
Chemistry	M
Civil Engineering	M
Communication—General	M
Computer and Information Systems Security	M,O
Computer Science	M
Conflict Resolution and Mediation/Peace Studies	M,D
Construction Management	M
Criminal Justice and Criminology	M
Curriculum and Instruction	O
Data Science/Data Analytics	M,D,O
Early Childhood Education	M
Education—General	M,D,O
Educational Leadership and Administration	M,D,O
Educational Media/Instructional Technology	M,D,O
Electrical Engineering	M
Engineering and Applied Sciences—General	M
Engineering Management	M
English as a Second Language	M
English Education	M
Environmental Engineering	M
Exercise and Sports Science	M
Geotechnical Engineering	M
Health Informatics	M,O
Health Services Management and Hospital Administration	M
Information Science	M,O
International Affairs	M
Management of Technology	M
Mathematics Education	M
Mechanical Engineering	M
Middle School Education	D,O
Nursing and Healthcare Administration	M
Nursing Education	M
Nursing—General	M,D
Public Administration	M
Reading Education	M
Science Education	M
Secondary Education	M,D,O
Social Work	M
Software Engineering	M,O
Special Education	M,D,O
Sports Management	M
Structural Engineering	M
Systems Engineering	M
Transportation and Highway Engineering	M
Water Resources Engineering	M
Writing	M

KENRICK-GLENNON SEMINARY

Theology	M

KENT STATE UNIVERSITY

Accounting	M,D
Adult Nursing	M,D
Advertising and Public Relations	M
Anthropology	M
Applied Mathematics	M,D
Architecture	M
Art Education	M
Art History	M
Art/Fine Arts	M
Athletic Training and Sports Medicine	M,D
Biological and Biomedical Sciences—General	M,D
Biological Anthropology	M,D
Biostatistics	M,D
Botany	M,D
Business Administration and Management—General	M
Cell Biology	M,D
Chemical Physics	M,D
Chemistry	M,D
Child and Family Studies	M
Clinical Psychology	M,D
Communication Disorders	M,D,O
Communication—General	M
Computer and Information Systems Security	M,D
Computer Education	M,D
Computer Science	M,D
Conflict Resolution and Mediation/Peace Studies	M,D
Counseling Psychology	M
Counselor Education	M,D,O
Criminal Justice and Criminology	M,D,O
Curriculum and Instruction	M,D,O
Early Childhood Education	M,D,O
Ecology	M,D
Economics	M,D
Education of the Gifted	M,D,O
Education—General	M,D,O
Educational Leadership and Administration	M,D,O
Educational Measurement and Evaluation	M,D
Educational Media/Instructional Technology	M,D
Educational Psychology	M,D
English as a Second Language	M,D
English Education	M,D
English	M,D
Environmental and Occupational Health	M,D
Environmental Design	M
Epidemiology	M,D
Exercise and Sports Science	M,D
Experimental Psychology	M,D
Family Nurse Practitioner Studies	M,D
Finance and Banking	D
Foundations and Philosophy of Education	M,D
French	M,D
Genetics	M,D
Geographic Information Systems	M,D
Geography	M,D
Geology	M,D
German	M,D
Gerontological Nursing	M,D
Gerontology	M,D
Graphic Design	M
Health Education	M,D
Health Informatics	M
Health Promotion	M,D
Health Services Management and Hospital Administration	M,D
Higher Education	M,D,O
History	M,D
Hospitality Management	M
Human Development	M,D
Human Services	M,D,O
Illustration	M
Information Science	M
Japanese	M,D
Journalism	M
Landscape Architecture	M
Liberal Studies	M
Library Science	M
Linguistics	M,D
Management Information Systems	D
Marketing	D
Mass Communication	M
Mathematics Education	M,D
Mathematics	M,D
Media Studies	M
Middle School Education	M,D
Molecular Biology	M,D
Music Education	M,D
Music	M,D
Near and Middle Eastern Languages	M,D
Neuroscience	M,D
Nursing and Healthcare Administration	M,D
Nursing Education	M,D
Nursing—General	M,D
Nutrition	M
Pediatric Nursing	M,D
Pharmacology	M,D
Philosophy	M
Photography	M
Physics	M,D
Physiology	M,D
Podiatric Medicine	D
Political Science	M,D
Psychiatric Nursing	M,D
Psychology—General	M,D
Public Administration	M,D
Public Health—General	M,D
Reading Education	M
Recreation and Park Management	M
Rehabilitation Counseling	M
Rhetoric	M,D
Russian	M,D
School Psychology	M,D,O
Secondary Education	M,D
Social Sciences Education	M,D
Sociology	M,D
Spanish	M,D
Special Education	M,D,O
Sports Management	M
Student Affairs	M
Textile Design	M
Theater	M
Translation and Interpretation	M,D
Travel and Tourism	M
Urban Design	M
Vocational and Technical Education	M
Writing	M,D

KENT STATE UNIVERSITY AT STARK

Business Administration and Management—General	M
Curriculum and Instruction	M
Education—General	M

KENTUCKY CHRISTIAN UNIVERSITY

Religion	M
Theology	M

KENTUCKY STATE UNIVERSITY

Aquaculture	M
Business Administration and Management—General	M
Computer Science	M
Environmental Management and Policy	M
Human Resources Development	M,D
Nursing—General	M,D
Psychology—General	M
Public Administration	M,D
Special Education	M,D

KETTERING COLLEGE

Physician Assistant Studies	M

KETTERING UNIVERSITY

Business Administration and Management—General	M
Electrical Engineering	M
Engineering Management	M
Manufacturing Engineering	M
Mechanical Engineering	M

KEUKA COLLEGE

Business Administration and Management—General	M
Criminal Justice and Criminology	M
Early Childhood Education	M
Elementary Education	M
Gerontological Nursing	M
Nursing Education	M
Nursing—General	M
Occupational Therapy	M
Secondary Education	M
Social Work	M

KEYSTONE COLLEGE
Accounting	M
Business Administration and Management—General	M
Early Childhood Education	M
Educational Leadership and Administration	M
Sports Management	M

KING'S COLLEGE
Education—General	M
Health Services Management and Hospital Administration	M
Physician Assistant Studies	M

THE KING'S UNIVERSITY
Pastoral Ministry and Counseling	M,D,O
Theology	M,D,O

KINGSWOOD UNIVERSITY
Pastoral Ministry and Counseling	M
Theology	M

KING UNIVERSITY
Accounting	M
Business Administration and Management—General	M
Family Nurse Practitioner Studies	M,D
Finance and Banking	M
Health Services Management and Hospital Administration	M
Human Resources Management	M
Marketing	M
Nursing and Healthcare Administration	M,D
Nursing Education	M,D
Nursing—General	M,D
Pediatric Nursing	M,D
Project Management	M

KNOX COLLEGE
Theology	M,D

KNOX THEOLOGICAL SEMINARY
Classics	M
Pastoral Ministry and Counseling	D
Religion	M
Theology	M

KUTZTOWN UNIVERSITY OF PENNSYLVANIA
Art Education	M
Arts Administration	M
Biological and Biomedical Sciences—General	M,D
Business Administration and Management—General	M
Clinical Psychology	M
Computer Science	M
Counseling Psychology	M
Counselor Education	M
Curriculum and Instruction	M,D
Education—General	M,D
Educational Leadership and Administration	M
Educational Media/Instructional Technology	M
Elementary Education	M
English Education	M,D
English	M
Internet and Interactive Multimedia	M
Library Science	M
Marriage and Family Therapy	M
Mathematics	M,D
Middle School Education	M,D
Public Administration	M,D
Reading Education	M
Secondary Education	M,D
Social Sciences Education	M,D
Social Work	M,D

LAGRANGE COLLEGE
Clinical Psychology	M
Curriculum and Instruction	M,O
Education—General	M,O
Middle School Education	M,O
Organizational Management	M
Secondary Education	M,O

LAGUNA COLLEGE OF ART & DESIGN
Art/Fine Arts	M

LAKE ERIE COLLEGE
Business Administration and Management—General	M
Education—General	M
Health Services Management and Hospital Administration	M
Management Information Systems	M

LAKE ERIE COLLEGE OF OSTEOPATHIC MEDICINE
Biological and Biomedical Sciences—General	M,D,O
Health Education	M,D,O
Osteopathic Medicine	M,D,O
Pharmacy	M,D,O

LAKE FOREST COLLEGE
American Studies	M
Art Education	M
Art/Fine Arts	M
Education—General	M
Elementary Education	M
English Education	M
Environmental Management and Policy	M
Film, Television, and Video Production	M
French	M
History	M
Liberal Studies	M
Mathematics Education	M
Music Education	M
Philosophy	M
Science Education	M
Secondary Education	M
Social Sciences Education	M
Spanish	M
Writing	M

LAKE FOREST GRADUATE SCHOOL OF MANAGEMENT
Business Administration and Management—General	M
Finance and Banking	M
Health Services Management and Hospital Administration	M
International Business	M
Marketing	M
Organizational Behavior	M

LAKEHEAD UNIVERSITY
Biological and Biomedical Sciences—General	M
Chemistry	M
Clinical Psychology	M,D
Computer Engineering	M
Computer Science	M
Economics	M
Education—General	M,D
Electrical Engineering	M
Engineering and Applied Sciences—General	M
English	M
Environmental Engineering	M
Exercise and Sports Science	M
Experimental Psychology	M,D
Forestry	M,D
Geology	M
Gerontology	M,D
Health Services Research	M
History	M
Kinesiology and Movement Studies	M
Mathematics	M
Physics	M
Psychology—General	M,D
Social Work	M
Sociology	M
Women's Studies	M,D

LAKELAND UNIVERSITY
Accounting	M
Business Administration and Management—General	M
Counselor Education	M
Education—General	M
Finance and Banking	M
Health Services Management and Hospital Administration	M
Project Management	M
Theology	M

LAMAR UNIVERSITY
Accounting	M
Biological and Biomedical Sciences—General	M
Business Administration and Management—General	M
Chemical Engineering	M,D
Chemistry	M
Clinical Psychology	M
Communication Disorders	M,D
Computer Science	M
Counseling Psychology	M
Counselor Education	M
Criminal Justice and Criminology	M
Education—General	M,D,O
Educational Leadership and Administration	M,D
Educational Media/Instructional Technology	M,D
Electrical Engineering	M,D
Engineering and Applied Sciences—General	M,D
Engineering Management	M,D
English	M
Entrepreneurship	M
Environmental Engineering	M,D
Environmental Management and Policy	M,D
Family and Consumer Sciences-General	M
Foreign Languages Education	M
Health Services Management and Hospital Administration	M
History	M
Industrial and Organizational Psychology	M
Industrial/Management Engineering	M,D
Kinesiology and Movement Studies	M
Mathematics	M
Mechanical Engineering	M,D
Music	M
Nursing and Healthcare Administration	M
Nursing Education	M
Nursing—General	M
Political Science	M
Psychology—General	M
Public Administration	M
Public Health—General	M
Spanish	M
Special Education	M,D

LANCASTER BIBLE COLLEGE
Counseling Psychology	M,D
Counselor Education	M,D
Elementary Education	M,D
Marriage and Family Therapy	M,D
Pastoral Ministry and Counseling	M,D,O
Secondary Education	M,D
Special Education	M,D
Theology	M,D,O

LANCASTER THEOLOGICAL SEMINARY
Art History	M,D,O
Ethics	M,D,O
Religion	M,D,O
Religious Education	M,D,O
Theology	M,D,O

LANDER UNIVERSITY
Early Childhood Education	M
Education—General	M
Emergency Management	M
Nursing—General	M

LANGSTON UNIVERSITY
Education—General	M
Elementary Education	M
English as a Second Language	M
Multilingual and Multicultural Education	M
Physical Therapy	D
Rehabilitation Counseling	M
Urban Education	M

LA ROCHE COLLEGE
Accounting	M
Human Resources Management	M,O
Nurse Anesthesia	M,D
Nursing and Healthcare Administration	M
Nursing Education	M
Nursing—General	M

LA SALLE UNIVERSITY
Accounting	M,O
Adult Nursing	M,D,O
Advertising and Public Relations	M,O
American Studies	M,O
Business Administration and Management—General	M,O
Business Analytics	M,O
Clinical Psychology	M,D
Communication Disorders	M
Communication—General	M,O
Community Health Nursing	M,D,O
Computer Science	M,O
Corporate and Organizational Communication	M,O
Counseling Psychology	M,D
Developmental Psychology	M,D
Early Childhood Education	M,O
Education—General	M,O
Educational Leadership and Administration	M,O
Educational Media/Instructional Technology	M,O
English as a Second Language	M,O
English	M,O
Family Nurse Practitioner Studies	M,D,O
Finance and Banking	M,O
Forensic Sciences	M,O
Gerontological Nursing	M,D,O
Gerontology	M,D,O
Health Psychology	M,D
Hispanic Studies	M,O
History	M,O
Human Resources Development	M,O
Human Resources Management	M,O
Industrial and Organizational Psychology	M
International Business	M,O
Latin American Studies	M,O
Management of Technology	M,O
Marketing	M,O
Marriage and Family Therapy	M
Media Studies	M,O
Middle School Education	M,O
Multilingual and Multicultural Education	M,O
Nonprofit Management	M
Nurse Anesthesia	M,D,O
Nursing and Healthcare Administration	M,D,O
Nursing Education	M,D,O
Nursing—General	M,D,O
Psychology—General	M,D
Public Health—General	M
Public History	M,O
Reading Education	M,O
School Nursing	M,D,O
Secondary Education	M,O
Social Sciences Education	M,O
Special Education	M,O
Translation and Interpretation	M,O
Western European Studies	M,O

LASELL COLLEGE
Advertising and Public Relations	M,O
Business Administration and Management—General	M,O
Communication—General	M,O
Corporate and Organizational Communication	M,O
Criminal Justice and Criminology	M,O
Curriculum and Instruction	M,O
Education—General	M,O
Educational Leadership and Administration	M,O
Elementary Education	M,O
Emergency Management	M,O
English as a Second Language	M,O
Health Communication	M,O
Health Services Management and Hospital Administration	M,O
Homeland Security	M,O
Hospitality Management	M,O
Human Resources Management	M,O
Marketing	M,O
Project Management	M,O
Recreation and Park Management	M,O
Rehabilitation Sciences	M
Special Education	M,O
Sports Management	M,O
Travel and Tourism	M,O

LA SIERRA UNIVERSITY
Accounting	M,O
Advertising and Public Relations	M
Business Administration and Management—General	M,O
Communication—General	M
Counselor Education	M,O
Curriculum and Instruction	M,D,O
Education—General	M,D,O
Educational Leadership and Administration	M,D,O
Educational Psychology	M,O
English	M
Finance and Banking	M,O
Human Resources Management	M,O
Marketing	M,O
Pastoral Ministry and Counseling	M
Religion	M
Religious Education	M
School Psychology	M,O
Writing	M

LAURENTIAN UNIVERSITY
Analytical Chemistry	M
Applied Physics	M
Applied Psychology	M
Applied Social Research	M
Biochemistry	M
Biological and Biomedical Sciences—General	M,D
Business Administration and Management—General	M
Chemistry	M
Ecology	M,D
Engineering and Applied Sciences—General	M,D
Environmental Sciences	M
Experimental Psychology	M
Geology	M,D
History	M
Human Development	M
Humanities	M
Mineral/Mining Engineering	M,D
Natural Resources	M,D
Nursing—General	M
Organic Chemistry	M
Physical Chemistry	M
Psychology—General	M
Public Health—General	D
Science Education	O
Social Work	M
Sociology	M
Technical Writing	O
Theoretical Chemistry	M

LAWRENCE TECHNOLOGICAL UNIVERSITY
Architectural Engineering	M,D
Architecture	M,O
Artificial Intelligence/Robotics	M,O
Automotive Engineering	M,D
Bioinformatics	M,O
Biomedical Engineering	M,D
Business Administration and Management—General	M,D,O
Civil Engineering	M,D
Communication—General	M,O
Computer and Information Systems Security	M,D,O
Computer Engineering	M,D
Computer Science	M,O
Construction Engineering	M,O
Data Science/Data Analytics	M,O
Educational Media/Instructional Technology	M,O
Electrical Engineering	M,D
Energy and Power Engineering	M,D
Engineering and Applied Sciences—General	M,D
Engineering Management	M,D
Finance and Banking	M,D,O
Health Services Management and Hospital Administration	M,D,O
Human Resources Development	M,O
Industrial and Manufacturing Management	M,D
Industrial/Management Engineering	M,D
Information Science	M,D,O
Interior Design	M,O
Management Strategy and Policy	M,D,O
Manufacturing Engineering	M,D
Marketing	M,D,O
Mechanical Engineering	M,D
Nonprofit Management	M,D,O
Project Management	M,D,O
Science Education	M,O
Technical Communication	M,O
Urban Design	M,O
Water Resources Engineering	M,D

LEBANESE AMERICAN UNIVERSITY
Business Administration and Management—General	M
Computer Science	M
International Affairs	M
Pharmacy	D

LEBANON VALLEY COLLEGE
Athletic Training and Sports Medicine	M
Business Administration and Management—General	M
Communication Disorders	M
Ethics	M
Health Services Management and Hospital Administration	M
Human Resources Management	M
Mathematics Education	M,O

*M—masters degree; D—doctorate; O—other advanced degree; *—Close-Up and/or Display*

Music Education	M
Physical Therapy	D
Project Management	M
Science Education	M,O
Social Sciences Education	M,O

LEE UNIVERSITY

Art/Fine Arts	M,O
Biological and Biomedical Sciences—General	M,O
Business Administration and Management—General	M
Child Development	M
Counseling Psychology	M
Counselor Education	M
Curriculum and Instruction	M,O
Early Childhood Education	M,O
Economics	M,O
Education—General	M,O
Educational Leadership and Administration	M,O
Elementary Education	M,O
English as a Second Language	M,O
English	M,O
Ethics	M
Higher Education	M,O
History	M,O
Marriage and Family Therapy	M
Mathematics Education	M,O
Mathematics	M,O
Middle School Education	M,O
Music Education	M
Music	M
Pastoral Ministry and Counseling	M
Religion	M
Secondary Education	M,O
Social Sciences Education	M,O
Spanish	M,O
Special Education	M,O
Theology	M

LEHIGH UNIVERSITY

Accounting	M
African Studies	M,O
American Studies	M,D,O
Applied Mathematics	M,D
Biochemical Engineering	M,D
Biochemistry	M,D
Bioengineering	M,D
Biological and Biomedical Sciences—General	M,D
Business Administration and Management—General	M
Cell Biology	M,D
Chemical Engineering	M,D
Chemistry	M,D
Civil Engineering	M,D
Computer Engineering	M,D
Computer Science	M,D
Counseling Psychology	M,D,O
Counselor Education	M,D,O
Curriculum and Instruction	M,D,O
Early Childhood Education	M,D,O
Economics	M,D
Education—General	M,D,O
Educational Leadership and Administration	M,D,O
Educational Media/Instructional Technology	M,D
Electrical Engineering	M,D
Elementary Education	M,D
Energy and Power Engineering	M
Engineering and Applied Sciences—General	M,D,O
Engineering Management	M,D,O
English	M,D
Entrepreneurship	M
Environmental and Occupational Health	M,O
Environmental Engineering	M,D
Environmental Law	M,O
Environmental Management and Policy	M,O
Environmental Sciences	M,D
Finance and Banking	M
Geology	M,D
Geosciences	M,D
Health Services Management and Hospital Administration	M,O
History	M,D
Human Services	M,D,O
Industrial/Management Engineering	M,D,O
Information Science	M
Interdisciplinary Studies	M,D
Materials Engineering	M,D
Materials Sciences	M,D
Mathematics	M,D
Mechanical Engineering	M,D
Mechanics	M,D
Molecular Biology	M,D
Photonics	M,D
Physics	M,D
Political Science	M
Polymer Science and Engineering	M,D
Project Management	M
Psychology—General	M,D
Public History	M,D
Quantitative Analysis	M
School Psychology	D,O
Sociology	M
Special Education	M,D
Statistics	M,D
Sustainable Development	M,O
Systems Engineering	M,D,O

LEHMAN COLLEGE OF THE CITY UNIVERSITY OF NEW YORK

Accounting	M
Adult Nursing	M
Art/Fine Arts	M
Biological and Biomedical Sciences—General	M
Business Education	M
Communication Disorders	M
Computer Science	M
Counselor Education	M
Early Childhood Education	M
Education—General	M
Elementary Education	M
English as a Second Language	M
English Education	M
English	M
Gerontological Nursing	M
Health Education	M
Health Promotion	M
History	M
Maternal and Child/Neonatal Nursing	M
Mathematics Education	M
Mathematics	M
Multilingual and Multicultural Education	M
Music Education	M
Nursing—General	M
Nutrition	M
Pediatric Nursing	M
Plant Sciences	D
Reading Education	M
Recreation and Park Management	M
Science Education	M
Social Sciences Education	M
Spanish	M
Special Education	M

LE MOYNE COLLEGE

Arts Administration	M
Business Administration and Management—General	M
Early Childhood Education	M,O
Education—General	M,O
Educational Leadership and Administration	M,O
Elementary Education	M,O
English as a Second Language	M,O
English Education	M,O
Family Nurse Practitioner Studies	M,O
Foreign Languages Education	M,O
Management Information Systems	M
Middle School Education	M,O
Nursing and Healthcare Administration	M,O
Nursing Education	M,O
Nursing Informatics	M,O
Nursing—General	M,O
Occupational Therapy	M
Physician Assistant Studies	M
Reading Education	M,O
Secondary Education	M,O
Social Sciences Education	M,O
Special Education	M,O
Urban Studies	M,O

LENOIR-RHYNE UNIVERSITY

Accounting	M
Addictions/Substance Abuse Counseling	M
Athletic Training and Sports Medicine	M
Business Administration and Management—General	M
Business Analytics	M
Clinical Psychology	M
Community College Education	M
Counseling Psychology	M
Counselor Education	M
Distance Education Development	M
Education—General	M
Educational Leadership and Administration	M
Educational Media/Instructional Technology	M
Entrepreneurship	M
Health Services Management and Hospital Administration	M
Human Services	M
International Business	M
Management Information Systems	M
Management Strategy and Policy	M
Nursing and Healthcare Administration	M
Nursing Education	M
Nursing—General	M
Occupational Therapy	M
Organizational Management	M
Physician Assistant Studies	M
Public Health—General	M
Secondary Education	M
Sustainable Development	M
Theology	M
Writing	M

LESLEY UNIVERSITY

Adult Education	M,D,O
Art Education	M,D,O
Art Therapy	M,D,O
Art/Fine Arts	M,D,O
Clinical Psychology	M,D,O
Computer Education	M,D,O
Conflict Resolution and Mediation/Peace Studies	M,D,O
Counseling Psychology	M,D,O
Curriculum and Instruction	M,D,O
Distance Education Development	M,D,O
Early Childhood Education	M,D,O
Ecology	M,D,O
Education—General	M,D,O
Educational Leadership and Administration	M,D,O
Educational Media/Instructional Technology	M,D,O
Elementary Education	M,D,O
English as a Second Language	M,D,O
Health Psychology	M,D,O
Interdisciplinary Studies	M,D,O
International Affairs	M,D,O
Mathematics Education	M,D,O
Middle School Education	M,D,O
Photography	M
Psychology—General	M,D,O
Reading Education	M,D,O
School Psychology	M,D,O
Science Education	M,D,O
Secondary Education	M,D,O
Social Psychology	M,D,O
Special Education	M,D,O
Sustainable Development	M,D,O
Therapies—Dance, Drama, and Music	M,D,O
Urban and Regional Planning	M,D,O
Women's Studies	M,D,O
Writing	M,D,O

LES ROCHES INTERNATIONAL SCHOOL OF HOTEL MANAGEMENT

Hospitality Management	M

LETOURNEAU UNIVERSITY

Business Administration and Management—General	M
Counseling Psychology	M
Curriculum and Instruction	M
Educational Leadership and Administration	M
Engineering and Applied Sciences—General	M
Engineering Management	M
Health Services Management and Hospital Administration	M
Management Strategy and Policy	M
Marriage and Family Therapy	M
Psychology—General	M
School Psychology	M

LEWIS & CLARK COLLEGE

Addictions/Substance Abuse Counseling	M
Communication Disorders	M
Counseling Psychology	M
Curriculum and Instruction	M
Educational Leadership and Administration	M,D,O
Elementary Education	M
Environmental Law	M,D
Law	M,D
Marriage and Family Therapy	M
School Psychology	M,O
Secondary Education	M
Special Education	M
Student Affairs	M,D,O

LEWIS UNIVERSITY

Accounting	M
Adult Nursing	M,D
Aviation Management	M
Aviation	M
Bioinformatics	M
Business Administration and Management—General	M
Business Analytics	M
Chemical Physics	M
Chemistry	M
Clinical Psychology	M
Computational Biology	M
Computer and Information Systems Security	M
Computer Science	M
Counseling Psychology	M
Counselor Education	M
Criminal Justice and Criminology	M
Curriculum and Instruction	M
Data Science/Data Analytics	M
Early Childhood Education	M
Education—General	M,D
Educational Leadership and Administration	M,D
Educational Media/Instructional Technology	M
Electronic Commerce	M
Elementary Education	M
English as a Second Language	M
English Education	M
Environmental and Occupational Health	M
Family Nurse Practitioner Studies	M,D
Finance and Banking	M
Foreign Languages Education	M
Health Services Management and Hospital Administration	M
Higher Education	M
Human Resources Management	M
International Business	M
Management Information Systems	M
Management of Technology	M
Marketing	M
Mathematics Education	M
Middle School Education	M
Nonprofit Management	M
Nursing and Healthcare Administration	M,D
Nursing Education	M,D
Nursing—General	M,D
Organizational Management	M
Physics	M
Project Management	M
Reading Education	M
School Nursing	M,D
Science Education	M
Secondary Education	M
Social Sciences Education	M
Social Work	M
Software Engineering	M
Special Education	M
Sports Management	M
Student Affairs	M

LEXINGTON THEOLOGICAL SEMINARY

Theology	M,D

LIBERTY UNIVERSITY

Accounting	M,D
Addictions/Substance Abuse Counseling	M,D,O
Advertising and Public Relations	M,D
Anatomy	M,D
Applied Psychology	M,D,O
Art/Fine Arts	M
Biological and Biomedical Sciences—General	M,D
Biopsychology	M,D
Business Administration and Management—General	M,D
Cell Biology	M,D
Child and Family Studies	M,D,O
Clinical Psychology	M,D,O
Communication—General	M
Computer and Information Systems Security	M,D
Counseling Psychology	M,D,O
Counselor Education	M,D,O
Criminal Justice and Criminology	M,D,O
Curriculum and Instruction	M,D,O
Developmental Psychology	M,D,O
Education of the Gifted	M,D,O
Education—General	M,D,O
Educational Leadership and Administration	M,D,O
Elementary Education	M,D,O
Emergency Management	M,D,O
English	M
Epidemiology	M,D
Exercise and Sports Science	M,D
Facilities Management	M,D
Family Nurse Practitioner Studies	M,D
Finance and Banking	M,D
Forensic Psychology	M
Graphic Design	M
Health Informatics	M,D
Health Promotion	M,D,O
History	M
Homeland Security	M
Human Services	M,D,O
Industrial and Organizational Psychology	M,D,O
International Affairs	M,D
International Business	M,D
International Health	M,D
Internet and Interactive Multimedia	M
Law	M
Legal and Justice Studies	M
Management Information Systems	M,D
Management of Technology	M,D
Marketing	M,D
Marriage and Family Therapy	M,D,O
Mathematics Education	M,D,O
Middle School Education	M,D,O
Military and Defense Studies	M,D
Missions and Missiology	M,D
Molecular Medicine	M,D
Music Education	M,D
Music	M,D
Nonprofit Management	M
Nursing and Healthcare Administration	M,D
Nursing Education	M,D
Nursing Informatics	M,D
Nursing—General	M,D
Nutrition	M,D
Osteopathic Medicine	D
Pastoral Ministry and Counseling	M,D,O
Political Science	M
Project Management	M,D
Psychology—General	M,D,O
Public Administration	M,D
Public Health—General	M,D
Public Policy	M
Reading Education	M,D,O
Religion	M,D
Religious Education	M,D
School Psychology	M,D,O
Secondary Education	M,D,O
Special Education	M,D,O
Sports Management	M,D,O
Taxation	M,D
Theology	M,D,O
Travel and Tourism	M,D,O

LIFE CHIROPRACTIC COLLEGE WEST

Chiropractic	D

LIFE UNIVERSITY

Athletic Training and Sports Medicine	M
Chiropractic	D
Exercise and Sports Science	M
Nutrition	M

LIM COLLEGE

Business Administration and Management—General	M
Clothing and Textiles	M
Marketing	M

LIMESTONE COLLEGE

Business Administration and Management—General	M

LINCOLN CHRISTIAN SEMINARY

Pastoral Ministry and Counseling	M,D
Religious Education	M,D
Theology	M,D

LINCOLN CHRISTIAN UNIVERSITY

Cultural Studies	M
Organizational Management	M
Pastoral Ministry and Counseling	M
Philosophy	M
Religion	M
Theology	M

LINCOLN MEMORIAL UNIVERSITY

Business Administration and Management—General	M
Counselor Education	M,D,O
Curriculum and Instruction	M,D,O
Education—General	M,D,O
Educational Leadership and Administration	M,D,O
English Education	M,D,O

Family Nurse Practitioner Studies M
Higher Education M,D,O
Human Resources Development M,D,O
Law D
Nurse Anesthesia M
Nursing—General M
Osteopathic Medicine D
Psychiatric Nursing M

LINCOLN UNIVERSITY (CA)
Business Administration and Management—General M,D
Finance and Banking M,D
Human Resources Management M,D
International Business M,D
Investment Management M,D
Management Information Systems M,D

LINCOLN UNIVERSITY (MO)
Accounting M
Business Administration and Management—General M
Counselor Education M
Criminal Justice and Criminology M
Elementary Education M
Environmental Sciences M
Higher Education M
History M
Management Information Systems M
Middle School Education M
Public Administration M
Public Policy M
Secondary Education M
Sociology M

LINCOLN UNIVERSITY (PA)
Early Childhood Education M
Educational Leadership and Administration M
Finance and Banking M
Human Resources Management M
Human Services M
Special Education M

LINDENWOOD UNIVERSITY
Accounting M
Advertising and Public Relations M
Applied Behavior Analysis M,D,O
Art History M
Business Administration and Management—General M,O
Communication Disorders M,D,O
Communication—General M,O
Computer and Information Systems Security M,O
Counseling Psychology M,D,O
Criminal Justice and Criminology M,O
Education of the Gifted M,D,O
Education—General M,D,O
Educational Leadership and Administration M,D,O
Educational Media/Instructional Technology M,D,O
English as a Second Language M,D,O
Entrepreneurship M
Film, Television, and Video Production M
Finance and Banking M
Health Promotion M
Health Services Management and Hospital Administration M,O
Human Resources Management M,O
International Business M
Internet and Interactive Multimedia M
Journalism M
Management Information Systems M,O
Marketing M,O
Mass Communication M
Media Studies M,O
Nonprofit Management M
Nursing—General M
Project Management M,O
Public Administration M
School Psychology M,D,O
Sports Management M
Supply Chain Management M
Writing M,O

LINDENWOOD UNIVERSITY–BELLEVILLE
Business Administration and Management—General M
Communication—General M
Computer Art and Design M
Counselor Education M
Criminal Justice and Criminology M
Education—General M
Educational Leadership and Administration M
Health Services Management and Hospital Administration M
Human Resources Management M
Internet and Interactive Multimedia M
Media Studies M

LINDSEY WILSON COLLEGE
Counseling Psychology M,D
Counselor Education M,D
Educational Leadership and Administration M
Human Development M,D
Internet and Interactive Multimedia M

LIPSCOMB UNIVERSITY
Accounting M,O
Applied Behavior Analysis M,D,O
Business Administration and Management—General M,O
Clinical Laboratory Sciences/Medical Technology M
Clinical Psychology M,O
Computer and Information Systems Security M,O
Conflict Resolution and Mediation/Peace Studies M,O
Counseling Psychology M,O
Data Science/Data Analytics M,O
Education—General M,D,O
Educational Leadership and Administration M,D,O
Educational Media/Instructional Technology M,D,O
English Education M,D,O
English M,D,O
Exercise and Sports Science M
Film, Television, and Video Production M
Finance and Banking M,O
Health Informatics M,D
Health Services Management and Hospital Administration M,O
International Affairs M,O
Management Information Systems M,O
Management of Technology M,O
Management Strategy and Policy M,O
Marriage and Family Therapy M,O
Molecular Biology M
Nonprofit Management M,O
Nutrition M
Organizational Management M,O
Pastoral Ministry and Counseling M,D
Pharmacy M,D
Psychology—General M,O
Public Administration M
Public Policy M
Reading Education M,D,O
School Psychology M,D,O
Software Engineering M,O
Special Education M,D,O
Sustainable Development M,O
Taxation M,O
Theology M,D
Writing M

LOCK HAVEN UNIVERSITY OF PENNSYLVANIA
Actuarial Science M
Athletic Training and Sports Medicine M
Business Education M
Clinical Psychology M
Counseling Psychology M
Education—General M
Educational Leadership and Administration M
Elementary Education M
Health Education M
Health Promotion M
Health Services Management and Hospital Administration M
Human Services M
Information Studies M
Physician Assistant Studies M
Sport Psychology M
Sports Management M

LOGAN UNIVERSITY
Chiropractic D
Exercise and Sports Science M,D
Health Education M,D
Health Informatics M,D
Nutrition M,D
Rehabilitation Sciences M,D

LOGOS EVANGELICAL SEMINARY
Theology M,D,O

LOMA LINDA UNIVERSITY
Addictions/Substance Abuse Counseling M,D,O
Adult Nursing M
Allied Health—General M,D
Allopathic Medicine M,D
Anatomy D
Applied Social Research M,D
Biochemistry M,D
Bioethics M,O
Biostatistics M,D
Child and Family Studies M,D,O
Clinical Psychology D
Communication Disorders M,D
Counselor Education M,D,O
Criminal Justice and Criminology M,D
Dentistry M,D,O
Environmental and Occupational Health M
Epidemiology M,D
Gerontological Nursing M
Gerontology M,D
Health Education M,D
Health Services Management and Hospital Administration M
International Health M
Marriage and Family Therapy M,D,O
Microbiology M,D
Nursing and Healthcare Administration M
Nursing Education M
Nursing—General D
Nutrition M,D
Occupational Therapy M,D
Oral and Dental Sciences M,O
Pathology D
Pediatric Nursing M
Pharmacology D
Pharmacy D
Physical Therapy M,D
Physician Assistant Studies M
Physiology D
Psychology—General D
Public Health—General M,D
Rehabilitation Sciences M,D
Religion M
Social Work M,D

LONDON METROPOLITAN UNIVERSITY
Applied Psychology M,D
Architecture M,D
Arts Administration M,D
Athletic Training and Sports Medicine M,D
Biological and Biomedical Sciences—General M,D
Child and Family Studies M,D
Clinical Psychology M,D
Computer and Information Systems Security M,D
Conflict Resolution and Mediation/Peace Studies M,D
Counseling Psychology M,D
Criminal Justice and Criminology M,D
Data Science/Data Analytics M,D
Early Childhood Education M,D
Education—General M,D
Emergency Management M,D
English Education M,D
Food Science and Technology M,D
Foreign Languages Education M,D
Forensic Psychology M,D
Health Services Management and Hospital Administration M,D
Higher Education M,D
Homeland Security M,D
Human Resources Management M,D
Immunology M,D
Industrial and Organizational Psychology M,D
International Affairs M,D
Internet and Interactive Multimedia M,D
Law M,D
Management Information Systems M,D
Management of Technology M,D
Military and Defense Studies M,D
Near and Middle Eastern Languages M,D
Nutrition M,D
Pharmacology M,D
Public Administration M,D
Public Health—General M,D
Public Policy M,D
Social Work M,D
Special Education M,D
Sports and Entertainment Law M,D
Translation and Interpretation M,D
Urban Design M,D
Women's Studies M,D
Writing M,D

LONG ISLAND UNIVERSITY–BRENTWOOD CAMPUS
Clinical Psychology M,O
Counseling Psychology M,O
Counselor Education M,O
Criminal Justice and Criminology M,O
Early Childhood Education M,O
Educational Leadership and Administration M,O
Elementary Education M,O
Family Nurse Practitioner Studies M,O
Health Services Management and Hospital Administration M,O
Library Science M,O
Reading Education M,O
Social Work M,O
Special Education M,O

LONG ISLAND UNIVERSITY–HUDSON
Addictions/Substance Abuse Counseling M,O
Counseling Psychology M,O
Counselor Education M,O
Early Childhood Education M,O
Educational Leadership and Administration M,O
Elementary Education M,O
English as a Second Language M,O
Health Services Management and Hospital Administration M,O
Marriage and Family Therapy M,O
Middle School Education M,O
Multilingual and Multicultural Education M,O
Pharmaceutical Sciences M,O
Pharmacy M,O
Public Administration M,O
Reading Education M,O
School Psychology M,O
Special Education M,O

LONG ISLAND UNIVERSITY–LIU BROOKLYN
Accounting M,O
Adult Nursing M,O
Applied Behavior Analysis M,O
Athletic Training and Sports Medicine M,D,O
Biological and Biomedical Sciences—General M,D,O
Business Administration and Management—General M,O
Chemistry M,D,O
Clinical Psychology M,D,O
Communication Disorders M,D,O
Community Health M,D,O
Computer Science M,O
Counseling Psychology M,O
Counselor Education M,O
Early Childhood Education M,O
Education—General M,O
Educational Leadership and Administration M,O
English as a Second Language M,O
English M,D,O
Exercise and Sports Science M,D,O
Family Nurse Practitioner Studies M,O
Forensic Sciences M,D,O
Gerontology M,O
Health Services Management and Hospital Administration M,O
Human Resources Management M,O
Marriage and Family Therapy M,O
Media Studies M,D,O
Multilingual and Multicultural Education M,O
Nonprofit Management M,O
Nursing Education M,O
Nursing—General M,O
Occupational Therapy M,D,O
Pharmaceutical Sciences M,D
Pharmacology M,D
Pharmacy M,D
Physical Therapy M,D,O
Physician Assistant Studies M,D,O
Political Science M,D,O
Psychology—General M,D,O
Public Administration M,O
Public Health—General M,D,O
Social Sciences Education M,D,O
Social Work M,D,O
Special Education M,O
Taxation M,O
Toxicology M,D
Urban Education M,D
Urban Studies M,D,O
Writing M,D,O

LONG ISLAND UNIVERSITY–LIU POST
Accounting M
Allied Health—General M,O
Applied Behavior Analysis M,O
Applied Mathematics M,O
Art Education M,D,O
Art Therapy M
Art/Fine Arts M
Biological and Biomedical Sciences—General M,O
Business Administration and Management—General M
Clinical Psychology M,D,O
Communication Disorders M,D,O
Counseling Psychology M,D,O
Criminal Justice and Criminology M,O
Early Childhood Education M,D,O
Education—General M,D,O
Educational Leadership and Administration M,D,O
Educational Media/Instructional Technology M,D,O
Engineering Management M
English as a Second Language M,D,O
English M,O
Environmental Management and Policy M,O
Family Nurse Practitioner Studies M,O
Finance and Banking M
Game Design and Development M
Genetic Counseling M,O
Geosciences M,O
Gerontology M,O
Health Services Management and Hospital Administration M,O
History M,O
Interdisciplinary Studies M,D,O
International Business M
Internet and Interactive Multimedia M
Library Science M,D,O
Management Information Systems M
Marketing M
Middle School Education M,D,O
Museum Studies M
Music Education M,D,O
Music M
Nonprofit Management M,O
Nursing Education M,O
Nutrition M,O
Political Science M,O
Psychology—General M,O
Public Administration M,O
Reading Education M,D,O
School Psychology M,D,O
Secondary Education M,D,O
Social Work M,O
Special Education M,D,O
Sustainable Development M,O
Taxation M
Theater M

LONG ISLAND UNIVERSITY–RIVERHEAD
Applied Behavior Analysis M,O
Computer and Information Systems Security M,O
Early Childhood Education M,O
Elementary Education M,O
English as a Second Language M,O
Homeland Security M,O
Reading Education M,O
Special Education M,O

LONGWOOD UNIVERSITY
Business Administration and Management—General M
Communication Disorders M
Counselor Education M
Education—General M
Educational Media/Instructional Technology M
Elementary Education M
Health Education M
Mathematics Education M
Middle School Education M
Physical Education M
Reading Education M

*M—masters degree; D—doctorate; O—other advanced degree; *—Close-Up and/or Display*

Real Estate	M
Special Education	M

LORAS COLLEGE

Applied Psychology	M
Educational Leadership and Administration	M
Pastoral Ministry and Counseling	M
Special Education	M
Theology	M

LOUISIANA COLLEGE

Education—General	M
Pastoral Ministry and Counseling	M
Theology	M

LOUISIANA STATE UNIVERSITY AND AGRICULTURAL & MECHANICAL COLLEGE

Accounting	M,D
Agricultural Economics and Agribusiness	M,D
Agricultural Education	M,D
Agricultural Engineering	M,D
Agricultural Sciences—General	M,D
Animal Sciences	M,D
Anthropology	M,D
Applied Arts and Design—General	M
Applied Science and Technology	M
Applied Statistics	M
Architecture	M
Art History	M
Art/Fine Arts	M
Astronomy	M,D
Astrophysics	M,D
Biochemistry	M,D
Bioengineering	M,D
Biological and Biomedical Sciences—General	M,D
Biopsychology	M,D
Business Administration and Management—General	M,D
Business Education	M,D
Chemical Engineering	M,D
Chemistry	M,D
Civil Engineering	M,D
Clinical Psychology	M,D
Cognitive Sciences	M,D
Communication Disorders	M,D
Communication—General	M,D
Comparative Literature	M,D
Computer Engineering	M,D
Computer Science	M,D
Construction Management	M,D
Counselor Education	M,D,O
Developmental Psychology	M,D
Economics	M,D
Education—General	M,D,O
Educational Leadership and Administration	M,D,O
Educational Measurement and Evaluation	M,D,O
Educational Media/Instructional Technology	M,D,O
Electrical Engineering	M,D
Elementary Education	M,D,O
Engineering and Applied Sciences—General	M,D
English	M,D
Entomology	M,D
Environmental Engineering	M,D
Environmental Management and Policy	M,D
Environmental Sciences	M,D
Family and Consumer Sciences-General	M,D
Finance and Banking	M,D
Fish, Game, and Wildlife Management	M,D
Food Science and Technology	M,D
Forestry	M,D
French	M,D
Geography	M,D
Geology	M,D
Geophysics	M,D
Geotechnical Engineering	M,D
Graphic Design	M
Higher Education	M,D,O
Hispanic Studies	M
History	M,D
Home Economics Education	M,D
Human Resources Development	M,D
Information Studies	M
International and Comparative Education	M,D
Internet and Interactive Multimedia	M
Kinesiology and Movement Studies	M,D
Landscape Architecture	M
Law	M,D
Liberal Studies	M
Library Science	M
Management Information Systems	M,D
Marine Affairs	M,D
Mass Communication	M,D
Mathematics	M,D
Mechanical Engineering	M,D
Mechanics	M,D
Media Studies	M,D
Medical Physics	M,D
Music Education	M,D
Music	M,D
Natural Resources	M,D
Nutrition	M,D
Oceanography	M,D
Petroleum Engineering	M,D
Philosophy	M
Photography	M
Physics	M,D
Plant Pathology	M,D
Political Science	M,D
Psychology—General	M,D
Public Administration	M,D
School Psychology	M,D
Secondary Education	M,D,O
Social Work	M,D
Sociology	M,D
Statistics	M
Structural Engineering	M,D
Systems Science	M,D
Theater	M,D
Toxicology	M,D
Transportation and Highway Engineering	M,D
Veterinary Medicine	D
Veterinary Sciences	M,D
Vocational and Technical Education	M,D
Water Resources Engineering	M,D
Writing	M,D

LOUISIANA STATE UNIVERSITY HEALTH SCIENCES CENTER

Allopathic Medicine	M,D
Anatomy	D
Biological and Biomedical Sciences—General	D
Biostatistics	M,D
Cell Biology	D
Communication Disorders	M,D
Community Health Nursing	M,D,O
Community Health	M,D
Dentistry	D
Developmental Biology	D
Environmental and Occupational Health	M,D
Epidemiology	M,D
Family Nurse Practitioner Studies	M,D,O
Gerontological Nursing	M,D,O
Health Services Management and Hospital Administration	M,D
Human Genetics	D
Immunology	D
Maternal and Child/Neonatal Nursing	M,D,O
Microbiology	D
Neurobiology	D
Neuroscience	D
Nurse Anesthesia	M,D,O
Nursing and Healthcare Administration	M,D,O
Nursing Education	M,D,O
Nursing—General	M,D,O
Occupational Therapy	M
Parasitology	D
Pharmacology	D
Physical Therapy	D
Physician Assistant Studies	M
Physiology	D
Public Health—General	M,D
Rehabilitation Counseling	M

LOUISIANA STATE UNIVERSITY HEALTH SCIENCES CENTER AT SHREVEPORT

Allopathic Medicine	D
Anatomy	M,D
Biochemistry	M,D
Biological and Biomedical Sciences—General	M
Cell Biology	M,D
Immunology	M,D
Microbiology	M,D
Molecular Biology	M,D
Pharmacology	M,D
Physiology	M,D

LOUISIANA STATE UNIVERSITY IN SHREVEPORT

Biological and Biomedical Sciences—General	M
Business Administration and Management—General	M
Computer Science	M
Counselor Education	M
Curriculum and Instruction	M,D
Education—General	M,D
Educational Leadership and Administration	M,D
Health Services Management and Hospital Administration	M
Liberal Studies	M
Nonprofit Management	M
Public Health—General	M
School Psychology	O
Systems Science	M

LOUISIANA TECH UNIVERSITY

Accounting	M,D
Agricultural Sciences—General	M,D,O
Applied Physics	M,D,O
Architecture	M,D,O
Art/Fine Arts	M,D,O
Biological and Biomedical Sciences—General	M,D,O
Biomedical Engineering	M,D,O
Business Administration and Management—General	M,D,O
Chemistry	M,D,O
Clinical Psychology	M,D,O
Communication Disorders	M,D,O
Computer and Information Systems Security	M,D
Computer Science	M,D,O
Counseling Psychology	M,D,O
Curriculum and Instruction	M,D,O
Early Childhood Education	M,D,O
Education—General	M,D,O
Educational Leadership and Administration	M,D,O
Elementary Education	M,D,O
Engineering and Applied Sciences—General	M,D,O
Engineering Management	M,D,O
Engineering Physics	M,D,O
English	M,D,O
Finance and Banking	M,D
Graphic Design	M,D,O
Health Informatics	M,D,O
Higher Education	M,D,O
History	M,D,O
Human Services	M,D,O
Industrial and Organizational Psychology	M,D,O
Kinesiology and Movement Studies	M,D,O
Management Information Systems	M,D
Management of Technology	M,D,O
Marketing	M,D
Materials Sciences	M,D,O
Mathematics	M,D,O
Middle School Education	M,D,O
Molecular Biology	M,D,O
Nanotechnology	M,D,O
Nutrition	M,D,O
Photography	M,D,O
Secondary Education	M,D,O
Special Education	M,D,O
Technical Writing	M,D,O

LOUISVILLE PRESBYTERIAN THEOLOGICAL SEMINARY

Religion	M,D
Theology	M,D

LOURDES UNIVERSITY

Business Administration and Management—General	M
Curriculum and Instruction	M
Educational Leadership and Administration	M
Nurse Anesthesia	M
Nursing and Healthcare Administration	M
Nursing Education	M
Organizational Management	M
Reading Education	M
Theology	M

LOYOLA MARYMOUNT UNIVERSITY

Accounting	M
Art/Fine Arts	M
Bioethics	M
Business Administration and Management—General	M
Civil Engineering	M
Communication—General	M
Counseling Psychology	M
Counselor Education	M
Education—General	M,D
Educational Leadership and Administration	M,D
Electrical Engineering	M
Elementary Education	M
Engineering Management	
English	M
Environmental Sciences	M
Film, Television, and Video Production	M
Higher Education	M
Law	M,D
Marriage and Family Therapy	M
Mathematics Education	M
Mechanical Engineering	M
Multilingual and Multicultural Education	M
Pastoral Ministry and Counseling	M
Philosophy	M
Reading Education	M
Recreation and Park Management	M
School Psychology	M
Secondary Education	M
Special Education	M
Systems Engineering	M
Theology	M
Urban Education	M
Writing	M

LOYOLA UNIVERSITY CHICAGO

Accounting	M
Adult Nursing	M,D,O
Applied Statistics	M
Biochemistry	M,D
Bioethics	M,D,O
Biological and Biomedical Sciences—General	M,D
Business Administration and Management—General	M,O
Business Analytics	M,O
Cell Biology	M,D
Chemistry	M,D
Clinical Psychology	M,D,O
Clinical Research	M
Communication—General	M
Computer Science	M
Corporate and Organizational Communication	M
Counseling Psychology	M,D,O
Counselor Education	M,O
Criminal Justice and Criminology	M
Curriculum and Instruction	M,D
Developmental Psychology	M,D
Economics	M
Education—General	M,D,O
Educational Leadership and Administration	M,D,O
Educational Measurement and Evaluation	M,D,O
Educational Policy	M,D
Elementary Education	M
English	M,D
Entrepreneurship	M
Ethics	M
Family Nurse Practitioner Studies	M,D,O
Finance and Banking	M
Health Law	M,D,O
Health Services Management and Hospital Administration	M
Higher Education	M,D
History	M,D
Human Resources Management	M
Humanities	M
Immunology	M,D
Infectious Diseases	M,D,O
Information Science	M
International and Comparative Education	M,D
International Business	M
Law	M,D,O
Legal and Justice Studies	M,O
Management Information Systems	M
Marketing	M
Mathematics	M
Medieval and Renaissance Studies	M,D
Microbiology	M,D
Molecular Biology	M,D
Molecular Pharmacology	M,D
Molecular Physiology	M,D
Neuroscience	M,D
Nursing and Healthcare Administration	M,D,O
Nursing—General	M,D,O
Nutrition	M,D,O
Pastoral Ministry and Counseling	M,O
Philosophy	M,D
Physiology	M,D
Political Science	M,D
Public Health—General	M,O
Public History	M,D
Public Policy	M
Religious Education	M,O
Risk Management	M
School Psychology	D,O
Secondary Education	M
Social Psychology	M,O
Social Work	M,D,O
Sociology	M,D
Software Engineering	M
Spanish	M
Special Education	M
Statistics	M
Supply Chain Management	M,O
Taxation	M,D,O
Theology	M,D,O
Urban Studies	M
Women's Health Nursing	M,D,O

LOYOLA UNIVERSITY MARYLAND

Business Administration and Management—General	M
Clinical Psychology	M,D,O
Communication Disorders	M
Counseling Psychology	M,D,O
Counselor Education	M,O
Curriculum and Instruction	M
Early Childhood Education	M,O
Education—General	M,O
Educational Leadership and Administration	M,O
Educational Media/Instructional Technology	M
Elementary Education	M,O
Finance and Banking	M
Investment Management	M
Management Information Systems	M
Marketing	M
Media Studies	M
Music Education	M
Psychology—General	M,D,O
Reading Education	M
Secondary Education	M
Theology	M

LOYOLA UNIVERSITY NEW ORLEANS

Business Administration and Management—General	M
Clinical Psychology	M
Criminal Justice and Criminology	M
Education—General	M
Family Nurse Practitioner Studies	M,D
Law	M,D
Marriage and Family Therapy	M
Music	M
Nursing—General	M,D
Organizational Management	M
Secondary Education	M
Theology	M,O
Therapies—Dance, Drama, and Music	M

LUBBOCK CHRISTIAN UNIVERSITY

Theology	M

LUTHERAN SCHOOL OF THEOLOGY AT CHICAGO

Pastoral Ministry and Counseling	M,D
Theology	M,D

LUTHERAN THEOLOGICAL SEMINARY SASKATOON

Ethics	M,D
Pastoral Ministry and Counseling	M,D
Religion	M,D
Theology	M,D

LUTHER RICE COLLEGE & SEMINARY

Pastoral Ministry and Counseling	M,D
Religion	M,D
Theology	M,D

LUTHER SEMINARY

Missions and Missiology	M,D
Pastoral Ministry and Counseling	M,D
Theology	M,D

LYNN UNIVERSITY

Applied Psychology	M
Aviation Management	M
Business Administration and Management—General	M
Communication—General	M,O
Computer Art and Design	M,O
Counseling Psychology	M
Criminal Justice and Criminology	M
Early Childhood Education	M,D
Education of the Gifted	M,D
Education—General	M,D
Educational Leadership and Administration	M,D

Entrepreneurship	M
Graphic Design	M,O
Hospitality Management	M
Human Resources Management	M
Industrial and Organizational Psychology	M
International Business	M
Internet and Interactive Multimedia	M,O
Investment Management	M
Marketing	M
Mass Communication	M,O
Media Studies	M,O
Middle School Education	M,D
Music	M,O
Psychology—General	M
Special Education	M,D
Sports Management	M

MAASTRICHT SCHOOL OF MANAGEMENT

Business Administration and Management—General	M,D
Facilities Management	M,D
Sustainability Management	M,D

MACHZIKEI HADATH RABBINICAL COLLEGE

Theology	O

MADONNA UNIVERSITY

Adult Nursing	M
Business Administration and Management—General	M
Clinical Psychology	M
Criminal Justice and Criminology	M
Education—General	M
Educational Leadership and Administration	M
English as a Second Language	M
Health Services Management and Hospital Administration	M
Hospice Nursing	M
International Business	M
Liberal Studies	M
Nursing and Healthcare Administration	M
Nursing—General	M
Pastoral Ministry and Counseling	M
Psychology—General	M
Quality Management	M
Reading Education	M
Special Education	M
Theology	M

MAHARISHI UNIVERSITY OF MANAGEMENT

Accounting	M,D
Asian Studies	M,D
Business Administration and Management—General	M,D
Computer Science	M
Physiology	D
Sustainability Management	M,D
Writing	M

MAINE COLLEGE OF ART

Art/Fine Arts	M

MAINE MARITIME ACADEMY

International Business	M
Supply Chain Management	M
Transportation Management	M

MALONE UNIVERSITY

Business Administration and Management—General	M
Counselor Education	M
Curriculum and Instruction	M
Education—General	M
Educational Leadership and Administration	M
Family Nurse Practitioner Studies	M
Nursing—General	M
Organizational Management	M
Special Education	M
Theology	M

MANCHESTER UNIVERSITY

Athletic Training and Sports Medicine	M
Genomic Sciences	M
Pharmacy	D

MANHATTAN COLLEGE

Applied Mathematics	M
Business Administration and Management—General	M
Chemical Engineering	M
Civil Engineering	M
Computer Engineering	M
Construction Management	M
Counseling Psychology	M,O
Counselor Education	M,O
Data Science/Data Analytics	M
Early Childhood Education	M,O
Education—General	M,O
Educational Leadership and Administration	M,O
Educational Media/Instructional Technology	M
Electrical Engineering	M
Elementary Education	M,O
Engineering and Applied Sciences—General	M
English	M,O
Environmental Engineering	M
Marriage and Family Therapy	M
Mathematics	M,O
Mechanical Engineering	M
Multilingual and Multicultural Education	M,O
Organizational Management	M
Special Education	M,O
Student Affairs	M,O

MANHATTAN SCHOOL OF MUSIC

Music	M,D,O

MANHATTANVILLE COLLEGE

Accounting	M,O
Art Education	M,O
Biological and Biomedical Sciences—General	M,O
Business Education	M,O
Chemistry	M,O
Classics	M,O
Corporate and Organizational Communication	M,O
Early Childhood Education	M,O
Education—General	M,D,O
Educational Leadership and Administration	M,D,O
Elementary Education	M,O
English as a Second Language	M,O
English Education	M,O
English	M,O
Entertainment Management	M,O
Entrepreneurship	M
Exercise and Sports Science	M,O
Finance and Banking	M,O
Foreign Languages Education	M,O
French	M,O
Geosciences	M,O
Health Promotion	M,O
Human Resources Management	M,O
International Business	M,O
Investment Management	M,O
Italian	M,O
Management Strategy and Policy	M,O
Marketing	M,O
Mathematics Education	M,O
Mathematics	M,O
Middle School Education	M,O
Multilingual and Multicultural Education	M,O
Music Education	M,O
Organizational Management	M,O
Physics	M,O
Reading Education	M,O
Science Education	M,O
Secondary Education	M,O
Social Sciences Education	M,O
Spanish	M,O
Special Education	M,O
Sports Management	M,O
Sustainable Development	M,O
Urban Education	M,O
Writing	M

MANSFIELD UNIVERSITY OF PENNSYLVANIA

Art Education	M
Education—General	M
Elementary Education	M
Information Studies	M
Library Science	M
Music	M
Nursing—General	M
Organizational Management	M
Psychology—General	M
Secondary Education	M
Special Education	M

MAPLE SPRINGS BAPTIST BIBLE COLLEGE AND SEMINARY

Pastoral Ministry and Counseling	M,D,O
Religious Education	M,D,O
Theology	M,D,O

MARANATHA BAPTIST UNIVERSITY

Cultural Studies	M
Education—General	M
Organizational Management	M
Pastoral Ministry and Counseling	M,D
Religion	M
Theology	M

MARCONI INTERNATIONAL UNIVERSITY

Business Administration and Management—General	M,D
Educational Leadership and Administration	M,D
Educational Media/Instructional Technology	M,D
International Business	M,D

MARIAN UNIVERSITY (IN)

Counseling Psychology	M
Counselor Education	M
Education—General	M
Family Nurse Practitioner Studies	M,D
Nurse Anesthesia	M,D
Nursing Education	M,D
Nursing—General	M,D
Osteopathic Medicine	M,D

MARIAN UNIVERSITY (WI)

Adult Nursing	M
Business Administration and Management—General	M
Curriculum and Instruction	M,D
Education—General	M,D
Educational Leadership and Administration	M,D
Educational Media/Instructional Technology	M,D
Nursing Education	M
Nursing—General	M
Organizational Management	M
Special Education	M,D
Thanatology	M

MARIETTA COLLEGE

Physician Assistant Studies	M
Psychology—General	M

MARIST COLLEGE

Business Administration and Management—General	M,O
Communication—General	M
Computer Science	M,O
Corporate and Organizational Communication	M
Counseling Psychology	M,O
Education—General	M,O
Management Information Systems	M,O
Management of Technology	M,O
Marketing	M
Museum Studies	M
Physical Therapy	D
Psychology—General	M,O
Public Administration	M
School Psychology	M,O
Software Engineering	M,O

MARLBORO COLLEGE

Business Administration and Management—General	M
Educational Media/Instructional Technology	M,O
English as a Second Language	M
Entrepreneurship	M
Legal and Justice Studies	M
Organizational Management	M
Project Management	M

MARQUETTE UNIVERSITY

Accounting	M
Acute Care/Critical Care Nursing	M,D,O
Adult Nursing	M,D,O
Advertising and Public Relations	M,O
Analytical Chemistry	M,D
Bioinformatics	M,D
Biological and Biomedical Sciences—General	M,D
Biomedical Engineering	M,D
Business Administration and Management—General	M,O
Cardiovascular Sciences	M
Cell Biology	M,D
Chemical Physics	M,D
Chemistry	M,D
Civil Engineering	M,D,O
Clinical Psychology	M,D
Communication Disorders	M,O
Communication—General	M,O
Computational Sciences	M,D
Computer Engineering	M,D,O
Computer Science	M,D
Construction Engineering	M,D,O
Construction Management	M,D,O
Counseling Psychology	M,D
Counselor Education	M,D
Curriculum and Instruction	M,D,O
Dentistry	D
Developmental Biology	M,D
Ecology	M,D
Economics	M,O
Education—General	M,D,O
Educational Leadership and Administration	M,D,O
Educational Policy	M,D,O
Electrical Engineering	M,D,O
Elementary Education	M,D,O
Engineering and Applied Sciences—General	M,D,O
Engineering Management	M,D,O
English	M,D
Entrepreneurship	M,O
Environmental Engineering	M,D,O
Ethics	M,D
Family Nurse Practitioner Studies	M,D,O
Finance and Banking	M,O
Foreign Languages Education	M
Foundations and Philosophy of Education	M,D,O
Genetics	M,D
Gerontological Nursing	M,D,O
Hazardous Materials Management	M,D,O
Health Communication	M,O
History	M,D
Human Resources Development	M
Human Resources Management	M,O
Industrial and Manufacturing Management	M,O
Inorganic Chemistry	M,D
Interdisciplinary Studies	D
International Affairs	M,D
International Business	M,O
Journalism	M,O
Law	D
Management Information Systems	M,O
Management of Technology	M,D
Marketing Research	M
Marketing	M,O
Mass Communication	M,O
Mathematics Education	M,D
Mathematics	M,D
Mechanical Engineering	M,D,O
Microbiology	M,D
Molecular Biology	M,D
Neuroscience	M,D
Nurse Midwifery	M,D,O
Nursing and Healthcare Administration	M,D,O
Nursing—General	M,D,O
Oral and Dental Sciences	M,O
Organic Chemistry	M,D
Pediatric Nursing	M,D,O
Philosophy	M,D
Physical Chemistry	M,D
Physical Therapy	D
Physician Assistant Studies	M
Physiology	M,D
Political Science	M
Psychology—General	D
Reading Education	M,D,O
Real Estate	M
Rehabilitation Sciences	M,D
Secondary Education	M,D,O
Social Psychology	M,D
Spanish	M
Speech and Interpersonal Communication	M,O
Sports Management	M,O
Structural Engineering	M,D,O
Student Affairs	M,D,O
Supply Chain Management	M,O
Theology	M,D
Transportation and Highway Engineering	M,D,O
Water Resources Engineering	M,D,O
Water Resources	M,D,O

MARSHALL B. KETCHUM UNIVERSITY

Optometry	M,D
Pharmacy	M,D
Vision Sciences	M,D

MARSHALL UNIVERSITY

Accounting	M
Adult Education	M
Advertising and Public Relations	M,O
Allopathic Medicine	D
Athletic Training and Sports Medicine	M
Biological and Biomedical Sciences—General	M,D
Business Administration and Management—General	M,O
Chemistry	M
Clinical Psychology	M,D,O
Communication Disorders	M
Communication—General	M
Computer Engineering	M
Computer Science	M
Counselor Education	M
Criminal Justice and Criminology	M
Education—General	M,D,O
Educational Leadership and Administration	M
Electrical Engineering	M
Engineering and Applied Sciences—General	M,O
Engineering Management	M
English	M,O
Environmental Engineering	M
Environmental Sciences	M
Exercise and Sports Science	M
Forensic Sciences	M,O
Geography	M,O
Health Education	M
Health Informatics	M
Health Services Management and Hospital Administration	M
History	M,O
Human Resources Management	M
Humanities	M,O
Information Science	M
Journalism	M,O
Management of Technology	M,O
Mathematics	M
Mechanical Engineering	M
Music	M
Nurse Anesthesia	D
Nursing—General	M,O
Nutrition	M,O
Pharmacy	D
Physical Therapy	D
Physics	M
Political Science	M
Psychology—General	M,D,O
Public Administration	M
Public Health—General	M
Reading Education	M
School Psychology	O
Social Work	M
Sociology	M
Special Education	M
Sports Management	M
Transportation and Highway Engineering	M

MARS HILL UNIVERSITY

Elementary Education	M

MARTIN LUTHER COLLEGE

Curriculum and Instruction	M
Early Childhood Education	M
Education—General	M
Educational Leadership and Administration	M
Educational Media/Instructional Technology	M
Special Education	M

MARTIN UNIVERSITY

Pastoral Ministry and Counseling	M
Psychology—General	M
Social Psychology	M

MARY BALDWIN UNIVERSITY

Education—General	M
Elementary Education	M
English	M
Middle School Education	M
Occupational Therapy	D
Theater	M

MARYGROVE COLLEGE

Curriculum and Instruction	M,O
Early Childhood Education	M,O
Educational Leadership and Administration	M,O
Educational Media/Instructional Technology	M,O
Elementary Education	M,O
Human Resources Management	M,O
Legal and Justice Studies	M,O

*M—masters degree; D—doctorate; O—other advanced degree; *—Close-Up and/or Display*

Mathematics	M,O
Middle School Education	M,O
Reading Education	M,O
Special Education	M,O

MARYLAND INSTITUTE COLLEGE OF ART

Applied Arts and Design—General	M
Art Education	M
Art/Fine Arts	M,O
Business Administration and Management—General	M
Film, Television, and Video Production	M
Graphic Design	M
Illustration	M
Museum Studies	M
Photography	M

MARYLAND UNIVERSITY OF INTEGRATIVE HEALTH

Acupuncture and Oriental Medicine	M,D,O
Health Promotion	M,O
Naturopathic Medicine	D
Nutrition	M,D,O

MARYMOUNT CALIFORNIA UNIVERSITY

Business Administration and Management—General	M
International Development	M
Social Psychology	M

MARYMOUNT UNIVERSITY

Allied Health—General	M,D,O
Business Administration and Management—General	M,O
Clinical Psychology	M
Community College Education	M,O
Computer and Information Systems Security	M,D,O
Counseling Psychology	M
Counselor Education	M
Curriculum and Instruction	M
Education—General	M
Elementary Education	M
English Education	M,O
English	M,O
Family Nurse Practitioner Studies	M,D,O
Forensic Psychology	M
Health Education	M
Health Informatics	M,O
Health Promotion	M
Health Services Management and Hospital Administration	M
Human Resources Management	O
Interior Design	M
Management Information Systems	M,O
Nonprofit Management	M,O
Nursing—General	M,D,O
Pastoral Ministry and Counseling	M
Physical Therapy	D
Project Management	M,O
Secondary Education	M
Software Engineering	M,O
Special Education	M

MARYVILLE UNIVERSITY OF SAINT LOUIS

Accounting	M,O
Actuarial Science	M
Acute Care/Critical Care Nursing	M,D
Addictions/Substance Abuse Counseling	M
Adult Nursing	M,D
Allied Health—General	M,D,O
Business Administration and Management—General	M,O
Business Education	M,O
Communication Disorders	M
Computer and Information Systems Security	M,O
Data Science/Data Analytics	M
Early Childhood Education	M,D
Education—General	M,D
Educational Leadership and Administration	M,D
Elementary Education	M,D
Family Nurse Practitioner Studies	M,D
Finance and Banking	M,O
Gerontological Nursing	M,D
Health Services Management and Hospital Administration	M,O
Higher Education	M,D
Human Resources Management	M,O
Information Science	M,O
Logistics	M,O
Marketing	M,O
Marriage and Family Therapy	M
Middle School Education	M,D
Nursing—General	M,D
Occupational Therapy	M
Pediatric Nursing	M,D
Physical Therapy	D
Project Management	M,O
Reading Education	M,D
Rehabilitation Counseling	M
Secondary Education	M,D
Sports Management	M,O
Supply Chain Management	M,O
Therapies—Dance, Drama, and Music	M

MARYWOOD UNIVERSITY

Architecture	M
Art Education	M
Art Therapy	M,O
Art/Fine Arts	M
Biotechnology	M
Business Administration and Management—General	M
Clinical Psychology	M,D
Communication Disorders	M
Communication—General	M
Computer and Information Systems Security	M
Counseling Psychology	M
Counselor Education	M
Criminal Justice and Criminology	M
Early Childhood Education	M
Education—General	M
Educational Leadership and Administration	M,D
Elementary Education	M
Exercise and Sports Science	M
Finance and Banking	M
Gerontology	M
Graphic Design	M
Health Education	D
Health Services Management and Hospital Administration	M
Higher Education	M,D
Human Development	D
Illustration	M
Interdisciplinary Studies	D
Interior Design	M
Investment Management	M
Management Information Systems	M
Music Education	M
Nutrition	M,O
Photography	M
Physician Assistant Studies	M
Psychology—General	M
Public Administration	M
Reading Education	M
Secondary Education	M
Social Work	M,D
Special Education	M

MASSACHUSETTS COLLEGE OF ART AND DESIGN

Applied Arts and Design—General	M,O
Architecture	M
Art Education	M,O
Art/Fine Arts	M,O
Film, Television, and Video Production	M,O
Interdisciplinary Studies	M,O
Media Studies	M,O
Photography	M,O
Textile Design	M,O

MASSACHUSETTS COLLEGE OF LIBERAL ARTS

Business Administration and Management—General	M,O
Curriculum and Instruction	M,O
Education—General	M,O
Educational Leadership and Administration	M,O
Educational Media/Instructional Technology	M,O
Health Education	M,O
Physical Education	M,O
Reading Education	M,O
Special Education	M,O

MASSACHUSETTS INSTITUTE OF TECHNOLOGY

Aerospace/Aeronautical Engineering	M,D,O
Archaeology	M,D,O
Architectural History	M,D
Architecture	M,D
Art History	M,D
Atmospheric Sciences	M,D
Biochemistry	D
Bioengineering	M,D
Bioinformatics	M,D
Biological and Biomedical Sciences—General	M,D
Biomedical Engineering	M,D
Business Administration and Management—General	M,D
Cell Biology	D
Chemical Engineering	M,D
Chemistry	D
Civil Engineering	M,D,O
Cognitive Sciences	D
Communication Disorders	M,D
Computational Biology	D
Computational Sciences	M
Computer Engineering	M,D,O
Computer Science	M,D,O
Construction Engineering	M,D,O
Developmental Biology	D
Economics	M,D
Electrical Engineering	M,D,O
Engineering and Applied Sciences—General	M,D,O
Engineering Management	M
Environmental Biology	M,D,O
Environmental Engineering	M,D,O
Environmental Sciences	M,D,O
Genetics	D
Genomic Sciences	M,D
Geochemistry	M,D
Geology	M,D
Geophysics	M,D
Geosciences	M,D
Geotechnical Engineering	M,D,O
History of Science and Technology	D
Hydrology	M,D,O
Immunology	D
Information Science	M,D,O
Inorganic Chemistry	D
Linguistics	D
Logistics	M
Manufacturing Engineering	M,D,O
Marine Geology	M,D
Materials Engineering	M,D,O
Materials Sciences	M,D,O
Mathematics	D
Mechanical Engineering	M,D,O
Media Studies	M,D
Medical Physics	M,D
Microbiology	D
Molecular Biology	M,D,O
Molecular Toxicology	D
Neurobiology	D
Neuroscience	D
Nuclear Engineering	M,D,O
Ocean Engineering	M,D,O
Oceanography	M,D,O
Operations Research	M,D
Organic Chemistry	M,D,O
Philosophy	D
Physical Chemistry	D
Physics	M,D
Planetary and Space Sciences	M,D
Political Science	M,D
Real Estate	M
Social Sciences	D
Structural Biology	D
Structural Engineering	M,D,O
Systems Biology	D
Systems Engineering	M,D
Technical Writing	M
Technology and Public Policy	M,D
Toxicology	M,D
Transportation and Highway Engineering	M,D,O
Urban and Regional Planning	M,D
Urban Studies	M,D
Writing	M

MASSACHUSETTS MARITIME ACADEMY

Emergency Management	M
Facilities Management	M

MASSACHUSETTS SCHOOL OF LAW AT ANDOVER

Law	D

THE MASTER'S UNIVERSITY

Pastoral Ministry and Counseling	M,D
Theology	M,D

MAYO CLINIC GRADUATE SCHOOL OF BIOMEDICAL SCIENCES

Biochemistry	M,D
Biomedical Engineering	M,D
Clinical Laboratory Sciences/Medical Technology	M,D
Genetics	D
Immunology	D
Molecular Biology	M,D
Molecular Pharmacology	M,D
Neuroscience	M,D
Physiology	M,D
Virology	D

MAYO CLINIC SCHOOL OF HEALTH SCIENCES

Nurse Anesthesia	D
Physical Therapy	D

MAYO CLINIC SCHOOL OF MEDICINE

Allopathic Medicine	D

MCCORMICK THEOLOGICAL SEMINARY

Pastoral Ministry and Counseling	M,D,O
Theology	M,D,O

MCDANIEL COLLEGE

Counselor Education	M
Curriculum and Instruction	M
Educational Leadership and Administration	M
Educational Media/Instructional Technology	M
Elementary Education	M,O
English as a Second Language	M
Gerontology	M,O
Human Resources Development	M
Human Services	M
Kinesiology and Movement Studies	M
Liberal Studies	M,O
Library Science	M
Mathematics Education	M,O
Reading Education	M
Science Education	M,O
Secondary Education	M,O
Special Education	M
Writing	M,O

MCGILL UNIVERSITY

Accounting	M,D,O
Aerospace/Aeronautical Engineering	M,D
Agricultural Economics and Agribusiness	M
Agricultural Engineering	M,D
Agricultural Sciences—General	M,D,O
Agronomy and Soil Sciences	M,D
Allopathic Medicine	M,D
Anatomy	M,D
Animal Sciences	M,D
Anthropology	M,D
Applied Mathematics	M,D
Architecture	M,D,O
Art History	M,D
Asian Studies	M,D
Atmospheric Sciences	M,D
Biochemistry	M,D
Bioengineering	M,D
Bioethics	M,D,O
Bioinformatics	M,D
Biological and Biomedical Sciences—General	M,D
Biomedical Engineering	M,D
Biostatistics	M,D,O
Biotechnology	M,D,O
Business Administration and Management—General	M,D,O
Cell Biology	M,D
Chemical Engineering	M,D
Chemistry	M,D
Civil Engineering	M,D
Clinical Psychology	M,D
Communication Disorders	M,D
Communication—General	M,D
Community Health	M,D,O
Computational Sciences	M,D
Computer Engineering	M,D
Computer Science	M,D
Counseling Psychology	M,D,O
Curriculum and Instruction	M,D,O
Dentistry	M,D,O
Developmental Psychology	M,D,O
Economics	M,D
Education—General	M,D,O
Educational Leadership and Administration	M,D,O
Educational Psychology	M,D,O
Electrical Engineering	M,D
Engineering and Applied Sciences—General	M,D,O
English	M,D
Entomology	M,D
Entrepreneurship	M,D,O
Environmental and Occupational Health	M,D,O
Environmental Engineering	M,D
Environmental Management and Policy	M,D
Epidemiology	M,D,O
Experimental Psychology	M,D
Family Nurse Practitioner Studies	M,D,O
Finance and Banking	M,D,O
Fish, Game, and Wildlife Management	M,D
Food Science and Technology	M,D
Foreign Languages Education	M,D,O
Forensic Sciences	M,D,O
Forestry	M,D
Foundations and Philosophy of Education	M,D,O
French	M,D
Genetic Counseling	M,D
Geography	M,D
Geosciences	M,D
Geotechnical Engineering	M,D
German	M,D
Health Services Management and Hospital Administration	M,D,O
Hispanic Studies	M,D
History of Medicine	M,D
History	M,D
Human Genetics	M,D
Hydraulics	M,D
Immunology	M,D
Industrial and Manufacturing Management	M,D,O
Information Studies	M,D,O
International Business	M,D,O
International Development	M,D,O
Italian	M,D
Jewish Studies	M
Kinesiology and Movement Studies	M,D,O
Law	M,D,O
Library Science	M,D,O
Linguistics	M,D
Management Information Systems	M,D,O
Management Strategy and Policy	M,D,O
Marketing	M,D,O
Materials Engineering	M,D,O
Mathematics	M,D
Mechanical Engineering	M,D
Mechanics	M,D
Medical Physics	M,D
Meteorology	M,D
Microbiology	M,D
Mineral/Mining Engineering	M,D,O
Music Education	M,D
Music	M,D
Natural Resources	M,D
Near and Middle Eastern Studies	M,D,O
Neuroscience	M,D
Nursing—General	M,D,O
Nutrition	M,D,O
Oceanography	M,D
Oral and Dental Sciences	M,D,O
Parasitology	M,D,O
Pathology	M,D
Pharmacology	M,D
Philosophy	M,D
Physical Education	M,D,O
Physics	M,D
Physiology	M,D
Planetary and Space Sciences	M,D
Plant Sciences	M,D,O
Political Science	M,D
Psychology—General	M,D
Rehabilitation Sciences	M,D,O
Religion	M,D
Russian	M,D
School Psychology	M,D,O
Social Work	M,D,O
Sociology	M,D,O
Statistics	M,D,O
Structural Engineering	M,D
Theology	M,D
Transportation Management	M,D
Urban and Regional Planning	M,D
Water Resources Engineering	M,D

MCKENDREE UNIVERSITY

Business Administration and Management—General	M
Clinical Psychology	M
Counseling Psychology	M
Curriculum and Instruction	M,D,O
Education—General	M,D,O
Educational Leadership and Administration	M,D,O
Higher Education	M,D,O
Human Resources Management	M
International Business	M
Music Education	M,D,O
Nursing and Healthcare Administration	M
Nursing Education	M
Nursing—General	M
Reading Education	M,D,O
Special Education	M,D,O

MCMASTER UNIVERSITY

Analytical Chemistry	M,D
Anthropology	M,D
Applied Statistics	M
Astrophysics	D
Biochemistry	M,D
Biological and Biomedical Sciences—General	M,D
Business Administration and Management—General	M,D
Cancer Biology/Oncology	M,D
Cardiovascular Sciences	M,D
Cell Biology	M,D
Chemical Engineering	M,D
Chemical Physics	M,D
Chemistry	M,D
Civil Engineering	M,D
Classics	M,D
Computer Science	M,D
Cultural Studies	M,D
Economics	M,D
Electrical Engineering	M,D
Engineering and Applied Sciences—General	M,D
Engineering Physics	M,D
English	M,D
French	M
Genetics	M,D
Geochemistry	M,D
Geography	M,D
Geology	M,D
Geosciences	M,D
Health Physics/Radiological Health	M,D
Health Services Research	M,D
History	M,D
Human Resources Management	M,D
Immunology	M,D
Industrial and Labor Relations	M
Inorganic Chemistry	M,D
International Affairs	M,D
Kinesiology and Movement Studies	M,D
Management Information Systems	D
Materials Engineering	M,D
Materials Sciences	M,D
Mathematics	M,D
Mechanical Engineering	M,D
Medical Physics	M,D
Molecular Biology	M,D
Neuroscience	M,D
Nuclear Engineering	M,D
Nursing—General	M,D
Nutrition	M,D
Occupational Therapy	M
Organic Chemistry	M,D
Pastoral Ministry and Counseling	M,D,O
Pharmacology	M,D
Philosophy	M,D
Physical Chemistry	M,D
Physical Therapy	M
Physics	D
Physiology	M,D
Political Science	M,D
Psychology—General	M,D
Public Administration	M,D
Public Affairs	M,D
Public Policy	M,D
Rehabilitation Sciences	M,D
Religion	M,D
Social Work	M
Sociology	M,D
Software Engineering	M,D
Statistics	M
Theology	M,D,O
Virology	M,D

MCMURRY UNIVERSITY

Family Nurse Practitioner Studies	M
Nursing Education	M
Nursing—General	M

MCNEESE STATE UNIVERSITY

Agricultural Sciences—General	M
Applied Behavior Analysis	M,O
Art Education	O
Business Administration and Management—General	M
Chemical Engineering	M
Chemistry	M
Civil Engineering	M
Computer Science	M
Counseling Psychology	M,O
Counselor Education	M
Criminal Justice and Criminology	M
Curriculum and Instruction	M
Early Childhood Education	O
Education of the Gifted	M
Education—General	O
Educational Leadership and Administration	M,O
Educational Measurement and Evaluation	M,O
Educational Media/Instructional Technology	M,O
Electrical Engineering	M
Elementary Education	M,O
Engineering and Applied Sciences—General	M
Engineering Management	M
English	M
Environmental Sciences	M
Exercise and Sports Science	M
Experimental Psychology	M,O
Family Nurse Practitioner Studies	M
Health Education	O
Health Promotion	M
Library Science	O
Mathematics Education	O
Mathematics	M
Mechanical Engineering	M
Middle School Education	O
Music Education	O
Nursing Education	M
Nursing—General	M,O
Nutrition	M
Physical Education	O
Psychiatric Nursing	M,O
Psychology—General	M,O
Reading Education	M
School Psychology	M,O
Science Education	O
Secondary Education	M,O
Special Education	M,O
Statistics	M
Writing	M

MCPHERSON COLLEGE

Education—General	M

MCPHS UNIVERSITY

Acupuncture and Oriental Medicine	M
Chemistry	M,D
Health Services Management and Hospital Administration	M
Nursing—General	M
Optometry	D
Pharmaceutical Sciences	M,D
Pharmacology	M,D
Pharmacy	D
Physical Therapy	D
Physician Assistant Studies	M

MEADVILLE LOMBARD THEOLOGICAL SCHOOL

Pastoral Ministry and Counseling	M,D
Theology	M,D

MEDAILLE COLLEGE

Business Administration and Management—General	M
Clinical Psychology	M,D
Counseling Psychology	M,D
Curriculum and Instruction	M
Education—General	M
Elementary Education	M
Marriage and Family Therapy	M,D
Organizational Management	M
Psychology—General	M,D
Reading Education	M
Secondary Education	M
Special Education	M

MEDICAL COLLEGE OF WISCONSIN

Allopathic Medicine	D
Biochemistry	D
Bioethics	M,O
Biological and Biomedical Sciences—General	M,D,O
Biostatistics	D
Clinical Laboratory Sciences/Medical Technology	M
Clinical Research	M
Community Health	D
Neuroscience	D
Pharmacology	D
Pharmacy	D
Physiology	D
Public Health—General	M,D,O
Toxicology	D

MEDICAL UNIVERSITY OF SOUTH CAROLINA

Adult Nursing	M,D
Allied Health—General	M,D
Allopathic Medicine	D
Biochemistry	M,D
Biological and Biomedical Sciences—General	M,D
Biostatistics	M,D
Cancer Biology/Oncology	D
Cardiovascular Sciences	D
Cell Biology	D
Clinical Research	M
Dentistry	D
Developmental Biology	D
Epidemiology	M,D
Family Nurse Practitioner Studies	M,D
Genetics	D
Gerontological Nursing	M,D
Health Services Management and Hospital Administration	M,D
Immunology	M,D
International Health	M
Marine Sciences	D
Maternal and Child/Neonatal Nursing	M,D
Medical Imaging	D
Medicinal and Pharmaceutical Chemistry	D
Microbiology	M,D
Molecular Biology	M,D
Molecular Pharmacology	M,D
Neuroscience	M,D
Nurse Anesthesia	M
Nursing and Healthcare Administration	M
Nursing Education	M
Nursing—General	D
Occupational Therapy	M
Pathobiology	D
Pathology	M,D
Pharmacy	D
Physical Therapy	D
Physician Assistant Studies	M
Rehabilitation Sciences	D
Toxicology	D

MEHARRY MEDICAL COLLEGE

Allopathic Medicine	D
Biochemistry	D
Biological and Biomedical Sciences—General	D
Cancer Biology/Oncology	D
Dentistry	D
Environmental and Occupational Health	M
Health Services Management and Hospital Administration	M
Immunology	D
Microbiology	D
Neuroscience	D
Pharmacology	D
Public Health—General	M

MELBOURNE BUSINESS SCHOOL

Business Administration and Management—General	M,D,O
Marketing	M,D,O

MEMORIAL UNIVERSITY OF NEWFOUNDLAND

Adult Education	M,D,O
Anthropology	M,D
Aquaculture	M
Archaeology	M,D
Biochemistry	M,D
Biological and Biomedical Sciences—General	M,D,O
Biopsychology	M,D
Business Administration and Management—General	M
Cancer Biology/Oncology	M,D
Cardiovascular Sciences	M,D
Chemistry	M,D
Civil Engineering	M,D
Classics	M
Clinical Psychology	M,D
Clinical Research	M
Community Health	M,D,O
Computational Sciences	M
Computer Engineering	M,D
Computer Science	M,D
Condensed Matter Physics	M,D
Cultural Anthropology	M,D
Curriculum and Instruction	M,D,O
Economics	M
Education—General	M,D,O
Educational Leadership and Administration	M,D,O
Educational Media/Instructional Technology	M,D,O
Educational Psychology	M,D,O
Electrical Engineering	M,D
Engineering and Applied Sciences—General	M,D
English	M,D
Environmental Engineering	M
Environmental Sciences	M,D
Epidemiology	M,D,O
Exercise and Sports Science	M
Experimental Psychology	M,D
Fish, Game, and Wildlife Management	M,O
Folklore	M,D
Food Science and Technology	M,D
French	M
Gender Studies	M,D
Geography	M,D
Geology	M,D
Geophysics	M,D
Geosciences	M,D
German	M
History	M,D
Human Genetics	M,D
Humanities	M
Immunology	M,D
Industrial and Labor Relations	M
Kinesiology and Movement Studies	M
Linguistics	M,D
Marine Affairs	M,D,O
Marine Sciences	M,O
Mathematics	M,D
Mechanical Engineering	M,D
Music	M,D
Neuroscience	M,D
Nursing—General	M,D
Ocean Engineering	M,D
Oceanography	M,D
Pharmaceutical Sciences	M,D
Philosophy	M,D
Physical Education	M
Physics	M,D
Political Science	M
Psychology—General	M,D
Religion	M
Social Work	M,D
Sociology	M,D
Statistics	M,D

MEMPHIS THEOLOGICAL SEMINARY

Theology	M,D

MERCER UNIVERSITY

Accounting	M
Allopathic Medicine	M,D
Athletic Training and Sports Medicine	M,D
Biomedical Engineering	M
Business Administration and Management—General	M
Clinical Psychology	M,D
Computer Engineering	M
Counselor Education	M,D
Criminal Justice and Criminology	M,D
Curriculum and Instruction	M,D,O
Early Childhood Education	M,D,O
Education—General	M,D,O
Educational Leadership and Administration	M,D,O
Electrical Engineering	M
Engineering and Applied Sciences—General	M
Engineering Management	M
Entrepreneurship	M
Environmental and Occupational Health	M,D
Environmental Engineering	M
Environmental Sciences	M
Family Nurse Practitioner Studies	M,D,O
Gerontological Nursing	M,D,O
Gerontology	M,D
Health Informatics	M,D
Higher Education	M,D,O
Human Services	M,D
Law	D
Management of Technology	M
Mathematics	M,D,O
Mechanical Engineering	M
Middle School Education	M,D,O
Music	M,D
Nonprofit Management	M,D
Nursing and Healthcare Administration	M,D
Nursing—General	M,D,O
Organizational Management	M,D
Pastoral Ministry and Counseling	M,D
Pharmaceutical Sciences	D
Pharmacy	D
Physical Therapy	M,D
Physician Assistant Studies	M,D
Public Health—General	M,D
Rehabilitation Counseling	M,D
School Psychology	M,D
Science Education	M,D,O
Secondary Education	M,D,O
Software Engineering	M
Theology	M,D

MERCY COLLEGE

Accounting	M
Allied Health—General	M,D
Business Administration and Management—General	M
Communication Disorders	M
Computer and Information Systems Security	M
Counseling Psychology	M,O
Counselor Education	M,O
Early Childhood Education	M
Education—General	M,O
Educational Leadership and Administration	M,O
Elementary Education	M
English as a Second Language	M,O
English	M
Health Services Management and Hospital Administration	M
Human Resources Management	M
Marriage and Family Therapy	M,O
Middle School Education	M,O
Nursing and Healthcare Administration	M
Nursing Education	M
Nursing—General	M
Occupational Therapy	M
Organizational Management	M
Physical Therapy	D
Physician Assistant Studies	M
Psychology—General	M
Reading Education	M,O
School Psychology	M
Secondary Education	M,O

MERCY COLLEGE OF OHIO

Health Services Management and Hospital Administration	M
Nursing—General	M

MERCYHURST UNIVERSITY

Accounting	M,O
Anthropology	M
Applied Behavior Analysis	M
Archaeology	M
Biological Anthropology	M
Computer and Information Systems Security	M
Criminal Justice and Criminology	M,O
Educational Leadership and Administration	M,O
Entrepreneurship	M,O
Forensic Sciences	M
Higher Education	M,O
Human Resources Management	M,O
Management Strategy and Policy	M,O
Organizational Management	M,O
Physician Assistant Studies	M
Secondary Education	M
Special Education	M
Sports Management	M,O

MEREDITH COLLEGE

Business Administration and Management—General	M
Education of the Gifted	M,O
Education—General	M,O
Elementary Education	M,O
English as a Second Language	M,O
Entrepreneurship	M
Health Education	M,O
Human Resources Management	M
Industrial and Organizational Psychology	M
Nutrition	M,O
Physical Education	M,O
Project Management	M
Psychology—General	M
Reading Education	M,O
Special Education	M,O

MERRIMACK COLLEGE

Accounting	M
Adult Education	M,O
Athletic Training and Sports Medicine	M
Business Administration and Management—General	M

*M—masters degree; D—doctorate; O—other advanced degree; *—Close-Up and/or Display*

Business Analytics M
Civil Engineering M
Clinical Psychology M,O
Computer Science M
Criminal Justice and Criminology M,O
Curriculum and Instruction M,O
Data Science/Data Analytics M
Early Childhood Education M,O
Education—General M,O
Educational Leadership and Administration M,O
Elementary Education M,O
Engineering and Applied Sciences—General M
Engineering Management M
English as a Second Language M,O
Exercise and Sports Science M
Health Education M
Health Promotion M
Higher Education M,O
Mechanical Engineering M
Middle School Education M,O
Public Affairs M,O
School Psychology M,O
Secondary Education M,O
Special Education M,O
Student Affairs M,O
Theology M,O

MESIVTA OF EASTERN PARKWAY–YESHIVA ZICHRON MEILECH
Theology

MESIVTA TORAH VODAATH RABBINICAL SEMINARY
Pastoral Ministry and Counseling O
Theology O

MESIVTHA TIFERETH JERUSALEM OF AMERICA
Theology

MESSIAH COLLEGE
Business Administration and Management—General M,O
Clinical Psychology M,O
Counseling Psychology M,O
Counselor Education M,O
Curriculum and Instruction M
English as a Second Language M,O
Higher Education M
Management Strategy and Policy M,O
Marriage and Family Therapy M,O
Music M
Nursing Education M
Organizational Management M,O
Special Education M
Sports Management M
Student Affairs M

METHODIST THEOLOGICAL SCHOOL IN OHIO
Theology M,D

METHODIST UNIVERSITY
Business Administration and Management—General M
Criminal Justice and Criminology M
Physician Assistant Studies M

METROPOLITAN COLLEGE OF NEW YORK
Business Administration and Management—General M
Elementary Education M
Emergency Management M
Finance and Banking M
Media Studies M
Public Administration M
Public Affairs M
Risk Management M
Special Education M

METROPOLITAN STATE UNIVERSITY
Business Administration and Management—General M,D,O
Business Analytics M,D,O
Computer and Information Systems Security M,D,O
Criminal Justice and Criminology M
Data Science/Data Analytics M,D,O
Information Studies M,D,O
Liberal Studies M
Management Information Systems M,D,O
Nursing and Healthcare Administration M,D
Nursing Education M,D
Nursing—General M,D
Oral and Dental Sciences M,D
Project Management M,D,O
Supply Chain Management M,D,O
Technical Writing M

METROPOLITAN STATE UNIVERSITY OF DENVER
Accounting M
Education—General M
Elementary Education M
Social Work M
Special Education M
Taxation M

MGH INSTITUTE OF HEALTH PROFESSIONS
Communication Disorders M,O
Gerontological Nursing M,D,O
Nursing Education M,D,O
Nursing—General M,D,O
Occupational Therapy D
Pediatric Nursing M,D,O
Physical Therapy M,D,O
Physician Assistant Studies M
Psychiatric Nursing M,D,O
Reading Education M,O
Women's Health Nursing M,D,O

MIAMI INTERNATIONAL UNIVERSITY OF ART & DESIGN
Applied Arts and Design—General M
Film, Television, and Video Production M

MIAMI REGIONAL UNIVERSITY
Nursing and Healthcare Administration M
Nursing Education M
Nursing—General M

MIAMI UNIVERSITY
Accounting M
Architecture M
Art Education M
Art/Fine Arts M
Biochemistry M,D
Biological and Biomedical Sciences—General M,D
Business Administration and Management—General M
Chemical Engineering M
Chemistry M,D
Child and Family Studies M
Communication Disorders M
Computer Engineering M
Demography and Population Studies M,D
Economics M
Education—General M,D,O
Educational Leadership and Administration M,D
Educational Psychology M,O
Electrical Engineering M
Engineering and Applied Sciences—General M
English M,D
Environmental Sciences M
Exercise and Sports Science M
French M
Geography M
Geology M,D
Gerontology M,D
History M
Interior Design M
Mathematics Education M
Mathematics M
Mechanical Engineering M
Microbiology M,D
Music Education M
Music M
Philosophy M
Physics M
Political Science M,D
Psychology—General M
Statistics M
Student Affairs M,D
Systems Science M
Theater M

MICHIGAN SCHOOL OF PROFESSIONAL PSYCHOLOGY
Clinical Psychology M,D
Educational Psychology M,D
Psychology—General M,D
Transpersonal and Humanistic Psychology M,D

MICHIGAN STATE UNIVERSITY
Accounting M,D
Adult Education M,D,O
Advertising and Public Relations M,D
African Studies M,D
African-American Studies M,D
Agricultural Economics and Agribusiness M,D
Agricultural Sciences—General M,D
Agronomy and Soil Sciences M,D
Allopathic Medicine D
American Studies M,D
Animal Sciences M,D
Anthropology M,D
Applied Mathematics M,D
Applied Statistics M
Art/Fine Arts M
Astronomy M,D
Astrophysics M,D
Biochemistry M,D
Biological and Biomedical Sciences—General M,D
Biosystems Engineering M,D
Business Administration and Management—General M,D
Business Analytics M
Cell Biology M,D
Chemical Engineering M,D
Chemical Physics M,D
Chemistry M,D
Child and Family Studies M,D
Child Development M,D
Civil Engineering M,D
Clinical Laboratory Sciences/Medical Technology M
Communication Disorders M,D
Communication—General M,D
Computer Art and Design M
Computer Science M,D
Construction Management M,D
Counselor Education M,D,O
Criminal Justice and Criminology M,D
Curriculum and Instruction M,D,O
Ecology D
Economics M,D
Education—General M,D,O
Educational Leadership and Administration M,D,O
Educational Measurement and Evaluation M,D,O
Educational Media/Instructional Technology M,D,O
Educational Policy D
Educational Psychology M,D,O
Electrical Engineering M,D
Engineering and Applied Sciences—General M,D
English as a Second Language M,D
English M,D
Entomology M,D
Environmental Design M,D
Environmental Engineering M,D
Environmental Sciences M,D
Epidemiology M,D
Evolutionary Biology D
Finance and Banking M,D
Fish, Game, and Wildlife Management M,D
Food Science and Technology M,D
Foreign Languages Education D
Forensic Sciences M,D
Forestry M,D
French M,D
Game Design and Development M
Genetics M,D
Geography M,D
Geosciences M,D
German M,D
Health Communication M
Higher Education M,D,O
Hispanic and Latin American Languages M,D
Hispanic Studies M,D
History M,D
Horticulture M,D
Hospitality Management M
Human Resources Management M,D
Industrial and Labor Relations M,D
Interior Design M,D
Journalism M
Kinesiology and Movement Studies M,D
Latin American Studies D
Linguistics M,D
Logistics M,D
Management Information Systems M,D
Management Strategy and Policy M,D
Manufacturing Engineering M,D
Marketing Research M,D
Marketing M,D
Marriage and Family Therapy M,D
Materials Engineering M,D
Materials Sciences M,D
Mathematics Education M,D
Mathematics M,D
Mechanical Engineering M,D
Mechanics M,D
Media Studies M,D
Microbiology M,D
Molecular Biology M,D
Molecular Genetics M,D
Music Education M,D
Music M,D
Natural Resources M,D
Neuroscience M,D
Nursing—General M,D
Nutrition M,D
Osteopathic Medicine D
Pathobiology M,D
Pathology M,D
Pharmacology M,D
Philosophy M,D
Physics M,D
Physiology M,D
Plant Biology M,D
Plant Pathology M,D
Plant Sciences M,D
Political Science M,D
Portuguese M,D
Psychology—General M,D
Public Health—General M
Reading Education M,D
Recreation and Park Management M,D
Rehabilitation Counseling M,D,O
Rhetoric M,D
Romance Languages M,D
School Psychology M,D,O
Science Education M,D
Social Sciences Education M,D
Social Work M,D
Sociology M,D
Spanish M,D
Special Education M,D,O
Statistics M,D
Structural Biology D
Supply Chain Management M,D
Systems Biology D
Taxation M,D
Telecommunications M
Theater M,D
Therapies—Dance, Drama, and Music M,D
Toxicology M,D
Urban and Regional Planning M,D
Veterinary Medicine D
Veterinary Sciences M,D
Writing M,D
Zoology M,D

MICHIGAN STATE UNIVERSITY COLLEGE OF LAW
Intellectual Property Law M,D
Law M,D
Legal and Justice Studies M,D

MICHIGAN TECHNOLOGICAL UNIVERSITY
Accounting M
Applied Mathematics M,D
Applied Physics M,D
Archaeology M,D
Atmospheric Sciences M,D,O
Automotive Engineering M,D,O
Biochemistry M,D,O
Biological and Biomedical Sciences—General M,D
Biomedical Engineering M,D
Biotechnology M,D
Business Administration and Management—General M
Chemical Engineering M,D
Chemistry M,D
Civil Engineering M,D
Cognitive Sciences M,D,O
Computational Sciences M,D,O
Computer and Information Systems Security M,D
Computer Engineering M,D,O
Computer Science M,D
Cultural Studies M,D
Data Science/Data Analytics M,D,O
Ecology M,D
Electrical Engineering M,D,O
Energy Management and Policy M,D
Engineering and Applied Sciences—General M,D,O
Environmental Engineering M,D,O
Environmental Management and Policy M,D
Ergonomics and Human Factors M,D,O
Forestry M,D
Geographic Information Systems M
Geophysics M,D
Interdisciplinary Studies M,D,O
Kinesiology and Movement Studies M,D
Materials Engineering M,D
Mathematics M,D
Mechanical Engineering M,D,O
Mechanics M,D,O
Medical Informatics M
Metallurgical Engineering and Metallurgy M,D
Mineral Economics M
Molecular Biology M,D,O
Nanotechnology M,D,O
Physics M,D
Rhetoric M,D
Science Education M,D,O
Statistics M,D
Sustainability Management M,D,O
Water Resources M,D,O

MID-AMERICA BAPTIST THEOLOGICAL SEMINARY
Missions and Missiology M,D
Pastoral Ministry and Counseling M,D
Theology M,D

MID-AMERICA BAPTIST THEOLOGICAL SEMINARY NORTHEAST BRANCH
Theology M

MID-AMERICA CHRISTIAN UNIVERSITY
Business Administration and Management—General M
Counseling Psychology M
Marriage and Family Therapy M
Organizational Management M
Pastoral Ministry and Counseling M
Public Administration M

MIDAMERICA NAZARENE UNIVERSITY
Business Administration and Management—General M
Clinical Psychology M
Education—General M
Educational Media/Instructional Technology M
English as a Second Language M
Marriage and Family Therapy M
Nursing and Healthcare Administration M
Nursing Education M
Nursing—General M
Public Health—General M
Reading Education M
School Psychology M

MID-AMERICA REFORMED SEMINARY
Theology M

MIDDLEBURY COLLEGE
Chinese M
English M
French M,D
German M,D
Italian M,D
Near and Middle Eastern Languages M
Russian M,D
Spanish M,D

MIDDLEBURY INSTITUTE OF INTERNATIONAL STUDIES AT MONTEREY
Conflict Resolution and Mediation/Peace Studies M
English as a Second Language M
Environmental Management and Policy M
Foreign Languages Education M
International Affairs M
International and Comparative Education M
International Development M
International Trade Policy M
Public Administration M
Translation and Interpretation M

MIDDLE GEORGIA STATE UNIVERSITY
Computer and Information Systems Security M
Forensic Sciences M
Gerontological Nursing M
Health Informatics M
Management Information Systems M

MIDDLE TENNESSEE SCHOOL OF ANESTHESIA
Nurse Anesthesia M,D

MIDDLE TENNESSEE STATE UNIVERSITY
Accounting M

Actuarial Science	M
Aerospace/Aeronautical Engineering	M
Archives/Archival Administration	M,D,O
Aviation Management	M
Biological and Biomedical Sciences—General	M
Biostatistics	M
Biotechnology	M
Business Administration and Management—General	M
Business Education	M
Chemistry	M
Clinical Psychology	M,O
Computational Sciences	D
Computer Science	M
Counseling Psychology	M
Counselor Education	M
Criminal Justice and Criminology	M
Curriculum and Instruction	M,O
Early Childhood Education	M,O
Economics	M,D
Education—General	M,D,O
Educational Leadership and Administration	M,O
Educational Media/Instructional Technology	M,O
Elementary Education	M,O
Engineering Management	M
English as a Second Language	M,O
English	M,D
Exercise and Sports Science	M,D
Experimental Psychology	M,O
Family Nurse Practitioner Studies	M,O
Foreign Languages Education	M
French	M
Gender Studies	O
Geosciences	O
German	M
Gerontology	O
Health Education	M
History	M
Human Resources Management	M
Industrial and Organizational Psychology	M,O
International Affairs	M
Management Information Systems	M
Management Strategy and Policy	M
Mass Communication	M
Mathematics Education	M,D
Mathematics	M
Medical Informatics	M
Middle School Education	M,O
Molecular Biology	D
Music	M
Nursing and Healthcare Administration	M
Nursing Education	M
Nursing—General	M,O
Physical Education	M
Political Science	M
Psychology—General	M,O
Public History	D
Reading Education	M,D
Recreation and Park Management	M
School Psychology	M,O
Science Education	M,D
Secondary Education	M,O
Social Work	M
Sociology	M
Spanish	M
Special Education	M
Vocational and Technical Education	M
Women's Studies	O

MIDWAY UNIVERSITY

Business Administration and Management—General	M
Education—General	M
Organizational Management	M

MIDWEST COLLEGE OF ORIENTAL MEDICINE

Acupuncture and Oriental Medicine	M,O

MIDWESTERN BAPTIST THEOLOGICAL SEMINARY

Music	M,D,O
Pastoral Ministry and Counseling	M,D,O
Religious Education	M,D,O
Theology	M,D,O

MIDWESTERN STATE UNIVERSITY

Biological and Biomedical Sciences—General	M
Business Administration and Management—General	M
Clinical Psychology	M
Community Health	M,O
Computer Science	M
Counseling Psychology	M
Counselor Education	M
Criminal Justice and Criminology	M,O
Curriculum and Instruction	M
Education—General	M
Educational Leadership and Administration	M
Educational Media/Instructional Technology	M
English	M,D
Exercise and Sports Science	M
Family Nurse Practitioner Studies	M
Health Informatics	M,O
Health Physics/Radiological Health	M
Health Services Management and Hospital Administration	M,O
History	M
Human Resources Development	M
Nursing Education	M
Nursing—General	M
Philosophy	M,D
Political Science	M
Psychiatric Nursing	M
Reading Education	M
Special Education	M
Sports Management	M

MIDWESTERN UNIVERSITY, DOWNERS GROVE CAMPUS

Biological and Biomedical Sciences—General	M
Clinical Psychology	D
Dentistry	D
Occupational Therapy	M
Optometry	D
Osteopathic Medicine	D
Pharmacy	D
Physical Therapy	D
Physician Assistant Studies	M

MIDWESTERN UNIVERSITY, GLENDALE CAMPUS

Allied Health—General	M,D
Biological and Biomedical Sciences—General	M
Cardiovascular Sciences	M
Clinical Psychology	D
Communication Disorders	M
Dentistry	D
Nurse Anesthesia	M
Occupational Therapy	M
Optometry	D
Osteopathic Medicine	D
Pharmacy	D
Physical Therapy	D
Physician Assistant Studies	M
Podiatric Medicine	D

MIDWIVES COLLEGE OF UTAH

Nurse Midwifery	M

MILLENNIA ATLANTIC UNIVERSITY

Accounting	M
Business Administration and Management—General	M
Health Informatics	M
Human Resources Management	M

MILLERSVILLE UNIVERSITY OF PENNSYLVANIA

Applied Arts and Design—General	M
Art Education	M
Art/Fine Arts	M
Atmospheric Sciences	M
Clinical Psychology	M
Distance Education Development	M
Early Childhood Education	M
Education of the Gifted	M
Education—General	M,D,O
Educational Leadership and Administration	M,D
Emergency Management	M
English as a Second Language	M
English Education	M
English	M,O
Environmental Management and Policy	M
Family Nurse Practitioner Studies	M,O
French	M
Geographic Information Systems	M
German	M
History	M
Mathematics Education	M
Meteorology	M
Nursing Education	M,O
Nursing—General	D
Physical Education	M,O
Psychology—General	M
Reading Education	M
School Psychology	M
Science Education	M,D
Social Work	M,D
Spanish	M
Special Education	M
Sports Management	M,O
Vocational and Technical Education	M
Writing	M,O

MILLIGAN COLLEGE

Business Administration and Management—General	M,O
Clinical Psychology	M,O
Counselor Education	M,O
Early Childhood Education	M,D,O
Education—General	M,D,O
Educational Leadership and Administration	M,D,O
Elementary Education	M,D,O
Health Services Management and Hospital Administration	M,O
Industrial and Manufacturing Management	M,O
Middle School Education	M,D,O
Missions and Missiology	M,D,O
Occupational Therapy	M
Pastoral Ministry and Counseling	M,D,O
Physician Assistant Studies	M
Religion	M,D,O
Religious Education	M,D,O
Secondary Education	M,D,O
Special Education	M,D,O
Theology	M,D,O

MILLIKIN UNIVERSITY

Business Administration and Management—General	M
Family Nurse Practitioner Studies	M,D
Nurse Anesthesia	M,D
Nursing Education	M,D
Nursing—General	M,D

MILLSAPS COLLEGE

Accounting	M
Business Administration and Management—General	M

MILLS COLLEGE

Applied Economics	M
Art/Fine Arts	M
Biological and Biomedical Sciences—General	O
Business Administration and Management—General	M
Computer Science	M,O
Dance	M
Early Childhood Education	M
Education—General	M,D,O
Educational Leadership and Administration	
English	M,O
Illustration	M,O
Interdisciplinary Studies	M,O
Music	M
Photography	M
Public Policy	M
Translation and Interpretation	M,O
Writing	M,O

MILWAUKEE SCHOOL OF ENGINEERING

Architectural Engineering	M
Business Administration and Management—General	M
Business Education	M
Cardiovascular Sciences	M
Civil Engineering	M
Clinical Laboratory Sciences/Medical Technology	M
Engineering and Applied Sciences—General	M
Engineering Management	M
Health Services Management and Hospital Administration	M
Industrial and Manufacturing Management	M
International Business	M
Marketing	M
Nursing and Healthcare Administration	M
Perfusion	M

MINNEAPOLIS COLLEGE OF ART AND DESIGN

Applied Arts and Design—General	M
Art/Fine Arts	M,O
Computer Art and Design	O
Film, Television, and Video Production	M
Graphic Design	M,O
Illustration	M
Internet and Interactive Multimedia	M
Photography	M
Sustainable Development	M,O

MINNESOTA STATE UNIVERSITY MANKATO

Accounting	M
Allied Health—General	M,D,O
Anthropology	M
Applied Statistics	M
Art Education	M
Art/Fine Arts	M
Astronomy	M
Automotive Engineering	M
Biological and Biomedical Sciences—General	M
Business Administration and Management—General	M
Clinical Psychology	M,D
Communication Disorders	M
Communication—General	M,O
Community Health	M,O
Computer Science	M,O
Corporate and Organizational Communication	M,O
Counseling Psychology	M,D
Counselor Education	M,D
Criminal Justice and Criminology	M
Education—General	M,D,O
Educational Leadership and Administration	M
English as a Second Language	M,O
English	M,O
Environmental Sciences	M
Ethnic Studies	M
Family Nurse Practitioner Studies	M,D
Foreign Languages Education	M
French	M
Gender Studies	M
Geography	M
Gerontology	M
Health Education	M,O
Higher Education	M
History	M
Human Services	M
Industrial and Organizational Psychology	M,D
Information Science	M,O
Interdisciplinary Studies	M
Manufacturing Engineering	M
Mathematics Education	M
Mathematics	M
Music Education	M
Music	M
Nonprofit Management	M,O
Nursing Education	M,D
Nursing—General	M,D
Physical Education	M
Physics	M
Psychology—General	M,D
Public Administration	M
Rehabilitation Counseling	M
School Psychology	M,D
Science Education	M
Social Sciences Education	M
Social Work	M
Sociology	M
Spanish	M
Special Education	M,O
Statistics	M
Student Affairs	M,D
Technical Communication	M,O
Theater	M
Urban and Regional Planning	M,O
Urban Studies	M,O
Women's Studies	M
Writing	M,O

MINNESOTA STATE UNIVERSITY MOORHEAD

Accounting	M
Business Administration and Management—General	M
Communication Disorders	M,D,O
Counselor Education	M,D,O
Curriculum and Instruction	M,D,O
Education—General	M,D,O
Educational Leadership and Administration	M,D,O
English as a Second Language	M
Finance and Banking	M
Health Services Management and Hospital Administration	M,O
Nursing—General	M,O
School Psychology	M,O
Special Education	M,D,O

MINOT STATE UNIVERSITY

Business Administration and Management—General	M
Communication Disorders	M
Elementary Education	M
Management Information Systems	M
Mathematics Education	M
Middle School Education	M
School Psychology	O
Science Education	M
Special Education	M

MIRRER YESHIVA CENTRAL INSTITUTE

Theology	

MISERICORDIA UNIVERSITY

Accounting	M
Allied Health—General	M,D
Business Administration and Management—General	M
Communication Disorders	M
Curriculum and Instruction	M
Education—General	M
Educational Media/Instructional Technology	M
Health Services Management and Hospital Administration	M
Human Resources Management	M
Nursing—General	M,D
Occupational Therapy	M,D
Organizational Management	M
Physical Therapy	D
Reading Education	M
Special Education	M
Sports Management	M

MISSISSIPPI COLLEGE

Accounting	M,O
Advertising and Public Relations	M
Art Education	M,D,O
Art/Fine Arts	M
Biochemistry	M
Biological and Biomedical Sciences—General	M
Business Administration and Management—General	M,O
Business Education	M,D,O
Chemistry	M
Communication—General	M
Computer Education	M,D,O
Computer Science	M
Corporate and Organizational Communication	M
Counseling Psychology	M,O
Counselor Education	M,O
Criminal Justice and Criminology	M,O
Curriculum and Instruction	M,D,O
Education—General	M,D,O
Educational Leadership and Administration	M,D,O
Elementary Education	M,D,O
English as a Second Language	M
English Education	M,D,O
English	M
Finance and Banking	M,O
Health Services Management and Hospital Administration	M
Higher Education	M,D,O
History	M,O
Kinesiology and Movement Studies	M
Law	D,O
Legal and Justice Studies	M,O
Liberal Studies	M
Marriage and Family Therapy	M,O
Mathematics Education	M,D,O
Mathematics	M
Music Education	M
Music	M
Political Science	M,O
Science Education	M,D,O
Secondary Education	M,D,O
Social Sciences Education	M,D,O
Social Sciences	M,O
Special Education	M,D,O

MISSISSIPPI STATE UNIVERSITY

Accounting	M
Aerospace/Aeronautical Engineering	M,D

*M—masters degree; D—doctorate; O—other advanced degree; *—Close-Up and/or Display*

Agricultural Economics and Agribusiness	M
Agricultural Education	M,D
Agricultural Sciences—General	M,D
Agronomy and Soil Sciences	M,D
Animal Sciences	M,D
Anthropology	M
Applied Psychology	M,D
Atmospheric Sciences	M,D
Biochemistry	M,D
Bioengineering	M,D
Biological and Biomedical Sciences—General	M,D
Biomedical Engineering	M,D
Business Administration and Management—General	M,D
Chemical Engineering	M,D
Chemistry	M,D
Child and Family Studies	M,D
Civil Engineering	M,D
Clinical Psychology	M,D,O
Clothing and Textiles	M,D
Cognitive Sciences	M,D
Communication—General	M,D
Community College Education	M,D,O
Computer Engineering	M,D
Computer Science	M,D
Counselor Education	M,D,O
Curriculum and Instruction	M,D,O
Early Childhood Education	M,D,O
Economics	M,D
Education—General	M,D,O
Educational Leadership and Administration	M,D,O
Educational Media/Instructional Technology	M,D,O
Educational Psychology	M,D,O
Electrical Engineering	M,D
Elementary Education	M,D,O
Engineering and Applied Sciences—General	M,D
English	M
Ergonomics and Human Factors	M,D
Exercise and Sports Science	M,D
Finance and Banking	M,D
Fish, Game, and Wildlife Management	M,D
Food Science and Technology	M,D
Foreign Languages Education	M
Forestry	M,D
Genetics	M,D
Geography	M,D
Geology	M,D
Geosciences	M,D
Higher Education	M,D,O
History	M,D
Horticulture	M,D
Human Development	M,D
Human Resources Development	M,D,O
Industrial and Manufacturing Management	M,D
Industrial/Management Engineering	M,D
Kinesiology and Movement Studies	M,D
Landscape Architecture	M
Management Information Systems	M,D
Marketing	D
Mathematics	M,D
Mechanical Engineering	M,D
Meteorology	M,D
Middle School Education	M,D,O
Molecular Biology	M,D
Nutrition	M,D
Operations Research	M,D
Physical Education	M,D
Physics	M,D
Plant Sciences	M,D
Political Science	M,D
Project Management	M,D
Psychology—General	M,D
Public Administration	M,D
Public Policy	M,D
Reading Education	M,D,O
Rehabilitation Counseling	M,D,O
School Psychology	M,D,O
Secondary Education	M,D,O
Sociology	M,D
Special Education	M,D,O
Sports Management	M,D
Statistics	M,D
Student Affairs	M,D,O
Sustainable Development	M,D
Systems Engineering	M,D
Taxation	M
Veterinary Medicine	D
Veterinary Sciences	M,D
Vocational and Technical Education	M,D,O

MISSISSIPPI UNIVERSITY FOR WOMEN

Communication Disorders	M,D,O
Curriculum and Instruction	M
Education of the Gifted	M
Education—General	M
Educational Leadership and Administration	M
Health Education	M,D,O
Nursing—General	M,D,O
Public Health—General	M,D,O
Reading Education	M

MISSISSIPPI VALLEY STATE UNIVERSITY

Criminal Justice and Criminology	M
Education—General	M
Environmental and Occupational Health	M

MISSOURI BAPTIST UNIVERSITY

Business Administration and Management—General	M,O
Counselor Education	M,O
Education—General	M,O
Educational Leadership and Administration	M,O
Pastoral Ministry and Counseling	M,O

MISSOURI SOUTHERN STATE UNIVERSITY

Business Administration and Management—General	M
Criminal Justice and Criminology	M
Dental Hygiene	M
Early Childhood Education	M
Education—General	M
Educational Media/Instructional Technology	M
Nursing—General	M

MISSOURI STATE UNIVERSITY

Accounting	M
Agricultural Sciences—General	M
Applied Behavior Analysis	M,O
Applied Science and Technology	M,O
Art/Fine Arts	M
Athletic Training and Sports Medicine	M
Biological and Biomedical Sciences—General	M
Business Administration and Management—General	M
Cell Biology	M
Chemistry	M
Child and Family Studies	M
Clinical Psychology	M,O
Communication Disorders	M,D
Communication—General	M,O
Computer Science	M
Construction Management	M
Counseling Psychology	M
Counselor Education	M
Criminal Justice and Criminology	M,O
Early Childhood Education	M
Educational Leadership and Administration	M,O
Educational Measurement and Evaluation	O
Educational Media/Instructional Technology	M
Elementary Education	M,O
English as a Second Language	M,O
English Education	M,O
English	M,O
Environmental Management and Policy	M,O
Experimental Psychology	M,O
Family Nurse Practitioner Studies	M,D
Film, Television, and Video Production	M,O
Geography	M,O
Geology	M,O
Geosciences	M,O
Health Services Management and Hospital Administration	M
Higher Education	M
History	M,O
Homeland Security	M,O
Industrial and Organizational Psychology	M,O
International Affairs	M
Kinesiology and Movement Studies	M
Materials Sciences	M
Mathematics Education	M
Mathematics	M
Military and Defense Studies	M,O
Molecular Biology	M
Music	M
Nurse Anesthesia	D
Nursing Education	M,D
Nursing—General	M,D
Nutrition	M,D,O
Occupational Therapy	M
Physical Education	M
Physical Therapy	D
Physician Assistant Studies	M
Physics	M
Plant Sciences	M
Political Science	M,O
Project Management	M
Psychology—General	M,O
Public Administration	M,O
Public Health—General	M
Reading Education	M,O
Religion	M,O
Science Education	M,O
Secondary Education	M,O
Social Sciences Education	M,O
Social Work	M
Special Education	M
Sports Management	M,O
Student Affairs	M
Theater	M
Urban and Regional Planning	M,O
Writing	M,O

MISSOURI UNIVERSITY OF SCIENCE AND TECHNOLOGY

Aerospace/Aeronautical Engineering	M,D
Applied Mathematics	M,D
Biological and Biomedical Sciences—General	M
Business Administration and Management—General	M
Ceramic Sciences and Engineering	M,D
Chemical Engineering	M,D
Chemistry	M,D
Civil Engineering	M,D
Computer Engineering	M,D
Computer Science	M,D
Electrical Engineering	M,D
Engineering Management	M,D
Environmental Biology	M
Environmental Engineering	M,D
Geochemistry	M,D
Geological Engineering	M,D
Geology	M,D
Geophysics	M,D
Industrial and Organizational Psychology	M
Information Science	M
Manufacturing Engineering	M,D
Materials Engineering	M,D
Materials Sciences	M,D
Mathematics Education	M,D
Mathematics	M,D
Mechanical Engineering	M,D
Metallurgical Engineering and Metallurgy	M,D
Mineral/Mining Engineering	M,D
Nuclear Engineering	M,D
Petroleum Engineering	M,D
Physics	M,D
Statistics	M,D
Systems Engineering	M,D
Technical Communication	M
Water Resources	M,D

MISSOURI VALLEY COLLEGE

Social Psychology	M

MISSOURI WESTERN STATE UNIVERSITY

Accounting	M
Animal Sciences	M
Biological and Biomedical Sciences—General	M
Business Administration and Management—General	M
Chemistry	M
Computer and Information Systems Security	M
Early Childhood Education	M,O
Educational Measurement and Evaluation	M,O
Engineering and Applied Sciences—General	M
English as a Second Language	M,O
Forensic Sciences	M,O
Information Studies	M
Media Studies	M,O
Nursing and Healthcare Administration	M,O
Nursing Education	M,O
Nursing—General	M,O
Rhetoric	M,O
Special Education	M,O
Sports Management	M
Technical Communication	M,O
Writing	M,O

MITCHELL HAMLINE SCHOOL OF LAW

Law	M,D

MOLLOY COLLEGE

Accounting	M,O
Business Administration and Management—General	M,O
Clinical Psychology	M
Communication Disorders	M
Criminal Justice and Criminology	M
Early Childhood Education	M,O
Education—General	M,O
Educational Media/Instructional Technology	M,O
English as a Second Language	M,O
English Education	M,O
Family Nurse Practitioner Studies	M,D,O
Finance and Banking	M,O
Foreign Languages Education	M,O
Gerontological Nursing	M,D,O
Health Services Management and Hospital Administration	M,D,O
Marketing	M,O
Mathematics Education	M,O
Multilingual and Multicultural Education	M,O
Nursing Education	M,D,O
Nursing—General	M,D,O
Pediatric Nursing	M,D,O
Psychiatric Nursing	M,D,O
Science Education	M,O
Social Sciences Education	M,O
Special Education	M,O
Therapies—Dance, Drama, and Music	M

MONMOUTH UNIVERSITY

Accounting	M,O
Addictions/Substance Abuse Counseling	M,O
Adult Nursing	M,D,O
Advertising and Public Relations	M,O
American Studies	M
Anthropology	M
Applied Behavior Analysis	M,D,O
Business Administration and Management—General	M,O*
Communication Disorders	M,D,O
Communication—General	M,O
Computer Science	M
Corporate and Organizational Communication	M,O
Counseling Psychology	M,O
Criminal Justice and Criminology	M,O
Early Childhood Education	M,D,O
Education—General	M,D,O
Educational Leadership and Administration	M,D,O
Elementary Education	M,D,O
English as a Second Language	M,D,O
English	M
Family Nurse Practitioner Studies	M,D,O
Finance and Banking	M,O
Forensic Nursing	M,D,O
Gerontological Nursing	M,D,O
History	M
Homeland Security	M,O
Human Resources Management	M,O
Information Studies	M
Marketing	M,O
Media Studies	M,O
Nursing and Healthcare Administration	M,D,O
Nursing Education	M,D,O
Nursing—General	M,D,O
Physician Assistant Studies	M,D,O
Psychiatric Nursing	M,D,O
Psychology—General	M,O
Reading Education	M,D,O
Real Estate	M,O
Rhetoric	M
School Nursing	M,D,O
School Psychology	M,D,O
Secondary Education	M,D,O
Social Work	M,O
Software Engineering	M,O
Special Education	M,D,O
Student Affairs	M,D,O
Western European Studies	M
Writing	M

MONROE COLLEGE

Accounting	M
Biostatistics	M
Business Administration and Management—General	M
Community Health	M
Computer Science	M
Criminal Justice and Criminology	M
Entrepreneurship	M
Epidemiology	M
Finance and Banking	M
Health Services Management and Hospital Administration	M
Hospitality Management	M
Human Resources Management	M
Information Science	M
Marketing	M
Public Health—General	M

MONTANA STATE UNIVERSITY

Accounting	M
Adult Education	M,D,O
Agricultural Education	M
Agricultural Sciences—General	M,D
American Indian/Native American Studies	M
Animal Sciences	M,D
Architecture	M
Art History	M
Art/Fine Arts	M
Biochemistry	M,D
Biological and Biomedical Sciences—General	M,D
Chemical Engineering	M,D
Chemistry	M,D
Civil Engineering	M,D
Computer Engineering	M,D
Computer Science	M,D
Construction Engineering	M,D
Curriculum and Instruction	M,D,O
Ecology	M,D
Education—General	M,D,O
Educational Leadership and Administration	M,D,O
Electrical Engineering	M,D
Engineering and Applied Sciences—General	M,D
English	M
Environmental Engineering	M,D
Environmental Sciences	M,D
Family Nurse Practitioner Studies	M,D,O
Film, Television, and Video Production	M
Fish, Game, and Wildlife Management	M,D
Geosciences	M,D
Health Education	M
Higher Education	M,D,O
History	M,D
Home Economics Education	M
Human Development	M
Immunology	M,D
Industrial/Management Engineering	M,D
Infectious Diseases	M,D
Mathematics Education	M,D
Mathematics	M,D
Mechanical Engineering	M,D
Mechanics	M,D
Microbiology	M,D
Natural Resources	M
Neuroscience	M,D
Nursing and Healthcare Administration	M,D,O
Nursing Education	M,D,O
Nursing—General	M,D,O
Physics	M,D
Plant Pathology	M,D
Plant Sciences	M,D
Psychiatric Nursing	M,D,O
Psychology—General	M
Public Administration	M
Range Science	M,D
School Psychology	M,D,O
Statistics	M,D
Vocational and Technical Education	M,D,O

MONTANA STATE UNIVERSITY BILLINGS

Advertising and Public Relations	M
Applied Behavior Analysis	M
Athletic Training and Sports Medicine	M
Communication—General	M
Counseling Psychology	M
Counselor Education	M
Curriculum and Instruction	M
Education—General	M,O
Educational Media/Instructional Technology	M
Elementary Education	M
Health Services Management and Hospital Administration	M

Interdisciplinary Studies	M
Psychology—General	M
Reading Education	M
Rehabilitation Counseling	M
Secondary Education	M
Special Education	M

MONTANA STATE UNIVERSITY–NORTHERN

Counselor Education	M
Education—General	M

MONTANA TECH OF THE UNIVERSITY OF MONTANA

Electrical Engineering	M
Engineering and Applied Sciences—General	M
Environmental Engineering	M
Geochemistry	M
Geological Engineering	M
Geology	M
Geosciences	M
Health Informatics	O
Hydrogeology	M
Industrial Hygiene	M
Industrial/Management Engineering	M
Interdisciplinary Studies	M
Materials Sciences	D
Metallurgical Engineering and Metallurgy	M
Mineral/Mining Engineering	M
Petroleum Engineering	M
Project Management	M
Technical Communication	M

MONTCLAIR STATE UNIVERSITY

Accounting	M,O
Addictions/Substance Abuse Counseling	O
Advertising and Public Relations	M
Applied Mathematics	M
Archives/Archival Administration	M
Art Education	M
Art/Fine Arts	M
Arts Administration	M
Biochemistry	M
Biological and Biomedical Sciences—General	M
Business Administration and Management—General	M,O
Chemistry	M
Child and Family Studies	M,D,O
Child Development	M,O
Clinical Psychology	M
Communication Disorders	M,D
Computer Science	M,O
Conflict Resolution and Mediation/Peace Studies	M,O
Corporate and Organizational Communication	M
Counselor Education	M,D
Curriculum and Instruction	M
Data Science/Data Analytics	O
Disability Studies	M,O
Ecology	M
Education—General	M,D,O
Educational Leadership and Administration	M,D
Educational Measurement and Evaluation	O
English as a Second Language	M,O
English Education	M,O
English	M
Environmental Education	M
Environmental Law	O
Environmental Management and Policy	M,D
Environmental Sciences	M
Evolutionary Biology	M
Exercise and Sports Science	M,O
Forensic Psychology	O
French	M
Geographic Information Systems	O
Geosciences	M
Health Education	M
Industrial and Organizational Psychology	M
Intellectual Property Law	M,O
Law	M,O
Legal and Justice Studies	O
Linguistics	M,O
Marine Biology	M
Mathematics Education	M,D,O
Mathematics	M
Molecular Biology	M,O
Music Education	M
Music	M,O
Nutrition	M,O
Pharmacology	M
Physical Education	M
Physiology	M
Political Science	M,O
Psychology—General	M
Public Health—General	M
Reading Education	M
Science Education	M
Social Sciences	M
Spanish	M
Special Education	M
Sports Management	M
Statistics	M
Sustainable Development	M
Theater	M
Therapies—Dance, Drama, and Music	M,O
Translation and Interpretation	O
Water Resources	O
Writing	O

MOODY BIBLE INSTITUTE

Pastoral Ministry and Counseling	M,O
Theology	M,O
Urban Studies	M,O

MOODY THEOLOGICAL SEMINARY–MICHIGAN

Counseling Psychology	M,O
Religion	M,O
Religious Education	M,O
Theology	M,O

MOORE COLLEGE OF ART & DESIGN

Art Education	M
Art/Fine Arts	M
Arts Administration	M
Communication—General	M
Interior Design	M

MORAVIAN COLLEGE

Accounting	M
Acute Care/Critical Care Nursing	M
Allied Health—General	M
Athletic Training and Sports Medicine	M,D
Business Administration and Management—General	M
Business Analytics	M
Curriculum and Instruction	M
Education—General	M
Health Services Management and Hospital Administration	M
Human Resources Development	M
Human Resources Management	M
Nursing and Healthcare Administration	M
Nursing Education	M
Nursing—General	M
Supply Chain Management	M

MORAVIAN THEOLOGICAL SEMINARY

Theology	M,O

MOREHEAD STATE UNIVERSITY

Adult Education	M,O
Agricultural Sciences—General	M
Art Education	M
Art/Fine Arts	M
Biological and Biomedical Sciences—General	M
Business Administration and Management—General	M
Business Education	M,O
Clinical Psychology	M
Communication—General	M
Counseling Psychology	M
Counselor Education	M,O
Criminal Justice and Criminology	M
Curriculum and Instruction	M,O
Education of the Gifted	M,O
Education—General	M,O
Educational Leadership and Administration	M,O
Educational Media/Instructional Technology	M,O
Elementary Education	M,O
English Education	M,O
English	M
Environmental Management and Policy	M
Exercise and Sports Science	M
Experimental Psychology	M
Foreign Languages Education	M
Gerontology	M
Graphic Design	M
Health Education	M
Higher Education	M,O
Industrial/Management Engineering	M
International and Comparative Education	M,O
Management Information Systems	M
Mathematics Education	M
Middle School Education	M,O
Music Education	M
Music	M
Physical Education	M
Psychology—General	M
Public Administration	M
Public Policy	M
Reading Education	M,O
Science Education	M
Secondary Education	M,O
Social Sciences Education	M,O
Sociology	M
Special Education	M,O
Sports Management	M
Vocational and Technical Education	M,O

MOREHOUSE SCHOOL OF MEDICINE

Allopathic Medicine	D
Biological and Biomedical Sciences—General	M,D
Clinical Research	M
Public Health—General	M

MORGAN STATE UNIVERSITY

Accounting	M,D
African-American Studies	M,D
Architecture	M
Bioinformatics	M
Biological and Biomedical Sciences—General	M,D
Business Administration and Management—General	M,D
Chemistry	M
Civil Engineering	M,D,O
Community College Education	D
Computational Sciences	M,D
Computer Science	M
Economics	M
Education—General	M,D
Educational Leadership and Administration	D
Electrical Engineering	M,D,O
Elementary Education	M
Engineering and Applied Sciences—General	M,D,O
English	M,D
Environmental Biology	D
Higher Education	M,D
Historic Preservation	M,D
History	M,D
Hospitality Management	M
Industrial/Management Engineering	M,D,O
International Affairs	M
Landscape Architecture	M
Management Information Systems	D
Marketing	D
Mathematics Education	M,D
Mathematics	M,D
Museum Studies	M,D
Music	M
Nursing—General	M,D
Project Management	M
Psychology—General	M,D
Science Education	M,D
Social Work	M
Sociology	M
Student Affairs	M,D
Transportation and Highway Engineering	M,D,O
Urban and Regional Planning	M
Urban Education	D

MORNINGSIDE COLLEGE

Education—General	M
Family Nurse Practitioner Studies	M
Gerontological Nursing	M
Nursing—General	M
Special Education	M

MOUNT ALLISON UNIVERSITY

Biochemistry	M
Biological and Biomedical Sciences—General	M
Chemistry	M

MOUNT ALOYSIUS COLLEGE

Accounting	M
Business Administration and Management—General	M
Health Services Management and Hospital Administration	M
Nonprofit Management	M
Project Management	M
Social Psychology	M

MOUNT ANGEL SEMINARY

Theology	M

MOUNT CARMEL COLLEGE OF NURSING

Acute Care/Critical Care Nursing	M,D
Adult Nursing	M,D
Family Nurse Practitioner Studies	M,D
Gerontological Nursing	M,D
Nursing and Healthcare Administration	M,D
Nursing Education	M,D
Nursing—General	M,D

MOUNT HOLYOKE COLLEGE

Educational Leadership and Administration	M
Mathematics Education	M

MOUNT MARTY COLLEGE

Business Administration and Management—General	M
Nurse Anesthesia	M
Nursing—General	M
Pastoral Ministry and Counseling	M

MOUNT MARY UNIVERSITY

Art Therapy	M,D
Business Administration and Management—General	M
Clinical Psychology	M,O
Counseling Psychology	M,O
Counselor Education	M,O
Education—General	M
English	M
Internet and Interactive Multimedia	M
Nursing and Healthcare Administration	M
Nutrition	M
Occupational Therapy	M,D
Rehabilitation Counseling	M,O
Writing	M

MOUNT MERCY UNIVERSITY

Business Administration and Management—General	M
Criminal Justice and Criminology	M
Education—General	M
Educational Leadership and Administration	M
Human Resources Management	M
Management Strategy and Policy	M
Marriage and Family Therapy	M
Nursing and Healthcare Administration	M
Nursing Education	M
Nursing—General	M
Quality Management	M
Reading Education	M
Special Education	M

MOUNT ST. JOSEPH UNIVERSITY

Business Administration and Management—General	M
Early Childhood Education	M,O
Education—General	M,O
Health Promotion	M,O
Health Services Management and Hospital Administration	D
Middle School Education	M,O
Multilingual and Multicultural Education	M,O
Nursing and Healthcare Administration	M
Nursing Education	M
Nursing—General	M,D
Organizational Management	M
Pastoral Ministry and Counseling	M,O
Physical Therapy	D
Reading Education	M,O
Religion	M,O
Secondary Education	M,O
Special Education	M,O
Theology	M,O

MOUNT SAINT MARY COLLEGE

Adult Nursing	M,O
Business Administration and Management—General	M
Child Development	M,O
Education—General	M,O
Family Nurse Practitioner Studies	M,O
Finance and Banking	M
Health Services Management and Hospital Administration	M
Middle School Education	M,O
Nursing and Healthcare Administration	M,O
Nursing Education	M,O
Nursing—General	M,O
Reading Education	M,O
Special Education	M,O

MOUNT SAINT MARY'S UNIVERSITY (CA)

Business Administration and Management—General	M,D,O
Counseling Psychology	M,D,O
Education—General	M,D,O
English	M,D,O
Film, Television, and Video Production	M,D,O
Health Services Management and Hospital Administration	M,D,O
Humanities	M,D,O
Nursing—General	M,D,O
Physical Therapy	M,D,O
Religion	M,D,O
Writing	M,D,O

MOUNT ST. MARY'S UNIVERSITY (MD)

Biotechnology	M
Business Administration and Management—General	M
Education—General	M
Health Services Management and Hospital Administration	M
Philosophy	M
Sports Management	M
Theology	M

MOUNT SAINT VINCENT UNIVERSITY

Adult Education	M
Child and Family Studies	M
Curriculum and Instruction	M
Education—General	M
Educational Psychology	M
Elementary Education	M
English as a Second Language	M
Foundations and Philosophy of Education	M
Gerontology	M
Middle School Education	M
Nutrition	M
Reading Education	M
School Psychology	M
Special Education	M
Women's Studies	M

MOUNT VERNON NAZARENE UNIVERSITY

Business Administration and Management—General	M
Education—General	M
Theology	M

MULTNOMAH UNIVERSITY

Education—General	M
English as a Second Language	M
Theology	M,D

MURRAY STATE UNIVERSITY

Accounting	M
Advertising and Public Relations	M
Agricultural Education	M,O
Agricultural Sciences—General	M,O
Biological and Biomedical Sciences—General	M
Business Administration and Management—General	M
Chemistry	M
Clinical Psychology	M,O
Communication Disorders	M,O
Computer Science	M
Corporate and Organizational Communication	M
Counselor Education	M,D,O
Early Childhood Education	M,O
Economic Development	M
Economics	M
Education—General	M,D,O
Educational Leadership and Administration	M,D,O
Educational Media/Instructional Technology	M,D,O
Elementary Education	M,O
English as a Second Language	M,D,O
English Education	M,D,O
English	M,D,O

*M—masters degree; D—doctorate; O—other advanced degree; *—Close-Up and/or Display*

Environmental and Occupational Health M
Environmental Sciences M,O
Experimental Psychology M,O
Family Nurse Practitioner Studies D
Finance and Banking M
Gender Studies M,D,O
Geosciences M,O
History M
Human Development M,D,O
Human Resources Management M
Human Services M,D,O
Interdisciplinary Studies M,O
Journalism M
Management Information Systems M
Marketing M
Mass Communication M
Mathematics Education M
Mathematics M
Middle School Education M,D,O
Music Education M
Music M
Nonprofit Management M,O
Nurse Anesthesia D
Nursing—General D
Nutrition M,O
Political Science M
Psychology—General M,O
Safety Engineering M
School Psychology M,D,O
Secondary Education M,D,O
Sociology M
Special Education M,O
Statistics M
Telecommunications Management M
Vocational and Technical Education M,O
Writing M,D,O

MUSKINGUM UNIVERSITY
Education—General M

NAROPA UNIVERSITY
Art Therapy M
Counseling Psychology M
Counselor Education M
Ecology M
Psychoanalysis and Psychotherapy M
Psychology—General M
Recreation and Park Management M
Religion M
Sustainability Management M
Theater M
Theology M
Therapies—Dance, Drama, and Music M
Writing M

NASHOTAH HOUSE THEOLOGICAL SEMINARY
Pastoral Ministry and Counseling M,D,O
Religion M,D,O
Theology M,D,O

NATIONAL AMERICAN UNIVERSITY (TX)
Accounting M,D
Aviation Management M,D
Business Administration and Management—General M,D
Community College Education M,D
Criminal Justice and Criminology M,D
Educational Leadership and Administration M,D
Health Services Management and Hospital Administration M,D
Higher Education M,D
Human Resources Management M,D
International Business M,D
Management Information Systems M,D
Marketing M,D
Nursing and Healthcare Administration M,D
Nursing Education M,D
Nursing Informatics M,D
Project Management M,D

NATIONAL COLLEGE OF MIDWIFERY
Nurse Midwifery M,D

NATIONAL DEFENSE UNIVERSITY
Homeland Security M
Military and Defense Studies M
National Security M

THE NATIONAL GRADUATE SCHOOL OF QUALITY MANAGEMENT
Homeland Security M,D
Quality Management M,D

NATIONAL INTELLIGENCE UNIVERSITY
Military and Defense Studies M

NATIONAL LOUIS UNIVERSITY
Adult Education M,D,O
Business Administration and Management—General M
Counselor Education M,D,O
Curriculum and Instruction M,D,O
Developmental Education M,D,O
Early Childhood Education M,D,O
Education—General M,D,O
Educational Leadership and Administration M,D,O
Educational Media/Instructional Technology M,D,O
Educational Psychology M,D,O
Elementary Education M,D,O
English Education M,D,O
Human Development M,D,O
Human Resources Development M
Human Resources Management M
Human Services M,D,O
Mathematics Education M,D,O
Middle School Education M,D,O
Psychology—General M,D,O
Public Policy M,D,O
Reading Education M,D,O
School Psychology M,D,O
Science Education M,D,O
Secondary Education M,D,O
Special Education M,D,O
Writing M,D,O

NATIONAL PARALEGAL COLLEGE
Legal and Justice Studies M
Taxation M

NATIONAL TEST PILOT SCHOOL
Aviation M

NATIONAL UNIVERSITY
Accounting M,O
Applied Behavior Analysis M,O
Biological and Biomedical Sciences—General M,O
Business Administration and Management—General M,O
Business Analytics M,O
Clinical Psychology M,O
Computer and Information Systems Security M
Computer Science M
Counseling Psychology M,O
Counselor Education M,O
Criminal Justice and Criminology M
Data Science/Data Analytics M
Distance Education Development M,O
Education—General M,O
Educational Leadership and Administration M,O
Educational Media/Instructional Technology M,O
Electrical Engineering M
Emergency Management M
Engineering and Applied Sciences—General M
Engineering Management M
English M,O
Family Nurse Practitioner Studies M,O
Film, Television, and Video Production M
Film, Television, and Video Theory and Criticism M,O
Forensic Sciences M,O
Health Informatics M,O
Health Promotion M,O
Health Services Management and Hospital Administration M,O
Higher Education M,O
Homeland Security M
Human Resources Management M,O
Human Services M,O
International Business M,O
Internet and Interactive Multimedia M
Journalism M
Legal and Justice Studies M
Management Information Systems M,O
Management of Technology M
Marketing M,O
Marriage and Family Therapy M,O
Mathematics Education M,O
Nurse Anesthesia M,O
Nursing and Healthcare Administration M,O
Nursing Informatics M,O
Organizational Management M,O
Psychiatric Nursing M,O
Public Administration M
Public Health—General M,O
School Psychology M,O
Special Education M,O
Sustainability Management M
Writing M,O

NATIONAL UNIVERSITY COLLEGE
Business Administration and Management—General M
Marketing M
Special Education M

NATIONAL UNIVERSITY OF HEALTH SCIENCES
Acupuncture and Oriental Medicine M,D
Chiropractic M,D
Medical Imaging M,D

NATIONAL UNIVERSITY OF NATURAL MEDICINE
Acupuncture and Oriental Medicine M,D
Clinical Research M
International Health M
Naturopathic Medicine M,D
Nutrition M

NAVAJO TECHNICAL UNIVERSITY
American Indian/Native American Studies M

NAVAL POSTGRADUATE SCHOOL
Acoustics M,D
Aerospace/Aeronautical Engineering M,D,O
Applied Mathematics M,D
Applied Physics M,D,O
Applied Science and Technology M,D
Business Administration and Management—General M
Computer and Information Systems Security M,D
Computer Engineering M,D,O
Computer Science M,D,O
Conflict Resolution and Mediation/Peace Studies M,D
Electrical Engineering M,D,O
Engineering Management M,D,O
Finance and Banking M,D
Geographic Information Systems M,D,O
Homeland Security M,D
Information Science M,D,O
Logistics M
Management Information Systems M,D,O
Mechanical Engineering M,D,O
Meteorology M,D
Military and Defense Studies M,D
Modeling and Simulation M,D
National Security M,D,O
Oceanography M,D
Operations Research M,D
Physics M,D
Software Engineering M,D
Supply Chain Management M
Systems Engineering M,D,O
Transportation Management M

NAVAL WAR COLLEGE
National Security M

NAZARENE THEOLOGICAL SEMINARY
Cultural Studies M,D,O
Theology M,D,O

NAZARETH COLLEGE OF ROCHESTER
Art Education M
Art Therapy M
Business Administration and Management—General M
Communication Disorders M
Early Childhood Education M
Education—General M
Educational Media/Instructional Technology M
Elementary Education M
English as a Second Language M
Human Resources Management M
Middle School Education M
Music Education M
Music M
Physical Therapy D
Reading Education M
Social Work M
Therapies—Dance, Drama, and Music M

NEBRASKA METHODIST COLLEGE
Health Promotion M
Health Services Management and Hospital Administration M
Nursing and Healthcare Administration M
Nursing Education M
Nursing—General M

NEBRASKA WESLEYAN UNIVERSITY
Forensic Sciences M
History M
Nursing—General M

NER ISRAEL RABBINICAL COLLEGE
Theology M,D,O

NER ISRAEL YESHIVA COLLEGE OF TORONTO
Theology M

NEUMANN UNIVERSITY
Accounting M
Adult Nursing M,O
Business Administration and Management—General M
Clinical Psychology M,D,O
Education—General M
Educational Leadership and Administration M,D
Elementary Education M
Gerontological Nursing M,O
Management Strategy and Policy M
Nursing—General M,O
Organizational Management M
Pastoral Ministry and Counseling M,D,O
Physical Therapy D
Secondary Education M
Special Education M
Sports Management M

NEW BRUNSWICK THEOLOGICAL SEMINARY
Pastoral Ministry and Counseling M,D
Theology M,D

NEW CHARTER UNIVERSITY
Business Administration and Management—General M
Criminal Justice and Criminology M
Finance and Banking M
Health Services Management and Hospital Administration M
Public Administration M

NEW COLLEGE OF FLORIDA
Data Science/Data Analytics M

NEW ENGLAND COLLEGE
Accounting M
Business Administration and Management—General M
Counseling Psychology M
Education—General M,D
Educational Leadership and Administration M,D
Health Services Management and Hospital Administration M
Higher Education M,D
Human Services M
International Affairs M
Management Strategy and Policy M
Marketing M
Nonprofit Management M
Project Management M
Public Policy M
Recreation and Park Management M
Special Education M,D
Sports Management M
Writing M

NEW ENGLAND COLLEGE OF BUSINESS AND FINANCE
Ethics M
Finance and Banking M

NEW ENGLAND COLLEGE OF OPTOMETRY
Optometry M,D
Vision Sciences M,D

NEW ENGLAND CONSERVATORY OF MUSIC
Music M,D,O

NEW ENGLAND INSTITUTE OF TECHNOLOGY
Applied Arts and Design—General M
Construction Management M
Engineering Management M
Management Information Systems M
Occupational Therapy M
Public Health—General M

NEW ENGLAND LAW–BOSTON
Law M,D

NEW HAMPSHIRE INSTITUTE OF ART
Art Education M
Art/Fine Arts M
Photography M
Writing M

NEW JERSEY CITY UNIVERSITY
Accounting M,O
Allied Health—General M
Art Education M
Art/Fine Arts M
Business Administration and Management—General M,O
Community Health M
Computer and Information Systems Security M,D,O
Counselor Education M
Criminal Justice and Criminology M,D,O
Early Childhood Education M
Education—General M,D
Educational Leadership and Administration M
Educational Media/Instructional Technology M,D
Elementary Education M
English as a Second Language M
Finance and Banking M,O
Health Education M
Health Services Management and Hospital Administration M
Marketing M
Mathematics Education M
Multilingual and Multicultural Education M
Music Education M
Music M
National Security M,D,O
Organizational Management M
Secondary Education M
Special Education M
Urban Education M
Urban Studies M

NEW JERSEY INSTITUTE OF TECHNOLOGY
Applied Mathematics M,D,O
Applied Physics M,D,O
Applied Statistics M,D,O
Architecture M,D
Bioinformatics M,D,O
Biological and Biomedical Sciences—General M,D,O
Biomedical Engineering M,D
Biostatistics M,D,O
Business Administration and Management—General M,D,O
Chemical Engineering M,D
Chemistry M,D,O
Computer and Information Systems Security M,D,O
Computer Engineering M,D
Computer Science M,D,O
Data Science/Data Analytics M,D,O
Electrical Engineering M,D
Emergency Management M,D,O
Energy and Power Engineering M,D
Engineering and Applied Sciences—General M,D
Engineering Management M,D
Environmental Engineering M,D
Environmental Management and Policy M,D,O
Environmental Sciences M,D,O
Health Services Management and Hospital Administration M,D
History M,D,O
Industrial/Management Engineering M,D
Information Science M,D,O
Internet Engineering M,D
Management Information Systems M,D,O
Management of Technology M,D,O
Manufacturing Engineering M,D
Materials Engineering M,D,O
Materials Sciences M,D,O
Mathematical and Computational Finance M,D,O
Mathematics M,D,O
Mechanical Engineering M,D
Medicinal and Pharmaceutical Chemistry M,D,O
Pharmaceutical Administration M,D
Pharmaceutical Engineering M,D
Pharmacology M,D
Safety Engineering M,D
Software Engineering M,D,O
Statistics M,D,O
Sustainable Development M,D,O
Systems Science M,D,O
Technical Communication M,D,O
Telecommunications M,D
Transportation and Highway Engineering M,D

Transportation Management	M,D
Urban Studies	M,D

NEWMAN THEOLOGICAL COLLEGE

Religious Education	M,O
Theology	M

NEWMAN UNIVERSITY

Business Administration and Management—General	M
Curriculum and Instruction	M
Education—General	M
Educational Leadership and Administration	M
English as a Second Language	M
Finance and Banking	M
International Business	M
Management Information Systems	M
Nurse Anesthesia	M
Organizational Management	M
Reading Education	M
Social Work	M
Theology	M

NEW MEXICO HIGHLANDS UNIVERSITY

American Studies	M
Anthropology	M
Business Administration and Management—General	M
Chemistry	M
Clinical Psychology	M
Computer Art and Design	M
Computer Science	M
Counseling Psychology	M
Counselor Education	M
Curriculum and Instruction	M
Education—General	M
Educational Leadership and Administration	M
English	M
Exercise and Sports Science	M
Health Education	M
History	M
Human Resources Management	M
International Business	M
Internet and Interactive Multimedia	M
Media Studies	M
Natural Resources	M
Political Science	M
Psychology—General	M
Public Affairs	M
Rhetoric	M
Social Work	M
Sociology	M
Special Education	M
Sports Management	M
Writing	M

NEW MEXICO INSTITUTE OF MINING AND TECHNOLOGY

Applied Mathematics	M,D
Astrophysics	M,D
Atmospheric Sciences	M,D
Biological and Biomedical Sciences—General	M,D
Chemistry	M,D
Computer Science	M,D
Electrical Engineering	M
Engineering Management	M
Environmental Engineering	M
Geochemistry	M,D
Geological Engineering	M
Geology	M,D
Geophysics	M,D
Geosciences	M,D
Hazardous Materials Management	M
Hydrology	M,D
Materials Engineering	M,D
Mathematical Physics	M,D
Mathematics	M,D
Mechanical Engineering	M
Mechanics	M
Mineral/Mining Engineering	M
Operations Research	M,D
Petroleum Engineering	M,D
Physics	M,D
Science Education	M
Statistics	M,D
Systems Engineering	M
Water Resources Engineering	M

NEW MEXICO STATE UNIVERSITY

Accounting	M
Aerospace/Aeronautical Engineering	M,D
Agricultural Economics and Agribusiness	M,D
Agricultural Education	M
Agricultural Sciences—General	M,D
Animal Sciences	M,D
Anthropology	M,O
Applied Statistics	M,D,O
Art History	M
Art/Fine Arts	M
Astronomy	M,D
Astrophysics	M,D
Bioinformatics	M,D
Biological and Biomedical Sciences—General	M,D
Biotechnology	M,D
Business Administration and Management—General	M,D
Chemical Engineering	M,D
Chemistry	M,D
Civil Engineering	M,D
Clothing and Textiles	M
Communication Disorders	M,D,O
Communication—General	M
Computer Engineering	M,D,O
Computer Science	M,D
Corporate and Organizational Communication	M,D
Counseling Psychology	M,D,O
Counselor Education	M,D,O
Criminal Justice and Criminology	M
Cultural Studies	M,D,O
Curriculum and Instruction	M,D,O
Dance	M,D,O
Distance Education Development	O
Early Childhood Education	M,D,O
Economic Development	M,D,O
Economics	M,D,O
Education—General	M,D,O
Educational Leadership and Administration	M,D
Educational Measurement and Evaluation	M,D,O
Electrical Engineering	M,D,O
Engineering and Applied Sciences—General	M,D,O
English as a Second Language	M,D,O
English Education	M,D
English	M,D
Entomology	M
Environmental Engineering	M,D
Environmental Sciences	M,D
Family and Consumer Sciences-General	M
Family Nurse Practitioner Studies	M,D,O
Finance and Banking	M,O
Fish, Game, and Wildlife Management	M
Food Science and Technology	M
Foreign Languages Education	M,D,O
Geography	M
Geological Engineering	M,D
Geology	M
Higher Education	M,D
History	M
Horticulture	M,D
Hydrology	M,D
Industrial/Management Engineering	M,D,O
Interdisciplinary Studies	M,D
Kinesiology and Movement Studies	D
Management Information Systems	M
Marketing	D
Mathematics	M,D
Mechanical Engineering	M,D
Molecular Biology	M,D
Multilingual and Multicultural Education	M,D,O
Museum Studies	M,O
Music Education	M
Music	M
Nursing and Healthcare Administration	M,D,O
Nursing—General	M,D,O
Physics	M,D
Plant Pathology	M
Plant Sciences	M
Political Science	M
Psychiatric Nursing	M,D,O
Psychology—General	M,D
Public Administration	M
Public Health—General	M,O
Range Science	M,D
Reading Education	M,D,O
Rhetoric	M,D
School Psychology	M,D,O
Social Work	M
Sociology	M
Spanish	M,D,O
Special Education	M,D,O
Systems Engineering	M,D,O
Travel and Tourism	M
Water Resources	M,D
Writing	M,D

NEW ORLEANS BAPTIST THEOLOGICAL SEMINARY

Music	M,D
Pastoral Ministry and Counseling	M,D
Religious Education	M,D
Theology	M,D

NEW SAINT ANDREWS COLLEGE

Religion	M,O
Theology	M,O
Writing	M,O

THE NEW SCHOOL

Anthropology	M,D
Applied Arts and Design—General	M
Applied Social Research	M,D
Architecture	M
Art/Fine Arts	M
Clinical Psychology	M,D
Clothing and Textiles	M
Cognitive Sciences	M,D
Computer Art and Design	M
Data Science/Data Analytics	M
Economics	M,D
English as a Second Language	M
Environmental Management and Policy	M
Finance and Banking	M,D
History	M,D
Industrial Design	M
Interior Design	M
International Affairs	M
International Economics	M,D
Internet and Interactive Multimedia	M
Liberal Studies	M
Lighting Design	M
Management Strategy and Policy	M,O
Media Studies	M,O
Museum Studies	M
Music	M,O
Nonprofit Management	M
Organizational Management	M,O
Philosophy	M,D
Photography	M
Political Science	M,D
Psychoanalysis and Psychotherapy	M,D
Psychology—General	M,D
Public Policy	M,D
Social Psychology	M,D
Social Sciences	M,D
Sociology	M,D
Sustainability Management	M
Textile Design	M
Theater	M
Urban Design	M
Writing	M

NEWSCHOOL OF ARCHITECTURE AND DESIGN

Architecture	M
Construction Management	M

NEW YORK ACADEMY OF ART

Anatomy	M
Art/Fine Arts	M

NEW YORK CHIROPRACTIC COLLEGE

Acupuncture and Oriental Medicine	M
Anatomy	M
Chiropractic	D*
Nutrition	M

NEW YORK COLLEGE OF HEALTH PROFESSIONS

Acupuncture and Oriental Medicine	M

NEW YORK COLLEGE OF PODIATRIC MEDICINE

Podiatric Medicine	D

NEW YORK COLLEGE OF TRADITIONAL CHINESE MEDICINE

Acupuncture and Oriental Medicine	M

NEW YORK FILM ACADEMY

Film, Television, and Video Production	M
Photography	M

NEW YORK INSTITUTE OF TECHNOLOGY

Applied Arts and Design—General	M
Architecture	M
Art/Fine Arts	M
Bioengineering	M
Business Administration and Management—General	M
Communication—General	M
Computer and Information Systems Security	M
Computer Art and Design	M
Computer Engineering	M
Computer Science	M
Counselor Education	M,O
Early Childhood Education	M
Education—General	M,O
Educational Leadership and Administration	O
Educational Media/Instructional Technology	M,O
Electrical Engineering	M
Elementary Education	M
Energy and Power Engineering	O
Energy Management and Policy	O
Engineering and Applied Sciences—General	M,O
English Education	M
Environmental Engineering	M
Environmental Management and Policy	O
Finance and Banking	M
Graphic Design	M
Human Resources Management	M,O
Industrial and Labor Relations	M,O
Interdisciplinary Studies	M,O
International Health	O
Marketing	M
Mathematics Education	M,O
Mechanical Engineering	M
Middle School Education	M
Nutrition	M
Occupational Therapy	M
Osteopathic Medicine	O
Physical Therapy	D
Physician Assistant Studies	M
Science Education	M,O
Secondary Education	M
Social Sciences Education	M
Supply Chain Management	M
Urban Design	M

NEW YORK LAW SCHOOL

Law	M,D

NEW YORK MEDICAL COLLEGE

Allopathic Medicine	D
Biochemistry	M,D
Biological and Biomedical Sciences—General	M,D
Biostatistics	M,D,O
Business Administration and Management—General	M,D,O
Cell Biology	M,D
Communication Disorders	M,D,O
Emergency Management	M,D,O
Environmental and Occupational Health	M,D,O
Epidemiology	M,D,O
Health Education	M,D,O
Health Services Management and Hospital Administration	M,D,O
Immunology	M,D
Industrial Hygiene	M,D,O
International Health	M,D,O
Microbiology	M,D
Molecular Biology	M,D
Pathology	M,D
Pharmacology	M,D
Physical Therapy	M,D,O
Physiology	M,D
Psychology—General	M,D,O
Public Health—General	M,D,O

NEW YORK SCHOOL OF INTERIOR DESIGN

Interior Design	M
Lighting Design	M
Sustainable Development	M

NEW YORK STUDIO SCHOOL OF DRAWING, PAINTING AND SCULPTURE

Art/Fine Arts	M,O*

NEW YORK THEOLOGICAL SEMINARY

Theology	M,D

NEW YORK UNIVERSITY

Accounting	M,D
Acute Care/Critical Care Nursing	M,D,O
Adult Nursing	M,D,O
Advertising and Public Relations	M
African Studies	M,D,O
Agricultural Engineering	M,D
Allopathic Medicine	M,D
American Studies	M,D
Anthropology	M,D
Applied Arts and Design—General	M
Applied Economics	M,D,O
Applied Physics	M
Applied Psychology	M,D,O
Applied Social Research	M
Applied Statistics	M
Archaeology	M,D
Architectural History	M
Archives/Archival Administration	M,D,O
Art Education	M,O
Art History	M,D
Art Therapy	M
Art/Fine Arts	M,D,O
Artificial Intelligence/Robotics	M
Arts Administration	M
Asian Studies	M,D
Bioethics	M
Bioinformatics	M
Biological and Biomedical Sciences—General	M,D,O
Biomedical Engineering	M,D
Biostatistics	D
Biotechnology	M
Business Administration and Management—General	M,D,O
Business Education	M,O
Cancer Biology/Oncology	M,D
Cell Biology	D
Chemical Engineering	M,D
Chemistry	M,D,O
Chinese	M,D,O
Civil Engineering	M,D
Classics	M,D,O
Clinical Research	M
Cognitive Sciences	M,D,O
Communication Disorders	M,D,O
Communication—General	M,D
Community Health	M,D
Comparative Literature	M,D
Computational Biology	D
Computer and Information Systems Security	M
Computer Engineering	M
Computer Science	M,D
Conflict Resolution and Mediation/Peace Studies	M
Construction Management	M
Corporate and Organizational Communication	M
Counseling Psychology	M,D,O
Counselor Education	M,D,O
Cultural Studies	M,D,O
Dance	M,D,O
Data Science/Data Analytics	M
Demography and Population Studies	M,D
Dentistry	D
Developmental Biology	M,D
Developmental Psychology	M,D
Early Childhood Education	M
Economics	M,D,O
Education—General	M,D,O
Educational Leadership and Administration	M,D,O
Educational Media/Instructional Technology	M,D,O
Educational Policy	M,D,O
Educational Psychology	M,D
Electrical Engineering	M,D
Elementary Education	M
Engineering and Applied Sciences—General	M,D,O
English as a Second Language	M,D,O
English Education	M,D,O
English	M,D
Entrepreneurship	M
Environmental and Occupational Health	M,D*
Environmental Education	M
Environmental Engineering	M
Environmental Management and Policy	M
Environmental Sciences	M
Epidemiology	M,D

*M—masters degree; D—doctorate; O—other advanced degree; *—Close-Up and/or Display*

Ergonomics and Human Factors	M,D
Family Nurse Practitioner Studies	M,D,O
Film, Television, and Video Production	M
Film, Television, and Video Theory and Criticism	M,D
Finance and Banking	M,D
Financial Engineering	M
Food Science and Technology	M,D
Foreign Languages Education	M,D,O
Foundations and Philosophy of Education	M,D
French	M,D,O
Game Design and Development	M
Gender Studies	M
Genetics	M,D
Genomic Sciences	D
German	M,D
Gerontological Nursing	M,D,O
Health Promotion	M,D,O
Health Services Management and Hospital Administration	M,D,O
Higher Education	M,D
Historic Preservation	M
History	M,D,O
Hospitality Management	M,D
Human Development	M,D,O
Human Resources Development	M
Human Resources Management	M
Humanities	M,O
Immunology	M,D
Industrial and Organizational Psychology	M,D,O
Industrial/Management Engineering	M
Interdisciplinary Studies	M
International Affairs	M,D
International and Comparative Education	M,D,O
International Business	M,D
International Health	M,D
Internet and Interactive Multimedia	M
Investment Management	M
Italian	M,D,O
Japanese	M,D,O
Jewish Studies	M,D,O
Journalism	M,D,O
Kinesiology and Movement Studies	M,D,O
Latin American Studies	M,O
Law	M,D,O
Legal and Justice Studies	M,D
Linguistics	M,D
Management Information Systems	M,D
Management of Technology	M,D
Management Strategy and Policy	M,D
Manufacturing Engineering	M
Marketing	M,D
Mathematical and Computational Finance	M,D
Mathematics Education	M
Mathematics	M,D*
Mechanical Engineering	M,D
Media Studies	M,D
Medical Imaging	D
Microbiology	M,D
Middle School Education	M,D,O
Molecular Biology	M,D
Molecular Genetics	M,D
Molecular Pharmacology	D
Molecular Toxicology	M,D
Multilingual and Multicultural Education	M,D,O
Museum Studies	M,O
Music Education	M,D,O
Music	M,D,O
Near and Middle Eastern Studies	M,D,O
Neurobiology	M,D
Neuroscience	D
Nonprofit Management	M,D,O
Nurse Midwifery	M,D,O
Nursing and Healthcare Administration	M,O
Nursing Education	M,O
Nursing Informatics	M,O
Nursing—General	M,D,O
Nutrition	M,D
Occupational Therapy	M,D
Oral and Dental Sciences	M,D,O
Organizational Behavior	M,D
Organizational Management	M,D
Pediatric Nursing	M,D,O
Philosophy	M,D
Physical Therapy	M,D,O
Physics	M,D,O
Physiology	D
Plant Biology	M,D
Political Science	M,D
Portuguese	M,D
Project Management	M
Psychiatric Nursing	M,D,O
Psychoanalysis and Psychotherapy	M,D,O
Psychology—General	M,D,O
Public Administration	M,D,O
Public Health—General	M,D
Public History	M,D,O
Public Policy	M
Publishing	M
Reading Education	M
Real Estate	M
Rehabilitation Sciences	M,D
Religion	M,O
Risk Management	M
Romance Languages	M,D
Russian	M
Science Education	M,D,O
Secondary Education	M,D,O
Slavic Languages	M
Social Psychology	M,D,O
Social Sciences Education	M,D,O
Social Sciences	M,D
Social Work	M,D
Sociology	M,D
Software Engineering	O
Spanish	M,D,O
Special Education	M
Speech and Interpersonal Communication	M,D
Sports and Entertainment Law	M
Statistics	M,D
Structural Biology	D
Student Affairs	M,D
Sustainable Development	M
Taxation	M,D,O
Theater	M,D,O
Therapies—Dance, Drama, and Music	M
Toxicology	M,D
Translation and Interpretation	M
Transportation and Highway Engineering	M,D
Transportation Management	M
Travel and Tourism	M
Urban and Regional Planning	M
Urban Studies	M
Western European Studies	M
Writing	M

NIAGARA UNIVERSITY

Accounting	M
Applied Behavior Analysis	M,D,O
Business Administration and Management—General	M
Computer and Information Systems Security	M
Counseling Psychology	M,D,O
Counselor Education	M,O
Criminal Justice and Criminology	M
Early Childhood Education	M,O
Education—General	M,D,O
Educational Leadership and Administration	M,D,O
Educational Policy	M,D,O
Elementary Education	M,O
English as a Second Language	M,O
Finance and Banking	M
Forensic Sciences	M
Health Services Management and Hospital Administration	M
Human Resources Management	M
Interdisciplinary Studies	M
International Business	M
Management Strategy and Policy	M
Marketing	M
Middle School Education	M,O
Reading Education	M
School Psychology	M
Secondary Education	M,O
Special Education	M,O
Supply Chain Management	M

NICHOLLS STATE UNIVERSITY

Business Administration and Management—General	M
Clinical Psychology	M,O
Counselor Education	M,O
Curriculum and Instruction	M
Education—General	M
Educational Leadership and Administration	M
Elementary Education	M
Environmental Biology	M
Family Nurse Practitioner Studies	M
Health Education	M
Marine Biology	M
Middle School Education	M
Nursing and Healthcare Administration	M
Nursing Education	M
Nursing—General	M
Psychiatric Nursing	M
School Psychology	M,O
Secondary Education	M

NICHOLS COLLEGE

Business Administration and Management—General	M
Homeland Security	M
Organizational Management	M

NIPISSING UNIVERSITY

Education—General	M,O

NORFOLK STATE UNIVERSITY

Art/Fine Arts	M
Clinical Psychology	M
Communication—General	M
Computer Engineering	M
Computer Science	M
Criminal Justice and Criminology	M
Early Childhood Education	M
Education of Students with Severe/Multiple Disabilities	M
Education—General	M
Educational Leadership and Administration	M
Electrical Engineering	M
Materials Sciences	M
Media Studies	M
Music Education	M
Music	M
Optical Sciences	M
Psychology—General	M,D
Secondary Education	M
Social Psychology	M
Social Work	M,D
Special Education	M
Urban Education	M
Urban Studies	M

NORTH AMERICAN UNIVERSITY

Educational Leadership and Administration	M

NORTH CAROLINA AGRICULTURAL AND TECHNICAL STATE UNIVERSITY

Accounting	M
Adult Education	M
African-American Studies	M
Agricultural Economics and Agribusiness	M
Agricultural Education	M
Agricultural Sciences—General	M
Agronomy and Soil Sciences	M
Animal Sciences	M
Applied Economics	M
Applied Mathematics	M
Bioengineering	M
Biological and Biomedical Sciences—General	M
Business Administration and Management—General	M
Business Education	M
Chemical Engineering	M
Chemistry	M,D
Child and Family Studies	M
Child Development	M
Civil Engineering	M
Computational Sciences	M
Computer Art and Design	M
Computer Engineering	M,D
Computer Science	M
Construction Management	M
Consumer Economics	M
Counselor Education	M
Early Childhood Education	M
Education—General	M
Educational Leadership and Administration	M
Educational Media/Instructional Technology	M
Electrical Engineering	M,D
Elementary Education	M
Energy and Power Engineering	M,D
Engineering and Applied Sciences—General	M,D
English Education	M
English	M
Environmental and Occupational Health	M
Environmental Sciences	M
Graphic Design	M
Health Education	M
Human Resources Management	M
Industrial/Management Engineering	M,D
Management Information Systems	M
Management of Technology	M
Mathematics	M
Mechanical Engineering	M,D
Nutrition	M
Optical Sciences	M,D
Physical Education	M
Physics	M
Plant Sciences	M
Reading Education	M
Science Education	M
Secondary Education	M
Social Work	M
Supply Chain Management	M
Systems Engineering	M,D
Vocational and Technical Education	M

NORTH CAROLINA CENTRAL UNIVERSITY

Biological and Biomedical Sciences—General	M
Business Administration and Management—General	M
Chemistry	M
Clinical Psychology	M
Communication Disorders	M
Counselor Education	M
Criminal Justice and Criminology	M
Education—General	M
Educational Leadership and Administration	M
Educational Media/Instructional Technology	M
English	M
Environmental Sciences	M
Geographic Information Systems	M
Geosciences	M
History	M
Information Studies	M
Law	D
Library Science	M
Mathematics	M
Music	M
Physical Education	M
Physics	M
Psychology—General	M
Public Administration	M
Recreation and Park Management	M
Special Education	M

NORTH CAROLINA STATE UNIVERSITY

Accounting	M
Adult Education	M,D
Aerospace/Aeronautical Engineering	M,D
Agricultural Economics and Agribusiness	M
Agricultural Education	M,O
Agricultural Engineering	M,D,O
Agricultural Sciences—General	M,D,O
Agronomy and Soil Sciences	M,D
Animal Sciences	M,D
Anthropology	M
Applied Arts and Design—General	M,D
Applied Mathematics	M,D
Architecture	M
Atmospheric Sciences	M,D
Biochemistry	D
Bioengineering	M,D,O
Bioinformatics	M,D
Biological and Biomedical Sciences—General	M,D,O
Biomathematics	M,D
Biomedical Engineering	M,D
Biotechnology	M
Botany	M,D
Business Administration and Management—General	M
Business Education	M
Cell Biology	M,D
Chemical Engineering	M,D
Chemistry	M,D
Civil Engineering	M,D
Clothing and Textiles	D
Communication—General	M
Community College Education	M,D
Computer Art and Design	D
Computer Engineering	M,D
Computer Science	M,D
Counselor Education	M,D
Cultural Anthropology	M
Curriculum and Instruction	M,D
Developmental Education	M,D,O
Developmental Psychology	D
Economics	M,D
Education—General	M,D,O
Educational Leadership and Administration	M,D
Educational Measurement and Evaluation	D
Educational Media/Instructional Technology	M,D
Electrical Engineering	M,D
Elementary Education	M
Engineering and Applied Sciences—General	M,D
English Education	M
English	M
Entomology	M,D
Entrepreneurship	M
Epidemiology	M,D
Ergonomics and Human Factors	D
Experimental Psychology	D
Financial Engineering	M
Fish, Game, and Wildlife Management	M,D
Food Science and Technology	M,D
Forestry	M,D
French	M
Genetics	M,D
Genomic Sciences	M,D
Geographic Information Systems	M,D
Geosciences	M,D
Graphic Design	M
Higher Education	M,D
History	M
Horticulture	M,D,O
Human Resources Development	M
Industrial and Organizational Psychology	D
Industrial Design	M
Industrial/Management Engineering	M,D
Infectious Diseases	M,D
International Affairs	M
Landscape Architecture	M
Liberal Studies	M
Management of Technology	D
Manufacturing Engineering	M
Marine Sciences	M,D
Materials Engineering	M,D
Materials Sciences	M,D
Mathematical and Computational Finance	M
Mathematics Education	M,D
Mathematics	M,D
Mechanical Engineering	M,D
Meteorology	M,D
Microbiology	M,D
Middle School Education	M
Molecular Toxicology	M,D
Natural Resources	M,D
Nonprofit Management	M,D,O
Nuclear Engineering	M,D
Nutrition	M,D
Oceanography	M,D
Operations Research	M,D
Paper and Pulp Engineering	M,D
Pathology	M,D
Pharmacology	M,D
Physics	M,D
Physiology	M,D
Plant Biology	M,D
Plant Pathology	M,D
Polymer Science and Engineering	D
Psychology—General	D
Public Administration	M,D
Public History	M
Recreation and Park Management	M,D
Rhetoric	D
School Psychology	M
Science Education	M,D
Secondary Education	M
Social Psychology	M
Social Sciences Education	M
Social Work	M
Sociology	M,D
Spanish	M
Special Education	M
Sports Management	M,D
Statistics	M,D
Supply Chain Management	M
Technical Communication	M
Textile Sciences and Engineering	M,D
Toxicology	M,D
Travel and Tourism	M,D
Veterinary Medicine	M,D
Veterinary Sciences	M,D
Writing	M
Zoology	M,D

NORTH CENTRAL COLLEGE

Business Administration and Management—General	M
Computer Science	M
Cultural Studies	M
Education—General	M
Educational Leadership and Administration	M
Finance and Banking	M
Human Resources Management	M
Liberal Studies	M
Management Strategy and Policy	M

NORTHCENTRAL UNIVERSITY

Business Administration and Management—General	M,D,O
Computer and Information Systems Security	M,D,O
Computer Science	M,D,O
Data Science/Data Analytics	M,D,O
Education—General	M,D,O
Marriage and Family Therapy	M,D,O
Psychology—General	M,D,O

NORTH DAKOTA STATE UNIVERSITY

Accounting	M
Agricultural Economics and Agribusiness	M
Agricultural Education	M
Agricultural Sciences—General	M,D*
Agronomy and Soil Sciences	M,D
Animal Sciences	M,D
Anthropology	M
Applied Mathematics	M,D
Architecture	M
Athletic Training and Sports Medicine	M,D
Biochemistry	M,D
Bioinformatics	M,D
Biological and Biomedical Sciences—General	M,D
Botany	M,D
Business Administration and Management—General	M*
Cell Biology	D
Chemistry	M,D
Child and Family Studies	M,D,O*
Child Development	M
Civil Engineering	M,D
Clinical Psychology	M,D
Cognitive Sciences	M,D
Communication—General	M,D
Community Health	M
Conservation Biology	M,D
Consumer Economics	M,O
Counseling Psychology	M,D
Counselor Education	M,D
Criminal Justice and Criminology	M,D
Developmental Psychology	D
Education—General	M,D,O
Educational Leadership and Administration	M,O
English	M,D
Entomology	M,D
Environmental Engineering	M,D
Environmental Sciences	M,D
Exercise and Sports Science	M,D
Family and Consumer Sciences-General	M
Food Science and Technology	M,D
Genomic Sciences	M,D
Gerontology	D,O
Health Psychology	M,D
Higher Education	O
History	M,D
Horticulture	M,D
Industrial/Management Engineering	M,D
Infectious Diseases	M
Landscape Architecture	M
Logistics	M,D
Manufacturing Engineering	M,D
Mass Communication	M,D
Materials Sciences	M,D
Mathematics Education	D
Mathematics	M,D*
Mechanical Engineering	M,D
Microbiology	M,D
Molecular Biology	D
Molecular Pathogenesis	M,D
Music Education	M,D
Music	M,D
Nanotechnology	M,D
Natural Resources	M,D
Nursing—General	D
Nutrition	M,D
Pathology	M,D
Pharmacy	M,D
Physics	M,D
Plant Pathology	M,D
Plant Sciences	M,D
Polymer Science and Engineering	M,D
Psychology—General	M,D
Public Health—General	M*
Rhetoric	M,D*
School Psychology	M,D
Science Education	D
Social Psychology	M,D
Sociology	M
Software Engineering	M,D,O
Speech and Interpersonal Communication	M,D
Statistics	M,D
Transportation and Highway Engineering	D
Transportation Management	M,D
Urban and Regional Planning	M
Urban Studies	M,D
Writing	M,D
Zoology	M,D

NORTHEASTERN ILLINOIS UNIVERSITY

Accounting	M
Applied Mathematics	M
Biological and Biomedical Sciences—General	M
Business Administration and Management—General	M
Cell Biology	M
Chemistry	M
Computer Science	M
Counselor Education	M
Early Childhood Education	M
Ecology	M
Education of the Gifted	M
Education—General	M
Educational Leadership and Administration	M
Elementary Education	M
English as a Second Language	M
English Education	M
English	M
Environmental Management and Policy	M,O
Exercise and Sports Science	M
Geographic Information Systems	M,O
Geography	M,O
Gerontology	M
History	M
Human Resources Development	M
Latin American Studies	M
Linguistics	M
Marriage and Family Therapy	M
Mathematics Education	M
Mathematics	M
Molecular Biology	M
Music Education	M
Music	M
Political Science	M
Reading Education	M
Rehabilitation Counseling	M
Science Education	M
Secondary Education	M
Social Sciences Education	M
Special Education	M
Speech and Interpersonal Communication	M
Urban Education	M

NORTHEASTERN SEMINARY AT ROBERTS WESLEYAN COLLEGE

Theology	M,D

NORTHEASTERN STATE UNIVERSITY

Accounting	M
American Indian/Native American Studies	M
Business Administration and Management—General	M
Communication Disorders	M
Communication—General	M
Criminal Justice and Criminology	M
Early Childhood Education	M
Education—General	M
Educational Leadership and Administration	M
Educational Media/Instructional Technology	M
English	M
Finance and Banking	M
Health Education	M
Kinesiology and Movement Studies	M
Mathematics Education	M
Natural Resources	M
Nursing and Healthcare Administration	M
Nursing Education	M
Occupational Therapy	M
Optometry	D
Psychology—General	M
Reading Education	M
Science Education	M
Special Education	M

NORTHEASTERN UNIVERSITY

Accounting	M
Acute Care/Critical Care Nursing	M,D,O
Allied Health—General	M,D,O
Applied Arts and Design—General	M
Applied Behavior Analysis	M,D,O
Applied Mathematics	M,D
Architecture	M
Art/Fine Arts	M
Bioengineering	M,D,O
Bioinformatics	M,D
Biological and Biomedical Sciences—General	M,D
Biotechnology	M,D
Business Administration and Management—General	M,D,O
Chemical Engineering	M,D,O
Chemistry	M,D
Civil Engineering	M,D,O
Communication Disorders	M,D,O
Computer and Information Systems Security	M,D,O
Computer Engineering	M,D,O
Computer Science	M,D
Corporate and Organizational Communication	M
Counseling Psychology	M,D,O
Criminal Justice and Criminology	M,D
Data Science/Data Analytics	M,D
Economic Development	M
Economics	M,D
Educational Leadership and Administration	M
Electrical Engineering	M,D,O
Elementary Education	M
Energy and Power Engineering	M,D,O
Engineering and Applied Sciences—General	M,D,O
Engineering Management	M,D,O
English	M,D
Entrepreneurship	M
Environmental Engineering	M,D,O
Environmental Management and Policy	M,D
Environmental Sciences	M,D
Exercise and Sports Science	M,D,O
Family Nurse Practitioner Studies	M,D,O
Finance and Banking	M
Geographic Information Systems	M
Gerontological Nursing	M,D,O
Health Informatics	M,D
Higher Education	M
History	M,D
Homeland Security	M,D
Human Services	M
Industrial/Management Engineering	M,D,O
Interdisciplinary Studies	M,D,O
International Affairs	M,D
International Business	M
Internet and Interactive Multimedia	M
Journalism	M
Law	M,D
Legal and Justice Studies	M,D
Management Information Systems	M,D,O
Marine Biology	M,D
Maternal and Child/Neonatal Nursing	M,D,O
Mathematics	M,D
Mechanical Engineering	M,D,O
Nonprofit Management	M
Nursing and Healthcare Administration	M,D,O
Nursing—General	M,D,O
Nutrition	M
Operations Research	M,D,O
Pediatric Nursing	M,D,O
Pharmaceutical Sciences	M,D,O
Pharmacology	M,D,O
Pharmacy	M,D,O
Physics	M,D
Political Science	M,D
Project Management	M
Psychiatric Nursing	M,D,O
Psychology—General	M,D
Public Administration	M,D
Public Policy	M,D,O
School Psychology	M,D,O
Sociology	M,D
Special Education	M
Sports Management	M
Systems Engineering	M,D,O
Taxation	M
Technical Communication	M
Telecommunications	M,D,O
Urban Studies	M,D

NORTHEAST OHIO MEDICAL UNIVERSITY

Allopathic Medicine	D
Bioethics	M,D,O
Health Services Management and Hospital Administration	M,D,O
Humanities	M,D,O
Pharmaceutical Administration	M,D,O
Pharmaceutical Sciences	M,D,O
Pharmacy	D
Public Health—General	M,D,O

NORTHERN ARIZONA UNIVERSITY

Allied Health—General	M,D,O
American Indian/Native American Studies	O
Anthropology	M
Applied Physics	M,D
Applied Statistics	M,O
Atmospheric Sciences	M,D,O
Bioengineering	M,D
Biological and Biomedical Sciences—General	M,D
Business Administration and Management—General	M,O
Chemistry	M
Civil Engineering	M
Communication Disorders	M
Communication—General	M,O
Community College Education	M,D,O
Computer Engineering	M,D
Computer Science	M,D
Counseling Psychology	M,D,O
Counselor Education	M,D,O
Criminal Justice and Criminology	M,O
Curriculum and Instruction	M,D
Early Childhood Education	M,D,O
Education—General	M,D,O
Educational Leadership and Administration	M,D,O
Educational Media/Instructional Technology	M,O
Educational Psychology	M,D,O
Electrical Engineering	M,D
Elementary Education	M,D
Engineering and Applied Sciences—General	M,D,O
English as a Second Language	M,D,O
English	M,D,O
Environmental Management and Policy	M,D,O
Environmental Sciences	M,D,O
Ethnic Studies	O
Family Nurse Practitioner Studies	M,D,O
Foreign Languages Education	M
Forestry	M,D
Foundations and Philosophy of Education	M,D,O
Gender Studies	O
Geographic Information Systems	M,O
Geography	M,O
Geology	M,D,O
Higher Education	M,D,O
History	M
Human Development	O
International Business	M
Liberal Studies	M
Linguistics	M,D,O
Mathematics Education	M,O
Mathematics	M,O
Mechanical Engineering	M,D
Meteorology	M,D,O
Multilingual and Multicultural Education	M,O
Music	M,O
Nursing—General	M,D,O
Occupational Therapy	D
Organizational Management	M
Physical Therapy	D
Physician Assistant Studies	M
Physics	M,D
Political Science	M,D,O
Psychology—General	M
Public Administration	M,D,O
Recreation and Park Management	M,O
Rhetoric	M,D,O
School Psychology	M,D,O
Science Education	M
Secondary Education	M,D,O
Sociology	M
Spanish	M
Special Education	M,O
Statistics	M,O
Student Affairs	M,D,O
Sustainable Development	M
Urban and Regional Planning	M,O
Vocational and Technical Education	M,O
Women's Studies	O
Writing	M,D,O

NORTHERN ILLINOIS UNIVERSITY

Accounting	M
Adult Education	M,D
Anthropology	M
Art/Fine Arts	M
Biochemistry	M,D
Biological and Biomedical Sciences—General	M,D
Business Administration and Management—General	M
Chemistry	M,D
Child and Family Studies	M
Communication Disorders	M,D
Communication—General	M
Computer Science	M
Counselor Education	M,D
Curriculum and Instruction	M,D
Dance	M
Early Childhood Education	M
Economics	M,D
Education—General	M,D,O
Educational Leadership and Administration	M,D,O
Educational Media/Instructional Technology	M,D
Educational Psychology	M,D,O
Electrical Engineering	M
Elementary Education	M
Engineering and Applied Sciences—General	M
English	M,D
Foundations and Philosophy of Education	M,D,O
French	M
Geography	M,D
Geology	M,D
Higher Education	M,D
History	M,D
Industrial and Manufacturing Management	M
Industrial/Management Engineering	M
Law	D
Management Information Systems	M
Mathematics	M,D
Mechanical Engineering	M
Music	M,O
Nursing—General	M,D
Nutrition	M
Philosophy	M
Physical Education	M
Physical Therapy	D
Physics	M,D
Political Science	M,D
Psychology—General	M,D
Public Administration	M
Public Health—General	M
Romance Languages	M
Sociology	M
Spanish	M
Special Education	M
Statistics	M
Taxation	M
Theater	M

NORTHERN KENTUCKY UNIVERSITY

Accounting	M,O
Advertising and Public Relations	M,O
Allied Health—General	M
Business Administration and Management—General	M,O
Clinical Psychology	M
Communication—General	M,O
Computer and Information Systems Security	M,O
Computer Science	M,O
Counseling Psychology	M

*M—masters degree; D—doctorate; O—other advanced degree; *—Close-Up and/or Display*

Counselor Education M
Cultural Studies M,O
Education—General M,D,O
Educational Leadership and Administration M,D,O
English M,O
Geographic Information Systems M,O
Health Informatics M,O
Health Psychology M,O
Industrial and Organizational Psychology M,O
Information Science M,O
Law D
Liberal Studies M
Management of Technology M
Marriage and Family Therapy M,O
Media Studies M,O
Nonprofit Management M,O
Nursing—General M,D,O
Organizational Management M
Public Administration M,O
Public History M
Rhetoric M,O
Social Work M
Software Engineering M,O
Special Education M,O
Taxation M,O
Writing M,O

NORTHERN MICHIGAN UNIVERSITY
Applied Behavior Analysis M
Biological and Biomedical Sciences—General M
Business Administration and Management—General M
Clinical Laboratory Sciences/Medical Technology M
Curriculum and Instruction M
Education—General M
Educational Leadership and Administration M
English as a Second Language M,O
English M,O
Exercise and Sports Science M
Molecular Genetics M
Nursing—General D
Psychology—General M
Reading Education M
Science Education M
Special Education M
Theater M,O
Writing M,O

NORTHERN SEMINARY
Missions and Missiology M,D
Pastoral Ministry and Counseling M,D
Religion M,D
Theology M,D

NORTHERN STATE UNIVERSITY
Clinical Psychology M
Counseling Psychology M
Counselor Education M
Curriculum and Instruction M
Education—General M
Educational Leadership and Administration M
Educational Media/Instructional Technology M
Finance and Banking M
Music Education M
Sports Management M

NORTHERN VERMONT UNIVERSITY–JOHNSON
Addictions/Substance Abuse Counseling M
Applied Behavior Analysis M
Art/Fine Arts M
Computer Art and Design M
Counselor Education M
Curriculum and Instruction M
Education—General M
Foundations and Philosophy of Education M
Photography M
School Psychology M
Special Education M

NORTHERN VERMONT UNIVERSITY–LYNDON
Counselor Education M
Curriculum and Instruction M
Education—General M
Reading Education M
Science Education M
Special Education M

NORTH GREENVILLE UNIVERSITY
Education—General M,D
Finance and Banking M,D
Human Resources Management M,D
Pastoral Ministry and Counseling M,D

NORTH PARK THEOLOGICAL SEMINARY
Pastoral Ministry and Counseling M,O
Theology M,D

NORTH PARK UNIVERSITY
Adult Nursing M
Business Administration and Management—General M
Education—General M
Music M
Nonprofit Management M
Nursing and Healthcare Administration M
Nursing—General M

NORTHWEST CHRISTIAN UNIVERSITY
Accounting M
Business Administration and Management—General M
Counseling Psychology M
Counselor Education M
Education—General M
Elementary Education M
English as a Second Language M
Secondary Education M
Special Education M

NORTHWESTERN COLLEGE
Early Childhood Education M,O
Education—General M,O
Educational Leadership and Administration M,O

NORTHWESTERN HEALTH SCIENCES UNIVERSITY
Acupuncture and Oriental Medicine M
Chiropractic D
Nutrition M

NORTHWESTERN OKLAHOMA STATE UNIVERSITY
Adult Education M
American Studies M
Counseling Psychology M
Counselor Education M
Curriculum and Instruction M
Education—General M
Educational Leadership and Administration M
Elementary Education M
Reading Education M
Secondary Education M

NORTHWESTERN POLYTECHNIC UNIVERSITY
Business Administration and Management—General M,D
Computer Engineering M,D
Computer Science M,D
Electrical Engineering M,D
Engineering and Applied Sciences—General M,D

NORTHWESTERN STATE UNIVERSITY OF LOUISIANA
Adult Education M
Art/Fine Arts M
Clinical Psychology M
Counselor Education M,O
Curriculum and Instruction M
Early Childhood Education M
Education—General M,O
Educational Leadership and Administration M,O
Educational Media/Instructional Technology M,O
Elementary Education M,O
English M
Health Education M
Health Physics/Radiological Health M
Homeland Security M
Middle School Education M
Music M
Nursing—General M
Psychology—General M
Reading Education M,O
Secondary Education M,O
Special Education M,O
Student Affairs M

NORTHWESTERN UNIVERSITY
Accounting M,D
African Studies O
African-American Studies D
Allopathic Medicine M
American Studies M
Anthropology D
Applied Mathematics M,D
Applied Physics D
Art History D
Art/Fine Arts M
Artificial Intelligence/Robotics M
Arts Administration M
Astronomy D
Biochemistry D
Bioengineering D
Biological and Biomedical Sciences—General D
Biomedical Engineering M,D
Biophysics D
Biopsychology D
Biostatistics D
Biotechnology M,D
Broadcast Journalism M
Business Administration and Management—General M,D
Business Analytics M,D
Cell Biology D
Chemical Engineering M,D
Chemistry D
Civil Engineering M,D
Clinical Laboratory Sciences/Medical Technology M
Clinical Psychology D
Clinical Research M,O
Cognitive Sciences D
Communication Disorders M,D
Communication—General M,D
Comparative Literature M,D
Computer and Information Systems Security M
Computer Engineering M,D
Computer Science M,D
Corporate and Organizational Communication M,D
Data Science/Data Analytics M
Developmental Biology D
Economics D
Education—General M,D
Educational Leadership and Administration M
Educational Media/Instructional Technology M,D
Electrical Engineering M,D
Electronic Commerce M
Elementary Education M
Engineering and Applied Sciences—General M,D,O
Engineering Design M
Engineering Management M
English M,D
Entrepreneurship M,D
Environmental Engineering M,D
Epidemiology D
Ethics M
Film, Television, and Video Production M,D
Finance and Banking M,D
French D,O
Gender Studies O
Genetic Counseling M
Geology D
Geosciences D
Geotechnical Engineering M,D
German D
Health Informatics M,D
Health Services Management and Hospital Administration M,D
Health Services Research D
History M,D
Human Development D
Human Resources Management M,D
Industrial and Manufacturing Management M,D
Industrial/Management Engineering M,D
Information Science M
International Affairs M,D,O
International Business M,D
International Health M
Internet and Interactive Multimedia M
Italian D,O
Journalism M
Kinesiology and Movement Studies D
Law M,D
Liberal Studies M
Linguistics D
Management Information Systems M
Management Strategy and Policy M,D
Marketing M,D
Marriage and Family Therapy M
Materials Engineering M,D,O
Materials Sciences M,D,O
Mathematics D
Mechanical Engineering M,D
Mechanics M,D
Media Studies M,D
Medical Informatics M,D
Molecular Biology D
Music Education M,D
Music M,D
Neurobiology M,D
Neuroscience D
Organizational Behavior M
Organizational Management M,D
Philosophy D
Physical Therapy D
Physics D
Physiology M
Plant Biology M,D
Political Science D
Portuguese D
Project Management M
Psychology—General D
Public Administration M
Public Health—General M
Public Policy M,D
Publishing M
Quality Management M
Real Estate M,D
Rehabilitation Sciences D
Religion M,D
Rhetoric M,D
Secondary Education M
Slavic Languages D
Social Psychology D
Sociology M,D
Software Engineering M
Spanish D
Speech and Interpersonal Communication M,D
Sports Management M
Statistics M,D
Structural Biology D
Structural Engineering M,D
Systems Biology D
Taxation M,D
Theater M,D
Transportation and Highway Engineering M,D
Writing M

NORTHWEST MISSOURI STATE UNIVERSITY
Agricultural Economics and Agribusiness M
Agricultural Education M
Agricultural Sciences—General M
Biological and Biomedical Sciences—General M,O
Business Administration and Management—General M
Business Analytics M
Computer Science M
Early Childhood Education M,D,O
Education—General M,D,O
Educational Leadership and Administration M,D,O
Educational Media/Instructional Technology M
Educational Policy M,D,O
Elementary Education M,D,O
English as a Second Language M,D,O
English Education M,O
English M,O
Exercise and Sports Science M
Geographic Information Systems M,O
Health Education M
Higher Education M,D,O
Human Resources Management M
Management Information Systems M
Marketing M
Mathematics Education M,D,O
Mathematics M,O
Middle School Education M,D,O
Physical Education M
Reading Education M,D,O
Recreation and Park Management M
Science Education M,O
Social Sciences Education M,O
Special Education M,D,O

NORTHWEST NAZARENE UNIVERSITY
Addictions/Substance Abuse Counseling M
Business Administration and Management—General M
Clinical Psychology M
Counselor Education M
Curriculum and Instruction M,D,O
Education—General M,D,O
Educational Leadership and Administration M,D,O
Marriage and Family Therapy M
Missions and Missiology M
Nursing and Healthcare Administration M
Pastoral Ministry and Counseling M
Religion M
School Psychology M
Social Work M
Special Education M,D,O
Theology M

NORTHWEST UNIVERSITY
Business Administration and Management—General M
Counseling Psychology M,D
Cultural Studies M
Education—General M
International Business M
Missions and Missiology M
Organizational Management M
Pastoral Ministry and Counseling M
Project Management M
Psychology—General M,D
Theology M
Urban and Regional Planning M,D

NORTHWOOD UNIVERSITY, MICHIGAN CAMPUS
Business Administration and Management—General M

NORWICH UNIVERSITY
Business Administration and Management—General M
Civil Engineering M
Computer and Information Systems Security M
Conflict Resolution and Mediation/Peace Studies M
Construction Management M
Criminal Justice and Criminology M
Emergency Management M
Energy Management and Policy M
Environmental Engineering M
Finance and Banking M
Geotechnical Engineering M
History M
Human Resources Management M
International Affairs M
International Business M
International Development M
Logistics M
Management Strategy and Policy M
Military and Defense Studies M
Nonprofit Management M
Nursing and Healthcare Administration M
Nursing Education M
Nursing—General M
Organizational Management M
Project Management M
Public Administration M
Public Policy M
Structural Engineering M
Supply Chain Management M

NOTRE DAME COLLEGE (OH)
Computer Science M,O
Homeland Security M,O
Reading Education M,O
Special Education M,O

NOTRE DAME DE NAMUR UNIVERSITY
Art Therapy M,D
Business Administration and Management—General M
Clinical Psychology M
Curriculum and Instruction M
Education—General M
Educational Leadership and Administration M
Finance and Banking M
Human Resources Management M
Marketing M
Marriage and Family Therapy M
Public Administration M
Public Affairs M
Special Education M

NOTRE DAME OF MARYLAND UNIVERSITY
Business Administration and Management—General M
Communication—General M
Education—General M
Educational Leadership and Administration M,D
English as a Second Language M
Liberal Studies M
Nonprofit Management M
Pharmacy D

NOTRE DAME SEMINARY

Theology	M

NOVA SOUTHEASTERN UNIVERSITY

Accounting	M
Addictions/Substance Abuse Counseling	M,D,O
Adult Nursing	M,D
Allied Health—General	M,D
Allopathic Medicine	D
Anesthesiologist Assistant Studies	M,D
Art/Fine Arts	M,D,O
Bioinformatics	M,D,O
Biological and Biomedical Sciences—General	M,D
Business Administration and Management—General	M
Business Analytics	M
Business Education	M
Clinical Psychology	M,D,O
Communication Disorders	M,D
Computer and Information Systems Security	M,D
Computer Science	M,D
Conflict Resolution and Mediation/Peace Studies	M,D,O
Counseling Psychology	M,D,O
Counselor Education	M,D,O
Criminal Justice and Criminology	M,D,O
Dentistry	M,D
Distance Education Development	M,D,O
Education—General	M,D,O
Educational Media/Instructional Technology	M,D,O
Emergency Management	M,D,O
Entrepreneurship	M
Experimental Psychology	M,D,O
Family Nurse Practitioner Studies	M,D
Finance and Banking	M
Forensic Psychology	M,D,O
Gerontological Nursing	M,D
Health Education	M,D,O
Health Informatics	M,D,O
Health Law	M,D
Human Resources Management	M
Humanities	M,D,O
Information Science	M,D
Interdisciplinary Studies	M,D,O
International Business	M
Law	M,D
Legal and Justice Studies	M,D
Management Information Systems	M,D
Management Strategy and Policy	M
Marine Biology	M,D
Marketing	M
Marriage and Family Therapy	M,D,O
Medical Informatics	M,D,O
Nursing Education	M,D
Nursing Informatics	M,D
Nursing—General	M,D
Nutrition	M,D,O
Occupational Therapy	M,D
Oceanography	M,D
Optometry	M,D
Osteopathic Medicine	M,D,O
Pharmacy	M,D*
Physical Therapy	M,D
Physician Assistant Studies	M,D
Psychiatric Nursing	M,D
Psychology—General	M,D,O
Public Administration	M
Public Health—General	M,D,O
School Psychology	M,D,O
Social Sciences	M,D,O
Student Affairs	M,D,O
Supply Chain Management	M

NSCAD UNIVERSITY

Applied Arts and Design—General	M
Art/Fine Arts	M

NYACK COLLEGE

Business Administration and Management—General	M
Counseling Psychology	M
Counselor Education	M
Elementary Education	M
English as a Second Language	M
Marriage and Family Therapy	M
Missions and Missiology	M,D
Organizational Management	M
Pastoral Ministry and Counseling	M,D
Religion	M
Social Work	M
Special Education	M
Theology	M,D

OAKLAND CITY UNIVERSITY

Business Administration and Management—General	M
Curriculum and Instruction	M,D
Education—General	M,D
Educational Leadership and Administration	M,D
Elementary Education	M,D
Management Strategy and Policy	M
Organizational Management	M,D
Pastoral Ministry and Counseling	M,D
Secondary Education	M,D
Theology	M,D

OAKLAND UNIVERSITY

Accounting	M,O
Allied Health—General	M,D,O
Applied Behavior Analysis	M,O
Applied Mathematics	M,D
Applied Statistics	M
Biological and Biomedical Sciences—General	M,D,O
Business Administration and Management—General	M,O
Chemistry	M,D
Computer Engineering	M,D
Computer Science	M,D
Counseling Psychology	M,D,O
Early Childhood Education	M,D,O
Economics	M,O
Education—General	M,D,O
Educational Leadership and Administration	M,D,O
Electrical Engineering	M,D
Elementary Education	M,O
Engineering and Applied Sciences—General	M,D,O
Engineering Management	M,D,O
English as a Second Language	M,O
English	M
Entrepreneurship	M,O
Environmental and Occupational Health	M
Environmental Sciences	M,D
Exercise and Sports Science	M,D,O
Family Nurse Practitioner Studies	M,O
Finance and Banking	M,O
Gerontological Nursing	M,O
Higher Education	M,D,O
History	M
Human Resources Management	M,O
Industrial and Manufacturing Management	M,O
International Business	M,O
Liberal Studies	M
Linguistics	M,O
Management Information Systems	M,D,O
Marketing	M,O
Maternal and Child Health	D,O
Mathematics	M
Mechanical Engineering	M,D
Medical Physics	M,D
Music Education	M,D
Music	M,D
Nonprofit Management	M,O
Nurse Anesthesia	M,O
Nursing—General	M,D,O
Organizational Management	M,D,O
Physical Therapy	D,O
Physics	M,D
Public Administration	M,O
Reading Education	M,D,O
Secondary Education	M,O
Software Engineering	M,D
Special Education	M,O
Statistics	O
Systems Engineering	M,D,O
Systems Science	M,D

OAKWOOD UNIVERSITY

Pastoral Ministry and Counseling	M

OBERLIN COLLEGE

Music	M,O

OBLATE SCHOOL OF THEOLOGY

African-American Studies	M,D,O
Pastoral Ministry and Counseling	M,D,O
Religion	M,D,O
Theology	M,D,O

OCCIDENTAL COLLEGE

Biological and Biomedical Sciences—General	M

OGLALA LAKOTA COLLEGE

Business Administration and Management—General	M
Educational Leadership and Administration	M

OHIO CHRISTIAN UNIVERSITY

Accounting	M
Business Administration and Management—General	M
Finance and Banking	M
Health Services Management and Hospital Administration	M
Human Resources Management	M
Marketing	M
Organizational Management	M
Pastoral Ministry and Counseling	M
Theology	M

OHIO DOMINICAN UNIVERSITY

Accounting	M
Business Administration and Management—General	M
Curriculum and Instruction	M
Data Science/Data Analytics	M
Education—General	M
Educational Leadership and Administration	M
Engineering Design	M
English as a Second Language	M
English	M
Finance and Banking	M
Health Services Management and Hospital Administration	M
Management Strategy and Policy	M
Physician Assistant Studies	M
Risk Management	M
Sports Management	M
Theology	M

OHIO NORTHERN UNIVERSITY

Accounting	M
Law	M,D
Pharmacy	D

THE OHIO STATE UNIVERSITY

Accounting	M
Actuarial Science	M,D
Aerospace/Aeronautical Engineering	M,D
African Studies	M,D
African-American Studies	M,D
Agricultural Economics and Agribusiness	M,D
Agricultural Education	M
Agricultural Engineering	M,D
Agricultural Sciences—General	M,D
Agronomy and Soil Sciences	M,D
Allied Health—General	M
Allopathic Medicine	D
Anatomy	M,D
Animal Sciences	M,D
Anthropology	M,D
Architecture	M,D
Art Education	M,D
Art History	M,D
Art/Fine Arts	M
Arts Administration	M
Asian Languages	M,D
Asian Studies	M
Astronomy	M,D
Atmospheric Sciences	M,D
Biochemistry	M,D
Bioengineering	M,D
Biological and Biomedical Sciences—General	M,D
Biomedical Engineering	M,D
Biophysics	M,D
Biostatistics	M,D
Business Administration and Management—General	M,D
Cell Biology	M,D
Chemical Engineering	M,D
Chemical Physics	M,D
Chemistry	M,D
Child and Family Studies	M,D
Chinese	M,D
Civil Engineering	M,D
Classics	M,D
Clinical Psychology	D
Cognitive Sciences	D
Communication Disorders	M,D
Communication—General	M,D
Computational Sciences	M,D
Computer Art and Design	M
Computer Engineering	M,D
Computer Science	M,D
Dance	M,D
Dental Hygiene	M,D
Dentistry	M,D
Developmental Biology	M,D
Developmental Psychology	D
East European and Russian Studies	M,D
Ecology	M,D
Economics	M,D
Education—General	M,D,O
Educational Leadership and Administration	M,D,O
Educational Policy	M,D,O
Electrical Engineering	M,D
Engineering and Applied Sciences—General	M,D
English	M,D
Entomology	M,D
Environmental Management and Policy	M,D
Environmental Sciences	M,D
Evolutionary Biology	M,D
Family and Consumer Sciences-General	M,D
Finance and Banking	M
Fish, Game, and Wildlife Management	M,D
Food Science and Technology	M,D
Forestry	M,D
French	M,D
Gender Studies	M,D
Genetics	M,D
Geodetic Sciences	M,D
Geography	M,D
Geology	M,D
Geosciences	M,D
German	M,D
Health Services Management and Hospital Administration	M,D
History	M,D
Horticulture	M,D
Human Development	M,D
Human Resources Management	M,D
Industrial and Labor Relations	M,D
Industrial Design	M
Industrial/Management Engineering	M,D
Interdisciplinary Studies	M,D
Interior Design	M
Internet and Interactive Multimedia	M
Italian	M,D
Japanese	M,D
Kinesiology and Movement Studies	M,D
Landscape Architecture	M,D
Latin American Studies	M
Law	M,D
Linguistics	M,D
Logistics	M
Management Information Systems	M,D
Materials Engineering	M,D
Materials Sciences	M,D
Mathematics Education	M,D
Mathematics	M,D
Mechanical Engineering	M,D
Metallurgical Engineering and Metallurgy	M,D
Microbiology	M,D
Molecular Biology	M,D
Molecular Genetics	M,D
Music	M,D
Natural Resources	M,D
Near and Middle Eastern Languages	M,D
Neuroscience	D
Nuclear Engineering	M,D
Nursing—General	M,D
Nutrition	M,D
Occupational Therapy	M
Operations Research	M
Optical Sciences	M,D
Optometry	M,D
Oral and Dental Sciences	M,D
Pharmaceutical Administration	M,D
Pharmacology	M,D
Pharmacy	M,D
Philosophy	M,D
Physical Education	M,D
Physical Therapy	D
Physics	M,D
Plant Pathology	M,D
Plant Sciences	D
Political Science	D
Portuguese	M,D
Psychology—General	D
Public Administration	M,D
Public Affairs	M,D
Public Health—General	M,D
Public Policy	M,D
Rehabilitation Sciences	D
Rural Sociology	M,D
Slavic Languages	M,D
Social Psychology	D
Social Sciences	M,D
Social Work	M,D
Sociology	D
Spanish	M,D
Special Education	D
Statistics	M,D
Systems Engineering	M,D
Theater	M,D
Urban and Regional Planning	M,D
Veterinary Sciences	M,D
Women's Studies	M,D

THE OHIO STATE UNIVERSITY AT LIMA

Social Work	M

THE OHIO STATE UNIVERSITY AT MANSFIELD

Education—General	M
Social Work	M

THE OHIO STATE UNIVERSITY AT MARION

Education—General	M

THE OHIO STATE UNIVERSITY AT NEWARK

Education—General	M
Social Work	M

OHIO UNIVERSITY

African Studies	M
Applied Economics	M
Art History	M
Art/Fine Arts	M
Asian Studies	M
Astronomy	M,D
Athletic Training and Sports Medicine	M
Biochemistry	M,D
Biological and Biomedical Sciences—General	M,D
Biomedical Engineering	M
Business Administration and Management—General	M
Cell Biology	M,D
Chemical Engineering	M,D
Child and Family Studies	M
Child Development	M
Civil Engineering	M,D
Clinical Psychology	D
Communication Disorders	M,D
Communication—General	M,D
Comparative and Interdisciplinary Arts	D
Computer Education	M,D
Computer Science	M,D
Construction Engineering	M,D
Consumer Economics	M
Corporate and Organizational Communication	M,D
Counselor Education	M,D
Curriculum and Instruction	M,D
Ecology	M,D
Economics	M
Education—General	M,D
Educational Leadership and Administration	M,D
Educational Measurement and Evaluation	M,D
Educational Media/Instructional Technology	M,D
Electrical Engineering	M,D
Engineering and Applied Sciences—General	M,D
English	M,D
Environmental Biology	M,D
Environmental Engineering	M,D
Environmental Management and Policy	M,O
Evolutionary Biology	M,D
Exercise and Sports Science	M,D
Experimental Psychology	D
Family Nurse Practitioner Studies	M,D
Film, Television, and Video Production	M
Film, Television, and Video Theory and Criticism	M
Finance and Banking	M
French	M
Geochemistry	M
Geography	M
Geology	M
Geotechnical Engineering	M,D
Graphic Design	M
Health Communication	M,D

*M—masters degree; D—doctorate; O—other advanced degree; *—Close-Up and/or Display*

Health Services Management and Hospital Administration	M
Higher Education	M,D
History	M,D
Industrial and Organizational Psychology	D
Industrial/Management Engineering	M,D
International Affairs	M
International Development	M
Internet and Interactive Multimedia	M
Journalism	M,D
Latin American Studies	M
Linguistics	M
Mathematics	M,D
Mechanical Engineering	M
Mechanics	M,D
Media Studies	M,D
Microbiology	M,D
Middle School Education	M,D
Molecular Biology	D
Music Education	M,O
Music	M,O
Neuroscience	M,D
Nursing and Healthcare Administration	M,D
Nursing Education	M,D
Nursing—General	M,D
Nutrition	M
Osteopathic Medicine	D
Philosophy	M
Photography	M
Physical Education	M
Physical Therapy	D
Physics	M,D
Physiology	M,D
Plant Biology	M,D
Political Science	M
Psychology—General	D
Public Administration	M,O
Public Health—General	M
Reading Education	M,D
Recreation and Park Management	M
Rehabilitation Counseling	M,D
Rhetoric	M,D
Secondary Education	M,D
Social Sciences	M
Social Work	M
Sociology	M
Spanish	M
Special Education	M,D
Speech and Interpersonal Communication	M,D
Sports Management	M
Structural Engineering	M,D
Student Affairs	M,D
Systems Engineering	M
Telecommunications	M
Theater	M
Therapies—Dance, Drama, and Music	M,O
Transportation and Highway Engineering	M,D
Water Resources Engineering	M,D

OHIO VALLEY UNIVERSITY

Curriculum and Instruction	M
Education—General	M

OHR HAMEIR THEOLOGICAL SEMINARY

Theology	

OKLAHOMA BAPTIST UNIVERSITY

Business Administration and Management—General	M
Energy Management and Policy	M
Marriage and Family Therapy	M
Nursing Education	M
Nursing—General	M

OKLAHOMA CHRISTIAN UNIVERSITY

Accounting	M
Business Administration and Management—General	M
Computer Engineering	M
Computer Science	M
Electrical Engineering	M
Engineering and Applied Sciences—General	M
Engineering Management	M
Finance and Banking	M
Health Services Management and Hospital Administration	M
Human Resources Management	M
International Business	M
Marketing	M
Mechanical Engineering	M
Nonprofit Management	M
Organizational Management	M
Project Management	M
Software Engineering	M
Theology	M

OKLAHOMA CITY UNIVERSITY

Applied Behavior Analysis	M
Business Administration and Management—General	M
Computer Science	M
Counselor Education	M
Criminal Justice and Criminology	M
Early Childhood Education	M
Elementary Education	M
Energy Management and Policy	M
English as a Second Language	M
Law	M,D
Music	M
Nursing Education	M,D
Nursing—General	M,D
Photography	M
Sociology	M
Writing	M

OKLAHOMA STATE UNIVERSITY

Accounting	M,D
Agricultural Economics and Agribusiness	M,D
Agricultural Education	M,D
Agricultural Engineering	M,D
Agricultural Sciences—General	M,D
Agronomy and Soil Sciences	M,D
Animal Sciences	M,D
Applied Arts and Design—General	M,D
Applied Behavior Analysis	M,D,O
Applied Mathematics	M,D
Applied Psychology	M,D,O
Art History	M
Aviation	M,D,O
Biochemistry	M,D
Bioengineering	M,D
Biological and Biomedical Sciences—General	M,D
Botany	M,D
Business Administration and Management—General	M,D
Chemical Engineering	M,D
Chemistry	M,D
Child and Family Studies	M,D
Civil Engineering	M,D
Clinical Psychology	M,D
Clothing and Textiles	M,D
Communication Disorders	M
Computer Engineering	M,D
Computer Science	M,D
Consumer Economics	M,D
Curriculum and Instruction	M,D
Ecology	M,D
Economics	M,D
Education—General	M,D,O
Educational Leadership and Administration	M,D
Educational Psychology	M,D,O
Electrical Engineering	M,D
Emergency Management	M,D
Engineering and Applied Sciences—General	M,D
English	M,D
Entomology	M,D
Entrepreneurship	M,D
Environmental Engineering	M,D
Environmental Sciences	M,D,O
Evolutionary Biology	M,D
Family and Consumer Sciences-General	M,D
Finance and Banking	M,D
Fire Protection Engineering	M,D
Food Science and Technology	M,D
Forestry	M,D
Geography	M,D
Geology	M,D
Graphic Design	M
Health Education	M,D,O
Health Psychology	M,D,O
Higher Education	M,D
History	M,D
Horticulture	M,D
Hospitality Management	M,D
Industrial/Management Engineering	M,D
Information Science	M,D
International Affairs	M,D,O
International Business	M,D
Landscape Architecture	M,D
Management Information Systems	M,D
Marketing	M,D
Mass Communication	M
Materials Engineering	M,D
Materials Sciences	M,D
Mathematics	M,D
Mechanical Engineering	M,D
Microbiology	M,D
Molecular Biology	M,D
Molecular Genetics	M,D
Music Education	M
Music	M
Natural Resources	M,D
Nonprofit Management	M,D,O
Nutrition	M,D
Philosophy	M
Photonics	M,D
Physics	M,D
Plant Biology	M,D
Plant Pathology	M,D
Plant Sciences	M,D
Political Science	M,D
Psychology—General	M,D
Sociology	M,D
Statistics	M,D
Sustainability Management	M,D,O
Telecommunications Management	M,D,O
Theater	M
Veterinary Medicine	D
Veterinary Sciences	M,D
Writing	M,D

OKLAHOMA STATE UNIVERSITY CENTER FOR HEALTH SCIENCES

Biological and Biomedical Sciences—General	M,D
Forensic Sciences	M
Health Services Management and Hospital Administration	M
Osteopathic Medicine	D
Toxicology	M

OKLAHOMA WESLEYAN UNIVERSITY

Management Strategy and Policy	M
Nursing and Healthcare Administration	M
Nursing Education	M
Theology	M

OLD DOMINION UNIVERSITY

Accounting	M
Adult Nursing	M,D
Aerospace/Aeronautical Engineering	M,D
Allied Health—General	M,D
Analytical Chemistry	M,D
Applied Mathematics	M,D
Applied Psychology	D
Athletic Training and Sports Medicine	M
Biochemistry	M,D
Biological and Biomedical Sciences—General	M,D
Biomedical Engineering	M,D
Biostatistics	M,D
Business Administration and Management—General	M,D
Business Education	M,D
Chemistry	M,D
Civil Engineering	M,D
Clinical Psychology	D
Communication Disorders	M
Communication—General	M,O
Community College Education	M,D
Community Health	M
Computer Art and Design	M
Computer Engineering	M,D
Computer Science	M,D
Conflict Resolution and Mediation/Peace Studies	M,D
Counseling Psychology	M,D,O
Counselor Education	M,D,O
Criminal Justice and Criminology	M,D
Cultural Studies	M,D,O
Curriculum and Instruction	M,D
Dental Hygiene	M
Early Childhood Education	M,D
Ecology	D
Economics	M
Education—General	M,D,O
Educational Leadership and Administration	M,D,O
Educational Measurement and Evaluation	D
Educational Media/Instructional Technology	M,D,O
Educational Psychology	D
Electrical Engineering	M,D
Elementary Education	M,O
Engineering and Applied Sciences—General	M,D
Engineering Management	D
English as a Second Language	M
English	M,D
Entrepreneurship	M,O
Environmental Engineering	M,D
Environmental Sciences	M,D
Ergonomics and Human Factors	D
Exercise and Sports Science	M,D
Family Nurse Practitioner Studies	M,D
Finance and Banking	D
Gender Studies	M,O
Geotechnical Engineering	M
Gerontological Nursing	M,D
Health Education	M,D
Health Promotion	M
Health Services Research	D
Higher Education	M,D,O
History	M
Humanities	M,O
Hydraulics	M
Immunology	M
Industrial and Organizational Psychology	D
Industrial Hygiene	M
Information Science	D
Inorganic Chemistry	M,D
International Affairs	M,D
International Business	M
International Development	M,D
Kinesiology and Movement Studies	M,D
Library Science	M,O
Linguistics	M
Management Information Systems	M,D
Marketing	M,D
Maternal and Child/Neonatal Nursing	M,D
Mathematics	M,D
Mechanical Engineering	M,D
Media Studies	M,O
Microbiology	M
Middle School Education	M,O
Modeling and Simulation	M,D
Music Education	M
Music	M
Nurse Anesthesia	D
Nursing and Healthcare Administration	M,D
Nursing Education	M,D
Nursing—General	D
Oceanography	M,D
Organic Chemistry	M,D
Pediatric Nursing	M,D
Philosophy	M,O
Physical Chemistry	M,D
Physical Education	M,D
Physical Therapy	D
Physics	M,D
Psychology—General	M,D
Public Administration	M,D
Public Health—General	M
Reading Education	M,D
Rehabilitation Sciences	D
Rhetoric	M
School Psychology	M,D,O
Secondary Education	M
Sociology	M
Special Education	M,D
Speech and Interpersonal Communication	M
Sports Management	M
Statistics	M,D
Structural Engineering	M
Supply Chain Management	M
Systems Engineering	M,D
Transportation and Highway Engineering	M
Vocational and Technical Education	M,D
Water Resources	M
Women's Studies	M
Writing	M

OLIVET COLLEGE

Insurance	M

OLIVET NAZARENE UNIVERSITY

Business Administration and Management—General	M
Curriculum and Instruction	M
Education—General	M
Educational Leadership and Administration	M
Elementary Education	M
Family Nurse Practitioner Studies	M
Library Science	M
Nursing—General	M
Organizational Management	M
Pastoral Ministry and Counseling	M
Reading Education	M
Religion	M
Secondary Education	M
Theology	M

OPEN UNIVERSITY

Business Administration and Management—General	M
Education—General	M
Engineering and Applied Sciences—General	M
History	M
Music	M
Philosophy	M

ORAL ROBERTS UNIVERSITY

Accounting	M
Addictions/Substance Abuse Counseling	M,D
Business Administration and Management—General	M
Curriculum and Instruction	M,D
Education—General	M,D
Educational Leadership and Administration	M,D
Entrepreneurship	M
Finance and Banking	M
Higher Education	M,D
International Business	M
Marketing	M
Marriage and Family Therapy	M,D
Missions and Missiology	M,D
Near and Middle Eastern Languages	M,D
Nonprofit Management	M
Pastoral Ministry and Counseling	M,D
Religious Education	M,D
Theology	M,D

OREGON COLLEGE OF ART AND CRAFT

Art/Fine Arts	M

OREGON COLLEGE OF ORIENTAL MEDICINE

Acupuncture and Oriental Medicine	M,D

OREGON HEALTH & SCIENCE UNIVERSITY

Allopathic Medicine	D
Biochemistry	M,D
Bioinformatics	M,D,O
Biological and Biomedical Sciences—General	M,D,O
Biomedical Engineering	M,D
Biopsychology	D
Cancer Biology/Oncology	D
Cell Biology	D
Clinical Research	M,O
Community Health Nursing	M,O
Computational Biology	M,D,O
Computer Engineering	M,D
Computer Science	M,D
Dentistry	D,O
Developmental Biology	D
Electrical Engineering	M,D
Environmental Engineering	M,D
Environmental Sciences	M,D
Family Nurse Practitioner Studies	M
Genetics	D
Gerontological Nursing	M,O
Gerontology	M,O
Health Informatics	M,D,O
Health Services Management and Hospital Administration	M,O
Immunology	D
Medical Informatics	M,D,O
Microbiology	D
Molecular Biology	M,D
Molecular Medicine	M,D
Neuroscience	D
Nurse Anesthesia	M
Nurse Midwifery	M
Nursing and Healthcare Administration	M
Nursing Education	M,O
Nursing—General	M,D,O
Nutrition	M,O
Oral and Dental Sciences	M,D,O
Pediatric Nursing	M
Pharmacology	D
Physician Assistant Studies	M
Physiology	D
Psychiatric Nursing	M

OREGON INSTITUTE OF TECHNOLOGY

Manufacturing Engineering	M

OREGON STATE UNIVERSITY

Accounting	M,D
Actuarial Science	M,D
Adult Education	M,D
Agricultural Education	M,D
Agricultural Engineering	M,D

- Agronomy and Soil Sciences M,D
- Allied Health—General M,D
- Analytical Chemistry M,D
- Animal Sciences M
- Anthropology M,D
- Applied Economics M,D
- Applied Mathematics M,D
- Aquaculture M,D
- Artificial Intelligence/Robotics M,D
- Athletic Training and Sports Medicine M
- Atmospheric Sciences M,D
- Biochemistry M,D
- Bioengineering M,D
- Bioinformatics D
- Biological and Biomedical Sciences—General M,D
- Biophysics M,D
- Biostatistics M,D
- Biotechnology M,D
- Botany M,D
- Business Administration and Management—General M,D
- Cell Biology M,D
- Chemical Engineering M,D
- Chemistry M,D
- Child and Family Studies M,D
- Civil Engineering M,D
- Clinical Psychology M,D
- Cognitive Sciences M,D
- Computational Biology M,D
- Computational Sciences M,D
- Computer Engineering M,D
- Computer Science M,D
- Conservation Biology M,D
- Construction Engineering M,D
- Counselor Education M,D
- Data Science/Data Analytics M
- Ecology M,D
- Education—General M,D
- Educational Leadership and Administration M,D
- Educational Policy M,D
- Electrical Engineering M,D
- Elementary Education M
- Engineering and Applied Sciences—General M,D
- Engineering Management M,D
- English Education M
- English M
- Environmental and Occupational Health M,D
- Environmental Biology M,D
- Environmental Education M,D
- Environmental Engineering M,D
- Environmental Management and Policy M,D
- Environmental Sciences M,D
- Epidemiology M,D
- Ethics M
- Finance and Banking M,D
- Fish, Game, and Wildlife Management M,D
- Food Science and Technology M,D
- Forestry M,D
- Gender Studies M,D
- Genetics M,D
- Genomic Sciences M,D
- Geochemistry M,D
- Geographic Information Systems M
- Geography M,D
- Geology M,D
- Geophysics M,D
- Geotechnical Engineering M,D
- Health Physics/Radiological Health M,D
- Health Promotion M,D
- Health Psychology M,D
- Health Services Management and Hospital Administration M,D
- Higher Education M,D
- Hispanic Studies M
- History of Science and Technology M,D
- Horticulture M,D
- Human Development M,D
- Hydrogeology M,D
- Hydrology M,D
- Immunology M,D
- Industrial/Management Engineering M,D
- Interdisciplinary Studies M
- International Health M,D
- Kinesiology and Movement Studies M,D
- Limnology M,D
- Manufacturing Engineering M,D
- Marine Affairs M
- Marine Sciences M
- Materials Sciences M,D
- Mathematical and Computational Finance M,D
- Mathematics Education M,D
- Mathematics M,D
- Mechanical Engineering M,D
- Medical Imaging M,D
- Medical Physics M,D
- Microbiology M,D
- Molecular Biology M,D
- Molecular Toxicology M,D
- Music Education M
- Natural Resources M,D
- Nuclear Engineering M,D
- Nutrition M,D
- Ocean Engineering M,D
- Oceanography M,D
- Parasitology M,D
- Pharmaceutical Sciences M,D
- Pharmacy D
- Physics M,D
- Physiology M,D
- Plant Molecular Biology D
- Plant Pathology M,D
- Plant Physiology M,D
- Psychology—General M,D
- Public Health—General M,D
- Public Policy M,D
- Range Science M,D
- Rhetoric M
- School Psychology M,D
- Science Education M,D
- Social Sciences Education M,D
- Social Sciences M,D
- Statistics M,D
- Structural Engineering M,D
- Student Affairs M
- Sustainability Management M,D
- Systems Biology M,D
- Systems Engineering M,D
- Toxicology M,D
- Transportation and Highway Engineering M,D
- Veterinary Medicine D
- Virology M,D
- Water Resources Engineering M,D
- Water Resources M,D
- Women's Studies M,D
- Writing M

OREGON STATE UNIVERSITY–CASCADES
- Education—General M
- School Psychology M
- Social Psychology M

OTIS COLLEGE OF ART AND DESIGN
- Art/Fine Arts M
- Graphic Design M
- Photography M
- Writing M

OTTAWA UNIVERSITY
- Art Therapy M
- Business Administration and Management—General M
- Counseling Psychology M
- Counselor Education M
- Curriculum and Instruction M
- Early Childhood Education M
- Education—General M
- Educational Leadership and Administration M
- Educational Media/Instructional Technology M
- Elementary Education M
- Finance and Banking M
- Human Resources Development M
- Human Resources Management M
- Marketing M
- Marriage and Family Therapy M
- Pastoral Ministry and Counseling M
- School Psychology M
- Special Education M

OTTERBEIN UNIVERSITY
- Business Administration and Management—General M
- Education—General M
- Family Nurse Practitioner Studies M,D,O
- Nurse Anesthesia M,D,O
- Nursing and Healthcare Administration M,D,O
- Nursing Education M,D,O
- Nursing—General M,D,O

OUR LADY OF THE LAKE UNIVERSITY
- Accounting M
- Business Administration and Management—General M
- Communication Disorders M
- Computer and Information Systems Security M
- Counseling Psychology D
- Counselor Education M
- Curriculum and Instruction M
- English M
- Finance and Banking M
- Health Services Management and Hospital Administration M
- Management Information Systems M
- Marriage and Family Therapy M
- Nonprofit Management M
- Organizational Management M,D
- Psychology—General M
- School Psychology M
- Science Education M
- Social Work M
- Sociology M
- Writing M

OXFORD GRADUATE SCHOOL
- Child and Family Studies M,D
- Organizational Management M,D
- Religion M,D
- Sociology M,D

PACE UNIVERSITY
- Accounting M,O
- Addictions/Substance Abuse Counseling M,D
- Biochemistry M
- Biological and Biomedical Sciences—General M,O
- Business Administration and Management—General M,D,O
- Chemistry M,O
- Clinical Psychology M,D
- Communication—General M
- Computer and Information Systems Security M,D,O
- Computer Science M,D,O
- Counseling Psychology M,D
- Developmental Psychology M,D
- Early Childhood Education M,O
- Economics O
- Education—General M,O
- Educational Media/Instructional Technology M,O
- Electronic Commerce O
- Elementary Education M,O
- Emergency Management M
- English M,O
- Entrepreneurship M
- Environmental Law M,D
- Environmental Management and Policy M
- Environmental Sciences M
- Family Nurse Practitioner Studies M,D,O
- Finance and Banking M,D,O
- Foreign Languages Education M,O
- Forensic Sciences M
- Geosciences M,O
- Health Services Management and Hospital Administration M
- Homeland Security M
- Human Resources Management M
- Information Science M,D,O
- International Business M,O
- International Economics O
- Internet and Interactive Multimedia M,D,O
- Investment Management M,O
- Law M,D
- Legal and Justice Studies M,D
- Management Information Systems M,D,O
- Management Strategy and Policy M
- Marketing M,D,O
- Mathematics M,O
- Media Studies M
- Molecular Biology M
- Nonprofit Management M
- Nursing and Healthcare Administration M,D,O
- Nursing—General M,D,O
- Physician Assistant Studies M
- Physics M,O
- Psychology—General M
- Public Administration M
- Publishing M,O
- Reading Education M,O
- Risk Management M
- School Psychology M,D
- Social Sciences Education M,O
- Software Engineering M,D,O
- Special Education M,O
- Taxation M
- Telecommunications M,D,O
- Theater M

PACIFICA GRADUATE INSTITUTE
- Clinical Psychology M,D
- Counseling Psychology M,D
- Psychology—General M,D

PACIFIC COLLEGE OF ORIENTAL MEDICINE
- Acupuncture and Oriental Medicine M,D

PACIFIC COLLEGE OF ORIENTAL MEDICINE–CHICAGO
- Acupuncture and Oriental Medicine M

PACIFIC COLLEGE OF ORIENTAL MEDICINE-NEW YORK
- Acupuncture and Oriental Medicine M

PACIFIC LUTHERAN UNIVERSITY
- Accounting M
- Business Administration and Management—General M
- Curriculum and Instruction M
- Education—General M
- Family Nurse Practitioner Studies D
- Finance and Banking M
- Marketing Research M
- Marriage and Family Therapy M
- Nursing—General M,D
- Writing M

PACIFIC NORTHWEST COLLEGE OF ART
- Applied Arts and Design—General M
- Art/Fine Arts M
- Cultural Studies M

PACIFIC NORTHWEST UNIVERSITY OF HEALTH SCIENCES
- Osteopathic Medicine D

PACIFIC OAKS COLLEGE
- Early Childhood Education M
- Education—General M
- Human Development M
- Marriage and Family Therapy M
- Special Education M

PACIFIC RIM CHRISTIAN UNIVERSITY
- Pastoral Ministry and Counseling M

PACIFIC SCHOOL OF RELIGION
- Religion M,D,O
- Theology M,D,O

PACIFIC STATES UNIVERSITY
- Accounting M,O
- Business Administration and Management—General M,O
- Computer Science M
- Finance and Banking M,O
- International Business M,O
- Management Information Systems M,O
- Management of Technology M,O
- Project Management M,O
- Real Estate M,O

PACIFIC UNION COLLEGE
- Education—General M
- Elementary Education M
- Secondary Education M

PACIFIC UNIVERSITY
- Athletic Training and Sports Medicine M,D
- Business Administration and Management—General M
- Clinical Psychology M,D
- Communication Disorders M,D
- Early Childhood Education M
- Education of the Gifted M
- Education—General M
- Elementary Education M
- English as a Second Language M
- Finance and Banking M
- Health Services Management and Hospital Administration M
- Middle School Education M
- Occupational Therapy D
- Optometry M,D
- Pharmacy D
- Physical Therapy M,D
- Physician Assistant Studies M
- Psychology—General M,D
- Science Education M
- Secondary Education M
- Social Work M
- Special Education M
- Vision Sciences M,D
- Writing M

PALM BEACH ATLANTIC UNIVERSITY
- Addictions/Substance Abuse Counseling M
- Business Administration and Management—General M
- Counseling Psychology M
- Counselor Education M
- Education—General M
- Family Nurse Practitioner Studies M,D
- Marriage and Family Therapy M
- Nursing and Healthcare Administration M,D
- Nursing—General M,D
- Organizational Management M
- Pharmacy D
- Religious Education M
- Theology M

PALMER COLLEGE OF CHIROPRACTIC
- Anatomy M
- Chiropractic D
- Clinical Research M

PALO ALTO UNIVERSITY
- Biopsychology D
- Clinical Psychology M,D
- Counseling Psychology M
- Marriage and Family Therapy M
- Psychology—General M,D

PARIS COLLEGE OF ART
- Art/Fine Arts M
- Interior Design M
- Media Studies M
- Photography M
- Textile Design M

PARKER UNIVERSITY
- Chiropractic D

PARK UNIVERSITY
- Business Administration and Management—General M,O
- Curriculum and Instruction M,O
- Education—General M,O
- Educational Leadership and Administration M,O
- Emergency Management M,O
- Finance and Banking M,O
- Health Services Management and Hospital Administration M,O
- International Business M,O
- International Health M,O
- Management Information Systems M,O
- Music M,O
- Nonprofit Management M,O
- Public Administration M,O
- Public Affairs M,O
- Reading Education M,O
- Social Work M,O
- Writing M,O

PAYNE THEOLOGICAL SEMINARY
- Theology M

PEIRCE COLLEGE
- Organizational Management M

PENN STATE ERIE, THE BEHREND COLLEGE
- Accounting M
- Applied Psychology M
- Business Administration and Management—General M
- Clinical Psychology M
- Industrial and Manufacturing Management M
- Quality Management M

PENN STATE GREAT VALLEY
- Business Administration and Management—General M,O
- Computer and Information Systems Security M,O
- Data Science/Data Analytics M,O
- Engineering and Applied Sciences—General M,O
- Engineering Management M,O
- Entrepreneurship M,O
- Finance and Banking M,O
- Health Services Management and Hospital Administration M,O
- Human Resources Development M,O
- Human Resources Management M,O
- Information Science M,O

*M—masters degree; D—doctorate; O—other advanced degree; *—Close-Up and/or Display*

Software Engineering	M,O
Sustainability Management	M,O
Systems Engineering	M,O

PENN STATE HARRISBURG

Accounting	M,O
Adult Education	M,D,O
American Studies	M,D,O
Applied Behavior Analysis	M,D,O
Applied Psychology	M,D,O
Business Administration and Management—General	M,O
Civil Engineering	M,O
Clinical Psychology	M,D,O
Communication—General	M,D,O
Computer Science	M,O
Criminal Justice and Criminology	M,D,O
Curriculum and Instruction	M,D,O
Developmental Education	M,D,O
Education—General	M,D,O
Electrical Engineering	M,O
Engineering and Applied Sciences—General	M,O
Engineering Management	M,O
English as a Second Language	M,D,O
Environmental Engineering	M,O
Environmental Sciences	M,O
Finance and Banking	M,D,O
Folklore	M,D,O
Health Education	M,D,O
Health Psychology	M,D,O
Health Services Management and Hospital Administration	M,D,O
Historic Preservation	M,D,O
Homeland Security	M,D,O
Human Resources Management	M,D,O
Humanities	M,D,O
Management Information Systems	M,O
Mechanical Engineering	M,O
Museum Studies	M,D,O
Nonprofit Management	M,D,O
Psychology—General	M,D,O
Public Administration	M,D,O
Public Affairs	M,D,O
Reading Education	M,D,O
Social Psychology	M,D,O
Structural Engineering	M,O
Supply Chain Management	M,O

PENN STATE HERSHEY MEDICAL CENTER

Allopathic Medicine	M,D
Anatomy	M,D
Biochemistry	M,D
Bioinformatics	
Biological and Biomedical Sciences—General	M,D
Biostatistics	D
Cell Biology	D
Developmental Biology	D
Genomic Sciences	
Health Services Research	M
Immunology	M,D
Molecular Genetics	M,D
Molecular Medicine	D
Molecular Toxicology	D
Neurobiology	D
Neuroscience	M,D
Public Health—General	M,D
Veterinary Sciences	M
Virology	M,D

PENN STATE UNIVERSITY–DICKINSON LAW

Law	M,D

PENN STATE UNIVERSITY PARK

Accounting	M,D
Acoustics	M,D
Adult Education	M,D,O
Aerospace/Aeronautical Engineering	M,D
Agricultural Economics and Agribusiness	M,D,O
Agricultural Education	M,D,O
Agricultural Engineering	M,D
Agricultural Sciences—General	M,D,O
Agronomy and Soil Sciences	M,D
Animal Sciences	M,D
Anthropology	M,D
Applied Statistics	M,D
Architectural Engineering	M,D
Architecture	M,D
Art Education	M,D,O
Art History	M,D
Art/Fine Arts	M,D,O
Astronomy	M,D
Astrophysics	M,D
Biochemistry	M,D
Bioengineering	M,D
Biological and Biomedical Sciences—General	M,D
Biopsychology	M,D
Biotechnology	M,D
Business Administration and Management—General	M,D
Cell Biology	M,D
Chemical Engineering	M,D
Chemistry	M,D
Child and Family Studies	M,D
Civil Engineering	M,D
Communication Disorders	M,D,O
Communication—General	M,D
Comparative Literature	M,D
Computer Engineering	M,D
Computer Science	M,D*
Counselor Education	M,D,O
Criminal Justice and Criminology	M,D
Curriculum and Instruction	M,D,O
Ecology	M,D
Economics	M,D
Education—General	M,D,O
Educational Leadership and Administration	M,D,O
Educational Media/Instructional Technology	M,D,O
Educational Policy	M,D,O
Educational Psychology	M,D,O
Electrical Engineering	M,D
Engineering and Applied Sciences—General	M,D
Engineering Design	M
English as a Second Language	M,D
English	M,D
Entomology	M,D
Entrepreneurship	M
Environmental Engineering	M,D
Environmental Management and Policy	M
Environmental Sciences	M
Fish, Game, and Wildlife Management	M,D
Food Science and Technology	M,D
Forensic Sciences	M
Forestry	M,D
Foundations and Philosophy of Education	M,D,O
French	M,D
Geography	M,D
Geosciences	M,D
Geotechnical Engineering	M,D
German	M,D
Health Services Management and Hospital Administration	M,D
Higher Education	M,D,O
History	M,D
Horticulture	M,D
Hospitality Management	M,D
Human Development	M,D
Human Resources Development	M
Human Resources Management	M
Industrial and Labor Relations	M
Industrial/Management Engineering	M,D
Information Science	M,D
International Affairs	M
Kinesiology and Movement Studies	M,D,O
Landscape Architecture	M,D
Law	M,D
Leisure Studies	M,D
Linguistics	M,D
Management Information Systems	M,D
Mass Communication	M,D
Materials Engineering	M,D
Materials Sciences	M,D
Mathematics	M,D
Mechanical Engineering	M,D
Mechanics	M,D
Media Studies	M,D
Meteorology	M,D
Mineral/Mining Engineering	M,D
Molecular Biology	M,D
Music Education	M,D,O
Music	M,D,O
Nuclear Engineering	M,D
Nursing—General	M,D
Nutrition	M,D
Organizational Management	M,D
Pathobiology	M,D
Philosophy	M,D
Physics	M,D
Physiology	M,D
Plant Biology	M,D
Plant Pathology	M,D
Plant Sciences	M,D
Political Science	M,D
Psychology—General	M,D
Recreation and Park Management	M,D
Rural Sociology	M,D,O
Russian	M,D
School Psychology	M,D,O
Sociology	M,D
Spanish	M,D
Special Education	M,D,O
Statistics	M,D
Sustainable Development	M
Theater	M
Travel and Tourism	M,D
Vocational and Technical Education	M,D,O

PENN STATE YORK

Curriculum and Instruction	M,O
Education—General	M,O
English as a Second Language	M,O

PENNSYLVANIA ACADEMY OF THE FINE ARTS

Art/Fine Arts	M,O

PENNSYLVANIA COLLEGE OF HEALTH SCIENCES

Health Education	M
Health Services Management and Hospital Administration	M
Nursing and Healthcare Administration	M
Nursing Education	M

PENSACOLA CHRISTIAN COLLEGE

Art/Fine Arts	M,D,O
Business Administration and Management—General	M,D,O
Curriculum and Instruction	M,D,O
Educational Leadership and Administration	M,D,O
Graphic Design	M,D,O
Music	M,D,O
Nursing—General	M,D,O
Theater	M,D,O

PENTECOSTAL THEOLOGICAL SEMINARY

Pastoral Ministry and Counseling	M,D
Theology	M,D

PEPPERDINE UNIVERSITY

Accounting	M
American Studies	M
Business Administration and Management—General	M
Business Education	M
Clinical Psychology	M,D
Communication—General	M
Conflict Resolution and Mediation/Peace Studies	M
Economics	M
Educational Leadership and Administration	M,D
Educational Media/Instructional Technology	M,D
Finance and Banking	M
Human Resources Management	M
Humanities	M
International Affairs	M,D
International Business	M
Law	M,D
Marriage and Family Therapy	M,D
Mathematics	M
Media Studies	M
Organizational Management	M,D
Pastoral Ministry and Counseling	M
Political Science	M
Psychology—General	M,D
Public Policy	M
Religion	M
Science Education	M,D
Sports and Entertainment Law	M
Writing	M

PERU STATE COLLEGE

Curriculum and Instruction	M
Economics	M
Education—General	M
Entrepreneurship	M
Organizational Management	M

PFEIFFER UNIVERSITY

Business Administration and Management—General	M
Elementary Education	M
Health Services Management and Hospital Administration	M
Organizational Management	M
Religious Education	M
Theology	M

PHILADELPHIA COLLEGE OF OSTEOPATHIC MEDICINE

Applied Behavior Analysis	M,D,O
Biological and Biomedical Sciences—General	M
Biopsychology	M,D,O
Clinical Psychology	M,D,O
Counseling Psychology	M,D,O
Educational Psychology	M,D,O
Forensic Sciences	M
Health Services Management and Hospital Administration	M,D,O
Industrial and Organizational Psychology	M,D,O
Osteopathic Medicine	D
Physician Assistant Studies	M
Psychology—General	M,D,O*
Public Health—General	M,D,O
School Psychology	M,D,O

PHILLIPS GRADUATE UNIVERSITY

Art Therapy	M
Counselor Education	M
Marriage and Family Therapy	M
Organizational Behavior	D
Psychology—General	M
School Psychology	M

PHILLIPS THEOLOGICAL SEMINARY

Business Administration and Management—General	M,D
Ethics	M,D
Higher Education	M,D
Missions and Missiology	M,D
Music	M,D
Pastoral Ministry and Counseling	D
Religious Education	M,D
Social Work	M,D
Theology	M,D

PHOENIX INSTITUTE OF HERBAL MEDICINE & ACUPUNCTURE

Acupuncture and Oriental Medicine	M

PHOENIX SEMINARY

Counseling Psychology	M,D,O
Pastoral Ministry and Counseling	M,D,O
Theology	M,D,O

PIEDMONT COLLEGE

Art Education	M,D,O
Business Administration and Management—General	M
Curriculum and Instruction	M,D,O
Early Childhood Education	M,D,O
Education—General	M,D,O
Educational Media/Instructional Technology	M,D,O
Middle School Education	M,D,O
Music Education	M,D,O
Secondary Education	M,D,O
Special Education	M,D,O

PIEDMONT INTERNATIONAL UNIVERSITY

Curriculum and Instruction	M,D
Educational Leadership and Administration	M,D
Pastoral Ministry and Counseling	M,D
Theology	M,D

PILLAR COLLEGE

Clinical Psychology	M
Marriage and Family Therapy	M

PITTSBURGH THEOLOGICAL SEMINARY

Pastoral Ministry and Counseling	M,D
Theology	M,D

PITTSBURG STATE UNIVERSITY

Accounting	M
Biological and Biomedical Sciences—General	M
Business Administration and Management—General	M
Chemistry	M
Clinical Psychology	M
Communication—General	M
Construction Engineering	M
Construction Management	M,O
Counselor Education	M
Education—General	M,O
Educational Leadership and Administration	M,O
Educational Media/Instructional Technology	M
Electrical Engineering	M
English as a Second Language	M,O
English	M
Exercise and Sports Science	M
Graphic Design	M,O
Health Education	M
History	M
Human Resources Development	M
International Business	M
Management of Technology	M,O
Manufacturing Engineering	M
Mathematics	M
Mechanical Engineering	M
Music Education	M
Music	M
Nursing Education	M,D
Nursing—General	M,D
Physical Education	M
Physics	M
Polymer Science and Engineering	M
Psychology—General	M
School Psychology	O
Secondary Education	M,O
Special Education	M,O
Sports Management	M
Vocational and Technical Education	M,O
Writing	M

PLYMOUTH STATE UNIVERSITY

Accounting	M
Addictions/Substance Abuse Counseling	M
Adult Education	D
Art Education	M
Athletic Training and Sports Medicine	M
Business Administration and Management—General	M
Clinical Psychology	O
Counselor Education	M
Cultural Studies	M
Curriculum and Instruction	D
Education—General	O
Educational Leadership and Administration	M,D,O
English Education	M
Health Education	M
Health Promotion	M,O
Higher Education	D,O
Historic Preservation	M,O
Marriage and Family Therapy	M
Mathematics Education	M
Music Education	M
School Psychology	O
Social Sciences Education	M

POINT LOMA NAZARENE UNIVERSITY

Acute Care/Critical Care Nursing	M
Biological and Biomedical Sciences—General	M
Business Administration and Management—General	M
Clinical Psychology	M
Counselor Education	M
Education—General	M
Educational Leadership and Administration	M
Entrepreneurship	M
Exercise and Sports Science	M
Family Nurse Practitioner Studies	M
Gerontological Nursing	M
Health Services Management and Hospital Administration	M
Kinesiology and Movement Studies	M
Marriage and Family Therapy	M
Nursing—General	M,D,O
Organizational Management	M
Pastoral Ministry and Counseling	M
Pediatric Nursing	M
Project Management	M
Special Education	M
Sports Management	M
Theology	M

POINT PARK UNIVERSITY

Adult Education	M,D
Business Administration and Management—General	M
Business Analytics	M
Clinical Psychology	M,D
Communication—General	M
Criminal Justice and Criminology	M
Curriculum and Instruction	M,D
Education—General	M,D
Educational Leadership and Administration	M,D
Elementary Education	M,D
Engineering Management	M
Entertainment Management	M
Environmental Management and Policy	M
Health Services Management and Hospital Administration	M
International Business	M
Journalism	M
Management Information Systems	M
Mass Communication	M

Media Studies	M
Middle School Education	M,D
Music	M
Organizational Management	M
Secondary Education	M,D
Special Education	M,D
Sports Management	M
Theater	M

POINT UNIVERSITY

Business Administration and Management—General	M
Pastoral Ministry and Counseling	M

POLYTECHNIC UNIVERSITY OF PUERTO RICO

Business Administration and Management—General	M
Civil Engineering	M
Computer Engineering	M
Computer Science	M
Electrical Engineering	M
Engineering Management	M
Environmental Management and Policy	M
Industrial and Manufacturing Management	M
International Business	M
Landscape Architecture	M
Management Information Systems	M
Management of Technology	M
Manufacturing Engineering	M
Mechanical Engineering	M

POLYTECHNIC UNIVERSITY OF PUERTO RICO, MIAMI CAMPUS

Accounting	M
Business Administration and Management—General	M
Construction Management	M
Environmental Engineering	M
Environmental Management and Policy	M
Finance and Banking	M
Human Resources Management	M
Industrial and Manufacturing Management	M
International Business	M
Logistics	M
Marketing	M
Project Management	M
Supply Chain Management	M

POLYTECHNIC UNIVERSITY OF PUERTO RICO, ORLANDO CAMPUS

Accounting	M
Business Administration and Management—General	M
Construction Management	M
Engineering Management	M
Environmental Engineering	M
Environmental Management and Policy	M
Finance and Banking	M
Human Resources Management	M
Industrial and Manufacturing Management	M
International Business	M
Management of Technology	M

PONCE HEALTH SCIENCES UNIVERSITY

Allopathic Medicine	D
Biological and Biomedical Sciences—General	D
Clinical Psychology	D
Epidemiology	M,D
Public Health—General	M,D

PONTIFICAL CATHOLIC UNIVERSITY OF PUERTO RICO

Accounting	M,O
Art/Fine Arts	M
Biological and Biomedical Sciences—General	M
Business Administration and Management—General	M,D,O
Business Education	M,D
Chemistry	M
Clinical Laboratory Sciences/Medical Technology	O
Clinical Psychology	D
Counselor Education	M
Criminal Justice and Criminology	M
Curriculum and Instruction	M,D
Education—General	M,D
Educational Leadership and Administration	D
Educational Psychology	M
English as a Second Language	M
Environmental Sciences	M
Finance and Banking	M
Hispanic Studies	M,O
History	M
Human Resources Management	M,O
Human Services	M,D
Industrial and Organizational Psychology	D
International Business	M
Law	D
Logistics	O
Management Information Systems	M,O
Marketing	M
Medical/Surgical Nursing	M
Nursing—General	M
Psychiatric Nursing	M
Psychology—General	M,D
Public Administration	M
Rehabilitation Counseling	M
Religious Education	M
Social Work	M
Spanish	M,O
Theology	M
Transportation Management	O

PONTIFICAL COLLEGE JOSEPHINUM

Theology	M

PONTIFICAL JOHN PAUL II INSTITUTE FOR STUDIES ON MARRIAGE AND FAMILY

Biotechnology	M,D,O
Ethics	M,D,O
Marriage and Family Therapy	M,D,O
Theology	M,D,O

PONTIFICIA UNIVERSIDAD CATOLICA MADRE Y MAESTRA

Allopathic Medicine	D
Architecture	M
Building Science	M
Business Administration and Management—General	M
Clinical Psychology	M
Criminal Justice and Criminology	M
Developmental Psychology	M
Early Childhood Education	M
Engineering and Applied Sciences—General	M
Entrepreneurship	M
Finance and Banking	M
Forensic Psychology	M
Hospitality Management	M
Human Resources Management	M
Insurance	M
Interior Design	M
International Affairs	M
International Business	M
Landscape Architecture	M
Law	M
Logistics	M
Management Strategy and Policy	M
Marketing	M
Psychology—General	M
Real Estate	M
Structural Engineering	M
Travel and Tourism	M

POPE ST. JOHN XXIII NATIONAL SEMINARY

Theology	M

PORTLAND STATE UNIVERSITY

American Studies	M
Anthropology	M,D,O
Applied Social Research	M,D
Applied Statistics	M,D,O
Architecture	M
Art/Fine Arts	M
Artificial Intelligence/Robotics	M,D,O
Biological and Biomedical Sciences—General	M,D
Business Administration and Management—General	M,D,O
Chemistry	M,D
Civil Engineering	M,D,O
Communication Disorders	M
Computer and Information Systems Security	M,D,O
Computer Engineering	M,D
Computer Science	M,D,O
Conflict Resolution and Mediation/Peace Studies	M
Criminal Justice and Criminology	M,D
Economics	M,D,O
Education—General	M,D
Electrical Engineering	M,D
Energy Management and Policy	M,D,O
Engineering and Applied Sciences—General	M,D,O
Engineering Management	M,D,O
English as a Second Language	M,O
English	M
Environmental Engineering	M,D
Environmental Management and Policy	M,D,O
Environmental Sciences	M,D,O
Finance and Banking	M
Food Science and Technology	M,D,O
Foreign Languages Education	M
French	M
Geography	M,D
Geology	M,D,O
German	M
Health Promotion	M,D
Health Services Management and Hospital Administration	M,D,O
History	M
Human Resources Management	M,D,O
Hydrology	M,D,O
International Affairs	M
International Business	M
Japanese	M
Management of Technology	M,D
Materials Engineering	M,D
Mathematics Education	M,D,O
Mathematics	M,D,O
Mechanical Engineering	M,D,O
Middle School Education	M,D,O
Modeling and Simulation	M,D,O
Music	M
Nonprofit Management	M,D,O
Physics	M,D
Political Science	M
Psychology—General	M,D,O
Public Administration	M,D,O
Public Affairs	M,D,O
Public Health—General	M,D
Public Policy	M,D,O
Real Estate	M,D,O
Science Education	M,D,O
Social Sciences Education	M
Social Work	M,D
Sociology	M,D,O
Spanish	M
Speech and Interpersonal Communication	M,O
Statistics	M,D,O
Supply Chain Management	M
Systems Science	M,D,O
Theater	M
Writing	M

POST UNIVERSITY

Accounting	M
Addictions/Substance Abuse Counseling	M
Business Administration and Management—General	M
Clinical Psychology	M
Curriculum and Instruction	M
Distance Education Development	M
Education—General	M
Educational Leadership and Administration	M
Educational Media/Instructional Technology	M
Emergency Management	M
English as a Second Language	M
Finance and Banking	M
Forensic Psychology	M
Health Services Management and Hospital Administration	M
Homeland Security	M
Human Services	M
Marketing	M
Nonprofit Management	M
Project Management	M
Public Administration	M

PRAIRIE VIEW A&M UNIVERSITY

Accounting	M
Agricultural Sciences—General	M
Architecture	M
Business Administration and Management—General	M
Chemistry	M
Clinical Psychology	M,D
Computer Science	M,D
Counselor Education	M,D
Curriculum and Instruction	M
Education—General	M,D
Educational Leadership and Administration	M,D
Electrical Engineering	M,D
Engineering and Applied Sciences—General	M,D
Forensic Psychology	M,D
Health Education	M
Kinesiology and Movement Studies	M
Legal and Justice Studies	M,D
Management Information Systems	M,D
Nursing—General	M,D
Sociology	M

PRATT INSTITUTE

Applied Arts and Design—General	M,O*
Architecture	M*
Art Education	M,O
Art History	M
Art Therapy	M
Art/Fine Arts	M*
Arts Administration	M
Facilities Management	M
Graphic Design	M
Historic Preservation	M
Industrial Design	M
Information Studies	M,O*
Interior Design	M
Internet and Interactive Multimedia	M
Library Science	M,O
Media Studies	M*
Music	M
Real Estate	M
Sustainable Development	M
Therapies—Dance, Drama, and Music	M
Urban and Regional Planning	M
Urban Design	M
Writing	M

PRESBYTERIAN COLLEGE

Pharmacy	D

PRESCOTT COLLEGE

Art Therapy	M
Art/Fine Arts	M
Counseling Psychology	M
Counselor Education	M,D
Early Childhood Education	M,D
Education—General	M,D
Educational Leadership and Administration	M,D
Elementary Education	M,D
Environmental Education	M,D
Environmental Management and Policy	M
Health Psychology	M
Humanities	M
Legal and Justice Studies	M
Leisure Studies	M
Psychoanalysis and Psychotherapy	M
Secondary Education	M,D
Special Education	M,D

PRESIDIO GRADUATE SCHOOL (CA)

Business Administration and Management—General	M,O
Sustainability Management	M,O

PRINCETON THEOLOGICAL SEMINARY

Religion	M,D
Theology	M,D

PRINCETON UNIVERSITY

Aerospace/Aeronautical Engineering	M,D
Anthropology	D
Applied Mathematics	D
Archaeology	D
Architecture	M,D
Asian Studies	D
Astronomy	D
Astrophysics	D
Atmospheric Sciences	D
Bioengineering	M,D
Chemical Engineering	M,D
Chemistry	M,D
Civil Engineering	M,D
Classics	D
Comparative Literature	D
Computational Biology	D
Computational Sciences	D
Computer Science	M,D
Demography and Population Studies	D,O
Ecology	D
Economics	D,O
Electrical Engineering	M,D
Electronic Materials	D
Engineering and Applied Sciences—General	M,D
English	D
Environmental Engineering	M,D
Evolutionary Biology	D
Finance and Banking	M
Financial Engineering	M,D
French	D
Geosciences	D
German	D
History of Science and Technology	D
History	D
International Affairs	M,D
Marine Biology	D
Materials Sciences	D
Mathematics	D
Mechanical Engineering	M,D
Molecular Biology	D
Music	D
Near and Middle Eastern Studies	M,D
Neuroscience	D
Ocean Engineering	D
Oceanography	D
Operations Research	M,D
Philosophy	D
Photonics	D
Physics	D
Plasma Physics	D
Political Science	D
Portuguese	D
Psychology—General	D
Public Affairs	M,D,O
Public Policy	M,D
Religion	D
Russian	D
Slavic Languages	D
Sociology	D,O
Spanish	D

PROVIDENCE COLLEGE

Accounting	M
American Studies	M
Business Administration and Management—General	M
Counselor Education	M
Educational Leadership and Administration	M
Elementary Education	M
Finance and Banking	M
History	M
International Business	M
Marketing	M
Mathematics Education	M
Reading Education	M
Secondary Education	M
Special Education	M
Theology	M
Urban Education	M

PROVIDENCE UNIVERSITY COLLEGE & THEOLOGICAL SEMINARY

Counseling Psychology	M,D,O
English as a Second Language	M,D,O
Missions and Missiology	M,D,O
Pastoral Ministry and Counseling	M,D,O
Religious Education	M,D,O
Student Affairs	M,D,O
Theology	M,D,O

PURCHASE COLLEGE, STATE UNIVERSITY OF NEW YORK

Art History	M
Art/Fine Arts	M
Arts Administration	M
Computer Art and Design	M
Entrepreneurship	M
Media Studies	M
Music	M

PURDUE UNIVERSITY

Aerospace/Aeronautical Engineering	M,D
Agricultural Economics and Agribusiness	M,D
Agricultural Education	M,D,O
Agricultural Engineering	M,D
Agricultural Sciences—General	M,D
Agronomy and Soil Sciences	M,D
Allied Health—General	M,D
American Studies	M,D
Analytical Chemistry	M,D
Anatomy	M,D
Animal Sciences	M,D
Anthropology	M,D
Applied Arts and Design—General	M,D

*M—masters degree; D—doctorate; O—other advanced degree; *—Close-Up and/or Display*

Aquaculture	M,D
Art Education	M,D,O
Art/Fine Arts	M,D
Atmospheric Sciences	M,D
Aviation Management	M
Biochemistry	M,D
Biological and Biomedical Sciences—General	M,D
Biomedical Engineering	M,D
Biophysics	M,D
Biotechnology	D
Botany	M,D
Business Administration and Management—General	M,D
Cancer Biology/Oncology	D
Cell Biology	M,D
Chemical Engineering	M,D
Chemistry	M,D
Child and Family Studies	M,D
Child Development	M,D
Civil Engineering	M,D
Clinical Psychology	D
Cognitive Sciences	D
Communication Disorders	M,D
Communication—General	M,D
Comparative Literature	M,D
Computational Sciences	D
Computer and Information Systems Security	M
Computer Art and Design	M,D
Computer Engineering	M,D
Computer Science	M,D
Construction Management	M
Consumer Economics	M,D
Counselor Education	M,D,O
Curriculum and Instruction	M,D,O
Developmental Biology	M,D
Ecology	M,D
Economics	D
Education of the Gifted	M,D,O
Education—General	M,D,O
Educational Leadership and Administration	M,D,O
Educational Media/Instructional Technology	M,D,O
Educational Psychology	M,D,O
Electrical Engineering	M,D
Elementary Education	M,D,O
Engineering and Applied Sciences—General	M,D,O
English Education	M,D,O
English	M,D
Entomology	M,D
Environmental and Occupational Health	M,D
Environmental Engineering	M,D
Environmental Management and Policy	M,D
Epidemiology	M,D
Ergonomics and Human Factors	M,D
Evolutionary Biology	M,D
Exercise and Sports Science	M,D
Family Nurse Practitioner Studies	M,D,O
Finance and Banking	M
Fish, Game, and Wildlife Management	M,D
Food Science and Technology	M,D
Foreign Languages Education	M,D,O
Forestry	M,D
Foundations and Philosophy of Education	M,D,O
French	M,D
Genetics	M,D
Genomic Sciences	D
Geosciences	M,D
German	M,D
Gerontological Nursing	M,D,O
Health Education	M,D
Health Physics/Radiological Health	M,D
Higher Education	M,D,O
History	M,D
Home Economics Education	M,D,O
Horticulture	M,D
Hospitality Management	M,D
Human Development	M,D
Human Resources Management	M,D
Immunology	M,D
Industrial and Organizational Psychology	D
Industrial Design	M,D
Industrial/Management Engineering	M,D
Inorganic Chemistry	M,D
Interior Design	M,D
International Business	M
Japanese	M,D
Kinesiology and Movement Studies	M,D
Linguistics	M,D
Management Information Systems	M
Management of Technology	M,D
Marriage and Family Therapy	M,D
Materials Engineering	M,D
Mathematics Education	M,D,O
Mathematics	M,D
Mechanical Engineering	M,D,O
Medical Physics	M,D
Medicinal and Pharmaceutical Chemistry	D
Microbiology	M,D
Molecular Biology	M,D
Molecular Pharmacology	D
Natural Resources	M,D
Neurobiology	M,D
Neuroscience	D
Nuclear Engineering	M,D
Nursing—General	M,D,O
Nutrition	M,D
Organic Chemistry	M,D
Organizational Behavior	D
Pathobiology	M,D
Pathology	M,D
Pediatric Nursing	M,D,O
Pharmaceutical Administration	M,D,O
Pharmaceutical Sciences	M,D
Pharmacology	M,D
Pharmacy	D
Philosophy	M,D
Photography	M,D
Physical Chemistry	M,D
Physical Education	M,D
Physics	M,D
Physiology	M,D
Plant Pathology	M,D
Plant Physiology	M,D
Plant Sciences	D
Political Science	M,D
Psychology—General	D
Public Health—General	M,D
Reading Education	M,D,O
Recreation and Park Management	M,D
Science Education	M,D,O
Social Sciences Education	M,D,O
Sociology	M,D
Spanish	M,D
Special Education	M,D,O
Sport Psychology	M,D
Sports Management	M,D
Statistics	M,D
Systems Biology	D
Theater	M
Toxicology	M,D
Travel and Tourism	M,D
Veterinary Medicine	D
Veterinary Sciences	M,D
Virology	M,D
Vocational and Technical Education	M,D,O
Writing	M,D

PURDUE UNIVERSITY GLOBAL

Business Administration and Management—General	M
Computer and Information Systems Security	M
Criminal Justice and Criminology	M
Education—General	M
Educational Leadership and Administration	M
Educational Media/Instructional Technology	M
Entrepreneurship	M
Finance and Banking	M
Health Services Management and Hospital Administration	M,O
Higher Education	M
Human Resources Management	M
International Business	M
Law	M
Legal and Justice Studies	M,O
Logistics	M
Management Information Systems	M
Marketing	M
Mathematics Education	M
Nursing and Healthcare Administration	M
Nursing Education	M
Nursing—General	M
Organizational Management	M
Political Science	M,O
Project Management	M
Reading Education	M
Science Education	M
Secondary Education	M
Special Education	M
Student Affairs	M
Supply Chain Management	M

PURDUE UNIVERSITY NORTHWEST

Accounting	M
Acute Care/Critical Care Nursing	M
Adult Nursing	M
Biological and Biomedical Sciences—General	M
Biotechnology	M
Business Administration and Management—General	M
Child and Family Studies	M
Child Development	M
Communication—General	M
Computer Engineering	M
Computer Science	M
Counseling Psychology	M
Counselor Education	M
Education—General	M
Educational Leadership and Administration	M
Educational Media/Instructional Technology	M
Electrical Engineering	M
Engineering and Applied Sciences—General	M
English	M
Family Nurse Practitioner Studies	M
History	M
Human Services	M
Marriage and Family Therapy	M
Mathematics Education	M
Mathematics	M
Mechanical Engineering	M
Nursing and Healthcare Administration	M
Nursing—General	M
School Psychology	M
Science Education	M
Special Education	M

QUEENS COLLEGE OF THE CITY UNIVERSITY OF NEW YORK

Accounting	M
Applied Behavior Analysis	M
Applied Mathematics	M
Applied Social Research	M
Archives/Archival Administration	M,O
Art Education	M,O
Art History	M
Art/Fine Arts	M
Biological and Biomedical Sciences—General	M,O
Chemistry	M
Child and Family Studies	M,O
Communication Disorders	M,O
Computer Science	M
Counseling Psychology	M,O
Counselor Education	M,O
Data Science/Data Analytics	M
Early Childhood Education	M,O
Education—General	M,O
Educational Leadership and Administration	M,O
Elementary Education	M,O
English as a Second Language	M,O
English Education	M,O
English	M
Environmental Sciences	M
Exercise and Sports Science	M,O
Family and Consumer Sciences-General	M,O
Finance and Banking	M
Foreign Languages Education	M,O
French	M
Geology	M
Geosciences	M
Hispanic and Latin American Languages	M
History	M
Information Studies	M,O
Italian	M
Liberal Studies	M
Library Science	M,O
Linguistics	M,O
Mathematics Education	M,O
Mathematics	M
Media Studies	M
Middle School Education	M,O
Multilingual and Multicultural Education	M,O
Music Education	M,O
Music	M,O
Neuroscience	M
Nutrition	M,O
Photonics	M
Physical Education	M,O
Physics	M
Psychology—General	M
Reading Education	M,O
Risk Management	M
Romance Languages	M
School Psychology	M,O
Science Education	M,O
Secondary Education	M,O
Social Sciences Education	M,O
Sociology	M
Spanish	M
Special Education	M,O
Urban Studies	M
Writing	M

QUEEN'S UNIVERSITY AT KINGSTON

Allopathic Medicine	D
Anatomy	M,D
Biochemistry	M,D
Biological and Biomedical Sciences—General	M,D
Business Administration and Management—General	M
Canadian Studies	M,D
Cancer Biology/Oncology	M,D
Cardiovascular Sciences	M,D
Cell Biology	M,D
Chemical Engineering	M,D
Chemistry	M,D
Civil Engineering	M,D
Classics	M
Clinical Psychology	M,D
Cognitive Sciences	M,D
Communication—General	M,D
Computer Engineering	M,D
Computer Science	M,D
Developmental Psychology	M,D
Education—General	M,D
Electrical Engineering	M,D
Engineering and Applied Sciences—General	M,D
English	M,D
Entrepreneurship	M
Epidemiology	M,D
Exercise and Sports Science	M,D
Family Nurse Practitioner Studies	M,D,O
Finance and Banking	M,D
French	M,D
Gender Studies	M,D
Geography	M,D
Geology	M,D
German	M,D
Health Services Management and Hospital Administration	M,D
Hispanic Studies	M
Immunology	M,D
Industrial and Labor Relations	M
Information Studies	M,D
International Affairs	M,D
Law	M,D
Legal and Justice Studies	M,D
Marketing	M
Mathematics	M,D
Mechanical Engineering	M,D
Microbiology	M,D
Mineral/Mining Engineering	M,D
Molecular Biology	M,D
Molecular Medicine	M,D
Neurobiology	M,D
Neuroscience	M,D
Nursing—General	M,D,O
Occupational Therapy	M,D
Pathology	M,D
Pediatric Nursing	M,D,O
Pharmaceutical Sciences	M,D
Pharmacology	M,D
Philosophy	M,D
Physical Therapy	M,D
Physics	M,D
Physiology	M,D
Political Science	M,D
Project Management	M
Psychology—General	M,D
Public Health—General	M,D
Public Policy	M
Rehabilitation Sciences	M,D
Religion	M
Reproductive Biology	M,D
Social Psychology	M,D
Sociology	M,D
Spanish	M
Sport Psychology	M,D
Statistics	M,D
Theology	M,O
Toxicology	M,D
Urban and Regional Planning	M
Women's Health Nursing	M,D,O
Women's Studies	M,D

QUEENS UNIVERSITY OF CHARLOTTE

Business Administration and Management—General	M
Communication—General	M
Education—General	M
Educational Leadership and Administration	M
Elementary Education	M
Interior Design	M
Nursing and Healthcare Administration	M
Nursing Education	M
Nursing—General	M
Organizational Management	M
Reading Education	M
Writing	M

QUINCY UNIVERSITY

Business Administration and Management—General	M
Clinical Psychology	M
Counselor Education	M
Curriculum and Instruction	M
Education—General	M
Educational Leadership and Administration	M
English as a Second Language	M
Multilingual and Multicultural Education	M
Reading Education	M
School Psychology	M
Student Affairs	M

QUINNIPIAC UNIVERSITY

Accounting	M
Adult Nursing	D
Advertising and Public Relations	M
Allied Health—General	M
Allopathic Medicine	D
Anesthesiologist Assistant Studies	M
Biological and Biomedical Sciences—General	M
Broadcast Journalism	M
Business Administration and Management—General	M
Cardiovascular Sciences	M
Cell Biology	M
Communication—General	M
Community Health	D
Education—General	M,O
Educational Leadership and Administration	M,O
Educational Media/Instructional Technology	M
Elementary Education	M
English Education	M
Family Nurse Practitioner Studies	D
Film, Television, and Video Production	M
Finance and Banking	M
Foreign Languages Education	M
Health Physics/Radiological Health	M
Health Services Management and Hospital Administration	M
Internet and Interactive Multimedia	M
Journalism	M
Law	M,D
Mathematics Education	M
Molecular Biology	M
Nurse Anesthesia	D
Nursing and Healthcare Administration	D
Nursing—General	D
Organizational Management	M
Pathology	M
Perfusion	M
Physician Assistant Studies	M
Science Education	M
Secondary Education	M
Social Sciences Education	M
Social Work	M
Supply Chain Management	M

RABBINICAL ACADEMY MESIVTA RABBI CHAIM BERLIN

Theology	O

RABBINICAL COLLEGE BETH SHRAGA

Theology	

RABBINICAL COLLEGE BOBOVER YESHIVA B'NEI ZION

Theology	O

RABBINICAL COLLEGE OF LONG ISLAND

Theology	

RABBINICAL SEMINARY OF AMERICA

Theology	

RADFORD UNIVERSITY

Art/Fine Arts	M
Business Administration and Management—General	M
Clinical Psychology	M
Communication Disorders	M

Corporate and Organizational Communication	M
Counseling Psychology	D
Counselor Education	M
Criminal Justice and Criminology	M,O
Data Science/Data Analytics	M
Early Childhood Education	M
Educational Leadership and Administration	M
English	M
Experimental Psychology	M
Industrial and Organizational Psychology	M
Management Information Systems	M
Mathematics Education	M
Music	M
Nursing—General	D
Occupational Therapy	M
Physical Therapy	D
Psychology—General	M
Reading Education	M
School Psychology	O
Social Work	M
Special Education	M,O

RAMAPO COLLEGE OF NEW JERSEY

Accounting	M
Business Administration and Management—General	M
Educational Leadership and Administration	M
Educational Media/Instructional Technology	M
Family Nurse Practitioner Studies	M
Nursing and Healthcare Administration	M
Nursing Education	M
Nursing—General	M
Social Work	M
Special Education	M

RANDALL UNIVERSITY

Pastoral Ministry and Counseling	M

RANDOLPH COLLEGE

Curriculum and Instruction	M
Education—General	M
Special Education	M
Writing	M

RECONSTRUCTIONIST RABBINICAL COLLEGE

Jewish Studies	M,D,O
Theology	M,D,O
Women's Studies	M,D,O

REED COLLEGE

Liberal Studies	M

REFORMED EPISCOPAL SEMINARY

Theology	M

REFORMED PRESBYTERIAN THEOLOGICAL SEMINARY

Theology	M,D

REFORMED THEOLOGICAL SEMINARY–ATLANTA CAMPUS

Theology	M,D,O

REFORMED THEOLOGICAL SEMINARY–CHARLOTTE CAMPUS

Pastoral Ministry and Counseling	M,D
Religion	M,D
Theology	M,D

REFORMED THEOLOGICAL SEMINARY–DALLAS CAMPUS

Theology	M

REFORMED THEOLOGICAL SEMINARY–HOUSTON CAMPUS

Religion	M

REFORMED THEOLOGICAL SEMINARY–JACKSON CAMPUS

Marriage and Family Therapy	M,D,O
Missions and Missiology	M,D,O
Pastoral Ministry and Counseling	M,D,O
Religion	M,D,O
Religious Education	M,D,O
Theology	M,D,O

REFORMED THEOLOGICAL SEMINARY–ORLANDO CAMPUS

Pastoral Ministry and Counseling	M,D,O
Theology	M,D,O

REFORMED THEOLOGICAL SEMINARY–WASHINGTON D.C.

Religion	M
Theology	M

REGENT COLLEGE

Theology	M,O

REGENT'S UNIVERSITY LONDON

Business Administration and Management—General	M
Finance and Banking	M
Human Resources Management	M
International Affairs	M
International Business	M
Management Information Systems	M
Marketing	M

REGENT UNIVERSITY

Accounting	M,D,O
Addictions/Substance Abuse Counseling	M,D,O
Adult Education	M,D,O
American Studies	M
Business Administration and Management—General	M,D,O
Business Analytics	M,D,O
Clinical Psychology	M,D,O
Communication—General	M,D
Computer and Information Systems Security	M
Conflict Resolution and Mediation/Peace Studies	M,D
Corporate and Organizational Communication	M,D
Counseling Psychology	M,D,O
Counselor Education	M,D,O
Criminal Justice and Criminology	M,D,O
Cultural Studies	M,D
Curriculum and Instruction	M,D,O
Distance Education Development	M,D,O
Early Childhood Education	M,D,O
Economics	M,D,O
Education of the Gifted	M,D,O
Education—General	M,D,O
Educational Leadership and Administration	M,D,O
Educational Media/Instructional Technology	M,D,O
Educational Psychology	M,D,O
Elementary Education	M,D,O
Emergency Management	M
English as a Second Language	M,D,O
Entrepreneurship	M,D,O
Film, Television, and Video Production	M,D
Finance and Banking	M,D,O
Health Services Management and Hospital Administration	M,D,O
Higher Education	M,D,O
Homeland Security	M
Human Resources Development	M,D,O
Human Resources Management	M,D,O
Human Services	M,D,O
Interdisciplinary Studies	M,D,O
International Affairs	M
Investment Management	M,D,O
Journalism	M,D
Law	M,D
Legal and Justice Studies	M,D
Management Strategy and Policy	M,D,O
Marketing	M,D,O
Marriage and Family Therapy	M,D,O
Mathematics	M,D,O
Missions and Missiology	M,D
National Security	M,D
Nonprofit Management	M,D,O
Organizational Management	M,D,O
Pastoral Ministry and Counseling	M,D,O
Political Science	M
Public Administration	M
Public Policy	M
Reading Education	M,D,O
Religion	M,D
Religious Education	M,D,O
Science Education	M,D,O
Special Education	M,D,O
Student Affairs	M,D,O
Theater	M,D
Theology	M,D
Writing	M,D

REGIS COLLEGE (CANADA)

Pastoral Ministry and Counseling	M,D,O
Philosophy	M,D,O
Theology	M,D,O

REGIS COLLEGE (MA)

Applied Behavior Analysis	M,D,O
Biotechnology	M
Corporate and Organizational Communication	M
Counseling Psychology	M,D,O
Education—General	M,D
Educational Leadership and Administration	M,D
Elementary Education	M,D
Family Nurse Practitioner Studies	M,D,O
Health Services Management and Hospital Administration	M,D,O
Higher Education	M,D
Nursing Education	M,D,O
Nursing—General	M,D,O
Occupational Therapy	M,D,O
Quality Management	M
Special Education	M,D

REGIS UNIVERSITY

Accounting	M,O
Allied Health—General	M,D,O
Biological and Biomedical Sciences—General	M
Business Education	M,O
Computer and Information Systems Security	M,O
Computer Science	M,O
Counselor Education	M,D,O
Criminal Justice and Criminology	M,O
Curriculum and Instruction	M,O
Data Science/Data Analytics	M,O
Developmental Psychology	M,D,O
Economics	M,O
Education—General	M
Educational Leadership and Administration	M,O
Elementary Education	M,O
Environmental Biology	M
Finance and Banking	M,O
Health Informatics	M,O
Health Services Management and Hospital Administration	M,D,O
Human Resources Management	M,O
Industrial and Manufacturing Management	M,O
Information Science	M,O
Management Information Systems	M,O
Management Strategy and Policy	M,O
Marketing	M,O
Marriage and Family Therapy	M,D,O
Maternal and Child/Neonatal Nursing	M,D,O
Medical Informatics	M,O
Nonprofit Management	M,O
Nursing and Healthcare Administration	M,D,O
Nursing Education	M,D,O
Occupational Therapy	M,D,O
Organizational Management	M,O
Pharmacy	M,D,O
Physical Therapy	M,D,O
Project Management	M,O
Reading Education	M,O
Secondary Education	M,O
Software Engineering	M,O
Special Education	M,O
Systems Engineering	M,O
Writing	M,O

REINHARDT UNIVERSITY

Business Administration and Management—General	M
Early Childhood Education	M
Education—General	M
Public Administration	M
Writing	M

RELAY GRADUATE SCHOOL OF EDUCATION

Education—General	M

RENSSELAER AT HARTFORD

Business Administration and Management—General	M
Computer Engineering	M
Computer Science	M
Electrical Engineering	M
Engineering and Applied Sciences—General	M
Information Science	M
Mechanical Engineering	M
Systems Science	M

RENSSELAER POLYTECHNIC INSTITUTE

Acoustics	D
Aerospace/Aeronautical Engineering	M,D
Applied Mathematics	M
Architecture	M
Art/Fine Arts	D
Astronomy	M
Biochemistry	M,D
Biological and Biomedical Sciences—General	M,D
Biomedical Engineering	M,D
Biophysics	M,D
Business Administration and Management—General	M,D
Business Analytics	M
Chemical Engineering	M,D
Chemistry	M,D
Civil Engineering	M,D
Cognitive Sciences	D
Computer Art and Design	D
Computer Engineering	M,D
Computer Science	M,D
Electrical Engineering	M,D
Engineering and Applied Sciences—General	M,D
Engineering Physics	M,D
Entrepreneurship	M
Environmental Engineering	M,D
Financial Engineering	M
Geology	M,D
History of Science and Technology	M,D
Industrial/Management Engineering	M,D
Information Science	M
Interdisciplinary Studies	M,D
Lighting Design	M,D
Materials Engineering	M,D
Mathematics	M,D
Mechanical Engineering	M,D
Nuclear Engineering	M,D
Physics	M,D
Rhetoric	M,D
Speech and Interpersonal Communication	M,D
Supply Chain Management	M
Systems Engineering	M,D
Technology and Public Policy	M,D
Transportation and Highway Engineering	M,D

RESEARCH COLLEGE OF NURSING

Adult Nursing	M
Family Nurse Practitioner Studies	M
Gerontological Nursing	M
Nursing and Healthcare Administration	M
Nursing—General	M

RESURRECTION UNIVERSITY

Nursing—General	M

RHODE ISLAND COLLEGE

Accounting	M,O
Art Education	M
Art/Fine Arts	M
Arts Administration	M
Biological and Biomedical Sciences—General	M,O
Counseling Psychology	M,O
Counselor Education	M,O
Early Childhood Education	M
Education—General	D
Educational Leadership and Administration	M,O
Elementary Education	M
English as a Second Language	M
English Education	M
English	M,O
Finance and Banking	M,O
Foreign Languages Education	M
Health Education	M,O
Health Psychology	M,O
Health Services Management and Hospital Administration	M
History	M
Legal and Justice Studies	M
Mathematics Education	M
Mathematics	M,O
Music Education	M
Nursing—General	M,D
Physical Education	M,O
Psychology—General	M,O
Public Administration	M
Reading Education	M
School Psychology	M,O
Secondary Education	M
Social Sciences Education	M
Social Work	M
Special Education	M,O
Writing	M,O

RHODE ISLAND SCHOOL OF DESIGN

Applied Arts and Design—General	M
Architecture	M
Art Education	M
Art/Fine Arts	M
Computer Art and Design	M
Graphic Design	M
Industrial Design	M
Interior Design	M
Landscape Architecture	M
Media Studies	M
Photography	M
Textile Design	M

RHODES COLLEGE

Accounting	M

RICE UNIVERSITY

African Studies	D
American Studies	D
Anthropology	M,D
Applied Mathematics	M,D
Applied Physics	M,D
Archaeology	M,D
Architecture	M,D
Art History	D
Astronomy	M,D
Biochemistry	M,D
Bioengineering	M,D
Bioinformatics	M,D
Biomedical Engineering	M,D
Biostatistics	M,D
Business Administration and Management—General	M
Cell Biology	M,D
Chemical Engineering	M,D
Chemistry	M,D
Civil Engineering	M,D
Cognitive Sciences	M,D
Computational Sciences	M,D
Computer Engineering	M,D
Computer Science	M,D
Cultural Anthropology	M,D
Ecology	M,D
Economics	M,D
Education—General	M
Electrical Engineering	M,D
Energy Management and Policy	M,D
Engineering and Applied Sciences—General	M,D
English	M,D
Environmental Engineering	M,D
Environmental Management and Policy	M
Environmental Sciences	M,D
Evolutionary Biology	M,D
Geophysics	M
Geosciences	M,D
Health Services Management and Hospital Administration	M
History	M,D
Industrial and Organizational Psychology	M,D
Inorganic Chemistry	M,D
Jewish Studies	D
Liberal Studies	M
Linguistics	M,D
Materials Sciences	M,D
Mathematical and Computational Finance	M,D
Mathematics	D
Mechanical Engineering	M,D
Music	M,D
Near and Middle Eastern Studies	D
Organic Chemistry	M,D
Philosophy	M,D
Physical Chemistry	M,D
Physics	M,D
Political Science	D
Psychology—General	M,D
Religion	D
Science Education	M,D
Sociology	D
Statistics	M,D
Urban Design	M,D

RICHMOND, THE AMERICAN INTERNATIONAL UNIVERSITY IN LONDON

Art History	M
International Affairs	M

RICHMONT GRADUATE UNIVERSITY

Clinical Psychology	M
Counselor Education	M
Marriage and Family Therapy	M
Pastoral Ministry and Counseling	M,O

*M—masters degree; D—doctorate; O—other advanced degree; *—Close-Up and/or Display*

RIDER UNIVERSITY

Accounting	M,O
Addictions/Substance Abuse Counseling	M,O
Business Administration and Management—General	M
Clinical Psychology	M,O
Corporate and Organizational Communication	M
Counselor Education	M,O
Early Childhood Education	M
Education—General	M,O
Elementary Education	M
English as a Second Language	M
Finance and Banking	M
Foreign Languages Education	M
Health Communication	M
Higher Education	M
Homeland Security	M
Multilingual and Multicultural Education	M
Music Education	M
Music	M
Organizational Management	M
School Psychology	O
Secondary Education	M
Special Education	M,O

RIVIER UNIVERSITY

Business Administration and Management—General	M
Clinical Psychology	M
Computer Science	M
Counseling Psychology	M,D,O
Counselor Education	M,D,O
Curriculum and Instruction	M,D,O
Early Childhood Education	M,D,O
Education—General	M,D,O
Educational Leadership and Administration	M,D,O
Elementary Education	M,D,O
English	M
Experimental Psychology	M
Family Nurse Practitioner Studies	M,D
Foreign Languages Education	M
Management Information Systems	M
Mathematics	M
Nursing and Healthcare Administration	M,D
Nursing Education	M,D
Nursing—General	M,D
Psychiatric Nursing	M,D
Psychology—General	M
Public Health—General	M,D
Reading Education	M,D,O
Social Sciences Education	M
Special Education	M,D,O
Writing	M

THE ROBERT E. WEBBER INSTITUTE FOR WORSHIP STUDIES

Religion	M,D

ROBERT MORRIS UNIVERSITY

Business Administration and Management—General	M
Business Education	M,D,O
Computer and Information Systems Security	M,D
Counseling Psychology	M,D,O
Data Science/Data Analytics	M,D
Education—General	M,D,O
Educational Leadership and Administration	M,D,O
Engineering and Applied Sciences—General	M
Engineering Management	M
Higher Education	M,D,O
Human Resources Management	M
Information Science	M,D
Internet and Interactive Multimedia	M,D
Management Information Systems	M,D
Nursing—General	M,D
Organizational Management	M,D
Project Management	M,D
Reading Education	M,D,O
Special Education	M,D,O
Taxation	M

ROBERT MORRIS UNIVERSITY ILLINOIS

Accounting	M
Business Administration and Management—General	M
Business Analytics	M
Computer and Information Systems Security	M
Criminal Justice and Criminology	M
Educational Leadership and Administration	M
Finance and Banking	M
Health Services Management and Hospital Administration	M
Higher Education	M
Human Resources Management	M
Management Information Systems	M
Sports Management	M

ROBERTS WESLEYAN COLLEGE

Business Administration and Management—General	M
Child and Family Studies	M
Clinical Psychology	M,D
Counselor Education	M,D
Early Childhood Education	M
Education—General	M
Health Informatics	M
Health Services Management and Hospital Administration	M
Human Services	M
Management Strategy and Policy	M
Marketing	M
Middle School Education	M
Nursing and Healthcare Administration	M
Nursing Education	M
Nursing Informatics	M
Nursing—General	M
Psychology—General	M,D
Reading Education	M
School Psychology	M,D
Secondary Education	M
Social Work	M
Special Education	M

ROCHESTER COLLEGE

Missions and Missiology	M
Religious Education	M

ROCHESTER INSTITUTE OF TECHNOLOGY

Accounting	M
Applied Mathematics	M
Applied Statistics	M,O
Architecture	M
Art Education	M
Art/Fine Arts	M
Astrophysics	M,D
Bioinformatics	M
Biological and Biomedical Sciences—General	M
Business Administration and Management—General	M
Chemistry	M
Cognitive Sciences	O
Communication—General	M
Computer and Information Systems Security	M,O
Computer Art and Design	M
Computer Engineering	M
Computer Science	M,D
Criminal Justice and Criminology	M
Data Science/Data Analytics	O
Electrical Engineering	M
Engineering and Applied Sciences—General	M,D,O
Engineering Design	M
Engineering Management	M
Entrepreneurship	M
Environmental and Occupational Health	M
Environmental Sciences	M
Experimental Psychology	M
Film, Television, and Video Production	M
Finance and Banking	M
Game Design and Development	M
Graphic Design	M
Health Informatics	M
Health Services Management and Hospital Administration	M,O
Hospitality Management	M
Human Resources Development	M
Human-Computer Interaction	M
Industrial and Manufacturing Management	M
Industrial Design	M
Industrial/Management Engineering	M
Information Science	M,D
Interdisciplinary Studies	M
International Business	M
Internet and Interactive Multimedia	O
Management Information Systems	O
Manufacturing Engineering	M
Materials Engineering	M
Materials Sciences	M
Mathematical and Computational Finance	M
Mathematics	M,D,O
Mechanical Engineering	M
Media Studies	M
Medical Illustration	M
Modeling and Simulation	D
Occupational Therapy	M
Optical Sciences	M,D
Organizational Management	O
Photography	M
Project Management	O
Psychology—General	M,O
Public Policy	M
Safety Engineering	M
School Psychology	M,O
Secondary Education	M
Software Engineering	M
Special Education	M
Statistics	O
Sustainability Management	M,D
Sustainable Development	M,D
Systems Engineering	M,D
Technology and Public Policy	M
Telecommunications	M
Translation and Interpretation	M
Travel and Tourism	M

THE ROCKEFELLER UNIVERSITY

Biological and Biomedical Sciences—General	M,D*

ROCKFORD UNIVERSITY

Business Administration and Management—General	M
Early Childhood Education	M
Education—General	M
Educational Media/Instructional Technology	M
Elementary Education	M
Reading Education	M
Secondary Education	M
Special Education	M

ROCKHURST UNIVERSITY

Accounting	M,O
Business Administration and Management—General	M,O
Business Analytics	M,O
Communication Disorders	M
Data Science/Data Analytics	M,O
Education—General	M
Entrepreneurship	M,O
Finance and Banking	M,O
Health Services Management and Hospital Administration	M,O
Human Resources Development	M,O
International Business	M,O
Management Strategy and Policy	M,O
Nonprofit Management	M,O
Occupational Therapy	M
Physical Therapy	D

ROCKY MOUNTAIN COLLEGE

Accounting	M
Educational Leadership and Administration	M
Physician Assistant Studies	M

ROCKY MOUNTAIN COLLEGE OF ART + DESIGN

Art Education	M
Arts Administration	M
Internet and Interactive Multimedia	M

ROCKY MOUNTAIN UNIVERSITY OF HEALTH PROFESSIONS

Communication Disorders	D
Family Nurse Practitioner Studies	D
Occupational Therapy	D
Physical Therapy	D
Physician Assistant Studies	M
Physiology	D

ROCKY VISTA UNIVERSITY

Biological and Biomedical Sciences—General	M
Osteopathic Medicine	D
Physician Assistant Studies	M

ROGERS STATE UNIVERSITY

Business Administration and Management—General	M

ROGER WILLIAMS UNIVERSITY

Architectural History	M,O
Architecture	M,O
Art History	M,O
Business Administration and Management—General	M
Clinical Psychology	M
Computer and Information Systems Security	M
Criminal Justice and Criminology	M
Education—General	M,O
Forensic Psychology	M
Health Services Management and Hospital Administration	M
Historic Preservation	M,O
Law	M,D
Middle School Education	M,O
Public Administration	M
Reading Education	M,O
Urban and Regional Planning	M,O

ROLLINS COLLEGE

Applied Behavior Analysis	M
Business Administration and Management—General	M
Counselor Education	M
Education—General	M
Elementary Education	M
Entrepreneurship	M
Finance and Banking	M
Human Resources Development	M
Human Resources Management	M
International Business	M
Liberal Studies	M
Public Health—General	M

ROOSEVELT UNIVERSITY

Accounting	M
Actuarial Science	M
Arts Administration	M,O
Biotechnology	M
Business Administration and Management—General	M
Chemistry	M
Clinical Psychology	M
Communication—General	M
Computer Science	M
Corporate and Organizational Communication	M
Early Childhood Education	M
Economics	M
Education—General	M,D
Educational Leadership and Administration	M
Elementary Education	M
History	M
Hospitality Management	M
Human Resources Development	M
Human Resources Management	M
Humanities	M
Industrial and Organizational Psychology	M,D
Marketing	M
Mathematics	M
Music	M,O
Organizational Management	M
Pharmacy	D
Philosophy	M
Psychology—General	M,D
Reading Education	M
Real Estate	M
School Psychology	M
Secondary Education	M
Sociology	M
Special Education	M
Theater	M
Writing	M

ROSALIND FRANKLIN UNIVERSITY OF MEDICINE AND SCIENCE

Allied Health—General	M,D,O
Allopathic Medicine	D
Anatomy	D
Biochemistry	D
Biological and Biomedical Sciences—General	M,D
Biophysics	M,D
Cell Biology	D
Clinical Psychology	M,D
Health Education	M,D
Health Promotion	M
Health Services Management and Hospital Administration	M,O
Immunology	D
Interdisciplinary Studies	D
Microbiology	D
Molecular Biology	D
Molecular Pharmacology	M,D
Neuroscience	D
Nurse Anesthesia	D
Nutrition	M
Pathology	M
Pharmacy	D
Physical Therapy	M,D
Physician Assistant Studies	M
Physiology	M,D
Podiatric Medicine	D
Psychology—General	M,D

ROSE-HULMAN INSTITUTE OF TECHNOLOGY

Biomedical Engineering	M
Chemical Engineering	M
Civil Engineering	M
Computer Engineering	M
Electrical Engineering	M
Engineering and Applied Sciences—General	M
Engineering Management	M
Environmental Engineering	M
Management Information Systems	M
Mechanical Engineering	M
Optical Sciences	M
Software Engineering	M
Systems Engineering	M

ROSEMAN UNIVERSITY OF HEALTH SCIENCES

Business Administration and Management—General	M,O
Dentistry	M,D,O
Pharmacy	D

ROSEMONT COLLEGE

Business Administration and Management—General	M
Counseling Psychology	M
Counselor Education	M
Education—General	M
Elementary Education	M
Human Services	M
Publishing	M
Writing	M

ROWAN UNIVERSITY

Advertising and Public Relations	M
Allopathic Medicine	D
Applied Behavior Analysis	M,O
Arts Administration	M
Bioinformatics	M
Biological and Biomedical Sciences—General	M
Business Administration and Management—General	M,O
Chemical Engineering	M
Civil Engineering	M
Clinical Psychology	M,O
Computer and Information Systems Security	O
Computer Science	M
Corporate and Organizational Communication	O
Counselor Education	M
Criminal Justice and Criminology	M
Education—General	M,D,O
Educational Leadership and Administration	M,D,O
Educational Media/Instructional Technology	M,O
Electrical Engineering	M
Engineering and Applied Sciences—General	M
English as a Second Language	O
English Education	O
Exercise and Sports Science	M
Health Promotion	M
Higher Education	M
History	M,O
Library Science	M,D,O
Marketing	O
Mathematics Education	M,O
Mathematics	M
Mechanical Engineering	M
Media Studies	O
Middle School Education	O
Music	M
Nursing—General	M
Osteopathic Medicine	D
Pharmaceutical Sciences	M
Psychology—General	M,O
Publishing	O
Reading Education	M,O
Rhetoric	O
School Nursing	M,D,O
School Psychology	M,O
Science Education	M,O
Special Education	M,O
Theater	M
Writing	M,O

ROYAL MILITARY COLLEGE OF CANADA

Business Administration and Management—General	M
Chemical Engineering	M,D
Chemistry	M,D
Civil Engineering	M,D
Computer Engineering	M,D
Computer Science	M

Electrical Engineering	M,D
Engineering and Applied Sciences—General	M,D
Environmental Engineering	M,D
Environmental Sciences	M,D
Materials Sciences	M,D
Mathematics	M
Mechanical Engineering	M,D
Military and Defense Studies	M,D
Nuclear Engineering	M,D
Physics	M
Software Engineering	M,D

ROYAL ROADS UNIVERSITY

Conflict Resolution and Mediation/Peace Studies	M,O
Emergency Management	M,O
Environmental Education	M,O
Environmental Management and Policy	M,O
Legal and Justice Studies	M,O
Sustainability Management	M,O
Travel and Tourism	M,O

RUSH UNIVERSITY

Adult Nursing	D,O
Allopathic Medicine	D
Anatomy	M,D
Biochemistry	M,D
Cell Biology	M,D
Clinical Laboratory Sciences/Medical Technology	M
Communication Disorders	M,D
Community Health Nursing	D
Family Nurse Practitioner Studies	D
Gerontological Nursing	D,O
Health Services Management and Hospital Administration	M,D
Immunology	M,D
Maternal and Child/Neonatal Nursing	D,O
Medical Physics	M,D
Microbiology	M,D
Neuroscience	M,D
Nurse Anesthesia	D,O
Nursing and Healthcare Administration	M
Nursing—General	D
Nutrition	M
Occupational Therapy	D
Pediatric Nursing	D,O
Perfusion	M
Pharmaceutical Sciences	M,D
Pharmacology	M,D
Physical Therapy	M
Physician Assistant Studies	M
Physiology	D
Psychiatric Nursing	D
Virology	M,D

RUTGERS UNIVERSITY–CAMDEN

Applied Mathematics	M
Biological and Biomedical Sciences—General	M
Business Administration and Management—General	M
Chemistry	M
Child Development	M,D
Computational Biology	M,D
Computer Science	M
Criminal Justice and Criminology	M
Educational Leadership and Administration	M
Educational Policy	M
English	M
Family Nurse Practitioner Studies	D
Gerontological Nursing	D
Health Services Management and Hospital Administration	M,O
History	M
International Affairs	M
International Development	M
Law	D
Liberal Studies	M
Mathematics Education	M
Mathematics	M
Nursing—General	D
Physical Therapy	D
Psychology—General	M
Public Administration	M
Public Health—General	M,O
Public History	M
Public Policy	M
Writing	M

RUTGERS UNIVERSITY–NEWARK

Accounting	M,D
Adult Nursing	M,D,O
Allied Health—General	M,D,O
Allopathic Medicine	D
American Studies	M,D
Analytical Chemistry	M,D
Applied Physics	M,D
Biochemistry	M,D
Bioinformatics	M,D
Biological and Biomedical Sciences—General	M,D,O
Biomedical Engineering	O
Biopsychology	D
Business Administration and Management—General	M,D
Cancer Biology/Oncology	D,O
Cell Biology	D
Chemistry	M,D
Clinical Laboratory Sciences/Medical Technology	M
Clothing and Textiles	M
Cognitive Sciences	D
Computational Biology	M
Criminal Justice and Criminology	M,D
Dentistry	M,D,O
Developmental Biology	D,O
Economics	M,D
English	M
Environmental Sciences	M,D
Epidemiology	M,O
Family Nurse Practitioner Studies	M,D,O
Finance and Banking	M,D
Geology	M
Health Education	M,D
Health Physics/Radiological Health	M
Health Services Management and Hospital Administration	M,D,O
History	M
Human Resources Management	M,D
Immunology	D
Infectious Diseases	D,O
Inorganic Chemistry	M,D
International Affairs	M,D
International Business	D
Law	D
Logistics	M
Management Information Systems	M,D
Management of Technology	D
Marketing	D
Mathematics	D
Medical Imaging	M
Medical Informatics	M,D,O
Microbiology	D
Molecular Biology	M,D
Molecular Genetics	D
Molecular Medicine	D
Molecular Pathology	D
Music	M
Neuroscience	D
Nurse Anesthesia	M,D,O
Nursing Informatics	M
Nursing—General	M,D,O
Nutrition	M,D,O
Occupational Health Nursing	M,D,O
Oral and Dental Sciences	M,D,O
Organic Chemistry	M,D
Organizational Management	D
Pathology	D
Pharmaceutical Administration	M
Pharmacology	D
Physical Chemistry	M,D
Physical Therapy	D
Physician Assistant Studies	M
Physiology	D
Political Science	M
Psychology—General	D
Public Administration	M,D
Public Health—General	M,O
Public Policy	M,D,O
Quantitative Analysis	M,O
Real Estate	M
Rehabilitation Counseling	M,D
Social Psychology	D
Supply Chain Management	D
Transcultural Nursing	M,D,O
Urban Studies	M,D
Women's Health Nursing	M,D,O
Writing	M

RUTGERS UNIVERSITY–NEW BRUNSWICK

Aerospace/Aeronautical Engineering	M,D
African Studies	D
African-American Studies	D
Agricultural Economics and Agribusiness	M
Allopathic Medicine	D
Animal Sciences	M,D
Anthropology	M,D
Applied Arts and Design—General	M
Applied Mathematics	M,D
Applied Psychology	M,D
Applied Statistics	M,D
Art History	M,D,O
Art/Fine Arts	M
Asian Studies	M,D
Astronomy	M,D
Atmospheric Sciences	M,D
Biochemical Engineering	M,D
Biochemistry	M,D
Biological and Biomedical Sciences—General	M,D
Biomedical Engineering	M,D
Biopsychology	D
Biostatistics	M,D,O
Cancer Biology/Oncology	M,D
Cell Biology	M,D
Chemical Engineering	M,D
Chemistry	M,D
Civil Engineering	M,D
Classics	M,D
Clinical Laboratory Sciences/Medical Technology	M
Clinical Psychology	M,D
Cognitive Sciences	D
Communication—General	D
Comparative Literature	M,D
Computational Biology	D
Computer Engineering	M,D
Computer Science	M,D
Condensed Matter Physics	M,D
Counseling Psychology	M
Counselor Education	M
Developmental Biology	M,D
Developmental Education	M
Early Childhood Education	M,D
Ecology	M,D
Economics	M,D
Education—General	M,D
Educational Leadership and Administration	M,D
Educational Measurement and Evaluation	M
Educational Policy	D
Educational Psychology	M,D
Electrical Engineering	M,D
Elementary Education	M,D
Emergency Management	M,D,O
English as a Second Language	M,D
English Education	M
English	D
Entomology	M,D
Environmental and Occupational Health	M,D,O
Environmental Biology	M,D
Environmental Engineering	M,D
Environmental Sciences	M,D
Epidemiology	M,D,O
Evolutionary Biology	M,D
Food Science and Technology	M,D
Foreign Languages Education	M,D
Foundations and Philosophy of Education	M,D
French	M,D
Gender Studies	M,D
Genetics	M,D
Geography	M,D
Geology	M,D
German	M,D
Hazardous Materials Management	M,D
Health Education	M,D,O
Health Psychology	D
Health Services Management and Hospital Administration	M,D,O
Historic Preservation	M,D,O
History of Medicine	D
History of Science and Technology	D
History	D
Horticulture	M,D
Human Resources Management	M,D
Immunology	M,D
Industrial and Labor Relations	M,D
Industrial/Management Engineering	M,D
Information Science	M
Information Studies	M,D
Inorganic Chemistry	M,D
Interdisciplinary Studies	D
International Affairs	M,D
Italian	M,D
Jewish Studies	M,O
Legal and Justice Studies	M,D
Library Science	D
Linguistics	D
Marine Biology	M,D
Materials Engineering	M,D
Materials Sciences	M,D
Mathematics Education	M,D
Mathematics	M,D
Mechanical Engineering	M,D
Mechanics	M,D
Medical Microbiology	M,D
Medicinal and Pharmaceutical Chemistry	M,D
Medieval and Renaissance Studies	D
Microbiology	M,D
Molecular Biology	M,D
Molecular Biophysics	D
Molecular Genetics	M,D
Molecular Pharmacology	M,D
Molecular Physiology	M,D
Multilingual and Multicultural Education	M,D
Music Education	M,D,O
Music	M,D,O
Neuroscience	M,D
Nutrition	M,D
Oceanography	M,D
Operations Research	D
Organic Chemistry	M,D
Pharmaceutical Sciences	M,D
Pharmacy	M,D
Philosophy	D
Physical Chemistry	M,D
Physics	M,D
Physiology	M,D
Plant Biology	M,D
Plant Molecular Biology	M,D
Plant Pathology	M,D
Political Science	M,D
Psychology—General	D
Public Health—General	M,D
Public Policy	M,D
Quality Management	M,D
Reading Education	M,D
Religion	M,D
Reproductive Biology	M,D
School Psychology	M,D
Science Education	M,D
Social Psychology	D
Social Sciences Education	M,D
Social Work	M,D
Sociology	M,D
Spanish	M,D
Special Education	M,D
Statistics	M,D
Student Affairs	M
Systems Biology	D
Systems Engineering	M,D
Theater	M
Theoretical Physics	M,D
Toxicology	M,D
Translation and Interpretation	M,D
Translational Biology	M
Urban and Regional Planning	M,D
Virology	M,D
Water Resources	M,D
Women's Studies	M,D
Writing	M

RYERSON UNIVERSITY

Arts Administration	M
Business Administration and Management—General	M
Management of Technology	M

SACRED HEART MAJOR SEMINARY

Pastoral Ministry and Counseling	M
Theology	M

SACRED HEART SEMINARY AND SCHOOL OF THEOLOGY

Theology	M,O

SACRED HEART UNIVERSITY

Accounting	M,O
Applied Psychology	M
Business Administration and Management—General	M,O
Chemistry	M
Communication Disorders	M
Communication—General	M
Computer and Information Systems Security	M
Computer Science	M
Criminal Justice and Criminology	M
Education—General	M,O
Educational Leadership and Administration	O
Exercise and Sports Science	M
Family Nurse Practitioner Studies	M,D,O
Film, Television, and Video Production	M
Finance and Banking	M,D,O
Game Design and Development	M
Health Informatics	M
Human Resources Management	M,O
Industrial and Organizational Psychology	M
Information Science	M
Investment Management	M,D,O
Journalism	M
Marketing	M,O
Molecular Biology	M
Nursing and Healthcare Administration	M,D,O
Nursing Education	M,D,O
Nursing—General	M,D,O
Nutrition	M
Occupational Therapy	M
Physical Therapy	D
Physician Assistant Studies	M
Public Administration	M
Public Health—General	M
Reading Education	O
Social Psychology	M
Social Work	M

SAGE GRADUATE SCHOOL

Applied Behavior Analysis	M,O
Business Administration and Management—General	M
Counseling Psychology	M
Counselor Education	M,O
Education—General	M,D,O
Educational Leadership and Administration	D
Elementary Education	M
Family Nurse Practitioner Studies	M
Forensic Psychology	M,O
Gerontological Nursing	M,O
Gerontology	M
Health Education	M
Health Services Management and Hospital Administration	M
Nursing Education	D
Nursing—General	M,D,O
Nutrition	M,O
Occupational Therapy	M
Organizational Management	M
Physical Therapy	D
Psychiatric Nursing	M,O
Psychology—General	M,O
Reading Education	M
Social Psychology	M
Special Education	M

SAGINAW VALLEY STATE UNIVERSITY

Business Administration and Management—General	M
Chinese	M
Communication—General	M
Early Childhood Education	M
Education—General	M,O
Educational Leadership and Administration	M,O
Educational Media/Instructional Technology	M
Engineering and Applied Sciences—General	M
Family Nurse Practitioner Studies	M,D
Foreign Languages Education	M
Health Services Management and Hospital Administration	M
Media Studies	M
Nursing—General	M
Occupational Therapy	M
Public Administration	M
Reading Education	M
Social Work	M
Special Education	M

ST. AMBROSE UNIVERSITY

Accounting	M
Business Administration and Management—General	M,D
Communication Disorders	M
Criminal Justice and Criminology	M
Early Childhood Education	M
Education—General	M
Educational Leadership and Administration	M
Exercise and Sports Science	M
Health Services Management and Hospital Administration	M,D
Human Resources Management	M,D

*M—masters degree; D—doctorate; O—other advanced degree; *—Close-Up and/or Display*

Management of Technology	M
Occupational Therapy	D
Organizational Management	M
Pastoral Ministry and Counseling	M
Physical Therapy	D
Physician Assistant Studies	M
Public Health—General	M
Social Work	M

ST. ANDREW'S COLLEGE

Theology	M,D,O

ST. ANDREW'S COLLEGE IN WINNIPEG

Theology	M

SAINT ANTHONY COLLEGE OF NURSING

Nursing—General	M

ST. AUGUSTINE'S SEMINARY OF TORONTO

Pastoral Ministry and Counseling	M,O
Religious Education	M,O
Theology	M,O

ST. BERNARD'S SCHOOL OF THEOLOGY AND MINISTRY

Pastoral Ministry and Counseling	M,O
Theology	M,O

ST. BONAVENTURE UNIVERSITY

Accounting	M
Business Administration and Management—General	M
Corporate and Organizational Communication	M
Counseling Psychology	M,O
Counselor Education	M,O
Early Childhood Education	M
Education of the Gifted	M,O
Education—General	M,O
Educational Leadership and Administration	M,O
Marketing	M
Middle School Education	M
Reading Education	M
Rehabilitation Counseling	M,O
Secondary Education	M
Social Psychology	M,O
Special Education	M,O

ST. CATHERINE UNIVERSITY

Adult Nursing	M,D
Business Administration and Management—General	M
Curriculum and Instruction	M
Early Childhood Education	M
Education—General	M,O
Gerontological Nursing	M,D
Health Informatics	M
Health Services Management and Hospital Administration	M
Information Studies	M
International Health	M
Library Science	M
Marketing	M
Nursing Education	M,D
Nursing—General	M,D
Occupational Therapy	M,D
Organizational Management	M
Pastoral Ministry and Counseling	M,O
Pediatric Nursing	M,D
Physical Therapy	D
Physician Assistant Studies	M
Public Health—General	M
Social Work	M,D
Theology	M,O

SAINT CHARLES BORROMEO SEMINARY, OVERBROOK

Philosophy	M
Theology	M

ST. CLOUD STATE UNIVERSITY

Applied Behavior Analysis	M
Applied Economics	M
Archaeology	M,O
Biological and Biomedical Sciences—General	M
Biomedical Engineering	M,O
Child and Family Studies	M
Communication Disorders	M
Computer and Information Systems Security	M
Computer Science	M,O
Counselor Education	M
Criminal Justice and Criminology	M
Economics	M
Education—General	M,D,O
Educational Leadership and Administration	M,D
Educational Media/Instructional Technology	M,O
Electrical Engineering	M
Engineering and Applied Sciences—General	M,O
English	M
Geography	M,O
Higher Education	D
Historic Preservation	M,O
History	M
Industrial and Organizational Psychology	M
Marriage and Family Therapy	M
Mass Communication	M
Psychology—General	M,D
Rhetoric	M
Special Education	M,O
Student Affairs	M
Writing	M

ST. EDWARD'S UNIVERSITY

Accounting	M
Counseling Psychology	M
Education—General	M,O
Environmental Management and Policy	M
Humanities	M,O
Liberal Studies	M,O
Organizational Management	M
Student Affairs	M
Sustainable Development	M

ST. FRANCIS COLLEGE

Accounting	M

SAINT FRANCIS MEDICAL CENTER COLLEGE OF NURSING

Family Nurse Practitioner Studies	M,D,O
Gerontological Nursing	M,D,O
Maternal and Child/Neonatal Nursing	M,D,O
Medical/Surgical Nursing	M,D,O
Nursing and Healthcare Administration	M,D,O
Nursing Education	M,D,O
Nursing—General	M,D,O
Psychiatric Nursing	M,D,O

SAINT FRANCIS UNIVERSITY

Biological and Biomedical Sciences—General	M
Business Administration and Management—General	M
Cancer Biology/Oncology	M
Education—General	M
Educational Leadership and Administration	M
Health Education	M
Human Resources Management	M
Nursing and Healthcare Administration	M
Nursing Education	M
Nursing—General	M
Occupational Therapy	M
Physical Therapy	D
Physician Assistant Studies	M
Reading Education	M

ST. FRANCIS XAVIER UNIVERSITY

Adult Education	M
Biological and Biomedical Sciences—General	M
Chemistry	M
Computer Science	M
Cultural Studies	M
Curriculum and Instruction	M
Education—General	M
Educational Leadership and Administration	M
Geology	M
Geosciences	M
Urban and Regional Planning	M

ST. JOHN FISHER COLLEGE

Biological and Biomedical Sciences—General	M
Business Administration and Management—General	M
Chemistry	M
Counseling Psychology	M
Education—General	M,D,O
Educational Leadership and Administration	M,D
Educational Media/Instructional Technology	M
Elementary Education	M,O
English Education	M
Foreign Languages Education	M
French	M
Mathematics Education	M
Middle School Education	M
Nursing—General	M,D,O
Pharmacy	D
Physics	M
Reading Education	M
Science Education	M
Social Sciences Education	M
Special Education	M,O

ST. JOHN'S COLLEGE (MD)

Liberal Studies	M

ST. JOHN'S COLLEGE (NM)

Asian Languages	M
Asian Studies	M
Liberal Studies	M

ST. JOHN'S SEMINARY (CA)

Pastoral Ministry and Counseling	M
Theology	M

SAINT JOHN'S SEMINARY (MA)

Religion	M
Theology	M

SAINT JOHN'S UNIVERSITY (MN)

Music	M
Pastoral Ministry and Counseling	M
Theology	M

ST. JOHN'S UNIVERSITY (NY)

Accounting	M
Actuarial Science	M
Applied Mathematics	M
Asian Studies	M
Biological and Biomedical Sciences—General	M,D
Biotechnology	M
Business Administration and Management—General	M
Business Analytics	M
Chemistry	M
Clinical Psychology	M,D,O
Communication Disorders	M,D
Computational Sciences	M
Counseling Psychology	M,O
Counselor Education	M,O
Criminal Justice and Criminology	M
Curriculum and Instruction	D
Data Science/Data Analytics	M
Early Childhood Education	M,D,O
Education of the Gifted	D,O
Education—General	M,D,O
Educational Leadership and Administration	M,D,O
Elementary Education	M
English as a Second Language	M,O
English	M,D
Finance and Banking	M
History	M,D
Homeland Security	M
Information Science	
Information Studies	M,O
Insurance	M
International and Comparative Education	D
International Business	M
Law	D
Legal and Justice Studies	M
Liberal Studies	M
Library Science	M,O
Management Information Systems	M
Management Strategy and Policy	M
Marketing	M
Mass Communication	M
Mathematics Education	D
Mathematics	M
Multilingual and Multicultural Education	M,O
Museum Studies	M
Pharmaceutical Administration	M
Pharmaceutical Sciences	M,D
Pharmacy	M,D
Political Science	M,O
Psychology—General	M
Public Administration	M,O
Public Health—General	M
Public History	M,D
Reading Education	M,D,O
Risk Management	M
School Psychology	M,D
Science Education	D
Secondary Education	M
Sociology	M
Spanish	M
Special Education	M,O
Sports Management	M
Statistics	M
Taxation	M
Theology	M
Toxicology	M

ST. JOSEPH'S COLLEGE, LONG ISLAND CAMPUS

Accounting	M
Adult Nursing	M
Business Administration and Management—General	M
Early Childhood Education	M
Educational Leadership and Administration	M
Forensic Sciences	M
Gerontological Nursing	M
Health Informatics	M
Health Services Management and Hospital Administration	M
Human Resources Management	M
Human Services	M
Mathematics Education	M
Nursing Education	M
Nursing—General	M
Organizational Management	M
Reading Education	M
Special Education	M

ST. JOSEPH'S COLLEGE, NEW YORK

Accounting	M
Adult Nursing	M
Business Administration and Management—General	M
Education—General	M
Educational Leadership and Administration	M
Forensic Sciences	M
Gerontological Nursing	M
Health Informatics	M
Health Services Management and Hospital Administration	M
Human Resources Management	M
Human Services	M
Nursing Education	M
Nursing—General	M
Organizational Management	M
Reading Education	M
Special Education	M
Writing	M

SAINT JOSEPH'S COLLEGE OF MAINE

Accounting	M
Adult Education	M
Business Administration and Management—General	M
Education—General	M
Educational Leadership and Administration	M
Family Nurse Practitioner Studies	M,O
Health Education	M
Health Services Management and Hospital Administration	M
Nursing and Healthcare Administration	M,O
Nursing Education	M,O
Nursing—General	M,O
Pastoral Ministry and Counseling	M

ST. JOSEPH'S SEMINARY

Pastoral Ministry and Counseling	M
Religion	M
Theology	M

SAINT JOSEPH'S UNIVERSITY

Accounting	M,O
Biological and Biomedical Sciences—General	M
Business Administration and Management—General	M,O*
Business Analytics	M*
Communication Disorders	M,D,O
Computer Science	M,O
Criminal Justice and Criminology	M,O
Curriculum and Instruction	M,D,O
Early Childhood Education	M,D,O
Education—General	M,D,O
Educational Leadership and Administration	M,D,O
Elementary Education	M,D,O
Finance and Banking	M,O*
Health Informatics	M
Health Services Management and Hospital Administration	M,O
Human Resources Management	M,O
International Business	M,O
Law	M,O
Marketing	M,O*
Mathematics	M,O
Middle School Education	M,D,O
Psychology—General	M,O
Reading Education	M,D,O
Secondary Education	M,D,O
Special Education	M,D,O
Writing	M

ST. LAWRENCE UNIVERSITY

Counselor Education	M,O
Education—General	M,O
Educational Leadership and Administration	M,O
Human Development	M,O

SAINT LEO UNIVERSITY

Accounting	M,D
Agricultural Education	M
Business Administration and Management—General	M,D
Computer and Information Systems Security	M,D
Criminal Justice and Criminology	M,D
Data Science/Data Analytics	M,D
Education of the Gifted	M,O
Education—General	M,O
Educational Leadership and Administration	M,O
Educational Media/Instructional Technology	M,O
Emergency Management	M
Forensic Sciences	M
Health Services Management and Hospital Administration	M,D
Human Resources Management	M,D
Human Services	M
International Business	M,D
Legal and Justice Studies	M
Marketing Research	M,D
Marketing	M,D
Project Management	M,D
Reading Education	M,O
Social Work	M
Supply Chain Management	M,D
Theology	M,O
Writing	M

ST. LOUIS COLLEGE OF PHARMACY

Pharmacy	D

SAINT LOUIS UNIVERSITY

Accounting	M
Allied Health—General	M,D,O
Allopathic Medicine	D
American Studies	M,D
Anatomy	M,D
Applied Behavior Analysis	M,D
Athletic Training and Sports Medicine	M,D
Biochemistry	D
Bioethics	D,O
Bioinformatics	M
Biological and Biomedical Sciences—General	M,D*
Biomedical Engineering	M,D
Business Administration and Management—General	M
Chemistry	M,D
Clinical Psychology	M,D
Communication Disorders	M
Communication—General	M
Community Health	M
Computational Biology	M
Computer Science	M
Criminal Justice and Criminology	M
Curriculum and Instruction	M,D
Dentistry	M
Education—General	M,D
Educational Leadership and Administration	M,D,O
Emergency Management	M
English	M,D
Experimental Psychology	M,D
Finance and Banking	M
Foundations and Philosophy of Education	M,D
French	M
Geophysics	M,D
Geosciences	M,D
Health Services Management and Hospital Administration	M,D
Higher Education	M,D,O
History	M,D
Immunology	D
Industrial and Organizational Psychology	M,D
International Business	M,D
Law	M,D
Mathematics	M,D
Meteorology	M,D
Microbiology	D
Molecular Biology	D
Nursing—General	M,D,O
Nutrition	M
Occupational Therapy	M
Oral and Dental Sciences	M
Pathology	D
Pharmacology	D
Philosophy	M,D
Physical Therapy	M,D

- Physician Assistant Studies M
- Physiology D
- Political Science M
- Psychology—General M,D
- Public Health—General M,D
- Social Work M,D
- Software Engineering M
- Spanish M
- Special Education M,D
- Student Affairs M,D,O
- Theology M,D
- Urban and Regional Planning M

SAINT LOUIS UNIVERSITY–MADRID CAMPUS
- English M
- Spanish M

SAINT MARTIN'S UNIVERSITY
- Business Administration and Management—General M
- Civil Engineering M
- Counseling Psychology M
- Education—General M
- Engineering Management M
- Mechanical Engineering M
- Social Psychology M

SAINT MARY-OF-THE-WOODS COLLEGE
- Art Therapy M,O
- Health Services Management and Hospital Administration M
- Management Strategy and Policy M
- Nonprofit Management M
- Nursing—General M
- Organizational Management M
- Therapies—Dance, Drama, and Music M

SAINT MARY'S COLLEGE
- Adult Nursing D
- Communication Disorders M
- Data Science/Data Analytics M
- Family Nurse Practitioner Studies D
- Gerontological Nursing D
- Nursing—General D

SAINT MARY'S COLLEGE OF CALIFORNIA
- Accounting M
- Business Administration and Management—General M
- Business Analytics M
- Conflict Resolution and Mediation/Peace Studies M
- Counselor Education M,O
- Dance M
- Early Childhood Education M
- Education—General M,D,O
- Educational Leadership and Administration M,D,O
- Exercise and Sports Science M
- Finance and Banking M
- Investment Management M
- Kinesiology and Movement Studies M
- Marriage and Family Therapy M,O
- Organizational Management M
- School Psychology M,O
- Special Education M
- Sports Management M
- Writing M

ST. MARY'S COLLEGE OF MARYLAND
- Education—General M

SAINT MARY SEMINARY AND GRADUATE SCHOOL OF THEOLOGY
- Theology M,D

ST. MARY'S SEMINARY AND UNIVERSITY
- Theology M,D,O

SAINT MARY'S UNIVERSITY (CANADA)
- Applied Psychology M,D
- Applied Science and Technology M
- Astronomy M,D
- Business Administration and Management—General M,D
- Canadian Studies M,O
- Criminal Justice and Criminology M
- Gender Studies M
- History M
- Industrial and Organizational Psychology M,D
- International Development M,O
- Philosophy M
- Psychology—General M,D
- Religion M
- Theology M
- Women's Studies M

ST. MARY'S UNIVERSITY (UNITED STATES)
- Business Administration and Management—General M
- Communication—General M
- Computer and Information Systems Security M,O
- Computer Engineering M
- Computer Science M
- Conflict Resolution and Mediation/Peace Studies M,O
- Counseling Psychology M
- Counselor Education D
- Criminal Justice and Criminology M
- Education—General M
- Educational Leadership and Administration M
- Electrical Engineering M
- Engineering Management M
- English M
- Environmental Law M
- Health Law M
- Homeland Security M,O
- Industrial and Organizational Psychology M
- Industrial/Management Engineering M
- Information Science M
- International Affairs M,O
- International Development M,O
- Law M,D
- Legal and Justice Studies M
- Public Administration M,O
- Software Engineering M,O
- Theology M

SAINT MARY'S UNIVERSITY OF MINNESOTA
- Accounting M
- Addictions/Substance Abuse Counseling M,O
- Business Administration and Management—General M,D
- Computer and Information Systems Security M
- Counseling Psychology M,D,O
- Data Science/Data Analytics M,O
- Education of the Gifted M,O
- Education—General M,O
- Educational Leadership and Administration M,D,O
- Educational Media/Instructional Technology M
- Elementary Education M
- Geographic Information Systems M,O
- Health Services Management and Hospital Administration M
- Human Development M
- Human Resources Management M
- International Development M
- Marriage and Family Therapy M
- Multilingual and Multicultural Education M,O
- Nurse Anesthesia M
- Organizational Management M
- Philanthropic Studies M
- Project Management M,O
- Public Administration M
- Reading Education M,O
- Religious Education M
- Secondary Education M
- Special Education M,O
- Telecommunications M

SAINT MEINRAD SCHOOL OF THEOLOGY
- Theology M

SAINT MICHAEL'S COLLEGE
- Art Education M,O
- Clinical Psychology M
- Education—General M,O
- Educational Leadership and Administration M,O
- English as a Second Language M,O
- Reading Education M,O
- Special Education M,O

ST. NORBERT COLLEGE
- Business Administration and Management—General M
- Health Services Management and Hospital Administration M
- Liberal Studies M
- Supply Chain Management M
- Theology M

ST. PATRICK'S SEMINARY & UNIVERSITY
- Theology M,O

SAINT PAUL SCHOOL OF THEOLOGY
- Theology M,D

SAINT PAUL UNIVERSITY
- Conflict Resolution and Mediation/Peace Studies M
- Counseling Psychology M
- Marriage and Family Therapy M
- Missions and Missiology M
- Pastoral Ministry and Counseling M,D,O
- Theology M,D,O

ST. PETER'S SEMINARY
- Theology M

SAINT PETER'S UNIVERSITY
- Accounting M
- Adult Nursing M,D,O
- Applied Behavior Analysis M,D,O
- Business Administration and Management—General M
- Counselor Education M,O
- Criminal Justice and Criminology M
- Data Science/Data Analytics M
- Education—General M,D,O
- Educational Leadership and Administration M,D
- Elementary Education M,O
- Finance and Banking M
- Health Services Management and Hospital Administration M
- Higher Education M,D
- Human Resources Management M
- International Business M
- Management Information Systems M
- Marketing M
- Mathematics Education M,D,O
- Middle School Education M,O
- Nursing and Healthcare Administration M,D,O
- Nursing—General M,D,O
- Public Administration M
- Reading Education M,O
- Risk Management M
- Secondary Education M,O
- Special Education M,O

SAINTS CYRIL AND METHODIUS SEMINARY
- Pastoral Ministry and Counseling M
- Religious Education M
- Theology M

ST. STEPHEN'S COLLEGE
- Pastoral Ministry and Counseling M,D
- Theology M,D

ST. THOMAS AQUINAS COLLEGE
- Business Administration and Management—General M
- Education—General M,O
- Educational Leadership and Administration M,O
- Elementary Education M,O
- Finance and Banking M
- Marketing M
- Middle School Education M,O
- Reading Education M,O
- Secondary Education M,O
- Special Education M,O

ST. THOMAS UNIVERSITY
- Accounting M,O
- Arts Administration M
- Business Administration and Management—General M,O
- Communication—General M,D,O
- Counseling Psychology M,O
- Counselor Education M,O
- Criminal Justice and Criminology M,O
- Education of the Gifted M,D,O
- Education—General M,D,O
- Educational Leadership and Administration M,D,O
- Educational Media/Instructional Technology M,D,O
- Elementary Education M,D,O
- English as a Second Language M,D,O
- Film, Television, and Video Production M
- Geosciences M,D,O
- Health Services Management and Hospital Administration M,O
- Hispanic Studies M,O
- Human Resources Management M,O
- International Business M,O
- Law M,D
- Marriage and Family Therapy M,O
- Pastoral Ministry and Counseling M,D,O
- Planetary and Space Sciences M,D,O
- Public Administration M,O
- Reading Education M,D,O
- Special Education M,D,O
- Sports Management M,O
- Taxation M,D
- Theology M,D,O

ST. TIKHON'S ORTHODOX THEOLOGICAL SEMINARY
- Theology M

SAINT VINCENT COLLEGE
- Business Administration and Management—General M
- Curriculum and Instruction M
- Education—General M
- Educational Leadership and Administration M
- Educational Media/Instructional Technology M
- Nurse Anesthesia M,D
- Special Education M

ST. VINCENT DE PAUL REGIONAL SEMINARY
- Theology M

SAINT VINCENT SEMINARY
- Pastoral Ministry and Counseling M
- Theology M

ST. VLADIMIR'S ORTHODOX THEOLOGICAL SEMINARY
- Theology M,D

SAINT XAVIER UNIVERSITY
- Business Administration and Management—General M,O
- Communication Disorders M
- Computer Science M
- Counselor Education M
- Curriculum and Instruction M
- Early Childhood Education M
- Education—General M
- Educational Leadership and Administration M
- Educational Media/Instructional Technology M
- Elementary Education M
- English as a Second Language M
- Finance and Banking M,O
- Foreign Languages Education M
- Health Services Management and Hospital Administration M,O
- Marketing M,O
- Music Education M
- Nursing—General M,O
- Project Management M,O
- Reading Education M
- Science Education M
- Secondary Education M
- Spanish M
- Special Education M

SALEM COLLEGE
- Art Education M
- Counselor Education M
- Education—General M
- Elementary Education M
- English as a Second Language M
- Middle School Education M
- Music M
- Reading Education M
- Secondary Education M
- Special Education M

SALEM INTERNATIONAL UNIVERSITY
- Business Administration and Management—General M
- Computer and Information Systems Security M
- Curriculum and Instruction M
- Education—General M
- Educational Leadership and Administration M
- International Business M

SALEM STATE UNIVERSITY
- Art Education M
- Business Administration and Management—General M
- Counseling Psychology M,O
- Counselor Education M
- Criminal Justice and Criminology M
- Early Childhood Education M
- Educational Leadership and Administration M
- Educational Media/Instructional Technology M
- Elementary Education M
- English as a Second Language M
- English M
- Geography M
- Gerontological Nursing M
- Higher Education M
- History M
- Mathematics Education M
- Mathematics M
- Middle School Education M
- Nursing and Healthcare Administration M
- Nursing Education M
- Nursing—General M
- Occupational Therapy M
- Physical Education M
- Psychology—General M,O
- Reading Education M
- Science Education M
- Secondary Education M
- Social Work M
- Spanish M
- Special Education M

SALISBURY UNIVERSITY
- American Studies M
- Athletic Training and Sports Medicine M
- Biological and Biomedical Sciences—General M
- Business Administration and Management—General M
- Conflict Resolution and Mediation/Peace Studies M
- Curriculum and Instruction M
- Educational Leadership and Administration M
- English as a Second Language M
- English M
- Family Nurse Practitioner Studies D
- Geographic Information Systems M
- History M
- Mathematics Education M
- Middle School Education M
- Nursing and Healthcare Administration M,D
- Nursing Education M
- Nursing—General M,D
- Physiology M
- Reading Education M,D
- Secondary Education M
- Social Work M

SALUS UNIVERSITY
- Communication Disorders M,D,O
- Occupational Therapy M,O
- Optometry D
- Physician Assistant Studies M
- Public Health—General M
- Rehabilitation Sciences M,O
- Special Education M,O
- Vision Sciences M,O

SALVE REGINA UNIVERSITY
- Addictions/Substance Abuse Counseling M,O
- Applied Behavior Analysis M,O
- Business Administration and Management—General M,O
- Business Education M,O
- Computer and Information Systems Security M,O
- Conflict Resolution and Mediation/Peace Studies M,D
- Counseling Psychology M,O
- Criminal Justice and Criminology M,O
- Educational Leadership and Administration O
- Entrepreneurship M
- Forensic Sciences M,O
- Health Services Management and Hospital Administration M,O
- Homeland Security M,O
- Human Resources Management M,O
- Humanities M,D
- International Affairs M,O
- Management Strategy and Policy M,O
- Nonprofit Management M,O
- Nursing—General D

*M—masters degree; D—doctorate; O—other advanced degree; *—Close-Up and/or Display*

Organizational Management	M,O
Rehabilitation Counseling	M,O
Religion	M,D
Writing	M

SAMFORD UNIVERSITY

Accounting	M
Athletic Training and Sports Medicine	M,D
Business Administration and Management—General	M
Communication Disorders	M,D
Education of the Gifted	M,D,O
Education—General	M,D,O
Educational Leadership and Administration	M,D,O
Educational Media/Instructional Technology	M,D,O
Elementary Education	M,D,O
Energy Management and Policy	M
Entrepreneurship	M
Environmental Management and Policy	M
Family Nurse Practitioner Studies	M,D
Finance and Banking	M
Health Informatics	M
Health Services Management and Hospital Administration	M
Law	M,D
Marketing	M
Music Education	M
Music	M
Nurse Anesthesia	M,D
Nursing and Healthcare Administration	M,D
Nursing Informatics	M,D
Nursing—General	M,D
Nutrition	M
Pharmacy	D
Physical Therapy	M,D
Public Health—General	M
Secondary Education	M,D,O
Social Work	M
Special Education	M,D,O
Theology	M,D

SAM HOUSTON STATE UNIVERSITY

Accounting	M
Agricultural Sciences—General	M
Allied Health—General	M
Biological and Biomedical Sciences—General	M
Business Administration and Management—General	M
Chemistry	M
Clinical Psychology	M,D,O
Communication—General	M
Computational Sciences	M,D
Computer and Information Systems Security	M,D
Computer Science	M,D
Counselor Education	M,D
Criminal Justice and Criminology	M,D
Curriculum and Instruction	M,D
Dance	M
Developmental Education	M,D
Education—General	M,D
Educational Leadership and Administration	M,D
English	M
Family and Consumer Sciences-General	M
Finance and Banking	M
Forensic Sciences	M,D
Geographic Information Systems	M,O
Higher Education	M,D
History	M
Homeland Security	M
Humanities	M,D,O
Information Science	M,D
Internet and Interactive Multimedia	M
Kinesiology and Movement Studies	M
Library Science	M
Mathematics	M
Music	M
Nutrition	M
Political Science	M
Project Management	M
Psychology—General	M,D,O
Public Administration	M
Publishing	M
Reading Education	M,D
School Psychology	M,D,O
Sociology	M
Spanish	M
Special Education	M,D
Sports Management	M
Statistics	M
Writing	M

SAMUEL MERRITT UNIVERSITY

Family Nurse Practitioner Studies	M,D,O
Nurse Anesthesia	M,D,O
Nursing and Healthcare Administration	M,D,O
Nursing—General	M,D,O
Occupational Therapy	D
Physical Therapy	D
Physician Assistant Studies	M
Podiatric Medicine	D

SAN DIEGO CHRISTIAN COLLEGE

Education—General	M
Organizational Management	M

SAN DIEGO STATE UNIVERSITY

Accounting	M
Advertising and Public Relations	M
Aerospace/Aeronautical Engineering	M,D
Anthropology	M
Applied Arts and Design—General	M
Applied Mathematics	M
Art History	M
Art/Fine Arts	M
Asian Studies	M
Astronomy	M
Biochemistry	M,D
Biological and Biomedical Sciences—General	M,D
Biometry	M
Biostatistics	M,D
Business Administration and Management—General	M
Cell Biology	M,D
Chemistry	M,D
Child and Family Studies	M
Child Development	M
Civil Engineering	M
Clinical Psychology	M,D
Communication Disorders	M,D
Communication—General	M
Computational Sciences	M,D
Computer Science	M
Counselor Education	M
Criminal Justice and Criminology	M
Curriculum and Instruction	M
Ecology	M,D
Economics	M
Education—General	M,D
Educational Leadership and Administration	M
Educational Media/Instructional Technology	M,D
Electrical Engineering	M
Elementary Education	M,D
Emergency Management	M,D
Emergency Medical Services	M,D
Engineering and Applied Sciences—General	M,D
Engineering Design	M,D
English as a Second Language	M,O
English	M
Entrepreneurship	M
Environmental and Occupational Health	M,D
Environmental Design	M
Epidemiology	M,D
Exercise and Sports Science	M
Film, Television, and Video Production	M
Finance and Banking	M
Gender Studies	O
Geography	M,D
Geology	M
Gerontology	M
Graphic Design	M
Health Physics/Radiological Health	M
Health Promotion	M,D
Health Psychology	M,D
Health Services Management and Hospital Administration	M,D
Higher Education	M
History	M
Human Resources Management	M
Industrial and Organizational Psychology	M,D
Interdisciplinary Studies	M
Interior Design	M
International Health	M,D
Internet and Interactive Multimedia	M
Kinesiology and Movement Studies	M
Latin American Studies	M
Liberal Studies	M
Linguistics	M,O
Management Information Systems	M
Marketing	M
Mathematics Education	M,D
Mathematics	M,D
Mechanical Engineering	M,D
Mechanics	M,D
Media Studies	M
Microbiology	M
Molecular Biology	M,D
Multilingual and Multicultural Education	M,D
Music Education	M
Music	M
Nursing—General	M
Nutrition	M
Pharmaceutical Administration	M
Philosophy	M
Physical Therapy	D
Physics	M
Political Science	M
Psychology—General	M,D
Public Administration	M
Public Health—General	M,D
Reading Education	M
Rehabilitation Counseling	M
Rhetoric	M
Romance Languages	M
School Psychology	M
Science Education	M,D
Secondary Education	M
Social Work	M
Sociology	M
Spanish	M
Special Education	M
Sports Management	M
Statistics	M
Telecommunications Management	M
Theater	M
Toxicology	M,D
Urban and Regional Planning	M
Western European Studies	M
Women's Studies	M
Writing	M

SANFORD BURNHAM PREBYS MEDICAL DISCOVERY INSTITUTE

Biological and Biomedical Sciences—General	D

SAN FRANCISCO ART INSTITUTE

Art History	M
Art/Fine Arts	M,O
Museum Studies	M

SAN FRANCISCO CONSERVATORY OF MUSIC

Music Education	M,O
Music	M,O

SAN FRANCISCO STATE UNIVERSITY

Accounting	M
Acute Care/Critical Care Nursing	M,O
Adult Education	M
Anthropology	M
Applied Arts and Design—General	M
Archaeology	M
Art/Fine Arts	M
Asian-American Studies	M
Astronomy	M
Biochemistry	M
Biological and Biomedical Sciences—General	M
Biotechnology	M
Business Administration and Management—General	M
Cell Biology	M
Chemistry	M
Chinese	M
Classics	M
Clinical Psychology	M,O
Communication Disorders	M
Community Health Nursing	M,O
Community Health	M
Comparative Literature	M
Computer Science	M
Criminal Justice and Criminology	M
Cultural Anthropology	M
Cultural Studies	M
Developmental Biology	M
Developmental Psychology	M,O
Early Childhood Education	M,D,O
Ecology	M
Economics	M
Education—General	M,D,O
Educational Leadership and Administration	M,D,O
Educational Media/Instructional Technology	M
Electrical Engineering	M
Elementary Education	M
Energy and Power Engineering	M
Engineering and Applied Sciences—General	M
English as a Second Language	M
English Education	M,O
English	M,O
Entrepreneurship	M
Environmental Management and Policy	M
Ethnic Studies	M
Family and Consumer Sciences-General	M
Family Nurse Practitioner Studies	M,O
Film, Television, and Video Production	M
Film, Television, and Video Theory and Criticism	M
Finance and Banking	M
French	M
Geographic Information Systems	M
Geography	M
Geosciences	M
German	M
Gerontology	M
Health Education	M
Health Services Management and Hospital Administration	M
History	M
Hospitality Management	M
Humanities	M
Industrial and Manufacturing Management	M
Industrial and Organizational Psychology	M,O
International Affairs	M
International Business	M
Italian	M
Japanese	M
Kinesiology and Movement Studies	M
Legal and Justice Studies	M
Leisure Studies	M
Liberal Studies	M
Linguistics	M
Management Information Systems	M
Marine Biology	M
Marine Sciences	M
Marketing	M
Marriage and Family Therapy	M
Mathematics Education	M,O
Mathematics	M
Media Studies	M
Microbiology	M
Molecular Biology	M
Museum Studies	M
Music Education	M
Music	M
Nonprofit Management	M
Nursing and Healthcare Administration	M,O
Nursing—General	M,O
Pediatric Nursing	M,O
Philosophy	M
Physical Therapy	D
Physics	M
Physiology	M
Political Science	M
Psychology—General	M,O
Public Administration	M
Public Health—General	M
Public Policy	M
Quantitative Analysis	M
Reading Education	M,O
Recreation and Park Management	M
School Psychology	M,O
Secondary Education	M,O
Social Psychology	M,O
Social Work	M
Spanish	M
Special Education	M,D,O
Speech and Interpersonal Communication	M
Sustainability Management	M
Theater	M
Travel and Tourism	M
Women's Health Nursing	M,O
Women's Studies	M
Writing	M

SAN FRANCISCO THEOLOGICAL SEMINARY

Theology	M,D

SAN IGNACIO UNIVERSITY

Business Administration and Management—General	M
Early Childhood Education	M
Education—General	M
Educational Leadership and Administration	M
Hospitality Management	M
Human Resources Management	M
International Business	M
Marketing	M
Special Education	M
Travel and Tourism	M

SAN JOAQUIN COLLEGE OF LAW

Law	D

SAN JOSE STATE UNIVERSITY

Accounting	M
Aerospace/Aeronautical Engineering	M
Anthropology	M
Art History	M
Athletic Training and Sports Medicine	M
Bioinformatics	M
Biological and Biomedical Sciences—General	M
Biomedical Engineering	M
Biotechnology	M
Business Administration and Management—General	M
Chemical Engineering	M
Chemistry	M
Child Development	M,D
Civil Engineering	M
Clinical Psychology	M
Communication Disorders	M,D
Communication—General	M
Computational Sciences	M
Computer and Information Systems Security	M
Computer Engineering	M
Computer Science	M
Counselor Education	M,D
Criminal Justice and Criminology	M
Curriculum and Instruction	M,D
Ecology	M
Economics	M
Education—General	M,D
Educational Leadership and Administration	M,D
Electrical Engineering	M
Elementary Education	M,D
Engineering and Applied Sciences—General	M
Engineering Management	M
English as a Second Language	M
English	M
Environmental Management and Policy	M
Ergonomics and Human Factors	M
Exercise and Sports Science	M
Experimental Psychology	M
Family Nurse Practitioner Studies	M
Geography	M
Geology	M
Hispanic Studies	M
History	M
Industrial and Organizational Psychology	M
Industrial/Management Engineering	M
Kinesiology and Movement Studies	M
Legal and Justice Studies	M
Library Science	M
Linguistics	M
Marine Sciences	M
Mass Communication	M
Materials Engineering	M
Mathematics Education	M
Mathematics	M
Mechanical Engineering	M
Media Studies	M
Meteorology	M
Molecular Biology	M
Music Education	M
Music	M
Nursing—General	M
Nutrition	M
Occupational Therapy	M
Philosophy	M
Photography	M
Physics	M
Physiology	M
Psychology—General	M
Public Administration	M
Public Health—General	M
Social Work	M
Sociology	M
Software Engineering	M
Spanish	M
Sports Management	M

Statistics M
Systems Engineering M
Taxation M
Transportation Management M
Writing M

SAN JUAN BAUTISTA SCHOOL OF MEDICINE
Allopathic Medicine M,D
Public Health—General M,D

THE SANS TECHNOLOGY INSTITUTE
Computer and Information Systems Security M

THE SANTA BARBARA AND VENTURA COLLEGES OF LAW–SANTA BARBARA
Law M,D
Legal and Justice Studies M,D

THE SANTA BARBARA AND VENTURA COLLEGES OF LAW–VENTURA
Law M,D
Legal and Justice Studies M,D

SANTA CLARA UNIVERSITY
Applied Mathematics M,D,O
Bioengineering M,D,O
Business Administration and Management—General M
Business Analytics M
Civil Engineering M,D,O
Computer Engineering M,D,O
Computer Science M,D,O
Counseling Psychology M,O
Counselor Education M,O
Education—General M,O
Educational Leadership and Administration M,O
Electrical Engineering M,D,O
Energy and Power Engineering M,D,O
Engineering and Applied Sciences—General M,D,O
Engineering Management M,D,O
Ethics M,D,O
Finance and Banking M,D,O
Intellectual Property Law M,D,O
Law M,D,O
Management Information Systems M
Mechanical Engineering M,D,O
Pastoral Ministry and Counseling M
Religion M,D,O
Software Engineering M,D,O
Supply Chain Management M
Theology M,D,O

SARAH LAWRENCE COLLEGE
Child Development M
Dance M
Education—General M
Genetic Counseling M
History M
Human Genetics M
Kinesiology and Movement Studies M
Public Health—General M
Theater M
Women's Studies M
Writing M

SAVANNAH COLLEGE OF ART AND DESIGN
Advertising and Public Relations M
Applied Arts and Design—General M
Architectural History M
Architecture M
Art History M
Art/Fine Arts M
Arts Administration M
Clothing and Textiles M
Computer Art and Design M
Film, Television, and Video Production M
Film, Television, and Video Theory and Criticism M
Game Design and Development M
Graphic Design M
Historic Preservation M
Illustration M
Industrial Design M
Interior Design M
Internet and Interactive Multimedia M
Media Studies M
Music M
Photography M
Sustainable Development M
Textile Design M
Theater M
Travel and Tourism M
Urban Design M
Writing M

SAVANNAH LAW SCHOOL
Law D

SAVANNAH STATE UNIVERSITY
Business Administration and Management—General M
Human Resources Management M
Marine Sciences M
Public Administration M
Social Work M
Urban and Regional Planning M
Urban Studies M

SAYBROOK UNIVERSITY
Clinical Psychology M
Counseling Psychology M
Health Psychology M,D
Marriage and Family Therapy M,D
Nutrition M,D,O
Organizational Behavior M,D
Organizational Management M,D
Psychology—General M,D
Sustainable Development M,D
Transpersonal and Humanistic Psychology M,D

SCHILLER INTERNATIONAL UNIVERSITY (GERMANY)
Business Administration and Management—General M
International Business M
Management Information Systems M

SCHILLER INTERNATIONAL UNIVERSITY
Business Administration and Management—General M
International Affairs M
International Business M

SCHILLER INTERNATIONAL UNIVERSITY (SPAIN)
Business Administration and Management—General M
International Business M

SCHILLER INTERNATIONAL UNIVERSITY (UNITED STATES)
Business Administration and Management—General M
Finance and Banking M
Hospitality Management M
International Business M
Management Information Systems M
Travel and Tourism M

SCHOOL OF ADVANCED AIR AND SPACE STUDIES
Military and Defense Studies M

SCHOOL OF ARCHITECTURE AT TALIESIN
Architecture M

SCHOOL OF THE ART INSTITUTE OF CHICAGO
Applied Arts and Design—General M
Architecture M
Art Education M
Art History M
Art Therapy M
Art/Fine Arts M
Arts Administration M
Arts Journalism M
Film, Television, and Video Production M
Graphic Design M
Historic Preservation M
Interior Design M
Journalism M
Materials Sciences M
Music M
Photography M
Textile Design M,O
Writing M,O

SCHOOL OF VISUAL ARTS (NY)
Applied Arts and Design—General M
Art Education M
Art History M
Art Therapy M
Art/Fine Arts M
Computer Art and Design M
Cultural Studies M
Film, Television, and Video Production M
Graphic Design M
Illustration M
Internet and Interactive Multimedia M
Photography M
Writing M

SCHREINER UNIVERSITY
Business Administration and Management—General M
Education—General M,O
Educational Leadership and Administration M,O
Ethics M

THE SCRIPPS RESEARCH INSTITUTE
Biological and Biomedical Sciences—General D
Chemistry D

SEATTLE INSTITUTE OF ORIENTAL MEDICINE
Acupuncture and Oriental Medicine M

SEATTLE PACIFIC UNIVERSITY
Adult Nursing M,O
Business Administration and Management—General M
Clinical Psychology D
Computer and Information Systems Security M
Counselor Education M,D,O
Data Science/Data Analytics M
Education—General D
Educational Leadership and Administration M,D,O
Educational Media/Instructional Technology M
English as a Second Language M
Family Nurse Practitioner Studies M,O
Gerontological Nursing M,O
Human Resources Management M
Industrial and Organizational Psychology M,D
Management Information Systems M
Marriage and Family Therapy M,O
Mathematics Education M
Nursing and Healthcare Administration M,O
Nursing Education M,O
Nursing Informatics M,O
Nursing—General M,O
Reading Education M
Religion M,O
Science Education M
Secondary Education M
Sustainability Management M
Theology M,O
Writing M

THE SEATTLE SCHOOL OF THEOLOGY AND PSYCHOLOGY
Counseling Psychology M
Psychology—General M
Religion M
Theology M

SEATTLE UNIVERSITY
Accounting M
Adult Education M,O
Arts Administration M
Business Administration and Management—General M,O
Computer Science M
Counselor Education M,O
Criminal Justice and Criminology M,O
Education—General M,D,O
Educational Leadership and Administration M,D,O
Engineering and Applied Sciences—General M
English as a Second Language M,O
Finance and Banking M,O
Forensic Sciences M,O
Health Law M,D
Law M,D
Marriage and Family Therapy M
Nursing—General D
Organizational Management M,O
Pastoral Ministry and Counseling M
Psychology—General M
Public Administration M
School Psychology M,O
Social Work M
Special Education M,O
Sports Management M
Theology M,D,O
Transpersonal and Humanistic Psychology M

SELMA UNIVERSITY
Pastoral Ministry and Counseling M
Religion M
Religious Education M

SEMINARY OF THE SOUTHWEST
Clinical Psychology M,O
Pastoral Ministry and Counseling M,O
Religion M,O
Theology M,O

SETON HALL UNIVERSITY
Accounting M,O
Adult Nursing M,D
Advertising and Public Relations M
Allied Health—General D
Allopathic Medicine D
Analytical Chemistry M,D
Asian Studies M
Athletic Training and Sports Medicine M
Biochemistry M,D
Biological and Biomedical Sciences—General M,D
Business Administration and Management—General M,O
Chemistry M,D
Communication Disorders M
Communication—General M
Corporate and Organizational Communication M
Counseling Psychology M,D
Counselor Education M,D
Education—General M,D,O
Educational Leadership and Administration D,O
Educational Measurement and Evaluation M,D,O
Educational Media/Instructional Technology M
English M
Entrepreneurship M,O
Experimental Psychology M
Finance and Banking M,O
Gerontological Nursing M,D
Health Law M,D
Health Services Management and Hospital Administration M,D
Higher Education D
History M
Inorganic Chemistry M,D
International Affairs M,O
International Business M,O
International Health M,O
Jewish Studies M,O
Law M,D
Management of Technology M,O
Marketing M,O
Marriage and Family Therapy M
Microbiology M,D
Molecular Biology M,D
Museum Studies M
Neuroscience M,D
Nonprofit Management M,O
Nursing and Healthcare Administration M,D
Nursing Education M,D
Nursing—General M,D
Occupational Therapy M
Organic Chemistry M,D
Pastoral Ministry and Counseling M,O
Pediatric Nursing M,D
Physical Chemistry M,D
Physical Therapy D
Physician Assistant Studies M
Psychology—General M,D
Public Administration M,O
Public Policy M,O
Religion M,O
School Nursing M,D
School Psychology M
Social Work M
Special Education M
Speech and Interpersonal Communication M
Sport Psychology M
Sports Management M,O
Student Affairs M
Supply Chain Management M,O
Taxation O
Theology M,O

SETON HILL UNIVERSITY
Accounting M
Art Therapy M
Business Administration and Management—General M
Educational Media/Instructional Technology M
Elementary Education M
Entrepreneurship M
Health Services Management and Hospital Administration M
Marriage and Family Therapy M
Middle School Education M
Oral and Dental Sciences M,O
Physician Assistant Studies M
Special Education M
Writing M

SHASTA BIBLE COLLEGE
Educational Leadership and Administration M
Pastoral Ministry and Counseling M
Religious Education M

SHAWNEE STATE UNIVERSITY
Curriculum and Instruction M
Education—General M
Occupational Therapy M

SHAW UNIVERSITY
Curriculum and Instruction M
Early Childhood Education M
Theology M

SHENANDOAH UNIVERSITY
Adult Nursing M,D,O
Allied Health—General M,D,O
Applied Behavior Analysis M
Athletic Training and Sports Medicine M,D,O
Business Administration and Management—General M,O
Early Childhood Education M,D,O
Education—General M,D,O
Educational Leadership and Administration M,D,O
Elementary Education M,D,O
Family Nurse Practitioner Studies M,D,O
Gerontological Nursing M,D,O
Health Education M,D,O
Health Services Management and Hospital Administration M,D,O
Middle School Education M,D,O
Music Education M,D,O
Music M,D,O
Nurse Midwifery M,D,O
Nursing and Healthcare Administration M,D,O
Nursing Education M,D,O
Nursing—General M,D,O
Pharmacy D
Physical Education M,D,O
Physical Therapy M,D,O
Physician Assistant Studies M,D,O
Psychiatric Nursing M,D,O
Public Health—General M,D,O
Reading Education M,D,O
Secondary Education M,D,O
Special Education M,D,O
Therapies—Dance, Drama, and Music M,D,O
Writing M,D,O

SHEPHERDS THEOLOGICAL SEMINARY
Pastoral Ministry and Counseling M
Theology M

SHEPHERD UNIVERSITY (WV)
Curriculum and Instruction M

SHERMAN COLLEGE OF CHIROPRACTIC
Chiropractic D

SHILOH UNIVERSITY
Pastoral Ministry and Counseling M,D
Theology M,D

SHIPPENSBURG UNIVERSITY OF PENNSYLVANIA
Biological and Biomedical Sciences—General M
Business Administration and Management—General M,D,O
Business Analytics M,D,O
Clinical Psychology M,D
Communication—General M
Computer and Information Systems Security M,O

*M—masters degree; D—doctorate; O—other advanced degree; *—Close-Up and/or Display*

Computer Science	M,O
Counselor Education	M,D
Criminal Justice and Criminology	M
Curriculum and Instruction	M
Early Childhood Education	M
Education—General	M,D
Educational Leadership and Administration	M,D
Elementary Education	M
Environmental Management and Policy	M
Finance and Banking	M,D,O
Foreign Languages Education	M
Geography	M
Health Services Management and Hospital Administration	M,D,O
Higher Education	M
History	M
Information Science	M,O
Logistics	M,D,O
Management Information Systems	M,D,O
Mathematics Education	M
Middle School Education	M
Organizational Management	M
Psychology—General	M
Public Administration	M
Public History	M
Reading Education	M
Science Education	M
Social Work	M
Sociology	M
Software Engineering	M,O
Special Education	M,D
Student Affairs	M,D
Supply Chain Management	M,D,O

SHORTER UNIVERSITY

Accounting	M
Business Administration and Management—General	M

SH'OR YOSHUV RABBINICAL COLLEGE

Theology	

SIENA COLLEGE

Accounting	M
Business Administration and Management—General	M

SIENA HEIGHTS UNIVERSITY

Clinical Psychology	M,O
Counseling Psychology	M,O
Early Childhood Education	M,O
Education—General	M,O
Educational Leadership and Administration	M,O
Elementary Education	M,O
Health Services Management and Hospital Administration	M,O
Higher Education	M,O
Organizational Management	M,O
Reading Education	M,O
Secondary Education	M,O
Special Education	M,O

SIERRA NEVADA COLLEGE

Education—General	M
Educational Leadership and Administration	M
Elementary Education	M
Secondary Education	M

SILVER LAKE COLLEGE OF THE HOLY FAMILY

Business Administration and Management—General	M
Education—General	M
Educational Leadership and Administration	M
Music	M

SIMMONS COLLEGE

Applied Behavior Analysis	M,D,O
Business Administration and Management—General	M
Communication—General	M
Cultural Studies	M
Education—General	M,D,O
Elementary Education	M,D,O
English	M
Family Nurse Practitioner Studies	M,D,O
Gender Studies	M,D
Health Education	M,D,O
Health Promotion	M,D,O
Health Services Management and Hospital Administration	M
History	M
Information Science	M,D,O
Library Science	M,D,O
Nonprofit Management	M
Nursing—General	M,D,O
Nutrition	M,D,O
Physical Therapy	M,D,O
Public Health—General	M
Public Policy	M
Reading Education	M,D,O
Social Work	M,D,O
Special Education	M,D,O
Writing	M,D,O

SIMON FRASER UNIVERSITY

Actuarial Science	M,D
Anthropology	M,D
Applied Mathematics	M,D
Archaeology	M,D
Art Education	M,D
Biochemistry	M,D,O
Bioinformatics	M,D,O
Biological and Biomedical Sciences—General	M,D,O
Biotechnology	M,D,O
Business Administration and Management—General	M,D,O
Chemistry	M,D
Communication—General	M,D
Comparative and Interdisciplinary Arts	M
Computational Sciences	M,D
Computer Science	M,D
Counselor Education	M
Criminal Justice and Criminology	M,D
Cultural Studies	D
Curriculum and Instruction	M,D
Economics	M,D
Education—General	M,D,O
Educational Leadership and Administration	M,D
Educational Media/Instructional Technology	M,D
Educational Psychology	M,D
Engineering and Applied Sciences—General	M,D
English as a Second Language	M
English Education	M,D
English	M,D
Entomology	M,D,O
Environmental Management and Policy	M,D,O
Finance and Banking	M,D,O
Fish, Game, and Wildlife Management	M,D,O
Foundations and Philosophy of Education	M,D
French	M
Gender Studies	M,D
Geography	M,D
Geosciences	M,D
Gerontology	M,D
History	M,D
Humanities	M
International Affairs	M
International Health	M,D,O
Kinesiology and Movement Studies	M,D
Latin American Studies	M,O
Legal and Justice Studies	M,D
Liberal Studies	M
Linguistics	M,D
Management of Technology	M,D,O
Mathematics Education	M,D
Mathematics	M,D
Mechanical Engineering	M,D
Molecular Biology	M,D,O
Operations Research	M,D
Philosophy	M,D
Physics	M,D
Political Science	M,D
Psychology—General	M,D
Public Health—General	M,D,O
Public Policy	M
Publishing	M
Reading Education	D
Sociology	M,D
Statistics	M,D
Systems Engineering	M,D
Toxicology	M,D,O
Urban Studies	M,D
Women's Studies	M,D

SIMPSON COLLEGE

Criminal Justice and Criminology	M
Education—General	M
Secondary Education	M

SIMPSON UNIVERSITY

Counseling Psychology	M
Curriculum and Instruction	M
Education—General	M
Educational Leadership and Administration	M
Missions and Missiology	M
Organizational Management	M
Pastoral Ministry and Counseling	M

SINTE GLESKA UNIVERSITY

Education—General	M
Elementary Education	M

SIOUX FALLS SEMINARY

Marriage and Family Therapy	M
Pastoral Ministry and Counseling	M
Religion	M
Theology	M,D,O

SIT GRADUATE INSTITUTE

Business Administration and Management—General	M
Conflict Resolution and Mediation/Peace Studies	M
Educational Leadership and Administration	M
Energy Management and Policy	M
English as a Second Language	M
Entrepreneurship	M
Environmental Management and Policy	M
International Affairs	M
International and Comparative Education	M
International Business	M
Meteorology	M
Organizational Management	M
Sustainability Management	M
Sustainable Development	M

SITTING BULL COLLEGE

Curriculum and Instruction	M
Environmental Sciences	M

SLIPPERY ROCK UNIVERSITY OF PENNSYLVANIA

Accounting	M
Business Administration and Management—General	M
Clinical Psychology	M
Counseling Psychology	M
Counselor Education	M
Criminal Justice and Criminology	M
Data Science/Data Analytics	M
Education—General	M,D
Educational Leadership and Administration	M,D
Educational Media/Instructional Technology	M,D
Elementary Education	M
English as a Second Language	M
English Education	M
English	M
Environmental Education	M
Environmental Management and Policy	M
Finance and Banking	M
Health Informatics	M
History	M
Marketing	M
Mathematics Education	M
Physical Education	M
Physical Therapy	D
Physician Assistant Studies	M
Public Health—General	M
Reading Education	M
Recreation and Park Management	M
School Psychology	M
Science Education	M
Secondary Education	M
Social Sciences Education	M
Special Education	M,D
Student Affairs	M
Therapies—Dance, Drama, and Music	M

SMITH COLLEGE

Biological and Biomedical Sciences—General	M
Chemistry	M
Dance	M
Education—General	M
Elementary Education	M
English Education	M
Exercise and Sports Science	M
History	M
Mathematics Education	M
Mathematics	O
Middle School Education	M
Science Education	M
Secondary Education	M
Social Sciences Education	M
Social Work	M,D
Theater	M
Women's Studies	O

SOFIA UNIVERSITY

Clinical Psychology	M,D
Computer Science	M,D
Counseling Psychology	M,D
Psychology—General	M,D
Transpersonal and Humanistic Psychology	M,D

SOKA UNIVERSITY OF AMERICA

Educational Leadership and Administration	M*

SONOMA STATE UNIVERSITY

Anthropology	M
Biochemistry	M
Biological and Biomedical Sciences—General	M
Business Administration and Management—General	M
Clinical Psychology	M
Counseling Psychology	M
Curriculum and Instruction	M,O
Early Childhood Education	M,O
Education—General	M,O
Educational Leadership and Administration	M,O
English	M
Exercise and Sports Science	M
Family Nurse Practitioner Studies	M
Health Promotion	M
History	M
Interdisciplinary Studies	M
Kinesiology and Movement Studies	M
Nursing—General	M
Occupational Therapy	M
Physical Therapy	M
Political Science	M
Public Administration	M
Public History	M
Reading Education	M,O
School Psychology	M
Special Education	M,O
Sports Management	M
Writing	M

SOTHEBY'S INSTITUTE OF ART–LONDON

Art/Fine Arts	M
Arts Administration	M
Decorative Arts	M

SOTHEBY'S INSTITUTE OF ART–NEW YORK

Art/Fine Arts	M
Arts Administration	M
Decorative Arts	M

SOUTH BAYLO UNIVERSITY

Acupuncture and Oriental Medicine	M

SOUTH CAROLINA STATE UNIVERSITY

Agricultural Economics and Agribusiness	M
Allied Health—General	M
Biological and Biomedical Sciences—General	M
Business Administration and Management—General	M
Business Education	M
Child and Family Studies	M
Civil Engineering	M
Communication Disorders	M
Counselor Education	M
Early Childhood Education	M
Education—General	M
Educational Leadership and Administration	D,O
Elementary Education	M
English Education	M
English	M
Entrepreneurship	M
Family and Consumer Sciences-General	M
Health Services Management and Hospital Administration	M
Home Economics Education	M
Human Services	M
Mathematics Education	M
Mathematics	M
Mechanical Engineering	M
Nutrition	M
Rehabilitation Counseling	M
Science Education	M
Secondary Education	M
Social Sciences Education	M
Special Education	M
Transportation and Highway Engineering	M
Vocational and Technical Education	M

SOUTH COLLEGE

Pharmacy	D
Physician Assistant Studies	M

SOUTH DAKOTA SCHOOL OF MINES AND TECHNOLOGY

Artificial Intelligence/Robotics	M
Atmospheric Sciences	M,D
Bioengineering	D
Biomedical Engineering	M,D
Chemical Engineering	M,D
Civil Engineering	M,D
Construction Management	M
Electrical Engineering	M
Engineering and Applied Sciences—General	M,D
Engineering Management	M
Environmental Sciences	D
Geological Engineering	M,D
Geology	M,D
Management of Technology	M
Materials Engineering	M,D
Materials Sciences	M,D
Mechanical Engineering	M,D
Mineral/Mining Engineering	M
Nanotechnology	D
Paleontology	M,D
Physics	M,D

SOUTH DAKOTA STATE UNIVERSITY

Agricultural Education	M
Agricultural Engineering	M,D
Agricultural Sciences—General	M,D
Agronomy and Soil Sciences	M,D
Animal Sciences	M,D
Athletic Training and Sports Medicine	M,D
Biological and Biomedical Sciences—General	M,D
Biosystems Engineering	M,D
Chemistry	M,D
Civil Engineering	M
Communication—General	M
Computational Sciences	M,D
Consumer Economics	M
Counselor Education	M
Curriculum and Instruction	M
Economics	M
Education—General	M,D
Educational Leadership and Administration	M
Electrical Engineering	M,D
Engineering and Applied Sciences—General	M,D
English	M
Exercise and Sports Science	M,D
Family and Consumer Sciences-General	M
Fish, Game, and Wildlife Management	M,D
Geography	M
Geosciences	D
Human Resources Development	M
Industrial and Organizational Psychology	M
Industrial/Management Engineering	M
Journalism	M
Mathematics	M,D
Mechanical Engineering	M,D
Microbiology	M,D
Nursing—General	M,D
Nutrition	M,D
Pharmaceutical Sciences	M,D
Pharmacy	D
Physics	M
Plant Sciences	M,D
Recreation and Park Management	M,D
Sociology	M,D
Statistics	M,D
Veterinary Sciences	M,D

SOUTHEASTERN BAPTIST THEOLOGICAL SEMINARY

Ethics	M,D
Missions and Missiology	M,D
Music	M,D
Philosophy	M,D
Psychology—General	M,D
Religious Education	M,D
Theology	M,D
Women's Studies	M,D

SOUTHEASTERN LOUISIANA UNIVERSITY

Advertising and Public Relations	M
Applied Science and Technology	M
Biological and Biomedical Sciences—General	M
Business Administration and Management—General	M

Communication Disorders	M
Communication—General	M
Counselor Education	M
Curriculum and Instruction	M
Education—General	M,D
Educational Leadership and Administration	M,D
Elementary Education	M
English Education	M
English	M
Health Communication	M
Health Education	M
History	M
Industrial and Organizational Psychology	M
Journalism	M
Kinesiology and Movement Studies	M
Marketing	M
Music	M
Nursing—General	M,D
Psychology—General	M
Reading Education	M
Sociology	M
Special Education	M
Sustainability Management	M
Writing	M

SOUTHEASTERN OKLAHOMA STATE UNIVERSITY

Aviation Management	M
Aviation	M
Biotechnology	M
Business Administration and Management—General	M
Clinical Psychology	M
Counseling Psychology	M
Counselor Education	M
Education—General	M
Educational Leadership and Administration	M
Environmental and Occupational Health	M
Management Information Systems	M
Mathematics Education	M
Reading Education	M

SOUTHEASTERN UNIVERSITY (FL)

Business Administration and Management—General	M,D
Counseling Psychology	M
Counselor Education	M
Curriculum and Instruction	M,D
Education of the Gifted	M,D
Education—General	M,D
Educational Leadership and Administration	M,D
Elementary Education	M,D
English as a Second Language	M,D
Entrepreneurship	M,D
Health Services Management and Hospital Administration	M,D
Human Services	M
International Business	M,D
Kinesiology and Movement Studies	M,D
Management Strategy and Policy	M,D
Marriage and Family Therapy	M
Organizational Management	M,D
Pastoral Ministry and Counseling	M,D
Reading Education	M,D
Social Work	M
Sports Management	M,D
Theology	M,D
Urban and Regional Planning	M

SOUTHEAST MISSOURI STATE UNIVERSITY

Accounting	M
Biological and Biomedical Sciences—General	M
Business Administration and Management—General	M
Chemistry	M
Communication Disorders	M
Counseling Psychology	M,O
Counselor Education	M,O
Criminal Justice and Criminology	M
Educational Leadership and Administration	M,D,O
Elementary Education	M,D,O
English as a Second Language	M
English	M
Entrepreneurship	M
Environmental Management and Policy	M
Environmental Sciences	M
Exercise and Sports Science	M
Finance and Banking	M
Higher Education	M,D,O
Historic Preservation	M,O
History	M,O
Leisure Studies	M
Management of Technology	M
Mathematics	M
Middle School Education	M
Nursing—General	M
Public Administration	M
Public History	M,O
Secondary Education	M,D,O
Special Education	M
Sports Management	M

SOUTHERN ADVENTIST UNIVERSITY

Accounting	M
Acute Care/Critical Care Nursing	M,D
Adult Nursing	M,D
Business Administration and Management—General	M
Counseling Psychology	M
Counselor Education	M
Education—General	M
Educational Leadership and Administration	M
Family Nurse Practitioner Studies	M,D
Finance and Banking	M
Gerontological Nursing	M,D
Health Services Management and Hospital Administration	M
Marketing	M
Missions and Missiology	M
Nursing Education	M,D
Nursing—General	M,D
Psychiatric Nursing	M,D
Psychology—General	M
Reading Education	M
Religion	M
Religious Education	M
Social Work	M
Theology	M

SOUTHERN ARKANSAS UNIVERSITY–MAGNOLIA

Adult Education	M
Agricultural Sciences—General	M
Business Administration and Management—General	M
Computer and Information Systems Security	M
Computer Science	M
Counselor Education	M
Curriculum and Instruction	M
Data Science/Data Analytics	M
Education of the Gifted	M
Education—General	M
Educational Leadership and Administration	M
Higher Education	M
Kinesiology and Movement Studies	M
Library Science	M
Organizational Management	M
Psychiatric Nursing	M
Public Administration	M
Student Affairs	M
Supply Chain Management	M

THE SOUTHERN BAPTIST THEOLOGICAL SEMINARY

Missions and Missiology	M,D
Pastoral Ministry and Counseling	M,D
Philosophy	M,D
Religion	M,D
Theology	M,D

SOUTHERN CALIFORNIA INSTITUTE OF ARCHITECTURE

Architecture	M*
Urban and Regional Planning	M
Urban Design	M

SOUTHERN CALIFORNIA SEMINARY

Counseling Psychology	M,D
Marriage and Family Therapy	M,D
Psychology—General	M,D
Religion	M,D
Theology	M,D

SOUTHERN CALIFORNIA UNIVERSITY OF HEALTH SCIENCES

Acupuncture and Oriental Medicine	M,D
Chiropractic	D

SOUTHERN COLLEGE OF OPTOMETRY

Optometry	D

SOUTHERN CONNECTICUT STATE UNIVERSITY

Art Education	M
Biological and Biomedical Sciences—General	M
Business Administration and Management—General	M
Chemistry	M
Communication Disorders	M
Computer Science	M
Counselor Education	M,O
Education—General	M,D,O
Educational Leadership and Administration	M,D,O
Educational Measurement and Evaluation	M,D,O
Elementary Education	M,O
English as a Second Language	M
English	M
Environmental Education	M,O
Environmental Sciences	M,O
Exercise and Sports Science	M
Family Nurse Practitioner Studies	M,D
Foreign Languages Education	M
Health Education	M
History	M
Information Studies	M,O
Leisure Studies	M
Library Science	M,O
Marine Sciences	M,O
Mathematics	M
Multilingual and Multicultural Education	M
Nursing Education	M,D
Nursing—General	M,D
Physical Education	M
Political Science	M
Psychology—General	M
Public Health—General	M
Reading Education	M,O
Recreation and Park Management	M
School Psychology	M,O
Science Education	M,O
Social Work	M
Sociology	M
Special Education	M
Women's Studies	M

SOUTHERN EVANGELICAL SEMINARY

Jewish Studies	M,D,O
Missions and Missiology	M,D,O
Near and Middle Eastern Studies	M,D,O
Pastoral Ministry and Counseling	M,D,O
Philosophy	M,D,O
Religion	M,D,O
Religious Education	M,D,O
Theology	M,D,O

SOUTHERN ILLINOIS UNIVERSITY CARBONDALE

Accounting	M,D
Agricultural Economics and Agribusiness	M
Agricultural Sciences—General	M
Agronomy and Soil Sciences	M
Animal Sciences	M
Anthropology	M,D
Applied Arts and Design—General	M
Applied Physics	M,D
Architecture	M
Art/Fine Arts	M
Biochemistry	M,D
Biological and Biomedical Sciences—General	M,D
Biomedical Engineering	M
Business Administration and Management—General	M,D
Chemistry	M,D
Civil Engineering	M,D
Clinical Psychology	M,D
Communication Disorders	M
Communication—General	M,D
Community Health	M
Computer Engineering	M,D
Computer Science	M,D
Counseling Psychology	M,D
Criminal Justice and Criminology	M,D
Cultural Studies	M,D
Curriculum and Instruction	M,D
Economics	M,D
Education—General	M,D
Educational Leadership and Administration	M,D
Educational Psychology	M,D
Electrical Engineering	M,D
Energy and Power Engineering	D
Engineering and Applied Sciences—General	M,D
Engineering Management	M
English as a Second Language	M
English	M,D
Environmental Engineering	D
Environmental Management and Policy	M,D
Environmental Sciences	D
Experimental Psychology	M,D
Forestry	M
Geography	M,D
Geology	M,D
Geosciences	M,D
Health Education	M,D
Health Law	M
Health Services Management and Hospital Administration	M
Higher Education	M
History	M,D
Homeland Security	M
Kinesiology and Movement Studies	M
Law	M,D
Legal and Justice Studies	M
Linguistics	M
Mass Communication	M,D
Mathematics	M,D
Mechanical Engineering	M,D
Mechanics	M
Media Studies	M,D
Medical Physics	M
Microbiology	M,D
Mineral/Mining Engineering	M,D
Molecular Biology	M,D
Music	M
Nutrition	M
Pharmacology	M,D
Philosophy	M,D
Physical Education	M
Physician Assistant Studies	M
Physics	M,D
Physiology	M,D
Plant Biology	M,D
Plant Sciences	M
Political Science	M,D
Psychology—General	M,D
Public Administration	M
Recreation and Park Management	M
Rhetoric	M,D
Social Work	M
Sociology	M,D
Special Education	M,D
Speech and Interpersonal Communication	M,D
Theater	M,D
Vocational and Technical Education	M,D
Writing	M
Zoology	M,D

SOUTHERN ILLINOIS UNIVERSITY EDWARDSVILLE

Accounting	M
Advertising and Public Relations	M
Applied Mathematics	M
Art Therapy	M
Art/Fine Arts	M
Biological and Biomedical Sciences—General	M
Business Administration and Management—General	M
Business Analytics	M
Chemistry	M
Civil Engineering	M
Clinical Psychology	M
Communication Disorders	M
Computational Sciences	M
Computer Science	M
Corporate and Organizational Communication	M
Cultural Anthropology	M
Curriculum and Instruction	M
Dentistry	D
Economics	M
Education—General	M,D,O
Educational Leadership and Administration	M,D,O
Educational Media/Instructional Technology	M,O
Electrical Engineering	M
Engineering and Applied Sciences—General	M
English as a Second Language	M,O
English Education	M,O
English	M,O
Environmental Engineering	M
Environmental Management and Policy	M
Environmental Sciences	M
Exercise and Sports Science	M
Family Nurse Practitioner Studies	M,D,O
Finance and Banking	M
Foundations and Philosophy of Education	M
Geography	M
Geotechnical Engineering	M
Health Communication	M
Health Education	M,D,O
Health Informatics	M
Higher Education	M
History	M
Industrial and Organizational Psychology	M
Industrial/Management Engineering	M
Interdisciplinary Studies	M
Kinesiology and Movement Studies	M
Management Information Systems	M
Marketing Research	M
Mass Communication	M
Mathematics Education	M
Mathematics	M
Mechanical Engineering	M
Media Studies	O
Museum Studies	O
Music Education	M,O
Music	M
Nurse Anesthesia	D
Nursing and Healthcare Administration	M,O
Nursing Education	M,O
Nursing—General	M,D,O
Operations Research	M
Pharmacy	D
Physical Education	M
Project Management	M
Psychology—General	M,O
Public Administration	M
Reading Education	M,O
School Psychology	O
Social Work	M
Sociology	M
Special Education	M,O
Speech and Interpersonal Communication	M
Sport Psychology	M
Statistics	M
Structural Engineering	M
Student Affairs	M
Sustainable Development	M
Taxation	M
Transportation and Highway Engineering	M
Writing	M

SOUTHERN METHODIST UNIVERSITY

Accounting	M
Advertising and Public Relations	M
Anthropology	M,D
Applied Economics	M,D
Applied Mathematics	M,D
Applied Statistics	M,D
Archaeology	M,D
Art History	M,D
Art/Fine Arts	M
Arts Administration	M
Biological and Biomedical Sciences—General	M,D
Biostatistics	M,D
Business Administration and Management—General	M
Business Analytics	M
Cell Biology	M,D
Chemistry	M,D
Civil Engineering	M,D
Clinical Psychology	D
Computational Sciences	M,D
Computer Engineering	M,D
Computer Science	M,D
Conflict Resolution and Mediation/Peace Studies	M,O
Counselor Education	M,O
Cultural Anthropology	M,D
Data Science/Data Analytics	M,D
Economics	M,D
Education of the Gifted	M,D
Education—General	M,D
Electrical Engineering	M,D
Engineering and Applied Sciences—General	M,D
Engineering Management	M,D
English as a Second Language	M,D
English	M,D
Entrepreneurship	M
Environmental Engineering	M,D

*M—masters degree; D—doctorate; O—other advanced degree; *—Close-Up and/or Display*

Finance and Banking	M
Geology	M,D
Geophysics	M,D
Geotechnical Engineering	M,D
Health Promotion	M,D
History	M,D
Information Science	M,D
Law	M,D
Liberal Studies	M,D
Management Information Systems	M
Management Strategy and Policy	M
Manufacturing Engineering	M,D
Marketing	M
Mathematics	M,D
Mechanical Engineering	M,D
Medieval and Renaissance Studies	M
Molecular Biology	M,D
Multilingual and Multicultural Education	M,D
Music Education	M
Music	M,D
Operations Research	M,D
Pastoral Ministry and Counseling	M,D
Physics	M,D
Physiology	M,D
Psychology—General	D
Reading Education	M,D
Real Estate	M
Religion	M,D
Software Engineering	M,D
Special Education	M,D
Sports Management	M,D
Statistics	M,D
Structural Engineering	M,D
Sustainable Development	M,D
Systems Engineering	M,D
Taxation	M,D
Telecommunications	M,D
Theater	M
Theology	M,D
Transportation and Highway Engineering	M,D

SOUTHERN NAZARENE UNIVERSITY

Business Administration and Management—General	M
Counseling Psychology	M
Health Services Management and Hospital Administration	M
Marriage and Family Therapy	M
Nursing and Healthcare Administration	M
Nursing Education	M
Nursing—General	M
Psychology—General	M
Sports Management	M

SOUTHERN NEW HAMPSHIRE UNIVERSITY

Accounting	M,D,O
Advertising and Public Relations	M,D,O
Applied Economics	M,D,O
Business Administration and Management—General	M,D,O
Business Analytics	M,D,O
Clinical Psychology	M
Computer and Information Systems Security	M
Criminal Justice and Criminology	M
Curriculum and Instruction	M,D,O
Data Science/Data Analytics	M,D,O
Early Childhood Education	M,D,O
Economic Development	M,D,O
Economics	M,D,O
Education—General	M,D,O
Educational Leadership and Administration	M,D,O
Educational Media/Instructional Technology	M,D,O
Elementary Education	M,D,O
Engineering Management	M,D,O
English as a Second Language	M,D,O
English	M
Entertainment Management	M,D,O
Entrepreneurship	M,D,O
Environmental Management and Policy	M,D,O
Finance and Banking	M,D,O
Health Informatics	M,D,O
Health Services Management and Hospital Administration	M,D,O
Higher Education	M,D,O
History	M
Human Resources Management	M,D,O
Industrial and Manufacturing Management	M,D,O
International Business	M,D,O
Internet and Interactive Multimedia	M,D,O
Investment Management	M,D,O
Legal and Justice Studies	M,D,O
Management Information Systems	M,D,O
Marketing	M,D,O
Nonprofit Management	M,D,O
Nursing and Healthcare Administration	M,O
Nursing Education	M,O
Nursing—General	M,O
Organizational Management	M,D,O
Political Science	M
Project Management	M,D,O
Psychology—General	M
Public Administration	M,D,O
Quality Management	M,D,O
Quantitative Analysis	M,D,O
Reading Education	M,D,O
Special Education	M,D,O
Sports Management	M,D,O
Supply Chain Management	M,D,O
Sustainability Management	M,D,O
Taxation	M,D,O
Writing	M

SOUTHERN OREGON UNIVERSITY

Accounting	M,O
Business Administration and Management—General	M,O
Computer Science	M
Counseling Psychology	M
Early Childhood Education	M
Education—General	M
Educational Leadership and Administration	M
Elementary Education	M
Environmental Education	M
Foreign Languages Education	M
French	M
Interdisciplinary Studies	M
International Business	M,O
Music	M
Psychology—General	M
Reading Education	M
Secondary Education	M
Spanish	M
Special Education	M
Theater	M

SOUTHERN UNIVERSITY AND AGRICULTURAL AND MECHANICAL COLLEGE

Agricultural Sciences—General	M
Analytical Chemistry	M
Biochemistry	M
Biological and Biomedical Sciences—General	M
Business Administration and Management—General	M
Chemistry	M
Communication Disorders	M
Computer Science	M
Counselor Education	M
Criminal Justice and Criminology	M
Education—General	M,D
Educational Leadership and Administration	M
Educational Media/Instructional Technology	M
Elementary Education	M
Engineering and Applied Sciences—General	M
Environmental Sciences	M
Family Nurse Practitioner Studies	M,D,O
Forestry	M
Gerontological Nursing	M,D,O
History	M
Inorganic Chemistry	M
Law	D
Mass Communication	M
Mathematics Education	D
Mathematics	M
Nursing and Healthcare Administration	M,D,O
Nursing Education	M,D,O
Nursing—General	M,D,O
Organic Chemistry	M
Physical Chemistry	M
Physics	M
Political Science	M
Psychology—General	M
Public Administration	M
Public Policy	D
Recreation and Park Management	M
Rehabilitation Counseling	M
Science Education	D
Secondary Education	M
Social Sciences	M
Special Education	M,D

SOUTHERN UNIVERSITY AT NEW ORLEANS

Criminal Justice and Criminology	M
Management Information Systems	M
Museum Studies	M
Social Work	M

SOUTHERN UTAH UNIVERSITY

Accounting	M
Arts Administration	M
Business Administration and Management—General	M
Communication—General	M
Computer and Information Systems Security	M
Education—General	M,O
Exercise and Sports Science	M
Interdisciplinary Studies	M
Music	M
Public Administration	M

SOUTHERN WESLEYAN UNIVERSITY

Business Administration and Management—General	M
Education—General	M
Pastoral Ministry and Counseling	M

SOUTH FLORIDA BIBLE COLLEGE AND THEOLOGICAL SEMINARY

Theology	M

SOUTH TEXAS COLLEGE OF LAW HOUSTON

Law	D

SOUTH UNIVERSITY (AL)

Business Administration and Management—General	M
Counseling Psychology	M
Criminal Justice and Criminology	M
Health Services Management and Hospital Administration	M
Management Information Systems	M
Nursing—General	M
Public Administration	M

SOUTH UNIVERSITY

Business Administration and Management—General	M
Counseling Psychology	M
Criminal Justice and Criminology	M
Family Nurse Practitioner Studies	M
Health Services Management and Hospital Administration	M
Management Information Systems	M
Nursing—General	D
Occupational Therapy	D
Public Administration	M

SOUTH UNIVERSITY

Adult Nursing	M
Business Administration and Management—General	M
Criminal Justice and Criminology	M
Family Nurse Practitioner Studies	M
Health Services Management and Hospital Administration	M
Management Information Systems	M
Nursing Education	M
Nursing—General	M
Physician Assistant Studies	M

SOUTH UNIVERSITY (GA)

Anesthesiologist Assistant Studies	M
Business Administration and Management—General	M
Counseling Psychology	M
Criminal Justice and Criminology	M
Entrepreneurship	M
Health Services Management and Hospital Administration	M
Hospitality Management	M
Nursing Education	M
Nursing—General	M
Organizational Management	M
Pastoral Ministry and Counseling	D
Pharmacy	
Physician Assistant Studies	M
Public Administration	M
Sustainability Management	M

SOUTH UNIVERSITY (SC)

Business Administration and Management—General	M
Counseling Psychology	M
Criminal Justice and Criminology	M
Health Services Management and Hospital Administration	M
Nursing—General	M
Organizational Management	M
Pharmacy	D

SOUTH UNIVERSITY (TX)

Business Administration and Management—General	M
Counseling Psychology	M
Management Information Systems	M

SOUTH UNIVERSITY

Business Administration and Management—General	M
Counseling Psychology	M
Nursing—General	M

SOUTH UNIVERSITY

Business Administration and Management—General	M
Counseling Psychology	M
Family Nurse Practitioner Studies	M
Management Information Systems	M
Nursing—General	M
Organizational Management	M

SOUTHWEST ACUPUNCTURE COLLEGE

Acupuncture and Oriental Medicine	M

SOUTHWEST BAPTIST UNIVERSITY

Business Administration and Management—General	M
Education—General	M,O
Educational Leadership and Administration	M,O
Health Services Management and Hospital Administration	M
Physical Therapy	D

SOUTHWEST COLLEGE OF NATUROPATHIC MEDICINE AND HEALTH SCIENCES

Naturopathic Medicine	D

SOUTHWESTERN ADVENTIST UNIVERSITY

Accounting	M
Business Administration and Management—General	M
Curriculum and Instruction	M
Education—General	M
Educational Leadership and Administration	M
Finance and Banking	M
Reading Education	M

SOUTHWESTERN ASSEMBLIES OF GOD UNIVERSITY

Counseling Psychology	M
Curriculum and Instruction	M
Education—General	M
Educational Leadership and Administration	M
History	M
Missions and Missiology	M
Pastoral Ministry and Counseling	M
Religion	M
Religious Education	M
Secondary Education	M
Theology	M

SOUTHWESTERN BAPTIST THEOLOGICAL SEMINARY

Missions and Missiology	M,D
Music	M,D
Near and Middle Eastern Studies	M,D
Pastoral Ministry and Counseling	M,D,O
Religious Education	M,D
Theology	M,D

SOUTHWESTERN CHRISTIAN UNIVERSITY

Missions and Missiology	M
Pastoral Ministry and Counseling	M

SOUTHWESTERN COLLEGE (KS)

Business Administration and Management—General	M
Criminal Justice and Criminology	M
Curriculum and Instruction	M,D
Early Childhood Education	M,D
Education—General	M,D
Educational Leadership and Administration	M,D
Elementary Education	M,D
Higher Education	M,D
Special Education	M,D

SOUTHWESTERN COLLEGE (NM)

Art Therapy	M
Counseling Psychology	M,O
Health Psychology	O
Psychology—General	O
Social Psychology	O
Thanatology	M,O

SOUTHWESTERN LAW SCHOOL

Law	M,D*
Sports and Entertainment Law	M,D

SOUTHWESTERN OKLAHOMA STATE UNIVERSITY

Allied Health—General	M
Art Education	M
Business Administration and Management—General	M
Counselor Education	M
Early Childhood Education	M
Education—General	M
Educational Leadership and Administration	M
Educational Measurement and Evaluation	M
Elementary Education	M
English Education	M
Kinesiology and Movement Studies	M
Mathematics Education	M
Microbiology	M
Music Education	M
Music	M
Pharmacy	D
Recreation and Park Management	M
School Psychology	M
Science Education	M
Secondary Education	M
Social Sciences Education	M
Special Education	M

SOUTHWEST MINNESOTA STATE UNIVERSITY

Business Administration and Management—General	M
Early Childhood Education	M
Education—General	M
Educational Leadership and Administration	M
English as a Second Language	M
Marketing	M
Mathematics Education	M
Reading Education	M
Special Education	M

SOUTHWEST UNIVERSITY

Business Administration and Management—General	M
Criminal Justice and Criminology	M
Organizational Management	M

SOUTHWEST UNIVERSITY OF VISUAL ARTS

Art/Fine Arts	M
Photography	M

SPALDING UNIVERSITY

Adult Nursing	M,D,O
Art Education	M
Athletic Training and Sports Medicine	M
Business Education	M
Clinical Psychology	M,D
Corporate and Organizational Communication	M
Counselor Education	M
Education—General	M,D
Educational Leadership and Administration	M,D
Elementary Education	M
Family Nurse Practitioner Studies	M,D,O
Foreign Languages Education	M
Middle School Education	M
Nursing and Healthcare Administration	M,D,O
Nursing Education	M,D,O
Nursing—General	M,D,O
Occupational Therapy	M
Pediatric Nursing	M,D,O
Psychology—General	M,D
Secondary Education	M
Social Work	M
Special Education	M
Writing	M

SPERTUS INSTITUTE FOR JEWISH LEARNING AND LEADERSHIP

Jewish Studies	M,D

SPRING ARBOR UNIVERSITY

Business Administration and Management—General	M
Child and Family Studies	M
Communication—General	M
Counseling Psychology	M
Education—General	M
Nursing—General	M
Pastoral Ministry and Counseling	M
Reading Education	M
Special Education	M
Theology	M

SPRINGFIELD COLLEGE

Art Therapy	M,O

Athletic Training and Sports Medicine	M
Business Administration and Management—General	M
Clinical Psychology	M,D,O
Counseling Psychology	M,D,O
Counselor Education	M,D,O
Early Childhood Education	M,O
Education—General	M,O
Educational Leadership and Administration	M,D,O
Elementary Education	M,O
Exercise and Sports Science	M,D,O
Health Promotion	M,D,O
Higher Education	M,D,O
Human Services	M
Industrial and Organizational Psychology	M,D,O
Occupational Therapy	M
Organizational Management	M
Physical Education	M,D,O
Physical Therapy	D
Physician Assistant Studies	M
Recreation and Park Management	M
Rehabilitation Counseling	M
Secondary Education	M,O
Social Work	M,O
Special Education	M,O
Sport Psychology	M,D,O
Sports Management	M,D,O
Student Affairs	M,D,O

SPRING HILL COLLEGE

Art/Fine Arts	M,O
Business Administration and Management—General	M
Early Childhood Education	M
Education—General	M
Elementary Education	M
English	M,O
Ethics	M,O
Foundations and Philosophy of Education	M
Liberal Studies	M,O
Nursing and Healthcare Administration	M,O
Nursing—General	M,O
Pastoral Ministry and Counseling	M,O
Secondary Education	M
Theology	M,O

STANBRIDGE UNIVERSITY

Nursing—General	M
Occupational Therapy	M

STANFORD UNIVERSITY

Aerospace/Aeronautical Engineering	M,D,O
Allopathic Medicine	D
Anthropology	M,D
Applied Arts and Design—General	M,D,O
Applied Physics	M,D
Archaeology	M,D
Art/Fine Arts	M,D
Asian Languages	M,D
Asian Studies	M
Biochemistry	D
Bioengineering	M,D
Biological and Biomedical Sciences—General	M,D
Biomedical Engineering	M,D,O
Biophysics	D
Biostatistics	M,D
Business Administration and Management—General	M,D
Chemical Engineering	M,D
Chemistry	D
Chinese	M,D
Civil Engineering	M,D,O
Classics	M,D
Clinical Research	M,D
Communication—General	M,D
Comparative Literature	D
Computational Sciences	M,D
Computer Science	M,D
Construction Engineering	M,D,O
Cultural Studies	M,D
Curriculum and Instruction	M
Developmental Biology	M,D
East European and Russian Studies	M
Ecology	M,D
Economics	D
Education—General	M,D
Educational Leadership and Administration	M
Educational Media/Instructional Technology	M
Educational Policy	M
Electrical Engineering	M,D
Elementary Education	M
Energy and Power Engineering	M,D,O
Engineering and Applied Sciences—General	M,D,O
Engineering Design	M
Engineering Management	M,D
Engineering Physics	M,D
English	M,D
Environmental Engineering	M,D,O
Environmental Law	M,D
Environmental Sciences	M,D,O
Epidemiology	M,D
Film, Television, and Video Production	M,D
French	M,D
Genetics	D
Geophysics	M,D
Geosciences	M,D,O
Geotechnical Engineering	M,D,O
German	M,D
Health Services Research	M,D
History	M,D
Hydrology	M,D,O
Immunology	D
Industrial/Management Engineering	M,D
International and Comparative Education	M,D
Italian	M,D
Japanese	M,D
Law	M,D
Legal and Justice Studies	M,D
Linguistics	M,D
Materials Engineering	M,D,O
Materials Sciences	M,D,O
Mathematics	M,D
Mechanical Engineering	M,D,O
Mechanics	M,D,O
Medical Informatics	M,D
Microbiology	D
Music	M,D
Philosophy	M,D
Physics	D
Physiology	D
Political Science	M,D
Psychology—General	D
Religion	D
Secondary Education	M
Slavic Languages	D
Sociology	D
Spanish	M,D
Statistics	M,D
Structural Biology	D
Structural Engineering	M,D,O
Sustainable Development	M,D,O
Systems Biology	D
Theater	D

STARR KING SCHOOL FOR THE MINISTRY

Theology	M

STATE UNIVERSITY OF NEW YORK AT FREDONIA

Biological and Biomedical Sciences—General	M,O
Communication Disorders	M,O
Curriculum and Instruction	M
Early Childhood Education	M
Education—General	M
English as a Second Language	M
English Education	M,O
English	M,O
Interdisciplinary Studies	M,O
Mathematics Education	M,O
Middle School Education	M,O
Music Education	M
Music	M
Reading Education	M
Secondary Education	M
Writing	M,O

STATE UNIVERSITY OF NEW YORK AT NEW PALTZ

Accounting	M
Art Education	M
Art/Fine Arts	M
Business Administration and Management—General	M
Chemistry	M,O
Clinical Psychology	M,O
Communication Disorders	M
Computer Science	M
Counseling Psychology	M,O
Counselor Education	M,O
Early Childhood Education	M,O
Education—General	M,O
Educational Leadership and Administration	M,O
Electrical Engineering	M
Elementary Education	M
English as a Second Language	M,O
English Education	M,O
English	M
French	M,O
Geosciences	M,O
Multilingual and Multicultural Education	M,O
Music	M
Psychology—General	M,O
Reading Education	M
Science Education	M
Secondary Education	M
Social Sciences Education	M,O
Spanish	M,O
Special Education	M
Therapies—Dance, Drama, and Music	M

STATE UNIVERSITY OF NEW YORK AT OSWEGO

Agricultural Education	M
Art Education	M
Art/Fine Arts	M
Bioinformatics	M
Business Administration and Management—General	M
Business Education	M
Chemistry	M
Child and Family Studies	M
Communication—General	M
Consumer Economics	M
Corporate and Organizational Communication	M
Counseling Psychology	M
Curriculum and Instruction	M
Early Childhood Education	M
Education—General	M,O
Educational Leadership and Administration	O
Elementary Education	M
English	M
Graphic Design	M
Health Communication	M
Health Informatics	M
History	M
Human-Computer Interaction	M
Internet and Interactive Multimedia	M
Middle School Education	M
Reading Education	M
Secondary Education	M
Special Education	M
Vocational and Technical Education	M

STATE UNIVERSITY OF NEW YORK AT PLATTSBURGH

Clinical Psychology	M,O
Communication Disorders	M
Counseling Psychology	M,O
Counselor Education	M,O
Curriculum and Instruction	M
Early Childhood Education	O
Educational Leadership and Administration	O
Elementary Education	M,O
English Education	M
Foreign Languages Education	M
Mathematics Education	M
Psychology—General	M,O
Reading Education	M
School Psychology	M,O
Science Education	M
Secondary Education	M
Social Sciences Education	M
Special Education	M
Student Affairs	M,O

STATE UNIVERSITY OF NEW YORK COLLEGE AT CORTLAND

Communication Disorders	M
Community Health	M
Early Childhood Education	M
Education—General	M,O
Educational Leadership and Administration	O
English as a Second Language	M
English Education	M
English	M
Environmental Education	M
Health Education	M
History	M
Mathematics Education	M
Mathematics	M
Physical Education	M
Physics	M
Reading Education	M
Recreation and Park Management	M
Science Education	M
Secondary Education	M
Special Education	M
Sports Management	M

STATE UNIVERSITY OF NEW YORK COLLEGE AT GENESEO

Accounting	M
Business Administration and Management—General	M
Education—General	M
English Education	M
French	M
Multilingual and Multicultural Education	M
Reading Education	M
Secondary Education	M
Social Sciences Education	M
Spanish	M

STATE UNIVERSITY OF NEW YORK COLLEGE AT OLD WESTBURY

Accounting	M
Business Administration and Management—General	M
Counseling Psychology	M
Education—General	M
English Education	M
Foreign Languages Education	M
Liberal Studies	M
Mathematics Education	M
Science Education	M
Social Sciences Education	M
Taxation	M

STATE UNIVERSITY OF NEW YORK COLLEGE AT ONEONTA

Biological and Biomedical Sciences—General	M
Counselor Education	M,O
Education—General	M,O
Educational Psychology	M,O
Elementary Education	M
Museum Studies	M
Nutrition	M
Reading Education	M
Special Education	M,O

STATE UNIVERSITY OF NEW YORK COLLEGE AT POTSDAM

Community Health	M
Curriculum and Instruction	M
Early Childhood Education	M
Educational Media/Instructional Technology	M
Elementary Education	M
English Education	M
Mathematics Education	M
Mathematics	M
Middle School Education	M
Music Education	M
Music	M
Reading Education	M
Science Education	M
Secondary Education	M
Social Sciences Education	M
Special Education	M

STATE UNIVERSITY OF NEW YORK COLLEGE OF ENVIRONMENTAL SCIENCE AND FORESTRY

Biochemistry	M,D
Chemistry	M,D
Conservation Biology	M,D
Ecology	M,D
Economics	M,D
Entomology	M,D
Environmental Biology	M,D
Environmental Engineering	M,D
Environmental Management and Policy	M,D
Environmental Sciences	M,D
Fish, Game, and Wildlife Management	M,D
Forestry	M,D
Geographic Information Systems	M,D
Landscape Architecture	M
Materials Sciences	M,D,O
Natural Resources	M,D
Organic Chemistry	M,D
Paper and Pulp Engineering	M,D,O
Plant Pathology	M,D
Plant Sciences	M,D
Sustainability Management	M,D,O
Sustainable Development	M,D,O
Urban and Regional Planning	M,D
Urban Design	M
Water Resources Engineering	M,D
Water Resources	M,D

STATE UNIVERSITY OF NEW YORK COLLEGE OF OPTOMETRY

Optometry	D
Vision Sciences	D

STATE UNIVERSITY OF NEW YORK COLLEGE OF TECHNOLOGY AT DELHI

Nursing and Healthcare Administration	M
Nursing Education	M
Nursing—General	M

STATE UNIVERSITY OF NEW YORK DOWNSTATE MEDICAL CENTER

Allopathic Medicine	M,D
Biological and Biomedical Sciences—General	M,D
Biomedical Engineering	M,D
Cell Biology	D
Community Health	M
Family Nurse Practitioner Studies	M,O
Medical/Surgical Nursing	M,O
Molecular Biology	D
Neuroscience	D
Nurse Anesthesia	M
Nurse Midwifery	M,O
Nursing—General	M,O
Occupational Therapy	M
Public Health—General	M

STATE UNIVERSITY OF NEW YORK EMPIRE STATE COLLEGE

Adult Education	M
Business Administration and Management—General	M
Economic Development	M
Education—General	M
Educational Media/Instructional Technology	M
Industrial and Labor Relations	M
International Business	M
Liberal Studies	M
Nursing Education	M
Public Policy	M

STATE UNIVERSITY OF NEW YORK MARITIME COLLEGE

Transportation Management	M

STATE UNIVERSITY OF NEW YORK POLYTECHNIC INSTITUTE

Accounting	M
Business Administration and Management—General	M
Computer and Information Systems Security	M
Computer Science	M
Family Nurse Practitioner Studies	M,O
Finance and Banking	M
Human Resources Management	M
Information Science	M
Management of Technology	M
Marketing	M
Nanotechnology	M,D
Nursing Education	M,O

STATE UNIVERSITY OF NEW YORK UPSTATE MEDICAL UNIVERSITY

Allopathic Medicine	D
Anatomy	M,D
Biochemistry	M,D
Biological and Biomedical Sciences—General	M,D
Cell Biology	M,D
Clinical Laboratory Sciences/Medical Technology	M
Family Nurse Practitioner Studies	M,O
Immunology	M,D
Microbiology	M,D
Molecular Biology	M,D
Neuroscience	D
Nursing—General	M,O
Pharmacology	D
Physical Therapy	D
Physiology	M,D

STEPHEN F. AUSTIN STATE UNIVERSITY

Accounting	M
Agricultural Education	M
Applied Arts and Design—General	M

*M—masters degree; D—doctorate; O—other advanced degree; *—Close-Up and/or Display*

Art/Fine Arts	M
Athletic Training and Sports Medicine	M
Biological and Biomedical Sciences—General	M
Biotechnology	M
Business Administration and Management—General	M
Chemistry	M
Communication Disorders	M
Communication—General	M
Computer Science	M
Counselor Education	M
Early Childhood Education	M
Education—General	M,D
Educational Leadership and Administration	M,D
Elementary Education	M
English	M
Environmental Sciences	M
Family and Consumer Sciences-General	M
Forestry	M,D
Geology	M
History	M
Interdisciplinary Studies	M
Kinesiology and Movement Studies	M
Marketing	M
Mass Communication	M
Mathematics Education	M
Mathematics	M
Music	M
Physics	M
Psychology—General	M
Public Administration	M
School Psychology	M
Secondary Education	M,D
Social Work	M
Special Education	M
Statistics	M

STEPHENS COLLEGE

Addictions/Substance Abuse Counseling	M,O
Clinical Psychology	M,O
Counselor Education	M,O
Health Informatics	M,O
Physician Assistant Studies	M,O
Writing	M,O

STETSON UNIVERSITY

Accounting	M
Business Administration and Management—General	M
Counseling Psychology	M
Counselor Education	M
Education—General	M
Educational Leadership and Administration	M
Law	M,D
Marriage and Family Therapy	M
Writing	M

STEVENS INSTITUTE OF TECHNOLOGY

Aerospace/Aeronautical Engineering	M,O
Analytical Chemistry	M,D,O
Applied Mathematics	M
Applied Statistics	O
Artificial Intelligence/Robotics	M,D,O
Atmospheric Sciences	M,D,O
Biochemistry	M,D,O
Bioinformatics	M,D,O
Biomedical Engineering	M,D,O
Business Administration and Management—General	M,O
Business Analytics	M,O
Chemical Engineering	M,D,O
Chemistry	M,D,O
Civil Engineering	M,D,O
Communication—General	M,D,O
Computer and Information Systems Security	M,D,O
Computer Art and Design	M,D,O
Computer Engineering	M,D,O
Computer Science	M,D,O
Construction Engineering	M,O
Construction Management	M,O
Corporate and Organizational Communication	O
Data Science/Data Analytics	M,D,O
Electrical Engineering	M,D,O
Electronic Commerce	M,O
Engineering and Applied Sciences—General	M,D,O
Engineering Design	M
Engineering Management	M,D,O
Entrepreneurship	M,D,O
Environmental Engineering	M,D,O
Ethics	M,O
Film, Television, and Video Production	M
Finance and Banking	M,O
Financial Engineering	M,D,O
Health Informatics	M,D,O
Human Resources Management	M,D
Hydrology	M,D,O
Industrial and Manufacturing Management	M
Information Science	M,O
International Business	M
Internet and Interactive Multimedia	M,D,O
Logistics	O
Management Information Systems	M,D,O
Management of Technology	M,D,O
Management Strategy and Policy	M
Manufacturing Engineering	M
Marine Affairs	M
Marketing	M,O
Materials Engineering	M,D
Materials Sciences	M,D
Mathematics	M,D
Mechanical Engineering	M,D,O
Media Studies	M
Modeling and Simulation	M,D,O
Nanotechnology	D
Nuclear Engineering	M,D,O
Ocean Engineering	M,D,O
Pharmaceutical Sciences	M,O
Photonics	M,D,O
Physics	M,D,O
Polymer Science and Engineering	M,D,O
Project Management	M,O
Quality Management	M,O
Software Engineering	M,O
Statistics	M,O
Structural Engineering	M,D,O
Systems Engineering	M,D,O
Systems Science	M,D,O
Telecommunications Management	M,D,O
Telecommunications	M,D,O
Transportation and Highway Engineering	M,D,O
Water Resources Engineering	M,D,O

STEVENSON UNIVERSITY

Biological and Biomedical Sciences—General	M
Chemistry	M
Communication—General	M
Computer and Information Systems Security	M
Education—General	M
Educational Leadership and Administration	M
Forensic Sciences	M
Health Services Management and Hospital Administration	M
Management of Technology	M
Mathematics Education	M
Nursing and Healthcare Administration	M
Nursing Education	M
Nursing—General	M
Project Management	M
Quality Management	M
Science Education	M

STOCKTON UNIVERSITY

American Studies	M,O
Business Administration and Management—General	M
Communication Disorders	M
Computational Sciences	M
Criminal Justice and Criminology	M
Data Science/Data Analytics	M
Education—General	M
Educational Media/Instructional Technology	M
Environmental Sciences	M
Holocaust and Genocide Studies	M
Management Strategy and Policy	M
Nursing—General	M
Occupational Therapy	M
Organizational Management	D
Physical Therapy	D
Quantitative Analysis	M
Social Work	M

STONY BROOK UNIVERSITY, STATE UNIVERSITY OF NEW YORK

Accounting	M,O
Addictions/Substance Abuse Counseling	M,O
Adult Nursing	M,D,O
African Studies	M,O
Allopathic Medicine	D
Anatomy	D
Anthropology	M,D
Applied Mathematics	M,D,O
Art History	M,D
Art/Fine Arts	M
Asian Studies	M
Asian-American Studies	M
Astronomy	D
Atmospheric Sciences	M,D
Biochemistry	M,D
Bioethics	M
Bioinformatics	M,D,O
Biological and Biomedical Sciences—General	M,D,O
Biomedical Engineering	M,D,O
Biophysics	D
Business Administration and Management—General	M,O
Cell Biology	M,D
Chemistry	M,D
Civil Engineering	M,D,O
Clinical Psychology	D
Cognitive Sciences	D
Community Health	M,D,O
Comparative Literature	M,D,O
Computer Education	M
Computer Engineering	M,D
Computer Science	M,D,O
Cultural Studies	M,D,O
Dentistry	D,O
Developmental Biology	M,D
Ecology	M,D
Economics	M,D
Educational Leadership and Administration	M,O
Educational Media/Instructional Technology	M,O
Electrical Engineering	M,D
Energy Management and Policy	M
Engineering and Applied Sciences—General	M,D,O
English as a Second Language	M
English Education	M,D,O
English	M,D,O
Entrepreneurship	M,O
Environmental Management and Policy	M,O
Evolutionary Biology	M,D
Family Nurse Practitioner Studies	M,D,O
Film, Television, and Video Production	M
Finance and Banking	M,O
Foreign Languages Education	M,O
French	M
Gender Studies	O
Genetics	D
Geographic Information Systems	O
Geosciences	M,D
Gerontological Nursing	M,D,O
Health Communication	M,O
Health Education	M,O
Health Informatics	M,D,O
Health Promotion	M,O
Health Psychology	D
Health Services Management and Hospital Administration	M,D,O
Higher Education	M,O
Hispanic and Latin American Languages	M,D
History	M,D
Human Resources Management	M,D
Immunology	M,D
Italian	M
Journalism	M,O
Liberal Studies	M,O
Linguistics	M,D
Management Information Systems	M,D,O
Management of Technology	M
Marine Affairs	M
Marine Sciences	M,D
Marketing	M,O
Materials Engineering	M,D
Materials Sciences	M,D
Maternal and Child/Neonatal Nursing	M,D,O
Mathematics Education	M,D
Mathematics	M,D
Mechanical Engineering	M,D
Medical Physics	M,D
Microbiology	D
Molecular Biology	M,D
Molecular Genetics	D
Molecular Physiology	D
Music	M,D
Neuroscience	M,D
Nurse Midwifery	M,D,O
Nursing and Healthcare Administration	M,D,O
Nursing Education	M,O
Nursing—General	M,D,O
Nutrition	M,O
Occupational Therapy	M,D,O
Oral and Dental Sciences	M,D,O
Pathology	M,D
Pediatric Nursing	M,D,O
Pharmacology	M,D
Pharmacy	D
Philosophy	M,D,O
Physical Education	M,O
Physical Therapy	M,D,O
Physician Assistant Studies	M,D,O
Physics	M,D
Physiology	D
Political Science	M,D
Psychiatric Nursing	M,D,O
Psychology—General	M,D
Public Health—General	M,D
Public Policy	M
Rehabilitation Sciences	M,D,O
Romance Languages	M
Science Education	M,D,O
Social Psychology	D
Social Sciences Education	M,O
Social Work	M,D
Sociology	M,D
Software Engineering	M,D,O
Statistics	M,D,O
Structural Biology	D
Systems Engineering	M,D
Technology and Public Policy	D
Telecommunications	M,D,O
Theater	M
Women's Health Nursing	M,D,O
Women's Studies	O
Writing	M,O

STRATFORD UNIVERSITY (MD)

Hospitality Management	M

STRATFORD UNIVERSITY (VA)

Accounting	M,D
Business Administration and Management—General	M,D
Computer and Information Systems Security	M,D
Computer Science	M,D
Forensic Sciences	M,D
Health Services Management and Hospital Administration	M,D
Management Information Systems	M,D
Management of Technology	M,D
Software Engineering	M,D
Telecommunications	M,D

STRAYER UNIVERSITY

Accounting	M
Business Administration and Management—General	M
Computer and Information Systems Security	M
Education—General	M
Educational Media/Instructional Technology	M
Finance and Banking	M
Health Services Management and Hospital Administration	M
Hospitality Management	M
Human Resources Management	M
Information Science	M
Management Information Systems	M
Marketing	M
Public Administration	M
Software Engineering	M
Supply Chain Management	M
Systems Science	M
Taxation	M
Telecommunications Management	M
Travel and Tourism	M

SUFFOLK UNIVERSITY

Accounting	M,O
Advertising and Public Relations	M
Applied Arts and Design—General	M
Business Administration and Management—General	M
Clinical Psychology	M,D,O
Community Health	M
Corporate and Organizational Communication	M
Counseling Psychology	M,D,O
Counselor Education	M,D,O
Criminal Justice and Criminology	M
Data Science/Data Analytics	M
Educational Leadership and Administration	M,O
Entrepreneurship	M
Ethics	M,O
Finance and Banking	M
Graphic Design	M
Health Law	M,D
Health Services Management and Hospital Administration	M
Intellectual Property Law	M,D
Interior Design	M
International Business	M
Law	M,D
Management Information Systems	M
Management Strategy and Policy	M
Marketing	M
Nonprofit Management	M
Organizational Behavior	M
Political Science	M,O
Psychology—General	M,D,O
Public Administration	M
Public Policy	M,O
Supply Chain Management	M
Taxation	M,O

SULLIVAN UNIVERSITY

Business Administration and Management—General	M,D
Pharmacy	D

SUL ROSS STATE UNIVERSITY

Animal Sciences	M
Art Education	M
Art History	M
Art/Fine Arts	M
Biological and Biomedical Sciences—General	M
Business Administration and Management—General	M
Counselor Education	M
Criminal Justice and Criminology	M
Education—General	M,O
Educational Leadership and Administration	M
Educational Measurement and Evaluation	M,O
Elementary Education	M
Emergency Management	M
English	M
Fish, Game, and Wildlife Management	M
Geology	M
History	M
Multilingual and Multicultural Education	M
Natural Resources	M
Physical Education	M
Political Science	M
Psychology—General	M
Range Science	M
Reading Education	M,O
Secondary Education	M

SUM BIBLE COLLEGE & THEOLOGICAL SEMINARY

Pastoral Ministry and Counseling	M
Religion	M
Theology	M

SWEDISH INSTITUTE, COLLEGE OF HEALTH SCIENCES

Acupuncture and Oriental Medicine	M

SWEET BRIAR COLLEGE

Education—General	M

SYRACUSE UNIVERSITY

Accounting	M
Addictions/Substance Abuse Counseling	M,O
Advertising and Public Relations	M
Aerospace/Aeronautical Engineering	M,D
African Studies	M
African-American Studies	M
Anthropology	M,D
Applied Arts and Design—General	M
Applied Statistics	M
Architecture	M
Art Education	M
Art History	M
Art/Fine Arts	M
Arts Journalism	M
Bioengineering	M,D
Biological and Biomedical Sciences—General	M,D
Broadcast Journalism	M
Business Administration and Management—General	M,D
Business Analytics	M
Chemical Engineering	M,D
Chemistry	M,D
Child and Family Studies	M,D
Civil Engineering	M,D

Clinical Psychology M,D
Cognitive Sciences D
Communication Disorders M,D
Communication—General M,D
Computer and Information Systems Security M,O
Computer Art and Design M
Computer Engineering M,D
Computer Science M
Conflict Resolution and Mediation/Peace Studies O
Counselor Education M,D
Curriculum and Instruction M,D,O
Data Science/Data Analytics M,O
Disability Studies O
Early Childhood Education M
Economics M,D
Education of Students with Severe/Multiple Disabilities M
Education—General M,D,O
Educational Leadership and Administration M,D,O
Educational Measurement and Evaluation M,D,O
Educational Media/Instructional Technology M,O
Electrical Engineering M,D
Emergency Management O
Engineering and Applied Sciences—General M,D,O
Engineering Management M
English as a Second Language M,O
English Education M
English M,D
Entertainment Management M
Entrepreneurship M
Environmental and Occupational Health O
Environmental Engineering M
Exercise and Sports Science M
Film, Television, and Video Production M
Finance and Banking M,D
Forensic Sciences M,O
Foundations and Philosophy of Education M,D,O
French M
Geography M,D
Geology M,D
Health Services Management and Hospital Administration O
Higher Education M,D
History M,D
Hospitality Management M,O
Human Development M,D
Illustration M
Information Science M,D
Information Studies M
International Affairs M
International Health M
Journalism M
Kinesiology and Movement Studies M,D,O
Law M,D
Library Science M*
Linguistics M
Management Information Systems M,D,O
Marketing M
Marriage and Family Therapy M,D
Mass Communication M,D
Mathematics Education M,D
Mathematics M,D
Mechanical Engineering M,D
Media Studies M
Museum Studies M
Music Education M
Music M
Neuroscience M,D
Nutrition M,D
Organizational Management O
Philosophy M,D
Photography M
Physics M,D
Political Science M,D,O
Psychology—General D
Public Administration M,D
Public Affairs
Reading Education M,D
Real Estate M
Religion M,D
Rhetoric M,D
School Psychology M,D,O
Science Education M,D
Social Psychology D
Social Sciences Education M
Social Sciences M,D
Social Work M
Sociology M,D
Spanish M
Special Education M,D
Sports Management M
Student Affairs M
Supply Chain Management M
Sustainability Management O
Travel and Tourism M
Urban and Regional Planning O
Writing M,D

TABOR COLLEGE
Accounting M
Business Administration and Management—General M

TAFT UNIVERSITY SYSTEM
Education—General M
Law M,D
Legal and Justice Studies M,D
Taxation M,D

TALMUDIC UNIVERSITY
Theology M

TARLETON STATE UNIVERSITY
Accounting M
Agricultural Sciences—General M
Applied Psychology M
Athletic Training and Sports Medicine M
Biological and Biomedical Sciences—General M
Business Administration and Management—General M
Clinical Laboratory Sciences/Medical Technology M
Communication—General M
Counseling Psychology M
Criminal Justice and Criminology M
Curriculum and Instruction M
Education—General M,D,O
Educational Leadership and Administration M,D,O
Educational Media/Instructional Technology M
Elementary Education M
Engineering Management M
English M
Environmental Sciences M
Fish, Game, and Wildlife Management M
History M
Human Resources Management M
Kinesiology and Movement Studies M
Management Information Systems M
Marketing M
Mathematics M
Music Education M
Natural Resources M
Nursing and Healthcare Administration M
Nursing Education M
Nursing—General M
Political Science M
Public Administration M
Public Health—General M
Secondary Education M
Social Work M
Special Education M

TAYLOR COLLEGE AND SEMINARY
Cultural Studies M,O
English as a Second Language M,O
Missions and Missiology M,O
Theology M,O

TAYLOR UNIVERSITY
Higher Education M

TEACHERS COLLEGE, COLUMBIA UNIVERSITY
Adult Education M,D
Anthropology M,D
Applied Behavior Analysis M,D,O
Applied Psychology M,D
Applied Statistics M,D
Art Education M,D,O
Arts Administration M,D,O
Biological and Biomedical Sciences—General M,D
Chemistry M,D
Clinical Psychology M,D
Communication Disorders M,D,O
Communication—General M,D
Community Health M,D,O
Computer Education M,D
Counseling Psychology M,D
Curriculum and Instruction M,D
Developmental Psychology M,D
Early Childhood Education M,D
Economics M,D
Education of Students with Severe/Multiple Disabilities M,D,O
Education of the Gifted M,D
Education—General M,D
Educational Leadership and Administration M,D
Educational Measurement and Evaluation M,D
Educational Media/Instructional Technology M,D
Educational Policy M,D
Educational Psychology M,D,O
Elementary Education M,D
English as a Second Language M,D,O
English Education M,D,O
Foundations and Philosophy of Education M,D,O
Geosciences M,D,O
Health Education M,D,O
Higher Education M,D
Industrial and Organizational Psychology M,D
Interdisciplinary Studies M,D
International Affairs M,D,O
International and Comparative Education M,D
Kinesiology and Movement Studies M,D
Linguistics M,D,O
Mathematics Education M,D
Multilingual and Multicultural Education M,D,O
Music Education M,D,O
Neuroscience M,D
Nursing and Healthcare Administration M,D
Nursing Education M,D,O
Nutrition M,D,O
Philosophy M,D,O
Physical Education M,D
Physics M,D
Physiology M,D
Political Science M,D
Psychology—General M,D
Reading Education M,D,O
School Psychology M,D,O
Science Education M,D
Secondary Education M,D
Social Psychology M,D
Social Sciences Education M,D,O
Sociology M,D
Special Education M,D,O
Urban Education M,D

TEACHERS COLLEGE OF SAN JOAQUIN
Early Childhood Education M
Education—General M
Educational Leadership and Administration M
Educational Measurement and Evaluation M
Mathematics Education M
Science Education M
Special Education M

TÉLÉ-UNIVERSITÉ
Computer Science M,D
Distance Education Development M,D
Finance and Banking M,D

TELSHE YESHIVA–CHICAGO
Jewish Studies O

TEMPLE UNIVERSITY
Accounting M,D
Actuarial Science M
Adult Nursing D
African-American Studies M,D
Allied Health—General M,D
Allopathic Medicine D
Anthropology D
Applied Behavior Analysis M,D,O
Applied Mathematics M,D
Architecture M
Art Education M
Art History M,D
Art/Fine Arts M
Artificial Intelligence/Robotics M,D
Arts Administration M
Athletic Training and Sports Medicine M,D
Bioengineering M,D
Biological and Biomedical Sciences—General M,D
Biotechnology M,D
Business Administration and Management—General M,D
Business Education M
Chemistry M,D
Civil Engineering M,D,O
Communication Disorders M,D
Communication—General M,D
Computer and Information Systems Security M,D
Computer Science M,D
Corporate and Organizational Communication M,D
Counseling Psychology M,D,O
Criminal Justice and Criminology M,D
Dance M,D
Dentistry D
Economics M,D
Education—General M,D,O
Educational Leadership and Administration M,D
Educational Psychology M,D,O
Electrical Engineering M,D
Engineering and Applied Sciences—General D*
Engineering Management M,O
English as a Second Language M
English Education M
English M,D
Entrepreneurship M,D
Environmental and Occupational Health M,D
Environmental Engineering M,D,O
Epidemiology M,D
Family Nurse Practitioner Studies D
Film, Television, and Video Production M
Finance and Banking M,D
Financial Engineering M
Geographic Information Systems M,D,O
Geography M,D,O
Geology M,D
Geosciences M,D
Gerontology D
Graphic Design M
Health Informatics M,D
Health Services Management and Hospital Administration M
History M,D
Hospitality Management M,D
Human Resources Management M
Hydrology M,O
Industrial and Labor Relations M,O
Information Science M,D
Insurance D
International Business M,D
Investment Management M,O
Journalism M
Kinesiology and Movement Studies M,D
Landscape Architecture M
Law M,D,O
Legal and Justice Studies M,D
Management Information Systems M,D
Management Strategy and Policy D
Marketing M,D
Mathematics Education M
Mathematics M,D
Mechanical Engineering M,D
Media Studies M
Medicinal and Pharmaceutical Chemistry M,D
Middle School Education M
Music Education M,D
Music M,D
Nursing—General D
Occupational Therapy M,D
Oral and Dental Sciences M,O
Pharmaceutical Administration M
Pharmaceutical Sciences M,D
Pharmacy M,D
Philosophy M,D
Photography M
Physical Education M,D
Physical Therapy D
Physics M,D
Podiatric Medicine D
Political Science M,D
Psychology—General M,D
Public Health—General M,D
Recreation and Park Management M,D
Rehabilitation Sciences M,D
Religion M,D
Risk Management D
School Psychology M,D,O
Science Education M
Secondary Education M
Social Psychology M,D,O
Social Sciences Education M
Social Work M
Sociology M,D
Spanish M,D
Sports Management M,D
Statistics M,D
Sustainable Development M,O
Taxation M,D
Textile Design M
Theater M
Therapies—Dance, Drama, and Music M,D
Transportation Management M,O
Travel and Tourism M,D
Urban and Regional Planning M,O
Urban Education M
Urban Studies M,D,O
Vocational and Technical Education M
Writing M,D

TENNESSEE STATE UNIVERSITY
Agricultural Education M,D
Agricultural Sciences—General M,D
Agronomy and Soil Sciences M,D
Allied Health—General M,D,O
Biological and Biomedical Sciences—General D
Biomedical Engineering M,D
Biotechnology M,D
Business Administration and Management—General M
Chemistry M
Civil Engineering M,D
Communication Disorders M
Computer Engineering M,D
Counseling Psychology M
Criminal Justice and Criminology M
Curriculum and Instruction M,D
Education—General M,D,O
Electrical Engineering M,D
Elementary Education M,D
Engineering and Applied Sciences—General M,D
Environmental Engineering M,D
Exercise and Sports Science M
Family and Consumer Sciences-General M,D
Family Nurse Practitioner Studies M,O
Human Resources Management M,D
Management Strategy and Policy M,D
Manufacturing Engineering M,D
Mathematics M,D
Mechanical Engineering M,D
Nursing—General M,O
Occupational Therapy M
Physical Education M
Physical Therapy D
Plant Sciences M,D
Psychology—General M
Public Administration M,D
Public Health—General M
Social Work M,D
Special Education M,D
Sports Management M
Systems Engineering M,D

TENNESSEE TECHNOLOGICAL UNIVERSITY
Accounting M
Acute Care/Critical Care Nursing D
Agricultural Sciences—General D
Applied Behavior Analysis D
Biological and Biomedical Sciences—General M,D
Business Administration and Management—General M
Chemical Engineering M
Chemistry M,D
Civil Engineering M
Computer Science M
Curriculum and Instruction M,O
Early Childhood Education M,O
Education of the Gifted D
Education—General M,D,O
Educational Leadership and Administration M,O
Educational Measurement and Evaluation D
Educational Media/Instructional Technology M,O
Educational Psychology M,O
Electrical Engineering M
Elementary Education M,O
Engineering and Applied Sciences—General M,D

*M—masters degree; D—doctorate; O—other advanced degree; *—Close-Up and/or Display*

English as a Second Language	M
English	M
Environmental Management and Policy	M
Environmental Sciences	M,D
Family Nurse Practitioner Studies	M,D
Finance and Banking	M
Fish, Game, and Wildlife Management	M
Geosciences	D
Gerontological Nursing	D
Health Education	M
Health Promotion	M
Human Resources Management	M
International Business	M
Internet and Interactive Multimedia	M
Kinesiology and Movement Studies	M
Library Science	M,O
Management Information Systems	M
Management Strategy and Policy	M
Mathematics Education	M,O
Mathematics	M
Mechanical Engineering	M
Middle School Education	M
Music Education	M
Nursing and Healthcare Administration	M,D
Nursing Education	M
Nursing—General	M,D
Physical Education	M
Psychiatric Nursing	D
Reading Education	M,D,O
Science Education	M,O
Secondary Education	M,O
Special Education	M,O
Sports Management	M
Women's Health Nursing	D

TENNESSEE WESLEYAN UNIVERSITY

Accounting	M
Business Administration and Management—General	M

TEXAS A&M INTERNATIONAL UNIVERSITY

Accounting	M
Biological and Biomedical Sciences—General	M
Business Administration and Management—General	M,D
Counseling Psychology	M
Counselor Education	M
Criminal Justice and Criminology	M
Curriculum and Instruction	M
Education—General	M
Educational Leadership and Administration	M
English	M
Family Nurse Practitioner Studies	M
Finance and Banking	M
Foreign Languages Education	M
History	M
International Business	M,D
Management Information Systems	M,D
Mathematics	M
Nursing—General	M
Political Science	M
Psychology—General	M
Public Administration	M
Social Sciences	M
Sociology	M
Special Education	M
Translation and Interpretation	M

TEXAS A&M UNIVERSITY

Accounting	M
Aerospace/Aeronautical Engineering	M,D
Agricultural Economics and Agribusiness	M,D
Agricultural Education	M,D
Agricultural Engineering	M,D
Agricultural Sciences—General	M,D
Agronomy and Soil Sciences	M,D
Allopathic Medicine	M,D
Animal Sciences	M,D
Anthropology	M,D
Applied Physics	M,D
Architecture	M,D
Art/Fine Arts	M
Astronomy	M,D
Athletic Training and Sports Medicine	M,D
Biochemistry	M,D
Bioengineering	M,D
Biological and Biomedical Sciences—General	M,D,O
Biomedical Engineering	M,D
Biostatistics	M,D
Business Administration and Management—General	M
Chemical Engineering	M,D
Chemistry	M,D
Civil Engineering	M,D
Clinical Psychology	M,D
Communication—General	M,D
Community Health	M,D
Computer Engineering	M,D
Computer Science	M,D
Construction Management	M
Counseling Psychology	M,D
Cultural Studies	M,D
Curriculum and Instruction	M,D
Dental Hygiene	M,D,O
Dentistry	M,D,O
Economics	M,D
Education—General	M,D
Educational Leadership and Administration	M,D
Educational Media/Instructional Technology	M,D
Educational Psychology	M,D
Electrical Engineering	M,D
Engineering Management	M,D
English	M,D
Entomology	M,D
Entrepreneurship	M
Environmental and Occupational Health	M,D
Epidemiology	M,D
Family Nurse Practitioner Studies	M
Finance and Banking	M
Fish, Game, and Wildlife Management	M,D
Food Science and Technology	M,D
Forensic Nursing	M
Forestry	M,D
Geography	M,D
Geology	M,D
Geophysics	M,D
Health Education	M,D
Health Promotion	M,D
Health Services Management and Hospital Administration	M,D
Health Services Research	M,D
History	M,D
Homeland Security	M,O
Horticulture	M,D
Human Resources Development	M,D
Human Resources Management	M
Industrial and Organizational Psychology	M,D
Industrial/Management Engineering	M,D
Intellectual Property Law	M,D
International Affairs	M,O
Kinesiology and Movement Studies	M,D
Landscape Architecture	M,D
Law	M,D
Management Information Systems	M
Management of Technology	M
Manufacturing Engineering	M
Marine Biology	M,D
Marine Sciences	M
Marketing	M
Materials Engineering	M,D
Materials Sciences	M,D
Mathematics	M,D
Mechanical Engineering	M,D
Meteorology	M,D
Microbiology	M,D
Multilingual and Multicultural Education	M,D
Music	M
National Security	M,O
Natural Resources	M,D
Nonprofit Management	M,O
Nuclear Engineering	M,D
Nursing and Healthcare Administration	M,D
Nursing Education	M,D
Nursing—General	M
Nutrition	M,D
Oceanography	M,D
Oral and Dental Sciences	M,D,O
Petroleum Engineering	M,D
Pharmacy	D
Philosophy	M,D
Physics	M,D
Plant Pathology	M,D
Political Science	M,D
Psychology—General	M,D
Public Administration	M,O
Public Affairs	M,O
Public Health—General	M,D,O
Real Estate	M
Recreation and Park Management	M,D
School Psychology	M,D
Sociology	M,D
Spanish	M,D
Special Education	M,D
Sports Management	M,D
Statistics	M,D
Transportation Management	M
Urban and Regional Planning	M,D
Veterinary Medicine	M,D
Veterinary Sciences	M,D

TEXAS A&M UNIVERSITY–CENTRAL TEXAS

Accounting	M,O
Business Administration and Management—General	M,O
Clinical Psychology	M,O
Counselor Education	M,O
Criminal Justice and Criminology	M,O
Curriculum and Instruction	M,O
Educational Leadership and Administration	M,O
Educational Psychology	M,O
Experimental Psychology	M,O
History	M,O
Human Resources Management	M,O
Liberal Studies	M,O
Management Information Systems	M,O
Marriage and Family Therapy	M,O
Mathematics	M,O
Political Science	M,O
School Psychology	M,O

TEXAS A&M UNIVERSITY–COMMERCE

Accounting	M
Agricultural Sciences—General	M
Art/Fine Arts	M,D,O
Biological and Biomedical Sciences—General	M,O
Business Administration and Management—General	M
Business Analytics	M
Chemistry	M,O
Computational Sciences	M,O
Counselor Education	M,D,O
Criminal Justice and Criminology	M,D,O
Curriculum and Instruction	M,D,O
Early Childhood Education	M,D,O
Education—General	M,D,O
Educational Leadership and Administration	M,D,O
Educational Media/Instructional Technology	M,D,O
Educational Psychology	M,D,O
Elementary Education	M,D,O
English as a Second Language	M,D,O
English	M,D,O
Environmental Sciences	M,O
Exercise and Sports Science	M,D,O
Film, Television, and Video Theory and Criticism	M,D,O
Finance and Banking	M
Higher Education	M,D,O
History	M,D,O
Holocaust and Genocide Studies	M,D,O
Homeland Security	M,D,O
Kinesiology and Movement Studies	M,D,O
Library Science	M,D,O
Linguistics	M,D,O
Management of Technology	M,O
Marketing	M
Mathematics	M,O
Music Education	M,D,O
Music	M,D,O
Physics	M,O
Political Science	M,D,O
Psychology—General	M,D,O
Public History	M,D,O
Reading Education	M,D,O
Secondary Education	M,D,O
Social Work	M,D,O
Sociology	M,D,O
Spanish	M,D,O
Special Education	M,D,O
Theater	M,D,O
Writing	M,D,O

TEXAS A&M UNIVERSITY–CORPUS CHRISTI

Accounting	M
Aquaculture	M
Art/Fine Arts	M
Biological and Biomedical Sciences—General	M,D
Business Administration and Management—General	M
Chemistry	M,D
Clinical Psychology	M
Communication—General	M
Computer Science	M
Counselor Education	M,D
Curriculum and Instruction	M,D
Early Childhood Education	M,D
Education—General	M,D
Educational Leadership and Administration	M,D
Educational Media/Instructional Technology	M,D
Elementary Education	M
English	M
Environmental Sciences	M
Family Nurse Practitioner Studies	M,D
Finance and Banking	M
Geographic Information Systems	M,D
Health Services Management and Hospital Administration	M,D
History	M
Human Development	M,D
International Business	M
Kinesiology and Movement Studies	M,D
Marine Biology	M,D
Marine Sciences	M,D
Mathematics	M
Nursing and Healthcare Administration	M,D
Nursing Education	M,D
Nursing—General	M,D
Psychology—General	M
Public Administration	M
Reading Education	M,D
Secondary Education	M
Special Education	M

TEXAS A&M UNIVERSITY–KINGSVILLE

Adult Education	M
Agricultural Economics and Agribusiness	M,D
Agricultural Sciences—General	M,D
Agronomy and Soil Sciences	M
Animal Sciences	M
Biological and Biomedical Sciences—General	M
Business Administration and Management—General	M
Chemical Engineering	M
Chemistry	M
Civil Engineering	M
Communication Disorders	M
Computer Science	M
Counselor Education	M
Criminal Justice and Criminology	M
Cultural Studies	M
Early Childhood Education	M
Education—General	M,D,O
Educational Leadership and Administration	M,D
Educational Media/Instructional Technology	M
Electrical Engineering	M
Energy and Power Engineering	D
Engineering and Applied Sciences—General	M,D
English as a Second Language	M,D
English	M
Environmental Engineering	M,D
Family and Consumer Sciences-General	M
Fish, Game, and Wildlife Management	M,D
Foreign Languages Education	M
Health Education	M
Hispanic Studies	D
Horticulture	M,D
Industrial and Manufacturing Management	M
Industrial/Management Engineering	M
Kinesiology and Movement Studies	M
Mathematics	M
Mechanical Engineering	M
Multilingual and Multicultural Education	M,D
Music Education	M
Music	M
Petroleum Engineering	M
Plant Sciences	M
Psychology—General	M
Range Science	M
Reading Education	M
Science Education	M
Sociology	M
Spanish	M
Special Education	M
Statistics	M
Sustainable Development	D
Systems Engineering	D

TEXAS A&M UNIVERSITY–SAN ANTONIO

Accounting	M
Business Administration and Management—General	M
Clinical Psychology	M
Counselor Education	M
Early Childhood Education	M
Education—General	M
Educational Leadership and Administration	M
Educational Measurement and Evaluation	M
English	M
Kinesiology and Movement Studies	M
Marriage and Family Therapy	M
Multilingual and Multicultural Education	M
Reading Education	M
Special Education	M

TEXAS A&M UNIVERSITY–TEXARKANA

Accounting	M
Adult Education	M
Business Administration and Management—General	M
Counseling Psychology	M
Curriculum and Instruction	M
Education—General	M
Educational Leadership and Administration	M
Educational Media/Instructional Technology	M
English	M
Interdisciplinary Studies	M
Psychology—General	M
Special Education	M

TEXAS CHIROPRACTIC COLLEGE

Chiropractic	D

TEXAS CHRISTIAN UNIVERSITY

Accounting	M
Adult Nursing	M,O
Allied Health—General	M,D,O
American Studies	M,D
Applied Mathematics	M,D
Art History	M
Art/Fine Arts	M
Astrophysics	M,D
Biochemistry	M,D
Biological and Biomedical Sciences—General	M,D
Biophysics	M,D
Business Administration and Management—General	M
Chemistry	M,D
Cognitive Sciences	M,D
Communication Disorders	M
Communication—General	M
Corporate and Organizational Communication	M
Counselor Education	M,D
Criminal Justice and Criminology	M
Curriculum and Instruction	M,D
Developmental Psychology	M,D
Education—General	M,D
Educational Leadership and Administration	M,D
English	M,D
Environmental Sciences	M
Experimental Psychology	M,D
Family Nurse Practitioner Studies	D
Geology	M
Gerontological Nursing	M,O
Gerontology	D
Health Services Management and Hospital Administration	M,O
History	M,D
Kinesiology and Movement Studies	M,D
Latin American Studies	M,D
Liberal Studies	M
Mass Communication	M
Mathematics Education	M
Mathematics	M,D
Music Education	M,D
Music	M,D
Neuroscience	M,D
Nurse Anesthesia	D
Nursing and Healthcare Administration	M,D,O
Nursing Education	M,O
Nursing—General	M,D,O
Pediatric Nursing	M,D,O
Physics	M,D
Psychology—General	M,D
Reading Education	M
Rhetoric	M,D
Science Education	M,D
Social Psychology	M,D

Social Work	M
Special Education	M
Speech and Interpersonal Communication	M
Taxation	M

TEXAS HEALTH AND SCIENCE UNIVERSITY

Acupuncture and Oriental Medicine	M,D
Business Administration and Management—General	M,D
Health Services Management and Hospital Administration	M,D

TEXAS LUTHERAN UNIVERSITY

Accounting	M

TEXAS SOUTHERN UNIVERSITY

Art/Fine Arts	M
Biological and Biomedical Sciences—General	M
Business Administration and Management—General	M
Chemistry	M
Communication—General	M
Computer Science	M
Counselor Education	M,D
Criminal Justice and Criminology	M,D
Curriculum and Instruction	M,D
Education—General	M,D
Educational Leadership and Administration	M,D
English	M
Environmental Management and Policy	M,D
Family and Consumer Sciences-General	M
Health Education	M
Health Services Management and Hospital Administration	M
Higher Education	M,D
History	M
Human Services	M
Industrial/Management Engineering	M
Law	D
Management Information Systems	M
Mathematics	M
Multilingual and Multicultural Education	M,D
Music	M
Pharmaceutical Sciences	M,D
Pharmacy	D
Physical Education	M
Psychology—General	M
Public Administration	M
Secondary Education	M,D
Sociology	M
Toxicology	M,D
Transportation and Highway Engineering	M
Transportation Management	M
Urban and Regional Planning	M,D

TEXAS STATE UNIVERSITY

Accounting	M
Adult Education	M,D
Agricultural Education	M
Allied Health—General	M,D
Anthropology	M
Applied Arts and Design—General	M
Applied Mathematics	M
Athletic Training and Sports Medicine	M
Biochemistry	M
Biological and Biomedical Sciences—General	M
Business Administration and Management—General	M
Chemistry	M
Child and Family Studies	M
Civil Engineering	M
Clinical Psychology	M
Communication Disorders	M
Communication—General	M
Computer Art and Design	M
Computer Science	M,D
Conservation Biology	M
Counselor Education	M
Criminal Justice and Criminology	M,D
Developmental Education	M,D
Early Childhood Education	M
Education—General	M,D,O
Educational Leadership and Administration	M,D
Educational Media/Instructional Technology	M
Electrical Engineering	M
Elementary Education	M
Engineering and Applied Sciences—General	M
English	M
Ethics	M
Family and Consumer Sciences-General	M
Family Nurse Practitioner Studies	M
Fish, Game, and Wildlife Management	M
Geographic Information Systems	M,D
Geography	M,D
Gerontology	M
Graphic Design	M
Health Education	M
Health Informatics	M
Health Services Management and Hospital Administration	M
Higher Education	M
History	M
Human Resources Management	M
Industrial/Management Engineering	M
Interdisciplinary Studies	M
International Affairs	M
Legal and Justice Studies	M
Leisure Studies	M
Management Information Systems	M
Management of Technology	M
Manufacturing Engineering	M
Marine Biology	M,D
Marriage and Family Therapy	M
Mass Communication	M
Materials Engineering	D
Materials Sciences	M,D
Mathematics Education	M,D
Mathematics	M
Mechanical Engineering	M
Multilingual and Multicultural Education	M
Music Education	M
Music	M
Nutrition	M
Philosophy	M
Physical Education	M
Physical Therapy	D
Physics	M
Political Science	M
Psychology—General	M
Public Administration	M
Reading Education	M
Recreation and Park Management	M
Rhetoric	M
School Psychology	O
Secondary Education	M
Social Work	M
Sociology	M
Software Engineering	M
Spanish	M
Special Education	M
Student Affairs	M
Sustainable Development	M
Technical Communication	M
Theater	M
Vocational and Technical Education	M
Writing	M

TEXAS TECH UNIVERSITY

Accounting	M,D
Agricultural Economics and Agribusiness	M,D
Agricultural Education	M,D
Agricultural Sciences—General	M,D
Agronomy and Soil Sciences	M,D
Animal Sciences	M,D
Anthropology	M
Applied Economics	M,D
Architecture	M,D
Art Education	M
Art History	M
Art/Fine Arts	M,D
Astronomy	M,D
Atmospheric Sciences	M,D
Bioengineering	M
Biological and Biomedical Sciences—General	M,D
Biotechnology	M,D
Business Administration and Management—General	M,D
Chemical Engineering	M,D
Chemistry	M,D
Child and Family Studies	M,D
Civil Engineering	M,D
Clinical Psychology	M,D
Communication—General	M,D
Computer Science	M,D
Construction Engineering	M,D
Consumer Economics	M,D
Counseling Psychology	M,D
Counselor Education	M,D
Cultural Studies	M,D
Curriculum and Instruction	M,D
Data Science/Data Analytics	M,D
Economics	M,D
Education—General	M,D
Educational Leadership and Administration	M,D
Educational Media/Instructional Technology	M,D
Educational Psychology	M,D
Electrical Engineering	M,D
Elementary Education	M,D
Energy and Power Engineering	M,D
Engineering and Applied Sciences—General	M,D
Engineering Management	M,D
English	M,D
Environmental Design	M,D
Environmental Engineering	M,D
Environmental Management and Policy	M,D
Environmental Sciences	M,D
Exercise and Sports Science	M
Experimental Psychology	M,D
Finance and Banking	M,D
Fish, Game, and Wildlife Management	M,D
Food Science and Technology	M,D
Forensic Sciences	M
Geography	M,D
Geosciences	M,D
Gerontology	M,D
Health Services Management and Hospital Administration	M,D
Higher Education	M,D
History	M,D
Home Economics Education	M,D
Horticulture	M,D
Hospitality Management	M,D
Human Development	M,D
Industrial/Management Engineering	M,D
Interdisciplinary Studies	M,D
Interior Design	M,D
Kinesiology and Movement Studies	M
Landscape Architecture	M
Law	M,D
Legal and Justice Studies	M,D
Management Information Systems	M,D
Marketing	M,D
Marriage and Family Therapy	M,D
Mass Communication	M,D
Mathematics	M,D
Mechanical Engineering	M,D
Media Studies	M,D
Microbiology	M,D
Multilingual and Multicultural Education	M,D
Museum Studies	M,D
Music Education	M,D
Music	M,D
Natural Resources	M,D
Nutrition	M,D
Petroleum Engineering	M,D
Philosophy	M
Physics	M,D
Plant Sciences	M,D
Political Science	M,D
Psychology—General	M,D
Public Administration	M,D
Reading Education	M,D
Rhetoric	M,D
Romance Languages	M,D
Science Education	M,D
Secondary Education	M,D
Social Sciences Education	M,D
Social Work	M
Sociology	M
Software Engineering	M,D
Spanish	M,D
Special Education	M,D
Sports Management	M
Statistics	M,D
Sustainable Development	M,D
Systems Engineering	M,D
Taxation	M,D
Technical Writing	M,D
Theater	M
Toxicology	M,D
Zoology	M,D

TEXAS TECH UNIVERSITY HEALTH SCIENCES CENTER

Acute Care/Critical Care Nursing	M,D,O
Addictions/Substance Abuse Counseling	M
Allopathic Medicine	D
Athletic Training and Sports Medicine	M
Biological and Biomedical Sciences—General	M,D
Biotechnology	M
Cell Biology	M,D
Clinical Psychology	M
Communication Disorders	M,D
Family Nurse Practitioner Studies	M,D,O
Gerontological Nursing	M,D,O
Health Services Management and Hospital Administration	M
Molecular Pathology	M
Nursing and Healthcare Administration	M,D,O
Nursing Education	M,D,O
Nursing—General	M,D,O
Occupational Therapy	M
Pediatric Nursing	M,D,O
Pharmaceutical Sciences	M,D
Physical Therapy	D
Physician Assistant Studies	M
Rehabilitation Counseling	M
Rehabilitation Sciences	D

TEXAS TECH UNIVERSITY HEALTH SCIENCES CENTER EL PASO

Allopathic Medicine	D
Biological and Biomedical Sciences—General	M
Nursing—General	M

TEXAS WESLEYAN UNIVERSITY

Business Administration and Management—General	M
Education—General	M,D
Nurse Anesthesia	M,D

TEXAS WOMAN'S UNIVERSITY

Accounting	M
Acute Care/Critical Care Nursing	M,D
Adult Nursing	M,D
Allied Health—General	M,D
Art Education	M
Art History	M
Art/Fine Arts	M
Biological and Biomedical Sciences—General	M,D
Business Administration and Management—General	M
Business Analytics	M
Chemistry	M
Child and Family Studies	M,D
Child Development	M,D
Communication Disorders	M
Counseling Psychology	M,D,O
Counselor Education	M,D
Curriculum and Instruction	M,D
Dance	M,D
Dental Hygiene	M,D
Early Childhood Education	M,D
Education—General	M,D,O
Educational Leadership and Administration	M,D
English Education	M,D
English	M,D
Exercise and Sports Science	M,D
Family Nurse Practitioner Studies	M,D
Food Science and Technology	M,D
Gender Studies	M,D
Gerontological Nursing	M,D
Graphic Design	M
Health Education	M,D
Health Services Management and Hospital Administration	M
History	M
Human Resources Management	M
Information Science	M
Internet and Interactive Multimedia	M
Kinesiology and Movement Studies	M,D
Library Science	M
Marriage and Family Therapy	M,D
Mathematics Education	M
Mathematics	M
Molecular Biology	M,D
Music Education	M
Music	M
Nursing and Healthcare Administration	M,D
Nursing Education	M,D
Nursing—General	M,D
Nutrition	M,D
Occupational Therapy	M,D
Pediatric Nursing	M,D
Photography	M
Physical Education	M,D
Physical Therapy	D
Political Science	M
Psychology—General	M,D,O
Reading Education	M,D,O
Rhetoric	M,D
School Psychology	M,D,O
Sociology	M,D
Special Education	M,D
Sports Management	M,D
Theater	M
Therapies—Dance, Drama, and Music	M
Women's Health Nursing	M,D
Women's Studies	M,D

THEOLOGICAL UNIVERSITY OF THE CARIBBEAN

Early Childhood Education	M,D
Middle School Education	M,D
Missions and Missiology	M,D
Pastoral Ministry and Counseling	M,D

THOMAS COLLEGE

Business Administration and Management—General	M
Business Education	M
Computer Education	M
Human Resources Management	M

THOMAS EDISON STATE UNIVERSITY

Accounting	M
Applied Science and Technology	M,O
Business Administration and Management—General	M
Computer and Information Systems Security	M,O
Distance Education Development	M,O
Economic Development	M
Educational Leadership and Administration	M,O
Educational Media/Instructional Technology	M,O
Environmental Management and Policy	M
Finance and Banking	M
Homeland Security	M
Hospitality Management	M
Human Resources Management	M
Industrial and Organizational Psychology	M,O
Information Science	M,O
International Business	M
Liberal Studies	M,O
Nonprofit Management	M
Nursing and Healthcare Administration	M
Nursing Education	M
Nursing Informatics	M
Nursing—General	M,D
Organizational Management	M
Project Management	M
Public Administration	M
Public Health—General	M
Urban and Regional Planning	M

THOMAS JEFFERSON SCHOOL OF LAW

Law	D

THOMAS JEFFERSON UNIVERSITY

Allopathic Medicine	D
Applied Economics	M,D,O
Architecture	M
Art/Fine Arts	M
Athletic Training and Sports Medicine	M
Biochemistry	D
Biological and Biomedical Sciences—General	M,D,O
Biotechnology	M
Business Administration and Management—General	M
Business Analytics	M
Cancer Biology/Oncology	D
Cell Biology	M,D
Clinical Laboratory Sciences/Medical Technology	M
Clinical Research	M,O
Clothing and Textiles	M

*M—masters degree; D—doctorate; O—other advanced degree; *—Close-Up and/or Display*

Construction Management	M
Developmental Biology	M
Emergency Management	M
Genetic Counseling	M
Genetics	D
Genomic Sciences	D
Geography	M
Health Education	M,D,O
Health Physics/Radiological Health	M
Health Services Management and Hospital Administration	M,D,O
Health Services Research	M,D,O
Human Genetics	M
Immunology	D
Industrial Design	M
Infectious Diseases	O
Interior Design	M
Internet and Interactive Multimedia	M
Management Strategy and Policy	M,D
Marketing	M
Marriage and Family Therapy	M
Microbiology	M,D
Molecular Pharmacology	D
Neuroscience	D
Nurse Midwifery	M
Nursing—General	M,D
Occupational Therapy	M,D
Pharmacology	M
Pharmacy	D
Physical Therapy	D
Physician Assistant Studies	M
Public Health—General	M,O
Real Estate	M
Social Psychology	M
Sustainable Development	M
Taxation	M
Textile Design	M
Textile Sciences and Engineering	M,D
Toxicology	M
Urban and Regional Planning	M

THOMAS MORE COLLEGE

Business Administration and Management—General	M
Education—General	M
Educational Leadership and Administration	M

THOMAS UNIVERSITY

Business Administration and Management—General	M
Education—General	M
Human Services	M
Nursing—General	M
Rehabilitation Counseling	M
Social Psychology	M

THOMPSON RIVERS UNIVERSITY

Business Administration and Management—General	M
Education—General	M
Environmental Sciences	M
Social Work	M

TIFFIN UNIVERSITY

Art/Fine Arts	M
Business Administration and Management—General	M
Communication—General	M
Criminal Justice and Criminology	M
Education—General	M
Educational Leadership and Administration	M
Educational Media/Instructional Technology	M
English	M
Film, Television, and Video Theory and Criticism	M
Finance and Banking	M
Forensic Psychology	M
Health Services Management and Hospital Administration	M
Higher Education	M
Homeland Security	M
Human Resources Management	M
Humanities	M
International Business	M
Marketing	M
Nonprofit Management	M
Psychology—General	M
Sports Management	M
Writing	M

TORONTO SCHOOL OF THEOLOGY

Theology	M,D

TOURO COLLEGE

Communication Disorders	M,D
Counseling Psychology	M,D
Education—General	M
Educational Leadership and Administration	M
Educational Media/Instructional Technology	M
English as a Second Language	M
Industrial and Organizational Psychology	M,D
Internet and Interactive Multimedia	M
Jewish Studies	M
Law	M,D
Legal and Justice Studies	M,D
Management Information Systems	M
Mathematics Education	M
Occupational Therapy	M,D
Physical Therapy	M,D
Physician Assistant Studies	M,D
Reading Education	M
Social Work	M
Special Education	M

TOURO UNIVERSITY CALIFORNIA

Education—General	M,D
Osteopathic Medicine	M,D
Pharmacy	M,D
Public Health—General	M,D

TOWSON UNIVERSITY

Accounting	M
Allied Health—General	M
Applied Mathematics	M
Applied Physics	M
Art Education	M,O
Art History	M
Art/Fine Arts	M
Biological and Biomedical Sciences—General	M
Child and Family Studies	M,O
Communication Disorders	M,D
Communication—General	M
Computer Science	M
Corporate and Organizational Communication	M
Counseling Psychology	M
Early Childhood Education	M,O
Education—General	M
Educational Leadership and Administration	M,O
Educational Media/Instructional Technology	M
Electronic Commerce	M,O
Elementary Education	M
Environmental and Occupational Health	D
Environmental Management and Policy	M
Environmental Sciences	M,O
Experimental Psychology	M
Forensic Sciences	M
Geography	M
Health Services Management and Hospital Administration	M,O
Homeland Security	M,O
Human Resources Development	M
Human Resources Management	M
Humanities	M
Information Science	M,D,O
Internet and Interactive Multimedia	M,O
Jewish Studies	M,O
Liberal Studies	M
Management of Technology	M,O
Marketing Research	M,O
Mathematics Education	M
Music Education	M
Music	M
Nursing Education	O
Nursing—General	O
Occupational Therapy	M
Physician Assistant Studies	M
Psychology—General	M
Reading Education	M,O
School Psychology	M
Secondary Education	M
Social Sciences	M
Special Education	M,O
Supply Chain Management	M,O
Theater	M
Women's Studies	M,O
Writing	M

TOYOTA TECHNOLOGICAL INSTITUTE AT CHICAGO

Computer Science	D

TRENT UNIVERSITY

American Indian/Native American Studies	M,D
Anthropology	M
Biological and Biomedical Sciences—General	M,D
Canadian Studies	M,D
Chemistry	M
Computer Science	M
Cultural Studies	D
Environmental Management and Policy	M,D
Geography	M,D
Materials Sciences	M
Modeling and Simulation	M,D
Physics	M

TREVECCA NAZARENE UNIVERSITY

Business Administration and Management—General	M
Counselor Education	M,D
Curriculum and Instruction	M,D
Education—General	M,O
Educational Leadership and Administration	M,D,O
Educational Media/Instructional Technology	M
Elementary Education	M,O
English as a Second Language	M,O
Health Services Management and Hospital Administration	M
Information Science	M,O
Library Science	M,O
Marriage and Family Therapy	M,D
Organizational Management	M,D
Pastoral Ministry and Counseling	M
Physician Assistant Studies	M
Religion	M
Secondary Education	M,O
Special Education	M,O

TRIDENT UNIVERSITY INTERNATIONAL

Adult Education	M
Business Administration and Management—General	M,D
Clinical Research	M,D,O
Computer and Information Systems Security	M,D
Conflict Resolution and Mediation/Peace Studies	M,D
Criminal Justice and Criminology	M,D
Early Childhood Education	M
Education—General	M,D
Educational Leadership and Administration	M,D
Educational Media/Instructional Technology	M,D
Emergency Management	M,D,O
Environmental and Occupational Health	M,D,O
Finance and Banking	M,D
Health Education	M,D,O
Health Informatics	M,D,O
Health Services Management and Hospital Administration	M,D,O
Higher Education	M,D
Human Resources Management	M,D
International Business	M,D
International Health	M,D,O
Legal and Justice Studies	M,D,O
Logistics	M,D
Management Information Systems	M,D,O
Marketing	M,D
Project Management	M,D
Public Administration	M,D
Public Health—General	M,D,O
Quality Management	M,D,O
Reading Education	M

TRINE UNIVERSITY

Business Administration and Management—General	M
Criminal Justice and Criminology	M
Emergency Management	M
Engineering Management	M
Management Information Systems	M
Organizational Management	M
Physical Therapy	D
Physician Assistant Studies	M

TRINITY BAPTIST COLLEGE

Curriculum and Instruction	M
Educational Leadership and Administration	M
Religion	M
Special Education	M

TRINITY BIBLE COLLEGE AND GRADUATE SCHOOL

Missions and Missiology	M
Pastoral Ministry and Counseling	M
Theology	M

TRINITY CHRISTIAN COLLEGE

Counseling Psychology	M
Special Education	M

TRINITY COLLEGE (CANADA)

Music	M,D,O
Pastoral Ministry and Counseling	M,D,O
Theology	M,D,O

TRINITY COLLEGE (UNITED STATES)

American Studies	M
Cultural Studies	M
English	M
Media Studies	M
Museum Studies	M
Public Policy	M
Writing	M

TRINITY INTERNATIONAL UNIVERSITY

Archaeology	M,D,O
Athletic Training and Sports Medicine	M
Bioethics	M,D
Business Administration and Management—General	M,D,O
Counseling Psychology	M,D,O
Education—General	M,D
Human Resources Management	M,D
Law	M,D
Missions and Missiology	M,D,O
Pastoral Ministry and Counseling	M,D,O
Religious Education	M,D,O
Theology	M,D,O

TRINITY INTERNATIONAL UNIVERSITY FLORIDA

Counseling Psychology	M
Religion	M,O

TRINITY LUTHERAN SEMINARY

African-American Studies	M
Missions and Missiology	M
Music	M
Pastoral Ministry and Counseling	M
Religious Education	M
Theology	M

TRINITY SCHOOL FOR MINISTRY

Missions and Missiology	M,D,O
Pastoral Ministry and Counseling	M,D,O
Religion	M,D,O
Theology	M,D,O

TRINITY UNIVERSITY

Accounting	M
Business Administration and Management—General	M
Education—General	M
Educational Leadership and Administration	M
Health Services Management and Hospital Administration	M
School Psychology	M

TRINITY WASHINGTON UNIVERSITY

Business Administration and Management—General	M
Clinical Psychology	M
Communication—General	M
Counseling Psychology	M
Counselor Education	M
Curriculum and Instruction	M
Early Childhood Education	M
Education—General	M
Educational Leadership and Administration	M
Elementary Education	M
English Education	M
Human Resources Management	M
National Security	M
Nonprofit Management	M
Organizational Management	M
Public Health—General	M
Reading Education	M
Secondary Education	M
Social Sciences Education	M
Special Education	M

TRINITY WESTERN UNIVERSITY

Business Administration and Management—General	M
Counseling Psychology	M
Educational Leadership and Administration	M,O
English as a Second Language	M
English	M
Health Services Management and Hospital Administration	M,O
History	M
Humanities	M
Interdisciplinary Studies	M
International Business	M
Linguistics	M
Nonprofit Management	M,O
Nursing—General	M
Organizational Management	M,O
Pastoral Ministry and Counseling	M,D
Philosophy	M
Theology	M,D

TRI-STATE BIBLE COLLEGE

Theology	M

TRI-STATE COLLEGE OF ACUPUNCTURE

Acupuncture and Oriental Medicine	M,O

TROPICAL AGRICULTURE RESEARCH AND HIGHER EDUCATION CENTER

Agricultural Economics and Agribusiness	M,D
Agricultural Sciences—General	M,D
Conservation Biology	M,D
Environmental Management and Policy	M,D
Forestry	M,D
Travel and Tourism	M,D
Water Resources	M,D

TROY UNIVERSITY

Accounting	M
Adult Education	M
Adult Nursing	M,D
Biological and Biomedical Sciences—General	M,O
Business Administration and Management—General	M
Communication—General	M
Computer Science	M
Corporate and Organizational Communication	M
Counselor Education	M,O
Criminal Justice and Criminology	M
Early Childhood Education	M,O
Economic Development	M
Economics	M
Education—General	M,O
Educational Leadership and Administration	M,O
Elementary Education	M,O
English as a Second Language	M
Environmental Management and Policy	M
Family Nurse Practitioner Studies	M,D
Finance and Banking	M
Health Services Management and Hospital Administration	M
History	M
Human Resources Management	M
International Affairs	M
Management Information Systems	M
Maternal and Child Health	M,D
Nursing Informatics	M,D
Nursing—General	M,D
Public Administration	M
Secondary Education	M
Social Sciences	M
Social Work	M
Sports Management	M,D

TRUETT MCCONNELL UNIVERSITY

Biological and Biomedical Sciences—General	M
Business Administration and Management—General	M
Counseling Psychology	M
Theology	M

TRUMAN STATE UNIVERSITY

Accounting	M
Biological and Biomedical Sciences—General	M
Communication Disorders	M
Education—General	M
English	M
Music	M

TUFTS UNIVERSITY

Allopathic Medicine	D
Animal Sciences	M
Art Education	M,D,O
Art History	M
Art/Fine Arts	M,O
Artificial Intelligence/Robotics	M,D
Astrophysics	M,D
Biochemistry	D
Bioengineering	M,D,O
Bioinformatics	M,D
Biological and Biomedical Sciences—General	M,D,O
Biomedical Engineering	M,D
Biostatistics	M,D,O
Biotechnology	M,D,O
Cancer Biology/Oncology	D
Cell Biology	D
Chemical Engineering	M,D

Chemical Physics M,D
Chemistry M,D
Child and Family Studies M,D
Child Development M,D
Civil Engineering M,D
Classics M
Clinical Laboratory Sciences/Medical Technology M,D,O
Cognitive Sciences M,D
Computer Science M,D,O
Data Science/Data Analytics M,D
Dentistry D
Developmental Biology D
Economics M,D
Education—General M,D,O
Electrical Engineering M,D,O
Elementary Education M,D
Engineering and Applied Sciences—General M,D*
Engineering Management M
English M,D
Entrepreneurship M
Environmental and Occupational Health M,D
Environmental Engineering M,D
Environmental Management and Policy M,D,O
Epidemiology M,D,O
Ergonomics and Human Factors M,D
Family and Consumer Sciences-General M,D
French M
Genetics D
Geotechnical Engineering M,D
German M
Health Communication M,D,O
Health Services Management and Hospital Administration M,D,O
History M,D
Human Development M,D
Human-Computer Interaction O
Immunology D
Infectious Diseases M,D
Interdisciplinary Studies D
International Affairs M,D
International Business M,D
International Development M
Law M,D
Management Strategy and Policy O
Manufacturing Engineering O
Mathematics Education M,D
Mathematics M,D
Mechanical Engineering M,D
Microbiology D
Middle School Education M,D
Molecular Biology D
Molecular Medicine D
Museum Education M,D
Museum Studies M,D,O
Music M
Neuroscience M,D
Nonprofit Management O
Nutrition M,D,O
Occupational Therapy M,D,O
Oral and Dental Sciences M,O
Organizational Management M
Pathology M,D
Philosophy M
Physician Assistant Studies M,D,O
Physics M,D
Psychology—General M,D
Public Administration O
Public Health—General M,D,O
Public Policy M,D
Reproductive Biology M,D
School Psychology M,O
Science Education M,D
Secondary Education M,D
Structural Biology D
Structural Engineering M,D
Theater M,D
Urban and Regional Planning M
Urban Studies M
Veterinary Medicine M,D
Water Resources Engineering M,D

TULANE UNIVERSITY
Accounting M,D
Allopathic Medicine D
Anthropology D
Architecture M
Art History M
Art/Fine Arts M
Biochemistry M
Biological and Biomedical Sciences—General M,D
Biomedical Engineering M,D
Biostatistics M,D
Business Administration and Management—General M,D
Business Analytics M,D
Cell Biology M,D
Chemical Engineering M,D
Chemistry M,D
Classics M
Community Health M,D
Dance M
Ecology M,D
Economics M,D
Emergency Management M,D
Energy Management and Policy M,D
English M
Entrepreneurship M,D
Environmental and Occupational Health M,D
Epidemiology M,D
Evolutionary Biology M,D
Finance and Banking M,D
French M,D
Health Promotion M
Health Services Management and Hospital Administration M,D
History M,D
Homeland Security M
Human Genetics M
Immunology M
Interdisciplinary Studies D
International Business M,D
International Development M,D
International Health M,D
Latin American Studies M,D
Law M,D
Liberal Studies M
Management Information Systems M
Management Strategy and Policy M,D
Mathematics M,D
Microbiology M
Molecular Biology M,D
Music M
Neuroscience M,D
Parasitology M,D,O
Pharmacology M
Philosophy M,D
Physics M,D
Physiology M
Political Science D
Portuguese M,D
Psychology—General M,D
Public Health—General M,D
Social Work M,D
Sociology M
Spanish M,D
Structural Biology M,D
Theater M

TUSCULUM COLLEGE
Business Administration and Management—General M
Curriculum and Instruction M
Education—General M
Family Nurse Practitioner Studies M
Human Resources Development M
Nursing—General M
Special Education M

TUSKEGEE UNIVERSITY
Agricultural Economics and Agribusiness M
Agronomy and Soil Sciences M
Animal Sciences M
Biological and Biomedical Sciences—General M,D
Chemistry M
Computer and Information Systems Security M
Electrical Engineering M
Engineering and Applied Sciences—General M,D
Environmental Sciences M
Food Science and Technology M
Management Information Systems M
Materials Engineering D
Mechanical Engineering M
Nutrition M
Occupational Therapy M
Plant Sciences M
Veterinary Medicine M,D
Veterinary Sciences M,D

TYNDALE UNIVERSITY COLLEGE & SEMINARY
Missions and Missiology M,O
Pastoral Ministry and Counseling M,O
Theology M,O

UNIFICATION THEOLOGICAL SEMINARY
Religious Education M,D
Theology M,D

UNIFORMED SERVICES UNIVERSITY OF THE HEALTH SCIENCES
Allopathic Medicine M,D
Biological and Biomedical Sciences—General M,D
Cell Biology M,D
Clinical Psychology D
Environmental and Occupational Health M,D
Family Nurse Practitioner Studies M,D
Gerontological Nursing M,D
Health Services Management and Hospital Administration M,D
Immunology D
Infectious Diseases D*
International Health M,D
Molecular Biology M,D*
Neuroscience D*
Nurse Anesthesia M,D
Nursing—General M,D
Psychiatric Nursing M,D
Psychology—General D
Public Health—General M,D
Women's Health Nursing M,D
Zoology M,D

UNION COLLEGE (KY)
Clinical Psychology M
Counseling Psychology M
Education—General M
Educational Leadership and Administration M
Elementary Education M
Health Education M
Middle School Education M
Music Education M
Physical Education M
Psychology—General M
Reading Education M
School Psychology M
Secondary Education M
Special Education M

UNION COLLEGE (NE)
Physician Assistant Studies M

UNION INSTITUTE & UNIVERSITY
Clinical Psychology M
Cultural Studies M,D
Education—General D
Health Promotion M
Health Services Management and Hospital Administration M
History M
Humanities D
Interdisciplinary Studies D
Organizational Management M
Public Policy M,D
Writing M

UNION PRESBYTERIAN SEMINARY
Religious Education M,D

UNION THEOLOGICAL SEMINARY IN THE CITY OF NEW YORK
Theology M,D

UNION UNIVERSITY
Accounting M
Business Administration and Management—General M
Cultural Studies M
Education—General M,D,O
Educational Leadership and Administration M,D,O
Family Nurse Practitioner Studies M,D,O
Higher Education M,D,O
Nurse Anesthesia M,D,O
Nursing and Healthcare Administration M,D,O
Nursing Education M,D,O
Nursing—General M,D,O
Pastoral Ministry and Counseling M,D
Pharmacy D
Religion M,D
Social Work M

UNITED LUTHERAN SEMINARY
Pastoral Ministry and Counseling M,D
Religion M,D
Theology M,D

UNITED LUTHERAN SEMINARY
Pastoral Ministry and Counseling M,D,O
Religion M,D,O
Theology M,D,O

UNITED STATES ARMY COMMAND AND GENERAL STAFF COLLEGE
Military and Defense Studies M

UNITED STATES INTERNATIONAL UNIVERSITY–AFRICA
Addictions/Substance Abuse Counseling M
Business Administration and Management—General M
Conflict Resolution and Mediation/Peace Studies M
Counseling Psychology M
Entrepreneurship M
Finance and Banking M
Health Psychology M
Human Resources Management M
International Affairs M
International Business M
Management Information Systems M
Management Strategy and Policy M
Marketing M
Organizational Management M

UNITED STATES MERCHANT MARINE ACADEMY
Civil Engineering M

UNITED STATES SPORTS ACADEMY
Exercise and Sports Science M
Physical Education M
Recreation and Park Management M
Sports Management M,D

UNITED STATES UNIVERSITY
Family Nurse Practitioner Studies M

UNITED TALMUDICAL SEMINARY
Theology

UNITED THEOLOGICAL SEMINARY
Pastoral Ministry and Counseling M,D
Theology M,D

UNITED THEOLOGICAL SEMINARY OF THE TWIN CITIES
Art/Fine Arts M,D,O
Asian Studies M,D,O
Conflict Resolution and Mediation/Peace Studies M,D,O
Ethnic Studies M,D,O
Humanities M,D,O
Pastoral Ministry and Counseling M,D,O
Religion M,D,O
Theology M,D,O
Women's Studies M,D,O

UNITY COLLEGE
Natural Resources M
Sustainable Development M

UNIVERSIDAD ADVENTISTA DE LAS ANTILLAS
Curriculum and Instruction M
Educational Leadership and Administration M
Medical/Surgical Nursing M

UNIVERSIDAD AUTONOMA DE GUADALAJARA
Advertising and Public Relations M,D
Allopathic Medicine D
Architecture M,D
Business Administration and Management—General M,D
Computer Art and Design M,D
Computer Science M,D
Corporate and Organizational Communication M,D
Education—General M,D
Energy and Power Engineering M,D
Entertainment Management M,D
Environmental and Occupational Health M,D
Environmental Management and Policy M,D
Film, Television, and Video Production M,D
International Business M,D
Internet and Interactive Multimedia M,D
Law M,D
Legal and Justice Studies M,D
Manufacturing Engineering M,D
Marketing Research M,D
Mathematics Education M,D
Philosophy M,D
Public Policy M,D
Spanish M,D
Systems Science M,D
Translation and Interpretation M,D

UNIVERSIDAD CENTRAL DEL CARIBE
Addictions/Substance Abuse Counseling M
Allopathic Medicine M,D
Anatomy M,D
Biochemistry M,D
Biological and Biomedical Sciences—General M,D
Cell Biology M,D
Immunology M,D
Microbiology M,D
Molecular Biology M,D
Pharmacology M,D
Physiology M,D

UNIVERSIDAD CENTRAL DEL ESTE
Allopathic Medicine D
Dentistry D
Environmental Engineering M
Finance and Banking M
Higher Education M
Human Resources Development M
Law D

UNIVERSIDAD DE CIENCIAS MEDICAS
Allopathic Medicine M,D,O
Anatomy M,D,O
Biological and Biomedical Sciences—General M,D,O
Community Health M,D,O
Environmental and Occupational Health M,D,O
Health Services Management and Hospital Administration M,D,O
Pharmacy M,D,O

UNIVERSIDAD DE IBEROAMERICA
Acute Care/Critical Care Nursing M,D
Allopathic Medicine M,D
Clinical Psychology M,D
Educational Psychology M,D
Forensic Psychology M,D
Health Services Management and Hospital Administration M,D
Neuroscience M,D

UNIVERSIDAD DE LAS AMERICAS, A.C.
Business Administration and Management—General M
Education—General M
Finance and Banking M
International Affairs M
Marketing Research M
Marriage and Family Therapy M
Organizational Behavior M
Psychology—General M
Quality Management M

UNIVERSIDAD DE LAS AMÉRICAS PUEBLA
American Studies M
Anthropology M
Archaeology M
Biotechnology M
Business Administration and Management—General M
Chemical Engineering M
Clinical Laboratory Sciences/Medical Technology M
Computer Art and Design M
Computer Science M,D
Construction Management M
Economics M
Education—General M
Electrical Engineering M
Engineering and Applied Sciences—General M,D
English M
Finance and Banking M
Food Science and Technology M
Industrial and Manufacturing Management M
Industrial/Management Engineering M
Linguistics M
Manufacturing Engineering M
Psychology—General M

UNIVERSIDAD DEL ESTE
Accounting M

*M—masters degree; D—doctorate; O—other advanced degree; *—Close-Up and/or Display*

Adult Education M
Agricultural Economics and Agribusiness M
Business Administration and Management—General M
Computer and Information Systems Security M
Criminal Justice and Criminology M
Electronic Commerce M
Elementary Education M
English as a Second Language M
Foreign Languages Education M
Human Resources Management M
Management Information Systems M
Management Strategy and Policy M
Public Policy M
Social Work M
Special Education M

UNIVERSIDAD DEL TURABO
Accounting M
Adult Nursing M,O
Art/Fine Arts M
Arts Administration M
Athletic Training and Sports Medicine M
Business Administration and Management—General M,D
Chemistry M,D
Communication Disorders M
Computer Engineering M
Conflict Resolution and Mediation/Peace Studies M
Counseling Psychology M,D,O
Counselor Education M
Criminal Justice and Criminology M
Curriculum and Instruction M,D
Early Childhood Education M
Education—General M,D
Educational Leadership and Administration M,D
Electrical Engineering M
Engineering and Applied Sciences—General M
English as a Second Language M
Environmental Biology M,D
Environmental Management and Policy M,D
Environmental Sciences M,D
Family Nurse Practitioner Studies M,O
Forensic Psychology M,D,O
Forensic Sciences M
Health Promotion M
Human Resources Management M
Human Services M
Information Studies M
Library Science M
Logistics M
Management Information Systems D
Marketing M
Mechanical Engineering M
Naturopathic Medicine D
Physical Education M
Project Management M
Quality Management M
Special Education M
Telecommunications M

UNIVERSIDAD IBEROAMERICANA
Allopathic Medicine D
Business Administration and Management—General M,D
Corporate and Organizational Communication M,D
Dentistry M,D
Educational Leadership and Administration M,D
Human Resources Development M,D
Law M,D
Marketing M,D
Real Estate M,D
Special Education M,D

UNIVERSIDAD METROPOLITANA
Accounting M
Adult Education M
Business Administration and Management—General M
Counseling Psychology M
Curriculum and Instruction M
Education—General M
Educational Leadership and Administration M
Elementary Education M
Environmental Management and Policy M
Finance and Banking M
Human Resources Management M
International Business M
Leisure Studies M
Management Information Systems M
Marketing M
Natural Resources M
Nursing and Healthcare Administration M,O
Nursing—General M,O
Oncology Nursing M,O
Physical Education M
Recreation and Park Management M
Secondary Education M
Special Education M

UNIVERSIDAD NACIONAL PEDRO HENRIQUEZ URENA
Agricultural Sciences—General M
Allopathic Medicine D
Animal Sciences M
Architecture M
Dentistry D
Ecology M
Environmental Engineering M
Environmental Sciences M
Historic Preservation M
Horticulture M
International Affairs M
Natural Resources M
Political Science M
Project Management M
Science Education M

UNIVERSITÉ DE MONCTON
Astronomy M
Biochemistry M
Biological and Biomedical Sciences—General M
Business Administration and Management—General M
Chemistry M
Civil Engineering M
Computer Science M,O
Counselor Education M
Economics M
Education—General M
Educational Leadership and Administration M
Educational Psychology M
Electrical Engineering M
Engineering and Applied Sciences—General M
Food Science and Technology M
French M,D
History M
Industrial/Management Engineering M
Mathematics M
Mechanical Engineering M
Nutrition M
Physics M
Public Administration M
Social Work M

UNIVERSITÉ DE MONTRÉAL
Allopathic Medicine D
Anthropology M,D
Art History M,D
Biochemistry M,D,O
Bioethics M,D,O
Bioinformatics M,D
Biological and Biomedical Sciences—General M,D
Biomedical Engineering M,D,O
Cell Biology M,D
Chemistry M,D
Classics M
Communication Disorders M,O
Communication—General M,D
Community Health M,D,O
Comparative Literature M,D
Computer Science M,D
Criminal Justice and Criminology M,D
Curriculum and Instruction M,D,O
Demography and Population Studies M,D
Dental Hygiene O
Developmental Psychology M,D
Economics M,D,O
Education—General M,D,O
Educational Leadership and Administration M,D,O
Educational Psychology M,D,O
Electronic Commerce M,D
Emergency Management O
English M,D
Environmental and Occupational Health M
Environmental Design M,D,O
Environmental Management and Policy O
Ergonomics and Human Factors O
Film, Television, and Video Theory and Criticism M,D
French M,D
Genetic Counseling O
Genetics O
Geography M,D,O
German M
Health Services Management and Hospital Administration M,O
Hispanic and Latin American Languages M,D
History M,D
Human Services D
Immunology M,D
Industrial and Labor Relations M,D,O
Information Studies M,D
International Affairs M,O
Kinesiology and Movement Studies M,D,O
Law M,D,O
Library Science M,D
Linguistics M,D,O
Mathematical and Computational Finance M,D,O
Mathematics M,D,O
Microbiology M,D
Molecular Biology M,D
Museum Studies M
Music M,D,O
Neuroscience M,D
Nursing—General M,D,O
Nutrition M,D,O
Occupational Therapy O
Optometry D
Oral and Dental Sciences M,O
Pathology M,D
Pharmaceutical Sciences M,D,O
Pharmacology M,D
Philosophy M,D
Physical Education M,D,O
Physics M,D
Physiology M,D
Political Science M,D
Psychology—General M,D
Public Health—General M,D,O
Public Policy O
Rehabilitation Sciences O
Religion M,D,O
Social Work O
Sociology M,D
Spanish M
Statistics M,D,O
Taxation M,D,O
Theology M,D,O
Toxicology O
Translation and Interpretation M,D,O
Urban and Regional Planning M,D,O
Veterinary Medicine D
Veterinary Sciences M,D
Virology D
Vision Sciences M,O

UNIVERSITÉ DE SAINT-BONIFACE
Canadian Studies M
Education—General M

UNIVERSITÉ DE SHERBROOKE
Accounting M
Allopathic Medicine D
Biochemistry M,D
Biological and Biomedical Sciences—General M,D,O
Biophysics M,D
Business Administration and Management—General M,D,O
Canadian Studies M,D
Cell Biology M,D
Chemical Engineering M,D
Chemistry M,D,O
Civil Engineering M,D
Clinical Laboratory Sciences/Medical Technology M,D
Comparative Literature M,D
Computer and Information Systems Security M
Conflict Resolution and Mediation/Peace Studies M,D,O
Corporate and Organizational Communication M
Economic Development D
Economics M
Education—General M,O
Educational Leadership and Administration M
Electrical Engineering M,D
Electronic Commerce M
Elementary Education M,O
Engineering and Applied Sciences—General M,D,O
Engineering Management M,O
Environmental Engineering M
Environmental Sciences M,O
Ethics M,D,O
Finance and Banking M
French M,D
Geography M,D
Gerontology M
Health Law M,D,O
Higher Education M,O
History M
Immunology M,D
Information Science M,D
International Business M
Kinesiology and Movement Studies M,O
Law M,D,O
Linguistics M,D
Management Information Systems M,O
Marketing M
Mathematics M,D
Mechanical Engineering M,D
Microbiology M,D
Organizational Behavior M
Pharmacology M,D
Philosophy M,D,O
Physical Education M,O
Physics M,D
Physiology M,D
Psychology—General M
Public Administration M
Radiation Biology M,D
Religion M,D,O
Social Work M
Special Education M,O
Taxation M,O
Theater M,D
Theology M,D,O

UNIVERSITÉ DU QUÉBEC À CHICOUTIMI
Art/Fine Arts M
Business Administration and Management—General M
Canadian Studies M
Comparative Literature M
Education—General M,D
Engineering and Applied Sciences—General M,D
Environmental Management and Policy M
Ethics O
French O
Genetics M
Geosciences M
Linguistics M
Mineralogy D
Project Management M
Theology M,D

UNIVERSITÉ DU QUÉBEC À MONTRÉAL
Accounting M,O
Actuarial Science O
Art History M,D
Art/Fine Arts M
Atmospheric Sciences M,D,O
Biological and Biomedical Sciences—General M,D
Business Administration and Management—General M,D,O
Chemistry M,D
Communication—General M,D
Comparative Literature M,D
Dance M
Economics M,D
Education—General M,D,O
Environmental and Occupational Health O
Environmental Education M,D,O
Environmental Sciences M,D,O
Ergonomics and Human Factors O
Finance and Banking O
Geographic Information Systems O
Geography M
Geology M,D,O
Geosciences M,D,O
History M,D,O
Kinesiology and Movement Studies M
Law O
Linguistics M,D
Management Information Systems M
Mathematics M,D
Meteorology M,D,O
Mineralogy M,D,O
Museum Studies M
Natural Resources M,D,O
Philosophy M,D
Political Science M,D
Project Management M,O
Psychology—General D
Public Administration M
Religion M,D
Social Work M
Sociology M,D
Urban Studies M,D

UNIVERSITÉ DU QUÉBEC À RIMOUSKI
Business Administration and Management—General M,O
Comparative Literature M,D
Education—General M,D,O
Engineering and Applied Sciences—General M
Ethics M,O
Fish, Game, and Wildlife Management M,D,O
Marine Affairs M,O
Nursing—General M,O
Oceanography M,D
Project Management M,O
Social Psychology M
Urban and Regional Planning M,D,O

UNIVERSITÉ DU QUÉBEC À TROIS-RIVIÈRES
Accounting M
Biophysics M,D
Business Administration and Management—General M,D
Chemistry M
Chiropractic D
Communication—General M,O
Comparative Literature M
Computer Science M
Education—General M,D
Educational Leadership and Administration O
Educational Psychology M,D
Electrical Engineering M,D
Environmental Sciences M,D
Finance and Banking O
Industrial and Labor Relations O
Industrial/Management Engineering M,O
Leisure Studies M,O
Mathematics M
Nursing—General M,O
Philosophy M,D
Physical Education M
Physics M,D
Psychology—General D,O
Travel and Tourism M,O

UNIVERSITÉ DU QUÉBEC, ÉCOLE DE TECHNOLOGIE SUPÉRIEURE
Engineering and Applied Sciences—General M,D,O

UNIVERSITÉ DU QUÉBEC, ÉCOLE NATIONALE D'ADMINISTRATION PUBLIQUE
International Business M,O
Public Administration D,O
Urban Studies M

UNIVERSITÉ DU QUÉBEC EN ABITIBI-TÉMISCAMINGUE
Biological and Biomedical Sciences—General M,D
Business Administration and Management—General M
Education—General M,D,O
Engineering and Applied Sciences—General M,O
Environmental Sciences M,O
Forestry M,D
Mineral/Mining Engineering M,O
Natural Resources M,D
Project Management M,O
Social Work M

UNIVERSITÉ DU QUÉBEC EN OUTAOUAIS
Accounting M,O
Computer Science M,D,O
Education—General M,D,O
Educational Psychology M
Finance and Banking M,O
Foreign Languages Education O
Industrial and Labor Relations M,D,O
Nursing—General M,O
Project Management M,O
Social Work M
Urban and Regional Planning M

UNIVERSITÉ DU QUÉBEC, INSTITUT NATIONAL DE LA RECHERCHE SCIENTIFIQUE
Biological and Biomedical Sciences—General M,D
Demography and Population Studies M,D,O
Energy Management and Policy M,D

Environmental Management and Policy	M,D
Geosciences	M,D
Hydrology	M,D
Immunology	M,D
Materials Sciences	M,D
Medical Microbiology	M,D
Microbiology	M,D
Telecommunications	M,D
Urban Studies	M,D,O
Virology	M,D

UNIVERSITÉ LAVAL

Accounting	M,O
Advertising and Public Relations	O
Aerospace/Aeronautical Engineering	M
Agricultural Economics and Agribusiness	M
Agricultural Engineering	M
Agricultural Sciences—General	M,D,O
Agronomy and Soil Sciences	M,D
Allopathic Medicine	D,O
Anatomy	O
Anesthesiologist Assistant Studies	O
Animal Sciences	M,D
Anthropology	M,D
Archaeology	M,D
Architecture	M
Art History	M,D
Art/Fine Arts	M
Biochemistry	M,D,O
Biological and Biomedical Sciences—General	M,D,O
Business Administration and Management—General	M,D,O
Cancer Biology/Oncology	O
Cardiovascular Sciences	O
Cell Biology	M,D
Chemical Engineering	M,D
Chemistry	M,D
Civil Engineering	M,D,O
Clinical Psychology	D
Communication Disorders	M
Community Health	M,D,O
Comparative Literature	M,D
Computer Science	M,D
Consumer Economics	O
Counselor Education	M,D
Curriculum and Instruction	M,D
Dentistry	D
Economics	M,D
Education—General	M,D,O
Educational Leadership and Administration	M,D,O
Educational Measurement and Evaluation	M,D,O
Educational Media/Instructional Technology	M,D
Educational Psychology	M,D
Electrical Engineering	M,D
Electronic Commerce	M,O
Emergency Medical Services	O
Engineering and Applied Sciences—General	M,D,O
English	M,D
Entrepreneurship	M,O
Environmental and Occupational Health	O
Environmental Engineering	M,D
Environmental Management and Policy	M,D,O
Environmental Sciences	M,D
Epidemiology	M,D
Ethics	O
Ethnic Studies	M,D
Facilities Management	M,O
Film, Television, and Video Theory and Criticism	M,D
Finance and Banking	M,O
Food Science and Technology	M,D
Forestry	M,D
Geodetic Sciences	M,D
Geographic Information Systems	M,O
Geography	M,D
Geology	M,D
Geosciences	M,D
Gerontology	O
Graphic Design	M
Health Physics/Radiological Health	O
History	M,D
Immunology	M,D
Industrial and Labor Relations	M,D
Industrial/Management Engineering	O
Infectious Diseases	O
International Affairs	M,D
International Business	M,O
Journalism	O
Kinesiology and Movement Studies	M,D
Law	M,D,O
Legal and Justice Studies	O
Linguistics	M,D
Management Information Systems	M,O
Marketing	M,O
Mass Communication	M,D
Mathematics	M,D
Mechanical Engineering	M,D
Metallurgical Engineering and Metallurgy	M,D
Microbiology	M,D
Mineral/Mining Engineering	M,D
Modeling and Simulation	M,O
Molecular Biology	M,D
Museum Studies	O
Music Education	M,D
Music	M,D
Neurobiology	M,D
Nursing—General	M,D,O
Nutrition	M,D
Oceanography	D
Oral and Dental Sciences	M,O
Organizational Management	M,O
Pathology	O
Pharmaceutical Sciences	M,D,O
Philosophy	M,D
Physics	M,D
Physiology	M,D
Plant Biology	M,D
Political Science	M,D
Psychology—General	D
Religion	M,D
Rural Planning and Studies	O
Social Psychology	D
Social Work	M,D
Sociology	M,D
Software Engineering	O
Spanish	M,D
Statistics	M
Theater	M,D
Theology	M,D
Translation and Interpretation	M,O
Urban and Regional Planning	M,D
Women's Studies	O

UNIVERSITÉ SAINTE-ANNE

Education—General	M

UNIVERSITY AT ALBANY, STATE UNIVERSITY OF NEW YORK

African Studies	M
African-American Studies	M
Anthropology	M,D
Art/Fine Arts	M
Atmospheric Sciences	M,D
Biological and Biomedical Sciences—General	M,D
Biostatistics	M,D
Business Administration and Management—General	M
Business Analytics	M
Chemistry	M,D
Clinical Psychology	M,D
Cognitive Sciences	M,D
Communication—General	M,D
Computer and Information Systems Security	M,D,O
Computer Science	M,D,O
Counseling Psychology	M,D,O
Criminal Justice and Criminology	M,D,O
Curriculum and Instruction	M,D,O
Demography and Population Studies	M,D,O
Economics	M,D,O
Education—General	M,D,O
Educational Leadership and Administration	M,D,O
Educational Media/Instructional Technology	M,D,O
Educational Policy	M,D,O
Emergency Management	M,D,O
Engineering and Applied Sciences—General	M,D,O
English	M,D
Entrepreneurship	M
Environmental and Occupational Health	M,D
Epidemiology	M,D
Finance and Banking	M,D,O
Forensic Sciences	M
Gender Studies	M
Geographic Information Systems	M,O
Geography	M,O
Health Services Management and Hospital Administration	M,D,O
Higher Education	M,D,O
History	M,D,O
Homeland Security	M,D,O
Human Resources Management	M,D,O
Industrial and Organizational Psychology	M,D
Information Science	M,D
International and Comparative Education	M,D,O
Latin American Studies	M,D,O
Liberal Studies	M
Management Information Systems	M,D,O
Marketing	M
Mathematics	M,D
Neuroscience	M,D
Nonprofit Management	M,D,O
Organizational Behavior	M,D,O
Philosophy	M,D
Physics	M,D
Political Science	M,D
Psychology—General	M,D
Public Administration	M,D,O
Public Health—General	M,D
Public History	M,D,O
Public Policy	M,D,O
Reading Education	M,D,O
Social Psychology	M,D
Social Work	M,D
Sociology	M,D,O
Spanish	M,D
Toxicology	M,D
Urban and Regional Planning	M,O
Urban Studies	M,D,O
Women's Studies	M,O

UNIVERSITY AT BUFFALO, THE STATE UNIVERSITY OF NEW YORK

Accounting	M,D
Adult Nursing	M,D,O
Aerospace/Aeronautical Engineering	M,D
Allied Health—General	M,D,O
Allopathic Medicine	D
American Studies	M,D
Anatomy	M,D
Anthropology	M,D
Architecture	M
Art History	M,D
Art/Fine Arts	M
Arts Administration	M
Biochemistry	M,D
Bioengineering	M,D,O
Bioinformatics	M,D
Biological and Biomedical Sciences—General	M,D
Biomedical Engineering	M,D
Biophysics	M,D
Biostatistics	M,D
Biotechnology	M
Business Administration and Management—General	M,D
Business Analytics	M,D
Canadian Studies	M,D
Cancer Biology/Oncology	M
Cell Biology	M,D
Chemical Engineering	M,D,O
Chemistry	M,D
Civil Engineering	M,D
Classics	M,D,O
Clinical Laboratory Sciences/Medical Technology	M
Communication Disorders	M,D
Communication—General	M,D
Community Health	M,D,O
Comparative Literature	M,D
Computational Sciences	D,O
Computer Science	M,D,O
Counseling Psychology	M,D,O
Counselor Education	M,D,O
Curriculum and Instruction	M,D,O
Dance	M,D
Data Science/Data Analytics	M,D
Dentistry	D
Distance Education Development	M,D,O
Early Childhood Education	M,D,O
Ecology	M,D,O
Economic Development	M,D,O
Economics	M,D,O
Education of the Gifted	M,D,O
Education—General	M,D,O
Educational Leadership and Administration	M,D,O
Educational Media/Instructional Technology	M,D,O
Educational Psychology	M,D,O
Electrical Engineering	M,D
Electronic Commerce	M,D,O
Elementary Education	M,D,O
Energy and Power Engineering	M,D
Engineering and Applied Sciences—General	M,D,O
Engineering Management	M,D,O
English as a Second Language	M,D,O
English Education	M,D,O
English	M,D,O
Environmental Engineering	M,D
Environmental Law	M,D
Environmental Sciences	M,D
Epidemiology	M,D
Evolutionary Biology	M,D,O
Exercise and Sports Science	M,D,O
Family Nurse Practitioner Studies	M,D,O
Film, Television, and Video Theory and Criticism	M,D,O
Finance and Banking	M,D
Food Science and Technology	M,D,O
Foreign Languages Education	M,D,O
Foundations and Philosophy of Education	M,D,O
French	M,D,O
Gender Studies	M,D
Genetics	M,D
Genomic Sciences	M,D
Geographic Information Systems	M,D
Geography	M,D
Geology	M,D
Geosciences	M,D
German	M,D,O
Gerontological Nursing	M,D,O
Health Services Management and Hospital Administration	M,D
Higher Education	M,D,O
Historic Preservation	M,D,O
History	M,D,O
Human Resources Management	M,D,O
Humanities	M
Immunology	M,D
Industrial/Management Engineering	M,D,O
Information Studies	M,O
Interdisciplinary Studies	M
International Business	M,D
Law	M,D
Legal and Justice Studies	M,D
Library Science	M,D
Linguistics	M,D
Logistics	M,D
Management Information Systems	M,D,O
Manufacturing Engineering	M,D,O
Marketing	M,D
Materials Sciences	M,D
Mathematics Education	M,D,O
Mathematics	M,D
Mechanical Engineering	M,D
Media Studies	M,D,O
Medical Informatics	M,D
Medical Physics	M,D
Medicinal and Pharmaceutical Chemistry	M,D
Microbiology	M,D
Modeling and Simulation	M,D
Molecular Biology	D
Molecular Biophysics	M,D
Molecular Pharmacology	D
Multilingual and Multicultural Education	M,D,O
Museum Studies	M,D
Music Education	M,D,O
Music	M,D,O
Nanotechnology	M,D,O
Neuroscience	M,D
Nurse Anesthesia	M,D,O
Nursing and Healthcare Administration	M,D,O
Nursing—General	M,D,O
Nutrition	M,D,O
Occupational Therapy	M
Oral and Dental Sciences	M,D,O
Pathology	M,D
Pharmaceutical Sciences	M,D
Pharmacology	M,D
Pharmacy	D
Philosophy	M,D
Physical Therapy	D
Physics	M,D
Physiology	M,D
Political Science	M,D
Psychiatric Nursing	M,D,O
Psychology—General	M,D
Public Health—General	M,D
Public History	M,D,O
Quantitative Analysis	M,D
Reading Education	M,D,O
Real Estate	M,D,O
Rehabilitation Counseling	M,D,O
Rehabilitation Sciences	O
Romance Languages	M,D
Science Education	M,D,O
Social Sciences Education	M,D,O
Social Sciences	M
Social Work	M,D
Sociology	M,D
Spanish	M,D,O
Special Education	M,D,O
Structural Biology	M,D
Structural Engineering	M,D
Supply Chain Management	M,D
Sustainable Development	M,D
Theater	M,D
Toxicology	M,D
Transportation Management	M
Urban and Regional Planning	M,D,O
Urban Design	M,D,O
Water Resources Engineering	M,D

UNIVERSITY OF ADVANCING TECHNOLOGY

Computer and Information Systems Security	M
Computer Science	M
Game Design and Development	M
Internet and Interactive Multimedia	M
Management of Technology	M

THE UNIVERSITY OF AKRON

Accounting	M
Applied Mathematics	M
Art Education	M
Arts Administration	M
Biological and Biomedical Sciences—General	M,D
Biomedical Engineering	M,D
Business Administration and Management—General	M
Chemical Engineering	M,D
Chemistry	M,D
Child and Family Studies	M
Child Development	M
Civil Engineering	M,D
Clinical Psychology	M
Clothing and Textiles	M
Communication Disorders	M,D
Communication—General	M
Computer Engineering	M,D
Computer Science	M
Counseling Psychology	M,D
Counselor Education	M,D
Curriculum and Instruction	M
Economics	M
Education—General	M
Educational Leadership and Administration	M,O
Educational Measurement and Evaluation	M,O
Educational Media/Instructional Technology	M
Electrical Engineering	M,D
Elementary Education	M
Engineering and Applied Sciences—General	M,D
English Education	M
English	M
Exercise and Sports Science	M
Finance and Banking	M
Geological Engineering	M
Geology	M
Geosciences	M
Gerontology	D
Health Services Management and Hospital Administration	M
Higher Education	M
History	M,D
Industrial and Organizational Psychology	M,D
International Business	M
Law	M,D
Management Information Systems	M
Marketing	M
Marriage and Family Therapy	M
Mathematics Education	M
Mathematics	M
Mechanical Engineering	M,D
Music Education	M
Music	M
Nursing—General	M,D

*M—masters degree; D—doctorate; O—other advanced degree; *—Close-Up and/or Display*

Physical Education	M
Physics	M
Political Science	M
Polymer Science and Engineering	M,D
Psychology—General	M,D
Public Administration	M
Reading Education	M
School Psychology	M
Science Education	M
Secondary Education	M
Social Sciences Education	M
Social Work	M
Sociology	M,D
Spanish	M
Special Education	M
Statistics	M
Supply Chain Management	M
Taxation	M
Theater	M
Writing	M

THE UNIVERSITY OF ALABAMA

Accounting	M,D
Aerospace/Aeronautical Engineering	M,D
American Studies	M
Anthropology	M,D
Applied Mathematics	M,D
Applied Statistics	M,D
Art History	M
Art/Fine Arts	M
Astronomy	M,D
Biological and Biomedical Sciences—General	M,D
Business Administration and Management—General	M,D
Chemical Engineering	M,D
Chemistry	M,D
Child and Family Studies	M
Civil Engineering	M,D
Clinical Psychology	D
Clothing and Textiles	M
Communication Disorders	M
Communication—General	M,D
Community Health	M
Computer Engineering	M,D
Computer Science	M,D
Construction Engineering	M,D
Consumer Economics	M
Counselor Education	M,D,O
Criminal Justice and Criminology	M
Economics	M,D
Education of the Gifted	M,D,O
Educational Leadership and Administration	M,D,O
Electrical Engineering	M,D
Elementary Education	M,D,O
Engineering and Applied Sciences—General	M,D
English as a Second Language	M,D
English	M,D
Environmental Engineering	M,D
Ergonomics and Human Factors	M
Exercise and Sports Science	M,D
Experimental Psychology	D
Family and Consumer Sciences-General	M,D
Finance and Banking	M,D
French	M,D
Geographic Information Systems	M,D
Geography	M,D
Geology	M,D
Geosciences	M,D
German	M,D
Health Education	M,D
Health Promotion	M,D
Higher Education	M,D
History	M,D
Hospitality Management	M
Human Development	M
Industrial and Manufacturing Management	M,D
Information Studies	M,D
Interdisciplinary Studies	D
Journalism	M
Kinesiology and Movement Studies	M,D
Law	M,D
Library Science	M,D
Marketing	M,D
Marriage and Family Therapy	M
Mass Communication	D
Materials Engineering	M,D
Materials Sciences	D
Mathematics	M,D
Mechanical Engineering	M,D
Mechanics	M,D
Metallurgical Engineering and Metallurgy	M,D
Music Education	M,D,O
Music	M,D
Nursing—General	M,D
Nutrition	M
Photography	M
Physical Education	M,D
Physics	M,D
Political Science	M,D
Psychology—General	D
Public Administration	M,D
Quality Management	M
Rhetoric	M,D
Romance Languages	M,D
Secondary Education	M,D,O
Social Work	M,D
Spanish	M,D
Special Education	M,D,O
Speech and Interpersonal Communication	M
Sports Management	M
Taxation	M,D
Theater	M
Women's Studies	M
Writing	M,D

THE UNIVERSITY OF ALABAMA AT BIRMINGHAM

Accounting	M
Adult Nursing	M,D
Allied Health—General	M,D,O
Allopathic Medicine	D
Anthropology	M
Applied Mathematics	D
Art Education	M
Art History	M
Biochemistry	D
Bioinformatics	D
Biological and Biomedical Sciences—General	M,D
Biomedical Engineering	M,D
Biostatistics	M,D
Biotechnology	M
Business Administration and Management—General	M
Cancer Biology/Oncology	D
Cell Biology	D
Chemistry	M,D
Civil Engineering	M,D
Clinical Laboratory Sciences/Medical Technology	M,D
Clinical Psychology	M,D
Communication—General	M
Community Health	M
Computational Sciences	D
Computer and Information Systems Security	M
Computer Engineering	M,D
Computer Science	M,D
Construction Engineering	M
Construction Management	M
Counselor Education	M
Criminal Justice and Criminology	M
Curriculum and Instruction	O
Dentistry	D
Developmental Biology	D
Developmental Psychology	M,D
Early Childhood Education	M,D
Education—General	M,D,O
Educational Leadership and Administration	M,D,O
Electrical Engineering	M,D
Elementary Education	M
Engineering and Applied Sciences—General	D
Engineering Design	M
Engineering Management	M
English as a Second Language	M,O
English	M
Environmental and Occupational Health	M,D
Epidemiology	M,D
Family Nurse Practitioner Studies	M,D
Finance and Banking	M
Forensic Sciences	M
Genetic Counseling	M
Genetics	D
Genomic Sciences	D
Gerontological Nursing	M,D
Health Education	D
Health Informatics	M
Health Promotion	D
Health Psychology	M,D
Health Services Management and Hospital Administration	M,D
Health Services Research	M,D
History	M
Immunology	D
Industrial Hygiene	M,D
Information Science	M,D
Management Information Systems	M
Marketing	M
Materials Engineering	M,D
Maternal and Child Health	M,D
Mathematics	M
Mechanical Engineering	M
Microbiology	D
Molecular Biology	D
Molecular Medicine	O
Neuroscience	M,D
Nurse Anesthesia	M,D
Nursing and Healthcare Administration	M,D
Nursing Informatics	M,D
Nursing—General	M,D
Nutrition	M,D
Occupational Therapy	M,O
Optometry	D
Oral and Dental Sciences	M
Pathobiology	D
Pediatric Nursing	M,D
Physical Therapy	D
Physician Assistant Studies	M
Physics	M,D
Psychiatric Nursing	M,D
Psychology—General	M,D
Public Administration	M
Public Health—General	M,D
Quantitative Analysis	M,D
Reading Education	M
Rehabilitation Sciences	D
Rhetoric	M
Secondary Education	M
Sociology	D
Special Education	M
Structural Biology	D
Structural Engineering	M
Sustainable Development	M
Toxicology	M,D
Vision Sciences	M,D
Women's Health Nursing	M,D
Writing	M

THE UNIVERSITY OF ALABAMA IN HUNTSVILLE

Accounting	M,O
Acute Care/Critical Care Nursing	M,D,O
Aerospace/Aeronautical Engineering	M,D
Applied Mathematics	M,D
Astronomy	M,D
Atmospheric Sciences	M,D
Biological and Biomedical Sciences—General	M,D
Biotechnology	M,D
Business Administration and Management—General	M,O
Business Analytics	M,O
Chemical Engineering	M,D
Chemistry	M,D
Civil Engineering	M,D
Computer and Information Systems Security	M,D,O
Computer Engineering	M,D
Computer Science	M,D,O
Education—General	M,O
Electrical Engineering	M,D
Engineering and Applied Sciences—General	M,D
English as a Second Language	M,O
English Education	M,O
English	M,O
Entrepreneurship	M,O
Environmental Engineering	M,D
Family Nurse Practitioner Studies	M,D,O
Finance and Banking	M,O
Geosciences	M,D
Gerontological Nursing	M,D,O
Health Services Management and Hospital Administration	M,D,O
History	M
Human Resources Management	M,O
Industrial and Organizational Psychology	M
Industrial/Management Engineering	M,D
Logistics	M,O
Management Information Systems	M,O
Management of Technology	M,O
Marketing	M,O
Materials Sciences	M,D
Mathematics Education	M,D,O
Mathematics	M,D
Mechanical Engineering	M,D
Modeling and Simulation	M,D,O
Nursing Education	M,D,O
Nursing—General	M,D,O
Operations Research	M,D
Optical Sciences	M,D
Photonics	M,D
Physics	M,D
Project Management	M,O
Psychology—General	M
Public Affairs	M
Reading Education	M,O
Science Education	M,D,O
Secondary Education	M,O
Social Sciences Education	M,O
Software Engineering	M,D,O
Special Education	M,O
Supply Chain Management	M,O
Systems Engineering	M,D
Taxation	M
Technical Writing	M,O

UNIVERSITY OF ALASKA ANCHORAGE

Anthropology	M
Biological and Biomedical Sciences—General	M
Business Administration and Management—General	M
Clinical Psychology	M,D
Early Childhood Education	M,O
Education—General	M,O
Educational Leadership and Administration	M,O
English	M
Health Services Management and Hospital Administration	M
Logistics	M
Psychology—General	M,D
Public Administration	M
Public Health—General	M
Social Psychology	M,D
Social Work	M,O
Special Education	M,O
Writing	M

UNIVERSITY OF ALASKA FAIRBANKS

Anthropology	M,D
Art/Fine Arts	M
Astrophysics	M,D
Atmospheric Sciences	M,D
Biochemistry	M,D
Biological and Biomedical Sciences—General	M,D,O
Business Administration and Management—General	M
Chemistry	M,D
Civil Engineering	M,D,O
Clinical Psychology	D
Communication—General	M
Computational Sciences	M,D
Computer Art and Design	M
Computer Science	M
Construction Management	M,D,O
Corporate and Organizational Communication	M
Counselor Education	M,O
Criminal Justice and Criminology	M
Cultural Studies	M
Economics	M
Education—General	M,O
Electrical Engineering	M
Emergency Management	M
Engineering and Applied Sciences—General	D
English	M
Environmental Engineering	M,D,O
Environmental Management and Policy	M
Finance and Banking	M
Fish, Game, and Wildlife Management	M,D,O
Geographic Information Systems	M
Geological Engineering	M
Geophysics	M
History	M
Homeland Security	M
Interdisciplinary Studies	M,D
Limnology	M,D
Linguistics	M
Marine Biology	M,D
Marine Sciences	M,D
Mathematics	M,D,O
Mechanical Engineering	M
Mineral/Mining Engineering	M
Multilingual and Multicultural Education	M
Music	M
Natural Resources	M,D
Neuroscience	M,D
Northern Studies	M
Oceanography	M,D
Petroleum Engineering	M
Photography	M
Physics	M,D
Psychology—General	D
Rural Planning and Studies	M
Social Psychology	M,D,O
Special Education	M
Statistics	M,D,O
Sustainable Development	M,D
Writing	M

UNIVERSITY OF ALASKA SOUTHEAST

Education—General	M
Educational Leadership and Administration	M
Educational Media/Instructional Technology	M
Elementary Education	M
Mathematics Education	M
Public Administration	M
Reading Education	M
Secondary Education	M
Special Education	M

UNIVERSITY OF ALBERTA

Accounting	D
Adult Education	M,D,O
Agricultural Economics and Agribusiness	M,D
Agricultural Sciences—General	M,D
Agronomy and Soil Sciences	M,D
Anthropology	M,D
Applied Arts and Design—General	M
Applied Mathematics	M,D,O
Archaeology	M,D
Art History	M
Art/Fine Arts	M
Asian Studies	M
Astrophysics	M,D
Biochemistry	M,D
Biological and Biomedical Sciences—General	M,D
Biomedical Engineering	M,D
Biostatistics	M,D,O
Biotechnology	M,D
Business Administration and Management—General	M,D
Cancer Biology/Oncology	M,D
Cell Biology	M,D
Chemical Engineering	M,D
Chemistry	M,D
Chinese	M
Civil Engineering	M,D
Classics	M,D
Clinical Laboratory Sciences/Medical Technology	M,D
Clothing and Textiles	M,D
Communication Disorders	M,D
Communication—General	M
Community Health	M,D
Computer Engineering	M,D
Computer Science	M,D
Condensed Matter Physics	M,D
Conservation Biology	M,D
Construction Engineering	M,D
Counseling Psychology	M,D
Counselor Education	M,D
Criminal Justice and Criminology	M,D
Demography and Population Studies	M,D
Dental Hygiene	O
Dentistry	D
East European and Russian Studies	M,D
Ecology	M,D
Economics	M,D
Educational Leadership and Administration	M,D,O
Educational Media/Instructional Technology	M,D
Educational Policy	M,D,O
Educational Psychology	M,D
Electrical Engineering	M,D
Elementary Education	M,D
Energy and Power Engineering	M,D
Engineering Management	M,D
English as a Second Language	M,D
English	M,D
Environmental and Occupational Health	M,D
Environmental Biology	M,D
Environmental Engineering	M,D
Environmental Management and Policy	M,D
Environmental Sciences	M,D
Epidemiology	M,D
Evolutionary Biology	M,D
Exercise and Sports Science	M,D
Family and Consumer Sciences-General	M,D
Finance and Banking	M,D
Folklore	M,D
Forestry	M,D
French	M,D
Genetics	M,D

Geophysics	M,D
Geosciences	M,D
Geotechnical Engineering	M,D
German	M,D
Health Physics/Radiological Health	M,D
Health Promotion	M,O
Health Services Management and Hospital Administration	M,D
Health Services Research	M,D
Hispanic Studies	M,D
History	M,D
Immunology	M,D
Industrial and Labor Relations	D
Information Studies	M
International Business	M
International Health	M,D
Italian	M,D
Japanese	M
Law	M,D
Library Science	M
Linguistics	M,D
Marketing	D
Materials Engineering	M,D
Maternal and Child/Neonatal Nursing	D
Mathematical and Computational Finance	M,D,O
Mathematical Physics	M,D,O
Mathematics	M,D,O
Mechanical Engineering	M,D
Medical Microbiology	M,D
Medical Physics	M,D
Microbiology	M,D
Mineral/Mining Engineering	M,D
Molecular Biology	M,D
Multilingual and Multicultural Education	M
Music	M,D
Nanotechnology	M,D
Natural Resources	M,D
Neuroscience	M,D
Nursing—General	M,D
Occupational Therapy	M,D
Oral and Dental Sciences	M,D
Organizational Management	D
Pathology	M,D
Petroleum Engineering	M,D
Pharmaceutical Sciences	M,D
Pharmacology	M,D
Pharmacy	M,D
Philosophy	M,D
Physical Education	M,D
Physical Therapy	M,D
Physics	M,D
Physiology	M,D
Plant Biology	M,D
Political Science	M,D
Psychology—General	M,D
Public Health—General	M,D
Recreation and Park Management	M,D
Rehabilitation Sciences	D
Rural Sociology	M,D
School Psychology	M,D
Secondary Education	M,D
Slavic Languages	M,D
Sociology	M,D
Special Education	M,D
Sports Management	M
Statistics	M,D,O
Structural Engineering	M,D
Systems Engineering	M,D
Telecommunications	M,D
Theater	M
Vision Sciences	M,D
Water Resources Engineering	M,D

UNIVERSITY OF ANTELOPE VALLEY

Business Administration and Management—General	M
Criminal Justice and Criminology	M

THE UNIVERSITY OF ARIZONA

Accounting	M
Aerospace/Aeronautical Engineering	M,D
African Studies	M,D,O
Agricultural Economics and Agribusiness	M
Agricultural Education	M,O
Agricultural Engineering	M,D
Agricultural Sciences—General	M,D,O
Agronomy and Soil Sciences	M,D,O
Allopathic Medicine	M,D
American Indian/Native American Studies	M,D
Animal Sciences	M,D
Anthropology	M,D,O
Applied Economics	M
Applied Mathematics	M,D
Architecture	M
Art Education	M,D
Art History	M,D
Art/Fine Arts	M
Asian Studies	M,D
Astronomy	D
Atmospheric Sciences	M,D
Biochemistry	M,D
Biological and Biomedical Sciences—General	M,D
Biomedical Engineering	M,D
Biostatistics	M,D
Biosystems Engineering	M,D
Business Administration and Management—General	M,D,O
Cancer Biology/Oncology	D
Cell Biology	D
Chemical Engineering	M,D
Chemistry	M,D
Child and Family Studies	M,D,O
Classics	M
Communication Disorders	M,D,O
Communication—General	M,D
Computer Engineering	M,D
Computer Science	M,D
Counseling Psychology	M
Counselor Education	M
Dance	M
Data Science/Data Analytics	M
Ecology	M,D
Economics	M,D
Education—General	M,D,O
Educational Leadership and Administration	M,D,O
Educational Psychology	M,D,O
Electrical Engineering	M,D
Elementary Education	M,D
Engineering and Applied Sciences—General	M,D,O
Engineering Management	M,D,O
English as a Second Language	M,D
English Education	M,D
English	M,D
Entomology	M,D
Environmental Engineering	M,D
Environmental Management and Policy	M,D
Environmental Sciences	M,D,O
Epidemiology	M,D
Evolutionary Biology	M,D
Family and Consumer Sciences-General	D
Family Nurse Practitioner Studies	M,D,O
Film, Television, and Video Theory and Criticism	M
Finance and Banking	M
Forestry	M,D
French	M
Gender Studies	M,D,O
Genetics	M,D
Geographic Information Systems	M,D,O
Geography	M,D,O
Geological Engineering	M,D,O
Geosciences	M,D
German	M,D
Higher Education	M,D
History	M,D,O
Human Development	M,D,O
Hydrology	D,O
Immunology	D
Industrial/Management Engineering	M,D,O
Information Studies	M,D
Interdisciplinary Studies	M,D
Journalism	M
Landscape Architecture	M
Latin American Studies	M
Law	M,D
Library Science	M,D
Linguistics	M,D
Management Information Systems	M,O
Management Strategy and Policy	M,D
Marketing	M,D
Materials Engineering	M,D
Materials Sciences	M,D
Mathematics Education	M
Mathematics	M,D
Mechanical Engineering	M,D
Medical Informatics	M,D,O
Medical Physics	M
Microbiology	D
Mineral/Mining Engineering	M,D,O
Molecular Biology	D
Molecular Medicine	M,D
Music Education	M,D
Music	M,D
Natural Resources	M,D
Near and Middle Eastern Studies	M,D,O
Neuroscience	D
Nursing—General	M,D,O
Nutrition	M,D
Optical Sciences	M,D,O
Organizational Management	M,D
Perfusion	M,D
Pharmaceutical Sciences	M,D
Pharmacology	M,D
Pharmacy	D
Philosophy	M,D
Physics	M,D
Physiology	M,D
Planetary and Space Sciences	M,D
Plant Pathology	M,D
Plant Sciences	M,D
Political Science	M,D
Psychology—General	M,D
Public Administration	M,D,O
Public Health—General	M,D
Public Policy	M,D,O
Range Science	M,D
Reading Education	M,D,O
Rehabilitation Counseling	M,D
Rhetoric	M,D
Russian	M
School Psychology	D,O
Secondary Education	M,D
Sociology	M,D
Spanish	M,D
Special Education	M,D
Statistics	M,D
Systems Engineering	M,D,O
Theater	M
Urban and Regional Planning	M
Water Resources	M,D,O
Women's Studies	M,D,O
Writing	M

UNIVERSITY OF ARKANSAS

Accounting	M
Adult Education	M,D
Agricultural Economics and Agribusiness	M
Agricultural Education	M
Agricultural Engineering	M,D
Agricultural Sciences—General	M,D
Agronomy and Soil Sciences	M,D
Animal Sciences	M,D
Anthropology	M,D
Applied Physics	M,D
Art/Fine Arts	M
Athletic Training and Sports Medicine	M
Bioengineering	M
Biological and Biomedical Sciences—General	M,D
Biomedical Engineering	M
Business Administration and Management—General	M,D
Cell Biology	M,D
Chemical Engineering	M,D
Chemistry	M,D
Civil Engineering	M,D
Communication Disorders	M
Communication—General	M
Community Health	M,D
Comparative Literature	M,D
Computer Engineering	M,D
Computer Science	M,D
Counselor Education	M,D
Cultural Studies	M,D
Curriculum and Instruction	M,D,O
Early Childhood Education	M
Economics	M,D
Education—General	M,D,O
Educational Leadership and Administration	M,D,O
Educational Measurement and Evaluation	M,D
Educational Media/Instructional Technology	M
Educational Policy	D
Electrical Engineering	M,D
Electronic Materials	M,D
Engineering and Applied Sciences—General	M,D
English	M,D
Entomology	M,D
Environmental Engineering	M,D
Family and Consumer Sciences-General	M
Food Science and Technology	M,D
French	M
Geography	M
Geology	M
German	M
Health Education	M,D
Health Promotion	M,D
Higher Education	M,D,O
History	M,D
Horticulture	M
Human Resources Development	M,D,O
Industrial and Manufacturing Management	M
Industrial/Management Engineering	M,D
Journalism	M
Kinesiology and Movement Studies	M,D
Law	M,D
Management Information Systems	M
Mathematics Education	M
Mathematics	M,D
Mechanical Engineering	M,D
Middle School Education	M,D,O
Molecular Biology	M,D
Music	M
Nursing—General	M
Operations Research	M,D
Philosophy	M,D
Photonics	M,D
Physical Education	M
Physics	M,D
Planetary and Space Sciences	M,D
Plant Pathology	M
Plant Sciences	D
Political Science	M
Psychology—General	M,D
Public Administration	M,D
Public Policy	D
Recreation and Park Management	M,D
Rehabilitation Counseling	M,D
Secondary Education	M,O
Social Work	M
Sociology	M
Spanish	M
Special Education	M
Sports Management	M,D
Statistics	M
Telecommunications	M,D
Theater	M
Transportation and Highway Engineering	M,D
Vocational and Technical Education	M,D,O
Writing	M

UNIVERSITY OF ARKANSAS AT LITTLE ROCK

Adult Education	M
Applied Mathematics	M,O
Applied Psychology	M
Applied Science and Technology	M,D
Applied Statistics	M,O
Art Education	M
Art History	M
Art/Fine Arts	M
Bioinformatics	M,D
Biological and Biomedical Sciences—General	M
Business Administration and Management—General	M,O
Chemistry	M
Community College Education	M,D
Computer Science	M,D
Conflict Resolution and Mediation/Peace Studies	O
Construction Management	M
Counselor Education	M
Criminal Justice and Criminology	M,D
Curriculum and Instruction	M
Education of the Gifted	M,O
Education—General	M,D,O
Educational Leadership and Administration	M,D,O
Educational Media/Instructional Technology	M
English as a Second Language	M
Entrepreneurship	O
Exercise and Sports Science	M
Foreign Languages Education	M
Geosciences	O
Gerontology	O
Health Education	M,D
Higher Education	M,D
Information Science	M,D,O
Interdisciplinary Studies	M
Law	D
Management Information Systems	M,O
Mass Communication	M
Mathematics	M,O
Middle School Education	M
Nonprofit Management	O
Psychology—General	M
Public Administration	M
Public Affairs	M,O
Public History	M
Reading Education	M,D,O
Rehabilitation Counseling	M,O
Rhetoric	M
Secondary Education	M
Social Work	M
Special Education	M,O
Speech and Interpersonal Communication	M
Sports Management	M
Student Affairs	M,D
Systems Engineering	M,D,O
Technical Writing	M
Writing	M

UNIVERSITY OF ARKANSAS AT MONTICELLO

Education—General	M
Educational Leadership and Administration	M
Forestry	M
Natural Resources	M

UNIVERSITY OF ARKANSAS AT PINE BLUFF

Aquaculture	M,D
Education—General	M
Elementary Education	M
English Education	M
Fish, Game, and Wildlife Management	M,D
Mathematics Education	M
Science Education	M
Secondary Education	M
Social Sciences Education	M

UNIVERSITY OF ARKANSAS FOR MEDICAL SCIENCES

Allopathic Medicine	D
Biochemistry	M,D,O
Bioinformatics	M,D,O
Biological and Biomedical Sciences—General	M,D,O
Biostatistics	M,D,O
Communication Disorders	M,D
Environmental and Occupational Health	M,D,O
Epidemiology	M,D,O
Genetic Counseling	M,D
Health Education	M,D,O
Health Physics/Radiological Health	M,D
Health Promotion	M,D,O
Health Services Management and Hospital Administration	M,D,O
Health Services Research	M,D,O
Immunology	M,D,O
Microbiology	M,D,O
Molecular Biology	M,D,O
Molecular Biophysics	M,D,O
Neurobiology	M,D,O
Nursing—General	D
Nutrition	M,D,O
Pharmacology	M,D,O
Pharmacy	M,D
Physician Assistant Studies	M,D
Physiology	M,D,O
Public Health—General	M,D,O
Toxicology	M,D,O

UNIVERSITY OF ARKANSAS–FORT SMITH

Health Services Management and Hospital Administration	M

UNIVERSITY OF BALTIMORE

Accounting	M,O
Applied Arts and Design—General	M
Applied Psychology	M
Business Administration and Management—General	M,O
Conflict Resolution and Mediation/Peace Studies	M
Counseling Psychology	M
Criminal Justice and Criminology	M
Entrepreneurship	M
Finance and Banking	M
Graphic Design	D

*M—masters degree; D—doctorate; O—other advanced degree; *—Close-Up and/or Display*

Health Services Management and Hospital Administration	M
Human Services	M
Human-Computer Interaction	M
Intellectual Property Law	M,D
International Business	M
Law	M,D
Legal and Justice Studies	M
Management Information Systems	M,O
Marketing	M
Public Administration	M,D
Public Affairs	M,D
Publishing	M
Taxation	M,D
Writing	M

UNIVERSITY OF BRIDGEPORT

Accounting	M
Acupuncture and Oriental Medicine	M
Applied Arts and Design—General	M
Asian Studies	M
Biomedical Engineering	M
Business Administration and Management—General	M
Chiropractic	D
Clinical Psychology	M
Communication—General	M
Computer Education	M,D,O
Computer Engineering	M,D
Computer Science	M,D
Conflict Resolution and Mediation/Peace Studies	M
Counseling Psychology	M
Dental Hygiene	M
Early Childhood Education	M,D,O
Education—General	M,D,O
Educational Leadership and Administration	M,D,O
Electrical Engineering	M
Elementary Education	M,D,O
Engineering and Applied Sciences—General	M,D
Entrepreneurship	M
Finance and Banking	M
Human Resources Development	M
Human Resources Management	M
Human Services	M
Industrial and Manufacturing Management	M
International Affairs	M
International and Comparative Education	M,D,O
International Business	M
Management Information Systems	M
Management of Technology	M,D
Marketing	M
Mechanical Engineering	M
Media Studies	M
Middle School Education	M,D,O
Music Education	M,D,O
Naturopathic Medicine	D
Nutrition	M
Physician Assistant Studies	M
Reading Education	M,D,O
Secondary Education	M,D,O
Social Psychology	M
Student Affairs	M

THE UNIVERSITY OF BRITISH COLUMBIA

Accounting	D
Adult Education	M,D
Agricultural Economics and Agribusiness	M
Agricultural Sciences—General	M,D
Agronomy and Soil Sciences	M,D
Allopathic Medicine	M,D
Animal Sciences	M,D
Anthropology	M,D
Archaeology	M
Architecture	M
Archives/Archival Administration	M,D
Art Education	M,D
Art History	M,D
Art/Fine Arts	M,D
Asian Studies	M,D
Astronomy	M,D
Atmospheric Sciences	M,D
Biochemistry	M,D
Bioengineering	M,D
Bioinformatics	M,D
Biomedical Engineering	M,D
Biopsychology	M,D
Botany	M,D
Business Administration and Management—General	M,D
Business Analytics	M
Cell Biology	M,D
Chemical Engineering	M,D
Chemistry	M,D
Civil Engineering	M,D
Classics	M,D
Clinical Psychology	M,D
Cognitive Sciences	M,D
Communication Disorders	M,D
Computer Engineering	M,D
Computer Science	M,D
Counseling Psychology	M,D,O
Curriculum and Instruction	M,D
Dentistry	D
Developmental Biology	M,D
Developmental Psychology	M,D
East European and Russian Studies	M,D
Economics	M,D
Education—General	M,D,O
Educational Leadership and Administration	M,D
Educational Measurement and Evaluation	M,D,O
Educational Policy	M,D
Electrical Engineering	M,D
Energy and Power Engineering	M
Engineering and Applied Sciences—General	M,D
English as a Second Language	M,D
English	M,D
Environmental Management and Policy	M,D
Ethnic Studies	M
Film, Television, and Video Production	M
Film, Television, and Video Theory and Criticism	M
Finance and Banking	D
Food Science and Technology	M,D
Forestry	M,D
Foundations and Philosophy of Education	M,D
French	M,D
Gender Studies	M,D
Genetic Counseling	M
Genetics	M,D
Geography	M,D
Geological Engineering	M,D
Geology	M,D
Geophysics	M,D
German	M,D
Health Psychology	M,D
Health Services Management and Hospital Administration	M,D
Higher Education	M,D
Hispanic Studies	M,D
History	M,D
Home Economics Education	M,D
Human Development	M,D,O
Immunology	M,D
Infectious Diseases	M,D
Information Studies	M,D
International Affairs	M
Internet and Interactive Multimedia	M
Journalism	M
Kinesiology and Movement Studies	M,D
Landscape Architecture	M
Law	M,D
Library Science	M,D
Linguistics	M,D
Management Information Systems	D
Management Strategy and Policy	D
Marine Sciences	M,D
Marketing	D
Materials Engineering	M,D
Mathematics Education	M,D
Mathematics	M,D
Mechanical Engineering	M,D
Microbiology	M,D
Mineral/Mining Engineering	M,D
Molecular Biology	M,D
Museum Studies	M,D
Music Education	M,D
Music	M,D
Natural Resources	M,D
Neuroscience	M,D
Nursing—General	M,D
Nutrition	M,D
Occupational Therapy	M
Oceanography	M,D
Oral and Dental Sciences	M,D
Organizational Behavior	D
Pacific Area/Pacific Rim Studies	M
Pathology	M,D
Pharmaceutical Sciences	M,D
Pharmacology	M,D
Pharmacy	M,D
Philosophy	M,D
Physical Education	M,D
Physical Therapy	M
Physics	M,D
Plant Sciences	M,D
Political Science	M,D
Psychology—General	M,D
Public Health—General	M,D
Public Policy	M
Quantitative Analysis	M,D
Reading Education	M,D
Rehabilitation Sciences	M,D
Religion	M,D
Reproductive Biology	M,D
School Psychology	M,D,O
Science Education	M,D
Social Psychology	M,D
Social Sciences Education	M,D
Social Work	M,D
Sociology	M,D
Special Education	M,D,O
Statistics	M,D
Sustainability Management	M,D
Sustainable Development	M
Taxation	M,D
Theater	M,D
Transportation Management	D
Urban and Regional Planning	M,D
Urban Design	M
Vocational and Technical Education	M,D
Water Resources	M
Writing	M,D
Zoology	M,D

UNIVERSITY OF CALGARY

Adult Education	M,D
Allopathic Medicine	D
Analytical Chemistry	M,D
Anthropology	M,D
Applied Psychology	M,D
Archaeology	M,D
Architecture	M
Art/Fine Arts	M
Astronomy	M,D
Biochemistry	M,D
Biological and Biomedical Sciences—General	M,D
Biomedical Engineering	M,D
Biotechnology	M
Business Administration and Management—General	M,D
Cancer Biology/Oncology	M,D
Cardiovascular Sciences	M,D
Chemical Engineering	M,D
Chemistry	M,D
Civil Engineering	M,D
Classics	M,D
Clinical Psychology	M,D
Communication—General	M,D
Community Health	M,D
Computer Engineering	M,D
Computer Science	M,D
Counseling Psychology	M,D
Curriculum and Instruction	M,D
Economics	M,D
Educational Leadership and Administration	M,D
Educational Measurement and Evaluation	M,D
Electrical Engineering	M,D
Energy and Power Engineering	M,D
Energy Management and Policy	M,D
Engineering and Applied Sciences—General	M,D
English	M,D
Environmental Design	M,D
Environmental Engineering	M,D
Environmental Law	M,O
Environmental Management and Policy	M,D,O
French	M,D
Genetics	M,D
Geography	M,D
Geology	M,D
Geophysics	M,D
Geosciences	M,D
Geotechnical Engineering	M,D
German	M,D
History	M,D
Hydrology	M,D
Immunology	M,D
Infectious Diseases	M,D
Inorganic Chemistry	M,D
Kinesiology and Movement Studies	M,D
Landscape Architecture	M,D
Law	M,D,O
Legal and Justice Studies	M,D
Linguistics	M,D
Management Strategy and Policy	M,D
Manufacturing Engineering	M,D
Materials Sciences	M,D
Mathematics	M,D
Mechanical Engineering	M,D
Mechanics	M,D
Microbiology	M,D
Military and Defense Studies	M,D
Molecular Biology	M,D
Molecular Genetics	M,D
Multilingual and Multicultural Education	M,D
Music	M,D
Neuroscience	M,D
Nursing—General	M,D,O
Organic Chemistry	M,D
Pathology	M,D
Petroleum Engineering	M,D
Philosophy	M,D
Physical Chemistry	M,D
Physics	M,D
Physiology	M,D
Political Science	M,D
Project Management	M,D
Psychology—General	M,D
Public Policy	M
Religion	M,D
School Psychology	M,D
Social Work	M,D,O
Sociology	M,D
Software Engineering	M,D
Spanish	M,D
Statistics	M,D
Structural Engineering	M,D
Sustainable Development	M,D
Theater	M
Theoretical Chemistry	M,D
Transportation and Highway Engineering	M,D
Water Resources	M,D

UNIVERSITY OF CALIFORNIA, BERKELEY

Accounting	D,O
Addictions/Substance Abuse Counseling	O
African-American Studies	D
Agricultural Economics and Agribusiness	D
Allopathic Medicine	
Anthropology	D
Applied Arts and Design—General	O
Applied Mathematics	M,D
Applied Science and Technology	D
Archaeology	M,D
Architectural History	M,D
Architecture	M,D
Art History	D
Art/Fine Arts	M,O
Asian Languages	M,D
Asian Studies	M,D
Astrophysics	D
Biochemistry	D
Bioengineering	M,D
Biological and Biomedical Sciences—General	D
Biophysics	D
Biostatistics	M,D
Building Science	M,D
Business Administration and Management—General	M,D,O
Cell Biology	D
Chemical Engineering	M,D
Chemistry	D
Chinese	D
Civil Engineering	M,D
Classics	M,D
Clinical Research	O
Comparative Literature	D
Computer Science	M,D
Construction Management	O
Counseling Psychology	O
Data Science/Data Analytics	M
Demography and Population Studies	M,D
Economics	D
Education—General	M,D,O
Educational Leadership and Administration	M,D
Electrical Engineering	M,D
Energy Management and Policy	M,D
Engineering and Applied Sciences—General	M,D,O
Engineering Management	M,D
English as a Second Language	O
English	D
Environmental and Occupational Health	M,D
Environmental Design	M,D
Environmental Engineering	M,D
Environmental Management and Policy	M,D,O
Environmental Sciences	M,D
Epidemiology	M,D
Ethnic Studies	D
Facilities Management	O
Film, Television, and Video Theory and Criticism	D
Finance and Banking	D,O
Financial Engineering	M
Folklore	M
Forestry	M,D
French	D
Geography	D
Geology	M,D
Geophysics	M,D
Geotechnical Engineering	M,D
German	D
Health Services Management and Hospital Administration	D
Hispanic and Latin American Languages	D
History of Science and Technology	D
History	M,D
Human Development	M,D
Human Resources Management	O
Immunology	D
Industrial and Labor Relations	D
Industrial/Management Engineering	M,D
Infectious Diseases	M,D
Information Studies	M,D
Interior Design	O
International Affairs	M
International Business	O
Italian	D
Japanese	D
Journalism	M
Landscape Architecture	M,D,O
Law	M,D
Legal and Justice Studies	D
Linguistics	D
Management Information Systems	M,D,O
Marketing	D,O
Materials Engineering	M,D
Materials Sciences	M,D
Mathematics Education	M,D
Mathematics	M,D
Mechanical Engineering	M,D
Mechanics	M,D
Microbiology	D
Molecular Biology	D
Molecular Toxicology	D
Music	D
Natural Resources	M,D
Near and Middle Eastern Studies	M,D
Neuroscience	D
Nuclear Engineering	M,D
Nutrition	M,D
Operations Research	M,D
Optometry	D,O
Organizational Behavior	D
Philosophy	D
Physics	D
Physiology	M,D
Plant Biology	D
Political Science	D
Project Management	O
Psychology—General	D
Public Affairs	M
Public Health—General	M,D
Public Policy	M,D
Range Science	M
Real Estate	D
Religion	D
Rhetoric	D
Romance Languages	D
Russian	D
Scandinavian Languages	D
Science Education	M,D
Slavic Languages	D
Social Work	M,D
Sociology	D
Spanish	D
Special Education	M,D
Statistics	M,D
Structural Engineering	M,D
Sustainability Management	O
Sustainable Development	M,O
Theater	D
Transportation and Highway Engineering	M,D
Urban and Regional Planning	M,D
Urban Design	M,D
Vision Sciences	M,D
Water Resources Engineering	M,D
Writing	O

UNIVERSITY OF CALIFORNIA, DAVIS

Accounting	M
Aerospace/Aeronautical Engineering	M,D,O
Agricultural Economics and Agribusiness	M,D
Agricultural Sciences—General	M
Agronomy and Soil Sciences	M,D
Allopathic Medicine	D
American Indian/Native American Studies	M,D
Animal Behavior	D
Animal Sciences	M,D
Anthropology	M,D
Applied Mathematics	M,D
Applied Science and Technology	M,D
Art History	M
Art/Fine Arts	M
Atmospheric Sciences	M,D
Biochemistry	M,D
Bioengineering	M,D
Biomedical Engineering	M,D
Biophysics	M,D
Biostatistics	M,D
Business Administration and Management—General	M
Business Analytics	M
Cell Biology	M,D
Chemical Engineering	M,D
Chemistry	M,D
Child Development	M
Civil Engineering	M,D,O
Clinical Research	M
Clothing and Textiles	M
Communication—General	M
Comparative Literature	D
Computer Engineering	M,D
Computer Science	M,D
Cultural Studies	M,D
Curriculum and Instruction	M,D
Developmental Biology	M,D
Ecology	M,D
Economics	M,D
Education—General	M,D
Educational Psychology	M,D
Electrical Engineering	M,D
Engineering and Applied Sciences—General	M,D,O
English	M,D
Entomology	M,D
Entrepreneurship	M
Environmental Engineering	M,D,O
Environmental Sciences	M,D
Epidemiology	M,D
Evolutionary Biology	D
Exercise and Sports Science	M
Finance and Banking	M
Food Science and Technology	M,D
Forensic Sciences	M
French	D
Genetics	M,D
Geography	M,D
Geology	M,D
German	M,D
History	M,D
Horticulture	M
Human Development	D
Hydrology	M,D
Immunology	M,D
Law	M,D
Linguistics	M,D
Management Strategy and Policy	M
Marketing	M
Materials Engineering	M,D
Materials Sciences	M,D
Maternal and Child Health	M
Mathematics	M,D
Mechanical Engineering	M,D,O
Medical Informatics	M
Microbiology	M,D
Molecular Biology	M,D
Music	M,D
Neuroscience	D
Nutrition	M,D
Organizational Behavior	M
Pathology	M,D
Pharmacology	M,D
Philosophy	M,D
Physics	M,D
Physiology	M,D
Plant Biology	M,D
Plant Pathology	M,D
Political Science	M,D
Psychology—General	D
Sociology	M,D
Spanish	M,D
Statistics	M,D
Textile Design	M
Theater	M,D
Toxicology	M,D
Transportation and Highway Engineering	M,D
Transportation Management	M,D
Urban and Regional Planning	M
Veterinary Medicine	D
Veterinary Sciences	M,O
Viticulture and Enology	M,D
Writing	M,D
Zoology	M

UNIVERSITY OF CALIFORNIA, HASTINGS COLLEGE OF THE LAW

Law	M,D

UNIVERSITY OF CALIFORNIA, IRVINE

Accounting	M
Aerospace/Aeronautical Engineering	M,D
Allopathic Medicine	D
Anatomy	M,D
Anthropology	M,D
Applied Mathematics	M,D
Art/Fine Arts	M,D
Asian Languages	M,D
Biochemical Engineering	M,D
Biochemistry	M,D
Biological and Biomedical Sciences—General	M,D
Biomedical Engineering	M,D
Biophysics	D
Biotechnology	M
Business Administration and Management—General	M,D
Cell Biology	M,D
Chemical Engineering	M,D
Chemistry	M,D
Chinese	M,D
Civil Engineering	M,D
Classics	M,D
Comparative Literature	M,D
Computational Biology	D
Computer Science	M,D
Criminal Justice and Criminology	M,D
Cultural Studies	D
Dance	M
Demography and Population Studies	M
Developmental Biology	M,D
Ecology	M,D
Economics	M,D
Education—General	M,D
Educational Leadership and Administration	M,D
Electrical Engineering	M,D
Elementary Education	M,D
Engineering and Applied Sciences—General	M,D
Engineering Management	M
English	M,D
Environmental and Occupational Health	M,D
Environmental Design	M,D
Environmental Engineering	M,D
Epidemiology	M,D
Evolutionary Biology	M,D
Foreign Languages Education	M,D
French	M,D
Genetic Counseling	M
Genetics	D
Geosciences	M,D
German	M,D
Health Services Management and Hospital Administration	M
History	M,D
Information Science	M,D
Japanese	M,D
Law	D
Manufacturing Engineering	M,D
Materials Engineering	M,D
Materials Sciences	M,D
Mathematics	M,D
Mechanical Engineering	M,D
Medicinal and Pharmaceutical Chemistry	D
Microbiology	M,D
Molecular Biology	M,D
Molecular Genetics	M,D
Music	M
Neurobiology	M,D
Neuroscience	D
Nursing—General	M
Pathology	D
Pharmaceutical Sciences	D
Philosophy	M,D
Physics	M,D
Physiology	D
Political Science	D
Psychology—General	D
Public Health—General	M,D
Secondary Education	M,D
Sociology	D
Spanish	M,D
Statistics	M,D
Systems Biology	D
Theater	M,D
Toxicology	M,D
Translational Biology	M
Transportation and Highway Engineering	M,D
Urban and Regional Planning	M,D
Urban Studies	M,D
Writing	M

UNIVERSITY OF CALIFORNIA, LOS ANGELES

Accounting	M,D
Aerospace/Aeronautical Engineering	M,D
African Studies	M
African-American Studies	M
Allopathic Medicine	D
American Indian/Native American Studies	M
Anatomy	M,D
Anthropology	M,D
Applied Arts and Design—General	M
Applied Economics	M
Archaeology	M,D
Architecture	M,D
Archives/Archival Administration	M,D,O
Art History	M,D
Art/Fine Arts	M
Asian Languages	M,D
Asian Studies	M,D
Asian-American Studies	M
Astronomy	M,D
Astrophysics	M,D
Atmospheric Sciences	M,D
Biochemistry	M,D
Bioengineering	M,D
Bioinformatics	M,D
Biological and Biomedical Sciences—General	M,D
Biomathematics	M,D
Biomedical Engineering	M,D
Biostatistics	M,D
Business Administration and Management—General	M,D
Business Analytics	M,D
Cell Biology	M,D
Chemical Engineering	M,D
Chemistry	M,D
Civil Engineering	M,D
Classics	M,D
Clinical Research	M
Community Health	M,D
Comparative Literature	M,D
Computer Engineering	M,D
Computer Science	M,D
Dance	M,D
Dentistry	D,O
Developmental Biology	M,D
Ecology	M,D
Economics	D*
Education—General	M,D
Educational Leadership and Administration	D
Electrical Engineering	M,D
Engineering and Applied Sciences—General	M,D
English as a Second Language	M,D,O
English	M,D
Environmental and Occupational Health	M,D
Environmental Engineering	M,D
Environmental Sciences	M,D
Epidemiology	M,D
Evolutionary Biology	M,D
Film, Television, and Video Production	M,D
Finance and Banking	M,D
Financial Engineering	M,D
French	M,D
Gender Studies	M,D
Geochemistry	M,D
Geography	M,D
Geology	M,D
Geophysics	M,D
Geosciences	M,D
German	M,D
Health Services Management and Hospital Administration	M,D
Hispanic and Latin American Languages	D
Historic Preservation	M
History	M,D
Human Genetics	M,D
Immunology	M,D
Information Studies	M,D,O
Italian	M,D
Latin American Studies	M
Law	M,D
Library Science	M,D,O
Linguistics	M,D
Management of Technology	M,D
Management Strategy and Policy	M,D
Manufacturing Engineering	M
Marketing	M,D
Materials Engineering	M,D
Materials Sciences	M,D
Mathematics	M,D
Mechanical Engineering	M,D
Media Studies	M,D
Medical Physics	M,D
Microbiology	M,D
Molecular Biology	M,D
Molecular Genetics	M,D
Molecular Physiology	D
Molecular Toxicology	D
Music	M,D
Near and Middle Eastern Languages	M,D
Near and Middle Eastern Studies	M,D
Neurobiology	M,D
Neuroscience	D
Nursing—General	M,D
Oceanography	M,D
Oral and Dental Sciences	M,D
Pathology	M,D
Pharmacology	M,D
Philosophy	M,D
Physics	M,D
Physiology	M,D
Planetary and Space Sciences	M,D
Political Science	M,D
Portuguese	M
Psychology—General	M,D
Public Affairs	M,D
Public Health—General	M,D
Public Policy	M
Scandinavian Languages	M
Slavic Languages	M,D
Social Work	M,D
Sociology	M,D
Spanish	M
Special Education	D
Statistics	M,D
Theater	M,D
Toxicology	D
Urban and Regional Planning	M,D
Urban Design	M

UNIVERSITY OF CALIFORNIA, MERCED

Applied Mathematics	M,D
Biochemistry	M,D
Bioengineering	M,D
Biological and Biomedical Sciences—General	M,D
Chemistry	M,D
Cognitive Sciences	M,D
Computer Science	M,D
Electrical Engineering	M,D
Engineering and Applied Sciences—General	M,D
Entrepreneurship	M,D
Environmental Engineering	M,D
Humanities	M,D
Information Science	M,D
Mechanical Engineering	M,D
Mechanics	M,D
Physics	M,D
Psychology—General	M,D
Social Sciences	M,D
Sociology	M,D
Sustainability Management	M,D
Systems Biology	M,D
Systems Engineering	M,D

UNIVERSITY OF CALIFORNIA, RIVERSIDE

Accounting	M,D
Agronomy and Soil Sciences	M,D
Allopathic Medicine	D
Anthropology	M,D
Applied Behavior Analysis	M,D,O
Archives/Archival Administration	M,D
Art History	M,D
Art/Fine Arts	M
Artificial Intelligence/Robotics	M,D
Asian Studies	M
Biochemistry	M,D
Bioengineering	M,D
Bioinformatics	D
Biological and Biomedical Sciences—General	M,D
Botany	M,D
Business Administration and Management—General	M,D
Cell Biology	M,D
Chemical Engineering	M,D
Chemistry	M,D
Classics	D
Comparative Literature	M,D
Computer Engineering	M
Computer Science	M,D
Cultural Studies	D
Dance	M
Developmental Biology	M,D
Economics	M
Education—General	M,D,O
Educational Leadership and Administration	M,D,O
Educational Measurement and Evaluation	M,D,O
Educational Policy	M,D,O
Educational Psychology	M,D,O
Electrical Engineering	M,D
English as a Second Language	M,D,O
English	M,D
Entomology	M,D
Environmental Engineering	M,D
Environmental Sciences	M
Ethnic Studies	D
Evolutionary Biology	M,D
Finance and Banking	M,D
Foundations and Philosophy of Education	M,D,O
Genetics	D
Genomic Sciences	D
Geology	M,D
Higher Education	M,D,O
Hispanic Studies	M,D
History	M,D
International Health	M,D
Materials Engineering	M
Materials Sciences	M
Mathematics	M,D
Mechanical Engineering	M,D
Microbiology	M,D
Molecular Biology	M,D
Multilingual and Multicultural Education	M,D,O
Music	M,D
Nanotechnology	M
Neuroscience	D
Philosophy	M,D
Physics	M,D
Plant Biology	M,D
Plant Molecular Biology	M,D
Plant Pathology	M,D
Plant Sciences	M,D
Political Science	M,D
Psychology—General	D
Public Policy	M,D
Religion	M,D
School Psychology	M,D,O
Sociology	M,D
Spanish	M,D
Special Education	M,D,O
Statistics	M
Toxicology	M,D
Water Resources	M,D
Writing	M

UNIVERSITY OF CALIFORNIA, SAN DIEGO

Aerospace/Aeronautical Engineering	M,D
Allopathic Medicine	D
Anthropology	D
Applied Mathematics	M,D
Applied Physics	M,D
Architectural Engineering	M
Art History	M,D
Art/Fine Arts	M,D
Artificial Intelligence/Robotics	M,D
Biochemistry	M,D
Bioengineering	M,D*
Bioinformatics	D
Biological and Biomedical Sciences—General	M,D*

*M—masters degree; D—doctorate; O—other advanced degree; *—Close-Up and/or Display*

Biophysics	M,D
Biostatistics	D
Business Administration and Management—General	M,D
Business Analytics	M,D
Chemical Engineering	M,D
Chemistry	M,D
Clinical Laboratory Sciences/Medical Technology	M,D
Clinical Psychology	D
Clinical Research	M
Cognitive Sciences	D
Communication Disorders	D
Communication—General	D
Computational Sciences	M,D
Computer Engineering	M,D
Computer Science	M,D
Curriculum and Instruction	M,D
Dance	M,D
Data Science/Data Analytics	M
Economics	D
Education—General	M,D
Educational Leadership and Administration	M,D
Electrical Engineering	M,D
Energy Management and Policy	M
Engineering Physics	M,D
English	M,D
Environmental Management and Policy	M
Epidemiology	D
Ethnic Studies	D
Finance and Banking	M,D
Geophysics	M,D
Geosciences	M,D
Health Services Management and Hospital Administration	M
History of Science and Technology	D
History	M,D
International Affairs	M,D
International Business	M
International Development	M
International Economics	M
International Health	D
Jewish Studies	M,D
Latin American Studies	M
Linguistics	D
Marine Sciences	M
Materials Sciences	M,D
Mathematics Education	D
Mathematics	M,D
Mechanical Engineering	M,D
Mechanics	M,D
Meteorology	M
Modeling and Simulation	M,D
Multilingual and Multicultural Education	M,D
Music	M,D
Nanotechnology	M,D
Neuroscience	M,D
Nonprofit Management	M
Ocean Engineering	M,D
Oceanography	M,D
Pharmacy	D
Philosophy	D
Photonics	M,D
Physics	M,D
Political Science	M,D
Psychology—General	D
Public Health—General	D
Public Policy	M
Science Education	D
Sociology	D
Statistics	M,D
Structural Engineering	M,D
Systems Biology	D*
Telecommunications	M,D
Theater	M,D
Writing	M,D

UNIVERSITY OF CALIFORNIA, SAN FRANCISCO

Allopathic Medicine	D
Anthropology	D
Biochemistry	D
Bioengineering	D
Bioinformatics	D
Biological and Biomedical Sciences—General	D
Biophysics	D
Cell Biology	D
Chemistry	D
Dentistry	D
Developmental Biology	D
Genetics	D
Genomic Sciences	D
Health Law	M
History of Science and Technology	M,D
Medical Imaging	M
Medicinal and Pharmaceutical Chemistry	D
Molecular Biology	D
Neuroscience	D
Nursing—General	M,D
Oral and Dental Sciences	M,D
Pharmaceutical Sciences	D
Pharmacology	D
Pharmacy	D
Physical Therapy	D
Sociology	D

UNIVERSITY OF CALIFORNIA, SANTA BARBARA

African-American Studies	D
Agricultural Economics and Agribusiness	M,D
Anthropology	M,D
Applied Mathematics	M,D
Applied Statistics	M,D
Art History	D
Art/Fine Arts	M
Asian Languages	M,D
Asian Studies	M,D
Biochemistry	D
Bioengineering	M,D
Biophysics	D
Cell Biology	M,D
Chemical Engineering	M,D
Chemistry	M,D
Classics	M,D
Clinical Psychology	M,D,O
Cognitive Sciences	M,D
Communication—General	D
Comparative Literature	D
Computational Sciences	M,D
Computer Engineering	M,D
Computer Science	M,D
Counseling Psychology	M,D,O
Cultural Anthropology	M,D
Cultural Studies	M,D
Developmental Biology	M,D
Ecology	M,D
Economics	M,D
Education—General	M,D,O
Electrical Engineering	M,D
Engineering and Applied Sciences—General	M,D
English	D
Environmental Management and Policy	M,D
Environmental Sciences	M,D
Evolutionary Biology	M,D
Film, Television, and Video Production	D
Finance and Banking	M,D
French	D
Geography	M,D
Geosciences	M,D
Hispanic and Latin American Languages	M,D
Hispanic Studies	M,D
History	D
Interdisciplinary Studies	D
International Affairs	M,D
Latin American Studies	M
Linguistics	M,D
Management of Technology	M
Marine Biology	M,D
Marine Sciences	M,D
Materials Engineering	M,D
Materials Sciences	M,D
Mathematical and Computational Finance	M,D
Mathematics	M,D
Mechanical Engineering	M,D
Media Studies	M,D
Medieval and Renaissance Studies	M,D
Molecular Biology	M,D
Music	M,D
Neuroscience	D
Philosophy	D
Photonics	M,D
Physics	D
Political Science	M,D
Portuguese	M,D
Psychology—General	D
Public History	D
Quantitative Analysis	M,D
Religion	M,D
School Psychology	M,D,O
Social Sciences	D
Sociology	D
Spanish	M,D
Speech and Interpersonal Communication	D
Statistics	M,D
Sustainable Development	M,D
Theater	M,D
Translation and Interpretation	M,D
Transportation Management	M,D
Women's Studies	M,D
Writing	M,D

UNIVERSITY OF CALIFORNIA, SANTA CRUZ

Anthropology	D
Applied Economics	M
Applied Mathematics	M,D
Art/Fine Arts	M,D
Astronomy	D
Astrophysics	D
Biochemistry	M,D
Bioinformatics	M,D
Cell Biology	M,D
Chemistry	M,D
Communication—General	O
Comparative Literature	M,D
Computer Art and Design	M,D
Computer Engineering	M,D
Computer Science	M,D
Cultural Anthropology	D
Developmental Biology	M,D
Ecology	M,D
Economics	D
Education—General	M,D
Electrical Engineering	M,D
Engineering and Applied Sciences—General	M,D
English	M,D
Environmental Biology	M,D
Environmental Management and Policy	D
Evolutionary Biology	M,D
Film, Television, and Video Theory and Criticism	D
Finance and Banking	M
Game Design and Development	M,D
Geosciences	M,D
History	M,D
Humanities	D
Interdisciplinary Studies	M,D
International Affairs	D
Internet and Interactive Multimedia	M,D
Linguistics	M,D
Management Information Systems	D
Management of Technology	D
Marine Sciences	M,D
Mathematics	M,D
Molecular Biology	M,D
Music	M,D
Philosophy	M,D
Physics	M,D*
Planetary and Space Sciences	M,D
Political Science	D
Psychology—General	D
Social Sciences Education	M
Social Sciences	D
Sociology	D
Statistics	M,D
Theater	O
Toxicology	M,D
Writing	M

UNIVERSITY OF CENTRAL ARKANSAS

Accounting	M
Adult Education	M,O
Adult Nursing	M,O
Applied Mathematics	M
Biological and Biomedical Sciences—General	M
Business Administration and Management—General	M
Communication Disorders	M,D
Computer Art and Design	M
Computer Science	M
Counseling Psychology	M
Counselor Education	M
Curriculum and Instruction	M,O
Economic Development	M,O
Education of the Gifted	M,O
Education—General	M,O
Educational Leadership and Administration	M,O
Educational Media/Instructional Technology	M
English	M
Family and Consumer Sciences-General	M
Family Nurse Practitioner Studies	M,O
Film, Television, and Video Production	M
Geographic Information Systems	M,O
Health Education	M
History	M
Kinesiology and Movement Studies	M
Library Science	M
Mathematics Education	M
Mathematics	M
Music Education	M,O
Music	M,O
Nursing and Healthcare Administration	M,O
Nursing Education	M,O
Nursing—General	M,O
Nutrition	M
Occupational Therapy	M
Organizational Management	D
Physical Therapy	D
Psychology—General	M,D,O
Reading Education	M
School Psychology	M,D,O
Social Psychology	M
Spanish	M
Special Education	M,O
Student Affairs	M
Urban and Regional Planning	M,O
Writing	M

UNIVERSITY OF CENTRAL FLORIDA

Accounting	M
Acute Care/Critical Care Nursing	M,D,O
Aerospace/Aeronautical Engineering	M
Allopathic Medicine	M,D
Anthropology	M
Art Education	M
Art/Fine Arts	M
Biological and Biomedical Sciences—General	M,D
Biotechnology	M,D
Business Administration and Management—General	M,D,O
Chemistry	M,D,O
Civil Engineering	M,D,O
Clinical Psychology	M,D
Cognitive Sciences	D
Communication Disorders	M,D,O
Communication—General	M,O
Community College Education	M,O
Computer Art and Design	M
Computer Engineering	M,D
Computer Science	M,D
Conservation Biology	M,D
Corporate and Organizational Communication	M,O
Counselor Education	M,D,O
Criminal Justice and Criminology	M,D,O
Curriculum and Instruction	M,D,O
Early Childhood Education	D
Educational Leadership and Administration	M,D,O
Educational Media/Instructional Technology	M,D,O
Electrical Engineering	M,D
Elementary Education	M,D
Emergency Management	M,O
Engineering and Applied Sciences—General	M,D,O
English as a Second Language	M,D,O
English Education	M
English	M,D,O
Entrepreneurship	M,O
Environmental Engineering	M,D
Exercise and Sports Science	M,D
Family Nurse Practitioner Studies	M,D,O
Film, Television, and Video Production	M
Foreign Languages Education	M,O
Forensic Sciences	M,D
Game Design and Development	M
Geographic Information Systems	M,O
Geotechnical Engineering	M,D,O
Gerontological Nursing	M,D,O
Health Informatics	M,O
Health Services Management and Hospital Administration	M,O
Higher Education	M,D,O
History	M
Homeland Security	M,O
Hospitality Management	M,D,O
Industrial and Organizational Psychology	M,D
Industrial/Management Engineering	M,D,O
Interdisciplinary Studies	M,O
Marriage and Family Therapy	M,O
Materials Engineering	M,D
Materials Sciences	M,D
Mathematics Education	M,D,O
Mathematics	M,D,O
Mechanical Engineering	M,D
Middle School Education	M
Modeling and Simulation	M,D,O
Music	M
Nanotechnology	M
National Security	M,D,O
Nonprofit Management	M,O
Nursing Education	M,D,O
Nursing—General	M,D,O
Optical Sciences	M,D
Photonics	M,D
Physical Therapy	D
Physics	M,D
Physiology	M
Political Science	M,D,O
Psychology—General	M,D
Public Administration	M,O
Public Affairs	D
Quality Management	M,D,O
Reading Education	M,D,O
Real Estate	M
School Psychology	O
Science Education	M,D,O
Social Sciences Education	M,D
Social Work	M,D
Sociology	M,D
Spanish	M
Special Education	M,O
Sports Management	M
Statistics	M,O
Structural Engineering	M,D,O
Student Affairs	M,O
Systems Engineering	M,D,O
Theater	M
Transportation and Highway Engineering	M,D,O
Travel and Tourism	M,O
Urban and Regional Planning	M,O
Vocational and Technical Education	M,D,O
Water Resources Engineering	M,D,O
Writing	M,D,O

UNIVERSITY OF CENTRAL MISSOURI

Accounting	M,D,O
Aerospace/Aeronautical Engineering	M,D,O
Applied Mathematics	M,D,O
Biological and Biomedical Sciences—General	M,D,O
Business Administration and Management—General	M,D,O
Communication Disorders	M,D,O
Communication—General	M,D,O
Computer Science	M,D,O
Counseling Psychology	M,D,O
Counselor Education	M,D,O
Criminal Justice and Criminology	M,D,O
Early Childhood Education	M,D,O
Education—General	M,D,O
Educational Leadership and Administration	M,D,O
Educational Media/Instructional Technology	M,D,O
Elementary Education	M,D,O
English as a Second Language	M,D,O
English	M,D,O
Environmental and Occupational Health	M,D,O
Environmental Management and Policy	M,D,O
Finance and Banking	M,D,O
Gerontology	M,D,O
History	M,D,O
Human Services	M,D,O
Industrial and Manufacturing Management	M,D,O
Industrial Hygiene	M,D,O
Information Science	M,D,O
Kinesiology and Movement Studies	M,D,O
Library Science	M,D,O
Management Information Systems	M,D,O
Management of Technology	M,D,O
Marketing	M,D,O
Mathematics	M,D,O
Music	M,D,O
Nursing—General	M,D,O
Psychology—General	M,D,O
Reading Education	M,D,O
Sociology	M,D,O
Special Education	M,D,O
Student Affairs	M,D,O
Theater	M,D,O
Vocational and Technical Education	M,D,O

UNIVERSITY OF CENTRAL OKLAHOMA

Addictions/Substance Abuse Counseling	M
Adult Education	M
Applied Arts and Design—General	M
Applied Mathematics	M
Athletic Training and Sports Medicine	M

Biological and Biomedical Sciences—General	M
Biomedical Engineering	M
Business Analytics	M
Child and Family Studies	M
Communication Disorders	M
Computational Sciences	M
Computer Science	M
Counseling Psychology	M
Counselor Education	M
Criminal Justice and Criminology	M
Early Childhood Education	M
Education—General	M
Educational Leadership and Administration	M
Educational Media/Instructional Technology	M
Electrical Engineering	M
Elementary Education	M
Engineering and Applied Sciences—General	M
Engineering Physics	M
English as a Second Language	M
English	M
Exercise and Sports Science	M
Experimental Psychology	M
Family and Consumer Sciences-General	M
Forensic Psychology	M
Forensic Sciences	M
Foundations and Philosophy of Education	M
Gerontology	M
Health Promotion	M
History	M
Human Development	M
Interdisciplinary Studies	M
Liberal Studies	M
Library Science	M
Marriage and Family Therapy	M
Mathematics	M
Mechanical Engineering	M
Museum Studies	M
Music Education	M
Music	M
Nonprofit Management	M
Nursing—General	M
Nutrition	M
Physics	M
Political Science	M
Psychology—General	M
Public Administration	M
Reading Education	M
Rhetoric	M
School Psychology	M
Secondary Education	M
Sociology	M
Special Education	M
Statistics	M
Student Affairs	M
Urban and Regional Planning	M
Writing	M

UNIVERSITY OF CHARLESTON

Accounting	M
Business Administration and Management—General	M
Forensic Sciences	M
Legal and Justice Studies	M
Management Strategy and Policy	M
Organizational Management	D
Pharmacy	D
Physician Assistant Studies	M

UNIVERSITY OF CHICAGO

Accounting	M,O
Allopathic Medicine	D
Anatomy	D
Anthropology	D
Applied Statistics	M
Archaeology	D
Art History	M,D
Art/Fine Arts	M
Asian Languages	D
Asian Studies	M,D
Astronomy	D
Astrophysics	D
Atmospheric Sciences	D
Bioengineering	D
Bioinformatics	M
Biological and Biomedical Sciences—General	D
Biophysics	D
Business Administration and Management—General	M,D,O
Cancer Biology/Oncology	D
Cell Biology	D
Chemistry	D
Classics	M,D
Comparative Literature	M,D
Computational Sciences	M
Computer Science	M,D
Developmental Biology	D
Ecology	D
Economics	M,D,O
Emergency Management	M
English	M,D
Entrepreneurship	M,O
Environmental Management and Policy	M
Environmental Sciences	M
Ethics	D
Evolutionary Biology	D
Film, Television, and Video Theory and Criticism	D
Finance and Banking	M,O
French	D
Gender Studies	M
Genetics	D
Genomic Sciences	D
Geophysics	D
Geosciences	D
German	M,D
Health Promotion	M,D
Health Services Management and Hospital Administration	M,O
History	D
Human Development	D
Human Genetics	D
Humanities	M
Immunology	D
Industrial and Manufacturing Management	M,O
International Affairs	M
International Business	M,O
Internet and Interactive Multimedia	M
Italian	D
Latin American Studies	M
Law	M,D
Liberal Studies	M
Linguistics	M,D
Management Strategy and Policy	M,O
Marketing	M,O
Mathematical and Computational Finance	M
Mathematics	D
Media Studies	M,D
Medical Physics	D
Medieval and Renaissance Studies	D
Microbiology	D
Molecular Biology	D
Molecular Biophysics	D
Music	M,D
Near and Middle Eastern Languages	D
Near and Middle Eastern Studies	M,D
Neurobiology	D
Neuroscience	D
Nutrition	D
Organizational Behavior	M,O
Paleontology	D
Pastoral Ministry and Counseling	M
Philosophy	M,D
Physics	M,D
Planetary and Space Sciences	D
Political Science	D
Psychology—General	D
Public Policy	M,D
Religion	M,D
Romance Languages	M,D
Science Education	D
Slavic Languages	M
Social Sciences	M,D
Social Work	M,D
Sociology	D
Spanish	D
Statistics	M,D,O
Systems Biology	D
Theater	M
Theology	D
Urban Education	M
Writing	M
Zoology	D

UNIVERSITY OF CINCINNATI

Accounting	M,D
Acute Care/Critical Care Nursing	M,D
Addictions/Substance Abuse Counseling	M,D,O
Adult Nursing	M,D
Aerospace/Aeronautical Engineering	M,D
Allopathic Medicine	D
Analytical Chemistry	M,D
Anthropology	M
Applied Arts and Design—General	M
Applied Economics	M
Applied Mathematics	M,D
Architecture	M
Art Education	M
Art History	M
Art/Fine Arts	M
Arts Administration	M,D
Biochemistry	M,D
Bioinformatics	D,O
Biological and Biomedical Sciences—General	M,D,O
Biomedical Engineering	M,D
Biophysics	D
Biostatistics	M,D
Business Administration and Management—General	M,D
Business Analytics	M,D
Cancer Biology/Oncology	D
Cell Biology	D
Chemical Engineering	M,D
Chemistry	M,D
Civil Engineering	M,D
Classics	M,D
Clinical Psychology	D
Communication Disorders	M,D
Communication—General	M
Computer Engineering	M,D
Computer Science	M,D
Counselor Education	M,D,O
Criminal Justice and Criminology	M,D
Curriculum and Instruction	M,D
Developmental Biology	D
Economics	D
Education—General	M,D,O
Educational Leadership and Administration	M,D,O
Electrical Engineering	M,D
Engineering and Applied Sciences—General	M,D
English as a Second Language	M,D
English	M,D
Environmental and Occupational Health	M,D
Environmental Engineering	M,D
Environmental Sciences	M,D
Epidemiology	M,D
Ergonomics and Human Factors	M,D
Experimental Psychology	D
Finance and Banking	M,D
Foundations and Philosophy of Education	M,D
French	M,D
Genetic Counseling	M
Genomic Sciences	M,D
Geography	M,D
Geology	M,D
German	M,D
Gerontological Nursing	M,D
Graphic Design	M
Health Education	M,D
Health Informatics	M
Health Physics/Radiological Health	M
Health Promotion	M
Health Services Research	M
History	M,D
Human Resources Management	M
Immunology	M,D
Industrial and Labor Relations	M
Industrial and Manufacturing Management	D
Industrial Design	M
Industrial Hygiene	M,D
Industrial/Management Engineering	M,D
Information Science	M,O
Inorganic Chemistry	M,D
Interdisciplinary Studies	D
Interior Design	M
Law	M,D
Management Information Systems	M,D
Marketing	M,D
Materials Engineering	M,D
Materials Sciences	M,D
Maternal and Child/Neonatal Nursing	M,D
Mathematics Education	M,D
Mathematics	M,D
Mechanical Engineering	M,D
Mechanics	M,D
Medical Imaging	M,D
Medical Physics	M
Microbiology	M,D
Molecular Biology	M,D
Molecular Genetics	M,D
Molecular Medicine	D
Molecular Toxicology	M,D
Music Education	M
Music	M,D,O
Neuroscience	D
Nuclear Engineering	M,D
Nurse Anesthesia	M,D
Nurse Midwifery	M,D
Nursing and Healthcare Administration	M,D
Nursing—General	M,D
Nutrition	M
Occupational Health Nursing	M,D
Organic Chemistry	M,D
Organizational Management	M
Pathobiology	D
Pathology	D
Pediatric Nursing	M,D
Pharmaceutical Sciences	M,D
Pharmacology	D
Pharmacy	D
Philosophy	M,D
Physical Chemistry	M,D
Physical Therapy	D
Physics	M,D
Political Science	M,D
Psychology—General	D
Public Health—General	M,O
Reading Education	M,D
Romance Languages	M,D
School Psychology	D,O
Social Work	M
Sociology	M,D
Spanish	M,D
Special Education	M,D
Sports Management	M
Statistics	M,D
Systems Biology	D
Taxation	M
Textile Design	M
Theater	M,D
Urban and Regional Planning	M
Women's Health Nursing	M,D
Women's Studies	M,O

UNIVERSITY OF COLORADO BOULDER

Advertising and Public Relations	M,D
Aerospace/Aeronautical Engineering	M,D
Anthropology	M,D
Applied Mathematics	M,D
Architectural Engineering	M,D
Art History	M
Art/Fine Arts	M
Asian Studies	M,D
Astrophysics	M,D
Atmospheric Sciences	M,D
Biochemistry	M,D
Business Administration and Management—General	M,D
Cell Biology	M,D
Chemical Engineering	M,D
Chemistry	M,D
Chinese	M,D
Civil Engineering	M,D
Classics	M,D
Communication Disorders	M,D
Communication—General	M,D
Computer Engineering	M,D
Computer Science	M,D
Curriculum and Instruction	M,D
Dance	M,D
Developmental Biology	M,D
East European and Russian Studies	M
Ecology	M,D
Economics	M,D
Education—General	M,D
Educational Measurement and Evaluation	D
Educational Policy	M,D
Educational Psychology	M,D
Electrical Engineering	M,D
Engineering and Applied Sciences—General	M,D
Engineering Management	M
English	M,D
Environmental Engineering	M,D
Environmental Management and Policy	M,D
Ethnic Studies	D
Evolutionary Biology	M,D
Film, Television, and Video Production	M
French	M,D
Geography	M,D
Geology	M,D
Geophysics	M,D
German	M
Hispanic and Latin American Languages	M,D
History	M,D
Information Science	D
Internet and Interactive Multimedia	D
Japanese	M,D
Journalism	M,D
Kinesiology and Movement Studies	M,D
Law	D
Linguistics	M,D
Mass Communication	M,D
Materials Engineering	M,D
Materials Sciences	M,D
Mathematical Physics	M,D
Mathematics	M,D
Mechanical Engineering	M,D
Media Studies	M,D
Molecular Biology	M,D
Multilingual and Multicultural Education	M,D
Museum Studies	M
Music Education	M,D
Music	M,D
Oceanography	M,D
Organizational Management	
Philosophy	M,D
Photography	M
Physics	M,D
Physiology	M,D
Plasma Physics	M,D
Political Science	M,D
Psychology—General	M,D
Religion	M
Sociology	D
Spanish	M,D
Telecommunications Management	M
Telecommunications	M
Theater	M,D
Writing	M,D

UNIVERSITY OF COLORADO COLORADO SPRINGS

Adult Nursing	M,D
Aerospace/Aeronautical Engineering	M,D
Applied Mathematics	M
Business Administration and Management—General	M
Communication—General	M
Computer and Information Systems Security	M,D
Computer Science	M,D
Counselor Education	M,D
Criminal Justice and Criminology	M
Curriculum and Instruction	M,D
Education—General	M,D
Educational Leadership and Administration	M,D
Electrical Engineering	M,D
Energy and Power Engineering	M,D
Engineering and Applied Sciences—General	M,D
Engineering Management	M,D
English as a Second Language	M,D
Environmental Sciences	M
Geography	M
Gerontological Nursing	M,D
History	M
Human Services	M,D
Interdisciplinary Studies	M
Mathematics	D
Mechanical Engineering	M,D
Nursing—General	M,D
Physics	D
Psychology—General	M,D
Public Administration	M
Public Affairs	M
Sociology	M
Software Engineering	M,D
Special Education	M,D
Systems Engineering	M,D

UNIVERSITY OF COLORADO DENVER

Accounting	M
Adult Education	M
Adult Nursing	M,D
Allopathic Medicine	D
American Studies	M
Anatomy	M,D
Anesthesiologist Assistant Studies	M

*M—masters degree; D—doctorate; O—other advanced degree; *—Close-Up and/or Display*

Anthropology	M
Applied Mathematics	M,D
Applied Science and Technology	M
Applied Statistics	M,D
Archaeology	M
Architectural History	D
Architecture	M
Art/Fine Arts	M,O
Biochemistry	D
Bioengineering	M,D
Bioinformatics	D
Biological and Biomedical Sciences—General	M,D
Biophysics	M
Biostatistics	M,D
Business Administration and Management—General	M
Cancer Biology/Oncology	D
Cell Biology	M,D
Chemistry	M
Child and Family Studies	M,D
Civil Engineering	M,D
Clinical Laboratory Sciences/Medical Technology	M,D
Clinical Psychology	M,D
Clinical Research	M,D
Communication—General	M
Community Health	M,D,O
Computational Biology	M,D
Computational Sciences	M,D
Computer Science	M,D
Corporate and Organizational Communication	M
Counseling Psychology	M
Counselor Education	M
Criminal Justice and Criminology	M,D
Data Science/Data Analytics	M
Demography and Population Studies	D
Dentistry	D,O
Developmental Biology	M,D
Distance Education Development	M
Early Childhood Education	M,D
Ecology	M
Economic Development	M
Economics	M
Education—General	M,D,O
Educational Leadership and Administration	M,D,O
Educational Measurement and Evaluation	M,D
Educational Media/Instructional Technology	M
Educational Policy	M,D,O
Electrical Engineering	M,D
Elementary Education	M
Emergency Management	M,D
Energy Management and Policy	M
Engineering and Applied Sciences—General	M,D
English Education	M
English	M
Entertainment Management	M
Entrepreneurship	M
Environmental and Occupational Health	M
Environmental Engineering	M,D
Environmental Law	M,D
Environmental Management and Policy	M,D,O
Environmental Sciences	M
Epidemiology	M,D
Ethnic Studies	M,O
Family and Consumer Sciences-General	M,D
Family Nurse Practitioner Studies	M,D
Finance and Banking	M
Forensic Sciences	M
Gender Studies	M,O
Genetic Counseling	M
Genetics	D
Genomic Sciences	D
Geographic Information Systems	M,D
Geotechnical Engineering	M,D
Hazardous Materials Management	M
Health Education	M,D
Health Informatics	M
Health Psychology	D
Health Services Management and Hospital Administration	M
Health Services Research	M,D
Historic Preservation	M
History	M
Homeland Security	M,D
Human Development	M,D
Human Resources Management	M
Humanities	M,O
Hydraulics	M,D
Hydrology	M,D
Immunology	D
Information Science	M,D
Insurance	M
International Affairs	M,O
International Business	M
International Health	M
Landscape Architecture	M
Linguistics	M
Management Information Systems	M,D
Management of Technology	M
Management Strategy and Policy	M
Marketing	M
Marriage and Family Therapy	M
Mathematics Education	M,D
Mathematics	M,D
Mechanical Engineering	M
Mechanics	M
Media Studies	M
Medical Informatics	M,D
Microbiology	D
Military and Defense Studies	M,D
Molecular Biology	D
Molecular Genetics	D
Multilingual and Multicultural Education	M
Music	M
Neuroscience	D
Nonprofit Management	M,D
Nurse Midwifery	M,D
Nursing and Healthcare Administration	M,D
Nursing—General	M,D
Operations Research	M,D
Oral and Dental Sciences	D,O
Pediatric Nursing	M,D
Pharmaceutical Sciences	D
Pharmacology	D
Pharmacy	D
Physical Therapy	D
Physician Assistant Studies	M
Political Science	M,D
Psychiatric Nursing	M,D
Public Administration	M,D
Public Affairs	M,D
Public Health—General	M,D
Public History	M
Reading Education	M
Rehabilitation Sciences	D
Risk Management	M
School Psychology	M
Science Education	M,D
Secondary Education	M
Sociology	M,O
Spanish	M
Special Education	M,D
Sports Management	M
Statistics	M,D
Structural Engineering	M,D
Sustainability Management	M
Sustainable Development	M,D
Systems Biology	M,D
Taxation	M
Toxicology	D
Transportation and Highway Engineering	M,D
Urban and Regional Planning	M,D
Urban Design	M,D
Water Resources	M
Western European Studies	M
Women's Health Nursing	M,D
Women's Studies	M,O
Writing	M

UNIVERSITY OF CONNECTICUT

Accounting	M,D
Adult Education	M,O
Agricultural Economics and Agribusiness	M,D
Agricultural Education	M,D
Agricultural Sciences—General	M,D
Agronomy and Soil Sciences	M,D
Animal Sciences	M,D
Anthropology	M,D
Applied Arts and Design—General	M
Applied Mathematics	M
Biomedical Engineering	M,D
Biophysics	M,D
Biopsychology	M,D
Botany	M,D
Business Administration and Management—General	M,D*
Business Analytics	M,D
Cell Biology	M,D
Chemical Engineering	M,D
Chemistry	M,D
Child and Family Studies	M,D
Civil Engineering	M,D
Clinical Psychology	M,D
Cognitive Sciences	M,D
Communication Disorders	M,D
Communication—General	M
Computer Science	M,D
Counseling Psychology	M,D
Counselor Education	M,D
Curriculum and Instruction	M,D
Developmental Biology	M,D
Developmental Psychology	M,D
Ecology	M,D
Economics	M,D
Education of the Gifted	O
Education—General	M,D
Educational Leadership and Administration	M
Educational Media/Instructional Technology	M,D
Educational Psychology	M,D,O
Electrical Engineering	M,D
Elementary Education	M,D
Engineering and Applied Sciences—General	M,D
English Education	M,D
English	M,D
Environmental and Occupational Health	O
Environmental Engineering	M,D
Exercise and Sports Science	M,D
Experimental Psychology	M,D
Finance and Banking	M,D,O
Foreign Languages Education	M,D
Genetics	M,D
Genomic Sciences	M,D
Geography	M,D
Geology	M,D
Gerontological Nursing	O
Health Services Management and Hospital Administration	M,D
Higher Education	M
History	M,D
Human Development	M,D
Human Resources Management	M,D
Industrial and Organizational Psychology	M,D
International Affairs	M
Jewish Studies	M
Latin American Studies	M
Law	D
Linguistics	M,D
Management Information Systems	M,D
Marketing	M,D
Materials Engineering	M
Materials Sciences	M,D
Maternal and Child/Neonatal Nursing	O
Mathematical and Computational Finance	M
Mathematics Education	M,D
Mechanical Engineering	M,D
Medicinal and Pharmaceutical Chemistry	M,D
Medieval and Renaissance Studies	M,D
Metallurgical Engineering and Metallurgy	M
Microbiology	M,D
Molecular Biology	M,D
Multilingual and Multicultural Education	M,D
Music Education	M,D
Music	M,D
Natural Resources	M,D
Neurobiology	M,D
Neuroscience	M,D
Nonprofit Management	M,O
Nursing—General	D,O*
Nutrition	M,D
Pathobiology	M,D
Pharmaceutical Sciences	M,D
Pharmacology	M,D
Pharmacy	D
Philosophy	M,D
Physical Therapy	D
Physics	M,D
Physiology	M,D
Plant Sciences	M,D
Political Science	M,D
Polymer Science and Engineering	M,D
Project Management	M,D
Psychology—General	M,D
Public Administration	M
Quantitative Analysis	M,O
Reading Education	M,D
Risk Management	M,D
Science Education	M,D
Secondary Education	M,D
Social Psychology	M,D
Social Sciences Education	M,D
Social Work	M,D
Sociology	M,D
Software Engineering	M,D
Sports Management	M
Statistics	M,D
Structural Biology	M,D
Theater	M
Toxicology	M,D
Western European Studies	M

UNIVERSITY OF CONNECTICUT HEALTH CENTER

Allopathic Medicine	D
Anatomy	D
Biochemistry	D
Biological and Biomedical Sciences—General	D
Cell Biology	D
Clinical Research	M
Dentistry	D,O
Developmental Biology	D
Genetics	D
Immunology	D
Molecular Biology	D
Neuroscience	D
Oral and Dental Sciences	M
Public Health—General	M

UNIVERSITY OF DALLAS

Accounting	M,D
American Studies	M
Art/Fine Arts	M
Business Administration and Management—General	M,D
Business Analytics	M,D
Classics	M
Clinical Psychology	M
Comparative Literature	D
Computer and Information Systems Security	M,D
English	M
Entertainment Management	M,D
Finance and Banking	M,D
Health Services Management and Hospital Administration	M,D
Human Resources Management	M,D
Humanities	M
International Business	M,D
Logistics	M,D
Management Information Systems	M,D
Management of Technology	M,D
Management Strategy and Policy	M,D
Marketing	M,D
Organizational Management	M,D
Pastoral Ministry and Counseling	M
Philosophy	M,D
Political Science	M,D
Project Management	M,D
Psychology—General	M
Sports Management	M,D
Supply Chain Management	M,D
Theology	M

UNIVERSITY OF DAYTON

Accounting	M
Aerospace/Aeronautical Engineering	M,D
Applied Mathematics	M
Art/Fine Arts	M
Biochemistry	M
Bioengineering	M
Biological and Biomedical Sciences—General	M,D
Business Administration and Management—General	M
Chemical Engineering	M
Chemistry	M
Civil Engineering	M
Clinical Psychology	M,O
Communication—General	M
Computer and Information Systems Security	M
Computer Engineering	M,D
Computer Science	M
Counseling Psychology	M,O
Counselor Education	M,O
Cultural Studies	M
Early Childhood Education	M
Educational Leadership and Administration	M,D,O
Educational Media/Instructional Technology	M
Electrical Engineering	M,D
Elementary Education	M
Engineering Management	M
English as a Second Language	M
English	M
Environmental Engineering	M
Environmental Management and Policy	M,D
Exercise and Sports Science	M
Finance and Banking	M
Foreign Languages Education	M
Geotechnical Engineering	M
Human Development	M,O
Interdisciplinary Studies	M
Law	M,D
Marketing	M
Materials Engineering	M,D
Mathematical and Computational Finance	M
Mathematics Education	M
Mechanical Engineering	M,D
Mechanics	M
Middle School Education	M
Music Education	M
Optical Sciences	M,D
Pastoral Ministry and Counseling	M,D
Photonics	M,D
Physical Education	M
Physical Therapy	D
Physician Assistant Studies	M
Psychology—General	M
Public Administration	M
Reading Education	M
Rhetoric	M
School Psychology	M,O
Secondary Education	M
Structural Engineering	M
Student Affairs	M,O
Theology	M,D
Transportation and Highway Engineering	M
Water Resources Engineering	M
Writing	M

UNIVERSITY OF DELAWARE

Accounting	M
Adult Nursing	M,O
Agricultural Economics and Agribusiness	M
Agricultural Education	M
Agricultural Sciences—General	M,D
Agronomy and Soil Sciences	M,D
American Studies	M,D
Animal Sciences	M,D
Applied Arts and Design—General	M
Applied Mathematics	M,D
Art History	M,D
Art/Fine Arts	M
Astronomy	M,D
Biochemistry	M,D
Biological and Biomedical Sciences—General	M,D
Biotechnology	M,D
Business Administration and Management—General	M,D
Business Education	M,D
Cancer Biology/Oncology	M,D
Cell Biology	M,D
Chemical Engineering	M,D
Chemistry	M,D
Child and Family Studies	M,D
Chinese	M
Civil Engineering	M,D
Clinical Psychology	D
Clothing and Textiles	M,D
Cognitive Sciences	M,D
Communication Disorders	M
Communication—General	M
Computer Engineering	M,D
Computer Science	M,D
Criminal Justice and Criminology	M,D
Curriculum and Instruction	M,D,O
Developmental Biology	M,D
Ecology	M,D
Economics	M,D
Education—General	M,D,O
Educational Leadership and Administration	M,D,O
Electrical Engineering	M,D
Emergency Management	M,D
Energy Management and Policy	M,D
Engineering and Applied Sciences—General	M,D
English as a Second Language	M,D,O
English	M,D
Entomology	M,D
Entrepreneurship	M,D
Environmental Engineering	M,D
Environmental Management and Policy	M,D
Evolutionary Biology	M,D
Family Nurse Practitioner Studies	M,O

Finance and Banking M
Fish, Game, and Wildlife Management M,D
Food Science and Technology M,D
Foreign Languages Education M
French M
Genetics M,D
Geography M,D
Geology M,D
Geotechnical Engineering M,D
German M
Gerontological Nursing M,O
Health Promotion M
Higher Education M,D,O
Historic Preservation M,D
History of Science and Technology M,D
History M,D
HIV/AIDS Nursing M,O
Horticulture M
Hospitality Management M
Human Development M,D
Information Science M,D
International Affairs M,D
Kinesiology and Movement Studies M,D
Liberal Studies M
Linguistics M,D
Management Information Systems M,D
Management of Technology M
Marine Affairs M,D
Marine Geology M,D
Marine Sciences M,D
Materials Engineering M,D
Materials Sciences M,D
Maternal and Child/Neonatal Nursing M,O
Mathematics M,D
Mechanical Engineering M,D
Microbiology M,D
Molecular Biology M,D
Multilingual and Multicultural Education M,D,O
Music Education M
Music M
Natural Resources M
Neuroscience D
Nursing and Healthcare Administration M,O
Nursing—General M,O
Nutrition M
Ocean Engineering M,D
Oceanography M,D
Oncology Nursing M,O
Operations Research M
Pediatric Nursing M,O
Physical Therapy D
Physics M,D
Physiology M,D
Plant Sciences M,D
Political Science M,D
Psychiatric Nursing M,O
Psychology—General D
Public Administration M*
Public Policy M,D
School Psychology M,D,O
Social Psychology D
Sociology M,D
Spanish M
Statistics M
Structural Engineering M,D
Theater M
Translation and Interpretation M
Transportation and Highway Engineering M,D
Urban Studies M,D
Water Resources Engineering M,D
Women's Health Nursing M,O

UNIVERSITY OF DENVER

Accounting M
Anthropology M
Archaeology M
Art Education M,O
Art History M
Art/Fine Arts M
Bioengineering M,D
Biological and Biomedical Sciences—General M,D
Business Administration and Management—General M
Cell Biology M,D
Chemistry M,D
Child and Family Studies M,D,O
Clinical Psychology M,D,O
Communication—General M,D,O
Computer and Information Systems Security M,D
Computer Art and Design M
Computer Engineering M,D
Computer Science M,D
Conflict Resolution and Mediation/Peace Studies M
Construction Management M
Counseling Psychology M,D,O
Criminal Justice and Criminology M,O
Cultural Anthropology M
Cultural Studies M,O
Curriculum and Instruction M,D,O
Data Science/Data Analytics M,D
Developmental Psychology D
Early Childhood Education M,D,O
Ecology M,D
Economics M
Education—General M,D,O
Educational Leadership and Administration M,D,O
Educational Measurement and Evaluation M,D,O
Educational Policy M,D,O
Electrical Engineering M,D
Emergency Management M,O
Engineering and Applied Sciences—General M,D
Engineering Management M,D
English M,D
Environmental Management and Policy M,O
Evolutionary Biology M,D
Finance and Banking M
Forensic Psychology M,D,O
Geographic Information Systems M,D,O
Geography M,D
Health Services Management and Hospital Administration M,O
Higher Education M,D,O
History M,O
Homeland Security M,D,O
Human Resources Management M,O
Information Science M,O
International Affairs M,D,O
International Development M,D,O
International Health M,D,O
Law M,D,O
Legal and Justice Studies M,O
Library Science M,D,O
Marketing M
Marriage and Family Therapy M,D,O
Mass Communication M
Materials Engineering M,D
Materials Sciences M,D
Mathematics M,D
Mechanical Engineering M,D
Media Studies M
Molecular Biology M,D
Museum Studies M
Music Education M,O
Music M,O
Organizational Management M,O
Physics M,D
Project Management M,O
Psychology—General M,D,O
Public Policy M
Real Estate M
Religion M,D,O
Rhetoric M,D
School Psychology M,D,O
Social Psychology D
Social Work M,D,O
Special Education M,D,O
Speech and Interpersonal Communication M,D
Sport Psychology M,D,O
Taxation M
Theology D,O
Translation and Interpretation M,O
Writing M,D,O

UNIVERSITY OF DETROIT MERCY

Accounting M,O
Addictions/Substance Abuse Counseling M,D,O
Allied Health—General M,D,O
Architectural Engineering M
Business Administration and Management—General M,O
Chemistry M,D
Civil Engineering M,D
Clinical Psychology M,D,O
Computer and Information Systems Security M,D,O
Computer Engineering M,D
Computer Science M,D,O
Criminal Justice and Criminology M,D,O
Curriculum and Instruction M,D,O
Dentistry M,D,O
Economics M,D,O
Educational Leadership and Administration M,D,O
Electrical Engineering M,D
Engineering and Applied Sciences—General M,D
Engineering Management M,D
Environmental Engineering M,D
Ethics M,O
Family Nurse Practitioner Studies M,D,O
Finance and Banking M,D,O
Forensic Sciences M,O
Health Services Management and Hospital Administration M,D,O
Industrial and Organizational Psychology M,D,O
Industrial Design M,D
Law D
Liberal Studies M,D,O
Management Information Systems M,D,O
Management Strategy and Policy M,O
Mathematics Education M,D
Mechanical Engineering M,D
Nurse Anesthesia M,D,O
Nursing Education M,D,O
Nursing—General M,D,O
Oral and Dental Sciences M,D,O
Physician Assistant Studies M,D,O
Religious Education M,D,O
School Psychology M,D,O
Software Engineering M,D
Special Education M,D,O
Urban and Regional Planning M

UNIVERSITY OF DUBUQUE

Business Administration and Management—General M
Communication—General M
Theology M,D

UNIVERSITY OF EAST-WEST MEDICINE

Acupuncture and Oriental Medicine M,D

UNIVERSITY OF EVANSVILLE

Athletic Training and Sports Medicine M
Health Services Management and Hospital Administration M
Physical Therapy D
Public Administration M

THE UNIVERSITY OF FINDLAY

Accounting M,D
Athletic Training and Sports Medicine M,D
Business Administration and Management—General M,D
Education—General M,D
Educational Leadership and Administration M,D
Educational Media/Instructional Technology M,D
English as a Second Language M,D
Environmental Management and Policy M,D
Health Informatics M,D
Health Services Management and Hospital Administration M,D
Hospitality Management M,D
Linguistics M,D
Mathematics M,D
Occupational Therapy M,D
Pharmacy M,D
Physical Therapy M,D
Physician Assistant Studies M,D
Public Administration M,D
Reading Education M,D
Rhetoric M,D
Science Education M,D
Writing M,D

UNIVERSITY OF FLORIDA

Accounting M,D
Advertising and Public Relations M,D
Aerospace/Aeronautical Engineering M,D
Agricultural Economics and Agribusiness M,D
Agricultural Education M,D
Agricultural Engineering M,D,O
Agricultural Sciences—General M,D,O
Agronomy and Soil Sciences M,D
Allied Health—General M,D,O
Allopathic Medicine D
Animal Sciences M,D
Anthropology M,D
Aquaculture M,D
Architecture M,D
Art Education M,D
Art History M,D
Art/Fine Arts M,D
Astronomy M,D
Athletic Training and Sports Medicine M,D
Biochemistry D
Bioengineering M,D,O
Biological and Biomedical Sciences—General M,D
Biomedical Engineering M,D,O
Biostatistics M,D,O
Botany M,D
Business Administration and Management—General M,D
Cell Biology M,D
Chemical Engineering M,D,O
Chemistry M,D
Child Development M
Civil Engineering M,D
Classics M,D
Clinical Laboratory Sciences/Medical Technology M,D
Clinical Psychology M,D
Clinical Research M,D,O
Communication Disorders M,D
Communication—General M,D
Computer Art and Design M,D
Computer Engineering M,D
Computer Science M,D
Construction Management M,D
Counseling Psychology M,D
Counselor Education M,D,O
Criminal Justice and Criminology M,D
Curriculum and Instruction M,D,O
Dentistry D,O
Early Childhood Education M,D,O
Ecology M,D,O
Economics M,D
Education—General M,D,O
Educational Leadership and Administration M,D,O
Educational Measurement and Evaluation M,D,O
Educational Policy M,D,O
Electrical Engineering M,D
Elementary Education M,D,O
Emergency Management M
Engineering and Applied Sciences—General M,D,O
English as a Second Language M,D,O
English Education M,D,O
English M,D
Entrepreneurship M,D,O
Environmental and Occupational Health M,D,O
Environmental Education M,D,O
Environmental Engineering M,D,O
Environmental Law M,D
Epidemiology M,D,O
Exercise and Sports Science M,D
Family and Consumer Sciences-General M
Finance and Banking M,D,O
Fish, Game, and Wildlife Management M,D,O
Food Science and Technology M,D
Foreign Languages Education M,D
Forensic Sciences M,O
Forestry M,D
French M,D
Gender Studies M,O
Genetics D
Geographic Information Systems M,D
Geography M,D
Geology M,D
Geosciences M,D
German M,D
Health Communication M,D,O
Health Education M,D,O
Health Psychology M,D
Health Services Management and Hospital Administration M,D
Health Services Research M,D
Higher Education M,D,O
Historic Preservation M,D
History M,D
Horticulture M,D
Human Resources Management M,D
Hydrology M,D
Immunology D
Industrial/Management Engineering M,D,O
Information Science M,D
Insurance M,D,O
Interdisciplinary Studies M,D
Interior Design M,D
International Affairs M
International Business M,D
International Development M,D,O
International Health M,D
Jewish Studies M,D
Journalism M,D
Kinesiology and Movement Studies M,D
Landscape Architecture M,D
Latin American Studies M,O
Law M,D
Limnology M,D
Linguistics M,D,O
Management Information Systems M,D,O
Marine Sciences M,D
Marketing M,D
Marriage and Family Therapy M,D,O
Mass Communication M,D
Materials Engineering M,D
Materials Sciences M,D
Mathematics Education M,D,O
Mathematics M,D
Mechanical Engineering M,D
Medical Physics M,D,O
Medicinal and Pharmaceutical Chemistry M,D
Microbiology M,D
Molecular Biology M,D
Molecular Genetics M
Museum Studies M,D
Music Education M,D
Music M,D
Natural Resources M,D
Neuroscience D
Nonprofit Management M
Nuclear Engineering M,D
Nursing—General M,D
Nutrition M,D
Occupational Therapy M
Ocean Engineering M,D
Oral and Dental Sciences M,D,O
Pharmaceutical Administration M,D
Pharmaceutical Sciences M,D
Pharmacology M,D
Pharmacy M,D
Philosophy M,D
Physical Education M,D
Physical Therapy D
Physician Assistant Studies M
Physics M,D
Physiology M,D
Plant Biology M,D
Plant Molecular Biology M,D
Plant Pathology M,D
Plant Sciences D
Political Science M,D,O
Psychology—General M,D
Public Affairs M,D,O
Public Health—General M,D,O
Quantitative Analysis M,D,O
Reading Education M,D,O
Real Estate M,D,O
Recreation and Park Management M,D,O
Rehabilitation Sciences D
Religion M,D
School Psychology M,D,O
Science Education M,D,O
Social Sciences Education M,D,O
Social Sciences M,D,O
Sociology M,D
Spanish M,D
Special Education M,D,O
Sports Management M,D
Statistics M,D
Student Affairs M,D,O
Supply Chain Management M,D,O
Sustainable Development M,O
Systems Engineering M,D,O
Taxation M,D
Telecommunications M,D
Theater M
Toxicology M,D,O
Travel and Tourism M,D
Urban and Regional Planning M,D
Veterinary Medicine D
Veterinary Sciences M,D,O
Water Resources M,D
Women's Studies M,D
Writing M,D
Zoology M,D

UNIVERSITY OF FORT LAUDERDALE

Pastoral Ministry and Counseling M

*M—masters degree; D—doctorate; O—other advanced degree; *—Close-Up and/or Display*

UNIVERSITY OF GEORGIA

Accounting	M
Adult Education	D,O
Agricultural Economics and Agribusiness	M,D
Agricultural Sciences—General	M,D
Agronomy and Soil Sciences	M,D
Analytical Chemistry	M,D
Animal Sciences	M,D
Anthropology	M,D
Applied Economics	M,D
Applied Mathematics	M,D
Art History	M,D
Art/Fine Arts	M,D
Artificial Intelligence/Robotics	M
Biochemical Engineering	M
Biochemistry	M,D
Bioinformatics	M,D
Biological and Biomedical Sciences—General	D
Business Administration and Management—General	M
Business Education	M,D,O
Cell Biology	M,D
Chemistry	M,D
Child and Family Studies	M
Classics	M
Clothing and Textiles	M,D
Communication Disorders	M,D,O
Communication—General	M,D
Comparative Literature	M,D
Computer Science	M,D
Counselor Education	M,D,O
Ecology	M,D
Economics	M,D
Education—General	M,D,O
Educational Leadership and Administration	D,O
Educational Media/Instructional Technology	M,D,O
Educational Policy	D,O
Educational Psychology	O
English Education	M,D
English	M,D
Entomology	M,D
Environmental and Occupational Health	M,D
Environmental Design	M
Environmental Engineering	M
Family and Consumer Sciences-General	M,D
Food Science and Technology	M,D
Forestry	M,D
French	M,D
Genetics	M,D
Genomic Sciences	M,D
Geography	M,D
Geology	M,D
German	M
Gerontology	O
Health Education	M,D
Health Promotion	M,D
Higher Education	M,D
Historic Preservation	M
History	M,D
Horticulture	M,D
Infectious Diseases	D
Interior Design	M,D
International Affairs	M,D
Italian	M,D
Journalism	M,D
Kinesiology and Movement Studies	M,D
Landscape Architecture	M
Law	M,D
Linguistics	M,D
Marine Sciences	M,D
Mass Communication	M,D
Mathematics Education	M,D,O
Mathematics	M,D
Microbiology	M,D
Molecular Biology	M,D
Music Education	M,D
Music	M,D
Natural Resources	M,D
Neuroscience	D
Nonprofit Management	M,D,O
Nutrition	M,D
Pathology	M,D
Pharmaceutical Administration	D
Pharmaceutical Sciences	M,D
Pharmacology	M,D
Pharmacy	M,D,O
Philosophy	M,D
Physical Education	M,D
Physics	M,D
Physiology	M,D
Plant Biology	M,D
Plant Pathology	M,D
Plant Sciences	M,D
Political Science	M,D
Portuguese	M,D
Psychology—General	D
Public Administration	M,D
Public Health—General	D
Public Policy	M,D
Reading Education	M,D
Religion	M
Science Education	M,D,O
Social Work	M,D,O
Sociology	M,D
Spanish	M,D
Special Education	M,D,O
Statistics	M,D
Student Affairs	M,D,O
Sustainable Development	M,D
Theater	M,D
Veterinary Medicine	M,D
Vocational and Technical Education	M,D,O
Women's Studies	O

UNIVERSITY OF GUAM

Art/Fine Arts	M
Biological and Biomedical Sciences—General	M
Business Administration and Management—General	M
Counselor Education	M
Education—General	M
Educational Leadership and Administration	M
English as a Second Language	M
English	M
Environmental Sciences	M
Graphic Design	M
Marine Biology	M
Pacific Area/Pacific Rim Studies	M
Public Administration	M
Reading Education	M
Secondary Education	M
Social Work	M
Special Education	M

UNIVERSITY OF GUELPH

Acute Care/Critical Care Nursing	M,D,O
Agricultural Economics and Agribusiness	M,D
Agricultural Sciences—General	M,D,O
Agronomy and Soil Sciences	M,D
Anatomy	M,D
Anesthesiologist Assistant Studies	M,D,O
Animal Sciences	M,D
Anthropology	M,D
Applied Mathematics	M,D
Applied Psychology	M,D
Applied Statistics	M,D
Aquaculture	M
Art/Fine Arts	M
Atmospheric Sciences	M,D
Biochemistry	M,D
Bioengineering	M,D
Biological and Biomedical Sciences—General	M,D
Biophysics	M,D
Biotechnology	M,D
Botany	M,D
Business Administration and Management—General	M,D
Cardiovascular Sciences	M,D,O
Cell Biology	M,D
Chemistry	M,D
Child and Family Studies	M,D
Clinical Psychology	M,D
Cognitive Sciences	M,D
Comparative Literature	D
Computer Science	M,D
Consumer Economics	M
Criminal Justice and Criminology	M,D
Demography and Population Studies	M,D
Ecology	M,D
Economics	M,D
Emergency Medical Services	M,D,O
Engineering and Applied Sciences—General	M,D
English	M
Entomology	M,D
Environmental Biology	M,D
Environmental Engineering	M,D
Environmental Management and Policy	M,D
Environmental Sciences	M,D
Epidemiology	M,D
Evolutionary Biology	M,D
Food Science and Technology	M,D
French	M
Geography	M,D
History	M,D
Horticulture	M,D
Hospitality Management	M
Human Development	M,D
Immunology	M,D,O
Industrial and Organizational Psychology	M,D
Infectious Diseases	M,D,O
International Development	M,D
Landscape Architecture	M
Marriage and Family Therapy	M,D
Mathematics	M,D
Medical Imaging	M,D,O
Medieval and Renaissance Studies	D
Microbiology	M,D
Molecular Biology	M,D
Molecular Genetics	M,D
Natural Resources	M,D
Neuroscience	M,D,O
Nutrition	M,D
Organizational Management	M
Pathology	M,D,O
Pharmacology	M,D
Philosophy	M,D
Physics	M,D
Physiology	M,D
Plant Pathology	M,D
Political Science	M
Psychology—General	M,D
Public Administration	M
Public Policy	M
Rural Planning and Studies	M,D
Social Psychology	M,D
Sociology	M,D
Statistics	M,D
Theater	M
Toxicology	M,D
Veterinary Medicine	M,D,O
Veterinary Sciences	M,D,O
Vision Sciences	M,D,O
Water Resources Engineering	M,D
Western European Studies	M
Zoology	M,D

UNIVERSITY OF HARTFORD

Accounting	M,O
Architecture	M
Art/Fine Arts	M
Biological and Biomedical Sciences—General	M
Business Administration and Management—General	M
Clinical Psychology	M,D
Communication—General	M
Community Health Nursing	M
Counselor Education	M,O
Early Childhood Education	M
Education—General	M,D,O
Educational Leadership and Administration	D,O
Educational Media/Instructional Technology	M
Elementary Education	M
Engineering and Applied Sciences—General	M
Experimental Psychology	M
Music Education	M,D,O
Music	M,D,O
Neuroscience	M
Nursing Education	M
Nursing—General	M
Organizational Behavior	M
Physical Therapy	M,D
Psychology—General	M,D
School Psychology	M
Taxation	M,O

UNIVERSITY OF HAWAII AT HILO

Conservation Biology	M
Counseling Psychology	M
Cultural Studies	M,D
Education—General	M
Environmental Sciences	M
Foreign Languages Education	M,D
Marine Biology	M
Nursing—General	D
Pharmaceutical Sciences	D*
Pharmacology	M
Pharmacy	D

UNIVERSITY OF HAWAII AT MANOA

Accounting	M,D
Adult Nursing	M,D,O
Agricultural Sciences—General	M,D
Allopathic Medicine	D
American Studies	M,D,O
Animal Sciences	M
Anthropology	M,D
Architecture	D
Art History	M
Art/Fine Arts	M
Asian Languages	M,D
Asian Studies	O
Astronomy	M,D
Bioengineering	M
Biological and Biomedical Sciences—General	M,D
Botany	M,D
Business Administration and Management—General	M
Chemistry	M,D
Chinese	M,D,O
Civil Engineering	M,D
Clinical Psychology	M,D,O
Communication Disorders	M
Communication—General	M,O
Community Health Nursing	M,D,O
Computer Science	M,D,O
Conflict Resolution and Mediation/Peace Studies	M,O
Cultural Studies	O
Curriculum and Instruction	M,D
Dance	M,D
Demography and Population Studies	O
Developmental Biology	M,D
Disability Studies	O
Early Childhood Education	M
Economics	M,D
Education—General	M,D,O
Educational Leadership and Administration	M,D
Educational Media/Instructional Technology	M,D
Educational Policy	D
Educational Psychology	M,D
Electrical Engineering	M,D
Emergency Management	O
Engineering and Applied Sciences—General	M,D
English as a Second Language	M,D,O
English	M,D
Entomology	M,D
Entrepreneurship	M,O
Environmental Engineering	M,D
Environmental Management and Policy	M,D,O
Epidemiology	D
Family Nurse Practitioner Studies	M,D,O
Finance and Banking	M,D
Food Science and Technology	M
Foreign Languages Education	M,D,O
Foundations and Philosophy of Education	M,D
French	M
Genetics	M,D
Geochemistry	M,D
Geography	M,D,O
Geological Engineering	M,D
Geology	M,D
Geophysics	M,D
Historic Preservation	O
History	M,D
Horticulture	M,D
Human Resources Management	M
Hydrogeology	M,D
Information Science	M,D
Information Studies	M,O
International Affairs	O
International Business	M,D
International Development	M,D,O
Japanese	M,D,O
Kinesiology and Movement Studies	M,D
Law	M,D,O
Library Science	M,O
Linguistics	M,D
Management Information Systems	M,D,O
Marine Biology	M,D
Marine Geology	M,D
Marine Sciences	O
Marketing	M,D
Mathematics	M,D
Mechanical Engineering	M,D
Medical Microbiology	M,D
Meteorology	M,D
Microbiology	M,D
Molecular Biology	M,D
Museum Studies	O
Music	M,D
Natural Resources	M,D
Nursing and Healthcare Administration	M,D,O
Nursing—General	M,D,O
Nutrition	M,D
Ocean Engineering	M,D
Oceanography	M,D
Organizational Behavior	M
Organizational Management	M,D
Pacific Area/Pacific Rim Studies	M,O
Philosophy	M,D
Physics	M,D
Physiology	M,D
Planetary and Space Sciences	M,D
Plant Pathology	M,D
Plant Sciences	M,D
Political Science	M,D
Psychology—General	M,D,O
Public Administration	M,O
Public Health—General	M,D,O
Public Policy	O
Real Estate	M
Religion	M
Reproductive Biology	M,D
Social Psychology	M,D,O
Social Work	M,D
Sociology	M,D
Spanish	M
Special Education	M,D
Speech and Interpersonal Communication	M
Sustainable Development	M,D,O
Taxation	M
Telecommunications	O
Theater	M,D
Transportation Management	M,D,O
Travel and Tourism	M
Urban and Regional Planning	M,D,O
Women's Studies	O
Zoology	M,D

UNIVERSITY OF HOLY CROSS

Biological and Biomedical Sciences—General	M,D
Business Administration and Management—General	M,D
Counselor Education	M,D
Education—General	M,D
Educational Leadership and Administration	M,D
Health Services Management and Hospital Administration	M,D
Marriage and Family Therapy	M,D
Theology	M,D

UNIVERSITY OF HOUSTON

Accounting	M,D
Advertising and Public Relations	M
Anthropology	M
Applied Economics	M,D
Applied Mathematics	M,D
Architecture	M
Art History	M
Art/Fine Arts	M
Atmospheric Sciences	M,D
Biochemistry	M,D
Biological and Biomedical Sciences—General	M,D
Biomedical Engineering	D
Business Administration and Management—General	M,D
Chemical Engineering	M,D
Chemistry	M,D
Civil Engineering	M,D
Clinical Psychology	M,D
Communication Disorders	M
Communication—General	M
Comparative Literature	M
Computer and Information Systems Security	M
Computer Science	M,D
Construction Management	M
Counseling Psychology	M,D
Cultural Studies	M
Curriculum and Instruction	M,D
Developmental Psychology	M,D
Economics	M,D
Education—General	M,D
Educational Leadership and Administration	M,D
Educational Psychology	M,D
Electrical Engineering	M,D
Engineering and Applied Sciences—General	M,D
Environmental Law	M,D
Exercise and Sports Science	M,D
Family and Consumer Sciences-General	M
Family Nurse Practitioner Studies	M
Finance and Banking	M
Foundations and Philosophy of Education	M,D
Geology	M,D
Geophysics	M,D
Health Communication	M
Health Education	M,D
Health Law	M,D
Higher Education	M,D
Hispanic Studies	M,D

History	M,D
Hospitality Management	M
Human Resources Development	M
Industrial and Organizational Psychology	M,D
Industrial/Management Engineering	M,D
Information Science	M,D
Intellectual Property Law	M,D
Kinesiology and Movement Studies	M,D
Law	M,D
Linguistics	M,D
Logistics	M
Marketing	D
Mass Communication	M
Mathematics	M,D
Mechanical Engineering	M,D
Music Education	M,D
Music	M,D
Nursing and Healthcare Administration	M
Nursing Education	M
Nursing—General	M
Nutrition	M,D
Optometry	D
Petroleum Engineering	M,D
Pharmaceutical Administration	M,D
Pharmaceutical Sciences	M,D
Pharmacology	M,D
Pharmacy	M,D
Philosophy	M
Physical Education	M,D
Physics	M,D
Planetary and Space Sciences	M,D
Political Science	M,D
Project Management	M
Psychology—General	M,D
Public Administration	M,D
Public Policy	M
Social Psychology	M,D
Social Work	M,D
Sociology	M
Spanish	M,D
Special Education	M,D
Speech and Interpersonal Communication	M
Supply Chain Management	M
Sustainable Development	M
Taxation	M,D
Telecommunications	M
Theater	M
Urban Design	M
Vision Sciences	M,D
Writing	M,D

UNIVERSITY OF HOUSTON–CLEAR LAKE

Accounting	M
Biological and Biomedical Sciences—General	M
Biotechnology	M
Business Administration and Management—General	M
Chemistry	M
Clinical Psychology	M
Computer Engineering	M
Computer Science	M
Counselor Education	M
Criminal Justice and Criminology	M
Cultural Studies	M
Curriculum and Instruction	M
Early Childhood Education	M
Education—General	M,D
Educational Leadership and Administration	M,D
Educational Media/Instructional Technology	M
English	M
Environmental Management and Policy	M
Environmental Sciences	M
Exercise and Sports Science	M
Finance and Banking	M
Foundations and Philosophy of Education	M
Health Services Management and Hospital Administration	M
History	M
Human Resources Management	M
Humanities	M
Information Science	M
Library Science	M
Management Information Systems	M
Marriage and Family Therapy	M
Mathematics	M
Multilingual and Multicultural Education	M
Physics	M
Psychology—General	M
Reading Education	M
School Psychology	M
Sociology	M
Software Engineering	M
Statistics	M
Systems Engineering	M

UNIVERSITY OF HOUSTON–DOWNTOWN

Accounting	M
Business Administration and Management—General	M
Criminal Justice and Criminology	M
Curriculum and Instruction	M
Data Science/Data Analytics	M
English	M
Finance and Banking	M
Human Resources Management	M
International Business	M
Investment Management	M
Nonprofit Management	M
Project Management	M
Rhetoric	M
Social Work	M
Supply Chain Management	M
Technical Communication	M
Urban Education	M

UNIVERSITY OF HOUSTON–VICTORIA

Accounting	M
Adult Education	M,O
Biological and Biomedical Sciences—General	M
Business Administration and Management—General	M
Computer Science	M
Counseling Psychology	M
Counselor Education	M,O
Curriculum and Instruction	M,O
Economic Development	M
Education—General	M,O
Educational Leadership and Administration	M,O
Educational Media/Instructional Technology	M,O
Entrepreneurship	M
Finance and Banking	M
Forensic Psychology	M
Forensic Sciences	M
Higher Education	M,O
Interdisciplinary Studies	M
International Business	M
Management Information Systems	M
Marketing	M
Psychology—General	M
Publishing	M
Reading Education	M,O
School Psychology	M
Special Education	M,O
Writing	M

UNIVERSITY OF IDAHO

Accounting	M
Agricultural Economics and Agribusiness	M
Animal Sciences	M,D
Anthropology	M
Architecture	M
Art/Fine Arts	M
Athletic Training and Sports Medicine	M,D
Biochemistry	M,D
Bioengineering	M,D
Bioinformatics	M,D
Biological and Biomedical Sciences—General	M,D
Business Administration and Management—General	M
Chemical Engineering	M,D
Chemistry	M,D
Civil Engineering	M,D
Computational Biology	M,D
Computer Science	M,D
Consumer Economics	M
Counselor Education	M,O
Curriculum and Instruction	M,O
Education—General	M,D,O
Educational Leadership and Administration	M,O
Electrical Engineering	M,D
Engineering and Applied Sciences—General	M,D
Entomology	M,D
Environmental Sciences	M,D
Exercise and Sports Science	M,D
Experimental Psychology	M,D
Food Science and Technology	M,D
Geography	M,D
Geological Engineering	M,D
Geology	M,D
History	M,D
Human Services	M,O
Interdisciplinary Studies	M
Kinesiology and Movement Studies	M,D
Law	M,D
Materials Sciences	M,D
Mathematics	M,D
Mechanical Engineering	M,D
Microbiology	M,D
Music	M
Natural Resources	M,D
Nuclear Engineering	M,D
Philosophy	M,D
Physical Education	M,D
Physics	M,D
Plant Pathology	M,D
Plant Sciences	M,D
Political Science	M,D
Psychology—General	M,D
Public Administration	M,D
Rehabilitation Counseling	M,O
Special Education	M,O
Sports Management	M,D
Statistics	M
Theater	M
Travel and Tourism	M,D
Urban and Regional Planning	M
Veterinary Sciences	M,D
Vocational and Technical Education	M,O
Water Resources Engineering	M,D
Water Resources	M,D
Writing	M

UNIVERSITY OF ILLINOIS AT CHICAGO

Accounting	M
Acute Care/Critical Care Nursing	M,O
Adult Nursing	M,O
Allied Health—General	M,D,O
Allopathic Medicine	D
Anatomy	M
Anthropology	M,D
Applied Arts and Design—General	M
Architecture	M
Art History	M,D
Art/Fine Arts	M,D
Biochemistry	D
Bioengineering	M,D
Bioinformatics	M,D
Biological and Biomedical Sciences—General	M,D
Biophysics	M,D
Biostatistics	M,D
Business Administration and Management—General	M,D
Cell Biology	M,D
Chemical Engineering	M,D
Chemistry	M,D
Civil Engineering	M,D
Communication—General	M,D
Community Health Nursing	M,O
Community Health	M,D
Computer Education	D
Computer Engineering	M,D
Computer Science	M,D
Criminal Justice and Criminology	M,D
Curriculum and Instruction	M,D
Dentistry	D
Developmental Psychology	M,D
Disability Studies	M,D
Early Childhood Education	M,D
East European and Russian Studies	M,D
Economics	M,D
Education—General	M,D
Educational Leadership and Administration	M,D
Educational Measurement and Evaluation	M,D
Educational Policy	M,D
Educational Psychology	M,D
Electrical Engineering	M,D
Elementary Education	M,D
Engineering and Applied Sciences—General	M,D
English as a Second Language	M,D
English	M,D
Environmental and Occupational Health	M,D
Epidemiology	M,D
Family Nurse Practitioner Studies	M,O
Finance and Banking	M
Foreign Languages Education	M,D
Forensic Sciences	M
French	M
Genetics	D
Geography	M
Geology	M,D
Geosciences	M,D
German	M,D
Gerontological Nursing	M,O
Graphic Design	M
Health Education	M
Health Informatics	M,O
Health Services Management and Hospital Administration	M,D
Health Services Research	M,D
Hispanic and Latin American Languages	M,D
Hispanic Studies	M,D
History	M,D
Human Development	M,D
Immunology	D
Industrial/Management Engineering	M,D
Interdisciplinary Studies	D
Kinesiology and Movement Studies	M,D
Latin American Studies	M
Linguistics	M
Management Information Systems	M,D
Materials Engineering	M,D
Maternal and Child/Neonatal Nursing	M,O
Mathematics Education	M,D
Mathematics	M,D
Mechanical Engineering	M,D
Medical Illustration	M
Medicinal and Pharmaceutical Chemistry	M,D
Microbiology	D
Molecular Biology	D
Molecular Genetics	D
Museum Studies	M,D
Neuroscience	M,D
Nurse Midwifery	M,O
Nursing and Healthcare Administration	M,O
Nursing—General	M,D,O
Nutrition	M,D
Occupational Health Nursing	M,O
Occupational Therapy	M,D
Operations Research	M,D
Oral and Dental Sciences	M,D
Pediatric Nursing	M,O
Pharmaceutical Administration	M,D
Pharmaceutical Sciences	M,D
Pharmacology	D
Pharmacy	D
Philosophy	M,D
Physical Therapy	M,D
Physics	M,D
Physiology	M,D
Political Science	M,D
Psychology—General	M,D
Public Administration	M,D
Public Health—General	M,D
Real Estate	M
School Nursing	M,O
Science Education	D
Secondary Education	M,D
Slavic Languages	M,D
Social Sciences Education	D
Social Work	M,D,O
Sociology	M,D
Spanish	M,D
Special Education	M,D
Statistics	M,D
Toxicology	M,D
Urban and Regional Planning	M,D
Urban Education	M,D
Women's Health Nursing	M,O

UNIVERSITY OF ILLINOIS AT SPRINGFIELD

Accounting	M
Addictions/Substance Abuse Counseling	M,O
Biological and Biomedical Sciences—General	M
Business Administration and Management—General	M
Child and Family Studies	M,O
Communication—General	M
Community Health	M,O
Computer Science	M
Data Science/Data Analytics	M
Distance Education Development	M,O
Education—General	M,O
Educational Leadership and Administration	M,O
Educational Media/Instructional Technology	M,O
Emergency Management	M,O
English as a Second Language	M,O
English Education	M,O
English	M,O
Environmental and Occupational Health	M,O
Environmental Management and Policy	M
Environmental Sciences	M
Epidemiology	M,O
Gerontology	M,O
Health Education	M,O
Higher Education	M,O
History	M
Homeland Security	M,O
Human Development	M
Human Services	M,O
Interdisciplinary Studies	M
Journalism	M
Legal and Justice Studies	M
Management Information Systems	M
Political Science	M
Public Administration	M,D,O
Public Health—General	M,O
Public History	M
Social Sciences	M,O

UNIVERSITY OF ILLINOIS AT URBANA–CHAMPAIGN

Accounting	M,D
Actuarial Science	M,D
Advertising and Public Relations	M
Aerospace/Aeronautical Engineering	M,D
African Studies	M
Agricultural Economics and Agribusiness	M,D
Agricultural Education	M
Agricultural Engineering	M,D
Agricultural Sciences—General	M
Agronomy and Soil Sciences	M,D
Animal Sciences	M,D
Anthropology	M,D
Applied Arts and Design—General	M,D
Applied Economics	M,D
Applied Mathematics	M,D
Applied Statistics	M,D
Architecture	M,D
Art Education	M,D
Art History	M,D
Art/Fine Arts	M
Asian Languages	M,D
Asian Studies	M,D
Astronomy	M,D
Atmospheric Sciences	M,D
Biochemistry	M,D
Bioengineering	M,D
Bioinformatics	M,D,O
Biological and Biomedical Sciences—General	M,D
Biophysics	M,D
Business Administration and Management—General	M,D
Cell Biology	D
Chemical Engineering	M,D
Chemical Physics	M,D
Chemistry	M,D
Civil Engineering	M,D
Classics	M,D
Communication Disorders	M,D
Communication—General	M,D
Community Health	M,D
Comparative Literature	M,D
Computational Biology	M,D
Computer Engineering	M,D
Computer Science	M,D
Conservation Biology	M,D
Consumer Economics	M,D
Corporate and Organizational Communication	M
Counselor Education	M,D,O
Curriculum and Instruction	M,D,O
Dance	M
Developmental Biology	D
East European and Russian Studies	M
Ecology	M,D
Economics	M,D
Education of Students with Severe/Multiple Disabilities	M,D,O
Education—General	M,D,O

*M—masters degree; D—doctorate; O—other advanced degree; *—Close-Up and/or Display*

Educational Leadership and Administration	M,D,O
Educational Policy	M,D,O
Educational Psychology	M,D,O
Electrical Engineering	M,D
Energy and Power Engineering	M,D
Energy Management and Policy	M
Engineering and Applied Sciences—General	M,D
English as a Second Language	M,D
English	M,D
Entomology	M,D
Environmental Engineering	M,D
Environmental Sciences	M,D
Evolutionary Biology	M,D
Finance and Banking	M,D
Financial Engineering	M
Food Science and Technology	M,D
Foreign Languages Education	M,D
French	M,D
Geography	M,D
Geology	M,D
Geosciences	M,D
German	M,D
Graphic Design	M
Health Informatics	M,D,O
Health Services Management and Hospital Administration	M,D
History	M,D
Human Development	M,D
Human Resources Management	M,D,O
Human Services	M,D
Human-Computer Interaction	M,D,O
Industrial and Labor Relations	M,D
Industrial Design	M
Industrial/Management Engineering	M,D
Information Science	M,D,O
Information Studies	M,D,O
Interdisciplinary Studies	D
Italian	M,D
Journalism	M
Kinesiology and Movement Studies	M,D
Landscape Architecture	M,D
Latin American Studies	M
Law	M,D
Leisure Studies	M,D
Library Science	M,D,O
Linguistics	M,D
Management Information Systems	M,D,O
Management of Technology	M,D
Management Strategy and Policy	M,D,O
Materials Engineering	M,D
Materials Sciences	M,D
Mathematics Education	M,D
Mathematics	M,D
Mechanical Engineering	M,D
Mechanics	M,D
Media Studies	M,D
Medical Informatics	M,D,O
Microbiology	M,D
Molecular Physiology	M,D
Music Education	M,D
Music	M,D
Natural Resources	M,D
Near and Middle Eastern Studies	M,D
Neuroscience	D
Nuclear Engineering	M,D
Nutrition	M,D
Pathobiology	M,D
Philosophy	M,D
Photography	M
Physics	M,D
Physiology	M,D
Plant Biology	M,D
Political Science	M,D
Portuguese	M,D
Psychology—General	M,D
Public Health—General	M,D
Rehabilitation Sciences	M,D
Religion	M
Romance Languages	D
Science Education	M,D
Slavic Languages	M,D
Social Work	M,D
Sociology	M,D
Spanish	M,D
Special Education	M,D,O
Statistics	M,D
Systems Engineering	M,D
Theater	M,D
Translation and Interpretation	M
Urban and Regional Planning	M,D
Veterinary Medicine	D
Veterinary Sciences	M,D
Western European Studies	M
Writing	M,D
Zoology	M,D

UNIVERSITY OF INDIANAPOLIS

Anthropology	M
Art Education	M
Art/Fine Arts	M
Biological and Biomedical Sciences—General	M
Business Administration and Management—General	M,O
Clinical Psychology	M,D
Counseling Psychology	M,D
Curriculum and Instruction	M
Education—General	M
Educational Leadership and Administration	M
Elementary Education	M
English Education	M
English	M
Family Nurse Practitioner Studies	M,D
Foreign Languages Education	M
Gerontology	M,D,O
History	M
International Affairs	M
Maternal and Child/Neonatal Nursing	M,D
Mathematics Education	M
Nurse Midwifery	M,D
Nursing and Healthcare Administration	M,D
Nursing Education	M,D
Nursing—General	M,D
Occupational Therapy	M,D
Physical Education	M
Physical Therapy	M,D
Psychology—General	M,D
Public Health—General	M
Science Education	M
Secondary Education	M
Social Sciences Education	M
Sociology	M
Sports Management	M
Women's Health Nursing	M,D

THE UNIVERSITY OF IOWA

Accounting	M,D
Actuarial Science	M,D
Agricultural Sciences—General	M,D,O
Allopathic Medicine	D
American Studies	M,D
Anatomy	D
Anthropology	M,D
Applied Mathematics	D
Art Education	M,D
Art History	M,D
Art/Fine Arts	M
Asian Languages	M
Asian Studies	M
Astronomy	M
Athletic Training and Sports Medicine	M,D
Bacteriology	M,D
Biochemical Engineering	M,D
Biochemistry	M,D
Bioinformatics	M,D
Biological and Biomedical Sciences—General	M,D
Biomedical Engineering	M,D
Biophysics	M,D
Biostatistics	M,D,O
Business Administration and Management—General	M,D
Business Analytics	M
Cell Biology	M,D
Chemical Engineering	M,D
Chemistry	D
Chinese	M
Civil Engineering	M,D
Classics	M,D
Clinical Research	M,D
Communication Disorders	M,D
Communication—General	M,D
Community Health	M,D
Computational Biology	M,D,O
Computational Sciences	D
Computer Engineering	M,D
Computer Science	M,D
Counseling Psychology	M,D,O
Counselor Education	M,D
Dance	M
Dentistry	M,D,O
Developmental Education	D
Economics	D
Education—General	M,D
Educational Leadership and Administration	M,D,O
Educational Measurement and Evaluation	M,D,O
Educational Policy	M,D,O
Educational Psychology	M,D,O
Electrical Engineering	M,D
Elementary Education	M,D
Energy and Power Engineering	M,D
Engineering and Applied Sciences—General	M,D*
English as a Second Language	M,D
English Education	M,D
English	M,D
Environmental and Occupational Health	M,D,O
Environmental Engineering	M,D
Epidemiology	M,D
Ergonomics and Human Factors	M,D,O
Evolutionary Biology	M,D
Exercise and Sports Science	M,D
Film, Television, and Video Production	M
Film, Television, and Video Theory and Criticism	M,D
Finance and Banking	M,D
Foreign Languages Education	M,D
Foundations and Philosophy of Education	M,D,O
French	M,D
Genetics	M,D
Geographic Information Systems	M,D,O
Geography	M,D,O
Geosciences	M,D
Health Informatics	M,D,O
Health Services Management and Hospital Administration	M,D
Higher Education	M,D
History	M,D
Immunology	M,D
Industrial Hygiene	M,D,O
Industrial/Management Engineering	M,D
Information Science	M,D,O
Information Studies	M,D
Journalism	M,D
Law	M,D
Leisure Studies	M,D
Library Science	M,D
Linguistics	M,D
Manufacturing Engineering	M,D
Marketing	M,D
Marriage and Family Therapy	M,D
Mass Communication	M,D
Materials Engineering	M,D
Mathematics Education	M,D
Mathematics	M,D
Mechanical Engineering	M,D
Media Studies	M,D
Medicinal and Pharmaceutical Chemistry	M,D
Microbiology	M,D
Molecular Biology	D
Music Education	M,D
Music	M,D
Neurobiology	M,D
Neuroscience	D
Nursing—General	M,D
Operations Research	M,D
Oral and Dental Sciences	M,D,O
Pathology	M
Pharmaceutical Sciences	M,D
Pharmacology	M,D
Pharmacy	M,D
Philosophy	D
Physical Therapy	M,D
Physician Assistant Studies	M
Physics	M,D
Physiology	M,D
Political Science	D
Psychology—General	M,D,O
Public Health—General	M,D,O
Quantitative Analysis	M,D,O
Radiation Biology	M
Recreation and Park Management	M,D
Rehabilitation Counseling	M,D
Rehabilitation Sciences	M,D
Religion	M,D
Rhetoric	M,D
School Psychology	M,D,O
Science Education	M,D
Secondary Education	M,D
Social Sciences Education	M,D
Social Work	M,D
Sociology	M,D
Spanish	M,D
Special Education	M,D
Speech and Interpersonal Communication	M,D
Sports Management	M,D
Statistics	M,D,O
Student Affairs	M,D
Sustainable Development	M,D
Theater	M
Toxicology	M,D
Translational Biology	M,D
Transportation and Highway Engineering	M,D
Urban and Regional Planning	M
Virology	M,D
Water Resources Engineering	M,D
Water Resources	M,D
Women's Studies	O
Writing	M,D

UNIVERSITY OF JAMESTOWN

Curriculum and Instruction	M
Education—General	M
Physical Therapy	D

THE UNIVERSITY OF KANSAS

Accounting	M
Acoustics	M,D,O
Adult Nursing	M,D,O
Aerospace/Aeronautical Engineering	M,D
African Studies	M,O
African-American Studies	M,O
Allied Health—General	M,D,O
Allopathic Medicine	D
American Indian/Native American Studies	M,O
American Studies	M,D
Anatomy	M,D
Anthropology	M,D
Applied Arts and Design—General	M
Applied Behavior Analysis	M,D,O
Applied Mathematics	M,D,O
Applied Statistics	M,D,O
Architectural Engineering	M
Architecture	M,D,O
Art Education	M
Art History	M,D
Art/Fine Arts	M
Asian Languages	M,O
Asian Studies	M,O
Astronomy	M,D
Atmospheric Sciences	M,D,O
Biochemistry	D
Bioengineering	M,D
Biological and Biomedical Sciences—General	D
Biophysics	D
Biostatistics	M,D,O
Biotechnology	M
Business Administration and Management—General	M,D
Cancer Biology/Oncology	M,D
Cell Biology	M,D
Chemical Engineering	M,D,O
Chemistry	M,D
Civil Engineering	M,D
Classics	M
Clinical Psychology	M,D
Clinical Research	M
Cognitive Sciences	M,D
Communication Disorders	M,D
Communication—General	M,D,O
Community Health Nursing	M,D,O
Community Health	M,D,O
Computational Biology	D
Computer Engineering	M,D
Computer Science	M,D
Construction Management	M
Counseling Psychology	M,D
Cultural Studies	M,D
Curriculum and Instruction	M,D
Developmental Biology	D
Developmental Psychology	M,D
Early Childhood Education	M,D,O
East European and Russian Studies	M,O
Ecology	M,D
Economics	M,D
Education—General	M,D,O
Educational Leadership and Administration	M,D
Educational Measurement and Evaluation	M,D
Educational Media/Instructional Technology	M,D
Educational Policy	M,D
Educational Psychology	M,D
Electrical Engineering	M,D
Engineering and Applied Sciences—General	M,D,O
Engineering Management	M,D,O
English	M,D
Environmental Engineering	M,D
Environmental Sciences	M,D
Epidemiology	M
Evolutionary Biology	M,D
Exercise and Sports Science	M,D
Film, Television, and Video Theory and Criticism	M,D
Finance and Banking	M,D
French	M,D
Geographic Information Systems	M,D,O
Geography	M,D,O
Geology	M,D
Gerontological Nursing	M,D,O
Gerontology	D
Health Education	M,D,O
Health Informatics	M,O
Health Promotion	M,D,O
Health Services Management and Hospital Administration	M,D
Higher Education	M,D
Historic Preservation	M,D,O
History	M,D
Human Resources Management	M,D
Interdisciplinary Studies	D
International Affairs	M
Journalism	M,D
Latin American Studies	M,O
Law	D
Linguistics	M,D
Logistics	M,D
Management Information Systems	M
Management Strategy and Policy	M,D
Marketing	M,D
Mathematics	M,D,O
Mechanical Engineering	M,D
Media Studies	M,D
Medical Informatics	M,D,O
Medicinal and Pharmaceutical Chemistry	M,D
Microbiology	M,D
Molecular Biology	D
Museum Studies	M,O
Music Education	M,D
Music	M,D
Near and Middle Eastern Studies	M,O
Neuroscience	M,D
Nurse Anesthesia	D
Nurse Midwifery	M,D,O
Nursing—General	M,D,O
Nutrition	M,D,O
Occupational Therapy	M,D
Organizational Behavior	M,D
Organizational Management	M,D,O
Pathology	M,D
Petroleum Engineering	M,D,O
Pharmacology	M,D
Pharmacy	M,D
Philosophy	M,D
Physical Education	M,D
Physical Therapy	D
Physics	M,D
Physiology	D
Political Science	M,D
Project Management	M
Psychiatric Nursing	M,D,O
Psychology—General	M,D,O
Public Administration	M,D,O
Public Health—General	M
Rehabilitation Sciences	M,D
Religion	M,O
School Psychology	D,O
Slavic Languages	M,D
Social Psychology	M,D
Social Work	M,D
Sociology	D
Spanish	M,D
Special Education	M,D,O
Sports Management	M,D
Statistics	M,D,O
Supply Chain Management	M,D
Textile Design	M
Theater	M,D
Therapies—Dance, Drama, and Music	M,D
Toxicology	M,D
Urban and Regional Planning	M
Urban Design	M,D,O
Writing	M,D

UNIVERSITY OF KENTUCKY

Accounting	M
Agricultural Economics and Agribusiness	M,D
Agricultural Engineering	M,D
Agricultural Sciences—General	M,D
Agronomy and Soil Sciences	M,D
Allied Health—General	M,D
Allopathic Medicine	D
Anatomy	D
Animal Sciences	M,D
Anthropology	M,D

Applied Arts and Design—General	M
Applied Mathematics	M,D
Architecture	M
Art Education	M
Art History	M
Art/Fine Arts	M
Arts Administration	M
Astronomy	M,D
Athletic Training and Sports Medicine	M
Biochemistry	D
Biological and Biomedical Sciences—General	M,D
Biomedical Engineering	M,D
Biostatistics	D
Business Administration and Management—General	M,D
Chemical Engineering	M,D
Chemistry	M,D
Child and Family Studies	M,D
Civil Engineering	M,D
Classics	M
Clinical Research	M
Communication Disorders	M
Communication—General	M,D
Computer Science	M,D
Counseling Psychology	M,D,O
Curriculum and Instruction	M,D
Dentistry	D
Early Childhood Education	M,D
Economics	M,D
Education—General	M,D,O
Educational Leadership and Administration	M,D,O
Educational Measurement and Evaluation	M,D
Educational Media/Instructional Technology	M,D
Educational Policy	M,D
Educational Psychology	M,D,O
Electrical Engineering	M,D
Elementary Education	M,D
Engineering and Applied Sciences—General	M,D
English	M,D
Entomology	M,D
Epidemiology	D
Exercise and Sports Science	M,D
Food Science and Technology	M,D
Foreign Languages Education	M
Forestry	M
Geography	M,D
Geology	M,D
German	M
Gerontology	D,O
Health Physics/Radiological Health	M
Health Promotion	M,D
Health Services Management and Hospital Administration	M
Higher Education	M,D
Hispanic Studies	M,D
Historic Preservation	M
History	M,D
Hospitality Management	M
Immunology	D
Information Science	M
Interior Design	M
International Affairs	M
International Business	M
Kinesiology and Movement Studies	M,D
Law	D
Library Science	M
Manufacturing Engineering	M
Materials Engineering	M,D
Materials Sciences	M,D
Mathematics	M,D
Mechanical Engineering	M,D
Medical Physics	M,D
Microbiology	D
Middle School Education	M,D
Mineral/Mining Engineering	M,D
Music Education	M,D
Music	M,D
Neurobiology	D
Nursing—General	M,D
Nutrition	M,D
Oral and Dental Sciences	M
Pharmaceutical Sciences	M,D
Pharmacology	D
Pharmacy	D
Philosophy	M,D
Physical Education	M,D
Physical Therapy	D
Physician Assistant Studies	M
Physics	M,D
Physiology	D
Plant Pathology	M,D
Plant Sciences	M,D
Political Science	M,D
Psychology—General	M,D
Public Administration	M,D,O
Public Health—General	M,D
Public Policy	M,D,O
Reading Education	M,D
Rehabilitation Counseling	M,D
Rehabilitation Sciences	D
School Psychology	M,D,O
Secondary Education	M,D
Social Work	M,D
Sociology	M,D
Special Education	M,D
Statistics	M,D
Therapies—Dance, Drama, and Music	M,D
Toxicology	M,D
Veterinary Sciences	M,D

UNIVERSITY OF KING'S COLLEGE

Journalism	M
Writing	M

UNIVERSITY OF LA VERNE

Accounting	M
Business Administration and Management—General	M,D,O
Child and Family Studies	M
Child Development	M
Clinical Psychology	D
Counselor Education	M,D,O
Education—General	M,O
Educational Leadership and Administration	M,D,O
Elementary Education	M,D,O
English	M,O
Finance and Banking	M
Gerontology	M,O
Health Services Management and Hospital Administration	M,D,O
Health Services Research	M
Higher Education	M
Human Resources Management	M,O
International Business	M
Law	D
Management Information Systems	M
Marketing	M
Marriage and Family Therapy	M
Nonprofit Management	M,O
Organizational Management	M,D,O
Psychology—General	M,D
Public Administration	M,D
Public Health—General	M
Reading Education	M,O
School Psychology	M,O
Secondary Education	M,D,O
Special Education	M,D,O
Student Affairs	M
Supply Chain Management	M

UNIVERSITY OF LETHBRIDGE

Accounting	M,D
Addictions/Substance Abuse Counseling	M,D
Agricultural Sciences—General	M,D
American Indian/Native American Studies	M,D
Anthropology	M,D
Archaeology	M,D
Art/Fine Arts	M,D
Biochemistry	M,D
Biological and Biomedical Sciences—General	M,D
Business Administration and Management—General	M,D
Canadian Studies	M,D
Chemistry	M,D
Computational Sciences	M,D
Computer Science	M,D
Counseling Psychology	M,D
Counselor Education	M,D
Economics	M,D
Education—General	M,D
Educational Leadership and Administration	M,D
English	M,D
Environmental Sciences	M,D
Exercise and Sports Science	M,D
Finance and Banking	M,D
French	M,D
Gender Studies	M,D
Geographic Information Systems	M,D
Geography	M,D
German	M,D
Human Resources Management	M,D
International Business	M,D
Kinesiology and Movement Studies	M,D
Management Information Systems	M,D
Management Strategy and Policy	M,D
Marketing	M,D
Mathematics	M,D
Media Studies	M,D
Molecular Biology	M,D
Music	M,D
Neuroscience	M,D
Nursing—General	M,D
Philosophy	M,D
Physics	M,D
Political Science	M,D
Psychology—General	M,D
Religion	M,D
Sociology	M,D
Spanish	M,D
Theater	M,D
Urban Studies	M,D
Women's Studies	M,D

UNIVERSITY OF LOUISIANA AT LAFAYETTE

Accounting	M
American Studies	M,D
Architectural Engineering	M
Biological and Biomedical Sciences—General	M,D
Business Administration and Management—General	M
Chemical Engineering	M
Civil Engineering	M
Cognitive Sciences	M
Communication Disorders	M,D
Communication—General	M,D
Computer Engineering	M,D
Counselor Education	M
Cultural Studies	M,D
Curriculum and Instruction	M
Early Childhood Education	M
Education of the Gifted	M
Education—General	M,D
Educational Leadership and Administration	M,D
Educational Media/Instructional Technology	M
English as a Second Language	M,D
English	M,D
Entrepreneurship	M
Environmental Biology	M,D
Environmental Sciences	M
Evolutionary Biology	M,D
Family Nurse Practitioner Studies	M,D
Finance and Banking	M
Folklore	M,D
French	M,D
Geosciences	M
History	M,D
Hospitality Management	M
Human Resources Management	M
International Business	M
Latin American Studies	M
Mathematics Education	M
Mathematics	M,D
Mechanical Engineering	M
Music Education	M
Music	M
Natural Resources	M
Nursing and Healthcare Administration	M
Nursing Education	M,D
Nursing—General	M,D
Petroleum Engineering	M
Physics	M
Project Management	M
Psychology—General	M
Public History	M
Rhetoric	M,D
Sociology	M,D
Special Education	M
Systems Engineering	M,D
Western European Studies	M
Writing	M,D

UNIVERSITY OF LOUISIANA AT MONROE

Biological and Biomedical Sciences—General	M
Business Administration and Management—General	M,O
Clinical Psychology	M
Communication Disorders	M
Communication—General	M
Counseling Psychology	M
Counselor Education	M
Criminal Justice and Criminology	M
Curriculum and Instruction	M,D
Education—General	M,D
Elementary Education	M
English	M
Exercise and Sports Science	M
Forensic Psychology	M
Gerontology	M,O
History	M
Marriage and Family Therapy	M,D
Occupational Therapy	M
Pharmacy	D
Psychology—General	M
Public Administration	M
Recreation and Park Management	M
Secondary Education	M
Special Education	M
Sports Management	M
Toxicology	D

UNIVERSITY OF LOUISVILLE

Accounting	M
Addictions/Substance Abuse Counseling	M,D,O
African Studies	M
African-American Studies	M
Allopathic Medicine	D
Analytical Chemistry	M,D
Anatomy	M,D
Anthropology	M
Applied Arts and Design—General	M,D
Applied Behavior Analysis	M,D,O
Applied Mathematics	M,D
Art Education	M,D,O
Art History	M,D
Art Therapy	M,D
Biochemistry	M,D
Bioengineering	M,D
Bioethics	M,D
Bioinformatics	M,D
Biological and Biomedical Sciences—General	M,D
Biostatistics	M,D
Business Administration and Management—General	M
Chemical Engineering	M,D
Chemical Physics	M,D
Chemistry	M,D
Civil Engineering	M,D
Clinical Psychology	D
Cognitive Sciences	D
Communication Disorders	M,D
Communication—General	M
Community Health	M
Computer and Information Systems Security	M,D,O
Computer Engineering	M,D,O
Computer Science	M,D,O
Counseling Psychology	M,D
Counselor Education	M,D
Criminal Justice and Criminology	M,D
Cultural Studies	M,D
Curriculum and Instruction	M,D,O
Data Science/Data Analytics	M,D,O
Dentistry	M,D
Developmental Psychology	D
Early Childhood Education	M,D,O
Education—General	M,D,O
Educational Leadership and Administration	M,D,O
Educational Measurement and Evaluation	M,D
Educational Psychology	M,D
Electrical Engineering	M,D
Elementary Education	M,D,O
Engineering and Applied Sciences—General	M,D,O
Engineering Management	M,D,O
English	M,D
Entrepreneurship	M,D
Environmental Biology	M,D
Epidemiology	M,D
Exercise and Sports Science	M,D,O
Experimental Psychology	D
Family Nurse Practitioner Studies	M,D
French	M
Geography	M
Gerontological Nursing	M,D
Gerontology	M,D,O
Health Education	M,D,O
Health Services Management and Hospital Administration	M
Higher Education	M,D,O
History	M,O
Human Resources Development	M,D,O
Human Resources Management	M,D,O
Humanities	M,D
Immunology	M,D
Industrial/Management Engineering	M,D,O
Inorganic Chemistry	M,D
Interdisciplinary Studies	M,D
International Business	M
Law	D
Linguistics	M,D
Logistics	M,D,O
Marriage and Family Therapy	M,D,O
Maternal and Child/Neonatal Nursing	M,D
Mathematics	M,D
Mechanical Engineering	M,D
Microbiology	M,D
Middle School Education	M,D,O
Molecular Genetics	M,D
Museum Studies	M,O
Music Education	M,D,O
Music	M
Neurobiology	M,D
Nonprofit Management	M,D
Nursing and Healthcare Administration	M,D
Nursing Education	M,D
Nursing—General	M,D
Oral and Dental Sciences	M,D
Organic Chemistry	M,D
Pharmacology	M,D
Philosophy	M,D
Physical Chemistry	M,D
Physical Education	M,D,O
Physics	M,D
Physiology	M,D
Political Science	M
Psychiatric Nursing	M,D
Psychology—General	D
Public Administration	M,D
Public Affairs	M,D
Public Health—General	M,D
Public History	M,O
Public Policy	M,D
Rhetoric	M,D
School Psychology	M,D
Secondary Education	M,D,O
Social Work	M,D,O
Sociology	M,D
Spanish	M,O
Special Education	M,D,O
Sports Management	M,D,O
Student Affairs	M,D
Supply Chain Management	M,D,O
Sustainability Management	M,D
Theater	M
Toxicology	M,D
Urban and Regional Planning	M,D
Urban Studies	M,D
Women's Health Nursing	M,O
Women's Studies	M,O
Writing	M,D

UNIVERSITY OF LYNCHBURG

Allopathic Medicine	D
Athletic Training and Sports Medicine	M
Business Administration and Management—General	M
Clinical Psychology	M
Counseling Psychology	M
Counselor Education	M
Criminal Justice and Criminology	M
Curriculum and Instruction	M
Educational Leadership and Administration	M,D
Geosciences	M
Health Informatics	O
Health Promotion	M
Higher Education	M
Mathematics	M
Nonprofit Management	M
Physical Therapy	D
Physician Assistant Studies	M
Public Health—General	M
Reading Education	M
School Psychology	M
Science Education	M
Special Education	M

UNIVERSITY OF MAINE

Agricultural Economics and Agribusiness	M
Agricultural Sciences—General	M,D,O
Anthropology	D

*M—masters degree; D—doctorate; O—other advanced degree; *—Close-Up and/or Display*

Art/Fine Arts	M
Bioinformatics	M,D
Biological and Biomedical Sciences—General	M,D
Biomedical Engineering	M,D
Botany	M,D
Business Administration and Management—General	M,O
Chemical Engineering	M,D
Chemistry	M,D
Civil Engineering	M,D
Communication Disorders	M
Communication—General	M,D
Computer Engineering	M,D
Computer Science	M,D,O
Early Childhood Education	M,D,O
Economics	M
Education—General	M,D,O
Educational Leadership and Administration	M,D,O
Educational Media/Instructional Technology	M,D,O
Electrical Engineering	M,D
Engineering and Applied Sciences—General	M,D
English	M
Entomology	M,D
Environmental Management and Policy	D
Exercise and Sports Science	M,D,O
Family Nurse Practitioner Studies	M,O
Finance and Banking	M
Fish, Game, and Wildlife Management	M,D
Foreign Languages Education	M,D
Forestry	M,D
French	M
Geology	M,O
Geosciences	M,D
Higher Education	M,D,O
History	M,D
Horticulture	M,D,O
Human Development	M,D,O
Information Science	M,D,O
Interdisciplinary Studies	M,D
International Affairs	M
Kinesiology and Movement Studies	M,D,O
Law	D
Marine Sciences	M,D
Mathematics	M
Mechanical Engineering	M,D
Microbiology	M,D
Molecular Biology	M,D
Music	M
Nursing Education	M,O
Nursing—General	M,O
Physical Education	M,D,O
Physics	M,D
Plant Pathology	M,D
Psychology—General	M,D
Reading Education	M,D,O
Social Sciences Education	M,D,O
Social Work	M,O
Special Education	M,D,O
Water Resources	M,D
Zoology	M,D

UNIVERSITY OF MAINE AT FARMINGTON

Early Childhood Education	M
Education—General	M
Educational Leadership and Administration	M
Educational Media/Instructional Technology	M

UNIVERSITY OF MANAGEMENT AND TECHNOLOGY

Business Administration and Management—General	M,D,O
Computer Science	M,O
Criminal Justice and Criminology	M,O
Engineering Management	M
Health Services Management and Hospital Administration	M
Homeland Security	M
Management Information Systems	M,O
Project Management	M,D,O
Public Administration	M,O
Software Engineering	M,O

THE UNIVERSITY OF MANCHESTER

Accounting	M
Actuarial Science	M,D
Aerospace/Aeronautical Engineering	M,D
Analytical Chemistry	M,D
Anthropology	M,D
Applied Mathematics	M,D
Archaeology	D
Architecture	M,D
Art History	D
Art/Fine Arts	M,D
Arts Administration	D
Asian Studies	D
Astronomy	M,D
Astrophysics	M,D
Atmospheric Sciences	M,D
Biochemical Engineering	M,D
Biochemistry	M,D
Bioinformatics	M,D
Biological and Biomedical Sciences—General	M,D
Biophysics	M,D
Biotechnology	M,D
Business Administration and Management—General	M
Business Analytics	M
Cancer Biology/Oncology	M,D
Cell Biology	M,D
Chemical Engineering	M,D
Chemistry	M,D
Chinese	D
Civil Engineering	M,D
Classics	D
Clinical Psychology	M,D
Clothing and Textiles	M,D
Communication Disorders	M,D
Computer Science	M,D
Condensed Matter Physics	M,D
Conflict Resolution and Mediation/Peace Studies	D
Counseling Psychology	M,D
Criminal Justice and Criminology	M,D
Cultural Studies	M,D
Dentistry	M,D
Developmental Biology	M,D
Developmental Psychology	M,D
East European and Russian Studies	D
Ecology	M,D
Education—General	M,D
Educational Psychology	M,D
Electrical Engineering	M,D
Engineering Management	M,D
English	D
Entrepreneurship	M
Environmental Biology	M,D
Environmental Design	M,D
Environmental Engineering	M,D
Environmental Management and Policy	M,D
Environmental Sciences	M,D
Evolutionary Biology	M,D
Finance and Banking	M
French	D
Genetics	M,D
Geochemistry	M,D
Geography	M,D
Geosciences	M,D
German	D
Hazardous Materials Management	M,D
Health Law	M,D
History of Medicine	M,D
History of Science and Technology	M,D
History	D
Human Resources Management	M
Immunology	M,D
Industrial and Labor Relations	M
Industrial and Manufacturing Management	M,D
Industrial and Organizational Psychology	M
Inorganic Chemistry	M,D
International Affairs	D
International Business	M
International Development	M,D
Japanese	D
Landscape Architecture	M,D
Latin American Studies	D
Law	M,D
Linguistics	D
Management Strategy and Policy	M
Marketing	M
Materials Sciences	M,D
Mathematical and Computational Finance	M,D
Mathematics	M,D
Mechanical Engineering	M,D
Metallurgical Engineering and Metallurgy	M,D
Microbiology	M,D
Modeling and Simulation	M,D
Molecular Biology	M,D
Molecular Genetics	M,D
Museum Studies	D
Music	D
Natural Resources	M,D
Near and Middle Eastern Studies	D
Neurobiology	M,D
Neuroscience	M,D
Nuclear Engineering	M,D
Nurse Midwifery	M,D
Nursing—General	M,D
Optometry	M,D
Oral and Dental Sciences	M,D
Organic Chemistry	M,D
Paleontology	M,D
Paper and Pulp Engineering	M,D
Pharmaceutical Sciences	M,D
Pharmacology	M,D
Pharmacy	M,D
Philosophy	M,D
Physical Chemistry	M,D
Physics	M,D
Physiology	M,D
Plant Sciences	M,D
Political Science	M,D
Polymer Science and Engineering	M,D
Portuguese	D
Project Management	M
Psychology—General	M,D
Public Health—General	M,D
Religion	D
Social Sciences	M,D
Social Work	M,D
Sociology	M,D
Spanish	D
Statistics	M,D
Structural Biology	M,D
Structural Engineering	M,D
Supply Chain Management	M
Textile Design	M,D
Theater	D
Theology	D
Theoretical Chemistry	M,D
Theoretical Physics	M,D
Toxicology	M,D
Translation and Interpretation	M,D
Vision Sciences	M,D
Writing	D

UNIVERSITY OF MANITOBA

Adult Education	M
Agricultural Economics and Agribusiness	M,D
Agricultural Sciences—General	M,D
Agronomy and Soil Sciences	M,D
Allopathic Medicine	M
American Indian/Native American Studies	M
Anatomy	M,D
Animal Sciences	M,D
Anthropology	M,D
Architecture	M
Archives/Archival Administration	M,D
Biochemistry	M,D
Biological and Biomedical Sciences—General	M,D,O
Biosystems Engineering	M,D
Botany	M,D
Business Administration and Management—General	M,D
Canadian Studies	M
Cancer Biology/Oncology	M
Chemistry	M,D
Civil Engineering	M,D
Classics	M
Clinical Psychology	M,D
Community Health	M,D,O
Computational Sciences	M
Computer Engineering	M,D
Computer Science	M,D
Counselor Education	M
Curriculum and Instruction	M
Dentistry	D
Disability Studies	M
Ecology	M,D
Economics	M,D
Education—General	M,D
Educational Leadership and Administration	M
Educational Psychology	M
Electrical Engineering	M,D
Engineering and Applied Sciences—General	M,D
English as a Second Language	M
English Education	M
English	M,D
Entomology	M,D
Environmental Sciences	M,D
Food Science and Technology	M,D
Foundations and Philosophy of Education	M
French	M,D
Genetic Counseling	M,D
Geography	M,D
Geology	M,D
Geophysics	M,D
German	M
Higher Education	M
History	M,D
Horticulture	M,D
Human Genetics	M,D
Immunology	M,D
Industrial/Management Engineering	M,D
Infectious Diseases	M,D
Interdisciplinary Studies	M,D
Interior Design	M
Kinesiology and Movement Studies	M
Landscape Architecture	M
Law	M
Linguistics	M,D
Manufacturing Engineering	M,D
Maternal and Child Health	M
Mathematics	M,D
Mechanical Engineering	M,D
Medical Microbiology	M,D
Microbiology	M,D
Music	M
Natural Resources	M,D
Northern Studies	M
Nursing—General	M
Nutrition	M,D
Occupational Therapy	M,D
Oral and Dental Sciences	M,D
Pathology	M
Pharmaceutical Sciences	M,D
Pharmacology	M,D
Philosophy	M
Physical Education	M
Physical Therapy	M,D
Physics	M,D
Physiology	M,D
Plant Physiology	M,D
Plant Sciences	M,D
Political Science	M
Psychoanalysis and Psychotherapy	M
Psychology—General	M,D
Public Administration	M
Recreation and Park Management	M
Rehabilitation Sciences	M,D
Religion	M,D
School Psychology	M,D
Slavic Languages	M
Social Work	M,D
Sociology	M,D
Special Education	M
Statistics	M,D
Urban and Regional Planning	M
Zoology	M,D

UNIVERSITY OF MARY

Bioethics	M
Business Administration and Management—General	M
Cardiovascular Sciences	M
Curriculum and Instruction	M,D
Education—General	M,D
Educational Leadership and Administration	M,D
Energy Management and Policy	M
Exercise and Sports Science	M
Family Nurse Practitioner Studies	M,D
Health Services Management and Hospital Administration	M
Human Resources Management	M
Kinesiology and Movement Studies	M
Nursing and Healthcare Administration	M,D
Nursing Education	M,D
Nursing—General	M,D
Occupational Therapy	M
Physical Education	M
Physical Therapy	D
Project Management	M
Reading Education	M,D
Special Education	M,D
Sports Management	M

UNIVERSITY OF MARY HARDIN-BAYLOR

Accounting	M
Business Administration and Management—General	M
Clinical Psychology	M
Counseling Psychology	M
Counselor Education	M
Curriculum and Instruction	M,D
Education—General	M,D
Educational Leadership and Administration	M,D
Elementary Education	M,D
Exercise and Sports Science	M
Family Nurse Practitioner Studies	M,D,O
Higher Education	M,D
International Business	M
Management Information Systems	M
Marriage and Family Therapy	M
Nursing Education	M,D,O
Nursing—General	M,D,O
Physical Therapy	D
Secondary Education	M,D
Sports Management	M

UNIVERSITY OF MARYLAND, BALTIMORE

Allied Health—General	M
Allopathic Medicine	D
Biochemistry	M,D
Biological and Biomedical Sciences—General	M,D,O
Biostatistics	M,D
Cancer Biology/Oncology	D
Cell Biology	M,D
Clinical Laboratory Sciences/Medical Technology	M
Clinical Research	M,D,O
Community Health Nursing	M,D,O
Dentistry	D,O
Environmental Sciences	M,D
Epidemiology	M,D,O
Ethics	O
Family Nurse Practitioner Studies	M,D,O
Forensic Sciences	M
Genetic Counseling	M
Genomic Sciences	M,D
Gerontological Nursing	M,D,O
Gerontology	M,D
Health Services Research	M,D
Human Genetics	M,D
Immunology	D
International Health	M,D,O
Law	M,D
Marine Sciences	M,D
Maternal and Child/Neonatal Nursing	M,D,O
Microbiology	D
Molecular Biology	M,D
Molecular Medicine	D
Neurobiology	D
Neuroscience	D
Nurse Anesthesia	M,D,O
Nursing and Healthcare Administration	M,D,O
Nursing Education	M,D,O
Nursing Informatics	M,D,O
Nursing—General	M,D,O
Oral and Dental Sciences	M,D,O
Pathology	M
Pediatric Nursing	M,D,O
Pharmaceutical Administration	M,D
Pharmaceutical Sciences	D
Pharmacology	M,D
Pharmacy	M,D
Physical Therapy	D
Psychiatric Nursing	M,D,O
Rehabilitation Sciences	D
Social Work	M,D
Thanatology	O
Toxicology	M,D

UNIVERSITY OF MARYLAND, BALTIMORE COUNTY

Applied Mathematics	M,D
Applied Psychology	D
Art Education	M
Atmospheric Sciences	M,D
Biochemical Engineering	M,D,O
Biological and Biomedical Sciences—General	M,D
Biostatistics	M,D
Biotechnology	M,O
Cell Biology	D
Chemical Engineering	M,D
Chemistry	M,D,O
Clinical Psychology	M,D
Cognitive Sciences	D
Communication—General	M
Computer and Information Systems Security	M,O
Computer Art and Design	M
Computer Engineering	M,D
Computer Science	M,D
Dance	M
Data Science/Data Analytics	M
Developmental Psychology	D
Distance Education Development	M,O
Early Childhood Education	M
Economics	M,D
Education—General	M,O
Educational Media/Instructional Technology	M,O
Educational Policy	M,D

Electrical Engineering	M,D
Elementary Education	M
Emergency Management	M,D,O
Engineering and Applied Sciences—General	M,D,O
Engineering Management	M,O
English as a Second Language	M,O
English Education	M
English	M
Environmental Engineering	M,D
Environmental Management and Policy	M,D
Environmental Sciences	M,D
Epidemiology	M,D,O
Foreign Languages Education	M
Geographic Information Systems	M,O
Geography	M,D
Gerontology	M,D
Health Informatics	M
Health Services Management and Hospital Administration	M,D,O
History	M
Human Services	M,D
Industrial and Organizational Psychology	M
Information Science	M,D
Linguistics	M
Management of Technology	M
Marine Sciences	M,D
Mathematics Education	M
Mechanical Engineering	M,D
Mechanics	O
Molecular Biology	M,D
Multilingual and Multicultural Education	M,D
Music Education	M
Music	O
Neuroscience	D
Nonprofit Management	M,O
Physics	M,D
Psychology—General	M,D
Public History	M,D
Public Policy	M,D,O
Science Education	M
Social Psychology	M,D
Social Sciences Education	M
Social Sciences	D
Sociology	M
Statistics	M,D
Systems Engineering	M,O
Theater	M
Urban Studies	M,D

UNIVERSITY OF MARYLAND, COLLEGE PARK

Advertising and Public Relations	M,D
Aerospace/Aeronautical Engineering	M,D
Agricultural Economics and Agribusiness	M,D
Agricultural Sciences—General	M,D
American Studies	M,D
Analytical Chemistry	M,D
Animal Sciences	M,D
Anthropology	M
Applied Mathematics	M,D
Architecture	M
Art History	M,D
Art Therapy	M,D,O
Art/Fine Arts	M
Astronomy	M,D
Biochemistry	M,D
Bioengineering	M,D
Bioinformatics	D
Biological and Biomedical Sciences—General	M,D
Biophysics	D
Biostatistics	M,D
Broadcast Journalism	M,D
Business Administration and Management—General	M,D
Cell Biology	M,D
Chemical Engineering	M,D
Chemical Physics	M,D
Chemistry	M,D
Child and Family Studies	M,D
Civil Engineering	M,D
Classics	M
Clinical Psychology	M,D
Cognitive Sciences	D
Communication Disorders	M,D
Communication—General	M,D
Comparative Literature	M,D
Computational Biology	D
Computer Engineering	M,D
Computer Science	M,D
Conservation Biology	M
Counseling Psychology	M,D,O
Counselor Education	M,D,O
Criminal Justice and Criminology	M,D
Curriculum and Instruction	M,D,O
Dance	M
Developmental Psychology	M,D
Ecology	M,D
Economics	M,D
Education—General	M,D,O
Educational Leadership and Administration	M,D,O
Educational Measurement and Evaluation	M,D
Educational Media/Instructional Technology	M,D,O
Electrical Engineering	M,D
Engineering and Applied Sciences—General	M
English as a Second Language	M,D,O
English	M,D
Entomology	M,D
Environmental and Occupational Health	M
Environmental Engineering	M,D
Environmental Sciences	M,D
Epidemiology	M,D
Evolutionary Biology	M,D
Experimental Psychology	M,D
Family and Consumer Sciences-General	M,D
Fire Protection Engineering	M
Food Science and Technology	M,D
Foreign Languages Education	D
Foundations and Philosophy of Education	M,D,O
French	M,D
Genomic Sciences	D
Geography	M,D
Geology	M,D
German	M,D
Health Education	M,D
Health Services Management and Hospital Administration	M,D
Historic Preservation	M,O
History	M,D
Horticulture	M,D
Human Development	M,D
Industrial and Organizational Psychology	M,D
Information Studies	M,D
Inorganic Chemistry	M,D
Jewish Studies	M
Journalism	M,D
Kinesiology and Movement Studies	M,D
Landscape Architecture	M
Law	
Library Science	
Linguistics	M,D
Manufacturing Engineering	M,D
Marine Sciences	M,D
Marriage and Family Therapy	M,D
Materials Engineering	M,D
Materials Sciences	M,D
Maternal and Child Health	M,D
Mathematics	M,D
Mechanical Engineering	M,D
Mechanics	M,D
Media Studies	M,D
Meteorology	M,D
Molecular Biology	D
Molecular Genetics	M,D
Music Education	M,D
Music	M,D
Natural Resources	M,D
Neuroscience	M,D
Nuclear Engineering	M,D
Nutrition	M,D
Oceanography	M,D
Organic Chemistry	M,D
Philosophy	M,D
Physical Chemistry	M,D
Physics	M,D
Plant Biology	M,D
Political Science	D
Portuguese	M,D
Psychology—General	M,D
Public Administration	M
Public Health—General	M,D
Public Policy	M,D
Quantitative Analysis	M,D
Reading Education	M,D,O
Real Estate	M
Rehabilitation Counseling	M,D,O
Reliability Engineering	M,D
School Psychology	M,D,O
Secondary Education	M,D,O
Social Psychology	M,D
Social Work	
Sociology	M,D
Spanish	M,D
Speech and Interpersonal Communication	M,D
Statistics	M,D
Student Affairs	M,D,O
Survey Methodology	M,D
Sustainable Development	M
Systems Engineering	M
Telecommunications	M
Theater	M,D
Urban and Regional Planning	M,D
Veterinary Medicine	D
Veterinary Sciences	M,D
Women's Studies	M,D
Writing	M,D

UNIVERSITY OF MARYLAND EASTERN SHORE

Agricultural Sciences—General	M,D
Chemistry	M
Computer Science	M
Counselor Education	M
Criminal Justice and Criminology	M
Education—General	M
Educational Leadership and Administration	D
Environmental Management and Policy	M,D
Environmental Sciences	M,D
Fish, Game, and Wildlife Management	M,D
Food Science and Technology	M,D
Marine Sciences	M,D
Organizational Management	D
Pharmaceutical Sciences	M,D
Physical Therapy	D
Rehabilitation Counseling	M
Rehabilitation Sciences	M
Special Education	M
Toxicology	M,D
Vocational and Technical Education	M

UNIVERSITY OF MARYLAND UNIVERSITY COLLEGE

Accounting	M
Biotechnology	M,O
Business Administration and Management—General	M,D,O
Computer and Information Systems Security	M,O
Data Science/Data Analytics	M,O
Distance Education Development	M
Education—General	M
Educational Media/Instructional Technology	M
Environmental Management and Policy	M
Finance and Banking	M
Health Informatics	M
Health Services Management and Hospital Administration	M
Information Science	M

UNIVERSITY OF MARY WASHINGTON

Business Administration and Management—General	M
Education—General	M
Elementary Education	M

UNIVERSITY OF MASSACHUSETTS AMHERST

Accounting	M,D
Adult Nursing	M,D
African-American Studies	M,D
Agricultural Economics and Agribusiness	M,D
American Studies	M,D
Animal Behavior	M,D
Animal Sciences	M,D
Anthropology	M,D
Applied Mathematics	M,D
Architectural Engineering	M,D
Architecture	M
Art Education	M
Art History	M
Art/Fine Arts	M
Astronomy	M,D
Biochemistry	M,D
Biological and Biomedical Sciences—General	M,D
Biostatistics	M,D
Biotechnology	M,D
Business Administration and Management—General	M,D
Cell Biology	M,D
Chemical Engineering	M,D
Chemistry	M,D
Child and Family Studies	M,D,O
Chinese	M
Civil Engineering	M,D
Classics	M
Clinical Psychology	M,D
Cognitive Sciences	M,D
Communication Disorders	M,D
Communication—General	M,D
Community Health Nursing	M,D
Community Health	M,D
Comparative Literature	M,D
Computer Engineering	M,D
Computer Science	M,D
Conflict Resolution and Mediation/Peace Studies	M,D
Counselor Education	M,D,O
Developmental Biology	D
Developmental Psychology	M,D
Early Childhood Education	M,D,O
Economics	M,D
Education—General	M,D,O
Educational Leadership and Administration	M,D,O
Educational Measurement and Evaluation	M,D,O
Educational Media/Instructional Technology	M,D,O
Educational Policy	M,D,O
Electrical Engineering	M,D
Elementary Education	M,D,O
Engineering and Applied Sciences—General	M,D
English as a Second Language	M,D,O
English	M,D
Entertainment Management	
Entrepreneurship	M,D
Environmental and Occupational Health	M,D
Environmental Biology	M,D
Environmental Engineering	M,D
Environmental Management and Policy	M,D
Epidemiology	M,D
Evolutionary Biology	M,D
Family Nurse Practitioner Studies	M,D
Finance and Banking	M,D
Fish, Game, and Wildlife Management	M,D
Food Science and Technology	M,D
Foreign Languages Education	M
Forestry	M,D
French	M
Genetics	M,D
Geography	M,D
Geosciences	M,D
Geotechnical Engineering	M,D
German	M,D
Gerontological Nursing	M,D
Health Education	M,D
Health Services Management and Hospital Administration	M,D
Higher Education	M,D,O
Hispanic and Latin American Languages	M,D
Historic Preservation	M
History	M,D
Hospitality Management	M,D
Industrial and Labor Relations	M
Industrial/Management Engineering	M,D
Interior Design	M
International and Comparative Education	M,D,O
Italian	M
Japanese	M
Kinesiology and Movement Studies	M,D
Landscape Architecture	M
Linguistics	M,D
Management Strategy and Policy	M,D
Marine Sciences	M,D
Marketing	M,D
Mathematics	M,D
Mechanical Engineering	M,D
Mechanics	M,D
Microbiology	M,D*
Molecular Biophysics	D
Multilingual and Multicultural Education	M,D,O
Music Education	M,D
Music	M,D
Neuroscience	M,D
Nursing and Healthcare Administration	M,D
Nursing—General	M,D
Nutrition	M,D
Operations Research	M,D
Organizational Management	M,D
Philosophy	M,D
Physics	M,D
Physiology	M,D
Plant Biology	M,D
Plant Molecular Biology	M,D
Plant Physiology	M,D
Plant Sciences	M,D
Political Science	M,D
Polymer Science and Engineering	M,D
Portuguese	M,D
Psychology—General	M,D
Public Administration	M
Public Health—General	M,D
Public Policy	M
Reading Education	M,D,O
Rhetoric	M,D
Scandinavian Languages	M,D
School Psychology	M,D,O
Science Education	M,D,O
Secondary Education	M,D,O
Social Psychology	M,D
Sociology	M,D
Spanish	M,D
Special Education	M,D,O
Sports Management	M,D
Statistics	M,D
Structural Engineering	M,D
Sustainable Development	M
Theater	M
Transportation and Highway Engineering	M,D
Travel and Tourism	M,D
Urban and Regional Planning	M,D
Water Resources Engineering	M,D
Water Resources	M,D
Writing	M,D

UNIVERSITY OF MASSACHUSETTS BOSTON

Accounting	M
American Studies	M
Applied Economics	M
Applied Physics	M
Archaeology	M
Archives/Archival Administration	M
Biological and Biomedical Sciences—General	M,D
Biomedical Engineering	D
Biotechnology	M,D
Business Administration and Management—General	M
Business Analytics	M
Chemistry	M,D
Classics	M
Clinical Psychology	D
Cognitive Sciences	M
Computational Sciences	D
Computer Science	M,D
Conflict Resolution and Mediation/Peace Studies	M,O
Counseling Psychology	M,D
Counselor Education	M
Cultural Studies	M
Early Childhood Education	D
Education—General	M,D,O
Educational Leadership and Administration	M,D,O
Educational Media/Instructional Technology	M,O
Educational Policy	D
English	M
Environmental Sciences	M,D
Exercise and Sports Science	M,D
Finance and Banking	M
Gerontology	M,D,O
Higher Education	D
History	M
Human Services	M
International Affairs	M
International Business	M
International Development	M,D
Linguistics	M,D
Management Information Systems	M
Marine Sciences	M,D
Marriage and Family Therapy	M
Nursing—General	M,D
Public Administration	M
Public Policy	M,D

*M—masters degree; D—doctorate; O—other advanced degree; *—Close-Up and/or Display*

Quality Management	M,O
Rehabilitation Counseling	M
School Psychology	M,D
Sociology	M,D
Special Education	M
Urban and Regional Planning	M
Urban Education	D
Vision Sciences	M
Writing	M

UNIVERSITY OF MASSACHUSETTS DARTMOUTH

Accounting	M,O
Applied Behavior Analysis	M,O
Art Education	M
Art History	M
Art/Fine Arts	M,O
Biochemistry	M,D
Biological and Biomedical Sciences—General	M,D
Biomedical Engineering	D
Biotechnology	D
Business Administration and Management—General	M,O
Chemistry	M,D
Civil Engineering	M
Clinical Psychology	M,O
Community Health Nursing	M,D
Computer Engineering	M,D,O
Computer Science	M,O
Data Science/Data Analytics	M
Education—General	M,D,O
Educational Leadership and Administration	D
Educational Policy	M,D,O
Electrical Engineering	M,D,O
Engineering and Applied Sciences—General	D
English as a Second Language	M,D,O
Environmental Management and Policy	M,O
Experimental Psychology	M,O
Finance and Banking	M,O
Health Services Management and Hospital Administration	M
Industrial/Management Engineering	M,O
Latin American Studies	M,D
Law	D
Management of Technology	M
Marine Affairs	M,D
Marine Biology	M,D
Marine Sciences	M,D
Mathematics Education	M,D,O
Mechanical Engineering	M,O
Media Studies	M
Middle School Education	M,D,O
Nursing—General	M,D
Physics	M
Portuguese	M,D
Psychology—General	M,O
Public Administration	M,O
Public Policy	M,O
Science Education	M,D,O
Secondary Education	M,D,O
Software Engineering	M,O
Special Education	M,O
Systems Engineering	M,O
Telecommunications	M,D,O
Writing	M,O

UNIVERSITY OF MASSACHUSETTS LOWELL

Allied Health—General	M,D
Analytical Chemistry	M,D
Biochemistry	M,D
Biological and Biomedical Sciences—General	M
Business Administration and Management—General	M,D
Chemical Engineering	M,D
Chemistry	M,D
Civil Engineering	M,D
Clinical Laboratory Sciences/Medical Technology	M
Computer Engineering	M,D
Computer Science	M,D
Conflict Resolution and Mediation/Peace Studies	M
Criminal Justice and Criminology	M
Curriculum and Instruction	M
Economic Development	M,O
Economics	M,O
Education—General	M
Electrical Engineering	M,D
Energy and Power Engineering	M,D
Engineering and Applied Sciences—General	M,D
Entrepreneurship	M,D
Environmental Engineering	M,D
Environmental Sciences	M,D
Family Nurse Practitioner Studies	M
Gerontological Nursing	M
Health Physics/Radiological Health	M
Health Promotion	D
Industrial/Management Engineering	D
Inorganic Chemistry	M,D
Legal and Justice Studies	M
Mathematics	D
Mechanical Engineering	M,D
Music Education	M
Music	M
Nuclear Engineering	M,D
Nursing—General	M,D
Organic Chemistry	M,D
Physical Therapy	D
Physics	M,D
Polymer Science and Engineering	M,D
Psychology—General	M
Social Psychology	M
Sociology	M,O
Urban and Regional Planning	M,O

UNIVERSITY OF MASSACHUSETTS MEDICAL SCHOOL

Adult Nursing	M,D,O
Allopathic Medicine	D
Biochemistry	M,D
Bioinformatics	M,D
Biological and Biomedical Sciences—General	M,D
Cancer Biology/Oncology	M,D
Clinical Research	M,D
Computational Biology	M,D
Family Nurse Practitioner Studies	M,D,O
Gerontological Nursing	M,D,O
Health Services Research	M,D
Immunology	M,D
Interdisciplinary Studies	M,D
Microbiology	M,D
Molecular Pharmacology	M,D
Neuroscience	M,D
Nursing and Healthcare Administration	M,D,O
Nursing Education	M,D,O
Nursing—General	M,D,O
Translational Biology	M,D

UNIVERSITY OF MEMPHIS

Accounting	M,D
Adult Education	M,D,O
African-American Studies	M,D,O
Allied Health—General	M,O
Analytical Chemistry	M,D
Anthropology	M
Applied Behavior Analysis	M,D,O
Applied Mathematics	M,D
Applied Statistics	M,D
Archaeology	M,D,O
Architecture	M
Art History	M,O
Art/Fine Arts	M,O
Bioinformatics	M,D
Biological and Biomedical Sciences—General	M,D
Biomedical Engineering	M,D
Biostatistics	M,D
Business Administration and Management—General	M,D
Chemistry	M,D
Civil Engineering	M,D,O
Clinical Psychology	M,D,O
Communication Disorders	M,D
Communication—General	M,D
Community College Education	M,D,O
Comparative Literature	M,D,O
Computational Sciences	M
Computer Engineering	M,D,O
Computer Science	M,D
Counseling Psychology	M,D
Counselor Education	M,D
Criminal Justice and Criminology	M
Curriculum and Instruction	M,D,O
Early Childhood Education	M,D,O
Economics	M,D
Education—General	M,D,O
Educational Leadership and Administration	M,D,O
Educational Measurement and Evaluation	M,D
Educational Media/Instructional Technology	M,D,O
Educational Psychology	M,D
Electrical Engineering	M,D,O
Electronic Materials	M,O
Elementary Education	M,D,O
Energy and Power Engineering	M,D,O
Engineering and Applied Sciences—General	M,D,O
English as a Second Language	M,D,O
English	M,D,O
Environmental and Occupational Health	M,D
Environmental Engineering	M,D,O
Epidemiology	M,D
Exercise and Sports Science	M,O
Experimental Psychology	M,D,O
Family Nurse Practitioner Studies	M,O
Film, Television, and Video Production	M,D
Finance and Banking	M,D
French	M
Gender Studies	O
Geographic Information Systems	M,D,O
Geography	M,D,O
Geology	M,D,O
Geophysics	M,D,O
Geotechnical Engineering	M,D,O
Graphic Design	M,O
Health Promotion	M,O
Health Services Management and Hospital Administration	M,D
Higher Education	M,D,O
History	M,D
Hospitality Management	M,D
Human Resources Management	M,O
Inorganic Chemistry	M,D
Interdisciplinary Studies	M,D,O
Journalism	M,O
Law	D
Liberal Studies	M,O
Linguistics	M,D,O
Management Information Systems	M,D,O
Management Strategy and Policy	M,D
Marketing	M,D
Mathematics Education	M,D
Mathematics	M,D,O
Mechanical Engineering	M,D,O
Museum Studies	M,O
Music Education	M,D
Music	M,D
Near and Middle Eastern Studies	M,D
Nonprofit Management	M,O
Nursing and Healthcare Administration	M,O
Nursing Education	M,O
Nursing—General	M,O
Nutrition	M,O
Organic Chemistry	M,D
Philosophy	M,D
Photography	M,O
Physical Chemistry	M,D
Physical Education	M,O
Physics	M
Political Science	M
Psychology—General	M,D,O
Public Administration	M,D
Public Health—General	M,D
Public Policy	M,O
Reading Education	M,D,O
Real Estate	M,D
Rehabilitation Counseling	M,D
School Psychology	M,D,O
Science Education	M,D,O
Secondary Education	M,D,O
Social Sciences	M,D
Social Work	M
Sociology	M
Spanish	M
Special Education	M,D,O
Statistics	M,D
Structural Engineering	M,D,O
Supply Chain Management	M,D
Theater	M
Transportation and Highway Engineering	M,D,O
Urban and Regional Planning	M
Urban Education	M,D,O
Water Resources Engineering	M,D,O
Writing	M,D,O

UNIVERSITY OF MIAMI

Acute Care/Critical Care Nursing	M,D
Adult Nursing	M,D
Advertising and Public Relations	M,D
Aerospace/Aeronautical Engineering	M,D
Allopathic Medicine	D
Architectural Engineering	M,D
Architecture	M
Art History	M
Art/Fine Arts	M
Athletic Training and Sports Medicine	M,D
Biochemistry	D
Biological and Biomedical Sciences—General	M,D
Biomedical Engineering	M,D
Biophysics	D
Broadcast Journalism	M,D
Business Administration and Management—General	M,D
Cancer Biology/Oncology	D
Cell Biology	D
Chemistry	M,D
Civil Engineering	M,D
Clinical Psychology	M,D
Communication—General	M,D
Community Health	D
Computer Engineering	M,D
Computer Science	M,D
Counseling Psychology	D
Counselor Education	M,O
Developmental Biology	D
Developmental Psychology	M,D
Early Childhood Education	M,O
Education—General	M,D,O
Educational Measurement and Evaluation	M,D
Electrical Engineering	M,D
Engineering and Applied Sciences—General	M,D
English	M,D
Environmental and Occupational Health	M
Epidemiology	M,D
Ergonomics and Human Factors	M
Evolutionary Biology	M,D
Exercise and Sports Science	M,D
Family Nurse Practitioner Studies	M,D
Film, Television, and Video Production	M,D
Film, Television, and Video Theory and Criticism	M,D
Fish, Game, and Wildlife Management	M,D
French	D
Genetics	M,D
Geography	M,D
Geophysics	M,D
Graphic Design	M
Higher Education	M,D,O
History	M,D
Immunology	D
Industrial/Management Engineering	M,D
Inorganic Chemistry	M,D
International Affairs	M,D
Internet and Interactive Multimedia	M
Journalism	M,D
Latin American Studies	M
Law	M,D*
Liberal Studies	M
Management of Technology	M,D
Marine Affairs	M
Marine Biology	M,D
Marine Geology	M,D
Marine Sciences	M,D
Marriage and Family Therapy	M,O
Mathematical and Computational Finance	M,D
Mathematics Education	D
Mathematics	M,D
Mechanical Engineering	M,D
Meteorology	M,D
Microbiology	D
Molecular Biology	D
Multilingual and Multicultural Education	D
Music Education	M,D,O
Music	M,D,O
Neuroscience	M,D
Nurse Anesthesia	M,D
Nurse Midwifery	M,D
Nursing—General	M,D
Nutrition	M
Oceanography	M,D
Organic Chemistry	M,D
Pharmacology	D
Philosophy	M,D
Photography	M
Physical Chemistry	M,D
Physical Therapy	D
Physics	M,D
Physiology	D
Political Science	M
Psychology—General	M,D
Public Health—General	M,D
Reading Education	D
Real Estate	M,D
Romance Languages	D
Science Education	D
Sociology	M,D
Spanish	M,D
Special Education	M,D,O
Sports and Entertainment Law	M,D
Sports Management	M
Taxation	M,D
Therapies—Dance, Drama, and Music	M,D,O
Urban Design	M
Writing	M,D

UNIVERSITY OF MICHIGAN

Accounting	M,D
Aerospace/Aeronautical Engineering	M,D
African Studies	M
Allopathic Medicine	D
American Studies	M,D
Analytical Chemistry	M,D
Anthropology	D
Applied Arts and Design—General	M,D
Applied Economics	M
Applied Physics	D
Applied Statistics	M,D
Archaeology	M,D
Architecture	M
Art History	M,D
Art/Fine Arts	M
Artificial Intelligence/Robotics	M,D
Asian Languages	D
Asian Studies	M,D,O
Astronomy	D
Astrophysics	D
Atmospheric Sciences	M,D
Automotive Engineering	M,D
Biochemistry	M,D
Bioinformatics	M,D
Biological and Biomedical Sciences—General	M,D
Biomedical Engineering	M,D
Biophysics	D
Biopsychology	D
Biostatistics	M,D
Business Administration and Management—General	M,D
Cancer Biology/Oncology	M,D
Cell Biology	M,D
Chemical Engineering	M,D,O
Chemistry	M,D
Civil Engineering	M,D,O
Classics	M,D,O
Clinical Psychology	D
Clinical Research	M
Cognitive Sciences	D
Communication—General	D
Comparative Literature	D
Computer Engineering	M,D
Computer Science	M,D
Construction Engineering	M,D,O
Cultural Anthropology	D
Dance	M
Data Science/Data Analytics	M,D,O
Dental Hygiene	M,O
Dentistry	D
Developmental Biology	M,D
Developmental Psychology	D
East European and Russian Studies	M,O
Ecology	M,D
Economics	M,D
Education—General	M,D
Electrical Engineering	M,D
Energy and Power Engineering	M,D
Engineering and Applied Sciences—General	M,D,O
Engineering Design	M,D
English Education	D
English	M,D,O
Environmental and Occupational Health	M,D,O
Environmental Engineering	M,D,O
Environmental Management and Policy	M,D
Environmental Sciences	M,D
Epidemiology	M,D
Evolutionary Biology	M,D
Film, Television, and Video Theory and Criticism	D,O
Foreign Languages Education	M,D
French	D
Genetic Counseling	M,D
Geosciences	M,D
German	M,D,O
Health Education	M,D
Health Informatics	M,D
Health Physics/Radiological Health	M,D,O
Health Promotion	M,D

Health Services Management and Hospital Administration	M,D
History	D,O
Human Genetics	M,D
Immunology	M,D
Industrial Hygiene	M,D
Industrial/Management Engineering	M,D
Information Science	M,D*
Information Studies	M,D
Inorganic Chemistry	M,D
International Health	M,D
Italian	D
Jewish Studies	M,D,O
Kinesiology and Movement Studies	M,D
Landscape Architecture	M
Law	M,D
Linguistics	D
Manufacturing Engineering	M,D
Materials Engineering	M,D
Materials Sciences	M,D
Mathematics	M,D
Mechanical Engineering	M,D
Media Studies	M
Medicinal and Pharmaceutical Chemistry	D
Microbiology	M,D
Molecular Biology	M,D
Molecular Pathology	D
Music Education	M,D,O
Music	M,D,O
Natural Resources	M,D
Near and Middle Eastern Languages	M,D
Near and Middle Eastern Studies	M,D
Neuroscience	D
Nuclear Engineering	M,D,O
Nursing—General	M,D,O
Nutrition	M,D
Ocean Engineering	M,D,O
Operations Research	M,D
Oral and Dental Sciences	M,D
Organic Chemistry	M,D
Pathology	D
Pediatric Nursing	M,D,O
Pharmaceutical Administration	D
Pharmaceutical Engineering	M,D
Pharmaceutical Sciences	D
Pharmacology	M,D
Pharmacy	D
Philosophy	M,D
Physical Chemistry	M,D
Physics	D
Physiology	M,D
Planetary and Space Sciences	M,D
Political Science	D
Psychology—General	D,O
Public Health—General	M,D
Public Policy	M,D
Quantitative Analysis	M,D
Religion	M,D
Risk Management	M,D
Slavic Languages	M,D
Social Psychology	D
Social Sciences	D
Social Work	M
Sociology	D
Spanish	D
Sports Management	M,D
Statistics	M,D,O
Structural Engineering	M,D,O
Supply Chain Management	M,D
Survey Methodology	M,D,O
Sustainable Development	M,D
Systems Engineering	M,D
Systems Science	M,D
Taxation	M,D
Toxicology	M,D
Urban and Regional Planning	M,D
Urban Design	M
Women's Studies	D,O
Writing	M

UNIVERSITY OF MICHIGAN–DEARBORN

Accounting	M
Applied Behavior Analysis	M
Applied Mathematics	M
Automotive Engineering	M,D
Bioengineering	M
Business Administration and Management—General	M
Clinical Psychology	M
Computational Sciences	M
Computer and Information Systems Security	D
Computer Engineering	M,D
Computer Science	D
Criminal Justice and Criminology	M
Curriculum and Instruction	D,O
Data Science/Data Analytics	M,D
Early Childhood Education	M
Education—General	M
Educational Leadership and Administration	M,D,O
Educational Measurement and Evaluation	M
Educational Media/Instructional Technology	M
Electrical Engineering	M,D
Energy and Power Engineering	M
Engineering and Applied Sciences—General	M,D
Engineering Management	M
Environmental Sciences	M
Finance and Banking	M
Health Informatics	M
Health Psychology	M
Industrial/Management Engineering	M,D
Information Science	M,D
Management Information Systems	M
Manufacturing Engineering	M
Mechanical Engineering	M,D
Project Management	M
Public Administration	M
Science Education	M
Software Engineering	M,D
Special Education	M
Supply Chain Management	M
Systems Engineering	M,D
Urban Education	M,D

UNIVERSITY OF MICHIGAN–FLINT

Accounting	M,O
American Studies	M
Art/Fine Arts	M
Arts Administration	M
Biological and Biomedical Sciences—General	M
Business Administration and Management—General	M,O
Communication—General	M
Computer Science	M
Criminal Justice and Criminology	M
Curriculum and Instruction	M,D,O
Early Childhood Education	M,D,O
Education—General	M,D,O
Educational Leadership and Administration	M,D,O
Educational Media/Instructional Technology	M,D,O
English	M
Family Nurse Practitioner Studies	M,D,O
Finance and Banking	M,O
Gender Studies	M
Gerontology	M,D,O
Health Education	M
Health Informatics	M
Health Services Management and Hospital Administration	M,O
Industrial and Manufacturing Management	M,O
Information Science	M
International Affairs	M
International Business	M,O
Liberal Studies	M
Management Information Systems	M,O
Marketing	M,O
Mathematics	M
Mechanical Engineering	M
Museum Studies	M
Music	M
Neuroscience	D,O
Nonprofit Management	M
Nurse Anesthesia	D
Nursing—General	M,D,O
Organizational Management	M,O
Physical Therapy	D,O
Political Science	M
Psychiatric Nursing	M,D,O
Public Administration	M
Public Health—General	M
Reading Education	M,D,O
Rhetoric	M
Secondary Education	M,D,O
Social Sciences	M
Writing	M

UNIVERSITY OF MINNESOTA, DULUTH

Allopathic Medicine	D
Anthropology	M
Applied Mathematics	M
Art/Fine Arts	M
Biochemistry	M,D
Biological and Biomedical Sciences—General	M,D
Biophysics	M,D
Business Administration and Management—General	M
Chemistry	M
Communication Disorders	M
Computational Sciences	M
Computer Engineering	M
Computer Science	M
Criminal Justice and Criminology	M
Education—General	M,D
Electrical Engineering	M
Engineering Management	M
English	M
Geology	M,D
Graphic Design	M
Immunology	M,D
Liberal Studies	M
Medical Microbiology	M,D
Molecular Biology	M,D
Music Education	M
Music	M
Pharmacology	M,D
Pharmacy	M,D
Physics	M
Physiology	M,D
Safety Engineering	M
Social Work	M
Sociology	M
Toxicology	M,D

UNIVERSITY OF MINNESOTA ROCHESTER

Bioinformatics	M,D
Business Administration and Management—General	M,D
Computational Biology	M,D
Occupational Therapy	M,D

UNIVERSITY OF MINNESOTA, TWIN CITIES CAMPUS

Accounting	M,D
Adult Education	M,D,O
Aerospace/Aeronautical Engineering	M,D
Agricultural Sciences—General	M,D
Agronomy and Soil Sciences	M,D
Allopathic Medicine	M,D
American Studies	D
Animal Behavior	M,D
Animal Sciences	M,D
Anthropology	M,D
Applied Arts and Design—General	M,D,O
Applied Economics	M,D
Archaeology	M,D
Architecture	M
Art Education	M
Art History	M,D
Art/Fine Arts	M
Asian Languages	D
Asian Studies	D
Astrophysics	M,D
Biochemistry	D
Biological and Biomedical Sciences—General	M
Biomedical Engineering	M,D
Biophysics	M,D
Biopsychology	D
Biostatistics	M,D
Biosystems Engineering	M,D
Biotechnology	M
Business Administration and Management—General	M,D
Cancer Biology/Oncology	D
Cell Biology	M,D
Chemical Engineering	M,D
Chemical Physics	M,D
Chemistry	M,D
Child and Family Studies	M,D
Child Development	M,D
Civil Engineering	M,D,O
Classics	M,D
Clinical Laboratory Sciences/Medical Technology	M
Clinical Psychology	D
Clinical Research	M
Clothing and Textiles	M,D,O
Cognitive Sciences	D
Communication Disorders	M,D
Communication—General	M,D,O
Community Health	M
Comparative Literature	D
Computational Sciences	M,D
Computer and Information Systems Security	M
Computer Engineering	M,D
Computer Science	M,D
Conservation Biology	M,D
Counseling Psychology	D
Counselor Education	M
Cultural Studies	D
Curriculum and Instruction	M,D
Data Science/Data Analytics	M
Dentistry	D
Developmental Biology	M,D
Early Childhood Education	M,D,O
Ecology	M,D
Economics	M,D
Education of the Gifted	M,D,O
Education—General	M,D,O
Educational Leadership and Administration	M,D
Educational Measurement and Evaluation	M,D
Educational Media/Instructional Technology	M,D,O
Educational Policy	M,D
Educational Psychology	M,D,O
Electrical Engineering	M,D
Elementary Education	M
Engineering and Applied Sciences—General	M,D,O
English as a Second Language	M,D,O
English Education	M
English	M,D
Entomology	M,D
Entrepreneurship	D
Environmental and Occupational Health	M,D,O
Environmental Management and Policy	M,D
Epidemiology	M,D
Evolutionary Biology	M,D
Exercise and Sports Science	M,D
Family Nurse Practitioner Studies	M,D
Finance and Banking	M,D
Food Science and Technology	M,D
Foreign Languages Education	M
Forestry	M,D
Foundations and Philosophy of Education	M,D
French	M,D
Genetic Counseling	M,D
Genetics	M,D
Geographic Information Systems	M,D
Geography	M,D
Geological Engineering	M,D,O
Geology	M,D
Geophysics	M,D
German	M,D
Gerontological Nursing	M,D
Health Informatics	M,D
Health Services Management and Hospital Administration	M,D
Health Services Research	M,D
Higher Education	M,D
Hispanic and Latin American Languages	M,D
History of Medicine	M,D
History of Science and Technology	M,D
History	M,D
Human Resources Development	M,D,O
Human Resources Management	M
Hydrology	M,D
Immunology	D
Industrial and Labor Relations	M
Industrial and Organizational Psychology	D
Industrial Hygiene	M,D
Industrial/Management Engineering	M,D
Infectious Diseases	M,D
Interdisciplinary Studies	D
Interior Design	M,D,O
International and Comparative Education	M,D
International Development	M
International Health	M,D
Kinesiology and Movement Studies	M,D
Landscape Architecture	M
Law	M,D
Linguistics	M,D
Management Information Systems	M,D
Management of Technology	M
Management Strategy and Policy	D
Marketing	M,D
Marriage and Family Therapy	M,D
Mass Communication	M,D
Materials Engineering	M,D
Materials Sciences	M,D
Maternal and Child Health	M
Mathematics Education	M,D,O
Mathematics	M,D,O
Mechanical Engineering	M,D
Mechanics	M,D
Medical Physics	M,D
Medicinal and Pharmaceutical Chemistry	M,D
Medieval and Renaissance Studies	M,D
Microbiology	D
Molecular Biology	M,D
Multilingual and Multicultural Education	M,D,O
Music	M,D
Natural Resources	M,D
Neurobiology	M,D
Neuroscience	M,D
Nurse Anesthesia	M,D
Nurse Midwifery	M,D
Nursing and Healthcare Administration	M,D
Nursing Informatics	M,D
Nursing—General	M,D
Nutrition	M,D
Occupational Health Nursing	M,D
Oral and Dental Sciences	M,D,O
Paper and Pulp Engineering	M,D
Pediatric Nursing	M,D
Pharmaceutical Administration	M,D
Pharmaceutical Sciences	M,D
Pharmacology	M,D
Pharmacy	D
Philosophy	M,D
Physical Therapy	M,D
Physics	M,D
Physiology	D
Plant Biology	M,D
Plant Pathology	M,D
Plant Sciences	M,D
Political Science	D
Portuguese	M,D
Psychiatric Nursing	M,D
Psychology—General	D
Public Affairs	M,D
Public Health—General	M,D,O
Public Policy	M,D
Quantitative Analysis	M,D,O
Reading Education	M,D,O
Religion	M,D
Scandinavian Languages	M,D
School Psychology	M,D,O
Science Education	M
Social Psychology	D
Social Sciences Education	M
Social Work	M,D
Sociology	M,D
Software Engineering	M
Spanish	M,D
Special Education	M,D
Sports Management	M,D
Statistics	M,D
Structural Biology	D
Student Affairs	M
Supply Chain Management	M,D
Taxation	M
Technology and Public Policy	M
Textile Design	M,D,O
Theater	M,D
Toxicology	M,D
Travel and Tourism	M,D
Urban and Regional Planning	M,D
Veterinary Medicine	D
Veterinary Sciences	M,D
Virology	D
Vocational and Technical Education	M,D,O
Water Resources	M,D
Women's Health Nursing	M,D
Women's Studies	D

UNIVERSITY OF MISSISSIPPI

Accounting	M,D
Anthropology	M,D
Applied Science and Technology	M,D
Art/Fine Arts	M,D
Biological and Biomedical Sciences—General	M,D
Business Administration and Management—General	M,D
Chemical Engineering	M,D
Chemistry	M,D
Civil Engineering	M,D
Communication Disorders	M,D
Computer Science	M,D
Counselor Education	M,D,O
Criminal Justice and Criminology	M,D

*M—masters degree; D—doctorate; O—other advanced degree; *—Close-Up and/or Display*

Data Science/Data Analytics	M,D
Early Childhood Education	M,D,O
Economics	M,D
Education—General	M,D,O
Educational Leadership and Administration	M,D,O
Electrical Engineering	M,D
Elementary Education	M,D,O
Engineering and Applied Sciences—General	M,D
English	M,D
Environmental Engineering	M,D
Exercise and Sports Science	M,D
Experimental Psychology	M,D
Film, Television, and Video Production	M,D
Finance and Banking	M,D
Food Science and Technology	M,D
Foreign Languages Education	M,D
Geological Engineering	M,D
Geology	M,D
Health Promotion	M,D
Higher Education	M,D,O
History	M,D
Hospitality Management	M,D
Hydrology	M,D
Journalism	M
Kinesiology and Movement Studies	M,D
Law	M,D
Management Information Systems	M,D
Marketing	M,D
Mathematics Education	M,D,O
Mathematics	M,D
Mechanical Engineering	M,D
Medicinal and Pharmaceutical Chemistry	M,D
Music	M,D
Nutrition	M,D
Pharmaceutical Administration	M,D
Pharmaceutical Sciences	M,D
Pharmacology	M,D
Pharmacy	M,D
Philosophy	M,D
Physics	M,D
Political Science	M,D
Reading Education	M,D,O
Recreation and Park Management	M,D
Secondary Education	M,D,O
Social Work	M,D
Special Education	M,D,O
Taxation	M,D
Telecommunications	M,D
Toxicology	M,D
Writing	M,D

UNIVERSITY OF MISSISSIPPI MEDICAL CENTER

Allied Health—General	M
Allopathic Medicine	D
Anatomy	M,D
Biochemistry	D
Biological and Biomedical Sciences—General	M,D
Biophysics	D
Dentistry	M,D
Materials Sciences	M,D
Microbiology	D
Neuroscience	D
Nursing—General	M,D
Occupational Therapy	M
Oral and Dental Sciences	M,D
Pathology	D
Pharmacology	D
Physical Therapy	M
Physiology	D
Toxicology	D

UNIVERSITY OF MISSOURI

Accounting	M,D,O
Adult Education	M,D,O
Adult Nursing	M,D,O
Aerospace/Aeronautical Engineering	M,D
Agricultural Economics and Agribusiness	M,D
Agricultural Education	M,D,O
Agricultural Engineering	M,D
Agricultural Sciences—General	M,D
Allopathic Medicine	D
Analytical Chemistry	M,D
Anatomy	M,D
Animal Sciences	M,D
Anthropology	M,D
Applied Mathematics	M,D
Art Education	M,D,O
Art/Fine Arts	M
Astronomy	M,D
Biochemistry	M,D
Bioengineering	M,D
Bioinformatics	M
Biological and Biomedical Sciences—General	M,D
Business Administration and Management—General	M,D
Business Education	M,D,O
Chemical Engineering	M,D
Chemistry	D
Child and Family Studies	M,D
Civil Engineering	M,D
Clothing and Textiles	M,D
Communication Disorders	M,D
Communication—General	M,D
Community Health	M,D
Conflict Resolution and Mediation/Peace Studies	M,D
Consumer Economics	D
Counseling Psychology	M,D,O
Curriculum and Instruction	M,D,O
Early Childhood Education	M,D,O
Ecology	M,D
Economics	M,D
Education—General	M,D,O
Educational Leadership and Administration	M,D,O
Educational Media/Instructional Technology	D
Educational Psychology	M,D,O
Elementary Education	M,D,O
Engineering and Applied Sciences—General	M,D,O
English Education	M,D,O
English	M,D
Environmental Engineering	M,D
Evolutionary Biology	M,D
Family and Consumer Sciences-General	M,D,O
Family Nurse Practitioner Studies	M,D,O
Finance and Banking	M,D
Food Science and Technology	M,D
Foreign Languages Education	M,D,O
French	M,D
Geographic Information Systems	M,O
Geography	M,O
Geology	M,D
German	M
Gerontological Nursing	M,D,O
Health Communication	M,D
Health Education	M,D,O
Health Physics/Radiological Health	M
Health Services Management and Hospital Administration	M,D
Higher Education	M,D,O
History	M,D
Hospitality Management	M,D
Human Development	M,D
Immunology	D
Industrial/Management Engineering	M,D
Information Studies	D
Journalism	M,D
Law	M,D
Library Science	D
Manufacturing Engineering	M,D
Mathematics Education	M,D,O
Mathematics	M,D
Mechanical Engineering	M,D
Microbiology	D
Music Education	M,D,O
Music	M,D
Nonprofit Management	M,D,O
Nursing and Healthcare Administration	M,D,O
Nursing—General	M,D,O
Nutrition	M,D
Occupational Therapy	M
Organizational Management	M,D,O
Pathobiology	M,D
Pathology	M,D
Pediatric Nursing	M,D,O
Pharmacology	M,D
Philosophy	M,D
Physical Therapy	D
Physics	M,D
Physiology	M,D
Political Science	M,D,O
Psychiatric Nursing	M,D,O
Psychology—General	M,D,O
Public Administration	M,D,O
Public Affairs	M,D,O
Public Policy	M,D,O
Reading Education	M,D,O
Religion	M
Romance Languages	M,D
Rural Sociology	M,D
Russian	M
School Psychology	M,D,O
Science Education	M,D,O
Social Sciences Education	M,D,O
Sociology	M,D
Special Education	D
Statistics	M,D
Taxation	M,D,O
Theater	M,D
Veterinary Medicine	M,D
Veterinary Sciences	M
Vocational and Technical Education	M,D,O

UNIVERSITY OF MISSOURI–KANSAS CITY

Accounting	M,D
Adult Nursing	M,D
Allopathic Medicine	M,D
Analytical Chemistry	M,D
Art/Fine Arts	M,D
Biochemistry	D
Bioinformatics	M,D,O
Biological and Biomedical Sciences—General	M,D
Biophysics	D
Business Administration and Management—General	M,D
Cell Biology	D
Chemistry	M,D
Civil Engineering	M,D,O
Computer Engineering	M,D,O
Computer Science	M,D,O
Construction Engineering	M,D,O
Counseling Psychology	M,D,O
Counselor Education	M,D,O
Criminal Justice and Criminology	M
Curriculum and Instruction	M,D,O
Dental Hygiene	M,D,O
Dentistry	M,D,O
Economics	M,D
Education—General	M,D,O
Educational Leadership and Administration	M,D,O
Electrical Engineering	M,D,O
Engineering and Applied Sciences—General	M,D,O
Engineering Management	M,D,O
English	M,D
Family Nurse Practitioner Studies	M,D
Finance and Banking	M,D
French	M
Geosciences	M,D
Gerontological Nursing	M,D
Health Education	M,D
Higher Education	M,D,O
History	M,D
Inorganic Chemistry	M,D
Interdisciplinary Studies	D
Law	M,D
Maternal and Child/Neonatal Nursing	M,D
Mathematics	M,D
Mechanical Engineering	M,D,O
Molecular Biology	D
Music Education	M,D
Music	M,D
Nursing and Healthcare Administration	M,D
Nursing Education	M,D
Nursing—General	M,D
Oral and Dental Sciences	M,D,O
Organic Chemistry	M,D
Pediatric Nursing	M,D
Pharmacy	D
Physical Chemistry	M,D
Physics	M,D
Political Science	M
Polymer Science and Engineering	M,D
Psychology—General	M,D
Public Administration	M,D
Public Affairs	M,D
Reading Education	M,D,O
Romance Languages	M
Social Psychology	M,D
Social Work	M
Sociology	M
Software Engineering	M,D,O
Spanish	M
Special Education	M,D,O
Statistics	M,D
Telecommunications	M,D,O
Theater	M
Therapies—Dance, Drama, and Music	M,D
Women's Health Nursing	M,D

UNIVERSITY OF MISSOURI–ST. LOUIS

Accounting	M,D,O
Adult Education	M,O
Adult Nursing	D,O
American Studies	M,O
Applied Physics	M,D
Astrophysics	M,D
Biochemistry	M,D
Biological and Biomedical Sciences—General	M,D,O
Biotechnology	M,D
Business Administration and Management—General	M,D,O
Chemistry	M,D
Clinical Psychology	M,D,O
Communication—General	M
Computer and Information Systems Security	M,D,O
Computer Science	M,D
Counselor Education	D
Criminal Justice and Criminology	M,D
Curriculum and Instruction	M
Early Childhood Education	M
Economics	M
Education—General	M,D,O
Educational Leadership and Administration	D
Educational Measurement and Evaluation	M,O
Educational Policy	D
Educational Psychology	D
Elementary Education	M
English as a Second Language	M
English	M
Family Nurse Practitioner Studies	D,O
Gerontological Nursing	D,O
Higher Education	M,O
History	M,O
Human Resources Management	M,D,O
Logistics	M,D,O
Management Information Systems	M,D,O
Marketing Research	M,D,O
Marketing	M,D,O
Mathematics	M,D
Middle School Education	M
Museum Studies	M,O
Neuroscience	M,D,O
Nonprofit Management	M,O
Nursing—General	D,O
Optometry	D
Pediatric Nursing	D,O
Philosophy	M
Physics	M,D
Political Science	M,D
Psychiatric Nursing	D,O
Psychology—General	M,D,O
Public Administration	M,D,O
Public Policy	M,D,O
Reading Education	M
School Psychology	M,O
Secondary Education	M
Social Sciences Education	M
Social Work	M
Special Education	M
Supply Chain Management	M,D,O
Women's Health Nursing	D,O
Writing	M

UNIVERSITY OF MOBILE

Business Administration and Management—General	M
Education—General	M
Educational Leadership and Administration	M
Educational Policy	M
Marriage and Family Therapy	M
Nursing and Healthcare Administration	M,D
Nursing Education	M,D
Nursing—General	M,D

UNIVERSITY OF MONTANA

Accounting	M
Analytical Chemistry	M,D
Animal Behavior	M,D,O
Anthropology	M,D
Art Education	M
Art History	M
Art/Fine Arts	M
Biochemistry	D
Biological and Biomedical Sciences—General	M,D
Business Administration and Management—General	M
Cell Biology	D
Chemistry	M,D
Child and Family Studies	M,D,O
Clinical Psychology	M,D,O
Communication Disorders	M,O
Communication—General	M
Community Health	M
Computer Art and Design	M
Computer Science	M
Counseling Psychology	M,D,O
Counselor Education	M,D,O
Criminal Justice and Criminology	M
Cultural Studies	M,D,O
Curriculum and Instruction	M,D
Developmental Biology	D
Developmental Psychology	M,D,O
Early Childhood Education	M,D
Ecology	M,D
Economics	M
Education—General	M,D,O
Educational Leadership and Administration	M,D,O
English Education	M
English	M
Environmental Management and Policy	M
Environmental Sciences	M
Exercise and Sports Science	M
Experimental Psychology	M,D,O
Film, Television, and Video Production	M
Fish, Game, and Wildlife Management	M,D
Forestry	M,D
French	M
Geography	M
Geology	M,D
Geosciences	M,D
German	M
Health Education	M
History	M,D
Immunology	D
Inorganic Chemistry	M,D
Interdisciplinary Studies	M,D
Internet and Interactive Multimedia	M
Journalism	M
Law	D
Legal and Justice Studies	M
Linguistics	M
Mathematics Education	M,D
Mathematics	M,D
Medicinal and Pharmaceutical Chemistry	M,D
Microbiology	D
Molecular Biology	D
Music	M
Natural Resources	M,D
Neuroscience	M,D
Organic Chemistry	M,D
Pharmaceutical Sciences	M,D
Pharmacy	M,D
Philosophy	M
Photography	M
Physical Chemistry	M,D
Physical Education	M
Physical Therapy	D
Political Science	M
Psychology—General	M,D,O
Public Administration	M
Public Health—General	M,O
Recreation and Park Management	M,D
Rural Planning and Studies	M
Rural Sociology	M
School Psychology	M,D,O
Social Work	M
Sociology	M
Spanish	M
Theater	M
Toxicology	M,D
Writing	M
Zoology	M,D

UNIVERSITY OF MONTEVALLO

Business Administration and Management—General	M
Communication Disorders	M
Counselor Education	M
Education—General	M,O
Educational Leadership and Administration	M,O
Elementary Education	M
English	M
Secondary Education	M

UNIVERSITY OF MOUNT OLIVE

Business Administration and Management—General	M
Nursing—General	M

UNIVERSITY OF MOUNT UNION

Educational Leadership and Administration	M
Physical Therapy	D
Physician Assistant Studies	M

UNIVERSITY OF NEBRASKA AT KEARNEY

Accounting	M
Art Education	M

Biological and Biomedical Sciences—General M
Business Administration and Management—General M
Communication Disorders M
Counseling Psychology M,O
Counselor Education M,O
Curriculum and Instruction M
Early Childhood Education M
Education of the Gifted M
Education—General M,O
Educational Leadership and Administration M,O
Educational Media/Instructional Technology M
Elementary Education M
English as a Second Language M
English M
Exercise and Sports Science M
Foreign Languages Education M
History M
Human Resources Management M
Human Services M
Leisure Studies M
Library Science M
Management Information Systems M
Marketing M
Mathematics Education M
Music Education M
Physical Education M
Reading Education M
Recreation and Park Management M
School Psychology M,O
Science Education M
Secondary Education M
Special Education M,O
Sports Management M
Student Affairs M,O
Writing M

UNIVERSITY OF NEBRASKA AT OMAHA

Accounting M
Applied Behavior Analysis M,D,O
Art/Fine Arts M
Artificial Intelligence/Robotics M,O
Athletic Training and Sports Medicine M,D
Bioinformatics M,D
Biological and Biomedical Sciences—General M,O
Business Administration and Management—General M,O
Communication Disorders M
Communication—General M,O
Computer and Information Systems Security M,D,O
Computer Science M,D,O
Counselor Education M
Criminal Justice and Criminology M,D,O
Data Science/Data Analytics M,D,O
Economics M
Education—General M,D,O
Educational Leadership and Administration M,D,O
Elementary Education M,O
English as a Second Language M,O
English M,O
Exercise and Sports Science M,D
Foreign Languages Education M
Geographic Information Systems M,O
Geography M,O
Gerontology M,D,O
Health Education M,D
History M
Human Resources Development M,D,O
Industrial and Organizational Psychology M,D,O
Information Science M,D,O
Kinesiology and Movement Studies M,D
Management Information Systems M,D,O
Mathematics M,O
Music M
National Security M,O
Organizational Management M
Political Science M,O
Project Management M,D,O
Psychology—General M,D,O
Public Administration M,D,O
School Psychology M,D,O
Science Education M,O
Secondary Education M,O
Social Work M
Sociology M
Software Engineering M,O
Special Education M
Systems Engineering M,O
Technical Communication M,O
Urban Education M,O
Writing M,O

UNIVERSITY OF NEBRASKA–LINCOLN

Accounting M,D
Actuarial Science M
Adult Education M,D,O
Advertising and Public Relations M,D
Agricultural Economics and Agribusiness M,D
Agricultural Education M
Agricultural Engineering M,D
Agricultural Sciences—General M,D
Agronomy and Soil Sciences M,D
Analytical Chemistry M,D
Animal Sciences M,D
Anthropology M
Archaeology M,D
Architectural Engineering M,D
Architecture M,D
Art History M
Art/Fine Arts M
Astronomy M,D
Biochemistry M,D
Bioengineering M,D
Bioinformatics M,D
Biological and Biomedical Sciences—General M,D
Biomedical Engineering M,D
Biopsychology M,D
Business Administration and Management—General M,D
Chemical Engineering M,D
Chemistry M,D
Child and Family Studies M,D
Child Development M,D
Civil Engineering M,D
Classics M
Clinical Psychology M,D
Clothing and Textiles M,D
Cognitive Sciences M,D,O
Communication Disorders M,D
Communication—General M,D
Comparative Literature M,D
Computer Engineering M,D
Computer Science M,D
Consumer Economics M,D
Corporate and Organizational Communication M,D
Counseling Psychology M,D,O
Curriculum and Instruction M,D,O
Developmental Psychology M,D,O
Early Childhood Education M,D
Economics M,D
Educational Leadership and Administration M,D,O
Educational Measurement and Evaluation M,D,O
Educational Psychology M,D,O
Electrical Engineering M,D
Engineering and Applied Sciences—General M,D
Engineering Management M,D
English M,D
Entomology M,D
Environmental Engineering M,D
Exercise and Sports Science M,D
Family and Consumer Sciences-General M,D
Finance and Banking M,D
Food Science and Technology M,D
French M,D
Geography M,D
Geosciences M,D
German M,D
Gerontology M,D
Health Promotion M,D
History M,D
Home Economics Education M,D
Horticulture M,D
Human Development M,D,O
Industrial/Management Engineering M,D
Information Science M,D
Inorganic Chemistry M,D
Interior Design M,D
Journalism M
Law M,D
Legal and Justice Studies M
Management Information Systems M
Manufacturing Engineering M,D
Marketing M,D
Marriage and Family Therapy M,D
Mass Communication M
Materials Engineering M,D
Materials Sciences M,D
Mathematics M,D
Mechanical Engineering M,D
Mechanics M,D
Metallurgical Engineering and Metallurgy M,D
Music Education M,D
Music M,D
Natural Resources M,D
Nutrition M,D
Organic Chemistry M,D
Philosophy M,D
Physical Chemistry M,D
Physics M,D
Political Science M,D,O
Psychology—General M,D
Public Policy M,D,O
Rhetoric M,D
School Psychology M,D,O
Social Psychology M,D
Sociology M,D
Spanish M,D
Special Education M,D,O
Speech and Interpersonal Communication M,D
Statistics M,D
Survey Methodology M,D
Theater M
Toxicology M,D
Urban and Regional Planning M,D
Veterinary Sciences M,D
Vocational and Technical Education M,D,O
Writing M,D

UNIVERSITY OF NEBRASKA MEDICAL CENTER

Allied Health—General M,D,O
Allopathic Medicine D,O
Anatomy M,D
Applied Behavior Analysis M,D
Biochemistry M
Bioinformatics M,D
Biological and Biomedical Sciences—General M,D
Biostatistics D
Cancer Biology/Oncology D
Cell Biology M,D
Clinical Laboratory Sciences/Medical Technology M,O
Dentistry M,D,O
Emergency Management M
Environmental and Occupational Health D
Epidemiology D
Genetics M,D
Health Promotion D
Health Services Management and Hospital Administration M,D
Health Services Research M,D
Immunology M,D
Infectious Diseases M,D
Molecular Biology M
Molecular Genetics M,D
Molecular Medicine D
Neuroscience D
Nursing—General D
Nutrition O
Oral and Dental Sciences M,D
Pathology D
Perfusion M
Pharmaceutical Sciences M,D
Pharmacology D
Pharmacy D
Physical Therapy D
Physician Assistant Studies M
Physiology D
Public Health—General M
Toxicology D

UNIVERSITY OF NEVADA, LAS VEGAS

Accounting M,O
Addictions/Substance Abuse Counseling M,D,O
Aerospace/Aeronautical Engineering M,D,O
Allied Health—General M,D,O
Anthropology M,D
Applied Economics M,O
Architecture M,O
Art/Fine Arts M
Astronomy M,D
Biochemistry M,D
Biological and Biomedical Sciences—General M,D
Biomedical Engineering M,D,O
Business Administration and Management—General M,O
Chemistry M,D
Civil Engineering M,D
Clinical Psychology M,D,O
Communication—General M
Community Health M,D,O
Computer and Information Systems Security M,D,O
Computer Engineering M,D
Computer Science M,D
Construction Management M,O
Counseling Psychology M,D,O
Counselor Education M,D,O
Criminal Justice and Criminology M,D,O
Curriculum and Instruction M,D,O
Data Science/Data Analytics M,D,O
Dentistry M,D,O
Distance Education Development M,D,O
Early Childhood Education M,D,O
Economics M
Education—General M,D,O
Educational Leadership and Administration M,D,O
Educational Media/Instructional Technology M,D,O
Electrical Engineering M,D,O
Elementary Education M,D,O
Emergency Management M,D,O
Engineering and Applied Sciences—General M,D,O
English as a Second Language M,D,O
English M,D,O
Environmental Engineering M,D,O
Environmental Sciences M,D,O
Exercise and Sports Science M,D,O
Family Nurse Practitioner Studies M,D,O
Film, Television, and Video Production M,O
Geosciences M,D
Health Physics/Radiological Health M,D,O
Health Services Management and Hospital Administration M
Higher Education M,D,O
Hispanic Studies M,O
History M,D
Hospitality Management M,D
Journalism M
Kinesiology and Movement Studies M,D
Law M,D
Management Information Systems M,O
Marriage and Family Therapy M
Materials Engineering M,D,O
Mathematics M,D
Mechanical Engineering M,D,O
Media Studies M
Music M,D
Nonprofit Management M,D,O
Nuclear Engineering M,D,O
Nursing Education M,D,O
Nursing—General M,D,O
Nutrition M,D
Oral and Dental Sciences M,D,O
Physical Therapy D
Physics M,D
Political Science M,D
Psychology—General M,D,O
Public Administration M,D,O
Public Affairs M,D,O
Public Health—General M,D,O
Public Policy M,D,O
Secondary Education M,D,O
Social Work M
Sociology M,D
Special Education M,D,O
Theater M
Translation and Interpretation M,O
Transportation and Highway Engineering M,D
Water Resources M,D
Writing M,D,O

UNIVERSITY OF NEVADA, RENO

Accounting M
Agricultural Economics and Agribusiness M,D
Agricultural Sciences—General M,D
Allopathic Medicine D
Animal Sciences M
Anthropology M,D
Applied Economics M,D
Art/Fine Arts M
Atmospheric Sciences M,D
Biochemistry M,D
Biological and Biomedical Sciences—General M
Biomedical Engineering M,D
Biotechnology M
Business Administration and Management—General M
Cell Biology M,D
Chemical Engineering M,D
Chemical Physics D
Chemistry M,D
Child and Family Studies M
Civil Engineering M,D
Clinical Psychology D
Cognitive Sciences M,D
Communication Disorders M,D
Computer Engineering M,D
Computer Science M,D
Conservation Biology D
Counselor Education M,D,O
Criminal Justice and Criminology M
Curriculum and Instruction M
Ecology D
Economics M,D
Education—General M,D,O
Educational Leadership and Administration M,D,O
Educational Psychology M,D,O
Electrical Engineering M,D
Elementary Education M
Engineering and Applied Sciences—General M,D
English as a Second Language M
English M,D
Environmental and Occupational Health M,D
Environmental Management and Policy M
Environmental Sciences M,D
Evolutionary Biology D
Finance and Banking M
Foreign Languages Education M
French M
Geochemistry M,D
Geography M,D
Geological Engineering M,D
Geology M,D
Geophysics M,D
German M
History M,D
Human Development M
Hydrogeology M,D
Hydrology M,D
Journalism M
Legal and Justice Studies M,D
Management Information Systems M
Materials Engineering M,D
Mathematics Education M
Mathematics M
Mechanical Engineering M,D
Metallurgical Engineering and Metallurgy M,D
Mineral/Mining Engineering M
Molecular Biology M,D
Molecular Pharmacology D
Music M
Nursing—General M,D
Nutrition M
Philosophy M
Physics M,D
Physiology D
Political Science M,D
Psychology—General M,D
Public Administration M
Public Health—General M,D
Reading Education M,D
Secondary Education M,D
Social Psychology D
Social Work M
Sociology M
Spanish M
Special Education M,D
Speech and Interpersonal Communication M
Western European Studies D

UNIVERSITY OF NEW BRUNSWICK FREDERICTON

Anthropology M
Applied Economics M
Biological and Biomedical Sciences—General M,D
Business Administration and Management—General M
Chemical Engineering M,D
Chemistry M,D
Civil Engineering M,D
Classics M
Computer Engineering M,D
Computer Science M,D

*M—masters degree; D—doctorate; O—other advanced degree; *—Close-Up and/or Display*

Conflict Resolution and Mediation/Peace Studies	M
Construction Engineering	M,D
Economics	M
Education—General	M,D
Electrical Engineering	M,D
Engineering and Applied Sciences—General	M,D,O
Engineering Management	M
English	M,D
Entrepreneurship	M
Environmental Engineering	M,D
Environmental Management and Policy	M,D
Exercise and Sports Science	M
Forestry	M,D
Geodetic Sciences	M,D
Geology	M,D
Geotechnical Engineering	M,D
Health Services Research	M
History	M,D
Hydrology	M,D
Interdisciplinary Studies	M,D
International Development	M
Marketing	M,D
Materials Sciences	M,D
Mathematics	M,D
Mechanical Engineering	M,D
Mechanics	M,D
Nursing Education	M
Nursing—General	M
Physical Education	M
Physics	M,D
Political Science	M
Psychology—General	M,D
Public Administration	M
Public Policy	M
Recreation and Park Management	M
Sociology	M,D
Sports Management	M
Statistics	M,D
Structural Engineering	M,D
Surveying Science and Engineering	M,D
Sustainable Development	M
Transportation and Highway Engineering	M,D
Urban and Regional Planning	M,D
Water Resources	M,D

UNIVERSITY OF NEW BRUNSWICK SAINT JOHN

Biological and Biomedical Sciences—General	M,D
Business Administration and Management—General	M
Clinical Psychology	M,D
Electronic Commerce	M
Experimental Psychology	M,D
International Business	M
Natural Resources	M
Psychology—General	M,D

UNIVERSITY OF NEW ENGLAND

Biological and Biomedical Sciences—General	M
Curriculum and Instruction	M,D,O
Dentistry	D
Early Childhood Education	M,D,O
Education—General	M,D,O
Educational Leadership and Administration	M,D,O
Health Informatics	M,D,O
Health Services Management and Hospital Administration	M,D,O
Marine Sciences	M
Nurse Anesthesia	M,D
Nutrition	M,D,O
Occupational Therapy	M,D
Osteopathic Medicine	D
Pharmacy	D
Physical Therapy	M,D
Physician Assistant Studies	M,D
Public Health—General	M,D,O
Reading Education	M,D,O
Social Work	M,D,O
Vocational and Technical Education	M,D,O

UNIVERSITY OF NEW HAMPSHIRE

Accounting	M
Addictions/Substance Abuse Counseling	M,O
Agricultural Sciences—General	M,D
Animal Sciences	M,D
Applied Mathematics	M,D,O
Biochemistry	M,D
Biological and Biomedical Sciences—General	M,D
Business Administration and Management—General	M,O
Chemical Engineering	M,D
Chemistry	M,D
Child and Family Studies	M,O
Civil Engineering	M,D
Communication Disorders	M
Computer and Information Systems Security	M,O
Computer Science	M,D
Conservation Biology	M
Curriculum and Instruction	D,O
Early Childhood Education	M
Economic Development	M
Economics	M,D
Education—General	M,D,O
Educational Leadership and Administration	M,O
Educational Media/Instructional Technology	M,O
Electrical Engineering	M,D,O
Elementary Education	M,O
English	M,D
Environmental Engineering	M,D
Environmental Management and Policy	M
Evolutionary Biology	D
Family Nurse Practitioner Studies	M,D,O
Fish, Game, and Wildlife Management	M
Forestry	M
Genetics	M,D
Geographic Information Systems	O
Geology	M
Geosciences	M
Higher Education	O
History	M,D
Hydrology	M
Intellectual Property Law	M,D,O
Kinesiology and Movement Studies	M,O
Law	M,D,O
Legal and Justice Studies	M,D,O
Liberal Studies	M
Linguistics	M,D
Management Information Systems	M,O
Marine Biology	M,D
Marriage and Family Therapy	M,O
Materials Engineering	M,D
Materials Sciences	M,D
Mathematics Education	M,D,O
Mathematics	M,D,O
Mechanical Engineering	M,D
Microbiology	M,D
Museum Studies	M,D
Music	M
Natural Resources	M,D
Nursing—General	M,D,O
Nutrition	M,D
Occupational Therapy	M,O
Ocean Engineering	M,D,O
Oceanography	M,D,O
Physical Education	M,O
Physics	M,D
Political Science	M,O
Psychiatric Nursing	M,D,O
Psychology—General	D
Public Administration	M,O
Public Health—General	M,O
Public Policy	M
Quantitative Analysis	M,O
Recreation and Park Management	M
Science Education	M,D
Secondary Education	M,O
Social Work	M,O
Sociology	M,D
Spanish	M,O
Special Education	M,O
Sports and Entertainment Law	M,D,O
Sustainability Management	M,O
Water Resources	M
Women's Studies	O
Writing	M,D

UNIVERSITY OF NEW HAVEN

Accounting	M,O
Biomedical Engineering	M
Business Administration and Management—General	M*
Cell Biology	M
Civil Engineering	M
Computer and Information Systems Security	M
Computer Engineering	M
Computer Science	M,O
Conflict Resolution and Mediation/Peace Studies	M,O
Criminal Justice and Criminology	M,D,O*
Ecology	M
Electrical Engineering	M
Emergency Management	M,O
Engineering and Applied Sciences—General	M,O*
Engineering Management	M,O
Environmental and Occupational Health	M
Environmental Engineering	M
Environmental Management and Policy	M
Environmental Sciences	M
Facilities Management	M,O
Finance and Banking	M,O
Fire Protection Engineering	M,O
Forensic Psychology	M,O
Forensic Sciences	M,O
Geographic Information Systems	M,O
Geosciences	M
Hazardous Materials Management	M
Health Services Management and Hospital Administration	M,O
Human Resources Management	M,O
Industrial and Manufacturing Management	M,O
Industrial and Organizational Psychology	M,O*
Industrial/Management Engineering	M,O
International Business	M
Management Strategy and Policy	M
Marketing	M
Mechanical Engineering	M
Molecular Biology	M
National Security	M,O
Nonprofit Management	M,O
Nutrition	M,O
Organizational Management	M,O
Public Administration	M,O
Social Psychology	M,O*
Software Engineering	M,O
Sports Management	M,O
Taxation	M,O
Water Resources Engineering	M

UNIVERSITY OF NEW MEXICO

Accounting	M
Allied Health—General	M,D,O
Allopathic Medicine	D
American Indian/Native American Studies	M,D
American Studies	M,D
Anthropology	M,D
Archaeology	M,D
Architecture	M,D
Art Education	M
Art History	M,D
Art/Fine Arts	M
Biochemistry	M,D
Biological and Biomedical Sciences—General	M,D
Biomedical Engineering	M,D
Business Administration and Management—General	M
Cell Biology	M,D
Chemical Engineering	M,D
Chemistry	M,D
Child and Family Studies	M,D
Civil Engineering	M,D
Clinical Laboratory Sciences/Medical Technology	M,O
Clinical Psychology	D
Cognitive Sciences	D
Communication Disorders	M
Communication—General	M,D
Community Health	M
Comparative Literature	M,D
Computer and Information Systems Security	M
Computer Engineering	M,D
Computer Science	M,D
Construction Management	M,D
Counselor Education	M,D
Cultural Studies	M,D
Dance	M
Dental Hygiene	M
Developmental Psychology	D
Early Childhood Education	D
Economics	M,D
Education—General	M,D,O
Educational Leadership and Administration	M,D,O
Educational Media/Instructional Technology	M,D,O
Educational Psychology	M,D
Electrical Engineering	M,D
Elementary Education	M
Engineering and Applied Sciences—General	M,D
English as a Second Language	M,D
English Education	M,D
English	M,D
Entrepreneurship	M
Environmental Management and Policy	M
Epidemiology	M
Ethnic Studies	M,D
Exercise and Sports Science	D
Finance and Banking	M
Foundations and Philosophy of Education	M,D
French	M,D
Genetics	M,D
Geography	M
Geosciences	M,D
German	M,D
Health Education	M
Health Psychology	D
Health Services Management and Hospital Administration	M
Higher Education	O
Historic Preservation	O
History	M,D
Human Development	M,D
Human Resources Management	M
Information Science	M
International Business	M
International Development	M,D
International Economics	M,D
Landscape Architecture	M
Latin American Studies	M,D
Law	D
Linguistics	M,D
Management Information Systems	M
Management of Technology	M
Management Strategy and Policy	M
Manufacturing Engineering	M
Marketing	M
Mathematics	M,D
Mechanical Engineering	M,D
Microbiology	M,D
Molecular Biology	M,D
Multilingual and Multicultural Education	M,D
Music Education	M
Music	M
Nanotechnology	M,D
Natural Resources	M,D
Neuroscience	M,D
Nuclear Engineering	M,D
Nursing—General	M,D
Nutrition	M
Occupational Therapy	M
Optical Sciences	M,D
Organizational Behavior	M
Organizational Management	M
Pathology	M,D
Pharmaceutical Sciences	M,D
Pharmacy	D
Philosophy	M,D
Photography	M,D
Photonics	M,D
Physical Education	D
Physical Therapy	D
Physician Assistant Studies	M
Physics	M,D
Physiology	M,D
Planetary and Space Sciences	M,D
Political Science	M,D
Portuguese	M,D
Psychology—General	D
Public Administration	M
Public Health—General	M
Quantitative Analysis	D
Reading Education	M,D
Science Education	O
Secondary Education	M
Sociology	M,D
Spanish	M,D
Special Education	M,D,O
Sports Management	D
Statistics	M,D
Systems Engineering	M,D
Taxation	M
Theater	M
Toxicology	M,D
Urban and Regional Planning	M
Water Resources	M
Writing	M

UNIVERSITY OF NEW ORLEANS

Accounting	M
Art/Fine Arts	M
Arts Administration	M
Biological and Biomedical Sciences—General	M
Business Administration and Management—General	M
Chemistry	M,D
Civil Engineering	M
Computer Science	M,D
Counselor Education	M,D
Economics	D
Educational Leadership and Administration	M,D
Electrical Engineering	M
Engineering and Applied Sciences—General	M,D
Engineering Management	M
English	M
Environmental Sciences	M,D
Film, Television, and Video Production	M
Finance and Banking	M
Geosciences	M,D
Health Services Management and Hospital Administration	M
Higher Education	M,D
History	M
Hospitality Management	M
Mathematics	M
Mechanical Engineering	M
Music	M
Physics	M,D
Political Science	M,D
Psychology—General	M,D
Public Administration	M
Romance Languages	M
Sociology	M
Taxation	M
Theater	M
Transportation Management	M
Travel and Tourism	M
Urban and Regional Planning	M
Urban Studies	M,D
Writing	M

UNIVERSITY OF NORTH ALABAMA

Accounting	M
Business Administration and Management—General	M
Child and Family Studies	M
Clinical Psychology	M
Counselor Education	M
Criminal Justice and Criminology	M
Economic Development	M
Education—General	M,O
Educational Leadership and Administration	M,O
Elementary Education	M,O
English	M
Exercise and Sports Science	M
Finance and Banking	M
Geographic Information Systems	M
Health Promotion	M
Health Services Management and Hospital Administration	M
Higher Education	M
Historic Preservation	M
History	M
Information Science	M
Interdisciplinary Studies	M
International Business	M
Kinesiology and Movement Studies	M
Law	M
Management Information Systems	M
Nursing—General	M
Physical Education	M
Political Science	M
Project Management	M
Public History	M
Rhetoric	M
Secondary Education	M
Special Education	M
Technical Writing	M
Writing	M

UNIVERSITY OF NORTH CAROLINA AT ASHEVILLE

Cultural Studies	M,O
Liberal Studies	M,O
Sustainable Development	M,O

THE UNIVERSITY OF NORTH CAROLINA AT CHAPEL HILL

Accounting	M,D
Adult Nursing	M,D,O
Allied Health—General	M,D
Allopathic Medicine	D
Anthropology	M,D
Archaeology	M,D
Art History	M,D
Art/Fine Arts	M
Astronomy	M,D
Astrophysics	M,D
Athletic Training and Sports Medicine	M
Biochemistry	M,D
Bioinformatics	D
Biological and Biomedical Sciences—General	M,D

Biomedical Engineering	M,D
Biophysics	M,D
Biopsychology	D
Biostatistics	M,D
Botany	M,D
Business Administration and Management—General	M,D
Cell Biology	M,D
Chemistry	M,D
Classics	M,D
Clinical Psychology	D
Clinical Research	M,D
Cognitive Sciences	D
Communication Disorders	M,D
Communication—General	M,D,O
Computational Biology	D
Computer Science	M,D
Counselor Education	M
Curriculum and Instruction	M,D
Dental Hygiene	M,D
Dentistry	D
Developmental Biology	M,D
Developmental Psychology	D
Early Childhood Education	M,D
East European and Russian Studies	M
Ecology	M,D
Economics	M,D
Education—General	M,D
Educational Leadership and Administration	M,D
Educational Measurement and Evaluation	M,D
Educational Psychology	M,D
English as a Second Language	M
English Education	M
English	M,D
Environmental and Occupational Health	M,D
Environmental Engineering	M,D
Environmental Sciences	M,D
Epidemiology	M,D
Evolutionary Biology	M,D
Exercise and Sports Science	M
Family Nurse Practitioner Studies	M,D,O
Finance and Banking	D
Folklore	M
Foreign Languages Education	M
French	M,D
Genetics	M,D
Geography	M,D
Geology	M,D
German	D
Gerontological Nursing	M,D,O
Health Communication	M,D,O
Health Promotion	M
Health Psychology	M,D
Health Services Management and Hospital Administration	M,D
History	M,D
Immunology	M,D
Information Studies	M,D,O
International Affairs	M
Italian	M,D
Journalism	M,D,O
Kinesiology and Movement Studies	D
Latin American Studies	M,D,O
Law	M,D
Library Science	M,D,O
Linguistics	M
Management Information Systems	D
Management Strategy and Policy	D
Marine Sciences	M,D
Marketing	D
Maternal and Child Health	M,D
Mathematics Education	M
Mathematics	M,D
Media Studies	M,D,O
Microbiology	M,D
Molecular Biology	M,D
Molecular Physiology	D
Music Education	M
Music	M,D
Neurobiology	D
Neuroscience	D
Nursing and Healthcare Administration	M,D,O
Nursing Education	M,D,O
Nursing Informatics	M,D,O
Nursing—General	M,D,O
Nutrition	M,D
Occupational Health Nursing	M
Occupational Therapy	M,D
Operations Research	M,D
Oral and Dental Sciences	M,D
Organizational Behavior	D
Pathology	D
Pediatric Nursing	M,D,O
Pharmaceutical Administration	M,D
Pharmaceutical Sciences	M,D
Pharmacology	D
Pharmacy	M,D
Philosophy	M,D
Physical Education	M
Physical Therapy	D
Physics	M,D
Political Science	M,D,O
Portuguese	M,D
Psychiatric Nursing	M,D,O
Psychology—General	D
Public Administration	M
Public Health—General	M,D
Public Policy	D
Reading Education	M,D
Rehabilitation Counseling	M
Religion	M,D
Romance Languages	M,D
School Psychology	M,D
Science Education	M
Secondary Education	M
Slavic Languages	D
Social Psychology	D
Social Sciences Education	M
Social Work	M,D
Sociology	M,D
Spanish	M,D
Sports Management	M
Statistics	M,D
Telecommunications	M,D,O
Theater	M
Toxicology	M,D
Urban and Regional Planning	M,D

THE UNIVERSITY OF NORTH CAROLINA AT CHARLOTTE

Accounting	M
Acute Care/Critical Care Nursing	M,D,O
Addictions/Substance Abuse Counseling	M,D,O
African Studies	O
Anthropology	M
Applied Economics	M,O
Applied Mathematics	M,D
Applied Physics	M,D
Architecture	M
Art Education	M,D,O
Arts Administration	M,O
Bioinformatics	M,D,O
Biological and Biomedical Sciences—General	M,D
Business Administration and Management—General	M,D,O
Business Analytics	M,D,O
Business Education	D
Chemistry	M,D
Child and Family Studies	M,D,O
Child Development	M,D,O
Civil Engineering	M,D
Cognitive Sciences	M,D,O
Communication—General	M
Community Health	M,D,O
Computer and Information Systems Security	M,D,O
Computer Engineering	M,D
Computer Science	M,D
Construction Management	M,O
Counselor Education	M,D,O
Criminal Justice and Criminology	M
Cultural Studies	M,O
Curriculum and Instruction	M,D,O
Early Childhood Education	M,D,O
Economics	M,O
Education of the Gifted	M,D,O
Education—General	M,D,O
Educational Leadership and Administration	M,D,O
Educational Media/Instructional Technology	M,D,O
Electrical Engineering	M,D
Elementary Education	M,O
Emergency Management	M,O
Energy and Power Engineering	M,O
Engineering and Applied Sciences—General	M,D,O
Engineering Management	M,O
English as a Second Language	M,D,O
English	M,O
Environmental Engineering	M,D
Ethics	M,O
Facilities Management	M,O
Family Nurse Practitioner Studies	M,D,O
Finance and Banking	M,O
Fire Protection Engineering	M,O
Foreign Languages Education	M,D,O
Game Design and Development	M,O
Gender Studies	M,D,O
Geographic Information Systems	M,D
Geography	M,D
Geosciences	M,D
Gerontological Nursing	M,D,O
Gerontology	M,D,O
Health Informatics	M,O
Health Psychology	M,D,O
Health Services Management and Hospital Administration	M,D,O
Health Services Research	D
History	M
Industrial and Manufacturing Management	M,D,O
Industrial and Organizational Psychology	M,D,O
Information Science	M,D,O
Interdisciplinary Studies	M,D,O
Kinesiology and Movement Studies	M
Latin American Studies	M,D,O
Liberal Studies	M,D,O
Linguistics	M,O
Logistics	M,O
Management Information Systems	M,D,O
Mathematical and Computational Finance	M,O
Mathematics	M,D,O
Mechanical Engineering	M,D
Middle School Education	M,D,O
Music	O
Nonprofit Management	M,O
Nurse Anesthesia	M,D,O
Nursing and Healthcare Administration	M,D,O
Nursing Education	M,D,O
Nursing—General	M,D,O
Optical Sciences	M,D
Philosophy	M,O
Psychology—General	M,D,O
Public Administration	M,D,O
Public Health—General	M,D,O
Public Policy	M,D,O
Reading Education	M,O
Real Estate	M,O
Religion	M
Secondary Education	M,D,O
Social Work	M
Sociology	M
Spanish	M,O
Special Education	M,D,O
Supply Chain Management	M,O
Systems Engineering	M,D,O
Technical Writing	M,O
Theater	M,D,O
Urban and Regional Planning	M,O
Urban Design	M
Women's Studies	M,D,O
Writing	M,O

THE UNIVERSITY OF NORTH CAROLINA AT GREENSBORO

Accounting	M,O
Adult Education	M,D,O
Adult Nursing	M,D,O
Applied Economics	M
Architecture	M,O
Art/Fine Arts	M
Athletic Training and Sports Medicine	M,D
Biochemistry	M
Biological and Biomedical Sciences—General	M
Business Administration and Management—General	M,O
Chemistry	M
Child and Family Studies	M,D
Classics	M
Clinical Psychology	M,D
Cognitive Sciences	M,D
Communication Disorders	M,D
Communication—General	M
Community Health	M,D
Computer Science	M
Conflict Resolution and Mediation/Peace Studies	M,O
Counseling Psychology	M,D,O
Counselor Education	M,D,O
Criminal Justice and Criminology	M
Curriculum and Instruction	M,D,O
Dance	M
Developmental Psychology	M,D
Early Childhood Education	M,D,O
Economic Development	M,D,O
Economics	D
Education—General	M,D,O
Educational Leadership and Administration	M,D,O
Educational Measurement and Evaluation	D
Educational Media/Instructional Technology	M,D,O
Elementary Education	D
English as a Second Language	M,D,O
English Education	M,D
English	M,D
Film, Television, and Video Production	M
Finance and Banking	M,O
Foreign Languages Education	M,D,O
French	M
Gender Studies	M,O
Genetic Counseling	M
Geographic Information Systems	M,D,O
Geography	M,D,O
Gerontological Nursing	M,D,O
Gerontology	M,O
Higher Education	D
Hispanic and Latin American Languages	M,O
Hispanic Studies	M,O
Historic Preservation	M,O
History	M,D,O
Human Development	M,D
Information Studies	M
Interior Design	M,D
Kinesiology and Movement Studies	M,D
Liberal Studies	M
Library Science	M
Management Information Systems	M,D,O
Marketing	M,D
Marriage and Family Therapy	M,D,O
Mathematics Education	M,D,O
Mathematics	M,D
Media Studies	M
Middle School Education	M,D,O
Multilingual and Multicultural Education	M,D,O
Museum Studies	M,D,O
Music Education	M,D
Music	M,D
Nonprofit Management	M,O
Nurse Anesthesia	M,D,O
Nursing and Healthcare Administration	M,D,O
Nursing Education	M,D,O
Nursing—General	M,D,O
Nutrition	M,D
Political Science	M,O
Psychology—General	M,D
Public Affairs	M,O
Reading Education	M,D,O
Recreation and Park Management	M
Rhetoric	M,D
School Psychology	M,D,O
Science Education	M,D,O
Social Psychology	M,D
Social Sciences Education	M,D,O
Social Work	M
Sociology	M
Spanish	M,O
Special Education	M,D,O
Supply Chain Management	M,D,O
Technical Writing	M,D,O
Textile Design	M,D
Theater	M
Women's Studies	M,D,O
Writing	M

THE UNIVERSITY OF NORTH CAROLINA AT PEMBROKE

Art Education	M
Business Administration and Management—General	M
Counseling Psychology	M
Counselor Education	M
Criminal Justice and Criminology	M
Education—General	M
Educational Leadership and Administration	M
Elementary Education	M
Emergency Management	M
English Education	M
Exercise and Sports Science	M
Health Education	M
Health Services Management and Hospital Administration	M
Mathematics Education	M
Nursing and Healthcare Administration	M
Nursing Education	M
Nursing—General	M
Physical Education	M
Public Administration	M
Reading Education	M
Science Education	M
Social Sciences Education	M
Social Work	M
Sports Management	M

UNIVERSITY OF NORTH CAROLINA SCHOOL OF THE ARTS

Film, Television, and Video Production	M
Music	M,O
Theater	M

THE UNIVERSITY OF NORTH CAROLINA WILMINGTON

Accounting	M
Applied Behavior Analysis	M,D
Applied Statistics	M,O
Biological and Biomedical Sciences—General	M,D
Business Administration and Management—General	M
Chemistry	M
Clinical Psychology	M,D
Clinical Research	M,D,O
Computer Science	M
Conflict Resolution and Mediation/Peace Studies	M
Criminal Justice and Criminology	M
Curriculum and Instruction	M,D
Data Science/Data Analytics	M
Early Childhood Education	M
Education—General	M,D
Educational Leadership and Administration	M,D
Educational Media/Instructional Technology	M
Educational Policy	M
Elementary Education	M
English as a Second Language	M
English	M
Environmental Management and Policy	M
Environmental Sciences	M
Family Nurse Practitioner Studies	M,D,O
Geographic Information Systems	M,O
Geosciences	M,O
Gerontology	M
Higher Education	M,D
Hispanic Studies	M,O
History	M
International Business	M
Liberal Studies	M
Management Information Systems	M
Marine Biology	M,D
Marine Sciences	M,D,O
Mathematics	M,O
Middle School Education	M
Nursing Education	M,D,O
Nursing—General	M,D,O
Psychology—General	M,D
Public Administration	M
Reading Education	M
Secondary Education	M
Social Work	M
Sociology	M
Spanish	M,O
Special Education	M
Statistics	M,O
Writing	M

UNIVERSITY OF NORTH DAKOTA

Applied Economics	M
Art/Fine Arts	M
Astrophysics	M,D
Atmospheric Sciences	M,D
Aviation	M
Biological and Biomedical Sciences—General	M,D
Business Administration and Management—General	M
Chemical Engineering	M,D
Chemistry	M,D
Civil Engineering	M,D
Clinical Laboratory Sciences/Medical Technology	M,D
Clinical Psychology	M,D
Communication Disorders	M
Communication—General	D
Community Health Nursing	M,D,O
Computer Science	M
Counseling Psychology	M,D
Criminal Justice and Criminology	D
Early Childhood Education	M
Education—General	M,D,O

*M—masters degree; D—doctorate; O—other advanced degree; *—Close-Up and/or Display*

Educational Leadership and Administration	M,D,O
Educational Media/Instructional Technology	M
Electrical Engineering	M,D
Elementary Education	M
Engineering and Applied Sciences—General	D
English	M,D
Environmental Engineering	M,D
Family Nurse Practitioner Studies	M,D,O
Fish, Game, and Wildlife Management	M,D
Forensic Psychology	M,D
Genetics	M,D
Geographic Information Systems	M
Geography	M
Geological Engineering	M,D
Geology	M,D
Geosciences	M,D
Gerontological Nursing	M,D,O
History	M,D
Kinesiology and Movement Studies	M
Law	D
Linguistics	M
Mathematics	M
Mechanical Engineering	M,D
Music Education	M,D
Music	M,D
Nurse Anesthesia	M,D,O
Nursing Education	M,D,O
Nursing—General	M,D,O
Occupational Therapy	M
Physical Therapy	D
Physician Assistant Studies	M
Physics	M,D
Planetary and Space Sciences	M
Psychiatric Nursing	M,D,O
Psychology—General	M,D
Public Administration	M
Public Health—General	M
Reading Education	M
Social Work	M
Sociology	M
Special Education	M
Zoology	M,D

UNIVERSITY OF NORTHERN BRITISH COLUMBIA

Community Health	M,D,O
Computer Science	M,D,O
Disability Studies	M,D,O
Education—General	M,D,O
Environmental Management and Policy	M,D,O
Gender Studies	M,D,O
History	M,D,O
Interdisciplinary Studies	M,D,O
International Affairs	M,D,O
Mathematics	M,D,O
Natural Resources	M,D,O
Political Science	M,D,O
Psychology—General	M,D,O
Social Work	M,D,O

UNIVERSITY OF NORTHERN COLORADO

Accounting	M
Acute Care/Critical Care Nursing	M,D
Applied Statistics	M,D
Art Education	M
Art History	M
Art/Fine Arts	M
Biological and Biomedical Sciences—General	M
Business Administration and Management—General	M
Chemistry	M,D
Clinical Psychology	M
Communication Disorders	M,D
Communication—General	M
Community Health	M
Counseling Psychology	D
Counselor Education	M,D
Criminal Justice and Criminology	M
Curriculum and Instruction	M,D
Education of the Gifted	M,D
Education—General	M,D,O
Educational Leadership and Administration	M,D,O
Educational Measurement and Evaluation	M,D
Educational Policy	M,D,O
Educational Psychology	M,D
Elementary Education	M
English as a Second Language	M,D
English Education	M,D
English	M
Exercise and Sports Science	M,D
Family Nurse Practitioner Studies	M,D
Foreign Languages Education	M,D
Geosciences	M
Gerontology	M,D
Health Education	M
Health Services Management and Hospital Administration	M
Higher Education	M,D
History	M
Human Resources Management	M
International Health	M
Mathematics Education	M,D
Mathematics	M,D
Multilingual and Multicultural Education	M,D
Music Education	M,D
Music	M,D
Nursing Education	M,D
Nursing—General	M,D
Physical Education	M,D
Public Health—General	M
Reading Education	M
Rehabilitation Counseling	M,D
Rehabilitation Sciences	M,D
School Psychology	O
Science Education	M,D
Sociology	M
Special Education	M,D
Sports Management	M,D
Student Affairs	M,D
Translation and Interpretation	M

UNIVERSITY OF NORTHERN IOWA

Accounting	M
Allied Health—General	M,D
Applied Mathematics	M
Art Education	M
Art/Fine Arts	M
Athletic Training and Sports Medicine	M
Biological and Biomedical Sciences—General	M
Business Administration and Management—General	M
Communication Disorders	M
Communication—General	M
Community College Education	M
Community Health	M
Counseling Psychology	M
Counselor Education	M
Curriculum and Instruction	D
Early Childhood Education	M
Education—General	M,D,O
Educational Leadership and Administration	M,D
Educational Measurement and Evaluation	M
Educational Media/Instructional Technology	M
Educational Psychology	M
Elementary Education	M
English as a Second Language	M
English Education	M
English	M
Foreign Languages Education	M
Gender Studies	M
Geography	M
Geosciences	M
Health Education	M
Health Promotion	M
Higher Education	M
History	M
Human Services	M
Kinesiology and Movement Studies	M
Mathematics Education	M
Mathematics	M
Middle School Education	M
Music Education	M
Music	M
Nonprofit Management	M
Physical Education	M
Physics	M
Psychology—General	M
Public History	M
Public Policy	M
Reading Education	M
School Psychology	M,O
Science Education	M
Secondary Education	M
Social Sciences	M
Social Work	M
Spanish	M
Special Education	M
Sports Management	M
Student Affairs	M
Vocational and Technical Education	M,D
Women's Studies	M
Writing	M

UNIVERSITY OF NORTH FLORIDA

Accounting	M
Adult Education	M
Allied Health—General	M,D,O
Applied Behavior Analysis	M
Biological and Biomedical Sciences—General	M
Business Administration and Management—General	M
Civil Engineering	M
Communication Disorders	M
Community Health	M,O
Computer Science	M
Construction Management	M
Counseling Psychology	M
Counselor Education	M,D
Criminal Justice and Criminology	M
Economics	M
Education—General	M,D
Educational Leadership and Administration	M,D
Educational Media/Instructional Technology	M,D
Electrical Engineering	M
Electronic Commerce	M
Elementary Education	M
English as a Second Language	M
English	M
Ethics	M,O
Exercise and Sports Science	M
Family Nurse Practitioner Studies	M,D,O
Finance and Banking	M
History	M
Human Resources Management	M
International Business	M
Logistics	M
Management Information Systems	M
Mathematics	M
Mechanical Engineering	M
Nonprofit Management	M,O
Nurse Anesthesia	M,D,O
Nursing—General	M,D,O
Nutrition	M
Philosophy	M,O
Physical Therapy	D
Psychology—General	M
Public Administration	M,O
Public Health—General	M,O
Reading Education	M
Secondary Education	M
Software Engineering	M
Special Education	M
Sports Management	M,D
Statistics	M
Translation and Interpretation	M
Writing	M

UNIVERSITY OF NORTH GEORGIA

Anthropology	M
Athletic Training and Sports Medicine	M
Business Administration and Management—General	M
Counseling Psychology	M
Criminal Justice and Criminology	M
Curriculum and Instruction	M
Early Childhood Education	M
Education—General	M
Educational Leadership and Administration	D,O
English Education	M
Family Nurse Practitioner Studies	M,O
Higher Education	D
History	M
Human Services	M
International Affairs	M
Kinesiology and Movement Studies	M
Mathematics Education	M
Middle School Education	M
Nursing Education	M
Philosophy	M
Physical Education	M
Physical Therapy	D
Public Administration	M
Science Education	M
Secondary Education	M
Social Sciences Education	M

UNIVERSITY OF NORTH TEXAS

Accounting	M,D,O
Advertising and Public Relations	M,D,O
Anthropology	M,D,O
Applied Arts and Design—General	M,D,O
Applied Behavior Analysis	M,D,O
Art Education	M,D,O
Art History	M,D,O
Art/Fine Arts	M,D,O
Biochemistry	M,D,O
Biological and Biomedical Sciences—General	M,D,O
Biomedical Engineering	M,D,O
Business Administration and Management—General	M,D,O
Chemistry	M,D,O
Child and Family Studies	M,D,O
Clinical Psychology	M,D,O
Communication Disorders	M,D,O
Communication—General	M,D,O
Computer Engineering	M,D,O
Computer Science	M,D,O
Counseling Psychology	M,D,O
Counselor Education	M,D,O
Criminal Justice and Criminology	M,D,O
Curriculum and Instruction	M,D,O
Early Childhood Education	M,D,O
Economics	M,D,O
Education of the Gifted	M,D,O
Education—General	M,D,O
Educational Leadership and Administration	M,D,O
Educational Measurement and Evaluation	M,D,O
Educational Psychology	M,D,O
Electrical Engineering	M,D,O
Emergency Management	M,D,O
Energy and Power Engineering	M,D,O
Engineering and Applied Sciences—General	M,D,O
English as a Second Language	M,D,O
English	M,D,O
Environmental Sciences	M,D,O
Film, Television, and Video Production	M,D,O
Finance and Banking	M,D,O
French	M,D,O
Geography	M,D,O
Gerontology	M,D,O
Health Services Management and Hospital Administration	M,D,O
Higher Education	M,D,O
History	M,D,O
Hospitality Management	M,D,O
Human Development	M,D,O
Human Resources Management	M,D,O
Industrial and Manufacturing Management	M,D,O
Information Science	M,D,O
Interdisciplinary Studies	M,D,O
Interior Design	M,D,O
International Affairs	M,D,O
Internet and Interactive Multimedia	M,D,O
Journalism	M,D,O
Kinesiology and Movement Studies	M,D,O
Linguistics	M,D,O
Logistics	M,D,O
Management Information Systems	M,D,O
Management Strategy and Policy	M,D,O
Marketing	M,D,O
Mathematics	M,D,O
Mechanical Engineering	M,D,O
Molecular Biology	M,D,O
Museum Studies	M,D,O
Music Education	M,D,O
Music	M,D,O
Nonprofit Management	M,D,O
Philosophy	M,D,O
Political Science	M,D,O
Psychology—General	M,D,O
Public Administration	M,D,O
Quantitative Analysis	M,D,O
Rehabilitation Counseling	M,D,O
Sociology	M,D,O
Spanish	M,D,O
Special Education	M,D,O
Supply Chain Management	M,D,O
Textile Design	M,D,O
Travel and Tourism	M,D,O
Vocational and Technical Education	M,D,O
Writing	M,D,O

UNIVERSITY OF NORTH TEXAS AT DALLAS

Accounting	M
Business Administration and Management—General	M
Clinical Psychology	M
Counselor Education	M
Criminal Justice and Criminology	M
Curriculum and Instruction	M
Educational Leadership and Administration	M
Human Resources Management	M
Law	D
Management Strategy and Policy	M
Organizational Behavior	M
Public Administration	M

UNIVERSITY OF NORTH TEXAS HEALTH SCIENCE CENTER AT FORT WORTH

Anatomy	M,D
Biochemistry	M,D
Biological and Biomedical Sciences—General	M,D
Biostatistics	M,D,O
Biotechnology	M,D
Cancer Biology/Oncology	M,D
Epidemiology	M,D,O
Forensic Sciences	M,D
Genetics	M,D
Geographic Information Systems	M,D,O
Health Services Management and Hospital Administration	M,D,O
Health Services Research	M,D,O
Immunology	M,D
International Health	M,D,O
Microbiology	M,D
Neuroscience	M,D
Osteopathic Medicine	D
Pharmaceutical Sciences	M,D
Pharmacology	M,D
Physical Therapy	M,D
Physician Assistant Studies	M,D
Physiology	M,D
Public Health—General	M,D,O
Rehabilitation Sciences	M,D

UNIVERSITY OF NORTHWESTERN OHIO

Business Administration and Management—General	M

UNIVERSITY OF NORTHWESTERN–ST. PAUL

Business Administration and Management—General	M
Education—General	M
Human Services	M
Organizational Management	M
Pastoral Ministry and Counseling	M
Theology	M

UNIVERSITY OF NOTRE DAME

Accounting	M
Aerospace/Aeronautical Engineering	M,D
Applied Arts and Design—General	M
Applied Mathematics	M,D
Applied Statistics	M,D
Architecture	M
Art History	M
Art/Fine Arts	M
Biochemistry	M,D
Bioengineering	M,D
Biological and Biomedical Sciences—General	M,D
Business Administration and Management—General	M
Business Analytics	M
Cell Biology	M,D
Chemical Engineering	M,D
Chemistry	M,D
Civil Engineering	M,D
Cognitive Sciences	D
Comparative Literature	D
Computational Sciences	M,D
Computer Engineering	M,D
Computer Science	M,D
Conflict Resolution and Mediation/Peace Studies	M,D
Counseling Psychology	D
Developmental Psychology	D
Ecology	M,D
Economics	M,D
Education—General	M
Electrical Engineering	M,D
Engineering and Applied Sciences—General	M,D
English	M,D
Entrepreneurship	M
Environmental Engineering	M,D
Evolutionary Biology	M,D
Finance and Banking	M
French	M
Genetics	M,D
Geosciences	M,D
Graphic Design	M
History of Science and Technology	M,D
History	M,D
Industrial Design	M
Inorganic Chemistry	M,D
International Affairs	M
Investment Management	M
Italian	M
Latin American Studies	M
Law	M,D
Marketing	M

Mathematical and Computational Finance	M,D
Mathematics	M,D
Mechanical Engineering	M,D
Medieval and Renaissance Studies	M,D
Molecular Biology	M,D
Nonprofit Management	M
Organic Chemistry	M,D
Parasitology	M,D
Philosophy	D
Photography	M
Physical Chemistry	M,D
Physics	M,D
Physiology	M,D
Political Science	D
Psychology—General	D
Religion	M
Romance Languages	M
Sociology	D
Spanish	M
Statistics	M,D
Sustainable Development	M
Taxation	M
Theology	M,D
Writing	M

UNIVERSITY OF OKLAHOMA

Accounting	M,D
Addictions/Substance Abuse Counseling	M
Adult Education	M,D
Aerospace/Aeronautical Engineering	M,D
American Indian/Native American Studies	M
Analytical Chemistry	M,D
Anthropology	M,D
Applied Arts and Design—General	M,D
Applied Behavior Analysis	M,D
Applied Economics	M,D
Archaeology	M,D
Architecture	M,D
Archives/Archival Administration	M,D,O
Art History	M,D
Art/Fine Arts	M
Biochemistry	M,D
Biological and Biomedical Sciences—General	D
Biomedical Engineering	M,D
Business Administration and Management—General	M,D
Business Analytics	M,O
Chemical Engineering	M,D
Chemistry	M,D
Civil Engineering	M,D
Clinical Psychology	M,O
Communication—General	M,D,O
Computer Engineering	M,D
Computer Science	M,D
Construction Management	M,D,O
Corporate and Organizational Communication	M,D
Counseling Psychology	M
Criminal Justice and Criminology	M,O
Cultural Studies	M,D
Curriculum and Instruction	M,D
Dance	M
Data Science/Data Analytics	M
Early Childhood Education	M,D
Ecology	M,D
Economic Development	M,D
Economics	M,D
Education—General	M,D,O
Educational Leadership and Administration	M,D
Educational Media/Instructional Technology	M,D,O
Educational Psychology	M,D
Electrical Engineering	M,D
Elementary Education	M,D
Engineering and Applied Sciences—General	M,D
Engineering Physics	M,D
English Education	M,D
English	M,D
Entrepreneurship	M,D
Environmental Engineering	M,D
Environmental Sciences	M,D
Evolutionary Biology	M,D
Exercise and Sports Science	M,D
Film, Television, and Video Theory and Criticism	M,D
Finance and Banking	M,D
Foreign Languages Education	M,D
French	M,D
Gender Studies	O
Geography	M,D
Geological Engineering	M,D
Geology	M,D
Geophysics	M,D
German	M
Health Communication	M,D
Health Promotion	M,D
Health Services Management and Hospital Administration	M,O
Higher Education	M,D
History of Science and Technology	M,D
History	M,D
Human Resources Management	M,O
Human Services	M,O
Industrial and Organizational Psychology	M,D
Industrial/Management Engineering	M,D
Information Studies	M,D,O
Inorganic Chemistry	M,D
Interdisciplinary Studies	M,D
Interior Design	M,O
International Affairs	M
International Business	M,D
Journalism	M,D
Landscape Architecture	M
Law	M,D
Library Science	M,D,O
Management Information Systems	M,D,O
Marketing	M,D
Mass Communication	M,D
Mathematics Education	M,D
Mathematics	M,D*
Mechanical Engineering	M,D
Media Studies	M,D
Meteorology	M,D
Microbiology	M,D
Museum Studies	M,O
Music Education	M,D,O
Music	M,D,O
Neurobiology	M,D
Nonprofit Management	M,O
Organic Chemistry	M,D
Organizational Behavior	M,O
Organizational Management	M,O
Petroleum Engineering	M,D,O
Philosophy	M,D
Photography	M,D
Physical Chemistry	M,D
Physics	M,D
Plant Biology	M,D
Political Science	M,D
Project Management	M,O
Psychology—General	M,D,O
Public Administration	M
Public Policy	M
Reading Education	M,D
Rhetoric	M,D
School Psychology	M
Science Education	M,D
Social Sciences Education	M,D
Social Work	M
Sociology	M,D
Spanish	M,D
Special Education	M,D
Structural Biology	M,D
Student Affairs	M,D
Supply Chain Management	M,D
Sustainable Development	M,D
Telecommunications	M
Urban and Regional Planning	M,D
Water Resources Engineering	M,D
Women's Studies	O
Writing	M,D

UNIVERSITY OF OKLAHOMA HEALTH SCIENCES CENTER

Allied Health—General	M,D,O
Allopathic Medicine	D
Biochemistry	M,D
Biological and Biomedical Sciences—General	M,D
Biopsychology	M,D
Biostatistics	M,D
Cell Biology	M,D
Communication Disorders	M,D,O
Dentistry	D,O
Environmental and Occupational Health	M,D
Epidemiology	M,D
Genetic Counseling	M
Health Education	D
Health Physics/Radiological Health	M,D
Health Promotion	M,D
Health Services Management and Hospital Administration	M,D
Homeland Security	M
Immunology	M,D
Medical Physics	M,D
Microbiology	M,D
Molecular Biology	M,D
Neuroscience	M,D
Nursing—General	M
Nutrition	M
Occupational Therapy	M
Oral and Dental Sciences	M
Pathology	D
Pharmaceutical Sciences	M,D
Pharmacy	D
Physical Therapy	M
Physician Assistant Studies	M
Physiology	M,D
Public Health—General	M,D
Radiation Biology	M,D
Reading Education	M,D,O
Rehabilitation Sciences	M
Special Education	M,D,O

UNIVERSITY OF OREGON

Accounting	M,D
Anthropology	M,D
Applied Arts and Design—General	M
Architecture	M
Art History	M,D
Art/Fine Arts	M
Asian Languages	M,D
Asian Studies	M
Biochemistry	M,D
Biological and Biomedical Sciences—General	M,D
Biopsychology	M,D
Business Administration and Management—General	M,D
Chemistry	M,D
Chinese	M,D
Classics	M
Clinical Psychology	D
Cognitive Sciences	M,D
Communication Disorders	M,D
Communication—General	M,D
Comparative Literature	M,D
Computer Science	M,D
Counseling Psychology	M,D
Curriculum and Instruction	M,D
Dance	M
Developmental Psychology	M,D
Ecology	M,D
Economics	M,D
Education—General	M,D
Educational Leadership and Administration	M,D
English	M,D
Environmental Management and Policy	M,D
Evolutionary Biology	M,D
Finance and Banking	D
Folklore	M
French	M
Genetics	M,D
Geography	M,D
Geology	M,D
German	M,D
Historic Preservation	M
History	M,D
Information Science	M,D
Interdisciplinary Studies	M
Interior Design	M
International Affairs	M
Italian	M
Japanese	M,D
Journalism	M,D
Landscape Architecture	M,D
Law	M,D
Linguistics	M,D
Management Information Systems	M
Marine Biology	M,D
Marketing	D
Marriage and Family Therapy	M,D
Mathematics	M,D
Media Studies	M,D
Molecular Biology	M,D
Music Education	M,D
Music	M,D
Neuroscience	M,D
Nonprofit Management	M,O
Philosophy	M,D
Physics	M,D
Physiology	M,D
Political Science	M,D
Psychology—General	M,D
Public Administration	M
Quantitative Analysis	M
Romance Languages	M,D
Russian	M
School Psychology	M,D
Social Psychology	M,D
Sociology	M,D
Spanish	M
Special Education	M,D
Sports Management	M
Theater	M,D
Urban and Regional Planning	M
Writing	M

UNIVERSITY OF OTTAWA

Aerospace/Aeronautical Engineering	M,D
Allopathic Medicine	M,D
Anthropology	M
Biochemistry	M,D
Bioengineering	M,D
Biological and Biomedical Sciences—General	M,D
Biomedical Engineering	M
Business Administration and Management—General	M
Canadian Studies	D
Cell Biology	M,D
Chemical Engineering	M,D
Chemistry	M,D
Civil Engineering	M,D
Classics	M,D
Communication Disorders	M
Communication—General	M,D
Community Health	D,O
Computer Engineering	M,D
Computer Science	M,D
Criminal Justice and Criminology	M,D
Economics	M,D
Education—General	M,D,O
Electrical Engineering	M,D
Electronic Commerce	M,D,O
Engineering and Applied Sciences—General	M,D,O
Engineering Management	M,O
English	M,D
Epidemiology	M,D
Finance and Banking	D,O
French	M,D
Geography	M,D
Geosciences	M,D
Health Services Management and Hospital Administration	M
Health Services Research	D,O
History	M,D
Immunology	M,D
Information Science	M,O
Interdisciplinary Studies	D,O
International Development	M
Kinesiology and Movement Studies	M
Law	M,D
Linguistics	M,D
Mathematics	M,D
Mechanical Engineering	M,D
Microbiology	M,D
Molecular Biology	M,D
Music Education	M,O
Music	M,O
Nursing—General	M,D,O
Philosophy	M,D
Physics	M,D
Political Science	M,D
Project Management	M,O
Psychology—General	D
Public Administration	D,O
Public Health—General	D
Rehabilitation Sciences	M
Religion	M,D
Social Work	M
Sociology	M
Spanish	M,D
Statistics	M,D
Systems Science	M,D,O
Theater	M
Translation and Interpretation	M,D
Women's Studies	M

UNIVERSITY OF PENNSYLVANIA

Accounting	M,D
Acute Care/Critical Care Nursing	M
Adult Nursing	M
African Studies	M,D
Allopathic Medicine	D
Anthropology	M,D
Applied Economics	D
Applied Mathematics	D
Applied Psychology	M
Archaeology	M,D
Architecture	M,D,O
Art History	M,D
Art/Fine Arts	M,O
Artificial Intelligence/Robotics	M
Asian Studies	M,D
Biochemistry	D
Bioengineering	M,D
Bioethics	M
Biological and Biomedical Sciences—General	M,D
Biostatistics	M,D
Biotechnology	M
Business Administration and Management—General	M,D
Cancer Biology/Oncology	D
Cell Biology	D
Chemical Engineering	M,D
Chemistry	M,D
Classics	M,D
Clinical Laboratory Sciences/Medical Technology	M
Communication—General	D
Comparative Literature	M,D
Computational Biology	D
Computational Sciences	M,D
Computer Art and Design	M,D
Computer Science	M,D
Counseling Psychology	M
Counselor Education	M
Criminal Justice and Criminology	M,D
Data Science/Data Analytics	M
Demography and Population Studies	M,D
Dentistry	D
Developmental Biology	D
Economic Development	M,O
Economics	M,D
Education—General	M,D,O*
Educational Leadership and Administration	M,D
Educational Measurement and Evaluation	M,D
Educational Media/Instructional Technology	M
Educational Policy	M,D
Electrical Engineering	M,D
Elementary Education	M
Engineering and Applied Sciences—General	M,D*
English as a Second Language	M
English Education	M,D
English	M,D
Entrepreneurship	M
Environmental and Occupational Health	M
Environmental Management and Policy	M
Environmental Sciences	M,D
Epidemiology	M
Ethics	M,D
Family Nurse Practitioner Studies	M,O
Finance and Banking	M,D
Foundations and Philosophy of Education	M,D
French	M,D
Game Design and Development	M,D
Genetics	D
Genomic Sciences	D
Geographic Information Systems	M,D,O
Geosciences	M,D
German	M,D
Gerontological Nursing	M
Graphic Design	M,O
Health Services Management and Hospital Administration	M,D
Health Services Research	M
Higher Education	M,D
Historic Preservation	M,O
History of Science and Technology	M,D
History	M,D
Human Development	M,D
Human Genetics	M
Immunology	D
Information Science	M,D
Insurance	M,D
International Affairs	M
International and Comparative Education	M
International Business	M
International Health	M
Internet and Interactive Multimedia	M,O
Italian	M,D
Landscape Architecture	M,O
Law	M,D
Legal and Justice Studies	M,D
Liberal Studies	M
Linguistics	M,D

*M—masters degree; D—doctorate; O—other advanced degree; *—Close-Up and/or Display*

- Management Information Systems M,D
- Marketing M,D
- Materials Engineering M,D
- Materials Sciences M,D
- Maternal and Child/Neonatal Nursing M
- Mathematics M,D
- Mechanical Engineering M,D
- Mechanics M,D
- Medical Physics M,D
- Microbiology D
- Molecular Biology D
- Molecular Biophysics D
- Multilingual and Multicultural Education M
- Music M,D
- Nanotechnology M
- Near and Middle Eastern Studies M,D
- Neuroscience D
- Nonprofit Management M,O
- Nurse Anesthesia M
- Nurse Midwifery M
- Nursing and Healthcare Administration M,D
- Nursing—General M,D,O
- Organizational Management M,O
- Pediatric Nursing M
- Pharmacology D
- Philosophy M,D
- Physics M,D
- Physiology D
- Political Science M,D,O
- Psychiatric Nursing M
- Psychology—General D
- Public Administration M,O
- Public Health—General M
- Public Policy M,D
- Reading Education M
- Real Estate M,D
- Religion D
- Risk Management M,D
- Romance Languages M,D
- Science Education M,D
- Secondary Education M
- Social Work M,D
- Sociology M,D
- Spanish M,D
- Statistics M,D
- Systems Engineering M,D
- Urban and Regional Planning M,D,O
- Urban Design M,D,O
- Urban Education M
- Veterinary Medicine D
- Virology D
- Women's Health Nursing M

UNIVERSITY OF PHILOSOPHICAL RESEARCH

- Psychology—General M
- Theology M

UNIVERSITY OF PHOENIX–BAY AREA CAMPUS

- Accounting M,D
- Adult Education M,D,O
- Business Administration and Management—General M,D
- Criminal Justice and Criminology M
- Early Childhood Education M,D,O
- Education—General M,D,O
- Educational Leadership and Administration M,D,O
- Elementary Education M,D,O
- Energy Management and Policy M,D
- Gerontological Nursing M,D
- Health Services Management and Hospital Administration M,D
- Higher Education M,D,O
- Human Resources Management M,D
- International Business M,D
- Management Information Systems M,D
- Management of Technology M,D
- Marketing M,D
- Marriage and Family Therapy M
- Nursing and Healthcare Administration M,D
- Nursing Education M,D
- Nursing Informatics M,D
- Nursing—General M,D
- Organizational Management M,D
- Project Management M,D
- Public Administration M,D
- Secondary Education M,D,O
- Special Education M,D,O

UNIVERSITY OF PHOENIX–CENTRAL VALLEY CAMPUS

- Accounting M
- Business Administration and Management—General M
- Community Health M
- Computer Education M
- Curriculum and Instruction M
- Education—General M
- Elementary Education M
- Gerontology M
- Health Services Management and Hospital Administration M
- Human Resources Management M
- International Business M
- Management Information Systems M
- Management of Technology M
- Marketing M
- Marriage and Family Therapy M
- Nursing—General M
- Public Administration M
- Secondary Education M

UNIVERSITY OF PHOENIX–DALLAS CAMPUS

- Accounting M
- Business Administration and Management—General M
- Criminal Justice and Criminology M
- Curriculum and Instruction M
- Education—General M
- Electronic Commerce M
- Human Resources Management M
- International Business M
- Management Information Systems M
- Management of Technology M
- Marketing M
- Public Administration M

UNIVERSITY OF PHOENIX–HAWAII CAMPUS

- Accounting M
- Business Administration and Management—General M
- Community Health M
- Curriculum and Instruction M
- Education—General M
- Educational Leadership and Administration M
- Elementary Education M
- Family Nurse Practitioner Studies M
- Gerontology M
- Health Services Management and Hospital Administration M
- Human Resources Management M
- International Business M
- Management Information Systems M
- Management of Technology M
- Marketing M
- Nursing Education M
- Nursing—General M
- Public Administration M
- Secondary Education M
- Special Education M

UNIVERSITY OF PHOENIX–HOUSTON CAMPUS

- Accounting M
- Business Administration and Management—General M
- Curriculum and Instruction M
- Education—General M
- Electronic Commerce M
- Health Services Management and Hospital Administration M
- Human Resources Management M
- International Business M
- Management Information Systems M
- Management of Technology M
- Marketing M
- Nursing—General M
- Public Administration M

UNIVERSITY OF PHOENIX–LAS VEGAS CAMPUS

- Accounting M
- Allied Health—General M
- Business Administration and Management—General M
- Counseling Psychology M
- Counselor Education M
- Curriculum and Instruction M
- Education—General M
- Educational Leadership and Administration M
- Elementary Education M
- Human Resources Management M
- International Business M
- Management Information Systems M
- Management of Technology M
- Marketing M
- Marriage and Family Therapy M
- Public Administration M
- School Psychology M

UNIVERSITY OF PHOENIX–ONLINE CAMPUS

- Accounting M,O
- Adult Education M,O
- Business Administration and Management—General M,D,O
- Computer Education M,O
- Conflict Resolution and Mediation/Peace Studies M,O
- Criminal Justice and Criminology M,O
- Curriculum and Instruction M,D,O
- Early Childhood Education M,O
- Education—General M,D,O
- Educational Leadership and Administration M,D,O
- Educational Media/Instructional Technology D,O
- Elementary Education M,O
- Energy Management and Policy M,O
- English as a Second Language M,O
- English Education M,O
- Family Nurse Practitioner Studies M,O
- Health Education M,O
- Health Informatics M,O
- Health Services Management and Hospital Administration M,D,O
- Higher Education D,O
- Homeland Security M,O
- Human Resources Management M,O
- Industrial and Organizational Psychology M,D,O
- International Business M,O
- Management Information Systems M
- Management of Technology M,O
- Marketing M,O
- Mathematics Education M,O
- Middle School Education M,O
- Nursing Education M,O
- Nursing—General M,D,O
- Organizational Management D,O
- Project Management M,O
- Psychology—General M,O
- Public Administration M,O
- Reading Education M,O
- Science Education M,O
- Secondary Education M,O
- Special Education M,O

UNIVERSITY OF PHOENIX–PHOENIX CAMPUS

- Accounting M,O
- Adult Education M
- Business Administration and Management—General M,O
- Clinical Psychology M
- Counseling Psychology M
- Counselor Education M
- Criminal Justice and Criminology M
- Curriculum and Instruction M
- Early Childhood Education M
- Education—General M
- Educational Leadership and Administration M
- Elementary Education M
- Energy Management and Policy M,O
- Family Nurse Practitioner Studies M,O
- Gerontological Nursing M,O
- Health Services Management and Hospital Administration M,O
- Homeland Security M
- Human Resources Management M,O
- International Business M,O
- Management of Technology M,O
- Marketing M,O
- Marriage and Family Therapy M
- Medical Informatics M,O
- Nursing Education M,O
- Nursing Informatics M,O
- Nursing—General M,O
- Project Management M,O
- Psychology—General M
- Public Administration M
- Reading Education M
- Secondary Education M
- Social Psychology M
- Special Education M
- Vocational and Technical Education M

UNIVERSITY OF PHOENIX–SACRAMENTO VALLEY CAMPUS

- Accounting M
- Adult Education M,O
- Business Administration and Management—General M
- Curriculum and Instruction M,O
- Education—General M,O
- Elementary Education M,O
- Family Nurse Practitioner Studies M
- Health Services Management and Hospital Administration M
- Human Resources Management M
- International Business M
- Management Information Systems M
- Management of Technology M
- Marketing M
- Nursing Education M
- Nursing—General M
- Public Administration M
- Secondary Education M,O

UNIVERSITY OF PHOENIX–SAN ANTONIO CAMPUS

- Accounting M
- Business Administration and Management—General M
- Criminal Justice and Criminology M
- Curriculum and Instruction M
- Electronic Commerce M
- Health Services Management and Hospital Administration M
- Human Resources Management M
- International Business M
- Management Information Systems M
- Management of Technology M
- Marketing M
- Nursing—General M
- Public Administration M

UNIVERSITY OF PHOENIX–SAN DIEGO CAMPUS

- Accounting M
- Business Administration and Management—General M
- Computer Education M
- Curriculum and Instruction M
- Education—General M
- Elementary Education M
- English as a Second Language M
- Human Resources Management M
- International Business M
- Management Information Systems M
- Management of Technology M
- Marketing M
- Nursing Education M
- Nursing—General M
- Public Administration M
- Secondary Education M

UNIVERSITY OF PIKEVILLE

- Business Administration and Management—General M
- Education—General M
- Educational Leadership and Administration M
- Entrepreneurship M
- Health Services Management and Hospital Administration M
- Optometry D
- Osteopathic Medicine D

UNIVERSITY OF PITTSBURGH

- Accounting M,D
- Acute Care/Critical Care Nursing M,D
- African Studies O
- Allopathic Medicine D
- Anthropology M,D
- Applied Behavior Analysis M,D
- Applied Mathematics M,D
- Applied Psychology M,D
- Applied Statistics M,D
- Architectural History M,D
- Art History M,D
- Artificial Intelligence/Robotics M,D
- Asian Studies M,O
- Athletic Training and Sports Medicine M
- Bioengineering M,D
- Bioethics M
- Bioinformatics M,D,O
- Biological and Biomedical Sciences—General M,D
- Biostatistics M,D
- Business Administration and Management—General M,D*
- Business Analytics D
- Cell Biology D
- Chemical Engineering M,D
- Chemistry M,D
- Chinese M
- Civil Engineering M,D
- Clinical Laboratory Sciences/Medical Technology D
- Clinical Psychology M,D
- Clinical Research M,O
- Communication Disorders M,D
- Communication—General M,D
- Community Health M,D,O
- Computational Biology D
- Computational Sciences M,D,O
- Computer Engineering M,D
- Computer Science M,D
- Criminal Justice and Criminology M
- Cultural Studies O
- Data Science/Data Analytics M,D,O
- Dentistry M,D,O
- Developmental Biology D
- Developmental Psychology M,D
- Disability Studies O
- Early Childhood Education M
- East European and Russian Studies O
- Ecology D
- Economics M,D
- Education—General M,D*
- Educational Leadership and Administration M,D
- Educational Measurement and Evaluation M,D
- Educational Policy D
- Electrical Engineering M,D
- Elementary Education M
- Energy Management and Policy M
- Engineering and Applied Sciences—General M,D
- English as a Second Language D,O
- English Education M,D
- English M,D
- Environmental and Occupational Health M,D
- Environmental Engineering M,D
- Environmental Law M
- Environmental Sciences M,D
- Epidemiology M,D
- Evolutionary Biology D
- Exercise and Sports Science M,D
- Family Nurse Practitioner Studies M,D
- Film, Television, and Video Theory and Criticism M,D,O
- Finance and Banking M,D
- Foreign Languages Education M,D
- Foundations and Philosophy of Education M,D
- French M,D
- Genetic Counseling M,D,O
- Geographic Information Systems M,D
- Geology M,D
- Gerontological Nursing M,D
- Health Education M,D
- Health Informatics M
- Health Law M
- Health Psychology D
- Health Services Management and Hospital Administration M,D,O
- Health Services Research M
- Higher Education M,D
- History of Science and Technology D
- History M,D
- Human Genetics M,D,O
- Human Resources Management M,D
- Immunology D
- Industrial and Manufacturing Management M
- Industrial/Management Engineering M,D
- Infectious Diseases M,D
- Information Science M,D,O
- Intellectual Property Law M
- Interdisciplinary Studies D
- International Affairs M,D,O
- International and Comparative Education M,D
- International Business O
- International Development M,D
- International Health M,D,O
- Italian M,D
- Japanese M
- Latin American Studies O
- Law M
- Legal and Justice Studies M
- Library Science M,D
- Linguistics M,D
- Management Information Systems M,D
- Management Strategy and Policy M,D
- Marketing M,D
- Materials Sciences M,D
- Maternal and Child/Neonatal Nursing M,D
- Mathematics Education M,D
- Mathematics M,D
- Mechanical Engineering M,D
- Medieval and Renaissance Studies O
- Microbiology M,D
- Military and Defense Studies M
- Modeling and Simulation M,D
- Molecular Biology D

Molecular Biophysics	D
Molecular Genetics	D
Molecular Pathology	D
Molecular Pharmacology	D
Molecular Physiology	D
Music	M,D
Neuroscience	D
Nonprofit Management	M
Nurse Anesthesia	D
Nurse Midwifery	D
Nursing and Healthcare Administration	M,D
Nursing Informatics	M,D
Nursing—General	D
Nutrition	M
Occupational Therapy	M,D
Oral and Dental Sciences	M,D,O
Organizational Behavior	M,D
Pathology	D
Pediatric Nursing	M,D
Petroleum Engineering	M,D
Pharmaceutical Administration	M
Pharmaceutical Sciences	M,D
Pharmacy	D
Philosophy	D
Physical Therapy	M,D
Physician Assistant Studies	M,D
Physics	M,D*
Political Science	M,D
Psychiatric Nursing	M,D
Psychology—General	D
Public Administration	M,D
Public Health—General	M,D,O
Public Policy	M,D
Reading Education	M,D
Rehabilitation Counseling	M,D
Rehabilitation Sciences	M,D
Science Education	M,D
Secondary Education	M,D
Slavic Languages	M,D
Social Psychology	D
Social Sciences Education	M,D
Social Work	M,D,O
Sociology	M,D
Spanish	D
Special Education	M,D
Statistics	M,D
Structural Biology	D
Supply Chain Management	M
Systems Biology	D
Theater	M,D
Urban and Regional Planning	M
Vision Sciences	M,D
Western European Studies	O
Women's Studies	O
Writing	M,D

UNIVERSITY OF PORTLAND

Biomedical Engineering	M
Business Administration and Management—General	M
Civil Engineering	M
Communication—General	M
Computer Science	M
Corporate and Organizational Communication	M
Education—General	M,D
Educational Leadership and Administration	M,D
Electrical Engineering	M
Engineering and Applied Sciences—General	M
English as a Second Language	M,D
Entrepreneurship	M
Family Nurse Practitioner Studies	M,D
Finance and Banking	M
Health Services Management and Hospital Administration	M
Industrial and Manufacturing Management	M
Management of Technology	M
Marketing	M
Mechanical Engineering	M
Nonprofit Management	M
Nursing Education	M,D
Nursing—General	M,D
Organizational Management	M,D
Pastoral Ministry and Counseling	M
Reading Education	M,D
Special Education	M,D
Sustainability Management	M
Theater	M

UNIVERSITY OF PRINCE EDWARD ISLAND

Anatomy	M,D
Bacteriology	M,D
Biological and Biomedical Sciences—General	M,D
Chemistry	M,D
Education—General	M,D
Educational Leadership and Administration	M,D
Environmental Sciences	M,D
Epidemiology	M,D
Geography	M
Immunology	M,D
Parasitology	M,D
Pathology	M,D
Pharmacology	M,D
Physiology	M,D
Toxicology	M,D
Veterinary Medicine	D
Veterinary Sciences	M,D
Virology	M,D

UNIVERSITY OF PROVIDENCE

Counseling Psychology	M
Criminal Justice and Criminology	M
Human Services	M

UNIVERSITY OF PUERTO RICO–MAYAGÜEZ

Aerospace/Aeronautical Engineering	M,D
Agricultural Economics and Agribusiness	M
Agricultural Education	M
Agricultural Sciences—General	M
Agronomy and Soil Sciences	M
Animal Sciences	M
Applied Mathematics	M
Bioengineering	M,D
Biological and Biomedical Sciences—General	M
Business Administration and Management—General	M
Chemical Engineering	M,D
Chemistry	M,D
Civil Engineering	M,D
Computational Sciences	M,D
Computer Engineering	M,D
Computer Science	M,D
Construction Engineering	M,D
Electrical Engineering	M,D
Energy and Power Engineering	M,D
Engineering and Applied Sciences—General	M,D
Engineering Management	M,D
English Education	M
English	M
Environmental Engineering	M,D
Environmental Sciences	M,D
Exercise and Sports Science	M
Finance and Banking	M
Food Science and Technology	M
Geology	M
Geotechnical Engineering	M,D
Higher Education	M
Hispanic Studies	M
Horticulture	M
Human Resources Management	M
Industrial and Manufacturing Management	M
Industrial/Management Engineering	M
Information Science	M,D
Kinesiology and Movement Studies	M
Manufacturing Engineering	M,D
Marine Sciences	M,D
Materials Engineering	M,D
Materials Sciences	M,D
Mathematics Education	M
Mathematics	M
Mechanical Engineering	M,D
Physical Chemistry	M,D
Physics	M
Rural Sociology	M
Structural Engineering	M,D
Transportation and Highway Engineering	M,D

UNIVERSITY OF PUERTO RICO–MEDICAL SCIENCES CAMPUS

Acute Care/Critical Care Nursing	M
Adult Nursing	M
Allied Health—General	M,D,O
Allopathic Medicine	D
Anatomy	M,D
Biochemistry	M,D
Biological and Biomedical Sciences—General	M,D
Biostatistics	M
Clinical Laboratory Sciences/Medical Technology	M,O
Clinical Research	M,O
Communication Disorders	M,D
Community Health Nursing	M
Demography and Population Studies	M
Dentistry	D
Environmental and Occupational Health	M,D
Epidemiology	M
Family Nurse Practitioner Studies	M
Gerontological Nursing	M
Gerontology	M,O
Health Education	M
Health Informatics	M
Health Promotion	O
Health Services Management and Hospital Administration	M
Health Services Research	M
Industrial Hygiene	M
Maternal and Child Health	M
Maternal and Child/Neonatal Nursing	M
Microbiology	M,D
Nurse Midwifery	M,O
Nursing—General	M
Nutrition	M,D,O
Occupational Therapy	M
Oral and Dental Sciences	O
Pediatric Nursing	M
Pharmaceutical Sciences	M,D
Pharmacology	M,D
Pharmacy	M,D
Physical Therapy	M
Physiology	M,D
Psychiatric Nursing	M
Special Education	O
Toxicology	M,D

UNIVERSITY OF PUERTO RICO–RÍO PIEDRAS

Accounting	M,D
Architecture	M
Biological and Biomedical Sciences—General	M,D
Business Administration and Management—General	M,D
Cell Biology	M,D
Chemistry	M,D
Clinical Psychology	M,D
Communication—General	M
Comparative Literature	M
Counselor Education	M
Curriculum and Instruction	M,D
Early Childhood Education	M
Ecology	M,D
Economic Development	M
Economics	M
Education—General	M,D
Educational Leadership and Administration	M,D
Educational Measurement and Evaluation	M
English as a Second Language	M
English	M,D
Environmental Management and Policy	M
Environmental Sciences	M,D
Evolutionary Biology	M,D
Exercise and Sports Science	M
Family and Consumer Sciences-General	M
Finance and Banking	M,D
Foreign Languages Education	M,D
Genetics	M,D
Hispanic Studies	M,D
History	M,D
Human Resources Management	M,D
Industrial and Manufacturing Management	M,D
Industrial and Organizational Psychology	M,D
Information Science	M,O
Information Studies	M,O
International Business	M,D
Journalism	M
Law	M,D
Library Science	M,O
Linguistics	M,O
Marketing	M,D
Mass Communication	M
Mathematics Education	M,D
Mathematics	M,D
Molecular Biology	M,D
Neuroscience	M,D
Nutrition	M
Philosophy	M
Physics	M,D
Psychology—General	M,D
Public Administration	M
Public Policy	M
Quantitative Analysis	M,D
Rehabilitation Counseling	M
Science Education	M,D
Social Psychology	M,D
Social Sciences Education	M,D
Social Work	M,D
Sociology	M
Special Education	M
Translation and Interpretation	M,O
Urban and Regional Planning	M

UNIVERSITY OF PUGET SOUND

Counseling Psychology	M
Counselor Education	M
Education—General	M
Elementary Education	M
Occupational Therapy	M,D
Physical Therapy	D
Secondary Education	M

UNIVERSITY OF REDLANDS

Business Administration and Management—General	M
Communication Disorders	M
Education—General	M,D,O
Geographic Information Systems	M
Management Information Systems	M
Music	M

UNIVERSITY OF REGINA

Adult Education	M
Analytical Chemistry	M,D
Anthropology	M
Applied Economics	M
Applied Psychology	M,D
Art/Fine Arts	M
Biochemistry	M,D
Biological and Biomedical Sciences—General	M,D
Biophysics	M,D
Business Administration and Management—General	M,O
Canadian Studies	M,D
Cancer Biology/Oncology	M,D
Chemistry	M,D
Clinical Psychology	M,D
Computer Engineering	M,D
Computer Science	M,D
Criminal Justice and Criminology	M
Curriculum and Instruction	M
Economics	M,D,O
Education—General	M,D,O
Educational Leadership and Administration	M
Educational Psychology	M
Engineering and Applied Sciences—General	M,D
Engineering Management	M,O
English	M
Environmental Engineering	M,D
Experimental Psychology	M,D
Film, Television, and Video Production	M
French	M
Geography	M,D
Geology	M,D
Gerontology	M
Health Services Management and Hospital Administration	M,D,O
History	M
Human Resources Development	M
Human Resources Management	M,O
Industrial/Management Engineering	M,D
Inorganic Chemistry	M,D
Interdisciplinary Studies	M
International Business	M,O
Journalism	M
Kinesiology and Movement Studies	M,D
Linguistics	M
Mathematics	M,D
Music	M
Nursing—General	M
Organic Chemistry	M,D
Organizational Management	M,O
Petroleum Engineering	M,D
Philosophy	M
Physics	M,D
Political Science	M
Project Management	M,O
Psychology—General	M,D
Public Administration	M,D,O
Public Policy	M,D,O
Religion	M
Social Sciences	M
Social Work	M,D
Sociology	M
Software Engineering	M,D
Statistics	M,D
Systems Engineering	M,D
Theoretical Chemistry	M,D
Women's Studies	M
Writing	M,D

UNIVERSITY OF RHODE ISLAND

Accounting	M
Acute Care/Critical Care Nursing	M,D,O
Adult Nursing	M,D,O
Animal Sciences	M,D
Anthropology	M
Applied Mathematics	M,D
Aquaculture	M,D
Archaeology	M
Biochemistry	M,D
Biological and Biomedical Sciences—General	M,D
Biomedical Engineering	M,D
Biotechnology	M,D
Business Administration and Management—General	M,D*
Cell Biology	M,D
Chemical Engineering	M,D,O
Chemistry	M,D
Child and Family Studies	M
Civil Engineering	M,D
Clinical Laboratory Sciences/Medical Technology	M,D
Clinical Psychology	M,D
Clothing and Textiles	M,O
Communication Disorders	M
Communication—General	M
Computer and Information Systems Security	M,D,O
Computer Art and Design	M
Computer Engineering	M,D
Computer Science	M,D,O
Counseling Psychology	M,D
Ecology	M,D
Economics	M,D
Education—General	M,D
Electrical Engineering	M,D
Engineering and Applied Sciences—General	M,D,O
English	M,D
Entrepreneurship	M,D,O
Environmental Engineering	M,D
Environmental Management and Policy	M,D
Environmental Sciences	M,D
Evolutionary Biology	M,D
Exercise and Sports Science	M
Family Nurse Practitioner Studies	M,D,O
Film, Television, and Video Production	M,D
Finance and Banking	M,D
Fish, Game, and Wildlife Management	M,D
Food Science and Technology	M,D
Forensic Sciences	M,D,O
Gender Studies	M,D,O
Geophysics	M,D
Geosciences	M,D,O
Geotechnical Engineering	M,D
Gerontological Nursing	M,D,O
Health Education	M
Health Services Management and Hospital Administration	M,D,O
History	M
Human Development	M
Human Resources Management	M,O
Hydrology	M,D,O
Industrial and Labor Relations	M,O
Industrial/Management Engineering	M,D
Information Studies	M
Library Science	M
Management Strategy and Policy	M,D,O
Marine Affairs	M,D
Marine Biology	M,D
Marine Geology	M,D
Marine Sciences	M,D
Marketing	M,D
Marriage and Family Therapy	M
Mathematics	M,D
Medical Physics	M,D

*M—masters degree; D—doctorate; O—other advanced degree; *—Close-Up and/or Display*

Medicinal and Pharmaceutical Chemistry	M,D
Microbiology	M,D
Molecular Biology	M,D
Molecular Genetics	M,D
Music Education	M
Music	M
Natural Resources	M,D
Nursing Education	M,D,O
Nursing—General	M,D,O
Nutrition	M
Ocean Engineering	M,D
Oceanography	M,D
Pharmaceutical Sciences	M,D
Pharmacology	M,D
Pharmacy	D
Physical Education	M
Physical Therapy	D
Physics	M,D
Political Science	M
Psychology—General	M,D
Public Administration	M
Public Policy	M
Reading Education	M,D
Recreation and Park Management	M
School Psychology	M,D
Spanish	M
Special Education	M,D
Sport Psychology	M
Statistics	M,D,O
Student Affairs	M
Supply Chain Management	M,D
Systems Engineering	M,D
Toxicology	M,D
Women's Studies	O
Writing	M,D

UNIVERSITY OF RICHMOND

Business Administration and Management—General	M
Law	D

UNIVERSITY OF RIO GRANDE

Art Education	M
Education—General	M
Educational Leadership and Administration	M
Physical Education	M
Special Education	M

UNIVERSITY OF ROCHESTER

Accounting	M,D
Acute Care/Critical Care Nursing	M,D
Adult Nursing	M,D
Allopathic Medicine	D
Anatomy	D
Archives/Archival Administration	M
Art History	D
Art/Fine Arts	D
Artificial Intelligence/Robotics	M,D
Astronomy	D
Biochemistry	D
Biological and Biomedical Sciences—General	M,D
Biomedical Engineering	M,D
Biophysics	D
Biostatistics	M
Business Administration and Management—General	M,D
Chemical Engineering	M,D*
Chemistry	D
Clinical Psychology	D
Clinical Research	M
Cognitive Sciences	D
Comparative Literature	M
Computational Biology	D
Computer Engineering	M,D
Computer Science	M,D
Counselor Education	M,D
Curriculum and Instruction	M,D
Data Science/Data Analytics	M
Developmental Psychology	D
Ecology	M,D
Economics	D
Education—General	M,D
Educational Leadership and Administration	M,D
Educational Policy	M,D
Electrical Engineering	M,D
Energy and Power Engineering	M
Engineering and Applied Sciences—General	M,D
English	M,D
Entrepreneurship	M
Epidemiology	D
Family Nurse Practitioner Studies	M,D
Finance and Banking	M,D
Foundations and Philosophy of Education	D
Genetics	M,D
Genomic Sciences	D
Geology	M,D
Geosciences	M,D
Gerontological Nursing	M,D
Health Services Management and Hospital Administration	M,D
Health Services Research	D
Higher Education	M,D
Historic Preservation	M
History	M,D
Human Development	M,D
Human-Computer Interaction	M,D
Immunology	M,D
Industrial and Manufacturing Management	D
Inorganic Chemistry	D
Linguistics	M
Management Information Systems	M,D
Management Strategy and Policy	M
Marketing Research	M
Marketing	M,D
Marriage and Family Therapy	M
Materials Sciences	M,D
Maternal and Child/Neonatal Nursing	M,D
Mathematics	D
Mechanical Engineering	M,D
Microbiology	M,D
Molecular Biology	M,D
Music Education	M,D
Music	M,D
Neurobiology	D
Neuroscience	D
Nursing and Healthcare Administration	M,D
Nursing Education	M,D
Nursing—General	M,D
Optical Sciences	M,D
Oral and Dental Sciences	M
Organic Chemistry	D
Pathology	D
Pediatric Nursing	M,D
Pharmacology	M,D
Philosophy	D
Photography	M
Physical Chemistry	D
Physics	D
Physiology	M,D
Political Science	D
Psychiatric Nursing	M,D
Psychology—General	D
Public Health—General	M
Social Psychology	M,D
Statistics	M,D
Structural Biology	D
Student Affairs	M
Toxicology	D
Translation and Interpretation	M,O

UNIVERSITY OF ST. AUGUSTINE FOR HEALTH SCIENCES

Athletic Training and Sports Medicine	M
Health Education	M,D
Health Informatics	M
Health Services Management and Hospital Administration	M
Nursing and Healthcare Administration	M
Nursing Education	M
Nursing Informatics	M
Nursing—General	M,D
Occupational Therapy	M,D
Physical Therapy	D

UNIVERSITY OF ST. FRANCIS (IL)

Art Education	M,D,O
Curriculum and Instruction	M,D,O
Education—General	M,D,O
Educational Leadership and Administration	M,D,O
Elementary Education	M,D,O
English as a Second Language	M,D,O
English Education	M,D,O
Family Nurse Practitioner Studies	M,D,O
Forensic Sciences	M,O
Mathematics Education	M,D,O
Nursing and Healthcare Administration	M,D,O
Nursing Education	M,D,O
Nursing—General	M,D,O
Physician Assistant Studies	M,O
Psychiatric Nursing	M,D,O
Reading Education	M,D,O
Science Education	M,D,O
Secondary Education	M,D,O
Social Sciences Education	M,D,O
Social Work	M,O
Special Education	M,D,O

UNIVERSITY OF SAINT FRANCIS (IN)

Art/Fine Arts	M
Business Administration and Management—General	M
Clinical Psychology	M,O
Counseling Psychology	M,O
Counselor Education	M,O
Education—General	M
Environmental and Occupational Health	M
Family Nurse Practitioner Studies	M,D,O
Health Services Management and Hospital Administration	M
Nurse Anesthesia	M,D,O
Nursing—General	M,D,O
Organizational Management	M
Physician Assistant Studies	M
Secondary Education	M
Special Education	M
Sustainability Management	M

UNIVERSITY OF SAINT JOSEPH

Biochemistry	M
Biological and Biomedical Sciences—General	M
Business Administration and Management—General	M
Chemistry	M
Clinical Psychology	M
Counseling Psychology	M
Counselor Education	M
Curriculum and Instruction	M
Education—General	M
Educational Media/Instructional Technology	M
Elementary Education	M
English as a Second Language	M
Family Nurse Practitioner Studies	M,D
Marriage and Family Therapy	M
Nursing Education	M,D
Nursing—General	M,D
Nutrition	M
Pharmacy	D
Psychiatric Nursing	M,D
Public Health—General	M
Reading Education	M
Secondary Education	M
Special Education	M,O

UNIVERSITY OF SAINT MARY

Advertising and Public Relations	M
Business Administration and Management—General	M
Counseling Psychology	M
Education—General	M
Elementary Education	M
Finance and Banking	M
Health Services Management and Hospital Administration	M
Human Resources Management	M
Marketing	M
Nursing and Healthcare Administration	M
Nursing Education	M
Nursing—General	M
Physical Therapy	D
Psychology—General	M
Risk Management	M
Special Education	M

UNIVERSITY OF SAINT MARY OF THE LAKE–MUNDELEIN SEMINARY

Pastoral Ministry and Counseling	M,D
Theology	M,D

UNIVERSITY OF ST. MICHAEL'S COLLEGE

Jewish Studies	M,D,O
Pastoral Ministry and Counseling	M,D,O
Religious Education	M,D,O
Theology	M,D,O

UNIVERSITY OF ST. THOMAS (MN)

Accounting	M
Art History	M,O
Business Administration and Management—General	M
Counseling Psychology	M,D
Data Science/Data Analytics	M,O
Education—General	M,D,O
Educational Leadership and Administration	M,D,O
Electrical Engineering	M,O
Engineering and Applied Sciences—General	M,O
Engineering Management	M,O
English	M,O
Ethics	M,D
Health Communication	M
Health Services Management and Hospital Administration	M
Higher Education	M,D
Human Development	D
Information Science	M,O
Law	M,O
Management of Technology	M,O
Manufacturing Engineering	M,O
Mechanical Engineering	M,O
Museum Studies	M,O
Music Education	M,D
Music	M,D
Organizational Management	D
Pastoral Ministry and Counseling	M
Publishing	M,O
Religion	M
Religious Education	M
Social Work	M
Software Engineering	M,O
Special Education	M,O
Student Affairs	M,D,O
Systems Engineering	M,O
Theology	M
Writing	M,O

UNIVERSITY OF ST. THOMAS (TX)

Accounting	M
Business Administration and Management—General	M
Counselor Education	M,D
Curriculum and Instruction	M,D
Education—General	M,D
Educational Leadership and Administration	M,D
Educational Measurement and Evaluation	M,D
Elementary Education	M,D
English as a Second Language	M,D
Finance and Banking	M
International Business	M
Liberal Studies	M
Multilingual and Multicultural Education	M,D
Music	M
Pastoral Ministry and Counseling	M,D
Philosophy	M
Public Administration	M
Public Policy	M
Reading Education	M,D
Religion	M
Religious Education	M,D
Secondary Education	M,D
Special Education	M,D
Theology	M

UNIVERSITY OF SAN DIEGO

Accounting	M
Adult Nursing	M,D
Business Administration and Management—General	M
Computer and Information Systems Security	M
Computer Engineering	M
Conflict Resolution and Mediation/Peace Studies	M
Counseling Psychology	M
Counselor Education	M
Criminal Justice and Criminology	M
Curriculum and Instruction	M
Education—General	M,D,O
Educational Leadership and Administration	M,D,O
English as a Second Language	M,D,O
Environmental Sciences	M
Family Nurse Practitioner Studies	M,D
Finance and Banking	M
Gerontological Nursing	M,D
Health Informatics	M,D
Higher Education	M,D,O
International Affairs	M
International Business	M
Law	M,D,O
Legal and Justice Studies	M,D,O
Marriage and Family Therapy	M
Mathematics	M
Nonprofit Management	M,D,O
Nursing and Healthcare Administration	M,D
Nursing—General	M,D
Oceanography	M
Pediatric Nursing	M,D
Psychiatric Nursing	M,D
Reading Education	M
Real Estate	M
School Psychology	M
Science Education	M
Special Education	M
Supply Chain Management	M,O
Taxation	M,D,O
Theater	M

UNIVERSITY OF SAN FRANCISCO

Applied Behavior Analysis	M
Asian Studies	M
Biological and Biomedical Sciences—General	M
Biotechnology	M
Business Administration and Management—General	M
Chemistry	M
Clinical Psychology	D
Communication—General	M
Computer Science	M
Counseling Psychology	M
Counselor Education	M
Curriculum and Instruction	M,D
Data Science/Data Analytics	M
Economics	M
Education—General	M,D
Educational Leadership and Administration	M,D
Educational Media/Instructional Technology	M,D
Energy Management and Policy	M
Entrepreneurship	M
Finance and Banking	M
Health Informatics	M
Health Services Management and Hospital Administration	M
Intellectual Property Law	M
International Affairs	M
International and Comparative Education	M,D
International Business	M
International Development	M
Law	D
Management Information Systems	M
Marketing	M
Marriage and Family Therapy	M
Multilingual and Multicultural Education	M,D
Museum Studies	M
Natural Resources	M
Nonprofit Management	M
Nursing—General	D
Organizational Management	M
Pacific Area/Pacific Rim Studies	M
Public Administration	M
Public Affairs	M
Public Health—General	M
Reading Education	M,D
Religious Education	M,D
Special Education	M,D
Sports Management	M
Urban Education	M
Urban Studies	M
Writing	M

UNIVERSITY OF SASKATCHEWAN

Accounting	M
Agricultural Economics and Agribusiness	M,D,O
Agricultural Sciences—General	M,D,O
Agronomy and Soil Sciences	M,D,O
Allopathic Medicine	D
Anatomy	M,D
Animal Sciences	M,D
Anthropology	M
Archaeology	M,D
Art/Fine Arts	M
Biochemistry	M,D
Bioengineering	M,D
Biological and Biomedical Sciences—General	M,D
Biomedical Engineering	M,D
Biotechnology	M
Business Administration and Management—General	M
Canadian Studies	M,D
Cell Biology	M,D
Chemical Engineering	M,D
Chemistry	M,D
Civil Engineering	M,D
Community Health	M,D
Computer Science	M,D
Curriculum and Instruction	M,D,O
Dentistry	D
East European and Russian Studies	M
Economics	M,O
Education—General	M,D,O
Educational Leadership and Administration	M,D,O
Educational Psychology	M,D,O
Electrical Engineering	M,D,O
Engineering and Applied Sciences—General	M,D,O
Engineering Physics	M,D
English	M,D

Environmental Sciences	M
Epidemiology	M,D
Finance and Banking	M
Food Science and Technology	M,D
Foundations and Philosophy of Education	M,D,O
French	M
Gender Studies	M,D
Geography	M,D
Geological Engineering	M,D
Geology	M,D,O
German	M
Health Services Management and Hospital Administration	M
History	M,D
Immunology	M,D
International Business	M,D
Kinesiology and Movement Studies	M,D,O
Law	M,D
Marketing	M
Mathematics	M,D
Mechanical Engineering	M,D
Microbiology	M,D
Music	M
Nursing—General	M
Pathology	M,D
Pharmaceutical Sciences	M,D
Pharmacology	M,D
Philosophy	M
Physics	M,D
Physiology	M,D
Plant Sciences	M,D
Political Science	M
Psychology—General	M,D
Public Affairs	M,D
Public Policy	M,D
Religion	M
Reproductive Biology	M,D
Sociology	M,D
Special Education	M,D,O
Statistics	M,D
Sustainability Management	M
Theater	M
Toxicology	M,D,O
Veterinary Medicine	M,D
Veterinary Sciences	M,D
Women's Studies	M,D

THE UNIVERSITY OF SCRANTON

Accounting	M
Art/Fine Arts	M
Biochemistry	M
Business Administration and Management—General	M
Chemistry	M
Clinical Psychology	M
Counseling Psychology	M
Counselor Education	M
Curriculum and Instruction	M
Education—General	M
Educational Leadership and Administration	M
Family Nurse Practitioner Studies	M,D,O
Finance and Banking	M
Health Services Management and Hospital Administration	M
Human Resources Development	M
International Business	M
Management Information Systems	M
Marketing	M
Nurse Anesthesia	M,D,O
Nursing and Healthcare Administration	M,D,O
Nursing—General	M,D,O
Occupational Therapy	M
Physical Therapy	D
Reading Education	M
Rehabilitation Counseling	M
Secondary Education	M
Software Engineering	M
Special Education	M
Theology	M

UNIVERSITY OF SIOUX FALLS

Business Administration and Management—General	M
Education—General	M,O
Educational Leadership and Administration	M,O
Educational Media/Instructional Technology	M,O
Entrepreneurship	M
Health Services Management and Hospital Administration	M
Marketing	M
Reading Education	M,O

UNIVERSITY OF SOUTH AFRICA

Accounting	M,D
Acute Care/Critical Care Nursing	M,D
Adult Education	M,D
Agricultural Sciences—General	M,D
Anthropology	M,D
Archaeology	M,D
Art History	M,D
Business Administration and Management—General	M,D
Chemical Engineering	M
Classics	M,D
Clinical Psychology	M,D
Communication—General	M,D
Counseling Psychology	M,D
Counselor Education	M,D
Criminal Justice and Criminology	M,D
Curriculum and Instruction	M,D
Economics	M,D
Education—General	M,D
Educational Leadership and Administration	M,D
Educational Media/Instructional Technology	M,D
Educational Psychology	M,D
Engineering and Applied Sciences—General	M
English as a Second Language	M,D
English	M,D
Environmental Education	M,D
Environmental Management and Policy	M,D
Environmental Sciences	M,D
Ethics	M,D
Family and Consumer Sciences-General	M,D
Foundations and Philosophy of Education	M,D
French	M,D
Geography	M,D
German	M,D
Health Education	M,D
Health Services Management and Hospital Administration	M,D
History	M,D
Horticulture	M,D
Human Development	M,D
Human Resources Development	M,D
Industrial and Organizational Psychology	M,D
Information Science	M,D
International and Comparative Education	M,D
Italian	M,D
Law	M,D
Linguistics	M,D
Logistics	M,D
Management Information Systems	M
Marketing	M,D
Maternal and Child/Neonatal Nursing	M,D
Mathematics Education	M,D
Medical/Surgical Nursing	M,D
Missions and Missiology	M,D
Music	M,D
Natural Resources	M,D
Near and Middle Eastern Languages	M,D
Near and Middle Eastern Studies	M,D
Nurse Midwifery	M,D
Pastoral Ministry and Counseling	M,D
Philosophy	M,D
Political Science	M,D
Portuguese	M,D
Psychology—General	M,D
Public Administration	M,D
Public Health—General	M,D
Quantitative Analysis	M,D
Real Estate	M,D
Religion	M,D
Romance Languages	M,D
Russian	M,D
Science Education	M,D
Social Work	M,D
Sociology	M,D
Spanish	M,D
Statistics	M,D
Technology and Public Policy	M,D
Telecommunications Management	M,D
Theology	M,D
Travel and Tourism	M,D
Vocational and Technical Education	M,D

UNIVERSITY OF SOUTH ALABAMA

Accounting	M
Allied Health—General	M,D
Allopathic Medicine	D
Art Education	M,D
Art/Fine Arts	M
Biological and Biomedical Sciences—General	M,D
Business Administration and Management—General	M,D
Chemical Engineering	M
Chemistry	M
Civil Engineering	M
Clinical Psychology	M,D,O
Communication Disorders	M,D
Communication—General	M
Computer Engineering	M
Computer Science	M
Counseling Psychology	M,D,O
Counselor Education	M,D,O
Early Childhood Education	M,D
Education—General	M,D,O
Educational Leadership and Administration	M,D
Educational Media/Instructional Technology	M,D,O
Electrical Engineering	M
Elementary Education	M,D
Engineering and Applied Sciences—General	M,D
English	M
Environmental and Occupational Health	M
Environmental Engineering	M
Environmental Management and Policy	M,D
Exercise and Sports Science	M
Health Education	M
History	M
Kinesiology and Movement Studies	M
Management Information Systems	M,D
Marine Sciences	M,D
Marketing	M,D
Mathematics	M
Mechanical Engineering	M
Music Education	M
Music	M
Nursing and Healthcare Administration	M,D,O
Nursing Education	M,D,O
Nursing—General	M,D,O
Occupational Therapy	M
Physical Education	M
Physical Therapy	D
Physician Assistant Studies	M
Psychology—General	M
Public Administration	M
Reading Education	M,D
Science Education	M,D
Secondary Education	M,D
Sociology	M
Special Education	M,D
Sports Management	M
Systems Engineering	D
Toxicology	M
Writing	M

UNIVERSITY OF SOUTH CAROLINA

Accounting	M
Acute Care/Critical Care Nursing	M,O
Adult Nursing	M
Allopathic Medicine	D
Anthropology	M,D
Applied Statistics	M,D,O
Archives/Archival Administration	M,O
Art Education	M,D
Art History	M
Art/Fine Arts	M
Astronomy	M,D
Biochemistry	M,D
Biological and Biomedical Sciences—General	M,D,O
Biostatistics	M,D
Business Administration and Management—General	M,D
Business Education	M,D
Cell Biology	M,D
Chemical Engineering	M,D
Chemistry	M,D
Civil Engineering	M,D
Clinical Psychology	M,D
Communication Disorders	M,D
Community Health Nursing	M
Comparative Literature	M,D
Computer Engineering	M,D
Computer Science	M,D
Consumer Economics	M
Counselor Education	D,O
Criminal Justice and Criminology	M,D
Curriculum and Instruction	D
Developmental Biology	M,D
Early Childhood Education	M,D
Ecology	M,D
Economics	M,D
Education—General	M,D,O
Educational Leadership and Administration	M,D,O
Educational Measurement and Evaluation	M,D
Educational Media/Instructional Technology	M
Educational Psychology	M,D
Electrical Engineering	M,D
Elementary Education	M,D
Engineering and Applied Sciences—General	M,D
English as a Second Language	M,D,O
English Education	M,D
English	M,D
Entertainment Management	M
Environmental and Occupational Health	M,D
Environmental Management and Policy	M
Epidemiology	M,D
Evolutionary Biology	M,D
Exercise and Sports Science	M,D
Experimental Psychology	M,D
Family Nurse Practitioner Studies	M
Foreign Languages Education	M,D
Foundations and Philosophy of Education	D
French	M,D
Genetic Counseling	M
Geography	M,D
Geology	M,D
Geosciences	M,D
German	M,D
Gerontology	O
Hazardous Materials Management	M,D
Health Education	M,D,O
Health Promotion	M,D,O
Health Services Management and Hospital Administration	M,D
Higher Education	M
Historic Preservation	M,O
History	M,D,O
Hospitality Management	M
Human Resources Management	M
Industrial Hygiene	M,D
Information Studies	M,D,O
International Affairs	M,D
International Business	M
Journalism	M,D
Law	D
Library Science	M,D,O
Linguistics	M,D,O
Marine Sciences	M,D
Mathematics Education	M,D
Mathematics	M,D
Mechanical Engineering	M,D
Media Studies	M
Medical/Surgical Nursing	M
Molecular Biology	M,D
Museum Studies	M,O
Music Education	M,D,O
Music	M,D,O
Nuclear Engineering	M,D
Nurse Anesthesia	M
Nursing and Healthcare Administration	M
Nursing—General	M,O
Pediatric Nursing	M
Pharmaceutical Sciences	M,D
Pharmacy	D
Philosophy	M,D
Physical Education	M,D
Physics	M,D
Political Science	M,D
Psychiatric Nursing	M,O
Psychology—General	M,D
Public Administration	M
Public Health—General	M
Public History	M,O
Reading Education	M,O
Rehabilitation Counseling	M,O
Rehabilitation Sciences	M,O
Religion	M
School Psychology	D
Science Education	M,D
Secondary Education	M,D
Social Psychology	M,D
Social Sciences Education	M,D
Social Work	M,D
Sociology	M,D
Software Engineering	M,D
Spanish	M,D
Special Education	M,D
Speech and Interpersonal Communication	M,D
Sports Management	M
Statistics	M,D,O
Student Affairs	M
Theater	M,D
Travel and Tourism	M
Women's Health Nursing	M
Women's Studies	O
Writing	M,D

UNIVERSITY OF SOUTH CAROLINA AIKEN

Applied Psychology	M
Business Administration and Management—General	M
Clinical Psychology	M
Educational Media/Instructional Technology	M

UNIVERSITY OF SOUTH CAROLINA UPSTATE

Early Childhood Education	M
Education—General	M
Elementary Education	M
Health Informatics	M
Information Science	M
Special Education	M

UNIVERSITY OF SOUTH DAKOTA

Accounting	M
Addictions/Substance Abuse Counseling	M
Adult Education	M,D,O
Allied Health—General	M,D,O
Allopathic Medicine	D,O
American Indian/Native American Studies	M,D,O
Art Education	M
Art/Fine Arts	M
Bioethics	D,O
Biological and Biomedical Sciences—General	M,D
Business Administration and Management—General	M,O
Business Analytics	M,O
Cardiovascular Sciences	M,D
Cell Biology	M,D
Chemistry	M,D
Clinical Psychology	M,D
Communication Disorders	M,D
Communication—General	M
Computer Science	M
Counseling Psychology	M,D,O
Counselor Education	M,D,O
Criminal Justice and Criminology	M
Curriculum and Instruction	M,D,O
Early Childhood Education	M,D,O
Education—General	M,D,O
Educational Leadership and Administration	M,D,O
Educational Media/Instructional Technology	M
Educational Psychology	M,D,O
Elementary Education	M
English as a Second Language	M
English	M,D
Exercise and Sports Science	M
Graphic Design	M
Health Services Management and Hospital Administration	M,O
Higher Education	M,D,O
History	M
Human Development	M,D,O
Human Resources Management	M
Immunology	M,D
Interdisciplinary Studies	M
Kinesiology and Movement Studies	M
Law	D
Marketing	M,O
Mathematics Education	M
Mathematics	M
Microbiology	M,D
Molecular Biology	M,D
Music Education	M
Music	M
Neuroscience	M,D
Occupational Therapy	M,D
Organizational Management	M
Pharmacology	M,D
Photography	M
Physical Therapy	D
Physician Assistant Studies	M

*M—masters degree; D—doctorate; O—other advanced degree; *—Close-Up and/or Display*

Physics	M,D
Physiology	M,D
Psychology—General	M,D
Public Health—General	M
Reading Education	M
School Psychology	M,D,O
Science Education	M
Secondary Education	M
Social Work	M
Special Education	M,D,O
Supply Chain Management	M,O
Sustainable Development	M,D
Theater	M

UNIVERSITY OF SOUTHERN CALIFORNIA

Accounting	M
Advertising and Public Relations	M
Aerospace/Aeronautical Engineering	M,D,O
Allopathic Medicine	D
American Studies	D
Applied Mathematics	M,D
Architecture	M,D
Art History	M,D,O
Art/Fine Arts	M,D,O
Artificial Intelligence/Robotics	M,D
Arts Administration	M
Asian Languages	M,D
Asian Studies	M,D
Biochemistry	M
Bioinformatics	D
Biological and Biomedical Sciences—General	M,D,O
Biomedical Engineering	M,D
Biophysics	M,D
Biostatistics	M,D
Biotechnology	M
Business Administration and Management—General	M,D
Cancer Biology/Oncology	D
Cell Biology	M,D
Chemical Engineering	M,D,O
Chemistry	D
Child and Family Studies	M,D
Civil Engineering	M,D,O
Classics	M,D
Clinical Psychology	M,D
Clinical Research	M,D,O
Cognitive Sciences	M,D
Communication—General	M,D
Comparative Literature	D
Computational Biology	D
Computer and Information Systems Security	M,D
Computer Art and Design	M
Computer Engineering	M,D,O
Computer Science	M,D
Construction Management	M,D,O
Corporate and Organizational Communication	M
Counselor Education	M
Cultural Studies	D
Dentistry	D
Developmental Biology	D
Developmental Psychology	M,D
Economic Development	M,D
Economics	M,D
Education—General	M,D
Educational Leadership and Administration	D
Educational Policy	D
Educational Psychology	D
Electrical Engineering	M,D,O
Engineering and Applied Sciences—General	M,D,O
Engineering Management	M,D,O
English as a Second Language	M
English	M,D
Entrepreneurship	M
Environmental and Occupational Health	M
Environmental Biology	M,D
Environmental Engineering	M,D,O
Epidemiology	M,D
Evolutionary Biology	D
Film, Television, and Video Production	M
Film, Television, and Video Theory and Criticism	M,D
Food Science and Technology	M,D,O
Game Design and Development	M,D
Genomic Sciences	D
Geographic Information Systems	M,O
Geography	M,O
Geosciences	M,D
Geotechnical Engineering	M,D,O
Gerontology	M,D,O*
Hazardous Materials Management	M,D,O
Health Communication	M,D
Health Education	M
Health Promotion	M
Health Services Management and Hospital Administration	M,O
Health Services Research	D
Higher Education	D
History	D
Homeland Security	M,O
Immunology	M
Industrial/Management Engineering	M,D,O
International Affairs	M,D
International Health	M,O
Internet and Interactive Multimedia	M,D,O
Journalism	M
Kinesiology and Movement Studies	M,D
Latin American Studies	D
Law	M,D
Linguistics	M,D
Manufacturing Engineering	M,D,O
Marine Biology	M,D
Marine Sciences	M,D
Marriage and Family Therapy	M
Materials Engineering	M,D,O
Materials Sciences	M,D,O
Mathematical and Computational Finance	M,D
Mathematics	M,D
Mechanical Engineering	M,D,O
Mechanics	M,D,O
Media Studies	M,D
Medical Imaging	M,D
Medical Microbiology	D
Microbiology	M
Modeling and Simulation	M,D
Molecular Biology	M,D
Molecular Pharmacology	M,D
Multilingual and Multicultural Education	D
Music Education	M,D,O
Music	M,D,O
Neurobiology	D
Neuroscience	M,D
Nonprofit Management	M,O
Nurse Anesthesia	D
Occupational Therapy	M,D
Oceanography	M,D
Operations Research	M,D,O
Oral and Dental Sciences	M,D,O
Organizational Management	M
Pathology	M
Petroleum Engineering	M,D,O
Pharmaceutical Administration	M
Pharmaceutical Sciences	M,D,O
Pharmacy	D
Philosophy	M,D
Photography	M
Physical Chemistry	D
Physical Therapy	M,D
Physician Assistant Studies	M
Physics	M,D
Physiology	M
Political Science	M,D
Psychology—General	M,D
Public Administration	M,O
Public Health—General	M
Public Policy	M,D,O
Quantitative Analysis	M,D
Real Estate	M
Rhetoric	D
Safety Engineering	M,D,O
Slavic Languages	M,D
Social Psychology	M,D
Social Work	M,D
Sociology	D
Software Engineering	M,D
Spanish	D
Statistics	M,D
Student Affairs	M
Supply Chain Management	M,D,O
Sustainable Development	M,D,O
Systems Engineering	M,D,O
Taxation	M
Telecommunications	M,D,O
Theater	M
Toxicology	M,D
Transportation and Highway Engineering	M,D,O
Urban and Regional Planning	M,D,O
Urban Education	D
Water Resources	M,D,O
Writing	M,D

UNIVERSITY OF SOUTHERN INDIANA

Accounting	M
Business Administration and Management—General	M
Communication—General	M
Cultural Studies	M
Data Science/Data Analytics	M
Education—General	M,D
Educational Leadership and Administration	M,D
Elementary Education	M
Engineering and Applied Sciences—General	M,D
Engineering Management	M
English as a Second Language	M
English	M
Family Nurse Practitioner Studies	M,D,O
Gerontology	M,D,O
Health Services Management and Hospital Administration	M
Human Resources Management	M
Industrial and Manufacturing Management	M
Liberal Studies	M
Mathematics Education	M
Nonprofit Management	M
Nursing and Healthcare Administration	M,D,O
Nursing Education	M,D,O
Nursing—General	M,D,O
Occupational Therapy	M
Psychiatric Nursing	M,D,O
Public Administration	M
Secondary Education	M
Social Work	M
Sports Management	M

UNIVERSITY OF SOUTHERN MAINE

Accounting	M
Addictions/Substance Abuse Counseling	M,O
Adult Education	M,O
Adult Nursing	M,D,O
American Studies	M,O
Applied Behavior Analysis	M,O
Biological and Biomedical Sciences—General	M
Business Administration and Management—General	M,O
Computer Science	M,O
Counseling Psychology	M,O
Counselor Education	M,O
Cultural Studies	M,O
Education of the Gifted	M,O
Education—General	M,D,O
Educational Leadership and Administration	M,O
Educational Psychology	M,O
English as a Second Language	M,O
Family Nurse Practitioner Studies	M,D,O
Finance and Banking	M
Gerontological Nursing	M,D,O
Health Services Management and Hospital Administration	M
Higher Education	M,O
Immunology	M
Molecular Biology	M
Music Education	M
Music	M
Nursing and Healthcare Administration	M,D,O
Nursing Education	M,D,O
Nursing—General	M,D,O
Occupational Therapy	M
Psychiatric Nursing	M,D,O
Public Health—General	M,O
Public Policy	M
Reading Education	M,O
Rehabilitation Counseling	M,O
School Psychology	M,D
Social Work	M
Software Engineering	M,O
Special Education	M,O
Statistics	M,O
Sustainability Management	M
Urban and Regional Planning	M,O
Writing	M

UNIVERSITY OF SOUTHERN MISSISSIPPI

Accounting	M
Anthropology	M
Biochemistry	M,D
Biological and Biomedical Sciences—General	M,D
Biostatistics	M
Business Administration and Management—General	M
Chemistry	M,D
Child and Family Studies	M
Clinical Laboratory Sciences/Medical Technology	M
Communication Disorders	M,D
Computational Sciences	M,D
Computer Science	M,D
Construction Engineering	M
Criminal Justice and Criminology	M,D
Curriculum and Instruction	M,D
Economic Development	M
Economics	M
Education—General	M,D,O
Educational Leadership and Administration	M,D,O
Educational Measurement and Evaluation	M,D,O
Educational Media/Instructional Technology	M,D
Elementary Education	M,D
English Education	M,D
English	M,D
Epidemiology	M
Food Science and Technology	M
Foreign Languages Education	M
Forensic Sciences	M,D
Geography	M,D
Geology	M,D
Health Services Management and Hospital Administration	M
Higher Education	M,D,O
History	M,D
Hydrology	M,D
Information Science	M,O
International Development	M,D
Library Science	M,O
Marine Sciences	M,D
Mathematics	M,D
Music Education	M,D
Music	M,D
Nursing—General	M,D,O
Nutrition	M
Physical Education	M,D
Physics	M,D
Political Science	M,D
Polymer Science and Engineering	M,D
Psychology—General	M,D
Public Health—General	M
Secondary Education	M,D
Social Work	M
Spanish	M
Special Education	M,D
Speech and Interpersonal Communication	M,D
Student Affairs	M,D,O
Theater	M
Writing	M,D

UNIVERSITY OF SOUTH FLORIDA

Accounting	M,D
Acute Care/Critical Care Nursing	M,D,O
Addictions/Substance Abuse Counseling	M,D
Adult Education	M,D,O
Adult Nursing	M,D,O
African Studies	M,D,O
Allopathic Medicine	M,D
American Studies	M,D
Anatomy	M,D
Anthropology	M,D,O
Applied Behavior Analysis	M,D
Applied Mathematics	M,D
Applied Physics	M,D
Archaeology	M,D,O
Architecture	M
Art History	M
Art/Fine Arts	M
Athletic Training and Sports Medicine	M,D
Bioethics	O
Bioinformatics	M,D,O
Biological and Biomedical Sciences—General	M,D
Biomedical Engineering	M,D,O
Biostatistics	M,D,O
Biotechnology	M,D,O
Business Administration and Management—General	M
Cancer Biology/Oncology	M,D
Cardiovascular Sciences	O
Cell Biology	M,D
Chemical Engineering	M,D,O
Chemistry	M,D
Child and Family Studies	M,D,O
Civil Engineering	M,D,O
Clinical Psychology	D
Clinical Research	M,D,O
Cognitive Sciences	D
Communication Disorders	M,D,O
Communication—General	M,D
Community College Education	M,D,O
Community Health	M,D,O
Comparative Literature	O
Computational Biology	M,D
Computer and Information Systems Security	M,D
Computer Engineering	M,D
Computer Science	M,D
Corporate and Organizational Communication	M,O
Counseling Psychology	M,D,O
Counselor Education	M,D,O
Criminal Justice and Criminology	M,D,O
Data Science/Data Analytics	M,D,O
Distance Education Development	O
Early Childhood Education	M,D,O
Ecology	M,D
Economics	M,D
Education—General	M,D,O
Educational Leadership and Administration	M,D,O
Educational Measurement and Evaluation	O
Educational Media/Instructional Technology	O
Educational Psychology	M,D,O
Electrical Engineering	M,D
Elementary Education	M,D,O
Emergency Management	O
Engineering and Applied Sciences—General	M,D,O
Engineering Management	M,D
English as a Second Language	M,D,O
English	M,D,O
Entrepreneurship	M,O
Environmental and Occupational Health	M,D,O
Environmental Biology	M,D
Environmental Engineering	M,D
Environmental Management and Policy	M,D,O
Environmental Sciences	M,D
Epidemiology	M,D,O
Evolutionary Biology	M,D
Family Nurse Practitioner Studies	M,D,O
Film, Television, and Video Theory and Criticism	M
Finance and Banking	M,D
Foreign Languages Education	O
Forensic Sciences	M,D,O
French	M,D
Gender Studies	M,O
Geographic Information Systems	M,D,O
Geography	O
Geology	M,D,O
Geosciences	M,D
Geotechnical Engineering	M,D
Gerontological Nursing	M,D,O
Gerontology	M,D,O
Health Education	M,D
Health Informatics	M,D,O
Health Services Management and Hospital Administration	M,D,O
Higher Education	M,D,O
History	M,D
Human Resources Development	O
Human Resources Management	M
Humanities	M
Hydrogeology	O
Immunology	M,D
Industrial and Organizational Psychology	D
Industrial/Management Engineering	M,D,O
Infectious Diseases	M,D
Information Science	M
Information Studies	M,O
Interdisciplinary Studies	M,D
International Affairs	O
International Health	M,D,O
Internet and Interactive Multimedia	M,O
Journalism	M,O
Latin American Studies	M,D,O
Legal and Justice Studies	O
Liberal Studies	M,D
Library Science	M
Linguistics	M,D
Management Information Systems	M,D,O
Management of Technology	O
Management Strategy and Policy	M,D,O
Marine Sciences	M,D
Marketing	M,D
Marriage and Family Therapy	M,D,O
Mass Communication	M,O
Materials Engineering	M,D,O
Materials Sciences	M,D,O
Maternal and Child Health	O
Mathematics	M,D,O
Mechanical Engineering	M,D
Media Studies	M

Medical Microbiology	M,D
Medical Physics	M,D
Microbiology	M,D
Molecular Biology	M,D
Molecular Medicine	M,D
Molecular Pharmacology	M,D
Museum Studies	O
Music Education	M,D
Music	M,D
Nanotechnology	M,D
Neuroscience	M,D,O
Nonprofit Management	O
Nurse Anesthesia	M,D,O
Nursing Education	M,D,O
Nursing—General	M,D,O
Nutrition	M,D,O
Occupational Health Nursing	M,D,O
Oceanography	M,D
Oncology Nursing	M,D,O
Pathology	M,D
Pediatric Nursing	M,D,O
Pharmaceutical Sciences	M,D
Pharmacy	M,D,O
Philosophy	M,D
Physical Therapy	D
Physics	M,D
Physiology	M,D
Political Science	M,D,O
Psychology—General	D
Public Administration	O
Public Affairs	O
Public Health—General	M,D,O*
Reading Education	M,D,O
Real Estate	M,D
Rehabilitation Counseling	M,D,O
Rehabilitation Sciences	D
Religion	M,D
Rhetoric	M,D
School Psychology	M,D,O
Secondary Education	O
Social Sciences Education	M,D,O
Social Work	M,D,O
Sociology	M,D
Spanish	M,D
Special Education	O
Sports Management	M,D
Statistics	M,D
Structural Engineering	M,D
Student Affairs	M,D,O
Sustainability Management	M,O
Sustainable Development	M,O
Systems Engineering	O
Taxation	M,D
Technical Communication	O
Toxicology	O
Transportation and Highway Engineering	M,D,O
Travel and Tourism	M,O
Urban and Regional Planning	O
Urban Design	O
Vocational and Technical Education	M,D,O
Water Resources Engineering	M,D,O
Western European Studies	M,D
Women's Studies	M
Writing	M,D,O

UNIVERSITY OF SOUTH FLORIDA, ST. PETERSBURG

Business Administration and Management—General	M
Computer Art and Design	M
Education—General	M
Educational Leadership and Administration	M
Elementary Education	M
English Education	M
Environmental Management and Policy	M
Environmental Sciences	M
Journalism	M
Liberal Studies	M
Mathematics Education	M
Media Studies	M
Middle School Education	M
Psychology—General	M
Reading Education	M
Science Education	M

UNIVERSITY OF SOUTH FLORIDA SARASOTA-MANATEE

Business Administration and Management—General	M
Criminal Justice and Criminology	M
Curriculum and Instruction	M
Educational Leadership and Administration	M
Elementary Education	M
English Education	M
Hospitality Management	M
Liberal Studies	M
Social Sciences	M
Social Work	M

THE UNIVERSITY OF TAMPA

Accounting	M,O
Adult Nursing	M
Business Administration and Management—General	M,O
Business Analytics	M,O
Computer and Information Systems Security	M,O
Criminal Justice and Criminology	M
Curriculum and Instruction	M
Education—General	M
Educational Leadership and Administration	M
Educational Media/Instructional Technology	M
Entrepreneurship	M,O
Exercise and Sports Science	M
Family Nurse Practitioner Studies	M
Finance and Banking	M,O
International Business	M,O
Management Information Systems	M,O
Marketing	M,O
Nonprofit Management	M,O
Nursing—General	M
Nutrition	M
Writing	M

THE UNIVERSITY OF TENNESSEE

Accounting	M,D
Adult Education	M,D
Advertising and Public Relations	M,D
Aerospace/Aeronautical Engineering	M,D
Agricultural Education	M
Agricultural Engineering	M
Agricultural Sciences—General	M,D
Analytical Chemistry	M,D
Anatomy	M,D
Animal Behavior	M,D
Animal Sciences	M,D
Anthropology	M,D
Applied Mathematics	M,D
Applied Psychology	M,D
Archaeology	M,D
Architecture	M
Art Education	M,D,O
Art/Fine Arts	M
Athletic Training and Sports Medicine	M,D
Aviation	M
Biochemistry	M,D
Bioethics	M,D
Biological and Biomedical Sciences—General	M,D
Biomedical Engineering	M,D
Biosystems Engineering	M,D
Business Administration and Management—General	M,D
Chemical Engineering	M,D
Chemical Physics	M,D
Chemistry	M,D
Child and Family Studies	M,D
Civil Engineering	M,D
Clinical Psychology	M,D
Clothing and Textiles	M,D
Communication Disorders	M,D,O
Communication—General	M,D
Community Health	M,D
Computer Engineering	M,D
Computer Science	M,D
Consumer Economics	M,D
Counseling Psychology	M,D
Counselor Education	M,D,O
Criminal Justice and Criminology	M,D
Cultural Anthropology	M,D
Curriculum and Instruction	M,D,O
Data Science/Data Analytics	D
Early Childhood Education	M,D,O
Ecology	M,D
Economics	M,D
Education—General	M,D,O
Educational Leadership and Administration	M,D,O
Educational Measurement and Evaluation	M,D,O
Educational Media/Instructional Technology	M,D,O
Educational Psychology	M,D,O
Electrical Engineering	M,D
Elementary Education	M,D,O
Energy and Power Engineering	D
Engineering and Applied Sciences—General	M,D
Engineering Management	M,D
English as a Second Language	M,D,O
English Education	M,D,O
English	M,D
Entomology	M,D
Environmental Engineering	M
Environmental Management and Policy	M,D
Evolutionary Biology	M,D
Exercise and Sports Science	M,D,O
Experimental Psychology	M,D
Family and Consumer Sciences-General	D
Finance and Banking	M,D
Fish, Game, and Wildlife Management	M
Food Science and Technology	M,D
Foreign Languages Education	M,D,O
Forestry	M
Foundations and Philosophy of Education	M,D,O
French	M,D
Genetics	M,D
Genomic Sciences	M,D
Geography	M,D
Geology	M,D
German	M,D
Gerontology	M
Graphic Design	M
Health Education	M
Health Promotion	M
Health Services Management and Hospital Administration	M
History	M,D
Hospitality Management	M
Human Resources Development	M
Industrial and Manufacturing Management	M,D
Industrial and Organizational Psychology	D
Industrial/Management Engineering	M,D
Information Science	M,D
Inorganic Chemistry	M,D
Italian	D
Journalism	M,D
Kinesiology and Movement Studies	M,D
Landscape Architecture	M
Law	D
Leisure Studies	M,D
Linguistics	D
Logistics	M,D
Marketing	M,D
Materials Engineering	M,D
Materials Sciences	M,D
Mathematics Education	M,D,O
Mathematics	M,D
Mechanical Engineering	M,D
Media Studies	M,D
Microbiology	M,D
Multilingual and Multicultural Education	M,D,O
Music Education	M
Music	M
Nuclear Engineering	M,D
Nursing—General	M,D
Nutrition	M
Organic Chemistry	M,D
Philosophy	M,D
Photography	M
Physical Chemistry	M,D
Physics	M,D
Physiology	M,D
Plant Pathology	M,D
Plant Physiology	M,D
Plant Sciences	M
Political Science	M,D
Portuguese	D
Psychology—General	M,D
Public Administration	M
Public Health—General	M
Reading Education	M,D,O
Recreation and Park Management	M,D
Rehabilitation Counseling	M,D
Reliability Engineering	M,D
Religion	M,D
Russian	D
School Psychology	M,D,O
Science Education	M,D,O
Secondary Education	M,D,O
Social Sciences Education	M,D,O
Social Work	M,D
Sociology	M,D
Spanish	M,D
Special Education	M,D,O
Speech and Interpersonal Communication	M,D
Sports Management	M,D
Statistics	M,D
Student Affairs	M
Theater	M
Theoretical Chemistry	M,D
Transportation Management	M,D
Travel and Tourism	M
Veterinary Medicine	D

THE UNIVERSITY OF TENNESSEE AT CHATTANOOGA

Accounting	M
Applied Mathematics	M
Applied Statistics	M
Athletic Training and Sports Medicine	M
Automotive Engineering	M
Bioinformatics	M,O
Business Administration and Management—General	M
Chemical Engineering	M
Civil Engineering	M
Computational Sciences	D
Computer Science	M,O
Construction Management	M,O
Counselor Education	M,D,O
Criminal Justice and Criminology	M
Education—General	M,D,O
Educational Leadership and Administration	M,D,O
Electrical Engineering	M
Elementary Education	M,D,O
Energy and Power Engineering	M,O
Engineering Management	M,O
English	M
Environmental Sciences	M
Ethics	M,O
Experimental Psychology	M
Family Nurse Practitioner Studies	M,D,O
Gerontological Nursing	M,D,O
Industrial and Organizational Psychology	M
Interior Design	M
Logistics	M,O
Mathematics Education	M
Mathematics	M
Mechanical Engineering	M
Music Education	M
Music	M
Nonprofit Management	M,O
Nurse Anesthesia	M,D,O
Nursing Education	M,D,O
Nursing—General	M,D,O
Occupational Therapy	D
Physical Education	M
Physical Therapy	D
Project Management	M,O
Psychology—General	M
Public Administration	M,O
Quality Management	M,O
Rhetoric	M
School Psychology	M,D,O
Secondary Education	M,D,O
Social Psychology	M,D,O
Social Work	M
Special Education	M,D,O
Supply Chain Management	M,O
Writing	M

THE UNIVERSITY OF TENNESSEE AT MARTIN

Addictions/Substance Abuse Counseling	M
Agricultural Economics and Agribusiness	M
Agricultural Sciences—General	M
Business Administration and Management—General	M
Child and Family Studies	M
Child Development	M
Communication—General	M
Counselor Education	M
Curriculum and Instruction	M
Education—General	M
Educational Leadership and Administration	M
Elementary Education	M
Family and Consumer Sciences-General	M
Finance and Banking	M
Food Science and Technology	M
Interdisciplinary Studies	M
Nutrition	M
Physical Education	M
Secondary Education	M
Social Psychology	M
Special Education	M
Student Affairs	M

THE UNIVERSITY OF TENNESSEE HEALTH SCIENCE CENTER

Allied Health—General	M,D
Allopathic Medicine	D
Biological and Biomedical Sciences—General	M,D
Biomedical Engineering	M,D
Clinical Laboratory Sciences/Medical Technology	M,D
Communication Disorders	M,D
Dentistry	D
Epidemiology	M,D
Family Nurse Practitioner Studies	D,O
Gerontological Nursing	D,O
Health Informatics	M,D
Health Services Research	M,D
Nursing—General	M,D,O
Occupational Therapy	M,D
Oral and Dental Sciences	M,D
Pathology	M,D
Pediatric Nursing	D,O
Pharmaceutical Sciences	M,D
Pharmacology	M,D
Pharmacy	M,D
Physical Therapy	M,D
Physician Assistant Studies	M,D
Psychiatric Nursing	D,O

THE UNIVERSITY OF TENNESSEE–OAK RIDGE NATIONAL LABORATORY

Biological and Biomedical Sciences—General	M,D
Genomic Sciences	M,D

THE UNIVERSITY OF TEXAS AT ARLINGTON

Accounting	M,D
Aerospace/Aeronautical Engineering	M,D
Anthropology	M
Applied Mathematics	M,D
Architecture	M
Art/Fine Arts	M
Athletic Training and Sports Medicine	M,D
Bioengineering	M,D
Biological and Biomedical Sciences—General	M,D
Chemistry	M,D
Civil Engineering	M,D
Communication—General	M
Computer Engineering	M,D
Computer Science	M,D
Construction Management	M,D
Criminal Justice and Criminology	M
Curriculum and Instruction	M
Economics	M
Education—General	M,D
Educational Leadership and Administration	M,D
Educational Policy	M,D
Electrical Engineering	M,D
Engineering and Applied Sciences—General	M,D
Engineering Management	M
English as a Second Language	M
English	M,D
Environmental Sciences	M,D
Exercise and Sports Science	M,D
Experimental Psychology	M,D
Family Nurse Practitioner Studies	M,D
Film, Television, and Video Production	M
Finance and Banking	M,D
French	M
Geology	M,D
Health Psychology	M,D
Health Services Management and Hospital Administration	M
Higher Education	M,D
History	M,D
Human Resources Management	M
Industrial and Organizational Psychology	M,D
Industrial/Management Engineering	M,D
Kinesiology and Movement Studies	M,D
Landscape Architecture	M

*M—masters degree; D—doctorate; O—other advanced degree; *—Close-Up and/or Display*

Linguistics	M,D
Logistics	M
Management Information Systems	M,D
Marketing Research	M
Marketing	M
Materials Engineering	M,D
Materials Sciences	M,D
Mathematics Education	M,D
Mathematics	M,D
Mechanical Engineering	M,D
Music Education	M
Music	M
Nursing and Healthcare Administration	M,D
Nursing Education	M,D
Nursing—General	M,D
Physics	M,D
Political Science	M
Psychology—General	M,D
Public Administration	M
Public Policy	M
Quantitative Analysis	M,D
Reading Education	M
Real Estate	M,D
Science Education	M
Social Work	M,D
Sociology	M
Software Engineering	M,D
Spanish	M
Systems Engineering	M
Taxation	M,D
Urban and Regional Planning	D

THE UNIVERSITY OF TEXAS AT AUSTIN

Accounting	M,D
Actuarial Science	M,D
Adult Nursing	M,D
Advertising and Public Relations	M,D
Aerospace/Aeronautical Engineering	M,D
African Studies	M,D
Allopathic Medicine	D
American Studies	M,D
Analytical Chemistry	D
Animal Behavior	D
Anthropology	M,D
Applied Arts and Design—General	M
Applied Mathematics	M,D
Applied Physics	M,D
Archaeology	M,D
Architectural Engineering	M
Architectural History	M,D
Architecture	M
Art Education	M
Art History	M,D
Art/Fine Arts	M
Asian Languages	M,D
Asian Studies	M,D
Astronomy	M,D
Biochemistry	D
Biological and Biomedical Sciences—General	M,D
Biomedical Engineering	M,D
Biopsychology	D
Business Administration and Management—General	M,D
Cell Biology	D
Chemical Engineering	M,D
Chemistry	D
Child and Family Studies	M,D
Child Development	M,D
Civil Engineering	M,D
Classics	M,D
Clinical Laboratory Sciences/Medical Technology	M,D
Clinical Psychology	D
Communication Disorders	M,D
Communication—General	M,D
Community Health Nursing	M,D
Comparative Literature	M,D
Computational Sciences	M,D
Computer and Information Systems Security	M,D
Computer Engineering	M,D
Computer Science	M,D
Counseling Psychology	M,D
Counselor Education	M,D
Cultural Studies	M,D
Curriculum and Instruction	M,D
Dance	M
Developmental Psychology	M,D
Early Childhood Education	M,D
East European and Russian Studies	M
Ecology	D
Economics	M,D
Education—General	M,D
Educational Leadership and Administration	M,D
Educational Media/Instructional Technology	M,D
Educational Psychology	M,D
Electrical Engineering	M,D
Engineering and Applied Sciences—General	M,D
English	M,D
Entrepreneurship	M
Environmental Engineering	M,D
Environmental Management and Policy	M
Evolutionary Biology	D
Exercise and Sports Science	M,D
Family and Consumer Sciences-General	M,D
Family Nurse Practitioner Studies	M,D
Film, Television, and Video Production	M,D
Finance and Banking	M,D
Folklore	M,D
French	M,D
Geography	M,D
Geology	M,D
Geosciences	M,D
Geotechnical Engineering	M,D
German	M,D
Gerontological Nursing	M,D
Health Education	M,D
Hispanic and Latin American Languages	M,D
Hispanic Studies	M
Historic Preservation	M
History	M,D
Human Development	M,D
Industrial and Manufacturing Management	M,D
Industrial/Management Engineering	M,D
Information Studies	M,D
Inorganic Chemistry	D
Interior Design	M
Italian	M,D
Journalism	M,D
Kinesiology and Movement Studies	M,D
Landscape Architecture	M
Latin American Studies	M,D
Law	M,D
Linguistics	M,D
Management Information Systems	M,D
Marine Sciences	M,D
Marketing	M,D
Materials Engineering	M,D
Materials Sciences	M,D
Maternal and Child/Neonatal Nursing	M,D
Mathematics	M,D
Mechanical Engineering	M,D
Mechanics	M,D
Media Studies	M,D
Medicinal and Pharmaceutical Chemistry	M,D
Microbiology	D
Mineral Economics	M
Mineral/Mining Engineering	M
Molecular Biology	D
Multilingual and Multicultural Education	M,D
Music Education	M,D
Music	M,D
Natural Resources	M,D
Near and Middle Eastern Languages	M,D
Near and Middle Eastern Studies	M,D
Neurobiology	D
Neuroscience	D
Nursing and Healthcare Administration	M,D
Nursing Education	M,D
Nursing—General	M,D
Nutrition	M,D
Operations Research	M,D
Organic Chemistry	D
Organizational Behavior	D
Pediatric Nursing	M,D
Petroleum Engineering	M,D
Pharmaceutical Sciences	M,D
Pharmacology	M,D
Pharmacy	D
Philosophy	D
Physical Chemistry	D
Physical Education	M,D
Physics	M,D
Plant Biology	M,D
Political Science	M,D
Portuguese	M,D
Psychiatric Nursing	M,D
Psychology—General	D
Public Administration	M,D
Public Affairs	M,D
Public History	M,D
Public Policy	M,D
Quantitative Analysis	M,D
Reading Education	M,D
Rehabilitation Counseling	M,D
Risk Management	M,D
Romance Languages	M,D
School Psychology	M,D
Slavic Languages	M,D
Social Work	M,D
Sociology	M,D
Spanish	M,D
Special Education	M,D
Sport Psychology	M,D
Statistics	M,D
Supply Chain Management	M,D
Sustainable Development	M
Technology and Public Policy	M
Textile Sciences and Engineering	M
Theater	M,D
Toxicology	M,D
Urban and Regional Planning	M,D
Urban Design	M
Water Resources Engineering	M,D
Writing	M,D

THE UNIVERSITY OF TEXAS AT DALLAS

Accounting	M
Actuarial Science	M,D
Applied Mathematics	M,D
Art History	M,D
Biochemistry	M,D
Biological and Biomedical Sciences—General	M,D
Biomedical Engineering	M,D
Biotechnology	M,D
Business Administration and Management—General	M,D
Cell Biology	M,D
Chemistry	M,D
Child and Family Studies	M,D
Cognitive Sciences	M,D
Communication Disorders	M,D
Communication—General	M,D
Comparative Literature	M,D
Computer Engineering	M,D
Computer Science	M,D
Criminal Justice and Criminology	M,D
Data Science/Data Analytics	M,D
Economics	M,D
Electrical Engineering	M,D
Engineering and Applied Sciences—General	M,D
Entrepreneurship	M,D
Finance and Banking	M
Geographic Information Systems	M,D
Geography	M,D
Geosciences	M,D
Health Services Management and Hospital Administration	M,D
History	M,D
Humanities	M,D
Industrial and Manufacturing Management	M,D
Interdisciplinary Studies	M
International Business	M,D
Internet and Interactive Multimedia	M,D
Latin American Studies	M,D
Law	M,D
Management Information Systems	M
Management of Technology	M
Management Strategy and Policy	M
Marketing	M
Materials Engineering	M,D
Materials Sciences	M,D
Mathematics Education	M
Mathematics	M,D
Mechanical Engineering	M,D
Mineralogy	M,D
Molecular Biology	M,D
Neuroscience	M,D
Nonprofit Management	M,D
Physics	M,D
Political Science	M,D
Project Management	M,D
Psychology—General	M,D
Public Administration	M,D
Public Policy	M,D
Real Estate	M
Science Education	M
Software Engineering	M,D
Statistics	M,D
Supply Chain Management	M
Systems Engineering	M,D
Telecommunications	M,D

THE UNIVERSITY OF TEXAS AT EL PASO

Accounting	M
Allied Health—General	D
Anthropology	M,O
Applied Psychology	M,O
Art Education	M
Art/Fine Arts	M
Biochemistry	M,D
Bioinformatics	M,D
Biological and Biomedical Sciences—General	M,D
Biomedical Engineering	M,D,O
Business Administration and Management—General	M,D,O
Chemistry	M,D
Civil Engineering	M,D,O
Clinical Psychology	M,D
Communication Disorders	M
Communication—General	M
Computer and Information Systems Security	M,D,O
Computer Science	M,D,O
Construction Management	M,D,O
Counselor Education	M
Curriculum and Instruction	M,D
Economics	M
Education—General	M,D
Educational Leadership and Administration	M,D
Educational Measurement and Evaluation	M
Educational Psychology	M
Energy and Power Engineering	M,D,O
English as a Second Language	M,D,O
English Education	M,D,O
English	M,D,O
Environmental Engineering	M,D,O
Environmental Sciences	M,D
Experimental Psychology	M,D
Family Nurse Practitioner Studies	M,D,O
Geology	M,D
Geophysics	M,D
Health Services Management and Hospital Administration	M,D,O
History	M,D
Information Science	M,D,O
Interdisciplinary Studies	M
International Business	M,D,O
Kinesiology and Movement Studies	M
Liberal Studies	M
Linguistics	M,O
Materials Engineering	M,D
Materials Sciences	M,D
Mathematics	M
Multilingual and Multicultural Education	M,D,O
Music Education	M
Music	M
Nursing and Healthcare Administration	M,D,O
Nursing Education	M,D,O
Nursing—General	M,D,O
Occupational Therapy	M,O
Philosophy	M
Physical Therapy	D
Physics	M
Political Science	M
Psychology—General	M,D
Public Health—General	M,O
Reading Education	M,D
Rehabilitation Counseling	M
Rhetoric	M,D,O
Social Work	M
Sociology	M,O
Software Engineering	M,D,O
Spanish	M,O
Special Education	M
Statistics	M
Writing	M,D,O

THE UNIVERSITY OF TEXAS AT SAN ANTONIO

Accounting	M,D
Anthropology	M,D
Applied Behavior Analysis	M,O
Applied Mathematics	M
Applied Statistics	M,D
Architecture	M
Art History	M
Art/Fine Arts	M
Biological and Biomedical Sciences—General	M,D
Biomedical Engineering	M,D
Biotechnology	M,D
Business Administration and Management—General	M,D,O
Cell Biology	M,D
Chemistry	M,D
Civil Engineering	M,D
Communication—General	M
Computer and Information Systems Security	M,D,O
Computer Engineering	M,D
Computer Science	M,D
Counselor Education	M,D
Criminal Justice and Criminology	M
Cultural Studies	M,D
Curriculum and Instruction	M,D
Demography and Population Studies	D
Early Childhood Education	M,D
Ecology	M
Economics	M
Educational Leadership and Administration	M,D
Educational Measurement and Evaluation	M,O
Educational Media/Instructional Technology	M,D
Educational Psychology	M,O
Electrical Engineering	M,D
Engineering and Applied Sciences—General	M,D
English as a Second Language	M,D,O
English	M,D
Environmental Engineering	M,D
Environmental Sciences	M,D
Finance and Banking	M,D
Geology	M
Health Education	M
Higher Education	M,D
History	M
Information Science	M,D,O
Interdisciplinary Studies	M,D
Kinesiology and Movement Studies	M
Management of Technology	M,D,O
Manufacturing Engineering	M,D
Marketing	M,D
Materials Engineering	M,D
Mathematics Education	M
Mathematics	M
Mechanical Engineering	M,D
Molecular Biology	M,D
Multilingual and Multicultural Education	M,D
Music	M
Neurobiology	M,D
Organizational Management	D
Philosophy	M
Physics	M,D
Political Science	M
Psychology—General	M,D
Public Administration	M
Reading Education	M,D
School Psychology	M,O
Social Work	M
Sociology	M
Spanish	M
Special Education	M,D
Statistics	M,D
Translational Biology	D
Urban and Regional Planning	M

THE UNIVERSITY OF TEXAS AT TYLER

Accounting	M
Art History	M
Art/Fine Arts	M
Biological and Biomedical Sciences—General	M
Business Administration and Management—General	M
Civil Engineering	M
Clinical Psychology	M
Communication—General	M
Computer and Information Systems Security	M
Computer Science	M
Counseling Psychology	M
Criminal Justice and Criminology	M
Early Childhood Education	M
Educational Leadership and Administration	M
Electrical Engineering	M
Energy Management and Policy	M
Engineering Management	M
English	M
Environmental and Occupational Health	M
Environmental Engineering	M
Family Nurse Practitioner Studies	M,D
Health Education	M
Health Services Management and Hospital Administration	M
History	M
Human Resources Development	M,D
Industrial and Manufacturing Management	M
Interdisciplinary Studies	M
Kinesiology and Movement Studies	M
Marketing	M

Marriage and Family Therapy M
Mathematics M
Mechanical Engineering M
Nursing and Healthcare Administration M,D
Nursing Education M,D
Nursing—General M,D
Organizational Management M
Pharmacy D
Political Science M
Psychology—General M
Public Administration M
Quality Management M
Reading Education M
School Psychology M
Social Sciences M
Sociology M
Special Education M
Structural Engineering M
Transportation and Highway Engineering M
Water Resources Engineering M

THE UNIVERSITY OF TEXAS HEALTH SCIENCE CENTER AT HOUSTON
Allopathic Medicine D
Biochemistry M,D
Bioinformatics M,D,O
Biological and Biomedical Sciences—General M,D
Biostatistics M,D,O
Cancer Biology/Oncology M,D
Cell Biology M,D
Community Health M,D,O
Data Science/Data Analytics M,D,O
Dentistry M,D
Environmental and Occupational Health M,D,O
Epidemiology M,D,O
Genetic Counseling M,D,O
Genetics M,D
Genomic Sciences M,D,O
Health Informatics M,D,O
Health Promotion M,D,O
Health Services Management and Hospital Administration M,D,O
Immunology M,D
Infectious Diseases M,D
Maternal and Child Health M,D,O
Medical Physics M,D
Microbiology M,D
Neuroscience M,D
Nursing—General M,D
Pharmacology M,D
Public Health—General M,D,O
Quantitative Analysis M,D

THE UNIVERSITY OF TEXAS HEALTH SCIENCE CENTER AT SAN ANTONIO
Acute Care/Critical Care Nursing M,D,O
Allopathic Medicine M,D
Biochemistry M,D
Biological and Biomedical Sciences—General D
Biomedical Engineering M,D
Cell Biology M,D
Clinical Laboratory Sciences/Medical Technology D
Clinical Research M
Communication Disorders M,D
Community Health Nursing M,D,O
Dentistry M,D,O
Family Nurse Practitioner Studies M,D,O
Gerontological Nursing M,D,O
Immunology M,D
Interdisciplinary Studies D
Medical Physics D
Microbiology M,D
Molecular Medicine M,D
Neuroscience D
Nursing and Healthcare Administration M,D,O
Nursing Education M,D,O
Nursing—General M,D,O
Occupational Therapy M,D
Pediatric Nursing M,D,O
Pharmacology D
Physical Therapy M,D
Physician Assistant Studies M,D
Psychiatric Nursing M,D,O
Special Education M,D
Structural Biology M,D
Toxicology M

THE UNIVERSITY OF TEXAS MD ANDERSON CANCER CENTER
Genetics M

THE UNIVERSITY OF TEXAS MEDICAL BRANCH
Allied Health—General M,D
Allopathic Medicine D
Biochemistry D
Bioinformatics D
Biological and Biomedical Sciences—General M,D
Biophysics D
Cell Biology M,D
Clinical Laboratory Sciences/Medical Technology M,D
Computational Biology M,D
Demography and Population Studies D
Humanities M,D
Immunology M,D
Microbiology M,D
Molecular Biophysics D
Neuroscience D
Nursing—General M,D
Occupational Therapy M
Pathology D
Pharmacology M,D
Physical Therapy M,D
Physician Assistant Studies M
Physiology M,D
Public Health—General M,D
Rehabilitation Sciences D
Structural Biology D
Toxicology M,D
Translational Biology M,D

THE UNIVERSITY OF TEXAS OF THE PERMIAN BASIN
Accounting M
Applied Psychology M
Biological and Biomedical Sciences—General M
Business Administration and Management—General M
Clinical Psychology M
Computer Science M
Counselor Education M
Criminal Justice and Criminology M
Early Childhood Education M
Education—General M
Educational Leadership and Administration M
English as a Second Language M
English M
Experimental Psychology M
Foundations and Philosophy of Education M
Geology M
History M
Kinesiology and Movement Studies M
Political Science M
Psychology—General M
Reading Education M
Spanish M
Special Education M

THE UNIVERSITY OF TEXAS RIO GRANDE VALLEY
Accounting M
Adult Nursing M,O
Agricultural Sciences—General M
Allopathic Medicine D
Art/Fine Arts M
Biological and Biomedical Sciences—General M
Business Administration and Management—General M,D
Chemistry M
Clinical Laboratory Sciences/Medical Technology M
Clinical Psychology M
Communication Disorders M
Communication—General M
Computer Science M
Counselor Education M
Criminal Justice and Criminology M
Curriculum and Instruction M,D
Early Childhood Education M
Education—General M,D
Educational Leadership and Administration M,D
Educational Media/Instructional Technology M,D
Educational Psychology M
Electrical Engineering M
Elementary Education M,D
Emergency Management M
Engineering Management M
English as a Second Language M
English M
Environmental Sciences M
Exercise and Sports Science M
Experimental Psychology M
Family Nurse Practitioner Studies M,O
Finance and Banking M,D
Geosciences M
Health Services Management and Hospital Administration M
History M
Interdisciplinary Studies M
Kinesiology and Movement Studies M
Management Information Systems M
Manufacturing Engineering M
Marketing M,D
Mathematics M
Mechanical Engineering M
Multilingual and Multicultural Education M
Music M
Nursing and Healthcare Administration M,O
Nursing Education M,O
Nursing—General M,O
Nutrition M
Occupational Therapy M
Oceanography M
Physician Assistant Studies M
Physics M
Psychiatric Nursing M,O
Psychology—General M
Public Administration M
Public Affairs M
Public Policy M
Reading Education M
Rehabilitation Counseling M,D
School Psychology M
Secondary Education M,D
Social Work M
Sociology M
Spanish M
Special Education M
Sustainable Development M
Systems Engineering M
Translation and Interpretation M
Writing M

THE UNIVERSITY OF TEXAS SOUTHWESTERN MEDICAL CENTER
Allopathic Medicine D
Biochemistry D
Biological and Biomedical Sciences—General M,D
Biomedical Engineering M,D
Cancer Biology/Oncology D
Cell Biology D
Clinical Psychology D
Developmental Biology D
Genetics D
Immunology D
Microbiology D
Molecular Biophysics D
Neuroscience D
Nutrition M
Physical Therapy D
Physician Assistant Studies M
Rehabilitation Counseling M

THE UNIVERSITY OF THE ARTS
Art Education M
Art/Fine Arts M
Industrial Design M
Museum Education M
Museum Studies M
Music Education M
Music M

UNIVERSITY OF THE CUMBERLANDS
Accounting M
Business Administration and Management—General M
Business Education M,D,O
Clinical Psychology D
Counseling Psychology M
Counselor Education M,D,O
Education—General M,D,O
Educational Leadership and Administration M,D,O
Elementary Education M,D,O
Marketing M,D,O
Middle School Education M,D,O
Physician Assistant Studies M
Reading Education M,D,O
Religion M
Secondary Education M,D,O
Special Education M,D,O
Student Affairs M,D,O
Theater M,D,O

UNIVERSITY OF THE DISTRICT OF COLUMBIA
Adult Education O
Architecture M
Business Administration and Management—General M
Cancer Biology/Oncology M
Communication Disorders M
Computer Science M
Counseling Psychology M
Early Childhood Education M
Electrical Engineering M
Elementary Education M
Engineering and Applied Sciences—General M
English Education M
Homeland Security M
Law M,D
Legal and Justice Studies M,D
Mathematics Education M
Middle School Education M
Nutrition M
Public Administration M
Rehabilitation Counseling M
Secondary Education M
Social Sciences Education M
Water Resources M

UNIVERSITY OF THE FRASER VALLEY
Criminal Justice and Criminology M
Social Work M

UNIVERSITY OF THE INCARNATE WORD
Applied Statistics M
Biological and Biomedical Sciences—General M
Business Administration and Management—General M,D
Clothing and Textiles M
Communication—General M,D
Education—General M,D
Health Services Management and Hospital Administration M,D
Industrial and Organizational Psychology M,D
Kinesiology and Movement Studies M,D
Mathematics Education M
Mathematics M
Nursing—General M,D
Nutrition M
Optometry D
Organizational Management M,D
Osteopathic Medicine M,D
Pastoral Ministry and Counseling M,D
Pharmacy D
Physical Therapy D
Sports Management M,D

UNIVERSITY OF THE PACIFIC
Biological and Biomedical Sciences—General M
Business Administration and Management—General M
Communication Disorders M,D
Communication—General M
Curriculum and Instruction M,D,O
Dentistry M,D,O
Education—General M,D,O
Educational Leadership and Administration M,D,O
Educational Psychology M,D,O
Engineering and Applied Sciences—General M
Exercise and Sports Science M,O
Hospitality Management M
International Affairs M,D
Law M,D
Music Education M
Music M
Pharmaceutical Sciences M,D
Pharmacy D
Physical Therapy M,D
Psychology—General M
Public Policy M,D
School Psychology M,D,O
Special Education M,D,O
Therapies—Dance, Drama, and Music M
Water Resources M,D

UNIVERSITY OF THE PEOPLE
Business Administration and Management—General M

UNIVERSITY OF THE POTOMAC
Business Administration and Management—General M

UNIVERSITY OF THE ROCKIES
Psychology—General M,D

UNIVERSITY OF THE SACRED HEART
Accounting M,O
Advertising and Public Relations M
Broadcast Journalism M,O
Business Administration and Management—General M,O
Communication—General M,O
Conflict Resolution and Mediation/Peace Studies M
Cultural Studies M
Early Childhood Education M,O
Education—General M,O
Educational Media/Instructional Technology M
English Education M,O
Environmental and Occupational Health M
Film, Television, and Video Production M,O
Foreign Languages Education M,O
Human Resources Management M
Information Science O
Internet and Interactive Multimedia M,O
Legal and Justice Studies M
Management Information Systems M
Marketing M
Mathematics Education M,O
Nonprofit Management M
Occupational Health Nursing M
Taxation M
Writing M,O

UNIVERSITY OF THE SCIENCES
Biochemistry M,D
Bioinformatics M
Biotechnology M
Cell Biology M
Chemistry M,D
Health Psychology M
Health Services Management and Hospital Administration M,D
Medicinal and Pharmaceutical Chemistry M,D
Occupational Therapy M,D
Pharmaceutical Administration M
Pharmaceutical Sciences M,D
Pharmacology M,D
Pharmacy D
Physical Therapy D
Public Health—General M
Technical Writing M,O
Toxicology M,D

THE UNIVERSITY OF THE SOUTH
English M
Theology M,D
Writing M

UNIVERSITY OF THE SOUTHWEST
Business Administration and Management—General M
Counseling Psychology M
Counselor Education M
Curriculum and Instruction M
Early Childhood Education M
Education—General M
Educational Leadership and Administration M
English as a Second Language M
Multilingual and Multicultural Education M
Special Education M
Sports Management M

UNIVERSITY OF THE VIRGIN ISLANDS
Business Administration and Management—General M
Education—General M,D,O
Educational Leadership and Administration M,D,O
Environmental Sciences M
Liberal Studies M
Marine Sciences M
Mathematics Education M
Mathematics M
School Psychology M,D,O
Secondary Education M
Social Sciences M

UNIVERSITY OF THE WEST
Business Administration and Management—General M
Finance and Banking M

*M—masters degree; D—doctorate; O—other advanced degree; *—Close-Up and/or Display*

International Business	M
Management Information Systems	M
Nonprofit Management	M
Psychology—General	M
Religion	M,D
Theology	M

THE UNIVERSITY OF TOLEDO

Accounting	M
Analytical Chemistry	M,D
Applied Mathematics	M,D
Art Education	M,D,O
Astrophysics	M,D
Athletic Training and Sports Medicine	M,D
Biochemistry	M,D
Bioengineering	M,D
Bioinformatics	M,O
Biological and Biomedical Sciences—General	M,D,O
Biomedical Engineering	D
Biostatistics	M,O
Business Administration and Management—General	M
Business Education	M,D,O
Cancer Biology/Oncology	M,D
Cardiovascular Sciences	M,D
Chemical Engineering	M,D
Chemistry	M,D
Civil Engineering	M,D
Clinical Psychology	M,D
Communication Disorders	M,D,O
Communication—General	O
Community Health Nursing	M,O
Computer Science	M,D
Counselor Education	M,D,O
Criminal Justice and Criminology	M,O
Curriculum and Instruction	M,D,O
Early Childhood Education	M,D,O
Ecology	M,D
Economics	M,D,O
Education of the Gifted	M,D,O
Education—General	M,D,O
Educational Leadership and Administration	M,D,O
Educational Measurement and Evaluation	M,D,O
Educational Media/Instructional Technology	M,D,O
Educational Psychology	M,D,O
Electrical Engineering	M,D
Elementary Education	M,D,O
Emergency Management	M,O
Engineering and Applied Sciences—General	M
English as a Second Language	M,D,O
English Education	M,D,O
English	M,O
Environmental and Occupational Health	M,D,O
Environmental Sciences	M,D
Epidemiology	M,O
Exercise and Sports Science	M,D
Experimental Psychology	M,D
Family Nurse Practitioner Studies	M,O
Finance and Banking	M
Foreign Languages Education	M,D,O
Foundations and Philosophy of Education	M,D,O
French	M
Gender Studies	O
Genomic Sciences	M,O
Geographic Information Systems	M,D,O
Geography	M,D,O
Geology	M,D
German	M
Gerontology	M,O
Health Education	M,D,O
Health Promotion	M,D,O
Health Services Management and Hospital Administration	M,O
Higher Education	M,D,O
History	M,D
Immunology	M,D
Industrial Hygiene	M,D,O
Industrial/Management Engineering	M,D
Inorganic Chemistry	M,D
International Business	M
International Health	M,O
Law	M,D,O
Leisure Studies	M,D
Liberal Studies	M
Marketing	M
Materials Sciences	M,D
Mathematics Education	M,D,O
Mathematics	M,D
Mechanical Engineering	M,D
Medical Physics	M,D
Medicinal and Pharmaceutical Chemistry	M,D
Middle School Education	M,D,O
Music Education	M,O
Music	M,O
Neuroscience	M,D
Nonprofit Management	M,O
Nursing and Healthcare Administration	M,O
Nursing Education	M,O
Nursing—General	M,D,O
Nutrition	M,O
Occupational Therapy	M,D
Oral and Dental Sciences	M
Organic Chemistry	M,D
Pathology	M,O
Pediatric Nursing	M,O
Pharmaceutical Administration	M
Pharmaceutical Sciences	M
Pharmacology	M,D
Pharmacy	M,D
Philosophy	M
Physical Chemistry	M,D
Physical Education	M
Physical Therapy	M,D
Physician Assistant Studies	M
Physics	M,D
Political Science	M,O
Psychology—General	M,D
Public Administration	M,O
Public Health—General	M,D,O
Recreation and Park Management	M,D
School Psychology	M,D,O
Science Education	M,D,O
Secondary Education	M,D,O
Social Sciences Education	M,D,O
Social Work	M,O
Sociology	M
Spanish	M
Special Education	M,D,O
Statistics	M,D
Urban and Regional Planning	M,D,O
Vocational and Technical Education	M,D,O
Women's Studies	O
Writing	M,O

UNIVERSITY OF TORONTO

Aerospace/Aeronautical Engineering	M,D
Allopathic Medicine	M,D
Anthropology	M,D
Architecture	M
Art History	M,D
Asian Studies	M,D
Astronomy	M,D
Astrophysics	M,D
Biochemistry	M,D
Bioethics	M,D
Biomedical Engineering	M,D
Biophysics	M,D
Biostatistics	M,D
Biotechnology	M
Business Administration and Management—General	M,D
Cell Biology	M,D
Chemical Engineering	M,D
Chemistry	M,D
Civil Engineering	M,D
Classics	M,D
Communication Disorders	M,D
Community Health	M,D
Comparative Literature	M,D
Computer Engineering	M,D
Computer Science	M,D
Criminal Justice and Criminology	M,D
Dentistry	D
East European and Russian Studies	M
Ecology	M,D
Economics	M,D
Education—General	M,D
Electrical Engineering	M,D
Engineering and Applied Sciences—General	M,D
English	M,D
Environmental and Occupational Health	M,D
Environmental Sciences	M,D
Epidemiology	M,D
Evolutionary Biology	M,D
Film, Television, and Video Theory and Criticism	M,D
Finance and Banking	M
Forestry	M,D
French	M,D
Gender Studies	M,D
Genetic Counseling	M,D
Geography	M,D
Geology	M,D
German	M,D
Health Informatics	M
Health Physics/Radiological Health	M,D
Health Promotion	M,D
Health Services Management and Hospital Administration	M
History of Science and Technology	M,D
History	M,D
Human Resources Management	M,D
Immunology	M,D
Industrial and Labor Relations	M,D
Industrial/Management Engineering	M,D
Information Studies	M,D
International Affairs	M
Italian	M,D
Kinesiology and Movement Studies	M,D
Landscape Architecture	M
Law	M,D
Linguistics	M,D
Management of Technology	M
Manufacturing Engineering	M
Materials Engineering	M,D
Materials Sciences	M,D
Mathematical and Computational Finance	M
Mathematics	M,D
Mechanical Engineering	M,D
Medieval and Renaissance Studies	M,D
Molecular Genetics	M,D
Museum Studies	M
Music Education	M,D
Music	M,D
Near and Middle Eastern Studies	M,D
Nursing—General	M,D
Nutrition	M,D
Occupational Therapy	M
Oral and Dental Sciences	M,D
Pathobiology	M,D
Pharmaceutical Sciences	M,D
Pharmacology	M,D
Philosophy	M,D
Physical Education	M,D
Physical Therapy	M
Physics	M,D
Physiology	M,D
Political Science	M,D
Portuguese	M,D
Psychology—General	M,D
Public Health—General	M,D
Rehabilitation Sciences	M,D
Religion	M,D
Slavic Languages	M,D
Social Sciences	M,D
Social Work	M,D
Sociology	M,D
Spanish	M,D
Statistics	M,D
Systems Biology	M,D
Theater	M,D
Urban and Regional Planning	M,D
Urban Design	M,D
Women's Studies	M,D
Writing	M,D

THE UNIVERSITY OF TULSA

Accounting	M
American Indian/Native American Studies	M,D,O
Anthropology	M,D
Applied Arts and Design—General	M
Applied Mathematics	
Art Education	M
Art History	M
Art/Fine Arts	M
Biochemistry	M,D
Biological and Biomedical Sciences—General	M,D
Business Administration and Management—General	M
Business Analytics	M
Chemical Engineering	M,D
Chemistry	M,D
Clinical Psychology	M,D
Communication Disorders	M
Computer and Information Systems Security	M,D
Computer Science	M,D
Education—General	M
Electrical Engineering	M,D
Energy Management and Policy	M
Engineering and Applied Sciences—General	M,D
Engineering Physics	M,D
English Education	M
English	M,D
Environmental Law	M,D,O
Family Nurse Practitioner Studies	D
Finance and Banking	M
Geophysics	M,D
Geosciences	M,D
Gerontological Nursing	D
Health Law	M,D,O
History	M
Industrial and Organizational Psychology	M,D
Kinesiology and Movement Studies	M
Law	M,D,O
Mathematics Education	M
Mathematics	M,D
Mechanical Engineering	M,D
Museum Studies	M
Nursing—General	D
Petroleum Engineering	M,D
Physics	M,D
Psychology—General	M,D
Rehabilitation Sciences	M
Risk Management	M
Science Education	M
Social Sciences Education	M

UNIVERSITY OF UTAH

Accounting	M,D
Allopathic Medicine	D
American Studies	M,D
Anatomy	D
Anthropology	M,D
Applied Behavior Analysis	M,D
Architecture	M
Art Education	M
Art History	M
Art/Fine Arts	M
Asian Studies	M
Atmospheric Sciences	M,D
Biochemistry	M,D
Bioengineering	M,D
Bioinformatics	M,D,O
Biological and Biomedical Sciences—General	M,D,O
Biostatistics	M,D
Biotechnology	M
Business Administration and Management—General	M,D,O
Cancer Biology/Oncology	M,D
Chemical Engineering	M,D
Chemical Physics	M,D
Chemistry	M,D
Child and Family Studies	M
Civil Engineering	M,D
Clinical Laboratory Sciences/Medical Technology	M
Clinical Psychology	M,D,O
Communication Disorders	M,D
Communication—General	M,D
Comparative Literature	M,D
Computational Sciences	M
Computer and Information Systems Security	M,O
Computer Engineering	M,D
Computer Science	M,D
Counseling Psychology	M,D,O
Counselor Education	M,D,O
Cultural Studies	M,D
Dance	M,O
Dentistry	D
Developmental Psychology	D
Early Childhood Education	M,D
Economics	M,D
Education—General	M,D,O
Educational Leadership and Administration	M,D
Educational Media/Instructional Technology	M,D,O
Educational Policy	M,D
Educational Psychology	M,D,O
Electrical Engineering	M,D
Elementary Education	M,D,O
Engineering and Applied Sciences—General	M,D
English	M,D
Environmental Engineering	M,D
Environmental Sciences	M
Film, Television, and Video Production	M
Finance and Banking	M,D
Foundations and Philosophy of Education	M,D
French	M,D
Game Design and Development	M
Geographic Information Systems	M,D
Geography	M,D
Geological Engineering	M,D
Geology	M,D
Geophysics	M,D
Gerontological Nursing	M,O
Gerontology	M,O
Graphic Design	M
Health Education	M,D
Health Promotion	M,D
Health Services Management and Hospital Administration	M,D
Health Services Research	M,D
Higher Education	M,D
History	M,D
Human Development	M
Human Genetics	M,D
Humanities	M
Industrial and Manufacturing Management	M,D,O
International Affairs	M,D
Internet and Interactive Multimedia	M,D
Kinesiology and Movement Studies	M,D
Latin American Studies	M
Law	M,D
Leisure Studies	M,D
Linguistics	M,D
Management Information Systems	M,D,O
Management Strategy and Policy	M,D,O
Marketing	M,D
Materials Engineering	M,D
Materials Sciences	M,D
Mathematics Education	M,D
Mathematics	M,D
Mechanical Engineering	M,D
Medical Physics	M,D
Medicinal and Pharmaceutical Chemistry	M,D
Metallurgical Engineering and Metallurgy	M,D
Mineral/Mining Engineering	M,D
Molecular Biology	D
Music Education	M,D
Music	M,D
Near and Middle Eastern Languages	M,D
Near and Middle Eastern Studies	M,D
Neurobiology	D
Neuroscience	D
Nuclear Engineering	M,D
Nursing—General	M,D
Nutrition	M,D
Occupational Therapy	M,D
Organizational Behavior	M,D
Pathology	M,D
Petroleum Engineering	M,D
Pharmaceutical Administration	M,D
Pharmaceutical Sciences	M,D
Pharmacology	D
Pharmacy	D
Philosophy	M,D
Photography	M
Physical Therapy	D
Physician Assistant Studies	M
Physics	M,D
Physiology	M,D
Political Science	M,D
Psychology—General	D
Public Administration	M,D
Public Health—General	M,D
Public Policy	M
Reading Education	M,D,O
Real Estate	M
Recreation and Park Management	M,D
Rehabilitation Sciences	D
Rhetoric	M,D
School Psychology	M,D,O
Science Education	M,D
Secondary Education	M,D
Social Psychology	D
Social Work	M,D
Sociology	M,D
Software Engineering	M,D,O
Spanish	M,D
Special Education	M,D
Statistics	M,D,O
Student Affairs	M,D
Systems Engineering	M,O
Toxicology	D
Urban and Regional Planning	M,D
Urban Design	M,D
Writing	M,D

UNIVERSITY OF VALLEY FORGE

Music	M
Religion	M
Theology	M

UNIVERSITY OF VERMONT

Accounting	M
Agricultural Economics and Agribusiness	M
Agricultural Sciences—General	M,D,O
Agronomy and Soil Sciences	M,D,O
Allied Health—General	M,D,O
Allopathic Medicine	M,D,O
Animal Sciences	M,D
Applied Economics	M

Biochemistry	M,D
Bioengineering	D
Biological and Biomedical Sciences—General	M,D
Biomedical Engineering	M
Biostatistics	M
Business Administration and Management—General	M
Cell Biology	D
Chemistry	M,D
Civil Engineering	M,D
Classics	M,O
Clinical Laboratory Sciences/Medical Technology	M,D,O
Clinical Psychology	M,D
Communication Disorders	M
Community Health	M
Computer Science	M,D
Counseling Psychology	M
Counselor Education	M
Curriculum and Instruction	M
Data Science/Data Analytics	M,D
Developmental Psychology	D
Early Childhood Education	M
Economics	M,D,O
Education—General	M,D
Educational Leadership and Administration	M,D
Educational Policy	D
Electrical Engineering	M,D
Elementary Education	M
Engineering and Applied Sciences—General	M,D
Engineering Management	M
English	M
Entomology	M,D,O
Environmental and Occupational Health	M,O
Environmental Engineering	M,D
Environmental Sciences	M
Epidemiology	M,O
Experimental Psychology	D
Food Science and Technology	M,D
Foreign Languages Education	M,O
Forestry	M,D,O
Geology	M
German	M
Health Promotion	M
Health Services Management and Hospital Administration	M,O
Higher Education	M
Historic Preservation	M
History	M
Horticulture	M,D,O
Interdisciplinary Studies	M
International Health	M,O
Materials Sciences	M,D
Mathematics	M,D
Mechanical Engineering	M,D
Middle School Education	M
Molecular Biology	D
Natural Resources	M,D,O
Neuroscience	D
Nursing—General	M,D,O
Nutrition	M
Pathology	M
Pharmacology	M,D
Physical Therapy	D
Physics	M
Plant Biology	M,D
Plant Pathology	M,D,O
Plant Sciences	M,D,O
Psychology—General	D
Public Administration	M
Public Health—General	M,O
Rehabilitation Sciences	D
School Psychology	M
Science Education	M,D
Secondary Education	M
Social Psychology	D
Social Work	M
Special Education	M
Statistics	M
Sustainability Management	M
Sustainable Development	M
Veterinary Sciences	M,D

UNIVERSITY OF VICTORIA

Anthropology	M
Art Education	M,D
Art History	M,D
Art/Fine Arts	M
Asian Studies	M
Astronomy	M,D
Astrophysics	M,D
Biochemistry	M,D
Biological and Biomedical Sciences—General	M,D
Business Administration and Management—General	M
Chemistry	M,D
Child and Family Studies	M,D
Classics	M,D
Clinical Psychology	M,D
Computer Art and Design	M
Computer Engineering	M,D
Computer Science	M,D
Condensed Matter Physics	M,D
Conflict Resolution and Mediation/Peace Studies	M,D
Counseling Psychology	M,D
Counselor Education	M,D
Curriculum and Instruction	M,D
Developmental Psychology	M,D
Early Childhood Education	M,D
Economics	M,D
Education—General	M,D
Educational Leadership and Administration	M,D
Educational Measurement and Evaluation	M,D
Educational Psychology	M,D
Electrical Engineering	M,D
Engineering and Applied Sciences—General	M,D
English Education	M,D
English	M,D
Environmental Education	M,D
Experimental Psychology	M,D
Family Nurse Practitioner Studies	M,D
Film, Television, and Video Production	M
Foreign Languages Education	M
Foundations and Philosophy of Education	M,D
French	M
Geography	M,D
Geosciences	M,D
German	M
Health Informatics	M
Hispanic Studies	M
History	M,D
Human Development	M,D
Italian	M
Kinesiology and Movement Studies	M
Law	M,D
Leisure Studies	M
Linguistics	M,D
Mathematics Education	M,D
Mathematics	M,D
Mechanical Engineering	M,D
Medical Physics	M,D
Microbiology	M,D
Music Education	M,D
Music	M,D
Nursing and Healthcare Administration	M,D
Nursing Education	M,D
Nursing—General	M,D
Oceanography	M,D
Pacific Area/Pacific Rim Studies	M
Philosophy	M
Photography	M
Physical Education	M
Physics	M,D
Political Science	M,D
Psychology—General	M,D
Public Administration	M,D
Reading Education	M,D
Science Education	M,D
Social Psychology	M,D
Social Sciences Education	M,D
Social Work	M
Sociology	M,D
Special Education	M,D
Statistics	M,D
Theater	M
Theoretical Physics	M,D
Vocational and Technical Education	M,D
Writing	M

UNIVERSITY OF VIRGINIA

Accounting	M
Acute Care/Critical Care Nursing	M,D
Aerospace/Aeronautical Engineering	M,D
Allopathic Medicine	M,D
Anthropology	M,D
Architectural History	M,D
Architecture	M
Art History	M,D
Asian Studies	M
Astronomy	M,D
Biochemistry	D
Biological and Biomedical Sciences—General	M,D
Biomedical Engineering	M,D
Biophysics	M,D
Business Administration and Management—General	M,D,O
Cell Biology	D
Chemical Engineering	M,D
Chemistry	M,D
Civil Engineering	M,D
Classics	M,D
Clinical Psychology	D
Clinical Research	M
Communication Disorders	M,D
Community Health	M,D
Computer Engineering	M,D
Computer Science	M,D
Construction Engineering	D
Counselor Education	M,D,O
Curriculum and Instruction	M,D,O
Data Science/Data Analytics	M
Early Childhood Education	M,D
Economics	M,D
Education of the Gifted	M,D,O
Education—General	M,D,O
Educational Leadership and Administration	M,D,O
Educational Measurement and Evaluation	M,D,O
Educational Media/Instructional Technology	M,D,O
Educational Policy	D
Educational Psychology	M,D,O
Electrical Engineering	M,D
Elementary Education	M,D,O
Engineering and Applied Sciences—General	M,D
Engineering Physics	M,D
English Education	M,D,O
English	M,D
Environmental Sciences	M,D
Finance and Banking	M
Foreign Languages Education	M,D,O
French	M,D
German	M
Health Informatics	M
Health Services Management and Hospital Administration	M
Health Services Research	M
Higher Education	M,D,O
History	M,D
Interdisciplinary Studies	M,D
International Affairs	M,D
International Business	M,O
Kinesiology and Movement Studies	M,D
Landscape Architecture	M
Law	M,D
Linguistics	M
Management of Technology	M
Management Strategy and Policy	M,O
Marketing	M
Materials Sciences	M,D
Mathematics Education	M,D,O
Mathematics	M,D
Mechanical Engineering	M,D
Microbiology	D
Molecular Genetics	D
Molecular Physiology	M,D
Music	M,D
Near and Middle Eastern Studies	M
Neuroscience	D
Nursing and Healthcare Administration	M,D
Nursing—General	M,D
Pathology	D
Pharmacology	D
Philosophy	M,D
Physical Education	M,D
Physics	M,D
Physiology	D
Political Science	M,D
Psychiatric Nursing	M,D
Psychology—General	M,D
Public Health—General	M,D
Public Policy	M
Reading Education	M,D
Religion	M,D
School Psychology	M,D
Science Education	M,D,O
Slavic Languages	M,D
Social Sciences Education	M,D,O
Sociology	M,D
Spanish	M,D
Special Education	M,D,O
Statistics	M,D
Student Affairs	M,D,O
Systems Engineering	M,D
Theater	M
Urban and Regional Planning	M
Western European Studies	M
Writing	M

UNIVERSITY OF WASHINGTON

Accounting	M,D
Aerospace/Aeronautical Engineering	M,D
Allopathic Medicine	D
Animal Behavior	M,D
Anthropology	M,D
Applied Arts and Design—General	M
Applied Mathematics	M,D
Applied Physics	M,D
Architecture	M,D,O
Art History	M,D
Art/Fine Arts	M
Asian Languages	M,D
Asian Studies	M,D
Astronomy	M,D
Atmospheric Sciences	M,D
Biochemistry	D
Bioengineering	M,D
Bioethics	M
Bioinformatics	M,D
Biological and Biomedical Sciences—General	M,D
Biophysics	D
Biostatistics	M,D
Biotechnology	D
Business Administration and Management—General	M,D
Cell Biology	D
Chemical Engineering	M,D
Chemistry	M,D
Chinese	M,D
Civil Engineering	M,D
Classics	M,D
Clinical Laboratory Sciences/Medical Technology	M
Clinical Psychology	M,D
Clinical Research	M,D
Cognitive Sciences	M,D
Communication Disorders	M,D
Communication—General	M,D
Community Health	M,D
Comparative Literature	M,D
Computational Sciences	M,D
Computer and Information Systems Security	M,D
Construction Engineering	M,D
Construction Management	M
Curriculum and Instruction	M,D
Dance	M
Data Science/Data Analytics	M,D
Dentistry	M,D,O
Developmental Psychology	M,D
East European and Russian Studies	M
Ecology	M,D
Economics	D
Education—General	M,D
Educational Leadership and Administration	M,D
Educational Measurement and Evaluation	M,D
Educational Media/Instructional Technology	M,D
Educational Policy	M,D
Educational Psychology	M,D
Electrical Engineering	M,D
Engineering and Applied Sciences—General	M,D,O
English as a Second Language	M,D
English Education	M,D
English	M,D
Entrepreneurship	M,D
Environmental and Occupational Health	M,D
Environmental Engineering	M,D
Environmental Management and Policy	M,D
Epidemiology	M,D
Fish, Game, and Wildlife Management	M,D
Forestry	M,D
Foundations and Philosophy of Education	M,D
French	M,D
Genetics	M,D,O
Genomic Sciences	D
Geography	M,D
Geology	M,D
Geophysics	M,D
Geotechnical Engineering	M,D
German	M,D
Health Informatics	M,D
Health Services Management and Hospital Administration	M
Health Services Research	M,D
Higher Education	M,D
Hispanic and Latin American Languages	M
Historic Preservation	O
History	M,D
Horticulture	M,D
Human Development	M,D
Human-Computer Interaction	M,D,O
Hydrology	M,D
Immunology	D
Industrial Design	M
Industrial/Management Engineering	M,D
Information Science	M,D
Intellectual Property Law	M,D
International Affairs	M,D
International Business	M,D,O
International Health	M,D
Italian	M,D
Japanese	M,D
Landscape Architecture	M
Law	M,D
Legal and Justice Studies	M,D
Library Science	M,D
Lighting Design	M,D,O
Linguistics	M,D
Logistics	O
Management Information Systems	M,D
Management of Technology	M,D
Marine Affairs	M,O
Marine Geology	M,D
Materials Engineering	M,D
Materials Sciences	M,D
Maternal and Child Health	M,D
Mathematics Education	M,D
Mathematics	M,D
Mechanical Engineering	M,D
Mechanics	M,D
Medical Informatics	M,D
Medicinal and Pharmaceutical Chemistry	D
Microbiology	D
Molecular Biology	D
Multilingual and Multicultural Education	M,D
Museum Studies	M
Music Education	M,D
Music	M,D
Nanotechnology	M,D
Natural Resources	M,D
Near and Middle Eastern Studies	M,D
Neurobiology	D
Neuroscience	M,D
Nursing—General	M,D,O
Nutrition	M,D
Occupational Therapy	M,D
Oceanography	M,D
Oral and Dental Sciences	M,D,O
Pathobiology	D
Pathology	D
Pharmaceutical Sciences	M,D
Pharmacology	D
Pharmacy	M,D
Philosophy	M,D
Photography	M
Physical Education	M,D
Physical Therapy	M,D
Physics	M,D
Physiology	D
Political Science	M,D
Portuguese	M
Psychology—General	M,D
Public Administration	M,D
Public Affairs	M,D
Public Health—General	M
Public Policy	M,D
Reading Education	M,D
Rehabilitation Sciences	M,D
Religion	M,D
Russian	M,D
Scandinavian Languages	M,D
School Psychology	M,D
Science Education	M,D
Slavic Languages	M,D
Social Psychology	M,D
Social Sciences Education	M,D
Social Sciences	M,D
Social Work	M,D
Sociology	M,D
Spanish	M

*M—masters degree; D—doctorate; O—other advanced degree; *—Close-Up and/or Display*

Special Education	M,D
Statistics	M,D
Structural Biology	D
Structural Engineering	M,D
Supply Chain Management	M,D
Sustainable Development	M,D
Systems Engineering	M,D
Taxation	M,D
Theater	M,D
Toxicology	M,D
Transportation and Highway Engineering	M,D
Transportation Management	O
Urban and Regional Planning	M,D
Urban Design	M,D,O
Veterinary Sciences	M
Women's Studies	D
Writing	M

UNIVERSITY OF WASHINGTON, BOTHELL

Business Administration and Management—General	M
Computer Engineering	M
Cultural Studies	M
Education—General	M
Educational Leadership and Administration	M
Middle School Education	M
Nursing—General	M
Public Policy	M
Secondary Education	M
Software Engineering	M
Writing	M

UNIVERSITY OF WASHINGTON, TACOMA

Accounting	M
Business Administration and Management—General	M
Community Health Nursing	M
Computer Engineering	M
Education—General	M
Educational Leadership and Administration	M
Elementary Education	M
Finance and Banking	M
Interdisciplinary Studies	M
Mathematics Education	M
Nursing and Healthcare Administration	M
Nursing Education	M
Nursing—General	M
Science Education	M
Social Work	M
Software Engineering	M
Special Education	M

UNIVERSITY OF WATERLOO

Accounting	M,D
Actuarial Science	M,D
Anthropology	M
Applied Mathematics	M,D
Architecture	M
Art/Fine Arts	M
Biochemistry	M,D
Biological and Biomedical Sciences—General	M,D
Biostatistics	M,D
Business Administration and Management—General	M
Chemical Engineering	M,D
Chemistry	M,D
Civil Engineering	M,D
Computer Engineering	M,D
Computer Science	M,D
Economic Development	M
Economics	M,D
Electrical Engineering	M,D
Engineering and Applied Sciences—General	M,D
Engineering Management	M,D
English	M,D
Entrepreneurship	M
Environmental Engineering	M,D
Environmental Management and Policy	M,D
Environmental Sciences	M,D
Finance and Banking	M,D
French	M,D
Geography	M,D
Geosciences	M,D
German	M,D
Health Education	M,D
Health Informatics	M,D
History	M,D
Information Science	M,D
International Affairs	M,D
Kinesiology and Movement Studies	M,D
Leisure Studies	M,D
Management of Technology	M,D
Mathematics	M,D
Mechanical Engineering	M,D
Near and Middle Eastern Studies	M
Operations Research	M,D
Optometry	M,D
Philosophy	M,D
Physics	M,D
Political Science	M,D
Psychology—General	M,D
Public Affairs	M
Public Health—General	M,D
Recreation and Park Management	M,D
Religion	D
Russian	M,D
Sociology	M,D
Software Engineering	M,D
Statistics	M,D
Systems Engineering	M,D
Taxation	M,D
Technical Writing	M,D
Urban and Regional Planning	M,D
Vision Sciences	M,D

THE UNIVERSITY OF WEST ALABAMA

Adult Education	M
Business Administration and Management—General	M
Child Development	M,O
Clinical Psychology	M
Conservation Biology	M
Counselor Education	M,O
Early Childhood Education	M,O
Education—General	M,O
Educational Leadership and Administration	M,O
Educational Media/Instructional Technology	M,O
Elementary Education	M,O
English Education	M
Experimental Psychology	M
Finance and Banking	M
Higher Education	M
History	M
Marriage and Family Therapy	M
Mathematics Education	M
Physical Education	M
Science Education	M
Secondary Education	M
Social Sciences Education	M
Special Education	M,O
Student Affairs	M

THE UNIVERSITY OF WESTERN ONTARIO

Allopathic Medicine	M,D
Anatomy	M,D
Anthropology	M,D
Applied Mathematics	M,D
Astronomy	M,D
Biochemical Engineering	M,D
Biochemistry	M,D
Biological and Biomedical Sciences—General	M,D
Biophysics	M,D
Biostatistics	M,D
Business Administration and Management—General	M,D
Cell Biology	M,D
Chemical Engineering	M,D
Chemistry	M,D
Civil Engineering	M,D
Classics	M
Communication Disorders	M
Comparative Literature	M,D
Computer Engineering	M,D
Computer Science	M,D
Counseling Psychology	M
Curriculum and Instruction	M
Dentistry	D
Economics	M,D
Education—General	M
Educational Policy	M
Educational Psychology	M
Electrical Engineering	M,D
Engineering and Applied Sciences—General	M,D
English	M,D
Entrepreneurship	M,D
Environmental Engineering	M,D
Environmental Sciences	M,D
Epidemiology	M,D
Finance and Banking	M,D
French	M,D
Geography	M,D
Geology	M,D
Geophysics	M,D
Geosciences	M,D
Health Services Management and Hospital Administration	M,D
History	M,D
Immunology	M,D
Information Studies	M,D
Interdisciplinary Studies	M,D
International Business	M,D
Journalism	M
Kinesiology and Movement Studies	M,D
Law	M,D,O
Library Science	M,D
Management Strategy and Policy	M,D
Marketing	M,D
Materials Engineering	M,D
Mathematics	M,D
Mechanical Engineering	M,D
Media Studies	M,D
Microbiology	M,D
Music	M,D
Neuroscience	M,D
Nursing—General	M,D
Occupational Therapy	M
Oral and Dental Sciences	M
Pathology	M,D
Philosophy	M,D
Physical Therapy	M,O
Physics	M,D
Physiology	M,D
Political Science	M,D
Psychology—General	M,D
Sociology	M,D
Spanish	M,D
Special Education	M
Statistics	M,D
Sustainable Development	M,D

UNIVERSITY OF WESTERN STATES

Chiropractic	D

UNIVERSITY OF WEST FLORIDA

Accounting	M
American Studies	M
Anthropology	M
Applied Behavior Analysis	M
Applied Psychology	M
Archaeology	M
Biological and Biomedical Sciences—General	M
Business Administration and Management—General	M
Communication—General	M
Computer and Information Systems Security	M
Computer Science	M
Counseling Psychology	M
Criminal Justice and Criminology	M
Curriculum and Instruction	M,O
Data Science/Data Analytics	M
Educational Leadership and Administration	M,D
Educational Media/Instructional Technology	M,D
Elementary Education	M
English	M
Environmental Sciences	M
Exercise and Sports Science	M
Experimental Psychology	M
Geographic Information Systems	M
Health Promotion	M
Health Services Management and Hospital Administration	M
History	M
Industrial and Organizational Psychology	M
Leisure Studies	M
Mathematics	M
Middle School Education	M
Nursing—General	M
Physical Education	M,D
Political Science	M
Psychology—General	M
Public Administration	M
Public Health—General	M
Public History	M
Reading Education	M
Secondary Education	M
Social Work	M
Software Engineering	M
Special Education	M
Student Affairs	M
Writing	M

UNIVERSITY OF WEST GEORGIA

Accounting	M
Biological and Biomedical Sciences—General	M,O
Business Administration and Management—General	M
Business Education	M,D,O
Communication Disorders	M,D,O
Computer Science	M,O
Counselor Education	M,D,O
Criminal Justice and Criminology	M,D,O
Early Childhood Education	M,D,O
Education—General	M,D,O
Educational Leadership and Administration	M,D,O
Educational Media/Instructional Technology	M,D,O
English	M,O
Geographic Information Systems	M,O
Health Services Management and Hospital Administration	M,D,O
History	M,O
Mathematics	M,O
Museum Studies	M,O
Music Education	M,O
Music	M,O
Nonprofit Management	M,D,O
Nursing Education	M,D,O
Nursing—General	M,D,O
Psychology—General	M,D,O
Public Administration	M,D,O
Public History	M,O
Reading Education	M,D,O
Secondary Education	M,D,O
Sociology	M,D,O
Special Education	M,D,O
Urban and Regional Planning	M,D,O

UNIVERSITY OF WINDSOR

Applied Psychology	M,D
Art/Fine Arts	M
Biochemistry	M,D
Biological and Biomedical Sciences—General	M,D
Biopsychology	M,D
Business Administration and Management—General	M
Chemistry	M,D
Civil Engineering	M,D
Clinical Psychology	M,D
Communication—General	M
Computer Science	M,D
Criminal Justice and Criminology	M,D
Economics	M
Education—General	M,D
Electrical Engineering	M,D
Engineering and Applied Sciences—General	M,D
English	M
Environmental Engineering	M,D
Environmental Sciences	M,D
Geosciences	M,D
History	M
Industrial/Management Engineering	M,D
Kinesiology and Movement Studies	M
Legal and Justice Studies	M
Manufacturing Engineering	M,D
Materials Engineering	M,D
Mathematics	M,D
Mechanical Engineering	M,D
Nursing—General	M
Philosophy	M
Physics	M,D
Political Science	M
Psychology—General	M,D
Social Psychology	M,D
Social Work	M
Sociology	M,D
Statistics	M,D
Writing	M

THE UNIVERSITY OF WINNIPEG

History	M
Marriage and Family Therapy	M,O
Public Administration	M
Religion	M
Theology	M,O

UNIVERSITY OF WISCONSIN–EAU CLAIRE

Adult Nursing	M,D
Business Administration and Management—General	M
Communication Disorders	M
Education—General	M
English	M
Family Nurse Practitioner Studies	M,D
Gerontological Nursing	M,D
History	M
Library Science	M
Nursing and Healthcare Administration	M,D
Nursing Education	M,D
Nursing—General	M,D
Psychology—General	M,O
Reading Education	M
School Psychology	M,O
Secondary Education	M
Special Education	M
Writing	M

UNIVERSITY OF WISCONSIN–GREEN BAY

Business Administration and Management—General	M
Education—General	M
Environmental Management and Policy	M
Environmental Sciences	M
Nursing and Healthcare Administration	M
Social Work	M
Sustainability Management	M

UNIVERSITY OF WISCONSIN–LA CROSSE

Athletic Training and Sports Medicine	M
Biological and Biomedical Sciences—General	M
Cancer Biology/Oncology	M
Cell Biology	M
Community Health	M
Data Science/Data Analytics	M
Education—General	M,O
English Education	M,O
Exercise and Sports Science	M
Health Education	M
Higher Education	M,D
Marine Sciences	M
Medical Microbiology	M
Microbiology	M
Molecular Biology	M
Nurse Anesthesia	M
Occupational Therapy	M
Physical Education	M
Physical Therapy	D
Physician Assistant Studies	M
Physiology	M
Psychology—General	M,O
Public Health—General	M
Reading Education	M,O
Recreation and Park Management	M
Rehabilitation Sciences	M
School Psychology	M,O
Software Engineering	M
Special Education	M,O
Student Affairs	M

UNIVERSITY OF WISCONSIN–MADISON

Accounting	M,D
Actuarial Science	D
Adult Nursing	D
African Studies	M,D
African-American Studies	M
Agricultural Economics and Agribusiness	M,D
Agricultural Engineering	M,D
Agricultural Sciences—General	M,D
Agronomy and Soil Sciences	M,D
Allopathic Medicine	D
American Studies	M,D
Animal Sciences	M,D
Anthropology	D
Applied Arts and Design—General	M,D
Applied Economics	M,D
Archaeology	D
Art History	M,D
Art/Fine Arts	M
Arts Administration	M
Asian Languages	M,D
Asian Studies	M,D
Astronomy	D
Atmospheric Sciences	M,D
Automotive Engineering	M,D
Bacteriology	M
Biochemistry	M,D
Bioinformatics	M,D
Biological and Biomedical Sciences—General	
Biomedical Engineering	M,D
Biometry	M
Biophysics	D
Biopsychology	D
Botany	M,D
Business Administration and Management—General	M
Cancer Biology/Oncology	D
Cell Biology	D
Chemical Engineering	D
Chemistry	M,D
Child and Family Studies	M,D
Chinese	M,D
Civil Engineering	M
Classics	M,D
Clinical Psychology	D

Clinical Research	M,D
Cognitive Sciences	D
Communication Disorders	M,D
Communication—General	M,D
Comparative Literature	M,D
Computer and Information Systems Security	M
Computer Science	M,D
Conservation Biology	M
Construction Engineering	M
Consumer Economics	M,D
Counseling Psychology	D
Counselor Education	M
Cultural Anthropology	D
Curriculum and Instruction	M,D
Demography and Population Studies	M,D
Developmental Psychology	D
Ecology	M
Economics	D
Education—General	M,D,O
Educational Leadership and Administration	M,D,O
Educational Policy	M,D,O
Educational Psychology	M,D
Electrical Engineering	M,D
Engineering and Applied Sciences—General	M,D
Engineering Physics	M,D
English as a Second Language	M,D
English	M,D
Entomology	M,D
Environmental Biology	M,D
Environmental Engineering	M
Environmental Sciences	M
Epidemiology	M,D
Ergonomics and Human Factors	M,D
Family and Consumer Sciences-General	M,D
Film, Television, and Video Theory and Criticism	M,D
Finance and Banking	M,D
Fish, Game, and Wildlife Management	M,D
Folklore	M,D
Food Science and Technology	M,D
Forestry	M,D
French	M,D,O
Genetic Counseling	M,D
Genetics	M,D
Geographic Information Systems	M,D,O
Geography	M,D,O
Geological Engineering	M,D
Geology	M,D
Geophysics	M,D
Geotechnical Engineering	M
German	M,D
Gerontological Nursing	D
Higher Education	M,D,O
History of Science and Technology	M,D
History	M,D
Horticulture	M,D
Human Development	M,D
Human Resources Management	M,D
Industrial/Management Engineering	M,D
Information Studies	M,D
Insurance	M,D
International and Comparative Education	M,D,O
Investment Management	D
Italian	M,D
Japanese	M,D
Jewish Studies	M,D
Journalism	M,D
Kinesiology and Movement Studies	M,D
Landscape Architecture	M,D
Latin American Studies	M,D
Law	M,D
Library Science	M,D
Linguistics	M,D
Management Information Systems	D
Management of Technology	M
Management Strategy and Policy	M,D
Manufacturing Engineering	M
Marine Sciences	M,D
Marketing Research	M
Marketing	D
Mass Communication	M,D
Materials Engineering	M,D
Mathematics	D
Mechanical Engineering	M,D
Mechanics	M,D
Media Studies	M,D
Medical Microbiology	D
Medical Physics	M,D
Microbiology	D
Molecular Biology	D
Molecular Pathology	D
Music Education	M,D
Music	M,D
Natural Resources	M,D
Near and Middle Eastern Languages	M,D
Near and Middle Eastern Studies	M,D
Neuroscience	D
Nuclear Engineering	M,D
Nursing—General	D
Nutrition	M,D
Occupational Therapy	M,D
Oceanography	M,D
Pathology	D
Pediatric Nursing	D
Pharmaceutical Administration	M,D
Pharmaceutical Sciences	M,D
Pharmacology	D
Pharmacy	D
Philosophy	M,D
Physical Therapy	D
Physician Assistant Studies	M
Physics	M,D
Physiology	M,D
Plant Pathology	M,D
Plant Sciences	M,D
Political Science	D
Portuguese	M,D
Psychiatric Nursing	D
Psychology—General	D
Public Affairs	M
Public Health—General	M,D
Real Estate	M,D
Rehabilitation Counseling	M,D
Rhetoric	M,D
Risk Management	M,D
Rural Sociology	M,D
Scandinavian Languages	M,D
Slavic Languages	M,D
Social Psychology	D
Social Work	M,D
Sociology	M,D
Spanish	M,D
Special Education	M,D
Speech and Interpersonal Communication	M,D
Statistics	M,D
Structural Engineering	M
Supply Chain Management	M
Sustainable Development	M
Systems Engineering	M,D
Taxation	M
Theater	M,D
Toxicology	M,D
Transportation and Highway Engineering	M
Urban and Regional Planning	M,D
Veterinary Medicine	M,D
Veterinary Sciences	M,D
Water Resources Engineering	M
Water Resources	M
Women's Studies	M,D
Writing	M,D
Zoology	M,D

UNIVERSITY OF WISCONSIN–MILWAUKEE

Actuarial Science	M,D
Adult Education	M,D,O
African Studies	D
Allied Health—General	M,D,O
Anthropology	M,D,O
Applied Arts and Design—General	M
Applied Mathematics	M,D
Architecture	M,D,O
Art Education	M,D,O
Art History	M
Athletic Training and Sports Medicine	M,D
Atmospheric Sciences	M,D
Biochemistry	M,D
Biological and Biomedical Sciences—General	M,D
Biomedical Engineering	M,D
Biostatistics	M,D,O
Business Administration and Management—General	M,D,O
Business Analytics	M,O
Cell Biology	M,D
Chemistry	M,D
Civil Engineering	M,D
Classics	M,O
Communication Disorders	M
Communication—General	M,D,O
Community Health	D
Comparative Literature	M,O
Computer Engineering	M,D
Computer Science	M,D
Conflict Resolution and Mediation/Peace Studies	M,D,O
Counseling Psychology	M,D,O
Criminal Justice and Criminology	M,O
Curriculum and Instruction	M,D,O
Developmental Psychology	M,D,O
Early Childhood Education	M
Economics	M,D
Education—General	M,D,O
Educational Leadership and Administration	M,D,O
Educational Measurement and Evaluation	M,D,O
Educational Media/Instructional Technology	M,O
Educational Policy	M,D
Educational Psychology	M,D,O
Electrical Engineering	M,D
Elementary Education	M
Engineering and Applied Sciences—General	M,D
English as a Second Language	M,D,O
English Education	M,D
English	M,D
Entrepreneurship	M,D,O
Environmental and Occupational Health	M,D,O
Environmental Sciences	M,D
Epidemiology	M,D,O
Ergonomics and Human Factors	M
Exercise and Sports Science	M,D
Family Nurse Practitioner Studies	M,D,O
Film, Television, and Video Theory and Criticism	M,O
Foreign Languages Education	M,D
Foundations and Philosophy of Education	M,D,O
French	M,O
Gender Studies	M,O
Geographic Information Systems	M,D,O
Geography	M,D
Geology	M,D
German	M,O
Gerontology	M,D,O
Health Informatics	M,D
Health Promotion	M,D,O
Health Services Management and Hospital Administration	M,D
Higher Education	M,O
History	M,D
Human Resources Management	M,O
Industrial and Labor Relations	M,O
Industrial/Management Engineering	M,D
Information Studies	M,D,O
Investment Management	M,O
Kinesiology and Movement Studies	M,D
Latin American Studies	M,O
Liberal Studies	M
Library Science	M,D,O
Linguistics	M,D,O
Management of Technology	M,O
Management Strategy and Policy	M,D,O
Manufacturing Engineering	M,D
Materials Engineering	M,D
Mathematics Education	M,D,O
Mathematics	M,D
Mechanical Engineering	M,D
Mechanics	M,D
Media Studies	M,D
Medical Imaging	D
Medical Informatics	M
Microbiology	M,D
Middle School Education	M
Molecular Biology	M,D
Multilingual and Multicultural Education	M,D,O
Museum Studies	M,D,O
Nonprofit Management	M,D,O
Nursing—General	M,D,O*
Nutrition	M,D
Occupational Therapy	M
Philosophy	M
Physical Therapy	M,D
Physics	M,D
Political Science	M,D
Portuguese	M
Psychology—General	M,D
Public Administration	M
Public Health—General	M,D,O
Reading Education	M
Recreation and Park Management	M
Rehabilitation Sciences	D
Rhetoric	M,D,O
School Psychology	M,D,O
Science Education	M
Secondary Education	M,D
Social Sciences Education	M
Social Work	M,D,O
Sociology	M,D
Spanish	M,O
Special Education	M,D,O
Statistics	M,D
Taxation	M,O
Translation and Interpretation	M,O
Urban and Regional Planning	M
Urban Education	M,D,O
Urban Studies	M,D
Water Resources	M,D
Women's Studies	M,O
Writing	M,D

UNIVERSITY OF WISCONSIN–OSHKOSH

Adult Nursing	M
Biological and Biomedical Sciences—General	M
Botany	M
Business Administration and Management—General	M
Counselor Education	M
Curriculum and Instruction	M
Early Childhood Education	M
Education—General	M
Educational Leadership and Administration	M
English	M
Experimental Psychology	M
Family Nurse Practitioner Studies	M
Health Services Management and Hospital Administration	M
Industrial and Organizational Psychology	M
International Business	M
Mathematics Education	M
Microbiology	M
Nursing—General	M
Psychology—General	M
Public Administration	M
Reading Education	M
Social Work	M
Special Education	M
Zoology	M

UNIVERSITY OF WISCONSIN–PARKSIDE

Business Administration and Management—General	M
Clinical Psychology	M
Computer Science	M
Health Promotion	M
Information Science	M
Molecular Biology	M
Sports Management	M
Sustainability Management	M

UNIVERSITY OF WISCONSIN–PLATTEVILLE

Adult Education	M
Computer Science	M
Criminal Justice and Criminology	M
Education—General	M
Engineering and Applied Sciences—General	M
Human Resources Management	M
Organizational Management	M
Project Management	M
Supply Chain Management	M

UNIVERSITY OF WISCONSIN–RIVER FALLS

Agricultural Education	M
Agricultural Sciences—General	M
Art/Fine Arts	M
Business Administration and Management—General	M
Communication Disorders	M
Counselor Education	M,O
Education—General	M
Elementary Education	M
English as a Second Language	M
Mathematics Education	M
Reading Education	M
School Psychology	M,O
Science Education	M
Social Sciences Education	M

UNIVERSITY OF WISCONSIN–STEVENS POINT

Advertising and Public Relations	M
Communication Disorders	M,D
Communication—General	M
Corporate and Organizational Communication	M
Education—General	M,D
Educational Leadership and Administration	M,D
Elementary Education	M
English Education	M
Family and Consumer Sciences-General	O
Health Promotion	M,O
Human Development	M,O
Media Studies	M
Music Education	M
Natural Resources	M
Nutrition	M
Reading Education	M
Science Education	M
Secondary Education	M
Social Sciences Education	M
Special Education	M
Speech and Interpersonal Communication	M
Sustainable Development	D

UNIVERSITY OF WISCONSIN–STOUT

Applied Mathematics	M
Applied Psychology	M
Art/Fine Arts	M
Clinical Psychology	M
Conservation Biology	M
Construction Management	M
Counseling Psychology	M
Education—General	M,D,O
Food Science and Technology	M
Human Resources Development	M
Industrial Hygiene	M
Industrial/Management Engineering	M
Information Science	M
Manufacturing Engineering	M
Marriage and Family Therapy	M
Nutrition	M
Project Management	M
Quality Management	M
Rehabilitation Counseling	M
School Psychology	M,O
Supply Chain Management	M
Sustainability Management	M
Technical Communication	M
Telecommunications Management	M
Vocational and Technical Education	M,D,O

UNIVERSITY OF WISCONSIN–SUPERIOR

Art Education	M
Art History	M
Art Therapy	M
Art/Fine Arts	M
Communication—General	M
Counselor Education	M
Curriculum and Instruction	M
Education—General	M
Educational Leadership and Administration	M,O
Mass Communication	M
Reading Education	M
School Psychology	M
Social Psychology	M
Special Education	M
Speech and Interpersonal Communication	M
Sustainability Management	M
Theater	M

UNIVERSITY OF WISCONSIN–WHITEWATER

Accounting	M
Business Administration and Management—General	M
Business Education	M
Communication Disorders	M
Communication—General	M
Corporate and Organizational Communication	M
Education—General	M,O
Educational Leadership and Administration	M
Environmental and Occupational Health	M
Finance and Banking	M
Marketing	M
Mass Communication	M
Psychology—General	M,O
School Psychology	M,O
Special Education	M,O

*M—masters degree; D—doctorate; O—other advanced degree; *—Close-Up and/or Display*

UNIVERSITY OF WYOMING

Accounting	M
Agricultural Economics and Agribusiness	M
Agricultural Sciences—General	M,D
Agronomy and Soil Sciences	M,D
American Studies	M
Animal Sciences	M,D
Anthropology	M,D
Applied Economics	M
Atmospheric Sciences	M,D
Biotechnology	D
Botany	M,D
Business Administration and Management—General	M
Cell Biology	D
Chemical Engineering	M,D
Chemistry	M,D
Child Development	M
Civil Engineering	M,D
Communication Disorders	M
Communication—General	M
Community Health	M,D
Computational Biology	D
Computer Science	M,D
Consumer Economics	M
Counselor Education	M,D
Curriculum and Instruction	M,D
Ecology	M,D
Economics	M,D
Educational Leadership and Administration	M,D,O
Educational Media/Instructional Technology	M,D
Electrical Engineering	M,D
Engineering and Applied Sciences—General	M,D
English	M
Entomology	M,D
Environmental Engineering	M
Exercise and Sports Science	M
Finance and Banking	M
Food Science and Technology	M
French	M
Genetics	D
Geography	M
Geology	M,D
Geophysics	M,D
German	M
Health Education	M
Health Promotion	M
Health Services Management and Hospital Administration	M,D
History	M
International Affairs	M
Kinesiology and Movement Studies	M
Law	D
Mathematics Education	M,D
Mathematics	M,D
Mechanical Engineering	M,D
Microbiology	D
Molecular Biology	M,D
Music Education	M
Music	M
Natural Resources	M,D
Nursing—General	M
Nutrition	M
Pathobiology	M
Petroleum Engineering	M,D
Pharmacy	M,D
Philosophy	M
Physical Education	M
Physiology	M,D
Political Science	M
Psychology—General	M,D
Public Administration	M
Range Science	M,D
Reproductive Biology	M,D
Rural Planning and Studies	M
Science Education	M
Social Work	M
Sociology	M
Spanish	M
Special Education	M,D,O
Statistics	M,D
Student Affairs	M,D
Water Resources	M,D
Writing	M
Zoology	M,D

UPPER IOWA UNIVERSITY

Accounting	M
Business Administration and Management—General	M
Early Childhood Education	M
Education—General	M
Educational Leadership and Administration	M
Emergency Management	M
English as a Second Language	M
Finance and Banking	M
Higher Education	M
Homeland Security	M
Human Resources Management	M
Human Services	M
Nonprofit Management	M
Organizational Management	M
Public Administration	M
Reading Education	M
Sports Management	M

URBANA UNIVERSITY–A BRANCH CAMPUS OF FRANKLIN UNIVERSITY

Business Administration and Management—General	M
Criminal Justice and Criminology	M
Education—General	M
Nursing—General	M

URSHAN GRADUATE SCHOOL OF THEOLOGY

Theology	M

URSULINE COLLEGE

Accounting	M
Adult Nursing	M,D
Art Therapy	M
Business Administration and Management—General	M
Early Childhood Education	M
Educational Leadership and Administration	M
Entrepreneurship	M
Family Nurse Practitioner Studies	M,D
Finance and Banking	M
Gerontological Nursing	M,D
Health Services Management and Hospital Administration	M
Historic Preservation	M
Liberal Studies	M
Marketing	M
Medical/Surgical Nursing	M,D
Middle School Education	M
Nursing Education	M,D
Nursing—General	M,D
Pastoral Ministry and Counseling	M
Secondary Education	M
Special Education	M
Theology	M

UTAH STATE UNIVERSITY

Accounting	M
Aerospace/Aeronautical Engineering	M,D
Agricultural Economics and Agribusiness	M,D
Agricultural Education	M
Agricultural Sciences—General	M,D
Agronomy and Soil Sciences	M,D
American Studies	M
Animal Sciences	M,D
Anthropology	M,D
Applied Economics	M,D
Applied Mathematics	M,D
Art/Fine Arts	M
Biochemistry	M,D
Bioengineering	M,D
Biological and Biomedical Sciences—General	M,D
Business Administration and Management—General	M
Business Education	D
Chemistry	M,D
Child and Family Studies	M,D
Civil Engineering	M,D,O
Clinical Psychology	M,D
Communication Disorders	M,D,O
Communication—General	M
Computer Science	M,D
Consumer Economics	M
Counseling Psychology	M,D
Counselor Education	M,D
Curriculum and Instruction	D
Disability Studies	M,D,O
Ecology	M,D
Economics	M,D
Education—General	M,D,O
Educational Measurement and Evaluation	M,D
Educational Media/Instructional Technology	M,D,O
Electrical Engineering	M,D
Elementary Education	M
Engineering and Applied Sciences—General	M,D,O
English	M
Environmental Engineering	M,D,O
Environmental Management and Policy	M,D
Family and Consumer Sciences-General	M,D
Finance and Banking	M
Fish, Game, and Wildlife Management	M,D
Folklore	M
Food Science and Technology	M,D
Forestry	M,D
Geography	M,D
Geology	M
Health Education	M,D
Health Promotion	M,D
History	M
Home Economics Education	M
Horticulture	M,D
Human Development	M,D
Human Resources Management	M
Kinesiology and Movement Studies	M,D
Landscape Architecture	M
Management Information Systems	M
Marriage and Family Therapy	M,D
Mathematics	M,D
Mechanical Engineering	M,D
Meteorology	M,D
Multilingual and Multicultural Education	M
Music Education	M
Music	M
Natural Resources	M
Nutrition	M,D
Physical Education	M,D
Physics	M,D
Plant Sciences	M,D
Political Science	M
Psychology—General	M,D
Public Health—General	M,D
Range Science	M,D
Recreation and Park Management	M,D
Rehabilitation Counseling	M
School Psychology	M,D
Secondary Education	M
Social Work	M,D
Sociology	M,D
Special Education	M,D,O
Statistics	M,D
Theater	M
Toxicology	M,D
Urban and Regional Planning	M,D
Veterinary Sciences	M,D
Vocational and Technical Education	D
Water Resources	M,D
Writing	M

UTAH VALLEY UNIVERSITY

Accounting	M
Business Administration and Management—General	M
Computer and Information Systems Security	O
Education—General	M
Educational Leadership and Administration	M
Educational Media/Instructional Technology	M
Elementary Education	M
English as a Second Language	M
Mathematics Education	M
Nursing—General	M
Reading Education	M

UTICA COLLEGE

Accounting	M
Computer and Information Systems Security	M
Criminal Justice and Criminology	M
Education—General	M,O
Health Services Management and Hospital Administration	M
Occupational Therapy	M
Physical Therapy	D

VALDOSTA STATE UNIVERSITY

Accounting	M
Business Administration and Management—General	M
Communication Disorders	M,D,O
Counselor Education	M,O
Educational Leadership and Administration	M,D,O
Elementary Education	M
English Education	M
English	M
Exercise and Sports Science	M
Family Nurse Practitioner Studies	M
Gerontological Nursing	M
Health Services Management and Hospital Administration	M
Industrial and Organizational Psychology	M,O
Information Studies	M
Library Science	M
Marriage and Family Therapy	M,O
Nursing—General	M
Psychiatric Nursing	M
Psychology—General	M,O
Public Administration	M,D
Social Work	M
Special Education	M,D,O

VALLEY CITY STATE UNIVERSITY

Education—General	M
Educational Media/Instructional Technology	M
Elementary Education	M
English as a Second Language	M
English Education	M
Library Science	M
Vocational and Technical Education	M

VALPARAISO UNIVERSITY

Arts Administration	M
Business Administration and Management—General	M,O
Clinical Psychology	M
Communication—General	M,O
Computational Sciences	M
Computer and Information Systems Security	M
Education—General	M,O
Educational Leadership and Administration	M,O
Elementary Education	M,O
Engineering Management	M,O
English as a Second Language	M,O
English	M
Entertainment Management	M
Ethics	M,O
Finance and Banking	M,O
Health Services Management and Hospital Administration	M
International Economics	M
International Trade Policy	M
Law	M,D
Management Information Systems	M
Management Strategy and Policy	M,O
Media Studies	M,O
Nursing Education	M,D,O
Nursing—General	M,D,O
Physician Assistant Studies	M,D,O
Public Health—General	M,D,O
School Psychology	M,O
Secondary Education	M,O
Sports Management	M

VAN ANDEL INSTITUTE GRADUATE SCHOOL

Genetics	D
Molecular Genetics	D

VANCOUVER ISLAND UNIVERSITY

Business Administration and Management—General	M
Finance and Banking	M
International Business	M
Marketing	M

VANCOUVER SCHOOL OF THEOLOGY

Religion	M,O
Religious Education	M,O
Theology	M,O

VANDERBILT UNIVERSITY

Accounting	M
Acute Care/Critical Care Nursing	M,D,O
Adult Nursing	M,D,O
Allopathic Medicine	M,D
Analytical Chemistry	M,D
Anthropology	M,D
Astronomy	M,D
Biochemistry	M,D
Bioinformatics	M,D
Biological and Biomedical Sciences—General	M,D
Biomedical Engineering	M,D
Biophysics	M,D
Business Administration and Management—General	M
Cell Biology	M,D
Chemical Engineering	M,D
Chemistry	M,D
Child and Family Studies	M
Civil Engineering	M,D
Classics	M
Communication Disorders	M,D
Computer and Information Systems Security	M
Computer Science	M,D
Counselor Education	M
Developmental Biology	M,D
Economic Development	M,D
Economics	M,D
Education—General	M,D*
Educational Leadership and Administration	M,D
Educational Policy	M,D
Electrical Engineering	M,D
Elementary Education	M
Engineering and Applied Sciences—General	M,D
English Education	M
English	M,D
Environmental Engineering	M,D
Environmental Management and Policy	M,D
Environmental Sciences	M
Family Nurse Practitioner Studies	M,D,O
Finance and Banking	M
Foreign Languages Education	M,D
French	M,D
Geology	M
German	M,D
Gerontological Nursing	M,D,O
Health Physics/Radiological Health	M,D
Health Services Management and Hospital Administration	M
Higher Education	M,D
History	M,D
Human Development	M
Human Genetics	D
Immunology	M,D
Inorganic Chemistry	M,D
International and Comparative Education	M,D
Latin American Studies	M
Law	M,D
Liberal Studies	M
Management Strategy and Policy	M
Marketing	M
Materials Sciences	M,D
Maternal and Child/Neonatal Nursing	M,D,O
Mathematics	M,D
Mechanical Engineering	M,D
Microbiology	M,D
Molecular Biology	M,D
Molecular Physiology	M,D
Multilingual and Multicultural Education	M,D
Nurse Midwifery	M,D,O
Nursing and Healthcare Administration	M,D,O
Nursing Informatics	M,D,O
Nursing—General	M,D,O
Organic Chemistry	M,D
Organizational Management	M,D
Pathology	D
Pediatric Nursing	M,D,O
Pharmacology	D
Philosophy	M,D
Physical Chemistry	M,D
Physics	M,D
Political Science	M,D
Portuguese	M,D
Psychiatric Nursing	M,D,O
Psychology—General	D
Public Health—General	M
Public Policy	D
Quantitative Analysis	M
Reading Education	M
Religion	M,D
Science Education	M,D
Secondary Education	M
Sociology	M,D
Spanish	M,D
Special Education	M,D
Theology	M
Theoretical Chemistry	M,D
Urban and Regional Planning	M
Urban Education	M
Women's Health Nursing	M,D,O
Writing	M

VANDERCOOK COLLEGE OF MUSIC

Music Education	M

VANGUARD UNIVERSITY OF SOUTHERN CALIFORNIA

Clinical Psychology	M
Curriculum and Instruction	M
Education—General	M
Educational Leadership and Administration	M
Nursing—General	M
Religion	M
Religious Education	M
Theology	M

VAUGHN COLLEGE OF AERONAUTICS AND TECHNOLOGY
Aviation Management M

VERMONT COLLEGE OF FINE ARTS
Art Education M
Art/Fine Arts M
Film, Television, and Video Production M
Graphic Design M
Music M
Publishing M
Writing M

VERMONT LAW SCHOOL
Energy Management and Policy M
Environmental Law M
Environmental Management and Policy M
Law D
Legal and Justice Studies M

VERMONT TECHNICAL COLLEGE
Software Engineering M

VICTORIA UNIVERSITY
Theology M,D,O

VILLANOVA UNIVERSITY
Accounting M
Adult Nursing M,D,O
Applied Statistics M
Artificial Intelligence/Robotics M,O
Biochemical Engineering M,O
Biological and Biomedical Sciences—General M
Business Administration and Management—General M
Chemical Engineering M,O
Chemistry M
Civil Engineering M
Classics M
Communication—General M
Computer Engineering M,O
Computer Science M,O
Counselor Education M
Education—General M
Educational Leadership and Administration M
Electrical Engineering M,O
Engineering and Applied Sciences—General M,D,O
English M
Environmental Engineering M,O
Family Nurse Practitioner Studies M,D,O
Finance and Banking M
Gerontological Nursing M,D,O
Health Services Management and Hospital Administration M
Hispanic Studies M
History M
Human Resources Development M
International Business M
Law D
Liberal Studies M
Management Strategy and Policy M
Manufacturing Engineering M,O
Marketing M
Mathematics M
Mechanical Engineering M,O
Missions and Missiology M
Nonprofit Management M,O
Nurse Anesthesia M,D,O
Nursing Education M,D,O
Nursing—General M,D,O
Pediatric Nursing M,D,O
Philosophy D
Political Science M
Psychology—General M
Public Administration M,O
Real Estate M
Taxation M
Theater M
Theology M,D
Water Resources Engineering M,O

VIRGINIA BAPTIST COLLEGE
Theology M

VIRGINIA BEACH THEOLOGICAL SEMINARY
Pastoral Ministry and Counseling M
Theology M

VIRGINIA COMMONWEALTH UNIVERSITY
Accounting M
Adult Education M
Adult Nursing M,D,O
Advertising and Public Relations M
Allied Health—General D
Allopathic Medicine D
Analytical Chemistry M,D
Anatomy M
Applied Mathematics M
Applied Physics M
Art Education M,D
Art History M,D
Art/Fine Arts M,D
Biochemistry M,D
Biological and Biomedical Sciences—General M,D,O
Biomedical Engineering M,D
Biostatistics M,D
Business Administration and Management—General M,D
Chemical Physics M,D
Chemistry M,D
Clinical Laboratory Sciences/Medical Technology M,D
Clinical Psychology D
Communication—General D
Computer Science M,D
Counseling Psychology M,D
Counselor Education M,D
Criminal Justice and Criminology M,O
Curriculum and Instruction D
Dentistry M,D
Early Childhood Education M
Economics M
Education—General M,D,O
Educational Leadership and Administration M,D
Educational Measurement and Evaluation D
Educational Media/Instructional Technology M
Educational Psychology D
Elementary Education M
Emergency Management M,O
Engineering and Applied Sciences—General M,D
English M
Environmental Management and Policy M
Exercise and Sports Science M
Family Nurse Practitioner Studies M
Film, Television, and Video Production M,D
Finance and Banking M
Forensic Sciences M
Geographic Information Systems O
Gerontology M,D
Health Physics/Radiological Health D
Health Psychology D
Health Services Management and Hospital Administration M,D
Health Services Research D
History M
Homeland Security M,O
Human Genetics M,D
Human Resources Development M
Human Resources Management M
Immunology M,D
Inorganic Chemistry M,D
Interdisciplinary Studies M
Interior Design M,D
Journalism M
Management Information Systems M
Mass Communication M
Mathematics M
Mechanical Engineering M,D
Media Studies M,D
Medical Physics M,D
Medicinal and Pharmaceutical Chemistry M,D
Microbiology M,D
Molecular Biology M,D
Molecular Genetics M,D
Museum Studies M,D
Music Education M
Music M
Nanotechnology M,D
Neurobiology M
Neuroscience M,D,O
Nonprofit Management O
Nuclear Engineering M,D
Nurse Anesthesia M,D
Nursing and Healthcare Administration M,D,O
Nursing Education M,D,O
Nursing—General M,D,O
Occupational Therapy M,D
Organic Chemistry M,D
Pediatric Nursing M,D,O
Pharmaceutical Administration M,D
Pharmaceutical Sciences M,D
Pharmacology M,D,O
Pharmacy D
Photography M,D
Physical Chemistry M,D
Physical Therapy M,D
Physics M
Physiology M,D
Political Science M,D,O
Psychiatric Nursing M,D,O
Public Administration M
Public Affairs M,D,O
Public Policy D
Reading Education M,O
Real Estate O
Recreation and Park Management M
Rehabilitation Counseling M
Rehabilitation Sciences D
Social Work M,D
Sociology M
Special Education M,D
Student Affairs M
Systems Biology D
Theater M
Toxicology M,D,O
Urban and Regional Planning M
Urban Education D
Women's Health Nursing M,D,O
Writing M

VIRGINIA INTERNATIONAL UNIVERSITY
Accounting M,O
Advertising and Public Relations M,O
Business Administration and Management—General M,O
Computer and Information Systems Security M,O
Computer Art and Design M,O
Computer Science M,O
Data Science/Data Analytics M,O
Education—General M
English as a Second Language M
Entrepreneurship M,O
Finance and Banking M,O
Game Design and Development M,O
Health Informatics M,O
Health Services Management and Hospital Administration M,O
Hospitality Management M,O
Human Resources Management M,O
International Affairs M
International Business M,O
Linguistics M
Logistics M,O
Management Information Systems M,O
Marketing M,O
Project Management M,O
Public Administration M
Software Engineering M,O

VIRGINIA POLYTECHNIC INSTITUTE AND STATE UNIVERSITY
Accounting M,D
Aerospace/Aeronautical Engineering M,D,O
Agricultural Economics and Agribusiness M,D
Agricultural Engineering M,D
Agricultural Sciences—General M,D,O
Agronomy and Soil Sciences M,D
Animal Sciences M,D
Applied Economics M,D
Applied Statistics M,D
Biochemistry M,D
Bioengineering M,D
Bioinformatics M,D
Biological and Biomedical Sciences—General M,D
Biomedical Engineering M,D
Biotechnology M,D
Business Administration and Management—General M,D
Business Analytics M,D
Chemical Engineering M,D
Chemistry M,D
Civil Engineering M,D,O
Communication—General M,D,O
Computer and Information Systems Security M,O
Computer Engineering M,D,O
Computer Science M,D,O
Counselor Education M,D,O
Curriculum and Instruction M,D,O
Distance Education Development M,O
Economics M,D
Education—General M,O
Educational Leadership and Administration M,D,O
Educational Measurement and Evaluation M,D,O
Educational Media/Instructional Technology M,O
Educational Policy M,D,O
Electrical Engineering M,D,O
Engineering and Applied Sciences—General M,D
Engineering Management M,O
English M,D,O
Entomology M,D
Environmental Design M,D
Environmental Engineering M,O
Environmental Management and Policy M,D,O
Environmental Sciences M,O
Exercise and Sports Science M,D
Finance and Banking M,D
Fish, Game, and Wildlife Management M,D
Forestry M,D
Genetics M,D
Geography M,D
Geosciences M,D
Horticulture M,D
Humanities M,D,O
Industrial/Management Engineering M,O
Interdisciplinary Studies M,D
International Affairs M,D
Internet and Interactive Multimedia M,D
Landscape Architecture M,D
Liberal Studies M,O
Management Information Systems M,D,O
Marketing M,D
Mathematics M,D
National Security M,O
Natural Resources M,D,O
Nonprofit Management M,O
Nutrition M,D
Ocean Engineering M,O
Physics M,D
Plant Pathology M,D
Plant Physiology M,D
Political Science M,D
Psychology—General M,D
Public Administration M,D
Public Affairs M,D
Public Health—General M,D
Public Policy M,D
Quantitative Analysis M,O
Social Sciences Education M,D,O
Software Engineering M,O
Statistics M,D
Systems Engineering M,O
Transportation and Highway Engineering M,O
Urban and Regional Planning M,D
Urban Studies M,D
Veterinary Medicine M,D
Veterinary Sciences M,D
Vocational and Technical Education M,D,O
Writing M,D,O

VIRGINIA STATE UNIVERSITY
Biological and Biomedical Sciences—General M
Clinical Psychology M,D
Community Health M,D
Computer Science M
Counselor Education M
Criminal Justice and Criminology M
Economics M
Education—General M,D
Educational Leadership and Administration M,D
Health Education M,D
Health Psychology M,D
Interdisciplinary Studies M
Mathematics Education M
Mathematics M
Media Studies M
Psychology—General M,D

VIRGINIA THEOLOGICAL SEMINARY
Educational Leadership and Administration M,D
Theology M,D

VIRGINIA UNION UNIVERSITY
Curriculum and Instruction M
Education—General M
Theology M,D

VIRGINIA UNIVERSITY OF LYNCHBURG
Pastoral Ministry and Counseling M,D
Religion M,D

VIRGINIA WESLEYAN UNIVERSITY
Business Administration and Management—General M
Education—General M
Secondary Education M

VITERBO UNIVERSITY
Addictions/Substance Abuse Counseling M
Business Administration and Management—General M
Counseling Psychology M
Developmental Psychology M
Early Childhood Education M,O
Education of the Gifted M,O
Education—General M,O
Educational Leadership and Administration M,O
Ethics M,O
Health Psychology M
Health Services Management and Hospital Administration M
International Business M
Nursing—General D
Organizational Management M,O
Pastoral Ministry and Counseling M,O
Project Management M
Reading Education M,O
Special Education M,O

WAGNER COLLEGE
Accounting M
Business Administration and Management—General M
Early Childhood Education M
Education—General M
Elementary Education M
English Education M
Family Nurse Practitioner Studies M,D,O
Finance and Banking M
Foreign Languages Education M
Higher Education M
Marketing M
Mathematics Education M
Media Studies M
Microbiology M
Middle School Education M
Nursing Education M,D,O
Nursing—General M,D,O
Science Education M
Secondary Education M
Social Sciences Education M
Special Education M

WAKE FOREST UNIVERSITY
Accounting M
Allopathic Medicine D
Analytical Chemistry M,D
Anatomy D
Biochemistry D
Biological and Biomedical Sciences—General M,D
Biomedical Engineering M,D
Business Administration and Management—General M
Business Analytics M
Cancer Biology/Oncology D
Chemistry M,D
Communication—General M
Computer Science M
Counselor Education M
Education—General M
English M
Exercise and Sports Science M
Genomic Sciences D
Health Services Research M
Immunology D
Inorganic Chemistry M,D
Law M,D
Liberal Studies M
Mathematics M
Microbiology D
Molecular Genetics D
Molecular Medicine M,D
Neurobiology D
Neuroscience D
Nurse Anesthesia M
Organic Chemistry M,D
Pathobiology M,D
Pharmacology D
Physical Chemistry M,D
Physics M,D

*M—masters degree; D—doctorate; O—other advanced degree; *—Close-Up and/or Display*

- Physiology D
- Psychology—General M
- Religion M
- Secondary Education M
- Speech and Interpersonal Communication M
- Taxation M

WALDEN UNIVERSITY

- Accounting M,D,O
- Addictions/Substance Abuse Counseling M,D
- Adult Education M,D,O
- Adult Nursing M,D,O
- Applied Psychology M,D,O
- Business Administration and Management—General M,D,O
- Child and Family Studies M,D,O
- Clinical Psychology M,D,O
- Clinical Research M,D,O
- Communication—General M,D,O
- Community Health M,D,O
- Computer and Information Systems Security M,D,O
- Conflict Resolution and Mediation/Peace Studies M,D,O
- Counseling Psychology M,D,O
- Counselor Education M,D
- Criminal Justice and Criminology M,D,O
- Curriculum and Instruction M,D,O
- Developmental Education M,D,O
- Distance Education Development M,D,O
- Early Childhood Education M,D,O
- Education—General M,D,O
- Educational Leadership and Administration M,D,O
- Educational Measurement and Evaluation M,D,O
- Educational Media/Instructional Technology M,D,O
- Educational Psychology M,D,O
- Elementary Education M,D,O
- Emergency Management M,D,O
- English as a Second Language M,D,O
- Entrepreneurship M,D,O
- Epidemiology M,D,O
- Family Nurse Practitioner Studies M,D,O
- Finance and Banking M,D,O
- Forensic Psychology M,D,O
- Gerontological Nursing M,D,O
- Gerontology M,D
- Health Education M,D,O
- Health Informatics M,D,O
- Health Promotion M,D,O
- Health Psychology M,D,O
- Health Services Management and Hospital Administration M,D,O
- Higher Education M,D,O
- Homeland Security M,D,O
- Human Resources Management M,D,O
- Human Services M,D
- Industrial and Organizational Psychology M,D,O
- Interdisciplinary Studies M,D,O
- International Affairs M,D,O
- International and Comparative Education M,D,O
- International Business M,D,O
- International Development M,D,O
- International Health M,D,O
- Law M,D,O
- Management Information Systems M,D,O
- Marketing M,D,O
- Marriage and Family Therapy M,D
- Mathematics Education M,D,O
- Multilingual and Multicultural Education M,D,O
- Nonprofit Management M,D,O
- Nursing and Healthcare Administration M,D,O
- Nursing Education M,D,O
- Nursing Informatics M,D,O
- Nursing—General M,D,O
- Organizational Management M,D,O
- Political Science M,D,O
- Project Management M,D,O
- Psychology—General M,D,O
- Public Administration M,D,O
- Public Health—General M,D,O
- Public Policy M,D,O
- Reading Education M,D,O
- Science Education M,D,O
- Social Psychology M,D,O
- Social Work M,D
- Special Education M,D,O
- Supply Chain Management M,D,O
- Sustainable Development M,D,O

WALDORF UNIVERSITY

- Criminal Justice and Criminology M
- Educational Leadership and Administration M
- Emergency Management M
- Human Resources Development M
- Organizational Management M
- Public Administration M
- Sports Management M

WALLA WALLA UNIVERSITY

- Biological and Biomedical Sciences—General M
- Communication—General M
- Curriculum and Instruction M
- Education—General M
- Educational Leadership and Administration M
- Film, Television, and Video Theory and Criticism M
- Internet and Interactive Multimedia M
- Pastoral Ministry and Counseling M
- Reading Education M
- Religion M
- Social Work M
- Special Education M

WALSH COLLEGE OF ACCOUNTANCY AND BUSINESS ADMINISTRATION

- Accounting M
- Business Administration and Management—General M
- Business Analytics M
- Computer and Information Systems Security M
- Data Science/Data Analytics M
- Finance and Banking M
- Human Resources Management M
- International Business M
- Investment Management M
- Management Information Systems M
- Management of Technology M
- Management Strategy and Policy M
- Marketing M
- Project Management M
- Taxation M

WALSH UNIVERSITY

- Adult Nursing M,D
- Business Administration and Management—General M
- Counseling Psychology M
- Counselor Education M
- Education—General M
- Health Services Management and Hospital Administration M
- Higher Education M
- Marketing M
- Nursing and Healthcare Administration M,D
- Nursing Education M,D
- Nursing—General M,D
- Pastoral Ministry and Counseling M
- Physical Therapy D
- Reading Education M
- Religious Education M
- Student Affairs M
- Theology M

WARNER PACIFIC UNIVERSITY

- Education—General M
- Human Services M
- Nonprofit Management M
- Organizational Management M

WARNER UNIVERSITY

- Accounting M
- Business Administration and Management—General M
- Curriculum and Instruction M
- Education—General M
- Educational Media/Instructional Technology M
- Elementary Education M
- Human Resources Management M
- International Business M
- Science Education M

WARREN WILSON COLLEGE

- Art/Fine Arts M
- Writing M

WARTBURG THEOLOGICAL SEMINARY

- Theology M

WASHBURN UNIVERSITY

- Accounting M
- Addictions/Substance Abuse Counseling M
- Business Administration and Management—General M
- Clinical Psychology M
- Criminal Justice and Criminology M
- Curriculum and Instruction M
- Education—General M
- Educational Leadership and Administration M
- Health Education M
- Human Services M
- Law M,D
- Legal and Justice Studies M,D
- Liberal Studies M
- Nursing and Healthcare Administration M,D,O
- Nursing—General M,D,O
- Psychology—General M
- Reading Education M
- Social Work M
- Special Education M

WASHINGTON ADVENTIST UNIVERSITY

- Business Administration and Management—General M
- Counseling Psychology M
- Health Services Management and Hospital Administration M
- Nursing and Healthcare Administration M
- Nursing Education M
- Nursing—General M
- Public Administration M
- Religion M

WASHINGTON & JEFFERSON COLLEGE

- Accounting M,O
- Applied Economics M,O
- Thanatology M,O
- Writing M,O

WASHINGTON AND LEE UNIVERSITY

- Law D

WASHINGTON STATE UNIVERSITY

- Accounting M
- Agricultural Economics and Agribusiness M,D,O
- Agricultural Engineering M,D
- Agronomy and Soil Sciences M,D,O
- Allopathic Medicine M,D
- American Studies M,D
- Animal Sciences M,D
- Anthropology M,D
- Applied Mathematics M,D
- Archaeology M,D
- Architecture M
- Art/Fine Arts M
- Biochemistry M,D
- Bioengineering M,D
- Bioethics M,D,O
- Biological and Biomedical Sciences—General M,D
- Biophysics M,D
- Business Administration and Management—General M,D
- Business Education M,D
- Chemical Engineering M,D
- Chemistry M,D
- Civil Engineering M,D
- Clinical Psychology M,D
- Clothing and Textiles M,D
- Communication Disorders M
- Communication—General M,D
- Community Health M,D,O
- Computer Engineering M,D
- Computer Science M,D
- Corporate and Organizational Communication M,D
- Counseling Psychology M,D
- Criminal Justice and Criminology M,D
- Cultural Anthropology M,D
- Cultural Studies M,D
- Curriculum and Instruction M,D
- Economics M,D,O
- Education—General M,D
- Educational Leadership and Administration M,D
- Educational Psychology M,D
- Electrical Engineering M,D
- Elementary Education M,D
- Energy and Power Engineering M,D
- Engineering and Applied Sciences—General M,D,O
- Engineering Management M,O
- English as a Second Language M,D
- English M,D
- Entomology M,D
- Environmental Engineering M,D
- Environmental Sciences M,D
- Exercise and Sports Science M
- Experimental Psychology M,D
- Family Nurse Practitioner Studies M,D,O
- Food Science and Technology M,D
- Foreign Languages Education M
- Genetics M,D
- Geology M,D
- Health Services Management and Hospital Administration M
- History M,D
- Horticulture M,D
- Human Development D
- Immunology M,D
- Infectious Diseases M,D
- Interdisciplinary Studies D
- Interior Design M
- Landscape Architecture M
- Management of Technology M,O
- Materials Engineering M,D
- Materials Sciences M,D
- Mathematics Education M,D
- Mathematics M,D
- Mechanical Engineering M,D
- Music M
- Natural Resources M,D
- Neuroscience M,D
- Nursing—General M,D,O
- Nutrition M
- Pharmacy M,D
- Physics M,D
- Plant Pathology M,D
- Political Science M,D,O
- Psychiatric Nursing M,D,O
- Psychology—General M,D
- Public Affairs M,D,O
- Reading Education M,D
- Secondary Education M,D
- Sociology M,D
- Special Education M,D
- Sports Management M,D
- Veterinary Medicine D
- Veterinary Sciences M,D
- Vocational and Technical Education M,D

WASHINGTON UNIVERSITY IN ST. LOUIS

- Accounting M
- Aerospace/Aeronautical Engineering M,D
- Allopathic Medicine D
- Anthropology D
- Archaeology M,D
- Architecture M
- Art History M,D
- Art/Fine Arts M
- Asian Languages M,D
- Asian Studies M,D
- Biochemistry D
- Bioethics M
- Biological and Biomedical Sciences—General D
- Biomedical Engineering M,D
- Biostatistics M,D,O
- Business Administration and Management—General M,D
- Cell Biology D
- Chemical Engineering M,D
- Chemistry D
- Child and Family Studies M,D
- Chinese M,D
- Classics M,D
- Clinical Research M
- Communication Disorders M,D
- Comparative Literature M,D
- Computational Biology D
- Computer Engineering M,D
- Computer Science M,D
- Dance M
- Data Science/Data Analytics M
- Developmental Biology D
- Developmental Psychology D
- Ecology D
- Economics D
- Education—General M,D
- Educational Measurement and Evaluation D
- Elementary Education M
- Engineering and Applied Sciences—General M,D
- English M,D
- Entrepreneurship M
- Environmental Biology D
- Environmental Engineering M,D
- Epidemiology M,D
- Evolutionary Biology D
- Finance and Banking M,D
- French D
- Genetics M,D
- Genomic Sciences M
- Geosciences D
- German D
- Gerontology M,D
- Health Services Research M,O
- History D
- Human Genetics D
- Immunology D
- International Health M,D
- Japanese M,D
- Jewish Studies M
- Kinesiology and Movement Studies D
- Law M,D
- Materials Sciences M,D
- Mathematics M,D
- Mechanical Engineering M,D
- Microbiology D
- Molecular Biology D
- Molecular Biophysics D
- Molecular Genetics D
- Molecular Pathogenesis D
- Music M,D
- Near and Middle Eastern Studies M
- Neuroscience D
- Occupational Therapy M,D
- Organizational Management M
- Philosophy D
- Physical Therapy D
- Physics D
- Planetary and Space Sciences D
- Plant Biology D
- Political Science D
- Psychology—General D
- Public Health—General M,D
- Rehabilitation Sciences D
- Religion M
- Romance Languages D
- Secondary Education M
- Social Work M,D
- Spanish D
- Special Education M,D
- Speech and Interpersonal Communication M,D
- Statistics M,D
- Supply Chain Management M
- Systems Biology D
- Theater M
- Urban Design M
- Writing M

WATKINS COLLEGE OF ART, DESIGN, & FILM

- Film, Television, and Video Production M

WAYLAND BAPTIST UNIVERSITY

- Accounting M,D
- Business Administration and Management—General M,D
- Counseling Psychology M
- Criminal Justice and Criminology M
- Education—General M
- Educational Leadership and Administration M
- Educational Measurement and Evaluation M
- Educational Media/Instructional Technology M
- Elementary Education M
- English as a Second Language M
- English Education M
- Health Services Management and Hospital Administration M,D
- Higher Education M
- History M
- Homeland Security M
- Human Resources Management M,D
- Humanities M
- International Business M,D
- Management Information Systems M,D
- Organizational Management M,D
- Pastoral Ministry and Counseling M
- Project Management M,D
- Religion M
- Science Education M
- Secondary Education M
- Social Sciences Education M
- Special Education M
- Sports Management M
- Theology M

WAYNESBURG UNIVERSITY

- Addictions/Substance Abuse Counseling M,D
- Business Administration and Management—General M,D
- Clinical Psychology M,D
- Counseling Psychology M,D
- Counselor Education M,D
- Criminal Justice and Criminology M,D
- Curriculum and Instruction M,D
- Distance Education Development M,D
- Educational Leadership and Administration M,D

Educational Media/Instructional Technology M,D
Energy Management and Policy M,D
Finance and Banking M,D
Health Services Management and Hospital Administration M,D
Human Resources Management M,D
Nursing and Healthcare Administration M,D
Nursing Education M,D
Nursing Informatics M,D
Nursing—General M,D
Organizational Management M,D
Special Education M,D

WAYNE STATE COLLEGE
Business Administration and Management—General M
Business Education M
Communication—General M
Counselor Education M
Curriculum and Instruction M
Early Childhood Education M
Education—General M,O
Educational Leadership and Administration M,O
Elementary Education M
English as a Second Language M
English Education M
Exercise and Sports Science M
Home Economics Education M
Mathematics Education M
Music Education M
Organizational Management M
Physical Education M
Science Education M
Social Sciences Education M
Special Education M
Sports Management M
Vocational and Technical Education M

WAYNE STATE UNIVERSITY
Accounting M,D,O
Acute Care/Critical Care Nursing M,D
Adult Nursing M,D
Advertising and Public Relations M,D,O
African-American Studies M,D,O
Allopathic Medicine D
Analytical Chemistry M,D
Anatomy M,D,O
Anthropology M,D
Applied Behavior Analysis M,D,O
Applied Mathematics M,D
Archives/Archival Administration M,O
Art Education M,D,O
Art History M
Art/Fine Arts M
Athletic Training and Sports Medicine M,D
Automotive Engineering M,O
Biochemistry M,D,O
Bioinformatics M,D
Biological and Biomedical Sciences—General M,D
Biomedical Engineering M,D,O
Biopsychology M,D,O
Business Administration and Management—General M,D,O
Cancer Biology/Oncology M,D,O
Cell Biology M,D,O
Chemical Engineering M,D,O
Chemistry M,D
Civil Engineering M,D
Clinical Psychology M,D
Clothing and Textiles M
Cognitive Sciences M,D
Communication Disorders M,D
Communication—General M,D,O
Community Health Nursing M,D
Computational Biology M,D
Computer Engineering M,D
Computer Science M,D
Conflict Resolution and Mediation/Peace Studies M,D,O
Counseling Psychology M,D,O
Counselor Education M,D,O
Criminal Justice and Criminology M
Cultural Studies M,D
Curriculum and Instruction M,D,O
Dance M,D,O
Data Science/Data Analytics M,D,O
Distance Education Development M,D,O
Early Childhood Education M,D,O
Economic Development M,D,O
Economics M,D
Education—General M,D,O
Educational Leadership and Administration M,D,O
Educational Measurement and Evaluation M,D,O
Educational Media/Instructional Technology M,D,O
Educational Policy M,D,O
Educational Psychology M,D,O
Electrical Engineering M,D
Electronic Materials M
Elementary Education M,D,O
Energy and Power Engineering M,O
Engineering and Applied Sciences—General M,D,O
Engineering Management M,D,O
English as a Second Language M,D,O
English Education M,D,O
English M,D
Entrepreneurship M,D,O
Exercise and Sports Science M,D
Film, Television, and Video Theory and Criticism M,D
Finance and Banking M,D,O
Food Science and Technology M,D,O
Foreign Languages Education M,D,O
Foundations and Philosophy of Education M,D,O
French M,D
Gender Studies M,D,O
Genetic Counseling M,D,O
Genomic Sciences M,D,O
Geology M
German M,D
Gerontological Nursing M,D
Gerontology M,D,O
Graphic Design M
Health Communication M,D,O
Health Education M,D,O
Health Services Management and Hospital Administration M,D
Health Services Research M,D
History M,D,O
Human Resources Management M,D,O
Immunology M,D,O
Industrial and Labor Relations M,D
Industrial and Manufacturing Management M,D
Industrial and Organizational Psychology M,D
Industrial Design M
Industrial/Management Engineering M,D,O
Information Studies M,O
Interior Design M
International Economics M,D
Italian M,D
Journalism M,D,O
Kinesiology and Movement Studies M,D
Law M,D
Library Science M,O
Linguistics M
Management Information Systems M,D,O
Management Strategy and Policy M,D,O
Manufacturing Engineering M,D,O
Materials Sciences M,D,O
Maternal and Child/Neonatal Nursing M,D
Mathematics Education M,D,O
Mathematics M,D,O
Mechanical Engineering M,D
Media Studies M,D,O
Medical Imaging M,D,O
Medical Physics M,D,O
Medicinal and Pharmaceutical Chemistry M,D
Microbiology M,D,O
Molecular Biology M,D,O
Molecular Genetics M,D,O
Molecular Medicine M,D,O
Multilingual and Multicultural Education M,D,O
Museum Studies M,D,O
Music Education M,O
Music M,O
Near and Middle Eastern Languages M,D
Near and Middle Eastern Studies M,D
Neuroscience M,D,O
Nonprofit Management M,D
Nurse Anesthesia M,D,O
Nurse Midwifery M,D
Nursing—General M,D
Nutrition M,D,O
Occupational Therapy M
Organizational Behavior M,D
Organizational Management M,D
Pathology M,D,O
Pediatric Nursing M,D,O
Pharmaceutical Sciences M,D
Pharmacology M,D,O
Pharmacy D
Philosophy M,D
Photography M
Physical Education M,D
Physical Therapy D
Physician Assistant Studies M
Physics M,D
Physiology M,D,O
Political Science M,D
Polymer Science and Engineering M,D,O
Psychiatric Nursing M,D
Psychology—General M,D
Public Administration M,D
Public Health—General M,D,O
Public History M,D,O
Public Policy M,D,O
Reading Education M,D,O
Rehabilitation Counseling M,D,O
Rhetoric M,D
Romance Languages M,D
School Psychology M,D,O
Science Education M,D,O
Secondary Education M,D,O
Social Psychology M,D,O
Social Sciences Education M,D,O
Social Work M,D,O
Sociology M,D
Spanish M,D
Special Education M,D,O
Sports Management M,D
Statistics M,D
Systems Engineering M,D,O
Taxation M,D,O
Textile Design M
Theater M
Toxicology M,D
Urban and Regional Planning M,O
Urban Studies M,D,O
Women's Health Nursing M,D
Women's Studies M,D,O
Writing M,D

WEBBER INTERNATIONAL UNIVERSITY
Accounting M
Business Administration and Management—General M
Criminal Justice and Criminology M
International Business M
Sports Management M

WEBER STATE UNIVERSITY
Accounting M
Athletic Training and Sports Medicine M
Business Administration and Management—General M,O
Communication—General M
Computer Engineering M
Curriculum and Instruction M
Education—General M
English M
Health Physics/Radiological Health M
Health Services Management and Hospital Administration M
Legal and Justice Studies M
Nursing and Healthcare Administration M
Nursing Education M
Nursing—General M
Taxation M

WEBSTER UNIVERSITY
Accounting M
Advertising and Public Relations M
Aerospace/Aeronautical Engineering M,D,O
Art History M
Art/Fine Arts M
Business Administration and Management—General M,D,O
Communication Disorders M
Communication—General M,O
Computer and Information Systems Security M
Computer Science M
Corporate and Organizational Communication M
Counseling Psychology M
Criminal Justice and Criminology M,D,O
Early Childhood Education M,O
Education—General M,O
Educational Media/Instructional Technology M,O
Educational Psychology M,O
Elementary Education M,O
English as a Second Language M,O
Environmental Management and Policy M
Finance and Banking M
Forensic Sciences M
Gerontology M
Health Services Management and Hospital Administration M,D,O
Human Resources Development M,D,O
Human Resources Management M,D,O
Human Services M
International Affairs M
International Business M
Internet and Interactive Multimedia M
Legal and Justice Studies M,O
Management Information Systems M,D,O
Management of Technology M,D,O
Marketing M,D,O
Mathematics Education M,O
Media Studies M
Middle School Education M,O
Music Education M
Music M
Nonprofit Management M,D,O
Nurse Anesthesia D
Nursing Education M
Nursing—General M
Psychology—General M
Public Administration M,D,O
Reading Education M,O
Secondary Education M,O
Special Education M,O

WEILL CORNELL MEDICINE
Biochemistry M,D
Biological and Biomedical Sciences—General M,D
Biophysics M,D
Cell Biology M,D
Computational Biology D
Epidemiology M
Health Informatics M
Health Services Research M
Immunology M,D
Molecular Biology M,D
Neuroscience M,D
Pharmacology M,D
Physician Assistant Studies M
Physiology M,D
Structural Biology M,D
Systems Biology M,D

WELCH COLLEGE
Pastoral Ministry and Counseling M
Theology M

WENTWORTH INSTITUTE OF TECHNOLOGY
Architecture M
Civil Engineering M
Computer Science M
Construction Engineering M
Construction Management M
Facilities Management M
Management of Technology M
Transportation and Highway Engineering M

WESLEYAN COLLEGE
Business Administration and Management—General M
Early Childhood Education M
Education—General M

WESLEYAN UNIVERSITY
Astronomy M
Biochemistry D
Bioinformatics D
Biological and Biomedical Sciences—General D
Cell Biology D
Chemical Physics D
Chemistry D
Computer Science M,D
Developmental Biology D
Ecology D
Environmental Sciences M
Evolutionary Biology D
Genetics D
Genomic Sciences D
Geosciences M
Inorganic Chemistry D
Liberal Studies M,O
Mathematics M,D
Molecular Biology D
Molecular Biophysics D
Music M,D
Neurobiology D
Organic Chemistry D
Physics D
Theoretical Chemistry D
Writing M,O

WESLEY BIBLICAL SEMINARY
Linguistics M
Missions and Missiology M
Pastoral Ministry and Counseling M
Religion M
Religious Education M
Theology M
Translation and Interpretation M

WESLEY COLLEGE
Business Administration and Management—General M
Education—General M
Environmental Management and Policy M
Nursing—General M

WESLEY THEOLOGICAL SEMINARY
Theology M,D

WEST CHESTER UNIVERSITY OF PENNSYLVANIA
Applied Mathematics M,O
Applied Statistics M,O
Astronomy M,O
Athletic Training and Sports Medicine M,O
Biological and Biomedical Sciences—General M,O
Business Administration and Management—General M,O
Business Analytics M,O
Business Education M,O
Chemistry O
Clinical Psychology M,D,O
Communication Disorders M
Communication—General M
Computer and Information Systems Security M,O
Computer Science M,O
Counselor Education M,O
Criminal Justice and Criminology M
Cultural Studies M,O
Early Childhood Education M,O
Education—General M,D,O
Educational Leadership and Administration M,D,O
Educational Media/Instructional Technology M,O
Educational Policy M,D,O
English as a Second Language M,O
English Education M,O
English M,O
Ethics M,O
Exercise and Sports Science M,O
Foreign Languages Education M,O
Foundations and Philosophy of Education M,O
French M,O
Geographic Information Systems M,O
Geography M,O
Geosciences M,O
German M,O
Gerontological Nursing M,D,O
Gerontology M,O
Health Services Management and Hospital Administration M,O
Higher Education M,O
History M
Holocaust and Genocide Studies M,O
Human Resources Management M,O
Industrial and Organizational Psychology M,D,O
Kinesiology and Movement Studies M,O
Management Information Systems M,O
Mathematics Education M,O
Mathematics M,O
Music Education M,O
Music M,O
Nonprofit Management M,O
Nursing Education M,D,O
Nursing—General M,D,O
Nutrition M
Philosophy M,O
Physical Education M,O
Psychology—General M,D,O
Public Administration M,O

*M—masters degree; D—doctorate; O—other advanced degree; *—Close-Up and/or Display*

Public Affairs	M,O
Public Health—General	M,O
Reading Education	M,O
School Nursing	M,D,O
Science Education	M,O
Social Work	M,O
Spanish	M,O
Special Education	M,O
Sports Management	M,O
Student Affairs	M,O
Sustainable Development	M,O
Urban and Regional Planning	M,O
Writing	M,O

WEST COAST UNIVERSITY

Family Nurse Practitioner Studies	M,D
Health Services Management and Hospital Administration	M,D
Nursing—General	M,D
Occupational Therapy	M,D
Pharmacy	M,D
Physical Therapy	M,D

WESTERN CAROLINA UNIVERSITY

Accounting	M
Applied Arts and Design—General	M
Art/Fine Arts	M
Biological and Biomedical Sciences—General	M
Business Administration and Management—General	M
Chemistry	M
Communication Disorders	M
Construction Management	M
Education—General	M
English as a Second Language	M,O
English	M,O
Entrepreneurship	M
Health Services Management and Hospital Administration	M
History	M
Industrial/Management Engineering	M
Nursing—General	M,D,O
Physical Therapy	D
Project Management	M,O
Psychology—General	M
Public Affairs	M
Rhetoric	M,O
Social Work	M
Technical Writing	M,O
Writing	M,O

WESTERN CONNECTICUT STATE UNIVERSITY

Accounting	M
Adult Nursing	M,D
Art/Fine Arts	M
Business Administration and Management—General	M
Clinical Psychology	M
Counselor Education	M
Curriculum and Instruction	M
Education—General	M,D
Educational Leadership and Administration	D
Educational Media/Instructional Technology	M
English	M
Geosciences	M
Gerontological Nursing	M,D
Health Services Management and Hospital Administration	M
History	M
Illustration	M
Mathematics	M
Music Education	M
Nursing Education	D
Nursing—General	M,D
Planetary and Space Sciences	M
Reading Education	M
Special Education	M
Writing	M

WESTERN GOVERNORS UNIVERSITY

Accounting	M
Business Administration and Management—General	M
Computer and Information Systems Security	M
Data Science/Data Analytics	M
Education—General	M,O
Educational Leadership and Administration	M,O
Educational Media/Instructional Technology	M,O
Elementary Education	M,O
English Education	M,O
Health Services Management and Hospital Administration	M
Information Science	M
Management Information Systems	M
Management Strategy and Policy	M
Mathematics Education	M,O
Nursing and Healthcare Administration	M
Nursing Education	M
Nursing Informatics	M
Science Education	M,O
Special Education	M,O

WESTERN ILLINOIS UNIVERSITY

Accounting	M
Applied Statistics	M
Biological and Biomedical Sciences—General	M,O
Business Administration and Management—General	M,O
Chemistry	M
Clinical Psychology	M,O
Communication Disorders	M
Communication—General	M
Computer Science	M
Counselor Education	M
Criminal Justice and Criminology	M,O
Curriculum and Instruction	M
Distance Education Development	M,O
Ecology	D
Economic Development	M
Economics	M
Education—General	M,D,O
Educational Leadership and Administration	M,D,O
Educational Media/Instructional Technology	M,O
English as a Second Language	M,O
English	M,O
Environmental Sciences	D
Experimental Psychology	M,O
Foundations and Philosophy of Education	M,O
Geographic Information Systems	M,O
Geography	M,O
Health Education	M
Higher Education	M
History	M
Kinesiology and Movement Studies	M
Liberal Studies	M
Manufacturing Engineering	M
Marine Biology	M,O
Mathematics	M
Museum Studies	M,O
Music	M
Physics	M
Political Science	M
Psychology—General	M,O
Public Health—General	M
Reading Education	M
Recreation and Park Management	M
School Psychology	M,O
Social Psychology	M,O
Social Work	M
Sociology	M
Special Education	M
Sports Management	M
Student Affairs	M
Supply Chain Management	M,O
Theater	M
Travel and Tourism	M
Zoology	M,O

WESTERN KENTUCKY UNIVERSITY

Adult Education	M,D,O
Agricultural Sciences—General	M
Anthropology	M
Applied Economics	M
Art Education	M
Biological and Biomedical Sciences—General	M
Business Administration and Management—General	M
Chemistry	M
Clinical Psychology	M,O
Communication Disorders	M
Communication—General	M,O
Comparative Literature	M
Computational Sciences	M
Computer Science	M
Corporate and Organizational Communication	M,O
Counseling Psychology	M
Counselor Education	M
Criminal Justice and Criminology	M
Early Childhood Education	M,O
Educational Leadership and Administration	M,D,O
Educational Media/Instructional Technology	M,O
Elementary Education	M,O
English as a Second Language	M
English Education	M
English	M
Experimental Psychology	M,O
Foreign Languages Education	M
French	M
Geology	M
Geosciences	M
German	M
Health Services Management and Hospital Administration	M
Higher Education	M
History	M
Homeland Security	M
Industrial and Organizational Psychology	M,O
Interdisciplinary Studies	M,O
Management of Technology	M
Marriage and Family Therapy	M
Mathematics	M
Middle School Education	M,O
Music Education	M
Nursing—General	M
Physical Education	M
Physical Therapy	D
Physics	M
Political Science	M
Psychology—General	M,O
Public Administration	M
Public Health—General	M
Reading Education	M,O
Recreation and Park Management	M
School Psychology	M,O
Secondary Education	M,O
Social Work	M
Sociology	M
Spanish	M
Special Education	M,O
Sports Management	M
Student Affairs	M
Writing	M

WESTERN MICHIGAN UNIVERSITY

Accounting	M
Aerospace/Aeronautical Engineering	M,D
Anthropology	M
Applied Arts and Design—General	M
Applied Economics	M,D
Applied Mathematics	M,D
Art Education	M
Athletic Training and Sports Medicine	M
Biological and Biomedical Sciences—General	M,D,O
Business Administration and Management—General	M
Chemical Engineering	M,D
Chemistry	M,D,O
Civil Engineering	M
Clinical Psychology	M,D
Communication Disorders	M,D
Communication—General	M
Computational Sciences	M,D
Computer Engineering	M,D
Computer Science	M,D
Counseling Psychology	M,D
Counselor Education	M,D
Economics	M,D
Education—General	M,D,O
Educational Leadership and Administration	M,D,O
Educational Measurement and Evaluation	M,D,O
Educational Media/Instructional Technology	M,D,O
Electrical Engineering	M,D
Engineering and Applied Sciences—General	M,D
Engineering Management	M,D
English Education	M,D
English	M,D
Exercise and Sports Science	M
Family and Consumer Sciences-General	M
Geographic Information Systems	M,O
Geography	M,D,O
Geosciences	M,D,O
Health Education	D,O
Health Services Management and Hospital Administration	M,D,O
Higher Education	M,D
History	M,D
Human Services	D,O
Industrial and Organizational Psychology	M,D
Industrial/Management Engineering	M,D
International Affairs	M,D
Manufacturing Engineering	M,D
Mathematics Education	M,D
Mathematics	M,D
Mechanical Engineering	M,D
Music Education	M,O
Music	M,O
Nonprofit Management	M,D,O
Nursing—General	M
Occupational Therapy	M
Paper and Pulp Engineering	M,D
Philosophy	M
Physical Education	M
Physician Assistant Studies	M
Physics	M,D,O
Physiology	M
Political Science	M,D
Psychology—General	M,D
Public Administration	M,D,O
Public Affairs	M,D,O
Reading Education	M,D
Rehabilitation Counseling	M
Rehabilitation Sciences	M
Religion	M,O
Science Education	M,D,O
Social Work	M
Sociology	M,D
Spanish	M,D
Special Education	M,D
Sports Management	M
Statistics	M,D,O
Therapies—Dance, Drama, and Music	M,O
Vocational and Technical Education	M
Writing	M,D

WESTERN MICHIGAN UNIVERSITY THOMAS M. COOLEY LAW SCHOOL

Environmental Law	M,D
Finance and Banking	M,D
Homeland Security	M,D
Insurance	M,D
Intellectual Property Law	M,D
Law	M,D
Legal and Justice Studies	M,D
National Security	M,D
Taxation	M,D

WESTERN NEW ENGLAND UNIVERSITY

Accounting	M
Advertising and Public Relations	M
Applied Behavior Analysis	M,D
Business Administration and Management—General	M
Civil Engineering	M
Communication—General	M
Curriculum and Instruction	M
Electrical Engineering	M
Engineering and Applied Sciences—General	M,D
Engineering Management	M,D
English Education	M
Industrial/Management Engineering	M
Law	M,D
Manufacturing Engineering	M
Mathematics Education	M
Mechanical Engineering	M
Occupational Therapy	D
Organizational Management	M
Pharmacy	D
Sports Management	M
Writing	M

WESTERN NEW MEXICO UNIVERSITY

Business Administration and Management—General	M
Education—General	M
Educational Leadership and Administration	M
Elementary Education	M
English as a Second Language	M
Interdisciplinary Studies	M
Multilingual and Multicultural Education	M
Occupational Therapy	M
Reading Education	M
Secondary Education	M
Social Work	M
Special Education	M

WESTERN OREGON UNIVERSITY

Criminal Justice and Criminology	M
Early Childhood Education	M
Education—General	M
Educational Media/Instructional Technology	M
Health Education	M
Mathematics Education	M
Multilingual and Multicultural Education	M
Music	M
Rehabilitation Counseling	M
Science Education	M
Secondary Education	M
Social Sciences Education	M
Special Education	M

WESTERN SEMINARY

Human Resources Development	M
Pastoral Ministry and Counseling	M,D,O
Religion	M,O
Theology	M,O
Women's Studies	M

WESTERN SEMINARY–SACRAMENTO CAMPUS

Marriage and Family Therapy	M
Pastoral Ministry and Counseling	M,O
Theology	M,O
Women's Studies	O

WESTERN SEMINARY–SAN JOSE CAMPUS

Marriage and Family Therapy	M,O
Pastoral Ministry and Counseling	M,O
Theology	M,O
Women's Studies	M,O

WESTERN STATE COLLEGE OF LAW AT ARGOSY UNIVERSITY

Law	D

WESTERN STATE COLORADO UNIVERSITY

Education—General	M
Educational Leadership and Administration	M
Environmental Management and Policy	M
Film, Television, and Video Production	M
Reading Education	M
Writing	M

WESTERN THEOLOGICAL SEMINARY

Pastoral Ministry and Counseling	M,D,O
Theology	M,D,O

WESTERN UNIVERSITY OF HEALTH SCIENCES

Allied Health—General	M,D
Biological and Biomedical Sciences—General	M
Dentistry	D
Health Education	M
Nursing and Healthcare Administration	M
Nursing—General	M,D
Optometry	D
Osteopathic Medicine	D
Pharmaceutical Sciences	M
Pharmacy	D
Physical Therapy	D
Physician Assistant Studies	M
Podiatric Medicine	D
Veterinary Medicine	D

WESTERN WASHINGTON UNIVERSITY

Adult Education	M
Anthropology	M
Biological and Biomedical Sciences—General	M
Business Administration and Management—General	M
Chemistry	M
Communication Disorders	M
Computer Science	M
Counseling Psychology	M
Counselor Education	M
Education of the Gifted	M
Education—General	M
Educational Leadership and Administration	M
Elementary Education	M
English	M
Environmental Education	M
Environmental Sciences	M
Exercise and Sports Science	M
Experimental Psychology	M
Geography	M
Geology	M
Higher Education	M
History	M
Marine Sciences	M
Mathematics	M
Music	M
Physical Education	M
Political Science	M
Psychology—General	M
Rehabilitation Counseling	M

Science Education	M
Secondary Education	M

WESTFIELD STATE UNIVERSITY

Accounting	M
Applied Behavior Analysis	M
Counseling Psychology	M
Counselor Education	M
Criminal Justice and Criminology	M
Early Childhood Education	M
Education—General	M
Elementary Education	M
English	M
Forensic Psychology	M
Mathematics Education	M
Nonprofit Management	M
Physical Education	M
Physician Assistant Studies	M
Psychology—General	M
Public Administration	M
Reading Education	M
Science Education	M
Secondary Education	M
Social Sciences Education	M
Social Work	M
Special Education	M
Vocational and Technical Education	M

WEST LIBERTY UNIVERSITY

Biological and Biomedical Sciences—General	M
Education of Students with Severe/Multiple Disabilities	M
Education—General	M
Educational Leadership and Administration	M
Organizational Management	M
Physical Education	M
Physician Assistant Studies	M
Reading Education	M
Special Education	M
Sports Management	M
Zoology	M

WESTMINSTER COLLEGE (PA)

Clinical Psychology	M
Counselor Education	M
Early Childhood Education	M
Educational Leadership and Administration	M
Reading Education	M
Special Education	M

WESTMINSTER COLLEGE (UT)

Accounting	M,O
Business Administration and Management—General	M,O
Communication—General	M
Counseling Psychology	M
Education—General	M
Family Nurse Practitioner Studies	M
Nurse Anesthesia	M
Nursing—General	M
Public Health—General	M
Writing	M

WESTMINSTER SEMINARY CALIFORNIA

Religion	M
Theology	M

WESTMINSTER THEOLOGICAL SEMINARY

Missions and Missiology	M,D,O
Pastoral Ministry and Counseling	M,D,O
Religion	M,D,O
Theology	M,D,O

WEST TEXAS A&M UNIVERSITY

Accounting	M
Agricultural Economics and Agribusiness	M
Agricultural Sciences—General	M,D
Animal Sciences	M
Art/Fine Arts	M
Biological and Biomedical Sciences—General	M
Business Administration and Management—General	M
Chemistry	M
Communication Disorders	M
Communication—General	M
Counselor Education	M
Criminal Justice and Criminology	M
Curriculum and Instruction	M
Economics	M
Education—General	M
Educational Leadership and Administration	M
Educational Measurement and Evaluation	M
Educational Media/Instructional Technology	M
Engineering and Applied Sciences—General	M
English	M
Environmental Sciences	M
Exercise and Sports Science	M
Family Nurse Practitioner Studies	M
Finance and Banking	M
History	M
Interdisciplinary Studies	M
Mathematics	M
Music	M
Nursing—General	M
Plant Sciences	M
Psychology—General	M
Reading Education	M
Social Work	M
Sports Management	M

WEST VIRGINIA SCHOOL OF OSTEOPATHIC MEDICINE

Osteopathic Medicine	D

WEST VIRGINIA STATE UNIVERSITY

Biotechnology	M
Criminal Justice and Criminology	M
Media Studies	M

WEST VIRGINIA UNIVERSITY

Accounting	M,D,O
Aerospace/Aeronautical Engineering	M,D
Agricultural Education	M,D
Agricultural Sciences—General	M,D
Agronomy and Soil Sciences	M,D
Allopathic Medicine	M,D
Animal Sciences	M,D
Art Education	M,D
Art History	M,D
Art/Fine Arts	M,D
Athletic Training and Sports Medicine	M,D
Biochemistry	M,D
Biological and Biomedical Sciences—General	M,D
Biostatistics	M,D
Business Administration and Management—General	M,D,O
Business Analytics	M,D,O
Cancer Biology/Oncology	M,D
Chemical Engineering	M,D
Chemistry	M,D
Civil Engineering	M,D
Clinical Psychology	M,D
Communication Disorders	M,D
Communication—General	M,D
Computer and Information Systems Security	M,D,O
Computer Engineering	M,D
Computer Science	M,D
Corporate and Organizational Communication	M,O
Counseling Psychology	M,D
Counselor Education	M,D
Curriculum and Instruction	M,D
Dental Hygiene	M,D
Dentistry	M,D
Developmental Biology	M,D
Early Childhood Education	M,D
Economics	M,D,O
Education of the Gifted	M,D
Education—General	M,D
Educational Leadership and Administration	M,D
Educational Media/Instructional Technology	M,D
Educational Psychology	M,D
Electrical Engineering	M,D
Elementary Education	M,D
Energy and Power Engineering	M,D
Engineering and Applied Sciences—General	M,D
English Education	M,D
English	M,D
Entomology	M,D
Environmental and Occupational Health	M,D
Epidemiology	M,D
Exercise and Sports Science	M,D
Finance and Banking	M,D,O
Fish, Game, and Wildlife Management	M,D
Food Science and Technology	M,D
Forensic Sciences	M,D
Forestry	M,D
Genetics	M,D
Geography	M,D
Geology	M,D
Graphic Design	M,D
Higher Education	M,D
History	M,D
Horticulture	M,D
Human Services	M,D
Immunology	M,D
Industrial and Labor Relations	M,D,O
Industrial Hygiene	M,D
Industrial/Management Engineering	M,D
Journalism	M,O
Landscape Architecture	M,D
Law	M,D
Legal and Justice Studies	M,D
Marketing	M,D,O
Materials Engineering	M,D
Materials Sciences	M,D
Mathematics	M,D
Mechanical Engineering	M,D
Media Studies	M,O
Mineral/Mining Engineering	M,D
Molecular Biology	M,D
Music Education	M,D
Music	M,D
Natural Resources	M,D
Nursing—General	M,D,O
Nutrition	M,D
Occupational Therapy	M,D
Oral and Dental Sciences	M,D
Pathology	M,D
Petroleum Engineering	M,D
Pharmaceutical Sciences	D
Pharmacy	D
Photography	M,D
Physical Education	M,D
Physical Therapy	M,D
Physics	M,D
Plant Pathology	M,D
Plant Sciences	M,D
Political Science	M,D
Psychology—General	M,D
Public Administration	M,D
Public Health—General	M,D
Reading Education	M,D
Recreation and Park Management	M,D
Rehabilitation Counseling	M,D
Safety Engineering	M,D
Secondary Education	M,D
Social Work	M
Sociology	M,D
Software Engineering	M,D
Special Education	M,D
Sport Psychology	M,D
Sports Management	M,D
Statistics	M,D
Theater	M,D
Travel and Tourism	M,D
Writing	M,D

WEST VIRGINIA WESLEYAN COLLEGE

Athletic Training and Sports Medicine	M
Business Administration and Management—General	M
Education—General	M
Family Nurse Practitioner Studies	M,O
Nurse Midwifery	M,O
Nursing and Healthcare Administration	M,O
Nursing Education	M,O
Nursing—General	M,O
Psychiatric Nursing	M,O
Writing	M

WHEATON COLLEGE

Archaeology	M,D
Clinical Psychology	M,D
Counseling Psychology	M,D
Cultural Studies	M,O
Education—General	M
Elementary Education	M
Emergency Management	M
English as a Second Language	M,O
Marriage and Family Therapy	M,D
Missions and Missiology	M
Psychology—General	M,D
Religious Education	M
Secondary Education	M
Theology	M,D

WHEELING JESUIT UNIVERSITY

Accounting	M
Business Administration and Management—General	M
Educational Leadership and Administration	M
Nursing—General	M
Organizational Management	M
Physical Therapy	D

WHITTIER COLLEGE

Child Development	M
Education—General	M
Educational Leadership and Administration	M
Elementary Education	M
Secondary Education	M

WHITWORTH UNIVERSITY

Business Administration and Management—General	M
Counselor Education	M
Education of the Gifted	M
Education—General	M
Educational Leadership and Administration	M
Elementary Education	M
Missions and Missiology	M
Pastoral Ministry and Counseling	M
Secondary Education	M
Special Education	M
Theology	M

WHU - OTTO BEISHEIM SCHOOL OF MANAGEMENT

Business Administration and Management—General	M

WICHITA STATE UNIVERSITY

Accounting	M
Aerospace/Aeronautical Engineering	M,D
Allied Health—General	M,D
Anthropology	M
Applied Mathematics	M,D
Art/Fine Arts	M
Biological and Biomedical Sciences—General	M
Biomedical Engineering	M
Business Administration and Management—General	M
Chemistry	M,D
Clinical Psychology	D
Communication Disorders	M,D
Communication—General	M
Computer Engineering	M,D
Computer Science	M,D
Counselor Education	M,D,O
Criminal Justice and Criminology	M
Curriculum and Instruction	M
Early Childhood Education	M
Economics	M
Education of the Gifted	M
Education—General	M,D,O
Educational Leadership and Administration	M,D,O
Educational Psychology	M,D,O
Electrical Engineering	M,D
Engineering and Applied Sciences—General	M,D
Engineering Management	M,D
English	M
Entrepreneurship	M
Environmental Sciences	M
Exercise and Sports Science	M
Geology	M
Gerontology	M
History	M
Human Services	M
Industrial/Management Engineering	M,D
International Economics	M
Liberal Studies	M
Management Information Systems	M
Manufacturing Engineering	M,D
Mathematics	M,D
Mechanical Engineering	M,D
Middle School Education	M
Music Education	M
Music	M
Nursing—General	M,D
Photography	M
Physical Therapy	D
Physician Assistant Studies	M
Physics	M,D
Psychology—General	D
Public Administration	M
School Psychology	M,D,O
Secondary Education	M
Social Psychology	D
Social Work	M
Sociology	M
Spanish	M
Special Education	M
Sports Management	M
Supply Chain Management	M
Taxation	M
Writing	M

WIDENER UNIVERSITY

Adult Education	M,D
Biomedical Engineering	M
Business Administration and Management—General	M
Chemical Engineering	M
Civil Engineering	M
Clinical Psychology	D
Counselor Education	M,D
Criminal Justice and Criminology	M
Early Childhood Education	M,D
Education—General	M,D
Educational Leadership and Administration	M,D
Educational Media/Instructional Technology	M,D
Educational Psychology	M,D
Electrical Engineering	M
Elementary Education	M,D
Engineering and Applied Sciences—General	M
Engineering Management	M
English Education	M,D
Foundations and Philosophy of Education	M,D
Health Education	M,D
Health Law	M,D
Health Services Management and Hospital Administration	M
Law	M,D
Mathematics Education	M,D
Mechanical Engineering	M
Middle School Education	M,D
Nursing—General	M,D,O
Physical Therapy	M,D
Psychology—General	
Public Administration	M
Reading Education	M,D
Science Education	M,D
Social Sciences Education	M,D
Social Work	M,D
Special Education	M,D
Taxation	M

WILBERFORCE UNIVERSITY

Rehabilitation Counseling	M

WILFRID LAURIER UNIVERSITY

Accounting	M,D
American Studies	M,D
Biological and Biomedical Sciences—General	M
Business Administration and Management—General	M,D
Canadian Studies	M,D
Chemistry	M
Cognitive Sciences	M,D
Communication—General	M
Conflict Resolution and Mediation/Peace Studies	D
Criminal Justice and Criminology	M
Cultural Studies	M
Developmental Psychology	M,D
Economics	M,D
English	M,D
Environmental Management and Policy	M,D
Environmental Sciences	M,D
Film, Television, and Video Theory and Criticism	M,D
Finance and Banking	M,D
Gender Studies	M
Geography	M,D
Health Promotion	M
History	M,D
Human Resources Management	M,D
International Affairs	M,D
International Economics	M
Kinesiology and Movement Studies	M
Legal and Justice Studies	D
Management of Technology	M,D
Marketing	M,D
Mathematics	M
Media Studies	M
Neuroscience	M,D

*M—masters degree; D—doctorate; O—other advanced degree; *—Close-Up and/or Display*

Organizational Behavior M,D
Organizational Management M,D
Pastoral Ministry and Counseling M,D,O
Philosophy M
Physical Education M
Political Science M,D
Psychology—General M,D
Public Policy M
Religion M,D
Social Psychology M,D
Social Sciences M
Social Work M,D
Sociology M,D
Supply Chain Management M,D
Theology M,D,O
Therapies—Dance, Drama, and Music M

WILKES UNIVERSITY
Accounting M
Bioengineering M
Business Administration and Management—General M
Distance Education Development M,D
Education—General M,D
Educational Leadership and Administration M,D
Educational Measurement and Evaluation M,D
Educational Media/Instructional Technology M,D
Electrical Engineering M
Engineering and Applied Sciences—General M
Engineering Management M
English as a Second Language M,D
Entrepreneurship M
Finance and Banking M
Health Services Management and Hospital Administration M
Human Resources Management M
Industrial and Manufacturing Management M
International and Comparative Education M,D
International Business M
Mathematics M
Mechanical Engineering M
Middle School Education M,D
Nursing—General M,D
Organizational Management M
Pharmacy D
Reading Education M,D
Special Education M,D
Writing M

WILLAMETTE UNIVERSITY
Business Administration and Management—General M
Conflict Resolution and Mediation/Peace Studies M,D
Law M,D

WILLIAM CAREY UNIVERSITY
Art Education M,O
Business Administration and Management—General M
Counseling Psychology M
Education of the Gifted M,O
Education—General M,D,O
Elementary Education M,D,O
English Education M,O
Nursing—General M
Osteopathic Medicine D
Psychology—General M
Secondary Education M,O
Social Sciences Education M,O
Special Education M,O

WILLIAM JAMES COLLEGE
Applied Psychology M,D,O
Clinical Psychology M,D,O
Community Health M,D,O
Counseling Psychology M,D,O
Forensic Psychology M,D,O
Industrial and Organizational Psychology M,D,O
International Health M,D,O
Psychology—General M,D,O
School Psychology M,D,O
Student Affairs M,D,O

WILLIAM JESSUP UNIVERSITY
Education—General M
English Education M
Mathematics Education M

WILLIAM JEWELL COLLEGE
Education—General M

WILLIAM PATERSON UNIVERSITY OF NEW JERSEY
Adult Nursing M,D,O
Biological and Biomedical Sciences—General M,D,O
Biotechnology M,D,O
Business Administration and Management—General M,O
Business Analytics M,O
Clinical Psychology M,D,O
Communication Disorders M,D,O
Counseling Psychology M,D,O
Counselor Education M,O
Early Childhood Education M,O
Education—General M,O
Educational Leadership and Administration M,O
Educational Media/Instructional Technology M,O
Elementary Education M,O
English as a Second Language M,D,O
English M,D,O
Exercise and Sports Science M,D,O
Foundations and Philosophy of Education M,D,O
Gerontological Nursing M,D,O
Higher Education M,O
History M,D,O
Materials Sciences M,D,O
Middle School Education M,O
Multilingual and Multicultural Education M,D,O
Music M
Nursing Education M,D,O
Nursing—General M,D,O
Public Policy M,D,O
Reading Education M,O
School Nursing M,D,O
Secondary Education M,O
Sociology M,D,O
Special Education M,O
Writing M,D,O

WILLIAM PENN UNIVERSITY
Organizational Management M

WILLIAMS BAPTIST COLLEGE
Education—General M

WILLIAMS COLLEGE
Art History M
Economic Development M

WILLIAMSON COLLEGE
Organizational Management M

WILLIAM WOODS UNIVERSITY
Advertising and Public Relations M,D,O
Business Administration and Management—General M,D,O
Curriculum and Instruction M,D,O
Educational Leadership and Administration M,D,O
Educational Media/Instructional Technology M,D,O
Health Services Management and Hospital Administration M,D,O
Human Resources Development M,D,O
Marketing M,D,O
Physical Education M,D,O

WILMINGTON COLLEGE
Education—General M
Reading Education M
Special Education M

WILMINGTON UNIVERSITY
Accounting M,D
Adult Nursing M,D
Business Administration and Management—General M,D
Clinical Psychology M
Computer and Information Systems Security M
Counseling Psychology M
Counselor Education M,D
Criminal Justice and Criminology M
Education of the Gifted M,D
Education—General M,D
Educational Leadership and Administration M,D
Educational Media/Instructional Technology M,D
Elementary Education M,D
English as a Second Language M,D
Environmental Management and Policy M,D
Family Nurse Practitioner Studies M,D
Finance and Banking M,D
Gerontological Nursing M,D
Health Services Management and Hospital Administration M,D
Higher Education M,D
Homeland Security M,D
Human Resources Management M,D
Human Services M
Internet and Interactive Multimedia M
Internet Engineering M
Management Information Systems M,D
Marketing M,D
Nursing and Healthcare Administration M,D
Nursing—General M,D
Organizational Management M,D
Project Management M
Public Administration M,D
Reading Education M,D
Secondary Education M,D
Special Education M,D
Vocational and Technical Education M,D

WILSON COLLEGE
Accounting M
Art/Fine Arts M
Business Administration and Management—General M
Cultural Studies M
Dance M
Education—General M
Educational Media/Instructional Technology M
Elementary Education M
English M
Health Services Management and Hospital Administration M
Humanities M
Nursing and Healthcare Administration M
Nursing Education M
Nursing—General M
Secondary Education M
Special Education M
Women's Studies M

WINEBRENNER THEOLOGICAL SEMINARY
Counseling Psychology M,D
Theology M,D

WINGATE UNIVERSITY
Accounting M
Business Administration and Management—General M
Community College Education M,D,O
Education—General M,D,O
Educational Leadership and Administration M,D,O
Elementary Education M,D,O
Entrepreneurship M
Finance and Banking M
Health Services Management and Hospital Administration M
Marketing M
Pharmacy D
Physical Therapy D
Physician Assistant Studies M
Project Management M
Sports Management M

WINONA STATE UNIVERSITY
Acute Care/Critical Care Nursing M,D,O
Addictions/Substance Abuse Counseling M,O
Adult Nursing M,D,O
Clinical Psychology M,O
Counselor Education M,O
Education—General O
Educational Leadership and Administration M,O
English as a Second Language M
English M
Family Nurse Practitioner Studies M,D,O
Gerontological Nursing M,D,O
Human Services M,O
Multilingual and Multicultural Education O
Nursing and Healthcare Administration M,D,O
Nursing Education M,D,O
Nursing—General M,D,O
Organizational Management M,D,O
Special Education M
Sports Management M,O

WINSTON-SALEM STATE UNIVERSITY
Business Administration and Management—General M
Computer Science M
Education—General M
Family Nurse Practitioner Studies M,D
Health Services Management and Hospital Administration M
Management Information Systems M
Middle School Education M
Nursing Education M,D
Nursing—General M,D
Occupational Therapy M
Physical Therapy D
Rehabilitation Counseling M
Special Education M

WINTHROP UNIVERSITY
Art Education M
Art/Fine Arts M
Arts Administration M
Biological and Biomedical Sciences—General M
Business Administration and Management—General M
Counselor Education M
Education—General M
Educational Leadership and Administration M
English M
History M
Liberal Studies M
Music Education M
Music M
Nutrition M,O
Physical Education M
Psychology—General M,O
Secondary Education M
Social Work M
Special Education M

WISCONSIN LUTHERAN COLLEGE
Curriculum and Instruction M
Educational Leadership and Administration M
Educational Media/Instructional Technology M
Science Education M

WISCONSIN SCHOOL OF PROFESSIONAL PSYCHOLOGY
Clinical Psychology M,D
Psychology—General M,D

WITTENBERG UNIVERSITY
Education—General M

WOLFORD COLLEGE
Nurse Anesthesia M,D

WON INSTITUTE OF GRADUATE STUDIES
Acupuncture and Oriental Medicine M,O
Religion M

WOODBURY UNIVERSITY
Architecture M
Business Administration and Management—General M
Organizational Management M

WOODS HOLE OCEANOGRAPHIC INSTITUTION
Marine Biology D
Marine Geology D
Ocean Engineering D
Oceanography D

WORCESTER POLYTECHNIC INSTITUTE
Aerospace/Aeronautical Engineering M,D
Applied Mathematics M,D,O
Applied Statistics M,D,O
Artificial Intelligence/Robotics M,D
Biochemistry M,D
Bioinformatics M,D
Biological and Biomedical Sciences—General M,D
Biomedical Engineering M,D,O
Biotechnology M,D
Business Administration and Management—General M,D,O
Chemical Engineering M,D
Chemistry M,D
Civil Engineering M,D,O
Computational Biology M,D
Computer Engineering M,D,O
Computer Science M,D,O
Construction Management M,D,O
Data Science/Data Analytics M,D,O
Educational Media/Instructional Technology M,D
Electrical Engineering M,D,O
Energy and Power Engineering M,D,O
Engineering and Applied Sciences—General M,D,O
Engineering Design M,D,O
Environmental Engineering M,D,O
Fire Protection Engineering M,D,O
Game Design and Development M
Interdisciplinary Studies M,D,O
Internet and Interactive Multimedia M
Management Information Systems M,D,O
Manufacturing Engineering M,D
Marketing M,D,O
Materials Engineering M,D
Materials Sciences M,D
Mathematics M,D,O
Mechanical Engineering M,D,O
Modeling and Simulation M,D,O
Nuclear Engineering M,D,O
Organizational Management M,D,O
Physics M,D
Social Sciences M,D,O
Supply Chain Management M,D,O
Systems Engineering M,D,O
Systems Science M,D,O

WORCESTER STATE UNIVERSITY
Accounting M
Biotechnology M
Business Administration and Management—General M
Communication Disorders M
Community Health Nursing M
Curriculum and Instruction M,O
Early Childhood Education M,O
Education—General M,O
Educational Leadership and Administration M
Elementary Education M,O
English as a Second Language M,O
English Education M
Foreign Languages Education M
Health Education M
Health Services Management and Hospital Administration M
History M
Marketing M
Middle School Education M,O
Nonprofit Management M
Nursing Education M
Occupational Therapy M
Organizational Management M
Reading Education M,O
School Psychology M,O
Secondary Education M,O
Social Sciences Education M
Spanish M
Special Education M,O

WORLD MEDICINE INSTITUTE
Acupuncture and Oriental Medicine M

WORLD MISSION UNIVERSITY
Music M,D
Pastoral Ministry and Counseling M,D
Theology M,D

THE WRIGHT INSTITUTE
Clinical Psychology D
Counseling Psychology M
Psychology—General D

WRIGHT STATE UNIVERSITY
Accounting M
Acute Care/Critical Care Nursing M
Adult Nursing M
Aerospace/Aeronautical Engineering M
Allopathic Medicine D
Anatomy M
Applied Behavior Analysis M
Applied Economics M
Applied Mathematics M
Applied Statistics M
Biochemistry M
Biological and Biomedical Sciences—General M,D
Biomedical Engineering M
Business Administration and Management—General M
Chemistry M
Clinical Psychology D
Computer Engineering M,D
Computer Science M,D
Counselor Education M
Criminal Justice and Criminology M
Curriculum and Instruction O
Economics M
Education—General M,O
Educational Leadership and Administration O
Electrical Engineering M
Elementary Education M
Engineering and Applied Sciences—General M,D
English M

Environmental Sciences	D
Ergonomics and Human Factors	M,D
Family Nurse Practitioner Studies	M
Geology	O
Geophysics	M
Gerontological Nursing	M
Health Education	M
Health Promotion	M
History	M
Humanities	M
Immunology	M
Industrial and Organizational Psychology	M,D
Industrial/Management Engineering	M
Logistics	M
Management Information Systems	M
Materials Engineering	M
Materials Sciences	M
Maternal and Child/Neonatal Nursing	M
Mathematics Education	D
Mathematics	M
Mechanical Engineering	M
Microbiology	M
Molecular Biology	M
Music Education	M
Neuroscience	M
Nursing and Healthcare Administration	M
Nursing—General	M
Pediatric Nursing	M
Pharmacology	M
Physics	M
Physiology	M
Psychiatric Nursing	M
Psychology—General	M,D
Public Administration	M
Public Health—General	M
Rehabilitation Counseling	M
School Nursing	M
Science Education	M,D
Secondary Education	M
Special Education	M
Supply Chain Management	M
Toxicology	M

WYCLIFFE COLLEGE

Religion	M,D,O
Theology	M,D,O

XAVIER UNIVERSITY

Accounting	M
Athletic Training and Sports Medicine	M
Business Administration and Management—General	M
Clinical Psychology	M,D
Counseling Psychology	M
Counselor Education	M
Criminal Justice and Criminology	M
Early Childhood Education	M
Education—General	M,D
Educational Leadership and Administration	M,D
Elementary Education	M
English	M
Ethics	M
Finance and Banking	M
Health Services Management and Hospital Administration	M*
Human Resources Development	M,D
Industrial and Organizational Psychology	M,D
International Business	M
Management Strategy and Policy	M
Marketing	M
Multilingual and Multicultural Education	M
Nursing—General	M,D,O
Occupational Therapy	M
Pastoral Ministry and Counseling	M
Psychology—General	M,D
Reading Education	M
Religious Education	M
Secondary Education	M
Special Education	M
Sports Management	M
Sustainable Development	M
Theology	M

XAVIER UNIVERSITY OF LOUISIANA

Counselor Education	M
Curriculum and Instruction	M
Education—General	M
Educational Leadership and Administration	M
Pastoral Ministry and Counseling	M
Pharmacy	D
Theology	M

YALE UNIVERSITY

Accounting	D
African Studies	M
African-American Studies	D
Allopathic Medicine	D
American Studies	D
Anthropology	M,D
Applied Arts and Design—General	M
Applied Mathematics	M,D
Applied Physics	M,D
Archaeology	M,D
Architecture	M,D
Art History	D
Art/Fine Arts	M
Asian Languages	D
Asian Studies	M
Astronomy	M,D
Astrophysics	M,D
Atmospheric Sciences	D
Biochemistry	D
Bioinformatics	D
Biological and Biomedical Sciences—General	D
Biomedical Engineering	M,D
Biophysics	D
Biostatistics	M,D
Business Administration and Management—General	M,D
Cell Biology	D
Chemical Engineering	M,D
Chemistry	D
Classics	M,D
Clinical Psychology	D
Cognitive Sciences	D
Comparative Literature	D
Computational Biology	D
Computer Science	M,D
Developmental Biology	D
Developmental Psychology	D
East European and Russian Studies	M,D
Ecology	D
Economic Development	M
Economics	M,D
Electrical Engineering	M,D
Engineering and Applied Sciences—General	M,D
Engineering Physics	M,D
English	M,D
Environmental and Occupational Health	M,D
Environmental Design	M,D
Environmental Engineering	M,D
Environmental Management and Policy	M,D
Environmental Sciences	M,D
Epidemiology	M,D
Evolutionary Biology	D
Film, Television, and Video Theory and Criticism	D
Finance and Banking	D
Forestry	M,D
French	M,D
Genetics	D
Genomic Sciences	D
Geochemistry	D
Geology	D
Geophysics	D
Geosciences	D
German	D
Graphic Design	M
Health Services Management and Hospital Administration	M,D
History of Medicine	M,D
History of Science and Technology	M,D
History	M,D
Immunology	D
Infectious Diseases	D
Inorganic Chemistry	D
International Affairs	M
International Economics	M
International Health	M,D
Italian	D
Latin American Studies	D
Law	M,D
Linguistics	D
Marketing	D
Mathematics	M,D
Mechanical Engineering	M,D
Medieval and Renaissance Studies	M,D
Meteorology	D
Microbiology	D
Molecular Biology	D
Molecular Biophysics	D
Molecular Medicine	D
Molecular Physiology	D
Music	M,D,O
Near and Middle Eastern Languages	M,D
Near and Middle Eastern Studies	M,D
Neurobiology	D
Neuroscience	D
Nursing—General	M,D,O
Oceanography	D
Organic Chemistry	D
Organizational Management	D
Paleontology	D
Pathology	M,D
Pharmacology	D
Philosophy	D
Photography	M
Physical Chemistry	D
Physician Assistant Studies	M
Physics	D
Physiology	D
Planetary and Space Sciences	M,D
Plant Biology	D
Political Science	D
Portuguese	D
Psychology—General	D
Public Health—General	M,D
Religion	D
Russian	D
Slavic Languages	D
Social Psychology	D
Social Sciences	M,D
Sociology	D
Spanish	D
Statistics	M,D
Theater	M,D,O
Theology	M
Theoretical Chemistry	D
Virology	D
Writing	M,D,O

YESHIVA BETH MOSHE

Theology	O

YESHIVA DERECH CHAIM

Religion	D

YESHIVA KARLIN STOLIN

Theology	O

YESHIVA OF NITRA RABBINICAL COLLEGE

Theology	O

YESHIVA SHAAR HATORAH TALMUDIC RESEARCH INSTITUTE

Theology	

YESHIVATH ZICHRON MOSHE

Theology	O

YESHIVA UNIVERSITY

Accounting	M
Biotechnology	M
Business Administration and Management—General	M
Clinical Psychology	D
Communication Disorders	M
Conflict Resolution and Mediation/Peace Studies	M,D
Counseling Psychology	M
Data Science/Data Analytics	M
Economics	M
Educational Leadership and Administration	M,D,O
Health Psychology	D
Intellectual Property Law	M,D
Jewish Studies	M,D
Law	M,D
Marketing	M
Mathematics	M
Psychology—General	M,D
Religious Education	M,D,O
Risk Management	M
School Psychology	D
Social Work	M,D
Taxation	M

YORK COLLEGE OF PENNSYLVANIA

Accounting	M
Business Administration and Management—General	M
Education—General	M
Educational Leadership and Administration	M
Educational Media/Instructional Technology	M
Finance and Banking	M
Gerontological Nursing	M
Health Services Management and Hospital Administration	M
Marketing	M
Nurse Anesthesia	M
Nursing—General	M
Reading Education	M

YORK COLLEGE OF THE CITY UNIVERSITY OF NEW YORK

Pharmaceutical Sciences	M
Physician Assistant Studies	M

YORK UNIVERSITY

Accounting	M,D
Anthropology	M,D
Applied Arts and Design—General	M
Applied Mathematics	M,D
Art History	M,D
Art/Fine Arts	M,D
Astronomy	M,D
Biological and Biomedical Sciences—General	M,D
Business Administration and Management—General	M,D
Business Analytics	M,D
Chemistry	M,D
Communication—General	M,D
Computer Science	M,D
Dance	M,D
Disability Studies	M,D
Economics	M,D
Education—General	M,D
Emergency Management	M
English	M,D
Environmental Management and Policy	M,D
Film, Television, and Video Production	M,D
Finance and Banking	M,D
French	M,D
Gender Studies	M,D
Geography	M,D
Geosciences	M,D
History	M,D
Human Resources Management	M,D
Humanities	M,D
Interdisciplinary Studies	M
International Affairs	M
International Business	M,D
Kinesiology and Movement Studies	M,D
Law	M,D
Linguistics	M,D
Mathematics	M,D
Music	M,D
Nursing—General	M
Philosophy	M,D
Physics	M,D
Planetary and Space Sciences	M,D
Political Science	M,D
Psychology—General	M,D
Public Administration	M
Public Affairs	M
Public Policy	M
Social Work	M,D
Sociology	M,D
Statistics	M,D
Theater	M,D
Translation and Interpretation	M
Women's Studies	M,D

YO SAN UNIVERSITY OF TRADITIONAL CHINESE MEDICINE

Acupuncture and Oriental Medicine	M

YOUNGSTOWN STATE UNIVERSITY

Accounting	M
Analytical Chemistry	M
Anatomy	M
Applied Behavior Analysis	M
Applied Mathematics	M
Biochemistry	M
Biological and Biomedical Sciences—General	M
Business Administration and Management—General	M,O
Chemistry	M
Civil Engineering	M
Computer Engineering	M
Computer Science	M
Counseling Psychology	M
Counselor Education	M
Criminal Justice and Criminology	M
Curriculum and Instruction	M
Early Childhood Education	M
Economics	M
Education of the Gifted	M
Education—General	M,D
Educational Leadership and Administration	M,D
Educational Media/Instructional Technology	M
Electrical Engineering	M
Engineering and Applied Sciences—General	M
English	M
Environmental Biology	M
Environmental Engineering	M
Environmental Management and Policy	M,O
Finance and Banking	M
Gerontology	M
Health Services Management and Hospital Administration	M
History	M
Human Services	M
Industrial/Management Engineering	M
Information Science	M
Inorganic Chemistry	M
Marketing	M
Mathematics Education	M
Mathematics	M
Mechanical Engineering	M
Microbiology	M
Middle School Education	M
Molecular Biology	M
Music Education	M
Music	M
Nursing—General	M
Organic Chemistry	M
Physical Chemistry	M
Physical Therapy	D
Physiology	M
Psychology—General	M
Reading Education	M
School Psychology	M
Science Education	M
Secondary Education	M
Special Education	M
Statistics	M

*M—masters degree; D—doctorate; O—other advanced degree; *—Close-Up and/or Display*

PROFILES OF INSTITUTIONS OFFERING GRADUATE AND PROFESSIONAL WORK

ABILENE CHRISTIAN UNIVERSITY, Abilene, TX 79699

General Information Independent-religious, coed, university. CGS member. *Enrollment:* 5,149 graduate, professional, and undergraduate students; 976 full-time matriculated graduate/professional students (697 women), 437 part-time matriculated graduate/professional students (235 women). *Enrollment by degree level:* 970 master's, 426 doctoral, 17 other advanced degrees. *Graduate faculty:* 42 full-time (18 women), 136 part-time/adjunct (60 women). *Tuition:* Full-time $20,664; part-time $1148 per contact hour. *Graduate housing:* On-campus housing not available. *Student services:* Campus employment opportunities, campus safety program, career counseling, exercise/wellness program, grant writing training, international student services, low-cost health insurance, multicultural affairs office, services for students with disabilities, teacher training, writing training. *Library facilities:* Brown Library. *Collection:* Books: 406,890 (physical), 347,095 (digital/electronic); Serial titles: 20,683 (physical), 52,058 (digital/electronic); Databases: 109. Weekly public service hours: 97; students can reserve study rooms. *Research affiliation:* Los Alamos National Laboratory (particle physics), Fermilab (peanut toxins).

Computer facilities: Computer purchase and lease plans are available. 466 computers available on campus for general student use. A campuswide network can be accessed from student residence rooms and from off campus. Online class registration is available.
Website: http://www.acu.edu/

General Application Contact: Graduate Admissions, 325-674-6911, Fax: 325-674-6717, E-mail: gradinfo@acu.edu.

GRADUATE UNITS

College of Graduate and Professional Studies Students: 673 full-time (462 women), 261 part-time (164 women); includes 340 minority (277 Black or African American, non-Hispanic/Latino; 8 American Indian or Alaska Native, non-Hispanic/Latino; 21 Asian, non-Hispanic/Latino; 34 Hispanic/Latino), 1 international. 709 applicants, 53% accepted, 293 enrolled. *Faculty:* 22 full-time (11 women), 43 part-time/adjunct (21 women). Expenses: Contact institution. *Financial support:* In 2017–18, 6 students received support. Application deadline: 4/1; applicants required to submit FAFSA. In 2017, 90 master's, 7 other advanced degrees awarded. *Program availability:* Part-time, online only. Offers advanced practice nurse (DNP); business analytics (MBA); child and adolescent therapy (MMFT); conflict management (M Ed, Certificate); conflict management and resolution (MA); corporate finance (MBA); enrollment management (M Ed); executive nursing leadership (DNP); general management (MBA); healthcare administration (MBA); human resource management (MBA); international business (MBA); learning with emerging technologies (M Ed, Certificate); management: business analytics (MS); management: healthcare administration (MS); management: international business (MS); management: marketing (MS); management: operations and supply chain management (MS); marketing (MBA); medical family therapy (MMFT); nonprofit leadership (MBA); nursing education (DNP); operations and supply chain management (MBA); organizational development (MS); organizational leadership (Ed D); therapy with military families (MMFT); treatment of trauma (MMFT). *Application deadline:* For fall admission, 8/15 for domestic students; for winter admission, 10/1 for domestic students; for spring admission, 12/15 for domestic students; for summer admission, 4/15 for domestic students. Applications are processed on a rolling basis. *Application fee:* $50. *Application Contact:* Graduate Advisor, 855-219-7300, E-mail: gradonline@acu.edu. *Dean*, Dr. Joe Cope, 214-305-9508, E-mail: gradonline@acu.edu.

Graduate Programs Students: 303 full-time (235 women), 176 part-time (71 women); includes 82 minority (42 Black or African American, non-Hispanic/Latino; 5 American Indian or Alaska Native, non-Hispanic/Latino; 6 Asian, non-Hispanic/Latino; 29 Hispanic/Latino), 15 international. 873 applicants, 42% accepted, 211 enrolled. *Faculty:* 20 full-time (7 women), 93 part-time/adjunct (39 women). Expenses: Contact institution. *Financial support:* In 2017–18, 197 students received support, including 39 research assistantships with partial tuition reimbursements available (averaging $5,800 per year), 12 teaching assistantships with partial tuition reimbursements available (averaging $5,800 per year); career-related internships or fieldwork, Federal Work-Study, and scholarships/grants also available. Support available to part-time students. Financial award application deadline: 4/1; financial award applicants required to submit FAFSA. In 2017, 168 master's, 3 doctorates awarded. *Program availability:* Part-time, evening/weekend, online learning. *Application deadline:* For fall admission, 4/1 priority date for domestic students; for spring admission, 11/1 priority date for domestic students. Applications are processed on a rolling basis. *Application fee:* $50. Electronic applications accepted. *Application Contact:* Graduate Admissions, 325-674-6911, Fax: 325-674-6717, E-mail: gradinfo@acu.edu. *Assistant Provost for Graduate Programs*, Dr. Donnie Snider, 325-674-2223, Fax: 325-674-6717, E-mail: gradinfo@acu.edu.

College of Arts and Sciences Students: 46 full-time (35 women), 12 part-time (8 women); includes 10 minority (4 Black or African American, non-Hispanic/Latino; 2 American Indian or Alaska Native, non-Hispanic/Latino; 4 Hispanic/Latino), 5 international. 117 applicants, 40% accepted, 23 enrolled. *Faculty:* 38 part-time/adjunct (13 women). Expenses: Contact institution. *Financial support:* In 2017–18, 39 students received support, including 21 research assistantships (averaging $5,800 per year), 12 teaching assistantships (averaging $5,800 per year); career-related internships or fieldwork, Federal Work-Study, and scholarships/grants also available. Support available to part-time students. Financial award application deadline: 4/1; financial award applicants required to submit FAFSA. In 2017, 32 master's awarded. *Program availability:* Part-time, online learning. Offers arts and sciences (MA, MLA, MS, Specialist); clinical psychology (MS); composition/rhetoric (MA); corporate communication (MA); counseling psychology (MS); liberal arts (MLA); literature (MA); psychology (MS, Specialist); school psychology (Specialist); writing (MA). *Application deadline:* For fall admission, 4/1 priority date for domestic students; for spring admission, 11/1 for domestic students. Applications are processed on a rolling basis. *Application fee:* $50. Electronic applications accepted. *Application Contact:* Graduate Admissions, 325-674-6911, Fax: 325-674-6717, E-mail: gradinfo@acu.edu. *Dean*, Dr. Greg Straughn, 325-674-2209, Fax: 325-674-6800, E-mail: cas@acu.edu.

College of Biblical Studies Students: 68 full-time (31 women), 123 part-time (24 women); includes 34 minority (25 Black or African American, non-Hispanic/Latino; 1 American Indian or Alaska Native, non-Hispanic/Latino; 1 Asian, non-Hispanic/Latino; 7 Hispanic/Latino), 7 international. 130 applicants, 53% accepted, 38 enrolled. *Faculty:* 16 full-time (4 women), 16 part-time/adjunct (3 women). Expenses: Contact institution. *Financial support:* In 2017–18, 41 students received support. Research assistantships, teaching assistantships, career-related internships or fieldwork, Federal Work-Study, and scholarships/grants available. Support available to part-time students. Financial award application deadline: 4/1; financial award applicants required to submit FAFSA. In 2017, 39 master's, 3 doctorates awarded. *Program availability:* Part-time, evening/weekend, blended/hybrid learning. Offers ancient and Oriental Christianity (MA); Biblical studies (M Div, MA, MACM, MMFT, D Min); Christian ministry (MACM); Christian spiritual formation (D Min); divinity (M Div); global service (MA); leadership for missional renewal (D Min); marriage and family therapy (MMFT); ministry (M Div, D Min); missions (M Div); modern and American Christianity (MA); New Testament (MA); Old Testament (MA); preaching for community transformation (D Min); theology (M Div, MA, MACM, D Min). *Application deadline:* For fall admission, 4/1 priority date for domestic students; for spring admission, 11/1 for domestic students. Applications are processed on a rolling basis. *Application fee:* $50. Electronic applications accepted. *Application Contact:* Graduate Admissions, 325-674-6911, Fax: 325-674-6717, E-mail: gradinfo@acu.edu. *Dean*, Dr. Ken Cukrowski, 325-674-3700, Fax: 325-674-3776, E-mail: cukrowski@bible.acu.edu.

College of Business Administration Students: 12 full-time (4 women), 1 (woman) part-time; includes 2 minority (1 American Indian or Alaska Native, non-Hispanic/Latino; 1 Hispanic/Latino). 26 applicants, 46% accepted, 9 enrolled. *Faculty:* 7 part-time/adjunct (0 women). Expenses: Contact institution. *Financial support:* In 2017–18, 7 students received support. Federal Work-Study and scholarships/grants available. Support available to part-time students. Financial award application deadline: 4/1; financial award applicants required to submit FAFSA. In 2017, 25 master's awarded. *Program availability:* Part-time, online learning. Offers accountancy (M Acc); business administration (M Acc). *Application deadline:* For fall admission, 8/11 for domestic students; for spring admission, 11/1 for domestic students. Applications are processed on a rolling basis. *Application fee:* $50. Electronic applications accepted. *Application Contact:* Graduate Admissions, 325-674-6911, Fax: 325-674-6717, E-mail: gradinfo@acu.edu. *Dean*, Dr. Brad Crisp, 325-674-2245, Fax: 325-674-2564, E-mail: coba@acu.edu.

College of Education and Human Services Students: 177 full-time (165 women), 40 part-time (38 women); includes 36 minority (13 Black or African American, non-Hispanic/Latino; 1 American Indian or Alaska Native, non-Hispanic/Latino; 5 Asian, non-Hispanic/Latino; 17 Hispanic/Latino), 3 international. 600 applicants, 41% accepted, 141 enrolled. *Faculty:* 4 full-time (3 women), 32 part-time/adjunct (23 women). Expenses: Contact institution. *Financial support:* In 2017–18, 110 students received support. Career-related internships or fieldwork and scholarships/grants available. Financial award application deadline: 4/1; financial award applicants required to submit FAFSA. In 2017, 72 master's awarded. Offers communication sciences and disorders (MS); dietetic internship (Certificate); education and human services (M Ed, MS, MSSW, Certificate); initial certification (M Ed); nutrition (MS); occupational therapy (MS); reading teacher (M Ed); social work (MSSW). *Application deadline:* For fall admission, 8/15 priority date for domestic students; for winter admission, 10/1 priority date for domestic students; for spring admission, 12/15 priority date for domestic students; for summer admission, 4/15 for domestic students. Applications are processed on a rolling basis. *Application fee:* $50. Electronic applications accepted. *Application Contact:* Graduate Admission, 325-674-6911, Fax: 325-674-6717, E-mail: gradinfo@acu.edu. *Dean*, Dr. Jennifer Shewmaker, 325-674-2700, Fax: 325-674-3707, E-mail: cehs@acu.edu.

ABRAHAM LINCOLN UNIVERSITY SCHOOL OF LAW, Los Angeles, CA 90010

General Information Proprietary, coed, comprehensive institution.

GRADUATE UNITS

Graduate and Professional Programs Offers law (JD).

ACACIA UNIVERSITY, Tempe, AZ 85284

General Information Private, coed, graduate-only institution.

GRADUATE UNITS

American Graduate School of Education Offers educational administration (M Ed); elementary education (MA); English as a second language (M Ed); secondary education (MA); special education (M Ed).

ACADEMY FOR FIVE ELEMENT ACUPUNCTURE, Gainesville, FL 32601

General Information Independent, coed, graduate-only institution.

GRADUATE UNITS

Graduate Program Offers acupuncture (M Ac).

ACADEMY FOR JEWISH RELIGION CALIFORNIA, Los Angeles, CA 90024

General Information Independent-religious, coed, graduate-only institution. *Graduate housing:* On-campus housing not available.
Website: http://www.ajrca.edu/

General Application Contact: Robin Federman, Director of Admissions, 213-884-4133, E-mail: rfederman@ajrca.edu.

GRADUATE UNITS

Graduate Programs Expenses: Contact institution. Offers Jewish studies (MJS). *Application fee:* $300. *Application Contact:* Robin Federman, Director of Admissions, 213-884-4133, E-mail: rfederman@ajrca.edu.

ACADEMY OF ART UNIVERSITY, San Francisco, CA 94105-3410

General Information Proprietary, coed, comprehensive institution. *Enrollment:* 11,672 graduate, professional, and undergraduate students; 2,357 full-time matriculated graduate/professional students (1,481 women), 1,661 part-time matriculated graduate/professional students (1,098 women). *Enrollment by degree level:* 4,018 master's. *Graduate faculty:* 188 full-time (73 women), 592 part-time/adjunct (252 women). *Tuition:* Part-time $982 per unit. *Graduate housing:* Room and/or apartments guaranteed to single students; on-campus housing not available to married students. *Student services:* Campus employment opportunities, campus safety program, career counseling, international student services, low-cost health insurance, services for students with disabilities, teacher training, writing training. *Library facilities:* Academy of Art University Library. *Collection:* Books: 35,255 (physical), 10,238 (digital/electronic); Serial titles: 197 (physical), 400,000 (digital/electronic); Databases: 20. Weekly public service hours: 83; students can reserve study rooms.

Computer facilities: 900 computers available on campus for general student use. A campuswide network can be accessed. Online class registration, support for students taking online courses are available.
Website: http://www.academyart.edu/

General Application Contact: 800-544-ARTS, E-mail: info@academyart.edu.

GRADUATE UNITS

Graduate Programs Students: 2,357 full-time (1,481 women), 1,661 part-time (1,098 women); includes 672 minority (218 Black or African American, non-Hispanic/Latino; 14 American Indian or Alaska Native, non-Hispanic/Latino; 178 Asian, non-Hispanic/Latino; 201 Hispanic/Latino; 12 Native Hawaiian or other Pacific Islander, non-Hispanic/Latino; 49 Two or more races, non-Hispanic/Latino), 2,186 international. Average age 31. 1,377 applicants, 100% accepted, 928 enrolled. *Faculty:* 188 full-time (73 women), 592 part-time/adjunct (252 women). Expenses: Contact institution. *Financial support:* Career-related internships or fieldwork, Federal Work-Study, and scholarships/grants available. Financial award application deadline: 8/10; financial award applicants required to submit FAFSA. In 2017, 1,270 master's awarded. *Program availability:* Part-time, 100% online. Offers costume design (MA, MFA); fashion journalism (MA). *Application deadline:* Applications are processed on a rolling basis. *Application fee:* $50. Electronic applications accepted. *Application Contact:* 800-544-ARTS, E-mail: info@academyart.edu.

School of Acting Students: 21 full-time (11 women), 1 part-time (0 women); includes 5 minority (3 Black or African American, non-Hispanic/Latino; 1 Asian, non-Hispanic/Latino; 1 Hispanic/Latino), 13 international. Average age 28. 45 applicants, 100% accepted, 13 enrolled. *Faculty:* 16 part-time/adjunct (10 women). Expenses: Contact institution. *Financial support:* Career-related internships or fieldwork, Federal Work-Study, and scholarships/grants available. Financial award application deadline: 8/10; financial award applicants required to submit FAFSA. In 2017, 13 master's awarded. *Program availability:* Part-time. Offers acting (MA, MFA). *Application deadline:* Applications are processed on a rolling basis. *Application fee:* $50. Electronic applications accepted. *Application Contact:* 800-544-ARTS, E-mail: info@academyart.edu.

School of Advertising Students: 59 full-time (41 women), 34 part-time (24 women); includes 16 minority (5 Black or African American, non-Hispanic/Latino; 6 Asian, non-Hispanic/Latino; 5 Hispanic/Latino), 57 international. Average age 28. 29 applicants, 100% accepted, 23 enrolled. *Faculty:* 5 full-time (2 women), 13 part-time/adjunct (6 women). Expenses: Contact institution. *Financial support:* Career-related internships or fieldwork, Federal Work-Study, and scholarships/grants available. Financial award application deadline: 8/10; financial award applicants required to submit FAFSA. In 2017, 61 master's awarded. *Program availability:* Part-time, 100% online. Offers advertising (MFA); advertising and branded media technology (MA). *Application deadline:* Applications are processed on a rolling basis. *Application fee:* $50. Electronic applications accepted. *Application Contact:* 800-544-ARTS, E-mail: info@academyart.edu.

School of Animation and Visual Effects Students: 273 full-time (130 women), 141 part-time (68 women); includes 72 minority (22 Black or African American, non-Hispanic/Latino; 1 American Indian or Alaska Native, non-Hispanic/Latino; 19 Asian, non-Hispanic/Latino; 23 Hispanic/Latino; 1 Native Hawaiian or other Pacific Islander, non-Hispanic/Latino; 6 Two or more races, non-Hispanic/Latino), 254 international. Average age 29. 131 applicants, 100% accepted, 99 enrolled. *Faculty:* 18 full-time (5 women), 54 part-time/adjunct (12 women). Expenses: Contact institution. *Financial support:* Career-related internships or fieldwork, Federal Work-Study, and scholarships/grants available. Financial award application deadline: 8/10; financial award applicants required to submit FAFSA. In 2017, 125 master's awarded. *Program availability:* Part-time, 100% online. Offers 3D animation (MFA). *Application deadline:* Applications are processed on a rolling basis. *Application fee:* $50. Electronic applications accepted. *Application Contact:* 800-544-ARTS, E-mail: info@academyart.edu.

School of Architecture Students: 98 full-time (43 women), 83 part-time (35 women); includes 39 minority (10 Black or African American, non-Hispanic/Latino; 8 Asian, non-Hispanic/Latino; 19 Hispanic/Latino; 2 Two or more races, non-Hispanic/Latino), 53 international. Average age 33. 87 applicants, 100% accepted, 34 enrolled. *Faculty:* 8 full-time (2 women), 32 part-time/adjunct (10 women). Expenses: Contact institution. *Financial support:* Career-related internships or fieldwork, Federal Work-Study, and scholarships/grants available. Financial award application deadline: 8/10; financial award applicants required to submit FAFSA. In 2017, 34 master's awarded. *Program availability:* Part-time, 100% online. Offers advanced architectural design (MA); architecture (M Arch). *Application deadline:* Applications are processed on a rolling basis. *Application fee:* $50. Electronic applications accepted. *Application Contact:* 800-544-ARTS, E-mail: info@academyart.edu.

School of Art Education Students: 26 full-time (all women), 14 part-time (12 women); includes 6 minority (2 Black or African American, non-Hispanic/Latino; 2 Asian, non-Hispanic/Latino; 2 Hispanic/Latino), 18 international. Average age 31. 27 applicants, 100% accepted, 16 enrolled. *Faculty:* 2 full-time (1 woman), 4 part-time/adjunct (all women). Expenses: Contact institution. *Financial support:* Career-related internships or fieldwork, Federal Work-Study, and scholarships/grants available. Financial award application deadline: 8/10; financial award applicants required to submit FAFSA. In 2017, 19 master's awarded. *Program availability:* Part-time, 100% online. Offers art education (MA, MAT). *Application deadline:* Applications are processed on a rolling basis. *Application fee:* $50. Electronic applications accepted. *Application Contact:* 800-544-ARTS, E-mail: info@academyart.edu.

School of Art History Students: 7 full-time (6 women), 41 part-time (37 women); includes 7 minority (1 Black or African American, non-Hispanic/Latino; 6 Hispanic/Latino), 3 international. Average age 37. 23 applicants, 100% accepted, 8 enrolled. *Faculty:* 1 (woman) full-time, 2 part-time/adjunct (1 woman). Expenses: Contact institution. *Financial support:* Career-related internships or fieldwork, Federal Work-Study, and scholarships/grants available. Financial award application deadline: 8/10; financial award applicants required to submit FAFSA. In 2017, 9 master's awarded. *Program availability:* Part-time, 100% online. Offers art history (MA). *Application deadline:* Applications are processed on a rolling basis. *Application fee:* $50. Electronic applications accepted. *Application Contact:* 800-544-ARTS, E-mail: info@academyart.edu.

School of Communications and Media Technologies Students: 45 full-time (29 women), 15 part-time (8 women); includes 7 minority (2 Black or African American, non-Hispanic/Latino; 2 Asian, non-Hispanic/Latino; 3 Hispanic/Latino), 40 international. Average age 29. 34 applicants, 100% accepted, 16 enrolled. *Faculty:* 2 full-time (0 women), 12 part-time/adjunct (4 women). Expenses: Contact institution. *Financial support:* Career-related internships or fieldwork, Federal Work-Study, and scholarships/grants available. Financial award application deadline: 8/10; financial award applicants required to submit FAFSA. In 2017, 44 master's awarded. *Program availability:* Part-time, 100% online. Offers communications and media technologies (MA). *Application deadline:* Applications are processed on a rolling basis. *Application fee:* $50. Electronic applications accepted. *Application Contact:* 800-544-ARTS, E-mail: info@academyart.edu.

School of Fashion Students: 325 full-time (297 women), 186 part-time (167 women); includes 115 minority (61 Black or African American, non-Hispanic/Latino; 2 American Indian or Alaska Native, non-Hispanic/Latino; 27 Asian, non-Hispanic/Latino; 17 Hispanic/Latino; 1 Native Hawaiian or other Pacific Islander, non-Hispanic/Latino; 7 Two or more races, non-Hispanic/Latino), 291 international. Average age 29. 157 applicants, 100% accepted, 110 enrolled. *Faculty:* 26 full-time (17 women), 54 part-time/adjunct (44 women). Expenses: Contact institution. *Financial support:* Career-related internships or fieldwork, Federal Work-Study, and scholarships/grants available. Financial award application deadline: 8/10; financial award applicants required to submit FAFSA. In 2017, 205 master's awarded. *Program availability:* Part-time, 100% online. Offers fashion (MA, MFA); fashion merchandising (MA); fashion merchandising and management (MFA); fashion product development (MFA); knitwear design (MFA); textile design (MFA). *Application deadline:* Applications are processed on a rolling basis. *Application fee:* $50. Electronic applications accepted. *Application Contact:* 800-544-ARTS, E-mail: info@academyart.edu.

School of Fine Art Students: 75 full-time (48 women), 143 part-time (112 women); includes 35 minority (7 Black or African American, non-Hispanic/Latino; 1 American Indian or Alaska Native, non-Hispanic/Latino; 7 Asian, non-Hispanic/Latino; 17 Hispanic/Latino; 2 Native Hawaiian or other Pacific Islander, non-Hispanic/Latino; 1 Two or more races, non-Hispanic/Latino), 54 international. Average age 41. 53 applicants, 100% accepted, 37 enrolled. *Faculty:* 19 full-time (9 women), 29 part-time/adjunct (16 women). Expenses: Contact institution. *Financial support:* Career-related internships or fieldwork, Federal Work-Study, and scholarships/grants available. Financial award application deadline: 8/10; financial award applicants required to submit FAFSA. In 2017, 55 master's awarded. *Program availability:* Part-time, 100% online. Offers figurative painting (MFA). *Application deadline:* Applications are processed on a rolling basis. *Application fee:* $50. Electronic applications accepted. *Application Contact:* 800-544-ARTS, E-mail: info@academyart.edu.

School of Game Development Students: 109 full-time (34 women), 47 part-time (9 women); includes 24 minority (9 Black or African American, non-Hispanic/Latino; 5 Asian, non-Hispanic/Latino; 8 Hispanic/Latino; 2 Two or more races, non-Hispanic/Latino), 82 international. Average age 29. 41 applicants, 100% accepted, 32 enrolled. *Faculty:* 12 full-time (0 women), 25 part-time/adjunct (2 women). Expenses: Contact institution. *Financial support:* Career-related internships or fieldwork, Federal Work-Study, and scholarships/grants available. Financial award application deadline: 8/10; financial award applicants required to submit FAFSA. In 2017, 28 master's awarded. *Program availability:* Part-time, 100% online. Offers game development (MA, MFA). *Application deadline:* Applications are processed on a rolling basis. *Application fee:* $50. Electronic applications accepted. *Application Contact:* 800-544-ARTS, E-mail: info@academyart.edu.

School of Graphic Design Students: 187 full-time (134 women), 188 part-time (142 women); includes 51 minority (12 Black or African American, non-Hispanic/Latino; 1 American Indian or Alaska Native, non-Hispanic/Latino; 14 Asian, non-Hispanic/Latino; 20 Hispanic/Latino; 2 Native Hawaiian or other Pacific Islander, non-Hispanic/Latino; 2 Two or more races, non-Hispanic/Latino), 239 international. Average age 29. 146 applicants, 100% accepted, 97 enrolled. *Faculty:* 6 full-time (2 women), 27 part-time/adjunct (13 women). Expenses: Contact institution. *Financial support:* Career-related internships or fieldwork, Federal Work-Study, and scholarships/grants available. Financial award application deadline: 8/10; financial award applicants required to submit FAFSA. In 2017, 82 master's awarded. *Program availability:* Part-time, 100% online. Offers graphic design (MFA); graphic design and digital media (MA). *Application deadline:* Applications are processed on a rolling basis. *Application fee:* $50. Electronic applications accepted. *Application Contact:* 800-544-ARTS, E-mail: info@academyart.edu.

School of Illustration Students: 123 full-time (82 women), 95 part-time (67 women); includes 39 minority (15 Black or African American, non-Hispanic/Latino; 7 Asian, non-Hispanic/Latino; 12 Hispanic/Latino; 5 Two or more races, non-Hispanic/Latino), 104 international. Average age 31. 67 applicants, 100% accepted, 46 enrolled. *Faculty:* 10 full-time (2 women), 39 part-time/adjunct (16 women). Expenses: Contact institution. *Financial support:* Career-related internships or fieldwork, Federal Work-Study, and scholarships/grants available. Financial award application deadline: 8/10; financial award applicants required to submit FAFSA. In 2017, 68 master's awarded. *Program availability:* Part-time, 100% online. Offers illustration (MA, MFA). *Application deadline:* Applications are processed on a rolling basis. *Application fee:* $50. Electronic applications accepted. *Application Contact:* 800-544-ARTS, E-mail: info@academyart.edu.

School of Industrial Design Students: 73 full-time (25 women), 56 part-time (21 women); includes 15 minority (2 Black or African American, non-Hispanic/Latino; 6 Asian, non-Hispanic/Latino; 6 Hispanic/Latino; 1 Native Hawaiian or other Pacific Islander, non-Hispanic/Latino), 96 international. Average age 28. 75 applicants, 100% accepted, 37 enrolled. *Faculty:* 5 full-time (0 women), 27 part-time/adjunct (5 women). Expenses: Contact institution. *Financial support:* Career-related internships or fieldwork, Federal Work-Study, and scholarships/grants available. Financial award application deadline: 8/10; financial award applicants required to submit FAFSA. In 2017, 52 master's awarded. *Program availability:* Part-time, 100% online. Offers industrial design (MA, MFA). *Application deadline:* Applications are processed on a rolling basis. *Application fee:* $50. Electronic applications accepted. *Application Contact:* 800-544-ARTS, E-mail: info@academyart.edu.

School of Interior Architecture and Design Students: 150 full-time (109 women), 136 part-time (121 women); includes 46 minority (20 Black or African American, non-Hispanic/Latino; 9 Asian, non-Hispanic/Latino; 13 Hispanic/Latino; 4 Two or more races, non-Hispanic/Latino), 127 international. Average age 32. 119 applicants, 100% accepted, 78 enrolled. *Faculty:* 3 full-time (2 women), 26 part-time/adjunct (10 women). Expenses: Contact institution. *Financial support:* Career-related internships or fieldwork, Federal Work-Study, and scholarships/grants available. Financial award application deadline: 8/10; financial award applicants required to submit FAFSA. In 2017, 53 master's awarded. *Program availability:* Part-time, 100% online. Offers interior architecture and design (MA, MFA). *Application deadline:* Applications are processed on a rolling basis. *Application fee:* $50. Electronic applications accepted. *Application Contact:* 800-544-ARTS, E-mail: info@academyart.edu.

School of Jewelry and Metal Arts Students: 22 full-time (21 women), 11 part-time (9 women); includes 3 minority (all Asian, non-Hispanic/Latino), 25 international. Average age 30. 12 applicants, 100% accepted, 4 enrolled. *Faculty:* 2 full-time (both women), 9 part-time/adjunct (5 women). Expenses: Contact institution. *Financial support:* Career-related internships or fieldwork, Federal Work-Study, and scholarships/grants available. Financial award application deadline: 8/10; financial award applicants required to submit FAFSA. In 2017, 12 master's awarded. *Program availability:* Part-time, 100% online. Offers jewelry and metal arts (MA, MFA). *Application deadline:* Applications are processed on a rolling basis. *Application fee:* $50. Electronic applications accepted. *Application Contact:* 800-544-ARTS, E-mail: info@academyart.edu.

School of Landscape Architecture Students: 25 full-time (15 women), 8 part-time (0 women); includes 1 minority (Hispanic/Latino), 30 international. Average age 28. 11 applicants, 100% accepted, 5 enrolled. *Faculty:* 2 full-time (1 woman), 11 part-time/adjunct (5 women). Expenses: Contact institution. *Financial support:* Career-related internships or fieldwork, Federal Work-Study, and scholarships/grants available. Financial award application deadline: 8/10; financial award applicants required to submit FAFSA. In 2017, 17 master's awarded. *Program availability:* Part-time, 100% online. Offers landscape architecture (MA, MFA). *Application deadline:* Applications are processed on a rolling basis. *Application fee:* $50. Electronic applications accepted. *Application Contact:* 800-544-ARTS, E-mail: info@academyart.edu.

School of Motion Pictures and Television Students: 147 full-time (73 women), 69 part-time (27 women); includes 24 minority (10 Black or African American, non-Hispanic/Latino; 1 American Indian or Alaska Native, non-Hispanic/Latino; 4 Asian, non-Hispanic/Latino; 5 Hispanic/Latino; 4 Two or more races, non-Hispanic/Latino), 148 international. Average age 29. 69 applicants, 100% accepted, 44 enrolled.

Faculty: 8 full-time (2 women), 37 part-time/adjunct (10 women). Expenses: Contact institution. *Financial support:* Career-related internships or fieldwork, Federal Work-Study, and scholarships/grants available. Financial award application deadline: 8/10; financial award applicants required to submit FAFSA. In 2017, 75 master's awarded. *Program availability:* Part-time, 100% online. Offers motion pictures and television (MFA); writing and directing for film (MA). *Application deadline:* Applications are processed on a rolling basis. *Application fee:* $50. Electronic applications accepted. *Application Contact:* 800-544-ARTS, E-mail: info@academyart.edu.

School of Music Production and Sound Design for Visual Media Students: 73 full-time (36 women), 35 part-time (11 women); includes 13 minority (7 Black or African American, non-Hispanic/Latino; 1 American Indian or Alaska Native, non-Hispanic/Latino; 3 Hispanic/Latino; 1 Native Hawaiian or other Pacific Islander, non-Hispanic/Latino; 1 Two or more races, non-Hispanic/Latino), 71 international. Average age 29. 37 applicants, 100% accepted, 29 enrolled. *Faculty:* 4 full-time (0 women), 18 part-time/adjunct (1 woman). Expenses: Contact institution. *Financial support:* Career-related internships or fieldwork, Federal Work-Study, and scholarships/grants available. Financial award application deadline: 8/10; financial award applicants required to submit FAFSA. In 2017, 52 master's awarded. *Program availability:* Part-time, 100% online. Offers music scoring and composition (MA, MFA); sound design (MA, MFA). *Application deadline:* Applications are processed on a rolling basis. *Application fee:* $50. Electronic applications accepted. *Application Contact:* 800-544-ARTS, E-mail: info@academyart.edu.

School of Photography Students: 128 full-time (62 women), 107 part-time (69 women); includes 43 minority (9 Black or African American, non-Hispanic/Latino; 5 American Indian or Alaska Native, non-Hispanic/Latino; 8 Asian, non-Hispanic/Latino; 13 Hispanic/Latino; 3 Native Hawaiian or other Pacific Islander, non-Hispanic/Latino; 5 Two or more races, non-Hispanic/Latino), 88 international. Average age 36. 65 applicants, 100% accepted, 48 enrolled. *Faculty:* 9 full-time (5 women), 23 part-time/adjunct (8 women). Expenses: Contact institution. *Financial support:* Career-related internships or fieldwork, Federal Work-Study, and scholarships/grants available. Financial award application deadline: 8/10; financial award applicants required to submit FAFSA. In 2017, 77 master's awarded. *Program availability:* Part-time, 100% online. Offers photography (MA, MFA). *Application deadline:* Applications are processed on a rolling basis. *Application fee:* $50. Electronic applications accepted. *Application Contact:* 800-544-ARTS, E-mail: info@academyart.edu.

School of Visual Development Students: 105 full-time (67 women), 79 part-time (40 women); includes 38 minority (8 Black or African American, non-Hispanic/Latino; 1 American Indian or Alaska Native, non-Hispanic/Latino; 14 Asian, non-Hispanic/Latino; 12 Hispanic/Latino; 3 Two or more races, non-Hispanic/Latino), 88 international. Average age 29. 37 applicants, 100% accepted, 33 enrolled. *Faculty:* 5 full-time (0 women), 13 part-time/adjunct (1 woman). Expenses: Contact institution. *Financial support:* Career-related internships or fieldwork, Federal Work-Study, and scholarships/grants available. Financial award application deadline: 8/10; financial award applicants required to submit FAFSA. In 2017, 48 master's awarded. *Program availability:* Part-time, 100% online. Offers visual development (MA, MFA). *Application deadline:* Applications are processed on a rolling basis. *Application fee:* $50. Electronic applications accepted. *Application Contact:* 800-544-ARTS, E-mail: info@academyart.edu.

School of Web Design and New Media Students: 272 full-time (183 women), 149 part-time (100 women); includes 60 minority (8 Black or African American, non-Hispanic/Latino; 36 Asian, non-Hispanic/Latino; 11 Hispanic/Latino; 1 Native Hawaiian or other Pacific Islander, non-Hispanic/Latino; 4 Two or more races, non-Hispanic/Latino), 298 international. Average age 29. 107 applicants, 100% accepted, 102 enrolled. *Faculty:* 8 full-time (3 women), 29 part-time/adjunct (9 women). Expenses: Contact institution. *Financial support:* Career-related internships or fieldwork, Federal Work-Study, and scholarships/grants available. Financial award application deadline: 8/10; financial award applicants required to submit FAFSA. In 2017, 138 master's awarded. *Program availability:* Part-time, 100% online. Offers Web design and new media (MA, MFA). *Application deadline:* Applications are processed on a rolling basis. *Application fee:* $50. Electronic applications accepted. *Application Contact:* 800-544-ARTS, E-mail: info@academyart.edu.

School of Writing for Film, Television and Digital Media Students: 14 full-time (9 women), 23 part-time (19 women); includes 13 minority (5 Black or African American, non-Hispanic/Latino; 1 American Indian or Alaska Native, non-Hispanic/Latino; 4 Hispanic/Latino; 3 Two or more races, non-Hispanic/Latino), 7 international. Average age 36. 15 applicants, 100% accepted, 9 enrolled. *Faculty:* 13 part-time/adjunct (4 women). Expenses: Contact institution. *Financial support:* Career-related internships or fieldwork, Federal Work-Study, and scholarships/grants available. Financial award application deadline: 8/10; financial award applicants required to submit FAFSA. In 2017, 3 master's awarded. *Program availability:* Part-time, 100% online. Offers writing for film, television and digital media (MFA). *Application deadline:* Applications are processed on a rolling basis. *Application fee:* $50. Electronic applications accepted. *Application Contact:* 800-544-ARTS, E-mail: info@academyart.edu.

See Display below and Close-Up on page 855.

ACADEMY OF CHINESE CULTURE AND HEALTH SCIENCES, Oakland, CA 94612

General Information Private, coed, graduate-only institution. *Graduate housing:* On-campus housing not available.

GRADUATE UNITS

Program in Traditional Chinese Medicine *Program availability:* Part-time, evening/weekend. Offers traditional Chinese medicine (MS).

ACADIA UNIVERSITY, Wolfville, NS B4P 2R6, Canada

General Information Province-supported, coed, comprehensive institution. *Graduate housing:* Room and/or apartments available on a first-come, first-served basis to single students; on-campus housing not available to married students. Housing application deadline: 5/31. *Student services:* Campus employment opportunities, campus safety program, career counseling, exercise/wellness program, free psychological counseling, international student services, low-cost health insurance, services for students with disabilities, writing training. *Library facilities:* Vaughan Memorial Library. *Research affiliation:* Atlantic Research Laboratory.

Computer facilities: Computer purchase and lease plans are available. A campuswide network can be accessed from student residence rooms and from off campus. Online class registration is available.
Website: http://www.acadiau.ca/

General Application Contact: Theresa Starratt, Graduate Studies Officer, 902-585-1914, Fax: 902-585-1096, E-mail: gradadmissions@acadiau.ca.

GRADUATE UNITS

Divinity College Expenses: Contact institution. *Financial support:* Application deadline: 8/12. *Program availability:* Part-time. Offers divinity (M Div); ministry (D Min); theology (MA). *Application deadline:* For fall admission, 6/30 priority date for domestic students, 4/1 priority date for international students; for spring admission, 4/30 priority date for domestic students. Applications are processed on a rolling basis. *Application fee:* $50. *Application Contact:* Shawna Peverill, Registrar, 902-585-2215, Fax: 902-585-2233, E-mail: shawna.peverill@acadiau.ca. *President/Dean of Theology,* Dr. Harry Gardner, 902-585-2213, Fax: 902-585-2233, E-mail: harry.gardner@acadiau.ca.

Faculty of Arts Expenses: Contact institution. *Financial support:* Application deadline: 2/1. Offers arts (MA); English (MA); political science (MA); social and political thought (MA); sociology (MA). *Application deadline:* For fall admission, 2/1 for domestic and international students. Applications are processed on a rolling basis. *Application fee:* $50. *Application Contact:* Theresa Starratt, Graduate Studies Officer, 902-585-1914, Fax: 902-585-1096, E-mail: gradadmissions@acadiau.ca. *Dean,* Bary Moody, 902-585-1485, Fax: 902-585-1070, E-mail: barry.moody@acadiau.ca.

Faculty of Professional Studies Expenses: Contact institution. *Financial support:* Application deadline: 2/1. Offers educational studies (PhD). *Application deadline:* Applications are processed on a rolling basis. *Application fee:* $50. *Application Contact:* Rosie Hare, Administrative Assistant, 902-585-1597, Fax: 902-585-1086, E-mail: rosie.hare@acadiau.ca. *Acting Dean,* Dr. Ann Vibert, 902-585-1597, Fax: 902-585-1086, E-mail: ann.vibert@acadiau.ca.

School of Education Expenses: Contact institution. *Financial support:* Application deadline: 2/1. Offers counseling (M Ed); curriculum studies (M Ed); inclusive education (M Ed); interprofessional health practice (M Ed); leadership (M Ed); music education (M Ed). *Application deadline:* Applications are processed on a rolling basis. *Application fee:* $50. *Application Contact:* Rosie Hare, Administrative Assistant, 902-585-1597, Fax: 902-585-1086, E-mail: rosie.hare@acadiau.ca. *Director,* Dr. John J. Guinney Yallop, 902-585-1229, Fax: 902-585-1071, E-mail: johnj.guiney.yallop@acadiau.ca.

School of Recreation Management and Community Development Expenses: Contact institution. *Financial support:* Application deadline: 2/1. Offers recreation management (MR). *Application deadline:* For fall admission, 2/1 priority date for domestic and international students. Applications are processed on a rolling basis. *Application fee:* $50. *Application Contact:* Rosie Hare, Administrative Assistant, 902-585-1597, Fax: 902-585-1086, E-mail: rosie.hare@acadiau.ca. *Program Head,* Dr. Glyn Bissix, 902-585-1123, Fax: 902-585-1702, E-mail: glyn.bissix@acadiau.ca.

Faculty of Pure and Applied Science Expenses: Contact institution. *Financial support:* Application deadline: 2/1. Offers applied geomatics (M Sc); applied mathematics and statistics (M Sc); biology (M Sc); chemistry (M Sc); clinical psychology (M Sc); geology (M Sc); pure and applied science (M Sc). *Application deadline:* For fall admission, 2/1 priority date for domestic and international students. Applications are processed on a rolling basis. *Application fee:* $50. *Application Contact:* Theresa Starratt, Graduate Studies Officer, 902-585-1914, Fax: 902-585-1096, E-mail: gradadmissions@acadiau.ca. *Dean,* Dr. Suzie Currie, E-mail: suzie.currie@acadiau.ca.

Jodrey School of Computer Science Expenses: Contact institution. *Financial support:* Application deadline: 2/1. Offers computer science (M Sc). *Application deadline:* For fall admission, 2/1 priority date for domestic and international students. Applications are processed on a rolling basis. *Application fee:* $50. *Application Contact:* Dr. Andre Trudel, Graduate Coordinator, 902-585-1136, E-mail: andre.trudel@acadiau.ca.

ACUPUNCTURE & INTEGRATIVE MEDICINE COLLEGE, BERKELEY, Berkeley, CA 94704

General Information Independent, coed, graduate-only institution. *Enrollment by degree level:* 86 master's. *Graduate faculty:* 24 part-time/adjunct (15 women). *Graduate housing:* On-campus housing not available. *Student services:* Campus employment opportunities, international student services, services for students with disabilities. *Library facilities:* AIMC Berkeley Library plus 1 other. *Collection:* Books: 1,959 (physical). Weekly public service hours: 40.

Computer facilities: 2 computers available on campus for general student use.
Website: http://aimc.edu/

General Application Contact: Raom Jordan, Admissions Manager, 510-666-8248 Ext. 121, Fax: 510-666-0111, E-mail: admissions@aimc.edu.

GRADUATE UNITS

Master of Science in Oriental Medicine Program Students: 58 full-time (44 women), 28 part-time (23 women); includes 27 minority (3 Black or African American, non-Hispanic/Latino; 10 Asian, non-Hispanic/Latino; 6 Hispanic/Latino; 8 Two or more races, non-Hispanic/Latino), 3 international. Average age 37. 40 applicants, 85% accepted, 29 enrolled. *Faculty:* 24 part-time/adjunct (15 women). Expenses: Contact institution. *Financial support:* Federal Work-Study available. Support available to part-time students. Financial award application deadline: 7/31; financial award applicants required to submit FAFSA. In 2017, 33 master's awarded. *Program availability:* Part-time. Offers Oriental medicine (MS). *Application deadline:* For fall admission, 3/15 priority date for domestic and international students; for winter admission, 7/15 priority date for domestic and international students; for spring admission, 11/15 priority date for domestic and international students. Applications are processed on a rolling basis. *Application fee:* $100. Electronic applications accepted. *Application Contact:* Rain Jordan, E-mail: admissions@aimc.edu. *President,* Yasou Tanaka, 510-666-8248, Fax: 510-666-0111, E-mail: ytanaka@aimc.edu.

ACUPUNCTURE AND MASSAGE COLLEGE, Miami, FL 33176

General Information Proprietary, coed, graduate-only institution.

GRADUATE UNITS

Program in Oriental Medicine Offers Oriental medicine (MOM).

ADAMS STATE UNIVERSITY, Alamosa, CO 81101

General Information State-supported, coed, comprehensive institution. CGS member. *Enrollment:* 3,308 graduate, professional, and undergraduate students; 959 full-time matriculated graduate/professional students (673 women), 336 part-time matriculated graduate/professional students (196 women). *Enrollment by degree level:* 1,295 master's. Tuition, state resident: full-time $4800; part-time $2400 per credit. Tuition, nonresident: full-time $7100; part-time $3550 per credit. *Required fees:* $213; $106 per credit. One-time fee: $100. Tuition and fees vary according to campus/location and program. *Graduate housing:* Rooms and/or apartments available on a first-come, first-served basis to single and married students. Typical cost: $4400 per year ($6600 including board) for single students; $1100 per year ($3300 including board) for married students. Room and board charges vary according to board plan, campus/location and housing facility selected. *Student services:* Campus employment opportunities, career counseling, child daycare facilities, exercise/wellness program, free psychological counseling, international student services, low-cost health insurance, multicultural affairs office, services for students with disabilities, writing training. *Library facilities:* Nielsen Library. *Collection:* Books: 252 (physical), 891 (digital/electronic); Serial titles: 102 (physical), 372 (digital/electronic); Databases: 60. Weekly public service hours: 84. *Research affiliation:* Sandia National Laboratories (science education).

Computer facilities: 322 computers available on campus for general student use. A campuswide network can be accessed from student residence rooms and from off campus. Online class registration is available.
Website: http://www.adams.edu/

General Application Contact: Information Contact, 719-587-8152, Fax: 719-587-8222, E-mail: graduatestudies@adams.edu.

GRADUATE UNITS

Office of Graduate Studies Expenses: Contact institution. *Financial support:* In 2017–18, teaching assistantships with partial tuition reimbursements (averaging $4,000 per year) were awarded; fellowships with partial tuition reimbursements, career-related internships or fieldwork, Federal Work-Study, institutionally sponsored loans, scholarships/grants, and unspecified assistantships also available. Financial award application deadline: 3/1; financial award applicants required to submit FAFSA. *Program availability:* Part-time, 100% online, summer residency. Offers counselor education (MA); counselor education and supervision (PhD); human performance and physical education (MA, MS); humanities (MA); music education (MA); teacher education (MA). *Application deadline:* Applications are processed on a rolling basis. *Application fee:* $30. Electronic applications accepted. *Application Contact:* Information Contact, 719-587-8152, Fax: 719-587-8222, E-mail: graduatestudies@adams.edu. *Assistant Vice President of Graduate Studies,* Dr. Penny Sanders, 719-587-8413, Fax: 719-587-8222, E-mail: pennysanders@adams.edu.

School of Business Offers business (MBA).

ADELPHI UNIVERSITY, Garden City, NY 11530-0701

General Information Independent, coed, university. *Enrollment:* 7,978 graduate, professional, and undergraduate students; 1,446 full-time matriculated graduate/professional students (1,070 women), 1,092 part-time matriculated graduate/professional students (833 women). *Enrollment by degree level:* 2,294 master's, 244 doctoral. *Graduate faculty:* 335 full-time (181 women), 727 part-time/adjunct (507 women). *Graduate housing:* Room and/or apartments available on a first-come, first-served basis to single students; on-campus housing not available to married students. Housing application deadline: 5/1. *Student services:* Campus employment opportunities, campus safety program, career counseling, child daycare facilities, exercise/wellness program, free psychological counseling, international student services, low-cost health insurance, multicultural affairs office, services for students with disabilities, teacher training, writing training. *Library facilities:* Swirbul Library. *Collection:* Books: 488,954 (physical), 29,258 (digital/electronic); Serial titles: 614 (physical); Databases: 272. Students can reserve study rooms. *Research affiliation:* The Hagedorn Foundation, North Shore Long Island Jewish Health System (medicine), National Science Foundation, The Research Corporation, Mount Sinai Medical Center, Albert Einstein College of Medicine.

Computer facilities: Computer purchase and lease plans are available. 880 computers available on campus for general student use. A campuswide network can be accessed from student residence rooms and from off campus. Online class registration, payment, drop/add classes, check application status are available.
Website: http://www.adelphi.edu/

General Application Contact: Kristen Capezza, Associate Vice President for Enrollment Management, 516-877-3050, Fax: 516-877-3039, E-mail: graduateadmissions@adelphi.edu.

GRADUATE UNITS

College of Arts and Sciences Students: 48 full-time (32 women), 26 part-time (17 women); includes 39 minority (9 Black or African American, non-Hispanic/Latino; 1 American Indian or Alaska Native, non-Hispanic/Latino; 15 Asian, non-Hispanic/Latino; 11 Hispanic/Latino; 3 Two or more races, non-Hispanic/Latino), 11 international. Average age 27. 185 applicants, 45% accepted, 22 enrolled. *Faculty:* 132 full-time (62 women), 194 part-time/adjunct (102 women). Expenses: Contact institution. *Financial support:* In 2017–18, 38 research assistantships with full and partial tuition reimbursements (averaging $14,269 per year) were awarded; fellowships, teaching assistantships, career-related internships or fieldwork, Federal Work-Study, scholarships/grants, traineeships, tuition waivers (partial), unspecified assistantships, and tuition remission for employees also available. Support available to part-time students. Financial award application deadline: 2/15; financial award applicants required to submit FAFSA. In 2017, 18 master's awarded. *Program availability:* Part-time. Offers arts and sciences (MA, MFA, MS); biology (MS); biotechnology (MS); creative writing (MFA); environmental studies (MS); studio art (MA). *Application deadline:* For fall admission, 5/1 priority date for international students; for spring admission, 11/1 priority date for international students. Applications are processed on a rolling basis. *Application fee:* $50. Electronic applications accepted. *Application Contact:* Kristen Capezza, Associate Vice President for Enrollment Management, 516-877-3050, Fax: 516-877-3039, E-mail: graduateadmissions@adelphi.edu. *Acting Dean,* Dr. Susan Briziarelli, 516-877-4118, E-mail: sbriziarelli@adelphi.edu.

College of Nursing and Public Health Students: 36 full-time (23 women), 395 part-time (337 women); includes 259 minority (123 Black or African American, non-Hispanic/Latino; 1 American Indian or Alaska Native, non-Hispanic/Latino; 88 Asian, non-Hispanic/Latino; 35 Hispanic/Latino; 12 Two or more races, non-Hispanic/Latino), 10 international. Average age 36. 388 applicants, 51% accepted, 122 enrolled. *Faculty:* 45 full-time (36 women), 234 part-time/adjunct (209 women). Expenses: Contact institution. *Financial support:* In 2017–18, 35 teaching assistantships with full and partial tuition reimbursements (averaging $5,178 per year) were awarded; fellowships, research assistantships, career-related internships or fieldwork, Federal Work-Study, scholarships/grants, traineeships, tuition waivers, unspecified assistantships, and tuition remission for employees also available. Support available to part-time students. Financial award application deadline: 2/15; financial award applicants required to submit FAFSA. In 2017, 73 master's, 6 doctorates, 3 other advanced degrees awarded. *Program availability:* Part-time, evening/weekend. Offers adult health nurse (MS); health information technology (MS, Advanced Certificate); nurse practitioner in adult health nursing (Certificate); nursing (PhD); nursing administration (MS, Certificate); nursing education (MS, Certificate); nutrition (MS); public health (MPH). *Application deadline:* For fall admission, 3/15 for domestic students, 4/1 for international students; for spring admission, 11/1 for international students. *Application fee:* $50. Electronic applications accepted. *Application Contact:* Kristen Capezza, Associate Vice President for Enrollment Management, 516-877-3021, Fax: 516-877-3039, E-mail: graduateadmissions@adelphi.edu. *Interim Dean,* Dr. Elaine Smith, 516-833-8181, E-mail: elsmith@adelphi.edu.

College of Professional and Continuing Studies Students: 6 full-time (4 women), 13 part-time (7 women); includes 10 minority (5 Black or African American, non-Hispanic/Latino; 4 Hispanic/Latino; 1 Two or more races, non-Hispanic/Latino). Average age 36. 48 applicants, 46% accepted, 6 enrolled. *Faculty:* 18 part-time/adjunct (8 women). Expenses: Contact institution. *Financial support:* In 2017–18, 1 teaching assistantship with full and partial tuition reimbursement (averaging $6,150 per year) was awarded; fellowships, research assistantships, career-related internships or fieldwork, Federal Work-Study, scholarships/grants, traineeships, tuition waivers (full and partial), unspecified assistantships, and tuition remission for employees also available. Support available to part-time students. In 2017, 2 Certificates awarded. Offers emergency management (Certificate). *Application deadline:* For fall admission, 5/1 for international students; for spring admission, 12/1 for international students. *Application fee:* $50. *Application Contact:* Kristen Capezza, Associate Vice President for Enrollment Management, 516-877-3021, Fax: 516-877-3039, E-mail: graduateadmissions@adelphi.edu. *Dean*, Dr. Shawn O'Riley, 516-877-3404, E-mail: oriley@adelphi.edu.

Gordon F. Derner School of Psychology Students: 230 full-time (186 women), 68 part-time (59 women); includes 95 minority (29 Black or African American, non-Hispanic/Latino; 2 American Indian or Alaska Native, non-Hispanic/Latino; 18 Asian, non-Hispanic/Latino; 39 Hispanic/Latino; 7 Two or more races, non-Hispanic/Latino), 21 international. Average age 28. 456 applicants, 45% accepted, 110 enrolled. *Faculty:* 24 full-time (11 women), 65 part-time/adjunct (41 women). Expenses: Contact institution. *Financial support:* In 2017–18, 121 research assistantships with full and partial tuition reimbursements (averaging $11,267 per year) were awarded; fellowships, teaching assistantships, career-related internships or fieldwork, Federal Work-Study, scholarships/grants, traineeships, unspecified assistantships, and tuition remission for employees also available. Support available to part-time students. Financial award application deadline: 2/15; financial award applicants required to submit FAFSA. In 2017, 70 master's, 20 doctorates awarded. *Program availability:* Part-time. Offers clinical psychology (PhD); general psychology (MA); mental health counseling (MA); psychology (MA, PhD); school psychology (MA). *Application deadline:* For fall admission, 4/1 priority date for domestic students, 5/1 priority date for international students; for spring admission, 11/1 priority date for international students. *Application fee:* $50. Electronic applications accepted. *Application Contact:* Kristen Capezza, Associate Vice President for Enrollment Management, 516-877-3021, Fax: 516-877-3039, E-mail: graduateadmissions@adelphi.edu. *Dean*, Dr. Jacques P. Barber, 516-877-4807, E-mail: sbarber@adelphi.edu.

Robert B. Willumstad School of Business Students: 282 full-time (120 women), 123 part-time (70 women); includes 80 minority (26 Black or African American, non-Hispanic/Latino; 22 Asian, non-Hispanic/Latino; 27 Hispanic/Latino; 1 Native Hawaiian or other Pacific Islander, non-Hispanic/Latino; 4 Two or more races, non-Hispanic/Latino), 184 international. Average age 30. 480 applicants, 58% accepted, 214 enrolled. *Faculty:* 42 full-time (13 women), 26 part-time/adjunct (7 women). Expenses: Contact institution. *Financial support:* In 2017–18, 65 teaching assistantships with full and partial tuition reimbursements (averaging $6,996 per year) were awarded; fellowships, research assistantships, career-related internships or fieldwork, Federal Work-Study, scholarships/grants, traineeships, tuition waivers (full and partial), unspecified assistantships, and tuition remission for employees also available. Support available to part-time students. Financial award application deadline: 3/1. In 2017, 147 master's, 11 other advanced degrees awarded. *Program availability:* Part-time, evening/weekend. Offers accounting (MBA); business (MBA, MS, Certificate); finance (MBA); health services administration (MBA); human resource management (Certificate); management (MBA); management information systems (MBA); marketing (MBA); sport management (MBA); supply chain management (MS). *Application deadline:* For fall admission, 4/1 for international students; for spring admission, 11/1 for international students. Applications are processed on a rolling basis. *Application fee:* $50. Electronic applications accepted. *Application Contact:* Kristen Capezza, Associate Vice President for Enrollment Management, 516-877-3021, Fax: 516-877-3039, E-mail: graduateadmissions@adelphi.edu. *Dean*, Dr. Rahib Sanyal, 516-877-4661, E-mail: rsanyal@adelphi.edu.

Ruth S. Ammon School of Education Students: 457 full-time (362 women), 226 part-time (150 women); includes 215 minority (55 Black or African American, non-Hispanic/Latino; 1 American Indian or Alaska Native, non-Hispanic/Latino; 28 Asian, non-Hispanic/Latino; 123 Hispanic/Latino; 8 Two or more races, non-Hispanic/Latino), 18 international. Average age 27. 1,162 applicants, 50% accepted, 249 enrolled. *Faculty:* 66 full-time (43 women), 92 part-time/adjunct (66 women). Expenses: Contact institution. *Financial support:* In 2017–18, 97 teaching assistantships with full and partial tuition reimbursements (averaging $11,015 per year) were awarded; fellowships, research assistantships, career-related internships or fieldwork, Federal Work-Study, scholarships/grants, traineeships, tuition waivers (full and partial), unspecified assistantships, and tuition remission for employees also available. Support available to part-time students. Financial award application deadline: 2/15; financial award applicants required to submit FAFSA. In 2017, 320 master's, 7 doctorates, 90 other advanced degrees awarded. *Program availability:* Part-time, evening/weekend. Offers adolescent education (MA); aging (Certificate); art education (MA); audiology (MS, DA); birth-grade 12 (MS); birth-grade 6 (MS); childhood education (MA); community health education (MA, Certificate); education (MA, MS, DA, Certificate); educational technology (MA); grades 5-12 (MS); physical/educational human performance science (MA); school health education (MA); special education (MS, Certificate); speech-language pathology (MS, DA); teaching English to speakers of other languages (MA, Certificate). *Application deadline:* For fall admission, 4/1 for international students; for spring admission, 11/1 for international students. Applications are processed on a rolling basis. *Application fee:* $50. Electronic applications accepted. *Application Contact:* Kristen Capezza, Associate Vice President for Enrollment Management, 516-877-3021, Fax: 516-877-3039, E-mail: graduateadmissions@adelphi.edu. *Interim Dean*, Dr. Anne Mungai, 516-877-4065, E-mail: mungai@adelphi.edu.

School of Social Work Students: 387 full-time (343 women), 240 part-time (193 women); includes 332 minority (178 Black or African American, non-Hispanic/Latino; 24 Asian, non-Hispanic/Latino; 117 Hispanic/Latino; 13 Two or more races, non-Hispanic/Latino), 6 international. Average age 33. 597 applicants, 68% accepted, 240 enrolled. *Faculty:* 26 full-time (16 women), 93 part-time/adjunct (69 women). Expenses: Contact institution. *Financial support:* In 2017–18, 39 teaching assistantships with full and partial tuition reimbursements (averaging $5,560 per year) were awarded; fellowships, research assistantships, career-related internships or fieldwork, Federal Work-Study, scholarships/grants, traineeships, tuition waivers (full and partial), unspecified assistantships, and tuition remission for employees also available. Support available to part-time students. Financial award application deadline: 2/15. In 2017, 268 master's, 1 doctorate awarded. *Program availability:* Part-time, evening/weekend. Offers social welfare (DSW); social work (MSW, DSW, PhD). *Application deadline:* For fall admission, 4/1 for international students; for spring admission, 12/1 for domestic students, 11/1 for international students. *Application fee:* $50. Electronic applications accepted. *Application Contact:* Kristen Capezza, Associate Vice President for Enrollment Management, 516-877-3021, Fax: 516-877-3039, E-mail: graduateadmissions@adelphi.edu. *Dean*, Dr. Andrew Safyer, 516-877-4354, E-mail: asafyer@adelphi.edu.

ADLER GRADUATE SCHOOL, Richfield, MN 55423

General Information Independent, coed, graduate-only institution. *Enrollment by degree level:* 317 master's. *Graduate faculty:* 71 part-time/adjunct (55 women). *Graduate housing:* On-campus housing not available. *Student services:* Campus employment opportunities, international student services, services for students with disabilities, writing training. *Library facilities:* Adler Graduate School Library.

Computer facilities: 12 computers available on campus for general student use. A campuswide network can be accessed. Online class registration is available.
Website: http://www.alfredadler.edu/

General Application Contact: Christina Hilpipre-Frischman, Director of Admissions, 612-767-7055, Fax: 612-861-7559, E-mail: christina@alfredadler.edu.

GRADUATE UNITS

Program in Adlerian Counseling and Psychotherapy Students: 317 part-time (259 women); includes 51 minority (40 Black or African American, non-Hispanic/Latino; 6 American Indian or Alaska Native, non-Hispanic/Latino; 5 Hispanic/Latino). *Faculty:* 71 part-time/adjunct (55 women). Expenses: Contact institution. *Financial support:* Career-related internships or fieldwork and tuition waivers available. Support available to part-time students. Financial award applicants required to submit FAFSA. *Program availability:* Part-time, evening/weekend. Offers Adlerian studies (MA); art therapy (MA); clinical mental health counseling (MA); co-occurring substance use and mental health disorders (MA); marriage and family therapy (MA); school counseling (MA). *Application deadline:* Applications are processed on a rolling basis. *Application fee:* $50. Electronic applications accepted. *Application Contact:* Christina Hilpipre-Frischman, Director of Admissions, 612-767-7055, Fax: 612-861-7559, E-mail: christina@alfredadler.edu. *President*, Dr. Jeffrey Allen, 612-767-7048, Fax: 612-861-7559, E-mail: jeffrey.allen@alfredadler.edu.

ADLER UNIVERSITY, Chicago, IL 60602

General Information Independent, coed, graduate-only institution. *Enrollment by degree level:* 500 master's, 456 doctoral. *Graduate faculty:* 40 full-time (18 women), 61 part-time/adjunct (31 women). *Graduate housing:* On-campus housing not available. *Student services:* Campus employment opportunities, campus safety program, career counseling, exercise/wellness program, international student services, low-cost health insurance, services for students with disabilities, writing training. *Library facilities:* Adler University Library plus 1 other. *Research affiliation:* LGBTQ Mental Health and Inclusion Center, Adler Child Guidance Center, Adler Institute on Social Exclusion, Adler Institute on Public Safety and Social Justice.

Computer facilities: 40 computers available on campus for general student use. Online class registration is available.
Website: http://www.adler.edu/

General Application Contact: Michelle Brice, Associate Vice President, Admissions, 312-288-2685, E-mail: admissions@adler.edu.

GRADUATE UNITS

Graduate Programs *Program availability:* Part-time, evening/weekend, online learning. Offers advanced Adlerian psychotherapy (Psy D); art therapy (MAC, MCP, PhD); child and adolescent clinical psychology (Psy D); clinical mental health counseling (MAC); community health (MPP); counseling psychology (MACP, MCP); counseling psychology: school and youth (MACP, MCP); counselor education and supervision (PhD); couple and family therapy (MA, PhD); criminal justice (MPA); criminology and criminal justice (MA); emergency management leadership (MA); forensic psychology (MAC); gender and sexuality studies (MA); human rights advocacy (MPP); immigration policy and practice (MPPA); industrial and organizational psychology (MA, PhD); media and communications (MA); military clinical psychology (Psy D); military psychology (MA); nonprofit management (MA); organizational psychology (MA); primary care psychology and behavioral medicine (Psy D); psychology (MA, MAC, MACP, MCP, MPA, MPP, MPPA, PhD, Psy D, Certificate); rehabilitation counseling (MAC); social change leadership (MPPA); sport and health psychology (MAC); student affairs and college counseling (MAC); substance abuse treatment (Psy D); sustainable communities (MPA); traumatic stress psychology (Psy D). Electronic applications accepted.

ADRIAN COLLEGE, Adrian, MI 49221-2575

General Information Independent-religious, coed, comprehensive institution. *Graduate housing:* On-campus housing not available.

GRADUATE UNITS

Graduate Programs Offers accounting (MS); athletic training (MS); criminal justice (MA).

ADVENTIST UNIVERSITY OF HEALTH SCIENCES, Orlando, FL 32803

General Information Independent, coed, comprehensive institution.

GRADUATE UNITS

Program in Healthcare Administration Offers healthcare administration (MHA).

Program in Nurse Anesthesia Offers nurse anesthesia (MS).

Program in Occupational Therapy Offers occupational therapy (MOT).

Program in Physical Therapy Offers physical therapy (DPT).

Program in Physician Assistant Studies Offers physician assistant studies (MS).

AIR FORCE INSTITUTE OF TECHNOLOGY, Dayton, OH 45433-7765

General Information Federally supported, coed, primarily men, graduate-only institution. *Graduate housing:* On-campus housing not available. *Research affiliation:* U.S. Air Force Office of Scientific Research, U.S. Air Force Research Laboratory (AFRL), Dayton Area Graduate Studies Institute (aerospace), U.S. Department of Energy, National Security Agency.

GRADUATE UNITS

Graduate School of Engineering and Management *Program availability:* Part-time. Offers aeronautical engineering (MS, PhD); applied mathematics (MS, PhD); applied physics (MS, PhD); astronautical engineering (MS, PhD); computer engineering (MS, PhD); computer systems/science (MS); cost analysis (MS); electrical engineering (MS, PhD); electro-optics (MS, PhD); engineering and management (MS, PhD); environmental and engineering management (MS); environmental engineering science (MS); information resource/systems management (MS); logistics management (MS); materials science (MS, PhD); nuclear engineering (MS, PhD); operations research (MS, PhD); space operations (MS); space physics (MS); systems engineering (MS, PhD).

ALABAMA AGRICULTURAL AND MECHANICAL UNIVERSITY, Huntsville, AL 35811

General Information State-supported, coed, university. CGS member. *Graduate housing:* Rooms and/or apartments available on a first-come, first-served basis to single and married students. Housing application deadline: 5/5. *Research affiliation:* NASA (utilization of space resources), Boeing Defense and Space Group (plant science), Lawrence Livermore National Laboratory (chemistry, physics), Alabama Supercomputer Network (computer services), Nichols Research Corporation (computer science), Hughes Aircraft Corporation (physics).

GRADUATE UNITS

School of Graduate Studies Electronic applications accepted.

College of Agricultural, Life and Natural Sciences *Program availability:* Part-time, evening/weekend. Offers agricultural, life and natural sciences (MS, MURP, PhD); apparel, merchandising and design (MS); biology (MS); family and consumer sciences (MS); food science (MS, PhD); human development and family studies (MS); nutrition and hospitality management (MS); plant and soil science (MS, PhD); urban and regional planning (MURP). Electronic applications accepted.

College of Business and Public Affairs *Program availability:* Part-time, evening/weekend. Offers business and public affairs (MBA). Electronic applications accepted.

College of Education, Humanities, and Behavioral Sciences *Program availability:* Part-time, evening/weekend. Offers art education (MS); biology (M Ed); business/marketing education (M Ed, Ed S); chemistry (M Ed); collaborative teacher secondary education (M Ed, Ed S); early childhood education (MS Ed, Ed S); education (M Ed, Ed S); education, humanities, and behavioral sciences (M Ed, MS, MS Ed, PhD, Ed S); elementary education (MS Ed, Ed S); English language arts (M Ed); family/consumer science education (M Ed, Ed S); general science (M Ed); general social science (M Ed); kinesiology (MS); mathematics (M Ed, Ed S); music education (M Ed); physical education (MS); physics (M Ed, Ed S); psychology and counseling (MS, Ed S); reading/literacy (PhD); social work (MSW); special education collaborative teacher training (MS Ed, Ed S); speech-language pathology (MS); technology education (M Ed). Electronic applications accepted.

College of Engineering, Technology, and Physical Sciences *Program availability:* Part-time, evening/weekend. Offers computer science (MS); engineering, technology, and physical sciences (M Eng, MS, PhD); material engineering (M Eng); physics (MS, PhD). Electronic applications accepted.

ALABAMA COLLEGE OF OSTEOPATHIC MEDICINE, Dothan, AL 36303

General Information Independent, coed, graduate-only institution.

GRADUATE UNITS

Graduate Program Offers osteophatic medicine (DO).

ALABAMA STATE UNIVERSITY, Montgomery, AL 36101-0271

General Information State-supported, coed, comprehensive institution. CGS member. *Enrollment:* 4,760 graduate, professional, and undergraduate students; 325 full-time matriculated graduate/professional students (232 women), 227 part-time matriculated graduate/professional students (165 women). *Enrollment by degree level:* 392 master's, 142 doctoral, 15 other advanced degrees. Tuition, state resident: part-time $412 per credit hour. Tuition, nonresident: part-time $824 per credit hour. *Required fees:* $685 per semester. *Graduate housing:* On-campus housing not available. *Student services:* Campus employment opportunities, campus safety program, career counseling, child daycare facilities, exercise/wellness program, free psychological counseling, international student services, low-cost health insurance, services for students with disabilities, teacher training, writing training. *Library facilities:* Levi Watkins Learning Center plus 1 other. *Collection:* Books: 436,536 (physical), 69,784 (digital/electronic); Serial titles: 1,607 (physical), 4,340 (digital/electronic); Databases: 182. Weekly public service hours: 78; study areas open 24 hours, 5–7 days a week; students can reserve study rooms.

Computer facilities: 805 computers available on campus for general student use. A campuswide network can be accessed from student residence rooms and from off campus. Online class registration is available.
Website: http://www.alasu.edu/

General Application Contact: Dr. William Person, Dean of Graduate Studies, 334-229-4274, Fax: 334-229-4928, E-mail: wperson@alasu.edu.

GRADUATE UNITS

College of Business Administration Students: 18 full-time (12 women), 6 part-time (4 women); includes 17 minority (15 Black or African American, non-Hispanic/Latino; 2 Hispanic/Latino), 5 international. Average age 22. 16 applicants, 63% accepted, 8 enrolled. *Faculty:* 4 full-time (1 woman), 1 part-time/adjunct (0 women). Expenses: Contact institution. *Financial support:* Fellowships and unspecified assistantships available. Financial award application deadline: 6/30; financial award applicants required to submit FAFSA. In 2017, 8 master's awarded. *Program availability:* Part-time. Offers accountancy (M Acc); business administration (M Acc). *Application deadline:* For fall admission, 4/15 for domestic and international students; for spring admission, 11/15 for domestic students, 11/1 for international students; for summer admission, 3/15 for domestic and international students. *Application fee:* $25. Electronic applications accepted. *Application Contact:* Dr. William Person, Dean of Graduate Studies, 334-229-4274, Fax: 334-229-4928, E-mail: wperson@alasu.edu. *Director, Master of Accountancy,* Dr. Dave Thompson, 334-229-6809, E-mail: dthompson@alasu.edu.

College of Education Students: 82 full-time (57 women), 190 part-time (146 women); includes 260 minority (259 Black or African American, non-Hispanic/Latino; 1 Two or more races, non-Hispanic/Latino), 2 international. Average age 22. 99 applicants, 68% accepted, 37 enrolled. *Faculty:* 7 full-time (4 women), 7 part-time/adjunct (4 women). Expenses: Contact institution. *Financial support:* In 2017–18, 4 students received support. Research assistantships and unspecified assistantships available. Financial award application deadline: 6/30; financial award applicants required to submit FAFSA. In 2017, 76 master's, 4 doctorates, 17 other advanced degrees awarded. *Program availability:* Part-time. Offers applied technology (MS); counselor education (M Ed, MS, Ed S); early childhood education (M Ed, Ed S); education (M Ed, MS, Ed D, PhD, Ed S); educational administration (M Ed, Ed D, PhD, Ed S); elementary education (M Ed, Ed S); health education (M Ed); library education media (M Ed, Ed S); physical education (M Ed); secondary education (M Ed, Ed S); special education (M Ed). *Application deadline:* For fall admission, 4/15 for domestic and international students; for spring admission, 11/15 for domestic and international students; for summer admission, 3/15 for domestic and international students. Applications are processed on a rolling basis. *Application fee:* $25. Electronic applications accepted. *Application Contact:* Dr. William Person, Dean of Graduate Studies, 334-229-4274, Fax: 334-229-4928, E-mail: wperson@alasu.edu. *Interim Dean,* Dr. Alma Freeman, 334-229-4250, E-mail: eduncan@alasu.edu.

College of Health Sciences Students: 168 full-time (117 women), 5 part-time (2 women); includes 71 minority (56 Black or African American, non-Hispanic/Latino; 10 Asian, non-Hispanic/Latino; 3 Hispanic/Latino; 2 Two or more races, non-Hispanic/Latino), 4 international. Average age 22. 172 applicants, 35% accepted, 58 enrolled. *Faculty:* 19 full-time (16 women), 19 part-time/adjunct (10 women). Expenses: Contact institution. *Financial support:* In 2017–18, 3 students received support. Research assistantships and unspecified assistantships available. Financial award application deadline: 6/30; financial award applicants required to submit FAFSA. In 2017, 21 master's, 21 doctorates awarded. Offers health sciences (MRC, MS, DPT); occupational therapy (MS); physical therapy (DPT); prosthetics and orthotics (MS); rehabilitation counseling (MRC). *Application deadline:* For fall admission, 4/15 for domestic and international students; for spring admission, 11/15 for domestic and international students; for summer admission, 3/15 for domestic and international students. Applications are processed on a rolling basis. *Application fee:* $25. Electronic applications accepted. *Application Contact:* Dr. William Person, Dean of Graduate Studies, 334-229-4274, Fax: 334-229-4928, E-mail: wperson@alasu.edu. *Dean, College of Health Sciences,* Dr. Cheryl E. Easley, 334-229-5053, E-mail: bdawson@alasu.edu.

College of Liberal Arts and Social Sciences Students: 37 full-time (31 women), 1 part-time (0 women); includes 36 minority (all Black or African American, non-Hispanic/Latino), 1 international. Average age 22. 19 applicants, 84% accepted, 9 enrolled. *Faculty:* 16 full-time (4 women). Expenses: Contact institution. *Financial support:* In 2017–18, 2 research assistantships (averaging $9,450 per year) were awarded. In 2017, 7 master's awarded. *Program availability:* Part-time. Offers history (MA); liberal arts and social sciences (MA, MSW); social work (MSW). *Application deadline:* For fall admission, 7/15 for domestic students; for spring admission, 12/15 for domestic students. Applications are processed on a rolling basis. *Application fee:* $25. *Application Contact:* Dr. William Person, Dean of Graduate Studies, 334-229-4274, Fax: 334-229-4928, E-mail: wperson@alasu.edu. *Dean,* Dr. Anthony Troy Adams, 334-229-5176, E-mail: atadams@alasu.edu.

College of Science, Mathematics and Technology Students: 19 full-time (14 women), 23 part-time (12 women); includes 40 minority (38 Black or African American, non-Hispanic/Latino; 1 Asian, non-Hispanic/Latino; 1 Hispanic/Latino), 2 international. Average age 22. 21 applicants, 71% accepted, 8 enrolled. *Faculty:* 11 full-time (4 women). Expenses: Contact institution. *Financial support:* In 2017–18, 22 students received support. Research assistantships and scholarships/grants available. Financial award application deadline: 6/30; financial award applicants required to submit CSS PROFILE or FAFSA. In 2017, 5 master's, 2 doctorates awarded. Offers biology (MS); forensic science (MS); mathematics (MS); microbiology (PhD); science, mathematics and technology (MS, PhD). *Application deadline:* For fall admission, 4/15 for domestic and international students; for spring admission, 11/15 for domestic and international students; for summer admission, 3/15 for domestic and international students. Applications are processed on a rolling basis. *Application fee:* $25. Electronic applications accepted. *Application Contact:* Dr. William Person, Dean of Graduate Studies, 334-229-4274, Fax: 334-229-4928, E-mail: wperson@alasu.edu. *Dean,* Dr. Kennedy Weskesa, 334-229-4316, Fax: 334-229-4916, E-mail: weskesa@alasu.edu.

ALASKA PACIFIC UNIVERSITY, Anchorage, AK 99508-4672

General Information Independent, coed, comprehensive institution. *Graduate housing:* Room and/or apartments available on a first-come, first-served basis to single students; on-campus housing not available to married students. Housing application deadline: 8/15.

GRADUATE UNITS

Graduate Programs *Program availability:* Part-time, evening/weekend. Offers business administration (MBA); counseling psychology (MSCP); environmental science (MSES, MSOEE); health services administration (MBA); information and communication technology (MBAICT); investment (CGS); outdoor and environmental education (MSOEE); self-designed study (MA); teaching (MAT); teaching (K-8) (MAT). Electronic applications accepted.

ALBANY COLLEGE OF PHARMACY AND HEALTH SCIENCES, Albany, NY 12208

General Information Independent, coed, comprehensive institution. *Graduate housing:* Room and/or apartments available on a first-come, first-served basis to single students; on-campus housing not available to married students. Housing application deadline: 7/1.

GRADUATE UNITS

School of Arts and Sciences Offers clinical laboratory sciences (MS); cytotechnology and molecular cytology (MS); health outcomes research (MS); molecular biosciences (MS). Electronic applications accepted.

School of Pharmacy and Pharmaceutical Sciences Offers health outcomes research (MS); pharmaceutical sciences (MS); pharmacy (Pharm D). Electronic applications accepted.

ALBANY LAW SCHOOL, Albany, NY 12208-3494

General Information Independent, coed, graduate-only institution. *Graduate housing:* On-campus housing not available.

GRADUATE UNITS

Professional Program *Program availability:* Part-time. Offers law (LL M, JD). JD/MBA offered jointly with The College of Saint Rose, The Sage Colleges, Union Graduate College, and University at Albany, State University of New York; JD/MPA, JD/MRP, and JD/MSW offered jointly with University at Albany, State University of New York.

ALBANY MEDICAL COLLEGE, Albany, NY 12208-3479

General Information Independent, coed, graduate-only institution. *Graduate housing:* On-campus housing not available. *Research affiliation:* X-Ray Optical Systems (diagnostic equipment), Integrated Tissue Dynamics INTIGYN (integrated tissue dynamics), Regenerative Research Foundation (biomedical research), Wadsworth Center for Laboratories and Research (biomedical research), ORDWAY Research Institute (biomedical research), General Electric Company (GE) (imaging).

GRADUATE UNITS

Alden March Bioethics Institute *Program availability:* Part-time, evening/weekend, online learning. Offers bioethics (MS, DPS); clinical ethics (Certificate); clinical ethics consultation (Certificate). Electronic applications accepted.

Center for Cardiovascular Sciences *Program availability:* Part-time. Offers cardiovascular sciences (MS, PhD).

Center for Cell Biology and Cancer Research *Program availability:* Part-time. Offers cell biology and cancer research (MS, PhD).

Center for Immunology and Microbial Disease *Program availability:* Part-time. Offers immunology and microbial disease (MS, PhD).

Center for Neuropharmacology and Neuroscience Offers neuropharmacology and neuroscience (MS, PhD).

Center for Nurse Anesthesiology Offers anesthesia (MS). Electronic applications accepted.

Center for Physician Assistant Studies Offers physician assistant studies (MS). Electronic applications accepted.

Professional Program Offers medicine (MD). Electronic applications accepted.

ALBANY STATE UNIVERSITY, Albany, GA 31705-2717

General Information State-supported, coed, comprehensive institution. *Graduate housing:* Room and/or apartments available on a first-come, first-served basis to single students; on-campus housing not available to married students. Housing application deadline: 6/30.

GRADUATE UNITS

College of Arts and Humanities *Program availability:* Part-time. Offers criminal justice (MS); English education (M Ed); public administration (MPA); social work (MSW). Electronic applications accepted.

College of Business *Program availability:* Part-time, evening/weekend. Offers accounting (MBA); general business administration (MBA); healthcare (MBA); public administration (MBA); supply chain and logistics (MBA). Electronic applications accepted.

College of Education *Program availability:* Part-time, evening/weekend, online learning. Offers early childhood education (M Ed); educational leadership (Ed S); health and physical education (M Ed); middle grades education (M Ed); school counseling (M Ed); special education (M Ed). Electronic applications accepted.

Darton College of Health Professions *Program availability:* Part-time, evening/weekend, online learning. Offers nursing (MSN). Electronic applications accepted.

ALBERT EINSTEIN COLLEGE OF MEDICINE, Bronx, NY 10461

General Information Independent, coed, graduate-only institution. *Graduate housing:* Room and/or apartments guaranteed to single students. *Library facilities:* D. Samuel Gottesman Library.
Website: http://www.einstein.yu.edu/

General Application Contact: Noreen Kerrigan, Associate Dean of Admissions, 718-430-2106, Fax: 718-430-8840, E-mail: noreen.kerrigan@einstein.yu.edu.

GRADUATE UNITS

Graduate Programs in the Biomedical Sciences Expenses: Contact institution. *Financial support:* Fellowships available. Offers anatomy (PhD); biochemistry (PhD); biomedical sciences (PhD); cell biology (PhD); clinical investigation (PhD); computational genetics (PhD); developmental and molecular biology (PhD); microbiology and immunology (PhD); molecular genetics (PhD); molecular pharmacology (PhD); neuroscience (PhD); pathology (PhD); physiology and biophysics (PhD); systems and computational biology (PhD); translational genetics (PhD). *Application deadline:* For fall admission, 12/15 for domestic students. Applications are processed on a rolling basis. *Application fee:* $75. Electronic applications accepted. *Application Contact:* Salvatore Calabro, Director of Graduate Admissions, 718-430-2345, Fax: 718-430-8655, E-mail: phd@einstein.yu.edu. *Associate Dean for Graduate Studies*, Dr. Victoria H. Freedman, 718-430-2872, Fax: 718-430-8655.

Medical Scientist Training Program Expenses: Contact institution. *Financial support:* Fellowships available. *Application deadline:* For fall admission, 11/1 for domestic students. *Application fee:* $75. *Application Contact:* Sheila Cleeton, Executive Director and Registrar, Einstein Graduate Division, 718-430-2128, Fax: 718-430-8655, E-mail: sheila.cleeton@einstein.yu.edu. *Director*, Dr. Myles Akabas, MD, 718-430-2128, Fax: 718-430-8655, E-mail: myles.akabas@einstein.yu.edu.

Professional Program in Medicine Expenses: Contact institution. *Financial support:* Research assistantships, career-related internships or fieldwork, Federal Work-Study, institutionally sponsored loans, and scholarships/grants available. Offers medicine (MD). *Application deadline:* Applications are processed on a rolling basis. *Application Contact:* Noreen Kerrigan, Associate Dean of Admissions, 718-430-2106, Fax: 718-430-8840, E-mail: noreen.kerrigan@einstein.yu.edu. *Senior Associate Dean for Medical Education*, Dr. Joshua D. Nosanchuk, 718-430-2801.

ALBERTUS MAGNUS COLLEGE, New Haven, CT 06511-1189

General Information Independent-religious, coed, comprehensive institution. *Enrollment:* 241 full-time matriculated graduate/professional students (175 women), 94 part-time matriculated graduate/professional students (68 women). *Enrollment by degree level:* 335 master's. *Graduate faculty:* 29 full-time (11 women), 59 part-time/adjunct (27 women). *Tuition:* Full-time $2530; part-time $2530 per course. Tuition and fees vary according to program and reciprocity agreements. *Graduate housing:* On-campus housing not available. *Student services:* Campus employment opportunities, career counseling, free psychological counseling, international student services, services for students with disabilities, teacher training, writing training. *Library facilities:* Rosary Hall. *Collection:* Books: 38,339 (physical), 148,500 (digital/electronic); Databases: 88.

Computer facilities: 117 computers available on campus for general student use. A campuswide network can be accessed from student residence rooms and from off campus. Online class registration, online class sessions are available.
Website: http://www.albertus.edu/

General Application Contact: Anthony Reich, Director of Admission, Division of Professional and Graduate Studies, 203-773-5032, E-mail: arreich@albertus.edu.

GRADUATE UNITS

Master of Arts in Art Therapy and Counseling Program Students: 20 full-time (19 women), 18 part-time (17 women); includes 2 minority (1 Asian, non-Hispanic/Latino; 1 Hispanic/Latino). Average age 28. 15 applicants, 80% accepted, 10 enrolled. *Faculty:* 3 full-time (all women), 13 part-time/adjunct (10 women). Expenses: Contact institution. *Financial support:* Federal Work-Study and unspecified assistantships available. Support available to part-time students. Financial award application deadline: 8/15; financial award applicants required to submit FAFSA. In 2017, 15 master's awarded. *Program availability:* Part-time. Offers art therapy and counseling (MA). *Application deadline:* For fall admission, 5/1 for domestic students; for spring admission, 11/1 for domestic students. Applications are processed on a rolling basis. *Application fee:* $50. Electronic applications accepted. *Application Contact:* Dr. Sean O'Connell, Vice President for Academic Affairs, 203-777-8539, Fax: 203-777-3701, E-mail: soconnell@albertus.edu. *Director*, Abbe Miller, 203-773-8543, Fax: 203-773-3117, E-mail: amiller@albertus.edu.

Master of Arts in Leadership Program Expenses: Contact institution. *Financial support:* Federal Work-Study and unspecified assistantships available. Support available to part-time students. Financial award applicants required to submit FAFSA. *Program availability:* Part-time, evening/weekend, blended/hybrid learning. Offers leadership (MA). *Application deadline:* Applications are processed on a rolling basis. *Application fee:* $50. Electronic applications accepted. *Application Contact:* Anthony Reich, Director of Admission, Division of Professional and Graduate Studies, 203-773-5032, Fax: 203-773-5257, E-mail: leadership@albertus.edu. *Director*, Dr. Howard Fero, 203-773-4424, E-mail: hfero@albertus.edu.

Master of Arts in Liberal Studies Program Expenses: Contact institution. *Financial support:* Federal Work-Study and unspecified assistantships available. Support available to part-time students. Financial award application deadline: 8/15; financial award applicants required to submit FAFSA. *Program availability:* Part-time, evening/weekend, blended/hybrid learning. Offers liberal studies (MALS). *Application deadline:* For fall admission, 8/31 for domestic students; for spring admission, 1/10 for domestic students. Applications are processed on a rolling basis. *Application fee:* $50. Electronic applications accepted. *Application Contact:* Anthony Reich, Director of Admission, Division of Professional and Graduate Studies, 203-773-5032, Fax: 203-773-5257, E-mail: arreich@albertus.edu. *Director*, Prof. Julia A. Coash, 203-773-8973, Fax: 203-773-5257, E-mail: jcoash@albertus.edu.

Master of Business Administration Program Expenses: Contact institution. *Financial support:* Federal Work-Study and unspecified assistantships available. Support available to part-time students. Financial award applicants required to submit FAFSA. *Program availability:* Part-time, evening/weekend, 100% online, blended/hybrid learning. Offers accounting (MBA); general management (MBA); health care management (MBA); human resource management (MBA); leadership (MBA); project management (MBA). Program also offered in East Hartford, CT. *Application deadline:* Applications are processed on a rolling basis. *Application fee:* $50. Electronic applications accepted. *Application Contact:* Anthony Reich, Director of Admission, Division of Professional and Graduate Studies, 203-773-5302, E-mail: arreich@albertus.edu. *Director*, Dr. Wayne Gineo, 203-672-6670, E-mail: wgineo@albertus.edu.

Master of Fine Arts in Writing Program Expenses: Contact institution. *Financial support:* Federal Work-Study and unspecified assistantships available. Support available to part-time students. Financial award applicants required to submit FAFSA. *Program availability:* Part-time, evening/weekend, 100% online, blended/hybrid learning. Offers writing (MFA). *Application deadline:* For fall admission, 8/15 for domestic students; for spring admission, 1/15 for domestic students. Applications are processed on a rolling basis. *Application fee:* $50. Electronic applications accepted. *Application Contact:* Prof. Sarah Wallman, Co-Director, 203-777-4473, Fax: 203-777-3701, E-mail: swallman@albertus.edu. *Director*, Charles Rafferty, 203-773-6901, Fax: 203-777-3701, E-mail: crafferty@albertus.edu.

Master of Science in Accounting Program Expenses: Contact institution. *Financial support:* Federal Work-Study and unspecified assistantships available. Support available to part-time students. Financial award applicants required to submit FAFSA. *Program availability:* Part-time, evening/weekend, 100% online, blended/hybrid learning. Offers accounting (MSA). *Application deadline:* Applications are processed on a rolling basis. *Application fee:* $50. Electronic applications accepted. *Application Contact:* Dr. Nancy Fallon, Director, 203-773-8567, E-mail: nfallon@albertus.edu. *Director*, Dr. Nancy Fallon, 203-773-8567, E-mail: nfallon@albertus.edu.

Master of Science in Criminal Justice Program Expenses: Contact institution. *Financial support:* Federal Work-Study and unspecified assistantships available. Support available to part-time students. Financial award applicants required to submit FAFSA. *Program availability:* Part-time, evening/weekend, 100% online, blended/hybrid learning. Offers corrections administration (MS); juvenile justice (MS). *Application fee:* $50. *Application Contact:* John Lawrie, Coordinator, 203-773-6142, E-mail: jnlawrie@albertus.edu. *Coordinator*, John Lawrie, 203-773-6142, E-mail: jnlawrie@albertus.edu.

Master of Science in Education Program Expenses: Contact institution. *Financial support:* Federal Work-Study and unspecified assistantships available. Support available to part-time students. Financial award applicants required to submit FAFSA. *Program availability:* Part-time, evening/weekend, blended/hybrid learning. Offers education (MS Ed). *Application deadline:* For fall admission, 8/15 for domestic students; for spring admission, 1/15 for domestic students. *Application fee:* $50. *Application Contact:* Anthony Reich, Director of Admission, Division of Professional and Graduate Studies, 203-773-5032, E-mail: arreich@albertus.edu. *Director, Education Programs*, Dr. Joan Venditto, 203-773-8087, Fax: 203-773-4422, E-mail: jvenditto@albertus.edu.

Master of Science in Human Services Program Expenses: Contact institution. *Financial support:* Federal Work-Study and unspecified assistantships available. Support available to part-time students. Financial award applicants required to submit FAFSA. *Program availability:* Part-time, evening/weekend, blended/hybrid learning. Offers human services (MS). *Application deadline:* For fall admission, 8/15 for domestic students; for spring admission, 1/15 for domestic students. Applications are processed on a rolling basis. *Application fee:* $50. Electronic applications accepted. *Application Contact:* Anthony Reich, Director of Admission, Division of Professional and Graduate Studies, 203-773-5032, E-mail: arreich@albertus.edu. *Director*, Ragaa Mazen, 203-773-8574, E-mail: rmazen@albertus.edu.

Master of Science in Management and Organizational Leadership Program Expenses: Contact institution. *Financial support:* Federal Work-Study and unspecified assistantships available. Support available to part-time students. Financial award applicants required to submit FAFSA. *Program availability:* Part-time, evening/weekend, blended/hybrid learning. Offers management and organizational leadership (MS). *Application deadline:* For fall admission, 8/14 for domestic students; for spring admission, 1/15 for domestic students. Applications are processed on a rolling basis. *Application fee:* $50. Electronic applications accepted. *Application Contact:* Anthony Reich, Director of Admission, Division of Professional and Graduate Studies, 203-773-5032, E-mail: arreich@albertus.edu. *Director of Leadership Programs*, Dr. Howard Fero, 203-773-4424, E-mail: hfero@albertus.edu.

ALBRIGHT COLLEGE, Reading, PA 19612-5234

General Information Independent-religious, coed, comprehensive institution. *Graduate housing:* On-campus housing not available.

GRADUATE UNITS

Graduate Division *Program availability:* Part-time, evening/weekend. Offers early childhood education (MS); elementary education (MS); English as a second language (MA); general education (MA); special education (MS). Electronic applications accepted.

ALCORN STATE UNIVERSITY, Lorman, MS 39096-7500

General Information State-supported, coed, comprehensive institution. CGS member. *Graduate housing:* Room and/or apartments available on a first-come, first-served basis to single students; on-campus housing not available to married students.

GRADUATE UNITS

School of Graduate Studies *Program availability:* Part-time. Offers workforce education leadership (MS). Electronic applications accepted.

School of Agriculture and Applied Science Offers agricultural economics (MS Ag); agronomy (MS Ag); animal science (MS Ag).

School of Arts and Sciences Offers arts and sciences (MS); biology (MS); computer and information sciences (MS).

School of Business Offers business (MBA).

School of Nursing Offers rural nursing (MSN).

School of Psychology and Education Offers agricultural education (MS Ed); elementary education (MS Ed, Ed S); guidance and counseling (MS Ed); industrial education (MS Ed); secondary education (MS Ed); special education (MS Ed).

ALDERSON BROADDUS UNIVERSITY, Philippi, WV 26416

General Information Independent-religious, coed, comprehensive institution. *Graduate housing:* Rooms and/or apartments available on a first-come, first-served basis to single and married students. Housing application deadline: 8/21.

GRADUATE UNITS

Program in Physician Assistant Studies Offers physician assistant studies (MPAS). Electronic applications accepted.

ALFRED UNIVERSITY, Alfred, NY 14802-1205

General Information Independent, coed, university. *Graduate housing:* Room and/or apartments available on a first-come, first-served basis to single students; on-campus housing not available to married students. Housing application deadline: 5/1. *Research affiliation:* Center for High Temperature Characterization (materials science), New York State Center for Advanced Ceramic Technology (ceramic engineering and materials science), Center for Glass Research (glass engineering and science), National Science Foundation Industry-University Center for Glass Research, Whitewares Research Center (whitewares processing, traditional ceramics), National Science Foundation Industry-University Center for Biosurfaces (bioceramics).

GRADUATE UNITS

Graduate School *Program availability:* Part-time. Offers mental health counseling (MS Ed); public administration (MPA); school counseling (MS Ed, CAS); school psychology (MA, Psy D, CAS). Electronic applications accepted.

College of Ceramics Offers biomaterials engineering (MS); ceramic art (MFA); ceramic engineering (MS, PhD); ceramics (MFA, MS, PhD); electrical engineering (MS); electronic integrated arts (MFA); glass science (MS, PhD); materials science and engineering (MS, PhD); mechanical engineering (MS); painting (MFA); sculpture/dimensional studies (MFA). Electronic applications accepted.

Division of Education *Program availability:* Part-time. Offers college student development (MS Ed); literacy (MS Ed). Electronic applications accepted.

School of Business *Program availability:* Part-time. Offers accounting (MBA); business administration (MBA). Electronic applications accepted.

ALLEN COLLEGE, Waterloo, IA 50703

General Information Independent, coed, primarily women, comprehensive institution. *Enrollment:* 622 graduate, professional, and undergraduate students; 106 full-time matriculated graduate/professional students (91 women), 187 part-time matriculated graduate/professional students (164 women). *Enrollment by degree level:* 254 master's, 39 doctoral. *Graduate faculty:* 24 full-time (all women), 8 part-time/adjunct (7 women). *Graduate housing:* On-campus housing not available. *Student services:* Campus safety program, career counseling, free psychological counseling. *Library facilities:* Barrett Library plus 1 other. *Collection:* Books: 13,226 (physical), 5,000 (digital/electronic); Serial titles: 211 (physical), 3,000 (digital/electronic); Databases: 45. Weekly public service hours: 50; study areas open 24 hours, 5–7 days a week; students can reserve study rooms.

Computer facilities: 32 computers available on campus for general student use. A campuswide network can be accessed from off campus. Online proctoring exams available.
Website: http://www.allencollege.edu/

General Application Contact: Molly Quinn, Director of Admissions, 319-226-2001, Fax: 319-226-2010, E-mail: molly.quinn@allencollege.edu.

GRADUATE UNITS

Graduate Programs Students: 106 full-time (91 women), 187 part-time (164 women); includes 22 minority (12 Black or African American, non-Hispanic/Latino; 1 American Indian or Alaska Native, non-Hispanic/Latino; 2 Asian, non-Hispanic/Latino; 3 Hispanic/Latino; 4 Two or more races, non-Hispanic/Latino), 2 international. Average age 33. 352 applicants, 56% accepted, 131 enrolled. *Faculty:* 24 full-time (all women), 8 part-time/adjunct (7 women). Expenses: Contact institution. *Financial support:* In 2017–18, 97 students received support. Federal Work-Study, institutionally sponsored loans, scholarships/grants, and traineeships available. Support available to part-time students. Financial award application deadline: 8/1; financial award applicants required to submit FAFSA. In 2017, 73 master's, 2 doctorates awarded. *Program availability:* Part-time, 100% online, blended/hybrid learning. Offers adult-gerontology acute care nurse practitioner (MSN); community/public health nursing (MSN); education (MSN); family nurse practitioner (MSN); health sciences (Ed D); leadership in health care delivery (MSN); leadership in health care informatics (MSN); nursing (DNP); occupational therapy (MS); psychiatric mental health nurse practitioner (MSN). MSN in leadership in healthcare informatics offered in partnership with University of Minnesota. *Application deadline:* For fall admission, 2/1 priority date for domestic students; for spring admission, 9/1 priority date for domestic students. Applications are processed on a rolling basis. *Application fee:* $50. Electronic applications accepted. *Application Contact:* Molly Quinn, Director of Admissions, 319-226-2001, Fax: 319-226-2010, E-mail: molly.quinn@allencollege.edu. *Vice Chancellor for Academic Affairs*, Dr. Nancy Kramer, 319-226-2040, Fax: 319-226-2070, E-mail: nancy.kramer@allencollege.edu.

ALLIANT INTERNATIONAL UNIVERSITY–FRESNO, Fresno, CA 93727

General Information Independent, coed, graduate-only institution. *Graduate housing:* On-campus housing not available.

GRADUATE UNITS

California School of Forensic Studies Offers clinical forensic psychology (PhD, Psy D); forensic studies (PhD, Psy D); victimology (Psy D). Electronic applications accepted.

California School of Professional Psychology Offers clinical psychology (PhD, Psy D); organizational behavior (MA); organizational development (Psy D); professional psychology (MA, PhD, Psy D). Electronic applications accepted.

ALLIANT INTERNATIONAL UNIVERSITY–IRVINE, Irvine, CA 92606

General Information Independent, coed, graduate-only institution. *Graduate housing:* On-campus housing not available.

GRADUATE UNITS

California School of Forensic Studies Offers forensic studies (Psy D). Electronic applications accepted.

California School of Professional Psychology *Program availability:* Part-time. Offers couple and family therapy (MA, Psy D); professional psychology (MA, Psy D). Electronic applications accepted.

Shirley M. Hufstedler School of Education *Program availability:* Part-time, evening/weekend, online learning. Offers education (MA, Psy D, Certificate, Credential); educational psychology (Psy D); pupil personnel services (Credential); school psychology (MA). Electronic applications accepted.

ALLIANT INTERNATIONAL UNIVERSITY–LOS ANGELES, Alhambra, CA 91803

General Information Independent, coed, graduate-only institution. *Graduate housing:* Room and/or apartments available to single students; on-campus housing not available to married students.

GRADUATE UNITS

California School of Forensic Studies Offers forensic psychology (Psy D).

California School of Professional Psychology Offers chemical dependency (MA); clinical health psychology (Psy D); clinical psychology (PhD, Psy D); family/child and couple clinical psychology (Psy D); gerontology (MA); Latin American family therapy (MA); multi-interest option (Psy D); multicultural community-clinical psychology (Psy D); professional psychology (MA, PhD, Psy D). Electronic applications accepted.

Organizational Psychology Division *Program availability:* Part-time. Offers organizational psychology (MA, PhD). Electronic applications accepted.

Marshall Goldsmith School of Management Offers management (DBA).

Business Division Offers business (DBA).

Shirley M. Hufstedler School of Education *Program availability:* Part-time, evening/weekend, online learning. Offers education (MA, Psy D, Credential); educational psychology (Psy D); pupil personnel services (Credential); school psychology (MA); teaching (MA, Credential). Electronic applications accepted.

ALLIANT INTERNATIONAL UNIVERSITY–SACRAMENTO, Sacramento, CA 95833

General Information Independent, coed, graduate-only institution. *Graduate housing:* On-campus housing not available.

GRADUATE UNITS

California School of Forensic Studies Offers clinical forensic psychology (Psy D); forensic studies (Psy D). Electronic applications accepted.

California School of Professional Psychology *Program availability:* Part-time. Offers clinical psychology (Psy D); couple and family therapy (MA, Psy D); professional psychology (MA, Psy D). Electronic applications accepted.

Shirley M. Hufstedler School of Education Offers education (MA, Credential); teaching (MA, Credential). Electronic applications accepted.

ALLIANT INTERNATIONAL UNIVERSITY–SAN DIEGO, San Diego, CA 92131

General Information Independent, coed, university. *Graduate housing:* Room and/or apartments available on a first-come, first-served basis to single students; on-campus housing not available to married students.

GRADUATE UNITS

Alliant School of Management *Program availability:* Part-time, evening/weekend. Offers management (MA, MBA). Electronic applications accepted.

Business and Management Division *Program availability:* Part-time, evening/weekend. Offers business administration (MBA). Electronic applications accepted.

California School of Forensic Studies Offers clinical forensic psychology (Psy D); forensic studies (Psy D).

California School of Professional Psychology *Program availability:* Part-time. Offers clinical psychology (PhD, Psy D); marital and family therapy (MA, Psy D); professional psychology (MA, MS, PhD, Psy D).

Organizational Psychology Division *Program availability:* Part-time, evening/weekend. Offers clinical/industrial organizational psychology (PhD); consulting psychology (PhD); industrial/organizational psychology (MA, MS, PhD); leadership (PhD). Electronic applications accepted.

Shirley M. Hufstedler School of Education *Program availability:* Part-time, evening/weekend, online learning. Offers education (MA, Ed D, Psy D, Certificate, Credential); educational administration (MA); educational leadership and management (K-12) (Ed D); educational psychology (Psy D); higher education (Ed D, Certificate); preliminary administrative services (Credential); preliminary single subject (Credential); professional clear multiple subject (Credential); professional clear single subject (Credential); pupil personnel services (Credential); school neuropsychology (Certificate); school psychology (MA); school-based mental health (Certificate); teacher education (MA); teaching English to speakers of other languages (MA, Ed D, Certificate). Electronic applications accepted.

ALLIANT INTERNATIONAL UNIVERSITY–SAN FRANCISCO, San Francisco, CA 94133

General Information Independent, coed, graduate-only institution. *Graduate housing:* On-campus housing not available.

GRADUATE UNITS

California School of Forensic Studies Offers applied criminology (MS); clinical forensic psychology (PhD, Psy D); victimology (MS).

California School of Professional Psychology Offers clinical counseling (MA); clinical psychology (PhD, Psy D, Certificate); professional psychology (MA, Post-Doctoral MS, PhD, Psy D, Certificate); psychopharmacology (Post-Doctoral MS). Electronic applications accepted.

Organizational Psychology Division *Program availability:* Part-time, evening/weekend. Offers organizational psychology (MA, PhD). Electronic applications accepted.

San Francisco Law School *Program availability:* Part-time, evening/weekend. Offers law (JD). Electronic applications accepted.

Shirley M. Hufstedler School of Education *Program availability:* Part-time, evening/weekend, online learning. Offers auditory oral education (Certificate); CLAD (Certificate); community college administration (Ed D); education (MA, Ed D, Psy D, Certificate, Credential); education specialist: mild/moderate disabilities (Credential); educational administration (MA); educational leadership and management (K-12) (Ed D); educational psychology (Psy D); higher education (Ed D); preliminary administrative services (Credential); preliminary multiple subject (Credential); preliminary single subject (Credential); professional clear multiple subject (Credential); professional clear single subject (Credential); pupil personnel services (Credential); school psychology (MA); special education (MA); teaching (MA); TESOL (Certificate). Electronic applications accepted.

ALVERNIA UNIVERSITY, Reading, PA 19607-1799

General Information Independent-religious, coed, comprehensive institution. *Graduate housing:* On-campus housing not available.

GRADUATE UNITS

School of Graduate Studies *Program availability:* Part-time, evening/weekend. Offers adult gerontology nurse practitioner (DNP); business (MBA); community counseling (MA); family nurse practitioner (DNP); leadership (PhD); liberal studies (MALS); nursing education (MSN); nursing leadership (Graduate Certificate); nursing leadership and healthcare administration (MSN); occupational therapy (MSOT); urban education (M Ed). Electronic applications accepted.

ALVERNO COLLEGE, Milwaukee, WI 53234-3922

General Information Independent-religious, Undergraduate: women only; graduate: coed, comprehensive institution. *Enrollment:* 1,942 graduate, professional, and undergraduate students; 298 full-time matriculated graduate/professional students (272 women), 190 part-time matriculated graduate/professional students (183 women). *Enrollment by degree level:* 481 master's, 7 doctoral. *Graduate faculty:* 23 full-time (21 women), 39 part-time/adjunct (27 women). *Graduate housing:* On-campus housing not available. *Student services:* Campus employment opportunities, campus safety program, career counseling, child daycare facilities, exercise/wellness program, free psychological counseling, low-cost health insurance, multicultural affairs office, services for students with disabilities. *Library facilities:* Alverno College Library. *Collection:* Books: 61,590 (physical), 233,437 (digital/electronic); Serial titles: 459 (physical), 53,337 (digital/electronic); Databases: 76.

Computer facilities: 706 computers available on campus for general student use. A campuswide network can be accessed from student residence rooms and from off campus. Online class registration is available.
Website: http://www.alverno.edu/

General Application Contact: Janet Stikel, Associate Director of Adult and Graduate Admissions, 414-382-6112, Fax: 414-382-6354, E-mail: janet.stikel@alverno.edu.

GRADUATE UNITS

JoAnn McGrath School of Nursing and Health Professions Students: 119 full-time (107 women), 103 part-time (101 women); includes 53 minority (22 Black or African American, non-Hispanic/Latino; 1 American Indian or Alaska Native, non-Hispanic/Latino; 11 Asian, non-Hispanic/Latino; 15 Hispanic/Latino; 4 Two or more races, non-Hispanic/Latino), 1 international. Average age 35. 80 applicants, 99% accepted, 56 enrolled. *Faculty:* 10 full-time (all women), 7 part-time/adjunct (4 women). Expenses: Contact institution. *Financial support:* Federal Work-Study and scholarships/grants available. Support available to part-time students. Financial award applicants required to submit FAFSA. In 2017, 47 master's awarded. *Program availability:* Part-time, evening/weekend. Offers clinical nurse specialist (MSN); family nurse practitioner (MSN); nursing practice (DNP); psychiatric mental health nurse practitioner (MSN). *Application deadline:* For fall admission, 7/15 priority date for domestic and international students; for spring admission, 12/15 priority date for domestic and international students. Applications are processed on a rolling basis. *Application fee:* $0. Electronic applications accepted. *Application Contact:* Karin Wasiullah, Associate Dean, Master of Science in Nursing, 414-382-6275, Fax: 414-382-6354, E-mail: karin.wasiullah@alverno.edu. *Dean,* Margaret Rauschenberger, 414-382-6276, Fax: 414-382-6354, E-mail: margaret.rauschenberger@alverno.edu.

School of Arts and Sciences Students: 78 full-time (76 women), 12 part-time (all women); includes 37 minority (24 Black or African American, non-Hispanic/Latino; 1 Asian, non-Hispanic/Latino; 11 Hispanic/Latino; 1 Two or more races, non-Hispanic/Latino), 2 international. Average age 34. 34 applicants, 100% accepted, 23 enrolled. *Faculty:* 6 full-time (all women), 6 part-time/adjunct (all women). Expenses: Contact institution. *Financial support:* Federal Work-Study and scholarships/grants available. Support available to part-time students. Financial award applicants required to submit FAFSA. In 2017, 20 master's awarded. *Program availability:* Part-time, evening/weekend. Offers community-based research and consultation (MSCP); professional counselor (MSCP). *Application deadline:* For fall admission, 7/15 priority date for domestic and international students; for spring admission, 12/15 priority date for domestic and international students. Applications are processed on a rolling basis. *Application fee:* $0. Electronic applications accepted. *Application Contact:* Katie Kipp, Graduate Admissions Counselor, 414-382-6045, Fax: 414-382-6354, E-mail: katie.kipp@alverno.edu. *Director, Master of Science in Community Psychology,* Dr. Kimberly Skerven, 414-382-6461, Fax: 414-382-6354, E-mail: kimberly.skerven@alverno.edu.

School of Professional Studies - Business Division Students: 53 full-time (45 women), 4 part-time (3 women); includes 24 minority (12 Black or African American, non-Hispanic/Latino; 3 Asian, non-Hispanic/Latino; 5 Hispanic/Latino; 4 Two or more races, non-Hispanic/Latino). Average age 34. 33 applicants, 100% accepted, 23 enrolled. *Faculty:* 4 full-time (3 women), 3 part-time/adjunct (0 women). Expenses: Contact institution. *Financial support:* Federal Work-Study and scholarships/grants available. Support available to part-time students. Financial award applicants required to submit FAFSA. In 2017, 24 master's awarded. *Program availability:* Part-time, evening/weekend. Offers business (MBA). *Application deadline:* For fall admission, 7/15 priority date for domestic and international students; for spring admission, 12/15 priority date for domestic and international students. Applications are processed on a rolling basis. *Application fee:* $0. Electronic applications accepted. *Application Contact:* Janet Stikel, Associate Director of Adult and Graduate Admissions, 414-382-6112, Fax: 414-382-6354, E-mail: janet.stikel@alverno.edu. *Dean, School of Professional Studies,* Dr. Patricia Luebke, 414-382-6368, E-mail: patricia.luebke@alverno.edu.

School of Professional Studies - Education Division Students: 37 full-time (34 women), 68 part-time (65 women); includes 27 minority (16 Black or African American, non-Hispanic/Latino; 1 American Indian or Alaska Native, non-Hispanic/Latino; 1 Asian, non-Hispanic/Latino; 7 Hispanic/Latino; 2 Two or more races, non-Hispanic/Latino). Average age 35. 67 applicants, 100% accepted, 51 enrolled. *Faculty:* 3 full-time (2 women), 23 part-time/adjunct (17 women). Expenses: Contact institution. *Financial support:* Federal Work-Study and scholarships/grants available. Support available to part-time students. Financial award applicants required to submit FAFSA. In 2017, 68 master's awarded. *Program availability:* Part-time, evening/weekend. Offers adaptive education (MA); administrative leadership (MA); adult education and organizational development (MA); adult educational and instructional design (MA); adult educational and instructional technology (MA); global connections in the humanities (MA); instructional leadership (MA); instructional technology for K-12 settings (MA); professional development (MA); reading education (MA); reading education with adaptive education (MA); science education (MA); special education (MA); teaching in alternative schools (MA). *Application deadline:* For fall admission, 7/15 priority date for domestic and international students; for spring admission, 12/15 priority date for domestic and international students. Applications are processed on a rolling basis. *Application fee:* $0. Electronic applications accepted. *Application Contact:* Katie Kipp, Graduate Admissions Counselor, 414-382-6045, Fax: 414-382-6354, E-mail: katie.kipp@alverno.edu. *Dean, School of Professional Studies,* Dr. Patricia Luebke, 414-382-6368, Fax: 414-382-6354, E-mail: patricia.luebke@alverno.edu.

AMBERTON UNIVERSITY, Garland, TX 75041-5595

General Information Independent-religious, coed, upper-level institution. *Enrollment:* 480 full-time matriculated graduate/professional students (296 women), 656 part-time matriculated graduate/professional students (451 women). *Enrollment by degree level:* 1,136 master's. *Graduate faculty:* 15 full-time (8 women), 41 part-time/adjunct (17 women). *Tuition:* Part-time $795 per course. *Graduate housing:* On-campus housing not available. *Library facilities:* Library Resource Center plus 1 other.

Computer facilities: 30 computers available on campus for general student use.
Website: http://www.amberton.edu/

General Application Contact: Adviser, 972-279-6511 Ext. 180, Fax: 972-279-9773, E-mail: advisor@amberton.edu.

GRADUATE UNITS

Graduate School Expenses: Contact institution. *Program availability:* Part-time, evening/weekend. Offers agile project management (MS); family studies (MS); general business (MBA); human relations and business (MS); human resources training and development (MS); international business (MBA); management (MBA); managerial science (MS); marriage and family therapy (MA); professional counseling (MA); professional development (MA); project management (MBA); school counseling (MA); strategic leadership (MBA). *Application deadline:* Applications are processed on a rolling basis. *Application fee:* $0. *Application Contact:* Adviser, 972-279-6511 Ext. 180, Fax: 972-279-9773, E-mail: advisor@amberton.edu. *Academic Dean,* 972-279-6511 Ext. 153, Fax: 972-279-9773.

AMBROSE UNIVERSITY, Calgary, AB T3H 0L5, Canada

General Information Independent-religious, coed, comprehensive institution. *Enrollment:* 922 graduate, professional, and undergraduate students; 64 full-time matriculated graduate/professional students (26 women), 126 part-time matriculated graduate/professional students (52 women). *Enrollment by degree level:* 124 master's, 66 other advanced degrees. *Graduate faculty:* 20 full-time (7 women), 48 part-time/adjunct (13 women). *Tuition:* Full-time $12,000 Canadian dollars; part-time $400 Canadian dollars per credit hour. *Required fees:* $810 Canadian dollars; $27 Canadian dollars per credit hour. $50 Canadian dollars per semester. Tuition and fees vary according to course load. *Graduate housing:* Room and/or apartments available on a first-come, first-served basis to single students; on-campus housing not available to married students. Typical cost: $2400 Canadian dollars per year. Room charges vary according to housing facility selected. Housing application deadline: 6/15. *Student services:* Campus employment opportunities, career counseling, international student services, low-cost health insurance, services for students with disabilities, writing training. *Library facilities:* Archibald Foundation Library. *Collection:* Books: 127,484 (physical), 150,000 (digital/electronic); Serial titles: 152 (physical), 60,338 (digital/electronic); Databases: 42. Weekly public service hours: 81; students can reserve study rooms.

Computer facilities: 20 computers available on campus for general student use. A campuswide network can be accessed from student residence rooms. Online class registration is available.
Website: http://www.ambrose.edu/

General Application Contact: Megan Silver, Enrollment Assistant, 403-410-2900, Fax: 403-571-2556, E-mail: enrolment@ambrose.edu.

GRADUATE UNITS

Ambrose Seminary Students: 64 full-time (26 women), 126 part-time (52 women). *Faculty:* 20 full-time (7 women), 48 part-time/adjunct (13 women). Expenses: Contact institution. *Financial support:* Career-related internships or fieldwork and scholarships/grants available. Support available to part-time students. Financial award application deadline: 3/30. In 2017, 21 master's, 1 other advanced degree awarded. *Program availability:* Part-time, blended/hybrid learning. Offers Biblical/theological studies (MA); Christian studies (MCS, Diploma); intercultural ministries (M Div, MA); leadership (Certificate); leadership and ministry (MA); pastoral ministry (M Div). *Application deadline:* For fall admission, 8/1 for domestic students, 7/15 for international students; for winter admission, 12/10 for domestic students, 11/15 for international students. Applications are processed on a rolling basis. *Application fee:* $70 ($100 for international students). Electronic applications accepted. *Application Contact:* Megan Silver, Enrollment Assistant, 403-410-2900, Fax: 403-571-2556, E-mail: enrolment@ambrose.edu. *Dean of Theology,* Dr. Jo-Ann Badley, 403-410-2000 Ext. 3994, Fax: 403-571-2556, E-mail: jbadley@ambrose.edu.

AMERICAN ACADEMY OF ACUPUNCTURE AND ORIENTAL MEDICINE, Roseville, MN 55113

General Information Proprietary, coed, graduate-only institution.

GRADUATE UNITS

Graduate Programs Offers acupuncture and Oriental medicine (MAOM, DAOM).

AMERICAN BAPTIST SEMINARY OF THE WEST, Berkeley, CA 94704-3029

General Information Independent-religious, coed, graduate-only institution. *Graduate housing:* Rooms and/or apartments available on a first-come, first-served basis to single and married students. Housing application deadline: 5/1.

GRADUATE UNITS

Graduate and Professional Programs *Program availability:* Part-time, evening/weekend, online learning. Offers community leadership (MA); theology (M Div, MA). MA program in theology offered jointly with Graduate Theological Union. Electronic applications accepted.

AMERICAN BUSINESS & TECHNOLOGY UNIVERSITY, Saint Joseph, MO 64506

General Information Proprietary, coed, comprehensive institution.

GRADUATE UNITS

Programs in Business Administration *Program availability:* Online learning. Offers business administration (MBA); financial management (MBA); global business management (MBA); information systems management (MBA); marketing and social media (MBA); project and operations management (MBA); public accounting (MBA).

AMERICAN COLLEGE DUBLIN, Dublin 2, Ireland

General Information Independent, coed, comprehensive institution.

GRADUATE UNITS

Graduate Programs

AMERICAN COLLEGE OF ACUPUNCTURE AND ORIENTAL MEDICINE, Houston, TX 77063

General Information Proprietary, coed, graduate-only institution. *Research affiliation:* Montrose Clinic (HIV/AIDS research and treatment), Rice University Wellness Center (student and staff care), Baylor College of Medicine (acupuncture for osteoarthritis of the knee), Memorial Herman Healthcare System, Tianjing Hospital, China (traditional Chinese medicine).

GRADUATE UNITS

Graduate Studies *Program availability:* Part-time.

AMERICAN COLLEGE OF EDUCATION, Indianapolis, IN 46204

General Information Proprietary, coed, graduate-only institution.

GRADUATE UNITS

Graduate Programs Offers curriculum and instruction (M Ed); educational leadership (M Ed); educational technology (M Ed).

THE AMERICAN COLLEGE OF FINANCIAL SERVICES, Bryn Mawr, PA 19010-2105

General Information Independent, coed, graduate-only institution. *Graduate housing:* On-campus housing not available.

GRADUATE UNITS

Graduate Programs *Program availability:* Part-time, evening/weekend, online learning. Offers financial services (MSFS); leadership (MSM). Electronic applications accepted.

AMERICAN COLLEGE OF HEALTHCARE SCIENCES, Portland, OR 97239-3719

General Information Independent, coed, comprehensive institution. *Graduate housing:* On-campus housing not available.

GRADUATE UNITS

Graduate Programs *Program availability:* Part-time, evening/weekend, online learning. Offers anatomy and physiology (Graduate Certificate); aromatherapy (MS, Graduate Certificate); botanical safety (Graduate Certificate); complementary alternative medicine (MS, Graduate Certificate); health and wellness (MS); herbal medicine (MS, Graduate Certificate); holistic nutrition (MS, Graduate Certificate); wellness coaching (Graduate Certificate).

AMERICAN COLLEGE OF THESSALONIKI, 55535 Pylaia, Greece

General Information Independent, coed, comprehensive institution.

GRADUATE UNITS

Department of Business Administration *Program availability:* Part-time, evening/weekend. Offers banking and finance (MBA); entrepreneurship (MBA, Certificate); finance (Certificate); management (MBA, Certificate); marketing (MBA, Certificate). Electronic applications accepted.

AMERICAN CONSERVATORY THEATER, San Francisco, CA 94108-5800

General Information Independent, coed, graduate-only institution. *Graduate housing:* On-campus housing not available.

GRADUATE UNITS

Program in Acting Offers acting (MFA, Certificate).

AMERICAN FILM INSTITUTE CONSERVATORY, Los Angeles, CA 90027-1657

General Information Independent, coed, graduate-only institution. *Enrollment by degree level:* 341 master's. *Graduate faculty:* 11 full-time (2 women), 64 part-time/adjunct (22 women). *Tuition:* Full-time $54,072. *Required fees:* $3268. *Graduate housing:* On-campus housing not available. *Student services:* Campus employment opportunities, campus safety program, career counseling, free psychological counseling, international student services, multicultural affairs office, services for students with disabilities. *Library facilities:* Louis B. Mayer Library. *Collection:* Books: 39,694 (physical), 519 (digital/electronic); Serial titles: 17 (physical), 4 (digital/electronic); Databases: 2. Weekly public service hours: 74.

Computer facilities: 31 computers available on campus for general student use. A campuswide network can be accessed. Online class registration is available.
Website: http://www.afi.com/Conservatory/

General Application Contact: Stacy Gaspard, Admissions Counselor, 323-856-7740, Fax: 323-856-7683, E-mail: admissions@afi.com.

GRADUATE UNITS

Graduate Program Students: 341 full-time (159 women); includes 65 minority (13 Black or African American, non-Hispanic/Latino; 2 American Indian or Alaska Native, non-Hispanic/Latino; 15 Asian, non-Hispanic/Latino; 27 Hispanic/Latino; 8 Two or more races, non-Hispanic/Latino), 117 international. Average age 26. *Faculty:* 11 full-time (2 women), 64 part-time/adjunct (22 women). Expenses: Contact institution. *Financial support:* Teaching assistantships, career-related internships or fieldwork, scholarships/grants, and unspecified assistantships available. Financial award applicants required to submit FAFSA. Offers cinematography (MFA); directing (MFA); editing (MFA); producing (MFA); production design (MFA); screenwriting (MFA). *Application deadline:* For fall admission, 11/30 for domestic and international students. *Application fee:* $90. Electronic applications accepted. *Application Contact:* Stacy Gaspard, Admissions Counselor, 323-856-7740, Fax: 323-856-7683, E-mail: admissions@afi.com.

AMERICAN GRADUATE SCHOOL IN PARIS, F-75006 Paris, France

General Information Independent, coed, graduate-only institution.

GRADUATE UNITS

Program in International Relations and Diplomacy Offers international relations and diplomacy (MA, PhD).

AMERICAN GRADUATE UNIVERSITY, Covina, CA 91724

General Information Proprietary, coed, graduate-only institution. *Graduate housing:* On-campus housing not available. *Research affiliation:* Library and Information Resources Network.

GRADUATE UNITS

Program in Acquisition Management *Program availability:* Part-time, online learning. Offers acquisition management (MAM, Certificate). Electronic applications accepted.

Program in Business Administration *Program availability:* Part-time, online learning. Offers acquisition and contracting (MBA); supply chain management (MBA). Electronic applications accepted.

Program in Contract Management *Program availability:* Part-time, online learning. Offers contract management (MCM, Certificate). Electronic applications accepted.

Program in Supply Chain Management *Program availability:* Part-time, online learning. Offers supply chain management (MSCM, Certificate).

AMERICAN INTERCONTINENTAL UNIVERSITY ATLANTA, Atlanta, GA 30328

General Information Proprietary, coed, comprehensive institution. *Graduate housing:* On-campus housing not available.

GRADUATE UNITS

Program in Global Technology Management *Program availability:* Part-time, evening/weekend, online learning. Offers global technology management (MBA). Electronic applications accepted.

Program in Information Technology *Program availability:* Part-time, evening/weekend. Offers information technology (MIT). Electronic applications accepted.

AMERICAN INTERCONTINENTAL UNIVERSITY HOUSTON, Houston, TX 77042

General Information Proprietary, coed, comprehensive institution.

GRADUATE UNITS

School of Business Offers management (MBA).

AMERICAN INTERCONTINENTAL UNIVERSITY ONLINE, Schaumburg, IL 60173

General Information Proprietary, coed, comprehensive institution.

GRADUATE UNITS

Program in Business Administration *Program availability:* Evening/weekend, online learning. Offers accounting and finance (MBA); finance (MBA); healthcare management (MBA); human resource management (MBA); international business (MBA); management (MBA); marketing (MBA); operations management (MBA); organizational psychology and development (MBA); project management (MBA). Electronic applications accepted.

Program in Education *Program availability:* Evening/weekend, online learning. Offers curriculum and instruction (M Ed); educational assessment and evaluation (M Ed); instructional technology (M Ed); leadership of educational organizations (M Ed). Electronic applications accepted.

Program in Information Technology *Program availability:* Evening/weekend, online learning. Offers Internet security (MIT); IT project management (MIT). Electronic applications accepted.

AMERICAN INTERNATIONAL COLLEGE, Springfield, MA 01109-3189

General Information Independent, coed, comprehensive institution. *Enrollment:* 3,283 graduate, professional, and undergraduate students; 1,716 full-time matriculated graduate/professional students (1,386 women), 195 part-time matriculated graduate/professional students (155 women). *Enrollment by degree level:* 1,361 master's, 224 doctoral, 242 other advanced degrees. *Graduate faculty:* 20 full-time (17 women), 190 part-time/adjunct (114 women). *Tuition:* Full-time $16,020; part-time $890 per credit. *Required fees:* $30 per semester. One-time fee: $50. Tuition and fees vary according to course load, program and student level. *Graduate housing:* Room and/or apartments available on a first-come, first-served basis to single students; on-campus housing not available to married students. Typical cost: $8920 per year ($15,540 including board). Room and board charges vary according to board plan and housing facility selected. Housing application deadline: 8/15. *Student services:* Campus employment opportunities, campus safety program, career counseling, exercise/wellness program, free psychological counseling, international student services, low-cost health insurance, multicultural affairs office, services for students with disabilities, writing training. *Library facilities:* James J. Shea Sr. Library. *Collection:* Books: 56,511 (physical), 179,160 (digital/electronic); Serial titles: 183 (physical), 962 (digital/electronic); Databases: 64. Weekly public service hours: 100; students can reserve study rooms.

Computer facilities: Computer purchase and lease plans are available. 230 computers available on campus for general student use. A campuswide network can be accessed from student residence rooms and from off campus. Online class registration is available.
Website: http://www.aic.edu/

General Application Contact: Kerry Barnes, Director of Graduate Admissions, 413-205-3703, Fax: 413-205-3051, E-mail: kerry.barnes@aic.edu.

GRADUATE UNITS

School of Business, Arts and Sciences Students: 178 full-time (120 women), 24 part-time (20 women); includes 94 minority (42 Black or African American, non-Hispanic/Latino; 1 American Indian or Alaska Native, non-Hispanic/Latino; 4 Asian, non-Hispanic/Latino; 39 Hispanic/Latino; 8 Two or more races, non-Hispanic/Latino), 13 international. Average age 28. 155 applicants, 83% accepted, 71 enrolled. *Faculty:* 4 full-time (2 women), 25 part-time/adjunct (13 women). Expenses: Contact institution. *Financial support:* In 2017–18, 6 students received support, including 6 research assistantships with full tuition reimbursements available (averaging $1,500 per year). Financial award application deadline: 4/1; financial award applicants required to submit FAFSA. In 2017, 87 master's, 3 doctorates awarded. *Program availability:* Part-time, evening/weekend. Offers accounting and taxation (MS); business administration (MBA); clinical psychology (MA); educational psychology (Ed D); forensic psychology (MS);

general psychology (MA, CAGS); management (CAGS); resort and casino management (MBA, CAGS). *Application deadline:* For fall admission, 8/15 for domestic and international students; for spring admission, 12/15 for domestic and international students. Applications are processed on a rolling basis. *Application fee:* $50. *Application Contact:* Kerry Barnes, Dean of Graduate Admissions, 413-205-3703, Fax: 413-205-3051, E-mail: kerry.barnes@aic.edu. *Dean,* Dr. Susanne Swanker, 413-205-3216, Fax: 413-205-3943, E-mail: susanne.swanker@aic.edu.

School of Education Students: 1,082 full-time (910 women), 143 part-time (113 women); includes 109 minority (19 Black or African American, non-Hispanic/Latino; 2 American Indian or Alaska Native, non-Hispanic/Latino; 10 Asian, non-Hispanic/Latino; 58 Hispanic/Latino; 1 Native Hawaiian or other Pacific Islander, non-Hispanic/Latino; 19 Two or more races, non-Hispanic/Latino). Average age 34. 537 applicants, 77% accepted, 327 enrolled. *Faculty:* 1 (woman) full-time, 151 part-time/adjunct (95 women). Expenses: Contact institution. *Financial support:* Applicants required to submit FAFSA. In 2017, 486 master's, 112 other advanced degrees awarded. *Program availability:* Evening/weekend. Offers early childhood education (M Ed, CAGS); education (MA, Ed D); elementary education (M Ed, CAGS); middle education/secondary education (M Ed, CAGS); moderate disabilities (M Ed, CAGS); reading specialist (M Ed, CAGS); school adjustment counseling (MAEP, CAGS); school guidance counseling (MAEP, CAGS); school leadership (M Ed, CAGS). *Application deadline:* Applications are processed on a rolling basis. *Application fee:* $50. Electronic applications accepted. *Application Contact:* Kerry Barnes, Dean of Graduate Admissions, 413-205-3703, Fax: 413-205-3051, E-mail: kerry.barnes@aic.edu. *Dean,* Sylvia Mason, 413-205-1743, Fax: 413-205-3943, E-mail: sylvia.mason@aic.edu.

Low Residency Programs Students: 117 full-time (90 women); includes 32 minority (22 Black or African American, non-Hispanic/Latino; 1 Asian, non-Hispanic/Latino; 7 Hispanic/Latino; 2 Two or more races, non-Hispanic/Latino). Average age 40. 35 applicants, 86% accepted, 20 enrolled. *Faculty:* 2 full-time (1 woman), 4 part-time/adjunct (all women). Expenses: Contact institution. In 2017, 8 master's, 12 doctorates awarded. *Program availability:* Evening/weekend. Offers counseling psychology (MA); educational leadership and supervision (Ed D); professional counseling and supervision (Ed D); teaching and learning (Ed D). *Application deadline:* For fall admission, 8/15 for domestic and international students; for spring admission, 1/3 for domestic and international students; for summer admission, 5/15 for domestic and international students. Applications are processed on a rolling basis. *Application fee:* $50. *Application Contact:* Kerry Barnes, Director of Graduate Admissions, 413-205-3703, Fax: 413-205-3051, E-mail: kerry.barnes@aic.edu. *Dean, Low Residency Programs,* Dr. Nicholas Young, 413-205-1726, E-mail: nicholas.young@aic.edu.

School of Health Sciences Students: 286 full-time (220 women), 11 part-time (9 women); includes 75 minority (30 Black or African American, non-Hispanic/Latino; 21 Asian, non-Hispanic/Latino; 19 Hispanic/Latino; 5 Two or more races, non-Hispanic/Latino), 2 international. Average age 27. 652 applicants, 49% accepted, 109 enrolled. *Faculty:* 14 full-time (13 women), 10 part-time/adjunct (all women). Expenses: Contact institution. In 2017, 48 master's, 28 doctorates, 2 other advanced degrees awarded. *Program availability:* Part-time, 100% online. Offers exercise science (MS); family nurse practitioner (MSN, Post-Master's Certificate); nursing administrator (MSN); nursing educator (MSN); occupational therapy (MSOT, OTD); physical therapy (DPT). *Application deadline:* For fall admission, 12/1 priority date for domestic and international students; for spring admission, 11/15 priority date for domestic and international students. *Application fee:* $50. Electronic applications accepted. *Application Contact:* Kerry Barnes, Director of Graduate Admissions, 413-205-3703, Fax: 413-205-3051, E-mail: kerry.barnes@aic.edu. *Dean,* Dr. Cesarina Thompson, 413-205-3056, Fax: 413-654-1430, E-mail: cesarina.thompson@aic.edu.

AMERICAN JEWISH UNIVERSITY, Bel Air, CA 90077-1599

General Information Independent-religious, coed, comprehensive institution. *Graduate housing:* Rooms and/or apartments available on a first-come, first-served basis to single and married students. Housing application deadline: 6/1.

GRADUATE UNITS

Graduate School of Education Offers education (MA Ed); education for working professionals (MA Ed).

Graduate School of Nonprofit Management *Program availability:* Part-time, evening/weekend. Offers general nonprofit administration (MBA); Jewish communal studies (MAJCS); Jewish nonprofit administration (MBA); nonprofit management (MAJCS, MBA).

Ziegler School of Rabbinic Studies Offers rabbinic studies (MARS).

AMERICAN MUSEUM OF NATURAL HISTORY–RICHARD GILDER GRADUATE SCHOOL, New York, NY 10024

General Information Independent, coed, graduate-only institution.

GRADUATE UNITS

Program in Comparative Biology Offers comparative biology (PhD).

AMERICAN NATIONAL UNIVERSITY, Salem, VA 24153

General Information Proprietary, coed, comprehensive institution.

GRADUATE UNITS

Program in Business Administration Offers business administration (MBA).

AMERICAN PUBLIC UNIVERSITY SYSTEM, Charles Town, WV 25414

General Information Proprietary, coed, comprehensive institution. CGS member. *Enrollment:* 46,420 graduate, professional, and undergraduate students; 455 full-time matriculated graduate/professional students (227 women), 7,939 part-time matriculated graduate/professional students (3,353 women). *Enrollment by degree level:* 8,078 master's, 315 other advanced degrees. *Tuition:* Full-time $6300; part-time $350 per credit. *Required fees:* $300; $50 per course. *Graduate housing:* On-campus housing not available. *Student services:* Career counseling, international student services, services for students with disabilities. *Library facilities:* APUS Online Library.

Computer facilities: Online class registration is available.
Website: http://www.apus.edu/

General Application Contact: Yoci Deal, Associate Vice President, Graduate and International Admissions, 877-468-6268, Fax: 304-724-3780, E-mail: info@apus.edu.

GRADUATE UNITS

AMU/APU Graduate Programs Students: 455 full-time (227 women), 7,939 part-time (3,353 women); includes 2,793 minority (1,429 Black or African American, non-Hispanic/Latino; 48 American Indian or Alaska Native, non-Hispanic/Latino; 205 Asian, non-Hispanic/Latino; 766 Hispanic/Latino; 62 Native Hawaiian or other Pacific Islander, non-Hispanic/Latino; 283 Two or more races, non-Hispanic/Latino), 101 international. Average age 37. Expenses: Contact institution. *Financial support:* Scholarships/grants available. Financial award applicants required to submit FAFSA. In 2017, 2,977 master's awarded. *Program availability:* Part-time, evening/weekend, online only, 100% online. Offers accounting (MS); applied business analytics (MS); business administration (MBA); criminal justice (MA); cybersecurity studies (MS); educational leadership (M Ed); environmental policy and management (MS); global security (DGS); health information management (MS); history (MA); information technology (MS); international relations and conflict resolution (MA); national security studies (MA); nursing (MSN); political science (MA); public policy (MPP); reverse logistics management (MA); space studies (MS); sports management (MS); strategic intelligence (DSI); teaching (M Ed); transportation and logistics management (MA). *Application deadline:* Applications are processed on a rolling basis. *Application fee:* $0. Electronic applications accepted. *Application Contact:* Yoci Deal, Associate Vice President, Graduate and International Admissions, 877-468-6268, Fax: 304-724-3764, E-mail: info@apus.edu. *President,* Dr. Wallace Boston, 877-468-6268, Fax: 304-728-2348, E-mail: president@apus.edu.

AMERICAN SENTINEL UNIVERSITY, Aurora, CO 80014

General Information Proprietary, coed, comprehensive institution.

GRADUATE UNITS

Graduate Programs *Program availability:* Part-time, evening/weekend, online learning. Electronic applications accepted.

AMERICAN UNIVERSITY, Washington, DC 20016-8001

General Information Independent-religious, coed, university. CGS member. *Enrollment:* 13,858 graduate, professional, and undergraduate students; 3,208 full-time matriculated graduate/professional students (2,022 women), 2,498 part-time matriculated graduate/professional students (1,477 women). *Enrollment by degree level:* 3,802 master's, 1,646 doctoral, 258 other advanced degrees. *Graduate faculty:* 808 full-time (398 women), 666 part-time/adjunct (284 women). *Tuition:* Full-time $29,556. *Required fees:* $690. Tuition and fees vary according to course load and program. *Graduate housing:* On-campus housing not available. *Student services:* Campus employment opportunities, campus safety program, career counseling, child daycare facilities, exercise/wellness program, free psychological counseling, grant writing training, international student services, multicultural affairs office, services for students with disabilities, teacher training, writing training. *Library facilities:* Bender Library plus 1 other. *Collection:* Books: 700,000 (physical), 800,000 (digital/electronic); Serial titles: 650 (physical), 145,000 (digital/electronic); Databases: 500. Study areas open 24 hours, 5–7 days a week; students can reserve study rooms.

Computer facilities: 700 computers available on campus for general student use. A campuswide network can be accessed from student residence rooms and from off campus. Online class registration, online e-support through learning management system are available.
Website: http://www.american.edu/

General Application Contact: Jonathan Tubman, Dean of Graduate Studies, 202-885-1000, E-mail: gradstudies@american.edu.

GRADUATE UNITS

College of Arts and Sciences Students: 544 full-time (363 women), 481 part-time (336 women); includes 248 minority (121 Black or African American, non-Hispanic/Latino; 2 American Indian or Alaska Native, non-Hispanic/Latino; 39 Asian, non-Hispanic/Latino; 62 Hispanic/Latino; 24 Two or more races, non-Hispanic/Latino), 111 international. Average age 31. 1,607 applicants, 62% accepted, 373 enrolled. *Faculty:* 385 full-time (212 women), 225 part-time/adjunct (121 women). Expenses: Contact institution. *Financial support:* Research assistantships, teaching assistantships, institutionally sponsored loans, scholarships/grants, and unspecified assistantships available. Financial award application deadline: 2/1; financial award applicants required to submit FAFSA. In 2017, 383 master's, 38 doctorates, 31 other advanced degrees awarded. *Program availability:* Part-time, evening/weekend, 100% online. Offers addiction and addictive behavior (Certificate); anthropology (PhD, Certificate); applied microeconomics (Certificate); applied statistics (Certificate); art history (MA); art management (MA); arts and sciences (MA, MAT, MFA, MS, PhD, Certificate, Graduate Certificate); audio production (Certificate); audio technology (MA); behavior, cognition, and neuroscience (PhD); biology (MS); biostatistics (MS); biotechnology (MA); chemistry (MS); clinical psychology (PhD); creative writing (MFA); data science (Certificate); economics (MA, PhD); environmental assessment (Graduate Certificate); environmental science (MS); ethics, peace, and global affairs (MA); gender analysis in economics (Certificate); health promotion management (MS); history (MA, PhD); international arts management (Certificate); international economic relations (Certificate); international economics (MA); literature (MA); mathematics (MA); nutrition education (MS, Certificate); philosophy (MA); professional science: environmental assessment (MS); professional science: quantitative analysis (MS); psychobiology of healing (Certificate); psychology (MA); public anthropology (MA); public sociology (Certificate); social research (Certificate); sociology (MA); Spanish: Latin American studies (MA); statistics (MS); studio art (MFA); teaching English as a foreign language (MA); teaching English to speakers of other languages (MA, Certificate); technology in arts management (Certificate); translation: French (Certificate); translation: Russian (Certificate); translation: Spanish (Certificate). *Application deadline:* Applications are processed on a rolling basis. *Application fee:* $55. Electronic applications accepted. *Application Contact:* Jonathan Harper, Assistant Director, Graduate Recruitment, 202-855-3622, E-mail: jharper@american.edu. *Dean,* Dr. Peter Starr, 202-885-2446, Fax: 202-885-2429, E-mail: pstarr@american.edu.

Critical Race, Gender, and Culture Studies Collaborative *Faculty:* 4 full-time (3 women), 10 part-time/adjunct (5 women). Expenses: Contact institution. In 2017, 3 Graduate Certificates awarded. Offers Asian studies (Graduate Certificate); women's, gender, and sexuality studies (Graduate Certificate). *Application deadline:* Applications are processed on a rolling basis. *Application Contact:* Jonathan Harper, Associate Director, Graduate Recruitment, 202-885-3622, Fax: 202-885-1505, E-mail: jharper@american.edu. *Dean,* Dr. Peter Starr, 202-885-2446, Fax: 202-885-2429, E-mail: pstarr@american.edu.

Kogod School of Business Students: 486 full-time (250 women), 427 part-time (197 women); includes 398 minority (201 Black or African American, non-Hispanic/Latino; 2 American Indian or Alaska Native, non-Hispanic/Latino; 68 Asian, non-Hispanic/Latino; 88 Hispanic/Latino; 2 Native Hawaiian or other Pacific Islander, non-Hispanic/Latino; 37 Two or more races, non-Hispanic/Latino), 116 international. Average age 31. 1,064 applicants, 81% accepted, 348 enrolled. *Faculty:* 73 full-time (26 women), 84 part-time/adjunct (36 women). Expenses: Contact institution. *Financial support:* Research assistantships, teaching assistantships, institutionally sponsored loans, scholarships/grants, and unspecified assistantships available. Financial award application deadline: 2/1; financial award applicants required to submit FAFSA. In 2017, 214 master's, 14 other advanced degrees awarded. *Program availability:* Part-time, evening/weekend, 100% online. Offers accounting (MS, Certificate); analytics (MS); business (MBA, MS, Certificate); business administration (MBA, Certificate); finance (MS, Certificate); marketing (MS); real estate (MS, Certificate); sustainability management (MS); taxation (MS, Certificate). *Application deadline:* For fall admission, 1/15 priority date for domestic students, 3/15 for international students; for winter admission, 10/15 priority date for domestic students, 10/15 for international students. Applications are processed on a rolling basis. *Application fee:* $100. Electronic applications accepted. *Application Contact:* Jason Garner, Director of Admissions, 202-885-1926, E-mail: jgarner@american.edu. *Dean*, John T. Delaney, 202-885-1908, Fax: 202-885-8044.

School of Communication Students: 188 full-time (117 women), 229 part-time (163 women); includes 144 minority (81 Black or African American, non-Hispanic/Latino; 2 American Indian or Alaska Native, non-Hispanic/Latino; 14 Asian, non-Hispanic/Latino; 35 Hispanic/Latino; 2 Native Hawaiian or other Pacific Islander, non-Hispanic/Latino; 10 Two or more races, non-Hispanic/Latino), 37 international. 955 applicants, 30% accepted, 139 enrolled. *Faculty:* 59 full-time (32 women), 33 part-time/adjunct (19 women). Expenses: Contact institution. *Financial support:* In 2017–18, 150 students received support, including 3 fellowships with partial tuition reimbursements available (averaging $20,000 per year), 46 research assistantships with partial tuition reimbursements available (averaging $10,000 per year), 45 teaching assistantships with partial tuition reimbursements available (averaging $10,000 per year); career-related internships or fieldwork, Federal Work-Study, institutionally sponsored loans, scholarships/grants, health care benefits, tuition waivers (partial), and unspecified assistantships also available. Support available to part-time students. Financial award application deadline: 2/1; financial award applicants required to submit FAFSA. In 2017, 137 master's, 2 doctorates awarded. *Program availability:* Part-time, evening/weekend, 100% online. Offers communication (MA, MFA, PhD); global media (MA). *Application deadline:* For fall admission, 2/1 priority date for domestic and international students; for spring admission, 11/1 for domestic and international students. Applications are processed on a rolling basis. *Application fee:* $55. Electronic applications accepted. *Application Contact:* Christine Rials, Assistant Director for Graduate Admissions, 202-885-2040, Fax: 202-885-2019, E-mail: gradcomm@american.edu. *Dean*, Dr. Jeffrey Rutenbeck, 202-885-2058, Fax: 202-885-2099, E-mail: jeff@american.edu.

Division of Communication Studies Students: 24 full-time (14 women); includes 5 minority (2 Black or African American, non-Hispanic/Latino; 3 Hispanic/Latino), 8 international. 136 applicants, 7% accepted, 6 enrolled. *Faculty:* 6 full-time (3 women), 2 part-time/adjunct (1 woman). Expenses: Contact institution. *Financial support:* In 2017–18, 5 students received support, including 15 research assistantships with full tuition reimbursements available (averaging $52,000 per year); scholarships/grants, health care benefits, and unspecified assistantships also available. Financial award application deadline: 12/15; financial award applicants required to submit FAFSA. In 2017, 3 doctorates awarded. Offers media industries and institutions (PhD); media, public issues, and engagement (PhD); media, technology, and culture (PhD). *Application deadline:* For fall admission, 12/15 priority date for domestic and international students. Applications are processed on a rolling basis. *Application fee:* $55. Electronic applications accepted. *Application Contact:* Leila Hernandez, Recruitment Coordinator, Graduate Programs, 202-885-2040, Fax: 202-885-2019, E-mail: leila@american.edu. *Division Director*, Prof. Kathryn Montgomery, 202-885-2680, Fax: 202-885-2099, E-mail: kcm@american.edu.

Division of Journalism Students: 30 full-time (20 women), 17 part-time (14 women); includes 31 minority (18 Black or African American, non-Hispanic/Latino; 3 Asian, non-Hispanic/Latino; 7 Hispanic/Latino; 3 Two or more races, non-Hispanic/Latino), 2 international. 277 applicants, 33% accepted, 39 enrolled. *Faculty:* 14 full-time (7 women), 4 part-time/adjunct (3 women). Expenses: Contact institution. *Financial support:* In 2017–18, 37 students received support, including 3 fellowships with tuition reimbursements available (averaging $27,000 per year), 6 research assistantships with partial tuition reimbursements available (averaging $10,000 per year), 5 teaching assistantships with partial tuition reimbursements available (averaging $10,000 per year); career-related internships or fieldwork, Federal Work-Study, institutionally sponsored loans, scholarships/grants, tuition waivers (partial), and unspecified assistantships also available. Financial award application deadline: 2/1; financial award applicants required to submit FAFSA. In 2017, 36 master's awarded. *Program availability:* Part-time, evening/weekend. Offers broadcast journalism (MA); international journalism (MA); investigative journalism (MA); journalism and digital storytelling (MA). *Application deadline:* For fall admission, 2/1 priority date for domestic and international students. Applications are processed on a rolling basis. *Application fee:* $55. Electronic applications accepted. *Application Contact:* Christine Rials, Assistant Director for Graduate Admissions, 202-885-2040, Fax: 202-885-2019, E-mail: crials@american.edu. *Division Director*, Prof. Amy Eisman, 202-885-2106, E-mail: aeisman@american.edu.

Division of Public Communication Students: 52 full-time (42 women), 34 part-time (20 women); includes 31 minority (19 Black or African American, non-Hispanic/Latino; 4 Asian, non-Hispanic/Latino; 7 Hispanic/Latino; 1 Two or more races, non-Hispanic/Latino), 6 international. 282 applicants, 38% accepted, 55 enrolled. *Faculty:* 23 full-time (15 women), 18 part-time/adjunct (10 women). Expenses: Contact institution. *Financial support:* In 2017–18, 45 students received support, including 11 research assistantships with partial tuition reimbursements available (averaging $13,000 per year), 15 teaching assistantships with partial tuition reimbursements available (averaging $13,000 per year); career-related internships or fieldwork, Federal Work-Study, institutionally sponsored loans, scholarships/grants, tuition waivers (partial), and unspecified assistantships also available. Financial award application deadline: 2/1; financial award applicants required to submit FAFSA. In 2017, 105 master's awarded. *Program availability:* Part-time, evening/weekend. Offers advocacy and social impact (MA); corporate communication and reputation management (MA); digital strategies and analytics (MA); poltical communication (MA); strategic communication (MA). *Application deadline:* For fall admission, 2/1 priority date for domestic and international students. Applications are processed on a rolling basis. *Application fee:* $50. Electronic applications accepted. *Application Contact:* Christine Rials, Assistant Director of Graduate Admissions, 202-885-2040, Fax: 202-885-2019, E-mail: gradcomm@american.edu. *Public Communication Division Director*, Pallavi Kumar, 202-885-2047, E-mail: kumar@american.edu.

Film and Media Arts Division Students: 57 full-time (32 women), 75 part-time (32 women); includes 71 minority (42 Black or African American, non-Hispanic/Latino; 8 Asian, non-Hispanic/Latino; 16 Hispanic/Latino; 5 Two or more races, non-Hispanic/Latino), 7 international. 258 applicants, 29% accepted, 41 enrolled. *Faculty:* 16 full-time (6 women), 9 part-time/adjunct (5 women). Expenses: Contact institution. *Financial support:* In 2017–18, 58 students received support, including 35 teaching assistantships with partial tuition reimbursements available (averaging $10,000 per year); career-related internships or fieldwork, Federal Work-Study, institutionally sponsored loans, scholarships/grants, tuition waivers (partial), and unspecified assistantships also available. Support available to part-time students. Financial award application deadline: 2/1; financial award applicants required to submit FAFSA. In 2017, 71 master's awarded. *Program availability:* Part-time, evening/weekend. Offers art in entertainment (MFA); environmental and wildlife filmmaking (MFA); film and media arts (MFA); game design (MA); games and interactive media (MFA); games and interactivity (MFA); political, cultural, and social impact (MFA); producing film, television and video (MA). *Application deadline:* For fall admission, 2/1 priority date for domestic and international students. Applications are processed on a rolling basis. *Application fee:* $50. Electronic applications accepted. *Application Contact:* Leila Hernandez, Recruitment Coordinator, Graduate Programs, 202-885-2040, Fax: 202-885-2019, E-mail: leila@american.edu. *Director, Film and Media Arts Division*, Prof. Brigid Maher, 202-885-2664, Fax: 202-885-2019, E-mail: bmaher@american.edu.

School of Education Students: 58 full-time (48 women), 122 part-time (94 women); includes 78 minority (53 Black or African American, non-Hispanic/Latino; 8 Asian, non-Hispanic/Latino; 13 Hispanic/Latino; 4 Two or more races, non-Hispanic/Latino), 2 international. Average age 29. 213 applicants, 99% accepted, 180 enrolled. *Faculty:* 14 full-time (11 women), 56 part-time/adjunct (37 women). Expenses: Contact institution. *Financial support:* Research assistantships, teaching assistantships, institutionally sponsored loans, scholarships/grants, and unspecified assistantships available. Financial award application deadline: 2/1; financial award applicants required to submit FAFSA. In 2017, 101 master's, 6 other advanced degrees awarded. *Program availability:* Part-time, evening/weekend. Offers education (M Ed, MA, MAT, Certificate). *Application deadline:* For fall admission, 2/1 priority date for domestic students. Applications are processed on a rolling basis. *Application fee:* $55. Electronic applications accepted. *Application Contact:* Graziella Covello, Graduate Program Coordinator, 202-885-3761, E-mail: gcovello@american.edu. *Dean*, Cheryl Holcomb-McCoy, 202-885-3720, E-mail: educate@american.edu.

School of International Service Students: 495 full-time (333 women), 518 part-time (276 women); includes 360 minority (95 Black or African American, non-Hispanic/Latino; 2 American Indian or Alaska Native, non-Hispanic/Latino; 60 Asian, non-Hispanic/Latino; 164 Hispanic/Latino; 39 Two or more races, non-Hispanic/Latino), 98 international. Average age 30. 1,559 applicants, 81% accepted, 356 enrolled. *Faculty:* 112 full-time (50 women), 46 part-time/adjunct (19 women). Expenses: Contact institution. *Financial support:* Research assistantships, teaching assistantships, institutionally sponsored loans, scholarships/grants, and unspecified assistantships available. Financial award application deadline: 1/15; financial award applicants required to submit FAFSA. In 2017, 427 master's, 9 doctorates, 5 other advanced degrees awarded. *Program availability:* Part-time, evening/weekend, 100% online. Offers comparative and regional studies (Certificate); cross-cultural communication (Certificate); development management (MS); ethics, peace, and global affairs (MA); European studies (Certificate); global environmental policy (MA, Certificate); global information technology (Certificate); global media (MA); international affairs (MA); international arts management (Certificate); international communication (MA, Certificate); international development (MA); international economic policy (Certificate); international economic relations (Certificate); international economics (MA); international peace and conflict resolution (MA, Certificate); international politics (Certificate); international relations (MA, PhD); international service (MIS); peacebuilding (Certificate); social enterprise (MA); the Americas (Certificate); United States foreign policy (Certificate). *Application deadline:* For fall admission, 1/15 for domestic students, 1/1 for international students; for spring admission, 10/1 for domestic students, 9/15 for international students. *Application fee:* $55. Electronic applications accepted. *Application Contact:* 202-885-1646, Fax: 202-885-1109, E-mail: sisgrad@american.edu.

School of Professional and Extended Studies Students: 17 full-time (8 women), 59 part-time (34 women); includes 9 minority (5 Black or African American, non-Hispanic/Latino; 2 Asian, non-Hispanic/Latino; 1 Hispanic/Latino; 1 Two or more races, non-Hispanic/Latino), 5 international. Average age 31. 55 applicants, 89% accepted, 38 enrolled. *Faculty:* 27 full-time (13 women), 21 part-time/adjunct (10 women). Expenses: Contact institution. *Financial support:* Applicants required to submit FAFSA. In 2017, 8 other advanced degrees awarded. *Program availability:* Part-time, evening/weekend, 100% online. Offers agile project management (MS); healthcare management (MS, Graduate Certificate); human resource analytics and management (MS, Graduate Certificate); instructional design and learning analytics (MS); measurement and evaluation (MS); project monitoring and evaluation (Graduate Certificate); sports analytics and management (MS, Graduate Certificate). *Application deadline:* Applications are processed on a rolling basis. *Application fee:* $55. Electronic applications accepted. *Application Contact:* Emily Aronoff, Assistant Director for Recruitment and Admission, 202-895-4953, E-mail: aronoff@american.edu. *Dean*, Carola Weil, 202-885-5990, Fax: 202-895-4960, E-mail: weil@american.edu.

School of Public Affairs Students: 357 full-time (212 women), 359 part-time (230 women); includes 181 minority (103 Black or African American, non-Hispanic/Latino; 4 American Indian or Alaska Native, non-Hispanic/Latino; 35 Asian, non-Hispanic/Latino; 27 Hispanic/Latino; 12 Two or more races, non-Hispanic/Latino), 46 international. Average age 30. 958 applicants, 80% accepted, 309 enrolled. *Faculty:* 88 full-time (35 women), 94 part-time/adjunct (30 women). Expenses: Contact institution. *Financial support:* Research assistantships, teaching assistantships, institutionally sponsored loans, and scholarships/grants available. Financial award application deadline: 2/1; financial award applicants required to submit FAFSA. In 2017, 228 master's, 18 doctorates, 19 other advanced degrees awarded. *Program availability:* Part-time, evening/weekend, 100% online. Offers justice, law and criminology (MS, PhD); organization development (MSOD, Certificate); political communication (MA); political science (MA, PhD); public administration (MPA, PhD, Certificate); public administration and policy (MPAP); public affairs (MA, MPA, MPAP, MPP, MS, MSOD, PhD, Certificate); public policy (MPP); public policy (Certificate); terrorism, homeland security and policy (MS); women, policy and political leadership (Certificate). *Application deadline:* For fall admission, 2/15 priority date for domestic students, 5/1 for international students; for spring admission, 11/1 priority date for domestic students, 9/15 for international students. *Application fee:* $55. Electronic applications accepted. *Application Contact:* Jennifer Forney, Assistant Dean, Graduate Enrollment, 202-885-6248, E-mail: forney@american.edu. *Dean*, Dr. Vicky Wilkins, 202-885-6443, E-mail: vwilkins@american.edu.

Washington College of Law Students: 1,034 full-time (697 women), 373 part-time (216 women); includes 523 minority (117 Black or African American, non-Hispanic/Latino; 1 American Indian or Alaska Native, non-Hispanic/Latino; 107 Asian, non-Hispanic/Latino; 234 Hispanic/Latino; 1 Native Hawaiian or other Pacific Islander, non-Hispanic/Latino; 63 Two or more races, non-Hispanic/Latino), 122 international. Average age 28. 5,138 applicants, 58% accepted, 550 enrolled. *Faculty:* 64 full-time (32 women), 134 part-time/adjunct (45 women). Expenses: Contact institution. *Financial support:* Institutionally sponsored loans and scholarships/grants available. Financial award application deadline: 3/1; financial award applicants required to submit FAFSA. In 2017, 95 master's, 374 doctorates awarded. *Program availability:* Part-time, evening/weekend.

Offers law (LL M, JD, SJD). *Application fee:* $70. Electronic applications accepted. *Application Contact:* Meghan Walter, Associate Director, Graduate Admissions, 202-274-4114, Fax: 202-274-4107, E-mail: mwalter@wcl.american.edu. *Dean*, Camille A. Nelson, 202-274-4004, Fax: 202-274-4005, E-mail: canelson@wcl.american.edu.

AMERICAN UNIVERSITY IN BULGARIA, Blagoevgrad 2700, Bulgaria

General Information Independent, coed, comprehensive institution.

GRADUATE UNITS

Executive MBA Program Offers business administration (EMBA).

THE AMERICAN UNIVERSITY IN CAIRO, 11835 New Cairo, Egypt

General Information Independent, coed, comprehensive institution. CGS member. *Enrollment:* 6,570 graduate, professional, and undergraduate students; 242 full-time matriculated graduate/professional students (152 women), 737 part-time matriculated graduate/professional students (475 women). *Enrollment by degree level:* 934 master's, 45 doctoral. *Graduate faculty:* 171 full-time (65 women), 31 part-time/adjunct (9 women). *Graduate housing:* Room and/or apartments available on a first-come, first-served basis to single students; on-campus housing not available to married students. *Student services:* Campus employment opportunities, campus safety program, career counseling, child daycare facilities, exercise/wellness program, free psychological counseling, grant writing training, international student services, low-cost health insurance, multicultural affairs office, services for students with disabilities, teacher training, writing training. *Library facilities:* American University in Cairo Library plus 1 other. *Collection:* Books: 546,020 (physical), 311,887 (digital/electronic); Databases: 123. Weekly public service hours: 80; students can reserve study rooms.

Computer facilities: 120 computers available on campus for general student use. A campuswide network can be accessed from student residence rooms and from off campus. Online class registration, learning management system, unofficial transcripts, ID creation are available.
Website: http://www.aucegypt.edu/

General Application Contact: Maha Hegazi, Director for Graduate Admissions, 20-2-2615-1462, E-mail: mahahegazi@aucegypt.edu.

GRADUATE UNITS

Graduate School of Education Students: 6 full-time (4 women), 77 part-time (65 women). Average age 33. 40 applicants, 48% accepted, 11 enrolled. *Faculty:* 9 full-time (6 women). Expenses: Contact institution. *Financial support:* Fellowships with partial tuition reimbursements, teaching assistantships, career-related internships or fieldwork, scholarships/grants, tuition waivers (partial), and unspecified assistantships available. Financial award application deadline: 3/10. In 2017, 24 master's awarded. *Program availability:* Part-time, evening/weekend. Offers educational leadership (MA); international and comparative education (MA). *Application deadline:* For fall admission, 2/1 priority date for domestic and international students; for spring admission, 10/15 priority date for domestic and international students. Applications are processed on a rolling basis. *Application fee:* $85. Electronic applications accepted. *Application Contact:* Maha Hegazi, Director for Graduate Admissions, 20-2-2615-1462, E-mail: mahahegazi@aucegypt.edu. *Dean*, Dr. Ted Purinton, 20-2-2615-1490, E-mail: tedpurinton@aucegypt.edu.

School of Business Students: 49 full-time (25 women), 67 part-time (38 women), 5 international. Average age 29. 112 applicants, 35% accepted, 26 enrolled. *Faculty:* 30 full-time (10 women), 8 part-time/adjunct (3 women). Expenses: Contact institution. *Financial support:* Fellowships with partial tuition reimbursements, scholarships/grants, tuition waivers (partial), and unspecified assistantships available. Financial award application deadline: 3/10. In 2017, 51 master's awarded. *Program availability:* Part-time, evening/weekend. Offers business administration (MBA); economics (MA); economics in international development (MA, Diploma); finance (MS). *Application deadline:* For fall admission, 2/1 priority date for domestic and international students; for spring admission, 10/15 priority date for domestic and international students. Applications are processed on a rolling basis. *Application fee:* $85. Electronic applications accepted. *Application Contact:* Maha Hegazi, Director of Graduate Admissions, 20-2-2615-1462, E-mail: mahahegazi@aucegypt.edu. *Dean*, Dr. Sherif Kamel, 20-2-2615-2118, E-mail: skamel@aucegypt.edu.

School of Global Affairs and Public Policy Students: 65 full-time (50 women), 201 part-time (136 women), 39 international. Average age 29. 357 applicants, 51% accepted, 72 enrolled. *Faculty:* 26 full-time (11 women), 4 part-time/adjunct (3 women). Expenses: Contact institution. *Financial support:* Fellowships with partial tuition reimbursements, scholarships/grants, and unspecified assistantships available. Financial award application deadline: 3/10. In 2017, 94 master's awarded. *Program availability:* Part-time, evening/weekend. Offers gender and women's studies (MA); global affairs (MGA); international and comparative law (LL M); international human rights law (MA); journalism and mass communication (MA); Middle East studies (MA); migration and refugee studies (MA, Diploma); public administration (MPA); public policy (MPP); television and digital journalism (MA). *Application deadline:* For fall admission, 2/1 for domestic and international students; for spring admission, 10/15 for domestic and international students. Applications are processed on a rolling basis. *Application fee:* $85. Electronic applications accepted. *Application Contact:* Maha Hegazi, Director for Graduate Admissions, 20-2-2615-1462, E-mail: mahahegazi@aucegypt.edu. *Dean*, Dr. Nabil Fahmy, 20-2-2615-2671, E-mail: nfahmy@aucegypt.edu.

School of Humanities and Social Sciences Students: 52 full-time (41 women), 159 part-time (119 women), 38 international. Average age 31. 209 applicants, 36% accepted, 39 enrolled. *Faculty:* 52 full-time (27 women), 7 part-time/adjunct (3 women). Expenses: Contact institution. *Financial support:* Fellowships with partial tuition reimbursements, scholarships/grants, tuition waivers (partial), and unspecified assistantships available. Financial award application deadline: 3/10. In 2017, 73 master's awarded. *Program availability:* Part-time, evening/weekend. Offers Arab and Islamic civilizations (Graduate Diploma); Arabic studies (MA); comparative literary studies (Graduate Diploma); Egyptology and Coptology (MA); English and comparative literature (MA); humanities and social sciences (Graduate Diploma); philosophy (MA); psychology (MA); sociology and anthropology (MA); teaching Arabic as a foreign language (MA); teaching English to speakers of other languages (MA). *Application deadline:* For fall admission, 2/1 priority date for domestic and international students; for spring admission, 10/15 priority date for domestic and international students. Applications are processed on a rolling basis. *Application fee:* $85. Electronic applications accepted. *Application Contact:* Maha Hegazi, Director for Graduate Admissions, 20-2-2615-1462, E-mail: mahahegazi@aucegypt.edu. *Interim Dean*, Dr. Robert Switzer, 20-2-2615-1068, E-mail: nbowditch@aucegypt.edu.

School of Sciences and Engineering Students: 62 full-time (26 women), 210 part-time (104 women), 14 international. Average age 28. 252 applicants, 39% accepted, 51 enrolled. *Faculty:* 53 full-time (8 women), 12 part-time/adjunct (0 women). Expenses: Contact institution. *Financial support:* Fellowships with partial tuition reimbursements, scholarships/grants, and unspecified assistantships available. Financial award application deadline: 3/10. In 2017, 71 master's, 10 doctorates awarded. *Program availability:* Part-time, evening/weekend. Offers biotechnology (MS); chemistry (MS); computer science (MS); computing (M Comp); construction engineering (M Eng, MS); electronics and communications engineering (M Eng); environmental engineering (MS); environmental system design (M Eng); mechanical engineering (M Eng, MS); nanotechnology (MS); physics (MS); robotics, control and smart systems (MS); sciences and engineering (PhD); sustainable development (MS, Graduate Diploma). *Application deadline:* For fall admission, 2/1 priority date for domestic and international students; for spring admission, 10/15 priority date for domestic and international students. Applications are processed on a rolling basis. *Application fee:* $85. Electronic applications accepted. *Application Contact:* Maha Hegazi, Director for Graduate Admissions, 20-2-2615-1462, E-mail: mahahegazi@aucegypt.edu. *Dean*, Dr. Hassan El Fawal, 20-2-2615-2926, E-mail: hassan.elfawal@aucegypt.edu.

THE AMERICAN UNIVERSITY IN DUBAI, Dubai, United Arab Emirates

General Information Proprietary, coed, comprehensive institution. *Graduate housing:* Room and/or apartments available on a first-come, first-served basis to single students; on-campus housing not available to married students. Housing application deadline: 7/31.

GRADUATE UNITS

Graduate Programs *Program availability:* Part-time, evening/weekend. Offers construction management (MS); education (M Ed); finance (MBA); generalist (MBA); marketing (MBA). Electronic applications accepted.

AMERICAN UNIVERSITY OF ARMENIA, Yerevan 3750198, Armenia

General Information Independent, coed, graduate-only institution. *Research affiliation:* Samsung (cryptography), Volkswagen Foundation (cryptography), Mentor Graphics (data compression algorithms), IBM (big data and data analytics), Johns Hopkins University Bloomberg School of Public Health (public health), Institut de Medecine Sociale et Preventive, Universite de Genève (Geneva, Switzerland) (tobacco control/health education).

GRADUATE UNITS

Graduate Programs *Program availability:* Part-time, evening/weekend. Offers business administration (MBA); computer and information science (MS); economics (MS); industrial engineering and systems management (ME); law (LL M); political science and international affairs (MPSIA); public health (MPH); teaching English as a foreign language (MA).

AMERICAN UNIVERSITY OF BEIRUT, 107 2020 Beirut, Lebanon

General Information Independent, coed, university. CGS member. *Enrollment:* 9,143 graduate, professional, and undergraduate students; 1,184 full-time matriculated graduate/professional students (691 women), 733 part-time matriculated graduate/professional students (499 women). *Enrollment by degree level:* 1,349 master's, 153 doctoral, 415 other advanced degrees. *Graduate faculty:* 567 full-time (194 women), 25 part-time/adjunct (10 women). *Tuition:* Full-time $17,244; part-time $958 per credit. *Required fees:* $740. Tuition and fees vary according to course load and program. *Graduate housing:* Room and/or apartments available on a first-come, first-served basis to single students; on-campus housing not available to married students. Typical cost: $2900 per year. Housing application deadline: 6/30. *Student services:* Campus employment opportunities, campus safety program, career counseling, exercise/wellness program, free psychological counseling, grant writing training, international student services, low-cost health insurance, services for students with disabilities, teacher training, writing training. *Library facilities:* Jafet Library plus 3 others. *Collection:* Books: 400,000 (physical), 1.6 million (digital/electronic); Serial titles: 190,000 (digital/electronic); Databases: 350. Weekly public service hours: 107; study areas open 24 hours, 5–7 days a week; students can reserve study rooms. *Research affiliation:* Qatar University (history and archeology), Ford Foundation (health promotion and community health), The University of Texas MD Anderson Cancer Center (medicine), Tech Hub s.a.l. (electrical and computer engineering), Open Society Foundations (public policy), UN Children's Fund (UNICEF) (nutrition and food sciences).

Computer facilities: 1,600 computers available on campus for general student use. A campuswide network can be accessed from student residence rooms and from off campus. Online class registration is available.
Website: http://www.aub.edu.lb/

General Application Contact: Dr. Salim Kanaan, Director, Admissions Office, 961-1-350000 Ext. 2594, Fax: 961-1-750775, E-mail: sk00@aub.edu.lb.

GRADUATE UNITS

Graduate Programs Students: 1,184 full-time (691 women), 733 part-time (499 women). Average age 26. 2,489 applicants, 47% accepted, 541 enrolled. *Faculty:* 567 full-time (194 women), 25 part-time/adjunct (10 women). Expenses: Contact institution. *Financial support:* In 2017–18, 426 students received support, including 1,302 research assistantships (averaging $6,191 per year); career-related internships or fieldwork, institutionally sponsored loans, scholarships/grants, health care benefits, and unspecified assistantships also available. Financial award application deadline: 12/20; financial award applicants required to submit CSS PROFILE. In 2017, 402 master's, 111 doctorates awarded. *Program availability:* Part-time, evening/weekend. *Application deadline:* For fall admission, 2/10 priority date for domestic and international students; for spring admission, 11/1 for domestic and international students; for summer admission, 2/10 for domestic and international students. *Application fee:* $50. Electronic applications accepted. *Application Contact:* Dr. Salim Kanaan, Director, Admissions Office, 961-1-350000 Ext. 2594, Fax: 961-1-750775, E-mail: sk00@aub.edu.lb. *Graduate Council Chairperson*, Prof. Zaher Dawy, 961-1-374374 Ext. 4386, E-mail: zd03@aub.edu.lb.

Faculty of Agricultural and Food Sciences Students: 76 full-time (58 women), 19 part-time (13 women); includes 6 minority (all Black or African American, non-Hispanic/Latino). Average age 25. 142 applicants, 72% accepted, 32 enrolled. *Faculty:* 16 full-time (4 women), 1 part-time/adjunct (0 women). Expenses: Contact institution. *Financial support:* In 2017–18, 9 research assistantships with partial tuition reimbursements (averaging $1,800 per year), 47 teaching assistantships with full and partial tuition reimbursements (averaging $1,400 per year) were awarded; scholarships/grants, health care benefits, and unspecified assistantships also available. Financial award application deadline: 2/2. In 2017, 20 master's awarded. *Program availability:* Part-time. Offers agricultural economics (MS); animal science (MS); ecosystem management (MSES); food safety (MS); food security (MS); food technology (MS); irrigation (MS); nutrition (MS); plant protection (MS); plant science (MS); poultry science (MS); public health nutrition (MS); rural community development

(MS). *Application deadline:* For fall admission, 2/10 for domestic and international students; for spring admission, 11/2 for domestic and international students. *Application fee:* $50. Electronic applications accepted. *Application Contact:* Prof. Zaher Dawy, Graduate Council Chairperson, 961-1-374374 Ext. 4386, Fax: 961-1-374376, E-mail: graduate.council@aub.edu.lb. *Dean of Faculty of Agricultural and Food Sciences*, Rabi Hassan Mohtar, 961-1-350000 Ext. 4400, Fax: 961-1-744460, E-mail: mohtar@aub.edu.lb.

Faculty of Arts and Sciences Students: 251 full-time (180 women), 233 part-time (172 women). Average age 26. 425 applicants, 65% accepted, 121 enrolled. *Faculty:* 108 full-time (36 women), 5 part-time/adjunct (4 women). Expenses: Contact institution. *Financial support:* In 2017–18, 29 fellowships, 40 research assistantships were awarded; teaching assistantships, scholarships/grants, tuition waivers (full and partial), and unspecified assistantships also available. Financial award application deadline: 4/4. In 2017, 47 master's, 2 doctorates awarded. *Program availability:* Part-time. *Application deadline:* For fall admission, 2/8 for domestic students; for spring admission, 11/3 for domestic students. *Application fee:* $50. Electronic applications accepted. *Application Contact:* Rima Rassi, Graduate Studies Officer, 961-1-350000 Ext. 3833, Fax: 961-1-744461, E-mail: rr46@aub.edu.lb. *Dean, Faculty of Arts and Sciences*, Dr. Nadia Maria El Cheikh, 961-1-374374 Ext. 3800, Fax: 961-1-744461, E-mail: nmcheikh@aub.edu.lb.

Faculty of Health Sciences Students: 75 full-time (60 women), 78 part-time (67 women). Average age 27. 274 applicants, 56% accepted, 47 enrolled. *Faculty:* 33 full-time (22 women), 5 part-time/adjunct (2 women). Expenses: Contact institution. *Financial support:* In 2017–18, 75 students received support. Scholarships/grants, health care benefits, and unspecified assistantships available. Financial award application deadline: 4/4. In 2017, 63 master's awarded. *Program availability:* Part-time. Offers environmental sciences (MS); epidemiology (MS, PhD); epidemiology and biostatistics (MPH); health care leadership (EMHCL); health management and policy (MPH); health promotion and community health (MPH); health research (MS); public health nutrition (MS). *Application deadline:* For fall admission, 4/4 for domestic and international students; for spring admission, 11/3 for domestic and international students. *Application fee:* $50. Electronic applications accepted. *Application Contact:* Mitra Tauk, Administrative Coordinator, 961-1-350000 Ext. 4687, E-mail: mt12@aub.edu.lb. *Dean/Professor*, Prof. Iman Adel Nuwayhid, 961-1-759683 Ext. 4600, Fax: 961-1-744470, E-mail: nuwayhid@aub.edu.lb.

Faculty of Medicine Students: 513 full-time (274 women). Average age 23. 527 applicants, 47% accepted, 169 enrolled. *Faculty:* 335 full-time (117 women), 54 part-time/adjunct (5 women). Expenses: Contact institution. *Financial support:* In 2017–18, 302 students received support. Fellowships, research assistantships, teaching assistantships, institutionally sponsored loans, scholarships/grants, tuition waivers, and unspecified assistantships available. In 2017, 18 master's, 98 doctorates awarded. *Program availability:* Part-time. Offers biochemistry (MS); biomedical engineering (MS); biomedical sciences (PhD); health research (MS); human morphology (MS); medicine (MD); microbiology and immunology (MS); neuroscience (MS); orthodontics (clinical) (MS); pharmacology and therapeutics (MS); physiology (MS). *Application deadline:* Applications are processed on a rolling basis. *Application fee:* $75. Electronic applications accepted. *Application Contact:* Dr. Salim Kanaan, Director, Admission's Office, 961-1-350000 Ext. 2594, Fax: 961-1-750775, E-mail: sk00@aub.edu.lb. *Dean*, Dr. Mohamed Sayegh, 961-1-135000 Ext. 4700, Fax: 961-1-744489, E-mail: msayegh@aub.edu.lb.

Maroun Semaan Faculty of Engineering and Architecture Students: 337 full-time (176 women), 114 part-time (42 women). Average age 26. 502 applicants, 65% accepted, 118 enrolled. *Faculty:* 98 full-time (21 women), 88 part-time/adjunct (27 women). Expenses: Contact institution. *Financial support:* In 2017–18, 26 students received support, including 92 fellowships with full tuition reimbursements available (averaging $14,400 per year), 65 research assistantships with full and partial tuition reimbursements available (averaging $5,000 per year), 129 teaching assistantships with full and partial tuition reimbursements available (averaging $1,326 per year); scholarships/grants, tuition waivers (full and partial), and unspecified assistantships also available. Financial award application deadline: 4/2. In 2017, 71 master's, 16 doctorates awarded. *Program availability:* Part-time, 100% online. Offers applied energy (ME); civil engineering (PhD); electrical and computer engineering (PhD); energy studies (MS); engineering management (MEM); environmental and water resources (ME); environmental technology (MSES); mechanical engineering (ME, PhD); urban design (MUD); urban planning and policy (MUPP). *Application deadline:* For fall admission, 4/4 for domestic and international students; for spring admission, 11/3 for domestic and international students; for summer admission, 4/4 for domestic and international students. Applications are processed on a rolling basis. *Application fee:* $50. Electronic applications accepted. *Application Contact:* Dr. Salim Kanaan, Director, Admissions Office, 961-1-374374 Ext. 2590, Fax: 961-1-750775, E-mail: sk00@aub.edu.lb. *Dean*, Prof. Alan Shihade, 961-1-374374 Ext. 3400, Fax: 961-1-744462, E-mail: as20@aub.edu.lb.

Rafic Hariri School of Nursing Students: 4 full-time (3 women), 40 part-time (34 women). Average age 28. 32 applicants, 81% accepted, 9 enrolled. *Faculty:* 13 full-time (12 women), 23 part-time/adjunct (18 women). Expenses: Contact institution. *Financial support:* In 2017–18, 7 students received support. Teaching assistantships, scholarships/grants, traineeships, and unspecified assistantships available. Financial award application deadline: 12/20. In 2017, 18 master's awarded. Offers adult gerontology clinical nurse specialist (MSN); community and public health nursing (MSN); nursing administration and management (MSN); psychiatric mental health clinical nurse specialist (MSN). *Application deadline:* For fall admission, 4/4 for domestic students. Applications are processed on a rolling basis. *Application fee:* $50. Electronic applications accepted. *Application Contact:* Nisreen Ghalayini, Administrative Assistant, 961-1-350000 Ext. 5951, E-mail: ng28@aub.edu.lb. *Director of the Hariri School of Nursing*, Dr. Huda Abu-Saad Huijer, 961-1-350000 Ext. 5953, Fax: 961-1-744476, E-mail: hh35@aub.edu.lb.

Suliman S. Olayan School of Business Students: 50 full-time (25 women), 27 part-time (18 women). Average age 26. 271 applicants, 58% accepted, 77 enrolled. *Faculty:* 23 full-time (7 women), 6 part-time/adjunct (1 woman). Expenses: Contact institution. *Financial support:* In 2017–18, 33 research assistantships with full tuition reimbursements (averaging $21,000 per year) were awarded; fellowships, teaching assistantships, scholarships/grants, health care benefits, tuition waivers, and unspecified assistantships also available. Financial award application deadline: 4/4. In 2017, 57 master's awarded. *Program availability:* Part-time, online learning. Offers business (M Fin, MBA, MHRM); business administration (MBA); finance (M Fin); human resource management (MHRM). *Application deadline:* For fall admission, 2/8 for domestic students; for spring admission, 4/4 for domestic students. *Application fee:* $50. Electronic applications accepted. *Dean*, Dr. Steve Harvey, 961-1-350000 Ext. 3934, E-mail: sh146@aub.edu.lb.

AMERICAN UNIVERSITY OF HEALTH SCIENCES, Signal Hill, CA 90755

General Information Proprietary, coed, comprehensive institution.

GRADUATE UNITS

School of Clinical Research Offers clinical research (MSCR).

THE AMERICAN UNIVERSITY OF PARIS, 75007 Paris, France

General Information Independent, coed, comprehensive institution. *Graduate housing:* Room and/or apartments available on a first-come, first-served basis to single students; on-campus housing not available to married students.

GRADUATE UNITS

Graduate Programs Offers cross-cultural and sustainable business management (MA); cultural translation (MA); global communications (MA); global communications and civil society (MA); international affairs (MA); international affairs, conflict resolution and civil society development (MA); Middle East and Islamic studies (MA); Middle East and Islamic studies and international affairs (MA); public policy and international affairs (MA); public policy and international law (MA). Electronic applications accepted.

AMERICAN UNIVERSITY OF PUERTO RICO, Bayamon, PR 00960-2037

General Information Independent, coed, comprehensive institution. *Enrollment:* 23 full-time matriculated graduate/professional students (18 women), 61 part-time matriculated graduate/professional students (45 women). *Enrollment by degree level:* 41 master's. *Graduate faculty:* 21 part-time/adjunct (8 women). Tuition and fees vary according to course load and degree level. *Graduate housing:* On-campus housing not available. *Student services:* Services for students with disabilities. *Library facilities:* Loida Figueroa Meacado.

Computer facilities: 359 computers available on campus for general student use. A campuswide network can be accessed.
Website: http://www.aupr.edu/

General Application Contact: Dr. Jose Ramirez-Figueroa, Vice President for Academic and Student Affairs, 787-620-2040 Ext. 2010, Fax: 787-620-2958, E-mail: jramirez@aupr.edu.

GRADUATE UNITS

Program in Criminal Justice Students: 1 full-time (0 women), 8 part-time (3 women); all minorities (all Hispanic/Latino). Average age 32. 2 applicants, 100% accepted, 2 enrolled. *Faculty:* 4 part-time/adjunct (1 woman). Expenses: Contact institution. *Financial support:* In 2017–18, 8 students received support, including 9 fellowships (averaging $500 per year). Financial award applicants required to submit FAFSA. In 2017, 2 master's awarded. *Program availability:* Part-time, evening/weekend. Offers criminal justice (MA). *Application deadline:* For fall admission, 8/1 for domestic students; for winter admission, 10/15 for domestic students; for spring admission, 3/22 for domestic students. Applications are processed on a rolling basis. *Application fee:* $25. *Application Contact:* Keren I. Llanos-Figueroa, Information Contact, 787-620-2040 Ext. 2021, Fax: 787-785-7377, E-mail: kllanos@aupr.edu. *Dean of Faculty*, Prof. Bolivar Ramirez-Carlo, III, 787-620-2040 Ext. 2011, Fax: 787-785-7377, E-mail: bramirez@aupr.edu.

Program in Education Students: 22 full-time (18 women), 54 part-time (42 women); all minorities (all Hispanic/Latino). Average age 33. 22 applicants, 86% accepted, 19 enrolled. *Faculty:* 17 part-time/adjunct (7 women). Expenses: Contact institution. *Financial support:* In 2017–18, 79 students received support, including 76 fellowships (averaging $400 per year), 55 teaching assistantships (averaging $1,741 per year). Financial award applicants required to submit FAFSA. In 2017, 53 master's awarded. *Program availability:* Part-time, evening/weekend. Offers art education (M Ed); elementary education 4-6 (M Ed); elementary education K-3 (M Ed); general science education (M Ed); physical education (M Ed); special education (M Ed). *Application deadline:* For fall admission, 8/1 for domestic students; for winter admission, 10/18 for domestic students; for spring admission, 3/15 for domestic students. Applications are processed on a rolling basis. *Application fee:* $25. *Application Contact:* Keren I. Llanos-Figueroa, Information Contact, 787-620-2040 Ext. 2021, Fax: 787-785-7377, E-mail: oficnaadmisiones@aupr.edu. *Dean of Faculty*, Prof. Bolivar Ramirez-Carlo, III, 787-620-2040 Ext. 2010, Fax: 787-620-2958, E-mail: bramirez@aupr.edu.

THE AMERICAN UNIVERSITY OF ROME, 00153 Rome, Italy

General Information Independent, coed, comprehensive institution. *Research affiliation:* ARCA - Association for Research into Crimes against Art (art crime prevention), ENFSI - European Network of Forensic Science Institutes (forensic archaeology), Conservation Science in Cultural Heritage.

GRADUATE UNITS

Graduate School Offers religious studies (MA); sustainable cultural heritage (MA). Electronic applications accepted.

See Display below and Close-Up on page 857.

AMERICAN UNIVERSITY OF SHARJAH, Sharjah, United Arab Emirates

General Information Independent, coed, comprehensive institution. *Enrollment:* 108 full-time matriculated graduate/professional students (73 women), 287 part-time matriculated graduate/professional students (207 women). *Enrollment by degree level:* 395 master's. *Graduate faculty:* 59 full-time (4 women), 5 part-time/adjunct (1 woman). *Tuition:* Full-time $20,000; part-time $1350 per credit. Tuition and fees vary according to degree level and program. *Graduate housing:* Room and/or apartments available on a first-come, first-served basis to single students; on-campus housing not available to married students. Housing application deadline: 8/16. *Student services:* Campus employment opportunities, campus safety program, career counseling, child daycare facilities, exercise/wellness program, free psychological counseling, international student services, low-cost health insurance. *Library facilities:* University Library. *Research affiliation:* Mohammed Bin Rashid Space Center (space), Advanced Technology Investment Company (technology and investment), Qatar National Research Foundation, Emirates Foundation (philanthropy), International Atomic Energy Agency (energy), National Research Foundation.

Computer facilities: 2,400 computers available on campus for general student use. A campuswide network can be accessed from student residence rooms. Online class registration is available.
Website: http://www.aus.edu/

General Application Contact: Hazim M. Numan, Student Recruitment Coordinator, 971-65151004, Fax: 971-6-5152040, E-mail: srecruitment@aus.edu.

GRADUATE UNITS

Graduate Programs Students: 108 full-time (73 women), 287 part-time (207 women). Average age 27. 203 applicants, 83% accepted, 121 enrolled. Expenses: Contact institution. *Financial support:* In 2017–18, 82 students received support, including 54 research assistantships, 54 teaching assistantships; scholarships/grants also available. Financial award application deadline: 6/3. In 2017, 114 master's awarded. *Program availability:* Part-time, evening/weekend. Offers accounting (MS); biomedical engineering (MSBME); business administration (MBA); chemical engineering (MS Ch E); civil engineering (MSCE); computer engineering (MS); electrical engineering (MSEE); engineering systems management (MS, PhD); mathematics (MS); mechanical engineering (MSME); mechatronics engineering (MS); teaching English to speakers of other languages (MA); translation and interpreting (MA); urban planning (MUP). *Application deadline:* For fall admission, 8/5 priority date for domestic students, 7/1 priority date for international students; for spring admission, 12/30 priority date for domestic students, 12/9 for international students; for summer admission, 5/21 for domestic and international students. Applications are processed on a rolling basis. *Application fee:* $110. Electronic applications accepted. *Office of Graduate Studies*, Salwa Mohammed, 971-6515-2934, E-mail: ogs@aus.edu.

AMRIDGE UNIVERSITY, Montgomery, AL 36117

General Information Independent-religious, coed, university. *Enrollment:* 674 graduate, professional, and undergraduate students; 105 full-time matriculated graduate/professional students (55 women), 250 part-time matriculated graduate/professional students (152 women). *Enrollment by degree level:* 241 master's, 114 doctoral. *Graduate faculty:* 23 full-time (3 women), 9 part-time/adjunct (5 women). *Graduate housing:* On-campus housing not available. *Student services:* Campus safety program, career counseling, services for students with disabilities. *Library facilities:* Southern Christian University Library. *Collection:* Weekly public service hours: 50.

Computer facilities: 5 computers available on campus for general student use. A campuswide network can be accessed from off campus. Online class registration is available.
Website: http://www.amridgeuniversity.edu/

General Application Contact: Brooks Housley, Student Services Coordinator, 888-790-8080 Ext. 1, Fax: 334-387-3878, E-mail: admissions@amridgeuniversity.edu.

GRADUATE UNITS

Graduate and Professional Programs Students: 105 full-time (55 women), 250 part-time (152 women); includes 217 minority (167 Black or African American, non-Hispanic/Latino; 4 Asian, non-Hispanic/Latino; 42 Hispanic/Latino; 4 Native Hawaiian or other Pacific Islander, non-Hispanic/Latino). Average age 42. 160 applicants, 100% accepted, 110 enrolled. *Faculty:* 23 full-time (3 women), 9 part-time/adjunct (5 women). Expenses: Contact institution. *Financial support:* In 2017–18, 33 students received support. Federal Work-Study and scholarships/grants available. Support available to part-time students. Financial award applicants required to submit FAFSA. *Program availability:* Part-time, evening/weekend, online learning. Offers Biblical studies (MA, PhD); Christian ministry (MS); family therapy (D Min); human services (MS); leadership and management (MS); marriage and family therapy (M Div, MA, PhD); ministerial leadership (M Div, MS); New Testament studies (MA); Old Testament studies (MA); professional counseling (M Div, MA, PhD); theology (M Div, D Min). *Application deadline:* Applications are processed on a rolling basis. *Application fee:* $50. Electronic applications accepted. *Application Contact:* Brooks Housley, Student Affairs Coordinator, 888-790-8080 Ext. 1, Fax: 334-387-3878, E-mail: admissions@amridgeuniversity.edu. *Vice President, Student Affairs*, Laina Costanza, 888-790-8080 Ext. 1, Fax: 334-387-3878, E-mail: cc@amridgeuniversity.edu.

ANABAPTIST MENNONITE BIBLICAL SEMINARY, Elkhart, IN 46517-1999

General Information Independent-religious, coed, graduate-only institution. *Graduate housing:* Rooms and/or apartments available on a first-come, first-served basis to single and married students. Housing application deadline: 5/1.

GRADUATE UNITS

Graduate and Professional Programs *Program availability:* Part-time, 100% online, blended/hybrid learning. Offers chaplaincy (M Div); Christian faith formation (M Div); Christian formation (MA); Christian spiritual formation (Certificate); divinity (M Div); pastoral ministry (M Div); pastoral theology for financial professionals (Certificate); peace studies (M Div); theological studies (M Div, Certificate); theology and peace studies (MA); United Methodist leadership (M Div). Conflict transformation and environmental sustainability leadership concentrations offered in cooperation with Goshen College; international development administration offered in cooperation with Andrews University. Electronic applications accepted.

ANAHEIM UNIVERSITY, Anaheim, CA 92806-5150

General Information Proprietary, coed, graduate-only institution.

GRADUATE UNITS

Program in Teaching English to Speakers of Other Languages *Program availability:* Part-time, evening/weekend, online only, 100% online. Offers teaching English to speakers of other languages (MA, Ed D, Certificate, Diploma).

Programs in Business Administration *Program availability:* Part-time, evening/weekend, online only, 100% online. Offers entrepreneurship (ME, DBA); global sustainable management (MBA); international business (MBA, DBA, Certificate, Diploma); management (DBA); sustainable management (DBA, Certificate, Diploma). Electronic applications accepted.

ANDERSON UNIVERSITY, Anderson, IN 46012-3495

General Information Independent-religious, coed, comprehensive institution. *Graduate housing:* Room and/or apartments available to single students; on-campus housing not available to married students. Housing application deadline: 6/1.

GRADUATE UNITS

Falls School of Business Offers accountancy (MA); business administration (MBA, DBA).

School of Education Offers education (M Ed).

School of Theology *Program availability:* Part-time. Offers missions (MA); theology (M Div, MTS, D Min).

ANDERSON UNIVERSITY, Anderson, SC 29621-4035

General Information Independent-religious, coed, comprehensive institution. *Enrollment:* 3,497 graduate, professional, and undergraduate students; 429 full-time matriculated graduate/professional students (239 women), 82 part-time matriculated graduate/professional students (33 women). *Enrollment by degree level:* 443 master's, 45 doctoral, 1 other advanced degree. *Tuition:* Full-time $24,290; part-time $650 per credit hour. Full-time tuition and fees vary according to degree level and program. *Graduate housing:* Room and/or apartments available on a first-come, first-served basis to single students; on-campus housing not available to married students. Housing application deadline: 5/1. *Student services:* Campus employment opportunities, campus safety program, career counseling, exercise/wellness program, free psychological counseling, multicultural affairs office, teacher training. *Library facilities:* Thrift Library. *Collection:* Books: 90,729 (physical), 99,204 (digital/electronic); Serial titles: 14,268 (physical), 174,052 (digital/electronic); Databases: 200. Weekly public service hours: 88; students can reserve study rooms.

Computer facilities: 192 computers available on campus for general student use. A campuswide network can be accessed from student residence rooms and from off campus. Online class registration is available.
Website: http://www.andersonuniversity.edu/

General Application Contact: Chris Woodlief, Associate Director of Adult and Graduate Programs, 864-231-5531, E-mail: cwoodlief@andersonuniversity.edu.

GRADUATE UNITS

Clamp Divinity School Expenses: Contact institution. *Financial support:* Tuition waivers available. Financial award application deadline: 3/1; financial award applicants required to submit FAFSA. *Program availability:* Online learning. Offers 21st-century ministry (D Min); Christian studies (M Div); ministry (M Min). *Application Contact:* Mallory Knight, Graduate Admission Counselor, 864-231-2182, Fax: 864-231-2115, E-mail: malloryknight@andersonuniversity.edu. *Dean*, Dr. Michael Duduit, 864-328-1809, E-mail: ministry@andersonuniversity.edu.

College of Business Expenses: Contact institution. *Financial support:* Tuition waivers available. Financial award application deadline: 3/1; financial award applicants required to submit FAFSA. Offers business administration (MBA); healthcare leadership (MBA); human resources (MBA); marketing (MBA); organizational leadership (MOL); supply chain management (MBA). *Application Contact:* Mallory Knight, Graduate Admission Counselor, 864-231-2182, Fax: 864-231-2115, E-mail: malloryknight@andersonuniversity.edu. *Dean*, Steve Nail, 864-MBA-6000.

College of Education Expenses: Contact institution. *Financial support:* Tuition waivers available. Financial award application deadline: 3/1; financial award applicants required to submit FAFSA. *Program availability:* 100% online. Offers administration and supervision (M Ed); education (M Ed); elementary education (MAT). *Application Contact:* Mallory Knight, Graduate Admission Counselor, 864-231-2182, Fax: 864-231-2115, E-mail: malloryknight@andersonuniversity.edu. *Dean*, Dr. Mark Butler, 864-231-2042.

College of Health Professions Expenses: Contact institution. *Program availability:* Online learning. Offers advanced practice (DNP); executive leadership (MSN, DNP); family nurse practitioner (MSN, DNP); nurse educator (MSN); psychiatric mental health nurse practitioner (MSN, DNP). *Application Contact:* Chris Woodlief, Associate Director of Adult and Graduate Programs, 864-231-5531, E-mail: cwoodlief@andersonuniversity.edu. *Dean*, Dr. Donald M. Peace, 864-231-5513, E-mail: dpeace@andersonuniversity.edu.

Command College of South Carolina Expenses: Contact institution. *Financial support:* Application deadline: 3/1; applicants required to submit FAFSA. *Program availability:* Blended/hybrid learning. Offers criminal justice (MCJ). *Application Contact:* Mallory Knight, Graduate Admission Counselor, 864-231-2182, Fax: 864-231-2115, E-mail: malloryknight@andersonuniversity.edu.

South Carolina School of the Arts Expenses: Contact institution. *Program availability:* Online learning. Offers music education (MM). *Application Contact:* Chris Woodlief, Associate Director of Adult and Graduate Programs, 864-231-5531, E-mail: cwoodlief@andersonuniversity.edu. *Dean*, David Larson, 864-231-2002, E-mail: dlarson@andersonuniversity.edu.

ANDREWS UNIVERSITY, Berrien Springs, MI 49104

General Information Independent-religious, coed, university. CGS member. *Enrollment:* 3,348 graduate, professional, and undergraduate students; 881 full-time matriculated graduate/professional students (301 women), 692 part-time matriculated graduate/professional students (241 women). *Enrollment by degree level:* 963 master's, 593 doctoral, 17 other advanced degrees. *Graduate faculty:* 168 full-time (62 women), 32 part-time/adjunct (11 women). *Graduate housing:* Rooms and/or apartments available on a first-come, first-served basis to single and married students. *Student services:* Campus employment opportunities, campus safety program, career counseling, child daycare facilities, free psychological counseling, international student services, low-cost health insurance, multicultural affairs office, teacher training. *Library facilities:* James White Library plus 2 others. *Collection:* Books: 950,014 (physical), 394,023 (digital/electronic); Serial titles: 1,229 (physical), 198,545 (digital/electronic); Databases: 187. *Research affiliation:* RAND Corporation (drug abuse), Argonne National Laboratory (physics), Deutches Electronen Synchroton (physics).

Computer facilities: Computer purchase and lease plans are available. 100 computers available on campus for general student use. A campuswide network can be accessed from student residence rooms and from off campus. Online class registration, degree audit are available.
Website: http://www.andrews.edu/

General Application Contact: Justina Clayburn, Supervisor of Graduate Admission, 800-253-2874, Fax: 269-471-3228, E-mail: graduate@andrews.edu.

GRADUATE UNITS

School of Graduate Studies Students: 881 full-time (301 women), 692 part-time (241 women); includes 717 minority (333 Black or African American, non-Hispanic/Latino; 8 American Indian or Alaska Native, non-Hispanic/Latino; 92 Asian, non-Hispanic/Latino; 260 Hispanic/Latino; 5 Native Hawaiian or other Pacific Islander, non-Hispanic/Latino; 19 Two or more races, non-Hispanic/Latino), 399 international. Average age 38. 1,173 applicants, 47% accepted, 435 enrolled. *Faculty:* 168 full-time (62 women), 32 part-time/adjunct (11 women). Expenses: Contact institution. *Financial support:* Fellowships, research assistantships, teaching assistantships, career-related internships or fieldwork, Federal Work-Study, institutionally sponsored loans, scholarships/grants, tuition waivers (partial), and unspecified assistantships available. Support available to part-time students. Financial award applicants required to submit FAFSA. In 2017, 292 master's, 114 doctorates, 26 other advanced degrees awarded. *Program availability:* Part-time, evening/weekend, online learning. *Application deadline:* Applications are processed on a rolling basis. *Application fee:* $40. *Application Contact:* Justina Clayburn, Supervisor of Graduate Admission, 800-253-2874, Fax: 269-471-6321, E-mail: graduate@andrews.edu. *Dean*, Dr. Christon Arthur, 269-471-3405.

College of Arts and Sciences Students: 69 full-time (51 women), 46 part-time (34 women); includes 50 minority (29 Black or African American, non-Hispanic/Latino; 3 Asian, non-Hispanic/Latino; 16 Hispanic/Latino; 2 Two or more races, non-Hispanic/Latino), 39 international. Average age 32. 124 applicants, 65% accepted, 47 enrolled. *Faculty:* 76 full-time (31 women), 3 part-time/adjunct (1 woman). Expenses: Contact institution. *Financial support:* Fellowships, research assistantships, teaching assistantships, career-related internships or fieldwork, Federal Work-Study, and institutionally sponsored loans available. Financial award applicants required to submit FAFSA. In 2017, 53 master's awarded. *Program availability:* Part-time, evening/weekend. Offers arts and sciences (M Mus, MA, MAT, MS, MSA, MSCID, MSW); biology (MAT, MS); communication (MA); community and international development (MSCID); English (MA, MAT); international development (MSCID); music (M Mus, MA); social work (MSW). *Application deadline:* Applications are processed on a rolling basis. *Application fee:* $40. *Application Contact:* Justina Clayburn, Supervisor of Graduate Admission, 800-253-2874, Fax: 269-471-6321, E-mail: graduate@andrews.edu. *Dean,* Dr. Keith Mattingly, 269-471-3411.

School of Architecture, Art and Design Students: 17 full-time (7 women), 1 part-time (0 women); includes 6 minority (3 Black or African American, non-Hispanic/Latino; 3 Hispanic/Latino), 5 international. Average age 26. 15 applicants, 100% accepted, 7 enrolled. *Faculty:* 9 full-time (3 women), 1 (woman) part-time/adjunct. Expenses: Contact institution. In 2017, 9 master's awarded. Offers architecture, art and design (M Arch). *Application deadline:* Applications are processed on a rolling basis. *Application fee:* $40. Electronic applications accepted. *Application Contact:* Justina Clayburn, Supervisor of Graduate Admission, 800-253-2874, Fax: 269-471-6321, E-mail: graduate@andrews.edu. *Dean,* Carey Carscallen, 269-471-6003.

School of Business Students: 23 full-time (13 women), 32 part-time (15 women); includes 21 minority (7 Black or African American, non-Hispanic/Latino; 6 Asian, non-Hispanic/Latino; 6 Hispanic/Latino; 2 Two or more races, non-Hispanic/Latino), 21 international. Average age 31. 83 applicants, 54% accepted, 28 enrolled. *Faculty:* 8 full-time (3 women). Expenses: Contact institution. *Financial support:* Fellowships, research assistantships, teaching assistantships, and Federal Work-Study available. In 2017, 23 master's awarded. *Program availability:* Part-time. Offers business (MBA, MSA). *Application deadline:* For fall admission, 8/15 for domestic students. Applications are processed on a rolling basis. *Application fee:* $40. *Application Contact:* Justina Clayburn, Supervisor of Graduate Admission, 800-253-2874, Fax: 269-471-6321, E-mail: graduate@andrews.edu. *Dean,* Dr. Ralph Trecartin, 269-471-3632.

School of Education Students: 131 full-time (84 women), 61 part-time (36 women); includes 64 minority (35 Black or African American, non-Hispanic/Latino; 4 Asian, non-Hispanic/Latino; 20 Hispanic/Latino; 5 Two or more races, non-Hispanic/Latino), 56 international. Average age 41. 166 applicants, 51% accepted, 42 enrolled. *Faculty:* 21 full-time (9 women), 5 part-time/adjunct (2 women). Expenses: Contact institution. *Financial support:* Fellowships, research assistantships, teaching assistantships, career-related internships or fieldwork, Federal Work-Study, institutionally sponsored loans, and tuition waivers (partial) available. Support available to part-time students. In 2017, 36 master's, 16 doctorates, 12 other advanced degrees awarded. *Program availability:* Part-time. Offers clinical mental health counseling (MA); community counseling (MA); counseling psychology (MA, PhD); curriculum and instruction (MA, Ed D, PhD, Ed S); education (MA, MAT, MS, Ed D, PhD, Ed S); educational administration and leadership (MA, Ed D, PhD, Ed S); educational and developmental psychology (MA, Ed D, PhD); educational psychology (Ed D, PhD); elementary education (MAT); higher education administration (MA, Ed D, PhD, Ed S); leadership (MA, Ed D, PhD, Ed S); school counseling (MA); school psychology (Ed S); secondary education (MAT); special education (MS); teacher education (MAT). *Application deadline:* Applications are processed on a rolling basis. *Application fee:* $40. *Application Contact:* Justina Clayburn, Supervisor of Graduate Admission, 800-253-2874, Fax: 269-471-6321, E-mail: graduate@andrews.edu. *Dean,* Dr. Robson Marinho, 269-471-3464.

Seventh-day Adventist Theological Seminary Students: 529 full-time (70 women), 419 part-time (69 women); includes 480 minority (217 Black or African American, non-Hispanic/Latino; 7 American Indian or Alaska Native, non-Hispanic/Latino; 53 Asian, non-Hispanic/Latino; 190 Hispanic/Latino; 5 Native Hawaiian or other Pacific Islander, non-Hispanic/Latino; 8 Two or more races, non-Hispanic/Latino), 242 international. Average age 40. 497 applicants, 46% accepted, 216 enrolled. *Faculty:* 40 full-time (5 women), 12 part-time/adjunct (2 women). Expenses: Contact institution. *Financial support:* Fellowships, research assistantships, teaching assistantships, career-related internships or fieldwork, Federal Work-Study, and institutionally sponsored loans available. In 2017, 147 master's, 46 doctorates awarded. Offers ministry (M Div, D Min); pastoral ministry (MA); religious education (MA, Ed D, PhD, Ed S); theology (M Th, Th D); youth ministry (MA). *Application deadline:* Applications are processed on a rolling basis. *Application fee:* $40. *Application Contact:* Justina Clayburn, Director, 800-253-2874, Fax: 269-471-6321. *Dean,* Dr. Jiri Moskala, 269-471-3537.

School of Health Professions Students: 112 full-time (76 women), 133 part-time (87 women); includes 96 minority (42 Black or African American, non-Hispanic/Latino; 1 American Indian or Alaska Native, non-Hispanic/Latino; 26 Asian, non-Hispanic/Latino; 25 Hispanic/Latino; 2 Two or more races, non-Hispanic/Latino), 36 international. Average age 31. 288 applicants, 65% accepted, 95 enrolled. *Faculty:* 13 full-time (10 women), 11 part-time/adjunct (5 women). Expenses: Contact institution. In 2017, 24 master's, 52 doctorates, 14 other advanced degrees awarded. Offers health professions (MPH, MS, MSMLS, DNP, DPT, Dr Sc PT, TDPT, Certificate); medical laboratory sciences (MSMLS); nursing (MS, DNP); nutrition (MS); nutrition and dietetics (Certificate); orthopedic manual therapy (Dr Sc PT); physical therapy (DPT, Dr Sc PT, TDPT); public health (MPH); speech-language pathology (MS). *Application fee:* $40. *Application Contact:* Justina Clayburn, Supervisor of Graduate Admission, 800-253-2874, Fax: 269-471-3228, E-mail: graduate@andrews.edu. *Dean,* Dr. Emmanuel Rudatsikira, 269-471-6649, E-mail: rudatsikira@andrews.edu.

ANGELO STATE UNIVERSITY, San Angelo, TX 76909

General Information State-supported, coed, comprehensive institution. *Enrollment:* 10,417 graduate, professional, and undergraduate students; 778 full-time matriculated graduate/professional students (545 women), 841 part-time matriculated graduate/professional students (577 women). *Enrollment by degree level:* 1,541 master's, 78 doctoral. *Graduate faculty:* 140 full-time (62 women). Tuition, state resident: full-time $3856. Tuition, nonresident: full-time $11,324. *Required fees:* $2650. *Graduate housing:* Room and/or apartments available on a first-come, first-served basis to single students; on-campus housing not available to married students. Housing application deadline: 7/15. *Student services:* Campus employment opportunities, campus safety program, career counseling, free psychological counseling, grant writing training, international student services, low-cost health insurance, multicultural affairs office, services for students with disabilities, writing training. *Library facilities:* Porter Henderson Library. *Collection:* Books: 487,297 (physical), 85,488 (digital/electronic); Serial titles: 108 (physical), 77,153 (digital/electronic); Databases: 237. Weekly public service hours: 137; study areas open 24 hours, 5–7 days a week; students can reserve study rooms. *Research affiliation:* Purina (animal nutrition), Zinpro Corporation (animal nutrition), Texas Space Consortium (space research and technology), TASCO (animal nutrition), Mannatech, Inc. (nutrition).

Computer facilities: Computer purchase and lease plans are available. 750 computers available on campus for general student use. A campuswide network can be accessed from student residence rooms and from off campus. Online class registration, online courses, tuition payments, book purchase, parking permits, university calendar, discounted hardware and software are available.
Website: http://www.angelo.edu/

General Application Contact: Jennifer Page McAndrews, Graduate Admissions Assistant, 325-942-2169, Fax: 325-942-2194, E-mail: graduate.studies@angelo.edu.

GRADUATE UNITS

College of Graduate Studies and Research Students: 757 full-time (529 women), 730 part-time (497 women); includes 433 minority (131 Black or African American, non-Hispanic/Latino; 5 American Indian or Alaska Native, non-Hispanic/Latino; 18 Asian, non-Hispanic/Latino; 267 Hispanic/Latino; 12 Two or more races, non-Hispanic/Latino), 19 international. Average age 32. Expenses: Contact institution. *Financial support:* Research assistantships, teaching assistantships, career-related internships or fieldwork, Federal Work-Study, scholarships/grants, and unspecified assistantships available. Support available to part-time students. Financial award application deadline: 3/1. *Program availability:* Part-time, evening/weekend, online learning. *Application deadline:* For fall admission, 7/15 priority date for domestic students, 6/10 for international students; for spring admission, 12/1 priority date for domestic students, 11/1 for international students. Applications are processed on a rolling basis. *Application fee:* $40 ($50 for international students). Electronic applications accepted. *Application Contact:* Jennifer Page McAndrews, Graduate Admissions Coordinator, 325-486-6481, Fax: 325-942-2194, E-mail: jennifer.mcandrews@angelo.edu. *Dean,* Dr. Susan E. Keith, 325-942-2169, Fax: 325-942-2194, E-mail: susan.keith@angelo.edu.

Archer College of Health and Human Services Students: 204 full-time (128 women), 140 part-time (104 women); includes 99 minority (20 Black or African American, non-Hispanic/Latino; 7 Asian, non-Hispanic/Latino; 68 Hispanic/Latino; 4 Two or more races, non-Hispanic/Latino), 8 international. Average age 30. Expenses: Contact institution. *Financial support:* Research assistantships available. Offers family nurse practitioner (MSN); health and human services (M Ed, MS, MSN, DPT); industrial-organizational psychology (MS); kinesiology (M Ed); nurse educator (MSN); physical therapy (DPT). *Application deadline:* For fall admission, 7/15 priority date for domestic students, 6/10 for international students; for spring admission, 12/1 priority date for domestic students, 11/1 for international students. *Application fee:* $40 ($50 for international students). *Dean,* Dr. Leslie M. Mayrand, 325-486-6258, Fax: 325-942-2631, E-mail: leslie.mayrand@angelo.edu.

College of Arts and Humanities Students: 73 full-time (39 women), 167 part-time (58 women); includes 95 minority (30 Black or African American, non-Hispanic/Latino; 2 American Indian or Alaska Native, non-Hispanic/Latino; 11 Asian, non-Hispanic/Latino; 45 Hispanic/Latino; 7 Two or more races, non-Hispanic/Latino), 7 international. Average age 31. Expenses: Contact institution. *Financial support:* Research assistantships, teaching assistantships, career-related internships or fieldwork, Federal Work-Study, scholarships/grants, and unspecified assistantships available. Support available to part-time students. Financial award application deadline: 3/1; financial award applicants required to submit FAFSA. *Program availability:* Part-time, evening/weekend. Offers arts and humanities (MA, MS, MSS); communication (MA); criminal justice (MS); English (MA); homeland security (MS); intelligence, security studies, and analysis (MSS); security studies (MSS); TESOL (MA). *Application deadline:* For fall admission, 7/15 priority date for domestic students, 6/10 for international students; for spring admission, 12/1 priority date for domestic students, 11/1 for international students. Applications are processed on a rolling basis. *Application fee:* $40 ($50 for international students). Electronic applications accepted. *Dean,* Dr. Carolyn Gascoigne, 325-942-2162, E-mail: cgascoigne@angelo.edu.

College of Business Students: 77 full-time (37 women), 66 part-time (24 women); includes 46 minority (9 Black or African American, non-Hispanic/Latino; 1 American Indian or Alaska Native, non-Hispanic/Latino; 1 Asian, non-Hispanic/Latino; 34 Hispanic/Latino; 1 Two or more races, non-Hispanic/Latino), 11 international. Average age 30. Expenses: Contact institution. *Financial support:* Career-related internships or fieldwork, Federal Work-Study, and scholarships/grants available. Support available to part-time students. Financial award application deadline: 3/1; financial award applicants required to submit FAFSA. *Program availability:* Part-time, evening/weekend. Offers business (MBA, MPAC); business administration (MBA); professional accountancy (MPAC). *Application deadline:* Applications are processed on a rolling basis. *Application fee:* $40 ($50 for international students). Electronic applications accepted. *Dean,* Dr. Clifton T. Jones, 325-942-2337, Fax: 325-942-2718, E-mail: clifton.jones@angelo.edu.

College of Education Students: 405 full-time (332 women), 449 part-time (380 women); includes 291 minority (98 Black or African American, non-Hispanic/Latino; 3 American Indian or Alaska Native, non-Hispanic/Latino; 3 Asian, non-Hispanic/Latino; 178 Hispanic/Latino; 9 Two or more races, non-Hispanic/Latino), 1 international. Average age 35. Expenses: Contact institution. *Financial support:* Career-related internships or fieldwork, Federal Work-Study, scholarships/grants, and unspecified assistantships available. Support available to part-time students. Financial award application deadline: 3/1; financial award applicants required to submit FAFSA. *Program availability:* Part-time, evening/weekend. Offers curriculum and instruction (MA); education (M Ed, MA); educational administration (M Ed); guidance and counseling (M Ed); student development and leadership in higher education (M Ed). *Application deadline:* For fall admission, 7/15 priority date for domestic students, 6/10 for international students; for spring admission, 12/1 priority date for domestic students, 11/1 for international students. Applications are processed on a rolling basis. *Application fee:* $40 ($50 for international students). Electronic applications accepted. *Dean,* Dr. John J. Miazga, Jr., 325-942-2212, E-mail: john.miazga@angelo.edu.

College of Science and Engineering Students: 22 full-time (12 women), 16 part-time (8 women); includes 7 minority (1 Black or African American, non-Hispanic/Latino; 1 Asian, non-Hispanic/Latino; 5 Hispanic/Latino), 1 international. Average age 25. Expenses: Contact institution. *Financial support:* Research assistantships, teaching assistantships, career-related internships or fieldwork, Federal Work-Study, scholarships/grants, and unspecified assistantships available. Support available to part-time students. Financial award application deadline: 8/1; financial award applicants required to submit FAFSA. *Program availability:* Part-time, evening/weekend. Offers agriculture (M Ag); biology (MS); science and engineering (M Ag, MS). *Application deadline:* For fall admission, 7/15 priority date for domestic students, 6/10 for international students; for spring admission, 12/1 priority date for domestic students, 11/1 for international students. Applications are processed on a rolling basis. *Application fee:* $40 ($50 for international students). Electronic applications accepted. *Application Contact:* Aly Hunter, Graduate Admissions Assistant, 325-942-2169, Fax: 325-942-2194, E-mail: aly.hunter@angelo.edu. *Dean,* Dr. Paul K. Swets, 325-942-2470, Fax: 325-942-2340, E-mail: paul.swets@angelo.edu.

ANNA MARIA COLLEGE, Paxton, MA 01612

General Information Independent-religious, coed, comprehensive institution. *Graduate housing:* On-campus housing not available.

GRADUATE UNITS

Graduate Division *Program availability:* Part-time, evening/weekend. Offers business administration (MBA, AC); counseling psychology (MA); criminal justice (MS); early childhood education (M Ed); education (CAGS); elementary education (M Ed); English language arts (M Ed); health emergency management (MS, Graduate Certificate); industrial/organizational psychology (MS); public administration (MPA); social work (MSW); visual arts (M Ed). Electronic applications accepted.

ANTIOCH UNIVERSITY LOS ANGELES, Culver City, CA 90230

General Information Independent, coed, upper-level institution. *Enrollment:* 628 graduate, professional, and undergraduate students; 517 full-time matriculated graduate/professional students (378 women), 37 part-time matriculated graduate/professional students (28 women). *Enrollment by degree level:* 553 master's, 1 other advanced degree. *Graduate housing:* On-campus housing not available. *Student services:* Campus employment opportunities, career counseling, grant writing training, international student services, low-cost health insurance, services for students with disabilities, writing training.

Computer facilities: A campuswide network can be accessed from off campus. Online class registration is available.
Website: http://www.antioch.edu/los-angeles/

General Application Contact: Information Contact, 310-578-1090, Fax: 310-822-4824, E-mail: admissions@antiochla.edu.

GRADUATE UNITS

Program in Education Students: 44 full-time (32 women), 1 (woman) part-time; includes 28 minority (8 Black or African American, non-Hispanic/Latino; 1 Asian, non-Hispanic/Latino; 14 Hispanic/Latino; 1 Native Hawaiian or other Pacific Islander, non-Hispanic/Latino; 4 Two or more races, non-Hispanic/Latino). Average age 34. 24 applicants, 79% accepted. *Faculty:* 3. Expenses: Contact institution. *Financial support:* Career-related internships or fieldwork, Federal Work-Study, and scholarships/grants available. Support available to part-time students. Financial award application deadline: 3/24; financial award applicants required to submit CSS PROFILE or FAFSA. *Program availability:* Evening/weekend. Offers education (MA). *Application deadline:* For fall admission, 5/4 priority date for domestic students. Applications are processed on a rolling basis. *Application fee:* $60. *Application Contact:* Information Contact, 310-578-1090, Fax: 310-822-4824, E-mail: admissions@antiochla.edu. *Head,* Dr. Cheryl Armon, 310-578-1080 Ext. 233, Fax: 310-822-4824, E-mail: cheryl_armon@antiochla.edu.

Program in Leadership, Management and Business Students: 25 full-time (20 women); includes 16 minority (5 Black or African American, non-Hispanic/Latino; 2 Asian, non-Hispanic/Latino; 7 Hispanic/Latino; 2 Two or more races, non-Hispanic/Latino), 1 international. Average age 33. *Faculty:* 7. Expenses: Contact institution. *Financial support:* In 2017–18, 23 students received support. Career-related internships or fieldwork, Federal Work-Study, and scholarships/grants available. Support available to part-time students. Financial award application deadline: 3/24; financial award applicants required to submit CSS PROFILE or FAFSA. In 2017, 8 master's awarded. *Program availability:* Part-time, evening/weekend. Offers human resource development (MA); leadership (MA); organizational development (MA). *Application deadline:* For fall admission, 8/4 for domestic students; for winter admission, 11/3 for domestic students; for spring admission, 2/2 for domestic students. *Application Contact:* Information Contact, 310-578-1090, Fax: 310-822-4824, E-mail: admissions@antiochla.edu. *Chair,* Dr. Susan Nero, 310-578-1080 Ext. 226, Fax: 310-882-4824, E-mail: susan_nero@antiochla.edu.

Program in Psychology Students: 428 full-time (312 women), 35 part-time (27 women); includes 140 minority (25 Black or African American, non-Hispanic/Latino; 13 Asian, non-Hispanic/Latino; 81 Hispanic/Latino; 1 Native Hawaiian or other Pacific Islander, non-Hispanic/Latino; 20 Two or more races, non-Hispanic/Latino), 1 international. Average age 36. *Faculty:* 19. Expenses: Contact institution. *Financial support:* In 2017–18, 167 students received support. Career-related internships or fieldwork, Federal Work-Study, scholarships/grants, and traineeships available. Support available to part-time students. Financial award application deadline: 3/24; financial award applicants required to submit FAFSA. In 2017, 118 master's awarded. *Program availability:* Part-time. Offers clinical psychology (MA); psychology (MA). *Application deadline:* For fall admission, 8/4 priority date for domestic students; for winter admission, 11/3 priority date for domestic students; for spring admission, 2/4 priority date for domestic students. Applications are processed on a rolling basis. *Application fee:* $60. *Application Contact:* Information Contact, 310-578-1090, Fax: 310-822-4824, E-mail: admissions@antiochla.edu. *Chair,* Joy Turek, 310-578-1080 Ext. 306, Fax: 310-822-4824, E-mail: joy_turek@antiochla.edu.

Program in Urban Sustainability Students: 20 full-time (14 women), 1 part-time (0 women); includes 15 minority (4 Black or African American, non-Hispanic/Latino; 1 Asian, non-Hispanic/Latino; 3 Hispanic/Latino; 7 Two or more races, non-Hispanic/Latino). Average age 43. Expenses: Contact institution. Offers urban sustainability (MA). *Application Contact:* Information Contact, 310-578-1090, Fax: 310-822-4824, E-mail: admissions@antiochla.edu. *President,* Dr. LucyAnn Gelselman, 310-578-1080 Ext. 112, Fax: 310-822-4824.

ANTIOCH UNIVERSITY MIDWEST, Yellow Springs, OH 45387-1609

General Information Independent, coed, upper-level institution. *Enrollment:* 135 graduate, professional, and undergraduate students; 49 full-time matriculated graduate/professional students (37 women), 35 part-time matriculated graduate/professional students (26 women). *Enrollment by degree level:* 61 master's, 20 other advanced degrees. *Graduate housing:* On-campus housing not available. *Student services:* International student services, low-cost health insurance, teacher training, writing training. *Library facilities:* Midwest Library.

Computer facilities: 10 computers available on campus for general student use. A campuswide network can be accessed. Online class registration, online bill pay and view/acceptance of financial aid award letter, narrative evaluations are available.
Website: http://www.antioch.edu/midwest/

General Application Contact: Deena Kent-Hummel, Director of Admissions, 937-769-1851, Fax: 937-769-1804, E-mail: dkent@antioch.edu.

GRADUATE UNITS

MBA Program in Healthcare Leadership Expenses: Contact institution. *Financial support:* Federal Work-Study available. Financial award applicants required to submit FAFSA. *Program availability:* Part-time, evening/weekend, online learning. Offers healthcare leadership (MBA). *Application deadline:* For fall admission, 9/1 for domestic students; for winter admission, 12/1 for domestic students; for spring admission, 3/10 for domestic students. Applications are processed on a rolling basis. *Application fee:* $50. Electronic applications accepted. *Application Contact:* Sarah Klemm, Enrollment Advisor, 937-769-1814, Fax: 937-769-1804, E-mail: sklemm@antioch.edu. *Chair, Graduate Management Programs,* Randolph Oliver, 937-769-1841, Fax: 937-769-1807, E-mail: roliver@antioch.edu.

ANTIOCH UNIVERSITY NEW ENGLAND, Keene, NH 03431-3552

General Information Independent, coed, graduate-only institution. *Graduate housing:* On-campus housing not available. *Research affiliation:* Cheshire Medical Center Cardiac Rehabilitation Program (clinical psychology), Northeast Foundation for Children (education), Pine Hill Waldorf School (education), Harris Center for Conservation Education (environmental studies).

GRADUATE UNITS

Graduate School *Program availability:* Evening/weekend. Offers advocacy for social justice and sustainability (MS); applied behavior analysis (Certificate); applied behavior analysis internship (Certificate); autism spectrum disorders (Certificate); clinical mental health counseling (MA); clinical psychology (Psy D); conservation biology (MS); dance/movement therapy and counseling (M Ed, MA, PMC); early childhood education (M Ed); elementary education (M Ed, Certificate); environmental education (MS); environmental studies (PhD); foundations of education (M Ed); integrated learning (M Ed); marriage and family therapy (MA, PhD, Certificate); principal certification (PMC); resource management and conservation (MS); science teacher certification (MS); self-designed studies (MS); special education (M Ed); substance abuse counseling (MA); sustainability (MBA); sustainable development and climate change (MS); teaching (M Ed, PMC); Waldorf teacher training (M Ed, Certificate). Electronic applications accepted.

ANTIOCH UNIVERSITY SANTA BARBARA, Santa Barbara, CA 93101-1581

General Information Independent, coed, upper-level institution. *Graduate housing:* On-campus housing not available.

GRADUATE UNITS

Program in Business Administration Offers non-profit management (MBA); social business (MBA); strategic leadership (MBA).

Program in Clinical Psychology Offers clinical psychology (MA, Psy D). Electronic applications accepted.

Program in Education/Teacher Credentialing *Program availability:* Part-time. Offers education/teacher credentialing (M Ed, MA). Electronic applications accepted.

Program in Writing and Contemporary Media *Program availability:* Part-time. Offers writing and contemporary media (MFA).

ANTIOCH UNIVERSITY SEATTLE, Seattle, WA 98121

General Information Independent, coed, university. *Enrollment:* 382 full-time matriculated graduate/professional students (311 women), 127 part-time matriculated graduate/professional students (107 women). *Enrollment by degree level:* 403 master's, 86 doctoral, 12 other advanced degrees. *Graduate housing:* On-campus housing not available. *Student services:* Campus employment opportunities, career counseling, free psychological counseling, international student services, services for students with disabilities, teacher training, writing training. *Library facilities:* Antioch Seattle Library. *Collection:* Books: 8,425 (physical), 264,631 (digital/electronic); Serial titles: 40,950 (digital/electronic); Databases: 222.
Website: http://www.antioch.edu/seattle/

General Application Contact: Eileen Knight, Recruitment and Admissions Director, 206-268-4200, Fax: 206-268-4242, E-mail: eknight@antioch.edu.

GRADUATE UNITS

Program in Clinical Psychology Students: 66 full-time (51 women), 12 part-time (11 women). Average age 40. Expenses: Contact institution. *Financial support:* Fellowships, research assistantships with tuition reimbursements, Federal Work-Study, scholarships/grants, and unspecified assistantships available. *Program availability:* Part-time, evening/weekend. Offers psychology (Psy D). *Application deadline:* Applications are processed on a rolling basis. Electronic applications accepted. *Application Contact:* Eileen Knight, Recruitment and Admissions Director, 206-268-4200, E-mail: eknight@antioch.edu. *Associate Chair,* Dana Waters, 206-268-4865, E-mail: dwaters@antioch.edu.

Program in Counseling, Therapy and Wellness Students: 258 full-time (220 women), 100 part-time (84 women); includes 81 minority (9 Black or African American, non-Hispanic/Latino; 3 American Indian or Alaska Native, non-Hispanic/Latino; 19 Asian, non-Hispanic/Latino; 30 Hispanic/Latino; 20 Two or more races, non-Hispanic/Latino), 1 international. Average age 35. Expenses: Contact institution. Offers clinical mental health counseling (MA); counselor education and supervision (PhD); couple and family therapy (MA). *Application Contact:* Eileen Knight, Recruitment and Admissions Director, 206-268-4200, E-mail: psmith-mentz@antiochsea.edu. *Vice President of Academic Affairs,* Peter Rojcewicz, 206-268-4108, E-mail: projcewicz@antioch.edu.

Program in Education Students: 58 full-time (40 women), 15 part-time (12 women); includes 12 minority (2 Asian, non-Hispanic/Latino; 6 Hispanic/Latino; 4 Two or more races, non-Hispanic/Latino). Average age 36. Expenses: Contact institution. *Financial support:* Research assistantships, Federal Work-Study, scholarships/grants, and unspecified assistantships available. Financial award application deadline: 6/15. *Program availability:* Part-time, evening/weekend. Offers adult education (MA); drama therapy (MA); individualized studies (MA); leadership in edible education (MA); teaching (MAT); urban environmental education (MA). *Application deadline:* Applications are processed on a rolling basis. *Application Contact:* Eileen Knight, Recruitment and Admissions Director, 206-268-4200, E-mail: eknight@antioch.edu. *Interim Dean,* Ed Mikel, 206-268-4617, E-mail: emikel@antioch.edu.

AOMA GRADUATE SCHOOL OF INTEGRATIVE MEDICINE, Austin, TX 78757

General Information Proprietary, coed, graduate-only institution. *Enrollment by degree level:* 127 master's, 31 doctoral. *Graduate faculty:* 9 full-time (3 women), 25 part-time/adjunct (14 women). *Graduate housing:* On-campus housing not available. *Student services:* Campus employment opportunities, campus safety program, career counseling, exercise/wellness program, international student services, services for students with disabilities. *Library facilities:* AOMA Library. *Collection:* Books: 4,768 (physical); Serial titles: 1,389 (physical). Weekly public service hours: 59; students can reserve study rooms.

Computer facilities: 8 computers available on campus for general student use. Online class registration is available.
Website: http://www.aoma.edu/

General Application Contact: Jessica Du, Director of Admissions, 512-492-3017, Fax: 512-454-7001, E-mail: admissions@aoma.edu.

GRADUATE UNITS

Doctor of Acupuncture and Oriental Medicine Program Students: 19 full-time (7 women), 12 part-time (9 women); includes 9 minority (4 Black or African American, non-Hispanic/Latino; 1 Asian, non-Hispanic/Latino; 4 Hispanic/Latino). Average age 39. *Faculty:* 2 full-time (1 woman), 7 part-time/adjunct (3 women). Expenses: Contact institution. *Financial support:* In 2017–18, 1 student received support. Application deadline: 6/30; applicants required to submit FAFSA. In 2017, 3 doctorates awarded. Offers acupuncture and Oriental medicine (DAOM). *Application deadline:* For fall admission, 8/25 for domestic students; for winter admission, 12/9 for domestic students; for spring admission, 3/17 for domestic students; for summer admission, 5/15 priority date for domestic students, 5/23 priority date for international students. Applications are processed on a rolling basis. *Application fee:* $75. Electronic applications accepted. *Application Contact:* Jessica Du, Director of Admissions, 512-492-3017, Fax: 512-454-7001, E-mail: admissions@aoma.edu. *Director, Doctoral Program and Research,* Dr. John S. Finnell, 512-492-3057, Fax: 512-454-7001, E-mail: jfinnell@aoma.edu.

Master of Acupuncture and Oriental Medicine Program Students: 100 full-time (81 women), 27 part-time (22 women); includes 19 minority (1 Black or African American, non-Hispanic/Latino; 16 Asian, non-Hispanic/Latino; 2 Hispanic/Latino). Average age 35. 39 applicants, 67% accepted, 24 enrolled. *Faculty:* 11 full-time (4 women), 20 part-time/adjunct (12 women). Expenses: Contact institution. *Financial support:* In 2017–18, 21 students received support. Federal Work-Study and scholarships/grants available. Financial award application deadline: 6/30; financial award applicants required to submit FAFSA. In 2017, 37 master's awarded. Offers acupuncture and Oriental medicine (MAcOM). *Application deadline:* For fall admission, 8/25 priority date for domestic students; for winter admission, 12/9 priority date for domestic students; for spring admission, 3/17 priority date for domestic students; for summer admission, 6/23 priority date for domestic students, 5/23 priority date for international students. Applications are processed on a rolling basis. *Application fee:* $75. Electronic applications accepted. *Application Contact:* Jessica Du, Director of Admissions, 512-492-3017, Fax: 512-454-7001, E-mail: admissions@aoma.edu. *Program Director,* Lesley Hamilton, 512-454-3040, Fax: 512-454-7001, E-mail: lhamilton@aoma.edu.

APEX SCHOOL OF THEOLOGY, Durham, NC 27703

General Information Independent-religious, coed, comprehensive institution. *Graduate housing:* On-campus housing not available.

GRADUATE UNITS

Graduate Programs

APOLLOS UNIVERSITY, Great Falls, MT 59401

General Information Proprietary, coed, comprehensive institution.

GRADUATE UNITS

School of Business and Management Offers business administration (MBA, DBA); organizational management (MS).

APPALACHIAN BIBLE COLLEGE, Mount Hope, WV 25880

General Information Independent-religious, coed, comprehensive institution. *Graduate housing:* Rooms and/or apartments guaranteed to single students and available on a first-come, first-served basis to married students. Housing application deadline: 9/1. *Student services:* Campus employment opportunities. *Library facilities:* John Van Pufflen Library.

Computer facilities: 15 computers available on campus for general student use. A campuswide network can be accessed from student residence rooms and from off campus.
Website: http://www.abc.edu/

General Application Contact: Benjamin Cale, Director of Admissions, 304-877-6428 Ext. 311, Fax: 304-877-5082, E-mail: admissions@abc.edu.

GRADUATE UNITS

Graduate Program Expenses: Contact institution. *Program availability:* Part-time, online learning. Offers ministry (MA). *Application fee:* $35. Electronic applications accepted. *Application Contact:* Benjamin Cale, Director of Admissions, 304-877-6428, Fax: 304-877-5082, E-mail: admissions@abc.edu. *Dean of Graduate Studies,* Dr. John Rinehart, 304-877-6428, E-mail: john.rinehart@abc.edu.

APPALACHIAN COLLEGE OF PHARMACY, Oakwood, VA 24631

General Information Independent, coed, graduate-only institution.

GRADUATE UNITS

Doctor of Pharmacy Program Offers pharmacy (Pharm D).

APPALACHIAN SCHOOL OF LAW, Grundy, VA 24614

General Information Independent, coed, graduate-only institution. *Enrollment by degree level:* 128 doctoral. *Graduate faculty:* 10 full-time (2 women), 10 part-time/adjunct (5 women). *Graduate housing:* On-campus housing not available. *Student services:* Campus employment opportunities, campus safety program, career counseling, services for students with disabilities, writing training. *Library facilities:* ASL Library. *Collection:* Students can reserve study rooms.

Computer facilities: 32 computers available on campus for general student use. Online class registration is available.
Website: http://www.asl.edu/

General Application Contact: Kelsea Wagner, Director of Admissions, 276-244-1245, Fax: 276-244-1298, E-mail: kwagner@asl.edu.

GRADUATE UNITS

Professional Program in Law Students: 128 full-time (63 women). *Faculty:* 10 full-time (2 women), 10 part-time/adjunct (5 women). Expenses: Contact institution. *Financial support:* Research assistantships, career-related internships or fieldwork, Federal Work-Study, institutionally sponsored loans, scholarships/grants, and tuition waivers (full and partial) available. Financial award application deadline: 7/1; financial award applicants required to submit FAFSA. Offers law (JD). *Application deadline:* For fall admission, 6/1 for domestic students. Applications are processed on a rolling basis. *Application fee:* $60. Electronic applications accepted. *Application Contact:* Glenna Owens, Student Services Coordinator, 276-935-4349 Ext. 1281, Fax: 276-935-8496, E-mail: gowens@asl.edu. *Dean,* Sandra Keen McGlothlin, 276-935-4349 Ext. 1265, Fax: 276-935-8261, E-mail: smcglothlin@asl.edu.

APPALACHIAN STATE UNIVERSITY, Boone, NC 28608

General Information State-supported, coed, comprehensive institution. CGS member. *Graduate housing:* On-campus housing not available.

GRADUATE UNITS

Cratis D. Williams Graduate School *Program availability:* Part-time, evening/weekend, online learning. Offers appropriate technology (MS); cell and molecular biology (MS); clinical health psychology (MA); clinical mental health counseling (MA); college student development (MA); computer science (MS); curriculum specialist (MA); educational administration (Ed S); educational media (MA); elementary education (MA); English (MA); exercise science (MS); general history (MA); general management (MBA); geography (MA); higher education (MA, Ed S); library science (MLS); marriage and family therapy (MA); mathematics (MA); middle grades education (MA); nutrition (MS); political science (MA); public administration (MPA); reading education (MA); renewable energy engineering (MS); romance languages (MA); school administration (MSA); school counseling (MA); social work (MSW); special education (MA); speech-language pathology (MS); taxation (MS). Electronic applications accepted.

Center for Appalachian Studies *Program availability:* Part-time. Offers culture (MA). Electronic applications accepted.

School of Music *Program availability:* Part-time. Offers music performance (MM); music therapy (MMT). Electronic applications accepted.

AQUINAS COLLEGE, Grand Rapids, MI 49506

General Information Independent-religious, coed, comprehensive institution. *Enrollment:* 1,716 graduate, professional, and undergraduate students; 29 full-time matriculated graduate/professional students (18 women), 136 part-time matriculated graduate/professional students (114 women). *Enrollment by degree level:* 158 master's. *Graduate faculty:* 14 full-time (9 women), 15 part-time/adjunct (8 women). *Tuition:* Full-time $10,260; part-time $570 per credit. *Required fees:* $120; $120 per credit. *Graduate housing:* On-campus housing not available. *Student services:* Campus employment opportunities, campus safety program, career counseling, exercise/wellness program, free psychological counseling, multicultural affairs office, services for students with disabilities, teacher training, writing training. *Library facilities:* Grace Hauenstein Library plus 1 other. *Collection:* Books: 85,348 (physical), 196,003 (digital/electronic); Serial titles: 231 (physical); Databases: 85. Weekly public service hours: 90; students can reserve study rooms.

Computer facilities: Computer purchase and lease plans are available. 210 computers available on campus for general student use. A campuswide network can be accessed from student residence rooms and from off campus. Online class registration is available.
Website: http://www.aquinas.edu/

General Application Contact: Lynn Atkins-Rykert, Graduate Programs Coordinator, 616-632-2924, Fax: 616-732-4465, E-mail: atkinlyn@aquinas.edu.

GRADUATE UNITS

School of Education Students: 4 full-time (1 woman), 104 part-time (92 women); includes 11 minority (2 Black or African American, non-Hispanic/Latino; 2 Asian, non-Hispanic/Latino; 6 Hispanic/Latino; 1 Two or more races, non-Hispanic/Latino). Expenses: Contact institution. *Financial support:* Scholarships/grants available. Support available to part-time students. Financial award application deadline: 3/15. *Program availability:* Part-time, evening/weekend. Offers education (M Ed, MAT). *Application deadline:* Applications are processed on a rolling basis. *Application fee:* $0. *Application Contact:* Administrative Assistant, 616-632-2440. *Dean,* Dr. Susan English, 616-632-2800, Fax: 616-732-4465, E-mail: englisus@aquinas.edu.

School of Management Students: 11 full-time (6 women), 30 part-time (20 women); includes 7 minority (2 Black or African American, non-Hispanic/Latino; 1 Asian, non-Hispanic/Latino; 4 Hispanic/Latino). Expenses: Contact institution. *Financial support:* Scholarships/grants available. Support available to part-time students. Financial award application deadline: 3/15; financial award applicants required to submit FAFSA. *Program availability:* Part-time, evening/weekend. Offers marketing management (MM); organizational leadership (MM); sustainable business (MM). *Application deadline:* Applications are processed on a rolling basis. *Application fee:* $0. *Application Contact:* Lynn Atkins-Rykert, Program Coordinator, 616-632-2925, Fax: 616-732-4489, E-mail: atkinlyn@aquinas.edu. *Interim Director,* Cynthia G. VanGelderen, 616-632-2922, Fax: 616-732-4489.

AQUINAS COLLEGE, Nashville, TN 37205-2005

General Information Independent-religious, coed, comprehensive institution. *Graduate housing:* On-campus housing not available.

GRADUATE UNITS

School of Education Offers elementary education (MAT); secondary education (MAT); teaching and learning (M Ed).

AQUINAS INSTITUTE OF THEOLOGY, St. Louis, MO 63108

General Information Independent-religious, coed, graduate-only institution. *Graduate housing:* On-campus housing not available.

GRADUATE UNITS

Graduate and Professional Programs *Program availability:* Part-time, evening/weekend, online learning. Offers biblical studies (Certificate); church music (MM); health care mission (MAHCM); ministry (M Div); pastoral care (Certificate); pastoral ministry (MAPM); pastoral studies (MAPS); preaching (D Min); spiritual direction (Certificate); theology (M Div, MA); Thomistic studies (Certificate).

ARCADIA UNIVERSITY, Glenside, PA 19038-3295

General Information Independent-religious, coed, comprehensive institution. CGS member. *Graduate housing:* On-campus housing not available.

GRADUATE UNITS

College of Arts and Sciences Offers applied behavior analysis (MAC); arts and sciences (MA, MAC, MAH, MFA, MSFS); autism (MAC); child/family therapy (MAC); community public health (MAC); counseling/international peace and conflict resolution dual degree (MAC); creative writing (MFA); English (MA); forensic science (MSFS); humanities (MAH); international peace and conflict resolution (MA); international public relations (MA); mental health counseling (MAC); trauma (MAC).

College of Health Sciences Offers genetic counseling (MSGC); health education (MSHE); health sciences (MMS, MPH, MSGC, MSHE, DPT); physical therapy (DPT); physician assistant (MMS); public health (MPH, MSHE).

Program in Business Administration Offers business administration (MBA).

School of Education *Program availability:* Part-time, evening/weekend, online learning. Offers art education (M Ed); computer education (CAS); curriculum (CAS); curriculum studies (M Ed); early childhood education (M Ed); educational leadership (M Ed, Ed D,

CAS); elementary education (M Ed); English education (MA Ed); environmental education (MA Ed); instructional technology (M Ed); language arts (M Ed); library science (M Ed); mathematics education (M Ed, MA Ed); music education (MA Ed); psychology (MA Ed); reading (M Ed, CAS); science education (M Ed, CAS); secondary education (M Ed, CAS); special education (M Ed, Ed D, CAS); theater arts (MA Ed); written communication (MA Ed). Electronic applications accepted.

ARGOSY UNIVERSITY, ATLANTA, Atlanta, GA 30328

General Information Proprietary, coed, university.

GRADUATE UNITS

College of Business Offers accounting (DBA); corporate compliance (MBA); customized professional concentration (MBA, DBA); finance (MBA); healthcare administration (MBA); information systems (DBA); information systems management (MBA); international business (MBA, DBA); management (MBA, MSM, DBA); marketing (MBA, DBA).

College of Education Offers educational leadership (MAEd, Ed D, Ed S); teaching and learning (MAEd, Ed D, Ed S).

College of Health Sciences Offers public health (MPH).

Georgia School of Professional Psychology Offers clinical psychology (MA, Psy D, Postdoctoral Respecialization Certificate); community counseling (MA); counselor education and supervision (Ed D); forensic psychology (MA); industrial organizational psychology (MA); marriage and family therapy (Certificate); sport-exercise psychology (MA).

ARGOSY UNIVERSITY, CHICAGO, Chicago, IL 60601

General Information Proprietary, coed, university.

GRADUATE UNITS

College of Business *Program availability:* Online learning. Offers accounting (DBA); customized professional concentration (MBA, DBA); finance (MBA); fraud examination (MBA); global business sustainability (DBA); healthcare administration (MBA); information systems (DBA); information systems management (MBA); international business (MBA, DBA); management (MBA, MSM, DBA); marketing (MBA, DBA); organizational leadership (Ed D); public administration (MBA); sustainable management (MBA).

College of Education *Program availability:* Online learning. Offers adult education and training (MA Ed); community college executive leadership (Ed D); educational leadership (MA Ed, Ed D, Ed S); instructional leadership (Ed D, Ed S).

College of Health Sciences Offers public health (MPH).

Illinois School of Professional Psychology *Program availability:* Online learning. Offers child and adolescent psychology (Psy D); client-centered and experiential psychotherapies (Psy D); clinical psychology (MA, Psy D); community counseling (MA); counseling psychology (Ed D); counselor education and supervision (Ed D); diversity and multicultural psychology (Psy D); family psychology (Psy D); forensic psychology (Psy D); health psychology (Psy D); industrial organizational psychology (MA); neuropsychology (Psy D); organizational consulting (Psy D); psychoanalytic psychology (Psy D); psychology and spirituality (Psy D).

ARGOSY UNIVERSITY, HAWAI`I, Honolulu, HI 96813

General Information Proprietary, coed, university.

GRADUATE UNITS

College of Business Offers accounting (DBA); corporate compliance (MBA); customized professional concentration (MBA, DBA); finance (MBA, Certificate); fraud examination (MBA); global business sustainability (DBA); healthcare administration (MBA, Certificate); information systems (DBA); information systems management (MBA, Certificate); international business (MBA, DBA, Certificate); management (MBA, MSM, DBA); marketing (MBA, DBA, Certificate); organizational leadership (Ed D); public administration (MBA); sustainable management (MBA).

College of Education Offers adult education and training (MAEd); educational leadership (Ed D); instructional leadership (Ed D); school psychology (MA).

College of Health Sciences Offers public health (MPH).

Hawai'i School of Professional Psychology Offers clinical psychology (MA, Psy D, Postdoctoral Respecialization Certificate); counseling psychology (Ed D); forensic psychology (MA); marriage and family therapy (MA); professional psychology (MA, MS, Ed D, Psy D, Certificate, Postdoctoral Respecialization Certificate); psychopharmacology (MS, Certificate); substance abuse counseling (Certificate).

ARGOSY UNIVERSITY, LOS ANGELES, Los Angeles, CA 90045

General Information Proprietary, coed, university.

GRADUATE UNITS

College of Business Offers accounting (DBA); corporate compliance (MBA); customized professional concentration (MBA, DBA); finance (MBA); fraud examination (MBA); global business sustainability (DBA); healthcare administration (MBA); information systems (DBA); information systems management (MBA); international business (MBA, DBA); management (MBA, MSM, DBA); marketing (MBA, DBA); organizational leadership (Ed D); public administration (MBA); sustainable management (MBA).

College of Education Offers community college executive leadership (Ed D); educational leadership (MA Ed, Ed D); instructional leadership (MA Ed, Ed D).

College of Health Sciences Offers public health (MPH).

College of Psychology and Behavioral Sciences Offers clinical psychology/marriage and family therapy (MA); counseling psychology (Ed D); counseling psychology/marriage and family therapy (MA); forensic psychology (MA).

ARGOSY UNIVERSITY, NORTHERN VIRGINIA, Arlington, VA 22209

General Information Proprietary, coed, university.

GRADUATE UNITS

American School of Professional Psychology Offers clinical psychology (MA, Psy D); community counseling (MA); counseling psychology (Ed D); counselor education and supervision (Ed D); forensic psychology (MA).

College of Business Offers accounting (DBA); customized professional concentration (MBA, DBA); finance (MBA); fraud examination (MBA); global business sustainability (DBA); healthcare administration (MBA); information systems (DBA); information systems management (MBA); international business (MBA, DBA, Certificate); management (MBA, MSM, DBA); marketing (MBA, DBA, Certificate); organizational leadership (Ed D); public administration (MBA); sustainable management (MBA).

College of Education Offers community college executive leadership (Ed D); educational leadership (MA Ed, Ed D, Ed S); instructional leadership (MA Ed, Ed D, Ed S).

College of Health Sciences Offers public health (MPH).

ARGOSY UNIVERSITY, ORANGE COUNTY, Orange, CA 92868

General Information Proprietary, coed, university.

GRADUATE UNITS

American School of Professional Psychology *Program availability:* Part-time, evening/weekend. Offers child and adolescent psychology (Psy D); counseling psychology (Ed D); forensic psychology (MA); marriage and family therapy (MA); professional psychology (MA, Ed D, Psy D); sport-exercise psychology (MA). Electronic applications accepted.

College of Business Offers accounting (DBA, Adv C); corporate compliance (MBA); customized professional concentration (MBA, DBA); finance (MBA, Certificate); fraud examination (MBA); global business sustainability (DBA); healthcare administration (MBA, Certificate); information systems (DBA, Adv C, Certificate); information systems management (MBA); international business (MBA, DBA, Adv C, Certificate); management (MBA, MSM, DBA, Adv C); marketing (MBA, DBA, Adv C, Certificate); organizational leadership (Ed D); public administration (MBA, Certificate); sustainable management (MBA).

College of Education Offers community college executive leadership (Ed D); educational leadership (MA Ed, Ed D); instructional leadership (MA Ed, Ed D).

College of Health Sciences Offers public health (MPH).

ARGOSY UNIVERSITY, PHOENIX, Phoenix, AZ 85021

General Information Proprietary, coed, university.

GRADUATE UNITS

Arizona School of Professional Psychology Offers clinical psychology (MA); forensic psychology (MA); industrial organizational psychology (MA); mental health counseling (MA); neuropsychology (Psy D); professional psychology (MA, Psy D); sport–exercise psychology (MA); sports-exercise psychology (Psy D).

College of Business Offers accounting (DBA); corporate compliance (MBA); customized professional concentration (MBA, DBA); finance (MBA); fraud examination (MBA); global business sustainability (DBA); healthcare administration (MBA); information systems (DBA); information systems management (MBA); international business (MBA, DBA); management (MBA, DBA); marketing (MBA, DBA); public administration (MBA); sustainable management (MBA).

College of Education Offers adult education and training (MA Ed); advanced educational administration (Ed D, Ed S); community college executive leadership (Ed D); educational administration (MA Ed); educational leadership (MA Ed, Ed D, Ed S); higher and postsecondary education (MA Ed); initial educational administration (Ed D, Ed S); school psychology (MA, Psy D); teaching and learning (MA Ed, Ed D, Ed S).

College of Health Sciences Offers public health (MPH).

ARGOSY UNIVERSITY, SEATTLE, Seattle, WA 98121

General Information Proprietary, coed, university.

GRADUATE UNITS

College of Business Offers accounting (DBA); corporate compliance (MBA); customized professional concentration (MBA, DBA); finance (MBA); fraud examination (MBA); global business sustainability (DBA); healthcare administration (MBA); information systems (DBA); information systems management (MBA); international business (MBA, DBA); management (MBA, MSM, DBA); marketing (MBA, DBA); organizational leadership (Ed D); public administration (MBA); sustainable management (MBA).

College of Education Offers adult education and training (MA Ed); community college executive leadership (Ed D); educational leadership (MA Ed, Ed D); higher and postsecondary education (MA Ed); instructional leadership (MA Ed, Ed D).

College of Health Sciences Offers public health (MPH).

College of Psychology and Behavioral Sciences Offers clinical psychology (MA, Psy D, Postdoctoral Respecialization Certificate); counseling psychology (MA, Ed D); psychology and behavioral sciences (MA, Ed D, Psy D, Postdoctoral Respecialization Certificate).

ARGOSY UNIVERSITY, TAMPA, Tampa, FL 33607

General Information Proprietary, coed, university.

GRADUATE UNITS

College of Business Offers accounting (DBA); corporate compliance (MBA); customized professional concentration (MBA, DBA); finance (MBA); fraud examination (MBA); global business sustainability (DBA); healthcare administration (MBA); information systems (DBA); information systems management (MBA); international business (MBA, DBA); management (MBA, MSM, DBA); marketing (MBA, DBA); organizational leadership (Ed D); public administration (MBA); sustainable management (MBA).

College of Education Offers community college executive leadership (Ed D); educational leadership (MA Ed, Ed D, Ed S); school counseling (MA); teaching and learning (MA Ed, Ed D, Ed S).

College of Health Sciences Offers public health (MPH).

Florida School of Professional Psychology Offers clinical psychology (MA, Psy D); counselor education and supervision (Ed D); industrial organizational psychology (MA); marriage and family therapy (MA); mental health counseling (MA).

ARGOSY UNIVERSITY, TWIN CITIES, Eagan, MN 55121

General Information Proprietary, coed, university.

GRADUATE UNITS

College of Business Offers accounting (DBA); customized professional concentration (MBA, DBA); finance (MBA); fraud examination (MBA); global business sustainability (DBA); healthcare administration (MBA); information systems (DBA); information systems management (MBA); international business (MBA, DBA); management (MBA, MSM, DBA); marketing (MBA, DBA); organizational leadership (Ed D); public administration (MBA); sustainable management (MBA).

College of Education Offers advanced educational administration (Ed D, Ed S); educational leadership (MA Ed, Ed D, Ed S); higher and postsecondary education (MA Ed); initial educational administration (Ed D, Ed S); instructional leadership (MA Ed, Ed D, Ed S).

College of Health Sciences Offers health services management (MS); public health (MPH).

Minnesota School of Professional Psychology Offers clinical psychology (MA, Psy D); forensic counseling (Post-Graduate Certificate); forensic psychology (MA); industrial organizational psychology (MA); marriage and family therapy (MA, DMFT).

ARIZONA SCHOOL OF ACUPUNCTURE AND ORIENTAL MEDICINE, Tucson, AZ 85712

General Information Proprietary, coed, graduate-only institution.

GRADUATE UNITS

Graduate Programs Offers acupuncture (M Ac, M Ac OM).

ARIZONA STATE UNIVERSITY AT THE TEMPE CAMPUS, Tempe, AZ 85287

General Information State-supported, coed, university. CGS member. *Graduate housing:* Room and/or apartments available to single students; on-campus housing not available to married students. *Research affiliation:* Mayo Clinic (healthcare, biomedical informatics), Raytheon Corporation (computer science and engineering), Translational Genomics Research Institute (TGen) (biomedicine), Arizona Public Service (electrical, computer and energy engineering), Banner Health (health, biomedical, and life sciences), Honeywell (mechanical and aerospace engineering).

GRADUATE UNITS

College of Health Solutions Offers audiology (Au D); behavioral health (DBH); biomedical informatics (MS, PhD); communication disorders (MS); health solutions (MS, Au D, DBH, PhD); speech and hearing science (PhD).

School of Nutrition and Health Promotion Offers clinical exercise physiology (MS); exercise and wellness (MS); nutrition (MS); obesity prevention and management (MS); physical activity, nutrition and wellness (PhD).

College of Liberal Arts and Sciences *Program availability:* Part-time, online learning. Offers American media and popular culture (MAS); applied behavior analysis (MS); applied linguistics (PhD); behavioral neuroscience (PhD); biochemistry (MS, PhD); chemistry (MS, PhD); clinical psychology (PhD); cognitive science (PhD); creative writing (MFA); developmental psychology (PhD); English (MA, PhD); film and media studies (MAS); liberal arts and sciences (MA, MAS, MFA, MLS, MNS, MS, MTESOL, MUEP, PSM, PSM, PhD, Graduate Certificate); liberal studies (MLS); linguistics (Graduate Certificate); nanoscience (PSM, PSM); physics (MNS, PhD); quantitative psychology (PhD); science and technology policy (MS); social psychology (PhD); teaching English to speakers of other languages (MTESOL); translation studies (Graduate Certificate). Electronic applications accepted.

Hugh Downs School of Human Communication *Program availability:* Evening/weekend. Offers communication (PhD). Electronic applications accepted.

School of Earth and Space Exploration Offers astrophysics (MS, PhD); exploration systems design (PhD); geological sciences (MS, PhD). PhD in exploration systems design is offered in collaboration with the Ira A. Fulton School of Engineering. Electronic applications accepted.

School of Geographical Sciences and Urban Planning Offers geographic information systems (MAS); geographical information science (Graduate Certificate); geography (MA, PhD); transportation systems (Graduate Certificate); urban and environmental planning (MUEP); urban planning (PhD). Electronic applications accepted.

School of Historical, Philosophical and Religious Studies *Program availability:* Part-time. Offers European history (MA, PhD); medieval studies (Graduate Certificate); North American history (MA, PhD); philosophy (MA, PhD); public history (MA); religious studies (MA, PhD); Renaissance studies (Graduate Certificate); scholarly publishing (Graduate Certificate). Electronic applications accepted.

School of Human Evolution and Social Change Offers anthropology (MA, PhD); applied mathematics for the life and social sciences (PhD); environmental social science (PhD); global health (MA, PhD); immigration studies (Graduate Certificate). Electronic applications accepted.

School of International Letters and Cultures Offers Asian languages and civilizations: Chinese (MA); Asian languages and civilizations: Japanese (MA); Chinese (MA, PhD); comparative literature (MA); cultural studies (PhD); French (MA); German (MA); Japanese (MA); language and culture (MA); linguistics (MA); literature (MA, PhD); literature and culture (MA); Spanish (MA, PhD). Electronic applications accepted.

School of Life Sciences Offers animal behavior (PhD); applied ethics (biomedical and health ethics) (MA); biology (MS, PhD); environmental life sciences (PhD); evolutionary biology (PhD); history and philosophy of science (PhD); human and social dimensions of science and technology (PhD); microbiology (PhD); molecular and cellular biology (PhD); neuroscience (PhD). Electronic applications accepted.

School of Mathematical and Statistical Sciences *Program availability:* Part-time. Offers applied mathematics (PhD); mathematics (MA, PhD); mathematics education (PhD); statistics (MS, PhD, Graduate Certificate). Electronic applications accepted.

School of Politics and Global Studies *Program availability:* Part-time. Offers political science (MA, PhD). Electronic applications accepted.

School of Social and Family Dynamics Offers family and human development (MS, PhD); infant-family practice (MAS); marriage and family therapy (MAS); sociology (MA, PhD). Electronic applications accepted.

School of Social Transformation *Program availability:* Part-time. Offers African studies (Graduate Certificate); gender studies (PhD, Graduate Certificate); justice studies (MS, PhD); social and cultural pedagogy (MA); socio-economic justice (Graduate Certificate). Electronic applications accepted.

College of Nursing and Health Innovation *Program availability:* Online learning. Offers advanced nursing practice (DNP); clinical research management (MS); community and public health practice (Graduate Certificate); family mental health nurse practitioner (Graduate Certificate); family nurse practitioner (Graduate Certificate); geriatric nursing (Graduate Certificate); healthcare innovation (MHI); nurse education in academic and practice settings (Graduate Certificate); nurse educator (MS); nursing and healthcare innovation (PhD). Electronic applications accepted.

College of Public Programs *Program availability:* Part-time, evening/weekend, online learning. Electronic applications accepted.

School of Community Resources and Development *Program availability:* Part-time, evening/weekend. Offers community resources and development (MS, PhD); nonprofit leadership and management (Graduate Certificate); nonprofit studies (MNpS); sustainable tourism (MAS). Electronic applications accepted.

School of Criminology and Criminal Justice *Program availability:* Part-time, evening/weekend, online learning. Offers corrections management (Graduate Certificate); criminal justice (MA); criminology and criminal justice (MS, PhD); law enforcement administration (Graduate Certificate). Electronic applications accepted.

School of Public Affairs *Program availability:* Part-time, evening/weekend. Offers emergency management and homeland security (MA); program evaluation (MS); public administration (MPA, PhD); public policy (MPP). Electronic applications accepted.

School of Social Work *Program availability:* Part-time. Offers advanced direct practice (MSW); assessment of integrative health modalities (Graduate Certificate); gerontology (Graduate Certificate); Latino cultural competency (Graduate Certificate); planning, administration and community practice (MSW); social work (PhD); trauma and bereavement (Graduate Certificate). Electronic applications accepted.

Graduate College *Program availability:* Part-time, evening/weekend, online learning. Offers human and social dimensions of science and technology (PhD); neuroscience (PhD). Electronic applications accepted.

Herberger Institute for Design and the Arts Offers design and the arts (M Arch, MA, MFA, MLA, MM, MS, MSD, MUD, DMA, PhD). Electronic applications accepted.

The Design School Offers architecture (M Arch); building design/built environment (MS); design (MSD, PhD); design, environment and the arts (PhD); digital culture (PhD); healthcare and healing environments (PhD); history, theory, and criticism (PhD); landscape architecture (MLA); urban design (MUD). Electronic applications accepted.

School of Art Offers art education (MA); art history (MA); ceramics (MFA); design, environment and the arts (PhD); drawing (MFA); fibers (MFA); intermedia (MFA); metals (MFA); museum studies (MFA); painting (MFA); printmaking (MFA); sculpture (MFA); wood (MFA). Electronic applications accepted.

School of Arts, Media and Engineering Offers media arts and sciences (PhD). Electronic applications accepted.

School of Film, Dance and Theatre Offers dance (MFA); interdisciplinary digital media and performance (MFA); theatre (MA, MFA, PhD). Electronic applications accepted.

School of Music Offers composition (MM, DMA); conducting (DMA); ethnomusicology (MA); interdisciplinary digital media/performance (DMA); music education (MM, PhD); music history and literature (MA); music therapy (MM); performance (MM, DMA). Electronic applications accepted.

Ira A. Fulton Schools of Engineering *Program availability:* Part-time, evening/weekend, online learning. Offers aerospace engineering (MS, PhD); chemical engineering (MS, PhD); construction (MS); embedded systems (M Eng); engineering (M Eng, MA, MCS, MS, MSE, PSM, PhD, Graduate Certificate); enterprise systems innovation and management (MSE); materials science and engineering (MS, PhD); mechanical engineering (MS, PhD); modeling and simulation (M Eng); quality and reliability engineering (M Eng); software engineering (MSE); solar energy engineering and commercialization (PSM); systems engineering (M Eng). Electronic applications accepted.

The Polytechnic School *Program availability:* Part-time, evening/weekend. Offers applied psychology (MS); aviation management and human factors (MS); environmental technology management (MS); global technology and development (MS); graphic information technology (MS); management of technology (MS); manufacturing engineering technology (MS); simulation, modeling, and applied cognitive science (PhD); technology and innovation (MS, PhD). Electronic applications accepted.

School of Biological and Health Systems Engineering *Program availability:* Part-time, evening/weekend. Offers biological design (PhD); biomedical engineering (MS, PhD). Electronic applications accepted.

School of Computing, Informatics, and Decision Systems Engineering *Program availability:* Part-time, evening/weekend, online learning. Offers computer engineering (MS, PhD); computer science (MCS, MS, PhD); industrial engineering (MS, PhD); software engineering (MS). Electronic applications accepted.

School of Electrical, Computer and Energy Engineering *Program availability:* Part-time, evening/weekend, online learning. Offers electrical engineering (MS, MSE, PhD); nuclear power generation (Graduate Certificate). Electronic applications accepted.

School of Sustainable Engineering and the Built Environment *Program availability:* Part-time, evening/weekend, online learning. Offers civil, environmental and sustainable engineering (MS, MSE, PhD); construction engineering (MSE); construction management (MS, PhD). Electronic applications accepted.

Mary Lou Fulton Teachers College *Program availability:* Part-time, evening/weekend, online learning. Offers autism spectrum disorder (Graduate Certificate); curriculum and instruction (M Ed, MA); education (M Ed, MA, MC, MPE, Ed D, PhD, Graduate Certificate); educational leadership (M Ed); educational policy and evaluation (PhD); educational technology (M Ed); elementary education (M Ed); higher and post-secondary education (M Ed); instructional design and performance improvement (Graduate Certificate); leadership and innovation (Ed D); online teaching for grades K-12 (Graduate Certificate); physical education (MPE); secondary education (M Ed); special education (M Ed). Electronic applications accepted.

New College of Interdisciplinary Arts and Sciences *Program availability:* Part-time, evening/weekend. Offers applied ethics and the professions (MA); communication studies (MA); interdisciplinary studies (MA); psychology (MS); social justice and human rights (MA). Electronic applications accepted.

Sandra Day O'Connor College of Law Students: 777 full-time (337 women); includes 207 minority (21 Black or African American, non-Hispanic/Latino; 14 American Indian or Alaska Native, non-Hispanic/Latino; 32 Asian, non-Hispanic/Latino; 104 Hispanic/Latino; 3 Native Hawaiian or other Pacific Islander, non-Hispanic/Latino; 33 Two or more races, non-Hispanic/Latino), 15 international. Average age 28. 2,056 applicants, 41% accepted, 215 enrolled. *Faculty:* 69 full-time (30 women), 115 part-time/adjunct (29 women). Expenses: Contact institution. *Financial support:* In 2017–18, 430 students received support. Institutionally sponsored loans and scholarships/grants available. Financial award application deadline: 3/15; financial award applicants required to submit FAFSA. In 2017, 52 master's, 198 doctorates awarded. *Program availability:* 100% online. Offers biotechnology and genomics (LL M); law (JD); legal studies (MLS); patent practice (MLS); sports law and business (MSLB); tribal policy, law and government (LL M). JD/MD offered jointly with Mayo Medical School. *Application deadline:* For fall admission, 3/1 priority date for domestic and international students. Applications are processed on a rolling basis. Electronic applications accepted. *Application Contact:* Chitra Damania, Director, 480-965-1474, Fax: 480-727-7930, E-mail: law.admissions@asu.edu. *Dean/Professor,* Douglas Sylvester, 480-965-6188, Fax: 480-965-6521, E-mail: douglas.sylvester@asu.edu.

School of Letters and Sciences *Program availability:* Part-time, evening/weekend, online learning. Offers biomedical and health ethics (MA); counseling (MC); counseling psychology (PhD); ethics and emerging technologies (MA); letters and sciences (MA, MC, PhD); public administration, policy and ethics (MA); science, technology and ethics (MA). Electronic applications accepted.

School of Sustainability *Program availability:* Part-time, evening/weekend. Offers sustainability (MA, MS, PhD); sustainable technology and management (Graduate Certificate). Electronic applications accepted.

Thunderbird School of Global Management *Program availability:* Online learning. Offers global affairs and management (MA); global management (MGM).

Walter Cronkite School of Journalism and Mass Communication Offers journalism and mass communication (PhD); mass communication (MMC). Electronic applications accepted.

W. P. Carey School of Business *Program availability:* Part-time, evening/weekend, online learning. Offers business (M Acc, M Tax, MBA, MRED, MS, PhD, Graduate Certificate); business administration (PhD); economics (PhD); entrepreneurship (MBA); finance (MBA); health sector management (MBA); information management (MS); international business (MBA); leadership (MBA); marketing (MBA); organizational behavior (PhD); real estate development (MRED); strategic management (PhD); supply chain management (MBA, PhD). Electronic applications accepted.

Morrison School of Agribusiness *Program availability:* Part-time, evening/weekend. Offers agribusiness (PhD). Electronic applications accepted.

School of Accountancy *Program availability:* Part-time, evening/weekend. Offers accountancy (M Acc, M Tax); business administration (PhD). Electronic applications accepted.

ARIZONA SUMMIT LAW SCHOOL, Phoenix, AZ 85004

General Information Proprietary, coed, graduate-only institution. *Enrollment by degree level:* 386 doctoral. *Graduate faculty:* 10 full-time (8 women), 7 part-time/adjunct (4 women). *Graduate housing:* On-campus housing not available. *Student services:* Campus employment opportunities, career counseling, free psychological counseling, international student services, services for students with disabilities, writing training.

Computer facilities: A campuswide network can be accessed from student residence rooms and from off campus.
Website: http://www.azsummitlaw.edu/

General Application Contact: Rick Jackson, Associate Dean of Admissions, 602-682-6817, E-mail: admissions@azsummitlaw.edu.

GRADUATE UNITS

JD Program Students: 184 full-time (91 women), 202 part-time (113 women); includes 165 minority (68 Black or African American, non-Hispanic/Latino; 11 American Indian or Alaska Native, non-Hispanic/Latino; 20 Asian, non-Hispanic/Latino; 63 Hispanic/Latino; 2 Native Hawaiian or other Pacific Islander, non-Hispanic/Latino; 1 Two or more races, non-Hispanic/Latino), 5 international. Average age 33. *Faculty:* 10 full-time (8 women), 7 part-time/adjunct (4 women). Expenses: Contact institution. *Financial support:* Applicants required to submit FAFSA. In 2017, 221 doctorates awarded. *Program availability:* Part-time, evening/weekend. Offers law (JD). *Application Contact:* Rick Jackson, Associate Dean of Admissions, 602-682-6817, E-mail: admissions@azsummitlaw.edu.

ARKANSAS STATE UNIVERSITY, State University, AR 72467

General Information State-supported, coed, comprehensive institution. CGS member. *Graduate housing:* Rooms and/or apartments available on a first-come, first-served basis to single and married students. *Research affiliation:* Oak Ridge Associated Universities (scientific research and education development), Applied Biotechnologies Institute (recombinant proteins), Biostrategies, LLC (biotechnology), Infinite Enzymes (plant biotechnology), Nature West (physical, engineering, and life sciences), GeneCoMe (biotechnology).

GRADUATE UNITS

Graduate School *Program availability:* Part-time, online learning. Electronic applications accepted.

College of Agriculture and Technology *Program availability:* Part-time. Offers agricultural education (SCCT); agriculture (MSA); vocational-technical administration (SCCT). Electronic applications accepted.

College of Business *Program availability:* Part-time, evening/weekend. Offers accountancy (M Acc); business (M Acc, MBA, SCCT); business administration (MBA); business administration education (SCCT); business technology education (SCCT). Electronic applications accepted.

College of Education and Behavioral Science *Program availability:* Part-time, online learning. Offers clinical mental health counseling (Graduate Certificate); college student personnel services (MS); community college administration (SCCT); curriculum and instruction (MSE); dyslexia therapy (Graduate Certificate); early childhood education (MSE); early childhood services (MS); education and behavioral science (MAT, MRC, MS, MSE, Ed D, Ed S, Graduate Certificate, SCCT); educational leadership (MSE, Ed D, Ed S); educational theory and practice (MSE); exercise science (MS); middle level education (MAT, MSE); physical education (MSE, SCCT); psychological science (MS); psychology and counseling (Ed S); reading (MSE, Ed S); rehabilitation counseling (MRC); school counseling (MSE); special education - gifted, talented, and creative (MSE); special education - instructional specialist grades 4-12 (MSE); special education - instructional specialist grades P-4 (MSE); special education, K-12 (MSE); sports administration (MS); student affairs (Graduate Certificate). Electronic applications accepted.

College of Engineering *Program availability:* Part-time. Offers engineering (MS Eng); engineering management (MEM). Electronic applications accepted.

College of Fine Arts *Program availability:* Part-time. Offers fine arts (MM, MME, SCCT); music education (MME, SCCT); music performance (MM). Electronic applications accepted.

College of Humanities and Social Sciences *Program availability:* Part-time. Offers criminal justice (MA); English (MA); English education (MSE, SCCT); heritage studies (MA, PhD); history (MA); history education (SCCT); humanities and social sciences (MA, MPA, MSE, PhD, SCCT); political science (MA); political science education (SCCT); public administration (MPA); social science education (MSE); sociology (MA); sociology education (SCCT). Electronic applications accepted.

College of Media and Communication *Program availability:* Part-time. Offers communication studies (MA, SCCT); health communications (Graduate Certificate); mass communications (MSMC); media and communication (MA, MSMC, Graduate Certificate, SCCT). Electronic applications accepted.

College of Nursing and Health Professions *Program availability:* Part-time. Offers addiction studies (Graduate Certificate); aging studies (Graduate Certificate); communication disorders (MCD); disaster preparedness and emergency management (MS); dyslexia therapy (Graduate Certificate); health care management (Graduate Certificate); health sciences (MS); health sciences education (Graduate Certificate); healthcare emergency management (Graduate Certificate); nurse anesthesia (MSN); nursing (MSN); nursing and health professions (MCD, MS, MSN, MSW, DNP, DOT, DPT, Graduate Certificate); nursing practice (DNP); occupational therapy (DOT); physical therapy (DPT); social work (MSW). Electronic applications accepted.

College of Sciences and Mathematics *Program availability:* Part-time. Offers biological sciences (MA); biology (MS); biology education (MSE, SCCT); biotechnology (PSM); chemistry (MS); chemistry education (MSE, SCCT); computer science (MS); environmental sciences (MS, PhD); mathematics (MS); mathematics education (MSE); molecular biosciences (MS, PhD); sciences and mathematics (MA, MS, MSE, PSM, PhD, SCCT). Electronic applications accepted.

ARKANSAS TECH UNIVERSITY, Russellville, AR 72801

General Information State-supported, coed, comprehensive institution. CGS member. *Enrollment:* 11,830 graduate, professional, and undergraduate students; 168 full-time matriculated graduate/professional students (78 women), 720 part-time matriculated graduate/professional students (506 women). *Enrollment by degree level:* 830 master's, 39 doctoral, 19 other advanced degrees. *Graduate faculty:* 88 full-time (37 women), 16 part-time/adjunct (13 women). Tuition, state resident: full-time $6816; part-time $284 per credit hour. Tuition, nonresident: full-time $13,632; part-time $568 per credit hour. *Required fees:* $420 per semester. Tuition and fees vary according to course load. *Graduate housing:* Room and/or apartments available on a first-come, first-served basis to single students; on-campus housing not available to married students. Typical cost: $4412 per year ($7654 including board). Room and board charges vary according to board plan and housing facility selected. Housing application deadline: 8/1. *Student services:* Campus employment opportunities, campus safety program, career counseling, exercise/wellness program, free psychological counseling, international student services, low-cost health insurance, multicultural affairs office, services for students with disabilities, teacher training. *Library facilities:* Ross Pendergraft Library and Technology Center. *Collection:* Books: 313,011 (physical), 47,410 (digital/electronic); Serial titles: 265 (physical), 151 (digital/electronic); Databases: 262. Students can reserve study rooms.

Computer facilities: Computer purchase and lease plans are available. 1,124 computers available on campus for general student use. A campuswide network can be accessed from student residence rooms and from off campus. Online class registration is available.
Website: http://www.atu.edu/

General Application Contact: Dr. Mary B. Gunter, Dean of Graduate College, 479-968-0398, Fax: 479-964-0542, E-mail: gradcollege@atu.edu.

GRADUATE UNITS

College of Arts and Humanities Students: 35 full-time (22 women), 122 part-time (94 women); includes 34 minority (11 Black or African American, non-Hispanic/Latino; 2 Asian, non-Hispanic/Latino; 19 Hispanic/Latino; 2 Two or more races, non-Hispanic/Latino), 19 international. Average age 34. Expenses: Contact institution. *Financial support:* In 2017–18, research assistantships with full and partial tuition reimbursements (averaging $4,800 per year), teaching assistantships with full and partial tuition reimbursements (averaging $4,800 per year) were awarded; career-related internships or fieldwork, Federal Work-Study, scholarships/grants, health care benefits, and unspecified assistantships also available. Support available to part-time students. Financial award application deadline: 4/15; financial award applicants required to submit FAFSA. In 2017, 85 master's awarded. *Program availability:* Part-time, 100% online, blended/hybrid learning. Offers applied sociology (MS); English (M Ed, MA); history (MA); liberal arts (MLA); multi-media journalism (MA); psychology (MS); teaching English as a second language (MA). *Application deadline:* For fall admission, 3/1 priority date for domestic students, 5/1 priority date for international students; for spring admission, 10/1 priority date for domestic and international students. Applications are processed on a rolling basis. *Application fee:* $40 ($90 for international students). Electronic applications accepted. *Application Contact:* Dr. Mary B. Gunter, Dean of Graduate College, 479-968-0398, Fax: 479-964-0542, E-mail: gradcollege@atu.edu. *Dean*, Dr. Jeffrey Woods, 479-968-0274, Fax: 479-964-0812, E-mail: jwoods@atu.edu.

College of Business Students: 2 full-time (0 women), 44 part-time (30 women); includes 4 minority (2 Black or African American, non-Hispanic/Latino; 2 Two or more races, non-Hispanic/Latino). Average age 31. Expenses: Contact institution. *Financial support:* In 2017–18, research assistantships with full and partial tuition reimbursements (averaging $4,800 per year), teaching assistantships with full and partial tuition reimbursements (averaging $4,800 per year) were awarded; career-related internships or fieldwork, Federal Work-Study, scholarships/grants, health care benefits, and unspecified assistantships also available. Support available to part-time students. Financial award application deadline: 4/15; financial award applicants required to submit FAFSA. In 2017, 15 master's awarded. *Program availability:* Part-time, evening/weekend, 100% online, blended/hybrid learning. Offers business (MBA). *Application deadline:* For fall admission, 3/1 priority date for domestic students, 5/1 priority date for international students; for spring admission, 10/1 priority date for domestic and international students. Applications are processed on a rolling basis. *Application fee:* $40 ($90 for international students). Electronic applications accepted. *Application Contact:* Dr. Mary B. Gunter, Dean of Graduate College, 479-968-0398, Fax: 479-964-0542, E-mail: gradcollege@atu.edu. *Dean*, Dr. Jeff Robertson, 479-968-0498, E-mail: jrobertson@atu.edu.

College of Education Students: 80 full-time (45 women), 433 part-time (328 women); includes 114 minority (81 Black or African American, non-Hispanic/Latino; 4 American Indian or Alaska Native, non-Hispanic/Latino; 1 Asian, non-Hispanic/Latino; 13 Hispanic/Latino; 15 Two or more races, non-Hispanic/Latino), 2 international. Average age 34. Expenses: Contact institution. *Financial support:* In 2017–18, research assistantships with full and partial tuition reimbursements (averaging $4,800 per year), teaching assistantships with full and partial tuition reimbursements (averaging $4,800 per year) were awarded; career-related internships or fieldwork, Federal Work-Study, scholarships/grants, health care benefits, and unspecified assistantships also available. Support available to part-time students. Financial award application deadline: 4/15; financial award applicants required to submit FAFSA. In 2017, 132 master's, 8 doctorates, 3 other advanced degrees awarded. *Program availability:* Part-time, evening/weekend, 100% online, blended/hybrid learning. Offers college student personnel (MS); educational leadership (M Ed, Ed S); instructional technology (M Ed); school counseling and leadership (M Ed); school leadership (Ed D); special education K-12 (M Ed); strength and conditioning studies (MS); teaching (MAT); teaching, learning, and leadership (M Ed). *Application deadline:* For fall admission, 3/1 priority date for domestic students, 5/1 priority date for international students; for spring admission, 10/1 priority date for domestic and international students. Applications are processed on a rolling basis. *Application fee:* $40 ($90 for international students). Electronic applications accepted. *Dean*, Dr. Mary Gunter, 479-964-3217, E-mail: mgunter@atu.edu.

College of Engineering and Applied Sciences Students: 45 full-time (8 women), 68 part-time (18 women); includes 22 minority (9 Black or African American, non-

Hispanic/Latino; 3 American Indian or Alaska Native, non-Hispanic/Latino; 4 Asian, non-Hispanic/Latino; 3 Hispanic/Latino; 3 Two or more races, non-Hispanic/Latino), 36 international. Average age 32. Expenses: Contact institution. *Financial support:* In 2017–18, research assistantships with full and partial tuition reimbursements (averaging $4,800 per year), teaching assistantships with full and partial tuition reimbursements (averaging $4,800 per year) were awarded; career-related internships or fieldwork, Federal Work-Study, scholarships/grants, health care benefits, and unspecified assistantships also available. Support available to part-time students. Financial award application deadline: 4/15; financial award applicants required to submit FAFSA. In 2017, 36 master's awarded. *Program availability:* Part-time, evening/weekend, 100% online, blended/hybrid learning. Offers electrical engineering (M Engr); emergency management (MS); information technology (MS); mechanical engineering (M Engr). *Application deadline:* For fall admission, 3/1 priority date for domestic students, 5/1 priority date for international students; for spring admission, 10/1 priority date for domestic and international students. Applications are processed on a rolling basis. *Application fee:* $40 ($90 for international students). Electronic applications accepted. *Application Contact:* Dr. Mary B. Gunter, Dean of Graduate College, 479-968-0398, Fax: 479-964-0542, E-mail: gradcollege@atu.edu. *Dean*, Dr. Douglas Barlow, 479-968-0353, E-mail: dbarlow@atu.edu.

College of Natural and Health Sciences Students: 6 full-time (3 women), 53 part-time (36 women); includes 14 minority (9 Black or African American, non-Hispanic/Latino; 1 Asian, non-Hispanic/Latino; 3 Hispanic/Latino; 1 Two or more races, non-Hispanic/Latino), 1 international. Average age 35. Expenses: Contact institution. *Financial support:* In 2017–18, research assistantships with full and partial tuition reimbursements (averaging $4,800 per year), teaching assistantships with full and partial tuition reimbursements (averaging $4,800 per year) were awarded; career-related internships or fieldwork, Federal Work-Study, scholarships/grants, health care benefits, and unspecified assistantships also available. Support available to part-time students. Financial award application deadline: 4/15; financial award applicants required to submit FAFSA. In 2017, 16 master's awarded. *Program availability:* Part-time, evening/weekend, 100% online, blended/hybrid learning. Offers fisheries and wildlife biology (MS); health informatics (MS); nursing (MSN). *Application deadline:* For fall admission, 3/1 priority date for domestic students, 5/1 priority date for international students; for spring admission, 10/1 priority date for domestic and international students. Applications are processed on a rolling basis. *Application fee:* $40 ($90 for international students). Electronic applications accepted. *Application Contact:* Dr. Mary B. Gunter, Dean of Graduate College, 479-968-0398, Fax: 479-964-0542, E-mail: gradcollege@atu.edu. *Dean*, Dr. Jeff Robertson, 479-968-0498, E-mail: jrobertson@atu.edu.

ARLINGTON BAPTIST UNIVERSITY, Arlington, TX 76012-3425

General Information Independent-religious, coed, comprehensive institution.

GRADUATE UNITS

Program in Biblical and Theological Studies Offers Biblical and theological studies (MA). Electronic applications accepted.

Program in Education Offers curriculum and instruction (M Ed); educational leadership (M Ed).

ART ACADEMY OF CINCINNATI, Cincinnati, OH 45202

General Information Independent, coed, comprehensive institution. *Graduate housing:* Rooms and/or apartments available on a first-come, first-served basis to single and married students. Housing application deadline: 5/1.

GRADUATE UNITS

Program in Art Education *Program availability:* Part-time. Offers art education (MAAE). Offered during summer only. Electronic applications accepted.

ARTCENTER COLLEGE OF DESIGN, Pasadena, CA 91103

General Information Independent, coed, comprehensive institution. *Graduate housing:* On-campus housing not available. *Library facilities:* James Lemont Fogg Memorial Library plus 1 other. *Collection:* Books: 101,955 (physical), 1 million (digital/electronic); Serial titles: 592 (physical), 36,738 (digital/electronic); Databases: 46. Weekly public service hours: 63.

Computer facilities: Computer purchase and lease plans are available. 470 computers available on campus for general student use. A campuswide network can be accessed from off campus. Online class registration is available.
Website: http://www.artcenter.edu/

GRADUATE UNITS

Graduate Art Program Expenses: Contact institution. Offers art (MFA).

Graduate Environmental Design Program Expenses: Contact institution. Offers furniture and fixtures (MS); spatial experience (MS).

Graduate Film Program Expenses: Contact institution. Offers film (MFA).

Graduate Graphic Design Program Expenses: Contact institution. Offers graphic design (MFA).

Graduate Industrial Design Program Expenses: Contact institution. Offers industrial design (MS).

Graduate Media Design Practices Program Expenses: Contact institution. Offers media design practices (MFA).

Graduate Transportation Systems and Design Program Expenses: Contact institution. Offers transportation systems (MS).

THE ART INSTITUTE OF DALLAS, A BRANCH OF MIAMI INTERNATIONAL UNIVERSITY OF ART & DESIGN, Dallas, TX 75231-5993

General Information Proprietary, coed, comprehensive institution.

GRADUATE UNITS

Program in Design and Media Management Offers design and media management (MA).

ASBURY THEOLOGICAL SEMINARY, Wilmore, KY 40390-1199

General Information Independent-religious, coed, primarily men, graduate-only institution. *Graduate housing:* Rooms and/or apartments available on a first-come, first-served basis to single and married students. Housing application deadline: 8/15.

GRADUATE UNITS

Graduate and Professional Programs *Program availability:* Part-time, online learning. Offers theology (M Div, MA, MAAS, MACE, MACL, MACM, MACP, MAMFC, MAMHC, MAPC, MASF, MAYM, Th M, D Min, PhD, Certificate). Electronic applications accepted.

ASBURY UNIVERSITY, Wilmore, KY 40390-1198

General Information Independent-religious, coed, comprehensive institution. *Graduate housing:* On-campus housing not available.

GRADUATE UNITS

School of Graduate and Professional Studies *Program availability:* Part-time. Offers biology: alternative certificate (MA Ed); chemistry: alternative certificate (MA Ed); child and family services (MSW); English (MA Ed); English as a second language (MA Ed); ESL (MA Ed); French (MA Ed); Latin: alternative certificate (MA Ed); mathematics: alternative certificate (MA Ed); reading/writing endorsement (MA Ed); social studies (MA Ed); social work (MSW); Spanish (MA Ed); special education (MA Ed); special education: alternative certificate (MA Ed); teacher as leader endorsement (MA Ed). Electronic applications accepted.

ASHLAND THEOLOGICAL SEMINARY, Ashland, OH 44805

General Information Independent-religious, coed, graduate-only institution. *Graduate housing:* Rooms and/or apartments available on a first-come, first-served basis to single and married students. Housing application deadline: 8/30. *Research affiliation:* Tel Gezer Excavation and Publication Program (archaeological studies), Tyndale House, Cambridge England (faculty study and research).

GRADUATE UNITS

Graduate Programs *Program availability:* Part-time. Offers Biblical studies (MA); Christian ministries (MACM); clinical mental health counseling (MA); counseling (MAC); historical and theological studies (MA); ministry (D Min); pastoral ministry (M Div). MAC program offered in Detroit, MI. Electronic applications accepted.

ASHLAND UNIVERSITY, Ashland, OH 44805-3702

General Information Independent-religious, coed, comprehensive institution. *Enrollment:* 6,579 graduate, professional, and undergraduate students; 1,059 full-time matriculated graduate/professional students (605 women), 586 part-time matriculated graduate/professional students (324 women). *Enrollment by degree level:* 1,520 master's, 125 doctoral. *Graduate faculty:* 71 full-time (35 women), 109 part-time/adjunct (45 women). *Tuition:* Full-time $9621; part-time $4707 per credit hour. *Required fees:* $15 per semester. *Graduate housing:* On-campus housing not available. *Student services:* Campus employment opportunities, campus safety program, career counseling, exercise/wellness program, free psychological counseling, international student services, low-cost health insurance, multicultural affairs office, services for students with disabilities, teacher training, writing training. *Library facilities:* Ashland University Library plus 2 others. *Collection:* Books: 223,607 (physical), 255,789 (digital/electronic); Serial titles: 1,070 (physical), 114,001 (digital/electronic); Databases: 200. Weekly public service hours: 102; students can reserve study rooms. *Research affiliation:* Teacher Quality Project (TQP) (education).

Computer facilities: Computer purchase and lease plans are available. 760 computers available on campus for general student use. A campuswide network can be accessed from student residence rooms and from off campus. Online class registration is available.
Website: http://www.ashland.edu/

General Application Contact: Bernie Bannin, Director, Graduate, Online, and Adult Admissions, 419-289-5291, E-mail: grad-admissions@ashland.edu.

GRADUATE UNITS

College of Arts and Sciences Expenses: Contact institution. *Financial support:* Application deadline: 4/1. Offers American history and government (MAHG); arts and sciences (MA, MAHG, MFA); communication (MA); creative writing (MFA). *Application deadline:* Applications are processed on a rolling basis. *Application fee:* $30. Electronic applications accepted. *Application Contact:* Dr. W. Gregory Gerrick, Dean, Graduate School, 419-289-5750, Fax: 419-289-5949, E-mail: ggerrick@ashland.edu. *Dean*, Dr. Dawn Weber, 419-289-5107.

Dauch College of Business and Economics Students: 458 full-time (210 women), 144 part-time (52 women); includes 88 minority (63 Black or African American, non-Hispanic/Latino; 1 American Indian or Alaska Native, non-Hispanic/Latino; 10 Asian, non-Hispanic/Latino; 14 Hispanic/Latino), 202 international. Average age 31. 216 applicants, 74% accepted, 115 enrolled. *Faculty:* 20 full-time (8 women), 13 part-time/adjunct (2 women). Expenses: Contact institution. *Financial support:* Scholarships/grants, tuition waivers (partial), and unspecified assistantships available. Financial award application deadline: 4/15; financial award applicants required to submit FAFSA. In 2017, 184 master's awarded. *Program availability:* Part-time, evening/weekend, 100% online, blended/hybrid learning. Offers accounting (MBA); business analytics (MBA); entrepreneurship (MBA); financial management (MBA); global management (MBA); health care management and leadership (MBA); human resource management (MBA); human resources (MBA); management information systems (MBA); project management (MBA); sport management (MBA); supply chain management (MBA). *Application deadline:* For fall admission, 8/1 priority date for domestic students; for spring admission, 12/1 priority date for domestic students. Applications are processed on a rolling basis. *Application fee:* $30. Electronic applications accepted. *Application Contact:* Stephen W. Krispinsky, Executive Director of MBA Program, 419-289-5236, Fax: 419-289-5910, E-mail: skrispin@ashland.edu. *Dean*, Dr. Elad Granot, 419-289-5932, E-mail: egranot@ashland.edu.

Dwight Schar College of Education Expenses: Contact institution. *Financial support:* Teaching assistantships with partial tuition reimbursements and scholarships/grants available. *Program availability:* Part-time. Offers education (M Ed, Ed D); educational leadership and administration (M Ed); executive leadership studies (Ed D); leadership studies (Ed D). *Application deadline:* Applications are processed on a rolling basis. *Application fee:* $30. Electronic applications accepted. *Application Contact:* Bernie Bannin, Director, Graduate, Online and Adult Admissions, 419-289-5291, E-mail: grad-admissions@ashland.edu. *Dean*, Dr. Donna Breault, 419-289-5377, E-mail: dbreault@ashland.edu.

Dwight Schar College of Nursing and Health Sciences Expenses: Contact institution. *Financial support:* Applicants required to submit FAFSA. *Program availability:* 100% online, blended/hybrid learning. Offers applied exercise science (MS); family nurse practitioner (DNP); nursing and health sciences (MS, DNP). *Application deadline:* Applications are processed on a rolling basis. Electronic applications accepted. *Application Contact:* Bernie Bannin, Director, Graduate, Online, and Adult Admissions, 419-289-5291, E-mail: grad-admissions@ashland.edu. *Dean and Administrative Officer*, Dr. Faye Grund, 419-521-6802, E-mail: fgrund@ashland.edu.

ASHWORTH COLLEGE, Norcross, GA 30092

General Information Proprietary, coed, comprehensive institution.

GRADUATE UNITS

Graduate Programs Offers business administration (MBA); criminal justice (MS); health care administration (MBA, MS); human resource management (MBA, MS); international business (MBA); management (MS); marketing (MBA, MS).

ASPEN UNIVERSITY, Denver, CO 80246-1930

General Information Independent, coed, comprehensive institution. *Graduate housing:* On-campus housing not available.

GRADUATE UNITS

Program in Business Administration *Program availability:* Part-time, evening/weekend, online learning. Offers business administration (MBA); finance (MBA); information management (MBA); project management (MBA, Certificate). Electronic applications accepted.

Program in Information Technology *Program availability:* Part-time, evening/weekend, online learning. Offers information technology (MS, Certificate). Electronic applications accepted.

Program in Nursing Offers forensic nursing (MSN); informatics (MSN); nursing (MSN); nursing administration and management (MSN); nursing education (MSN); public health (MSN).

Programs in Information Management *Program availability:* Part-time, evening/weekend, online learning. Offers information management (MS); information systems (Certificate). Electronic applications accepted.

ASSEMBLIES OF GOD THEOLOGICAL SEMINARY, Springfield, MO 65802

General Information Independent-religious, coed, graduate-only institution. *Enrollment by degree level:* 152 master's, 160 doctoral. *Graduate faculty:* 12 full-time (3 women), 15 part-time/adjunct (4 women). *Graduate housing:* On-campus housing not available. *Student services:* Campus employment opportunities, campus safety program, career counseling, exercise/wellness program, free psychological counseling, international student services, services for students with disabilities, writing training. *Library facilities:* Cordas C. Burnett Library plus 2 others.

Computer facilities: 18 computers available on campus for general student use. A campuswide network can be accessed. Online class registration is available.
Website: http://www.agts.edu/

General Application Contact: Erin Leonard, Seminary Enrollment Coordinator, 417-268-1000, Fax: 417-268-1001, E-mail: info@agts.edu.

GRADUATE UNITS

Graduate and Professional Programs Students: 153 full-time (48 women), 159 part-time (41 women); includes 62 minority (20 Black or African American, non-Hispanic/Latino; 4 American Indian or Alaska Native, non-Hispanic/Latino; 14 Asian, non-Hispanic/Latino; 18 Hispanic/Latino; 6 Two or more races, non-Hispanic/Latino), 12 international. Average age 46. 69 applicants, 88% accepted, 48 enrolled. *Faculty:* 12 full-time (3 women), 15 part-time/adjunct (4 women). Expenses: Contact institution. *Financial support:* Career-related internships or fieldwork and scholarships/grants available. Support available to part-time students. Financial award application deadline: 7/15; financial award applicants required to submit FAFSA. In 2017, 35 master's, 22 doctorates awarded. *Program availability:* Part-time, evening/weekend, 100% online. Offers Biblical interpretation and theology (PhD); Christian ministries (MA); divinity (M Div); intercultural studies (MA, PhD); leadership and ministry (MLM); ministry (D Min); missiology (DAIS); pastoral studies (MPL); theological studies (MA, Th M). *Application deadline:* For fall admission, 7/1 priority date for domestic students, 6/1 priority date for international students; for spring admission, 12/1 priority date for domestic students, 11/1 priority date for international students. Applications are processed on a rolling basis. *Application fee:* $75. Electronic applications accepted. *Application Contact:* Erin Leonard, Seminary Enrollment Coordinator, 417-268-1000, Fax: 417-268-1001, E-mail: info@agts.edu. *Dean*, Dr. Timothy A. Hager, 417-268-1000, Fax: 417-268-1001.

ASSUMPTION COLLEGE, Worcester, MA 01609-1296

General Information Independent-religious, coed, comprehensive institution. *Enrollment:* 2,334 graduate, professional, and undergraduate students; 143 full-time matriculated graduate/professional students (99 women), 230 part-time matriculated graduate/professional students (178 women). *Enrollment by degree level:* 341 master's, 32 other advanced degrees. *Graduate faculty:* 17 full-time (8 women), 59 part-time/adjunct (29 women). *Tuition:* Full-time $11,952; part-time $664 per credit. *Required fees:* $70 per term. *Graduate housing:* On-campus housing not available. *Student services:* Campus employment opportunities, campus safety program, career counseling, exercise/wellness program, international student services, low-cost health insurance, multicultural affairs office, services for students with disabilities. *Library facilities:* Emmanuel d'Alzon Library. *Collection:* Books: 131,961 (physical), 159,279 (digital/electronic); Serial titles: 2,163 (physical), 45,363 (digital/electronic); Databases: 78. Weekly public service hours: 102; students can reserve study rooms.

Computer facilities: Computer purchase and lease plans are available. 361 computers available on campus for general student use. A campuswide network can be accessed from student residence rooms and from off campus. Online class registration is available.
Website: http://www.assumption.edu/

General Application Contact: Karen Stoyanoff, Director of Recruitment for Graduate Enrollment, 508-767-7442, Fax: 508-799-4412, E-mail: graduate@assumption.edu.

GRADUATE UNITS

Addiction Counseling Program Expenses: Contact institution. *Program availability:* Part-time, evening/weekend. Offers addiction counseling (CGS). *Application deadline:* Applications are processed on a rolling basis. *Application fee:* $30. Electronic applications accepted. *Application Contact:* Karen Stoyanoff, Director of Recruitment for Graduate Enrollment, 508-767-7442, Fax: 508-799-4412, E-mail: graduate@assumption.edu. *Director*, Dr. Leonard A. Doerfler, 508-767-7549, Fax: 508-767-7263, E-mail: doerfler@assumption.edu.

Applied Behavior Analysis Program Students: 7 full-time (6 women), 15 part-time (11 women); includes 3 minority (1 Black or African American, non-Hispanic/Latino; 1 Asian, non-Hispanic/Latino; 1 Hispanic/Latino), 1 international. Average age 32. 27 applicants, 81% accepted, 15 enrolled. *Faculty:* 1 (woman) full-time, 3 part-time/adjunct (2 women). Expenses: Contact institution. *Financial support:* In 2017–18, 8 students received support. Tuition waivers (full and partial) and institutional discounts available. Financial award application deadline: 6/15; financial award applicants required to submit FAFSA. *Program availability:* Part-time, evening/weekend. Offers applied behavior analysis (MA, CAGS). *Application deadline:* For fall admission, 6/15 for domestic and international students. *Application fee:* $30. Electronic applications accepted. *Application Contact:* Karen Stoyanoff, Director of Recruitment for Graduate Enrollment, 508-767-7442, Fax: 508-799-4412, E-mail: graduate@assumption.edu. *Director*, Dr. Karen Lionello-DeNolf, 508-767-7498, E-mail: k.lionellodenolf@assumption.edu.

Business Studies Program Students: 29 full-time (13 women), 87 part-time (50 women); includes 15 minority (1 Black or African American, non-Hispanic/Latino; 4 Asian, non-Hispanic/Latino; 8 Hispanic/Latino; 2 Two or more races, non-Hispanic/Latino), 4 international. Average age 29. 34 applicants, 100% accepted, 26 enrolled. *Faculty:* 5 full-time (1 woman), 21 part-time/adjunct (6 women). Expenses: Contact institution. *Financial support:* In 2017–18, 19 students received support. Tuition waivers (full and partial), unspecified assistantships, and institutional discounts available. Financial award applicants required to submit FAFSA. In 2017, 81 master's, 2 other advanced degrees awarded. *Program availability:* Part-time, evening/weekend. Offers accounting (MBA); business studies (CAGS); finance/economics (MBA); human resources (MBA); international business (MBA); management (MBA); marketing (MBA); nonprofit leadership (MBA). *Application deadline:* For fall admission, 8/10 priority date for domestic and international students; for spring admission, 1/4 priority date for domestic and international students; for summer admission, 5/10 priority date for domestic and international students. *Application fee:* $30. Electronic applications accepted. *Application Contact:* Karen Stoyanoff, Director of Recruitment for Graduate Enrollment, 508-767-7442, Fax: 508-799-4412, E-mail: graduate@assumption.edu. *Director*, Dr. Robin Frkal, 508-767-7622, E-mail: ra.frkal@assumption.edu.

Clinical Counseling Psychology Program Students: 47 full-time (34 women), 19 part-time (all women); includes 9 minority (3 Black or African American, non-Hispanic/Latino; 2 Asian, non-Hispanic/Latino; 3 Hispanic/Latino; 1 Two or more races, non-Hispanic/Latino), 1 international. Average age 27. 59 applicants, 80% accepted, 19 enrolled. *Faculty:* 4 full-time (2 women), 7 part-time/adjunct (2 women). Expenses: Contact institution. *Financial support:* In 2017–18, 18 students received support, including 10 fellowships with full tuition reimbursements available; tuition waivers (full and partial), unspecified assistantships, and institutional discounts also available. Financial award application deadline: 3/1; financial award applicants required to submit FAFSA. In 2017, 20 master's awarded. *Program availability:* Part-time, evening/weekend. Offers child and family interventions (MA); clinical counseling psychology (CAGS); cognitive-behavioral therapies (MA). *Application deadline:* For fall admission, 3/1 priority date for domestic and international students; for spring admission, 10/5 for domestic and international students; for summer admission, 2/8 for domestic and international students. *Application fee:* $30. Electronic applications accepted. *Application Contact:* Karen Stoyanoff, Director of Recruitment for Graduate Enrollment, 508-767-7442, Fax: 508-799-4412, E-mail: graduate@assumption.edu. *Director*, Dr. Leonard A. Doerfler, 508-767-7549, Fax: 508-767-7263, E-mail: doerfler@assumption.edu.

Health Advocacy Program Students: 15 part-time (all women). Average age 50. 8 applicants, 88% accepted, 7 enrolled. *Faculty:* 1 (woman) full-time, 5 part-time/adjunct (3 women). Expenses: Contact institution. *Financial support:* In 2017–18, 1 student received support. Tuition waivers (full and partial) and institutional discounts available. Financial award applicants required to submit FAFSA. In 2017, 2 other advanced degrees awarded. *Program availability:* Part-time, evening/weekend, online only, 100% online. Offers health advocacy (MA, Professional Certificate). *Application deadline:* For fall admission, 7/1 for domestic and international students; for spring admission, 12/1 for domestic and international students. *Application fee:* $30. Electronic applications accepted. *Application Contact:* Karen Stoyanoff, Director of Recruitment for Graduate Enrollment, 508-767-7442, Fax: 508-799-4412, E-mail: graduate@assumption.edu. *Director*, Lea Christo, 508-767-7503, Fax: 508-798-2872, E-mail: l.christo@assumption.edu.

Healthcare Management Program Expenses: Contact institution. *Financial support:* Tuition waivers (full and partial), unspecified assistantships, and institutional discounts available. Financial award applicants required to submit FAFSA. *Program availability:* Part-time, evening/weekend, online only, 100% online, blended/hybrid learning. Offers healthcare management (MBA, CAGS, CGS). *Application deadline:* For fall admission, 8/10 priority date for domestic and international students; for spring admission, 1/4 priority date for domestic and international students; for summer admission, 5/10 priority date for domestic and international students. *Application fee:* $30. Electronic applications accepted. *Application Contact:* Karen Stoyanoff, Director of Recruitment for Graduate Enrollment, 508-767-7442, Fax: 508-799-4412, E-mail: graduate@assumption.edu. *Co-Director*, Dr. Robin Frkal, 508-767-7622, E-mail: ra.frkal@assumption.edu.

Rehabilitation Counseling Program Students: 26 full-time (18 women), 35 part-time (30 women); includes 15 minority (10 Black or African American, non-Hispanic/Latino; 1 American Indian or Alaska Native, non-Hispanic/Latino; 3 Hispanic/Latino; 1 Two or more races, non-Hispanic/Latino). Average age 35. 19 applicants, 89% accepted, 14 enrolled. *Faculty:* 2 full-time (0 women), 15 part-time/adjunct (10 women). Expenses: Contact institution. *Financial support:* In 2017–18, 12 students received support. Scholarships/grants, tuition waivers (full and partial), unspecified assistantships, and institutional discounts available. Financial award application deadline: 4/15; financial award applicants required to submit FAFSA. In 2017, 33 master's awarded. *Program availability:* Part-time, evening/weekend, blended/hybrid learning. Offers rehabilitation counseling (MA, CAGS). *Application deadline:* For fall admission, 7/1 for domestic and international students; for spring admission, 12/1 for domestic and international students; for summer admission, 4/15 for domestic and international students. *Application fee:* $30. Electronic applications accepted. *Application Contact:* Karen Stoyanoff, Director of Recruitment for Graduate Enrollment, 508-767-7442, Fax: 508-799-4915, E-mail: graduate@assumption.edu. *Director*, Dr. Nicholas Cioe, 508-767-7370, Fax: 508-798-2872, E-mail: nj.cioe@assumption.edu.

Resiliency in the Helping Professions Program Students: 6 part-time (all women); includes 1 minority (American Indian or Alaska Native, non-Hispanic/Latino). Average age 42. 4 applicants, 75% accepted, 2 enrolled. *Faculty:* 1 (woman) full-time, 1 (woman) part-time/adjunct. Expenses: Contact institution. *Financial support:* In 2017–18, 1 student received support. Tuition waivers (full and partial) and institutional discounts available. Financial award applicants required to submit FAFSA. In 2017, 2 CAGSs awarded. *Program availability:* Part-time, evening/weekend. Offers resiliency in the helping professions (CAGS, CGS). *Application deadline:* Applications are processed on a rolling basis. *Application fee:* $30. *Application Contact:* Karen Stoyanoff, Director of Recruitment for Graduate Enrollment, 508-767-7442, Fax: 508-799-4412, E-mail: graduate@assumption.edu. *Director*, Lea Christo, 508-767-7503, Fax: 508-798-2872, E-mail: l.christo@assumption.edu.

School Counseling Program Students: 29 full-time (24 women), 32 part-time (26 women); includes 8 minority (3 Black or African American, non-Hispanic/Latino; 4 Hispanic/Latino; 1 Two or more races, non-Hispanic/Latino). Average age 28. 29 applicants, 83% accepted, 15 enrolled. *Faculty:* 3 full-time (2 women), 5 part-time/adjunct (2 women). Expenses: Contact institution. *Financial support:* In 2017–18, 11 students received support. Tuition waivers (full and partial), unspecified assistantships, and institutional discounts available. Financial award applicants required to submit FAFSA. In 2017, 20 master's, 10 other advanced degrees awarded. *Program availability:* Part-time, evening/weekend. Offers school counseling (MA, CAGS). *Application deadline:* Applications are processed on a rolling basis. *Application fee:* $30. Electronic applications accepted. *Application Contact:* Karen Stoyanoff, Director of Recruitment for Graduate Enrollment, 508-767-7442, Fax: 508-799-4915, E-mail: graduate@assumption.edu. *Director,* Dr. Susan Scully-Hill, 508-767-7319, Fax: 508-798-2872, E-mail: sscully@assumption.edu.

Special Education Program Students: 32 full-time (26 women), 45 part-time (39 women); includes 11 minority (4 Black or African American, non-Hispanic/Latino; 6 Hispanic/Latino; 1 Two or more races, non-Hispanic/Latino). Average age 28. 8 applicants, 88% accepted, 6 enrolled. *Faculty:* 2 full-time (both women), 3 part-time/adjunct (all women). Expenses: Contact institution. *Financial support:* In 2017–18, 4 students received support. Tuition waivers (full and partial), unspecified assistantships, and institutional discounts available. Financial award applicants required to submit FAFSA. In 2017, 9 master's, 12 other advanced degrees awarded. *Program availability:* Part-time, evening/weekend. Offers positive behavior support (CAGS); special education (MA). *Application deadline:* Applications are processed on a rolling basis. *Application fee:* $30. Electronic applications accepted. *Application Contact:* Karen Stoyanoff, Director of Recruitment for Graduate Enrollment, 508-767-7442, Fax: 508-799-4915, E-mail: graduate@assumption.edu. *Director,* Dr. Nanho Vander Hart, 508-767-7380, Fax: 508-767-7263, E-mail: nvanderh@assumption.edu.

ATHABASCA UNIVERSITY, Athabasca, AB T9S 3A3, Canada

General Information Province-supported, coed, comprehensive institution. *Graduate housing:* On-campus housing not available. *Research affiliation:* SAP (software), IBM (software).

GRADUATE UNITS

Centre for Distance Education *Program availability:* Part-time, online learning. Offers distance education (MDE, Ed D); distance education technology (Advanced Diploma). Electronic applications accepted.

Centre for Interdisciplinary Studies *Program availability:* Part-time, evening/weekend, online learning. Offers adult education (MA); community studies (MA); cultural studies (MA); educational studies (MA); global change (MA); heritage resource management (Postbaccalaureate Certificate); legislative drafting (Postbaccalaureate Certificate); work, organization, and leadership (MA). Electronic applications accepted.

Faculty of Business *Program availability:* Part-time, evening/weekend, online learning. Offers business administration (MBA); information technology management (MBA); innovative management (DBA); management (GDM); project management (MBA, GDM). Electronic applications accepted.

Faculty of Health Disciplines *Program availability:* Part-time, online learning. Offers advanced nursing practice (MN, Advanced Diploma); generalist (MN); health studies (MHS). Electronic applications accepted.

Faculty of Science and Technology *Program availability:* Part-time, online learning. Offers architecture (Postgraduate Diploma); information systems (M Sc). Electronic applications accepted.

Program in Counseling Offers applied psychology (Post Master's Certificate); art therapy (MC); career counseling (MC); counseling (Advanced Certificate); counseling psychology (MC); school counseling (MC).

THE ATHENAEUM OF OHIO, Cincinnati, OH 45230-5900

General Information Independent-religious, coed, graduate-only institution. *Enrollment by degree level:* 110 master's, 77 other advanced degrees. *Graduate housing:* On-campus housing not available. *Library facilities:* Eugene H. Maly Memorial Library. *Collection:* Students can reserve study rooms.

Computer facilities: 3 computers available on campus for general student use. A campuswide network can be accessed from student residence rooms.
Website: http://www.mtsm.org/

General Application Contact: Nicholas Jobe, Registrar, 513-231-2223, Fax: 513-231-3254, E-mail: njobe@athenaeum.edu.

GRADUATE UNITS

Graduate Programs Students: 80 full-time (1 woman), 62 part-time (31 women); includes 12 minority (1 Black or African American, non-Hispanic/Latino; 3 Asian, non-Hispanic/Latino; 6 Hispanic/Latino; 2 Two or more races, non-Hispanic/Latino), 10 international. Expenses: Contact institution. *Financial support:* Scholarships/grants available. Support available to part-time students. Financial award application deadline: 8/1. In 2017, 16 master's awarded. *Program availability:* Part-time, evening/weekend. Offers theology (M Div, MA, MA Th, MABS, Certificate). *Application deadline:* For fall admission, 4/15 priority date for domestic students; for spring admission, 11/1 priority date for domestic students. Applications are processed on a rolling basis. *Application fee:* $30. *Application Contact:* Nicholas Jobe, Registrar, 513-231-2223, Fax: 513-231-3254, E-mail: njobe@athenaeum.edu. *Dean,* Fr. David J. Endres, 513-231-2223, Fax: 513-231-3254, E-mail: dendres@athenaeum.edu.

ATHENS STATE UNIVERSITY, Athens, AL 35611

General Information State-supported, coed, upper-level institution. *Enrollment:* 3,001 graduate, professional, and undergraduate students; 28 full-time matriculated graduate/professional students (19 women), 119 part-time matriculated graduate/professional students (55 women). *Enrollment by degree level:* 147 master's. Tuition, state resident: full-time $3900; part-time $325 per credit hour. Tuition, nonresident: full-time $3900; part-time $325 per credit hour. *Graduate housing:* On-campus housing not available. *Library facilities:* Athens State University Library. *Collection:* Books: 83,092 (physical), 255,950 (digital/electronic); Serial titles: 289 (physical), 296,023 (digital/electronic); Databases: 23,955. Students can reserve study rooms.

Computer facilities: 210 computers available on campus for general student use. A campuswide network can be accessed. Online class registration, transcripts, e-mail are available.
Website: http://www.athens.edu/

GRADUATE UNITS

Graduate Programs Students: 28 full-time (19 women), 119 part-time (55 women). Expenses: Contact institution. Offers career and technical education (M Ed); global logistics and supply chain management (MS); religious studies (MA).

ATLANTA'S JOHN MARSHALL LAW SCHOOL, Atlanta, GA 30309

General Information Private, coed, graduate-only institution.

GRADUATE UNITS

JD and LL M Programs *Program availability:* Part-time, evening/weekend, online learning. Offers American legal studies (LL M); employment law (LL M); law (JD). Electronic applications accepted.

ATLANTIC INSTITUTE OF ORIENTAL MEDICINE, Fort Lauderdale, FL 33301

General Information Independent, coed, graduate-only institution. *Enrollment by degree level:* 107 master's, 38 doctoral. *Graduate faculty:* 7 full-time (1 woman), 15 part-time/adjunct (6 women). *Tuition:* Full-time $17,000. *Required fees:* $250. One-time fee: $250 full-time. *Graduate housing:* On-campus housing not available. *Student services:* Campus employment opportunities, campus safety program, career counseling, exercise/wellness program, international student services. *Collection:* Books: 3,700 (physical). Weekly public service hours: 50.

Computer facilities: 4 computers available on campus for general student use. A campuswide network can be accessed. Online class registration is available.
Website: http://www.atom.edu/

General Application Contact: Karen Gemignani, Admissions Counselor, 954-763-9840 Ext. 213, Fax: 954-763-9844, E-mail: admissions@atom.edu.

GRADUATE UNITS

Graduate Program Students: 145 full-time (103 women); includes 66 minority (8 Black or African American, non-Hispanic/Latino; 13 Asian, non-Hispanic/Latino; 45 Hispanic/Latino), 8 international. Average age 37. 30 applicants, 53% accepted, 16 enrolled. *Faculty:* 7 full-time (1 woman), 15 part-time/adjunct (6 women). Expenses: Contact institution. *Financial support:* Applicants required to submit FAFSA. In 2017, 29 master's, 15 doctorates awarded. *Program availability:* Evening/weekend. Offers Oriental medicine (MS, DAOM). *Application deadline:* For fall admission, 7/1 for domestic students, 5/1 for international students; for spring admission, 11/30 for domestic students, 2/28 for international students. Applications are processed on a rolling basis. *Application fee:* $20 ($30 for international students). *Application Contact:* Karen Gemignani, Admissions Counselor, 954-763-9840 Ext. 213, Fax: 954-763-9844, E-mail: admissions@atom.edu. *President,* Dr. Johanna C. Yen, 954-763-9840 Ext. 202, Fax: 954-763-9844, E-mail: president@atom.edu.

ATLANTIC SCHOOL OF THEOLOGY, Halifax, NS B3H 3B5, Canada

General Information Independent, coed, graduate-only institution. *Graduate housing:* Rooms and/or apartments available on a first-come, first-served basis to single and married students. Housing application deadline: 6/1.

GRADUATE UNITS

Graduate and Professional Programs *Program availability:* Part-time, online learning. Offers ministry (M Div); theological studies (Graduate Certificate).

ATLANTIC UNIVERSITY, Virginia Beach, VA 23451-2061

General Information Independent, coed, primarily women, graduate-only institution. *Tuition:* Full-time $1080; part-time $1080 per course. *Required fees:* $100; $100 per course. *Graduate housing:* On-campus housing not available. *Library facilities:* A.R.E. Library plus 1 other.

Computer facilities: 2 computers available on campus for general student use. Online class registration is available.
Website: http://www.atlanticuniv.edu/

General Application Contact: Rachel Alvidrez, Associate Vice President of Enrollment Management Services, 757-631-8101, Fax: 757-631-8096, E-mail: rachel.alvidrez@atlanticuniv.edu.

GRADUATE UNITS

Program in Integrated Imagery: Regression Hypnosis Expenses: Contact institution. *Program availability:* Blended/hybrid learning. Offers integrated imagery: regression hypnosis (Graduate Certificate). *Application deadline:* For fall admission, 9/3 for domestic students; for winter admission, 3/12 for domestic students; for spring admission, 12/4 for domestic students; for summer admission, 6/11 for domestic students. Applications are processed on a rolling basis. *Application fee:* $50. Electronic applications accepted. *Application Contact:* Rachel Alvidrez, Educational Services Manager, 757-631-8101, Fax: 757-631-8096, E-mail: info@atlanticuniv.edu.

Program in Mindful Leadership Expenses: Contact institution. *Program availability:* Online learning. Offers global leadership (MA). *Application fee:* $50. *Application Contact:* Rachel Alvidrez, Associate Vice President of Enrollment Management Services, 757-631-8101, Fax: 757-631-8096, E-mail: rachel.alvidrez@atlanticuniv.edu.

Program in Transpersonal Psychology Expenses: Contact institution. *Program availability:* Part-time, evening/weekend, online learning. Offers applied spirituality (MA); consciousness (MA); creativity (MA); general studies (MA); leadership and conflict transformation (MA). *Application deadline:* For fall admission, 9/3 for domestic students; for winter admission, 6/11 for domestic students; for spring admission, 12/4 for domestic students; for summer admission, 3/12 for domestic students. Applications are processed on a rolling basis. *Application fee:* $50. Electronic applications accepted. *Application Contact:* Rachel Alvidrez, Associate Vice President of Enrollment Management Services, 757-631-8101, Fax: 757-631-8096, E-mail: info@atlanticuniv.edu.

Spiritual Guidance Mentor Program Expenses: Contact institution. *Program availability:* Online learning. Offers spiritual guidance mentor (Certificate). *Application deadline:* For fall admission, 9/17 for domestic students; for winter admission, 3/26 for domestic students; for spring admission, 12/18 for domestic students; for summer admission, 6/25 for domestic students. Applications are processed on a rolling basis. *Application fee:* $35. Electronic applications accepted. *Application Contact:* Rachel Alvidrez, Educational Services Manager, 757-631-8101, Fax: 757-631-8096, E-mail: info@atlanticuniv.edu.

ATLANTIC UNIVERSITY COLLEGE, Guaynabo, PR 00970

General Information Independent, coed, comprehensive institution.

GRADUATE UNITS

Program in Graphic Arts *Program availability:* Part-time. Offers digital graphic design (MGD).

ATLANTIS UNIVERSITY, Miami, FL 33132

General Information Proprietary, coed, comprehensive institution.

GRADUATE UNITS

School of Business Offers business (MBA, DBA).

School of Computer Science and Information Technology Offers information technology (MIT).

School of Engineering Offers computer engineering (MS).

School of Health Care Offers healthcare management (MS).

A.T. STILL UNIVERSITY, Kirksville, MO 63501

General Information Independent, coed, graduate-only institution. *Enrollment by degree level:* 758 master's, 2,807 doctoral, 158 other advanced degrees. *Graduate faculty:* 230 full-time (113 women), 504 part-time/adjunct (260 women). *Graduate housing:* Rooms and/or apartments available on a first-come, first-served basis to single and married students. Typical cost: $5460 per year for single students; $5460 per year for married students. Housing application deadline: 4/1. *Student services:* Campus employment opportunities, campus safety program, career counseling, exercise/wellness program, free psychological counseling, multicultural affairs office, services for students with disabilities. *Library facilities:* A.T. Still Memorial Library plus 1 other. *Collection:* Books: 13,285 (physical), 219,033 (digital/electronic); Serial titles: 1,281 (physical), 55,498 (digital/electronic); Databases: 75. Weekly public service hours: 156. *Research affiliation:* Truman State University (osteopathic clinical research), Arizona State University (clinical/translational research/bioengineering), Fresenius University of Applied Sciences, Germany (osteopathic clinical research), Diers Medical Systems (biomechanics, posture and osteopathic clinical research), University of Missouri, Columbia (osteopathic clinical research), Translational Genomics Research Institute (TGen) (genetics research).

Computer facilities: 45 computers available on campus for general student use. A campuswide network can be accessed from student residence rooms and from off campus.
Website: http://www.atsu.edu/

General Application Contact: Donna Sparks, Director, Admissions Processing, 660-626-2117, Fax: 660-626-2969, E-mail: admissions@atsu.edu.

GRADUATE UNITS

Arizona School of Dentistry & Oral Health Students: 311 full-time (164 women); includes 129 minority (5 Black or African American, non-Hispanic/Latino; 4 American Indian or Alaska Native, non-Hispanic/Latino; 83 Asian, non-Hispanic/Latino; 20 Hispanic/Latino; 17 Two or more races, non-Hispanic/Latino), 1 international. Average age 28. 2,433 applicants, 6% accepted, 76 enrolled. *Faculty:* 50 full-time (26 women), 101 part-time/adjunct (36 women). Expenses: Contact institution. *Financial support:* In 2017–18, 49 students received support. Federal Work-Study and scholarships/grants available. Financial award application deadline: 6/1; financial award applicants required to submit FAFSA. In 2017, 74 doctorates, 4 other advanced degrees awarded. Offers dental medicine (DMD); orthodontics (MS, Certificate). *Application deadline:* For fall admission, 11/15 for domestic and international students; for summer admission, 11/15 for domestic and international students. Applications are processed on a rolling basis. *Application fee:* $70. Electronic applications accepted. *Application Contact:* Donna Sparks, Director, Admissions Processing, 660-626-2117, Fax: 660-626-2969, E-mail: admissions@atsu.edu. *Dean*, Dr. Robert Trombly, 480-248-8105, Fax: 623-223-7063, E-mail: rtrombly@atsu.edu.

Arizona School of Health Sciences Students: 608 full-time (405 women), 431 part-time (310 women); includes 247 minority (54 Black or African American, non-Hispanic/Latino; 13 American Indian or Alaska Native, non-Hispanic/Latino; 151 Asian, non-Hispanic/Latino; 2 Hispanic/Latino; 1 Native Hawaiian or other Pacific Islander, non-Hispanic/Latino; 26 Two or more races, non-Hispanic/Latino), 1 international. Average age 33. 4,882 applicants, 9% accepted, 278 enrolled. *Faculty:* 59 full-time (39 women), 221 part-time/adjunct (155 women). Expenses: Contact institution. *Financial support:* In 2017–18, 161 students received support. Federal Work-Study and scholarships/grants available. Financial award application deadline: 6/1; financial award applicants required to submit FAFSA. In 2017, 132 master's, 270 doctorates awarded. *Program availability:* Part-time, 100% online. Offers advanced occupational therapy (MS); advanced physician assistant studies (MS); athletic training (MS, DAT); audiology (Au D); clinical decision making in athletic training (Graduate Certificate); occupational therapy (MS, OTD); orthopedic rehabilitation (Graduate Certificate); physical therapy (DPT); physician assistant studies (MS); transitional audiology (Au D); transitional physical therapy (DPT). *Application deadline:* For fall admission, 7/7 for domestic and international students; for winter admission, 10/3 for domestic and international students; for spring admission, 1/16 for domestic and international students; for summer admission, 4/17 for domestic and international students. Applications are processed on a rolling basis. *Application fee:* $70. Electronic applications accepted. *Application Contact:* Donna Sparks, Director, Admissions Processing, 660-626-2117, Fax: 660-626-2969, E-mail: admissions@atsu.edu. *Dean*, Dr. Randy Danielsen, 480-219-6009, Fax: 480-219-6110, E-mail: rdanielsen@atsu.edu.

College of Graduate Health Studies Students: 537 full-time (334 women), 516 part-time (316 women); includes 397 minority (171 Black or African American, non-Hispanic/Latino; 14 American Indian or Alaska Native, non-Hispanic/Latino; 84 Asian, non-Hispanic/Latino; 106 Hispanic/Latino; 1 Native Hawaiian or other Pacific Islander, non-Hispanic/Latino; 21 Two or more races, non-Hispanic/Latino), 43 international. Average age 36. 392 applicants, 84% accepted, 270 enrolled. *Faculty:* 28 full-time (18 women), 83 part-time/adjunct (43 women). Expenses: Contact institution. *Financial support:* In 2017–18, 18 students received support. Scholarships/grants available. Financial award applicants required to submit FAFSA. In 2017, 138 master's, 102 doctorates, 116 other advanced degrees awarded. *Program availability:* Part-time, evening/weekend, online only, 100% online, blended/hybrid learning. Offers dental public health (MPH); exercise and sport psychology (Certificate); fundamentals of education (Certificate); geriatric exercise science (Certificate); global health (Certificate); health administration (MHA, DHA); health professions (Ed D); health sciences (DH Sc); kinesiology (MS); leadership and organizational behavior (Certificate); public health (MPH); sports conditioning (Certificate). *Application deadline:* For fall admission, 6/26 for domestic students, 5/20 for international students; for winter admission, 9/11 for domestic students, 9/12 for international students; for spring admission, 12/11 for domestic students, 12/12 for international students; for summer admission, 3/5 for domestic students, 3/6 for international students. Applications are processed on a rolling basis. *Application fee:* $70. Electronic applications accepted. *Application Contact:* Amie Waldemer, Associate Director, Online Admissions, 480-219-6146, E-mail: awaldemer@atsu.edu. *Dean*, Dr. Donald Altman, 480-219-6008, Fax: 660-626-2826, E-mail: daltman@atsu.edu.

Kirksville College of Osteopathic Medicine Students: 716 full-time (309 women), 10 part-time (5 women); includes 133 minority (18 Black or African American, non-Hispanic/Latino; 1 American Indian or Alaska Native, non-Hispanic/Latino; 43 Asian, non-Hispanic/Latino; 36 Hispanic/Latino; 35 Two or more races, non-Hispanic/Latino), 1 international. Average age 27. 4,481 applicants, 9% accepted, 183 enrolled. *Faculty:* 37 full-time (6 women), 30 part-time/adjunct (6 women). Expenses: Contact institution. *Financial support:* In 2017–18, 142 students received support, including 22 fellowships with full tuition reimbursements available (averaging $55,455 per year); Federal Work-Study and scholarships/grants also available. Financial award application deadline: 6/1; financial award applicants required to submit FAFSA. In 2017, 13 master's, 172 doctorates awarded. Offers biomedical sciences (MS); osteopathic medicine (DO). *Application deadline:* For fall admission, 2/1 for domestic students; for summer admission, 2/1 for domestic students. Applications are processed on a rolling basis. *Application fee:* $70. Electronic applications accepted. *Application Contact:* Donna Sparks, Director, Admissions Processing, 660-626-2117, Fax: 660-626-2969, E-mail: admissions@atsu.edu. *Dean*, Dr. Margaret Wilson, 660-626-2354, Fax: 660-626-2080, E-mail: mwilson@atsu.edu.

Missouri School of Dentistry & Oral Health Students: 167 full-time (88 women); includes 43 minority (1 American Indian or Alaska Native, non-Hispanic/Latino; 29 Asian, non-Hispanic/Latino; 11 Hispanic/Latino; 2 Two or more races, non-Hispanic/Latino). Average age 27. 1,430 applicants, 8% accepted, 42 enrolled. *Faculty:* 17 full-time (4 women), 42 part-time/adjunct (12 women). Expenses: Contact institution. *Financial support:* In 2017–18, 33 students received support. Federal Work-Study and scholarships/grants available. Financial award application deadline: 6/1; financial award applicants required to submit FAFSA. In 2017, 42 doctorates awarded. Offers dental medicine (DMD). *Application deadline:* For fall admission, 12/1 for domestic students; for summer admission, 12/1 for domestic students. Applications are processed on a rolling basis. *Application fee:* $70. Electronic applications accepted. *Application Contact:* Donna Sparks, Director, Admissions Processing, 660-626-2237, Fax: 660-626-2969, E-mail: admissions@atsu.edu. *Dean*, Dr. Dwight McLeod, 660-626-2969, Fax: 660-626-2969, E-mail: dmcleod@atsu.edu.

School of Osteopathic Medicine in Arizona Students: 427 full-time (237 women); includes 212 minority (7 Black or African American, non-Hispanic/Latino; 1 American Indian or Alaska Native, non-Hispanic/Latino; 142 Asian, non-Hispanic/Latino; 32 Hispanic/Latino; 2 Native Hawaiian or other Pacific Islander, non-Hispanic/Latino; 28 Two or more races, non-Hispanic/Latino). Average age 28. 5,555 applicants, 5% accepted, 108 enrolled. *Faculty:* 39 full-time (19 women), 27 part-time/adjunct (19 women). Expenses: Contact institution. *Financial support:* In 2017–18, 50 students received support, including 3 fellowships with full tuition reimbursements available (averaging $55,972 per year); Federal Work-Study and scholarships/grants also available. Financial award application deadline: 6/1; financial award applicants required to submit FAFSA. In 2017, 103 doctorates awarded. Offers osteopathic medicine (DO). *Application deadline:* For fall admission, 3/1 for domestic students; for summer admission, 3/1 for domestic students. Applications are processed on a rolling basis. *Application fee:* $70. Electronic applications accepted. *Application Contact:* Donna Sparks, Director, Admissions Processing, 660-626-2117, Fax: 660-626-2969, E-mail: admissions@atsu.edu. *Dean*, Dr. Jeffrey Morgan, 480-265-8017, Fax: 480-219-6159, E-mail: jeffreymorgan@atsu.edu.

AUBURN UNIVERSITY, Auburn University, AL 36849

General Information State-supported, coed, university. *Enrollment:* 29,776 graduate, professional, and undergraduate students; 3,391 full-time matriculated graduate/professional students (1,917 women), 2,308 part-time matriculated graduate/professional students (1,106 women). *Enrollment by degree level:* 2,748 master's, 2,785 doctoral, 166 other advanced degrees. *Graduate faculty:* 1,205 full-time (473 women), 145 part-time/adjunct (60 women). Tuition, state resident: full-time $10,974; part-time $519 per credit hour. Tuition, nonresident: full-time $29,658; part-time $1557 per credit hour. *Required fees:* $816 per semester. Tuition and fees vary according to degree level and program. *Graduate housing:* Rooms and/or apartments available on a first-come, first-served basis to single and married students. Typical cost: $7860 per year ($13,332 including board) for single students; $7860 per year ($13,332 including board) for married students. *Student services:* Campus employment opportunities, campus safety program, career counseling, exercise/wellness program, free psychological counseling, international student services, low-cost health insurance, multicultural affairs office, services for students with disabilities, teacher training, writing training. *Library facilities:* R. B. Draughon Library plus 3 others. *Collection:* Books: 4.6 million (physical), 1 million (digital/electronic); Serial titles: 76,272 (physical), 83,255 (digital/electronic); Databases: 253. Study areas open 24 hours, 5–7 days a week. *Research affiliation:* National Center of Excellence for Airliner Cabin Environmental Research (aerospace, polymer and fibers engineering), National Textile Center Consortium (polymer and fibers engineering), National Asphalt Pavement Association (asphalt technology, civil engineering), Consortium for Vehicle Electronics (mechanical and automotive engineering, electrical engineering), Tay-Sachs Gene Therapy Consortium (veterinary medicine, clinical sciences), Higher Education Consortium for Special Education (special and rehabilitative education).

Computer facilities: Computer purchase and lease plans are available. 1,722 computers available on campus for general student use. A campuswide network can be accessed. Online class registration, bursar payments, course materials are available.
Website: http://www.auburn.edu/

General Application Contact: Dr. George Flowers, Dean of the Graduate School, 334-844-2125, E-mail: flowegt@auburn.edu.

GRADUATE UNITS

College of Veterinary Medicine Students: 503 full-time (408 women), 101 part-time (74 women); includes 50 minority (9 Black or African American, non-Hispanic/Latino; 7 Asian, non-Hispanic/Latino; 26 Hispanic/Latino; 1 Native Hawaiian or other Pacific Islander, non-Hispanic/Latino; 7 Two or more races, non-Hispanic/Latino), 27 international. Average age 26. 1,013 applicants, 18% accepted, 135 enrolled. *Faculty:* 100 full-time (41 women), 3 part-time/adjunct (1 woman). Expenses: Contact institution. *Financial support:* Fellowships, research assistantships, teaching assistantships, and Federal Work-Study available. Support available to part-time students. Financial award application deadline: 3/15; financial award applicants required to submit FAFSA. In 2017, 11 master's, 122 doctorates awarded. *Program availability:* Part-time. Offers veterinary medicine (MS, DVM, PhD). *Application deadline:* Applications are processed on a rolling basis. *Application fee:* $50 ($60 for international students). *Application Contact:* Dr. George Flowers, Interim Dean of the Graduate School, 334-844-4700. *Acting Dean*, Dr. Calvin Johnson, 334-844-2650.

Graduate School Students: 3,391 full-time (1,917 women), 2,308 part-time (1,106 women); includes 851 minority (430 Black or African American, non-Hispanic/Latino; 15 American Indian or Alaska Native, non-Hispanic/Latino; 131 Asian, non-Hispanic/Latino; 193 Hispanic/Latino; 6 Native Hawaiian or other Pacific Islander, non-Hispanic/Latino; 76 Two or more races, non-Hispanic/Latino), 1,224 international. Average age 29. 6,110 applicants, 44% accepted, 1566 enrolled. *Faculty:* 1,214 full-time (474 women), 146 part-time/adjunct (61 women). Expenses: Contact institution. *Financial support:* Fellowships, research assistantships, teaching assistantships, career-related internships or fieldwork, and Federal Work-Study available. Support available to part-time students. Financial award applicants required to submit FAFSA. In 2017, 1,237 master's, 567 doctorates, 177 other advanced degrees awarded. *Program availability:* Part-time, evening/weekend. Offers applied economics (PhD); cell and molecular biology (PhD); real estate development (MRED); sociology and rural sociology (MA, MS). *Application fee:* $50 ($60 for international students). *Dean*, Dr. George Flowers, 334-844-4700, E-mail: gradadm@auburn.edu.

College of Agriculture Students: 126 full-time (77 women), 151 part-time (67 women); includes 18 minority (6 Black or African American, non-Hispanic/Latino; 1 Asian, non-Hispanic/Latino; 8 Hispanic/Latino; 3 Two or more races, non-Hispanic/Latino), 94 international. Average age 28. 207 applicants, 48% accepted, 79 enrolled. *Faculty:* 115 full-time (34 women). Expenses: Contact institution. *Financial support:* Fellowships, research assistantships, teaching assistantships, and Federal Work-Study available. Support available to part-time students. Financial award application deadline: 3/1; financial award applicants required to submit FAFSA. In 2017, 63 master's, 21 doctorates awarded. *Program availability:* Part-time. Offers agricultural economics (M Ag); agriculture (M Ag, M Aq, MS, PhD); agronomy and soils (M Ag, MS, PhD); animal sciences (M Ag, MS, PhD); entomology (M Ag, MS); fisheries and allied aquacultures (M Aq, MS, PhD); horticulture (M Ag, MS, PhD); plant pathology (M Ag, MS, PhD); poultry science (M Ag, MS, PhD). *Application deadline:* Applications are processed on a rolling basis. *Application fee:* $50 ($60 for international students). Electronic applications accepted. *Application Contact:* Dr. George Flowers, Dean of the Graduate School, 334-844-2125. *Dean*, Paul Patterson, 334-844-3254.

College of Architecture, Design, and Construction Students: 66 full-time (34 women), 71 part-time (20 women); includes 23 minority (8 Black or African American, non-Hispanic/Latino; 5 Asian, non-Hispanic/Latino; 8 Hispanic/Latino; 1 Native Hawaiian or other Pacific Islander, non-Hispanic/Latino; 1 Two or more races, non-Hispanic/Latino), 51 international. Average age 32. 144 applicants, 69% accepted, 60 enrolled. *Faculty:* 61 full-time (15 women), 15 part-time/adjunct (3 women). Expenses: Contact institution. *Financial support:* Fellowships and Federal Work-Study available. Support available to part-time students. Financial award application deadline: 3/15; financial award applicants required to submit FAFSA. In 2017, 63 master's awarded. *Program availability:* Part-time. Offers architecture, design, and construction (MBC, MCP, MID, ML Arch); building science (MBC); community planning (MCP); industrial design (MID); landscape architecture (ML Arch). *Application deadline:* Applications are processed on a rolling basis. *Application fee:* $50 ($60 for international students). Electronic applications accepted. *Application Contact:* Dr. George Flowers, Dean of the Graduate School, 334-844-2125. *Dean/Chair*, Dr. Vini Nathan, 334-844-4285.

College of Business Students: 263 full-time (84 women), 504 part-time (155 women); includes 130 minority (44 Black or African American, non-Hispanic/Latino; 3 American Indian or Alaska Native, non-Hispanic/Latino; 29 Asian, non-Hispanic/Latino; 42 Hispanic/Latino; 12 Two or more races, non-Hispanic/Latino), 44 international. Average age 32. 685 applicants, 55% accepted, 259 enrolled. *Faculty:* 77 full-time (25 women), 12 part-time/adjunct (5 women). Expenses: Contact institution. *Financial support:* Fellowships, research assistantships, teaching assistantships, career-related internships or fieldwork, and Federal Work-Study available. Support available to part-time students. Financial award application deadline: 3/15; financial award applicants required to submit FAFSA. In 2017, 336 master's, 2 doctorates awarded. *Program availability:* Part-time. Offers accountancy (M Acc); business (M Acc, MBA, MRED, MS, PhD); business administration (MBA); finance (MS); management (PhD). *Application deadline:* Applications are processed on a rolling basis. *Application fee:* $50 ($60 for international students). Electronic applications accepted. *Application Contact:* Dr. George Flowers, Dean of the Graduate School, 334-844-2125. *Interim Dean*, Dr. Jow Hanna, 334-844-6848, E-mail: bch0014@auburn.edu.

College of Education Students: 501 full-time (357 women), 526 part-time (373 women); includes 258 minority (191 Black or African American, non-Hispanic/Latino; 3 American Indian or Alaska Native, non-Hispanic/Latino; 7 Asian, non-Hispanic/Latino; 36 Hispanic/Latino; 2 Native Hawaiian or other Pacific Islander, non-Hispanic/Latino; 19 Two or more races, non-Hispanic/Latino), 47 international. Average age 32. 800 applicants, 61% accepted, 327 enrolled. *Faculty:* 99 full-time (63 women), 30 part-time/adjunct (20 women). Expenses: Contact institution. *Financial support:* Fellowships, research assistantships, teaching assistantships, career-related internships or fieldwork, and Federal Work-Study available. Support available to part-time students. Financial award application deadline: 3/15; financial award applicants required to submit FAFSA. In 2017, 291 master's, 80 doctorates, 75 other advanced degrees awarded. *Program availability:* Part-time. Offers adult education (PhD, Ed S); curriculum and instruction (M Ed, MS, Ed S); curriculum supervision (M Ed, PhD); education (M Ed, MS, Ed D, PhD, Ed S, Graduate Certificate); exercise science (M Ed); higher education administration (PhD); library media (Ed S); school administration (M Ed, PhD); special education, rehabilitation, counseling and school psychology (M Ed, MS, PhD). *Application fee:* $50 ($60 for international students). Electronic applications accepted. *Application Contact:* Dr. George Flowers, Dean of the Graduate School, 334-844-2125. *Dean*, Dr. Betty Lou Whitford, 334-844-4446.

College of Human Sciences Students: 68 full-time (60 women), 83 part-time (51 women); includes 26 minority (12 Black or African American, non-Hispanic/Latino; 1 American Indian or Alaska Native, non-Hispanic/Latino; 2 Asian, non-Hispanic/Latino; 6 Hispanic/Latino; 1 Native Hawaiian or other Pacific Islander, non-Hispanic/Latino; 4 Two or more races, non-Hispanic/Latino), 27 international. Average age 31. 158 applicants, 52% accepted, 62 enrolled. *Faculty:* 56 full-time (38 women). Expenses: Contact institution. *Financial support:* Fellowships, research assistantships, teaching assistantships, career-related internships or fieldwork, and Federal Work-Study available. Support available to part-time students. Financial award application deadline: 3/15; financial award applicants required to submit FAFSA. In 2017, 24 master's, 20 doctorates, 5 other advanced degrees awarded. *Program availability:* Part-time. Offers consumer affairs (MS, PhD); human development and family studies (MS, PhD); human sciences (MS, PhD, Graduate Certificate); nutrition and food science (MS, PhD, Graduate Certificate). *Application deadline:* Applications are processed on a rolling basis. *Application fee:* $50 ($60 for international students). Electronic applications accepted. *Application Contact:* Dr. George Flowers, Dean of the Graduate School, 334-844-2125. *Dean*, Dr. June Henton, 334-844-3790, E-mail: jhenton@humsci.auburn.edu.

College of Liberal Arts Students: 334 full-time (226 women), 135 part-time (70 women); includes 69 minority (39 Black or African American, non-Hispanic/Latino; 2 American Indian or Alaska Native, non-Hispanic/Latino; 7 Asian, non-Hispanic/Latino; 15 Hispanic/Latino; 6 Two or more races, non-Hispanic/Latino), 85 international. Average age 29. 910 applicants, 25% accepted, 140 enrolled. *Faculty:* 255 full-time (136 women), 42 part-time/adjunct (23 women). Expenses: Contact institution. *Financial support:* Fellowships, research assistantships, teaching assistantships, career-related internships or fieldwork, and Federal Work-Study available. Support available to part-time students. Financial award application deadline: 3/15; financial award applicants required to submit FAFSA. In 2017, 95 master's, 39 doctorates, 12 other advanced degrees awarded. *Program availability:* Part-time. Offers applied economics (PhD); audiology (MCD, Au D); communication and journalism (MA, Graduate Certificate); economics (MS); English (MA, MTPC, PhD, Graduate Certificate); foreign languages and literatures (MA, MHS); history (MA, PhD, Graduate Certificate); liberal arts (MA, MCD, MHS, MPA, MS, MTPC, Au D, PhD, Graduate Certificate); psychology (MS, PhD); public administration (MPA, PhD, Graduate Certificate). *Application deadline:* Applications are processed on a rolling basis. *Application fee:* $50 ($60 for international students). Electronic applications accepted. *Application Contact:* Dr. George Flowers, Dean of the Graduate School, 334-844-2125. *Dean*, Dr. Joe Aistrup, 334-844-2183.

College of Sciences and Mathematics Students: 214 full-time (70 women), 163 part-time (81 women); includes 40 minority (16 Black or African American, non-Hispanic/Latino; 10 Asian, non-Hispanic/Latino; 7 Hispanic/Latino; 7 Two or more races, non-Hispanic/Latino), 150 international. Average age 28. 319 applicants, 57% accepted, 87 enrolled. *Faculty:* 162 full-time (41 women), 26 part-time/adjunct (6 women). Expenses: Contact institution. *Financial support:* Fellowships, research assistantships, teaching assistantships, career-related internships or fieldwork, and Federal Work-Study available. Support available to part-time students. Financial award applicants required to submit FAFSA. In 2017, 74 master's, 37 doctorates awarded. *Program availability:* Part-time. Offers analytical chemistry (MS, PhD); applied mathematics (MAM, MS); biochemistry (MS, PhD); botany (MS); geology and geography (MS); inorganic chemistry (MS); mathematics (MS, PhD); organic chemistry (PhD); physical chemistry (MS, PhD); physics (MS, PhD); probability and statistics (M Prob S); sciences and mathematics (M Prob S, MAM, MS, PhD); statistics (MS); zoology (MS). *Application deadline:* Applications are processed on a rolling basis. *Application fee:* $50 ($60 for international students). *Application Contact:* Dr. George Flowers, Dean of the Graduate School, 334-844-2125. *Dean*, Nicholas Giordano, 334-844-5737.

Ginn College of Engineering Students: 605 full-time (153 women), 371 part-time (77 women); includes 66 minority (25 Black or African American, non-Hispanic/Latino; 1 American Indian or Alaska Native, non-Hispanic/Latino; 15 Asian, non-Hispanic/Latino; 20 Hispanic/Latino; 5 Two or more races, non-Hispanic/Latino), 608 international. Average age 27. 1,309 applicants, 43% accepted, 187 enrolled. *Faculty:* 177 full-time (17 women), 16 part-time/adjunct (1 woman). Expenses: Contact institution. *Financial support:* Fellowships, research assistantships, teaching assistantships, and Federal Work-Study available. Support available to part-time students. Financial award application deadline: 3/15; financial award applicants required to submit FAFSA. In 2017, 184 master's, 71 doctorates, 5 other advanced degrees awarded. *Program availability:* Part-time. Offers aerospace engineering (MAE, MS, PhD); biosystems engineering (MS, PhD); chemical engineering (M Ch E, MS, PhD); civil engineering (MCE, MS, PhD); computer science and software engineering (MS, MSWE, PhD); electrical and computer engineering (MEE, MS, PhD); engineering (M Ch E, M Mtl E, MAE, MCE, MEE, MISE, MME, MS, MSWE, PhD, Graduate Certificate); industrial and systems engineering (MISE, MS, PhD, Graduate Certificate); materials engineering (M Mtl E, MS, PhD); mechanical engineering (M Mtl E, MME, MS, PhD); polymer and fiber engineering (MS, PhD). *Application deadline:* Applications are processed on a rolling basis. *Application fee:* $50 ($60 for international students). Electronic applications accepted. *Application Contact:* Dr. George Flowers, Dean of the Graduate School, 334-844-2125. *Dean*, Dr. Chris Roberts, 334-844-2308.

School of Forestry and Wildlife Sciences Students: 42 full-time (18 women), 30 part-time (14 women); includes 6 minority (1 Asian, non-Hispanic/Latino; 4 Hispanic/Latino; 1 Two or more races, non-Hispanic/Latino), 28 international. Average age 29. 41 applicants, 59% accepted, 22 enrolled. *Faculty:* 28 full-time (7 women), 1 (woman) part-time/adjunct. Expenses: Contact institution. *Financial support:* Fellowships, research assistantships, teaching assistantships, and Federal Work-Study available. Support available to part-time students. Financial award application deadline: 3/15; financial award applicants required to submit FAFSA. In 2017, 19 master's, 7 doctorates awarded. *Program availability:* Part-time. Offers forestry (MS); natural resource conservation (MNR); wildlife sciences (MS, PhD). *Application deadline:* Applications are processed on a rolling basis. *Application fee:* $50 ($60 for international students). Electronic applications accepted. *Application Contact:* Dr. George Flowers, Dean of the Graduate School, 334-844-2125. *Dean*, Dr. Janaki Alavalapati, 334-844-1004, Fax: 334-844-1084, E-mail: jra0024@auburn.edu.

School of Nursing Students: 9 full-time (all women), 116 part-time (105 women); includes 25 minority (18 Black or African American, non-Hispanic/Latino; 1 American Indian or Alaska Native, non-Hispanic/Latino; 3 Hispanic/Latino; 3 Two or more races, non-Hispanic/Latino). Average age 33. 67 applicants, 81% accepted, 43 enrolled. *Faculty:* 26 full-time (24 women). Expenses: Contact institution. In 2017, 55 master's awarded. Offers nursing educator (MSN); primary care practitioner (MSN). *Application Contact:* Dr. George Flowers, Dean of the Graduate School, 334-844-4700, E-mail: gradadm@auburn.edu. *Dean*, Dr. Gregg Newschwander, 334-844-3658, E-mail: gen0002@auburn.edu.

Harrison School of Pharmacy Students: 629 full-time (403 women), 13 part-time (8 women); includes 124 minority (53 Black or African American, non-Hispanic/Latino; 4 American Indian or Alaska Native, non-Hispanic/Latino; 46 Asian, non-Hispanic/Latino; 13 Hispanic/Latino; 1 Native Hawaiian or other Pacific Islander, non-Hispanic/Latino; 7 Two or more races, non-Hispanic/Latino), 46 international. Average age 25. 580 applicants, 54% accepted, 156 enrolled. *Faculty:* 58 full-time (33 women), 1 (woman) part-time/adjunct. Expenses: Contact institution. *Financial support:* Fellowships, research assistantships, teaching assistantships, and Federal Work-Study available. Support available to part-time students. Financial award application deadline: 3/15; financial award applicants required to submit FAFSA. In 2017, 4 master's, 159 doctorates awarded. *Program availability:* Part-time. Offers pharmacal sciences (MS, PhD); pharmaceutical sciences (PhD); pharmacy (MS, PhD, Pharm D); pharmacy care systems (MS, PhD). *Application deadline:* Applications are processed on a rolling basis. *Application fee:* $50 ($60 for international students). Electronic applications accepted. *Application Contact:* Dr. George Flowers, Dean of the Graduate School, 334-844-2125. *Dean*, Dr. Richard Hansen, 334-844-8307.

AUBURN UNIVERSITY AT MONTGOMERY, Montgomery, AL 36124-4023

General Information State-supported, coed, comprehensive institution. *Enrollment:* 4,894 graduate, professional, and undergraduate students; 211 full-time matriculated graduate/professional students (127 women), 370 part-time matriculated graduate/professional students (262 women). *Graduate faculty:* 93 full-time (39 women), 21 part-time/adjunct (17 women). Tuition, state resident: full-time $6930; part-time $385 per credit hour. Tuition, nonresident: full-time $15,588; part-time $866 per credit hour. *Required fees:* $640. *Graduate housing:* Rooms and/or apartments available on a first-come, first-served basis to single and married students. Typical cost: $4580 per year ($6980 including board) for single students. Housing application deadline: 5/1. *Student services:* Campus employment opportunities, campus safety program, career counseling, exercise/wellness program, free psychological counseling, international student services, low-cost health insurance, multicultural affairs office, services for students with disabilities. *Library facilities:* Auburn University at Montgomery Library. *Collection:* Books: 502,246 (physical), 722,903 (digital/electronic). Weekly public service hours: 84; students can reserve study rooms.

Computer facilities: 500 computers available on campus for general student use. A campuswide network can be accessed from student residence rooms. Online class registration is available.
Website: http://www.aum.edu/

General Application Contact: Ashley Warren, Administrative Coordinator, Provost's Office, 334-244-3623, Fax: 334-244-3947, E-mail: awarren3@aum.edu.

GRADUATE UNITS

College of Arts and Sciences Students: 35 full-time (20 women), 65 part-time (43 women); includes 26 minority (25 Black or African American, non-Hispanic/Latino; 1 Asian, non-Hispanic/Latino), 16 international. Average age 32. 71 applicants, 85% accepted, 29 enrolled. *Faculty:* 32 full-time (15 women), 2 part-time/adjunct (1 woman). Expenses: Contact institution. *Financial support:* Teaching assistantships, career-related internships or fieldwork, and scholarships/grants available. Support available to part-time students. Financial award application deadline: 3/1; financial award applicants required to submit FAFSA. In 2017, 34 master's awarded. *Program availability:* Part-time, evening/weekend. Offers arts and sciences (MLA, MS, MTW); clinical psychology (MS); liberal arts (MLA); teaching writing (MTW). *Application deadline:* For fall admission, 7/15 for international students; for spring admission, 11/15 for international students; for summer admission, 4/15 for international students. Applications are processed on a rolling basis. *Application fee:* $25 ($0 for international students). Electronic applications accepted. *Application Contact:* Ashley Warren, Graduate Admissions Coordinator, 334-244-3623, E-mail: awarren3@aum.edu. *Associate Provost for Graduate Studies and Faculty Services/Acting Dean, College of Arts and Sciences,* Dr. Matthew Ragland, 334-244-3138, E-mail: mragland@aum.edu.

Department of Mathematics and Computer Science Students: 8 full-time (2 women), 10 part-time (3 women), 15 international. Average age 26. 29 applicants, 76% accepted, 6 enrolled. *Faculty:* 3 full-time (0 women), 1 part-time/adjunct (0 women). Expenses: Contact institution. *Financial support:* In 2017–18, 1 teaching assistantship was awarded. Financial award application deadline: 3/1; financial award applicants required to submit FAFSA. In 2017, 10 master's awarded. Offers cybersystems and information security (MS). *Application deadline:* For fall admission, 7/15 for international students; for spring admission, 11/15 for international students; for summer admission, 4/15 for international students. Applications are processed on a rolling basis. *Application fee:* $25 ($0 for international students). Electronic applications accepted. *Application Contact:* Dr. Luis Cueva-Parra, Associate Dean, 334-244-3321, Fax: 334-244-3826, E-mail: lcuevapa@aum.edu. *Chair,* Dr. Yi Wang, 334-244-3318, Fax: 334-244-3826, E-mail: ywang2@aum.edu.

College of Business Students: 57 full-time (22 women), 76 part-time (45 women); includes 31 minority (21 Black or African American, non-Hispanic/Latino; 1 American Indian or Alaska Native, non-Hispanic/Latino; 7 Asian, non-Hispanic/Latino; 1 Hispanic/Latino; 1 Two or more races, non-Hispanic/Latino), 27 international. Average age 32. 129 applicants, 77% accepted, 65 enrolled. *Faculty:* 11 full-time (3 women), 1 part-time/adjunct (0 women). Expenses: Contact institution. *Financial support:* Research assistantships, career-related internships or fieldwork, and scholarships/grants available. Support available to part-time students. Financial award application deadline: 3/1; financial award applicants required to submit FAFSA. In 2017, 67 master's awarded. *Program availability:* Part-time, evening/weekend. Offers business (M Acc, MBA, MS); business and management (MBA); information systems management (MS). *Application deadline:* For fall admission, 7/15 for international students; for spring admission, 11/15 for international students; for summer admission, 4/15 for international students. Applications are processed on a rolling basis. *Application fee:* $25 ($0 for international students). Electronic applications accepted. *Application Contact:* Jennifer Taylor, Assistant Director of Graduate Programs, 334-244-3587, Fax: 334-244-3137, E-mail: jtaylor5@aum.edu. *Dean,* Dr. Rhea Ingram, 334-244-3476, Fax: 334-244-3792, E-mail: wingram4@aum.edu.

School of Accountancy Students: 13 full-time (7 women), 31 part-time (18 women); includes 8 minority (4 Black or African American, non-Hispanic/Latino; 1 American Indian or Alaska Native, non-Hispanic/Latino; 2 Asian, non-Hispanic/Latino; 1 Two or more races, non-Hispanic/Latino), 9 international. Average age 28. 34 applicants, 85% accepted, 23 enrolled. *Faculty:* 4 full-time (3 women), 1 part-time/adjunct (0 women). Expenses: Contact institution. *Financial support:* Scholarships/grants available. Financial award applicants required to submit FAFSA. In 2017, 10 master's awarded. *Program availability:* Part-time. Offers accountancy (M Acc). *Application deadline:* Applications are processed on a rolling basis. *Application fee:* $25 ($0 for international students). Electronic applications accepted. *Application Contact:* Rhonda Seay, Graduate Advisor, 334-244-3115, E-mail: rseay@aum.edu.

College of Education Students: 82 full-time (66 women), 156 part-time (127 women); includes 91 minority (87 Black or African American, non-Hispanic/Latino; 4 Hispanic/Latino), 2 international. Average age 33. 198 applicants, 71% accepted, 73 enrolled. *Faculty:* 26 full-time (15 women), 11 part-time/adjunct (all women). Expenses: Contact institution. *Financial support:* Teaching assistantships, career-related internships or fieldwork, and scholarships/grants available. Support available to part-time students. Financial award application deadline: 3/1; financial award applicants required to submit FAFSA. In 2017, 102 master's awarded. *Program availability:* Part-time, evening/weekend. Offers counselor education (M Ed, Ed S); early childhood special education (M Ed); education (M Ed, Ed S); elementary education (M Ed, Ed S); exercise science (M Ed); instructional leadership (M Ed, Ed S); instructional technology (Ed S); physical education (Ed S); secondary education (M Ed); special education/collaborative teacher (M Ed, Ed S); sport management (M Ed). *Application deadline:* For fall admission, 7/1 for international students; for spring admission, 11/1 for international students; for summer admission, 4/15 for international students. Applications are processed on a rolling basis. *Application fee:* $25. Electronic applications accepted. *Application Contact:* Dr. Rhonda Morton, Associate Dean/Graduate Coordinator, 334-224-3287, Fax: 334-244-3978, E-mail: rmorton@aum.edu. *Dean,* Dr. Sheila Austin, 334-244-3425, Fax: 334-244-3102, E-mail: saustin1@aum.edu.

College of Nursing and Health Sciences Students: 23 full-time (14 women), 19 part-time (9 women); includes 10 minority (9 Black or African American, non-Hispanic/Latino; 1 Hispanic/Latino), 2 international. Expenses: Contact institution. Offers family nurse practitioner (MSN); nurse educator for interprofessional practice (MSN). Programs offered jointly with Auburn University. *Application deadline:* For fall admission, 7/1 for domestic students; for spring admission, 10/1 for domestic students; for summer admission, 3/1 for domestic students. Applications are processed on a rolling basis. *Application fee:* $25 ($0 for international students). Electronic applications accepted. *Application Contact:* Dr. Barbara Wilder, Graduate Program Director, 334-844-6766, E-mail: wildebf@auburn.edu. *Dean,* Dr. Jean Leuner, 334-244-3658, E-mail: jleuner@aum.edu.

College of Public Policy and Justice Students: 36 full-time (17 women), 65 part-time (40 women); includes 49 minority (46 Black or African American, non-Hispanic/Latino; 2 Asian, non-Hispanic/Latino; 1 Two or more races, non-Hispanic/Latino), 8 international. Average age 31. 71 applicants, 83% accepted, 35 enrolled. *Faculty:* 19 full-time (3 women), 2 part-time/adjunct (1 woman). Expenses: Contact institution. *Financial support:* Teaching assistantships, career-related internships or fieldwork, and scholarships/grants available. Support available to part-time students. Financial award application deadline: 3/1; financial award applicants required to submit FAFSA. In 2017, 29 master's awarded. *Program availability:* Part-time, evening/weekend. Offers applied economics (MS); criminal studies (MSJPS); geographic information systems (MS); homeland security (MSJPS); homeland security and emergency management (MS); legal studies (MSJPS); organizational leadership (MSJPS); political science (MPS); public administration (MPA); public administration and public policy (PhD); public policy and justice (MPA, MPS, MS, MSJPS, PhD). *Application deadline:* For fall admission, 7/15 for international students; for spring admission, 11/15 for international students; for summer admission, 4/15 for international students. Applications are processed on a rolling basis. *Application fee:* $25. Electronic applications accepted. *Dean,* Dr. Keivan Deravi, 334-244-3422, Fax: 334-244-3920, E-mail: mderavi@aum.edu.

AUGSBURG UNIVERSITY, Minneapolis, MN 55454-1351

General Information Independent-religious, coed, comprehensive institution. *Graduate housing:* On-campus housing not available.

GRADUATE UNITS

Program in Business Administration *Program availability:* Evening/weekend. Offers business administration (MBA). Electronic applications accepted.

Program in Education *Program availability:* Part-time, evening/weekend. Offers education (MAE). Electronic applications accepted.

Program in Leadership *Program availability:* Part-time, evening/weekend. Offers leadership (MA).

Program in Physician Assistant Studies Offers physician assistant studies (MS).

Program in Social Work *Program availability:* Part-time, evening/weekend. Offers social work (MSW).

Programs in Nursing Offers nursing (MA, DNP).

AUGUSTANA UNIVERSITY, Sioux Falls, SD 57197

General Information Independent-religious, coed, comprehensive institution. *Enrollment:* 2,080 graduate, professional, and undergraduate students; 25 full-time matriculated graduate/professional students (16 women), 306 part-time matriculated graduate/professional students (254 women). *Enrollment by degree level:* 331 master's. *Graduate faculty:* 14 full-time (8 women), 14 part-time/adjunct (12 women). *Tuition:* Full-time $16,500; part-time $2940 per credit hour. Tuition and fees vary according to program. *Graduate housing:* Rooms and/or apartments available on a first-come, first-served basis to single and married students. Typical cost: $5082 per year ($9422 including board) for single students; $5598 per year ($9938 including board) for married students. Room and board charges vary according to board plan, campus/location and housing facility selected. Housing application deadline: 9/1. *Student services:* Campus employment opportunities, campus safety program, career counseling, child daycare facilities, exercise/wellness program, free psychological counseling, international student services, low-cost health insurance, multicultural affairs office, services for students with disabilities, teacher training, writing training. *Library facilities:* Mikkelsen Library. *Collection:* Students can reserve study rooms. *Research affiliation:* Binghamton University, State University of New York (chemistry), Sanford Underground Science and Engineering Lab (physics), J.R. Macdonald Laboratory (physics), NASA (computer science), Labratori Nazionalidd Gran Sasso, Italy (physics), Sanford Research (biology, biochemistry, genetic counseling).

Computer facilities: Computer purchase and lease plans are available. 295 computers available on campus for general student use. A campuswide network can be accessed from student residence rooms and from off campus. Online class registration is available.
Website: http://www.augie.edu/

General Application Contact: Julia Paluch, Administrative Assistant, Graduate Education, 605-274-4043, Fax: 605-274-4450, E-mail: julia.paluch@augie.edu.

GRADUATE UNITS

Augustana-Sanford Genetic Counseling Program Students: 16 full-time (14 women); includes 1 minority (Asian, non-Hispanic/Latino). Average age 25. 114 applicants, 7% accepted, 8 enrolled. *Faculty:* 1 full-time (0 women), 9 part-time/adjunct (8 women). Expenses: Contact institution. *Financial support:* Application deadline: 7/1; applicants required to submit FAFSA. Offers genetic counseling (MS). Program offered in collaboration with Sanford Health. *Application deadline:* For fall admission, 2/5 for domestic students. *Application fee:* $60. Electronic applications accepted. *Application Contact:* Julia Paluch, Administrative Assistant, Graduate Education, 605-274-4043, Fax: 605-274-4450, E-mail: julia.paluch@augie.edu. *Associate Professor and Chair of the Department of Genetic Counseling,* Dr. Quinn Stein, E-mail: quinn.stein@augie.edu.

MA in Education Program Students: 288 part-time (250 women); includes 20 minority (2 Black or African American, non-Hispanic/Latino; 2 American Indian or Alaska Native, non-Hispanic/Latino; 1 Asian, non-Hispanic/Latino; 11 Hispanic/Latino; 1 Native Hawaiian or other Pacific Islander, non-Hispanic/Latino; 3 Two or more races, non-Hispanic/Latino), 3 international. Average age 32. 47 applicants, 77% accepted, 35 enrolled. *Faculty:* 7 full-time (5 women), 6 part-time/adjunct (5 women). Expenses: Contact institution. *Financial support:* Application deadline: 3/1; applicants required to submit FAFSA. In 2017, 84 master's awarded. *Program availability:* Part-time-only, evening/weekend, online only, 100% online. Offers instructional strategies (MA); reading (MA); special populations (MA); STEM (MA); technology (MA). *Application deadline:* For fall admission, 8/1 for domestic and international students; for spring admission, 11/1 for domestic and international students; for summer admission, 4/1 for domestic and international students. Applications are processed on a rolling basis. *Application fee:* $60. Electronic applications accepted. *Application Contact:* Julia Paulich, Graduate Coordinator, 605-274-4043, Fax: 605-274-4450, E-mail: graduate@augie.edu. *Chair,* Dr. Laurie Daily, 605-274-5211, E-mail: laurie.daily@augie.edu.

Master of Professional Accountancy Program Students: 6 full-time (2 women), 1 part-time (0 women); includes 1 minority (Hispanic/Latino). Average age 23. 11 applicants, 100% accepted, 10 enrolled. *Faculty:* 5 full-time (3 women), 1 (woman) part-time/adjunct. Expenses: Contact institution. *Financial support:* In 2017–18, 6 students received support. Scholarships/grants available. Financial award applicants required to submit FAFSA. In 2017, 2 master's awarded. *Program availability:* Part-time. Offers professional accountancy (MPA). *Application deadline:* For fall admission, 4/1 for domestic students. *Application fee:* $60. Electronic applications accepted. *Application Contact:* Julia Paluch, Administrative Assistant, Graduate Education, 605-274-4043, Fax: 605-274-4450, E-mail: julia.paluch@augie.edu. *Associate Professor,* Laura Hybertson, 605-274-5495, E-mail: laura.hybertson@augie.edu.

Sports Administration and Leadership Program Students: 3 full-time (0 women), 17 part-time (4 women); includes 1 minority (Black or African American, non-Hispanic/Latino). Average age 25. 9 applicants, 100% accepted, 8 enrolled. *Faculty:* 2 full-time (0 women), 4 part-time/adjunct (1 woman). Expenses: Contact institution. *Financial support:* Unspecified assistantships available. Financial award application deadline: 3/1; financial award applicants required to submit FAFSA. In 2017, 5 master's awarded. *Program availability:* Part-time. Offers sports administration and leadership (MA). *Application deadline:* For fall admission, 4/1 priority date for domestic students, 6/1 priority date for international students. Applications are processed on a rolling basis. *Application fee:* $60. Electronic applications accepted. *Application Contact:* Julia Paulich, Graduate Education Assistant, 605-274-4043, Fax: 605-274-4450, E-mail: graduate@augie.edu. *Program Coordinator,* Shelly Gardner, 605-274-5318, E-mail: shelly.gardner@augie.edu.

AUGUSTA UNIVERSITY, Augusta, GA 30912

General Information State-supported, coed, university. CGS member. *Graduate housing:* Rooms and/or apartments available on a first-come, first-served basis to single and married students. *Research affiliation:* Georgia Cancer Coalition (cancer research programs), Advanced Technology Development Center (biotechnology transfer), Medical College of Georgia Research Institute, Inc. (biomedical research), Georgia Center of Innovation for Life Sciences (research commercialization and economic development), Georgia Research Alliance (science and technology development).

GRADUATE UNITS

College of Allied Health Sciences *Program availability:* Online learning. Offers allied health sciences (MHS, MPA, MPH, MS, DPT, PhD); clinical laboratory sciences (MHS); diagnostic sciences (PhD); environmental health (MPH); health care outcomes (PhD); health informatics (MPH); health management (MPH); medical illustration (MS); occupational therapy (MHS); physical therapy (DPT); physician assistant (MPA); rehabilitation science (PhD); social and behavioral sciences (MPH).

College of Education *Program availability:* Part-time, evening/weekend. Offers counselor education (M Ed, Ed S); curriculum and instruction (Ed S); education (M Ed, MAT, Ed D, Ed S); educational innovation (Ed D); elementary education (MAT); foreign language education (MAT); instruction (M Ed); leadership (Ed S); middle grades education (MAT); music education (MAT); school administration (M Ed); secondary education (MAT); special education (MAT); teacher leadership (M Ed).

College of Nursing Offers adult gerontology acute care nurse practitioner (DNP); clinical nurse leader (MSN); family nurse practitioner (DNP); nurse executive (DNP); nursing (DNP); nursing anesthesia (DNP); pediatric nurse practitioner (DNP); psychiatric mental health nurse practitioner (DNP).

College of Science and Mathematics Offers psychological sciences (MS); science and mathematics (MS).

The Dental College of Georgia Offers dentistry (DMD). Electronic applications accepted.

Hull College of Business *Program availability:* Part-time, evening/weekend. Offers business administration (MBA); information security management (MS).

Medical College of Georgia Offers medicine (MD).

Program in Biochemistry and Cancer Biology Offers biochemistry and cancer biology (PhD). Electronic applications accepted.

Program in Cellular Biology and Anatomy Offers cellular biology and anatomy (PhD).

Program in Genomic Medicine Offers genomic medicine (PhD). Electronic applications accepted.

Program in Molecular Medicine Offers molecular medicine (PhD). Electronic applications accepted.

Program in Neuroscience Offers neuroscience (PhD). Electronic applications accepted.

Program in Oral Biology *Program availability:* Part-time. Offers oral biology (MS, PhD). Electronic applications accepted.

Program in Pharmacology Offers pharmacology (PhD). Electronic applications accepted.

Program in Physiology Offers physiology (PhD). Electronic applications accepted.

Program in Vascular Biology Offers vascular biology (PhD).

AURORA UNIVERSITY, Aurora, IL 60506-4892

General Information Independent, coed, comprehensive institution. *Enrollment:* 5,833 graduate, professional, and undergraduate students; 1,524 full-time matriculated graduate/professional students (1,197 women), 308 part-time matriculated graduate/professional students (213 women). *Enrollment by degree level:* 1,556 master's, 254 doctoral, 22 other advanced degrees. *Graduate faculty:* 43 full-time (23 women), 141 part-time/adjunct (99 women). *Tuition:* Full-time $10,800; part-time $600 per credit hour. Tuition and fees vary according to degree level, campus/location and program. *Graduate housing:* On-campus housing not available. *Student services:* Campus employment opportunities, campus safety program, career counseling, exercise/wellness program, free psychological counseling, international student services, multicultural affairs office, services for students with disabilities, teacher training, writing training. *Library facilities:* Charles B. Phillips Library plus 1 other. *Collection:* Books: 14,969 (physical), 160,012 (digital/electronic); Serial titles: 46,444 (digital/electronic); Databases: 61. Weekly public service hours: 96; students can reserve study rooms.

Computer facilities: 254 computers available on campus for general student use. A campuswide network can be accessed from student residence rooms and from off campus. Online class registration, learning management system are available.
Website: http://www.aurora.edu/

General Application Contact: Judson Curry, Dean of Adult and Graduate Studies, 630-947-8946, E-mail: jcurry@aurora.edu.

GRADUATE UNITS

College of Arts and Sciences Students: 47 full-time (28 women), 45 part-time (10 women); includes 12 minority (5 Black or African American, non-Hispanic/Latino; 4 Asian, non-Hispanic/Latino; 3 Hispanic/Latino). Average age 36. 68 applicants, 96% accepted, 15 enrolled. *Faculty:* 3 full-time (2 women), 6 part-time/adjunct (3 women). Expenses: Contact institution. *Financial support:* Federal Work-Study, scholarships/grants, and unspecified assistantships available. Support available to part-time students. Financial award application deadline: 4/1; financial award applicants required to submit FAFSA. *Program availability:* Part-time, evening/weekend, 100% online. Offers homeland security (MS); mathematics (MS); mathematics and science education for elementary teachers (MA); mathematics educaton (MA); science education (MA). *Application deadline:* For fall admission, 6/1 for international students; for spring admission, 10/1 for international students. Applications are processed on a rolling basis. *Application fee:* $0. Electronic applications accepted. *Application Contact:* Judson Curry, Dean of Adult and Graduate Studies, 630-947-8946, E-mail: jcurry@aurora.edu. *Vice President for Academic Affairs,* Dr. Frank Buscher, 630-844-5252, E-mail: fbuscher@aurora.edu.

Dunham School of Business and Public Policy Students: 193 full-time (106 women), 34 part-time (20 women); includes 83 minority (31 Black or African American, non-Hispanic/Latino; 6 Asian, non-Hispanic/Latino; 36 Hispanic/Latino; 1 Native Hawaiian or other Pacific Islander, non-Hispanic/Latino; 9 Two or more races, non-Hispanic/Latino), 2 international. Average age 33. 135 applicants, 100% accepted, 52 enrolled. *Faculty:* 4 full-time (0 women), 22 part-time/adjunct (9 women). Expenses: Contact institution. *Financial support:* In 2017–18, 58 students received support. Federal Work-Study, scholarships/grants, and unspecified assistantships available. Support available to part-time students. Financial award applicants required to submit FAFSA. In 2017, 122 master's awarded. *Program availability:* Part-time, evening/weekend, 100% online. Offers accountancy (MS); business (MBA). *Application deadline:* For fall admission, 6/1 for international students; for spring admission, 10/1 for international students. Applications are processed on a rolling basis. *Application fee:* $0. Electronic applications accepted. *Application Contact:* Tom Gergits, Recruiter for Graduate Programs, 630-947-8945, E-mail: tgergits@aurora.edu. *Dean, School of Business and Policy,* Dr. Toby Arquette, 630-844-5614, E-mail: tarquett@aurora.edu.

School of Education and Human Performance Students: 421 full-time (299 women), 142 part-time (89 women); includes 90 minority (25 Black or African American, non-Hispanic/Latino; 7 Asian, non-Hispanic/Latino; 50 Hispanic/Latino; 2 Native Hawaiian or other Pacific Islander, non-Hispanic/Latino; 6 Two or more races, non-Hispanic/Latino). Average age 37. 169 applicants, 95% accepted, 59 enrolled. *Faculty:* 15 full-time (8 women), 39 part-time/adjunct (20 women). Expenses: Contact institution. *Financial support:* In 2017–18, 34 students received support. Federal Work-Study, scholarships/grants, and unspecified assistantships available. Support available to part-time students. Financial award applicants required to submit FAFSA. In 2017, 175 master's, 36 doctorates awarded. *Program availability:* Part-time, evening/weekend. Offers applied behavioral analysis (MS); bilingual-ESL education (MA); educational leadership with principal endorsement (MA); educational technology (MA); leadership in adult learning higher education (Ed D); leadership in curriculum and instruction (Ed D); leadership in educational administration (Ed D); reading instruction (MA); special education (MA). *Application deadline:* For fall admission, 6/1 for international students; for spring admission, 10/1 for international students. Applications are processed on a rolling basis. *Application fee:* $0. Electronic applications accepted. *Application Contact:* Elizabeth Botica, Graduate Education Recruiter, 630-947-8918, E-mail: ebotica@aurora.edu. *Dean, School of Education and Human Performance,* Dr. Jen Buckley, 630-844-1542, Fax: 630-844-6155, E-mail: jbuckley@aurora.edu.

School of Social Work Students: 862 full-time (764 women), 80 part-time (63 women); includes 316 minority (147 Black or African American, non-Hispanic/Latino; 1 American Indian or Alaska Native, non-Hispanic/Latino; 18 Asian, non-Hispanic/Latino; 125 Hispanic/Latino; 25 Two or more races, non-Hispanic/Latino), 1 international. Average age 31. 602 applicants, 98% accepted, 227 enrolled. *Faculty:* 17 full-time (10 women), 72 part-time/adjunct (65 women). Expenses: Contact institution. *Financial support:* In 2017–18, 521 students received support. Federal Work-Study, scholarships/grants, and unspecified assistantships available. Support available to part-time students. Financial award applicants required to submit FAFSA. In 2017, 379 master's, 7 doctorates awarded. *Program availability:* Part-time, evening/weekend, 100% online. Offers social work (MSW, DSW). *Application deadline:* For fall admission, 6/1 for international students; for spring admission, 10/1 for international students. Applications are processed on a rolling basis. *Application fee:* $0. Electronic applications accepted. *Application Contact:* Luke Kerber, Director of Graduate Recruitment, 630-947-8904, E-mail: lkerber@aurora.edu. *Dean, School of Social Work,* Dr. Brenda Barnwell, 630-947-8933, E-mail: mckenzie@aurora.edu.

AUSTIN COLLEGE, Sherman, TX 75090-4400

General Information Independent-religious, coed, comprehensive institution. *Enrollment:* 1,237 graduate, professional, and undergraduate students; 14 full-time matriculated graduate/professional students (5 women). *Enrollment by degree level:* 14 master's. *Graduate faculty:* 3 full-time (all women), 3 part-time/adjunct (all women). *Graduate housing:* Room and/or apartments available on a first-come, first-served basis to single students; on-campus housing not available to married students. Housing application deadline: 5/1. *Student services:* Campus employment opportunities, campus safety program, career counseling, free psychological counseling, teacher training. *Library facilities:* Abell Library. *Collection:* Books: 227,390 (physical). Study areas open 24 hours, 5–7 days a week; students can reserve study rooms.

Computer facilities: 160 computers available on campus for general student use. A campuswide network can be accessed from student residence rooms and from off campus. Online class registration is available.
Website: http://www.austincollege.edu/

General Application Contact: Nikki Christensen, Administrative Assistant, Academic Affairs, 903-813-2327, E-mail: nchristensen@austincollege.edu.

GRADUATE UNITS

Austin Teacher Program Students: 14 full-time (5 women); includes 4 minority (1 Black or African American, non-Hispanic/Latino; 1 American Indian or Alaska Native, non-Hispanic/Latino; 1 Asian, non-Hispanic/Latino; 1 Hispanic/Latino). Average age 22. *Faculty:* 3 full-time (all women), 3 part-time/adjunct (all women). Expenses: Contact institution. *Financial support:* Career-related internships or fieldwork, Federal Work-Study, scholarships/grants, and unspecified assistantships available. Support available to part-time students. Financial award application deadline: 4/1; financial award applicants required to submit FAFSA. In 2017, 15 master's awarded. *Program availability:* Part-time. Offers teaching (MAT). *Application deadline:* For fall admission, 5/1 priority date for domestic students; for spring admission, 1/15 priority date for domestic students. Applications are processed on a rolling basis. *Application fee:* $35. Electronic applications accepted. *Application Contact:* Nikki Christensen, Administrative Assistant, 903-813-2327, E-mail: nchristensen@austincollege.edu. *Department Chair,* Julia Shahid, 903-813-2457, E-mail: jshahid@austincollege.edu.

AUSTIN GRADUATE SCHOOL OF THEOLOGY, Austin, TX 78752

General Information Independent-religious, coed, upper-level institution. *Enrollment:* 36 graduate, professional, and undergraduate students; 6 full-time matriculated graduate/professional students (1 woman), 8 part-time matriculated graduate/professional students (4 women). *Enrollment by degree level:* 14 master's. *Graduate faculty:* 4 full-time (0 women), 4 part-time/adjunct (0 women). *Graduate housing:* On-campus housing not available. *Student services:* Campus employment opportunities, international student services, services for students with disabilities. *Library facilities:* David Worley Library.

Computer facilities: 6 computers available on campus for general student use. A campuswide network can be accessed.
Website: http://www.austingrad.edu/

General Application Contact: Dawn Bond, Director of Admissions/Registrar, 512-476-2772 Ext. 103, Fax: 512-476-3919, E-mail: dbond@austingrad.edu.

GRADUATE UNITS

Program in Theological Studies Students: 6 full-time (1 woman), 8 part-time (4 women). *Faculty:* 4 full-time (0 women), 4 part-time/adjunct (0 women). Expenses: Contact institution. *Financial support:* Federal Work-Study and scholarships/grants available. Support available to part-time students. Financial award application deadline: 7/1. *Program availability:* Part-time. Offers theological studies (MATS). *Application deadline:* For fall admission, 7/1 priority date for domestic and international students; for spring admission, 10/1 priority date for domestic and international students. Applications are processed on a rolling basis. *Application fee:* $25. Electronic applications accepted. *Application Contact:* Dawn Bond, Director of Admissions/Registrar, 512-476-2772 Ext. 103, Fax: 512-476-3919, E-mail: dbond@austingrad.edu. *Graduate Student Advisor,* Dr. Keith Stanglin, 512-476-2772, Fax: 512-476-3919, E-mail: stanglin@austingrad.edu.

AUSTIN PEAY STATE UNIVERSITY, Clarksville, TN 37044

General Information State-supported, coed, comprehensive institution. CGS member. *Enrollment:* 10,463 graduate, professional, and undergraduate students; 274 full-time matriculated graduate/professional students (175 women), 575 part-time matriculated graduate/professional students (403 women). *Enrollment by degree level:* 832 master's, 17 other advanced degrees. *Graduate faculty:* 131 full-time (62 women), 23 part-time/adjunct (19 women). Tuition, state resident: full-time $7686; part-time $427 per credit hour. Tuition, nonresident: full-time $20,268; part-time $1126 per credit hour. *Required fees:* $1529; $76.45 per credit hour. *Graduate housing:* Rooms and/or apartments available on a first-come, first-served basis to single and married students. Typical cost: $6700 per year ($10,180 including board) for single students; $6700 per year ($10,180 including board) for married students. Room and board charges vary according to board plan and housing facility selected. *Student services:* Campus employment opportunities, campus safety program, career counseling, child daycare facilities, exercise/wellness program, free psychological counseling, international student services, low-cost health insurance, multicultural affairs office, services for students with disabilities, teacher training, writing training. *Library facilities:* Felix G. Woodward Library. *Collection:* Books: 195,467 (physical), 317,822 (digital/electronic); Serial titles: 2,800 (physical), 54,971 (digital/electronic); Databases: 294. Weekly public service hours: 109.

Computer facilities: Computer purchase and lease plans are available. 1,400 computers available on campus for general student use. A campuswide network can be accessed from student residence rooms and from off campus. Online class registration is available.
Website: http://www.apsu.edu/

General Application Contact: Megan Mitchell, Coordinator of Graduate Admissions and Recruitment, 800-859-4723, Fax: 931-221-7641, E-mail: gradadmissions@apsu.edu.

GRADUATE UNITS

College of Graduate Studies Students: 274 full-time (175 women), 575 part-time (403 women); includes 189 minority (105 Black or African American, non-Hispanic/Latino; 1 American Indian or Alaska Native, non-Hispanic/Latino; 10 Asian, non-Hispanic/Latino; 40 Hispanic/Latino; 33 Two or more races, non-Hispanic/Latino), 15 international. Average age 33. 493 applicants, 82% accepted, 291 enrolled. *Faculty:* 131 full-time (62 women), 23 part-time/adjunct (19 women). Expenses: Contact institution. *Financial support:* In 2017–18, 136 students received support, including 136 research assistantships with full tuition reimbursements available (averaging $5,184 per year); career-related internships or fieldwork, Federal Work-Study, institutionally sponsored loans, scholarships/grants, and unspecified assistantships also available. Support available to part-time students. Financial award applicants required to submit FAFSA. In 2017, 373 master's, 12 other advanced degrees awarded. *Program availability:* Part-time, evening/weekend, online learning. *Application deadline:* For fall admission, 8/8 priority date for domestic students. Applications are processed on a rolling basis. *Application fee:* $45 ($50 for international students). Electronic applications accepted. *Application Contact:* Megan Mitchell, Coordinator of Graduate Admissions, 931-221-6189, Fax: 931-221-7641, E-mail: mitchellm@apsu.edu. *Associate Provost of Research and Dean of the College of Graduate Studies,* Dr. Chad Brooks, 931-221-7415, Fax: 931-221-7641, E-mail: brooksc@apsu.edu.

College of Arts and Letters Students: 33 full-time (14 women), 82 part-time (43 women); includes 18 minority (14 Black or African American, non-Hispanic/Latino; 2 Hispanic/Latino; 2 Two or more races, non-Hispanic/Latino), 3 international. Average age 31. 74 applicants, 88% accepted, 48 enrolled. *Faculty:* 42 full-time (17 women), 6 part-time/adjunct (4 women). Expenses: Contact institution. *Financial support:* Research assistantships with full tuition reimbursements, teaching assistantships, career-related internships or fieldwork, Federal Work-Study, institutionally sponsored loans, scholarships/grants, and unspecified assistantships available. Support available to part-time students. Financial award application deadline: 4/1; financial award applicants required to submit FAFSA. In 2017, 42 master's awarded. *Program availability:* Part-time, evening/weekend, online learning. Offers arts and letters (M Mu, MA); English (MA); marketing communication (MA); media management (MA); military history (MA); music education (M Mu); music performance (M Mu). *Application deadline:* For fall admission, 8/8 priority date for domestic students. Applications are processed on a rolling basis. *Application fee:* $45 ($55 for international students). Electronic applications accepted. *Application Contact:* Megan Mitchell, Coordinator of Graduate Admissions, 931-221-6189, Fax: 931-221-7641, E-mail: mitchellm@apsu.edu. *Interim Dean,* Dr. Barry Jones, 931-221-7330, Fax: 931-221-1024, E-mail: jonesb@apsu.edu.

College of Behavioral and Health Sciences Students: 126 full-time (92 women), 232 part-time (197 women); includes 84 minority (56 Black or African American, non-Hispanic/Latino; 1 American Indian or Alaska Native, non-Hispanic/Latino; 1 Asian, non-Hispanic/Latino; 18 Hispanic/Latino; 8 Two or more races, non-Hispanic/Latino), 1 international. Average age 33. 225 applicants, 76% accepted, 145 enrolled. *Faculty:* 35 full-time (23 women), 11 part-time/adjunct (all women). Expenses: Contact institution. *Financial support:* Research assistantships with full tuition reimbursements, career-related internships or fieldwork, Federal Work-Study, institutionally sponsored loans, scholarships/grants, and unspecified assistantships available. Support available to part-time students. Financial award application deadline: 4/1; financial award applicants required to submit FAFSA. In 2017, 181 master's awarded. *Program availability:* Part-time, evening/weekend, online learning. Offers behavioral and health sciences (MA, MPS, MS, MSN, MSW); family nurse practitioner (MSN); industrial-organizational psychology (MS); mental health counseling (MS); nursing administration (MSN); nursing education (MSN); nursing informatics (MSN); public health education (MS); school counseling (MS); social work (MSW); sports and wellness leadership (MS); strategic leadership (MPS). *Application deadline:* For fall admission, 8/8 priority date for domestic students. Applications are processed on a rolling basis. *Application fee:* $45 ($55 for international students). Electronic applications accepted. *Application Contact:* Megan Mitchell, Coordinator of Graduate Admissions, 931-221-6189, Fax: 931-221-7641, E-mail: mitchellm@apsu.edu. *Interim Dean,* Dr. Rebecca Corvey, 931-221-1040, Fax: 931-221-6382, E-mail: corveyr@apsu.edu.

College of Business Students: 17 full-time (9 women), 46 part-time (26 women); includes 14 minority (5 Black or African American, non-Hispanic/Latino; 2 Asian, non-Hispanic/Latino; 2 Hispanic/Latino; 5 Two or more races, non-Hispanic/Latino). Average age 35. 44 applicants, 73% accepted, 16 enrolled. *Faculty:* 6 full-time (2 women). Expenses: Contact institution. *Financial support:* Research assistantships with full tuition reimbursements, career-related internships or fieldwork, Federal Work-Study, institutionally sponsored loans, scholarships/grants, and unspecified assistantships available. Support available to part-time students. Financial award application deadline: 4/1; financial award applicants required to submit FAFSA. In 2017, 32 master's awarded. *Program availability:* Part-time, evening/weekend, online learning. Offers management (MS). *Application deadline:* For fall admission, 8/8 priority date for domestic students. Applications are processed on a rolling basis. *Application fee:* $45 ($55 for international students). Electronic applications accepted. *Application Contact:* Megan Mitchell, Coordinator of Graduate Admissions, 931-221-6189, Fax: 931-221-7641, E-mail: mitchellm@apsu.edu. *Dean,* Dr. Mickey Hepner, 931-221-7675, Fax: 931-221-7355, E-mail: hepnerm@apsu.edu.

College of Education Students: 73 full-time (54 women), 139 part-time (106 women); includes 49 minority (23 Black or African American, non-Hispanic/Latino; 4 Asian, non-Hispanic/Latino; 12 Hispanic/Latino; 10 Two or more races, non-Hispanic/Latino), 1 international. Average age 34. 72 applicants, 96% accepted, 42 enrolled. *Faculty:* 16 full-time (10 women), 5 part-time/adjunct (4 women). Expenses: Contact institution. *Financial support:* Research assistantships with full tuition reimbursements, career-related internships or fieldwork, Federal Work-Study, institutionally sponsored loans, scholarships/grants, and unspecified assistantships available. Support available to part-time students. Financial award application deadline: 4/1; financial award applicants required to submit FAFSA. In 2017, 94 master's, 12 Ed Ss awarded. *Program availability:* Part-time, evening/weekend, online learning. Offers administration and supervision (Ed S); counseling and guidance (Ed S); curriculum and instruction (MA Ed); education (MA Ed, Ed S); education leadership (MA Ed); elementary education (Ed S); reading (MA Ed); secondary education (Ed S). *Application deadline:* For fall admission, 8/8 priority date for domestic students. Applications are processed on a rolling basis. *Application fee:* $45 ($55 for international students). Electronic applications accepted. *Application Contact:* Megan Mitchell, Coordinator of Graduate Admissions, 931-221-6189, Fax: 931-221-7641, E-mail: mitchellm@apsu.edu. *Dean,* Dr. Prentice Chandler, 931-221-7511, Fax: 931-221-1292, E-mail: chandlerp@apsu.edu.

College of Science, Technology, Engineering and Mathematics Students: 25 full-time (6 women), 76 part-time (31 women); includes 24 minority (7 Black or African American, non-Hispanic/Latino; 3 Asian, non-Hispanic/Latino; 6 Hispanic/Latino; 8 Two or more races, non-Hispanic/Latino), 10 international. Average age 33. 78 applicants, 90% accepted, 49 enrolled. *Faculty:* 32 full-time (10 women), 1 part-time/adjunct (0 women). Expenses: Contact institution. *Financial support:* Research assistantships with full tuition reimbursements, career-related internships or fieldwork, Federal Work-Study, institutionally sponsored loans, scholarships/grants, and unspecified assistantships available. Support available to part-time students. Financial award application deadline: 4/1; financial award applicants required to submit FAFSA. In 2017, 24 master's awarded. *Program availability:* Part-time, online learning. Offers clinical laboratory science (MS); data management and analysis (MS, PSM); engineering technology (MS); information assurance and security (MS, PSM); mathematical finance (MS, PSM); mathematics instruction (MS); predictive analytics (MS, PSM); science, technology, engineering and mathematics (MS, PSM). *Application deadline:* For fall admission, 8/8 priority date for domestic students. Applications are processed on a rolling basis. *Application fee:* $45 ($50 for international students). Electronic applications accepted. *Application Contact:* Megan Mitchell, Coordinator of Graduate Admissions, 931-221-6189, Fax: 931-221-7641, E-mail: mitchellm@apsu.edu. *Interim Dean,* Dr. Karen Meisch, 931-221-7780, Fax: 931-221-7984, E-mail: meischk@apsu.edu.

AUSTIN PRESBYTERIAN THEOLOGICAL SEMINARY, Austin, TX 78705-5797

General Information Independent-religious, coed, graduate-only institution. *Enrollment by degree level:* 116 master's, 41 doctoral. *Graduate faculty:* 21 full-time (6 women), 4 part-time/adjunct (0 women). *Tuition:* Full-time $13,500; part-time $6750 per credit. *Required fees:* $120; $120 per credit. One-time fee: $150. Tuition and fees vary according to program. *Graduate housing:* Rooms and/or apartments available on a first-come, first-served basis to single and married students. Typical cost: $2700 (including board) for single students; $6750 (including board) for married students. Room and board charges vary according to housing facility selected. Housing application deadline: 5/31. *Student services:* Campus employment opportunities, campus safety program, career counseling, free psychological counseling, international student services, services for students with disabilities, writing training. *Library facilities:* Stitt Library. *Collection:* Books: 112,022 (physical), 306,370 (digital/electronic); Serial titles: 1,127 (physical), 53,206 (digital/electronic); Databases: 103. Weekly public service hours: 37; students can reserve study rooms.

Computer facilities: 20 computers available on campus for general student use. A campuswide network can be accessed from student residence rooms and from off campus.
Website: http://www.austinseminary.edu/

General Application Contact: Dr. Jack Barden, Vice President for Enrollment Management, 512-404-4827, Fax: 512-472-7089, E-mail: admissions@austinseminary.edu.

GRADUATE UNITS

Graduate and Professional Programs Students: 80 full-time (50 women), 77 part-time (45 women). *Faculty:* 21 full-time (6 women), 4 part-time/adjunct (0 women). Expenses: Contact institution. *Financial support:* Fellowships, career-related internships or fieldwork, institutionally sponsored loans, and scholarships/grants available. Support available to part-time students. Financial award application deadline: 2/1; financial award applicants required to submit FAFSA. Offers divinity (M Div); ministry (D Min); ministry practice (MA); theological studies (MA); youth ministry (MA). M Div/MSSW offered in collaboration with The University of Texas at Austin School of Social Work. *Application deadline:* For fall admission, 5/1 for domestic students, 1/1 for international students; for winter admission, 9/6 for domestic students; for summer admission, 2/2 for domestic students. Applications are processed on a rolling basis. *Application fee:* $50. Electronic applications accepted. *Application Contact:* Dr. Jack Barden, Vice President for Enrollment Management, 512-404-4827, Fax: 512-472-7089, E-mail: admissions@austinseminary.edu. *Academic Dean*, Dr. David Jensen, 512-404-4821, Fax: 512-479-0738, E-mail: dean@austinseminary.edu.

AVE MARIA SCHOOL OF LAW, Naples, FL 34119

General Information Independent-religious, coed, graduate-only institution. *Enrollment by degree level:* 241 doctoral. *Graduate faculty:* 22 full-time (7 women), 18 part-time/adjunct (7 women). *Tuition:* Full-time $39,450. *Required fees:* $2256. *Graduate housing:* Rooms and/or apartments available on a first-come, first-served basis to single and married students. Typical cost: $10,350 per year ($14,562 including board) for single students; $10,350 per year ($14,562 including board) for married students. Housing application deadline: 4/15. *Student services:* Campus employment opportunities, campus safety program, career counseling, exercise/wellness program, international student services, services for students with disabilities, writing training. *Library facilities:* Veterans Memorial Law Library. *Collection:* Books: 53,471 (physical), 48,624 (digital/electronic); Serial titles: 2,330 (physical), 29,769 (digital/electronic); Databases: 206. Weekly public service hours: 168; study areas open 24 hours, 5–7 days a week; students can reserve study rooms.

Computer facilities: 20 computers available on campus for general student use. A campuswide network can be accessed from student residence rooms. Online class registration is available.
Website: http://www.avemarialaw.edu/

General Application Contact: Claire T. O'Keefe, Associate Dean of Admissions and Student Engagement, 239-687-5423, Fax: 239-352-2890, E-mail: info@avemarialaw.edu.

GRADUATE UNITS

Professional Program Students: 241 full-time (132 women); includes 67 minority (13 Black or African American, non-Hispanic/Latino; 1 American Indian or Alaska Native, non-Hispanic/Latino; 1 Asian, non-Hispanic/Latino; 52 Hispanic/Latino), 7 international. Average age 26. 568 applicants, 55% accepted, 97 enrolled. *Faculty:* 22 full-time (7 women), 18 part-time/adjunct (7 women). Expenses: Contact institution. *Financial support:* In 2017–18, 182 students received support. Research assistantships, career-related internships or fieldwork, Federal Work-Study, and scholarships/grants available. Financial award application deadline: 6/30; financial award applicants required to submit FAFSA. In 2017, 81 doctorates awarded. Offers law (JD). *Application deadline:* For fall admission, 7/15 priority date for domestic and international students. Applications are processed on a rolling basis. *Application fee:* $0. Electronic applications accepted. *Application Contact:* Claire T. O'Keefe, Associate Dean of Admissions and Student Engagement, 239-687-5423, Fax: 239-352-2890, E-mail: info@avemarialaw.edu. *President/Dean*, Kevin Cieply, 239-687-5300, E-mail: kcieply@avemarialaw.edu.

AVE MARIA UNIVERSITY, Ave Maria, FL 34142

General Information Independent-religious, coed, comprehensive institution. *Graduate housing:* Room and/or apartments available on a first-come, first-served basis to single students; on-campus housing not available to married students. Housing application deadline: 7/15.

GRADUATE UNITS

Graduate Programs

AVERETT UNIVERSITY, Danville, VA 24541-3692

General Information Independent-religious, coed, comprehensive institution. *Enrollment:* 929 graduate, professional, and undergraduate students; 91 full-time matriculated graduate/professional students (60 women), 181 part-time matriculated graduate/professional students (115 women). *Enrollment by degree level:* 272 master's. *Graduate faculty:* 11 full-time (2 women), 27 part-time/adjunct (16 women). *Graduate housing:* On-campus housing not available. *Student services:* Campus employment opportunities, campus safety program, career counseling, free psychological counseling, services for students with disabilities, teacher training, writing training. *Library facilities:* Mary B. Blount Library. *Collection:* Books: 88,079 (physical), 307,115 (digital/electronic); Serial titles: 2,490 (physical), 32,577 (digital/electronic); Databases: 93. Weekly public service hours: 81; students can reserve study rooms.

Computer facilities: 150 computers available on campus for general student use. A campuswide network can be accessed from student residence rooms. Online class registration is available.
Website: http://www.averett.edu/

General Application Contact: Melissa Anderson, Director of Admissions, Graduate and Professional Studies, 804-729-8285, E-mail: manderson@averett.edu.

GRADUATE UNITS

Master in Education Program Students: 38 full-time (32 women), 46 part-time (28 women); includes 33 minority (29 Black or African American, non-Hispanic/Latino; 1 Hispanic/Latino; 3 Two or more races, non-Hispanic/Latino). Average age 38. 155 applicants, 52% accepted, 59 enrolled. *Faculty:* 2 full-time (1 woman), 14 part-time/adjunct (11 women). Expenses: Contact institution. *Financial support:* Application deadline: 3/1; applicants required to submit FAFSA. In 2017, 50 master's awarded. *Program availability:* Part-time, online only, 100% online. Offers administration and supervision (M Ed); curriculum and instruction (M Ed); special education with endorsement (M Ed); special education with licensure (M Ed). *Application deadline:* Applications are processed on a rolling basis. Electronic applications accepted. *Education Chair*, Dr. Sue Davis, 434-791-5741, Fax: 434-791-5020, E-mail: suedavis@averett.edu.

Master of Accountancy Program Students: 6 part-time (4 women); includes 1 minority (Black or African American, non-Hispanic/Latino). Average age 24. 1 applicant, 100% accepted, 1 enrolled. *Faculty:* 2 full-time (1 woman). Expenses: Contact institution. *Financial support:* In 2017–18, 1 student received support. Application deadline: 3/1; applicants required to submit FAFSA. *Program availability:* Part-time, online only, 100% online. Offers accountancy (M Acc). *Application deadline:* Applications are processed on a rolling basis. Electronic applications accepted. *Application Contact:* Melissa Anderson, Director of Admissions, Graduate and Professional Studies, 804-729-8285, E-mail: manderson@averett.edu. *Director of the Master in Accountancy Program*, Dr. Peggy C. Wright, 434-791-7118, E-mail: pwright@averett.edu.

Master of Business Administration Program Students: 53 full-time (28 women), 129 part-time (83 women); includes 82 minority (65 Black or African American, non-Hispanic/Latino; 1 American Indian or Alaska Native, non-Hispanic/Latino; 5 Asian, non-Hispanic/Latino; 4 Hispanic/Latino; 7 Two or more races, non-Hispanic/Latino). Average age 38. 88 applicants, 81% accepted, 65 enrolled. *Faculty:* 7 full-time (0 women), 12 part-time/adjunct (4 women). Expenses: Contact institution. *Financial support:* Application deadline: 3/1; applicants required to submit FAFSA. In 2017, 129 master's awarded. *Program availability:* Part-time, evening/weekend, 100% online, blended/hybrid learning. Offers business administration (MBA); human resources management (MBA); leadership (MBA); marketing (MBA). *Application deadline:* Applications are processed on a rolling basis. Electronic applications accepted. *Application Contact:* Melissa Anderson, Director of Admissions, Graduate and Professional Studies, 804-729-8285, E-mail: manderson@averett.edu. *Chair, Business Department*, Dr. Peggy C. Wright, 434-791-7118, E-mail: pwright@averett.edu.

AVILA UNIVERSITY, Kansas City, MO 64145-1698

General Information Independent-religious, coed, comprehensive institution. *Enrollment:* 1,703 graduate, professional, and undergraduate students; 319 full-time matriculated graduate/professional students (231 women), 111 part-time matriculated graduate/professional students (70 women). *Enrollment by degree level:* 357 master's, 73 other advanced degrees. *Graduate faculty:* 19 full-time (13 women), 33 part-time/adjunct (19 women). *Tuition:* Full-time $7200; part-time $600 per credit hour. Tuition and fees vary according to program. *Graduate housing:* Room and/or apartments available on a first-come, first-served basis to single students; on-campus housing not available to married students. Typical cost: $3300 (including board). Room and board charges vary according to board plan and housing facility selected. *Student services:* Campus employment opportunities, campus safety program, career counseling, child daycare facilities, exercise/wellness program, free psychological counseling, international student services, low-cost health insurance, multicultural affairs office, services for students with disabilities, teacher training, writing training. *Library facilities:* Hooley-Bundshu Library plus 1 other. *Collection:* Books: 39,963 (physical), 309,288 (digital/electronic); Serial titles: 205 (physical), 389,497 (digital/electronic); Databases: 72. Weekly public service hours: 91; students can reserve study rooms.

Computer facilities: 141 computers available on campus for general student use. A campuswide network can be accessed from student residence rooms and from off campus. Online class registration, laptop checkout through library are available.
Website: http://www.avila.edu/

General Application Contact: Jamie McConnell, Director of Graduate and Advantage Admission, 816-501-0428, E-mail: jamie.mcconnell@avila.edu.

GRADUATE UNITS

Department of Psychology Students: 104 full-time (88 women), 17 part-time (12 women); includes 39 minority (25 Black or African American, non-Hispanic/Latino; 2 American Indian or Alaska Native, non-Hispanic/Latino; 2 Asian, non-Hispanic/Latino; 6 Hispanic/Latino; 4 Two or more races, non-Hispanic/Latino), 3 international. Average age 33. 69 applicants, 65% accepted, 34 enrolled. *Faculty:* 7 full-time (6 women), 4 part-time/adjunct (1 woman). Expenses: Contact institution. *Financial support:* In 2017–18, 17 students received support, including 5 research assistantships with partial tuition reimbursements available; career-related internships or fieldwork, scholarships/grants, and unspecified assistantships also available. Support available to part-time students. Financial award applicants required to submit FAFSA. In 2017, 24 master's awarded. *Program availability:* Part-time. Offers counseling psychology (MS); psychology (MS). *Application deadline:* Applications are processed on a rolling basis. *Application fee:* $0. Electronic applications accepted. *Application Contact:* Tamika Doolin, Graduate Admissions Advisor, 816-501-3661, Fax: 816-501-2455, E-mail: gradpsych@avila.edu. *Director of Graduate Psychology Enrollment Management*, Phil Gebauer, 816-501-0419, Fax: 816-501-2455, E-mail: philip.gebauer@avila.edu.

School of Business Students: 49 full-time (19 women), 29 part-time (14 women); includes 16 minority (12 Black or African American, non-Hispanic/Latino; 1 Asian, non-Hispanic/Latino; 3 Hispanic/Latino), 19 international. Average age 32. 51 applicants, 47% accepted, 20 enrolled. *Faculty:* 6 full-time (2 women), 6 part-time/adjunct (2 women). Expenses: Contact institution. *Financial support:* In 2017–18, 18 students received support. Career-related internships or fieldwork and scholarships/grants available. Support available to part-time students. Financial award applicants required to submit FAFSA. In 2017, 31 master's awarded. *Program availability:* Part-time, evening/weekend. Offers accounting (MBA); finance (MBA); health care administration (MBA); international business (MBA); management (MBA); management information systems (MBA); marketing (MBA). *Application deadline:* For fall admission, 7/30 priority date for domestic and international students; for winter admission, 11/30 priority date for domestic and international students; for spring admission, 2/28 priority date for domestic and international students; for summer admission, 6/1 priority date for domestic and international students. Applications are processed on a rolling basis. *Application fee:* $0. Electronic applications accepted. *Application Contact:* Brandon Black, MBA Admission Advisor, 816-501-3601, Fax: 816-501-2463, E-mail: brandon.black@avila.edu. *Interim Dean*, Dr. Wendy L. Acker, 816-501-3720, Fax: 816-501-2463, E-mail: wendy.acker@avila.edu.

School of Education Students: 81 full-time (63 women), 20 part-time (11 women); includes 14 minority (8 Black or African American, non-Hispanic/Latino; 2 Asian, non-Hispanic/Latino; 3 Hispanic/Latino; 1 Two or more races, non-Hispanic/Latino), 4 international. Average age 35. 92 applicants, 62% accepted, 40 enrolled. *Faculty:* 6 full-time (5 women), 9 part-time/adjunct (8 women). Expenses: Contact institution. *Financial support:* In 2017–18, 14 students received support. Unspecified assistantships available. Financial award applicants required to submit FAFSA. In 2017, 24 master's awarded. *Program availability:* Part-time, evening/weekend, online learning. Offers advanced classroom management (MA); art K-12 (Teaching Certificate); educational technology (MA, Certificate); elementary education (Teaching Certificate); English as a second language (MA); English language learners (Advanced Certificate); middle school (Teaching Certificate); physical education K-12 (Teaching Certificate); secondary education (Teaching Certificate); special education (Teaching Certificate); special reading (Advanced Certificate); teaching and learning (MA). *Application deadline:* Applications are processed on a rolling basis. Electronic applications accepted. *Application Contact:* Cory Roup, Graduate Education Enrollment and Academic Advisor, 816-501-2464, E-mail: cory.roup@avila.edu. *Director of Graduate Education*, Dr. Stacy Keith, 816-501-2446, Fax: 816-501-2915, E-mail: stacy.keith@avila.edu.

School of Professional Studies Students: 85 full-time (61 women), 45 part-time (33 women); includes 42 minority (35 Black or African American, non-Hispanic/Latino; 2 Asian, non-Hispanic/Latino; 4 Hispanic/Latino; 1 Two or more races, non-Hispanic/Latino), 3 international. Average age 37. 63 applicants, 60% accepted, 29 enrolled. *Faculty:* 14 part-time/adjunct (8 women). Expenses: Contact institution. *Financial support:* In 2017–18, 14 students received support. Unspecified assistantships available. Support available to part-time students. Financial award applicants required to submit FAFSA. In 2017, 39 master's awarded. *Program availability:* Part-time-only, evening/weekend, 100% online, blended/hybrid learning. Offers executive leadership (MS); fundraising (MA); instructional design and technology (MA, MS); leadership coaching (MS); project management (MA); strategic human resources (MS). *Application deadline:* Applications are processed on a rolling basis. *Application fee:* $0. Electronic applications accepted. *Application Contact:* Jessica Burson, Graduate Admission Advisor, 816-501-2482, Fax: 816-941-4650, E-mail: advantage@avila.edu. *Associate Dean/Director*, Kari Clevenger, 816-501-3675, Fax: 816-941-4650, E-mail: advantage@avila.edu.

AZUSA PACIFIC UNIVERSITY, Azusa, CA 91702-7000

General Information Independent-religious, coed, university. CGS member. *Graduate housing:* On-campus housing not available.

GRADUATE UNITS

Azusa Pacific Seminary *Program availability:* Part-time, evening/weekend. Offers Biblical studies (M Div, MA); church leadership and development (MAPS); ministry (D Min); theology (M Div, MA, MAPS, D Min); theology and ethics (MA); urban studies (MAPS).

College of Liberal Arts and Sciences *Program availability:* Part-time, evening/weekend, online learning. Offers biotechnology (MS); English (MA); liberal arts and sciences (MA, MS); teaching English to speakers of other languages (MA).

Haggard Graduate School of Theology Offers theology (MA).

College of Music and the Arts *Program availability:* Part-time, evening/weekend. Offers composition (M Mus); conducting (M Mus); education (M Mus); modern art history, theory, and criticism (MA); music entrepreneurial studies (MA); performance (M Mus); screenwriting (MA); visual art (MFA).

School of Behavioral and Applied Sciences Offers athletic training (MS); behavioral and applied sciences (MA, MS, MSW, DPT, Ed D, PhD, Psy D); child life (MS); college counseling and student development (MS); executive leadership (MA); family psychology (Psy D); higher education (PhD); higher education leadership (Ed D); leadership (MA); leadership development (MA); leadership studies (MA); organizational psychology (MS); physical education (MA, MS); physical therapy (DPT); research psychology and data analytics (MS); social work (MSW); sport management (MA).

School of Business and Management *Program availability:* Part-time, evening/weekend. Offers accounting (MBA); business administration (MBA); entrepreneurship (MBA); finance (MBA); international business (MBA); marketing (MBA); organizational science (MBA); professional accountancy (M Acc); sport management (MBA).

School of Education *Program availability:* Part-time, evening/weekend. Offers education (M Ed, MA, MA Ed, Ed D); educational counseling (MA Ed); educational leadership (MA, Ed D); educational psychology (MA Ed); educational technology (MA); learning and technology (MA Ed); special education (MA Ed); teaching (MA Ed).

School of Nursing *Program availability:* Part-time, evening/weekend. Offers adult clinical nurse specialist (MSN); adult-gerontology nurse practitioner (MSN); family nurse practitioner (MSN); healthcare administration and leadership (MSN); nursing (MSN, DNP, PhD); nursing education (MSN); parent-child clinical nurse specialist (MSN); psychiatric mental health nurse practitioner (MSN).

University College *Program availability:* Online learning. Offers leadership and organizational studies (MA); public health (MPH).

BABEL UNIVERSITY PROFESSIONAL SCHOOL OF TRANSLATION, Honolulu, HI 96815

General Information Proprietary, coed, primarily women, graduate-only institution. *Graduate housing:* On-campus housing not available.

GRADUATE UNITS

Program in Translation *Program availability:* Part-time, evening/weekend, online learning. Offers translation (MS).

BABSON COLLEGE, Babson Park, MA 02457-0310

General Information Independent, coed, comprehensive institution. *Graduate housing:* Rooms and/or apartments available on a first-come, first-served basis to single and married students. Housing application deadline: 5/1.

GRADUATE UNITS

F. W. Olin Graduate School of Business *Program availability:* Part-time, evening/weekend, online learning. Offers accounting (MSA); advanced management (Certificate); business administration (MBA); business analytics (MS); finance (MS); global entrepreneurship (MS); technological entrepreneurship (MS). Electronic applications accepted.

BAKER COLLEGE CENTER FOR GRADUATE STUDIES–ONLINE, Flint, MI 48507

General Information Independent, coed, graduate-only institution. *Graduate housing:* On-campus housing not available.

GRADUATE UNITS

Graduate Programs *Program availability:* Part-time, evening/weekend, online learning. Offers accounting (MBA); business administration (DBA); finance (MBA); general business (MBA); health care management (MBA); human resources management (MBA); information management (MBA); leadership studies (MBA); management information systems (MSIS); marketing (MBA). Electronic applications accepted.

BAKER UNIVERSITY, Baldwin City, KS 66006-0065

General Information Independent-religious, coed, comprehensive institution. *Enrollment:* 1,159 graduate, professional, and undergraduate students; 34 full-time matriculated graduate/professional students (23 women), 889 part-time matriculated graduate/professional students (553 women). *Enrollment by degree level:* 720 master's, 203 doctoral. *Graduate housing:* On-campus housing not available. *Student services:* Campus safety program, international student services, services for students with disabilities. *Library facilities:* Baker University Library. *Collection:* Books: 69,073 (physical), 170,620 (digital/electronic); Serial titles: 1,285 (physical), 276 (digital/electronic); Databases: 48. Weekly public service hours: 73; study areas open 24 hours, 5–7 days a week; students can reserve study rooms.

Computer facilities: 140 computers available on campus for general student use. A campuswide network can be accessed from student residence rooms. Online class registration is available.
Website: http://www.bakeru.edu/

General Application Contact: Kelly Belk, Vice President of Enrollment Management, 913-491-4432, E-mail: kbelk@bakeru.edu.

GRADUATE UNITS

School of Education Students: 11 full-time (9 women), 492 part-time (350 women); includes 79 minority (43 Black or African American, non-Hispanic/Latino; 5 American Indian or Alaska Native, non-Hispanic/Latino; 3 Asian, non-Hispanic/Latino; 18 Hispanic/Latino; 2 Native Hawaiian or other Pacific Islander, non-Hispanic/Latino; 8 Two or more races, non-Hispanic/Latino), 1 international. Average age 36. Expenses: Contact institution. *Financial support:* Applicants required to submit FAFSA. In 2017, 173 master's, 42 doctorates awarded. *Program availability:* Part-time, evening/weekend, 100% online. Offers education (MA Ed, MSSE, MSSL, Ed D). Master's-level programs also offered in Wichita, KS. *Application deadline:* Applications are processed on a rolling basis. Electronic applications accepted. *Application Contact:* Linda Reynolds, Director of Graduate Education Enrollment, 913-344-6037, E-mail: linda.reynolds@bakeru.edu. *Dean of the School of Education*, Dr. Marc Childress, 913-344-1235, E-mail: marcus.childress@bakeru.edu.

School of Professional and Graduate Studies Students: 23 full-time (14 women), 384 part-time (191 women); includes 116 minority (44 Black or African American, non-Hispanic/Latino; 20 American Indian or Alaska Native, non-Hispanic/Latino; 11 Asian, non-Hispanic/Latino; 28 Hispanic/Latino; 13 Two or more races, non-Hispanic/Latino), 1 international. Average age 35. Expenses: Contact institution. *Financial support:* Applicants required to submit FAFSA. In 2017, 213 master's awarded. *Program availability:* Part-time, evening/weekend, 100% online. Offers business (MAOL, MBA, MSM, MSSM); liberal arts (MLA). *Application deadline:* Applications are processed on a rolling basis. *Application Contact:* Kelly Belk, Vice President of Enrollment Management, 913-491-4432, E-mail: kelly.belk@learn.bakeru.edu. *Interim Dean of the School of Professional and Graduate Studies*, Dr. Emily Ford, 785-594-8475, E-mail: emily.ford@bakeru.edu.

BAKKE GRADUATE UNIVERSITY, Dallas, TX 75243-7039

General Information Independent-religious, coed, primarily men, graduate-only institution. *Enrollment by degree level:* 45 master's, 129 doctoral. *Graduate faculty:* 5 full-time (3 women), 27 part-time/adjunct (12 women). *Tuition:* Full-time $6120; part-time $3000 per credit. *Required fees:* $50 per course. $50 per quarter. *Graduate housing:* On-campus housing not available. *Student services:* Career counseling, writing training. *Library facilities:* Bakke Graduate University Library plus 1 other. *Collection:* Books: 43,788 (physical), 4,625 (digital/electronic); Serial titles: 5,000 (digital/electronic); Databases: 3,000. Weekly public service hours: 40.

Computer facilities: 4 computers available on campus for general student use. Online class registration is available.
Website: https://www.bgu.edu/

General Application Contact: Traci Tucker, Director of Admissions, 214-329-4447 Ext. 122, Fax: 214-347-9367, E-mail: traci.tucker@bgu.edu.

GRADUATE UNITS

Programs in Pastoral Ministry and Business Students: 120 full-time (48 women), 54 part-time (24 women). *Faculty:* 5 full-time (3 women), 27 part-time/adjunct (12 women). Expenses: Contact institution. *Financial support:* Scholarships/grants and tuition waivers (partial) available. Financial award applicants required to submit FAFSA. *Program availability:* Part-time, online learning. Offers business administration (MBA); church and ministry multiplication (D Min); global urban leadership (MA); leadership (D Min); ministry in complex contexts (D Min); social and civic entrepreneurship (MA); theology of work (D Min); theology reflection (D Min); transformational leadership (DTL); urban youth ministry (D Min). *Application deadline:* For fall admission, 7/1 priority date for domestic students; for winter admission, 12/1 for domestic students; for spring admission, 3/15 for domestic students. Applications are processed on a rolling basis. *Application fee:* $50. Electronic applications accepted. *Application Contact:* Traci Tucker, Director of Admissions, 214-329-4447 Ext. 122, Fax: 214-347-9367, E-mail: traci.tucker@bgu.edu. *Senior Vice President of International Partnerships*, Dr. Gwen Dewey, 214-329-4447 Ext. 119, E-mail: gwen.dewey@bgu.edu.

BALDWIN WALLACE UNIVERSITY, Berea, OH 44017-2088

General Information Independent-religious, coed, comprehensive institution. *Enrollment:* 3,812 graduate, professional, and undergraduate students; 403 full-time matriculated graduate/professional students (260 women), 196 part-time matriculated graduate/professional students (126 women). *Enrollment by degree level:* 599 master's. *Graduate faculty:* 46 full-time (24 women), 41 part-time/adjunct (12 women). *Graduate housing:* Room and/or apartments available to single students; on-campus housing not available to married students. *Student services:* Campus employment opportunities, campus safety program, career counseling, exercise/wellness program, free psychological counseling, international student services, low-cost health insurance, multicultural affairs office, services for students with disabilities, teacher training, writing training. *Library facilities:* Ritter Library plus 2 others. *Collection:* Books: 109,038 (physical), 387,882 (digital/electronic); Serial titles: 174 (physical), 73,946 (digital/electronic); Databases: 265. Weekly public service hours: 90; study areas open 24 hours, 5–7 days a week; students can reserve study rooms. *Research affiliation:* Cuyahoga Community College (early childhood education), Berea City Schools (co-teaching models), Head Start Programs (early childhood education).

Computer facilities: 500 computers available on campus for general student use. A campuswide network can be accessed from student residence rooms. Online class registration is available.
Website: http://www.bw.edu/

General Application Contact: Winnie W. Gerhardt, Director of Transfer, Adult and Graduate Admission, 440-826-2222, Fax: 440-826-3830, E-mail: admission@bw.edu.

GRADUATE UNITS

Graduate Programs Students: 403 full-time (260 women), 196 part-time (126 women); includes 105 minority (51 Black or African American, non-Hispanic/Latino; 17 Asian, non-Hispanic/Latino; 21 Hispanic/Latino; 16 Two or more races, non-Hispanic/Latino), 6 international. Average age 32. 970 applicants, 28% accepted, 163 enrolled. *Faculty:* 46 full-time (24 women), 41 part-time/adjunct (12 women). Expenses: Contact institution. In 2017, 250 master's awarded. *Program availability:* Part-time, evening/weekend, 100% online, blended/hybrid learning. Offers health education and disease prevention (MPH); physician assistant (MMS); population health leadership and management (MPH); speech-language pathology (MS). *Application deadline:* Applications are processed on a rolling basis. *Application fee:* $25. Electronic applications accepted. *Application Contact:* Winnie W. Gerhardt, Director of Transfer, Adult and Graduate Admission, 440-826-2222, Fax: 440-826-3830, E-mail: admission@bw.edu. *Provost, Academic Affairs*, Stephen D. Stahl, 440-826-2251, Fax: 440-826-2329, E-mail: sstahl@bw.edu.

School of Business Students: 198 full-time (98 women), 114 part-time (61 women); includes 65 minority (33 Black or African American, non-Hispanic/Latino; 12 Asian, non-Hispanic/Latino; 15 Hispanic/Latino; 5 Two or more races, non-Hispanic/Latino), 4 international. Average age 34. 161 applicants, 64% accepted, 59 enrolled. *Faculty:* 21 full-time (8 women), 24 part-time/adjunct (6 women). Expenses: Contact institution. *Financial support:* Applicants required to submit FAFSA. In 2017, 135 master's awarded. *Program availability:* Part-time, evening/weekend, blended/hybrid learning. Offers accounting (MBA); analytics (MBA); health care (MBA); human resources (MBA); international management (MBA); management (MAM, MBA). *Application deadline:* For fall admission, 7/25 priority date for domestic students, 4/30 priority date for international students; for spring admission, 12/15 priority date for domestic students, 9/30 priority date for international students; for summer admission, 4/15 for domestic students. Applications are processed on a rolling basis. Electronic applications accepted. *Application Contact:* Laura Spencer, Graduate Application

Specialist, 440-826-2191, Fax: 440-826-3868, E-mail: lspencer@bw.edu. *Dean of School of Business*, John Lanigan, 440-826-3566, Fax: 440-826-3868, E-mail: jlanigan@bw.edu.

School of Education Students: 84 full-time (63 women), 81 part-time (64 women); includes 21 minority (14 Black or African American, non-Hispanic/Latino; 1 Hispanic/Latino; 6 Two or more races, non-Hispanic/Latino). Average age 31. 89 applicants, 62% accepted, 40 enrolled. *Faculty:* 10 full-time (4 women), 8 part-time/adjunct (1 woman). Expenses: Contact institution. *Financial support:* Career-related internships or fieldwork available. Financial award applicants required to submit FAFSA. In 2017, 69 master's awarded. *Program availability:* Part-time, evening/weekend, 100% online, blended/hybrid learning. Offers leadership in higher education (MA Ed); leadership in technology for teaching and learning (MA Ed); literacy (MA Ed); mild/moderate educational needs (MA Ed); school leadership (MA Ed). *Application deadline:* For fall admission, 8/15 priority date for domestic students; for spring admission, 12/15 priority date for domestic students. Applications are processed on a rolling basis. *Application fee:* $25. Electronic applications accepted. *Application Contact:* Winnie W. Gerhardt, Director of Transfer, Adult and Graduate Admission, 440-826-2222, Fax: 440-826-3830, E-mail: admission@bw.edu. *Dean*, Dr. Karen Kaye, 440-826-2168, Fax: 440-826-3779, E-mail: kkaye@bw.edu.

BALL STATE UNIVERSITY, Muncie, IN 47306

General Information State-supported, coed, university. CGS member. *Enrollment:* 22,513 graduate, professional, and undergraduate students; 1,229 full-time matriculated graduate/professional students (794 women), 4,100 part-time matriculated graduate/professional students (3,223 women). *Enrollment by degree level:* 4,458 master's, 338 doctoral, 533 other advanced degrees. *Graduate faculty:* 477 full-time (239 women), 91 part-time/adjunct (58 women). *Graduate housing:* Rooms and/or apartments available on a first-come, first-served basis to single and married students. Housing application deadline: 6/1. *Student services:* Campus employment opportunities, campus safety program, career counseling, child daycare facilities, exercise/wellness program, free psychological counseling, grant writing training, international student services, low-cost health insurance, multicultural affairs office, services for students with disabilities, teacher training, writing training. *Library facilities:* Bracken Library plus 2 others. *Collection:* Books: 822,983 (physical), 15,244 (digital/electronic); Serial titles: 13,599 (physical), 103,640 (digital/electronic); Databases: 296. Weekly public service hours: 123; students can reserve study rooms. *Research affiliation:* DowAgro (biochemistry), Lilly Company (biochemistry), Cisco (networking, information management), Element (biochemistry), ConforMIS (biomechanics), Monell (chemistry).

Computer facilities: Computer purchase and lease plans are available. 578 computers available on campus for general student use. A campuswide network can be accessed from student residence rooms and from off campus. Online class registration, room reservations, testing and test results, manage and pay tuition, order/buy textbooks, request room repairs, order transcripts, manage meal plan, manage and prepay long distance service, undergraduate degree progress report are available.
Website: http://www.bsu.edu/

General Application Contact: Dr. Adam Beach, Dean of the Graduate School, 765-285-1300, Fax: 765-285-1994, E-mail: arbeach@bsu.edu.

GRADUATE UNITS

Graduate School Students: 1,229 full-time (794 women), 4,100 part-time (3,223 women); includes 868 minority (337 Black or African American, non-Hispanic/Latino; 123 Asian, non-Hispanic/Latino; 307 Hispanic/Latino; 4 Native Hawaiian or other Pacific Islander, non-Hispanic/Latino; 97 Two or more races, non-Hispanic/Latino), 210 international. Average age 30. 3,667 applicants, 60% accepted, 1618 enrolled. *Faculty:* 477 full-time (239 women), 101 part-time/adjunct (68 women). Expenses: Contact institution. *Financial support:* In 2017–18, 859 students received support, including 283 research assistantships with partial tuition reimbursements available (averaging $10,818 per year), 334 teaching assistantships with partial tuition reimbursements available (averaging $10,503 per year); health care benefits and unspecified assistantships also available. Financial award application deadline: 3/1; financial award applicants required to submit FAFSA. In 2017, 1,747 master's, 65 doctorates, 373 other advanced degrees awarded. *Program availability:* Part-time, evening/weekend, 100% online, blended/hybrid learning. *Application deadline:* For fall admission, 3/1 priority date for domestic students, 1/1 priority date for international students; for spring admission, 12/1 priority date for domestic students, 7/1 priority date for international students. Applications are processed on a rolling basis. *Application fee:* $60. Electronic applications accepted. *Dean of the Graduate School*, Dr. Adam Beach, 765-285-1300, Fax: 765-285-1994, E-mail: arbeach@bsu.edu.

College of Architecture and Planning Students: 114 full-time (54 women), 36 part-time (21 women); includes 13 minority (6 Black or African American, non-Hispanic/Latino; 2 Asian, non-Hispanic/Latino; 4 Hispanic/Latino; 1 Two or more races, non-Hispanic/Latino), 29 international. Average age 26. 135 applicants, 76% accepted, 57 enrolled. *Faculty:* 25 full-time (13 women), 2 part-time/adjunct (1 woman). Expenses: Contact institution. *Financial support:* In 2017–18, 68 students received support, including 11 research assistantships with partial tuition reimbursements available (averaging $6,073 per year), 28 teaching assistantships with partial tuition reimbursements available (averaging $3,448 per year); unspecified assistantships also available. Financial award application deadline: 3/1; financial award applicants required to submit FAFSA. In 2017, 72 master's, 15 other advanced degrees awarded. *Program availability:* Part-time. Offers architecture (M Arch, M Arch II); architecture and planning (M Arch, M Arch II, MLA, MS, MUD, MURP, Certificate); digital fabrication (Certificate); historic preservation (MS); landscape architecture (MLA); urban and regional planning (MURP); urban design (MUD). *Application deadline:* For fall admission, 1/15 for domestic students. Applications are processed on a rolling basis. *Application fee:* $60. Electronic applications accepted. *Application Contact:* Stephanie D. Wilson, Graduate Recruiter, 765-285-6130, Fax: 765-285-1328, E-mail: shuffman@bsu.edu. *Dean*, Dr. Phil Repp, 765-285-5863, Fax: 765-285-3726, E-mail: prepp@bsu.edu.

College of Communication, Information, and Media Students: 115 full-time (66 women), 100 part-time (59 women); includes 42 minority (21 Black or African American, non-Hispanic/Latino; 1 Asian, non-Hispanic/Latino; 11 Hispanic/Latino; 9 Two or more races, non-Hispanic/Latino), 15 international. Average age 28. 202 applicants, 71% accepted, 117 enrolled. Expenses: Contact institution. *Financial support:* In 2017–18, 68 students received support, including 26 research assistantships with partial tuition reimbursements available (averaging $8,911 per year), 38 teaching assistantships with partial tuition reimbursements available (averaging $11,503 per year); unspecified assistantships also available. Financial award application deadline: 3/1; financial award applicants required to submit FAFSA. In 2017, 97 master's, 10 other advanced degrees awarded. *Program availability:* Part-time, 100% online, blended/hybrid learning. Offers communication studies (MA); communication, information, and media (MA, MS, Certificate); emerging media and visual reporting (Certificate); emerging media design and development (MA); information and communication sciences (MS); information and communication technologies (Certificate); journalism (MA); literary journalism (Certificate); public relations (MA); telecommunications (MA). *Application deadline:* For fall admission, 1/1 priority date for international students; for spring admission, 7/1 priority date for international students. Applications are processed on a rolling basis. *Application fee:* $60. Electronic applications accepted. *Dean*, Roger Lavery, 765-285-6000, Fax: 765-285-6002, E-mail: rlavery@bsu.edu.

College of Fine Arts Students: 72 full-time (38 women), 39 part-time (22 women); includes 16 minority (7 Black or African American, non-Hispanic/Latino; 4 Asian, non-Hispanic/Latino; 4 Hispanic/Latino; 1 Two or more races, non-Hispanic/Latino), 27 international. Average age 29. 101 applicants, 57% accepted, 41 enrolled. *Faculty:* 70 full-time (28 women), 3 part-time/adjunct (2 women). Expenses: Contact institution. *Financial support:* In 2017–18, 77 students received support, including 1 research assistantship with partial tuition reimbursement available (averaging $10,667 per year), 53 teaching assistantships with partial tuition reimbursements available (averaging $10,473 per year); unspecified assistantships also available. Financial award application deadline: 3/1; financial award applicants required to submit FAFSA. In 2017, 18 master's, 6 doctorates, 2 other advanced degrees awarded. *Program availability:* Part-time. Offers fine arts (MFA); music (MA, MM, DA, Artist Diploma); visual arts studio (MA). *Application deadline:* For fall admission, 1/1 priority date for international students; for spring admission, 6/1 priority date for international students. Applications are processed on a rolling basis. *Application fee:* $60. Electronic applications accepted. *Application Contact:* Stephanie D. Wilson, Graduate Recruiter, 765-285-6130, Fax: 765-285-1328, E-mail: shuffman@bsu.edu. *Dean*, Dr. Robert Kvam, 765-285-5495, Fax: 765-285-3790, E-mail: rkvam@bsu.edu.

College of Health Students: 107 full-time (74 women), 493 part-time (391 women); includes 40 minority (17 Black or African American, non-Hispanic/Latino; 9 Asian, non-Hispanic/Latino; 10 Hispanic/Latino; 4 Two or more races, non-Hispanic/Latino), 16 international. Average age 31. 353 applicants, 46% accepted, 136 enrolled. *Faculty:* 44 full-time (25 women), 16 part-time/adjunct (12 women). Expenses: Contact institution. *Financial support:* In 2017–18, 94 students received support, including 61 research assistantships with partial tuition reimbursements available (averaging $12,405 per year), 2 teaching assistantships with partial tuition reimbursements available (averaging $12,151 per year); unspecified assistantships also available. Financial award application deadline: 3/1; financial award applicants required to submit FAFSA. In 2017, 215 master's, 12 doctorates, 1 other advanced degree awarded. *Program availability:* Part-time, evening/weekend, 100% online. Offers adult/gerontology nurse practitioner (Post Master's Certificate); athletic coaching education (Certificate); audiology (Au D); counseling (MA); counseling psychology (MA, PhD); evidence-based clinical practice (Postbaccalaureate Certificate); exercise science (MA, MS); family nurse practitioner (Post Master's Certificate); health (MA, MS, Au D, DNP, PhD, Certificate, Post Master's Certificate, Postbaccalaureate Certificate); human bioenergetics (PhD); identity and leadership development for counselors (Certificate); nurse educator (Post Master's Certificate); nursing (MS); nursing education (Postbaccalaureate Certificate); nursing practice (DNP); physical education (MS); physical education and sport (MA, MS); social psychology (MA); social psychology and clinical mental health counseling (MA); speech-language pathology (MA); wellness management (MA, MS). *Application deadline:* For fall admission, 3/1 priority date for domestic students, 1/1 priority date for international students; for spring admission, 1/1 priority date for domestic students, 7/1 priority date for international students. Applications are processed on a rolling basis. *Application fee:* $60. Electronic applications accepted. *Dean*, Dr. Mitchell Whaley, 765-285-5818, Fax: 765-285-1071, E-mail: mwhaley@bsu.edu.

College of Sciences and Humanities Students: 217 full-time (109 women), 265 part-time (139 women); includes 50 minority (15 Black or African American, non-Hispanic/Latino; 9 Asian, non-Hispanic/Latino; 17 Hispanic/Latino; 9 Two or more races, non-Hispanic/Latino), 84 international. Average age 29. 733 applicants, 51% accepted, 223 enrolled. *Faculty:* 144 full-time (57 women), 4 part-time/adjunct (3 women). Expenses: Contact institution. *Financial support:* In 2017–18, 198 students received support, including 66 research assistantships with partial tuition reimbursements available (averaging $11,915 per year), 129 teaching assistantships with partial tuition reimbursements available (averaging $12,102 per year); unspecified assistantships also available. Financial award application deadline: 3/1; financial award applicants required to submit FAFSA. In 2017, 188 master's, 9 doctorates, 16 other advanced degrees awarded. *Program availability:* Part-time, 100% online, blended/hybrid learning. Offers actuarial science (MA); anthropology (MA); biology (MA, MS); chemistry (MA, MS); clinical psychology (MA); cognitive and social processes (MA); computer science (MA, MS); elementary mathematics teacher leadership (Certificate); emergency management and homeland security (Certificate); English (MA, PhD); environmental science (PhD); geographic information systems (Certificate); geography (MS); geology (MA, MS); history (MA); interpretive ethnography (Certificate); linguistics (MA); mathematics (MA, MS); mathematics education (MA); middle school mathematics education (Certificate); natural resources and environmental management (MA, MS); physics (MA, MAE, MS); physiology (MA, MS); political science (MA); post-secondary foundational mathematics teaching (MA, Certificate); professional meteorology and climatology (Certificate); public administration (MPA, Certificate); sciences and humanities (MA, MAE, MPA, MS, PhD, Certificate); sociology (MA); statistical modeling (Certificate); statistics (MA, MS); teaching English to speakers of other languages (TESOL) and linguistics (MA). *Application deadline:* For fall admission, 1/1 priority date for international students; for spring admission, 7/1 priority date for international students. Applications are processed on a rolling basis. *Application fee:* $60. Electronic applications accepted. *Dean*, Dr. Maureen McCarthy, 765-285-1042, Fax: 765-285-8980, E-mail: mamcarthy@bsu.edu.

Miller College of Business Students: 70 full-time (30 women), 259 part-time (101 women); includes 27 minority (6 Black or African American, non-Hispanic/Latino; 11 Asian, non-Hispanic/Latino; 5 Hispanic/Latino; 1 Native Hawaiian or other Pacific Islander, non-Hispanic/Latino; 4 Two or more races, non-Hispanic/Latino), 11 international. Average age 30. 272 applicants, 52% accepted, 104 enrolled. *Faculty:* 23 full-time (7 women). Expenses: Contact institution. *Financial support:* In 2017–18, 40 students received support, including 18 research assistantships with partial tuition reimbursements available (averaging $10,366 per year), 21 teaching assistantships with partial tuition reimbursements available (averaging $10,966 per year); unspecified assistantships also available. Financial award application deadline: 3/1; financial award applicants required to submit FAFSA. In 2017, 100 master's, 35 other advanced degrees awarded. *Program availability:* Part-time, evening/weekend, 100% online, blended/hybrid learning. Offers accounting (MS); business administration (MBA, Certificate, Graduate Certificate); business education (MA); business essentials (Graduate Certificate); community and economic development

(Certificate); health economics, policy and administration (Certificate); information systems and operations management (MA, Certificate); information systems security management (Certificate); selling and sales management (Certificate). *Application deadline:* For fall admission, 7/1 for domestic students; for spring admission, 12/1 for domestic students; for summer admission, 4/1 for domestic students. Applications are processed on a rolling basis. *Application fee:* $60. Electronic applications accepted. *Application Contact:* Stephanie D. Wilson, Graduate Recruiter, 765-285-6130, Fax: 765-285-1328, E-mail: shuffman@bsu.edu. *Dean*, Dr. Jennifer Bott, 765-285-5323, Fax: 765-285-5323, E-mail: jpbott@bsu.edu.

Teachers College Students: 389 full-time (306 women), 2,873 part-time (2,450 women); includes 647 minority (259 Black or African American, non-Hispanic/Latino; 86 Asian, non-Hispanic/Latino; 239 Hispanic/Latino; 3 Native Hawaiian or other Pacific Islander, non-Hispanic/Latino; 60 Two or more races, non-Hispanic/Latino), 39 international. Average age 31. 1,873 applicants, 65% accepted, 947 enrolled. *Faculty:* 95 full-time (75 women), 68 part-time/adjunct (48 women). Expenses: Contact institution. *Financial support:* In 2017–18, 120 students received support, including 81 research assistantships with partial tuition reimbursements available (averaging $10,472 per year), 19 teaching assistantships with partial tuition reimbursements available (averaging $8,704 per year); unspecified assistantships also available. Financial award application deadline: 3/1; financial award applicants required to submit FAFSA. In 2017, 1,002 master's, 29 doctorates, 286 other advanced degrees awarded. *Program availability:* Part-time, evening/weekend, 100% online, blended/hybrid learning. Offers adult and community education (MA); adult education (MA, Ed D, Certificate); adult, higher and community education (Ed D); applied behavior analysis (MA, Certificate); autism (Certificate); charter school leadership (Certificate); college and university teaching (Certificate); community college leadership (Certificate); community education (Certificate); computer education (Certificate); curriculum and educational technology (MA); diversity studies (Certificate); early childhood administration (Certificate); education (MA, MAE, MS, Ed D, PhD, Certificate, Ed S); educational administration and supervision (MA, Ed D); educational psychology (MA, MS, PhD, Certificate, Ed S); educational psychology (PhD); educational studies (PhD); elementary education (MAE, Ed D, PhD); enhanced teaching practices for elementary teachers (Certificate); executive development for public service (MA); family and consumer science (MS); family and consumer sciences (MA); gifted and talented education (Certificate); human development and learning (Certificate); instructional design and assessment (Certificate); literacy instruction (Certificate); middle-level education (Certificate); neuropsychology (Certificate); nutrition and dietetics (MA, MS); qualitative research in education (Certificate); quantitative psychology (MS); response to intervention (Certificate); school psychology (MA, PhD, Ed S); school psychology (Ed S); school superintendency (Ed S); secondary education (MA); special education (MA, MAE, Ed D); student affairs administration in higher education (MA). *Application deadline:* For fall admission, 1/1 priority date for international students. Applications are processed on a rolling basis. *Application fee:* $60. Electronic applications accepted. *Application Contact:* Stephanie D. Wilson, Graduate Recruiter, 765-285-6130, Fax: 765-285-1328, E-mail: shuffman@bsu.edu. *Interim Dean*, Dr. Roy Weaver, 765-285-5452, Fax: 765-285-5455, E-mail: rweaver@bsu.edu.

BANK STREET COLLEGE OF EDUCATION, New York, NY 10025

General Information Independent, coed, graduate-only institution. *Research affiliation:* Annenberg Institute (education), Stanford University (education), Educational Development Center (education), Mathematica Policy Research, Inc. (education), Center for Teaching Quality (education).

GRADUATE UNITS

Graduate School Offers advanced literacy specialization (Ed M); bilingual childhood special education (Ed M); bilingual early childhood general education (MS Ed); bilingual early childhood special and general education (MS Ed); bilingual early childhood special education (Ed M, MS Ed); bilingual elementary/childhood general education (MS Ed); bilingual elementary/childhood special and general education (MS Ed); bilingual elementary/childhood special education (MS Ed); child life (MS); early childhood and elementary/childhood education (MS Ed); early childhood education (MS Ed); early childhood leadership (MS Ed); early childhood special and general education (MS Ed); early childhood special education (Ed M, MS Ed); education (Ed M, MS, MS Ed); educational leadership (MS Ed); elementary/childhood education (MS Ed); elementary/childhood special and general education (MS Ed); elementary/childhood special education (MS Ed); elementary/childhood special education certification (Ed M); infant and family development (MS Ed); infant and family early childhood special and general education (MS Ed); infant and family/early childhood special education (Ed M); leadership for educational change (Ed M, MS Ed); leadership in community-based learning (MS Ed); leadership in mathematics education (MS Ed); leadership in museum education (MS Ed); leadership in the arts: creative writing (MS Ed); leadership in the arts: visual arts (MS Ed); museum education (MS Ed); museum education: elementary education certification (MS Ed); reading and literacy (MS Ed); teaching literacy (MS Ed); teaching literacy and childhood general education (MS Ed). Electronic applications accepted.

BAPTIST BIBLE COLLEGE, Springfield, MO 65803-3498

General Information Independent-religious, coed, comprehensive institution. *Enrollment:* 2 full-time matriculated graduate/professional students, 27 part-time matriculated graduate/professional students (4 women). *Enrollment by degree level:* 29 master's. *Graduate faculty:* 1 full-time (0 women), 6 part-time/adjunct (0 women). *Graduate housing:* Rooms and/or apartments available on a first-come, first-served basis to single and married students. Typical cost: $7500 (including board) for single students. *Student services:* Campus employment opportunities, campus safety program, free psychological counseling, international student services. *Library facilities:* G. B. Vick Memorial Library plus 1 other.

Computer facilities: 50 computers available on campus for general student use. Website: http://www.gobbc.edu/

General Application Contact: Terry Allcorn, Registrar, 417-268-6003, Fax: 800-819-8330, E-mail: tallcorn@gobbc.edu.

GRADUATE UNITS

Graduate and Professional Programs Students: 2 full-time (0 women), 27 part-time (4 women); includes 5 minority (2 Black or African American, non-Hispanic/Latino; 1 Asian, non-Hispanic/Latino; 2 Hispanic/Latino), 3 international. *Faculty:* 1 full-time (0 women), 6 part-time/adjunct (0 women). Expenses: Contact institution. *Financial support:* Application deadline: 3/6; applicants required to submit FAFSA. *Program availability:* Part-time. Offers biblical counseling (MA); church ministry (MA); theology (M Div). *Application deadline:* For fall admission, 8/1 priority date for domestic students; for spring admission, 1/14 for domestic students. Applications are processed on a rolling basis. *Application fee:* $40. Electronic applications accepted. *Application Contact:* Mark Milioni, President, 417-268-6008, Fax: 800-819-8330. *President*, Mark Milioni, 417-268-6008, Fax: 800-819-8330.

THE BAPTIST COLLEGE OF FLORIDA, Graceville, FL 32440

General Information Independent-religious, coed, comprehensive institution. *Enrollment:* 448 graduate, professional, and undergraduate students; 33 full-time matriculated graduate/professional students (6 women). *Enrollment by degree level:* 33 master's. *Graduate faculty:* 12 full-time (0 women). *Graduate housing:* Rooms and/or apartments available on a first-come, first-served basis to single and married students. Housing application deadline: 8/13. *Student services:* Campus employment opportunities, campus safety program, exercise/wellness program, free psychological counseling, services for students with disabilities, writing training. *Library facilities:* Ida J. MacMillan Library plus 1 other. *Collection:* Books: 90,006 (physical), 88,931 (digital/electronic); Serial titles: 5,602 (physical), 5,602 (digital/electronic); Databases: 16. Weekly public service hours: 66.

Computer facilities: 25 computers available on campus for general student use. A campuswide network can be accessed from student residence rooms. Online class registration is available.
Website: http://www.baptistcollege.edu/

General Application Contact: Sandra Richards, Director of Student Life and Marketing, 850-263-3261 Ext. 415, E-mail: skrichards@baptistcollege.edu.

GRADUATE UNITS

Graduate Programs Students: 33 full-time (6 women); includes 2 minority (1 Black or African American, non-Hispanic/Latino; 1 Hispanic/Latino). Average age 28. 10 applicants, 100% accepted, 10 enrolled. *Faculty:* 12 full-time (0 women). Expenses: Contact institution. *Financial support:* In 2017–18, 2 students received support. In 2017, 3 master's awarded. *Program availability:* Part-time, 100% online, blended/hybrid learning. Offers Christian ministry (MA); Christian studies (MA); music and worship leadership (MA). *Application deadline:* For fall admission, 8/15 for domestic students; for spring admission, 1/15 for domestic students. Applications are processed on a rolling basis. *Application fee:* $25. Electronic applications accepted. *Application Contact:* Sandra Richards, Director of Student Life and Marketing, 850-263-3261 Ext. 415. *Chair of the Graduate Division*, Dr. Ed Scott, 850-263-3261 Ext. 488, E-mail: eescott@baptistcollege.edu.

BAPTIST MISSIONARY ASSOCIATION THEOLOGICAL SEMINARY, Jacksonville, TX 75766-5407

General Information Independent-religious, coed, primarily men, comprehensive institution. *Graduate housing:* Rooms and/or apartments available on a first-come, first-served basis to single and married students. Housing application deadline: 6/1.

GRADUATE UNITS

Graduate and Professional Programs *Program availability:* Part-time. Offers theology (M Div, MAR). Electronic applications accepted.

BAPTIST THEOLOGICAL SEMINARY AT RICHMOND, Richmond, VA 23228

General Information Independent-religious, coed, graduate-only institution. *Enrollment by degree level:* 46 master's, 20 doctoral, 3 other advanced degrees. *Graduate faculty:* 2 full-time (1 woman), 8 part-time/adjunct (2 women). *Graduate housing:* Rooms and/or apartments available on a first-come, first-served basis to single and married students. Housing application deadline: 2/15. *Student services:* Campus employment opportunities, campus safety program, free psychological counseling, international student services, services for students with disabilities, writing training. *Library facilities:* Morton Library. *Collection:* Students can reserve study rooms.

Computer facilities: 2 computers available on campus for general student use. Online class registration is available.
Website: http://www.btsr.edu/

General Application Contact: Melissa Fallen, Director of Admissions and Recruitment, 804-204-1208, E-mail: admissions@btsr.edu.

GRADUATE UNITS

Graduate and Professional Programs Students: 38 full-time (14 women), 31 part-time (22 women); includes 15 minority (11 Black or African American, non-Hispanic/Latino; 4 Asian, non-Hispanic/Latino). Average age 46. *Faculty:* 2 full-time (1 woman), 8 part-time/adjunct (2 women). Expenses: Contact institution. *Financial support:* In 2017–18, 46 students received support, including 9 teaching assistantships (averaging $3,300 per year); scholarships/grants also available. Financial award application deadline: 2/1. In 2017, 15 master's, 2 doctorates awarded. *Program availability:* Part-time, 100% online, blended/hybrid learning. Offers Biblical interpretation (M Div); Christian education formation (M Div); Christian ministry (MCM); justice and peacebuilding (M Div); ministry (D Min); religious freedom (M Div); theological studies (MTS, Graduate Certificate); theology (M Div); youth and student ministries (M Div). *Application deadline:* For fall admission, 7/1 for domestic students, 5/1 for international students; for winter admission, 12/15 for domestic students, 9/1 for international students; for spring admission, 1/15 for domestic students, 10/1 for international students. Applications are processed on a rolling basis. *Application fee:* $35. Electronic applications accepted. *Application Contact:* Melissa Fallen, Director of Admissions and Recruitment, 804-204-1208, E-mail: admissions@btsr.edu. *President*, Dr. Linda M. Bridges, 804-204-1201, Fax: 804-355-8182, E-mail: lmbridges@btsr.edu.

BARCLAY COLLEGE, Haviland, KS 67059-0288

General Information Independent-religious, coed, comprehensive institution.

GRADUATE UNITS

Master of Arts Program *Program availability:* Online learning. Offers transformational leadership (MA). Electronic applications accepted.

BARD COLLEGE, Annandale-on-Hudson, NY 12504

General Information Independent, coed, comprehensive institution. *Graduate housing:* On-campus housing not available.

GRADUATE UNITS

Bard Center for Environmental Policy *Program availability:* Part-time. Offers climate science and policy (MS, Professional Certificate); environmental policy (MS, Professional Certificate); sustainability (MBA). Electronic applications accepted.

Center for Curatorial Studies Offers curatorial studies (MA). Electronic applications accepted.

Conservatory of Music Offers music (MM); vocal arts (MM).

The Conductors Institute Offers choral conducting (MM); orchestral conducting (MM).

International Center of Photography Offers advanced photographic studies (MFA).

Levy Economics Institute Offers economic theory and policy (MS).

Longy School of Music *Program availability:* Part-time. Offers chamber music (Artist Diploma); collaborative piano (MM, Artist Diploma, GPD); composition (MM); opera

(MM, GPD); organ (MM, Artist Diploma, GPD); piano (MM, Artist Diploma, GPD); voice (MM, Artist Diploma, GPD). MAT offered in partnership with the Los Angeles Philharmonic at the Los Angeles campus only. Electronic applications accepted.

Master of Arts in Teaching Program *Program availability:* Part-time. Offers secondary education (MAT). Electronic applications accepted.

Milton Avery Graduate School of the Arts Offers film/video (MFA); music/sound (MFA); painting (MFA); photography (MFA); sculpture (MFA); writing (MFA). Electronic applications accepted.

BARD GRADUATE CENTER, New York, NY 10024-3602

General Information Independent, coed, primarily women, graduate-only institution. *Graduate housing:* Rooms and/or apartments available on a first-come, first-served basis to single and married students. Housing application deadline: 4/1. *Research affiliation:* Association of Research Institutes in Art History, Metropolitan Museum of Art, Brooklyn Museum, American Museum of Natural History, Museum of Arts and Design, The Frick Collection.

GRADUATE UNITS

Graduate Studies *Program availability:* Part-time. Offers decorative arts, design history, and material culture (MA, PhD).

BARRY UNIVERSITY, Miami Shores, FL 33161-6695

General Information Independent-religious, coed, university. *Graduate housing:* On-campus housing not available. *Research affiliation:* Baxter Corporation (immunology, diagnostics), Coulter Corporation (immunology, cytology), Cordis Corporation (cardiac product development), Diamedix (immunological diagnostics), Noven Pharmaceutical, Sano Pharmaceuticals.

GRADUATE UNITS

Andreas School of Business *Program availability:* Part-time, evening/weekend. Offers accounting (MSA); business (MBA, MSA, MSM, Certificate); business administration (MBA); finance (Certificate); health services administration (Certificate); international business (Certificate); management (MSM); management information systems (Certificate); marketing (Certificate). Electronic applications accepted.

College of Arts and Sciences *Program availability:* Part-time, evening/weekend. Offers arts and sciences (MA, MFA, MS, D Min, Certificate, SSP); broadcasting (Certificate); clinical psychology (MS); communication (MA); liberal studies (MA); ministry (D Min); organizational communication (MS); pastoral ministry for Hispanics (MA); pastoral theology (MA); photography (MA, MFA); practical theology (MA); school psychology (MS, SSP). Electronic applications accepted.

College of Health Sciences *Program availability:* Part-time, evening/weekend. Offers anesthesiology (MS); biology (MS); biomedical sciences (MS); health care leadership (Certificate); health care planning and informatics (Certificate); health sciences (MS, Certificate); health services administration (MS); histotechnology (Certificate); long term care management (Certificate); medical group practice management (Certificate); occupational therapy (MS); quality improvement and outcomes management (Certificate). Electronic applications accepted.

Dwayne O. Andreas School of Law Offers law (JD).

Ellen Whiteside McDonnell School of Social Work *Program availability:* Part-time, evening/weekend. Offers social work (MSW, PhD). Electronic applications accepted.

Physician Assistant Program Offers physician assistant (MCMS). Electronic applications accepted.

School of Adult and Continuing Education *Program availability:* Part-time, evening/weekend. Offers administrative studies (MA); adult and continuing education (MA, MPA, MS, MSN, PhD, Certificate); information technology (MS); public administration (MPA). Electronic applications accepted.

Division of Nursing *Program availability:* Part-time, evening/weekend. Offers acute care nurse practitioner (MSN); family nurse practitioner (MSN); nurse practitioner (Certificate); nursing (MSN, PhD, Certificate); nursing administration (MSN, PhD, Certificate); nursing education (MSN, Certificate). Electronic applications accepted.

School of Education *Program availability:* Part-time, evening/weekend, online learning. Offers accomplished teacher (Ed S); advanced teaching and learning with technology (Certificate); counseling (MS, PhD, Ed S); culture, language and literacy (TESOL) (PhD); curriculum evaluation and research (PhD); distance education (Certificate); early childhood (Ed S); early childhood education (PhD); education (MS, Ed D, PhD, Certificate, Ed S); education for teachers of students with hearing impairments (MS); educational computing and technology (MS, Ed S); educational leadership (MS, Ed D, Certificate, Ed S); educational technology (PhD); elementary (Ed S); elementary education (MS, PhD); elementary education/ESOL (MS); ESOL (Ed S); exceptional student education (PhD); gifted (Ed S); higher education administration (PhD); higher education technology integration (Certificate); human resource development (PhD); human resource development and administration (MS); human resources: not for profit and religious organizations (Certificate); K-12 technology integration (Certificate); leadership (PhD); marital, couple and family counseling/therapy (MS, Ed S); mental health counseling (MS, Ed S); Montessori (Ed S); Montessori education (MS, Ed S); PKP/elementary (Ed S); pre-k/primary (MS); pre-k/primary/ESOL (MS); reading (Ed S); reading, language and cognition (PhD); rehabilitation counseling (MS, Ed S); school counseling (MS, Ed S); technology and TESOL (MS, Ed S); TESOL (MS); TESOL international (MS). Electronic applications accepted.

School of Human Performance and Leisure Sciences *Program availability:* Part-time, evening/weekend. Offers athletic training (MS); biomechanics (MS); exercise science (MS); general movement science (MS); human performance and leisure sciences (MS); sport and exercise psychology (MS); sport management (MS). Electronic applications accepted.

School of Podiatric Medicine Offers anatomy (MS); podiatric medicine (MS, DPM); podiatric medicine and surgery (DPM). Electronic applications accepted.

BARTON COLLEGE, Wilson, NC 27893-7000

General Information Independent-religious, coed, comprehensive institution.

GRADUATE UNITS

Program in Elementary Education Offers elementary education (M Ed). Electronic applications accepted.

BARUCH COLLEGE OF THE CITY UNIVERSITY OF NEW YORK, New York, NY 10010-5585

General Information State and locally supported, coed, comprehensive institution. *Graduate housing:* On-campus housing not available.

GRADUATE UNITS

Austin W. Marxe School of Public and International Affairs *Program availability:* Part-time, evening/weekend. Offers educational leadership (MS Ed); general public administration (MPA); health care policy (MPA); higher education administration (MS Ed); international nongovernmental organizations (MIA); nonprofit administration (MPA); policy analysis and evaluation (MPA); public and international affairs (MIA, MPA, MS Ed, Advanced Certificate); public management (MPA); school building leadership (Advanced Certificate); school district leadership (Advanced Certificate); trade policy and global economic governance (MIA); urban development and sustainability (MPA); Western Hemisphere affairs (MIA). Electronic applications accepted.

Weissman School of Arts and Sciences *Program availability:* Part-time, evening/weekend. Offers arts administration (MA); arts and sciences (MA, MS); corporate communication (MA); financial engineering (MS); industrial/organizational psychology (MS); mental health counseling (MA). Electronic applications accepted.

Zicklin School of Business *Program availability:* Part-time, evening/weekend. Offers accounting (MBA, MS, PhD); business (MBA, MS, PhD, Certificate); business administration (MBA); decision sciences (MBA); economics (MBA); entrepreneurship (MBA, MS); finance (MBA, MS, PhD); general business administration (MBA); health care administration (MBA); industrial and labor relations (MS); industrial and organizational psychology (MBA, MS, PhD); information systems (MBA, MS, PhD); international business (MBA); management (PhD); marketing (MBA, MS, PhD); operations management (MBA); organizational behavior/human resources management (MBA); quantitative methods and modeling (MBA, MS); real estate (MBA, MS); statistics (MBA, MS); sustainable business (MBA); taxation (MBA, MS). JD/MBA offered jointly with Brooklyn Law School and New York Law School. Electronic applications accepted.

BASTYR UNIVERSITY, Kenmore, WA 98028-4966

General Information Independent, coed, upper-level institution. *Enrollment:* 824 full-time matriculated graduate/professional students (697 women), 174 part-time matriculated graduate/professional students (152 women). *Enrollment by degree level:* 370 master's, 609 doctoral, 19 other advanced degrees. *Tuition:* Part-time $714 per credit hour. *Required fees:* $75. *Graduate housing:* Room and/or apartments available on a first-come, first-served basis to single students; on-campus housing not available to married students. Typical cost: $7590 per year. Housing application deadline: 5/1. *Student services:* Campus employment opportunities, campus safety program, career counseling, child daycare facilities, exercise/wellness program, free psychological counseling, international student services, low-cost health insurance, services for students with disabilities, writing training. *Library facilities:* Bastyr University Library. *Research affiliation:* University of Washington (health), Fred Hutchinson Cancer Research Center (oncology), Seattle Cancer Care Alliance (oncology), Benaroya Research Institute at Virginia Mason (health).

Computer facilities: A campuswide network can be accessed from student residence rooms and from off campus.
Website: http://www.bastyr.edu/

General Application Contact: Chris Masterson, Associate Vice President of Enrollment Management, Admissions, 425-602-3087, Fax: 425-602-3015, E-mail: admissions@bastyr.edu.

GRADUATE UNITS

School of Natural Health Arts and Sciences Expenses: Contact institution. *Financial support:* Career-related internships or fieldwork, Federal Work-Study, and scholarships/grants available. Support available to part-time students. Financial award application deadline: 4/15; financial award applicants required to submit FAFSA. *Program availability:* Part-time. Offers counseling psychology (MA); maternal-child health systems (MA); midwifery (MS); nutrition (Certificate); nutrition and clinical health psychology (MS); nutrition and wellness (MS). *Application deadline:* For fall admission, 3/15 priority date for domestic and international students. Applications are processed on a rolling basis. *Application fee:* $75. *Application Contact:* Admissions Office, 425-602-3330, Fax: 425-602-3090, E-mail: admissions@bastyr.edu. *Dean*, Dr. Lynelle Golden, 425-602-3110, Fax: 425-823-6222, E-mail: lgolden@bastyr.edu.

School of Naturopathic Medicine Expenses: Contact institution. *Financial support:* Career-related internships or fieldwork, Federal Work-Study, and scholarships/grants available. Support available to part-time students. Financial award application deadline: 4/15; financial award applicants required to submit FAFSA. *Program availability:* Part-time. Offers naturopathic medicine (ND, Postbaccalaureate Certificate). *Application deadline:* For fall admission, 2/1 priority date for domestic and international students. Applications are processed on a rolling basis. *Application fee:* $75. Electronic applications accepted. *Application Contact:* Alexis Rush, Associate Director of Admissions, 425-602-3330, Fax: 425-602-3090, E-mail: ndadvise@bastyr.edu. *Dean*, Dr. Jane Guiltinan, 425-823-1300, Fax: 425-823-6222, E-mail: jguiltin@bastyr.edu.

School of Traditional World Medicines Expenses: Contact institution. *Financial support:* Career-related internships or fieldwork, Federal Work-Study, and scholarships/grants available. Support available to part-time students. Financial award application deadline: 4/15; financial award applicants required to submit FAFSA. *Program availability:* Evening/weekend. Offers acupuncture and Oriental medicine (MS, DAOM); Ayurvedic sciences (MS). *Application deadline:* For fall admission, 3/15 priority date for domestic and international students. Applications are processed on a rolling basis. *Application fee:* $75. Electronic applications accepted. *Application Contact:* Admissions Office, 425-602-3330, Fax: 425-602-3090, E-mail: admissions@bastyr.edu. *Dean*, 425-602-3151, Fax: 425-823-6222.

BAYAMÓN CENTRAL UNIVERSITY, Bayamón, PR 00960-1725

General Information Independent-religious, coed, comprehensive institution. *Graduate housing:* On-campus housing not available.

GRADUATE UNITS

Graduate Programs *Program availability:* Part-time, evening/weekend. Offers accounting (MBA); administration and supervision (MA Ed); commercial education (MA Ed); elementary education (K–3) (MA Ed); family counseling (Graduate Certificate); finance (MBA); general business (MBA); guidance and counseling (MA Ed); management (MBA); marketing (MBA); organizational psychology (MA); pre-elementary teacher (MA Ed); rehabilitation counseling (MA Ed); special education (MA Ed).

BAYLOR COLLEGE OF MEDICINE, Houston, TX 77030-3498

General Information Independent, coed, graduate-only institution. CGS member. *Graduate housing:* On-campus housing not available. *Research affiliation:* Veterans Affairs Medical Center (biomedical research), Texas Children's Hospital (pediatric biomedical research), St. Luke's Episcopal Hospital (biomedical research), National Space Biomedical Research Institute (biomedical research), Harris Health System (biomedical research), Children's Nutrition Research Center (pediatric nutrition).

GRADUATE UNITS

Graduate School of Biomedical Sciences Offers biochemistry (PhD); biochemistry and molecular biology (PhD); biomedical sciences (MS, PhD); cardiovascular sciences (PhD); cell and molecular biology (PhD); clinical scientist training (MS, PhD);

developmental biology (PhD); genetics (PhD); human genetics (PhD); immunology (PhD); microbiology (PhD); molecular and cellular biology (PhD); molecular and human genetics (PhD); molecular physiology and biophysics (PhD); molecular virology and microbiology (PhD); neuroscience (PhD); pharmacology (PhD); structural and computational biology and molecular biophysics (PhD); translational biology and molecular medicine (PhD); virology (PhD). Electronic applications accepted.

Medical School Offers medicine (MD). Electronic applications accepted.

School of Allied Health Sciences Offers allied health sciences (MS, DNP); genetic counseling (MS); nurse anesthesia (DNP); physician assistant (MS). Electronic applications accepted.

BAYLOR UNIVERSITY, Waco, TX 76798

General Information Independent-religious, coed, university. CGS member. *Enrollment:* 17,059 graduate, professional, and undergraduate students; 2,286 full-time matriculated graduate/professional students (1,130 women), 331 part-time matriculated graduate/professional students (151 women). *Enrollment by degree level:* 1,381 master's, 1,217 doctoral, 19 other advanced degrees. *Graduate faculty:* 789. *Graduate housing:* Rooms and/or apartments available to single and married students. *Student services:* Campus employment opportunities, campus safety program, career counseling, exercise/wellness program, free psychological counseling, international student services, low-cost health insurance, multicultural affairs office, services for students with disabilities. *Library facilities:* Moody Memorial Library plus 8 others. *Research affiliation:* Sandia National Laboratories (physics), Zyvex Corporation (physics), OXiGENE, Inc. (pharmaceuticals), Brookhaven National Laboratory (physics), Fermi National Accelerator Laboratory (physics), National Center for Supercomputing Applications (physics).

Computer facilities: Computer purchase and lease plans are available. A campuswide network can be accessed from student residence rooms and from off campus. Online class registration is available.
Website: http://www.baylor.edu/

General Application Contact: Lori McNamara, Admissions Coordinator, 254-710-3588, Fax: 254-710-3870.

GRADUATE UNITS

Diana R. Garland School of Social Work Students: 121 full-time (112 women), 20 part-time (17 women); includes 47 minority (16 Black or African American, non-Hispanic/Latino; 6 Asian, non-Hispanic/Latino; 18 Hispanic/Latino; 7 Two or more races, non-Hispanic/Latino), 6 international. Average age 27. 190 applicants, 72% accepted, 71 enrolled. *Faculty:* 11 full-time (5 women), 13 part-time/adjunct (7 women). Expenses: Contact institution. *Financial support:* In 2017–18, 138 students received support, including 12 research assistantships with tuition reimbursements available (averaging $6,800 per year); career-related internships or fieldwork, Federal Work-Study, institutionally sponsored loans, scholarships/grants, traineeships, tuition waivers (full and partial), and unspecified assistantships also available. Support available to part-time students. Financial award application deadline: 6/1; financial award applicants required to submit FAFSA. In 2017, 69 master's awarded. *Program availability:* Part-time, blended/hybrid learning. Offers social work (MSW, PhD). *Application deadline:* For spring admission, 3/15 for domestic and international students. Applications are processed on a rolling basis. *Application fee:* $45. Electronic applications accepted. *Application Contact:* Dr. Crystal Diaz-Espinoza, Director of Recruitment and Career Services, 254-710-4479, Fax: 254-710-6455, E-mail: crystal_diaz-espinoza@baylor.edu. *Associate Dean for Academic Affairs*, Dr. David Pooler, 254-710-3884, Fax: 254-710-7412, E-mail: david_pooler@baylor.edu.

George W. Truett Theological Seminary Students: 267 full-time (94 women), 75 part-time (22 women); includes 102 minority (55 Black or African American, non-Hispanic/Latino; 1 American Indian or Alaska Native, non-Hispanic/Latino; 6 Asian, non-Hispanic/Latino; 24 Hispanic/Latino; 16 Two or more races, non-Hispanic/Latino), 18 international. Average age 30. 129 applicants, 95% accepted, 91 enrolled. *Faculty:* 21 full-time (2 women), 14 part-time/adjunct (4 women). Expenses: Contact institution. *Financial support:* In 2017–18, 342 students received support, including 38 research assistantships with partial tuition reimbursements available (averaging $5,130 per year); career-related internships or fieldwork, Federal Work-Study, scholarships/grants, and unspecified assistantships also available. Support available to part-time students. Financial award application deadline: 8/1; financial award applicants required to submit FAFSA. In 2017, 67 master's, 7 doctorates awarded. *Program availability:* Part-time. Offers theology (M Div, MACM, MTS, D Min). *Application deadline:* For fall admission, 5/1 priority date for domestic students, 6/10 for international students; for spring admission, 11/15 for domestic students, 10/10 for international students; for summer admission, 4/1 for domestic students, 3/10 for international students. Applications are processed on a rolling basis. *Application fee:* $35. Electronic applications accepted. *Application Contact:* Carley Lund, Administrative Associate, Admission Services, 254-710-7334, Fax: 254-710-7233, E-mail: carley_lund@baylor.edu. *Dean*, Dr. Todd D. Still, 254-710-6080, Fax: 254-710-7234, E-mail: todd_still@baylor.edu.

Graduate School Students: 1,524 full-time (741 women), 240 part-time (114 women); includes 357 minority (62 Black or African American, non-Hispanic/Latino; 3 American Indian or Alaska Native, non-Hispanic/Latino; 69 Asian, non-Hispanic/Latino; 128 Hispanic/Latino; 3 Native Hawaiian or other Pacific Islander, non-Hispanic/Latino; 92 Two or more races, non-Hispanic/Latino), 217 international. 1,692 applicants. *Faculty:* 789. Expenses: Contact institution. *Financial support:* Fellowships, research assistantships with tuition reimbursements, teaching assistantships with tuition reimbursements, career-related internships or fieldwork, Federal Work-Study, institutionally sponsored loans, scholarships/grants, health care benefits, tuition waivers (full and partial), and unspecified assistantships available. Support available to part-time students. Financial award applicants required to submit FAFSA. In 2017, 680 master's, 136 doctorates, 7 other advanced degrees awarded. *Program availability:* Part-time, evening/weekend, 100% online, blended/hybrid learning. Offers emergency medicine (D Sc PA); health care administration (MHA); health sciences (MHA, MS, D Sc, D Sc PA, DPT, DScPT); nutrition (MS); orthopedics (D Sc); physical therapy (DPT, DScPT). *Application deadline:* For fall admission, 2/15 for domestic students; for spring admission, 12/1 for domestic students; for summer admission, 5/1 for domestic students. Applications are processed on a rolling basis. *Application fee:* $50. Electronic applications accepted. *Application Contact:* Lori McNamara, Graduate Admissions Coordinator, 254-710-3588, Fax: 254-710-3870, E-mail: lori_mcnamara@baylor.edu. *Dean*, Dr. Larry Lyon, 254-710-3588, Fax: 254-710-3870, E-mail: larry_lyon@baylor.edu.

College of Arts and Sciences Students: 568 full-time (263 women), 73 part-time (28 women); includes 106 minority (13 Black or African American, non-Hispanic/Latino; 18 Asian, non-Hispanic/Latino; 37 Hispanic/Latino; 38 Two or more races, non-Hispanic/Latino), 102 international. Expenses: Contact institution. *Financial support:* Fellowships, research assistantships with partial tuition reimbursements, teaching assistantships, career-related internships or fieldwork, Federal Work-Study, institutionally sponsored loans, scholarships/grants, tuition waivers (full and partial), and laboratory assistantships, practicum stipends available. Support available to part-time students. In 2017, 71 master's, 98 doctorates awarded. *Program availability:* Part-time, evening/weekend. Offers American studies (MA); arts and sciences (IMES, MA, MES, MFA, MIJ, MPPA, MS, MSCSD, MSW, PhD, Psy D); biochemistry (MS, PhD); biology (MA, MS, PhD); chemistry (MS, PhD); clinical psychology (Psy D); communication (MA); community analytics (PhD); ecological, earth and environmental sciences (PhD); English (MA, PhD); environmental biology (MS); environmental science (MES, MS, PhD); geosciences (MS, PhD); health and society (PhD); history (MA, PhD); international studies (MA); journalism, public relations and new media (MIJ); limnology (MS); mathematics (MS, PhD); museum studies (MA); news editorial public relations (MA); philosophy (MA, PhD); physics (MA, MS, PhD); political science (MA, PhD); psychology (MA, PhD); public policy and administration (MPPA); religion (MA, PhD); sociology (MA); sociology of religion (PhD); Spanish (MA); statistical science (MA, PhD); theatre arts (MA, MFA). *Application deadline:* Applications are processed on a rolling basis. *Application fee:* $25. Electronic applications accepted. *Application Contact:* Lori McNamara, Admissions Coordinator, 254-710-3588, Fax: 254-710-3870. *Dean*, Dr. Larry Lyon, 254-710-3588, Fax: 254-710-3870, E-mail: larry_lyon@baylor.edu.

Hankamer School of Business Students: 306 full-time (120 women), 36 part-time (18 women); includes 88 minority (17 Black or African American, non-Hispanic/Latino; 1 American Indian or Alaska Native, non-Hispanic/Latino; 22 Asian, non-Hispanic/Latino; 28 Hispanic/Latino; 1 Native Hawaiian or other Pacific Islander, non-Hispanic/Latino; 19 Two or more races, non-Hispanic/Latino), 38 international. Expenses: Contact institution. *Financial support:* Research assistantships, teaching assistantships, career-related internships or fieldwork, Federal Work-Study, and institutionally sponsored loans available. In 2017, 312 master's, 2 doctorates awarded. *Program availability:* Part-time. Offers accounting and business law (M Acc, MT); business (M Acc, MBA, MS Eco, MSIS, MT, PhD); business administration (MBA); economics (MS Eco); entrepreneurship (PhD); information systems (MSIS, PhD); information systems management (MBA). *Application deadline:* Applications are processed on a rolling basis. *Application fee:* $25. *Application Contact:* Laurie Wilson, Director, Graduate Business Programs, 254-710-4163, Fax: 254-710-1066, E-mail: laurie_wilson@baylor.edu. *Associate Dean*, Dr. Gary Carini, 254-710-3718, Fax: 254-710-1092, E-mail: gary_carini@baylor.edu.

Institute of Biomedical Studies Students: 22 full-time (8 women); includes 4 minority (1 Black or African American, non-Hispanic/Latino; 1 Asian, non-Hispanic/Latino; 2 Hispanic/Latino), 11 international. Average age 24. 69 applicants, 10% accepted, 5 enrolled. *Faculty:* 19 part-time/adjunct (4 women). Expenses: Contact institution. *Financial support:* In 2017–18, 22 students received support. Research assistantships, teaching assistantships, and tuition waivers available. In 2017, 2 master's, 5 doctorates awarded. Offers biomedical studies (MS, PhD). *Application deadline:* For spring admission, 2/15 for domestic and international students. Applications are processed on a rolling basis. *Application fee:* $25. Electronic applications accepted. *Application Contact:* Rhonda Bellert, Administrative Associate, 254-710-2514, Fax: 254-710-2199, E-mail: rhonda_bellert@baylor.edu. *Acting Graduate Program Director*, Dr. Bob Kane, 254-710-4556, Fax: 254-710-2199, E-mail: bob_kane@baylor.edu.

Louise Herrington School of Nursing Students: 35 full-time (34 women), 11 part-time (all women); includes 21 minority (5 Black or African American, non-Hispanic/Latino; 1 American Indian or Alaska Native, non-Hispanic/Latino; 5 Asian, non-Hispanic/Latino; 8 Hispanic/Latino; 2 Two or more races, non-Hispanic/Latino). Average age 35. 47 applicants, 70% accepted, 26 enrolled. *Faculty:* 11 full-time (all women), 3 part-time/adjunct (2 women). Expenses: Contact institution. *Financial support:* In 2017–18, 66 students received support. Teaching assistantships, Federal Work-Study, scholarships/grants, and unspecified assistantships available. Support available to part-time students. Financial award application deadline: 6/30; financial award applicants required to submit FAFSA. In 2017, 13 master's, 4 doctorates awarded. *Program availability:* Part-time, online learning. Offers family nurse practitioner (MSN); neonatal nurse practitioner (MSN); nurse-midwifery (DNP). *Application deadline:* For fall admission, 2/1 for domestic students. *Application fee:* $50. Electronic applications accepted. *Application Contact:* Elaine Lark, Coordinator of Recruitment and Enrollment, 214-818-7839, Fax: 214-820-3835, E-mail: elaine_lark@baylor.edu. *Graduate Program Director*, Dr. Barbara Camune, 214-367-3754, Fax: 214-820-3375, E-mail: barbara_camune@baylor.edu.

Robbins College of Health and Human Sciences Students: 157 full-time (122 women), 10 part-time (7 women); includes 38 minority (7 Black or African American, non-Hispanic/Latino; 4 Asian, non-Hispanic/Latino; 15 Hispanic/Latino; 1 Native Hawaiian or other Pacific Islander, non-Hispanic/Latino; 11 Two or more races, non-Hispanic/Latino), 9 international. Expenses: Contact institution. In 2017, 66 master's, 3 doctorates awarded. Offers athletic training (MS); communication sciences and disorders (MS); community health (MPH); exercise physiology (MS); health and human sciences (MA, MPH, MS, MS Ed, PhD); kinesiology, exercise nutrition, and health promotion (PhD); nutrition sciences (MS); sport pedagogy (MS). *Application Contact:* Lori McNamara, Graduate Admissions Coordinator, 254-710-3588, Fax: 254-710-3870, E-mail: lori_mcnamara@baylor.edu. *Interim Dean*, Dr. Rodney G. Bowden, 254-710-6111, Fax: 254-710-3699, E-mail: rodney_bowden@baylor.edu.

School of Education Students: 140 full-time (94 women), 42 part-time (23 women); includes 47 minority (11 Black or African American, non-Hispanic/Latino; 5 Asian, non-Hispanic/Latino; 20 Hispanic/Latino; 1 Native Hawaiian or other Pacific Islander, non-Hispanic/Latino; 10 Two or more races, non-Hispanic/Latino), 7 international. 248 applicants, 35% accepted, 28 enrolled. *Faculty:* 42 full-time (26 women), 10 part-time/adjunct (6 women). Expenses: Contact institution. *Financial support:* In 2017–18, 181 students received support, including 38 research assistantships (averaging $12,050 per year), 68 teaching assistantships (averaging $12,050 per year); career-related internships or fieldwork, Federal Work-Study, institutionally sponsored loans, scholarships/grants, health care benefits, tuition waivers (partial), unspecified assistantships, and stipends also available. Support available to part-time students. Financial award application deadline: 2/1; financial award applicants required to submit FAFSA. In 2017, 66 master's, 4 doctorates, 7 other advanced degrees awarded. *Program availability:* Part-time. Offers applied behavior analysis (MS Ed); curriculum and instruction (MA, MS Ed, Ed D, PhD); education (MA, MS Ed, Ed D, PhD, Ed S); educational leadership (MS Ed, Ed S); educational psychology (MA, MS Ed, PhD); exceptionalities (PhD); gifted and talented studies (MS Ed); learning and development (PhD); quantitative methods (MA); school psychology (Ed S). *Application deadline:* For fall admission, 2/1 priority date for domestic and international students. Applications are processed on a rolling basis. *Application fee:* $25. Electronic applications accepted. *Dean*, Dr. Terrill F. Saxon, 254-710-3111, Fax: 254-710-3987, E-mail: terrill_saxon@baylor.edu.

School of Engineering and Computer Science Students: 99 full-time (15 women), 8 part-time (0 women); includes 15 minority (2 Black or African American, non-Hispanic/Latino; 6 Asian, non-Hispanic/Latino; 5 Hispanic/Latino; 2 Two or more races, non-Hispanic/Latino), 44 international. Expenses: Contact institution. *Financial support:* Research assistantships and teaching assistantships available. Financial award application deadline: 3/15. In 2017, 27 master's, 3 doctorates awarded. *Program availability:* Part-time. Offers biomedical engineering (MSBME); computer science (MS, PhD); electrical and computer engineering (MS, PhD); engineering (ME); engineering and computer science (ME, MS, MSBME, PhD); mechanical engineering (MS, PhD). *Application deadline:* Applications are processed on a rolling basis. *Application fee:* $25. *Application Contact:* 254-710-3588, Fax: 254-710-3870. *Dean,* Dr. Dennis L. O'Neal, 254-710-3871, Fax: 254-710-3839, E-mail: dennis_oneal@baylor.edu.

School of Music Students: 17 full-time (8 women), 48 part-time (18 women); includes 11 minority (2 Asian, non-Hispanic/Latino; 7 Hispanic/Latino; 2 Two or more races, non-Hispanic/Latino), 17 international. Expenses: Contact institution. *Financial support:* Teaching assistantships, Federal Work-Study, and institutionally sponsored loans available. In 2017, 35 master's awarded. Offers church music (MM, DMA); collaborative piano (MM); composition (MM); conducting (MM); music history and literature (MM); music theory (MM); performance (MM); piano pedagogy and performance (MM). *Application deadline:* Applications are processed on a rolling basis. *Application fee:* $25. *Application Contact:* Melinda Coates, Administrative Assistant, 254-710-2360, Fax: 254-710-3870, E-mail: melinda_coats@baylor.edu. *Graduate Program Director,* Dr. David Music, 254-710-2360, Fax: 254-710-1191, E-mail: david_music@baylor.edu.

School of Law Students: 377 full-time (186 women), 8 part-time (7 women); includes 104 minority (8 Black or African American, non-Hispanic/Latino; 6 American Indian or Alaska Native, non-Hispanic/Latino; 22 Asian, non-Hispanic/Latino; 57 Hispanic/Latino; 2 Native Hawaiian or other Pacific Islander, non-Hispanic/Latino; 9 Two or more races, non-Hispanic/Latino), 1 international. Average age 24. 1,597 applicants, 48% accepted, 86 enrolled. *Faculty:* 28 full-time (9 women), 20 part-time/adjunct (2 women). Expenses: Contact institution. *Financial support:* In 2017–18, 343 students received support. Federal Work-Study and scholarships/grants available. Financial award application deadline: 2/1; financial award applicants required to submit FAFSA. In 2017, 144 doctorates awarded. Offers law (JD). *Application deadline:* For fall admission, 7/15 for domestic and international students; for spring admission, 11/15 for domestic and international students; for summer admission, 3/15 for domestic and international students. Applications are processed on a rolling basis. *Application fee:* $0. Electronic applications accepted. *Application Contact:* Jenny Branson, Assistant Dean of Admissions and Financial Aid, 254-710-1911, Fax: 254-710-2316, E-mail: jenny_branson@baylor.edu. *Dean,* Bradley J. B. Toben, 254-710-1911, Fax: 254-710-2316.

BAY PATH UNIVERSITY, Longmeadow, MA 01106-2292

General Information Independent, Undergraduate: women only; graduate: coed, comprehensive institution. *Enrollment:* 3,298 graduate, professional, and undergraduate students; 556 full-time matriculated graduate/professional students (482 women), 795 part-time matriculated graduate/professional students (687 women). *Enrollment by degree level:* 1,246 master's, 13 doctoral, 56 other advanced degrees. *Graduate faculty:* 39 full-time (34 women), 155 part-time/adjunct (118 women). Tuition and fees vary according to degree level and program. *Graduate housing:* Room and/or apartments available on a first-come, first-served basis to single students; on-campus housing not available to married students. Housing application deadline: 7/2. *Student services:* Campus employment opportunities, campus safety program, career counseling, exercise/wellness program, free psychological counseling, international student services, low-cost health insurance, multicultural affairs office, services for students with disabilities. *Library facilities:* Hatch Library. *Collection:* Books: 52,565 (physical), 408,000 (digital/electronic); Serial titles: 80 (physical), 55,000 (digital/electronic); Databases: 110. Weekly public service hours: 86; students can reserve study rooms.

Computer facilities: 235 computers available on campus for general student use. A campuswide network can be accessed from student residence rooms and from off campus. Online class registration is available.
Website: http://www.baypath.edu/

General Application Contact: Diane Ranaldi, Dean of Graduate Admissions, 413-565-1332, Fax: 413-565-1250, E-mail: dranaldi@baypath.edu.

GRADUATE UNITS

Program in Accounting Students: 3 full-time (1 woman), 17 part-time (all women); includes 5 minority (2 Black or African American, non-Hispanic/Latino; 1 Asian, non-Hispanic/Latino; 2 Hispanic/Latino). Average age 29. Expenses: Contact institution. *Financial support:* In 2017–18, 2 students received support. Scholarships/grants and unspecified assistantships available. Financial award applicants required to submit FAFSA. In 2017, 3 master's awarded. *Program availability:* Part-time, online only, 100% online. Offers forensic accounting (MS); private accounting (MS); public accounting (tax and audit) (MS). *Application deadline:* Applications are processed on a rolling basis. *Application fee:* $45. Electronic applications accepted. *Application Contact:* Diane Ranaldi, Dean of Graduate Admissions, 413-565-1332, Fax: 413-565-1250, E-mail: dranaldi@baypath.edu. *Director,* Kara Stevens, 413-565-1344, E-mail: kastevens@baypath.edu.

Program in Applied Behavior Analysis Students: 2 full-time (both women), 159 part-time (139 women); includes 27 minority (9 Black or African American, non-Hispanic/Latino; 2 Asian, non-Hispanic/Latino; 12 Hispanic/Latino; 4 Two or more races, non-Hispanic/Latino), 1 international. Average age 31. *Faculty:* 39 full-time (34 women), 155 part-time/adjunct (118 women). Expenses: Contact institution. *Financial support:* Unspecified assistantships available. Financial award applicants required to submit FAFSA. In 2017, 18 master's awarded. *Program availability:* Part-time, online learning. Offers applied behavior analysis (MS); autism spectrum disorders (MS). *Application deadline:* Applications are processed on a rolling basis. *Application fee:* $45. Electronic applications accepted. *Application Contact:* Diane Ranaldi, Dean of Graduate Admissions, 413-565-1332, Fax: 413-565-1250, E-mail: dranaldi@baypath.edu. *Director,* Susan Ainsleigh, E-mail: sainsleigh@baypath.edu.

Program in Applied Data Science Students: 2 full-time (both women), 8 part-time (2 women); includes 3 minority (1 Black or African American, non-Hispanic/Latino; 1 Asian, non-Hispanic/Latino; 1 Hispanic/Latino). Average age 34. *Faculty:* 42 full-time (37 women), 155 part-time/adjunct (118 women). Expenses: Contact institution. *Financial support:* Applicants required to submit FAFSA. *Program availability:* Part-time, 100% online. Offers applied data science (MS). *Application deadline:* Applications are processed on a rolling basis. *Application fee:* $45. Electronic applications accepted. *Application Contact:* Diane Ranaldi, Dean of Graduate Admissions, 413-565-1332, Fax: 413-565-1250, E-mail: dranaldi@baypath.edu. *Director,* Ning Jia, E-mail: njia@baypath.edu.

Program in Applied Laboratory Science and Operations Students: 9 full-time (all women), 5 part-time (all women); includes 5 minority (1 Black or African American, non-Hispanic/Latino; 3 Hispanic/Latino; 1 Two or more races, non-Hispanic/Latino). Average age 32. *Faculty:* 39 full-time (34 women), 155 part-time/adjunct (118 women). Expenses: Contact institution. *Financial support:* Unspecified assistantships available. Financial award applicants required to submit FAFSA. *Program availability:* Part-time, evening/weekend. Offers applied laboratory science and operations (MS). *Application deadline:* Applications are processed on a rolling basis. *Application fee:* $45. Electronic applications accepted. *Application Contact:* Diane Ranaldi, Dean of Graduate Admissions, 413-565-1332, Fax: 413-565-1250, E-mail: dranaldi@baypath.edu. *Program Director,* Dr. Thomas Mennella, 413-565-1318, E-mail: tmennella@baypath.edu.

Program in Clinical Mental Health Counseling Students: 68 full-time (59 women), 82 part-time (75 women); includes 42 minority (21 Black or African American, non-Hispanic/Latino; 19 Hispanic/Latino; 2 Two or more races, non-Hispanic/Latino), 11 international. Average age 32. Expenses: Contact institution. *Financial support:* Unspecified assistantships available. Financial award applicants required to submit FAFSA. In 2017, 21 master's awarded. *Program availability:* Part-time, blended/hybrid learning. Offers clinical mental health counseling (MS). Program also offered in Sturbridge and Burlington, MA. *Application deadline:* Applications are processed on a rolling basis. *Application fee:* $45. Electronic applications accepted. *Application Contact:* Diane Ranaldi, Dean of Graduate Admissions, 413-565-1332, Fax: 413-565-1250, E-mail: dranaldi@baypath.edu. *Director,* Dr. Mark Benander, 413-565-1332, E-mail: mbenander@baypath.edu.

Program in Communications and Information Management Students: 4 full-time (3 women), 18 part-time (13 women); includes 9 minority (4 Black or African American, non-Hispanic/Latino; 1 Asian, non-Hispanic/Latino; 3 Hispanic/Latino; 1 Two or more races, non-Hispanic/Latino). Average age 40. Expenses: Contact institution. *Financial support:* Unspecified assistantships available. Financial award applicants required to submit FAFSA. In 2017, 27 master's awarded. *Program availability:* Part-time, evening/weekend, 100% online. Offers communications and information management (MS). *Application deadline:* Applications are processed on a rolling basis. *Application fee:* $45. Electronic applications accepted. *Application Contact:* Diane Ranaldi, Dean of Graduate Admissions, 413-565-1332, Fax: 413-565-1250, E-mail: dranaldi@baypath.edu. *Program Director,* Robin Saunders, 413-565-1009.

Program in Creative Nonfiction Students: 3 full-time (all women), 34 part-time (29 women); includes 6 minority (2 Black or African American, non-Hispanic/Latino; 2 Hispanic/Latino; 2 Two or more races, non-Hispanic/Latino). Average age 48. Expenses: Contact institution. *Financial support:* Applicants required to submit FAFSA. In 2017, 7 master's awarded. *Program availability:* Part-time, evening/weekend, online only, 100% online. Offers creative nonfiction (MFA). *Application deadline:* Applications are processed on a rolling basis. *Application fee:* $45. Electronic applications accepted. *Application Contact:* Diane Ranaldi, Dean of Graduate Admissions, 413-565-1332, Fax: 413-565-1250, E-mail: dranaldi@baypath.edu. *Director,* Leanne James Blackwell, 413-565-1232, E-mail: ljblackwell@baypath.edu.

Program in Curriculum and Instruction Students: 17 full-time (all women), 37 part-time (35 women); includes 4 minority (3 Black or African American, non-Hispanic/Latino; 1 Hispanic/Latino). Average age 31. Expenses: Contact institution. *Financial support:* Unspecified assistantships available. Financial award applicants required to submit FAFSA. In 2017, 4 master's awarded. *Program availability:* Part-time, 100% online. Offers curriculum and instruction (MS Ed). *Application deadline:* Applications are processed on a rolling basis. *Application fee:* $45. Electronic applications accepted. *Application Contact:* Diane Ranaldi, Dean of Graduate Admissions, 413-565-1332, Fax: 413-565-1250, E-mail: dranaldi@baypath.edu. *Program Director,* Andrea Hickson, E-mail: ahickson@baypath.edu.

Program in Cybersecurity Management Students: 7 full-time (3 women), 27 part-time (15 women); includes 14 minority (5 Black or African American, non-Hispanic/Latino; 2 Asian, non-Hispanic/Latino; 6 Hispanic/Latino; 1 Two or more races, non-Hispanic/Latino). Average age 34. Expenses: Contact institution. *Financial support:* Unspecified assistantships available. Financial award applicants required to submit FAFSA. In 2017, 4 master's awarded. *Program availability:* Part-time, evening/weekend, online only, 100% online. Offers cybersecurity management (MS). *Application deadline:* Applications are processed on a rolling basis. *Application fee:* $45. Electronic applications accepted. *Application Contact:* Diane Ranaldi, Dean of Graduate Admissions, 413-565-1332, Fax: 413-565-1250, E-mail: dranaldi@baypath.edu. *Director,* Dr. Larry Snyder, 413-565-1294, E-mail: lsnyder@baypath.edu.

Program in Developmental Psychology Students: 6 full-time (all women), 12 part-time (all women); includes 9 minority (3 Black or African American, non-Hispanic/Latino; 5 Hispanic/Latino; 1 Two or more races, non-Hispanic/Latino). Average age 35. Expenses: Contact institution. *Financial support:* Unspecified assistantships available. Financial award applicants required to submit FAFSA. In 2017, 7 master's awarded. *Program availability:* Part-time, 100% online. Offers developmental psychology (MS). *Application deadline:* Applications are processed on a rolling basis. *Application fee:* $45. Electronic applications accepted. *Application Contact:* Diane Ranaldi, Dean of Graduate Admissions, 413-565-1332, Fax: 413-565-1250, E-mail: dranaldi@baypath.edu. *Program Director,* Dr. Mark Benander, 413-565-1332, E-mail: mbenander@baypath.edu.

Program in Education Students: 37 full-time (34 women), 100 part-time (84 women); includes 14 minority (7 Black or African American, non-Hispanic/Latino; 1 Asian, non-Hispanic/Latino; 5 Hispanic/Latino; 1 Two or more races, non-Hispanic/Latino). Average age 32. Expenses: Contact institution. *Financial support:* Unspecified assistantships available. Financial award applicants required to submit FAFSA. *Program availability:* Part-time, 100% online. Offers education. *Application deadline:* Applications are processed on a rolling basis. *Application fee:* $45. Electronic applications accepted. *Application Contact:* Diane Ranaldi, Dean of Graduate Admissions, 413-565-1332, Fax: 413-565-1250, E-mail: dranaldi@baypath.edu. *Program Coordinator,* Dr. Karen DeAngelis, E-mail: kdeangelis@baypath.edu.

Program in Entrepreneurial Thinking and Innovative Practices Students: 19 full-time (16 women), 57 part-time (53 women); includes 20 minority (11 Black or African American, non-Hispanic/Latino; 1 Asian, non-Hispanic/Latino; 5 Hispanic/Latino; 3 Two or more races, non-Hispanic/Latino). Average age 34. Expenses: Contact institution. *Financial support:* Unspecified assistantships available. Financial award applicants required to submit FAFSA. In 2017, 34 master's awarded. *Program availability:* Part-time, 100% online. Offers entrepreneurial thinking and innovative practices (MBA). *Application deadline:* Applications are processed on a rolling basis. *Application fee:* $45. Electronic applications accepted. *Application Contact:* Diane Ranaldi, Dean of Graduate Admissions, 413-565-1332, Fax: 413-565-1250, E-mail: dranaldi@baypath.edu. *Program Director,* Mo Sattar, 413-565-1228, E-mail: msattar@baypath.edu.

Program in Genetic Counseling Students: 11 full-time (10 women), 1 (woman) part-time. Average age 31. Expenses: Contact institution. *Financial support:* Scholarships/grants available. Financial award applicants required to submit FAFSA.

Program availability: Evening/weekend, blended/hybrid learning. Offers genetic counseling (MS). *Application deadline:* For fall admission, 2/1 for domestic students. Applications are processed on a rolling basis. *Application fee:* $45. Electronic applications accepted. *Application Contact:* Diane Ranaldi, Dean of Graduate Admissions, 413-565-1332, Fax: 413-565-1250, E-mail: dranaldi@baypath.edu. *Associate Provost/Dean*, Dr. Liz Fleming, 413-565-1332, E-mail: lfleming@baypath.edu.

Program in Higher Education Administration Students: 3 full-time (all women), 47 part-time (33 women); includes 19 minority (9 Black or African American, non-Hispanic/Latino; 8 Hispanic/Latino; 2 Two or more races, non-Hispanic/Latino). Average age 34. Expenses: Contact institution. *Financial support:* Unspecified assistantships available. Financial award applicants required to submit FAFSA. In 2017, 15 master's awarded. *Program availability:* Part-time, online only, 100% online. Offers enrollment management (MS); general administration (MS); institutional advancement (MS); online teaching and program administration (MS). *Application deadline:* Applications are processed on a rolling basis. *Application fee:* $45. Electronic applications accepted. *Application Contact:* Diane Ranaldi, Dean of Graduate Admissions, 413-565-1332, Fax: 413-565-1250, E-mail: dranaldi@baypath.edu. *Program Director*, Dr. Lauren Way, 413-565-1193, E-mail: lway@baypath.edu.

Program in Information Management Students: 4 full-time (1 woman), 2 part-time (both women); includes 1 minority (Black or African American, non-Hispanic/Latino). Average age 49. Expenses: Contact institution. *Financial support:* Unspecified assistantships available. Financial award applicants required to submit FAFSA. *Program availability:* Part-time, 100% online. Offers information management (MS). *Application deadline:* Applications are processed on a rolling basis. *Application fee:* $45. Electronic applications accepted. *Application Contact:* Diane Ranaldi, Dean of Graduate Admissions, 413-565-1332, Fax: 413-565-1250, E-mail: dranaldi@baypath.edu. *Director*, Robin Saunders, 413-565-1009, E-mail: rsaunders@baypath.edu.

Program in Leadership and Negotiation Students: 3 full-time (all women), 26 part-time (23 women); includes 5 minority (4 Black or African American, non-Hispanic/Latino; 1 Hispanic/Latino). Average age 42. Expenses: Contact institution. *Financial support:* Unspecified assistantships available. Financial award applicants required to submit FAFSA. *Program availability:* Part-time, 100% online, blended/hybrid learning. Offers leadership and negotiation (MS). *Application deadline:* Applications are processed on a rolling basis. *Application fee:* $45. Electronic applications accepted. *Application Contact:* Diane Ranaldi, Dean of Graduate Admissions, 413-565-1332, Fax: 413-565-1250, E-mail: dranaldi@baypath.edu. *Director*, Dr. Joshua Weiss, E-mail: joweiss@baypath.edu.

Program in Nonprofit Management and Philanthropy Students: 2 full-time (1 woman), 43 part-time (42 women); includes 16 minority (8 Black or African American, non-Hispanic/Latino; 6 Hispanic/Latino; 2 Two or more races, non-Hispanic/Latino). Average age 35. Expenses: Contact institution. *Financial support:* Unspecified assistantships available. Financial award applicants required to submit FAFSA. In 2017, 13 master's awarded. *Program availability:* Part-time, 100% online. Offers nonprofit management and philanthropy (MS). *Application deadline:* Applications are processed on a rolling basis. *Application fee:* $45. Electronic applications accepted. *Application Contact:* Diane Ranaldi, Dean of Graduate Admissions, 413-565-1332, Fax: 413-565-1250, E-mail: dranaldi@baypath.edu. *Program Director*, Silvia de Haas-Phillips, E-mail: sdphillips@baypath.edu.

Program in Occupational Therapy Students: 280 full-time (256 women), 36 part-time (33 women); includes 56 minority (20 Black or African American, non-Hispanic/Latino; 2 American Indian or Alaska Native, non-Hispanic/Latino; 13 Asian, non-Hispanic/Latino; 14 Hispanic/Latino; 7 Two or more races, non-Hispanic/Latino), 1 international. Average age 28. Expenses: Contact institution. *Financial support:* Unspecified assistantships available. Financial award applicants required to submit FAFSA. In 2017, 81 master's, 36 doctorates awarded. *Program availability:* Part-time. Offers occupational therapy (MOT, OTD). *Application deadline:* Applications are processed on a rolling basis. *Application fee:* $45. Electronic applications accepted. *Application Contact:* Diane Ranaldi, Dean of Graduate Admissions, 413-565-1332, Fax: 413-565-1250, E-mail: dranaldi@baypath.edu. *Program Director*, Dr. Beverly St. Pierre, E-mail: bstpierre@baypath.edu.

Program in Physician Assistant Studies Students: 61 full-time (39 women); includes 13 minority (4 Black or African American, non-Hispanic/Latino; 1 American Indian or Alaska Native, non-Hispanic/Latino; 5 Asian, non-Hispanic/Latino; 2 Hispanic/Latino; 1 Two or more races, non-Hispanic/Latino). Average age 30. Expenses: Contact institution. *Financial support:* Unspecified assistantships available. Financial award applicants required to submit FAFSA. In 2017, 23 master's awarded. Offers physician assistant studies (MS). *Application deadline:* Applications are processed on a rolling basis. *Application fee:* $60. Electronic applications accepted. *Application Contact:* Diane Ranaldi, Dean of Graduate Admissions, 413-565-1332, Fax: 413-565-1250, E-mail: dranaldi@baypath.edu. *Director*, Theresa Riethle, 413-565-1206, E-mail: triethle@baypath.edu.

Program in Strategic Fundraising and Philanthropy Students: 2 full-time (both women), 9 part-time (7 women); includes 2 minority (1 Black or African American, non-Hispanic/Latino; 1 Native Hawaiian or other Pacific Islander, non-Hispanic/Latino). Average age 36. Expenses: Contact institution. *Financial support:* Unspecified assistantships available. Financial award applicants required to submit FAFSA. In 2017, 4 master's awarded. *Program availability:* Part-time, 100% online. Offers higher education fundraising (MS); nonprofit fundraising (MS). *Application deadline:* Applications are processed on a rolling basis. *Application fee:* $45. Electronic applications accepted. *Application Contact:* Diane Ranaldi, Dean of Graduate Admissions, 413-565-1332, Fax: 413-565-1250, E-mail: dranaldi@baypath.edu. *Program Director*, Silvia de Haas-Phillips, E-mail: sdphillips@baypath.edu.

BECKER COLLEGE, Worcester, MA 01609

General Information Independent, coed, comprehensive institution.

GRADUATE UNITS

Program in Mental Health Counseling Offers community mental health (MA); school consultation (MA). Electronic applications accepted.

BELHAVEN UNIVERSITY, Jackson, MS 39202-1789

General Information Independent-religious, coed, comprehensive institution. *Enrollment:* 4,458 graduate, professional, and undergraduate students; 26 full-time matriculated graduate/professional students (18 women), 1,950 part-time matriculated graduate/professional students (1,477 women). *Enrollment by degree level:* 1,921 master's, 14 doctoral, 41 other advanced degrees. *Graduate faculty:* 24 full-time (17 women), 128 part-time/adjunct (62 women). *Tuition:* Full-time $15,255; part-time $565 per credit. Tuition and fees vary according to degree level, campus/location and program. *Graduate housing:* On-campus housing not available. *Student services:* Career counseling, free psychological counseling. *Library facilities:* Warren A. Hood Library plus 1 other. *Collection:* Books: 42,425 (physical), 106,114 (digital/electronic); Serial titles: 160 (physical), 75,718 (digital/electronic); Databases: 96. Weekly public service hours: 104.

Computer facilities: 36 computers available on campus for general student use. A campuswide network can be accessed from student residence rooms and from off campus. Online class registration is available.
Website: http://www.belhaven.edu/

General Application Contact: Suzanne Sullivan, Assistant Vice President for Jackson and Online, 601-968-5940, E-mail: ssullivan@belhaven.edu.

GRADUATE UNITS

School of Business Students: 20 full-time (12 women), 1,441 part-time (1,061 women); includes 1,168 minority (1,100 Black or African American, non-Hispanic/Latino; 22 American Indian or Alaska Native, non-Hispanic/Latino; 2 Asian, non-Hispanic/Latino; 23 Hispanic/Latino; 1 Native Hawaiian or other Pacific Islander, non-Hispanic/Latino; 20 Two or more races, non-Hispanic/Latino), 21 international. Average age 35. 501 applicants, 74% accepted, 261 enrolled. *Faculty:* 11 full-time (4 women), 93 part-time/adjunct (39 women). Expenses: Contact institution. *Financial support:* Applicants required to submit FAFSA. In 2017, 326 master's awarded. *Program availability:* Part-time, evening/weekend, 100% online. Offers business administration (MBA); health administration (MBA, MHA); human resources (MBA, MSL); leadership (MBA); public administration (MPA); sports administration (MBA, MSA). *Application deadline:* Applications are processed on a rolling basis. *Application fee:* $25. Electronic applications accepted. *Application Contact:* Dr. Audrey Kelleher, Vice President of Adult and Graduate Marketing and Development, 407-804-1424, Fax: 407-620-5210, E-mail: akelleher@belhaven.edu. *Dean*, Dr. Ralph Mason, 601-968-8949, Fax: 601-968-8951, E-mail: cmason@belhaven.edu.

School of Education Students: 4 full-time (all women), 505 part-time (413 women); includes 273 minority (257 Black or African American, non-Hispanic/Latino; 1 Asian, non-Hispanic/Latino; 5 Hispanic/Latino; 10 Two or more races, non-Hispanic/Latino). Average age 35. 203 applicants, 48% accepted, 92 enrolled. *Faculty:* 7 full-time (all women), 34 part-time/adjunct (23 women). Expenses: Contact institution. *Financial support:* Applicants required to submit FAFSA. In 2017, 82 master's awarded. *Program availability:* Part-time, evening/weekend, 100% online, blended/hybrid learning. Offers education (M Ed, MAT); educational leadership (Ed D, Ed S); reading literacy (M Ed). *Application deadline:* Applications are processed on a rolling basis. *Application fee:* $25. Electronic applications accepted. *Application Contact:* Sean Kirnan, Assistant Vice President for Adult and Graduate Enrollment and Student Services, 601-968-8727, Fax: 601-968-5953, E-mail: gradadmission@belhaven.edu. *Dean*, Dr. David Hand, 601-965-7020, E-mail: dhand@belhaven.edu.

BELLARMINE UNIVERSITY, Louisville, KY 40205

General Information Independent-religious, coed, comprehensive institution. *Enrollment:* 3,757 graduate, professional, and undergraduate students; 319 full-time matriculated graduate/professional students (197 women), 393 part-time matriculated graduate/professional students (281 women). *Enrollment by degree level:* 389 master's, 311 doctoral, 12 other advanced degrees. *Graduate faculty:* 82 full-time (50 women), 71 part-time/adjunct (52 women). Tuition and fees vary according to program. *Graduate housing:* Rooms and/or apartments available on a first-come, first-served basis to single and married students. Typical cost: $3150 per year for single students; $7650 per year for married students. Room charges vary according to board plan and housing facility selected. Housing application deadline: 5/1. *Student services:* Campus employment opportunities, campus safety program, career counseling, exercise/wellness program, free psychological counseling, international student services, multicultural affairs office, services for students with disabilities, teacher training, writing training. *Library facilities:* W. L. Lyons Brown Library. *Collection:* Books: 121,125 (physical), 233,857 (digital/electronic); Serial titles: 207 (physical), 88,144 (digital/electronic); Databases: 145. Weekly public service hours: 140; study areas open 24 hours, 5–7 days a week.

Computer facilities: 440 computers available on campus for general student use. A campuswide network can be accessed from student residence rooms and from off campus. Online class registration, mobile app are available.
Website: http://www.bellarmine.edu/

General Application Contact: Dr. Sara Pettingill, Dean of Graduate Admission, 502-272-8401, Fax: 502-272-8002, E-mail: spettingill@bellarmine.edu.

GRADUATE UNITS

Annsley Frazier Thornton School of Education Students: 34 full-time (27 women), 204 part-time (158 women); includes 60 minority (43 Black or African American, non-Hispanic/Latino; 7 Asian, non-Hispanic/Latino; 7 Hispanic/Latino; 3 Two or more races, non-Hispanic/Latino). Average age 33. *Faculty:* 19 full-time (10 women), 36 part-time/adjunct (29 women). Expenses: Contact institution. *Financial support:* Scholarships/grants available. Financial award applicants required to submit FAFSA. In 2017, 50 master's, 8 doctorates, 42 other advanced degrees awarded. *Program availability:* Part-time, evening/weekend. Offers education and district leadership (Ed D); education and social change (PhD); elementary education (MA Ed, MAT); leadership in higher education (PhD); middle school education (MA Ed, MAT); principalship (Ed S); reading and writing (MA Ed); secondary education (MAT); teacher leadership (MA Ed). *Application deadline:* For fall admission, 8/1 priority date for domestic and international students; for spring admission, 12/1 priority date for domestic and international students; for summer admission, 4/10 priority date for domestic and international students. Applications are processed on a rolling basis. *Application fee:* $40. Electronic applications accepted. *Application Contact:* Sarah Schuble, Senior Graduate Admissions Recruiter, 502-272-8271, Fax: 502-272-8002, E-mail: sschuble@bellarmine.edu. *Interim Dean*, Dr. Elizabeth Dinkins, 502-272-7958, Fax: 502-272-8189, E-mail: edinkins@bellarmine.edu.

College of Health Professions Offers health professions (MHS, MSAT, MSN, DNP, DPT).

Donna and Allan Lansing School of Nursing and Clinical Sciences Students: 10 full-time (6 women), 101 part-time (89 women); includes 10 minority (5 Black or African American, non-Hispanic/Latino; 2 Asian, non-Hispanic/Latino; 1 Hispanic/Latino; 2 Two or more races, non-Hispanic/Latino), 1 international. Average age 34. *Faculty:* 20 full-time (17 women), 7 part-time/adjunct (6 women). Expenses: Contact institution. *Financial support:* Career-related internships or fieldwork and scholarships/grants available. Financial award applicants required to submit FAFSA. In 2017, 42 master's, 5 doctorates awarded. *Program availability:* Part-time, evening/weekend. Offers family nurse practitioner (MSN); health science (MHS); nursing administration (MSN); nursing education (MSN); nursing practice (DNP). *Application deadline:* Applications are processed on a rolling basis. *Application fee:* $40. Electronic applications accepted. *Application Contact:* Julie Armstrong-Binnix, Health Science Recruiter, 800-274-4723 Ext. 8364, E-mail: julieab@bellarmine.edu. *Dean*, Dr. Nancy York, 502-272-8639, E-mail: nyork@bellarmine.edu.

School of Movement and Rehabilitation Sciences Students: 212 full-time (136 women), 2 part-time (both women); includes 18 minority (2 Black or African American, non-Hispanic/Latino; 4 Asian, non-Hispanic/Latino; 2 Hispanic/Latino; 10 Two or more races, non-Hispanic/Latino), 1 international. Average age 25. *Faculty:* 22 full-time (15 women), 27 part-time/adjunct (17 women). Expenses: Contact institution. *Financial support:* Applicants required to submit FAFSA. In 2017, 62 doctorates awarded. *Program availability:* Part-time. Offers athletic training (MSAT); physical therapy (DPT). *Application deadline:* Applications are processed on a rolling basis. *Application fee:* $40. Electronic applications accepted. *Application Contact:* Dr. Sara Pettingill, Dean of Graduate Admission, 502-272-8401, Fax: 502-272-8002, E-mail: spettingill@bellarmine.edu. *Dean*, Dr. Tony Brosky, 502-272-8375, E-mail: jbrosky@bellarmine.edu.

School of Communication Students: 9 full-time (6 women), 29 part-time (15 women); includes 4 minority (all Black or African American, non-Hispanic/Latino), 5 international. Average age 26. *Faculty:* 6 full-time (3 women). Expenses: Contact institution. *Financial support:* Applicants required to submit FAFSA. In 2017, 10 master's awarded. *Program availability:* Part-time, evening/weekend. Offers communication (MA, MSDM). *Application deadline:* Applications are processed on a rolling basis. *Application fee:* $40. Electronic applications accepted. *Application Contact:* Dr. Sara Pettingill, Dean of Graduate Admission, 502-272-8401, Fax: 502-272-8002, E-mail: spettingill@bellarmine.edu. *Dean*, Dr. Lara Needham, 502-272-7965, E-mail: lneedham@bellarmine.edu.

W. Fielding Rubel School of Business Students: 54 full-time (22 women), 42 part-time (13 women); includes 17 minority (6 Black or African American, non-Hispanic/Latino; 6 Asian, non-Hispanic/Latino; 3 Hispanic/Latino; 2 Two or more races, non-Hispanic/Latino), 2 international. Average age 30. *Faculty:* 15 full-time (5 women), 1 part-time/adjunct (0 women). Expenses: Contact institution. *Financial support:* Career-related internships or fieldwork, scholarships/grants, and unspecified assistantships available. Support available to part-time students. Financial award applicants required to submit FAFSA. In 2017, 54 master's awarded. *Program availability:* Part-time, evening/weekend. Offers business (MBA). *Application deadline:* Applications are processed on a rolling basis. *Application fee:* $40. Electronic applications accepted. *Application Contact:* Dr. Sara Pettingill, Dean of Graduate Admission, 800-274-4723 Ext. 8258, Fax: 502-272-8002, E-mail: spettingill@bellarmine.edu. *Dean*, Dr. Sharon Kerrick, 800-272-8249, Fax: 502-272-7443, E-mail: skerrick@bellarmine.edu.

BELLEVUE UNIVERSITY, Bellevue, NE 68005-3098

General Information Independent, coed, comprehensive institution. *Graduate housing:* Room and/or apartments available on a first-come, first-served basis to single students; on-campus housing not available to married students.

GRADUATE UNITS

Graduate School *Program availability:* Part-time, evening/weekend, online learning.

College of Arts and Sciences *Program availability:* Online learning. Offers clinical counseling (MS); healthcare administration (MHA); human services (MA); international security and intelligence studies (MS); managerial communication (MA).

College of Business Offers acquisition and contract management (MS); business administration (MBA); finance (MS); human capital management (PhD); management (MSM).

College of Information Technology Offers computer information systems (MS); cybersecurity (MS); management of information systems (MS); project management (MPM).

College of Professional Studies

BELLIN COLLEGE, Green Bay, WI 54305

General Information Independent, coed, primarily women, comprehensive institution. *Enrollment:* 13 full-time matriculated graduate/professional students (12 women), 29 part-time matriculated graduate/professional students (27 women). *Enrollment by degree level:* 42 master's. *Graduate faculty:* 10 part-time/adjunct (all women). *Tuition:* Part-time $728 per credit. *Graduate housing:* On-campus housing not available. *Library facilities:* Phil and Betsy Hendrickson Library. *Collection:* Weekly public service hours: 63; students can reserve study rooms.

Computer facilities: 41 computers available on campus for general student use. A campuswide network can be accessed from off campus.
Website: http://www.bellincollege.edu/

General Application Contact: Ann Wasmund, Administrative Assistant, 920-433-6628, Fax: 920-433-1921, E-mail: ann.wasmund@bellincollege.edu.

GRADUATE UNITS

School of Nursing Students: 13 full-time (12 women), 29 part-time (27 women). *Faculty:* 10 part-time/adjunct (all women). Expenses: Contact institution. Offers family nurse practitioner (MSN); nurse educator (MSN). *Graduate Program Director*, Dr. Amber B. Carriveau, 920-433-6694, Fax: 920-433-1921, E-mail: amber.carriveau@bellincollege.edu.

BELMONT UNIVERSITY, Nashville, TN 37212

General Information Independent-religious, coed, university. *Enrollment:* 8,012 graduate, professional, and undergraduate students; 1,426 full-time matriculated graduate/professional students (920 women), 89 part-time matriculated graduate/professional students (50 women). *Enrollment by degree level:* 635 master's, 880 doctoral. *Graduate faculty:* 164 full-time (85 women), 67 part-time/adjunct (30 women). *Graduate housing:* On-campus housing not available. *Student services:* Campus employment opportunities, campus safety program, career counseling, exercise/wellness program, free psychological counseling, international student services, low-cost health insurance, multicultural affairs office, services for students with disabilities. *Library facilities:* Lila D. Bunch Library plus 1 other. *Collection:* Books: 184,352 (physical), 224,292 (digital/electronic); Serial titles: 1,033 (physical), 94,560 (digital/electronic); Databases: 288. Weekly public service hours: 127; students can reserve study rooms.

Computer facilities: Computer purchase and lease plans are available. 500 computers available on campus for general student use. A campuswide network can be accessed from student residence rooms and from off campus. Online class registration, individual student information via course management system are available.
Website: http://www.belmont.edu/

General Application Contact: David Mee, Dean of Enrollment Services, 615-460-6785, Fax: 615-460-5434, E-mail: david.mee@belmont.edu.

GRADUATE UNITS

College of Health Sciences Students: 394 full-time (330 women), 9 part-time (8 women); includes 34 minority (9 Black or African American, non-Hispanic/Latino; 12 Asian, non-Hispanic/Latino; 7 Hispanic/Latino; 6 Two or more races, non-Hispanic/Latino). Average age 26. *Faculty:* 29 full-time (25 women), 16 part-time/adjunct (11 women). Expenses: Contact institution. *Financial support:* Teaching assistantships with full tuition reimbursements, career-related internships or fieldwork, scholarships/grants, and traineeships available. Financial award application deadline: 3/1; financial award applicants required to submit FAFSA. In 2017, 52 master's, 79 doctorates awarded. *Program availability:* Part-time, blended/hybrid learning. Offers nursing (MSN, DNP); occupational therapy (MSOT, OTD); physical therapy (DPT). *Application deadline:* Applications are processed on a rolling basis. *Application fee:* $50. Electronic applications accepted. *Application Contact:* Bill Nichols, Director of Enrollment Services, 615-460-6107, E-mail: bill.nichols@belmont.edu. *Dean*, Dr. Cathy Taylor, 615-460-6916, Fax: 615-460-6750.

College of Law Students: 276 full-time (146 women); includes 40 minority (12 Black or African American, non-Hispanic/Latino; 4 Asian, non-Hispanic/Latino; 10 Hispanic/Latino; 1 Native Hawaiian or other Pacific Islander, non-Hispanic/Latino; 13 Two or more races, non-Hispanic/Latino). Average age 26. 760 applicants, 47% accepted, 113 enrolled. *Faculty:* 18 full-time (8 women), 9 part-time/adjunct (3 women). Expenses: Contact institution. *Financial support:* In 2017–18, 180 students received support. Career-related internships or fieldwork and scholarships/grants available. Financial award applicants required to submit FAFSA. In 2017, 82 doctorates awarded. Offers law (JD). *Application deadline:* For fall admission, 7/15 priority date for domestic and international students. Applications are processed on a rolling basis. *Application fee:* $50. Electronic applications accepted. *Application Contact:* Drew Ford, Recruiting Coordinator, Fax: 615-460-8250, E-mail: drew.ford@belmont.edu. *Dean*, Judge Alberto R. Gonzales, 615-460-8259, E-mail: alberto.gonzales@belmont.edu.

College of Pharmacy Students: 323 full-time (216 women); includes 90 minority (37 Black or African American, non-Hispanic/Latino; 38 Asian, non-Hispanic/Latino; 10 Hispanic/Latino; 5 Two or more races, non-Hispanic/Latino), 1 international. Average age 25. 638 applicants, 34% accepted, 94 enrolled. *Faculty:* 25 full-time (16 women), 3 part-time/adjunct (2 women). Expenses: Contact institution. *Financial support:* In 2017–18, 112 students received support. Career-related internships or fieldwork and scholarships/grants available. Financial award applicants required to submit FAFSA. In 2017, 65 doctorates awarded. Offers advanced pharmacotherapy (Pharm D); health care informatics (Pharm D); management (Pharm D); missions/public health (Pharm D). Pharm D/MBA offered in collaboration with Jack C. Massey Graduate School of Business. *Application deadline:* For fall admission, 8/31 priority date for domestic students; for spring admission, 3/1 for domestic students. Applications are processed on a rolling basis. *Application fee:* $50. Electronic applications accepted. *Dean*, Dr. David Gregory, 615-460-6746, Fax: 615-460-6741, E-mail: david.gregory@belmont.edu.

Jack C. Massey Graduate School of Business Students: 163 full-time (72 women), 42 part-time (19 women); includes 36 minority (13 Black or African American, non-Hispanic/Latino; 9 Asian, non-Hispanic/Latino; 5 Hispanic/Latino; 9 Two or more races, non-Hispanic/Latino), 10 international. Average age 30. 135 applicants, 96% accepted, 102 enrolled. *Faculty:* 29 full-time (9 women), 7 part-time/adjunct (3 women). Expenses: Contact institution. *Financial support:* In 2017–18, 86 students received support. Scholarships/grants, tuition waivers (partial), and unspecified assistantships available. Financial award application deadline: 7/1; financial award applicants required to submit FAFSA. In 2017, 110 master's awarded. *Program availability:* Part-time, evening/weekend. Offers accounting (M Acc); business (AMBA, PMBA); healthcare (MBA). *Application deadline:* For fall admission, 7/1 for domestic and international students; for spring admission, 11/1 for domestic and international students. Applications are processed on a rolling basis. *Application fee:* $50. Electronic applications accepted. *Application Contact:* 615-460-6480, E-mail: masseyadmissions@belmont.edu. *Dean*, Dr. Patrick Raines, 615-460-6480, Fax: 615-460-6455, E-mail: pat.raines@belmont.edu.

BEMIDJI STATE UNIVERSITY, Bemidji, MN 56601-2699

General Information State-supported, coed, comprehensive institution. CGS member. *Graduate housing:* Room and/or apartments available on a first-come, first-served basis to single students; on-campus housing not available to married students. Housing application deadline: 8/1. *Research affiliation:* National Interscholastic Athletic Administrators Association, Sanford Research, Mossy Oak, Bass Pro Shops.

GRADUATE UNITS

School of Graduate Studies *Program availability:* Part-time, online learning. Offers biology (MS); education (MS); English (MA, MS); environmental studies (MS); mathematics (MS); mathematics (elementary and middle level education) (MS); special education (M Sp Ed). Electronic applications accepted.

BENEDICTINE COLLEGE, Atchison, KS 66002-1499

General Information Independent-religious, coed, comprehensive institution. *Enrollment:* 2,167 graduate, professional, and undergraduate students; 55 full-time matriculated graduate/professional students (13 women), 26 part-time matriculated graduate/professional students (19 women). *Enrollment by degree level:* 74 master's, 7 other advanced degrees. *Graduate faculty:* 10 part-time/adjunct (1 woman). *Tuition:* Full-time $14,000; part-time $7000 per credit hour. *Required fees:* $1200; $750 per credit hour. Tuition and fees vary according to course load and program. *Graduate housing:* Room and/or apartments available on a first-come, first-served basis to single students; on-campus housing not available to married students. Typical cost: $5320 per year ($9820 including board). Room and board charges vary according to board plan and housing facility selected. *Student services:* Campus employment opportunities, campus safety program, career counseling, exercise/wellness program, free psychological counseling, international student services, services for students with disabilities, teacher training. *Library facilities:* Benedictine College Library. *Collection:* Books: 198,277 (physical), 139,987 (digital/electronic); Serial titles: 45,794 (physical), 400 (digital/electronic); Databases: 88. Weekly public service hours: 85.

Computer facilities: Computer purchase and lease plans are available. 100 computers available on campus for general student use. A campuswide network can be accessed from student residence rooms and from off campus. Online class registration is available.
Website: http://www.benedictine.edu/

General Application Contact: Dr. Cheryl Reding, Director, Graduate Programs in Education, 913-360-7384, E-mail: creding@benedictine.edu.

GRADUATE UNITS

Master of Arts in Education Program Students: 1 (woman) part-time. Average age 24. Expenses: Contact institution. *Financial support:* Unspecified assistantships available. Financial award applicants required to submit FAFSA. *Program availability:* Part-time, evening/weekend. Offers education (MA). *Application deadline:* Applications are processed on a rolling basis. *Application fee:* $50. Electronic applications accepted. *Application Contact:* Dr. Cheryl Reding, Director, Graduate Programs in Education, 913-360-7384, E-mail: creding@benedictine.edu.

Master of Arts in School Leadership Program Students: 11 full-time (4 women), 14 part-time (9 women). Average age 33. *Faculty:* 3 part-time/adjunct (1 woman). Expenses: Contact institution. *Financial support:* Scholarships/grants and unspecified assistantships available. Financial award applicants required to submit FAFSA. In 2017, 8 master's awarded. *Program availability:* Part-time, evening/weekend. Offers school leadership (MA). *Application deadline:* Applications are processed on a rolling basis. *Application fee:* $50. Electronic applications accepted. *Application Contact:* Dr. Cheryl Reding, Director, Graduate Programs in Education, 913-360-7384, E-mail: creding@benedictine.edu.

Master of Business Administration Program Students: 44 full-time (9 women), 4 part-time (2 women); includes 8 minority (4 Black or African American, non-Hispanic/Latino; 1 Asian, non-Hispanic/Latino; 3 Hispanic/Latino), 3 international. Average age 28. *Faculty:* 6 part-time/adjunct (0 women). Expenses: Contact institution. *Financial support:* Unspecified assistantships available. Financial award application deadline: 3/15; financial award applicants required to submit FAFSA. In 2017, 12 master's awarded. *Program availability:* Part-time, evening/weekend. Offers business administration (MBA). *Application deadline:* Applications are processed on a rolling basis. *Application fee:* $50. Electronic applications accepted. *Chair, School of Business,* Michael King, 913-360-7160, E-mail: mking@benedictine.edu.

BENEDICTINE UNIVERSITY, Lisle, IL 60532

General Information Independent-religious, coed, comprehensive institution. *Graduate housing:* On-campus housing not available.

GRADUATE UNITS

Graduate Programs *Program availability:* Part-time, evening/weekend, online learning. Offers accountancy (MS); accounting (MBA); administration of health care institutions (MPH); clinical exercise physiology (MS); clinical psychology (MS); curriculum and instruction and collaborative teaching (M Ed); dietetics (MPH); disaster management (MPH); elementary education (MA Ed); entrepreneurship and managing innovation (MBA); financial management (MBA); health administration (MBA); health education (MPH); health information systems (MPH); higher education and organizational change (Ed D); human resource management (MBA); information systems security (MBA); international business (MBA); leadership (MS); leadership and administration (M Ed); management and organizational behavior (MS, PhD); management consulting (MBA); management information systems (MS); marketing management (MBA); nursing (MSN); nutrition and wellness (MS); operations management and logistics (MBA); organization development (PhD); organizational leadership (MBA); reading and literacy (M Ed); science content and process (MS); secondary education (MA Ed); special education (MA Ed); values-driven leadership (DBA, PhD). Electronic applications accepted.

BENNINGTON COLLEGE, Bennington, VT 05201

General Information Independent, coed, comprehensive institution. *Graduate housing:* Room and/or apartments available on a first-come, first-served basis to single students; on-campus housing not available to married students.

GRADUATE UNITS

Graduate Programs *Program availability:* Part-time, online learning. Offers allied and health sciences (Certificate); dance (MFA); music (MFA); writing (MFA).

BENTLEY UNIVERSITY, Waltham, MA 02452-4705

General Information Independent, coed, comprehensive institution. *Enrollment:* 5,543 graduate, professional, and undergraduate students; 736 full-time matriculated graduate/professional students (458 women), 529 part-time matriculated graduate/professional students (270 women). *Enrollment by degree level:* 1,229 master's, 29 doctoral, 7 other advanced degrees. *Graduate faculty:* 71 full-time (25 women), 33 part-time/adjunct (15 women). *Tuition:* Part-time $4445 per course. *Required fees:* $170 per unit. *Graduate housing:* Room and/or apartments available on a first-come, first-served basis to single students; on-campus housing not available to married students. Typical cost: $12,260 per year ($18,540 including board). *Student services:* Campus employment opportunities, campus safety program, career counseling, exercise/wellness program, free psychological counseling, international student services, low-cost health insurance, multicultural affairs office, services for students with disabilities. *Library facilities:* Bentley Library. *Collection:* Books: 187,590 (physical), 206,692 (digital/electronic); Serial titles: 2,550 (physical), 101,266 (digital/electronic); Databases: 106. Weekly public service hours: 110; students can reserve study rooms.

Computer facilities: Computer purchase and lease plans are available. 4,620 computers available on campus for general student use. A campuswide network can be accessed from student residence rooms and from off campus. Online class registration, grade checking; online admission; blackboard; resume review; student employment; interlibrary loan; free software are available.
Website: http://www.bentley.edu/

General Application Contact: Graduate Admissions, 781-891-2108, Fax: 781-891-2464, E-mail: applygrad@bentley.edu.

GRADUATE UNITS

McCallum Graduate School of Business Students: 736 full-time (458 women), 529 part-time (270 women); includes 159 minority (35 Black or African American, non-Hispanic/Latino; 1 American Indian or Alaska Native, non-Hispanic/Latino; 83 Asian, non-Hispanic/Latino; 26 Hispanic/Latino; 14 Two or more races, non-Hispanic/Latino), 579 international. Average age 28. 1,687 applicants, 72% accepted, 545 enrolled. *Faculty:* 71 full-time (25 women), 33 part-time/adjunct (15 women). Expenses: Contact institution. *Financial support:* In 2017–18, 388 students received support. Scholarships/grants, tuition waivers (partial), and unspecified assistantships available. Financial award application deadline: 6/1; financial award applicants required to submit FAFSA. In 2017, 566 master's, 6 doctorates, 58 other advanced degrees awarded. *Program availability:* Part-time, evening/weekend, 100% online, blended/hybrid learning. Offers accountancy (PhD); accounting (GBC); audit analytics (MS); business (MBA, MS, MSA, MSF, MSFP, MSHFID, MSIT, MSMA, MST, PhD, Certificate, GBC, GSS); business administration (MBA); business analytics (GBC); business ethics (GBC); finance (MSF); financial planning (GBC); fraud and forensic accounting (GBC); human factors (MSHFID); information technology (MSIT); marketing analytics (MSMA); taxation (GBC). *Application deadline:* Applications are processed on a rolling basis. *Application fee:* $75. Electronic applications accepted. *Application Contact:* Graduate Admissions, 781-891-2108, Fax: 781-891-2464, E-mail: applygrad@bentley.edu. *Acting Co-Provost, Dean of Business,* Dr. Roy A. Wiggins, III, 781-891-3166.

BERGIN UNIVERSITY OF CANINE STUDIES, Rohnert Park, CA 94928

General Information Independent, coed, comprehensive institution. *Enrollment by degree level:* 24 master's. *Graduate faculty:* 1 (woman) full-time, 5 part-time/adjunct (4 women). *Tuition:* Full-time $17,600. *Required fees:* $300. Full-time tuition and fees vary according to program. *Graduate housing:* On-campus housing not available. *Student services:* Career counseling, free psychological counseling, international student services, services for students with disabilities.
Website: http://www.berginu.edu/

General Application Contact: Connie Van Guilder, Director, Student Services, 707-545-3647 Ext. 21, Fax: 707-545-0800, E-mail: connie@berginu.edu.

GRADUATE UNITS

Program in Canine Life Sciences Students: 24 full-time (23 women). *Faculty:* 1 (woman) full-time, 5 part-time/adjunct (4 women). Expenses: Contact institution. *Program availability:* Online learning. Offers canine life sciences (MS). *Application Contact:* Connie Van Guilder, Director, Student Services, 707-545-3647 Ext. 21, Fax: 707-545-0800, E-mail: connie@berginu.edu.

BERKELEY COLLEGE–WOODLAND PARK CAMPUS, Woodland Park, NJ 07424

General Information Proprietary, coed, comprehensive institution.

GRADUATE UNITS

MBA Program Offers management (MBA).

BERKLEE COLLEGE OF MUSIC, Boston, MA 02215-3693

General Information Independent, coed, comprehensive institution. *Enrollment:* 433 full-time matriculated graduate/professional students (216 women), 47 part-time matriculated graduate/professional students (37 women). *Enrollment by degree level:* 386 master's, 94 other advanced degrees. *Graduate faculty:* 78 full-time (25 women), 60 part-time/adjunct (19 women). *Tuition:* Full-time $47,500. *Required fees:* $1255. Tuition and fees vary according to campus/location and program. *Graduate housing:* On-campus housing not available. *Student services:* Campus employment opportunities, campus safety program, career counseling, exercise/wellness program, free psychological counseling, grant writing training, international student services, low-cost health insurance, multicultural affairs office, services for students with disabilities, teacher training, writing training. *Library facilities:* The Stan Getz Media Center and Library.

Computer facilities: Computer purchase and lease plans are available. A campuswide network can be accessed from student residence rooms. Online class registration is available.
Website: http://www.berklee.edu/

General Application Contact: 617-747-2221, Fax: 617-747-2047, E-mail: admissions@berklee.edu.

GRADUATE UNITS

Berklee Graduate Programs Students: 196 full-time (75 women), 24 part-time (22 women); includes 36 minority (5 Black or African American, non-Hispanic/Latino; 9 Asian, non-Hispanic/Latino; 17 Hispanic/Latino; 5 Two or more races, non-Hispanic/Latino), 109 international. Average age 27. 735 applicants, 38% accepted, 162 enrolled. *Faculty:* 45 full-time (12 women), 41 part-time/adjunct (6 women). Expenses: Contact institution. *Financial support:* In 2017–18, 153 students received support, including 123 fellowships with full and partial tuition reimbursements available (averaging $15,943 per year), 30 research assistantships (averaging $5,429 per year); career-related internships or fieldwork, scholarships/grants, and tuition waivers (full and partial) also available. Support available to part-time students. Financial award application deadline: 1/15; financial award applicants required to submit CSS PROFILE or FAFSA. In 2017, 170 master's awarded. *Program availability:* Part-time, blended/hybrid learning. Offers contemporary performance (MM); global entertainment and music business (MA); music production, technology, and innovation (MM); scoring for film, television, and video games (MM). Production; global entertainment and music business; music production, technology, and innovation; and scoring for film, television, and video games programs offered at Valencia, Spain campus. *Application deadline:* For fall admission, 1/15 for domestic and international students. *Application fee:* $150. Electronic applications accepted. *Application Contact:* Office of Admissions, 617-747-2221, E-mail: admissions@berklee.edu. *Dean, Institutional Research and Assessment/Graduate Studies,* Camille Colatosti, PhD, 617-536-6340, E-mail: ccolatosti@berklee.edu.

The Boston Conservatory at Berklee Students: 237 full-time (141 women), 23 part-time (15 women); includes 43 minority (9 Black or African American, non-Hispanic/Latino; 1 American Indian or Alaska Native, non-Hispanic/Latino; 9 Asian, non-Hispanic/Latino; 13 Hispanic/Latino; 11 Two or more races, non-Hispanic/Latino), 73 international. Average age 25. 668 applicants, 48% accepted, 154 enrolled. *Faculty:* 33 full-time (13 women), 19 part-time/adjunct (13 women). Expenses: Contact institution. *Financial support:* In 2017–18, 247 students received support, including 2 research assistantships (averaging $4,000 per year), 10 teaching assistantships (averaging $2,000 per year); scholarships/grants also available. Financial award application deadline: 12/15; financial award applicants required to submit FAFSA. In 2017, 85 master's, 31 other advanced degrees awarded. *Program availability:* Part-time. Offers bassoon performance (MM); cello performance (MM); choral conducting (MM); clarinet performance (MM); collaborative piano (MM); composition (MM); contemporary music performance (MM); double bass performance (MM); flute performance (MM); harp performance (MM); horn performance (MM); marimba performance (MM); music and autism (Certificate); music education (MM); music education and autism (MM); music performance (ADP); musical theater (MFA); oboe performance (MM); opera performance (MM); orchestral conducting (MM); percussion performance (MM); piano performance (MM); saxophone performance (MM); trombone performance (MM); trumpet performance (MM). *Application deadline:* For fall admission, 12/15 for domestic and international students. *Application fee:* $110. Electronic applications accepted. *Application Contact:* Director of Admissions, 617-912-9153, Fax: 617-912-9217, E-mail: admissions@bostonconservatory.edu. *Dean, Institutional Research and Assessment/Graduate Studies,* Camille Colatosti, PhD, 617-536-6340, E-mail: ccolatosti@berklee.edu.

BERRY COLLEGE, Mount Berry, GA 30149-0159

General Information Independent-religious, coed, comprehensive institution. *Enrollment:* 2,110 graduate, professional, and undergraduate students; 17 full-time matriculated graduate/professional students (10 women), 115 part-time matriculated graduate/professional students (77 women). *Enrollment by degree level:* 30 master's, 102 other advanced degrees. *Graduate faculty:* 1 full-time (0 women), 11 part-time/adjunct (6 women). *Tuition:* Full-time $11,430; part-time $635 per credit hour. *Required fees:* $176. Tuition and fees vary according to program. *Graduate housing:* On-campus housing not available. *Student services:* Campus employment opportunities, campus safety program, career counseling, child daycare facilities, exercise/wellness program, free psychological counseling, international student services, low-cost health insurance, multicultural affairs office, services for students with disabilities, teacher training, writing training. *Library facilities:* Memorial Library plus 1 other. *Collection:* Books: 246,222 (physical), 664,520 (digital/electronic); Serial titles: 7,978 (physical), 44,764 (digital/electronic); Databases: 224. Weekly public service hours: 106; students can reserve study rooms. *Research affiliation:* Georgia Professional Standards Commission (education), Koch Foundation (business and economics), South Rome

Early Learning Center (education), Marcus Autism Center (psychology and education), South Rome Development Corporation (education), Rome-Floyd County Commission on Children and Youth (education and psychology).

Computer facilities: 200 computers available on campus for general student use. A campuswide network can be accessed from student residence rooms and from off campus. Online class registration is available.
Website: http://www.berry.edu/

General Application Contact: Brett Kennedy, Assistant Vice President of Enrollment Management, 706-236-2215, Fax: 706-290-2178, E-mail: admissions@berry.edu.

GRADUATE UNITS

Graduate Programs Students: 17 full-time (10 women), 115 part-time (77 women); includes 23 minority (20 Black or African American, non-Hispanic/Latino; 3 Hispanic/Latino). Average age 39. *Faculty:* 1 full-time (0 women), 11 part-time/adjunct (6 women). Expenses: Contact institution. *Financial support:* In 2017–18, 24 students received support, including 10 research assistantships with full tuition reimbursements available (averaging $6,096 per year); scholarships/grants, tuition waivers (partial), and unspecified assistantships also available. Support available to part-time students. Financial award application deadline: 3/1; financial award applicants required to submit FAFSA. In 2017, 22 master's, 46 other advanced degrees awarded. *Program availability:* Part-time, evening/weekend. Offers curriculum and instruction (M Ed, Ed S); early childhood education (M Ed, MAT); educational leadership (Ed S); middle grades education (MAT); middle-grades education (M Ed); middle-grades education and reading (M Ed, MAT); reading (M Ed); secondary education (MAT). *Application deadline:* For fall admission, 7/20 for domestic students, 5/1 for international students; for spring admission, 12/1 for domestic students, 2/1 for international students. Applications are processed on a rolling basis. *Application fee:* $25 ($30 for international students). Electronic applications accepted. *Application Contact:* Brett Kennedy, Assistant Vice President of Enrollment Management, 706-236-2215, Fax: 706-290-2178, E-mail: admissions@berry.edu. *Provost,* Dr. Mary K Boyd, 706-236-2216, Fax: 706-290-2179, E-mail: provostoffice@berry.edu.

Campbell School of Business Students: 1 full-time (0 women), 29 part-time (10 women); includes 3 minority (all Black or African American, non-Hispanic/Latino). Average age 32. *Faculty:* 4 part-time/adjunct (1 woman). Expenses: Contact institution. *Financial support:* In 2017–18, 21 students received support, including 10 research assistantships with full tuition reimbursements available (averaging $6,096 per year); scholarships/grants, tuition waivers (partial), and unspecified assistantships also available. Support available to part-time students. Financial award application deadline: 3/1; financial award applicants required to submit FAFSA. In 2017, 10 master's awarded. *Program availability:* Part-time, evening/weekend. Offers business (MBA). *Application deadline:* For fall admission, 7/20 for domestic students; for spring admission, 12/1 for domestic students. Applications are processed on a rolling basis. *Application fee:* $25 ($30 for international students). Electronic applications accepted. *Application Contact:* Brett Kennedy, Assistant Vice President of Enrollment Management, 706-236-2215, Fax: 706-290-2178, E-mail: admissions@berry.edu. *Dean,* Dr. Joyce Heames, 706-236-2233, Fax: 706-802-6728, E-mail: jheames@berry.edu.

BETHANY COLLEGE, Bethany, WV 26032

General Information Independent-religious, coed, comprehensive institution. *Graduate housing:* Room and/or apartments available on a first-come, first-served basis to single students; on-campus housing not available to married students.

GRADUATE UNITS

Master of Arts in Teaching Program *Program availability:* Part-time. Offers teaching (MAT). Electronic applications accepted.

BETHANY GLOBAL UNIVERSITY, Bloomington, MN 55438

General Information Independent-religious, coed, comprehensive institution. *Graduate housing:* On-campus housing not available.

GRADUATE UNITS

Graduate Programs *Program availability:* Part-time, evening/weekend, online only, 100% online. Offers intercultural ministry education (MA); intercultural ministry leadership (MA); intercultural ministry studies (MA). Electronic applications accepted.

BETHANY THEOLOGICAL SEMINARY, Richmond, IN 47374-4019

General Information Independent-religious, coed, graduate-only institution. *Graduate housing:* On-campus housing not available.

GRADUATE UNITS

Graduate and Professional Programs *Program availability:* Part-time, online learning. Offers biblical studies (MA Th); ministry studies (M Div); peace studies (M Div, MA Th); theological studies (MA Th, CATS); youth ministry (M Div).

BETHEL COLLEGE, Mishawaka, IN 46545-5591

General Information Independent-religious, coed, comprehensive institution. *Enrollment:* 1,513 graduate, professional, and undergraduate students; 50 full-time matriculated graduate/professional students (34 women), 169 part-time matriculated graduate/professional students (104 women). *Enrollment by degree level:* 183 master's, 36 other advanced degrees. *Graduate faculty:* 11 full-time (5 women), 25 part-time/adjunct (11 women). Tuition and fees vary according to program. *Graduate housing:* On-campus housing not available. *Student services:* Campus employment opportunities, campus safety program, career counseling, free psychological counseling, international student services, services for students with disabilities, writing training. *Library facilities:* Otis and Elizabeth Bowen Library. *Collection:* Books: 80,904 (physical), 174,107 (digital/electronic); Serial titles: 473 (physical), 58,644 (digital/electronic); Databases: 89. Weekly public service hours: 79.

Computer facilities: 160 computers available on campus for general student use. A campuswide network can be accessed from student residence rooms.
Website: http://www.bethelcollege.edu/

General Application Contact: Dr. Terence Linhart, Dean of Adult and Graduate Studies, 574-807-7394, Fax: 574-807-7551, E-mail: linhart@bethelcollege.edu.

GRADUATE UNITS

Adult and Graduate Programs Students: 50 full-time (34 women), 169 part-time (104 women); includes 53 minority (29 Black or African American, non-Hispanic/Latino; 2 Asian, non-Hispanic/Latino; 10 Hispanic/Latino; 12 Two or more races, non-Hispanic/Latino), 4 international. Average age 37. 185 applicants, 51% accepted, 90 enrolled. *Faculty:* 11 full-time (5 women), 25 part-time/adjunct (11 women). Expenses: Contact institution. *Financial support:* Career-related internships or fieldwork available. Financial award applicants required to submit FAFSA. In 2017, 69 master's awarded. *Program availability:* Part-time, evening/weekend, 100% online, blended/hybrid learning. Offers business administration (MBA); education (M Ed, MAT); ministries (M Min); nursing (MSN); theological studies (MATS). *Application deadline:* For fall admission, 5/1 for international students; for spring admission, 10/1 for international students. Applications are processed on a rolling basis. *Application fee:* $0. Electronic applications accepted. *Dean for Adult and Graduate Studies,* Dr. Terence Linhart, 574-807-7394, Fax: 574-807-7551, E-mail: linhart@bethelcollege.edu.

BETHEL SEMINARY, St. Paul, MN 55112-6998

General Information Independent-religious, coed, graduate-only institution. *Enrollment by degree level:* 482 master's, 57 doctoral, 8 other advanced degrees. *Graduate faculty:* 16 full-time (4 women), 31 part-time/adjunct (15 women). *Graduate housing:* On-campus housing not available. *Student services:* Campus employment opportunities, campus safety program, career counseling, child daycare facilities, exercise/wellness program, free psychological counseling, international student services, multicultural affairs office, services for students with disabilities, writing training. *Library facilities:* Carl H. Lundquist Library plus 2 others. *Collection:* Books: 262,412 (physical), 150,147 (digital/electronic); Serial titles: 25,812 (physical), 30,657 (digital/electronic); Databases: 120. Weekly public service hours: 57; students can reserve study rooms.

Computer facilities: 19 computers available on campus for general student use. Online class registration is available.
Website: http://seminary.bethel.edu/

General Application Contact: Director of Admissions, 651-638-8000, Fax: 651-638-6002, E-mail: seminary-admissions@bethel.edu.

GRADUATE UNITS

Graduate and Professional Programs Students: 380 full-time (170 women), 167 part-time (55 women); includes 161 minority (65 Black or African American, non-Hispanic/Latino; 52 Asian, non-Hispanic/Latino; 31 Hispanic/Latino; 1 Native Hawaiian or other Pacific Islander, non-Hispanic/Latino; 12 Two or more races, non-Hispanic/Latino), 5 international. Average age 38. 356 applicants, 62% accepted, 156 enrolled. *Faculty:* 16 full-time (4 women), 31 part-time/adjunct (15 women). Expenses: Contact institution. *Financial support:* Teaching assistantships, career-related internships or fieldwork, Federal Work-Study, and scholarships/grants available. Financial award applicants required to submit FAFSA. In 2017, 120 master's, 15 doctorates, 4 other advanced degrees awarded. *Program availability:* Part-time, evening/weekend, 100% online, blended/hybrid learning. Offers Anglican studies (Certificate); children's and family ministry (MA); Christian studies (Certificate); Christian thought (MA); church planting (Certificate); Greek and Hebrew language (M Div); Greek language (M Div); Hebrew language (M Div); marriage and family therapy (MA, Certificate); mental health counseling (MA); ministry (MA, D Min); ministry practice (Certificate); theological studies (MA, Certificate); transformational leadership (MA); young life youth ministry (Certificate). *Application deadline:* For fall admission, 8/1 priority date for domestic students, 8/1 for international students; for winter admission, 12/1 priority date for domestic students; for spring admission, 1/1 priority date for domestic students. Applications are processed on a rolling basis. *Application fee:* $0. Electronic applications accepted. *Application Contact:* Director of Admissions, 651-638-8000, Fax: 651-638-6002, E-mail: seminary-admissions@bethel.edu. *Associate Provost,* Dr. Randy Bergen, 651-635-8000, E-mail: r-bergen@bethel.edu.

BETHEL UNIVERSITY, St. Paul, MN 55112-6999

General Information Independent-religious, coed, comprehensive institution. *Enrollment:* 4,591 graduate, professional, and undergraduate students; 611 full-time matriculated graduate/professional students (431 women), 393 part-time matriculated graduate/professional students (249 women). *Enrollment by degree level:* 749 master's, 213 doctoral, 42 other advanced degrees. *Graduate faculty:* 22 full-time (16 women), 70 part-time/adjunct (44 women). *Graduate housing:* On-campus housing not available. *Student services:* Campus employment opportunities, campus safety program, career counseling, child daycare facilities, exercise/wellness program, international student services, low-cost health insurance, multicultural affairs office, services for students with disabilities, teacher training, writing training. *Library facilities:* Bethel University Library plus 1 other. *Collection:* Books: 141,904 (physical), 153,597 (digital/electronic); Serial titles: 890 (physical), 31,538 (digital/electronic); Databases: 93. Weekly public service hours: 96; students can reserve study rooms.

Computer facilities: Computer purchase and lease plans are available. 203 computers available on campus for general student use. A campuswide network can be accessed from student residence rooms and from off campus. Online class registration is available.
Website: http://www.bethel.edu/

General Application Contact: Director of Admissions, 651-635-8000, Fax: 651-635-8004, E-mail: gs@bethel.edu.

GRADUATE UNITS

Graduate School Students: 611 full-time (431 women), 393 part-time (249 women); includes 176 minority (82 Black or African American, non-Hispanic/Latino; 4 American Indian or Alaska Native, non-Hispanic/Latino; 31 Asian, non-Hispanic/Latino; 39 Hispanic/Latino; 2 Native Hawaiian or other Pacific Islander, non-Hispanic/Latino; 18 Two or more races, non-Hispanic/Latino), 9 international. Average age 36. 668 applicants, 42% accepted, 223 enrolled. *Faculty:* 22 full-time (16 women), 70 part-time/adjunct (44 women). Expenses: Contact institution. *Financial support:* Teaching assistantships, career-related internships or fieldwork, and scholarships/grants available. Support available to part-time students. Financial award applicants required to submit FAFSA. In 2017, 287 master's, 30 doctorates, 172 other advanced degrees awarded. *Program availability:* Part-time, evening/weekend, 100% online, blended/hybrid learning. Offers business administration (MBA); classroom management (Certificate); counseling (MA); K-12 education (MA); leadership (Ed D); leadership foundations (Certificate); nurse educator (MS, Certificate); nurse-midwifery (MS); physician assistant (MS); special education (MA); strategic leadership (MA); teaching (MA); teaching and learning (Certificate). *Application deadline:* Applications are processed on a rolling basis. *Application fee:* $0. Electronic applications accepted. *Application Contact:* Director of Admissions, 651-635-8000, Fax: 651-635-8004, E-mail: gs@bethel.edu. *Associate Provost,* Dr. Randy Bergen, 651-635-8000, Fax: 651-635-8004, E-mail: r-bergen@bethel.edu.

BETHEL UNIVERSITY, McKenzie, TN 38201

General Information Independent-religious, coed, comprehensive institution. *Graduate housing:* Room and/or apartments available on a first-come, first-served basis to single students; on-campus housing not available to married students. Housing application deadline: 7/31.

GRADUATE UNITS

Graduate Programs *Program availability:* Part-time, evening/weekend. Offers administration and supervision (MA Ed); business administration (MBA); conflict resolution (MA); physician assistant studies (MS).

BETHESDA UNIVERSITY, Anaheim, CA 92801

General Information Independent-religious, coed, comprehensive institution.

GRADUATE UNITS

Graduate and Professional Programs Offers biblical studies (MA); music (MA); theology (M Div).

BETH HAMEDRASH SHAAREI YOSHER INSTITUTE, Brooklyn, NY 11204

General Information Independent-religious, men only, comprehensive institution.

GRADUATE UNITS

Graduate Programs

BETH HATALMUD RABBINICAL COLLEGE, Brooklyn, NY 11214

General Information Independent-religious, men only, comprehensive institution.

GRADUATE UNITS

Graduate Programs

BETHLEHEM COLLEGE & SEMINARY, Minneapolis, MN 55415

General Information Independent-religious, coed, comprehensive institution. *Enrollment by degree level:* 66 master's. *Graduate faculty:* 16 full-time (0 women), 26 part-time/adjunct (4 women). *Tuition:* Full-time $6000. One-time fee: $275 full-time. Tuition and fees vary according to class time and program. *Graduate housing:* On-campus housing not available. *Student services:* Campus employment opportunities, international student services, services for students with disabilities.
Website: http://www.bcsmn.edu/

General Application Contact: Daniel Kleven, Director of Admissions, 612-455-3420 Ext. 418, E-mail: admissions@bcsmn.edu.

GRADUATE UNITS

Graduate and Professional Programs Students: 56 full-time (0 women), 14 part-time (0 women). *Faculty:* 16 full-time (0 women), 26 part-time/adjunct (4 women). Expenses: Contact institution. Offers church planting and revitalization (M Div); exegesis and theology (MA); theology (Th M); worship pastor (M Div). *Application Contact:* Daniel Kleven, Director of Admissions, 612-455-3420 Ext. 418, E-mail: admissions@bcsmn.edu.

BETH MEDRASH GOVOHA, Lakewood, NJ 08701-2797

General Information Independent-religious, men only, comprehensive institution.

GRADUATE UNITS

Graduate Programs

BETHUNE-COOKMAN UNIVERSITY, Daytona Beach, FL 32114-3099

General Information Independent-religious, coed, comprehensive institution.

GRADUATE UNITS

School of Graduate Studies *Program availability:* Online learning. Offers transformative leadership (MS). Electronic applications accepted.

BEULAH HEIGHTS UNIVERSITY, Atlanta, GA 30316

General Information Independent-religious, coed, comprehensive institution.

GRADUATE UNITS

Graduate School Offers biblical studies (MA); leadership studies (MA). Electronic applications accepted.

BEXLEY SEABURY SEMINARY, Chicago, IL 60637

General Information Independent-religious, coed, graduate-only institution. *Enrollment by degree level:* 28 doctoral, 17 other advanced degrees. *Graduate faculty:* 2 full-time (1 woman), 10 part-time/adjunct (3 women). *Graduate housing:* On-campus housing not available. *Student services:* Career counseling, low-cost health insurance. *Library facilities:* United Library.
Website: http://www.bexleyseabury.edu/

General Application Contact: Jaime Briceno, Recruiter and Digital Missioner, 773-380-7045, Fax: 773-380-6788, E-mail: jbriceno@bexleyseabury.edu.

GRADUATE UNITS

Graduate Programs Students: 45 part-time (20 women); includes 6 minority (2 Black or African American, non-Hispanic/Latino; 2 American Indian or Alaska Native, non-Hispanic/Latino; 2 Hispanic/Latino), 2 international. *Faculty:* 2 full-time (1 woman), 10 part-time/adjunct (3 women). Expenses: Contact institution. *Financial support:* Career-related internships or fieldwork, institutionally sponsored loans, and scholarships/grants available. Financial award application deadline: 5/1; financial award applicants required to submit FAFSA. In 2017, 3 master's, 2 doctorates, 3 other advanced degrees awarded. *Program availability:* Part-time. Offers Anglican studies (Diploma); congregational development (D Min); preaching (D Min); theology (M Div). *Application deadline:* Applications are processed on a rolling basis. *Application fee:* $25. *Application Contact:* Jaime Briceno, Recruiter and Digital Missioner, 773-380-7045, Fax: 773-380-5788, E-mail: jbriceno@bexleyseabury.edu. *Acting President*, Therese DeLisio, 773-380-6787, E-mail: tdelisio@bexleyseabury.edu.

BIBLICAL THEOLOGICAL SEMINARY, Hatfield, PA 19440-2499

General Information Independent-religious, coed, graduate-only institution. *Enrollment by degree level:* 177 master's, 27 doctoral, 12 other advanced degrees. *Graduate faculty:* 9 full-time (1 woman), 20 part-time/adjunct (5 women). *Tuition:* Full-time $12,360; part-time $6180 per credit. *Required fees:* $50 per semester. One-time fee: $30. *Graduate housing:* On-campus housing not available. *Student services:* Campus employment opportunities, career counseling, international student services. *Library facilities:* BTS Library plus 1 other. *Collection:* Books: 43,390 (physical), 140,000 (digital/electronic); Serial titles: 13,572 (physical), 220 (digital/electronic); Databases: 10. Weekly public service hours: 36. *Research affiliation:* Christian Counseling and Education Foundation (psychology).

Computer facilities: 20 computers available on campus for general student use. A campuswide network can be accessed from off campus.
Website: http://www.biblical.edu/

General Application Contact: Patsy Byrd, Administrative Coordinator for Student Advancement, 215-368-5000 Ext. 106, Fax: 215-368-7002, E-mail: pbyrd@biblical.edu.

GRADUATE UNITS

Graduate and Professional Programs Students: 138 full-time (41 women), 78 part-time (31 women); includes 83 minority (51 Black or African American, non-Hispanic/Latino; 1 American Indian or Alaska Native, non-Hispanic/Latino; 26 Asian, non-Hispanic/Latino; 3 Hispanic/Latino; 2 Two or more races, non-Hispanic/Latino), 65 international. Average age 41. 83 applicants, 64% accepted, 49 enrolled. *Faculty:* 9 full-time (1 woman), 20 part-time/adjunct (5 women). Expenses: Contact institution. *Financial support:* In 2017–18, 194 students received support. Career-related internships or fieldwork, institutionally sponsored loans, and scholarships/grants available. Support available to part-time students. Financial award application deadline: 8/30; financial award applicants required to submit FAFSA. In 2017, 50 master's, 12 doctorates awarded. *Program availability:* Part-time, evening/weekend. Offers advanced missional leadership (D Min); advanced pastoral studies (Certificate); biblical counseling (Certificate); biblical studies (MA, Certificate); counseling (MA); ministry (M Div, MA); missional theology (MA). *Application deadline:* Applications are processed on a rolling basis. *Application fee:* $30. Electronic applications accepted. *Application Contact:* Rev. Michael Heath, Student Advancement Counselor, 215-368-5000 Ext. 152, Fax: 215-368-7002, E-mail: mheath@biblical.edu.

BINGHAMTON UNIVERSITY, STATE UNIVERSITY OF NEW YORK, Binghamton, NY 13902-6000

General Information State-supported, coed, university. CGS member. *Enrollment:* 17,322 graduate, professional, and undergraduate students; 2,063 full-time matriculated graduate/professional students (973 women), 1,483 part-time matriculated graduate/professional students (760 women). *Enrollment by degree level:* 2,013 master's, 1,479 doctoral, 54 other advanced degrees. *Graduate faculty:* 754 full-time (328 women). *Graduate housing:* Room and/or apartments available on a first-come, first-served basis to single students; on-campus housing not available to married students. *Student services:* Campus employment opportunities, campus safety program, career counseling, child daycare facilities, exercise/wellness program, free psychological counseling, grant writing training, international student services, low-cost health insurance, multicultural affairs office, services for students with disabilities, teacher training, writing training. *Library facilities:* Glenn G. Bartle Library plus 4 others. *Collection:* Books: 2.3 million (physical), 1.1 million (digital/electronic); Serial titles: 683 (physical), 125,064 (digital/electronic); Databases: 358. Weekly public service hours: 136; study areas open 24 hours, 5–7 days a week; students can reserve study rooms. *Research affiliation:* United Health Services Hospitals (health care, engineering), Mount Sinai Hospital (health care, engineering), Lockheed Martin Corporation (engineering, management, mathematics), Matco Company (engineering), IBM (engineering), Universal Instruments (engineering).

Computer facilities: 1,184 computers available on campus for general student use. A campuswide network can be accessed from student residence rooms and from off campus. Online class registration, course management system, personal Web space, wiki, virtual desktop are available.
Website: http://www.binghamton.edu/

General Application Contact: Dr. Aondover Tarhule, Vice Provost and Dean of the Graduate School, 607-777-2151, Fax: 607-777-2501, E-mail: gradadmission@binghamton.edu.

GRADUATE UNITS

Graduate School Students: 2,063 full-time (973 women), 1,483 part-time (760 women); includes 561 minority (141 Black or African American, non-Hispanic/Latino; 5 American Indian or Alaska Native, non-Hispanic/Latino; 181 Asian, non-Hispanic/Latino; 163 Hispanic/Latino; 2 Native Hawaiian or other Pacific Islander, non-Hispanic/Latino; 69 Two or more races, non-Hispanic/Latino), 1,444 international. Average age 29. 4,904 applicants, 68% accepted, 1263 enrolled. *Faculty:* 754 full-time (328 women). Expenses: Contact institution. *Financial support:* In 2017–18, 1,157 students received support, including 7 fellowships with full tuition reimbursements available (averaging $11,000 per year), 180 research assistantships with full tuition reimbursements available (averaging $15,000 per year), 543 teaching assistantships with full tuition reimbursements available (averaging $15,000 per year); career-related internships or fieldwork, Federal Work-Study, institutionally sponsored loans, scholarships/grants, traineeships, health care benefits, tuition waivers (full and partial), and unspecified assistantships also available. Support available to part-time students. Financial award applicants required to submit FAFSA. In 2017, 1,212 master's, 153 doctorates, 62 other advanced degrees awarded. *Program availability:* Part-time, evening/weekend, online learning. Offers materials science and engineering (MS, PhD); sustainable communities (MA, MS). *Application deadline:* Applications are processed on a rolling basis. *Application fee:* $75. Electronic applications accepted. *Application Contact:* Ben Balkaya, Assistant Dean and Director, 607-777-2151, Fax: 607-777-2501, E-mail: balkaya@binghamton.edu. *Vice Provost and Dean of the Graduate School*, Dr. Susan Strehle, 607-777-2070, Fax: 607-777-2501, E-mail: sstrehle@binghamton.edu.

College of Community and Public Affairs Students: 350 full-time (243 women), 285 part-time (222 women); includes 126 minority (41 Black or African American, non-Hispanic/Latino; 1 American Indian or Alaska Native, non-Hispanic/Latino; 14 Asian, non-Hispanic/Latino; 46 Hispanic/Latino; 1 Native Hawaiian or other Pacific Islander, non-Hispanic/Latino; 23 Two or more races, non-Hispanic/Latino), 33 international. Average age 31. 599 applicants, 65% accepted, 221 enrolled. *Faculty:* 67 full-time (50 women). Expenses: Contact institution. *Financial support:* In 2017–18, 132 students received support. Fellowships, research assistantships, career-related internships or fieldwork, Federal Work-Study, institutionally sponsored loans, scholarships/grants, health care benefits, and unspecified assistantships available. Financial award applicants required to submit FAFSA. In 2017, 212 master's, 7 doctorates, 28 other advanced degrees awarded. *Program availability:* Part-time, evening/weekend. Offers adolescence education (MAT, MS Ed); biology education (MAT, MS Ed); chemistry education (MAT, MS Ed); childhood and early childhood education (MS Ed); community and public affairs (MA, MAT, MPA, MS, MS Ed, MSW, Ed D, PhD, Certificate); community research and action (PhD); earth science education (MAT, MS Ed); educational leadership (Certificate); educational studies (MS); educational theory and practice (Ed D); English education (MAT, MS Ed); French education (MAT, MS Ed); literacy education (MS Ed); mathematical sciences education (MAT, MS Ed); physics (MAT, MS Ed); public administration (MPA); social studies (MAT, MS Ed); social work (MSW); Spanish education (MAT, MS Ed); special education (MS Ed); student affairs administration (MS); TESOL education (MA, MS Ed). *Application deadline:* Applications are processed on a rolling basis. *Application fee:* $75. Electronic applications accepted. *Application Contact:* Ben Balkaya, Assistant Dean and Director, 607-777-2151, Fax: 607-777-2501, E-mail: balkaya@binghamton.edu. *Dean*, Dr. Laura Bronstein, 607-777-5572, Fax: 607-777-2406, E-mail: lbronst@binghamton.edu.

Decker School of Nursing Students: 94 full-time (79 women), 109 part-time (94 women); includes 43 minority (21 Black or African American, non-Hispanic/Latino; 10

Asian, non-Hispanic/Latino; 7 Hispanic/Latino; 5 Two or more races, non-Hispanic/Latino), 13 international. Average age 36. 111 applicants, 95% accepted, 63 enrolled. *Faculty:* 52 full-time (45 women). Expenses: Contact institution. *Financial support:* In 2017–18, 33 students received support, including 1 fellowship with partial tuition reimbursement available (averaging $16,500 per year), research assistantships with full tuition reimbursements available (averaging $12,500 per year), 1 teaching assistantship with full tuition reimbursement available (averaging $16,500 per year); career-related internships or fieldwork, Federal Work-Study, institutionally sponsored loans, traineeships, health care benefits, tuition waivers (full and partial), and unspecified assistantships also available. Financial award applicants required to submit FAFSA. In 2017, 53 master's, 5 doctorates, 20 other advanced degrees awarded. *Program availability:* Part-time, evening/weekend. Offers adult-gerontological nursing (MS, DNP, Certificate); community health nursing (MS, DNP, Certificate); family health nursing (MS, DNP, Certificate); family psychiatric mental health nursing (MS, DNP, Certificate); nursing (PhD). *Application fee:* $75. Electronic applications accepted. *Application Contact:* Ben Balkaya, Assistant Dean and Director, 607-777-2151, Fax: 607-777-2501, E-mail: balkaya@binghamton.edu. *Dean*, Dr. Mario R. Ortiz, 607-777-2311, E-mail: mortiz@binghamton.edu.

Harpur College of Arts and Sciences Students: 528 full-time (276 women), 584 part-time (310 women); includes 154 minority (27 Black or African American, non-Hispanic/Latino; 3 American Indian or Alaska Native, non-Hispanic/Latino; 41 Asian, non-Hispanic/Latino; 61 Hispanic/Latino; 1 Native Hawaiian or other Pacific Islander, non-Hispanic/Latino; 21 Two or more races, non-Hispanic/Latino), 400 international. Average age 30. 1,197 applicants, 55% accepted, 236 enrolled. *Faculty:* 448 full-time (177 women). Expenses: Contact institution. *Financial support:* In 2017–18, 592 students received support, including 2 fellowships with full tuition reimbursements available (averaging $8,000 per year), 42 research assistantships with full tuition reimbursements available (averaging $16,500 per year), 429 teaching assistantships with full tuition reimbursements available (averaging $15,000 per year); career-related internships or fieldwork, Federal Work-Study, institutionally sponsored loans, scholarships/grants, health care benefits, tuition waivers (full and partial), and unspecified assistantships also available. Financial award applicants required to submit FAFSA. In 2017, 167 master's, 93 doctorates, 2 other advanced degrees awarded. *Program availability:* Part-time, evening/weekend. Offers analytical chemistry (PhD); anthropology (MA, PhD); applied liberal studies (MA); art history (MA, PhD); arts and sciences (MA, MM, MS, PhD, Certificate); Asian and Asian American studies (MA, Certificate); biological sciences (MA, MS, PhD); biomedical anthropology (MS); chemistry (MA, MS); comparative literature (MA, PhD); creative writing (MA); economics (MA, PhD); English (PhD); English/American literature (MA); environmental studies (MS); French (MA); geography (MA); geological sciences (MS, PhD); history (MA, PhD); inorganic chemistry (PhD); Italian (MA); mathematical sciences (MA, PhD); music (MM); philosophy (MA, PhD); physical chemistry (PhD); physics, applied physics, and astronomy (MS, PhD); political science (MA, PhD); psychology - behavioral neuroscience (PhD); psychology - clinical psychology (PhD); psychology - cognitive and behavioral science (PhD); social, political, ethical and legal philosophy (MA, PhD); sociology (MA, PhD); Spanish (MA); statistics (MA); theatre (MA); translation (Certificate); translation studies (PhD). *Application deadline:* Applications are processed on a rolling basis. *Application fee:* $75. Electronic applications accepted. *Application Contact:* Ben Balkaya, Assistant Dean and Director, 607-777-2151, Fax: 607-777-2501, E-mail: balkaya@binghamton.edu. *Dean*, Dr. Terrence Deak, 607-777-2145, E-mail: tdeak@binghamton.edu.

School of Management Students: 298 full-time (149 women), 38 part-time (26 women); includes 71 minority (4 Black or African American, non-Hispanic/Latino; 41 Asian, non-Hispanic/Latino; 14 Hispanic/Latino; 12 Two or more races, non-Hispanic/Latino), 132 international. Average age 24. 599 applicants, 65% accepted, 221 enrolled. *Faculty:* 43 full-time (13 women), 32 part-time/adjunct (4 women). Expenses: Contact institution. *Financial support:* In 2017–18, 39 students received support, including 16 teaching assistantships with full tuition reimbursements available (averaging $17,000 per year); career-related internships or fieldwork, Federal Work-Study, institutionally sponsored loans, scholarships/grants, health care benefits, tuition waivers (full and partial), and unspecified assistantships also available. Financial award applicants required to submit FAFSA. In 2017, 316 master's, 3 doctorates awarded. *Program availability:* Part-time, evening/weekend. Offers accounting (MS); business administration (MBA); corporate executive (MBA); executive business administration (MBA); finance (PhD); health care professional executive (MBA); management (MBA, MS, PhD); management information systems (PhD); marketing (PhD); organizational studies (PhD); professional business administration (MBA); supply chain management (PhD). *Application deadline:* Applications are processed on a rolling basis. *Application fee:* $75. Electronic applications accepted. *Application Contact:* Ben Balkaya, Assistant Dean and Director, 607-777-2151, Fax: 607-777-2501, E-mail: balkaya@binghamton.edu. *Dean*, Dr. Upinder Dhillon, 607-777-2314, E-mail: dhillon@binghamton.edu.

School of Pharmacy and Pharmaceutical Sciences Students: 65 full-time (35 women); includes 44 minority (9 Black or African American, non-Hispanic/Latino; 30 Asian, non-Hispanic/Latino; 3 Hispanic/Latino; 2 Two or more races, non-Hispanic/Latino). Average age 24. 277 applicants, 52% accepted, 65 enrolled. *Faculty:* 18 full-time (12 women). Expenses: Contact institution. *Financial support:* In 2017–18, 2 students received support. Offers pharmacy (Pharm D). *Application deadline:* For fall admission, 3/1 for domestic students. *Application Contact:* Ben Balkaya, Assistant Dean and Director, 607-777-2151, Fax: 607-777-2501, E-mail: balkaya@binghamton.edu. *Dean*, Dr. Gloria E. Meredith, 607-777-2761, E-mail: gmeredith@binghamton.edu.

Thomas J. Watson School of Engineering and Applied Science Students: 707 full-time (181 women), 440 part-time (101 women); includes 118 minority (37 Black or African American, non-Hispanic/Latino; 1 American Indian or Alaska Native, non-Hispanic/Latino; 42 Asian, non-Hispanic/Latino; 31 Hispanic/Latino; 1 Native Hawaiian or other Pacific Islander, non-Hispanic/Latino; 6 Two or more races, non-Hispanic/Latino), 893 international. Average age 27. 2,028 applicants, 74% accepted, 408 enrolled. *Faculty:* 108 full-time (19 women). Expenses: Contact institution. *Financial support:* In 2017–18, 323 students received support, including 2 fellowships with full tuition reimbursements available (averaging $10,000 per year), 138 research assistantships with full tuition reimbursements available (averaging $16,500 per year), 94 teaching assistantships with full tuition reimbursements available (averaging $16,500 per year); career-related internships or fieldwork, Federal Work-Study, institutionally sponsored loans, scholarships/grants, health care benefits, tuition waivers (full and partial), and unspecified assistantships also available. Financial award application deadline: 2/15; financial award applicants required to submit FAFSA. In 2017, 454 master's, 33 doctorates awarded. *Program availability:* Part-time, evening/weekend, online learning. Offers biomedical engineering (MS, PhD); computer science (MS, PhD); electrical and computer engineering (MS, PhD); engineering and applied science (M Eng, MS, PhD); executive health systems (MS); industrial and systems engineering (M Eng); mechanical engineering (M Eng, MS, PhD); systems science and industrial engineering (MS, PhD). *Application deadline:* Applications are processed on a rolling basis. *Application fee:* $75. Electronic applications accepted. *Application Contact:* Ben Balkaya, Assistant Dean and Director, 607-777-2151, Fax: 607-777-2501, E-mail: balkaya@binghamton.edu. *Coordinator of Graduate Programs, The Watson School*, Ellen Tilden, 607-777-2873, E-mail: etilden@binghamton.edu.

BIOLA UNIVERSITY, La Mirada, CA 90639-0001

General Information Independent-religious, coed, university. *Enrollment:* 6,095 graduate, professional, and undergraduate students; 895 full-time matriculated graduate/professional students (389 women), 1,227 part-time matriculated graduate/professional students (494 women). *Graduate faculty:* 167. *Graduate housing:* Rooms and/or apartments available on a first-come, first-served basis to single and married students. *Student services:* Campus employment opportunities, campus safety program, career counseling, exercise/wellness program, international student services, low-cost health insurance, multicultural affairs office, services for students with disabilities, teacher training, writing training. *Library facilities:* Biola University Library plus 1 other. *Collection:* Books: 550,000 (physical); Databases: 259. Weekly public service hours: 100; students can reserve study rooms.

Computer facilities: A campuswide network can be accessed from student residence rooms and from off campus. Online class registration is available.
Website: http://www.biola.edu/

General Application Contact: Graduate Admissions, 562-903-4752, E-mail: graduate.admissions@biola.edu.

GRADUATE UNITS

Cook School of Intercultural Studies Students: 127 full-time (64 women), 123 part-time (70 women); includes 72 minority (9 Black or African American, non-Hispanic/Latino; 2 American Indian or Alaska Native, non-Hispanic/Latino; 41 Asian, non-Hispanic/Latino; 17 Hispanic/Latino; 3 Two or more races, non-Hispanic/Latino), 26 international. *Faculty:* 19. Expenses: Contact institution. *Financial support:* Scholarships/grants available. Support available to part-time students. Financial award applicants required to submit FAFSA. In 2017, 28 master's, 16 doctorates awarded. *Program availability:* Part-time, 100% online. Offers anthropology (MA); applied linguistics (MA); intercultural education (PhD); intercultural studies (MA, PhD); linguistics (Certificate); linguistics and Biblical languages (MA); missiology (D Miss); missions (MA); teaching English to speakers of other languages (MA, Certificate). *Application deadline:* For fall admission, 7/1 for domestic students, 6/1 for international students; for spring admission, 12/1 for domestic students; for summer admission, 5/1 for domestic students. Applications are processed on a rolling basis. *Application fee:* $65. Electronic applications accepted. *Application Contact:* Graduate Admissions Office, 562-903-4752, E-mail: graduate.admissions@biola.edu. *Dean*, Dr. Bulus Y. Galadima, 562-903-4844.

Crowell School of Business Students: 36 full-time (19 women), 40 part-time (18 women); includes 27 minority (5 Black or African American, non-Hispanic/Latino; 13 Asian, non-Hispanic/Latino; 9 Hispanic/Latino), 1 international. *Faculty:* 11. Expenses: Contact institution. *Financial support:* Scholarships/grants available. Support available to part-time students. Financial award applicants required to submit FAFSA. In 2017, 10 master's awarded. *Program availability:* Part-time, evening/weekend. Offers business (MBA, MP Acc). *Application deadline:* For fall admission, 4/15 priority date for domestic and international students; for spring admission, 12/1 for domestic students. Applications are processed on a rolling basis. *Application fee:* $65. Electronic applications accepted. *Application Contact:* Christina Gramenz, MBA Coordinator, 562-777-4015, E-mail: mba@biola.edu. *Dean*, Dr. Gary Lindblad, 562-777-4015, Fax: 562-906-4545, E-mail: mba@biola.edu.

Rosemead School of Psychology Students: 122 full-time (92 women), 46 part-time (39 women); includes 69 minority (7 Black or African American, non-Hispanic/Latino; 1 American Indian or Alaska Native, non-Hispanic/Latino; 31 Asian, non-Hispanic/Latino; 23 Hispanic/Latino; 7 Two or more races, non-Hispanic/Latino), 3 international. 96 applicants, 41% accepted, 21 enrolled. *Faculty:* 24. Expenses: Contact institution. *Financial support:* Scholarships/grants and unspecified assistantships available. Financial award applicants required to submit FAFSA. In 2017, 19 doctorates awarded. Offers clinical psychology (PhD, Psy D). *Application deadline:* For fall admission, 12/1 priority date for domestic students, 12/1 for international students. *Application fee:* $65. Electronic applications accepted. *Application Contact:* Jon Garcia, Graduate Admissions Counselor, 562-903-4752, E-mail: graduate.admissions@biola.edu. *Dean*, Dr. Clark Campbell, 562-903-4867, Fax: 562-903-4864.

School of Arts and Sciences Students: 24 full-time (7 women), 251 part-time (49 women); includes 80 minority (21 Black or African American, non-Hispanic/Latino; 1 American Indian or Alaska Native, non-Hispanic/Latino; 31 Asian, non-Hispanic/Latino; 19 Hispanic/Latino; 8 Two or more races, non-Hispanic/Latino), 15 international. 168 applicants, 70% accepted, 77 enrolled. *Faculty:* 20. Expenses: Contact institution. *Financial support:* Scholarships/grants and unspecified assistantships available. Support available to part-time students. Financial award applicants required to submit FAFSA. In 2017, 64 master's awarded. *Program availability:* Part-time, evening/weekend, online learning. Offers Christian apologetics (MA, Certificate); science and religion (MA); speech language pathology (MA). *Application deadline:* For fall admission, 7/1 for domestic students, 6/1 for international students; for spring admission, 12/1 for domestic students. Applications are processed on a rolling basis. *Application fee:* $65. Electronic applications accepted. *Application Contact:* Graduate Admissions Office, 562-903-4752, E-mail: graduate.admissions@biola.edu.

School of Education Students: 67 full-time (52 women), 164 part-time (142 women); includes 97 minority (8 Black or African American, non-Hispanic/Latino; 1 American Indian or Alaska Native, non-Hispanic/Latino; 51 Asian, non-Hispanic/Latino; 30 Hispanic/Latino; 7 Two or more races, non-Hispanic/Latino), 4 international. 164 applicants, 87% accepted, 116 enrolled. *Faculty:* 16. Expenses: Contact institution. *Financial support:* Scholarships/grants available. Support available to part-time students. Financial award applicants required to submit FAFSA. In 2017, 25 master's awarded. *Program availability:* Part-time, evening/weekend, online learning. Offers curriculum and instruction (Certificate); early childhood (MA Ed, MAT); multiple subject (MAT); single subject (MAT); special education (MA Ed, MAT, Certificate). *Application deadline:* For fall admission, 7/1 for domestic students, 6/1 for international students; for spring admission, 12/1 for domestic students; for summer admission, 5/1 for domestic students. Applications are processed on a rolling basis. *Application fee:* $65. Electronic applications accepted. *Application Contact:* Graduate Admissions Office, 562-903-4752, E-mail: graduate.admissions@biola.edu. *Dean*, Dr. June Hetzel, 562-903-4715.

Talbot School of Theology Students: 475 full-time (113 women), 603 part-time (176 women); includes 541 minority (39 Black or African American, non-Hispanic/Latino; 2 American Indian or Alaska Native, non-Hispanic/Latino; 378 Asian, non-Hispanic/Latino;

84 Hispanic/Latino; 1 Native Hawaiian or other Pacific Islander, non-Hispanic/Latino; 37 Two or more races, non-Hispanic/Latino), 105 international. 437 applicants, 78% accepted, 241 enrolled. Expenses: Contact institution. *Financial support:* Scholarships/grants and unspecified assistantships available. Support available to part-time students. Financial award applicants required to submit FAFSA. In 2017, 177 master's, 24 doctorates awarded. *Program availability:* Part-time, evening/weekend. Offers adult/family ministry (MACE); Bible exposition (MA, Th M); Biblical and theological studies (Certificate); children's ministry (MACE); Christian education (M Div); cross-cultural education ministry (MACE); educational studies (Ed D, PhD); evangelism and discipleship (M Div); general Christian education (MACE); Messianic Jewish studies (M Div, Certificate); missions and intercultural studies (M Div); New Testament (MA, Th M); Old Testament (MA); Old Testament and Semitics (Th M); pastoral and general ministry (M Div); pastoral care and counseling (M Div, MACML); philosophy (MA); preaching and pastoral ministry (MACML); spiritual formation (M Div, Certificate); spiritual formation and soul care (MA); sports ministry (MACML); theology (MA, Th M, D Min, Certificate); youth ministry (MACE). *Application deadline:* For fall admission, 7/1 for domestic students, 6/1 for international students; for spring admission, 12/1 priority date for domestic students. Applications are processed on a rolling basis. *Application fee:* $65. Electronic applications accepted. *Application Contact:* Graduate Admissions Office, 562-903-4752, E-mail: graduate.admissions@biola.edu. *Dean*, Dr. Clint Arnold, 562-903-4816, Fax: 562-903-4748.

BISHOP'S UNIVERSITY, Sherbrooke, QC J1M 1Z7, Canada

General Information Province-supported, coed, comprehensive institution. *Graduate housing:* Room and/or apartments available on a first-come, first-served basis to single students; on-campus housing not available to married students. Housing application deadline: 7/1.

GRADUATE UNITS

School of Education *Program availability:* Part-time, online learning. Offers advanced studies in education (Diploma); education (M Ed, MA); teaching English as a second language (Certificate).

BLACK HILLS STATE UNIVERSITY, Spearfish, SD 57799

General Information State-supported, coed, comprehensive institution. *Graduate housing:* Room and/or apartments available on a first-come, first-served basis to single students; on-campus housing not available to married students. Housing application deadline: 4/1.

GRADUATE UNITS

Graduate Studies *Program availability:* Part-time, evening/weekend, online learning. Offers business administration (MBA); curriculum and instruction (MS); integrative genomics (MS); strategic leadership (MS). Electronic applications accepted.

BLESSING-RIEMAN COLLEGE OF NURSING & HEALTH SCIENCES, Quincy, IL 62305-7005

General Information Independent, coed, primarily women, comprehensive institution. *Enrollment:* 16 part-time matriculated graduate/professional students (14 women). *Enrollment by degree level:* 16 master's. *Graduate faculty:* 7 full-time (all women). *Tuition:* Part-time $500 per credit hour. *Required fees:* $300 per unit. $150 per semester. One-time fee: $20 part-time. *Graduate housing:* On-campus housing not available. *Student services:* Campus safety program, services for students with disabilities. *Library facilities:* Blessing Health Professions Library plus 1 other.

Computer facilities: 28 computers available on campus for general student use. A campuswide network can be accessed.
Website: http://www.brcn.edu/

General Application Contact: Heather Mutter, Admissions Counselor, 217-228-5520 Ext. 6964, Fax: 217-223-4661, E-mail: hmutter@brcn.edu.

GRADUATE UNITS

Master of Science in Nursing Program Students: 16 part-time (14 women). Average age 35. *Faculty:* 7 full-time (all women). Expenses: Contact institution. *Financial support:* Scholarships/grants available. Financial award application deadline: 4/30; financial award applicants required to submit FAFSA. *Program availability:* Part-time-only, evening/weekend, online only, 100% online. Offers nursing education (MSN); nursing leadership (MSN). *Application deadline:* Applications are processed on a rolling basis. Electronic applications accepted. *Application Contact:* Heather Mutter, Admissions Counselor, 217-228-5520 Ext. 6964, Fax: 217-223-4661, E-mail: hmutter@brcn.edu. *Administrative Coordinator, Assessment*, Dr. Karen Mayville, 217-228-5520 Ext. 6968, Fax: 217-223-1781, E-mail: kmayville@brcn.edu.

BLOOMFIELD COLLEGE, Bloomfield, NJ 07003-9981

General Information Independent-religious, coed, comprehensive institution.

GRADUATE UNITS

Program in Accounting Offers accounting (MS).

BLOOMSBURG UNIVERSITY OF PENNSYLVANIA, Bloomsburg, PA 17815-1301

General Information State-supported, coed, comprehensive institution. *Enrollment:* 9,287 graduate, professional, and undergraduate students; 335 full-time matriculated graduate/professional students (241 women), 335 part-time matriculated graduate/professional students (237 women). *Enrollment by degree level:* 590 master's, 63 doctoral, 17 other advanced degrees. *Graduate faculty:* 75 full-time (37 women), 21 part-time/adjunct (15 women). Tuition, state resident: full-time $10,000; part-time $500 per credit hour. Tuition, nonresident: full-time $15,000; part-time $750 per credit hour. *Required fees:* $2484; $110.75 per credit hour. $75 per term. Tuition and fees vary according to program. *Graduate housing:* Room and/or apartments available on a first-come, first-served basis to single students; on-campus housing not available to married students. *Student services:* Campus employment opportunities, campus safety program, career counseling, child daycare facilities, exercise/wellness program, free psychological counseling, international student services, low-cost health insurance, multicultural affairs office, services for students with disabilities, teacher training, writing training. *Library facilities:* Andruss Library. *Collection:* Books: 374,393 (physical), 269,435 (digital/electronic); Serial titles: 5,838 (physical), 84,065 (digital/electronic); Databases: 165. Weekly public service hours: 98; students can reserve study rooms. *Research affiliation:* Merck & Company, Inc. (biology), Marine Science Consortium (biology), Consortium of Big Ten Universities Research and Training Reactors (physics), Melanoma Research Fund (biology).

Computer facilities: Computer purchase and lease plans are available. 1,571 computers available on campus for general student use. A campuswide network can be accessed. Online class registration is available.
Website: http://www.bloomu.edu/

General Application Contact: Jennifer Kessler, Administrative Assistant, 570-389-4015, Fax: 570-389-3054, E-mail: jkessler@bloomu.edu.

GRADUATE UNITS

School of Graduate Studies Students: 335 full-time (241 women), 335 part-time (237 women); includes 76 minority (26 Black or African American, non-Hispanic/Latino; 16 Asian, non-Hispanic/Latino; 22 Hispanic/Latino; 2 Native Hawaiian or other Pacific Islander, non-Hispanic/Latino; 10 Two or more races, non-Hispanic/Latino), 5 international. Average age 29. 794 applicants, 46% accepted, 255 enrolled. *Faculty:* 75 full-time (37 women), 21 part-time/adjunct (15 women). Expenses: Contact institution. *Financial support:* Research assistantships, Federal Work-Study, scholarships/grants, and unspecified assistantships available. Financial award application deadline: 3/15; financial award applicants required to submit FAFSA. In 2017, 243 master's, 9 doctorates, 2 other advanced degrees awarded. *Program availability:* Part-time, evening/weekend. *Application deadline:* Applications are processed on a rolling basis. *Application fee:* $35 ($60 for international students). Electronic applications accepted. *Application Contact:* Jennifer Kessler, Administrative Assistant, 570-389-4015, Fax: 570-389-3054, E-mail: jkessler@bloomu.edu. *Interim Assistant Vice President/Dean of Graduate Studies and Sponsored Research*, Dr. Mark Tapsak, 570-389-4015, Fax: 570-389-3054, E-mail: mtapsak@bloomu.edu.

College of Education *Program availability:* Part-time. Offers college student affairs (M Ed); curriculum and instruction (M Ed, Certificate); early childhood education (M Ed); education (M Ed, MS, Certificate); education of the deaf/hard of hearing (MS); educational leadership (M Ed); language arts (M Ed); math (M Ed); middle level education grades 4-8 (M Ed); PreK-12 curriculum and instruction (M Ed); PreK-12 school counseling (M Ed); PreK-12 school principal (M Ed); reading (M Ed); school principal (Certificate); science (M Ed); social studies (M Ed); special education (M Ed, MS, Certificate). Electronic applications accepted.

College of Science and Technology Offers adult and family nurse practitioner (MSN); audiology (Au D); biology (MS); clinical athletic training (MS); community health (MSN); corporate instructional technology (MS); eLearning developer (Certificate); exercise science (MS); intraoperative neurophysiological monitoring (Certificate); nurse anesthesia (MSN); nursing (MSN, DNP); nursing administration (MSN); science and technology (M Ed, MS, MSN, Au D, Certificate); speech pathology (MS); speech-language pathology (MS). Electronic applications accepted.

Zeigler College of Business *Program availability:* Part-time, evening/weekend. Offers accounting (M Acc); business (M Acc, M Ed, MBA, Certificate); business administration (MBA); business education (M Ed); management (Certificate). Electronic applications accepted.

BLUEFIELD COLLEGE, Bluefield, VA 24605-1799

General Information Independent-religious, coed, comprehensive institution. *Graduate housing:* On-campus housing not available.

GRADUATE UNITS

School of Education *Program availability:* Part-time, online only, 100% online. Offers education (MA Ed). Electronic applications accepted.

BLUE MOUNTAIN COLLEGE, Blue Mountain, MS 38610

General Information Independent-religious, coed, comprehensive institution. *Enrollment:* 601 graduate, professional, and undergraduate students; 3 full-time matriculated graduate/professional students (all women), 10 part-time matriculated graduate/professional students (all women). *Enrollment by degree level:* 13 master's. *Graduate faculty:* 5 part-time/adjunct (3 women). *Tuition:* Full-time $6030; part-time $335 per semester hour. *Required fees:* $790; $790 per semester hour. *Graduate housing:* Room and/or apartments available on a first-come, first-served basis to single students; on-campus housing not available to married students. Typical cost: $6046 (including board). Housing application deadline: 7/1. *Student services:* Campus employment opportunities, international student services, services for students with disabilities, teacher training. *Library facilities:* Guyton Library plus 1 other. *Collection:* Books: 41,725 (physical), 35,897 (digital/electronic); Serial titles: 143 (physical); Databases: 24. Weekly public service hours: 70.

Computer facilities: 95 computers available on campus for general student use. A campuswide network can be accessed from student residence rooms.
Website: http://www.bmc.edu/

General Application Contact: Jean Harrington, Administrative Assistant, Department of Education, 662-685-4771 Ext. 238, Fax: 662-815-2919, E-mail: jharrington@bmc.edu.

GRADUATE UNITS

Program in Elementary Education Students: 1 (woman) part-time. Average age 28. 2 applicants, 100% accepted. *Faculty:* 2 part-time/adjunct (1 woman). Expenses: Contact institution. *Financial support:* Scholarships/grants available. Financial award application deadline: 6/30; financial award applicants required to submit FAFSA. In 2017, 5 master's awarded. *Program availability:* Part-time, evening/weekend. Offers elementary education (M Ed). *Application deadline:* For fall admission, 7/15 priority date for domestic students; for spring admission, 12/1 priority date for domestic students; for summer admission, 5/1 priority date for domestic students. Applications are processed on a rolling basis. Electronic applications accepted. *Application Contact:* Jean Harrington, Administrative Assistant, Department of Education, 662-685-4771 Ext. 238, Fax: 662-815-2919, E-mail: jharrington@bmc.edu. *Dean of Graduate Studies*, Dr. Jenetta R. Waddell, 662-685-4771 Ext. 118, Fax: 662-815-2919, E-mail: jwaddell@bmc.edu.

Program in Literacy/Reading (K-12) Students: 3 full-time (all women), 8 part-time (all women); includes 1 minority (Black or African American, non-Hispanic/Latino). Average age 34. 3 applicants, 33% accepted. *Faculty:* 3 part-time/adjunct (2 women). Expenses: Contact institution. *Financial support:* Scholarships/grants available. Financial award application deadline: 6/30; financial award applicants required to submit FAFSA. In 2017, 13 master's awarded. *Program availability:* Part-time, evening/weekend. Offers literacy/reading (K-12) (M Ed). *Application deadline:* For fall admission, 7/15 priority date for domestic students; for spring admission, 12/1 priority date for domestic students; for summer admission, 5/1 priority date for domestic students. Applications are processed on a rolling basis. Electronic applications accepted. *Application Contact:* Jean Harrington, Administrative Assistant, Department of Education, 662-685-4771 Ext. 238, Fax: 662-815-2919, E-mail: jharrington@bmc.edu. *Dean of Graduate Studies*, Dr. Jenetta R. Waddell, 662-685-4771 Ext. 118, Fax: 662-815-2919, E-mail: jwaddell@bmc.edu.

Program in Secondary Education - Biology Students: 1 (woman) part-time. Average age 31. *Faculty:* 1 part-time/adjunct (0 women). Expenses: Contact institution. *Financial support:* Scholarships/grants available. Financial award application deadline: 6/30; financial award applicants required to submit FAFSA. *Program availability:* Part-time, evening/weekend. Offers secondary education - biology (M Ed). *Application deadline:* For fall admission, 7/15 priority date for domestic students; for spring admission, 12/1 priority date for domestic students; for summer admission, 5/1 priority date for domestic students. Applications are processed on a rolling basis. Electronic applications accepted. *Application Contact:* Jean Harrington, Administrative Assistant in Department of Education, 662-685-4771 Ext. 238, Fax: 662-815-2919, E-mail: jharrington@bmc.edu. *Dean of Graduate Studies*, Dr. Jenetta R. Waddell, 662-685-4771 Ext. 118, Fax: 662-815-2919, E-mail: jwaddell@bmc.edu.

BLUFFTON UNIVERSITY, Bluffton, OH 45817

General Information Independent-religious, coed, comprehensive institution. *Enrollment:* 824 graduate, professional, and undergraduate students; 55 full-time matriculated graduate/professional students (35 women), 11 part-time matriculated graduate/professional students (10 women). *Enrollment by degree level:* 66 master's. *Graduate faculty:* 7 full-time (3 women), 9 part-time/adjunct (2 women). *Graduate housing:* Room and/or apartments available on a first-come, first-served basis to single students; on-campus housing not available to married students. *Student services:* Campus employment opportunities, career counseling, exercise/wellness program, free psychological counseling, international student services, multicultural affairs office, services for students with disabilities, writing training. *Library facilities:* Musselman Library plus 1 other. *Collection:* Books: 73,648 (physical), 283,031 (digital/electronic); Serial titles: 1,001 (physical), 46,672 (digital/electronic); Databases: 258. Weekly public service hours: 74; students can reserve study rooms.

Computer facilities: 175 computers available on campus for general student use. A campuswide network can be accessed from student residence rooms and from off campus. Online class registration is available.
Website: http://www.bluffton.edu/

General Application Contact: Rebecca Cox, Administrative Assistant, 419-488-3257, Fax: 419-358-3399.

GRADUATE UNITS

Programs in Business Students: 48 full-time (31 women); includes 11 minority (5 Black or African American, non-Hispanic/Latino; 1 Asian, non-Hispanic/Latino; 3 Hispanic/Latino; 2 Two or more races, non-Hispanic/Latino), 1 international. Average age 33. 44 applicants, 70% accepted, 26 enrolled. *Faculty:* 5 full-time (2 women), 8 part-time/adjunct (2 women). Expenses: Contact institution. *Financial support:* Unspecified assistantships and faculty/staff grants available. Financial award applicants required to submit FAFSA. In 2017, 41 master's awarded. *Program availability:* Evening/weekend, blended/hybrid learning, videoconference. Offers accounting and financial management (MBA); health care management (MBA); leadership (MAOM, MBA); production and operations management (MBA); sustainability management (MBA). *Application deadline:* For fall admission, 7/31 priority date for domestic and international students. Applications are processed on a rolling basis. *Application fee:* $0. Electronic applications accepted. *Application Contact:* Carrie Mast, Administrative Assistant, Graduate Programs in Business, 419-358-3065, E-mail: mastc@bluffton.edu. *Director of Graduate Programs in Business*, Dr. Melissa Green, 419-358-3447, E-mail: greenm@bluffton.edu.

Programs in Education Students: 7 full-time (4 women), 11 part-time (10 women); includes 1 minority (Black or African American, non-Hispanic/Latino). Average age 29. 14 applicants, 64% accepted, 9 enrolled. *Faculty:* 2 full-time (1 woman), 1 part-time/adjunct (0 women). Expenses: Contact institution. *Financial support:* In 2017–18, 2 students received support. Unspecified assistantships available. Financial award application deadline: 9/15; financial award applicants required to submit FAFSA. In 2017, 7 master's awarded. *Program availability:* Part-time, 100% online, blended/hybrid learning, videoconference. Offers intervention specialist (MA Ed); leadership (MA Ed); reading (MA Ed). *Application deadline:* For fall admission, 8/15 priority date for domestic students, 6/15 priority date for international students; for spring admission, 12/15 priority date for domestic students, 9/15 priority date for international students. Applications are processed on a rolling basis. Electronic applications accepted. *Application Contact:* Nancey Schortgen, Program Representative, 419-358-3202, Fax: 419-358-3399, E-mail: schortgenn@bluffton.edu. *Director of Graduate Programs in Education*, Dr. Amy K. Mullins, 419-358-3457, E-mail: mullinsa@bluffton.edu.

BOB JONES UNIVERSITY, Greenville, SC 29614

General Information Independent-religious, coed, university.

GRADUATE UNITS

Graduate Programs

BOISE STATE UNIVERSITY, Boise, ID 83725-0399

General Information State-supported, coed, university. CGS member. *Enrollment:* 24,154 graduate, professional, and undergraduate students; 1,059 full-time matriculated graduate/professional students (609 women), 1,653 part-time matriculated graduate/professional students (985 women). *Enrollment by degree level:* 1,922 master's, 281 doctoral, 509 other advanced degrees. *Graduate faculty:* 457. Tuition, state resident: full-time $6471; part-time $390 per credit. Tuition, nonresident: full-time $21,787; part-time $685 per credit. *Required fees:* $2283; $100 per term. Part-time tuition and fees vary according to course load and program. *Graduate housing:* Rooms and/or apartments available on a first-come, first-served basis to single and married students. Typical cost: $4437 per year for single students; $4437 per year for married students. Room charges vary according to board plan, campus/location and housing facility selected. Housing application deadline: 6/1. *Student services:* Campus employment opportunities, campus safety program, career counseling, child daycare facilities, exercise/wellness program, free psychological counseling, grant writing training, international student services, low-cost health insurance, multicultural affairs office, services for students with disabilities, teacher training, writing training. *Library facilities:* Albertson's Library plus 1 other. *Collection:* Books: 644,899 (physical), 60,977 (digital/electronic); Serial titles: 112,213 (digital/electronic); Databases: 303. Weekly public service hours: 115; study areas open 24 hours, 5–7 days a week; students can reserve study rooms. *Research affiliation:* Federal Aviation Administration (airliner cabin environment research), Lee Pesky Learning Center (elementary mathematics education), Prewitt & Associates, Inc. (C-130 drop zones), Bechtel BWXT Idaho, LLC (energy policy analysis), Argonne National Laboratory (energy policy analysis), American Chemical Society (petroleum research).

Computer facilities: 900 computers available on campus for general student use. A campuswide network can be accessed from student residence rooms and from off campus. Online class registration is available.
Website: http://www.boisestate.edu/

General Application Contact: Katie Stone, Director of Graduate Recruiting, 208-426-3903, Fax: 208-426-2789, E-mail: gradcoll@boisestate.edu.

GRADUATE UNITS

College of Arts and Sciences Expenses: Contact institution. *Financial support:* Research assistantships, teaching assistantships, scholarships/grants, and unspecified assistantships available. Financial award applicants required to submit FAFSA. *Program availability:* Part-time. Offers anthropology (MA); applied anthropology (MAA); applied historical research (MAHR); arts and sciences (M E Sci, MA, MAA, MAHR, MFA, MM, MS, PhD); biology (MA, MS); biomolecular sciences (PhD); chemistry (MS); communication (MA); earth science (M E Sci); English literature (MA); English, rhetoric and composition (MA); geoscience (MS); geosciences (PhD); history (MA); interdisciplinary studies (MA, MS); mathematics (MS); mathematics education (MS); music education (MM); music performance (MM); raptor biology (MS); teaching English language (MA); technical communication (MA); visual arts (MFA). *Application deadline:* For fall admission, 5/1 for domestic and international students. Electronic applications accepted. *Dean*, Dr. Tony Roark, 208-426-1414, Fax: 208-426-3006.

College of Business and Economics Students: 146 full-time (52 women), 187 part-time (59 women); includes 33 minority (3 Black or African American, non-Hispanic/Latino; 1 American Indian or Alaska Native, non-Hispanic/Latino; 8 Asian, non-Hispanic/Latino; 16 Hispanic/Latino; 5 Two or more races, non-Hispanic/Latino), 12 international. Average age 33. 234 applicants, 63% accepted, 116 enrolled. *Faculty:* 22. Expenses: Contact institution. *Financial support:* Research assistantships, scholarships/grants, and unspecified assistantships available. Financial award applicants required to submit FAFSA. In 2017, 125 master's awarded. *Program availability:* Part-time, online learning. Offers accountancy (MSA); accountancy taxation (MSAT); business administration (MBA); business and economics (M Ec, MBA, MSA, MSAT, MSE); economics (M Ec, MSE). *Application deadline:* For fall admission, 5/1 for domestic and international students. Applications are processed on a rolling basis. *Application fee:* $65 ($95 for international students). Electronic applications accepted. *Application Contact:* Scott Lowe, Program Coordinator, 208-426-5439, E-mail: scottlowe@boisestate.edu. *Dean*, Dr. Kenneth J. Petersen, 208-426-1125, E-mail: kenpetersen@boisestate.edu.

College of Education Students: 131 full-time (106 women), 762 part-time (486 women); includes 88 minority (13 Black or African American, non-Hispanic/Latino; 4 American Indian or Alaska Native, non-Hispanic/Latino; 19 Asian, non-Hispanic/Latino; 46 Hispanic/Latino; 4 Native Hawaiian or other Pacific Islander, non-Hispanic/Latino; 2 Two or more races, non-Hispanic/Latino), 32 international. Average age 37. 399 applicants, 61% accepted, 146 enrolled. *Faculty:* 106. Expenses: Contact institution. *Financial support:* Teaching assistantships, scholarships/grants, and unspecified assistantships available. Financial award applicants required to submit FAFSA. In 2017, 234 master's, 12 doctorates awarded. *Program availability:* Part-time, 100% online, blended/hybrid learning. Offers bilingual education (M Ed); counselor education (MA, Graduate Certificate); curriculum and instruction (MA Ed, Ed D); early and special education (M Ed); education (M Ed, MA, MET, MPE, MS, MS Ed, Ed D, Ed S, Graduate Certificate); educational leadership (M Ed); educational technology (MET, MS, Ed D); English as a new language (M Ed); executive educational leadership (Ed S); literacy (MA); online teaching (Graduate Certificate); school technology coordination (Graduate Certificate); technology integration (Graduate Certificate). *Application fee:* $65 ($95 for international students). Electronic applications accepted. *Dean*, Dr. Rich Osguthorpe, 208-426-1611, E-mail: richardosguthorpe@boisestate.edu.

College of Engineering Students: 136 full-time (42 women), 231 part-time (117 women); includes 52 minority (15 Black or African American, non-Hispanic/Latino; 17 Asian, non-Hispanic/Latino; 15 Hispanic/Latino; 5 Two or more races, non-Hispanic/Latino), 78 international. Average age 34. 309 applicants, 51% accepted, 81 enrolled. *Faculty:* 78. Expenses: Contact institution. *Financial support:* Research assistantships, teaching assistantships with partial tuition reimbursements, scholarships/grants, and unspecified assistantships available. Financial award applicants required to submit FAFSA. In 2017, 72 master's, 1 doctorate awarded. *Program availability:* Part-time, online learning. Offers civil engineering (M Engr, MS); computer science (MS); computer science teacher endorsement (Graduate Certificate); electrical and computer engineering (M Engr, MS, PhD); engineering (M Engr, MS, PhD, Graduate Certificate); mechanical engineering (M Engr, MS); organizational performance and workplace learning (MS); STEM education (MS); workplace e-learning and performance support (Graduate Certificate); workplace instructional design (Graduate Certificate); workplace performance improvement (Graduate Certificate). *Application fee:* $65 ($95 for international students). Electronic applications accepted. *Application Contact:* Hao Chen, Program Coordinator, 208-426-1020, E-mail: haochen@boisestate.edu. *Dean*, Dr. JoAnn Lighty, 208-426-4844, E-mail: joannlighty@boisestate.edu.

Micron School of Materials Science and Engineering Students: 37 full-time (13 women), 6 part-time (3 women); includes 6 minority (5 Asian, non-Hispanic/Latino; 1 Hispanic/Latino), 8 international. Average age 29. 61 applicants, 36% accepted, 7 enrolled. *Faculty:* 16. Expenses: Contact institution. *Financial support:* Research assistantships, scholarships/grants, and unspecified assistantships available. Financial award application deadline: 1/15; financial award applicants required to submit FAFSA. In 2017, 10 master's, 1 doctorate awarded. Offers materials science and engineering (M Engr, MS, PhD). *Application deadline:* For fall admission, 1/15 priority date for domestic and international students. *Application fee:* $65 ($95 for international students). Electronic applications accepted. *Application Contact:* Jessica Economy, Academic Program Manager, 208-426-4896, E-mail: msegrad@boisestate.edu. *Department Chair*, Dr. Janet Callahan, 208-426-5983, E-mail: janetcallahan@boisestate.edu.

College of Health Sciences Students: 221 full-time (174 women), 183 part-time (138 women); includes 42 minority (11 Black or African American, non-Hispanic/Latino; 3 Asian, non-Hispanic/Latino; 24 Hispanic/Latino; 1 Native Hawaiian or other Pacific Islander, non-Hispanic/Latino; 3 Two or more races, non-Hispanic/Latino). Average age 35. 246 applicants, 49% accepted, 85 enrolled. *Faculty:* 72. Expenses: Contact institution. *Financial support:* Research assistantships, scholarships/grants, and unspecified assistantships available. Financial award applicants required to submit FAFSA. In 2017, 151 master's, 13 other advanced degrees awarded. *Program availability:* Part-time, 100% online. Offers athletic leadership (MAL); community and environmental health (MHS); health science (MHS); health sciences (MAL, MHS, MK, MS, MSN, MSW, DNP, Graduate Certificate); health services leadership (Graduate Certificate); kinesiology (MK, MS). *Application deadline:* Applications are processed on a rolling basis. *Application fee:* $65 ($95 for international students). Electronic applications accepted. *Application Contact:* Alicia Anderson, Project Director, 208-426-2425, E-mail: aliciaanderson@boisestate.edu. *Dean*, Dr. Tim Dunnagan, 208-426-4150, E-mail: timdunnagan@boisestate.edu.

School of Nursing Students: 1 (woman) full-time, 91 part-time (73 women); includes 11 minority (5 Black or African American, non-Hispanic/Latino; 2 Asian, non-Hispanic/Latino; 3 Hispanic/Latino; 1 Native Hawaiian or other Pacific Islander, non-Hispanic/Latino). Average age 43. 32 applicants, 44% accepted, 12 enrolled. Expenses: Contact institution. *Financial support:* Scholarships/grants and unspecified assistantships available. Financial award application deadline: 10/15; financial award applicants required to submit FAFSA. In 2017, 3 master's awarded. Offers acute care adult gerontology (Graduate Certificate); adult gerontology acute care (MSN); adult gerontology primary care (MSN); healthcare simulation (Graduate Certificate); nursing practice (DNP); primary care adult gerontology (Graduate Certificate). *Application deadline:* For spring admission, 10/15 priority date for domestic and international students. Applications are processed on a rolling basis. *Application fee:* $65 ($95 for international students). Electronic applications accepted. *Application Contact:* Dr. Nancy Loftus, Program Coordinator, 208-426-3819, E-mail: nancyloftus@boisestate.edu. *Director,* Dr. Ann Hubbert, 208-426-3404, E-mail: annhubbert@boisestate.edu.

School of Social Work Students: 177 full-time (146 women), 23 part-time (22 women); includes 13 minority (2 Black or African American, non-Hispanic/Latino; 10 Hispanic/Latino; 1 Two or more races, non-Hispanic/Latino). Average age 34. 139 applicants, 46% accepted, 47 enrolled. *Faculty:* 33. Expenses: Contact institution. *Financial support:* Research assistantships, scholarships/grants, and unspecified assistantships available. Financial award applicants required to submit FAFSA. In 2017, 104 master's awarded. *Program availability:* Part-time, 100% online. Offers social work (MSW). *Application deadline:* For fall admission, 1/10 for domestic and international students. *Application fee:* $65 ($95 for international students). Electronic applications accepted. *Application Contact:* Dr. Cynthia Sanders, Program Coordinator, 208-426-1780, E-mail: cynthiasanders@boisestate.edu. *Director,* Dr. Randy Magen, 208-426-1789, E-mail: randymagen@boisestate.edu.

School of Public Service Students: 63 full-time (32 women), 111 part-time (68 women); includes 21 minority (1 American Indian or Alaska Native, non-Hispanic/Latino; 2 Asian, non-Hispanic/Latino; 16 Hispanic/Latino; 1 Native Hawaiian or other Pacific Islander, non-Hispanic/Latino; 1 Two or more races, non-Hispanic/Latino), 2 international. Average age 36. 114 applicants, 48% accepted, 44 enrolled. *Faculty:* 28. Expenses: Contact institution. *Financial support:* Research assistantships, scholarships/grants, and unspecified assistantships available. Financial award applicants required to submit FAFSA. In 2017, 44 master's awarded. *Program availability:* Part-time. Offers criminal justice (MA); political science (MA); public policy and administration (MPA, PhD, Graduate Certificate); public service (MA, MPA, PhD, Graduate Certificate). *Application fee:* $65 ($95 for international students). Electronic applications accepted. *Dean,* Dr. Corey Cook, 208-426-3349, E-mail: coreydcook@boisestate.edu.

BORICUA COLLEGE, New York, NY 10032-1560

General Information Independent, coed, comprehensive institution.

GRADUATE UNITS

Program in Human Services *Program availability:* Evening/weekend. Offers human services (MS). Program offered in Brooklyn and Manhattan.

Program in Latin American and Caribbean Studies *Program availability:* Evening/weekend. Offers Latin American and Caribbean studies (MA). Program offered in Brooklyn and Manhattan.

Program in TESOL Education (K-12) *Program availability:* Evening/weekend. Offers TESOL education (MS).

BOSTON ARCHITECTURAL COLLEGE, Boston, MA 02115-2795

General Information Independent, coed, comprehensive institution.

GRADUATE UNITS

Graduate Programs Offers architecture (M Arch); historic preservation (MDS); interior design (MID); landscape architecture (MLA); sustainable design (MDS). Electronic applications accepted.

BOSTON COLLEGE, Chestnut Hill, MA 02467-3800

General Information Independent-religious, coed, university. CGS member. *Graduate housing:* On-campus housing not available.

GRADUATE UNITS

Carroll School of Management *Program availability:* Part-time, evening/weekend. Offers accounting (MSA); business administration (MBA); finance (MSF, PhD); management (MBA, MSA, MSF, PhD); management and organization (PhD). Electronic applications accepted.

Graduate School of Arts and Sciences *Program availability:* Part-time. Offers arts and sciences (MA, MS, MST, PhD); biochemistry (PhD); biology (PhD); classics (MA); earth and environmental sciences (MS); economics (PhD); English (MA, PhD); European national studies (MA); French (MA); Greek (MA); history (MA, PhD); inorganic chemistry (PhD); Irish studies (MA, PhD); Italian (MA); Latin (MA); linguistics (MA); mathematics (PhD); medieval studies (MA); organic chemistry (PhD); philosophy (MA, PhD); philosophy and theology (MA); physical chemistry (PhD); physics (MS, PhD); political science (MA, PhD); psychology (PhD); Russian (MA); science education (MST); Slavic studies (MA); sociology (MA, PhD); Spanish (MA); theology (PhD). Electronic applications accepted.

Law School Offers law (JD). Electronic applications accepted.

Lynch School of Education Students: 345 full-time (277 women), 422 part-time (318 women); includes 157 minority (50 Black or African American, non-Hispanic/Latino; 36 Asian, non-Hispanic/Latino; 50 Hispanic/Latino; 1 Native Hawaiian or other Pacific Islander, non-Hispanic/Latino; 20 Two or more races, non-Hispanic/Latino), 103 international. Average age 28. 1,385 applicants, 58% accepted, 322 enrolled. *Faculty:* 56 full-time (33 women). Expenses: Contact institution. *Financial support:* Fellowships with tuition reimbursements, research assistantships with tuition reimbursements, teaching assistantships with tuition reimbursements, career-related internships or fieldwork, Federal Work-Study, scholarships/grants, traineeships, health care benefits, tuition waivers (partial), and unspecified assistantships available. Support available to part-time students. Financial award applicants required to submit FAFSA. In 2017, 375 master's, 56 doctorates, 7 other advanced degrees awarded. *Program availability:* Part-time. Offers applied developmental and educational psychology (MA, PhD); applied statistics and psychometrics (MS); counseling psychology (PhD); curriculum and instruction (M Ed, PhD, CAES); early childhood education (M Ed); education (M Ed, MA, MAT, MS, MST, Ed D, PhD, CAES); educational leadership (M Ed, Ed D, CAES); educational research methodology (M Ed); elementary education (M Ed, MAT); higher education (MA, PhD); international higher education (MA); measurement, evaluation, statistics, and assessment (PhD); mental health counseling (MA); moderate special needs (M Ed, CAES); reading and literacy (M Ed, MAT, CAES); secondary education (M Ed, MAT, MST); severe special needs (M Ed, CAES). *Application deadline:* For fall admission, 1/10 priority date for domestic and international students; for spring admission, 11/1 for domestic and international students; for summer admission, 5/15 for domestic and international students. Applications are processed on a rolling basis. *Application fee:* $65. Electronic applications accepted. *Application Contact:* Jamie Grenon, Associate Dean for Graduate Admissions and Financial Aid, 617-552-4214, Fax: 617-552-0398, E-mail: grenonj@bc.edu. *Dean,* Dr. Stanton Wortham, 617-552-4200, Fax: 617-552-0812.

School of Social Work *Program availability:* Part-time. Offers social work (MSW, PhD). Electronic applications accepted.

School of Theology and Ministry *Program availability:* Part-time. Offers church leadership (MA); divinity (M Div); pastoral ministry (MA); religious education (MA, PhD); sacred theology (STD, STL); social justice/social ministry (MA); spiritual direction (MA); theological studies (MTS); theology (Th M, PhD); youth ministry (MA). Electronic applications accepted.

William F. Connell School of Nursing Students: 170 full-time (153 women), 90 part-time (83 women); includes 39 minority (8 Black or African American, non-Hispanic/Latino; 10 Asian, non-Hispanic/Latino; 12 Hispanic/Latino; 9 Two or more races, non-Hispanic/Latino), 3 international. Average age 28. 360 applicants, 56% accepted, 94 enrolled. *Faculty:* 54 full-time (48 women). Expenses: Contact institution. *Financial support:* In 2017–18, 152 students received support, including 11 fellowships with full tuition reimbursements available (averaging $24,504 per year), 29 teaching assistantships (averaging $3,768 per year); scholarships/grants, health care benefits, tuition waivers (partial), and unspecified assistantships also available. Support available to part-time students. Financial award application deadline: 4/18; financial award applicants required to submit FAFSA. In 2017, 104 master's, 5 doctorates awarded. *Program availability:* Part-time. Offers adult-gerontology primary care nurse practitioner (MS); family health nursing (MS); nurse anesthesia (MS); nursing (PhD); pediatric primary care nurse practitioner (MS); psychiatric-mental health nursing (MS); women's health nursing (MS). MS/MBA offered jointly with Carroll School of Management, MS/MA with School of Theology and Ministry. *Application deadline:* For fall admission, 9/30 for domestic and international students; for winter admission, 1/15 for domestic and international students; for spring admission, 3/15 for domestic and international students. *Application fee:* $40. Electronic applications accepted. *Application Contact:* Sean Sendall, Assistant Dean, Graduate Enrollment and Data Analytics, 617-552-4745, Fax: 617-552-2121, E-mail: sean.sendall@bc.edu. *Dean,* Dr. Susan Gennaro, 617-552-4251, Fax: 617-552-0931, E-mail: susan.gennaro@bc.edu.

BOSTON GRADUATE SCHOOL OF PSYCHOANALYSIS, Brookline, MA 02446-4602

General Information Independent, coed, graduate-only institution. *Graduate housing:* On-campus housing not available. *Research affiliation:* Boston Institute for Psychotherapy (psychotherapy).

GRADUATE UNITS

BGSP-New Jersey Offers psychoanalysis (MA); psychoanalytic counseling (MA). Programs offered in conjunction with Academic of Clinical and Applied Psychoanalysis in Livingston, NJ.

CAGS and Certificate Programs *Program availability:* Part-time. Offers child and adolescent intervention (CAGS); psychoanalysis (Certificate); psychoanalytic psychotherapy (CAGS).

Doctoral Programs *Program availability:* Part-time. Offers psychoanalysis (Psya D); psychoanalysis, society and culture (Psya D).

Master's Programs *Program availability:* Part-time. Offers mental health counseling (MA); psychoanalysis (MA); psychoanalysis, society and culture (MA).

New York Graduate School of Psychoanalysis *Program availability:* Part-time. Offers psychoanalysis (MA).

BOSTON UNIVERSITY, Boston, MA 02215

General Information Independent, coed, university. CGS member. *Enrollment:* 33,355 graduate, professional, and undergraduate students; 10,221 full-time matriculated graduate/professional students (5,784 women), 5,017 part-time matriculated graduate/professional students (2,757 women). *Enrollment by degree level:* 9,948 master's, 5,110 doctoral, 180 other advanced degrees. *Graduate housing:* On-campus housing not available. *Student services:* Campus employment opportunities, campus safety program, career counseling, child daycare facilities, exercise/wellness program, free psychological counseling, international student services, low-cost health insurance, services for students with disabilities, writing training. *Library facilities:* Mugar Memorial Library plus 20 others. *Collection:* Books: 1.2 million (physical), 1.7 million (digital/electronic); Serial titles: 227,677 (physical), 103,216 (digital/electronic); Databases: 591. Weekly public service hours: 123; students can reserve study rooms. *Research affiliation:* NASA-Ames Research Center, Society for the Preservation of New England Antiquities, Massachusetts Historical Society, Woods Hole Oceanographic Institution-Marine Biological Laboratory.

Computer facilities: Computer purchase and lease plans are available. 250 computers available on campus for general student use. A campuswide network can be accessed from student residence rooms and from off campus. Online class registration, research and educational networks are available.
Website: http://www.bu.edu/

GRADUATE UNITS

College of Communication Students: 417 full-time (321 women), 19 part-time (13 women); includes 66 minority (25 Black or African American, non-Hispanic/Latino; 10 Asian, non-Hispanic/Latino; 22 Hispanic/Latino; 9 Two or more races, non-Hispanic/Latino), 231 international. Average age 24. 975 applicants, 61% accepted, 222 enrolled. *Faculty:* 67 full-time, 73 part-time/adjunct. Expenses: Contact institution. *Financial support:* In 2017–18, 125 students received support, including 5 research assistantships (averaging $10,000 per year), 50 teaching assistantships (averaging $8,000 per year); career-related internships or fieldwork, Federal Work-Study, institutionally sponsored loans, scholarships/grants, health care benefits, and unspecified assistantships also available. Support available to part-time students. Financial award application deadline: 5/1; financial award applicants required to submit FAFSA. In 2017, 258 master's awarded. *Program availability:* Part-time. Offers advertising (MS); communication (MA, MFA, MS, PhD); film and television (MFA, MS); journalism (MS); mass communication (MS); public relations (MS). *Application deadline:* For fall admission, 5/1 for domestic and international students. Applications are processed on a rolling basis. *Application fee:* $95. Electronic applications accepted. *Application Contact:* Manny Dotel, Assistant Director, Graduate Affairs, 617-353-3481, E-mail: comgrad@bu.edu. *Dean,* Thomas Fiedler, 617-353-3450, Fax: 617-358-0399, E-mail: comdean@bu.edu.

Division of Emerging Media Studies Students: 29 full-time (21 women), 4 part-time (3 women); includes 3 minority (2 Hispanic/Latino; 1 Two or more races, non-Hispanic/Latino), 21 international. Average age 25. 143 applicants, 32% accepted, 20 enrolled. *Faculty:* 4 full-time (1 woman). Expenses: Contact institution. *Financial support:* In 2017–18, 3 fellowships with full tuition reimbursements were awarded; research assistantships, teaching assistantships, career-related internships or fieldwork, Federal Work-Study, scholarships/grants, health care benefits, and unspecified assistantships also available. Financial award application deadline: 5/1; financial award applicants required to submit FAFSA. In 2017, 36 master's awarded.

Program availability: Part-time. Offers emerging media studies (MA, PhD). *Application deadline:* For fall admission, 5/1 for domestic and international students. Applications are processed on a rolling basis. *Application fee:* $95. Electronic applications accepted. *Application Contact:* Jackie Cummings, Admission and Financial Aid Counselor, 617-353-3481, E-mail: comgrad@bu.edu. *Professor of Emerging Media/Chair of the Division of Emerging Media Studies*, Dr. James Katz, 617-353-7733, E-mail: dems@bu.edu.

College of Engineering Students: 814 full-time (245 women), 188 part-time (54 women); includes 140 minority (5 Black or African American, non-Hispanic/Latino; 84 Asian, non-Hispanic/Latino; 27 Hispanic/Latino; 24 Two or more races, non-Hispanic/Latino), 560 international. Average age 26. 3,337 applicants, 42% accepted, 402 enrolled. *Faculty:* 112 full-time (12 women), 9 part-time/adjunct (1 woman). Expenses: Contact institution. *Financial support:* In 2017–18, 458 students received support, including 115 fellowships with full tuition reimbursements available (averaging $33,000 per year), 246 research assistantships with full tuition reimbursements available (averaging $33,000 per year), 7 teaching assistantships with full tuition reimbursements available (averaging $22,000 per year); scholarships/grants and unspecified assistantships also available. Support available to part-time students. Financial award application deadline: 1/15; financial award applicants required to submit FAFSA. In 2017, 288 master's, 55 doctorates awarded. *Program availability:* Part-time, blended/hybrid learning. Offers biomedical engineering (M Eng, MS, PhD); computer engineering (M Eng, MS, PhD); engineering (M Eng, MS, PhD); manufacturing engineering (MS); materials science and engineering (M Eng, MS, PhD); mechanical engineering (PhD); systems engineering (M Eng, MS, PhD). *Application deadline:* For fall admission, 12/15 for domestic and international students; for spring admission, 10/1 for domestic and international students. *Application fee:* $95. Electronic applications accepted. *Application Contact:* Andrew Butler, Assistant Director, Enrollment Operations, 617-353-9760, E-mail: enggrad@bu.edu. *Dean*, Dr. Kenneth R. Lutchen, 617-353-2800, Fax: 617-358-3468, E-mail: klutch@bu.edu.

College of Fine Arts Students: 874 full-time (532 women), 24 part-time (11 women); includes 129 minority (29 Black or African American, non-Hispanic/Latino; 3 American Indian or Alaska Native, non-Hispanic/Latino; 34 Asian, non-Hispanic/Latino; 40 Hispanic/Latino; 1 Native Hawaiian or other Pacific Islander, non-Hispanic/Latino; 22 Two or more races, non-Hispanic/Latino), 211 international. Average age 31. 2,276 applicants, 22% accepted, 161 enrolled. Expenses: Contact institution. *Financial support:* Fellowships, teaching assistantships, Federal Work-Study, and scholarships/grants available. Support available to part-time students. Financial award application deadline: 1/1. In 2017, 227 master's, 57 doctorates, 10 other advanced degrees awarded. *Program availability:* Part-time. Offers ethnomusicology (PhD); fine arts (MA, MFA, MM, DMA, PhD, CAS, Certificate, Performance Diploma); historical musicology (PhD); musicology (MA). *Application deadline:* For fall admission, 1/15 for domestic and international students. *Application fee:* $95. Electronic applications accepted. *Application Contact:* Mark Krone, Assistant Director of Graduate Affairs, 617-353-3350, E-mail: arts@bu.edu. *Dean*, Harvey Young, 617-353-3350.

School of Music Students: 301 full-time (175 women), 8 part-time (4 women); includes 36 minority (3 Black or African American, non-Hispanic/Latino; 14 Asian, non-Hispanic/Latino; 10 Hispanic/Latino; 9 Two or more races, non-Hispanic/Latino), 151 international. Average age 27. 1,590 applicants, 21% accepted, 101 enrolled. *Faculty:* 36 full-time, 21 part-time/adjunct. Expenses: Contact institution. *Financial support:* Fellowships, teaching assistantships, scholarships/grants, and unspecified assistantships available. Financial award application deadline: 12/1. In 2017, 128 master's, 57 doctorates, 10 other advanced degrees awarded. *Program availability:* Part-time. Offers choral conducting (MM); composition and theory (DMA); conducting (Performance Diploma); music education (MM, DMA); musicology (MA, PhD). *Application deadline:* For fall admission, 12/1 priority date for domestic and international students. *Application fee:* $95. Electronic applications accepted. *Application Contact:* Katie Luellen, Director of Admissions, 617-353-3341, E-mail: arts@bu.edu. *Director*, Shiela Kibbe, 617-353-3341, Fax: 617-353-7455, E-mail: cfamusic@bu.edu.

School of Theatre Students: 53 full-time (35 women), 4 part-time (1 woman); includes 7 minority (1 Black or African American, non-Hispanic/Latino; 1 American Indian or Alaska Native, non-Hispanic/Latino; 3 Asian, non-Hispanic/Latino; 1 Hispanic/Latino; 1 Two or more races, non-Hispanic/Latino), 2 international. Average age 27. 212 applicants, 14% accepted, 17 enrolled. *Faculty:* 16 full-time, 9 part-time/adjunct. Expenses: Contact institution. *Financial support:* In 2017–18, 16 students received support. Fellowships, teaching assistantships, scholarships/grants, unspecified assistantships, and stipends available. Financial award application deadline: 2/1. In 2017, 14 master's awarded. Offers design (MFA); lighting crafts (Certificate); management (MFA); production (MFA); scenic painting (Certificate). *Application deadline:* For fall admission, 2/1 priority date for domestic and international students. *Application fee:* $95. Electronic applications accepted. *Application Contact:* Mark Krone, Assistant Director of Graduate Affairs, 617-353-3350, E-mail: arts@bu.edu. *Director*, Jim Petosa, 617-353-3390.

School of Visual Arts Students: 161 full-time (139 women), 3 part-time (all women); includes 19 minority (2 Black or African American, non-Hispanic/Latino; 6 Asian, non-Hispanic/Latino; 9 Hispanic/Latino; 2 Two or more races, non-Hispanic/Latino), 37 international. Average age 30. 365 applicants, 27% accepted, 21 enrolled. *Faculty:* 17 full-time, 4 part-time/adjunct. Expenses: Contact institution. *Financial support:* In 2017–18, 36 students received support. Fellowships, teaching assistantships, scholarships/grants, and unspecified assistantships available. Financial award application deadline: 2/1. In 2017, 85 master's awarded. Offers art education (MA); graphic design (MFA); painting (MFA); sculpture (MFA); studio teaching (MA). *Application deadline:* For fall admission, 2/1 for domestic and international students. Applications are processed on a rolling basis. *Application fee:* $95. *Application Contact:* Jessica Caccamo, Assistant Director of Admissions, 617-353-3371, E-mail: visuarts@bu.edu. *Director*, Lynne Allen, 617-353-3371.

College of Health and Rehabilitation Sciences: Sargent College Students: 459 full-time (380 women), 74 part-time (65 women); includes 91 minority (5 Black or African American, non-Hispanic/Latino; 47 Asian, non-Hispanic/Latino; 26 Hispanic/Latino; 13 Two or more races, non-Hispanic/Latino), 39 international. Average age 26. 1,687 applicants, 24% accepted, 146 enrolled. *Faculty:* 54 full-time (42 women), 44 part-time/adjunct (28 women). Expenses: Contact institution. *Financial support:* In 2017–18, 300 students received support, including 30 research assistantships with full tuition reimbursements available (averaging $22,000 per year), 18 teaching assistantships (averaging $2,500 per year); career-related internships or fieldwork, Federal Work-Study, institutionally sponsored loans, scholarships/grants, and health care benefits also available. Support available to part-time students. Financial award application deadline: 1/1; financial award applicants required to submit FAFSA. In 2017, 118 master's, 85 doctorates awarded. *Program availability:* Blended/hybrid learning. Offers athletic training (MS); health and rehabilitation sciences (MS, DPT, OTD, PhD); human physiology (MS, PhD); nutrition (MS); occupational therapy (OTD); physical therapy (DPT); rehabilitation sciences (PhD); speech, language and hearing sciences (PhD); speech-language pathology (MS). *Application deadline:* For fall admission, 1/1 priority date for domestic and international students. Applications are processed on a rolling basis. *Application fee:* $95. Electronic applications accepted. *Application Contact:* Sharon Sankey, Assistant Dean, Student Services, 617-353-2713, Fax: 617-353-7500, E-mail: ssankey@bu.edu. *Dean*, Dr. Christopher Moore, 617-353-2705, Fax: 617-353-7500, E-mail: mooreca@bu.edu.

Graduate School of Arts and Sciences Students: 1,773 full-time (858 women), 218 part-time (107 women); includes 238 minority (32 Black or African American, non-Hispanic/Latino; 95 Asian, non-Hispanic/Latino; 83 Hispanic/Latino; 1 Native Hawaiian or other Pacific Islander, non-Hispanic/Latino; 27 Two or more races, non-Hispanic/Latino), 859 international. Average age 25. 8,572 applicants, 29% accepted, 588 enrolled. Expenses: Contact institution. *Financial support:* In 2017–18, 1,351 students received support, including 210 fellowships with full tuition reimbursements available (averaging $22,000 per year), 400 research assistantships with full tuition reimbursements available (averaging $22,000 per year), 575 teaching assistantships with full tuition reimbursements available (averaging $22,000 per year); career-related internships or fieldwork, Federal Work-Study, scholarships/grants, traineeships, health care benefits, and unspecified assistantships also available. In 2017, 419 master's, 168 doctorates awarded. Offers African American studies (MA); American and New England studies (PhD); anthropology (PhD); applied anthropology (MA); archaeology (MA, PhD); arts and sciences (MA, MAEP, MFA, MS, PhD, Certificate); astronomy (MA, PhD); bioinformatics (MS, PhD); biology (MA, PhD); biostatistics (MA, PhD); chemistry (MA, PhD); classical studies (MA, PhD); computer science (MS, PhD); creative writing (MFA); cyber security (MS); data-centric computing (MS); earth and environment (MA, PhD); economic policy (MAEP); energy and environment (MA); English (MA, PhD); global development economics (MA); Hispanic language and literature (MA, PhD); history (MA, PhD); history of art and architecture (MA, PhD); linguistics (MA, PhD); mathematics (MA, PhD); molecular biology, cell biology, and biochemistry (MA, PhD); museum studies (Certificate); philosophy (MA, PhD); physics (PhD); playwriting (MFA); political science (PhD); preservation studies (MA); psychological and brain sciences (MA, PhD); religion (MA, PhD); remote sensing and geospatial sciences (MA); sociology (MA, PhD); statistical practice (MS); statistics (MA, PhD). *Application deadline:* For fall admission, 1/15 priority date for domestic and international students; for spring admission, 10/15 priority date for domestic and international students. *Application fee:* $95. Electronic applications accepted. *Application Contact:* Martin Gastmann, Assistant Director of Admissions and Financial Aid, 617-353-2696, Fax: 617-358-5492, E-mail: grs@bu.edu. *Associate Dean*, Dr. Emily Barman, 617-353-2696, Fax: 617-358-5492.

Editorial Institute Students: 13 full-time (8 women), 4 part-time (2 women); includes 3 minority (2 Hispanic/Latino; 1 Two or more races, non-Hispanic/Latino), 1 international. Average age 31. 3 applicants. Expenses: Contact institution. *Financial support:* In 2017–18, 16 students received support, including fellowships with full tuition reimbursements available (averaging $22,000 per year), 5 research assistantships with full tuition reimbursements available (averaging $22,000 per year), 5 teaching assistantships with full tuition reimbursements available (averaging $22,000 per year); Federal Work-Study, scholarships/grants, and health care benefits also available. Financial award application deadline: 1/15. In 2017, 1 master's awarded. Offers editorial studies (MA). *Application deadline:* For fall admission, 4/15 for domestic and international students. *Application fee:* $95. Electronic applications accepted. *Application Contact:* Ellen Wrigley, Administrative Assistant, 617-353-6631, Fax: 617-353-6917, E-mail: ellen@bu.edu. *Director*, Archie Burnett, 617-353-6631, E-mail: burnetta@bu.edu.

Frederick S. Pardee School of Global Studies Students: 100 full-time (62 women), 10 part-time (4 women); includes 17 minority (5 Black or African American, non-Hispanic/Latino; 6 Asian, non-Hispanic/Latino; 5 Hispanic/Latino; 1 Two or more races, non-Hispanic/Latino), 45 international. Average age 25. 377 applicants, 79% accepted, 41 enrolled. *Faculty:* 33 full-time (8 women), 10 part-time/adjunct (4 women). Expenses: Contact institution. *Financial support:* In 2017–18, 55 students received support. Federal Work-Study, scholarships/grants, and unspecified assistantships available. Financial award application deadline: 1/15. In 2017, 31 master's awarded. Offers global policy (MA); international affairs (MA); international relations (MA); Latin American studies (MA). *Application deadline:* For fall admission, 1/15 priority date for domestic and international students; for spring admission, 12/15 for domestic and international students. Applications are processed on a rolling basis. *Application fee:* $95. Electronic applications accepted. *Application Contact:* Holly Chase, Graduate Affairs Manager, 617-358-8625, Fax: 617-353-9290, E-mail: psgsgrad@bu.edu. *Dean*, Adil Najam, 617-358-0988, Fax: 617-353-9290, E-mail: anajam@bu.edu.

Henry M. Goldman School of Dental Medicine Students: 770 full-time (371 women); includes 273 minority (12 Black or African American, non-Hispanic/Latino; 3 American Indian or Alaska Native, non-Hispanic/Latino; 178 Asian, non-Hispanic/Latino; 65 Hispanic/Latino; 15 Two or more races, non-Hispanic/Latino), 231 international. Average age 28. 6,401 applicants, 8% accepted, 259 enrolled. *Faculty:* 137 full-time (58 women), 91 part-time/adjunct (36 women). Expenses: Contact institution. *Financial support:* In 2017–18, 91 students received support. Institutionally sponsored loans, scholarships/grants, and stipends (for oral surgery residents) available. Financial award application deadline: 4/15; financial award applicants required to submit FAFSA. In 2017, 18 master's, 209 doctorates, 62 other advanced degrees awarded. Offers dental medicine (MS, MSD, D Sc, D Sc D, DMD, CAGS). *Application deadline:* For fall admission, 12/15 for domestic and international students. Applications are processed on a rolling basis. *Application fee:* $75. Electronic applications accepted. *Application Contact:* Admissions Representative, 617-638-4787, Fax: 617-638-4798, E-mail: applydmd@bu.edu. *Dean*, Dr. Jeffrey W. Hutter, 617-638-4780, E-mail: jhutter@bu.edu.

Metropolitan College Students: 516 full-time (254 women), 2,169 part-time (949 women); includes 645 minority (189 Black or African American, non-Hispanic/Latino; 7 American Indian or Alaska Native, non-Hispanic/Latino; 213 Asian, non-Hispanic/Latino; 191 Hispanic/Latino; 3 Native Hawaiian or other Pacific Islander, non-Hispanic/Latino; 42 Two or more races, non-Hispanic/Latino), 780 international. Average age 31. 2,679 applicants, 70% accepted, 727 enrolled. *Faculty:* 36 full-time (12 women), 199 part-time/adjunct (57 women). Expenses: Contact institution. *Financial support:* In 2017–18, 68 research assistantships (averaging $8,400 per year), 8 teaching assistantships (averaging $5,000 per year) were awarded; career-related internships or fieldwork, scholarships/grants, and unspecified assistantships also available. Support available to part-time students. Financial award applicants required to submit FAFSA. In 2017, 1,118 master's awarded. *Program availability:* Part-time, evening/weekend, 100% online, blended/hybrid learning. Offers actuarial science (MS); advertising (MS); applied business analytics (MS); arts administration (MS, Graduate Certificate); city planning (MCP); communications (MLA); computer information systems (MS); computer networks (Certificate); computer science (MS); cybercrime investigation and cybersecurity (MCJ);

data analytics (Certificate); digital forensics (Certificate); economic development and tourism management (MSAS); enterprise risk management (MS); financial management (MS); fundraising management (Graduate Certificate); global marketing management (MS); health communication (MS); health informatics (Certificate); history and culture (MLA); information technology project management (Certificate); innovation and technology (MSAS); insurance management (MS); leadership (MS); project management (MS); software development (MS); software engineering in health care systems (Certificate); strategic management (MCJ); supply chain management (MS); telecommunications (MS); urban affairs (MUA). *Application deadline:* Applications are processed on a rolling basis. *Application fee:* $85. Electronic applications accepted. *Application Contact:* Kristin McAullife, Director, Enrollment Services, 617-353-6000, E-mail: met@bu.edu. *Dean*, Dr. Tanya Zlateva, 617-353-3010, Fax: 617-353-6066.

Questrom School of Business Students: 690 full-time (320 women), 650 part-time (278 women); includes 241 minority (41 Black or African American, non-Hispanic/Latino; 1 American Indian or Alaska Native, non-Hispanic/Latino; 119 Asian, non-Hispanic/Latino; 58 Hispanic/Latino; 22 Two or more races, non-Hispanic/Latino), 427 international. Average age 27. 1,069 applicants, 40% accepted, 164 enrolled. *Faculty:* 85 full-time (23 women), 28 part-time/adjunct (10 women). Expenses: Contact institution. *Financial support:* Career-related internships or fieldwork, Federal Work-Study, institutionally sponsored loans, scholarships/grants, and tuition waivers (partial) available. Support available to part-time students. Financial award applicants required to submit FAFSA. In 2017, 496 master's, 15 doctorates awarded. *Program availability:* Part-time, evening/weekend. Offers business (EMBA); digital innovation (MS); management (PhD); management studies (MSMS); mathematical finance (MS, PhD). *Application deadline:* For fall admission, 3/18 for domestic and international students; for spring admission, 11/7 for domestic and international students. *Application fee:* $125. Electronic applications accepted. *Application Contact:* Meredith C. Siegel, Assistant Dean, Graduate Admissions Office, 617-353-2670, Fax: 617-353-7368, E-mail: mba@bu.edu. *Professor/Dean*, Kenneth W. Freeman, 617-353-9720, Fax: 617-353-5581, E-mail: kfreeman@bu.edu.

School of Hospitality Administration Students: 30 full-time (21 women), 3 part-time (2 women); includes 6 minority (4 Black or African American, non-Hispanic/Latino; 1 Asian, non-Hispanic/Latino; 1 Hispanic/Latino), 20 international. Average age 26. *Faculty:* 9 full-time, 17 part-time/adjunct. Expenses: Contact institution. *Financial support:* In 2017–18, 32 students received support. Scholarships/grants and unspecified assistantships available. Financial award application deadline: 3/1; financial award applicants required to submit FAFSA. *Program availability:* Part-time. Offers hospitality administration (MMH). *Application deadline:* For summer admission, 3/1 priority date for domestic and international students. Applications are processed on a rolling basis. *Application fee:* $95. Electronic applications accepted. *Application Contact:* Micah Sieber, Director of Graduate Affairs, 617-353-1011, E-mail: shagrad@bu.edu. *Dean*, Dr. Arun Upneja, 617-353-3261, E-mail: aupneja@bu.edu.

School of Law Students: 923 full-time (528 women), 122 part-time (62 women); includes 201 minority (30 Black or African American, non-Hispanic/Latino; 2 American Indian or Alaska Native, non-Hispanic/Latino; 60 Asian, non-Hispanic/Latino; 84 Hispanic/Latino; 1 Native Hawaiian or other Pacific Islander, non-Hispanic/Latino; 24 Two or more races, non-Hispanic/Latino), 241 international. Average age 26. 5,450 applicants, 29% accepted, 233 enrolled. *Faculty:* 63 full-time (28 women), 138 part-time/adjunct (45 women). Expenses: Contact institution. *Financial support:* In 2017–18, 650 students received support. Career-related internships or fieldwork, Federal Work-Study, institutionally sponsored loans, scholarships/grants, and resident assistantships available. Financial award application deadline: 3/1; financial award applicants required to submit FAFSA. In 2017, 236 master's, 216 doctorates awarded. *Program availability:* 100% online, blended/hybrid learning. Offers law (LL M, JD). MD/JD offered jointly with the School of Medicine. *Application deadline:* For fall admission, 4/1 for domestic and international students. Applications are processed on a rolling basis. *Application fee:* $85. Electronic applications accepted. *Application Contact:* Alissa Leonard, Director of Admissions and Financial Aid, 617-353-3100, Fax: 617-353-0578, E-mail: bulawadm@bu.edu. *Dean*, Maureen A. O'Rourke, 617-353-3112, Fax: 617-358-4706, E-mail: lawdean@bu.edu.

School of Medicine Students: 1,535 full-time (873 women), 117 part-time (47 women); includes 514 minority (59 Black or African American, non-Hispanic/Latino; 2 American Indian or Alaska Native, non-Hispanic/Latino; 294 Asian, non-Hispanic/Latino; 117 Hispanic/Latino; 1 Native Hawaiian or other Pacific Islander, non-Hispanic/Latino; 41 Two or more races, non-Hispanic/Latino), 141 international. Average age 25. Expenses: Contact institution. *Financial support:* In 2017–18, 388 students received support. Fellowships, teaching assistantships, career-related internships or fieldwork, Federal Work-Study, institutionally sponsored loans, and scholarships/grants available. Support available to part-time students. Financial award application deadline: 2/15; financial award applicants required to submit CSS PROFILE or FAFSA. In 2017, 367 master's, 213 doctorates awarded. *Program availability:* Part-time, evening/weekend. Offers medicine (MA, MS, MD, PhD). *Application Contact:* Dr. Kristen Goodell, Associate Dean/Director of Admissions, 617-414-4465, E-mail: kgoodell@bu.edu. *Dean*, Dr. Karen H. Antman, 617-638-5300.

Division of Graduate Medical Sciences Students: 861 full-time (520 women), 92 part-time (40 women); includes 310 minority (42 Black or African American, non-Hispanic/Latino; 2 American Indian or Alaska Native, non-Hispanic/Latino; 162 Asian, non-Hispanic/Latino; 75 Hispanic/Latino; 29 Two or more races, non-Hispanic/Latino), 98 international. Average age 25. Expenses: Contact institution. *Financial support:* Fellowships, research assistantships, teaching assistantships, Federal Work-Study, scholarships/grants, and traineeships available. Financial award applicants required to submit FAFSA. In 2017, 367 master's, 54 doctorates awarded. *Program availability:* Part-time. Offers anatomy and neurobiology (MA, PhD); behavioral neuroscience (PhD); biochemistry (MA, PhD); bioimaging (MS); biomedical forensic sciences (MS); biomedical sciences (PhD); cell and molecular biology (PhD); clinical research (MA); forensic anthropology (MS); genetic counseling (MS); genetics and genomics (PhD); health sciences education (MS); healthcare emergency management (MS); immunology (PhD); medical anthropology and cross cultural practice (MS); medical sciences (MA, MS, PhD); mental health counseling and behavioral medicine (MA); microbiology (PhD); molecular and translational medicine (PhD); neuroscience (PhD); nutrition and metabolism (MS, PhD); oral biology (PhD); oral health sciences (MS); pathology and laboratory medicine (MS, PhD); pharmacology and experimental therapeutics (PhD); physician assistant (MS); physiology and biophysics (MA, PhD). *Application deadline:* For fall admission, 1/31 for domestic and international students; for spring admission, 10/15 for domestic and international students. *Application fee:* $95. Electronic applications accepted. *Application Contact:* GMS Admissions Office, 617-638-5255, Fax: 617-638-5740, E-mail: askgms@bu.edu. *Associate Provost*, Dr. Linda Hyman, 617-638-5255, Fax: 617-638-5740.

School of Public Health Students: 688 full-time (560 women), 318 part-time (271 women); includes 296 minority (66 Black or African American, non-Hispanic/Latino; 2 American Indian or Alaska Native, non-Hispanic/Latino; 124 Asian, non-Hispanic/Latino; 78 Hispanic/Latino; 1 Native Hawaiian or other Pacific Islander, non-Hispanic/Latino; 25 Two or more races, non-Hispanic/Latino), 125 international. Average age 26. 2,594 applicants, 43% accepted, 396 enrolled. *Faculty:* 153 full-time, 271 part-time/adjunct. Expenses: Contact institution. *Financial support:* In 2017–18, 421 students received support. Fellowships, teaching assistantships, career-related internships or fieldwork, Federal Work-Study, institutionally sponsored loans, scholarships/grants, traineeships, and tuition waivers (partial) available. Support available to part-time students. Financial award application deadline: 5/31; financial award applicants required to submit FAFSA. In 2017, 489 master's, 22 doctorates awarded. *Program availability:* Part-time, evening/weekend. Offers biostatistics (MA, MPH, PhD); community health sciences (MPH, Dr PH); environmental health (MPH, MS, PhD); epidemiology (MPH, MS, PhD); global health (MPH, Dr PH); health law, policy and management (MPH); health services and systems research (MS); health services research (PhD); public health (MA, MPH, MS, Dr PH, PhD). *Application deadline:* For fall admission, 1/1 priority date for domestic and international students; for spring admission, 10/1 priority date for domestic and international students. Applications are processed on a rolling basis. *Application fee:* $120. Electronic applications accepted. *Application Contact:* LePhan Quan, Associate Director of Admissions, 617-638-4640, Fax: 617-638-5299, E-mail: asksph@bu.edu. *Dean*, Dr. Sandro Galea, 617-638-4640, Fax: 617-638-5299, E-mail: asksph@bu.edu.

School of Social Work Students: 197 full-time (178 women), 587 part-time (528 women); includes 229 minority (73 Black or African American, non-Hispanic/Latino; 2 American Indian or Alaska Native, non-Hispanic/Latino; 26 Asian, non-Hispanic/Latino; 111 Hispanic/Latino; 2 Native Hawaiian or other Pacific Islander, non-Hispanic/Latino; 15 Two or more races, non-Hispanic/Latino), 7 international. Average age 30. 988 applicants, 75% accepted, 254 enrolled. *Faculty:* 29 full-time (18 women), 39 part-time/adjunct (31 women). Expenses: Contact institution. *Financial support:* In 2017–18, 165 students received support. Career-related internships or fieldwork, Federal Work-Study, scholarships/grants, and stipends available. Support available to part-time students. Financial award application deadline: 3/1; financial award applicants required to submit FAFSA. In 2017, 204 master's awarded. *Program availability:* Part-time, evening/weekend, 100% online. Offers social work (MSW, PhD). *Application deadline:* For fall admission, 2/15 for domestic students, 1/15 for international students. *Application fee:* $95. Electronic applications accepted. *Application Contact:* Julie Billings, Admissions and Financial Aid Coordinator, 617-353-3750, Fax: 617-353-5612, E-mail: busswad@bu.edu. *Dean*, Dr. Jorge Delva, 617-353-3760, Fax: 617-353-5612.

School of Theology Students: 256 full-time (135 women), 87 part-time (40 women); includes 82 minority (38 Black or African American, non-Hispanic/Latino; 10 Asian, non-Hispanic/Latino; 23 Hispanic/Latino; 1 Native Hawaiian or other Pacific Islander, non-Hispanic/Latino; 10 Two or more races, non-Hispanic/Latino), 66 international. Average age 34. 334 applicants, 69% accepted, 106 enrolled. *Faculty:* 39 full-time (17 women), 11 part-time/adjunct (5 women). Expenses: Contact institution. *Financial support:* In 2017–18, 236 students received support, including 102 fellowships with full tuition reimbursements available (averaging $7,500 per year), 11 research assistantships with full tuition reimbursements available (averaging $22,000 per year), 12 teaching assistantships with full tuition reimbursements available (averaging $22,000 per year); career-related internships or fieldwork, Federal Work-Study, scholarships/grants, and health care benefits also available. Support available to part-time students. Financial award application deadline: 7/15. In 2017, 62 master's, 9 doctorates awarded. *Program availability:* Part-time, blended/hybrid learning. Offers chaplaincy (M Div); choral conducting (MSM); church and the arts (M Div); community and global engagement (M Div); constructive theology and ethics (PhD); history and hermeneutics (PhD); organ (MSM); pastoral ministry (M Div); practical theology (PhD); religion and the academy (M Div); transformational leadership (D Min). PhD in mission studies offered in collaboration with Gordon-Conwell Theological Seminary. *Application deadline:* For fall admission, 1/15 priority date for domestic and international students; for spring admission, 10/15 priority date for domestic and international students. Applications are processed on a rolling basis. *Application fee:* $95. Electronic applications accepted. *Application Contact:* Rev. Dr. Anastasia Kidd, Director of Enrollment, 617-353-3036, Fax: 617-358-0140, E-mail: sthadmis@bu.edu. *Dean*, Rev. Dr. Mary Elizabeth Moore, 617-353-3050, Fax: 617-353-3061, E-mail: memoore@bu.edu.

Wheelock College of Education and Human Development Students: 234 full-time (183 women), 444 part-time (331 women); includes 168 minority (38 Black or African American, non-Hispanic/Latino; 46 Asian, non-Hispanic/Latino; 63 Hispanic/Latino; 1 Native Hawaiian or other Pacific Islander, non-Hispanic/Latino; 20 Two or more races, non-Hispanic/Latino), 53 international. Average age 27. 1,303 applicants, 65% accepted, 346 enrolled. Expenses: Contact institution. *Financial support:* Fellowships with full tuition reimbursements, research assistantships, teaching assistantships with partial tuition reimbursements, career-related internships or fieldwork, Federal Work-Study, and scholarships/grants available. Support available to part-time students. Financial award applicants required to submit FAFSA. In 2017, 286 master's, 26 doctorates, 6 other advanced degrees awarded. *Program availability:* Part-time, evening/weekend. Offers education and human development (Ed M, MAT, Ed D, PhD, CAGS). *Application deadline:* For fall admission, 1/15 priority date for domestic and international students; for spring admission, 9/15 priority date for domestic and international students. Applications are processed on a rolling basis. *Application fee:* $95. Electronic applications accepted. *Application Contact:* Katharine Nelson, Director of Graduate Student Services, 617-353-4237, E-mail: sedgrad@bu.edu. *Interim Dean*, Dr. David J. Chard, 617-353-3213.

BOWIE STATE UNIVERSITY, Bowie, MD 20715-9465

General Information State-supported, coed, comprehensive institution. CGS member. *Graduate housing:* Room and/or apartments available on a first-come, first-served basis to single students; on-campus housing not available to married students. Housing application deadline: 8/1.

GRADUATE UNITS

Graduate Programs *Program availability:* Part-time, evening/weekend. Offers administration of nursing services (MS); applied and computational mathematics (MS); business administration (MBA); computer science (MS, App Sc D); counseling psychology (MA); educational leadership (Ed D); elementary and secondary school administration (M Ed); elementary education (M Ed); English (MA); family nurse practitioner (MS); guidance and counseling (M Ed); human resource development (MA); information systems analyst (Certificate); management information systems (MS); mental health counseling (MA); nursing education (MS); organizational communication (MA, Certificate); public administration (MPA); reading education (M Ed); school administration and supervision (M Ed); secondary education (M Ed); special education (M Ed); teaching (MAT). Electronic applications accepted.

BOWLING GREEN STATE UNIVERSITY, Bowling Green, OH 43403

General Information State-supported, coed, university. CGS member. *Graduate housing:* Rooms and/or apartments available to single and married students. *Research affiliation:* Spectra Group, Inc. (photoscience).

GRADUATE UNITS

Graduate College *Program availability:* Part-time, evening/weekend. Electronic applications accepted.

College of Arts and Sciences *Program availability:* Part-time. Offers 2-D studio art (MA, MFA); 3-D studio art (MA, MFA); American culture studies (MA, PhD); applied philosophy (PhD); art education (MA); art history (MA); arts and sciences (MA, MAT, MFA, MPA, MS, PhD); biological sciences (MS, PhD); chemistry (MS, PhD); clinical psychology (MA, PhD); computer art (MA); computer science (MS); creative writing (MFA); demography and population studies (MA); design (MFA); developmental psychology (MA, PhD); digital arts (MFA); English (MA, PhD); experimental psychology (MA, PhD); fiction (MFA); French (MA); geology (MS); geophysics (MS); German (MA); graphics (MFA); history (MA, MAT, PhD); industrial/organizational psychology (MA, PhD); institutional theory and history (PhD); literature (MA); mathematics (MA, MAT, PhD); media and communication (MA, PhD); philosophy (MA); photochemical sciences (PhD); physics (MAT, MS); poetry (MFA); popular culture (MA); public administration (MPA); public history (MA); quantitative psychology (MA, PhD); rhetoric and writing (PhD); scientific and technical communication (MA); social psychology (MA); sociology (PhD); Spanish (MA); statistics (PhD); strategic communication (MA); theatre and film (MA, PhD). Electronic applications accepted.

College of Business *Program availability:* Part-time, evening/weekend. Offers accountancy (M Acc); applied statistics (MS); business (M Acc, MA, MBA, MOD, MS); business administration (MBA); financial economics (MA); organization development (MOD). Electronic applications accepted.

College of Education and Human Development *Program availability:* Part-time, evening/weekend. Offers assistive technology (M Ed); autism spectrum disorders (M Ed); classroom technology (M Ed); clinical mental health counseling (M Ed, MA); college student personnel (MA); cross-cultural and international education (MA); curriculum and teaching (M Ed); developmental kinesiology (M Ed); education and human development (M Ed, MA, Ed D, PhD, Ed S); educational administration and supervision (M Ed, Ed D, Ed S); educational leadership (M Ed, Ed S); general special education (M Ed); higher education administration (PhD); intervention specialist: mild/moderate disabilities (M Ed); intervention specialist: moderate/intensive disabilities (M Ed); leadership studies (Ed D); reading (M Ed, Ed S); recreation and leisure (M Ed); school counseling (M Ed); secondary transition/transition-to-work (M Ed); special education (M Ed); sport administration (M Ed); workforce education and development (M Ed). Electronic applications accepted.

College of Health and Human Services *Program availability:* Part-time, evening/weekend. Offers communication disorders (PhD); criminal justice (MSCJ); health and human services (MPH, MS, MSCJ, PhD); public health (MPH); speech-language pathology (MS). Electronic applications accepted.

College of Musical Arts *Program availability:* Part-time. Offers composition (MM); contemporary music (DMA); ethnomusicology (MM); music education (MM); music history (MM); music theory (MM); performance (MM). Electronic applications accepted.

College of Technology *Program availability:* Part-time. Offers career and technology education (M Ed); technology (M Ed). Electronic applications accepted.

Interdisciplinary Studies *Program availability:* Part-time. Offers interdisciplinary studies (M Ed, MA, MS, PhD). Electronic applications accepted.

BRADLEY UNIVERSITY, Peoria, IL 61625-0002

General Information Independent, coed, comprehensive institution. CGS member. *Graduate housing:* On-campus housing not available. *Research affiliation:* Illinois Manufacturing Extension Center, Northern Research Laboratory, Peoria School of Medicine, Caterpillar, Inc., Ford Motor Credit/Visteon.

GRADUATE UNITS

The Graduate School *Program availability:* Part-time, evening/weekend. Electronic applications accepted.

Caterpillar College of Engineering and Technology *Program availability:* Part-time, evening/weekend. Offers civil engineering and construction (MSCE); electrical and computer engineering (MSEE); engineering and technology (MS, MSCE, MSEE, MSME); industrial engineering (MS); manufacturing engineering (MS); mechanical engineering (MSME). Electronic applications accepted.

College of Education and Health Sciences *Program availability:* Part-time, evening/weekend. Offers counseling (MA); curriculum and instruction (MA); dietetic internship (MS); education and health sciences (MA, MS, MSN, DNP, DPT, Certificate); family nurse practitioner (MSN, DNP, Certificate); leadership (DNP); leadership in educational administration (MA); nonprofit leadership (MA); nursing administration (MSN); nursing education (MSN, Certificate); physical therapy (DPT). Electronic applications accepted.

College of Liberal Arts and Sciences *Program availability:* Part-time, evening/weekend. Offers biochemistry (MS); biology (MS); chemistry (MS); computer information systems (MS); computer science (MS); English (MA); liberal arts and sciences (MA, MS). Electronic applications accepted.

Foster College of Business *Program availability:* Part-time, evening/weekend. Offers accounting (MSA); business (MBA, MSA); business administration (MBA). Electronic applications accepted.

Slane College of Communications and Fine Arts *Program availability:* Part-time, evening/weekend. Offers ceramics (MA, MFA); communications and fine arts (MA, MFA); drawing (MA, MFA); graphic design (MA, MFA); painting (MA, MFA); photography (MA, MFA); printmaking (MA, MFA); sculpture (MA, MFA). Electronic applications accepted.

BRANDEIS UNIVERSITY, Waltham, MA 02454-9110

General Information Independent, coed, university. CGS member. *Enrollment:* 5,722 graduate, professional, and undergraduate students; 1,494 full-time matriculated graduate/professional students (841 women), 487 part-time matriculated graduate/professional students (286 women). *Enrollment by degree level:* 1,367 master's, 580 doctoral, 34 other advanced degrees. *Graduate faculty:* 361 full-time (156 women), 208 part-time/adjunct (88 women). *Tuition:* Full-time $48,720. *Required fees:* $88. Tuition and fees vary according to course load, degree level, program and student level. *Graduate housing:* On-campus housing not available. *Student services:* Campus employment opportunities, career counseling, exercise/wellness program, free psychological counseling, grant writing training, international student services, low-cost health insurance, multicultural affairs office, services for students with disabilities, teacher training, writing training. *Library facilities:* Goldfarb Library plus 1 other. *Collection:* Books: 993,533 (physical), 1.1 million (digital/electronic); Serial titles: 10,606 (physical), 38,001 (digital/electronic); Databases: 310. Students can reserve study rooms.

Computer facilities: Computer purchase and lease plans are available. 130 computers available on campus for general student use. A campuswide network can be accessed from student residence rooms and from off campus. Online class registration, educational software are available.
Website: http://www.brandeis.edu/

General Application Contact: Emily Goldberg, Department Coordinator, 781-736-3410, E-mail: gradschool@brandeis.edu.

GRADUATE UNITS

Graduate School of Arts and Sciences Students: 761 full-time (388 women), 70 part-time (53 women); includes 123 minority (21 Black or African American, non-Hispanic/Latino; 2 American Indian or Alaska Native, non-Hispanic/Latino; 38 Asian, non-Hispanic/Latino; 46 Hispanic/Latino; 16 Two or more races, non-Hispanic/Latino), 237 international. Average age 28. 2,549 applicants, 32% accepted, 286 enrolled. *Faculty:* 306 full-time (132 women), 125 part-time/adjunct (62 women). Expenses: Contact institution. *Financial support:* In 2017–18, 780 students received support, including 298 fellowships with tuition reimbursements available, 108 research assistantships with tuition reimbursements available, 162 teaching assistantships with partial tuition reimbursements available; Federal Work-Study, scholarships/grants, health care benefits, tuition waivers (full and partial), and unspecified assistantships also available. Support available to part-time students. Financial award application deadline: 4/15; financial award applicants required to submit FAFSA. In 2017, 227 master's, 66 doctorates, 21 other advanced degrees awarded. *Program availability:* Part-time, blended/hybrid learning. Offers acting (MFA); ancient Greek and Roman studies (classical studies) (MA); anthropology/women's, gender, and sexuality studies (MA); arts and sciences (Ed M, MA, MAT, MFA, MS, PSM, PhD, AGC, Postbaccalaureate Certificate); biochemistry and biophysics (MS, PhD); biotechnology (PSM); brain, body and behavior (PhD); cognitive neuroscience (PhD); comparative humanities (MA); composition and theory (MA, MFA, PhD); computational linguistics (MS); computer science (MA, PhD); English (MA, PhD); English/women's, gender, and sexuality studies (MA); general psychology (MA); genetic counseling (MS); genetics (PhD); global studies (MA); history (MA, PhD); inorganic chemistry (MA, MS, PhD); Jewish day schools (MAT); Jewish professional leadershipmathematics (MA, PhD); Mesoamerican archaeology (MA, PhD); microbiology (PhD); molecular and cell biology (MS, PhD); molecular biology (PhD); musicology (MA, MFA, PhD); Near Eastern and Judaic studies (MA, PhD); near Eastern and Judaic studies /women's, gender, and sexuality studies (MA); near Eastern and Judaic studies/conflict resolution and coexistence (MA); near Eastern and Judaic studies/Jewish professional leadership (MA); near Eastern and Judaic studies/women's, gender, and sexuality studies (MA); neurobiology (PhD); neuroscience (MS, PhD); organic chemistry (MA, MS, PhD); philosophy (MA); physical chemistry (MS, PhD); physics (MS, PhD); politics (MA, PhD); premedical studies (Postbaccalaureate Certificate); public elementary education (MAT); public policy/women's, gender, and sexuality studies (MA); quantitative biology (PhD); secondary education (MAT); social policy and sociology (PhD); social/developmental psychology (PhD); sociocultural anthropology (MA, PhD); sociology (PhD); sociology/women's, gender, and sexuality studies (MA); studio art (Postbaccalaureate Certificate); sustainable international development/women's, gender, and sexuality studies (MA); teacher leadership (Ed M, AGC); teaching Chinese language and culture (MA); teaching of Hebrew (MAT); women's, gender, and sexuality studies (MA). Offered jointly with The Heller School of Social Policy and Management. *Application deadline:* For fall admission, 1/15 priority date for domestic and international students; for spring admission, 11/1 for domestic and international students. Applications are processed on a rolling basis. *Application fee:* $75. Electronic applications accepted. *Application Contact:* Emily Goldberg, Department Coordinator, 781-736-3410, Fax: 781-736-3412, E-mail: gradschool@brandeis.edu. *Dean*, Dr. Eric Chasalow, 781-736-3410, Fax: 781-736-3412, E-mail: gradschool@brandeis.edu.

The Heller School for Social Policy and Management *Program availability:* Part-time. Offers aging (MPP); assets and inequalities (PhD); behavioral health (MPP); child, youth, and family management (MBA); children, youth and families (MPP, PhD); coexistence and conflict (MA); general social policy (MPP); global health and development (PhD); health (MPP); health and behavioral health (PhD); health care management (MBA); international development (MA); international health policy and management (MS); poverty alleviation and development (MPP); social impact management (MBA); social policy and management (MBA); sustainable development (MBA). Electronic applications accepted.

International Business School (IBS) Students: 328 full-time (187 women), 72 part-time (52 women); includes 14 minority (1 Black or African American, non-Hispanic/Latino; 2 American Indian or Alaska Native, non-Hispanic/Latino; 9 Asian, non-Hispanic/Latino; 2 Hispanic/Latino), 360 international. 1,652 applicants, 39% accepted, 218 enrolled. *Faculty:* 40 full-time (16 women), 31 part-time/adjunct (7 women). Expenses: Contact institution. *Financial support:* In 2017–18, 188 students received support. Institutionally sponsored loans, health care benefits, and scholarships (averaging $17,578 annually) available. Financial award application deadline: 4/15. In 2017, 171 master's, 3 doctorates awarded. Offers advanced macroeconomics (PhD); applied economic analysis (MA); applied microeconomics (PhD); asset management (MSF); corporate finance (MSF); data analytics (MBA); finance (MBA); international business (MA, MBA, MSF, PhD); marketing (MBA); real estate (MBA); risk management (MSF). *Application deadline:* For fall admission, 11/1 for domestic and international students; for winter admission, 1/15 for domestic and international students; for spring admission, 3/15 for domestic students, 3/15 priority date for international students; for summer admission, 4/15 for domestic and international students. *Application fee:* $100. Electronic applications accepted. *Application Contact:* Kelly Sugrue, Assistant Dean of Admissions, 781-736-2252, Fax: 781-736-2263, E-mail: globaladmissions@brandeis.edu. *Interim Dean*, Peter Petri, 781-736-2256.

Rabb School of Continuing Studies, Division of Graduate Professional Studies Students: 511 part-time (243 women); includes 138 minority (58 Black or African American, non-Hispanic/Latino; 61 Asian, non-Hispanic/Latino; 13 Hispanic/Latino; 6 Two or more races, non-Hispanic/Latino). Average age 37. 73 applicants, 97% accepted, 55 enrolled. *Faculty:* 55 part-time/adjunct (18 women). Expenses: Contact institution. *Financial support:* Applicants required to submit FAFSA. In 2017, 114 master's awarded. *Program availability:* Part-time-only. Offers bioinformatics (MS); digital innovation for finance technology (MS); digital marketing and design (MS); health and medical informatics (MS); information security leadership (MS); instructional design and technology (MS); learning analytics (Graduate Certificate); project and program management (MS); robotic software engineering (MS); software engineering (MSE); strategic analytics (MS); technology management (MS); user-centered design (MS). *Application deadline:* For fall admission, 6/20 priority date for domestic and international students; for winter admission, 9/12 priority date for domestic and international students;

for spring admission, 12/19 priority date for domestic and international students; for summer admission, 3/13 priority date for domestic and international students. Applications are processed on a rolling basis. *Application fee:* $75. Electronic applications accepted. *Application Contact:* Frances Stearns, Director of Student and Faculty Operations, 781-736-8785, E-mail: fstearns@brandeis.edu. *Executive Director,* Anne M. Marando, 781-736-8782, E-mail: marando@brandeis.edu.

BRANDMAN UNIVERSITY, Irvine, CA 92618

General Information Independent, coed, comprehensive institution. *Enrollment:* 7,812 graduate, professional, and undergraduate students; 1,711 full-time matriculated graduate/professional students (1,264 women), 2,424 part-time matriculated graduate/professional students (1,637 women). *Enrollment by degree level:* 3,719 master's, 379 doctoral, 37 other advanced degrees. *Graduate faculty:* 48 full-time (29 women), 454 part-time/adjunct (275 women). *Tuition:* Part-time $640 per credit hour. Tuition and fees vary according to degree level and program. *Student services:* Career counseling, services for students with disabilities, writing training. *Library facilities:* Leatherby Library plus 1 other. *Collection:* Weekly public service hours: 65; study areas open 24 hours, 5–7 days a week; students can reserve study rooms.

Computer facilities: 837 computers available on campus for general student use. A campuswide network can be accessed. Online class registration is available.
Website: http://www.brandman.edu/

GRADUATE UNITS

Marybelle and S. Paul Musco School of Nursing and Health Professions Expenses: Contact institution. Offers nursing (DNP). *Application Contact:* Dr. Tyke Hanisch, Dean, 949-341-9815. *Dean,* Dr. Tyke Hanisch, 949-341-9815.

School of Arts and Sciences Expenses: Contact institution. Offers psychology (MA); social work (MSW). *Application Contact:* Dr. Jeremy Korr, Dean, 949-341-9831. *Dean,* Dr. Jeremy Korr, 949-341-9831.

School of Business and Professional Studies Expenses: Contact institution. Offers accounting (MBA); business administration (MBA); business intelligence and data analytics (MBA); e-business strategic management (MBA); entrepreneurship (MBA); finance (MBA); health administration (MBA); human resources (MBA, MS); international business (MBA); marketing (MBA); organizational leadership (MA, MBA, MPA); public administration (MPA). *Application Contact:* Dr. Glenn Worthington, Dean, 253-861-1024, E-mail: gworthin@brandman.edu. *Dean,* Dr. Glenn Worthington, 253-861-1024, E-mail: gworthin@brandman.edu.

School of Education Expenses: Contact institution. Offers curriculum and instruction (MAE); educational administration (MAE); educational leadership (MAE); educational leadership and administration (MA); elementary education (MAT); instructional technology: teaching the 21st century learner (MAE); leadership in early childhood education (MAE); organizational leadership (Ed D); school counseling (MA); secondary education (MAT); special education (MA); teaching and learning (MAE). *Application Contact:* Dr. Christine G. Zeppos, Dean, 949-341-9948, E-mail: zeppos@brandman.edu. *Dean,* Dr. Christine G. Zeppos, 949-341-9948, E-mail: zeppos@brandman.edu.

BRANDON UNIVERSITY, Brandon, MB R7A 6A9, Canada

General Information Province-supported, coed, comprehensive institution. *Graduate housing:* Room and/or apartments available on a first-come, first-served basis to single students; on-campus housing not available to married students.

GRADUATE UNITS

Department of Rural Development Offers rural development (MRD, Diploma). Electronic applications accepted.

Faculty of Education Offers curriculum and instruction (M Ed, Diploma); educational administration (M Ed, Diploma); guidance and counseling (M Ed, Diploma); special education (M Ed, Diploma).

School of Music *Program availability:* Part-time. Offers composition (M Mus); music education (M Mus); performance and literature (M Mus). Electronic applications accepted.

BRENAU UNIVERSITY, Gainesville, GA 30501

General Information Independent, coed, primarily women, comprehensive institution. *Graduate housing:* Room and/or apartments available on a first-come, first-served basis to single students; on-campus housing not available to married students.

GRADUATE UNITS

Sydney O. Smith Graduate School *Program availability:* Part-time, evening/weekend, online learning. Electronic applications accepted.

College of Business and Mass Communication *Program availability:* Part-time, evening/weekend, online learning. Offers accounting (MBA); business administration (MBA); healthcare management (MBA); organizational leadership (MS); project management (MBA). Electronic applications accepted.

College of Education *Program availability:* Part-time, evening/weekend, online learning. Offers early childhood (Ed S); early childhood education (M Ed, MAT); middle grades (Ed S); middle grades education (M Ed, MAT); secondary education (MAT); special education (M Ed, MAT). Electronic applications accepted.

College of Fine Arts and Humanities *Program availability:* Part-time. Offers interior design (MID). Electronic applications accepted.

College of Health Sciences *Program availability:* Part-time, evening/weekend. Offers family nurse practitioner (MSN); nurse educator (MSN); nursing management (MSN); occupational therapy (MS); psychology (MS). Electronic applications accepted.

BRESCIA UNIVERSITY, Owensboro, KY 42301-3023

General Information Independent-religious, coed, comprehensive institution. *Graduate housing:* Room and/or apartments available on a first-come, first-served basis to single students; on-campus housing not available to married students.

GRADUATE UNITS

Program in Business Administration *Program availability:* Part-time, evening/weekend. Offers business administration (MBA). Electronic applications accepted.

Program in Management *Program availability:* Part-time, evening/weekend. Offers management (MSM).

Program in Social Work *Program availability:* Online learning. Offers social work (MSW). Electronic applications accepted.

Program in Teacher Leadership *Program availability:* Part-time, evening/weekend. Offers teacher leadership (MSTL). Electronic applications accepted.

BRIAR CLIFF UNIVERSITY, Sioux City, IA 51104-0100

General Information Independent-religious, coed, comprehensive institution. *Graduate housing:* Room and/or apartments available on a first-come, first-served basis to single students; on-campus housing not available to married students. Housing application deadline: 6/1.

GRADUATE UNITS

Graduate Nursing Programs *Program availability:* Part-time, online only, 100% online, blended/hybrid learning. Offers nursing (MSN, DNP, Post-Master's Certificate). Electronic applications accepted.

BRIDGEWATER COLLEGE, Bridgewater, VA 22812-1599

General Information Independent-religious, coed, comprehensive institution.

GRADUATE UNITS

Program in Athletic Training Offers athletic training (MS). Electronic applications accepted.

BRIDGEWATER STATE UNIVERSITY, Bridgewater, MA 02325

General Information State-supported, coed, comprehensive institution. CGS member. *Graduate housing:* On-campus housing not available.

GRADUATE UNITS

College of Graduate Studies *Program availability:* Part-time, evening/weekend.

Bartlett College of Science and Mathematics Offers biology (MAT); computer science (MS); mathematics (MAT); physics (MAT); science and mathematics (MAT, MS).

College of Education and Allied Studies *Program availability:* Part-time, evening/weekend. Offers counseling (M Ed, CAGS); early childhood education (M Ed); education and allied studies (M Ed, MAT, MS, CAGS); educational leadership (M Ed, CAGS); elementary education (M Ed); health promotion (M Ed); instructional technology (M Ed); physical education (MS); reading (M Ed, CAGS); secondary education (MAT); special education (M Ed); speech/language pathology (MS).

College of Humanities and Social Sciences *Program availability:* Part-time, evening/weekend. Offers art (MAT); criminal justice (MS); English (MA, MAT); history (MAT); humanities and social sciences (MA, MAT, MPA, MS, MSW); physical sciences (MAT); psychology (MA); public administration (MPA); social work (MSW).

Ricciardi College of Business *Program availability:* Part-time, evening/weekend. Offers accounting and finance (MSM); business (MSM); management (MSM).

BRIERCREST SEMINARY, Caronport, SK S0H 0S0, Canada

General Information Independent-religious, coed, graduate-only institution. *Graduate housing:* Rooms and/or apartments guaranteed to single students and available on a first-come, first-served basis to married students.

GRADUATE UNITS

Graduate Programs *Program availability:* Part-time. Offers Biblical studies (M Div); leadership (MA); leadership and management (M Div); marriage and family counseling (MA); missions (MA); New Testament (MATS); Old Testament (MATS); organizational leadership (MA); pastoral counseling (M Div, MA); pastoral ministry (M Div); theological studies (M Div); theology (MATS); worship (M Div, MA); youth and family ministry (M Div, MA).

BRIGHAM YOUNG UNIVERSITY, Provo, UT 84602-1001

General Information Independent-religious, coed, university. CGS member. *Enrollment:* 34,334 graduate, professional, and undergraduate students; 2,002 full-time matriculated graduate/professional students (755 women), 1,137 part-time matriculated graduate/professional students (429 women). *Enrollment by degree level:* 2,166 master's, 925 doctoral, 48 other advanced degrees. *Graduate faculty:* 1,027 full-time (174 women), 5 part-time/adjunct (0 women). *Tuition:* Full-time $6880; part-time $405 per credit hour. Tuition and fees vary according to course load, program and student's religious affiliation. *Graduate housing:* Rooms and/or apartments available on a first-come, first-served basis to single and married students. Typical cost: $3435 per year ($7530 including board) for single students; $5680 per year ($12,392 including board) for married students. Room and board charges vary according to board plan, campus/location and housing facility selected. Housing application deadline: 2/1. *Student services:* Campus employment opportunities, campus safety program, career counseling, exercise/wellness program, free psychological counseling, grant writing training, international student services, low-cost health insurance, multicultural affairs office, services for students with disabilities, teacher training, writing training. *Library facilities:* Harold B. Lee Library plus 2 others.

Computer facilities: Computer purchase and lease plans are available. A campuswide network can be accessed from student residence rooms and from off campus. Online class registration is available.
Website: http://www.byu.edu/

General Application Contact: Graduate Studies, 801-422-4091, Fax: 801-422-0270, E-mail: gradstudies@byu.edu.

GRADUATE UNITS

Graduate Studies Students: 2,002 full-time (755 women), 1,137 part-time (429 women); includes 358 minority (16 Black or African American, non-Hispanic/Latino; 9 American Indian or Alaska Native, non-Hispanic/Latino; 57 Asian, non-Hispanic/Latino; 162 Hispanic/Latino; 14 Native Hawaiian or other Pacific Islander, non-Hispanic/Latino; 100 Two or more races, non-Hispanic/Latino), 309 international. Average age 30. 2,194 applicants, 50% accepted, 1070 enrolled. *Faculty:* 1,027 full-time (174 women), 5 part-time/adjunct (0 women). Expenses: Contact institution. *Financial support:* Fellowships, research assistantships, teaching assistantships, career-related internships or fieldwork, institutionally sponsored loans, scholarships/grants, health care benefits, and tuition waivers (full and partial) available. Support available to part-time students. Financial award applicants required to submit FAFSA. In 2017, 1,042 master's, 219 doctorates, 12 other advanced degrees awarded. *Program availability:* Part-time, evening/weekend. *Application deadline:* For fall admission, 12/1 priority date for domestic and international students; for winter admission, 6/30 priority date for domestic and international students; for spring admission, 1/15 priority date for domestic and international students; for summer admission, 2/1 for domestic and international students. Applications are processed on a rolling basis. *Application fee:* $50. Electronic applications accepted. *Application Contact:* Logan Gillette, Director of Graduate Admissions and Recruitment, 801-422-7308, E-mail: logangillette@byu.edu. *Dean,* Dr. Wynn Stirling, 801-422-4465, Fax: 801-422-0089, E-mail: gradstudies@byu.edu.

BYU Marriott School of Business Students: 408 full-time (115 women), 264 part-time (82 women); includes 59 minority (6 Black or African American, non-Hispanic/Latino; 3 American Indian or Alaska Native, non-Hispanic/Latino; 16 Asian, non-Hispanic/Latino; 21 Hispanic/Latino; 13 Native Hawaiian or other Pacific Islander, non-Hispanic/Latino), 84 international. Average age 33. 610 applicants, 61% accepted,

300 enrolled. *Faculty:* 134 full-time (15 women), 65 part-time/adjunct (16 women). Expenses: Contact institution. *Financial support:* Research assistantships, teaching assistantships, career-related internships or fieldwork, institutionally sponsored loans, and scholarships/grants available. Financial award applicants required to submit FAFSA. In 2017, 315 master's awarded. *Program availability:* Part-time, evening/weekend. Offers business (EMBA, MBA, MPA); business administration (MBA); entrepreneurship (MBA); finance (MBA); global supply chain management (MBA); healthcare (MPA); local government (MPA); marketing (MBA); nonprofit management (MPA); public administration (MPA); state and federal government (MPA); strategic human resources (MBA). *Application fee:* $50. Electronic applications accepted. *Dean*, Dr. Lee Perry, 801-422-4121, Fax: 801-422-4501.

College of Family, Home, and Social Sciences Students: 217 full-time (151 women); includes 29 minority (5 Black or African American, non-Hispanic/Latino; 2 American Indian or Alaska Native, non-Hispanic/Latino; 6 Asian, non-Hispanic/Latino; 11 Hispanic/Latino; 3 Native Hawaiian or other Pacific Islander, non-Hispanic/Latino; 2 Two or more races, non-Hispanic/Latino), 7 international. Average age 27. 296 applicants. *Faculty:* 94 full-time (22 women), 24 part-time/adjunct (12 women). Expenses: Contact institution. *Financial support:* In 2017–18, 176 students received support, including 60 fellowships with tuition reimbursements available (averaging $3,249 per year), 124 research assistantships with tuition reimbursements available (averaging $10,018 per year), 15 teaching assistantships with tuition reimbursements available (averaging $7,015 per year); career-related internships or fieldwork, institutionally sponsored loans, scholarships/grants, tuition waivers (partial), unspecified assistantships, and administrative aides, paid field practicum, AmeriCorps education awards also available. Financial award application deadline: 3/27; financial award applicants required to submit FAFSA. In 2017, 77 master's, 15 doctorates awarded. Offers anthropology (MA); clinical psychology (PhD); cognitive and behavioral neuroscience (PhD); family, home, and social sciences (MA, MS, MSW, PhD); marriage and family therapy (MS, PhD); marriage, family and human development (MS, PhD); social work (MSW); sociology (MS). *Application deadline:* For fall admission, 1/15 for domestic and international students. *Application fee:* $50. Electronic applications accepted. *Application Contact:* Adviser, 801-422-4541, Fax: 801-378-5238, E-mail: gradstudies@byu.edu. *Dean*, Dr. Benjamin M. Ogles, 801-422-2083, Fax: 801-422-2084, E-mail: ben_ogles@byu.edu.

College of Fine Arts and Communications Students: 68 full-time (44 women), 40 part-time (25 women); includes 16 minority (8 Asian, non-Hispanic/Latino; 7 Hispanic/Latino; 1 Native Hawaiian or other Pacific Islander, non-Hispanic/Latino), 4 international. Average age 31. 85 applicants, 55% accepted, 40 enrolled. *Faculty:* 100 full-time (20 women), 60 part-time/adjunct (38 women). Expenses: Contact institution. *Financial support:* In 2017–18, 87 students received support, including 73 research assistantships with full and partial tuition reimbursements available (averaging $3,051 per year), 61 teaching assistantships with full and partial tuition reimbursements available (averaging $3,126 per year); career-related internships or fieldwork, institutionally sponsored loans, scholarships/grants, tuition waivers (full and partial), unspecified assistantships, and supplementary awards also available. Support available to part-time students. Financial award applicants required to submit FAFSA. In 2017, 38 master's awarded. Offers art education (MA); composition (MM); conducting (MM); fine arts and communications (MA, MFA, MM); mass communications (MA); music education (MA, MM); performance (MM); studio arts (MFA); theatre and media arts (MA). *Application deadline:* Applications are processed on a rolling basis. *Application fee:* $50. Electronic applications accepted. *Dean*, Edward E. Adams, 801-422-8271, Fax: 801-422-0253, E-mail: francie_jenson@byu.edu.

College of Humanities Students: 158 full-time (99 women), 36 part-time (23 women); includes 36 minority (1 American Indian or Alaska Native, non-Hispanic/Latino; 8 Asian, non-Hispanic/Latino; 22 Hispanic/Latino; 1 Native Hawaiian or other Pacific Islander, non-Hispanic/Latino; 4 Two or more races, non-Hispanic/Latino), 12 international. Average age 31. 110 applicants, 72% accepted, 67 enrolled. *Faculty:* 169 full-time (37 women), 11 part-time/adjunct (7 women). Expenses: Contact institution. *Financial support:* In 2017–18, 157 students received support, including 21 research assistantships (averaging $4,566 per year), 21 teaching assistantships (averaging $4,244 per year); fellowships, career-related internships or fieldwork, institutionally sponsored loans, scholarships/grants, and student instructorships, travel money for conference presentations also available. In 2017, 59 master's awarded. Offers comparative studies (MA); creative writing (MFA); French studies (MA); humanities (MA, MFA); linguistics (MA); literature (MA); Portuguese (MA); rhetoric/composition (MA); second language teaching (MA); Spanish (MA); teaching English as a second language (MA). *Application fee:* $50. Electronic applications accepted. *Application Contact:* Adviser, 801-422-4541, Fax: 801-378-5238, E-mail: gradstudies@byu.edu. *Dean*, Scott J. Miller, 801-422-2779, Fax: 801-422-0308, E-mail: scott_miller@byu.edu.

College of Life Sciences Students: 166 full-time (91 women), 76 part-time (33 women); includes 35 minority (2 Black or African American, non-Hispanic/Latino; 2 American Indian or Alaska Native, non-Hispanic/Latino; 14 Asian, non-Hispanic/Latino; 17 Hispanic/Latino), 6 international. Average age 29. 130 applicants, 55% accepted, 59 enrolled. *Faculty:* 143 full-time (22 women), 11 part-time/adjunct (9 women). Expenses: Contact institution. *Financial support:* In 2017–18, 214 students received support, including 38 fellowships with tuition reimbursements available (averaging $10,700 per year), 181 research assistantships with tuition reimbursements available (averaging $12,578 per year), 136 teaching assistantships with tuition reimbursements available (averaging $12,310 per year); career-related internships or fieldwork, institutionally sponsored loans, scholarships/grants, health care benefits, tuition waivers (full and partial), and unspecified assistantships also available. Financial award application deadline: 2/1; financial award applicants required to submit FAFSA. In 2017, 55 master's, 10 doctorates awarded. Offers athletic training (MS); biological science education (MS); biology (MS, PhD); environmental science (MS); exercise physiology (MS, PhD); exercise sciences (MS); food science (MS); genetics and biotechnology (MS); health promotion (MS, PhD); life sciences (MPH, MS, PhD); microbiology and molecular biology (MS, PhD); neuroscience (MS, PhD); nutrition (MS); physical medicine and rehabilitation (PhD); physiology and developmental biology (MS, PhD); public health (MPH); wildlife and wildlands conservation (MS, PhD). *Application deadline:* For fall admission, 2/1 for domestic and international students; for winter admission, 2/1 for international students. *Application fee:* $50. Electronic applications accepted. *Application Contact:* Sue Pratley, Application Contact, 801-422-3963, Fax: 801-422-0050, E-mail: sue_pratley@byu.edu. *Dean*, James P. Porter, 801-422-3963, Fax: 801-422-0050, E-mail: james_porter@byu.edu.

College of Nursing Students: 29 full-time (20 women); includes 1 minority (Hispanic/Latino). Average age 33. 40 applicants, 45% accepted, 14 enrolled. *Faculty:* 17 full-time (11 women). Expenses: Contact institution. *Financial support:* In 2017–18, 27 students received support, including 1 research assistantship (averaging $12,800 per year); teaching assistantships, institutionally sponsored loans, and scholarships/grants also available. Financial award application deadline: 4/13; financial award applicants required to submit FAFSA. In 2017, 14 master's awarded. Offers family nurse practitioner (MS). *Application deadline:* For spring admission, 12/1 for domestic and international students. *Application fee:* $50. Electronic applications accepted. *Application Contact:* Cherie Top, Graduate Secretary, 801-422-4142, Fax: 801-422-0538, E-mail: cherie-top@byu.edu. *Dean*, Dr. Patricia Ravert, 801-422-1167, Fax: 801-422-0536, E-mail: patricia_ravert@byu.edu.

College of Physical and Mathematical Sciences Students: 294 full-time (62 women), 38 part-time (11 women); includes 42 minority (1 Black or African American, non-Hispanic/Latino; 25 Asian, non-Hispanic/Latino; 10 Hispanic/Latino; 3 Native Hawaiian or other Pacific Islander, non-Hispanic/Latino; 3 Two or more races, non-Hispanic/Latino), 56 international. Average age 28. 216 applicants, 66% accepted, 108 enrolled. *Faculty:* 167 full-time (15 women), 23 part-time/adjunct (7 women). Expenses: Contact institution. *Financial support:* In 2017–18, 184 students received support, including 14 fellowships with full tuition reimbursements available (averaging $21,660 per year), 162 research assistantships with tuition reimbursements available (averaging $16,778 per year), 140 teaching assistantships with tuition reimbursements available (averaging $16,191 per year); career-related internships or fieldwork, institutionally sponsored loans, scholarships/grants, health care benefits, tuition waivers (full and partial), and unspecified assistantships also available. Support available to part-time students. Financial award applicants required to submit CSS PROFILE or FAFSA. In 2017, 81 master's, 18 doctorates awarded. *Program availability:* Part-time. Offers applied statistics (MS); biochemistry (MS, PhD); chemistry (MS, PhD); computer science (MS, PhD); geological sciences (MS); mathematics (MS, PhD); mathematics education (MA); physical and mathematical sciences (MA, MS, PhD); physics (MS, PhD); physics and astronomy (PhD). *Application deadline:* For fall admission, 2/1 for domestic and international students. Applications are processed on a rolling basis. *Application fee:* $50. Electronic applications accepted. *Application Contact:* Michelle Prososki, Executive Secretary, 801-422-2290, E-mail: michelle_prososki@byu.edu. *Dean*, Dr. Shane Reese, 801-422-9250, E-mail: shane_reese@byu.edu.

College of Religious Education Students: 17 full-time (2 women); includes 1 minority (Two or more races, non-Hispanic/Latino). Average age 32. 16 applicants, 75% accepted, 12 enrolled. *Faculty:* 42 full-time (4 women), 2 part-time/adjunct (0 women). Expenses: Contact institution. *Financial support:* In 2017–18, 4 students received support. Scholarships/grants available. In 2017, 7 master's awarded. Offers religious education (MA). *Application deadline:* For fall admission, 12/1 for domestic and international students. *Application fee:* $50. Electronic applications accepted. *Application Contact:* Dr. Terry B. Ball, Professor of Ancient Scripture, 801-422-3357, Fax: 801-422-0616, E-mail: terry_ball@byu.edu. *Dean*, Dr. Brent L. Top, 801-422-2736, Fax: 801-422-0616, E-mail: brent_top@byu.edu.

David O. McKay School of Education Students: 171 full-time (98 women), 136 part-time (84 women); includes 30 minority (1 Black or African American, non-Hispanic/Latino; 4 American Indian or Alaska Native, non-Hispanic/Latino; 6 Asian, non-Hispanic/Latino; 10 Hispanic/Latino; 9 Native Hawaiian or other Pacific Islander, non-Hispanic/Latino), 6 international. Average age 34. 312 applicants, 30% accepted, 86 enrolled. *Faculty:* 82 full-time (28 women), 11 part-time/adjunct (4 women). Expenses: Contact institution. *Financial support:* In 2017–18, 168 students received support, including 64 fellowships (averaging $9,270 per year), 20 research assistantships with tuition reimbursements available (averaging $1,701 per year), 18 teaching assistantships with tuition reimbursements available (averaging $2,786 per year); career-related internships or fieldwork, Federal Work-Study, institutionally sponsored loans, scholarships/grants, traineeships, health care benefits, tuition waivers, and unspecified assistantships also available. Support available to part-time students. Financial award applicants required to submit FAFSA. In 2017, 85 master's, 20 doctorates, 10 other advanced degrees awarded. Offers counseling psychology (PhD); education (M Ed, MA, MS, Ed D, PhD, Ed S); educational inquiry, measurement, and evaluation (PhD); educational leadership and foundations (Ed D); educational leadership: education policy studies (M Ed); educational leadership: school leadership (M Ed); instructional psychology and technology (MS, PhD); school psychology (Ed S); special education (MS); speech language pathology (MS); teacher education (MA). *Application fee:* $50. Electronic applications accepted. *Application Contact:* Brandan Beerli, Director, Education Student Services, 801-422-9199, Fax: 801-422-0195. *Dean*, Dr. Mary Anne Prater, 801-422-1592, Fax: 801-422-0200, E-mail: prater@byu.edu.

Ira A. Fulton College of Engineering and Technology Students: 378 full-time (50 women); includes 15 minority (3 American Indian or Alaska Native, non-Hispanic/Latino; 7 Asian, non-Hispanic/Latino; 3 Hispanic/Latino; 2 Native Hawaiian or other Pacific Islander, non-Hispanic/Latino), 56 international. Average age 28. 192 applicants, 54% accepted, 90 enrolled. *Faculty:* 108 full-time (4 women), 40 part-time/adjunct (11 women). Expenses: Contact institution. *Financial support:* In 2017–18, 279 students received support, including 18 fellowships with full and partial tuition reimbursements available (averaging $18,465 per year), 232 research assistantships with full and partial tuition reimbursements available (averaging $16,947 per year), 70 teaching assistantships with full and partial tuition reimbursements available (averaging $12,226 per year); scholarships/grants and health care benefits also available. Financial award application deadline: 1/1; financial award applicants required to submit FAFSA. In 2017, 93 master's, 15 doctorates awarded. Offers chemical engineering (MS, PhD); civil engineering (MS, PhD); construction management (MS); electrical and computer engineering (MS, PhD); engineering and technology (MS, PhD); information technology (MS); manufacturing engineering technology (MS); mechanical engineering (MS, PhD); technology and engineering education (MS). *Application deadline:* For fall admission, 1/15 for domestic and international students; for winter admission, 6/15 for domestic and international students; for spring admission, 2/5 for domestic and international students; for summer admission, 2/5 for domestic and international students. *Application fee:* $50. Electronic applications accepted. *Application Contact:* Claire A. DeWitt, Adviser, 801-422-4541, Fax: 801-422-0270, E-mail: gradstudies@byu.edu. *Dean*, Dr. Michael A. Jensen, 801-422-5736, Fax: 801-422-0218, E-mail: college@et.byu.edu.

J. Reuben Clark Law School Students: 381 full-time (138 women); includes 61 minority (6 Black or African American, non-Hispanic/Latino; 4 American Indian or Alaska Native, non-Hispanic/Latino; 9 Asian, non-Hispanic/Latino; 18 Hispanic/Latino; 4 Native Hawaiian or other Pacific Islander, non-Hispanic/Latino; 20 Two or more races, non-Hispanic/Latino), 2 international. Average age 28. 394 applicants, 44% accepted, 101 enrolled. Expenses: Contact institution. *Financial support:* In 2017–18, 227 students received support, including 12 fellowships (averaging $29,905 per year); career-related internships or fieldwork, institutionally sponsored loans, scholarships/grants, unspecified assistantships, and student employment also available. Financial award application deadline: 6/1; financial award applicants required to submit FAFSA. In 2017, 6 master's, 130 doctorates awarded. Offers law (LL M, JD). *Application deadline:* For fall admission, 3/1 priority date for domestic students, 3/1 for international students. Applications are processed on a rolling basis. *Application fee:* $50. Electronic applications accepted. *Application Contact:* Rebeca Welch, Admissions Coordinator, 801-422-4356, Fax: 801-422-0389, E-mail: welchr@law.byu.edu. *Dean*, D. Gordon Smith, 801-422-6383, Fax: 801-422-0389, E-mail: smithg@law.byu.edu.

BRITE DIVINITY SCHOOL, Fort Worth, TX 76109

General Information Independent-religious, coed, graduate-only institution. *Graduate housing:* Rooms and/or apartments available on a first-come, first-served basis to single and married students. Housing application deadline: 4/1.

GRADUATE UNITS

Graduate and Professional Programs *Program availability:* Part-time, evening/weekend. Offers Biblical interpretation (PhD); divinity (M Div); ministry (D Min); pastoral theology (PhD); theological studies (MTS, CTS); theology (Th M); theology and ministry (MA).

BROADVIEW UNIVERSITY–WEST JORDAN, West Jordan, UT 84088

General Information Proprietary, coed, comprehensive institution.

GRADUATE UNITS

Graduate Programs

BROCK UNIVERSITY, St. Catharines, ON L2S 3A1, Canada

General Information Province-supported, coed, university. *Graduate housing:* Room and/or apartments available on a first-come, first-served basis to single students; on-campus housing not available to married students. *Research affiliation:* Fly Fishing Canada/Trout Unlimited Canada (fisheries management), Henry Ford Health Centre (cancer epidemiology), Registered Nurses Association of Ontario (nursing best practices), Canadian Honey Council (agriculture, therapeutic product development).

GRADUATE UNITS

Faculty of Graduate Studies *Program availability:* Part-time, evening/weekend. Electronic applications accepted.

Faculty of Applied Health Sciences Offers applied health sciences (M Sc, MA, PhD). Electronic applications accepted.

Faculty of Business *Program availability:* Part-time. Offers accountancy (M Acc); business (M Acc, M Sc, MBA); business administration (MBA); management (M Sc). Electronic applications accepted.

Faculty of Education *Program availability:* Part-time, evening/weekend. Offers education (M Ed, PhD). Electronic applications accepted.

Faculty of Humanities *Program availability:* Part-time. Offers applied linguistics (MA); classics (MA); English (MA); history (MA); humanities (MA); philosophy (MA); studies in comparative literatures and arts (MA). Electronic applications accepted.

Faculty of Mathematics and Science *Program availability:* Part-time. Offers biological sciences (M Sc, PhD); biotechnology (M Sc, PhD); chemistry (M Sc, PhD); computer science (M Sc); earth sciences (M Sc); mathematics and science (M Sc, PhD); mathematics and statistics (M Sc); physics (M Sc). Electronic applications accepted.

Faculty of Social Sciences *Program availability:* Part-time. Offers applied disability studies (MA, MADS, Diploma); behavioral neuroscience (MA, PhD); business economics (MBE); Canadian politics (MA); child and youth studies (MA); comparative politics (MA); critical sociology (MA); geography (MA); international relations (MA); life span development (MA, PhD); political theory or philosophy (MA); popular culture (MA); public policy (MA); social justice and equity studies (MA); social personality (MA, PhD); social sciences (MA, MADS, MBE, PhD, Diploma). Electronic applications accepted.

BROOKLINE COLLEGE, Phoenix, AZ 85021

General Information Proprietary, coed, comprehensive institution.

GRADUATE UNITS

Nursing Programs *Program availability:* Part-time, online learning. Offers health systems administration (MSN); nursing (MSN).

BROOKLYN COLLEGE OF THE CITY UNIVERSITY OF NEW YORK, Brooklyn, NY 11210-2889

General Information State and locally supported, coed, comprehensive institution. *Graduate housing:* Room and/or apartments available on a first-come, first-served basis to single students; on-campus housing not available to married students. *Research affiliation:* Biothera Inc. (biology), Silicon Valley Community Foundation (computer and information science), Jessie Smith Noyes Foundation (sustainability), Sloan-Kettering Memorial Cancer Center (health/biology), Community Health Care Association of New York State (health and nutrition sciences), Welfare Research Inc. (education).

GRADUATE UNITS

School of Business *Program availability:* Part-time, evening/weekend. Offers accounting (MS); business administration (MS). Electronic applications accepted.

School of Education *Program availability:* Part-time, evening/weekend. Offers adolescence science education (MAT); art teacher (K-12) (MA); autism spectrum disorders (AC); bilingual education (MS Ed); biology (MA); biology teacher (7-12) (MA); birth-grade 2 (MS Ed); chemistry (MA); chemistry teacher (7-12) (MA); earth science (MA); earth science teacher (7-12) (MAT); education (MA, MAT, MS Ed, AC); English teacher (7-12) (MA); French teacher (7-12) (MA); general science (MA); liberal arts (MS Ed); mathematics (MS Ed); mathematics teacher (7-12) (MA); middle childhood mathematics education (MS Ed); music teacher (MA); physics (MA); physics teacher (7-12) (MA); play therapy (AC); school building leader (MS Ed); school counseling (MS Ed); school district leader (MS Ed); school psychologist (MS Ed); science and environmental education (MS Ed); social studies teacher (7-12) (MA); Spanish teacher (7-12) (MA); teacher of students with disabilities (MS Ed). Electronic applications accepted.

School of Humanities and Social Sciences *Program availability:* Part-time, evening/weekend. Offers audiology (Au D); creative writing (MFA); English (MA); French (MA); history (MA); humanities and social sciences (MA, MFA, MS, Au D, PhD); international affairs (MA); Judaic studies (MA); political science (MA); sociology (MA, PhD); Spanish (MA); speech (MA); speech-language pathology (MS); urban policy and administration (MA). Electronic applications accepted.

School of Natural and Behavioral Sciences *Program availability:* Part-time, evening/weekend. Offers biology (MA); chemistry (MA, MS, PhD); community health (MA); community health education (MA); computer science (MA); earth and environmental sciences (MA, PhD); exercise and sports science (MS); experimental psychology (MA); general public health (MPH); grief counseling (CAS); health care policy and administration (MPH); health informatics (MS); industrial and organizational psychology (MA); information systems (MS); mathematics (MA); mental health counseling (MA); natural and behavioral sciences (MA, MPH, MS, PhD, AC, Advanced Certificate); nutrition (MS); parallel and distributed computing (Advanced Certificate); physical education teacher (MS); physics (MA); psychology (PhD); public health (MPH); sport management (MS); thanatology (MA). Electronic applications accepted.

School of Visual, Media and Performing Arts *Program availability:* Part-time, evening/weekend. Offers acting (MFA); art history (MA); cinema arts (MFA); cinema studies (MA); design and technical theater (MFA); digital art (MFA); directing (MFA); drawing and painting (MFA); media studies (MS); performance and interactive media arts (MFA); performing arts management (MFA); photography (MFA); printmaking (MFA); sculpture (MFA); television production (MFA); theater history and criticism (MA); visual, media and performing arts (M Mus, MA, MFA, MS). Electronic applications accepted.

Conservatory of Music *Program availability:* Part-time. Offers composition (MM); music teacher (MA); musicology (MA); performance (MM). Electronic applications accepted.

BROOKLYN LAW SCHOOL, Brooklyn, NY 11201-3798

General Information Independent, coed, graduate-only institution. *Graduate housing:* Rooms and/or apartments available to single students and guaranteed to married students. Housing application deadline: 5/1.

GRADUATE UNITS

Graduate and Professional Programs *Program availability:* Part-time, evening/weekend. Offers law (LL M, JD). JD/MBA offered jointly with Bernard M. Baruch College of the City University of New York; JD/MS with Pratt Institute; JD/MUP with Hunter College of the City University of New York; and JD/MA with Brooklyn College of the City University of New York. Electronic applications accepted.

BROWN UNIVERSITY, Providence, RI 02912

General Information Independent, coed, university. CGS member. *Graduate housing:* Room and/or apartments available to single students; on-campus housing not available to married students. *Research affiliation:* Woods Hole Oceanographic Institution-Marine Biological Laboratory, Rhode Island Reactor, International Center for Numismatic Studies, Meeting Street School.

GRADUATE UNITS

Graduate School *Program availability:* Part-time. Offers acting and directing (MFA); American studies (PhD); American studies for international students (MA); ancient western Asian studies (PhD); anthropology (MA, PhD); Asian religious traditions (PhD); Brazilian studies (AM); chemistry (PhD); classics (MA, PhD); cognitive science (Sc M, PhD); comparative literature (PhD); computer music and multimedia (PhD); computer science (Sc M, PhD); earth, environmental and planetary sciences (PhD); economics (PhD); Egyptology (PhD); elementary education (MAT); English (MAT, PhD); English as a second language and cross-cultural studies (AM); ethnomusicology (PhD); French studies (PhD); German (PhD); Hispanic studies (PhD); history (MA, PhD); history of art and architecture (PhD); history of the exact sciences in antiquity (PhD); history/social studies (MAT); Islam, society and culture (PhD); Italian studies (PhD); linguistics (AM, PhD); literary arts (MFA); mathematics (PhD); philosophy (PhD); physics (Sc M, PhD); playwriting (MFA); political science (PhD); Portuguese and Brazilian studies (AM, PhD); Portuguese bilingual education and cross-cultural studies (AM); psychology (PhD); public humanities (MA); religion and critical thought (PhD); religions of the ancient Mediterranean (PhD); Russian language and literature (AM); science (MAT); secondary education (MAT); Slavic linguistics (AM); Slavic studies (PhD); sociology (MA, PhD); teaching (MAT); theatre and performance studies (PhD); urban education policy (AM).

A. Alfred Taubman Center for Public Policy and American Institutions Offers public policy and American institutions (MPA, MPP).

Division of Applied Mathematics Offers applied mathematics (Sc M, PhD).

Division of Biology and Medicine *Program availability:* Part-time. Offers behavioral and social sciences intervention (M Sc); biology and medicine (AM, M Sc, MA, MPH, Sc M, MD, PhD); biomedical engineering (Sc M, PhD); biostatistics (AM, Sc M, PhD); biotechnology (PhD); ecology and evolutionary biology (PhD); epidemiology (Sc M); health services, policy and practice (PhD); medicine (MD); molecular biology, cell biology, and biochemistry (MA, PhD); molecular pharmacology and physiology (PhD); neuroscience (PhD); pathology and laboratory medicine (Sc M, PhD); public health (MPH). Electronic applications accepted.

Joukowsky Institute for Archaeology and the Ancient World Offers archaeology and the ancient world (PhD).

School of Engineering Offers biomedical engineering (Sc M, PhD); chemical and biochemical engineering (Sc M, PhD); electrical sciences and computer engineering (Sc M, PhD); fluid and thermal sciences (Sc M, PhD); materials science and engineering (Sc M, PhD); mechanics of solids and structures (Sc M, PhD).

National Institutes of Health Sponsored Programs Offers neuroscience (PhD).

BRYAN COLLEGE, Dayton, TN 37321

General Information Independent-religious, coed, comprehensive institution. *Tuition:* Part-time $575 per credit hour. *Required fees:* $65 per semester. *Graduate housing:* On-campus housing not available. *Library facilities:* Bryan College Library.

Computer facilities: A campuswide network can be accessed from student residence rooms and from off campus. Online class registration is available.
Website: http://www.bryan.edu/

General Application Contact: Mandi K. Sullivan, Director of Academic Programs, 423-634-9880, E-mail: mandi.sullivan@bryan.edu.

GRADUATE UNITS

MBA Program Expenses: Contact institution. *Financial support:* Scholarships/grants available. Financial award applicants required to submit FAFSA. *Program availability:* Online only, 100% online. Offers business administration (MBA); healthcare administration (MBA); human resources (MBA); marketing (MBA); ministry (MBA); sports management (MBA). *Application deadline:* For fall admission, 7/1 for domestic and international students; for winter admission, 11/15 for domestic and international students; for spring admission, 12/1 for domestic and international students; for summer admission, 5/1 for domestic and international students. Applications are processed on a rolling basis. *Application fee:* $50. Electronic applications accepted. *Application Contact:* Mandi K Sullivan, Director of Academic Programs, 423-634-9880, E-mail: mandi.sullivan@bryan.edu. *Dean of Adult and Graduate Studies*, Dr. Adina Scruggs, 423-634-2057, E-mail: adina.scruggs@bryan.edu.

BRYAN COLLEGE OF HEALTH SCIENCES, Lincoln, NE 68506-1398

General Information Independent, coed, comprehensive institution. CGS member.

GRADUATE UNITS

School of Nurse Anesthesia Offers nurse anesthesia (MS).

BRYANT UNIVERSITY, Smithfield, RI 02917

General Information Independent, coed, comprehensive institution. *Enrollment:* 3,751 graduate, professional, and undergraduate students; 135 full-time matriculated graduate/professional students (67 women), 138 part-time matriculated graduate/professional students (68 women). *Enrollment by degree level:* 273 master's. *Graduate faculty:* 41 full-time (11 women), 12 part-time/adjunct (4 women). *Tuition:* Full-time $40,248; part-time $1118 per credit hour. Part-time tuition and fees vary according to course load, degree level and program. *Graduate housing:* Room and/or apartments available on a first-come, first-served basis to single students; on-campus housing not available to married students. Typical cost: $11,212 per year ($17,392 including board). Room and board charges vary according to board plan and housing facility selected. Housing application deadline: 8/1. *Student services:* Campus employment opportunities, campus safety program, career counseling, exercise/wellness program, free psychological counseling, international student services, low-cost health insurance, multicultural affairs office, services for students with disabilities, teacher training, writing training. *Library facilities:* Douglas and Judith Krupp Library plus 1 other. *Collection:* Books: 121,623 (physical), 16,854 (digital/electronic); Serial titles: 3,183 (physical), 299 (digital/electronic); Databases: 80. Weekly public service hours: 107; students can reserve study rooms.

Computer facilities: Computer purchase and lease plans are available. 526 computers available on campus for general student use. A campuswide network can be accessed from student residence rooms and from off campus. Online class registration, e-mail, online library, student Web hosts are available.
Website: http://www.bryant.edu/

General Application Contact: Terri Rogers, Admissions Assistant, 401-232-6230, E-mail: graduateprograms@bryant.edu.

GRADUATE UNITS

College of Arts and Sciences Students: 8 full-time (4 women), 10 part-time (8 women); includes 3 minority (2 Black or African American, non-Hispanic/Latino; 1 Two or more races, non-Hispanic/Latino), 2 international. Average age 25. 25 applicants, 32% accepted, 6 enrolled. *Faculty:* 3 full-time (0 women), 2 part-time/adjunct (0 women). Expenses: Contact institution. *Financial support:* In 2017–18, 15 fellowships with full and partial tuition reimbursements (averaging $10,483 per year) were awarded; research assistantships, scholarships/grants, and unspecified assistantships also available. Financial award application deadline: 2/15; financial award applicants required to submit FAFSA. In 2017, 4 master's awarded. *Program availability:* Part-time-only, evening/weekend. Offers applied economics (MS, Graduate Certificate); communication (MA, Graduate Certificate); organizational communication (Graduate Certificate); sustainability practices (Graduate Certificate). *Application deadline:* For fall admission, 8/15 for domestic and international students; for spring admission, 1/15 for domestic and international students; for summer admission, 5/15 for domestic and international students. Applications are processed on a rolling basis. *Application fee:* $80. Electronic applications accepted. *Application Contact:* Terri Rogers, Admission Assistant, Graduate School, 401-232-6230, E-mail: graduateprograms@bryant.edu. *Dean, College of Arts and Sciences,* Bradford Martin, 401-232-6929, E-mail: bmartin@bryant.edu.

Graduate School of Business Students: 84 full-time (31 women), 91 part-time (35 women); includes 24 minority (4 Black or African American, non-Hispanic/Latino; 1 American Indian or Alaska Native, non-Hispanic/Latino; 6 Asian, non-Hispanic/Latino; 8 Hispanic/Latino; 5 Two or more races, non-Hispanic/Latino), 6 international. Average age 26. 215 applicants, 66% accepted, 96 enrolled. *Faculty:* 30 full-time (5 women), 7 part-time/adjunct (2 women). Expenses: Contact institution. *Financial support:* In 2017–18, 95 fellowships with full and partial tuition reimbursements (averaging $9,825 per year), 9 research assistantships with full and partial tuition reimbursements (averaging $7,100 per year) were awarded; scholarships/grants and unspecified assistantships also available. Support available to part-time students. Financial award application deadline: 2/15; financial award applicants required to submit FAFSA. In 2017, 118 master's awarded. *Program availability:* Part-time, 100% online. Offers accounting (MPAC); business administration (MBA); taxation (MST). *Application deadline:* For fall admission, 7/15 for domestic and international students; for spring admission, 11/15 for domestic and international students; for summer admission, 4/15 for domestic and international students. Applications are processed on a rolling basis. *Application fee:* $80. Electronic applications accepted. *Application Contact:* Terri Rogers, Admissions Assistant, 401-232-6230, Fax: 401-232-6494, E-mail: graduateprograms@bryant.edu. *Graduate Program Director,* Bjorn Carlsson, 401-232-6707, E-mail: bcarlsson@bryant.edu.

School of Health Sciences Students: 43 full-time (32 women), 37 part-time (25 women); includes 9 minority (2 American Indian or Alaska Native, non-Hispanic/Latino; 2 Asian, non-Hispanic/Latino; 2 Hispanic/Latino; 3 Two or more races, non-Hispanic/Latino). Average age 28. 811 applicants, 7% accepted, 43 enrolled. *Faculty:* 8 full-time (6 women), 3 part-time/adjunct (2 women). Expenses: Contact institution. *Financial support:* Fund for a Healthy Rhode Island awards available. Financial award application deadline: 10/1; financial award applicants required to submit FAFSA. In 2017, 30 master's awarded. Offers physician assistant studies (MPAS). *Application deadline:* For winter admission, 10/1 for domestic and international students. Applications are processed on a rolling basis. *Application fee:* $80. Electronic applications accepted. *Application Contact:* Kayla Cetrone, Director, Physician Assistant Admissions, 401-232-6404, E-mail: pa_program@bryant.edu. *Program Director,* Jay Amrien, 401-232-6556, E-mail: jamrien@bryant.edu.

BRYAN UNIVERSITY, Springfield, MO 65804

General Information Proprietary, coed, comprehensive institution.

GRADUATE UNITS

Program in Business Administration *Program availability:* Online learning. Offers business administration (MBA).

BRYN ATHYN COLLEGE OF THE NEW CHURCH, Bryn Athyn, PA 19009-0717

General Information Independent-religious, coed, comprehensive institution. *Graduate housing:* Room and/or apartments available on a first-come, first-served basis to single students; on-campus housing not available to married students. Housing application deadline: 1/31.

GRADUATE UNITS

Academy of the New Church Theological School *Program availability:* Part-time, online learning. Offers divinity (M Div); religious studies (MA).

BRYN MAWR COLLEGE, Bryn Mawr, PA 19010-2899

General Information Independent, Undergraduate: women only; graduate: coed, university. CGS member. *Enrollment:* 1,640 graduate, professional, and undergraduate students; 261 full-time matriculated graduate/professional students (196 women), 45 part-time matriculated graduate/professional students (38 women). *Enrollment by degree level:* 141 master's, 89 doctoral, 76 other advanced degrees. *Graduate faculty:* 56 full-time (32 women), 8 part-time/adjunct (5 women). *Graduate housing:* On-campus housing not available. *Student services:* Campus employment opportunities, career counseling, exercise/wellness program, international student services, low-cost health insurance, multicultural affairs office, services for students with disabilities, teacher training. *Library facilities:* Canaday Library plus 2 others. *Collection:* Books: 740,887 (physical), 754,968 (digital/electronic); Serial titles: 9,146 (physical), 123,010 (digital/electronic); Databases: 170. Weekly public service hours: 105; study areas open 24 hours, 5–7 days a week.

Computer facilities: 125 computers available on campus for general student use. A campuswide network can be accessed from student residence rooms and from off campus. Online class registration is available.
Website: http://www.brynmawr.edu/

GRADUATE UNITS

Graduate School of Arts and Sciences Students: 55 full-time (39 women), 18 part-time (12 women); includes 6 minority (2 Black or African American, non-Hispanic/Latino; 2 Hispanic/Latino; 1 Native Hawaiian or other Pacific Islander, non-Hispanic/Latino; 1 Two or more races, non-Hispanic/Latino), 5 international. Average age 30. 122 applicants, 22% accepted, 10 enrolled. *Faculty:* 42 full-time (24 women), 1 part-time/adjunct (0 women). Expenses: Contact institution. *Financial support:* In 2017–18, 69 students received support, including 46 fellowships with tuition reimbursements available (averaging $15,886 per year), 3 research assistantships with tuition reimbursements available (averaging $21,695 per year), 19 teaching assistantships with tuition reimbursements available (averaging $17,000 per year); career-related internships or fieldwork, Federal Work-Study, institutionally sponsored loans, scholarships/grants, health care benefits, unspecified assistantships, and tuition awards also available. Support available to part-time students. Financial award application deadline: 12/15. In 2017, 9 master's, 13 doctorates awarded. *Program availability:* Part-time. Offers arts and sciences (MA, PhD); chemistry (MA, PhD); classical and Near Eastern archaeology (MA, PhD); Greek, Latin, and classical studies (MA, PhD); history of art (MA, PhD); mathematics (MA, PhD); physics (MA, PhD). *Application deadline:* For fall admission, 12/15 for domestic and international students. *Application fee:* $50. Electronic applications accepted. *Application Contact:* Maria Dantis, Graduate Program Administrator, 610-526-5074, E-mail: gsas@brynmawr.edu. *Dean of Graduate Studies,* Sharon Burgmayer, 610-526-5106, E-mail: sburgmay@brynmawr.edu.

Graduate School of Social Work and Social Research Students: 134 full-time (111 women), 27 part-time (26 women); includes 30 minority (16 Black or African American, non-Hispanic/Latino; 3 Asian, non-Hispanic/Latino; 4 Hispanic/Latino; 7 Two or more races, non-Hispanic/Latino). Average age 33. 128 applicants, 77% accepted, 74 enrolled. *Faculty:* 14 full-time (8 women), 7 part-time/adjunct (5 women). Expenses: Contact institution. *Financial support:* In 2017–18, 131 students received support. Fellowships, research assistantships, teaching assistantships, career-related internships or fieldwork, Federal Work-Study, institutionally sponsored loans, scholarships/grants, tuition waivers, and dissertation awards (for PhD) available. Support available to part-time students. Financial award application deadline: 4/15; financial award applicants required to submit FAFSA. In 2017, 68 master's, 6 doctorates awarded. *Program availability:* Part-time, evening/weekend. Offers social work and social research (MSS, PhD). *Application deadline:* For fall admission, 4/15 for domestic and international students. Applications are processed on a rolling basis. *Application fee:* $50. Electronic applications accepted. *Application Contact:* Sheila Gillin, Director of Graduate Admissions, 610-520-7533, E-mail: sgillin@brynmawr.edu. *Dean,* Dr. Darlyne Bailey, 610-520-2610, Fax: 610-520-2613, E-mail: dbailey01@brynmawr.edu.

BUCKNELL UNIVERSITY, Lewisburg, PA 17837

General Information Independent, coed, comprehensive institution. CGS member. *Graduate housing:* On-campus housing not available.

GRADUATE UNITS

Graduate Studies *Program availability:* Part-time.

College of Arts and Sciences *Program availability:* Part-time. Offers animal behavior (MS); arts and sciences (MA, MS, MS Ed); biology (MS); chemistry (MA, MS); college student personnel (MS Ed); English (MA); mathematics (MA, MS); psychology (MS).

College of Engineering *Program availability:* Part-time. Offers chemical engineering (MS Ch E); civil and environmental engineering (MSCE, MSEV); electrical and computer engineering (MSEE); engineering (MS Ch E, MSCE, MSEE, MSEV, MSME); mechanical engineering (MSME).

BUENA VISTA UNIVERSITY, Storm Lake, IA 50588

General Information Independent-religious, coed, comprehensive institution. *Graduate housing:* Room and/or apartments available on a first-come, first-served basis to single students; on-campus housing not available to married students. Housing application deadline: 5/1.

GRADUATE UNITS

School of Education *Program availability:* Part-time, evening/weekend, online learning. Offers curriculum and instruction (M Ed); school guidance and counseling (MS Ed). Program offered in summer only. Electronic applications accepted.

BUFFALO STATE COLLEGE, STATE UNIVERSITY OF NEW YORK, Buffalo, NY 14222-1095

General Information State-supported, coed, comprehensive institution. CGS member. *Graduate housing:* Room and/or apartments available on a first-come, first-served basis to single students; on-campus housing not available to married students. Housing application deadline: 8/15. *Research affiliation:* Friends of Buffalo River, Research Institute on Addictions at the University of Buffalo, Roswell Park Memorial Institute, Hauptman-Woodward Medical Research Institute, Ecology and Environment Corporation, Phillip Morris Foundation.

GRADUATE UNITS

The Graduate School *Program availability:* Part-time, evening/weekend, online learning. Offers multidisciplinary studies (MA, MS).

Faculty of Applied Science and Education *Program availability:* Part-time, evening/weekend, online learning. Offers adult education (MS, Certificate); applied science and education (MPS, MS, MS Ed, CAS, Certificate); business and marketing education (MS Ed); career and technical education (MS Ed); childhood education (grades 1-6) (MS Ed); creative studies (MS); criminal justice (MS); early childhood and childhood curriculum and instruction (MS Ed); early childhood education (birth-grade 2) (MS Ed); educational computing (MS Ed); educational leadership (CAS); elementary education (MS Ed); human resources development (Certificate); industrial technology (MS); literacy specialist (MPS, MS Ed); literacy specialist (birth-grade 6) (MS Ed); literacy specialist (grades 5-12) (MPS); special education (MS Ed); special education: adolescents (MS Ed); special education: childhood (MS Ed); special education: early childhood (MS Ed); speech-language pathology (MS Ed); student personnel administration (MS); teaching bilingual exceptional individuals (MS Ed); technology education (MS Ed).

Faculty of Arts and Humanities *Program availability:* Part-time, evening/weekend. Offers art conservation (CAS); art education (MS Ed); arts and humanities (MA, MS Ed, CAS); conservation of historic works and art works (MA); English (MA); secondary education (MS Ed).

Faculty of Natural and Social Sciences *Program availability:* Part-time, evening/weekend. Offers applied economics (MA); biology (MA); chemistry (MA); history (MA); mathematics education (MS Ed); natural and social sciences (MA, MS Ed); secondary education (MS Ed); secondary education physics (MS Ed).

BUTLER UNIVERSITY, Indianapolis, IN 46208-3485

General Information Independent, coed, comprehensive institution. *Enrollment:* 5,081 graduate, professional, and undergraduate students; 447 full-time matriculated graduate/professional students (325 women), 342 part-time matriculated graduate/professional students (195 women). *Enrollment by degree level:* 523 master's, 248 doctoral, 18 other advanced degrees. *Graduate faculty:* 130 full-time (66 women), 59 part-time/adjunct (29 women). *Tuition:* Full-time $15,080; part-time $3480 per credit hour. Tuition and fees vary according to degree level, program and student level. *Graduate housing:* Room and/or apartments available on a first-come, first-served basis to single students; on-campus housing not available to married students. Typical cost: $7660 per year ($14,690 including board). Room and board charges vary according to board plan, campus/location and housing facility selected. Housing application deadline: 8/1. *Student services:* Campus employment opportunities, campus safety program, career counseling, exercise/wellness program, free psychological counseling, international student services, low-cost health insurance, multicultural affairs office, services for students with disabilities. *Library facilities:* Irwin Library plus 2 others. *Collection:* Books: 197,610 (physical), 307,297 (digital/electronic); Serial titles: 2,327 (physical), 59,443 (digital/electronic); Databases: 265. Weekly public service hours: 106; students can reserve study rooms.

Computer facilities: Computer purchase and lease plans are available. 490 computers available on campus for general student use. A campuswide network can be accessed from student residence rooms and from off campus. Online class registration is available.
Website: http://www.butler.edu/

General Application Contact: Diane Dubord, Graduate Student Services Specialist, 317-940-8107, Fax: 317-940-8250, E-mail: ddubord@butler.edu.

GRADUATE UNITS

College of Education Students: 3 full-time (2 women), 131 part-time (102 women); includes 13 minority (7 Black or African American, non-Hispanic/Latino; 2 Asian, non-Hispanic/Latino; 2 Hispanic/Latino; 2 Two or more races, non-Hispanic/Latino). Average age 31. 65 applicants, 75% accepted, 41 enrolled. *Faculty:* 12 full-time (8 women), 10 part-time/adjunct (7 women). Expenses: Contact institution. *Financial support:* In 2017–18, 64 students received support. Scholarships/grants, tuition waivers (full and partial), and unspecified assistantships available. Financial award application deadline: 7/15; financial award applicants required to submit FAFSA. In 2017, 45 master's, 10 other advanced degrees awarded. *Program availability:* Part-time. Offers applied educational neuroscience (Certificate); educational administration (MS); effective teaching and leadership (MS); licensed mental health counselor (Certificate); school counseling (MS); wellness and sport leadership (Certificate). *Application deadline:* For fall admission, 2/1 for domestic and international students; for spring admission, 11/1 for domestic and international students; for summer admission, 4/1 for domestic and international students. Applications are processed on a rolling basis. *Application fee:* $0. Electronic applications accepted. *Application Contact:* Diane Dubord, Graduate Student Services Specialist, 317-940-8100, Fax: 317-940-8250, E-mail: ddubord@butler.edu. *Dean,* Dr. Ena Shelley, 317-940-9752, Fax: 317-940-6481.

College of Liberal Arts and Sciences Students: 7 full-time (2 women), 47 part-time (28 women); includes 7 minority (3 Black or African American, non-Hispanic/Latino; 1 Hispanic/Latino; 3 Two or more races, non-Hispanic/Latino), 1 international. Average age 34. 55 applicants, 69% accepted, 14 enrolled. *Faculty:* 17 full-time (5 women), 5 part-time/adjunct (2 women). Expenses: Contact institution. *Financial support:* In 2017–18, 20 students received support. Scholarships/grants, tuition waivers (full and partial), and unspecified assistantships available. Financial award application deadline: 7/15; financial award applicants required to submit FAFSA. In 2017, 20 master's awarded. *Program availability:* Part-time, evening/weekend. Offers creative writing (MFA); English (MA); history (MA); liberal arts and sciences (MA, MFA). *Application deadline:* For fall admission, 2/15 for domestic and international students; for spring admission, 9/15 for domestic and international students. Applications are processed on a rolling basis. *Application fee:* $0. Electronic applications accepted. *Application Contact:* Diane Dubord, Graduate Student Services Specialist, 317-940-8107, Fax: 317-940-8250, E-mail: ddubord@butler.edu. *Dean,* Dr. Jay Howard, 317-940-9874, E-mail: jrhoward@butler.edu.

College of Pharmacy and Health Sciences Students: 390 full-time (302 women), 10 part-time (6 women); includes 35 minority (3 Black or African American, non-Hispanic/Latino; 21 Asian, non-Hispanic/Latino; 7 Hispanic/Latino; 4 Two or more races, non-Hispanic/Latino), 3 international. Average age 24. 581 applicants, 25% accepted, 131 enrolled. *Faculty:* 62 full-time (42 women). Expenses: Contact institution. *Financial support:* In 2017–18, 8 students received support. Scholarships/grants, tuition waivers (full and partial), and unspecified assistantships available. Financial award application deadline: 7/15; financial award applicants required to submit FAFSA. In 2017, 75 master's, 116 doctorates awarded. Offers pharmaceutical science (MS); pharmacy (Pharm D); physician assistant studies (MS). *Application deadline:* For fall admission, 4/1 for domestic and international students. *Application fee:* $0. Electronic applications accepted. *Application Contact:* Diane Dubord, Graduate Student Services Specialist, 317-940-8107, E-mail: ddubord@butler.edu. *Dean,* Dr. Robert Soltis, 317-940-8056, E-mail: rsoltis@butler.edu.

Jordan College of the Arts Students: 12 full-time (3 women), 25 part-time (9 women); includes 8 minority (3 Black or African American, non-Hispanic/Latino; 2 Asian, non-Hispanic/Latino; 1 Hispanic/Latino; 2 Two or more races, non-Hispanic/Latino), 1 international. Average age 27. 36 applicants, 67% accepted, 14 enrolled. *Faculty:* 25 full-time (7 women), 35 part-time/adjunct (18 women). Expenses: Contact institution. *Financial support:* In 2017–18, 19 students received support. Scholarships/grants, tuition waivers (full and partial), and unspecified assistantships available. Financial award application deadline: 7/15; financial award applicants required to submit FAFSA. In 2017, 10 master's awarded. *Program availability:* Part-time. Offers composition (MM); conducting (MM); music education (MM); musicology (MA); performance (MM); piano pedagogy (MM). *Application deadline:* For fall admission, 2/1 for domestic and international students; for spring admission, 12/15 for domestic and international students; for summer admission, 4/15 for domestic and international students. Applications are processed on a rolling basis. *Application fee:* $0. Electronic applications accepted. *Application Contact:* Diane Dubord, Graduate Student Services Specialist, 317-940-8107, E-mail: ddubord@butler.edu. *Dean,* Wendy Meaden, 317-940-9229, E-mail: wmeaden@butler.edu.

Lacy School of Business Students: 35 full-time (16 women), 111 part-time (38 women); includes 15 minority (2 Black or African American, non-Hispanic/Latino; 5 Asian, non-Hispanic/Latino; 8 Hispanic/Latino), 6 international. Average age 30. 149 applicants, 64% accepted, 43 enrolled. *Faculty:* 14 full-time (4 women), 9 part-time/adjunct (2 women). Expenses: Contact institution. *Financial support:* In 2017–18, 22 students received support. Scholarships/grants, tuition waivers (full and partial), and unspecified assistantships available. Financial award application deadline: 7/15; financial award applicants required to submit FAFSA. In 2017, 90 master's awarded. *Program availability:* Part-time. Offers entrepreneurship and innovation (MBA); finance (MBA); international business (MBA); leadership (MBA); marketing (MBA); professional accounting (MP Acc). *Application deadline:* For fall admission, 8/1 for domestic and international students; for spring admission, 12/1 for domestic and international students; for summer admission, 4/1 for domestic and international students. Applications are processed on a rolling basis. *Application fee:* $0. Electronic applications accepted. *Application Contact:* Diane Dubord, Graduate Student Service Specialist, 317-940-8107, Fax: 317-940-8250, E-mail: ddubord@butler.edu. *Dean,* Dr. Stephen Standifird, 317-940-6307.

BYZANTINE CATHOLIC SEMINARY OF SAINTS CYRIL AND METHODIUS, Pittsburgh, PA 15214

General Information Independent-religious, coed, graduate-only institution.

GRADUATE UNITS

Graduate and Professional Programs Offers theology (M Div, MAT).

CABARRUS COLLEGE OF HEALTH SCIENCES, Concord, NC 28025

General Information Independent, coed, primarily women, comprehensive institution.

GRADUATE UNITS

Program in Occupational Therapy Offers occupational therapy (MOT).

CABRINI UNIVERSITY, Radnor, PA 19087

General Information Independent-religious, coed, comprehensive institution. *Enrollment:* 111 full-time matriculated graduate/professional students (72 women), 678 part-time matriculated graduate/professional students (524 women). *Enrollment by degree level:* 685 master's, 104 doctoral. *Graduate faculty:* 12 full-time (9 women), 77 part-time/adjunct (60 women). *Graduate housing:* On-campus housing not available. *Student services:* Campus employment opportunities, campus safety program, career counseling, exercise/wellness program, free psychological counseling, international student services, low-cost health insurance, multicultural affairs office, services for students with disabilities, teacher training, writing training. *Library facilities:* Holy Spirit Library. *Collection:* Books: 143,980 (digital/electronic); Serial titles: 67 (physical), 68,500 (digital/electronic); Databases: 47. Weekly public service hours: 97.

Computer facilities: 575 computers available on campus for general student use. A campuswide network can be accessed from student residence rooms and from off campus. Online class registration, account balances are available.
Website: http://www.cabrini.edu/

General Application Contact: Diane Greenwood, Director of Graduate Admissions, 610-902-8291, Fax: 610-902-8522, E-mail: dgreenwood@cabrini.edu.

GRADUATE UNITS

Academic Affairs Students: 60 full-time (35 women), 559 part-time (435 women); includes 93 minority (66 Black or African American, non-Hispanic/Latino; 1 American Indian or Alaska Native, non-Hispanic/Latino; 8 Asian, non-Hispanic/Latino; 15 Hispanic/Latino; 3 Two or more races, non-Hispanic/Latino), 4 international. Average age 33. 290 applicants, 82% accepted, 154 enrolled. *Faculty:* 23 full-time (17 women), 46 part-time/adjunct (38 women). Expenses: Contact institution. *Financial support:* In 2017–18, 1,459 students received support. Tuition waivers and unspecified assistantships available. Financial award application deadline: 5/1; financial award applicants required to submit FAFSA. In 2017, 283 master's awarded. *Program availability:* Part-time, evening/weekend. Offers accounting (M Acc); autism spectrum disorder (M Ed); biological sciences (MS); criminology and criminal justice (MA); curriculum, instruction, and assessment (M Ed); educational leadership (M Ed, Ed D); English as a second language (M Ed); organizational leadership (DBA, PhD); preK to 4 (M Ed); reading specialist (M Ed); secondary education (M Ed); special education grades 7-12 (M Ed); special education preK-8 (M Ed); teaching and learning (M Ed). *Application deadline:* For fall admission, 8/26 for domestic students, 8/1 for international students; for winter admission, 1/13 for domestic students, 12/20 for international students; for spring admission, 1/13 for domestic students, 12/20 for international students; for summer admission, 5/20 for domestic students, 4/30 for international students. Applications are processed on a rolling basis. *Application fee:* $50. Electronic applications accepted. *Application Contact:* Diane Greenwood, Director of Graduate Admissions, 610-902-8291, E-mail: diane.l.greenwood@cabrini.edu.

CAIRN UNIVERSITY, Langhorne, PA 19047-2990

General Information Independent-religious, coed, comprehensive institution. *Graduate housing:* Rooms and/or apartments available on a first-come, first-served basis to single and married students.

GRADUATE UNITS

Department of Counseling *Program availability:* Part-time, evening/weekend. Offers counseling (MS). Electronic applications accepted.

School of Business *Program availability:* Part-time, evening/weekend, 100% online, blended/hybrid learning. Offers accounting (MBA); business administration (MBA); international entrepreneurship (MBA); nonprofit leadership (MBA); organizational leadership (MSOL, Postbaccalaureate Certificate). Electronic applications accepted.

School of Divinity *Program availability:* Part-time, evening/weekend, 100% online, blended/hybrid learning. Offers divinity (M Div); religion (MA); theology (Th M). Electronic applications accepted.

School of Education *Program availability:* Part-time, evening/weekend, 100% online, blended/hybrid learning. Offers applied behavior analysis (MS Sp Ed, Certificate); educational leadership and administration (MS El); instruction (MS Sp Ed); teacher education (MS Ed). Electronic applications accepted.

CALDWELL UNIVERSITY, Caldwell, NJ 07006-6195

General Information Independent-religious, coed, comprehensive institution. CGS member. *Enrollment:* 2,200 graduate, professional, and undergraduate students; 166 full-time matriculated graduate/professional students (140 women), 431 part-time matriculated graduate/professional students (356 women). *Enrollment by degree level:* 407 master's, 66 doctoral, 124 other advanced degrees. *Graduate faculty:* 31 full-time (15 women), 41 part-time/adjunct (25 women). *Tuition:* Part-time $975 per credit hour. *Required fees:* $225 per semester. Tuition and fees vary according to degree level and campus/location. *Graduate housing:* Room and/or apartments available on a first-come, first-served basis to single students; on-campus housing not available to married students. Typical cost: $12,025 (including board). Room and board charges vary according to board plan and housing facility selected. Housing application deadline: 5/1. *Student services:* Career counseling, free psychological counseling, international student services, services for students with disabilities, writing training. *Library facilities:* Jennings Library plus 1 other. *Collection:* Books: 143,853 (physical), 151,660 (digital/electronic); Serial titles: 104 (physical), 419,719 (digital/electronic); Databases: 68. Students can reserve study rooms.

Computer facilities: 286 computers available on campus for general student use. A campuswide network can be accessed from student residence rooms. Online class registration is available.
Website: http://www.caldwell.edu/

General Application Contact: Tom Disch, Senior Graduate Admissions Counselor, 973-618-3544, Fax: 973-618-3640, E-mail: graduate@caldwell.edu.

GRADUATE UNITS

Department of Applied Behavior Analysis Students: 18 full-time (17 women), 66 part-time (59 women); includes 18 minority (3 Black or African American, non-Hispanic/Latino; 3 Asian, non-Hispanic/Latino; 11 Hispanic/Latino; 1 Two or more races, non-Hispanic/Latino). Average age 31. 57 applicants, 67% accepted, 17 enrolled. *Faculty:* 6 full-time (4 women). Expenses: Contact institution. *Financial support:* In 2017–18, 4 fellowships (averaging $35,000 per year) were awarded; 10 clinical assistantships (averaging $23,000 annually) also available. Financial award applicants required to submit FAFSA. In 2017, 12 master's, 1 doctorate awarded. *Program availability:* Part-time. Offers applied behavior analysis (MA, PhD, Post-Master's Certificate). *Application deadline:* For fall admission, 6/1 for domestic students; for spring admission, 12/1 for domestic students; for summer admission, 4/1 for domestic students. Applications are processed on a rolling basis. *Application fee:* $50. Electronic applications accepted. *Application Contact:* Tom Disch, Senior Graduate Admissions Counselor, 973-618-3544, E-mail: graduate@caldwell.edu. *Department Chair and Co-Coordinator,* Dr. Sharon Reeve, 973-618-3315, Fax: 973-615-3580, E-mail: sreeve@caldwell.edu.

School of Business and CIS Students: 23 full-time (14 women), 54 part-time (37 women); includes 25 minority (11 Black or African American, non-Hispanic/Latino; 2 Asian, non-Hispanic/Latino; 11 Hispanic/Latino; 1 Two or more races, non-Hispanic/Latino), 4 international. Average age 31. 39 applicants, 100% accepted, 23 enrolled. *Faculty:* 8 full-time (4 women), 12 part-time/adjunct (2 women). Expenses: Contact institution. *Financial support:* 1 general assistantship available. In 2017, 20 master's awarded. *Program availability:* Part-time. Offers accounting (MS); business administration (MBA). *Application deadline:* Applications are processed on a rolling basis. *Application fee:* $50. Electronic applications accepted. *Application Contact:* Tom Disch, Senior Admissions Counselor, 973-618-3544, E-mail: graduate@caldwell.edu. *Associate Dean,* Bernard O'Rourke, 973-618-3409, Fax: 973-618-3355, E-mail: borourke@caldwell.edu.

School of Education Students: 37 full-time (30 women), 225 part-time (177 women); includes 47 minority (19 Black or African American, non-Hispanic/Latino; 3 Asian, non-Hispanic/Latino; 23 Hispanic/Latino; 2 Two or more races, non-Hispanic/Latino). Average age 35. 189 applicants, 57% accepted, 85 enrolled. *Faculty:* 10 full-time (6 women), 21 part-time/adjunct (12 women). Expenses: Contact institution. *Financial support:* Unspecified assistantships available. Financial award applicants required to submit FAFSA. In 2017, 47 master's awarded. *Program availability:* Part-time, evening/weekend. Offers curriculum and instruction (MA); education leadership (Ed D); educational administration (MA); elementary, secondary or preschool endorsement, special ed, ESL (Postbaccalaureate Certificate); learning disabilities teacher-consultant (Post-Master's Certificate); literacy instruction (MA); principal (Post-Master's Certificate); reading specialist (Post-Master's Certificate); special education (MA); superintendent (Post-Master's Certificate); supervisor (Post-Master's Certificate). *Application deadline:* For fall admission, 6/1 for domestic students; for spring admission, 12/1 for domestic students; for summer admission, 4/1 for domestic students. Applications are processed on a rolling basis. *Application fee:* $50. Electronic applications accepted. *Application Contact:* Tom Disch, Senior Admissions Counselor, 973-618-3544, E-mail: graduate@caldwell.edu. *Associate Dean,* Dr. Joan Moriarity, 973-618-3626, E-mail: jmoriarity@caldwell.edu.

School of Psychology and Counseling Students: 88 full-time (79 women), 84 part-time (82 women); includes 33 minority (12 Black or African American, non-Hispanic/Latino; 6 Asian, non-Hispanic/Latino; 15 Hispanic/Latino). Average age 30. 104 applicants, 100% accepted, 44 enrolled. *Faculty:* 16 full-time (13 women), 13 part-time/adjunct (7 women). Expenses: Contact institution. *Financial support:* 2 general assistantships available. Financial award applicants required to submit FAFSA. In 2017, 31 master's awarded. *Program availability:* Part-time. Offers art therapy (MA); counseling (MA); director of school counseling (Post-Master's Certificate); professional counselor (Post-Master's Certificate); school counselor (Post-Master's Certificate). *Application deadline:* For fall admission, 6/1 for domestic students, 7/1 for international students; for spring admission, 12/1 for domestic and international students; for summer admission, 4/1 for domestic and international students. Applications are processed on a rolling basis. *Application fee:* $50. Electronic applications accepted. *Application Contact:* Tom Disch, Senior Graduate Admissions Counselor, 973-618-3544, E-mail: graduate@caldwell.edu. *Associate Dean,* Dr. Thomson Ling, 973-618-3596, E-mail: tling@caldwell.edu.

CALIFORNIA BAPTIST UNIVERSITY, Riverside, CA 92504-3206

General Information Independent-religious, coed, comprehensive institution. *Enrollment:* 9,941 graduate, professional, and undergraduate students; 1,406 full-time matriculated graduate/professional students (1,018 women), 1,121 part-time matriculated graduate/professional students (823 women). *Enrollment by degree level:* 2,451 master's, 76 doctoral. *Graduate faculty:* 171 full-time (93 women), 84 part-time/adjunct (42 women). *Tuition:* Full-time $14,700; part-time $700 per credit hour. *Required fees:* $175 per semester. Tuition and fees vary according to course load, degree level and program. *Graduate housing:* Room and/or apartments available on a first-come, first-served basis to single students; on-campus housing not available to married students. Typical cost: $8440 per year ($13,540 including board). Room and board charges vary according to board plan. Housing application deadline: 8/1. *Student services:* Campus employment opportunities, campus safety program, career counseling, exercise/wellness program, free psychological counseling, international student services, low-cost health insurance, multicultural affairs office, services for students with disabilities, teacher training, writing training. *Library facilities:* Annie Gabriel Library. *Collection:* Books: 130,837 (physical), 190,918 (digital/electronic); Serial titles: 59,915 (physical), 21,548 (digital/electronic); Databases: 83. Weekly public service hours: 101; students can reserve study rooms.

Computer facilities: Computer purchase and lease plans are available. 279 computers available on campus for general student use. A campuswide network can be accessed from student residence rooms and from off campus. Online class registration, online course evaluations are available.
Website: http://www.calbaptist.edu/

General Application Contact: Alma Salazar, Director of Graduate Admissions, 951-552-8086, Fax: 951-552-8700, E-mail: graduateadmissions@calbaptist.edu.

GRADUATE UNITS

Doctor of Nursing Practice Program Students: 1 full-time (0 women), 5 part-time (3 women); includes 4 minority (1 Black or African American, non-Hispanic/Latino; 1 American Indian or Alaska Native, non-Hispanic/Latino; 2 Hispanic/Latino). Average age 49. 4 applicants, 100% accepted, 3 enrolled. *Faculty:* 6 full-time (5 women). Expenses: Contact institution. *Financial support:* Federal Work-Study and scholarships/grants available. Financial award applicants required to submit CSS PROFILE or FAFSA. *Program availability:* Part-time. Offers nursing (DNP). *Application deadline:* For fall admission, 8/1 priority date for domestic students, 7/1 priority date for international students; for spring admission, 12/1 priority date for domestic students, 11/1 priority date for international students. Applications are processed on a rolling basis. *Application fee:* $45. Electronic applications accepted. *Application Contact:* Dr. Lisa Bursch, DNP Program Director, 951-343-4940, E-mail: lbursch@calbaptist.edu. *Dean, School of Nursing,* Dr. Geneva Oaks, 951-343-4702, E-mail: goaks@calbaptist.edu.

Program in Accounting Students: 11 full-time (6 women), 15 part-time (11 women); includes 11 minority (1 Black or African American, non-Hispanic/Latino; 9 Hispanic/Latino; 1 Two or more races, non-Hispanic/Latino). Average age 31. 48 applicants, 56% accepted, 10 enrolled. *Faculty:* 8 full-time (2 women). Expenses: Contact institution. *Financial support:* In 2017–18, 7 students received support. Federal Work-Study and scholarships/grants available. Financial award applicants required to submit CSS PROFILE or FAFSA. In 2017, 12 master's awarded. *Program availability:* Part-time, evening/weekend, online only, 100% online. Offers accounting (MS). *Application deadline:* For fall admission, 8/1 priority date for domestic students, 7/1 priority date for international students; for spring admission, 12/1 priority date for domestic students, 11/1 priority date for international students. Applications are processed on a rolling basis. *Application fee:* $45. Electronic applications accepted. *Application Contact:* Karin Nelson, Program Director, Accounting, 951-552-8777, E-mail: knelson@calbaptist.edu. *Vice President, Online and Professional Studies,* Dr. David Poole, 951-343-3902, E-mail: dpoole@calbaptist.edu.

Program in Applied Mathematics Students: 5 full-time (4 women), 5 part-time (3 women); includes 5 minority (1 Black or African American, non-Hispanic/Latino; 4 Hispanic/Latino), 1 international. Average age 25. 6 applicants, 83% accepted, 5 enrolled. *Faculty:* 8 full-time (3 women). Expenses: Contact institution. *Financial support:* In 2017–18, 2 students received support. Scholarships/grants and unspecified assistantships available. Financial award applicants required to submit CSS PROFILE or FAFSA. In 2017, 4 master's awarded. *Program availability:* Part-time. Offers applied mathematics (MS). *Application deadline:* For fall admission, 8/1 priority date for domestic students, 7/1 priority date for international students; for spring admission, 12/1 priority date for domestic students, 11/1 priority date for international students. Applications are processed on a rolling basis. *Application fee:* $45. Electronic applications accepted. *Application Contact:* Dr. Ricardo J. Cordero-Soto, Associate Professor of Mathematics, 951-552-8632, E-mail: rcordero@calbaptist.edu. *Dean of the College of Arts and Science,* Dr. Gayne Anacker, 951-343-4682.

Program in Architecture Students: 9 full-time (5 women), 1 (woman) part-time; includes 7 minority (2 Black or African American, non-Hispanic/Latino; 5 Hispanic/Latino). Average age 25. 12 applicants, 100% accepted, 10 enrolled. *Faculty:* 5 full-time (1 woman). Expenses: Contact institution. *Financial support:* Federal Work-Study and scholarships/grants available. Financial award applicants required to submit CSS PROFILE or FAFSA. Offers architecture (M Arch). *Application deadline:* For fall admission, 8/1 priority date for domestic students, 7/1 for international students; for spring admission, 12/1 priority date for domestic students, 11/1 for international students. Applications are processed on a rolling basis. *Application fee:* $45. Electronic applications accepted. *Dean, College of Architecture, Visual Arts and Design,* Mark Roberson, 951-552-8652, E-mail: maroberson@calbaptist.edu.

Program in Athletic Training Students: 36 full-time (20 women); includes 21 minority (2 Black or African American, non-Hispanic/Latino; 3 Asian, non-Hispanic/Latino; 16 Hispanic/Latino). Average age 25. 2 applicants. *Faculty:* 4 full-time (3 women). Expenses: Contact institution. *Financial support:* In 2017–18, 3 students received support. Research assistantships, Federal Work-Study, and scholarships/grants available. Financial award applicants required to submit CSS PROFILE or FAFSA. In 2017, 19 master's awarded. *Program availability:* Part-time. Offers athletic training (MS). *Application deadline:* For fall admission, 8/1 priority date for domestic students, 7/1 for international students; for spring admission, 12/1 priority date for domestic students, 11/1 for international students. Applications are processed on a rolling basis. *Application fee:* $45. Electronic applications accepted. *Application Contact:* Dr. Nicole MacDonald, Director, Athletic Training Program, 951-343-4379, E-mail: nmacdona@calbaptist.edu. *Dean of the College of Health Science,* Dr. David Pearson, 951-343-4298, E-mail: dpearson@calbaptist.edu.

Program in Business Administration Students: 123 full-time (64 women), 101 part-time (55 women); includes 108 minority (22 Black or African American, non-Hispanic/Latino; 15 Asian, non-Hispanic/Latino; 62 Hispanic/Latino; 1 Native Hawaiian or other Pacific Islander, non-Hispanic/Latino; 8 Two or more races, non-Hispanic/Latino), 29 international. Average age 30. 285 applicants, 62% accepted, 142 enrolled. *Faculty:* 19 full-time (7 women), 18 part-time/adjunct (6 women). Expenses: Contact institution. *Financial support:* In 2017–18, 38 students received support. Federal Work-Study and scholarships/grants available. Financial award applicants required to submit CSS PROFILE or FAFSA. In 2017, 147 master's awarded. *Program* *availability:* Part-time, evening/weekend, 100% online, blended/hybrid learning. Offers accounting (MBA); construction management (MBA); healthcare management (MBA); management (MBA). *Application deadline:* For fall admission, 8/1 priority date for domestic students, 7/1 for international students; for spring admission, 12/1 priority date for domestic students, 11/1 for international students. Applications are processed on a rolling basis. *Application fee:* $45. Electronic applications accepted. *Application Contact:* Deanna Meyer, Graduate Admissions Counselor, 951-343-4463, E-mail: dmeyer@calbaptist.edu. *Dean, School of Business*, Dr. Andrea Scott, 951-343-4701, Fax: 951-343-4361, E-mail: ascott@calbaptist.edu.

Program in Civil Engineering Students: 2 full-time (0 women), 7 part-time (4 women); includes 3 minority (all Hispanic/Latino), 4 international. Average age 25. 6 applicants, 50% accepted, 2 enrolled. *Faculty:* 6 full-time (1 woman), 1 part-time/adjunct (0 women). Expenses: Contact institution. *Financial support:* Federal Work-Study and scholarships/grants available. Financial award applicants required to submit CSS PROFILE or FAFSA. *Program availability:* Part-time. Offers civil engineering (MS). *Application deadline:* For fall admission, 8/1 priority date for domestic students, 7/1 priority date for international students; for spring admission, 12/1 priority date for domestic students, 11/1 priority date for international students. Applications are processed on a rolling basis. *Application fee:* $45. Electronic applications accepted. *Application Contact:* Taylor Neece, Director of Graduate Admissions, 951-343-4871, Fax: 877-228-8877, E-mail: graduateadmissions@calbaptist.edu. *Associate Dean, College of Engineering*, Dr. Helen Jung, 951-343-4510.

Program in Communication Students: 10 full-time (9 women), 4 part-time (3 women); includes 10 minority (3 Black or African American, non-Hispanic/Latino; 1 Asian, non-Hispanic/Latino; 3 Hispanic/Latino; 3 Two or more races, non-Hispanic/Latino). Average age 28. 14 applicants, 71% accepted, 4 enrolled. *Faculty:* 2 full-time (both women), 1 (woman) part-time/adjunct. Expenses: Contact institution. *Financial support:* In 2017–18, 2 students received support. Federal Work-Study and scholarships/grants available. Financial award applicants required to submit CSS PROFILE or FAFSA. In 2017, 13 master's awarded. *Program availability:* Part-time, evening/weekend. Offers communication (MA). *Application deadline:* For fall admission, 8/1 priority date for domestic students, 7/1 priority date for international students; for spring admission, 12/1 priority date for domestic students, 11/1 priority date for international students. Applications are processed on a rolling basis. *Application fee:* $45. Electronic applications accepted. *Application Contact:* Ted Meyer, Dean of Enrollment Services, Online and Professional Studies, 951-343-3909, E-mail: tmeyer@calbaptist.edu. *Program Director, MA in Communication*, Dr. Sandra Romo, 951-343-2173, E-mail: sromo@calbaptist.edu.

Program in Counseling Ministry Students: 6 full-time (5 women), 3 part-time (1 woman); includes 3 minority (all Hispanic/Latino). Average age 35. 2 applicants, 50% accepted, 1 enrolled. *Faculty:* 2 full-time (0 women), 1 part-time/adjunct (0 women). Expenses: Contact institution. *Financial support:* In 2017–18, 2 students received support. Federal Work-Study and scholarships/grants available. Financial award applicants required to submit CSS PROFILE or FAFSA. In 2017, 5 master's awarded. *Program availability:* Part-time, evening/weekend. Offers professional ministry (MA); research in counseling ministry (MA). *Application deadline:* For fall admission, 8/1 priority date for domestic students, 7/1 for international students; for spring admission, 12/1 priority date for domestic students, 11/1 for international students. Applications are processed on a rolling basis. *Application fee:* $45. Electronic applications accepted. *Application Contact:* Deanna Meyer, Graduate Admissions Counselor, 951-343-4463, E-mail: dmeyer@calbaptist.edu. *Dean, School of Behavioral Sciences*, Dr. Jacqueline Gustafson, 951-343-4487, E-mail: jcraig@calbaptist.edu.

Program in Counseling Ministry and Counseling Psychology (Dual Master's) Students: 12 full-time (9 women), 1 part-time (0 women); includes 8 minority (2 Black or African American, non-Hispanic/Latino; 1 Asian, non-Hispanic/Latino; 5 Hispanic/Latino). Average age 29. 7 applicants, 57% accepted, 3 enrolled. *Faculty:* 18 full-time (11 women), 10 part-time/adjunct (7 women). Expenses: Contact institution. *Financial support:* In 2017–18, 2 students received support. Federal Work-Study and scholarships/grants available. Financial award applicants required to submit CSS PROFILE or FAFSA. *Program availability:* Part-time, evening/weekend. *Application deadline:* For fall admission, 8/1 priority date for domestic students, 7/1 for international students; for spring admission, 12/1 priority date for domestic students, 11/1 for international students. Applications are processed on a rolling basis. *Application fee:* $45. Electronic applications accepted. *Application Contact:* Mischa Routon, Director of Counseling Psychology Program, 951-343-4206, Fax: 877-228-8877, E-mail: mrouton@calbaptist.edu. *Dean, School of Behavioral Sciences*, Dr. Jacqueline Gustafson, 951-343-4487, E-mail: jcraig@calbaptist.edu.

Program in Counseling Psychology Students: 249 full-time (211 women), 91 part-time (76 women); includes 234 minority (58 Black or African American, non-Hispanic/Latino; 2 American Indian or Alaska Native, non-Hispanic/Latino; 11 Asian, non-Hispanic/Latino; 149 Hispanic/Latino; 1 Native Hawaiian or other Pacific Islander, non-Hispanic/Latino; 13 Two or more races, non-Hispanic/Latino), 2 international. Average age 31. 136 applicants, 69% accepted, 77 enrolled. *Faculty:* 15 full-time (8 women), 17 part-time/adjunct (12 women). Expenses: Contact institution. *Financial support:* In 2017–18, 79 students received support. Federal Work-Study and scholarships/grants available. Financial award applicants required to submit CSS PROFILE or FAFSA. In 2017, 114 master's awarded. *Program availability:* Part-time, evening/weekend. Offers counseling psychology (MS); forensic psychology (MS); professional clinical counseling (MS). *Application deadline:* For fall admission, 8/1 priority date for domestic students, 7/1 for international students; for spring admission, 12/1 priority date for domestic students, 11/1 for international students. Applications are processed on a rolling basis. *Application fee:* $45. Electronic applications accepted. *Application Contact:* Deanna Meyer, Graduate Admission Counselor, 951-343-4463, E-mail: dmeyer@calbaptist.edu. *Dean, School of Behavioral Sciences*, Dr. Jacqueline Gustafson, 951-343-4487, E-mail: jcraig@calbaptist.edu.

Program in Disability Studies *Faculty:* 1 full-time (0 women). Expenses: Contact institution. *Financial support:* Federal Work-Study and scholarships/grants available. Financial award applicants required to submit CSS PROFILE or FAFSA. In 2017, 1 master's awarded. *Program availability:* Part-time, evening/weekend, 100% online. Offers disability ministry (MA); disability policy (MA). *Application deadline:* For fall admission, 8/1 priority date for domestic students, 7/1 for international students; for spring admission, 12/1 priority date for domestic students, 11/1 for international students. Applications are processed on a rolling basis. *Application fee:* $45. Electronic applications accepted. *Application Contact:* Gavin Andrew, Assistant Director, Graduate Admissions, 951-552-8437, E-mail: gandrew@calbaptist.edu. *Program Director, MA in Disability Studies*, Dr. Jeff McNair, 951-343-4489, E-mail: jmcnair@calbaptist.edu.

Program in Education Students: 232 full-time (182 women), 315 part-time (247 women); includes 264 minority (33 Black or African American, non-Hispanic/Latino; 4 American Indian or Alaska Native, non-Hispanic/Latino; 11 Asian, non-Hispanic/Latino; 186 Hispanic/Latino; 7 Native Hawaiian or other Pacific Islander, non-Hispanic/Latino; 23 Two or more races, non-Hispanic/Latino). Average age 31. 217 applicants, 64% accepted, 129 enrolled. *Faculty:* 19 full-time (11 women), 36 part-time/adjunct (22 women). Expenses: Contact institution. *Financial support:* In 2017–18, 162 students received support. Federal Work-Study and scholarships/grants available. Financial award applicants required to submit CSS PROFILE or FAFSA. In 2017, 196 master's awarded. *Program availability:* Part-time, evening/weekend, 100% online, blended/hybrid learning. Offers educational leadership (MS); educational leadership for faith-based institutions (MS); educational leadership for public institutions (MS); educational technology (MS); instructional computer applications (MS); international education (MS); leadership and adult learning (MS); leadership and organizational studies (MS); online teaching and learning (MS); reading (MS); science education (MA); special education in mild/moderate disabilities (MS); special education in moderate/severe disabilities (MS); teacher leadership (MS); teaching (MS); teaching and learning (MS). *Application deadline:* For fall admission, 8/1 priority date for domestic students, 7/1 for international students; for spring admission, 12/1 priority date for domestic students, 11/1 for international students. Applications are processed on a rolling basis. *Application fee:* $45. Electronic applications accepted. *Application Contact:* Gavin Andrew, Graduate Admissions Counselor, 951-552-8437, E-mail: gandrew@calbaptist.edu. *Dean, School of Education*, Dr. John Shoup, 951-343-4516, E-mail: jshoup@calbaptist.edu.

Program in English Students: 3 full-time (2 women), 26 part-time (19 women); includes 14 minority (4 Black or African American, non-Hispanic/Latino; 1 Asian, non-Hispanic/Latino; 9 Hispanic/Latino), 3 international. Average age 28. 11 applicants, 45% accepted, 4 enrolled. *Faculty:* 13 full-time (8 women), 1 (woman) part-time/adjunct. Expenses: Contact institution. *Financial support:* In 2017–18, 5 students received support. Federal Work-Study and scholarships/grants available. Financial award applicants required to submit CSS PROFILE or FAFSA. In 2017, 8 master's awarded. *Program availability:* Part-time, evening/weekend. Offers English pedagogy (MA); literature (MA); teaching English to speakers of other languages (TESOL) (MA). *Application deadline:* For fall admission, 8/1 priority date for domestic students, 7/1 for international students; for spring admission, 12/1 priority date for domestic students, 11/1 for international students. Applications are processed on a rolling basis. *Application fee:* $45. Electronic applications accepted. *Application Contact:* Dr. Laura Veltman, Director, Master of Arts Program in English, 951-343-4276, Fax: 951-343-4661, E-mail: lveltman@calbaptist.edu. *Dean, College of Arts and Sciences*, Dr. Gayne Anacker, 951-343-4682, E-mail: ganacker@calbaptist.edu.

Program in Forensic Psychology Students: 60 full-time (53 women), 11 part-time (all women); includes 41 minority (8 Black or African American, non-Hispanic/Latino; 27 Hispanic/Latino; 3 Native Hawaiian or other Pacific Islander, non-Hispanic/Latino; 3 Two or more races, non-Hispanic/Latino). Average age 25. 33 applicants, 73% accepted, 21 enrolled. *Faculty:* 4 full-time (3 women), 1 (woman) part-time/adjunct. Expenses: Contact institution. *Financial support:* In 2017–18, 12 students received support. Federal Work-Study and scholarships/grants available. Financial award applicants required to submit CSS PROFILE or FAFSA. In 2017, 28 master's awarded. *Program availability:* Part-time, evening/weekend. Offers forensic psychology (MA). *Application deadline:* For fall admission, 8/1 priority date for domestic students, 7/1 for international students; for spring admission, 12/1 priority date for domestic students, 11/1 for international students. Applications are processed on a rolling basis. *Application fee:* $45. Electronic applications accepted. *Application Contact:* Rudy Villarruel, Graduate Admission Counselor, 951-552-8132, E-mail: rvillarruel@calbaptist.edu. *Dean, School of Behavioral Sciences*, Dr. Jacqueline Gustafson, 951-343-4487, E-mail: jcraig@calbaptist.edu.

Program in Higher Education Leadership and Student Development Students: 30 part-time (21 women); includes 19 minority (6 Black or African American, non-Hispanic/Latino; 13 Hispanic/Latino), 1 international. Average age 29. 22 applicants, 77% accepted, 15 enrolled. *Faculty:* 9 full-time (3 women), 4 part-time/adjunct (1 woman). Expenses: Contact institution. *Financial support:* In 2017–18, 5 students received support. Federal Work-Study and scholarships/grants available. Financial award applicants required to submit CSS PROFILE or FAFSA. In 2017, 3 master's awarded. *Program availability:* Part-time, evening/weekend. Offers higher education leadership and student development (MS). *Application deadline:* For fall admission, 8/1 priority date for domestic students, 7/1 for international students; for spring admission, 12/1 priority date for domestic students, 11/1 for international students. Applications are processed on a rolling basis. *Application fee:* $45. Electronic applications accepted. *Application Contact:* David Little, Graduate Admissions Counselor, 951-552-8093, E-mail: dlittle@calbaptist.edu. *Dean, School of Education*, Dr. John Shoup, 951-343-4205, E-mail: jshoup@calbaptist.edu.

Program in Kinesiology Students: 86 full-time (43 women), 45 part-time (21 women); includes 63 minority (20 Black or African American, non-Hispanic/Latino; 5 Asian, non-Hispanic/Latino; 35 Hispanic/Latino; 3 Two or more races, non-Hispanic/Latino), 20 international. Average age 28. 47 applicants, 62% accepted, 24 enrolled. *Faculty:* 11 full-time (6 women), 5 part-time/adjunct (0 women). Expenses: Contact institution. *Financial support:* In 2017–18, 11 students received support. Federal Work-Study, scholarships/grants, and unspecified assistantships available. Financial award applicants required to submit CSS PROFILE or FAFSA. In 2017, 55 master's awarded. *Program availability:* Part-time, 100% online, blended/hybrid learning. Offers exercise science (MS); physical education (MS); sport management (MS). *Application deadline:* For fall admission, 8/1 priority date for domestic students, 7/1 for international students; for spring admission, 12/1 priority date for domestic students, 11/1 for international students. Applications are processed on a rolling basis. *Application fee:* $45. Electronic applications accepted. *Application Contact:* Dr. Sean Sullivan, Chair, Department of Kinesiology, 951-343-4528, Fax: 951-343-5095, E-mail: ssullivan@calbaptist.edu. *Dean, College of Allied Health*, Dr. David Pearson, 951-343-4298, E-mail: dpearson@calbaptist.edu.

Program in Leadership and Adult Learning *Faculty:* 1 full-time (0 women). Expenses: Contact institution. *Financial support:* Applicants required to submit CSS PROFILE or FAFSA. *Program availability:* Part-time, evening/weekend. Offers leadership and adult learning (MA). *Application deadline:* For fall admission, 8/1 priority date for domestic students, 7/1 priority date for international students; for spring admission, 12/1 priority date for domestic students, 11/1 priority date for international students. Applications are processed on a rolling basis. *Application fee:* $45. Electronic applications accepted. *Dean, School of Education*, Dr. John Shoup, 951-343-4205, E-mail: jshoup@calbaptist.edu.

Program in Leadership and Community Development 1 applicant, 100% accepted. Expenses: Contact institution. *Financial support:* In 2017–18, 1 student received support. Applicants required to submit CSS PROFILE or FAFSA. In 2017, 2 master's awarded. *Program availability:* Part-time, evening/weekend. Offers leadership and community development (MA). *Application deadline:* For fall admission, 8/1 priority date for domestic students, 7/1 priority date for international students; for spring admission, 12/1 for domestic students, 11/1 priority date for international students. Applications are processed on a rolling basis. *Application fee:* $45. Electronic applications accepted. *Dean, School of Education*, Dr. John Shoup, 951-343-4205, E-mail: jshoup@calbaptist.edu.

Program in Leadership and Organizational Studies Students: 1 full-time (0 women), 22 part-time (14 women); includes 13 minority (3 Black or African American, non-Hispanic/Latino; 1 Asian, non-Hispanic/Latino; 7 Hispanic/Latino; 2 Two or more races, non-Hispanic/Latino), 1 international. Average age 39. 33 applicants, 55% accepted, 12 enrolled. *Faculty:* 3 full-time (0 women), 3 part-time/adjunct (0 women). Expenses: Contact institution. *Financial support:* In 2017–18, 7 students received support. Federal Work-Study and scholarships/grants available. Financial award applicants required to submit CSS PROFILE or FAFSA. In 2017, 7 master's awarded. *Program availability:* Part-time, evening/weekend. Offers leadership and organizational studies (MA). *Application deadline:* For fall admission, 8/1 priority date for domestic students, 7/1 for international students; for spring admission, 11/1 priority date for domestic students, 11/1 for international students. Applications are processed on a rolling basis. *Application fee:* $45. Electronic applications accepted. *Application Contact:* David Little, Graduate Admissions Counselor, 951-552-8093, E-mail: dlittle@calbaptist.edu. *Dean, School of Education*, Dr. John Shoup, 951-343-4205, E-mail: jshoup@calbaptist.edu.

Program in Mechanical Engineering Students: 14 full-time (0 women); includes 1 minority (Asian, non-Hispanic/Latino), 9 international. Average age 25. 3 applicants, 100% accepted, 2 enrolled. *Faculty:* 9 full-time (4 women). Expenses: Contact institution. *Financial support:* Federal Work-Study and scholarships/grants available. Financial award applicants required to submit CSS PROFILE or FAFSA. *Program availability:* Part-time. Offers mechanical engineering (MS). *Application deadline:* For fall admission, 8/1 priority date for domestic students, 7/1 priority date for international students; for spring admission, 12/1 priority date for domestic students, 11/1 priority date for international students. Applications are processed on a rolling basis. *Application fee:* $45. Electronic applications accepted. *Application Contact:* Felicia Tasabia, Administrative Assistant, 951-343-4972, E-mail: ftasabia@calbaptist.edu. *Chair, Aerospace, Industrial and Mechanical Engineering*, Dr. Xiuhua Si, 951-552-8479, E-mail: asi@calbaptist.edu.

Program in Music Students: 13 full-time (6 women), 6 part-time (5 women); includes 5 minority (2 Black or African American, non-Hispanic/Latino; 2 Asian, non-Hispanic/Latino; 1 Hispanic/Latino), 9 international. Average age 27. 10 applicants, 70% accepted, 5 enrolled. *Faculty:* 13 full-time (6 women), 18 part-time/adjunct (9 women). Expenses: Contact institution. *Financial support:* In 2017–18, 8 students received support. Federal Work-Study and scholarships/grants available. Financial award applicants required to submit CSS PROFILE or FAFSA. In 2017, 8 master's awarded. *Program availability:* Part-time, evening/weekend. Offers conducting (MM); music education (MM); performance (MM). *Application deadline:* For fall admission, 8/1 priority date for domestic students, 7/1 for international students; for spring admission, 12/1 priority date for domestic students, 11/1 for international students. Applications are processed on a rolling basis. *Application fee:* $45. Electronic applications accepted. *Application Contact:* Rudy Villarruel, Graduate Admissions Counselor, 951-552-8132, E-mail: rvillarruel@calbaptist.edu. *Dean, School of Music*, Dr. Joseph Bolin, 951-343-4714, Fax: 951-343-4570, E-mail: jbolin@calbaptist.edu.

Program in Nursing Students: 78 full-time (59 women), 130 part-time (106 women); includes 114 minority (25 Black or African American, non-Hispanic/Latino; 3 American Indian or Alaska Native, non-Hispanic/Latino; 34 Asian, non-Hispanic/Latino; 47 Hispanic/Latino; 2 Native Hawaiian or other Pacific Islander, non-Hispanic/Latino; 3 Two or more races, non-Hispanic/Latino), 2 international. Average age 32. 25 applicants, 84% accepted, 14 enrolled. *Faculty:* 19 full-time (18 women), 12 part-time/adjunct (11 women). Expenses: Contact institution. *Financial support:* In 2017–18, 38 students received support. Federal Work-Study and scholarships/grants available. Financial award applicants required to submit CSS PROFILE or FAFSA. In 2017, 49 master's awarded. *Program availability:* Part-time. Offers clinical nurse specialist (MSN); family nurse practitioner (MSN); healthcare systems management (MSN); teaching-learning (MSN). *Application deadline:* For fall admission, 8/1 priority date for domestic students, 7/1 for international students; for spring admission, 12/1 priority date for domestic students, 11/1 for international students. Applications are processed on a rolling basis. *Application fee:* $45. Electronic applications accepted. *Application Contact:* Tamakia King, Graduate Admissions Counselor, 951-552-8138, Fax: 951-343-5095, E-mail: tking@calbaptist.edu. *Dean, School of Nursing*, Dr. Geneva Oaks, 951-343-4702, E-mail: goaks@calbaptist.edu.

Program in Organizational Leadership Students: 49 full-time (34 women), 29 part-time (22 women); includes 35 minority (11 Black or African American, non-Hispanic/Latino; 2 Asian, non-Hispanic/Latino; 21 Hispanic/Latino; 1 Two or more races, non-Hispanic/Latino). Average age 37. 34 applicants, 88% accepted, 25 enrolled. *Faculty:* 5 full-time (2 women), 2 part-time/adjunct (1 woman). Expenses: Contact institution. *Financial support:* In 2017–18, 36 students received support. Federal Work-Study and scholarships/grants available. Financial award applicants required to submit CSS PROFILE or FAFSA. In 2017, 52 master's awarded. *Program availability:* Part-time, evening/weekend. Offers organizational leadership (MA). *Application deadline:* For fall admission, 8/1 priority date for domestic students, 7/1 for international students; for spring admission, 12/1 priority date for domestic students, 11/1 for international students. Applications are processed on a rolling basis. *Application fee:* $45. Electronic applications accepted. *Application Contact:* Ted Meyer, Dean of Enrollment Services, Online and Professional Studies, 951-343-3909, E-mail: tmeyer@calbaptist.edu. *Director, MA in Organizational Leadership*, Dr. Alfred Greg Bowden, 951-343-5560, E-mail: abowden@calbaptist.edu.

Program in Physician Assistant Studies Students: 60 full-time (44 women); includes 33 minority (1 Black or African American, non-Hispanic/Latino; 15 Asian, non-Hispanic/Latino; 12 Hispanic/Latino; 1 Native Hawaiian or other Pacific Islander, non-Hispanic/Latino; 4 Two or more races, non-Hispanic/Latino). Average age 26. 1,134 applicants, 4% accepted, 30 enrolled. *Faculty:* 5 full-time (3 women). Expenses: Contact institution. *Financial support:* In 2017–18, 2 students received support. Federal Work-Study and scholarships/grants available. Financial award applicants required to submit CSS PROFILE or FAFSA. *Program availability:* Part-time. Offers physician assistant studies (MS). *Application deadline:* For fall admission, 12/1 priority date for domestic students, 11/1 priority date for international students; for spring admission, 8/1 priority date for domestic students, 7/1 priority date for international students. Applications are processed on a rolling basis. *Application fee:* $45. Electronic applications accepted. *Application Contact:* Stephanie Fluitt, Graduate Admissions Counselor, 951-343-4696, Fax: 877-228-8877, E-mail: sfluitt@calbaptist.edu. *Director*, Dr. Allan M. Bedashi, 951-552-8838, E-mail: abedashi@calbaptist.edu.

Program in Public Administration Students: 39 full-time (24 women), 71 part-time (32 women); includes 71 minority (13 Black or African American, non-Hispanic/Latino; 1 American Indian or Alaska Native, non-Hispanic/Latino; 8 Asian, non-Hispanic/Latino; 42 Hispanic/Latino; 2 Native Hawaiian or other Pacific Islander, non-Hispanic/Latino; 5 Two or more races, non-Hispanic/Latino), 1 international. Average age 37. 35 applicants, 60% accepted, 19 enrolled. *Faculty:* 4 full-time (all women), 2 part-time/adjunct (0 women). Expenses: Contact institution. *Financial support:* In 2017–18, 37 students received support. Federal Work-Study and scholarships/grants available. Financial award applicants required to submit CSS PROFILE or FAFSA. In 2017, 60 master's awarded. *Program availability:* Part-time, evening/weekend. Offers public administration (MPA). *Application deadline:* For fall admission, 8/1 priority date for domestic students, 7/1 for international students; for spring admission, 12/1 priority date for domestic students, 11/1 for international students. Applications are processed on a rolling basis. *Application fee:* $45. Electronic applications accepted. *Application Contact:* Dr. Elaine Ahumada, Director, MPA Program, 951-343-3929, Fax: 951-343-4661, E-mail: eahumada@calbaptist.edu. *Vice President, Online and Professional Studies*, Dr. David Poole, 951-343-3902, E-mail: dpoole@calbaptist.edu.

Program in Public Health Students: 56 full-time (47 women), 37 part-time (30 women); includes 72 minority (18 Black or African American, non-Hispanic/Latino; 8 Asian, non-Hispanic/Latino; 38 Hispanic/Latino; 8 Two or more races, non-Hispanic/Latino), 4 international. Average age 28. 83 applicants, 64% accepted, 39 enrolled. *Faculty:* 9 full-time (5 women), 4 part-time/adjunct (2 women). Expenses: Contact institution. *Financial support:* In 2017–18, 22 students received support. Federal Work-Study and scholarships/grants available. Financial award applicants required to submit CSS PROFILE or FAFSA. In 2017, 4 master's awarded. *Program availability:* Part-time, evening/weekend. Offers health education and promotion (MPH); health policy and administration (MPH). *Application deadline:* For fall admission, 8/1 priority date for domestic students, 7/1 for international students; for spring admission, 12/1 priority date for domestic students, 11/1 for international students. Applications are processed on a rolling basis. *Application fee:* $45. Electronic applications accepted. *Application Contact:* Tamakia King, Graduate Admissions Counselor, 951-552-8138, E-mail: tking@calbaptist.edu. *Dean, College of Health Science*, Dr. David Pearson, 951-343-4298, E-mail: dpearson@calbaptist.edu.

Program in Public Relations Students: 16 full-time (14 women), 8 part-time (all women); includes 17 minority (5 Black or African American, non-Hispanic/Latino; 1 Asian, non-Hispanic/Latino; 9 Hispanic/Latino; 2 Two or more races, non-Hispanic/Latino). Average age 33. 19 applicants, 68% accepted, 11 enrolled. *Faculty:* 2 full-time (both women). Expenses: Contact institution. *Financial support:* Applicants required to submit CSS PROFILE or FAFSA. In 2017, 10 master's awarded. *Program availability:* Part-time, evening/weekend. Offers public relations (MA). *Application deadline:* For fall admission, 8/1 priority date for domestic students, 7/1 for international students; for spring admission, 12/1 priority date for domestic students, 11/1 priority date for international students. Applications are processed on a rolling basis. *Application fee:* $45. Electronic applications accepted. *Application Contact:* Ted Meyer, Dean of Enrollment Services, Online and Professional Studies, 951-343-3909, E-mail: tmeyer@calbaptist.edu. *Program Director, MA in Public Relations*, Dr. Mary Ann Pearson, 951-343-3967, E-mail: mpearson@calbaptist.edu.

Program in School Counseling Students: 58 part-time (49 women); includes 31 minority (2 Black or African American, non-Hispanic/Latino; 1 American Indian or Alaska Native, non-Hispanic/Latino; 1 Asian, non-Hispanic/Latino; 26 Hispanic/Latino; 1 Two or more races, non-Hispanic/Latino). Average age 32. 46 applicants, 50% accepted, 22 enrolled. *Faculty:* 2 full-time (both women), 6 part-time/adjunct (3 women). Expenses: Contact institution. *Financial support:* In 2017–18, 17 students received support. Federal Work-Study and scholarships/grants available. Financial award applicants required to submit CSS PROFILE or FAFSA. In 2017, 9 master's awarded. *Program availability:* Part-time, evening/weekend. Offers school counseling (MS). *Application deadline:* For fall admission, 8/1 priority date for domestic students, 7/7 priority date for international students; for spring admission, 12/1 priority date for domestic students, 11/1 priority date for international students. Applications are processed on a rolling basis. *Application fee:* $45. Electronic applications accepted. *Application Contact:* David Little, Graduate Admissions Counselor, 951-552-8093, E-mail: dlittle@calbaptist.edu. *Dean, School of Education*, Dr. John Shoup, 951-343-4205, E-mail: jshoup@calbaptist.edu.

Program in School Psychology Students: 39 full-time (34 women), 30 part-time (29 women); includes 35 minority (5 Black or African American, non-Hispanic/Latino; 6 Asian, non-Hispanic/Latino; 23 Hispanic/Latino; 1 Two or more races, non-Hispanic/Latino). Average age 29. 62 applicants, 66% accepted, 39 enrolled. *Faculty:* 2 full-time (both women), 6 part-time/adjunct (3 women). Expenses: Contact institution. *Financial support:* In 2017–18, 16 students received support. Federal Work-Study and scholarships/grants available. Financial award applicants required to submit CSS PROFILE or FAFSA. In 2017, 14 master's awarded. *Program availability:* Part-time, evening/weekend. Offers school psychology (MS). *Application deadline:* For fall admission, 7/1 priority date for domestic and international students; for spring admission, 12/1 priority date for domestic students, 11/1 priority date for international students. Applications are processed on a rolling basis. *Application fee:* $45. Electronic applications accepted. *Application Contact:* David Little, Graduate Admissions Counselor, 951-552-8093, E-mail: dlittle@calbaptist.edu. *Dean, School of Education*, Dr. John Shoup, 951-343-4205, E-mail: jshoup@calbaptist.edu.

Program in Social Work Students: 68 full-time (60 women); includes 54 minority (14 Black or African American, non-Hispanic/Latino; 1 Asian, non-Hispanic/Latino; 33 Hispanic/Latino; 6 Two or more races, non-Hispanic/Latino). Average age 30. 136 applicants, 71% accepted, 72 enrolled. *Faculty:* 5 full-time (4 women). Expenses: Contact institution. *Financial support:* Federal Work-Study and scholarships/grants available. *Program availability:* Part-time. Offers clinical social work (MSW); community social work practice (MSW). *Application deadline:* For fall admission, 8/1 priority date for domestic students, 7/1 for international students; for spring admission, 12/1 priority date for domestic students, 11/1 for international students. Applications are processed on a rolling basis. *Application fee:* $45. Electronic applications accepted. *Application Contact:* Debbie Passalacqua, Associate Director of Graduate Admissions, 951-343-4527, Fax: 877-228-8877, E-mail: dpassala@calbaptist.edu. *Director, Social Work Program*, Dr. Satara Armstrong, 951-552-8442, E-mail: sarmstrong@calbaptist.edu.

Program in Software Engineering Students: 24 full-time (6 women), 1 (woman) part-time; includes 3 minority (2 Asian, non-Hispanic/Latino; 1 Two or more races, non-Hispanic/Latino), 22 international. Average age 25. 5 applicants, 60% accepted, 2 enrolled. *Faculty:* 8 full-time (3 women). Expenses: Contact institution. *Financial support:* In 2017–18, 2 students received support. Federal Work-Study and scholarships/grants available. Financial award applicants required to submit CSS PROFILE or FAFSA. In 2017, 2 master's awarded. *Program availability:* Part-time. Offers software engineering (MS). *Application deadline:* For fall admission, 8/1 priority date for domestic students, 7/1 priority date for international students; for spring admission, 12/1 priority date for domestic students, 11/1 priority date for international students. Applications are processed on a rolling basis. *Application fee:* $45. Electronic applications accepted. *Application Contact:* Rudy Villarruel, Graduate Admissions Counselor, 951-552-8132, Fax: 877-228-8877, E-mail: rvillarruel@calbaptist.edu. *Chair, Computer Science and Software Engineering*, Dr. Arlene Perkins, 951-552-8630, E-mail: aperkins@calbaptist.edu.

Program in Speech Language Pathology Students: 48 full-time (44 women); includes 25 minority (2 Black or African American, non-Hispanic/Latino; 5 Asian, non-

Hispanic/Latino; 16 Hispanic/Latino; 2 Two or more races, non-Hispanic/Latino). Average age 25. 148 applicants, 29% accepted, 24 enrolled. *Faculty:* 6 full-time (5 women), 5 part-time/adjunct (3 women). Expenses: Contact institution. *Financial support:* In 2017–18, 1 student received support. Federal Work-Study and scholarships/grants available. Financial award applicants required to submit CSS PROFILE or FAFSA. *Program availability:* Part-time. Offers speech language pathology (MS). *Application deadline:* For fall admission, 12/1 priority date for domestic students, 11/1 priority date for international students; for spring admission, 8/1 priority date for domestic students, 7/1 priority date for international students. Applications are processed on a rolling basis. *Application fee:* $45. Electronic applications accepted. *Application Contact:* Stephanie Fluitt, Graduate Admissions Counselor, 951-343-4696, Fax: 877-228-8877, E-mail: sfluitt@calbaptist.edu. *Director*, Dr. Candace Vickers, 951-552-8129, E-mail: cvickers@calbaptist.edu.

CALIFORNIA COAST UNIVERSITY, Santa Ana, CA 92701

General Information Proprietary, coed, comprehensive institution.

GRADUATE UNITS

School of Administration and Management *Program availability:* Online learning. Offers business marketing (MBA); health care management (MBA); human resource management (MBA); management (MBA, MS). Electronic applications accepted.

School of Behavioral Science *Program availability:* Online learning. Offers psychology (MS).

School of Criminal Justice Offers criminal justice (MS).

School of Education *Program availability:* Online learning. Offers administration (M Ed); curriculum and instruction (M Ed); educational administration (Ed D); educational psychology (Ed D); organizational leadership (Ed D).

CALIFORNIA COLLEGE OF THE ARTS, San Francisco, CA 94107

General Information Independent, coed, comprehensive institution. *Enrollment:* 1,983 graduate, professional, and undergraduate students; 414 full-time matriculated graduate/professional students (271 women), 29 part-time matriculated graduate/professional students (14 women). *Enrollment by degree level:* 443 master's. *Graduate faculty:* 58 full-time (31 women), 107 part-time/adjunct (45 women). *Tuition:* Full-time $49,230; part-time $1641 per credit. *Required fees:* $490; $490 per credit. Part-time tuition and fees vary according to course load and program. *Graduate housing:* Room and/or apartments available on a first-come, first-served basis to single students; on-campus housing not available to married students. Typical cost: $10,136 per year. Room charges vary according to housing facility selected. Housing application deadline: 5/15. *Student services:* Campus employment opportunities, campus safety program, career counseling, exercise/wellness program, free psychological counseling, grant writing training, international student services, low-cost health insurance, multicultural affairs office, services for students with disabilities, writing training. *Library facilities:* Meyer Library plus 1 other.

Computer facilities: Computer purchase and lease plans are available. 400 computers available on campus for general student use. A campuswide network can be accessed from student residence rooms and from off campus. Online class registration, online course evaluations, learning management system, media applications, software training, print payments are available.
Website: http://www.cca.edu/

General Application Contact: Wes Fanelli, Assistant Director of Graduate Admissions, 415-703-9533, Fax: 415-703-9539, E-mail: graduateprograms@cca.edu.

GRADUATE UNITS

Graduate Programs Students: 395 full-time (250 women), 9 part-time (5 women); includes 108 minority (18 Black or African American, non-Hispanic/Latino; 2 American Indian or Alaska Native, non-Hispanic/Latino; 41 Asian, non-Hispanic/Latino; 46 Hispanic/Latino; 1 Native Hawaiian or other Pacific Islander, non-Hispanic/Latino), 162 international. Average age 31. 1,164 applicants, 48% accepted, 210 enrolled. *Faculty:* 99 full-time (48 women), 143 part-time/adjunct (65 women). Expenses: Contact institution. *Financial support:* Teaching assistantships, Federal Work-Study, scholarships/grants, and unspecified assistantships available. Financial award applicants required to submit FAFSA. *Program availability:* Part-time. Offers advanced architecture design (MAAD); architecture (M Arch); comics (MFA); creative non-fiction (MFA); curatorial practice (MA); design strategy (MBA); fiction (MFA); film (MFA); fine arts (MFA); graphic design (MFA); industrial design (MFA); interaction design (MFA); poetry (MFA); visual and critical studies (MA). *Application deadline:* For fall admission, 1/31 priority date for domestic and international students. Applications are processed on a rolling basis. *Application fee:* $70. Electronic applications accepted. *Application Contact:* Wes Fanelli, Assistant Director of Graduate Admissions, 415-703-9533, Fax: 415-703-9539, E-mail: wfanelli@cca.edu. *Director of Graduate Admissions*, Noel Dahl, 415-703-9537, Fax: 415-703-9539, E-mail: ndahl@cca.edu.

CALIFORNIA HEALTH SCIENCES UNIVERSITY, Clovis, CA 93612

General Information Proprietary, coed, graduate-only institution.

GRADUATE UNITS

College of Pharmacy Offers pharmacy (Pharm D).

CALIFORNIA INSTITUTE OF ADVANCED MANAGEMENT, El Monte, CA 91731

General Information Private, coed, graduate-only institution.

GRADUATE UNITS

The MBA Program Offers executive management and entrepreneurship (MBA).

CALIFORNIA INSTITUTE OF INTEGRAL STUDIES, San Francisco, CA 94103

General Information Independent, coed, upper-level institution. CGS member. *Enrollment:* 1,417 graduate, professional, and undergraduate students; 1,065 full-time matriculated graduate/professional students (784 women), 314 part-time matriculated graduate/professional students (235 women). *Enrollment by degree level:* 698 master's, 672 doctoral. *Tuition:* Full-time $20,970. *Required fees:* $430. Tuition and fees vary according to course load, degree level and program. *Graduate housing:* On-campus housing not available. *Student services:* Campus employment opportunities, campus safety program, career counseling, grant writing training, international student services, low-cost health insurance, multicultural affairs office, services for students with disabilities, writing training. *Library facilities:* The Laurance S. Rockefeller Library plus 1 other. *Research affiliation:* Bay Area Reference Service.

Computer facilities: 25 computers available on campus for general student use. A campuswide network can be accessed from off campus. Online class registration is available.
Website: http://www.ciis.edu/

General Application Contact: Ellen Durst, Interim Director of Admissions, 415-575-6153, Fax: 415-575-1264, E-mail: admissions@ciis.edu.

GRADUATE UNITS

American College of Traditional Chinese Medicine Students: 157 full-time (118 women), 68 part-time (53 women); includes 84 minority (3 Black or African American, non-Hispanic/Latino; 54 Asian, non-Hispanic/Latino; 13 Hispanic/Latino; 3 Native Hawaiian or other Pacific Islander, non-Hispanic/Latino; 11 Two or more races, non-Hispanic/Latino), 9 international. Average age 37. 56 applicants, 100% accepted, 44 enrolled. Expenses: Contact institution. In 2017, 33 master's, 29 doctorates awarded. Offers acupuncture and Chinese medicine (DACM, tDACM); acupuncture and Oriental medicine (DAOM); traditional Chinese medicine (MSTCM). *Application deadline:* For fall admission, 8/1 priority date for domestic students; for spring admission, 12/1 priority date for domestic students; for summer admission, 4/1 priority date for domestic students. *Application fee:* $65. Electronic applications accepted. *Application Contact:* Yuwen Chiu, Associate Director of Admissions, 415-828-7600, E-mail: yuwenchiu@actcm.edu. *Academic Dean*, Dr. Bingzen Zou, 415-828-7600, E-mail: bingzou@actcm.edu.

School of Consciousness and Transformation Students: 392 full-time (265 women), 141 part-time (98 women); includes 145 minority (40 Black or African American, non-Hispanic/Latino; 1 American Indian or Alaska Native, non-Hispanic/Latino; 19 Asian, non-Hispanic/Latino; 54 Hispanic/Latino; 31 Two or more races, non-Hispanic/Latino), 61 international. Average age 43. 212 applicants, 96% accepted, 153 enrolled. Expenses: Contact institution. *Financial support:* Fellowships, research assistantships, teaching assistantships, career-related internships or fieldwork, Federal Work-Study, and scholarships/grants available. Support available to part-time students. Financial award application deadline: 4/15; financial award applicants required to submit FAFSA. In 2017, 49 master's, 36 doctorates awarded. *Program availability:* Part-time, evening/weekend, 100% online, blended/hybrid learning. Offers anthropology and social change (MA, PhD); Asian philosophies and cultures (MA); creative inquiry/interdisciplinary arts (MFA); East-West psychology (MA, PhD); integral and transpersonal psychology (PhD); philosophy and religion (PhD); philosophy, cosmology, and consciousness (Certificate); transformative leadership (MA); transformative studies (PhD); women, gender, spirituality and social justice (MA); writing and consciousness (MFA). *Application deadline:* For fall admission, 2/1 priority date for domestic and international students; for spring admission, 10/15 priority date for domestic and international students. Applications are processed on a rolling basis. *Application fee:* $65. Electronic applications accepted. *Application Contact:* Ellen Durst, Director of Admissions, 415-575-6100, Fax: 415-575-1268, E-mail: admissions@ciis.edu. *Academic Dean*, Kathy Littles, 415-575-6100, E-mail: klittles@ciis.edu.

School of Professional Psychology and Health Students: 507 full-time (401 women), 96 part-time (77 women); includes 167 minority (29 Black or African American, non-Hispanic/Latino; 3 American Indian or Alaska Native, non-Hispanic/Latino; 32 Asian, non-Hispanic/Latino; 62 Hispanic/Latino; 2 Native Hawaiian or other Pacific Islander, non-Hispanic/Latino; 39 Two or more races, non-Hispanic/Latino), 60 international. Average age 34. 302 applicants, 89% accepted, 171 enrolled. Expenses: Contact institution. *Financial support:* Research assistantships with tuition reimbursements, teaching assistantships with tuition reimbursements, career-related internships or fieldwork, Federal Work-Study, and scholarships/grants available. Support available to part-time students. Financial award application deadline: 4/15; financial award applicants required to submit FAFSA. In 2017, 194 master's, 18 doctorates awarded. *Program availability:* Part-time, evening/weekend, 100% online, blended/hybrid learning. Offers clinical psychology (Psy D); community mental health (MA); drama therapy (MA); expressive arts therapy (MA); integral counseling psychology (MA); integrative health studies (MA); psychological studies (MA); somatic psychology (MA). *Application deadline:* For fall admission, 2/1 priority date for domestic and international students; for spring admission, 10/15 priority date for domestic and international students. Applications are processed on a rolling basis. *Application fee:* $65. Electronic applications accepted. *Application Contact:* Ellen Durst, Director of Admissions, 415-575-6100, Fax: 415-575-1268, E-mail: admissions@ciis.edu. *Academic Dean*, Nicolle Zapien, 415-575-5577, E-mail: nzapien@ciis.edu.

CALIFORNIA INSTITUTE OF TECHNOLOGY, Pasadena, CA 91125-0001

General Information Independent, coed, university. CGS member. *Graduate housing:* Rooms and/or apartments available on a first-come, first-served basis to single students and available to married students. Housing application deadline: 5/1. *Research affiliation:* Scripps Institute of Oceanography, Stanford Linear Accelerator Center (high-energy physics), European Center for Nuclear Research (high-energy physics), National Science Foundation Center for Research in Parallel Computing, Cosmic Gravitational Waves Observatory (laser interferometer gravitational waves).

GRADUATE UNITS

Division of Biology Offers biochemistry and molecular biophysics (PhD); cell biology and biophysics (PhD); developmental biology (PhD); genetics (PhD); immunology (PhD); molecular biology (PhD); neurobiology (PhD). Electronic applications accepted.

Division of Chemistry and Chemical Engineering Students: 295 full-time (115 women); includes 79 minority (3 Black or African American, non-Hispanic/Latino; 41 Asian, non-Hispanic/Latino; 21 Hispanic/Latino; 14 Two or more races, non-Hispanic/Latino), 80 international. Average age 25. 638 applicants, 23% accepted, 43 enrolled. *Faculty:* 42 full-time (10 women). Expenses: Contact institution. *Financial support:* In 2017–18, 309 students received support, including fellowships (averaging $33,000 per year), research assistantships (averaging $25,900 per year), teaching assistantships (averaging $5,100 per year); Federal Work-Study, institutionally sponsored loans, scholarships/grants, traineeships, health care benefits, and unspecified assistantships also available. Financial award application deadline: 12/15. In 2017, 14 master's, 59 doctorates awarded. Offers biochemistry and molecular biophysics (MS, PhD); chemical engineering (MS, PhD); chemistry (MS, PhD). *Application deadline:* For fall admission, 12/15 for domestic and international students. *Application fee:* $100. Electronic applications accepted. *Application Contact:* Natalie Gilmore, Graduate Office, 626-395-3812, Fax: 626-577-9246, E-mail: ngilmore@its.caltech.edu. *Chair, Division of Chemistry and Chemical Engineering*, Prof. Jacqueline K. Barton, 626-395-3646, Fax: 626-395-6948, E-mail: jkbarton@caltech.edu.

Division of Engineering and Applied Science Offers aeronautics (MS, PhD, Engr); applied and computational mathematics (MS, PhD); applied mechanics (MS, PhD); applied physics (MS, PhD); bioengineering (MS, PhD); civil engineering (MS, PhD, Engr); computation and neural systems (MS, PhD); computer science (MS, PhD); control and dynamical systems (MS, PhD); electrical engineering (MS, PhD, Engr); environmental science and engineering (MS, PhD); materials science (MS, PhD); mechanical engineering (MS, PhD, Engr). Electronic applications accepted.

Division of Geological and Planetary Sciences Offers environmental science and engineering (MS, PhD); geobiology (MS, PhD); geochemistry (MS, PhD); geology (MS, PhD); geophysics (MS, PhD); planetary science (MS, PhD). Electronic applications accepted.

Division of Physics, Mathematics and Astronomy Offers astronomy (PhD); mathematics (PhD); physics (PhD).

Division of the Humanities and Social Sciences Offers humanities and social sciences (MS, PhD); social science (MS, PhD). Electronic applications accepted.

CALIFORNIA INSTITUTE OF THE ARTS, Valencia, CA 91355-2340

General Information Independent, coed, comprehensive institution. *Graduate housing:* Room and/or apartments available on a first-come, first-served basis to single students; on-campus housing not available to married students. Housing application deadline: 7/1.

GRADUATE UNITS

The Herb Alpert School of Music *Program availability:* Part-time. Offers African music (MFA, Adv C); composition (MFA, Adv C); composition/new media (MFA, Adv C); Indonesian music (MFA, Adv C); jazz (MFA, Adv C); North Indian music (MFA, Adv C); performance (MFA, Adv C); performer/composer (MFA, Adv C); voice (MFA, Adv C); world music performance (MFA). Electronic applications accepted.

School of Art Offers art (MFA, Adv C); graphic design (MFA, Adv C); photography (MFA, Adv C). Electronic applications accepted.

School of Critical Studies Offers writing (MFA, Adv C).

School of Film/Video Offers experimental animation (MFA); film directing (MFA, Adv C); film/video (Adv C). Electronic applications accepted.

School of Theater Offers acting (MFA, Adv C); creative producing and management (MFA); design and production (MFA); design and technology (Adv C); directing (MFA); theater management (Adv C). Electronic applications accepted.

The Sharon Disney Lund School of Dance Offers dance (MFA, Adv C).

CALIFORNIA INTERCONTINENTAL UNIVERSITY, Irvine, CA 92614

General Information Proprietary, coed, comprehensive institution.

GRADUATE UNITS

Hollywood College of the Entertainment Industry Offers Hollywood and entertainment management (MBA).

School of Business Offers banking and finance (MBA); entrepreneurship and business management (DBA); global business leadership (DBA); international management and marketing (MBA); organizational management and human resource management (MBA).

School of Healthcare Offers healthcare management and leadership (MBA, DBA).

School of Information Technology Offers information systems and enterprise resource management (DBA); information systems and knowledge management (MBA); project and quality management (MBA).

CALIFORNIA INTERNATIONAL BUSINESS UNIVERSITY, San Diego, CA 92101

General Information Independent, coed, graduate-only institution.

GRADUATE UNITS

Graduate Programs Offers business (MBA, MSIM, DBA).

CALIFORNIA LUTHERAN UNIVERSITY, Thousand Oaks, CA 91360-2787

General Information Independent-religious, coed, comprehensive institution. CGS member. *Enrollment:* 4,236 graduate, professional, and undergraduate students; 1,010 full-time matriculated graduate/professional students (620 women), 263 part-time matriculated graduate/professional students (159 women). *Enrollment by degree level:* 1,154 master's, 112 doctoral, 7 other advanced degrees. *Graduate faculty:* 56 full-time (34 women), 102 part-time/adjunct (52 women). *Tuition:* Full-time $15,000. Full-time tuition and fees vary according to degree level and program. *Graduate housing:* Room and/or apartments available on a first-come, first-served basis to single students; on-campus housing not available to married students. *Student services:* Campus employment opportunities, career counseling, free psychological counseling, international student services, low-cost health insurance, multicultural affairs office, services for students with disabilities, writing training. *Library facilities:* Pearson Library. *Collection:* Books: 120,019 (physical), 246,484 (digital/electronic); Serial titles: 27 (physical), 34 (digital/electronic); Databases: 163. Weekly public service hours: 102; students can reserve study rooms.

Computer facilities: 334 computers available on campus for general student use. A campuswide network can be accessed from student residence rooms and from off campus. Online class registration is available.
Website: http://www.callutheran.edu/

General Application Contact: Information Contact, 805-493-3325, Fax: 805-493-3861, E-mail: clugrad@callutheran.edu.

GRADUATE UNITS

Graduate Studies Students: 926 full-time (556 women), 228 part-time (133 women); includes 436 minority (22 Black or African American, non-Hispanic/Latino; 6 American Indian or Alaska Native, non-Hispanic/Latino; 39 Asian, non-Hispanic/Latino; 324 Hispanic/Latino; 1 Native Hawaiian or other Pacific Islander, non-Hispanic/Latino; 44 Two or more races, non-Hispanic/Latino), 302 international. Average age 31. 952 applicants, 65% accepted, 309 enrolled. *Faculty:* 56 full-time (34 women), 102 part-time/adjunct (52 women). Expenses: Contact institution. *Financial support:* Scholarships/grants and unspecified assistantships available. Support available to part-time students. Financial award applicants required to submit FAFSA. In 2017, 472 master's, 26 doctorates awarded. *Program availability:* Part-time, evening/weekend. Offers clinical psychology (MS, Psy D); marital and family therapy (MS). *Application deadline:* Applications are processed on a rolling basis. *Application fee:* $50. Electronic applications accepted. *Application Contact:* 805-493-3325, Fax: 805-493-3861, E-mail: clugrad@callutheran.edu. *Provost/Vice President for Academic Affairs,* Dr. Leanne Neilson, 805-493-3145, E-mail: neilson@callutheran.edu.

Graduate School of Education Students: 390 full-time (303 women), 61 part-time (51 women); includes 228 minority (6 Black or African American, non-Hispanic/Latino; 2 American Indian or Alaska Native, non-Hispanic/Latino; 13 Asian, non-Hispanic/Latino; 186 Hispanic/Latino; 1 Native Hawaiian or other Pacific Islander, non-Hispanic/Latino; 20 Two or more races, non-Hispanic/Latino). Average age 31. 201 applicants, 76% accepted, 121 enrolled. *Faculty:* 21 full-time (18 women), 40 part-time/adjunct (27 women). Expenses: Contact institution. In 2017, 129 master's, 19 doctorates awarded. *Program availability:* Part-time, evening/weekend. Offers counseling and guidance (MS); educational leadership (MA, Ed D); special education (MS); teacher leadership (M Ed); teaching (M Ed). *Application deadline:* For fall admission, 7/1 priority date for domestic students; for spring admission, 11/1 priority date for domestic students; for summer admission, 4/1 priority date for domestic students. Applications are processed on a rolling basis. *Application fee:* $50. Electronic applications accepted. *Application Contact:* 805-493-3325, Fax: 805-493-3861, E-mail: clugrad@callutheran.edu. *Dean,* Dr. Michael Hillis, 805-493-3421.

Pacific Lutheran Theological Seminary Students: 41 full-time (26 women), 8 part-time (3 women); includes 9 minority (1 Black or African American, non-Hispanic/Latino; 1 Asian, non-Hispanic/Latino; 3 Hispanic/Latino; 4 Two or more races, non-Hispanic/Latino), 2 international. Average age 34. 23 applicants, 74% accepted, 14 enrolled. *Faculty:* 8 full-time (6 women), 3 part-time/adjunct (1 woman). Expenses: Contact institution. *Financial support:* In 2017–18, 104 students received support. Teaching assistantships, career-related internships or fieldwork, Federal Work-Study, institutionally sponsored loans, and scholarships/grants available. Support available to part-time students. Financial award application deadline: 3/15; financial award applicants required to submit FAFSA. In 2017, 7 master's awarded. *Program availability:* Part-time. Offers theology (M Div, MA, MCM, MTS, PhD, Th D, Certificate). MA, Th D, PhD offered jointly with Graduate Theological Union; PhD with University of California, Berkeley. *Application deadline:* For fall admission, 8/1 priority date for domestic students; for spring admission, 1/1 priority date for domestic students. Applications are processed on a rolling basis. *Application fee:* $25. Electronic applications accepted. *Application Contact:* 805-493-3325, Fax: 805-493-3861, E-mail: clugrad@callutheran.edu. *Dean,* Alica Vargas, 510-559-2732, E-mail: avargas@plts.edu.

School of Management Students: 423 full-time (168 women), 153 part-time (72 women); includes 124 minority (11 Black or African American, non-Hispanic/Latino; 1 American Indian or Alaska Native, non-Hispanic/Latino; 21 Asian, non-Hispanic/Latino; 75 Hispanic/Latino; 16 Two or more races, non-Hispanic/Latino), 294 international. Average age 31. 467 applicants, 72% accepted, 108 enrolled. *Faculty:* 17 full-time (4 women), 40 part-time/adjunct (9 women). Expenses: Contact institution. In 2017, 306 master's awarded. *Program availability:* Part-time, evening/weekend, 100% online, blended/hybrid learning. Offers business (IMBA); entrepreneurship (MBA, Certificate); finance (MBA, Certificate); financial planning (MBA, MS, Certificate); human capital management (MBA, Certificate); information technology (MS); information technology management (MBA, Certificate); international business (MBA, Certificate); marketing (MBA, Certificate); public policy and administration (MPPA); quantitative economics (MS). *Application deadline:* Applications are processed on a rolling basis. *Application fee:* $50. Electronic applications accepted. *Application Contact:* 805-493-3325, Fax: 805-493-3861, E-mail: clugrad@callutheran.edu. *Dean,* Dr. Gerhard Apfelthaler, 805-493-3360.

CALIFORNIA MIRAMAR UNIVERSITY, San Diego, CA 92108

General Information Proprietary, coed, comprehensive institution.

GRADUATE UNITS

Program in Business Administration Offers business administration (MBA).

Program in Strategic Leadership Offers strategic leadership (MS).

Program in Taxation and Trade for Executives Offers taxation and trade for executives (MT).

Program in Telecommunications Management Offers telecommunications management (MST).

CALIFORNIA NORTHSTATE UNIVERSITY, Elk Grove, CA 95757

General Information Proprietary, coed, comprehensive institution.

GRADUATE UNITS

College of Medicine Offers medicine (MD).

College of Pharmacy Offers pharmacy (Pharm D).

CALIFORNIA POLYTECHNIC STATE UNIVERSITY, SAN LUIS OBISPO, San Luis Obispo, CA 93407

General Information State-supported, coed, comprehensive institution. CGS member. *Enrollment:* 22,188 graduate, professional, and undergraduate students; 538 full-time matriculated graduate/professional students (246 women), 189 part-time matriculated graduate/professional students (79 women). *Enrollment by degree level:* 727 master's. *Graduate faculty:* 171 full-time (51 women), 20 part-time/adjunct (9 women). Tuition, state resident: full-time $7176; part-time $4164 per year. *Required fees:* $3690; $3219 per year. $1073 per trimester. *Graduate housing:* Room and/or apartments available on a first-come, first-served basis to single students; on-campus housing not available to married students. *Student services:* Campus employment opportunities, campus safety program, career counseling, child daycare facilities, exercise/wellness program, free psychological counseling, grant writing training, international student services, low-cost health insurance, multicultural affairs office, services for students with disabilities, teacher training, writing training. *Library facilities:* Robert E. Kennedy Library.

Computer facilities: A campuswide network can be accessed from student residence rooms and from off campus. Online class registration is available.
Website: http://www.calpoly.edu/

General Application Contact: Dr. James Maraviglia, Associate Vice Provost for Marketing and Enrollment Development, 805-756-2311, Fax: 805-756-5400, E-mail: admissions@calpoly.edu.

GRADUATE UNITS

College of Agriculture, Food and Environmental Sciences Students: 63 full-time (45 women), 24 part-time (16 women); includes 23 minority (2 Asian, non-Hispanic/Latino; 15 Hispanic/Latino; 6 Two or more races, non-Hispanic/Latino), 3 international. Average age 26. 87 applicants, 52% accepted, 31 enrolled. *Faculty:* 29 full-time (10 women), 2 part-time/adjunct (0 women). Expenses: Contact institution. *Financial support:* Fellowships, research assistantships, teaching assistantships, career-related internships or fieldwork, institutionally sponsored loans, scholarships/grants, and health care benefits available. Financial award application deadline: 3/2; financial award applicants required to submit FAFSA. In 2017, 46 master's awarded. *Program availability:* Part-time. Offers agricultural education and communication (MAE); agriculture (MS); agriculture, food and environmental sciences (MAE, MS); food science and nutrition (MS); forestry sciences (MS); nutrition (MS). *Application deadline:* For fall admission, 4/1 for domestic students, 11/30 for international students; for winter admission, 10/1 for domestic students; for spring admission, 1/1 for domestic students. Applications are processed on a rolling basis. *Application fee:* $55. Electronic applications accepted. *Application Contact:* Dr. Jim Prince, Associate Dean, Research and Graduate Programs, 805-756-5104, E-mail: jpprince@calpoly.edu. *Dean,* Dr. Andrew Thulin, 805-756-2161, Fax: 805-756-6577, E-mail: athulin@calpoly.edu.

College of Architecture and Environmental Design Students: 42 full-time (17 women), 4 part-time (2 women); includes 12 minority (5 Asian, non-Hispanic/Latino; 5 Hispanic/Latino; 2 Two or more races, non-Hispanic/Latino), 4 international. Average age 25. 79 applicants, 61% accepted, 23 enrolled. *Faculty:* 10 full-time (5 women), 2 part-time/adjunct (1 woman). Expenses: Contact institution. *Financial support:* Research assistantships, teaching assistantships, career-related internships or fieldwork, and institutionally sponsored loans available. Financial award application deadline: 3/2; financial award applicants required to submit FAFSA. In 2017, 22 master's awarded. *Program availability:* Part-time. Offers architectural engineering (MS); architecture (MS); architecture and environmental design (MCRP, MS); city and regional planning (MCRP). *Application deadline:* For fall admission, 6/1 for domestic students, 11/30 for international students; for winter admission, 11/1 for domestic students, 6/30 for international students. Applications are processed on a rolling basis. *Application fee:* $55. Electronic applications accepted. *Associate Dean*, Dr. Michael Lucas, E-mail: mlucas@calpoly.edu.

College of Engineering Students: 228 full-time (52 women), 97 part-time (14 women); includes 110 minority (4 Black or African American, non-Hispanic/Latino; 53 Asian, non-Hispanic/Latino; 32 Hispanic/Latino; 21 Two or more races, non-Hispanic/Latino), 20 international. Average age 25. 400 applicants, 50% accepted, 142 enrolled. *Faculty:* 68 full-time (15 women), 3 part-time/adjunct (0 women). Expenses: Contact institution. *Financial support:* Fellowships, research assistantships, teaching assistantships, career-related internships or fieldwork, institutionally sponsored loans, and unspecified assistantships available. Financial award application deadline: 3/2; financial award applicants required to submit FAFSA. In 2017, 206 master's awarded. *Program availability:* Part-time. Offers aerospace engineering (MS); biomedical engineering (MS); civil and environmental engineering (MS); computer science (MS); electrical engineering (MS); engineering (MS); general engineering (MS); industrial engineering (MS); mechanical engineering (MS). *Application deadline:* For fall admission, 4/1 for domestic students, 3/1 for international students; for winter admission, 10/1 for domestic students; for spring admission, 1/1 for domestic students. Applications are processed on a rolling basis. *Application fee:* $55. Electronic applications accepted. *Associate Dean*, Dr. Rakesh Goel, 805-756-6402, E-mail: rgoel@calpoly.edu.

College of Liberal Arts Students: 40 full-time (31 women), 52 part-time (32 women); includes 25 minority (1 Asian, non-Hispanic/Latino; 18 Hispanic/Latino; 6 Two or more races, non-Hispanic/Latino). Average age 28. 112 applicants, 54% accepted, 36 enrolled. *Faculty:* 18 full-time (6 women), 1 (woman) part-time/adjunct. Expenses: Contact institution. *Financial support:* Fellowships, teaching assistantships, career-related internships or fieldwork, Federal Work-Study, institutionally sponsored loans, scholarships/grants, and tutorships, writing laboratory assistantships available. Support available to part-time students. Financial award application deadline: 3/2; financial award applicants required to submit FAFSA. In 2017, 27 master's awarded. *Program availability:* Part-time. Offers English (MA); history (MA); liberal arts (MA, MPP, MS); political science (MPP); psychology (MS). *Application deadline:* For fall admission, 4/1 for domestic students, 3/1 for international students. *Application fee:* $55. *Associate Dean*, Dr. Debra Valencia-Laver, 805-756-2706, Fax: 805-756-5748, E-mail: dlvalenc@calpoly.edu.

College of Science and Mathematics Students: 139 full-time (93 women), 28 part-time (13 women); includes 54 minority (1 Black or African American, non-Hispanic/Latino; 10 Asian, non-Hispanic/Latino; 40 Hispanic/Latino; 3 Two or more races, non-Hispanic/Latino), 3 international. Average age 28. 298 applicants, 38% accepted, 93 enrolled. *Faculty:* 42 full-time (14 women), 10 part-time/adjunct (7 women). Expenses: Contact institution. *Financial support:* Fellowships, research assistantships, teaching assistantships, career-related internships or fieldwork, and Federal Work-Study available. Support available to part-time students. Financial award application deadline: 3/2; financial award applicants required to submit FAFSA. In 2017, 88 master's awarded. *Program availability:* Part-time. Offers biological sciences (MA, MS); mathematics (MS); polymers and coating science (MS); science and mathematics (MA, MS). *Application deadline:* For fall admission, 4/1 for domestic students, 3/1 for international students. Applications are processed on a rolling basis. *Application fee:* $55. Electronic applications accepted. *Associate Dean*, Dr. Kellie G. Hall, 805-756-2226, Fax: 805-756-1670, E-mail: kghall@calpoly.edu.

School of Education Students: 92 full-time (67 women), 4 part-time (1 woman); includes 32 minority (1 Black or African American, non-Hispanic/Latino; 5 Asian, non-Hispanic/Latino; 25 Hispanic/Latino; 1 Two or more races, non-Hispanic/Latino). Average age 30. 155 applicants, 42% accepted, 57 enrolled. *Faculty:* 10 full-time (5 women), 8 part-time/adjunct (5 women). Expenses: Contact institution. *Financial support:* Fellowships, research assistantships, career-related internships or fieldwork, Federal Work-Study, and institutionally sponsored loans available. Support available to part-time students. Financial award application deadline: 3/2; financial award applicants required to submit FAFSA. In 2017, 42 master's awarded. *Program availability:* Part-time, evening/weekend. Offers education (MA). *Application deadline:* For fall admission, 4/1 for domestic students, 3/1 for international students. Applications are processed on a rolling basis. *Application fee:* $55. Electronic applications accepted. *Application Contact:* E-mail: soe@calpoly.edu. *Director*, Dr. Kevin Taylor, 805-756-1503, E-mail: jktaylor@calpoly.edu.

Orfalea College of Business Students: 103 full-time (48 women), 14 part-time (7 women); includes 32 minority (13 Asian, non-Hispanic/Latino; 13 Hispanic/Latino; 6 Two or more races, non-Hispanic/Latino), 9 international. Average age 24. 81 applicants, 53% accepted, 37 enrolled. *Faculty:* 4 full-time (1 woman), 1 part-time/adjunct (0 women). Expenses: Contact institution. *Financial support:* Fellowships, career-related internships or fieldwork, Federal Work-Study, institutionally sponsored loans, scholarships/grants, and unspecified assistantships available. Support available to part-time students. Financial award application deadline: 3/2; financial award applicants required to submit FAFSA. In 2017, 78 master's awarded. Offers accounting (MS); business (MBA, MS); business administration (MBA); business analytics (MS); economics (MS); packaging value chain (MS); taxation (MS). *Application deadline:* For fall admission, 4/1 for domestic students, 3/1 for international students. Applications are processed on a rolling basis. *Application fee:* $55. Electronic applications accepted. *Application Contact:* Dr. Beena Khurana, Associate Dean, 805-756-7519, E-mail: bkhurana@calpoly.edu. *Associate Dean*, Dr. Sanjiv Jaggia, 805-756-2705, E-mail: sjaggia@calpoly.edu.

CALIFORNIA STATE POLYTECHNIC UNIVERSITY, POMONA, Pomona, CA 91768-2557

General Information State-supported, coed, comprehensive institution. *Enrollment:* 25,894 graduate, professional, and undergraduate students; 395 full-time matriculated graduate/professional students (202 women), 889 part-time matriculated graduate/professional students (378 women). *Enrollment by degree level:* 1,238 master's, 46 doctoral. *Graduate faculty:* 607 full-time (246 women), 637 part-time/adjunct (263 women). Tuition, state resident: full-time $7176. Tuition, nonresident: full-time $13,512. *Required fees:* $1555. Tuition and fees vary according to program. *Graduate housing:* Room and/or apartments available on a first-come, first-served basis to single students; on-campus housing not available to married students. Housing application deadline: 5/1. *Student services:* Campus employment opportunities, campus safety program, career counseling, child daycare facilities, free psychological counseling, international student services, low-cost health insurance, multicultural affairs office, services for students with disabilities. *Library facilities:* University Library. *Collection:* Books: 576,734 (physical), 246,874 (digital/electronic); Serial titles: 278,011 (physical), 13,335 (digital/electronic); Databases: 143. Weekly public service hours: 92; study areas open 24 hours, 5–7 days a week; students can reserve study rooms.

Computer facilities: Computer purchase and lease plans are available. 2,117 computers available on campus for general student use. A campuswide network can be accessed from student residence rooms and from off campus.
Website: http://www.cpp.edu/

General Application Contact: Deborah L. Brandon, Executive Director of Admissions and Enrollment Planning, 909-869-3427, Fax: 909-869-5315, E-mail: dlbrandon@cpp.edu.

GRADUATE UNITS

Ed D Program in Educational Leadership Students: 1 (woman) full-time, 45 part-time (34 women); includes 33 minority (8 Black or African American, non-Hispanic/Latino; 5 Asian, non-Hispanic/Latino; 18 Hispanic/Latino; 2 Two or more races, non-Hispanic/Latino), 1 international. Average age 43. 23 applicants, 87% accepted, 13 enrolled. Expenses: Contact institution. *Financial support:* Applicants required to submit FAFSA. In 2017, 14 doctorates awarded. *Program availability:* Part-time, evening/weekend. Offers educational leadership (Ed D). *Application deadline:* Applications are processed on a rolling basis. *Application fee:* $55. Electronic applications accepted. *Application Contact:* Dr. Nancy M. Sanders, Professor/Doctoral Program Co-Director, 909-869-2579, Fax: 909-869-5416, E-mail: nmsanders@cpp.edu. *Professor/Doctoral Program Co-Director*, Dr. Betty T Alford, 909-869-5369, Fax: 909-869-4822, E-mail: btalford@cpp.edu.

John T. Lyle Center for Regenerative Studies Students: 7 full-time (4 women), 11 part-time (9 women); includes 11 minority (2 Black or African American, non-Hispanic/Latino; 1 Asian, non-Hispanic/Latino; 7 Hispanic/Latino; 1 Two or more races, non-Hispanic/Latino), 2 international. Average age 28. 13 applicants, 92% accepted, 5 enrolled. Expenses: Contact institution. *Financial support:* Application deadline: 3/2; applicants required to submit FAFSA. In 2017, 4 master's awarded. *Program availability:* Part-time. Offers regenerative studies (MS). *Application deadline:* Applications are processed on a rolling basis. *Application fee:* $55. Electronic applications accepted. *Application Contact:* Deborah L. Brandon, Executive Director of Admissions and Enrollment Planning, 909-869-3427, Fax: 909-869-5315, E-mail: dlbrandon@cpp.edu. *Interim Director*, Dr. Pablo La Roche, 909-869-2700, Fax: 909-869-4331, E-mail: pmlaroche@cpp.edu.

Master of Science in Business Administration Program Students: 5 part-time (2 women); includes 3 minority (1 Asian, non-Hispanic/Latino; 2 Hispanic/Latino), 1 international. Average age 28. 24 applicants, 38% accepted, 5 enrolled. Expenses: Contact institution. *Financial support:* Application deadline: 3/2; applicants required to submit FAFSA. In 2017, 4 master's awarded. *Program availability:* Part-time, evening/weekend. Offers information systems auditing (MS). *Application deadline:* Applications are processed on a rolling basis. *Application fee:* $55. Electronic applications accepted. *Application Contact:* Deborah L. Brandon, Executive Director of Admissions and Enrollment Planning, 909-869-3427, Fax: 909-869-5315, E-mail: dlbrandon@cpp.edu. *Associate Professor/Director of Graduate Programs*, Dr. Tarique Hossain, 909-869-2362, Fax: 909-869-4559, E-mail: tmhossain@cpp.edu.

Master's Programs in Education Students: 19 full-time (14 women), 71 part-time (43 women); includes 58 minority (6 Black or African American, non-Hispanic/Latino; 10 Asian, non-Hispanic/Latino; 39 Hispanic/Latino; 3 Two or more races, non-Hispanic/Latino), 5 international. Average age 35. 45 applicants, 56% accepted, 13 enrolled. Expenses: Contact institution. *Financial support:* Application deadline: 3/2; applicants required to submit FAFSA. In 2017, 43 master's awarded. *Program availability:* Part-time, evening/weekend. Offers curriculum and instruction (MA). *Application deadline:* Applications are processed on a rolling basis. *Application fee:* $55. Electronic applications accepted. *Application Contact:* Deborah L. Brandon, Executive Director of Admissions and Enrollment Planning, 909-869-3427, Fax: 909-869-5315, E-mail: dlbrandon@cpp.edu. *Professor/Graduate Coordinator*, Dr. Richard A. Navarro, 909-869-2081, Fax: 909-869-4822, E-mail: ranavarro@cpp.edu.

MBA Program Students: 45 part-time (18 women); includes 29 minority (2 Black or African American, non-Hispanic/Latino; 9 Asian, non-Hispanic/Latino; 18 Hispanic/Latino), 4 international. Average age 30. 73 applicants, 44% accepted, 21 enrolled. Expenses: Contact institution. *Financial support:* Application deadline: 3/2; applicants required to submit FAFSA. In 2017, 13 master's awarded. *Program availability:* Part-time, evening/weekend. Offers business administration (MBA). *Application deadline:* Applications are processed on a rolling basis. *Application fee:* $55. Electronic applications accepted. *Application Contact:* Deborah L. Brandon, Executive Director of Admissions and Enrollment Planning, 909-869-3427, Fax: 909-869-5315, E-mail: dlbrandon@cpp.edu. *Associate Professor/Director of Graduate Programs*, Dr. Tarique Hossain, 909-869-2362, Fax: 909-869-4559, E-mail: tmhossain@cpp.edu.

Program in Accountancy Students: 14 full-time (5 women), 7 part-time (4 women); includes 10 minority (5 Asian, non-Hispanic/Latino; 5 Hispanic/Latino), 6 international. Average age 27. 51 applicants, 51% accepted, 14 enrolled. Expenses: Contact institution. *Financial support:* Application deadline: 3/2; applicants required to submit FAFSA. In 2017, 12 master's awarded. *Program availability:* Part-time, evening/weekend. Offers accountancy (MS). *Application deadline:* Applications are processed on a rolling basis. *Application fee:* $55. Electronic applications accepted. *Application Contact:* Deborah L. Brandon, Executive Director of Admissions and Enrollment Planning, 909-869-3427, Fax: 909-869-5315, E-mail: dlbrandon@cpp.edu. *Assistant Professor/MSA Coordinator*, Dr. Meihua Koo, 909-869-4531, Fax: 909-869-4511, E-mail: mkoo@cpp.edu.

Program in Agriculture Students: 16 full-time (10 women), 31 part-time (16 women); includes 28 minority (2 Black or African American, non-Hispanic/Latino; 6 Asian, non-Hispanic/Latino; 19 Hispanic/Latino; 1 Two or more races, non-Hispanic/Latino), 3 international. Average age 29. 40 applicants, 45% accepted, 12 enrolled. Expenses: Contact institution. *Financial support:* Application deadline: 3/2; applicants required to submit FAFSA. In 2017, 11 master's awarded. *Program availability:* Part-time, evening/weekend. Offers agricultural science (MS). *Application deadline:* Applications are processed on a rolling basis. *Application fee:* $55. Electronic applications accepted. *Application Contact:* Deborah L. Brandon, Executive Director of Admissions and Enrollment Planning, 909-869-3427, Fax: 909-869-5315, E-mail: dlbrandon@cpp.edu. *Associate Professor/Director of Research and Graduate Studies*, Dr. Harmit Singh, 909-869-3023, Fax: 909-869-5078, E-mail: harmitsingh@cpp.edu.

Program in Architecture Students: 37 full-time (19 women), 7 part-time (5 women); includes 23 minority (9 Asian, non-Hispanic/Latino; 14 Hispanic/Latino), 3 international. Average age 30. 88 applicants, 51% accepted, 14 enrolled. Expenses: Contact institution. *Financial support:* Application deadline: 3/2; applicants required to submit FAFSA. In 2017, 12 master's awarded. *Program availability:* Part-time, evening/weekend. Offers architecture (M Arch). *Application deadline:* Applications are processed on a rolling basis. *Application fee:* $55. Electronic applications accepted. *Application Contact:* Deborah L. Brandon, Executive Director of Admissions and Enrollment Planning, 909-869-3427, Fax: 909-869-5315, E-mail: dlbrandon@cpp.edu. *Professor/Graduate Coordinator,* Prof. Kip A. Dickson, 909-869-2682, Fax: 909-869-4331, E-mail: kadickson@cpp.edu.

Program in Biological Sciences Students: 37 full-time (21 women), 45 part-time (21 women); includes 51 minority (1 Black or African American, non-Hispanic/Latino; 16 Asian, non-Hispanic/Latino; 29 Hispanic/Latino; 5 Two or more races, non-Hispanic/Latino), 7 international. Average age 27. 47 applicants, 60% accepted, 20 enrolled. Expenses: Contact institution. *Financial support:* Application deadline: 3/2; applicants required to submit FAFSA. In 2017, 24 master's awarded. *Program availability:* Part-time, evening/weekend. Offers biological sciences (MS). *Application deadline:* Applications are processed on a rolling basis. *Application fee:* $55. Electronic applications accepted. *Application Contact:* Deborah L. Brandon, Executive Director of Admissions and Enrollment Planning, 909-869-3427, Fax: 909-869-5315, E-mail: dlbrandon@cpp.edu. *Professor/Graduate Coordinator,* Dr. Robert J. Talmadge, 909-869-3025, Fax: 909-869-4078, E-mail: rjtalmadge@cpp.edu.

Program in Chemistry Students: 5 full-time (2 women), 18 part-time (2 women); includes 11 minority (8 Asian, non-Hispanic/Latino; 3 Hispanic/Latino), 4 international. Average age 28. 24 applicants, 42% accepted, 6 enrolled. Expenses: Contact institution. *Financial support:* Application deadline: 3/2; applicants required to submit FAFSA. In 2017, 5 master's awarded. *Program availability:* Part-time, evening/weekend. Offers chemistry (MS). *Application deadline:* Applications are processed on a rolling basis. *Application fee:* $55. Electronic applications accepted. *Application Contact:* Deborah L. Brandon, Executive Director of Admissions and Enrollment Planning, 909-869-3427, Fax: 909-869-5315, E-mail: dlbrandon@cpp.edu. *Graduate Coordinator,* Dr. Gregory Barding, 909-869-3681, Fax: 909-869-4344, E-mail: gabarding@cpp.edu.

Program in Civil Engineering Students: 25 full-time (9 women), 76 part-time (15 women); includes 61 minority (4 Black or African American, non-Hispanic/Latino; 30 Asian, non-Hispanic/Latino; 25 Hispanic/Latino; 2 Two or more races, non-Hispanic/Latino), 13 international. Average age 28. 65 applicants, 66% accepted, 18 enrolled. Expenses: Contact institution. *Financial support:* Application deadline: 3/2; applicants required to submit FAFSA. In 2017, 38 master's awarded. *Program availability:* Part-time, evening/weekend. Offers civil engineering (MS). *Application deadline:* Applications are processed on a rolling basis. *Application fee:* $55. Electronic applications accepted. *Application Contact:* Deborah L. Brandon, Executive Director of Admissions and Enrollment Planning, 909-869-3427, Fax: 909-869-5315, E-mail: dlbrandon@cpp.edu. *Professor/Graduate Coordinator,* Dr. Lisa Wang, 909-869-4641, Fax: 909-869-4342, E-mail: ylwang@cpp.edu.

Program in Computer Science Students: 27 full-time (6 women), 66 part-time (16 women); includes 39 minority (1 Black or African American, non-Hispanic/Latino; 28 Asian, non-Hispanic/Latino; 10 Hispanic/Latino), 39 international. Average age 28. 171 applicants, 38% accepted, 21 enrolled. Expenses: Contact institution. *Financial support:* Application deadline: 3/2; applicants required to submit FAFSA. In 2017, 22 master's awarded. *Program availability:* Part-time, evening/weekend. Offers computer science (MS). *Application deadline:* Applications are processed on a rolling basis. *Application fee:* $55. Electronic applications accepted. *Application Contact:* Deborah L. Brandon, Executive Director of Admissions and Enrollment Planning, 909-869-3427, Fax: 909-869-5315, E-mail: dlbrandon@cpp.edu. *Professor/Graduate Coordinator,* Dr. Gilbert S. Young, 909-869-4413, Fax: 909-869-4733, E-mail: gsyoung@cpp.edu.

Program in Economics Students: 6 full-time (3 women), 36 part-time (15 women); includes 15 minority (2 Black or African American, non-Hispanic/Latino; 6 Asian, non-Hispanic/Latino; 5 Hispanic/Latino; 2 Two or more races, non-Hispanic/Latino), 21 international. Average age 29. 40 applicants, 80% accepted, 12 enrolled. Expenses: Contact institution. *Financial support:* Application deadline: 3/2; applicants required to submit FAFSA. In 2017, 8 master's awarded. *Program availability:* Part-time, evening/weekend. Offers economics (MS). *Application deadline:* Applications are processed on a rolling basis. *Application fee:* $55. Electronic applications accepted. *Application Contact:* Deborah L. Brandon, Executive Director of Admissions and Enrollment Planning, 909-869-3427, Fax: 909-869-5315, E-mail: dlbrandon@cpp.edu. *Professor/Graduate Coordinator,* Dr. Carsten Lange, 909-869-3843, Fax: 909-869-6987, E-mail: clange@cpp.edu.

Program in Electrical Engineering Students: 17 full-time (2 women), 41 part-time (6 women); includes 29 minority (1 American Indian or Alaska Native, non-Hispanic/Latino; 21 Asian, non-Hispanic/Latino; 7 Hispanic/Latino), 6 international. Average age 29. 79 applicants, 39% accepted, 15 enrolled. Expenses: Contact institution. *Financial support:* Application deadline: 3/2; applicants required to submit FAFSA. In 2017, 28 master's awarded. *Program availability:* Part-time, evening/weekend. Offers communication systems (MSEE). *Application deadline:* Applications are processed on a rolling basis. *Application fee:* $55. Electronic applications accepted. *Application Contact:* Deborah L. Brandon, Executive Director of Admissions and Enrollment Planning, 909-869-3427, Fax: 909-869-5315, E-mail: dlbrandon@cpp.edu. *Assistant Professor/MSEE Coordinator,* Dr. Ha T. Le, 909-869-2523, Fax: 909-869-4687, E-mail: hatle@cpp.edu.

Program in Engineering Students: 2 full-time (0 women), 27 part-time (5 women); includes 11 minority (1 Black or African American, non-Hispanic/Latino; 4 Asian, non-Hispanic/Latino; 5 Hispanic/Latino; 1 Two or more races, non-Hispanic/Latino), 4 international. Average age 28. 39 applicants, 49% accepted, 13 enrolled. Expenses: Contact institution. *Financial support:* Application deadline: 3/2; applicants required to submit FAFSA. In 2017, 4 master's awarded. *Program availability:* Part-time, evening/weekend. Offers engineering (MSE). *Application deadline:* Applications are processed on a rolling basis. *Application fee:* $55. Electronic applications accepted. *Application Contact:* Deborah L. Brandon, Executive Director of Admissions and Enrollment Planning, 909-869-3427, Fax: 909-869-5315, E-mail: dlbrandon@cpp.edu. *Department Chair/Professor,* Dr. Ali R. Ahmadi, 909-869-2470, Fax: 909-869-6920, E-mail: arahmadi@cpp.edu.

Program in Engineering Management Students: 12 full-time (2 women), 24 part-time (4 women); includes 11 minority (2 Asian, non-Hispanic/Latino; 7 Hispanic/Latino; 2 Two or more races, non-Hispanic/Latino), 15 international. Average age 30. 22 applicants, 68% accepted, 6 enrolled. Expenses: Contact institution. *Financial support:* Application deadline: 3/2; applicants required to submit FAFSA. In 2017, 9 master's awarded. *Program availability:* Part-time, evening/weekend. Offers engineering management (MS). *Application deadline:* Applications are processed on a rolling basis. *Application fee:* $55. Electronic applications accepted. *Application Contact:* Deborah L. Brandon, Executive Director of Admissions and Enrollment Planning, 909-869-3427, Fax: 909-869-5315, E-mail: dlbrandon@cpp.edu. *Chair/Graduate Coordinator,* Dr. Kamran Abedini, 909-869-2569, Fax: 909-869-2564, E-mail: kabedini@cpp.edu.

Program in English Students: 12 full-time (7 women), 60 part-time (42 women); includes 34 minority (2 Black or African American, non-Hispanic/Latino; 1 American Indian or Alaska Native, non-Hispanic/Latino; 8 Asian, non-Hispanic/Latino; 21 Hispanic/Latino; 2 Two or more races, non-Hispanic/Latino), 1 international. Average age 29. 33 applicants, 88% accepted, 16 enrolled. Expenses: Contact institution. *Financial support:* Application deadline: 3/2; applicants required to submit FAFSA. In 2017, 19 master's awarded. *Program availability:* Part-time, evening/weekend. Offers English (MA). *Application deadline:* Applications are processed on a rolling basis. *Application fee:* $55. Electronic applications accepted. *Application Contact:* Deborah L. Brandon, Executive Director of Admissions and Enrollment Planning, 909-869-3427, Fax: 909-869-5315, E-mail: dlbrandon@cpp.edu. *Associate Professor/Graduate Coordinator,* Dr. Lise-Hélène V. Smith, 909-869-3979, Fax: 909-869-4896, E-mail: lvtrouilloud@cpp.edu.

Program in Geology Students: 9 full-time (3 women), 20 part-time (9 women); includes 15 minority (1 Black or African American, non-Hispanic/Latino; 3 Asian, non-Hispanic/Latino; 9 Hispanic/Latino; 2 Two or more races, non-Hispanic/Latino), 1 international. Average age 29. 14 applicants, 86% accepted, 9 enrolled. Expenses: Contact institution. *Financial support:* Application deadline: 3/2; applicants required to submit FAFSA. In 2017, 2 master's awarded. *Program availability:* Part-time, evening/weekend. Offers geology (MS). *Application deadline:* Applications are processed on a rolling basis. Electronic applications accepted. *Application Contact:* Deborah L. Brandon, Executive Director of Admissions and Enrollment Planning, 909-869-3427, Fax: 909-869-5315, E-mail: dlbrandon@cpp.edu. *Department Chair/Coordinator,* Dr. Jonathan A. Nourse, 909-869-3460, Fax: 909-869-2920, E-mail: janourse@cpp.edu.

Program in History Students: 1 full-time (0 women), 15 part-time (6 women); includes 9 minority (1 Asian, non-Hispanic/Latino; 7 Hispanic/Latino; 1 Two or more races, non-Hispanic/Latino). Average age 34. 12 applicants, 58% accepted, 6 enrolled. Expenses: Contact institution. *Financial support:* Application deadline: 3/2; applicants required to submit FAFSA. In 2017, 4 master's awarded. *Program availability:* Part-time, evening/weekend. Offers history (MA). *Application deadline:* Applications are processed on a rolling basis. *Application fee:* $55. Electronic applications accepted. *Application Contact:* Deborah L. Brandon, Executive Director of Admissions and Enrollment Planning, 909-869-3427, Fax: 909-869-5315, E-mail: dlbrandon@cpp.edu. *Professor/Graduate Coordinator,* Dr. Amanda H. Podany, 909-869-3875, Fax: 909-869-4724, E-mail: ahpodany@cpp.edu.

Program in Hospitality Management Students: 14 full-time (12 women), 24 part-time (16 women); includes 10 minority (2 Black or African American, non-Hispanic/Latino; 6 Asian, non-Hispanic/Latino; 2 Two or more races, non-Hispanic/Latino), 21 international. Average age 30. 22 applicants, 45% accepted, 6 enrolled. Expenses: Contact institution. *Financial support:* Application deadline: 3/2; applicants required to submit FAFSA. In 2017, 16 master's awarded. *Program availability:* Part-time, evening/weekend. Offers hospitality management (MS). *Application deadline:* Applications are processed on a rolling basis. *Application fee:* $55. Electronic applications accepted. *Application Contact:* Deborah L. Brandon, Executive Director of Admissions and Enrollment Planning, 909-869-3427, Fax: 909-869-5315, E-mail: dlbrandon@cpp.edu. *Associate Professor/MSHM Program Director,* Dr. Neha Singh, 909-869-4565, Fax: 909-869-4805, E-mail: nsingh@cpp.edu.

Program in Interior Architecture Students: 17 full-time (15 women), 32 part-time (29 women); includes 12 minority (2 Black or African American, non-Hispanic/Latino; 9 Asian, non-Hispanic/Latino; 1 Two or more races, non-Hispanic/Latino), 22 international. Average age 30. 41 applicants, 54% accepted, 18 enrolled. Expenses: Contact institution. *Financial support:* Application deadline: 3/2; applicants required to submit FAFSA. In 2017, 39 master's awarded. *Program availability:* Part-time, evening/weekend. Offers interior architecture (MIA). Program offered in partnership with UCLA Extension. *Application deadline:* Applications are processed on a rolling basis. *Application fee:* $55. Electronic applications accepted. *Application Contact:* Deborah L. Brandon, Executive Director of Admissions and Enrollment Planning, 909-869-3427, Fax: 909-869-5315, E-mail: dlbrandon@cpp.edu. *Professor/Coordinator,* Prof. Irma Ramirez, 909-869-5355, Fax: 909-869-4331, E-mail: ieramirez@cpp.edu.

Program in Kinesiology Students: 6 full-time (3 women), 7 part-time (4 women); includes 8 minority (4 Asian, non-Hispanic/Latino; 2 Hispanic/Latino; 2 Two or more races, non-Hispanic/Latino). Average age 27. 20 applicants, 60% accepted, 7 enrolled. Expenses: Contact institution. *Financial support:* Application deadline: 3/2; applicants required to submit FAFSA. In 2017, 12 master's awarded. *Program availability:* Part-time, evening/weekend. Offers kinesiology (MS). *Application deadline:* Applications are processed on a rolling basis. *Application fee:* $55. Electronic applications accepted. *Application Contact:* Deborah L. Brandon, Executive Director of Admissions and Enrollment Planning, 909-869-3427, Fax: 909-869-5315, E-mail: dlbrandon@cpp.edu. *Professor/Graduate Coordinator,* Dr. Ken Hansen, 909-869-4638, Fax: 909-869-4797, E-mail: kahansen@cpp.edu.

Program in Landscape Architecture Students: 31 full-time (19 women); includes 14 minority (6 Asian, non-Hispanic/Latino; 8 Hispanic/Latino), 5 international. Average age 30. 45 applicants, 67% accepted, 18 enrolled. Expenses: Contact institution. *Financial support:* Application deadline: 3/2; applicants required to submit FAFSA. In 2017, 11 master's awarded. *Program availability:* Part-time, evening/weekend. Offers landscape architecture (M Land Arch). *Application deadline:* Applications are processed on a rolling basis. *Application fee:* $55. Electronic applications accepted. *Application Contact:* Deborah L. Brandon, Executive Director of Admissions and Enrollment Planning, 909-869-3427, Fax: 909-869-5315, E-mail: dlbrandon@cpp.edu. *Graduate Coordinator,* Prof. Gerald O. Taylor, 909-869-6891, Fax: 909-869-2580, E-mail: jotaylor@cpp.edu.

Program in Mathematics Students: 13 full-time (4 women), 36 part-time (12 women); includes 27 minority (2 Black or African American, non-Hispanic/Latino; 7 Asian, non-Hispanic/Latino; 16 Hispanic/Latino; 2 Two or more races, non-Hispanic/Latino), 3 international. Average age 26. 60 applicants, 52% accepted, 18 enrolled. Expenses: Contact institution. *Financial support:* Application deadline: 3/2; applicants required to submit FAFSA. In 2017, 15 master's awarded. *Program availability:* Part-time, evening/weekend. Offers applied mathematics (MS). *Application deadline:* Applications are processed on a rolling basis. *Application fee:* $55. Electronic applications accepted. *Application Contact:* Deborah L. Brandon, Executive Director of Admissions and Enrollment Planning, 909-869-3427, Fax: 909-869-5315, E-mail: dlbrandon@cpp.edu. *Assistant Professor/Graduate Coordinator,* Dr. John A. Rock, 909-869-2404, Fax: 909-869-4904, E-mail: jarock@cpp.edu.

Program in Mechanical Engineering Students: 5 full-time (1 woman), 72 part-time (12 women); includes 47 minority (1 Black or African American, non-Hispanic/Latino; 26 Asian, non-Hispanic/Latino; 17 Hispanic/Latino; 3 Two or more races, non-Hispanic/Latino), 10 international. Average age 28. 65 applicants, 63% accepted, 16 enrolled. Expenses: Contact institution. *Financial support:* Application deadline: 3/2; applicants required to submit FAFSA. In 2017, 17 master's awarded. *Program availability:* Part-time, evening/weekend. Offers mechanical engineering (MS).

Application deadline: Applications are processed on a rolling basis. *Application fee:* $55. Electronic applications accepted. *Application Contact:* Deborah L. Brandon, Executive Director of Admissions and Enrollment Planning, 909-869-3427, Fax: 909-869-5315, E-mail: dlbrandon@cpp.edu. *Graduate Coordinator*, Dr. Henry Xue, 909-869-4304, Fax: 909-869-4341, E-mail: hxue@cpp.edu.

Program in Psychology Students: 30 full-time (23 women), 1 (woman) part-time; includes 23 minority (4 Asian, non-Hispanic/Latino; 16 Hispanic/Latino; 3 Two or more races, non-Hispanic/Latino), 1 international. Average age 26. 96 applicants, 16% accepted, 15 enrolled. Expenses: Contact institution. *Financial support:* Application deadline: 3/2; applicants required to submit FAFSA. In 2017, 15 master's awarded. *Program availability:* Part-time, evening/weekend. Offers psychology (MS). *Application deadline:* Applications are processed on a rolling basis. *Application fee:* $55. Electronic applications accepted. *Application Contact:* Deborah L. Brandon, Executive Director of Admissions and Enrollment Planning, 909-869-3427, Fax: 909-869-5315, E-mail: dlbrandon@cpp.edu. *Director of Graduate Studies*, Dr. Jeffery Mio, 909-869-3899, Fax: 909-869-4930, E-mail: jsmio@cpp.edu.

Program in Public Administration Students: 6 full-time (2 women), 36 part-time (23 women); includes 28 minority (3 Black or African American, non-Hispanic/Latino; 6 Asian, non-Hispanic/Latino; 18 Hispanic/Latino; 1 Two or more races, non-Hispanic/Latino), 3 international. Average age 33. 29 applicants, 52% accepted, 11 enrolled. Expenses: Contact institution. *Financial support:* Application deadline: 3/2; applicants required to submit FAFSA. In 2017, 11 master's awarded. *Program availability:* Part-time, evening/weekend. Offers public administration (MPA). *Application deadline:* Applications are processed on a rolling basis. *Application fee:* $55. Electronic applications accepted. *Application Contact:* Deborah L. Brandon, Executive Director of Admissions and Enrollment Planning, 909-869-3427, Fax: 909-869-5315, E-mail: dlbrandon@cpp.edu. *Professor/MPA Coordinator*, Dr. Sandra M. Emerson, 909-869-3879, Fax: 909-869-6995, E-mail: smemerson@cpp.edu.

Program in Systems Engineering Students: 14 part-time (4 women); includes 5 minority (1 Asian, non-Hispanic/Latino; 4 Hispanic/Latino), 5 international. Average age 26. 12 applicants, 58% accepted, 6 enrolled. Expenses: Contact institution. *Financial support:* Application deadline: 3/2. In 2017, 4 master's awarded. *Program availability:* Part-time, evening/weekend. Offers systems engineering (MS). *Application deadline:* Applications are processed on a rolling basis. *Application fee:* $55. Electronic applications accepted. *Application Contact:* Deborah L. Brandon, Executive Director of Admissions and Enrollment Planning, 909-869-3427, Fax: 909-869-5315, E-mail: dlbrandon@cpp.edu. *Professor/Coordinator*, Dr. Kamran Abedini, 909-869-2569, Fax: 909-869-2564, E-mail: kabedini@cpp.edu.

Program in Urban and Regional Planning Students: 26 full-time (15 women), 17 part-time (5 women); includes 29 minority (1 Black or African American, non-Hispanic/Latino; 10 Asian, non-Hispanic/Latino; 18 Hispanic/Latino), 1 international. Average age 30. 76 applicants, 75% accepted, 43 enrolled. Expenses: Contact institution. *Financial support:* Application deadline: 3/2; applicants required to submit FAFSA. In 2017, 14 master's awarded. *Program availability:* Part-time, evening/weekend. Offers urban and regional planning (MURP). *Application deadline:* Applications are processed on a rolling basis. *Application fee:* $55. Electronic applications accepted. *Application Contact:* Deborah L. Brandon, Executive Director of Admissions and Enrollment Planning, 909-869-3427, Fax: 909-869-5315, E-mail: dlbrandon@cpp.edu. *Graduate Coordinator*, Dr. Do-Hyung Kim, 909-869-4645, Fax: 909-869-4688, E-mail: dohyungkim@cpp.edu.

CALIFORNIA STATE UNIVERSITY, BAKERSFIELD, Bakersfield, CA 93311

General Information State-supported, coed, comprehensive institution. *Enrollment:* 482 full-time matriculated graduate/professional students (363 women), 160 part-time matriculated graduate/professional students (101 women). *Enrollment by degree level:* 616 master's, 26 doctoral. *Graduate faculty:* 55 full-time (20 women), 48 part-time/adjunct (32 women). Tuition, state resident: full-time $7176; part-time $4164 per year. *Graduate housing:* Room and/or apartments available on a first-come, first-served basis to single students; on-campus housing not available to married students. Housing application deadline: 7/15. *Student services:* Campus employment opportunities, campus safety program, career counseling, child daycare facilities, exercise/wellness program, free psychological counseling, grant writing training, international student services, multicultural affairs office, services for students with disabilities, teacher training, writing training. *Library facilities:* Walter W. Stiern Library.

Computer facilities: A campuswide network can be accessed from student residence rooms and from off campus. Online class registration is available.
Website: http://www.csub.edu/

General Application Contact: Dr. Vandana Kohli, Director, Graduate Programs, 661-654-2786, E-mail: vkohli@csub.edu.

GRADUATE UNITS

Division of Graduate Studies Expenses: Contact institution. *Financial support:* Fellowships, research assistantships with partial tuition reimbursements, teaching assistantships with partial tuition reimbursements, career-related internships or fieldwork, Federal Work-Study, institutionally sponsored loans, scholarships/grants, and traineeships available. Support available to part-time students. Financial award application deadline: 1/15; financial award applicants required to submit CSS PROFILE. *Program availability:* Part-time, evening/weekend, online learning. Offers administration (MSA); interdisciplinary studies (MA). *Application deadline:* For fall admission, 8/1 priority date for domestic students; for winter admission, 11/1 priority date for domestic students; for spring admission, 3/1 priority date for domestic students. Applications are processed on a rolling basis. *Application fee:* $55. *Application Contact:* Debbie Blowers, Assistant Director, Admissions and Evaluations, 661-654-3381, Fax: 661-654-3389, E-mail: dblowers@csub.edu. *Associate Vice President for Academic Programs*, Dr. Vernon B. Harper, Jr., 661-664-3420, Fax: 661-664-6911, E-mail: vharper@csub.edu.

School of Arts and Humanities Students: 15 full-time (7 women), 25 part-time (15 women); includes 22 minority (1 Black or African American, non-Hispanic/Latino; 3 Asian, non-Hispanic/Latino; 16 Hispanic/Latino; 2 Two or more races, non-Hispanic/Latino). Average age 36. 25 applicants, 72% accepted, 14 enrolled. Expenses: Contact institution. *Financial support:* Fellowships, career-related internships or fieldwork, institutionally sponsored loans, scholarships/grants, and traineeships available. *Program availability:* Part-time, evening/weekend. Offers arts and humanities (MA); English (MA); history (MA); Spanish (MA). *Application deadline:* Applications are processed on a rolling basis. *Application fee:* $55. *Application Contact:* Debbie Blowers, Assistant Director of Admissions, 661-664-3381, E-mail: dblowers@csub.edu. *Dean*, Dr. Robert Frakes, 661-654-3986, Fax: 661-654-2132, E-mail: rfrakes1@csub.edu.

School of Business and Public Administration Students: 95 full-time (58 women), 74 part-time (40 women); includes 90 minority (20 Black or African American, non-Hispanic/Latino; 12 Asian, non-Hispanic/Latino; 53 Hispanic/Latino; 5 Two or more races, non-Hispanic/Latino), 14 international. Average age 30. 161 applicants, 57% accepted, 77 enrolled. Expenses: Contact institution. *Financial support:* Career-related internships or fieldwork available. Offers business administration (MBA); business and public administration (MBA, MPA, MS); health care administration (MS); public administration (MPA). *Application deadline:* Applications are processed on a rolling basis. *Application fee:* $55. *Application Contact:* Debbie Blowers, Assistant Director of Admissions, 661-664-3381, E-mail: dblowers@csub.edu. *Dean*, Dr. Angappa Gunasekaran, 661-654-2184, Fax: 661-654-2207, E-mail: agunasekaran@csub.edu.

School of Natural Sciences, Mathematics, and Engineering Students: 19 full-time (7 women), 33 part-time (13 women); includes 25 minority (2 Black or African American, non-Hispanic/Latino; 7 Asian, non-Hispanic/Latino; 15 Hispanic/Latino; 1 Two or more races, non-Hispanic/Latino). Average age 29. 16 applicants, 88% accepted, 10 enrolled. Expenses: Contact institution. Offers biology (MS); family nurse practitioner (MSN); geological sciences (MS); hydrogeology (MS); natural sciences, mathematics, and engineering (MA, MS, MSN); petroleum geology (MS); science education (MS); teaching mathematics (MA). *Application fee:* $55. *Application Contact:* Debbie Blowers, Assistant Director of Admissions, 661-664-3381, E-mail: dblowers@csub.edu. *Dean*, Dr. Kathleen Madden, 661-654-3450, Fax: 661-654-6959, E-mail: kmadden2@csub.edu.

School of Social Sciences and Education Students: 239 full-time (206 women), 74 part-time (57 women); includes 222 minority (23 Black or African American, non-Hispanic/Latino; 4 American Indian or Alaska Native, non-Hispanic/Latino; 18 Asian, non-Hispanic/Latino; 161 Hispanic/Latino; 16 Two or more races, non-Hispanic/Latino), 8 international. Average age 33. 312 applicants, 64% accepted, 156 enrolled. Expenses: Contact institution. Offers anthropology (MA); counseling psychology (MS); educational administration (MA); educational leadership (Ed D); school counseling (MS); social sciences and education (MA, MS, MSW, Ed D); social work (MSW); sociology (MA); special education (MA); student affairs (MS). *Application deadline:* Applications are processed on a rolling basis. *Application fee:* $55. *Application Contact:* Debbie Blowers, Assistant Director of Admissions, 661-664-3381, E-mail: dblowers@csub.edu. *Dean*, Dr. Steve Bacon, 661-664-2210, Fax: 661-664-2016, E-mail: sbacon@csub.edu.

CALIFORNIA STATE UNIVERSITY CHANNEL ISLANDS, Camarillo, CA 93012

General Information State-supported, coed, comprehensive institution. *Enrollment:* 400 matriculated graduate/professional students. *Enrollment by degree level:* 400 master's. *Graduate housing:* Room and/or apartments available on a first-come, first-served basis to single students; on-campus housing not available to married students. Housing application deadline: 6/1. *Student services:* Campus employment opportunities, campus safety program, career counseling, exercise/wellness program, international student services, low-cost health insurance, multicultural affairs office, services for students with disabilities, teacher training, writing training. *Library facilities:* John Spoor Broome Library at Channel Islands.
Website: http://www.csuci.edu/

GRADUATE UNITS

Extended University and International Programs Students: 500. Expenses: Contact institution. *Financial support:* Career-related internships or fieldwork, Federal Work-Study, and scholarships/grants available. *Program availability:* Part-time-only, evening/weekend. Offers biotechnology and bioinformatics (MS); business administration (MBA); computer science (MS); mathematics (MS). *Application Contact:* Emma Guetter, Application Specialist, 805-437-2748, Fax: 805-437-8859, E-mail: emma.battles@csuci.edu. *Dean of Extended Education and Associate Vice President for International Programs*, Dr. Osman Ozturgut, 805-437-8580, Fax: 805-437-8859, E-mail: osman.ozturgut@csuci.edu.

CALIFORNIA STATE UNIVERSITY, CHICO, Chico, CA 95929-0722

General Information State-supported, coed, comprehensive institution. CGS member. *Graduate housing:* Room and/or apartments available on a first-come, first-served basis to single students; on-campus housing not available to married students. Housing application deadline: 3/22. *Research affiliation:* Sierra Nevada Brewery (nutrition, food sciences, agriculture), Lawrence Livermore Labs - Inspection and Surveillance Robots (engineering and computer science), California Department of Transportation Pavement Preservation and Recycling (engineering, computer science, construction management), U.S. Navy Office of Naval Research (engineering), Verizon Wireless/Samsung (business).

GRADUATE UNITS

Office of Graduate Studies *Program availability:* Part-time, 100% online, blended/hybrid learning. Electronic applications accepted.

College of Agriculture Offers agricultural education (MS).

College of Behavioral and Social Sciences Offers anthropology (MA); applied/school psychology (MA); behavioral and social sciences (MA, MPA, MS, MSW); health administration (MPA); local government management (MPA); marriage and family therapy (MS); museum studies (MA); political science (MA); psychological science (MA); public administration (MPA); social science (MA); social work (MSW). Electronic applications accepted.

College of Business *Program availability:* Part-time. Offers business (MBA). Electronic applications accepted.

College of Communication and Education *Program availability:* Part-time. Offers communication and education (MA, MS); communication sciences and disorders (MA); communication studies (MA); curriculum and instruction (MA); kinesiology (MA); recreation, parks, and tourism (MS); teaching English learners and special education advising patterns (MA). Electronic applications accepted.

College of Engineering, Computer Science, and Construction Management *Program availability:* Part-time, online learning. Offers computer engineering (MS); computer science (MS); electronic engineering (MS); electronics engineering (MS); engineering, computer science, and construction management (MS). Electronic applications accepted.

College of Humanities and Fine Arts Offers art history (MA); art studio (MFA); English (MA); fine arts (MFA); history (MA); humanities and fine arts (MA, MFA). Electronic applications accepted.

College of Natural Sciences *Program availability:* Part-time. Offers biological sciences (MS); environmental science (MS, PSM); general nutritional science (MS); geosciences (MS); mathematics in education (MS); natural sciences (MS, MSN, PSM); nursing (MSN); nutrition education (MS). Electronic applications accepted.

CALIFORNIA STATE UNIVERSITY, DOMINGUEZ HILLS, Carson, CA 90747-0001

General Information State-supported, coed, comprehensive institution. CGS member. *Graduate housing:* Rooms and/or apartments available on a first-come, first-served basis to single and married students. Housing application deadline: 4/15. *Research affiliation:* Los Angeles Biomedical Research Institute at Harbor UCLA Medical Center (biomedical science), Hewlett Packard (catalyst initiative grants).

GRADUATE UNITS

College of Arts and Humanities *Program availability:* Part-time, evening/weekend, 100% online. Offers arts and humanities (MA, Certificate); English literature (MA); negotiation, conflict resolution and peacebuilding (MA); rhetoric and composition (Certificate); teaching English as a second language (MA, Certificate).

College of Business Administration and Public Policy *Program availability:* Part-time, evening/weekend, online learning. Offers business administration (MBA); business administration and public policy (MBA, MPA); public administration (MPA).

College of Education *Program availability:* Part-time, evening/weekend. Offers education (MA, MS).

Division of Graduate Education *Program availability:* Part-time, evening/weekend. Offers college counseling (MS); counseling (MS); school counseling (MS).

Division of Teacher Education *Program availability:* Part-time, evening/weekend. Offers early childhood special education (MA); special education (MA).

College of Extended and International Education *Program availability:* Part-time, evening/weekend, online learning. Offers extended and international education (MA, MS); humanities (MA); quality assurance (MS). Electronic applications accepted.

College of Health, Human Services and Nursing Offers health, human services and nursing (MS, MSN, MSW); marital and family therapy (MS); nursing (MSN); occupational therapy (MS); social work (MSW). Electronic applications accepted.

College of Natural and Behavioral Sciences Offers biology (MS); clinical psychology (MA); computer science (MS); health psychology (MA); natural and behavioral sciences (MA, MS, Certificate); social research (MA); sociology (MA).

CALIFORNIA STATE UNIVERSITY, EAST BAY, Hayward, CA 94542-3000

General Information State-supported, coed, comprehensive institution. *Enrollment:* 15,435 graduate, professional, and undergraduate students; 946 full-time matriculated graduate/professional students (621 women), 1,119 part-time matriculated graduate/professional students (662 women). *Enrollment by degree level:* 2,003 master's, 62 doctoral. *Graduate faculty:* 388 full-time (199 women), 494 part-time/adjunct (297 women). *Graduate housing:* On-campus housing not available. *Student services:* Campus employment opportunities, campus safety program, career counseling, exercise/wellness program, free psychological counseling, international student services, low-cost health insurance, services for students with disabilities. *Library facilities:* Hayward Campus Library. *Collection:* Books: 630,855 (physical), 233,485 (digital/electronic); Serial titles: 10,905 (physical), 107,791 (digital/electronic); Databases: 133. Weekly public service hours: 101; students can reserve study rooms. *Research affiliation:* Bayer USA Foundation (STEM), Chevron (STEM), Hearst Foundation (STEM), NASA (earth and environmental sciences), Irvine Foundation (education: teacher preparation), Carnegie Foundation (statistics for non-STEM majors).

Computer facilities: Computer purchase and lease plans are available. 700 computers available on campus for general student use. A campuswide network can be accessed from student residence rooms and from off campus. Online class registration is available.
Website: http://www.csueastbay.edu/

General Application Contact: Philip Cole-Regis, Administrative Support Coordinator, 510-885-3286, Fax: 510-885-4777, E-mail: philip.coleregis@csueastbay.edu.

GRADUATE UNITS

Office of Graduate Studies Students: 949 full-time (622 women), 1,182 part-time (677 women); includes 973 minority (201 Black or African American, non-Hispanic/Latino; 5 American Indian or Alaska Native, non-Hispanic/Latino; 392 Asian, non-Hispanic/Latino; 285 Hispanic/Latino; 16 Native Hawaiian or other Pacific Islander, non-Hispanic/Latino; 74 Two or more races, non-Hispanic/Latino), 569 international. Average age 32. 3,725 applicants, 42% accepted, 697 enrolled. Expenses: Contact institution. *Financial support:* Fellowships, teaching assistantships, career-related internships or fieldwork, Federal Work-Study, institutionally sponsored loans, and scholarships/grants available. Support available to part-time students. Financial award application deadline: 3/2; financial award applicants required to submit FAFSA. In 2017, 1,088 master's, 16 doctorates awarded. *Program availability:* Part-time, evening/weekend, online learning. Offers interdisciplinary studies (MA, MS). *Application deadline:* For fall admission, 6/30 for domestic and international students. Applications are processed on a rolling basis. *Application fee:* $55. Electronic applications accepted. *Interim Associate Vice President,* Dr. Donna Wiley, 510-885-3716, Fax: 510-885-4777, E-mail: donna.wiley@csueastbay.edu.

College of Business and Economics Students: 191 full-time (91 women), 249 part-time (126 women); includes 172 minority (21 Black or African American, non-Hispanic/Latino; 112 Asian, non-Hispanic/Latino; 23 Hispanic/Latino; 3 Native Hawaiian or other Pacific Islander, non-Hispanic/Latino; 13 Two or more races, non-Hispanic/Latino), 196 international. Average age 32. 648 applicants, 49% accepted, 137 enrolled. *Faculty:* 61 full-time (22 women), 24 part-time/adjunct (3 women). Expenses: Contact institution. *Financial support:* Fellowships, career-related internships or fieldwork, Federal Work-Study, institutionally sponsored loans, and scholarships/grants available. Support available to part-time students. Financial award application deadline: 3/2; financial award applicants required to submit FAFSA. In 2017, 228 master's awarded. *Program availability:* Part-time, evening/weekend, online learning. Offers accountancy (MS); business analytics (MS); business and economics (MA, MBA, MS); economics (MA); finance (MBA); human resources and organizational behavior (MBA); marketing management (MBA); operations and supply chain management (MBA); strategy and innovation (MBA). *Application deadline:* For fall admission, 6/1 for domestic students, 5/1 for international students. Applications are processed on a rolling basis. *Application fee:* $55. Electronic applications accepted. *Application Contact:* Nancy Flinn, Graduate Programs Manager, 510-885-3912, E-mail: nancy.flinn@csueastbay.edu. *Interim Associate Dean,* Dr. Eric Fricke, 510-885-3290, E-mail: eric.fricke@csueastbay.edu.

College of Education and Allied Studies Students: 274 full-time (221 women), 126 part-time (86 women); includes 216 minority (48 Black or African American, non-Hispanic/Latino; 1 American Indian or Alaska Native, non-Hispanic/Latino; 61 Asian, non-Hispanic/Latino; 79 Hispanic/Latino; 1 Native Hawaiian or other Pacific Islander, non-Hispanic/Latino; 26 Two or more races, non-Hispanic/Latino), 13 international. Average age 35. 398 applicants, 56% accepted, 174 enrolled. *Faculty:* 61 full-time (22 women), 24 part-time/adjunct (3 women). Expenses: Contact institution. *Financial support:* Career-related internships or fieldwork, Federal Work-Study, and institutionally sponsored loans available. Support available to part-time students. Financial award application deadline: 3/2; financial award applicants required to submit FAFSA. In 2017, 246 master's, 12 doctorates awarded. *Program availability:* Part-time, evening/weekend, online learning. Offers counseling (MS); education (MS); education and allied studies (MS, Ed D); educational leadership (MS, Ed D); kinesiology (MS); mild-moderate disabilities (MS); moderate-severe disabilities (MS); recreation and tourism (MS); special education (MS). *Application deadline:* For fall admission, 6/1 for domestic students, 5/1 for international students. *Application fee:* $55. Electronic applications accepted. *Application Contact:* Philip Cole-Regis, Administrative Support Coordinator, 510-885-3286, E-mail: philip.coleregis@csueastbay.edu. *Dean,* Dr. Carolyn Nelson, 510-885-3942, Fax: 510-885-2283, E-mail: carolyn.nelson@csueastbay.edu.

College of Letters, Arts, and Social Sciences Students: 276 full-time (221 women), 384 part-time (275 women); includes 435 minority (100 Black or African American, non-Hispanic/Latino; 4 American Indian or Alaska Native, non-Hispanic/Latino; 135 Asian, non-Hispanic/Latino; 157 Hispanic/Latino; 5 Native Hawaiian or other Pacific Islander, non-Hispanic/Latino; 34 Two or more races, non-Hispanic/Latino), 55 international. Average age 32. 1,098 applicants, 34% accepted, 240 enrolled. *Faculty:* 137 full-time (71 women), 171 part-time/adjunct (102 women). Expenses: Contact institution. *Financial support:* Fellowships, research assistantships, teaching assistantships, career-related internships or fieldwork, Federal Work-Study, institutionally sponsored loans, and scholarships/grants available. Support available to part-time students. Financial award application deadline: 3/2; financial award applicants required to submit FAFSA. In 2017, 426 master's awarded. *Program availability:* Part-time, evening/weekend, online learning. Offers anthropology (MA); children, youth, and family services (MSW); communication (MA); community mental health services (MSW); English (MA); geography (MA); health care administration (MPA, MS); history (MA); letters, arts, and social sciences (MA, MPA, MS, MSW); management and change in health care (MS); multimedia (MA); music (MA); public administration (MPA); public history (MA); public management and policy analysis (MPA); speech-language pathology (MS); teaching (MA); teaching English to speaker of other languages (MA). *Application deadline:* For fall admission, 6/1 for domestic students, 5/1 for international students. Applications are processed on a rolling basis. *Application fee:* $55. Electronic applications accepted. *Application Contact:* Philip Cole-Regis, Administrative Support Coordinator, 510-885-3286, E-mail: philip.coleregis@csueastbay.edu. *Dean,* Dr. Kathleen Rountree, 510-885-3161, Fax: 510-885-3164, E-mail: kathleen.rountree@csueastbay.edu.

College of Science Students: 206 full-time (89 women), 360 part-time (175 women); includes 148 minority (17 Black or African American, non-Hispanic/Latino; 83 Asian, non-Hispanic/Latino; 37 Hispanic/Latino; 2 Native Hawaiian or other Pacific Islander, non-Hispanic/Latino; 9 Two or more races, non-Hispanic/Latino), 323 international. Average age 28. 1,345 applicants, 38% accepted, 180 enrolled. *Faculty:* 119 full-time (59 women), 146 part-time/adjunct (84 women). Expenses: Contact institution. *Financial support:* Career-related internships or fieldwork, Federal Work-Study, and institutionally sponsored loans available. Support available to part-time students. Financial award application deadline: 3/2; financial award applicants required to submit FAFSA. In 2017, 270 master's awarded. *Program availability:* Part-time, evening/weekend. Offers actuarial science (MS); applied statistics (MS); biochemistry (MS); biostatistics (MS); computational statistics (MS); computer networks (MS); computer science (MS); construction management (MS); engineering management (MS); geology (MS); marine science (MA, MS); mathematical statistics (MS); mathematics teaching (MS); pure mathematics (MS); science (MA, MS); statistics (MS). *Application deadline:* For fall admission, 6/1 for domestic students, 5/1 for international students. *Application fee:* $55. Electronic applications accepted. *Application Contact:* Philip Cole-Regis, Administrative Support Coordinator, 510-885-3286, E-mail: philip.coleregis@csueastbay.edu. *Dean,* Dr. Jason Singley, 510-885-3441, Fax: 510-885-2035, E-mail: jason.singley@csueastbay.edu.

CALIFORNIA STATE UNIVERSITY, FRESNO, Fresno, CA 93740-8027

General Information State-supported, coed, comprehensive institution. CGS member. *Graduate housing:* Room and/or apartments available on a first-come, first-served basis to single students; on-campus housing not available to married students. Housing application deadline: 4/1. *Research affiliation:* Coleman Foundation (administration), Starburst Foundation (engineering), Garabedian Foundation (agribusiness), California Endowment (arts and humanities).

GRADUATE UNITS

Division of Research and Graduate Studies *Program availability:* Part-time, evening/weekend. Electronic applications accepted.

College of Arts and Humanities *Program availability:* Part-time, evening/weekend. Offers art (MA); arts and humanities (MA, MFA); communication (MA); creative writing (MFA); linguistics (MA); literature (MA); music (MA); music education (MA); performance (MA); rhetoric and writing studies (MA); Spanish (MA). Electronic applications accepted.

College of Health and Human Services *Program availability:* Part-time, evening/weekend. Offers communicative disorders (MA); exercise science (MA); general kinesiology (MA); health and human services (MA, MPH, MS, MSW, DNP, DPT); health policy and management (MPH); health promotion (MPH); nursing (MS, DNP); physical therapy (DPT); social work education (MSW); sport administration (MA); sport psychology (MA). Electronic applications accepted.

College of Science and Mathematics *Program availability:* Part-time, evening/weekend. Offers applied behavior analysis (MA); biology (MS); biotechnology (MBT); chemistry (MS); computer science (MS); general/experimental psychology (MA); geology (MS); marine science (MS); mathematics (MA); mathematics teaching (MA); physics (MS); school psychology (Ed S); science and mathematics (MA, MBT, MS, Ed S). Electronic applications accepted.

College of Social Sciences *Program availability:* Part-time, evening/weekend. Offers criminology (MS); history (MA); history teaching (MA); public administration (MPA); social sciences (MA, MPA, MS). Electronic applications accepted.

Craig School of Business *Program availability:* Part-time, blended/hybrid learning. Offers business (MBA). Electronic applications accepted.

Jordan College of Agricultural Sciences and Technology *Program availability:* Part-time, evening/weekend. Offers agricultural sciences and technology (MS); animal science (MS); industrial technology (MS); plant science (MS); viticulture and enology (MS). Electronic applications accepted.

Kremen School of Education and Human Development *Program availability:* Part-time, evening/weekend. Offers clinical rehabilitation and mental health counseling

(MS); clinical rehabilitation and mental health counseling (MS); education (MA); education and human development (MA, MS, Ed D); educational leadership (MA, Ed D); marriage, family and child counseling (MS); special education (MA); student affairs and college counseling (MS). Electronic applications accepted.

Lyles College of Engineering *Program availability:* Part-time, evening/weekend. Offers civil and geomatics engineering (MS); computer engineering (MSE); electrical engineering (MSE); engineering (MS, MSE); mechanical engineering (MS). Electronic applications accepted.

CALIFORNIA STATE UNIVERSITY, FULLERTON, Fullerton, CA 92831-3599

General Information State-supported, coed, comprehensive institution. CGS member. *Enrollment:* 70,681 graduate, professional, and undergraduate students; 2,556 full-time matriculated graduate/professional students (1,707 women), 2,963 part-time matriculated graduate/professional students (1,677 women). *Enrollment by degree level:* 3,761 master's, 897 doctoral, 861 other advanced degrees. *Graduate faculty:* 799 full-time (375 women), 42 part-time/adjunct (19 women). *Graduate housing:* Rooms and/or apartments available on a first-come, first-served basis to single and married students. Housing application deadline: 6/30. *Student services:* Campus employment opportunities, campus safety program, career counseling, child daycare facilities, exercise/wellness program, free psychological counseling, international student services, low-cost health insurance, multicultural affairs office, services for students with disabilities, teacher training, writing training. *Library facilities:* Pollak Library. *Research affiliation:* U.S. Department of Interior (desert studies), County of Orange (demographic research), Department of Literacy and Reading Education, SchoolsFirst Federal Credit Union (creativity and critical thinking), California Office of Historic Preservation and the State Historic Resources Commission (South Central coastal information).

Computer facilities: 2,000 computers available on campus for general student use. A campuswide network can be accessed from student residence rooms and from off campus. Online class registration is available.
Website: http://www.fullerton.edu/

General Application Contact: Admissions/Applications, 657-278-2371, E-mail: admissions@fullerton.edu.

GRADUATE UNITS

Graduate Studies Students: 1,925 full-time (1,231 women), 2,733 part-time (1,490 women); includes 2,139 minority (137 Black or African American, non-Hispanic/Latino; 6 American Indian or Alaska Native, non-Hispanic/Latino; 734 Asian, non-Hispanic/Latino; 1,095 Hispanic/Latino; 5 Native Hawaiian or other Pacific Islander, non-Hispanic/Latino; 162 Two or more races, non-Hispanic/Latino), 943 international. Average age 30. 6,361 applicants, 46% accepted, 1700 enrolled. *Faculty:* 389 full-time (186 women), 143 part-time/adjunct (74 women). Expenses: Contact institution. *Financial support:* Research assistantships, teaching assistantships, career-related internships or fieldwork, Federal Work-Study, institutionally sponsored loans, and scholarships/grants available. Support available to part-time students. Financial award application deadline: 3/1; financial award applicants required to submit FAFSA. *Program availability:* Part-time, evening/weekend, online learning. *Application deadline:* For fall admission, 3/1 for domestic and international students; for spring admission, 10/1 for domestic and international students. Applications are processed on a rolling basis. *Application fee:* $55. Electronic applications accepted. *Application Contact:* Admissions/Applications, 657-278-2371, Fax: 657-278-2356, E-mail: admissions@fullerton.edu. *Director,* Dr. Katherine Powers, 657-278-2618, E-mail: gradstudiesrecept@fullerton.edu.

College of Business and Economics Students: 365 full-time (198 women), 304 part-time (115 women); includes 244 minority (5 Black or African American, non-Hispanic/Latino; 137 Asian, non-Hispanic/Latino; 85 Hispanic/Latino; 17 Two or more races, non-Hispanic/Latino), 292 international. Average age 28. 1,028 applicants, 50% accepted, 198 enrolled. *Faculty:* 46 full-time (15 women), 10 part-time/adjunct (3 women). Expenses: Contact institution. *Financial support:* Career-related internships or fieldwork, Federal Work-Study, institutionally sponsored loans, and scholarships/grants available. Support available to part-time students. Financial award application deadline: 3/1; financial award applicants required to submit FAFSA. *Program availability:* Part-time. Offers accounting (MBA, MS); business administration (MBA); business analytics (MBA); business and economics (MA, MBA, MS); decision science (MBA); economics (MA, MBA); finance (MBA); information systems (MBA, MS); information systems and decision sciences (MS); information systems and e-commerce (MS); information technology (MS); international business (MBA); organizational leadership (MBA); risk management and insurance (MBA). *Application deadline:* Applications are processed on a rolling basis. *Application fee:* $55. Electronic applications accepted. *Application Contact:* Admissions/Applications, 657-278-2371. *Interim Dean,* Dr. Morteza Rahmatian, 657-773-2592.

College of Communications Students: 118 full-time (90 women), 57 part-time (41 women); includes 93 minority (12 Black or African American, non-Hispanic/Latino; 22 Asian, non-Hispanic/Latino; 49 Hispanic/Latino; 2 Native Hawaiian or other Pacific Islander, non-Hispanic/Latino; 8 Two or more races, non-Hispanic/Latino), 8 international. Average age 29. 475 applicants, 16% accepted, 55 enrolled. *Faculty:* 24 full-time (14 women), 7 part-time/adjunct (3 women). Expenses: Contact institution. *Financial support:* Teaching assistantships, career-related internships or fieldwork, Federal Work-Study, institutionally sponsored loans, and scholarships/grants available. Support available to part-time students. Financial award application deadline: 3/1; financial award applicants required to submit FAFSA. *Program availability:* Part-time. Offers communication studies (MA); communications (MA, MFA); communications in tourism and entertainment (MA); communicative disorders (MA); mass communications research and theory (MA); professional communications (MA); screenwriting (MFA). *Application fee:* $55. *Application Contact:* Admissions/Applications, 657-278-2371. *Dean,* Dr. William G. Briggs, 657-278-3355.

College of Education Students: 251 full-time (220 women), 819 part-time (654 women); includes 566 minority (48 Black or African American, non-Hispanic/Latino; 3 American Indian or Alaska Native, non-Hispanic/Latino; 152 Asian, non-Hispanic/Latino; 317 Hispanic/Latino; 2 Native Hawaiian or other Pacific Islander, non-Hispanic/Latino; 44 Two or more races, non-Hispanic/Latino), 13 international. Average age 34. 804 applicants, 59% accepted, 419 enrolled. *Faculty:* 38 full-time (26 women), 33 part-time/adjunct (18 women). Expenses: Contact institution. *Financial support:* Research assistantships and teaching assistantships available. Financial award application deadline: 3/1; financial award applicants required to submit FAFSA. Offers bilingual/bicultural education (MS); education (MS, Ed D); educational administration (MS); educational leadership (Ed D); educational technology (MS); elementary curriculum and instruction (MS); instructional design and technology (MS); literacy and reading education (MS); special education (MS); teacher instruction (MS); teaching foundational mathematics (MS). *Application fee:* $55. *Application Contact:* Admissions/Applications, 657-278-2371. *Dean,* Dr. Claire Cavallaro, 657-278-4021.

College of Engineering and Computer Science Students: 335 full-time (87 women), 679 part-time (177 women); includes 326 minority (18 Black or African American, non-Hispanic/Latino; 154 Asian, non-Hispanic/Latino; 128 Hispanic/Latino; 26 Two or more races, non-Hispanic/Latino), 531 international. Average age 27. 1,744 applicants, 51% accepted, 379 enrolled. *Faculty:* 42 full-time (7 women), 14 part-time/adjunct (2 women). Expenses: Contact institution. *Financial support:* Career-related internships or fieldwork, Federal Work-Study, institutionally sponsored loans, and scholarships/grants available. Support available to part-time students. Financial award application deadline: 3/1; financial award applicants required to submit FAFSA. *Program availability:* Part-time. Offers civil engineering (MS); computer engineering (MS); computer science (MS); electrical engineering (MS); engineering and computer science (MS); mechanical engineering (MS); software engineering (MS); systems engineering (MS). *Application fee:* $55. *Application Contact:* Admissions/Applications, 657-278-2371. *Dean,* Dr. Raman Unnikrishnan, 657-278-3362.

College of Health and Human Development Students: 508 full-time (411 women), 232 part-time (168 women); includes 424 minority (24 Black or African American, non-Hispanic/Latino; 2 American Indian or Alaska Native, non-Hispanic/Latino; 155 Asian, non-Hispanic/Latino; 209 Hispanic/Latino; 1 Native Hawaiian or other Pacific Islander, non-Hispanic/Latino; 33 Two or more races, non-Hispanic/Latino), 14 international. Average age 31. 1,307 applicants, 32% accepted, 305 enrolled. *Faculty:* 64 full-time (42 women), 43 part-time/adjunct (35 women). Expenses: Contact institution. *Financial support:* Career-related internships or fieldwork, Federal Work-Study, institutionally sponsored loans, and scholarships/grants available. Support available to part-time students. Financial award application deadline: 3/1; financial award applicants required to submit FAFSA. *Program availability:* Part-time. Offers aging (MSW); child welfare (MSW); community mental health (MSW); counseling (MS); environmental and occupational health and safety (MPH); gerontological health (MPH); health and human development (MPH, MS, MSW, DNP); health promotion and disease (MPH); kinesiology (MS); leadership (MS); nurse anesthesia (MS); nurse educator (MS); nursing (DNP); school nursing (MS); women's health care (MS). *Application fee:* $55. *Application Contact:* Admissions/Applications, 657-278-2371. *Dean,* Dr. Shari McMahan, 657-278-3311.

College of Humanities and Social Sciences Students: 266 full-time (180 women), 371 part-time (211 women); includes 337 minority (22 Black or African American, non-Hispanic/Latino; 53 Asian, non-Hispanic/Latino; 239 Hispanic/Latino; 23 Two or more races, non-Hispanic/Latino), 47 international. Average age 30. 560 applicants, 55% accepted, 208 enrolled. *Faculty:* 86 full-time (49 women), 12 part-time/adjunct (7 women). Expenses: Contact institution. *Financial support:* Career-related internships or fieldwork, Federal Work-Study, institutionally sponsored loans, and scholarships/grants available. Support available to part-time students. Financial award application deadline: 3/1; financial award applicants required to submit FAFSA. *Program availability:* Part-time. Offers American studies (MA); anthropology (MA); clinical psychology (MS); English (MA); environmental studies (MS); geography (MA); gerontology (MS); history (MA); humanities and social sciences (MA, MPA, MS); linguistics (MA); political science (MA); psychology (MA); public administration (MPA); sociology (MA); Spanish (MA). *Application fee:* $55. *Application Contact:* Admissions/Applications, 657-278-2371. *Dean,* Dr. Angela Della-Volpe, 657-278-3528.

College of Natural Science and Mathematics Students: 22 full-time (11 women), 214 part-time (101 women); includes 103 minority (4 Black or African American, non-Hispanic/Latino; 45 Asian, non-Hispanic/Latino; 48 Hispanic/Latino; 6 Two or more races, non-Hispanic/Latino), 23 international. Average age 28. 319 applicants, 55% accepted, 95 enrolled. *Faculty:* 54 full-time (22 women), 1 part-time/adjunct (0 women). Expenses: Contact institution. *Financial support:* Research assistantships, teaching assistantships, career-related internships or fieldwork, Federal Work-Study, institutionally sponsored loans, and scholarships/grants available. Support available to part-time students. Financial award application deadline: 3/1; financial award applicants required to submit FAFSA. *Program availability:* Part-time. Offers applied mathematics (MA); biology (MS); biotechnology (MBT); chemistry (MA, MS); geological sciences (MS); mathematics education (MA); natural science and mathematics (MA, MBT, MS); physics (MS). *Application fee:* $55. *Application Contact:* Admissions/Applications, 657-278-2371. *Acting Dean,* Dr. Robert Koch, 657-278-2638.

College of the Arts Students: 60 full-time (34 women), 57 part-time (23 women); includes 46 minority (4 Black or African American, non-Hispanic/Latino; 1 American Indian or Alaska Native, non-Hispanic/Latino; 16 Asian, non-Hispanic/Latino; 20 Hispanic/Latino; 5 Two or more races, non-Hispanic/Latino), 14 international. Average age 31. 157 applicants, 38% accepted, 41 enrolled. *Faculty:* 35 full-time (11 women), 23 part-time/adjunct (6 women). Expenses: Contact institution. *Financial support:* Teaching assistantships, career-related internships or fieldwork, Federal Work-Study, institutionally sponsored loans, and scholarships/grants available. Support available to part-time students. Financial award application deadline: 3/1; financial award applicants required to submit FAFSA. *Program availability:* Part-time. Offers art (MA, MFA); arts (MA, MFA, MM); music education (MA); performance (MM); theatre arts (MFA). *Application fee:* $55. *Director,* Larry M. Timm, 657-278-3511, E-mail: ltimm@fullerton.edu.

CALIFORNIA STATE UNIVERSITY, LONG BEACH, Long Beach, CA 90840

General Information State-supported, coed, comprehensive institution. *Graduate housing:* Room and/or apartments available on a first-come, first-served basis to single students; on-campus housing not available to married students. Housing application deadline: 4/1. *Research affiliation:* Boeing (aerospace engineering and manufacturing).

GRADUATE UNITS

Graduate Studies *Program availability:* Part-time, evening/weekend, online learning. Electronic applications accepted.

College of Business Administration *Program availability:* Part-time, evening/weekend. Offers business administration (MS). Electronic applications accepted.

College of Education *Program availability:* Part-time, evening/weekend. Offers counseling (MS); education (MA, Ed D); educational administration (MA, Ed D); educational psychology (MA); elementary education (MA); secondary education (MA); special education (MS). Electronic applications accepted.

College of Engineering *Program availability:* Part-time, evening/weekend. Offers aerospace engineering (MSAE); civil engineering (MSCE); computer engineering (MSCS); computer science (MSCS); electrical engineering (MSEE); engineering (MS, MSAE, MSCE, MSCS, MSE, MSEE, MSME, PhD); engineering and industrial applied mathematics (PhD); interdisciplinary engineering (MSE); management engineering (MSE); mechanical engineering (MSME). Electronic applications accepted.

College of Health and Human Services *Program availability:* Part-time, evening/weekend, online learning. Offers adapted physical education (MA); coaching and student athlete development (MA); criminal justice (MS); emergency services administration (MS); exercise physiology and nutrition (MS); exercise science (MS); gerontology (MS); health and human services (MA, MPA, MPH, MS, MSN, MSW, DNP, DPT, Graduate Certificate); health care administration (MS); health science (MPH); individualized studies (MA); kinesiology (MA); nursing (MSN, DNP, Graduate Certificate); pedagogical studies (MA); physical therapy (DPT); public policy and administration (MPA, Graduate Certificate); recreation administration (MS); social work (MSW); speech-language pathology (MA); sport and exercise psychology (MS); sport management (MA); sports medicine and injury studies (MS). Electronic applications accepted.

College of Liberal Arts *Program availability:* Part-time, evening/weekend. Offers Africa and the Middle East (MA); anthropology (MA); applied anthropology (MA); Asian studies (MA); communication studies (MA); creative writing (MFA); economics (MA); English (MA); French and Francophone studies (MA); general linguistics (MA); geography (MA, MS); German (MA); human factors (MS); industrial/organizational psychology (MS); language and culture (MA); liberal arts (MA, MFA, MS, Graduate Certificate); philosophy (MA); political science (MA); psychology (MA); religious studies (MA); Spanish (MA); special concentration (MA); teaching English to speakers of other languages (MA, Graduate Certificate). Electronic applications accepted.

College of Natural Sciences and Mathematics *Program availability:* Part-time. Offers biochemistry (MS); biology (MS); chemistry (MS); geology (MS); mathematics (MS); microbiology (MS); natural sciences and mathematics (MS); physics (MS); science education (MS). Electronic applications accepted.

College of the Arts *Program availability:* Part-time. Offers acting (MFA); art education (MA); arts (MA, MFA, MM); composition (MM); dance (MA, MFA); music (MA); studio art (MFA). Electronic applications accepted.

CALIFORNIA STATE UNIVERSITY, LOS ANGELES, Los Angeles, CA 90032-8530

General Information State-supported, coed, comprehensive institution. CGS member. *Graduate housing:* Room and/or apartments available on a first-come, first-served basis to single students; on-campus housing not available to married students. *Research affiliation:* NASA (engineering), General Motors (engineering).

GRADUATE UNITS

Graduate Studies *Program availability:* Part-time, evening/weekend. Electronic applications accepted.

Charter College of Education *Program availability:* Part-time, evening/weekend. Offers applied and advanced studies in education (Graduate Certificate); counseling (MS); education (MA, MS, Ed D, PhD, Graduate Certificate); elementary teaching (MA); special education (MA, PhD). Electronic applications accepted.

College of Arts and Letters *Program availability:* Part-time, evening/weekend. Offers art (MA); arts and letters (MA, MFA, MM, Certificate, Graduate Certificate); communication studies (MA, MFA); English (MA, Certificate); fine arts (MFA); French (MA); music composition (MM); music education (MA); musicology (MA); performance (MM); philosophy (MA, Graduate Certificate); Spanish (MA); theater arts (MA). Electronic applications accepted.

College of Business and Economics *Program availability:* Part-time, evening/weekend. Offers accounting (MBA); business and economics (MA, MBA, MS, Postbaccalaureate Certificate); finance and banking (MBA, MS); financial economics (MA); global economics (MA); health care management (MS); international business (MBA, MS); management (MBA, MS). Electronic applications accepted.

College of Engineering, Computer Science, and Technology *Program availability:* Part-time, evening/weekend. Offers civil engineering (MS); computer science (MS); electrical engineering (MS); engineering, computer science, and technology (MA, MS); industrial and technical studies (MA); mechanical engineering (MS). Electronic applications accepted.

College of Health and Human Services *Program availability:* Part-time, evening/weekend. Offers child development (MA); criminal justice (MS); criminalistics (MS); health and human services (MA, MS, MSW, Certificate, Post Master's Certificate); nursing (MS, Post Master's Certificate); nutritional science (MS); physical education and kinesiology (MA); social work (MSW); speech and hearing (MA); speech-language pathology (MA). Electronic applications accepted.

College of Natural and Social Sciences *Program availability:* Part-time, evening/weekend. Offers analytical chemistry (MS); anthropology (MA); biology (MS); geography (MA); geological sciences (MS); history (MA); Latin American studies (MA); mathematics (MS); Mexican-American studies (MA); natural and social sciences (MA, MS); physics (MS); political science (MA); psychology (MA, MS); public administration (MS); sociology (MA).

CALIFORNIA STATE UNIVERSITY MARITIME ACADEMY, Vallejo, CA 94590

General Information State-supported, coed, comprehensive institution. *Enrollment:* 1,090 graduate, professional, and undergraduate students; 41 full-time matriculated graduate/professional students (7 women). *Enrollment by degree level:* 41 master's. *Graduate faculty:* 16 part-time/adjunct (2 women). *Graduate housing:* On-campus housing not available. *Student services:* Career counseling, services for students with disabilities.

Computer facilities: A campuswide network can be accessed. Online class registration is available.
Website: http://www.csum.edu/

General Application Contact: Kathy Arnold, Graduate Program Coordinator, 707-654-1271, Fax: 707-654-1158, E-mail: karnold@csum.edu.

GRADUATE UNITS

Graduate Studies Students: 41 full-time (7 women); includes 10 minority (2 Black or African American, non-Hispanic/Latino; 5 Asian, non-Hispanic/Latino; 2 Hispanic/Latino; 1 Native Hawaiian or other Pacific Islander, non-Hispanic/Latino), 2 international. Average age 33. 32 applicants, 84% accepted, 22 enrolled. *Faculty:* 16 part-time/adjunct (2 women). Expenses: Contact institution. *Financial support:* Applicants required to submit FAFSA. In 2017, 16 master's awarded. *Program availability:* Evening/weekend, online only, 100% online. Offers transportation and engineering management (MS). *Application deadline:* Applications are processed on a rolling basis. *Application fee:* $55. Electronic applications accepted. *Application Contact:* Kathy Arnold, Program Coordinator, 707-654-1271, Fax: 707-654-1158, E-mail: karnold@csum.edu. *Associate Vice President, Academic Affairs,* Dr. Graham Benton, 707-654-1147.

CALIFORNIA STATE UNIVERSITY, MONTEREY BAY, Seaside, CA 93955-8001

General Information State-supported, coed, comprehensive institution. *Graduate housing:* Rooms and/or apartments available on a first-come, first-served basis to single and married students.

GRADUATE UNITS

College of Business *Program availability:* Part-time, evening/weekend, online learning. Offers business (MBA). Electronic applications accepted.

College of Education *Program availability:* Part-time, evening/weekend. Offers education (MAE). Electronic applications accepted.

College of Health Sciences and Human Services *Program availability:* Part-time. Offers social work (MSW). Electronic applications accepted.

College of Science *Program availability:* Part-time. Offers applied marine and watershed science (MS); marine science (MS); science (MS, MSMIT). Electronic applications accepted.

School of Computing and Design Offers computing and design (MS, MSMIT). MSMIT offered in conjunction with College of Business. Electronic applications accepted.

CALIFORNIA STATE UNIVERSITY, NORTHRIDGE, Northridge, CA 91330

General Information State-supported, coed, comprehensive institution. *Enrollment:* 39,916 graduate, professional, and undergraduate students; 1,659 full-time matriculated graduate/professional students (1,074 women), 1,562 part-time matriculated graduate/professional students (966 women). *Enrollment by degree level:* 3,081 master's, 140 doctoral. *Graduate housing:* Room and/or apartments available to single students; on-campus housing not available to married students. *Student services:* Campus employment opportunities, campus safety program, career counseling, child daycare facilities, free psychological counseling, international student services, low-cost health insurance, multicultural affairs office, services for students with disabilities, teacher training. *Library facilities:* Oviatt Library plus 1 other. *Collection:* Students can reserve study rooms. *Research affiliation:* Haagen Company (archaeology), Northridge Hospital (biology), Warner Center Institute (child care), Jet Propulsion Laboratory (engineering), Hughes Aircraft Corporation (engineering), California Institute of Technology (science).

Computer facilities: A campuswide network can be accessed from student residence rooms and from off campus. Online class registration is available.
Website: http://www.csun.edu/

General Application Contact: Dr. Crist Khachikian, Associate Vice President, 818-677-2138.

GRADUATE UNITS

Graduate Studies Students: 1,659 full-time (1,074 women), 1,562 part-time (966 women); includes 1,513 minority (115 Black or African American, non-Hispanic/Latino; 7 American Indian or Alaska Native, non-Hispanic/Latino; 289 Asian, non-Hispanic/Latino; 980 Hispanic/Latino; 6 Native Hawaiian or other Pacific Islander, non-Hispanic/Latino; 116 Two or more races, non-Hispanic/Latino), 332 international. Average age 31. 5,150 applicants, 41% accepted, 1106 enrolled. Expenses: Contact institution. *Financial support:* Fellowships, research assistantships, teaching assistantships, career-related internships or fieldwork, Federal Work-Study, institutionally sponsored loans, scholarships/grants, tuition waivers (partial), and unspecified assistantships available. Support available to part-time students. Financial award applicants required to submit FAFSA. In 2017, 1,786 master's awarded. *Program availability:* Part-time, evening/weekend. *Application deadline:* For fall admission, 3/31 for domestic students; for spring admission, 10/31 for domestic students. Applications are processed on a rolling basis. *Application fee:* $55. Electronic applications accepted. *Application Contact:* 818-677-3755. *Associate Vice President,* Dr. Crist Khachikian, 818-677-2138.

College of Engineering and Computer Science 908 applicants, 32% accepted, 124 enrolled. Expenses: Contact institution. *Financial support:* Teaching assistantships, career-related internships or fieldwork, and Federal Work-Study available. Support available to part-time students. Financial award application deadline: 3/1. In 2017, 242 master's awarded. *Program availability:* Part-time, evening/weekend. Offers computer science (MS); electrical engineering (MS); engineering (MS); engineering and computer science (MS); engineering automation (MS); engineering management (MS); manufacturing systems engineering (MS); materials engineering (MS); mechanical engineering (MS); software engineering (MS). *Application deadline:* For fall admission, 11/30 for domestic students. *Application fee:* $55. *Dean,* Dr. Hamid Johari, 818-677-4501, E-mail: hamid.johari@csun.edu.

College of Health and Human Development Students: 431 full-time (299 women), 194 part-time (145 women); includes 305 minority (19 Black or African American, non-Hispanic/Latino; 1 American Indian or Alaska Native, non-Hispanic/Latino; 82 Asian, non-Hispanic/Latino; 167 Hispanic/Latino; 3 Native Hawaiian or other Pacific Islander, non-Hispanic/Latino; 33 Two or more races, non-Hispanic/Latino), 38 international. Average age 29. 767 applicants, 35% accepted, 175 enrolled. Expenses: Contact institution. *Financial support:* Teaching assistantships, career-related internships or fieldwork, Federal Work-Study, and institutionally sponsored loans available. Support available to part-time students. Financial award application deadline: 3/1. In 2017, 277 master's awarded. *Program availability:* Part-time, evening/weekend. Offers audiology (MS); environmental and occupational health (MS); family and consumer sciences (MS); health administration (MS); health and human development (MPH, MPT, MS); hospitality and tourism (MS); industrial hygiene (MS); kinesiology (MS); physical therapy (MPT); public health (MPH); recreational sport management/campus recreation (MS); speech language pathology (MS). *Application deadline:* For fall admission, 11/30 for domestic students. *Application fee:* $55. *Application Contact:* 818-677-3755. *Dean,* Farrell J. Webb, 818-677-3001.

College of Humanities Students: 91 full-time (56 women), 115 part-time (78 women). Average age 33. 205 applicants, 76% accepted, 77 enrolled. Expenses: Contact institution. *Financial support:* Teaching assistantships and Federal Work-Study available. Support available to part-time students. Financial award application deadline: 3/1. In 2017, 80 master's awarded. *Program availability:* Part-time, evening/weekend. Offers Chicana and Chicano studies (MA); creative writing (MA); humanities (MA); linguistics (MA); literature (MA); rhetoric and composition theory (MA); Spanish (MA). *Application deadline:* For fall admission, 11/30 for domestic students. *Application fee:* $55. *Dean,* Dr. Elizabeth Say, 818-677-3301.

College of Science and Mathematics Students: 54 full-time (14 women), 150 part-time (65 women); includes 81 minority (4 Black or African American, non-Hispanic/Latino; 24 Asian, non-Hispanic/Latino; 48 Hispanic/Latino; 5 Two or more races, non-Hispanic/Latino), 15 international. Average age 29. 195 applicants, 43% accepted, 55 enrolled. Expenses: Contact institution. *Financial support:* Research assistantships, teaching assistantships, Federal Work-Study, institutionally sponsored loans, tuition waivers (partial), and unspecified assistantships available. Support available to part-time students. Financial award applicants required to submit FAFSA. In 2017, 63 master's awarded. *Program availability:* Part-time, evening/weekend. Offers applied mathematics (MS); biochemistry (MS); biology (MS); chemistry (MS); geology (MS); mathematics (MS); physics (MS); science and mathematics (MS). *Application fee:* $55. *Dean*, Dr. Jerry Stinner, 818-677-2004, E-mail: jerry.stinner@csun.edu.

College of Social and Behavioral Sciences Students: 357 full-time (268 women), 142 part-time (91 women); includes 302 minority (35 Black or African American, non-Hispanic/Latino; 2 American Indian or Alaska Native, non-Hispanic/Latino; 27 Asian, non-Hispanic/Latino; 220 Hispanic/Latino; 18 Two or more races, non-Hispanic/Latino), 16 international. Average age 30. 1,630 applicants, 41% accepted, 226 enrolled. Expenses: Contact institution. *Financial support:* Teaching assistantships, career-related internships or fieldwork, Federal Work-Study, and institutionally sponsored loans available. Support available to part-time students. Financial award application deadline: 3/1. In 2017, 615 master's awarded. *Program availability:* Part-time, evening/weekend. Offers clinical psychology (MA); general anthropology (MA); general experimental psychology (MA); geography (MA); history (MA); political science (MA); public archaeology (MA); social and behavioral sciences (MA, MSW); social work (MSW); sociology (MA). *Application deadline:* For fall admission, 11/30 for domestic students. *Application fee:* $55. *Interim Dean*, Dr. Matthew Cahn, 818-677-3317.

David Nazarian College of Business and Economics Students: 61 full-time (27 women), 95 part-time (47 women); includes 58 minority (7 Black or African American, non-Hispanic/Latino; 25 Asian, non-Hispanic/Latino; 21 Hispanic/Latino; 5 Two or more races, non-Hispanic/Latino), 22 international. Average age 32. 374 applicants, 39% accepted, 64 enrolled. Expenses: Contact institution. *Financial support:* Teaching assistantships and Federal Work-Study available. Support available to part-time students. Financial award application deadline: 3/1. In 2017, 85 master's awarded. *Program availability:* Part-time. Offers business and economics (MBA). *Application deadline:* For fall admission, 11/30 for domestic students. *Application fee:* $55. *Application Contact:* Dr. Deborah Heisley, Director of Graduate Programs, 818-677-2467. *Dean*, Dr. Kenneth Lord, 818-677-2455.

Michael D. Eisner College of Education Students: 351 full-time (296 women), 553 part-time (441 women); includes 477 minority (33 Black or African American, non-Hispanic/Latino; 2 American Indian or Alaska Native, non-Hispanic/Latino; 57 Asian, non-Hispanic/Latino; 355 Hispanic/Latino; 1 Native Hawaiian or other Pacific Islander, non-Hispanic/Latino; 29 Two or more races, non-Hispanic/Latino), 19 international. Average age 33. 703 applicants, 48% accepted, 300 enrolled. Expenses: Contact institution. *Financial support:* Fellowships, career-related internships or fieldwork, Federal Work-Study, institutionally sponsored loans, scholarships/grants, and tuition waivers (partial) available. Support available to part-time students. Financial award application deadline: 3/1. In 2017, 284 master's awarded. *Program availability:* Part-time, evening/weekend. Offers counseling (MS); curriculum and instruction (MA); early childhood special education (MA); education (MA, MA Ed, MS, Ed D); education of the deaf and hard of hearing (MA); educational administration (MA); educational leadership (Ed D); educational psychology (MA Ed); educational technology (MA); educational therapy (MA); English education (MA); language and literacy (MA); mathematics education (MA); mild/moderate disabilities (MA); moderate/severe disabilities (MA); multilingual/multicultural education (MA); secondary science education (MA); teaching and learning (MA). *Application deadline:* For fall admission, 11/30 for domestic students. *Application fee:* $55. *Dean*, Dr. Shari Tarver Behring, 818-677-2590, E-mail: coe.educ@csun.edu.

Mike Curb College of Arts, Media, and Communication Students: 121 full-time (69 women), 79 part-time (45 women); includes 75 minority (9 Black or African American, non-Hispanic/Latino; 1 American Indian or Alaska Native, non-Hispanic/Latino; 14 Asian, non-Hispanic/Latino; 40 Hispanic/Latino; 11 Two or more races, non-Hispanic/Latino), 33 international. Average age 31. 368 applicants, 42% accepted, 85 enrolled. Expenses: Contact institution. *Financial support:* Teaching assistantships, career-related internships or fieldwork, Federal Work-Study, and unspecified assistantships available. Support available to part-time students. Financial award application deadline: 3/1. *Program availability:* Part-time, evening/weekend. Offers art education (MA); art history (MA); arts, media, and communication (MA, MFA, MM); communication studies (MA); composition (MM); conducting (MM); mass communication (MA); music education (MA); performance (MM); screenwriting (MA); studio art (MA, MFA); theatre (MA); visual communications (MA, MFA). *Application deadline:* For fall admission, 11/30 for domestic students. *Application fee:* $55. *Dean*, Dan Hosken, 818-677-2246.

Tseng College Students: 4 part-time (all women); includes 1 minority (Black or African American, non-Hispanic/Latino). Average age 37. Expenses: Contact institution. In 2017, 2 master's awarded. Offers business administration (Graduate Certificate); health administration (MPA); health education (MPH); knowledge management (MKM); music industry administration (MA); nonprofit-sector management (Graduate Certificate); public administration (MPA); public sector management and leadership (MPA); social work (MSW); taxation (MS); tourism, hospitality and recreation management (MS). *Dean*, Joyce Feucht-Haviar, 866-873-6439.

CALIFORNIA STATE UNIVERSITY, SACRAMENTO, Sacramento, CA 95819

General Information State-supported, coed, comprehensive institution. CGS member. *Enrollment:* 30,670 graduate, professional, and undergraduate students; 1,129 full-time matriculated graduate/professional students (587 women), 1,656 part-time matriculated graduate/professional students (1,207 women). *Enrollment by degree level:* 2,255 master's, 145 doctoral, 385 other advanced degrees. *Graduate housing:* Room and/or apartments available on a first-come, first-served basis to single students; on-campus housing not available to married students. *Student services:* Campus employment opportunities, career counseling, child daycare facilities, free psychological counseling, grant writing training, international student services, low-cost health insurance, multicultural affairs office, services for students with disabilities, teacher training, writing training. *Library facilities:* California State University, Sacramento Library. *Collection:* Students can reserve study rooms.

Computer facilities: Computer purchase and lease plans are available. A campuswide network can be accessed from student residence rooms and from off campus. Online class registration, online transcripts are available.
Website: http://www.csus.edu/

General Application Contact: Dr. Chevelle Newsome, Dean of Graduate Admissions, 916-278-6470, Fax: 916-278-5669, E-mail: cnewsome@skymail.csus.edu.

GRADUATE UNITS

College of Arts and Letters Students: 86 full-time (46 women), 118 part-time (70 women); includes 70 minority (7 Black or African American, non-Hispanic/Latino; 3 American Indian or Alaska Native, non-Hispanic/Latino; 10 Asian, non-Hispanic/Latino; 50 Hispanic/Latino). Average age 31. Expenses: Contact institution. *Financial support:* Teaching assistantships, career-related internships or fieldwork, Federal Work-Study, and scholarships/grants available. Support available to part-time students. Financial award application deadline: 3/1; financial award applicants required to submit FAFSA. In 2017, 55 master's awarded. *Program availability:* Part-time, evening/weekend. Offers arts and letters (MA, MM, PhD); communication studies (MA); composition (MA, MM); conducting (MM); creative writing (MA); history (MA); literature (MA); performance (MM); public historical studies (PhD); public history (MA); studio art (MA); teaching English to speakers of other languages (MA); world languages and literatures (MA). *Application deadline:* For fall admission, 3/1 for domestic students, 2/1 for international students; for spring admission, 9/15 for domestic students, 8/15 for international students. Applications are processed on a rolling basis. *Application fee:* $55. Electronic applications accepted. *Application Contact:* Jose Martinez, Graduate Admissions Supervisor, 916-278-7871, E-mail: martinj@skymail.csus.edu. *Dean*, Dr. Sheree Meyer, 916-278-6502.

College of Business Administration Students: 122 full-time (62 women), 153 part-time (75 women); includes 114 minority (10 Black or African American, non-Hispanic/Latino; 2 American Indian or Alaska Native, non-Hispanic/Latino; 73 Asian, non-Hispanic/Latino; 25 Hispanic/Latino; 4 Native Hawaiian or other Pacific Islander, non-Hispanic/Latino), 6 international. Average age 34. 230 applicants, 75% accepted, 134 enrolled. Expenses: Contact institution. *Financial support:* Teaching assistantships, career-related internships or fieldwork, Federal Work-Study, and scholarships/grants available. Support available to part-time students. Financial award application deadline: 3/1; financial award applicants required to submit FAFSA. In 2017, 123 master's awarded. *Program availability:* Part-time, evening/weekend, 100% online, blended/hybrid learning. Offers accountancy (MS); business administration (IMBA, MBA); human resources (MBA); urban land development (MBA). *Application deadline:* For fall admission, 2/1 for domestic students, 3/1 for international students; for spring admission, 9/15 for domestic students, 9/30 for international students. Applications are processed on a rolling basis. *Application fee:* $55. Electronic applications accepted. *Application Contact:* Jose Martinez, Graduate Admissions Supervisor, 916-278-7871, E-mail: martinj@skymail.csus.edu. *Dean*, Dr. Pierre A. Balthazard, 916-278-6578, Fax: 916-278-5793, E-mail: cba@csus.edu.

College of Education Students: 381 full-time (294 women), 135 part-time (101 women); includes 296 minority (44 Black or African American, non-Hispanic/Latino; 1 American Indian or Alaska Native, non-Hispanic/Latino; 94 Asian, non-Hispanic/Latino; 153 Hispanic/Latino; 4 Native Hawaiian or other Pacific Islander, non-Hispanic/Latino). Average age 32. 550 applicants, 53% accepted, 292 enrolled. Expenses: Contact institution. *Financial support:* Teaching assistantships, career-related internships or fieldwork, and Federal Work-Study available. Support available to part-time students. Financial award application deadline: 3/1; financial award applicants required to submit FAFSA. In 2017, 147 master's, 13 doctorates, 10 other advanced degrees awarded. *Program availability:* Part-time, evening/weekend, blended/hybrid learning. Offers behavioral science and gender equity (MA); child development (MA); counseling (MS); curriculum and instruction (MA); education (MA, MS, Ed D, Ed S); education leadership and policy studies (MA); education specialist (Ed S); educational technology (MA); language and literacy (MA); multicultural education (MA); school psychology (MA); special education (MA); workforce development advocacy (MA). *Application deadline:* For fall admission, 2/15 for domestic and international students; for spring admission, 9/15 for domestic and international students. Applications are processed on a rolling basis. *Application fee:* $55. Electronic applications accepted. *Application Contact:* Jose Martinez, Graduate Admissions Supervisor, 916-278-7871, E-mail: martinj@skymail.csus.edu. *Dean*, Dr. Alexander Sidorkin, 916-278-6639, E-mail: sidorkin@csus.edu.

College of Engineering and Computer Science Students: 182 full-time (61 women), 178 part-time (42 women); includes 109 minority (16 Black or African American, non-Hispanic/Latino; 1 American Indian or Alaska Native, non-Hispanic/Latino; 59 Asian, non-Hispanic/Latino; 33 Hispanic/Latino), 162 international. Average age 28. 705 applicants, 32% accepted, 191 enrolled. Expenses: Contact institution. *Financial support:* Teaching assistantships, career-related internships or fieldwork, Federal Work-Study, and scholarships/grants available. Support available to part-time students. Financial award application deadline: 3/1; financial award applicants required to submit FAFSA. In 2017, 143 master's awarded. *Program availability:* Part-time, evening/weekend. Offers civil engineering (MS); computer science (MS); electrical and electronic engineering (MS); engineering and computer science (MS); mechanical engineering (MS); software engineering (MS). *Application deadline:* Applications are processed on a rolling basis. *Application fee:* $55. Electronic applications accepted. *Application Contact:* Jose Martinez, Graduate Admissions Supervisor, 916-278-7871, E-mail: martinj@skymail.csus.edu. *Dean*, Dr. Lorenzo M. Smith, 916-278-6127, Fax: 916-278-5949, E-mail: lsmith@csus.edu.

College of Health and Human Services Students: 487 full-time (395 women), 162 part-time (139 women); includes 237 minority (37 Black or African American, non-Hispanic/Latino; 5 American Indian or Alaska Native, non-Hispanic/Latino; 88 Asian, non-Hispanic/Latino; 105 Hispanic/Latino; 2 Native Hawaiian or other Pacific Islander, non-Hispanic/Latino), 2 international. Average age 32. 749 applicants, 36% accepted, 237 enrolled. Expenses: Contact institution. *Financial support:* Teaching assistantships, career-related internships or fieldwork, Federal Work-Study, and scholarships/grants available. Support available to part-time students. Financial award application deadline: 3/1; financial award applicants required to submit FAFSA. In 2017, 223 master's, 29 doctorates awarded. *Program availability:* Part-time, evening/weekend. Offers communication sciences and disorders (MS); exercise science (MS); health and human services (MS, MSW, DPT); movement studies (MS); physical therapy (DPT); recreation, parks and tourism administration (MS). *Application deadline:* Applications are processed on a rolling basis. *Application fee:* $55. Electronic applications accepted. *Application Contact:* Jose Martinez, Graduate Admissions Supervisor, 916-278-7871, E-mail: martinj@skymail.csus.edu. *Dean*, Dr. Fred Baldini, 916-278-7255, Fax: 916-278-7421, E-mail: baldinif@csus.edu.

Division of Criminal Justice Students: 6 full-time (5 women), 17 part-time (11 women); includes 10 minority (2 Black or African American, non-Hispanic/Latino; 3 Asian, non-Hispanic/Latino; 5 Hispanic/Latino). Average age 27. 18 applicants, 44% accepted, 8 enrolled. Expenses: Contact institution. *Financial support:* Teaching assistantships, career-related internships or fieldwork, Federal Work-Study, and scholarships/grants available. Support available to part-time students. Financial award application deadline: 3/1; financial award applicants required to submit FAFSA. In 2017, 8 master's awarded. *Program availability:* Part-time. Offers criminal justice (MS). *Application deadline:* For fall admission, 3/1 for domestic and international students; for spring admission, 9/15 for domestic students, 9/30 for international students. Applications are processed on a rolling basis. *Application fee:* $55. Electronic applications accepted. *Application Contact:* Jose Martinez, Graduate Admissions Supervisor, 916-278-7871, E-mail: martinj@skymail.csus.edu. *Chair*, Dr. Ernest Uwazie, 916-278-6282, E-mail: uwazieee@csus.edu.

Division of Nursing Students: 70 full-time (65 women), 84 part-time (79 women); includes 41 minority (5 Black or African American, non-Hispanic/Latino; 2 American Indian or Alaska Native, non-Hispanic/Latino; 23 Asian, non-Hispanic/Latino; 11 Hispanic/Latino). Average age 40. 41 applicants, 93% accepted, 32 enrolled. Expenses: Contact institution. *Financial support:* Teaching assistantships, career-related internships or fieldwork, Federal Work-Study, and scholarships/grants available. Support available to part-time students. Financial award application deadline: 3/1; financial award applicants required to submit FAFSA. In 2017, 43 master's awarded. *Program availability:* Part-time. Offers nursing (MS). *Application deadline:* For fall admission, 3/1 for domestic and international students; for spring admission, 12/1 for domestic and international students. Applications are processed on a rolling basis. *Application fee:* $55. Electronic applications accepted. *Application Contact:* Jose Martinez, Graduate Admissions Supervisor, 916-278-7871, E-mail: martinj@skymail.csus.edu. *Chair*, Dr. Tanya Altmann, 916-278-1504, E-mail: altmannt@csus.edu.

Division of Social Work Students: 230 full-time (202 women), 14 part-time (10 women); includes 125 minority (24 Black or African American, non-Hispanic/Latino; 3 American Indian or Alaska Native, non-Hispanic/Latino; 28 Asian, non-Hispanic/Latino; 69 Hispanic/Latino; 1 Native Hawaiian or other Pacific Islander, non-Hispanic/Latino). Average age 31. 306 applicants, 41% accepted, 109 enrolled. Expenses: Contact institution. *Financial support:* Career-related internships or fieldwork, Federal Work-Study, and scholarships/grants available. Support available to part-time students. Financial award application deadline: 3/1; financial award applicants required to submit FAFSA. In 2017, 107 master's awarded. *Program availability:* Part-time, evening/weekend. Offers family and children's services (MSW). *Application deadline:* For fall admission, 1/18 for domestic and international students. Applications are processed on a rolling basis. *Application fee:* $55. Electronic applications accepted. *Application Contact:* Jose Martinez, Graduate Admissions Supervisor, 916-278-7871, E-mail: martinj@skymail.csus.edu. *Chair*, Dr. Dale Russell, 916-278-6943, E-mail: drussell@csus.edu.

College of Natural Sciences and Mathematics Students: 35 full-time (20 women), 69 part-time (28 women); includes 30 minority (2 Black or African American, non-Hispanic/Latino; 2 American Indian or Alaska Native, non-Hispanic/Latino; 20 Asian, non-Hispanic/Latino; 6 Hispanic/Latino), 2 international. Average age 31. 160 applicants, 38% accepted, 46 enrolled. Expenses: Contact institution. *Financial support:* Teaching assistantships, career-related internships or fieldwork, Federal Work-Study, and scholarships/grants available. Support available to part-time students. Financial award application deadline: 3/1; financial award applicants required to submit FAFSA. In 2017, 18 master's awarded. *Program availability:* Part-time. Offers biochemistry (MS); biological conservation (MS); chemistry (MS); mathematics (MA); molecular and cellular biology (MS); natural sciences and mathematics (MA, MS); stem cell (MA). *Application deadline:* For fall admission, 3/1 for domestic and international students. Applications are processed on a rolling basis. *Application fee:* $55. Electronic applications accepted. *Application Contact:* Jose Martinez, Graduate Admissions Supervisor, 916-278-7871, E-mail: martinj@skymail.csus.edu. *Dean*, Dr. Jill Trainer, 916-278-4655, E-mail: jill.trainer@csus.edu.

College of Social Sciences and Interdisciplinary Studies Students: 63 full-time (32 women), 132 part-time (83 women); includes 79 minority (10 Black or African American, non-Hispanic/Latino; 3 American Indian or Alaska Native, non-Hispanic/Latino; 19 Asian, non-Hispanic/Latino; 43 Hispanic/Latino; 4 Native Hawaiian or other Pacific Islander, non-Hispanic/Latino), 2 international. Average age 30. 205 applicants, 51% accepted, 68 enrolled. Expenses: Contact institution. *Financial support:* Teaching assistantships, career-related internships or fieldwork, Federal Work-Study, and scholarships/grants available. Support available to part-time students. Financial award application deadline: 3/1; financial award applicants required to submit FAFSA. In 2017, 33 master's awarded. *Program availability:* Part-time. Offers anthropology (MA); applied behavior analysis (MA); government (MA); industrial/organizational psychology (MA); public policy and administration (MPPA); social sciences and interdisciplinary studies (MA, MPPA); sociology (MA). *Application deadline:* Applications are processed on a rolling basis. *Application fee:* $55. Electronic applications accepted. *Application Contact:* Jose Martinez, Graduate Admissions Supervisor, 916-278-7871, E-mail: martinj@skymail.csus.edu. *Interim Dean*, Dr. Ted Lascher, 916-278-6504, Fax: 916-278-4678, E-mail: tedl@csus.edu.

CALIFORNIA STATE UNIVERSITY, SAN BERNARDINO, San Bernardino, CA 92407

General Information State-supported, coed, comprehensive institution. CGS member. *Enrollment:* 20,461 graduate, professional, and undergraduate students; 1,037 full-time matriculated graduate/professional students (738 women), 1,181 part-time matriculated graduate/professional students (749 women). *Enrollment by degree level:* 1,689 master's, 73 doctoral. *Graduate faculty:* 141 full-time (62 women), 75 part-time/adjunct (54 women). *Graduate housing:* Room and/or apartments available on a first-come, first-served basis to single students; on-campus housing not available to married students. *Student services:* Campus employment opportunities, campus safety program, career counseling, child daycare facilities, exercise/wellness program, free psychological counseling, international student services, low-cost health insurance, multicultural affairs office, services for students with disabilities, teacher training. *Library facilities:* Pfau Library.

Computer facilities: Computer purchase and lease plans are available. A campuswide network can be accessed from student residence rooms and from off campus. Online class registration is available.
Website: http://www.csusb.edu/

General Application Contact: Dr. Dorota Huizinga, Dean of Graduate Studies, 909-537-5058, Fax: 909-537-5078, E-mail: dorota.huizinga@csusb.edu.

GRADUATE UNITS

Graduate Studies Students: 712 full-time (526 women), 1,050 part-time (665 women); includes 1,040 minority (133 Black or African American, non-Hispanic/Latino; 3 American Indian or Alaska Native, non-Hispanic/Latino; 87 Asian, non-Hispanic/Latino; 762 Hispanic/Latino; 4 Native Hawaiian or other Pacific Islander, non-Hispanic/Latino; 51 Two or more races, non-Hispanic/Latino), 174 international. Average age 33. 1,769 applicants, 49% accepted, 606 enrolled. *Faculty:* 141 full-time (62 women), 75 part-time/adjunct (54 women). Expenses: Contact institution. In 2017, 767 master's, 7 doctorates awarded. *Program availability:* Part-time, evening/weekend. Offers integrative studies (MA). *Application deadline:* For fall admission, 7/17 for domestic students. *Application fee:* $55. *Application Contact:* Olivia Rosas, Director of Admissions, 909-537-7577, Fax: 909-537-7034, E-mail: orosas@csusb.edu. *Dean*, Dr. Dorota Huizinga, 909-537-5058, Fax: 909-537-5078, E-mail: dorota.huizinga@csusb.edu.

College of Arts and Letters Students: 23 full-time (16 women), 110 part-time (80 women); includes 81 minority (11 Black or African American, non-Hispanic/Latino; 3 Asian, non-Hispanic/Latino; 62 Hispanic/Latino; 5 Two or more races, non-Hispanic/Latino). Average age 32. 77 applicants, 58% accepted, 33 enrolled. *Faculty:* 18 full-time (10 women), 1 (woman) part-time/adjunct. Expenses: Contact institution. *Financial support:* Application deadline: 3/1. In 2017, 24 master's awarded. *Program availability:* Part-time, evening/weekend. Offers arts and letters (MA, MFA); communication studies (MA); creative writing (MFA); English composition (MA); integrated marketing communication (MA); Spanish (MA); studio art (MA). *Application deadline:* For fall admission, 7/17 priority date for domestic students. Applications are processed on a rolling basis. *Application fee:* $55. Electronic applications accepted. *Application Contact:* Dr. Dorota Huizinga, Dean of Graduate Studies, 909-537-3064, Fax: 909-537-5078, E-mail: dorota.huizinga@csusb.edu. *Dean*, Dr. Terry L. Ballman, 909-537-5800, Fax: 909-537-5926, E-mail: tballman@csusb.edu.

College of Business and Public Administration Students: 81 full-time (46 women), 340 part-time (159 women); includes 237 minority (41 Black or African American, non-Hispanic/Latino; 2 American Indian or Alaska Native, non-Hispanic/Latino; 40 Asian, non-Hispanic/Latino; 144 Hispanic/Latino; 1 Native Hawaiian or other Pacific Islander, non-Hispanic/Latino; 9 Two or more races, non-Hispanic/Latino), 89 international. Average age 32. 396 applicants, 50% accepted, 112 enrolled. *Faculty:* 19 full-time (4 women), 9 part-time/adjunct (6 women). Expenses: Contact institution. *Financial support:* Application deadline: 3/1. In 2017, 263 master's awarded. *Program availability:* Part-time, evening/weekend. Offers accountancy (MSA); accounting (MBA); business and public administration (MBA, MPA, MSA); entrepreneurship (MBA); finance (MBA); global business (MBA); information management (MBA); information security (MBA); management (MBA); public administration (MPA); supply chain management (MBA). *Application deadline:* For fall admission, 7/17 for domestic students. Applications are processed on a rolling basis. *Application fee:* $55. *Application Contact:* Dr. Dorota Huizinga, Dean of Graduate Studies, 909-537-3064, Fax: 909-537-5078, E-mail: dorota.huizinga@csusb.edu. *Dean*, Dr. Lawrence C. Rose, 909-537-3703, E-mail: lrose@csusb.edu.

College of Education Students: 299 full-time (234 women), 343 part-time (259 women); includes 378 minority (58 Black or African American, non-Hispanic/Latino; 1 American Indian or Alaska Native, non-Hispanic/Latino; 23 Asian, non-Hispanic/Latino; 277 Hispanic/Latino; 19 Two or more races, non-Hispanic/Latino), 52 international. Average age 35. 402 applicants, 75% accepted, 224 enrolled. *Faculty:* 33 full-time (20 women), 45 part-time/adjunct (33 women). Expenses: Contact institution. In 2017, 242 master's, 7 doctorates awarded. *Program availability:* Part-time, evening/weekend. Offers counseling and guidance (MS); education (MA, MS, Ed D); educational administration (MA); educational leadership: community college (MA); educational leadership: P-12 (Ed D); rehabilitation counseling (MA). *Application deadline:* For fall admission, 7/17 for domestic students. *Application fee:* $55. *Application Contact:* Dr. Dorota Huizinga, Dean of Graduate Studies, 909-537-3604, E-mail: dorota.huizinga@csusb.edu. *Dean*, Dr. Jay Fiene, 909-537-5600, Fax: 909-537-7011, E-mail: jfiene@csusb.edu.

College of Natural Sciences Students: 56 full-time (37 women), 107 part-time (64 women); includes 78 minority (8 Black or African American, non-Hispanic/Latino; 1 American Indian or Alaska Native, non-Hispanic/Latino; 67 Hispanic/Latino; 2 Native Hawaiian or other Pacific Islander, non-Hispanic/Latino), 40 international. Average age 30. 297 applicants, 35% accepted, 56 enrolled. *Faculty:* 30 full-time (10 women), 10 part-time/adjunct (5 women). Expenses: Contact institution. *Financial support:* Fellowships, research assistantships, and teaching assistantships available. In 2017, 64 master's awarded. *Program availability:* Part-time. Offers biology (MS); computer science (MS); earth and environmental sciences (MS); health services administration (MS); mathematics (MA); natural sciences (MA, MAT, MPH, MS, MSN); nursing (MSN); public health (MPH); teaching mathematics (MAT). *Application fee:* $55. *Application Contact:* Dr. Dorota Huizinga, Dean of Graduate Studies, 909-537-3064, E-mail: dorota.huizinga@csusb.edu. *Interim Dean*, Dr. Sally McGill, 909-537-3304, Fax: 909-537-7005, E-mail: smcgill@csusb.edu.

College of Social and Behavioral Sciences Students: 253 full-time (193 women), 144 part-time (100 women); includes 242 minority (23 Black or African American, non-Hispanic/Latino; 3 American Indian or Alaska Native, non-Hispanic/Latino; 12 Asian, non-Hispanic/Latino; 184 Hispanic/Latino; 20 Two or more races, non-Hispanic/Latino), 11 international. Average age 29. 594 applicants, 38% accepted, 162 enrolled. *Faculty:* 33 full-time (14 women), 18 part-time/adjunct (13 women). Expenses: Contact institution. *Financial support:* Career-related internships or fieldwork, Federal Work-Study, institutionally sponsored loans, and unspecified assistantships available. Support available to part-time students. In 2017, 173 master's awarded. *Program availability:* Part-time, evening/weekend. Offers child development (MA); clinical psychology (MS); clinical/counseling psychology (MS); criminal justice (MA); industrial/organizational psychology (MS); national cyber security studies (MA); national security studies (MA); psychological science (MA); psychology-life span (MA); social and behavioral sciences (MA, MS, MSW); social sciences and globalization (MA); social work (MSW). *Application deadline:* For fall admission, 7/17 for domestic students. *Application fee:* $55. *Application Contact:* Dr. Dorota Huizinga, Dean of Graduate Studies, 909-537-3064, E-mail: dorota.huizinga@csusb.edu. *Dean*, Dr. Rafik Mohamed, 909-537-7500, Fax: 909-537-7107, E-mail: rafik.mohamed@csusb.edu.

CALIFORNIA STATE UNIVERSITY, SAN MARCOS, San Marcos, CA 92096-0001

General Information State-supported, coed, comprehensive institution. *Enrollment:* 13,887 graduate, professional, and undergraduate students; 391 full-time matriculated graduate/professional students (262 women), 180 part-time matriculated graduate/professional students (114 women). *Enrollment by degree level:* 571 master's. *Graduate faculty:* 186 full-time (93 women), 377 part-time/adjunct (246 women). Tuition, state resident: full-time $7176. Tuition, nonresident: full-time $9504. *Graduate housing:* Room and/or apartments available on a first-come, first-served basis to single students; on-campus housing not available to married students. Housing application deadline: 10/1. *Student services:* Campus employment opportunities, campus safety program, career counseling, child daycare facilities, exercise/wellness program, free psychological counseling, international student services, low-cost health insurance, multicultural affairs office, services for students with disabilities, teacher training, writing training. *Library facilities:* Kellogg Library. *Collection:* Books: 215,402 (physical), 268,189 (digital/electronic); Serial titles: 3,130 (physical), 81,643 (digital/electronic); Databases: 100. Weekly public service hours: 100; students can reserve study rooms.

Computer facilities: A campuswide network can be accessed from student residence rooms and from off campus. Online class registration is available.
Website: http://www.csusm.edu/

General Application Contact: Dr. Wesley Schultz, Dean of Office of Graduate Studies and Research, 760-750-8045, Fax: 760-750-8045, E-mail: apply@csusm.edu.

GRADUATE UNITS

College of Business Administration Expenses: Contact institution. *Financial support:* Applicants required to submit FAFSA. *Program availability:* Evening/weekend. Offers business administration (MBA). *Application deadline:* For fall admission, 4/30 priority date for domestic students. Applications are processed on a rolling basis. *Application fee:* $55. *Director of Graduate Programs*, Dr. Mohammad Oskoorouchi, 760-750-4267, Fax: 760-750-4263, E-mail: mba@csusm.edu.

College of Education, Health and Human Services Expenses: Contact institution. Offers behavioral health (MSW); children, youth and families (MSW); education, health and human services (MA, MPH, MS, MSN, MSW, Ed D); kinesiology (MS); public health (MPH); speech-language pathology (MS). *Assistant Dean*, Shannon Cody, 760-750-4289, E-mail: scody@csusm.edu.

School of Education Expenses: Contact institution. *Financial support:* Applicants required to submit FAFSA. *Program availability:* Part-time, evening/weekend. Offers education (MA); educational administration (MA); educational leadership (Ed D); literacy education (MA); special education (MA). *Application deadline:* For fall admission, 2/1 priority date for domestic students. Applications are processed on a rolling basis. *Application fee:* $55. *Director*, Pat Stall, 760-750-4386, E-mail: pstall@csusm.edu.

School of Nursing Expenses: Contact institution. Offers advanced practice nursing (MSN); clinical nurse leader (MSN); nursing education (MSN). *Director*, Lorna Kendrick, 760-750-7580, E-mail: lkendrick@csusm.edu.

College of Humanities, Arts, Behavioral and Social Sciences Expenses: Contact institution. *Program availability:* Part-time, evening/weekend. Offers Hispanic cultures and society (MA); Hispanic language and linguistics (MA); Hispanic literatures and literary theory (MA); history (MA); humanities, arts, behavioral and social sciences (MA); literature and writing studies (MA); psychological science (MA); sociological practice (MA). *Application deadline:* For fall admission, 11/30 priority date for domestic students; for spring admission, 8/31 priority date for domestic students. Applications are processed on a rolling basis. *Application fee:* $55. Electronic applications accepted. *Dean*, Dr. Julia Johnson, 760-750-4195, E-mail: jjohnson@csusm.edu.

College of Science and Mathematics Expenses: Contact institution. Offers biology (MS); computer science (MS); cybersecurity (MS); mathematics (MS); science and mathematics (MS). *Dean*, Dr. Katherine Kantardjieff, 760-750-7240, E-mail: kkantard@csusm.edu.

Program in Biotechnology Offers biotechnology (PSM).

CALIFORNIA STATE UNIVERSITY, STANISLAUS, Turlock, CA 95382

General Information State-supported, coed, comprehensive institution. CGS member. *Graduate housing:* Room and/or apartments available on a first-come, first-served basis to single students; on-campus housing not available to married students. Housing application deadline: 7/15. *Research affiliation:* California Campus Compact-Carnegie Fellowship Program (teaching development for faculty), Valley Mountain Regional Center (development disability), Friends of Turlock Library, EDAW, Inc. (environmental sustainable development), Mathematical Association of America (mathematics), Kaiser Permanente (health care).

GRADUATE UNITS

College of Business Administration *Program availability:* Part-time, evening/weekend. Offers business administration (EMBA, MBA).

College of Education, Kinesiology and Social Work *Program availability:* Part-time, evening/weekend. Offers community college leadership (Ed D); curriculum and instruction (MA); education, kinesiology and social work (MA, MSW, Ed D); P-12 leadership (Ed D); school administration (MA); school counseling (MA); social work (MSW).

College of Natural Sciences Offers ecological conservation (MS); genetic counseling (MS); natural sciences (MS).

College of Science Offers behavior analysis (MA, MS); counseling psychology (MS); general psychology (MA); gerontological nursing (MS); nursing education (MS); science (MA, MS).

College of the Arts, Humanities and Social Sciences Offers arts, humanities and social sciences (MA, MPA, MS, Certificate); criminal justice (MA); history (MA); interdisciplinary studies (MA, MS); literature (Certificate); public administration (MPA); rhetoric and teaching writing (MA); teaching English to speakers of other languages (MA).

CALIFORNIA UNIVERSITY OF MANAGEMENT AND SCIENCES, Anaheim, CA 92801

General Information Independent, coed, comprehensive institution.

GRADUATE UNITS

Graduate Programs Offers business administration (MBA, DBA); computer information systems (MS); economics (MS); international business (MS); sports management (MS).

CALIFORNIA UNIVERSITY OF PENNSYLVANIA, California, PA 15419-1394

General Information State-supported, coed, comprehensive institution. CGS member. *Enrollment:* 7,788 graduate, professional, and undergraduate students; 890 full-time matriculated graduate/professional students (576 women), 1,299 part-time matriculated graduate/professional students (823 women). *Enrollment by degree level:* 1,780 master's, 36 doctoral, 373 other advanced degrees. *Graduate faculty:* 87 full-time (49 women), 58 part-time/adjunct (21 women). *Graduate housing:* Room and/or apartments available on a first-come, first-served basis to single students; on-campus housing not available to married students. Typical cost: $6592 per year ($10,344 including board). *Student services:* Campus employment opportunities, campus safety program, career counseling, exercise/wellness program, free psychological counseling, grant writing training, international student services, low-cost health insurance, multicultural affairs office, services for students with disabilities, teacher training, writing training. *Library facilities:* Manderino Library. *Collection:* Books: 219,774 (physical), 273,898 (digital/electronic); Serial titles: 22,098 (physical), 48,610 (digital/electronic); Databases: 97. Students can reserve study rooms. *Research affiliation:* The Center for Rural Pennsylvania (agriculture), The Technology Collaborative (robotics), International Technical Education Association (curricular development), National Collegiate Athletic Association (NCAA) (tobacco use), Gettysburg Travel Council (travel and tourism), NASA.

Computer facilities: 1,300 computers available on campus for general student use. Online class registration is available.
Website: http://www.calu.edu/

General Application Contact: Nicole Popielarcheck, Assistant Director of Graduate Admissions and Recruitment, 724-938-4029, Fax: 724-938-5712, E-mail: popielarcheck@calu.edu.

GRADUATE UNITS

School of Graduate Studies and Research Students: 890 full-time (576 women), 1,299 part-time (823 women); includes 321 minority (188 Black or African American, non-Hispanic/Latino; 2 American Indian or Alaska Native, non-Hispanic/Latino; 16 Asian, non-Hispanic/Latino; 62 Hispanic/Latino; 4 Native Hawaiian or other Pacific Islander, non-Hispanic/Latino; 49 Two or more races, non-Hispanic/Latino), 21 international. Average age 33. 715 applicants, 77% accepted, 355 enrolled. *Faculty:* 87 full-time (49 women), 58 part-time/adjunct (21 women). Expenses: Contact institution. *Financial support:* Scholarships/grants, tuition waivers (partial), and unspecified assistantships available. Financial award applicants required to submit FAFSA. In 2017, 1,095 master's awarded. *Program availability:* Part-time, evening/weekend, 100% online. *Application deadline:* For fall admission, 8/1 priority date for domestic and international students; for winter admission, 12/1 priority date for domestic and international students; for spring admission, 5/1 priority date for domestic and international students. Applications are processed on a rolling basis. *Application fee:* $25. Electronic applications accepted. *Application Contact:* Stephanie Franks, Dean of Graduate Admissions, 724-938-4301, Fax: 724-938-4270, E-mail: franks_s@calu.edu. *Dean of Graduate Studies and Research*, Dr. William B. Biddington, 724-938-1589, Fax: 724-938-4648, E-mail: biddington_w@calu.edu.

College of Education and Human Services Expenses: Contact institution. *Financial support:* Applicants required to submit FAFSA. *Program availability:* Part-time, evening/weekend, online learning. Offers advanced studies in secondary education and teacher leadership (M Ed); applied sport science (MS); athletic training (MS); autism (M Ed); clinical mental health counseling (MS); communication disorders (MS); early childhood education (M Ed); education administration and leadership (Ed D); education and human services (M Ed, MAT, MS, MSW, Ed D); educational leadership (M Ed); elementary education (M Ed); exercise science (MS); general special education (M Ed); group fitness leadership (MS); nutrition (MS); reading specialist (M Ed); school counseling (M Ed); secondary education (MAT); social work (MSW); sport management studies (MS); STEM education (M Ed); strategic sport analysis (MS); technology education (M Ed); wellness coaching (MS). *Application deadline:* For fall admission, 8/1 priority date for domestic and international students; for winter admission, 12/1 priority date for domestic and international students; for spring admission, 5/1 priority date for domestic and international students. Applications are processed on a rolling basis. *Application fee:* $25. Electronic applications accepted. *Application Contact:* Suzanne C. Powers, Director of Graduate Admissions and Recruitment, 724-938-4029, Fax: 724-938-5712, E-mail: powers_s@cup.edu. *Dean*, Geraldine Jones, 724-938-4125, E-mail: jones_gm@cup.edu.

College of Liberal Arts Expenses: Contact institution. *Program availability:* Part-time, evening/weekend. Offers conflict resolution (MA); criminal justice studies (MA); legal studies (MS); liberal arts (MA, MS); school psychology (MS); social science (MA). *Application deadline:* For fall admission, 8/1 priority date for domestic and international students; for winter admission, 12/1 priority date for domestic and international students; for spring admission, 5/1 priority date for domestic and international students. Applications are processed on a rolling basis. *Application fee:* $25. Electronic applications accepted. *Application Contact:* Stephanie Franks, Dean of Graduate Admissions and Global Online Enrollment Management, 724-938-4301, Fax: 724-938-4270, E-mail: franks_s@calu.edu. *Dean*, Dr. Mohamed Yamba, 724-938-4240, E-mail: yamba@calu.edu.

Eberly College of Science and Technology Expenses: Contact institution. *Program availability:* Part-time, evening/weekend, online learning. Offers business analytics (MBA); cybersecurity (PSM); entrepreneurship (MBA); healthcare management (MBA); nursing administration and leadership (MSN); nursing education (MSN); science and technology (MBA, MSN, PSM). *Application deadline:* For fall admission, 8/1 priority date for domestic and international students; for winter admission, 12/1 priority date for domestic and international students; for spring admission, 5/1 priority date for domestic and international students. Applications are processed on a rolling basis. *Application fee:* $25. Electronic applications accepted. *Application Contact:* Suzanne C. Powers, Director of Graduate Admissions and Recruitment, 724-938-4029, Fax: 724-938-5712, E-mail: powers_s@cup.edu. *Dean*, Dr. Leonard Colelli, 724-938-4169, Fax: 724-938-5743, E-mail: colelli@cup.edu.

CALIFORNIA WESTERN SCHOOL OF LAW, San Diego, CA 92101-3090

General Information Independent, coed, graduate-only institution. *Graduate housing:* On-campus housing not available.

GRADUATE UNITS

Graduate and Professional Programs *Program availability:* Part-time. Offers law (JD); Spanish language in trial advocacy (LL M). JD/MSW and JD/MBA offered jointly with San Diego State University. Electronic applications accepted.

CALUMET COLLEGE OF SAINT JOSEPH, Whiting, IN 46394-2195

General Information Independent-religious, coed, comprehensive institution.

GRADUATE UNITS

Program in Leadership in Teaching Offers leadership in teaching (MS Ed).

Program in Public Safety Administration Offers public safety administration (MS).

Program in Quality Assurance Offers quality assurance (MS).

CALVARY UNIVERSITY, Kansas City, MO 64147

General Information Independent-religious, coed, comprehensive institution. *Enrollment:* 271 graduate, professional, and undergraduate students; 11 full-time matriculated graduate/professional students (3 women), 29 part-time matriculated graduate/professional students (15 women). *Enrollment by degree level:* 40 master's. *Graduate faculty:* 6 full-time (2 women), 2 part-time/adjunct (1 woman). *Graduate housing:* Rooms and/or apartments available on a first-come, first-served basis to single and married students. *Student services:* Campus employment opportunities, services for students with disabilities, writing training. *Library facilities:* Hilda Kroeker Library. *Collection:* Books: 41,841 (physical), 420 (digital/electronic); Serial titles: 268 (physical); Databases: 4.

Computer facilities: 32 computers available on campus for general student use. A campuswide network can be accessed from student residence rooms. Online class registration is available.
Website: http://www.calvary.edu/

General Application Contact: Ann Rogers, Admissions Office Assistant, 800-326-3960 Ext. 1321, Fax: 816-331-4474, E-mail: admissions@calvary.edu.

GRADUATE UNITS

Graduate School and Seminary Students: 11 full-time (3 women), 29 part-time (15 women); includes 12 minority (4 Black or African American, non-Hispanic/Latino; 1 American Indian or Alaska Native, non-Hispanic/Latino; 6 Asian, non-Hispanic/Latino; 1 Native Hawaiian or other Pacific Islander, non-Hispanic/Latino). Average age 39. *Faculty:* 6 full-time (2 women), 2 part-time/adjunct (1 woman). Expenses: Contact institution. *Financial support:* Scholarships/grants available. Financial award application deadline: 11/5; financial award applicants required to submit FAFSA. *Program availability:* Part-time, evening/weekend. Offers Bible and theology (MS); Biblical counseling (MA); education (MS); organizational development (MS); pastoral studies (M Div); worship arts (MS). *Application deadline:* Applications are processed on a rolling basis. *Application fee:* $0. Electronic applications accepted. *Application Contact:* Ann Rogers, Admissions Office Assistant, 800-326-3960 Ext. 1321, Fax: 816-331-4474, E-mail: admissions@calvary.edu. *Director of Seminary*, Dr. Thomas Baurain, 816-322-0110 Ext. 1502, Fax: 816-331-4474, E-mail: thomas.baurain@calvary.edu.

CALVIN COLLEGE, Grand Rapids, MI 49546-4388

General Information Independent-religious, coed, comprehensive institution. *Graduate housing:* Room and/or apartments available on a first-come, first-served basis to single students; on-campus housing not available to married students. Housing application deadline: 4/1.

GRADUATE UNITS

Graduate Programs in Education *Program availability:* Part-time. Offers curriculum and instruction (M Ed). Electronic applications accepted.

Program in Accounting *Program availability:* Part-time. Offers accounting (M Acc).

CALVIN THEOLOGICAL SEMINARY, Grand Rapids, MI 49546-4387

General Information Independent-religious, coed, graduate-only institution. *Graduate housing:* Rooms and/or apartments available on a first-come, first-served basis to single and married students. Housing application deadline: 4/1.

GRADUATE UNITS

Graduate and Professional Programs *Program availability:* Part-time. Offers Bible and theology (MA); divinity (M Div); educational ministry (MA); historical theology (PhD); missions and evangelism (MA); pastoral care (MA); philosophical and moral theology (PhD); systematic theology (PhD); theological studies (MTS); theology (Th M); worship (MA); youth and family ministries (MA). Electronic applications accepted.

CAMBRIDGE COLLEGE, Boston, MA 02129

General Information Independent, coed, comprehensive institution. CGS member. *Tuition:* Part-time $554 per credit. Part-time tuition and fees vary according to degree level and program. *Graduate housing:* On-campus housing not available. *Student services:* Career counseling, free psychological counseling, international student services, services for students with disabilities, writing training. *Library facilities:* Cambridge College Online Library.

Computer facilities: Computer purchase and lease plans are available. A campuswide network can be accessed from off campus. Online class registration is available. Website: http://www.cambridgecollege.edu/

General Application Contact: Robyn Shahid-Bellot, Interim Director of Admissions, 800-877-4723 Ext. 1191, Fax: 617-349-3561, E-mail: robyn.shahid-bellot@cambridgecollege.edu.

GRADUATE UNITS

School of Education Expenses: Contact institution. *Financial support:* Career-related internships or fieldwork, Federal Work-Study, and scholarships/grants available. Financial award applicants required to submit FAFSA. *Program availability:* Part-time, evening/weekend, online learning. Offers autism specialist (M Ed); autism/behavior analyst (M Ed); behavior analyst (Post-Master's Certificate); curriculum and instruction (CAGS); early childhood teacher (M Ed); educational leadership (M Ed, Ed D); elementary teacher (M Ed); English as a second language (M Ed, Certificate); general science (M Ed); health education (Post-Master's Certificate); interdisciplinary studies (M Ed); library teacher (M Ed); mathematics education (M Ed); mathematics specialist (Certificate); school administration (M Ed, CAGS); school nurse education (M Ed); teacher of students with moderate disabilities (M Ed); teaching skills and methodologies (M Ed). *Application deadline:* Applications are processed on a rolling basis. *Application fee:* $30. Electronic applications accepted. *Application Contact:* Robyn Shahid-Bellot, Interim Director of Admissions, 800-877-4723 Ext. 1191, Fax: 617-349-3561, E-mail: robyn.shahid-bellot@cambridgecollege.edu. *Interim Dean*, Dr. Mary Garrity, 617-873-0168, E-mail: mary.garrity@cambridgecollege.edu.

School of Management Expenses: Contact institution. *Financial support:* Career-related internships or fieldwork, Federal Work-Study, and scholarships/grants available. Financial award applicants required to submit FAFSA. *Program availability:* Part-time, evening/weekend. Offers business administration (MBA); business negotiation and conflict resolution (M Mgt); general business (M Mgt); health care (MBA); health care management (M Mgt); small business development (M Mgt); technology management (M Mgt). *Application deadline:* Applications are processed on a rolling basis. *Application fee:* $30. Electronic applications accepted. *Application Contact:* Robyn Shahid-Bellot, Interim Director of Admissions, 800-877-4723, Fax: 617-349-3561, E-mail: robyn.shahid-bellot@cambridgecollege.edu. *Dean*, Dr. Mary Ann Joseph, 617-873-0227, E-mail: maryann.joseph@cambridgecollege.edu.

School of Psychology and Counseling Expenses: Contact institution. *Financial support:* Career-related internships or fieldwork, Federal Work-Study, and scholarships/grants available. Financial award applicants required to submit FAFSA. *Program availability:* Part-time, evening/weekend. Offers alcohol and drug counseling (Certificate); behavioral health care management (CAGS); marriage and family therapy (M Ed); mental health and school counseling (M Ed); mental health counseling (M Ed); psychological studies (M Ed); rehabilitation counseling (Certificate); school adjustment and mental health counseling (M Ed); school adjustment counseling for mental health counselors (Certificate); school counseling (M Ed); trauma studies (Certificate). *Application deadline:* Applications are processed on a rolling basis. *Application fee:* $30. Electronic applications accepted. *Application Contact:* Robyn Shahid-Bellot, Interim Director of Admissions, 800-877-4723 Ext. 1191, Fax: 617-349-3561, E-mail: robyn.shahid-bellot@cambridgecollege.edu. *Dean*, Dr. Niti Seth, 617-873-0208, Fax: 617-349-3561, E-mail: niti.seth@cambridgecollege.edu.

CAMERON UNIVERSITY, Lawton, OK 73505-6377

General Information State-supported, coed, comprehensive institution. *Graduate housing:* Room and/or apartments available on a first-come, first-served basis to single students; on-campus housing not available to married students. *Research affiliation:* Army Research Institute (human factors), Advanced Systems Technology, Inc. (informational systems), Dynamics Research Corporation (multimedia systems), Eagle Systems, Inc. (multimedia systems), Halliburton (energy systems), Telos OK, LLC (simulations).

GRADUATE UNITS

Office of Graduate Studies *Program availability:* Part-time, evening/weekend, online learning. Offers behavioral sciences (MS); business administration (MBA); education (M Ed); educational leadership (MS); entrepreneurial studies (MS); teaching (MAT). Electronic applications accepted.

CAMPBELLSVILLE UNIVERSITY, Campbellsville, KY 42718-2799

General Information Independent-religious, coed, comprehensive institution. *Enrollment:* 8,056 graduate, professional, and undergraduate students; 1,273 full-time matriculated graduate/professional students (545 women), 2,684 part-time matriculated graduate/professional students (641 women). *Enrollment by degree level:* 3,949 master's, 8 doctoral. *Graduate faculty:* 90 full-time (41 women), 61 part-time/adjunct (40 women). *Tuition:* Full-time $11,970; part-time $399 per credit hour. Tuition and fees vary according to degree level, campus/location and program. *Graduate housing:* Rooms and/or apartments available on a first-come, first-served basis to single and married students. Typical cost: $8000 (including board) for single students. Room and board charges vary according to housing facility selected. Housing application deadline: 6/30. *Student services:* Campus employment opportunities, campus safety program, career counseling, exercise/wellness program, international student services, services for students with disabilities, teacher training, writing training. *Library facilities:* Montgomery Library. *Collection:* Books: 173,113 (physical), 239,581 (digital/electronic); Serial titles: 67 (physical); Databases: 77. Weekly public service hours: 77; students can reserve study rooms.

Computer facilities: 220 computers available on campus for general student use. A campuswide network can be accessed from student residence rooms and from off campus. Online class registration is available. Website: http://www.campbellsville.edu/

General Application Contact: Monica Bamwine, Assistant Director of Graduate Admissions, 270-789-5221, Fax: 270-789-5071, E-mail: mkbamwine@campbellsville.edu.

GRADUATE UNITS

Carver School of Social Work Students: 80 full-time (76 women), 243 part-time (223 women); includes 44 minority (39 Black or African American, non-Hispanic/Latino; 1 American Indian or Alaska Native, non-Hispanic/Latino; 1 Asian, non-Hispanic/Latino; 2 Hispanic/Latino; 1 Two or more races, non-Hispanic/Latino), 3 international. Average age 33. 328 applicants, 68% accepted, 170 enrolled. *Faculty:* 15 full-time (14 women), 25 part-time/adjunct (23 women). Expenses: Contact institution. *Financial support:* Unspecified assistantships available. Financial award applicants required to submit FAFSA. In 2017, 71 master's awarded. *Program availability:* Part-time, evening/weekend, 100% online, blended/hybrid learning. Offers social work (MSW). *Application deadline:* Applications are processed on a rolling basis. *Application fee:* $25. Electronic applications accepted. *Application Contact:* Monica Bamwine, Assistant Director of Graduate Admissions, 270-789-5221, Fax: 270-789-5071, E-mail: mkbamwine@campbellsville.edu. *Program Director*, Dr. Helen K. Mudd, 270-789-5045, Fax: 270-789-5542, E-mail: hkmudd@campbellsville.edu.

College of Arts and Sciences Students: 6 full-time (3 women), 28 part-time (12 women); includes 9 minority (all Black or African American, non-Hispanic/Latino), 1 international. Average age 29. 38 applicants, 66% accepted, 25 enrolled. *Faculty:* 12 full-time (4 women), 2 part-time/adjunct (1 woman). Expenses: Contact institution. *Financial support:* In 2017–18, 2 students received support. Unspecified assistantships and employee tuition waivers available. Financial award application deadline: 6/1; financial award applicants required to submit FAFSA. In 2017, 5 master's awarded. *Program availability:* Part-time, evening/weekend, 100% online, blended/hybrid learning. Offers justice studies (MS); sport management (MA). *Application deadline:* Applications are processed on a rolling basis. *Application fee:* $25. Electronic applications accepted. *Application Contact:* Monica Bamwine, Assistant Director of Graduate Admissions, 270-789-5221, Fax: 270-789-5071, E-mail: mkbamwine@campbellsville.edu. *Dean*, Dr. Mike Page, 270-789-5394.

School of Business, Economics, and Technology Students: 74 full-time (16 women), 3,218 part-time (642 women); includes 28 minority (16 Black or African American, non-Hispanic/Latino; 9 Asian, non-Hispanic/Latino; 3 Hispanic/Latino), 3,164 international. Average age 27. 3,261 applicants, 95% accepted, 2220 enrolled. *Faculty:* 20 full-time (4 women), 9 part-time/adjunct (3 women). Expenses: Contact institution. *Financial support:* In 2017–18, 7 students received support. Unspecified assistantships and employee tuition waivers available. Financial award application deadline: 6/1; financial award applicants required to submit FAFSA. In 2017, 89 master's awarded. *Program availability:* Part-time, evening/weekend, 100% online, blended/hybrid learning. Offers business administration (MBA, Professional MBA); information technology management (MS); management (PhD); management and leadership (MML). *Application deadline:* Applications are processed on a rolling basis. *Application fee:* $25. Electronic applications accepted. *Application Contact:* Monica Bamwine, Assistant Director of Graduate Admissions, 270-789-5221, Fax: 270-789-5071, E-mail: mkbamwine@campbellsville.edu. *Dean*, Dr. Patricia H. Cowherd, 270-789-5553, Fax: 270-789-5066, E-mail: phcowherd@campbellsville.edu.

School of Education Students: 26 full-time (20 women), 155 part-time (122 women); includes 14 minority (13 Black or African American, non-Hispanic/Latino; 1 Hispanic/Latino). Average age 35. 199 applicants, 34% accepted, 57 enrolled. *Faculty:* 15 full-time (10 women), 14 part-time/adjunct (9 women). Expenses: Contact institution. *Financial support:* Unspecified assistantships and employee tuition waivers available. Financial award applicants required to submit FAFSA. In 2017, 96 master's awarded. *Program availability:* Part-time, evening/weekend, 100% online, blended/hybrid learning. Offers education (MA); school counseling (MA); school improvement (MA); special education (MASE); special education-teacher leader (MA); teacher leader (MA); teaching (MAT). *Application deadline:* Applications are processed on a rolling basis. *Application fee:* $25. Electronic applications accepted. *Application Contact:* Monica Bamwine, Assistant Director of Graduate Admissions, 270-789-5221, Fax: 270-789-5071, E-mail: mkbamwine@campbellsville.edu. *Dean*, Dr. Beverly Ennis, 270-789-5344, Fax: 270-789-5206, E-mail: bcennis@campbellsville.edu.

School of Music Students: 25 part-time (11 women); includes 1 minority (Black or African American, non-Hispanic/Latino), 6 international. Average age 31. 13 applicants, 38% accepted, 5 enrolled. *Faculty:* 14 full-time (6 women), 9 part-time/adjunct (4 women). Expenses: Contact institution. *Financial support:* In 2017–18, 14 students received support. Unspecified assistantships and employee tuition waivers available. Financial award application deadline: 6/1; financial award applicants required to submit FAFSA. In 2017, 3 master's awarded. *Program availability:* Part-time, 100% online, blended/hybrid learning. Offers music (MA, MM); musicology (MA); worship (MA). *Application deadline:* Applications are processed on a rolling basis. *Application fee:* $25. Electronic applications accepted. *Application Contact:* Monica Bamwine, Assistant Director of Graduate Admissions, 270-789-5221, Fax: 270-789-5071, E-mail: mkbamwine@campbellsville.edu. *Dean*, Dr. Tony Cunha, 270-789-5240, Fax: 270-789-5524, E-mail: accunha@campbellsville.edu.

School of Theology Students: 7 full-time (6 women), 83 part-time (44 women); includes 32 minority (30 Black or African American, non-Hispanic/Latino; 2 Hispanic/Latino). Average age 43. 58 applicants, 64% accepted, 29 enrolled. *Faculty:* 14 full-time (3 women), 2 part-time/adjunct (0 women). Expenses: Contact institution. *Financial support:* In 2017–18, 22 students received support. Unspecified assistantships and employee tuition waivers available. Financial award application deadline: 6/1; financial award applicants required to submit FAFSA. In 2017, 32 master's awarded. *Program availability:* Part-time, evening/weekend, 100% online, blended/hybrid learning. Offers marriage and family therapy (MMFT); theology (M Th). *Application deadline:* Applications are processed on a rolling basis. *Application fee:* $25. Electronic applications accepted. *Application Contact:* Monica Bamwine, Assistant Director of Graduate Admissions, 270-789-5221, Fax: 270-789-5071, E-mail: mkbamwine@campbellsville.edu. *Dean*, Dr. John E. Hurtgen, 270-789-5077, Fax: 270-789-5050, E-mail: jehurtgen@campbellsville.edu.

CAMPBELL UNIVERSITY, Buies Creek, NC 27506

General Information Independent-religious, coed, university. *Graduate housing:* Rooms and/or apartments available on a first-come, first-served basis to single and married students. Housing application deadline: 6/2.

GRADUATE UNITS

Graduate and Professional Programs *Program availability:* Part-time, evening/weekend.

College of Pharmacy and Health Sciences *Program availability:* Part-time, evening/weekend. Offers clinical research (MS); pharmaceutical sciences (MS); pharmacy (Pharm D); physician assistant (MPAP); public health (MS). Electronic applications accepted.

Divinity School Offers Christian ministry (MA); divinity (M Div); ministry (D Min).

Jerry M. Wallace School of Osteopathic Medicine Offers osteopathic medicine (DO).

Lundy-Fetterman School of Business *Program availability:* Part-time, evening/weekend. Offers business (MBA, MTWM).

Norman Adrian Wiggins School of Law Offers law (JD). JD/MPA offered in partnership with North Carolina State University. Electronic applications accepted.

School of Education *Program availability:* Part-time, evening/weekend. Offers elementary education (M Ed); interdisciplinary studies (M Ed); middle grades education (M Ed); physical education (M Ed); school administration (MSA); school counseling (M Ed); secondary education (M Ed).

CANADIAN COLLEGE OF NATUROPATHIC MEDICINE, Toronto, ON M2K 1E2, Canada

General Information Independent, coed, primarily women, graduate-only institution. *Graduate housing:* Room and/or apartments available on a first-come, first-served basis to single students; on-campus housing not available to married students. Housing application deadline: 4/30. *Research affiliation:* Ottawa Regional Cancer Centre, McMaster University, University of Oxford, Hospital for Sick Children, Mayo Clinic, Johns Hopkins University.

GRADUATE UNITS

Bachelor of Naturopathy Program Offers naturopathy (BN). Electronic applications accepted.

CANADIAN MEMORIAL CHIROPRACTIC COLLEGE, Toronto, ON M2H 3J1, Canada

General Information Independent, coed, graduate-only institution. *Graduate housing:* On-campus housing not available. *Research affiliation:* University of Waterloo, University of Calgary, University of Toronto.

GRADUATE UNITS

Certificate Programs Offers chiropractic clinical sciences (Certificate); chiropractic radiology (Certificate); chiropractic sports sciences (Certificate); clinical acupuncture (Certificate).

Professional Program Offers chiropractic (DC).

CANADIAN SOUTHERN BAPTIST SEMINARY, Cochrane, AB T4C 2G1, Canada

General Information Independent-religious, coed, graduate-only institution. *Enrollment by degree level:* 39 master's. *Graduate faculty:* 5 full-time (0 women), 5 part-time/adjunct (1 woman). *Tuition:* Full-time $7500 Canadian dollars; part-time $375 Canadian dollars per credit hour. *Required fees:* $450 Canadian dollars; $20 Canadian dollars per credit hour. *Graduate housing:* Rooms and/or apartments available on a first-come, first-served basis to single and married students. Typical cost: $4950 Canadian dollars per year for single students; $6500 Canadian dollars per year for married students. Room charges vary according to housing facility selected. Housing application deadline: 7/1. *Student services:* Campus employment opportunities, free psychological counseling, international student services. *Library facilities:* Keith C. Wills Library. *Collection:* Books: 40,100 (physical), 1,970 (digital/electronic). Weekly public service hours: 65.

Computer facilities: 6 computers available on campus for general student use. A campuswide network can be accessed from student residence rooms. Online class registration is available.
Website: http://www.csbs.ca/

General Application Contact: David Ong, Director of Admissions, 403-932-6622 Ext. 251, Fax: 403-932-7049, E-mail: admissions@csbs.ca.

GRADUATE UNITS

Graduate Programs Students: 20 full-time (6 women), 19 part-time (3 women); includes 7 minority (2 Black or African American, non-Hispanic/Latino; 5 Asian, non-Hispanic/Latino), 9 international. Average age 29. 16 applicants, 63% accepted, 10 enrolled. *Faculty:* 5 full-time (0 women), 5 part-time/adjunct (1 woman). Expenses: Contact institution. *Financial support:* Scholarships/grants available. Financial award application deadline: 7/1. In 2017, 7 master's awarded. *Program availability:* Part-time, 100% online, blended/hybrid learning. Offers Biblical studies (MBS); Christian ministry (MCMin); Christian studies (MCS); ministry (M Div). *Application deadline:* For fall admission, 7/1 priority date for domestic students, 3/1 priority date for international students; for winter admission, 11/15 priority date for domestic students. Applications are processed on a rolling basis. *Application fee:* $50 ($150 for international students). *Application Contact:* David Ong, Director of Admissions, 403-932-6622 Ext. 251, E-mail: admissions@csbs.ca. *Academic Dean*, Dr. Steve Booth, 403-932-6622 Ext. 232, E-mail: steve.booth@csbs.ca.

CANISIUS COLLEGE, Buffalo, NY 14208-1098

General Information Independent-religious, coed, comprehensive institution. *Enrollment:* 3,464 graduate, professional, and undergraduate students; 488 full-time matriculated graduate/professional students (305 women), 569 part-time matriculated graduate/professional students (353 women). *Enrollment by degree level:* 973 master's, 84 other advanced degrees. *Graduate faculty:* 57 full-time (25 women), 78 part-time/adjunct (47 women). *Tuition:* Full-time $22,860; part-time $820 per credit. *Required fees:* $720; $25 per credit. $65 per semester. One-time fee: $425. *Graduate housing:* Room and/or apartments available on a first-come, first-served basis to single students; on-campus housing not available to married students. Housing application deadline: 5/1. *Student services:* Campus employment opportunities, campus safety program, career counseling, exercise/wellness program, free psychological counseling, international student services, multicultural affairs office, services for students with disabilities, teacher training. *Library facilities:* Andrew L. Bouwhuis Library plus 1 other. *Collection:* Books: 222,252 (physical), 1.7 million (digital/electronic); Serial titles: 1,143 (physical), 303,210 (digital/electronic); Databases: 108. Weekly public service hours: 110; students can reserve study rooms. *Research affiliation:* Eduventures (enrollment management).

Computer facilities: Computer purchase and lease plans are available. 700 computers available on campus for general student use. A campuswide network can be accessed from student residence rooms and from off campus. Online class registration, online accounts are available.
Website: http://www.canisius.edu/

General Application Contact: Julie A Zulewski, Director of Graduate Enrollment, 716-888-2548, Fax: 716-888-3290, E-mail: zulewskj@canisius.edu.

GRADUATE UNITS

Graduate Division Students: 488 full-time (305 women), 569 part-time (353 women); includes 135 minority (79 Black or African American, non-Hispanic/Latino; 5 American Indian or Alaska Native, non-Hispanic/Latino; 8 Asian, non-Hispanic/Latino; 27 Hispanic/Latino; 3 Native Hawaiian or other Pacific Islander, non-Hispanic/Latino; 13 Two or more races, non-Hispanic/Latino), 46 international. Average age 29. 730 applicants, 79% accepted, 339 enrolled. *Faculty:* 57 full-time (25 women), 78 part-time/adjunct (47 women). Expenses: Contact institution. *Financial support:* Career-related internships or fieldwork, Federal Work-Study, scholarships/grants, tuition waivers (partial), and unspecified assistantships available. Support available to part-time students. Financial award application deadline: 4/30; financial award applicants required to submit FAFSA. In 2017, 532 master's, 39 other advanced degrees awarded. *Program availability:* Part-time, evening/weekend, 100% online, blended/hybrid learning. *Application deadline:* Applications are processed on a rolling basis. *Application fee:* $0. Electronic applications accepted. *Vice President for Academic Affairs*, Dr. Margaret C. McCarthy, 716-888-2120, Fax: 716-888-2120, E-mail: mmccarth@canisius.edu.

College of Arts and Sciences Students: 29 full-time (27 women), 45 part-time (35 women); includes 6 minority (3 Black or African American, non-Hispanic/Latino; 2 Hispanic/Latino; 1 Two or more races, non-Hispanic/Latino), 1 international. Average age 33. 102 applicants, 33% accepted, 25 enrolled. *Faculty:* 6 full-time (4 women), 8 part-time/adjunct (6 women). Expenses: Contact institution. *Financial support:* Career-related internships or fieldwork, Federal Work-Study, scholarships/grants, tuition waivers (partial), and unspecified assistantships available. Financial award application deadline: 4/30; financial award applicants required to submit FAFSA. In 2017, 274 master's awarded. *Program availability:* Part-time, evening/weekend, 100% online, blended/hybrid learning. Offers anthrozoology (MS); arts and sciences (MS); communication and leadership (MS). *Application deadline:* For fall admission, 7/15 priority date for domestic students; for spring admission, 4/15 priority date for domestic students. Applications are processed on a rolling basis. *Application fee:* $0. Electronic applications accepted. *Dean of Arts and Sciences*, Dr. Beth A. Gill, 716-888-2150, E-mail: gille@canisius.edu.

Richard J. Wehle School of Business Students: 132 full-time (59 women), 135 part-time (47 women); includes 27 minority (10 Black or African American, non-Hispanic/Latino; 2 American Indian or Alaska Native, non-Hispanic/Latino; 4 Asian, non-Hispanic/Latino; 6 Hispanic/Latino; 3 Native Hawaiian or other Pacific Islander, non-Hispanic/Latino; 2 Two or more races, non-Hispanic/Latino), 32 international. Average age 28. 172 applicants, 84% accepted, 95 enrolled. *Faculty:* 25 full-time (6 women), 12 part-time/adjunct (2 women). Expenses: Contact institution. *Financial support:* Career-related internships or fieldwork, Federal Work-Study, scholarships/grants, tuition waivers (partial), and unspecified assistantships available. Support available to part-time students. Financial award application deadline: 4/30; financial award applicants required to submit FAFSA. In 2017, 152 master's awarded. *Program availability:* Part-time, evening/weekend. Offers accounting (MBA); business (MBA, MS); business administration (MBA); forensic accounting (MS); international business (MS); professional accounting (MBA). *Application deadline:* For fall admission, 7/1 priority date for domestic students; for spring admission, 11/1 priority date for domestic students. Applications are processed on a rolling basis. *Application fee:* $0. Electronic applications accepted. *Dean*, Dr. Denise M. Rotundo, 716-888-2164, Fax: 716-888-2145, E-mail: rotundod@canisius.edu.

School of Education and Human Services Students: 328 full-time (219 women), 388 part-time (271 women); includes 102 minority (66 Black or African American, non-Hispanic/Latino; 3 American Indian or Alaska Native, non-Hispanic/Latino; 4 Asian, non-Hispanic/Latino; 19 Hispanic/Latino; 10 Two or more races, non-Hispanic/Latino), 13 international. Average age 31. 490 applicants, 86% accepted, 315 enrolled. *Faculty:* 26 full-time (15 women), 58 part-time/adjunct (39 women). Expenses: Contact institution. *Financial support:* Career-related internships or fieldwork, Federal Work-Study, scholarships/grants, tuition waivers (partial), and unspecified assistantships available. Support available to part-time students. Financial award application deadline: 4/30; financial award applicants required to submit FAFSA. In 2017, 449 master's awarded. *Program availability:* Part-time, evening/weekend, 100% online, blended/hybrid learning. Offers adolescence education (MS Ed); applied nutrition (MS, Certificate); business and marketing education (MS Ed); childhood education (MS Ed); college student personnel (MS Ed); community and school health (MS); community mental health counseling (MS); counseling and human services (MS); deaf education (MS Ed); deaf/adolescent education, grades 7-12 (MS Ed); deaf/childhood education, grades 1-6 (MS Ed); differentiated instruction (MS Ed); education administration (MS); education and human services (MS, MS Ed, MSA, Certificate); educational administration (MS Ed); educational technologies (Certificate); general education (MS Ed); gifted education extension (Certificate); health and human performance (MS); health information technology (MS); literacy (MS Ed); physical education (MS Ed); physical education birth - 12 (MS Ed); reading (Certificate); respiratory care (MS); school agency counseling (MS); school building leadership (MS Ed, Certificate); school district leadership (Certificate); special education (MS); sport administration (MSA); teacher leader (Certificate); TESOL (MS Ed). *Application deadline:* Applications are processed on a rolling basis. *Application fee:* $0. Electronic applications accepted. *Dean*, Dr. Jeffrey R. Lindauer, 716-888-3294, Fax: 716-888-3164, E-mail: lindauej@canisius.edu.

CAPE BRETON UNIVERSITY, Sydney, NS B1P 6L2, Canada

General Information Province-supported, coed, comprehensive institution. *Graduate housing:* Room and/or apartments available on a first-come, first-served basis to single students; on-campus housing not available to married students. Housing application deadline: 3/31. *Research affiliation:* Hyperspectral Data International (marine remote sensing), Sable Offshore Energy, Inc. (petroleum resources), Fortress Louisbourg National Historic Park (museum/heritage projects), Dynagen Industrial Mine Technology (mining industry equipment), Atlantic Geomatics (computer networking and software development), Advanced Glazing, Limited (transparent insulation).

GRADUATE UNITS

Shannon School of Business *Program availability:* Part-time. Offers business (MBA). Electronic applications accepted.

CAPELLA UNIVERSITY, Minneapolis, MN 55402

General Information Proprietary, coed, upper-level institution. CGS member.

GRADUATE UNITS

Harold Abel School of Social and Behavioral Science *Program availability:* Part-time, evening/weekend, online learning. Offers addiction psychology (PhD); applied behavior analysis (MS); child and adolescent development (MS); clinical psychology (MS, Psy D); counseling psychology (MS); educational psychology (MS, PhD); evaluation, research, and measurement (MS); general addiction counseling (MS); general advanced studies in human behavior (MS, PhD); general counselor education and supervision (PhD); general marriage and family counseling/therapy (MS); general mental health counseling (MS); general psychology (MS, PhD); general school counseling (MS); general social work (DSW); industrial/organizational psychology (MS, PhD); leadership coaching psychology (MS); school psychology (MS, Psy D); social and behavioral science (MS, PhD, Psy D); sport psychology (MS). Electronic applications accepted.

School of Business and Technology *Program availability:* Part-time, evening/weekend, online learning. Offers accounting (MBA, DBA, PhD); business analysis (MS); business and technology (MBA, MS, DBA, PhD); business intelligence (MBA, DBA); enterprise software architecture (MS); entrepreneurship (MBA); finance (MBA, DBA, PhD); general business administration (MBA); general business management (PhD); general human resource management (MS); general information systems and technology management (MS); general information technology (PhD); general leadership (MS); global operations and supply chain management (MBA, DBA); health care management (MBA); human resource management (MBA, DBA, PhD); information assurance and security (MS, PhD); information technology education (PhD); information technology management (MBA, DBA, PhD); leadership (DBA, PhD); management education (PhD); marketing (MBA, DBA, PhD); network management (MS); project management (MBA, MS, DBA, PhD); strategy and innovation (DBA, PhD). Electronic applications accepted.

School of Education *Program availability:* Part-time, evening/weekend, online learning. Offers adult education (MS); curriculum and instruction (MS, PhD); early childhood education (MS); education (MS, Ed D, PhD); educational leadership and management (Ed D); enrollment management (MS); higher education leadership and management (MS); instructional design for online learning (MS, PhD); integrative studies (MS); K-12 studies in education (MS, PhD); leadership for higher education (PhD); leadership in educational administration (MS, PhD); postsecondary and adult education (PhD); professional studies in education (PhD); reading and literacy (MS, Ed D); special education leadership (PhD); special education teaching (MS); training and performance improvement (PhD). Electronic applications accepted.

School of Public Service Leadership Offers criminal justice (MS, PhD); diabetes nursing (MSN); emergency management (MS, PhD); epidemiology (Dr PH); general health administration (DHA); general nursing (MSN); general public administration (DPA); general public health (MPH); gerontology (MS); gerontology nursing (MSN); health administration (MHA); health advocacy and leadership (Dr PH); health care administration (PhD); health care leadership (DHA); health care operations (MHA); health information management (MS); health management policy (MPH); health policy (MHA); health policy advocacy (DHA); homeland security (MS); multidisciplinary human services (MS, PhD); nonprofit management and leadership (PhD); nurse educator (MSN); nursing education (PhD); nursing leadership and administration (MSN); nursing practice (DNP); public administration (MPA); public safety leadership (MS, PhD); public service leadership (MHA, MPA, MPH, MS, DHA, DPA, Dr PH, PhD); social and community services (MS, PhD); social behavioral sciences (MPH).

CAPITAL UNIVERSITY, Columbus, OH 43209-2394

General Information Independent-religious, coed, comprehensive institution. *Graduate housing:* On-campus housing not available.

GRADUATE UNITS

Conservatory of Music *Program availability:* Part-time. Offers music education (MM). Program offered only in summer. Electronic applications accepted.

Law School *Program availability:* Part-time, evening/weekend. Offers business (LL M); business and taxation (LL M); law (LL M, MT, JD); taxation (LL M, MT). Electronic applications accepted.

School of Management *Program availability:* Part-time, evening/weekend. Offers leadership (MBA). Electronic applications accepted.

School of Nursing *Program availability:* Part-time, evening/weekend. Offers administration (MSN); legal studies (MSN); theological studies (MSN).

CAPITOL TECHNOLOGY UNIVERSITY, Laurel, MD 20708-9759

General Information Independent, coed, comprehensive institution. *Graduate housing:* On-campus housing not available.

GRADUATE UNITS

Graduate Programs *Program availability:* Part-time, evening/weekend, online learning. Offers business administration (MBA); computer science (MS); electrical engineering (MS); information and telecommunications systems management (MS); information architecture (MS); network security (MS). Electronic applications accepted.

CARDINAL STRITCH UNIVERSITY, Milwaukee, WI 53217-3985

General Information Independent-religious, coed, university. *Enrollment:* 2,355 graduate, professional, and undergraduate students; 245 full-time matriculated graduate/professional students (160 women), 554 part-time matriculated graduate/professional students (365 women). *Enrollment by degree level:* 637 master's, 114 doctoral. *Tuition:* Full-time $9520; part-time $680 per credit. Tuition and fees vary according to course load, degree level, program and student's religious affiliation. *Graduate housing:* Room and/or apartments available on a first-come, first-served basis to single students; on-campus housing not available to married students. Typical cost: $8292 (including board). Room and board charges vary according to board plan. *Student services:* Campus employment opportunities, career counseling, exercise/wellness program, free psychological counseling, international student services, multicultural affairs office, services for students with disabilities, teacher training, writing training. *Library facilities:* Cardinal Stritch University Library. *Collection:* Books: 122,184 (physical), 146,127 (digital/electronic); Serial titles: 66 (physical), 68 (digital/electronic); Databases: 71. Weekly public service hours: 90.

Computer facilities: Computer purchase and lease plans are available. 458 computers available on campus for general student use. A campuswide network can be accessed from student residence rooms and from off campus. Online class registration is available. Website: http://www.stritch.edu/

General Application Contact: Nate D. Dehne, Vice President for Admissions and Enrollment Services, 800-347-8822 Ext. 4060, E-mail: admissions@stritch.edu.

GRADUATE UNITS

College of Arts and Sciences Students: 23 full-time (17 women), 38 part-time (23 women); includes 14 minority (7 Black or African American, non-Hispanic/Latino; 2 American Indian or Alaska Native, non-Hispanic/Latino; 1 Asian, non-Hispanic/Latino; 2 Hispanic/Latino; 1 Native Hawaiian or other Pacific Islander, non-Hispanic/Latino; 1 Two or more races, non-Hispanic/Latino), 12 international. Average age 31. 70 applicants, 100% accepted, 14 enrolled. Expenses: Contact institution. *Financial support:* Research assistantships with partial tuition reimbursements, career-related internships or fieldwork, Federal Work-Study, scholarships/grants, and unspecified assistantships available. Financial award applicants required to submit FAFSA. In 2017, 32 master's awarded. *Program availability:* Part-time, evening/weekend. Offers arts and sciences (MA, MS); clinical psychology (MA); ministry (MA); religious studies (MA); sport management (MS). *Application deadline:* For fall admission, 7/15 priority date for domestic students; for spring admission, 12/15 priority date for domestic students. Applications are processed on a rolling basis. *Application fee:* $0. Electronic applications accepted. *Application Contact:* 800-347-8822 Ext. 4042, E-mail: admissions@stritch.edu. *Interim Dean*, Dr. Carl D. Mueller, 414-410-4376, E-mail: cd2mueller@stritch.edu.

College of Business and Management Students: 133 full-time (72 women), 98 part-time (54 women); includes 88 minority (64 Black or African American, non-Hispanic/Latino; 1 American Indian or Alaska Native, non-Hispanic/Latino; 12 Asian, non-Hispanic/Latino; 10 Hispanic/Latino; 1 Two or more races, non-Hispanic/Latino), 8 international. Average age 36. 144 applicants, 100% accepted, 57 enrolled. Expenses: Contact institution. *Financial support:* Career-related internships or fieldwork, Federal Work-Study, and scholarships/grants available. Financial award applicants required to submit FAFSA. In 2017, 118 master's awarded. *Program availability:* Part-time, evening/weekend, 100% online, blended/hybrid learning. Offers cyber security (MBA); healthcare management (MBA); justice administration (MBA); marketing (MBA). *Application deadline:* Applications are processed on a rolling basis. *Application fee:* $0. Electronic applications accepted. *Application Contact:* Graduate Admissions, 414-410-4042, E-mail: admissions@stritch.edu. *Dean*, Janette Braverman, 414-410-4004, E-mail: jmbraverman1@stritch.edu.

College of Education and Leadership Students: 226 part-time (146 women); includes 55 minority (32 Black or African American, non-Hispanic/Latino; 6 Asian, non-Hispanic/Latino; 14 Hispanic/Latino; 1 Native Hawaiian or other Pacific Islander, non-Hispanic/Latino; 2 Two or more races, non-Hispanic/Latino), 7 international. Average age 38. 356 applicants, 100% accepted, 189 enrolled. Expenses: Contact institution. *Financial support:* Fellowships, research assistantships with partial tuition reimbursements, career-related internships or fieldwork, Federal Work-Study, and scholarships/grants available. Financial award applicants required to submit FAFSA. In 2017, 152 master's, 28 doctorates awarded. *Program availability:* Part-time, evening/weekend, 100% online. Offers education and leadership (MA, MS, Ed D, PhD); educational leadership (MS); higher education student affairs leadership (MS); language and literacy (MA, PhD); leadership for the advancement of learning and service (Ed D, PhD); leadership for the advancement of learning and service in higher education (Ed D, PhD); special education (PhD); teaching (MAT); urban education (MA); urban special education (MA). *Application deadline:* For fall admission, 7/15 priority date for domestic students; for spring admission, 12/15 priority date for domestic students. Applications are processed on a rolling basis. Electronic applications accepted. *Application Contact:* Graduate Admissions, 800-347-8822 Ext. 4042, E-mail: admissions@stritch.edu. *Dean*, Dr. Freda Russell, 414-410-4735, E-mail: frrussell@stritch.edu.

Ruth S. Coleman College of Nursing and Health Sciences 17 applicants, 100% accepted. Expenses: Contact institution. *Financial support:* Federal Work-Study and scholarships/grants available. Financial award applicants required to submit FAFSA. In 2017, 8 master's awarded. *Program availability:* Part-time, evening/weekend. Offers nursing and health sciences (MSN). *Application deadline:* For fall admission, 6/15 priority date for domestic students; for spring admission, 11/15 priority date for domestic students. Applications are processed on a rolling basis. Electronic applications accepted. *Application Contact:* Graduate Admissions, 800-347-8822 Ext. 4042, E-mail: admissions@stritch.edu. *Dean*, Dr. Kelly J. Dries, 414-410-4397, E-mail: kjdries@stritch.edu.

CAREY THEOLOGICAL COLLEGE, Vancouver, BC V6T 1J6, Canada

General Information Independent-religious, coed, graduate-only institution. *Graduate housing:* Rooms and/or apartments available on a first-come, first-served basis to single and married students. Housing application deadline: 5/31.

GRADUATE UNITS

Graduate Programs *Program availability:* Part-time. Offers theology (M Div, MASF, D Min). Electronic applications accepted.

CARIBBEAN UNIVERSITY, Bayamón, PR 00960-0493

General Information Independent, coed, comprehensive institution.

GRADUATE UNITS

Graduate School

CARLETON UNIVERSITY, Ottawa, ON K1S 5B6, Canada

General Information Province-supported, coed, university. *Graduate housing:* Room and/or apartments guaranteed to single students; on-campus housing not available to married students. Housing application deadline: 5/31.

GRADUATE UNITS

Faculty of Graduate Studies *Program availability:* Part-time, evening/weekend. Electronic applications accepted.

Faculty of Arts and Social Sciences *Program availability:* Part-time, evening/weekend. Offers anthropology (MA); applied language studies (MA); art history: art and its institutions (MA); arts and social sciences (M Sc, MA, PhD); Canadian studies (MA, PhD); cognitive science (PhD); cultural mediations (PhD); English (MA, PhD); film studies (MA); French (MA); geography (M Sc, MA, PhD); history (MA, PhD); music and culture (MA); neuroscience (M Sc); philosophy (MA); psychology (MA, PhD); sociology (MA, PhD).

Faculty of Business Offers business (MBA, PhD); business administration (MBA); management (PhD).

Faculty of Engineering and Design Offers aerospace engineering (M Eng, MA Sc, PhD); biomedical engineering (MA Sc); civil and environmental engineering (M Eng, MA Sc, PhD); design studies (M Arch); electrical engineering (M Eng, M Sc, MA Sc, PhD); engineering and design (M Arch, M Des, M Eng, M Sc, MA Sc, PhD); industrial design (M Des); information and systems science (M Sc); materials engineering (M Eng, MA Sc); mechanical engineering (M Eng, MA Sc, PhD); technology innovation management (M Eng, MA Sc).

Faculty of Public Affairs and Management *Program availability:* Part-time. Offers communication (MA, PhD); conflict resolution (Certificate); economics (MA, PhD); European and European Union studies (MA); European integration studies (Diploma); international affairs (MA, PhD); journalism (MJ); legal studies (MA); political economy (MA, PhD); political science (MA, PhD); public administration (MA, DPA); public affairs and management (MA, MJ, MSW, DPA, PhD, Certificate, Diploma); public policy (PhD); Russian, Eurasian and transition studies (MA); social work (MSW).

Faculty of Science *Program availability:* Part-time, evening/weekend. Offers biology (M Sc, PhD); chemistry (M Sc, PhD); computer science (MCS, PhD); earth sciences (M Sc, PhD); information and system science (M Sc); information and systems science (M Sc); mathematics (M Sc, PhD); physics (M Sc, PhD); science (M Sc, MCS, PhD).

CARLOS ALBIZU UNIVERSITY, San Juan, PR 00901

General Information Independent, coed, university. *Graduate housing:* On-campus housing not available.

GRADUATE UNITS

Graduate Programs *Program availability:* Part-time, evening/weekend. Offers clinical psychology (MS, PhD, Psy D); general psychology (PhD); industrial/organizational psychology (MS, PhD); speech and language pathology (MS).

CARLOS ALBIZU UNIVERSITY, MIAMI CAMPUS, Miami, FL 33172-2209

General Information Independent, coed, comprehensive institution. *Enrollment:* 411 full-time matriculated graduate/professional students (345 women), 248 part-time matriculated graduate/professional students (215 women). *Enrollment by degree level:* 410 master's, 248 doctoral, 1 other advanced degree. *Graduate faculty:* 32 full-time (24 women), 29 part-time/adjunct (17 women). *Tuition:* Full-time $11,160; part-time $5580 per credit hour. *Required fees:* $322 per term. Tuition and fees vary according to course load, degree level and program. *Graduate housing:* On-campus housing not available. *Student services:* Campus employment opportunities, campus safety program, career counseling, exercise/wellness program, international student services, services for students with disabilities, teacher training, writing training. *Library facilities:* Albizu Library. *Collection:* Books: 27,760 (physical), 22,900 (digital/electronic); Serial titles: 295 (physical), 17,034 (digital/electronic); Databases: 73. Weekly public service hours: 66.

Computer facilities: 268 computers available on campus for general student use. A campuswide network can be accessed from off campus. Online class registration, campus portal, virtual library, 24/7 support, Cloud computing, learning center are available.
Website: http://www.albizu.edu/

General Application Contact: Chantel Caraza-Garcia, Administrative Assistant, 305-593-1223 Ext. 3137, Fax: 305-593-1854, E-mail: ccaraza@albizu.edu.

GRADUATE UNITS

Graduate Programs Students: 411 full-time (345 women), 248 part-time (215 women); includes 562 minority (53 Black or African American, non-Hispanic/Latino; 4 Asian, non-Hispanic/Latino; 498 Hispanic/Latino; 7 Two or more races, non-Hispanic/Latino), 23 international. Average age 34. 391 applicants, 42% accepted, 154 enrolled. *Faculty:* 32 full-time (24 women), 27 part-time/adjunct (15 women). Expenses: Contact institution. *Financial support:* In 2017–18, 145 students received support. Federal Work-Study, scholarships/grants, unspecified assistantships, and tuition discounts available. Financial award application deadline: 6/1; financial award applicants required to submit FAFSA. In 2017, 96 master's, 54 doctorates awarded. *Program availability:* Part-time, evening/weekend, 100% online, blended/hybrid learning. Offers clinical psychology (PhD, Psy D); entrepreneurship (MBA); exceptional student education (MS); human services (PhD); industrial/organizational psychology (MS); marriage and family therapy (MS); mental health counseling (MS); nonprofit management (MBA); organizational management (MBA); psychology (MS); speech and language pathology (MS); teaching English for speakers of other languages (MS). *Application deadline:* For fall admission, 4/1 priority date for domestic students, 5/1 priority date for international students; for spring admission, 11/1 priority date for domestic students, 9/1 priority date for international students. Applications are processed on a rolling basis. *Application fee:* $50. Electronic applications accepted. *Application Contact:* Sonia Feliciano, Institutional Director of Student Recruitment, 305-593-1223 Ext. 3108, Fax: 305-477-8983, E-mail: sfeliciano@albizu.edu. *Provost*, Dr. Etiony Aldarondo, 305-593-1223 Ext. 3138, Fax: 305-592-7930, E-mail: ealdarondo@albizu.edu.

CARLOW UNIVERSITY, Pittsburgh, PA 15213-3165

General Information Independent-religious, coed, primarily women, comprehensive institution. *Enrollment:* 2,140 graduate, professional, and undergraduate students; 651 full-time matriculated graduate/professional students (571 women), 194 part-time matriculated graduate/professional students (163 women). *Enrollment by degree level:* 758 master's, 70 doctoral, 17 other advanced degrees. *Graduate faculty:* 25 full-time, 86 part-time/adjunct. *Tuition:* Full-time $12,103; part-time $825 per credit hour. Tuition and fees vary according to program. *Graduate housing:* Room and/or apartments available on a first-come, first-served basis to single students; on-campus housing not available to married students. *Student services:* Campus employment opportunities, campus safety program, career counseling, exercise/wellness program, free psychological counseling, international student services, multicultural affairs office, services for students with disabilities, teacher training, writing training. *Library facilities:* Grace Library.

Computer facilities: A campuswide network can be accessed. Online class registration is available.
Website: http://www.carlow.edu/

General Application Contact: Wendy Phillips, Director, Graduate Admissions, 412-578-8861, Fax: 412-578-6321, E-mail: gradstudies@carlow.edu.

GRADUATE UNITS

College of Health and Wellness Students: 236 full-time (209 women), 100 part-time (95 women); includes 26 minority (12 Black or African American, non-Hispanic/Latino; 1 American Indian or Alaska Native, non-Hispanic/Latino; 7 Asian, non-Hispanic/Latino; 5 Hispanic/Latino; 1 Two or more races, non-Hispanic/Latino). Average age 36. 141 applicants, 96% accepted, 93 enrolled. Expenses: Contact institution. *Financial support:* Application deadline: 4/1; applicants required to submit FAFSA. In 2017, 103 master's, 16 doctorates, 4 other advanced degrees awarded. *Program availability:* Part-time, evening/weekend, 100% online, blended/hybrid learning, low-residency. Offers family nurse practitioner (MSN, Certificate); health and wellness (MSN, DNP, Certificate); nursing leadership and education (MSN); nursing practice (DNP); women's health nurse practitioner (MSN, Certificate). *Application deadline:* For fall admission, 6/15 priority date for domestic and international students; for spring admission, 11/15 priority date for domestic and international students. Applications are processed on a rolling basis. Electronic applications accepted. *Application Contact:* E-mail: gradstudies@carlow.edu. *Dean*, Dr. Lynn George, Fax: 412-578-6114.

College of Leadership and Social Change Students: 273 full-time (225 women), 70 part-time (51 women); includes 98 minority (75 Black or African American, non-Hispanic/Latino; 1 American Indian or Alaska Native, non-Hispanic/Latino; 6 Asian, non-Hispanic/Latino; 8 Hispanic/Latino; 8 Two or more races, non-Hispanic/Latino), 1 international. Average age 36. 210 applicants, 87% accepted, 109 enrolled. Expenses: Contact institution. *Financial support:* Application deadline: 4/1; applicants required to submit FAFSA. In 2017, 130 master's, 6 doctorates, 1 other advanced degree awarded. *Program availability:* Part-time, evening/weekend, 100% online, blended/hybrid learning. Offers child and family (MS); counseling psychology (Psy D); fraud and forensics (MS, Certificate); healthcare management (MBA); human resource management (MBA); leadership and management (MBA); leadership and social change (MA, MBA, MS, MSW, Psy D, Certificate); project management (MBA); psychology (MA); social work (MSW); student affairs (MA). *Application deadline:* For fall admission, 6/15 priority date for domestic and international students; for spring admission, 11/15 priority date for domestic and international students. Applications are processed on a rolling basis. *Application fee:* $0. Electronic applications accepted. *Application Contact:* 412-578-6059, Fax: 412-578-6321, E-mail: gradstudies@carlow.edu. *Dean*, Dr. Allyson M. Lowe, 412-578-6663, Fax: 412-578-6357, E-mail: amlowe@carlow.edu.

College of Learning and Innovation Students: 51 full-time (47 women), 41 part-time (37 women); includes 16 minority (10 Black or African American, non-Hispanic/Latino; 1 American Indian or Alaska Native, non-Hispanic/Latino; 2 Asian, non-Hispanic/Latino; 3 Two or more races, non-Hispanic/Latino), 1 international. Average age 31. 23 applicants, 100% accepted, 19 enrolled. Expenses: Contact institution. *Financial support:* Application deadline: 4/1; applicants required to submit FAFSA. In 2017, 57 master's, 9 other advanced degrees awarded. *Program availability:* Part-time, evening/weekend, 100% online, blended/hybrid learning, low-residency. Offers art (MA); autism (M Ed); early childhood education (M Ed); early childhood leadership (M Ed); education (M Ed); fiction (MFA); learning and innovation (M Ed, MA, MFA, Certificate, Graduate Certificate); non-fiction (MFA); online instructional design and technology (Certificate); online learning instructional design (M Ed); poetry (MFA); special education (M Ed); STEM (M Ed). *Application deadline:* Applications are processed on a rolling basis. *Application fee:* $0. Electronic applications accepted. *Application Contact:* 412-578-6059, E-mail: gradstudies@carlow.edu. *Dean*, Dr. Matthew Gordley, 412-578-6262, E-mail: megordley@carlow.edu.

CARNEGIE MELLON UNIVERSITY, Pittsburgh, PA 15213-3891

General Information Independent, coed, university. CGS member. *Graduate housing:* On-campus housing not available. *Research affiliation:* National Census Data Research Center (public policy), Robotics Engineering Consortium (computer science and engineering), Software Engineering Institute (computer science and engineering), Carnegie Bosch Institute for Applied Studies in International Management (business and management), Pittsburgh Supercomputer Center.

GRADUATE UNITS

Carnegie Institute of Technology *Program availability:* Part-time, evening/weekend. Offers advanced infrastructure systems (MS, PhD); advanced infrastructure systems technology development and application (MS); air quality engineering and science (MS); bioengineering (MS, PhD); chemical engineering (M Ch E, MS, PhD); civil and environmental engineering (MS, PhD); civil and environmental engineering/engineering and public policy (PhD); civil engineering (MS, PhD); colloids, polymers and surfaces (MS); computational mechanics (MS, PhD); computational modeling and monitoring for resilient structural and material systems (MS); electrical and computer engineering (MS, PhD); energy infrastructure systems (MS); engineering and public policy (PhD); environmental engineering (MS, PhD); environmental management and science (MS, PhD); IT-based sustainable global infrastructure and construction management (MS); materials science and engineering (MS, PhD); mechanical engineering (MS, PhD); product development (MPD); sustainability and green design (MS); technology (M Ch E, MPD, MS, PhD); water quality engineering and science (MS).

Information Networking Institute Offers information networking (MS); information security (MS); information technology - information security (MS); information technology - mobility (MS); information technology - software management (MS).

Center for the Neural Basis of Cognition Offers neural basis of cognition (PhD).

College of Fine Arts *Program availability:* Part-time. Offers fine arts (M Des, M Sc, MAM, MET, MFA, MM, MPD, MS, MSA, MTID, MUD, D Des, PhD). Electronic applications accepted.

School of Architecture Offers architecture (MSA); architecture, engineering, and construction management (PhD); building performance and diagnostics (MS, PhD); computational design (MS, PhD); engineering construction management (MSA); tangible interaction design (MTID); urban design (MUD).

School of Art Offers art (MFA).

School of Design Offers design (M Des, MA, MPD, D Des, PhD); design for interaction (M Des); design for interactions (M Des); design theory (PhD); new product development (PhD); product development (MPD); typography and information design (PhD).

School of Drama Offers design (MFA); directing (MFA); dramatic writing (MFA); production technology and management (MFA); video and media design (MFA).

School of Music *Program availability:* Part-time. Offers collaborative piano (MM); composition (MM); instrumental performance (MM); music and technology (MS); music education (MM); vocal performance (MM).

Dietrich College of Humanities and Social Sciences *Program availability:* Part-time. Offers African and African-American diaspora (PhD); behavioral decision research (PhD); cognitive neuroscience (PhD); cognitive psychology (PhD); communication planning and design (M Des); culture and power (PhD); developmental psychology (PhD); editing and publishing (MAPW); humanities and social sciences (M Des, MA, MAPW, MS, PhD); labor, politics and social movements (PhD); literary and cultural studies (MA, PhD); logic, computation and methodology (MS, PhD); machine learning and statistics (PhD); mathematical finance (PhD); philosophy (MA, PhD); policy and non-profit communication (MAPW); professional writing (MAPW); public and media relations/corporate communications (MAPW); pure and applied logic (PhD); rhetoric

(MA, PhD); science or healthcare communication (MAPW); second language acquisition (MA, PhD); social and decision science (PhD); social/personality/health psychology (PhD); statistics (MS, PhD); statistics and public policy (PhD); strategy, entrepreneurship, and technological change (PhD); technical writing (MAPW); technology, environment, science and health (PhD); women, gender and the family (PhD); writing for new media (MAPW); writing for print media (MAPW). Electronic applications accepted.

Heinz College *Program availability:* Part-time, evening/weekend. Offers information systems, public policy, and management (MAM, MEIM, MISM, MMM, MPM, MSBTM, MSHCPM, MSISPM, MSIT, MSPPM, PhD). Electronic applications accepted.

Heinz College Australia Offers information technology (MSIT); public policy and management (MS).

School of Information Systems and Management Offers information security policy and management (MSISPM); information systems and management (MISM, MSISPM, MSIT); information systems management (MISM); information technology (MSIT).

School of Public Policy and Management Offers arts management (MAM); biotechnology and management (MS); entertainment industry management (MEIM); health care policy and management (MSHCPM); medical management (MMM); public management (MPM); public policy and management (MMM, MPM, MS, MSHCPM, PhD).

Joint CMU-Pitt PhD Program in Computational Biology Offers computational biology (PhD).

Mellon College of Science *Program availability:* Part-time. Offers algorithms, combinatorics, and optimization (PhD); applied physics (PhD); atmospheric chemistry (PhD); biochemistry (PhD); bioinorganic chemistry (PhD); bioorganic chemistry and chemical biology (PhD); biophysical chemistry (PhD); biophysics (PhD); catalysis (PhD); cell and developmental biology (PhD); computational biology (MS, PhD); computational finance (MS); genetics (PhD); green and environmental chemistry (PhD); materials and nanoscience (PhD); mathematical finance (PhD); mathematical sciences (DA, PhD); molecular biology (PhD); molecular biophysics and structural biology (PhD); neuroscience (PhD); physics (MS, PhD); pure and applied logic (PhD); renewable energy (PhD); science (MS, DA, PhD); sensors, probes, and imaging (PhD); spectroscopy and single molecule analysis (PhD); structural biology (PhD); theoretical and computational chemistry (PhD). Electronic applications accepted.

School of Computer Science Offers algorithms, combinatorics, and optimization (PhD); computer science (MS, PhD); entertainment technology (MET); human-computer interaction (MHCI, PhD); machine learning (MS, PhD); pure and applied logic (PhD); software engineering (MSE, PhD).

Language Technologies Institute Offers language technologies (MLT, MS, PhD).

Robotics Institute Offers computer vision (MS); robotic systems development (MS); robotics (MS, PhD); robotics technology (MS).

Tepper School of Business *Program availability:* Part-time. Offers accounting (PhD); business management and software engineering (MBMSE); business technologies (PhD); civil engineering and industrial management (MS); computational finance (MSCF); economics (PhD); environmental engineering and management (MEEM); financial economics (PhD); industrial administration (MBA); marketing (PhD); mathematical finance (PhD); operations management (PhD); operations research (PhD); organizational behavior and theory (PhD); production and operations management (PhD); public policy and management (MS, MSED); software engineering and business management (MS). JD/MSIA offered jointly with University of Pittsburgh.

CAROLINA CHRISTIAN COLLEGE, Winston-Salem, NC 27102-0777

General Information Independent-religious, coed, comprehensive institution.

GRADUATE UNITS

Program in Religious Education Offers Christian education (MRE); pastoral care (MRE).

CARROLL UNIVERSITY, Waukesha, WI 53186-5593

General Information Independent-religious, coed, comprehensive institution. *Graduate housing:* On-campus housing not available.

GRADUATE UNITS

Graduate Programs in Education *Program availability:* Part-time, evening/weekend. Offers adult and continuing education (M Ed); educational leadership (MS); PK-12 (M Ed). Electronic applications accepted.

Program in Business Administration *Program availability:* Part-time. Offers business administration (MBA). Electronic applications accepted.

Program in Exercise Physiology Offers exercise physiology (MS).

Program in Occupational Therapy Offers occupational therapy (MOT).

Program in Physical Therapy Offers physical therapy (DPT).

Program in Physician Assistant Studies Offers physician assistant studies (MS).

Program in Software Engineering *Program availability:* Part-time, evening/weekend. Offers software engineering (MSE). Electronic applications accepted.

CARSON-NEWMAN UNIVERSITY, Jefferson City, TN 37760

General Information Independent-religious, coed, comprehensive institution. *Enrollment:* 2,514 graduate, professional, and undergraduate students; 187 full-time matriculated graduate/professional students (106 women), 600 part-time matriculated graduate/professional students (439 women). *Enrollment by degree level:* 586 master's, 175 doctoral, 26 other advanced degrees. *Graduate faculty:* 33 full-time (18 women), 24 part-time/adjunct (14 women). *Tuition:* Full-time $10,516; part-time $478 per credit hour. *Required fees:* $240; $120 per semester. One-time fee: $150. *Graduate housing:* Rooms and/or apartments available to single and married students. Housing application deadline: 7/15. *Student services:* Campus employment opportunities, career counseling, free psychological counseling, international student services, low-cost health insurance, services for students with disabilities. *Library facilities:* Stephens-Burnett Library plus 3 others. *Collection:* Study areas open 24 hours, 5–7 days a week; students can reserve study rooms.

Computer facilities: 200 computers available on campus for general student use. A campuswide network can be accessed from student residence rooms and from off campus. Online class registration is available.
Website: http://www.cn.edu/

General Application Contact: Nilma Stewart, Graduate Admissions and Services Adviser, 865-471-3230, Fax: 865-471-3875, E-mail: adults@cn.edu.

GRADUATE UNITS

Department of Nursing Students: 7 full-time (6 women), 33 part-time (30 women), 2 international. Average age 33. 18 applicants, 100% accepted, 13 enrolled. *Faculty:* 4 full-time (3 women). Expenses: Contact institution. *Financial support:* Federal Work-Study and tuition waivers (full and partial) available. Financial award applicants required to submit FAFSA. In 2017, 14 master's awarded. *Program availability:* Part-time. Offers family nurse practitioner (MSN); nurse educator (MSN). *Application deadline:* For fall admission, 3/15 for domestic students; for spring admission, 10/15 for domestic students. Applications are processed on a rolling basis. *Application fee:* $50. *Application Contact:* Nilma Stewart, Graduate Admissions and Services Adviser, 865-471-3230, Fax: 865-471-3875, E-mail: adults@cn.edu. *Director,* Dr. Kimberly Bolton, 865-471-4056, E-mail: kbolton@cn.edu.

Graduate Program in Education Students: 63 full-time (37 women), 488 part-time (362 women); includes 60 minority (46 Black or African American, non-Hispanic/Latino; 2 American Indian or Alaska Native, non-Hispanic/Latino; 1 Asian, non-Hispanic/Latino; 5 Hispanic/Latino; 1 Native Hawaiian or other Pacific Islander, non-Hispanic/Latino; 5 Two or more races, non-Hispanic/Latino), 29 international. Average age 35. 204 applicants, 100% accepted, 188 enrolled. *Faculty:* 20 full-time (11 women), 16 part-time/adjunct (13 women). Expenses: Contact institution. *Financial support:* Federal Work-Study and unspecified assistantships available. Financial award applicants required to submit FAFSA. In 2017, 211 master's awarded. *Program availability:* Part-time, evening/weekend, 100% online, blended/hybrid learning. Offers curriculum and instruction (M Ed); educational leadership (M Ed); elementary education (MAT); school counseling (MS); secondary education (MAT); teaching English as a second language (MATESL). *Application deadline:* For fall admission, 7/15 priority date for domestic students. Applications are processed on a rolling basis. *Application fee:* $50. *Application Contact:* Nilma Stewart, Graduate Admissions and Services Adviser, 865-471-3230, Fax: 865-471-3875, E-mail: adults@cn.edu. *Chair,* Dr. Kim Hawkins, 865-471-3314, E-mail: khawkins@cn.edu.

Program in Applied Theology Students: 6 part-time (3 women); includes 2 minority (1 Black or African American, non-Hispanic/Latino; 1 Hispanic/Latino). Average age 49. 3 applicants, 100% accepted, 2 enrolled. *Faculty:* 2 full-time (0 women). Expenses: Contact institution. *Financial support:* Federal Work-Study and tuition waivers (full and partial) available. Financial award applicants required to submit FAFSA. In 2017, 1 master's awarded. *Program availability:* Part-time, evening/weekend. Offers applied theology (MAAT). *Application deadline:* For fall admission, 7/15 priority date for domestic students. Applications are processed on a rolling basis. *Application fee:* $50. *Application Contact:* Nilma Stewart, Graduate Admissions and Services Adviser, 865-473-3468, Fax: 865-471-3875, E-mail: adults@cn.edu. *Dean, School of Religion,* Dr. David E. Crutchley, 865-471-3277, E-mail: dcruthley@cn.edu.

Program in Business Administration Students: 75 full-time (30 women), 33 part-time (13 women); includes 12 minority (10 Black or African American, non-Hispanic/Latino; 2 Hispanic/Latino), 21 international. Average age 29. 47 applicants, 100% accepted, 44 enrolled. *Faculty:* 4 full-time (2 women), 6 part-time/adjunct (1 woman). Expenses: Contact institution. *Financial support:* Federal Work-Study and tuition waivers (full and partial) available. Financial award applicants required to submit FAFSA. In 2017, 34 master's awarded. *Program availability:* Part-time, evening/weekend, 100% online, blended/hybrid learning. Offers business administration (MBA). *Application deadline:* For fall admission, 7/15 priority date for domestic students. Applications are processed on a rolling basis. *Application fee:* $50. *Application Contact:* Nilma Stewart, Graduate Admissions and Services Adviser, 865-471-3230, Fax: 865-471-3875, E-mail: adults@cn.edu. *Director,* Dr. Kyle J. Kaplan, 865-471-7124, E-mail: kkaplan@cn.edu.

Program in Counseling Students: 40 full-time (33 women), 34 part-time (29 women); includes 2 minority (1 Black or African American, non-Hispanic/Latino; 1 Hispanic/Latino), 2 international. Average age 29. 19 applicants, 100% accepted, 14 enrolled. *Faculty:* 3 full-time (2 women), 1 part-time/adjunct (0 women). Expenses: Contact institution. *Financial support:* Federal Work-Study and tuition waivers (full and partial) available. Financial award applicants required to submit FAFSA. In 2017, 18 master's awarded. *Program availability:* Part-time, evening/weekend. Offers counseling (MSC). *Application deadline:* Applications are processed on a rolling basis. *Application fee:* $50. *Application Contact:* Nilma Stewart, Graduate Admissions and Services Adviser, 865-471-3230, Fax: 865-471-3875, E-mail: adults@cn.edu. *Director,* Dr. Michael L. Bundy, 865-471-2087, E-mail: mbundy@cn.edu.

Program in Social Entrepreneurship Students: 2 full-time (0 women), 6 part-time (2 women); includes 1 minority (Two or more races, non-Hispanic/Latino), 2 international. Average age 27. 3 applicants, 100% accepted, 3 enrolled. *Faculty:* 1 part-time/adjunct (0 women). Expenses: Contact institution. *Financial support:* Federal Work-Study and tuition waivers (full and partial) available. Financial award applicants required to submit FAFSA. In 2017, 3 master's awarded. *Program availability:* Part-time, evening/weekend, 100% online, blended/hybrid learning. Offers social entrepreneurship (MAASJ). *Application deadline:* For fall admission, 7/15 for domestic students. Applications are processed on a rolling basis. *Application fee:* $50. *Application Contact:* Nilma Stewart, Graduate Admissions and Services Adviser, 865-471-3223, Fax: 865-471-3875, E-mail: adults@cn.edu. *Department Chair,* Dr. Laura Wadlington, 865-471-3270.

CARTHAGE COLLEGE, Kenosha, WI 53140

General Information Independent-religious, coed, comprehensive institution. *Graduate housing:* On-campus housing not available.

GRADUATE UNITS

Division of Teacher Education *Program availability:* Part-time, evening/weekend. Offers classroom guidance and counseling (M Ed); creative arts (M Ed); gifted and talented children (M Ed); language arts (M Ed); modern language (M Ed); natural sciences (M Ed); reading (M Ed, Certificate); social sciences (M Ed); teacher leadership (M Ed).

CASE WESTERN RESERVE UNIVERSITY, Cleveland, OH 44106

General Information Independent, coed, university. CGS member. *Enrollment:* 11,824 graduate, professional, and undergraduate students; 5,446 full-time matriculated graduate/professional students (2,935 women), 1,031 part-time matriculated graduate/professional students (650 women). *Enrollment by degree level:* 3,360 master's, 3,079 doctoral, 38 other advanced degrees. *Graduate faculty:* 3,501 full-time (1,326 women). *Tuition:* Full-time $43,854; part-time $1827 per credit hour. *Required fees:* $50; $50 per credit hour. Tuition and fees vary according to course load and program. *Graduate housing:* On-campus housing not available. *Student services:* Campus employment opportunities, campus safety program, career counseling, exercise/wellness program, free psychological counseling, grant writing training, international student services, low-cost health insurance, multicultural affairs office, services for students with disabilities, teacher training, writing training. *Library facilities:* Kelvin Smith Library plus 6 others. *Collection:* Books: 3.4 million (physical); Serial titles: 196,361 (physical); Databases: 470. Students can reserve study rooms. *Research affiliation:* Bayer Materials Science (wind materials research), Cleveland Clinic Foundation (biomedical science), Johnson and Johnson Services, Inc. (human health), Cleveland Botanical Garden (plant sciences and ecology), Swagelok Company (surface analysis and materials technology), University Hospitals of Cleveland (biomedical science).

Computer facilities: Computer purchase and lease plans are available. 357 computers available on campus for general student use. A campuswide network can be accessed from student residence rooms and from off campus. Online class registration, software library, online reference databases, electronic books and journals, research computing, training are available.
Website: http://www.case.edu/

GRADUATE UNITS

Frances Payne Bolton School of Nursing Students: 256 full-time (211 women), 232 part-time (189 women); includes 104 minority (46 Black or African American, non-Hispanic/Latino; 32 Asian, non-Hispanic/Latino; 13 Hispanic/Latino; 2 Native Hawaiian or other Pacific Islander, non-Hispanic/Latino; 11 Two or more races, non-Hispanic/Latino), 38 international. Average age 37. 328 applicants, 67% accepted, 141 enrolled. *Faculty:* 85 full-time (76 women), 29 part-time/adjunct (26 women). Expenses: Contact institution. *Financial support:* In 2017–18, 304 students received support, including 10 fellowships with full tuition reimbursements available (averaging $10,598 per year), 7 research assistantships with partial tuition reimbursements available (averaging $16,674 per year), 20 teaching assistantships with partial tuition reimbursements available (averaging $18,100 per year); scholarships/grants, traineeships, and nurse faculty loan program also available. Financial award application deadline: 5/15; financial award applicants required to submit FAFSA. In 2017, 134 master's, 51 doctorates awarded. *Program availability:* Part-time. Offers acute care pediatric nurse practitioner (MSN); acute care/cardiovascular nursing (MSN); acute care/flight nurse (MSN); adult gerontology acute care nurse practitioner (MSN); adult gerontology primary care nurse practitioner (MSN); educational leadership (DNP); family nurse practitioner (MSN); family systems psychiatric mental health nursing (MSN); neonatal nurse practitioner (MSN); nurse anesthesia (MSN); nurse education (MSN); nurse midwifery (MSN); nurse practitioner (MSN); nursing (MN); palliative care (MSN); pediatric nurse practitioner (MSN); practice leadership (DNP); women's health nurse practitioner (MSN). *Application deadline:* For fall admission, 3/1 for domestic and international students; for spring admission, 10/1 for domestic and international students; for summer admission, 3/1 for domestic and international students. Applications are processed on a rolling basis. *Application fee:* $75. Electronic applications accepted. *Application Contact:* Jackie Tepale, Admissions Coordinator, Graduate Programs, 216-368-5253, Fax: 216-368-0124, E-mail: yyd@case.edu. *Dean/Professor*, Dr. Mary E. Kerr, 216-368-2545, Fax: 216-368-5050, E-mail: mek55@case.edu.

Jack, Joseph and Morton Mandel School of Applied Social Sciences Students: 630 full-time (544 women), 61 part-time (54 women); includes 253 minority (187 Black or African American, non-Hispanic/Latino; 2 American Indian or Alaska Native, non-Hispanic/Latino; 10 Asian, non-Hispanic/Latino; 34 Hispanic/Latino; 1 Native Hawaiian or other Pacific Islander, non-Hispanic/Latino; 19 Two or more races, non-Hispanic/Latino), 34 international. Average age 32. 848 applicants, 78% accepted, 320 enrolled. Expenses: Contact institution. *Financial support:* In 2017–18, 650 students received support, including 650 fellowships with full tuition reimbursements available (averaging $10,000 per year); career-related internships or fieldwork, Federal Work-Study, institutionally sponsored loans, scholarships/grants, tuition waivers (partial), and paid field placements (for MSSA students) also available. Support available to part-time students. Financial award application deadline: 4/15; financial award applicants required to submit FAFSA. In 2017, 184 master's, 3 doctorates awarded. *Program availability:* Part-time, evening/weekend, 100% online. Offers nonprofit management (MNO); social welfare (PhD); social work (MSSA). *Application deadline:* For fall admission, 4/15 for domestic and international students; for spring admission, 11/2 for domestic students; for summer admission, 3/1 for domestic students. Applications are processed on a rolling basis. *Application fee:* $0. Electronic applications accepted. *Application Contact:* Richard Sigg, Director of Recruitment and Enrollment, 216-368-1655, E-mail: richard.sigg@case.edu. *Dean*, Dr. Grover Cleveland Gilmore, 216-368-2256, E-mail: msassdean@case.edu.

School of Dental Medicine Offers advanced general dentistry (Certificate); dental medicine (MSD, DMD, Certificate); dentistry (MSD, DMD, Certificate); endodontics (MSD, Certificate); oral surgery (Certificate); orthodontics (MSD, Certificate); pedodontics (MSD, Certificate); periodontics (MSD, Certificate). Electronic applications accepted.

School of Graduate Studies Students: 2,144 full-time (1,011 women), 375 part-time (205 women); includes 590 minority (155 Black or African American, non-Hispanic/Latino; 261 Asian, non-Hispanic/Latino; 123 Hispanic/Latino; 2 Native Hawaiian or other Pacific Islander, non-Hispanic/Latino; 49 Two or more races, non-Hispanic/Latino), 757 international. Average age 29. 4,724 applicants, 41% accepted, 808 enrolled. *Faculty:* 256 full-time (111 women), 89 part-time/adjunct (42 women). Expenses: Contact institution. *Financial support:* Fellowships with tuition reimbursements, research assistantships with tuition reimbursements, teaching assistantships with tuition reimbursements, career-related internships or fieldwork, Federal Work-Study, institutionally sponsored loans, scholarships/grants, traineeships, health care benefits, tuition waivers (full and partial), and unspecified assistantships available. Support available to part-time students. Financial award applicants required to submit CSS PROFILE or FAFSA. In 2017, 621 master's, 196 doctorates awarded. *Program availability:* Part-time, evening/weekend, online learning. Offers acting (MFA); anthropology (MA, PhD); applied mathematics (MS, PhD); art education (MA); art history (MA, PhD); art history and museum studies (MA); astronomy (MS, PhD); biology (MS, PhD); chemistry (MS, PhD); clinical psychology (PhD); cognitive linguistics (MA); communication sciences (MA, PhD); dance (MA, MFA); early music (MA, D Mus A); earth, environmental, and planetary sciences (MS, PhD); English (MA, PhD); experimental psychology (PhD); French (MA); historical musicology (MA, PhD); historical performance practice (DMA, PhD); history (MA, PhD); mathematics (MS, PhD); music education (MA, PhD); music history (MA); physics (MS, PhD); political science (MA, PhD); sociology (MA, PhD); speech-language pathology (MA, PhD); theater (MA); world literature (MA). *Application deadline:* For fall admission, 3/1 for domestic students; for spring admission, 11/1 for domestic students. *Application fee:* $50. Electronic applications accepted. *Vice Provost and Dean*, Dr. Charles E. Rozek, 216-368-4390, Fax: 216-368-4250, E-mail: charles.rozek@case.edu.

Case School of Engineering Students: 650 full-time (183 women), 55 part-time (18 women); includes 83 minority (11 Black or African American, non-Hispanic/Latino; 50 Asian, non-Hispanic/Latino; 16 Hispanic/Latino; 6 Two or more races, non-Hispanic/Latino), 422 international. 1,350 applicants, 43% accepted, 199 enrolled. *Faculty:* 111 full-time (17 women). Expenses: Contact institution. *Financial support:* In 2017–18, 345 students received support, including 33 fellowships with tuition reimbursements available, 280 research assistantships with tuition reimbursements available, 32 teaching assistantships; career-related internships or fieldwork, Federal Work-Study, and institutionally sponsored loans also available. Support available to part-time students. Financial award applicants required to submit FAFSA. In 2017, 192 master's, 60 doctorates awarded. *Program availability:* Part-time, evening/weekend, 100% online, blended/hybrid learning. Offers biomedical engineering (MS, PhD); chemical and biomolecular engineering (MS, PhD); civil engineering (MS, PhD); computer engineering (MS, PhD); computing and information sciences (MS, PhD); electrical engineering (MS, PhD); engineering (ME, MEM, MS, PhD); macromolecular science and engineering (MS, PhD); management and engineering (MEM); materials science and engineering (MS, PhD); mechanical and aerospace engineering (MS, PhD); systems and control engineering (MS, PhD). *Application deadline:* Applications are processed on a rolling basis. *Application fee:* $50. Electronic applications accepted. *Application Contact:* Dr. Marc Buchner, Associate Dean, Academics, 216-368-4096, Fax: 216-368-6939, E-mail: marc.buchner@case.edu. *Interim Dean/Professor of Engineering*, James McGuffin-Cawley, 216-368-4436, Fax: 216-368-6939, E-mail: jxc41@case.edu.

School of Law Students: 412 full-time (216 women); includes 80 minority (39 Black or African American, non-Hispanic/Latino; 14 Asian, non-Hispanic/Latino; 24 Hispanic/Latino; 3 Two or more races, non-Hispanic/Latino), 36 international. Average age 24. 1,488 applicants, 39% accepted, 131 enrolled. *Faculty:* 37 full-time (13 women), 26 part-time/adjunct (10 women). Expenses: Contact institution. *Financial support:* In 2017–18, 395 students received support. Career-related internships or fieldwork, Federal Work-Study, institutionally sponsored loans, and scholarships/grants available. Financial award application deadline: 5/1; financial award applicants required to submit FAFSA. In 2017, 138 master's awarded. Offers financial integrity (MA); health law (SJD); intellectual property law (LL M, ML); international business law (LL M, ML); international criminal law (LL M); law (JD, SJD); patent practice (MA); U.S. and global legal studies (LL M, ML). *Application deadline:* For fall admission, 4/1 priority date for domestic and international students. Applications are processed on a rolling basis. *Application fee:* $40. Electronic applications accepted. *Application Contact:* Kelli Curtis, Associate Dean for Admissions, 216-368-3600, Fax: 216-368-0185, E-mail: lawadmissions@case.edu. *Co-Dean*, Jessica Berg, 216-368-3283.

School of Medicine *Program availability:* Part-time. Offers clinical research (MS, PhD); medicine (MA, MPH, MS, MD, PhD); physician assistant (MS).

Graduate Programs in Medicine *Program availability:* Part-time. Offers anesthesiologist assistant (MS); applied anatomy (MS); biochemistry (MS, PhD); bioethics (MA); biostatistics (MS); cancer biology (PhD); cell biology (PhD); dietetics (MS); epidemiology and biostatistics (PhD); genetic counseling (MS); genetics and genome sciences (PhD); immunology (PhD); medical physiology (MS); medicine (MA, MPH, MS, PhD); molecular and cellular basis of disease (PhD); molecular biology (PhD); molecular medicine (PhD); molecular nutrition (MS); molecular virology (PhD); neuroscience (PhD); nutrition (MS, PhD); nutritional biochemistry and metabolism (MS); pathology (MS); pharmacology (PhD); physiology and biophysics (PhD); public health (MPH); public health nutrition (MS). Electronic applications accepted.

Weatherhead School of Management *Program availability:* Part-time, evening/weekend. Offers accountancy (M Acc, PhD); business administration (EMBA, MBA); business analytics (MSM); designing sustainable systems (PhD); finance (MSM); healthcare (MSM); management (EMBA, M Acc, MBA, MNO, MPOD, MS, MSM, EDM, PhD, CNM); operations and supply chain management (MSM); operations research (PhD); organizational behavior (PhD); positive organization development and change (MS). Electronic applications accepted.

Mandel Center for Nonprofit Organizations Offers nonprofit management (MNO, CNM).

CASTLETON UNIVERSITY, Castleton, VT 05735

General Information State-supported, coed, comprehensive institution. *Graduate housing:* Room and/or apartments available on a first-come, first-served basis to single students; on-campus housing not available to married students. Housing application deadline: 5/19.

GRADUATE UNITS

Division of Graduate Studies *Program availability:* Part-time, evening/weekend. Offers curriculum and instruction (MA Ed); educational leadership (MA Ed, CAGS); forensic psychology (MA); language arts and reading (MA Ed, CAGS); special education (MA Ed, CAGS).

CATAWBA COLLEGE, Salisbury, NC 28144-2488

General Information Independent-religious, coed, comprehensive institution. *Enrollment:* 1,331 graduate, professional, and undergraduate students; 14 part-time matriculated graduate/professional students (13 women). *Enrollment by degree level:* 14 master's. *Graduate faculty:* 3 full-time (2 women), 4 part-time/adjunct (3 women). *Tuition:* Part-time $190 per credit hour. *Required fees:* $25 per semester. *Graduate housing:* On-campus housing not available. *Student services:* Campus safety program, career counseling, exercise/wellness program, teacher training. *Library facilities:* Corriher-Linn-Black Memorial Library plus 1 other. *Collection:* Books: 149,877 (physical), 228,252 (digital/electronic); Serial titles: 12,505 (physical), 112,726 (digital/electronic); Databases: 100. Weekly public service hours: 83; students can reserve study rooms.

Computer facilities: 175 computers available on campus for general student use. A campuswide network can be accessed from student residence rooms and from off campus. Online class registration is available.
Website: http://www.catawba.edu/

General Application Contact: Dr. Kimberly Creamer, Director, Graduate Program, 704-637-4462, Fax: 704-637-4732, E-mail: kcreamer14@catawba.edu.

GRADUATE UNITS

Department of Teacher Education Students: 14 part-time (13 women); includes 1 minority (Black or African American, non-Hispanic/Latino). Average age 30. 7 applicants, 100% accepted, 7 enrolled. *Faculty:* 3 full-time (2 women), 4 part-time/adjunct (3 women). Expenses: Contact institution. *Financial support:* In 2017–18, 12 students received support. Scholarships/grants and free tuition (for Rowan-Salisbury teachers only) available. Financial award application deadline: 10/1. *Program availability:* Part-time-only. Offers STEM education (M Ed). *Application deadline:* For spring admission, 10/1 for domestic students. Applications are processed on a rolling basis. *Application fee:* $25. Electronic applications accepted. *Application Contact:* Jane V. Snider, Administrative Assistant, 704-637-4461, Fax: 704-637-4732, E-mail: jvsnider@catawba.edu. *Director, Graduate Program*, Dr. Kimberly Creamer, 704-637-4462, Fax: 704-637-4732, E-mail: kcreamer14@catawba.edu.

CATHOLIC DISTANCE UNIVERSITY, Charles Town, WV 25414

General Information Independent-religious, coed, graduate-only institution. *Graduate housing:* On-campus housing not available.

GRADUATE UNITS

Graduate Programs *Program availability:* Part-time, evening/weekend, online learning. Offers religious studies (MRS); theology (MA).

CATHOLIC THEOLOGICAL UNION, Chicago, IL 60615-5698

General Information Independent-religious, coed, graduate-only institution. *Graduate housing:* Rooms and/or apartments available on a first-come, first-served basis to single and married students. Housing application deadline: 7/1.

GRADUATE UNITS

Graduate and Professional Programs *Program availability:* Part-time, evening/weekend. Offers biblical spirituality (Certificate); cross-cultural ministries (D Min); cross-cultural missions (Certificate); divinity (M Div); liturgical studies (Certificate); liturgy (D Min); pastoral studies (MAPS, Certificate); spiritual formation (Certificate); spirituality (D Min); theology (MA). M Div/PhD offered jointly with University of Chicago; M Div/MSW with Loyola University Chicago and University of Chicago.

THE CATHOLIC UNIVERSITY OF AMERICA, Washington, DC 20064

General Information Independent-religious, coed, university. CGS member. *Enrollment:* 6,023 graduate, professional, and undergraduate students; 1,013 full-time matriculated graduate/professional students (467 women), 1,695 part-time matriculated graduate/professional students (979 women). *Enrollment by degree level:* 1,387 master's, 1,219 doctoral, 102 other advanced degrees. *Graduate faculty:* 400 full-time (152 women), 355 part-time/adjunct (155 women). *Tuition:* Full-time $44,400; part-time $1770 per credit. *Required fees:* $620; $205 per semester. One-time fee: $440. *Graduate housing:* Room and/or apartments available on a first-come, first-served basis to single students; on-campus housing not available to married students. Typical cost: $16,372 (including board). Housing application deadline: 5/15. *Student services:* Campus employment opportunities, campus safety program, career counseling, free psychological counseling, international student services, low-cost health insurance, multicultural affairs office, services for students with disabilities, teacher training, writing training. *Library facilities:* Mullen Library plus 1 other. *Collection:* Books: 734,247 (physical), 390,119 (digital/electronic); Serial titles: 342,482 (physical), 135,001 (digital/electronic); Databases: 482. Weekly public service hours: 102. *Research affiliation:* EnergySolutions (waste vitrification research), National Rehabilitation Hospital (rehabilitation engineering research), Samsung (building environmental control), Space Telescope Science Institute (astronomy and space physics research), Better Way Foundation (early childhood education), Eco-Convergence Group, Inc. (concrete materials research).

Computer facilities: 542 computers available on campus for general student use. A campuswide network can be accessed from student residence rooms and from off campus. Online class registration is available.
Website: http://www.catholic.edu/

General Application Contact: Dr. Steven Brown, Vice Provost and Dean of Graduate Studies, 202-319-5057, Fax: 202-319-6533, E-mail: cua-admissions@cua.edu.

GRADUATE UNITS

Benjamin T. Rome School of Music Students: 30 full-time (19 women), 61 part-time (27 women); includes 25 minority (7 Black or African American, non-Hispanic/Latino; 10 Asian, non-Hispanic/Latino; 5 Hispanic/Latino; 3 Two or more races, non-Hispanic/Latino), 22 international. Average age 33. 104 applicants, 76% accepted, 26 enrolled. *Faculty:* 19 full-time (4 women), 43 part-time/adjunct (18 women). Expenses: Contact institution. *Financial support:* Fellowships, research assistantships, teaching assistantships, Federal Work-Study, scholarships/grants, tuition waivers (full and partial), and unspecified assistantships available. Financial award application deadline: 2/1; financial award applicants required to submit FAFSA. In 2017, 14 master's, 18 doctorates awarded. *Program availability:* Part-time. Offers cello (Artist Diploma); chamber music (piano) (MM, DMA); composition (MM, DMA); music (MAT); musicology (MA, PhD); orchestral conducting (MM, DMA, Artist Diploma); orchestral instruments/guitar (MM, DMA); piano (Artist Diploma); piano pedagogy (MM, DMA); piano performance (MM, DMA); sacred music (MMSM, DMA); violin (Artist Diploma); vocal accompanying (MM, DMA); vocal pedagogy (MM, DMA); vocal performance (MM, DMA); voice (Artist Diploma). MA/MSLIS offered in partnership with Department of Library and Information Science. *Application deadline:* For fall admission, 7/15 priority date for domestic students, 7/1 for international students; for spring admission, 11/15 priority date for domestic students, 11/1 for international students. Applications are processed on a rolling basis. *Application fee:* $55. Electronic applications accepted. *Application Contact:* Dr. Steven Brown, Director of Graduate Admissions, 202-319-5247, Fax: 202-319-6174, E-mail: cua-graduatestudies@cua.edu. *Dean,* Dr. Grayson Wagstaff, 202-319-5417, Fax: 202-319-6280, E-mail: cua-music@cua.edu.

Busch School of Business and Economics Students: 74 full-time (50 women), 9 part-time (3 women); includes 26 minority (5 Black or African American, non-Hispanic/Latino; 1 American Indian or Alaska Native, non-Hispanic/Latino; 3 Asian, non-Hispanic/Latino; 9 Hispanic/Latino; 8 Two or more races, non-Hispanic/Latino), 18 international. Average age 31. 99 applicants, 86% accepted, 61 enrolled. *Faculty:* 27 full-time (6 women), 45 part-time/adjunct (12 women). Expenses: Contact institution. *Financial support:* Fellowships, research assistantships, teaching assistantships, Federal Work-Study, scholarships/grants, tuition waivers (full and partial), and unspecified assistantships available. Financial award application deadline: 2/1; financial award applicants required to submit FAFSA. In 2017, 46 master's awarded. *Program availability:* Part-time. Offers accounting (MS); business analysis (MSBA); integral economic development management (MA); integral economic development policy (MA); management (MS). *Application deadline:* For fall admission, 7/15 priority date for domestic students, 7/1 for international students; for spring admission, 11/15 priority date for domestic students, 11/1 for international students. Applications are processed on a rolling basis. *Application fee:* $55. Electronic applications accepted. *Application Contact:* Dr. Steven Brown, Director of Graduate Admissions, 202-319-5057, Fax: 202-319-6533, E-mail: cua-admissions@cua.edu. *Dean,* Dr. William Bowman, 202-319-5290, Fax: 202-319-4426, E-mail: otey@cua.edu.

Columbus School of Law *Program availability:* Part-time, evening/weekend. Offers law (MLS, JD). Electronic applications accepted.

Metropolitan School of Professional Studies Students: 14 full-time (8 women), 36 part-time (20 women); includes 26 minority (16 Black or African American, non-Hispanic/Latino; 1 Asian, non-Hispanic/Latino; 4 Hispanic/Latino; 5 Two or more races, non-Hispanic/Latino), 3 international. Average age 36. 45 applicants, 80% accepted, 21 enrolled. *Faculty:* 20 part-time/adjunct (6 women). Expenses: Contact institution. *Financial support:* Scholarships/grants available. Financial award application deadline: 3/15; financial award applicants required to submit FAFSA. In 2017, 100 master's awarded. *Program availability:* Part-time, evening/weekend, 100% online. Offers emergency service administration (MS); health administration (MHA); social service administration (MS). *Application deadline:* For fall admission, 7/15 priority date for domestic students, 7/1 for international students; for spring admission, 11/15 priority date for domestic students, 11/1 for international students. Applications are processed on a rolling basis. *Application fee:* $55. Electronic applications accepted. *Application Contact:* Dr. Steven Brown, Director of Graduate Admissions, 202-319-5057, Fax: 202-319-6533, E-mail: cua-admissions@cua.edu. *Dean,* Dr. Vince Kiernan, 202-319-5256, Fax: 202-319-6260, E-mail: kiernan@cua.edu.

National Catholic School of Social Service Students: 126 full-time (102 women), 447 part-time (385 women); includes 273 minority (161 Black or African American, non-Hispanic/Latino; 14 Asian, non-Hispanic/Latino; 53 Hispanic/Latino; 1 Native Hawaiian or other Pacific Islander, non-Hispanic/Latino; 44 Two or more races, non-Hispanic/Latino), 7 international. Average age 36. 301 applicants, 78% accepted, 141 enrolled. *Faculty:* 16 full-time (13 women), 38 part-time/adjunct (32 women). Expenses: Contact institution. *Financial support:* Fellowships, research assistantships, teaching assistantships, Federal Work-Study, scholarships/grants, tuition waivers (full and partial), and unspecified assistantships available. Financial award application deadline: 3/15; financial award applicants required to submit FAFSA. In 2017, 76 master's, 3 doctorates awarded. *Program availability:* Part-time, 100% online. Offers clinical (MSW); combined (clinical and social change) (MSW); social change (MSW); social work (PhD). MSW/JD offered with Columbus School of Law. *Application deadline:* For fall admission, 7/15 priority date for domestic students, 7/1 for international students; for spring admission, 11/15 priority date for domestic students, 11/1 for international students. Applications are processed on a rolling basis. *Application fee:* $60. Electronic applications accepted. *Application Contact:* Dr. Steven Brown, Director of Graduate Admissions, 202-319-5057, Fax: 202-319-6533, E-mail: cua-admissions@cua.edu. *Dean,* Dr. Will Rainford, 202-319-5454, Fax: 202-319-5093, E-mail: rainford@cua.edu.

School of Architecture and Planning Students: 61 full-time (24 women), 13 part-time (7 women); includes 31 minority (12 Black or African American, non-Hispanic/Latino; 1 American Indian or Alaska Native, non-Hispanic/Latino; 3 Asian, non-Hispanic/Latino; 8 Hispanic/Latino; 7 Two or more races, non-Hispanic/Latino), 11 international. Average age 28. 61 applicants, 90% accepted, 28 enrolled. *Faculty:* 19 full-time (7 women), 9 part-time/adjunct (1 woman). Expenses: Contact institution. *Financial support:* Fellowships, research assistantships, teaching assistantships, Federal Work-Study, scholarships/grants, tuition waivers (full and partial), and unspecified assistantships available. Financial award application deadline: 2/1; financial award applicants required to submit FAFSA. In 2017, 46 master's awarded. *Program availability:* Part-time. Offers architecture and planning (M Arch, MS Arch St); city and regional planning (M Arch); facilities management (MS Arch); regional development (Certificate); sustainable design (M Arch, Certificate). *Application deadline:* For fall admission, 1/15 priority date for domestic students, 7/1 for international students; for spring admission, 10/15 priority date for domestic students, 11/1 for international students. Applications are processed on a rolling basis. *Application fee:* $55. Electronic applications accepted. *Application Contact:* Dr. Steven Brown, Director of Graduate Admissions, 202-319-5057, Fax: 202-319-6533, E-mail: cua-admissions@cua.edu. *Dean,* Randall Ott, 202-319-5784, Fax: 202-319-2023, E-mail: ott@cua.edu.

School of Arts and Sciences Students: 153 full-time (88 women), 358 part-time (195 women); includes 91 minority (21 Black or African American, non-Hispanic/Latino; 15 Asian, non-Hispanic/Latino; 21 Hispanic/Latino; 34 Two or more races, non-Hispanic/Latino), 100 international. Average age 32. 484 applicants, 51% accepted, 107 enrolled. *Faculty:* 160 full-time (72 women), 72 part-time/adjunct (32 women). Expenses: Contact institution. *Financial support:* Fellowships, research assistantships, teaching assistantships, Federal Work-Study, scholarships/grants, tuition waivers (full and partial), and unspecified assistantships available. Financial award application deadline: 2/1; financial award applicants required to submit FAFSA. In 2017, 107 master's, 34 doctorates, 1 other advanced degree awarded. *Program availability:* Part-time. Offers acting (MFA); American government (MA, PhD); ancient Near East (Biblical Hebrew/Aramaic) (MA, PhD); anthropology (MA); applied experimental psychology (PhD); Arabic (PhD); arts and sciences (MA, MFA, MS, MSBA, MSLS, PhD, Certificate); biotechnology (MS); Byzantine and Orthodox studies (MA); Catholic school leadership (MA); cell and microbial biology (MS, PhD); Christian Near East (Biblical Hebrew/Aramaic) (MA); clinical laboratory science (MS, PhD); clinical psychology (PhD); Congressional and Presidential studies (MA); Coptic (MA, PhD); creative teaching through drama (Certificate); crime and justice studies (MA); directing (MFA); early Christian studies (MA, PhD); education (Certificate); English (MA, PhD); general psychology (MA); global and comparative sociology (MA); Greek (MA, Certificate); Greek and Latin (MA, PhD, Certificate); Hispanic studies (MA, PhD); history (MA, PhD); human development psychology (PhD); human factors (MA); international affairs (MA); international political economics (MA); Latin (MA, Certificate); library and information science (MSLS, Certificate); Medieval and Byzantine studies (PhD, Certificate); nuclear environmental protection (MS); physics (MS, PhD); playwriting (MFA); political theory (MA, PhD); public policy (MA); religion and society in the late medieval and early modern world (MA); rhetoric (Certificate); secondary education (MA); special education (MA); Syriac (MA, PhD); the Islamic world (MA); the Medieval West (MA); theatre education (MA); theatre history and criticism (MA); world politics (MA, PhD). *Application deadline:* For fall admission, 2/1 priority date for domestic students, 7/1 for international students; for spring admission, 11/15 priority date for domestic students, 11/1 for international students. Applications are processed on a rolling basis. *Application fee:* $55. Electronic applications accepted. *Application Contact:* Dr. Steven Brown, Director of Graduate Admissions, 202-319-5057, Fax: 202-319-6533, E-mail: cua-admissions@cua.edu. *Dean,* Dr. Aaron Dominguez, 202-319-5115, Fax: 202-319-4463, E-mail: artsandsciences@cua.edu.

School of Canon Law Students: 32 full-time (6 women), 49 part-time (6 women); includes 9 minority (2 Black or African American, non-Hispanic/Latino; 3 Asian, non-Hispanic/Latino; 2 Hispanic/Latino; 2 Two or more races, non-Hispanic/Latino), 13 international. Average age 38. 36 applicants, 89% accepted, 27 enrolled. *Faculty:* 7 full-time (1 woman), 2 part-time/adjunct (0 women). Expenses: Contact institution. *Financial support:* Fellowships, research assistantships, teaching assistantships, Federal Work-Study, scholarships/grants, tuition waivers (full and partial), and unspecified assistantships available. Financial award application deadline: 2/1; financial award applicants required to submit FAFSA. In 2017, 10 master's, 3 doctorates awarded. *Program availability:* Part-time. Offers Canon law (JCD, JCL); church administration (MCA). JD/JCL offered jointly with Columbus School of Law. *Application deadline:* For fall admission, 7/15 priority date for domestic students, 7/1 for international students; for spring admission, 11/15 priority date for domestic students, 11/1 for international students. Applications are processed on a rolling basis. *Application fee:* $55. Electronic applications accepted. *Application Contact:* Dr. Steven Brown, Director of Graduate Admissions, 202-319-5057, Fax: 202-319-6533, E-mail: cua-admissions@cua.edu. *Dean,* Msgr. Ronny Jenkins, 202-319-5492, Fax: 202-319-4187, E-mail: cua-canonlaw@cua.edu.

School of Engineering Students: 72 full-time (26 women), 147 part-time (45 women); includes 43 minority (15 Black or African American, non-Hispanic/Latino; 7 Asian, non-Hispanic/Latino; 5 Hispanic/Latino; 16 Two or more races, non-Hispanic/Latino), 97 international. Average age 31. 155 applicants, 75% accepted, 57 enrolled. *Faculty:* 32 full-time (3 women), 31 part-time/adjunct (5 women). Expenses: Contact institution.

Financial support: Fellowships, research assistantships, teaching assistantships, Federal Work-Study, scholarships/grants, tuition waivers (full and partial), and unspecified assistantships available. Financial award application deadline: 2/1; financial award applicants required to submit FAFSA. In 2017, 63 master's, 6 doctorates awarded. *Program availability:* Part-time. Offers biomedical engineering (MBE, PhD); civil engineering (MS, PhD); computer science (MSCS, PhD); electrical engineering (MEE, PhD); energy and environment (MME); engineering (MBE, MCE, MEE, MME, MS, MSCS, MSE, PhD, Certificate); engineering management (MSE, Certificate); general (MME); materials science and engineering (MS); mechanical engineering (MSE, PhD); program management (Certificate); systems engineering and management of information technology (Certificate); transportation and infrastructure systems (Certificate). *Application deadline:* For fall admission, 7/15 priority date for domestic students, 7/1 for international students; for spring admission, 11/15 priority date for domestic students, 11/1 for international students. Applications are processed on a rolling basis. *Application fee:* $55. Electronic applications accepted. *Application Contact:* Dr. Steven Brown, Director of Graduate Admissions, 202-319-5057, Fax: 202-319-6533, E-mail: cua-admissions@cua.edu. *Dean*, Dr. John Judge, 202-319-5127, Fax: 202-319-4499, E-mail: judge@cua.edu.

School of Nursing Students: 22 full-time (all women), 177 part-time (162 women); includes 67 minority (40 Black or African American, non-Hispanic/Latino; 6 Asian, non-Hispanic/Latino; 7 Hispanic/Latino; 14 Two or more races, non-Hispanic/Latino), 13 international. Average age 42. 125 applicants, 72% accepted, 49 enrolled. *Faculty:* 21 full-time (all women), 42 part-time/adjunct (36 women). Expenses: Contact institution. *Financial support:* Fellowships, research assistantships, teaching assistantships, Federal Work-Study, scholarships/grants, tuition waivers (full and partial), and unspecified assistantships available. Financial award application deadline: 2/1; financial award applicants required to submit FAFSA. In 2017, 47 master's, 9 doctorates, 3 other advanced degrees awarded. *Program availability:* Part-time, 100% online. Offers nursing (MSN, DNP, PhD, Certificate). *Application deadline:* For fall admission, 7/15 priority date for domestic students, 7/1 for international students; for spring admission, 11/15 priority date for domestic students, 11/1 for international students. Applications are processed on a rolling basis. *Application fee:* $55. Electronic applications accepted. *Application Contact:* Dr. Steven Brown, Director of Graduate Admissions, 202-319-5057, Fax: 202-319-6533, E-mail: cua-admissions@cua.edu. *Dean*, Dr. Patricia McMullen, 202-319-5403, Fax: 202-319-6485, E-mail: mcmullep@cua.edu.

School of Philosophy Students: 51 full-time (6 women), 58 part-time (12 women); includes 12 minority (2 Asian, non-Hispanic/Latino; 5 Hispanic/Latino; 5 Two or more races, non-Hispanic/Latino), 6 international. Average age 31. 92 applicants, 47% accepted, 30 enrolled. *Faculty:* 23 full-time (5 women), 5 part-time/adjunct (2 women). Expenses: Contact institution. *Financial support:* Fellowships, research assistantships, teaching assistantships, Federal Work-Study, scholarships/grants, tuition waivers (full and partial), and unspecified assistantships available. Financial award application deadline: 2/1; financial award applicants required to submit FAFSA. In 2017, 18 master's, 11 doctorates awarded. *Program availability:* Part-time. Offers philosophy (MA, PhD, Ph L). MA/JD offered in combination with Columbus School of Law. *Application deadline:* For fall admission, 7/15 priority date for domestic students, 7/1 for international students; for spring admission, 11/15 priority date for domestic students, 11/1 for international students. Applications are processed on a rolling basis. *Application fee:* $55. Electronic applications accepted. *Application Contact:* Dr. Steven Brown, Director of Graduate Admissions, 202-319-5057, Fax: 202-319-6533, E-mail: cua-admissions@cua.edu. *Dean*, Dr. John McCarthy, 202-319-6649, Fax: 202-319-4731, E-mail: mccartjc@cua.edu.

School of Theology and Religious Studies Students: 146 full-time (11 women), 201 part-time (44 women); includes 70 minority (9 Black or African American, non-Hispanic/Latino; 1 American Indian or Alaska Native, non-Hispanic/Latino; 9 Asian, non-Hispanic/Latino; 25 Hispanic/Latino; 26 Two or more races, non-Hispanic/Latino), 53 international. Average age 36. 180 applicants, 67% accepted, 66 enrolled. *Faculty:* 42 full-time (3 women), 11 part-time/adjunct (1 woman). Expenses: Contact institution. *Financial support:* Fellowships, research assistantships, teaching assistantships, Federal Work-Study, scholarships/grants, tuition waivers (full and partial), and unspecified assistantships available. Financial award application deadline: 2/1; financial award applicants required to submit FAFSA. In 2017, 59 master's, 25 doctorates awarded. *Program availability:* Part-time. Offers theology and religious studies (M Cat, M Div, MA, D Min, PhD, STD, Certificate, STB, STL). MSLA/MA offered in conjunction with Department of Library and Information Science. *Application deadline:* For fall admission, 7/15 priority date for domestic students, 7/1 for international students; for spring admission, 11/15 priority date for domestic students, 11/1 for international students. Applications are processed on a rolling basis. *Application fee:* $55. Electronic applications accepted. *Application Contact:* Dr. Steven Brown, Director of Graduate Admissions, 202-319-5057, Fax: 202-319-6533, E-mail: cua-admissions@cua.edu. *Dean*, Very Rev. Mark Morozowich, 202-319-5684, Fax: 202-319-4967, E-mail: morozowich@cua.edu.

CEDAR CREST COLLEGE, Allentown, PA 18104-6196

General Information Independent-religious, coed, primarily women, comprehensive institution. *Enrollment:* 1,664 graduate, professional, and undergraduate students; 67 full-time matriculated graduate/professional students (53 women), 164 part-time matriculated graduate/professional students (143 women). *Enrollment by degree level:* 200 master's, 31 other advanced degrees. *Graduate faculty:* 18 full-time (14 women), 31 part-time/adjunct (18 women). *Graduate housing:* On-campus housing not available. *Student services:* Campus employment opportunities, campus safety program, career counseling, exercise/wellness program, free psychological counseling, international student services, multicultural affairs office, services for students with disabilities, teacher training. *Library facilities:* Frank M. Cressman Library.

Computer facilities: Computer purchase and lease plans are available. A campuswide network can be accessed from student residence rooms and from off campus. Online class registration is available.
Website: http://www.cedarcrest.edu/

General Application Contact: Nancy Wunderly, Director of School of Adult and Graduate Education, 610-437-4471, E-mail: sage@cedarcrest.edu.

GRADUATE UNITS

Department of Education Students: 9 full-time (7 women), 57 part-time (50 women); includes 7 minority (3 Black or African American, non-Hispanic/Latino; 3 Hispanic/Latino; 1 Two or more races, non-Hispanic/Latino). Average age 34. *Faculty:* 3 full-time (all women), 8 part-time/adjunct (5 women). Expenses: Contact institution. *Financial support:* In 2017–18, 60 students received support. Available to part-time students. Applicants required to submit FAFSA. In 2017, 38 master's awarded. *Program availability:* Part-time, evening/weekend, 100% online, blended/hybrid learning. Offers education (M Ed). *Application deadline:* For fall admission, 8/7 priority date for domestic and international students; for winter admission, 11/7 priority date for domestic and international students; for spring admission, 1/8 priority date for domestic and international students. Applications are processed on a rolling basis. Electronic applications accepted. *Application Contact:* Nancy Wunderly, Director of School of Adult and Graduate Education, 610-606-4666, E-mail: sage@cedarcrest.edu. *Graduate Program Director*, Dr. Jill Purdy, 610-606-4666 Ext. 3419, E-mail: jepurdy@cedarcrest.edu.

Dietetic Internship Certificate Program Students: 27 part-time (24 women). Average age 26. *Faculty:* 3 full-time (all women), 3 part-time/adjunct (2 women). Expenses: Contact institution. In 2017, 26 Graduate Certificates awarded. *Program availability:* Part-time, evening/weekend, blended/hybrid learning. Offers dietetic internship (Graduate Certificate). *Application deadline:* Applications are processed on a rolling basis. Electronic applications accepted. *Application Contact:* Nancy Wunderly, Director of School of Adult and Graduate Education, 610-437-4471, E-mail: sage@cedarcrest.edu. *Director*, Marilou Wieder, 610-606-4666 Ext. 3445, E-mail: mwieder@cedarcrest.edu.

Program in Art Therapy Students: 12 full-time (all women), 10 part-time (all women); includes 3 minority (1 Black or African American, non-Hispanic/Latino; 1 Asian, non-Hispanic/Latino; 1 Hispanic/Latino). Average age 30. *Faculty:* 2 full-time (both women), 4 part-time/adjunct (all women). Expenses: Contact institution. In 2017, 8 master's awarded. *Program availability:* Part-time, evening/weekend, blended/hybrid learning. Offers art therapy (MA). *Application deadline:* Applications are processed on a rolling basis. Electronic applications accepted. *Application Contact:* Nancy Wunderly, Director of School of Adult and Graduate Education, 610-437-4471, E-mail: sage@cedarcrest.edu. *Director*, Rebecca Arnold, 610-437-4471 Ext. 3594, E-mail: rarnold@cedarcrest.edu.

Program in Business Administration Students: 22 full-time (15 women), 13 part-time (10 women); includes 10 minority (3 Black or African American, non-Hispanic/Latino; 2 Asian, non-Hispanic/Latino; 5 Hispanic/Latino), 1 international. Average age 36. *Faculty:* 2 full-time (1 woman), 9 part-time/adjunct (4 women). Expenses: Contact institution. In 2017, 21 master's awarded. *Program availability:* Part-time, evening/weekend, blended/hybrid learning. Offers business administration (MBA). *Application deadline:* Applications are processed on a rolling basis. Electronic applications accepted. *Application Contact:* Nancy Wunderly, Director of School of Adult and Graduate Education, 610-437-4471, E-mail: sage@cedarcrest.edu. *Chair*, Stephanie Colbry, 610-437-4471 Ext. 4453, E-mail: slcolbry@cedarcrest.edu.

Program in Creative Writing Students: 8 part-time (7 women). Average age 33. *Faculty:* 3 part-time/adjunct (1 woman). Expenses: Contact institution. In 2017, 6 master's awarded. *Program availability:* Part-time, evening/weekend, blended/hybrid learning. Offers creative writing (MFA). *Application deadline:* Applications are processed on a rolling basis. Electronic applications accepted. *Application Contact:* Nancy Wunderly, Director of School of Adult and Graduate Education, 610-437-4471, E-mail: sage@cedarcrest.edu. *Director of Writing Program*, Allison Wellford, 610-606-4666 Ext. 3474, E-mail: acwellfo@cedarcrest.edu.

Program in Forensic Science Students: 19 full-time (14 women), 7 part-time (5 women); includes 4 minority (1 American Indian or Alaska Native, non-Hispanic/Latino; 3 Asian, non-Hispanic/Latino). Average age 25. *Faculty:* 4 full-time (2 women), 2 part-time/adjunct (1 woman). Expenses: Contact institution. *Financial support:* In 2017–18, 4 students received support. Unspecified assistantships available. In 2017, 11 master's awarded. Offers forensic science (MS). *Application deadline:* For fall admission, 1/2 priority date for domestic students. Applications are processed on a rolling basis. Electronic applications accepted. *Application Contact:* Nancy Wunderly, Director of School of Adult and Graduate Education, 610-606-4666, E-mail: sage@cedarcrest.edu. *Director and Associate Professor*, Dr. Lawrence A. Quarino, 610-606-4666 Ext. 3507, Fax: 610-740-3787, E-mail: laquarin@cedarcrest.edu.

Program in Nursing Students: 25 part-time (23 women); includes 7 minority (2 Black or African American, non-Hispanic/Latino; 2 Asian, non-Hispanic/Latino; 3 Hispanic/Latino). Average age 36. *Faculty:* 4 full-time (3 women), 2 part-time/adjunct (1 woman). Expenses: Contact institution. In 2017, 8 master's awarded. *Program availability:* Part-time. Offers nursing administration (MS); nursing education (MS). *Application deadline:* Applications are processed on a rolling basis. Electronic applications accepted. *Application Contact:* Nancy Wunderly, Director of School of Adult and Graduate Education, 610-606-4666, E-mail: sage@cedarcrest.edu. *Director*, Dr. Wendy Robb, 610-606-4666, E-mail: wjrobb@cedarcrest.edu.

CEDARS-SINAI MEDICAL CENTER, Los Angeles, CA 90048

General Information Independent, coed, graduate-only institution. *Enrollment by degree level:* 24 master's, 40 doctoral. *Graduate faculty:* 60 full-time (15 women), 6 part-time/adjunct (3 women). *Graduate housing:* On-campus housing not available. *Student services:* Exercise/wellness program, free psychological counseling, grant writing training, low-cost health insurance. *Library facilities:* Cedars-Sinai Medical Library.

Computer facilities: 15 computers available on campus for general student use. A campuswide network can be accessed from off campus. Online class registration is available.
Website: http://www.cedars-sinai.edu/Education/

General Application Contact: Emma Yates Casler, Program Coordinator, 310-423-8294, E-mail: yatese@cshs.org.

GRADUATE UNITS

Graduate Programs Students: 40 full-time (26 women); includes 12 minority (2 Black or African American, non-Hispanic/Latino; 4 Asian, non-Hispanic/Latino; 4 Hispanic/Latino; 2 Native Hawaiian or other Pacific Islander, non-Hispanic/Latino). Average age 29. 55 applicants, 15% accepted, 8 enrolled. *Faculty:* 60 full-time (15 women). Expenses: Contact institution. *Financial support:* Health care benefits and annual stipends (averaging $36,000) available. Offers biomedical and translational sciences (PhD); magnetic resonance in medicine (MS). *Application deadline:* For fall admission, 1/31 for domestic students. *Application fee:* $35. Electronic applications accepted. *Application Contact:* Emma Yates Casler, Program Coordinator, 310-423-8294, E-mail: yatese@cshs.org.

CEDARVILLE UNIVERSITY, Cedarville, OH 45314

General Information Independent-religious, coed, comprehensive institution. *Enrollment:* 3,886 graduate, professional, and undergraduate students; 202 full-time matriculated graduate/professional students (123 women), 146 part-time matriculated graduate/professional students (96 women). *Enrollment by degree level:* 178 master's, 167 doctoral, 3 other advanced degrees. *Graduate faculty:* 23 full-time (9 women), 48 part-time/adjunct (21 women). *Tuition:* Full-time $12,594; part-time $566 per credit. One-time fee: $100 full-time. Tuition and fees vary according to degree level and program. *Graduate housing:* On-campus housing not available. *Student services:* Campus employment opportunities, campus safety program, career counseling, exercise/wellness program, free psychological counseling, international student services, low-cost health insurance, services for students with disabilities, writing training. *Library facilities:* Centennial Library. *Collection:* Books: 182,543 (physical), 128,348 (digital/electronic); Serial titles: 737 (physical), 26,199 (digital/electronic); Databases: 199. Weekly public service hours: 91; students can reserve study rooms.

Computer facilities: 1,500 computers available on campus for general student use. A campuswide network can be accessed from student residence rooms and from off campus. Online class registration, over 70 software packages are available.
Website: http://www.cedarville.edu/

General Application Contact: Jim Amstutz, Director of Graduate Admissions, 937-766-8000, Fax: 937-766-7575, E-mail: gradadmissions@cedarville.edu.

GRADUATE UNITS

Graduate Programs Students: 202 full-time (123 women), 146 part-time (96 women); includes 63 minority (39 Black or African American, non-Hispanic/Latino; 3 American Indian or Alaska Native, non-Hispanic/Latino; 15 Asian, non-Hispanic/Latino; 2 Hispanic/Latino; 1 Native Hawaiian or other Pacific Islander, non-Hispanic/Latino; 3 Two or more races, non-Hispanic/Latino), 3 international. Average age 24. 345 applicants, 37% accepted, 91 enrolled. *Faculty:* 23 full-time (9 women), 48 part-time/adjunct (21 women). Expenses: Contact institution. *Financial support:* Scholarships/grants and unspecified assistantships available. Support available to part-time students. Financial award application deadline: 1/30; financial award applicants required to submit FAFSA. In 2017, 53 master's, 47 doctorates awarded. *Program availability:* Part-time, evening/weekend, 100% online, blended/hybrid learning. Offers business administration (MBA); family nurse practitioner (MSN); global ministry (M Div); global public health nursing (MSN); healthcare administration (MBA); ministry (M Min); nurse educator (MSN); operations management (MBA); pharmacy (Pharm D). *Application deadline:* For fall admission, 5/1 priority date for domestic and international students; for spring admission, 11/1 priority date for domestic and international students. Applications are processed on a rolling basis. *Application fee:* $0. Electronic applications accepted. *Application Contact:* Jim Amstutz, Director of Graduate Admissions, 937-766-7878, Fax: 937-766-7575, E-mail: amstutzj@cedarville.edu. *Dean of Graduate Studies*, Dr. Janice Supplee, 937-766-7700, E-mail: suppleej@cedarville.edu.

CENTENARY COLLEGE OF LOUISIANA, Shreveport, LA 71104

General Information Independent-religious, coed, comprehensive institution. *Graduate housing:* Room and/or apartments available on a first-come, first-served basis to single students; on-campus housing not available to married students.

GRADUATE UNITS

Graduate Programs *Program availability:* Part-time, evening/weekend. Offers elementary education (MAT); secondary education (MAT).

Frost School of Business *Program availability:* Part-time, evening/weekend. Offers business (MBA).

CENTENARY UNIVERSITY, Hackettstown, NJ 07840-2100

General Information Independent-religious, coed, comprehensive institution. *Graduate housing:* Room and/or apartments available on a first-come, first-served basis to single students; on-campus housing not available to married students. Housing application deadline: 6/1.

GRADUATE UNITS

Program in Business Administration *Program availability:* Part-time, evening/weekend, online learning. Offers business administration (MBA).

Program in Counseling Psychology *Program availability:* Part-time, evening/weekend, online learning. Offers counseling (MA); counseling psychology (MA).

Program in Education *Program availability:* Part-time, evening/weekend, online learning. Offers education practice (M Ed); educational leadership (MA, Ed D); instructional leadership (MA); reading (M Ed); special education (MA).

Program in Professional Accounting *Program availability:* Part-time, evening/weekend, online learning. Offers professional accounting (MS).

CENTRAL BAPTIST THEOLOGICAL SEMINARY, Shawnee, KS 66226

General Information Independent-religious, coed, graduate-only institution. *Graduate housing:* On-campus housing not available.

GRADUATE UNITS

Graduate and Professional Programs *Program availability:* Part-time. Offers missional church studies (MA); theological studies (MA); theology (M Div, Diploma). Electronic applications accepted.

CENTRAL CONNECTICUT STATE UNIVERSITY, New Britain, CT 06050-4010

General Information State-supported, coed, comprehensive institution. *Enrollment:* 11,880 graduate, professional, and undergraduate students; 646 full-time matriculated graduate/professional students (405 women), 1,523 part-time matriculated graduate/professional students (985 women). *Enrollment by degree level:* 1,674 master's, 84 doctoral, 411 other advanced degrees. *Graduate faculty:* 185 full-time (88 women), 77 part-time/adjunct (48 women). *Tuition, area resident:* Full-time $6757. Tuition, state resident: full-time $9750; part-time $374 per credit. Tuition, nonresident: full-time $18,102; part-time $374 per credit. *Required fees:* $4635; $255 per credit. *Graduate housing:* Room and/or apartments available on a first-come, first-served basis to single students; on-campus housing not available to married students. Typical cost: $6820 per year ($11,816 including board). Room and board charges vary according to board plan and housing facility selected. Housing application deadline: 5/1. *Student services:* Campus employment opportunities, campus safety program, career counseling, child daycare facilities, exercise/wellness program, free psychological counseling, international student services, low-cost health insurance, multicultural affairs office, services for students with disabilities, teacher training, writing training. *Library facilities:* Elihu Burritt Library plus 1 other. *Collection:* Books: 451,499 (physical), 160,771 (digital/electronic); Serial titles: 4,177 (physical), 87,138 (digital/electronic); Databases: 147. Weekly public service hours: 84.

Computer facilities: 750 computers available on campus for general student use. A campuswide network can be accessed from student residence rooms and from off campus. Online class registration is available.
Website: http://www.ccsu.edu/

General Application Contact: Patricia Gardner, Associate Director of Graduate Studies, 860-832-2350, Fax: 860-832-2362.

GRADUATE UNITS

School of Graduate Studies Students: 646 full-time (405 women), 1,523 part-time (985 women); includes 537 minority (224 Black or African American, non-Hispanic/Latino; 2 American Indian or Alaska Native, non-Hispanic/Latino; 71 Asian, non-Hispanic/Latino; 190 Hispanic/Latino; 2 Native Hawaiian or other Pacific Islander, non-Hispanic/Latino; 48 Two or more races, non-Hispanic/Latino), 41 international. Average age 32. 1,218 applicants, 76% accepted, 623 enrolled. *Faculty:* 185 full-time (88 women), 77 part-time/adjunct (48 women). Expenses: Contact institution. *Financial support:* In 2017–18, 281 students received support. Career-related internships or fieldwork, Federal Work-Study, scholarships/grants, and unspecified assistantships available. Support available to part-time students. Financial award application deadline: 3/1; financial award applicants required to submit FAFSA. In 2017, 604 master's, 13 doctorates, 152 other advanced degrees awarded. *Program availability:* Part-time, evening/weekend, 100% online. *Application deadline:* For fall admission, 8/1 for domestic students, 5/1 for international students; for spring admission, 11/1 for domestic and international students. Applications are processed on a rolling basis. *Application fee:* $50. Electronic applications accepted. *Associate Director of Graduate Studies*, Patricia Gardner, 860-832-2350, Fax: 860-832-2362.

College of Liberal Arts and Social Sciences Students: 126 full-time (80 women), 202 part-time (138 women); includes 81 minority (30 Black or African American, non-Hispanic/Latino; 8 Asian, non-Hispanic/Latino; 36 Hispanic/Latino; 1 Native Hawaiian or other Pacific Islander, non-Hispanic/Latino; 6 Two or more races, non-Hispanic/Latino), 5 international. Average age 31. 229 applicants, 72% accepted, 104 enrolled. *Faculty:* 72 full-time (38 women), 4 part-time/adjunct (1 woman). Expenses: Contact institution. *Financial support:* In 2017–18, 65 students received support. Career-related internships or fieldwork, Federal Work-Study, scholarships/grants, and unspecified assistantships available. Support available to part-time students. Financial award application deadline: 3/1; financial award applicants required to submit FAFSA. In 2017, 111 master's, 11 other advanced degrees awarded. *Program availability:* Part-time, evening/weekend. Offers art education (MS, Certificate); communication (MS); criminal justice (MS); English (MA); English education (MAT); geography (MS); history (MA, Certificate); information design (MA); international studies (MS); liberal arts and social sciences (MA, MAT, MS, Certificate); modern language (MA, Certificate); music education (MS, Certificate); psychological science (MA); public relations/promotions (Certificate); Spanish (MS, Certificate); teaching English to speakers of other languages (MS, Certificate). *Application deadline:* For fall admission, 8/1 for domestic students, 5/1 for international students; for spring admission, 11/1 for domestic and international students. Applications are processed on a rolling basis. *Application fee:* $50. Electronic applications accepted. *Application Contact:* Patricia Gardner, Associate Director of Graduate Studies, 860-832-2350, Fax: 860-832-2362. *Interim Dean*, Dr. Brian Sommers, 860-832-2604, E-mail: sommersb@ccsu.edu.

School of Business Students: 29 full-time (14 women), 240 part-time (118 women); includes 93 minority (44 Black or African American, non-Hispanic/Latino; 22 Asian, non-Hispanic/Latino; 24 Hispanic/Latino; 3 Two or more races, non-Hispanic/Latino), 3 international. Average age 31. 192 applicants, 81% accepted, 98 enrolled. *Faculty:* 12 full-time (5 women), 4 part-time/adjunct (0 women). Expenses: Contact institution. *Financial support:* In 2017–18, 22 students received support. Career-related internships or fieldwork, Federal Work-Study, scholarships/grants, and unspecified assistantships available. Support available to part-time students. Financial award application deadline: 3/1; financial award applicants required to submit FAFSA. In 2017, 45 master's awarded. *Program availability:* Part-time, evening/weekend. Offers accounting (MSA); business (MBA, MSA); business administration (MBA). *Application deadline:* For fall admission, 8/1 for domestic students, 5/1 for international students; for spring admission, 11/1 for domestic and international students. Applications are processed on a rolling basis. *Application fee:* $50. Electronic applications accepted. *Application Contact:* Patricia Gardner, Associate Director of Graduate Admissions, 860-832-2350, Fax: 860-832-2362. *Dean*, Dr. Ken Colwell, 860-832-3209, E-mail: colwell@ccsu.edu.

School of Education and Professional Studies Students: 289 full-time (209 women), 824 part-time (622 women); includes 248 minority (98 Black or African American, non-Hispanic/Latino; 2 American Indian or Alaska Native, non-Hispanic/Latino; 9 Asian, non-Hispanic/Latino; 108 Hispanic/Latino; 1 Native Hawaiian or other Pacific Islander, non-Hispanic/Latino; 30 Two or more races, non-Hispanic/Latino), 3 international. Average age 33. 492 applicants, 74% accepted, 265 enrolled. *Faculty:* 50 full-time (29 women), 61 part-time/adjunct (44 women). Expenses: Contact institution. *Financial support:* In 2017–18, 121 students received support. Career-related internships or fieldwork, Federal Work-Study, scholarships/grants, and unspecified assistantships available. Support available to part-time students. Financial award application deadline: 3/1; financial award applicants required to submit FAFSA. In 2017, 257 master's, 13 doctorates, 126 other advanced degrees awarded. *Program availability:* Part-time, evening/weekend. Offers education and professional studies (MAT, MS, MSN, Ed D, AC, Certificate, Sixth Year Certificate); educational leadership, policy and instructional technology (MS, Ed D, AC, Sixth Year Certificate); hospice and palliative care (MSN); literacy, elementary, and early childhood education (MS, AC, Sixth Year Certificate); marriage and family therapy (MS); physical education (MS); professional counseling (MS, AC, Certificate); school counseling (MS); special education and interventions (MS, Certificate); student development in higher education (MS). *Application deadline:* For fall admission, 8/1 for domestic students, 5/1 for international students; for spring admission, 11/1 for domestic and international students. Applications are processed on a rolling basis. *Application fee:* $50. Electronic applications accepted. *Application Contact:* Patricia Gardner, Associate Director of Graduate Studies, 860-832-2350, Fax: 860-832-2362. *Interim Dean*, Dr. Kimberly Kostelis, 860-832-2101, E-mail: kimberly.kostelis@ccsu.edu.

School of Engineering, Science and Technology Students: 202 full-time (102 women), 257 part-time (107 women); includes 115 minority (52 Black or African American, non-Hispanic/Latino; 32 Asian, non-Hispanic/Latino; 22 Hispanic/Latino; 9 Two or more races, non-Hispanic/Latino), 30 international. Average age 32. 305 applicants, 77% accepted, 156 enrolled. *Faculty:* 51 full-time (16 women), 8 part-time/adjunct (3 women). Expenses: Contact institution. *Financial support:* In 2017–18, 73 students received support. Career-related internships or fieldwork, Federal Work-Study, scholarships/grants, and unspecified assistantships available. Support available to part-time students. Financial award application deadline: 3/1; financial award applicants required to submit FAFSA. In 2017, 191 master's, 15 other advanced degrees awarded. *Program availability:* Part-time, evening/weekend, 100% online. Offers biological sciences (MA); biology (DNP-A); biomolecular sciences (MS, Certificate); computer information technology (MS); construction management (MS, Certificate); data mining (MS, Certificate); engineering (MS); engineering, science and technology (MA, MS, DNP-A, Certificate, Sixth Year Certificate); environmental and occupational safety (Certificate); lean manufacturing and Six Sigma (Certificate); mathematics (MA, MS); mathematics education leadership (Sixth Year Certificate); mathematics for secondary education (Certificate); science education (Certificate);

STEM education (MS); supply chain and logistics (Certificate); technology management (MS). *Application deadline:* For fall admission, 8/1 for domestic students, 5/1 for international students; for spring admission, 11/1 for domestic and international students. Applications are processed on a rolling basis. *Application fee:* $50. Electronic applications accepted. *Application Contact:* Patricia Gardner, Associate Director of Graduate Studies, 860-832-2350, Fax: 860-832-2362. *Interim Dean*, Dr. Zdzislaw Kremens, 860-832-1800, E-mail: kremensz@ccsu.edu.

CENTRAL EUROPEAN UNIVERSITY, H-1051 Budapest, Hungary

General Information Independent, coed, graduate-only institution. CGS member. *Enrollment by degree level:* 886 master's, 420 doctoral. *Graduate faculty:* 161 full-time (50 women), 95 part-time/adjunct (23 women). *Tuition:* Full-time 12,000 euros. *Required fees:* 230 euros. One-time fee: 30 euros full-time. Tuition and fees vary according to course level, course load, degree level and program. *Graduate housing:* Room and/or apartments guaranteed to single students; on-campus housing not available to married students. Housing application deadline: 2/4. *Student services:* Campus employment opportunities, campus safety program, career counseling, exercise/wellness program, free psychological counseling, grant writing training, international student services, low-cost health insurance, multicultural affairs office, services for students with disabilities, teacher training, writing training. *Library facilities:* CEU Library plus 1 other. *Collection:* Books: 184,083 (physical), 164,176 (digital/electronic); Serial titles: 208 (physical), 44,700 (digital/electronic); Databases: 95. Weekly public service hours: 89; students can reserve study rooms. *Research affiliation:* Institute of Human Sciences Vienna (social sciences), Open Society Institute (social sciences), Alfréd Rényi Institute of Mathematics.

Computer facilities: 290 computers available on campus for general student use. A campuswide network can be accessed from student residence rooms and from off campus. Online class registration is available.
Website: http://www.ceu.hu/

General Application Contact: Zsuzsanna Jaszberenyi, Admissions Officer, 361-327-3009, Fax: 361-327-3211, E-mail: admissions@ceu.edu.

GRADUATE UNITS

Center for Network Science Students: 13 full-time (5 women). Average age 30. 45 applicants, 18% accepted, 5 enrolled. *Faculty:* 3 full-time (1 woman). Expenses: Contact institution. *Financial support:* In 2017–18, 10 students received support. Fellowships, research assistantships, teaching assistantships, scholarships/grants, health care benefits, and tuition waivers (full) available. Financial award applicants required to submit FAFSA. Offers network science (PhD). *Application deadline:* For fall admission, 2/4 for domestic and international students. *Application fee:* $30. Electronic applications accepted. *Application Contact:* Janos Kertesz, Program Director, 36-1-327-3000 Ext. 2655, E-mail: cns@ceu.edu. *Director*, Balazs Vedres, 36-1-327-3000.

Department of Cognitive Science Students: 32 full-time (19 women). Average age 29. 62 applicants, 13% accepted, 6 enrolled. *Faculty:* 24 full-time (8 women), 5 part-time/adjunct (2 women). Expenses: Contact institution. *Financial support:* In 2017–18, 6 students received support. Fellowships, career-related internships or fieldwork, scholarships/grants, and health care benefits available. In 2017, 3 doctorates awarded. Offers cognitive science (PhD). *Application deadline:* For fall admission, 2/4 priority date for domestic and international students. *Application fee:* $30. Electronic applications accepted. *Application Contact:* Zsuzsanna Jaszberenyi, Admissions Officer, 361-324-3009, Fax: 367-327-3211, E-mail: admissions@ceu.edu. *Head of Department*, Dr. Christophe Heintz, 36 1 887-5137, E-mail: heintzc@ceu.edu.

Department of Economics Students: 177 full-time (77 women), 125 part-time (39 women). Average age 31. 530 applicants, 49% accepted, 144 enrolled. *Faculty:* 23 full-time (2 women), 25 part-time/adjunct (4 women). Expenses: Contact institution. *Financial support:* Fellowships, teaching assistantships, career-related internships or fieldwork, institutionally sponsored loans, scholarships/grants, health care benefits, and tuition waivers (full and partial) available. In 2017, 150 master's, 6 doctorates awarded. *Program availability:* Part-time. Offers business administration (PhD); business analytics (M Sc); economic policy in global markets (MA); economics (MA, PhD); finance (MS); global economic relations (MA); technology management and innovation (MS). *Application deadline:* For fall admission, 2/4 for domestic and international students. *Application fee:* $30. Electronic applications accepted. *Application Contact:* Zsuzsanna Jaszberenyi, Admissions Officer, 361-324-3009, Fax: 367-327-3211, E-mail: admissions@ceu.edu. *Head of Department*, Miklos Koren, 36 1 327-3000 Ext. 2212, E-mail: econbusi@ceu.edu.

Department of Environmental Sciences and Policy Students: 89 full-time (53 women), 5 part-time (2 women). Average age 29. 460 applicants, 36% accepted, 57 enrolled. *Faculty:* 11 full-time (3 women), 2 part-time/adjunct (both women). Expenses: Contact institution. *Financial support:* Fellowships, teaching assistantships, career-related internships or fieldwork, institutionally sponsored loans, scholarships/grants, health care benefits, and tuition waivers (full and partial) available. Financial award application deadline: 2/4. In 2017, 37 master's, 3 doctorates awarded. *Program availability:* Part-time. Offers environmental sciences and policy (MS, PhD). *Application deadline:* For fall admission, 2/4 for domestic and international students. *Application fee:* $30. Electronic applications accepted. *Application Contact:* Zsuzsanna Jaszberenyi, Head of Admissions Services, 361-327-3009, E-mail: admissions@ceu.edu. *Head of Department*, Dr. Laszlo Pinter, 36 1 327-3021, Fax: 36-1-327-3031, E-mail: envsci@ceu.edu.

Department of Gender Studies Students: 77 full-time (60 women). Average age 29. 353 applicants, 14% accepted, 35 enrolled. *Faculty:* 12 full-time (11 women), 4 part-time/adjunct (all women). Expenses: Contact institution. *Financial support:* Fellowships, career-related internships or fieldwork, scholarships/grants, health care benefits, and tuition waivers (full and partial) available. Financial award application deadline: 2/4. In 2017, 39 master's, 2 doctorates awarded. Offers gender studies (MA, PhD). *Application deadline:* For fall admission, 2/4 for domestic and international students. *Application fee:* $30. Electronic applications accepted. *Application Contact:* Zsuzsanna Jaszberenyi, Admissions Officer, 361-324-3009, Fax: 367-327-3211, E-mail: admissions@ceu.edu. *Head of Department*, Jasmina Lukic, 36 1 327-3034, Fax: 36-1-327-3296, E-mail: gender@ceu.edu.

Department of History Students: 92 full-time (41 women). Average age 28. 169 applicants, 41% accepted, 41 enrolled. *Faculty:* 13 full-time (3 women), 8 part-time/adjunct (2 women). Expenses: Contact institution. *Financial support:* Fellowships, career-related internships or fieldwork, institutionally sponsored loans, scholarships/grants, and tuition waivers (full and partial) available. In 2017, 34 master's, 5 doctorates awarded. Offers history (MA, PhD). *Application deadline:* For fall admission, 2/4 for domestic and international students. *Application fee:* $30. Electronic applications accepted. *Application Contact:* Agnes Bendik, Coordinator, 361-327-3000 Ext. 2591, Fax: 361-235-6145, E-mail: history@ceu.edu. *Head*, Dr. Balazs Trencsenyi, 36 1 327-3022, Fax: 36-1-327-3191, E-mail: history@ceu.edu.

Department of International Relations Students: 96 full-time (49 women), 3 part-time (1 woman). Average age 27. 575 applicants, 23% accepted, 67 enrolled. *Faculty:* 10 full-time (2 women), 4 part-time/adjunct (2 women). Expenses: Contact institution. *Financial support:* In 2017–18, 71 students received support. Fellowships, career-related internships or fieldwork, scholarships/grants, health care benefits, and tuition waivers (full and partial) available. In 2017, 31 master's, 6 doctorates awarded. Offers global economic relations (MA); international relations (MA, PhD). *Application deadline:* For fall admission, 2/4 for domestic and international students. *Application fee:* $30. Electronic applications accepted. *Application Contact:* Zsuzsanna Jaszberenyi, Admissions Officer, 361-324-3009, Fax: 367-327-3211, E-mail: admissions@ceu.edu. *Head of Department*, Alexander Astrov, 36 1 327-3243 Ext. 2219, E-mail: ir@ceu.edu.

Department of Legal Studies Students: 90 full-time (52 women). Average age 28. 384 applicants, 33% accepted, 71 enrolled. *Faculty:* 10 full-time (5 women), 9 part-time/adjunct (1 woman). Expenses: Contact institution. *Financial support:* Fellowships, career-related internships or fieldwork, institutionally sponsored loans, scholarships/grants, and tuition waivers (full and partial) available. Financial award application deadline: 2/4. In 2017, 53 master's, 3 doctorates awarded. Offers comparative Constitutional law (LL M); human rights (LL M, MA); international business law (LL M); juridical sciences (SJD). *Application deadline:* For fall admission, 2/4 for domestic and international students. *Application fee:* $30. Electronic applications accepted. *Application Contact:* Zsuzsanna Jaszberenyi, Department Coordinator, 361-327-3272, Fax: 361-327-3198, E-mail: admissions@ceu.edu. *Head of Department*, Dr. Karoly Bard, 36 1 327-3294, Fax: 361-327-3198, E-mail: legalst@ceu.edu.

Department of Mathematics and its Applications Students: 37 full-time (6 women). Average age 27. 71 applicants, 23% accepted, 11 enrolled. *Faculty:* 2 full-time (0 women), 11 part-time/adjunct (0 women). Expenses: Contact institution. *Financial support:* Fellowships, career-related internships or fieldwork, scholarships/grants, health care benefits, and tuition waivers (full and partial) available. Financial award application deadline: 2/4. In 2017, 9 master's, 4 doctorates awarded. Offers mathematics and its applications (MS, PhD). *Application deadline:* For fall admission, 2/4 for domestic and international students. *Application fee:* $30. Electronic applications accepted. *Application Contact:* Zsuzsanna Jaszberenyi, Admissions Officer, 361-324-3009, Fax: 367-327-3211, E-mail: admissions@ceu.edu. *Head*, Dr. Karoly Boroczky, 36 1 327-3053, E-mail: mathematics@ceu.edu.

Department of Medieval Studies Students: 89 full-time (50 women). Average age 30. 132 applicants, 38% accepted, 34 enrolled. *Faculty:* 14 full-time (4 women), 7 part-time/adjunct (2 women). Expenses: Contact institution. *Financial support:* In 2017–18, 74 students received support. Fellowships, scholarships/grants, health care benefits, and tuition waivers (full and partial) available. In 2017, 32 master's, 6 doctorates awarded. Offers comparative history: interdisciplinary Medieval studies (MA); cultural heritage studies (MA); Medieval studies (MA, PhD). *Application deadline:* For fall admission, 2/4 for domestic and international students. *Application fee:* $30. Electronic applications accepted. *Application Contact:* Zsuzsanna Jaszberenyi, Admissions Officer, 361-324-3009, Fax: 367-327-3211, E-mail: admissions@ceu.edu. *Head*, Dr. Katalin Szende, 36 1 327-3046, E-mail: medstud@ceu.edu.

Department of Philosophy Students: 49 full-time (10 women). Average age 28. 177 applicants, 26% accepted, 25 enrolled. *Faculty:* 9 full-time (2 women), 4 part-time/adjunct (1 woman). Expenses: Contact institution. *Financial support:* In 2017–18, 45 students received support. Fellowships, teaching assistantships, scholarships/grants, health care benefits, and tuition waivers (full and partial) available. In 2017, 20 master's awarded. Offers philosophy (MA, PhD). *Application deadline:* For fall admission, 2/4 for domestic and international students. *Application fee:* $30. Electronic applications accepted. *Application Contact:* Zsuzsanna Jaszberenyi, Admissions Officer, 361-324-3009, Fax: 367-327-3211, E-mail: admissions@ceu.edu. *Head of Department*, Dr. Hanoch Ben-Yami, 36 1 327-3806, Fax: 36-1-327-3072, E-mail: philosophy@ceu.edu.

Department of Political Science Students: 112 full-time (41 women). Average age 27. 390 applicants, 27% accepted, 68 enrolled. *Faculty:* 17 full-time (4 women), 8 part-time/adjunct (1 woman). Expenses: Contact institution. *Financial support:* Fellowships, teaching assistantships, career-related internships or fieldwork, scholarships/grants, health care benefits, and tuition waivers (full and partial) available. In 2017, 35 master's, 9 doctorates awarded. Offers political science (MA, PhD). *Application deadline:* For fall admission, 2/4 for domestic and international students. *Application fee:* $30. Electronic applications accepted. *Application Contact:* Zsuzsanna Jaszberenyi, Admissions Officer, 361-324-3009, Fax: 367-327-3211, E-mail: admissions@ceu.edu. *Head of Department*, Dr. Zoltan Miklosi, 36 1 235-6164, E-mail: polsci@ceu.edu.

Department of Sociology and Social Anthropology Students: 65 full-time (37 women). Average age 29. 288 applicants, 19% accepted, 33 enrolled. *Faculty:* 9 full-time (3 women), 4 part-time/adjunct (2 women). Expenses: Contact institution. *Financial support:* Fellowships, career-related internships or fieldwork, scholarships/grants, health care benefits, and tuition waivers (full and partial) available. In 2017, 30 master's, 6 doctorates awarded. Offers sociology and social anthropology (MA, PhD). *Application deadline:* For fall admission, 2/4 for domestic and international students. *Application fee:* $30. Electronic applications accepted. *Application Contact:* Zsuzsanna Jaszberenyi, Admissions Officer, 361-324-3009, Fax: 367-327-3211, E-mail: admissions@ceu.edu. *Head of Department*, Dr. Dorit Geva, 36 1 327-3000 Ext. 2131, E-mail: sociology@ceu.edu.

Nationalism Studies Program Students: 32 full-time (18 women). Average age 26. 114 applicants, 32% accepted, 23 enrolled. *Faculty:* 4 full-time (2 women), 4 part-time/adjunct (0 women). Expenses: Contact institution. *Financial support:* In 2017–18, 32 students received support. Fellowships, scholarships/grants, health care benefits, and tuition waivers (full and partial) available. In 2017, 20 master's awarded. Offers nationalism studies (MA). *Application deadline:* For fall admission, 2/4 for domestic and international students. *Application fee:* $30. Electronic applications accepted. *Application Contact:* Zsuzsanna Jaszberenyi, Admissions Officer, 361-324-3009, Fax: 367-327-3211, E-mail: admissions@ceu.edu. *Program Director*, Dr. Michael Laurence Miller, 36 1 327-3081, E-mail: nationalism@ceu.edu.

School of Public Policy Students: 123 full-time (76 women). Average age 28. 696 applicants, 32% accepted, 62 enrolled. *Faculty:* 22 full-time (7 women), 7 part-time/adjunct (5 women). Expenses: Contact institution. *Financial support:* Fellowships, career-related internships or fieldwork, scholarships/grants, health care benefits, and tuition waivers (full and partial) available. In 2017, 74 master's, 4 doctorates awarded. Offers public administration (MPA); public policy (MA, PhD). *Application deadline:* For fall admission, 2/4 for domestic and international students. *Application fee:* $30. Electronic applications accepted. *Application Contact:* Zsuzsanna Jaszberenyi, Admissions Officer, 361-324-3009, Fax: 367-327-3211, E-mail: admissions@ceu.edu. *Head*, Dr. Martin Kahanec, 36 1 327-3110, E-mail: spp@ceu.edu.

CENTRAL METHODIST UNIVERSITY, Fayette, MO 65248-1198

General Information Independent-religious, coed, comprehensive institution. *Graduate housing:* Rooms and/or apartments available on a first-come, first-served basis to single and married students.

GRADUATE UNITS

College of Graduate and Extended Studies *Program availability:* Part-time, evening/weekend, online learning. Offers clinical counseling (MS); clinical nurse leader (MSN); education (M Ed); music education (MME); nurse educator (MSN). Electronic applications accepted.

CENTRAL MICHIGAN UNIVERSITY, Mount Pleasant, MI 48859

General Information State-supported, coed, university. CGS member. *Graduate housing:* Rooms and/or apartments available on a first-come, first-served basis to single and married students. *Research affiliation:* IBM (information technology), Dendritic Nanotechnologies, Inc. (chemistry, physics), Dow Corning Corporation (silicon-based technology), Dow Chemical Company (chemicals and plastics), SAS Business Analytics (business analysis), SAP (information technology).

GRADUATE UNITS

Central Michigan University Global Campus *Program availability:* Part-time, evening/weekend, online learning. Offers acquisitions administration (MSA, Certificate); college teaching (Graduate Certificate); community college (MA); curriculum and instruction (MA); cybersecurity (Certificate); educational technology (MA, DET); engineering management administration (MSA, Certificate); enterprise resource planning (MBA, Certificate); general administration (MSA, Certificate); general public administration (MPA); health administration (DHA); health services administration (MSA, Certificate); human resource management (MBA); human resources administration (MSA, Certificate); information resource management (MSA); information resource management administration (Certificate); international administration (MSA, Certificate); international health (Certificate); K-12 leadership (Ed D); leadership (MSA, Certificate); logistics management (MBA, Certificate); marketing (MBA); nutrition and dietetics (MS); philanthropy and fundraising administration (MSA, Certificate); professional counseling (MA); public administration (MSA, Certificate); public management (MPA); reading and literacy K-12 (MA); recreation and park administration (MSA); research administration (MSA, Certificate); school counseling (MA); school principalship (MA); state and local government (MPA); training and development (MA); value-driven organization (MBA). Electronic applications accepted.

College of Graduate Studies *Program availability:* Part-time, evening/weekend, online learning. Offers acquisitions administration (MSA, Graduate Certificate); general administration (MSA, Graduate Certificate); health services administration (MSA, Graduate Certificate); human resource administration (Graduate Certificate); human resources administration (MSA); information resource management (MSA, Graduate Certificate); international administration (MSA, Graduate Certificate); leadership (MSA, Graduate Certificate); public administration (MSA, Graduate Certificate); research administration (Graduate Certificate); sport administration (MSA). Electronic applications accepted.

College of Business Administration *Program availability:* Part-time, evening/weekend. Offers accounting (MBA); business administration (MA, MBA, MS, Graduate Certificate); business computing (Graduate Certificate); business economics (MBA); consulting (MBA); economics (MA); finance (MBA); general business (MBA); human resource management (MBA); information systems (MBA, MS); international business (MBA); logistics management (MBA); marketing (MBA); value-driven organization (MBA). Electronic applications accepted.

College of Communication and Fine Arts *Program availability:* Part-time. Offers communication (MA); communication and fine arts (MA, MM); composition (MM); conducting (MM); electronic media management (MA); electronic media production (MA); electronic media studies (MA); film theory and criticism (MA); music education (MM); performance (MM). Electronic applications accepted.

College of Education and Human Services *Program availability:* Part-time, evening/weekend. Offers apparel product development and merchandising technology (MS); autism (Graduate Certificate); counseling (MA); education and human services (MA, MS, Ed D, Ed S, Graduate Certificate); educational leadership (Ed D); educational technology (MA, Graduate Certificate); elementary education (MA); general educational administration (Ed S); gerontology (Graduate Certificate); human development and family studies (MA); nutrition and dietetics (MS); reading and literacy K-12 (MA); school principalship (MA); secondary education (MA); special education (MA, Graduate Certificate); student affairs administration (MA); teacher leadership (MA). Electronic applications accepted.

College of Humanities and Social and Behavioral Sciences *Program availability:* Part-time, evening/weekend. Offers American politics (MA); applied experimental psychology (PhD); clinical psychology (PhD); English composition and communication (MA); English language and literature (MA); European history (Graduate Certificate); experimental psychology (MS, PhD); history (MA); humanities (MA); humanities and social and behavioral sciences (MA, MPA, MS, PhD, Graduate Certificate, S Psy S); industrial and organizational psychology (MA, PhD); modern history (Graduate Certificate); neuroscience (MS, PhD); occupational health psychology (PhD); political science (MA); professional development in public administration (Graduate Certificate); public administration (MPA, Graduate Certificate); public management (MPA); school psychology (PhD, S Psy S); Spanish (MA); state and local government (MPA); TESOL: teaching English to speakers of other languages (MA); United States history (Graduate Certificate). Electronic applications accepted.

College of Science and Technology *Program availability:* Part-time, evening/weekend. Offers biology (MS); chemistry (MS); computer science (MS); conservation biology (MS); geographic information sciences (MS); industrial management and technology (MA); mathematics (MA, PhD); physics (MS); science and technology (MA, MAT, MS, PhD, Graduate Certificate); science of advanced materials (PhD); teaching chemistry (MA). Electronic applications accepted.

The Herbert H. and Grace A. Dow College of Health Professions *Program availability:* Part-time. Offers audiology (Au D); exercise science (MA); health administration (DHA); health professions (MA, MS, Au D, DHA, DPT, Graduate Certificate); physical therapy (DPT); physician assistant (MS); speech-language pathology (MA); sport administration (MA). Electronic applications accepted.

CENTRAL PENN COLLEGE, Summerdale, PA 17093-0309

General Information Proprietary, coed, comprehensive institution.

GRADUATE UNITS

Graduate Programs *Program availability:* Evening/weekend. Offers information systems management (MPS); organizational development (MPS). Programs offered in Harrisburg, PA.

CENTRAL WASHINGTON UNIVERSITY, Ellensburg, WA 98926

General Information State-supported, coed, comprehensive institution. CGS member. *Graduate housing:* Rooms and/or apartments available on a first-come, first-served basis to single and married students. *Student services:* Campus employment opportunities, campus safety program, career counseling, child daycare facilities, exercise/wellness program, free psychological counseling, grant writing training, international student services, low-cost health insurance, multicultural affairs office, services for students with disabilities, teacher training, writing training. *Library facilities:* James E. Brooks Library plus 2 others. *Collection:* Books: 900,981 (physical), 251,073 (digital/electronic); Serial titles: 327 (physical), 72,453 (digital/electronic); Databases: 112. Weekly public service hours: 101; students can reserve study rooms. *Research affiliation:* Associated Western Universities (science and engineering), East-West Center (Pacific area studies), Jet Propulsion Laboratory (engineering).

Computer facilities: Computer purchase and lease plans are available. 791 computers available on campus for general student use. A campuswide network can be accessed from student residence rooms and from off campus. Online class registration, online data storage, office software are available.
Website: http://www.cwu.edu/

General Application Contact: Justine Eason, Communication Consultant III, 509-963-3103, Fax: 509-963-1799, E-mail: masters@cwu.edu.

GRADUATE UNITS

School of Graduate Studies and Research Expenses: Contact institution. *Financial support:* Application deadline: 3/1; applicants required to submit FAFSA. *Program availability:* Part-time, evening/weekend. Offers individual studies (M Ed, MA, MFA, MS). *Application deadline:* For fall admission, 2/1 priority date for domestic students; for winter admission, 10/1 priority date for domestic students; for spring admission, 1/1 priority date for domestic students. Applications are processed on a rolling basis. *Application fee:* $50. Electronic applications accepted. *Application Contact:* Justine Eason, Admissions Program Coordinator, 509-963-3103, Fax: 509-963-1799, E-mail: masters@cwu.edu. *Interim Dean, Graduate Studies and Research,* Kevin Archer, 509-963-3101, Fax: 509-963-1799, E-mail: masters@cwu.edu.

College of Arts and Humanities Expenses: Contact institution. *Financial support:* Application deadline: 3/1; applicants required to submit FAFSA. *Program availability:* Part-time. Offers arts and humanities (MA, MFA, MM); ceramics (MFA); composition (MM); computer arts (MFA); conducting (MM); history (MA); jewelry and metalsmithing (MFA); literature (MA); music education (MM); painting and drawing (MFA); pedagogy (MM); performance (MM); photography (MFA); professional and creative writing (MA); sculpture (MFA); teaching English to speakers of other languages (MA); theatre production (MA); theatre studies (MA). *Application deadline:* For fall admission, 2/1 for domestic students; for winter admission, 10/1 priority date for domestic students; for spring admission, 1/1 priority date for domestic students. Applications are processed on a rolling basis. *Application fee:* $50. Electronic applications accepted. *Application Contact:* Justine Eason, Admissions Program Coordinator, 509-963-3103, Fax: 509-963-1799, E-mail: masters@cwu.edu. *Interim Dean,* Dr. Todd Shiver, E-mail: todd.shiver@cwu.edu.

College of Education and Professional Studies Expenses: Contact institution. *Financial support:* Application deadline: 3/1; applicants required to submit FAFSA. *Program availability:* Part-time. Offers athletic administration (MS); career and technical education (MS); education and professional studies (M Ed, MS); family and child life (MS); family and consumer sciences education (MS); health and physical education (MS); higher education (M Ed); integrative human physiology (MS); literacy (M Ed); master teacher (M Ed); nutrition (MS). *Application deadline:* For fall admission, 2/1 priority date for domestic students; for winter admission, 10/1 for domestic students; for spring admission, 1/1 for domestic students. Applications are processed on a rolling basis. *Application fee:* $50. Electronic applications accepted. *Application Contact:* Justine Eason, Admissions Program Coordinator, 509-963-3103, Fax: 509-963-1799, E-mail: masters@cwu.edu. *Dean,* Dr. Paul Ballard, 509-963-1411, E-mail: paul.ballard@cwu.edu.

College of the Sciences Expenses: Contact institution. *Financial support:* Application deadline: 3/1; applicants required to submit FAFSA. *Program availability:* Part-time, evening/weekend. Offers active and regional tectonics (MS); anthropology (MS); botany (MS); chemistry (MS); continental dynamics and seismology (MS); environmental geochemistry (MS); experimental psychology (MS); geography (MS); geomorphology (MS); geomorphology and climate change (MS); mental health counseling (MS); microbiology and parasitology (MS); paleohydrology and volcanology (MS); school psychology (Ed S); sciences (MS, Ed S); stream ecology and fisheries (MS); terrestrial ecology (MS). *Application deadline:* For fall admission, 2/1 priority date for domestic students. Applications are processed on a rolling basis. *Application fee:* $50. Electronic applications accepted. *Application Contact:* Justine Eason, Admissions Program Coordinator, 509-963-3103, Fax: 509-963-1799, E-mail: masters@cwu.edu. *Dean,* Dr. Tim Englund, 509-963-1866, E-mail: timothy.englund@cwu.edu.

CENTRAL YESHIVA TOMCHEI TMIMIM-LUBAVITCH, Brooklyn, NY 11230

General Information Independent-religious, men only, comprehensive institution.

GRADUATE UNITS

Graduate Programs Offers Jewish/Judaic studies (MA); Talmudic studies (MA).

CENTRO DE ESTUDIOS AVANZADOS DE PUERTO RICO Y EL CARIBE, Old San Juan, PR 00902-3970

General Information Independent, coed, graduate-only institution. *Graduate housing:* On-campus housing not available. *Research affiliation:* Museo de las Americas, Museo Hombre Dominicano, Archivo General, Museo Universidad del Turabo.

GRADUATE UNITS

Graduate Program in Puerto Rican and Caribbean Studies *Program availability:* Part-time, evening/weekend. Offers Puerto Rican and Caribbean history (MA, PhD); Puerto Rican and Caribbean literature (MA, PhD); Puerto Rican studies (MA).

CHADRON STATE COLLEGE, Chadron, NE 69337

General Information State-supported, coed, comprehensive institution. *Graduate housing:* Rooms and/or apartments available on a first-come, first-served basis to single and married students. Housing application deadline: 6/1.

GRADUATE UNITS

School of Professional and Graduate Studies *Program availability:* Part-time, evening/weekend, online learning. Offers business (MA Ed); business and economics (MBA); community counseling (MA Ed); educational administration (MS Ed, Sp Ed); elementary education (MS Ed); history (MA Ed); language and literature (MA Ed); secondary administration (MS Ed); secondary education (MS Ed). Electronic applications accepted.

CHAMINADE UNIVERSITY OF HONOLULU, Honolulu, HI 96816-1578

General Information Independent-religious, coed, comprehensive institution. *Enrollment:* 1,719 graduate, professional, and undergraduate students; 365 full-time matriculated graduate/professional students (250 women), 197 part-time matriculated graduate/professional students (141 women). *Enrollment by degree level:* 562 master's. *Graduate faculty:* 20 full-time (8 women), 36 part-time/adjunct (18 women). *Tuition:* Full-time $20,640; part-time $860 per credit hour. Tuition and fees vary according to course load, campus/location and program. *Graduate housing:* On-campus housing not available. *Student services:* Campus safety program, career counseling, free psychological counseling, international student services, services for students with disabilities, teacher training, writing training. *Library facilities:* Sullivan Library. *Collection:* Books: 47,508 (physical), 133,757 (digital/electronic); Serial titles: 142 (physical), 36,441 (digital/electronic); Databases: 99.

Computer facilities: 200 computers available on campus for general student use. A campuswide network can be accessed from student residence rooms and from off campus. Online class registration is available.
Website: http://www.chaminade.edu/

General Application Contact: 808-735-4755, E-mail: gradserv@chaminade.edu.

GRADUATE UNITS

Office of Professional and Continuing Education Students: 365 full-time (250 women), 197 part-time (141 women); includes 386 minority (32 Black or African American, non-Hispanic/Latino; 6 American Indian or Alaska Native, non-Hispanic/Latino; 166 Asian, non-Hispanic/Latino; 37 Hispanic/Latino; 138 Native Hawaiian or other Pacific Islander, non-Hispanic/Latino; 7 Two or more races, non-Hispanic/Latino), 14 international. Average age 33. 162 applicants, 96% accepted, 117 enrolled. *Faculty:* 20 full-time (8 women), 36 part-time/adjunct (18 women). Expenses: Contact institution. *Financial support:* Applicants required to submit FAFSA. In 2017, 249 master's awarded. *Program availability:* Part-time, evening/weekend, 100% online, blended/hybrid learning. Offers accounting (MBA); business (MBA); child development (M Ed); correctional (MSCJA); criminal justice (MSCJA); diaconate education (MPT); early childhood education (Montessori) (MAT); early childhood education (PK-3) (MAT); educational leadership (M Ed); elementary education (MAT); instructional leadership (M Ed); island business (MBA); law enforcement (MSCJA); marriage and family counseling (MSCP); mental health counseling (MSCP); Montessori (M Ed); not-for-profit (MBA); pastoral counseling and spiritual direction (MPT); school counseling (MSCP); secondary education (MAT); special education (MAT); teacher leader (M Ed). *Application deadline:* Applications are processed on a rolling basis. *Application fee:* $40. Electronic applications accepted.

CHAMPLAIN COLLEGE, Burlington, VT 05402-0670

General Information Independent, coed, comprehensive institution. *Graduate housing:* Rooms and/or apartments available on a first-come, first-served basis to single and married students.

GRADUATE UNITS

Graduate Studies *Program availability:* Part-time, online learning. Offers business (MBA); digital forensic science (MS); early childhood education (M Ed); emergent media (MFA, MS); executive leadership (MS); health care administration (MS); information security operations (MS); law (MS); mediation and applied conflict studies (MS). MS in emergent media program held in Shanghai. Electronic applications accepted.

CHAPMAN UNIVERSITY, Orange, CA 92866

General Information Independent-religious, coed, comprehensive institution. CGS member. *Enrollment:* 9,392 graduate, professional, and undergraduate students; 1,778 full-time matriculated graduate/professional students (1,044 women), 590 part-time matriculated graduate/professional students (357 women). *Enrollment by degree level:* 1,242 master's, 1,114 doctoral, 12 other advanced degrees. *Graduate faculty:* 345 full-time (145 women), 361 part-time/adjunct (156 women). *Graduate housing:* Rooms and/or apartments available on a first-come, first-served basis to single and married students. Housing application deadline: 6/1. *Student services:* Campus employment opportunities, campus safety program, career counseling, exercise/wellness program, free psychological counseling, grant writing training, international student services, low-cost health insurance, multicultural affairs office, services for students with disabilities, teacher training, writing training. *Library facilities:* Leatherby Libraries plus 1 other. *Collection:* Books: 339,051 (physical), 17,371 (digital/electronic); Serial titles: 267 (physical), 69,372 (digital/electronic); Databases: 287. Weekly public service hours: 127; students can reserve study rooms. *Research affiliation:* National Science Foundation (science, engineering), National Endowment for the Arts (NEA) (art), U.S. Department of Education (DOE) (education), U.S. Geological Survey (USGS) (earth sciences), U.S. Department of Agriculture (USDA) (agriculture, food, nutrition).

Computer facilities: Computer purchase and lease plans are available. A campuswide network can be accessed from student residence rooms and from off campus. Online class registration is available.
Website: http://www.chapman.edu/

General Application Contact: Eva Yen, Director of Graduate Admissions, 888-CU-APPLY, Fax: 714-997-6713, E-mail: eyen@chapman.edu.

GRADUATE UNITS

Crean College of Health and Behavioral Sciences Students: 283 full-time (189 women), 191 part-time (115 women); includes 228 minority (5 Black or African American, non-Hispanic/Latino; 124 Asian, non-Hispanic/Latino; 69 Hispanic/Latino; 30 Two or more races, non-Hispanic/Latino), 7 international. Average age 27. *Faculty:* 35 full-time (25 women), 9 part-time/adjunct (7 women). Expenses: Contact institution. *Financial support:* Application deadline: 3/2; applicants required to submit FAFSA. In 2017, 63 master's, 57 doctorates awarded. Offers athletic training (MS); communication sciences and disorders (MS); health and behavioral sciences (MA, MMS, MS, DPT, TDPT); marriage and family therapy (MA); physical therapy (DPT, TDPT); physician assistant studies (MMS). *Application fee:* $60. Electronic applications accepted. *Dean,* Dr. Janeen Hill, 714-628-7223, E-mail: jhill@chapman.edu.

Dale E. Fowler School of Law Students: 478 full-time (262 women), 37 part-time (24 women); includes 217 minority (9 Black or African American, non-Hispanic/Latino; 1 American Indian or Alaska Native, non-Hispanic/Latino; 69 Asian, non-Hispanic/Latino; 104 Hispanic/Latino; 34 Two or more races, non-Hispanic/Latino), 11 international. Average age 26. 1,499 applicants, 50% accepted, 190 enrolled. *Faculty:* 44 full-time (18 women), 34 part-time/adjunct (9 women). Expenses: Contact institution. *Financial support:* Fellowships, Federal Work-Study, and scholarships/grants available. Financial award applicants required to submit FAFSA. In 2017, 17 master's, 149 doctorates awarded. *Program availability:* Part-time. Offers advocacy and dispute resolution (JD); business law (LL M, JD); criminal law (JD); entertainment and media law (LL M); entertainment law (JD); environmental, land use, and real estate law (JD); international and comparative law (LL M); international law (JD); law (JD); prosecutorial science (LL M); tax law (JD); taxation (LL M); trial advocacy (LL M). *Application deadline:* For fall admission, 4/17 priority date for domestic students. Applications are processed on a rolling basis. Electronic applications accepted. *Application Contact:* Justin Cruz, Assistant Dean of Admissions and Diversity Initiatives, 714-628-2594, E-mail: lawadmission@chapman.edu. *Dean,* Matthew J. Parlow, 714-628-2678, E-mail: parlow@chapman.edu.

Dodge College of Film and Media Arts Students: 273 full-time (129 women), 1 part-time (0 women); includes 58 minority (14 Black or African American, non-Hispanic/Latino; 9 Asian, non-Hispanic/Latino; 21 Hispanic/Latino; 14 Two or more races, non-Hispanic/Latino), 127 international. Average age 26. 467 applicants, 50% accepted, 113 enrolled. *Faculty:* 49 full-time (13 women), 95 part-time/adjunct (31 women). Expenses: Contact institution. *Financial support:* Fellowships, Federal Work-Study, and scholarships/grants available. Financial award applicants required to submit FAFSA. In 2017, 82 master's awarded. Offers documentary filmmaking (MFA); film and television producing (MFA); film production (MFA); film studies (MA); production design (MFA); screenwriting (MFA); television writing and producing (MFA). *Application deadline:* For fall admission, 12/1 for domestic students. *Application fee:* $60. Electronic applications accepted. *Application Contact:* Lauren Kacura, Assistant Director of Admissions, 714-744-7856, E-mail: kacura@chapman.edu. *Dean,* Robert Bassett, 714-997-6715, E-mail: bassett@chapman.edu.

Donna Ford Attallah College of Educational Studies Students: 170 full-time (140 women), 180 part-time (129 women); includes 164 minority (6 Black or African American, non-Hispanic/Latino; 38 Asian, non-Hispanic/Latino; 101 Hispanic/Latino; 1 Native Hawaiian or other Pacific Islander, non-Hispanic/Latino; 18 Two or more races, non-Hispanic/Latino), 10 international. Average age 28. 143 applicants, 63% accepted, 64 enrolled. *Faculty:* 32 full-time (18 women), 37 part-time/adjunct (26 women). Expenses: Contact institution. *Financial support:* Fellowships and scholarships/grants available. Financial award application deadline: 3/2; financial award applicants required to submit FAFSA. In 2017, 126 master's, 18 doctorates awarded. *Program availability:* Part-time, evening/weekend. Offers counseling (MA); curriculum and instruction (MA); education (PhD); educational psychology (MA); leadership development (MA); multiple subjects (Credential); pupil personnel services (Credential); school psychology (Ed S); single subject (Credential); special education (MA, Credential); teaching (MA). *Application deadline:* Applications are processed on a rolling basis. *Application fee:* $60. Electronic applications accepted. *Application Contact:* Shannon McCance, Graduate Admission Counselor, 714-516-5236, E-mail: smccance@chapman.edu. *Dean,* Dr. Margaret Grogan, 714-516-5968, E-mail: grogan@chapman.edu.

The George L. Argyros School of Business and Economics Students: 180 full-time (87 women), 100 part-time (45 women); includes 86 minority (4 Black or African American, non-Hispanic/Latino; 1 American Indian or Alaska Native, non-Hispanic/Latino; 39 Asian, non-Hispanic/Latino; 28 Hispanic/Latino; 1 Native Hawaiian or other Pacific Islander, non-Hispanic/Latino; 13 Two or more races, non-Hispanic/Latino), 89 international. Average age 28. 250 applicants, 75% accepted, 94 enrolled. *Faculty:* 60 full-time (16 women), 46 part-time/adjunct (8 women). Expenses: Contact institution. *Financial support:* Fellowships, Federal Work-Study, and scholarships/grants available. Financial award applicants required to submit FAFSA. In 2017, 119 master's awarded. *Program availability:* Part-time, evening/weekend. Offers accounting (MS); behavioral and computational economics (MS); business administration (Exec MBA, MBA). *Application fee:* $60. Electronic applications accepted. *Application Contact:* Debra Gonda, Associate Dean, 714-997-6894, E-mail: gonda@chapman.edu. *Interim Dean,* Thomas Turk, 714-997-6819, E-mail: turk@chapman.edu.

Schmid College of Science and Technology Students: 52 full-time (23 women), 57 part-time (29 women); includes 41 minority (3 Black or African American, non-Hispanic/Latino; 16 Asian, non-Hispanic/Latino; 14 Hispanic/Latino; 8 Two or more races, non-Hispanic/Latino), 25 international. Average age 27. 104 applicants, 61% accepted, 43 enrolled. *Faculty:* 18 full-time (5 women), 40 part-time/adjunct (27 women). Expenses: Contact institution. In 2017, 25 master's awarded. *Program availability:* Part-time, evening/weekend. Offers computational and data sciences (MS, PhD); food science (MS); science and technology (MS, PhD). *Application fee:* $60. Electronic applications accepted. *Dean,* Dr. L. Andrew Lyon, 714-997-6730, E-mail: lyon@chapman.edu.

School of Communication Students: 6 full-time (all women), 3 part-time (2 women); includes 2 minority (1 Asian, non-Hispanic/Latino; 1 Hispanic/Latino), 2 international. Average age 24. 10 applicants, 100% accepted, 7 enrolled. *Faculty:* 18 full-time (12 women), 14 part-time/adjunct (7 women). Expenses: Contact institution. *Financial support:* Fellowships, research assistantships, Federal Work-Study, scholarships/grants, and unspecified assistantships available. Financial award applicants required to submit FAFSA. In 2017, 6 master's awarded. *Program availability:* Evening/weekend. Offers communication (MS). *Application deadline:* Applications are processed on a rolling basis. *Application fee:* $60. Electronic applications accepted. *Application Contact:* Shannon McCance, Admission Counselor, 714-997-6711, E-mail: smccance@chapman.edu. *Dean,* Dr. Lisa Sparks, 714-744-7088, E-mail: ditommas@chapman.edu.

School of Pharmacy Students: 290 full-time (177 women), 1 part-time (0 women); includes 192 minority (12 Black or African American, non-Hispanic/Latino; 1 American Indian or Alaska Native, non-Hispanic/Latino; 146 Asian, non-Hispanic/Latino; 24 Hispanic/Latino; 1 Native Hawaiian or other Pacific Islander, non-Hispanic/Latino; 8 Two or more races, non-Hispanic/Latino), 24 international. Average age 27. 725 applicants, 26% accepted, 107 enrolled. *Faculty:* 37 full-time (17 women), 7 part-time/adjunct (1 woman). Expenses: Contact institution. *Financial support:* Fellowships, research assistantships, Federal Work-Study, and scholarships/grants available. In 2017, 5 master's awarded. Offers pharmaceutical sciences (MS, PhD); pharmacy (Pharm D). *Application deadline:* Applications are processed on a rolling basis. Electronic applications accepted. *Application Contact:* Dr. Lawrence Brown, Associate Dean of Student and Academic Affairs, 714-516-5600, E-mail: pharmacyadmissions@chapman.edu. *Dean,* Ronald P. Jordan, 714-516-5486, E-mail: rpjordan@chapman.edu.

Wilkinson College of Arts, Humanities, and Social Sciences Students: 70 full-time (42 women), 25 part-time (15 women); includes 24 minority (3 Black or African American, non-Hispanic/Latino; 6 Asian, non-Hispanic/Latino; 13 Hispanic/Latino; 2 Two or more races, non-Hispanic/Latino), 7 international. Average age 30. 110 applicants, 87% accepted, 32 enrolled. *Faculty:* 32 full-time (14 women), 54 part-time/adjunct (32 women). Expenses: Contact institution. In 2017, 30 master's awarded. *Program availability:* Part-time, evening/weekend. Offers arts, humanities, and social sciences (MA, MFA); creative writing (MFA); English (MA); international studies (MA); war and society (MA). *Application fee:* $60. Electronic applications accepted. *Dean,* Dr. Patrick Fuery, 714-516-4580, E-mail: fuery@chapman.edu.

CHARLES R. DREW UNIVERSITY OF MEDICINE AND SCIENCE, Los Angeles, CA 90059

General Information Independent, coed, comprehensive institution. *Graduate housing:* On-campus housing not available.

GRADUATE UNITS

College of Science and Health

Professional Program in Medicine Offers medicine (MD).

CHARLESTON SCHOOL OF LAW, Charleston, SC 29403

General Information Proprietary, coed, graduate-only institution. *Enrollment by degree level:* 564 doctoral. *Graduate faculty:* 18 full-time (9 women), 58 part-time/adjunct (27 women). *Tuition:* Full-time $40,596; part-time $32,618 per year. *Required fees:* $942; $942 per unit. *Graduate housing:* On-campus housing not available. *Student services:* Campus employment opportunities, campus safety program, career counseling, free psychological counseling, services for students with disabilities, writing training. *Library facilities:* Sol Blatt Jr. Law Library. *Collection:* Books: 7,186 (physical), 301,765 (digital/electronic). Weekly public service hours: 105; students can reserve study rooms.

Computer facilities: A campuswide network can be accessed. Online class registration is available.
Website: http://www.charlestonlaw.edu/

General Application Contact: Jacqueline B. Bell, Assistant Dean of Admission, 843-377-2143, Fax: 843-329-4091, E-mail: info@charlestonlaw.edu.

GRADUATE UNITS

Graduate and Professional Programs Students: 514 full-time (275 women), 50 part-time (32 women). *Faculty:* 18 full-time (9 women), 58 part-time/adjunct (27 women). Expenses: Contact institution. *Financial support:* Scholarships/grants available. Offers law (JD). *Application deadline:* For fall admission, 6/1 for domestic students; for spring admission, 11/1 for domestic students. Applications are processed on a rolling basis. Electronic applications accepted. *Application Contact:* Jacqueline B. Bell, Assistant Dean of Admission, 843-377-2143, Fax: 843-329-4091, E-mail: info@charlestonlaw.edu.

CHARLESTON SOUTHERN UNIVERSITY, Charleston, SC 29423-8087

General Information Independent-religious, coed, comprehensive institution. *Enrollment:* 3,493 graduate, professional, and undergraduate students; 56 full-time matriculated graduate/professional students (35 women), 375 part-time matriculated graduate/professional students (225 women). *Enrollment by degree level:* 431 master's. *Graduate faculty:* 12 full-time (6 women), 10 part-time/adjunct (3 women). *Tuition:* Part-time $500 per credit hour. One-time fee: $30. Tuition and fees vary according to program. *Graduate housing:* On-campus housing not available. *Student services:* Campus employment opportunities, campus safety program, career counseling, free psychological counseling, international student services, services for students with disabilities, writing training. *Library facilities:* L. Mendel Rivers Library plus 1 other. *Collection:* Books: 117,095 (physical), 303,641 (digital/electronic); Serial titles: 4,761 (physical), 53,688 (digital/electronic); Databases: 177. Weekly public service hours: 83; students can reserve study rooms. *Research affiliation:* Waccamaw Regional Planning and Development Council (economic forecasting), Metro Charleston Chamber of Commerce (economic forecasting), Santee Lynches Council of Governments (economic forecasting).

Computer facilities: 250 computers available on campus for general student use. A campuswide network can be accessed from student residence rooms and from off campus. Online class registration, online course work are available.
Website: http://www.charlestonsouthern.edu/

General Application Contact: Janie Cogdill, Graduate Enrollment Counselor, 843-863-7050, Fax: 843-863-7070, E-mail: jcogdill@csuniv.edu.

GRADUATE UNITS

College of Business Expenses: Contact institution. *Financial support:* Research assistantships with full tuition reimbursements available. Financial award application deadline: 4/15; financial award applicants required to submit FAFSA. *Program availability:* Part-time, evening/weekend. Offers accounting (MBA); finance (MBA); general management (MBA); human resource management (MS); leadership (MBA); management information systems (MBA); organizational leadership (MA). *Application deadline:* Applications are processed on a rolling basis. *Application fee:* $40. Electronic applications accepted. *Application Contact:* Dr. Darin L. Gerdes, Associate Professor of Management, 843-863-7814, Fax: 843-863-7922, E-mail: dgerdes@csuniv.edu. *Dean*, Dr. David Palmer, 843-863-7025, Fax: 843-863-7922, E-mail: dpalmer@csuniv.edu.

College of Education Expenses: Contact institution. *Financial support:* Research assistantships with full tuition reimbursements, career-related internships or fieldwork, and Federal Work-Study available. Financial award application deadline: 4/15; financial award applicants required to submit FAFSA. *Program availability:* Part-time, evening/weekend. Offers elementary administration and supervision (M Ed); elementary education (M Ed); secondary administration and supervision (M Ed). *Application deadline:* Applications are processed on a rolling basis. *Application fee:* $40. Electronic applications accepted. *Dean*, Dr. George Metz, 843-863-7765, Fax: 843-863-7784, E-mail: gmetz@csuniv.edu.

Department of Criminal Justice Expenses: Contact institution. *Financial support:* Research assistantships with full tuition reimbursements available. Financial award application deadline: 4/15; financial award applicants required to submit FAFSA. *Program availability:* Part-time, evening/weekend, online learning. Offers criminal justice (MSCJ). *Application deadline:* Applications are processed on a rolling basis. *Application fee:* $40. Electronic applications accepted. *Interim Chair*, Gary Metts, 843-863-7330, Fax: 843-863-7198, E-mail: gmetts@csuniv.edu.

CHARLOTTE CHRISTIAN COLLEGE AND THEOLOGICAL SEMINARY, Charlotte, NC 28205

General Information Independent-religious, coed, comprehensive institution. *Enrollment:* 97 graduate, professional, and undergraduate students; 17 full-time matriculated graduate/professional students (8 women), 21 part-time matriculated graduate/professional students (11 women). *Graduate faculty:* 5 full-time (0 women), 6 part-time/adjunct (0 women). *Tuition:* Part-time $1278 per course. *Graduate housing:* On-campus housing not available. *Student services:* Campus employment opportunities, grant writing training, writing training. *Library facilities:* CCCTS Library. *Collection:* Books: 26,489 (physical), 1,100 (digital/electronic); Serial titles: 30 (physical). Weekly public service hours: 50.

Computer facilities: A campuswide network can be accessed from off campus. Online class registration, class syllabi are available.
Website: http://www.charlottechristian.edu/

General Application Contact: George Shears, Director of Admissions, 704-334-6882 Ext. 115, Fax: 704-334-6885, E-mail: gshears@charlottechristian.edu.

GRADUATE UNITS

Graduate Program Students: 17 full-time (8 women), 21 part-time (11 women); includes 31 minority (29 Black or African American, non-Hispanic/Latino; 1 Asian, non-Hispanic/Latino; 1 Two or more races, non-Hispanic/Latino), 2 international. Average age 48. 13 applicants, 100% accepted, 9 enrolled. *Faculty:* 5 full-time (0 women), 6 part-time/adjunct (0 women). Expenses: Contact institution. *Financial support:* In 2017–18, 2 students received support. Teaching assistantships, Federal Work-Study, and scholarships/grants available. Financial award application deadline: 4/1; financial award applicants required to submit FAFSA. In 2017, 2 master's awarded. *Program availability:* Part-time, evening/weekend. Offers Biblical studies (MA); chaplaincy (M Div); general pastoral studies (M Div); ministry (D Min); pastoral counseling (M Div); urban Christian ministry (MA). *Application deadline:* For fall admission, 8/3 for domestic and international students; for spring admission, 12/8 for domestic and international students; for summer admission, 4/7 for domestic and international students. *Application fee:* $50. Electronic applications accepted. *Application Contact:* George Shears, Director of Admissions, 704-334-6882 Ext. 115, Fax: 704-334-6885, E-mail: gshears@charlottechristian.edu. *President*, Dr. Eddie G. Grigg, 704-344-6882 Ext. 101, Fax: 704-334-6885, E-mail: egrigg@charlottechristian.edu.

CHARTER COLLEGE, Vancouver, WA 98683

General Information Proprietary, coed, comprehensive institution.

GRADUATE UNITS

Program in Business Administration *Program availability:* Online learning. Offers business administration (MBA).

CHARTER OAK STATE COLLEGE, New Britain, CT 06053-2142

General Information State-supported, coed, comprehensive institution. *Enrollment:* 1,500 graduate, professional, and undergraduate students; 6 full-time matriculated graduate/professional students (3 women), 78 part-time matriculated graduate/professional students (47 women). *Enrollment by degree level:* 84 master's. *Graduate faculty:* 7 part-time/adjunct (3 women). Tuition, state resident: full-time $8748; part-time $5832 per credit. Tuition, nonresident: full-time $9144; part-time $6096 per credit. *Required fees:* $401 per semester. Tuition and fees vary according to course load. *Graduate housing:* On-campus housing not available. *Student services:* Services for students with disabilities.

Computer facilities: A campuswide network can be accessed from off campus. Online class registration is available.
Website: http://www.charteroak.edu/

General Application Contact: Dr. Thomas Barron, Director of Organizatioinal Effectiveness and Leadership Program, 860-515-3838, E-mail: tbarron@charteroak.edu.

GRADUATE UNITS

Program in Organizational Effectiveness and Leadership Students: 6 full-time (3 women), 78 part-time (47 women); includes 29 minority (19 Black or African American, non-Hispanic/Latino; 3 Asian, non-Hispanic/Latino; 7 Hispanic/Latino). *Faculty:* 7 part-time/adjunct (3 women). Expenses: Contact institution. *Financial support:* Scholarships/grants available. Financial award applicants required to submit FAFSA. *Program availability:* Part-time, evening/weekend, online only, 100% online. Offers organizational effectiveness and leadership (MS). *Application deadline:* Applications are processed on a rolling basis. *Application fee:* $75. Electronic applications accepted. *Director of Organizational Effectiveness and Leadership Program*, Dr. Thomas Barron, 860-515-3838, E-mail: tbarron@charteroak.edu.

CHATHAM UNIVERSITY, Pittsburgh, PA 15232-2826

General Information Independent, coed, primarily women, university. CGS member. *Enrollment:* 2,269 graduate, professional, and undergraduate students; 731 full-time matriculated graduate/professional students (568 women), 315 part-time matriculated graduate/professional students (248 women). *Enrollment by degree level:* 686 master's, 360 doctoral. *Graduate faculty:* 91 full-time (67 women), 112 part-time/adjunct (86 women). *Tuition:* Full-time $16,740; part-time $930 per credit. *Required fees:* $486; $27 per credit. $243 per semester. *Graduate housing:* Rooms and/or apartments available on a first-come, first-served basis to single and married students. Typical cost: $5803 per year ($11,373 including board) for single students; $6833 per year ($12,403 including board) for married students. Housing application deadline: 3/26. *Student services:* Campus employment opportunities, campus safety program, career counseling, exercise/wellness program, free psychological counseling, international student services, low-cost health insurance, services for students with disabilities, teacher training, writing training. *Library facilities:* Jennie King Mellon Library. *Collection:* Books: 88,368 (physical), 1,200 (digital/electronic); Serial titles: 92 (physical), 32,874 (digital/electronic); Databases: 65. Weekly public service hours: 99; study areas open 24 hours, 5–7 days a week; students can reserve study rooms.

Computer facilities: Computer purchase and lease plans are available. 202 computers available on campus for general student use. A campuswide network can be accessed from student residence rooms and from off campus. Online class registration is available.
Website: http://www.chatham.edu/

General Application Contact: Monique Moreland, Assistant Director of Graduate Admission, 412-365-2989; Fax: 412-365-1609, E-mail: mmoreland@chatham.edu.

GRADUATE UNITS

Nursing Programs Students: 49 full-time (41 women), 95 part-time (80 women); includes 68 minority (51 Black or African American, non-Hispanic/Latino; 7 Asian, non-Hispanic/Latino; 8 Hispanic/Latino; 2 Two or more races, non-Hispanic/Latino), 11 international. Average age 42. 209 applicants, 51% accepted, 76 enrolled. *Faculty:* 12 full-time (all women), 12 part-time/adjunct (10 women). Expenses: Contact institution. *Financial support:* Application deadline: 8/1; applicants required to submit FAFSA. In 2017, 13 master's, 82 doctorates awarded. *Program availability:* Online learning. Offers education/leadership (MSN); nursing (DNP). *Application deadline:* For fall admission, 5/1 priority date for domestic and international students. Applications are processed on a rolling basis. *Application fee:* $35. Electronic applications accepted. *Application Contact:* Patricia Golla, Assistant Director of Graduate Admissions, 412-365-1386, Fax: 412-365-1720, E-mail: pgolla@chatham.edu. *Director*, Dr. Diane Hunker, 412-365-1738, E-mail: dhunker@chatham.edu.

Program in Accounting Students: 4 full-time (3 women), 12 part-time (7 women); includes 4 minority (1 Black or African American, non-Hispanic/Latino; 2 Asian, non-Hispanic/Latino; 1 Hispanic/Latino), 2 international. Average age 31. 13 applicants, 54% accepted, 6 enrolled. *Faculty:* 1 full-time (0 women), 1 part-time/adjunct (0 women). Expenses: Contact institution. *Financial support:* Applicants required to submit FAFSA.

In 2017, 10 master's awarded. *Program availability:* Part-time, evening/weekend. Offers accounting (M Acc, MAC). *Application deadline:* For fall admission, 4/1 for domestic and international students; for spring admission, 11/1 for domestic students, 10/1 for international students. Applications are processed on a rolling basis. *Application fee:* $45. Electronic applications accepted. *Application Contact:* 412-365-1141, Fax: 412-365-1609, E-mail: gradadmissions@chatham.edu. *Director of Business and Entrepreneurship Program,* Dr. Rachel Chung, 412-365-2433, E-mail: rchung@chatham.edu.

Program in Biology Students: 51 full-time (39 women), 9 part-time (6 women); includes 23 minority (10 Black or African American, non-Hispanic/Latino; 1 American Indian or Alaska Native, non-Hispanic/Latino; 9 Asian, non-Hispanic/Latino; 3 Hispanic/Latino), 5 international. Average age 25. 180 applicants, 60% accepted, 39 enrolled. *Faculty:* 1 full-time (0 women), 2 part-time/adjunct (1 woman). Expenses: Contact institution. *Financial support:* Applicants required to submit FAFSA. In 2017, 52 master's awarded. *Program availability:* Part-time. Offers environmental biology (MS); human biology (MS). *Application deadline:* For fall admission, 4/1 priority date for domestic and international students; for spring admission, 11/1 priority date for domestic students, 10/1 priority date for international students. Applications are processed on a rolling basis. *Application fee:* $45. Electronic applications accepted. *Application Contact:* Ashlee Bartko, Senior Assistant Director of Graduate Admission, 412-365-1115, Fax: 412-365-1609, E-mail: gradadmissions@chatham.edu. *Director,* Dr. Lisa Lambert, 412-365-1217, E-mail: lambert@chatham.edu.

Program in Business Administration Students: 19 full-time (12 women), 36 part-time (20 women); includes 8 minority (4 Black or African American, non-Hispanic/Latino; 3 Asian, non-Hispanic/Latino; 1 Hispanic/Latino), 5 international. Average age 31. 57 applicants, 56% accepted, 24 enrolled. *Faculty:* 6 part-time/adjunct (2 women). Expenses: Contact institution. *Financial support:* Applicants required to submit FAFSA. In 2017, 20 master's awarded. *Program availability:* Part-time, evening/weekend. Offers business administration (MBA); healthcare management (MBA); sustainability (MBA); women's leadership (MBA). *Application deadline:* For fall admission, 4/1 for domestic and international students; for spring admission, 11/1 for domestic students, 10/1 for international students. Applications are processed on a rolling basis. *Application fee:* $45. Electronic applications accepted. *Application Contact:* Katie Noel, Assistant Director of Graduate Admission, 412-365-2758, Fax: 412-365-1609, E-mail: gradadmissions@chatham.edu. *Director of Business and Entrepreneurship Program,* Dr. Rachel Chung, 412-365-2433.

Program in Communication Students: 4 full-time (1 woman), 9 part-time (all women); includes 1 minority (Black or African American, non-Hispanic/Latino), 1 international. Average age 28. 16 applicants, 50% accepted, 7 enrolled. *Faculty:* 3 part-time/adjunct (2 women). Expenses: Contact institution. *Financial support:* Applicants required to submit FAFSA. *Program availability:* Part-time, online learning. Offers environmental communication (M Comm); health communication (M Comm); strategic communication (M Comm). *Application deadline:* Applications are processed on a rolling basis. *Application fee:* $35. Electronic applications accepted. *Application Contact:* Athena Wintruba, Graduate Admission Recruiter, 412-365-1141, E-mail: awintruba@chatham.edu.

Program in Counseling Psychology Students: 61 full-time (46 women), 25 part-time (22 women); includes 12 minority (9 Black or African American, non-Hispanic/Latino; 2 Hispanic/Latino; 1 Two or more races, non-Hispanic/Latino), 3 international. Average age 30. 124 applicants, 62% accepted, 45 enrolled. *Faculty:* 11 full-time (10 women). Expenses: Contact institution. *Financial support:* Career-related internships or fieldwork available. Financial award applicants required to submit FAFSA. In 2017, 38 master's awarded. *Program availability:* Part-time, evening/weekend. Offers child, adolescent and family (MSCP); counseling psychology (Psy D); health and holistic (MSCP); organization and supervision (MSCP); sport and exercise (MSCP). *Application deadline:* For fall admission, 4/1 priority date for domestic and international students; for spring admission, 11/1 for domestic students, 10/1 for international students. Applications are processed on a rolling basis. *Application fee:* $45. Electronic applications accepted. *Application Contact:* Katie Noel, Assistant Director of Graduate Admission, 412-365-2758, Fax: 412-365-1609, E-mail: gradadmissions@chatham.edu. *Director,* Dr. Mary Beth Mannarino, 412-365-1196, Fax: 412-365-1505, E-mail: mmannarino@chatham.edu.

Program in Education Students: 31 full-time (23 women), 3 part-time (1 woman); includes 9 minority (8 Black or African American, non-Hispanic/Latino; 1 Hispanic/Latino). Average age 30. 25 applicants, 60% accepted, 9 enrolled. *Faculty:* 1 (woman) full-time, 15 part-time/adjunct (13 women). Expenses: Contact institution. *Financial support:* Career-related internships or fieldwork available. Financial award applicants required to submit FAFSA. In 2017, 23 master's awarded. Offers early childhood education (MAT); elementary education (MAT); environmental education (K-12) (MAT); secondary art (MAT); secondary biology education (MAT); secondary chemistry education (MAT); secondary English education (MAT); secondary math education (MAT); secondary physics education (MAT); secondary social studies education (MAT); special education (MAT). *Application deadline:* For fall admission, 4/1 priority date for domestic and international students; for spring admission, 11/1 priority date for domestic students, 10/1 priority date for international students. Applications are processed on a rolling basis. *Application fee:* $45. Electronic applications accepted. *Application Contact:* Katie Noel, Assistant Director of Graduate Admission, 412-365-2758, Fax: 412-365-1609, E-mail: gradadmissions@chatham.edu.

Program in Film and Digital Technology Students: 7 full-time (3 women), 1 (woman) part-time; includes 3 minority (all Black or African American, non-Hispanic/Latino), 2 international. Average age 28. 10 applicants, 60% accepted, 5 enrolled. *Faculty:* 3 full-time (2 women), 2 part-time/adjunct (1 woman). Expenses: Contact institution. *Financial support:* Applicants required to submit FAFSA. In 2017, 4 master's awarded. *Program availability:* Part-time, evening/weekend. Offers film and digital technology (MFA). *Application deadline:* For fall admission, 4/1 priority date for domestic and international students; for spring admission, 11/1 priority date for domestic students, 10/1 priority date for international students. Applications are processed on a rolling basis. *Application fee:* $45. Electronic applications accepted. *Application Contact:* Katie Noel, Assistant Director of Graduate Admission, 412-365-2758, Fax: 412-365-1609, E-mail: gradadmissions@chatham.edu. *Director,* Dr. Prajna Parasher, 412-365-1182, E-mail: parasher@chatham.edu.

Program in Healthcare Informatics Students: 11 part-time (9 women); includes 4 minority (all Black or African American, non-Hispanic/Latino). Average age 36. 18 applicants, 33% accepted, 6 enrolled. *Faculty:* 2 part-time/adjunct (1 woman). Expenses: Contact institution. *Financial support:* Applicants required to submit FAFSA. *Program availability:* Online learning. Offers healthcare informatics (MHI). *Application fee:* $45. *Application Contact:* Monique Moreland, Assistant Director of Graduate Admissions, 412-365-2989, E-mail: mmoreland@chatham.edu. *Coordinator,* Dr. Debra M. Wolf, RN, E-mail: dwolf@chatham.edu.

Program in Interior Architecture Students: 19 full-time (18 women), 5 part-time (all women); includes 2 minority (1 Black or African American, non-Hispanic/Latino; 1 Asian, non-Hispanic/Latino), 5 international. Average age 31. 32 applicants, 53% accepted, 11 enrolled. *Faculty:* 1 (woman) full-time, 5 part-time/adjunct (2 women). Expenses: Contact institution. *Financial support:* Applicants required to submit FAFSA. In 2017, 14 master's awarded. *Program availability:* Part-time, evening/weekend, online learning. Offers interior architecture (MIA). *Application deadline:* For fall admission, 4/1 priority date for domestic and international students; for spring admission, 11/1 priority date for domestic students, 10/1 priority date for international students. Applications are processed on a rolling basis. *Application fee:* $45. Electronic applications accepted. *Director,* Dr. Thelma Lazo-Flores, 412-365-2977, E-mail: tlazoflores@chatham.edu.

Program in Occupational Therapy Students: 100 full-time (91 women), 30 part-time (28 women); includes 11 minority (7 Black or African American, non-Hispanic/Latino; 2 Hispanic/Latino; 2 Two or more races, non-Hispanic/Latino). Average age 31. 501 applicants, 23% accepted, 65 enrolled. *Faculty:* 7 full-time (all women), 11 part-time/adjunct (all women). Expenses: Contact institution. *Financial support:* Applicants required to submit FAFSA. In 2017, 40 master's, 35 doctorates awarded. Offers occupational therapy (MOT, OTD). *Application deadline:* For fall admission, 12/5 priority date for domestic and international students. Applications are processed on a rolling basis. *Application fee:* $45. Electronic applications accepted. *Application Contact:* Ashlee Bartko, Senior Assistant Director of Graduate Admission, 412-365-1115, Fax: 412-365-1609, E-mail: gradadmissions@chatham.edu. *Director,* Dr. Joyce Salls, 412-365-1177, E-mail: salls@chatham.edu.

Program in Physical Therapy Students: 114 full-time (76 women), 1 part-time (0 women); includes 8 minority (1 Black or African American, non-Hispanic/Latino; 4 Asian, non-Hispanic/Latino; 3 Hispanic/Latino). Average age 25. 415 applicants, 21% accepted, 40 enrolled. *Faculty:* 8 full-time (5 women), 3 part-time/adjunct (2 women). Expenses: Contact institution. *Financial support:* Career-related internships or fieldwork available. Financial award applicants required to submit FAFSA. In 2017, 41 doctorates awarded. Offers physical therapy (DPT, TDPT). *Application deadline:* For fall admission, 12/1 priority date for domestic and international students. *Application fee:* $45. Electronic applications accepted. *Application Contact:* Ashlee Bartko, Senior Assistant Director of Graduate Admission, 412-365-2988, Fax: 412-365-1609, E-mail: gradadmissions@chatham.edu. *Director,* Dr. Patricia Downey, 412-365-1199, Fax: 412-365-1505, E-mail: downey@chatham.edu.

Program in Physician Assistant Studies Students: 135 full-time (112 women); includes 14 minority (1 Black or African American, non-Hispanic/Latino; 3 Asian, non-Hispanic/Latino; 6 Hispanic/Latino; 4 Two or more races, non-Hispanic/Latino). Average age 25. 723 applicants, 15% accepted, 73 enrolled. *Faculty:* 8 full-time (all women), 16 part-time/adjunct (15 women). Expenses: Contact institution. *Financial support:* Career-related internships or fieldwork available. Financial award applicants required to submit FAFSA. In 2017, 67 master's awarded. Offers physician assistant studies (MPAS). *Application deadline:* For fall admission, 10/1 priority date for domestic and international students. *Application fee:* $45. Electronic applications accepted. *Application Contact:* Maureen Stokan, Assistant Director of Graduate Admission, 412-365-2988, Fax: 412-365-1609, E-mail: gradadmissions@chatham.edu. *Director,* Carl Garrubba, 412-365-1425, Fax: 412-365-1213, E-mail: cgarrubba@chatham.edu.

Program in Writing Students: 36 full-time (26 women), 36 part-time (28 women); includes 12 minority (7 Black or African American, non-Hispanic/Latino; 4 Hispanic/Latino; 1 Two or more races, non-Hispanic/Latino). Average age 32. 90 applicants, 80% accepted, 30 enrolled. *Faculty:* 14 part-time/adjunct (11 women). Expenses: Contact institution. *Financial support:* Career-related internships or fieldwork available. Financial award applicants required to submit FAFSA. In 2017, 36 master's awarded. *Program availability:* Part-time, evening/weekend, online learning. Offers children's writing (MFA); fiction (MFA); non-fiction (MFA); poetry (MFA); professional writing (MPW); screenwriting (MFA). *Application deadline:* For fall admission, 1/15 priority date for domestic and international students; for spring admission, 11/1 priority date for domestic students, 10/1 priority date for international students. Applications are processed on a rolling basis. *Application fee:* $45. Electronic applications accepted. *Application Contact:* Katie Noel, Assistant Director of Graduate Admission, 412-365-2758, Fax: 412-365-1609, E-mail: gradadmissions@chatham.edu. *Director,* Dr. Sheryl St. Germain, 412-365-1190, Fax: 412-365-1505, E-mail: sstgermain@chatham.edu.

CHESTNUT HILL COLLEGE, Philadelphia, PA 19118-2693

General Information Independent-religious, coed, comprehensive institution. *Graduate housing:* On-campus housing not available.

GRADUATE UNITS

School of Graduate Studies *Program availability:* Part-time, evening/weekend. Offers administration of human services (MS, CAS); early education (M Ed); educational leadership (M Ed); elementary/middle education (M Ed); instructional technology (MS, CAS); reading (M Ed); reading specialist (M Ed); secondary education (M Ed); special education (M Ed). Electronic applications accepted.

Division of Psychology *Program availability:* Part-time, evening/weekend. Offers clinical and counseling psychology (MS, CAS); clinical psychology (Psy D).

CHEYNEY UNIVERSITY OF PENNSYLVANIA, Cheyney, PA 19319

General Information State-supported, coed, comprehensive institution. *Graduate housing:* On-campus housing not available.

GRADUATE UNITS

Graduate Programs *Program availability:* Part-time, evening/weekend. Offers educational leadership (M Ed, Certificate); elementary education (M Ed); principal certification (Certificate); public administration (MPA); special education (M Ed); urban education (M Ed). Electronic applications accepted.

THE CHICAGO SCHOOL OF PROFESSIONAL PSYCHOLOGY, Chicago, IL 60610

General Information Independent, coed, primarily women, graduate-only institution. CGS member. *Graduate housing:* On-campus housing not available.

GRADUATE UNITS

Program in Applied Behavior Analysis Offers applied behavior analysis (MS, PhD).

Program in Business Psychology Offers business psychology (PhD); industrial and organizational business psychology (Psy D); industrial and organizational psychology (MA); organizational leadership (MA, PhD).

Program in Clinical Forensic Psychology Offers clinical forensic psychology (Psy D).

Program in Clinical Mental Health Counseling *Program availability:* Part-time. Offers clinical mental health counseling (MA).

Program in Clinical Psychology Offers clinical psychology (Psy D). Electronic applications accepted.

Program in Forensic Psychology Offers forensic psychology (MA).

Program in Industrial and Organizational Psychology *Program availability:* Part-time, evening/weekend. Offers business psychology (Psy D); industrial and organizational psychology (MA).

Program in School Psychology *Program availability:* Part-time. Offers school psychology (Ed D, Psy D, Ed S).

THE CHICAGO SCHOOL OF PROFESSIONAL PSYCHOLOGY AT DOWNTOWN LOS ANGELES, Los Angeles, CA 90017

General Information Independent, coed, graduate-only institution.

GRADUATE UNITS

Program in Applied Behavior Analysis Offers applied behavior analysis (Psy D).

Program in Clinical Forensic Psychology Offers clinical forensic psychology (Psy D).

Program in Clinical Psychology Offers applied behavior analysis (MA); clinical psychology (Psy D); marital and family therapy (MA).

Program in Industrial and Organizational Psychology Offers industrial and organizational psychology (MA).

THE CHICAGO SCHOOL OF PROFESSIONAL PSYCHOLOGY AT IRVINE, Irvine, CA 92612

General Information Independent, coed, graduate-only institution.

GRADUATE UNITS

Program in Clinical Forensic Psychology Offers clinical forensic psychology (Psy D).

Program in Marital and Family Therapy Offers clinical psychology (MA); management practice (Psy D); psychodynamic psychotherapy (Psy D).

Program in Psychology Offers generalist (Psy D); psychodynamic psychotherapy (Psy D).

THE CHICAGO SCHOOL OF PROFESSIONAL PSYCHOLOGY AT WASHINGTON DC, Washington, DC 20005

General Information Independent, coed.

GRADUATE UNITS

Program in School Psychology *Program availability:* Part-time. Offers school psychology (Ed S).

THE CHICAGO SCHOOL OF PROFESSIONAL PSYCHOLOGY: ONLINE, Chicago, IL 60654

General Information Independent, coed, graduate-only institution. *Graduate housing:* On-campus housing not available.

GRADUATE UNITS

PhD Program in Organizational Leadership Offers organizational leadership (PhD).

Program in Applied Industrial and Organizational Psychology Offers applied industrial and organizational psychology (MA, Certificate).

Program in Clinical Psychopharmacology *Program availability:* Online learning. Offers clinical psychopharmacology (MS).

Program in Forensic Psychology Offers forensic psychology (MA, Certificate).

Program in Health Services Administration *Program availability:* Online learning. Offers health services administration (MHSA).

Program in International Psychology Offers international psychology (PhD).

Program in Psychology Offers child and adolescent psychology (MA); generalist (MA); gerontology (MA); international psychology (MA); organizational leadership (MA); sport and exercise psychology (MA).

CHICAGO STATE UNIVERSITY, Chicago, IL 60628

General Information State-supported, coed, comprehensive institution. *Graduate housing:* Room and/or apartments available on a first-come, first-served basis to single students; on-campus housing not available to married students. *Student services:* Campus employment opportunities, career counseling, child daycare facilities, free psychological counseling, international student services, low-cost health insurance, services for students with disabilities, teacher training, writing training. *Library facilities:* New Academic Library.

Computer facilities: Computer purchase and lease plans are available. 75 computers available on campus for general student use. A campuswide network can be accessed from student residence rooms and from off campus. Online class registration is available.
Website: http://www.csu.edu/

General Application Contact: Stephen Powenski, Interim Director of Admissions, 773-995-3526, Fax: 773-995-3671, E-mail: g-studies1@csu.edu.

GRADUATE UNITS

College of Pharmacy Expenses: Contact institution. Offers pharmacy (Pharm D). *Application deadline:* For fall admission, 2/3 for domestic students. *Application fee:* $50. *Application Contact:* Daphne G. Townsend, Admissions and Records Officer II, 773-995-2404, Fax: 773-995-3671, E-mail: g-studies1@csu.edu. *Interim Dean*, Carmita A. Coleman, E-mail: ccolem30@csu.edu.

School of Graduate and Professional Studies Expenses: Contact institution. *Financial support:* Applicants required to submit FAFSA. *Program availability:* Part-time, evening/weekend. *Application deadline:* For fall admission, 3/15 for domestic students; for spring admission, 10/15 for domestic students. Applications are processed on a rolling basis. *Application fee:* $25. Electronic applications accepted. *Application Contact:* Daphne G. Townsend, Admissions and Records Officer II, 773-995-2404, Fax: 773-995-3671, E-mail: g-studies1@csu.edu. *Dean of Graduate Studies*, Dr. Ellen F. Rosen, 773-995-2404, Fax: 773-995-3671, E-mail: ef-rosen@csu.edu.

College of Arts and Sciences Expenses: Contact institution. *Program availability:* Part-time, evening/weekend. Offers arts and sciences (MA, MFA, MS, MSW); biological sciences (MS); computer science (MS); counseling (MA); creative writing (MFA); criminal justice (MS); English (MA); geographic information systems (MA); history (MA); mathematics (MS); social work (MSW). *Application Contact:* Anika Miller, Graduate Studies Office, 773-995-2404, E-mail: g-studies1@csu.edu. *Interim Dean*, David Kanis, 773-995-2339, Fax: 773-995-3767, E-mail: dkanis@csu.edu.

College of Education Expenses: Contact institution. *Program availability:* Part-time. Offers bilingual education (MS Ed); curriculum and instruction (MS Ed); early childhood education (MAT, MS Ed); education (M Ed, MA, MAT, MS Ed, Ed D); educational leadership (MA, Ed D); elementary education (MAT); higher education administration (MA); instructional foundations (MS Ed); library science (MS); middle school education (MAT); physical education (MS Ed); principal preparation (MA); reading (MS Ed); special education (MS Ed); teaching of reading (MS Ed); technology and performance improvement studies (MS). *Application deadline:* For fall admission, 7/1 for domestic students; for spring admission, 11/10 for domestic students. *Application fee:* $25. *Application Contact:* Daphne G. Townsend, Admissions and Records Officer II, 773-995-2404, Fax: 773-995-3671, E-mail: g-studies1@csu.edu. *Acting Dean*, Dr. Sandra Westbrooks, 773-995-2472, Fax: 773-995-2473.

College of Health Sciences Expenses: Contact institution. Offers health sciences (MOT, MPH, MSN); nursing (MSN); occupational therapy (MOT); public health (MPH). *Application Contact:* Daphne G. Townsend, Admissions and Records Officer II, 773-995-2404, Fax: 773-995-3671, E-mail: g-studies1@csu.edu. *Dean*, Leslie K. Roundtree, 773-995-2525, E-mail: lroundtr@csu.edu.

CHICAGO THEOLOGICAL SEMINARY, Chicago, IL 60637-1507

General Information Independent-religious, coed, graduate-only institution. *Graduate housing:* On-campus housing not available.

GRADUATE UNITS

Graduate and Professional Programs *Program availability:* Part-time. Offers Bible, culture and hermeneutics (PhD); preaching (D Min); religion and health (D Min); religious studies (MA); spirituality and spiritual direction (D Min); theology (M Div); theology, ethics and the human sciences (PhD).

CHOWAN UNIVERSITY, Murfreesboro, NC 27855

General Information Independent-religious, coed, comprehensive institution. *Tuition:* Part-time $400 per hour. *Graduate housing:* Room and/or apartments available to single students; on-campus housing not available to married students. *Student services:* Campus employment opportunities, campus safety program, career counseling, exercise/wellness program, free psychological counseling, international student services, low-cost health insurance, multicultural affairs office, services for students with disabilities, teacher training, writing training. *Library facilities:* Whitaker Library plus 1 other. *Collection:* Books: 163,497 (physical), 405,678 (digital/electronic); Serial titles: 1,310 (physical), 69,556 (digital/electronic); Databases: 135. Weekly public service hours: 84; students can reserve study rooms.

Computer facilities: Computer purchase and lease plans are available. 251 computers available on campus for general student use. A campuswide network can be accessed from student residence rooms. Online class registration is available.
Website: http://www.chowan.edu/

GRADUATE UNITS

School of Graduate Studies Expenses: Contact institution. Offers education (M Ed). *Application fee:* $50. Electronic applications accepted. *Application Contact:* Crystal Powell, Assistant Director of Graduate Admission, 252-398-6214, E-mail: powellcc@chowan.edu. *Dean*, Dr. John Dilustro, 252-398-6528, E-mail: dilusj@chowan.edu.

CHRISTENDOM COLLEGE, Front Royal, VA 22630-5103

General Information Independent-religious, coed, comprehensive institution. *Tuition:* Part-time $390 per credit. Part-time tuition and fees vary according to program. *Graduate housing:* On-campus housing not available. *Student services:* Campus employment opportunities, campus safety program. *Library facilities:* St. John the Evangelist Library. *Collection:* Books: 100,000 (physical), 1,000 (digital/electronic); Serial titles: 250 (physical), 1,000 (digital/electronic); Databases: 45. Weekly public service hours: 97.

Computer facilities: A campuswide network can be accessed.
Website: http://www.christendom.edu/

General Application Contact: Sam Phillips, Director of Admissions, 703-658-4304, E-mail: graduate.school@christendom.edu.

GRADUATE UNITS

Graduate School of Theology Expenses: Contact institution. *Program availability:* Part-time, evening/weekend, 100% online, blended/hybrid learning. Offers theological studies (MA). *Application deadline:* For fall admission, 6/1 priority date for domestic students; for spring admission, 11/1 priority date for domestic students. Applications are processed on a rolling basis. *Application fee:* $100. Electronic applications accepted. *Application Contact:* Sam Phillips, Director of Admissions, 703-658-4304, E-mail: graduate.school@christendom.edu. *Dean*, Dr. Robert J. Matava, 703-658-4304.

CHRISTIAN BROTHERS UNIVERSITY, Memphis, TN 38104-5581

General Information Independent-religious, coed, comprehensive institution. *Graduate housing:* On-campus housing not available.

GRADUATE UNITS

School of Arts *Program availability:* Part-time, evening/weekend. Offers Catholic studies (MACS); educational leadership (MSEL); teacher-leadership (M Ed); teaching (MAT).

School of Business *Program availability:* Part-time, evening/weekend. Offers accountancy (M Acc); business (MBA); international business (MIB); project management (Certificate).

School of Engineering *Program availability:* Part-time, evening/weekend, online learning. Offers engineering (MEM, MSEM).

School of Sciences Offers physician assistant studies (MS).

CHRISTIAN THEOLOGICAL SEMINARY, Indianapolis, IN 46208-3301

General Information Independent-religious, coed, graduate-only institution. *Graduate housing:* Rooms and/or apartments available on a first-come, first-served basis to single and married students.

GRADUATE UNITS

Graduate and Professional Programs *Program availability:* Part-time. Offers educational and arts ministries (MA); marriage and family therapy (MA); pastoral care and counseling (D Min); psychotherapy and faith (MA); theological studies (MTS); theology (M Div). Electronic applications accepted.

CHRISTIE'S EDUCATION, New York, NY 10020

General Information Proprietary, coed, primarily women, graduate-only institution. *Enrollment by degree level:* 41 master's, 9 other advanced degrees. *Graduate faculty:* 6 full-time (4 women). *Graduate housing:* On-campus housing not available. *Student services:* Campus employment opportunities, career counseling, international student services, services for students with disabilities, writing training. *Library facilities:* Christie's Education Library. *Collection:* Books: 6,000 (physical); Databases: 20.

Computer facilities: 11 computers available on campus for general student use.
Website: http://www.christies.edu/

General Application Contact: Hilary Smith, Recruitment and Admissions Officer, 212-355-1501 Ext. 3309, Fax: 212-355-7370, E-mail: hsmith@christies.edu.

GRADUATE UNITS

Certificate Program in Art Business Expenses: Contact institution. Offers art business (Certificate). *Application deadline:* Applications are processed on a rolling basis. Electronic applications accepted. *Application Contact:* Catherine Warden, Academic Coordinator, 212-355-1501, Fax: 212-355-7370, E-mail: shortcoursesus@christies.edu. *Director of Continuing Education*, Dr. Marisa Kayyem, 212-355-1501, Fax: 212-355-7370, E-mail: mkayyem@christies.edu.

Certificate Program in Modern and Contemporary Art in New York Students: 9. *Faculty:* 4 full-time (3 women). Expenses: Contact institution. *Program availability:* Part-time. Offers modern and contemporary art (Certificate). *Application deadline:* Applications are processed on a rolling basis. *Application fee:* $95. *Application Contact:* Hilary Smith, Recruitment and Admissions Officer, 212-355-1501 Ext. 3309, Fax: 212-355-7370, E-mail: hsmith@christies.edu. *Program Director*, Dr. Julie Reiss, 212-355-1501 Ext. 3307, E-mail: jreiss@christies.edu.

MA Program in Art, Law and Business Students: 17 full-time (15 women). *Faculty:* 3 full-time (2 women). Expenses: Contact institution. *Financial support:* In 2017–18, 1 student received support. Scholarships/grants and unspecified assistantships available. Financial award applicants required to submit FAFSA. In 2017, 13 master's awarded. Offers art, law and business (MA). *Application deadline:* For fall admission, 1/12 priority date for domestic and international students. Applications are processed on a rolling basis. *Application fee:* $95. *Application Contact:* Hilary Smith, Recruitment and Admissions Officer, 212-355-1501 Ext. 3309, Fax: 212-355-7370, E-mail: hsmith@christies.edu. *Program Director*, Noah Kupferman, 212-355-1501 Ext. 7101, E-mail: nkupferman@christies.edu.

MA Program in Modern and Contemporary Art and the Market Students: 23 full-time (21 women), 1 (woman) part-time. *Faculty:* 4 full-time (3 women). Expenses: Contact institution. *Financial support:* In 2017–18, 3 students received support. Scholarships/grants and unspecified assistantships available. Financial award applicants required to submit FAFSA. In 2017, 25 master's awarded. *Program availability:* Part-time. Offers modern and contemporary art and the market (MA). *Application deadline:* For fall admission, 1/12 priority date for domestic and international students. Applications are processed on a rolling basis. *Application fee:* $95. *Application Contact:* Hilary Smith, Recruitment and Admissions Officer, 212-355-1501 Ext. 3309, Fax: 212-355-7370, E-mail: hsmith@christies.edu. *Program Director*, Dr. Julie Reiss, 212-355-1501 Ext. 3307, Fax: 212-355-7370, E-mail: jreiss@christies.edu.

CHRISTOPHER NEWPORT UNIVERSITY, Newport News, VA 23606-3072

General Information State-supported, coed, comprehensive institution. *Enrollment:* 5,081 graduate, professional, and undergraduate students; 99 full-time matriculated graduate/professional students (73 women), 26 part-time matriculated graduate/professional students (7 women). *Enrollment by degree level:* 125 master's. *Graduate faculty:* 28 full-time (8 women), 16 part-time/adjunct (14 women). Tuition, state resident: full-time $6984; part-time $388 per credit hour. Tuition, nonresident: full-time $15,588; part-time $866 per credit hour. *Required fees:* $3906; $225 per credit hour. Tuition and fees vary according to course load. *Graduate housing:* On-campus housing not available. *Student services:* Campus employment opportunities, campus safety program, career counseling, exercise/wellness program, free psychological counseling, grant writing training, multicultural affairs office, services for students with disabilities, writing training. *Library facilities:* Paul and Rosemary Trible Library. *Collection:* Books: 229,577 (physical), 578,114 (digital/electronic); Serial titles: 745 (physical), 65,202 (digital/electronic); Databases: 282. Weekly public service hours: 101; study areas open 24 hours, 5–7 days a week; students can reserve study rooms. *Research affiliation:* Thomas Jefferson National Accelerator Facility (instrument and nuclear physics), Langley Research Center, Center for Distance Learning (flow visualization), National Science Foundation (science).

Computer facilities: 540 computers available on campus for general student use. A campuswide network can be accessed from student residence rooms and from off campus. Online class registration is available.
Website: http://www.cnu.edu/

General Application Contact: Lyn Sawyer, Associate Director, Graduate Admissions, 757-594-7544, Fax: 757-594-7649, E-mail: gradstdy@cnu.edu.

GRADUATE UNITS

Graduate Studies Students: 99 full-time (73 women), 26 part-time (7 women); includes 7 minority (1 American Indian or Alaska Native, non-Hispanic/Latino; 2 Asian, non-Hispanic/Latino; 1 Hispanic/Latino; 3 Two or more races, non-Hispanic/Latino), 2 international. Average age 23. 118 applicants, 92% accepted, 95 enrolled. *Faculty:* 28 full-time (8 women), 16 part-time/adjunct (14 women). Expenses: Contact institution. *Financial support:* In 2017–18, 13 students received support, including 9 research assistantships with full tuition reimbursements available (averaging $2,000 per year), 3 teaching assistantships (averaging $1,000 per year); scholarships/grants and unspecified assistantships also available. Financial award application deadline: 3/1; financial award applicants required to submit FAFSA. In 2017, 86 master's awarded. *Program availability:* Part-time. Offers applied physics and computer science (MS); environmental science (MS); teacher preparation (MAT). *Application deadline:* For fall admission, 7/15 for domestic students, 3/1 for international students; for spring admission, 10/15 for domestic students, 10/1 for international students; for summer admission, 12/1 for domestic and international students. Applications are processed on a rolling basis. *Application fee:* $65. Electronic applications accepted. *Application Contact:* Lyn Sawyer, Associate Director, Graduate Admissions and Records, 757-594-7544, Fax: 757-594-7649, E-mail: gradstdy@cnu.edu. *Vice Provost for Research, Graduate Studies and Assessment*, Dr. Geoffrey C. Klein, 757-594-7477, E-mail: geoffrey.klein@cnu.edu.

CHRIST THE KING SEMINARY, East Aurora, NY 14052

General Information Independent-religious, coed, graduate-only institution. *Graduate housing:* On-campus housing not available.

GRADUATE UNITS

Graduate and Professional Programs *Program availability:* Part-time, evening/weekend. Offers divinity (M Div); pastoral ministry (MA); theology (MA).

CHURCH DIVINITY SCHOOL OF THE PACIFIC, Berkeley, CA 94709-1217

General Information Independent-religious, coed, graduate-only institution. *Graduate housing:* Rooms and/or apartments available on a first-come, first-served basis to single and married students. Housing application deadline: 5/1.

GRADUATE UNITS

Graduate and Professional Programs *Program availability:* Part-time. Offers theology (M Div, MA, MTS, D Min, Certificate). MA program offered jointly with Graduate Theological Union. Electronic applications accepted.

CINCINNATI CHRISTIAN UNIVERSITY, Cincinnati, OH 45204-3200

General Information Independent-religious, coed, comprehensive institution. *Graduate housing:* On-campus housing not available.

GRADUATE UNITS

Graduate School *Program availability:* Part-time. Offers biblical studies (MA); church history (MA); counseling (MAC); divinity (M Div); ministry (M Min); practical ministries (MA); theological studies (MA). Electronic applications accepted.

THE CITADEL, THE MILITARY COLLEGE OF SOUTH CAROLINA, Charleston, SC 29409

General Information State-supported, coed, primarily men, comprehensive institution. *Enrollment:* 3,717 graduate, professional, and undergraduate students; 194 full-time matriculated graduate/professional students (110 women), 686 part-time matriculated graduate/professional students (366 women). *Enrollment by degree level:* 831 master's, 49 other advanced degrees. *Graduate faculty:* 74 full-time (22 women), 20 part-time/adjunct (6 women). Tuition, state resident: part-time $587 per credit hour. Tuition, nonresident: part-time $988 per credit hour. *Required fees:* $90 per term. *Graduate housing:* On-campus housing not available. *Student services:* Campus employment opportunities, career counseling, exercise/wellness program, free psychological counseling, international student services, low-cost health insurance, multicultural affairs office, services for students with disabilities, teacher training, writing training. *Library facilities:* Daniel Library. *Collection:* Books: 182,744 (physical), 225,852 (digital/electronic); Serial titles: 97 (physical); Databases: 250. Students can reserve study rooms.

Computer facilities: 350 computers available on campus for general student use. A campuswide network can be accessed from student residence rooms and from off campus. Online class registration is available.
Website: http://www.citadel.edu/

General Application Contact: Dr. Tara Hornor, Associate Provost for Planning, Assessment and Evaluation/Dean of Enrollment Management, 843-953-5089, E-mail: cgc@citadel.edu.

GRADUATE UNITS

Citadel Graduate College *Program availability:* Part-time, evening/weekend, 100% online, blended/hybrid learning. Offers leadership studies (MS, Graduate Certificate). Electronic applications accepted.

School of Engineering *Program availability:* Part-time, evening/weekend. Offers aeronautical engineering (Graduate Certificate); built environment and public health (Graduate Certificate); civil engineering (MS); composites engineering (Graduate Certificate); computer engineering (Graduate Certificate); electrical engineering (MS); engineering (MS, Graduate Certificate); geotechnical engineering (Graduate Certificate); manufacturing engineering (Graduate Certificate); mechanical engineering (MS); mechatronics engineering (Graduate Certificate); power and energy (Graduate Certificate); project management (MS); structural engineering (Graduate Certificate); systems engineering management (Graduate Certificate); technical program management (Graduate Certificate); technical project management (Graduate Certificate); transportation engineering (Graduate Certificate). Electronic applications accepted.

School of Humanities and Social Sciences *Program availability:* Part-time, evening/weekend, 100% online, blended/hybrid learning. Offers English (MA); Hispanic studies (Graduate Certificate); history (MA); history and teaching content (Graduate Certificate); homeland security (Graduate Certificate); humanities and social sciences (MA, Ed S, Graduate Certificate); intelligence analysis (Graduate Certificate); intelligence and security studies (MA); international politics and military affairs (MA); psychology (MA); school psychology (Ed S); social science (MA). Electronic applications accepted.

School of Science and Mathematics *Program availability:* Part-time, evening/weekend. Offers biology (MA); computer and information sciences (MS); environmental studies (Graduate Certificate); health, exercise, and sport science (MS); science and mathematics (MA, MA Ed, MAT, MS, Graduate Certificate); sport management (MA, Graduate Certificate). Electronic applications accepted.

Tommy and Victoria Baker School of Business *Program availability:* Part-time, evening/weekend, 100% online, blended/hybrid learning. Offers business (MBA). Electronic applications accepted.

Zucker Family School of Education *Program availability:* Part-time, evening/weekend, 100% online, blended/hybrid learning. Offers elementary/secondary school administration and supervision (M Ed); elementary/secondary school counseling (M Ed); interdisciplinary STEM education (M Ed); literacy education (M Ed, Graduate Certificate); middle grades (MAT); physical education (grades K-12) (MAT); school superintendency (Ed S); secondary education (MAT); student affairs (Graduate Certificate); student affairs and college counseling (M Ed). Electronic applications accepted.

CITY COLLEGE OF THE CITY UNIVERSITY OF NEW YORK, New York, NY 10031-9198

General Information State and locally supported, coed, comprehensive institution. CGS member. *Graduate housing:* Room and/or apartments available on a first-come, first-served basis to single students; on-campus housing not available to married students. *Research affiliation:* New York Center for Biological Structures, Lucent Laboratories (engineering), Hospital for Joint Diseases (biomedical engineering), Museum of Natural History.

GRADUATE UNITS

Graduate School *Program availability:* Part-time, evening/weekend. Offers sustainability in the urban environment (MS).

The Bernard and Anne Spitzer School of Architecture *Program availability:* Part-time. Offers architecture (M Arch); landscape architecture (MLA); urban design (MUP).

Colin Powell School for Civic and Global Leadership *Program availability:* Part-time. Offers clinical psychology (PhD); economics (MA); economics and business (MA); general psychology (MA); international relations (MA); mental health counseling (MA); psychology (MA, PhD); public service management (MPA); sociology (MA). Electronic applications accepted.

Division of Humanities and the Arts *Program availability:* Part-time. Offers advertising design (MFA); art history (MA); art history and museum studies (MA); art museum education (MA); branding and integrated communications (MPS); ceramic design

(MFA); creative writing (MFA); digital and interdisciplinary art practice (MFA); film (MFA); fine arts (MFA); history (MA); humanities and the arts (MA, MFA, MPS); language and literacy (MA); literature (MA); museum studies (MA); painting (MFA); printmaking (MFA); sculpture (MFA); Spanish (MA); wood and metal design (MFA). Electronic applications accepted.

Division of Science *Program availability:* Part-time. Offers biochemistry (MS, PhD); biology (MS, PhD); chemistry (MS, PhD); geology (MS); mathematics (MS); physics (MS, PhD); science (MS, PhD). Electronic applications accepted.

Grove School of Engineering *Program availability:* Part-time. Offers biomedical engineering (MS, PhD); chemical engineering (ME, PhD); civil engineering (ME, MS, PhD); computer science (MS, PhD); electrical engineering (ME, MS, PhD); engineering (ME, MIS, MS, PhD); information systems (MIS); mechanical engineering (ME, MS, PhD).

School of Education *Program availability:* Part-time, evening/weekend. Offers adolescent mathematics education (MA, AC); bilingual education (MS); childhood education (MS); early childhood education (MS); education (MA, MS, MS Ed, AC); educational leadership (MS, AC); educational theatre (MS); English education (MA); literacy (MS); middle school mathematics education (MS); science education (MA); social studies education (AC); teacher of students with disabilities in adolescent education (MS Ed); teacher of students with disabilities in childhood education (MS Ed); TESOL (MS).

CITY UNIVERSITY OF NEW YORK SCHOOL OF LAW, Long Island City, NY 11101-4356

General Information State and locally supported, coed, graduate-only institution. *Enrollment by degree level:* 480 doctoral. *Graduate faculty:* 51 full-time (34 women), 12 part-time/adjunct (8 women). Tuition, state resident: full-time $14,550. Tuition, nonresident: full-time $24,160. *Graduate housing:* On-campus housing not available. *Student services:* Campus employment opportunities, campus safety program, career counseling, exercise/wellness program, free psychological counseling, services for students with disabilities, writing training. *Library facilities:* CUNY School of Law Library. *Collection:* Books: 62,088 (physical), 611,977 (digital/electronic); Serial titles: 1,931 (physical), 105,425 (digital/electronic); Databases: 333. Weekly public service hours: 61; study areas open 24 hours, 5–7 days a week; students can reserve study rooms.

Computer facilities: 105 computers available on campus for general student use. A campuswide network can be accessed from off campus. Online class registration is available.
Website: http://www.law.cuny.edu/

General Application Contact: Degna P. Levister, Assistant Dean of Admissions and Enrollment Management, 718-340-4210, Fax: 718-340-4435, E-mail: admissions@law.cuny.edu.

GRADUATE UNITS

Professional Program Students: 342 full-time (214 women), 138 part-time (79 women); includes 230 minority (68 Black or African American, non-Hispanic/Latino; 1 American Indian or Alaska Native, non-Hispanic/Latino; 49 Asian, non-Hispanic/Latino; 100 Hispanic/Latino; 1 Native Hawaiian or other Pacific Islander, non-Hispanic/Latino; 11 Two or more races, non-Hispanic/Latino), 16 international. Average age 29. 1,427 applicants, 46% accepted, 193 enrolled. *Faculty:* 51 full-time (34 women), 12 part-time/adjunct (8 women). Expenses: Contact institution. *Financial support:* In 2017–18, 148 students received support, including 42 fellowships (averaging $14,813 per year), 18 research assistantships (averaging $839 per year); Federal Work-Study, scholarships/grants, tuition waivers (full and partial), and unspecified assistantships also available. Support available to part-time students. Financial award application deadline: 7/15; financial award applicants required to submit FAFSA. In 2017, 94 doctorates awarded. *Program availability:* Part-time, evening/weekend. Offers law (JD). *Application deadline:* For fall admission, 6/15 priority date for domestic students. Applications are processed on a rolling basis. *Application fee:* $60. Electronic applications accepted. *Application Contact:* Degna P. Levister, Assistant Dean of Admissions and Enrollment Management, 718-340-4210, Fax: 718-340-4435, E-mail: admissions@law.cuny.edu. *Dean/Professor of Law,* Mary Lu Bilek, 718-340-4201, Fax: 718-340-4482.

CITY UNIVERSITY OF SEATTLE, Seattle, WA 98121

General Information Independent, coed, comprehensive institution. *Graduate housing:* Room and/or apartments available on a first-come, first-served basis to single students; on-campus housing not available to married students.

GRADUATE UNITS

Graduate Division *Program availability:* Part-time, evening/weekend, online learning. Electronic applications accepted.

Albright School of Education *Program availability:* Part-time, evening/weekend, online learning. Offers administrator certification (Certificate); curriculum and instruction (M Ed); elementary education (MIT); guidance and counseling (M Ed); leadership (M Ed); reading and literacy (M Ed); school counseling (M Ed); special education (MIT); superintendent certification (Certificate). Electronic applications accepted.

Division of Arts and Sciences *Program availability:* Part-time, evening/weekend, online learning. Offers counseling psychology (MA). Electronic applications accepted.

Division of Doctoral Studies *Program availability:* Online learning. Offers leadership (Ed D).

School of Management *Program availability:* Part-time, evening/weekend, online learning. Offers accounting (Certificate); change leadership (MBA, Certificate); computer systems (MS); finance (Certificate); financial management (MBA); general management (MBA); general management-Europe (MBA); global marketing (MBA); human resources management (Certificate); individualized study (MBA); information security (MS); information systems (MBA); leadership (MA); marketing (MBA, Certificate); project management (MBA, MS, Certificate); sustainable business (Certificate); technology management (MBA, Certificate). Electronic applications accepted.

CITY VISION UNIVERSITY, Kansas City, MO 64109-1845

General Information Independent-religious, coed, comprehensive institution.

GRADUATE UNITS

Program in Technology and Ministry *Program availability:* Online learning. Offers technology and ministry (MS).

CLAFLIN UNIVERSITY, Orangeburg, SC 29115

General Information Independent-religious, coed, comprehensive institution. *Graduate housing:* Room and/or apartments available on a first-come, first-served basis to single students; on-campus housing not available to married students. Housing application deadline: 4/15.

GRADUATE UNITS

Graduate Programs *Program availability:* Part-time. Offers biotechnology (MS); business administration (MBA).

CLAREMONT GRADUATE UNIVERSITY, Claremont, CA 91711-6160

General Information Independent, coed, graduate-only institution. CGS member. *Graduate housing:* Rooms and/or apartments available on a first-come, first-served basis to single and married students. Housing application deadline: 5/15. *Research affiliation:* Claremont School of Theology (religion), Rancho Santa Ana Botanic Garden (botany, native plants).

GRADUATE UNITS

Graduate Programs *Program availability:* Part-time, evening/weekend. Offers arts management (MA); botany (MS, PhD); financial engineering (MSFE). Electronic applications accepted.

Center for Information Systems and Technology *Program availability:* Part-time. Offers cybersecurity and networking (MS); data science and analytics (MS); electronic commerce (PhD); geographic information systems (MS); health informatics (MS); information systems (Certificate); IT strategy and innovation (MS); knowledge management (PhD); systems development (PhD); telecommunications and networking (PhD). Electronic applications accepted.

Institute of Mathematical Sciences *Program availability:* Part-time. Offers computational and systems biology (PhD); computational mathematics and numerical analysis (MA, MS); computational science (PhD); engineering and industrial applied mathematics (PhD); mathematics (PhD); operations research and statistics (MA, MS); physical applied mathematics (MA, MS); pure mathematics (MA, MS); scientific computing (MA, MS); systems and control theory (MA, MS). PhD programs offered jointly with San Diego State University and California State University, Long Beach. Electronic applications accepted.

Peter F. Drucker and Masatoshi Ito Graduate School of Management *Program availability:* Part-time. Offers advanced management (MS); art business (MA); executive management (EMBA); leadership (Certificate); management (EMBA, MA, MBA, MS, PhD, Certificate); strategy (Certificate). Electronic applications accepted.

School of Arts and Humanities *Program availability:* Part-time. Offers Africana history (Certificate); Africana studies (Certificate); American studies (MA, PhD); American studies and U.S. history (MA, PhD); applied women's studies (MA); archival studies (MA); arts and humanities (M Phil, MA, MFA, DCM, DMA, PhD, Certificate); church music (MA, DCM); composition (MA, DMA); critical theory (MA, PhD); cultural studies (MA, PhD); digital media (MFA); drawing (MFA); early modern studies (MA, PhD); English (M Phil, MA, PhD); European studies (MA, PhD); Hebrew Bible (MA, PhD); historical performance practices (MA, DMA); history of Christianity and religions of North America (MA, PhD); installation (MFA); literary theory (PhD); literature (MA, PhD); literature and creative writing (MA); literature and film (MA); media studies (MA, PhD); museum studies (MA); musicology (MA, PhD); New Testament (MA, PhD); oral history (MA, PhD); painting (MFA); performance (MA, MFA, DMA); philosophy (MA, PhD); philosophy of religion and theology (MA, PhD); photography (MFA); sculpture (MFA); studio (MFA); theology, ethics and culture (MA, PhD); women's studies in religion (MA, PhD). Electronic applications accepted.

School of Community and Global Health Offers health promotion science (PhD); public health (MPH). Electronic applications accepted.

School of Educational Studies *Program availability:* Part-time. Offers Africana education (Certificate); education and policy (MA, PhD); higher education/student affairs (MA, PhD); human development (MA, PhD); public school administration (MA, PhD); quantitative evaluation (MA, PhD); special education (MA, PhD); teacher education (MA); teaching and learning (MA, PhD); urban leadership (PhD). PhD program offered jointly with San Diego State University. Electronic applications accepted.

School of Social Science, Policy and Evaluation Offers advanced study in evaluation (Certificate); American politics (MA, PhD); behavioral economics and neuroeconomics (PhD); business and financial economics (MA, PhD); cognitive psychology (MA, PhD); comparative politics (PhD); developmental psychology (MA, PhD); economic development (Certificate); evaluation and applied research methods (MA, PhD); health behavior research and evaluation (MA, PhD); human resource development and evaluation (MA); human resource management (MS); industrial/organizational psychology (MA, PhD); international economic and development policy (PhD); international economics policy and development (MA); international money and finance (PhD); international political economy (MA); international studies (MA); organizational behavior (MA, PhD); organizational psychology (MA, PhD); political economy and public economics (PhD); political economy and public policy (MA); political philosophy (PhD); political science (PhD); politics, economics and business (MA); politics, economics, and business (MA); public policy (MA, PhD); public policy and evaluation (MA); social psychology (MA, PhD); social science, policy and evaluation (MA, MS, PhD, Certificate); world politics (PhD).

CLAREMONT LINCOLN UNIVERSITY, Claremont, CA 91711

General Information Independent, coed, graduate-only institution.

GRADUATE UNITS

Graduate Programs Offers ethical leadership (MA); interfaith action (MA); social impact (MA).

CLAREMONT SCHOOL OF THEOLOGY, Claremont, CA 91711-3199

General Information Independent-religious, coed, graduate-only institution. *Graduate housing:* Rooms and/or apartments available on a first-come, first-served basis to single students and guaranteed to married students. Housing application deadline: 5/1. *Research affiliation:* Moore Multicultural Resource and Research Center, Institute for Antiquity and Christianity, Center for Process Studies, National United Methodist Native American Center, Center for Pacific and Asian-American Ministries, Ancient Biblical Manuscript Center.

GRADUATE UNITS

Graduate and Professional Programs *Program availability:* Part-time. Offers interfaith chaplaincy (M Div); Islamic chaplaincy (M Div); ministerial leadership (M Div); practical theology (PhD); practical theology of conflict, healing and transformation in Korean contexts (D Min); religion (MA, PhD); spiritual renewal, contemplative practice, and strategic leadership (D Min). Electronic applications accepted.

CLARION UNIVERSITY OF PENNSYLVANIA, Clarion, PA 16214

General Information State-supported, coed, comprehensive institution. *Enrollment:* 5,225 graduate, professional, and undergraduate students; 250 full-time matriculated graduate/professional students (208 women), 654 part-time matriculated graduate/professional students (506 women). *Enrollment by degree level:* 881 master's, 10 doctoral, 13 other advanced degrees. *Graduate faculty:* 51 full-time (27 women), 27 part-time/adjunct (16 women). Tuition, state resident: part-time $500 per credit hour. Tuition, nonresident: part-time $750 per credit hour. *Required fees:* $155 per credit hour. One-time fee: $50 part-time. Tuition and fees vary according to degree level, campus/location and program. *Graduate housing:* Room and/or apartments available on a first-come, first-served basis to single students; on-campus housing not available to married students. Typical cost: $3596 per year ($10,946 including board). Room and board charges vary according to board plan, campus/location and housing facility selected. *Student services:* Campus employment opportunities, campus safety program, career counseling, exercise/wellness program, free psychological counseling, international student services, multicultural affairs office, services for students with disabilities, teacher training, writing training. *Library facilities:* Carlson Library plus 1 other. *Collection:* Books: 447,921 (physical), 250,647 (digital/electronic); Serial titles: 177 (physical), 53,762 (digital/electronic); Databases: 102. Weekly public service hours: 94; students can reserve study rooms.

Computer facilities: 950 computers available on campus for general student use. A campuswide network can be accessed from student residence rooms and from off campus. Online class registration, Online Learning Management System, web-based personal disk space, other online student services (financial aid, billing etc.) are available.
Website: http://www.clarion.edu/

General Application Contact: Dana Bearer, Associate Director, Transfer, Adult, and Graduate Admissions Office, 814-393-2337, Fax: 814-393-2722, E-mail: gradstudies@clarion.edu.

GRADUATE UNITS

College of Arts, Education and Sciences Students: 31 full-time (28 women), 115 part-time (92 women); includes 11 minority (8 Black or African American, non-Hispanic/Latino; 1 Asian, non-Hispanic/Latino; 1 Hispanic/Latino; 1 Two or more races, non-Hispanic/Latino). Average age 34. 107 applicants, 93% accepted, 43 enrolled. *Faculty:* 19 full-time (13 women), 3 part-time/adjunct (all women). Expenses: Contact institution. *Financial support:* Application deadline: 3/1; applicants required to submit FAFSA. In 2017, 66 master's, 2 other advanced degrees awarded. Offers arts, education and sciences (M Ed, MS, Certificate); curriculum and instruction (M Ed); early childhood (M Ed); mass media arts and journalism (MS); math education (M Ed); public relations (Certificate); reading (M Ed); science education (M Ed); special education (M Ed); technology (M Ed). *Application deadline:* Applications are processed on a rolling basis. *Application fee:* $40. Electronic applications accepted. *Application Contact:* Dana Bearer, Associate Director for Transfer, Adult and Graduate Admissions, 814-393-2337, Fax: 814-393-2772, E-mail: gradstudies@clarion.edu. *Interim Dean*, Dr. Steven Harris, 814-393-2328, E-mail: harris@clarion.edu.

College of Business Administration and Information Sciences Students: 116 full-time (84 women), 358 part-time (264 women); includes 66 minority (29 Black or African American, non-Hispanic/Latino; 1 American Indian or Alaska Native, non-Hispanic/Latino; 9 Asian, non-Hispanic/Latino; 19 Hispanic/Latino; 8 Two or more races, non-Hispanic/Latino), 4 international. Average age 31. 418 applicants, 84% accepted, 162 enrolled. *Faculty:* 13 full-time (6 women), 11 part-time/adjunct (3 women). Expenses: Contact institution. *Financial support:* Federal Work-Study available. Financial award application deadline: 3/1; financial award applicants required to submit FAFSA. In 2017, 173 master's, 1 other advanced degree awarded. Offers accounting (MS); applied data analytics (MS); business administration and information sciences (MBA, MS, MSLS, Certificate); finance (MBA); health care administration (MBA); information and library science (MSLS); innovation and entrepreneurship (MBA); library science (Certificate); non-profit business (MBA); school library media (MSLS). *Application deadline:* Applications are processed on a rolling basis. *Application fee:* $40. Electronic applications accepted. *Application Contact:* Dana Bearer, Associate Director for Transfer, Adult and Graduate Admissions, 814-393-2337, Fax: 814-393-2772, E-mail: gradstudies@clarion.edu. *Dean*, Dr. Phillip Frese, 814-393-2600, E-mail: pfrese@clarion.edu.

College of Health and Human Services Students: 103 full-time (96 women), 170 part-time (141 women); includes 20 minority (7 Black or African American, non-Hispanic/Latino; 2 Asian, non-Hispanic/Latino; 4 Hispanic/Latino; 7 Two or more races, non-Hispanic/Latino). Average age 33. 325 applicants, 57% accepted, 110 enrolled. *Faculty:* 20 full-time (17 women), 13 part-time/adjunct (11 women). Expenses: Contact institution. *Financial support:* Application deadline: 3/1; applicants required to submit FAFSA. In 2017, 93 master's, 7 doctorates awarded. Offers clinical mental health counseling (MS); family nurse practitioner (MSN); health and human services (MS, MSN, DNP); nursing (MSN, DNP); speech language pathology (MS). *Application deadline:* Applications are processed on a rolling basis. *Application fee:* $40. Electronic applications accepted. *Application Contact:* Dana Bearer, Associate Director for Transfer, Adult and Graduate Admissions, 814-393-2337, Fax: 814-393-2772, E-mail: gradstudies@clarion.edu. *Dean*, Dr. Jeffery Allen, 814-393-2163.

CLARK ATLANTA UNIVERSITY, Atlanta, GA 30314

General Information Independent-religious, coed, university. CGS member. *Enrollment:* 3,992 graduate, professional, and undergraduate students; 459 full-time matriculated graduate/professional students (328 women), 231 part-time matriculated graduate/professional students (143 women). *Enrollment by degree level:* 477 master's, 210 doctoral, 3 other advanced degrees. *Graduate faculty:* 140 full-time (62 women), 73 part-time/adjunct (37 women). *Graduate housing:* Room and/or apartments available on a first-come, first-served basis to single students; on-campus housing not available to married students. Housing application deadline: 6/1. *Student services:* Campus employment opportunities, campus safety program, career counseling, free psychological counseling, international student services, low-cost health insurance, services for students with disabilities. *Library facilities:* Robert W. Woodruff Library.

Computer facilities: 741 computers available on campus for general student use. A campuswide network can be accessed from student residence rooms. Online class registration is available.
Website: http://www.cau.edu/

GRADUATE UNITS

School of Arts and Sciences Students: 165 full-time (100 women), 129 part-time (79 women); includes 179 minority (178 Black or African American, non-Hispanic/Latino; 1 Asian, non-Hispanic/Latino), 96 international. Average age 32. 134 applicants, 82% accepted, 49 enrolled. *Faculty:* 82 full-time (33 women), 55 part-time/adjunct (26 women). Expenses: Contact institution. *Financial support:* Fellowships, research assistantships, teaching assistantships, career-related internships or fieldwork, Federal Work-Study, institutionally sponsored loans, scholarships/grants, and unspecified assistantships available. Support available to part-time students. Financial award application deadline: 4/30; financial award applicants required to submit FAFSA. In 2017, 74 master's, 19 doctorates awarded. *Program availability:* Part-time. Offers African American studies, Africana women's studies, and history (MA, PhD); arts and sciences (MA, MPA, MS, PhD); biology (MS, PhD); chemistry (MS, PhD); computer and information science (MS); English and modern languages (MA, PhD); mathematical sciences (MS); physics (MS); political science (MA, PhD); public administration (MPA); sociology (MA). *Application deadline:* For fall admission, 4/1 for domestic and international students; for spring admission, 11/1 for domestic and international students. Applications are processed on a rolling basis. *Application fee:* $40 ($55 for international students). *Dean*, Dr. Danille K. Taylor, 404-880-6774, E-mail: dtaylor3@cau.edu.

School of Business Administration Students: 41 full-time (25 women), 8 part-time (4 women); includes 33 minority (31 Black or African American, non-Hispanic/Latino; 1 Asian, non-Hispanic/Latino; 1 Hispanic/Latino), 10 international. Average age 27. 61 applicants, 59% accepted, 18 enrolled. *Faculty:* 27 full-time (12 women), 3 part-time/adjunct (all women). Expenses: Contact institution. *Financial support:* Career-related internships or fieldwork, scholarships/grants, and unspecified assistantships available. Support available to part-time students. Financial award application deadline: 4/30; financial award applicants required to submit FAFSA. In 2017, 48 master's awarded. *Program availability:* Part-time. Offers accounting (MA); business administration (MA, MBA); economics (MA). *Application deadline:* For fall admission, 4/1 for domestic and international students; for spring admission, 11/1 for domestic and international students. Applications are processed on a rolling basis. *Application fee:* $40 ($55 for international students). Electronic applications accepted. *Interim Dean*, Dr. Edward L. Davis, 404-880-8475, E-mail: edavis@cau.edu.

School of Education Students: 84 full-time (57 women), 67 part-time (36 women); includes 112 minority (110 Black or African American, non-Hispanic/Latino; 1 Asian, non-Hispanic/Latino; 1 Hispanic/Latino), 31 international. Average age 32. 72 applicants, 96% accepted, 37 enrolled. *Faculty:* 13 full-time (7 women), 12 part-time/adjunct (5 women). Expenses: Contact institution. *Financial support:* Career-related internships or fieldwork, Federal Work-Study, scholarships/grants, and unspecified assistantships available. Support available to part-time students. Financial award application deadline: 4/30; financial award applicants required to submit FAFSA. In 2017, 33 master's, 21 doctorates, 1 other advanced degree awarded. *Program availability:* Part-time, evening/weekend. Offers counseling and psychological studies (MA); education (MA, MAT, Ed D, Ed S); educational leadership (MA, Ed D, Ed S); special education general curriculum (MA); teaching math and science (MAT). *Application deadline:* For fall admission, 4/1 for domestic and international students; for spring admission, 11/1 for domestic and international students. Applications are processed on a rolling basis. *Application fee:* $40 ($55 for international students). Electronic applications accepted. *Dean*, Dr. Moses C. Norman, 404-880-8495, E-mail: mnorman@cau.edu.

School of Social Work Students: 169 full-time (146 women), 26 part-time (23 women); includes 150 minority (148 Black or African American, non-Hispanic/Latino; 1 American Indian or Alaska Native, non-Hispanic/Latino; 1 Hispanic/Latino), 21 international. Average age 31. 75 applicants, 87% accepted, 37 enrolled. *Faculty:* 18 full-time (10 women), 3 part-time/adjunct (all women). Expenses: Contact institution. *Financial support:* Career-related internships or fieldwork, Federal Work-Study, scholarships/grants, and unspecified assistantships available. Support available to part-time students. Financial award application deadline: 4/30; financial award applicants required to submit FAFSA. In 2017, 89 master's, 3 doctorates awarded. *Program availability:* Part-time. Offers social work (MSW, PhD). *Application deadline:* For fall admission, 4/1 for domestic and international students; for spring admission, 11/1 for domestic and international students. Applications are processed on a rolling basis. *Application fee:* $40 ($55 for international students). Electronic applications accepted. *Dean*, Dr. Jenny Jones, 404-880-8549, E-mail: jjones@cau.edu.

CLARKE UNIVERSITY, Dubuque, IA 52001-3198

General Information Independent-religious, coed, comprehensive institution. *Enrollment:* 1,032 graduate, professional, and undergraduate students; 178 full-time matriculated graduate/professional students (141 women), 61 part-time matriculated graduate/professional students (43 women). *Enrollment by degree level:* 101 master's, 138 doctoral. *Graduate faculty:* 28 full-time (23 women), 11 part-time/adjunct (5 women). *Tuition:* Part-time $550 per credit. *Required fees:* $35 per credit. Tuition and fees vary according to degree level and program. *Graduate housing:* On-campus housing not available. *Student services:* Career counseling, exercise/wellness program, free psychological counseling, international student services, multicultural affairs office, services for students with disabilities, writing training. *Library facilities:* Nicholas J. Schrupp Library. *Collection:* Books: 76,525 (physical), 136,800 (digital/electronic); Serial titles: 150 (physical), 53,000 (digital/electronic); Databases: 60. Weekly public service hours: 90.

Computer facilities: 237 computers available on campus for general student use. A campuswide network can be accessed from student residence rooms and from off campus. Online class registration is available.
Website: http://www.clarke.edu/

General Application Contact: Kimberly Roush, Director of Admission, Graduate and Adult Programs, 563-588-6635, Fax: 563-552-7994, E-mail: graduate@clarke.edu.

GRADUATE UNITS

Department of Nursing and Health Students: 55 full-time (54 women), 11 part-time (10 women); includes 3 minority (1 Black or African American, non-Hispanic/Latino; 1 Asian, non-Hispanic/Latino; 1 Two or more races, non-Hispanic/Latino). Average age 32. 62 applicants, 40% accepted, 22 enrolled. *Faculty:* 6 full-time (all women). Expenses: Contact institution. *Financial support:* Applicants required to submit FAFSA. In 2017, 36 doctorates awarded. *Program availability:* Part-time. Offers family nurse practitioner (DNP); health leadership and practice (DNP); psychiatric mental health nurse practitioner (DNP). *Application deadline:* For fall admission, 2/1 priority date for domestic students. *Application fee:* $35. Electronic applications accepted. *Application Contact:* Kimberly Roush, Director of Admission, Graduate and Adult Programs, 563-588-6539, Fax: 563-552-7994, E-mail: graduate@clarke.edu. *Chair*, Dr. Jan Lee, 563-588-6339, E-mail: jan.lee@clarke.edu.

Department of Social Work Students: 30 full-time (25 women), 2 part-time (both women); includes 3 minority (2 Hispanic/Latino; 1 Two or more races, non-Hispanic/Latino). Average age 28. 61 applicants, 38% accepted, 20 enrolled. *Faculty:* 7 full-time (all women). Expenses: Contact institution. *Financial support:* Applicants required to submit FAFSA. In 2017, 4 master's awarded. *Program availability:* Part-time, evening/weekend. Offers social work (MSW). *Application deadline:* For fall admission, 2/1 priority date for domestic students. *Application fee:* $35. Electronic applications accepted. *Application Contact:* Kimberly Roush, Director of Admission, Graduate and Adult Programs, 563-588-6539, Fax: 563-552-7994, E-mail: graduate@clarke.edu. *Chair*, Regina Boarman, 888-825-2753 Ext. 6583, E-mail: regina.boarman@clarke.edu.

Graduate Business Programs Students: 13 full-time (9 women), 26 part-time (16 women); includes 5 minority (2 Black or African American, non-Hispanic/Latino; 1 Asian, non-Hispanic/Latino; 2 Hispanic/Latino), 1 international. Average age 33. 19 applicants, 100% accepted, 13 enrolled. *Faculty:* 4 full-time (2 women), 3 part-time/adjunct (1 woman). Expenses: Contact institution. *Financial support:* Applicants required to submit FAFSA. In 2017, 19 master's awarded. *Program availability:* Part-time, evening/weekend, blended/hybrid learning. Offers business (MBA, MOL). *Application deadline:* Applications are processed on a rolling basis. *Application fee:* $35. Electronic applications accepted. *Application Contact:* Kimberly Roush, Director of Admission, Graduate and Adult Programs, 563-588-6539, Fax: 563-552-7994, E-mail: graduate@clarke.edu. *Director of Graduate Business Studies*, Jody Wolfe, 563-588-8143, E-mail: jody.wolfe@clarke.edu.

Physical Therapy Program Students: 72 full-time (46 women); includes 2 minority (1 Hispanic/Latino; 1 Two or more races, non-Hispanic/Latino). Average age 24. 221 applicants, 20% accepted, 20 enrolled. *Faculty:* 8 full-time (5 women), 6 part-time/adjunct (3 women). Expenses: Contact institution. *Financial support:* Applicants required to submit FAFSA. In 2017, 27 doctorates awarded. Offers physical therapy (DPT). *Application deadline:* For fall admission, 11/2 for domestic students. *Application fee:* $0. Electronic applications accepted. *Application Contact:* Kimberly Roush, Director of Admission, Graduate and Adult Programs, 563-588-6539, Fax: 563-552-7994, E-mail: graduate@clarke.edu. *Chair*, Dr. Bill O'Dell, 563-588-6618, E-mail: bill.odell@clarke.edu.

Program in Education Students: 3 full-time (all women), 27 part-time (19 women); includes 3 minority (1 Black or African American, non-Hispanic/Latino; 1 Hispanic/Latino; 1 Two or more races, non-Hispanic/Latino). Average age 29. 39 applicants, 87% accepted, 21 enrolled. *Faculty:* 3 full-time (all women), 2 part-time/adjunct (1 woman). Expenses: Contact institution. *Financial support:* Applicants required to submit FAFSA. In 2017, 15 master's awarded. *Program availability:* Part-time, 100% online, blended/hybrid learning. Offers instructional leadership (MAE). *Application deadline:* Applications are processed on a rolling basis. *Application fee:* $35. Electronic applications accepted. *Application Contact:* Kimberly Roush, Director of Admission, Graduate and Adult Programs, 563-588-6539, Fax: 563-552-7994, E-mail: graduate@clarke.edu. *Director of Graduate Education*, Beth Putnam, 563-588-6573, E-mail: beth.putnam@clarke.edu.

CLARKSON COLLEGE, Omaha, NE 68131-2739

General Information Independent, coed, primarily women, comprehensive institution. *Graduate housing:* Room and/or apartments available on a first-come, first-served basis to single students; on-campus housing not available to married students. Housing application deadline: 6/30.

GRADUATE UNITS

Master of Science in Nursing Program *Program availability:* Part-time, evening/weekend, online learning. Offers adult nurse practitioner (MSN, Post-Master's Certificate); family nurse practitioner (MSN, Post-Master's Certificate); nursing education (MSN, Post-Master's Certificate); nursing health care leadership (MSN, Post-Master's Certificate). Electronic applications accepted.

Program in Health Care Administration *Program availability:* Part-time, evening/weekend, online learning. Offers health care administration (MHCA). Electronic applications accepted.

CLARKSON UNIVERSITY, Potsdam, NY 13699

General Information Independent, coed, university. *Enrollment:* 4,233 graduate, professional, and undergraduate students; 621 full-time matriculated graduate/professional students (276 women), 380 part-time matriculated graduate/professional students (129 women). *Enrollment by degree level:* 737 master's, 253 doctoral, 11 other advanced degrees. *Graduate faculty:* 251 full-time (74 women), 111 part-time/adjunct (45 women). *Tuition:* Full-time $24,210; part-time $1345 per credit hour. Tuition and fees vary according to campus/location and program. *Graduate housing:* On-campus housing not available. *Student services:* Campus employment opportunities, campus safety program, career counseling, free psychological counseling, international student services, low-cost health insurance, multicultural affairs office, services for students with disabilities, teacher training. *Library facilities:* Harriet Call Burnap Memorial Library plus 1 other. *Collection:* Books: 104,973 (physical), 193,399 (digital/electronic); Serial titles: 1,948 (physical), 69,072 (digital/electronic); Databases: 148. Weekly public service hours: 97; students can reserve study rooms. *Research affiliation:* Trudeau Institute (biomedical sciences).

Computer facilities: 350 computers available on campus for general student use. A campuswide network can be accessed from student residence rooms and from off campus. Online class registration is available.
Website: http://www.clarkson.edu/

General Application Contact: Dan Capogna, Graduate Admissions Contact, 518-631-9910, E-mail: graduate@clarkson.edu.

GRADUATE UNITS

David D. Reh School of Business Students: 135 full-time (54 women), 85 part-time (45 women); includes 32 minority (9 Black or African American, non-Hispanic/Latino; 1 American Indian or Alaska Native, non-Hispanic/Latino; 14 Asian, non-Hispanic/Latino; 7 Hispanic/Latino; 1 Two or more races, non-Hispanic/Latino), 16 international. *Faculty:* 66 full-time (15 women), 39 part-time/adjunct (6 women). Expenses: Contact institution. In 2017, 132 master's, 4 other advanced degrees awarded. Offers business (MBA, MS, Advanced Certificate); business fundamentals (Advanced Certificate); clinical leadership in healthcare management (MS); global supply chain management (Advanced Certificate); healthcare data analytics (MS); healthcare management (MBA, Advanced Certificate); human resource management (Advanced Certificate); management and leadership (Advanced Certificate). *Application Contact:* Dan Capogna, Director of Graduate Admissions, 518-631-9910, E-mail: graduate@clarkson.edu. *Dean of Business*, Dr. Dayle Smith, 315-268-2300, E-mail: dsmith@clarkson.edu.

Department of Bioethics Students: 10 full-time (7 women), 22 part-time (18 women); includes 5 minority (2 Black or African American, non-Hispanic/Latino; 1 Asian, non-Hispanic/Latino; 1 Hispanic/Latino; 1 Two or more races, non-Hispanic/Latino), 10 international. 26 applicants, 81% accepted, 16 enrolled. *Faculty:* 1 full-time (0 women), 5 part-time/adjunct (4 women). Expenses: Contact institution. *Financial support:* Scholarships/grants available. In 2017, 19 master's, 3 other advanced degrees awarded. *Program availability:* Part-time, evening/weekend, 100% online, blended/hybrid learning. Offers bioethics (MS, Advanced Certificate). Offered jointly with Icahn School of Medicine at Mount Sinai. *Application deadline:* Applications are processed on a rolling basis. *Application fee:* $50. Electronic applications accepted. *Application Contact:* Ann Nolte, Assistant Chair of Bioethics, 518-631-9860, E-mail: anolte@clarkson.edu. *Chair of Bioethics*, Dr. Sean Philpott, 518-631-9860, E-mail: sphilpott@clarkson.edu.

Division of Health Sciences Students: 167 full-time (126 women), 2 part-time (both women); includes 27 minority (3 Black or African American, non-Hispanic/Latino; 16 Asian, non-Hispanic/Latino; 6 Hispanic/Latino; 2 Two or more races, non-Hispanic/Latino), 1 international. *Faculty:* 43 full-time (28 women), 23 part-time/adjunct (17 women). Expenses: Contact institution. In 2017, 19 master's, 24 doctorates awarded. Offers health sciences (MS, DPT); occupational therapy (MS); physical therapy (DPT); physician assistant studies (MS). *Application Contact:* Lisa Hayes, Office Manager, 315-268-4352, E-mail: lhayes@clarkson.edu. *Chair of Physical Therapy/Associate Dean of Health Sciences*, Dr. George Fulk, 315-268-3786, E-mail: gfulk@clarkson.edu.

Institute for a Sustainable Environment Students: 22 full-time (9 women), 12 international. *Faculty:* 5 full-time (2 women), 6 part-time/adjunct (2 women). Expenses: Contact institution. In 2017, 4 master's, 1 doctorate awarded. Offers environmental politics and governance (MS); environmental science and engineering (MS, PhD); sustainable environment (MS, PhD). *Application Contact:* Dan Capogna, Director of Graduate Admissions, 518-631-9910, E-mail: graduate@clarkson.edu. *Director of the Institute for a Sustainable Environment/Associate Director of Sustainability*, Dr. Susan Powers, 315-268-6542, E-mail: spowers@clarkson.edu.

Program in Data Analytics Students: 12 full-time (5 women), 7 part-time (2 women); includes 1 minority (Black or African American, non-Hispanic/Latino), 6 international. 57 applicants, 58% accepted, 13 enrolled. Expenses: Contact institution. *Financial support:* Scholarships/grants and unspecified assistantships available. In 2017, 11 master's awarded. *Program availability:* Part-time, evening/weekend, 100% online. Offers data analytics (MS). *Application deadline:* Applications are processed on a rolling basis. *Application fee:* $50. Electronic applications accepted. *Application Contact:* Dan Capogna, Director of Graduate Admissions, 518-631-9910, E-mail: graduate@clarkson.edu. *Director of Business Analytics*, Dr. Boris Jukic, 315-268-3884, E-mail: bjukic@clarkson.edu.

Program in Education Students: 22 full-time (13 women), 12 part-time (8 women); includes 4 minority (1 Black or African American, non-Hispanic/Latino; 3 Asian, non-Hispanic/Latino), 6 international. 39 applicants, 72% accepted, 21 enrolled. *Faculty:* 3 full-time (all women), 23 part-time/adjunct (14 women). Expenses: Contact institution. *Financial support:* Scholarships/grants available. In 2017, 28 master's awarded. Offers adolescence education 7-12 (MAT); teaching of English to speakers of other languages (MAT); technology education K-12 (MAT). *Application deadline:* Applications are processed on a rolling basis. *Application fee:* $50. Electronic applications accepted. *Application Contact:* Dan Capogna, Director of Graduate Admissions, 518-631-9910, E-mail: graduate@clarkson.edu. *Chair of Education*, Dr. Catherine Snyder, 518-631-9870, E-mail: csnyder@clarkson.edu.

Program in Engineering Management Students: 1 (woman) full-time, 129 part-time (33 women); includes 21 minority (5 Black or African American, non-Hispanic/Latino; 8 Asian, non-Hispanic/Latino; 8 Hispanic/Latino), 10 international. 51 applicants, 96% accepted, 48 enrolled. *Faculty:* 2 full-time (0 women), 6 part-time/adjunct (0 women). Expenses: Contact institution. *Financial support:* Scholarships/grants available. In 2017, 17 master's awarded. *Program availability:* Part-time-only, evening/weekend, blended/hybrid learning. Offers engineering management (MS). *Application deadline:* Applications are processed on a rolling basis. *Application fee:* $50. Electronic applications accepted. *Application Contact:* Dan Capogna, Director of Graduate Admissions, 518-631-9910, E-mail: graduate@clarkson.edu. *Executive Director of the Engineering Management Program*, Mike Walsh, 518-631-9846, E-mail: mwalsh@clarkson.edu.

School of Arts and Sciences Students: 113 full-time (39 women), 28 part-time (20 women); includes 14 minority (3 Black or African American, non-Hispanic/Latino; 6 Asian, non-Hispanic/Latino; 3 Hispanic/Latino; 2 Two or more races, non-Hispanic/Latino), 63 international. *Faculty:* 102 full-time (32 women), 49 part-time/adjunct (26 women). Expenses: Contact institution. In 2017, 26 master's, 15 doctorates awarded. Offers arts and sciences (MS, DPT, PhD); basic science (MS); chemistry (MS, PhD); computer science (MS, PhD); interdisciplinary bioscience and biotechnology (PhD); mathematics (MS, PhD); physics (MS, PhD). *Application Contact:* Dan Capogna, Director of Graduate Admissions, 518-631-9910, E-mail: graduate@clarkson.edu. *Interim Dean of Arts and Sciences*, Dr. Charles Thorpe, 315-268-6544, E-mail: cthorpe@clarkson.edu.

Wallace H. Coulter School of Engineering Students: 149 full-time (29 women), 117 part-time (19 women); includes 25 minority (4 Black or African American, non-Hispanic/Latino; 7 Asian, non-Hispanic/Latino; 9 Hispanic/Latino; 5 Two or more races, non-Hispanic/Latino), 97 international. *Faculty:* 108 full-time (16 women), 34 part-time/adjunct (8 women). Expenses: Contact institution. In 2017, 59 master's, 16 doctorates, 6 other advanced degrees awarded. Offers business of energy (MS, Advanced Certificate); chemical engineering (ME, MS, PhD); civil and environmental engineering (ME, MS, PhD); electrical and computer engineering (PhD); electrical engineering (ME, MS); energy systems (MS); engineering (ME, MS, PhD, Advanced Certificate); engineering and management systems (MS); interdisciplinary engineering science (MS, PhD); materials science and engineering (PhD); mechanical engineering (ME, MS, PhD). *Application Contact:* Dan Capogna, Director of Graduate Admissions, 518-631-9910, E-mail: graduate@clarkson.edu. *Dean of Engineering*, Dr. William Jemison, 315-268-6446, E-mail: wjemison@clarkson.edu.

CLARKS SUMMIT UNIVERSITY, South Abington Township, PA 18411

General Information Independent-religious, coed, comprehensive institution. *Graduate housing:* Room and/or apartments available on a first-come, first-served basis to single students; on-campus housing not available to married students. *Student services:* Campus employment opportunities, campus safety program, career counseling, free psychological counseling, international student services. *Library facilities:* Murphy Memorial Library.

Computer facilities: 25 computers available on campus for general student use. A campuswide network can be accessed from student residence rooms. Online class registration is available.
Website: http://www.clarkssummitu.edu/

General Application Contact: Howard Hicks, Registrar, 570-585-9345, Fax: 570-586-1753, E-mail: hhicks@clarkssummitu.edu.

GRADUATE UNITS

Baptist Bible Seminary Expenses: Contact institution. *Financial support:* Career-related internships or fieldwork and scholarships/grants available. Support available to part-time students. *Program availability:* Part-time, evening/weekend, online learning. Offers Biblical apologetics (MA); Biblical studies (MA); church education (M Min); church planting (M Div, M Min); communication (D Min); counseling and spiritual development (D Min); global ministry (M Min, D Min); ministry (PhD); missions (M Min); organizational leadership (M Min); outreach pastor (M Min); pastoral counseling (M Min); pastoral leadership (M Div, M Min); pastoral ministry (D Min); theological studies (D Min); theology (Th M); youth pastor (M Min). M Min in missions available only for Association of Baptists for World Evangelism missionary personnel. *Application deadline:* Applications are processed on a rolling basis. *Application fee:* $30. Electronic applications accepted. *Application Contact:* Dr. Wayne Slusser, Dean, 570-585-9348, Fax: 570-585-4057, E-mail: wslusser@clarkssummitu.edu. *Dean*, Dr. Wayne Slusser, 570-585-9348, Fax: 570-585-4057, E-mail: wslusser@clarkssummitu.edu.

Online Master's Programs Expenses: Contact institution. *Financial support:* Institutionally sponsored loans and scholarships/grants available. Financial award application deadline: 8/20; financial award applicants required to submit FAFSA. *Program availability:* Part-time, evening/weekend, online learning. Offers Bible (MA); counseling (MA, MS); curriculum and instruction (M Ed); educational administration (M Ed); literature (MA); organizational leadership (MA). *Application deadline:* Applications are processed on a rolling basis. *Application fee:* $30. *Application Contact:* Drew Whipple, Vice President for Enrollment Management, 570-585-9370, Fax: 570-585-9299, E-mail: awhipple@clarkssummitu.edu. *President*, Dr. James Lytle, 570-586-2400 Ext. 9222, Fax: 570-586-1753.

CLARK UNIVERSITY, Worcester, MA 01610-1477

General Information Independent, coed, university. CGS member. *Enrollment:* 3,153 graduate, professional, and undergraduate students; 760 full-time matriculated graduate/professional students (437 women), 218 part-time matriculated graduate/professional students (116 women). *Enrollment by degree level:* 769 master's, 207 doctoral, 2 other advanced degrees. *Graduate faculty:* 209 full-time (93 women), 142 part-time/adjunct (65 women). *Graduate housing:* Rooms and/or apartments available on a first-come, first-served basis to single and married students. *Student services:* Campus employment opportunities, campus safety program, career counseling, exercise/wellness program, free psychological counseling, grant writing training, international student services, low-cost health insurance, multicultural affairs office, services for students with disabilities, teacher training, writing training. *Library facilities:* Robert Hutchings Goddard Library plus 8 others. *Collection:* Students can reserve study rooms. *Research affiliation:* Worcester Area Computation Center, Worcester Foundation for Experimental Biology, Massachusetts Biotechnology Research Institute.

Computer facilities: A campuswide network can be accessed from student residence rooms and from off campus. Online class registration, online course support are available.
Website: http://www.clarku.edu/

General Application Contact: Jeremiah Czub, Director of Graduate Admissions, 508-793-7676, Fax: 508-793-8834, E-mail: jczub@clarku.edu.

GRADUATE UNITS

Graduate School Average age 28. 2,048 applicants, 72% accepted, 388 enrolled. *Faculty:* 209 full-time (93 women), 142 part-time/adjunct (65 women). Expenses: Contact institution. *Financial support:* In 2017–18, 10 fellowships with tuition reimbursements (averaging $17,000 per year), 39 research assistantships with tuition reimbursements (averaging $17,000 per year), 84 teaching assistantships with tuition reimbursements (averaging $17,000 per year) were awarded; career-related internships or fieldwork, Federal Work-Study, institutionally sponsored loans, scholarships/grants, and tuition waivers (full and partial) also available. Support available to part-time students. In 2017, 491 master's, 38 doctorates awarded. *Program availability:* Part-time, evening/weekend. Offers biology (MA, PhD); community and global health (MHS); community development and planning (MA); economics (PhD); English (MA); environmental science and policy (MS); genocide studies (PhD); geographic information science for development and environment (MS); history of the Atlantic world (PhD); history of the Holocaust (PhD); history of the United States (PhD); Holocaust history and genocide studies (PhD); international development and social change (MA); physics (PhD); United States and Atlantic history (PhD). *Application deadline:* Applications are processed on a rolling basis. *Application fee:* $75. Electronic applications accepted. *Application Contact:* Ethan Bernstein, Director of Graduate Admission, 508-793-7373, E-mail: gradadmissions@clarku.edu. *Associate Provost and Dean of Graduate Studies*, Dr. William Fisher, 508-793-7676.

Adam Institute for Urban Teaching and School Practice Students: 34 full-time (27 women); includes 7 minority (1 Black or African American, non-Hispanic/Latino; 3 Asian, non-Hispanic/Latino; 1 Hispanic/Latino; 2 Two or more races, non-Hispanic/Latino). Average age 24. 73 applicants, 52% accepted, 33 enrolled. *Faculty:* 11 full-time (7 women), 8 part-time/adjunct (6 women). Expenses: Contact institution. *Financial support:* Fellowships with tuition reimbursements, research assistantships with tuition reimbursements, teaching assistantships with tuition reimbursements, institutionally sponsored loans, and tuition waivers (partial) available. In 2017, 28 master's awarded. Offers urban teaching and school practice (MAT, PhD). *Application deadline:* For fall admission, 1/15 priority date for domestic students. *Application fee:* $75. Electronic applications accepted. *Application Contact:* Andrea Allen, Program Administrator, 508-793-7685, E-mail: aallen@clarku.edu. *Co-Chair*, Dr. Thomas Del Prete, 508-793-7197, E-mail: tdelprete@clarku.edu.

Graduate School of Management Students: 244 full-time (129 women), 49 part-time (29 women); includes 22 minority (11 Black or African American, non-Hispanic/Latino; 7 Asian, non-Hispanic/Latino; 4 Hispanic/Latino), 193 international. Average age 27. 1,183 applicants, 79% accepted, 183 enrolled. *Faculty:* 25 full-time (11 women), 17 part-time/adjunct (6 women). Expenses: Contact institution. *Financial support:* Fellowships, research assistantships, teaching assistantships, career-related internships or fieldwork, Federal Work-Study, institutionally sponsored loans, and tuition waivers (partial) available. Support available to part-time students. In 2017, 202 master's awarded. *Program availability:* Part-time, evening/weekend. Offers accounting (MSA); business analytics (MSBA); finance (MBA); information management and business analytics (MBA); management (MBA); marketing (MBA); social change (MBA); sustainability (MBA). *Application deadline:* For fall admission, 6/1 priority date for domestic students; for spring admission, 12/1 priority date for domestic students. Applications are processed on a rolling basis. *Application fee:* $75. Electronic applications accepted. *Application Contact:* Jeremiah Czub, Director of Graduate Enrollment Management, 508-793-7559, E-mail: graduateadmissions@clarku.edu. *Dean*, Dr. Catherine Usoff, 508-793-7670, Fax: 508-793-8822, E-mail: cusoff@clarku.edu.

Gustav H. Carlson School of Chemistry Students: 10 full-time (3 women); includes 3 minority (2 Asian, non-Hispanic/Latino; 1 Hispanic/Latino), 6 international. Average age 27. 75 applicants, 23% accepted, 10 enrolled. *Faculty:* 9 full-time (1 woman). Expenses: Contact institution. *Financial support:* Fellowships, research assistantships, teaching assistantships, and tuition waivers (full) available. Offers biochemistry (PhD); chemistry (PhD). *Application deadline:* For fall admission, 1/15 priority date for domestic students. *Application fee:* $75. Electronic applications accepted. *Application Contact:* Rene Baril, Managerial Secretary, 508-793-7130, Fax: 528-793-7117, E-mail: mbaril@clarku.edu.

Hiatt School of Psychology Students: 37 full-time (31 women); includes 9 minority (2 Black or African American, non-Hispanic/Latino; 2 Asian, non-Hispanic/Latino; 5 Hispanic/Latino), 7 international. Average age 28. 272 applicants, 6% accepted, 6 enrolled. *Faculty:* 17 full-time (12 women), 2 part-time/adjunct (both women). Expenses: Contact institution. *Financial support:* Fellowships, research assistantships, teaching assistantships, career-related internships or fieldwork, and tuition waivers (full and partial) available. In 2017, 5 doctorates awarded. Offers clinical psychology (PhD); developmental psychology (PhD); social psychology (PhD). *Application deadline:* For fall admission, 12/15 priority date for domestic and international students. *Application fee:* $75. Electronic applications accepted.

School of Geography Students: 55 full-time (29 women); includes 8 minority (1 Black or African American, non-Hispanic/Latino; 3 Asian, non-Hispanic/Latino; 4 Hispanic/Latino), 21 international. Average age 32. 135 applicants, 13% accepted, 9 enrolled. *Faculty:* 19 full-time (7 women), 3 part-time/adjunct (2 women). Expenses: Contact institution. *Financial support:* Fellowships, research assistantships, teaching assistantships, career-related internships or fieldwork, and tuition waivers (full) available. In 2017, 11 doctorates awarded. Offers geography (PhD). *Application deadline:* For fall admission, 12/31 priority date for domestic and international students. *Application fee:* $75. Electronic applications accepted. *Director*, Dr. Deb Martin, 508-793-7104, E-mail: dmartin@clarku.edu.

School of Professional Studies Students: 109 full-time (67 women), 31 part-time (16 women); includes 14 minority (3 Black or African American, non-Hispanic/Latino; 2 Asian, non-Hispanic/Latino; 9 Hispanic/Latino), 78 international. Average age 29. 245 applicants, 80% accepted, 82 enrolled. *Faculty:* 46 part-time/adjunct (16 women). Expenses: Contact institution. *Financial support:* Career-related internships or fieldwork available. Support available to part-time students. In 2017, 86 master's awarded. *Program availability:* Part-time, evening/weekend. Offers information technology (MSIT); professional communication (MSPC); public administration (MPA, Certificate). *Application deadline:* Applications are processed on a rolling basis. *Application fee:* $75. Electronic applications accepted. *Assistant Dean*, Mary Piecewicz, 508-793-7212, E-mail: mpiecewicz@clarku.edu.

CLAYTON STATE UNIVERSITY, Morrow, GA 30260-0285

General Information State-supported, coed, comprehensive institution. *Graduate housing:* On-campus housing not available.

GRADUATE UNITS

School of Graduate Studies Electronic applications accepted.

College of Arts and Sciences Offers administration of justice (MS); applied developmental psychology (MS); arts and sciences (MA, MAT, MS); biology (MAT); clinical/counseling psychology (MS); criminology, law, and society (MS); English (MAT); history (MAT); liberal studies (MA); mathematics (MAT).

College of Business Offers accounting (MBA); business (MBA); human resource leadership (MBA); international business (MBA); sports and entertainment management (MBA); supply chain management (MBA).

College of Health Offers family nurse practitioner (MSN); health (MHA, MSN).

College of Information and Mathematical Sciences Offers archival studies (MAS); information and mathematical sciences (MAS).

CLEARY UNIVERSITY, Howell, MI 48843

General Information Independent, coed, comprehensive institution. *Graduate housing:* On-campus housing not available.

GRADUATE UNITS

Online Program in Business Administration *Program availability:* Part-time, evening/weekend, online learning. Offers analytics, technology, and innovation (MBA, Graduate Certificate); financial planning (Graduate Certificate); global leadership (MBA, Graduate Certificate); health care leadership (MBA, Graduate Certificate). Electronic applications accepted.

CLEMSON UNIVERSITY, Clemson, SC 29634

General Information State-supported, coed, university. CGS member. *Enrollment:* 24,387 graduate, professional, and undergraduate students; 4,622 full-time matriculated graduate/professional students (1,910 women), 2,880 part-time matriculated graduate/professional students (1,486 women). *Enrollment by degree level:* 5,192 master's, 2,174 doctoral, 136 other advanced degrees. *Graduate faculty:* 1,268 full-time (481 women), 116 part-time/adjunct (44 women). Tuition, state resident: full-time $10,380; part-time $636 per semester hour. Tuition, nonresident: full-time $20,682; part-time $1290 per semester hour. *Required fees:* $1154; $459 per semester. Tuition and fees vary according to course load, campus/location and program. *Graduate housing:* On-campus housing not available. *Student services:* Campus employment opportunities, campus safety program, career counseling, exercise/wellness program, free psychological counseling, grant writing training, international student services, low-cost health insurance, multicultural affairs office, services for students with disabilities, teacher training, writing training. *Library facilities:* Robert Muldrow Cooper Library plus 1 other. *Collection:* Study areas open 24 hours, 5–7 days a week; students can reserve study rooms. *Research affiliation:* Savannah National Research Lab (energy), Fluor Corporation (supply chain logistics), Greenville Hospital System (biological sciences), South Carolina Universities Research and Education Foundation (energy), Oak Ridge National Laboratory (materials science, physics), BMW (automotive, electrical and mechanical engineering).

Computer facilities: Computer purchase and lease plans are available. 1,250 computers available on campus for general student use. A campuswide network can be accessed. Online class registration is available.
Website: http://www.clemson.edu/

General Application Contact: Kathleen Costello, Director of Admissions and Recruitment, 864-656-2561, E-mail: kcostel@clemson.edu.

GRADUATE UNITS

Graduate School Students: 4,673 full-time (1,935 women), 3,490 part-time (1,900 women); includes 938 minority (434 Black or African American, non-Hispanic/Latino; 9 American Indian or Alaska Native, non-Hispanic/Latino; 131 Asian, non-Hispanic/Latino; 235 Hispanic/Latino; 6 Native Hawaiian or other Pacific Islander, non-Hispanic/Latino; 123 Two or more races, non-Hispanic/Latino), 2,157 international. Average age 30. 8,402 applicants, 53% accepted, 2519 enrolled. *Faculty:* 1,267 full-time (480 women), 116 part-time/adjunct (44 women). Expenses: Contact institution. *Financial support:* In 2017–18, 1,702 students received support, including 309 fellowships with partial tuition reimbursements available (averaging $6,648 per year), 451 research assistantships with partial tuition reimbursements available (averaging $18,395 per year), 569 teaching assistantships with partial tuition reimbursements available (averaging $16,846 per year); career-related internships or fieldwork and unspecified assistantships also available. In 2017, 2,243 master's, 485 doctorates, 205 other advanced degrees awarded. *Program availability:* Part-time, evening/weekend, 100% online, blended/hybrid learning. *Application deadline:* For fall admission, 4/15 for international students; for spring admission, 10/15 for international students. Applications are processed on a rolling basis. *Application fee:* $80 ($90 for international students). Electronic applications accepted. *Application Contact:* Kathleen Costello, Director of Graduate Admissions and Recruitment, 864-656-2561, E-mail: kcostel@clemson.edu. *Associate Provost and Dean of the Graduate School*, Dr. Jason Osborne, 864-656-4172, Fax: 864-656-5344, E-mail: jwo@clemson.edu.

College of Agriculture, Forestry and Life Sciences Students: 203 full-time (102 women), 55 part-time (25 women); includes 19 minority (4 Black or African American, non-Hispanic/Latino; 1 Asian, non-Hispanic/Latino; 7 Hispanic/Latino; 7 Two or more races, non-Hispanic/Latino), 52 international. Average age 29. 259 applicants, 58% accepted, 101 enrolled. *Faculty:* 117 full-time (28 women), 2 part-time/adjunct (1 woman). Expenses: Contact institution. *Financial support:* In 2017–18, 208 students received support, including 31 fellowships with partial tuition reimbursements available (averaging $8,242 per year), 111 research assistantships with partial tuition reimbursements available (averaging $16,586 per year), 84 teaching assistantships with partial tuition reimbursements available (averaging $15,112 per year); career-related internships or fieldwork and unspecified assistantships also available. In 2017, 18 master's, 15 doctorates awarded. *Program availability:* 100% online, blended/hybrid learning. Offers agricultural education (M Ag Ed); agriculture, forestry and life sciences (M Ag Ed, MFR, MS, PhD); animal and veterinary sciences (MS, PhD); applied economics (PhD); applied economics and statistics (MS); entomology (MS, PhD); food technology (PhD); food, nutrition and culinary sciences (MS); forest resources (MFR, MS, PhD); packaging science (MS); plant and environmental sciences (MS, PhD); wildlife and fisheries biology (MS, PhD). *Application deadline:* Applications are processed on a rolling basis. *Application fee:* $80 ($90 for international students). Electronic applications accepted. *Application Contact:* Dr. Paula Agudelo, Interim Associate Dean for Research and Graduate Studies, 864-656-2810, E-mail: pagudel@clemson.edu. *Dean*, Dr. Keith Belli, 864-656-3013, E-mail: caflsdean-l@clemson.edu.

College of Architecture, Arts, and Humanities Students: 323 full-time (178 women), 14 part-time (4 women); includes 38 minority (10 Black or African American, non-Hispanic/Latino; 6 Asian, non-Hispanic/Latino; 19 Hispanic/Latino; 3 Two or more races, non-Hispanic/Latino), 59 international. Average age 26. 597 applicants, 63% accepted, 133 enrolled. *Faculty:* 159 full-time (67 women), 34 part-time/adjunct (15 women). Expenses: Contact institution. *Financial support:* In 2017–18, 245 students received support, including 77 fellowships with partial tuition reimbursements available (averaging $2,386 per year), 41 research assistantships with partial tuition reimbursements available (averaging $6,624 per year), 42 teaching assistantships with partial tuition reimbursements available (averaging $15,845 per year); career-related internships or fieldwork and unspecified assistantships also available. In 2017, 144 master's, 12 doctorates, 12 other advanced degrees awarded. *Program availability:* Part-time, 100% online. Offers architecture (M Arch, MS, Certificate); architecture and health (M Arch); architecture, arts, and humanities (M Arch, MA, MCSM, MFA, MLA, MRED, MRUD, MS, PhD, Certificate); construction science and management (MCSM); digital ecologies (Certificate); English (MA); historic preservation (MS, Certificate); history (MA); integrated project delivery (Certificate); landscape architecture (MLA); planning, design and the built environment (PhD); real estate development (MRED); resilient urban design (MRUD); rhetoric, communication and information design (PhD); visual arts (MFA); writing, rhetoric and media (MA). *Application deadline:* For fall admission, 4/15 for international students; for spring admission, 9/15 for international students. Applications are processed on a rolling basis. *Application fee:* $80 ($90 for international students). Electronic applications accepted. *Application Contact:* Dr. James Spencer, Associate Dean for Research and Graduate Studies, 864-656-0377, E-mail: jhspenc@clemson.edu. *Dean*, Dr. Richard Goodstein, 864-656-3084, Fax: 864-656-0204, E-mail: regst@clemson.edu.

College of Behavioral, Social and Health Sciences Students: 264 full-time (186 women), 341 part-time (239 women); includes 94 minority (63 Black or African American, non-Hispanic/Latino; 1 American Indian or Alaska Native, non-Hispanic/Latino; 4 Asian, non-Hispanic/Latino; 20 Hispanic/Latino; 6 Two or more races, non-Hispanic/Latino), 48 international. Average age 32. 723 applicants, 53% accepted, 261 enrolled. *Faculty:* 188 full-time (110 women), 12 part-time/adjunct (3 women). Expenses: Contact institution. *Financial support:* In 2017–18, 178 students received support, including 10 fellowships with partial tuition reimbursements available (averaging $7,600 per year), 31 research assistantships with partial tuition reimbursements available (averaging $16,379 per year), 129 teaching assistantships with partial tuition reimbursements available (averaging $8,791 per year); unspecified assistantships also available. In 2017, 235 master's, 17 doctorates, 21 other advanced degrees awarded. *Program availability:* Part-time, evening/weekend, 100% online, blended/hybrid learning. Offers applied health research and evaluation (MS, PhD); applied psychology (MS); applied sociology (MS); behavioral, social and health sciences (MA, MPA, MS, DNP, PhD, Certificate); biomedical data science and informatics (PhD); clinical and translational research (PhD, Certificate); communication, technology and society (MA); global health (Certificate); healthcare genetics (PhD); human factors psychology (PhD); industrial-organizational psychology (PhD); international family and community studies (PhD, Certificate); international parks and tourism (Certificate); nursing (MS, DNP); parks, recreation and tourism management (MS, PhD); policy studies (PhD, Certificate); public administration (MPA, Certificate); recreational therapy (MS); youth development leadership (MS, Certificate). *Application deadline:* Applications are processed on a rolling basis. *Application fee:* $80 ($90 for international students). Electronic applications accepted. *Application Contact:* Dr. Eric Muth, Associate Dean for Research and Graduate Programs, 864-656-6741, E-mail: muth@clemson.edu. *Dean*, Dr. Leslie Hossfeld, 864-656-7640.

College of Business Students: 667 full-time (280 women), 773 part-time (240 women); includes 194 minority (98 Black or African American, non-Hispanic/Latino; 26 Asian, non-Hispanic/Latino; 48 Hispanic/Latino; 2 Native Hawaiian or other Pacific Islander, non-Hispanic/Latino; 20 Two or more races, non-Hispanic/Latino), 188 international. Average age 31. 937 applicants, 70% accepted, 375 enrolled. *Faculty:* 144 full-time (47 women), 27 part-time/adjunct (8 women). Expenses: Contact institution. *Financial support:* In 2017–18, 105 students received support, including 20 fellowships with partial tuition reimbursements available (averaging $7,400 per year), 2 research assistantships with partial tuition reimbursements available (averaging $13,392 per year), 18 teaching assistantships with partial tuition reimbursements available (averaging $18,778 per year); career-related internships or fieldwork and unspecified assistantships also available. In 2017, 626 master's, 27 doctorates awarded. *Program availability:* Part-time, evening/weekend. Offers accounting (MP Acc); applied economics (PhD); applied economics and statistics (MS); business (MA, MBA, MP Acc, MS, PhD); business administration (MBA, PhD); business analytics (MBA); economics (MA, PhD); entrepreneurship and innovation (MBA); graphic communications (MS); management (MS); marketing (MS). *Application deadline:* Applications are processed on a rolling basis. *Application fee:* $80 ($90 for international students). Electronic applications accepted. *Application Contact:* Dr. Gregory Pickett, Senior Associate Dean, 864-656-3975, E-mail: pgregor@clemson.edu. *Dean*, Wendy York, 864-656-3178.

College of Education Students: 546 full-time (407 women), 616 part-time (467 women); includes 206 minority (118 Black or African American, non-Hispanic/Latino; 16 Asian, non-Hispanic/Latino; 44 Hispanic/Latino; 2 Native Hawaiian or other Pacific Islander, non-Hispanic/Latino; 26 Two or more races, non-Hispanic/Latino), 7 international. Average age 32. 797 applicants, 65% accepted, 343 enrolled. *Faculty:* 74 full-time (53 women), 1 part-time/adjunct (0 women). Expenses: Contact institution. *Financial support:* In 2017–18, 118 students received support, including 15 fellowships with partial tuition reimbursements available (averaging $7,689 per year), 2 research assistantships with partial tuition reimbursements available (averaging $13,689 per year), 24 teaching assistantships with partial tuition reimbursements available (averaging $14,822 per year); unspecified assistantships also available. In 2017, 327 master's, 154 doctorates awarded. *Program availability:* Part-time, evening/weekend, 100% online. Offers administration and supervision (M Ed, Ed S); athletic leadership (MS, Certificate); counselor education (M Ed, Ed S); curriculum and instruction (PhD); education (M Ed, MAT, MHRD, MS, Ed D, PhD, Certificate, Ed S); education systems improvement science (Ed D); educational leadership (PhD); human resource development (MHRD); leadership (Certificate); learning sciences (PhD); literacy (M Ed); literacy, language and culture (PhD); middle level education (MAT); secondary math and science (MAT); special education (M Ed, MAT, PhD); STEAM education (Certificate); student affairs (M Ed); teaching and learning (M Ed). *Application deadline:* Applications are processed on a rolling basis. *Application fee:* $80 ($90 for international students). Electronic applications accepted. *Application Contact:* Julie Jones, Graduate Programs Coordinator, 864-656-5096, E-mail: jgambre@clemson.edu. *Founding Dean*, Dr. George Petersen, 864-656-4444, E-mail: soedean@clemson.edu.

College of Engineering, Computing and Applied Sciences Students: 2,007 full-time (478 women), 493 part-time (105 women); includes 194 minority (66 Black or African American, non-Hispanic/Latino; 4 American Indian or Alaska Native, non-Hispanic/Latino; 42 Asian, non-Hispanic/Latino; 50 Hispanic/Latino; 2 Native Hawaiian or other Pacific Islander, non-Hispanic/Latino; 30 Two or more races, non-Hispanic/Latino), 1,461 international. Average age 27. 3,793 applicants, 36% accepted, 539 enrolled. *Faculty:* 255 full-time (52 women), 15 part-time/adjunct (4 women). Expenses: Contact institution. *Financial support:* In 2017–18, 610 students received support, including 95 fellowships with partial tuition reimbursements available (averaging $11,000 per year), 428 research assistantships with partial tuition reimbursements available (averaging $20,710 per year), 141 teaching assistantships with partial tuition reimbursements available (averaging $19,326 per year); career-related internships or fieldwork and unspecified assistantships also available. In 2017, 750 master's, 188 doctorates, 35 other advanced degrees awarded. *Program availability:* Part-time, 100% online. Offers automotive engineering (MS, PhD, Certificate); bioengineering (MS, PhD); biomedical engineering (M Engr); biosystems engineering (MS, PhD); chemical engineering (MS, PhD); civil engineering (MS, PhD); computer engineering (MS, PhD); computer science (MS, PhD); digital production arts (MFA); electrical engineering (M Engr, MS, PhD); engineering and science education (PhD, Certificate); engineering, computing and applied sciences (M Engr, MFA, MS, PhD, Certificate); environmental engineering and science (MS, PhD); environmental health physics (MS); human centered computing (PhD); hydrogeology (MS); industrial engineering (M Engr, MS, PhD); materials science and engineering (MS, PhD); mechanical engineering (MS, PhD); medical device recycling and reprocessing (Certificate). *Application deadline:* Applications are processed on a rolling basis. *Application fee:* $80 ($90 for international students). Electronic applications accepted. *Application Contact:* Dr. Douglas Hirt, Associate Dean for Research and Graduate Studies, 864-656-3201, E-mail: hirtd@clemson.edu. *Dean*, Dr. Anand Gramopadhye, 864-656-3200, E-mail: agrampo@clemson.edu.

College of Science Students: 710 full-time (328 women), 560 part-time (388 women); includes 112 minority (32 Black or African American, non-Hispanic/Latino; 2 American Indian or Alaska Native, non-Hispanic/Latino; 20 Asian, non-Hispanic/Latino; 32 Hispanic/Latino; 26 Two or more races, non-Hispanic/Latino), 326 international. Average age 32. 628 applicants, 64% accepted, 231 enrolled. *Faculty:* 216 full-time (66 women), 16 part-time/adjunct (7 women). Expenses: Contact institution. *Financial support:* In 2017–18, 221 students received support, including 19 fellowships with partial tuition reimbursements available (averaging $12,142 per year), 35 research assistantships with partial tuition reimbursements available (averaging $23,360 per year), 154 teaching assistantships with partial tuition reimbursements available (averaging $22,594 per year); career-related internships or fieldwork also available. In 2017, 238 master's, 84 doctorates awarded. *Program availability:* Part-time, 100% online. Offers biochemistry and molecular biology (PhD); biological sciences (MS, PhD); biological sciences for science educators (MBS); chemistry (MS, PhD); environmental toxicology (MS, PhD); genetics (PhD); mathematical sciences (MS, PhD); microbiology (MS, PhD); physics (MS, PhD); science (MBS, MS, PhD). *Application deadline:* Applications are processed on a rolling basis. *Application fee:* $80 ($90 for international students). Electronic applications accepted. *Application Contact:* Dr. Julia Frugoli, Associate Dean for Inclusive Excellence and Graduate Education, 864-656-1859, E-mail: jfrugol@clemson.edu. *Founding Dean*, Dr. Cynthia Young, 864-656-3642, E-mail: sciencedean@clemson.edu.

CLEVELAND INSTITUTE OF MUSIC, Cleveland, OH 44106-1776

General Information Independent, coed, comprehensive institution. *Graduate housing:* Room and/or apartments available on a first-come, first-served basis to single students; on-campus housing not available to married students. Housing application deadline: 5/30.

GRADUATE UNITS

Graduate Programs Offers performance (MM, DMA, AD, CPS). DMA and MM programs offered jointly with Case Western Reserve University. Electronic applications accepted.

CLEVELAND STATE UNIVERSITY, Cleveland, OH 44115

General Information State-supported, coed, university. CGS member. *Enrollment:* 16,607 graduate, professional, and undergraduate students; 2,016 full-time matriculated graduate/professional students (1,212 women), 2,000 part-time matriculated graduate/professional students (1,182 women). *Enrollment by degree level:* 3,015 master's, 776 doctoral, 225 other advanced degrees. *Graduate faculty:* 273 full-time (125 women), 316 part-time/adjunct (162 women). *Graduate housing:* Room and/or apartments available on a first-come, first-served basis to single students; on-campus housing not available to married students. Housing application deadline: 7/15. *Student* *services:* Campus employment opportunities, campus safety program, career counseling, exercise/wellness program, international student services, low-cost health insurance, multicultural affairs office, services for students with disabilities, teacher training, writing training. *Library facilities:* Michael Schwartz Library plus 1 other. *Collection:* Books: 524,556 (physical), 228,146 (digital/electronic); Serial titles: 6,155 (physical), 194 (digital/electronic); Databases: 733. Students can reserve study rooms. *Research affiliation:* Cleveland Clinic Foundation, Metro Health System.

Computer facilities: Computer purchase and lease plans are available. 736 computers available on campus for general student use. A campuswide network can be accessed from student residence rooms and from off campus. Online class registration, each general purpose computer lab has a scanner and printer, students are allowed free black and white printing up to 2,000 pages per semester are available.
Website: http://www.csuohio.edu/

General Application Contact: Dianne C. Oloff, Graduate Student Services Specialist, 216-687-5230, Fax: 216-875-9933, E-mail: d.oloff@csuohio.edu.

GRADUATE UNITS

Cleveland-Marshall College of Law Students: 226 full-time (113 women), 126 part-time (75 women); includes 62 minority (30 Black or African American, non-Hispanic/Latino; 8 Asian, non-Hispanic/Latino; 15 Hispanic/Latino; 9 Two or more races, non-Hispanic/Latino), 5 international. Average age 28. 711 applicants, 44% accepted, 118 enrolled. *Faculty:* 34 full-time (17 women), 61 part-time/adjunct (16 women). Expenses: Contact institution. *Financial support:* In 2017–18, 198 students received support, including 17 fellowships (averaging $2,500 per year), 34 research assistantships, 7 teaching assistantships with partial tuition reimbursements available (averaging $6,700 per year); career-related internships or fieldwork, Federal Work-Study, scholarships/grants, and unspecified assistantships also available. Support available to part-time students. Financial award application deadline: 5/1; financial award applicants required to submit FAFSA. In 2017, 9 master's, 118 doctorates, 5 Certificates awarded. *Program availability:* Part-time, evening/weekend. Offers law (LL M, MLS, JD, Certificate). *Application deadline:* For fall admission, 5/1 for domestic and international students. Applications are processed on a rolling basis. *Application fee:* $0. Electronic applications accepted. *Application Contact:* Christopher Lucak, Assistant Dean for Admission and Financial Aid, 216-687-4692, Fax: 216-687-6881, E-mail: law.admissions@csuohio.edu. *Dean,* Lee Fisher, 216-687-2300, Fax: 216-687-6881, E-mail: lee.fisher@csuohio.edu.

College of Graduate Studies Students: 1,790 full-time (1,099 women), 1,874 part-time (1,107 women); includes 770 minority (493 Black or African American, non-Hispanic/Latino; 3 American Indian or Alaska Native, non-Hispanic/Latino; 103 Asian, non-Hispanic/Latino; 112 Hispanic/Latino; 1 Native Hawaiian or other Pacific Islander, non-Hispanic/Latino; 58 Two or more races, non-Hispanic/Latino), 619 international. Average age 30. 4,931 applicants, 46% accepted, 966 enrolled. Expenses: Contact institution. *Financial support:* In 2017–18, 306 research assistantships with tuition reimbursements (averaging $3,480 per year), 123 teaching assistantships with tuition reimbursements (averaging $3,480 per year) were awarded; career-related internships or fieldwork, scholarships/grants, tuition waivers (full and partial), and unspecified assistantships also available. Financial award applicants required to submit FAFSA. In 2017, 1,362 master's, 86 doctorates, 10 other advanced degrees awarded. *Program availability:* Part-time, evening/weekend, 100% online, blended/hybrid learning. *Application deadline:* For fall admission, 7/1 priority date for domestic students, 5/15 priority date for international students; for spring admission, 11/15 priority date for domestic students, 11/1 priority date for international students; for summer admission, 4/1 for domestic students, 3/15 for international students. Applications are processed on a rolling basis. *Application fee:* $30. Electronic applications accepted. *Application Contact:* Dianne C. Oloff, Graduate Student Services Specialist, 216-523-7572, Fax: 216-875-9933, E-mail: d.oloff@csuohio.edu. *Dean, College of Graduate Studies,* Dr. Jianping Zhu, 216-687-3595, Fax: 216-875-9933, E-mail: j.zhu94@csuohio.edu.

College of Education and Human Services Students: 266 full-time (199 women), 763 part-time (562 women); includes 324 minority (252 Black or African American, non-Hispanic/Latino; 1 American Indian or Alaska Native, non-Hispanic/Latino; 15 Asian, non-Hispanic/Latino; 34 Hispanic/Latino; 1 Native Hawaiian or other Pacific Islander, non-Hispanic/Latino; 21 Two or more races, non-Hispanic/Latino), 37 international. Average age 34. 487 applicants, 58% accepted, 178 enrolled. *Faculty:* 86 full-time (60 women), 106 part-time/adjunct (81 women). Expenses: Contact institution. *Financial support:* In 2017–18, 64 students received support, including 38 research assistantships with full tuition reimbursements available (averaging $6,960 per year), 2 teaching assistantships with full tuition reimbursements available (averaging $7,800 per year); career-related internships or fieldwork, Federal Work-Study, scholarships/grants, tuition waivers (partial), and unspecified assistantships also available. Support available to part-time students. Financial award application deadline: 8/1; financial award applicants required to submit FAFSA. In 2017, 280 master's, 14 doctorates awarded. *Program availability:* Part-time, evening/weekend, 100% online, blended/hybrid learning. Offers adult learning and development (M Ed); adult, continuing, and higher education (PhD); art education (M Ed); counseling psychology (PhD); counselor education (PhD); early childhood education (M Ed); early childhood mental health counseling (Certificate); education and human services (M Ed, MPH, PhD, Certificate, Ed S); educational administration and supervision (M Ed); foreign language education (M Ed); learning and development (PhD); middle childhood mathematics and science education (M Ed); nursing education (PhD); physical education pedagogy (M Ed); policy studies (PhD); public health (MPH); school administration (PhD); special education (M Ed); teaching English to speakers of other languages (M Ed); urban education (PhD). *Application deadline:* For fall admission, 7/1 priority date for domestic students, 5/15 for international students; for spring admission, 11/15 priority date for domestic students, 11/1 for international students; for summer admission, 4/1 for domestic students, 3/15 for international students. Applications are processed on a rolling basis. *Application fee:* $30. Electronic applications accepted. *Application Contact:* Patricia Sokolowski, Office Coordinator/Assistant to the Dean, 216-523-7143, Fax: 216-687-5415, E-mail: p.sokolowski@csuohio.edu. *Dean,* Dr. Sajit Zachariah, 216-523-7143, Fax: 216-687-5415, E-mail: sajit.zachariah@csuohio.edu.

College of Liberal Arts and Social Sciences Students: 212 full-time (162 women), 127 part-time (82 women); includes 105 minority (77 Black or African American, non-Hispanic/Latino; 3 Asian, non-Hispanic/Latino; 13 Hispanic/Latino; 12 Two or more races, non-Hispanic/Latino), 18 international. Average age 32. 499 applicants, 46% accepted, 123 enrolled. *Faculty:* 156 full-time (64 women), 184 part-time/adjunct (79 women). Expenses: Contact institution. *Financial support:* Fellowships, research assistantships, teaching assistantships, career-related internships or fieldwork, Federal Work-Study, institutionally sponsored loans, tuition waivers (full and partial), and unspecified assistantships available. Support available to part-time students. Financial award applicants required to submit FAFSA. In 2017, 184 master's awarded. *Program availability:* Part-time, evening/weekend. Offers applied communication theory and methodology (MA); art history (MA); bioethics (MA, Certificate); composition (MM); creative writing (MFA); economics (MA); global interactions (MA); liberal arts and social sciences (M Ed, MA, MFA, MM, MSW, Certificate); museum studies (MA); music education (MM); philosophy (MA); social work (MSW); Spanish (MA). *Application deadline:* Applications are processed on a rolling basis. *Application fee:* $30. Electronic applications accepted. *Application Contact:* Deborah L. Brown, Interim Assistant Director, Graduate Admissions, 216-523-7572, Fax: 216-687-5400, E-mail: d.l.brown@csuohio.edu. *Dean,* Dr. Gregory M. Sadlek, 216-687-3660.

College of Sciences and Health Professions Students: 579 full-time (413 women), 181 part-time (134 women); includes 102 minority (46 Black or African American, non-Hispanic/Latino; 1 American Indian or Alaska Native, non-Hispanic/Latino; 19 Asian, non-Hispanic/Latino; 27 Hispanic/Latino; 9 Two or more races, non-Hispanic/Latino), 98 international. Average age 28. 912 applicants, 34% accepted, 204 enrolled. *Faculty:* 107 full-time (35 women), 76 part-time/adjunct (43 women). Expenses: Contact institution. *Financial support:* In 2017–18, 174 students received support, including 47 research assistantships with full tuition reimbursements available (averaging $17,000 per year), 127 teaching assistantships with tuition reimbursements available (averaging $10,700 per year); unspecified assistantships also available. Financial award applicants required to submit FAFSA. In 2017, 190 master's, 55 doctorates, 10 other advanced degrees awarded. *Program availability:* Part-time, evening/weekend, online learning. Offers applied statistics (MS); biological, geological, and environmental sciences (MS, PhD); clinical chemistry (PhD); health sciences (MS); mathematics (MS); occupational therapy (MOT); organic chemistry (MS); physical chemistry (MS); physical therapy (DPT); physician assistant science (MS); physics (MS); psychology (MA, PhD, Psy S); sciences and health professions (MA, MOT, MS, DPT, PhD, Psy S); speech pathology and audiology (MA). *Application deadline:* For fall admission, 7/1 priority date for domestic students, 5/15 priority date for international students; for spring admission, 11/15 priority date for domestic students, 11/1 priority date for international students; for summer admission, 4/1 for domestic students, 3/15 for international students. Applications are processed on a rolling basis. *Application fee:* $30. Electronic applications accepted. *Application Contact:* Dianne C. Oloff, Graduate Student Services Specialist, 216-687-5230, Fax: 216-875-9933, E-mail: d.oloff@csuohio.edu. *Dean of the College of Graduate Studies,* Dr. Jianping Zhu, 216-687-3595, Fax: 216-875-9933, E-mail: j.zhu94@csuohio.edu.

Fenn College of Engineering Students: 290 full-time (71 women), 191 part-time (39 women); includes 29 minority (8 Black or African American, non-Hispanic/Latino; 17 Asian, non-Hispanic/Latino; 3 Hispanic/Latino; 1 Two or more races, non-Hispanic/Latino), 306 international. Average age 26. 1,037 applicants, 48% accepted, 143 enrolled. *Faculty:* 54 full-time (5 women), 12 part-time/adjunct (0 women). Expenses: Contact institution. *Financial support:* In 2017–18, 93 students received support. Fellowships, research assistantships, teaching assistantships, career-related internships or fieldwork, institutionally sponsored loans, scholarships/grants, tuition waivers (full and partial), and unspecified assistantships available. Support available to part-time students. Financial award application deadline: 3/30; financial award applicants required to submit FAFSA. In 2017, 312 master's, 6 doctorates awarded. *Program availability:* Part-time, evening/weekend. Offers applied biomedical engineering (D Eng); chemical and biomedical engineering (MS, D Eng); civil and environmental engineering (MS, D Eng); electrical engineering (MS, D Eng); engineering (MS, D Eng); mechanical engineering (MS, D Eng); software engineering (MS). *Application deadline:* Applications are processed on a rolling basis. *Application fee:* $30. Electronic applications accepted. *Application Contact:* Deborah L. Brown, Interim Assistant Director, Graduate Admissions, 216-523-7572, Fax: 216-687-9214, E-mail: d.l.brown@csuohio.edu. *Associate Dean,* Dr. Paul P. Lin, 216-687-2556, Fax: 216-687-9280, E-mail: p.lin@csuohio.edu.

Maxine Goodman Levin College of Urban Affairs Students: 63 full-time (35 women), 122 part-time (66 women); includes 41 minority (29 Black or African American, non-Hispanic/Latino; 1 Asian, non-Hispanic/Latino; 6 Hispanic/Latino; 5 Two or more races, non-Hispanic/Latino), 11 international. Average age 33. 195 applicants, 47% accepted, 38 enrolled. *Faculty:* 22 full-time (9 women), 8 part-time/adjunct (4 women). Expenses: Contact institution. *Financial support:* In 2017–18, 60 students received support, including 40 research assistantships with full tuition reimbursements available (averaging $8,000 per year), 15 teaching assistantships with tuition reimbursements available (averaging $7,000 per year); career-related internships or fieldwork, Federal Work-Study, institutionally sponsored loans, scholarships/grants, and unspecified assistantships also available. Support available to part-time students. Financial award application deadline: 3/1; financial award applicants required to submit FAFSA. In 2017, 71 master's, 4 doctorates awarded. *Program availability:* Part-time, evening/weekend. Offers communication (PhD); economic development (MPA, MUPD); environmental nonprofit management (MAES); environmental planning (MAES); environmental sustainability (MUPD); historic preservation (MUPD); housing and neighborhood development (MUPD); local and urban management (Certificate); non-profit management (MPA); nonprofit administration and leadership (MNAL); nonprofit management (Certificate); policy and administration (MAES); public administration (PhD); public management (MPA); real estate development and finance (MUPD); sustainable economic development (MAES); urban affairs (MAES, MNAL, MPA, MS, MUPD, PhD, Certificate); urban economic development (Certificate); urban geographic information systems (MUPD); urban policy and development (PhD); urban studies (MS, Certificate). *Application deadline:* For fall admission, 7/1 priority date for domestic students, 5/15 for international students; for spring admission, 11/15 for domestic students, 11/1 for international students; for summer admission, 4/1 for domestic students, 3/15 for international students. Applications are processed on a rolling basis. *Application fee:* $30. Electronic applications accepted. *Application Contact:* Graduate Program Coordinator, 216-523-7522, Fax: 216-687-5398, E-mail: urbanprograms@csuohio.edu. *Dean,* Dr. Roland V. Anglin, 216-687-2135, E-mail: r.anglin@csuohio.edu.

Monte Ahuja College of Business Students: 351 full-time (182 women), 461 part-time (216 women); includes 161 minority (82 Black or African American, non-Hispanic/Latino; 1 American Indian or Alaska Native, non-Hispanic/Latino; 46 Asian, non-Hispanic/Latino; 25 Hispanic/Latino; 7 Two or more races, non-Hispanic/Latino), 151 international. Average age 29. 1,052 applicants, 46% accepted, 258 enrolled. *Faculty:* 48 full-time (16 women), 33 part-time/adjunct (12 women). Expenses: Contact institution. *Financial support:* In 2017–18, 110 students received support, including 45 research assistantships with full tuition reimbursements available (averaging $6,960 per year), 1 teaching assistantship with full tuition reimbursement available (averaging $7,800 per year); career-related internships or fieldwork, scholarships/grants, tuition waivers (full), and unspecified assistantships also available. Financial award application deadline: 5/15; financial award applicants required to submit FAFSA. In 2017, 307 master's, 7 doctorates awarded. *Program availability:* Part-time, evening/weekend. Offers business (AMBA, EMBA, M Acc,

MBA, MLRHR, DBA); business administration (AMBA, EMBA, MBA, DBA); financial accounting/audit (M Acc); health care administration (MBA); information systems (DBA); labor relations and human resources (MLRHR); marketing (DBA). *Application deadline:* For fall admission, 7/1 priority date for domestic students, 5/15 for international students; for spring admission, 11/15 priority date for domestic students, 11/1 for international students; for summer admission, 4/1 for domestic students, 3/15 for international students. Applications are processed on a rolling basis. *Application fee:* $30. Electronic applications accepted. *Application Contact:* Kenneth Dippong, Director, Student Services, 216-523-7545, Fax: 216-687-9354, E-mail: k.dippong@csuohio.edu.

School of Nursing Students: 10 full-time (9 women), 57 part-time (51 women); includes 15 minority (10 Black or African American, non-Hispanic/Latino; 2 Asian, non-Hispanic/Latino; 3 Hispanic/Latino). Average age 36. 60 applicants, 62% accepted, 26 enrolled. *Faculty:* 7 full-time (all women). Expenses: Contact institution. *Financial support:* Tuition waivers (full) and unspecified assistantships available. Financial award application deadline: 5/1; financial award applicants required to submit FAFSA. In 2017, 14 master's awarded. *Program availability:* Part-time, 100% online. Offers nursing (MSN, PhD). *Application deadline:* For fall admission, 3/1 priority date for domestic and international students. *Application fee:* $55. Electronic applications accepted. *Application Contact:* Maureen Mitchell, Assistant Professor and Graduate Program Director, 216-523-7128, Fax: 216-687-3556, E-mail: m.m.mitchell1@csuohio.edu. *Dean,* Dr. Vida Lock, 216-523-7237, Fax: 216-687-3556, E-mail: v.lock@csuohio.edu.

CLEVELAND UNIVERSITY–KANSAS CITY, Overland Park, KS 66210

General Information Independent, coed, comprehensive institution. *Graduate housing:* On-campus housing not available. *Student services:* Campus employment opportunities, campus safety program, career counseling, child daycare facilities, exercise/wellness program, free psychological counseling, international student services, low-cost health insurance, services for students with disabilities. *Library facilities:* Ruth R. Cleveland Memorial Library.

Computer facilities: 30 computers available on campus for general student use. A campuswide network can be accessed. Educational software available.
Website: http://www.cleveland.edu/

General Application Contact: Melissa Denton, Director of Admissions, 913-234-0744, Fax: 913-234-0906, E-mail: kc.admissions@cleveland.edu.

GRADUATE UNITS

Doctor of Chiropractic Program Expenses: Contact institution. *Financial support:* Federal Work-Study and scholarships/grants available. Financial award applicants required to submit FAFSA. *Program availability:* Part-time. Offers chiropractic (DC). *Application deadline:* For fall admission, 7/1 priority date for domestic and international students; for winter admission, 11/1 priority date for domestic and international students; for spring admission, 3/1 priority date for domestic and international students. Applications are processed on a rolling basis. Electronic applications accepted. *Application Contact:* Melissa Denton, Director of Admissions, 913-234-0744, Fax: 913-234-0906, E-mail: kc.admissions@cleveland.edu.

Program in Health Education and Promotion Expenses: Contact institution. *Financial support:* Applicants required to submit FAFSA. *Program availability:* Part-time. Offers health education and promotion (MS). *Application deadline:* For fall admission, 7/1 for domestic and international students; for winter admission, 10/1 for domestic and international students. Applications are processed on a rolling basis. Electronic applications accepted. *Application Contact:* Melissa Denton, Director of Admissions, 913-234-0744, Fax: 913-234-0906, E-mail: kc.admissions@cleveland.edu.

COASTAL CAROLINA UNIVERSITY, Conway, SC 29528-6054

General Information State-supported, coed, comprehensive institution. *Enrollment:* 10,663 graduate, professional, and undergraduate students; 188 full-time matriculated graduate/professional students (89 women), 430 part-time matriculated graduate/professional students (333 women). *Enrollment by degree level:* 563 master's, 10 doctoral, 45 other advanced degrees. *Graduate faculty:* 77 full-time (34 women), 27 part-time/adjunct (17 women). Tuition, state resident: full-time $5184; part-time $576 per credit hour. Tuition, nonresident: full-time $9369; part-time $1041 per credit hour. *Required fees:* $90; $5 per credit hour. *Graduate housing:* Room and/or apartments available on a first-come, first-served basis to single students; on-campus housing not available to married students. Typical cost: $5440 per year ($9140 including board). Room and board charges vary according to board plan and housing facility selected. Housing application deadline: 5/1. *Student services:* Campus employment opportunities, campus safety program, career counseling, exercise/wellness program, free psychological counseling, grant writing training, international student services, low-cost health insurance, multicultural affairs office, services for students with disabilities, teacher training, writing training. *Library facilities:* Kimbel Library. *Collection:* Books: 137,543 (physical), 417,526 (digital/electronic); Serial titles: 588 (physical), 127,240 (digital/electronic); Databases: 175. Weekly public service hours: 168; study areas open 24 hours, 5–7 days a week.

Computer facilities: Computer purchase and lease plans are available. 1,322 computers available on campus for general student use. A campuswide network can be accessed from student residence rooms and from off campus. Online class registration is available.
Website: http://www.coastal.edu/

General Application Contact: Dr. James O. Luken, Associate Provost/Interim Vice Dean of the School of the Coastal Environment, 843-349-2235, Fax: 843-349-6444, E-mail: joluken@coastal.edu.

GRADUATE UNITS

College of Science Students: 58 full-time (19 women), 38 part-time (19 women); includes 19 minority (14 Black or African American, non-Hispanic/Latino; 1 American Indian or Alaska Native, non-Hispanic/Latino; 2 Hispanic/Latino; 2 Two or more races, non-Hispanic/Latino), 8 international. Average age 27. 104 applicants, 62% accepted, 42 enrolled. *Faculty:* 29 full-time (7 women), 2 part-time/adjunct (1 woman). Expenses: Contact institution. *Financial support:* Fellowships, research assistantships, teaching assistantships, and tuition waivers available. Financial award application deadline: 3/1; financial award applicants required to submit FAFSA. In 2017, 9 master's awarded. *Program availability:* Part-time, evening/weekend, 100% online. Offers applied computing and information systems (Certificate); coastal marine and wetland studies (MS); information systems technology (MS); marine science (PhD); sports management (MS). *Application deadline:* For fall admission, 1/15 priority date for domestic and international students; for spring admission, 11/1 priority date for domestic and international students. Applications are processed on a rolling basis. *Application fee:* $45. Electronic applications accepted. *Application Contact:* Dr. James O. Luken, Associate Provost for Graduate Program/Vice-Dean of the Coastal Environment, 843-349-2235, Fax: 843-349-6444, E-mail: joluken@coastal.edu. *Dean/Vice President for Research and Emerging Initiatives,* Dr. Michael H. Roberts, 843-349-2282, Fax: 843-349-2545, E-mail: mroberts@coastal.edu.

E. Craig Wall, Sr. College of Business Administration Students: 58 full-time (31 women), 34 part-time (16 women); includes 26 minority (19 Black or African American, non-Hispanic/Latino; 2 Asian, non-Hispanic/Latino; 1 Hispanic/Latino; 1 Native Hawaiian or other Pacific Islander, non-Hispanic/Latino; 3 Two or more races, non-Hispanic/Latino), 9 international. Average age 27. 103 applicants, 74% accepted, 54 enrolled. *Faculty:* 11 full-time (5 women), 2 part-time/adjunct (0 women). Expenses: Contact institution. *Financial support:* Fellowships, research assistantships, teaching assistantships, and tuition waivers available. Financial award application deadline: 3/1; financial award applicants required to submit FAFSA. In 2017, 68 master's awarded. *Program availability:* Part-time, evening/weekend, 100% online, blended/hybrid learning. Offers accounting (M Acc); business administration (MBA); business foundations (Certificate); fraud examination (Certificate). *Application deadline:* For fall admission, 6/15 priority date for domestic and international students; for spring admission, 11/15 priority date for domestic and international students; for summer admission, 4/15 priority date for domestic and international students. Applications are processed on a rolling basis. *Application fee:* $45. Electronic applications accepted. *Application Contact:* Dr. James O. Luken, Associate Provost for Graduate Program/Interim Vice-Dean of the Coastal Environment, 843-349-2235, Fax: 843-349-6444, E-mail: joluken@coastal.edu. *Associate Dean/Professor/Director of Graduate Programs and Executive Education,* Dr. Mark Mitchell, 843-349-2392, Fax: 843-349-2455, E-mail: mmitchel@coastal.edu.

Spadoni College of Education Students: 43 full-time (22 women), 345 part-time (290 women); includes 70 minority (51 Black or African American, non-Hispanic/Latino; 3 American Indian or Alaska Native, non-Hispanic/Latino; 3 Asian, non-Hispanic/Latino; 8 Hispanic/Latino; 1 Native Hawaiian or other Pacific Islander, non-Hispanic/Latino; 4 Two or more races, non-Hispanic/Latino). Average age 33. 288 applicants, 77% accepted, 157 enrolled. *Faculty:* 16 full-time (9 women), 22 part-time/adjunct (15 women). Expenses: Contact institution. *Financial support:* Fellowships, research assistantships, teaching assistantships, and tuition waivers available. Financial award application deadline: 3/1; financial award applicants required to submit FAFSA. In 2017, 151 master's, 28 other advanced degrees awarded. *Program availability:* Part-time, evening/weekend, 100% online, blended/hybrid learning. Offers education (MAT); educational leadership (M Ed, Ed S); English for speakers of other languages (Certificate); instructional technology (M Ed, Ed S); language, literacy and culture (M Ed); learning and teaching (M Ed); online teaching and training (Certificate); special education (M Ed). *Application deadline:* For fall admission, 5/1 priority date for domestic and international students; for spring admission, 11/1 priority date for domestic and international students; for summer admission, 3/1 priority date for domestic and international students. Applications are processed on a rolling basis. *Application fee:* $45. Electronic applications accepted. *Application Contact:* Dr. James O. Luken, Associate Provost for Graduate Program/Vice-Dean of the Coastal Environment, 843-349-2235, Fax: 843-349-6444, E-mail: joluken@coastal.edu. *Dean/Vice President for Online Education and Teaching Excellence,* Dr. Edward Jadallah, 843-349-2773, Fax: 843-349-2106, E-mail: ejadalla@coastal.edu.

Thomas W. and Robin W. Edwards College of Humanities and Fine Arts Students: 29 full-time (17 women), 13 part-time (8 women); includes 7 minority (6 Black or African American, non-Hispanic/Latino; 1 Two or more races, non-Hispanic/Latino), 2 international. Average age 32. 32 applicants, 72% accepted, 19 enrolled. *Faculty:* 20 full-time (12 women), 1 (woman) part-time/adjunct. Expenses: Contact institution. *Financial support:* Fellowships, research assistantships, teaching assistantships, and tuition waivers available. Financial award application deadline: 3/1; financial award applicants required to submit FAFSA. In 2017, 18 master's awarded. *Program availability:* Part-time, evening/weekend. Offers liberal studies (MA); writing (MA). *Application deadline:* For fall admission, 5/15 priority date for domestic and international students; for spring admission, 11/15 priority date for domestic and international students. Applications are processed on a rolling basis. *Application fee:* $45. Electronic applications accepted. *Application Contact:* Dr. James O. Luken, Associate Provost for Graduate Program/Vice-Dean of the Coastal Environment, 843-349-2235, Fax: 843-349-6444, E-mail: joluken@coastal.edu. *Dean/Vice President for Academic Outreach,* Dr. Daniel J. Ennis, 843-349-2746, E-mail: dennis@coastal.edu.

COGSWELL POLYTECHNICAL COLLEGE, San Jose, CA 95134

General Information Proprietary, coed, comprehensive institution.

GRADUATE UNITS

Program in Entrepreneurship and Innovation Offers entrepreneurship and innovation (MA).

COKER COLLEGE, Hartsville, SC 29550

General Information Independent, coed, comprehensive institution. *Enrollment:* 1,093 graduate, professional, and undergraduate students; 77 full-time matriculated graduate/professional students (47 women), 9 part-time matriculated graduate/professional students (4 women). *Enrollment by degree level:* 86 master's. *Graduate faculty:* 9 full-time (4 women), 3 part-time/adjunct (2 women). *Tuition:* Full-time $14,424; part-time $601 per credit hour. *Required fees:* $176; $176 per credit hour. Tuition and fees vary according to course load and program. *Graduate housing:* On-campus housing not available. *Student services:* Campus employment opportunities, campus safety program, career counseling, free psychological counseling, services for students with disabilities, writing training. *Library facilities:* The Charles W. and Joan S. Coker Library-Information Technology Center plus 1 other. *Collection:* Books: 81,626 (physical), 15,760 (digital/electronic). Weekly public service hours: 87; students can reserve study rooms.

Computer facilities: 116 computers available on campus for general student use. A campuswide network can be accessed from student residence rooms. Online class registration is available.
Website: http://www.coker.edu/

General Application Contact: Lacey Rice-Serafin, Director of Graduate Programs, 843-857-4128, E-mail: lriceserafin@coker.edu.

GRADUATE UNITS

Graduate Programs Students: 77 full-time (47 women), 9 part-time (4 women); includes 21 minority (15 Black or African American, non-Hispanic/Latino; 1 American Indian or Alaska Native, non-Hispanic/Latino; 1 Hispanic/Latino; 4 Two or more races, non-Hispanic/Latino), 1 international. Average age 30. *Faculty:* 9 full-time (4 women), 3 part-time/adjunct (2 women). Expenses: Contact institution. *Financial support:* Unspecified assistantships available. Financial award application deadline: 6/30; financial award applicants required to submit FAFSA. *Program availability:* Part-time, 100% online. Offers college athletic administration (MS); criminal and social justice policy (MS); curriculum and instructional technology (M Ed); literacy studies (M Ed); management and leadership (MS). *Application deadline:* Applications are processed on a rolling basis. *Application fee:* $25. Electronic applications accepted. *Application Contact:* Lacey Rice-Serafin, Director of Graduate Programs, 843-857-4128, E-mail: lriceserafin@coker.edu.

THE COLBURN SCHOOL CONSERVATORY OF MUSIC, Los Angeles, CA 90012

General Information Independent, coed, comprehensive institution.

GRADUATE UNITS

Graduate Programs Offers music (AD); performance (MM).

COLD SPRING HARBOR LABORATORY, Cold Spring Harbor, NY 11724

General Information Independent, coed, graduate-only institution. *Enrollment by degree level:* 44 doctoral. *Graduate faculty:* 55 full-time (11 women). *Graduate housing:* Rooms and/or apartments guaranteed to single students and available on a first-come, first-served basis to married students. Housing application deadline: 8/1. *Student services:* Campus safety program, career counseling, child daycare facilities, exercise/wellness program, free psychological counseling, grant writing training, international student services, low-cost health insurance, services for students with disabilities, teacher training, writing training. *Library facilities:* Cold Spring Harbor Laboratory Library. *Collection:* Study areas open 24 hours, 5–7 days a week; students can reserve study rooms.

Computer facilities: A campuswide network can be accessed from student residence rooms and from off campus.
Website: http://www.cshl.edu/gradschool/

General Application Contact: Kimberly Creteur, Admissions and Recruitment Manager, 516-367-6890, Fax: 516-367-6919, E-mail: gradschool@cshl.edu.

GRADUATE UNITS

Watson School of Biological Sciences Students: 44 full-time (22 women); includes 7 minority (1 Black or African American, non-Hispanic/Latino; 2 Asian, non-Hispanic/Latino; 3 Hispanic/Latino; 1 Two or more races, non-Hispanic/Latino), 22 international. Average age 27. 202 applicants, 13% accepted, 8 enrolled. *Faculty:* 55 full-time (11 women). Expenses: Contact institution. *Financial support:* In 2017–18, 44 students received support, including 44 fellowships with full tuition reimbursements available (averaging $34,000 per year); scholarships/grants, traineeships, health care benefits, and tuition waivers (full) also available. Financial award application deadline: 12/1. In 2017, 9 doctorates awarded. Offers biological sciences (PhD). *Application deadline:* For fall admission, 12/1 for domestic and international students. *Application fee:* $60. Electronic applications accepted. *Application Contact:* Admissions and Recruitment Manager, 516-367-6890, E-mail: gradschool@cshl.edu. *Dean,* Dr. Alexander Gann, 516-367-6890.

COLGATE ROCHESTER CROZER DIVINITY SCHOOL, Rochester, NY 14620-2530

General Information Independent-religious, coed, graduate-only institution. *Enrollment by degree level:* 42 master's, 50 doctoral, 2 other advanced degrees. *Graduate faculty:* 7 full-time (3 women), 15 part-time/adjunct (7 women). *Tuition:* Full-time $10,770; part-time $1795 per course. *Required fees:* $260; $35 per course. One-time fee: $50 full-time. Tuition and fees vary according to course load, degree level and program. *Graduate housing:* On-campus housing not available. *Student services:* Campus employment opportunities, campus safety program, services for students with disabilities. *Library facilities:* Ambrose Swasey Library plus 1 other. *Collection:* Books: 19,227 (physical); Serial titles: 57 (physical). Weekly public service hours: 41.

Computer facilities: 8 computers available on campus for general student use. A campuswide network can be accessed.
Website: http://www.crcds.edu/

General Application Contact: Rev. Melissa M. Morral, Vice President for Enrollment Services, 585-340-9500, Fax: 585-340-9644, E-mail: mmorral@crcds.edu.

GRADUATE UNITS

Graduate and Professional Programs Students: 70 full-time, 24 part-time; includes 58 minority (48 Black or African American, non-Hispanic/Latino; 3 Asian, non-Hispanic/Latino; 3 Hispanic/Latino; 4 Two or more races, non-Hispanic/Latino). Average age 43. 23 applicants, 96% accepted, 21 enrolled. *Faculty:* 7 full-time (3 women), 15 part-time/adjunct (7 women). Expenses: Contact institution. *Financial support:* In 2017–18, 26 students received support. Scholarships/grants available. Financial award application deadline: 9/1; financial award applicants required to submit FAFSA. In 2017, 21 master's, 3 doctorates awarded. *Program availability:* Part-time, evening/weekend. Offers divinity (M Div, MA, Certificate); peace building and interfaith dialogue (D Min); prophetic preaching (D Min); transformative leadership (D Min). *Application deadline:* For fall admission, 7/1 priority date for domestic students, 3/1 for international students; for spring admission, 12/1 priority date for domestic students, 9/1 for international students. Applications are processed on a rolling basis. *Application fee:* $35. Electronic applications accepted. *Application Contact:* Rev. Melissa M. Morral, Vice President for Enrollment Services, 585-340-9633, Fax: 585-340-9644, E-mail: mmorral@crcds.edu. *President,* Rev. Marvin A. McMickle, PhD, 585-271-1320 Ext. 680, Fax: 585-271-8013.

COLGATE UNIVERSITY, Hamilton, NY 13346-1386

General Information Independent, coed, comprehensive institution. *Graduate housing:* On-campus housing not available.

GRADUATE UNITS

Master of Arts in Teaching Program Offers teaching (MAT).

THE COLLEGE AT BROCKPORT, STATE UNIVERSITY OF NEW YORK, Brockport, NY 14420-2997

General Information State-supported, coed, comprehensive institution. CGS member. *Enrollment:* 8,313 graduate, professional, and undergraduate students; 350 full-time matriculated graduate/professional students (227 women), 749 part-time matriculated graduate/professional students (524 women). *Enrollment by degree level:* 1,099 master's. *Graduate faculty:* 121 full-time (62 women), 39 part-time/adjunct (23 women). Tuition, state resident: full-time $10,870; part-time $453 per credit hour. Tuition, nonresident: full-time $22,210. *Required fees:* $988; $246 per semester. *Graduate housing:* On-campus housing not available. *Student services:* Campus employment opportunities, campus safety program, career counseling, child daycare facilities, exercise/wellness program, free psychological counseling, grant writing training, international student services, low-cost health insurance, multicultural affairs office, services for students with disabilities, teacher training, writing training. *Library facilities:* Drake Memorial Library. *Collection:* Books: 500,461 (physical), 185,000 (digital/electronic); Serial titles: 4,747 (physical), 113,396 (digital/electronic); Databases: 270. Weekly public service hours: 93; students can reserve study rooms.

Computer facilities: 1,000 computers available on campus for general student use. A campuswide network can be accessed from student residence rooms and from off campus. Online class registration is available.
Website: http://www.brockport.edu/

General Application Contact: Danielle A. Welch, Graduate Admissions Counselor, 585-395-2525, Fax: 585-395-2515, E-mail: dwelch@brockport.edu.

GRADUATE UNITS

School of Arts and Sciences Students: 92 full-time (55 women), 104 part-time (61 women); includes 21 minority (10 Black or African American, non-Hispanic/Latino; 2 Asian, non-Hispanic/Latino; 4 Hispanic/Latino; 5 Two or more races, non-Hispanic/Latino), 6 international. 71 applicants, 44% accepted, 21 enrolled. *Faculty:* 27 full-time (11 women), 2 part-time/adjunct (both women). Expenses: Contact institution. *Financial support:* Research assistantships, teaching assistantships, Federal Work-Study, scholarships/grants, and unspecified assistantships available. Support available to part-time students. Financial award applicants required to submit FAFSA. In 2017, 66 master's, 1 other advanced degree awarded. *Program availability:* Part-time. Offers arts and sciences (MA, MFA, MS, PSM, AGC); biology (MS, PSM); clinical psychology (with applied emphasis) (MA); clinical psychology (with research emphasis) (MA); communication (MA); creative writing (AGC); dance (MA, MFA); English (MA); environmental science and biology (MS); general psychology (MA); history (MA); liberal studies (MA); mathematics (MA); visual studies (MFA). *Application Contact:* Danielle A. Welch, Graduate Admissions Counselor, 585-395-2525, Fax: 585-395-2515. *Dean,* Dr. Jose Maliekal, 585-395-5806, E-mail: jmalieka@brockport.edu.

School of Business and Management Students: 76 full-time (49 women), 106 part-time (64 women); includes 45 minority (22 Black or African American, non-Hispanic/Latino; 6 Asian, non-Hispanic/Latino; 11 Hispanic/Latino; 6 Two or more races, non-Hispanic/Latino), 6 international. 29 applicants, 79% accepted, 19 enrolled. *Faculty:* 6 full-time (2 women), 5 part-time/adjunct (3 women). Expenses: Contact institution. *Financial support:* Career-related internships or fieldwork, Federal Work-Study, scholarships/grants, and unspecified assistantships available. Financial award application deadline: 3/15; financial award applicants required to submit FAFSA. In 2017, 75 master's, 6 other advanced degrees awarded. *Program availability:* Part-time. Offers accounting (MS); arts administration (AGC); nonprofit management (AGC); public administration (MPA, AGC). *Application deadline:* For fall admission, 7/1 priority date for domestic and international students; for spring admission, 12/1 priority date for domestic and international students. *Application fee:* $50. Electronic applications accepted. *Application Contact:* Danielle A. Welch, Graduate Counselor, 585-395-5430, Fax: 585-395-2515, E-mail: dwelch@brockport.edu. *School Dean,* Dr. Joy Bhadury, 585-395-2623, Fax: 585-395-2542.

School of Education, Health, and Human Services Students: 182 full-time (123 women), 539 part-time (399 women); includes 102 minority (47 Black or African American, non-Hispanic/Latino; 1 American Indian or Alaska Native, non-Hispanic/Latino; 10 Asian, non-Hispanic/Latino; 26 Hispanic/Latino; 1 Native Hawaiian or other Pacific Islander, non-Hispanic/Latino; 17 Two or more races, non-Hispanic/Latino), 1 international. 523 applicants, 72% accepted, 275 enrolled. *Faculty:* 33 full-time (20 women), 35 part-time/adjunct (23 women). Expenses: Contact institution. *Financial support:* In 2017–18, 3 teaching assistantships with full tuition reimbursements (averaging $3,000 per year) were awarded; institutionally sponsored loans, scholarships/grants, and unspecified assistantships also available. Financial award applicants required to submit FAFSA. In 2017, 246 master's, 44 other advanced degrees awarded. *Program availability:* Part-time, 100% online. Offers adapted physical education (AGC); adolescence biology education (MS Ed); adolescence chemistry education (MS Ed); adolescence education (MS Ed); adolescence English (MS Ed); adolescence mathematics (MS Ed); adolescence physics (MS Ed); adolescence social studies education (MS Ed); bilingual education (MS Ed, AGC); biology (MS Ed, AGC); chemistry (MS Ed, AGC); childhood curriculum specialist (MS Ed); college counseling (MS Ed, CAS); community health education (MS Ed); education, health, and human services (MPA, MS, MS Ed, MSW, AGC, Advanced Certificate, CAS, Graduate Certificate); English (MS Ed, Advanced Certificate); family and community practice (MSW); gerontology (AGC); health education (MS Ed); inclusive generalist education (MS Ed, AGC, Advanced Certificate); interdisciplinary health practice (MSW); literacy education B-12 (MS Ed); mathematics (MS Ed, Advanced Certificate); mental health counseling (MS, CAS); physical education (MS Ed); school building leader (CAS); school building leader/school district leader (CAS); school counseling (MS Ed, CAS); school counselor supervision (CAS); school district business leader (CAS); school district leader (CAS); science (MS Ed, Advanced Certificate); social studies (MS Ed, Advanced Certificate); teacher leadership (Graduate Certificate). *Application Contact:* Danielle A. Welch, Graduate Admissions Counselor, 585-395-2525, Fax: 585-395-2515. *Dean,* Dr. Thomas Hernandez, 585-395-2510, Fax: 585-395-2172, E-mail: thernandez@brockport.edu.

COLLÈGE DOMINICAIN DE PHILOSOPHIE ET DE THÉOLOGIE, Ottawa, ON K1R 7G3, Canada

General Information Independent-religious, coed, university. *Graduate housing:* Room and/or apartments available on a first-come, first-served basis to single students; on-campus housing not available to married students.

GRADUATE UNITS

Graduate Programs *Program availability:* Part-time, evening/weekend.

Faculty of Philosophy Offers philosophy (MA Ph, PhD).

Faculty of Theology *Program availability:* Part-time, evening/weekend. Offers theology (M Th, MA Th, PhD, Th D, L Th).

COLLEGE FOR CREATIVE STUDIES, Detroit, MI 48202-4034

General Information Independent, coed, comprehensive institution.

GRADUATE UNITS

Graduate Programs

COLLEGE FOR FINANCIAL PLANNING, Centennial, CO 80112

General Information Proprietary, coed, primarily men, graduate-only institution. *Enrollment by degree level:* 250 master's, 4,750 other advanced degrees. *Graduate faculty:* 9 full-time (2 women), 24 part-time/adjunct (4 women). *Tuition:* Full-time $7000; part-time $1400 per course. *Graduate housing:* On-campus housing not available. *Student services:* Services for students with disabilities. *Library facilities:* Apollo University Library. *Collection:* Books: 190,000 (digital/electronic); Databases: 7. Study areas open 24 hours, 5–7 days a week.

Computer facilities: Online class registration is available.
Website: http://www.cffp.edu/

General Application Contact: Alicia Christensen, Director of Enrollment, 303-220-4835, Fax: 303-220-1810, E-mail: alicia.mead@cffp.edu.

GRADUATE UNITS

Graduate Programs Students: 5,000 full-time. *Faculty:* 9 full-time (2 women), 24 part-time/adjunct (4 women). Expenses: Contact institution. *Program availability:* Part-time, evening/weekend, online only, 100% online. Offers finance (MSF); personal financial planning (MS). *Application deadline:* Applications are processed on a rolling basis. Electronic applications accepted. *Application Contact:* Alicia Christensen, Director of Enrollment, 303-220-4835, Fax: 303-220-1810, E-mail: alicia.mead@cffp.edu. *President*, John Sears, 303-220-4918, E-mail: john.sears@cffp.edu.

COLLEGE OF CHARLESTON, Charleston, SC 29424-0001

General Information State-supported, coed, comprehensive institution. CGS member. *Graduate housing:* On-campus housing not available. *Research affiliation:* Oak Ridge Associated Universities (science), South Carolina Department of Natural Resources, Marine Resources Division (marine biology, environmental studies), National Institute of Standards and Technology (NIST) (marine biology, environmental studies), National Oceanic and Atmospheric Administration (NOAA) (marine biology, environmental studies), U.S. Department of Agriculture (USDA) (environmental studies), South Carolina Aquarium (marine biology, environmental studies).

GRADUATE UNITS

Graduate School *Program availability:* Part-time, evening/weekend. Electronic applications accepted.

School of Business Offers accountancy (MS); business (MBA, MS); business administration (MBA). Electronic applications accepted.

School of Education, Health, and Human Performance *Program availability:* Part-time, evening/weekend. Offers early childhood education (MAT); education, health, and human performance (M Ed, MAT, Certificate); elementary education (MAT); English to speakers of other languages (Certificate); languages (M Ed); performing arts education (MAT); science and mathematics for teachers (M Ed); special education (MAT); teaching, learning and advocacy (M Ed). Electronic applications accepted.

School of Humanities and Social Sciences *Program availability:* Part-time, evening/weekend. Offers creative writing (MFA); English (MA); history (MA); humanities and social sciences (MA, MFA, MPA, Certificate); public administration (MPA); urban and regional planning (Certificate). Electronic applications accepted.

School of Sciences and Mathematics *Program availability:* Part-time, evening/weekend. Offers computer and information sciences (MS); environmental studies (MS); marine biology (MS); mathematics (MS); sciences and mathematics (MS). Electronic applications accepted.

School of the Arts Offers arts (MS, Certificate); arts management (Certificate); historic preservation (MS).

COLLEGE OF EMMANUEL AND ST. CHAD, Saskatoon, SK S7N 0W6, Canada

General Information Independent-religious, coed, graduate-only institution. *Graduate housing:* Room and/or apartments available to single students; on-campus housing not available to married students. Housing application deadline: 6/15.

GRADUATE UNITS

Bachelor of Theology Program *Program availability:* Part-time, online learning. Offers theology (B Th).

Graduate Programs *Program availability:* Part-time. Offers theology (M Div, MTS, STM, D Min, L Th). STM and D Min programs offered jointly with Lutheran Theological Seminary and St. Andrew's College.

THE COLLEGE OF IDAHO, Caldwell, ID 83605

General Information Independent, coed, comprehensive institution. *Graduate housing:* Room and/or apartments available on a first-come, first-served basis to single students; on-campus housing not available to married students. Housing application deadline: 5/1.

GRADUATE UNITS

Department of Education Offers curriculum and instruction (M Ed); teaching (MAT).

COLLEGE OF MOUNT SAINT VINCENT, Riverdale, NY 10471-1093

General Information Independent, coed, comprehensive institution. *Graduate housing:* On-campus housing not available.

GRADUATE UNITS

School of Professional and Graduate Studies Offers family nurse practitioner (MSN, PMC); instructional technology and global perspectives (Certificate); middle level education (Certificate); multicultural studies (Certificate); nurse educator (PMC); nursing administration (MSN); nursing education (MSN); teaching English to speakers of other languages (MS Ed); urban and multicultural education (MS Ed).

THE COLLEGE OF NEW JERSEY, Ewing, NJ 08628

General Information State-supported, coed, comprehensive institution. CGS member.

GRADUATE UNITS

Office of Graduate and Advancing Education Students: 348 full-time (272 women), 841 part-time (673 women); includes 207 minority (64 Black or African American, non-Hispanic/Latino; 3 American Indian or Alaska Native, non-Hispanic/Latino; 63 Asian, non-Hispanic/Latino; 71 Hispanic/Latino; 2 Native Hawaiian or other Pacific Islander, non-Hispanic/Latino; 4 Two or more races, non-Hispanic/Latino). 541 applicants, 82% accepted, 411 enrolled. Expenses: Contact institution. *Financial support:* Tuition waivers (partial) and unspecified assistantships available. Financial award application deadline: 5/1; financial award applicants required to submit FAFSA. In 2017, 375 master's, 129 other advanced degrees awarded. *Program availability:* Part-time, evening/weekend. Offers overseas education (M Ed, Certificate). *Application deadline:* For fall admission, 2/1 priority date for domestic students; for spring admission, 10/1 priority date for domestic students. *Application fee:* $75. Electronic applications accepted. *Application Contact:* Deidre Queen, Program Assistant, 609-771-2300, Fax: 609-637-5105, E-mail: graduate@tcnj.edu. *Assistant Director, Office of Graduate and Advancing Education*, Michael Ellard, 609-771-3121, E-mail: ellardm@tcnj.edu.

School of Education *Program availability:* Part-time, evening/weekend. Offers community counseling: human services (MA); community counseling: substance abuse and addiction (MA, Certificate); developmental reading (M Ed); early childhood education (M Ed, MAT); education (M Ed, MA, MAT, Certificate, Ed S); educational leadership (M Ed, Certificate); elementary education (M Ed, MAT); elementary teaching (MAT); English as a second language (M Ed); marriage and family therapy (Ed S); reading certification (Certificate); school counseling (MA); school personnel: preschool-grade 3 (M Ed); secondary education (MAT); special education (M Ed, MAT); special education with learning disabilities (Certificate); teaching English as a second language (M Ed, Certificate). Electronic applications accepted.

School of Humanities and Social Sciences *Program availability:* Part-time. Offers English (MA); gender studies (Certificate); humanities and social sciences (MA, Certificate). Electronic applications accepted.

School of Nursing, Health, and Exercise Science *Program availability:* Part-time. Offers global health (MPH); health communications (MPH); nursing (MSN, Certificate); nursing, health, and exercise science (M Ed, MAT, MPH, MSN, Certificate); precision health (MPH). Electronic applications accepted.

See Display on the next page and Close-Up on page 859.

THE COLLEGE OF NEW ROCHELLE, New Rochelle, NY 10805-2308

General Information Independent, coed, comprehensive institution. *Enrollment:* 2,023 graduate, professional, and undergraduate students; 99 full-time matriculated graduate/professional students (83 women), 597 part-time matriculated graduate/professional students (491 women). *Enrollment by degree level:* 551 master's, 145 other advanced degrees. *Graduate faculty:* 19 full-time (13 women), 38 part-time/adjunct (25 women). *Tuition:* Full-time $17,406. *Required fees:* $1120. *Graduate housing:* On-campus housing not available. *Student services:* Campus employment opportunities, campus safety program, career counseling, exercise/wellness program, free psychological counseling, international student services, services for students with disabilities, teacher training, writing training. *Library facilities:* Gill Library plus 1 other. *Collection:* Books: 93,999 (physical), 153,914 (digital/electronic); Serial titles: 886 (physical), 94,336 (digital/electronic); Databases: 133. Weekly public service hours: 86; students can reserve study rooms.

Computer facilities: 86 computers available on campus for general student use. A campuswide network can be accessed from student residence rooms and from off campus. Online class registration is available.
Website: http://www.cnr.edu/

General Application Contact: Michael Petri, Interim Director of Graduate Admission, 914-654-5256, E-mail: mpetri@cnr.edu.

GRADUATE UNITS

Graduate School *Program availability:* Part-time, evening/weekend. Offers acute care nurse practitioner (MS, Certificate); clinical specialist in holistic nursing (MS, Certificate); family nurse practitioner (MS, Certificate); nursing and health care management (MS); nursing education (Certificate). Electronic applications accepted.

Division of Art and Communication Studies *Program availability:* Part-time, evening/weekend. Offers art therapy (MS); art therapy/counseling (MS); communication studies (MS, Certificate).

Division of Education *Program availability:* Part-time, evening/weekend. Offers art education (MS); bilingual education (Certificate); childhood education (MS Ed); childhood education/early childhood education (MS Ed); early childhood education (MS Ed); educational leadership (MS, Advanced Certificate, Advanced Diploma); gifted education (Certificate); literacy education (MS Ed); multilingual/multicultural education (MS Ed, Certificate); school building leader (MS, Advanced Certificate); school district leader (MS, Advanced Diploma); special education (MS Ed); teaching English to speakers of other languages (MS Ed, Certificate). Electronic applications accepted.

Division of Human Services *Program availability:* Part-time, evening/weekend. Offers career development (MS, Advanced Certificate); guidance and counseling (MS, Advanced Certificate); long term care administration (MPA); marriage and family therapy (MMFT); mental health counseling (MS, Certificate); public administration (MPA); school psychology (MS); thanatology (Certificate). Electronic applications accepted.

COLLEGE OF SAINT ELIZABETH, Morristown, NJ 07960-6989

General Information Independent-religious, coed, comprehensive institution. *Enrollment:* 1,149 graduate, professional, and undergraduate students; 77 full-time matriculated graduate/professional students (67 women), 306 part-time matriculated graduate/professional students (245 women). *Enrollment by degree level:* 269 master's, 89 doctoral, 25 other advanced degrees. *Graduate faculty:* 24 full-time (17 women), 41 part-time/adjunct (24 women). *Graduate housing:* Room and/or apartments available on a first-come, first-served basis to single students; on-campus housing not available to married students. Housing application deadline: 7/1. *Student services:* Campus employment opportunities, campus safety program, career counseling, exercise/wellness program, free psychological counseling, international student services, low-cost health insurance, multicultural affairs office, services for students with disabilities, teacher training, writing training. *Library facilities:* Mahoney Library plus 1 other. *Collection:* Books: 113,292 (physical), 1.1 million (digital/electronic); Serial titles: 240 (physical), 26,767 (digital/electronic); Databases: 122. Weekly public service hours: 75. *Research affiliation:* National Figure Skating Association (sports nutrition), National Institute of Mental Health (NIMH) (mental health service), Cornell University/The University of Texas at Houston (food biotechnology (attitude research)).

Computer facilities: 127 computers available on campus for general student use. A campuswide network can be accessed from student residence rooms and from off campus. Online class registration, online course evaluations; online system for registering for student activities, clubs, and events are available.
Website: http://www.cse.edu/

General Application Contact: Lori J. Fragoso, Director of Graduate and Continuing Studies Admissions, 973-290-4413, Fax: 973-290-4710, E-mail: apply@cse.edu.

GRADUATE UNITS

Department of Business Administration and Management Students: 5 full-time (all women), 19 part-time (14 women); includes 8 minority (4 Black or African American, non-Hispanic/Latino; 1 Asian, non-Hispanic/Latino; 2 Hispanic/Latino; 1 Two or more races, non-Hispanic/Latino), 3 international. Average age 37. 11 applicants, 100% accepted, 5 enrolled. *Faculty:* 1 (woman) full-time, 5 part-time/adjunct (3 women). Expenses: Contact institution. *Financial support:* Career-related internships or fieldwork, scholarships/grants, tuition waivers (partial), and unspecified assistantships available. Financial award applicants required to submit FAFSA. In 2017, 5 master's awarded. *Program availability:* Part-time. Offers human resource management (MS); organizational change (MS). *Application deadline:* For fall admission, 5/1 for international students. Applications are processed on a rolling basis. *Application fee:* $35. Electronic applications accepted. *Application Contact:* Lori J. Fragoso, Director of Graduate and Continuing Studies Admissions, 973-290-4413, Fax: 973-290-4710, E-mail: apply@cse.edu. *Program Chair and Director*, Dr. Regina Riccioni, 973-290-4271, E-mail: rriccioni@cse.edu.

Department of Educational Leadership Students: 4 full-time (3 women), 74 part-time (51 women); includes 34 minority (20 Black or African American, non-Hispanic/Latino; 2 Asian, non-Hispanic/Latino; 11 Hispanic/Latino; 1 Two or more races, non-

Hispanic/Latino). Average age 44. 33 applicants, 97% accepted, 28 enrolled. *Faculty:* 3 full-time (0 women), 8 part-time/adjunct (3 women). Expenses: Contact institution. *Financial support:* Career-related internships or fieldwork, scholarships/grants, and unspecified assistantships available. Financial award applicants required to submit FAFSA. In 2017, 15 master's, 6 doctorates awarded. *Program availability:* Part-time. Offers educational leadership (MA, Ed D); supervisor (Certificate). *Application deadline:* For fall admission, 5/1 for international students. Applications are processed on a rolling basis. *Application fee:* $35. Electronic applications accepted. *Application Contact:* Lori J. Fragoso, Director of Graduate and Continuing Studies Admissions, 973-290-4413, Fax: 973-290-4710, E-mail: apply@cse.edu. *Program Chair,* Dr. Joseph Ciccone, 973-290-4383, Fax: 973-290-4389, E-mail: jciccone@cse.edu.

Department of Foods and Nutrition Students: 23 full-time (21 women), 52 part-time (49 women); includes 14 minority (2 Asian, non-Hispanic/Latino; 10 Hispanic/Latino; 2 Two or more races, non-Hispanic/Latino), 1 international. Average age 26. 39 applicants, 100% accepted, 35 enrolled. *Faculty:* 4 full-time (all women), 2 part-time/adjunct (both women). Expenses: Contact institution. *Financial support:* Career-related internships or fieldwork, scholarships/grants, and unspecified assistantships available. Financial award applicants required to submit FAFSA. In 2017, 31 master's awarded. *Program availability:* Part-time, blended/hybrid learning. Offers dietetics verification (Certificate); nutrition (MS); nutrition/dietetic internship (MS). *Application deadline:* For fall admission, 5/1 for international students. Applications are processed on a rolling basis. *Application fee:* $35. Electronic applications accepted. *Application Contact:* Lori J. Fragoso, Director of Graduate and Continuing Studies Admissions, 973-290-4413, Fax: 973-290-4710, E-mail: apply@cse.edu. *Program Chair,* Dr. Anne Buison Pellizzon, 973-290-4065, Fax: 973-290-4167, E-mail: apellizzon@cse.edu.

Department of Nursing Students: 1 (woman) full-time, 26 part-time (23 women); includes 9 minority (1 Black or African American, non-Hispanic/Latino; 3 Asian, non-Hispanic/Latino; 5 Hispanic/Latino). Average age 41. 10 applicants, 100% accepted, 7 enrolled. *Faculty:* 3 full-time (all women), 1 (woman) part-time/adjunct. Expenses: Contact institution. *Financial support:* Career-related internships or fieldwork, scholarships/grants, tuition waivers (partial), and unspecified assistantships available. Financial award applicants required to submit FAFSA. In 2017, 19 master's awarded. *Program availability:* Part-time. Offers nursing (MSN). *Application deadline:* For fall admission, 5/1 for international students. Applications are processed on a rolling basis. *Application fee:* $35. Electronic applications accepted. *Application Contact:* Lori J. Fragoso, Director of Graduate and Continuing Studies Admissions, 973-290-4413, Fax: 973-290-4710, E-mail: apply@cse.edu. *Interim Nursing Administrator,* Dr. Sarah Arnold, 973-290-4037, E-mail: sarnold@cse.edu.

Department of Psychology Students: 37 full-time (32 women), 40 part-time (37 women); includes 30 minority (12 Black or African American, non-Hispanic/Latino; 1 Asian, non-Hispanic/Latino; 16 Hispanic/Latino; 1 Two or more races, non-Hispanic/Latino). Average age 31. 37 applicants, 81% accepted, 24 enrolled. *Faculty:* 4 full-time (3 women), 7 part-time/adjunct (all women). Expenses: Contact institution. *Financial support:* Career-related internships or fieldwork, scholarships/grants, tuition waivers (partial), and unspecified assistantships available. Support available to part-time students. Financial award applicants required to submit FAFSA. In 2017, 17 master's, 3 doctorates awarded. *Program availability:* Part-time. Offers counseling psychology (MA, Psy D). *Application deadline:* For fall admission, 5/1 for international students. Applications are processed on a rolling basis. *Application fee:* $35. Electronic applications accepted. *Application Contact:* Lori J. Fragoso, Director of Graduate and Continuing Studies Admissions, 973-290-4413, Fax: 973-290-4710, E-mail: apply@cse.edu. *Director, Graduate and Doctoral Programs in Psychology,* Dr. Michelle M. Barrett, 973-290-4027, Fax: 973-290-4676, E-mail: mbarrett01@cse.edu.

Department of Theology and Philosophy Students: 10 part-time (8 women); includes 2 minority (1 Black or African American, non-Hispanic/Latino; 1 Asian, non-Hispanic/Latino). Average age 56. 4 applicants, 100% accepted, 3 enrolled. *Faculty:* 1 (woman) full-time, 2 part-time/adjunct (0 women). Expenses: Contact institution. *Financial support:* Career-related internships or fieldwork, scholarships/grants, tuition waivers (partial), and unspecified assistantships available. Financial award applicants required to submit FAFSA. In 2017, 1 master's awarded. *Program availability:* Part-time. Offers Catholic studies (Certificate); pastoral care (Certificate); spirituality (Certificate); theology (MA). *Application deadline:* For fall admission, 5/1 for international students. Applications are processed on a rolling basis. *Application fee:* $35. Electronic applications accepted. *Application Contact:* Lori J. Fragoso, Director of Graduate and Continuing Studies Admissions, 973-290-4413, Fax: 973-290-4710, E-mail: apply@cse.edu. *Chairperson,* Dr. Anthony Santamaria, 973-290-4338, Fax: 973-290-4312, E-mail: asantamaria@cse.edu.

Health Administration Program Students: 1 (woman) full-time, 21 part-time (16 women); includes 9 minority (5 Black or African American, non-Hispanic/Latino; 3 Asian, non-Hispanic/Latino; 1 Hispanic/Latino). Average age 42. 11 applicants, 100% accepted, 4 enrolled. *Faculty:* 2 full-time (both women), 3 part-time/adjunct (0 women). Expenses: Contact institution. *Financial support:* Career-related internships or fieldwork, scholarships/grants, tuition waivers (partial), and unspecified assistantships available. Financial award applicants required to submit FAFSA. In 2017, 5 master's awarded. *Program availability:* Part-time. Offers health administration (MS). *Application deadline:* For fall admission, 5/1 for international students. Applications are processed on a rolling basis. *Application fee:* $35. Electronic applications accepted. *Application Contact:* Lori J. Fragoso, Director of Graduate and Continuing Studies Admissions, 973-290-4413, Fax: 973-290-4710, E-mail: apply@cse.edu. *Program Chair and Director, Health Care Administration,* Dr. Regina Riccioni, 973-290-4271, Fax: 973-290-4167, E-mail: rriccioni@cse.edu.

Program in Applied Behavior Analysis Students: 1 (woman) full-time, 1 (woman) part-time. Average age 35. 4 applicants, 75% accepted, 2 enrolled. *Faculty:* 1 part-time/adjunct (0 women). Expenses: Contact institution. *Financial support:* Career-related internships or fieldwork, scholarships/grants, and unspecified assistantships available. Financial award applicants required to submit FAFSA. *Program availability:* Part-time. Offers applied behavior analysis (MA, Certificate). *Application deadline:* For fall admission, 5/1 for international students. Applications are processed on a rolling basis. *Application fee:* $35. Electronic applications accepted. *Application Contact:* Lori J. Fragoso, Director of Graduate and Continuing Studies Admissions, 973-290-4413, Fax: 973-290-4710, E-mail: apply@cse.edu. *Coordinator,* Dr. Brian S. Friedlander, 973-290-4386, E-mail: bfriedlander@cse.edu.

Program in Data Analytics Students: 3 part-time (0 women); includes 1 minority (Asian, non-Hispanic/Latino). Average age 41. 3 applicants, 100% accepted, 3 enrolled. *Faculty:* 1 full-time (0 women). Expenses: Contact institution. *Financial support:* Career-related internships or fieldwork, scholarships/grants, and unspecified assistantships available. Financial award applicants required to submit FAFSA. *Program availability:* Part-time. Offers data analytics (MS). *Application deadline:* For fall admission, 5/1 for international students. Applications are processed on a rolling basis. *Application fee:* $35. Electronic applications accepted. *Application Contact:* Lori J. Fragoso, Director of

Graduate and Continuing Studies Admissions, 973-290-4413, Fax: 973-290-4710, E-mail: apply@cse.edu. *Director*, Dr. Jesse Yu, 973-290-4067, E-mail: jyu@cse.edu.

Program in Education Students: 1 (woman) full-time, 34 part-time (29 women); includes 1 minority (Hispanic/Latino). Average age 32. 25 applicants, 100% accepted, 24 enrolled. *Faculty:* 3 full-time (2 women), 8 part-time/adjunct (6 women). Expenses: Contact institution. *Financial support:* Career-related internships or fieldwork, scholarships/grants, and unspecified assistantships available. Financial award applicants required to submit FAFSA. In 2017, 23 master's awarded. *Program availability:* Part-time. Offers assistive technology (Certificate); education (MA); ESL (Certificate); Holocaust/genocide education (Certificate); middle school science (Certificate); online teaching in the 21st century (Certificate); teaching (Certificate). *Application deadline:* For fall admission, 5/1 for international students. Applications are processed on a rolling basis. *Application fee:* $35. Electronic applications accepted. *Application Contact:* Lori J. Fragoso, Director of Graduate and Continuing Studies Admissions, 973-290-4413, Fax: 973-290-4710, E-mail: apply@cse.edu.

Program in Justice Administration and Public Service Students: 4 full-time (2 women), 21 part-time (12 women); includes 12 minority (8 Black or African American, non-Hispanic/Latino; 1 Asian, non-Hispanic/Latino; 2 Hispanic/Latino; 1 Two or more races, non-Hispanic/Latino). Average age 31. 15 applicants, 100% accepted, 10 enrolled. *Faculty:* 3 full-time (1 woman), 1 (woman) part-time/adjunct. Expenses: Contact institution. *Financial support:* Career-related internships or fieldwork, scholarships/grants, and unspecified assistantships available. Support available to part-time students. Financial award applicants required to submit FAFSA. In 2017, 13 master's awarded. *Program availability:* Part-time, 100% online, blended/hybrid learning. Offers counter terrorism (Certificate); cyber security investigation (Certificate); justice administration and public service (MA); leadership in community policing (Certificate). *Application deadline:* For fall admission, 5/1 for international students. Applications are processed on a rolling basis. *Application fee:* $35. Electronic applications accepted. *Application Contact:* Lori J. Fragoso, Director of Graduate and Continuing Studies Admissions, 973-290-4413, Fax: 973-290-4710, E-mail: apply@cse.edu. *Associate Professor*, Dr. James Ford, 973-290-4324, E-mail: jford@cse.edu.

Program in Public Health Students: 5 part-time (all women); includes 4 minority (2 Black or African American, non-Hispanic/Latino; 2 Hispanic/Latino). Average age 34. 5 applicants, 100% accepted, 5 enrolled. *Faculty:* 1 (woman) part-time/adjunct. Expenses: Contact institution. *Financial support:* Career-related internships or fieldwork, scholarships/grants, and unspecified assistantships available. Financial award applicants required to submit FAFSA. *Program availability:* Part-time. Offers public health (MPH). *Application deadline:* For fall admission, 5/1 for international students. Applications are processed on a rolling basis. *Application fee:* $35. Electronic applications accepted. *Application Contact:* Lori J. Fragoso, Director of Graduate and Continuing Studies Admissions, 973-290-4194, Fax: 973-290-4710, E-mail: apply@cse.edu. *Chair*, Dr. Regina Riccioni, 973-290-4271, E-mail: rriccioni@cse.edu.

Program in Social Media Design and Management Expenses: Contact institution. *Financial support:* Career-related internships or fieldwork, scholarships/grants, and unspecified assistantships available. Financial award applicants required to submit FAFSA. *Program availability:* Part-time. Offers social media design and management (MA). *Application deadline:* For fall admission, 5/1 for international students. Applications are processed on a rolling basis. *Application fee:* $35. Electronic applications accepted. *Application Contact:* Lori J. Fragoso, Director of Graduate and Continuing Studies Admissions, Fax: 973-290-4710, E-mail: apply@cse.edu. *Chair*, Dr. Virginia Butera, 973-290-4315, E-mail: vbutera@cse.edu.

COLLEGE OF ST. JOSEPH, Rutland, VT 05701-3899

General Information Independent-religious, coed, comprehensive institution. *Graduate housing:* Room and/or apartments guaranteed to single students; on-campus housing not available to married students. Housing application deadline: 7/1.

GRADUATE UNITS

Graduate Programs *Program availability:* Part-time, evening/weekend. Electronic applications accepted.

Division of Business *Program availability:* Part-time, evening/weekend. Offers business administration (MBA). Electronic applications accepted.

Division of Education *Program availability:* Part-time, evening/weekend. Offers elementary education (M Ed); English (M Ed); general education (M Ed); reading (M Ed); secondary education (M Ed); social studies (M Ed); special education (M Ed). Electronic applications accepted.

Division of Psychology and Human Services *Program availability:* Part-time, evening/weekend. Offers alcohol and substance abuse counseling (MS); clinical mental health counseling (MS); clinical psychology (MS); community counseling (MS); school guidance counseling (MS). Electronic applications accepted.

COLLEGE OF SAINT MARY, Omaha, NE 68106

General Information Independent-religious, women only, comprehensive institution.

GRADUATE UNITS

Program in Education *Program availability:* Part-time. Offers assessment leadership (MSE); English as a second language (MSE).

Program in Health Professions Education *Program availability:* Part-time. Offers health professions education (Ed D).

Program in Nursing *Program availability:* Part-time. Offers nursing (MSN).

Program in Occupational Therapy Offers occupational therapy (MOT).

Program in Organizational Leadership *Program availability:* Part-time, evening/weekend. Offers organizational leadership (MOL). Electronic applications accepted.

Program in Teaching *Program availability:* Evening/weekend. Offers teaching (MAT).

THE COLLEGE OF SAINT ROSE, Albany, NY 12203-1419

General Information Independent, coed, comprehensive institution. CGS member. *Enrollment:* 3,950 graduate, professional, and undergraduate students; 418 full-time matriculated graduate/professional students (324 women), 997 part-time matriculated graduate/professional students (744 women). *Enrollment by degree level:* 612 master's, 803 other advanced degrees. *Graduate faculty:* 58 full-time (33 women), 86 part-time/adjunct (46 women). *Tuition:* Full-time $7191; part-time $799 per credit hour. *Required fees:* $924; $462 per credit hour. Tuition and fees vary according to course load. *Graduate housing:* Room and/or apartments available on a first-come, first-served basis to single students; on-campus housing not available to married students. Typical cost: $6624 per year ($12,766 including board). Housing application deadline: 3/15. *Student services:* Campus employment opportunities, campus safety program, career counseling, child daycare facilities, exercise/wellness program, free psychological counseling, international student services, multicultural affairs office, services for students with disabilities, teacher training, writing training. *Library facilities:* Neil Hellman Library plus 2 others. *Collection:* Books: 241,000 (physical), 116,500 (digital/electronic); Serial titles: 1,201 (physical), 10 (digital/electronic); Databases: 104. Students can reserve study rooms.

Computer facilities: 787 computers available on campus for general student use. A campuswide network can be accessed from student residence rooms and from off campus. Online class registration is available.
Website: http://www.strose.edu/

General Application Contact: Cris Murray, Assistant Vice President for Graduate Recruitment and Enrollment, 518-485-3390, Fax: 518-458-5479, E-mail: grad@strose.edu.

GRADUATE UNITS

Graduate Studies Students: 418 full-time (324 women), 997 part-time (744 women); includes 380 minority (168 Black or African American, non-Hispanic/Latino; 5 American Indian or Alaska Native, non-Hispanic/Latino; 27 Asian, non-Hispanic/Latino; 138 Hispanic/Latino; 1 Native Hawaiian or other Pacific Islander, non-Hispanic/Latino; 41 Two or more races, non-Hispanic/Latino), 61 international. Average age 32. 818 applicants, 68% accepted, 506 enrolled. *Faculty:* 58 full-time (33 women), 86 part-time/adjunct (46 women). Expenses: Contact institution. *Financial support:* Career-related internships or fieldwork, scholarships/grants, tuition waivers (partial), and unspecified assistantships available. Support available to part-time students. Financial award application deadline: 4/15. In 2017, 486 master's, 713 other advanced degrees awarded. *Program availability:* Part-time, evening/weekend, 100% online. *Application deadline:* For fall admission, 4/1 priority date for domestic and international students; for spring admission, 10/15 priority date for domestic and international students; for summer admission, 3/15 priority date for domestic and international students. Applications are processed on a rolling basis. *Application fee:* $40. Electronic applications accepted. *Application Contact:* Cris Murray, Assistant Vice President for Recruitment and Enrollment, 518-485-3390, Fax: 518-458-5479, E-mail: grad@strose.edu.

Huether School of Business Students: 60 full-time (15 women), 59 part-time (36 women); includes 17 minority (11 Black or African American, non-Hispanic/Latino; 1 Hispanic/Latino; 5 Two or more races, non-Hispanic/Latino), 10 international. Average age 28. 75 applicants, 84% accepted, 42 enrolled. *Faculty:* 12 full-time (6 women), 6 part-time/adjunct (2 women). Expenses: Contact institution. *Financial support:* Career-related internships or fieldwork, scholarships/grants, tuition waivers (partial), and unspecified assistantships available. Support available to part-time students. Financial award application deadline: 4/15. In 2017, 71 master's, 6 other advanced degrees awarded. *Program availability:* Part-time, evening/weekend. Offers accounting (MS); business administration (MBA); business analytics (MS); financial planning (Advanced Certificate); organizational leadership and change management (Advanced Certificate). *Application deadline:* For fall admission, 4/1 priority date for domestic and international students; for spring admission, 10/15 priority date for domestic and international students; for summer admission, 3/15 priority date for domestic and international students. Applications are processed on a rolling basis. *Application fee:* $40. Electronic applications accepted. *Application Contact:* Cris Murray, Assistant Vice President for Graduate Recruitment and Enrollment, 518-485-3390, Fax: 518-458-5479, E-mail: grad@strose.edu. *Interim Dean*, Mike Mathews, 518-454-5272, E-mail: mathewsm@strose.edu.

School of Mathematics and Sciences Students: 41 full-time (24 women), 27 part-time (13 women); includes 10 minority (3 Black or African American, non-Hispanic/Latino; 2 Asian, non-Hispanic/Latino; 1 Hispanic/Latino; 4 Two or more races, non-Hispanic/Latino), 37 international. Average age 27. 59 applicants, 85% accepted, 28 enrolled. *Faculty:* 12 full-time (6 women), 6 part-time/adjunct (2 women). Expenses: Contact institution. *Financial support:* Career-related internships or fieldwork, scholarships/grants, tuition waivers (partial), and unspecified assistantships available. Support available to part-time students. Financial award application deadline: 4/15. In 2017, 83 master's, 7 other advanced degrees awarded. *Program availability:* Part-time, evening/weekend, 100% online. Offers computer information systems (MS, Advanced Certificate); mathematics and sciences (MS, MSSW, Advanced Certificate); social work (MSSW). *Application deadline:* For fall admission, 4/1 priority date for domestic and international students; for spring admission, 10/15 priority date for domestic and international students; for summer admission, 3/15 priority date for domestic and international students. Applications are processed on a rolling basis. *Application fee:* $40. Electronic applications accepted. *Application Contact:* Cris Murray, Assistant Vice President for Graduate Recruitment and Enrollment, 518-485-3390, Fax: 518-458-5479, E-mail: grad@strose.edu. *Interim Dean*, Dr. Ian MacDonald, 518-458-5396, E-mail: macdonai@strose.edu.

Thelma P. Lally School of Education Students: 317 full-time (285 women), 907 part-time (694 women); includes 353 minority (154 Black or African American, non-Hispanic/Latino; 5 American Indian or Alaska Native, non-Hispanic/Latino; 25 Asian, non-Hispanic/Latino; 136 Hispanic/Latino; 1 Native Hawaiian or other Pacific Islander, non-Hispanic/Latino; 32 Two or more races, non-Hispanic/Latino), 14 international. Average age 33. 674 applicants, 65% accepted, 436 enrolled. *Faculty:* 29 full-time (18 women), 78 part-time/adjunct (45 women). Expenses: Contact institution. *Financial support:* Career-related internships or fieldwork, scholarships/grants, tuition waivers (partial), and unspecified assistantships available. Support available to part-time students. Financial award application deadline: 4/15. In 2017, 312 master's, 695 other advanced degrees awarded. *Program availability:* Part-time, evening/weekend, 100% online. Offers adolescence education (MS Ed, Advanced Certificate); adolescence education/special education (MS Ed, Advanced Certificate); childhood education (MS Ed); childhood education/special education (MS Ed); childhood special education (MS Ed); clinical mental health counseling (Certificate); college student services administration (MS Ed); communication sciences and disorders (MS Ed); curriculum and instruction (MS Ed); early childhood education (MS Ed); early childhood special education (MS Ed); education (MS, MS Ed, Advanced Certificate, Certificate); educational leadership (MS Ed); educational psychology (MS Ed, Certificate); higher education leadership and administration (MS Ed, Advanced Certificate); literacy: birth-grade 6 (MS Ed, Advanced Certificate); literacy: grades 5-12 (MS Ed, Advanced Certificate); school building leader (Certificate); school counseling (MS Ed, Certificate); school district business leader (Certificate); school district leader (Certificate); school psychology (MS Ed); special education (Certificate); special education professional (MS Ed). *Application deadline:* For fall admission, 4/1 priority date for domestic and international students; for spring admission, 10/15 priority date for domestic and international students; for summer admission, 3/15 priority date for domestic and international students. Applications are processed on a rolling basis. *Application fee:* $40. Electronic applications accepted. *Application Contact:* Cris Murray, Assistant Vice President for Graduate Recruitment and Enrollment, 518-454-5136, Fax: 518-458-5479, E-mail: grad@strose.edu. *Acting Associate Dean*, Dr. Theresa Ward, 518-454-5125.

THE COLLEGE OF ST. SCHOLASTICA, Duluth, MN 55811-4199

General Information Independent-religious, coed, comprehensive institution. *Graduate housing:* On-campus housing not available.

GRADUATE UNITS

Graduate Studies *Program availability:* Part-time, evening/weekend, online learning. Offers athletic training (MS); computer information systems (MA, Certificate); education (M Ed, MS, Certificate); exercise physiology (MA); health information management (MA, Certificate); management (MA, Certificate); nursing (MA, PMC); occupational therapy (MA); physical therapy (DPT); social work (MSW). Electronic applications accepted.

COLLEGE OF STATEN ISLAND OF THE CITY UNIVERSITY OF NEW YORK, Staten Island, NY 10314-6600

General Information State and locally supported, coed, comprehensive institution. *Enrollment:* 13,594 graduate, professional, and undergraduate students; 200 full-time matriculated graduate/professional students (130 women), 734 part-time matriculated graduate/professional students (510 women). *Enrollment by degree level:* 812 master's, 62 doctoral, 60 other advanced degrees. *Graduate faculty:* 73 full-time (48 women), 100 part-time/adjunct (58 women). Tuition, state resident: full-time $10,450; part-time $440 per credit. Tuition, nonresident: full-time $19,320; part-time $440 per credit. *Required fees:* $181.10 per semester. Tuition and fees vary according to program. *Graduate housing:* Room and/or apartments available on a first-come, first-served basis to single students; on-campus housing not available to married students. Typical cost: $13,900 per year ($17,850 including board). Room and board charges vary according to housing facility selected. *Student services:* Career counseling, child daycare facilities, international student services. *Library facilities:* College of Staten Island Library. *Collection:* Weekly public service hours: 112; students can reserve study rooms. *Research affiliation:* Alfred P. Sloan Foundation, Craig H. Neilson Foundation, Northfield Bank Foundation, Simons Foundation, Eurasia Foundation, Richmond Foundation Bank.

Computer facilities: 1,700 computers available on campus for general student use. A campuswide network can be accessed from off campus. Online class registration, MyInfo app are available.
Website: http://www.csi.cuny.edu/

General Application Contact: Sasha Spence, Associate Director for Graduate Recruitment and Admissions, 718-982-2019, Fax: 718-982-2500, E-mail: sasha.spence@csi.cuny.edu.

GRADUATE UNITS

Graduate Programs Students: 200 full-time (130 women), 734 part-time (510 women); includes 239 minority (49 Black or African American, non-Hispanic/Latino; 1 American Indian or Alaska Native, non-Hispanic/Latino; 102 Asian, non-Hispanic/Latino; 87 Hispanic/Latino). Average age 30. Expenses: Contact institution. In 2017, 215 master's, 17 doctorates, 21 other advanced degrees awarded. *Application Contact:* Sasha Spence, Associate Director for Graduate Admissions, 718-982-2019, Fax: 718-982-2500, E-mail: sasha.spence@csi.cuny.edu. *Provost/Senior Vice President for Academic Affairs*, Dr. Gary Reichard, 718-982-2440, Fax: 718-982-2442, E-mail: provost@csi.cuny.edu.

Division of Humanities and Social Sciences Students: 162. 307 applicants, 47% accepted, 91 enrolled. *Faculty:* 21 full-time, 16 part-time/adjunct. Expenses: Contact institution. In 2017, 49 master's, 3 other advanced degrees awarded. Offers autism spectrum disorders (Advanced Certificate); cinema and media studies (MA); clinical mental health counseling (MA); English (MA); history (MA); liberal studies (MA); public history (Advanced Certificate). *Application Contact:* Sasha Spence, Associate Director for Graduate Admissions, 718-982-2019, Fax: 718-982-2500, E-mail: sasha.spence@csi.cuny.edu. *Dean of Humanities and Social Sciences*, Dr. Gerry Milligan, 718-982-2315, Fax: 718-982-2316, E-mail: gerry.milligan@csi.cuny.edu.

Division of Science and Technology Students: 112. 138 applicants, 49% accepted, 36 enrolled. *Faculty:* 21 full-time, 6 part-time/adjunct. Expenses: Contact institution. In 2017, 34 master's awarded. Offers biology (MS); computer science (MS); environmental science (MS); neuroscience and developmental disabilities (MS). *Application Contact:* Sasha Spence, Associate Director for Graduate Admissions, 718-982-2019, Fax: 718-982-2500, E-mail: sasha.spence@csi.cuny.edu. *Dean*, Dr. Vivian Incera, 718-982-2430, E-mail: vivian.incera@csi.cuny.edu.

School of Business Students: 69. 73 applicants, 47% accepted, 27 enrolled. *Faculty:* 8 full-time, 4 part-time/adjunct. Expenses: Contact institution. In 2017, 23 master's awarded. Offers accounting (MS); business (MS, Advanced Certificate); business analytics of large-scale data (Advanced Certificate); healthcare management (MS); large scale data analysis (MS); strategic management (MS). *Application Contact:* Sasha Spence, Associate Director for Graduate Admissions, 718-982-2019, Fax: 718-982-2500, E-mail: sasha.spence@csi.cuny.edu. *Dean of School of Business*, Dr. Susan L. Holak, 718-982-2920, Fax: 718-982-3183, E-mail: susan.holak@csi.cuny.edu.

School of Education Students: 409. 212 applicants, 66% accepted, 113 enrolled. *Faculty:* 30 full-time, 28 part-time/adjunct. Expenses: Contact institution. In 2017, 90 master's, 11 Advanced Certificates awarded. Offers adolescence education (MS Ed); bilingual education (Advanced Certificate); childhood (MS Ed); education (MS Ed, Advanced Certificate, Post-Master's Certificate); leadership in education (Post-Master's Certificate); special education (MS Ed); teaching of English to speakers of other languages (MS Ed, Advanced Certificate). *Application Contact:* Sasha Spence, Associate Director for Graduate Admissions, 718-982-2019, Fax: 718-982-2500, E-mail: sasha.spence@csi.cuny.edu. *Dean of School of Education*, Dr. Kenneth Gold, 718-982-3737, Fax: 718-982-3743, E-mail: kenneth.gold@csi.cuny.edu.

School of Health Sciences Students: 182. 316 applicants, 25% accepted, 51 enrolled. *Faculty:* 16 full-time, 17 part-time/adjunct. Expenses: Contact institution. In 2017, 19 master's, 17 doctorates, 6 other advanced degrees awarded. Offers adult-gerontological health nursing (DNP); adult-gerontological nursing (MS, Post Master's Certificate); health sciences (MS, MSW, DNP, DPT, Post Master's Certificate); physical therapy (DPT); social work (MSW). *Application Contact:* Sasha Spence, Associate Director for Graduate Admissions, 718-982-2019, Fax: 718-982-2500, E-mail: sasha.spence@csi.cuny.edu. *Dean of School of Health Sciences*, Dr. Marcus C. Tye, 718-982-3690, E-mail: marcus.tye@csi.cuny.edu.

See Display on the next page and Close-Up on page 861.

COLLEGE OF THE ATLANTIC, Bar Harbor, ME 04609-1198

General Information Independent, coed, comprehensive institution. *Graduate housing:* Room and/or apartments available to single students; on-campus housing not available to married students. Housing application deadline: 6/1. *Research affiliation:* Acadia National Park, National Park Service (research management, environmental education), Mount Desert Island Biological Laboratory, Jackson Laboratory (genetics), Society for Human Ecology (ecological decision making in society).

GRADUATE UNITS

Program in Human Ecology Offers human ecology (M Phil).

THE COLLEGE OF WILLIAM AND MARY, Williamsburg, VA 23187-8795

General Information State-supported, coed, university. CGS member. *Enrollment:* 8,740 graduate, professional, and undergraduate students; 1,766 full-time matriculated graduate/professional students (901 women), 584 part-time matriculated graduate/professional students (247 women). *Enrollment by degree level:* 1,303 master's, 1,035 doctoral, 9 other advanced degrees. *Graduate faculty:* 735 full-time (307 women), 188 part-time/adjunct (81 women). *Graduate housing:* Room and/or apartments available on a first-come, first-served basis to single students; on-campus housing not available to married students. Housing application deadline: 2/14. *Student services:* Campus employment opportunities, campus safety program, career counseling, child daycare facilities, exercise/wellness program, free psychological counseling, grant writing training, international student services, low-cost health insurance, multicultural affairs office, services for students with disabilities, teacher training, writing training. *Library facilities:* Earl Gregg Swem Library plus 7 others. *Collection:* Books: 1.3 million (physical), 2.5 million (digital/electronic); Serial titles: 40,439 (physical), 132,861 (digital/electronic); Databases: 533. Weekly public service hours: 110; study areas open 24 hours, 5–7 days a week; students can reserve study rooms. *Research affiliation:* Colonial Williamsburg (archaeology, history), Thomas Jefferson National Accelerator Facility (nuclear physics), Court Records Solutions (law and technology), AidData (global aid flows and development finance), James City County Business and Technology Incubator (economic development), Center for Excellence in Aging and Geriatric Health (public policy, kinesiology).

Computer facilities: Computer purchase and lease plans are available. 400 computers available on campus for general student use. A campuswide network can be accessed from student residence rooms. Online class registration is available.
Website: http://www.wm.edu/

GRADUATE UNITS

Faculty of Arts and Sciences Students: 365 full-time (160 women), 9 part-time (3 women); includes 42 minority (15 Black or African American, non-Hispanic/Latino; 1 American Indian or Alaska Native, non-Hispanic/Latino; 7 Asian, non-Hispanic/Latino; 10 Hispanic/Latino; 9 Two or more races, non-Hispanic/Latino), 111 international. Average age 26. 657 applicants, 33% accepted, 119 enrolled. *Faculty:* 526 full-time (220 women), 92 part-time/adjunct (41 women). Expenses: Contact institution. *Financial support:* Fellowships, research assistantships, teaching assistantships, career-related internships or fieldwork, Federal Work-Study, institutionally sponsored loans, and unspecified assistantships available. Financial award applicants required to submit FAFSA. In 2017, 111 master's, 54 doctorates awarded. *Program availability:* Part-time. Offers accelerator science (PhD); American studies (MA, PhD); anthropology (MA, PhD); applied mathematics (PhD); applied mechanics (PhD); applied robotics (PhD); applied science (MS); arts and sciences (MA, MPP, MS, PhD); atmospheric and environmental science (PhD); biology (MS); chemistry (MA, MS); computational neuroscience (PhD); computational operations research (MS); computer science (MS, PhD); history (MA, PhD); interface, thin film and surface science (PhD); international development and policy (MPP); lasers and optics (PhD); magnetic resonance (PhD); materials science and engineering (PhD); mathematical and computational biology (PhD); medical imaging (PhD); nanotechnology (PhD); neuroscience (PhD); non-destructive evaluation (PhD); physics (MS, PhD); polymer chemistry (PhD); psychological sciences (MS); public policy analysis (MPP); remote sensing (PhD). *Application fee:* $45. Electronic applications accepted. *Application Contact:* Wanda Carter, Graduate Registrar, 757-221-2467, Fax: 757-221-4874, E-mail: wdcart@wm.edu. *Dean of Graduate Studies and Research*, Dr. Virginia Torczon, 757-221-2468, E-mail: vjtorc@wm.edu.

Raymond A. Mason School of Business Students: 458 full-time (171 women), 402 part-time (127 women); includes 210 minority (81 Black or African American, non-Hispanic/Latino; 2 American Indian or Alaska Native, non-Hispanic/Latino; 47 Asian, non-Hispanic/Latino; 50 Hispanic/Latino; 2 Native Hawaiian or other Pacific Islander, non-Hispanic/Latino; 28 Two or more races, non-Hispanic/Latino), 131 international. Average age 29. 1,323 applicants, 56% accepted, 447 enrolled. *Faculty:* 61 full-time (22 women), 13 part-time/adjunct (2 women). Expenses: Contact institution. *Financial support:* Scholarships/grants and unspecified assistantships available. Financial award applicants required to submit FAFSA. In 2017, 345 master's awarded. *Program availability:* Part-time, evening/weekend, 100% online. Offers accounting (M Acc); business (EMBA, M Acc, MBA, MS); business analytics (MS). *Application deadline:* For fall admission, 11/16 for domestic and international students; for winter admission, 1/18 for domestic and international students; for spring admission, 5/16 for domestic and international students; for summer admission, 7/15 for domestic students. *Application fee:* $100. Electronic applications accepted. *Application Contact:* Amanda K. Barth, Director, Full-time MBA Admissions, 757-221-2944, Fax: 757-221-2958, E-mail: amanda.barth@mason.wm.edu. *Dean*, Dr. Lawrence Pulley, 757-221-2891, Fax: 757-221-2937, E-mail: larry.pulley@mason.wm.edu.

School of Education Students: 220 full-time (163 women), 192 part-time (131 women); includes 103 minority (48 Black or African American, non-Hispanic/Latino; 7 Asian, non-Hispanic/Latino; 33 Hispanic/Latino; 15 Two or more races, non-Hispanic/Latino), 7 international. Average age 34. 538 applicants, 63% accepted, 242 enrolled. *Faculty:* 54 full-time (31 women), 80 part-time/adjunct (40 women). Expenses: Contact institution. *Financial support:* In 2017–18, 143 students received support, including 1 fellowship with full tuition reimbursement available (averaging $20,000 per year), 93 research assistantships (averaging $17,316 per year); scholarships/grants and unspecified assistantships also available. Financial award application deadline: 1/15; financial award applicants required to submit FAFSA. In 2017, 129 master's, 33 doctorates, 6 other advanced degrees awarded. *Program availability:* Part-time, evening/weekend. Offers addictions counseling (M Ed); community counseling (M Ed); counselor education (PhD); curriculum and educational technology (PhD); curriculum leadership (Ed D, PhD); education (M Ed, MA Ed, Ed D, PhD, Ed S); educational leadership (M Ed); educational policy, planning, and leadership (Ed D, PhD); elementary education (MA Ed); English as a second language/bilingual education (MA Ed); family counseling (M Ed); gifted education (MA Ed); literacy leadership (MA Ed); math specialist (MA Ed); school counseling (M Ed); school psychology (M Ed, Ed S); secondary education (MA Ed); special education (MA Ed). *Application deadline:* For fall admission, 1/15 for domestic and international students; for spring admission, 10/1 for domestic and international students. *Application fee:* $50. Electronic applications accepted. *Application Contact:* Dorothy Smith Osborne, Assistant Dean for Academic Programs and Student Services, 757-221-2317, E-mail: dsosbo@wm.edu. *Dean*, Dr. Spencer G. Niles, 757-221-2317, E-mail: sgniles@wm.edu.

Virginia Institute of Marine Science Students: 81 full-time (53 women), 6 part-time (3 women); includes 9 minority (1 Black or African American, non-Hispanic/Latino; 2 Asian,

non-Hispanic/Latino; 2 Hispanic/Latino; 4 Two or more races, non-Hispanic/Latino), 18 international. Average age 26. 100 applicants, 24% accepted, 18 enrolled. *Faculty:* 54 full-time (18 women), 2 part-time/adjunct (0 women). Expenses: Contact institution. *Financial support:* In 2017–18, 64 students received support, including fellowships with full tuition reimbursements available (averaging $25,000 per year), research assistantships with full tuition reimbursements available (averaging $20,452 per year), teaching assistantships with full tuition reimbursements available (averaging $20,452 per year); health care benefits also available. Financial award application deadline: 1/5. In 2017, 8 master's, 6 doctorates awarded. Offers marine science (MS, PhD). *Application deadline:* For fall admission, 1/5 for domestic and international students. *Application fee:* $53. Electronic applications accepted. *Application Contact:* Dr. Linda C. Schaffner, Associate Dean of Academic Studies, 804-684-7105, Fax: 804-684-7881, E-mail: admissions@vims.edu. *Dean/Director,* Dr. John T. Wells, 804-684-7102, Fax: 804-684-7009, E-mail: wells@vims.edu.

William and Mary Law School Students: 638 full-time (351 women), 3 part-time (1 woman); includes 113 minority (39 Black or African American, non-Hispanic/Latino; 2 American Indian or Alaska Native, non-Hispanic/Latino; 25 Asian, non-Hispanic/Latino; 30 Hispanic/Latino; 17 Two or more races, non-Hispanic/Latino), 57 international. Average age 23. 4,225 applicants, 38% accepted, 209 enrolled. *Faculty:* 47 full-time (20 women), 64 part-time/adjunct (23 women). Expenses: Contact institution. *Financial support:* In 2017–18, 560 students received support, including 85 fellowships (averaging $3,858 per year), 224 research assistantships (averaging $1,842 per year), 47 teaching assistantships (averaging $3,957 per year); career-related internships or fieldwork, Federal Work-Study, and scholarships/grants also available. Financial award application deadline: 2/15; financial award applicants required to submit FAFSA. In 2017, 59 master's, 208 doctorates awarded. Offers law (LL M, JD). *Application deadline:* For fall admission, 3/1 priority date for domestic and international students. *Application fee:* $0. Electronic applications accepted. *Application Contact:* Faye F. Shealy, Associate Dean for Admission, 757-221-3785, Fax: 757-221-3261, E-mail: ffshea@wm.edu. *Dean/Professor,* Davison M. Douglas, 757-221-3790, Fax: 757-221-3261, E-mail: dmdoug@wm.edu.

COLORADO CHRISTIAN UNIVERSITY, Lakewood, CO 80226

General Information Independent-religious, coed, comprehensive institution. *Graduate housing:* On-campus housing not available.

GRADUATE UNITS

Program in Business Administration *Program availability:* Part-time, evening/weekend, online learning. Offers corporate training (MBA); information security (MA); leadership (MBA); project management (MBA). Electronic applications accepted.

Program in Counseling *Program availability:* Part-time, evening/weekend. Offers counseling (MAC). Electronic applications accepted.

Program in Curriculum and Instruction *Program availability:* Part-time, evening/weekend. Offers corporate education (MACI); early childhood educator (MACI); elementary educator (MACI); instructional technology (MACI); master educator (MACI); online course developer (MACI); online teaching and learning (MACI); special education generalist (MACI). Electronic applications accepted.

THE COLORADO COLLEGE, Colorado Springs, CO 80903-3294

General Information Independent, coed, comprehensive institution. *Graduate housing:* On-campus housing not available.

GRADUATE UNITS

Education Department Offers art teaching (K-12) (MAT); arts and humanities (MAT); elementary education (MAT); elementary school teaching (MAT); English teaching (MAT); foreign language teaching (MAT); integrated natural sciences (MAT); liberal arts (MAT); mathematics teaching (MAT); music teaching (MAT); science teaching (MAT); secondary education (MAT); social studies teaching (MAT); Southwest studies (MAT); teaching (MAT). Electronic applications accepted.

COLORADO MESA UNIVERSITY, Grand Junction, CO 81501-3122

General Information State-supported, coed, comprehensive institution. *Graduate housing:* Room and/or apartments available on a first-come, first-served basis to single students; on-campus housing not available to married students. Housing application deadline: 8/1.

GRADUATE UNITS

Center for Teacher Education *Program availability:* Part-time. Offers educational leadership (MAEd); English for speakers of other languages (MAEd); exceptional learner/special education (MAEd); teacher education (Graduate Certificate); teacher leader (MAEd). Electronic applications accepted.

Department of Business *Program availability:* Part-time, evening/weekend. Offers business (MBA). Electronic applications accepted.

Department of Health Sciences *Program availability:* Part-time, evening/weekend, 100% online, blended/hybrid learning. Offers advanced nursing practice (MSN); family nurse practitioner (DNP); health information technology systems (Graduate Certificate); nursing education (MSN). Electronic applications accepted.

COLORADO SCHOOL OF MINES, Golden, CO 80401-1887

General Information State-supported, coed, university. CGS member. *Enrollment:* 1,115 full-time matriculated graduate/professional students (325 women), 171 part-time matriculated graduate/professional students (40 women). *Enrollment by degree level:* 702 master's, 584 doctoral. *Graduate faculty:* 426 full-time (135 women), 181 part-time/adjunct (64 women). Tuition, state resident: full-time $16,170. Tuition, nonresident: full-time $35,220. *Required fees:* $2216. *Graduate housing:* Rooms and/or apartments available on a first-come, first-served basis to single and married students. Typical cost: $10,800 per year for single students; $11,700 per year for married students. Room charges vary according to board plan and housing facility selected. Housing application deadline: 5/1. *Student services:* Campus employment opportunities, campus safety program, career counseling, exercise/wellness program, free psychological counseling, international student services, low-cost health insurance, multicultural affairs office, services for students with disabilities, teacher training, writing training. *Library facilities:* Arthur Lakes Library. *Collection:* Books: 503,801 (physical), 134,211 (digital/electronic); Serial titles: 578 (physical), 104,424 (digital/electronic); Databases: 128. Weekly public service hours: 107; students can reserve study rooms.

Computer facilities: Computer purchase and lease plans are available. 1,000 computers available on campus for general student use. A campuswide network can be accessed from student residence rooms and from off campus. Online class registration is available.
Website: http://www.mines.edu/

General Application Contact: Angel Dotson, Graduate Admissions Coordinator, 303-273-3348, E-mail: grad-app@mines.edu.

GRADUATE UNITS

Office of Graduate Studies Students: 1,115 full-time (325 women), 171 part-time (40 women); includes 159 minority (14 Black or African American, non-Hispanic/Latino; 3 American Indian or Alaska Native, non-Hispanic/Latino; 36 Asian, non-Hispanic/Latino; 70 Hispanic/Latino; 1 Native Hawaiian or other Pacific Islander, non-Hispanic/Latino; 35 Two or more races, non-Hispanic/Latino), 398 international. Average age 28. 2,016 applicants, 52% accepted, 425 enrolled. *Faculty:* 426 full-time (135 women), 181 part-time/adjunct (64 women). Expenses: Contact institution. *Financial support:* In 2017–18, 439 research assistantships with full tuition reimbursements, 194 teaching assistantships with full tuition reimbursements were awarded; fellowships, career-related internships or fieldwork, Federal Work-Study, institutionally sponsored loans, scholarships/grants, health care benefits, and unspecified assistantships also available. Financial award application deadline: 12/15; financial award applicants required to submit FAFSA. In 2017, 296 master's, 86 doctorates awarded. *Program availability:* Part-time. Offers applied physics (MS, PhD); chemical engineering (MS, PhD); chemistry (MS, PhD); civil and environmental engineering (MS, PhD); computational and applied mathematics (MS, PhD); electrical engineering (MS, PhD); engineering and technology management (MS); environmental engineering science (MS, PhD); environmental geochemistry (PMS); geochemistry (MS, PhD); geological engineering (ME, MS, PhD); geology (MS, PhD); geophysical engineering (ME, MS, PhD); geophysics (MS, PhD); hydrologic science and engineering (MS, PhD); hydrology (MS, PhD); international political economy (Graduate Certificate); materials science (MS, PhD); mechanical engineering (MS, PhD); metallurgical and materials engineering (ME, MS, PhD); mineral and energy economics (MS, PhD); mineral exploration (PMS); mineral exploration and mining geosciences (PMS); mining and earth systems engineering (MS); mining engineering (PhD); nuclear engineering (ME, MS, PhD); operations research and engineering (PhD); petroleum economics and management with mineral and energy economics (MS); petroleum engineering (ME, MS, PhD); petroleum reservoir systems (PMS); science and technology policy (Graduate Certificate); statistics (MS, PhD); underground construction and tunneling (MS, PhD). *Application deadline:* For fall admission, 12/15 priority date for domestic and international students; for spring admission, 9/1 priority date for domestic and international students. *Application fee:* $60 ($80 for international students). Electronic applications accepted. *Application Contact:* Angel Dotson, Graduate Admissions Coordinator, 303-273-3348, Fax: 303-273-3247, E-mail: grad-app@mines.edu. *Dean of Graduate Studies,* Dr. Wendy Zhou, 303-384-2181, E-mail: wzhou@mines.edu.

See Display below and Close-Up on page 863.

COLORADO SCHOOL OF TRADITIONAL CHINESE MEDICINE, Denver, CO 80206-2127

General Information Independent, coed, graduate-only institution. *Enrollment by degree level:* 96 master's. *Graduate faculty:* 52 part-time/adjunct (20 women). *Tuition:* Full-time $17,000; part-time $12,500 per trimester. *Required fees:* $495; $1020 per year. $340 per trimester. Part-time tuition and fees vary according to course load. *Graduate housing:* On-campus housing not available. *Student services:* Campus employment opportunities, exercise/wellness program. *Library facilities:* CSTCM Library. *Collection:* Books: 8,000 (physical), 200 (digital/electronic).

Computer facilities: 4 computers available on campus for general student use. X available.
Website: http://www.cstcm.edu/

General Application Contact: Chris Duxbury-Edwards, Recruiting Director, 303-329-6355 Ext. 21, Fax: 303-388-8165, E-mail: recruiting@cstcm.edu.

GRADUATE UNITS

Graduate Programs Students: 96 full-time (77 women). Average age 33. 50 applicants, 54% accepted, 23 enrolled. *Faculty:* 52 part-time/adjunct (20 women). Expenses: Contact institution. *Financial support:* Scholarships/grants available. Financial award applicants required to submit FAFSA. In 2017, 61 master's awarded. Offers acupuncture (MS); traditional Chinese medicine (MS). *Application deadline:* For fall admission, 8/18 for domestic students, 8/19 for international students; for winter admission, 12/29 for domestic and international students; for summer admission, 4/21 for domestic and international students. Applications are processed on a rolling basis. *Application fee:* $50. *Application Contact:* Chris Duxbury-Edwards, Recruiting Director, 303-329-6355 Ext. 21, Fax: 303-388-8165, E-mail: recruiting@cstcm.edu. *Administrative Director,* Vladimir Dibrigida, 303-329-6355 Ext. 11, Fax: 303-388-8165, E-mail: director@cstcm.edu.

COLORADO STATE UNIVERSITY, Fort Collins, CO 80523

General Information State-supported, coed, university. CGS member. *Enrollment:* 33,237 graduate, professional, and undergraduate students; 2,769 full-time matriculated graduate/professional students (1,694 women), 4,094 part-time matriculated graduate/professional students (1,972 women). *Enrollment by degree level:* 4,396 master's, 2,310 doctoral, 157 other advanced degrees. *Graduate faculty:* 1,080 full-time (428 women), 237 part-time/adjunct (111 women). Tuition, state resident: full-time $9917. Tuition, nonresident: full-time $24,312. *Required fees:* $2284. Tuition and fees vary according to course load and program. *Graduate housing:* Rooms and/or apartments available on a first-come, first-served basis to single and married students. Typical cost: $5578 per year ($11,514 including board) for single students. Room and board charges vary according to board plan and housing facility selected. *Student services:* Campus employment opportunities, campus safety program, career counseling, child daycare facilities, exercise/wellness program, free psychological counseling, grant writing training, international student services, low-cost health insurance, multicultural affairs office, services for students with disabilities, teacher training, writing training. *Library facilities:* William E. Morgan Library plus 1 other. *Collection:* Books: 2 million (physical), 537,992 (digital/electronic); Serial titles: 40,446 (physical), 84,523 (digital/electronic); Databases: 322. Weekly public service hours: 108; study areas open 24 hours, 5–7 days a week; students can reserve study rooms. *Research affiliation:* U.S. Department of Commerce/National Oceanic and Atmospheric Administration (NOAA) Joint Institutes (meteorological satellite imagery), Natural Resources Research Center/Agencies of U.S. Departments of Agriculture (USDA) and Interior (infectious disease), National Center for Genetic Resources Preservation (genetic resources of crops), National Wildlife Research Center (interactions of wild animals and society), National Centers for Atmospheric Research (climate, meteorology), Solix (algae-produced biofuels).

Computer facilities: Computer purchase and lease plans are available. 1,700 computers available on campus for general student use. A campuswide network can be accessed from student residence rooms and from off campus. Online class registration, personalized portal services including transcripts and financials (billing, financial aid) are available.
Website: http://www.colostate.edu/

General Application Contact: Sandra Dailey, Academic Progress and Special Admissions Coordinator, Graduate School, 970-491-6817, Fax: 970-491-2194, E-mail: gradschool@colostate.edu.

GRADUATE UNITS

College of Agricultural Sciences Students: 134 full-time (74 women), 174 part-time (105 women); includes 26 minority (2 Black or African American, non-Hispanic/Latino; 2 American Indian or Alaska Native, non-Hispanic/Latino; 1 Asian, non-Hispanic/Latino; 13 Hispanic/Latino; 8 Two or more races, non-Hispanic/Latino), 67 international. Average age 31. 246 applicants, 52% accepted, 63 enrolled. *Faculty:* 98 full-time (31 women), 11 part-time/adjunct (6 women). Expenses: Contact institution. *Financial support:* In 2017–18, 116 research assistantships with tuition reimbursements (averaging $19,699 per year), 36 teaching assistantships (averaging $16,090 per year) were awarded; fellowships with full tuition reimbursements, Federal Work-Study, scholarships/grants, tuition waivers (full and partial), and unspecified assistantships also available. Financial award application deadline: 1/15; financial award applicants required to submit FAFSA. In 2017, 70 master's, 15 doctorates awarded. *Program availability:* Part-time, evening/weekend, 100% online, blended/hybrid learning. Offers agricultural and resource economics (MS, PhD); agricultural sciences (M Agr, M Ext Ed, MAEE, MLA, MS, PhD); animal sciences (MS, PhD); entomology (MS, PhD); extension education (M Ext Ed); horticulture and landscape architecture (MLA, MS, PhD); pest management (MS); plant pathology (MS, PhD); soil and crop sciences (MS, PhD); weed science (MS, PhD). *Application fee:* $60 ($70 for international students). Electronic applications accepted. *Application Contact:* Administrative Assistant, 970-491-7401, Fax: 970-491-4895. *Dean*, Dr. Ajay Menon, 970-491-6274, Fax: 970-491-4895, E-mail: ajay.menon@colostate.edu.

College of Business Students: 235 full-time (104 women), 901 part-time (342 women); includes 216 minority (30 Black or African American, non-Hispanic/Latino; 4 American Indian or Alaska Native, non-Hispanic/Latino; 62 Asian, non-Hispanic/Latino; 90 Hispanic/Latino; 1 Native Hawaiian or other Pacific Islander, non-Hispanic/Latino; 29 Two or more races, non-Hispanic/Latino), 125 international. Average age 34. 644 applicants, 73% accepted, 318 enrolled. *Faculty:* 43 full-time (11 women), 7 part-time/adjunct (1 woman). Expenses: Contact institution. *Financial support:* In 2017–18, 62 fellowships with partial tuition reimbursements (averaging $7,128 per year), 1 research assistantship with partial tuition reimbursement (averaging $7,128 per year) were awarded; career-related internships or fieldwork, scholarships/grants, and unspecified assistantships also available. In 2017, 441 master's awarded. *Program availability:* Part-time, evening/weekend, 100% online, blended/hybrid learning. Offers accounting (M Acc); business (M Acc, M Fin, MBA, MCIS, MS); business administration (MBA); computer information systems (MCIS); finance (M Fin). *Application deadline:* Applications are processed on a rolling basis. *Application fee:* $60 ($70 for international students). Electronic applications accepted. *Application Contact:* Graduate Programs Admissions Contact, 970-491-4622, E-mail: cobgradinfo@colostate.edu. *Dean*, Dr. Beth Walker, 970-491-6471, E-mail: beth.walker@colostate.edu.

College of Health and Human Sciences Students: 383 full-time (310 women), 750 part-time (519 women); includes 224 minority (49 Black or African American, non-Hispanic/Latino; 4 American Indian or Alaska Native, non-Hispanic/Latino; 21 Asian, non-Hispanic/Latino; 117 Hispanic/Latino; 33 Two or more races, non-Hispanic/Latino), 48 international. Average age 34. 1,557 applicants, 25% accepted, 244 enrolled. *Faculty:* 112 full-time (79 women), 40 part-time/adjunct (28 women). Expenses: Contact institution. *Financial support:* In 2017–18, 11 fellowships with full tuition reimbursements (averaging $8,384 per year), 50 research assistantships with tuition reimbursements (averaging $15,180 per year), 68 teaching assistantships with tuition reimbursements (averaging $12,175 per year) were awarded; Federal Work-Study, scholarships/grants, and unspecified assistantships also available. In 2017, 336 master's, 30 doctorates awarded. *Program availability:* Part-time, evening/weekend, 100% online, blended/hybrid learning. Offers apparel and merchandising (MS); applied developmental science (PhD); construction management (MS); dietetics (MS); exercise science and nutrition (MS); family and developmental studies (MS); food science and human nutrition (PhD); food science and nutrition (MS); health and human sciences (M Ed, MA, MOT, MS, MSW, PhD); human bioenergetics (PhD); marriage and family therapy (MS); nutrition and exercise science (MS); occupational therapy (MOT, MS, PhD). *Application fee:* $60 ($70 for international students). Electronic applications accepted. *Application Contact:* Patricia Davies, Associate Dean for Research and Graduate Programs, 970-491-7294, Fax: 970-491-7859, E-mail: patricia.davies@colostate.edu. *Dean*, Dr. Jeff McCubbin, 970-491-6331, Fax: 970-491-7859, E-mail: jeff.mccubbin@colostate.edu.

School of Education Students: 74 full-time (53 women), 548 part-time (357 women); includes 151 minority (37 Black or African American, non-Hispanic/Latino; 4 American Indian or Alaska Native, non-Hispanic/Latino; 14 Asian, non-Hispanic/Latino; 71 Hispanic/Latino; 25 Two or more races, non-Hispanic/Latino), 16 international. Average age 37. 456 applicants, 31% accepted, 123 enrolled. *Faculty:* 33 full-time (23 women), 19 part-time/adjunct (11 women). Expenses: Contact institution. *Financial support:* In 2017–18, 4 students received support, including 8 research assistantships with full and partial tuition reimbursements available (averaging $12,758 per year), 4 teaching assistantships with full and partial tuition reimbursements available (averaging $14,256 per year); fellowships with full and partial tuition reimbursements available, Federal Work-Study, scholarships/grants, tuition waivers (full and partial), and unspecified assistantships also available. Financial award applicants required to submit FAFSA. In 2017, 177 master's, 22 doctorates awarded. *Program availability:* Part-time, online only, 100% online, blended/hybrid learning. Offers adult education and training (M Ed); counseling and career development (MA); education and human resources (M Ed); education, equity, and transformation (PhD); higher education leadership (PhD); organizational learning, performance, and change (M Ed, PhD); student affairs in higher education (MS). *Application deadline:* Applications are processed on a rolling basis. *Application fee:* $60 ($70 for international students). Electronic applications accepted. *Application Contact:* Kelli Clark, Graduate Programs Coordinator, 970-491-2093, Fax: 970-491-1317, E-mail: kelli.clark@colostate.edu. *Co-Director*, Dr. Louise Jennings, 970-491-6317, Fax: 970-491-1317, E-mail: louise.jennings@colostate.edu.

School of Social Work Students: 69 full-time (62 women), 113 part-time (98 women); includes 42 minority (12 Black or African American, non-Hispanic/Latino; 3 American Indian or Alaska Native, non-Hispanic/Latino; 26 Hispanic/Latino; 1 Two or more races, non-Hispanic/Latino), 2 international. Average age 34. 108 applicants, 41% accepted, 21 enrolled. *Faculty:* 8 full-time (7 women), 10 part-time/adjunct (9 women). Expenses: Contact institution. *Financial support:* In 2017–18, 7 students received support, including 3 fellowships (averaging $7,128 per year), 3 research assistantships (averaging $9,504 per year), 1 teaching assistantship (averaging $9,001 per year); scholarships/grants and unspecified assistantships also available. Financial award applicants required to submit FAFSA. In 2017, 57 master's, 3 doctorates awarded. *Program availability:* Part-time, evening/weekend, 100% online, blended/hybrid learning. Offers social work (MSW, PhD). *Application deadline:* For fall admission, 1/2 for domestic and international students; for spring admission, 5/31 for domestic and international students; for summer admission, 1/2 for domestic and international students. *Application fee:* $60 ($70 for international students). Electronic applications accepted. *Application Contact:* Timothy Frank, Graduate Program Coordinator, 970-491-2536, Fax: 970-491-7280, E-mail: timothy.frank@colostate.edu. *Director*, Dr. Audrey Shillington, 970-491-2378, Fax: 970-491-7280, E-mail: audrey.shillington@colostate.edu.

College of Liberal Arts Students: 335 full-time (207 women), 380 part-time (252 women); includes 92 minority (10 Black or African American, non-Hispanic/Latino; 3 American Indian or Alaska Native, non-Hispanic/Latino; 17 Asian, non-Hispanic/Latino; 48 Hispanic/Latino; 1 Native Hawaiian or other Pacific Islander, non-Hispanic/Latino; 13 Two or more races, non-Hispanic/Latino), 87 international. Average age 30. 866 applicants, 50% accepted, 198 enrolled. *Faculty:* 150 full-time (64 women), 37 part-time/adjunct (26 women). Expenses: Contact institution. *Financial support:* In 2017–18, 2 fellowships (averaging $19,008 per year), 4 research assistantships with tuition reimbursements (averaging $15,261 per year), 259 teaching assistantships with tuition reimbursements (averaging $14,445 per year) were awarded; career-related internships or fieldwork, Federal Work-Study, scholarships/grants, and unspecified assistantships also available. Support available to part-time students. In 2017, 170 master's, 11 doctorates awarded. *Program availability:* Part-time. Offers anthropology (MA, PhD); communication (PhD); communication studies (MA); communications and media management (MCMM); creative writing (MFA); economics (MA, PhD); environmental politics and policy (PhD); ethnic studies (MA); French (MA); liberal arts (MA); philosophy (MA); political science (MA); public communication and technology (MS, PhD); public history (MA); rhetoric and composition (MA); sociology (MA, PhD); studio art (MFA). *Application fee:* $60 ($70 for international students). Electronic applications accepted. *Application Contact:* Dr. Bruce Ronda, Associate Dean for Faculty and Graduate Studies, 970-491-5421, Fax: 970-491-0528, E-mail: bruce.ronda@colostate.edu. *Dean*, Dr. Ben Withers, 970-491-5421, Fax: 970-491-0528, E-mail: ben.withers@colostate.edu.

LEAP Institute for the Arts Students: 4 full-time (all women), 65 part-time (53 women); includes 14 minority (2 Black or African American, non-Hispanic/Latino; 4 Asian, non-Hispanic/Latino; 6 Hispanic/Latino; 2 Two or more races, non-Hispanic/Latino), 6 international. Average age 31. 50 applicants, 82% accepted, 24 enrolled. *Faculty:* 6 part-time/adjunct (3 women). Expenses: Contact institution. *Financial support:* Career-related internships or fieldwork, scholarships/grants, and unspecified assistantships available. Financial award application deadline: 1/1; financial award applicants required to submit FAFSA. In 2017, 9 master's awarded. *Program availability:* Part-time, evening/weekend, 100% online. Offers arts leadership and cultural management (MALCM). *Application deadline:* For fall admission, 6/30 for domestic and international students; for spring admission, 11/15 for domestic and international students; for summer admission, 4/1 for domestic and international students. Applications are processed on a rolling basis. *Application fee:* $60 ($70 for international students). Electronic applications accepted. *Application Contact:* Erica Pepmeyer, Recruitment Coordinator, 970-491-1194, E-mail: erika.pepmeyer@colostate.edu. *Director*, Dr. Constance DeVereaux, 970-491-3902, E-mail: constance.devereaux@colostate.edu.

School of Music, Theatre and Dance Students: 66 full-time (38 women), 99 part-time (73 women); includes 20 minority (1 Black or African American, non-Hispanic/Latino; 4 Asian, non-Hispanic/Latino; 13 Hispanic/Latino; 2 Two or more races, non-Hispanic/Latino), 16 international. Average age 29. 140 applicants, 57% accepted, 37 enrolled. *Faculty:* 24 full-time (6 women), 10 part-time/adjunct (7 women). Expenses: Contact institution. *Financial support:* In 2017–18, 40 students received support, including 25 teaching assistantships with full and partial tuition reimbursements available (averaging $8,839 per year); fellowships with full and partial tuition reimbursements available, scholarships/grants, health care benefits, and unspecified assistantships also available. Financial award application deadline: 2/15. In 2017, 46 master's awarded. *Program availability:* Part-time. Offers collaborative piano (MM). *Application deadline:* For fall admission, 2/15 for domestic and international students; for summer admission, 2/1 for domestic and international students. *Application fee:* $60 ($70 for international students). Electronic applications accepted. *Application Contact:* Dr. G. Murray Oliver, Graduate Program Coordinator, 970-491-5193, Fax: 970-491-7541, E-mail: murray.oliver@colostate.edu. *Director*, Dr. Daniel Goble, 970-491-5529, E-mail: dan.goble@colostate.edu.

College of Natural Sciences Students: 357 full-time (141 women), 571 part-time (231 women); includes 131 minority (11 Black or African American, non-Hispanic/Latino; 2 American Indian or Alaska Native, non-Hispanic/Latino; 37 Asian, non-Hispanic/Latino; 53 Hispanic/Latino; 28 Two or more races, non-Hispanic/Latino), 145 international. Average age 29. 815 applicants, 43% accepted, 247 enrolled. *Faculty:* 192 full-time (68 women), 35 part-time/adjunct (15 women). Expenses: Contact institution. *Financial support:* In 2017–18, 8 fellowships (averaging $13,283 per year), 202 research assistantships with full and partial tuition reimbursements (averaging $22,388 per year), 373 teaching assistantships with full and partial tuition reimbursements (averaging $19,261 per year) were awarded; scholarships/grants and unspecified assistantships also available. In 2017, 139 master's, 64 doctorates awarded. *Program availability:* Part-time, 100% online, blended/hybrid learning. Offers biochemistry and molecular biology (MS, PhD); botany (MS, PhD); chemistry (MS, PhD); computer science (MCS, MS, PhD); material science and engineering (PhD); mathematics (MS, PhD); natural science education (MNSE); natural sciences (MAC, MAIOP, MAS, MCS, MNSE, MS, PhD); physics (MS, PhD); psychology (PhD); statistics (MAS, MS, PhD); zoo, aquarium, and animal shelter management (MS). *Application fee:* $60 ($70 for international students). Electronic applications accepted. *Application Contact:* Dr. Simon Tavener, Associate Dean for Academics, 970-491-1300, Fax: 970-491-6639, E-mail: cns@colostate.edu. *Dean*, Dr. Janice Nerger, 970-491-1300, Fax: 970-491-6639, E-mail: janice.nerger@colostate.edu.

College of Veterinary Medicine and Biomedical Sciences Students: 853 full-time (667 women), 175 part-time (112 women); includes 200 minority (15 Black or African American, non-Hispanic/Latino; 2 American Indian or Alaska Native, non-Hispanic/Latino; 53 Asian, non-Hispanic/Latino; 88 Hispanic/Latino; 42 Two or more races, non-Hispanic/Latino), 56 international. Average age 27. 2,673 applicants, 16% accepted, 354 enrolled. *Faculty:* 233 full-time (110 women), 33 part-time/adjunct (19 women). Expenses: Contact institution. *Financial support:* In 2017–18, 82 research assistantships with tuition reimbursements (averaging $23,608 per year), 22 teaching assistantships with tuition reimbursements (averaging $20,605 per year) were awarded; fellowships with full tuition reimbursements, career-related internships or fieldwork, scholarships/grants, traineeships, and unspecified assistantships also available. In 2017, 188 master's, 20 doctorates awarded. Offers biomedical sciences (PhD); clinical sciences (MS, PhD); environmental health (MS, PhD); microbiology, immunology and pathology (MS, PhD); pathology (PhD); reproductive technology (MS); veterinary medicine (DVM); veterinary medicine and biomedical sciences (MS, DVM, PhD). *Application fee:* $60 ($70 for international students). Electronic applications accepted. *Application Contact:* Graduate Program Coordinator. *Dean*, Dr. Mark Stetter, 970-491-7051, E-mail: mark.stetter@colostate.edu.

Interdisciplinary College Students: 66 full-time (46 women), 136 part-time (80 women); includes 29 minority (2 Black or African American, non-Hispanic/Latino; 10 Asian, non-Hispanic/Latino; 8 Hispanic/Latino; 9 Two or more races, non-Hispanic/Latino), 30 international. Average age 32. 181 applicants, 24% accepted, 32 enrolled. Expenses: Contact institution. In 2017, 25 master's, 21 doctorates awarded. *Application fee:* $60 ($70 for international students). Electronic applications accepted. *Application Contact:* Sandra Dailey, Graduate School Academic Progress and Special Admissions Coordinator, 970-491-6817, Fax: 970-491-2194, E-mail: gradschool@colostate.edu.

School of Global Environmental Sustainability Students: 11 part-time (9 women); includes 2 minority (1 Black or African American, non-Hispanic/Latino; 1 Two or more races, non-Hispanic/Latino). Average age 35. Expenses: Contact institution. *Program availability:* Part-time-only, online only, 100% online. Offers applied global stability: agriculture (Graduate Certificate). *Application deadline:* For fall admission, 7/15 for domestic and international students; for spring admission, 12/15 for domestic and international students; for summer admission, 4/15 for domestic and international students. Applications are processed on a rolling basis. *Application fee:* $60 ($70 for international students). Electronic applications accepted. *Application Contact:* Sandra Dailey, Graduate School Academic Progress and Special Admissions Coordinator, 970-491-6817, Fax: 970-491-2194, E-mail: gradschool@colostate.edu. *Director, School of Global Environmental Sustainability,* Dr. Diana Wall, E-mail: diana.wall@colostate.edu.

Walter Scott, Jr. College of Engineering Students: 290 full-time (85 women), 652 part-time (144 women); includes 102 minority (16 Black or African American, non-Hispanic/Latino; 1 American Indian or Alaska Native, non-Hispanic/Latino; 35 Asian, non-Hispanic/Latino; 34 Hispanic/Latino; 16 Two or more races, non-Hispanic/Latino), 341 international. Average age 30. 1,001 applicants, 43% accepted, 181 enrolled. *Faculty:* 178 full-time (41 women), 42 part-time/adjunct (8 women). Expenses: Contact institution. *Financial support:* In 2017–18, 286 research assistantships (averaging $24,266 per year), 63 teaching assistantships (averaging $17,198 per year) were awarded; fellowships, scholarships/grants, traineeships, health care benefits, and unspecified assistantships also available. In 2017, 223 master's, 49 doctorates awarded. *Program availability:* Part-time, evening/weekend, 100% online, blended/hybrid learning. Offers atmospheric science (MS, PhD); chemical and biological engineering (MS, PhD); civil and environmental engineering (MS, PhD); computer engineering (ME, PhD); electrical engineering (MS); engineering (ME, MS, PhD); engineering education (ME); mechanical engineering (MS, PhD). *Application fee:* $60 ($70 for international students). Electronic applications accepted. *Application Contact:* Dr. Anthony Marchese, Associate Dean of Academic and Student Affairs, 970-491-6220, Fax: 970-491-3429, E-mail: anthony.marchese@colostate.edu. *Dean,* Dr. David McLean, 970-491-3366, E-mail: david.mclean@colostate.edu.

School of Biomedical Engineering Students: 18 full-time (3 women), 24 part-time (12 women); includes 7 minority (3 Asian, non-Hispanic/Latino; 2 Hispanic/Latino; 2 Two or more races, non-Hispanic/Latino), 5 international. Average age 27. 59 applicants, 19% accepted, 8 enrolled. *Faculty:* 1 (woman) part-time/adjunct. Expenses: Contact institution. *Financial support:* In 2017–18, 35 students received support, including 23 research assistantships (averaging $24,376 per year), 2 teaching assistantships (averaging $18,225 per year); fellowships, scholarships/grants, and health care benefits also available. In 2017, 5 master's, 4 doctorates awarded. *Program availability:* Part-time, online learning. Offers bioengineering (MS, PhD). *Application deadline:* For fall admission, 1/15 for domestic and international students; for spring admission, 9/1 for domestic and international students. *Application fee:* $60 ($70 for international students). Electronic applications accepted. *Application Contact:* Sara Mattern, Graduate Academic Adviser, 970-491-7157, Fax: 970-491-5569, E-mail: sara.mattern@colostate.edu. *Director and Professor,* Dr. Stu Tobet, 970-491-7157, Fax: 970-491-5569, E-mail: stuart.tobet@colostate.edu.

Warner College of Natural Resources Students: 116 full-time (60 women), 355 part-time (187 women); includes 64 minority (7 Black or African American, non-Hispanic/Latino; 6 American Indian or Alaska Native, non-Hispanic/Latino; 3 Asian, non-Hispanic/Latino; 34 Hispanic/Latino; 14 Two or more races, non-Hispanic/Latino), 32 international. Average age 30. 438 applicants, 54% accepted, 170 enrolled. *Faculty:* 74 full-time (24 women), 32 part-time/adjunct (8 women). Expenses: Contact institution. *Financial support:* In 2017–18, 93 research assistantships (averaging $24,217 per year), 45 teaching assistantships (averaging $13,549 per year) were awarded; fellowships, career-related internships or fieldwork, Federal Work-Study, scholarships/grants, and unspecified assistantships also available. In 2017, 109 master's, 13 doctorates awarded. *Program availability:* Part-time, evening/weekend, 100% online, blended/hybrid learning. Offers earth sciences (PhD); ecological restoration (MNRS); fish, wildlife, and conservation biology (MFWCB, MS, PhD); forest sciences (MS); greenhouse gas management and accounting (MGMA); human dimensions of natural resources (MS, PhD); natural resources (MFWCB, MGMA, MNRS, MS, MTM, PhD); rangeland ecosystem science (PhD); tourism management (MTM); watershed science (MS). *Application fee:* $60 ($70 for international students). Electronic applications accepted. *Application Contact:* Dr. Rich Conant, Associate Dean for Academic Affairs, 970-491-1919, Fax: 970-491-0279, E-mail: conant@nrel.colostate.edu. *Dean and Professor,* John P. Hayes, 970-491-6675, Fax: 970-491-0279, E-mail: wcnr_deans_office@mail.colostate.edu.

COLORADO STATE UNIVERSITY–GLOBAL CAMPUS, Greenwood Village, CO 80111

General Information State-supported, coed, comprehensive institution.

GRADUATE UNITS

Graduate Programs *Program availability:* Online learning.

COLORADO STATE UNIVERSITY–PUEBLO, Pueblo, CO 81001-4901

General Information State-supported, coed, comprehensive institution. *Graduate housing:* Room and/or apartments available on a first-come, first-served basis to single students; on-campus housing not available to married students. Housing application deadline: 8/1.

GRADUATE UNITS

College of Education, Engineering and Professional Studies *Program availability:* Part-time, evening/weekend. Offers art education (M Ed); education, engineering and professional studies (M Ed, MS); foreign language education (M Ed); health and physical education (M Ed); industrial and systems engineering (MS); instructional technology (M Ed); linguistically diverse education (M Ed); music education (M Ed); nursing (MS); special education (M Ed). Electronic applications accepted.

College of Science and Mathematics *Program availability:* Part-time, evening/weekend. Offers applied natural science (MS).

Malik and Seeme Hasan School of Business *Program availability:* Part-time, evening/weekend. Offers business (MBA).

COLORADO TECHNICAL UNIVERSITY AURORA, Aurora, CO 80014

General Information Proprietary, coed, comprehensive institution. *Graduate housing:* On-campus housing not available.

GRADUATE UNITS

Program in Computer Engineering Offers computer engineering (MS).

Program in Computer Science *Program availability:* Part-time, evening/weekend. Offers computer systems security (MSCS); database systems (MSCS); software engineering (MSCS).

Program in Electrical Engineering Offers electrical engineering (MS).

Program in Information Science Offers information systems security (MSM).

Program in Systems Engineering Offers systems engineering (MS).

Programs in Business Administration and Management *Program availability:* Part-time, evening/weekend. Offers accounting (MBA); business administration (MBA); business administration and management (EMBA); finance (MBA); human resource management (MBA); marketing (MBA); mediation and dispute resolution (MBA); operations management (MBA); project management (MBA); technology management (MBA).

COLORADO TECHNICAL UNIVERSITY COLORADO SPRINGS, Colorado Springs, CO 80907

General Information Proprietary, coed, university. *Graduate housing:* On-campus housing not available.

GRADUATE UNITS

Graduate Studies *Program availability:* Part-time, evening/weekend. Offers accounting (MBA, MSA); business administration (MBA); computer engineering (MSCE); computer science (DCS); computer systems security (MSCS); criminal justice (MSM); database systems (MSCS); electrical engineering (MSEE); finance (MBA); human resources management (MBA); information systems security (MSM); logistics/supply chain management (MBA); management (DM); marketing (MBA); mediation and dispute resolution (MBA); operations management (MBA); project management (MBA); software engineering (MSCS); systems engineering (MS); technology management (MBA).

COLUMBIA COLLEGE, Columbia, MO 65216-0002

General Information Independent-religious, coed, comprehensive institution. *Enrollment:* 1,196 graduate, professional, and undergraduate students; 91 full-time matriculated graduate/professional students (63 women), 650 part-time matriculated graduate/professional students (421 women). *Enrollment by degree level:* 741 master's. *Graduate faculty:* 34 full-time (15 women), 150 part-time/adjunct (70 women). *Tuition:* Full-time $12,450; part-time $415 per credit hour. *Graduate housing:* On-campus housing not available. *Student services:* Campus employment opportunities, campus safety program, career counseling, exercise/wellness program, free psychological counseling, international student services, low-cost health insurance, services for students with disabilities, teacher training, writing training. *Library facilities:* J. W. and Lois Stafford Library. *Collection:* Books: 61,727 (physical), 212,036 (digital/electronic); Serial titles: 108 (physical), 93,017 (digital/electronic); Databases: 61. Weekly public service hours: 94; students can reserve study rooms.

Computer facilities: Computer purchase and lease plans are available. 134 computers available on campus for general student use. A campuswide network can be accessed from student residence rooms and from off campus. Online class registration is available.

Website: http://www.ccis.edu/

General Application Contact: Stephanie Johnson, Director of Admissions, 573-875-7352, Fax: 573-875-7506, E-mail: sjohnson@ccis.edu.

GRADUATE UNITS

Master of Arts in Teaching Program Students: 14 full-time (10 women), 73 part-time (60 women); includes 22 minority (12 Black or African American, non-Hispanic/Latino; 1 Asian, non-Hispanic/Latino; 6 Hispanic/Latino; 3 Two or more races, non-Hispanic/Latino), 2 international. Average age 34. 99 applicants, 91% accepted, 56 enrolled. *Faculty:* 24 full-time (15 women), 48 part-time/adjunct (31 women). Expenses: Contact institution. *Financial support:* In 2017–18, 16 students received support. Career-related internships or fieldwork, Federal Work-Study, and scholarships/grants available. Financial award application deadline: 3/15; financial award applicants required to submit FAFSA. In 2017, 61 master's awarded. *Program availability:* Part-time, evening/weekend, 100% online, blended/hybrid learning. Offers teaching (MAT). *Application deadline:* For fall admission, 8/9 priority date for domestic and international students; for spring admission, 12/27 priority date for domestic and international students. Applications are processed on a rolling basis. *Application fee:* $55. Electronic applications accepted. *Application Contact:* Stephanie Johnson, Director of Admissions, 573-875-7352, Fax: 573-875-7506, E-mail: sjohnson@ccis.edu. *Dean of School of Humanities,* Dr. David Roebuck, 573-875-7570, E-mail: cdroebuck@ccis.edu.

Master of Business Administration Program Students: 53 full-time (37 women), 389 part-time (241 women); includes 114 minority (60 Black or African American, non-Hispanic/Latino; 2 American Indian or Alaska Native, non-Hispanic/Latino; 7 Asian, non-Hispanic/Latino; 28 Hispanic/Latino; 1 Native Hawaiian or other Pacific Islander, non-Hispanic/Latino; 16 Two or more races, non-Hispanic/Latino), 22 international. Average age 37. 368 applicants, 99% accepted, 111 enrolled. *Faculty:* 7 full-time (0 women), 76 part-time/adjunct (26 women). Expenses: Contact institution. *Financial support:* In 2017–18, 27 students received support. Federal Work-Study and scholarships/grants available. Financial award application deadline: 3/1; financial award applicants required to submit FAFSA. In 2017, 209 master's awarded. *Program availability:* Part-time, evening/weekend, 100% online, blended/hybrid learning. Offers accounting (MBA); business administration (MBA); human resources (MBA). *Application deadline:* For fall admission, 8/9 priority date for domestic and international students; for spring admission, 12/27 priority date for domestic and international students. Applications are processed on a rolling basis. *Application fee:* $55. Electronic applications accepted. *Application Contact:* Stephanie Johnson, Director of Admissions, 573-875-7352, Fax: 573-875-7506, E-mail: sjohnson@ccis.edu. *Dean, School of Business Administration,* Dr. Shanda Davis, 573-875-7561, Fax: 573-876-4493, E-mail: sdavis19@ccis.edu.

Master of Education in Educational Leadership Program Students: 7 full-time (all women), 49 part-time (33 women); includes 4 minority (3 Black or African American, non-Hispanic/Latino; 1 Hispanic/Latino). Average age 35. 30 applicants, 100% accepted, 21 enrolled. *Faculty:* 24 full-time (15 women), 7 part-time/adjunct (all women). Expenses: Contact institution. *Financial support:* In 2017–18, 20 students received support. Federal Work-Study and scholarships/grants available. Financial award application deadline: 3/1; financial award applicants required to submit FAFSA. In 2017, 9 master's awarded. *Program availability:* Part-time, evening/weekend, 100% online, blended/hybrid learning. Offers educational leadership (M Ed). *Application deadline:* For fall admission, 8/9 priority date for domestic and international students; for spring admission, 12/27 priority date for domestic and international students. Applications are processed on a rolling basis. *Application fee:* $55. Electronic applications accepted. *Application Contact:* Stephanie Johnson, Director of Admissions, 573-875-7352, Fax: 573-875-7506, E-mail: sjohnson@ccis.edu. *Dean of the School of Humanities*, Dr. David Roebuck, 573-875-7570, E-mail: cdroebuck@ccis.edu.

Master of Science in Criminal Justice Program Students: 10 full-time (4 women), 100 part-time (62 women); includes 42 minority (27 Black or African American, non-Hispanic/Latino; 1 American Indian or Alaska Native, non-Hispanic/Latino; 12 Hispanic/Latino; 2 Two or more races, non-Hispanic/Latino). Average age 40. 80 applicants, 76% accepted, 27 enrolled. *Faculty:* 3 full-time (0 women), 26 part-time/adjunct (13 women). Expenses: Contact institution. *Financial support:* In 2017–18, 9 students received support. Federal Work-Study and scholarships/grants available. Financial award application deadline: 3/1; financial award applicants required to submit FAFSA. In 2017, 42 master's awarded. *Program availability:* Part-time, evening/weekend, 100% online, blended/hybrid learning. Offers criminal justice (MSCJ). *Application deadline:* For fall admission, 8/9 priority date for domestic and international students; for spring admission, 12/27 priority date for domestic and international students. Applications are processed on a rolling basis. *Application fee:* $55. Electronic applications accepted. *Application Contact:* Stephanie Johnson, Director of Admissions, 573-875-7352, Fax: 573-875-7506, E-mail: sgjohnson@ccis.edu. *Dean of the School of Humanities*, Dr. David Roebuck, 573-875-7570, E-mail: cdroebuck@ccis.edu.

COLUMBIA COLLEGE, Columbia, SC 29203-5998

General Information Independent-religious, coed, primarily women, comprehensive institution. *Enrollment:* 1,513 graduate, professional, and undergraduate students; 130 full-time matriculated graduate/professional students (92 women), 4 part-time matriculated graduate/professional students (2 women). *Enrollment by degree level:* 134 master's. *Graduate faculty:* 3 full-time (2 women), 16 part-time/adjunct (6 women). *Tuition:* Full-time $15,840; part-time $480 per semester hour. Full-time tuition and fees vary according to course load. *Graduate housing:* On-campus housing not available. *Student services:* Campus safety program, career counseling, free psychological counseling, multicultural affairs office. *Library facilities:* J. Edens Drake Library. *Collection:* Books: 128,000 (physical), 92 (digital/electronic); Serial titles: 310 (physical); Databases: 84. Weekly public service hours: 70; students can reserve study rooms.

Computer facilities: Computer purchase and lease plans are available. 165 computers available on campus for general student use. A campuswide network can be accessed. Online class registration is available.
Website: http://www.columbiasc.edu/

General Application Contact: Myles Hacking, Associate Dean of Admissions, 803-786-3419, Fax: 803-786-3674, E-mail: mhacking@columbiasc.edu.

GRADUATE UNITS

Graduate Programs Students: 95 full-time (88 women), 2 part-time (1 woman); includes 38 minority (36 Black or African American, non-Hispanic/Latino; 1 Asian, non-Hispanic/Latino; 1 Hispanic/Latino). Average age 26. Expenses: Contact institution. *Financial support:* Available to part-time students. Application deadline: 7/1; applicants required to submit FAFSA. *Program availability:* Part-time, evening/weekend. Offers criminal justice (MA); organizational change and leadership (MA). *Application deadline:* For fall admission, 8/22 priority date for domestic students, 8/22 for international students. Applications are processed on a rolling basis. *Application fee:* $50. Electronic applications accepted. *Application Contact:* Myles Hacking, Associate Dean of Admissions, 803-786-3419, Fax: 803-786-3674, E-mail: mhacking@columbiasc.edu. *Provost and Vice President for Academic Affairs*, Dr. Robin Rosenthal, 803-786-3142, Fax: 803-754-3178, E-mail: rrosenthal@columbiasc.edu.

Education Division Expenses: Contact institution. *Financial support:* Available to part-time students. Application deadline: 7/1; applicants required to submit FAFSA. *Program availability:* Part-time, evening/weekend, online learning. Offers divergent learning (M Ed); higher education administration (M Ed). *Application deadline:* For fall admission, 8/22 for domestic students. *Application fee:* $50. Electronic applications accepted. *Application Contact:* Myles Hacking, Associate Dean of Admissions, 803-786-3871, Fax: 803-786-3674, E-mail: mhacking@columbiasc.edu.

COLUMBIA COLLEGE CHICAGO, Chicago, IL 60605-1996

General Information Independent, coed, comprehensive institution. CGS member. *Enrollment:* 7,312 graduate, professional, and undergraduate students; 227 full-time matriculated graduate/professional students (148 women), 58 part-time matriculated graduate/professional students (39 women). *Tuition:* Full-time $26,808; part-time $1117 per credit. *Required fees:* $572; $155 per credit. *Graduate housing:* Room and/or apartments available on a first-come, first-served basis to single students; on-campus housing not available to married students. Housing application deadline: 5/1. *Student services:* Campus employment opportunities, campus safety program, career counseling, exercise/wellness program, free psychological counseling, international student services, low-cost health insurance, multicultural affairs office, services for students with disabilities, teacher training, writing training. *Library facilities:* Columbia College Chicago Library. *Collection:* Books: 295,362 (physical), 61,291 (digital/electronic); Serial titles: 553 (physical); Databases: 180. Weekly public service hours: 87; students can reserve study rooms.

Computer facilities: Computer purchase and lease plans are available. A campuswide network can be accessed from student residence rooms and from off campus. Online class registration is available.
Website: http://www.colum.edu/

General Application Contact: David Marts, Graduate Counselor, 312-369-7942, Fax: 312-369-8047, E-mail: gradstudy@colum.edu.

GRADUATE UNITS

School of Graduate Studies Students: 227 full-time (148 women), 58 part-time (39 women); includes 75 minority (38 Black or African American, non-Hispanic/Latino; 13 Asian, non-Hispanic/Latino; 19 Hispanic/Latino; 5 Two or more races, non-Hispanic/Latino), 52 international. 584 applicants, 63% accepted, 147 enrolled. Expenses: Contact institution. *Financial support:* In 2017–18, 90 students received support. Fellowships, career-related internships or fieldwork, Federal Work-Study, scholarships/grants, and unspecified assistantships available. Financial award application deadline: 1/15. In 2017, 149 master's awarded. *Program availability:* Part-time, evening/weekend. Offers arts, entertainment and media management (MAM); cinema directing (MFA); civic media (MA); creative producing (MFA); fiction (MFA); fine arts (MFA); music (MFA); nonfiction (MFA); photography (MFA); poetry (MFA). *Application deadline:* For fall admission, 1/15 priority date for domestic and international students. Applications are processed on a rolling basis. *Application fee:* $55 ($100 for international students). Electronic applications accepted. *Application Contact:* David Marts, Graduate Admissions Counselor, 312-369-7945, Fax: 312-369-8004, E-mail: gradstudy@colum.edu. *Senior Vice President/Provost for Academic Affairs*, Dr. Stanley Wearden, 312-369-7495, Fax: 312-369-8466, E-mail: swearden@colum.edu.

COLUMBIA COLLEGE OF NURSING, Glendale, WI 53212

General Information Independent, coed, primarily women, upper-level institution.

GRADUATE UNITS

Graduate Program Offers nursing (MSN).

COLUMBIA INTERNATIONAL UNIVERSITY, Columbia, SC 29203

General Information Independent-religious, coed, university. *Graduate housing:* Rooms and/or apartments available on a first-come, first-served basis to single and married students. Housing application deadline: 8/1.

GRADUATE UNITS

Columbia Graduate School *Program availability:* Part-time, evening/weekend, online learning. Offers Bible teaching (MABT); counseling (MACN); early childhood and elementary education (MAT); educational administration (M Ed); educational leadership (PhD); instruction and learning (M Ed); teaching English as a foreign language (Certificate); teaching English as a foreign language and intercultural studies (MATF). Electronic applications accepted.

Seminary and School of Ministry *Program availability:* Part-time, evening/weekend. Offers academic ministries (M Div); Bible and theology (Certificate); bible exposition (M Div, MABE); Biblical ministry (Certificate); chaplaincy (M Div); intercultural studies (MAIS); leadership (D Min); member care (D Min); missions (D Min); preaching (D Min); theological studies (MA). Electronic applications accepted.

COLUMBIA SOUTHERN UNIVERSITY, Orange Beach, AL 36561

General Information Proprietary, coed, comprehensive institution. *Graduate housing:* On-campus housing not available.

GRADUATE UNITS

College of Safety and Emergency Services *Program availability:* Part-time, evening/weekend, online learning. Offers criminal justice administration (MS); emergency services management (MS); occupational safety and health (MS). Electronic applications accepted.

DBA Program *Program availability:* Part-time, evening/weekend, online learning. Offers business administration (DBA). Electronic applications accepted.

MBA Program *Program availability:* Part-time, evening/weekend, online learning. Offers finance (MBA); health care management (MBA); human resource management (MBA); marketing (MBA); project management (MBA); public administration (MBA). Electronic applications accepted.

Program in Organizational Leadership Offers organizational leadership (MS).

COLUMBIA THEOLOGICAL SEMINARY, Decatur, GA 30031-0520

General Information Independent-religious, coed, graduate-only institution. *Graduate housing:* Rooms and/or apartments available on a first-come, first-served basis to single students and available to married students. Housing application deadline: 4/30.

GRADUATE UNITS

Graduate and Professional Programs Offers theology (M Div, MATS, Th M, D Min, Th D). Th D program offered jointly with Emory University; D Min with Interdenominational Theological Center.

COLUMBIA UNIVERSITY, New York, NY 10027

General Information Independent, coed, university. CGS member. *Enrollment by degree level:* 16,858 master's, 4,855 doctoral, 571 other advanced degrees. *Graduate faculty:* 4,114 full-time (1,786 women), 1,587 part-time/adjunct (653 women). *Tuition:* Full-time $44,864; part-time $1704 per credit. *Required fees:* $2370 per semester. One-time fee: $105. *Graduate housing:* Rooms and/or apartments available to single and married students. Typical cost: $15,300 per year for single students; $22,750 per year for married students. Room charges vary according to campus/location and housing facility selected. Housing application deadline: 10/15. *Student services:* Campus employment opportunities, campus safety program, career counseling, free psychological counseling, international student services, low-cost health insurance, multicultural affairs office, services for students with disabilities, writing training. *Library facilities:* Butler plus 18 others. *Collection:* Books: 11.5 million (physical), 2.5 million (digital/electronic); Databases: 1,689. Weekly public service hours: 86; study areas open 24 hours, 5–7 days a week; students can reserve study rooms. *Research affiliation:* Long Island Biological Laboratory, Brookhaven National Laboratory, New York Botanical Gardens, American Museum of Natural History, Marine Biological Laboratory, Goddard Space Flight Center.

Computer facilities: Computer purchase and lease plans are available. 460 computers available on campus for general student use. A campuswide network can be accessed from student residence rooms and from off campus. Online class registration is available.
Website: http://www.columbia.edu/

General Application Contact: General Information, 212-854-1754.

GRADUATE UNITS

College of Dental Medicine Offers advanced education in general dentistry (Certificate); biomedical informatics (MA, PhD); dental and oral surgery (DDS); dental medicine (MA, MS, DDS, PhD, Certificate); endodontics (Certificate); orthodontics (MS, Certificate); periodontics (MS, Certificate); prosthodontics (MS, Certificate); science education (MA).

College of Physicians and Surgeons *Program availability:* Part-time. Offers anatomy (M Phil, MA, PhD); anatomy and cell biology (PhD); biochemistry and molecular biophysics (M Phil, PhD); biomedical informatics (M Phil, MA, PhD); biomedical sciences (M Phil, MA, PhD); biophysics (PhD); cellular, molecular, structural and genetic studies (PhD); genetics (M Phil, MA, PhD); medicine (M Phil, MA, MS, DN Sc, DPT, Ed D, MD, OTD, PhD, Adv C); movement science (Ed D); neurobiology and behavior (PhD); occupational therapy (MS); occupational therapy and cognition (OTD); pathobiology (M Phil, MA, PhD); pharmacology (M Phil, MA, PhD); pharmacology-toxicology (M Phil, MA, PhD); physical therapy (DPT); physiology and cellular biophysics (M Phil, MA, PhD).

Institute of Human Nutrition *Program availability:* Part-time. Offers nutrition (MS, PhD). Electronic applications accepted.

Columbia School of Social Work Students: 992 full-time (855 women), 124 part-time (107 women); includes 432 minority (123 Black or African American, non-Hispanic/Latino; 1 American Indian or Alaska Native, non-Hispanic/Latino; 108 Asian, non-Hispanic/Latino; 163 Hispanic/Latino; 2 Native Hawaiian or other Pacific Islander, non-Hispanic/Latino; 35 Two or more races, non-Hispanic/Latino), 118 international. Average age 26. 1,683 applicants. *Faculty:* 40 full-time (28 women), 116 part-time/adjunct (88 women). Expenses: Contact institution. *Financial support:* Teaching assistantships, Federal Work-Study, scholarships/grants, and unspecified assistantships available. Financial award application deadline: 2/15; financial award applicants required to submit FAFSA. In 2017, 454 master's, 2 doctorates awarded. *Program availability:* 100% online, blended/hybrid learning. Offers advanced clinical practice (MSSW); advanced generalist practice and programming (MSSW); policy practice (MSSW); social enterprise administration (MSSW). *Application deadline:* For fall admission, 2/1 for domestic and international students; for spring admission, 10/15 for domestic and international students. *Application fee:* $75. Electronic applications accepted. *Application Contact:* Andrew Rapin, Director of Admissions, 212-851-2400, E-mail: cssw-admit@columbia.edu. *Assistant Dean, Enrollment and Student Services*, Michael Lovaglio, 212-851-2359, E-mail: ml3992@columbia.edu.

Columbia University Mailman School of Public Health Students: 913 full-time (707 women), 483 part-time (346 women); includes 518 minority (91 Black or African American, non-Hispanic/Latino; 3 American Indian or Alaska Native, non-Hispanic/Latino; 272 Asian, non-Hispanic/Latino; 111 Hispanic/Latino; 41 Two or more races, non-Hispanic/Latino), 282 international. Average age 28. 3,146 applicants, 55% accepted, 644 enrolled. Expenses: Contact institution. *Financial support:* Fellowships, research assistantships, teaching assistantships, career-related internships or fieldwork, Federal Work-Study, and traineeships available. Support available to part-time students. Financial award application deadline: 2/1; financial award applicants required to submit FAFSA. In 2017, 601 master's, 22 doctorates awarded. *Program availability:* Part-time, evening/weekend. Offers biostatistics (MPH, MS, Dr PH, PhD); environmental health sciences (MPH, Dr PH, PhD); epidemiology (MPH, MS, Dr PH, PhD); health policy and management (Exec MHA, Exec MPH, MHA, MPH); population and family health (MPH, Dr PH); public health (Exec MHA, Exec MPH, MHA, MPH, MS, Dr PH, PhD); radiological sciences (MS); sociomedical sciences (MPH, MS, Dr PH, PhD); toxicology (MS). PhD offered in cooperation with the Graduate School of Arts and Sciences. *Application deadline:* For fall admission, 12/1 priority date for domestic and international students. *Application fee:* $120. Electronic applications accepted. *Application Contact:* Clare Norton, Associate Dean for Enrollment Management, 212-305-8698, Fax: 212-342-1861, E-mail: ph-admit@columbia.edu. *Dean/Professor*, Dr. Linda P. Fried, 212-305-9300, Fax: 212-305-9342, E-mail: lpfried@columbia.edu.

Fu Foundation School of Engineering and Applied Science *Program availability:* Part-time, 100% online. Offers applied mathematics (MS, Eng Sc D, PhD); applied physics (MS, Eng Sc D, PhD); biomedical engineering (MS, Eng Sc D, PhD); business analytics (MS); chemical engineering (MS, PhD); civil engineering (MS, Eng Sc D, PhD); computer engineering (MS); computer science (MS, Eng Sc D, PhD); construction engineering and management (MS); earth and environmental engineering (Eng Sc D, PhD); earth resources engineering (MS); electrical engineering (MS, PhD); engineering and applied science (MS, Eng Sc D, PhD); engineering mechanics (MS, Eng Sc D, PhD); financial engineering (MS); industrial engineering (MS); industrial engineering and operations research (PhD); management science and engineering (MS); materials science and engineering (MS, Eng Sc D, PhD); mechanical engineering (MS, Eng Sc D, PhD); medical physics (MS); operations research (MS). Electronic applications accepted.

Data Science Institute *Program availability:* Part-time. Offers data science (MS).

Graduate School of Architecture, Planning, and Preservation Offers advanced architectural design (MS); architecture (M Arch, PhD); architecture, planning, and preservation (M Arch, MS, PhD, Certificate); historic preservation (MS, PhD, Certificate); real estate development (MS); urban planning (MS, PhD).

Graduate School of Arts and Sciences *Program availability:* Part-time. Offers African-American studies (MA); American studies (MA); anthropology (MA, PhD); art history and archaeology (MA, PhD); astronomy (PhD); biological sciences (PhD); biotechnology (MA); chemical physics (PhD); chemistry (PhD); classical studies (MA, PhD); classics (MA, PhD); climate and society (MA); conservation biology (MA); earth and environmental sciences (PhD); East Asia: regional studies (MA); East Asian languages and cultures (MA, PhD); ecology, evolution and environmental biology (MA); ecology, evolution, and environmental biology (PhD); economics (MA, PhD); English and comparative literature (MA, PhD); French and Romance philology (MA, PhD); Germanic languages (MA, PhD); global French studies (MA); global thought (MA); Hispanic cultural studies (MA); history (PhD); history and literature (MA); human rights studies (MA); Islamic studies (MA); Italian (MA, PhD); Japanese pedagogy (MA); Jewish studies (MA); Latin America and the Caribbean: regional studies (MA); Latin American and Iberian cultures (PhD); mathematics (MA, PhD); medieval and Renaissance studies (MA); Middle Eastern, South Asian, and African studies (MA, PhD); modern art: critical and curatorial studies (MA); modern European studies (MA); museum anthropology (MA); music (DMA, PhD); oral history (MA); philosophical foundations of physics (MA); philosophy (MA, PhD); physics (PhD); political science (MA, PhD); psychology (PhD); quantitative methods in the social sciences (MA); religion (MA, PhD); Russia, Eurasia and East Europe: regional studies (MA); Russian translation (MA); Slavic cultures (MA); Slavic languages (MA, PhD); sociology (MA, PhD); South Asian studies (MA); statistics (MA, PhD); theatre (PhD). Dual-degree programs require admission to both Graduate School of Arts and Sciences and another Columbia school. Electronic applications accepted.

Graduate School of Business Offers accounting (MBA); business (EMBA, MBA, PhD); business administration (EMBA, MBA); decision, risk, and operations (MBA); entrepreneurship (MBA); finance and economics (MBA); global business administration (EMBA); healthcare and pharmaceutical management (MBA); human resource management (MBA); international business (MBA); leadership and ethics (MBA); management (MBA); marketing (MBA); media (MBA); private equity (MBA); real estate (MBA); social enterprise (MBA); value investing (MBA). Electronic applications accepted.

Graduate School of Journalism *Program availability:* Part-time. Offers journalism (MA, MS, PhD).

School of International and Public Affairs Students: 1,188 full-time (721 women), 196 part-time (108 women); includes 273 minority (42 Black or African American, non-Hispanic/Latino; 122 Asian, non-Hispanic/Latino; 77 Hispanic/Latino; 1 Native Hawaiian or other Pacific Islander, non-Hispanic/Latino; 31 Two or more races, non-Hispanic/Latino), 765 international. Average age 28. 2,082 applicants, 65% accepted, 670 enrolled. *Faculty:* 72 full-time (18 women), 315 part-time/adjunct (109 women). Expenses: Contact institution. *Financial support:* Fellowships, research assistantships, teaching assistantships, career-related internships or fieldwork, Federal Work-Study, institutionally sponsored loans, and scholarships/grants available. Financial award application deadline: 1/5; financial award applicants required to submit FAFSA. In 2017, 749 master's awarded. *Program availability:* Part-time, evening/weekend. Offers development practice (MPA); environmental science and policy (MPA); international affairs (MIA); international and public affairs (MA, MIA, MPA, Certificate); public policy and administration (MPA). *Application deadline:* For fall admission, 2/5 for domestic and international students; for spring admission, 10/15 for domestic and international students. *Application fee:* $95. Electronic applications accepted. *Application Contact:* Grace Han, Executive Director of Admissions and Financial Aid, 212-854-6216, Fax: 212-854-3010, E-mail: sipa_admission@columbia.edu. *Dean*, Merit Janow, 212-854-4604, Fax: 212-864-4847, E-mail: njc2138@sipa.columbia.edu.

School of Law Students: 1,239 full-time (554 women); includes 360 minority (111 Black or African American, non-Hispanic/Latino; 8 American Indian or Alaska Native, non-Hispanic/Latino; 160 Asian, non-Hispanic/Latino; 81 Hispanic/Latino), 124 international. Average age 24. Expenses: Contact institution. *Financial support:* Fellowships, research assistantships, teaching assistantships, career-related internships or fieldwork, Federal Work-Study, institutionally sponsored loans, scholarships/grants, and tuition waivers (full and partial) available. Financial award application deadline: 3/1; financial award applicants required to submit FAFSA. Offers law (LL M, JD, JSD). *Application deadline:* For fall admission, 2/15 for domestic students. Applications are processed on a rolling basis. *Application fee:* $85. Electronic applications accepted. *Application Contact:* E. Nkonye Iwerebon, Dean of Admissions, 212-854-2674, Fax: 212-854-1109, E-mail: niwere@law.columbia.edu. *Dean of Faculty*, Gillian L. Lester, 212-854-2675, E-mail: glester@law.columbia.edu.

School of Nursing Offers adult-gerontology acute care nurse practitioner (MS, Adv C); adult-gerontology primary care nurse practitioner (MS, Adv C); family nurse practitioner (MS, Adv C); nurse anesthesia (MS, Adv C); nurse midwifery (MS); nursing (MS, DNP, PhD, Adv C); pediatric nurse practitioner (MS, Adv C); psychiatric mental health nursing (MS, Adv C). Electronic applications accepted.

School of Professional Studies *Program availability:* Part-time, evening/weekend. Offers actuarial science (MS); bioethics (MS); communications practice (MS); construction administration (MS); fundraising management (MS); information and archive management (MS); landscape design (MS); narrative medicine (MS); negotiation and conflict resolution (MS); sports management (MS); strategic communications (MS); sustainability management (MS); technology management (Exec MS). Electronic applications accepted.

School of the Arts Students: 869 full-time (491 women), 9 part-time (all women); includes 228 minority (60 Black or African American, non-Hispanic/Latino; 4 American Indian or Alaska Native, non-Hispanic/Latino; 52 Asian, non-Hispanic/Latino; 70 Hispanic/Latino; 42 Two or more races, non-Hispanic/Latino), 217 international. Average age 27. 2,144 applicants, 25% accepted, 311 enrolled. *Faculty:* 78 full-time (28 women), 204 part-time/adjunct (102 women). Expenses: Contact institution. *Financial support:* In 2017–18, 546 students received support, including 367 fellowships, 109 teaching assistantships with full and partial tuition reimbursements available; research assistantships, career-related internships or fieldwork, Federal Work-Study, and scholarships/grants also available. Financial award application deadline: 2/1; financial award applicants required to submit FAFSA. In 2017, 276 master's awarded. *Program availability:* Part-time. Offers arts (MA, MFA); film (MFA); film and media studies (MA); new genres (MFA); sound art (MFA); theatre (MFA); writing (MFA). JD/MFA offered in cooperation with Columbia Law School. *Application fee:* $110. Electronic applications accepted. *Application Contact:* Kenny Wong, Director of Admissions and Financial Aid, 212-854-2134, E-mail: admissions-arts@columbia.edu. *Dean*, Carol Becker, 212-854-9847.

South Asia Institute Students: 6 full-time (4 women); includes 4 minority (all Asian, non-Hispanic/Latino). Average age 28. 18 applicants, 44% accepted, 1 enrolled. *Faculty:* 22 full-time (11 women), 3 part-time/adjunct (1 woman). Expenses: Contact institution. *Financial support:* In 2017–18, 2 students received support, including 3 fellowships (averaging $33,000 per year); Federal Work-Study and tuition waivers (partial) also available. Financial award application deadline: 4/6; financial award applicants required to submit FAFSA. In 2017, 8 master's awarded. *Program availability:* Part-time. Offers South Asian studies (MA, Certificate). Students must be enrolled in a separate graduate degree program at Columbia University. *Application deadline:* For fall admission, 4/6 for domestic and international students; for spring admission, 11/17 for domestic students, 11/18 for international students. *Application fee:* $100. Electronic applications accepted. *MA Coordinator*, Prof. Katherine Pratt Ewing, E-mail: ke2131@columbia.edu.

COLUMBUS COLLEGE OF ART & DESIGN, Columbus, OH 43215-1758

General Information Independent, coed, comprehensive institution. *Enrollment:* 50 full-time matriculated graduate/professional students (35 women), 1 part-time matriculated graduate/professional student. *Enrollment by degree level:* 51 master's. *Graduate faculty:* 64 full-time (28 women), 111 part-time/adjunct (52 women). *Tuition:* Full-time $34,920. *Graduate housing:* Rooms and/or apartments available on a first-come, first-served basis to single and married students. Typical cost: $8740 per year ($12,340 including board) for single students. Housing application deadline: 5/1. *Student services:* Campus employment opportunities, campus safety program, career counseling, exercise/wellness program, free psychological counseling, grant writing training, international student services, services for students with disabilities, teacher training, writing training. *Library facilities:* Packard Library. *Collection:* Books: 40,836 (physical), 28,701 (digital/electronic); Serial titles: 434 (physical), 253,828 (digital/electronic).

Computer facilities: 485 computers available on campus for general student use. A campuswide network can be accessed. Online class registration is available.
Website: http://www.ccad.edu/

General Application Contact: John Cairns, Senior Graduate Admissions Counselor, 614-222-3249, E-mail: jcairns.1@ccad.edu.

GRADUATE UNITS

Graduate Programs Students: 50 full-time (35 women), 1 part-time (0 women); includes 21 minority (4 Black or African American, non-Hispanic/Latino; 14 Asian, non-Hispanic/Latino; 2 Hispanic/Latino; 1 Two or more races, non-Hispanic/Latino). Average age 32. 61 applicants, 77% accepted, 31 enrolled. *Faculty:* 64 full-time (28 women), 111 part-time/adjunct (52 women). Expenses: Contact institution. *Financial support:* In 2017–18, 30 students received support. Teaching assistantships, scholarships/grants, and unspecified assistantships available. Support available to part-time students. Financial award application deadline: 2/1; financial award applicants required to submit FAFSA. In 2017, 20 master's awarded. *Program availability:* Part-time. Offers integrative design (M Des); visual arts (MFA). *Application deadline:* For fall admission, 2/1 priority date for domestic and international students. Applications are processed on a rolling basis. *Application fee:* $65. Electronic applications accepted. *Application Contact:* John Cairns, Senior Admissions Counselor, Graduate Studies, 614-222-3249, E-mail: jcairns.1@ccad.edu. *Director of Graduate Studies/MFA Professor*, Ric Petry, 614-222-3227, E-mail: rpetry@ccad.edu.

COLUMBUS STATE UNIVERSITY, Columbus, GA 31907-5645

General Information State-supported, coed, comprehensive institution. CGS member. *Enrollment:* 8,452 graduate, professional, and undergraduate students; 612 full-time matriculated graduate/professional students (370 women), 1,039 part-time matriculated graduate/professional students (641 women). *Enrollment by degree level:* 1,168 master's, 181 doctoral, 302 other advanced degrees. *Graduate faculty:* 120 full-time (53 women), 66 part-time/adjunct (33 women). *International tuition:* $19,218 full-time. Tuition, state resident: full-time $3708; part-time $2472 per year. Tuition, nonresident: full-time $14,418; part-time $9612 per year. *Required fees:* $1605. Tuition and fees vary according to program. *Graduate housing:* Rooms and/or apartments available on a first-come, first-served basis to single and married students. Typical cost: $5790 (including board) for single students; $11,580 (including board) for married students. Room and board charges vary according to board plan, campus/location and housing facility selected. Housing application deadline: 6/30. *Student services:* Campus employment opportunities, campus safety program, career counseling, exercise/wellness program, free psychological counseling, international student services, low-cost health insurance, multicultural affairs office, services for students with disabilities, teacher training, writing training. *Library facilities:* Simon Schwob Memorial Library plus 1 other. *Collection:* Books: 379,660 (physical); Serial titles: 1,103 (physical).

Computer facilities: 3,053 computers available on campus for general student use. A campuswide network can be accessed from student residence rooms and from off campus. Online class registration is available.

Website: http://www.columbusstate.edu/

General Application Contact: Kristin Williams, Assistant Director for Graduate and Global Admission, 706-507-8824, Fax: 706-568-5091, E-mail: smithedmond_catrina@columbusstate.edu.

GRADUATE UNITS

Graduate Studies Students: 612 full-time (370 women), 1,039 part-time (641 women); includes 730 minority (581 Black or African American, non-Hispanic/Latino; 5 American Indian or Alaska Native, non-Hispanic/Latino; 39 Asian, non-Hispanic/Latino; 65 Hispanic/Latino; 3 Native Hawaiian or other Pacific Islander, non-Hispanic/Latino; 37 Two or more races, non-Hispanic/Latino), 55 international. Average age 36. 948 applicants, 52% accepted, 199 enrolled. *Faculty:* 120 full-time (53 women), 66 part-time/adjunct (33 women). Expenses: Contact institution. *Financial support:* In 2017–18, 157 students received support, including 95 research assistantships with partial tuition reimbursements available (averaging $3,000 per year); career-related internships or fieldwork, Federal Work-Study, institutionally sponsored loans, scholarships/grants, tuition waivers (partial), and unspecified assistantships also available. Support available to part-time students. Financial award application deadline: 5/1; financial award applicants required to submit FAFSA. In 2017, 462 master's, 18 doctorates, 123 other advanced degrees awarded. *Program availability:* Part-time, evening/weekend, 100% online, blended/hybrid learning. *Application deadline:* For fall admission, 6/30 for domestic and international students; for spring admission, 11/1 for domestic and international students; for summer admission, 5/1 for domestic and international students. Applications are processed on a rolling basis. *Application fee:* $50. Electronic applications accepted. *Application Contact:* Catrina Smith-Edmund, Assistant Director for Graduate and Global Admission, 706-507-8824, Fax: 706-568-5091, E-mail: smithedmond_catrina@columbusstate.edu. *Assistant Vice President for Academic Affairs*, Dr. Ellen Roberts, 706-507-8573, Fax: 706-569-3168, E-mail: roberts_ellen@columbusstate.edu.

College of Education and Health Professions Students: 409 full-time (290 women), 632 part-time (503 women); includes 525 minority (445 Black or African American, non-Hispanic/Latino; 1 American Indian or Alaska Native, non-Hispanic/Latino; 20 Asian, non-Hispanic/Latino; 34 Hispanic/Latino; 1 Native Hawaiian or other Pacific Islander, non-Hispanic/Latino; 24 Two or more races, non-Hispanic/Latino), 2 international. Average age 37. 452 applicants, 50% accepted, 117 enrolled. *Faculty:* 50 full-time (31 women), 46 part-time/adjunct (30 women). Expenses: Contact institution. *Financial support:* In 2017–18, 84 students received support, including 29 research assistantships with partial tuition reimbursements available (averaging $3,000 per year); career-related internships or fieldwork, Federal Work-Study, institutionally sponsored loans, scholarships/grants, tuition waivers (partial), and unspecified assistantships also available. Support available to part-time students. Financial award application deadline: 5/1; financial award applicants required to submit FAFSA. In 2017, 202 master's, 18 doctorates, 118 other advanced degrees awarded. *Program availability:* Part-time, evening/weekend, 100% online, blended/hybrid learning. Offers clinical mental health counseling (MS); curriculum and instruction in accomplished teaching (M Ed); curriculum and leadership (Ed D); early childhood education (M Ed, MAT, Ed S); education and health professions (M Ed, MAT, MS, MSN, Ed D, Ed S); educational leadership (M Ed, Ed S); exercise science (MS); family nurse practitioner (MSN); health and physical education (M Ed, MAT); middle grades education (M Ed, MAT, Ed S); nursing (MSN); school counseling (M Ed, Ed S); secondary education (M Ed, MAT, Ed S); special education (M Ed, MAT, Ed S); teacher leadership (M Ed). *Application deadline:* For fall admission, 6/30 for domestic students, 5/1 for international students; for spring admission, 11/1 for domestic and international students; for summer admission, 3/1 for domestic and international students. Applications are processed on a rolling basis. *Application fee:* $50. Electronic applications accepted. *Application Contact:* Catrina Smith-Edmond, Assistant Director for Graduate and Global Admission, 706-507-8824, Fax: 706-568-5091, E-mail: smithedmond_catrina@columbusstate.edu. *Dean*, Dr. Deirdre Greer, 706-507-8505, Fax: 706-569-3134, E-mail: greer_deirdre@columbusstate.edu.

College of Letters and Sciences Students: 81 full-time (37 women), 227 part-time (64 women); includes 101 minority (83 Black or African American, non-Hispanic/Latino; 2 American Indian or Alaska Native, non-Hispanic/Latino; 3 Asian, non-Hispanic/Latino; 8 Hispanic/Latino; 1 Native Hawaiian or other Pacific Islander, non-Hispanic/Latino; 4 Two or more races, non-Hispanic/Latino), 3 international. Average age 40. 139 applicants, 60% accepted, 66 enrolled. *Faculty:* 16 full-time (5 women), 15 part-time/adjunct (0 women). Expenses: Contact institution. *Financial support:* In 2017–18, 8 students received support, including 27 research assistantships with partial tuition reimbursements available (averaging $3,000 per year); fellowships, career-related internships or fieldwork, Federal Work-Study, institutionally sponsored loans, scholarships/grants, tuition waivers (partial), and unspecified assistantships also available. Support available to part-time students. Financial award application deadline: 5/1; financial award applicants required to submit FAFSA. In 2017, 128 master's, 1 other advanced degree awarded. *Program availability:* Part-time, evening/weekend, 100% online, blended/hybrid learning. Offers history (MA); letters and sciences (MA, MPA, MPSA, MS, Certificate); natural sciences (MS); public administration (MPA); public safety administration (MPSA); teaching English to speakers of other languages (Certificate). *Application deadline:* For fall admission, 6/30 for domestic students, 5/1 for international students; for spring admission, 11/1 for domestic students, 10/1 for international students; for summer admission, 3/1 for domestic and international students. Applications are processed on a rolling basis. *Application fee:* $50. Electronic applications accepted. *Application Contact:* Catrina Smith-Edmond, Assistant Director for Graduate and Global Admission, 706-507-8824, Fax: 706-568-5091, E-mail: smithedmond_catrina@columbusstate.edu. *Dean*, Dr. Dennis Rome, 706-568-2056, E-mail: rome_dennis@columbusstate.edu.

College of the Arts Students: 49 full-time (20 women), 22 part-time (13 women); includes 16 minority (9 Black or African American, non-Hispanic/Latino; 4 Asian, non-Hispanic/Latino; 2 Hispanic/Latino; 1 Native Hawaiian or other Pacific Islander, non-Hispanic/Latino), 20 international. Average age 28. 68 applicants, 43% accepted, 19 enrolled. *Faculty:* 28 full-time (11 women), 4 part-time/adjunct (2 women). Expenses: Contact institution. *Financial support:* In 2017–18, 43 students received support, including 28 research assistantships with partial tuition reimbursements available (averaging $3,000 per year); career-related internships or fieldwork, Federal Work-Study, institutionally sponsored loans, scholarships/grants, tuition waivers (partial), and unspecified assistantships also available. Support available to part-time students. Financial award application deadline: 5/1; financial award applicants required to submit FAFSA. In 2017, 13 master's, 5 other advanced degrees awarded. *Program availability:* Part-time, evening/weekend. Offers art education (M Ed, MAT); arts (M Ed, MAT, MM, Artist Diploma); music (Artist Diploma); music education (MM); music performance (MM); theatre education (M Ed, MAT). *Application deadline:* For fall admission, 6/30 for domestic students, 5/1 for international students; for spring admission, 11/1 for domestic and international students; for summer admission, 3/1 for domestic and international students. Applications are processed on a rolling basis. *Application fee:* $50. Electronic applications accepted. *Application Contact:* Catrina Smith-Edmond, Assistant Director for Graduate and Global Admission, 706-507-8824, Fax: 706-568-5091, E-mail: smithedmond_catrina@columbusstate.edu. *Dean*, Dr. Richard Baxter, 706-507-8043, E-mail: baxter_richard@columbusstate.edu.

Turner College of Business Students: 70 full-time (20 women), 134 part-time (44 women); includes 76 minority (34 Black or African American, non-Hispanic/Latino; 2 American Indian or Alaska Native, non-Hispanic/Latino; 11 Asian, non-Hispanic/Latino; 20 Hispanic/Latino; 9 Two or more races, non-Hispanic/Latino), 30 international. Average age 30. 218 applicants, 56% accepted, 73 enrolled. *Faculty:* 20 full-time (5 women), 1 (woman) part-time/adjunct. Expenses: Contact institution. *Financial support:* In 2017–18, 20 students received support, including 18 research assistantships (averaging $3,000 per year); Federal Work-Study also available. Financial award application deadline: 5/1; financial award applicants required to submit FAFSA. In 2017, 110 master's, 1 other advanced degree awarded. *Program availability:* Part-time, evening/weekend, 100% online, blended/hybrid learning. Offers applied computer science (MS); business administration (MBA); cyber security (MS); human resource management (Certificate); information systems security (Certificate); modeling and simulation (Certificate); organizational leadership (MS); servant leadership (Certificate). *Application deadline:* For fall admission, 6/30 for domestic students, 5/1 for international students; for spring admission, 11/1 for domestic and international students; for summer admission, 3/1 for domestic and international students. Applications are processed on a rolling basis. *Application fee:* $50. Electronic applications accepted. *Application Contact:* Catrina Smith-Edmond, Assistant Director for Graduate and Global Admission, 706-507-8824, Fax: 706-568-5091, E-mail: smithedmond_catrina@columbusstate.edu. *Dean*, Dr. Linda U. Hadley, 706-507-8153, Fax: 706-568-2184, E-mail: hadley_linda@columbusstate.edu.

CONCORDIA COLLEGE, Moorhead, MN 56562

General Information Independent-religious, coed, comprehensive institution.

GRADUATE UNITS

Program in Education Offers world language instruction (M Ed).

CONCORDIA COLLEGE–NEW YORK, Bronxville, NY 10708-1998

General Information Independent-religious, coed, comprehensive institution.

GRADUATE UNITS

Program in Business Leadership Offers business leadership (MS).

Program in Childhood Special Education Offers childhood special education (MS Ed).

CONCORDIA LUTHERAN SEMINARY, Edmonton, AB T5B 4E3, Canada

General Information Independent-religious, coed, primarily men, graduate-only institution. *Graduate housing:* On-campus housing not available.

GRADUATE UNITS

Graduate and Professional Programs *Program availability:* Part-time. Offers theology (M Div, Graduate Certificate).

CONCORDIA SEMINARY, St. Louis, MO 63105-3199

General Information Independent-religious, coed, primarily men, graduate-only institution. *Graduate housing:* Rooms and/or apartments guaranteed to single students and available to married students. Housing application deadline: 3/4. *Research affiliation:* Center for Reformation Research, Concordia Historical Institute.

GRADUATE UNITS

Graduate Programs Offers theology (M Div, MA, STM, D Min, PhD, Certificate).

CONCORDIA THEOLOGICAL SEMINARY, Fort Wayne, IN 46825-4996

General Information Independent-religious, coed, primarily men, graduate-only institution. *Graduate housing:* Room and/or apartments available to single students; on-campus housing not available to married students.

GRADUATE UNITS

Graduate and Professional Programs *Program availability:* Part-time. Offers theology (M Div, MA, STM, D Min, PhD).

CONCORDIA UNIVERSITY, Montréal, QC H3G 1M8, Canada

General Information Province-supported, coed, university. CGS member. *Graduate housing:* Room and/or apartments available on a first-come, first-served basis to single students; on-campus housing not available to married students. *Research affiliation:* Canadian Rural Revitalization Foundation (sociology), Blue Metropolis Literary Series (English), Canadian Journalism Project (journalism), Centre de Recherche en Plasturgie et Composites (CREPEC) (mechanical and industrial engineering), Centre de Recherche Informatique de Montreal (CRIM) (computer science), Center d'experise et de services en application Multimedia (multimedia).

GRADUATE UNITS

School of Graduate Studies *Program availability:* Part-time, evening/weekend. Offers individualized research (M Sc, MA, PhD).

Faculty of Arts and Science Offers adult education (Certificate, Diploma); Anglais-Français en langue et techniques de localization (Certificate); applied linguistics (MA, Certificate); arts and science (M Env, M Sc, MA, MTM, PhD, Certificate, Diploma, Graduate Diploma); biology (M Sc, PhD); biotechnology and genomics (Diploma); chemistry (M Sc, PhD); child studies (MA); communication (PhD); communication studies (Diploma); community economic development (Diploma); creative writing (MA); economics (MA, PhD, Diploma); educational studies (MA); educational technology (MA); English literature (MA, PhD); environmental assessment (M Env, Diploma); exercise science (M Sc); geography, urban and environmental studies (M Sc, PhD); history (MA, PhD); human systems intervention (MA); humanities (PhD); instructional technology (Diploma); journalism (Graduate Diploma); journalism studies (MA); Judaic studies (MA); littératures Francophones et résonances médiatiques (MA); mathematics (PhD); mathematics and statistics (M Sc, MA); media studies (MA); philosophy (MA); physics (M Sc, PhD); political science (PhD); psychology (MA, PhD, Certificate); public policy and public administration (MA); religion (MA, PhD); social and cultural analysis (PhD); social and cultural anthropology (MA); sociology (MA); teaching English as a second language (Certificate); teaching of mathematics (MTM); theological studies (MA); translation (Diploma); translation studies (MA); visual journalism (Diploma); youth work (Graduate Diploma).

Faculty of Engineering and Computer Science Offers 3D graphics and game development (Certificate); aerospace engineering (M Eng); building engineering (M Eng, MA Sc, PhD, Certificate); civil engineering (M Eng, MA Sc, PhD); computer science (M App Comp Sc, M Comp Sc, PhD, Diploma); electrical and computer engineering (M Eng, MA Sc, PhD); engineering and computer science (M App Comp Sc, M Comp Sc, M Eng, MA Sc, PhD, Certificate, Diploma); environmental engineering (Certificate); industrial engineering (M Eng, MA Sc, PhD); information and systems engineering (PhD); information systems security (M Eng, MA Sc); mechanical engineering (M Eng, MA Sc, PhD, Certificate); quality systems engineering (M Eng, MA Sc); service engineering and network management (Certificate); software engineering (M Eng, MA Sc).

Faculty of Fine Arts *Program availability:* Part-time. Offers advanced music performance studies (Diploma); art education (MA, PhD); art history (MA, PhD); art therapy (MA); design (M Des); digital technologies in design art practice (Certificate); drama therapy (MA); film and moving image studies (PhD); film production (MFA); film studies (MA); fine arts (M Des, MA, MFA, PhD, Certificate, Diploma); music therapy (MA); studio arts (MFA).

John Molson School of Business *Program availability:* Part-time, evening/weekend. Offers administration (M Sc); business administration (MBA, PhD, Certificate, Diploma); executive business administration (EMBA); supply chain management (MSCM). PhD program offered jointly with HEC Montreal, McGill University, and Université du Québec à Montréal. Electronic applications accepted.

CONCORDIA UNIVERSITY, Portland, OR 97211-6099

General Information Independent-religious, coed, comprehensive institution. *Graduate housing:* Room and/or apartments available on a first-come, first-served basis to single students; on-campus housing not available to married students. Housing application deadline: 8/1. *Student services:* Campus employment opportunities, campus safety program, career counseling, exercise/wellness program, free psychological counseling, international student services, low-cost health insurance, writing training. *Library facilities:* Concordia University Library plus 2 others.

Computer facilities: 100 computers available on campus for general student use. A campuswide network can be accessed from student residence rooms and from off campus. Online class registration is available.
Website: http://www.cu-portland.edu/

General Application Contact: Amy Gehrke, Director of Graduate Admission, 503-493-6416, Fax: 503-280-8531, E-mail: agehrke@cu-portland.edu.

GRADUATE UNITS

College of Arts and Sciences Offers community psychology (MA); teaching English to speakers of other languages (MA).

College of Education Expenses: Contact institution. *Financial support:* Scholarships/grants available. Financial award applicants required to submit FAFSA. *Program availability:* Part-time, online learning. Offers administrative leadership (Ed D); career and technical education (M Ed); curriculum and instruction (M Ed); educational administration (M Ed); educational leadership (M Ed); elementary education (MAT); higher education (Ed D); instructional leadership (Ed D); professional leadership, inquiry, and transformation (Ed D); secondary education (MAT); transformational leadership (Ed D). *Application deadline:* For fall admission, 7/1 for domestic and international students. Applications are processed on a rolling basis. *Application fee:* $50. Electronic applications accepted. *Application Contact:* Amy Gehrke, Director of Graduate Admission, 503-493-6416, Fax: 503-280-8531, E-mail: agehrke@cu-portland.edu. *Dean*, Sheryl Reinisch, 503-493-6539.

School of Law Expenses: Contact institution. *Financial support:* Scholarships/grants available. Offers law (JD). Electronic applications accepted. *Application Contact:* Amy Gehrke, Director of Graduate Admission, 503-493-6416, Fax: 503-280-8531, E-mail: agehrke@cu-portland.edu. *Dean*, Elena Langan, 208-639-5401.

School of Management Expenses: Contact institution. *Financial support:* Applicants required to submit FAFSA. *Program availability:* Evening/weekend. Offers management (MBA). *Application deadline:* For fall admission, 6/1 priority date for domestic students; for spring admission, 11/1 priority date for domestic students. *Application fee:* $35. *Application Contact:* Amy Gehrke, Director of Graduate Admission, 503-493-6416, Fax: 503-280-8531, E-mail: agehrke@cu-portland.edu. *Dean*, Dr. Michelle M. Cowing, 503-493-6455, E-mail: mcowing@cu-portland.edu.

CONCORDIA UNIVERSITY ANN ARBOR, Ann Arbor, MI 48105-2797

General Information Independent-religious, coed, comprehensive institution. *Graduate housing:* On-campus housing not available.

GRADUATE UNITS

Graduate Programs *Program availability:* Part-time, evening/weekend. Offers curriculum and instruction (MS); educational leadership (MS); organizational leadership and administration (MS). Electronic applications accepted.

CONCORDIA UNIVERSITY CHICAGO, River Forest, IL 60305-1499

General Information Independent-religious, coed, comprehensive institution. CGS member. *Graduate housing:* Rooms and/or apartments available on a first-come, first-served basis to single and married students.

GRADUATE UNITS

College of Education Offers Christian education (MA); curriculum and instruction (MA); early childhood education (MA, Ed D); elementary education (MAT); reading education (MA); school leadership (MA, Ed D, CAS); secondary education (MAT).

College of Graduate and Innovative Programs Offers business administration (MBA); church music (MCM); community counseling (MA); educational technology (MA); gerontology (MA); human services (MA); liberal studies (MA); music (MA); psychology (MA); religion (MA); school counseling (MA, CAS).

CONCORDIA UNIVERSITY IRVINE, Irvine, CA 92612-3299

General Information Independent-religious, coed, comprehensive institution. *Graduate housing:* Room and/or apartments available on a first-come, first-served basis to single students; on-campus housing not available to married students. Housing application deadline: 6/1.

GRADUATE UNITS

School of Arts and Sciences *Program availability:* Part-time, evening/weekend, online learning. Offers coaching and athletic administration (MA). Electronic applications accepted.

School of Business *Program availability:* Part-time, evening/weekend. Offers business administration (MBA). Electronic applications accepted.

School of Education *Program availability:* Part-time, evening/weekend, online learning. Offers curriculum and instruction (MA); education and preliminary teaching credential (M Ed); educational administration and preliminary administrative services credential (MA); educational technology (MA); school counseling with pupil personnel services credential (MA). Electronic applications accepted.

School of Professional Studies

School of Theology *Program availability:* Part-time, evening/weekend. Offers Christian leadership (MA); research in theology (MA); theology and culture (MA). Electronic applications accepted.

CONCORDIA UNIVERSITY, NEBRASKA, Seward, NE 68434

General Information Independent-religious, coed, comprehensive institution. *Graduate housing:* Rooms and/or apartments available on a first-come, first-served basis to single and married students.

GRADUATE UNITS

Graduate Programs in Education *Program availability:* Part-time, evening/weekend. Offers early childhood education (M Ed); education (M Ed, MPE, MS); elementary and secondary education (M Ed); elementary education (M Ed); family life ministry (MS); parish education (MPE); reading education (M Ed); secondary education (M Ed). Electronic applications accepted.

Program in Computer Science *Program availability:* Online learning. Offers cyber operations (MS).

CONCORDIA UNIVERSITY OF EDMONTON, Edmonton, AB T5B 4E4, Canada

General Information Independent-religious, coed, comprehensive institution.

GRADUATE UNITS

Program in Biblical and Christian Studies Offers Biblical and Christian studies (MA).

Program in Information Systems Security Management Offers information systems security management (MA).

CONCORDIA UNIVERSITY, ST. PAUL, St. Paul, MN 55104-5494

General Information Independent-religious, coed, comprehensive institution. CGS member. *Enrollment:* 4,792 graduate, professional, and undergraduate students; 1,833 full-time matriculated graduate/professional students (1,255 women), 108 part-time matriculated graduate/professional students (62 women). *Enrollment by degree level:* 1,724 master's, 136 doctoral, 81 other advanced degrees. *Graduate faculty:* 35 full-time (17 women), 156 part-time/adjunct (88 women). *Tuition:* Full-time $7200. Tuition and fees vary according to degree level and program. *Graduate housing:* Rooms and/or apartments available on a first-come, first-served basis to single and married students. Housing application deadline: 6/1. *Student services:* Campus employment opportunities, campus safety program, career counseling, child daycare facilities, exercise/wellness program, free psychological counseling, international student services, multicultural affairs office, services for students with disabilities, teacher training, writing training. *Library facilities:* Library Technology Center. *Collection:* Books: 108,345 (physical), 226,902 (digital/electronic); Serial titles: 917 (physical), 98,931 (digital/electronic); Databases: 178. Weekly public service hours: 74; students can reserve study rooms.

Computer facilities: 10 computers available on campus for general student use. A campuswide network can be accessed from student residence rooms and from off campus. Online class registration is available.
Website: http://www.csp.edu/

General Application Contact: Amber Faletti, Director of Enrollment Management, 651-641-8230, Fax: 651-603-6320, E-mail: faletti@csp.edu.

GRADUATE UNITS

College of Business and Technology Students: 475 full-time (293 women), 35 part-time (17 women); includes 122 minority (57 Black or African American, non-Hispanic/Latino; 1 American Indian or Alaska Native, non-Hispanic/Latino; 34 Asian, non-Hispanic/Latino; 12 Hispanic/Latino; 1 Native Hawaiian or other Pacific Islander, non-Hispanic/Latino; 17 Two or more races, non-Hispanic/Latino), 47 international. Average age 33. 203 applicants, 70% accepted, 136 enrolled. *Faculty:* 12 full-time (5 women), 33 part-time/adjunct (16 women). Expenses: Contact institution. *Financial support:* In 2017–18, 292 students received support. Scholarships/grants and unspecified assistantships available. Financial award applicants required to submit FAFSA. In 2017, 172 master's awarded. *Program availability:* Part-time, evening/weekend, 100% online, blended/hybrid learning. Offers business administration (MBA); health care management (MBA); human resource management (MA); information technology (MBA); leadership and management (MA); strategic communication management (MA). *Application deadline:* For fall admission, 8/1 for domestic and international students; for spring admission, 12/1 for domestic and international students; for summer admission, 5/1 for domestic and international students. Applications are processed on a rolling basis. *Application fee:* $0. Electronic applications accepted. *Application Contact:* Amber Faletti, Director of Enrollment Management, 651-641-8838, Fax: 651-603-6320, E-mail: faletti@csp.edu. *Dean*, Dr. Kevin Hall, 651-603-6165, Fax: 651-641-8807, E-mail: khall@csp.edu.

College of Education Students: 955 full-time (731 women), 42 part-time (28 women); includes 105 minority (35 Black or African American, non-Hispanic/Latino; 5 American Indian or Alaska Native, non-Hispanic/Latino; 31 Asian, non-Hispanic/Latino; 19 Hispanic/Latino; 15 Two or more races, non-Hispanic/Latino), 9 international. Average

age 34. 409 applicants, 87% accepted, 347 enrolled. *Faculty:* 15 full-time (8 women), 86 part-time/adjunct (56 women). Expenses: Contact institution. *Financial support:* In 2017–18, 105 students received support. Scholarships/grants and unspecified assistantships available. Financial award applicants required to submit FAFSA. In 2017, 386 master's, 104 other advanced degrees awarded. *Program availability:* Part-time, evening/weekend, 100% online, blended/hybrid learning. Offers classroom instruction (MA Ed); differentiated instruction (MA Ed); early childhood education (MA Ed); education (Ed D); educational leadership (MA Ed); educational technology (MA Ed, Certificate); K-12 principal licensure (Ed S); special education (MA Ed); superintendent (Ed S); teaching (MAT). *Application deadline:* For fall admission, 8/1 for domestic and international students; for spring admission, 12/1 for domestic and international students; for summer admission, 5/1 for domestic and international students. Applications are processed on a rolling basis. *Application fee:* $0. Electronic applications accepted. *Application Contact:* Amber Faletti, Director of Enrollment Management, 651-641-8838, Fax: 651-603-6320, E-mail: faletti@csp.edu. *Dean,* Lonn Maly, 651-641-8203, E-mail: maly@csp.edu.

College of Health and Science Students: 260 full-time (127 women), 20 part-time (6 women); includes 48 minority (24 Black or African American, non-Hispanic/Latino; 5 Asian, non-Hispanic/Latino; 11 Hispanic/Latino; 1 Native Hawaiian or other Pacific Islander, non-Hispanic/Latino; 7 Two or more races, non-Hispanic/Latino), 4 international. Average age 28. 218 applicants, 43% accepted, 84 enrolled. *Faculty:* 14 full-time (8 women), 22 part-time/adjunct (8 women). Expenses: Contact institution. *Financial support:* In 2017–18, 60 students received support. Scholarships/grants and unspecified assistantships available. Financial award applicants required to submit FAFSA. In 2017, 57 master's, 26 doctorates awarded. *Program availability:* Part-time, evening/weekend, 100% online, blended/hybrid learning. Offers exercise science (MS); orthotics and prosthetics (MS); physical therapy (DPT); sports management (MA). *Application deadline:* For fall admission, 4/1 for domestic students. Applications are processed on a rolling basis. *Application fee:* $0. Electronic applications accepted. *Application Contact:* Amber Faletti, Director of Enrollment Management, 651-641-8838, Fax: 651-603-6320, E-mail: faletti@csp.edu. *Dean,* Dr. Katie Fischer, 651-641-8735, E-mail: fischer@csp.edu.

CONCORDIA UNIVERSITY TEXAS, Austin, TX 78726

General Information Independent-religious, coed, comprehensive institution.

GRADUATE UNITS

College of Education *Program availability:* Part-time, evening/weekend. Offers education (M Ed).

CONCORDIA UNIVERSITY WISCONSIN, Mequon, WI 53097-2402

General Information Independent-religious, coed, comprehensive institution. *Graduate housing:* Room and/or apartments available to single students; on-campus housing not available to married students. Housing application deadline: 8/1.

GRADUATE UNITS

Graduate Programs *Program availability:* Part-time, evening/weekend, online learning. Offers art education (MS Ed); early childhood (MS Ed); educational administration (MS Ed); environmental education (MS Ed); family studies (MS Ed); literacy (MS Ed); school counseling (MS Ed); special education (MS Ed). Electronic applications accepted.

School of Arts and Sciences Offers arts and sciences (MCM); church music (MCM).

School of Business Administration Offers business administration (MBA, MS); finance (MBA); health care administration (MBA); human resource management (MBA); international business (MBA); international business-bilingual English/Chinese (MBA); management (MBA); management information systems (MBA); managerial communications (MBA); marketing (MBA); organizational leadership administration (MS); public administration (MBA); risk management (MBA).

School of Health Professions Offers health professions (MOT, MSRS, DPT); occupational therapy (MOT); physical therapy (DPT); rehabilitation science (MSRS).

School of Nursing *Program availability:* Online learning. Offers family nurse practitioner (MSN).

School of Pharmacy Offers pharmaceutical/chemical product development (MPD); pharmacy (Pharm D).

CONCORD LAW SCHOOL, Los Angeles, CA 90024

General Information Proprietary, coed, graduate-only institution.

GRADUATE UNITS

Program in Law *Program availability:* Part-time, evening/weekend, online learning. Offers law (EJD, JD). Electronic applications accepted.

CONCORD UNIVERSITY, Athens, WV 24712-1000

General Information State-supported, coed, comprehensive institution. *Enrollment:* 2,194 graduate, professional, and undergraduate students; 146 full-time matriculated graduate/professional students (117 women), 195 part-time matriculated graduate/professional students (161 women). *Enrollment by degree level:* 341 master's. *Graduate faculty:* 16 full-time (10 women), 7 part-time/adjunct (4 women). Tuition, state resident: full-time $8132; part-time $453 per semester hour. Tuition, nonresident: full-time $14,180; part-time $788 per semester hour. *Graduate housing:* Room and/or apartments available on a first-come, first-served basis to single students; on-campus housing not available to married students. *Student services:* Campus employment opportunities, career counseling, child daycare facilities, free psychological counseling, international student services, multicultural affairs office, services for students with disabilities. *Library facilities:* J. Frank Marsh Library. *Collection:* Books: 162,020 (physical), 34,329 (digital/electronic); Serial titles: 68 (physical), 110 (digital/electronic); Databases: 14. Weekly public service hours: 77; study areas open 24 hours, 5–7 days a week; students can reserve study rooms.

Computer facilities: 350 computers available on campus for general student use. A campuswide network can be accessed. Online class registration is available.
Website: http://www.concord.edu/

General Application Contact: Debra Moore, Special Events Assistant, 304-384-5113, E-mail: dlm@concord.edu.

GRADUATE UNITS

Graduate Studies Students: 146 full-time (117 women), 195 part-time (161 women); includes 26 minority (15 Black or African American, non-Hispanic/Latino; 1 American Indian or Alaska Native, non-Hispanic/Latino; 4 Asian, non-Hispanic/Latino; 1 Hispanic/Latino; 5 Two or more races, non-Hispanic/Latino). Average age 34. 591 applicants, 99% accepted, 144 enrolled. *Faculty:* 16 full-time (10 women), 7 part-time/adjunct (4 women). Expenses: Contact institution. *Financial support:* Tuition waivers and unspecified assistantships available. Financial award applicants required to submit FAFSA. In 2017, 114 master's awarded. *Program availability:* Part-time, evening/weekend, 100% online. Offers educational leadership and supervision (M Ed); health promotion (MA); reading specialist (M Ed); social work (MSW); special education (M Ed); teaching (MAT). *Application deadline:* Applications are processed on a rolling basis. *Application fee:* $30. Electronic applications accepted. *Application Contact:* Debra Moore, Special Events Assistant, 304-384-5113, E-mail: dlm@concord.edu. *Director,* Dr. Cheryl Barnes, 304-384-6306, E-mail: cbarnes@concord.edu.

CONSERVATORIO DE MUSICA DE PUERTO RICO, San Juan, PR 00907

General Information Commonwealth-supported, coed, comprehensive institution.

GRADUATE UNITS

Program in Musical Performance Offers guitar (Diploma); orchestral instruments (Diploma); piano (Diploma); vocal performance (Diploma).

Program in Music Education Offers music education (MM Ed).

CONVERSE COLLEGE, Spartanburg, SC 29302

General Information Independent, Undergraduate: women only; graduate: coed, comprehensive institution. *Enrollment:* 1,319 graduate, professional, and undergraduate students; 108 full-time matriculated graduate/professional students (85 women), 341 part-time matriculated graduate/professional students (288 women). *Enrollment by degree level:* 416 master's, 33 other advanced degrees. *Graduate housing:* Room and/or apartments available to single students; on-campus housing not available to married students. *Student services:* Campus employment opportunities, campus safety program, career counseling, international student services, teacher training. *Library facilities:* Mickel Library. *Collection:* Books: 165,873 (physical), 252,047 (digital/electronic); Databases: 30.

Computer facilities: 140 computers available on campus for general student use. A campuswide network can be accessed from student residence rooms and from off campus. Online class registration is available.
Website: http://www.converse.edu/

General Application Contact: Graduate Admissions, 864-596-9404, E-mail: graduate@converse.edu.

GRADUATE UNITS

Education Specialist Program Expenses: Contact institution. *Program availability:* Part-time. Offers administration and leadership (Ed S); administration and supervision (Ed S); literacy (Ed S). *Application deadline:* For fall admission, 8/1 for domestic and international students; for winter admission, 11/15 for domestic and international students; for spring admission, 1/15 for domestic and international students. Applications are processed on a rolling basis. *Application fee:* $40. Electronic applications accepted. *Application Contact:* Kimberly Newton-Burgess, Director of Post-Traditional and Online Admissions, 864-596-9746, E-mail: kimberly.newton-burgess@converse.edu. *Dean of Graduate Studies and Distance Education,* Lienne Medford, 864-596-9082, E-mail: lienne.medford@converse.edu.

Petrie School of Music Expenses: Contact institution. *Financial support:* Career-related internships or fieldwork, Federal Work-Study, institutionally sponsored loans, and unspecified assistantships available. Support available to part-time students. Financial award application deadline: 4/15. *Program availability:* Part-time, evening/weekend. Offers music education (M Mus); performance (M Mus). *Application deadline:* For spring admission, 3/1 priority date for domestic and international students. Applications are processed on a rolling basis. *Application fee:* $40. Electronic applications accepted. *Head, Petrie School of Music/Associate Professor of Flute and Musicology,* Chris Vaneman, 864-596-9038, E-mail: chris.vaneman@converse.edu.

Program in Art Education Expenses: Contact institution. Offers art education (M Ed, MAT). *Application Contact:* 864-596-9404, E-mail: graduate@converse.edu. *Department Chair,* Susanne Gunter, 864-596-9126, E-mail: susanne.gunter@converse.edu.

Program in Creative Writing Expenses: Contact institution. Offers creative writing (MFA). *Director,* Rick Mulkey, 864-596-9685, E-mail: rick.mulkey@converse.edu.

Program in Educational Administration and Supervision Expenses: Contact institution. Offers administration and supervision (M Ed). *Application deadline:* For fall admission, 8/1 for domestic and international students; for winter admission, 11/15 for domestic and international students; for spring admission, 1/15 for domestic and international students. *Application fee:* $40. Electronic applications accepted. *Application Contact:* 864-596-9404, E-mail: graduate@converse.edu. *Dean of Graduate Studies and Distance Education,* Lienne Medford, 864-596-9082, E-mail: lienne.medford@converse.edu.

Program in Elementary Education Expenses: Contact institution. *Financial support:* Available to part-time students. Applicants required to submit FAFSA. *Program availability:* Part-time. Offers elementary education (M Ed, MAT). *Application deadline:* For fall admission, 8/1 for domestic and international students; for winter admission, 11/15 for domestic and international students; for spring admission, 1/15 for domestic and international students. Applications are processed on a rolling basis. *Application fee:* $40. Electronic applications accepted. *Application Contact:* 864-596-9404, E-mail: graduate@converse.edu. *Dean of Graduate Studies and Distance Education,* 864-596-9082, E-mail: lienne.medford@converse.edu.

Program in Gifted Education Expenses: Contact institution. *Financial support:* Career-related internships or fieldwork available. Support available to part-time students. Financial award applicants required to submit FAFSA. *Program availability:* Part-time. Offers gifted education (M Ed). *Application deadline:* For fall admission, 8/1 for domestic and international students; for winter admission, 11/15 for domestic and international students; for spring admission, 1/15 for domestic and international students. Applications are processed on a rolling basis. *Application fee:* $40. Electronic applications accepted. *Application Contact:* E-mail: graduate@converse.edu. *Department Chair,* Lee Givens, 864-596-9476, E-mail: lee.givens@converse.edu.

Program in Liberal Arts Expenses: Contact institution. Offers English (MLA); history (MLA); political science (MLA). *Application deadline:* For fall admission, 5/1 priority date for domestic students; for spring admission, 1/30 for domestic students. *Application fee:* $40. *Dean of Graduate Studies and Distance Education,* Lienne Medford, 864-596-9082, E-mail: lienne.medford@converse.edu.

Program in Marriage and Family Therapy Expenses: Contact institution. Offers marriage and family therapy (MMFT). *Application Contact:* 864-596-9404, E-mail: graduate@converse.edu. *Dean of Graduate Studies and Distance Education,* Lienne Medford, 864-596-9082, E-mail: lienne.medford@converse.edu.

Program in Middle Level Education Expenses: Contact institution. Offers language arts/English (MAT); mathematics (MAT); middle level education (M Ed); science (MAT); social studies (MAT). *Application Contact:* 864-596-9404, E-mail: graduate@converse.edu. *Dean of Graduate Studies and Distance Education,* Lienne Medford, 864-596-9082, E-mail: lienne.medford@converse.edu.

Program in Secondary Education Expenses: Contact institution. *Financial support:* Available to part-time students. Applicants required to submit FAFSA. *Program availability:* Part-time. Offers biology (MAT); chemistry (MAT); English (M Ed, MAT); mathematics (M Ed, MAT); natural sciences (M Ed); social sciences (M Ed, MAT). *Application deadline:* For fall admission, 8/1 for domestic and international students; for winter admission, 11/15 for domestic and international students; for spring admission, 1/15 for domestic and international students. Applications are processed on a rolling basis. *Application fee:* $40. Electronic applications accepted. *Application Contact:* 864-596-9404, E-mail: graduate@converse.edu. *Dean of Graduate Studies and Distance Education*, Lienne Medford, 864-596-9082, E-mail: lienne.medford@converse.edu.

Program in Special Education Expenses: Contact institution. *Financial support:* Available to part-time students. Applicants required to submit FAFSA. *Program availability:* Part-time. Offers intellectual disabilities (MAT); learning disabilities (MAT); special education (M Ed). *Application deadline:* For fall admission, 8/1 for domestic and international students; for winter admission, 11/15 for domestic and international students; for spring admission, 1/15 for domestic and international students. Applications are processed on a rolling basis. *Application fee:* $40. Electronic applications accepted. *Application Contact:* 864-596-9404, E-mail: graduate@converse.edu. *Dean of Graduate Studies and Distance Education*, Lienne Medford, 864-596-9082, E-mail: lienne.medford@converse.edu.

THE CONWAY SCHOOL, Conway, MA 01341-0179

General Information Independent, coed, graduate-only institution. *Enrollment by degree level:* 18 master's. *Graduate faculty:* 2 full-time (1 woman), 10 part-time/adjunct (6 women). *Graduate housing:* On-campus housing not available. *Collection:* Books: 4,000 (physical). Study areas open 24 hours, 5–7 days a week; students can reserve study rooms.

Computer facilities: 2 computers available on campus for general student use.
Website: http://www.csld.edu/

General Application Contact: Kate Cholakis, Director of Admissions, 413-369-4044, E-mail: admissions@csld.edu.

GRADUATE UNITS

Program in Ecological Design Students: 18 full-time (9 women). Average age 41. *Faculty:* 2 full-time (1 woman), 10 part-time/adjunct (6 women). Expenses: Contact institution. *Financial support:* Career-related internships or fieldwork, institutionally sponsored loans, and scholarships/grants available. Financial award application deadline: 11/9; financial award applicants required to submit FAFSA. Offers ecological design (MS). *Application deadline:* For fall admission, 2/1 priority date for domestic students. Applications are processed on a rolling basis. *Application fee:* $50. *Application Contact:* Kate Cholakis, Director of Admissions, 413-369-4044, E-mail: admissions@csld.edu. *Academic Coordinator*, Ken Byrne, 413-369-4044.

COOPER UNION FOR THE ADVANCEMENT OF SCIENCE AND ART, New York, NY 10003-7120

General Information Independent, coed, comprehensive institution. *Enrollment:* 941 graduate, professional, and undergraduate students; 48 full-time matriculated graduate/professional students (14 women), 26 part-time matriculated graduate/professional students (4 women). *Enrollment by degree level:* 74 master's. *Graduate faculty:* 29 full-time (3 women), 19 part-time/adjunct (6 women). *Tuition:* Full-time $33,072; part-time $1272 per credit. *Required fees:* $1850; $925 per semester. One-time fee: $250. *Graduate housing:* On-campus housing not available. *Student services:* Campus employment opportunities, campus safety program, career counseling, international student services, low-cost health insurance, services for students with disabilities, writing training. *Library facilities:* Cooper Union Library. *Collection:* Books: 98,400 (physical), 213,578 (digital/electronic); Serial titles: 71 (physical), 40,306 (digital/electronic); Databases: 48. Weekly public service hours: 69. *Research affiliation:* National Science Foundation, National Institutes of Health, Defense Advanced Research Projects Agency, Naval Postgraduate School, U.S. Department of Homeland Security, U.S. Department of Defense.

Computer facilities: Computer purchase and lease plans are available. 100 computers available on campus for general student use. A campuswide network can be accessed from student residence rooms and from off campus. Online class registration is available.
Website: http://www.cooper.edu/

General Application Contact: Chabeli Lajara, Administrative Assistant, 212-353-4120, E-mail: admissions@cooper.edu.

GRADUATE UNITS

Albert Nerken School of Engineering Students: 39 full-time (11 women), 26 part-time (4 women); includes 23 minority (2 Black or African American, non-Hispanic/Latino; 11 Asian, non-Hispanic/Latino; 3 Hispanic/Latino; 7 Two or more races, non-Hispanic/Latino), 3 international. Average age 24. 77 applicants, 65% accepted, 38 enrolled. *Faculty:* 22 full-time (4 women), 21 part-time/adjunct (0 women). Expenses: Contact institution. *Financial support:* In 2017–18, 58 students received support, including 4 fellowships with tuition reimbursements available (averaging $11,000 per year); career-related internships or fieldwork, tuition waivers (full and partial), and tuition scholarships offered to exceptional students also available. Support available to part-time students. Financial award application deadline: 5/1; financial award applicants required to submit FAFSA. In 2017, 33 master's awarded. *Program availability:* Part-time. Offers chemical engineering (ME); civil engineering (ME); electrical engineering (ME); mechanical engineering (ME). *Application deadline:* For fall admission, 3/31 for domestic and international students. *Application fee:* $75. Electronic applications accepted. *Application Contact:* Chabeli Lajara, Administrative Assistant, 212-353-4120, E-mail: admissions@cooper.edu. *Acting Dean of Albert Nerken School of Engineering*, Richard Stock, 212-353-4285, E-mail: stock@cooper.edu.

Irwin S. Chanin School of Architecture Students: 9 full-time (3 women); includes 1 minority (Asian, non-Hispanic/Latino), 7 international. Average age 27. 75 applicants, 31% accepted, 10 enrolled. *Faculty:* 3 full-time (2 women), 14 part-time/adjunct (6 women). Expenses: Contact institution. *Financial support:* In 2017–18, 9 students received support. Tuition waivers (partial) and tuition scholarships offered to exceptional students available. Financial award application deadline: 5/1; financial award applicants required to submit FAFSA. In 2017, 11 master's awarded. Offers architecture (M Arch II). *Application deadline:* For fall admission, 1/31 for domestic and international students. *Application fee:* $75. Electronic applications accepted. *Application Contact:* Chabeli Lajara, Administrative Assistant, 212-353-4120, E-mail: admissions@cooper.edu. *Dean*, Nader Tehrani, 212-353-4220, E-mail: ntehrani@cooper.edu.

COPPIN STATE UNIVERSITY, Baltimore, MD 21216-3698

General Information State-supported, coed, comprehensive institution. CGS member. *Graduate housing:* On-campus housing not available.

GRADUATE UNITS

Division of Graduate Studies *Program availability:* Part-time, evening/weekend, online learning.

Division of Arts and Sciences *Program availability:* Part-time, evening/weekend. Offers alcohol and substance abuse counseling (MS); arts and sciences (M Ed, MA, MS); criminal justice (MS); human services administration (MS); rehabilitation counseling (M Ed).

Division of Education *Program availability:* Part-time, evening/weekend, online learning. Offers adult and general education (MS); curriculum and instruction (M Ed); education (M Ed, MAT, MS); reading education (MS); special education (M Ed); teacher education (MAT); teaching (MAT).

Helene Fuld School of Nursing *Program availability:* Part-time, evening/weekend. Offers family nurse practitioner (PMC); nursing (MSN).

CORBAN UNIVERSITY, Salem, OR 97301-9392

General Information Independent-religious, coed, comprehensive institution.

GRADUATE UNITS

Graduate School Offers counseling (MA); education (MS Ed); management (MBA); non-profit management (MBA).

School of Ministry *Program availability:* Part-time, evening/weekend. Offers Biblical languages (M Div); Biblical leadership (Certificate); Christian leadership (MA); Church ministry (M Div); ministry (D Min).

CORNELL UNIVERSITY, Ithaca, NY 14853

General Information Independent, coed, university. CGS member. *Graduate housing:* Rooms and/or apartments available on a first-come, first-served basis to single and married students. Housing application deadline: 7/1. *Research affiliation:* Brookhaven National Laboratory (physics, biology, medicine, chemistry, energy, engineering, environmental science), Fermi National Accelerator Laboratory, Boyce Thompson Institute for Plant Research (plant research).

GRADUATE UNITS

College of Veterinary Medicine Students: 413 full-time (321 women); includes 94 minority (8 Black or African American, non-Hispanic/Latino; 23 Asian, non-Hispanic/Latino; 17 Hispanic/Latino; 1 Native Hawaiian or other Pacific Islander, non-Hispanic/Latino; 45 Two or more races, non-Hispanic/Latino), 6 international. Average age 26. 1,205 applicants, 15% accepted, 116 enrolled. *Faculty:* 202 full-time (96 women). Expenses: Contact institution. *Financial support:* In 2017–18, 371 students received support. Federal Work-Study, institutionally sponsored loans, and scholarships/grants available. Financial award application deadline: 2/1; financial award applicants required to submit CSS PROFILE or FAFSA. In 2017, 99 doctorates awarded. Offers veterinary medicine (DVM). *Application deadline:* For fall admission, 9/15 for domestic and international students. Electronic applications accepted. *Application Contact:* Jennifer A. Mailey, Director of Admissions, 607-253-3700, Fax: 607-253-3709, E-mail: jam333@cornell.edu. *Dean*, Dr. Lorin Warnick, 607-253-3771, Fax: 607-253-3701.

Cornell Law School Offers law (LL M, JD, JSD). JD/MLLP offered jointly with Humboldt University, Berlin; JD/DESS offered jointly with Institut d'etudes Politiques de Paris ("Sciences Po") and Paris I. Electronic applications accepted.

Graduate School Offers 19th century art (PhD); acarology (MS, PhD); adult and extension education (MPS, MS, PhD); advanced composites and structures (M Eng); advanced materials processing (M Eng, MS, PhD); aerospace engineering (M Eng, MS, PhD); African history (MA, PhD); African studies (MPS); African, African American and African diaspora (PhD); African-American literature (PhD); African-American studies (MPS); Africana studies (PhD); agricultural finance (MS, PhD); agriculture and life sciences (M Eng, MFS, MLA, MPS, MS, PhD); agronomy (MS, PhD); algorithms (M Eng, PhD); American art (PhD); American history (MA, PhD); American literature after 1865 (PhD); American literature to 1865 (PhD); American politics (PhD); American studies (PhD); analytical chemistry (PhD); ancient art and archaeology (PhD); ancient Greek history (PhD); ancient history (MA, PhD); ancient Near Eastern studies (MA, PhD); ancient philosophy (PhD); ancient Roman history (PhD); animal genetics (MPS, MS, PhD); animal genomics (MPS, MS, PhD); animal nutrition (MPS, MS, PhD); animal science (MPS, MS); apiculture (MS, PhD); apparel design (MA, MPS); applied econometrics and qualitative analysis (MS, PhD); applied economics (PhD); applied entomology (MS, PhD); applied linguistics (MA, PhD); applied logic and automated reasoning (M Eng, PhD); applied mathematics (PhD); applied mathematics and computational methods (M Eng, MS, PhD); applied physics (PhD); applied probability and statistics (PhD); applied research in human-environment relations (MS); applied statistics (MPS); aquatic entomology (MS, PhD); Arabic and Islamic studies (MA, PhD); archaeological anthropology (PhD); architectural design (M Arch); architectural science (MS); architecture, art and planning (M Arch, MA, MFA, MPS, MRP, MS, PhD); artificial intelligence (M Eng, PhD); arts and sciences (MA, MFA, MPA, MPS, MS, DMA, PhD); Asian American art (PhD); Asian religions (MA, PhD); astronomy (PhD); astrophysics (PhD); atmospheric science (MS, PhD); Baroque art (PhD); basic analytical economics (PhD); behavioral biology (PhD); biblical studies (MA, PhD); bio-organic chemistry (PhD); biochemical engineering (M Eng, MS, PhD); biochemistry (PhD); bioenergy and integrated energy systems (M Eng, MPS, MS, PhD); biological anthropology (PhD); biological control (MS, PhD); biological engineering (M Eng, MPS, MS, PhD); biomechanical engineering (M Eng, MS, PhD); biomedical and biological sciences (PhD); biomedical engineering (M Eng, MS, PhD); biometry (MS, PhD); biophysical chemistry (PhD); biophysics (PhD); bioprocess engineering (M Eng, MPS, MS, PhD); biopsychology (PhD); breeding of horticultural crops (MPS); cell biology (PhD); cellular and molecular toxicology (MS, PhD); chemical biology (PhD); chemical physics (PhD); chemical reaction engineering (M Eng, MS, PhD); Chinese philosophy (PhD); city and regional planning (MRP, PhD); classical and statistical thermodynamics (M Eng, MS, PhD); classical archaeology (PhD); classical Chinese literature (PhD); classical Japanese literature (PhD); classical literature and philology (PhD); classical myth (PhD); classical rhetoric (PhD); cognition (PhD); collective bargaining, labor law and labor history (MILR, MPS, MS, PhD); colonial and postcolonial literatures (PhD); combustion (M Eng, MS, PhD); communication (MS, PhD); community nutrition (MPS, PhD); community-based natural resources management (MS, PhD); comparative literature (PhD); comparative modernities (PhD); comparative politics (PhD); composition (DMA); computational behavioral biology (PhD); computational biology (PhD); computational cell biology (PhD); computational ecology (PhD); computational genetics (PhD); computational macromolecular biology (PhD); computational organismal biology (PhD); computer engineering (M Eng, PhD); computer graphics (M Eng, MS, PhD); computer science (M Eng, PhD); computer vision (M Eng, PhD); concurrency and distributed computing (M Eng, PhD); conservation biology (MS, PhD); consumer policy (PhD); creative visual arts (MFA); creative writing (MFA); cultural studies (PhD); cytology (MS, PhD); dairy science (MPS, MS, PhD); decision theory (MS, PhD); development policy (MPS); developmental biology (PhD); developmental psychology (MA, PhD); digital art

(PhD); drama and the theatre (PhD); dramatic literature (PhD); dynamics and space mechanics (MS, PhD); early modern European history (MA, PhD); East Asian art (PhD); East Asian linguistics (MA, PhD); East Asian literature and culture (PhD); East Asian studies (MA); ecohydrology (M Eng, MPS, MS, PhD); ecology (PhD); econometrics and economic statistics (PhD); economic and social statistics (MILR, MS, PhD); economic development and planning (PhD); economic geology (M Eng, MS, PhD); economic theory (PhD); economics of development (MS, PhD); economy and society (MA, PhD); ecosystem biology and biogeochemistry (MPS, MS, PhD); ecotoxicology and environmental chemistry (MS, PhD); electrical engineering (M Eng, PhD); electrical systems (M Eng, PhD); electrophysics (M Eng, PhD); energy and power systems (M Eng, MS, PhD); engineering (M Eng, MPS, MS, PhD); engineering geology (M Eng, MS, PhD); engineering management (M Eng, MS, PhD); engineering physics (M Eng); engineering statistics (MS, PhD); English history (MA, PhD); English linguistics (MA, PhD); English poetry (PhD); English Renaissance to 1660 (PhD); enology (MS, PhD); environmental archaeology (MA); environmental economics (MS, PhD); environmental engineering (M Eng, MPS, MS, PhD); environmental fluid mechanics and hydrology (M Eng, MS, PhD); environmental geophysics (M Eng, MS, PhD); environmental information science (MS, PhD); environmental management (MPS); environmental planning and design (MRP, PhD); environmental studies (MA, MS, PhD); environmental systems engineering (M Eng, MS, PhD); evolutionary biology (PhD); experimental design (MS, PhD); experimental physics (MS, PhD); facilities planning and management (MS); family and social welfare policy (PhD); farm management and production economics (MS, PhD); fiber science (MS, PhD); field crop science (MS, PhD); fishery and aquatic science (MPS, MS, PhD); fluid dynamics, rheology and biorheology (M Eng, MS, PhD); fluid mechanics (M Eng, MS, PhD); food chemistry (MPS, MS, PhD); food engineering (M Eng, MPS, MS, PhD); food microbiology (MPS, MS, PhD); food processing waste technology (MPS, MS, PhD); food science (MFS, MPS, MS, PhD); forest science (MPS, MS, PhD); French history (MA, PhD); French linguistics (PhD); French literature (PhD); fungal and oomycete biology (MPS, MS, PhD); gender and life course (MA, PhD); general geology (M Eng, MS, PhD); general linguistics (MA, PhD); general space sciences (PhD); genetics (PhD); genomics (PhD); geobiology (M Eng, MS, PhD); geochemistry and isotope geology (M Eng, MS, PhD); geohydrology (M Eng, MS, PhD); geomorphology (M Eng, MS, PhD); geophysics (M Eng, MS, PhD); geotechnical engineering (M Eng, MS, PhD); geotectonics (M Eng, MS, PhD); German area studies (MA, PhD); German history (MA, PhD); German intellectual history (MA, PhD); Germanic linguistics (MA, PhD); Germanic literature (MA, PhD); Greek and Latin language and linguistics (PhD); health administration (MHA); health management and policy (PhD); heat and mass transfer (M Eng, MS, PhD); heat transfer (M Eng, MS, PhD); Hebrew and Judaic studies (MA, PhD); Hispanic literature (PhD); historic preservation planning (MA); historical archaeology (MA); history and philosophy of science and technology (MA, PhD); history of architecture (MA, PhD); history of photography (PhD); history of science (MA, PhD); history of urban development (MA, PhD); horticultural crop management systems (MPS); housing and design (MS); human computer interaction (PhD); human development and family studies (MA, PhD); human dimensions of natural resources management (MPS, MS, PhD); human ecology (MA, MHA, MPA, MPS, MS, PhD); human experimental psychology (PhD); human factors and ergonomics (MS); human nutrition (MPS, MS, PhD); human resource studies (MILR, MPS, MS, PhD); human-computer interaction (MS, PhD); human-environment relations (MS); human-plant interactions (MPS, PhD); Indo-European linguistics (MA, PhD); industrial and labor relations problems (MILR, MPS, MS, PhD); industrial biotechnology (M Eng, MPS, MS, PhD); industrial organization and control (PhD); information organization and retrieval (M Eng, PhD); information science (PhD); information systems (PhD); infrared astronomy (PhD); inorganic chemistry (PhD); insect behavior (MS, PhD); insect biochemistry (MS, PhD); insect ecology (MS, PhD); insect genetics (MS, PhD); insect morphology (MS, PhD); insect pathology (MS, PhD); insect physiology (MS, PhD); insect systematics (MS, PhD); insect toxicology and insecticide chemistry (MS, PhD); integrated pest management (MS, PhD); interior design (MA, MPS); international agriculture and development (MPS); international and comparative labor (MILR, MPS, MS, PhD); international development (MPS); international development planning (MRP, PhD); international economics (PhD); international food science (MPS, MS, PhD); international nutrition (MPS, PhD); international planning (MPS); international population (MPS); international relations (PhD); international spatial problems (MA, MS, PhD); Islamic art (PhD); Italian linguistics (PhD); Italian literature (PhD); kinetics and catalysis (M Eng, MS, PhD); Korean history (PhD); Korean literature (PhD); labor economics (MILR, MPS, MS, PhD); landscape architecture (MLA, MPS); language and communication (MS, PhD); Latin American archaeology (MA); Latin American art (PhD); Latin American history (MA, PhD); learning, teaching, and social policy (MPS, MS, PhD); lesbian, bisexual, and gay literary studies (PhD); literary criticism and theory (PhD); location theory (MA, MS, PhD); manufacturing systems engineering (PhD); marine geology (MS, PhD); marketing and food distribution (MS, PhD); materials and manufacturing engineering (M Eng, MS, PhD); materials chemistry (PhD); materials engineering (M Eng, PhD); materials science (M Eng, PhD); mathematical programming (PhD); mathematical statistics (MS, PhD); mathematics (PhD); mathematics 7-12 (MS); mechanical systems and design (M Eng, MS, PhD); mechanics of materials (MS, PhD); media communication and society (MS, PhD); medical and veterinary entomology (MS, PhD); medieval and Renaissance Latin literature (PhD); medieval archaeology (MA, PhD); medieval art (PhD); medieval Chinese history (MA, PhD); medieval history (MA, PhD); medieval literature (PhD); medieval music (PhD); medieval philology and linguistics (PhD); medieval philosophy (PhD); Mediterranean and Near Eastern archaeology (MA); methodology (MA, PhD); microbiology (PhD); mineralogy (M Eng, MS, PhD); modern art (PhD); modern Chinese history (MA, PhD); modern Chinese literature (PhD); modern European history (MA, PhD); modern Japanese history (MA, PhD); modern Japanese literature (PhD); modern Middle Eastern history (PhD); molecular biochemistry (MPS, PhD); molecular biology (PhD); monetary and macro economics (PhD); multiphase flows (M Eng, MS, PhD); multiregional economic analysis (MA, MS, PhD); musicology (PhD); nanobiotechnology (M Eng, MPS, MS, PhD); neurobiology (PhD); nutritional and food toxicology (MS, PhD); Old and Middle English (PhD); old Norse (MA, PhD); operating systems (M Eng, PhD); operations research and industrial engineering (M Eng); organic chemistry (PhD); organizational behavior (MILR, MPS, MS, PhD); organizational communication (MS, PhD); organizations (MA, PhD); organometallic chemistry (PhD); paleobotany (MS, PhD); paleontology (M Eng, MS, PhD); parallel computing (M Eng, PhD); peace science (MA, MS, PhD); performance practice (DMA); personality and social psychology (PhD); petroleum geology (M Eng, MS, PhD); petrology (M Eng, MS, PhD); philosophy (PhD); phonetics (MA, PhD); phonological theory (MA, PhD); physical chemistry (PhD); physics (MS, PhD); physiology and ecology of horticultural crops (MPS, MS, PhD); physiology of reproduction (MPS, MS, PhD); planetary geology (M Eng, MS, PhD); planetary studies (PhD); planning methods (MA, MS, PhD); planning theory and systems analysis (MRP, PhD); plant biochemistry (MS, PhD); plant breeding (MPS, MS, PhD); plant cell biology (MS, PhD); plant ecology (MS, PhD); plant genetics (MPS, MS, PhD); plant microbe pathology (MPS, MS, PhD); plant molecular biology (MS, PhD); plant morphology, anatomy and biomechanics (MS, PhD); plant pathology (MPS, MS, PhD); plant physiology (MS, PhD); plant protection (MPS); policy analysis (MA, PhD); policy and institutional analysis (MS, PhD); political methodology (PhD); political sociology/social movements (MA, PhD); political thought (PhD); polymer chemistry (PhD); polymer science (MS, PhD); polymers (M Eng, MS, PhD); population and development (MS, PhD); Precambrian geology (M Eng, MS, PhD); premodern Islamic history (MA, PhD); premodern Japanese history (MA, PhD); probability (MS, PhD); program development and evaluation (MPS, MS, PhD); programming environments (M Eng, PhD); programming languages and methodology (M Eng, PhD); prose fiction (PhD); public affairs (MPA); public finance (PhD); public policy (PhD); public policy analysis (MS, PhD); quantitative ecology (MS, PhD); Quaternary geology (M Eng, MS, PhD); racial and ethnic relations (MA, PhD); radio astronomy (PhD); radiophysics (PhD); real estate (MPS); regional economics and development planning (MRP, PhD); regional science (MRP, PhD); remote sensing (M Eng, MS, PhD); Renaissance art (PhD); Renaissance history (MA, PhD); resource economics (PhD); Restoration and the eighteenth-century (PhD); risk assessment, management and public policy (MS, PhD); robotics (M Eng, PhD); rock mechanics (M Eng, MS, PhD); Romance linguistics (MA, PhD); rural and environmental sociology (MS, PhD); Russian history (MA, PhD); sampling (MS, PhD); science and technology policy (MPS); science, environment and health communication (MS, PhD); scientific computing (M Eng, PhD); second language acquisition (MA, PhD); sedimentology (M Eng, MS, PhD); seismology (M Eng, MS, PhD); semantics (MA, PhD); sensory evaluation (MPS, MS, PhD); Slavic linguistics (MA, PhD); social and health systems planning (MRP, PhD); social aspects of information (PhD); social networks (MA, PhD); social psychology (MA, PhD); social psychology of communication (MS, PhD); social stratification (MA, PhD); social studies of science and technology (MA, PhD); sociocultural anthropology (PhD); sociolinguistics (MA, PhD); soil science (MS, PhD); solid mechanics (MS, PhD); South Asian history (PhD); South Asian linguistics (MA, PhD); South Asian literature and culture (PhD); South Asian studies (MA); Southeast Asian art (PhD); Southeast Asian history (MA, PhD); Southeast Asian linguistics (MA, PhD); Southeast Asian literature and culture (PhD); Southeast Asian studies (MA); Spanish linguistics (PhD); state, economy, and society (MS, PhD); statistical computing (MS, PhD); stochastic processes (MS, PhD); Stone Age archaeology (MA); stratigraphy (M Eng, MS, PhD); structural engineering (M Eng, MS, PhD); structural geology (M Eng, MS, PhD); structural mechanics (M Eng, MS); surface science (M Eng, MS, PhD); sustainable systems (M Eng, MPS, MS, PhD); syntactic theory (MA, PhD); synthetic biology (MS); syntheticbiology (M Eng, MPS, PhD); systematic botany (MS, PhD); systems engineering (M Eng, PhD); textile science (MS, PhD); the nineteenth century (PhD); the twentieth century (PhD); theatre history (PhD); theatre theory and aesthetics (PhD); theoretical astrophysics (PhD); theoretical chemistry (PhD); theoretical physics (MS, PhD); theory and criticism (PhD); theory and criticism of architecture (M Arch); theory of computation (M Eng, PhD); theory of music (MA); transportation engineering (MS, PhD); transportation systems engineering (M Eng); urban and regional economics (MA, MS, PhD); urban and regional theory (MRP, PhD); urban design (M Arch); urban planning history (MRP, PhD); visual studies (PhD); water resource systems (M Eng, MS, PhD); wildlife science (MPS, MS, PhD); women's literature (PhD). Electronic applications accepted.

Field of Hotel Administration Offers hospitality management (MMH); hotel administration (MS, PhD). Electronic applications accepted.

Graduate Field in the Law School Offers law (JSD). Electronic applications accepted.

Graduate Field of Management Offers accounting (PhD); finance (PhD); marketing (PhD); organizational behavior (PhD); production and operations management (PhD). Electronic applications accepted.

Samuel Curtis Johnson Graduate School of Management Students: 573 full-time (165 women); includes 72 minority (11 Black or African American, non-Hispanic/Latino; 1 American Indian or Alaska Native, non-Hispanic/Latino; 36 Asian, non-Hispanic/Latino; 16 Hispanic/Latino; 8 Two or more races, non-Hispanic/Latino), 189 international. Average age 28. 1,653 applicants, 30% accepted, 277 enrolled. *Faculty:* 65 full-time (17 women). Expenses: Contact institution. *Financial support:* Fellowships, institutionally sponsored loans, and scholarships/grants available. Financial award applicants required to submit FAFSA. In 2017, 283 master's awarded. Offers business administration (Exec MBA); management (MBA, PhD); management - accounting (MPS). *Application deadline:* For fall admission, 10/5 for domestic and international students; for winter admission, 11/15 for domestic and international students; for spring admission, 1/10 for domestic and international students; for summer admission, 4/5 for domestic and international students. *Application fee:* $200. Electronic applications accepted. *Application Contact:* Admissions Office, 800-847-2082, Fax: 607-255-0065, E-mail: mba@johnson.cornell.edu. *Dean*, Dr. Mark Nelson, 607-255-6418, E-mail: dean@johnson.cornell.edu.

CORNERSTONE UNIVERSITY, Grand Rapids, MI 49525-5897

General Information Independent-religious, coed, comprehensive institution. *Graduate housing:* Rooms and/or apartments available on a first-come, first-served basis to single and married students.

GRADUATE UNITS

Graduate Programs *Program availability:* Part-time, online learning. Offers business administration (MBA); education (MA Ed); management (MSM); teaching English to speakers of other languages (MA, Graduate Certificate). Programs also offered at Holland, Kalamazoo, and Troy, MI campuses. Electronic applications accepted.

COVENANT COLLEGE, Lookout Mountain, GA 30750

General Information Independent-religious, coed, comprehensive institution. *Graduate housing:* Room and/or apartments available on a first-come, first-served basis to single students; on-campus housing not available to married students. Housing application deadline: 5/1.

GRADUATE UNITS

Program in Education *Program availability:* Part-time. Offers education (M Ed, MAT).

COVENANT THEOLOGICAL SEMINARY, St. Louis, MO 63141-8697

General Information Independent-religious, coed, graduate-only institution. *Graduate housing:* Rooms and/or apartments available on a first-come, first-served basis to single and married students.

GRADUATE UNITS

Graduate and Professional Programs *Program availability:* Part-time, evening/weekend, online learning. Offers theology (M Div, MA, MAC, MAEM, Th M, D Min, Certificate). Electronic applications accepted.

COX COLLEGE, Springfield, MO 65802

General Information Independent, coed, primarily women, comprehensive institution.

GRADUATE UNITS

Programs in Nursing Offers clinical nurse leader (MSN); family nurse practitioner (MSN); nurse educator (MSN). Electronic applications accepted.

CRANBROOK ACADEMY OF ART, Bloomfield Hills, MI 48303-0801

General Information Independent, coed, graduate-only institution. *Graduate housing:* Room and/or apartments available on a first-come, first-served basis to single students; on-campus housing not available to married students. Housing application deadline: 4/1.

GRADUATE UNITS

Program in Architecture Offers architecture (M Arch). Electronic applications accepted.

Program in Fine Arts Offers 2d design (MFA); 3d design (MFA); ceramics (MFA); fiber (MFA); metalsmithing (MFA); painting (MFA); photography (MFA); print media (MFA); sculpture (MFA). Electronic applications accepted.

CRANDALL UNIVERSITY, Moncton, NB E1C 9L7, Canada

General Information Independent-religious, coed, comprehensive institution.

GRADUATE UNITS

Graduate Programs

CREIGHTON UNIVERSITY, Omaha, NE 68178-0001

General Information Independent-religious, coed, university. CGS member. *Enrollment:* 8,654 graduate, professional, and undergraduate students; 2,828 full-time matriculated graduate/professional students (1,679 women), 1,520 part-time matriculated graduate/professional students (971 women). *Enrollment by degree level:* 1,005 master's, 3,215 doctoral, 128 other advanced degrees. *Graduate faculty:* 807 full-time (366 women). Part-time tuition and fees vary according to course load, degree level, campus/location and program. *Graduate housing:* Rooms and/or apartments available on a first-come, first-served basis to single and married students. Typical cost: $8856 per year for single students; $8712 per year for married students. Housing application deadline: 5/1. *Student services:* Campus employment opportunities, campus safety program, career counseling, child daycare facilities, exercise/wellness program, free psychological counseling, grant writing training, international student services, low-cost health insurance, multicultural affairs office, services for students with disabilities, teacher training, writing training. *Library facilities:* Reinert Alumni Memorial Library plus 2 others. *Collection:* Study areas open 24 hours, 5–7 days a week. *Research affiliation:* U.S. Department of Education (DOE) (student support services), National Institutes of Health (asthma), U.S. Department of Commerce (atmospheric science), National Science Foundation (business and education).

Computer facilities: Computer purchase and lease plans are available. 404 computers available on campus for general student use. A campuswide network can be accessed from student residence rooms and from off campus. Online class registration, financial aid information are available.
Website: http://www.creighton.edu/

General Application Contact: Lindsay Johnson, Director of Graduate and Adult Recruitment, 402-280-2703, Fax: 402-280-2423, E-mail: gradschool@creighton.edu.

GRADUATE UNITS

College of Nursing *Program availability:* Part-time, blended/hybrid learning. Offers adult gerontology acute care nurse practitioner (DNP, Post-Master's Certificate); adult gerontology nurse practitioner (DNP); clinical nurse leader (MSN, Post-Graduate Certificate); clinical systems administration (MSN, DNP); family nurse practitioner (DNP, Post-Master's Certificate); neonatal nurse practitioner (DNP, Post-Master's Certificate); nursing (Post-Graduate Certificate); pediatric acute care nurse practitioner (DNP, Post-Master's Certificate); psychiatric mental health nurse practitioner (DNP). Electronic applications accepted.

Graduate School Students: 327 full-time (198 women), 1,191 part-time (671 women); includes 124 minority (68 Black or African American, non-Hispanic/Latino; 11 American Indian or Alaska Native, non-Hispanic/Latino; 28 Asian, non-Hispanic/Latino; 14 Hispanic/Latino; 3 Native Hawaiian or other Pacific Islander, non-Hispanic/Latino), 88 international. Average age 35. 920 applicants, 87% accepted, 574 enrolled. *Faculty:* 323 full-time (119 women). Expenses: Contact institution. *Financial support:* In 2017–18, fellowships with tuition reimbursements (averaging $23,000 per year), research assistantships with tuition reimbursements (averaging $15,700 per year), teaching assistantships with tuition reimbursements (averaging $15,700 per year) were awarded; career-related internships or fieldwork, institutionally sponsored loans, scholarships/grants, tuition waivers (partial), and unspecified assistantships also available. Support available to part-time students. Financial award application deadline: 3/1; financial award applicants required to submit FAFSA. In 2017, 492 master's, 51 doctorates awarded. *Program availability:* Part-time, evening/weekend, 100% online, blended/hybrid learning. Offers emergency medical services (MS); health and wellness coaching (MS); health care ethics (MS); healthcare management (MHM); leadership (Ed D); negotiation and conflict resolution (MS); organizational leadership (MS); public health (MPH). *Application deadline:* For fall admission, 3/1 priority date for domestic and international students; for winter admission, 10/1 for domestic students, 7/1 for international students; for spring admission, 4/1 for domestic students, 10/1 for international students. Applications are processed on a rolling basis. *Application fee:* $50. Electronic applications accepted. *Application Contact:* Lindsay Johnson, Director of Graduate and Adult Recruitment, 402-280-2703, Fax: 402-280-2423, E-mail: gradschool@creighton.edu. *Dean,* Dr. Gail M. Jensen, 402-280-2424, Fax: 402-280-2423, E-mail: gjensen@creighton.edu.

College of Arts and Sciences Students: 55 full-time (38 women), 203 part-time (144 women); includes 7 minority (2 Black or African American, non-Hispanic/Latino; 2 American Indian or Alaska Native, non-Hispanic/Latino; 2 Asian, non-Hispanic/Latino; 1 Native Hawaiian or other Pacific Islander, non-Hispanic/Latino), 11 international. Average age 33. 58 applicants, 76% accepted, 17 enrolled. *Faculty:* 119 full-time (37 women). Expenses: Contact institution. *Financial support:* In 2017–18, 8 fellowships with full and partial tuition reimbursements (averaging $12,000 per year), 3 teaching assistantships with full and partial tuition reimbursements (averaging $12,000 per year) were awarded; scholarships/grants and tuition waivers (partial) also available. Financial award applicants required to submit FAFSA. In 2017, 118 master's awarded. *Program availability:* Part-time, 100% online, blended/hybrid learning. Offers arts and sciences (M Ed, MA, MFA, MS); creative writing (MA, MFA); educational leadership (MS); elementary school guidance (MS); elementary teaching (M Ed); medical anthropology (MA); medical physics (MS); physics (MS); school counseling and preventive mental health (MS); secondary school guidance (MS); secondary teaching (M Ed); teaching (M Ed); theology (MA). *Application deadline:* For fall admission, 3/1 for domestic and international students; for winter admission, 10/1 for domestic students, 7/1 for international students; for spring admission, 4/1 for domestic students, 10/1 for international students. Applications are processed on a rolling basis. *Application fee:* $50. Electronic applications accepted. *Application Contact:* Lindsay Johnson, Director of Graduate and Adult Recruitment, 402-280-2703, Fax: 402-280-2423, E-mail: gradschool@creighton.edu. *Dean,* Dr. Bridget M. Keegan, 402-280-4015, E-mail: bridgetkeegan@creighton.edu.

Heider College of Business Students: 60 full-time (24 women), 308 part-time (95 women); includes 31 minority (14 Black or African American, non-Hispanic/Latino; 1 American Indian or Alaska Native, non-Hispanic/Latino; 9 Asian, non-Hispanic/Latino; 3 Hispanic/Latino; 2 Native Hawaiian or other Pacific Islander, non-Hispanic/Latino; 2 Two or more races, non-Hispanic/Latino), 28 international. Average age 32. 253 applicants, 74% accepted, 123 enrolled. *Faculty:* 33 full-time (10 women), 22 part-time/adjunct (3 women). Expenses: Contact institution. *Financial support:* In 2017–18, 10 fellowships with partial tuition reimbursements (averaging $8,448 per year) were awarded; career-related internships or fieldwork, tuition waivers (partial), and unspecified assistantships also available. Financial award application deadline: 3/1. In 2017, 139 master's awarded. *Program availability:* Part-time, evening/weekend, 100% online, blended/hybrid learning. Offers accounting (MAC); business administration (MBA, DBA); business intelligence and analytics (MS); finance (M Fin); investment management and financial analysis (MIMFA). *Application deadline:* For fall admission, 7/1 priority date for domestic students, 3/1 for international students; for winter admission, 10/1 priority date for domestic students, 7/1 for international students; for spring admission, 4/1 priority date for domestic students, 10/1 for international students; for summer admission, 5/1 for domestic and international students. Applications are processed on a rolling basis. *Application fee:* $50. Electronic applications accepted. *Application Contact:* Chris Karasek, Assistant Dean, 402-280-2829, Fax: 402-280-2172, E-mail: chriskarasek@creighton.edu. *Associate Dean for Graduate Programs,* Dr. Deborah Wells, 402-280-2841, E-mail: deborahwells@creighton.edu.

School of Dentistry Offers dentistry (DDS).

School of Law *Program availability:* Part-time. Offers law (MS, JD, Certificate); negotiation and conflict resolution (MS, Certificate). Electronic applications accepted.

School of Medicine Offers biomedical sciences (MS, PhD); clinical anatomy (MS); medical microbiology and immunology (MS, PhD); medicine (MS, MD, PhD); pharmaceutical sciences (MS); pharmacology (MS, PhD). Electronic applications accepted.

School of Pharmacy and Health Professions *Program availability:* Online learning. Offers occupational therapy (OTD); pharmaceutical sciences (MS); pharmacy (Pharm D); pharmacy and health professions (MS, DPT, OTD, Pharm D); physical therapy (DPT). Electronic applications accepted.

CRISWELL COLLEGE, Dallas, TX 75246-1537

General Information Independent-religious, coed, comprehensive institution. *Graduate housing:* On-campus housing not available.

GRADUATE UNITS

Graduate School of the Bible *Program availability:* Part-time. Offers biblical studies (M Div); Christian leadership (MA); counseling (MA); Jewish studies (MA); ministry (MA); theological and biblical studies (MA). Electronic applications accepted.

CROWN COLLEGE, St. Bonifacius, MN 55375-9001

General Information Independent-religious, coed, comprehensive institution. *Graduate housing:* Room and/or apartments available on a first-come, first-served basis to married students; on-campus housing not available to single students. Housing application deadline: 7/1.

GRADUATE UNITS

Adult and Graduate Studies *Program availability:* Part-time, evening/weekend, online learning. Offers Christian studies (MA); instructional leadership (MA); international leadership (MA); ministry leadership (MA); organizational leadership (MA). Electronic applications accepted.

CULVER-STOCKTON COLLEGE, Canton, MO 63435-1299

General Information Independent-religious, coed, comprehensive institution.

GRADUATE UNITS

MBA Program Offers accounting and finance (MBA).

CUMBERLAND UNIVERSITY, Lebanon, TN 37087

General Information Independent, coed, comprehensive institution. *Graduate housing:* Room and/or apartments available on a first-come, first-served basis to single students; on-campus housing not available to married students.

GRADUATE UNITS

Program in Business Administration *Program availability:* Part-time, evening/weekend. Offers business administration (MBA).

Program in Education *Program availability:* Part-time, evening/weekend, online learning. Offers education (MAE).

Program in Public Service Administration *Program availability:* Part-time, evening/weekend. Offers public service administration (MS).

CUNY GRADUATE SCHOOL OF JOURNALISM, New York, NY 10018

General Information City-supported, coed, graduate-only institution.

GRADUATE UNITS

Graduate Program Offers entrepreneurial journalism (MA); journalism (MA); social journalism (MA). Electronic applications accepted.

CURRY COLLEGE, Milton, MA 02186-9984

General Information Independent, coed, comprehensive institution. *Graduate housing:* On-campus housing not available. *Research affiliation:* Literacy Centers/GED Programs.

GRADUATE UNITS

Graduate Studies *Program availability:* Part-time, evening/weekend. Offers business administration (MBA); criminal justice (MA); elementary education (M Ed); finance (Certificate); foundations (non-license) (M Ed); nursing (MSN); reading (M Ed, Certificate); special education (M Ed).

CURTIS INSTITUTE OF MUSIC, Philadelphia, PA 19103-6107

General Information Independent, coed, comprehensive institution. *Graduate housing:* On-campus housing not available.

GRADUATE UNITS

Graduate Studies Offers opera (MM).

DAEMEN COLLEGE, Amherst, NY 14226-3592

General Information Independent, coed, comprehensive institution. *Graduate housing:* Room and/or apartments available on a first-come, first-served basis to single students; on-campus housing not available to married students. Housing application deadline: 7/15.

GRADUATE UNITS

Department of Accounting/Information Systems *Program availability:* Part-time, evening/weekend. Offers global business (MS). Electronic applications accepted.

Department of Nursing *Program availability:* Part-time. Offers adult nurse practitioner (MS, Post Master's Certificate); nurse executive leadership (Post Master's Certificate); nursing education (MS, Post Master's Certificate); nursing executive leadership (MS); nursing practice (DNP); palliative care nursing (Post Master's Certificate). Electronic applications accepted.

Department of Physical Therapy *Program availability:* Part-time. Offers orthopedic manual physical therapy (Advanced Certificate); physical therapy-direct entry (DPT); transitional (DPT). Electronic applications accepted.

Department of Visual and Performing Arts Offers arts administration (MS).

Education Department *Program availability:* Part-time. Offers adolescence education (MS); childhood education (MS); childhood special education (MS); childhood special-alternative certification (MS); early childhood special-alternative certification (MS). Electronic applications accepted.

Physician Assistant Department Offers physician assistant (MS). Electronic applications accepted.

Program in Executive Leadership and Change *Program availability:* Part-time, evening/weekend. Offers business (MS); health professions (MS); not-for-profit organizations (MS). Electronic applications accepted.

Program in Public Health *Program availability:* Part-time, online learning. Offers community health education (MPH); epidemiology (MPH); generalist (MPH).

Program in Social Work Offers social work (MSW).

DAKOTA STATE UNIVERSITY, Madison, SD 57042-1799

General Information State-supported, coed, comprehensive institution. CGS member. *Enrollment:* 3,307 graduate, professional, and undergraduate students; 72 full-time matriculated graduate/professional students (12 women), 236 part-time matriculated graduate/professional students (66 women). *Enrollment by degree level:* 185 master's, 110 doctoral, 13 other advanced degrees. *Graduate faculty:* 28 full-time (6 women), 1 (woman) part-time/adjunct. Tuition, state resident: full-time $5749. Tuition, nonresident: full-time $10,733. *Required fees:* $715. Tuition and fees vary according to campus/location and reciprocity agreements. *Graduate housing:* Room and/or apartments available on a first-come, first-served basis to single students; on-campus housing not available to married students. Typical cost: $3062 per year ($4580 including board). Room and board charges vary according to board plan and housing facility selected. *Student services:* Campus employment opportunities, campus safety program, career counseling, exercise/wellness program, free psychological counseling, grant writing training, international student services, low-cost health insurance, multicultural affairs office, services for students with disabilities, teacher training, writing training. *Library facilities:* Karl E. Mundt Library & Learning Commons plus 1 other. *Collection:* Books: 43,699 (physical), 162,866 (digital/electronic); Serial titles: 200 (physical); Databases: 121. Weekly public service hours: 85. *Research affiliation:* SBS-Secure Banking Solutions, LLC (information security), Secure Healthcare Solutions (information security), Chenega Logistics (information security).

Computer facilities: 135 computers available on campus for general student use. A campuswide network can be accessed from student residence rooms and from off campus. Online class registration is available.
Website: http://www.dsu.edu/

General Application Contact: Erin Blankespoor, Senior Secretary, Office of Graduate Studies and Research, 605-256-5799, E-mail: erin.blankespoor@dsu.edu.

GRADUATE UNITS

Beacom College of Computer and Cyber Sciences Students: 35 full-time (3 women), 66 part-time (11 women); includes 23 minority (8 Black or African American, non-Hispanic/Latino; 6 Asian, non-Hispanic/Latino; 5 Hispanic/Latino; 4 Two or more races, non-Hispanic/Latino), 5 international. Average age 35. 110 applicants, 33% accepted, 26 enrolled. *Faculty:* 13 full-time (2 women). Expenses: Contact institution. *Financial support:* Research assistantships with partial tuition reimbursements, teaching assistantships with partial tuition reimbursements, scholarships/grants, and unspecified assistantships available. Financial award applicants required to submit FAFSA. In 2017, 34 master's, 2 doctorates, 5 other advanced degrees awarded. *Program availability:* Part-time, evening/weekend, 100% online, blended/hybrid learning. Offers applied computer science (MSACS); banking security (Graduate Certificate); cyber security (D Sc); ethical hacking (Graduate Certificate); information assurance and computer security (MSIA). *Application deadline:* For fall admission, 6/15 for domestic students, 4/15 for international students; for spring admission, 11/15 for domestic students, 10/15 priority date for international students; for summer admission, 4/15 for domestic students. Applications are processed on a rolling basis. *Application fee:* $35. Electronic applications accepted. *Application Contact:* Erin Blankespoor, Senior Secretary, Office of Graduate Studies and Research, 605-256-5799, E-mail: erin.blankespoor@dsu.edu. *Dean of College of Computing*, Dr. Richard Hanson, 605-256-5838, E-mail: richard.hanson@dsu.edu.

College of Business and Information Systems Students: 37 full-time (9 women), 168 part-time (52 women); includes 60 minority (29 Black or African American, non-Hispanic/Latino; 3 American Indian or Alaska Native, non-Hispanic/Latino; 15 Asian, non-Hispanic/Latino; 10 Hispanic/Latino; 1 Native Hawaiian or other Pacific Islander, non-Hispanic/Latino; 2 Two or more races, non-Hispanic/Latino), 40 international. Average age 38. 179 applicants, 57% accepted, 59 enrolled. *Faculty:* 22 full-time (6 women), 1 (woman) part-time/adjunct. Expenses: Contact institution. *Financial support:* Research assistantships with partial tuition reimbursements, teaching assistantships with partial tuition reimbursements, and unspecified assistantships available. Financial award applicants required to submit FAFSA. In 2017, 49 master's, 8 doctorates, 5 other advanced degrees awarded. *Program availability:* Part-time, evening/weekend, 100% online, blended/hybrid learning. Offers analytics (MSA); business analytics (Graduate Certificate); general management (MBA); health informatics (MSHI); information systems (MSIS, D Sc IS); information technology (Graduate Certificate). *Application deadline:* For fall admission, 6/15 for domestic students, 4/15 priority date for international students; for spring admission, 11/15 for domestic students, 10/15 priority date for international students; for summer admission, 4/15 for domestic students. Applications are processed on a rolling basis. *Application fee:* $35. Electronic applications accepted. *Application Contact:* Erin Blankespoor, Senior Secretary, Office of Graduate Studies and Research, 605-256-5799, E-mail: erin.blankespoor@dsu.edu. *Dean of College of Business and Information Systems*, Dr. Dorine Bennett, 605-256-5165, E-mail: dorine.bennett@dsu.edu.

College of Education Students: 8 part-time (5 women). Average age 32. 3 applicants, 100% accepted, 2 enrolled. *Faculty:* 4 full-time (0 women). Expenses: Contact institution. *Financial support:* Unspecified assistantships and administrative assistantships available. Financial award applicants required to submit FAFSA. In 2017, 5 master's awarded. *Program availability:* Part-time-only, evening/weekend, online only, 100% online. Offers educational technology (MSET). *Application deadline:* For fall admission, 6/15 for domestic students; for spring admission, 11/15 for domestic students; for summer admission, 4/15 for domestic students. Applications are processed on a rolling basis. *Application fee:* $35. Electronic applications accepted. *Application Contact:* Dr. Kevin Smith, Program Coordinator, 605-256-5175, Fax: 605-256-7300, E-mail: kevin.smith@dsu.edu. *Dean of College of Education*, Dr. Crystal Pauli, 605-256-5799.

DAKOTA WESLEYAN UNIVERSITY, Mitchell, SD 57301-4398

General Information Independent-religious, coed, comprehensive institution.

GRADUATE UNITS

Program in Education *Program availability:* Part-time, evening/weekend. Offers curriculum and instruction (MA Ed); educational policy and administration (MA Ed); preK-12 principal certification (MA Ed); secondary certification (MA Ed). Electronic applications accepted.

DALHOUSIE UNIVERSITY, Halifax, NS B3H 4R2, Canada

General Information Province-supported, coed, university. *Graduate housing:* Rooms and/or apartments available on a first-come, first-served basis to single and married students. Housing application deadline: 8/1.

GRADUATE UNITS

Faculty of Agriculture *Program availability:* Part-time. Offers agriculture (M Sc).

Faculty of Architecture and Planning Offers architecture and planning (M Arch, M Eng, M Plan, MEDS, MPS). Electronic applications accepted.

School of Planning Offers planning (M Eng, M Plan, MPS). Electronic applications accepted.

Faculty of Arts and Social Science *Program availability:* Part-time. Offers arts and social science (MA, PhD); classics (MA, PhD); English (MA, PhD); French (MA, PhD); German (MA); history (MA, PhD); international development studies (MA); musicology (MA); philosophy (MA, PhD); political science (MA, PhD); social anthropology (MA, PhD); sociology (MA, PhD). Electronic applications accepted.

Faculty of Computer Science Offers computational biology and bioinformatics (M Sc); computer science (MA Sc, MC Sc, PhD); electronic commerce (MEC); health informatics (MHI). Electronic applications accepted.

Faculty of Dentistry Offers dentistryoral and maxillofacial surgery.

Faculty of Engineering Offers biological engineering (M Eng, MA Sc, PhD); biomedical engineering (MA Sc, PhD); chemical engineering (M Eng, MA Sc, PhD); civil and resource engineering (M Eng, MA Sc, PhD); electrical and computer engineering (M Eng, MA Sc, PhD); engineering (M Eng, M Sc, MA Sc, PhD); engineering mathematics (M Sc, PhD); environmental engineering (M Eng, MA Sc, PhD); food science and technology (M Sc, PhD); industrial engineering (M Eng, MA Sc, PhD); internetworking (M Eng); materials engineering (M Eng, MA Sc, PhD); mechanical engineering (M Eng, MA Sc, PhD); mineral resource engineering (M Eng, MA Sc, PhD).

Faculty of Graduate Studies *Program availability:* Part-time, online learning. Offers anatomy and neurobiology (M Sc, PhD); interdisciplinary studies (PhD); medicine (M Sc, PhD); neuroscience (M Sc, PhD); pathology (M Sc, PhD); pharmacology (M Sc, PhD). Electronic applications accepted.

Dalhousie Law School *Program availability:* Part-time. Offers law (LL M, JSD). Electronic applications accepted.

Faculty of Health Professions *Program availability:* Part-time, online learning. Offers health professions (M Sc, MA, MAHSR, MHA, MN, MPH, MSW, PhD).

School of Health Administration *Program availability:* Part-time, online learning. Offers health administration (MAHSR, MHA, MPH, PhD). Electronic applications accepted.

School of Health and Human Performance *Program availability:* Part-time. Offers health and human performance (M Sc, MA); health promotion (MA); kinesiology (M Sc); leisure studies (MA). Electronic applications accepted.

School of Human Communication Disorders Offers audiology (M Sc); speech-language pathology (M Sc). Electronic applications accepted.

School of Nursing *Program availability:* Part-time, online learning. Offers nursing (MN, PhD). Electronic applications accepted.

School of Occupational Therapy *Program availability:* Part-time, evening/weekend, online learning. Offers occupational therapy (entry to profession) (M Sc); occupational therapy (post-professional) (M Sc). Electronic applications accepted.

School of Physiotherapy Offers physiotherapy (entry to profession) (M Sc); physiotherapy (rehabilitation research) (M Sc). Electronic applications accepted.

School of Social Work *Program availability:* Part-time, online learning. Offers social work (MSW). Electronic applications accepted.

Faculty of Management *Program availability:* Part-time. Offers management (MBA, MEC, MES, MIM, MLIS, MMM, MPA, MREM, GDPA); marine affairs (MMM). Electronic applications accepted.

Centre for Advanced Management Education *Program availability:* Part-time, online learning. Offers financial services (MBA); information management (MIM); management (MPA); natural resources (MBA). Electronic applications accepted.

Rowe School of Business *Program availability:* Part-time. Offers business administration (MBA); financial services (MBA). Electronic applications accepted.

School for Resource and Environmental Studies *Program availability:* Part-time. Offers resource and environmental studies (MES, MREM). Electronic applications accepted.

School of Information Management *Program availability:* Part-time. Offers information management (MIM, MLIS). Electronic applications accepted.

School of Public Administration *Program availability:* Part-time. Offers management (MPA); public administration (MPA, GDPA). Electronic applications accepted.

Faculty of Medicine Offers biochemistry and molecular biology (M Sc, PhD); community health and epidemiology (M Sc); medicine (M Sc, MD, PhD); microbiology and immunology (M Sc, PhD); physiology and biophysics (M Sc, PhD). Electronic applications accepted.

Faculty of Science Offers biology (M Sc, PhD); chemistry (M Sc, PhD); clinical psychology (PhD); earth sciences (M Sc, PhD); economics (MA, MDE, PhD); mathematics (M Sc, PhD); oceanography (M Sc, PhD); physics and atmospheric science (M Sc, PhD); psychology (M Sc, PhD); psychology/neuroscience (M Sc, PhD); science (M Sc, MA, MDE, PhD); statistics (M Sc, PhD). Electronic applications accepted.

DALLAS BAPTIST UNIVERSITY, Dallas, TX 75211-9299

General Information Independent-religious, coed, comprehensive institution. *Enrollment:* 5,067 graduate, professional, and undergraduate students; 745 full-time matriculated graduate/professional students (431 women), 1,161 part-time matriculated graduate/professional students (711 women). *Enrollment by degree level:* 1,614 master's, 292 doctoral. *Graduate faculty:* 80 full-time (26 women), 215 part-time/adjunct (91 women). *Tuition:* Full-time $16,308; part-time $906 per credit hour. *Required fees:* $900; $450 per semester. Tuition and fees vary according to course load and degree level. *Graduate housing:* Room and/or apartments available on a first-come, first-served basis to single students; on-campus housing not available to married students. Typical cost: $3790 per year ($7740 including board). Room and board charges vary according to board plan and housing facility selected. *Student services:* Campus employment opportunities, campus safety program, career counseling, free psychological counseling, international student services, low-cost health insurance, services for students with disabilities, writing training. *Library facilities:* Vance Memorial Library plus 3 others. *Collection:* Books: 237,744 (physical), 156,156 (digital/electronic); Serial titles: 567 (physical), 35,666 (digital/electronic); Databases: 194. Weekly public service hours: 108.

Computer facilities: 214 computers available on campus for general student use. A campuswide network can be accessed from student residence rooms and from off campus. Online class registration is available.
Website: http://www.dbu.edu/

General Application Contact: Bobby Soto, Director of Admissions, 214-333-5242, Fax: 214-333-5579, E-mail: graduate@dbu.edu.

GRADUATE UNITS

College of Business Expenses: Contact institution. *Program availability:* Part-time, evening/weekend, online learning. Offers accounting (MBA); business (MA, MBA, MS); business communication (MBA); conflict resolution management (MA, MBA); entrepreneurship (MBA); finance (MBA); general management (MA, MS); health care management (MA, MBA); human resource management (MA); international business (MBA); leading the non-profit organization (MBA); management (MBA); management information systems (MBA); marketing (MBA); organizational communication (MA); performance management (MA); professional sales and management optimization (MA); project management (MBA); technology and engineering management (MBA). *Application deadline:* Applications are processed on a rolling basis. *Application fee:* $25. Electronic applications accepted. *Application Contact:* Dr. Sandra Reid, Chair of Graduate Business Programs, 214-333-6860, E-mail: sandra@dbu.edu. *Dean*, Dr. Dale Sims, 214-333-5244, E-mail: graduate@dbu.edu.

College of Fine Arts Expenses: Contact institution. *Program availability:* Part-time, evening/weekend. Offers worship studies (MA). *Application deadline:* Applications are processed on a rolling basis. *Application fee:* $25. Electronic applications accepted. *Application Contact:* Dr. Joanne Morgan, Program Director, 214-333-6854, E-mail: joannem@dbu.edu. *Dean*, Dr. Ronald Bowles, 214-333-5316, E-mail: ronb@dbu.edu.

College of Humanities and Social Sciences Expenses: Contact institution. Offers professional counseling (MA). *Application Contact:* Dr. Mary Becerril, Program Director, 214-333-5265, Fax: 214-333-6819, E-mail: maryb@dbu.edu. *Dean*, Dr. Rob Sullivan, 214-333-5238.

Dorothy M. Bush College of Education Expenses: Contact institution. *Program availability:* Part-time, evening/weekend, online learning. Offers bilingual education (M Ed); charter school administration (M Ed); Christian school administration (M Ed); diagnostician (M Ed); distance learning (M Ed, MAT); early childhood through grade 6 certification (MAT); early childhood-12 (MAT); education (M Ed, MA, MAT, MS, Ed D); educational leadership (M Ed); educational leadership K-12 (Ed D); elementary (MAT); English as a second language (M Ed, MAT); instructional technology (M Ed); kinesiology (M Ed); Montessori (MAT); multisensory (MAT); professional life coaching (M Ed); reading and English as a second language (M Ed); school counseling (M Ed); secondary (MAT); special education (M Ed); sport management (MA); supervision (M Ed). *Application deadline:* Applications are processed on a rolling basis. *Application fee:* $25. Electronic applications accepted. *Application Contact:* Bobby Soto, Director of Admissions, 214-333-5242, E-mail: graduate@dbu.edu. *Dean*, Dr. Neil Dugger, 214-333-5413, E-mail: graduate@dbu.edu.

Gary Cook School of Leadership Expenses: Contact institution. *Program availability:* Part-time, evening/weekend, online learning. Offers East Asian studies (MA); European studies (MA); general international studies (MA); global business (MA); higher education leadership (Ed D); international immersion (MA); international ministry (MA); international relations (MA); leadership (M Ed, MA, Ed D, PhD); leadership studies (M Ed, PhD); student affairs leadership (M Ed). *Application deadline:* Applications are processed on a rolling basis. *Application fee:* $25. Electronic applications accepted. *Application Contact:* Bobby Soto, Director of Admissions, 214-333-5242, Fax: 214-333-5447, E-mail: bobby@dbu.edu. *Dean*, Dr. Jack Goodyear, 214-333-5595, Fax: 214-333-5323, E-mail: jackg@dbu.edu.

Graduate School of Ministry Expenses: Contact institution. *Program availability:* Part-time. Offers chaplaincy (MA); Christian counseling (MA); Christian heritage (MA); Christian ministry (MA); Christian scriptures (MA); church planting (MA); counseling ministry (MA); discipleship for the family (MA); discipleship through communications (MA); East Asian Studies (MA); English as a second language (MA); family ministry (MA); general (MA); general ministry (MA); general studies (MA); global communication (MA); global studies (MA); international business (MA); leadership (MA); leading the nonprofit organization (MA); local church discipleship (MA); ministry (MA); ministry leadership (MA); missions (MA); professional life coaching (MA); small group ministry (MA); special needs children ministry (MA); special needs family ministry (MA); student ministry (MA); urban ministry (MA); worship leadership (MA); worship theology (MA). *Application deadline:* Applications are processed on a rolling basis. *Application fee:* $25. Electronic applications accepted. *Application Contact:* Bobby Soto, Director of Admissions, 214-333-5242, Fax: 214-333-5447, E-mail: bobby@dbu.edu. *Dean*, Dr. Robert R. Brooks, 214-333-5390, Fax: 214-333-5673, E-mail: bobb@dbu.edu.

Liberal Arts Program Expenses: Contact institution. *Program availability:* Part-time, evening/weekend. Offers art (MLA); Christian studies (MLA); commercial art (MLA); East Asian studies (MLA); English (MLA); English as a second language (MLA); fine arts (MLA); history (MLA); missions (MLA); political science (MLA). *Application deadline:* Applications are processed on a rolling basis. *Application fee:* $25. Electronic applications accepted. *Application Contact:* Bobby Soto, Director of Admissions, 214-333-5242, E-mail: bobby@dbu.edu. *Director*, Jared Ingram, 214-333-5584, E-mail: jaredi@dbu.edu.

Professional Development Program Expenses: Contact institution. *Program availability:* Part-time, evening/weekend. Offers accounting (MA); church leadership (MA); communication (MA); counseling (MA); criminal justice (MA); English as a second language (MA); finance (MA); higher education (MA); leadership studies (MA); management (MA). *Application deadline:* Applications are processed on a rolling basis. *Application fee:* $25. Electronic applications accepted. *Application Contact:* Bobby Soto, Director of Admissions, 214-333-5242, E-mail: bobby@dbu.edu. *Program Director*, Jared Ingram, 214-333-5584, E-mail: jaredi@dbu.edu.

DALLAS THEOLOGICAL SEMINARY, Dallas, TX 75204-6499

General Information Independent, coed, graduate-only institution. *Graduate housing:* Rooms and/or apartments available on a first-come, first-served basis to single and married students.

GRADUATE UNITS

Graduate Programs *Program availability:* Part-time, online learning. Offers adult education (Th M); apologetics (Th M); Bible backgrounds (Th M); Bible translation (Th M); Biblical and theological studies (Certificate); biblical counseling (MA); biblical exegesis and linguistics (MA); biblical exposition (PhD); biblical studies (MA); Biblical theology (Th M); children's education (Th M); Christian education (MA, D Min); Christian leadership (MA); cross-cultural ministries (MA); educational administration (Th M); educational leadership (Th M); evangelism and discipleship (Th M); exposition of Biblical books (Th M); family life education (Th M); general studies (Th M); Hebrew and cognate studies (Th M); hermeneutics (Th M); historical theology (Th M); homiletics (Th M); intercultural ministries (Th M); Jesus studies (Th M); leadership studies (Th M); media and communication (MA); media arts (Th M); ministry (D Min); ministry with women (Th M); New Testament studies (Th M, PhD); Old Testament studies (Th M, PhD); parachurch ministries (Th M); pastoral care and counseling (Th M); pastoral theology and practice (Th M); philosophy (Th M); sacred theology (STM); spiritual formation (Th M); systematic theology (Th M); teaching in Christian institutions (Th M); theological studies (PhD); urban ministries (Th M); worship studies (Th M); youth education (Th M). Electronic applications accepted.

DANIEL MORGAN GRADUATE SCHOOL OF NATIONAL SECURITY, Washington, DC 20036

General Information Independent, coed, graduate-only institution.

GRADUATE UNITS

Graduate Programs Offers integrated risk value communications (MA); national security (MA).

★ DARTMOUTH COLLEGE, Hanover, NH 03755

General Information Independent, coed, university. CGS member. *Enrollment:* 6,509 graduate, professional, and undergraduate students; 1,942 full-time matriculated graduate/professional students (895 women), 99 part-time matriculated graduate/professional students (62 women). *Enrollment by degree level:* 993 master's, 962 doctoral, 86 other advanced degrees. *Graduate faculty:* 460 full-time (142 women), 119 part-time/adjunct (47 women). *Graduate housing:* Rooms and/or apartments available on a first-come, first-served basis to single and married students. Housing application deadline: 5/15. *Student services:* Campus safety program, career counseling, free psychological counseling, international student services, low-cost health insurance, services for students with disabilities, teacher training, writing training. *Library facilities:* Baker-Berry Library plus 8 others. *Collection:* Books: 2.6 million (physical), 880,374 (digital/electronic); Serial titles: 75,548 (physical). Study areas open 24 hours, 5–7 days a week; students can reserve study rooms.

Computer facilities: Computer purchase and lease plans are available. 200 computers available on campus for general student use. A campuswide network can be accessed from student residence rooms and from off campus. Online class registration is available.
Website: http://www.dartmouth.edu/

General Application Contact: Jane Seibel, Assistant Dean of Recruiting and Diversity, School of Graduate and Advanced Studies, 603-646-6578, Fax: 603-646-3488, E-mail: jane.b.seibel@dartmouth.edu.

GRADUATE UNITS

The Dartmouth Institute Students: 77 full-time (39 women), 59 part-time (40 women); includes 20 minority (3 Black or African American, non-Hispanic/Latino; 2 American Indian or Alaska Native, non-Hispanic/Latino; 11 Asian, non-Hispanic/Latino; 1 Hispanic/Latino; 3 Two or more races, non-Hispanic/Latino), 7 international. Average age 33. 331 applicants, 54% accepted, 83 enrolled. *Faculty:* 51 full-time (26 women), 95 part-time/adjunct (41 women). Expenses: Contact institution. *Financial support:* In 2017–18, fellowships with full tuition reimbursements (averaging $28,200 per year) were awarded; scholarships/grants also available. *Program availability:* Part-time. Offers evaluative clinical sciences (MS, PhD); public health (MPH). *Application deadline:* For fall admission, 1/15 for domestic students. *Application fee:* $135. *Application Contact:* Marc Aquila, Senior Director of Recruitment and Admissions, 603-650-1539. *Director*, Dr. Elliot S. Fisher, 603-653-0802.

Geisel School of Medicine Students: 380 full-time (223 women), 4 part-time (3 women); includes 173 minority (27 Black or African American, non-Hispanic/Latino; 5 American Indian or Alaska Native, non-Hispanic/Latino; 79 Asian, non-Hispanic/Latino; 47 Hispanic/Latino; 15 Two or more races, non-Hispanic/Latino), 31 international. Average age 27. 6,781 applicants, 4% accepted, 92 enrolled. *Faculty:* 148 full-time (54 women), 40 part-time/adjunct (18 women). Expenses: Contact institution. *Financial support:* Institutionally sponsored loans and scholarships/grants available. In 2017, 72 doctorates awarded. Offers medicine (MD). *Application deadline:* For fall admission, 11/1 for domestic students. *Application fee:* $130. Electronic applications accepted. *Application Contact:* Rand S. Swenson, Chair, Geisel Admissions Committee, 603-650-1505, Fax: 603-650-1560, E-mail: geisel.admissions@dartmouth.edu. *Senior Associate Dean for Faculty Affairs*, Dr. Leslie Henderson, 603-650-1574, E-mail: leslie.p.henderson@dartmouth.edu.

Graduate Program in Molecular and Cellular Biology Students: 62 full-time (28 women); includes 12 minority (2 Asian, non-Hispanic/Latino; 9 Hispanic/Latino; 1 Two or more races, non-Hispanic/Latino), 22 international. Average age 26. 161 applicants, 38% accepted, 30 enrolled. *Faculty:* 70 full-time (16 women), 6 part-time/adjunct (3 women). Expenses: Contact institution. *Financial support:* Fellowships and health care benefits available. In 2017, 9 doctorates awarded. Offers biochemistry (PhD); biological sciences (PhD); genetics (PhD); immunology (PhD); microbiology and molecular pathogenesis (PhD); molecular and cellular biology (PhD). *Application deadline:* For fall admission, 12/8 for domestic students. Applications are processed on a rolling basis. *Application fee:* $75. Electronic applications accepted. *Application Contact:* Janet Cheney, Program Coordinator, 603-650-1612, E-mail: mcb@dartmouth.edu. *Vice Chair*, Dr. Patrick J. Dolph, 603-650-1092, E-mail: mcb@dartmouth.edu.

Program in Experimental and Molecular Medicine Students: 44 full-time (26 women); includes 8 minority (5 Asian, non-Hispanic/Latino; 3 Hispanic/Latino), 4 international. Average age 26. 72 applicants, 25% accepted, 5 enrolled. *Faculty:* 35 full-time (6 women), 15 part-time/adjunct (6 women). Expenses: Contact institution. *Financial support:* Fellowships and health care benefits available. Offers experimental and molecular medicine. *Application deadline:* For fall admission, 1/1 for domestic and international students. *Application fee:* $75. Electronic applications accepted. *Application Contact:* Gail Egner, Program Administrator, 603-650-4933, Fax: 603-650-4932, E-mail: gail.p.egner@dartmouth.edu. *Director*, Dr. Michael Spinella, 603-650-1126, Fax: 603-650-4932.

School of Graduate and Advanced Studies Students: 574 full-time (243 women), 31 part-time (17 women); includes 99 minority (10 Black or African American, non-Hispanic/Latino; 3 American Indian or Alaska Native, non-Hispanic/Latino; 42 Asian, non-Hispanic/Latino; 26 Hispanic/Latino; 18 Two or more races, non-Hispanic/Latino), 198 international. Average age 30. 1,360 applicants, 31% accepted, 200 enrolled. *Faculty:* 172 full-time (55 women), 60 part-time/adjunct (25 women). Expenses: Contact institution. *Financial support:* Fellowships, research assistantships, teaching assistantships, career-related internships or fieldwork, institutionally sponsored loans, scholarships/grants, traineeships, tuition waivers (full and partial), and unspecified assistantships available. Support available to part-time students. Financial award application deadline: 4/1; financial award applicants required to submit CSS PROFILE or FAFSA. In 2017, 120 master's, 72 doctorates awarded. Offers biophysical chemistry (MS); chemistry (PhD); cognitive neuroscience (PhD); comparative literature (MA); computer science (MS, PhD); digital music (MA); earth sciences (MS, PhD); ecology and evolutionary biology (PhD); liberal studies (MALS); mathematics (AM, PhD); physics and astronomy (PhD); psychology (PhD); sustainability, ecosystems, and environment (PhD). *Application deadline:* For fall admission, 1/15 for domestic students. Electronic applications accepted. *Application Contact:* Gary Hutchins, Assistant Dean, School of Graduate and Advanced Studies, 603-646-2107, Fax: 603-646-3488, E-mail: g.hutchins@dartmouth.edu. *Dean of Graduate Studies,* Dr. Jon Kull, 603-646-1552, E-mail: f.jon.kull@dartmouth.edu.

Institute for Quantitative Biomedical Sciences Students: 30 full-time (18 women); includes 7 minority (1 Black or African American, non-Hispanic/Latino; 4 Asian, non-Hispanic/Latino; 2 Hispanic/Latino), 12 international. Average age 27. 40 applicants, 35% accepted, 9 enrolled. Expenses: Contact institution. *Financial support:* Fellowships available. In 2017, 1 doctorate awarded. Offers epidemiology (MS); health data science (MS); quantitative biomedical sciences (PhD). PhD offered in collaboration with the Department of Genetics and the Department of Community and Family Medicine. *Application deadline:* For fall admission, 3/1 for domestic students. Applications are processed on a rolling basis. *Application fee:* $75. Electronic applications accepted. *Application Contact:* Gary Hutchins, Assistant Dean, School of Arts and Sciences, 603-646-2107, Fax: 603-646-3488, E-mail: g.hutchins@dartmouth.edu. *Director,* Dr. Micheal Whitfield, 603-650-1109.

Thayer School of Engineering Students: 221 full-time (78 women); includes 27 minority (3 Black or African American, non-Hispanic/Latino; 20 Asian, non-Hispanic/Latino; 3 Hispanic/Latino; 1 Two or more races, non-Hispanic/Latino), 127 international. Average age 24. 632 applicants, 26% accepted, 95 enrolled. *Faculty:* 56 full-time (10 women), 10 part-time/adjunct (0 women). Expenses: Contact institution. *Financial support:* In 2017–18, 195 students received support, including 23 fellowships with full tuition reimbursements available (averaging $27,120 per year), 92 research assistantships with full tuition reimbursements available (averaging $27,120 per year), 22 teaching assistantships with partial tuition reimbursements available (averaging $8,640 per year); career-related internships or fieldwork, institutionally sponsored loans, scholarships/grants, and tuition waivers (full and partial) also available. Financial award application deadline: 2/15; financial award applicants required to submit CSS PROFILE. In 2017, 59 master's, 11 doctorates awarded. Offers biological and chemical engineering (MS, PhD); electrical and computer engineering (MS, PhD); energy engineering (MS, PhD); engineering (M Eng, MEM, MS, PhD); engineering in medicine/biomedical engineering (M Eng, MS, PhD); engineering management (MEM); innovation (PhD); materials sciences and engineering (MS, PhD); mechanical and systems engineering (MS, PhD). *Application deadline:* For fall admission, 1/1 priority date for domestic and international students. Applications are processed on a rolling basis. *Application fee:* $45. Electronic applications accepted. *Application Contact:* Candace S. Potter, Graduate Admissions and Financial Aid Administrator, 603-646-3844, Fax: 603-646-1620, E-mail: candace.s.potter@dartmouth.edu. *Dean,* Dr. Joseph J. Helbie, 603-646-2238, Fax: 603-646-2580, E-mail: joseph.j.helbie@dartmouth.edu.

Tuck School of Business at Dartmouth Students: 582 full-time (259 women); includes 118 minority (27 Black or African American, non-Hispanic/Latino; 1 American Indian or Alaska Native, non-Hispanic/Latino; 52 Asian, non-Hispanic/Latino; 30 Hispanic/Latino; 1 Native Hawaiian or other Pacific Islander, non-Hispanic/Latino; 7 Two or more races, non-Hispanic/Latino), 172 international. Average age 28. 2,610 applicants, 23% accepted, 293 enrolled. *Faculty:* 53 full-time (11 women). Expenses: Contact institution. *Financial support:* Institutionally sponsored loans and scholarships/grants available. Financial award application deadline: 4/1; financial award applicants required to submit FAFSA. In 2017, 282 master's awarded. Offers business (MBA). *Application deadline:* For fall admission, 10/1 for domestic and international students; for winter admission, 1/1 for domestic and international students; for spring admission, 4/1 for domestic and international students. *Application fee:* $250. Electronic applications accepted. *Application Contact:* Luke Anthony Pena, Executive Director of Admissions and Financial Aid, 603-646-3162, Fax: 603-646-1441, E-mail: tuck.admissions@tuck.dartmouth.edu. *Dean,* Matthew J. Slaughter, 603-646-2460, E-mail: tuck.public.relations@tuck.dartmouth.edu.

DAVENPORT UNIVERSITY, Grand Rapids, MI 49512

General Information Independent, coed, comprehensive institution. *Graduate housing:* Room and/or apartments available on a first-come, first-served basis to single students; on-campus housing not available to married students. *Research affiliation:* Human Synergistic Center for Applied Research, Inc. (leadership, organizational culture, strategy).

GRADUATE UNITS

Sneden Graduate School *Program availability:* Evening/weekend. Offers accounting (MBA); business administration (EMBA); finance (MBA); health care management (MBA); human resources (MBA); information assurance (MS); public health (MPH); strategic management (MBA). Electronic applications accepted.

DEFIANCE COLLEGE, Defiance, OH 43512-1610

General Information Independent-religious, coed, comprehensive institution. *Graduate housing:* On-campus housing not available. *Student services:* Career counseling, exercise/wellness program, low-cost health insurance, multicultural affairs office, services for students with disabilities, teacher training. *Library facilities:* Pilgrim Library plus 1 other. *Collection:* Books: 62,576 (physical), 271,510 (digital/electronic); Serial titles: 308 (physical), 79,914 (digital/electronic); Databases: 162. Weekly public service hours: 90; students can reserve study rooms.

Computer facilities: Computer purchase and lease plans are available. 200 computers available on campus for general student use. A campuswide network can be accessed from student residence rooms and from off campus. Online class registration is available.
Website: http://www.defiance.edu/

General Application Contact: Sally Bissell, Director of Career Development, 419-783-2366, Fax: 419-784-0426, E-mail: sbissell@defiance.edu.

GRADUATE UNITS

Program in Business Administration Expenses: Contact institution. *Program availability:* Part-time, evening/weekend. Offers leadership (MBA). *Application deadline:* For fall admission, 8/1 for domestic and international students. Applications are processed on a rolling basis. *Application fee:* $25. Electronic applications accepted. *Application Contact:* William Sholl, Assistant Professor, 419-783-2441, Fax: 419-784-0426, E-mail: wsholl@defiance.edu. *Assistant Professor,* William Sholl, 419-783-2441, Fax: 419-784-0426, E-mail: wsholl@defiance.edu.

Program in Education *Faculty:* 5 full-time (all women), 2 part-time/adjunct (both women). Expenses: Contact institution. In 2017, 5 master's awarded. *Program availability:* Part-time-only. Offers education (MAE); sport coaching (MAE). *Application deadline:* For fall admission, 8/1 for domestic students. Electronic applications accepted. *Application Contact:* Teresa Watkins, Administrative Assistant, 419-783-2323, Fax: 419-784-0426, E-mail: twatkins@defiance.edu. *Assistant Professor of Education,* Dr. Carla Higgins, 419-783-2571, E-mail: chiggins@defiance.edu.

DELAWARE STATE UNIVERSITY, Dover, DE 19901-2277

General Information State-supported, coed, university. *Graduate housing:* Room and/or apartments available on a first-come, first-served basis to single students; on-campus housing not available to married students.

GRADUATE UNITS

Graduate Programs *Program availability:* Part-time, evening/weekend. Offers applied chemistry (MS, PhD); applied mathematics (MS); applied mathematics and theoretical physics (PhD); applied optics (MS); biological sciences (MA, MS, PhD); biology education (MS); chemistry (MS); French (MA); historic preservation (MA); mathematics (MS); mathematics education (MS); molecular and cellular neuroscience (MS); natural resources (MS); neuroscience (PhD); optics (PhD); physics (MS); physics teaching (MS); plant science (MS); Spanish (MA).

College of Business *Program availability:* Part-time, evening/weekend. Offers business administration (MBA). Electronic applications accepted.

College of Education, Health and Public Policy *Program availability:* Part-time, evening/weekend. Offers adult literacy and basic education (MA); art education (MA); curriculum and instruction (MA); education, health and public policy (MA, MS, MSW, Ed D); educational leadership (MA, Ed D); nursing (MS); science education (MA); social work (MSW); special education (MA); sport administration (MS); teaching (MA). Electronic applications accepted.

DELAWARE VALLEY UNIVERSITY, Doylestown, PA 18901-2697

General Information Independent, coed, comprehensive institution. *Graduate housing:* On-campus housing not available.

GRADUATE UNITS

MBA Program *Program availability:* Part-time, evening/weekend, online learning. Offers accounting (MBA); entrepreneurship (MBA); finance (MBA); food and agribusiness (MBA); general business (MBA); global executive leadership (MBA); human resource management (MBA); supply chain management (MBA). Electronic applications accepted.

Program in Counseling Psychology Offers child and adolescent therapy (MA); social justice community counseling (MA).

Program in Educational Leadership *Program availability:* Part-time, evening/weekend. Offers instruction, curriculum and technology (MS); school administration and leadership (MS).

DELL'ARTE INTERNATIONAL SCHOOL OF PHYSICAL THEATRE, Blue Lake, CA 95525

General Information Independent, coed, graduate-only institution. *Graduate housing:* Rooms and/or apartments available on a first-come, first-served basis to single and married students.

GRADUATE UNITS

MFA Program Offers ensemble based physical theatre (MFA). Electronic applications accepted.

DELTA STATE UNIVERSITY, Cleveland, MS 38733-0001

General Information State-supported, coed, comprehensive institution. *Graduate housing:* Rooms and/or apartments available on a first-come, first-served basis to single and married students. Housing application deadline: 6/1.

GRADUATE UNITS

Graduate Programs *Program availability:* Part-time, evening/weekend, online learning. Electronic applications accepted.

College of Arts and Sciences *Program availability:* Part-time. Offers arts and sciences (M Ed, MALS, MSCD, MSCJ, MSJC, MSNS); community development (MS); evolving human voices (MALS); gender and diversity studies (MALS); globalization studies (MALS); Mississippi Delta studies (MALS); natural sciences (MSNS); philosophy (MALS); religious studies (MALS); secondary education (M Ed); social justice and criminology (MSJC); social science secondary education (M Ed).

College of Business *Program availability:* Part-time, evening/weekend, online learning. Offers accountancy (MPA); business (MBA, MCA, MPA); business administration (MBA); commercial aviation (MCA).

College of Education *Program availability:* Part-time, evening/weekend. Offers counseling (M Ed); counselor education (Ed D); education (M Ed, MAT, MS, Ed D, Ed S); educational administration and supervision (M Ed, Ed S); elementary education (M Ed, MAT, Ed S); health, physical education, and recreation (M Ed); higher education (Ed D); professional studies (Ed D); secondary education (MAT); special education (M Ed); sport and human performance (MS).

Robert E. Smith School of Nursing *Program availability:* Part-time. Offers family nurse practitioner (MSN); nurse administrator (MSN); nurse educator (MSN). Electronic applications accepted.

DENVER SEMINARY, Littleton, CO 80120

General Information Independent-religious, coed, graduate-only institution. *Graduate housing:* Rooms and/or apartments available on a first-come, first-served basis to single and married students. Housing application deadline: 6/1.

GRADUATE UNITS

Graduate and Professional Programs *Program availability:* Part-time, evening/weekend, online learning. Offers apologetics (Certificate); biblical studies (MA); Christian formation and soul care (MA, Certificate); Christian studies (MA, Certificate); church and parachurch leadership (D Min); counseling licensure (MA); counseling ministry (MA); intercultural ministry (Certificate); leadership (MA, Certificate); marriage and family counseling (D Min); pastoral ministry (D Min); philosophy of religion (MA); spiritual guidance (Certificate); theology (M Div, Certificate); worship (Certificate); youth and family ministry (MA). Electronic applications accepted.

DEPAUL UNIVERSITY, Chicago, IL 60604-2287

General Information Independent-religious, coed, university. CGS member. *Enrollment:* 22,769 graduate, professional, and undergraduate students; 5,450 full-time matriculated graduate/professional students (3,008 women), 2,429 part-time matriculated graduate/professional students (1,215 women). *Enrollment by degree level:* 6,534 master's, 1,266 doctoral, 79 other advanced degrees. *Graduate faculty:* 418 full-time (177 women), 320 part-time/adjunct (141 women). *Graduate housing:* Room and/or apartments available on a first-come, first-served basis to single students; on-campus housing not available to married students. Typical cost: $10,965 per year ($14,169 including board). Room and board charges vary according to board plan and housing facility selected. *Student services:* Campus employment opportunities, campus safety program, career counseling, exercise/wellness program, free psychological counseling, international student services, low-cost health insurance, multicultural affairs office, services for students with disabilities, writing training. *Library facilities:* John T. Richardson Library plus 2 others. *Collection:* Books: 1.1 million (physical), 335,025 (digital/electronic); Serial titles: 12,015 (physical), 80,609 (digital/electronic). Students can reserve study rooms. *Research affiliation:* Civic Federation (public services), Metro Chicago Information Center (public services), International Institute of Higher Studies in the Criminal Sciences (law).

Computer facilities: Computer purchase and lease plans are available. A campuswide network can be accessed from student residence rooms and from off campus. Online class registration, tuition payments, degree progress, financial aid, transcript requests, housing services, student employment information are available.
Website: http://www.depaul.edu/

GRADUATE UNITS

College of Communication Expenses: Contact institution. *Financial support:* Applicants required to submit FAFSA. *Program availability:* Part-time, evening/weekend. Offers digital communication and media arts (MA); health communication (MA); journalism (MA); media and cinema studies (MA); multicultural communication (MA); organizational communication (MA); public relations and advertising (MA); relational communication (MA). *Application deadline:* For fall admission, 6/1 priority date for domestic students; for winter admission, 10/1 priority date for domestic students; for spring admission, 2/15 priority date for domestic students. Applications are processed on a rolling basis. *Application fee:* $40. Electronic applications accepted. *Application Contact:* Ann Spittle, Director of Graduate Admission, 773-325-7315, Fax: 312-362-8620, E-mail: graddepaul@depaul.edu. *Dean*, Salma Ghanem, 312-362-8600, Fax: 312-362-8620.

College of Computing and Digital Media Expenses: Contact institution. *Financial support:* Fellowships with full tuition reimbursements, research assistantships with full and partial tuition reimbursements, teaching assistantships with full and partial tuition reimbursements, Federal Work-Study, scholarships/grants, tuition waivers (full and partial), and unspecified assistantships available. Support available to part-time students. Financial award application deadline: 4/20; financial award applicants required to submit FAFSA. *Program availability:* Part-time, evening/weekend, online learning. Offers animation (MA, MFA); applied technology (MS); business information technology (MS); computational finance (MS); computer and information sciences (PhD); computer science (MS); creative producing (MFA); cybersecurity (MS); data science (MS); digital communication and media arts (MA); documentary (MFA); e-commerce technology (MS); experience design (MA); film and television (MS); film and television directing (MFA); game design (MFA); game programming (MS); health informatics (MS); human centered design (PhD); human-computer interaction (MS); information systems (MS); network engineering and security (MS); product innovation and computing (MS); screenwriting (MFA); software engineering (MS). *Application deadline:* For fall admission, 8/1 priority date for domestic students, 6/15 priority date for international students; for winter admission, 12/1 priority date for domestic students, 10/15 priority date for international students; for spring admission, 3/1 priority date for domestic students, 1/15 priority date for international students; for summer admission, 5/1 for domestic students, 4/15 for international students. Applications are processed on a rolling basis. *Application fee:* $25. Electronic applications accepted. *Application Contact:* Office of Admission, 312-362-8714, E-mail: admission@cdm.depaul.edu. *Communications Manager*, Elly Kafritsas-Wessels, 312-362-5816, Fax: 312-362-5185, E-mail: ekafrits@cdm.depaul.edu.

College of Education Expenses: Contact institution. *Financial support:* Application deadline: 12/31; applicants required to submit FAFSA. *Program availability:* Part-time, evening/weekend, online learning. Offers bilingual-bicultural education (M Ed, MA); counseling (M Ed, MA); curriculum studies (M Ed, MA, Ed D); early childhood education (M Ed, MA, Ed D); educational leadership (M Ed, MA, Ed D); elementary education (M Ed, MA); middle grades education (M Ed); middle school mathematics education (MS); reading specialist (M Ed, MA); secondary education (M Ed, MA); social and cultural foundations in education (M Ed, MA); special education (M Ed); sport, fitness and recreation leadership (MS); value-creating education for global citizenship (M Ed); world languages education (M Ed, MA). *Application deadline:* Applications are processed on a rolling basis. *Application fee:* $40. Electronic applications accepted. *Application Contact:* Dr. Paul Zionts, Dean, 773-325-7581, Fax: 773-325-7713, E-mail: pzionts@depaul.edu. *Dean*, Dr. Paul Zionts, 773-325-7581, Fax: 773-325-7713, E-mail: pzionts@depaul.edu.

College of Law Expenses: Contact institution. *Financial support:* Application deadline: 3/1; applicants required to submit FAFSA. *Program availability:* Part-time, evening/weekend. Offers business law and taxation (MJ); criminal law (MJ); health and intellectual property law (MJ); health care compliance (MJ); health law (LL M, MJ); intellectual property law (LL M); international and comparative law (MJ); international law (LL M); law (JD); public interest law (MJ); taxation (LL M); U.S. legal studies (LL M). *Application deadline:* For fall admission, 3/1 for domestic and international students. Applications are processed on a rolling basis. Electronic applications accepted. *Application Contact:* Amanda Noascono, Director of Law Admissions/Assistant Dean, 312-362-8807, Fax: 312-362-5280, E-mail: lawinfo@depaul.edu. *Dean*, Jennifer Rosato Perea, 312-362-8701, E-mail: jrosato@depaul.edu.

College of Liberal Arts and Social Sciences Expenses: Contact institution. *Financial support:* Applicants required to submit FAFSA. *Program availability:* Part-time, evening/weekend, online learning. Offers Arabic (MA); Chinese (MA); critical ethnic studies (MA); English (MA); French (MA); German (MA); history (MA); interdisciplinary studies (MA, MS); international public service (MS); international studies (MA); Italian (MA); Japanese (MA); liberal studies (MA); nonprofit management (MNM); public administration (MPA); public health (MPH); public policy (MPP); public service management (MS); refugee and forced migration studies (MS); social work (MSW); sociology (MA); Spanish (MA); sustainable urban development (MA); women's and gender studies (MA); writing and publishing (MA); writing, rhetoric and discourse (MA). *Application deadline:* Applications are processed on a rolling basis. *Application fee:* $40. Electronic applications accepted. *Application Contact:* Ann Spittle, Director of Graduate Admission, 773-325-8369, Fax: 312-476-3244, E-mail: graddepaul@depaul.edu. *Dean*, Dr. Guillermo Vasquez de Velasco, 773-325-7305.

College of Science and Health Expenses: Contact institution. *Financial support:* Applicants required to submit FAFSA. Offers applied mathematics (MS); applied statistics (MS); biological sciences (MA, MS); chemistry (MS); environmental science (MS); mathematics education (MA); mathematics for teaching (MS); nursing (MS); nursing practice (DNP); physics (MS); polymer and coatings science (MS); psychology (MS); pure mathematics (MS); science education (MS). *Application deadline:* Applications are processed on a rolling basis. *Application fee:* $40. Electronic applications accepted. *Application Contact:* Ann Spittle, Director of Graduate Admission, 773-325-7315, Fax: 312-476-3244, E-mail: graddepaul@depaul.edu. *Dean*, Dr. Gerald P. Koocher, 773-325-8300.

Kellstadt Graduate School of Business Expenses: Contact institution. *Financial support:* Application deadline: 4/1; applicants required to submit FAFSA. *Program availability:* Part-time, evening/weekend, online learning. Offers accountancy (MBA, MSA); applied economics (MBA); audit and advisory services (MS); business administration (DBA); business analytics (MS); business strategy and decision-making (MBA); computational finance (MS); economics and policy analysis (MS); enterprise risk management (MS); entrepreneurship (MBA, MS); finance (MBA, MS); general business (MBA); hospitality leadership (MBA); hospitality leadership and operational performance (MS); human resources (MS); international business (MBA); management (MBA, MS); management information systems (MBA); marketing (MBA, MS); marketing analysis (MS); marketing strategy and planning (MBA); real estate (MS); real estate finance and investment (MBA); strategy, execution and valuation (MBA); supply chain management (MS); sustainable management (MS); taxation (MS). *Application deadline:* For fall admission, 7/1 for domestic students, 6/1 for international students; for winter admission, 10/1 for domestic students, 9/1 for international students; for spring admission, 2/1 for domestic students, 1/1 for international students. Applications are processed on a rolling basis. *Application fee:* $60. Electronic applications accepted. *Application Contact:* Garry Cooke, Director of Recruitment and Admissions, 312-362-8810, Fax: 312-362-6677, E-mail: kgsb@depaul.edu. *Assistant Dean and Director*, Christa Hinton, 312-362-8810, Fax: 312-362-6677, E-mail: chinton@depaul.edu.

School for New Learning Expenses: Contact institution. *Financial support:* Applicants required to submit FAFSA. *Program availability:* Part-time, evening/weekend. Offers applied professional studies (MA); applied technology (MS); educating adults (MA). *Application deadline:* Applications are processed on a rolling basis. *Application fee:* $25. Electronic applications accepted. *Application Contact:* Russ Rogers, Director, Graduate Programs, 312-362-8512, Fax: 312-362-8809, E-mail: rrogers@depaul.edu. *Interim Dean*, Dr. Don Opitz, 312-362-8512, Fax: 312-362-8809.

School of Music Expenses: Contact institution. *Financial support:* Application deadline: 12/1; applicants required to submit FAFSA. *Program availability:* Part-time, evening/weekend. Offers composition (MM); jazz studies (MM); music education (MM); music performance (MM); performance (Certificate). *Application deadline:* For fall admission, 12/1 priority date for domestic and international students. Applications are processed on a rolling basis. *Application fee:* $40. Electronic applications accepted. *Application Contact:* Ross Beacraft, Director of Admission, 773-325-7444, Fax: 773-325-7429, E-mail: musicadmissions@depaul.edu. *Dean*, Ronald Caltabiano, 773-325-7256, Fax: 773-325-7429, E-mail: rcalt@depaul.edu.

The Theatre School Expenses: Contact institution. *Financial support:* Application deadline: 2/15; applicants required to submit FAFSA. Offers acting (MFA); arts leadership (MFA); directing (MFA). *Application deadline:* For fall admission, 12/15 priority date for domestic students, 1/1 priority date for international students. *Application fee:* $25. Electronic applications accepted. *Application Contact:* Tracee Duerson, Director of Admissions, 773-325-7999, Fax: 773-325-7744, E-mail: theatreadmissions@depaul.edu. *Dean*, John Culbert, 773-325-7917, Fax: 773-325-7920, E-mail: theatreadmissions@depaul.edu.

DEREE - THE AMERICAN COLLEGE OF GREECE, GR-153-42 Aghia Paraskevi, Athens, Greece

General Information Independent, coed, comprehensive institution.

GRADUATE UNITS

Graduate Programs

DESALES UNIVERSITY, Center Valley, PA 18034-9568

General Information Independent-religious, coed, comprehensive institution. *Enrollment:* 3,315 graduate, professional, and undergraduate students; 422 full-time matriculated graduate/professional students (290 women), 548 part-time matriculated graduate/professional students (323 women). *Enrollment by degree level:* 855 master's, 93 doctoral, 22 other advanced degrees. *Graduate faculty:* 30 full-time (20 women), 54 part-time/adjunct (21 women). *Tuition:* Part-time $840 per credit. Full-time tuition and fees vary according to course load, degree level and program. *Graduate housing:* Room and/or apartments available on a first-come, first-served basis to single students; on-campus housing not available to married students. Housing application deadline: 3/15. *Student services:* Campus safety program, career counseling, free psychological counseling, international student services, low-cost health insurance, multicultural affairs office, services for students with disabilities, teacher training. *Library facilities:* Trexler Library. *Collection:* Books: 155,243 (physical), 135,000 (digital/electronic); Serial titles: 260 (physical), 19,000 (digital/electronic); Databases: 87. Weekly public service hours: 102; students can reserve study rooms.

Computer facilities: 245 computers available on campus for general student use. A campuswide network can be accessed from student residence rooms and from off campus. Online class registration is available.
Website: http://www.desales.edu/

General Application Contact: Julia Ferraro, Director of Graduate Admissions, 610-282-1100 Ext. 1768, E-mail: gradadmissions@desales.edu.

GRADUATE UNITS

Division of Business Students: 78 full-time (44 women), 323 part-time (164 women); includes 71 minority (22 Black or African American, non-Hispanic/Latino; 17 Asian, non-Hispanic/Latino; 24 Hispanic/Latino; 8 Two or more races, non-Hispanic/Latino), 1 international. Average age 34. 213 applicants, 40% accepted, 64 enrolled. *Faculty:* 9 full-time (3 women), 32 part-time/adjunct (8 women). Expenses: Contact institution. *Financial support:* Applicants required to submit FAFSA. In 2017, 123 master's awarded. *Program availability:* Part-time, evening/weekend, 100% online, blended/hybrid learning. Offers accounting (MBA); computer information systems (MBA); finance (MBA); health care systems management (MBA); human resources management

(MBA); management (MBA); marketing (MBA); project management (MBA); self-design (MBA); supply chain management (MBA). *Application deadline:* Applications are processed on a rolling basis. *Application fee:* $50. Electronic applications accepted. *Application Contact:* Julia Ferraro, Director of Graduate Admissions, 610-282-1100 Ext. 1768, E-mail: gradadmissions@desales.edu. *Director, MBA Program*, Dr. David M. Gilfoil, 610-282-1100 Ext. 1828, Fax: 610-282-2869, E-mail: david.gilfoil@desales.edu.

Division of Healthcare Students: 282 full-time (210 women), 101 part-time (85 women); includes 39 minority (12 Black or African American, non-Hispanic/Latino; 11 Asian, non-Hispanic/Latino; 12 Hispanic/Latino; 4 Two or more races, non-Hispanic/Latino), 1 international. Average age 29. 2,884 applicants, 5% accepted, 114 enrolled. *Faculty:* 26 full-time (20 women), 30 part-time/adjunct (19 women). Expenses: Contact institution. *Financial support:* Applicants required to submit FAFSA. In 2017, 76 master's, 6 doctorates awarded. *Program availability:* Part-time. Offers adult-gerontology acute care (Post Master's Certificate); adult-gerontology acute care nurse practitioner (MSN); adult-gerontology acute certified nurse practitioner (Post Master's Certificate); adult-gerontology clinical nurse specialist (MSN, Post Master's Certificate); clinical leadership (DNP); family nurse practitioner (MSN, Post Master's Certificate); general nursing practice (DNP); nurse anesthetist (MSN); nurse educator (Post Master's Certificate, Postbaccalaureate Certificate); nurse midwife (MSN); nurse practitioner (MSN); psychiatric-mental health nurse practitioner (MSN, Post Master's Certificate). *Application deadline:* Applications are processed on a rolling basis. *Application fee:* $50. Electronic applications accepted. *Application Contact:* Julia Ferraro, Director of Graduate Admissions, 610-282-1100 Ext. 1768, E-mail: gradadmissions@desales.edu. *Dean of Graduate Education*, Ronald Nordone, 610-282-1100 Ext. 1289, E-mail: ronald.nordone@desales.edu.

Division of Liberal Arts and Social Sciences Students: 54 full-time (36 women), 112 part-time (68 women); includes 23 minority (3 Black or African American, non-Hispanic/Latino; 1 Asian, non-Hispanic/Latino; 17 Hispanic/Latino; 2 Two or more races, non-Hispanic/Latino), 1 international. Average age 33. 114 applicants, 64% accepted, 41 enrolled. *Faculty:* 5 full-time (3 women), 15 part-time/adjunct (9 women). Expenses: Contact institution. *Financial support:* Applicants required to submit FAFSA. In 2017, 41 master's awarded. *Program availability:* Part-time, 100% online, blended/hybrid learning. Offers criminal justice (MCJ); digital forensics (MCJ, Postbaccalaureate Certificate); education (M Ed); investigative forensics (MCJ, Postbaccalaureate Certificate). *Application deadline:* Applications are processed on a rolling basis. *Application fee:* $50. Electronic applications accepted. *Application Contact:* Julia Ferraro, Director of Graduate Admissions, 610-282-1100 Ext. 1768, E-mail: gradadmissions@desales.edu. *Dean of Graduate Education*, Ronald Nordone, 610-282-1100 Ext. 1289, E-mail: ronald.nordone@desales.edu.

Division of Science and Mathematics Students: 8 full-time (0 women), 12 part-time (6 women); includes 3 minority (1 Asian, non-Hispanic/Latino; 1 Hispanic/Latino; 1 Two or more races, non-Hispanic/Latino), 1 international. Average age 35. 35 applicants, 31% accepted, 5 enrolled. *Faculty:* 1 (woman) full-time, 2 part-time/adjunct (0 women). Expenses: Contact institution. *Financial support:* Applicants required to submit FAFSA. In 2017, 6 master's awarded. *Program availability:* Part-time, evening/weekend, 100% online, blended/hybrid learning. Offers cyber security (Postbaccalaureate Certificate); data analytics (Postbaccalaureate Certificate); information systems (MS). *Application deadline:* Applications are processed on a rolling basis. *Application fee:* $50. Electronic applications accepted. *Application Contact:* Julia Ferraro, Director of Graduate Admissions, 610-282-1100 Ext. 1768, E-mail: gradadmissions@desales.edu. *Director/Assistant Professor of Computer Science*, Dr. Patricia Riola, 610-282-1100 Ext. 1647, E-mail: patricia.riola@desales.edu.

DES MOINES UNIVERSITY, Des Moines, IA 50312-4104

General Information Independent, coed, graduate-only institution. *Graduate housing:* On-campus housing not available.

GRADUATE UNITS

College of Health Sciences *Program availability:* Part-time, evening/weekend. Offers health sciences (MHA, MPH, MS, DPT); healthcare administration (MHA); physical therapy (DPT); physician assistant (MS); public health (MPH). Electronic applications accepted.

College of Osteopathic Medicine Offers anatomy (MS); biomedical sciences (MS); osteopathic medicine (DO). Electronic applications accepted.

College of Podiatric Medicine and Surgery Offers podiatric medicine and surgery (DPM). Electronic applications accepted.

DEVRY COLLEGE OF NEW YORK–MIDTOWN MANHATTAN CAMPUS, New York, NY 10016

General Information Proprietary, coed, comprehensive institution.

GRADUATE UNITS

Keller Graduate School of Management Offers management (M Acc, MAFM, MBA, MHRM, MISM, MNCM, MPA, MPM).

DEVRY UNIVERSITY–ALPHARETTA CAMPUS, Alpharetta, GA 30009

General Information Proprietary, coed, comprehensive institution.

GRADUATE UNITS

Keller Graduate School of Management Offers management (MAFM, MBA, MHRM, MISM, MNCM, MPA, MPM).

DEVRY UNIVERSITY–ARLINGTON CAMPUS, Arlington, VA 22202

General Information Proprietary, coed, comprehensive institution.

GRADUATE UNITS

Keller Graduate School of Management Offers management (M Acc, MAFM, MBA, MHRM, MISM, MPM).

DEVRY UNIVERSITY–CHARLOTTE CAMPUS, Charlotte, NC 28273

General Information Proprietary, coed, comprehensive institution.

GRADUATE UNITS

Keller Graduate School of Management Offers management (MAFM, MBA, MHRM, MISM, MNCM, MPA, MPM).

DEVRY UNIVERSITY–CHESAPEAKE CAMPUS, Chesapeake, VA 23320

General Information Proprietary, coed, comprehensive institution.

GRADUATE UNITS

Keller Graduate School of Management Offers management (MAFM, MBA, MHRM, MISM, MNCM, MPA, MPM).

DEVRY UNIVERSITY–CHICAGO CAMPUS, Chicago, IL 60618

General Information Proprietary, coed, comprehensive institution.

GRADUATE UNITS

Keller Graduate School of Management Offers management (M Acc, MAFM, MBA, MHRM, MISM, MPM).

DEVRY UNIVERSITY–CHICAGO LOOP CAMPUS, Chicago, IL 60606

General Information Proprietary, coed, comprehensive institution.

GRADUATE UNITS

Keller Graduate School of Management Offers management (MAFM, MBA, MHRM, MISM, MNCM, MPM).

DEVRY UNIVERSITY–CINCINNATI CAMPUS, Cincinnati, OH 45249

General Information Proprietary, coed, comprehensive institution.

GRADUATE UNITS

Keller Graduate School of Management Offers management (MAFM, MBA, MHRM, MISM, MNCM, MPA, MPM).

DEVRY UNIVERSITY–COLUMBUS CAMPUS, Columbus, OH 43209

General Information Proprietary, coed, comprehensive institution.

GRADUATE UNITS

Keller Graduate School of Management Offers management (MAFM, MBA, MHRM, MISM, MPM).

DEVRY UNIVERSITY–DECATUR CAMPUS, Decatur, GA 30030

General Information Proprietary, coed, comprehensive institution.

GRADUATE UNITS

Keller Graduate School of Management Offers management (MAFM, MBA, MHRM, MISM, MNCM, MPA, MPM, MSA).

DEVRY UNIVERSITY–FOLSOM CAMPUS, Folsom, CA 95630

General Information Proprietary, coed, comprehensive institution.

GRADUATE UNITS

Graduate Programs

DEVRY UNIVERSITY–FREMONT CAMPUS, Fremont, CA 94555

General Information Proprietary, coed, comprehensive institution.

GRADUATE UNITS

Keller Graduate School of Management Offers management (MAFM, MBA, MHRM, MISM, MNCM, MPA, MPM).

DEVRY UNIVERSITY–FT. WASHINGTON CAMPUS, Fort Washington, PA 19034

General Information Proprietary, coed, comprehensive institution.

GRADUATE UNITS

Keller Graduate School of Management Offers management (MAFM, MBA, MHRM, MISM, MNCM, MPA, MPM).

DEVRY UNIVERSITY–HENDERSON CAMPUS, Henderson, NV 89074

General Information Proprietary, coed, comprehensive institution.

GRADUATE UNITS

Keller Graduate School of Management Offers management (MAFM, MBA, MHRM, MISM, MNCM, MPA, MPM).

DEVRY UNIVERSITY–IRVING CAMPUS, Irving, TX 75063

General Information Proprietary, coed, comprehensive institution.

GRADUATE UNITS

Keller Graduate School of Management Offers management (M Acc, MAFM, MBA, MHRM, MISM, MPM).

DEVRY UNIVERSITY–JACKSONVILLE CAMPUS, Jacksonville, FL 32256

General Information Proprietary, coed, comprehensive institution.

GRADUATE UNITS

Keller Graduate School of Management Offers management (MAFM, MBA, MHRM, MISM, MNCM, MPA, MPM).

DEVRY UNIVERSITY–LONG BEACH CAMPUS, Long Beach, CA 90806

General Information Proprietary, coed, comprehensive institution.

GRADUATE UNITS

Keller Graduate School of Management Offers management (MAFM, MBA, MHRM, MISM, MNCM, MPA, MPM).

DEVRY UNIVERSITY–MIRAMAR CAMPUS, Miramar, FL 33027

General Information Proprietary, coed, comprehensive institution.

GRADUATE UNITS

Keller Graduate School of Management Offers management (MAFM, MBA, MHRM, MISM, MPM, MSA).

DEVRY UNIVERSITY–MORRISVILLE CAMPUS, Morrisville, NC 27560

General Information Proprietary, coed, comprehensive institution.

GRADUATE UNITS

Keller Graduate School of Management Offers management (MBA, MHRM, MISM, MNCM, MPA, MPM).

DEVRY UNIVERSITY–NASHVILLE CAMPUS, Nashville, TN 37211

General Information Proprietary, coed, comprehensive institution.

GRADUATE UNITS

Keller Graduate School of Management Offers management (MAFM, MBA, MHRM, MISM, MNCM, MPA, MPM).

DEVRY UNIVERSITY–NORTH BRUNSWICK CAMPUS, North Brunswick, NJ 08902
General Information Proprietary, coed, comprehensive institution.
GRADUATE UNITS
Keller Graduate School of Management Offers management (MBA).

DEVRY UNIVERSITY ONLINE, Addison, IL 60101
General Information Proprietary, coed, comprehensive institution.
GRADUATE UNITS
Keller Graduate School of Management

DEVRY UNIVERSITY–ORLANDO CAMPUS, Orlando, FL 32819
General Information Proprietary, coed, comprehensive institution.
GRADUATE UNITS
Keller Graduate School of Management Offers management (MAFM, MBA, MHRM, MISM, MPA, MPM, MSA).

DEVRY UNIVERSITY–PHOENIX CAMPUS, Phoenix, AZ 85021
General Information Proprietary, coed, comprehensive institution.
GRADUATE UNITS
Keller Graduate School of Management Offers management (MAFM, MBA, MISM, MPM, MSA).

DEVRY UNIVERSITY–POMONA CAMPUS, Pomona, CA 91768
General Information Proprietary, coed, comprehensive institution.
GRADUATE UNITS
Keller Graduate School of Management Offers management (MAFM, MBA, MHRM, MISM, MPM, MSA).

DEVRY UNIVERSITY–SAN DIEGO CAMPUS, San Diego, CA 92108
General Information Proprietary, coed, comprehensive institution.
GRADUATE UNITS
Keller Graduate School of Management Offers management (MAFM, MBA, MHRM, MISM, MNCM, MPA, MPM, Graduate Certificate).

DEVRY UNIVERSITY–SEVEN HILLS CAMPUS, Seven Hills, OH 44131
General Information Proprietary, coed, comprehensive institution.
GRADUATE UNITS
Keller Graduate School of Management Offers management (MAFM, MBA, MHRM, MISM, MNCM, MPA, MPM, Graduate Certificate).

DEVRY UNIVERSITY–TINLEY PARK CAMPUS, Tinley Park, IL 60477
General Information Proprietary, coed, comprehensive institution.
GRADUATE UNITS
Keller Graduate School of Management Offers management (MAFM, MBA, MHRM, MISM, MNCM, MPA, MPM).

DIGIPEN INSTITUTE OF TECHNOLOGY, Redmond, WA 98052
General Information Proprietary, coed, comprehensive institution. *Enrollment:* 1,102 graduate, professional, and undergraduate students; 44 full-time matriculated graduate/professional students (7 women), 30 part-time matriculated graduate/professional students (6 women). *Enrollment by degree level:* 74 master's. *Graduate faculty:* 36 full-time (8 women), 16 part-time/adjunct (1 woman). *Tuition:* Full-time $18,540; part-time $1030 per credit hour. *Required fees:* $200; $100 per semester. Tuition and fees vary according to program. *Graduate housing:* Room and/or apartments available on a first-come, first-served basis to single students; on-campus housing not available to married students. Housing application deadline: 6/1. *Student services:* Campus employment opportunities, career counseling, free psychological counseling, international student services, multicultural affairs office, services for students with disabilities. *Library facilities:* DigiPen Library plus 1 other. *Collection:* Books: 4,484 (physical), 186,538 (digital/electronic); Serial titles: 1,235 (physical), 5,028 (digital/electronic); Databases: 11. Weekly public service hours: 72. *Research affiliation:* NorthWest Research Associates (NWRA) (atmospheric modeling), Andretti Autosport (software development), Boeing (simulations), Lotus Formula 1 (software development).
Computer facilities: 794 computers available on campus for general student use. A campuswide network can be accessed from student residence rooms and from off campus. Online class registration is available.
Website: http://www.digipen.edu/
General Application Contact: Danial Powers, Director of Admissions, 425-629-5071, Fax: 425-558-0378, E-mail: dpowers@digipen.edu.
GRADUATE UNITS
Graduate Programs Students: 44 full-time (7 women), 30 part-time (6 women); includes 31 minority (1 Black or African American, non-Hispanic/Latino; 23 Asian, non-Hispanic/Latino; 5 Hispanic/Latino; 2 Two or more races, non-Hispanic/Latino), 15 international. Average age 28. 122 applicants, 37% accepted, 30 enrolled. *Faculty:* 36 full-time (8 women), 16 part-time/adjunct (1 woman). Expenses: Contact institution. *Financial support:* Fellowships, career-related internships or fieldwork, and scholarships/grants available. Financial award application deadline: 5/1; financial award applicants required to submit FAFSA. In 2017, 17 master's awarded. *Program availability:* Part-time. Offers computer science (MS); digital art and animation (MFA). *Application deadline:* For fall admission, 2/1 priority date for domestic and international students; for spring admission, 7/1 for domestic and international students. Applications are processed on a rolling basis. *Application fee:* $60. Electronic applications accepted. *Application Contact:* Danial Powers, Director of Admissions, 425-629-5071, Fax: 425-558-0378, E-mail: dpowers@digipen.edu. *Senior Vice President*, Angela Kugler, 425-895-4438, Fax: 425-558-0378, E-mail: akugler@digipen.edu.

DIVINE MERCY UNIVERSITY, Arlington, VA 30327
General Information Independent-religious, coed, graduate-only institution.
GRADUATE UNITS
Institute for the Psychological Sciences *Program availability:* Part-time. Offers clinical psychology (Psy D).
School of Counseling *Program availability:* Online learning. Offers clinical mental health counseling (MS); psychology (MS).

DOANE UNIVERSITY, Crete, NE 68333-2430
General Information Independent-religious, coed, comprehensive institution. *Enrollment:* 1,069 graduate, professional, and undergraduate students; 398 full-time matriculated graduate/professional students (288 women), 614 part-time matriculated graduate/professional students (476 women). *Enrollment by degree level:* 829 master's, 75 doctoral, 108 other advanced degrees. *Graduate faculty:* 15 full-time (10 women), 102 part-time/adjunct (70 women). *Graduate housing:* On-campus housing not available. *Student services:* Career counseling, teacher training. *Library facilities:* Perkins Library plus 1 other. *Collection:* Study areas open 24 hours, 5–7 days a week; students can reserve study rooms.
Computer facilities: Computer purchase and lease plans are available. 250 computers available on campus for general student use. A campuswide network can be accessed from student residence rooms and from off campus. Online class registration is available.
Website: http://www.doane.edu/
General Application Contact: 402-466-4774, Fax: 402-466-4228, E-mail: enrollment@doane.edu.
GRADUATE UNITS
Program in Counseling Students: 61 full-time (48 women), 20 part-time (14 women); includes 9 minority (1 Black or African American, non-Hispanic/Latino; 1 American Indian or Alaska Native, non-Hispanic/Latino; 6 Hispanic/Latino; 1 Two or more races, non-Hispanic/Latino), 4 international. Average age 34. *Faculty:* 2 full-time (1 woman), 15 part-time/adjunct (11 women). Expenses: Contact institution. *Financial support:* Unspecified assistantships available. Financial award application deadline: 6/1; financial award applicants required to submit FAFSA. In 2017, 37 master's awarded. *Program availability:* Evening/weekend. Offers counseling (MAC). *Application deadline:* Applications are processed on a rolling basis. *Application fee:* $25. Electronic applications accepted. *Application Contact:* Jean Kilnoski, Assistant Dean, 402-466-4774, Fax: 404-466-4228, E-mail: jean.kilnoski@doane.edu. *Associate Dean/Director of the Counseling Program*, 402-466-4774, Fax: 402-466-4228.
Program in Education Students: 228 full-time (172 women), 541 part-time (433 women); includes 51 minority (21 Black or African American, non-Hispanic/Latino; 4 American Indian or Alaska Native, non-Hispanic/Latino; 4 Asian, non-Hispanic/Latino; 12 Hispanic/Latino; 1 Native Hawaiian or other Pacific Islander, non-Hispanic/Latino; 9 Two or more races, non-Hispanic/Latino). Average age 33. *Faculty:* 10 full-time (7 women), 66 part-time/adjunct (50 women). Expenses: Contact institution. *Financial support:* Applicants required to submit FAFSA. In 2017, 284 master's, 1 other advanced degree awarded. *Program availability:* Part-time, evening/weekend. Offers curriculum and instruction (M Ed); curriculum leadership (Ed S); education (Ed D); educational leadership (M Ed); school counseling (M Ed). *Application deadline:* Applications are processed on a rolling basis. Electronic applications accepted. *Application Contact:* Leah Schaber, Assistant Dean, 402-464-1223, Fax: 402-466-4228, E-mail: leah.schaber@doane.edu. *Dean*, Dr. Lyn C. Forester, 402-826-8604, Fax: 402-826-8278.
Program in Management Students: 109 full-time (68 women), 53 part-time (29 women); includes 26 minority (13 Black or African American, non-Hispanic/Latino; 1 American Indian or Alaska Native, non-Hispanic/Latino; 5 Asian, non-Hispanic/Latino; 5 Hispanic/Latino; 2 Two or more races, non-Hispanic/Latino), 6 international. Average age 36. *Faculty:* 3 full-time (2 women), 21 part-time/adjunct (9 women). Expenses: Contact institution. *Financial support:* Application deadline: 6/1; applicants required to submit FAFSA. In 2017, 54 master's awarded. *Program availability:* Part-time, evening/weekend. Offers management (MA, MBA). *Application deadline:* Applications are processed on a rolling basis. *Application fee:* $25. Electronic applications accepted. *Application Contact:* Cathy Dillon, Director of Academic Advising, 402-466-4774, Fax: 404-466-4228, E-mail: cathy.dillon@doane.edu. *Director of Graduate Business Program*, Dr. Debora Sepich, 880-333-6263, E-mail: deb.sepich@doane.edu.

DOMINICAN COLLEGE, Orangeburg, NY 10962-1210
General Information Independent, coed, comprehensive institution. *Enrollment:* 1,954 graduate, professional, and undergraduate students; 175 full-time matriculated graduate/professional students (130 women), 354 part-time matriculated graduate/professional students (245 women). *Enrollment by degree level:* 265 master's, 264 doctoral. *Graduate faculty:* 14 full-time (6 women), 26 part-time/adjunct (18 women). *Tuition:* Part-time $900 per credit. One-time fee: $200. Tuition and fees vary according to degree level and program. *Graduate housing:* Room and/or apartments available on a first-come, first-served basis to single students; on-campus housing not available to married students. Housing application deadline: 5/1. *Student services:* Campus employment opportunities, campus safety program, career counseling, free psychological counseling, services for students with disabilities, teacher training, writing training. *Library facilities:* Sullivan Library plus 1 other. *Collection:* Books: 74,226 (physical), 117,187 (digital/electronic); Serial titles: 610 (physical), 75,067 (digital/electronic); Databases: 85. Weekly public service hours: 89; students can reserve study rooms.
Computer facilities: 150 computers available on campus for general student use. A campuswide network can be accessed from student residence rooms and from off campus. Online class registration, Web portal, learning management system are available.
Website: http://www.dc.edu/
General Application Contact: Christina Lifshey, Assistant Director of Graduate Admissions, 845-848-7908, Fax: 845-365-3150, E-mail: graduate.admissions@dc.edu.
GRADUATE UNITS
Division of Allied Health Students: 152 full-time (108 women), 191 part-time (116 women); includes 146 minority (11 Black or African American, non-Hispanic/Latino; 1 American Indian or Alaska Native, non-Hispanic/Latino; 97 Asian, non-Hispanic/Latino; 26 Hispanic/Latino; 3 Native Hawaiian or other Pacific Islander, non-Hispanic/Latino; 8 Two or more races, non-Hispanic/Latino), 36 international. Average age 37. *Faculty:* 10 full-time (4 women), 26 part-time/adjunct (18 women). Expenses: Contact institution. *Financial support:* Applicants required to submit FAFSA. In 2017, 54 master's, 112 doctorates awarded. *Program availability:* Part-time, evening/weekend, online learning. Offers allied health (MS, DPT); occupational therapy (MS); physical therapy (MS, DPT). *Application deadline:* Applications are processed on a rolling basis. *Application fee:* $50. Electronic applications accepted. *Application Contact:* Christina Lifshey, Assistant Director of Graduate Admissions, 845-848-7900, Fax: 845-365-3150, E-mail: admissions@dc.edu. *Coordinator of Academic Study and Fieldwork*, Margaret Boyd, 845-848-6033, Fax: 845-398-4893, E-mail: margaret.boyd@dc.edu.
Division of Nursing Students: 19 full-time (18 women), 94 part-time (84 women); includes 59 minority (17 Black or African American, non-Hispanic/Latino; 20 Asian, non-Hispanic/Latino; 20 Hispanic/Latino; 2 Two or more races, non-Hispanic/Latino), 2 international. *Faculty:* 1 (woman) full-time. Expenses: Contact institution. *Financial*

support: Application deadline: 2/1; applicants required to submit FAFSA. In 2017, 16 master's, 7 doctorates awarded. *Program availability:* Part-time, evening/weekend. Offers nursing (MSN, DNP). *Application deadline:* Applications are processed on a rolling basis. *Application fee:* $50. Electronic applications accepted. *Application Contact:* Heather Bergling, Assistant Director of Graduate Admissions, 845-848-7908, Fax: 845-365-3150, E-mail: admissions@dc.edu. *Director*, Dr. Nancy DiDona, 845-848-6051, Fax: 845-398-4891, E-mail: nancy.didona@dc.edu.

Division of Teacher Education Students: 3 full-time (all women), 48 part-time (30 women); includes 9 minority (1 Black or African American, non-Hispanic/Latino; 1 Asian, non-Hispanic/Latino; 7 Hispanic/Latino). *Faculty:* 2 full-time (1 woman), 7 part-time/adjunct (all women). Expenses: Contact institution. *Financial support:* Application deadline: 2/1; applicants required to submit FAFSA. In 2017, 18 master's awarded. *Program availability:* Part-time, evening/weekend, online learning. Offers education/teaching of individuals with multiple disabilities (MS Ed). *Application deadline:* Applications are processed on a rolling basis. *Application Contact:* Christina Lifshey, Assistant Director of Graduate Admissions, 845-848-7908 Ext. 15, Fax: 845-365-3150, E-mail: admissions@dc.edu. *Director*, Dr. Mike Kelly, 845-848-4090, Fax: 845-359-7802, E-mail: mike.kelly@dc.edu.

MBA Program Students: 1 (woman) full-time, 21 part-time (15 women); includes 11 minority (6 Black or African American, non-Hispanic/Latino; 1 Asian, non-Hispanic/Latino; 3 Hispanic/Latino; 1 Two or more races, non-Hispanic/Latino), 1 international. *Faculty:* 1 full-time (0 women). Expenses: Contact institution. *Financial support:* Application deadline: 2/1; applicants required to submit FAFSA. In 2017, 14 master's awarded. *Program availability:* Part-time, evening/weekend. Offers accounting (MBA); healthcare management (MBA); management (MBA). *Application deadline:* Applications are processed on a rolling basis. *Application fee:* $50. Electronic applications accepted. *Application Contact:* Christina Lifshey, Assistant Director of Graduate Admissions, 845-848-7908, Fax: 845-365-3150, E-mail: admissions@dc.edu. *MBA Director*, Ken Mias, 845-848-4102, E-mail: ken.mias@dc.edu.

DOMINICAN HOUSE OF STUDIES, PONTIFICAL FACULTY OF THE IMMACULATE CONCEPTION, Washington, DC 20017-1585

General Information Independent-religious, coed, primarily men, graduate-only institution. *Enrollment by degree level:* 88 master's. *Graduate faculty:* 19 full-time (1 woman), 3 part-time/adjunct (2 women). *Tuition:* Full-time $16,080; part-time $670 per credit hour. *Required fees:* $280; $140 per semester. Part-time tuition and fees vary according to course load. *Graduate housing:* On-campus housing not available. *Student services:* Campus employment opportunities, career counseling, international student services. *Library facilities:* Dominican Theological Library. *Collection:* Books: 77,000 (physical); Serial titles: 219 (physical), 18 (digital/electronic); Databases: 6. Weekly public service hours: 61; students can reserve study rooms. *Research affiliation:* Washington Theological Consortium (theology, ecumenism), The Thomist (theology).

Computer facilities: 8 computers available on campus for general student use. A campuswide network can be accessed.
Website: http://www.dhs.edu/

General Application Contact: Rev. Albert Trudel, Registrar, 202-495-3836, Fax: 202-495-3873, E-mail: registrar@dhs.edu.

GRADUATE UNITS

Graduate and Professional Programs in Theology Students: 75 full-time (7 women), 9 part-time (3 women); includes 2 minority (both Asian, non-Hispanic/Latino), 13 international. Average age 33. 36 applicants, 100% accepted, 33 enrolled. *Faculty:* 18 full-time (1 woman), 6 part-time/adjunct (3 women). Expenses: Contact institution. *Financial support:* In 2017–18, 3 students received support. Career-related internships or fieldwork and Federal Work-Study available. Support available to part-time students. Financial award application deadline: 6/30; financial award applicants required to submit FAFSA. In 2017, 32 master's awarded. *Program availability:* Part-time. Offers moral theology (STL); sacred scripture (STL); systematic theology (STL); theology (M Div, MA, STB); Thomistic studies (MA, STD, STL). *Application deadline:* For fall admission, 7/1 for domestic and international students; for spring admission, 12/1 for domestic and international students. Applications are processed on a rolling basis. *Application fee:* $150. Electronic applications accepted. *Application Contact:* Rev. Albert Trudel, Registrar, 202-495-3836, Fax: 202-495-3873, E-mail: registrar@dhs.edu. *Vice-President/Academic Dean*, Rev. Thomas Petri, OP, 202-495-3832, Fax: 202-495-3873, E-mail: dean@dhs.edu.

DOMINICAN SCHOOL OF PHILOSOPHY AND THEOLOGY, Berkeley, CA 94708

General Information Independent-religious, coed, graduate-only institution. *Graduate housing:* Rooms and/or apartments available on a first-come, first-served basis to single and married students. Housing application deadline: 5/1.

GRADUATE UNITS

Graduate Programs *Program availability:* Part-time. Offers philosophy (MA); theology (M Div, MA, MTS, Certificate). Electronic applications accepted.

DOMINICAN UNIVERSITY, River Forest, IL 60305-1099

General Information Independent-religious, coed, comprehensive institution. *Enrollment:* 3,127 graduate, professional, and undergraduate students; 319 full-time matriculated graduate/professional students (271 women), 637 part-time matriculated graduate/professional students (497 women). *Enrollment by degree level:* 784 master's, 16 doctoral, 13 other advanced degrees. *Graduate faculty:* 62 full-time (38 women), 133 part-time/adjunct (101 women). *Tuition:* Part-time $850 per credit hour. Tuition and fees vary according to program. *Graduate housing:* Room and/or apartments available on a first-come, first-served basis to single students; on-campus housing not available to married students. Typical cost: $6335 (including board). Room and board charges vary according to campus/location and housing facility selected. Housing application deadline: 7/1. *Student services:* Campus employment opportunities, campus safety program, career counseling, child daycare facilities, exercise/wellness program, free psychological counseling, international student services, low-cost health insurance, multicultural affairs office, services for students with disabilities, teacher training, writing training. *Library facilities:* Rebecca Crown Library. *Collection:* Books: 247,967 (physical), 9,389 (digital/electronic); Serial titles: 280 (physical), 53,047 (digital/electronic); Databases: 114. Weekly public service hours: 100; students can reserve study rooms.

Computer facilities: Computer purchase and lease plans are available. 550 computers available on campus for general student use. A campuswide network can be accessed from student residence rooms and from off campus. Online class registration is available.
Website: http://www.dom.edu/

General Application Contact: Cathering Galarza-Espino, Coordinator of Graduate Marketing and Recruitment, 708-524-6983, E-mail: cgalarza@dom.edu.

GRADUATE UNITS

Brennan School of Business Students: 68 full-time (52 women), 79 part-time (48 women); includes 34 minority (10 Black or African American, non-Hispanic/Latino; 7 Asian, non-Hispanic/Latino; 14 Hispanic/Latino; 1 Native Hawaiian or other Pacific Islander, non-Hispanic/Latino; 2 Two or more races, non-Hispanic/Latino), 25 international. Average age 29. 80 applicants, 78% accepted, 40 enrolled. *Faculty:* 20 full-time (8 women), 17 part-time/adjunct (6 women). Expenses: Contact institution. *Financial support:* Research assistantships, career-related internships or fieldwork, scholarships/grants, tuition waivers (partial), and unspecified assistantships available. Financial award application deadline: 3/1; financial award applicants required to submit FAFSA. In 2017, 77 master's awarded. *Program availability:* Part-time, evening/weekend, 100% online, blended/hybrid learning. Offers business (MBA, MSA). JD/MBA offered jointly with John Marshall Law School. *Application deadline:* Applications are processed on a rolling basis. *Application fee:* $25. Electronic applications accepted. *Application Contact:* Dr. Kathleen Odell, Associate Dean, Brennan School of Business, 708-488-5394, Fax: 708-524-6939, E-mail: kodell@dom.edu. *Dean*, Dr. Roberto Curci, 708-524-6321, Fax: 708-524-6939, E-mail: rcurci@dom.edu.

School of Education Students: 5 full-time (all women), 261 part-time (206 women); includes 45 minority (16 Black or African American, non-Hispanic/Latino; 1 American Indian or Alaska Native, non-Hispanic/Latino; 5 Asian, non-Hispanic/Latino; 18 Hispanic/Latino; 5 Two or more races, non-Hispanic/Latino), 1 international. Average age 32. 95 applicants, 98% accepted, 72 enrolled. *Faculty:* 8 full-time (6 women), 42 part-time/adjunct (38 women). Expenses: Contact institution. *Financial support:* Career-related internships or fieldwork, scholarships/grants, tuition waivers (partial), and unspecified assistantships available. Support available to part-time students. Financial award application deadline: 8/15; financial award applicants required to submit FAFSA. In 2017, 206 master's awarded. *Program availability:* Part-time, evening/weekend, 100% online, blended/hybrid learning. Offers child life studies (MS); early childhood education (MS); education (MAT); elementary education (MA Ed); English as a second language (MA Ed); reading (MA Ed); secondary education (MAT); special education (MS). *Application deadline:* Applications are processed on a rolling basis. *Application fee:* $25. *Application Contact:* Benjamin Mueller, Senior Graduate Marketing and Recruitment Coordinator, 708-524-6456, Fax: 708-524-6665, E-mail: bmueller@dom.edu. *Interim Executive Director, School of Education*, Dr. Colleen Reardon, 708-524-6643, Fax: 708-524-6665, E-mail: creardon@dom.edu.

School of Information Studies Students: 58 full-time (49 women), 184 part-time (145 women); includes 53 minority (29 Black or African American, non-Hispanic/Latino; 2 Asian, non-Hispanic/Latino; 21 Hispanic/Latino; 1 Two or more races, non-Hispanic/Latino), 5 international. Average age 34. 84 applicants, 94% accepted, 52 enrolled. *Faculty:* 11 full-time (7 women), 16 part-time/adjunct (10 women). Expenses: Contact institution. *Financial support:* Fellowships, research assistantships, career-related internships or fieldwork, scholarships/grants, and unspecified assistantships available. Support available to part-time students. Financial award application deadline: 4/15; financial award applicants required to submit FAFSA. In 2017, 86 master's awarded. *Program availability:* Part-time, evening/weekend, 100% online, blended/hybrid learning. Offers information management (MSIM); knowledge management (Certificate); library and information science (MLIS, MPS, PhD); special studies (CSS). MLIS/M Div offered jointly with McCormick Theological Seminary, MLIS/MA with Loyola University Chicago, MLIS/MM with Northwestern University. *Application deadline:* For fall admission, 6/1 priority date for domestic students; for winter admission, 3/1 priority date for domestic students; for spring admission, 10/1 priority date for domestic students. Applications are processed on a rolling basis. *Application fee:* $25. *Application Contact:* Catherine Galarza-Espino, Coordinator of Graduate Marketing and Recruiting, 708-524-6983, E-mail: cgalarza@dom.edu. *Director*, Dr. Kate Marek, 708-524-6648, Fax: 708-524-6657, E-mail: kmarek@dom.edu.

School of Social Work Students: 126 full-time (112 women), 80 part-time (72 women); includes 92 minority (36 Black or African American, non-Hispanic/Latino; 4 Asian, non-Hispanic/Latino; 46 Hispanic/Latino; 2 Native Hawaiian or other Pacific Islander, non-Hispanic/Latino; 4 Two or more races, non-Hispanic/Latino), 4 international. Average age 33. 134 applicants, 81% accepted, 72 enrolled. *Faculty:* 7 full-time (4 women), 18 part-time/adjunct (15 women). Expenses: Contact institution. *Financial support:* Research assistantships with partial tuition reimbursements, Federal Work-Study, scholarships/grants, and unspecified assistantships available. Financial award applicants required to submit FAFSA. In 2017, 115 master's awarded. *Program availability:* Part-time. Offers social work (MSW). *Application deadline:* For fall admission, 7/1 for domestic and international students; for spring admission, 11/1 for domestic and international students. Applications are processed on a rolling basis. *Application fee:* $25. Electronic applications accepted. *Application Contact:* Catherine Galarza-Espino, Coordinator of Graduate Marketing and Recruiting, 708-524-6983, E-mail: cgalarza@dom.edu. *Executive Director, School of Social Work*, Dr. Julie Bach, 708-714-9102, E-mail: jbach@dom.edu.

DOMINICAN UNIVERSITY OF CALIFORNIA, San Rafael, CA 94901-2298

General Information Independent-religious, coed, comprehensive institution. *Enrollment:* 1,750 graduate, professional, and undergraduate students; 263 full-time matriculated graduate/professional students (210 women), 185 part-time matriculated graduate/professional students (135 women). *Enrollment by degree level:* 448 master's. *Graduate faculty:* 47 full-time (29 women), 34 part-time/adjunct (26 women). *Tuition:* Full-time $17,370; part-time $965 per credit. *Required fees:* $150 per semester. Tuition and fees vary according to course load and program. *Graduate housing:* Room and/or apartments available on a first-come, first-served basis to single students; on-campus housing not available to married students. Typical cost: $11,760 per year. Housing application deadline: 5/1. *Student services:* Campus employment opportunities, career counseling, exercise/wellness program, free psychological counseling, international student services, low-cost health insurance, services for students with disabilities. *Library facilities:* Archbishop Alemany Library. *Collection:* Books: 110,523 (physical); Databases: 84.

Computer facilities: 195 computers available on campus for general student use. A campuswide network can be accessed from student residence rooms. Online class registration, office software are available.
Website: http://www.dominican.edu/

General Application Contact: Graduate Admissions, 415-485-3280, Fax: 415-485-3214, E-mail: gradmissions@dominican.edu.

GRADUATE UNITS

Barowsky School of Business Students: 14 full-time (7 women), 24 part-time (13 women); includes 19 minority (4 Black or African American, non-Hispanic/Latino; 5 Asian, non-Hispanic/Latino; 7 Hispanic/Latino; 1 Native Hawaiian or other Pacific

Islander, non-Hispanic/Latino; 2 Two or more races, non-Hispanic/Latino), 3 international. Average age 36. 35 applicants, 71% accepted, 15 enrolled. *Faculty:* 9 full-time (2 women). Expenses: Contact institution. *Financial support:* In 2017–18, 18 students received support. Scholarships/grants available. Support available to part-time students. Financial award application deadline: 3/2; financial award applicants required to submit FAFSA. In 2017, 36 master's awarded. *Program availability:* Part-time, evening/weekend. Offers business (MBA); healthcare leadership (MBA). MBA in healthcare leadership offered jointly with School of Health and Natural Sciences. *Application deadline:* For fall admission, 5/15 priority date for domestic and international students; for spring admission, 11/15 priority date for domestic and international students. Applications are processed on a rolling basis. *Application fee:* $0. Electronic applications accepted. *Application Contact:* Michael Lavigna, Assistant Director, Graduate Admissions, 415-485-3253, Fax: 415-485-3214, E-mail: gradmissions@dominican.edu. *Dean,* Dr. Sam Beldona, 415-458-3737, E-mail: sriam.beldona@dominican.edu.

Programs in Education plus Teacher Preparation Students: 51 full-time (38 women), 79 part-time (59 women); includes 29 minority (1 Black or African American, non-Hispanic/Latino; 1 American Indian or Alaska Native, non-Hispanic/Latino; 4 Asian, non-Hispanic/Latino; 16 Hispanic/Latino; 2 Native Hawaiian or other Pacific Islander, non-Hispanic/Latino; 5 Two or more races, non-Hispanic/Latino). Average age 35. 44 applicants, 98% accepted, 35 enrolled. *Faculty:* 9 full-time (7 women), 10 part-time/adjunct (9 women). Expenses: Contact institution. *Financial support:* In 2017–18, 61 students received support. Scholarships/grants available. Support available to part-time students. Financial award application deadline: 3/2; financial award applicants required to submit FAFSA. In 2017, 37 master's awarded. *Program availability:* Part-time, evening/weekend. Offers multiple subject (MS); single subject (MS). *Application deadline:* For fall admission, 5/15 priority date for domestic and international students; for spring admission, 11/15 priority date for domestic and international students. Applications are processed on a rolling basis. *Application fee:* $0. Electronic applications accepted. *Application Contact:* Michael Lavigna, Assistant Director, Graduate Admissions, 415-485-3246, Fax: 415-485-3253, E-mail: gradmissions@dominican.edu. *Director of Operations,* Pauline Camp, 415-458-3779, E-mail: pauline.camp@dominican.edu.

School of Health and Natural Sciences Students: 192 full-time (160 women), 56 part-time (42 women); includes 111 minority (6 Black or African American, non-Hispanic/Latino; 59 Asian, non-Hispanic/Latino; 33 Hispanic/Latino; 2 Native Hawaiian or other Pacific Islander, non-Hispanic/Latino; 11 Two or more races, non-Hispanic/Latino), 3 international. Average age 32. 165 applicants, 96% accepted, 105 enrolled. *Faculty:* 22 full-time (16 women), 23 part-time/adjunct (16 women). Expenses: Contact institution. *Financial support:* In 2017–18, 32 students received support. Career-related internships or fieldwork and scholarships/grants available. Financial award application deadline: 3/2; financial award applicants required to submit FAFSA. In 2017, 68 master's awarded. Offers biological sciences (MS); clinical laboratory sciences (MS); general (MS); health and natural sciences (MS); marriage and family therapy (MS); occupational therapy (MS). *Application deadline:* For fall admission, 3/15 for domestic and international students. Applications are processed on a rolling basis. *Application fee:* $0. Electronic applications accepted. *Application Contact:* Michael Lavigna, Associate Director of Graduate Admissions, 415-485-3253, Fax: 415-485-3214, E-mail: gradmissions@dominican.edu. *Dean,* Dr. Ruth Ramsey, 415-257-1393, E-mail: ruth.ramsey@dominican.edu.

School of Liberal Arts and Education Students: 57 full-time (43 women), 99 part-time (75 women); includes 37 minority (4 Black or African American, non-Hispanic/Latino; 1 American Indian or Alaska Native, non-Hispanic/Latino; 4 Asian, non-Hispanic/Latino; 20 Hispanic/Latino; 2 Native Hawaiian or other Pacific Islander, non-Hispanic/Latino; 6 Two or more races, non-Hispanic/Latino), 2 international. Average age 37. 63 applicants, 98% accepted, 41 enrolled. *Faculty:* 17 full-time (11 women), 11 part-time/adjunct (10 women). Expenses: Contact institution. *Financial support:* In 2017–18, 69 students received support. Scholarships/grants available. Support available to part-time students. Financial award application deadline: 3/2; financial award applicants required to submit FAFSA. In 2017, 51 master's awarded. *Program availability:* Part-time, evening/weekend. Offers applied music (MA); art history (MA); creative writing (MA); gender studies (MA); history (MA); liberal arts and education (MA); philosophy (MA); political theory (MA); religion (MA). *Application deadline:* For fall admission, 5/15 for domestic and international students; for spring admission, 11/15 for domestic and international students. Applications are processed on a rolling basis. *Application fee:* $0. Electronic applications accepted. *Application Contact:* Michael Lavigna, Assistant Director of Graduate Admissions, 415-485-3253, Fax: 415-485-3214, E-mail: gradmissions@dominican.edu. *Dean,* Laura Stivers, 415-458-3734, E-mail: laura.stivers@dominican.edu.

DONGGUK UNIVERSITY LOS ANGELES, Los Angeles, CA 90020

General Information Independent, coed, graduate-only institution. *Graduate housing:* On-campus housing not available.

GRADUATE UNITS

Program in Oriental Medicine *Program availability:* Part-time, evening/weekend. Offers Oriental medicine (MS).

DORDT COLLEGE, Sioux Center, IA 51250-1697

General Information Independent-religious, coed, comprehensive institution. *Graduate housing:* Rooms and/or apartments available to single and married students.

GRADUATE UNITS

Program in Education *Program availability:* Part-time, online learning. Offers education (M Ed). Electronic applications accepted.

DRAGON RISES COLLEGE OF ORIENTAL MEDICINE, Gainesville, FL 32601

General Information Proprietary, coed, graduate-only institution. *Enrollment by degree level:* 45 master's. *Graduate faculty:* 2 full-time (0 women), 12 part-time/adjunct (7 women). *Tuition:* Full-time $11,000. *Required fees:* $365. One-time fee: $75 full-time. *Student services:* Career counseling. *Library facilities:* Ewa Hammer Library plus 1 other. *Collection:* Books: 1,743 (physical), 559 (digital/electronic); Serial titles: 89 (physical). Weekly public service hours: 20.

Computer facilities: 2 computers available on campus for general student use. Website: http://www.dragonrises.edu/

General Application Contact: Chantay Moxley, Director of Admissions, 352-371-2833 Ext. 27, Fax: 352-244-0003, E-mail: admissions@dragonrises.edu.

GRADUATE UNITS

Graduate Program Students: 45 full-time (35 women). *Faculty:* 2 full-time (0 women), 12 part-time/adjunct (7 women). Expenses: Contact institution. Offers Oriental medicine (MAOM). *Application fee:* $50. Electronic applications accepted. *Application Contact:* Chantay Moxley, Director of Admissions, 352-371-2833 Ext. 27, Fax: 352-244-0003, E-mail: admissions@dragonrises.edu.

DRAKE UNIVERSITY, Des Moines, IA 50311-4516

General Information Independent, coed, university. *Enrollment:* 4,904 graduate, professional, and undergraduate students; 879 full-time matriculated graduate/professional students (552 women), 927 part-time matriculated graduate/professional students (655 women). *Enrollment by degree level:* 819 master's, 578 doctoral, 95 other advanced degrees. *Graduate faculty:* 107 full-time (60 women), 70 part-time/adjunct (43 women). *Tuition:* Part-time $600 per credit hour. *Required fees:* $120 per credit hour. Tuition and fees vary according to course load and program. *Graduate housing:* Room and/or apartments available on a first-come, first-served basis to single students; on-campus housing not available to married students. Typical cost: $5486 per year ($10,158 including board). Housing application deadline: 8/1. *Student services:* Campus employment opportunities, campus safety program, career counseling, exercise/wellness program, free psychological counseling, international student services, low-cost health insurance, services for students with disabilities, teacher training, writing training. *Library facilities:* Cowles Library plus 1 other. *Collection:* Study areas open 24 hours, 5–7 days a week; students can reserve study rooms. *Research affiliation:* NASA through Iowa State University of Science and Technology (arts and sciences), Albertson's Inc. (pharmacy), U.S. Department of Agriculture (USDA) (agriculture), U.S. Department of Education (DOE) (education), Iowa Department of Education (education), National Science Foundation (biology, physics).

Computer facilities: A campuswide network can be accessed from student residence rooms and from off campus. Online class registration is available. Website: http://www.drake.edu/

General Application Contact: Jennifer Reitano, Director, Graduate Student Programs, 515-271-2188, Fax: 515-271-2831, E-mail: jennifer.reitano@drake.edu.

GRADUATE UNITS

College of Business and Public Administration Expenses: Contact institution. *Financial support:* Fellowships with tuition reimbursements, teaching assistantships, career-related internships or fieldwork, and institutionally sponsored loans available. Support available to part-time students. Financial award application deadline: 3/1; financial award applicants required to submit FAFSA. *Program availability:* Part-time, evening/weekend. Offers accounting (M Acc); business administration (MBA); public administration (MPA). *Application deadline:* For fall admission, 8/15 priority date for domestic students; for winter admission, 12/20 priority date for domestic students; for spring admission, 12/1 priority date for domestic students. Applications are processed on a rolling basis. *Application fee:* $25. Electronic applications accepted. *Application Contact:* Danette Kenne, Assistant Dean, 515-271-2188, Fax: 515-271-4518, E-mail: cbpa.gradprograms@drake.edu. *Dean,* Dr. Daniel J. Connolly, 515-271-2872, Fax: 515-271-4518, E-mail: daniel.connolly@drake.edu.

College of Pharmacy and Health Sciences Expenses: Contact institution. *Financial support:* Teaching assistantships, career-related internships or fieldwork, Federal Work-Study, institutionally sponsored loans, and scholarships/grants available. Support available to part-time students. Financial award application deadline: 3/1; financial award applicants required to submit FAFSA. Offers athletic training (MAT); occupational therapy (OTD); pharmacy (Pharm D). *Application deadline:* For fall admission, 2/1 priority date for domestic students. *Application fee:* $135. Electronic applications accepted. *Dean,* Dr. Renae Chesnut, 515-271-3018, Fax: 515-271-4171, E-mail: renae.chesnut@drake.edu.

Law School Expenses: Contact institution. *Financial support:* Research assistantships, teaching assistantships, career-related internships or fieldwork, Federal Work-Study, institutionally sponsored loans, scholarships/grants, and tuition waivers (full and partial) available. Support available to part-time students. Financial award application deadline: 3/1; financial award applicants required to submit FAFSA. *Program availability:* Part-time. Offers law (LL M, MJ, JD). *Application deadline:* For fall admission, 4/1 priority date for domestic and international students. Applications are processed on a rolling basis. *Application fee:* $40. Electronic applications accepted. *Application Contact:* Kara Blanchard, Assistant Dean for Admission and Financial Aid, 515-271-2953, Fax: 515-271-2530, E-mail: kara.blanchard@drake.edu. *Dean,* Jerry Anderson, 515-271-2658, Fax: 515-271-4118, E-mail: jerry.anderson@drake.edu.

School of Education Expenses: Contact institution. *Financial support:* Research assistantships, career-related internships or fieldwork, and unspecified assistantships available. Support available to part-time students. *Program availability:* Part-time, evening/weekend. Offers applied behavior analysis (MS); counseling (MS); education (PhD); education administration (Ed D); educational leadership (MSE, Ed D); effective teaching (MSE); leadership development (MS); literacy (Ed S); literacy education (MSE); rehabilitation administration (MS); rehabilitation placement (MS); special education (MSE); STEM education (MSE); teacher education (5-12) (MAT); teacher education (K-8) (MST); teacher effectiveness and professional development (MSE). *Application deadline:* For fall admission, 7/1 priority date for domestic students, 6/1 priority date for international students; for spring admission, 11/1 priority date for domestic students, 10/1 priority date for international students. Applications are processed on a rolling basis. *Application fee:* $25. Electronic applications accepted. *Dean,* Dr. Janet McMahill, 515-271-3829, E-mail: janet.mcmahill@drake.edu.

School of Journalism and Mass Communication Expenses: Contact institution. *Program availability:* Part-time, evening/weekend. Offers brand communication (MCL); communication leadership (MCL); public affairs and advocacy (MCL). *Dean,* Dr. Kathleen Richardson, 515-271-2295, Fax: 515-271-4518, E-mail: kathleen.richardson@drake.edu.

DREW UNIVERSITY, Madison, NJ 07940-1493

General Information Independent-religious, coed, university. CGS member. *Enrollment:* 2,117 graduate, professional, and undergraduate students; 263 full-time matriculated graduate/professional students (139 women), 309 part-time matriculated graduate/professional students (173 women). *Enrollment by degree level:* 257 master's, 295 doctoral, 20 other advanced degrees. *Graduate faculty:* 26 full-time (11 women), 53 part-time/adjunct (25 women). *Graduate housing:* Rooms and/or apartments available on a first-come, first-served basis to single and married students. Housing application deadline: 7/1. *Student services:* Campus employment opportunities, campus safety program, career counseling, child daycare facilities, exercise/wellness program, free psychological counseling, international student services, low-cost health insurance, multicultural affairs office, services for students with disabilities, teacher training, writing training. *Library facilities:* Rose Memorial Library plus 1 other. *Collection:* Books: 662,733 (physical), 288,268 (digital/electronic); Serial titles: 8,820 (physical), 121,021 (digital/electronic); Databases: 196. Weekly public service hours: 107; students can reserve study rooms. *Research affiliation:* Center for Research Libraries (humanities), Dana Rise Institute (science), St. Barnabas Medical Center (medical humanities), Overlook Hospital (medical humanities), Methodist Archives (religion).

Computer facilities: Computer purchase and lease plans are available. A campuswide network can be accessed from student residence rooms and from off campus. Online class registration is available.
Website: http://www.drew.edu/

General Application Contact: Leanne Horinko, Interim Director of Graduate Admissions, 973-408-3111, E-mail: gradm@drew.edu.

GRADUATE UNITS

Caspersen School of Graduate Studies Students: 77 full-time (42 women), 175 part-time (114 women); includes 39 minority (12 Black or African American, non-Hispanic/Latino; 6 Asian, non-Hispanic/Latino; 16 Hispanic/Latino; 5 Two or more races, non-Hispanic/Latino), 11 international. Average age 41. 126 applicants, 75% accepted, 52 enrolled. *Faculty:* 4 full-time (2 women), 29 part-time/adjunct (15 women). Expenses: Contact institution. *Financial support:* Fellowships, research assistantships, teaching assistantships, career-related internships or fieldwork, Federal Work-Study, scholarships/grants, and unspecified assistantships available. Support available to part-time students. Financial award applicants required to submit FAFSA. In 2017, 38 master's, 23 doctorates, 35 other advanced degrees awarded. *Program availability:* Part-time, evening/weekend. Offers conflict resolution and leadership (Certificate); education (M Ed); finance (MA); history and culture (MA, PhD); K-12 education (MAT); liberal studies (M Litt, D Litt); medical humanities (MMH, DMH, CMH); poetry (MFA). *Application deadline:* For fall admission, 8/1 for domestic students, 6/1 for international students; for spring admission, 12/1 for domestic students, 10/1 for international students. Applications are processed on a rolling basis. *Application fee:* $35. Electronic applications accepted. *Application Contact:* Leanne Horinko, Director of Caspersen Admissions, 973-408-3280, E-mail: gradm@drew.edu.

Theological School Students: 186 full-time (97 women), 134 part-time (59 women); includes 128 minority (85 Black or African American, non-Hispanic/Latino; 1 American Indian or Alaska Native, non-Hispanic/Latino; 17 Asian, non-Hispanic/Latino; 19 Hispanic/Latino; 6 Two or more races, non-Hispanic/Latino), 84 international. Average age 41. 201 applicants, 78% accepted, 94 enrolled. *Faculty:* 21 full-time (9 women), 20 part-time/adjunct (9 women). Expenses: Contact institution. *Financial support:* Fellowships, career-related internships or fieldwork, Federal Work-Study, institutionally sponsored loans, and scholarships/grants available. Support available to part-time students. Financial award application deadline: 2/15; financial award applicants required to submit FAFSA. In 2017, 58 master's, 33 doctorates awarded. *Program availability:* Part-time, blended/hybrid learning. Offers theology (M Div, MA, MA Min, STM, D Min, PhD, Certificate). *Application deadline:* For fall admission, 8/1 for domestic students, 4/1 for international students; for spring admission, 12/1 for domestic students, 10/1 for international students. Applications are processed on a rolling basis. *Application fee:* $35. Electronic applications accepted. *Application Contact:* Rev. Dr. Kevin D. Miller, Director of Theological Admissions, 973-408-3111, E-mail: kmiller@drew.edu. *Dean of the Theological School*, Dr. Javier Viera, 973-408-3418, E-mail: jviera@drew.edu.

DREXEL UNIVERSITY, Philadelphia, PA 19104-2875

General Information Independent, coed, university. CGS member. *Graduate housing:* Room and/or apartments available on a first-come, first-served basis to single students; on-campus housing not available to married students. Housing application deadline: 1/9.

GRADUATE UNITS

College of Arts and Sciences *Program availability:* Part-time, evening/weekend. Offers arts and sciences (MA, MS, PhD); biological sciences (MS, PhD); chemistry (MS, PhD); clinical psychology (PhD); communication (MS); environmental policy (MS); environmental science (MS, PhD); forensic psychology (PhD); health psychology (PhD); law-psychologymathematics (MS, PhD); neuropsychology (PhD); physics (MS, PhD); psychology (MS); public communication (MS); science communication (MS); science, technology and society (MS); technical communication (MS). Electronic applications accepted.

College of Computing and Informatics Students: 228 full-time (112 women), 280 part-time (160 women); includes 92 minority (35 Black or African American, non-Hispanic/Latino; 21 Asian, non-Hispanic/Latino; 26 Hispanic/Latino; 10 Two or more races, non-Hispanic/Latino), 118 international. Average age 32. 609 applicants, 63% accepted, 157 enrolled. *Faculty:* 40 full-time (16 women), 15 part-time/adjunct (7 women). Expenses: Contact institution. *Financial support:* In 2017–18, 122 students received support, including 3 fellowships with full tuition reimbursements available (averaging $33,111 per year), 42 research assistantships with full tuition reimbursements available (averaging $27,342 per year), 14 teaching assistantships with full tuition reimbursements available (averaging $27,500 per year); career-related internships or fieldwork, institutionally sponsored loans, scholarships/grants, health care benefits, and tuition waivers (partial) also available. Support available to part-time students. Financial award application deadline: 3/1; financial award applicants required to submit FAFSA. In 2017, 210 master's, 8 doctorates, 17 other advanced degrees awarded. *Program availability:* Part-time, evening/weekend, 100% online. Offers computer science (MS, PhD, Postbaccalaureate Certificate); computing and informatics (MS, PhD, Post-Master's Certificate, Postbaccalaureate Certificate); health informatics (MS); information science (PhD, Post-Master's Certificate, Postbaccalaureate Certificate); information systems (MS); library and information science (MS); software engineering (MS). *Application deadline:* For fall admission, 8/15 for domestic students, 7/15 for international students; for spring admission, 3/1 for domestic students, 2/1 for international students. Applications are processed on a rolling basis. *Application fee:* $65. Electronic applications accepted. *Application Contact:* Matthew Lechtenberg, Director, Recruitment, 215-895-2474, Fax: 215-895-2303, E-mail: cciinfo@drexel.edu. *Dean/Professor*, Dr. Yi Deng, 215-895-2475, Fax: 215-895-2494, E-mail: yd362@drexel.edu.

College of Engineering *Program availability:* Part-time, evening/weekend. Offers architectural/building systems engineering (MS, PhD); biochemical engineering (MS); chemical engineering (MS, PhD); civil engineering (MS, PhD); computer engineering (MS); electrical and computer engineering (PhD); electrical engineering (MSEE); engineering (MS, MSEE, MSSE, PhD, Certificate); engineering management (MS, Certificate); environmental engineering (MS, PhD); geotechnical, geoenvironmental and geosynthetics engineering (MS, PhD); hydraulics, hydrology and water resources engineering (MS, PhD); materials engineering (MS, PhD); mechanical engineering (MS, PhD); software engineering (MSSE); structures (MS); telecommunications engineering (MSEE). Electronic applications accepted.

College of Medicine *Program availability:* Part-time. Offers medicine (MLAS, MMS, MS, MD, PhD, Certificate). Electronic applications accepted.

Biomedical Graduate Programs *Program availability:* Part-time. Offers biochemistry (MS, PhD); biomedical sciences (MLAS, MMS, MS, PhD, Certificate); drug discovery and development (MS); laboratory animal science (MLAS); medical science (MMS, Certificate); microbiology and immunology (MS, PhD); molecular and cell biology and genetics (MS, PhD); molecular medicine (MS); molecular pathobiology (MS, PhD); neuroscience (MS, PhD); pharmacology and physiology (MS, PhD). Electronic applications accepted.

College of Nursing and Health Professions *Program availability:* Part-time, evening/weekend. Offers art therapy (MA, PMC); clinical biomechanics and orthopedics (PhD); couple and family therapy (MFT, PhD); creative arts therapies (PhD); dance/movement therapy (MA, PMC); emergency and public safety services (MS); hand and upper quarter rehabilitation (Certificate); hand therapy (MHS, PPDPT); music therapy (MA, PMC); nurse anesthesia (MSN); nursing and health professions (MA, MFT, MHS, MS, MSN, DPT, Dr NP, PPDPT, PhD, Certificate, PMC); nursing studies (Dr NP); orthopedics (MHS, PPDPT); pediatric rehabilitation (Certificate); pediatrics (MHS, PPDPT, PhD); physical therapy (DPT); physician assistant (MHS). Electronic applications accepted.

Division of Graduate Nursing Offers adult acute care (MSN); adult psychiatric/mental health (MSN); advanced practice nursing (MSN); clinical trials research (MSN); family nurse practitioner (MSN); leadership in health systems management (MSN); nursing education (MSN); pediatric primary care (MSN); women's health (MSN). Electronic applications accepted.

Dornsife School of Public Health Offers biostatistics (MS); epidemiology (PhD); epidemiology and biostatistics (Certificate); public health (MPH, MS, PhD, Certificate). Electronic applications accepted.

Goodwin College of Professional Studies

School of Education *Program availability:* Part-time, evening/weekend, online learning. Offers applied behavior analysis (MS); creativity and innovation (MS); education improvement and transformation (MS); educational administration (MS); educational leadership and management (Ed D); educational leadership development and learning technologies (PhD); global and international education (MS); higher education (MS); human resources development (MS); learning technologies (MS); mathematics, learning and teaching (MS); special education (MS); teaching, learning and curriculum (MS). Electronic applications accepted.

School of Technology and Professional Studies *Program availability:* Part-time, evening/weekend. Offers construction management (MS); creativity and innovation (MS); engineering technology (MS); food science (MS); hospitality management (MS); professional studies: creativity studies (MS); professional studies: e-learning leadership (MS); professional studies: homeland security management (MS); project management (MS); property management (MS); sport management (MS). Electronic applications accepted.

LeBow College of Business *Program availability:* Part-time, evening/weekend. Offers accounting (MS); business (MBA, MS, PhD, APC); business administration (MBA, PhD, APC); finance (MS). Electronic applications accepted.

School of Biomedical Engineering, Science and Health Systems Offers biomedical engineering (MS, PhD); biomedical science (MS, PhD); biostatistics (MS); clinical/rehabilitation engineering (MS). Electronic applications accepted.

Thomas R. Kline School of Law Offers business and entrepreneurship law (JD); criminal law (MLS, JD); cybersecurity and information privacy compliance (MLS); entrepreneurship and law (MLS); financial regulatory compliance (MLS); health care compliance (MLS); health law (JD); higher education compliance (MLS); human resources compliance (MLS); intellectual property law (JD); NCAA compliance and sports law (MLS).

Westphal College of Media Arts and Design *Program availability:* Part-time, evening/weekend. Offers arts administration (MS); design research (MS); digital media (MS, PhD); fashion design (MS); interior architecture and design (MS); museum leadership (MS); retail and merchandising (MS); television management (MS); urban strategy (MS). Electronic applications accepted.

DRURY UNIVERSITY, Springfield, MO 65802

General Information Independent, coed, comprehensive institution. *Enrollment:* 1,659 graduate, professional, and undergraduate students; 237 full-time matriculated graduate/professional students (165 women). *Enrollment by degree level:* 237 master's. *Graduate faculty:* 14 full-time (7 women), 9 part-time/adjunct (6 women). *Graduate housing:* On-campus housing not available. *Student services:* Campus employment opportunities, campus safety program, career counseling, grant writing training, international student services, multicultural affairs office, services for students with disabilities, teacher training, writing training. *Library facilities:* F. W. Olin Library plus 1 other. *Collection:* Books: 149,706 (physical), 185,811 (digital/electronic); Serial titles: 751 (physical), 38 (digital/electronic); Databases: 44. Weekly public service hours: 92; students can reserve study rooms. *Research affiliation:* Yale University (child development).

Computer facilities: 385 computers available on campus for general student use. A campuswide network can be accessed from student residence rooms and from off campus. Online class registration, digital imaging lab, online bill payment/student information are available.
Website: http://www.drury.edu/

General Application Contact: Regina Waters, Dean, Graduate Programs, 417-873-7251, E-mail: grad@drury.edu.

GRADUATE UNITS

Cybersecurity Leadership Certificate Program Students: 3 full-time (1 woman); includes 1 minority (Hispanic/Latino). Average age 33. 3 applicants, 100% accepted, 3 enrolled. *Faculty:* 3 full-time (1 woman), 2 part-time/adjunct (0 women). Expenses: Contact institution. *Financial support:* Career-related internships or fieldwork, scholarships/grants, and unspecified assistantships available. Financial award application deadline: 6/30; financial award applicants required to submit FAFSA. *Program availability:* Part-time, evening/weekend. Offers cybersecurity leadership (Certificate). *Application deadline:* For fall admission, 8/4 for domestic and international students; for spring admission, 1/5 for domestic and international students; for summer admission, 5/26 for domestic and international students. Applications are processed on a rolling basis. *Application fee:* $25 ($50 for international students). Electronic applications accepted. *Application Contact:* Dr. Robin Soster, Director, 417-873-7612, E-mail: rsoster@drury.edu. *Director*, Dr. Robin Soster, 417-873-7612, E-mail: rsoster@drury.edu.

Master in Education Program Students: 146 full-time (111 women); includes 6 minority (1 Asian, non-Hispanic/Latino; 3 Hispanic/Latino; 2 Two or more races, non-Hispanic/Latino), 1 international. Average age 34. 42 applicants, 74% accepted. Expenses: Contact institution. *Financial support:* In 2017–18, 20 students received support. Career-related internships or fieldwork, scholarships/grants, tuition waivers (partial), and unspecified assistantships available. Financial award application deadline: 6/30; financial award applicants required to submit FAFSA. In 2017, 74 master's awarded. *Program availability:* Part-time, evening/weekend, 100% online, blended/hybrid learning. Offers curriculum and instruction (M Ed); instructional leadership (M Ed); instructional technology (M Ed); integrated learning (M Ed); special education (M Ed); special reading (M Ed). *Application deadline:* For fall admission, 8/4 priority date for domestic and international students; for spring admission, 1/5 priority date for domestic and international students; for summer admission, 5/26 priority date for domestic and international students. Applications are processed on a rolling basis. *Application fee:* $25 ($50 for international students). Electronic applications accepted. *Application Contact:* Dr. Asikaa Cosgrove, Director, Master in Education Program, 417-873-7806, E-mail: acosgrov@drury.edu. *Director, Master in Education Program,* Dr. Asikaa Cosgrove, 417-873-7806, E-mail: acosgrov@drury.edu.

Master of Arts in Communication Program Students: 39 full-time (32 women); includes 4 minority (1 Black or African American, non-Hispanic/Latino; 2 Hispanic/Latino; 1 Two or more races, non-Hispanic/Latino), 2 international. Average age 27. 8 applicants, 88% accepted, 7 enrolled. *Faculty:* 3 full-time (1 woman), 2 part-time/adjunct (0 women). Expenses: Contact institution. *Financial support:* Career-related internships or fieldwork, scholarships/grants, and unspecified assistantships available. Financial award application deadline: 6/30; financial award applicants required to submit FAFSA. In 2017, 8 master's awarded. *Program availability:* Part-time, evening/weekend. Offers integrated marketing communications (MAC); organizational leadership and change (MAC). *Application deadline:* For fall admission, 8/4 priority date for domestic and international students; for spring admission, 1/5 priority date for domestic and international students; for summer admission, 5/26 priority date for domestic and international students. Applications are processed on a rolling basis. *Application fee:* $25 ($50 for international students). Electronic applications accepted. *Application Contact:* Dr. Charles Taylor, Director, Master of Arts in Communication Program, 417-873-7391, E-mail: ctaylor@drury.edu. *Director, Master of Arts in Communication Program,* Dr. Charles Taylor, 417-873-7391, E-mail: ctaylor@drury.edu.

Master of Business Administration Program Students: 38 full-time (13 women). Average age 25. 38 applicants, 61% accepted, 21 enrolled. *Faculty:* 3 full-time (1 woman), 2 part-time/adjunct (0 women). Expenses: Contact institution. *Financial support:* In 2017–18, 4 students received support. Career-related internships or fieldwork, scholarships/grants, and unspecified assistantships available. Financial award application deadline: 6/30; financial award applicants required to submit FAFSA. In 2017, 26 master's awarded. *Program availability:* Part-time, evening/weekend. Offers business administration (MBA). *Application deadline:* For fall admission, 8/4 priority date for domestic and international students; for spring admission, 1/6 priority date for domestic and international students; for summer admission, 5/26 priority date for domestic and international students. Applications are processed on a rolling basis. *Application fee:* $25 ($50 for international students). Electronic applications accepted. *Application Contact:* Dr. Robin Soster, Director, MBA Program, 417-873-7612, E-mail: rsoster@drury.edu. *Director, MBA Program,* Dr. Robin Soster, 417-873-7612, E-mail: rsoster@drury.edu.

Master of Nonprofit and Civic Leadership Program Students: 39 full-time (32 women); includes 4 minority (1 Black or African American, non-Hispanic/Latino; 2 Hispanic/Latino; 1 Two or more races, non-Hispanic/Latino), 2 international. Average age 27. 7 applicants, 86% accepted, 5 enrolled. *Faculty:* 3 full-time (1 woman), 2 part-time/adjunct (0 women). Expenses: Contact institution. *Financial support:* Career-related internships or fieldwork, institutionally sponsored loans, scholarships/grants, and unspecified assistantships available. Financial award application deadline: 6/30; financial award applicants required to submit FAFSA. *Program availability:* Part-time, evening/weekend. Offers nonprofit and civic leadership (MNCL). *Application deadline:* For fall admission, 8/4 for domestic and international students; for spring admission, 1/6 for domestic and international students; for summer admission, 5/24 for domestic and international students. Applications are processed on a rolling basis. *Application fee:* $25 ($50 for international students). Electronic applications accepted. *Application Contact:* Dr. Charles Taylor, Director, 417-873-7391, E-mail: ctaylor@drury.edu. *Director,* Dr. Charles Taylor, 417-873-7391, E-mail: ctaylor@drury.edu.

DUKE UNIVERSITY, Durham, NC 27708-0586

General Information Independent-religious, coed, university. CGS member. *Graduate housing:* Rooms and/or apartments available on a first-come, first-served basis to single and married students. Housing application deadline: 5/8. *Research affiliation:* Highlands Biological Station, U.S. Forest Sciences Laboratory, Organization for Tropical Studies.

GRADUATE UNITS

Divinity School *Program availability:* Part-time, online learning. Offers theology (M Div, MACP, MACS, MTS, Th M, D Min, Th D). Electronic applications accepted.

The Fuqua School of Business Students: 1,594 full-time (591 women); includes 339 minority (67 Black or African American, non-Hispanic/Latino; 5 American Indian or Alaska Native, non-Hispanic/Latino; 175 Asian, non-Hispanic/Latino; 78 Hispanic/Latino; 14 Two or more races, non-Hispanic/Latino), 655 international. Average age 29. *Faculty:* 96 full-time (19 women), 48 part-time/adjunct (15 women). Expenses: Contact institution. *Financial support:* In 2017–18, 665 students received support. In 2017, 730 master's, 14 doctorates awarded. Offers academic excellence in finance (Certificate); accounting (PhD); business (EMBA, GEMBA, MBA, MMS, MQM, WEMBA, PhD, Certificate); business administration (MBA); decision sciences (MBA, PhD); energy and environment (MBA); energy finance (MBA); entrepreneurship and innovation (MBA); finance (MBA, MQM, PhD); financial analysis (MBA); forensics (MQM); foundations of business (MMS); health analytics (MQM); health sector management (Certificate); leadership and ethics (MBA); management (MBA); management and organizations (PhD); management science and technology management (Certificate); management studies (MMS); marketing (MBA, MQM, PhD); operations management (MBA, PhD); social entrepreneurship (MBA); strategy (MBA, MQM, PhD). Electronic applications accepted. *Application Contact:* Shari Hubert, Associate Dean, Office of Admissions, Fax: 919-681-8026, E-mail: admissions-info@fuqua.duke.edu. *Dean,* William Boulding.

Graduate School *Program availability:* Part-time, evening/weekend. Offers bioethics and science policy (MA); biological psychology (PhD); biology (PhD); business administration (PhD); cell and molecular biology (Certificate); cell biology (PhD); cellular and molecular biology (PhD); chemistry (PhD); classical studies (PhD); clinical psychology (PhD); cognitive neuroscience (PhD, Certificate); cognitive psychology (PhD); computational biology and bioinformatics (PhD, Certificate); computer science (MS, PhD); crystallography of macromolecules (PhD); developmental and stem cell biology (Certificate); developmental psychology (PhD); East Asian studies (AM, Certificate); ecology (PhD, Certificate); econometrics (MS); economics (AM, PhD); economics and computation (MS); English (PhD); environment (PhD); environmental policy (PhD); enzyme mechanisms (PhD); experimental and documentary arts (MFA); experimental psychology (PhD); financial economics (MS); French (PhD); genetics and genomics (PhD); German studies (PhD); gross anatomy and physical anthropology (PhD); health psychology (PhD); historical and cultural visualization (MA); history (AM, PhD); history of art (PhD); human social development (PhD); humanities (AM); immunology (PhD); integrated toxicology and environmental health (Certificate); Italian (PhD); Latin American studies (PhD); liberal studies (AM); lipid biochemistry (PhD); literature (PhD); marine science and conservation (PhD); mathematics (PhD); medical physics (MS, PhD); membrane structure and function (PhD); molecular cancer biology (PhD); molecular genetics (PhD); molecular genetics and microbiology (PhD); music composition (PhD); musicology (PhD); neuroanatomy (PhD); neurobiology (PhD); neurochemistry (PhD); nucleic acid structure and function (PhD); pathology (PhD); performance practice (PhD); pharmacology (PhD); philosophy (PhD); physical anthropology (PhD); physics (PhD); political science (AM, PhD); protein structure and function (PhD); public policy (PhD); religion (MA, PhD); Slavic and Eurasian studies (AM, Certificate); social/cultural anthropology (PhD); sociology (AM, PhD); Spanish (PhD); statistical science (MSS, PhD); structural biology and biophysics (Certificate); teaching (MAT). Electronic applications accepted.

Division of Earth and Ocean Sciences *Program availability:* Part-time. Offers earth and ocean sciences (MS, PhD). Electronic applications accepted.

Duke Global Health Institute Offers global health (MS).

Pratt School of Engineering Students: 1,293 full-time (334 women), 76 part-time (17 women); includes 141 minority (22 Black or African American, non-Hispanic/Latino; 2 American Indian or Alaska Native, non-Hispanic/Latino; 80 Asian, non-Hispanic/Latino; 37 Hispanic/Latino), 655 international. Average age 25. 2,805 applicants, 28% accepted, 371 enrolled. Expenses: Contact institution. *Financial support:* Fellowships, research assistantships, teaching assistantships, and Federal Work-Study available. Financial award application deadline: 12/31. *Program availability:* Part-time, online learning. Offers biomedical engineering (M Eng, MS, PhD); civil and environmental engineering (MS, PhD); civil engineering (M Eng); computational mechanics and scientific computing (M Eng); electrical and computer engineering (M Eng, MS, PhD); engineering (M Eng, MEM, MS, PhD); engineering management (MEM); environmental engineering (M Eng, MS, PhD); materials science (M Eng, MS, PhD); materials science and engineering (M Eng); mechanical engineering (M Eng, MS, PhD); photonics and optical sciences (M Eng); risk engineering (M Eng). *Application Contact:* Duke Graduate School Admissions, 919-684-3913, Fax: 919-684-2277, E-mail: grad-admissions@duke.edu. *Dean,* Ravi V. Bellamkonda, 919-660-5386.

Nicholas School of the Environment Students: 135 full-time (94 women). Average age 25. *Faculty:* 50. Expenses: Contact institution. *Financial support:* In 2017–18, research assistantships (averaging $3,000 per year) were awarded; career-related internships or fieldwork, Federal Work-Study, institutionally sponsored loans, scholarships/grants, and unspecified assistantships also available. Financial award application deadline: 12/15; financial award applicants required to submit CSS PROFILE or FAFSA. In 2017, 130 master's, 25 doctorates awarded. *Program availability:* Blended/hybrid learning. Offers earth and ocean sciences (PhD); environment (MEM, MF, PhD); marine science and conservation (PhD). Application deadline for PhD program is December 8. *Application deadline:* For fall admission, 12/15 priority date for domestic and international students. Applications are processed on a rolling basis. *Application fee:* $80. Electronic applications accepted. *Application Contact:* Benjamin Spain, Associate Director of Enrollment Services, 919-684-1155, E-mail: admissions@nicholas.duke.edu. *Associate Dean, Student Services,* Sherri Nevius, 919-613-8063, E-mail: sherri.nevius@duke.edu.

Sanford School of Public Policy Students: 257 full-time (150 women); includes 77 minority (22 Black or African American, non-Hispanic/Latino; 1 American Indian or Alaska Native, non-Hispanic/Latino; 37 Asian, non-Hispanic/Latino; 15 Hispanic/Latino; 1 Native Hawaiian or other Pacific Islander, non-Hispanic/Latino; 1 Two or more races, non-Hispanic/Latino), 70 international. Average age 29. 704 applicants, 126 enrolled. *Faculty:* 70 full-time (24 women), 34 part-time/adjunct (9 women). Expenses: Contact institution. *Financial support:* Fellowships, research assistantships, teaching assistantships, career-related internships or fieldwork, Federal Work-Study, scholarships/grants, and unspecified assistantships available. Financial award application deadline: 1/5; financial award applicants required to submit FAFSA. In 2017, 113 master's awarded. Offers international development policy (MIDP); public policy (MIDP, MPP). *Application deadline:* For fall admission, 1/5 for domestic and international students. *Application fee:* $80. Electronic applications accepted. *Application Contact:* Jessica Pan, Director of Admissions, 919-613-9244, E-mail: jessica.pan@duke.edu. *Dean, Sanford School of Public Policy,* Judith Kelley, 919-613-7401.

School of Law Students: 666; includes 161 minority (46 Black or African American, non-Hispanic/Latino; 1 American Indian or Alaska Native, non-Hispanic/Latino; 66 Asian, non-Hispanic/Latino; 43 Hispanic/Latino; 1 Native Hawaiian or other Pacific Islander, non-Hispanic/Latino; 4 Two or more races, non-Hispanic/Latino), 49 international. Average age 24. 4,672 applicants, 23% accepted, 207 enrolled. *Faculty:* 92 full-time (40 women), 102 part-time/adjunct (30 women). Expenses: Contact institution. *Financial support:* In 2017–18, 580 students received support. Institutionally sponsored loans, scholarships/grants, and unspecified assistantships available. Financial award application deadline: 3/15; financial award applicants required to submit FAFSA. In 2017, 225 doctorates awarded. Offers American law (LL M); judicial studies (MJS); law (JD, SJD); law and entrepreneurship (LL M). *Application deadline:* For fall admission, 2/15 for domestic and international students. Applications are processed on a rolling basis. *Application fee:* $70. Electronic applications accepted. *Application Contact:* William J. Hoye, Associate Dean for Admissions and Student Affairs, 919-613-7020, Fax: 919-613-7257, E-mail: hoye@law.duke.edu. *Dean/Professor of Law,* David F. Levi, 919-613-7001, Fax: 919-613-7158.

School of Medicine Students: 1,038 full-time, 126 part-time; includes 461 minority (93 Black or African American, non-Hispanic/Latino; 14 American Indian or Alaska Native, non-Hispanic/Latino; 302 Asian, non-Hispanic/Latino; 48 Hispanic/Latino; 4 Native Hawaiian or other Pacific Islander, non-Hispanic/Latino), 51 international. 10,182 applicants, 6% accepted, 446 enrolled. *Faculty:* 1,541 full-time (550 women), 118 part-time/adjunct (59 women). Expenses: Contact institution. *Financial support:* In 2017–18, 438 students received support. Institutionally sponsored loans and scholarships/grants available. Financial award application deadline: 5/1; financial award applicants required to submit FAFSA. In 2017, 229 master's, 179 doctorates awarded. Offers biomedical sciences (MS); biostatistics (MS); clinical informatics (MS); clinical leadership (MHS); clinical research (MHS); medicine (MHS, MS, DPT, MD); pathologists' assistant (MHS); physician assistant (MHS). *Application Contact:* Andrea Liu, Director of Admissions, 919-684-2985, Fax: 919-684-8893, E-mail: medadm@mc.duke.edu. *Vice Dean, Medical Education,* Dr. Edward G. Buckley, 919-668-3381, Fax: 919-660-7040, E-mail: buckl002@mc.duke.edu.

Physical Therapy Division Students: 226 full-time (152 women); includes 53 minority (12 Black or African American, non-Hispanic/Latino; 1 American Indian or Alaska Native, non-Hispanic/Latino; 23 Asian, non-Hispanic/Latino; 13 Hispanic/Latino; 4 Native Hawaiian or other Pacific Islander, non-Hispanic/Latino). 924 applicants, 15% accepted, 80 enrolled. *Faculty:* 17 full-time (8 women). Expenses: Contact institution. *Financial support:* In 2017–18, 22 students received support. Application deadline: 5/1; applicants required to submit FAFSA. In 2017, 73 doctorates awarded. Offers physical therapy (DPT). *Application deadline:* For fall admission, 11/1 priority date for domestic and international students. Applications are processed on a rolling basis. *Application fee:* $50. Electronic applications accepted. *Application Contact:* Mya Shackleford, Admissions Coordinator, 919-668-5206, Fax: 919-684-1846, E-mail: mya.shackleford@duke.edu. *Program Director,* Dr. Chad Cook, 919-684-8905, Fax: 919-684-1846, E-mail: chad.cook@duke.edu.

School of Nursing Students: 155 full-time (137 women), 613 part-time (548 women); includes 177 minority (64 Black or African American, non-Hispanic/Latino; 2 American Indian or Alaska Native, non-Hispanic/Latino; 47 Asian, non-Hispanic/Latino; 34 Hispanic/Latino; 30 Two or more races, non-Hispanic/Latino), 10 international. Average age 34. 631 applicants, 47% accepted, 211 enrolled. *Faculty:* 72 full-time (61 women). Expenses: Contact institution. *Financial support:* Institutionally sponsored loans, scholarships/grants, and traineeships available. Support available to part-time students. Financial award applicants required to submit FAFSA. In 2017, 221 master's, 71 doctorates, 26 other advanced degrees awarded. *Program availability:* Part-time, evening/weekend, online with on-campus intensives. Offers acute care pediatric nurse practitioner (MSN, Post-Graduate Certificate); adult-gerontology nurse practitioner (MSN, Post-Graduate Certificate); family nurse practitioner (MSN, Post-Graduate Certificate); neonatal nurse practitioner (MSN, Post-Graduate Certificate); nurse anesthesia (DNP); nurse practitioner (DNP); nursing (MSN, DNP, PhD, Post-Graduate Certificate); nursing and health care leadership (MSN, Post-Graduate Certificate); nursing education (MSN, Post-Graduate Certificate); nursing informatics (MSN, Post-Graduate Certificate); pediatric nurse practitioner (MSN, Post-Graduate Certificate); psychiatric mental health nurse practitioner (MSN, Post-Graduate Certificate); women's health nurse practitioner (MSN, Post-Graduate Certificate). *Application deadline:* For fall admission, 12/1 for domestic and international students; for spring admission, 5/1 for domestic and international students. *Application fee:* $50. Electronic applications accepted. *Application Contact:* Dr. Ernie Rushing, Director of Admissions and Recruitment, 919-668-6274, Fax: 919-668-4693, E-mail: ernie.rushing@dm.duke.edu. *Dean/Vice Chancellor for Nursing Affairs/Associate Vice President for Academic Affairs for Nursing*, Dr. Marion E. Broome, 919-684-9446, Fax: 919-684-9414, E-mail: marion.broome@duke.edu.

DUNLAP-STONE UNIVERSITY, Phoenix, AZ 85024

General Information Proprietary, coed, comprehensive institution.

GRADUATE UNITS

Graduate Law Center Offers regulatory trade compliance (M Sc); U.S. regulatory trade law (LL M).

DUQUESNE UNIVERSITY, Pittsburgh, PA 15282-0001

General Information Independent-religious, coed, university. CGS member. *Enrollment:* 9,190 graduate, professional, and undergraduate students; 2,870 full-time matriculated graduate/professional students (1,760 women), 360 part-time matriculated graduate/professional students (240 women). *Enrollment by degree level:* 1,315 master's, 1,870 doctoral, 45 other advanced degrees. *Graduate faculty:* 448 full-time (203 women), 325 part-time/adjunct (152 women). *Tuition:* Full-time $22,662; part-time $1259 per credit. Tuition and fees vary according to program. *Graduate housing:* Rooms and/or apartments available on a first-come, first-served basis to single and married students. Typical cost: $6658 per year ($12,114 including board) for single students; $6658 per year ($12,114 including board) for married students. Room and board charges vary according to board plan and housing facility selected. Housing application deadline: 5/1. *Student services:* Campus employment opportunities, campus safety program, career counseling, child daycare facilities, exercise/wellness program, free psychological counseling, international student services, low-cost health insurance, multicultural affairs office, services for students with disabilities, teacher training, writing training. *Library facilities:* Gumberg Library plus 1 other. *Collection:* Books: 562,257 (physical), 305,837 (digital/electronic); Serial titles: 142 (physical), 83,995 (digital/electronic); Databases: 205. Weekly public service hours: 112; students can reserve study rooms.

Computer facilities: Computer purchase and lease plans are available. 1,000 computers available on campus for general student use. A campuswide network can be accessed from student residence rooms and from off campus. Online class registration is available.
Website: http://www.duq.edu/

General Application Contact: Todd Eicker, Director of Graduate Admission, 412-396-6219, E-mail: eickert@duq.edu.

GRADUATE UNITS

Bayer School of Natural and Environmental Sciences Students: 113 full-time (61 women), 17 part-time (11 women); includes 14 minority (3 Black or African American, non-Hispanic/Latino; 4 Asian, non-Hispanic/Latino; 4 Hispanic/Latino; 3 Two or more races, non-Hispanic/Latino), 13 international. Average age 27. 78 applicants, 71% accepted, 35 enrolled. *Faculty:* 39 full-time (12 women), 29 part-time/adjunct (11 women). Expenses: Contact institution. *Financial support:* In 2017–18, 119 students received support, including 3 fellowships with full tuition reimbursements available, 18 research assistantships with full tuition reimbursements available, 54 teaching assistantships with full tuition reimbursements available; career-related internships or fieldwork, scholarships/grants, tuition waivers (partial), and unspecified assistantships also available. Financial award application deadline: 5/31. In 2017, 53 master's, 4 doctorates, 2 other advanced degrees awarded. *Program availability:* Part-time. Offers biological sciences (PhD); biotechnology (MS); chemistry (PhD); environmental science and management (MS, Certificate); forensic science and law (MS); natural and environmental sciences (MS, PhD, Certificate). *Application deadline:* For fall admission, 2/15 priority date for domestic students, 2/15 for international students; for spring admission, 10/1 priority date for domestic students, 10/1 for international students. Applications are processed on a rolling basis. *Application fee:* $0. Electronic applications accepted. *Application Contact:* Heather Costello, Senior Graduate Academic Advisor, 412-396-6339, Fax: 412-396-4881, E-mail: costelloh@duq.edu. *Dean*, Dr. Philip Reeder, 412-396-4877, Fax: 412-396-4881, E-mail: reederp@duq.edu.

Graduate School of Liberal Arts Students: 431 full-time (214 women), 75 part-time (41 women); includes 68 minority (37 Black or African American, non-Hispanic/Latino; 8 Asian, non-Hispanic/Latino; 13 Hispanic/Latino; 10 Two or more races, non-Hispanic/Latino), 96 international. Average age 33. 433 applicants, 53% accepted, 121 enrolled. *Faculty:* 134 full-time (49 women), 37 part-time/adjunct (18 women). Expenses: Contact institution. *Financial support:* In 2017–18, research assistantships with full tuition reimbursements (averaging $11,000 per year), teaching assistantships with full tuition reimbursements (averaging $17,500 per year) were awarded; career-related internships or fieldwork, Federal Work-Study, institutionally sponsored loans, scholarships/grants, and tuition waivers (full and partial) also available. Support available to part-time students. Financial award application deadline: 5/1. In 2017, 235 master's, 36 doctorates awarded. *Program availability:* Part-time, evening/weekend, 100% online, blended/hybrid learning. Offers clinical psychology (PhD); communication (MA); computational mathematics (MS); English (MA, PhD); historical studies (MA); leadership (MS); liberal arts (MA, MS, DHCE, PhD, Certificate); media (MS, Certificate); pastoral ministry (MA); philosophy (MA, PhD); public history (MA); religious education (MA); rhetoric (PhD); systematic theology (PhD); theology (MA). *Application deadline:* For fall admission, 8/1 for domestic students, 5/1 for international students; for spring admission, 11/1 for domestic students, 9/1 for international students. Applications are processed on a rolling basis. *Application fee:* $0. Electronic applications accepted. *Application Contact:* Linda Rendulic, Assistant to the Dean, 412-396-6400, Fax: 412-396-5265, E-mail: rendulic@duq.edu. *Dean*, Dr. James Swindal, 412-396-6400.

Center for Healthcare Ethics Students: 44 full-time (25 women), 1 (woman) part-time; includes 9 minority (4 Black or African American, non-Hispanic/Latino; 4 Asian, non-Hispanic/Latino; 1 Two or more races, non-Hispanic/Latino), 14 international. Average age 37. 18 applicants, 89% accepted, 8 enrolled. *Faculty:* 3 full-time (0 women). Expenses: Contact institution. *Financial support:* In 2017–18, 7 students received support, including 5 teaching assistantships with full and partial tuition reimbursements available (averaging $18,000 per year); Federal Work-Study and tuition waivers (full and partial) also available. Support available to part-time students. Financial award application deadline: 5/1. In 2017, 1 master's, 11 doctorates awarded. *Program availability:* Part-time, 100% online. Offers healthcare ethics (MA, DHCE, PhD, Certificate). *Application deadline:* For fall admission, 8/1 for domestic students, 5/1 for international students. *Application fee:* $0. Electronic applications accepted. *Application Contact:* Linda Rendulic, Assistant to the Dean, 412-396-6400, Fax: 412-396-5265, E-mail: rendulic@duq.edu. *Director*, Dr. Henk Ten Have, 412-396-1585, E-mail: tenhaveh@duq.edu.

John G. Rangos, Sr. School of Health Sciences Students: 247 full-time (199 women), 11 part-time (7 women); includes 15 minority (2 Black or African American, non-Hispanic/Latino; 7 Asian, non-Hispanic/Latino; 3 Hispanic/Latino; 3 Two or more races, non-Hispanic/Latino), 42 international. Average age 23. 283 applicants, 31% accepted, 54 enrolled. *Faculty:* 51 full-time (38 women), 33 part-time/adjunct (17 women). Expenses: Contact institution. *Financial support:* Federal Work-Study available. Financial award applicants required to submit FAFSA. In 2017, 134 master's, 39 doctorates awarded. *Program availability:* Part-time, minimal on-campus study. Offers health management systems (MHMS); occupational therapy (MS, OTD); physical therapy (DPT); physician assistant studies (MPAS); rehabilitation science (MS, PhD); speech-language pathology (MS). *Application deadline:* For fall admission, 2/1 for domestic and international students; for spring admission, 7/1 for domestic and international students. Applications are processed on a rolling basis. *Application fee:* $0. Electronic applications accepted. *Application Contact:* Christopher R. Hilf, Director of Enrollment Management, 412-396-5653, Fax: 412-396-5554, E-mail: hilfc@duq.edu. *Dean*, Dr. Fevzi Akinci, 412-396-5303, Fax: 412-396-5554, E-mail: akincif@duq.edu.

Mary Pappert School of Music Students: 54 full-time (21 women), 9 part-time (3 women); includes 4 minority (1 Black or African American, non-Hispanic/Latino; 1 Asian, non-Hispanic/Latino; 2 Hispanic/Latino), 23 international. Average age 26. 76 applicants, 95% accepted, 31 enrolled. *Faculty:* 26 full-time (9 women), 77 part-time/adjunct (22 women). Expenses: Contact institution. *Financial support:* In 2017–18, 76 students received support. Scholarships/grants and unspecified assistantships available. Financial award application deadline: 4/1. In 2017, 47 master's, 12 ADs awarded. *Program availability:* Part-time. Offers music education (MM). *Application deadline:* For fall admission, 7/1 for domestic and international students; for spring admission, 12/1 for domestic and international students; for summer admission, 6/1 for domestic students, 5/1 for international students. Applications are processed on a rolling basis. *Application fee:* $50. Electronic applications accepted. *Application Contact:* Thomas Carsecka, Director of Music Admissions, 412-396-5983, Fax: 412-396-5719, E-mail: carseckat@duq.edu. *Dean/Professor*, Dr. Seth Beckman, 412-396-6082, Fax: 412-396-1524, E-mail: beckmans@duq.edu.

Palumbo-Donahue School of Business Students: 232 full-time (83 women), 46 part-time (18 women); includes 28 minority (14 Black or African American, non-Hispanic/Latino; 8 Asian, non-Hispanic/Latino; 4 Hispanic/Latino; 2 Two or more races, non-Hispanic/Latino), 24 international. Average age 29. 220 applicants, 83% accepted, 121 enrolled. *Faculty:* 59 full-time (23 women), 25 part-time/adjunct (6 women). Expenses: Contact institution. *Financial support:* In 2017–18, 211 students received support, including 12 fellowships with partial tuition reimbursements available (averaging $14,200 per year), 20 research assistantships with partial tuition reimbursements available (averaging $22,662 per year); career-related internships or fieldwork, scholarships/grants, and unspecified assistantships also available. Support available to part-time students. Financial award application deadline: 7/1; financial award applicants required to submit FAFSA. In 2017, 113 master's awarded. *Program availability:* Part-time, evening/weekend, minimal on-campus study. Offers accounting (M Acc); finance (MBA); information systems management (MSISM); management (MBA, MS); marketing (MBA); sports business (MS); supply chain management (MS); sustainability (MBA). *Application deadline:* For fall admission, 7/1 priority date for domestic and international students; for spring admission, 12/1 for domestic and international students; for summer admission, 4/1 for domestic and international students. Applications are processed on a rolling basis. *Application fee:* $0. Electronic applications accepted. *Application Contact:* Jeff Jewett, Director of Admissions and Enrollment Management, 412-396-6244, Fax: 412-396-1726, E-mail: decrostam@duq.edu. *Associate Dean of Graduate Programs and Executive Education*, Dr. Karen Donovan, 412-396-6276, Fax: 412-396-1726, E-mail: donovan6@duq.edu.

Post-Baccalaureate Pre-Medical and Health Professions Program Students: 6 full-time (4 women); includes 3 minority (2 Black or African American, non-Hispanic/Latino; 1 Hispanic/Latino). Average age 23. 40 applicants, 38% accepted, 3 enrolled. *Faculty:* 1 (woman) full-time. Expenses: Contact institution. *Financial support:* Applicants required to submit FAFSA. In 2017, 6 Postbaccalaureate Certificates awarded. Offers pre-medical studies and health professions (Postbaccalaureate Certificate). *Application deadline:* For fall admission, 5/15 for domestic students. Applications are processed on a rolling basis. *Application fee:* $0. Electronic applications accepted. *Application Contact:* Todd Eicker, Director of Graduate Admission, 412-396-6219, E-mail: eickert@duq.edu. *Director*, Dr. Paula Sammarone-Turocy, 412-396-6335, Fax: 412-396-5587, E-mail: turocyp@duq.edu.

School of Education Students: 488 full-time (354 women), 52 part-time (35 women); includes 87 minority (51 Black or African American, non-Hispanic/Latino; 1 American Indian or Alaska Native, non-Hispanic/Latino; 12 Asian, non-Hispanic/Latino; 12 Hispanic/Latino; 11 Two or more races, non-Hispanic/Latino), 54 international. Average age 30. 439 applicants, 84% accepted, 180 enrolled. *Faculty:* 52 full-time (31 women), 83 part-time/adjunct (63 women). Expenses: Contact institution. *Financial support:* In 2017–18, 53 research assistantships with full and partial tuition reimbursements (averaging $3,603 per year) were awarded; teaching assistantships, career-related internships or fieldwork, Federal Work-Study, institutionally sponsored loans, and tuition waivers also available. Support available to part-time students. In 2017, 138 master's, 36 doctorates, 7 other advanced degrees awarded. *Program availability:* Part-time, evening/weekend, 100% online, blended/hybrid learning. Offers biology (MS Ed); chemistry (MS Ed); child psychology (MS Ed); clinical mental health counseling (MS Ed, Post-Master's Certificate); cognitive, behavior, physical/health disabilities (MS Ed); community and special education support (MS Ed); counselor education (MS Ed, Ed D, Post-Master's Certificate); counselor education and supervision (Ed D); counselor licensure (Post-Master's Certificate); curriculum and instruction (Post-Master's Certificate); early level (PreK-4) education (MS Ed); education (MS Ed, Ed D, PhD, Psy D, Post-Master's Certificate); educational leadership (Ed D); educational studies (MS Ed); English (MS Ed); English as a second language (MS Ed); instructional technology (MS Ed, Ed D, Post-Master's Certificate); K-12 education (MS Ed); marriage and family counseling (MS Ed); mathematics (MS Ed); middle level (4-8) education (MS Ed); physics (MS Ed); program evaluation (MS Ed); reading and language arts (MS Ed); school administration and supervision (MS Ed, Post-Master's Certificate); school administration K-12 (MS Ed, Post-Master's Certificate); school counseling (MS Ed); school psychology (MS Ed, PhD, Psy D); school supervision (MS Ed); secondary education (MS Ed); social studies (MS Ed); special education (MS Ed, PhD); special education 7-12 (MS Ed); special education PreK-8 (MS Ed). *Application deadline:* For fall admission, 3/1 for domestic students; for spring admission, 9/1 for domestic students. Applications are processed on a rolling basis. *Application fee:* $0. Electronic applications accepted. *Application Contact:* Kelly McGinley, Graduate Admissions Assistant, 412-396-1559, Fax: 412-296-5585, E-mail: mcginleyk@duq.edu. *Dean*, Dr. Cindy Walker, 412-396-6102, Fax: 412-396-5585.

School of Law Students: 404 full-time (214 women); includes 33 minority (7 Black or African American, non-Hispanic/Latino; 2 American Indian or Alaska Native, non-Hispanic/Latino; 6 Asian, non-Hispanic/Latino; 11 Hispanic/Latino; 1 Native Hawaiian or other Pacific Islander, non-Hispanic/Latino; 6 Two or more races, non-Hispanic/Latino), 4 international. Average age 26. 796 applicants, 62% accepted, 149 enrolled. *Faculty:* 30 full-time (16 women), 35 part-time/adjunct (9 women). Expenses: Contact institution. *Financial support:* In 2017–18, 338 students received support, including 25 research assistantships with partial tuition reimbursements available (averaging $2,500 per year), 20 teaching assistantships with partial tuition reimbursements available (averaging $2,500 per year); career-related internships or fieldwork, scholarships/grants, tuition waivers (partial), and library assistants also available. Support available to part-time students. Financial award application deadline: 5/1; financial award applicants required to submit FAFSA. In 2017, 3 master's, 126 doctorates awarded. *Program availability:* Part-time, evening/weekend. Offers American law for foreign lawyers (LL M); law (JD). JD/M Div offered jointly with Pittsburgh Theological Seminary. *Application deadline:* For fall admission, 3/1 priority date for domestic and international students. Applications are processed on a rolling basis. *Application fee:* $0. Electronic applications accepted. *Application Contact:* Office of Admissions, 412-396-6296, Fax: 412-396-6659, E-mail: lawadmissions@duq.edu. *Dean*, Maureen Lally-Green, 412-396-6280, Fax: 412-396-6283, E-mail: lallygreen@duq.edu.

School of Nursing Students: 179 full-time (165 women), 102 part-time (94 women); includes 45 minority (18 Black or African American, non-Hispanic/Latino; 3 American Indian or Alaska Native, non-Hispanic/Latino; 5 Asian, non-Hispanic/Latino; 13 Hispanic/Latino; 6 Two or more races, non-Hispanic/Latino), 4 international. Average age 38. 244 applicants, 70% accepted, 119 enrolled. *Faculty:* 29 full-time (24 women), 3 part-time/adjunct (all women). Expenses: Contact institution. *Financial support:* In 2017–18, 31 students received support, including 31 teaching assistantships with partial tuition reimbursements available (averaging $5,396 per year); institutionally sponsored loans, scholarships/grants, traineeships, tuition waivers (partial), and unspecified assistantships also available. Support available to part-time students. Financial award application deadline: 5/1; financial award applicants required to submit FAFSA. In 2017, 50 master's, 23 doctorates, 6 other advanced degrees awarded. *Program availability:* Part-time, evening/weekend, online only, 100% online. Offers family (individual across the life span) nurse practitioner (MSN, Post-Master's Certificate); forensic nursing (MSN, Post-Master's Certificate); nursing (MSN, DNP, PhD, Post-Master's Certificate); nursing education and faculty role (MSN, Post-Master's Certificate); nursing ethics (PhD); nursing practice (DNP). *Application deadline:* For fall admission, 7/10 for domestic and international students; for spring admission, 11/29 for domestic and international students; for summer admission, 4/2 for domestic and international students. *Application fee:* $0. Electronic applications accepted. *Application Contact:* Devon George, Nurse Recruiter, 412-396-1009, Fax: 412-396-6346, E-mail: nursing@duq.edu. *Dean/Professor*, Dr. Mary Ellen Glasgow, 412-396-6554, Fax: 412-396-5974, E-mail: glasgowm@duq.edu.

School of Pharmacy Students: 718 full-time (447 women), 48 part-time (31 women); includes 83 minority (20 Black or African American, non-Hispanic/Latino; 34 Asian, non-Hispanic/Latino; 17 Hispanic/Latino; 12 Two or more races, non-Hispanic/Latino), 51 international. Average age 23. 492 applicants, 56% accepted, 206 enrolled. *Faculty:* 49 full-time (21 women), 3 part-time/adjunct (0 women). Expenses: Contact institution. *Financial support:* In 2017–18, 113 students received support. Federal Work-Study and scholarships/grants available. Financial award application deadline: 6/1; financial award applicants required to submit FAFSA. In 2017, 5 master's, 191 doctorates awarded. *Program availability:* Evening/weekend. Offers pharmacy (MS, PhD, Pharm D). *Application deadline:* For fall admission, 2/1 for domestic and international students; for spring admission, 12/1 for domestic and international students. Applications are processed on a rolling basis. *Application fee:* $50. Electronic applications accepted. *Dean*, Dr. J. Douglas Bricker, 412-396-6377, Fax: 412-396-5130.

Graduate School of Pharmaceutical Sciences Students: 56 full-time (29 women), 1 part-time (0 women); includes 2 minority (1 Asian, non-Hispanic/Latino; 1 Hispanic/Latino), 45 international. Average age 27. 124 applicants, 43% accepted, 6 enrolled. *Faculty:* 22 full-time (7 women). Expenses: Contact institution. *Financial support:* In 2017–18, 57 students received support, including 13 research assistantships with full tuition reimbursements available, 44 teaching assistantships with full tuition reimbursements available; unspecified assistantships also available. In 2017, 5 master's, 4 doctorates awarded. Offers medicinal chemistry (MS, PhD); pharmaceutics (MS, PhD); pharmacology (MS, PhD); pharmacy administration (MS). *Application deadline:* For fall admission, 12/1 priority date for domestic and international students; for spring admission, 10/1 priority date for domestic and international students. Applications are processed on a rolling basis. Electronic applications accepted. *Application Contact:* Information Contact, 412-396-1172, E-mail: gsps-adm@duq.edu. *Associate Dean for Research and Graduate Programs*, Dr. James K. Drennen, III, 412-396-5520.

D'YOUVILLE COLLEGE, Buffalo, NY 14201-1084

General Information Independent, coed, comprehensive institution. *Graduate housing:* Room and/or apartments available on a first-come, first-served basis to single students. Housing application deadline: 8/1.

GRADUATE UNITS

Department of Business *Program availability:* Part-time, evening/weekend. Offers business administration (MBA); international business (MS). Electronic applications accepted.

Department of Chiropractic Offers chiropractic (DC). Electronic applications accepted.

Department of Dietetics Offers dietetics (MS). Five-year program begins at freshman entry. Electronic applications accepted.

Department of Education *Program availability:* Part-time, evening/weekend. Offers educational leadership (Ed D); elementary education (MS Ed); secondary education (MS Ed); special education (MS Ed). Electronic applications accepted.

Department of Health Services Administration *Program availability:* Part-time, evening/weekend. Offers clinical research associate (Certificate); health administration (Ed D); health services administration (MS, Certificate); long term care administration (Certificate). Electronic applications accepted.

Department of Physical Therapy *Program availability:* Part-time, online learning. Offers advanced orthopedic physical therapy (Certificate); manual physical therapy (Certificate); physical therapy (DPT). Electronic applications accepted.

Occupational Therapy Department Offers occupational therapy (MS). Electronic applications accepted.

Physician Assistant Department Offers physician assistant (MS). Electronic applications accepted.

Program in Anatomy Offers anatomy (MS).

School of Nursing *Program availability:* Part-time. Offers advanced practice nursing (DNP); family nurse practitioner (MSN, Certificate); nursing and health-related professions education (Certificate). Electronic applications accepted.

School of Pharmacy Offers pharmacy (Pharm D). Electronic applications accepted.

EARLHAM COLLEGE, Richmond, IN 47374-4095

General Information Independent-religious, coed, comprehensive institution. *Graduate housing:* On-campus housing not available.

GRADUATE UNITS

Graduate Programs Offers education (M Ed, MAT).

EARLHAM SCHOOL OF RELIGION, Richmond, IN 47374-5360

General Information Independent-religious, coed, graduate-only institution. *Enrollment by degree level:* 57 master's, 1 other advanced degree. *Graduate faculty:* 8 full-time (2 women), 2 part-time/adjunct (1 woman). *Tuition:* Full-time $15,741; part-time $1741 per course. *Required fees:* $450. *Graduate housing:* On-campus housing not available. *Student services:* Campus employment opportunities, campus safety program, career counseling, exercise/wellness program, international student services, teacher training, writing training. *Library facilities:* Lilly Library plus 2 others. *Collection:* Books: 351,561 (physical); Serial titles: 292 (physical). Weekly public service hours: 112; students can reserve study rooms.

Computer facilities: 125 computers available on campus for general student use. Online class registration is available.
Website: http://www.esr.earlham.edu/

General Application Contact: Matthew Hisrich, Director of Recruitment and Admissions, 765-983-1523, Fax: 765-983-1688, E-mail: hisrima@earlham.edu.

GRADUATE UNITS

Graduate Programs Students: 26 full-time (15 women), 32 part-time (21 women). *Faculty:* 8 full-time (2 women), 2 part-time/adjunct (1 woman). Expenses: Contact institution. *Financial support:* Scholarships/grants and tuition waivers (full and partial) available. Financial award application deadline: 4/15; financial award applicants required to submit FAFSA. *Program availability:* Part-time, online learning. Offers ministry (M Min); religion (MA); theology (M Div). *Application deadline:* For fall admission, 7/15 priority date for domestic students; for winter admission, 12/15 priority date for domestic students. Applications are processed on a rolling basis. *Application fee:* $35. Electronic applications accepted. *Application Contact:* Matthew Hisrich, Director of Recruitment and Admissions, 765-983-1523, Fax: 765-983-1688, E-mail: hisrima@earlham.edu. *Dean*, Jay W. Marshall, 800-432-1377, Fax: 765-983-1688, E-mail: marshja@earlham.edu.

EAST CAROLINA UNIVERSITY, Greenville, NC 27858-4353

General Information State-supported, coed, university. CGS member. *Enrollment:* 29,131 graduate, professional, and undergraduate students; 2,643 full-time matriculated graduate/professional students (1,690 women), 2,953 part-time matriculated graduate/professional students (1,993 women). *Enrollment by degree level:* 3,986 master's, 1,233 doctoral, 377 other advanced degrees. *Graduate faculty:* 966 full-time (444 women), 98 part-time/adjunct (55 women). Tuition, state resident: full-time $4749; part-time $297 per credit hour. Tuition, nonresident: full-time $17,898; part-time $1119 per credit hour. *Required fees:* $2691; $224 per credit hour. Part-time tuition and fees vary according to course load and program. *Graduate housing:* Room and/or apartments available on a first-come, first-served basis to single students; on-campus housing not available to married students. Housing application deadline: 5/1. *Student services:* Campus employment opportunities, campus safety program, career counseling, exercise/wellness program, free psychological counseling, grant writing training, international student services, low-cost health insurance, multicultural affairs office, services for students with disabilities, teacher training, writing training. *Library facilities:* Joyner Library plus 1 other. *Collection:* Books: 1.2 million (physical), 827,747 (digital/electronic); Serial titles: 8,311 (physical), 91,772 (digital/electronic); Databases: 507. Weekly public service hours: 143; study areas open 24 hours, 5–7 days a week; students can reserve study rooms.

Computer facilities: Computer purchase and lease plans are available. 2,760 computers available on campus for general student use. A campuswide network can be accessed from student residence rooms and from off campus. Online class registration is available.
Website: http://www.ecu.edu/

General Application Contact: Dr. Heidi Puckett, Director of Admissions, 252-328-5400, Fax: 252-328-6071, E-mail: gradschool@ecu.edu.

GRADUATE UNITS

Brody School of Medicine Students: 499 full-time (261 women), 23 part-time (18 women); includes 155 minority (61 Black or African American, non-Hispanic/Latino; 7 American Indian or Alaska Native, non-Hispanic/Latino; 61 Asian, non-Hispanic/Latino; 21 Hispanic/Latino; 5 Two or more races, non-Hispanic/Latino), 15 international. Average age 26. 1,100 applicants, 19% accepted, 134 enrolled. *Faculty:* 90 full-time (41 women), 13 part-time/adjunct (8 women). Expenses: Contact institution. *Financial support:* Fellowships, institutionally sponsored loans, and unspecified assistantships available. Financial award application deadline: 6/1. In 2017, 44 master's, 87 doctorates awarded. *Program availability:* Part-time, 100% online, blended/hybrid learning. Offers anatomy and cell biology (PhD); biochemistry and molecular biology (PhD); biomedical science (MS); medicine (MPH, MS, Dr PH, MD, PhD); microbiology and immunology (PhD); pharmacology and toxicology (PhD); physiology (PhD); public health (Dr PH). *Application fee:* $70. Electronic applications accepted.

Graduate School Students: 1,768 full-time (1,167 women), 2,539 part-time (1,612 women); includes 1,096 minority (689 Black or African American, non-Hispanic/Latino;

34 American Indian or Alaska Native, non-Hispanic/Latino; 116 Asian, non-Hispanic/Latino; 174 Hispanic/Latino; 2 Native Hawaiian or other Pacific Islander, non-Hispanic/Latino; 81 Two or more races, non-Hispanic/Latino), 78 international. Average age 33. 3,333 applicants, 60% accepted, 1485 enrolled. *Faculty:* 879 full-time (409 women), 85 part-time/adjunct (53 women). Expenses: Contact institution. *Financial support:* Fellowships with partial tuition reimbursements, research assistantships with partial tuition reimbursements, teaching assistantships with partial tuition reimbursements, career-related internships or fieldwork, Federal Work-Study, scholarships/grants, traineeships, and unspecified assistantships available. Support available to part-time students. Financial award application deadline: 3/1; financial award applicants required to submit FAFSA. In 2017, 1,269 master's, 133 doctorates, 360 other advanced degrees awarded. *Program availability:* Part-time, evening/weekend, online learning. *Application deadline:* For fall admission, 8/15 for domestic students, 2/1 for international students; for spring admission, 12/20 for domestic students, 10/1 for international students; for summer admission, 5/5 for domestic students. Applications are processed on a rolling basis. *Application fee:* $75. Electronic applications accepted. *Dean*, Dr. Paul Gemperline, 252-328-6073, E-mail: gemperlinep@ecu.edu.

College of Allied Health Sciences Students: 472 full-time (400 women), 194 part-time (165 women); includes 116 minority (65 Black or African American, non-Hispanic/Latino; 2 American Indian or Alaska Native, non-Hispanic/Latino; 19 Asian, non-Hispanic/Latino; 20 Hispanic/Latino; 10 Two or more races, non-Hispanic/Latino), 2 international. Average age 29. 1,173 applicants, 27% accepted, 203 enrolled. Expenses: Contact institution. *Financial support:* Research assistantships with partial tuition reimbursements, teaching assistantships with partial tuition reimbursements, career-related internships or fieldwork, Federal Work-Study, scholarships/grants, and unspecified assistantships available. Support available to part-time students. Financial award application deadline: 3/1; financial award applicants required to submit FAFSA. In 2017, 144 master's, 39 doctorates, 65 other advanced degrees awarded. *Program availability:* Part-time, evening/weekend, online learning. Offers allied health sciences (MS, MSOT, Au D, DPT, PhD, Certificate); clinical counseling (MS); communication sciences and disorders (MS, Au D, PhD); health care administration (Certificate); health care management (Certificate); health informatics (Certificate); health informatics and information management (MS); health information management (Certificate); military and trauma counseling (Certificate); nutrition science (MS); occupational therapy (MSOT); physical therapy (DPT); physician assistant studies (MS); rehabilitation and career counseling (MS); rehabilitation counseling (Certificate); rehabilitation counseling and administration (PhD); substance abuse counseling (Certificate); vocational evaluation (Certificate). *Application deadline:* For fall admission, 2/1 for domestic and international students; for spring admission, 9/1 for domestic students, 10/1 for international students. Applications are processed on a rolling basis. *Application fee:* $75. Electronic applications accepted. *Interim Dean*, Dr. Greg Hassler, 252-744-6010, E-mail: hasslerg@ecu.edu.

College of Business Students: 263 full-time (123 women), 623 part-time (293 women); includes 203 minority (122 Black or African American, non-Hispanic/Latino; 3 American Indian or Alaska Native, non-Hispanic/Latino; 28 Asian, non-Hispanic/Latino; 41 Hispanic/Latino; 9 Two or more races, non-Hispanic/Latino), 11 international. Average age 33. 418 applicants, 89% accepted, 299 enrolled. Expenses: Contact institution. *Financial support:* Research assistantships with partial tuition reimbursements, teaching assistantships with partial tuition reimbursements, Federal Work-Study, scholarships/grants, and unspecified assistantships available. Support available to part-time students. Financial award application deadline: 3/1. In 2017, 251 master's, 68 other advanced degrees awarded. *Program availability:* Part-time, evening/weekend. Offers accounting (MSA); business (MBA, MS, MSA, Postbaccalaureate Certificate); business administration (MBA); hospitality management (Postbaccalaureate Certificate); sustainable tourism and hospitality (MS). *Application deadline:* For fall admission, 6/1 priority date for domestic students, 2/1 for international students; for spring admission, 11/15 for domestic students, 10/1 for international students; for summer admission, 3/15 for domestic students. Applications are processed on a rolling basis. *Application fee:* $75. Electronic applications accepted. *Interim Director of Graduate Programs*, Paul Russell, 252-328-6970, E-mail: gradbus@ecu.edu.

College of Education Students: 186 full-time (145 women), 959 part-time (778 women); includes 266 minority (184 Black or African American, non-Hispanic/Latino; 13 American Indian or Alaska Native, non-Hispanic/Latino; 11 Asian, non-Hispanic/Latino; 33 Hispanic/Latino; 25 Two or more races, non-Hispanic/Latino), 6 international. Average age 37. 397 applicants, 96% accepted, 326 enrolled. Expenses: Contact institution. *Financial support:* Research assistantships with partial tuition reimbursements, teaching assistantships with partial tuition reimbursements, and Federal Work-Study available. Support available to part-time students. Financial award application deadline: 6/1. In 2017, 317 master's, 23 doctorates, 71 other advanced degrees awarded. *Program availability:* Part-time, evening/weekend, online learning. Offers adult education (MA Ed); assistive technology (Certificate); autism (Certificate); business and marketing education (MA Ed); community college instruction (Certificate); counselor education (MS); curriculum and instruction (MA Ed); distance learning and administration (Certificate); education (MA, MA Ed, MAT, MLS, MS, MSA, Ed D, Certificate, Ed S); education in the healthcare professions (Certificate); educational administration and supervision (Ed S); educational leadership (Ed D); elementary education (MA Ed, MAT); elementary mathematics education (Certificate); English education (MAT); history education (MAT); instructional technology (MA Ed, MS); library science (MLS); mathematics education (MA Ed); middle grades education (MA Ed, MAT); reading education (MA Ed); school administration (MSA); science education (MA Ed, MAT); special education (MA Ed, MAT); special endorsement in computer education (Certificate); student affairs in higher education (Certificate); vocational education (MS). *Application deadline:* For fall admission, 8/15 for domestic students, 2/1 for international students; for spring admission, 12/20 for domestic students, 10/1 for international students. Applications are processed on a rolling basis. *Application fee:* $75. Electronic applications accepted. *Dean*, Dr. Linda Ann Patriarca, 252-328-1000, Fax: 252-328-4219, E-mail: patriarcal@ecu.edu.

College of Engineering and Technology Students: 70 full-time (15 women), 223 part-time (54 women); includes 68 minority (38 Black or African American, non-Hispanic/Latino; 3 American Indian or Alaska Native, non-Hispanic/Latino; 12 Asian, non-Hispanic/Latino; 9 Hispanic/Latino; 6 Two or more races, non-Hispanic/Latino), 30 international. Average age 36. 119 applicants, 89% accepted, 80 enrolled. Expenses: Contact institution. *Financial support:* Fellowships, research assistantships, teaching assistantships, and Federal Work-Study available. Support available to part-time students. Financial award application deadline: 6/1. In 2017, 65 master's, 31 other advanced degrees awarded. *Program availability:* Part-time, evening/weekend, online learning. Offers biomedical engineering (MS); computer network professional (Certificate); computer science (MS); construction management (MCM); cyber security professional (Certificate); engineering and technology (MCM, MS, PhD, Certificate); information assurance (Certificate); Lean Six Sigma Black Belt (Certificate); network technology (MS); occupational safety (MS); residential construction management (Certificate); software engineering (MS); technology management (MS, PhD); Website developer (Certificate). *Application deadline:* For fall admission, 6/1 priority date for domestic students. Applications are processed on a rolling basis. *Application fee:* $75. Electronic applications accepted. *Dean*, Dr. David White, 252-328-9604.

College of Fine Arts and Communication Students: 67 full-time (41 women), 62 part-time (43 women); includes 31 minority (15 Black or African American, non-Hispanic/Latino; 9 Asian, non-Hispanic/Latino; 3 Hispanic/Latino; 4 Two or more races, non-Hispanic/Latino), 2 international. Average age 31. 85 applicants, 80% accepted, 46 enrolled. Expenses: Contact institution. In 2017, 38 master's, 5 other advanced degrees awarded. Offers advanced performance studies (Certificate); art education (MA Ed); ceramics (MFA); communication (MA); composition (MM); fine arts and communication (MA, MA Ed, MFA, MM, Certificate); graphic design (MFA); health communication (Certificate); illustration (MFA); metal design (MFA); music education (MM); music therapy (MM); painting and drawing (MFA); photography (MFA); printmaking (MFA); sculpture (MFA); Suzuki pedagogy (Certificate); textile design (MFA); theory (MM); wood design (MFA); woodwind specialist (MM). *Application fee:* $75. *Dean*, J. Christopher Buddo, 252-328-1283, E-mail: buddoj@ecu.edu.

College of Health and Human Performance Students: 290 full-time (222 women), 137 part-time (103 women); includes 132 minority (90 Black or African American, non-Hispanic/Latino; 5 American Indian or Alaska Native, non-Hispanic/Latino; 8 Asian, non-Hispanic/Latino; 19 Hispanic/Latino; 1 Native Hawaiian or other Pacific Islander, non-Hispanic/Latino; 9 Two or more races, non-Hispanic/Latino), 6 international. Average age 29. 333 applicants, 71% accepted, 163 enrolled. Expenses: Contact institution. *Financial support:* Research assistantships, teaching assistantships, and Federal Work-Study available. Support available to part-time students. Financial award application deadline: 6/1. In 2017, 163 master's, 8 doctorates, 39 other advanced degrees awarded. *Program availability:* Part-time, evening/weekend. Offers adapted physical education (MS); aquatic therapy (Certificate); bioenergetics and exercise science (PhD); biofeedback (Certificate); biomechanics and motor control (MS); birth through kindergarten education (MA Ed); environmental health (MS); exercise physiology (MS); gerontology (Certificate); health and human performance (MA, MA Ed, MAT, MS, MSEH, MSW, PhD, Certificate); health education (MA Ed); health education and promotion (MA); human development and family science (MS); marriage and family therapy (MS); medical family therapy (PhD); physical activity promotion (MS); physical education (MA Ed, MAT); physical education clinical supervision (Certificate); physical education pedagogy (MS); recreation services and interventions (MS); social work (MSW); sport and exercise psychology (MS); sport management (MS, Certificate); substance abuse (Certificate). *Application deadline:* For fall admission, 6/1 priority date for domestic students. Applications are processed on a rolling basis. *Application fee:* $75. *Dean*, Dr. Glen Gilbert, 252-328-0038, E-mail: gilbertg@ecu.edu.

College of Nursing Students: 163 full-time (147 women), 391 part-time (363 women); includes 115 minority (78 Black or African American, non-Hispanic/Latino; 5 American Indian or Alaska Native, non-Hispanic/Latino; 13 Asian, non-Hispanic/Latino; 11 Hispanic/Latino; 1 Native Hawaiian or other Pacific Islander, non-Hispanic/Latino; 7 Two or more races, non-Hispanic/Latino), 2 international. Average age 38. 234 applicants, 79% accepted, 162 enrolled. Expenses: Contact institution. *Financial support:* Research assistantships with partial tuition reimbursements, teaching assistantships with partial tuition reimbursements, and Federal Work-Study available. Support available to part-time students. Financial award application deadline: 6/1. In 2017, 119 master's, 47 doctorates awarded. *Program availability:* Part-time. Offers nursing (MSN, DNP, PhD). *Application deadline:* For fall admission, 3/15 priority date for domestic students; for spring admission, 10/15 priority date for domestic students. Applications are processed on a rolling basis. *Application fee:* $70. *Dean*, Dr. Sylvia Brown, 252-744-6372, E-mail: brownsy@ecu.edu.

Thomas Harriot College of Arts and Sciences Students: 403 full-time (212 women), 329 part-time (171 women); includes 161 minority (96 Black or African American, non-Hispanic/Latino; 2 American Indian or Alaska Native, non-Hispanic/Latino; 15 Asian, non-Hispanic/Latino; 37 Hispanic/Latino; 11 Two or more races, non-Hispanic/Latino), 16 international. Average age 30. 560 applicants, 61% accepted, 202 enrolled. Expenses: Contact institution. *Financial support:* Fellowships with partial tuition reimbursements, research assistantships with partial tuition reimbursements, teaching assistantships with partial tuition reimbursements, career-related internships or fieldwork, Federal Work-Study, scholarships/grants, traineeships, and unspecified assistantships available. Support available to part-time students. Financial award application deadline: 3/1. In 2017, 172 master's, 12 doctorates, 80 other advanced degrees awarded. *Program availability:* Part-time, evening/weekend, online learning. Offers American history (MA); anthropology (MA); applied physics (MS); arts and sciences (MA, MPA, MS, PhD, Certificate); Atlantic world (MA); biology (MS); biomedical physics (PhD); chemistry (MS); creative writing (MA); criminal justice (MS); criminal justice education (Certificate); development and environmental planning (Certificate); economic development (Certificate); English studies (MA); European history (MA); geographic information science and technology (Certificate); geography (MA); geology (MS); health physics (MS); health psychology (PhD); hydrogeology and environmental geology (Certificate); industrial and organizational psychology (MA); international studies (MA); international teaching (Certificate); linguistics (MA); literature (MA); maritime studies (MA); mathematics (MA); medical physics (MS); military history (MA); molecular biology and biotechnology (MS); multicultural and transnational literatures (MA, Certificate); professional communication (Certificate); public administration (MPA); public history (MA); quantitative economics and econometrics (MS); quantitative methods for the social and behavioral sciences (Certificate); rhetoric and composition (MA); rhetoric, writing, and professional communication (PhD); security studies (MS, Certificate); sociology (MA); teaching English in the two-year college (Certificate); teaching English to speakers of other languages (MA, Certificate); technical and professional communication (MA). *Application deadline:* For fall admission, 8/15 priority date for domestic students, 2/1 priority date for international students; for spring admission, 12/20 priority date for domestic students, 10/1 priority date for international students. Applications are processed on a rolling basis. *Application fee:* $75. Electronic applications accepted. *Dean*, Dr. William M. Downs, 252-328-6249, E-mail: downsw14@ecu.edu.

School of Dental Medicine Students: 213 full-time (115 women); includes 81 minority (41 Black or African American, non-Hispanic/Latino; 4 American Indian or Alaska Native, non-Hispanic/Latino; 16 Asian, non-Hispanic/Latino; 14 Hispanic/Latino; 6 Two or more races, non-Hispanic/Latino). Average age 26. 94 applicants, 81% accepted, 52 enrolled. Expenses: Contact institution. In 2017, 46 doctorates awarded. Offers dental medicine (DMD). *Application deadline:* For fall admission, 6/30 for domestic students. Applications are processed on a rolling basis. *Application fee:* $80. Electronic applications accepted. *Dean*, Dr. Greg Chadwick, 252-737-7703.

EAST CENTRAL UNIVERSITY, Ada, OK 74820

General Information State-supported, coed, comprehensive institution. *Graduate housing:* On-campus housing not available. *Student services:* Campus employment opportunities, career counseling, child daycare facilities, exercise/wellness program, free psychological counseling, grant writing training, international student services, multicultural affairs office, services for students with disabilities, teacher training, writing training. *Library facilities:* Linscheid Library. *Collection:* Books: 159,582 (physical), 25,548 (digital/electronic); Serial titles: 24,879 (physical), 825 (digital/electronic); Databases: 73. Weekly public service hours: 71; students can reserve study rooms.

Computer facilities: 800 computers available on campus for general student use. A campuswide network can be accessed from student residence rooms. Online class registration is available.
Website: http://www.ecok.edu/

General Application Contact: Brenda Sherbourne, Acting Dean, 580-559-5350, Fax: 580-332-8691, E-mail: bsherbrn@ecok.edu.

GRADUATE UNITS

School of Graduate Studies Expenses: Contact institution. *Financial support:* Career-related internships or fieldwork, Federal Work-Study, institutionally sponsored loans, and tuition waivers (partial) available. Support available to part-time students. *Program availability:* Part-time, evening/weekend. Offers accounting (MS); clinical rehabilitation and clinical mental health counseling (MSHR); criminal justice (MSHR); education (M Ed); human resources (MSHR); psychology (MSPS). *Application deadline:* Applications are processed on a rolling basis. *Application fee:* $0 ($50 for international students). Electronic applications accepted. *Application Contact:* Brenda Sherbourne, Acting Dean, 580-559-5350, E-mail: bsherbrn@ecok.edu. *Acting Dean*, Brenda Sherbourne, 580-559-5350, E-mail: bsherbrn@ecok.edu.

EASTERN CONNECTICUT STATE UNIVERSITY, Willimantic, CT 06226-2295

General Information State-supported, coed, comprehensive institution. *Enrollment:* 90 full-time matriculated graduate/professional students (57 women), 124 part-time matriculated graduate/professional students (94 women). *Enrollment by degree level:* 214 master's. *Graduate faculty:* 27 full-time (12 women), 14 part-time/adjunct (8 women). *Tuition, area resident:* Full-time $12,252. Tuition, state resident: full-time $15,245; part-time $582 per credit hour. Tuition, nonresident: full-time $24,828; part-time $582 per credit hour. *Required fees:* $40 per semester. Full-time tuition and fees vary according to reciprocity agreements. *Graduate housing:* Room and/or apartments available on a first-come, first-served basis to single students; on-campus housing not available to married students. Typical cost: $12,064 per year. Housing application deadline: 4/3. *Student services:* Campus employment opportunities, campus safety program, career counseling, child daycare facilities, exercise/wellness program, free psychological counseling, grant writing training, international student services, multicultural affairs office, services for students with disabilities, teacher training, writing training. *Library facilities:* J. Eugene Smith Library. *Research affiliation:* Spencer Foundation (early childhood education), CEEDAR Center (early childhood, physical education, elementary education, secondary education).

Computer facilities: Computer purchase and lease plans are available. 2,500 computers available on campus for general student use. A campuswide network can be accessed from student residence rooms and from off campus. Online class registration is available.
Website: http://www.easternct.edu/

General Application Contact: Paula Goyette, Graduate Division, School of Education and Professional Studies, 860-465-5292, Fax: 860-465-4538, E-mail: graduateadmissions@easternct.edu.

GRADUATE UNITS

School of Education and Professional Studies/Graduate Division Students: 90 full-time (57 women), 124 part-time (94 women); includes 46 minority (12 Black or African American, non-Hispanic/Latino; 4 American Indian or Alaska Native, non-Hispanic/Latino; 11 Asian, non-Hispanic/Latino; 15 Hispanic/Latino; 1 Native Hawaiian or other Pacific Islander, non-Hispanic/Latino; 3 Two or more races, non-Hispanic/Latino). Average age 34. 91 applicants, 74% accepted, 52 enrolled. *Faculty:* 27 full-time (12 women), 14 part-time/adjunct (8 women). Expenses: Contact institution. *Financial support:* Research assistantships, teaching assistantships, career-related internships or fieldwork, scholarships/grants, and unspecified assistantships available. Financial award application deadline: 3/1; financial award applicants required to submit FAFSA. In 2017, 61 master's awarded. *Program availability:* Part-time, evening/weekend. Offers accounting (MS); early childhood education (MS); education and professional studies (MS); educational technology (MS); elementary education (MS); organizational management (MS); secondary education (MS). *Application deadline:* For fall admission, 7/6 priority date for domestic and international students; for spring admission, 11/3 priority date for domestic and international students; for summer admission, 4/5 priority date for domestic and international students. Applications are processed on a rolling basis. *Application fee:* $50. Electronic applications accepted. *Application Contact:* Paula Goyette, Secretary II, 860-465-5292, Fax: 860-465-4538, E-mail: graduateadmissions@easternct.edu. *Dean*, Dr. Jacob Easley, II, 860-465-5293, Fax: 860-465-4538, E-mail: easleyj@easternct.edu.

EASTERN ILLINOIS UNIVERSITY, Charleston, IL 61920

General Information State-supported, coed, comprehensive institution. CGS member. *Enrollment:* 677 full-time matriculated graduate/professional students (433 women), 785 part-time matriculated graduate/professional students (495 women). *Graduate faculty:* 310. *Graduate housing:* Rooms and/or apartments available on a first-come, first-served basis to single and married students. *Student services:* Campus employment opportunities, campus safety program, career counseling, exercise/wellness program, free psychological counseling, international student services, low-cost health insurance, multicultural affairs office, services for students with disabilities, teacher training, writing training. *Library facilities:* Booth Library. *Collection:* Books: 1 million (physical), 1.3 million (digital/electronic); Serial titles: 161 (physical), 45,276 (digital/electronic); Databases: 244. Weekly public service hours: 98.

Computer facilities: Computer purchase and lease plans are available. 706 computers available on campus for general student use. A campuswide network can be accessed from student residence rooms and from off campus. Online class registration is available.
Website: http://www.eiu.edu/

General Application Contact: Dr. Ryan Hendrickson, Dean of Graduate School, 217-581-2220, Fax: 217-581-6020, E-mail: graduate@eiu.edu.

GRADUATE UNITS

Graduate School Expenses: Contact institution. *Financial support:* Fellowships with full tuition reimbursements, research assistantships with full tuition reimbursements, teaching assistantships with full tuition reimbursements, career-related internships or fieldwork, Federal Work-Study, and unspecified assistantships available. Support available to part-time students. Financial award application deadline: 3/1; financial award applicants required to submit FAFSA. *Program availability:* Part-time, evening/weekend, 100% online, blended/hybrid learning. *Application deadline:* For fall admission, 5/15 for domestic and international students; for spring admission, 10/15 for domestic and international students. Applications are processed on a rolling basis. *Application fee:* $30. Electronic applications accepted. *Application Contact:* Tracey S. Hutchison, Admissions Officer, 217-581-7488, Fax: 217-581-6020, E-mail: tshutchison@eiu.edu. *Dean*, Dr. Ryan Hendrickson, 217-581-2220, Fax: 217-581-6020, E-mail: rchendrickson@eiu.edu.

College of Education and Professional Studies Expenses: Contact institution. *Financial support:* In 2017–18, 245 students received support. Research assistantships with full tuition reimbursements available, teaching assistantships with full tuition reimbursements available, career-related internships or fieldwork, Federal Work-Study, and unspecified assistantships available. Support available to part-time students. Financial award application deadline: 3/1; financial award applicants required to submit FAFSA. *Program availability:* Part-time, evening/weekend. Offers college student affairs (MS); counseling (MS); curriculum and instruction (MS Ed); education and professional studies (MS, MS Ed, Ed S); educational administration (Ed S); educational leadership (MS Ed); special education (MS Ed). *Application deadline:* For fall admission, 5/15 for domestic and international students; for spring admission, 10/15 for domestic and international students. Applications are processed on a rolling basis. *Application fee:* $30. Electronic applications accepted. *Application Contact:* Douglas J. Bower, Dean, 217-581-2200, Fax: 217-581-2518, E-mail: djbower@eiu.edu. *Dean*, Douglas J. Bower, 217-581-2200, Fax: 217-581-2518, E-mail: djbower@eiu.edu.

College of Health and Human Services Expenses: Contact institution. *Financial support:* Research assistantships with tuition reimbursements, teaching assistantships with tuition reimbursements, and career-related internships or fieldwork available. *Program availability:* Part-time. Offers aging studies (MA); communication disorders and sciences (MS); health and human services (MA, MHS, MS); human services program development (MHS); kinesiology and sports studies (MS); nutrition and dietetics (MS). *Application deadline:* For fall admission, 3/31 priority date for domestic students. Applications are processed on a rolling basis. *Application fee:* $30.

College of Liberal Arts and Sciences Expenses: Contact institution. *Financial support:* Research assistantships with full tuition reimbursements, teaching assistantships with full tuition reimbursements, career-related internships or fieldwork, Federal Work-Study, scholarships/grants, and unspecified assistantships available. Support available to part-time students. Financial award applicants required to submit FAFSA. *Program availability:* Part-time, evening/weekend, 100% online, blended/hybrid learning. Offers art (MA); art education (MA); biological sciences (MS); chemistry (MS); clinical psychology (MA); communication pedagogy (MA); community arts (MA); composition (MA); conducting (MA); economics (MA); elementary/middle school mathematics education (MA); English (MA); geographic information sciences (PSM); history (MA); liberal arts and sciences (MA, MS, PSM, SSP); mathematics (MA); music education (MA); performance (MA); political science (MA); school psychology (SSP); secondary mathematics education (MA). *Application deadline:* For fall admission, 5/15 for domestic and international students; for spring admission, 10/15 for domestic and international students. Applications are processed on a rolling basis. *Application fee:* $30. Electronic applications accepted. *Application Contact:* JoAnn Ingle, Admissions Officer, 217-581-7488, Fax: 217-581-6020, E-mail: ljingle@eiu.edu. *Dean*, 217-581-2922, Fax: 217-581-7085.

Lumpkin College of Business and Technology Expenses: Contact institution. *Financial support:* Research assistantships with tuition reimbursements, teaching assistantships with tuition reimbursements, career-related internships or fieldwork, Federal Work-Study, and unspecified assistantships available. Support available to part-time students. Financial award application deadline: 3/1; financial award applicants required to submit FAFSA. *Program availability:* Part-time, evening/weekend, online learning. Offers accountancy (MBA); applied management (MBA); business and technology (MA, MBA, MS, Certificate); computer technology (Certificate); cybersecurity (MS); geographic information systems (MBA); quality systems (Certificate); research (MBA); sustainable energy (MS); technology (MS, Certificate); technology security (Certificate); work performance improvement (Certificate). *Application deadline:* For fall admission, 5/15 for domestic and international students; for spring admission, 10/15 for domestic and international students. Applications are processed on a rolling basis. *Application fee:* $30. Electronic applications accepted. *Application Contact:* Deborah D. Endsley, Assistant to the Dean for Administration, 217-581-7816, Fax: 217-581-6029, E-mail: ddendsley@eiu.edu. *Interim Dean*, Dr. William C. Minnis, 217-581-3526, Fax: 217-581-6029.

EASTERN KENTUCKY UNIVERSITY, Richmond, KY 40475-3102

General Information State-supported, coed, comprehensive institution. CGS member. *Graduate housing:* Rooms and/or apartments guaranteed to single students and available to married students.

GRADUATE UNITS

The Graduate School *Program availability:* Part-time, evening/weekend, online learning. Electronic applications accepted.

College of Arts and Sciences *Program availability:* Part-time, evening/weekend. Offers arts and sciences (MA, MFA, MM, MPA, MS, PhD, Psy S); biological sciences (MS); chemistry (MS); choral conducting (MM); clinical psychology (MS); community development (MPA); community health administration (MPA); creative writing (MFA); ecology (MS); English (MA); general public administration (MPA); geology (MS, PhD); history (MA); industrial/organizational psychology (MS); mathematical sciences (MS); performance (MM); political science (MA); school psychology (Psy S); theory/composition (MM).

College of Business and Technology *Program availability:* Part-time. Offers business administration (MBA); business and technology (MBA, MS); industrial education (MS); industrial technology (MS); occupational training and development (MS); technical administration (MS); technology education (MS).

College of Education *Program availability:* Part-time, online learning. Offers communication disorders (MA Ed); education (MA, MA Ed, MAT); elementary education (MA Ed); human services (MA); instructional leadership (MA Ed); library science (MA Ed); mental health counseling (MA); music education (MA Ed); school counseling (MA Ed); secondary and higher education (MA Ed); secondary education (MA Ed); teaching (MAT).

College of Health Sciences *Program availability:* Part-time. Offers community health education (MPH); environmental health science (MPH); exercise and sport science (MS); exercise and wellness (MS); family and consumer sciences (M Ed); health sciences (MPH, MS, MSN); industrial hygiene (MPH); occupational therapy (MS); public health nutrition (MPH); recreation and park administration (MS); rural community health care (MSN); rural health family nurse practitioner (MSN); sports administration (MS).

College of Justice and Safety *Program availability:* Part-time. Offers correctional and juvenile justice studies (MS); criminal justice (MS); criminal justice education (MS); justice and safety (MS); loss prevention and safety (MS); police studies (MS).

EASTERN MENNONITE UNIVERSITY, Harrisonburg, VA 22802-2462

General Information Independent-religious, coed, comprehensive institution. *Enrollment:* 1,530 graduate, professional, and undergraduate students; 125 full-time matriculated graduate/professional students (78 women), 307 part-time matriculated graduate/professional students (211 women). *Enrollment by degree level:* 407 master's, 25 other advanced degrees. *Graduate faculty:* 45 full-time (27 women), 14 part-time/adjunct (10 women). *Graduate housing:* Rooms and/or apartments available on a first-come, first-served basis to single and married students. Housing application deadline: 4/15. *Student services:* Campus employment opportunities, campus safety program, career counseling, exercise/wellness program, free psychological counseling, international student services, low-cost health insurance, multicultural affairs office, services for students with disabilities, teacher training, writing training. *Library facilities:* Sadie Hartzler Library. *Collection:* Books: 166,455 (physical), 179,434 (digital/electronic); Serial titles: 69,668 (physical), 34,489 (digital/electronic); Databases: 94. Weekly public service hours: 92.

Computer facilities: 154 computers available on campus for general student use. A campuswide network can be accessed from student residence rooms and from off campus. Online class registration is available.
Website: http://www.emu.edu/

General Application Contact: Shirley Ewald, Assistant to the Dean of Graduate Studies, 540-432-4026, Fax: 540-432-4444, E-mail: shirley.ewald@emu.edu.

GRADUATE UNITS

Eastern Mennonite Seminary Expenses: Contact institution. *Financial support:* Application deadline: 6/30; applicants required to submit FAFSA. *Program availability:* Part-time. Offers Christian leadership (MA); divinity (M Div); ministry studies (Certificate); religion (MA); theological studies (Certificate). *Application deadline:* For fall admission, 6/15 priority date for domestic and international students; for winter admission, 11/15 priority date for domestic and international students; for spring admission, 3/15 priority date for domestic and international students. Applications are processed on a rolling basis. *Application fee:* $25. *Application Contact:* Laura Lehman, Director of Seminary Admissions, 540-432-4268, Fax: 540-432-4598, E-mail: semadmiss@emu.edu. *Dean*, Sue Cockley, 540-432-4984, Fax: 540-432-4444, E-mail: cockleys@emu.edu.

Master of Arts in Counseling Program Expenses: Contact institution. *Financial support:* Scholarships/grants available. Financial award application deadline: 6/30; financial award applicants required to submit FAFSA. *Program availability:* Part-time. Offers counseling (MA). *Application deadline:* For fall admission, 3/1 for domestic and international students. *Application fee:* $50. Electronic applications accepted. *Application Contact:* Amanda Williams, Administrative Assistant, 540-432-4243, Fax: 540-432-4444, E-mail: amanda.k.williams@emu.edu. *Director*, Dr. Teresa J. Haase, 540-432-4248, Fax: 540-432-4444, E-mail: teresa.haase@emu.edu.

Program in Biomedicine Expenses: Contact institution. Offers biomedicine (MA). *Application deadline:* For fall admission, 7/31 for domestic students; for spring admission, 11/9 for domestic students. Applications are processed on a rolling basis. *Application fee:* $50. Electronic applications accepted. *Application Contact:* Don A. Yoder, Director of Seminary and Graduate Admissions, 540-432-4257, Fax: 540-432-4598, E-mail: yoderda@emu.edu. *Chair*, Kim Gingerich Brenneman, 540-432-4429, E-mail: brennkg@emu.edu.

Program in Business Administration Expenses: Contact institution. *Financial support:* Application deadline: 6/30; applicants required to submit FAFSA. *Program availability:* Part-time, evening/weekend. Offers general management (MBA); health services administration (MBA); non-profit leadership (MBA). *Application deadline:* For fall admission, 3/1 priority date for domestic and international students. Applications are processed on a rolling basis. *Application fee:* $25. Electronic applications accepted. *Application Contact:* Patricia S. Eckard, Administrative Coordinator, 540-432-4150, Fax: 540-432-4071, E-mail: eckardp@emu.edu. *Department Chair*, Dr. James M. Leaman, 540-432-4152, Fax: 540-432-4071, E-mail: james.leaman@emu.edu.

Program in Conflict Transformation Expenses: Contact institution. *Financial support:* Scholarships/grants available. Financial award application deadline: 6/30; financial award applicants required to submit FAFSA. *Program availability:* Part-time. Offers conflict transformation (MA, Graduate Certificate). *Application deadline:* For fall admission, 2/15 priority date for domestic and international students. Applications are processed on a rolling basis. *Application fee:* $50. Electronic applications accepted. *Application Contact:* Lora Steiner, Coordinator of Admissions and Marketing, 540-432-4689, Fax: 540-432-4449, E-mail: lora.steiner@emu.edu. *Program Director*, Dr. Jayne Docherty, 540-432-4627, Fax: 540-432-4449, E-mail: jayne.docherty@emu.edu.

Program in Nursing Expenses: Contact institution. *Financial support:* Federal Work-Study and scholarships/grants available. Financial award applicants required to submit FAFSA. *Program availability:* Part-time, online learning. Offers leadership and management (MSN); leadership and school nursing (MSN); nursing management (DNP). *Application deadline:* For fall admission, 6/1 for domestic students. Applications are processed on a rolling basis. *Application fee:* $25. *Application Contact:* Don A. Yoder, Director of Seminary and Graduate Admissions, 540-432-4257, Fax: 540-432-4598, E-mail: yoderda@emu.edu. *Coordinator*, Ann Hershberger, 540-432-4192, E-mail: hershbea@emu.edu.

Program in Organizational Leadership Expenses: Contact institution. Offers organizational leadership (MA). *Application fee:* $50. *Application Contact:* Lois Shank, Assistant to the Provost, 540-432-4105, Fax: 540-432-4444, E-mail: graduate@emu.edu. *Director*, David Brubaker, 540-432-4423, E-mail: mol@emu.edu.

Program in Teacher Education Expenses: Contact institution. *Financial support:* Federal Work-Study and scholarships/grants available. Financial award application deadline: 6/30; financial award applicants required to submit FAFSA. *Program availability:* Part-time. Offers curriculum and instruction (MA Ed); diverse needs (MA Ed); literacy (MA Ed); restorative justice in education (MA Ed). *Application deadline:* Applications are processed on a rolling basis. *Application fee:* $50. Electronic applications accepted. *Application Contact:* Yvonne Martin, Office Assistant, 540-432-4350, Fax: 540-432-4071, E-mail: yvonne.martin@emu.edu. *Chair*, Cathy Smeltzer Erb, 540-432-4638.

EASTERN MICHIGAN UNIVERSITY, Ypsilanti, MI 48197

General Information State-supported, coed, comprehensive institution. CGS member. *Enrollment:* 20,313 graduate, professional, and undergraduate students; 955 full-time matriculated graduate/professional students (645 women), 2,360 part-time matriculated graduate/professional students (1,524 women). *Enrollment by degree level:* 2,768 master's, 219 doctoral, 328 other advanced degrees. *Graduate faculty:* 659 full-time (333 women). *Graduate housing:* Rooms and/or apartments available on a first-come, first-served basis to single and married students. *Student services:* Campus employment opportunities, campus safety program, career counseling, child daycare facilities, exercise/wellness program, free psychological counseling, grant writing training, international student services, low-cost health insurance, multicultural affairs office, services for students with disabilities, teacher training, writing training. *Library facilities:* Bruce T. Halle Library. *Research affiliation:* Dima-Shield (coatings research), Signal Medical Corporation (textiles research), TRACO (coatings research), 3M Corporation (coatings research), Toyota Motor Company (coatings research), Beckers-Fusion (coatings research).

Computer facilities: 1,600 computers available on campus for general student use. A campuswide network can be accessed from student residence rooms. Online class registration is available.
Website: http://www.emich.edu/

General Application Contact: Graduate Admissions, 734-487-2400, Fax: 734-487-6559, E-mail: graduate.admissions@emich.edu.

GRADUATE UNITS

Graduate School Students: 955 full-time (645 women), 2,360 part-time (1,524 women); includes 773 minority (436 Black or African American, non-Hispanic/Latino; 11 American Indian or Alaska Native, non-Hispanic/Latino; 100 Asian, non-Hispanic/Latino; 138 Hispanic/Latino; 1 Native Hawaiian or other Pacific Islander, non-Hispanic/Latino; 87 Two or more races, non-Hispanic/Latino), 283 international. Average age 33. 2,952 applicants, 57% accepted, 835 enrolled. *Faculty:* 659 full-time (333 women). Expenses: Contact institution. *Financial support:* Fellowships, research assistantships with full tuition reimbursements, teaching assistantships with full tuition reimbursements, career-related internships or fieldwork, Federal Work-Study, institutionally sponsored loans, scholarships/grants, tuition waivers (partial), and unspecified assistantships available. Support available to part-time students. Financial award applicants required to submit FAFSA. In 2017, 1,154 master's, 58 doctorates, 156 other advanced degrees awarded. *Program availability:* Part-time, evening/weekend, online learning. *Application deadline:* For fall admission, 5/15 priority date for domestic students, 2/15 priority date for international students; for winter admission, 10/15 priority date for domestic students, 9/1 priority date for international students; for summer admission, 3/15 priority date for domestic students, 3/1 priority date for international students. Applications are processed on a rolling basis. *Application fee:* $45. Electronic applications accepted. *Application Contact:* Graduate Admissions, 734-487-2400, Fax: 734-487-6559, E-mail: graduate.admissions@emich.edu. *Interim Dean, Graduate School*, Dr. Wade Tornquist, 734-487-0042, Fax: 734-487-0050, E-mail: wade.tornquist@emich.edu.

Academic and Student Affairs Division Students: 4 full-time (2 women), 36 part-time (25 women); includes 6 minority (2 Asian, non-Hispanic/Latino; 1 Hispanic/Latino; 3 Two or more races, non-Hispanic/Latino). Average age 35. 64 applicants, 84% accepted, 26 enrolled. Expenses: Contact institution. In 2017, 1 master's awarded. Offers individualized studies (MA, MS); integrated marketing communications (MS). *Application fee:* $45. *Application Contact:* Graduate Admissions, 734-487-2400, Fax: 734-487-6559, E-mail: graduate.admissions@emich.edu. *Interim Dean*, Dr. Wade Tornquist, 734-487-0042, Fax: 734-487-0050, E-mail: wade.tornquist@emich.edu.

College of Arts and Sciences Students: 240 full-time (148 women), 554 part-time (338 women); includes 181 minority (87 Black or African American, non-Hispanic/Latino; 1 American Indian or Alaska Native, non-Hispanic/Latino; 27 Asian, non-Hispanic/Latino; 39 Hispanic/Latino; 27 Two or more races, non-Hispanic/Latino), 91 international. Average age 31. 899 applicants, 53% accepted, 216 enrolled. *Faculty:* 343 full-time (149 women). Expenses: Contact institution. *Financial support:* Fellowships, research assistantships with full tuition reimbursements, teaching assistantships with full tuition reimbursements, career-related internships or fieldwork, Federal Work-Study, institutionally sponsored loans, and tuition waivers (partial) available. Support available to part-time students. Financial award applicants required to submit FAFSA. In 2017, 260 master's, 9 doctorates, 12 other advanced degrees awarded. *Program availability:* Part-time, evening/weekend. Offers Africology and African-American studies (Graduate Certificate); applied drama/theatre for the young (MFA); arts administration (MA); arts and sciences (MA, MFA, MLS, MM, MPA, MS, PhD, Graduate Certificate); chemistry (MS); children's literature (MA); clinical behavioral psychology (MS); clinical psychology (PhD); communication (MA); community college biology teaching (MS); computer science (MS, Graduate Certificate); creative writing (MA); criminology and criminal justice (MA); cultural museum studies (Graduate Certificate); earth science education (MS); economics (MA, Graduate Certificate); English linguistics (MA); English studies for teachers (MA); general biology (MS); general clinical psychology (MS); general experimental psychology (MS); general public management (Graduate Certificate); geographic information systems (MS, Graduate Certificate); geographic information systems for educators (Graduate Certificate); geographic information systems for professionals (Graduate Certificate); heritage interpretation and museum practice (MS); historic preservation (MS, Graduate Certificate); history (MA); interpretation/performance studies (MA); language and international trade (MA); literature (MA); local government management (Graduate Certificate); management of public healthcare services (Graduate Certificate); mathematics (MA); music and dance (MM); nonprofit management (Graduate Certificate); philosophy (MA); physics (MS); preservation planning and administration (MS); public administration (MPA, Graduate Certificate); public budget management (Graduate Certificate); public land planning and development management (Graduate Certificate); public personnel management (Graduate Certificate); public policy analysis (Graduate Certificate); recording, documentation and digital cultural heritage (MS); schools, society and violence (MA); social science (MA); sociology (MA); sociology - applied research specialty (MA); studio art (MA, MFA); teaching English to speakers of other languages (MA, Graduate Certificate); technical communication (Graduate Certificate); theatre arts (MA); transportation planning and modeling (Graduate Certificate); urban and regional planning (MS, Graduate Certificate); visual art education (MA); women's and gender studies (MA, Graduate Certificate); world languages (MA, Graduate Certificate); written communication (MA, Graduate Certificate). *Application deadline:* Applications are processed on a rolling basis. *Application fee:* $45. *Interim Dean*, Dr. Kathleen Stacey, 734-487-4344, Fax: 734-485-9592, E-mail: kstacey@emich.edu.

College of Business Students: 150 full-time (89 women), 460 part-time (274 women); includes 174 minority (95 Black or African American, non-Hispanic/Latino; 5 American Indian or Alaska Native, non-Hispanic/Latino; 29 Asian, non-Hispanic/Latino; 30 Hispanic/Latino; 15 Two or more races, non-Hispanic/Latino), 57 international. Average age 31. 428 applicants, 69% accepted, 163 enrolled. *Faculty:* 75 full-time (30 women). Expenses: Contact institution. *Financial support:* Fellowships, research assistantships with full tuition reimbursements, teaching assistantships with full tuition reimbursements, career-related internships or fieldwork, Federal Work-Study, institutionally sponsored loans, traineeships, tuition waivers (partial), and unspecified assistantships available. Support available to part-time students. Financial award applicants required to submit FAFSA. In 2017, 253 master's, 35 other advanced degrees awarded. *Program availability:* Part-time, evening/weekend, online learning. Offers accounting (MS); accounting information systems (MS); business (MBA, MS, MSHROD, Graduate Certificate, Postbaccalaureate Certificate); business administration (MBA, Graduate Certificate); computer information systems (Graduate Certificate); e-business (MBA, Graduate Certificate); enterprise business intelligence (MBA); entrepreneurship (MBA, Graduate Certificate, Postbaccalaureate Certificate); finance (MBA, Graduate Certificate); human resources (MBA); human resources management (Graduate Certificate); human resources management and organizational development (MSHROD); information systems (MBA); integrated marketing communications (MS, Postbaccalaureate Certificate); internal auditing (MBA); international business (MBA, Graduate Certificate); marketing management (MBA, Graduate Certificate); nonprofit management (MBA); organizational development (Graduate Certificate); supply chain management (MBA, Graduate Certificate). *Application deadline:* Applications are processed on a rolling basis. *Application fee:* $45. *Application Contact:* K. Michelle Henry, Director, Graduate Business Programs, 734-487-4444, Fax: 734-483-1316, E-mail: cob.graduate@emich.edu. *Interim Dean*, Dr. Anne Balazs, 734-487-4140, Fax: 734-487-7099, E-mail: cob_dean@emich.edu.

College of Education Students: 193 full-time (163 women), 681 part-time (523 women); includes 201 minority (136 Black or African American, non-Hispanic/Latino; 3 American Indian or Alaska Native, non-Hispanic/Latino; 11 Asian, non-Hispanic/Latino; 30 Hispanic/Latino; 21 Two or more races, non-Hispanic/Latino), 30 international. Average age 34. 693 applicants, 54% accepted, 196 enrolled. *Faculty:* 69 full-time (48 women). Expenses: Contact institution. *Financial support:* Fellowships, research assistantships with full tuition reimbursements, teaching assistantships with full tuition reimbursements, career-related internships or fieldwork, Federal Work-Study, institutionally sponsored loans, scholarships/grants, tuition waivers (partial), and unspecified assistantships available. Support available to part-time students. Financial award applicants required to submit FAFSA. In 2017, 253 master's, 34 doctorates, 87 other advanced degrees awarded. *Program availability:* Part-time, evening/weekend, online learning. Offers advanced teaching and learning (MA); autism spectrum disorders (MA); clinical mental health counseling (MA); cognitive impairment (M Ed); college counseling (MA); community college leadership (Graduate Certificate); counseling (MA, Graduate Certificate, Post Master's Certificate); curriculum and instruction (MA, Certificate, Graduate Certificate); early childhood education (MA); early literacy instruction (Graduate Certificate); education (M Ed, MA, Ed D, PhD, Graduate Certificate, Post Master's Certificate, SPA); educational assessment (Graduate Certificate); educational leadership (MA, Ed D, Graduate Certificate, Post Master's Certificate, SPA); educational media and technology (MA); educational psychology and assessment (Graduate Certificate); educational studies (PhD); emotional impairment (M Ed); helping interventions in a multicultural society (Graduate Certificate); higher education/general administration (MA); higher education/student affairs (MA); instructional leadership (MA); K-12 administration (MA); K-12 basic administration (Post Master's Certificate); K-12 education (MA); learning disabilities (MA); learning technology and design (MA); learning, motivation and creativity (Graduate Certificate); literacy coaching (Graduate Certificate); middle school education (MA); online teaching (Certificate); physical/other health impairment (M Ed); reading (MA); school counseling (MA); school counselor licensure (Post Master's Certificate); secondary literacy instruction (Graduate Certificate); secondary school education (MA); social foundations (MA); special education (M Ed, MA, SPA); speech-language pathology (MA); urban and diversity education (MA); urban/diversity education (MA); visual impairment (M Ed). *Application deadline:* Applications are processed on a rolling basis. *Application fee:* $45. *Dean*, Dr. Michael Sayler, 734-487-1414, Fax: 734-484-6471, E-mail: msayler@emich.edu.

College of Health and Human Services Students: 254 full-time (197 women), 352 part-time (279 women); includes 144 minority (78 Black or African American, non-Hispanic/Latino; 1 American Indian or Alaska Native, non-Hispanic/Latino; 21 Asian, non-Hispanic/Latino; 29 Hispanic/Latino; 1 Native Hawaiian or other Pacific Islander, non-Hispanic/Latino; 14 Two or more races, non-Hispanic/Latino), 14 international. Average age 31. 549 applicants, 50% accepted, 140 enrolled. *Faculty:* 114 full-time (85 women). Expenses: Contact institution. *Financial support:* Fellowships, research assistantships with full tuition reimbursements, teaching assistantships with full tuition reimbursements, career-related internships or fieldwork, Federal Work-Study, institutionally sponsored loans, scholarships/grants, tuition waivers (partial), and unspecified assistantships available. Support available to part-time students. Financial award applicants required to submit FAFSA. In 2017, 286 master's, 21 other advanced degrees awarded. *Program availability:* Part-time, evening/weekend, online learning. Offers adapted physical education (MS); clinical research administration (MS, Graduate Certificate); dementia (Graduate Certificate); dietetics (MS); exercise physiology (MS); gerontology (Graduate Certificate); health administration (MHA, MS, Graduate Certificate); health and human services (MHA, MOT, MS, MSN, MSW, Graduate Certificate); health education (MS, Graduate Certificate); health promotion and human performance (MS, Graduate Certificate); health sciences (MHA, MOT, MS, Graduate Certificate); human nutrition (MS); non-profit management (Graduate Certificate); nursing (MSN); occupational therapy (MOT, MS); orthotics and prosthetics (MS, Graduate Certificate); physical education pedagogy (MS); physician assistant studies (MS); social work (MSW); sports management (MS); sports medicine-biomechanics (MS); sports medicine-corporate adult fitness (MS); sports medicine-exercise physiology (MS); teaching in health care systems (MSN, Graduate Certificate). *Application deadline:* For fall admission, 5/15 priority date for domestic students, 2/15 priority date for international students; for winter admission, 10/15 priority date for domestic students, 9/1 priority date for international students; for summer admission, 3/15 priority date for domestic students, 3/1 priority date for international students. Applications are processed on a rolling basis. *Application fee:* $45. *Dean*, Dr. Murali Nair, 734-487-0077, Fax: 734-487-8536, E-mail: mnair@emich.edu.

College of Technology Students: 85 full-time (30 women), 277 part-time (85 women); includes 67 minority (40 Black or African American, non-Hispanic/Latino; 1 American Indian or Alaska Native, non-Hispanic/Latino; 10 Asian, non-Hispanic/Latino; 9 Hispanic/Latino; 7 Two or more races, non-Hispanic/Latino), 91 international. Average age 35. 319 applicants, 60% accepted, 94 enrolled. *Faculty:* 55 full-time (18 women). Expenses: Contact institution. *Financial support:* Fellowships, research assistantships with full tuition reimbursements, teaching assistantships with full tuition reimbursements, career-related internships or fieldwork, Federal Work-Study, institutionally sponsored loans, scholarships/grants, tuition waivers (partial), and unspecified assistantships available. Support available to part-time students. Financial award applicants required to submit FAFSA. In 2017, 101 master's, 15 doctorates, 1 other advanced degree awarded. *Program availability:* Part-time, evening/weekend, online learning. Offers apparel textiles and merchandising (MS); CAD/CAM (MS); computer-aided technology (MS); construction (Certificate); construction management (MS, Certificate); engineering management (MS); engineering technology (MS, Graduate Certificate, Postbaccalaureate Certificate); hotel and restaurant management (Graduate Certificate); information assurance (Graduate Certificate); information security and applied computing (Graduate Certificate); interior design (MS); polymers and coatings technology (MS, Postbaccalaureate Certificate); project leadership (Certificate); quality management (MS, Graduate Certificate); sustainable construction (Certificate); technology (MLS, MS, PhD, Graduate Certificate); technology studies (MS). *Application deadline:* For fall admission, 5/15 priority date for domestic students, 2/15 priority date for international students; for winter admission, 10/15 priority date for domestic students, 9/1 priority date for international students; for summer admission, 3/15 priority date for domestic students, 3/1 priority date for international students. Applications are processed on a rolling basis. *Application fee:* $45. *Dean*, Dr. Mohamad Qatu, 734-487-0354, Fax: 734-487-0843, E-mail: mqatu@emich.edu.

EASTERN NAZARENE COLLEGE, Quincy, MA 02170

General Information Independent-religious, coed, comprehensive institution. *Graduate housing:* Rooms and/or apartments available to single students and available on a first-come, first-served basis to married students.

GRADUATE UNITS

Adult and Graduate Studies *Program availability:* Part-time, evening/weekend. Offers management (MSM); marriage and family therapy (MS).

Division of Teacher Education *Program availability:* Part-time, evening/weekend. Offers administration (M Ed); early childhood education (M Ed, Certificate); elementary education (M Ed, Certificate); English as a second language (Certificate); instructional enrichment and development (Certificate); middle school education (M Ed, Certificate); moderate special needs education (Certificate); principal (Certificate); program development and supervision (Certificate); secondary education (M Ed, Certificate); special education administrator (Certificate); special needs (M Ed); supervisor (Certificate); teacher of reading (M Ed, Certificate). M Ed also available through weekend program for administration, special needs, and teacher of reading only.

EASTERN NEW MEXICO UNIVERSITY, Portales, NM 88130

General Information State-supported, coed, comprehensive institution. *Graduate housing:* Rooms and/or apartments available on a first-come, first-served basis to single and married students. Housing application deadline: 8/1. *Student services:* Campus employment opportunities, campus safety program, career counseling, child daycare facilities, exercise/wellness program, free psychological counseling, international student services, low-cost health insurance, multicultural affairs office, services for students with disabilities, writing training. *Library facilities:* Golden Library plus 2 others. *Research affiliation:* National Institutes of Health.

Computer facilities: 453 computers available on campus for general student use. A campuswide network can be accessed. Online class registration is available. Website: http://www.enmu.edu/

General Application Contact: Dr. Linda Weems, Dean, Graduate School, 575-562-2147, Fax: 575-562-2500, E-mail: linda.weems@enmu.edu.

GRADUATE UNITS

Graduate School Expenses: Contact institution. *Financial support:* Application deadline: 7/1; applicants required to submit FAFSA. *Program availability:* Part-time, evening/weekend, online learning. *Application deadline:* For fall admission, 7/20 priority date for domestic students, 6/20 priority date for international students; for spring admission, 12/15 priority date for domestic students, 11/15 priority date for international students. Applications are processed on a rolling basis. *Application fee:* $10. Electronic applications accepted. *Application Contact:* Gail Crozier, Receptionist/Records Clerk, 575-562-2147, Fax: 575-562-2500, E-mail: gail.crozier@enmu.edu. *Dean*, Dr. Linda Weems, 575-562-2147, Fax: 575-562-2500, E-mail: linda.weems@enmu.edu.

College of Business Expenses: Contact institution. *Financial support:* Applicants required to submit FAFSA. *Program availability:* Part-time, evening/weekend, online learning. Offers business (MBA). *Application deadline:* For fall admission, 7/20 priority date for domestic students, 6/20 priority date for international students; for spring admission, 12/15 priority date for domestic students, 11/15 priority date for international students. Applications are processed on a rolling basis. *Application fee:* $10. Electronic applications accepted. *Application Contact:* Gail Crozier, Receptionist/Records Clerk, 575-562-2147, Fax: 575-562-2500, E-mail: gail.crozier@enmu.edu. *Graduate Coordinator*, Dr. Pattarapong Burusnukul, 575-562-2366, E-mail: pattarapong.burusnukul@enmu.edu.

College of Education and Technology Expenses: Contact institution. *Financial support:* Applicants required to submit FAFSA. *Program availability:* Part-time, online learning. Offers alternative licensure in elementary education (M Ed); bilingual education (M Ed); career and technical education (M Ed); counseling (MA); early childhood special education (M Sp Ed); education (M Ed); education and technology (M Ed, M Sp Ed, MA, MS); educational technology (M Ed); elementary education (M Ed); English as a second language (M Ed); general special education (M Sp Ed); gifted education pedagogy (M Ed); pedagogy and learning (M Ed); reading/literacy (M Ed); school counseling (M Ed); special education (M Ed, M Sp Ed); special education pedagogy (M Ed); sport administration (MS). *Application deadline:* For fall admission, 7/20 priority date for domestic students, 6/20 priority date for international students; for spring admission, 12/15 priority date for domestic students, 11/15 priority date for international students. Applications are processed on a rolling basis. *Application fee:* $10. Electronic applications accepted. *Application Contact:* Cheryl Reeves, Senior Secretary, 575-562-2443, Fax: 575-562-2559, E-mail: cheryl.reeves@enmu.edu. *Dean*, Dr. Jerry Harmon, 575-562-2443, Fax: 575-562-2559, E-mail: jerry.harmon@enmu.edu.

College of Fine Arts Expenses: Contact institution. *Financial support:* Applicants required to submit FAFSA. *Program availability:* Part-time, online learning. Offers communication (MA). *Application deadline:* For fall admission, 7/20 priority date for domestic students, 6/20 priority date for international students; for spring admission,

12/15 priority date for domestic students, 11/15 priority date for international students. Applications are processed on a rolling basis. *Application fee:* $10. Electronic applications accepted. *Application Contact:* Gail Crozier, Receptionist/Records Clerk, 575-562-2147, Fax: 575-562-2500, E-mail: gail.crozier@enmu.edu. *Graduate Coordinator*, Dr. Patricia Dobson, 575-562-2778, E-mail: patricia.dobson@enmu.edu.

College of Liberal Arts and Sciences Expenses: Contact institution. *Financial support:* Applicants required to submit FAFSA. *Program availability:* Part-time, evening/weekend, online learning. Offers anthropology (MA); biology (MS); chemistry (MS); communicative disorders (MS); English (MA); liberal arts and sciences (MA, MS, MSN); nursing (MSN). *Application deadline:* For fall admission, 7/20 priority date for domestic students, 6/20 priority date for international students; for spring admission, 12/15 priority date for domestic students, 11/15 priority date for international students. Applications are processed on a rolling basis. *Application fee:* $10. Electronic applications accepted. *Application Contact:* Maggie Gardels, Dean's Secretary, 575-562-2421, Fax: 575-562-2555, E-mail: mary.gardels@enmu.edu. *Dean*, Dr. Mary Ayala, 575-562-2421, Fax: 575-562-2555, E-mail: mary.ayala@enmu.edu.

EASTERN OREGON UNIVERSITY, La Grande, OR 97850-2899

General Information State-supported, coed, comprehensive institution. *Enrollment:* 3,016 graduate, professional, and undergraduate students; 94 full-time matriculated graduate/professional students (66 women), 133 part-time matriculated graduate/professional students (91 women). *Enrollment by degree level:* 227 master's. *Graduate faculty:* 20 full-time (12 women), 13 part-time/adjunct (6 women). Tuition, state resident: full-time $12,510; part-time $347 per quarter hour. Tuition, nonresident: full-time $15,768; part-time $438 per quarter hour. *Required fees:* $1434. One-time fee: $350. Tuition and fees vary according to campus/location and program. *Graduate housing:* Room and/or apartments available on a first-come, first-served basis to single students; on-campus housing not available to married students. Typical cost: $5500 per year ($9250 including board). Room and board charges vary according to board plan and housing facility selected. *Student services:* Campus employment opportunities, campus safety program, career counseling, exercise/wellness program, free psychological counseling, international student services, low-cost health insurance, multicultural affairs office, services for students with disabilities, writing training. *Library facilities:* Pierce Library. *Collection:* Students can reserve study rooms.

Computer facilities: Computer purchase and lease plans are available. A campuswide network can be accessed from student residence rooms and from off campus. Online class registration is available.
Website: http://www.eou.edu/

General Application Contact: Dr. Danny Ray Mielke, Coordinator of Graduate Studies, 541-962-3399, Fax: 541-962-3701, E-mail: danny.mielke@eou.edu.

GRADUATE UNITS

Master of Arts in Teaching Program Students: 53 full-time (41 women), 2 part-time (both women); includes 6 minority (5 Hispanic/Latino; 1 Two or more races, non-Hispanic/Latino), 1 international. Average age 29. *Faculty:* 12 full-time (9 women), 4 part-time/adjunct (1 woman). Expenses: Contact institution. *Financial support:* In 2017–18, 24 students received support. Federal Work-Study, scholarships/grants, and tuition waivers (full and partial) available. Support available to part-time students. In 2017, 32 master's awarded. Offers elementary education (MAT); secondary education (MAT). *Application deadline:* For fall admission, 3/1 for domestic students. Applications are processed on a rolling basis. Electronic applications accepted. *Application Contact:* Janet Frye, Administrative Support, MAT/MS Graduate Admission, 541-962-3772, Fax: 541-962-3701, E-mail: jfrye@eou.edu. *Dean of College of Business and Education*, Dr. Danny Ray Mielke, 541-962-3399, Fax: 541-962-3701, E-mail: dmeilke@eou.edu.

Master of Science Program Students: 9 full-time (all women), 52 part-time (44 women); includes 2 minority (both Hispanic/Latino). Average age 37. *Faculty:* 10 full-time (6 women), 4 part-time/adjunct (2 women). Expenses: Contact institution. *Financial support:* In 2017–18, 8 students received support. Federal Work-Study, scholarships/grants, and tuition waivers (full and partial) available. Support available to part-time students. In 2017, 22 master's awarded. *Program availability:* Part-time, online only, 100% online. Offers education (MS). *Application deadline:* Applications are processed on a rolling basis. Electronic applications accepted. *Coordinator*, Dr. Danny Ray Mielke, 541-962-3349, Fax: 541-962-3701, E-mail: danny.mielke@eou.edu.

Program in Business Administration Students: 30 full-time (15 women), 59 part-time (33 women); includes 20 minority (2 Black or African American, non-Hispanic/Latino; 4 American Indian or Alaska Native, non-Hispanic/Latino; 3 Asian, non-Hispanic/Latino; 10 Hispanic/Latino; 1 Two or more races, non-Hispanic/Latino), 1 international. Average age 31. *Faculty:* 6 full-time (2 women), 4 part-time/adjunct (1 woman). Expenses: Contact institution. *Financial support:* In 2017–18, 7 students received support. Federal Work-Study, scholarships/grants, and tuition waivers (full and partial) available. Support available to part-time students. In 2017, 43 master's awarded. *Program availability:* Part-time, 100% online. Offers business administration (MBA). *Application deadline:* For fall admission, 5/15 priority date for domestic students. Applications are processed on a rolling basis. Electronic applications accepted. *Application Contact:* Kristin Johnson, MAT Advisor/Recruiter, 541-962-3529, Fax: 541-962-3701, E-mail: kristin.johnson@eou.edu. *Program Coordinator*, Les Mueller, 541-962-3225, E-mail: lmueller@eou.edu.

EASTERN UNIVERSITY, St. Davids, PA 19087-3696

General Information Independent-religious, coed, university. *Enrollment:* 3,291 graduate, professional, and undergraduate students; 441 full-time matriculated graduate/professional students (294 women), 619 part-time matriculated graduate/professional students (399 women). *Enrollment by degree level:* 882 master's, 178 doctoral. *Tuition:* Full-time $16,560; part-time $8280 per credit. *Required fees:* $95 per term. One-time fee: $65. Tuition and fees vary according to course load, degree level and program. *Graduate housing:* Room and/or apartments available on a first-come, first-served basis to single students; on-campus housing not available to married students. Typical cost: $8200 per year ($13,340 including board). Room and board charges vary according to campus/location and housing facility selected. *Student services:* Campus employment opportunities, career counseling, international student services, low-cost health insurance, services for students with disabilities. *Library facilities:* Warner Memorial Library plus 1 other. *Collection:* Books: 172,820 (physical), 1.5 million (digital/electronic); Serial titles: 94 (physical), 48,564 (digital/electronic); Databases: 155. Weekly public service hours: 83; students can reserve study rooms.

Computer facilities: 98 computers available on campus for general student use. A campuswide network can be accessed from student residence rooms and from off campus. Online class registration, BRIGHTSPACE are available.
Website: http://www.eastern.edu/

General Application Contact: Michael Dziedziak, Executive Director of Enrollment, 800-452-0996, E-mail: gpsadmissions@eastern.edu.

GRADUATE UNITS

Department of Counseling Psychology Students: 66 full-time (58 women), 64 part-time (50 women); includes 56 minority (43 Black or African American, non-Hispanic/Latino; 1 Asian, non-Hispanic/Latino; 9 Hispanic/Latino; 3 Two or more races, non-Hispanic/Latino), 2 international. Average age 29. Expenses: Contact institution. In 2017, 26 master's, 9 other advanced degrees awarded. *Program availability:* Part-time. Offers applied behavior analysis (Certificate); counseling (MA); professional counseling (Certificate). *Application deadline:* Applications are processed on a rolling basis. *Application fee:* $35. Electronic applications accepted. *Executive Director of Enrollment*, Michael Dziedziak, 800-452-0996, E-mail: gpsadmissions@eastern.edu.

Department of Global Studies and Mission Students: 23 full-time (11 women), 26 part-time (15 women); includes 11 minority (8 Black or African American, non-Hispanic/Latino; 1 Asian, non-Hispanic/Latino; 2 Hispanic/Latino), 1 international. Average age 35. Expenses: Contact institution. In 2017, 19 master's awarded. Offers international development (MA); theological and cultural anthropology (MA). *Application deadline:* Applications are processed on a rolling basis. *Application fee:* $35. Electronic applications accepted. *Executive Director of Enrollment*, Michael Dziedziak, 800-452-0996, E-mail: gpsadmissions@eastern.edu.

Department of Marriage and Family Therapy Students: 63 full-time (45 women); includes 42 minority (33 Black or African American, non-Hispanic/Latino; 2 Asian, non-Hispanic/Latino; 5 Hispanic/Latino; 2 Two or more races, non-Hispanic/Latino), 1 international. Average age 43. Expenses: Contact institution. In 2017, 7 doctorates awarded. *Program availability:* Evening/weekend, online learning. Offers marriage and family therapy (PhD); marriage and family therapy studies (DA). *Application deadline:* Applications are processed on a rolling basis. *Application fee:* $75. Electronic applications accepted. *Executive Director of Enrollment*, Michael Dziedziak, 800-452-0996, E-mail: gpsadmissions@eastern.edu.

Department of Nursing Students: 1 (woman) full-time, 41 part-time (40 women); includes 5 minority (4 Black or African American, non-Hispanic/Latino; 1 Asian, non-Hispanic/Latino). Average age 43. Expenses: Contact institution. In 2017, 8 master's awarded. Offers nursing (MSN); school health services (M Ed); school health supervisor (K-12) (Certificate); school nurse (K-12) (Certificate). *Application deadline:* Applications are processed on a rolling basis. *Application fee:* $35. Electronic applications accepted. *Executive Director of Enrollment*, Michael Dziedziak, 800-452-0996, E-mail: gpsadmissions@eastern.edu.

Department of Social Transformation Students: 12 full-time (10 women), 17 part-time (14 women); includes 14 minority (10 Black or African American, non-Hispanic/Latino; 2 Hispanic/Latino; 2 Two or more races, non-Hispanic/Latino), 2 international. Average age 32. Expenses: Contact institution. In 2017, 15 master's awarded. Offers urban studies (MA). *Application deadline:* Applications are processed on a rolling basis. *Application fee:* $35. Electronic applications accepted. *Executive Director of Enrollment*, Michael Dziedziak, 800-452-0996, E-mail: gpsadmissions@eastern.edu.

Graduate Education Programs Students: 46 full-time (40 women), 115 part-time (93 women); includes 65 minority (42 Black or African American, non-Hispanic/Latino; 3 Asian, non-Hispanic/Latino; 14 Hispanic/Latino; 6 Two or more races, non-Hispanic/Latino), 1 international. Average age 32. Expenses: Contact institution. In 2017, 72 master's awarded. *Program availability:* Part-time, evening/weekend, online learning. Offers ESL program specialist (K-12) (Certificate); general supervisor (PreK-12) (Certificate); health and physical education (K-12) (Certificate); middle level (4-8) (Certificate); multicultural education (M Ed); music (K-12) (Certificate); Pre K-4 (Certificate); Pre K-4 with special education (Certificate); reading (M Ed); reading specialist (K-12) (Certificate); reading supervisor (K-12) (Certificate); school counseling (MA, CAGS); school principalship (preK-12) (Certificate); school psychology (MS, CAGS); secondary biology education (7-12) (Certificate); secondary chemistry education (7-12) (Certificate); secondary communication education (7-12) (Certificate); secondary English education (7-12) (Certificate); secondary math education (7-12) (Certificate); secondary social studies education (7-12) (Certificate); special education (M Ed); special education (7-12) (Certificate); special education (Pre K-8) (Certificate); special education supervisor (K-12) (Certificate); TESOL (M Ed); world language (Certificate). *Application deadline:* Applications are processed on a rolling basis. *Application fee:* $35. Electronic applications accepted. *Executive Director of Enrollment*, Michael Dziedziak, 800-452-0996, E-mail: gpsadmissions@eastern.edu.

Graduate Programs in Business and Leadership Students: 55 full-time (34 women), 195 part-time (126 women); includes 123 minority (93 Black or African American, non-Hispanic/Latino; 1 American Indian or Alaska Native, non-Hispanic/Latino; 12 Asian, non-Hispanic/Latino; 12 Hispanic/Latino; 5 Two or more races, non-Hispanic/Latino), 23 international. Average age 34. Expenses: Contact institution. *Financial support:* Applicants required to submit FAFSA. In 2017, 123 master's awarded. *Program availability:* Part-time, evening/weekend, online learning. Offers health administration (MBA); health services management (MS); management (MBA); organizational leadership (MA); social impact (MBA). *Application deadline:* Applications are processed on a rolling basis. *Application fee:* $35. Electronic applications accepted. *Executive Director of Enrollment*, Michael Dziedziak, 800-452-0996, E-mail: gpsadmissions@eastern.edu.

Palmer Theological Seminary Students: 77 full-time (35 women), 161 part-time (61 women); includes 95 minority (82 Black or African American, non-Hispanic/Latino; 4 Asian, non-Hispanic/Latino; 9 Hispanic/Latino), 9 international. Average age 45. Expenses: Contact institution. In 2017, 41 master's awarded. *Program availability:* Part-time, online learning. Offers divinity (M Div); theological studies (MTS). *Application deadline:* Applications are processed on a rolling basis. *Application fee:* $30. Electronic applications accepted. *Executive Director of Enrollment*, Michael Dziedziak, 800-452-0996, E-mail: semadmis@eastern.edu.

Program in Organizational Leadership Students: 98 full-time (60 women); includes 31 minority (26 Black or African American, non-Hispanic/Latino; 2 Asian, non-Hispanic/Latino; 2 Hispanic/Latino; 1 Two or more races, non-Hispanic/Latino), 4 international. Average age 47. Expenses: Contact institution. In 2017, 8 doctorates, 10 other advanced degrees awarded. Offers leadership studies (CAGS); organizational leadership (PhD). *Application deadline:* Applications are processed on a rolling basis. *Application fee:* $75. Electronic applications accepted. *Executive Director of Enrollment*, Michael Dziedziak, 800-452-0996, E-mail: gpsadmissions@eastern.edu.

EASTERN VIRGINIA MEDICAL SCHOOL, Norfolk, VA 23501-1980

General Information Independent, coed, graduate-only institution. *Graduate housing:* On-campus housing not available.

GRADUATE UNITS

Biotechnology Program Offers biotechnology (MS). Electronic applications accepted.

Doctoral Program in Biomedical Sciences Offers biomedical sciences (PhD). Electronic applications accepted.

Graduate Art Therapy and Counseling Program Offers art therapy and counseling (MS). Electronic applications accepted.

Master of Physician Assistant Program Offers physician assistant (MPA). Electronic applications accepted.

Master of Public Health Program *Program availability:* Evening/weekend. Offers public health (MPH). Program offered jointly with Old Dominion University. Electronic applications accepted.

Master of Surgical Assisting Program Offers surgical assisting (MSA). Electronic applications accepted.

Master's Program in Biomedical Sciences Research Offers biomedical sciences research (MS). Electronic applications accepted.

Master's Program in Clinical Embryology and Andrology *Program availability:* Online learning. Offers clinical embryology and andrology (MS). Electronic applications accepted.

Medical Master's Program in Biomedical Sciences Offers biomedical sciences (MS). Electronic applications accepted.

Ophthalmic Technology Program Offers ophthalmic technology (Certificate). Electronic applications accepted.

Professional Program in Medicine Offers medicine (MD). Electronic applications accepted.

The Virginia Consortium Program in Clinical Psychology Offers clinical psychology (Psy D). Program offered jointly with The College of William and Mary, Norfolk State University, and Old Dominion University.

EASTERN WASHINGTON UNIVERSITY, Cheney, WA 99004-2431

General Information State-supported, coed, comprehensive institution. CGS member. *Enrollment:* 12,607 graduate, professional, and undergraduate students; 436 full-time matriculated graduate/professional students (304 women), 226 part-time matriculated graduate/professional students (172 women). *Enrollment by degree level:* 549 master's, 48 doctoral, 65 other advanced degrees. *Graduate faculty:* 209. Tuition, state resident: full-time $11,191; part-time $373.06 per credit. Tuition, nonresident: full-time $25,995; part-time $866.52 per credit. *Graduate housing:* Rooms and/or apartments available on a first-come, first-served basis to single and married students. Housing application deadline: 5/1. *Student services:* Campus employment opportunities, campus safety program, career counseling, child daycare facilities, exercise/wellness program, free psychological counseling, international student services, low-cost health insurance, multicultural affairs office, services for students with disabilities, teacher training, writing training. *Library facilities:* John F. Kennedy Library. *Collection:* Students can reserve study rooms.

Computer facilities: Computer purchase and lease plans are available. A campuswide network can be accessed. Online class registration, network disk storage; discounted software; laptops, still and video cameras, projectors for checkout; print credit; black white laser, color laser, and color photo options, large format print service are available.
Website: http://www.ewu.edu/

General Application Contact: Roberta Brooke, Director of Graduate Programs, 509-359-6297, Fax: 509-359-6044, E-mail: gradprograms@ewu.edu.

GRADUATE UNITS

Graduate Studies Students: 777 full-time (550 women), 344 part-time (260 women); includes 78 minority (11 Black or African American, non-Hispanic/Latino; 17 American Indian or Alaska Native, non-Hispanic/Latino; 11 Asian, non-Hispanic/Latino; 39 Hispanic/Latino), 33 international. Average age 32. 1,465 applicants, 28% accepted, 347 enrolled. *Faculty:* 199. Expenses: Contact institution. *Financial support:* Teaching assistantships with partial tuition reimbursements, career-related internships or fieldwork, Federal Work-Study, institutionally sponsored loans, scholarships/grants, health care benefits, tuition waivers (full and partial), and unspecified assistantships available. Support available to part-time students. Financial award application deadline: 2/1. In 2017, 452 master's, 38 doctorates, 43 other advanced degrees awarded. *Program availability:* Part-time, evening/weekend. Offers interdisciplinary studies (MA, MS). *Application deadline:* For fall admission, 3/1 priority date for domestic students. *Application fee:* $50. Electronic applications accepted. *Application Contact:* E-mail: gradprograms@ewu.edu. *Executive Director of Graduate Department*, Roberta Brooke, 509-359-6566, E-mail: rbrooke@ewu.edu.

College of Arts, Letters and Education Students: 118 full-time (75 women), 52 part-time (35 women); includes 10 minority (1 Black or African American, non-Hispanic/Latino; 2 Asian, non-Hispanic/Latino; 7 Hispanic/Latino), 13 international. Average age 34. 175 applicants, 48% accepted, 64 enrolled. *Faculty:* 51. Expenses: Contact institution. *Financial support:* Teaching assistantships with partial tuition reimbursements, career-related internships or fieldwork, Federal Work-Study, institutionally sponsored loans, scholarships/grants, health care benefits, tuition waivers (partial), and unspecified assistantships available. Support available to part-time students. Financial award application deadline: 2/1; financial award applicants required to submit FAFSA. In 2017, 69 master's awarded. *Program availability:* Part-time. Offers adult education (M Ed); arts, letters and education (M Ed, MA, MFA, MS); composition (MA); curriculum development (M Ed); early childhood education (M Ed); educational foundations (M Ed); educational leadership (M Ed); exercise science (MS); instrumental/vocal performance (MA); jazz pedagogy (MA); liberal arts (MA); literacy (M Ed); literature (MA); music education (MA); rhetoric, composition, and technical communication (MA); sports and recreation administration (MS); teaching English as a second language (MA); teaching K-8 (M Ed). *Application deadline:* Applications are processed on a rolling basis. Electronic applications accepted. *Application Contact:* Kathy White, Advisor/Recruiter for Graduate Studies, 509-359-2491, Fax: 509-359-6044, E-mail: gradprograms@ewu.edu. *Dean*, Dr. Roy Sonnema, 509-359-2227, E-mail: rsonnema1@ewu.edu.

College of Business and Public Administration Students: 75 full-time (41 women), 51 part-time (29 women); includes 17 minority (1 Black or African American, non-Hispanic/Latino; 6 American Indian or Alaska Native, non-Hispanic/Latino; 4 Asian, non-Hispanic/Latino; 6 Hispanic/Latino), 10 international. Average age 34. 130 applicants, 61% accepted, 62 enrolled. *Faculty:* 21. Expenses: Contact institution. *Financial support:* In 2017–18, 9 students received support. Teaching assistantships with partial tuition reimbursements available, career-related internships or fieldwork, Federal Work-Study, institutionally sponsored loans, scholarships/grants, health care benefits, tuition waivers (partial), and unspecified assistantships available. Support available to part-time students. Financial award application deadline: 2/1. In 2017, 76 master's awarded. *Program availability:* Part-time, evening/weekend. Offers business administration (MBA); business and public administration (MBA, MCR, MPA); professional accounting (MP Acc); public administration (MPA). *Application deadline:* For fall admission, 4/1 priority date for domestic students; for spring admission, 1/15 for domestic students. Applications are processed on a rolling basis. *Application fee:* $75. Electronic applications accepted. *Application Contact:* Dr. Jill Ericson, Director of Graduate Programs, College of Business and Administration, 509-828-1248, Fax: 509-828-1275, E-mail: jericson1@ewu.edu. *Interim Dean, College of Business and Public Administration*, Dr. Ahmad Tootoonchi, 509-828-1224, Fax: 509-828-1274, E-mail: tootoonchi@ewu.edu.

College of Health Science and Public Health Students: 300 full-time (228 women), 37 part-time (27 women); includes 14 minority (2 Black or African American, non-Hispanic/Latino; 2 American Indian or Alaska Native, non-Hispanic/Latino; 3 Asian, non-Hispanic/Latino; 7 Hispanic/Latino), 3 international. Average age 29. 790 applicants, 12% accepted, 95 enrolled. *Faculty:* 43. Expenses: Contact institution. *Financial support:* Teaching assistantships with partial tuition reimbursements, career-related internships or fieldwork, Federal Work-Study, institutionally sponsored loans, scholarships/grants, health care benefits, tuition waivers (partial), and unspecified assistantships available. Support available to part-time students. Financial award application deadline: 2/1; financial award applicants required to submit FAFSA. In 2017, 104 master's awarded. *Program availability:* Part-time. Offers communication sciences and disorders (MS); dental hygiene (MS); health science and public health (MOT, MPH, MS, DPT); occupational therapy (MOT); physical therapy (DPT); public health (MPH). *Application deadline:* Applications are processed on a rolling basis. *Application fee:* $75. Electronic applications accepted. *Application Contact:* Kathy White, Advisor/Recruiter for Graduate Studies, 509-359-2491, Fax: 509-359-6044, E-mail: gradprograms@ewu.edu. *Dean*, Dr. Laureen O'Hanlon, 509-359-1456, E-mail: lohanlon@ewu.edu.

College of Science, Technology, Engineering and Mathematics Students: 32 full-time (13 women), 9 part-time (3 women); includes 4 minority (1 American Indian or Alaska Native, non-Hispanic/Latino; 1 Asian, non-Hispanic/Latino; 2 Hispanic/Latino), 2 international. Average age 30. 54 applicants, 39% accepted, 17 enrolled. *Faculty:* 22. Expenses: Contact institution. *Financial support:* Teaching assistantships and unspecified assistantships available. Financial award application deadline: 2/15; financial award applicants required to submit FAFSA. In 2017, 12 master's awarded. *Program availability:* Part-time. Offers biology (MS); computer science (MS); science, technology, engineering and mathematics (MS). *Application fee:* $75. Electronic applications accepted. *Application Contact:* Kathy White, Advisor/Recruiter for Graduate Studies, 509-359-2491, Fax: 509-359-6044, E-mail: gradprograms@ewu.edu. *Dean*, Dr. David Bowman, 509-359-6244, Fax: 509-359-6950, E-mail: dbowman@ewu.edu.

College of Social Sciences Students: 252 full-time (193 women), 194 part-time (165 women); includes 33 minority (7 Black or African American, non-Hispanic/Latino; 8 American Indian or Alaska Native, non-Hispanic/Latino; 1 Asian, non-Hispanic/Latino; 17 Hispanic/Latino), 4 international. Average age 34. 314 applicants, 41% accepted, 107 enrolled. *Faculty:* 72. Expenses: Contact institution. *Financial support:* Research assistantships, teaching assistantships with partial tuition reimbursements, career-related internships or fieldwork, Federal Work-Study, institutionally sponsored loans, scholarships/grants, health care benefits, tuition waivers (partial), and unspecified assistantships available. Support available to part-time students. Financial award application deadline: 2/1; financial award applicants required to submit FAFSA. In 2017, 226 master's, 35 other advanced degrees awarded. *Program availability:* Part-time, evening/weekend. Offers applied psychology (MS); clinical psychology (MS); communication studies (MSC); experimental psychology (MS); history (MA); mental health counseling (MS); school counseling (MS); school psychology respecialization (Ed S); social sciences (MA, MS, MSC, MSW, Ed S); social work (MSW). *Application deadline:* Applications are processed on a rolling basis. *Application fee:* $75. Electronic applications accepted. *Application Contact:* Kathy White, Advisor/Recruiter for Graduate Studies, 509-359-6297, Fax: 509-359-6044, E-mail: gradprograms@ewu.edu. *Dean*, Dr. Jonathan Anderson, 509-359-6707, E-mail: janderson@ewu.edu.

EAST STROUDSBURG UNIVERSITY OF PENNSYLVANIA, East Stroudsburg, PA 18301-2999

General Information State-supported, coed, comprehensive institution. CGS member. *Enrollment:* 6,742 graduate, professional, and undergraduate students; 289 full-time matriculated graduate/professional students (173 women), 402 part-time matriculated graduate/professional students (296 women). *Graduate faculty:* 88 full-time (47 women), 14 part-time/adjunct (10 women). Tuition, state resident: full-time $4500; part-time $3000 per credit. Tuition, nonresident: full-time $6750; part-time $4500 per credit. *Required fees:* $2642; $1756 per credit. $878 per semester. Tuition and fees vary according to course load, campus/location and program. *Graduate housing:* Room and/or apartments available on a first-come, first-served basis to single students; on-campus housing not available to married students. Typical cost: $4500 per year ($7172 including board). Room and board charges vary according to board plan and housing facility selected. Housing application deadline: 6/1. *Student services:* Campus employment opportunities, campus safety program, career counseling, child daycare facilities, exercise/wellness program, free psychological counseling, international student services, low-cost health insurance, multicultural affairs office, services for students with disabilities. *Library facilities:* Kemp Library. *Collection:* Books: 306,633 (physical), 408,082 (digital/electronic); Serial titles: 4,066 (physical), 22,666 (digital/electronic); Databases: 93. Weekly public service hours: 99.

Computer facilities: 500 computers available on campus for general student use. A campuswide network can be accessed. Online class registration, online classes are available.
Website: http://www.esu.edu/

General Application Contact: Kevin Quintero, Associate Director, Graduate and Extended Studies, 570-422-3536, Fax: 570-422-3711, E-mail: kquintero@esu.edu.

GRADUATE UNITS

Graduate and Extended Studies Students: 289 full-time (173 women), 402 part-time (296 women); includes 98 minority (35 Black or African American, non-Hispanic/Latino; 2 American Indian or Alaska Native, non-Hispanic/Latino; 6 Asian, non-Hispanic/Latino; 37 Hispanic/Latino; 1 Native Hawaiian or other Pacific Islander, non-Hispanic/Latino; 17 Two or more races, non-Hispanic/Latino), 33 international. Average age 31. 540 applicants, 61% accepted, 223 enrolled. *Faculty:* 72 full-time (39 women), 23 part-time/adjunct (16 women). Expenses: Contact institution. *Financial support:* Research assistantships with tuition reimbursements, teaching assistantships, career-related internships or fieldwork, Federal Work-Study, and unspecified assistantships available. Support available to part-time students. Financial award application deadline: 6/30; financial award applicants required to submit FAFSA. In 2017, 191 master's, 2 doctorates awarded. *Program availability:* Part-time, evening/weekend, 100% online, blended/hybrid learning. *Application deadline:* For fall admission, 7/31 priority date for domestic students, 6/30 priority date for international students; for spring admission, 11/30 for domestic students, 10/31 for international students. Applications are processed on a rolling basis. *Application fee:* $50. Electronic applications accepted. *Application Contact:* Kevin Quintero, Associate Director, Graduate and Extended Studies, 570-422-3890, Fax: 570-422-3711, E-mail: kquintero@esu.edu. *Director, Graduate and Extended Studies*, Dr. William Bajor, 570-422-3536, Fax: 570-422-3711, E-mail: wbajor@esu.edu.

College of Arts and Sciences Students: 39 full-time (18 women), 42 part-time (20 women); includes 11 minority (3 Black or African American, non-Hispanic/Latino; 1 Asian, non-Hispanic/Latino; 6 Hispanic/Latino; 1 Two or more races, non-Hispanic/Latino), 15 international. Average age 29. 55 applicants, 85% accepted, 30 enrolled. *Faculty:* 30 full-time (12 women), 3 part-time/adjunct (all women). Expenses: Contact institution. *Financial support:* Research assistantships with tuition reimbursements, career-related internships or fieldwork, Federal Work-Study, and unspecified assistantships available. Support available to part-time students. Financial award application deadline: 3/1; financial award applicants required to submit FAFSA. In 2017, 31 master's awarded. *Program availability:* Part-time, evening/weekend. Offers arts and sciences (M Ed, MA, MS); biology (MS); computer science (MS); history and geography (M Ed, MA); management and leadership in public administration (MS); political science (MA). *Application deadline:* For fall admission, 7/31 for domestic students, 6/30 priority date for international students; for spring admission, 11/30 for domestic students, 10/31 for international students. Applications are processed on a rolling basis. *Application fee:* $50. Electronic applications accepted. *Application Contact:* Kevin Quintero, Associate Director, Graduate and Extended Studies, 570-422-3890, Fax: 570-422-3711, E-mail: kquintero@esu.edu. *Dean of Arts and Sciences,* Dr. Peter Hawkes, 570-422-3494, Fax: 570-422-3949, E-mail: phawkes@esu.edu.

College of Business and Management Students: 35 full-time (16 women), 39 part-time (21 women); includes 16 minority (12 Black or African American, non-Hispanic/Latino; 1 Hispanic/Latino; 1 Native Hawaiian or other Pacific Islander, non-Hispanic/Latino; 2 Two or more races, non-Hispanic/Latino), 9 international. Average age 29. 52 applicants, 77% accepted, 29 enrolled. *Faculty:* 10 full-time (5 women), 4 part-time/adjunct (1 woman). Expenses: Contact institution. *Financial support:* Research assistantships, career-related internships or fieldwork, Federal Work-Study, and unspecified assistantships available. Support available to part-time students. Financial award application deadline: 3/1; financial award applicants required to submit FAFSA. In 2017, 15 master's awarded. *Program availability:* Part-time, evening/weekend, online learning. Offers business and management (MS); sport management (MS). *Application deadline:* For fall admission, 7/31 for domestic students, 6/30 priority date for international students; for spring admission, 11/30 for domestic students, 10/31 for international students. Applications are processed on a rolling basis. *Application fee:* $50. Electronic applications accepted. *Application Contact:* Kevin Quintero, Associate Director, Graduate and Extended Studies, 570-422-3890, Fax: 570-422-2711, E-mail: kquintero@esu.edu. *Dean,* Tribhuvan Puri, 570-422-3589, Fax: 570-422-2704, E-mail: tpuri@esu.edu.

College of Education Students: 34 full-time (22 women), 244 part-time (196 women); includes 37 minority (13 Black or African American, non-Hispanic/Latino; 1 American Indian or Alaska Native, non-Hispanic/Latino; 2 Asian, non-Hispanic/Latino; 17 Hispanic/Latino; 4 Two or more races, non-Hispanic/Latino), 2 international. Average age 35. 146 applicants, 88% accepted, 90 enrolled. *Faculty:* 12 full-time (10 women), 9 part-time/adjunct (6 women). Expenses: Contact institution. *Financial support:* Research assistantships with tuition reimbursements, career-related internships or fieldwork, Federal Work-Study, and unspecified assistantships available. Support available to part-time students. Financial award application deadline: 3/1; financial award applicants required to submit FAFSA. In 2017, 37 master's, 2 doctorates awarded. *Program availability:* Part-time, evening/weekend, online learning. Offers digital media technologies (M Ed); early childhood and elementary education (M Ed); education (M Ed, Ed D); professional and secondary education (Ed D); reading (M Ed); secondary education (M Ed); special education (M Ed). *Application deadline:* For fall admission, 7/31 priority date for domestic students, 6/30 priority date for international students; for spring admission, 11/30 for domestic students, 10/31 for international students. Applications are processed on a rolling basis. *Application fee:* $50. Electronic applications accepted. *Application Contact:* Kevin Quintero, Associate Director, Graduate and Extended Studies, 570-422-3890, Fax: 570-422-3711, E-mail: kquintero@esu.edu. *Dean,* Dr. Terry Barry, 570-422-3377, Fax: 570-422-3506, E-mail: tbarry1@esu.edu.

College of Health Sciences Students: 177 full-time (113 women), 35 part-time (27 women); includes 32 minority (7 Black or African American, non-Hispanic/Latino; 3 Asian, non-Hispanic/Latino; 13 Hispanic/Latino; 9 Two or more races, non-Hispanic/Latino), 4 international. Average age 26. 271 applicants, 36% accepted, 59 enrolled. *Faculty:* 20 full-time (12 women), 8 part-time/adjunct (7 women). Expenses: Contact institution. *Financial support:* Research assistantships with tuition reimbursements, career-related internships or fieldwork, Federal Work-Study, and institutionally sponsored loans available. Financial award application deadline: 3/1; financial award applicants required to submit FAFSA. In 2017, 108 master's awarded. *Program availability:* Part-time, evening/weekend, online learning. Offers athletic training (MS); communication sciences and disorders (MS); exercise science (MS); health sciences (MPH, MS); health studies (MPH, MS). *Application deadline:* For fall admission, 7/31 priority date for domestic students, 6/30 priority date for international students; for spring admission, 11/30 for domestic students, 10/31 for international students. Applications are processed on a rolling basis. *Application fee:* $50. Electronic applications accepted. *Application Contact:* Kevin Quintero, Associate Director, Graduate and Extended Studies, 570-422-3890, Fax: 570-422-2711, E-mail: kquintero@esu.edu. *Dean,* Dr. Denise Seigart, 570-422-3425, Fax: 570-422-3347, E-mail: dseigart@esu.edu.

EAST TENNESSEE STATE UNIVERSITY, Johnson City, TN 37614

General Information State-supported, coed, university. CGS member. *Enrollment:* 14,353 graduate, professional, and undergraduate students; 1,309 full-time matriculated graduate/professional students (823 women), 1,132 part-time matriculated graduate/professional students (832 women). *Enrollment by degree level:* 1,691 master's, 547 doctoral, 203 other advanced degrees. *Graduate housing:* Rooms and/or apartments available on a first-come, first-served basis to single and married students. Housing application deadline: 8/1. *Student services:* Campus employment opportunities, campus safety program, career counseling, child daycare facilities, exercise/wellness program, free psychological counseling, grant writing training, international student services, low-cost health insurance, multicultural affairs office, services for students with disabilities, teacher training. *Library facilities:* Charles C. Sherrod Library plus 2 others. *Collection:* Books: 731,960 (physical), 98,312 (digital/electronic); Databases: 210. Study areas open 24 hours, 5–7 days a week; students can reserve study rooms. *Research affiliation:* Puckett Institute (education), Cyberonics (biomedical science), Mountain Home VA Medical Center (clinical and biomedical science), Mountain States Health Alliance; Wellmont Health System; State of Franklin Healthcare Associates (clinical, nursing, and biomedical science), Oak Ridge National Laboratory (biomedical physical science and computer science), Frontier Health, Inc./Cherokee Health Systems (clinical and education).

Computer facilities: Computer purchase and lease plans are available. 1,400 computers available on campus for general student use. A campuswide network can be accessed. Online class registration is available.
Website: http://www.etsu.edu/

General Application Contact: Dr. Karin Bartoszuk, Associate Dean, 423-439-4221, Fax: 423-439-5624, E-mail: gradsch@etsu.edu.

GRADUATE UNITS

Bill Gatton College of Pharmacy Students: 311 full-time (178 women); includes 33 minority (14 Black or African American, non-Hispanic/Latino; 11 Asian, non-Hispanic/Latino; 5 Hispanic/Latino; 3 Two or more races, non-Hispanic/Latino), 6 international. Average age 25. 470 applicants, 37% accepted, 74 enrolled. *Faculty:* 52 full-time (30 women). Expenses: Contact institution. In 2017, 76 doctorates awarded. *Program availability:* Part-time. Offers pharmacy (Pharm D). *Application deadline:* For fall admission, 6/1 for domestic students, 4/29 for international students; for spring admission, 11/1 for domestic students, 9/29 for international students; for summer admission, 3/15 for domestic students, 2/1 for international students. Applications are processed on a rolling basis. *Application fee:* $55 ($65 for international students). Electronic applications accepted. *Application Contact:* Admissions and Records Office, 423-439-6300, Fax: 423-439-6320, E-mail: pharmacy@etsu.edu. *Dean,* Dr. Debbie C. Byrd, 423-439-2068, Fax: 423-439-6310, E-mail: byrdc1@etsu.edu.

Quillen College of Medicine Students: 65 (32 women). Average age 24. Expenses: Contact institution. *Financial support:* Career-related internships or fieldwork, Federal Work-Study, institutionally sponsored loans, scholarships/grants, and tuition waivers (full) available. Financial award applicants required to submit FAFSA. *Program availability:* Part-time. Offers anatomy (PhD); biochemistry (PhD); medicine (MD, PhD); microbiology (PhD); pharmaceutical sciences (PhD); pharmacology (PhD); physiology (PhD); quantitative biosciences (PhD). *Application deadline:* For fall admission, 6/1 for domestic students, 4/29 for international students; for spring admission, 11/1 for domestic students, 9/29 for international students; for summer admission, 3/15 for domestic students, 2/1 for international students. Applications are processed on a rolling basis. *Application fee:* $55 ($65 for international students). Electronic applications accepted. *Application Contact:* Doug Taylor, Assistant Dean for Admissions and Records, 423-439-2033, Fax: 423-439-2110, E-mail: dougt@etsu.edu. *Interim Dean,* Dr. William A. Block, Jr., 423-439-6316, Fax: 423-439-8090, E-mail: deanofmedicine@etsu.edu.

School of Graduate Studies Expenses: Contact institution. *Financial support:* Fellowships with tuition reimbursements, research assistantships with tuition reimbursements, and teaching assistantships with tuition reimbursements available. Financial award application deadline: 7/1; financial award applicants required to submit FAFSA. Offers global sport leadership (Ed D). *Application deadline:* For fall admission, 6/1 for domestic students, 4/29 for international students; for spring admission, 11/1 for domestic students, 9/29 for international students; for summer admission, 3/15 for domestic students, 2/1 for international students. *Application fee:* $55 ($65 for international students). Electronic applications accepted. *Application Contact:* Dr. Cecilia McIntosh, Dean, 423-439-4221, Fax: 423-439-5624, E-mail: gradsch@etsu.edu. *Dean,* Dr. Cecilia McIntosh, 423-439-4221, Fax: 423-439-5624, E-mail: gradsch@etsu.edu.

College of Arts and Sciences Expenses: Contact institution. *Financial support:* Research assistantships with tuition reimbursements, teaching assistantships with tuition reimbursements, career-related internships or fieldwork, institutionally sponsored loans, traineeships, and unspecified assistantships available. Financial award application deadline: 7/1; financial award applicants required to submit FAFSA. Offers Appalachian communities (MA); Appalachian heritage and culture (MA); Appalachian studies (Postbaccalaureate Certificate); applied sociology (MA); arts and sciences (MA, MFA, MPA, MS, PhD, Postbaccalaureate Certificate); biology (MS); biomedical sciences (MS); chemistry (MS); clinical psychology (PhD); communication and storytelling studies (MA); criminal justice and criminology (MA); economic development (Postbaccalaureate Certificate); economic development and planning (MPA); experimental psychology (PhD); forensic document examination (Postbaccalaureate Certificate); general sociology (MA); geographic information systems (Postbaccalaureate Certificate); geospatial analysis (MS); healthcare translation and interpreting (Postbaccalaureate Certificate); history (MA); literature (MA); local government management (MPA); mathematical modeling in bioscience (Postbaccalaureate Certificate); mathematical sciences (MS); microbiology (MS); nonprofit and public financial management (MPA); paleontology (MS); storytelling (Postbaccalaureate Certificate); studio art (MFA); teaching English to speakers of other languages (Postbaccalaureate Certificate); urban planning (Postbaccalaureate Certificate). *Application fee:* $55 ($65 for international students). Electronic applications accepted. *Application Contact:* School of Graduate Studies, 423-439-4221, Fax: 423-439-5624, E-mail: gradsch@etsu.edu. *Dean,* Dr. Gordon K. Anderson, 423-439-5671, Fax: 423-439-4645, E-mail: andersgk@etsu.edu.

College of Business and Technology Expenses: Contact institution. *Financial support:* Research assistantships with tuition reimbursements and teaching assistantships with tuition reimbursements available. Financial award application deadline: 7/1; financial award applicants required to submit FAFSA. In 2017, 118 master's, 1 other advanced degree awarded. Offers accountancy (M Acc); applied computer science (MS); business administration (MBA, Postbaccalaureate Certificate); business and technology (M Acc, MBA, MS, Postbaccalaureate Certificate); digital marketing (MS); emerging technologies (Postbaccalaureate Certificate); entrepreneurial leadership (Postbaccalaureate Certificate); health care management (Postbaccalaureate Certificate); information technology (MS); technology (MS). *Application fee:* $55 ($65 for international students). Electronic applications accepted. *Application Contact:* School of Graduate Studies, 423-439-4221, Fax: 423-439-5624, E-mail: gradsch@etsu.edu. *Dean,* Dr. Dennis Depew, 423-439-4289, Fax: 423-439-5274, E-mail: depewd@etsu.edu.

College of Clinical and Rehabilitative Health Sciences Expenses: Contact institution. *Financial support:* Research assistantships with tuition reimbursements and teaching assistantships with tuition reimbursements available. In 2017, 48 master's, 44 doctorates awarded. Offers allied health (MSAH); audiology (Au D); clinical and rehabilitative health sciences (MS, MSAH, MSW, Au D, DPT); clinical nutrition (MS); physical therapy (DPT); social work (MSW); speech-language pathology (MS). *Application fee:* $55 ($65 for international students). Electronic applications accepted. *Application Contact:* School of Graduate Studies, 423-439-4221, Fax: 423-439-5624, E-mail: gradsch@etsu.edu. *Dean,* Dr. Don Samples, 423-439-7454, Fax: 423-439-4240, E-mail: carhs@etsu.edu.

College of Education Expenses: Contact institution. *Financial support:* Fellowships with full tuition reimbursements, research assistantships with full tuition reimbursements, teaching assistantships with full tuition reimbursements, career-related internships or fieldwork, institutionally sponsored loans, scholarships/grants, and unspecified assistantships available. Financial award application deadline: 7/1;

financial award applicants required to submit FAFSA. In 2017, 198 master's, 51 doctorates, 12 other advanced degrees awarded. Offers administrative endorsement (Ed D, Ed S); advanced studies in teaching and learning (M Ed); classroom leadership (Ed D); clinical mental health counseling (MA); college counseling/student affairs higher education (MA); community college leadership (Postbaccalaureate Certificate); community leadership (Post-Master's Certificate); counselor leadership (Ed S); couples and family therapy (MA); early childhood education (MA, PhD); early childhood education emergent inquiry (Postbaccalaureate Certificate); education (M Ed, MA, MAT, MS, Ed D, PhD, Ed S, Post-Master's Certificate, Postbaccalaureate Certificate); educational technology (M Ed); elementary education (M Ed); human services (MS); postsecondary and private sector leadership (Ed D); reading (M Ed, MA); response to intervention (Post-Master's Certificate); school and administrator leadership (M Ed); school counseling (MA); school library professional (Post-Master's Certificate); school system leadership (Ed D, Ed S); secondary education (M Ed); special education (M Ed, Post-Master's Certificate); sport management (MA); sport physiology and performance (PhD); sport science and coach education (MS); STEAM K-12 education (Postbaccalaureate Certificate); storytelling (Postbaccalaureate Certificate); student personnel leadership (M Ed); teacher education (MAT); teacher leadership (M Ed, Ed S). *Application fee:* $55 ($65 for international students). Electronic applications accepted. *Application Contact:* School of Graduate Studies, 423-439-4221, Fax: 423-439-5624, E-mail: gradsch@etsu.edu. *Dean,* Dr. Gregory F. Aloia, 423-439-7616, Fax: 423-439-7560, E-mail: aloiag@etsu.edu.

College of Nursing Expenses: Contact institution. *Financial support:* Research assistantships with tuition reimbursements, teaching assistantships, career-related internships or fieldwork, institutionally sponsored loans, scholarships/grants, and unspecified assistantships available. Financial award application deadline: 7/1; financial award applicants required to submit FAFSA. In 2017, 126 master's, 30 doctorates, 4 other advanced degrees awarded. *Program availability:* Part-time, evening/weekend, online learning. Offers acute care nurse practitioner (DNP); adult-gerontology primary care nurse practitioner (DNP); adult/gerontological nurse practitioner (Postbaccalaureate Certificate); executive leadership in nursing (DNP, Postbaccalaureate Certificate); family nurse practitioner (MSN, DNP, Post-Master's Certificate, Postbaccalaureate Certificate); nursing (PhD); nursing administration (MSN); nursing education (MSN); pediatric primary care nurse practitioner (DNP); psychiatric mental health nurse practitioner (Postbaccalaureate Certificate); psychiatric/mental health nurse practitioner (MSN, DNP, Post-Master's Certificate); women's health care nurse practitioner (DNP). *Application deadline:* For fall admission, 4/15 priority date for domestic and international students; for spring admission, 10/15 priority date for domestic and international students; for summer admission, 2/1 for domestic and international students. *Application fee:* $55 ($65 for international students). Electronic applications accepted. *Application Contact:* Dr. Myra Clark, Director of Graduate Programs, 423-439-4396, Fax: 423-439-4100, E-mail: clarkml2@etsu.edu. *Dean,* Dr. Wendy Nehring, 423-439-7051, Fax: 423-439-4543, E-mail: nursing@etsu.edu.

College of Public Health Expenses: Contact institution. *Financial support:* Research assistantships with tuition reimbursements, teaching assistantships with tuition reimbursements, career-related internships or fieldwork, institutionally sponsored loans, scholarships/grants, and unspecified assistantships available. Financial award application deadline: 7/1; financial award applicants required to submit FAFSA. In 2017, 48 master's, 9 doctorates, 20 other advanced degrees awarded. *Program availability:* Part-time, online learning. Offers biostatistics (MPH, Postbaccalaureate Certificate); community health (MPH, DPH); environmental health (MSEH, PhD); epidemiology (MPH, DPH, Postbaccalaureate Certificate); gerontology (Postbaccalaureate Certificate); global health (Postbaccalaureate Certificate); health care management (Postbaccalaureate Certificate); health management and policy (DPH); public health (Postbaccalaureate Certificate); public health services administration (MPH); rural health (Postbaccalaureate Certificate). *Application fee:* $55 ($65 for international students). Electronic applications accepted. *Application Contact:* Dr. Randy Wykoff, Dean, 423-439-4243, Fax: 423-439-5238, E-mail: wykoff@etsu.edu. *Dean,* Dr. Randy Wykoff, 423-439-4243, Fax: 423-439-5238, E-mail: wykoff@etsu.edu.

School of Continuing Studies and Academic Outreach Expenses: Contact institution. *Financial support:* Research assistantships with full tuition reimbursements, teaching assistantships with full tuition reimbursements, institutionally sponsored loans, scholarships/grants, tuition waivers, and unspecified assistantships available. Financial award application deadline: 7/1; financial award applicants required to submit FAFSA. In 2017, 9 master's, 1 other advanced degree awarded. *Program availability:* Part-time, online learning. Offers archival studies (Postbaccalaureate Certificate); liberal studies (MALS); reinforcing education through artistic learning (Postbaccalaureate Certificate); strategic leadership (MPS); training and development (MPS). *Application deadline:* For fall admission, 6/1 for domestic students, 4/29 for international students; for spring admission, 11/1 for domestic students, 9/29 for international students. *Application fee:* $55 ($65 for international students). Electronic applications accepted. *Application Contact:* Dr. Rick E. Osborn, Dean, 423-439-4223, Fax: 423-439-7091, E-mail: osbornr@etsu.edu. *Dean,* Dr. Rick E. Osborn, 423-439-4223, Fax: 423-439-7091, E-mail: osbornr@etsu.edu.

EAST TEXAS BAPTIST UNIVERSITY, Marshall, TX 75670-1498

General Information Independent-religious, coed, comprehensive institution. *Enrollment:* 1,533 graduate, professional, and undergraduate students; 38 full-time matriculated graduate/professional students (26 women), 74 part-time matriculated graduate/professional students (44 women). *Enrollment by degree level:* 112 master's. *Graduate faculty:* 14 full-time (6 women), 6 part-time/adjunct (3 women). *Graduate housing:* Rooms and/or apartments available on a first-come, first-served basis to single and married students. Typical cost: $4784 per year ($8105 including board) for single students; $5000 per year for married students. Room and board charges vary according to board plan and housing facility selected. *Student services:* Campus employment opportunities, campus safety program, career counseling, free psychological counseling, international student services, services for students with disabilities, teacher training, writing training. *Library facilities:* Mamye Jarrett Library. *Collection:* Books: 92,020 (physical), 3.7 million (digital/electronic); Serial titles: 695 (physical), 47,336 (digital/electronic); Databases: 217. Weekly public service hours: 88.

Computer facilities: 301 computers available on campus for general student use. A campuswide network can be accessed from student residence rooms. Online class registration is available.
Website: http://www.etbu.edu/

General Application Contact: Den Murley, Director of Graduate Admissions, 903-923-2079, Fax: 903-934-8115, E-mail: gradadmissions@etbu.edu.

GRADUATE UNITS

Master of Arts in Counseling Program Students: 14 full-time (11 women), 19 part-time (16 women); includes 22 minority (20 Black or African American, non-Hispanic/Latino; 2 Hispanic/Latino). Average age 34. 20 applicants, 55% accepted, 8 enrolled. *Faculty:* 4 full-time (3 women), 1 (woman) part-time/adjunct. Expenses: Contact institution. *Financial support:* In 2017–18, 7 students received support. Scholarships/grants, unspecified assistantships, and staff grants available. Financial award applicants required to submit FAFSA. In 2017, 9 master's awarded. *Program availability:* Part-time, evening/weekend. Offers counseling (MA). *Application deadline:* For fall admission, 8/13 for domestic students; for spring admission, 1/7 for domestic students; for summer admission, 5/10 for domestic students. Applications are processed on a rolling basis. *Application fee:* $50. Electronic applications accepted. *Application Contact:* Den Murley, Director of Graduate Admissions, 903-923-2079, Fax: 903-934-8115, E-mail: gradadmissions@etbu.edu. *Director,* Dr. LaShondra Manning, 903-923-2088, E-mail: macounsel@etbu.edu.

Master of Business Administration Program Students: 15 full-time (11 women), 12 part-time (7 women); includes 13 minority (10 Black or African American, non-Hispanic/Latino; 2 Hispanic/Latino; 1 Two or more races, non-Hispanic/Latino). Average age 26. 20 applicants, 65% accepted, 13 enrolled. *Faculty:* 2 full-time (1 woman), 2 part-time/adjunct (0 women). Expenses: Contact institution. *Financial support:* In 2017–18, 16 students received support. Federal Work-Study, scholarships/grants, unspecified assistantships, and staff grants available. Financial award applicants required to submit FAFSA. In 2017, 16 master's awarded. *Program availability:* Part-time, evening/weekend, 100% online. Offers business administration (MBA). *Application deadline:* For fall admission, 8/13 for domestic students; for spring admission, 1/7 for domestic students; for summer admission, 5/10 for domestic students. Applications are processed on a rolling basis. *Application fee:* $50. Electronic applications accepted. *Director of Graduate Admissions,* Den Murley, 903-923-2079, Fax: 903-934-8115, E-mail: dmurley@etbu.edu.

Master of Education Program Students: 32 part-time (18 women); includes 12 minority (8 Black or African American, non-Hispanic/Latino; 1 American Indian or Alaska Native, non-Hispanic/Latino; 1 Hispanic/Latino; 2 Two or more races, non-Hispanic/Latino). Average age 28. 70 applicants, 41% accepted, 21 enrolled. *Faculty:* 3 full-time (1 woman), 4 part-time/adjunct (3 women). Expenses: Contact institution. *Financial support:* In 2017–18, 18 students received support. Federal Work-Study, scholarships/grants, unspecified assistantships, and staff grants available. Financial award applicants required to submit FAFSA. In 2017, 20 master's awarded. *Program availability:* Part-time, evening/weekend, 100% online, blended/hybrid learning. Offers education (M Ed). *Application deadline:* For fall admission, 8/13 for domestic students; for spring admission, 1/7 for domestic students; for summer admission, 5/10 for domestic students. Applications are processed on a rolling basis. *Application fee:* $50. Electronic applications accepted. *Application Contact:* Den Murley, Director of Graduate Admissions, 903-923-2079, Fax: 903-934-8115, E-mail: gradadmissions@etbu.edu. *Director,* Dr. PJ Winters, 903-923-2276, Fax: 903-935-4318, E-mail: med@etbu.edu.

Master of Science in Kinesiology Program Students: 6 part-time (2 women); includes 3 minority (1 Black or African American, non-Hispanic/Latino; 1 Hispanic/Latino; 1 Two or more races, non-Hispanic/Latino). Average age 24. 9 applicants, 56% accepted, 5 enrolled. *Faculty:* 2 full-time (0 women). Expenses: Contact institution. *Financial support:* In 2017–18, 3 students received support. Federal Work-Study, scholarships/grants, unspecified assistantships, and staff grants available. Financial award applicants required to submit FAFSA. *Program availability:* Part-time, evening/weekend. Offers kinesiology (MS). *Application deadline:* For fall admission, 8/13 for domestic students; for spring admission, 1/7 for domestic students; for summer admission, 5/10 for domestic students. Applications are processed on a rolling basis. *Application fee:* $50. Electronic applications accepted. *Application Contact:* Den Murley, Director of Graduate Admissions, 903-923-2079, Fax: 903-934-8115, E-mail: gradadmissions@etbu.edu. *Dean, Frank S. Groner School of Professional Studies,* Dr. Joseph D. Brown, 903-923-2270, Fax: 903-935-4318, E-mail: jbrown@etbu.edu.

School of Christian Studies Students: 9 full-time (4 women), 5 part-time (1 woman); includes 4 minority (2 Black or African American, non-Hispanic/Latino; 1 Hispanic/Latino; 1 Two or more races, non-Hispanic/Latino). Average age 26. 13 applicants, 62% accepted, 7 enrolled. *Faculty:* 4 full-time (0 women), 1 part-time/adjunct (0 women). Expenses: Contact institution. *Financial support:* In 2017–18, 6 students received support. Federal Work-Study, scholarships/grants, unspecified assistantships, and staff grants available. Financial award applicants required to submit FAFSA. In 2017, 3 master's awarded. *Program availability:* Part-time, evening/weekend, blended/hybrid learning. Offers Christian studies (MA, MACM). *Application deadline:* For fall admission, 8/13 for domestic students; for spring admission, 1/7 for domestic students; for summer admission, 5/10 for domestic students. Applications are processed on a rolling basis. *Application fee:* $50. Electronic applications accepted. *Application Contact:* Den Murley, Director of Graduate Admissions, 903-923-2079, Fax: 903-934-8115, E-mail: gradadmissions@etbu.edu. *Director,* Dr. Warren Johnson, 903-923-2182, Fax: 903-923-2077, E-mail: christianstudiesma@etbu.edu.

EAST WEST COLLEGE OF NATURAL MEDICINE, Sarasota, FL 34234

General Information Proprietary, coed, graduate-only institution.

GRADUATE UNITS

Graduate Programs Offers Oriental medicine (MSOM).

ECCLESIA COLLEGE, Springdale, AR 72762

General Information Independent-religious, coed, comprehensive institution.

GRADUATE UNITS

Graduate School *Program availability:* Online learning.

EC-COUNCIL UNIVERSITY, Albuquerque, NM 87109

General Information Proprietary, coed, upper-level institution. *Enrollment by degree level:* 74 master's. *Graduate faculty:* 28 part-time/adjunct (9 women). *Graduate housing:* On-campus housing not available.
Website: http://www.eccu.edu/

General Application Contact: David Valdez, Enrollment Counselor, 505-922-2886, Fax: 505-856-8267, E-mail: david.valdez@eccu.edu.

GRADUATE UNITS

Master of Science in Cyber Security Program Students: 74 full-time (13 women). *Faculty:* 28 part-time/adjunct (9 women). Expenses: Contact institution. *Financial support:* Scholarships/grants available. *Program availability:* Part-time, online only, 100% online. Offers information assurance management (MSCS). *Application deadline:* For fall admission, 9/15 for domestic and international students; for winter admission, 12/15 for domestic and international students; for spring admission, 3/15 for domestic and international students; for summer admission, 6/15 for domestic and international students. Applications are processed on a rolling basis. *Application fee:* $65. Electronic applications accepted. *Application Contact:* David Valdez, Enrollment Counselor, 505-922-2886, Fax: 505-856-8267, E-mail: david.valdez@eccu.edu.

ECOLE HÔTELIÈRE DE LAUSANNE, CH-1000 Lausanne 25, Switzerland

General Information Independent, coed, comprehensive institution.

GRADUATE UNITS

Program in Hospitality Administration Offers hospitality administration (MHA).

ÉCOLE POLYTECHNIQUE DE MONTRÉAL, Montréal, QC H3C 3A7, Canada

General Information Province-supported, coed, university. *Graduate housing:* Room and/or apartments available on a first-come, first-served basis to single students; on-campus housing not available to married students. Housing application deadline: 2/1. *Research affiliation:* Hydro-Quebec (energy), Bell Canada (telecommunications), Bombardier, Inc. (aircraft and aviation), IBM (computer research), Pratt and Whitney (aircraft and aviation), Ubisoft (video games).

GRADUATE UNITS

Graduate Programs *Program availability:* Part-time, evening/weekend. Offers aerothermics (M Eng, M Sc A, PhD); applied mechanics (M Eng, M Sc A, PhD); automation (M Eng, M Sc A, PhD); chemical engineering (M Eng, M Sc A, PhD, DESS); civil, geological and mining engineering (DESS); computer science (M Eng, M Sc A, PhD); electrical engineering (DESS); electrotechnology (M Eng, M Sc A, PhD); environmental engineering (M Eng, M Sc A, PhD); ergonomy (M Eng, M Sc A, DESS); geotechnical engineering (M Eng, M Sc A, PhD); hydraulics engineering (M Eng, M Sc A, PhD); mathematical method in CA engineering (M Eng, M Sc A, PhD); microelectronics (M Eng, M Sc A, PhD); microwave technology (M Eng, M Sc A, PhD); operational research (M Eng, M Sc A, PhD); optical engineering (M Eng, M Sc A, PhD); production (M Eng, M Sc A); solid-state physics and engineering (M Eng, M Sc A, PhD); structural engineering (M Eng, M Sc A, PhD); technology management (M Eng, M Sc A); tool design (M Eng, M Sc A, PhD); transportation engineering (M Eng, M Sc A, PhD). Electronic applications accepted.

Institute of Biomedical Engineering *Program availability:* Part-time. Offers biomedical engineering (M Sc A, PhD, DESS). M Sc A and PhD programs offered jointly with Université de Montréal.

Institute of Nuclear Engineering Offers nuclear engineering (M Eng, PhD, DESS); nuclear engineering, socio-economics of energy (M Sc A).

ECUMENICAL THEOLOGICAL SEMINARY, Detroit, MI 48201

General Information Independent-religious, coed, graduate-only institution. *Graduate housing:* On-campus housing not available.

GRADUATE UNITS

Professional Program Offers theology (M Div).

Program in Ministry Offers ministry (D Min).

EDEN THEOLOGICAL SEMINARY, St. Louis, MO 63119-3192

General Information Independent-religious, coed, graduate-only institution. *Graduate housing:* Rooms and/or apartments available on a first-come, first-served basis to single and married students. Housing application deadline: 7/30.

GRADUATE UNITS

Graduate and Professional Programs Offers theology (M Div, MAPS, MTS, D Min). Electronic applications accepted.

EDGEWOOD COLLEGE, Madison, WI 53711-1997

General Information Independent-religious, coed, comprehensive institution. *Enrollment:* 2,221 graduate, professional, and undergraduate students; 232 full-time matriculated graduate/professional students (167 women), 360 part-time matriculated graduate/professional students (253 women). *Enrollment by degree level:* 434 master's, 158 doctoral. *Tuition:* Part-time $930 per credit. *Graduate housing:* On-campus housing not available. *Student services:* Campus employment opportunities, career counseling, free psychological counseling, international student services, low-cost health insurance, multicultural affairs office, services for students with disabilities, writing training. *Library facilities:* Oscar Rennebohm Library. *Collection:* Books: 82,008 (physical), 140,319 (digital/electronic); Serial titles: 219 (physical), 38,116 (digital/electronic); Databases: 90. Weekly public service hours: 98; students can reserve study rooms.

Computer facilities: Computer purchase and lease plans are available. 180 computers available on campus for general student use. A campuswide network can be accessed from student residence rooms and from off campus. Online class registration is available.

Website: http://www.edgewood.edu/

General Application Contact: Joann Eastman, Admissions Counselor, 608-663-3250, Fax: 608-663-2214, E-mail: gps@edgewood.edu.

GRADUATE UNITS

Henry Predolin School of Nursing Expenses: Contact institution. Offers nursing (MSN, DNP). *Application deadline:* For fall admission, 8/15 priority date for domestic students, 5/1 for international students; for spring admission, 1/8 priority date for domestic students, 11/1 for international students. Applications are processed on a rolling basis. *Application fee:* $30. Electronic applications accepted. *Dean*, Dr. Margaret Noreuil, 608-663-2820, Fax: 608-663-3291, E-mail: mnoreuil@edgewood.edu.

Program in Business Students: 19 full-time (12 women), 107 part-time (63 women); includes 16 minority (3 Black or African American, non-Hispanic/Latino; 5 Asian, non-Hispanic/Latino; 4 Hispanic/Latino; 4 Two or more races, non-Hispanic/Latino), 13 international. Average age 34. Expenses: Contact institution. *Financial support:* Career-related internships or fieldwork and scholarships/grants available. In 2017, 47 master's awarded. *Program availability:* Part-time, evening/weekend. Offers accountancy (MS); sustainability leadership (MBA). *Application deadline:* For fall admission, 8/15 for domestic students, 5/1 for international students; for spring admission, 1/8 for domestic students, 11/1 for international students. Applications are processed on a rolling basis. *Application fee:* $30. Electronic applications accepted. *Application Contact:* Joann Eastman, Admissions Counselor, 608-663-3250, Fax: 608-663-2214, E-mail: gps@edgewood.edu. *Dean*, Dr. Stevie Watson, 608-663-2224, Fax: 608-663-3291, E-mail: swatson@edgewood.edu.

Program in Social Innovation and Sustainability Leadership Students: 5 full-time (4 women), 7 part-time (4 women); includes 2 minority (1 Hispanic/Latino; 1 Two or more races, non-Hispanic/Latino). Average age 37. 15 applicants, 100% accepted, 12 enrolled. *Faculty:* 1 full-time (0 women), 2 part-time/adjunct (1 woman). Expenses: Contact institution. *Financial support:* In 2017–18, 14 students received support. Scholarships/grants available. Support available to part-time students. Financial award application deadline: 5/1; financial award applicants required to submit FAFSA. In 2017, 5 master's awarded. *Program availability:* Part-time, evening/weekend. Offers social innovation and sustainability leadership (MA). *Application deadline:* For fall admission, 7/1 for domestic students. *Application fee:* $30. *Director*, Dr. Stephan Gilchrist, 608-663-6991, E-mail: sgilchrist@edgewood.edu.

School of Education Students: 157 full-time (106 women), 188 part-time (133 women); includes 65 minority (26 Black or African American, non-Hispanic/Latino; 1 American Indian or Alaska Native, non-Hispanic/Latino; 8 Asian, non-Hispanic/Latino; 23 Hispanic/Latino; 7 Two or more races, non-Hispanic/Latino), 14 international. Average age 37. *Faculty:* 13 full-time (9 women), 15 part-time/adjunct (10 women). Expenses: Contact institution. *Financial support:* Applicants required to submit FAFSA. In 2017, 68 master's, 34 doctorates awarded. *Program availability:* Part-time, evening/weekend. Offers adult learning (MA Ed); director of special education and pupil services (Certificate); education (MA Ed); teaching and learning (MA Ed). *Application deadline:* For fall admission, 8/15 for domestic students, 5/1 for international students; for spring admission, 1/8 for domestic students, 11/1 for international students. Applications are processed on a rolling basis. *Application fee:* $30. Electronic applications accepted. *Application Contact:* Joann Eastman, Admissions Counselor, 608-663-3250, Fax: 608-663-2214, E-mail: gps@edgewood.edu. *Dean*, Dr. Timothy D. Slekar, 608-663-2293, E-mail: tslekar@edgewood.edu.

EDINBORO UNIVERSITY OF PENNSYLVANIA, Edinboro, PA 16444

General Information State-supported, coed, comprehensive institution. *Graduate housing:* Room and/or apartments available on a first-come, first-served basis to single students; on-campus housing not available to married students. Housing application deadline: 4/3. *Research affiliation:* Arts Erie (art), State Higher Education Executive Officers Association (education and learning), Preventative Aftercare, Inc. (social work), CampusEAI (computing), Northwest Institute of Research (training and education), College Board (disability education).

GRADUATE UNITS

Department of Art *Program availability:* Evening/weekend. Offers art education (MA); fine arts (MFA); studio art (MA). Electronic applications accepted.

Department of Communication Studies *Program availability:* Part-time, evening/weekend. Offers communication studies (MA). Electronic applications accepted.

Department of Counseling, School Psychology and Special Education *Program availability:* Part-time, evening/weekend. Offers counseling (MA); educational psychology (M Ed); school psychology (Ed S); special education (M Ed). Electronic applications accepted.

Department of Early Childhood and Reading *Program availability:* Part-time, evening/weekend. Offers arts infusion (Graduate Certificate); early childhood education (M Ed); reading (M Ed); reading specialist (Graduate Certificate). Electronic applications accepted.

Department of History, Politics, Languages and Cultures *Program availability:* Part-time, evening/weekend. Offers social sciences (MA). Electronic applications accepted.

Department of Middle and Secondary Education and Educational Leadership *Program availability:* Part-time, evening/weekend. Offers educational leadership (M Ed); middle and secondary instruction (M Ed). Electronic applications accepted.

Department of Nursing *Program availability:* Part-time, evening/weekend. Offers advanced practice nursing (DNP); family nurse practitioner (MSN); nurse educator (MSN). Electronic applications accepted.

Department of Social Work *Program availability:* Evening/weekend. Offers social work (MSW). Electronic applications accepted.

Department of Speech, Language and Hearing *Program availability:* Part-time, evening/weekend. Offers speech language pathology (MA). Electronic applications accepted.

EDP UNIVERSITY OF PUERTO RICO–SAN SEBASTIAN, San Sebastian, PR 00685

General Information Independent, coed, comprehensive institution.

GRADUATE UNITS

Graduate School

EDWARD VIA COLLEGE OF OSTEOPATHIC MEDICINE–CAROLINAS CAMPUS, Spartanburg, SC 29303

General Information Independent, coed, graduate-only institution.

GRADUATE UNITS

Graduate Program Offers osteopathic medicine (DO).

EDWARD VIA COLLEGE OF OSTEOPATHIC MEDICINE–VIRGINIA CAMPUS, Blacksburg, VA 24060

General Information Independent, coed, graduate-only institution. *Research affiliation:* Virginia Polytechnic Institute and State University (biomedical research).

GRADUATE UNITS

Graduate Program Offers osteopathic medicine (DO).

ELIZABETH CITY STATE UNIVERSITY, Elizabeth City, NC 27909-7806

General Information State-supported, coed, comprehensive institution. CGS member. *Enrollment:* 43 full-time matriculated graduate/professional students (37 women), 2 part-time matriculated graduate/professional students (1 woman). *Enrollment by degree level:* 45 master's. *Graduate faculty:* 19 full-time (5 women), 2 part-time/adjunct (both women). Tuition and fees vary according to course load and program. *Graduate housing:* Room and/or apartments available on a first-come, first-served basis to single students; on-campus housing not available to married students. Housing application deadline: 5/31. *Student services:* Campus employment opportunities, campus safety program, career counseling, child daycare facilities, exercise/wellness program, free psychological counseling, grant writing training, international student services, low-cost health insurance, services for students with disabilities, teacher training, writing training. *Library facilities:* G. R. Little Library plus 1 other. *Collection:* Books: 231,406 (physical), 184,579 (digital/electronic); Serial titles: 1,923 (physical), 22,828 (digital/electronic); Databases: 101. Weekly public service hours: 82.

Computer facilities: Computer purchase and lease plans are available. A campuswide network can be accessed from student residence rooms and from off campus. Online class registration is available.

Website: http://www.ecsu.edu/

General Application Contact: Dr. Sharon D. Raynor, Director, Graduate Education Program, 252-335-3945, E-mail: sdraynor@ecsu.edu.

GRADUATE UNITS

Department of Education, Psychology and Health Students: 3 full-time (2 women), 42 part-time (33 women); includes 21 minority (20 Black or African American, non-Hispanic/Latino; 1 Two or more races, non-Hispanic/Latino). Average age 37. 3 applicants, 100% accepted, 2 enrolled. *Faculty:* 7 full-time (4 women), 1 (woman) part-time/adjunct. Expenses: Contact institution. *Financial support:* In 2017–18, 25 students received support. Scholarships/grants and tuition waivers (partial) available. In 2017, 51 master's awarded. *Program availability:* Part-time, evening/weekend. Offers education, psychology and health (M Ed, MSA); elementary education (M Ed); school administration (MSA). *Application deadline:* For fall admission, 11/1 priority date for domestic students; for spring admission, 3/15 priority date for domestic students. Applications are processed on a rolling basis. *Application fee:* $30. Electronic applications accepted. *Director, Graduate Education Program,* Dr. Sharon D. Raynor, 252-335-3945, E-mail: sdraynor@ecsu.edu.

Department of Mathematics and Computer Science Students: 3 full-time (1 woman), 42 part-time (24 women); includes 33 minority (31 Black or African American, non-Hispanic/Latino; 1 Asian, non-Hispanic/Latino; 1 Two or more races, non-Hispanic/Latino). Average age 28. 15 applicants, 73% accepted, 9 enrolled. *Faculty:* 15 full-time (3 women), 1 (woman) part-time/adjunct. Expenses: Contact institution. *Financial support:* In 2017–18, 40 students received support, including 3 research assistantships, 2 teaching assistantships with partial tuition reimbursements available; fellowships also available. In 2017, 28 master's awarded. *Program availability:* Part-time, evening/weekend. Offers applied mathematics (MS); community college teaching (MS); mathematics (MS); mathematics education (MS); remote sensing (MS). *Application deadline:* For fall admission, 11/1 priority date for domestic and international students; for spring admission, 3/15 priority date for domestic and international students. *Application fee:* $30. Electronic applications accepted. *Application Contact:* Dr. Sharon D. Raynor, Director of Graduate Education, 252-335-3945, E-mail: sdraynor@ecsu.edu. *Chair,* Dr. Kenneth L. Jones, 252-335-3858, Fax: 252-335-3858, E-mail: kljones@ecsu.edu.

Master of Science in Biology Program Students: 3 full-time (1 woman), 17 part-time (11 women); includes 14 minority (12 Black or African American, non-Hispanic/Latino; 1 Asian, non-Hispanic/Latino; 1 Two or more races, non-Hispanic/Latino). Average age 30. 10 applicants, 70% accepted, 5 enrolled. *Faculty:* 8 full-time (1 woman), 1 (woman) part-time/adjunct. Expenses: Contact institution. *Financial support:* In 2017–18, 18 students received support. Scholarships/grants available. Financial award application deadline: 6/30; financial award applicants required to submit FAFSA. In 2017, 10 master's awarded. *Program availability:* Part-time, evening/weekend. Offers biological sciences (MS); biology education (MS). *Application deadline:* For fall admission, 7/15 priority date for domestic and international students; for spring admission, 11/15 priority date for domestic and international students; for summer admission, 3/15 priority date for domestic and international students. Applications are processed on a rolling basis. *Application fee:* $30. Electronic applications accepted. *Chair,* Dr. Gloria Payne, 252-335-3595, Fax: 252-335-3697, E-mail: gepayne@ecsu.edu.

ELIZABETHTOWN COLLEGE, Elizabethtown, PA 17022-2298

General Information Independent-religious, coed, comprehensive institution.

GRADUATE UNITS

Department of Occupational Therapy Offers occupational therapy (MS).

ELMEZZI GRADUATE SCHOOL OF MOLECULAR MEDICINE, Manhasset, NY 11030

General Information Independent, coed, graduate-only institution. *Enrollment by degree level:* 8 doctoral. *Graduate faculty:* 41 full-time (13 women). *Graduate housing:* On-campus housing not available. *Student services:* Campus employment opportunities, campus safety program, career counseling, exercise/wellness program, free psychological counseling, grant writing training, low-cost health insurance. *Library facilities:* North Shore University Hospital Library plus 3 others. *Research affiliation:* Feinstein Institute for Medical Research (biomedical research), North Shore Long Island Jewish Health System (medicine).

Computer facilities: 20 computers available on campus for general student use. Website: http://www.elmezzigraduateschool.org/

General Application Contact: Emilia C. Hristis, Education Coordinator, 516-562-3405, Fax: 516-562-1022, E-mail: ehristis@nshs.edu.

GRADUATE UNITS

Graduate Program Students: 8 full-time (2 women); includes 2 minority (both Asian, non-Hispanic/Latino). Average age 30. *Faculty:* 41 full-time (13 women). Expenses: Contact institution. *Financial support:* Fellowships with full tuition reimbursements, health care benefits, and tuition waivers (full) available. Offers molecular medicine (PhD). *Application deadline:* Applications are processed on a rolling basis. *Application fee:* $100. *Application Contact:* Emilia C. Hristis, Education Coordinator, 516-562-3405, Fax: 516-562-1022, E-mail: ehristis@nshs.edu. *Provost,* Dr. Bettie M. Steinberg, 516-562-1159, Fax: 516-562-1022, E-mail: bsteinbe@lij.edu.

ELMHURST COLLEGE, Elmhurst, IL 60126-3296

General Information Independent-religious, coed, comprehensive institution. *Enrollment:* 3,483 graduate, professional, and undergraduate students; 150 full-time matriculated graduate/professional students (132 women), 456 part-time matriculated graduate/professional students (273 women). *Enrollment by degree level:* 606 master's. *Graduate faculty:* 39 full-time (29 women), 43 part-time/adjunct (16 women). *Tuition:* Part-time $775 per semester hour. *Required fees:* $150 per term. *Graduate housing:* On-campus housing not available. *Student services:* Campus employment opportunities, campus safety program, career counseling, exercise/wellness program, free psychological counseling, international student services, low-cost health insurance, multicultural affairs office, services for students with disabilities, teacher training, writing training. *Library facilities:* Buehler Library.

Computer facilities: 800 computers available on campus for general student use. A campuswide network can be accessed. Online class registration is available. Website: http://www.elmhurst.edu/

General Application Contact: Timothy J. Panfil, Director of Enrollment Management, School for Professional Studies, 630-617-3300 Ext. 3256, Fax: 630-617-6471, E-mail: panfilt@elmhurst.edu.

GRADUATE UNITS

Graduate Programs Students: 150 full-time (132 women), 456 part-time (273 women); includes 139 minority (30 Black or African American, non-Hispanic/Latino; 3 American Indian or Alaska Native, non-Hispanic/Latino; 34 Asian, non-Hispanic/Latino; 64 Hispanic/Latino; 2 Native Hawaiian or other Pacific Islander, non-Hispanic/Latino; 6 Two or more races, non-Hispanic/Latino), 12 international. Average age 30. 1,141 applicants, 37% accepted, 284 enrolled. *Faculty:* 39 full-time (29 women), 43 part-time/adjunct (16 women). Expenses: Contact institution. *Financial support:* In 2017–18, 279 students received support. Fellowships, scholarships/grants, and unspecified assistantships available. Support available to part-time students. Financial award application deadline: 3/1; financial award applicants required to submit FAFSA. In 2017, 203 master's awarded. *Program availability:* Part-time, evening/weekend, 100% online. Offers business administration (MBA); communication sciences and disorders (MS); computer information systems (MS); data science (MS); early childhood special education (M Ed); geographic information systems (MS); health care management and administration (MHCA); industrial/organizational psychology (MA); nursing (MS, MSN); occupational therapy (MOT); project management (MPM); public health (MPH); special education (MS Ed); supply chain management (MS); teacher leadership (M Ed). *Application deadline:* For fall admission, 7/1 priority date for domestic and international students; for spring admission, 12/1 priority date for domestic students; for summer admission, 4/1 priority date for domestic students. Applications are processed on a rolling basis. *Application fee:* $0. Electronic applications accepted. *Application Contact:* Timothy J. Panfil, Director of Enrollment Management, 630-617-3300 Ext. 3256, Fax: 630-617-6471, E-mail: panfilt@elmhurst.edu. *Vice President for Admission,* Dr. Timothy Ricordati, 630-617-3089, E-mail: timothy.ricordati@elmhurst.edu.

ELMS COLLEGE, Chicopee, MA 01013-2839

General Information Independent-religious, coed, comprehensive institution. *Enrollment:* 1,580 graduate, professional, and undergraduate students; 103 full-time matriculated graduate/professional students (69 women), 286 part-time matriculated graduate/professional students (231 women). *Enrollment by degree level:* 257 master's, 61 doctoral, 71 other advanced degrees. *Graduate faculty:* 24 full-time (19 women), 32 part-time/adjunct (20 women). *Tuition:* Full-time $13,860; part-time $770 per credit hour. *Required fees:* $200. Tuition and fees vary according to degree level and program. *Graduate housing:* On-campus housing not available. *Student services:* Career counseling, low-cost health insurance. *Library facilities:* Alumnae Library.

Computer facilities: 175 computers available on campus for general student use. A campuswide network can be accessed from student residence rooms and from off campus. Online class registration is available. Website: http://www.elms.edu/

General Application Contact: Dr. Elizabeth Teahan Hukowicz, Dean, School of Graduate and Professional Studies, 413-265-2360 Ext. 238, Fax: 413-265-2459, E-mail: hukowicze@elms.edu.

GRADUATE UNITS

Division of Business Students: 51 part-time (30 women); includes 9 minority (4 Black or African American, non-Hispanic/Latino; 2 Asian, non-Hispanic/Latino; 3 Hispanic/Latino), 2 international. Average age 33. 14 applicants, 93% accepted, 10 enrolled. *Faculty:* 5 full-time (all women), 7 part-time/adjunct (4 women). Expenses: Contact institution. In 2017, 28 master's awarded. *Program availability:* Part-time, evening/weekend. Offers accounting (MBA); accounting and finance (MS); financial planning (MBA, Certificate); healthcare leadership (MBA); lean entrepreneurship (MBA); management (MBA). *Application deadline:* Applications are processed on a rolling basis. *Application fee:* $30. Electronic applications accepted. *Application Contact:* MBA Program Coordinator, 413-265-2592, E-mail: mba@elms.edu. *Chair, Division of Business,* Dr. David Kimball, 413-265-2300, E-mail: kimballd@elms.edu.

Division of Education Students: 6 full-time (4 women), 127 part-time (107 women); includes 8 minority (2 Asian, non-Hispanic/Latino; 6 Hispanic/Latino). Average age 33. 42 applicants, 88% accepted, 36 enrolled. *Faculty:* 4 full-time (all women), 8 part-time/adjunct (7 women). Expenses: Contact institution. *Financial support:* In 2017–18, 2 teaching assistantships with partial tuition reimbursements were awarded. Financial award applicants required to submit FAFSA. In 2017, 50 master's, 6 other advanced degrees awarded. *Program availability:* Part-time, evening/weekend. Offers early childhood education (MAT); education (M Ed, CAGS); elementary education (MAT); English as a second language (MAT); reading (MAT); secondary education (MAT); special education (MAT). *Application deadline:* For fall admission, 7/1 priority date for domestic students; for spring admission, 11/1 priority date for domestic students. Applications are processed on a rolling basis. *Application fee:* $30. *Application Contact:* School of Graduate and Professional Studies, 413-265-2445, E-mail: graduateeducation@elms.edu. *Chair, Division of Education,* Dr. Mary Janeczek, 413-594-2761, Fax: 413-592-4871, E-mail: janeczeke@elms.edu.

Division of Natural Sciences, Mathematics and Technology Students: 16 full-time (10 women); includes 9 minority (5 Black or African American, non-Hispanic/Latino; 4 Asian, non-Hispanic/Latino), 1 international. Average age 24. 21 applicants, 95% accepted, 16 enrolled. *Faculty:* 4 full-time (2 women), 1 (woman) part-time/adjunct. Expenses: Contact institution. *Financial support:* Applicants required to submit FAFSA. Offers biomedical sciences (MS). *Application deadline:* Applications are processed on a rolling basis. *Application fee:* $30. *Application Contact:* School of Graduate and Professional Studies, 413-265-2445, E-mail: graduateeducation@elms.edu. *Chair, Division of Natural Sciences and Mathematics,* Dr. Goose Gosselin, 413-265-2216, E-mail: gosseling@elms.edu.

Division of Social Sciences Students: 3 full-time (all women), 22 part-time (19 women); includes 1 minority (Black or African American, non-Hispanic/Latino). Average age 31. 24 applicants, 75% accepted, 15 enrolled. *Faculty:* 2 full-time (1 woman), 3 part-time/adjunct (1 woman). Expenses: Contact institution. *Financial support:* Applicants required to submit FAFSA. In 2017, 6 master's, 3 other advanced degrees awarded. *Program availability:* Part-time. Offers applied behavior analysis (MS); autism spectrum disorders (MS, CAGS); communication sciences and disorders (CAGS). *Application deadline:* Applications are processed on a rolling basis. *Application fee:* $30. Electronic applications accepted. *Application Contact:* School of Graduate and Professional Studies, 413-265-2445, E-mail: graduateeducation@elms.edu. *Chair, Division of Social Sciences,* Dr. John Lambdin, 413-265-2442, E-mail: lambdinj@elms.edu.

Religious Studies Department Students: 1 full-time (0 women), 3 part-time (2 women). Average age 55. 2 applicants, 100% accepted, 2 enrolled. *Faculty:* 1 full-time (0 women), 3 part-time/adjunct (1 woman). Expenses: Contact institution. *Financial support:* Applicants required to submit FAFSA. In 2017, 32 master's awarded. *Program availability:* Part-time, evening/weekend. Offers religious studies (MAAT). *Application deadline:* For fall admission, 7/1 priority date for domestic students; for spring admission, 11/1 priority date for domestic students. Applications are processed on a rolling basis. *Application fee:* $30. *Application Contact:* School of Graduate and Professional Studies, 413-265-2445, E-mail: graduateeducation@elms.edu. *Director of Religious Studies,* Dr. Martin Pion, 413-265-3581, Fax: 413-594-3951, E-mail: pionm@elms.edu.

School of Nursing Students: 20 full-time (16 women), 79 part-time (70 women); includes 12 minority (2 Black or African American, non-Hispanic/Latino; 2 American

Indian or Alaska Native, non-Hispanic/Latino; 8 Hispanic/Latino). Average age 40. 33 applicants, 94% accepted, 28 enrolled. *Faculty:* 5 full-time (all women), 9 part-time/adjunct (6 women). Expenses: Contact institution. *Financial support:* Applicants required to submit FAFSA. In 2017, 14 master's, 30 doctorates awarded. *Program availability:* Part-time, evening/weekend. Offers adult-gerontology acute care nurse practitioner (DNP); family nurse practitioner (DNP); health systems innovation and leadership (DNP); nursing and health services management (MSN); nursing education (MSN). *Application deadline:* For fall admission, 7/1 priority date for domestic students; for spring admission, 11/1 priority date for domestic students. Applications are processed on a rolling basis. *Application fee:* $30. *Application Contact:* Dr. Cynthia L. Dakin, Director of Graduate Nursing Studies, 413-265-2455, Fax: 413-265-2335, E-mail: dakinc@elms.edu. *Dean, School of Nursing*, Dr. Kathleen Scoble, 413-265-2204, E-mail: scoblek@elms.edu.

ELON UNIVERSITY, Elon, NC 27244-2010

General Information Independent-religious, coed, comprehensive institution. *Enrollment:* 6,791 graduate, professional, and undergraduate students; 654 full-time matriculated graduate/professional students (410 women), 92 part-time matriculated graduate/professional students (52 women). *Enrollment by degree level:* 254 master's, 492 doctoral. *Graduate faculty:* 96 full-time (51 women), 82 part-time/adjunct (39 women). *Graduate housing:* On-campus housing not available. *Student services:* Campus employment opportunities, campus safety program, career counseling, exercise/wellness program, free psychological counseling, international student services, low-cost health insurance, multicultural affairs office, services for students with disabilities, teacher training, writing training. *Library facilities:* Carol Grotnes Belk. *Collection:* Books: 401,760 (physical), 1.3 million (digital/electronic); Serial titles: 217 (physical), 64,848 (digital/electronic); Databases: 179. Weekly public service hours: 143; study areas open 24 hours, 5–7 days a week; students can reserve study rooms.

Computer facilities: Computer purchase and lease plans are available. 1,200 computers available on campus for general student use. A campuswide network can be accessed from student residence rooms and from off campus. Online class registration is available.
Website: http://www.elon.edu/

General Application Contact: Art Fadde, Director of Graduate Admissions, 800-334-8448 Ext. 3, Fax: 336-278-7699, E-mail: afadde@elon.edu.

GRADUATE UNITS

Program in Business Administration Students: 60 full-time (25 women), 68 part-time (30 women); includes 25 minority (13 Black or African American, non-Hispanic/Latino; 6 Asian, non-Hispanic/Latino; 4 Hispanic/Latino; 2 Two or more races, non-Hispanic/Latino). Average age 33. 126 applicants, 75% accepted, 73 enrolled. *Faculty:* 20 full-time (10 women), 7 part-time/adjunct (3 women). Expenses: Contact institution. *Financial support:* Federal Work-Study and scholarships/grants available. Support available to part-time students. Financial award application deadline: 3/15; financial award applicants required to submit FAFSA. In 2017, 40 master's awarded. *Program availability:* Part-time, evening/weekend. Offers business (MBA); management (M Sc). *Application deadline:* For fall admission, 8/15 priority date for domestic students; for spring admission, 2/15 priority date for domestic students. Applications are processed on a rolling basis. *Application fee:* $50. Electronic applications accepted. *Application Contact:* Art Fadde, Director of Graduate Admissions, 800-334-8448 Ext. 3, Fax: 336-278-7699, E-mail: afadde@elon.edu. *Associate Dean of the Love School of Business/Associate Professor of Economics*, Dr. Jen Platania, 336-278-5938, E-mail: jplatania@elon.edu.

Program in Education Students: 24 part-time (22 women); includes 13 minority (2 Black or African American, non-Hispanic/Latino; 2 Asian, non-Hispanic/Latino; 8 Hispanic/Latino; 1 Two or more races, non-Hispanic/Latino). Average age 23. 29 applicants, 69% accepted, 16 enrolled. *Faculty:* 8 full-time (6 women), 2 part-time/adjunct (both women). Expenses: Contact institution. *Financial support:* Federal Work-Study and scholarships/grants available. Support available to part-time students. Financial award application deadline: 6/1; financial award applicants required to submit FAFSA. In 2017, 10 master's awarded. *Program availability:* Part-time. Offers elementary education (M Ed); gifted education (M Ed); special education (M Ed). *Application deadline:* For fall admission, 5/1 for domestic students. Applications are processed on a rolling basis. *Application fee:* $50. Electronic applications accepted. *Application Contact:* Art Fadde, Director of Graduate Admissions, 800-334-8448 Ext. 3, Fax: 336-278-7699, E-mail: afadde@elon.edu. *Dean of the School of Education/Professor*, Dr. Ann Bullock, 336-278-5900, E-mail: abullock9@elon.edu.

Program in Interactive Media Students: 26 full-time (15 women); includes 13 minority (11 Black or African American, non-Hispanic/Latino; 2 Hispanic/Latino). Average age 23. 41 applicants, 85% accepted, 26 enrolled. *Faculty:* 10 full-time (3 women). Expenses: Contact institution. *Financial support:* Federal Work-Study and scholarships/grants available. Support available to part-time students. Financial award application deadline: 3/15; financial award applicants required to submit FAFSA. In 2017, 24 master's awarded. Offers interactive media (MA). *Application deadline:* For fall admission, 5/1 priority date for domestic students. Applications are processed on a rolling basis. *Application fee:* $50. Electronic applications accepted. *Application Contact:* Art Fadde, Director of Graduate Admissions, 800-334-8448 Ext. 3, Fax: 336-278-7699, E-mail: afadde@elon.edu. *Dean of the School of Communications*, Dr. Paul Parsons, 336-278-5724, E-mail: pparsons@elon.edu.

Program in Law Students: 353 full-time (211 women); includes 81 minority (59 Black or African American, non-Hispanic/Latino; 5 American Indian or Alaska Native, non-Hispanic/Latino; 2 Asian, non-Hispanic/Latino; 15 Hispanic/Latino), 1 international. Average age 25. 819 applicants, 42% accepted, 138 enrolled. *Faculty:* 36 full-time (16 women), 55 part-time/adjunct (20 women). Expenses: Contact institution. *Financial support:* Scholarships/grants available. Financial award applicants required to submit FAFSA. In 2017, 91 doctorates awarded. Offers law (JD). *Application deadline:* For fall admission, 7/30 for domestic students; for spring admission, 4/1 priority date for domestic students. Applications are processed on a rolling basis. *Application fee:* $50. Electronic applications accepted. *Application Contact:* Alan Woodlief, Associate Dean of School of Law/Director of Law School Admissions, 336-279-9203, E-mail: awoodlief@elon.edu. *Dean*, Dr. Luke Bierman, 336-279-9201, E-mail: lbierman@elon.edu.

Program in Physical Therapy Students: 139 full-time (99 women); includes 17 minority (5 Black or African American, non-Hispanic/Latino; 2 Asian, non-Hispanic/Latino; 2 Hispanic/Latino; 8 Two or more races, non-Hispanic/Latino), 2 international. Average age 26. 916 applicants, 10% accepted, 47 enrolled. *Faculty:* 14 full-time (9 women), 16 part-time/adjunct (13 women). Expenses: Contact institution. *Financial support:* Federal Work-Study and scholarships/grants available. Financial award application deadline: 10/1; financial award applicants required to submit FAFSA. In 2017, 48 doctorates awarded. Offers physical therapy (DPT). *Application deadline:* For fall admission, 11/1 for domestic students. Applications are processed on a rolling basis. *Application fee:* $50. Electronic applications accepted. *Application Contact:* Art Fadde, Director of Graduate Admissions, 800-334-8448 Ext. 3, Fax: 336-278-7699, E-mail: afadde@elon.edu. *Dean of the School of Health Sciences*, Dr. Becky Neiduski, 336-278-6350, E-mail: bneiduski@elon.edu.

Program in Physician Assistant Studies Students: 76 full-time (60 women); includes 9 minority (2 Black or African American, non-Hispanic/Latino; 5 Asian, non-Hispanic/Latino; 1 Hispanic/Latino; 1 Two or more races, non-Hispanic/Latino). Average age 27. 1,286 applicants, 4% accepted, 38 enrolled. *Faculty:* 8 full-time (7 women), 2 part-time/adjunct (1 woman). Expenses: Contact institution. *Financial support:* Federal Work-Study and scholarships/grants available. Financial award application deadline: 10/1; financial award applicants required to submit FAFSA. In 2017, 38 master's awarded. Offers physician assistant studies (MS). *Application deadline:* For spring admission, 11/1 for domestic students. Applications are processed on a rolling basis. *Application fee:* $50. Electronic applications accepted. *Application Contact:* Art Fadde, Director of Graduate Admissions, 800-334-8448 Ext. 3, Fax: 336-278-7699, E-mail: afadde@elon.edu. *Dean of the School of Health Sciences*, Dr. Becky Neiduski, 336-278-6350, E-mail: bneiduski@elon.edu.

EMBRY-RIDDLE AERONAUTICAL UNIVERSITY–DAYTONA, Daytona Beach, FL 32114-3900

General Information Independent, coed, university. *Enrollment:* 6,338 graduate, professional, and undergraduate students; 539 full-time matriculated graduate/professional students (149 women), 129 part-time matriculated graduate/professional students (36 women). *Enrollment by degree level:* 504 master's, 164 doctoral. *Graduate faculty:* 107 full-time (15 women), 4 part-time/adjunct (1 woman). *Tuition:* Full-time $16,704; part-time $1392 per credit hour. *Required fees:* $1314; $657 per semester. Tuition and fees vary according to degree level. *Graduate housing:* On-campus housing not available. *Student services:* Campus employment opportunities, campus safety program, career counseling, exercise/wellness program, international student services, low-cost health insurance, multicultural affairs office, services for students with disabilities. *Library facilities:* Jack R. Hunt Memorial Library. *Collection:* Books: 53,612 (physical), 92,114 (digital/electronic); Serial titles: 459 (physical), 69,595 (digital/electronic); Databases: 98. Students can reserve study rooms. *Research affiliation:* United Space Alliance, SpaceX, The Boeing Company, Honeywell, Virgin Galactic, NASA.

Computer facilities: A campuswide network can be accessed from student residence rooms and from off campus. Online class registration is available.
Website: http://www.daytonabeach.erau.edu/

General Application Contact: Graduate Admissions, 800-388-3728, Fax: 386-226-7070, E-mail: graduate.admissions@erau.edu.

GRADUATE UNITS

College of Business Students: 95 full-time (31 women), 19 part-time (8 women); includes 15 minority (5 Black or African American, non-Hispanic/Latino; 1 Asian, non-Hispanic/Latino; 1 Hispanic/Latino; 8 Two or more races, non-Hispanic/Latino), 65 international. Average age 27. 141 applicants, 38% accepted, 41 enrolled. *Faculty:* 14 full-time (2 women). Expenses: Contact institution. *Financial support:* Research assistantships, teaching assistantships, career-related internships or fieldwork, scholarships/grants, unspecified assistantships, and on-campus employment available. Financial award application deadline: 3/15; financial award applicants required to submit FAFSA. In 2017, 49 master's awarded. Offers airline management (MBA); airport management (MBA); aviation finance (MSAF); aviation human resources (MBA); aviation management (MBA-AM); aviation system management (MBA); finance (MBA). *Application deadline:* For fall admission, 1/15 priority date for domestic students; for spring admission, 11/1 priority date for domestic students; for summer admission, 4/1 priority date for domestic students. Applications are processed on a rolling basis. *Application fee:* $50. Electronic applications accepted. *Application Contact:* Graduate Admissions, 386-226-6176, E-mail: graduate.admissions@erau.edu. *Dean of the College of Business and Professor of Information Systems*, Michael J. Williams, PhD, 386-226-6293, E-mail: michael.williams@erau.edu.

Department of Aerospace Engineering Students: 125 full-time (24 women), 8 part-time (3 women); includes 11 minority (2 Black or African American, non-Hispanic/Latino; 1 American Indian or Alaska Native, non-Hispanic/Latino; 3 Asian, non-Hispanic/Latino; 2 Hispanic/Latino; 3 Two or more races, non-Hispanic/Latino), 95 international. Average age 25. 184 applicants, 28% accepted, 36 enrolled. *Faculty:* 28 full-time (2 women). Expenses: Contact institution. *Financial support:* Research assistantships, teaching assistantships, career-related internships or fieldwork, scholarships/grants, unspecified assistantships, and on-campus employment available. Financial award application deadline: 3/15; financial award applicants required to submit FAFSA. In 2017, 45 master's, 3 doctorates awarded. Offers aerodynamics and propulsion (MS, PhD); dynamics and control (MS, PhD); structures and materials (MS, PhD). *Application deadline:* For fall admission, 1/15 priority date for domestic students; for spring admission, 9/15 priority date for domestic students; for summer admission, 4/1 priority date for domestic students. Applications are processed on a rolling basis. *Application fee:* $50. Electronic applications accepted. *Application Contact:* Graduate Admissions, 386-226-6176, E-mail: graduate.admissions@erau.edu. *Professor/Chair, Aerospace Engineering*, Dr. Anastasios Lyrintzis, 386-226-7007, Fax: 386-226-6747, E-mail: lyrintzi@erau.edu.

Department of Civil Engineering Students: 5 full-time (0 women); includes 2 minority (both Asian, non-Hispanic/Latino), 2 international. Average age 27. 4 applicants, 25% accepted, 1 enrolled. *Faculty:* 2 full-time (0 women), 1 part-time/adjunct (0 women). Expenses: Contact institution. *Financial support:* Research assistantships, teaching assistantships, career-related internships or fieldwork, scholarships/grants, unspecified assistantships, and on-campus employment available. Financial award application deadline: 3/15; financial award applicants required to submit FAFSA. Offers civil engineering (MS). *Application deadline:* For fall admission, 1/15 priority date for domestic students; for spring admission, 11/1 priority date for domestic students; for summer admission, 4/1 priority date for domestic students. Applications are processed on a rolling basis. *Application fee:* $50. Electronic applications accepted. *Application Contact:* Graduate Admissions, 800-388-3728, Fax: 386-226-7070, E-mail: graduate.admissions@erau.edu. *Professor and Chair, Department of Civil Engineering*, Dr. Ashok Gurjar, 386-226-6757, E-mail: gurjara@erau.edu.

Department of Electrical, Computer, Software and Systems Engineering Students: 69 full-time (23 women), 15 part-time (3 women); includes 8 minority (2 Black or African American, non-Hispanic/Latino; 1 Asian, non-Hispanic/Latino; 1 Hispanic/Latino; 4 Two or more races, non-Hispanic/Latino), 51 international. Average age 26. 96 applicants, 45% accepted, 25 enrolled. *Faculty:* 15 full-time (1 woman), 2 part-time/adjunct (1 woman). Expenses: Contact institution. *Financial support:* Research assistantships, teaching assistantships, career-related internships or fieldwork, unspecified assistantships, and on-campus employment available. Financial award application deadline: 3/15; financial award applicants required to submit FAFSA. In 2017, 23 master's awarded. Offers cybersecurity engineering (MS); electrical and computer engineering (MSECE); software engineering (MSSE); systems engineering (MS). *Application deadline:* For fall admission, 1/15 priority date for domestic students; for spring admission, 11/1 priority date for domestic students; for summer admission, 4/1 priority date for domestic students. Applications are processed on a rolling basis. *Application fee:* $50. Electronic applications accepted. *Application Contact:* Graduate Admissions, 386-226-6176, Fax: 386-226-7070, E-mail: graduate.admissions@erau.edu. *Professor of Electrical and Computer Engineering/Chair, Department of Electrical, Computer, Software and Systems Engineering*, Timothy Wilson, PhD, 386-226-6100, E-mail: timothy.wilson@erau.edu.

Department of Human Factors and Behavioral Neurobiology Students: 69 full-time (27 women), 40 part-time (13 women); includes 19 minority (2 Black or African American, non-Hispanic/Latino; 4 Asian, non-Hispanic/Latino; 7 Hispanic/Latino; 6 Two or more races, non-Hispanic/Latino), 10 international. 59 applicants, 42% accepted, 21 enrolled. *Faculty:* 6 full-time (2 women). Expenses: Contact institution. *Financial support:* Research assistantships, teaching assistantships, career-related internships or fieldwork, scholarships/grants, unspecified assistantships, and on-campus employment available. Financial award application deadline: 3/15; financial award applicants required to submit FAFSA. In 2017, 14 master's, 3 doctorates awarded. Offers human factors (PhD). *Application deadline:* For fall admission, 1/15 priority date for domestic students; for spring admission, 11/1 priority date for domestic students; for summer admission, 4/1 priority date for domestic students. Applications are processed on a rolling basis. *Application fee:* $50. Electronic applications accepted. *Application Contact:* Graduate Admissions, 800-862-2416, E-mail: graduate.admissions@erau.edu. *Professor/Department Chair*, Scott Shappell, PhD, E-mail: scott.shappell@erau.edu.

Department of Mechanical Engineering Students: 46 full-time (6 women), 12 part-time (4 women); includes 6 minority (1 Asian, non-Hispanic/Latino; 5 Two or more races, non-Hispanic/Latino), 23 international. Average age 26. 53 applicants, 36% accepted, 13 enrolled. *Faculty:* 12 full-time (3 women). Expenses: Contact institution. *Financial support:* Research assistantships, teaching assistantships, career-related internships or fieldwork, scholarships/grants, unspecified assistantships, and on-campus employment available. Financial award application deadline: 3/15; financial award applicants required to submit FAFSA. In 2017, 23 master's, 1 doctorate awarded. Offers high performance vehicles (MSME); mechanical engineering (PhD); mechanical systems (MSME). *Application deadline:* For fall admission, 1/15 priority date for domestic students; for spring admission, 11/1 priority date for domestic students; for summer admission, 4/1 priority date for domestic students. Applications are processed on a rolling basis. *Application fee:* $50. Electronic applications accepted. *Application Contact:* Graduate Admissions, 386-226-6176, Fax: 386-226-7070, E-mail: graduate.admissions@erau.edu. *Associate Professor/Interim Department Chair/PhD Program Coordinator*, Eduardo Divo, PhD, 386-226-7987, E-mail: eduardo.divo@erau.edu.

Department of Physical Sciences Students: 29 full-time (9 women), 4 part-time (1 woman); includes 6 minority (2 Hispanic/Latino; 4 Two or more races, non-Hispanic/Latino), 10 international. Average age 27. 29 applicants, 28% accepted, 6 enrolled. *Faculty:* 12 full-time (2 women). Expenses: Contact institution. *Financial support:* Research assistantships, teaching assistantships, career-related internships or fieldwork, scholarships/grants, unspecified assistantships, and on-campus employment available. Financial award application deadline: 3/15; financial award applicants required to submit FAFSA. In 2017, 5 master's, 4 doctorates awarded. Offers engineering physics (MS, PhD). *Application deadline:* For fall admission, 1/15 priority date for domestic students; for spring admission, 11/1 priority date for domestic students; for summer admission, 4/1 priority date for domestic students. Applications are processed on a rolling basis. *Application fee:* $50. Electronic applications accepted. *Application Contact:* Graduate Admissions, 386-226-6176, E-mail: graduate.admissions@erau.edu. *Professor of Engineering Physics/Chair, Department of Physical Sciences*, Terry Oswalt, PhD, 386-226-6100, E-mail: terry.oswalt@erau.edu.

Program in Unmanned and Autonomous Systems Engineering Students: 11 full-time (3 women), 7 international. Average age 27. 19 applicants, 26% accepted, 4 enrolled. *Faculty:* 2 full-time (1 woman). Expenses: Contact institution. *Financial support:* Research assistantships, career-related internships or fieldwork, scholarships/grants, unspecified assistantships, and on-campus employment available. Financial award application deadline: 3/15; financial award applicants required to submit FAFSA. In 2017, 5 master's awarded. Offers systems engineering (MSUASE); technical (MSUASE); unmanned aircraft systems (MSUASE). *Application deadline:* For fall admission, 1/15 priority date for domestic students; for spring admission, 11/1 priority date for domestic students; for summer admission, 4/1 priority date for domestic students. Applications are processed on a rolling basis. *Application fee:* $50. Electronic applications accepted. *Application Contact:* Graduate Admissions, 386-226-6176, E-mail: graduate.admissions@erau.edu. *Associate Professor of Computer Engineering and Computer Science/Master's Program Coordinator, Unmanned and Autonomous Systems Engineering*, Richard Stansbury, PhD, 800-862-2416, E-mail: richard.stansbury@erau.edu.

School of Graduate Studies Students: 105 full-time (29 women), 48 part-time (13 women); includes 27 minority (7 Black or African American, non-Hispanic/Latino; 6 Asian, non-Hispanic/Latino; 7 Hispanic/Latino; 7 Two or more races, non-Hispanic/Latino), 53 international. Average age 35. 115 applicants, 46% accepted, 41 enrolled. *Faculty:* 19 full-time (2 women), 1 part-time/adjunct (0 women). Expenses: Contact institution. *Financial support:* Research assistantships, career-related internships or fieldwork, scholarships/grants, unspecified assistantships, and on-campus employment available. Financial award application deadline: 3/15; financial award applicants required to submit FAFSA. In 2017, 23 master's, 5 doctorates awarded. Offers aeronautics (MSA); aviation (PhD). Application fee for PhD is $100. *Application deadline:* For fall admission, 1/15 priority date for domestic students; for spring admission, 11/1 priority date for domestic students; for summer admission, 4/1 priority date for domestic students. Applications are processed on a rolling basis. *Application fee:* $50. Electronic applications accepted. *Application Contact:* Graduate Admissions, 386-226-6176, E-mail: graduate.admissions@erau.edu. *Professor of Doctoral Studies, Dean of the College of Aviation School of Graduate Studies*, Dr. Alan Stolzer, 386-226-7352, E-mail: stolzera@erau.edu.

EMBRY-RIDDLE AERONAUTICAL UNIVERSITY–PRESCOTT, Prescott, AZ 86301-3720

General Information Independent, coed, comprehensive institution. *Enrollment:* 53 full-time matriculated graduate/professional students (17 women), 4 part-time matriculated graduate/professional students (3 women). *Enrollment by degree level:* 57 master's. *Graduate faculty:* 11 full-time (2 women), 1 part-time/adjunct (0 women). *Tuition:* Full-time $16,704; part-time $1358 per credit hour. *Required fees:* $1254; $627 per semester. *Graduate housing:* On-campus housing not available. *Student services:* Campus employment opportunities, campus safety program, career counseling, exercise/wellness program, free psychological counseling, international student services, low-cost health insurance, multicultural affairs office, services for students with disabilities. *Library facilities:* Christine & Steven F. Udvar-Hazy Library & Learning Center. *Collection:* Books: 30,076 (physical), 179,675 (digital/electronic); Serial titles: 149 (physical), 51,589 (digital/electronic); Databases: 101. Students can reserve study rooms. *Research affiliation:* Boeing/Intelligent Light/Pointwise (CFD analysis on aerospace vehicles and energy systems), University of Alaska, Anchorage (development of field deployed multi-spectral computer vision systems), NASA (optimization ideas for aircraft design), Federal Aviation Administration (human factors, air traffic control interoperability, air traffic management, low-altitude operations, wake separation and noise reduction), NATO Modelling & Simulation Centre of Excellence (operational requirements, training and interoperability), Flight Research Inc. (production of world-class training and curriculum programs for aircraft loss-of-control situations).

Computer facilities: Computer purchase and lease plans are available. 730 computers available on campus for general student use. A campuswide network can be accessed from student residence rooms and from off campus. Online class registration is available.
Website: http://www.prescott.erau.edu/

General Application Contact: Graduate Admissions, 928-777-6600, E-mail: prescott@erau.edu.

GRADUATE UNITS

Behavioral and Safety Sciences Department Students: 19 full-time (6 women); includes 1 minority (Two or more races, non-Hispanic/Latino), 5 international. Average age 35. 24 applicants, 50% accepted, 5 enrolled. *Faculty:* 5 full-time (2 women). Expenses: Contact institution. *Financial support:* In 2017–18, 22 students received support. Research assistantships, teaching assistantships, scholarships/grants, unspecified assistantships, and athletic scholarships available. Financial award application deadline: 3/15; financial award applicants required to submit FAFSA. In 2017, 12 master's awarded. Offers aviation safety (MSSS). *Application deadline:* For fall admission, 1/15 priority date for domestic students; for spring admission, 11/1 priority date for domestic students; for summer admission, 4/1 priority date for domestic students. Applications are processed on a rolling basis. *Application fee:* $50. Electronic applications accepted. *Application Contact:* Graduate Admissions, 928-777-6600, E-mail: prescott@erau.edu. *Dean and Professor, College of Arts and Sciences*, Kathleen Lustyk, PhD, 928-777-3928, E-mail: lustykm@erau.edu.

Security and Intelligence Program Students: 33 full-time (10 women), 4 part-time (3 women); includes 11 minority (1 Black or African American, non-Hispanic/Latino; 2 Asian, non-Hispanic/Latino; 3 Hispanic/Latino; 5 Two or more races, non-Hispanic/Latino), 1 international. Average age 29. 40 applicants, 70% accepted, 12 enrolled. *Faculty:* 6 full-time (0 women), 1 part-time/adjunct (0 women). Expenses: Contact institution. *Financial support:* Research assistantships, teaching assistantships, scholarships/grants, and unspecified assistantships available. Financial award application deadline: 3/15; financial award applicants required to submit FAFSA. In 2017, 12 master's awarded. Offers security and intelligence studies (MSSIS). *Application deadline:* For fall admission, 1/15 priority date for domestic students; for spring admission, 11/1 priority date for domestic students; for summer admission, 4/1 priority date for domestic students. Applications are processed on a rolling basis. *Application fee:* $50. Electronic applications accepted. *Application Contact:* Graduate Admissions, 928-777-6600, E-mail: prescott@erau.edu. *Dean and Professor, College of Security and Intelligence*, Philip Jones, PhD, 928-777-6992, E-mail: philip.e.jones@erau.edu.

EMBRY-RIDDLE AERONAUTICAL UNIVERSITY–WORLDWIDE, Daytona Beach, FL 32114-3900

General Information Independent, coed, comprehensive institution. *Enrollment:* 2,064 full-time matriculated graduate/professional students (509 women), 2,128 part-time matriculated graduate/professional students (452 women). *Enrollment by degree level:* 4,192 master's. *Graduate faculty:* 66 full-time (20 women), 318 part-time/adjunct (63 women). *Tuition:* Full-time $7680; part-time $640 per credit hour. Tuition and fees vary according to program. *Graduate housing:* On-campus housing not available. *Student services:* Career counseling, services for students with disabilities. *Library facilities:* Jack R. Hunt Memorial Library located in Daytona Beach. *Collection:* Books: 54,106 (physical), 76,328 (digital/electronic); Serial titles: 1,521 (physical), 48,948 (digital/electronic); Databases: 106. *Research affiliation:* The Society for Protective Coatings and Honda Aircraft (creation of standards for training and certification program for higher paint quality).

Computer facilities: Online class registration, ERAU Worldwide does not have a physical campus; courses are offered online and at military bases worldwide are available.
Website: http://www.worldwide.erau.edu/

General Application Contact: Worldwide Campus, 800-522-6787, E-mail: worldwide@erau.edu.

GRADUATE UNITS

Department of Aeronautics, Graduate Studies Students: 821 full-time (175 women), 972 part-time (146 women); includes 403 minority (136 Black or African American, non-Hispanic/Latino; 5 American Indian or Alaska Native, non-Hispanic/Latino; 65 Asian, non-Hispanic/Latino; 90 Hispanic/Latino; 8 Native Hawaiian or other Pacific Islander, non-Hispanic/Latino; 99 Two or more races, non-Hispanic/Latino), 128 international. Average age 37. 515 applicants, 75% accepted, 329 enrolled. *Faculty:* 31 full-time (9 women), 145 part-time/adjunct (18 women). Expenses: Contact institution. *Financial support:* Career-related internships or fieldwork and scholarships/grants available. Financial award applicants required to submit FAFSA. In 2017, 514 master's awarded. *Program availability:* Part-time, evening/weekend. Offers aeronautics (MSA); aeronautics and design (MS); aviation maintenance (MAM); aviation/aerospace management (MS); aviation/aerospace research (MS); education (MS); human factors (MSHFS); occupational safety management (MS); operations (MS); safety/emergency response (MS); space systems (MS); unmanned systems (MS). *Application deadline:* Applications are processed on a rolling basis. *Application fee:* $50. Electronic applications accepted. *Application Contact:* Worldwide Campus, 800-522-6787, E-mail: worldwide@erau.edu. *Associate Professor and Dean, College of Aeronautics*, Kenneth Witcher, PhD, E-mail: kenneth.witcher@erau.edu.

Department of Business Administration Students: 374 full-time (77 women), 292 part-time (65 women); includes 163 minority (54 Black or African American, non-Hispanic/Latino; 3 American Indian or Alaska Native, non-Hispanic/Latino; 27 Asian, non-Hispanic/Latino; 43 Hispanic/Latino; 4 Native Hawaiian or other Pacific Islander, non-Hispanic/Latino; 32 Two or more races, non-Hispanic/Latino), 55 international. Average age 35. 166 applicants, 74% accepted, 115 enrolled. *Faculty:* 12 full-time (5 women), 60 part-time/adjunct (18 women). Expenses: Contact institution. *Financial support:* Career-related internships or fieldwork and scholarships/grants available. Financial award applicants required to submit FAFSA. In 2017, 214 master's awarded.

Program availability: Part-time, evening/weekend, online only, EagleVision Classroom (between classrooms), EagleVision Home (faculty and students at home), and a blend of Classroom or Home. Offers aviation (MBAA). *Application deadline:* Applications are processed on a rolling basis. *Application fee:* $50. Electronic applications accepted. *Application Contact:* Worldwide Campus, 800-522-6787, E-mail: worldwide@erau.edu. *Department Chair,* Ronald Mau, PhD, E-mail: ronald.mau@erau.edu.

Department of Decision Sciences Students: 514 full-time (141 women), 476 part-time (111 women); includes 337 minority (136 Black or African American, non-Hispanic/Latino; 6 American Indian or Alaska Native, non-Hispanic/Latino; 39 Asian, non-Hispanic/Latino; 81 Hispanic/Latino; 4 Native Hawaiian or other Pacific Islander, non-Hispanic/Latino; 71 Two or more races, non-Hispanic/Latino), 21 international. Average age 36. 297 applicants, 72% accepted, 209 enrolled. *Faculty:* 12 full-time (3 women), 53 part-time/adjunct (10 women). Expenses: Contact institution. *Financial support:* Career-related internships or fieldwork and scholarships/grants available. Financial award applicants required to submit FAFSA. In 2017, 292 master's awarded. *Program availability:* Part-time, evening/weekend, EagleVision Classroom (between classrooms), EagleVision Home (faculty and students at home), and a blend of Classroom or Home. Offers aviation and aerospace (MSPM); aviation/aerospace management (MSEM); financial management (MSEM, MSPM); general management (MSPM); global management (MSPM); human resources management (MSPM); information systems (MSPM); leadership (MSEM, MSPM); logistics and supply chain management (MSEM, MSLSCM, MSPM); management (MSEM, MSPM); project management (MSEM); systems engineering (MSEM, MSPM); technical management (MSPM). *Application deadline:* Applications are processed on a rolling basis. *Application fee:* $50. Electronic applications accepted. *Application Contact:* Worldwide Campus, 800-522-6787, E-mail: worldwide@erau.edu. *Department Chair,* Aman Gupta, PhD, E-mail: aman.gupta@erau.edu.

Department of Engineering and Technology Students: 29 full-time (5 women), 39 part-time (6 women); includes 16 minority (3 Black or African American, non-Hispanic/Latino; 4 Asian, non-Hispanic/Latino; 5 Hispanic/Latino; 4 Two or more races, non-Hispanic/Latino). Average age 32. 76 applicants, 28% accepted, 15 enrolled. *Faculty:* 6 full-time (1 woman), 5 part-time/adjunct (0 women). Expenses: Contact institution. *Financial support:* Career-related internships or fieldwork and scholarships/grants available. Financial award applicants required to submit FAFSA. In 2017, 34 master's awarded. *Program availability:* Part-time, evening/weekend, 100% online, blended/hybrid learning. Offers aerospace engineering (MS); entrepreneurship in technology (MS); systems engineering (M Sys E). *Application deadline:* Applications are processed on a rolling basis. *Application fee:* $50. Electronic applications accepted. *Application Contact:* Worldwide Campus, 800-522-6787, E-mail: worldwide@erau.edu. *Department Chair,* Brian Sanders, PhD, E-mail: brian.sanders1@erau.edu.

Department of Management Students: 148 full-time (48 women), 192 part-time (52 women); includes 91 minority (46 Black or African American, non-Hispanic/Latino; 1 American Indian or Alaska Native, non-Hispanic/Latino; 11 Asian, non-Hispanic/Latino; 16 Hispanic/Latino; 17 Two or more races, non-Hispanic/Latino), 7 international. Average age 39. Expenses: Contact institution. *Financial support:* Career-related internships or fieldwork and scholarships/grants available. Financial award applicants required to submit FAFSA. In 2017, 104 master's awarded. *Program availability:* Part-time, evening/weekend, EagleVision Classroom (between classrooms), EagleVision Home (faculty and students at home), and a blend of Classroom or Home. Offers global management (MS); human resources management (MS); leadership (MS); operations management (MS); project management (MS). *Application deadline:* Applications are processed on a rolling basis. *Application fee:* $50. Electronic applications accepted. *Application Contact:* Worldwide Campus, 800-522-6787, E-mail: worldwide@erau.edu. *Department Chair,* Thomas Henkel, PhD, E-mail: thomas.henkel@erau.edu.

Department of Organizational Leadership Students: 64 full-time (27 women), 70 part-time (35 women); includes 25 minority (10 Black or African American, non-Hispanic/Latino; 3 Asian, non-Hispanic/Latino; 6 Hispanic/Latino; 6 Two or more races, non-Hispanic/Latino), 1 international. Average age 38. 38 applicants, 66% accepted, 20 enrolled. *Faculty:* 4 full-time (2 women), 33 part-time/adjunct (12 women). Expenses: Contact institution. *Financial support:* Career-related internships or fieldwork and scholarships/grants available. Financial award applicants required to submit FAFSA. In 2017, 44 master's awarded. *Program availability:* Part-time, evening/weekend, EagleVision Classroom (between classrooms), EagleVision Home (faculty and students at home), and a blend of Classroom or Home. Offers leadership (MS). *Application deadline:* Applications are processed on a rolling basis. *Application fee:* $50. Electronic applications accepted. *Application Contact:* Worldwide Campus, 800-522-6787, E-mail: worldwide@erau.edu. *Department Chair,* Matt P. Earnhardt, PhD, E-mail: matthew.earnhardt@erau.edu.

Department of Security and Emergency Services Students: 53 full-time (19 women), 66 part-time (23 women); includes 51 minority (16 Black or African American, non-Hispanic/Latino; 8 Asian, non-Hispanic/Latino; 12 Hispanic/Latino; 15 Two or more races, non-Hispanic/Latino), 2 international. Average age 36. 58 applicants, 66% accepted, 34 enrolled. *Faculty:* 3 full-time (0 women), 12 part-time/adjunct (4 women). Expenses: Contact institution. *Financial support:* Career-related internships or fieldwork and scholarships/grants available. Financial award applicants required to submit FAFSA. In 2017, 6 master's awarded. *Program availability:* Part-time, evening/weekend, EagleVision Classroom (between classrooms), EagleVision Home (faculty and students at home), and a blend of Classroom or Home. Offers cybersecurity management and policy (MSCMP); human security and resilience (MSHSR). *Application deadline:* Applications are processed on a rolling basis. *Application fee:* $50. Electronic applications accepted. *Application Contact:* Worldwide Campus, 800-522-6787, E-mail: worldwide@erau.edu. *Department Chair,* Dr. Ronald Wakeham, E-mail: ronald.wakeham@erau.edu.

Department of Technology Management Students: 58 full-time (11 women), 51 part-time (18 women); includes 39 minority (15 Black or African American, non-Hispanic/Latino; 2 American Indian or Alaska Native, non-Hispanic/Latino; 5 Asian, non-Hispanic/Latino; 8 Hispanic/Latino; 9 Two or more races, non-Hispanic/Latino). Average age 38. 53 applicants, 68% accepted, 25 enrolled. *Faculty:* 2 full-time (1 woman), 20 part-time/adjunct (5 women). Expenses: Contact institution. *Financial support:* Career-related internships or fieldwork and scholarships/grants available. Financial award applicants required to submit FAFSA. In 2017, 12 master's awarded. *Program availability:* Part-time, evening/weekend, EagleVision Classroom (between classrooms), EagleVision Home (faculty and students at home), and a blend of Classroom or Home. Offers information and security assurance (MS); management information systems (MS). *Application deadline:* Applications are processed on a rolling basis. *Application fee:* $50. Electronic applications accepted. *Application Contact:* Worldwide Campus, 800-522-6787, E-mail: worldwide@erau.edu. *Department Chair,* Dr. Aaron Glassman, E-mail: aaron.glassman@erau.edu.

EMERSON COLLEGE, Boston, MA 02116-4624

General Information Independent, coed, comprehensive institution. *Enrollment:* 4,466 graduate, professional, and undergraduate students; 571 full-time matriculated graduate/professional students (423 women), 82 part-time matriculated graduate/professional students (60 women). *Enrollment by degree level:* 653 master's. *Graduate faculty:* 202 full-time (86 women), 252 part-time/adjunct (125 women). *Tuition:* Full-time $20,016; part-time $1251 per credit. *Required fees:* $624; $232 per credit. $116 per semester. *Graduate housing:* On-campus housing not available. *Student services:* Campus employment opportunities, campus safety program, career counseling, exercise/wellness program, free psychological counseling, grant writing training, international student services, low-cost health insurance, multicultural affairs office, services for students with disabilities, writing training. *Library facilities:* Iwasaki Library plus 1 other. *Collection:* Books: 336,669 (physical), 2,484 (digital/electronic); Serial titles: 67,760 (digital/electronic); Databases: 125. Weekly public service hours: 93; students can reserve study rooms.

Computer facilities: Computer purchase and lease plans are available. 480 computers available on campus for general student use. A campuswide network can be accessed from student residence rooms and from off campus. Online class registration is available.
Website: http://www.emerson.edu/

General Application Contact: Office of Graduate Admission, 617-824-8610, Fax: 617-824-8614, E-mail: gradadmission@emerson.edu.

GRADUATE UNITS

Graduate Studies Students: 571 full-time (423 women), 82 part-time (60 women); includes 102 minority (24 Black or African American, non-Hispanic/Latino; 19 Asian, non-Hispanic/Latino; 38 Hispanic/Latino; 1 Native Hawaiian or other Pacific Islander, non-Hispanic/Latino; 20 Two or more races, non-Hispanic/Latino), 170 international. Average age 27. 1,578 applicants, 57% accepted, 297 enrolled. *Faculty:* 202 full-time (86 women), 252 part-time/adjunct (125 women). Expenses: Contact institution. *Financial support:* In 2017–18, 382 students received support, including 382 fellowships with partial tuition reimbursements available (averaging $7,551 per year); research assistantships with partial tuition reimbursements available, Federal Work-Study, scholarships/grants, and unspecified assistantships also available. Financial award application deadline: 3/1; financial award applicants required to submit FAFSA. In 2017, 271 master's awarded. *Program availability:* Part-time, evening/weekend. Offers civic media (MA); communication disorders (MS); creative writing (MFA); digital marketing (MA); film and media art (MFA); journalism (MA); popular fiction writing and publishing (MFA); public relations (MA); publishing and writing (MA); strategic communication for marketing (MA); theatre education (MA); writing for film and television (MFA). *Application deadline:* Applications are processed on a rolling basis. *Application fee:* $60 ($75 for international students). Electronic applications accepted. *Application Contact:* Leanda Ferland, Director of Graduate Admission, 617-824-8610, Fax: 617-824-8614, E-mail: gradadmission@emerson.edu.

EMILY CARR UNIVERSITY OF ART + DESIGN, Vancouver, BC V6H 3R9, Canada

General Information Province-supported, coed, comprehensive institution. *Graduate housing:* On-campus housing not available. *Research affiliation:* Children's Hospital, Vancouver BC (health care research), Aldrich Pears and Associates (experience design), Kodak Communications Group (interaction design), Donat Group (e-learning), Paperny Films (television and film production), Fuel Cell Research Centre, National Research Council (clean technology).

GRADUATE UNITS

Program in Applied Arts Offers design (M Des); media arts (MAA); visual arts (MAA). Electronic applications accepted.

Program in Digital Media Offers digital media (MDM). Electronic applications accepted.

EMMANUEL COLLEGE, Boston, MA 02115

General Information Independent-religious, coed, comprehensive institution. *Enrollment:* 2,083 graduate, professional, and undergraduate students; 9 full-time matriculated graduate/professional students (7 women), 112 part-time matriculated graduate/professional students (91 women). *Enrollment by degree level:* 114 master's, 7 other advanced degrees. *Graduate faculty:* 4 full-time (all women), 22 part-time/adjunct (14 women). *Graduate housing:* On-campus housing not available. *Student services:* Campus safety program, career counseling, exercise/wellness program, multicultural affairs office, services for students with disabilities, writing training. *Library facilities:* Cardinal Cushing Library. *Collection:* Books: 64,408 (physical), 186,664 (digital/electronic); Serial titles: 119 (physical), 3,967 (digital/electronic); Databases: 60. Weekly public service hours: 112; students can reserve study rooms.

Computer facilities: 284 computers available on campus for general student use. A campuswide network can be accessed from student residence rooms. Online class registration is available.
Website: http://www.emmanuel.edu/

General Application Contact: Helen Muterperl, Director of Graduate and Professional Programs, 617-735-9700, Fax: 617-507-0434, E-mail: gpp@emmanuel.edu.

GRADUATE UNITS

Graduate and Professional Programs Students: 9 full-time (7 women), 112 part-time (91 women); includes 33 minority (15 Black or African American, non-Hispanic/Latino; 5 Asian, non-Hispanic/Latino; 13 Hispanic/Latino). Average age 36. 88 applicants, 33% accepted, 18 enrolled. *Faculty:* 4 full-time (all women), 22 part-time/adjunct (14 women). Expenses: Contact institution. *Financial support:* Application deadline: 2/15; applicants required to submit FAFSA. In 2017, 77 master's, 10 other advanced degrees awarded. *Program availability:* Part-time, evening/weekend, blended/hybrid learning. Offers education (MSN, Graduate Certificate); human resource management (MS, Graduate Certificate); management (MSM, MSN, Graduate Certificate); management and leadership (Graduate Certificate); moderate learning disabilities (Certificate); research administration (MSM, Graduate Certificate); urban education (M Ed). *Application deadline:* Applications are processed on a rolling basis. Electronic applications accepted. *Application Contact:* Helen Muterperl, Director of Graduate and Professional Programs, 617-735-9700, Fax: 617-507-0434, E-mail: gpp@emmanuel.edu. *Dean of Academic Administration and Graduate and Professional Programs,* Cindy O'Callaghan, 617-735-9700, E-mail: gpp@emmanuel.edu.

EMORY & HENRY COLLEGE, Emory, VA 24327-0947

General Information Independent-religious, coed, comprehensive institution. *Enrollment:* 1,226 graduate, professional, and undergraduate students; 194 full-time matriculated graduate/professional students (128 women), 4 part-time matriculated graduate/professional students (2 women). *Graduate faculty:* 7 full-time (3 women). *Graduate housing:* Room and/or apartments available on a first-come, first-served basis to single students; on-campus housing not available to married students. *Student services:* Campus employment opportunities, campus safety program, career counseling, child daycare facilities, exercise/wellness program, free psychological counseling, services for students with disabilities, teacher training, writing training. *Library facilities:* Kelly Library plus 1 other. *Collection:* Books: 225,739 (physical), 126,654 (digital/electronic); Serial titles: 728 (physical), 113,345 (digital/electronic); Databases: 105. Weekly public service hours: 90; students can reserve study rooms.

Computer facilities: 200 computers available on campus for general student use. A campuswide network can be accessed. Online class registration is available.
Website: http://www.ehc.edu/

General Application Contact: Mary Bolt, Director of Transfer and Graduate Admission, 276-944-6135, E-mail: mbolt@ehc.edu.

GRADUATE UNITS

Graduate Programs Students: 194 full-time (128 women), 4 part-time (2 women); includes 6 minority (2 Black or African American, non-Hispanic/Latino; 1 American Indian or Alaska Native, non-Hispanic/Latino; 1 Asian, non-Hispanic/Latino; 2 Hispanic/Latino). Average age 25. 525 applicants, 21% accepted, 74 enrolled. *Faculty:* 7 full-time (3 women). Expenses: Contact institution. *Financial support:* Application deadline: 10/15; applicants required to submit FAFSA. In 2017, 24 master's awarded. *Program availability:* Part-time. Offers American history (MA Ed); education professional studies (M Ed); occupational therapy (MOT); organizational leadership (MCOL); physical therapy (DPT); physician assistant studies (MPAS); reading specialist (MA Ed). *Application deadline:* Applications are processed on a rolling basis. Electronic applications accepted. *Application Contact:* Mary Bolt, Director of Transfer and Graduate Admission, 276-944-6135, E-mail: mbolt@ehc.edu. *Associate Dean for Academic Affairs,* Dr. Michael Puglisi, 276-944-6662, E-mail: mpuglisi@ehc.edu.

EMORY UNIVERSITY, Atlanta, GA 30322-1100

General Information Independent-religious, coed, university. CGS member. *Graduate housing:* Rooms and/or apartments available on a first-come, first-served basis to single and married students. *Research affiliation:* Bill and Melinda Gates Foundation, Children's Pediatric Research Trust, International AIDS Vaccine Initiative, Garden City Group, Georgia Cancer Coalition, The Wistar Institute.

GRADUATE UNITS

Candler School of Theology *Program availability:* Part-time. Offers formation and witness (M Div); history, scripture and tradition (MTS); leadership in church and community (M Div); modern religious thought and experience (MTS); pastoral counseling (Th D); religion and race (M Div); religion, health and science (M Div); scripture and interpretation (M Div); society and personality (M Div); theology (Th M); theology and ethics (M Div); theology and the arts (M Div); traditions of the church (M Div); women and religion (M Div). Electronic applications accepted.

Goizueta Business School Students: 512 full-time (147 women), 250 part-time (86 women); includes 224 minority (56 Black or African American, non-Hispanic/Latino; 2 American Indian or Alaska Native, non-Hispanic/Latino; 103 Asian, non-Hispanic/Latino; 50 Hispanic/Latino; 1 Native Hawaiian or other Pacific Islander, non-Hispanic/Latino; 12 Two or more races, non-Hispanic/Latino), 148 international. Average age 34. 2,044 applicants, 37% accepted, 329 enrolled. *Faculty:* 161 full-time (29 women), 48 part-time/adjunct (11 women). Expenses: Contact institution. *Financial support:* Fellowships with full tuition reimbursements, research assistantships, teaching assistantships, career-related internships or fieldwork, Federal Work-Study, institutionally sponsored loans, and scholarships/grants available. Support available to part-time students. Financial award application deadline: 4/1; financial award applicants required to submit FAFSA. *Program availability:* Part-time, evening/weekend. Offers accounting (MBA, PhD); alternative investments (MBA); business (MBA, PhD); business administration (MBA); business process consulting (MBA); business technology management (MBA); capital markets (MBA); corporate finance (MBA); customer relationship management (MBA); decision analytics (MBA); entrepreneurship (MBA); finance (MBA, PhD); global management (MBA); information systems and operations management (PhD); investment banking (MBA); management consulting (MBA); marketing (MBA, PhD); marketing analytics (MBA); marketing consulting (MBA); operations management (MBA); organization and management (MBA, PhD); product and brand management (MBA); real estate (MBA); social enterprise (MBA); strategy consulting (MBA). *Application deadline:* For fall admission, 10/5 for domestic and international students; for winter admission, 11/30 for domestic and international students; for spring admission, 1/18 for domestic and international students. Applications are processed on a rolling basis. Electronic applications accepted. *Application Contact:* Erika H. James, Dean, 404-727-6369, Fax: 404-727-0868. *Dean,* Erika H. James, 404-727-6369, Fax: 404-727-0868.

Laney Graduate School Offers anthropology (PhD); art history (PhD); biophysics (PhD); chemistry (PhD); choral conducting (MM, MSM); clinical psychology (PhD); clinical research (MS); cognition and development (PhD); comparative literature (PhD, Certificate); computer science (MS); computer science and informatics (PhD); development practice (MDP); economics (PhD); English (PhD, Graduate Certificate); experimental condensed matter physics (PhD); film studies (MA); French (PhD); French and educational studies (PhD); history (PhD); mathematics (MS, PhD); neuroscience and animal behavior (PhD); nursing (PhD); organ performance (MM, MSM); philosophy (PhD); political science (PhD); psychoanalytic studies (PhD); sociology (PhD); Spanish (PhD); theoretical and computational statistical physics (PhD); women's studies (Certificate); women's, gender, and sexuality studies (PhD). Electronic applications accepted.

Division of Biological and Biomedical Sciences Offers biochemistry, cell and developmental biology (PhD); biological and biomedical sciences (PhD); cancer biology (PhD); genetics and molecular biology (PhD); immunology and molecular pathogenesis (PhD); microbiology and molecular genetics (PhD); molecular and systems pharmacology (PhD); neuroscience (PhD); nutrition and health sciences (PhD); population biology, ecology and evolution (PhD). Electronic applications accepted.

Division of Educational Studies Offers educational studies (MA, PhD); middle grades teaching (MAT); secondary teaching (MAT). Electronic applications accepted.

Division of Religion Offers religion (PhD). Electronic applications accepted.

Emory Center for Ethics Offers bioethics (MA). Electronic applications accepted.

Graduate Institute of the Liberal Arts Offers liberal arts (PhD). Electronic applications accepted.

Nell Hodgson Woodruff School of Nursing *Program availability:* Part-time. Offers adult nurse practitioner (MSN); emergency nurse practitioner (MSN); family nurse practitioner (MSN); family nurse-midwife (MSN); health systems leadership (MSN); nurse-midwifery (MSN); pediatric nurse practitioner acute and primary care (MSN); women's health care (Title X) (MSN); women's health nurse practitioner (MSN). Electronic applications accepted.

Rollins School of Public Health *Program availability:* Part-time, evening/weekend, online learning. Offers applied epidemiology (MPH); applied public health informatics (MPH); behavioral sciences and health education (MPH, PhD); bioinformatics (PhD); biostatistics (MPH, MSPH); environmental health (MPH); environmental health and epidemiology (MSPH); environmental health sciences (PhD); epidemiology (MPH, MSPH, PhD); global environmental health (MPH); global health (MPH); health policy (MPH); health policy research (MSPH); health services management (MPH); health services research and health policy (PhD); prevention science (MPH); public health (MPH, MSPH, PhD); public health informatics (MSPH); public nutrition (MSPH). Electronic applications accepted.

School of Law Offers law (LL M, JD, Certificate). Electronic applications accepted.

School of Medicine Offers anesthesiology assistant (MM Sc); genetic counseling (MM Sc); medicine (MM Sc, DPT, MD); physical therapy (DPT); physician assistant (MM Sc). Electronic applications accepted.

EMPEROR'S COLLEGE OF TRADITIONAL ORIENTAL MEDICINE, Santa Monica, CA 90403

General Information Private, coed, graduate-only institution. *Graduate housing:* On-campus housing not available. *Research affiliation:* UCLA Ashe Center (student health), Lotus Herbs (herbs), LA Free Clinic (herbs).

GRADUATE UNITS

Graduate Programs *Program availability:* Part-time, evening/weekend. Offers oriental medicine (MTOM, DAOM).

EMPIRE COLLEGE, Santa Rosa, CA 95403

General Information Proprietary, coed.

GRADUATE UNITS

School of Law Offers law (MLS, JD).

EMPORIA STATE UNIVERSITY, Emporia, KS 66801-5415

General Information State-supported, coed, comprehensive institution. CGS member. *Enrollment:* 5,732 graduate, professional, and undergraduate students; 405 full-time matriculated graduate/professional students (263 women), 1,456 part-time matriculated graduate/professional students (1,018 women). *Enrollment by degree level:* 1,843 master's, 18 doctoral. *Graduate faculty:* 206 full-time (98 women), 23 part-time/adjunct (14 women). Tuition, state resident: full-time $6084; part-time $253.50 per credit hour. Tuition, nonresident: full-time $18,924; part-time $788.50 per credit hour. *Required fees:* $1943; $80.95 per credit hour. Tuition and fees vary according to campus/location. *Graduate housing:* Room and/or apartments available on a first-come, first-served basis to single students; on-campus housing not available to married students. Housing application deadline: 8/1. *Student services:* Campus employment opportunities, campus safety program, career counseling, child daycare facilities, exercise/wellness program, free psychological counseling, grant writing training, international student services, low-cost health insurance, multicultural affairs office, services for students with disabilities, teacher training, writing training. *Library facilities:* William Allen White Library plus 1 other. *Collection:* Books: 389,595 (physical), 153,016 (digital/electronic); Serial titles: 35,153 (physical), 278 (digital/electronic); Databases: 97. Weekly public service hours: 79; study areas open 24 hours, 5–7 days a week; students can reserve study rooms.

Computer facilities: 410 computers available on campus for general student use. A campuswide network can be accessed from student residence rooms and from off campus. Online class registration is available.
Website: http://www.emporia.edu/

General Application Contact: Kerri Jackson, Recruitment and Development Specialist, 800-950-GRAD, Fax: 620-341-5403, E-mail: kjacks20@emporia.edu.

GRADUATE UNITS

Department of Biological Sciences Students: 20 full-time (11 women), 15 part-time (3 women); includes 3 minority (2 Hispanic/Latino; 1 Two or more races, non-Hispanic/Latino), 17 international. 17 applicants, 59% accepted, 8 enrolled. *Faculty:* 13 full-time (3 women), 1 part-time/adjunct (0 women). Expenses: Contact institution. *Financial support:* In 2017–18, 7 research assistantships with full tuition reimbursements (averaging $9,747 per year), 15 teaching assistantships with full tuition reimbursements (averaging $7,499 per year) were awarded; career-related internships or fieldwork, Federal Work-Study, institutionally sponsored loans, health care benefits, and unspecified assistantships also available. Financial award application deadline: 3/15; financial award applicants required to submit FAFSA. In 2017, 21 master's awarded. *Program availability:* Part-time. Offers botany (MS); environmental biology (MS); forensic science (MS); general biology (MS); microbial and cellular biology (MS); zoology (MS). *Application deadline:* For fall admission, 8/15 priority date for domestic students. Applications are processed on a rolling basis. *Application fee:* $30 ($75 for international students). Electronic applications accepted. *Interim Chair,* Dr. Tim Burnett, 620-341-5910, Fax: 620-341-5608, E-mail: tburnett@emporia.edu.

Department of Health, Physical Education and Recreation Students: 37 full-time (14 women), 157 part-time (74 women); includes 13 minority (5 Black or African American, non-Hispanic/Latino; 1 American Indian or Alaska Native, non-Hispanic/Latino; 3 Hispanic/Latino; 4 Two or more races, non-Hispanic/Latino). 49 applicants, 67% accepted, 31 enrolled. *Faculty:* 16 full-time (8 women), 2 part-time/adjunct (both women). Expenses: Contact institution. *Financial support:* In 2017–18, 5 teaching assistantships with full tuition reimbursements (averaging $6,610 per year) were awarded; research assistantships with full tuition reimbursements, career-related internships or fieldwork, Federal Work-Study, institutionally sponsored loans, health care benefits, and unspecified assistantships also available. Financial award application deadline: 3/15; financial award applicants required to submit FAFSA. In 2017, 90 master's awarded. *Program availability:* Part-time, 100% online. Offers health, physical education and recreation (MS). *Application deadline:* For fall admission, 8/15 priority date for domestic students. Applications are processed on a rolling basis. *Application fee:* $30 ($75 for international students). Electronic applications accepted. *Application Contact:* Mary Sewell, Admissions Coordinator, 800-950-GRAD, Fax: 620-341-5909, E-mail: msewell@emporia.edu. *Chair,* Dr. Paul Luebbers, 620-341-5653, E-mail: pluebber@emporia.edu.

Department of Instructional Design and Technology Students: 25 full-time (20 women), 40 part-time (30 women); includes 6 minority (2 Black or African American, non-Hispanic/Latino; 2 Asian, non-Hispanic/Latino; 1 Hispanic/Latino; 1 Two or more races, non-Hispanic/Latino), 24 international. 26 applicants, 77% accepted, 11 enrolled. *Faculty:* 7 full-time (4 women). Expenses: Contact institution. *Financial support:* In 2017–18, 7 teaching assistantships with full tuition reimbursements (averaging $6,295 per year) were awarded; Federal Work-Study, institutionally sponsored loans, health care benefits, and unspecified assistantships also available. Financial award application deadline: 3/15; financial award applicants required to submit FAFSA. In 2017, 43 master's, 31 other advanced degrees awarded. *Program availability:* Part-time, online only, 100% online. Offers elearning/online teaching (Certificate); teaching with technology (Certificate). *Application deadline:* For fall admission, 8/15 priority date for domestic students. Applications are processed on a rolling basis. *Application fee:* $30 ($75 for international students). Electronic applications accepted. *Application Contact:* Mary Sewell, Admissions Coordinator, 800-950-GRAD, Fax: 620-341-5909, E-mail: msewell@emporia.edu. *Chair,* Dr. Zeni Colorado Resa, 620-341-5477, E-mail: jcolorad@emporia.edu.

Department of Mathematics and Economics Students: 8 full-time (2 women), 126 part-time (63 women); includes 9 minority (2 Black or African American, non-Hispanic/Latino; 1 American Indian or Alaska Native, non-Hispanic/Latino; 5 Hispanic/Latino; 1 Two or more races, non-Hispanic/Latino), 12 international. 49 applicants, 59% accepted, 20 enrolled. *Faculty:* 14 full-time (4 women), 2 part-time/adjunct (1 woman). Expenses: Contact institution. *Financial support:* In 2017–18, 6 teaching assistantships with full tuition reimbursements (averaging $5,566 per year) were awarded; research assistantships, career-related internships or fieldwork, Federal Work-Study, institutionally sponsored loans, health care benefits, and unspecified assistantships also available. Financial award application deadline: 3/15; financial award applicants required to submit FAFSA. In 2017, 21 master's awarded. *Program availability:* Part-time, evening/weekend, online only, 100% online. Offers mathematics (MS). *Application deadline:* For fall admission, 8/15 priority date for domestic students. Applications are processed on a rolling basis. *Application fee:* $30 ($75 for international students). Electronic applications accepted. *Application Contact:* Mary Sewell, Admissions Coordinator, 800-950-GRAD, Fax: 620-341-5909, E-mail: msewell@emporia.edu. *Chair,* Dr. Brian Hollenbeck, 620-341-5281, Fax: 620-341-6055, E-mail: bhollenb@emporia.edu.

Department of Music Students: 12 full-time (8 women), 8 part-time (1 woman); includes 1 minority (Black or African American, non-Hispanic/Latino), 8 international. 8 applicants, 63% accepted, 5 enrolled. *Faculty:* 13 full-time (4 women), 4 part-time/adjunct (all women). Expenses: Contact institution. *Financial support:* In 2017–18, 4 teaching assistantships with full tuition reimbursements (averaging $6,526 per year) were awarded; Federal Work-Study, institutionally sponsored loans, health care benefits, and unspecified assistantships also available. Financial award application deadline: 3/15; financial award applicants required to submit FAFSA. In 2017, 2 master's awarded. *Program availability:* Part-time. Offers music (MM). *Application deadline:* For fall admission, 8/15 priority date for domestic students. Applications are processed on a rolling basis. *Application fee:* $30 ($75 for international students). Electronic applications accepted. *Application Contact:* Dr. Andrew Houchins, Graduate Coordinator, 620-341-6089, E-mail: ahouchin@emporia.edu. *Chair,* Dr. Allan D. Comstock, 620-341-5431, E-mail: acomstoc@emporia.edu.

Department of Physical Sciences Students: 7 full-time (5 women), 15 part-time (8 women); includes 3 minority (all Two or more races, non-Hispanic/Latino), 7 international. 18 applicants, 50% accepted, 5 enrolled. *Faculty:* 14 full-time (6 women), 3 part-time/adjunct (0 women). Expenses: Contact institution. *Financial support:* In 2017–18, 6 teaching assistantships with full tuition reimbursements (averaging $7,190 per year) were awarded; research assistantships with full tuition reimbursements, Federal Work-Study, institutionally sponsored loans, health care benefits, and unspecified assistantships also available. Financial award application deadline: 3/15; financial award applicants required to submit FAFSA. In 2017, 15 master's, 1 other advanced degree awarded. *Program availability:* Part-time, online learning. Offers forensic science (MS); geospatial analysis (Postbaccalaureate Certificate); physical science (MS). *Application deadline:* For fall admission, 8/15 priority date for domestic students. Applications are processed on a rolling basis. *Application fee:* $30 ($75 for international students). Electronic applications accepted. *Application Contact:* Mary Sewell, Admissions Coordinator, 800-950-GRAD, Fax: 620-341-5909, E-mail: msewell@emporia.edu. *Chair,* Dr. Kim Simons, 620-341-5330, Fax: 620-341-6055, E-mail: ksimons@emporia.edu.

Program in Accountancy Students: 13 full-time (10 women), 33 part-time (15 women); includes 1 minority (Hispanic/Latino), 6 international. 26 applicants, 73% accepted, 18 enrolled. *Faculty:* 29 full-time (8 women). Expenses: Contact institution. *Financial support:* In 2017–18, 1 research assistantship with full tuition reimbursement (averaging $7,344 per year), 9 teaching assistantships with full tuition reimbursements (averaging $4,488 per year) were awarded; unspecified assistantships also available. Financial award applicants required to submit FAFSA. In 2017, 23 master's awarded. *Program availability:* Part-time, 100% online, blended/hybrid learning. Offers accountancy (M Acc). *Application deadline:* Applications are processed on a rolling basis. *Application fee:* $40. Electronic applications accepted. *Application Contact:* April Huddleston, Recruitment and Development Specialist, 800-950-GRAD, Fax: 620-341-5909, E-mail: ahuddles@emporia.edu. *Chair of the Faculty,* Dr. Shawn Keough, 620-341-5408, E-mail: skeough@emporia.edu.

Program in Art Therapy Students: 30 full-time (29 women), 4 part-time (3 women); includes 5 minority (1 American Indian or Alaska Native, non-Hispanic/Latino; 2 Hispanic/Latino; 2 Two or more races, non-Hispanic/Latino), 1 international. 28 applicants, 29% accepted, 5 enrolled. *Faculty:* 13 full-time (9 women). Expenses: Contact institution. *Financial support:* In 2017–18, 1 research assistantship with full tuition reimbursement (averaging $7,344 per year), 3 teaching assistantships with full tuition reimbursements (averaging $7,344 per year) were awarded; career-related internships or fieldwork, Federal Work-Study, institutionally sponsored loans, health care benefits, and unspecified assistantships also available. Financial award application deadline: 3/15; financial award applicants required to submit FAFSA. In 2017, 9 master's awarded. *Program availability:* Part-time. Offers art therapy (MS). *Application deadline:* For fall admission, 6/1 for domestic students; for spring admission, 10/1 for domestic students. Applications are processed on a rolling basis. *Application fee:* $30 ($75 for international students). Electronic applications accepted. *Application Contact:* Mary Sewell, Admissions Coordinator, 800-950-GRAD, Fax: 620-341-5909, E-mail: msewell@emporia.edu. *Chair,* Dr. Katrina Miller, 620-341-5231, E-mail: kmille12@emporia.edu.

Program in Business Administration Students: 49 full-time (18 women), 44 part-time (24 women); includes 11 minority (3 Black or African American, non-Hispanic/Latino; 1 American Indian or Alaska Native, non-Hispanic/Latino; 3 Asian, non-Hispanic/Latino; 2 Hispanic/Latino; 2 Two or more races, non-Hispanic/Latino), 29 international. 51 applicants, 63% accepted, 17 enrolled. *Faculty:* 29 full-time (8 women). Expenses: Contact institution. *Financial support:* In 2017–18, 1 research assistantship with full tuition reimbursement (averaging $7,344 per year), 9 teaching assistantships with full tuition reimbursements (averaging $4,488 per year) were awarded; career-related internships or fieldwork, health care benefits, and unspecified assistantships also available. Financial award applicants required to submit FAFSA. In 2017, 45 master's awarded. *Program availability:* Part-time, evening/weekend, blended/hybrid learning. Offers business administration (MBA). *Application deadline:* For fall admission, 8/15 for domestic students. Applications are processed on a rolling basis. *Application fee:* $30 ($75 for international students). Electronic applications accepted. *Application Contact:* Mary Sewell, Admissions Coordinator, 800-950-GRAD, Fax: 620-341-5909, E-mail: msewell@emporia.edu. *Coordinator, Graduate and Career Services,* James Willingham, 620-341-5456, E-mail: jwilling@emporia.edu.

Program in Clinical Counseling Students: 25 full-time (21 women), 5 part-time (3 women); includes 6 minority (2 Black or African American, non-Hispanic/Latino; 2 Asian, non-Hispanic/Latino; 1 Hispanic/Latino; 1 Two or more races, non-Hispanic/Latino), 1 international. 24 applicants, 58% accepted, 6 enrolled. *Faculty:* 13 full-time (9 women). Expenses: Contact institution. *Financial support:* In 2017–18, 4 research assistantships with full tuition reimbursements (averaging $7,344 per year) were awarded; Federal Work-Study, institutionally sponsored loans, health care benefits, and unspecified assistantships also available. Financial award application deadline: 3/15; financial award applicants required to submit FAFSA. In 2017, 18 master's awarded. *Program availability:* Part-time. Offers clinical counseling (MS). *Application deadline:* For fall admission, 8/15 for domestic students. Applications are processed on a rolling basis. *Application fee:* $30 ($75 for international students). Electronic applications accepted. *Application Contact:* Mary Sewell, Admissions Coordinator, 800-950-GRAD, Fax: 620-341-5909, E-mail: msewell@emporia.edu. *Chair,* Dr. Katrina Miller, 620-341-5791, E-mail: kmille12@emporia.edu.

Program in Clinical Psychology Students: 29 full-time (21 women), 4 part-time (3 women); includes 5 minority (3 Black or African American, non-Hispanic/Latino; 1 Hispanic/Latino; 1 Two or more races, non-Hispanic/Latino), 3 international. 34 applicants, 62% accepted, 5 enrolled. *Faculty:* 8 full-time (4 women). Expenses: Contact institution. *Financial support:* In 2017–18, 11 teaching assistantships with full tuition reimbursements (averaging $7,344 per year) were awarded; research assistantships with full tuition reimbursements, career-related internships or fieldwork, Federal Work-Study, institutionally sponsored loans, health care benefits, and unspecified assistantships also available. Support available to part-time students. Financial award application deadline: 3/15; financial award applicants required to submit FAFSA. In 2017, 7 master's awarded. *Program availability:* Part-time. Offers clinical psychology (MS). *Application deadline:* For fall admission, 8/15 for domestic students. Applications are processed on a rolling basis. *Application fee:* $30 ($75 for international students). Electronic applications accepted. *Application Contact:* Mary Sewell, Admissions Coordinator, 800-950-GRAD, Fax: 620-341-5909, E-mail: msewell@emporia.edu. *Chair,* Dr. Jim Persinger, 620-341-5317, E-mail: jpersing@emporia.edu.

Program in Curriculum and Instruction Students: 6 full-time (all women), 105 part-time (91 women); includes 7 minority (2 Black or African American, non-Hispanic/Latino; 2 Hispanic/Latino; 3 Two or more races, non-Hispanic/Latino). 19 applicants, 95% accepted, 15 enrolled. *Faculty:* 10 full-time (3 women). Expenses: Contact institution. *Financial support:* Career-related internships or fieldwork, Federal Work-Study, institutionally sponsored loans, health care benefits, and unspecified assistantships available. Financial award application deadline: 3/15; financial award applicants required to submit FAFSA. In 2017, 60 master's awarded. *Program availability:* Part-time, online only, 100% online. Offers curriculum leadership (MS); effective practitioner (MS); national board certification (MS). *Application deadline:* For fall admission, 8/15 priority date for domestic students. Applications are processed on a rolling basis. *Application fee:* $30 ($75 for international students). Electronic applications accepted. *Application Contact:* Mary Sewell, Admissions Coordinator, 800-950-GRAD, Fax: 620-341-5909, E-mail: msewell@emporia.edu. *Chair,* Dr. Daniel Stiffler, 620-341-5776, E-mail: dstiffle@emporia.edu.

Program in Early Childhood Education Students: 2 full-time (both women), 48 part-time (all women); includes 2 minority (both Hispanic/Latino). 12 applicants, 50% accepted, 4 enrolled. *Faculty:* 30 full-time (24 women), 1 part-time/adjunct (0 women). Expenses: Contact institution. *Financial support:* In 2017–18, 4 research assistantships (averaging $7,344 per year), 4 teaching assistantships (averaging $7,344 per year) were awarded; Federal Work-Study, institutionally sponsored loans, health care benefits, and unspecified assistantships also available. Financial award application deadline: 3/15; financial award applicants required to submit FAFSA. In 2017, 23 master's awarded. *Program availability:* Part-time, online learning. Offers early childhood education (MS). *Application deadline:* For fall admission, 8/15 priority date for domestic students. Applications are processed on a rolling basis. *Application fee:* $30 ($75 for international students). Electronic applications accepted. *Application Contact:* Mary Sewell, Admissions Coordinator, 800-950-GRAD, Fax: 620-341-5909, E-mail: msewell@emporia.edu. *Chair,* Dr. Matt Siemears, 620-341-6057, E-mail: mseimear@emporia.edu.

Program in Educational Administration Students: 3 full-time (0 women), 100 part-time (53 women); includes 6 minority (3 Black or African American, non-Hispanic/Latino; 1 Hispanic/Latino; 2 Two or more races, non-Hispanic/Latino). 19 applicants, 79% accepted, 12 enrolled. *Faculty:* 10 full-time (3 women). Expenses: Contact institution. *Financial support:* In 2017–18, 1 research assistantship with partial tuition reimbursement (averaging $7,344 per year) was awarded; career-related internships or fieldwork, Federal Work-Study, institutionally sponsored loans, health care benefits, and unspecified assistantships also available. Financial award application deadline: 3/15; financial award applicants required to submit FAFSA. In 2017, 45 master's awarded. *Program availability:* Part-time. Offers elementary administration (MS); elementary/secondary administration (MS); secondary administration (MS). *Application deadline:* For fall admission, 8/15 priority date for domestic students. Applications are processed on a rolling basis. *Application fee:* $30 ($75 for international students). Electronic applications accepted. *Application Contact:* Mary Sewell, Admissions Coordinator, 800-950-GRAD, Fax: 620-341-5909, E-mail: msewell@emporia.edu. *Chair,* Dr. Daniel Stiffler, 620-341-5776, E-mail: dstiffle@emporia.edu.

Program in English Students: 10 full-time (5 women), 39 part-time (25 women); includes 2 minority (1 Black or African American, non-Hispanic/Latino; 1 Hispanic/Latino), 5 international. 26 applicants, 54% accepted, 7 enrolled. *Faculty:* 17 full-time (10 women), 8 part-time/adjunct (6 women). Expenses: Contact institution. *Financial support:* In 2017–18, 3 research assistantships with full tuition reimbursements (averaging $7,344 per year), 4 teaching assistantships with full tuition reimbursements (averaging $7,344 per year) were awarded; Federal Work-Study, health care benefits, and unspecified assistantships also available. Financial award application deadline: 2/15; financial award applicants required to submit FAFSA. In 2017, 7 master's awarded. *Program availability:* Part-time. Offers English (MA). *Application deadline:* For fall admission, 8/15 for domestic students. *Application fee:* $30 ($75 for international students). *Application Contact:* Mary Sewell, Admissions Coordinator, 800-950-GRAD, Fax: 620-341-5909, E-mail: msewell@emporia.edu. *Chair,* Dr. Kevin Rabas, 620-341-5216, E-mail: krabas@emporia.edu.

Program in Forensic Science Students: 21 full-time (13 women), 1 (woman) part-time; includes 2 minority (1 Hispanic/Latino; 1 Two or more races, non-Hispanic/Latino), 7 international. 22 applicants, 82% accepted, 13 enrolled. *Faculty:* 13 full-time (3 women), 1 part-time/adjunct (0 women). Expenses: Contact institution. *Financial support:* In 2017–18, 7 research assistantships (averaging $9,747 per year), 15 teaching assistantships with full tuition reimbursements (averaging $7,499 per year) were awarded; unspecified assistantships also available. Financial award applicants required to submit FAFSA. In 2017, 10 master's awarded. *Program availability:* Part-time. Offers forensic science (MS). *Application deadline:* For fall admission, 4/15 for domestic students. Applications are processed on a rolling basis. *Application fee:* $40. Electronic applications accepted. *Application Contact:* April Huddleston, Recruitment and Development Specialist, 800-950-GRAD, Fax: 620-341-5909, E-mail: ahuddles@emporia.edu. *Interim Director,* Dr. Melissa M. Bailey, 620-341-5619, E-mail: mbailey4@emporia.edu.

Program in History Students: 5 full-time (0 women), 23 part-time (11 women); includes 2 minority (1 Black or African American, non-Hispanic/Latino; 1 Two or more races, non-Hispanic/Latino). 9 applicants, 100% accepted, 9 enrolled. *Faculty:* 13 full-time (6 women), 1 part-time/adjunct (0 women). Expenses: Contact institution. *Financial support:* In 2017–18, 1 research assistantship with full tuition reimbursement (averaging $7,344 per year), 4 teaching assistantships with full tuition reimbursements (averaging $6,426 per year) were awarded; Federal Work-Study, institutionally sponsored loans, health care benefits, and unspecified assistantships also available. Financial award application deadline: 3/15; financial award applicants required to submit FAFSA. In 2017, 8 master's awarded. *Program availability:* Part-time. Offers American history (MA); world history (MA). *Application deadline:* For fall admission, 8/15 priority date for domestic students. Applications are processed on a rolling basis. *Application fee:* $30 ($75 for international students). Electronic applications accepted. *Chair,* Dr. Michael Smith, 620-341-5566, E-mail: msmith3@emporia.edu.

Program in Instructional Specialist Students: 2 full-time (1 woman), 88 part-time (80 women); includes 3 minority (1 Black or African American, non-Hispanic/Latino; 1 Asian, non-Hispanic/Latino; 1 Two or more races, non-Hispanic/Latino). 14 applicants, 93% accepted, 11 enrolled. *Faculty:* 30 full-time (24 women), 1 part-time/adjunct (0 women). Expenses: Contact institution. *Financial support:* Federal Work-Study, institutionally sponsored loans, health care benefits, and unspecified assistantships available. Financial award application deadline: 3/15; financial award applicants required to submit FAFSA. In 2017, 15 master's awarded. *Program availability:* Part-time. Offers elementary subject matter (MS); reading (MS). *Application deadline:* For fall admission, 8/15 priority date for domestic students. Applications are processed on a rolling basis. *Application fee:* $30 ($75 for international students). Electronic applications accepted. *Application Contact:* Mary Sewell, Admissions Coordinator, 800-950-GRAD, Fax: 620-341-5909, E-mail: msewell@emporia.edu. *Chair,* Dr. Matt Siemears, 620-341-6057, E-mail: msiemear@emporia.edu.

Program in Psychology Students: 9 full-time (5 women), 4 part-time (2 women); includes 1 minority (Black or African American, non-Hispanic/Latino), 2 international. 20 applicants, 75% accepted, 5 enrolled. *Faculty:* 8 full-time (4 women). Expenses: Contact institution. *Financial support:* In 2017–18, 11 teaching assistantships with full tuition reimbursements (averaging $7,344 per year) were awarded; career-related internships or fieldwork, Federal Work-Study, institutionally sponsored loans, health care benefits, and unspecified assistantships also available. Financial award application deadline: 3/15; financial award applicants required to submit FAFSA. In 2017, 3 master's awarded. *Program availability:* Part-time. Offers general psychology (MS); industrial/organizational psychology (MS). *Application deadline:* For fall admission, 6/1 priority date for domestic students; for spring admission, 10/1 for domestic students. Applications are processed on a rolling basis. *Application fee:* $30 ($75 for international students). Electronic applications accepted. *Application Contact:* Mary Sewell, Admissions Coordinator, 800-950-GRAD, Fax: 620-341-5909, E-mail: msewell@emporia.edu. *Chair,* Dr. Jim Persinger, 620-341-5317, E-mail: jpersing@emporia.edu.

Program in Rehabilitation Counseling Students: 13 full-time (10 women), 2 part-time (1 woman); includes 1 minority (Hispanic/Latino). 6 applicants, 67% accepted, 2 enrolled. *Faculty:* 13 full-time (9 women). Expenses: Contact institution. *Financial support:* Career-related internships or fieldwork, Federal Work-Study, institutionally sponsored loans, health care benefits, and unspecified assistantships available. Financial award application deadline: 3/15; financial award applicants required to submit FAFSA. In 2017, 17 master's awarded. *Program availability:* Part-time. Offers rehabilitation counseling (MS). *Application deadline:* For fall admission, 8/15 priority date for domestic students. Applications are processed on a rolling basis. *Application fee:* $30 ($75 for international students). Electronic applications accepted. *Application Contact:* Mary Sewell, Admissions Coordinator, 800-950-GRAD, Fax: 620-341-5909, E-mail: msewell@emporia.edu. *Chair/Graduate Co-Coordinator,* Dr. Katrina Miller, 620-341-5791, E-mail: kmille12@emporia.edu.

Program in School Counseling Students: 19 full-time (16 women), 73 part-time (67 women); includes 6 minority (1 Asian, non-Hispanic/Latino; 3 Hispanic/Latino; 2 Two or more races, non-Hispanic/Latino). 28 applicants, 50% accepted, 12 enrolled. *Faculty:* 13 full-time (9 women). Expenses: Contact institution. *Financial support:* In 2017–18, 4 research assistantships with full tuition reimbursements (averaging $7,344 per year) were awarded; career-related internships or fieldwork, Federal Work-Study, institutionally sponsored loans, health care benefits, and unspecified assistantships also available. Financial award application deadline: 3/15; financial award applicants required to submit FAFSA. In 2017, 23 master's awarded. *Program availability:* Part-time. Offers school counseling (MS). *Application deadline:* For fall admission, 8/15 priority date for domestic students. Applications are processed on a rolling basis. *Application fee:* $30 ($75 for international students). Electronic applications accepted. *Application Contact:* Mary Sewell, Admissions Coordinator, 800-950-GRAD, Fax: 620-341-5909, E-mail: msewell@emporia.edu. *Chair,* Dr. Katrina Miller, 620-341-5791, E-mail: kmille12@emporia.edu.

Program in School Psychology Students: 26 full-time (23 women), 7 part-time (all women); includes 2 minority (1 Hispanic/Latino; 1 Two or more races, non-Hispanic/Latino). 38 applicants, 74% accepted, 14 enrolled. *Faculty:* 8 full-time (4 women). Expenses: Contact institution. *Financial support:* Career-related internships or fieldwork, Federal Work-Study, institutionally sponsored loans, health care benefits, and unspecified assistantships available. Financial award application deadline: 3/15; financial award applicants required to submit FAFSA. In 2017, 16 master's awarded. *Program availability:* Part-time. Offers school psychology (MS, Ed S). *Application deadline:* For fall admission, 8/15 priority date for domestic students. Applications are processed on a rolling basis. *Application fee:* $30 ($75 for international students). Electronic applications accepted. *Application Contact:* Mary Sewell, Admissions Coordinator, 800-950-GRAD, Fax: 620-341-5909, E-mail: msewell@emporia.edu. *Chair,* Dr. Jim Persinger, 620-341-5317, E-mail: jpersing@emporia.edu.

Program in Special Education Students: 4 full-time (2 women), 160 part-time (119 women); includes 9 minority (3 Black or African American, non-Hispanic/Latino; 1 Asian, non-Hispanic/Latino; 3 Hispanic/Latino; 2 Two or more races, non-Hispanic/Latino). 29 applicants, 72% accepted, 21 enrolled. *Faculty:* 30 full-time (24 women), 1 part-time/adjunct (0 women). Expenses: Contact institution. *Financial support:* In 2017–18, 4 teaching assistantships with full tuition reimbursements (averaging $7,344 per year) were awarded; Federal Work-Study, institutionally sponsored loans, health care benefits, and unspecified assistantships also available. Financial award application deadline: 3/15; financial award applicants required to submit FAFSA. In 2017, 55 master's awarded. *Program availability:* Part-time. Offers behavior disorders (MS); gifted, talented, and creative (MS); interrelated special education (MS). *Application deadline:* For fall admission, 8/15 priority date for domestic students. Applications are processed on a rolling basis. *Application fee:* $30 ($75 for international students). Electronic applications accepted. *Application Contact:* Mary Sewell, Admissions Coordinator, 800-950-GRAD, Fax: 620-341-5909, E-mail: msewell@emporia.edu. *Chair,* Dr. Matt Siemears, 620-341-6057, E-mail: msiemear@emporia.edu.

Program in Teaching Students: 6 full-time (4 women), 19 part-time (15 women); includes 1 minority (Black or African American, non-Hispanic/Latino). 14 applicants, 64% accepted, 6 enrolled. *Faculty:* 10 full-time (3 women). Expenses: Contact institution. In 2017, 18 master's awarded. *Program availability:* Part-time, online learning. Offers teaching (M Ed). *Application fee:* $40. *Application Contact:* Mary Sewell, Admissions Coordinator, 800-950-GRAD, Fax: 620-341-5909, E-mail: msewell@emporia.edu. *Chair,* Dr. Daniel Stiffler, 620-341-5776, E-mail: dstiffle@emporia.edu.

Program in Teaching English to Speakers of Other Languages Students: 15 part-time (13 women); includes 4 minority (1 Asian, non-Hispanic/Latino; 1 Hispanic/Latino; 2 Two or more races, non-Hispanic/Latino), 1 international. 10 applicants, 40% accepted, 4 enrolled. *Faculty:* 7 full-time (3 women). Expenses: Contact institution. *Financial support:* Federal Work-Study, institutionally sponsored loans, health care benefits, and unspecified assistantships available. Financial award application deadline: 2/15. In 2017, 17 master's, 2 other advanced degrees awarded. *Program availability:* Part-time. Offers TESOL (Certificate). *Application deadline:* For fall admission, 8/15 priority date for domestic students. Applications are processed on a rolling basis. *Application fee:* $30 ($75 for international students). Electronic applications accepted. *Application Contact:* Mary Sewell, Admissions Coordinator, 800-950-GRAD, Fax: 620-341-5909, E-mail: msewell@emporia.edu. *Professor,* Dr. Abdelilah Salim Sehlaoui, 620-341-5237, E-mail: asehlaou@emporia.edu.

School of Library and Information Management Students: 23 full-time (17 women), 310 part-time (250 women); includes 14 minority (2 Black or African American, non-Hispanic/Latino; 10 Hispanic/Latino; 2 Two or more races, non-Hispanic/Latino), 4 international. 137 applicants, 76% accepted, 85 enrolled. *Faculty:* 9 full-time (5 women), 1 (woman) part-time/adjunct. Expenses: Contact institution. *Financial support:* Federal Work-Study, institutionally sponsored loans, and unspecified assistantships available. Financial award application deadline: 3/15; financial award applicants required to submit FAFSA. In 2017, 145 master's, 1 doctorate, 27 other advanced degrees awarded. *Program availability:* Part-time, evening/weekend, online learning. Offers archives studies (Certificate); information technology and science literacy (Certificate); library and information management (MLS, PhD). *Application deadline:* For fall admission, 8/15 priority date for domestic students. Applications are processed on a rolling basis. *Application fee:* $30 ($75 for international students). Electronic applications accepted. *Application Contact:* Candace Boardman, Director, Kansas MLS Program, 620-341-6159, E-mail: cboardma@emporia.edu. *Dean,* Dr. Wooseob Jeong, 620-341-5203, Fax: 620-341-5203, E-mail: wjeong1@emporia.edu.

ENDICOTT COLLEGE, Beverly, MA 01915-2096

General Information Independent, coed, comprehensive institution. *Enrollment:* 5,058 graduate, professional, and undergraduate students; 504 full-time matriculated graduate/professional students (311 women), 490 part-time matriculated graduate/professional students (362 women). *Enrollment by degree level:* 923 master's, 71 doctoral. *Graduate faculty:* 24 full-time (14 women), 146 part-time/adjunct (77 women). Tuition and fees vary according to program. *Graduate housing:* Room and/or apartments available on a first-come, first-served basis to single students; on-campus housing not available to married students. Typical cost: $10,272 per year ($14,900 including board). Room and board charges vary according to board plan, campus/location and housing facility selected. Housing application deadline: 5/1. *Student services:* Campus employment opportunities, campus safety program, career counseling, free psychological counseling, international student services, low-cost health insurance, multicultural affairs office, services for students with disabilities, teacher training, writing training. *Library facilities:* Diane M. Halle Library. *Collection:* Books: 104,213 (physical), 172,731 (digital/electronic); Serial titles: 47 (physical), 154,538 (digital/electronic); Databases: 175. Weekly public service hours: 97; students can reserve study rooms. *Research affiliation:* Peabody Essex Museum (history), North Shore Consortium (special needs).

Computer facilities: Computer purchase and lease plans are available. 285 computers available on campus for general student use. A campuswide network can be accessed from student residence rooms and from off campus. Online class registration is available.
Website: http://www.endicott.edu/

General Application Contact: Dr. Mary Huegel, Vice President and Dean of the School of Graduate and Professional Studies, 978-232-2084, Fax: 978-232-3000, E-mail: mhuegel@endicott.edu.

GRADUATE UNITS

Van Loan School of Graduate and Professional Studies Students: 482 full-time (324 women), 514 part-time (373 women); includes 121 minority (39 Black or African American, non-Hispanic/Latino; 24 Asian, non-Hispanic/Latino; 42 Hispanic/Latino; 16 Two or more races, non-Hispanic/Latino), 19 international. Average age 32. 334 applicants, 99% accepted, 280 enrolled. *Faculty:* 24 full-time (14 women), 146 part-time/adjunct (77 women). Expenses: Contact institution. *Financial support:* Fellowships, research assistantships, teaching assistantships, career-related internships or fieldwork, Federal Work-Study, tuition waivers (partial), and unspecified assistantships available. Financial award applicants required to submit FAFSA. In 2017, 542 master's, 16 doctorates, 10 other advanced degrees awarded. *Program availability:* Part-time, evening/weekend, 100% online, blended/hybrid learning. Offers administrative leadership (M Ed); applied behavior analysis (M Ed, PhD, Post-Master's Certificate); athletic administration (M Ed); autism (Certificate); autism and applied behavior analysis (M Ed); business administration (MBA); cybersecurity (MS, Postbaccalaureate Certificate); early childhood and elementary education (M Ed); early childhood education (M Ed); educational leadership (Ed D); elementary education (M Ed); emergency management (MS); family nurse practitioner (MSN, Post-Master's Certificate); global health (MSN); information technology (MSIT); integrative education (M Ed); interior architecture (MA, MFA); nursing administration (MSN); nursing administrator (Post-Master's Certificate); nursing educator (MSN, Post-Master's Certificate); organizational leadership (MBA); organizational management (M Ed); reading and literacy (M Ed); secondary education (M Ed); special education (M Ed). *Application deadline:* Applications are processed on a rolling basis. *Application fee:* $50. Electronic applications accepted. *Application Contact:* Ian Menchini, Director, Graduate Enrollment and Advising, 978-232-5292. *Dean,* Dr. Mary Huegel, 978-232-2084, Fax: 978-232-3000, E-mail: mhuegel@endicott.edu.

ERIKSON INSTITUTE, Chicago, IL 60654

General Information Independent, coed, primarily women, graduate-only institution.

GRADUATE UNITS

Academic Programs *Program availability:* Part-time, evening/weekend. Offers administration (Certificate); bilingual/ESL (Certificate); child development (MS); early childhood education (MS); infant mental health (Certificate); infant studies (Certificate). MS/MSW offered jointly with Loyola University Chicago.

ERSKINE THEOLOGICAL SEMINARY, Due West, SC 29639-0668

General Information Independent-religious, coed, graduate-only institution. *Graduate housing:* Room and/or apartments available on a first-come, first-served basis to single students; on-campus housing not available to married students. Housing application deadline: 6/1.

GRADUATE UNITS

Graduate and Professional Programs *Program availability:* Part-time, evening/weekend. Offers theology (M Div, MAPM, MATS, Th M, D Min). Electronic applications accepted.

EVANGELICAL SEMINARY, Myerstown, PA 17067-1212

General Information Independent-religious, coed, graduate-only institution. *Graduate housing:* Rooms and/or apartments available on a first-come, first-served basis to single and married students. Housing application deadline: 6/1.

GRADUATE UNITS

Graduate and Professional Programs *Program availability:* Part-time, online learning. Offers Biblical studies (MAR); congregational ministry (M Div); global and contextual studies (M Div, MAR); historical and theological studies (MAR); interdisciplinary studies (MAR); marriage and family counseling (M Div); marriage and family therapy (MA); New Testament (MAR); Old Testament (MAR); spiritual formation (MAR); teaching ministry (M Div); youth ministry (M Div).

EVANGELICAL SEMINARY OF PUERTO RICO, San Juan, PR 00925-2207

General Information Independent-religious, coed, graduate-only institution. *Graduate housing:* Rooms and/or apartments available on a first-come, first-served basis to single and married students. Housing application deadline: 12/15.

GRADUATE UNITS

Graduate and Professional Programs *Program availability:* Part-time. Offers theology (M Div, MAR, D Min).

EVANGEL UNIVERSITY, Springfield, MO 65802

General Information Independent-religious, coed, comprehensive institution. *Enrollment:* 2,112 graduate, professional, and undergraduate students; 104 full-time matriculated graduate/professional students (75 women), 103 part-time matriculated graduate/professional students (86 women). *Enrollment by degree level:* 168 master's, 39 doctoral. *Graduate faculty:* 19 full-time (12 women), 14 part-time/adjunct (9 women). *Tuition:* Full-time $7200; part-time $4800 per credit hour. *Required fees:* $210; $155 per semester. *Graduate housing:* Room and/or apartments available on a first-come, first-served basis to single students; on-campus housing not available to married students. *Student services:* Campus employment opportunities, campus safety program, career counseling, exercise/wellness program, free psychological counseling, international student services, multicultural affairs office, services for students with disabilities, teacher training, writing training. *Library facilities:* Claude Kendrick Library.

Computer facilities: A campuswide network can be accessed from student residence rooms. Online class registration, online payment are available.
Website: http://www.evangel.edu/

General Application Contact: Karen Benitez, Admissions Representative, Graduate Studies, 417-865-2815 Ext. 7416, Fax: 417-575-5484, E-mail: benitezk@evangel.edu.

GRADUATE UNITS

Department of Behavioral and Social Sciences Students: 33 full-time (27 women), 6 part-time (5 women); includes 3 minority (all Hispanic/Latino). Average age 31. 30 applicants, 70% accepted, 16 enrolled. *Faculty:* 6 full-time (4 women), 2 part-time/adjunct (1 woman). Expenses: Contact institution. *Financial support:* In 2017–18, 12 students received support. Unspecified assistantships available. Financial award application deadline: 4/1; financial award applicants required to submit FAFSA. In 2017, 14 master's awarded. *Program availability:* Part-time. Offers clinical mental health counseling (MS). *Application deadline:* For fall admission, 7/15 priority date for domestic students, 8/1 for international students; for spring admission, 11/15 priority date for domestic students, 12/1 for international students. Applications are processed on a rolling basis. *Application fee:* $25. Electronic applications accepted. *Application Contact:* Michael Mann, Enrollment Coordinator, Graduate Studies, 417-865-2815 Ext. 8276, Fax: 417-575-5484, E-mail: mannm@evangel.edu. *Program Coordinator,* Dr. Christine Arnzen, 417-865-2815 Ext. 8618, E-mail: arnzenc@evangel.edu.

Department of Education Students: 1 (woman) full-time, 47 part-time (41 women); includes 2 minority (both Hispanic/Latino). Average age 37. 16 applicants, 100% accepted, 14 enrolled. *Faculty:* 8 full-time (5 women), 8 part-time/adjunct (5 women). Expenses: Contact institution. *Financial support:* In 2017–18, 23 students received support. Scholarships/grants and unspecified assistantships available. Financial award application deadline: 4/1; financial award applicants required to submit FAFSA. In 2017, 14 master's awarded. *Program availability:* Part-time, evening/weekend, 100% online, blended/hybrid learning. Offers curriculum and instruction (M Ed); educational leadership (M Ed); literacy (M Ed); secondary teaching (M Ed). *Application deadline:* For fall admission, 7/15 priority date for domestic students, 8/1 for international students; for spring admission, 11/15 priority date for domestic students, 12/1 for international students. Applications are processed on a rolling basis. *Application fee:* $25. Electronic applications accepted. *Application Contact:* Michael Mann, Enrollment Coordinator, Graduate Studies, 417-865-2815 Ext. 8276, Fax: 417-575-5484, E-mail: mannm@evangel.edu. *Program Coordinator,* Dr. Susan Langston, 417-865-2815 Ext. 8552, E-mail: langstons@evangel.edu.

Doctor of Education in Educational Leadership, Curriculum, and Instruction Program Students: 14 full-time (12 women), 25 part-time (17 women); includes 3 minority (1 Black or African American, non-Hispanic/Latino; 1 American Indian or Alaska Native, non-Hispanic/Latino; 1 Two or more races, non-Hispanic/Latino). Average age 40. 13 applicants, 85% accepted, 8 enrolled. *Faculty:* 5 full-time (3 women), 6 part-time/adjunct (3 women). Expenses: Contact institution. *Financial support:* In 2017–18, 15 students received support. Scholarships/grants available. Support available to part-time students. Financial award application deadline: 4/1; financial award applicants required to submit FAFSA. *Program availability:* Part-time, evening/weekend. Offers educational leadership, curriculum, and instruction (Ed D). *Application deadline:* For fall admission, 7/15 priority date for domestic students, 8/1 for international students; for spring admission, 11/15 priority date for domestic students, 12/1 for international students. Applications are processed on a rolling basis. *Application fee:* $25. Electronic applications accepted. *Application Contact:* Michael Mann, Enrollment Coordinator, Graduate Studies, 417-865-2811 Ext. 8276, Fax: 417-575-5484, E-mail: mannm@evangel.edu. *Program Coordinator,* Dr. Susan Langston, 417-865-2815 Ext. 8552, E-mail: langstons@evangel.edu.

Organizational Leadership Program Students: 32 full-time (15 women); includes 2 minority (1 American Indian or Alaska Native, non-Hispanic/Latino; 1 Hispanic/Latino). Average age 38. 14 applicants, 93% accepted, 13 enrolled. *Faculty:* 2 full-time (0 women), 2 part-time/adjunct (1 woman). Expenses: Contact institution. *Financial support:* In 2017–18, 13 students received support. Scholarships/grants available. Financial award application deadline: 4/1; financial award applicants required to submit FAFSA. In 2017, 16 master's awarded. *Program availability:* Part-time, evening/weekend, 100% online, blended/hybrid learning. Offers organizational leadership (MOL). *Application deadline:* For fall admission, 7/15 priority date for domestic students, 8/1 for international students; for spring admission, 11/15 priority date for domestic students, 12/1 for international students. Applications are processed on a rolling basis. *Application fee:* $25. Electronic applications accepted. *Application Contact:* Michael Mann, Enrollment Coordinator, Graduate Studies, 417-865-2815 Ext. 8276, Fax: 417-575-5484, E-mail: mannm@evangel.edu. *Program Coordinator,* Dr. Jeff Fulks, 417-865-2815 Ext. 8212, Fax: 417-575-5484, E-mail: fulksj@evangel.edu.

School Counseling Program Students: 24 full-time (19 women), 21 part-time (19 women); includes 3 minority (2 Black or African American, non-Hispanic/Latino; 1 Hispanic/Latino). Average age 31. 16 applicants, 100% accepted, 11 enrolled. *Faculty:* 17 full-time (12 women), 4 part-time/adjunct (3 women). Expenses: Contact institution. *Financial support:* In 2017–18, 6 students received support. Scholarships/grants and unspecified assistantships available. Financial award application deadline: 4/1; financial award applicants required to submit FAFSA. In 2017, 14 master's awarded. *Program availability:* Part-time, evening/weekend. Offers school counseling (MS). *Application deadline:* For fall admission, 7/15 priority date for domestic students, 7/1 for international students; for spring admission, 11/15 priority date for domestic students, 12/1 for international students. Applications are processed on a rolling basis. *Application fee:* $25. Electronic applications accepted. *Application Contact:* Michael Mann, Enrollment Coordinator, Graduate Studies, 417-865-2815 Ext. 8276, Fax: 417-575-5484, E-mail: mannm@evangel.edu. *Program Coordinator,* Dr. Christine Arnzen, 417-865-2815 Ext. 8678, Fax: 417-575-5484, E-mail: arnzenc@evangel.edu.

EVERGLADES UNIVERSITY, Boca Raton, FL 33431

General Information Independent, coed, comprehensive institution. *Graduate housing:* On-campus housing not available.

GRADUATE UNITS

Graduate Programs *Program availability:* Part-time, evening/weekend, 100% online. Offers accounting for managers (MBA); aviation management (MBA); aviation operations management (MSA); aviation security (MSA); business administration (MSA); complementary and alternative medicine (MPH); entrepreneurship (MS); human resource management (MBA); project management (MBA). Electronic applications accepted.

THE EVERGREEN STATE COLLEGE, Olympia, WA 98505

General Information State-supported, coed, comprehensive institution. *Enrollment:* 3,907 graduate, professional, and undergraduate students; 182 full-time matriculated graduate/professional students (124 women), 111 part-time matriculated graduate/professional students (80 women). *Enrollment by degree level:* 293 master's. *Graduate faculty:* 16 full-time (10 women), 14 part-time/adjunct (6 women). Tuition, state resident: full-time $10,038; part-time $334.60 per credit. Tuition, nonresident: full-time $23,226; part-time $774.20 per credit. *Required fees:* $637; $9.25 per credit. $5 per quarter. *Graduate housing:* Rooms and/or apartments available on a first-come, first-served basis to single and married students. Typical cost: $6471 per year ($9681 including board) for single students. Housing application deadline: 6/15. *Student services:* Campus employment opportunities, campus safety program, career counseling, child daycare facilities, exercise/wellness program, free psychological counseling, grant writing training, international student services, multicultural affairs office, services for students with disabilities, teacher training, writing training. *Library facilities:* Daniel J. Evans Library. *Collection:* Books: 326,129 (physical), 160,427 (digital/electronic); Serial titles: 69 (physical), 65,977 (digital/electronic); Databases: 64. Weekly public service hours: 83; students can reserve study rooms. *Research affiliation:* Washington State Institute for Public Policy (public policy).

Computer facilities: 556 computers available on campus for general student use. A campuswide network can be accessed from student residence rooms and from off campus. Online class registration, online payment, student accounts history, financial aid records, academic history, housing application, evaluations are available.
Website: http://www.evergreen.edu/

General Application Contact: Admissions, 360-867-6170, E-mail: admissions@evergreen.edu.

GRADUATE UNITS

Graduate Programs Students: 182 full-time (117 women), 113 part-time (84 women); includes 78 minority (8 Black or African American, non-Hispanic/Latino; 25 American Indian or Alaska Native, non-Hispanic/Latino; 2 Asian, non-Hispanic/Latino; 21 Hispanic/Latino; 2 Native Hawaiian or other Pacific Islander, non-Hispanic/Latino; 20 Two or more races, non-Hispanic/Latino), 2 international. Average age 32. 309 applicants, 73% accepted, 157 enrolled. *Faculty:* 14 full-time (9 women), 17 part-time/adjunct (7 women). Expenses: Contact institution. *Financial support:* In 2017–18, 170 students received support, including 51 fellowships with partial tuition reimbursements available (averaging $1,313 per year); career-related internships or fieldwork, Federal Work-Study, institutionally sponsored loans, scholarships/grants, health care benefits, and tuition waivers (partial) also available. Support available to part-time students. Financial award application deadline: 2/1; financial award applicants required to submit FAFSA. In 2017, 141 master's awarded. *Program availability:* Part-time, evening/weekend. Offers environmental studies (MES); public administration (MPA); teaching (MIT). *Application deadline:* For fall admission, 2/1 priority date for domestic and international students. Applications are processed on a rolling basis. *Application fee:* $50. Electronic applications accepted. *Application Contact:* Amanda Mobbs, Graduate Admission Coordinator, 360-867-6856, E-mail: graduateadmissions@evergreen.edu. *Vice President and Provost,* Dr. Jennifer Drake, 360-867-6400, Fax: 360-867-6745, E-mail: drakej@evergreen.edu.

EXCELSIOR COLLEGE, Albany, NY 12203-5159

General Information Independent, coed, comprehensive institution. *Enrollment:* 31,095 graduate, professional, and undergraduate students; 1,974 part-time matriculated graduate/professional students (821 women). *Enrollment by degree level:* 1,957 master's, 17 other advanced degrees. *Graduate faculty:* 78 part-time/adjunct (48 women). *Tuition:* Part-time $645 per credit. *Required fees:* $265 per credit. *Student services:* Career counseling, services for students with disabilities, writing training. *Library facilities:* Excelsior College Library.

Computer facilities: A campuswide network can be accessed from off campus. Online class registration is available.
Website: http://www.excelsior.edu/

General Application Contact: Admissions Counselor, 518-464-8500, Fax: 518-464-8777, E-mail: admissions@excelsior.edu.

GRADUATE UNITS

School of Business and Technology Students: 1,204 part-time (333 women); includes 560 minority (310 Black or African American, non-Hispanic/Latino; 7 American Indian or Alaska Native, non-Hispanic/Latino; 42 Asian, non-Hispanic/Latino; 140 Hispanic/Latino; 10 Native Hawaiian or other Pacific Islander, non-Hispanic/Latino; 51 Two or more races, non-Hispanic/Latino). Average age 40. *Faculty:* 30 part-time/adjunct (12 women). Expenses: Contact institution. *Financial support:* Scholarships/grants available. In 2017, 294 master's awarded. *Program availability:* Part-time, evening/weekend, online learning. Offers business administration (MBA); cybersecurity - information assurance (MS); cybersecurity - medical data security (MS); cybersecurity - policy administration (MS); cybersecurity management (MBA, Graduate Certificate); general business management (MS); health care management (MBA); human performance technology (MBA); human resource management (MS); human resources management (MBA); leadership (MBA, MS); mediation and arbitration (MBA, MS); social media management (MBA); technology management (MBA). *Application deadline:* Applications are processed on a rolling basis. *Application fee:* $50. Electronic applications accepted. *Application Contact:* Admissions, 888-647-2388 Ext. 133, Fax: 518-464-8777, E-mail: admissions@excelsior.edu. *Dean*, Dr. Lifang Shih, 888-647-2388.

School of Health Sciences Students: 133 part-time (92 women); includes 84 minority (49 Black or African American, non-Hispanic/Latino; 4 American Indian or Alaska Native, non-Hispanic/Latino; 8 Asian, non-Hispanic/Latino; 13 Hispanic/Latino; 2 Native Hawaiian or other Pacific Islander, non-Hispanic/Latino; 8 Two or more races, non-Hispanic/Latino). Average age 40. *Faculty:* 4 part-time/adjunct (all women). Expenses: Contact institution. *Financial support:* Scholarships/grants available. In 2017, 38 master's awarded. *Program availability:* Part-time, evening/weekend, online learning. Offers health care administration (MS); health professions education (MSHS); healthcare informatics (MS); organizational development (MS); public health (MSHS). *Application deadline:* Applications are processed on a rolling basis. *Application fee:* $50. Electronic applications accepted. *Application Contact:* Admissions Counselor, 518-464-8500, Fax: 518-464-8777, E-mail: gradadmissions@excelsior.edu. *Dean*, Dr. Barbara Pieper, 518-464-8500, Fax: 518-464-8777.

School of Liberal Arts Students: 76 part-time (34 women); includes 33 minority (19 Black or African American, non-Hispanic/Latino; 2 American Indian or Alaska Native, non-Hispanic/Latino; 5 Hispanic/Latino; 7 Two or more races, non-Hispanic/Latino). Average age 45. *Faculty:* 25 part-time/adjunct (17 women). Expenses: Contact institution. *Financial support:* Scholarships/grants available. In 2017, 16 master's awarded. *Program availability:* Part-time, evening/weekend, online learning. Offers liberal studies (MA). *Application deadline:* Applications are processed on a rolling basis. *Application fee:* $50. Electronic applications accepted. *Application Contact:* Admissions Counselor, 518-464-8500, Fax: 518-464-8777, E-mail: gradadmissions@excelsior.edu. *Dean*, Dr. George Timmons, 518-464-8500, Fax: 518-464-8777, E-mail: mlsadmin@excelsior.edu.

School of Nursing Students: 388 part-time (313 women); includes 122 minority (63 Black or African American, non-Hispanic/Latino; 4 American Indian or Alaska Native, non-Hispanic/Latino; 18 Asian, non-Hispanic/Latino; 28 Hispanic/Latino; 2 Native Hawaiian or other Pacific Islander, non-Hispanic/Latino; 7 Two or more races, non-Hispanic/Latino). Average age 44. *Faculty:* 12 part-time/adjunct (9 women). Expenses: Contact institution. *Financial support:* Scholarships/grants available. In 2017, 173 master's awarded. *Program availability:* Part-time, evening/weekend, online learning. Offers nursing (MS); nursing education (MS); nursing informatics (MS); nursing leadership and administration of health care systems (MS). *Application deadline:* Applications are processed on a rolling basis. *Application fee:* $50. Electronic applications accepted. *Application Contact:* Admissions Counselor, 888-647-2388, Fax: 518-464-8777, E-mail: gradadmissions@excelsior.edu. *Dean, School of Nursing*, Dr. Mary Lee Pollard, 518-464-8500, Fax: 518-464-8777, E-mail: msn@excelsior.edu.

School of Public Service Students: 173 part-time (49 women); includes 70 minority (32 Black or African American, non-Hispanic/Latino; 1 American Indian or Alaska Native, non-Hispanic/Latino; 3 Asian, non-Hispanic/Latino; 28 Hispanic/Latino; 1 Native Hawaiian or other Pacific Islander, non-Hispanic/Latino; 5 Two or more races, non-Hispanic/Latino). Average age 40. *Faculty:* 6 part-time/adjunct (5 women). Expenses: Contact institution. *Financial support:* Scholarships/grants available. In 2017, 45 master's awarded. *Program availability:* Part-time, evening/weekend, online learning. Offers criminal justice (MSCI); homeland security and emergency management (MSCJ); justice administration (MSCI); mediation and arbitration (MPA); public administration (MPA). *Application deadline:* Applications are processed on a rolling basis. *Application fee:* $50. Electronic applications accepted. *Application Contact:* Admissions Counselor, 888-647-2388, Fax: 518-464-8777, E-mail: gradadmissions@excelsior.edu. *Dean, School of Public Service*, Dr. Robert Waters, 518-464-8500, Fax: 518-464-8777.

FAIRFIELD UNIVERSITY, Fairfield, CT 06824

General Information Independent-religious, coed, comprehensive institution. *Enrollment:* 5,192 graduate, professional, and undergraduate students; 476 full-time matriculated graduate/professional students (325 women), 604 part-time matriculated graduate/professional students (427 women). *Enrollment by degree level:* 876 master's, 130 doctoral, 74 other advanced degrees. *Graduate faculty:* 75 full-time (42 women), 77 part-time/adjunct (46 women). *Tuition:* Part-time $775 per credit hour. *Required fees:* $35 per term. One-time fee: $55 part-time. Tuition and fees vary according to degree level and program. *Graduate housing:* Room and/or apartments available on a first-come, first-served basis to single students; on-campus housing not available to married students. Typical cost: $12,370 per year ($14,280 including board). Room and board charges vary according to housing facility selected. *Student services:* Campus employment opportunities, campus safety program, career counseling, child daycare facilities, exercise/wellness program, free psychological counseling, international student services, low-cost health insurance, multicultural affairs office, services for students with disabilities, teacher training, writing training. *Library facilities:* DiMenna-Nyselius Library. *Collection:* Books: 376,556 (physical), 892,810 (digital/electronic); Serial titles: 1,292 (physical), 58,084 (digital/electronic); Databases: 183. Weekly public service hours: 104; study areas open 24 hours, 5–7 days a week; students can reserve study rooms.

Computer facilities: Computer purchase and lease plans are available. 131 computers available on campus for general student use. A campuswide network can be accessed from student residence rooms and from off campus. Online class registration is available.
Website: http://www.fairfield.edu/

General Application Contact: Marianne Gumpper, Director of Graduate Admission, 203-254-4184, Fax: 203-254-4073, E-mail: gradadmis@fairfield.edu.

GRADUATE UNITS

College of Arts and Sciences Students: 67 full-time (46 women), 64 part-time (35 women); includes 27 minority (8 Black or African American, non-Hispanic/Latino; 1 Asian, non-Hispanic/Latino; 14 Hispanic/Latino; 4 Two or more races, non-Hispanic/Latino), 10 international. Average age 32. 80 applicants, 81% accepted, 43 enrolled. *Faculty:* 16 full-time (8 women), 12 part-time/adjunct (8 women). Expenses: Contact institution. *Financial support:* In 2017–18, 11 students received support. Scholarships/grants and unspecified assistantships available. Financial award applicants required to submit FAFSA. In 2017, 38 master's awarded. *Program availability:* Part-time, evening/weekend, online learning. Offers American studies (MA); communication (MA); creative writing (MFA); mathematics (MS); public administration (MPA). *Application deadline:* For fall admission, 5/15 for international students; for spring admission, 10/15 for international students. Applications are processed on a rolling basis. *Application fee:* $60. Electronic applications accepted. *Application Contact:* Marianne Gumpper, Director of Graduate Admission, 203-254-4184, Fax: 203-254-4073, E-mail: gradadmis@fairfield.edu. *Dean*, Dr. Richard Greenwald, 203-254-4000 Ext. 2221, Fax: 203-254-4119, E-mail: rgreenwald@fairfield.edu.

Dolan School of Business Students: 120 full-time (57 women), 67 part-time (27 women); includes 20 minority (3 Black or African American, non-Hispanic/Latino; 1 American Indian or Alaska Native, non-Hispanic/Latino; 3 Asian, non-Hispanic/Latino; 11 Hispanic/Latino; 2 Two or more races, non-Hispanic/Latino), 33 international. Average age 26. 195 applicants, 87% accepted, 112 enrolled. *Faculty:* 18 full-time (6 women), 6 part-time/adjunct (2 women). Expenses: Contact institution. *Financial support:* In 2017–18, 31 students received support. Scholarships/grants and unspecified assistantships available. Financial award applicants required to submit FAFSA. In 2017, 93 master's awarded. *Program availability:* Part-time, evening/weekend. Offers accounting (MBA, MS, CAS); business analytics (MS); finance (MBA, MS, CAS); information systems and business analytics (MBA); management (MBA, CAS); marketing (MBA, CAS); taxation (CAS). *Application deadline:* For fall admission, 5/15 for international students; for spring admission, 10/15 for international students. Applications are processed on a rolling basis. *Application fee:* $60. Electronic applications accepted. *Application Contact:* Marianne Gumpper, Director of Graduate and Continuing Studies Admission, 203-254-4184, Fax: 203-254-4073, E-mail: gradadmis@fairfield.edu. *Interim Dean*, Dr. Mark Ligas, 203-254-4070, Fax: 203-254-4105, E-mail: mligas@fairfield.edu.

Graduate School of Education and Allied Professions Students: 199 full-time (168 women), 251 part-time (206 women); includes 85 minority (21 Black or African American, non-Hispanic/Latino; 9 Asian, non-Hispanic/Latino; 49 Hispanic/Latino; 6 Two or more races, non-Hispanic/Latino), 4 international. Average age 32. 370 applicants, 56% accepted, 125 enrolled. *Faculty:* 23 full-time (17 women), 39 part-time/adjunct (28 women). Expenses: Contact institution. *Financial support:* In 2017–18, 34 students received support. Career-related internships or fieldwork and unspecified assistantships available. Support available to part-time students. Financial award applicants required to submit FAFSA. In 2017, 136 master's, 28 other advanced degrees awarded. *Program availability:* Part-time, evening/weekend. Offers applied behavior analysis (ATC); applied psychology (MA); clinical mental health counseling (MA, CAS); educational technology (MA); elementary education (MA, CAS); family studies (MA); integration of spirituality and religion in counseling (ATC); marriage and family therapy (MA); reading and language development (Sixth Year Certificate); school counseling (MA, CAS); school psychology (MA, CAS); school-based marriage and family therapy (ATC); secondary education (MA); special education (MA, CAS); substance abuse counseling (ATC); teaching (Certificate); teaching and foundations (MA, CAS); TESOL, world languages, and bilingual education (MA, CAS). *Application deadline:* For fall admission, 2/15 for international students; for spring admission, 10/1 for international students. *Application fee:* $60. Electronic applications accepted. *Application Contact:* Marianne Gumpper, Director of Graduate Admission, 203-254-4184, Fax: 203-254-4073, E-mail: gradadmis@fairfield.edu. *Dean*, Dr. Robert D. Hannafin, 203-254-4250, Fax: 203-254-4241, E-mail: rhannafin@fairfield.edu.

Marion Peckham Egan School of Nursing and Health Studies Students: 50 full-time (42 women), 153 part-time (140 women); includes 48 minority (15 Black or African American, non-Hispanic/Latino; 1 American Indian or Alaska Native, non-Hispanic/Latino; 10 Asian, non-Hispanic/Latino; 19 Hispanic/Latino; 3 Two or more races, non-Hispanic/Latino), 2 international. Average age 34. 160 applicants, 50% accepted, 55 enrolled. *Faculty:* 9 full-time (all women), 11 part-time/adjunct (8 women). Expenses: Contact institution. *Financial support:* In 2017–18, 45 students received support. Scholarships/grants and unspecified assistantships available. Financial award applicants required to submit FAFSA. In 2017, 26 master's, 36 doctorates awarded. *Program availability:* Part-time, evening/weekend. Offers advanced practice (DNP); family nurse practitioner (MSN, DNP); nurse anesthesia (DNP); nursing leadership (MSN); psychiatric nurse practitioner (MSN, DNP). *Application deadline:* For fall admission, 5/15 for international students; for spring admission, 10/15 for international students. Applications are processed on a rolling basis. *Application fee:* $60. Electronic applications accepted. *Application Contact:* Marianne Gumpper, Director of Graduate and Continuing Studies Admission, 203-254-4184, Fax: 203-254-4073, E-mail: gradadmis@fairfield.edu. *Dean*, Dr. Meredith Wallace Kazer, 203-254-4000 Ext. 2701, Fax: 203-254-4126, E-mail: mkazer@fairfield.edu.

School of Engineering Students: 40 full-time (12 women), 69 part-time (19 women); includes 23 minority (10 Black or African American, non-Hispanic/Latino; 7 Asian, non-Hispanic/Latino; 5 Hispanic/Latino; 1 Two or more races, non-Hispanic/Latino), 51 international. Average age 28. 91 applicants, 78% accepted, 30 enrolled. *Faculty:* 9 full-time (2 women), 9 part-time/adjunct (0 women). Expenses: Contact institution. *Financial support:* In 2017–18, 20 students received support. Scholarships/grants and unspecified assistantships available. Financial award applicants required to submit FAFSA. In 2017, 100 master's awarded. *Program availability:* Part-time, evening/weekend. Offers database management (CAS); electrical and computer engineering (MS); information security (CAS); management of technology (MS); mechanical engineering (MS); network technology (CAS); software engineering (MS); Web application development (CAS). *Application deadline:* For fall admission, 5/15 for international students; for spring admission, 10/15 for international students. Applications are processed on a rolling basis. *Application fee:* $60. Electronic applications accepted. *Application Contact:* Marianne Gumpper, Director of Graduate and Continuing Studies Admission, 203-254-4184, Fax: 203-254-4073, E-mail: gradadmis@fairfield.edu. *Dean*, Dr. Bruce Berdanier, 203-254-4147, Fax: 203-254-4013, E-mail: bberdanier@fairfield.edu.

FAIRLEIGH DICKINSON UNIVERSITY, FLORHAM CAMPUS, Madison, NJ 07940-1099

General Information Independent, coed, comprehensive institution. *Enrollment:* 3,512 graduate, professional, and undergraduate students; 553 full-time matriculated graduate/professional students (358 women), 212 part-time matriculated graduate/professional students (116 women). *Enrollment by degree level:* 431 master's,

328 doctoral, 6 other advanced degrees. *Tuition:* Full-time $22,410; part-time $1245 per credit. *Required fees:* $888; $414 per unit. Tuition and fees vary according to course load, degree level and program. *Graduate housing:* Room and/or apartments available on a first-come, first-served basis to single students; on-campus housing not available to married students. Housing application deadline: 5/1. *Student services:* Campus employment opportunities, career counseling, exercise/wellness program, free psychological counseling, international student services, teacher training, writing training. *Library facilities:* Monninger Center for Learning and Research. *Collection:* Books: 131,212 (physical), 158,628 (digital/electronic); Serial titles: 1,423 (physical), 126,248 (digital/electronic); Databases: 144. Weekly public service hours: 83.

Computer facilities: Computer purchase and lease plans are available. A campuswide network can be accessed. Online class registration is available.
Website: http://www.fdu.edu/

General Application Contact: Susan Brooman, University Director, Graduate Admissions, 973-443-8905, Fax: 973-443-8088, E-mail: grad@fdu.edu.

GRADUATE UNITS

Anthony J. Petrocelli College of Continuing Studies Offers continuing studies (MAS, MPA, MS, MSA); sports administration (MSA).

International School of Hospitality and Tourism Management Offers hospitality management studies (MS).

Public Administration Institute Offers public administration (MPA).

School of Administrative Science Offers administrative science (MAS).

Maxwell Becton College of Arts and Sciences Offers arts and sciences (MA, MFA, MS, Certificate); biology (MS); chemistry (MS); clinical mental health counseling (MA); computer science (MS); corporate and organizational communication (MA); counseling (MA); creative nonfiction (MFA); creative writing (MFA); creative writing and literature for educators (MA); fiction (MFA); industrial/organizational psychology (MA); literary translation (MFA); organizational behavior (MA, Certificate); organizational leadership (Certificate); poetry (MFA); writing for young adults (MFA).

School of Pharmacy Offers pharmacy (Pharm D).

Silberman College of Business *Program availability:* Part-time, evening/weekend. Offers accounting (MS); business (EMBA, MBA, MS, Certificate); business administration (MBA); entrepreneurial studies (MBA, Certificate); evolving technology (Certificate); finance (MBA, Certificate); health care and life sciences (EMBA); international business (MBA, Certificate); international taxation (Certificate); management (EMBA, MBA, Certificate); managing sustainability (Certificate); marketing (MBA, Certificate); pharmaceutical studies (MBA, Certificate); supply chain management (MS); taxation (MS, Certificate).

Center for Human Resource Management Studies Offers human resource management (MBA); human resource management studies (MBA).

University College: Arts, Sciences, and Professional Studies Offers arts, sciences, and professional studies (MA, MAT, MSN, Certificate).

The Henry P. Becton School of Nursing and Allied Health *Program availability:* Part-time, evening/weekend. Offers adult gerontology primary care nurse practitioner (MSN); family psychiatric/mental health nurse practitioner (MSN).

Peter Sammartino School of Education Offers education for certified teachers (MA, Certificate); educational leadership (MA); instructional technology (Certificate); literacy/reading (Certificate); PreK - 3 certification (MA, MAT); teaching (MAT).

FAIRLEIGH DICKINSON UNIVERSITY, METROPOLITAN CAMPUS, Teaneck, NJ 07666-1914

General Information Independent, coed, university. *Enrollment:* 7,846 graduate, professional, and undergraduate students; 745 full-time matriculated graduate/professional students (392 women), 1,627 part-time matriculated graduate/professional students (1,110 women). *Enrollment by degree level:* 1,817 master's, 206 doctoral, 349 other advanced degrees. *Tuition:* Full-time $22,410; part-time $1245 per credit. *Required fees:* $888; $414 per unit. Tuition and fees vary according to course load, degree level and program. *Graduate housing:* Room and/or apartments available on a first-come, first-served basis to single students; on-campus housing not available to married students. Housing application deadline: 5/1. *Student services:* Campus employment opportunities, career counseling, exercise/wellness program, free psychological counseling, international student services, teacher training, writing training. *Library facilities:* Giovatto Library. *Collection:* Books: 157,566 (physical); Serial titles: 1,217 (physical), 126,248 (digital/electronic); Databases: 144. Weekly public service hours: 87.

Computer facilities: Computer purchase and lease plans are available. A campuswide network can be accessed. Online class registration is available.
Website: http://www.fdu.edu/

General Application Contact: Susan Brooman, University Director of Graduate Admissions, 201-692-2554, Fax: 201-692-2560, E-mail: globaleducation@fdu.edu.

GRADUATE UNITS

Anthony J. Petrocelli College of Continuing Studies Offers continuing studies (MAS, MPA, MS, MSA, MSHS, Certificate); sports administration (MSA).

International School of Hospitality and Tourism Management Offers hospitality management (MS).

Public Administration Institute Offers public administration (MPA, Certificate); public non-profit management (Certificate).

School of Administrative Science Offers administrative science (MAS, MSHS, Certificate); homeland security (MSHS).

Silberman College of Business Offers accounting (MBA, MS, Certificate); business (EMBA, MBA, MS, Certificate); business administration (MBA); chemical studies (Certificate); entrepreneurial studies (MBA, Certificate); executive management (EMBA); finance (MBA, Certificate); healthcare and life sciences (EMBA); international business (MBA); management (MBA, Certificate); management information systems (Certificate); marketing (MBA, Certificate); pharmaceutical studies (MBA, Certificate); taxation (MS).

Center for Human Resources Management Studies Offers human resource management (MBA, Certificate).

University College: Arts, Sciences, and Professional Studies Offers arts, sciences, and professional studies (MA, MAT, MS, MSEE, MSN, DNP, PhD, Psy D, Certificate); English and literature (MA); systems science (MS).

Henry P. Becton School of Nursing and Allied Health Offers medical technology (MS); nursing (MSN, Certificate); nursing practice (DNP).

Peter Sammartino School of Education *Program availability:* Part-time. Offers dyslexia specialist (Certificate); education for certified teachers (MA); educational leadership (MA); instructional technology (Certificate); learning disabilities (MA); literacy/reading (Certificate); multilingual education (MA); PreK - 3 certification (MA, MAT); teacher of the handicapped (Certificate); teaching (MAT).

School of Art and Media Studies Offers art and media studies (MA); media and communications (MA).

School of Computer Sciences and Engineering Offers computer engineering (MS); computer science (MS); e-commerce (MS); electrical engineering (MSEE); management information systems (MS); mathematical foundation (MS).

School of Criminal Justice and Legal Studies Offers criminal justice (MA).

School of History, Political and International Studies Offers history (MA); international studies (MA); political science (MA).

School of Natural Sciences Offers biology (MS); chemistry (MS); cosmetic science (MS); science (MA).

School of Psychology Offers clinical psychology (MA, PhD); clinical psychopharmacology (MA); forensic psychology (MA); general-theoretical psychology (MA, Certificate); school psychology (MA, Psy D).

FAIRMONT STATE UNIVERSITY, Fairmont, WV 26554

General Information State-supported, coed, comprehensive institution. CGS member. *Graduate housing:* Room and/or apartments available on a first-come, first-served basis to single students; on-campus housing not available to married students.

GRADUATE UNITS

Program in Business Administration *Program availability:* Part-time, evening/weekend. Offers business administration (MBA). Electronic applications accepted.

Program in Criminal Justice *Program availability:* Part-time, evening/weekend, 100% online. Offers criminal justice (MS). Electronic applications accepted.

Programs in Education *Program availability:* Part-time, evening/weekend, 100% online. Offers digital media, new literacies and learning (M Ed); education (MAT); exercise science, fitness and wellness (M Ed); professional studies (M Ed); reading (M Ed); special education (M Ed). Electronic applications accepted.

FAITH BAPTIST BIBLE COLLEGE AND THEOLOGICAL SEMINARY, Ankeny, IA 50023

General Information Independent-religious, coed, comprehensive institution. *Graduate housing:* Rooms and/or apartments available on a first-come, first-served basis to single and married students. Housing application deadline: 8/1.

GRADUATE UNITS

Graduate Program *Program availability:* Part-time. Offers Biblical studies (MA); pastoral studies (M Div); pastoral training (MA); religion (MA); theological studies (MA). Electronic applications accepted.

FAITH INTERNATIONAL UNIVERSITY, Tacoma, WA 98407

General Information Independent-religious, coed, graduate-only institution.

GRADUATE UNITS

Graduate and Professional Programs *Program availability:* Part-time, evening/weekend, online learning. Offers theology (M Div, MACM, MTS, D Min).

FAITH THEOLOGICAL SEMINARY, Baltimore, MD 21212

General Information Independent-religious, coed, comprehensive institution.

GRADUATE UNITS

Graduate Programs Offers theology (M Div, D Min, Th D).

FARMINGDALE STATE COLLEGE, Farmingdale, NY 11735

General Information State-supported, coed, comprehensive institution.

GRADUATE UNITS

Program in Technology Management Offers construction management (MS); electrical and mechanical engineering (MS).

FASHION INSTITUTE OF TECHNOLOGY, New York, NY 10001-5992

General Information State and locally supported, coed, primarily women, comprehensive institution. *Graduate housing:* Room and/or apartments available on a first-come, first-served basis to single students; on-campus housing not available to married students. *Research affiliation:* Exhibition Designers and Producers Association (exhibition design), Society for Environmental Graphic Design (exhibition design), Lolita S. A. (global fashion management), IDEO (design and management innovation), Grove Dictionary of Art, Oxford University Press (costume history).

GRADUATE UNITS

School of Graduate Studies *Program availability:* Part-time, evening/weekend. Offers art market studies (MA); cosmetics and fragrance marketing and management (MPS); exhibition and experience design (MA); fashion and textile studies: history, theory, museum practice (MA); fashion design (MFA); global fashion management (MPS); illustration (MFA). Electronic applications accepted.

FAULKNER UNIVERSITY, Montgomery, AL 36109-3398

General Information Independent-religious, coed, university. *Enrollment:* 3,350 graduate, professional, and undergraduate students; 570 full-time matriculated graduate/professional students (329 women), 108 part-time matriculated graduate/professional students (43 women). *Enrollment by degree level:* 454 master's, 224 doctoral. *Graduate faculty:* 24 full-time (16 women), 24 part-time/adjunct (18 women). *Tuition:* Full-time $9720; part-time $540 per semester hour. *Required fees:* $560; $280 per semester. Tuition and fees vary according to course load, degree level and program. *Graduate housing:* On-campus housing not available. *Student services:* Campus employment opportunities, career counseling, free psychological counseling, low-cost health insurance, services for students with disabilities, writing training. *Library facilities:* Gus Nichols Library System plus 4 others. *Collection:* Books: 121,708 (physical), 159,003 (digital/electronic); Serial titles: 2,098 (physical), 142,578 (digital/electronic); Databases: 134. Weekly public service hours: 74.

Computer facilities: 496 computers available on campus for general student use. A campuswide network can be accessed. Online class registration, student account access are available.
Website: http://www.faulkner.edu/

General Application Contact: Alison R. Cahoon, Director of Graduate Admissions, 334-386-7343, Fax: 334-386-7143, E-mail: acahoon@faulkner.edu.

GRADUATE UNITS

Alabama Christian College of Arts and Sciences Students: 84 full-time (46 women), 68 part-time (21 women); includes 139 minority (39 Black or African American, non-Hispanic/Latino; 2 American Indian or Alaska Native, non-Hispanic/Latino; 5 Hispanic/Latino; 92 Native Hawaiian or other Pacific Islander, non-Hispanic/Latino; 1

Two or more races, non-Hispanic/Latino), 1 international. Average age 38. 116 applicants, 52% accepted, 50 enrolled. *Faculty:* 2 full-time (0 women), 6 part-time/adjunct (1 woman). Expenses: Contact institution. *Financial support:* Application deadline: 7/15; applicants required to submit FAFSA. In 2017, 38 master's, 4 doctorates awarded. *Program availability:* Part-time, evening/weekend, 100% online, blended/hybrid learning. Offers arts and sciences (MA, MJA, PhD); humanities (MA, PhD); justice administration (MJA). *Application deadline:* For fall admission, 6/1 for domestic students; for spring admission, 11/1 for domestic students; for summer admission, 4/1 for domestic students. *Application fee:* $35. Electronic applications accepted. *Dean,* Dr. Jeffrey E. Arrington, 334-386-7105, Fax: 334-386-7147, E-mail: jarrington@faulkner.edu.

College of Biblical Studies Students: 28 full-time (9 women), 16 part-time (2 women); includes 21 minority (18 Black or African American, non-Hispanic/Latino; 2 Hispanic/Latino; 1 Two or more races, non-Hispanic/Latino), 1 international. Average age 39. 42 applicants, 45% accepted, 15 enrolled. *Faculty:* 7 full-time (1 woman). Expenses: Contact institution. *Financial support:* Applicants required to submit FAFSA. In 2017, 5 master's awarded. *Program availability:* Part-time, evening/weekend, 100% online, blended/hybrid learning, synchronous online/on-ground. Offers Biblical studies (MA, PhD); Christian counseling and family ministry (MA); Christian ministry (MA). *Application deadline:* For fall admission, 6/1 for domestic students; for spring admission, 11/1 for domestic students; for summer admission, 4/1 for domestic students. *Application fee:* $35. Electronic applications accepted. *Application Contact:* Dr. Randall C. Bailey, Director, Kearly Graduate School of Theology, 334-386-7663, Fax: 334-386-7203, E-mail: rbailey@faulkner.edu. *Dean/Vice President, Black College of Biblical Studies,* Dr. G. Scott Gleaves, 334-386-7660, Fax: 334-386-7203, E-mail: sgleaves@faulkner.edu.

College of Education Students: 140 full-time (107 women), 16 part-time (13 women); includes 97 minority (92 Black or African American, non-Hispanic/Latino; 1 American Indian or Alaska Native, non-Hispanic/Latino; 1 Asian, non-Hispanic/Latino; 3 Hispanic/Latino). Average age 37. 92 applicants, 55% accepted, 48 enrolled. *Faculty:* 13 full-time (8 women), 6 part-time/adjunct (1 woman). Expenses: Contact institution. *Financial support:* Applicants required to submit FAFSA. In 2017, 51 master's awarded. *Program availability:* Part-time, evening/weekend, 100% online, blended/hybrid learning. Offers counseling (MS); curriculum and instruction (M Ed); elementary education (M Ed); school counseling (M Ed). *Application deadline:* For fall admission, 8/1 for domestic students; for spring admission, 12/1 for domestic students; for summer admission, 5/1 for domestic students. *Application fee:* $35. Electronic applications accepted. *Application Contact:* Rebecca L. Horn, Director, Graduate Education, 334-386-7264, Fax: 334-386-7194, E-mail: rhorn@faulkner.edu. *Dean, College of Education,* Dr. Leslie S. Cowell, 334-386-7224, Fax: 334-386-7194, E-mail: lcowell@faulkner.edu.

Harris College of Business and Executive Education Students: 95 full-time (60 women), 8 part-time (7 women); includes 52 minority (47 Black or African American, non-Hispanic/Latino; 1 American Indian or Alaska Native, non-Hispanic/Latino; 1 Hispanic/Latino; 3 Two or more races, non-Hispanic/Latino), 2 international. Average age 36. 148 applicants, 59% accepted, 67 enrolled. *Faculty:* 4 full-time (1 woman), 1 part-time/adjunct (0 women). Expenses: Contact institution. *Financial support:* Applicants required to submit FAFSA. In 2017, 61 master's awarded. *Program availability:* Part-time, evening/weekend, 100% online, blended/hybrid learning. Offers business administration (MBA); management (MSM). *Application deadline:* For fall admission, 9/1 for domestic students; for spring admission, 1/15 for domestic students. Applications are processed on a rolling basis. *Application fee:* $35. Electronic applications accepted. *Application Contact:* Ralph W. Aisnworth, Director, MSM Program, 334-386-7571, Fax: 334-386-7569, E-mail: rainsworth@faulkner.edu. *Dean, Harris College of Business,* Dr. Dave A. Khadanga, 334-386-7112, E-mail: dkhadanga@faulkner.edu.

Thomas Goode Jones School of Law Offers law (JD). Electronic applications accepted.

FAYETTEVILLE STATE UNIVERSITY, Fayetteville, NC 28301-4298

General Information State-supported, coed, comprehensive institution. *Enrollment:* 6,226 graduate, professional, and undergraduate students; 456 full-time matriculated graduate/professional students (289 women), 384 part-time matriculated graduate/professional students (223 women). *Enrollment by degree level:* 761 master's, 79 doctoral. *Graduate faculty:* 50 full-time (24 women), 24 part-time/adjunct (15 women). Tuition, state resident: full-time $8604. Tuition, nonresident: full-time $19,669. *Graduate housing:* On-campus housing not available. *Student services:* Campus employment opportunities, career counseling, child daycare facilities, free psychological counseling, low-cost health insurance, services for students with disabilities. *Library facilities:* Charles W. Chestnut Library. *Collection:* Books: 218,500 (physical), 225,740 (digital/electronic); Serial titles: 298 (physical), 30,747 (digital/electronic); Databases: 427. Weekly public service hours: 97; students can reserve study rooms. *Research affiliation:* Research Triangle Park.

Computer facilities: Computer purchase and lease plans are available. 600 computers available on campus for general student use. A campuswide network can be accessed from student residence rooms and from off campus. Online class registration is available.
Website: http://www.uncfsu.edu/

General Application Contact: Melissa Wells, Assistant Director of Admissions, 910-672-1412, Fax: 910-672-2600, E-mail: mwells@uncfsu.edu.

GRADUATE UNITS

Graduate School Students: 456 full-time (289 women), 384 part-time (223 women); includes 505 minority (402 Black or African American, non-Hispanic/Latino; 12 American Indian or Alaska Native, non-Hispanic/Latino; 38 Asian, non-Hispanic/Latino; 45 Hispanic/Latino; 3 Native Hawaiian or other Pacific Islander, non-Hispanic/Latino; 5 Two or more races, non-Hispanic/Latino), 12 international. Average age 35. 549 applicants, 82% accepted, 368 enrolled. *Faculty:* 50 full-time (24 women), 24 part-time/adjunct (15 women). Expenses: Contact institution. *Financial support:* Research assistantships, institutionally sponsored loans, and unspecified assistantships available. Support available to part-time students. Financial award application deadline: 3/1; financial award applicants required to submit FAFSA. In 2017, 150 master's, 17 doctorates awarded. *Program availability:* Part-time, evening/weekend. Offers business administration (MBA); criminal justice (MA); middle grades (MA Ed); psychology (MA); school administration (MSA); social work (MSW); sociology (MA Ed); special education (MA Ed). *Application deadline:* For fall admission, 4/1 for domestic students, 3/1 for international students; for spring admission, 10/15 for domestic students. Applications are processed on a rolling basis. *Application fee:* $40. Electronic applications accepted. *Application Contact:* Melissa Wells, Assistant Director of Admissions, 910-672-1412, Fax: 910-672-2600. *Office of Admissions,* 910-672-1371, Fax: 910-672-2600.

FELICIAN UNIVERSITY, Lodi, NJ 07644-2117

General Information Independent-religious, coed, comprehensive institution. *Enrollment:* 1,996 graduate, professional, and undergraduate students; 83 full-time matriculated graduate/professional students (60 women), 287 part-time matriculated graduate/professional students (230 women). *Enrollment by degree level:* 312 master's, 48 doctoral, 8 other advanced degrees. *Graduate faculty:* 29 full-time (14 women), 22 part-time/adjunct (11 women). *Graduate housing:* Room and/or apartments available on a first-come, first-served basis to single students; on-campus housing not available to married students. Typical cost: $12,630 (including board). Housing application deadline: 5/1. *Student services:* Campus employment opportunities, campus safety program, career counseling, child daycare facilities, free psychological counseling, international student services, low-cost health insurance, services for students with disabilities, teacher training, writing training. *Library facilities:* Felician University Library plus 1 other. *Collection:* Books: 68,565 (physical), 158,952 (digital/electronic); Serial titles: 178 (physical), 51,874 (digital/electronic); Databases: 56. Weekly public service hours: 137; students can reserve study rooms.

Computer facilities: 190 computers available on campus for general student use. A campuswide network can be accessed from student residence rooms and from off campus. Online class registration is available.
Website: http://www.felician.edu/

General Application Contact: Michael Szarek, Assistant Vice-President of Graduate Admissions, 201-355-1450, E-mail: szarekm@felician.edu.

GRADUATE UNITS

Doctor of Nursing Practice Program Students: 9 part-time (all women); includes 4 minority (2 Black or African American, non-Hispanic/Latino; 2 Hispanic/Latino). Average age 55. 3 applicants, 67% accepted. *Faculty:* 4 full-time (all women). Expenses: Contact institution. *Financial support:* Federal Work-Study and scholarships/grants available. Financial award applicants required to submit FAFSA. In 2017, 2 doctorates awarded. *Program availability:* Evening/weekend, online only, 100% online, blended/hybrid learning. Offers advanced practice (DNP); executive leadership (DNP). *Application deadline:* Applications are processed on a rolling basis. *Application fee:* $40. Electronic applications accepted. *Application Contact:* Michael Szarek, Assistant Vice-President of Graduate Admissions, 201-355-1450, E-mail: szarekm@felician.edu. *Associate Dean of Graduate Nursing,* Dr. Ann Tritak, 201-559-6151, E-mail: tritaka@felician.edu.

Master of Science in Nursing Program Students: 96 part-time (90 women); includes 48 minority (17 Black or African American, non-Hispanic/Latino; 1 American Indian or Alaska Native, non-Hispanic/Latino; 16 Asian, non-Hispanic/Latino; 12 Hispanic/Latino; 1 Native Hawaiian or other Pacific Islander, non-Hispanic/Latino; 1 Two or more races, non-Hispanic/Latino). Average age 37. 49 applicants, 86% accepted, 23 enrolled. *Faculty:* 9 full-time (8 women), 1 (woman) part-time/adjunct. Expenses: Contact institution. *Financial support:* Federal Work-Study, scholarships/grants, and traineeships available. Financial award applicants required to submit FAFSA. In 2017, 35 master's, 3 other advanced degrees awarded. *Program availability:* Evening/weekend, online only, 100% online, blended/hybrid learning. Offers adult-gerontology nurse practitioner (MSN, PMC); executive leadership (MSN, PMC); family nurse practitioner (MSN, PMC); nursing education (MSN, PMC). *Application deadline:* Applications are processed on a rolling basis. *Application fee:* $40. Electronic applications accepted. *Application Contact:* Michael Szarek, Assistant Vice-President, Graduate Admissions, 201-355-1450, E-mail: szarekm@felician.edu. *Associate Dean of Graduate Nursing,* Dr. Ann Tritak, 201-559-6151, E-mail: tritaka@felician.edu.

Program in Business Students: 17 full-time (11 women), 94 part-time (59 women); includes 59 minority (25 Black or African American, non-Hispanic/Latino; 10 Asian, non-Hispanic/Latino; 24 Hispanic/Latino), 5 international. Average age 34. 68 applicants, 81% accepted, 34 enrolled. *Faculty:* 5 full-time (0 women), 17 part-time/adjunct (3 women). Expenses: Contact institution. *Financial support:* Federal Work-Study and scholarships/grants available. Financial award applicants required to submit FAFSA. In 2017, 20 master's awarded. *Program availability:* Part-time-only, evening/weekend, online learning. Offers business administration (DBA); innovation and entrepreneurial leadership (MBA). *Application deadline:* Applications are processed on a rolling basis. *Application fee:* $40. Electronic applications accepted. *Application Contact:* Michael Szarek, Assistant Vice-President of Graduate Admissions, 201-355-1450, E-mail: szarekm@felician.edu. *Associate Dean/Associate Professor, School of Business,* Dr. David M. Turi, 201-559-3327, E-mail: turid@felician.edu.

Program in Counseling Psychology Students: 58 full-time (45 women), 18 part-time (13 women); includes 46 minority (11 Black or African American, non-Hispanic/Latino; 3 Asian, non-Hispanic/Latino; 30 Hispanic/Latino; 1 Native Hawaiian or other Pacific Islander, non-Hispanic/Latino; 1 Two or more races, non-Hispanic/Latino), 3 international. Average age 31. 39 applicants, 82% accepted, 20 enrolled. *Faculty:* 4 full-time (1 woman), 8 part-time/adjunct (7 women). Expenses: Contact institution. *Financial support:* Federal Work-Study and scholarships/grants available. Financial award applicants required to submit FAFSA. In 2017, 12 master's awarded. *Program availability:* Part-time, evening/weekend. Offers counseling psychology (MA, Psy D). *Application deadline:* Applications are processed on a rolling basis. *Application fee:* $40. Electronic applications accepted. *Application Contact:* Michael Szarek, Assistant Vice-President of Graduate Admissions, 201-355-1450, E-mail: szarekm@felician.edu. *Director of the Master's in Counseling Program,* Dr. Daniel Mahoney, 201-559-6161, E-mail: mahoneyd@felician.edu.

Program in Education Students: 3 full-time (2 women), 51 part-time (48 women); includes 15 minority (4 Black or African American, non-Hispanic/Latino; 3 Asian, non-Hispanic/Latino; 8 Hispanic/Latino), 2 international. Average age 36. 29 applicants, 86% accepted, 12 enrolled. *Faculty:* 2 full-time (1 woman), 7 part-time/adjunct (2 women). Expenses: Contact institution. *Financial support:* Federal Work-Study and scholarships/grants available. Financial award applicants required to submit FAFSA. In 2017, 23 master's, 11 other advanced degrees awarded. *Program availability:* Part-time, evening/weekend. Offers education (MA); educational leadership (principal/supervision) (MA); educational supervision (PMC); principal (PMC). *Application deadline:* Applications are processed on a rolling basis. *Application fee:* $40. Electronic applications accepted. *Application Contact:* Michael Szarek, Assistant Vice-President, Graduate Admissions, 201-355-1450, E-mail: szarekm@felician.edu. *Dean of Education,* Stephanie McGowan, 201-559-3551, E-mail: mcgowans@felician.edu.

Program in Health Care Administration Students: 9 full-time (8 women), 36 part-time (29 women); includes 30 minority (14 Black or African American, non-Hispanic/Latino; 5 Asian, non-Hispanic/Latino; 11 Hispanic/Latino), 2 international. Average age 33. 28 applicants, 93% accepted, 16 enrolled. *Faculty:* 1 full-time (0 women), 6 part-time/adjunct (2 women). Expenses: Contact institution. *Financial support:* Federal Work-Study and scholarships/grants available. Financial award applicants required to submit FAFSA. In 2017, 6 master's awarded. *Program availability:* Part-time, evening/weekend. Offers health care administration (MSHA). *Application deadline:* Applications are processed on a rolling basis. *Application fee:* $40. Electronic applications accepted. *Application Contact:* Michael Szarek, Assistant Vice-President of Graduate Admissions, 201-355-1450, E-mail: szarekm@felician.edu. *Associate Dean/Associate Professor, School of Business*, Dr. David M. Turi, 201-559-3327, E-mail: turid@felician.edu.

Program in Religious Education Students: 1 (woman) full-time, 12 part-time (8 women); includes 2 minority (1 Asian, non-Hispanic/Latino; 1 Hispanic/Latino), 2 international. Average age 45. 5 applicants, 100% accepted, 5 enrolled. *Faculty:* 1 (woman) full-time, 5 part-time/adjunct (2 women). Expenses: Contact institution. *Financial support:* In 2017–18, 12 students received support. Federal Work-Study, scholarships/grants, and tuition waivers (partial) available. Financial award applicants required to submit FAFSA. In 2017, 7 master's awarded. *Program availability:* Part-time, evening/weekend, online only, 100% online. Offers religious education (MA, Certificate). *Application deadline:* Applications are processed on a rolling basis. *Application fee:* $40. Electronic applications accepted. *Application Contact:* Michael Szarek, Director of Graduate Admissions, 201-355-1450, E-mail: szarekm@felician.edu. *Dean of Academic Success Programs*, Dr. Dolores M. Henchy, 201-355-1133, E-mail: henchyd@felician.edu.

FERRIS STATE UNIVERSITY, Big Rapids, MI 49307

General Information State-supported, coed, comprehensive institution. CGS member. *Enrollment:* 13,798 graduate, professional, and undergraduate students; 895 full-time matriculated graduate/professional students (527 women), 309 part-time matriculated graduate/professional students (219 women). *Enrollment by degree level:* 413 master's, 690 doctoral, 101 other advanced degrees. *Graduate faculty:* 149 full-time (89 women), 167 part-time/adjunct (82 women). *Graduate housing:* Rooms and/or apartments available on a first-come, first-served basis to single and married students. Typical cost: $9894 (including board) for single students. *Student services:* Campus employment opportunities, campus safety program, career counseling, child daycare facilities, exercise/wellness program, free psychological counseling, international student services, low-cost health insurance, multicultural affairs office, services for students with disabilities, teacher training. *Library facilities:* Ferris Library for Information, Technology and Education. *Collection:* Books: 267,897 (physical), 214,655 (digital/electronic); Serial titles: 161 (physical), 160,936 (digital/electronic); Databases: 183. Weekly public service hours: 93; study areas open 24 hours, 5–7 days a week; students can reserve study rooms. *Research affiliation:* Allergan-Hydron (optometry), Bausch & Lomb (optometry), Ciba Vision (optometry), American Education Research Association (education), Vistakon-Johnson & Johnson (optometry).

Computer facilities: 1,723 computers available on campus for general student use. A campuswide network can be accessed from student residence rooms and from off campus. Online class registration is available.
Website: http://www.ferris.edu/

General Application Contact: Dr. Kristen Salomonson, Dean, Enrollment Services/Director, Admissions and Records, 231-591-2100, Fax: 231-591-3944, E-mail: admissions@ferris.edu.

GRADUATE UNITS

College of Arts and Sciences Students: 32 full-time (29 women), 30 part-time (28 women); includes 7 minority (3 Black or African American, non-Hispanic/Latino; 1 American Indian or Alaska Native, non-Hispanic/Latino; 2 Hispanic/Latino; 1 Two or more races, non-Hispanic/Latino), 1 international. Average age 32. 60 applicants, 77% accepted, 38 enrolled. *Faculty:* 7 full-time (all women), 5 part-time/adjunct (4 women). Expenses: Contact institution. *Financial support:* Federal Work-Study available. Financial award application deadline: 4/15; financial award applicants required to submit FAFSA. In 2017, 43 master's awarded. *Program availability:* Part-time, evening/weekend. Offers social work (MSW). *Application deadline:* For fall admission, 3/1 for domestic students. Electronic applications accepted. *Application Contact:* Dr. Janet Vizina-Roubal, MSW Coordinator, 231-357-2816, E-mail: janetvizinaroubal@ferris.edu. *Director of Social Work Program*, Dr. Wendy Samuels, 231-591-5896, E-mail: wendysamuels@ferris.edu.

College of Business Students: 19 full-time (10 women), 73 part-time (45 women); includes 8 minority (1 Black or African American, non-Hispanic/Latino; 2 Asian, non-Hispanic/Latino; 3 Hispanic/Latino; 2 Two or more races, non-Hispanic/Latino), 12 international. Average age 32. 52 applicants, 77% accepted, 16 enrolled. *Faculty:* 18 full-time (7 women), 6 part-time/adjunct (3 women). Expenses: Contact institution. *Financial support:* Career-related internships or fieldwork, Federal Work-Study, scholarships/grants, and unspecified assistantships available. Support available to part-time students. Financial award application deadline: 3/15; financial award applicants required to submit FAFSA. In 2017, 88 master's awarded. *Program availability:* Part-time, evening/weekend, 100% online, blended/hybrid learning. Offers business intelligence (MBA); design and innovation management (MBA); incident response (MBA); information security and intelligence (MS); lean systems and leadership (MBA); performance metrics (MBA); project management (MBA); supply chain management and lean logistics (MBA). *Application deadline:* For fall admission, 7/1 priority date for domestic students, 6/15 for international students; for winter admission, 11/1 priority date for domestic students, 10/15 for international students; for spring admission, 3/1 priority date for domestic students, 2/15 for international students. Applications are processed on a rolling basis. *Application fee:* $0 ($30 for international students). Electronic applications accepted. *Application Contact:* Dr. Greg Gogolin, Professor, 231-591-3159, Fax: 231-591-3521, E-mail: greggogolin@ferris.edu. *College of Business Dean*, Dr. David Nicol, 231-591-2168, Fax: 231-591-3521, E-mail: davidnicol@ferris.edu.

College of Education and Human Services Students: 10 full-time (6 women), 72 part-time (41 women); includes 21 minority (12 Black or African American, non-Hispanic/Latino; 4 Hispanic/Latino; 5 Two or more races, non-Hispanic/Latino), 4 international. Average age 35. 36 applicants, 97% accepted, 24 enrolled. *Faculty:* 15 full-time (6 women), 9 part-time/adjunct (6 women). Expenses: Contact institution. *Financial support:* In 2017–18, 1 research assistantship (averaging $4,850 per year) was awarded; career-related internships or fieldwork, Federal Work-Study, scholarships/grants, and unspecified assistantships also available. Support available to part-time students. Financial award applicants required to submit FAFSA. In 2017, 63 master's awarded. *Program availability:* Part-time, evening/weekend, blended/hybrid learning. Offers education and human services (M Ed, MS, MSCJ, MSCTE). *Application deadline:* For fall admission, 7/1 priority date for domestic and international students; for winter admission, 12/15 priority date for domestic and international students; for spring admission, 11/1 priority date for domestic and international students; for summer admission, 3/1 priority date for domestic and international students. Applications are processed on a rolling basis. *Application fee:* $30. Electronic applications accepted. *Application Contact:* Dr. Kristen Salomonson, Dean, Enrollment Services/Director, Admissions and Records, 231-591-2100, Fax: 231-591-3944, E-mail: admissions@ferris.edu. *Dean*, Arrick L. Jackson, 231-591-2702, Fax: 231-592-3792, E-mail: arrickjackson@ferris.edu.

School of Criminal Justice Students: 6 full-time (5 women), 32 part-time (18 women); includes 14 minority (9 Black or African American, non-Hispanic/Latino; 2 Hispanic/Latino; 3 Two or more races, non-Hispanic/Latino). Average age 35. 23 applicants, 100% accepted, 17 enrolled. *Faculty:* 8 full-time (2 women). Expenses: Contact institution. *Financial support:* In 2017–18, 1 research assistantship (averaging $4,850 per year) was awarded; Federal Work-Study and unspecified assistantships also available. Support available to part-time students. Financial award applicants required to submit FAFSA. In 2017, 17 master's awarded. *Program availability:* Part-time, evening/weekend. Offers criminal justice administration (MSCJ). *Application deadline:* For fall admission, 8/15 for domestic students; for winter admission, 12/15 for domestic students; for spring admission, 3/15 for domestic students. Applications are processed on a rolling basis. *Application fee:* $0. Electronic applications accepted. *Application Contact:* Sara P. Rasmussen, Secretary, 231-591-3652, Fax: 231-591-3792, E-mail: sararasmussen@ferris.edu. *Professor/Graduate Program Coordinator*, Dr. Nancy L. Hogan, 231-591-2664, Fax: 231-591-3792, E-mail: hogann@ferris.edu.

School of Education Students: 4 full-time (1 woman), 40 part-time (23 women); includes 7 minority (3 Black or African American, non-Hispanic/Latino; 2 Hispanic/Latino; 2 Two or more races, non-Hispanic/Latino), 4 international. Average age 37. 13 applicants, 92% accepted, 7 enrolled. *Faculty:* 7 full-time (4 women), 9 part-time/adjunct (6 women). Expenses: Contact institution. *Financial support:* Career-related internships or fieldwork and scholarships/grants available. Support available to part-time students. Financial award applicants required to submit FAFSA. In 2017, 36 master's awarded. *Program availability:* Part-time, evening/weekend, blended/hybrid learning. Offers curriculum and instruction (M Ed); educational leadership (MS); instructor (MSCTE); post-secondary administration (MSCTE); training and development (MSCTE). *Application deadline:* For fall admission, 7/1 priority date for domestic and international students; for spring admission, 11/1 priority date for domestic and international students; for summer admission, 3/1 priority date for domestic and international students. Applications are processed on a rolling basis. *Application fee:* $30. Electronic applications accepted. *Application Contact:* Liza Ing, Graduate Program Coordinator, 231-591-5362, Fax: 231-591-2043, E-mail: lizaIng@ferris.edu. *Dean*, Arrick L. Jackson, 231-591-2702, Fax: 231-591-2043, E-mail: arrickjackson@ferris.edu.

College of Health Professions Students: 28 full-time (25 women), 129 part-time (116 women); includes 22 minority (4 Black or African American, non-Hispanic/Latino; 6 American Indian or Alaska Native, non-Hispanic/Latino; 3 Asian, non-Hispanic/Latino; 3 Hispanic/Latino; 1 Native Hawaiian or other Pacific Islander, non-Hispanic/Latino; 5 Two or more races, non-Hispanic/Latino). Average age 34. 64 applicants, 91% accepted, 54 enrolled. *Faculty:* 16 full-time (13 women), 2 part-time/adjunct (both women). Expenses: Contact institution. *Financial support:* In 2017–18, 3 students received support. Career-related internships or fieldwork and scholarships/grants available. Financial award application deadline: 4/15; financial award applicants required to submit FAFSA. In 2017, 25 master's awarded. *Program availability:* Part-time, evening/weekend, 100% online. Offers health professions (MHA, MPH, MSN); healthcare administration (MHA); public health (MPH). *Application deadline:* For fall admission, 4/15 priority date for domestic students; for spring admission, 10/15 for domestic students. Applications are processed on a rolling basis. *Application fee:* $0. Electronic applications accepted. *Application Contact:* Dr. Kristen Salomonson, Dean of Enrollment Services and Director of Admissions and Records, 231-591-3963, Fax: 231-591-3179, E-mail: kristensalomonson@ferris.edu. *Dean*, Dr. Matthew Adeyanju, 231-591-2342, E-mail: matthewadeyanju@ferris.edu.

School of Nursing Students: 3 full-time (all women), 104 part-time (95 women); includes 15 minority (3 Black or African American, non-Hispanic/Latino; 5 American Indian or Alaska Native, non-Hispanic/Latino; 2 Asian, non-Hispanic/Latino; 3 Hispanic/Latino; 1 Native Hawaiian or other Pacific Islander, non-Hispanic/Latino; 1 Two or more races, non-Hispanic/Latino). Average age 40. 36 applicants, 92% accepted, 31 enrolled. *Faculty:* 7 full-time (all women), 2 part-time/adjunct (both women). Expenses: Contact institution. *Financial support:* In 2017–18, 3 students received support. Career-related internships or fieldwork and scholarships/grants available. Financial award application deadline: 4/15; financial award applicants required to submit FAFSA. In 2017, 25 master's awarded. *Program availability:* Part-time, evening/weekend, online only, 100% online. Offers nursing (MSN); nursing administration (MSN); nursing education (MSN); nursing informatics (MSN). *Application deadline:* For fall admission, 4/15 priority date for domestic students; for spring admission, 10/15 for domestic students. *Application fee:* $0. Electronic applications accepted. *Application Contact:* Sharon Colley, MSN Program Coordinator, 231-591-2288, Fax: 231-591-2325, E-mail: colleys@ferris.edu. *Chair, School of Nursing*, Dr. Susan Owens, 231-591-2267, Fax: 231-591-2325, E-mail: owenss3@ferris.edu.

College of Pharmacy Students: 547 full-time (305 women), 18 part-time (8 women); includes 38 minority (5 Black or African American, non-Hispanic/Latino; 1 American Indian or Alaska Native, non-Hispanic/Latino; 12 Asian, non-Hispanic/Latino; 14 Hispanic/Latino; 6 Two or more races, non-Hispanic/Latino), 16 international. Average age 24. 404 applicants, 44% accepted, 143 enrolled. *Faculty:* 35 full-time (24 women), 4 part-time/adjunct (2 women). Expenses: Contact institution. *Financial support:* Career-related internships or fieldwork, Federal Work-Study, institutionally sponsored loans, and scholarships/grants available. Financial award application deadline: 4/15; financial award applicants required to submit FAFSA. In 2017, 147 doctorates awarded. *Program availability:* Part-time, evening/weekend, online learning. Offers pharmacy (Pharm D). *Application deadline:* For fall admission, 2/1 for domestic and international students. *Application fee:* $150. *Application Contact:* Tara M. Lee, Director of Admissions, 231-591-2249, Fax: 231-591-3829, E-mail: leet@ferris.edu. *Dean*, Dr. Stephen Durst, 231-591-2254, Fax: 231-591-3829, E-mail: dursts@ferris.edu.

Extended and International Operations Students: 103 full-time (72 women), 2 part-time (0 women); includes 29 minority (19 Black or African American, non-Hispanic/Latino; 1 Asian, non-Hispanic/Latino; 9 Hispanic/Latino). Average age 46. 41 applicants, 73% accepted, 27 enrolled. *Faculty:* 25 part-time/adjunct (15 women). Expenses: Contact institution. *Financial support:* In 2017–18, 4 teaching assistantships (averaging $1,000 per year) were awarded. Financial award application deadline: 5/1; financial award applicants required to submit FAFSA. In 2017, 11 doctorates awarded. *Program availability:* Evening/weekend, blended/hybrid learning. Offers community college leadership (Ed D). *Application deadline:* For fall admission, 12/15 for domestic and international students; for winter admission, 1/27 for domestic and international students; for spring admission, 4/15 for domestic students, 4/18 for international students. Applications are processed on a rolling basis. *Application fee:* $0. Electronic applications accepted. *Application Contact:* Megan Biller, Coordinator, 231-591-2710, Fax: 231-591-3539, E-mail: meganbiller@ferris.edu. *Director*, Dr. Roberta Teahen, 231-591-3805, E-mail: robertateahen@ferris.edu.

Kendall College of Art and Design Students: 39 full-time (29 women), 15 part-time (9 women); includes 12 minority (4 Black or African American, non-Hispanic/Latino; 1 American Indian or Alaska Native, non-Hispanic/Latino; 3 Asian, non-Hispanic/Latino; 4 Hispanic/Latino), 6 international. Average age 31. 48 applicants, 60% accepted, 17 enrolled. *Faculty:* 21 full-time (15 women), 6 part-time/adjunct (2 women). Expenses: Contact institution. *Financial support:* In 2017–18, 32 students received support, including 8 fellowships (averaging $16,781 per year); scholarships/grants and unspecified assistantships also available. Financial award application deadline: 2/1; financial award applicants required to submit FAFSA. In 2017, 12 master's awarded. *Program availability:* Part-time. Offers architecture (M Arch); art education (MAE); design (MA); drawing (MFA); painting (MFA); photography (MFA); printmaking (MFA); visual and critical studies (MA). *Application deadline:* For fall admission, 2/1 priority date for domestic and international students; for spring admission, 11/1 priority date for domestic and international students. Applications are processed on a rolling basis. *Application fee:* $0. Electronic applications accepted. *Application Contact:* Thomas Post, Graduate Recruitment Specialist, 616-451-2787, Fax: 616-831-9689, E-mail: thomaspost@ferris.edu. *President,* Leslie Bellavance, 616-451-2787.

Michigan College of Optometry Students: 149 full-time (80 women); includes 4 minority (2 Asian, non-Hispanic/Latino; 2 Hispanic/Latino), 5 international. Average age 24. 177 applicants, 31% accepted, 37 enrolled. *Faculty:* 19 full-time (9 women), 115 part-time/adjunct (52 women). Expenses: Contact institution. *Financial support:* In 2017–18, 38 students received support. Career-related internships or fieldwork, Federal Work-Study, and scholarships/grants available. Financial award application deadline: 3/30; financial award applicants required to submit FAFSA. In 2017, 35 doctorates awarded. Offers optometry (OD). *Application deadline:* For fall admission, 2/1 for domestic and international students. Applications are processed on a rolling basis. *Application fee:* $165. Electronic applications accepted. *Application Contact:* Amy Parks, Health College Administrative Specialist, 231-591-3703, Fax: 231-591-2394, E-mail: amyparks@ferris.edu. *Dean,* Dr. David Damari, 231-591-3706, Fax: 231-591-2394, E-mail: damarid@ferris.edu.

FIELDING GRADUATE UNIVERSITY, Santa Barbara, CA 93105-3814

General Information Independent, coed, graduate-only institution. CGS member. *Enrollment by degree level:* 60 master's, 752 doctoral, 145 other advanced degrees. *Graduate faculty:* 52 full-time (34 women), 138 part-time/adjunct (86 women). Tuition and fees vary according to course load, degree level and program. *Graduate housing:* On-campus housing not available. *Student services:* Grant writing training, international student services, services for students with disabilities, writing training. *Library facilities:* Fielding Graduate University Library Services. *Collection:* Books: 203,776 (digital/electronic); Serial titles: 50,341 (digital/electronic); Databases: 94.

Computer facilities: Online class registration is available.
Website: http://www.fielding.edu/

General Application Contact: Admission Office, 800-340-1099, Fax: 805-687-9793, E-mail: admission@fielding.edu.

GRADUATE UNITS

Graduate Programs Students: 815 full-time (621 women), 142 part-time (101 women); includes 355 minority (136 Black or African American, non-Hispanic/Latino; 7 American Indian or Alaska Native, non-Hispanic/Latino; 34 Asian, non-Hispanic/Latino; 116 Hispanic/Latino; 2 Native Hawaiian or other Pacific Islander, non-Hispanic/Latino; 60 Two or more races, non-Hispanic/Latino), 9 international. Average age 44. 448 applicants, 65% accepted, 180 enrolled. *Faculty:* 52 full-time (34 women), 138 part-time/adjunct (86 women). Expenses: Contact institution. *Financial support:* In 2017–18, 215 students received support, including 2 research assistantships (averaging $300 per year), 9 teaching assistantships (averaging $1,900 per year); scholarships/grants also available. Support available to part-time students. Financial award applicants required to submit FAFSA. In 2017, 40 master's, 143 doctorates, 100 other advanced degrees awarded. *Program availability:* Part-time, evening/weekend, 100% online, blended/hybrid learning. *Application deadline:* For fall admission, 7/15 for domestic and international students; for spring admission, 11/1 for domestic and international students; for summer admission, 3/1 for domestic and international students. *Application fee:* $75. Electronic applications accepted. *Application Contact:* Enrollment Coordinator, 800-340-1099 Ext. 4098, Fax: 805-687-9793, E-mail: admissions@fielding.edu. *President,* Dr. Katrina Rogers, 805-898-2924, Fax: 805-687-9793, E-mail: krogers@fielding.edu.

School of Leadership Studies Students: 341 full-time (256 women), 72 part-time (53 women); includes 151 minority (64 Black or African American, non-Hispanic/Latino; 5 American Indian or Alaska Native, non-Hispanic/Latino; 15 Asian, non-Hispanic/Latino; 38 Hispanic/Latino; 2 Native Hawaiian or other Pacific Islander, non-Hispanic/Latino; 27 Two or more races, non-Hispanic/Latino), 5 international. Average age 49. 101 applicants, 94% accepted, 62 enrolled. *Faculty:* 19 full-time (12 women), 94 part-time/adjunct (63 women). Expenses: Contact institution. *Financial support:* In 2017–18, 70 students received support, including 1 research assistantship; scholarships/grants and tuition waivers (partial) also available. Support available to part-time students. Financial award applicants required to submit FAFSA. In 2017, 21 master's, 67 doctorates, 50 other advanced degrees awarded. *Program availability:* Part-time, evening/weekend, 100% online, blended/hybrid learning. Offers clinical mental health counseling (MA); comprehensive evidence based coaching (Graduate Certificate); couples/marriage and family therapy (MA); digital teaching and learning (MA); evidence based coaching for organizational leadership (Graduate Certificate); human development (PhD); infant and early childhood development (MA, PhD, Graduate Certificate); leadership for change (Ed D); leadership studies (MA, Ed D, PhD, Graduate Certificate); organizational consulting (Graduate Certificate); organizational development and change (PhD); organizational development and leadership (MA, Graduate Certificate). *Application deadline:* For fall admission, 7/1 for domestic and international students; for spring admission, 9/1 for domestic and international students; for summer admission, 3/1 for domestic and international students. *Application fee:* $75. Electronic applications accepted. *Application Contact:* Enrollment Coordinator, 800-340-1099 Ext. 4098, Fax: 805-687-9793, E-mail: hodadmission@fielding.edu. *Provost and Senior Vice President,* Dr. Gerald Porter, 805-898-2940, Fax: 805-687-9793, E-mail: gporter@fielding.edu.

School of Psychology Students: 474 full-time (365 women), 70 part-time (48 women); includes 204 minority (72 Black or African American, non-Hispanic/Latino; 2 American Indian or Alaska Native, non-Hispanic/Latino; 19 Asian, non-Hispanic/Latino; 78 Hispanic/Latino; 33 Two or more races, non-Hispanic/Latino), 4 international. Average age 41. 347 applicants, 57% accepted, 118 enrolled. *Faculty:* 33 full-time (22 women), 44 part-time/adjunct (23 women). Expenses: Contact institution. *Financial support:* In 2017–18, 104 students received support, including 1 research assistantship (averaging $400 per year), 9 teaching assistantships (averaging $1,900 per year); scholarships/grants also available. Support available to part-time students. Financial award applicants required to submit FAFSA. In 2017, 19 master's, 56 doctorates, 50 other advanced degrees awarded. *Program availability:* Part-time, evening/weekend, 100% online, blended/hybrid learning. Offers clinical psychology (PhD, Postbaccalaureate Certificate); media psychology (MA, PhD, Graduate Certificate); neuropsychology (Post-Doctoral Certificate); psychology (MA, PhD, Graduate Certificate, Post-Doctoral Certificate, Postbaccalaureate Certificate); respecialization in clinical psychology (Post-Doctoral Certificate). *Application deadline:* For fall admission, 1/24 for domestic and international students; for spring admission, 11/1 for domestic and international students; for summer admission, 3/1 for domestic and international students. *Application fee:* $75. Electronic applications accepted. *Application Contact:* Enrollment Coordinator, 800-340-1099 Ext. 4098, Fax: 805-687-9793, E-mail: psyadmission@fielding.edu. *Provost and Senior Vice President,* Dr. Gerald Porter, 805-898-2940, E-mail: gporter@fielding.edu.

FISHER COLLEGE, Boston, MA 02116-1500

General Information Independent, coed, comprehensive institution. *Enrollment:* 1,923 graduate, professional, and undergraduate students; 12 full-time matriculated graduate/professional students (6 women), 29 part-time matriculated graduate/professional students (16 women). *Enrollment by degree level:* 41 master's. *Graduate faculty:* 5 full-time (1 woman), 6 part-time/adjunct (1 woman). *Tuition:* Full-time $28,512; part-time $14,256 per semester. *Required fees:* $4800. Tuition and fees vary according to class time. *Graduate housing:* Room and/or apartments available on a first-come, first-served basis to single students; on-campus housing not available to married students. Typical cost: $15,768 (including board). Housing application deadline: 8/1. *Student services:* Campus employment opportunities, campus safety program, career counseling, free psychological counseling, international student services, low-cost health insurance, multicultural affairs office, services for students with disabilities, writing training. *Library facilities:* Fisher College Library. *Collection:* Books: 23,902 (physical), 105,119 (digital/electronic); Serial titles: 40 (physical); Databases: 104. Weekly public service hours: 72; study areas open 24 hours, 5–7 days a week; students can reserve study rooms.

Computer facilities: 208 computers available on campus for general student use. A campuswide network can be accessed from student residence rooms and from off campus. Online class registration is available.
Website: http://www.fisher.edu/

General Application Contact: Dr. Neil Trotta, Dean, 617-236-8867, Fax: 617-236-5462, E-mail: ntrotta@fisher.edu.

GRADUATE UNITS

Master of Business Administration Program Students: 12 full-time (6 women), 29 part-time (16 women); includes 13 minority (2 Black or African American, non-Hispanic/Latino; 1 Asian, non-Hispanic/Latino; 9 Hispanic/Latino; 1 Two or more races, non-Hispanic/Latino), 5 international. Average age 31. 57 applicants, 56% accepted, 19 enrolled. *Faculty:* 5 full-time (1 woman), 6 part-time/adjunct (1 woman). Expenses: Contact institution. *Financial support:* In 2017–18, 2 students received support. Scholarships/grants and unspecified assistantships available. Financial award applicants required to submit FAFSA. In 2017, 8 master's awarded. *Program availability:* Part-time, evening/weekend, online only, 100% online. Offers strategic leadership (MBA). *Application deadline:* For fall admission, 8/1 for domestic and international students; for winter admission, 11/1 for domestic and international students. Applications are processed on a rolling basis. Electronic applications accepted. *Assistant Dean, School of Graduate Studies/MBA Program Director,* Neil Trotta, 617-236-8867, Fax: 617-236-5462, E-mail: ntrotta@fisher.edu.

FISK UNIVERSITY, Nashville, TN 37208-3051

General Information Independent-religious, coed, comprehensive institution. *Graduate housing:* Rooms and/or apartments available on a first-come, first-served basis to single and married students. Housing application deadline: 4/6. *Research affiliation:* Oak Ridge Associated Universities (physics).

GRADUATE UNITS

Division of Graduate Studies *Program availability:* Part-time. Offers biology (MA); chemistry (MA); clinical psychology (MA); physics (MA); psychology (MA). Electronic applications accepted.

FITCHBURG STATE UNIVERSITY, Fitchburg, MA 01420-2697

General Information State-supported, coed, comprehensive institution. *Enrollment:* 7,075 graduate, professional, and undergraduate students; 916 full-time matriculated graduate/professional students (620 women), 516 part-time matriculated graduate/professional students (378 women). *Enrollment by degree level:* 1,369 master's, 63 other advanced degrees. *Graduate faculty:* 49 full-time (21 women), 194 part-time/adjunct (147 women). Tuition, state resident: part-time $167 per credit. Tuition, nonresident: part-time $167 per credit. *Required fees:* $137 per credit. *Graduate housing:* On-campus housing not available. *Student services:* Campus employment opportunities, campus safety program, career counseling, exercise/wellness program, free psychological counseling, international student services, low-cost health insurance, multicultural affairs office, services for students with disabilities, teacher training, writing training. *Library facilities:* Amelia V. Galucci-Cirio Library. *Collection:* Books: 222,517 (physical); Databases: 150. Weekly public service hours: 77.

Computer facilities: 500 computers available on campus for general student use. A campuswide network can be accessed from student residence rooms and from off campus. Online class registration is available.
Website: http://www.fitchburgstate.edu/

General Application Contact: Jinawa McNeil, Director of Admissions, 978-665-3140, Fax: 978-665-4540, E-mail: admissions@fitchburgstate.edu.

GRADUATE UNITS

Division of Graduate and Continuing Education Students: 916 full-time (620 women), 516 part-time (378 women); includes 182 minority (73 Black or African American, non-Hispanic/Latino; 5 American Indian or Alaska Native, non-Hispanic/Latino; 10 Asian, non-Hispanic/Latino; 69 Hispanic/Latino; 1 Native Hawaiian or other Pacific Islander, non-Hispanic/Latino; 24 Two or more races, non-Hispanic/Latino), 56 international. Average age 34. 665 applicants, 96% accepted, 528 enrolled. *Faculty:* 49 full-time (21 women), 147,177 part-time/adjunct (147,130 women). Expenses: Contact institution. *Financial support:* In 2017–18, research assistantships with partial tuition reimbursements (averaging $5,500 per year) were awarded; Federal Work-Study, scholarships/grants, and unspecified assistantships also available. Support available to part-time students. Financial award application deadline: 3/1; financial award applicants required to submit FAFSA. In 2017, 387 master's, 35 other advanced degrees awarded. *Program availability:* Part-time, evening/weekend, online learning. Offers accounting (MBA); applied communication studies (MS); applied communications (CAGS); arts education (M Ed); biology (MA); clinical mental health counseling (MS); computer science (MS); counseling/psychology (CAGS); curriculum and teaching (M Ed); data science (MS); early childhood education (M Ed); education technology (Certificate); educational leadership and management (M Ed, CAGS); elementary education (M Ed); English (M Ed); English and teaching English (secondary level) (MA, MAT, Certificate); fine arts director (Certificate); forensic nursing (MS, Certificate); general science (M Ed); guided studies: dyslexia specialist (M Ed); guided studies: individualized (M Ed); guided studies: professional (M Ed); higher education administration (CAGS); history (M Ed); history and teaching history (secondary level) (MA); human resources management (MBA); individualized track (CAGS); management (MBA); math (M Ed); moderate disabilities: initial licensure (5-12) (M Ed); moderate disabilities: initial licensure (PK-8) (M Ed); occupational education (M Ed); reading specialist (CAGS); school guidance counseling (MS); school principal (M Ed, CAGS); science education (M Ed); supervisor/director (M Ed, CAGS); teacher of students with severe disabilities (M Ed); technical and professional writing (MS); technology education (M Ed). *Application deadline:* For fall admission, 7/15 for international students; for spring admission, 12/1 for international students. Applications are processed on a rolling basis. *Application fee:* $50. Electronic applications accepted. *Application Contact:* Jinawa McNeil, Director of Admissions, 978-665-3140, Fax: 978-665-4540, E-mail: admissions@fitchburgstate.edu. *Dean*, Becky Copper Glenz, 978-665-3564, Fax: 978-665-3658, E-mail: gce@fitchburgstate.edu.

FIVE BRANCHES UNIVERSITY, Santa Cruz, CA 95062

General Information Independent, coed, graduate-only institution. *Graduate housing:* On-campus housing not available. *Research affiliation:* Highland Hospital (healthcare).

GRADUATE UNITS

Graduate School of Traditional Chinese Medicine Offers acupuncture (M Ac); acupuncture and Oriental medicine (DAOM); traditional Chinese medicine (MTCM, PhD). Electronic applications accepted.

FIVE TOWNS COLLEGE, Dix Hills, NY 11746-6055

General Information Independent, coed, comprehensive institution. *Enrollment:* 21 full-time matriculated graduate/professional students (7 women), 6 part-time matriculated graduate/professional students (2 women). *Enrollment by degree level:* 10 master's, 14 doctoral, 3 other advanced degrees. *Graduate faculty:* 12 full-time (3 women), 6 part-time/adjunct (0 women). *Graduate housing:* Room and/or apartments available on a first-come, first-served basis to single students; on-campus housing not available to married students. *Student services:* Campus employment opportunities, campus safety program, career counseling, international student services, low-cost health insurance, services for students with disabilities, teacher training, writing training. *Library facilities:* Five Towns College Library plus 1 other.

Computer facilities: 110 computers available on campus for general student use. A campuswide network can be accessed from student residence rooms.
Website: http://www.ftc.edu/

General Application Contact: Ronnie MacDonald, Director of Admissions, 631-656-2110, Fax: 631-656-2172, E-mail: admissions@ftc.edu.

GRADUATE UNITS

Graduate Programs Students: 18 full-time (7 women), 6 part-time (2 women); includes 9 minority (3 Black or African American, non-Hispanic/Latino; 4 Asian, non-Hispanic/Latino; 1 Hispanic/Latino; 1 Two or more races, non-Hispanic/Latino), 1 international. Average age 35. 63 applicants, 11% accepted, 7 enrolled. *Faculty:* 12 full-time (3 women), 6 part-time/adjunct (0 women). Expenses: Contact institution. *Financial support:* Fellowships with tuition reimbursements, teaching assistantships with tuition reimbursements, and tuition waivers (partial) available. Financial award applicants required to submit FAFSA. In 2017, 4 master's, 2 doctorates awarded. *Program availability:* Part-time. Offers childhood education (MS Ed); composition and arranging (DMA); jazz/commercial music (MM); music education (MM, DMA); music history and literature (DMA); music performance (DMA). *Application deadline:* For fall admission, 9/1 for domestic and international students; for spring admission, 1/25 for domestic and international students. Applications are processed on a rolling basis. *Application fee:* $50. Electronic applications accepted. *Application Contact:* Ronnie MacDonald, Director of Admissions, 631-656-2110, Fax: 631-656-2172, E-mail: admissions@ftc.edu.

FLAGLER COLLEGE, St. Augustine, FL 32085-1027

General Information Independent, coed, comprehensive institution.

GRADUATE UNITS

Program in Deaf Education Offers deaf education (MA).

FLORIDA AGRICULTURAL AND MECHANICAL UNIVERSITY, Tallahassee, FL 32307-3200

General Information State-supported, coed, university. CGS member. *Graduate housing:* Rooms and/or apartments available on a first-come, first-served basis to single and married students. Housing application deadline: 6/1. *Research affiliation:* Boeing (aerospace science), Minority Health Professions Foundation (health science), Pfizer, Inc.

GRADUATE UNITS

College of Law *Program availability:* Part-time, evening/weekend. Offers law (JD).

Division of Graduate Studies, Research, and Continuing Education *Program availability:* Part-time, evening/weekend.

College of Education *Program availability:* Part-time, evening/weekend. Offers administration and supervision (M Ed, MS, PhD); adult education (M Ed, MS); biology (M Ed); business education (MBE); chemistry (MS Ed); education (M Ed, MBE, MS, MS Ed, PhD); educational leadership (PhD); elementary education (M Ed, MS); English (MS Ed); guidance and counseling (M Ed, MS); history (MS Ed); industrial education (MS Ed); math (MS Ed); physics (MS Ed); sport management (MS); technology education (M Ed).

College of Pharmacy and Pharmaceutical Sciences Offers environmental toxicology (PhD); health outcomes research and pharmacoeconomics (PhD); medicinal chemistry (MS, PhD); pharmaceutics (MS, PhD); pharmacology/toxicology (MS, PhD); pharmacy administration (MS); pharmacy and pharmaceutical sciences (MPH, MS, DPH, PhD, Pharm D); public health (MPH, DPH).

College of Science and Technology Offers chemistry (MS); physics (MS, PhD); science and technology (MS, PhD); software engineering (MS).

College of Social Sciences, Arts and Humanities *Program availability:* Part-time. Offers community psychology (MS); criminal justice (MASS); history (MASS); history and political science (MASS, MSW); political science (MASS); public administration (MASS); social sciences, arts and humanities (MASS, MS, MSW); social work (MSW).

FAMU-FSU College of Engineering Offers biomedical engineering (MS, PhD); chemical engineering (MS, PhD); civil engineering (M Eng, MS, PhD); electrical engineering (MS, PhD); engineering (M Eng, MS, PhD); industrial engineering (MS, PhD); mechanical engineering (MS, PhD). College administered jointly by Florida State University.

School of Allied Health Sciences Offers health administration (MS); occupational therapy (MOT); physical therapy (DPT).

School of Architecture *Program availability:* Part-time. Offers architectural studies (MS Arch); architecture (professional) (M Arch); landscape architecture (MLA).

School of Business and Industry Offers accounting (MBA); finance (MBA); management information systems (MBA); marketing (MBA).

School of Journalism and Graphic Communication Offers journalism (MS).

School of Nursing Offers nursing (MSN, PhD).

School of the Environment Students: 31 full-time (14 women), 2 part-time (1 woman); includes 28 minority (23 Black or African American, non-Hispanic/Latino; 1 Asian, non-Hispanic/Latino; 4 Hispanic/Latino). Average age 25. 23 applicants, 78% accepted, 13 enrolled. *Faculty:* 10 full-time (1 woman), 3 part-time/adjunct (1 woman). Expenses: Contact institution. *Financial support:* In 2017–18, 27 students received support, including 11 fellowships, 21 research assistantships (averaging $18,000 per year); career-related internships or fieldwork, institutionally sponsored loans, scholarships/grants, health care benefits, tuition waivers (partial), and unspecified assistantships also available. Financial award application deadline: 6/10; financial award applicants required to submit FAFSA. In 2017, 3 master's, 2 doctorates awarded. Offers the environment (MS, PhD). *Application deadline:* For fall admission, 6/30 priority date for domestic students, 3/30 priority date for international students; for spring admission, 11/1 priority date for domestic students, 10/1 priority date for international students. *Application fee:* $30. Electronic applications accepted. *Application Contact:* Diane Hall, Coordinator, Research Programs and Services, 850-561-2641, Fax: 850-599-8183, E-mail: diane.hall@famu.edu. *Dean*, Dr. Victor M. Ibeanusi, 850-599-3550, Fax: 850-599-8183, E-mail: victor.ibeanusi@famu.edu.

FLORIDA ATLANTIC UNIVERSITY, Boca Raton, FL 33431-0991

General Information State-supported, coed, university. CGS member. *Enrollment:* 30,203 graduate, professional, and undergraduate students; 2,174 full-time matriculated graduate/professional students (1,189 women), 2,727 part-time matriculated graduate/professional students (1,710 women). *Enrollment by degree level:* 3,718 master's, 1,145 doctoral, 38 other advanced degrees. *Graduate faculty:* 644 full-time (244 women), 58 part-time/adjunct (31 women). Tuition, state resident: full-time $7400; part-time $369.82 per credit. Tuition, nonresident: full-time $20,496; part-time $1042.81 per credit. *Graduate housing:* Room and/or apartments guaranteed to single students; on-campus housing not available to married students. Typical cost: $8320 per year. *Student services:* Campus employment opportunities, campus safety program, career counseling, exercise/wellness program, free psychological counseling, international student services, low-cost health insurance, multicultural affairs office, services for students with disabilities, teacher training. *Library facilities:* S. E. Wimberly Library plus 2 others. *Collection:* Books: 1.4 million (physical), 1.2 million (digital/electronic); Serial titles: 29,249 (physical), 105,472 (digital/electronic); Databases: 581. Study areas open 24 hours, 5–7 days a week. *Research affiliation:* Max Planck Florida Institute for Neuroscience (neuroscience), The Vaccine and Gene Institute of Florida (biomedical sciences), Torrey Pines Institute for Molecular Studies (medical research), The Scripps Research Institute (biomedical sciences).

Computer facilities: 1,350 computers available on campus for general student use. A campuswide network can be accessed from student residence rooms and from off campus. Online class registration is available.
Website: http://www.fau.edu/

General Application Contact: Jordan Hession, Assistant Director, Graduate Orientation and Admissions, 561-297-1213, Fax: 561-297-1212, E-mail: jparks3@fau.edu.

GRADUATE UNITS

Charles E. Schmidt College of Medicine Students: 277 full-time (127 women), 17 part-time (12 women); includes 109 minority (25 Black or African American, non-Hispanic/Latino; 43 Asian, non-Hispanic/Latino; 36 Hispanic/Latino; 5 Two or more races, non-Hispanic/Latino), 2 international. Average age 25. 3,714 applicants, 2% accepted, 84 enrolled. Expenses: Contact institution. *Financial support:* Fellowships and research assistantships available. Financial award applicants required to submit FAFSA. In 2017, 25 master's, 62 doctorates awarded. *Program availability:* Part-time. Offers biomedical science (MS); medicine (MD). *Application deadline:* For fall admission, 5/1 for domestic students, 3/15 for international students; for spring admission, 10/1 for domestic and international students. *Application fee:* $30. Electronic applications accepted. *Senior Director of Administration*, Deborah Roski, 561-297-2142, E-mail: dsalerno@health.fau.edu.

Charles E. Schmidt College of Science Students: 237 full-time (111 women), 182 part-time (78 women); includes 113 minority (18 Black or African American, non-Hispanic/Latino; 19 Asian, non-Hispanic/Latino; 59 Hispanic/Latino; 17 Two or more races, non-Hispanic/Latino), 80 international. Average age 29. 350 applicants, 37% accepted, 111 enrolled. *Faculty:* 150 full-time (40 women), 9 part-time/adjunct (2 women). Expenses: Contact institution. *Financial support:* Fellowships with partial tuition reimbursements, research assistantships with partial tuition reimbursements, teaching assistantships with partial tuition reimbursements, career-related internships or fieldwork, Federal Work-Study, institutionally sponsored loans, scholarships/grants, tuition waivers (partial), and unspecified assistantships available. Financial award applicants required to submit FAFSA. In 2017, 94 master's, 30 doctorates awarded. *Program availability:* Part-time. Offers applied mathematics and statistics (MS); biology (MS, MST); chemistry (MS, MST, PhD); geology (MS); geosciences (PhD); mathematics (MST, PhD); physics (MS, MST, PhD); psychology (MA); science (MA, MS, MSMP, MST, PhD). *Application deadline:* For fall admission, 6/1 for domestic students, 2/15 for international students; for spring admission, 11/1 for domestic students, 8/15 for international students. Applications are processed on a rolling basis. *Application fee:* $30. Electronic applications accepted. *Dean*, Ata Sarejedini, 561-297-3301, E-mail: ata@fau.edu.

Center for Complex Systems and Brain Sciences Students: 8 full-time (1 woman), 6 part-time (2 women); includes 4 minority (1 Black or African American, non-Hispanic/Latino; 1 Asian, non-Hispanic/Latino; 1 Hispanic/Latino; 1 Two or more races, non-Hispanic/Latino), 2 international. Average age 31. 10 applicants, 10% accepted, 1 enrolled. *Faculty:* 1 full-time (0 women). Expenses: Contact institution. *Financial support:* Fellowships with full tuition reimbursements, research assistantships with partial tuition reimbursements, teaching assistantships with partial tuition reimbursements, Federal Work-Study, and traineeships available. In 2017, 1 doctorate awarded. Offers complex systems and brain sciences (PhD). *Application deadline:* For fall admission, 1/15 priority date for domestic and international students. *Application fee:* $30. *Graduate Coordinator*, Dr. Armin Fuchs, 561-297-0125, E-mail: fuchs@ccs.fau.edu.

Christine E. Lynn College of Nursing Students: 61 full-time (57 women), 443 part-time (405 women); includes 265 minority (133 Black or African American, non-Hispanic/Latino; 33 Asian, non-Hispanic/Latino; 87 Hispanic/Latino; 1 Native Hawaiian or other Pacific Islander, non-Hispanic/Latino; 11 Two or more races, non-Hispanic/Latino), 6 international. Average age 37. 569 applicants, 28% accepted, 128 enrolled. *Faculty:* 32 full-time (31 women), 7 part-time/adjunct (6 women). Expenses: Contact institution. *Financial support:* Research assistantships with partial tuition reimbursements, teaching assistantships with partial tuition reimbursements, career-related internships or fieldwork, Federal Work-Study, institutionally sponsored loans, scholarships/grants, and traineeships available. Support available to part-time students. In 2017, 131 master's, 28 doctorates awarded. *Program availability:* Part-time. Offers administrative and financial leadership in nursing and health care (Post Master's Certificate); nursing (MSN, PhD); nursing practice (DNP). *Application deadline:* For fall admission, 6/1 for domestic students, 2/15 for international students; for spring admission, 10/1 for domestic students, 7/15 for international students. Applications are processed on a rolling basis. *Application fee:* $30. *Dean,* Marlaine Smith, 561-297-3206, E-mail: msmit230@health.fau.edu.

College for Design and Social Inquiry Students: 202 full-time (142 women), 238 part-time (174 women); includes 203 minority (104 Black or African American, non-Hispanic/Latino; 10 Asian, non-Hispanic/Latino; 72 Hispanic/Latino; 17 Two or more races, non-Hispanic/Latino), 7 international. Average age 32. 544 applicants, 44% accepted, 183 enrolled. *Faculty:* 45 full-time (15 women), 1 part-time/adjunct (0 women). Expenses: Contact institution. *Financial support:* Fellowships with partial tuition reimbursements, research assistantships with partial tuition reimbursements, teaching assistantships with partial tuition reimbursements, career-related internships or fieldwork, Federal Work-Study, and institutionally sponsored loans available. Support available to part-time students. Financial award application deadline: 4/1. In 2017, 248 master's, 6 doctorates awarded. *Program availability:* Part-time, evening/weekend. Offers design and social inquiry (MNM, MPA, MS, MSW, MURP, DSW, PhD). *Application deadline:* For fall admission, 5/1 for domestic students, 2/15 for international students; for spring admission, 11/1 for domestic students, 7/15 for international students. Applications are processed on a rolling basis. *Application fee:* $30. *Dean,* Dr. Wesley Hawkins, 561-297-4168, E-mail: whawkins@fau.edu.

Phyllis and Harvey Sandler School of Social Work Students: 137 full-time (105 women), 120 part-time (103 women); includes 106 minority (49 Black or African American, non-Hispanic/Latino; 5 Asian, non-Hispanic/Latino; 39 Hispanic/Latino; 13 Two or more races, non-Hispanic/Latino), 1 international. Average age 32. 371 applicants, 49% accepted, 140 enrolled. *Faculty:* 12 full-time (7 women), 1 (woman) part-time/adjunct. Expenses: Contact institution. *Financial support:* Fellowships with tuition reimbursements, research assistantships with tuition reimbursements, career-related internships or fieldwork, Federal Work-Study, institutionally sponsored loans, and tuition waivers (partial) available. Financial award application deadline: 4/1. In 2017, 130 master's awarded. *Program availability:* Part-time, evening/weekend. Offers social work (MSW, DSW). *Application deadline:* For fall admission, 5/1 priority date for domestic students, 2/15 for international students. Applications are processed on a rolling basis. *Application fee:* $30. *Program Coordinator,* Joy McClellan, 561-297-3234, E-mail: jmcclel2@fau.edu.

School of Criminology and Criminal Justice Students: 20 full-time (16 women), 29 part-time (22 women); includes 33 minority (21 Black or African American, non-Hispanic/Latino; 1 Asian, non-Hispanic/Latino; 10 Hispanic/Latino; 1 Two or more races, non-Hispanic/Latino). Average age 27. 57 applicants, 35% accepted, 15 enrolled. *Faculty:* 9 full-time (2 women). Expenses: Contact institution. *Financial support:* Research assistantships, institutionally sponsored loans, scholarships/grants, and unspecified assistantships available. Financial award application deadline: 4/1. In 2017, 38 master's awarded. *Program availability:* Part-time, evening/weekend, online learning. Offers criminology and criminal justice (MS). *Application deadline:* For fall admission, 5/1 priority date for domestic students, 2/15 for international students; for spring admission, 11/1 priority date for domestic students, 7/15 for international students. Applications are processed on a rolling basis. *Application fee:* $30. Electronic applications accepted. *Assistant Graduate Coordinator,* Sigal Rubin, 561-297-4936, E-mail: rubins@fau.edu.

School of Public Administration Students: 28 full-time (14 women), 77 part-time (44 women); includes 48 minority (24 Black or African American, non-Hispanic/Latino; 3 Asian, non-Hispanic/Latino; 19 Hispanic/Latino; 2 Two or more races, non-Hispanic/Latino), 5 international. Average age 34. 80 applicants, 31% accepted, 16 enrolled. *Faculty:* 12 full-time (4 women), 1 part-time/adjunct (0 women). Expenses: Contact institution. *Financial support:* Fellowships with full tuition reimbursements, research assistantships with partial tuition reimbursements, teaching assistantships with partial tuition reimbursements, career-related internships or fieldwork, Federal Work-Study, institutionally sponsored loans, and tuition waivers (partial) available. Support available to part-time students. Financial award application deadline: 4/1. In 2017, 56 master's, 6 doctorates awarded. *Program availability:* Part-time, evening/weekend. Offers public administration (MPA, PhD). *Application deadline:* For fall admission, 5/1 priority date for domestic students, 2/15 for international students; for spring admission, 11/1 for domestic students, 7/15 for international students. Applications are processed on a rolling basis. *Application fee:* $30. *Program Coordinator,* Leslie Leip, 954-924-8818, E-mail: lleip@fau.edu.

School of Urban and Regional Planning Students: 17 full-time (7 women), 12 part-time (5 women); includes 16 minority (10 Black or African American, non-Hispanic/Latino; 1 Asian, non-Hispanic/Latino; 4 Hispanic/Latino; 1 Two or more races, non-Hispanic/Latino), 1 international. Average age 30. 36 applicants, 33% accepted, 12 enrolled. *Faculty:* 3 full-time (1 woman). Expenses: Contact institution. *Financial support:* Fellowships with full tuition reimbursements, research assistantships, career-related internships or fieldwork, Federal Work-Study, institutionally sponsored loans, and tuition waivers (partial) available. Financial award application deadline: 4/1. In 2017, 24 master's awarded. *Program availability:* Part-time, evening/weekend. Offers urban and regional planning (MURP). *Application deadline:* For fall admission, 5/1 priority date for domestic students, 2/15 for international students; for spring admission, 11/1 priority date for domestic students, 7/15 for international students. Applications are processed on a rolling basis. *Application fee:* $30. *Application Contact:* Alejandra Quintero, E-mail: mquinte5@fau.edu.

College of Business Students: 664 full-time (326 women), 1,026 part-time (554 women); includes 808 minority (277 Black or African American, non-Hispanic/Latino; 3 American Indian or Alaska Native, non-Hispanic/Latino; 98 Asian, non-Hispanic/Latino; 386 Hispanic/Latino; 1 Native Hawaiian or other Pacific Islander, non-Hispanic/Latino; 43 Two or more races, non-Hispanic/Latino), 93 international. Average age 32. 1,211 applicants, 65% accepted, 620 enrolled. *Faculty:* 106 full-time (34 women), 4 part-time/adjunct (3 women). Expenses: Contact institution. *Financial support:* Fellowships with partial tuition reimbursements, research assistantships with partial tuition reimbursements, teaching assistantships with full tuition reimbursements, career-related internships or fieldwork, Federal Work-Study, institutionally sponsored loans, tuition waivers (full and partial), and unspecified assistantships available. Support available to part-time students. Financial award application deadline: 3/1. In 2017, 562 master's, 10 doctorates awarded. *Program availability:* Part-time, evening/weekend, online learning. Offers business (M Tax, MAC, MBA, MHA, MS, PhD); business administration (MBA); economics (MS); entrepreneurship (MBA); health administration (MBA); information technology management (MS); international business (MBA); sport management (MBA). *Application deadline:* For fall admission, 5/1 priority date for domestic students, 2/15 priority date for international students; for spring admission, 4/1 priority date for domestic students, 1/15 priority date for international students. Applications are processed on a rolling basis. *Application fee:* $30. *Dean,* Daniel Gropper, 561-297-3635, E-mail: dgropper@fau.edu.

School of Accounting Students: 145 full-time (62 women), 455 part-time (247 women); includes 288 minority (63 Black or African American, non-Hispanic/Latino; 1 American Indian or Alaska Native, non-Hispanic/Latino; 42 Asian, non-Hispanic/Latino; 158 Hispanic/Latino; 24 Two or more races, non-Hispanic/Latino), 23 international. Average age 31. 504 applicants, 63% accepted, 247 enrolled. *Faculty:* 15 full-time (5 women), 3 part-time/adjunct (2 women). Expenses: Contact institution. *Financial support:* Fellowships, research assistantships with partial tuition reimbursements, teaching assistantships, career-related internships or fieldwork, Federal Work-Study, institutionally sponsored loans, scholarships/grants, and tuition waivers (partial) available. Support available to part-time students. Financial award application deadline: 3/1. In 2017, 242 master's awarded. *Program availability:* Part-time, evening/weekend, online learning. Offers accounting (MAC). *Application deadline:* For fall admission, 7/1 priority date for domestic students, 2/15 priority date for international students; for spring admission, 11/1 priority date for domestic students, 7/15 priority date for international students. Applications are processed on a rolling basis. *Application fee:* $30. *Director,* George Young, 561-297-3636, E-mail: soa@fau.edu.

College of Education Students: 324 full-time (242 women), 495 part-time (372 women); includes 344 minority (168 Black or African American, non-Hispanic/Latino; 13 Asian, non-Hispanic/Latino; 146 Hispanic/Latino; 17 Two or more races, non-Hispanic/Latino), 17 international. Average age 33. 986 applicants, 38% accepted, 259 enrolled. *Faculty:* 76 full-time (44 women), 22 part-time/adjunct (13 women). Expenses: Contact institution. *Financial support:* Fellowships with partial tuition reimbursements, research assistantships with partial tuition reimbursements, teaching assistantships with partial tuition reimbursements, career-related internships or fieldwork, Federal Work-Study, and unspecified assistantships available. In 2017, 205 master's, 25 doctorates, 20 other advanced degrees awarded. *Program availability:* Part-time, evening/weekend. Offers adult and community education (M Ed, PhD, Ed S); counselor education (MS, PhD); curriculum and instruction (M Ed, PhD, Ed S); early childhood education (M Ed); education (M Ed, MA, MS, Ed D, PhD, Ed S); educational leadership (M Ed, PhD, Ed S); elementary education (M Ed); environmental education (M Ed); exceptional student education (M Ed, Ed D); exercise science and health promotion (MS); higher education (M Ed, PhD); instructional technology (M Ed); K-12 school leadership (M Ed, PhD, Ed S); multicultural education (M Ed); reading education (M Ed); secondary education (M Ed); speech-language pathology (MS); TESOL and bilingual education (MA). *Application deadline:* For fall admission, 5/1 for domestic students. Applications are processed on a rolling basis. *Application fee:* $30. Electronic applications accepted. *Dean,* Dr. Valerie Bristor, 561-297-3357, E-mail: bristor@fau.edu.

College of Engineering and Computer Science Students: 184 full-time (49 women), 203 part-time (43 women); includes 117 minority (19 Black or African American, non-Hispanic/Latino; 22 Asian, non-Hispanic/Latino; 65 Hispanic/Latino; 11 Two or more races, non-Hispanic/Latino), 138 international. Average age 31. 339 applicants, 47% accepted, 116 enrolled. *Faculty:* 77 full-time (8 women), 3 part-time/adjunct (0 women). Expenses: Contact institution. *Financial support:* Fellowships, research assistantships with partial tuition reimbursements, teaching assistantships with partial tuition reimbursements, career-related internships or fieldwork, Federal Work-Study, and unspecified assistantships available. Support available to part-time students. Financial award applicants required to submit FAFSA. In 2017, 95 master's, 22 doctorates awarded. *Program availability:* Part-time, evening/weekend, online learning. Offers bioengineering (MS); civil engineering (MS); computer engineering (MS, PhD); computer science (MS, PhD); electrical engineering (MS, PhD); engineering and computer science (MS, PhD); environmental engineering (MS); mechanical engineering (MS, PhD). *Application deadline:* For fall admission, 7/1 for domestic students, 2/15 for international students; for spring admission, 11/1 for domestic students, 7/15 for international students. Applications are processed on a rolling basis. *Application fee:* $30. *Dean,* Dr. Stella Batalama, 561-297-3454, E-mail: sbatalama@fau.edu.

Dorothy F. Schmidt College of Arts and Letters Students: 225 full-time (135 women), 123 part-time (72 women); includes 130 minority (36 Black or African American, non-Hispanic/Latino; 1 American Indian or Alaska Native, non-Hispanic/Latino; 9 Asian, non-Hispanic/Latino; 74 Hispanic/Latino; 10 Two or more races, non-Hispanic/Latino), 26 international. Average age 33. 245 applicants, 53% accepted, 106 enrolled. *Faculty:* 157 full-time (72 women), 10 part-time/adjunct (6 women). Expenses: Contact institution. *Financial support:* Fellowships with partial tuition reimbursements, research assistantships, teaching assistantships, career-related internships or fieldwork, Federal Work-Study, institutionally sponsored loans, and tuition waivers (partial) available. Support available to part-time students. In 2017, 110 master's, 4 doctorates awarded. *Program availability:* Part-time. Offers acting (MFA); American literature (MA); anthropology (MA, MAT); arts and letters (MA, MAT, MFA, MM, PhD, Certificate); comparative literature (MA); comparative studies (PhD); design and technology (MFA); French (MA); history (MA); linguistics (MA); music (MM); political science (MA); sociology (MA); Spanish (MA); visual art (MFA). *Application deadline:* For fall admission, 6/1 priority date for domestic students. Applications are processed on a rolling basis. *Application fee:* $30. Electronic applications accepted. *Dean,* Michael Horswell, 561-297-3803, E-mail: horswell@fau.edu.

Center for Women, Gender and Sexuality Studies Students: 6 full-time (4 women), 3 part-time (2 women); includes 4 minority (2 Hispanic/Latino; 2 Two or more races, non-Hispanic/Latino). Average age 28. 6 applicants, 67% accepted, 4 enrolled. *Faculty:* 2 full-time (both women). Expenses: Contact institution. *Financial support:* Fellowships with tuition reimbursements, teaching assistantships with tuition reimbursements, career-related internships or fieldwork, Federal Work-Study, institutionally sponsored loans, scholarships/grants, and unspecified assistantships available. Support available to part-time students. Financial award applicants required to submit FAFSA. In 2017, 5 master's awarded. *Program availability:* Part-time. Offers women, gender and sexuality studies (MA). *Application deadline:* For fall admission, 7/1 for domestic students, 2/15 for international students; for spring admission, 11/1 for domestic students, 7/15 for international students. Applications are processed on a rolling basis. *Application fee:* $30. Electronic applications accepted. *Associate Dean/Director,* Barclay Barrious, 561-297-4573, E-mail: bbarrios@fau.edu.

School of Communication and Multimedia Studies Students: 21 full-time (15 women), 16 part-time (9 women); includes 19 minority (11 Black or African American, non-Hispanic/Latino; 1 Asian, non-Hispanic/Latino; 6 Hispanic/Latino; 1 Two or more races, non-Hispanic/Latino), 2 international. Average age 32. 29 applicants, 52% accepted, 13 enrolled. *Faculty:* 24 full-time (8 women). Expenses: Contact institution. *Financial support:* Teaching assistantships with partial tuition reimbursements, Federal Work-Study, institutionally sponsored loans, scholarships/grants, and unspecified assistantships available. Support available to part-time students. Financial award application deadline: 3/1; financial award applicants required to submit FAFSA. In 2017, 15 master's awarded. *Program availability:* Part-time. Offers communication studies (MA); film and video (Certificate); media, technology and entertainment (MFA). *Application deadline:* For fall admission, 7/1 priority date for domestic students, 4/1 for international students; for spring admission, 11/1 for domestic students, 10/1 for international students. Applications are processed on a rolling basis. *Application fee:* $30. Electronic applications accepted. *Application Contact:* Dr. Stephen Charbonneau, Graduate Director, 561-297-3856, Fax: 561-297-2615, E-mail: efreedma@fau.edu. *Director,* Dr. David Williams, 561-297-0045, Fax: 561-297-2615, E-mail: dcwill@fau.edu.

FLORIDA COASTAL SCHOOL OF LAW, Jacksonville, FL 32256

General Information Proprietary, coed, graduate-only institution.

GRADUATE UNITS

Professional Program *Program availability:* Part-time. Offers law (JD). Electronic applications accepted.

FLORIDA COLLEGE OF INTEGRATIVE MEDICINE, Orlando, FL 32809

General Information Proprietary, coed, graduate-only institution. *Graduate housing:* On-campus housing not available.

GRADUATE UNITS

Graduate Program *Program availability:* Evening/weekend. Offers Oriental medicine (MSOM). Electronic applications accepted.

FLORIDA GULF COAST UNIVERSITY, Fort Myers, FL 33965-6565

General Information State-supported, coed, comprehensive institution. CGS member. *Enrollment:* 14,983 graduate, professional, and undergraduate students; 449 full-time matriculated graduate/professional students (298 women), 565 part-time matriculated graduate/professional students (379 women). *Enrollment by degree level:* 822 master's, 67 doctoral. *Graduate faculty:* 465 full-time (213 women), 420 part-time/adjunct (220 women). Tuition, state resident: part-time $290 per credit hour. Tuition, nonresident: part-time $1173 per credit hour. *Required fees:* $127 per credit hour. Tuition and fees vary according to course load. *Graduate housing:* Room and/or apartments available on a first-come, first-served basis to single students; on-campus housing not available to married students. Typical cost: $4820 per year ($8619 including board). Room and board charges vary according to board plan and housing facility selected. Housing application deadline: 4/1. *Student services:* Campus employment opportunities, campus safety program, career counseling, child daycare facilities, exercise/wellness program, free psychological counseling, international student services, low-cost health insurance, multicultural affairs office, services for students with disabilities, teacher training. *Library facilities:* Library Services plus 1 other. *Collection:* Books: 242,131 (physical), 73,000 (digital/electronic); Serial titles: 128,865 (digital/electronic); Databases: 389. Students can reserve study rooms. *Research affiliation:* Department of Education (education), Small Business Administration (business), Department of Commerce, U.S. Fish and Wildlife Service (biological sciences), Florida Department of Environmental Protection (biological sciences), National Institute of Standards and Technology.

Computer facilities: Computer purchase and lease plans are available. 1,029 computers available on campus for general student use. A campuswide network can be accessed from student residence rooms and from off campus. Online class registration, online admissions and advising are available.
Website: http://www.fgcu.edu/

General Application Contact: Francisco Marquez, Graduate Studies Admissions, 239-590-7908, E-mail: graduate@fgcu.edu.

GRADUATE UNITS

College of Arts and Sciences Students: 79 full-time (53 women), 156 part-time (102 women); includes 52 minority (12 Black or African American, non-Hispanic/Latino; 2 Asian, non-Hispanic/Latino; 33 Hispanic/Latino; 1 Native Hawaiian or other Pacific Islander, non-Hispanic/Latino; 4 Two or more races, non-Hispanic/Latino), 3 international. Average age 31. 109 applicants, 70% accepted, 61 enrolled. *Faculty:* 245 full-time (104 women), 155 part-time/adjunct (71 women). Expenses: Contact institution. *Financial support:* In 2017–18, 29 students received support. Research assistantships, Federal Work-Study, scholarships/grants, and unspecified assistantships available. Financial award application deadline: 6/30; financial award applicants required to submit FAFSA. In 2017, 60 master's awarded. *Program availability:* Part-time, blended/hybrid learning. Offers arts and sciences (MA, MPA, MS); criminal justice (MS); English (MA); environmental policy (MPA); environmental science (MS); environmental studies (MA); forensic studies (MS); history (MA); management (MPA); mathematics (MS). *Application deadline:* For fall admission, 2/15 priority date for domestic students, 5/1 for international students; for spring admission, 12/1 for domestic students, 9/15 for international students. Applications are processed on a rolling basis. *Application fee:* $30. Electronic applications accepted. *Application Contact:* Patricia Rice, Executive Secretary, 239-590-7196, Fax: 239-590-7200, E-mail: price@fgcu.edu. *Dean,* Dr. Robert Gregerson, 239-590-7156, Fax: 239-590-7200, E-mail: rgregerson@fgcu.edu.

College of Education Students: 13 full-time (11 women), 84 part-time (70 women). Average age 36. 62 applicants, 94% accepted, 46 enrolled. *Faculty:* 27 full-time (19 women), 44 part-time/adjunct (30 women). Expenses: Contact institution. *Financial support:* In 2017–18, 17 students received support. Application deadline: 6/30; applicants required to submit FAFSA. In 2017, 49 master's awarded. *Program availability:* Part-time, evening/weekend, online learning. Offers behavior disorders (M Ed); education (M Ed, MA); educational leadership (M Ed, MA); elementary education (M Ed); English education (M Ed); English speakers of other languages endorsement (M Ed); gifted education (M Ed); mathematics education (M Ed); mental retardation (M Ed); middle school education (M Ed); reading education (M Ed); science education (M Ed); social science education (M Ed); special education (M Ed); specific learning disabilities (M Ed); varying exceptionalities (M Ed). *Application deadline:* For fall admission, 2/15 priority date for domestic students, 5/1 for international students; for spring admission, 12/1 for domestic students, 9/15 for international students. Applications are processed on a rolling basis. *Application fee:* $30. Electronic applications accepted. *Application Contact:* Shannon Acosta, Graduate Studies Admissions, 239-590-7027, Fax: 239-590-7843, E-mail: sacosta@fgcu.edu. *Dean,* Dr. Eunny Hyun, 239-590-7791, Fax: 239-590-7801, E-mail: ehyun@fgcu.edu.

Elaine Nicpon Marieb College of Health and Human Services Students: 187 full-time (147 women), 133 part-time (98 women); includes 114 minority (33 Black or African American, non-Hispanic/Latino; 12 Asian, non-Hispanic/Latino; 61 Hispanic/Latino; 8 Two or more races, non-Hispanic/Latino), 3 international. Average age 29. 473 applicants, 51% accepted, 186 enrolled. *Faculty:* 71 full-time (49 women), 49 part-time/adjunct (32 women). Expenses: Contact institution. *Financial support:* In 2017–18, 62 students received support. Career-related internships or fieldwork, Federal Work-Study, and institutionally sponsored loans available. Financial award application deadline: 6/30; financial award applicants required to submit FAFSA. In 2017, 111 master's, 32 doctorates awarded. *Program availability:* Part-time, evening/weekend, online learning. Offers clinical mental health counseling (MA); health and human services (MA, MPAS, MS, MSN, MSW, DNP, DPT); health science (MS); nurse anesthesia (MSN); nurse educator (MSN); occupational therapy (MS); physical therapy (DPT); physician assistant studies (MPAS); school counseling (MA); social work (MSW). *Application deadline:* For fall admission, 2/15 priority date for domestic students; for spring admission, 12/1 for domestic students. Applications are processed on a rolling basis. *Application fee:* $30. Electronic applications accepted. *Application Contact:* Susan Baurer, Administrative Assistant, 239-590-7451, E-mail: sbaurer@fgcu.edu. *Interim Dean,* Dr. Joan Glacken, 239-590-7498, E-mail: jglacken@fgcu.edu.

Lutgert College of Business Students: 50 full-time (29 women), 108 part-time (53 women); includes 34 minority (5 Black or African American, non-Hispanic/Latino; 1 American Indian or Alaska Native, non-Hispanic/Latino; 4 Asian, non-Hispanic/Latino; 21 Hispanic/Latino; 3 Two or more races, non-Hispanic/Latino), 8 international. Average age 29. 119 applicants, 61% accepted, 56 enrolled. *Faculty:* 60 full-time (24 women), 31 part-time/adjunct (7 women). Expenses: Contact institution. *Financial support:* In 2017–18, 15 students received support. Application deadline: 6/30; applicants required to submit FAFSA. In 2017, 60 master's awarded. *Program availability:* Part-time, evening/weekend. Offers accounting and taxation (MS); business (MBA, MS); business administration (MBA); information systems and analytics (MS). *Application deadline:* For fall admission, 2/15 priority date for domestic students, 5/1 for international students; for spring admission, 12/1 priority date for domestic students, 9/15 for international students. Applications are processed on a rolling basis. *Application fee:* $30. Electronic applications accepted. *Application Contact:* Judy Wynekoop, Associate Dean and Professor of Computer Information Systems, 239-590-7387, Fax: 239-590-7330, E-mail: jwynekoo@fgcu.edu. *Dean, Lutgert College of Business,* Robert Beatty, 239-590-7300, Fax: 239-590-7330, E-mail: rbeatty@fgcu.edu.

FLORIDA INSTITUTE OF TECHNOLOGY, Melbourne, FL 32901-6975

General Information Independent, coed, university. *Enrollment:* 6,402 graduate, professional, and undergraduate students; 1,299 full-time matriculated graduate/professional students (631 women), 1,451 part-time matriculated graduate/professional students (480 women). *Enrollment by degree level:* 2,133 master's, 617 doctoral. *Graduate faculty:* 236 full-time (41 women), 130 part-time/adjunct (31 women). *Tuition:* Part-time $1241 per credit hour. Part-time tuition and fees vary according to campus/location. *Graduate housing:* Room and/or apartments available on a first-come, first-served basis to single students; on-campus housing not available to married students. Typical cost: $7000 per year ($12,880 including board). Room and board charges vary according to board plan, campus/location and housing facility selected. Housing application deadline: 6/1. *Student services:* Campus employment opportunities, campus safety program, career counseling, exercise/wellness program, free psychological counseling, international student services, low-cost health insurance, multicultural affairs office, services for students with disabilities, writing training. *Library facilities:* Evans Library. *Collection:* Books: 131,564 (physical), 728,454 (digital/electronic); Serial titles: 1,605 (physical), 56,994 (digital/electronic); Databases: 161. Weekly public service hours: 96; students can reserve study rooms. *Research affiliation:* Boeing (digital signal processing aeronautics), Siemens (mechanical and aerospace engineering), General Electric-Harris (software testing), IBM (software technology, information assurance), Microsoft Corporation (simulation software development), Lockheed Martin Corporation (biological sciences).

Computer facilities: 254 computers available on campus for general student use. A campuswide network can be accessed from student residence rooms and from off campus. Online class registration is available.
Website: http://www.fit.edu/

General Application Contact: Cheryl A. Brown, Associate Director of Graduate Admissions, 321-674-7581, Fax: 321-723-9468, E-mail: cbrown@fit.edu.

GRADUATE UNITS

College of Aeronautics Students: 50 full-time (14 women), 67 part-time (18 women); includes 17 minority (9 Black or African American, non-Hispanic/Latino; 1 Asian, non-Hispanic/Latino; 6 Hispanic/Latino; 1 Two or more races, non-Hispanic/Latino), 43 international. Average age 33. 63 applicants, 52% accepted, 17 enrolled. *Faculty:* 13 full-time (5 women), 1 part-time/adjunct (0 women). Expenses: Contact institution. *Financial support:* In 2017–18, 6 research assistantships with partial tuition reimbursements were awarded; teaching assistantships with partial tuition reimbursements, career-related internships or fieldwork, institutionally sponsored loans, tuition waivers (partial), and tuition remissions also available. Financial award application deadline: 3/1; financial award applicants required to submit FAFSA. In 2017, 51 master's, 4 doctorates awarded. *Program availability:* Part-time, evening/weekend, 100% online. Offers airport development and management (MSA); applied aviation safety (MSA); aviation human factors (MS); aviation safety (MSA); aviation sciences (PhD); human factors in aeronautics (MS). *Application deadline:* For fall admission, 4/1 for international students; for spring admission, 9/30 for international students. Applications are processed on a rolling basis. Electronic applications accepted. *Application Contact:* Cheryl A. Brown, Associate Director of Graduate Admissions, 321-674-7581, Fax: 321-723-9468, E-mail: cbrown@fit.edu. *Dean,* Dr. Korhan Oyman, 321-674-8971, Fax: 321-674-7368, E-mail: koyman@fit.edu.

College of Engineering Average age 28. 2,952 applicants, 42% accepted, 252 enrolled. Expenses: Contact institution. *Financial support:* In 2017–18, 74 research assistantships with partial tuition reimbursements, 65 teaching assistantships with partial tuition reimbursements were awarded; career-related internships or fieldwork, institutionally sponsored loans, unspecified assistantships, and tuition remissions also available. Support available to part-time students. Financial award application deadline: 3/1; financial award applicants required to submit FAFSA. In 2017, 412 master's, 25 doctorates awarded. *Program availability:* Part-time. Offers aerospace engineering (MS, PhD); biological oceanography (MS); biomedical engineering (MS, PhD); chemical engineering (MS, PhD); chemical oceanography (MS); civil engineering (MS, PhD); coastal management (MS); computer engineering (MS, PhD); computer information systems (MS); computer science (MS, PhD); earth remote sensing (MS); electrical engineering (MS, PhD); engineering (MS, PhD); engineering management (MS); environmental resource management (MS); environmental science (MS, PhD); flight test engineering (MS); geological oceanography (MS); information assurance and cybersecurity (MS); mechanical engineering (MS, PhD); meteorology (MS); ocean engineering (MS, PhD); oceanography (PhD); physical oceanography (MS); software engineering (MS); systems engineering (MS, PhD). *Application deadline:* For fall admission, 4/1 for international students; for spring admission, 9/30 for international students. Applications are processed on a rolling basis. Electronic applications accepted. *Application Contact:* Cheryl A. Brown, Associate Director of Graduate Admissions, 321-674-7581, Fax: 321-723-9468, E-mail: cbrown@fit.edu. *Dean*, Dr. Martin Glicksman, 321-674-8020, Fax: 321-674-7270, E-mail: coe@fit.edu.

College of Psychology and Liberal Arts Average age 29. 735 applicants, 36% accepted, 138 enrolled. *Faculty:* 34 full-time (17 women), 9 part-time/adjunct (4 women). Expenses: Contact institution. *Financial support:* In 2017–18, 68 research assistantships with partial tuition reimbursements, 31 teaching assistantships with partial tuition reimbursements (averaging $8,002 per year) were awarded; fellowships, career-related internships or fieldwork, institutionally sponsored loans, tuition waivers (partial), unspecified assistantships, and tuition remissions also available. Support available to part-time students. Financial award application deadline: 3/1; financial award applicants required to submit FAFSA. In 2017, 144 master's, 28 doctorates awarded. *Program availability:* Part-time, evening/weekend, 100% online. Offers applied behavior analysis (MS); applied behavior analysis and organizational behavior management (MS); behavior analysis (PhD); clinical psychology (Psy D); global strategic communication (MS); industrial/organizational psychology (MS, PhD); organizational behavior management (MS); professional behavior analysis (MA); psychology and liberal arts (MA, MS, PhD, Psy D). *Application deadline:* For fall admission, 4/1 for international students; for spring admission, 9/30 for international students. Applications are processed on a rolling basis. Electronic applications accepted. *Application Contact:* Cheryl A. Brown, Associate Director of Graduate Admissions, 321-674-7581, Fax: 321-723-9468, E-mail: cbrown@fit.edu. *Dean*, Dr. Mary Beth Kenkel, 321-674-8142, Fax: 321-674-7105, E-mail: mkenkel@fit.edu.

College of Science Average age 30. 715 applicants, 41% accepted, 85 enrolled. Expenses: Contact institution. *Financial support:* In 2017–18, 23 research assistantships with partial tuition reimbursements, 74 teaching assistantships with partial tuition reimbursements were awarded; career-related internships or fieldwork, institutionally sponsored loans, tuition waivers (partial), unspecified assistantships, and tuition remissions also available. Support available to part-time students. Financial award application deadline: 3/1; financial award applicants required to submit FAFSA. In 2017, 75 master's, 13 doctorates awarded. *Program availability:* Part-time, evening/weekend. Offers applied mathematics (MS, PhD); biochemistry (MS); biological science (PhD); biotechnology (MS); cell and molecular biology (MS); chemistry (MS, PhD); computer education (MS); conservation technology (MS); ecology (MS); educational technology (MS); elementary science education (M Ed); environmental education (MS); interdisciplinary science (MS); marine biology (MS); mathematics education (MS, PhD, Ed S); operations research (MS, PhD); physics (MS, PhD); science (M Ed, MAT, MS, PhD, Ed S); science education (MS, PhD, Ed S); science education: informal science education (MS); space sciences (MS, PhD); teaching (MAT). *Application deadline:* For fall admission, 3/1 for domestic students, 4/1 for international students; for spring admission, 9/1 for domestic students, 9/30 for international students. Applications are processed on a rolling basis. Electronic applications accepted. *Application Contact:* Cheryl A. Brown, Associate Director of Graduate Admissions, 321-674-7581, Fax: 321-723-9468, E-mail: cbrown@fit.edu. *Dean*, Dr. Hamid K. Rassoul, 321-674-7273, Fax: 321-674-8864, E-mail: rassoul@fit.edu.

Extended Studies Division Average age 36. 962 applicants, 48% accepted, 323 enrolled. Expenses: Contact institution. *Financial support:* Application deadline: 3/1; applicants required to submit FAFSA. In 2017, 403 master's awarded. *Program availability:* Part-time, evening/weekend, online learning. Offers acquisition and contract management (MS); aerospace engineering (MS); business administration (MBA, DBA); computer information systems (MS); computer science (MS); electrical engineering (MS); engineering management (MS); human resources management (MS); logistics management (MS); management (MS); material acquisition management (MS); mechanical engineering (MS); operations research (MS); project management (MS); public administration (MPA); quality management (MS); software engineering (MS); space systems (MS); space systems management (MS); supply chain management (MS); systems management (MS); technology management (MS). *Application deadline:* For fall admission, 4/1 for international students; for spring admission, 9/30 for international students. Applications are processed on a rolling basis. Electronic applications accepted. *Application Contact:* Carolyn Farrior, Director of Graduate Admissions, Online Learning and Off-Campus Programs, 321-674-7118, Fax: 321-674-8216, E-mail: cfarrior@fit.edu. *Dean*, Dr. Theodore R. Richardson, III, 321-674-8123, Fax: 321-674-7597, E-mail: trichardson@fit.edu.

Nathan M. Bisk College of Business Average age 33. 206 applicants, 40% accepted, 18 enrolled. Expenses: Contact institution. *Financial support:* Research assistantships with partial tuition reimbursements, career-related internships or fieldwork, institutionally sponsored loans, and unspecified assistantships available. Support available to part-time students. Financial award application deadline: 3/1; financial award applicants required to submit FAFSA. In 2017, 192 master's awarded. *Program availability:* Part-time, online learning. Offers business (MBA, MS); business administration (MBA); healthcare management (MBA); innovation and entrepreneurship (MS). *Application deadline:* For fall admission, 4/1 for international students; for spring admission, 9/30 for international students. Applications are processed on a rolling basis. Electronic applications accepted. *Application Contact:* Cheryl A. Brown, Associate Director of Graduate Admissions, 321-674-7581, Fax: 321-723-9468, E-mail: cbrown@fit.edu. *Dean*, Dr. Theodore R. Richardson, III, 321-674-8123, Fax: 321-674-7597, E-mail: trichardson@fit.edu.

School of Human-Centered Design, Innovation and Art Average age 35. 21 applicants, 57% accepted, 4 enrolled. Expenses: Contact institution. *Financial support:* In 2017–18, 5 research assistantships with partial tuition reimbursements were awarded; career-related internships or fieldwork, institutionally sponsored loans, tuition waivers (partial), unspecified assistantships, and tuition remissions also available. Financial award application deadline: 3/1; financial award applicants required to submit FAFSA. In 2017, 4 master's, 1 doctorate awarded. *Program availability:* Part-time, evening/weekend. Offers human-centered design (MS, PhD). *Application deadline:* For fall admission, 4/1 for international students; for spring admission, 9/30 for international students. Applications are processed on a rolling basis. Electronic applications accepted. *Application Contact:* Cheryl A. Brown, Associate Director of Graduate Admissions, 321-674-7581, Fax: 321-723-9468, E-mail: cbrown@fit.edu. *Director*, Dr. Guy Boy, 321-674-7631, Fax: 321-984-8461, E-mail: gboy@fit.edu.

FLORIDA INTERNATIONAL UNIVERSITY, Miami, FL 33199

General Information State-supported, coed, university. CGS member. *Enrollment:* 56,851 graduate, professional, and undergraduate students; 6,271 full-time matriculated graduate/professional students (3,755 women), 2,429 part-time matriculated graduate/professional students (1,431 women). *Enrollment by degree level:* 5,980 master's, 2,720 doctoral. *Graduate faculty:* 1,182 full-time (510 women), 1,100 part-time/adjunct (530 women). Tuition, state resident: full-time $8912; part-time $446 per credit hour. Tuition, nonresident: full-time $21,393; part-time $992 per credit hour. *Required fees:* $390; $195 per semester. *Graduate housing:* Rooms and/or apartments available on a first-come, first-served basis to single and married students. Typical cost: $13,248 per year ($18,712 including board) for single students. *Student services:* Campus employment opportunities, campus safety program, career counseling, child daycare facilities, exercise/wellness program, free psychological counseling, international student services, low-cost health insurance, multicultural affairs office, services for students with disabilities, writing training. *Library facilities:* Steven and Dorothea Green Library plus 4 others. *Collection:* Books: 1.5 million (physical), 443,863 (digital/electronic); Serial titles: 63,945 (physical), 111,662 (digital/electronic); Databases: 808. Weekly public service hours: 112; students can reserve study rooms. *Research affiliation:* National Institute of Justice (law), National Science Foundation (biological sciences), Howard Hughes Medical Institute (physics), National Institute of Child Health and Human Development (social work), Boeing (mechanical engineering), American Heart Association (biomedical engineering).

Computer facilities: A campuswide network can be accessed from student residence rooms and from off campus. Online class registration, online financial and cashier's information; financial, campus maps information available on cell phones are available. Website: http://www.fiu.edu/

General Application Contact: Nanett Rojas, Assistant Director of Graduate Admissions, 305-348-7442, Fax: 305-348-7441, E-mail: gradadm@fiu.edu.

GRADUATE UNITS

Chaplin School of Hospitality and Tourism Management Students: 193 full-time (124 women), 89 part-time (67 women); includes 94 minority (20 Black or African American, non-Hispanic/Latino; 3 Asian, non-Hispanic/Latino; 67 Hispanic/Latino; 4 Two or more races, non-Hispanic/Latino), 150 international. Average age 27. 216 applicants, 82% accepted, 115 enrolled. *Faculty:* 22 full-time (6 women), 36 part-time/adjunct (11 women). Expenses: Contact institution. *Financial support:* Institutionally sponsored loans and scholarships/grants available. Financial award application deadline: 3/1; financial award applicants required to submit FAFSA. In 2017, 143 master's awarded. *Program availability:* Part-time, evening/weekend, online learning. Offers hospitality and tourism management (MS). *Application deadline:* For fall admission, 6/1 for domestic students, 4/1 for international students; for spring admission, 10/1 for domestic students, 9/1 for international students. Applications are processed on a rolling basis. *Application fee:* $30. Electronic applications accepted. *Application Contact:* Nanett Rojas, Manager, Admissions Operations, 305-348-7464, Fax: 305-348-7441, E-mail: gradadm@fiu.edu. *Interim Dean*, Dr. Michael Cheng, 305-919-4506, E-mail: michael.cheng@fiu.edu.

Chapman Graduate School of Business Students: 1,412 full-time (794 women), 696 part-time (341 women); includes 1,519 minority (273 Black or African American, non-Hispanic/Latino; 68 Asian, non-Hispanic/Latino; 1,133 Hispanic/Latino; 5 Native Hawaiian or other Pacific Islander, non-Hispanic/Latino; 40 Two or more races, non-Hispanic/Latino), 267 international. Average age 31. 2,332 applicants, 47% accepted, 744 enrolled. *Faculty:* 135 full-time (47 women), 92 part-time/adjunct (27 women). Expenses: Contact institution. *Financial support:* Institutionally sponsored loans and scholarships/grants available. Financial award application deadline: 3/1; financial award applicants required to submit FAFSA. In 2017, 1,255 master's, 13 doctorates awarded. *Program availability:* Part-time, evening/weekend. Offers business (EMBA, IMBA, M Acc, MBA, MIB, MS, MSF, MSHRM, MST, PhD); decision sciences and information systems (PhD); finance (MSF); health information management systems (MS); human resources management (MSHRM); international business (MIB); management and international business (EMBA, IMBA, MBA, PhD); marketing (MS); systems management (MS). *Application deadline:* For fall admission, 6/1 for domestic students, 4/1 for international students; for spring admission, 10/1 for domestic students, 9/1 for international students. Applications are processed on a rolling basis. *Application fee:* $30. Electronic applications accepted. *Application Contact:* Nanett Rojas, Manager, Admissions Operations, 305-348-7464, Fax: 305-348-7441, E-mail: gradadm@fiu.edu. *Dean*, Dr. Joanne Li, 305-348-2751, Fax: 305-919-5478, E-mail: gradadm@fiu.edu.

Hollo School of Real Estate Students: 82 full-time (32 women), 7 part-time (3 women); includes 56 minority (10 Black or African American, non-Hispanic/Latino; 2 Asian, non-Hispanic/Latino; 42 Hispanic/Latino; 2 Two or more races, non-Hispanic/Latino), 15 international. Average age 33. 138 applicants, 60% accepted, 56 enrolled. *Faculty:* 5 full-time (1 woman), 4 part-time/adjunct (2 women). Expenses: Contact institution. *Financial support:* Institutionally sponsored loans and scholarships/grants available. Financial award application deadline: 3/1; financial award applicants required to submit FAFSA. In 2017, 83 master's awarded. *Program availability:* Part-time, evening/weekend. Offers international real estate (MS). *Application deadline:* For fall admission, 4/1 for domestic and international students. *Application fee:* $30. Electronic applications accepted. *Application Contact:* Isabel Lopez, Associate Director for Academic Support Services, 305-348-4198, E-mail: isabel.lopez@fiu.edu. *Director*, Eli Beracha, 305-779-7898, E-mail: eli.beracha@fiu.edu.

School of Accounting Students: 84 full-time (41 women), 19 part-time (8 women); includes 87 minority (5 Black or African American, non-Hispanic/Latino; 9 Asian, non-Hispanic/Latino; 72 Hispanic/Latino; 1 Two or more races, non-Hispanic/Latino), 4 international. Average age 26. 202 applicants, 48% accepted, 71 enrolled. *Faculty:* 25 full-time (9 women), 18 part-time/adjunct (2 women). Expenses: Contact institution. *Financial support:* Institutionally sponsored loans and scholarships/grants available. Financial award application deadline: 3/1; financial award applicants required to submit FAFSA. In 2017, 139 master's awarded. *Program availability:* Part-time, evening/weekend. Offers accounting (M Acc). *Application deadline:* For fall admission, 6/1 for domestic students, 4/1 for international students; for spring admission, 10/1 for domestic students, 9/1 for international students. Applications are processed on a rolling basis. *Application fee:* $30. Electronic applications accepted. *Application Contact:* Cynthia Teijeiro, Program Manager, 305-348-7564, E-mail: cteijeir@fiu.edu. *Director*, Ruth Ann McEwen, 305-348-2581, E-mail: rmcewen@fiu.edu.

College of Arts, Sciences, and Education Students: 932 full-time (610 women), 588 part-time (431 women); includes 980 minority (222 Black or African American, non-Hispanic/Latino; 32 Asian, non-Hispanic/Latino; 691 Hispanic/Latino; 35 Two or more races, non-Hispanic/Latino), 153 international. Average age 31. 1,380 applicants, 40% accepted, 360 enrolled. *Faculty:* 372 full-time (165 women), 314 part-time/adjunct (180 women). Expenses: Contact institution. *Financial support:* Career-related internships or fieldwork, Federal Work-Study, institutionally sponsored loans, and scholarships/grants available. Financial award application deadline: 3/1; financial award applicants required to submit FAFSA. In 2017, 555 master's, 77 doctorates awarded. *Program availability:* Part-time, evening/weekend. Offers adult education and human resource development (MS, Ed D); art education (MA, MS); arts, sciences, and education (MA, MFA, MS, PSM,

Ed D, PhD, Certificate, Ed S); behavioral analysis (MS); biological sciences (MS, PhD); chemistry (MS, PhD); clinical science (PhD); cognitive neuroscience (PhD); counseling (MS); counseling psychology (MS); counselor education (MS); creative writing (MFA); curriculum and instruction (MS, Ed D, PhD, Ed S); developmental science (MS, PhD); early childhood education (MS); earth science (PhD); educational administration and supervision (Ed D); educational leadership (MS, Certificate, Ed S); English (MA); environmental studies (MS); exceptional student education (Ed D); foreign language education (MS); forensic science (MS, PSM, PhD); geosciences (MS, PhD); higher education (Ed D); higher education administration (MS); international and comparative education (MS); language, literacy and culture (PhD); legal psychology (MS, PhD); liberal studies (MA); linguistics (MA); mathematical sciences (MS); mathematics, science, and learning technologies (PhD); natural resources management and policy (PSM); organizational psychology (MS, PhD); physical education (MS); physics (MS, PhD); reading education (MS); recreation and sport management (MS); school psychology (Ed S); statistics (MS); urban education (MS). *Application deadline:* For fall admission, 6/1 for domestic students, 4/1 for international students; for spring admission, 10/1 for domestic students, 9/1 for international students. Applications are processed on a rolling basis. *Application fee:* $30. Electronic applications accepted. *Application Contact:* Nanett Rojas, Assistant Director, Graduate Admissions, 305-348-7464, Fax: 305-348-7441, E-mail: gradadm@fiu.edu. *Dean*, Dr. Michael Heithaus, 305-348-2866, Fax: 305-348-4172, E-mail: casdean@fiu.edu.

College of Communication, Architecture and The Arts Students: 351 full-time (217 women), 119 part-time (82 women); includes 317 minority (43 Black or African American, non-Hispanic/Latino; 7 Asian, non-Hispanic/Latino; 258 Hispanic/Latino; 9 Two or more races, non-Hispanic/Latino), 82 international. Average age 28. 354 applicants, 53% accepted, 127 enrolled. *Faculty:* 100 full-time (42 women), 135 part-time/adjunct (72 women). Expenses: Contact institution. *Financial support:* Institutionally sponsored loans and scholarships/grants available. Financial award application deadline: 3/1; financial award applicants required to submit FAFSA. In 2017, 253 master's awarded. *Program availability:* Part-time, evening/weekend. Offers architecture (M Arch, MA); communication, architecture and the arts (M Arch, MA, MFA, MIA, MLA, MM, MS, Certificate, Graduate Certificate); interior architecture (MA, MIA, Certificate); landscape architecture (MLA); museum studies (Graduate Certificate); studio art (MFA). *Application deadline:* For fall admission, 6/1 for domestic students, 4/1 for international students; for spring admission, 10/1 for domestic students, 9/1 for international students. Applications are processed on a rolling basis. *Application fee:* $30. Electronic applications accepted. *Application Contact:* Nanett Rojas, Manager, Admissions Operations, 305-348-7464, Fax: 305-348-7441, E-mail: gradadm@fiu.edu. *Dean*, Dr. Brian Schriner, 305-348-3176, Fax: 305-348-6716, E-mail: schriner@fiu.edu.

School of Communication and Journalism Students: 91 full-time (63 women), 65 part-time (47 women); includes 112 minority (20 Black or African American, non-Hispanic/Latino; 3 Asian, non-Hispanic/Latino; 84 Hispanic/Latino; 5 Two or more races, non-Hispanic/Latino), 31 international. Average age 28. 122 applicants, 68% accepted, 67 enrolled. *Faculty:* 35 full-time (24 women), 59 part-time/adjunct (38 women). Expenses: Contact institution. *Financial support:* Institutionally sponsored loans and scholarships/grants available. Financial award application deadline: 3/1; financial award applicants required to submit FAFSA. In 2017, 86 master's awarded. *Program availability:* Part-time, evening/weekend. Offers mass communication (MS). *Application deadline:* For fall admission, 6/1 for domestic students, 4/1 for international students; for spring admission, 10/1 for domestic students, 9/1 for international students. Applications are processed on a rolling basis. *Application fee:* $30. Electronic applications accepted. *Application Contact:* Nanett Rojas, Assistant Director, Graduate Admissions, 305-348-7442, Fax: 305-348-7441, E-mail: gradadm@fiu.edu. *Chair*, Dr. Maria Elena Villar, 305-919-5795, Fax: 305-919-5215, E-mail: mariaelena.villar@fiu.edu.

School of Music Students: 27 full-time (11 women), 10 part-time (5 women); includes 23 minority (6 Black or African American, non-Hispanic/Latino; 1 Asian, non-Hispanic/Latino; 15 Hispanic/Latino; 1 Two or more races, non-Hispanic/Latino), 4 international. Average age 32. 46 applicants, 61% accepted, 14 enrolled. *Faculty:* 22 full-time (4 women), 27 part-time/adjunct (7 women). Expenses: Contact institution. *Financial support:* Institutionally sponsored loans and scholarships/grants available. Financial award application deadline: 3/1; financial award applicants required to submit FAFSA. In 2017, 24 master's awarded. *Program availability:* Part-time, evening/weekend. Offers music (MM); music education (MS). *Application deadline:* For fall admission, 6/1 for domestic students, 4/1 for international students; for spring admission, 10/1 for domestic students, 9/1 for international students. Applications are processed on a rolling basis. *Application fee:* $30. Electronic applications accepted. *Application Contact:* Joel Galand, Graduate Program Director, 305-348-7078, E-mail: galandj@fiu.edu. *Interim Chair*, Robert Dundas, 305-348-3587, Fax: 305-348-4073, E-mail: robert.dundas@fiu.edu.

College of Engineering and Computing Students: 530 full-time (162 women), 308 part-time (80 women); includes 375 minority (57 Black or African American, non-Hispanic/Latino; 1 American Indian or Alaska Native, non-Hispanic/Latino; 16 Asian, non-Hispanic/Latino; 291 Hispanic/Latino; 10 Two or more races, non-Hispanic/Latino), 384 international. Average age 30. 1,231 applicants, 44% accepted, 220 enrolled. *Faculty:* 137 full-time (26 women), 73 part-time/adjunct (12 women). Expenses: Contact institution. *Financial support:* Career-related internships or fieldwork, Federal Work-Study, institutionally sponsored loans, scholarships/grants, and unspecified assistantships available. Financial award application deadline: 3/1; financial award applicants required to submit FAFSA. In 2017, 317 master's, 50 doctorates awarded. *Program availability:* Part-time, evening/weekend, online learning. Offers biomedical engineering (MS, PhD); civil engineering (MS, PhD); computer engineering (MS); electrical engineering (MS, PhD); engineering and computing (MS, PMS, PhD); engineering management (MS); environmental engineering (MS); materials science and engineering (MS, PhD); mechanical engineering (MS, PhD). *Application deadline:* For fall admission, 6/1 for domestic students, 4/1 for international students; for spring admission, 10/1 for domestic students, 9/1 for international students. Applications are processed on a rolling basis. *Application fee:* $30. Electronic applications accepted. *Application Contact:* Sara-Michelle Lemus, Engineering Admissions Officer, 305-348-1890, E-mail: grad_eng@fiu.edu. *Dean*, Dr. John Volakis, 305-348-0273, Fax: 305-348-0127, E-mail: grad_eng@fiu.edu.

School of Computing and Information Sciences Students: 143 full-time (38 women), 127 part-time (20 women); includes 151 minority (16 Black or African American, non-Hispanic/Latino; 1 American Indian or Alaska Native, non-Hispanic/Latino; 7 Asian, non-Hispanic/Latino; 123 Hispanic/Latino; 4 Two or more races, non-Hispanic/Latino), 101 international. Average age 29. 403 applicants, 49% accepted, 84 enrolled. *Faculty:* 48 full-time (10 women), 29 part-time/adjunct (5 women). Expenses: Contact institution. *Financial support:* Research assistantships, teaching assistantships, institutionally sponsored loans, scholarships/grants, and unspecified assistantships available. Financial award application deadline: 3/1; financial award applicants required to submit FAFSA. In 2017, 74 master's, 8 doctorates awarded. *Program availability:* Part-time, evening/weekend. Offers computer science (MS, PhD); cybersecurity (MS); data science (MS); information technology (MS); telecommunications and networking (MS). *Application deadline:* For fall admission, 6/1 for domestic students, 4/1 for international students; for spring admission, 10/1 for domestic students, 9/1 for international students. Applications are processed on a rolling basis. *Application fee:* $30. Electronic applications accepted. *Application Contact:* Sara-Michelle Lemus, Engineering Admissions Officer, 305-348-1890, E-mail: grad_eng@fiu.edu. *Director*, Dr. S. S. Iyengar, 305-348-3947, E-mail: iyengar@cis.fiu.edu.

School of Construction Students: 31 full-time (7 women), 39 part-time (16 women); includes 32 minority (6 Black or African American, non-Hispanic/Latino; 26 Hispanic/Latino), 23 international. Average age 32. 144 applicants, 37% accepted, 19 enrolled. *Faculty:* 8 full-time (1 woman), 6 part-time/adjunct (0 women). Expenses: Contact institution. *Financial support:* In 2017–18, 5 students received support. Institutionally sponsored loans, scholarships/grants, and unspecified assistantships available. Financial award application deadline: 3/1; financial award applicants required to submit FAFSA. In 2017, 38 master's awarded. *Program availability:* Part-time, evening/weekend. Offers construction management (MS, PMS). *Application deadline:* For fall admission, 6/1 for domestic students, 4/1 for international students; for spring admission, 10/1 for domestic students, 9/1 for international students. Applications are processed on a rolling basis. *Application fee:* $30. Electronic applications accepted. *Application Contact:* Sara-Michelle Lemus, Engineering Admissions Officer, 305-348-1890, Fax: 305-348-7441, E-mail: grad_eng@fiu.edu. *Director*, Dr. Irtishad Ahmad, 305-348-3172, Fax: 305-348-6255, E-mail: ahmadi@fiu.edu.

College of Law Students: 484 full-time (269 women), 28 part-time (18 women); includes 315 minority (35 Black or African American, non-Hispanic/Latino; 3 American Indian or Alaska Native, non-Hispanic/Latino; 11 Asian, non-Hispanic/Latino; 261 Hispanic/Latino; 5 Two or more races, non-Hispanic/Latino), 25 international. Average age 27. 1,778 applicants, 32% accepted, 204 enrolled. *Faculty:* 29 full-time (14 women), 48 part-time/adjunct (8 women). Expenses: Contact institution. *Financial support:* Application deadline: 3/1; applicants required to submit FAFSA. In 2017, 14 master's, 154 doctorates awarded. *Program availability:* Part-time, evening/weekend. Offers American law for foreign lawyers (LL M); law (JD). *Application deadline:* For fall admission, 5/1 for domestic and international students. Applications are processed on a rolling basis. *Application fee:* $20. Electronic applications accepted. *Acting Dean*, Tawia B Ansah, 305-348-1118, Fax: 305-348-1159, E-mail: tawia.ansah@fiu.edu.

Herbert Wertheim College of Medicine Students: 638 full-time (364 women); includes 418 minority (42 Black or African American, non-Hispanic/Latino; 124 Asian, non-Hispanic/Latino; 228 Hispanic/Latino; 24 Two or more races, non-Hispanic/Latino), 13 international. Average age 26. 5,410 applicants, 7% accepted, 170 enrolled. *Faculty:* 84 full-time (45 women), 83 part-time/adjunct (28 women). Expenses: Contact institution. *Financial support:* Institutionally sponsored loans and scholarships/grants available. Financial award application deadline: 3/1; financial award applicants required to submit FAFSA. In 2017, 115 doctorates awarded. Offers biomedical sciences (PhD); medicine (MD); physician assistant studies (MPAS). *Application deadline:* For fall admission, 12/15 for domestic students. *Application fee:* $160. Electronic applications accepted. *Application Contact:* Cristina M. Arabatzis, Assistant Director of Admissions, 305-348-0639, Fax: 305-348-0650, E-mail: carabatz@fiu.edu. *Dean*, Dr. John Rock, 305-348-0570, E-mail: med.admissions@fiu.edu.

Nicole Wertheim College of Nursing and Health Sciences Students: 861 full-time (660 women), 104 part-time (84 women); includes 751 minority (160 Black or African American, non-Hispanic/Latino; 1 American Indian or Alaska Native, non-Hispanic/Latino; 59 Asian, non-Hispanic/Latino; 513 Hispanic/Latino; 3 Native Hawaiian or other Pacific Islander, non-Hispanic/Latino; 15 Two or more races, non-Hispanic/Latino), 17 international. Average age 29. 1,538 applicants, 27% accepted, 348 enrolled. *Faculty:* 69 full-time (50 women), 150 part-time/adjunct (108 women). Expenses: Contact institution. *Financial support:* Career-related internships or fieldwork, Federal Work-Study, institutionally sponsored loans, and scholarships/grants available. Financial award application deadline: 3/1; financial award applicants required to submit FAFSA. In 2017, 256 master's, 61 doctorates awarded. *Program availability:* Part-time, evening/weekend. Offers adult health nursing (MSN); athletic training (MS); family health (MSN); health services administration (MHSA); nurse anesthetist (MSN); nursing and health sciences (MHSA, MS, MSN, MSOT, DNP, DPT, PhD); nursing practice (DNP); nursing science research (PhD); occupational therapy (MSOT); pediatric nurse (MSN); physical therapy (DPT); psychiatric and mental health nursing (MSN); registered nurse (MSN); speech-language pathology (MS). *Application fee:* $30. Electronic applications accepted. *Application Contact:* Nanett Rojas, Manager, Admissions Operations, 305-348-7464, Fax: 305-348-7441, E-mail: gradadm@fiu.edu. *Dean*, Dr. Ora Strickland, 305-348-0407, E-mail: olstrick@fiu.edu.

Robert Stempel College of Public Health and Social Work Students: 353 full-time (275 women), 174 part-time (142 women); includes 388 minority (111 Black or African American, non-Hispanic/Latino; 25 Asian, non-Hispanic/Latino; 236 Hispanic/Latino; 16 Two or more races, non-Hispanic/Latino), 50 international. Average age 30. 466 applicants, 51% accepted, 145 enrolled. *Faculty:* 62 full-time (40 women), 24 part-time/adjunct (20 women). Expenses: Contact institution. *Financial support:* Institutionally sponsored loans, scholarships/grants, and unspecified assistantships available. Financial award application deadline: 3/1; financial award applicants required to submit FAFSA. In 2017, 160 master's, 17 doctorates awarded. *Program availability:* Part-time, evening/weekend, online learning. Offers biostatistics (MPH); dietetics and nutrition (MS, PhD); environmental and occupational health (MPH, PhD); epidemiology (MPH, PhD); health policy and management (MPH); health promotion and disease prevention (MPH, PhD); public health and social work (MPH, MS, MSW, PhD). *Application deadline:* For fall admission, 6/1 for domestic students, 4/1 for international students; for spring admission, 10/1 for domestic students, 9/1 for international students. Applications are processed on a rolling basis. *Application fee:* $30. Electronic applications accepted. *Application Contact:* Nanett Rojas, Manager, Admissions Operations, 305-348-7464, Fax: 305-348-7441, E-mail: gradadm@fiu.edu. *Dean*, Dr. Tomas Guilarte, 305-348-1158, Fax: 305-348-1691, E-mail: tomas.guilarte@fiu.edu.

School of Social Work Students: 139 full-time (117 women), 70 part-time (59 women); includes 176 minority (51 Black or African American, non-Hispanic/Latino; 1 Asian, non-Hispanic/Latino; 117 Hispanic/Latino; 7 Two or more races, non-Hispanic/Latino), 5 international. Average age 31. 143 applicants, 48% accepted, 55 enrolled. *Faculty:* 17 full-time (12 women), 14 part-time/adjunct (10 women). Expenses: Contact institution. *Financial support:* Institutionally sponsored loans and scholarships/grants available. Financial award application deadline: 3/1; financial award applicants required to submit FAFSA. In 2017, 85 master's, 1 doctorate awarded. *Program availability:* Part-time, evening/weekend. Offers social welfare (PhD); social work (MSW). *Application deadline:* For fall admission, 6/1 for domestic students, 4/1 for international students; for spring admission, 10/1 for domestic students, 9/1 for international students. Applications are processed on a rolling basis. *Application fee:* $30. Electronic applications accepted. *Application Contact:* Gladys Ramos, Program Assistant, 305-348-5887, E-mail: gladys.ramos@fiu.edu. *Director,* Dr. Mary Helen Hayden, 305-348-1208, E-mail: haydenm@fiu.edu.

Steven J. Green School of International and Public Affairs Students: 517 full-time (280 women), 323 part-time (186 women); includes 547 minority (122 Black or African American, non-Hispanic/Latino; 2 American Indian or Alaska Native, non-Hispanic/Latino; 12 Asian, non-Hispanic/Latino; 394 Hispanic/Latino; 17 Two or more races, non-Hispanic/Latino), 131 international. Average age 32. 821 applicants, 52% accepted, 286 enrolled. *Faculty:* 161 full-time (67 women), 181 part-time/adjunct (75 women). Expenses: Contact institution. *Financial support:* Career-related internships or fieldwork, Federal Work-Study, institutionally sponsored loans, and scholarships/grants available. Financial award application deadline: 3/1; financial award applicants required to submit FAFSA. In 2017, 247 master's, 41 doctorates awarded. *Program availability:* Part-time, evening/weekend. Offers African and African diaspora studies (MA); Asian studies (MA); Atlantic history (PhD); criminal justice (MS); disaster management (MA); economics (MA, PhD); global and sociocultural studies (MA, PhD); history (MA); international and public affairs (MA, MPA, MS, PhD); international crime and justice (PhD); international relations (MA, PhD); Latin American and Caribbean studies (MA); political science (MA, PhD); public administration (MPA); public affairs (PhD); religious studies (MA); Spanish (MA, PhD). *Application deadline:* For fall admission, 6/1 for domestic students, 4/1 for international students; for winter admission, 10/1 for domestic students, 9/1 for international students. Applications are processed on a rolling basis. *Application fee:* $30. Electronic applications accepted. *Application Contact:* Nanett Rojas, Assistant Director of Graduate Admissions, 305-348-7442, Fax: 305-348-7441, E-mail: gradadm@fiu.edu. *Dean,* Dr. John F. Stack, Jr., 305-348-7266, Fax: 305-348-1013, E-mail: john.stack@fiu.edu.

FLORIDA MEMORIAL UNIVERSITY, Miami-Dade, FL 33054

General Information Independent-religious, coed, comprehensive institution.

GRADUATE UNITS

School of Business *Program availability:* Part-time. Offers business (MBA).

School of Education Offers elementary education (MS); exceptional student education (MS); reading (MS).

FLORIDA NATIONAL UNIVERSITY, Hialeah, FL 33012

General Information Proprietary, coed, comprehensive institution. *Enrollment:* 4,169 graduate, professional, and undergraduate students; 34 full-time matriculated graduate/professional students (18 women), 112 part-time matriculated graduate/professional students (71 women). *Enrollment by degree level:* 146 master's. *Graduate faculty:* 11 full-time (6 women), 10 part-time/adjunct (6 women). *Tuition:* Full-time $15,600. *Required fees:* $650. *Student services:* Campus employment opportunities, campus safety program, career counseling, child daycare facilities, international student services. *Library facilities:* Hialeah Campus Library plus 1 other. *Collection:* Books: 21,521 (physical), 144,218 (digital/electronic); Serial titles: 55 (physical), 196,357 (digital/electronic); Databases: 32. Weekly public service hours: 69; students can reserve study rooms.

Computer facilities: 300 computers available on campus for general student use. A campuswide network can be accessed from off campus. Online class registration is available.
Website: http://www.fnu.edu/

General Application Contact: Virginia Rabelo, Admissions Supervisor, 305-821-3333 Ext. 1016, Fax: 305-362-0595, E-mail: vrabelo@fnu.edu.

GRADUATE UNITS

Program in Business Administration Expenses: Contact institution. *Financial support:* Federal Work-Study, institutionally sponsored loans, scholarships/grants, and tuition waivers available. Financial award applicants required to submit FAFSA. *Program availability:* Part-time, blended/hybrid learning. Offers accounting (MBA); finance (MBA); general management (MBA); health services administration (MBA); marketing (MBA); public management and leadership (MBA). *Application deadline:* Applications are processed on a rolling basis. Electronic applications accepted. *Business and Economics Department Head,* Dr. Ernesto Gonzalez, 305-821-3333 Ext. 1070, Fax: 305-362-0595, E-mail: egonzalez@fnu.edu.

Program in Health Services Administration Expenses: Contact institution. *Financial support:* Scholarships/grants available. Financial award applicants required to submit FAFSA. *Program availability:* Part-time, evening/weekend, 100% online, blended/hybrid learning. Offers health services administration (MHSA). *Application deadline:* Applications are processed on a rolling basis. Electronic applications accepted. *Allied Health Division Head,* Dr. Loreto Almonte, 305-821-3333 Ext. 1074, Fax: 305-362-0595, E-mail: lalmonte@fnu.edu.

Program in Nursing Expenses: Contact institution. *Program availability:* 100% online, blended/hybrid learning. Offers family nurse practitioner (MSN); nurse educator (MSN); nurse leadership and management (MSN).

FLORIDA SOUTHERN COLLEGE, Lakeland, FL 33801-5698

General Information Independent-religious, coed, comprehensive institution. *Enrollment:* 3,073 graduate, professional, and undergraduate students; 421 full-time matriculated graduate/professional students (343 women), 48 part-time matriculated graduate/professional students (43 women). *Enrollment by degree level:* 313 master's, 66 doctoral. *Graduate faculty:* 27 full-time (14 women), 14 part-time/adjunct (9 women). *Tuition:* Full-time $16,426; part-time $618 per credit hour. *Required fees:* $50 per semester. *Graduate housing:* On-campus housing not available. *Student services:* Campus employment opportunities, campus safety program, career counseling, exercise/wellness program, free psychological counseling, international student services, multicultural affairs office, services for students with disabilities, teacher training. *Library facilities:* Roux Library plus 1 other. *Collection:* Books: 160,667 (physical), 167,731 (digital/electronic); Serial titles: 22 (physical), 97,772 (digital/electronic); Databases: 118. Weekly public service hours: 104; students can reserve study rooms.

Computer facilities: Computer purchase and lease plans are available. 490 computers available on campus for general student use. A campuswide network can be accessed from student residence rooms. Online class registration, campus portal are available.
Website: http://www.flsouthern.edu/

General Application Contact: Kristen Placek, Director, Office of Adult and Graduate Education, 863-680-4205, Fax: 863-680-3872, E-mail: kplacek@flsouthern.edu.

GRADUATE UNITS

Program in Accounting Students: 23 full-time (14 women), 3 part-time (1 woman); includes 6 minority (2 Black or African American, non-Hispanic/Latino; 4 Hispanic/Latino), 4 international. Average age 28. 25 applicants, 80% accepted, 18 enrolled. *Faculty:* 4 full-time (2 women). Expenses: Contact institution. *Financial support:* Federal Work-Study and unspecified assistantships available. Financial award applicants required to submit FAFSA. In 2017, 8 master's awarded. *Program availability:* Part-time, blended/hybrid learning. Offers accounting (M Acc). *Application deadline:* For fall admission, 6/1 for domestic and international students; for spring admission, 10/1 for domestic and international students. Applications are processed on a rolling basis. *Application fee:* $30. Electronic applications accepted. *Application Contact:* Jared Welling, Director, Office of Adult and Graduate Education, 863-680-4914, Fax: 863-680-3872, E-mail: jwelling@flsouthern.edu. *Director,* Dr. Lynn Clements, 863-680-5022, E-mail: lclements@flsouthern.edu.

Program in Business Administration Students: 73 full-time (41 women), 4 part-time (1 woman); includes 12 minority (4 Black or African American, non-Hispanic/Latino; 2 Asian, non-Hispanic/Latino; 6 Hispanic/Latino), 7 international. Average age 29. 86 applicants, 60% accepted, 37 enrolled. *Faculty:* 7 full-time (3 women), 1 part-time/adjunct (0 women). Expenses: Contact institution. *Financial support:* Scholarships/grants and unspecified assistantships available. Support available to part-time students. Financial award application deadline: 3/1; financial award applicants required to submit FAFSA. In 2017, 37 master's awarded. *Program availability:* Part-time, 100% online, blended/hybrid learning. Offers business administration (MBA). *Application deadline:* For fall admission, 6/1 for domestic and international students; for spring admission, 10/1 for domestic and international students. Applications are processed on a rolling basis. *Application fee:* $30. Electronic applications accepted. *Application Contact:* Kamalie Morales, Senior Assistant Director of Adult and Graduate Education, 863-680-4205, Fax: 863-680-3872, E-mail: kmorales@flsouthern.edu. *Program Coordinator,* Dr. Charles DuVal, 863-680-4280, Fax: 863-680-4355, E-mail: cduval@flsouthern.edu.

Program in Nursing Students: 142 full-time (126 women), 9 part-time (all women); includes 70 minority (39 Black or African American, non-Hispanic/Latino; 1 American Indian or Alaska Native, non-Hispanic/Latino; 11 Asian, non-Hispanic/Latino; 13 Hispanic/Latino; 1 Native Hawaiian or other Pacific Islander, non-Hispanic/Latino; 5 Two or more races, non-Hispanic/Latino), 1 international. Average age 40. 83 applicants, 93% accepted, 72 enrolled. *Faculty:* 5 full-time (all women), 2 part-time/adjunct (both women). Expenses: Contact institution. *Financial support:* In 2017–18, 1 student received support. Scholarships/grants and traineeships available. Support available to part-time students. Financial award applicants required to submit FAFSA. In 2017, 41 master's awarded. *Program availability:* Part-time. Offers adult gerontology clinical nurse specialist (MSN); adult gerontology primary care nurse practitioner (MSN); family nurse practitioner (MSN); nurse educator (MSN); nursing administration (MSN). *Application deadline:* For fall admission, 6/1 for domestic and international students; for spring admission, 10/1 for domestic and international students. Applications are processed on a rolling basis. *Application fee:* $30. Electronic applications accepted. *Application Contact:* Kathy Connelly, Evening Program Assistant Director, 863-680-4205, Fax: 863-680-3872, E-mail: kconnelly@flsouthern.edu. *Dean,* Dr. Linda Comer, 863-680-4310, Fax: 863-680-3872, E-mail: lcomer@flsouthern.edu.

Programs in Teaching Students: 41 full-time (36 women), 23 part-time (all women); includes 11 minority (6 Black or African American, non-Hispanic/Latino; 1 American Indian or Alaska Native, non-Hispanic/Latino; 2 Hispanic/Latino; 1 Native Hawaiian or other Pacific Islander, non-Hispanic/Latino; 1 Two or more races, non-Hispanic/Latino), 2 international. Average age 40. 130 applicants, 92% accepted, 95 enrolled. *Faculty:* 11 full-time (4 women), 11 part-time/adjunct (7 women). Expenses: Contact institution. *Financial support:* In 2017–18, 3 students received support. Scholarships/grants available. Support available to part-time students. Financial award applicants required to submit FAFSA. In 2017, 1 master's awarded. *Program availability:* Part-time, evening/weekend, 100% online, blended/hybrid learning. Offers collaborative teaching and learning (M Ed); educational leadership (M Ed, Ed D); teaching (MAT). *Application deadline:* For fall admission, 8/1 for domestic and international students; for winter admission, 4/1 for domestic and international students; for spring admission, 12/1 for domestic and international students. Applications are processed on a rolling basis. *Application fee:* $30. Electronic applications accepted. *Application Contact:* Kathy Connelly, Evening Program Assistant Director, 863-680-4205, Fax: 863-680-3872, E-mail: kconnelly@flsouthern.edu. *Dean,* Dr. Tracey Tedder, 863-680-4177, Fax: 863-680-4102, E-mail: ttedder@flsouthern.edu.

FLORIDA STATE UNIVERSITY, Tallahassee, FL 32306

General Information State-supported, coed, university. CGS member. *Enrollment:* 41,447 graduate, professional, and undergraduate students; 5,715 full-time matriculated graduate/professional students (3,002 women), 2,148 part-time matriculated graduate/professional students (1,363 women). *Enrollment by degree level:* 4,026 master's, 3,733 doctoral, 104 other advanced degrees. *Graduate faculty:* 1,795 full-time (726 women), 60 part-time/adjunct (31 women). *Graduate housing:* Room and/or apartments available on a first-come, first-served basis to single students; on-campus housing not available to married students. Housing application deadline: 5/1. *Student services:* Campus employment opportunities, campus safety program, career counseling, child daycare facilities, exercise/wellness program, free psychological counseling, grant writing training, international student services, low-cost health insurance, multicultural affairs office, services for students with disabilities, teacher training, writing training. *Library facilities:* Robert Manning Strozier Library plus 8 others. *Collection:* Books: 2.3 million (physical), 1.6 million (digital/electronic); Serial titles: 125,007 (digital/electronic); Databases: 1,144. Weekly public service hours: 134; study areas open 24 hours, 5–7 days a week; students can reserve study rooms. *Research affiliation:* University Corporation for Atmospheric Research (atmospheric research), Oak Ridge National Laboratory (materials science), Southeastern Universities Research Association (energy), University Research Association (energy), Bruker, Inc. (nuclear magnetic resonance), Oak Ridge Associated Universities (education, environmental assessment).

Computer facilities: 1,100 computers available on campus for general student use. A campuswide network can be accessed from student residence rooms and from off campus. Online class registration, course home pages, course search, online fee payment are available.
Website: http://www.fsu.edu/

General Application Contact: Jermaine Williams, Associate Director for Graduate Admissions, 850-644-7145, Fax: 850-644-0197, E-mail: jawilliams@fsu.edu.

GRADUATE UNITS

College of Law Students: 520 full-time (268 women), 79 part-time (45 women); includes 184 minority (53 Black or African American, non-Hispanic/Latino; 2 American Indian or Alaska Native, non-Hispanic/Latino; 13 Asian, non-Hispanic/Latino; 71 Hispanic/Latino; 45 Two or more races, non-Hispanic/Latino), 13 international. Average age 26. 1,805 applicants, 36% accepted, 225 enrolled. *Faculty:* 57 full-time (29 women), 36 part-time/adjunct (11 women). Expenses: Contact institution. *Financial support:* In 2017–18,

400 students received support, including 2 fellowships with full tuition reimbursements available (averaging $20,683 per year), 30 research assistantships (averaging $1,205 per year), 10 teaching assistantships (averaging $1,354 per year); career-related internships or fieldwork, scholarships/grants, and unspecified assistantships also available. Financial award application deadline: 3/1; financial award applicants required to submit FAFSA. In 2017, 18 master's, 218 doctorates awarded. *Program availability:* Part-time, 100% online. Offers American law for foreign lawyers (LL M); business law (LL M); environmental law and policy (LL M); financial regulation and compliance (JM); health law compliance (JM); law (JM, JD); legal risk management and HR compliance (JM). *Application deadline:* For fall admission, 6/30 for domestic and international students; for spring admission, 12/1 for domestic students; for summer admission, 4/15 for domestic students. Applications are processed on a rolling basis. *Application fee:* $30. Electronic applications accepted. *Application Contact:* Jennifer L. Kessinger, Director of Admissions and Records, 850-644-3787, Fax: 850-644-7284, E-mail: jkessing@law.fsu.edu. *Dean,* Erin O'Hara O'Connor, 850-644-3400, Fax: 850-644-5487, E-mail: eoconnor@law.fsu.edu.

College of Medicine Students: 480 full-time (250 women); includes 200 minority (53 Black or African American, non-Hispanic/Latino; 59 Asian, non-Hispanic/Latino; 80 Hispanic/Latino; 8 Two or more races, non-Hispanic/Latino). Average age 26. 5,866 applicants, 3% accepted, 120 enrolled. *Faculty:* 165 full-time (83 women), 56 part-time/adjunct (19 women). Expenses: Contact institution. *Financial support:* In 2017–18, 123 students received support. Scholarships/grants and tuition waivers (partial) available. Financial award application deadline: 6/30; financial award applicants required to submit FAFSA. In 2017, 116 doctorates awarded. Offers medicine (MD, PhD). *Application deadline:* Applications are processed on a rolling basis. Electronic applications accepted. *Application Contact:* Dana Urrutia, Admissions Coordinator, 850-644-1857, Fax: 850-645-2846, E-mail: medadmissions@med.fsu.edu. *Dean,* Dr. John Patrick Fogarty, MD, 850-644-1346, Fax: 850-645-1420, E-mail: john.fogarty@med.fsu.edu.

Division of Research and Graduate Programs Students: 41 full-time (26 women); includes 10 minority (2 Black or African American, non-Hispanic/Latino; 1 Asian, non-Hispanic/Latino; 1 Hispanic/Latino; 6 Two or more races, non-Hispanic/Latino), 3 international. Average age 27. 30 applicants, 50% accepted, 7 enrolled. *Faculty:* 28 full-time (8 women). Expenses: Contact institution. *Financial support:* In 2017–18, 39 students received support, including 41 research assistantships with full tuition reimbursements available (averaging $29,900 per year). Financial award application deadline: 12/1; financial award applicants required to submit FAFSA. In 2017, 6 doctorates awarded. Offers biomedical sciences (PhD); neuroscience (PhD). *Application deadline:* For fall admission, 12/1 for domestic and international students. *Application fee:* $30. Electronic applications accepted. *Application Contact:* Robin Ryan, Academic Program Specialist, 850-645-6420, Fax: 850-644-5781, E-mail: robin.ryan@med.fsu.edu. *Senior Associate Dean for Research and Graduate Programs,* Dr. Jeffrey N. Joyce, 850-644-2190, Fax: 850-644-9399, E-mail: jeffrey.joyce@med.fsu.edu.

The Graduate School Students: 5,715 full-time (3,002 women), 2,148 part-time (1,363 women); includes 1,973 minority (657 Black or African American, non-Hispanic/Latino; 10 American Indian or Alaska Native, non-Hispanic/Latino; 243 Asian, non-Hispanic/Latino; 866 Hispanic/Latino; 6 Native Hawaiian or other Pacific Islander, non-Hispanic/Latino; 191 Two or more races, non-Hispanic/Latino), 1,247 international. Average age 29. 9,419 applicants, 39% accepted, 2132 enrolled. *Faculty:* 1,795 full-time (726 women), 60 part-time/adjunct (31 women). Expenses: Contact institution. *Financial support:* In 2017–18, 40 fellowships with full tuition reimbursements (averaging $10,000 per year), 1,887 research assistantships with full tuition reimbursements (averaging $12,000 per year), 4,282 teaching assistantships with full tuition reimbursements (averaging $12,000 per year) were awarded; career-related internships or fieldwork, Federal Work-Study, institutionally sponsored loans, scholarships/grants, traineeships, health care benefits, tuition waivers (full and partial), and unspecified assistantships also available. Support available to part-time students. Financial award applicants required to submit FAFSA. In 2017, 2,076 master's, 417 doctorates, 387 other advanced degrees awarded. *Program availability:* Part-time, evening/weekend, 100% online, blended/hybrid learning. Offers materials science and engineering (MS, PhD). *Application deadline:* For fall admission, 7/1 for domestic and international students; for spring admission, 11/1 for domestic and international students. *Application fee:* $35. Electronic applications accepted. *Application Contact:* Jermaine Williams, Associate Director for Graduate Admissions, 850-644-7145, Fax: 850-644-0197, E-mail: jawilliams@fsu.edu. *Dean,* Dr. Mark Riley, 850-644-3501, Fax: 850-644-2969, E-mail: mriley@admin.fsu.edu.

College of Arts and Sciences Students: 1,644 full-time (942 women), 153 part-time (76 women); includes 248 minority (39 Black or African American, non-Hispanic/Latino; 53 Asian, non-Hispanic/Latino; 113 Hispanic/Latino; 1 Native Hawaiian or other Pacific Islander, non-Hispanic/Latino; 42 Two or more races, non-Hispanic/Latino), 578 international. Average age 29. *Faculty:* 588 full-time, 8 part-time/adjunct. Expenses: Contact institution. *Financial support:* Fellowships, research assistantships, teaching assistantships, career-related internships or fieldwork, institutionally sponsored loans, scholarships/grants, traineeships, and unspecified assistantships available. Support available to part-time students. Financial award applicants required to submit FAFSA. In 2017, 292 master's, 181 doctorates awarded. *Program availability:* Part-time. Offers analytical chemistry (MS, PhD); ancient history (MA); applied and computational mathematics (MS, PhD); applied behavior analysis (MS); applied statistics (MS); aquatic environmental science (MS, PSM); arts and sciences (MA, MFA, MS, MST, PSM, PhD); biochemistry (MS, PhD); biomathematics (MS, PhD); biostatistics (MS, PhD); cell and molecular biology (MS, PhD); classical archaeology (MA); classical civilization (MA); classics (PhD); clinical psychology (PhD); cognitive psychology (PhD); computational science (MS, PhD); computational sciences (PhD); computer network and system administration (MS); computer science (MS, PhD); cyber criminology (MS); cyber security (MS); developmental psychology (PhD); ecology and evolutionary biology (MS, PhD); English (MA, MFA, PhD); financial mathematics (MS, PhD); French (MA, PhD); geological sciences (MS, PhD); German (MA); Greek (MA); Greek and Latin (MA); history (MA, MS, PhD); history and philosophy of science (MA); humanities (PhD); inorganic chemistry (MS, PhD); Italian (MA); Italian studies (MA); Latin (MA); materials chemistry (PhD); mathematical statistics (MS, PhD); meteorology (MS, PhD); neuroscience (PhD); oceanography (MS, PSM, PhD); organic chemistry (MS, PhD); philosophy (MA, PhD); physical chemistry (MS, PhD); physics (MS, PhD); psychobiology (MS); public history (MA); pure mathematics (MS, PhD); religion (MA, PhD); science teaching (MST); Slavic languages and literatures (MA); Slavic languages/Russian (MA); social psychology (PhD); Spanish (MA, PhD); statistical data science (MS); structural biology (PhD). *Application deadline:* Applications are processed on a rolling basis. *Application fee:* $30. Electronic applications accepted. *Application Contact:* Ginger Martin, Assistant Dean for Student Affairs, 850-644-1081, Fax: 850-644-9656, E-mail: vmartin@fsu.edu. *Dean,* Dr. Sam Huckaba, 850-644-1081.

College of Business Students: 229 full-time (96 women), 423 part-time (154 women); includes 159 minority (44 Black or African American, non-Hispanic/Latino; 24 Asian, non-Hispanic/Latino; 75 Hispanic/Latino; 1 Native Hawaiian or other Pacific Islander, non-Hispanic/Latino; 15 Two or more races, non-Hispanic/Latino), 48 international. Average age 31. 300 applicants, 61% accepted, 133 enrolled. *Faculty:* 93 full-time (23 women), 2 part-time/adjunct (1 woman). Expenses: Contact institution. *Financial support:* In 2017–18, 146 students received support, including 26 fellowships (averaging $1,500 per year), 77 research assistantships with full tuition reimbursements available (averaging $20,000 per year), 43 teaching assistantships with full tuition reimbursements available (averaging $20,000 per year); career-related internships or fieldwork, scholarships/grants, health care benefits, tuition waivers (full and partial), and unspecified assistantships also available. Support available to part-time students. Financial award application deadline: 1/1; financial award applicants required to submit FAFSA. In 2017, 268 master's, 9 doctorates awarded. *Program availability:* Part-time, 100% online. Offers accounting (M Acc); business administration (MBA, PhD); finance (MS); management information systems (MS); risk management and insurance (MS). *Application deadline:* For fall admission, 6/1 for domestic and international students; for spring admission, 10/1 for domestic and international students; for summer admission, 3/1 for domestic and international students. Applications are processed on a rolling basis. *Application fee:* $30. Electronic applications accepted. *Application Contact:* Jennifer Clark, Director, 850-644-6458, E-mail: gradprograms@business.fsu.edu. *Dean,* Dr. Michael Hartline, 850-644-4405, Fax: 850-644-0915, E-mail: mhartline@business.fsu.edu.

College of Communication and Information Students: 227 full-time (174 women), 371 part-time (290 women); includes 241 minority (59 Black or African American, non-Hispanic/Latino; 42 Asian, non-Hispanic/Latino; 101 Hispanic/Latino; 1 Native Hawaiian or other Pacific Islander, non-Hispanic/Latino; 38 Two or more races, non-Hispanic/Latino), 16 international. Average age 31. 709 applicants, 45% accepted, 195 enrolled. *Faculty:* 52 full-time (26 women), 9 part-time/adjunct (5 women). Expenses: Contact institution. *Financial support:* In 2017–18, 188 students received support, including 3 fellowships with full tuition reimbursements available (averaging $21,000 per year), 57 research assistantships with full tuition reimbursements available (averaging $10,604 per year), 125 teaching assistantships with full tuition reimbursements available (averaging $11,564 per year); career-related internships or fieldwork, Federal Work-Study, institutionally sponsored loans, scholarships/grants, health care benefits, tuition waivers (full and partial), and unspecified assistantships also available. Support available to part-time students. Financial award application deadline: 1/1; financial award applicants required to submit FAFSA. In 2017, 229 master's, 12 doctorates, 2 other advanced degrees awarded. *Program availability:* Part-time, evening/weekend, 100% online. Offers communication and information (MA, MS, PhD, Specialist); communication science and disorders (MS, PhD); communication theory and research (PhD); information (MA, MS, PhD, Specialist); information technology (MS); integrated marketing communication (MA, MS); media and communication studies (MA, MS); public interest media and communication (MA, MS). *Application deadline:* For fall admission, 7/1 for domestic students, 5/1 for international students; for spring admission, 11/1 for domestic and international students. Applications are processed on a rolling basis. *Application fee:* $30. Electronic applications accepted. *Application Contact:* Betsy Crawford, Development and Recruiting Coordinator, 850-645-9661, Fax: 850-644-0611, E-mail: betsy.crawford@cci.fsu.edu. *Dean,* Dr. Lawrence C. Dennis, 850-644-9698, Fax: 850-644-0611, E-mail: larry.dennis@cci.fsu.edu.

College of Criminology and Criminal Justice Students: 92 full-time (59 women), 123 part-time (60 women); includes 80 minority (37 Black or African American, non-Hispanic/Latino; 1 American Indian or Alaska Native, non-Hispanic/Latino; 7 Asian, non-Hispanic/Latino; 29 Hispanic/Latino; 6 Two or more races, non-Hispanic/Latino). Average age 33. 201 applicants, 57% accepted, 59 enrolled. *Faculty:* 18 full-time (7 women). Expenses: Contact institution. *Financial support:* In 2017–18, 44 students received support, including 3 fellowships with full tuition reimbursements available (averaging $12,000 per year), 29 research assistantships with full tuition reimbursements available (averaging $17,100 per year), 15 teaching assistantships with full tuition reimbursements available (averaging $16,000 per year); career-related internships or fieldwork, institutionally sponsored loans, scholarships/grants, health care benefits, tuition waivers (full), and unspecified assistantships also available. Financial award application deadline: 1/15; financial award applicants required to submit FAFSA. In 2017, 83 master's, 3 doctorates awarded. *Program availability:* Part-time, 100% online. Offers criminology and criminal justice (MA, MSC, PhD). *Application deadline:* For fall admission, 7/1 for domestic and international students; for spring admission, 11/1 for domestic and international students; for summer admission, 3/1 for domestic and international students. Applications are processed on a rolling basis. *Application fee:* $30. Electronic applications accepted. *Application Contact:* Meghan Martinez, Graduate Coordinator, 850-645-9169, Fax: 850-644-9614, E-mail: mhm1991@fsu.edu. *Dean,* Dr. Thomas G. Blomberg, 850-644-7365, Fax: 850-644-9614.

College of Education Students: 706 full-time (470 women), 438 part-time (311 women); includes 332 minority (135 Black or African American, non-Hispanic/Latino; 5 American Indian or Alaska Native, non-Hispanic/Latino; 13 Asian, non-Hispanic/Latino; 130 Hispanic/Latino; 49 Two or more races, non-Hispanic/Latino), 215 international. Average age 32. 937 applicants, 47% accepted, 238 enrolled. *Faculty:* 97 full-time (68 women), 46 part-time/adjunct (34 women). Expenses: Contact institution. *Financial support:* In 2017–18, 307 students received support, including 23 fellowships with tuition reimbursements available, 334 research assistantships with tuition reimbursements available, 248 teaching assistantships with tuition reimbursements available; scholarships/grants, tuition waivers (full and partial), and unspecified assistantships also available. Financial award application deadline: 1/15; financial award applicants required to submit FAFSA. In 2017, 283 master's, 50 doctorates, 56 other advanced degrees awarded. *Program availability:* Part-time, evening/weekend, blended/hybrid learning, asynchronous, minimal on-campus study. Offers counseling and human systems (PhD); curriculum and instruction (MS, PhD, Ed S); education (MS, Ed D, PhD, Certificate, Ed S); educational leadership and administration (Certificate); educational leadership and policy (MS, Ed D, PhD, Ed S); educational psychology (MS, PhD); foundations of education (MS, PhD); higher education (MS, PhD); human performance and technology (Certificate); institutional research (Certificate); instructional systems and learning technologies (MS, PhD); measurement and statistics (MS, PhD, Certificate); online instructional development (Certificate); program evaluation (Certificate); sport management (MS, PhD); teaching English to speakers of other languages (Certificate). *Application fee:* $30. Electronic applications accepted. *Application Contact:* Jennie H. Kroeger, Assistant Director, Office of Communication and Recruitment, 850-644-6885, Fax: 850-644-2725, E-mail: jennie.kroeger@fsu.edu. *Dean,* Marcy P. Driscoll, 850-644-6885, Fax: 850-644-2725, E-mail: mdriscoll@fsu.edu.

College of Fine Arts Students: 268 full-time (200 women), 33 part-time (23 women); includes 93 minority (23 Black or African American, non-Hispanic/Latino; 1 American Indian or Alaska Native, non-Hispanic/Latino; 15 Asian, non-Hispanic/Latino; 41 Hispanic/Latino; 13 Two or more races, non-Hispanic/Latino), 16 international. Average age 25. 381 applicants, 89% accepted. *Faculty:* 67 full-time (40 women), 17 part-time/adjunct (12 women). Expenses: Contact institution. *Financial support:* In 2017–18, 257 students received support, including 5 fellowships with partial tuition reimbursements available (averaging $18,000 per year), 90 research assistantships with partial tuition reimbursements available (averaging $4,957 per year), 78 teaching assistantships with partial tuition reimbursements available (averaging $8,001 per year); career-related internships or fieldwork, Federal Work-Study, institutionally sponsored loans, scholarships/grants, and unspecified assistantships also available. Support available to part-time students. Financial award application deadline: 4/15; financial award applicants required to submit FAFSA. In 2017, 101 master's, 4 doctorates awarded. *Program availability:* Part-time. Offers acting (MFA); American dance studies (MA); art (MFA); art education (MA, MS, Ed D, PhD); art history (MA, PhD); art therapy (PhD); arts administration (PhD); costume design (MFA); dance (MFA); directing (MFA); fine arts (MA, MFA, MS, Ed D, PhD, Graduate Certificate); interior architecture and design (MFA, MS); museum and cultural heritage studies (MA); studio and related studies (MA); technical production (MFA); theatre (MA, PhD); theatre management (MFA). *Application deadline:* For fall admission, 7/1 priority date for domestic students; for spring admission, 11/1 priority date for domestic students. Applications are processed on a rolling basis. *Application fee:* $30. Electronic applications accepted. *Application Contact:* Jermaine Williams, Assistant Director for Graduate Admissions, 850-644-7145, Fax: 850-644-0197, E-mail: jawilliams@fsu.edu. *Interim Dean*, Dr. Scott Shamp, 850-664-5244, Fax: 850-644-2604, E-mail: sshamp@fsu.edu.

College of Human Sciences Students: 117 full-time (80 women), 5 part-time (2 women); includes 26 minority (8 Black or African American, non-Hispanic/Latino; 3 Asian, non-Hispanic/Latino; 3 Hispanic/Latino; 12 Two or more races, non-Hispanic/Latino), 19 international. 137 applicants, 53% accepted, 34 enrolled. *Faculty:* 40 full-time (20 women). Expenses: Contact institution. *Financial support:* In 2017–18, 89 students received support, including 36 research assistantships with full tuition reimbursements available (averaging $8,312 per year), 69 teaching assistantships with full tuition reimbursements available (averaging $15,247 per year); career-related internships or fieldwork, Federal Work-Study, scholarships/grants, and unspecified assistantships also available. Financial award application deadline: 1/15; financial award applicants required to submit FAFSA. In 2017, 33 master's, 16 doctorates awarded. *Program availability:* Part-time. Offers exercise physiology (MS, PhD); family and child sciences (MS); human development and family sciences (PhD); human sciences (MS, PhD); marriage and family therapy (PhD); nutrition and food science (MS, PhD); retail, merchandising and product development (MS); sports nutrition (MS); sports sciences (MS). *Application deadline:* For fall admission, 4/1 for domestic and international students; for spring admission, 10/1 for domestic and international students. Applications are processed on a rolling basis. *Application fee:* $30. Electronic applications accepted. *Application Contact:* Tara L. Hartman, Academic Program Specialist, 850-644-7221, Fax: 850-644-0700, E-mail: thartman@fsu.edu. *Dean*, Dr. Michael D. Delp, 850-644-1281, Fax: 850-644-0700, E-mail: mdelp@fsu.edu.

College of Motion Picture Arts Students: 62 full-time (26 women); includes 20 minority (10 Black or African American, non-Hispanic/Latino; 1 American Indian or Alaska Native, non-Hispanic/Latino; 4 Asian, non-Hispanic/Latino; 3 Hispanic/Latino; 2 Two or more races, non-Hispanic/Latino), 14 international. Average age 25. 217 applicants, 15% accepted, 32 enrolled. *Faculty:* 28 full-time (8 women), 3 part-time/adjunct (1 woman). Expenses: Contact institution. *Financial support:* In 2017–18, 20 students received support, including 20 teaching assistantships with partial tuition reimbursements available (averaging $5,500 per year); institutionally sponsored loans and unspecified assistantships also available. Financial award application deadline: 12/1; financial award applicants required to submit FAFSA. In 2017, 28 master's awarded. Offers film production (MFA); screenwriting (MFA). *Application deadline:* For fall admission, 12/1 for domestic and international students. *Application fee:* $30. Electronic applications accepted. *Application Contact:* Gloria McElroy, Staff Director of Admissions and Recruitment, 850-644-8524, Fax: 850-644-2626, E-mail: gmcelroy@fsu.edu. *Dean*, Reb Braddock, 850-644-8712, Fax: 850-644-2626.

College of Music Students: 331 full-time (169 women); includes 100 minority (29 Black or African American, non-Hispanic/Latino; 40 Asian, non-Hispanic/Latino; 29 Hispanic/Latino; 2 Native Hawaiian or other Pacific Islander, non-Hispanic/Latino). Average age 26. 760 applicants, 47% accepted, 173 enrolled. Expenses: Contact institution. *Financial support:* In 2017–18, 233 students received support, including 2 fellowships with full tuition reimbursements available (averaging $15,000 per year), 14 research assistantships with full and partial tuition reimbursements available (averaging $6,458 per year), 201 teaching assistantships with full and partial tuition reimbursements available (averaging $6,458 per year); career-related internships or fieldwork, scholarships/grants, tuition waivers (full and partial), and unspecified assistantships also available. Support available to part-time students. Financial award application deadline: 2/28; financial award applicants required to submit FAFSA. In 2017, 94 master's, 45 doctorates awarded. *Program availability:* Part-time. Offers accompanying (MM); arts administration (MA); choral conducting (MM); composition (MM, DM); ethnomusicology (MM); general music (MA); instrumental accompanying (MM); instrumental conducting (MM); jazz studies (MM); music theory (MM, PhD); music therapy (MM); musicology (MM, PhD); opera (MM); performance (MM, DM); piano pedagogy (MM); piano technology (MA); vocal accompanying (MM). *Application deadline:* For fall admission, 7/1 for domestic and international students; for spring admission, 11/1 for domestic and international students; for summer admission, 3/1 for domestic students. Applications are processed on a rolling basis. *Application fee:* $30. Electronic applications accepted. *Application Contact:* Kris Watson, Director of Admissions, 850-645-2126, Fax: 850-644-2033, E-mail: krwatson@fsu.edu. *Dean*, Dr. Patricia Flowers, 850-644-4361, Fax: 850-644-2033, E-mail: pjflowers@fsu.edu.

College of Nursing Students: 82 full-time (72 women), 26 part-time (25 women); includes 29 minority (9 Black or African American, non-Hispanic/Latino; 8 Asian, non-Hispanic/Latino; 10 Hispanic/Latino; 2 Two or more races, non-Hispanic/Latino). Average age 38. 123 applicants, 48% accepted, 41 enrolled. *Faculty:* 20 full-time (19 women), 3 part-time/adjunct (all women). Expenses: Contact institution. *Financial support:* In 2017–18, 29 students received support, including fellowships with partial tuition reimbursements available (averaging $6,300 per year), research assistantships with partial tuition reimbursements available (averaging $3,000 per year), 3 teaching assistantships with partial tuition reimbursements available (averaging $3,000 per year); career-related internships or fieldwork, Federal Work-Study, institutionally sponsored loans, scholarships/grants, traineeships, and tuition waivers (partial) also available. Financial award application deadline: 4/1; financial award applicants required to submit FAFSA. In 2017, 20 doctorates awarded. *Program availability:* Part-time, 100% online. Offers family nurse practitioner (DNP); psychiatric mental health (Certificate). *Application deadline:* For fall admission, 4/1 for domestic and international students. *Application fee:* $30. Electronic applications accepted. *Application Contact:* Carlos Urrutia, Assistant Director for Student Services, 850-644-5638, Fax: 850-645-7249, E-mail: currutia@fsu.edu. *Dean*, Dr. Judith McFetridge-Durdle, 850-644-6846, Fax: 850-644-7660, E-mail: jdurdle@nursing.fsu.edu.

College of Social Sciences and Public Policy Students: 443 full-time (216 women), 183 part-time (95 women); includes 145 minority (66 Black or African American, non-Hispanic/Latino; 29 Asian, non-Hispanic/Latino; 32 Hispanic/Latino; 18 Two or more races, non-Hispanic/Latino), 100 international. Average age 26. 743 applicants, 64% accepted, 225 enrolled. *Faculty:* 134 full-time (47 women), 44 part-time/adjunct (7 women). Expenses: Contact institution. *Financial support:* In 2017–18, 273 students received support, including 33 fellowships with full tuition reimbursements available (averaging $21,828 per year), 85 research assistantships with full tuition reimbursements available (averaging $13,487 per year), 126 teaching assistantships with full tuition reimbursements available (averaging $18,710 per year); career-related internships or fieldwork, Federal Work-Study, institutionally sponsored loans, scholarships/grants, health care benefits, tuition waivers (full and partial), and unspecified assistantships also available. Support available to part-time students. Financial award application deadline: 1/15; financial award applicants required to submit FAFSA. In 2017, 294 master's, 31 doctorates awarded. *Program availability:* Part-time, evening/weekend. Offers applied American politics and policy (MS); applied economics (MS); applied social research (MS); Asian studies (MA); demography (MS); economics (PhD); geographic information science (MS); geography (MA, MS, PhD); international affairs (MA, MS); planning (MSP); political science (MS, PhD); public administration (MPA, PhD); public administration and policy (Certificate); public health (MPH); Russian and East European studies (MA); social sciences and public policy (MA, MPA, MPH, MS, MSP, PhD, Certificate); sociology (MS, PhD); sociology of health and aging (MS); urban and regional planning (PhD). *Application deadline:* For fall admission, 7/1 priority date for domestic and international students; for spring admission, 11/1 priority date for domestic and international students; for summer admission, 3/1 priority date for domestic and international students. Applications are processed on a rolling basis. *Application fee:* $30. Electronic applications accepted. *Application Contact:* Jermaine Williams, Assistant Director for Graduate Admissions, 850-644-7145, Fax: 850-644-0197, E-mail: jawilliams@fsu.edu. *Dean*, Dr. Timothy Chapin, 850-644-5488, Fax: 850-645-4923, E-mail: tchapin@fsu.edu.

College of Social Work Students: 224 full-time (191 women), 300 part-time (263 women); includes 205 minority (112 Black or African American, non-Hispanic/Latino; 2 American Indian or Alaska Native, non-Hispanic/Latino; 10 Asian, non-Hispanic/Latino; 57 Hispanic/Latino; 24 Two or more races, non-Hispanic/Latino). Average age 31. 324 applicants, 70% accepted, 197 enrolled. *Faculty:* 34 full-time (24 women), 8 part-time/adjunct (4 women). Expenses: Contact institution. *Financial support:* In 2017–18, 77 students received support, including 26 research assistantships with full tuition reimbursements available, 6 teaching assistantships with full tuition reimbursements available; fellowships with full tuition reimbursements available, career-related internships or fieldwork, scholarships/grants, health care benefits, tuition waivers (full and partial), and unspecified assistantships also available. Financial award application deadline: 5/1; financial award applicants required to submit FAFSA. In 2017, 270 master's, 3 doctorates awarded. *Program availability:* Part-time, evening/weekend, 100% online coursework with face to face internship requirements. Offers clinical social work (MSW); social leadership (MSW); social work (PhD). *Application deadline:* For fall admission, 6/1 for domestic and international students; for spring admission, 10/1 for domestic and international students; for summer admission, 3/1 for domestic and international students. Applications are processed on a rolling basis. *Application fee:* $30. Electronic applications accepted. *Application Contact:* Dana DeBoer, Coordinator of MSW Admissions, 800-378-9550, Fax: 850-644-9591, E-mail: ddeboer2@admin.fsu.edu. *Dean*, Dr. James Clark, 850-644-4752, Fax: 850-644-9750, E-mail: jclark5@fsu.edu.

FAMU-FSU College of Engineering Students: 324 full-time (75 women); includes 60 minority (26 Black or African American, non-Hispanic/Latino; 10 Asian, non-Hispanic/Latino; 19 Hispanic/Latino; 5 Two or more races, non-Hispanic/Latino), 187 international. Average age 25. 489 applicants, 39% accepted, 80 enrolled. *Faculty:* 97 full-time (12 women), 8 part-time/adjunct (3 women). Expenses: Contact institution. *Financial support:* In 2017–18, 359 students received support, including 2 fellowships with full tuition reimbursements available, 92 research assistantships with full tuition reimbursements available, 127 teaching assistantships with full tuition reimbursements available; career-related internships or fieldwork, scholarships/grants, tuition waivers (full), and unspecified assistantships also available. Financial award application deadline: 1/15; financial award applicants required to submit FAFSA. In 2017, 78 master's, 31 doctorates awarded. *Program availability:* Part-time. Offers biomedical engineering (MS, PhD); chemical engineering (MS, PhD); civil and environmental engineering (M Eng, MS, PhD); electrical engineering (MS, PhD); engineering (M Eng, MS, PhD); industrial engineering (MS, PhD); mechanical engineering (MS, PhD); sustainable energy (MS). *Application deadline:* For fall admission, 3/1 for domestic and international students; for spring admission, 11/1 for domestic and international students. Applications are processed on a rolling basis. *Application fee:* $30. Electronic applications accepted. *Application Contact:* Frederika Manciagli, Director, Student Services, 850-410-6361, E-mail: manciagl@eng.famu.fsu.edu. *Dean/Professor*, Dr. John Murray Gibson, 850-410-6161, Fax: 850-410-6546, E-mail: dean@eng.famu.fsu.edu.

FONTBONNE UNIVERSITY, St. Louis, MO 63105-3098

General Information Independent-religious, coed, comprehensive institution. *Graduate housing:* Room and/or apartments available on a first-come, first-served basis to single students; on-campus housing not available to married students. Housing application deadline: 5/1.

GRADUATE UNITS

Graduate Programs *Program availability:* Part-time, evening/weekend, online learning. Offers accounting (MBA, MS); art (MA); art (K-12) (MAT); business (MBA); computer science (MS); deaf education (MA); early intervention in deaf education (MA); education (MA); elementary education (MAT); family and consumer sciences (MA); fine arts (MFA); instructional design and technology (MS); management and leadership (MM); middle school education (MAT); secondary education (MAT); special education (MAT); speech-language pathology (MS); supply chain management (MS); theatre (MA). Electronic applications accepted.

FORDHAM UNIVERSITY, New York, NY 10458

General Information Independent-religious, coed, university. CGS member. *Graduate housing:* Room and/or apartments available on a first-come, first-served basis to single students; on-campus housing not available to married students. Housing application deadline: 4/10. *Research affiliation:* New York Ocean Science Library, Wildlife Conservation Society, Memorial Sloan-Kettering Cancer Center, Equator Initiative/United Nations Development Programme, Folger Shakespeare Library, New York Botanical Gardens.

GRADUATE UNITS

Gabelli School of Business Students: 1,051 full-time (570 women), 563 part-time (313 women); includes 190 minority (48 Black or African American, non-Hispanic/Latino; 72 Asian, non-Hispanic/Latino; 69 Hispanic/Latino; 1 Native Hawaiian or other Pacific Islander, non-Hispanic/Latino), 1,106 international. Average age 27. 4,577 applicants, 58% accepted, 794 enrolled. *Faculty:* 130 full-time (46 women), 42 part-time/adjunct (5 women). Expenses: Contact institution. *Financial support:* Career-related internships or fieldwork, institutionally sponsored loans, scholarships/grants, and unspecified assistantships available. Support available to part-time students. Financial award application deadline: 6/30; financial award applicants required to submit FAFSA. In 2017, 937 master's awarded. *Program availability:* Part-time, evening/weekend. Offers accounting (MBA, MS); applied statistics and decision-making (MS); business economics (DPS); capital markets (DPS); communications and media management (MBA); electronic business (MBA); entrepreneurship (MBA); finance (MBA, PhD); global finance (MS); global sustainability (MBA); health administration (MS); healthcare management (MBA); information systems (MBA, MS); investor relations (MS); management (EMBA, MBA, MS, PhD); marketing (MBA); marketing intelligence (MS); media management (MS); nonprofit leadership (MS); quantitative finance (MS); strategy and decision-making (DPS); taxation (MS). *Application deadline:* For fall admission, 11/15 priority date for domestic and international students; for winter admission, 1/19 priority date for domestic students, 1/1 priority date for international students; for spring admission, 4/15 for domestic students, 3/1 for international students; for summer admission, 6/1 for domestic students. *Application fee:* $130. Electronic applications accepted. *Application Contact:* Lawrence Murray, Senior Assistant Dean of Graduate Admissions and Advising, 212-636-6200, Fax: 212-636-7076, E-mail: admissionsgb@fordham.edu. *Dean,* Dr. Donna Rapaccioli, 212-636-6165, Fax: 212-307-1779, E-mail: rapaccioli@fordham.edu.

Graduate School of Arts and Sciences Students: 609 full-time (298 women), 190 part-time (88 women); includes 167 minority (45 Black or African American, non-Hispanic/Latino; 4 American Indian or Alaska Native, non-Hispanic/Latino; 46 Asian, non-Hispanic/Latino; 71 Hispanic/Latino; 1 Native Hawaiian or other Pacific Islander, non-Hispanic/Latino), 181 international. Average age 31. 2,504 applicants, 38% accepted, 392 enrolled. *Faculty:* 249 full-time (81 women). Expenses: Contact institution. *Financial support:* In 2017–18, 29 fellowships with tuition reimbursements (averaging $22,844 per year), 106 research assistantships with tuition reimbursements (averaging $16,516 per year), 280 teaching assistantships with tuition reimbursements (averaging $19,927 per year) were awarded; career-related internships or fieldwork, Federal Work-Study, institutionally sponsored loans, scholarships/grants, health care benefits, tuition waivers (full and partial), and unspecified assistantships also available. Support available to part-time students. Financial award application deadline: 1/4; financial award applicants required to submit FAFSA. In 2017, 145 master's, 56 doctorates, 87 other advanced degrees awarded. *Program availability:* Part-time, evening/weekend. Offers applied developmental psychology (PhD); applied psychological methods (MS); arts and sciences (MA, MFA, MS, PhD, Advanced Certificate, Certificate, Graduate Certificate); biological sciences (MS, PhD); classical languages and literatures (MA, PhD); clinical psychology (PhD); clinical research methods (MS); computer science (MS); conservation biology (Graduate Certificate); cyber security (MS); data analytics (MS); economics (MA, PhD); elections and campaign management (MA); English language and literature (MA, PhD); history (MA, PhD); international humanitarian action (MA); international political economy and development (MA, Certificate); philosophy (MA, PhD); playwriting (MFA); psychometrics and quantitative psychology (PhD); public media (MA); theology (MA, PhD); urban studies (MA). *Application deadline:* For fall admission, 1/4 priority date for domestic and international students; for spring admission, 10/31 for domestic and international students. Applications are processed on a rolling basis. *Application fee:* $70. Electronic applications accepted. *Application Contact:* Travis Strattion, Interim Director of Graduate Admissions, 718-817-4417, Fax: 718-817-3566, E-mail: tstrattion@fordham.edu. *Dean,* Dr. Eva Badowska, 718-817-4400, Fax: 718-817-4474, E-mail: badowska@fordham.edu.

Program in Ethics and Society Students: 13 full-time (8 women), 7 part-time (2 women); includes 8 minority (3 Asian, non-Hispanic/Latino; 5 Hispanic/Latino), 1 international. Average age 34. 37 applicants, 59% accepted, 8 enrolled. Expenses: Contact institution. *Financial support:* In 2017–18, 1 student received support. Teaching assistantships, Federal Work-Study, institutionally sponsored loans, scholarships/grants, tuition waivers (partial), and unspecified assistantships available. Financial award application deadline: 1/4. In 2017, 8 master's awarded. *Program availability:* Part-time. Offers ethics and society (MA); health care ethics (Certificate). *Application deadline:* For fall admission, 1/4 priority date for domestic students; for spring admission, 10/31 for domestic students. Applications are processed on a rolling basis. *Application fee:* $70. Electronic applications accepted. *Application Contact:* Bernadette Valentino-Morrison, Director of Graduate Admissions, 718-817-4419, Fax: 718-817-3566, E-mail: valentinomor@fordham.edu. *Director of Academic Programs, Fordham University Center for Ethics Education,* Dr. Bryan Pilkington, 718-817-3775, Fax: 212-759-2009, E-mail: afried@fordham.edu.

Program in Medieval Studies Students: 9 full-time (7 women), 14 part-time (7 women); includes 2 minority (both Hispanic/Latino). Average age 27. 17 applicants, 94% accepted, 9 enrolled. Expenses: Contact institution. *Financial support:* In 2017–18, 4 students received support. Institutionally sponsored loans, tuition waivers (full and partial), and unspecified assistantships available. Financial award application deadline: 1/4; financial award applicants required to submit FAFSA. In 2017, 8 master's, 2 other advanced degrees awarded. *Program availability:* Part-time, evening/weekend. Offers medieval studies (MA, Certificate). *Application deadline:* For fall admission, 1/4 priority date for domestic students; for spring admission, 11/1 for domestic students. Applications are processed on a rolling basis. *Application fee:* $70. Electronic applications accepted. *Application Contact:* Bernadette Valentino-Morrison, Director of Graduate Admissions, 718-817-4419, Fax: 718-817-3566, E-mail: valentinomor@fordham.edu. *Director,* Dr. Susanne Hafner, 718-817-4655, E-mail: hafner@fordham.edu.

Graduate School of Education *Program availability:* Part-time, evening/weekend. Offers education (MSE, MST, Ed D, PhD, Adv C). Electronic applications accepted.

Division of Curriculum and Teaching *Program availability:* Part-time, evening/weekend. Offers curriculum and teaching (MSE); early childhood education (MSE); elementary education (MST); special education (MSE, Adv C); teaching English as a second language (MSE). Electronic applications accepted.

Division of Educational Leadership, Administration and Policy *Program availability:* Part-time, evening/weekend. Offers administration and supervision (MSE, Adv C); administration and supervision for church leaders (PhD); educational administration and supervision (Ed D, PhD). Electronic applications accepted.

Division of Psychological and Educational Services *Program availability:* Part-time, evening/weekend. Offers counseling and personnel services (MSE); counseling psychology (PhD); school psychology (PhD). Electronic applications accepted.

Graduate School of Religion and Religious Education *Program availability:* Part-time. Offers pastoral counseling and spiritual care (MA); pastoral ministry/spirituality/pastoral counseling (D Min); religion and religious education (MA); religious education (MS, PhD, PD); spiritual direction (Certificate). Electronic applications accepted.

Graduate School of Social Service Students: 1,026 full-time (891 women), 636 part-time (560 women); includes 881 minority (377 Black or African American, non-Hispanic/Latino; 3 American Indian or Alaska Native, non-Hispanic/Latino; 52 Asian, non-Hispanic/Latino; 411 Hispanic/Latino; 7 Native Hawaiian or other Pacific Islander, non-Hispanic/Latino; 31 Two or more races, non-Hispanic/Latino), 24 international. Average age 32. *Faculty:* 37 full-time (25 women), 106 part-time/adjunct (29 women). Expenses: Contact institution. *Financial support:* In 2017–18, 838 students received support, including 39 research assistantships with partial tuition reimbursements available (averaging $1,980 per year); fellowships with partial tuition reimbursements available, career-related internships or fieldwork, Federal Work-Study, scholarships/grants, tuition waivers (partial), and unspecified assistantships also available. Support available to part-time students. Financial award application deadline: 2/1. In 2017, 697 master's, 5 doctorates awarded. *Program availability:* Part-time, evening/weekend, 100% online, blended/hybrid learning. Offers nonprofit leadership (MS); social work (MSW, PhD). MS program jointly sponsored with Graduate School of Business and conducted through the Fordham Center for Nonprofit Leaders; MSW/MPH offered with Ichan School of Public Health at Mount Sinai. *Application deadline:* For fall admission, 2/1 priority date for domestic students; for spring admission, 11/1 priority date for domestic students. Applications are processed on a rolling basis. *Application fee:* $60. Electronic applications accepted. *Application Contact:* Melba Remice, Assistant Dean of Admissions, 212-636-6600, Fax: 212-636-6613, E-mail: gssadmission@fordham.edu. *Dean,* Dr. Debra McPhee, 212-636-6616, E-mail: dmcphee1@fordham.edu.

School of Law *Program availability:* Part-time, evening/weekend. Offers banking, corporate and finance law (LL M); corporate compliance (MSL); fashion law (MSL); intellectual property and information law (LL M); international business and trade law (LL M); law (JD). Electronic applications accepted.

FORT HAYS STATE UNIVERSITY, Hays, KS 67601-4099

General Information State-supported, coed, comprehensive institution. CGS member. *Graduate housing:* Rooms and/or apartments available to single and married students. Housing application deadline: 8/1.

GRADUATE UNITS

Graduate School *Program availability:* Part-time. Electronic applications accepted.

College of Arts and Sciences *Program availability:* Part-time. Offers arts and sciences (MA, MFA, MLS, MS, Ed S); communication (MS); English (MA); history (MA); liberal studies (MLS); psychology (MS); school psychology (Ed S); studio art (MFA). Electronic applications accepted.

College of Business and Entrepreneurship *Program availability:* Part-time. Offers business and entrepreneurship (MBA); management (MBA). Electronic applications accepted.

College of Education *Program availability:* Part-time. Offers counseling (MS); education (MS, MSE, Ed S); educational administration (MS, Ed S); instructional technology (MS); special education (MS). Electronic applications accepted.

College of Health and Life Sciences *Program availability:* Part-time. Offers health and human performance (MS); health and life sciences (MS, MSN); nursing (MSN); speech-language pathology (MS). Electronic applications accepted.

College of Science, Technology and Mathematics Offers biology (MS); geography (MS); geology (MS); geosciences (MS); science, technology and mathematics (MS).

FORT LEWIS COLLEGE, Durango, CO 81301-3999

General Information State-supported, coed, comprehensive institution.

GRADUATE UNITS

Program in Teacher Leadership Offers teacher leadership (MA, Certificate).

FORT VALLEY STATE UNIVERSITY, Fort Valley, GA 31030

General Information State-supported, coed, comprehensive institution. *Graduate housing:* Room and/or apartments available on a first-come, first-served basis to single students; on-campus housing not available to married students. Housing application deadline: 7/1.

GRADUATE UNITS

College of Graduate Studies and Extended Education *Program availability:* Part-time. Offers animal science (MS); environmental health (MPH); guidance and counseling (Ed S); mental health counseling (MS); rehabilitation counseling (MS).

FRAMINGHAM STATE UNIVERSITY, Framingham, MA 01701-9101

General Information State-supported, coed, comprehensive institution. *Graduate housing:* On-campus housing not available. *Student services:* Career counseling, child daycare facilities, free psychological counseling, grant writing training, low-cost health insurance, multicultural affairs office, services for students with disabilities, teacher training, writing training. *Library facilities:* Henry Whittemore Library. *Collection:* Books: 155,690 (physical), 28,774 (digital/electronic); Serial titles: 120 (physical); Databases: 65. Weekly public service hours: 100.

Computer facilities: Computer purchase and lease plans are available. 216 computers available on campus for general student use. A campuswide network can be accessed from student residence rooms and from off campus. Online class registration is available.
Website: http://www.framingham.edu/

General Application Contact: Graduate and Continuing Education Office, 508-626-4550, Fax: 508-626-4030, E-mail: dgce@framingham.edu.

GRADUATE UNITS

Graduate Studies Expenses: Contact institution. *Program availability:* Part-time, evening/weekend, online learning. Offers art (M Ed); biotechnology operations (MBA); counseling psychology (MA); curriculum and instructional technology (M Ed); dietetics (MS); early childhood education (M Ed); educational leadership (MA); elementary education (M Ed); English (MA); healthcare administration (MHA); human resource management (MHR); literacy and language (M Ed); management (MBA); mathematics (M Ed); nursing education (MSN); nursing leadership (MSN); nutrition science and informatics (MS); public administration (MPA); special education (M Ed); teaching of English as a second language (M Ed, Graduate Certificate). *Application deadline:* For fall admission, 7/1 priority date for domestic students, 7/1 for international students; for spring admission, 11/1 for domestic and international students. Applications are processed on a rolling basis. *Application fee:* $50. *Associate Vice President of Academic Affairs and Dean of Continuing Education*, Dr. Scott Greenberg, 508-626-4603, E-mail: sgreenberg@framingham.edu.

FRANCISCAN MISSIONARIES OF OUR LADY UNIVERSITY, Baton Rouge, LA 70808

General Information Independent-religious, coed, comprehensive institution. *Graduate housing:* On-campus housing not available. *Student services:* Career counseling, exercise/wellness program, free psychological counseling, services for students with disabilities, writing training. *Collection:* Students can reserve study rooms.

Computer facilities: 150 computers available on campus for general student use. A campuswide network can be accessed. Online class registration is available.
Website: http://www.franu.edu/

GRADUATE UNITS

School of Health Professions Expenses: Contact institution. Offers health administration (MHA); nutritional sciences (MS); physical therapy (DPT); physician assistant studies (MMS). *Application Contact:* Dr. Susan K. Steele-Moses, Dean, 225-768-1676. *Dean*, Dr. Susan K. Steele-Moses, 225-768-1676.

School of Nursing Expenses: Contact institution. Offers family nurse practitioner (MSN); nurse anesthesia (DNP); nursing (MSN, DNP). *Application Contact:* Dr. Amy M. Hall, RN, Dean, 225-768-1753. *Dean*, Dr. Amy M. Hall, RN, 225-768-1753.

FRANCISCAN SCHOOL OF THEOLOGY, Oceanside, CA 92057

General Information Independent-religious, coed, graduate-only institution. *Graduate housing:* Rooms and/or apartments available on a first-come, first-served basis to single and married students. Housing application deadline: 5/15.

GRADUATE UNITS

Graduate and Professional Programs *Program availability:* Part-time. Offers theology (M Div, MA, MAMC, MTS).

FRANCISCAN UNIVERSITY OF STEUBENVILLE, Steubenville, OH 43952-1763

General Information Independent-religious, coed, comprehensive institution. *Enrollment:* 157 full-time matriculated graduate/professional students (70 women), 572 part-time matriculated graduate/professional students (332 women). *Enrollment by degree level:* 722 master's. *Graduate faculty:* 9 full-time (3 women), 46 part-time/adjunct (11 women). *Tuition:* Full-time $9000; part-time $500 per semester hour. *Required fees:* $16 per semester hour. Tuition and fees vary according to program. *Graduate housing:* On-campus housing not available. *Student services:* Campus employment opportunities, career counseling, exercise/wellness program, free psychological counseling, international student services, services for students with disabilities. *Library facilities:* St. John Paul II Library. *Collection:* Books: 143,662 (physical), 254,496 (digital/electronic); Serial titles: 590 (physical), 51,894 (digital/electronic); Databases: 131. Weekly public service hours: 93.

Computer facilities: Computer purchase and lease plans are available. 126 computers available on campus for general student use. A campuswide network can be accessed from student residence rooms. Online class registration is available.
Website: http://www.franciscan.edu/

General Application Contact: Tom Weishaar, Director of Online and Graduate Enrollment, 800-783-6220, Fax: 740-284-5456, E-mail: tweishaar@franciscan.edu.

GRADUATE UNITS

Graduate Programs *Program availability:* Part-time, evening/weekend, online learning. Offers administration (MS Ed); business (MBA); clinical mental health counseling (MA); nursing (MSN); philosophy (MA); teaching (MS Ed); theology and Christian ministry (MA). Electronic applications accepted.

FRANCIS MARION UNIVERSITY, Florence, SC 29502-0547

General Information State-supported, coed, comprehensive institution. *Graduate housing:* Room and/or apartments available on a first-come, first-served basis to single students; on-campus housing not available to married students. Housing application deadline: 5/1.

GRADUATE UNITS

Graduate Programs *Program availability:* Part-time, evening/weekend. Offers applied psychology (MS); family nurse practitioner (MSN); family nurse practitioner with nurse educator certificate (MSN); nurse educator (MSN); physician assistant (MPAS); school psychology (SSP). Electronic applications accepted.

School of Business *Program availability:* Part-time, evening/weekend. Offers business (MBA); health executive management (MBA).

School of Education *Program availability:* Part-time. Offers learning disabilities (M Ed, MAT).

FRANKLIN COLLEGE, Franklin, IN 46131

General Information Independent-religious, coed, comprehensive institution.

GRADUATE UNITS

Program in Athletic Training Offers athletic training (MSAT).

FRANKLIN PIERCE UNIVERSITY, Rindge, NH 03461-0060

General Information Independent, coed, university. *Graduate housing:* On-campus housing not available.

GRADUATE UNITS

Graduate and Professional Studies *Program availability:* Part-time, 100% online, blended/hybrid learning. Offers curriculum and instruction (M Ed); elementary education (MS Ed); emerging network technologies (Graduate Certificate); energy and sustainability studies (MBA, Graduate Certificate); health administration (MBA, Graduate Certificate); human resource management (MBA, Graduate Certificate); information technology (MBA); leadership (MBA); nursing education (MS); nursing leadership (MS); physical therapy (DPT); physician assistant studies (MPAS); special education (M Ed); sports management (MBA). Electronic applications accepted.

FRANKLIN UNIVERSITY, Columbus, OH 43215-5399

General Information Independent, coed, comprehensive institution. *Graduate housing:* On-campus housing not available.

GRADUATE UNITS

Accounting Program *Program availability:* Online learning. Offers accounting (MSA).

Computer Science Program *Program availability:* Part-time, evening/weekend. Offers computer science (MS). Electronic applications accepted.

Criminal Justice Administration Program Offers criminal justice administration (MA).

Instructional Design and Learning Technology Program Offers instructional design and learning technology (MS).

Marketing and Communication Program *Program availability:* Part-time, evening/weekend. Offers marketing and communication (MS). Electronic applications accepted.

MBA Program *Program availability:* Part-time, evening/weekend, online learning. Offers business administration (MBA). Electronic applications accepted.

FRANKLIN UNIVERSITY SWITZERLAND, CH-6924 Sorengo, Switzerland

General Information Independent, coed, comprehensive institution.

GRADUATE UNITS

The Taylor Institute for Global Enterprise Management Offers international management (MS).

FREDERICK S. PARDEE RAND GRADUATE SCHOOL, Santa Monica, CA 90407-2138

General Information Independent, coed, graduate-only institution. *Enrollment by degree level:* 107 doctoral. *Tuition:* Full-time $26,500. *Graduate housing:* On-campus housing not available. *Student services:* Campus employment opportunities, career counseling, exercise/wellness program, free psychological counseling, grant writing training, international student services, low-cost health insurance, writing training. *Library facilities:* RAND Library plus 1 other. *Collection:* Books: 17,327 (physical), 46,457 (digital/electronic); Serial titles: 1,271 (physical), 55,438 (digital/electronic); Databases: 61. Weekly public service hours: 65; study areas open 24 hours, 5–7 days a week; students can reserve study rooms. *Research affiliation:* RAND Corporation (not-for-profit research).

Computer facilities: 107 computers available on campus for general student use. Online class registration is available.
Website: http://www.prgs.edu/

General Application Contact: Mary Parker, Registrar/Admissions Manager, 310-393-0411 Ext. 7690, Fax: 310-451-6978, E-mail: mfparker@prgs.edu.

GRADUATE UNITS

Program in Policy Analysis Students: 107; includes 20 minority (3 Black or African American, non-Hispanic/Latino; 9 Asian, non-Hispanic/Latino; 8 Hispanic/Latino), 38 international. Average age 31. 136 applicants, 29% accepted, 22 enrolled. Expenses: Contact institution. *Financial support:* In 2017–18, 107 students received support, including 107 fellowships (averaging $46,000 per year), 30 teaching assistantships (averaging $2,000 per year); scholarships/grants and health care benefits also available. Financial award application deadline: 7/1. In 2017, 19 doctorates awarded. Offers policy analysis (PhD). *Application deadline:* For fall admission, 1/10 for domestic and international students. *Application fee:* $50. Electronic applications accepted. *Application Contact:* Mary Parker, Registrar/Admissions Manager, 310-393-0411 Ext. 7690, Fax: 310-451-6978, E-mail: mfparker@prgs.edu. *Dean*, Dr. Susan L. Marquis, 310-393-0411 Ext. 7075, Fax: 310-451-6978.

FREED-HARDEMAN UNIVERSITY, Henderson, TN 38340-2399

General Information Independent-religious, coed, comprehensive institution. *Graduate housing:* Room and/or apartments available on a first-come, first-served basis to single students; on-campus housing not available to married students. Housing application deadline: 8/22.

GRADUATE UNITS

Program in Business Administration *Program availability:* Part-time, evening/weekend, online learning. Offers accounting (MBA); corporate responsibility (MBA); leadership (MBA).

Program in Counseling *Program availability:* Part-time, evening/weekend. Offers counseling (MS).

Program in Education *Program availability:* Part-time, evening/weekend. Offers curriculum and instruction (M Ed); school counseling (M Ed); school leadership (Ed S).

School of Biblical Studies *Program availability:* Part-time. Offers biblical studies (M Div, M Min, MA); divinity (M Div); ministry (M Min); New Testament (MA).

FRESNO PACIFIC UNIVERSITY, Fresno, CA 93702-4709

General Information Independent-religious, coed, comprehensive institution. *Graduate housing:* Rooms and/or apartments available on a first-come, first-served basis to single and married students. Housing application deadline: 4/20.

GRADUATE UNITS

Biblical Seminary *Program availability:* Part-time, online learning. Offers Christian ministry (MA); community leadership and transformation (MA); divinity (M Div); marriage and family therapy (MA); New Testament (MA); Old Testament (MA); theology (MA); urban mission (MA).

Graduate Programs *Program availability:* Part-time, evening/weekend. Offers business administration (MBA); church conflict and peacemaking (Certificate); family nurse practitioner (MSN); individualized study (MA); kinesiology (MA); leadership and organizational studies (MA); mediation (Certificate); peacemaking and conflict studies (MA); restorative justice (Certificate). Electronic applications accepted.

School of Education *Program availability:* Part-time, evening/weekend. Offers administrative services (MA); board certified associate behavior analyst (Certificate); curriculum and teaching (MA); education (MA, MA Ed, Certificate); educational technology (MA); reading (Certificate); reading/English as a second language (MA Ed); reading/language arts (MA Ed); school counseling (MA); school library and information technology (MA Ed); school psychology (MA); special education (MA); STEM education (MA Ed). Electronic applications accepted.

FRIENDS UNIVERSITY, Wichita, KS 67213

General Information Independent-religious, coed, comprehensive institution.

GRADUATE UNITS

Graduate School *Program availability:* Part-time, evening/weekend, online learning. Offers family therapy (MSFT); global business administration (MBA); health care leadership (MHCL); management information systems (MMIS); professional business administration (MBA). Electronic applications accepted.

FRONTIER NURSING UNIVERSITY, Hyden, KY 41749

General Information Independent, coed, primarily women, graduate-only institution.

GRADUATE UNITS

Graduate Programs Offers family nurse practitioner (MSN, DNP, Post Master's Certificate); nurse-midwifery (MSN, DNP, Post Master's Certificate); psychiatric-mental health nurse practitioner (MSN, DNP, Post Master's Certificate); women's health care nurse practitioner (MSN, DNP, Post Master's Certificate).

FROSTBURG STATE UNIVERSITY, Frostburg, MD 21532-1099

General Information State-supported, coed, comprehensive institution. *Enrollment:* 5,396 graduate, professional, and undergraduate students; 176 full-time matriculated graduate/professional students (110 women), 495 part-time matriculated graduate/professional students (317 women). *Enrollment by degree level:* 589 master's, 82 doctoral. *Graduate faculty:* 84 full-time (40 women), 38 part-time/adjunct (28 women). Tuition, state resident: part-time $433 per credit hour. Tuition, nonresident: part-time $557 per credit hour. *Required fees:* $121 per credit hour. $27 per term. *Graduate housing:* Room and/or apartments available to single students; on-campus housing not available to married students. Typical cost: $5980 per year ($10,670 including board). Housing application deadline: 6/1. *Student services:* Career counseling, child daycare facilities, free psychological counseling, international student services, services for students with disabilities. *Library facilities:* Lewis J. Ort Library.

Computer facilities: Computer purchase and lease plans are available. 577 computers available on campus for general student use. A campuswide network can be accessed from student residence rooms and from off campus. Online class registration is available.
Website: http://www.frostburg.edu/

General Application Contact: Vickie Mazer, Director, Graduate Services, 301-687-7053, Fax: 301-687-4597, E-mail: vmmazer@frostburg.edu.

GRADUATE UNITS

College of Business Students: 33 full-time (14 women), 143 part-time (77 women); includes 38 minority (20 Black or African American, non-Hispanic/Latino; 9 Asian, non-Hispanic/Latino; 6 Hispanic/Latino; 3 Two or more races, non-Hispanic/Latino), 3 international. Average age 34. 55 applicants, 60% accepted, 22 enrolled. *Faculty:* 12 full-time (5 women), 2 part-time/adjunct (1 woman). Expenses: Contact institution. *Financial support:* In 2017–18, 8 research assistantships with full tuition reimbursements (averaging $5,000 per year) were awarded; career-related internships or fieldwork and Federal Work-Study also available. Financial award application deadline: 4/1; financial award applicants required to submit FAFSA. In 2017, 75 master's awarded. *Program availability:* Part-time, evening/weekend. Offers business (MBA); business administration (MBA). *Application deadline:* For fall admission, 7/15 priority date for domestic students. Applications are processed on a rolling basis. *Application fee:* $45. Electronic applications accepted. *Application Contact:* Vickie Mazer, Director, Graduate Services, 301-687-7053, Fax: 301-687-4597, E-mail: vmmazer@frostburg.edu. *Dean*, Dr. Sudhir Singh, 301-687-4019, E-mail: ssingh@frostburg.edu.

College of Education Students: 89 full-time (63 women), 273 part-time (193 women); includes 31 minority (20 Black or African American, non-Hispanic/Latino; 1 Asian, non-Hispanic/Latino; 4 Hispanic/Latino; 6 Two or more races, non-Hispanic/Latino), 3 international. Average age 30. 210 applicants, 74% accepted, 103 enrolled. *Faculty:* 24 full-time (17 women), 33 part-time/adjunct (26 women). Expenses: Contact institution. *Financial support:* In 2017–18, 29 research assistantships with full tuition reimbursements (averaging $5,000 per year) were awarded; career-related internships or fieldwork and Federal Work-Study also available. Financial award application deadline: 4/1; financial award applicants required to submit FAFSA. In 2017, 96 master's, 12 doctorates awarded. *Program availability:* Part-time, evening/weekend. Offers curriculum and instruction (M Ed, Ed D); education (M Ed, MAT, MS, Ed D); educational administration and supervision (M Ed, Ed D); educational technology (M Ed); elementary (M Ed); elementary education (M Ed); elementary teaching (MAT); interdisciplinary education (M Ed, Ed D); parks and recreational management (MS); reading (M Ed, Ed D); school counseling (M Ed); secondary (M Ed); secondary education (M Ed); secondary teaching (MAT); special education (M Ed). *Application deadline:* For fall admission, 7/15 priority date for domestic students. Applications are processed on a rolling basis. *Application fee:* $45. Electronic applications accepted. *Application Contact:* Vickie Mazer, Director, Graduate Services, 301-687-7053, Fax: 301-687-4597, E-mail: vmmazer@frostburg.edu. *Interim Dean*, Dr. Boyce Williams, 301-687-4759, E-mail: bcwilliams@frostburg.edu.

College of Liberal Arts and Sciences Students: 52 full-time (32 women), 59 part-time (35 women); includes 10 minority (5 Black or African American, non-Hispanic/Latino; 2 Asian, non-Hispanic/Latino; 3 Hispanic/Latino), 15 international. Average age 29. 110 applicants, 49% accepted, 34 enrolled. *Faculty:* 30 full-time (14 women), 1 part-time/adjunct (0 women). Expenses: Contact institution. *Financial support:* In 2017–18, 31 research assistantships with full tuition reimbursements (averaging $5,000 per year) were awarded; career-related internships or fieldwork and Federal Work-Study also available. Financial award application deadline: 4/1; financial award applicants required to submit FAFSA. In 2017, 97 master's awarded. *Program availability:* Part-time, evening/weekend. Offers applied computer science (MS); applied ecology and conservation biology (MS); counseling psychology (MS); fisheries and wildlife management (MS); liberal arts and sciences (MS, MSN); nursing administration (MSN); nursing education (MSN). *Application deadline:* Applications are processed on a rolling basis. *Application fee:* $45. Electronic applications accepted. *Application Contact:* Vickie Mazer, Director, Graduate Services, 301-687-7053, Fax: 301-687-4597, E-mail: vmmazer@frostburg.edu. *Interim Dean*, Dr. Dorothy Campbell, 301-687-3165, E-mail: dicampbell@frostburg.edu.

FULLER THEOLOGICAL SEMINARY, Pasadena, CA 91182

General Information Independent-religious, coed, graduate-only institution. *Graduate housing:* Rooms and/or apartments available on a first-come, first-served basis to single and married students.

GRADUATE UNITS

Graduate Programs Offers Christian leadership (MACL); clinical psychology (PhD, Psy D); family studies (MA); global leadership (MA); global ministries (D Min); global ministries (Korean language) (D Min); intercultural studies (MA, Th M, PhD); intercultural studies (Korean language) (MA); marital and family therapy (MS); marriage and family enrichment (Certificate); ministry (M Div, D Min); missiology (D Miss); missiology (Korean language) (Th M); theology (MA, Th M, PhD); theology and ministry (MA).

FULL SAIL UNIVERSITY, Winter Park, FL 32792-7437

General Information Proprietary, coed, primarily men, comprehensive institution. *Graduate housing:* On-campus housing not available.

GRADUATE UNITS

Creative Writing Master of Fine Arts Program - Online *Program availability:* Online learning. Offers creative writing (MFA).

Education Media Design and Technology Master of Science Program - Online *Program availability:* Online learning. Offers education media design and technology (MS).

Entertainment Business Master of Science Program - Campus Offers entertainment business (MS).

Entertainment Business Master of Science Program - Online *Program availability:* Online learning. Offers entertainment business (MS).

Game Design Master of Science Program - Campus Offers game design (MS).

Internet Marketing Master of Science Program - Online *Program availability:* Online learning. Offers Internet marketing (MS).

Media Design Master of Fine Arts Program - Online *Program availability:* Online learning. Offers media design (MFA).

New Media Journalism Master of Arts Program - Online Offers new media journalism (MA).

FURMAN UNIVERSITY, Greenville, SC 29613

General Information Independent, coed, comprehensive institution. CGS member. *Graduate housing:* On-campus housing not available.

GRADUATE UNITS

Graduate Division *Program availability:* Part-time, online learning. Offers chemistry (MS); curriculum and instruction (MA); early childhood education (MA); educational leadership (Ed S); English as a second language (MA); literacy (MA); school leadership (MA); special education (MA).

FUTURE GENERATIONS UNIVERSITY, Franklin, WV 26807

General Information Independent, coed, graduate-only institution. *Enrollment by degree level:* 20 master's. *Graduate faculty:* 4 full-time (1 woman), 4 part-time/adjunct (2 women). *Graduate housing:* On-campus housing not available. *Student services:* Campus safety program, international student services, services for students with disabilities.

Computer facilities: Online class registration is available.
Website: http://www.future.edu/

General Application Contact: Christie Hand, Chief Academic Officer, 304-358-2000, E-mail: christie@future.edu.

GRADUATE UNITS

Program in Applied Community Change Students: 16 full-time (7 women); includes 13 minority (6 Black or African American, non-Hispanic/Latino; 4 Asian, non-Hispanic/Latino; 3 Hispanic/Latino). *Faculty:* 9 full-time (3 women), 12 part-time/adjunct (4 women). Expenses: Contact institution. *Financial support:* Scholarships/grants and tuition waivers (partial) available. Financial award applicants required to submit FAFSA. In 2017, 11 master's awarded. *Program availability:* Blended/hybrid learning. Offers conservation (MA). *Application deadline:* Applications are processed on a rolling basis. *Application fee:* $0. Electronic applications accepted. *Application Contact:* Jodie Wimer, Registrar, 304-358-2000, E-mail: jwimer@future.edu. *Chief Academic Officer*, Christie Hand, 304-358-2000.

GALLAUDET UNIVERSITY, Washington, DC 20002-3625

General Information Independent, coed, university. CGS member. *Graduate housing:* Rooms and/or apartments available on a first-come, first-served basis to single and married students. Housing application deadline: 4/1. *Research affiliation:* National Science Foundation/Howard University (linguistics, visual language and visual learning, integrated quantum materials), Maryland Sea Grant/University of Maryland/National Oceanic and Atmospheric Administration (NOAA) (advanced recruitment and retention in geosciences), U.S. Department of Education/Vcom3D Inc. (signing math dictionaries with mouth morphemes; accessibility and usability technologies for deaf and hard of hearing), Spencer Foundation (deaf legal discourse), University of Wisconsin-Madison/U.S. Department of Education (DOE) (telecommunications access), University of California Los Angeles/National Institutes of Health (cancer genetics).

GRADUATE UNITS

The Graduate School *Program availability:* Part-time. Offers American Sign Language/English bilingual early childhood deaf education: birth to 5 (Certificate); audiology (Au D); clinical psychology (PhD); deaf and hard of hearing infants, toddlers, and their families (Certificate); deaf education (MA, Ed S); deaf history (Certificate); deaf studies (Certificate); educating deaf students with disabilities (Certificate); education: teacher preparation (MA); educational neuroscience (PhD); hearing, speech and language sciences (MS, PhD); international development (MA); interpretation (MA, PhD); linguistics (MA, PhD); mental health counseling (MA); peer mentoring (Certificate); public administration (MPA); school counseling (MA); school psychology (Psy S); sign language teaching (MA); social work (MSW); speech-language pathology (MS). Electronic applications accepted.

GANNON UNIVERSITY, Erie, PA 16541-0001

General Information Independent-religious, coed, university. *Graduate housing:* Rooms and/or apartments available on a first-come, first-served basis to single and married students. *Research affiliation:* GE Global Research (nanotechnology), LifeLink Technologies (postural stability of flooring), Erie Insurance, Precision Rehabilitation Manufacturing (software development), AirBorn (PPS software enhancer).

GRADUATE UNITS

School of Graduate Studies *Program availability:* Part-time, evening/weekend, 100% online, blended/hybrid learning. Electronic applications accepted.

College of Engineering and Business *Program availability:* Part-time, evening/weekend, 100% online, blended/hybrid learning. Offers business administration (MBA, MPA); computer and information science (MSCIS); electrical and computer engineering (MSEE, MSES); engineering and business (MBA, MPA, MS, MSCIS, MSEE, MSEH, MSEM, MSES, MSME, Certificate); engineering management (MSEM); environmental health (MSEH); environmental health and engineering (MS); environmental science and engineering (MS, MSEH); finance (MBA); human resources management (MBA); information analytics (MSCIS, MSCIS); marketing (MBA); mechanical engineering (MSME); public administration (MPA); software engineering (MSCIS). Electronic applications accepted.

College of Humanities, Education, and Social Sciences *Program availability:* Part-time, evening/weekend, 100% online, blended/hybrid learning. Offers clinical mental health counseling (MS); criminalistics (MSC); curriculum and instruction (M Ed); curriculum supervisor (Certificate); English (MA); English as a second language (Certificate); health communication (MA); humanities, education, and social sciences

(M Ed, MA, MS, MSC, PhD, Certificate); organizational learning and leadership (PhD); pastoral studies (MA, Certificate); principal certification (Certificate); reading (M Ed); reading specialist (Certificate); superintendent letter of eligibility (Certificate); theological studies (Certificate). Electronic applications accepted.

Morosky College of Health Professions and Sciences *Program availability:* Part-time, evening/weekend, 100% online. Offers athletic training (MAT); family nurse practitioner (MSN, Certificate); health professions and sciences (MAT, MPAS, MS, MSN, DNP, DPT, OTD, Certificate); human performance (MS); nurse anesthesia (MSN, Certificate); nursing administration (MSN); nursing practice (DNP); occupational therapy (MS, OTD); physical therapy (DPT); physician assistant science (MPAS); sport and exercise science (MS). Electronic applications accepted.

GARDNER-WEBB UNIVERSITY, Boiling Springs, NC 28017

General Information Independent-religious, coed, university. *Enrollment:* 204 full-time matriculated graduate/professional students (115 women), 1,399 part-time matriculated graduate/professional students (1,030 women). *Enrollment by degree level:* 1,102 master's, 472 doctoral, 29 other advanced degrees. *Graduate faculty:* 69 full-time (36 women), 54 part-time/adjunct (33 women). *Tuition:* Part-time $455 per credit hour. *Graduate housing:* Room and/or apartments available on a first-come, first-served basis to single students; on-campus housing not available to married students. Typical cost: $5100 per year ($10,080 including board). *Student services:* Campus employment opportunities, campus safety program, career counseling, exercise/wellness program, free psychological counseling, international student services, low-cost health insurance, services for students with disabilities, teacher training, writing training. *Library facilities:* Dover Memorial Library plus 1 other.

Computer facilities: Computer purchase and lease plans are available. 121 computers available on campus for general student use. A campuswide network can be accessed from student residence rooms and from off campus. Online class registration is available. Website: http://www.gardner-webb.edu/

General Application Contact: Office of Graduate Admissions, 877-498-4723, Fax: 704-406-3895, E-mail: gradinfo@gardner-webb.edu.

GRADUATE UNITS

Graduate School Students: 204 full-time (115 women), 1,399 part-time (1,030 women); includes 542 minority (469 Black or African American, non-Hispanic/Latino; 11 American Indian or Alaska Native, non-Hispanic/Latino; 17 Asian, non-Hispanic/Latino; 27 Hispanic/Latino; 1 Native Hawaiian or other Pacific Islander, non-Hispanic/Latino; 17 Two or more races, non-Hispanic/Latino), 3 international. Average age 27. 1,319 applicants, 51% accepted, 131 enrolled. *Faculty:* 69 full-time (36 women), 52 part-time/adjunct (32 women). Expenses: Contact institution. *Financial support:* Fellowships, Federal Work-Study, institutionally sponsored loans, and unspecified assistantships available. Support available to part-time students. In 2017, 385 master's, 94 doctorates awarded. *Program availability:* Part-time, evening/weekend. Offers English (MA); English education (MA); physician assistant studies (MPAS); sport science and pedagogy (MA). *Application deadline:* Applications are processed on a rolling basis. *Application fee:* $0. Electronic applications accepted. *Application Contact:* Michael Utsman, Office of Graduate Admissions, 704-406-4490, Fax: 704-406-3972, E-mail: gradinfo@gardner-webb.edu. *Dean,* Dr. Jeff Rogers, 704-406-4724, E-mail: gradschool@gardner-webb.edu.

Graduate School of Business Students: 27 full-time (13 women), 236 part-time (126 women); includes 63 minority (45 Black or African American, non-Hispanic/Latino; 1 American Indian or Alaska Native, non-Hispanic/Latino; 3 Asian, non-Hispanic/Latino; 10 Hispanic/Latino; 4 Two or more races, non-Hispanic/Latino), 1 international. Average age 26. *Faculty:* 11 full-time (3 women), 5 part-time/adjunct (1 woman). Expenses: Contact institution. *Financial support:* In 2017–18, 23 students received support. Unspecified assistantships available. Support available to part-time students. Financial award applicants required to submit FAFSA. *Program availability:* Part-time, evening/weekend, online learning. Offers business (IMBA, M Acc, MBA). *Application deadline:* For spring admission, 1/15 for domestic students. Applications are processed on a rolling basis. Electronic applications accepted. *Dean,* Mischia Taylor, 704-406-2324, E-mail: mtaylor@gardner-webb.edu.

School of Education Students: 13 full-time (10 women), 736 part-time (567 women); includes 332 minority (306 Black or African American, non-Hispanic/Latino; 6 American Indian or Alaska Native, non-Hispanic/Latino; 4 Asian, non-Hispanic/Latino; 9 Hispanic/Latino; 1 Native Hawaiian or other Pacific Islander, non-Hispanic/Latino; 6 Two or more races, non-Hispanic/Latino). Average age 33. *Faculty:* 15 full-time (7 women), 33 part-time/adjunct (20 women). Expenses: Contact institution. *Financial support:* Unspecified assistantships available. *Program availability:* Part-time, evening/weekend. Offers curriculum and instruction (Ed D); educational leadership (Ed D); executive leadership studies (MA, Ed S); organizational leadership (Ed D); school administration (MA). *Application deadline:* For fall admission, 8/1 priority date for domestic students. Applications are processed on a rolling basis. Electronic applications accepted. *Application Contact:* Office of Graduate Admissions, 877-498-4723, Fax: 704-406-3895, E-mail: gradinfo@gardner-webb.edu.

School of Nursing Students: 1 (woman) full-time, 223 part-time (206 women); includes 41 minority (31 Black or African American, non-Hispanic/Latino; 2 American Indian or Alaska Native, non-Hispanic/Latino; 4 Asian, non-Hispanic/Latino; 2 Hispanic/Latino; 2 Two or more races, non-Hispanic/Latino), 2 international. Average age 37. *Faculty:* 13 full-time (11 women), 8 part-time/adjunct (all women). Expenses: Contact institution. *Program availability:* Part-time, online learning. Offers family nurse practitioner (MSN, DNP). *Application Contact:* Office of Graduate Admissions, 877-498-4723, Fax: 704-406-3895, E-mail: gradinfo@gardner-webb.edu. *Dean,* Nicole Waters, 704-406-4358, Fax: 704-406-4329, E-mail: gradschool@gardner-webb.edu.

School of Psychology Students: 1 full-time (0 women), 88 part-time (76 women); includes 19 minority (13 Black or African American, non-Hispanic/Latino; 1 American Indian or Alaska Native, non-Hispanic/Latino; 3 Hispanic/Latino; 2 Two or more races, non-Hispanic/Latino). Average age 31. *Faculty:* 5 full-time (4 women), 4 part-time/adjunct (2 women). Expenses: Contact institution. *Financial support:* Unspecified assistantships available. *Program availability:* Part-time, evening/weekend. Offers mental health counseling (MA); school counseling (MA). *Application deadline:* For fall admission, 7/1 priority date for domestic students. Applications are processed on a rolling basis. Electronic applications accepted. *Application Contact:* Office of Graduate Admissions, 877-498-4723, Fax: 704-406-3895, E-mail: gradinfo@gardner-webb.edu. *Chair,* Dr. David Carscaddon, 704-406-4437, Fax: 704-406-4329, E-mail: dcarscaddon@gardner-webb.edu.

School of Divinity Students: 102 full-time (47 women), 56 part-time (15 women); includes 67 minority (63 Black or African American, non-Hispanic/Latino; 3 Asian, non-Hispanic/Latino; 1 Hispanic/Latino). Average age 38. *Faculty:* 10 full-time (1 woman), 4 part-time/adjunct (2 women). Expenses: Contact institution. *Financial support:* Fellowships, institutionally sponsored loans, and unspecified assistantships available. Support available to part-time students. Financial award application deadline: 5/15. *Program availability:* Part-time. Offers biblical studies (M Div); Christian education and formation (M Div); intercultural studies (M Div); ministry (D Min); missiology (M Div); pastoral care and counseling (M Div); pastoral care and counseling/member care for missionaries (D Min); pastoral studies (M Div). *Application deadline:* Applications are processed on a rolling basis. Electronic applications accepted. *Application Contact:* Kheresa Harmon, Director of Admissions, 704-406-3205, Fax: 704-406-3895, E-mail: kharmon@gardner-webb.edu. *Dean,* Dr. Robert W. Canoy, Sr., 704-406-4400, Fax: 704-406-3935, E-mail: rcanoy@gardner-webb.edu.

GARRETT-EVANGELICAL THEOLOGICAL SEMINARY, Evanston, IL 60201-3298

General Information Independent-religious, coed, graduate-only institution. *Graduate housing:* Rooms and/or apartments guaranteed to single students and available to married students. Housing application deadline: 4/1.

GRADUATE UNITS

Graduate and Professional Programs *Program availability:* Part-time. Offers Bible and culture (PhD); Christian education (MA); Christian education and congregational studies (PhD); contemporary theology and culture (PhD); divinity (M Div); ethics, church, and society (MA); liturgical studies (PhD); ministry (D Min); music ministry (MA); pastoral care and counseling (MA); pastoral theology, personality, and culture (PhD); spiritual formation and evangelism (MA); theological studies (MTS). M Div/MSW offered jointly with Loyola University Chicago. Electronic applications accepted.

GATEWAY SEMINARY, Ontario, CA 91761-8642

General Information Independent-religious, coed, graduate-only institution. *Graduate housing:* Rooms and/or apartments available on a first-come, first-served basis to single and married students. Housing application deadline: 6/15.

GRADUATE UNITS

Graduate and Professional Programs *Program availability:* Part-time, evening/weekend. Offers divinity (M Div); early childhood education (Certificate); education leadership (MAEL, Diploma); ministry (D Min); theological studies (MTS); theology (Th M); youth ministry (Certificate). Electronic applications accepted.

GEISINGER COMMONWEALTH SCHOOL OF MEDICINE, Scranton, PA 18509

General Information Independent, coed, graduate-only institution.

GRADUATE UNITS

Graduate Programs in Medicine *Program availability:* Part-time, evening/weekend. Offers biomedical sciences (MBS). Electronic applications accepted.

Professional Program in Medicine Offers medicine (MD).

GENERAL THEOLOGICAL SEMINARY, New York, NY 10011-4977

General Information Independent-religious, coed, graduate-only institution. *Graduate housing:* Rooms and/or apartments available to single and married students. Housing application deadline: 6/1.

GRADUATE UNITS

Graduate and Professional Programs *Program availability:* Part-time, evening/weekend. Offers Anglican studies (STM, Th D, Certificate); ascetical theology (Certificate); biblical studies (Certificate); congregational development (Certificate); divinity (M Div); historical and theological studies (Certificate); spiritual direction (MASD, STM, Certificate); theology (MA).

GENEVA COLLEGE, Beaver Falls, PA 15010-3599

General Information Independent-religious, coed, comprehensive institution. *Enrollment:* 1,599 graduate, professional, and undergraduate students; 143 full-time matriculated graduate/professional students (88 women), 38 part-time matriculated graduate/professional students (24 women). *Enrollment by degree level:* 181 master's. *Graduate faculty:* 12 full-time (4 women), 16 part-time/adjunct (3 women). *Tuition:* Full-time $11,570; part-time $5785 per credit. *Required fees:* $34; $34 per credit. *Graduate housing:* On-campus housing not available. *Student services:* Campus employment opportunities, campus safety program, career counseling, free psychological counseling, international student services, low-cost health insurance, multicultural affairs office, services for students with disabilities, teacher training. *Library facilities:* McCartney Library plus 3 others. *Collection:* Books: 139,301 (physical), 12,739 (digital/electronic); Serial titles: 438 (physical), 20 (digital/electronic); Databases: 53. Weekly public service hours: 84. *Research affiliation:* INOVA Fairfax Hospital (cardiovascular science).

Computer facilities: 150 computers available on campus for general student use. A campuswide network can be accessed from student residence rooms and from off campus. Online class registration is available.
Website: http://www.geneva.edu/

General Application Contact: Information Contact, 724-846-5100.

GRADUATE UNITS

Master of Arts in Counseling Program Students: 34 full-time (26 women), 20 part-time (16 women); includes 12 minority (11 Black or African American, non-Hispanic/Latino; 1 Hispanic/Latino), 1 international. Average age 33. *Faculty:* 6 full-time (3 women), 3 part-time/adjunct (1 woman). Expenses: Contact institution. *Financial support:* Research assistantships, teaching assistantships, career-related internships or fieldwork, and unspecified assistantships available. Financial award application deadline: 8/1; financial award applicants required to submit FAFSA. In 2017, 34 master's awarded. *Program availability:* Part-time, evening/weekend. Offers clinical mental health counseling (MA); marriage and family counseling (MA); school counseling (MA). *Application deadline:* For fall admission, 9/1 for domestic students; for spring admission, 1/10 for domestic students. Applications are processed on a rolling basis. Electronic applications accepted. *Application Contact:* Marina Frazier, Graduate Program Manager, 724-847-6697, E-mail: counseling@geneva.edu. *Program Director,* Dr. Shannan Shiderly, 724-847-6649, Fax: 724-847-6101, E-mail: slshider@geneva.edu.

Master of Arts in Higher Education Program Students: 44 full-time (27 women), 10 part-time (6 women); includes 8 minority (5 Black or African American, non-Hispanic/Latino; 2 Hispanic/Latino; 1 Two or more races, non-Hispanic/Latino), 1 international. Average age 27. 40 applicants, 75% accepted, 21 enrolled. *Faculty:* 1 full-time (0 women), 6 part-time/adjunct (1 woman). Expenses: Contact institution. *Financial support:* Unspecified assistantships available. Financial award application deadline: 8/1; financial award applicants required to submit FAFSA. In 2017, 18 master's awarded. *Program availability:* Part-time, evening/weekend, blended/hybrid learning. Offers campus ministry (MA); college teaching (MA); educational leadership (MA); student affairs administration (MA). *Application deadline:* Applications are processed on a rolling basis. *Application fee:* $0. Electronic applications accepted. *Application Contact:* Allison Davis, Assistant Director, 724-847-6510, Fax: 724-847-6696, E-mail: hed@geneva.edu. *Program Director,* Dr. Keith Martel, 724-847-6884, Fax: 724-847-6107, E-mail: hed@geneva.edu.

Program in Business Administration Students: 33 full-time (13 women), 8 part-time (2 women); includes 6 minority (4 Black or African American, non-Hispanic/Latino; 1 American Indian or Alaska Native, non-Hispanic/Latino; 1 Asian, non-Hispanic/Latino). Average age 37. 25 applicants, 52% accepted, 10 enrolled. *Faculty:* 5 full-time (1 woman), 3 part-time/adjunct (0 women). Expenses: Contact institution. *Financial support:* In 2017–18, 1 student received support. Scholarships/grants available. Financial award application deadline: 8/1; financial award applicants required to submit FAFSA. In 2017, 14 master's awarded. *Program availability:* Part-time, evening/weekend. Offers business administration (MBA); finance (MBA); marketing (MBA); operations (MBA). *Application deadline:* For fall admission, 3/1 priority date for domestic students; for spring admission, 11/1 priority date for domestic students. Applications are processed on a rolling basis. Electronic applications accepted. *Application Contact:* Marina Frazier, Director of Graduate Enrollment, 724-847-6697, E-mail: mba@geneva.edu. *Director of the MBA Program*, Dr. Gary Vander Plaats, 724-847-6619, E-mail: gpvander@geneva.edu.

Program in Leadership Studies Students: 32 full-time (22 women); includes 10 minority (8 Black or African American, non-Hispanic/Latino; 1 Asian, non-Hispanic/Latino; 1 Hispanic/Latino). Average age 43. 25 applicants, 60% accepted, 11 enrolled. *Faculty:* 4 part-time/adjunct (1 woman). Expenses: Contact institution. *Financial support:* Scholarships/grants available. Financial award application deadline: 8/1; financial award applicants required to submit FAFSA. In 2017, 35 master's awarded. *Program availability:* Online only, 100% online. Offers business management (MS); ministry leadership (MS); non-profit leadership (MS); organizational management (MS); project management (MS). *Application deadline:* For fall admission, 9/21 for domestic students; for spring admission, 2/23 for domestic students; for summer admission, 7/22 for domestic students. Applications are processed on a rolling basis. Electronic applications accepted. *Application Contact:* Graduate Enrollment Representative, 800-576-3111, Fax: 724-847-6839, E-mail: msls@geneva.edu. *Dean of Graduate, Adult and Online Programs*, John D. Gallo, 800-576-3111, Fax: 724-847-6839, E-mail: msls@geneva.edu.

GEORGE FOX UNIVERSITY, Newberg, OR 97132-2697

General Information Independent-religious, coed, university. *Graduate housing:* On-campus housing not available.

GRADUATE UNITS

College of Business *Program availability:* Part-time, evening/weekend, online learning. Offers accounting (DBA); finance (MBA); management (DBA); management and leadership (MBA); marketing (DBA); organizational strategy (MBA); strategic human resource management (MBA). MBA offered in Newberg, OR and in Portland, OR. Electronic applications accepted.

College of Education Offers administrative leadership (Ed S); clinical mental health counseling (MA); continuing administrator license (Certificate); education (M Ed, MA, MAT, Ed D, Certificate, Ed S); educational leadership (M Ed); educational technology (M Ed); English for speakers of other languages (M Ed); ESOL (Certificate); initial administrator license (Certificate); marriage, couple and family counseling (MA, Certificate); reading (M Ed, Certificate); school counseling (MA, Certificate); school psychology (Ed S); special education (M Ed); teaching (MAT).

Portland Seminary *Program availability:* Part-time, evening/weekend, online learning. Offers Biblical studies (M Div, MA); chaplaincy (M Div); Christian history and theology (M Div, MA); creation care (M Div, MA); intercultural studies (M Div, MA); leadership (M Div, MA); leadership and global perspectives (D Min); leadership and spiritual formation (D Min); semiotics and future studies (D Min); spiritual direction (MA, Certificate); spiritual direction supervision (M Div, MA, Certificate); spiritual formation and discipleship (M Div, MA, Certificate). Electronic applications accepted.

Program in Clinical Psychology Offers clinical psychology (Psy D). Electronic applications accepted.

Program in Physical Therapy Offers physical therapy (DPT). Electronic applications accepted.

School of Social Work Offers social work (MSW).

GEORGE MASON UNIVERSITY, Fairfax, VA 22030

General Information State-supported, coed, university. CGS member. *Enrollment:* 35,960 graduate, professional, and undergraduate students; 4,108 full-time matriculated graduate/professional students (2,240 women), 5,977 part-time matriculated graduate/professional students (3,650 women). *Enrollment by degree level:* 6,883 master's, 2,707 doctoral, 495 other advanced degrees. *Graduate faculty:* 1,421 full-time (592 women), 1,199 part-time/adjunct (538 women). Tuition, state resident: full-time $11,228; part-time $459.50 per credit. Tuition, nonresident: full-time $30,932; part-time $1280.50 per credit. *Required fees:* $3252; $135.50 per credit. Part-time tuition and fees vary according to course load and program. *Graduate housing:* Room and/or apartments available on a first-come, first-served basis to single students; on-campus housing not available to married students. Typical cost: $11,180 per year. Housing application deadline: 5/1. *Student services:* Campus employment opportunities, campus safety program, career counseling, child daycare facilities, exercise/wellness program, free psychological counseling, grant writing training, international student services, low-cost health insurance, multicultural affairs office, services for students with disabilities, teacher training, writing training. *Library facilities:* Fenwick Library plus 3 others. *Collection:* Books: 1.4 million (physical), 1.8 million (digital/electronic); Serial titles: 1,177 (physical), 189,776 (digital/electronic); Databases: 775. Weekly public service hours: 87; study areas open 24 hours, 5–7 days a week; students can reserve study rooms. *Research affiliation:* Science Applications International Corporation (science and technology), Lockheed Martin Corporation (science and technology), Inova Health System (health care and medical research), CIT Center for Innovative Technology (nonprofit technology company), Alion Science and Technology Corporation (science and technology research), Northrop Grumman Corporation (high-tech communication technology).

Computer facilities: Computer purchase and lease plans are available. 622 computers available on campus for general student use. A campuswide network can be accessed from student residence rooms and from off campus. Online class registration is available.
Website: http://www.gmu.edu/

General Application Contact: Graduate Admissions Office, 703-993-9700, Fax: 703-993-2392, E-mail: masongrad@gmu.edu.

GRADUATE UNITS

Antonin Scalia Law School Students: 401 full-time (199 women), 138 part-time (56 women); includes 115 minority (17 Black or African American, non-Hispanic/Latino; 40 Asian, non-Hispanic/Latino; 38 Hispanic/Latino; 20 Two or more races, non-Hispanic/Latino), 7 international. Average age 26. 2,452 applicants, 25% accepted, 175 enrolled. *Faculty:* 44 full-time (9 women), 157 part-time/adjunct (41 women). Expenses: Contact institution. *Financial support:* Fellowships, research assistantships, career-related internships or fieldwork, scholarships/grants, and tuition waivers (full and partial) available. Support available to part-time students. Financial award applicants required to submit FAFSA. In 2017, 142 doctorates awarded. *Program availability:* Part-time, evening/weekend. Offers global antitrust law and economics (LL M); intellectual property (LL M); law (JD); law and economics (LL M); U.S. law (LL M). *Application deadline:* For fall admission, 6/15 for domestic and international students. Applications are processed on a rolling basis. *Application fee:* $0. Electronic applications accepted. *Application Contact:* Tiffany J. Williams, Assistant Dean for Admissions and Enrollment Management, 703-993-8010, Fax: 703-993-8088, E-mail: lawadmit@gmu.edu. *Dean*, Henry N. Butler, 703-993-8644, Fax: 703-993-8088.

College of Education and Human Development Students: 476 full-time (377 women), 2,154 part-time (1,751 women); includes 773 minority (286 Black or African American, non-Hispanic/Latino; 9 American Indian or Alaska Native, non-Hispanic/Latino; 195 Asian, non-Hispanic/Latino; 221 Hispanic/Latino; 5 Native Hawaiian or other Pacific Islander, non-Hispanic/Latino; 57 Two or more races, non-Hispanic/Latino), 90 international. Average age 34. 1,321 applicants, 82% accepted, 788 enrolled. *Faculty:* 122 full-time (86 women), 211 part-time/adjunct (144 women). Expenses: Contact institution. *Financial support:* In 2017–18, 95 students received support, including 5 fellowships (averaging $6,080 per year), 75 research assistantships with tuition reimbursements available (averaging $13,826 per year), 32 teaching assistantships with tuition reimbursements available (averaging $5,037 per year); career-related internships or fieldwork, Federal Work-Study, scholarships/grants, unspecified assistantships, and health care benefits (for full-time research or teaching assistantship recipients) also available. Support available to part-time students. Financial award application deadline: 3/1; financial award applicants required to submit FAFSA. In 2017, 786 master's, 40 doctorates, 250 other advanced degrees awarded. *Program availability:* Part-time, evening/weekend, 100% online, blended/hybrid learning. Offers advanced international baccalaureate (M Ed); assessment, evaluation, and testing (MS); assistive technology (M Ed); athletic training (MS); community agency counseling (M Ed); data-driven decision-making for continuous improvement (Certificate); designing digital learning in schools (M Ed); early childhood education (M Ed); early childhood education for diverse learners (M Ed); education and human development (M Ed, MS, PhD, Certificate); education leadership (M Ed, Certificate); elementary education (M Ed); English as a second language (M Ed); exercise, fitness, and health promotion (MS); gifted child education (M Ed); higher education (PhD); history (M Ed); international sport management (Certificate); learning and decision-making in leadership (MS); learning, cognition, and motivation (MS); literacy (M Ed); literacy leadership for diverse schools (M Ed); physical education (M Ed); recreation, health and tourism (Certificate); school counseling PK-12 (M Ed); science K-12 (M Ed); secondary education (M Ed); special education (M Ed, Certificate); sport management (MS); teacher leadership (M Ed); teacher preparation (MS); teaching culturally, linguistically diverse and exceptional learners (M Ed); transformative teaching (M Ed). *Application deadline:* For fall admission, 4/2 for domestic and international students; for spring admission, 11/1 for domestic and international students. *Application fee:* $75 ($80 for international students). Electronic applications accepted. *Application Contact:* Nicole Mariam, Graduate Admissions Coordinator, 703-993-3832, Fax: 703-993-2020, E-mail: nwhite5@gmu.edu. *Dean*, Mark Ginsberg, 703-993-2004, Fax: 703-993-2001, E-mail: mginsber@gmu.edu.

College of Health and Human Services Students: 408 full-time (343 women), 411 part-time (352 women); includes 352 minority (152 Black or African American, non-Hispanic/Latino; 1 American Indian or Alaska Native, non-Hispanic/Latino; 106 Asian, non-Hispanic/Latino; 75 Hispanic/Latino; 1 Native Hawaiian or other Pacific Islander, non-Hispanic/Latino; 17 Two or more races, non-Hispanic/Latino), 75 international. Average age 32. 860 applicants, 76% accepted, 307 enrolled. *Faculty:* 95 full-time (68 women), 144 part-time/adjunct (109 women). Expenses: Contact institution. *Financial support:* In 2017–18, 79 students received support, including 8 fellowships (averaging $10,000 per year), 60 research assistantships with tuition reimbursements available (averaging $16,270 per year), 12 teaching assistantships with tuition reimbursements available (averaging $5,592 per year); career-related internships or fieldwork, Federal Work-Study, scholarships/grants, unspecified assistantships, and health care benefits (for full-time research or teaching assistantship recipients) also available. Support available to part-time students. Financial award application deadline: 3/1; financial award applicants required to submit FAFSA. In 2017, 215 master's, 26 doctorates, 23 other advanced degrees awarded. *Program availability:* Part-time, evening/weekend, 100% online, blended/hybrid learning. Offers food security (Certificate); global and community health (Certificate); global health (MS); health and human services (MHA, MPH, MS, MSN, MSW, DNP, PhD, Certificate); health and medical policy (MS); health informatics (MS); health informatics and data analytics (Certificate); health services research (PhD); health systems management (MHA); nutrition (MS); public health (MPH, Certificate); quality improvement and outcomes management in health care systems (Certificate); rehabilitation science (PhD, Certificate); social work (MSW). *Application fee:* $75 ($80 for international students). Electronic applications accepted. *Application Contact:* Kelly Benedicto, Administrative Office Specialist, Graduate Admissions, 703-993-8246, Fax: 703-993-3606, E-mail: kbenedi2@gmu.edu. *Dean*, Dr. Thomas Prohaska, 703-993-1918, Fax: 703-993-1943, E-mail: tprohask@gmu.edu.

School of Nursing Students: 51 full-time (40 women), 182 part-time (162 women); includes 110 minority (59 Black or African American, non-Hispanic/Latino; 1 American Indian or Alaska Native, non-Hispanic/Latino; 36 Asian, non-Hispanic/Latino; 10 Hispanic/Latino; 4 Two or more races, non-Hispanic/Latino), 8 international. Average age 37. 159 applicants, 70% accepted, 73 enrolled. *Faculty:* 28 full-time (27 women), 51 part-time/adjunct (47 women). Expenses: Contact institution. *Financial support:* In 2017–18, 7 students received support, including 5 research assistantships with tuition reimbursements available (averaging $20,500 per year), 2 teaching assistantships; career-related internships or fieldwork, Federal Work-Study, scholarships/grants, unspecified assistantships, and health care benefits (for full-time research or teaching assistantship recipients) also available. Financial award application deadline: 3/1; financial award applicants required to submit FAFSA. In 2017, 33 master's, 24 doctorates, 1 other advanced degree awarded. *Program availability:* Part-time, evening/weekend, blended/hybrid learning. Offers adult gerontology (DNP); adult/gerontological nurse practitioner (MSN); family nurse practitioner (MSN, DNP); nurse educator (MSN); nursing (PhD); nursing administration (MSN, DNP); nursing education (Certificate); psychiatric mental health (DNP). *Application deadline:* For fall admission, 2/1 for domestic and international students. *Application fee:* $75 ($80 for international students). Electronic applications accepted. *Application Contact:* Susan Eckis, Office Manager, 703-993-1938, Fax: 703-993-1949, E-mail: seckis@gmu.edu. *Director*, Carol Urban, 703-993-2991, Fax: 703-993-1949, E-mail: curban@gmu.edu.

College of Humanities and Social Sciences Students: 670 full-time (399 women), 672 part-time (409 women); includes 276 minority (77 Black or African American, non-Hispanic/Latino; 7 American Indian or Alaska Native, non-Hispanic/Latino; 62 Asian, non-

Hispanic/Latino; 95 Hispanic/Latino; 4 Native Hawaiian or other Pacific Islander, non-Hispanic/Latino; 31 Two or more races, non-Hispanic/Latino), 97 international. Average age 31. 1,757 applicants, 51% accepted, 381 enrolled. *Faculty:* 375 full-time (179 women), 238 part-time/adjunct (121 women). Expenses: Contact institution. *Financial support:* In 2017–18, 441 students received support, including 42 fellowships (averaging $3,264 per year), 195 research assistantships with tuition reimbursements available (averaging $16,008 per year), 261 teaching assistantships with tuition reimbursements available (averaging $10,196 per year); career-related internships or fieldwork, Federal Work-Study, scholarships/grants, unspecified assistantships, and health care benefits (for full-time research or teaching assistantship recipients) also available. Support available to part-time students. Financial award application deadline: 3/1; financial award applicants required to submit FAFSA. In 2017, 338 master's, 74 doctorates, 38 other advanced degrees awarded. *Program availability:* Part-time, evening/weekend. Offers anthropology (MA); applied developmental psychology (MA, PhD); art history (MA); clinical psychology (PhD); cognitive and behavioral neuroscience (MA, PhD); cognitive neuroscience (Certificate); college teaching (Certificate); communication (MA, PhD, Certificate); computational social science (MAIS); creative writing (MFA); criminal justice (MS); criminology, law, and society (MA, PhD); cultural studies (PhD); digital public humanities (Certificate); economics (MA, PhD); energy and sustainability (MAIS); English (MA); English pedagogy (Certificate); ethics and public affairs (MA); fiction (MFA); folklore studies (MAIS, Certificate); foreign languages (MA); global affairs (MA); higher education (MAIS); higher education administration (Certificate); higher education and student development (MA); history (MA, PhD, Certificate); human factors/applied cognition (MA, PhD, Certificate); humanities and social sciences (MA, MAIS, MFA, MS, PhD, Certificate); individualized studies (MAIS); industrial/organizational psychology (MA, PhD); linguistics (PhD); Middle East and Islamic studies (MA, Certificate); nonfiction writing (MFA); philosophy and cultural theory (MA); poetry (MFA); religion, culture, and values (MAIS); science communication (Certificate); social entrepreneurship (MAIS); social justice and human rights (MAIS); sociology (MA, PhD); war and the military in society (MAIS); women and gender studies (MAIS); writing and rhetoric (PhD). *Application fee:* $75 ($80 for international students). Electronic applications accepted. *Application Contact:* Stephanie Hinnenkamp, Graduate Admissions Coordinator, 703-993-2409, E-mail: shinnenk@gmu.edu. *Dean*, Deborah A. Boehm-Davis, 703-993-8715, Fax: 703-993-8714, E-mail: dbdavis@gmu.edu.

College of Science Students: 510 full-time (266 women), 464 part-time (207 women); includes 303 minority (101 Black or African American, non-Hispanic/Latino; 117 Asian, non-Hispanic/Latino; 58 Hispanic/Latino; 1 Native Hawaiian or other Pacific Islander, non-Hispanic/Latino; 26 Two or more races, non-Hispanic/Latino), 143 international. Average age 32. 932 applicants, 73% accepted, 337 enrolled. *Faculty:* 296 full-time (95 women), 91 part-time/adjunct (30 women). Expenses: Contact institution. *Financial support:* In 2017–18, 250 students received support, including 20 fellowships (averaging $5,259 per year), 108 research assistantships with tuition reimbursements available (averaging $17,382 per year), 142 teaching assistantships with tuition reimbursements available (averaging $15,694 per year); career-related internships or fieldwork, Federal Work-Study, scholarships/grants, and health care benefits (for full-time research or teaching assistantship recipients) also available. Support available to part-time students. Financial award application deadline: 3/1; financial award applicants required to submit FAFSA. In 2017, 131 master's, 64 doctorates, 112 other advanced degrees awarded. *Program availability:* Part-time, evening/weekend, 100% online. Offers applied and engineering physics (MS); chemistry (MS); chemistry and biochemistry (PhD); climate dynamics (PhD); computational science (MS); computational sciences and informatics (PhD); computational social science (PhD, Certificate); data science (Certificate); earth system science (MS); earth systems and geoinformation sciences (PhD); environmental geoinformation science and biodiversity conservation (Certificate); environmental science and policy (MS, PhD); forensic science (MS); geography and geoinformation science (Certificate); mathematical sciences (MS, PhD); neuroscience (PhD); physics (PhD); science (MS, PSM, PhD, Certificate). *Application fee:* $75 ($80 for international students). Electronic applications accepted. *Application Contact:* Melissa C. Hayes, Graduate Programs Director, 703-993-3430, Fax: 703-993-9033, E-mail: mhayes5@gmu.edu. *Dean*, Peggy Agouris, 703-993-1362, Fax: 703-993-9614, E-mail: pagouris@gmu.edu.

School of Systems Biology Students: 107 full-time (54 women), 89 part-time (44 women); includes 64 minority (6 Black or African American, non-Hispanic/Latino; 35 Asian, non-Hispanic/Latino; 14 Hispanic/Latino; 9 Two or more races, non-Hispanic/Latino), 37 international. Average age 31. 141 applicants, 79% accepted, 64 enrolled. *Faculty:* 12 full-time (4 women), 2 part-time/adjunct (0 women). Expenses: Contact institution. *Financial support:* In 2017–18, 51 students received support, including 15 fellowships (averaging $3,902 per year), 14 research assistantships with tuition reimbursements available (averaging $16,679 per year), 38 teaching assistantships with tuition reimbursements available (averaging $15,754 per year); career-related internships or fieldwork, Federal Work-Study, scholarships/grants, unspecified assistantships, and health care benefits (for full-time research or teaching assistantship recipients) also available. Support available to part-time students. Financial award application deadline: 3/1; financial award applicants required to submit FAFSA. In 2017, 27 master's, 8 doctorates, 4 other advanced degrees awarded. Offers bioinformatics and computational biology (MS, PhD, Certificate); bioinformatics management (MS, PSM); biology (MS); biosciences (PhD); personalized medicine (Certificate). *Application fee:* $75 ($80 for international students). Electronic applications accepted. *Application Contact:* Diane St. Germain, Graduate Student Services Coordinator, 703-993-4263, Fax: 703-993-8976, E-mail: dstgerma@gmu.edu. *Director*, Dr. Iosif Vaisman, 703-993-8431, Fax: 703-993-8976, E-mail: ivaisman@gmu.edu.

College of Visual and Performing Arts Students: 86 full-time (65 women), 127 part-time (81 women); includes 49 minority (12 Black or African American, non-Hispanic/Latino; 18 Asian, non-Hispanic/Latino; 12 Hispanic/Latino; 1 Native Hawaiian or other Pacific Islander, non-Hispanic/Latino; 6 Two or more races, non-Hispanic/Latino), 52 international. Average age 30. 188 applicants, 60% accepted, 49 enrolled. *Faculty:* 77 full-time (34 women), 146 part-time/adjunct (70 women). Expenses: Contact institution. *Financial support:* In 2017–18, 21 students received support, including 1 research assistantship with tuition reimbursement available, 20 teaching assistantships with tuition reimbursements available (averaging $3,161 per year); career-related internships or fieldwork, Federal Work-Study, scholarships/grants, unspecified assistantships, and health care benefits (for full-time research or teaching assistantship recipients) also available. Support available to part-time students. Financial award application deadline: 3/1; financial award applicants required to submit FAFSA. In 2017, 72 master's, 5 doctorates, 14 other advanced degrees awarded. *Program availability:* Part-time, evening/weekend. Offers art education (MAT); arts management (MA); dance (MFA); graphic design (MFA); theater (MFA); visual and performing arts (MA, MAT, MFA, MM, DMA, PhD, Certificate); visual art (MFA). *Application fee:* $75 ($80 for international students). Electronic applications accepted. *Application Contact:* Stevie Otto, Assistant Director, Graduate Admissions and Recruitment, 703-993-5576, Fax: 703-993-9037, E-mail: sotto2@gmu.edu. *Dean*, Rick Davis, 703-993-8624, Fax: 703-993-8883, E-mail: rdavi4@gmu.edu.

School of Music Students: 26 full-time (13 women), 49 part-time (23 women); includes 20 minority (4 Black or African American, non-Hispanic/Latino; 9 Asian, non-Hispanic/Latino; 5 Hispanic/Latino; 2 Two or more races, non-Hispanic/Latino), 5 international. Average age 33. 79 applicants, 59% accepted, 24 enrolled. *Faculty:* 23 full-time (10 women), 56 part-time/adjunct (20 women). Expenses: Contact institution. *Financial support:* In 2017–18, 16 students received support, including 16 teaching assistantships with tuition reimbursements available (averaging $3,100 per year); career-related internships or fieldwork, Federal Work-Study, scholarships/grants, unspecified assistantships, and health care benefits (for full-time research or teaching assistantship recipients) also available. Support available to part-time students. Financial award application deadline: 3/1; financial award applicants required to submit FAFSA. In 2017, 17 master's, 5 doctorates awarded. Offers composition (MM, DMA); conducting (MM, DMA); instrumental performance artist (Certificate); jazz studies (MM); music (MM); music education (MM, PhD); musical arts (DMA); pedagogy (MM); performance (MM, DMA). *Application fee:* $75 ($80 for international students). Electronic applications accepted. *Application Contact:* Dr. Lisa A. Billingham, Director of Graduate Studies, 703-993-3778, Fax: 703-993-1394, E-mail: lbillin1@gmu.edu. *Managing Director*, Dr. Linda Apple Monson, 703-993-3580, Fax: 703-993-1394, E-mail: lmonson@gmu.edu.

Schar School of Policy and Government Students: 323 full-time (161 women), 667 part-time (360 women); includes 330 minority (128 Black or African American, non-Hispanic/Latino; 69 Asian, non-Hispanic/Latino; 96 Hispanic/Latino; 2 Native Hawaiian or other Pacific Islander, non-Hispanic/Latino; 35 Two or more races, non-Hispanic/Latino), 68 international. Average age 32. 733 applicants, 81% accepted, 272 enrolled. *Faculty:* 74 full-time (24 women), 48 part-time/adjunct (13 women). Expenses: Contact institution. *Financial support:* In 2017–18, 55 students received support, including 2 fellowships, 37 research assistantships with tuition reimbursements available (averaging $17,051 per year), 17 teaching assistantships (averaging $16,544 per year); career-related internships or fieldwork, Federal Work-Study, scholarships/grants, unspecified assistantships, and health care benefits (for full-time research or teaching assistantship recipients) also available. Support available to part-time students. Financial award application deadline: 3/1; financial award applicants required to submit FAFSA. In 2017, 329 master's, 19 doctorates, 27 other advanced degrees awarded. *Program availability:* Part-time, evening/weekend, 100% online. Offers biodefense (MS, PhD, Certificate); international commerce and policy (MA); international security (MA); organization development and knowledge management (MS); policy and government (MA, MPA, MPP, MS, PhD, Certificate); political science (MA, PhD); public administration (MPA); public policy (MPP, PhD); transportation policy, operations and logistics (MA). *Application fee:* $75 ($80 for international students). Electronic applications accepted. *Application Contact:* Travis Major, Director of Graduate Admissions, 703-993-3183, Fax: 703-993-4876, E-mail: tmajor@gmu.edu. *Dean*, Mark Rozell, 703-993-8171, Fax: 703-993-8215, E-mail: mrozell@gmu.edu.

School for Conflict Analysis and Resolution Students: 119 full-time (68 women), 154 part-time (89 women); includes 84 minority (37 Black or African American, non-Hispanic/Latino; 13 Asian, non-Hispanic/Latino; 24 Hispanic/Latino; 1 Native Hawaiian or other Pacific Islander, non-Hispanic/Latino; 9 Two or more races, non-Hispanic/Latino), 34 international. Average age 35. 231 applicants, 51% accepted, 50 enrolled. *Faculty:* 19 full-time (10 women), 24 part-time/adjunct (11 women). Expenses: Contact institution. *Financial support:* In 2017–18, 29 students received support, including 21 research assistantships with tuition reimbursements available (averaging $14,607 per year), 8 teaching assistantships with tuition reimbursements available (averaging $11,298 per year); career-related internships or fieldwork, Federal Work-Study, scholarships/grants, unspecified assistantships, and health care benefits (for full-time research or teaching assistantship recipients) also available. Support available to part-time students. Financial award application deadline: 3/1; financial award applicants required to submit FAFSA. In 2017, 75 master's, 13 doctorates, 5 other advanced degrees awarded. *Program availability:* Part-time, evening/weekend, blended/hybrid learning. Offers conflict analysis and resolution (MS, PhD, Certificate). *Application fee:* $75 ($80 for international students). Electronic applications accepted. *Application Contact:* Monique Barner, Assistant Director for Graduate Admissions, 703-993-1300, Fax: 703-993-1302, E-mail: mwilli43@gmu.edu. *Dean*, Kevin Avruch, 703-993-3607, Fax: 703-993-1302, E-mail: kavruch@gmu.edu.

School of Business Students: 403 full-time (176 women), 137 part-time (72 women); includes 212 minority (77 Black or African American, non-Hispanic/Latino; 78 Asian, non-Hispanic/Latino; 48 Hispanic/Latino; 2 Native Hawaiian or other Pacific Islander, non-Hispanic/Latino; 7 Two or more races, non-Hispanic/Latino), 74 international. Average age 32. 558 applicants, 77% accepted, 221 enrolled. *Faculty:* 105 full-time (40 women), 79 part-time/adjunct (26 women). Expenses: Contact institution. *Financial support:* In 2017–18, 16 students received support, including 11 research assistantships with tuition reimbursements available (averaging $7,250 per year), 9 teaching assistantships with tuition reimbursements available (averaging $4,272 per year); career-related internships or fieldwork, Federal Work-Study, scholarships/grants, unspecified assistantships, and health care benefits (for full-time research or teaching assistantship recipients) also available. Support available to part-time students. Financial award application deadline: 3/1; financial award applicants required to submit FAFSA. In 2017, 246 master's awarded. *Program availability:* Part-time, evening/weekend, 100% online. Offers accounting (MS); business (EMBA, MBA, MS); business administration (MBA); management (MS); management of secure information systems (MS); technology management (MS). *Application fee:* $75 ($80 for international students). Electronic applications accepted. *Application Contact:* Paige Wolf, Senior Assistant Dean of Graduate Programs, 703-993-1758, Fax: 703-993-1870, E-mail: pwolf1@gmu.edu. *Interim Dean*, Anne Magro, 703-993-1765, Fax: 703-993-2472, E-mail: amagro@gmu.edu.

Volgenau School of Engineering Students: 801 full-time (271 women), 949 part-time (261 women); includes 433 minority (85 Black or African American, non-Hispanic/Latino; 228 Asian, non-Hispanic/Latino; 85 Hispanic/Latino; 2 Native Hawaiian or other Pacific Islander, non-Hispanic/Latino; 33 Two or more races, non-Hispanic/Latino), 675 international. Average age 30. 1,754 applicants, 71% accepted, 500 enrolled. *Faculty:* 210 full-time (55 women), 166 part-time/adjunct (26 women). Expenses: Contact institution. *Financial support:* In 2017–18, 338 students received support, including 4 fellowships (averaging $5,372 per year), 130 research assistantships with tuition reimbursements available (averaging $18,462 per year), 207 teaching assistantships with tuition reimbursements available (averaging $13,335 per year); career-related internships or fieldwork, Federal Work-Study, scholarships/grants, unspecified assistantships, and health care benefits (for full-time research or teaching assistantship recipients) also available. Support available to part-time students. Financial award application deadline: 3/1; financial award applicants required to submit FAFSA. In 2017, 550 master's, 42 doctorates, 104 other advanced degrees awarded. *Program availability:* Part-time, evening/weekend, 100% online. Offers applied information technology (MS); bioengineering (PhD); biostatistics (MS); computer engineering (MS); computer science

(MS, PhD, Certificate); construction project management (MS); data analytics engineering (MS); electrical and computer engineering (PhD, Certificate); engineering (MS, PhD, Certificate); information sciences and technology (Certificate); information technology (PhD); operations research (MS); statistical science (MS, PhD); statistics (Certificate); systems engineering and operations research (PhD, Certificate); transportation engineering (PhD). *Application fee:* $75 ($80 for international students). Electronic applications accepted. *Application Contact:* Suddaf Ismail, Director, Graduate Admissions and Recruitment, 703-993-9115, Fax: 703-993-1242, E-mail: sismail@gmu.edu. *Dean*, Kenneth S. Ball, 703-993-1498, Fax: 703-993-1734, E-mail: vsdean@gmu.edu.

GEORGETOWN COLLEGE, Georgetown, KY 40324-1696

General Information Independent-religious, coed, comprehensive institution. *Graduate housing:* On-campus housing not available.

GRADUATE UNITS

Department of Education *Program availability:* Part-time. Offers reading and writing (MA Ed); special education (MA Ed); teaching (MA Ed).

GEORGETOWN UNIVERSITY, Washington, DC 20057

General Information Independent-religious, coed, university. CGS member. *Graduate housing:* On-campus housing not available.

GRADUATE UNITS

Graduate School of Arts and Sciences Offers American government (MA); analytical chemistry (PhD); arts and sciences (EMBA, EML, EMPL, GEMBA, MA, MAE, MALS, MAT, MBA, MDSPP, MIPM, MPM, MPP, MPS, MS, DLS, DNP, PhD, Certificate); biochemistry (PhD); biochemistry and molecular and cellular biology (MS, PhD); bioethics (MA); biohazardous threat agents and emerging infectious diseases (MS); biology (PhD); biomedical science policy and advocacy (MS); biostatistics (MS, Certificate); British and American literature (MA); communication, culture, and technology (MA); computational chemistry (PhD); computer science (MS, PhD); conflict resolution (MA); democracy and governance (MA); development, management and policy (MA); econometrics (PhD); economic development (PhD); economic theory (PhD); epidemiology (Certificate); general microbiology and immunology (MS); German (MA, PhD); global history (MA); global infectious diseases (PhD); global, international and comparative history (MA); government (PhD); health physics (MS); history (MA, PhD); human development and public policy (PhD); industrial organization (PhD); inorganic chemistry (PhD); international macro and finance (PhD); international trade (PhD); labor economics (PhD); language and communication (MA); lifespan cognitive neuroscience (PhD); linguistics (MS, PhD); macroeconomics (PhD); materials chemistry (PhD); mathematics (MS); microbiology and immunology (PhD); neuroscience (PhD); nuclear nonproliferation (MS); organic chemistry (PhD); pharmacology (MS, PhD); philosophy (PhD); physiology (MS); public economics and political economy (PhD); Spanish (MS, PhD); statistics (MS); theology (PhD); theoretical chemistry (PhD).

McDonough School of Business Offers business administration (EMBA, GEMBA, MBA); finance (MS); leadership (EML).

School of Continuing Studies Offers American studies (MALS); applied intelligence (MPS); Catholic studies (MALS); classical civilizations (MALS); emergency and disaster management (MPS); ethics and the professions (MALS); global strategic communications (MPS); hospitality management (MPS); human resources management (MPS); humanities (MALS); individualized study (MALS); integrated marketing communications (MPS); international affairs (MALS); Islam and Muslim-Christian relations (MALS); journalism (MPS); liberal studies (DLS); literature and society (MALS); medieval and early modern European studies (MALS); public relations and corporate communications (MPS); real estate (MPS); religious studies (MALS); social and public policy (MALS); sports industry management (MPS); systems engineering management (MPS); technology management (MPS); the theory and practice of American democracy (MALS); urban and regional planning (MPS); visual culture (MALS). MPS in systems engineering management offered jointly with Stevens Institute of Technology.

School of Nursing and Health Studies Offers acute care nurse practitioner (MS); clinical nurse specialist (MS); family nurse practitioner (MS); nurse anesthesia (MS); nurse-midwifery (MS); nursing (DNP); nursing education (MS).

Walsh School of Foreign Service Offers Asian studies (MA); contemporary Arab studies (MA, Certificate); Eurasian, Russian and East European studies (MA); foreign service (MA, MS, Certificate); German and European studies (MA); global business and finance (MS); global human development (MA); global politics and security (MS); international development (MS); Latin American studies (MA); security studies (MA); self-designed studies (MS).

Law Center *Program availability:* Part-time, evening/weekend. Offers environmental law (LL M); global health law (LL M); global health law and international institutions (LL M); individualized study (LL M); international business and economic law (LL M); law (JD, SJD); national security law (LL M); securities and financial regulation (LL M); taxation (LL M).

Master of Arts in Learning and Design Program Average age 27. Expenses: Contact institution. *Financial support:* Scholarships/grants and unspecified assistantships available. Financial award application deadline: 4/1; financial award applicants required to submit FAFSA. *Program availability:* Part-time, evening/weekend. Offers learning and design (MA). *Application deadline:* For fall admission, 4/1 priority date for domestic students. Applications are processed on a rolling basis. *Application fee:* $90. Electronic applications accepted. *Application Contact:* Kimberly Luciano, Program Coordinator, 202-687-1882, E-mail: kl791@georgetown.edu. *Founding Director*, Dr. Edward J. Maloney.

McCourt School of Public Policy Expenses: Contact institution. *Financial support:* Research assistantships, teaching assistantships, career-related internships or fieldwork, scholarships/grants, and unspecified assistantships available. Financial award application deadline: 2/1; financial award applicants required to submit FAFSA. *Program availability:* Part-time. Offers data science for public policy (MDSPP); international development policy (MIDP); policy leadership (EMPL); policy management (MPM); public policy (MPP). *Application deadline:* For fall admission, 1/15 priority date for domestic students. Applications are processed on a rolling basis. *Application fee:* $90. Electronic applications accepted. *Application Contact:* Dr. Adam Thomas, Director of Admissions, 202-687-9186, E-mail: mccourtadmissions@georgetown.edu. *Dean, McCourt School of Public Policy*, Dr. Michael A. Bailey, 202-687-6163.

National Institutes of Health Sponsored Programs Offers biomedical sciences (MS, PhD).

School of Medicine Offers medicine (MD).

THE GEORGE WASHINGTON UNIVERSITY, Washington, DC 20052

General Information Independent, coed, university. CGS member. *Enrollment:* 27,973 graduate, professional, and undergraduate students; 7,753 full-time matriculated graduate/professional students (4,414 women), 8,054 part-time matriculated graduate/professional students (4,974 women). *Enrollment by degree level:* 10,975 master's, 4,322 doctoral, 510 other advanced degrees. *Graduate faculty:* 1,413 full-time (656 women), 1,622 part-time/adjunct (752 women). *Tuition:* Full-time $28,800; part-time $1655 per credit hour. *Required fees:* $45; $2.75 per credit hour. *Graduate housing:* Room and/or apartments available on a first-come, first-served basis to single students; on-campus housing not available to married students. *Student services:* Campus employment opportunities, campus safety program, career counseling, exercise/wellness program, free psychological counseling, international student services, low-cost health insurance, multicultural affairs office, services for students with disabilities, teacher training, writing training. *Library facilities:* Gelman Library. *Research affiliation:* Goddard Space Flight Center (radar modeling analysis, space systems technologies), Library of Congress, Smithsonian Institution, National Institutes of Health (biostatistics), NASA Langley Research Center (aeroacoustics, aeronautics, astronautics), Children's Hospital National Medical Center.

Computer facilities: A campuswide network can be accessed from student residence rooms and from off campus.
Website: http://www.gwu.edu/

General Application Contact: Jeanne Fiander, Executive Director, Graduate Enrollment Management, 202-994-5136, Fax: 202-994-0371, E-mail: jfian@gwu.edu.

GRADUATE UNITS

College of Professional Studies Students: 280 full-time (114 women), 716 part-time (435 women); includes 365 minority (165 Black or African American, non-Hispanic/Latino; 7 American Indian or Alaska Native, non-Hispanic/Latino; 34 Asian, non-Hispanic/Latino; 132 Hispanic/Latino; 27 Two or more races, non-Hispanic/Latino), 57 international. Average age 34. 914 applicants, 86% accepted, 481 enrolled. *Faculty:* 26 full-time (9 women), 89 part-time/adjunct (27 women). Expenses: Contact institution. In 2017, 428 master's, 58 other advanced degrees awarded. Offers healthcare corporate compliance (Graduate Certificate); law firm management (MPS, Graduate Certificate); paralegal studies (MPS, Graduate Certificate); publishing (MPS). *Application Contact:* Kristin Williams, Associate Provost, Graduate Enrollment, 202-994-0467, Fax: 202-994-0371, E-mail: ksw@gwu.edu. *Dean*, Christopher J. Deering, 571-553-5004.

Graduate School of Political Management Students: 54 full-time (24 women), 228 part-time (105 women); includes 107 minority (36 Black or African American, non-Hispanic/Latino; 5 American Indian or Alaska Native, non-Hispanic/Latino; 5 Asian, non-Hispanic/Latino; 54 Hispanic/Latino; 7 Two or more races, non-Hispanic/Latino), 32 international. Average age 31. 204 applicants, 91% accepted, 117 enrolled. *Faculty:* 8 full-time (2 women), 6 part-time/adjunct (1 woman). Expenses: Contact institution. *Financial support:* In 2017–18, 18 students received support. Fellowships with tuition reimbursements available, scholarships/grants, and tuition waivers available. Financial award application deadline: 2/1. In 2017, 110 master's, 5 other advanced degrees awarded. Offers community advocacy (Graduate Certificate); legislative affairs (MPS); PACs and political management (Graduate Certificate); political management (MPS). *Application deadline:* For fall admission, 6/15 priority date for domestic students, 4/1 priority date for international students; for spring admission, 11/15 priority date for domestic students, 10/1 priority date for international students. Applications are processed on a rolling basis. *Application fee:* $75. Electronic applications accepted. *Application Contact:* Information Contact, 202-994-6000, Fax: 202-994-6006. *Director*, Lara M. Brown, 202-994-4545.

Columbian College of Arts and Sciences Students: 1,705 full-time (1,123 women), 1,034 part-time (621 women); includes 606 minority (192 Black or African American, non-Hispanic/Latino; 4 American Indian or Alaska Native, non-Hispanic/Latino; 151 Asian, non-Hispanic/Latino; 188 Hispanic/Latino; 4 Native Hawaiian or other Pacific Islander, non-Hispanic/Latino; 67 Two or more races, non-Hispanic/Latino), 729 international. Average age 28. 7,223 applicants, 46% accepted, 1090 enrolled. *Faculty:* 560 full-time (253 women), 507 part-time/adjunct (232 women). Expenses: Contact institution. *Financial support:* Fellowships with tuition reimbursements, research assistantships, teaching assistantships with tuition reimbursements, career-related internships or fieldwork, Federal Work-Study, scholarships/grants, tuition waivers, and unspecified assistantships available. Support available to part-time students. Financial award application deadline: 2/1. In 2017, 856 master's, 126 doctorates, 120 other advanced degrees awarded. *Program availability:* Part-time, evening/weekend. Offers American studies (PhD); analytical chemistry (MS, PhD); anthropology (MA, PhD); applied mathematics (MS); applied social psychology (PhD); art and the book (MA); art education (MA, MAT); art history (MA); art therapy (MA, Graduate Certificate); arts and sciences (MA, MAT, MFA, MFS, MPA, MPP, MS, PhD, Psy D, Certificate, Graduate Certificate); biological sciences (MS, PhD); biostatistics (MS, PhD); ceramics (MFA); classical acting (MFA); clinical psychology (PhD); cognitive neuroscience (PhD); crime scene investigation (MFS); criminology (MA); dance (MFA); decorative arts and design history (MA); drawing/painting (MFA); economics (MA, PhD); English (MA, PhD); environmental and resource policy (MA); exhibit design (Graduate Certificate); exhibition design (MA); financial mathematics (Graduate Certificate); folk life (MA); forensic chemistry (MFS); forensic molecular biology (MFS); forensic toxicology (MFS); geography (MA, Graduate Certificate); high-technology crime investigation (MS); historic preservation (MA); history (MA, PhD); human resources management (MA); inorganic chemistry (MS, PhD); interior design (MA, MFA); international development (MA); Islam (MA); legal institutions and theory (MA); material culture (MA); materials science (MS, PhD); mathematics (MA, PhD, Graduate Certificate); medical anthropology (MA); museum collections management and care (Graduate Certificate); museum studies (MA); museum training (MA); new media (MFA); new media photojournalism (MA); non-profit management (Graduate Certificate); organic chemistry (MS, PhD); organizational management (Graduate Certificate); philosophy and social policy (MA); photography (MFA); physical chemistry (MS, PhD); physics (MA, PhD); political science (MA); production design (MFA); professional psychology (MA, Psy D, Graduate Certificate); sculpture (MFA); security management (MFS); sociology (MA); speech-language pathology (MA); statistics (MS, PhD); survey design and data analysis (Graduate Certificate); women's studies (MA, Certificate). *Application deadline:* For fall admission, 1/15 priority date for domestic and international students; for spring admission, 10/1 priority date for domestic and international students. Applications are processed on a rolling basis. *Application fee:* $75. Electronic applications accepted. *Application Contact:* Linda Wilkerson, Executive Assistant, 202-994-6210, Fax: 202-994-6213, E-mail: askccas@gwu.edu. *Dean*, Ben Vinson, III, 202-994-6130, E-mail: bvinson3@gwu.edu.

Institute for Biomedical Sciences Average age 27. Expenses: Contact institution. *Financial support:* In 2017–18, 24 students received support. Fellowships with full tuition reimbursements available, Federal Work-Study, institutionally sponsored loans, and tuition waivers available. *Program availability:* Part-time, evening/weekend. Offers biochemistry and systems biology (PhD); microbiology and immunology (PhD); molecular and cellular oncology (PhD); molecular medicine (PhD); neurosciences (PhD); pharmacology and physiology (PhD). *Application deadline:* For fall admission, 12/15 priority date for domestic and international students. Applications are processed on a rolling basis. *Application fee:* $60. Electronic applications accepted. *Application Contact:* 202-994-2179, Fax: 202-994-0967, E-mail: gwibs@gwu.edu. *Director,* Dr. Linda L. Werling, 202-994-2918, Fax: 202-994-0967, E-mail: lwerling@gwu.edu.

School of Media and Public Affairs Students: 33 full-time (20 women), 17 part-time (13 women); includes 11 minority (4 Black or African American, non-Hispanic/Latino; 5 Hispanic/Latino; 2 Two or more races, non-Hispanic/Latino), 7 international. Average age 27. 98 applicants, 55% accepted, 20 enrolled. *Faculty:* 24 full-time (10 women), 27 part-time/adjunct (7 women). Expenses: Contact institution. *Financial support:* In 2017–18, fellowships with tuition reimbursements (averaging $10,000 per year), teaching assistantships with tuition reimbursements (averaging $5,000 per year) were awarded. Financial award application deadline: 1/15. In 2017, 23 master's, 13 other advanced degrees awarded. Offers media and public affairs (MA, Graduate Certificate). *Application deadline:* For fall admission, 4/1 priority date for domestic students, 1/15 priority date for international students; for spring admission, 10/1 priority date for domestic students, 9/1 priority date for international students. Applications are processed on a rolling basis. *Application fee:* $75. Electronic applications accepted. *Application Contact:* Information Contact, 202-994-6227, Fax: 202-994-5806, E-mail: smpa@gwu.edu. *Director,* Frank Sesno, 202-994-9553, E-mail: sesno@gwu.edu.

Trachtenberg School of Public Policy and Public Administration Students: 102 full-time (63 women), 127 part-time (76 women); includes 66 minority (25 Black or African American, non-Hispanic/Latino; 10 Asian, non-Hispanic/Latino; 24 Hispanic/Latino; 2 Native Hawaiian or other Pacific Islander, non-Hispanic/Latino; 5 Two or more races, non-Hispanic/Latino), 28 international. Average age 30. 630 applicants, 59% accepted, 91 enrolled. *Faculty:* 13 full-time (7 women), 20 part-time/adjunct (8 women). Expenses: Contact institution. *Financial support:* In 2017–18, 57 students received support. Fellowships, research assistantships, teaching assistantships, Federal Work-Study, scholarships/grants, health care benefits, and unspecified assistantships available. Financial award application deadline: 1/5; financial award applicants required to submit FAFSA. In 2017, 122 master's, 13 doctorates awarded. *Program availability:* Part-time, evening/weekend, online learning. Offers environmental resource policy (MA); public administration (MPA); public policy (MPP); public policy and administration (PhD). *Application deadline:* For fall admission, 1/5 priority date for domestic and international students; for spring admission, 10/1 priority date for domestic students, 10/1 for international students. *Application fee:* $75. Electronic applications accepted. *Application Contact:* Denee' Bottoms, Assistant Director of Graduate Studies, 202-994-6662, Fax: 202-994-6792, E-mail: dbottoms@gwu.edu. *Director,* Dr. Kathyrn E. Newcomer, 202-994-3959, Fax: 202-994-6792, E-mail: newcomer@gwu.edu.

Elliott School of International Affairs Students: 549 full-time (317 women), 255 part-time (146 women); includes 223 minority (60 Black or African American, non-Hispanic/Latino; 49 Asian, non-Hispanic/Latino; 85 Hispanic/Latino; 29 Two or more races, non-Hispanic/Latino), 101 international. Average age 27. 1,543 applicants, 79% accepted, 326 enrolled. *Faculty:* 74 full-time (25 women), 110 part-time/adjunct (36 women). Expenses: Contact institution. *Financial support:* In 2017–18, 155 students received support. Fellowships with partial tuition reimbursements available and Federal Work-Study available. Financial award application deadline: 1/15; financial award applicants required to submit FAFSA. In 2017, 361 master's, 3 other advanced degrees awarded. *Program availability:* Part-time. Offers Asian studies (MA); European and Eurasian studies (MA); global communication (MA); global gender policy (Graduate Certificate); international affairs (MA, MIPP, MIS, Graduate Certificate); international development studies (MA); international policy and practice (MIPP); international science and technology policy (MA, Graduate Certificate); international studies (MIS); international trade and investment policy (MA); Latin American and hemispheric studies (MA); Middle East studies (MA); security policy studies (MA). *Application deadline:* For fall admission, 1/15 priority date for domestic students, 1/15 for international students; for spring admission, 10/1 for domestic and international students. *Application fee:* $75. Electronic applications accepted. *Application Contact:* Nicole A. Campbell, Director of Graduate Admissions, 202-994-7050, Fax: 202-994-9537, E-mail: esiagrad@gwu.edu. *Dean,* Rueben E. Brigety, 202-994-6240, Fax: 202-994-0335, E-mail: esiadean@gwu.edu.

Graduate School of Education and Human Development Students: 411 full-time (327 women), 1,048 part-time (794 women); includes 526 minority (286 Black or African American, non-Hispanic/Latino; 7 American Indian or Alaska Native, non-Hispanic/Latino; 82 Asian, non-Hispanic/Latino; 111 Hispanic/Latino; 40 Two or more races, non-Hispanic/Latino), 115 international. Average age 36. 1,735 applicants, 65% accepted, 550 enrolled. *Faculty:* 87 full-time (55 women), 96 part-time/adjunct (61 women). Expenses: Contact institution. *Financial support:* In 2017–18, 279 students received support. Fellowships with tuition reimbursements available, research assistantships with tuition reimbursements available, teaching assistantships with tuition reimbursements available, career-related internships or fieldwork, Federal Work-Study, and tuition waivers (full and partial) available. Support available to part-time students. Financial award application deadline: 1/15. In 2017, 388 master's, 68 doctorates, 108 other advanced degrees awarded. *Program availability:* Part-time, evening/weekend, online learning. Offers adolescents with emotional and behavioral disabilities (MA Ed/HD); adolescents with learning disabilities (MA Ed/HD); Arabic (M Ed); art education (MA); autism spectrum disorder (MA Ed/HD); bilingual special education (MA Ed, Certificate); brain injury special education (MA Ed/HD); brain injury specialist (MA Ed/HD); clinical mental health counseling (MA); college teaching and academic leadership (MA Ed/HD, Ed S); counseling (PhD, Ed S); counseling culturally and linguistically diverse persons (MA Ed/HD, Certificate); curriculum and instruction (MA Ed, Ed D, Ed S, Graduate Certificate); design and assessment of adult learning (Graduate Certificate); e-learning (Graduate Certificate); early childhood special education (MA Ed/HD); education and human development (M Ed, MA, MA Ed, MA Ed/HD, MAT, Ed D, PhD, Certificate, Ed S, Graduate Certificate, Teaching Certificate); education policy (Ed D); education policy studies (MA Ed); educational administration (Ed D); educational administration and policy studies (Ed D); educational leadership and administration (MA Ed, Certificate, Ed S); educational technology leadership (MA Ed); elementary education (MA Ed/HD); forensic rehabilitation counseling (Graduate Certificate); general administration (MA Ed/HD, Ed S); higher education administration (MA Ed/HD, Ed D, Ed S); higher education finance (MA Ed/HD, Ed S); human and organizational learning (Ed D, Ed S); human resource development (MA); infant special education (MA Ed/HD); instructional design (Graduate Certificate); integrating technology into education (Graduate Certificate); interdisciplinary transition services (MA Ed/HD); international education (MA Ed); Italian (M Ed); job development and placement (Graduate Certificate); leadership development (Graduate Certificate); leadership in educational technology (Graduate Certificate); math (M Ed); multimedia development (Graduate Certificate); museum education (MAT); organizational learning and change (Graduate Certificate); physics (M Ed); policy (MA Ed/HD, Ed S); rehabilitation counseling (MA Ed/HD); Russian (M Ed); school counseling (MA Ed, Graduate Certificate); secondary education (M Ed); secondary special education and transition services (MA Ed/HD); special education (Ed D, Ed S); special education and transition services (Certificate); special education for children with emotional and behavioral disabilities (MA Ed/HD); special education for culturally and linguistically diverse persons (MA Ed/HD, Certificate); student affairs administration (MA Ed/HD, Ed S); substance abuse and psychiatric disabilities (MA Ed/HD); training and educational technology (Graduate Certificate); transition special education (Teaching Certificate); traumatic brain injury (MA Ed/HD). *Application deadline:* For fall admission, 1/15 priority date for domestic students; for spring admission, 10/1 for domestic students. Applications are processed on a rolling basis. *Application fee:* $75. Electronic applications accepted. *Application Contact:* Sarah Lang, Director of Graduate Admissions, 202-994-1447, Fax: 202-994-7207, E-mail: slang@gwu.edu. *Dean,* Michael Feuer, 202-994-6161, Fax: 202-994-7207, E-mail: mjfeuer@gwu.edu.

Law School Students: 1,444 full-time (760 women), 249 part-time (118 women); includes 422 minority (157 Black or African American, non-Hispanic/Latino; 11 American Indian or Alaska Native, non-Hispanic/Latino; 198 Asian, non-Hispanic/Latino; 38 Hispanic/Latino; 4 Native Hawaiian or other Pacific Islander, non-Hispanic/Latino; 14 Two or more races, non-Hispanic/Latino), 190 international. Average age 27. 191 applicants, 100% accepted, 128 enrolled. *Faculty:* 84 full-time (33 women), 233 part-time/adjunct (65 women). Expenses: Contact institution. *Financial support:* Research assistantships, career-related internships or fieldwork, Federal Work-Study, institutionally sponsored loans, scholarships/grants, and tuition waivers (full and partial) available. Support available to part-time students. Financial award application deadline: 3/1; financial award applicants required to submit CSS PROFILE or FAFSA. In 2017, 167 master's, 4 doctorates awarded. *Program availability:* Part-time, evening/weekend. Offers law (SJD); national security and U.S. foreign relations (LL M). *Application deadline:* For fall admission, 3/1 for domestic students. Applications are processed on a rolling basis. *Application fee:* $75. *Application Contact:* Sophia Sim, Assistant Dean of Admissions and Financial Aid, 202-994-7235, Fax: 202-739-0624, E-mail: ssim@law.gwu.edu. *Dean,* Blake D. Morant, E-mail: bmorant@law.gwu.edu.

Milken Institute School of Public Health Students: 506 full-time (401 women), 1,578 part-time (1,208 women); includes 983 minority (386 Black or African American, non-Hispanic/Latino; 5 American Indian or Alaska Native, non-Hispanic/Latino; 345 Asian, non-Hispanic/Latino; 159 Hispanic/Latino; 5 Native Hawaiian or other Pacific Islander, non-Hispanic/Latino; 83 Two or more races, non-Hispanic/Latino), 45 international. Average age 31. 3,369 applicants, 64% accepted, 705 enrolled. *Faculty:* 132 full-time (84 women), 207 part-time/adjunct (142 women). Expenses: Contact institution. *Financial support:* In 2017–18, 71 students received support. Career-related internships or fieldwork, Federal Work-Study, institutionally sponsored loans, scholarships/grants, and tuition waivers (partial) available. Support available to part-time students. Financial award application deadline: 2/15. In 2017, 630 master's, 9 doctorates, 7 other advanced degrees awarded. *Program availability:* Part-time, evening/weekend. Offers biostatistics (MPH); environmental and occupational health (Dr PH); epidemiology (MPH); exercise and nutrition sciences (MS); global health (Dr PH); global health communication (MPH); health policy and management (EMHA, MHA, MPH, MS, Graduate Certificate); microbiology and emerging infectious diseases (MSPH); prevention and community health (MPH, Dr PH); public health (EMHA, MHA, MPH, MS, MSPH, Dr PH, Graduate Certificate). *Application deadline:* For fall admission, 2/15 priority date for domestic students, 2/15 for international students. Applications are processed on a rolling basis. *Application Contact:* Director of Admissions, 202-994-2160, Fax: 202-994-1860, E-mail: sphhsinfo@gwumc.edu. *Dean,* Dr. Lynn Goldman, 202-994-5179, E-mail: goldmanl@gwu.edu.

School of Business Students: 930 full-time (458 women), 850 part-time (436 women); includes 525 minority (212 Black or African American, non-Hispanic/Latino; 4 American Indian or Alaska Native, non-Hispanic/Latino; 164 Asian, non-Hispanic/Latino; 103 Hispanic/Latino; 4 Native Hawaiian or other Pacific Islander, non-Hispanic/Latino; 38 Two or more races, non-Hispanic/Latino), 686 international. Average age 32. 4,247 applicants, 49% accepted, 665 enrolled. *Faculty:* 126 full-time (35 women), 65 part-time/adjunct (15 women). Expenses: Contact institution. *Financial support:* In 2017–18, 194 students received support. Fellowships, teaching assistantships, career-related internships or fieldwork, Federal Work-Study, institutionally sponsored loans, and tuition waivers (partial) available. Financial award application deadline: 4/1. In 2017, 817 master's, 3 doctorates, 94 other advanced degrees awarded. *Program availability:* Part-time, evening/weekend, online learning. Offers accountancy (M Accy); business (M Accy, MBA, MS, MSF, MSIST, MTA, PMBA, PhD, Certificate, Professional Certificate); business administration (MBA); business analytics (MS, Certificate); destination management (Professional Certificate); event and meeting management (MTA); event management (Professional Certificate); finance (MSF, PhD); finance and investments (MBA); government contracts (MS); hospitality management (MTA); individualized studies (MTA); information and decision systems (PhD); information systems (MSIST); information systems development (MSIST); information systems management (MBA); information systems project management (MSIST); international business (PhD); management information systems (MSIST); management of science, technology, and innovation (MBA, PhD); marketing (MBA, PhD); project management (MS); sport management (MTA); strategic management and public policy (MBA, PhD); sustainable tourism destination management (MTA); tourism and hospitality management (MBA); walkable urban real estate development (Professional Certificate). PMBA also offered in Alexandria and Ashburn, VA. *Application deadline:* For fall admission, 4/1 priority date for domestic students; for spring admission, 10/1 for domestic students. Applications are processed on a rolling basis. *Application fee:* $75. Electronic applications accepted. *Application Contact:* Christopher Storer, Executive Director, Graduate Admissions, 202-994-1212, E-mail: gwmba@gwu.edu. *Dean,* Dr. Vivek Choudhury, 202-994-6380, E-mail: vchoudhury@gwu.edu.

School of Engineering and Applied Science Students: 875 full-time (220 women), 1,278 part-time (352 women); includes 465 minority (258 Black or African American, non-Hispanic/Latino; 5 American Indian or Alaska Native, non-Hispanic/Latino; 140 Asian, non-Hispanic/Latino; 42 Hispanic/Latino; 4 Native Hawaiian or other Pacific Islander, non-Hispanic/Latino; 16 Two or more races, non-Hispanic/Latino), 873 international. Average age 32. 3,267 applicants, 68% accepted, 765 enrolled. *Faculty:* 92 full-time (19 women), 101 part-time/adjunct (17 women). Expenses: Contact institution. *Financial support:* In 2017–18, 216 students received support. Fellowships, research assistantships, teaching assistantships, career-related internships or fieldwork, Federal Work-Study, institutionally sponsored loans, and tuition waivers (full and partial) available. Financial award application deadline: 3/1; financial award applicants required to submit FAFSA. In 2017, 523 master's, 134 doctorates, 31 other advanced degrees awarded. *Program availability:* Part-time, evening/weekend. Offers biomedical engineering (MS, PhD); civil and environmental engineering (MS, PhD, App Sc, Engr, Graduate Certificate); computer science (MS, D Sc); cybersecurity (MS); electrical engineering (MS, PhD); engineering and applied science (MS, D Sc, PhD, App Sc, Engr, Graduate Certificate); mechanical and aerospace engineering (MS, PhD, App Sc, Engr, Graduate Certificate); regulatory biomedical engineering (MS); system engineering (PhD); telecommunication and computers (MS). *Application deadline:* For fall admission, 3/1 for domestic students; for spring admission, 10/1 for domestic students. Applications are processed on a rolling basis. *Application fee:* $75. *Application Contact:* Adina Lav, Marketing, Recruiting and Admissions, 202-994-5827, Fax: 202-994-0909, E-mail: engineering@gwu.edu. *Dean*, David S. Dolling, 202-994-6080, E-mail: dolling@gwu.edu.

School of Medicine and Health Sciences Students: 1,015 full-time (660 women), 476 part-time (354 women); includes 616 minority (155 Black or African American, non-Hispanic/Latino; 7 American Indian or Alaska Native, non-Hispanic/Latino; 270 Asian, non-Hispanic/Latino; 139 Hispanic/Latino; 9 Native Hawaiian or other Pacific Islander, non-Hispanic/Latino; 36 Two or more races, non-Hispanic/Latino), 41 international. Average age 30. 2,516 applicants, 22% accepted, 315 enrolled. *Faculty:* 158 full-time (81 women), 92 part-time/adjunct (45 women). Expenses: Contact institution. *Financial support:* Career-related internships or fieldwork, Federal Work-Study, and institutionally sponsored loans available. In 2017, 197 master's, 49 doctorates, 186 other advanced degrees awarded. Offers clinical practice management (MSHS); clinical research administration (MSHS); emergency services management (MSHS); end-of-life care (MSHS); immunohematology (MSHS); immunohematology and biotechnology (MSHS); medicine (MD); medicine and health sciences (MSHS, DPT, MD, OTD, Graduate Certificate); physical therapy (DPT); physician assistant (MSHS). *Application deadline:* Applications are processed on a rolling basis. *Application fee:* $75. *Application Contact:* Admissions, 202-994-3748, Fax: 202-994-1753, E-mail: medadmit@gwu.edu. *Dean*, Dr. Jeffrey Akman, 202-994-3727, E-mail: akman@gwu.edu.

School of Nursing Students: 38 full-time (34 women), 570 part-time (510 women); includes 197 minority (92 Black or African American, non-Hispanic/Latino; 2 American Indian or Alaska Native, non-Hispanic/Latino; 63 Asian, non-Hispanic/Latino; 28 Hispanic/Latino; 1 Native Hawaiian or other Pacific Islander, non-Hispanic/Latino; 11 Two or more races, non-Hispanic/Latino), 2 international. Average age 31. 507 applicants, 76% accepted, 185 enrolled. *Faculty:* 58 full-time (56 women), 119 part-time/adjunct (111 women). Expenses: Contact institution. In 2017, 155 master's, 32 doctorates awarded. Offers adult nurse practitioner (MSN, DNP, Post-Master's Certificate); clinical research administration (MSN); family nurse practitioner (MSN, Post-Master's Certificate); health care quality (MSN, Post-Master's Certificate); nursing leadership and management (MSN); nursing practice (DNP); palliative care nurse practitioner (Post-Master's Certificate). *Application Contact:* Kristin Williams, Associate Provost for Graduate Enrollment Management, 202-994-0467, Fax: 202-994-0371, E-mail: ksw@gwu.edu. *Dean*, Pamela R. Jeffries, 202-994-3725, E-mail: pjeffries@gwu.edu.

GEORGIA CAMPUS–PHILADELPHIA COLLEGE OF OSTEOPATHIC MEDICINE, Suwanee, GA 30024

General Information Independent, coed, graduate-only institution. *Graduate housing:* On-campus housing not available.

GRADUATE UNITS

Doctor of Osteopathic Medicine Program Offers osteopathic medicine (DO). Electronic applications accepted.

Doctor of Physical Therapy Program Offers physical therapy (DPT).

School of Pharmacy Offers pharmacy (Pharm D). Electronic applications accepted.

GEORGIA COLLEGE & STATE UNIVERSITY, Milledgeville, GA 31061

General Information State-supported, coed, comprehensive institution. *Enrollment:* 6,952 graduate, professional, and undergraduate students; 306 full-time matriculated graduate/professional students (198 women), 649 part-time matriculated graduate/professional students (444 women). *Enrollment by degree level:* 761 master's, 37 doctoral, 157 other advanced degrees. *Graduate faculty:* 330 full-time (185 women). Tuition and fees vary according to course load, campus/location and program. *Graduate housing:* Room and/or apartments available on a first-come, first-served basis to single students; on-campus housing not available to married students. Housing application deadline: 5/1. *Student services:* Campus employment opportunities, campus safety program, career counseling, free psychological counseling, grant writing training, international student services, low-cost health insurance, multicultural affairs office, services for students with disabilities, teacher training, writing training. *Library facilities:* Ina Dillard Russell Library plus 1 other. *Collection:* Books: 175,159 (physical), 576,315 (digital/electronic); Serial titles: 4,951 (physical), 232,257 (digital/electronic); Databases: 379. Weekly public service hours: 102; students can reserve study rooms.

Computer facilities: 900 computers available on campus for general student use. A campuswide network can be accessed from student residence rooms and from off campus. Online class registration is available.
Website: http://www.gcsu.edu/

General Application Contact: Kate Marshall, Graduate Admissions Coordinator, 478-445-1184, Fax: 478-445-1336, E-mail: grad-admit@gcsu.edu.

GRADUATE UNITS

Graduate School Students: 306 full-time (198 women), 649 part-time (444 women); includes 318 minority (234 Black or African American, non-Hispanic/Latino; 1 American Indian or Alaska Native, non-Hispanic/Latino; 20 Asian, non-Hispanic/Latino; 40 Hispanic/Latino; 2 Native Hawaiian or other Pacific Islander, non-Hispanic/Latino; 21 Two or more races, non-Hispanic/Latino), 9 international. Average age 33. 318 applicants, 90% accepted, 220 enrolled. Expenses: Contact institution. *Financial support:* In 2017–18, 115 students received support. Unspecified assistantships available. Support available to part-time students. Financial award application deadline: 3/1; financial award applicants required to submit FAFSA. In 2017, 294 master's, 5 doctorates, 91 other advanced degrees awarded. *Program availability:* Part-time, evening/weekend, 100% online, blended/hybrid learning. *Application deadline:* For fall admission, 7/1 priority date for domestic students, 4/1 priority date for international students; for spring admission, 11/1 priority date for domestic students, 9/1 priority date for international students; for summer admission, 4/1 priority date for domestic students. Applications are processed on a rolling basis. *Application fee:* $40. Electronic applications accepted. *Application Contact:* Kate Marshall, Graduate Admissions Coordinator, 478-445-1184, Fax: 478-445-1336, E-mail: grad-admit@gcsu.edu. *Associate Provost/Dean of Graduate Studies*, Dr. Costas Spirou, 478-445-4715, Fax: 478-445-5151, E-mail: costas.spirou@gcsu.edu.

College of Arts and Sciences Students: 66 full-time (44 women), 105 part-time (71 women); includes 54 minority (34 Black or African American, non-Hispanic/Latino; 5 Asian, non-Hispanic/Latino; 9 Hispanic/Latino; 6 Two or more races, non-Hispanic/Latino), 1 international. Average age 30. 98 applicants, 82% accepted, 56 enrolled. *Faculty:* 190 full-time (91 women). Expenses: Contact institution. *Financial support:* In 2017–18, 53 students received support. Unspecified assistantships available. Support available to part-time students. Financial award application deadline: 3/1; financial award applicants required to submit FAFSA. In 2017, 48 master's awarded. *Program availability:* Part-time, evening/weekend, 100% online. Offers arts and sciences (MA, MFA, MM Ed, MPA, MS, MSCJ); biology (MS); creative writing (MFA); criminal justice (MSCJ); English (MA, MFA); music (MM Ed); public administration (MPA). *Application deadline:* For fall admission, 7/1 priority date for domestic students, 4/1 priority date for international students; for spring admission, 11/1 priority date for domestic students, 9/1 priority date for international students; for summer admission, 4/1 priority date for domestic students. Applications are processed on a rolling basis. *Application fee:* $40. Electronic applications accepted. *Application Contact:* Kate Marshall, Graduate Admissions Coordinator, 478-445-1184, Fax: 478-445-1336, E-mail: grad-admit@gcsu.edu. *Dean*, Kenneth Proctor, 478-445-4441, E-mail: ken.proctor@gcsu.edu.

College of Health Sciences Students: 68 full-time (47 women), 146 part-time (130 women); includes 73 minority (52 Black or African American, non-Hispanic/Latino; 5 Asian, non-Hispanic/Latino; 14 Hispanic/Latino; 2 Two or more races, non-Hispanic/Latino), 2 international. Average age 35. 50 applicants, 100% accepted, 45 enrolled. *Faculty:* 49 full-time (39 women). Expenses: Contact institution. *Financial support:* In 2017–18, 24 students received support. Unspecified assistantships available. Support available to part-time students. Financial award application deadline: 3/1; financial award applicants required to submit FAFSA. In 2017, 54 master's, 5 doctorates, 3 other advanced degrees awarded. *Program availability:* Part-time, evening/weekend. Offers art therapy (MA); health and human performance (MS); health sciences (M Ed, MA, MAT, MMT, MS, MSN, DNP, Post-MSN Certificate); kinesiology/health education (MAT); music therapy (MMT); nursing (MSN, Post-MSN Certificate); nursing practice (DNP). *Application deadline:* For fall admission, 7/1 priority date for domestic students, 4/1 priority date for international students; for spring admission, 11/1 priority date for domestic students, 9/1 priority date for international students; for summer admission, 4/1 priority date for domestic students. Applications are processed on a rolling basis. *Application fee:* $40. Electronic applications accepted. *Application Contact:* Kate Marshall, Graduate Admissions Coordinator, 478-445-1184, Fax: 478-445-1336, E-mail: grad-admit@gcsu.edu. *Dean*, Dr. Sandra Gangstead, 478-445-4092, Fax: 478-445-1913, E-mail: sandra.gangstead@gcsu.edu.

The John H. Lounsbury College of Education Students: 68 full-time (47 women), 146 part-time (130 women); includes 73 minority (52 Black or African American, non-Hispanic/Latino; 5 Asian, non-Hispanic/Latino; 14 Hispanic/Latino; 2 Two or more races, non-Hispanic/Latino), 2 international. Average age 35. 72 applicants, 100% accepted, 58 enrolled. *Faculty:* 29 full-time (25 women). Expenses: Contact institution. *Financial support:* In 2017–18, 33 students received support. Unspecified assistantships available. Support available to part-time students. Financial award application deadline: 3/1; financial award applicants required to submit FAFSA. In 2017, 78 master's, 87 other advanced degrees awarded. *Program availability:* Evening/weekend, 100% online, blended/hybrid learning. Offers curriculum and instruction (M Ed); early childhood education (M Ed); education (M Ed, MAT, Ed S); educational leadership (M Ed, Ed S); instructional technology (M Ed); library media (M Ed); middle grades education (M Ed, MAT); secondary education (MAT); special education (M Ed, MAT, Ed S); teacher education (Ed S). *Application deadline:* For fall admission, 7/1 priority date for domestic students; for spring admission, 11/1 priority date for domestic students; for summer admission, 4/1 priority date for domestic students. Applications are processed on a rolling basis. *Application fee:* $40. Electronic applications accepted. *Application Contact:* Shanda Brand, Graduate Admissions Advisor, 478-445-1383, Fax: 478-445-6582, E-mail: shanda.brand@gcsu.edu. *Dean, College of Education*, Dr. Joseph Peters, 478-445-2518, Fax: 478-445-6582, E-mail: joseph.peters@gcsu.edu.

The J. Whitney Bunting School of Business Students: 28 full-time (10 women), 187 part-time (81 women); includes 63 minority (37 Black or African American, non-Hispanic/Latino; 9 Asian, non-Hispanic/Latino; 9 Hispanic/Latino; 1 Native Hawaiian or other Pacific Islander, non-Hispanic/Latino; 7 Two or more races, non-Hispanic/Latino), 4 international. Average age 33. 90 applicants, 86% accepted, 59 enrolled. *Faculty:* 54 full-time (24 women). Expenses: Contact institution. *Financial support:* In 2017–18, 22 students received support. Unspecified assistantships available. Financial award application deadline: 3/1; financial award applicants required to submit FAFSA. In 2017, 95 master's awarded. *Program availability:* Part-time, evening/weekend, 100% online, blended/hybrid learning. Offers accounting (M Acc); business (M Acc, MBA, MLSCM, MMIS); business administration (MBA); logistics (MLSCM); management information systems (MMIS). *Application deadline:* For fall admission, 7/1 priority date for domestic students, 4/1 priority date for international students; for spring admission, 11/1 priority date for domestic students, 8/1 priority date for international students; for summer admission, 4/1 priority date for domestic students. Applications are processed on a rolling basis. *Application fee:* $40. Electronic applications accepted. *Application Contact:* Lynn Hanson, Director of Graduate Programs, 478-445-5115, E-mail: lynn.hanson@gcsu.edu. *Dean, School of Business*, Dr. Dale Young, 478-445-5497, E-mail: dael.young@gcsu.edu.

GEORGIA INSTITUTE OF TECHNOLOGY, Atlanta, GA 30332-0001

General Information State-supported, coed, university. CGS member. *Graduate housing:* Rooms and/or apartments available on a first-come, first-served basis to single and married students. Housing application deadline: 6/1. *Research affiliation:* Oak Ridge National Laboratory (energy, health, environment), Children's Healthcare of Atlanta (pediatric biomedical and device research), Georgia State University (brain imaging), Southeastern Universities Research Association (high-energy physics), Emory University Medical School (biomedical engineering), Zoo Atlanta (environmental design, environmental psychology).

GRADUATE UNITS

Graduate Studies Students: 8,985 full-time (2,346 women), 4,810 part-time (815 women); includes 2,525 minority (647 Black or African American, non-Hispanic/Latino; 5 American Indian or Alaska Native, non-Hispanic/Latino; 654 Asian, non-Hispanic/Latino; 886 Hispanic/Latino; 6 Native Hawaiian or other Pacific Islander, non-Hispanic/Latino; 327 Two or more races, non-Hispanic/Latino), 5,186 international. 22,927 applicants, 39% accepted, 8477 enrolled. Expenses: Contact institution. *Financial support:* Fellowships, research assistantships, teaching assistantships, career-related internships or fieldwork, Federal Work-Study, institutionally sponsored loans, traineeships, tuition waivers (partial), and unspecified assistantships available. Support available to part-time students. Financial award application deadline: 5/1; financial award applicants required to submit FAFSA. *Program availability:* Part-time, evening/weekend, 100% online. Offers algorithms, combinatorics, and optimization (PhD); analytics (MS); bioengineering (MS, PhD); bioinformatics (MS, PhD); computational science and engineering (MS, PhD); human computer interaction (MS); paper science and engineering (MS, PhD); quantitative and computational finance (MS); statistics (MS). *Application deadline:* Applications are processed on a rolling basis. *Application fee:* $75 ($85 for international students). Electronic applications accepted. *Application Contact:* E-mail: gradinfo@gatech.edu. *Director, Graduate Studies*, Marla S. Bruner, 404-894-0099, E-mail: marla.bruner@grad.gatech.edu.

College of Computing *Program availability:* Part-time, online learning. Offers computer science (MS, PhD); computing (MS, PhD); human-centered computing (MS, PhD); information security (MS); robotics (PhD). Electronic applications accepted.

College of Design Offers architecture (M Arch, MS, PhD); building construction (PhD); city and regional planning (PhD); design (M Arch, MCRP, MS, PhD); economic development (MCRP); environmental planning and management (MCRP); geographic information systems (MCRP); industrial design (MID); integrated facility and property management (MS); integrated project delivery systems (MS); land and community development (MCRP); land use planning (MCRP); music technology (MS, PhD); program management (MS); residential construction development (MS); transportation (MCRP); urban design (MCRP). Electronic applications accepted.

College of Engineering *Program availability:* Part-time, online learning. Offers aerospace engineering (MS, PhD); applied systems engineering (PMS); biomedical engineering (PhD); chemical engineering (MS, PhD); civil engineering (MS, PhD); electrical and computer engineering (MS, PhD); engineering (MS, MSMP, MSNE, PhD); engineering science and mechanics (MS, PhD); environmental engineering (MS); health systems (MS); industrial and systems engineering (MS, PhD); industrial engineering (MS, PhD); international logistics (MS); materials science and engineering (MS, PhD); mechanical engineering (MS, MSME, MSMP, MSNE, PhD); medical physics (MS, MSMP); nuclear and radiological engineering (PhD); nuclear and radiological engineering and medical physics (MS, MSMP, MSNE, PhD); nuclear engineering (MSNE); operations research (MS, PhD). Electronic applications accepted.

College of Sciences *Program availability:* Part-time. Offers applied physiology (PhD); biology (MS, PhD); chemistry and biochemistry (MS, PhD); earth and atmospheric sciences (MS, PhD); mathematics (MS, PhD); physics (MS, PhD); prosthetics and orthotics (MS); psychology (MS, PhD); sciences (MS, PhD). Electronic applications accepted.

Ivan Allen College of Liberal Arts *Program availability:* Part-time. Offers digital media (MS, PhD); economics (MS, PhD); history and sociology of technology and science (MS, PhD); international affairs (MS); liberal arts (MS, PhD); public policy (MS, PhD). Electronic applications accepted.

Scheller College of Business *Program availability:* Part-time, evening/weekend. Offers business (MBA, MS, PhD); business administration (MBA); global business (MBA); management (MS, PhD); management of technology (MBA). Electronic applications accepted.

GEORGIAN COURT UNIVERSITY, Lakewood, NJ 08701-2697

General Information Independent-religious, coed, comprehensive institution. *Enrollment:* 2,390 graduate, professional, and undergraduate students; 178 full-time matriculated graduate/professional students (147 women), 599 part-time matriculated graduate/professional students (483 women). *Enrollment by degree level:* 638 master's, 135 other advanced degrees. *Graduate faculty:* 35 full-time (21 women), 59 part-time/adjunct (29 women). *Tuition:* Part-time $839 per credit. *Required fees:* $248 per semester. Tuition and fees vary according to campus/location and program. *Graduate housing:* On-campus housing not available. *Student services:* Campus employment opportunities, campus safety program, career counseling, exercise/wellness program, free psychological counseling, low-cost health insurance, services for students with disabilities, teacher training. *Library facilities:* The Sister Mary Joseph Cunningham Library. *Collection:* Books: 129,447 (physical), 117,590 (digital/electronic); Serial titles: 2,898 (physical), 33,651 (digital/electronic); Databases: 115. Weekly public service hours: 85; students can reserve study rooms.

Computer facilities: 221 computers available on campus for general student use. A campuswide network can be accessed from student residence rooms and from off campus. Online class registration is available.
Website: http://www.georgian.edu/

General Application Contact: Patrick Givens, Director of Graduate and Professional Studies Admissions, 732-987-2736, Fax: 732-987-2000, E-mail: gps@georgian.edu.

GRADUATE UNITS

School of Arts and Sciences Students: 100 full-time (86 women), 92 part-time (67 women); includes 34 minority (9 Black or African American, non-Hispanic/Latino; 1 Asian, non-Hispanic/Latino; 20 Hispanic/Latino; 4 Two or more races, non-Hispanic/Latino), 2 international. Average age 34. 187 applicants, 56% accepted, 78 enrolled. *Faculty:* 18 full-time (11 women), 8 part-time/adjunct (4 women). Expenses: Contact institution. *Financial support:* Scholarships/grants, health care benefits, and unspecified assistantships available. Financial award application deadline: 4/15; financial award applicants required to submit FAFSA. In 2017, 58 master's, 20 other advanced degrees awarded. *Program availability:* Part-time, evening/weekend. Offers applied behavior analysis (MA); autism spectrum disorders (Certificate); clinical mental health counseling (MA); criminal justice and human rights (MS); holistic health studies (MA, Certificate); homeland security (Certificate); instructional technology (CPC); mercy spirituality (Certificate); parish business management (Certificate); professional counselor (Certificate); school psychology (MA, Certificate); theology (MA, Certificate). *Application deadline:* For fall admission, 8/15 for domestic students, 5/1 for international students; for spring admission, 1/15 for domestic students, 10/1 for international students. Applications are processed on a rolling basis. *Application fee:* $40. Electronic applications accepted. *Application Contact:* Patrick Givens, Director of Graduate and Professional Studies Admissions, 732-987-2736, Fax: 732-987-2000, E-mail: gps@georgian.edu. *Dean*, Dr. Mary Chinery, 732-987-2493, Fax: 732-987-2007, E-mail: mchinery@georgian.edu.

School of Business and Digital Media Students: 29 full-time (19 women), 31 part-time (24 women); includes 17 minority (7 Black or African American, non-Hispanic/Latino; 3 Asian, non-Hispanic/Latino; 4 Hispanic/Latino; 3 Two or more races, non-Hispanic/Latino), 2 international. Average age 31. 54 applicants, 65% accepted, 21 enrolled. *Faculty:* 6 full-time (3 women), 11 part-time/adjunct (3 women). Expenses: Contact institution. *Financial support:* Scholarships/grants, health care benefits, and unspecified assistantships available. Financial award application deadline: 4/15; financial award applicants required to submit FAFSA. In 2017, 33 master's, 7 other advanced degrees awarded. *Program availability:* Part-time, evening/weekend. Offers business (MBA); business essentials (Certificate); nonprofit management (Certificate). *Application deadline:* For fall admission, 8/15 priority date for domestic students, 5/1 for international students; for spring admission, 1/15 priority date for domestic students, 10/1 for international students. Applications are processed on a rolling basis. *Application fee:* $40. Electronic applications accepted. *Application Contact:* Patrick Givens, Director of Graduate and Professional Studies Admissions, 732-987-2736, Fax: 732-987-2000, E-mail: gps@georgian.edu. *Dean*, Dr. Cathleen McQuillen, 732-987-2623, Fax: 732-987-2024, E-mail: cmcquillen@georgian.edu.

School of Education Students: 49 full-time (42 women), 472 part-time (388 women); includes 101 minority (42 Black or African American, non-Hispanic/Latino; 12 Asian, non-Hispanic/Latino; 44 Hispanic/Latino; 3 Two or more races, non-Hispanic/Latino). Average age 34. 412 applicants, 56% accepted, 153 enrolled. *Faculty:* 11 full-time (7 women), 40 part-time/adjunct (22 women). Expenses: Contact institution. *Financial support:* Scholarships/grants, health care benefits, and unspecified assistantships available. Financial award application deadline: 4/15; financial award applicants required to submit FAFSA. In 2017, 81 master's awarded. *Program availability:* Part-time, evening/weekend. Offers administration and leadership (MA); autism spectrum disorders (Certificate); education (M Ed, MA, MAT); instructional technology (M Mat SE, Certificate). *Application deadline:* For fall admission, 8/15 priority date for domestic students, 5/1 for international students; for spring admission, 1/15 priority date for domestic students, 10/1 for international students. Applications are processed on a rolling basis. *Application fee:* $40. Electronic applications accepted. *Application Contact:* Patrick Givens, Director of Graduate and Professional Studies Admissions, 732-987-2736, Fax: 732-987-2000, E-mail: gps@georgian.edu. *Dean*, Dr. Lynn DeCapua, 732-987-2729, E-mail: ldecapua@georgian.edu.

GEORGIA SOUTHERN UNIVERSITY, Statesboro, GA 30458

General Information State-supported, coed, university. CGS member. *Enrollment:* 20,418 graduate, professional, and undergraduate students; 1,112 full-time matriculated graduate/professional students (704 women), 1,491 part-time matriculated graduate/professional students (1,036 women). *Enrollment by degree level:* 1,845 master's, 521 doctoral, 237 other advanced degrees. *Graduate faculty:* 723 full-time (304 women), 24 part-time/adjunct (12 women). Tuition, state resident: full-time $4986; part-time $3324 per year. Tuition, nonresident: full-time $21,982; part-time $15,352 per year. *Required fees:* $2092; $1802 per credit hour. $901 per semester. Tuition and fees vary according to course load, campus/location and program. *Graduate housing:* Room and/or apartments available on a first-come, first-served basis to single students; on-campus housing not available to married students. Typical cost: $3500 per year. Housing application deadline: 5/1. *Student services:* Campus employment opportunities, campus safety program, exercise/wellness program, free psychological counseling, grant writing training, international student services, low-cost health insurance, multicultural affairs office, services for students with disabilities, teacher training, writing training. *Library facilities:* Henderson Library. *Collection:* Books: 1 million (physical), 374,473 (digital/electronic); Serial titles: 14,993 (physical), 94,948 (digital/electronic); Databases: 332. Weekly public service hours: 143; study areas open 24 hours, 5–7 days a week; students can reserve study rooms. *Research affiliation:* Oak Ridge National Laboratory (physical sciences), Mount Desert Island Biological Laboratory (marine biology), Space Telescope Science Institute (astronomy, physics), St. Catherine's Island Foundation (marine science, life sciences), Skidaway Institute of Oceanography (marine sciences).

Computer facilities: Computer purchase and lease plans are available. 3,743 computers available on campus for general student use. A campuswide network can be accessed from student residence rooms and from off campus. Online class registration, online degree audit, online career services, and online healthcare are available.
Website: http://www.georgiasouthern.edu/

General Application Contact: Naronda C. Wright, Office of Graduate Admissions, 912-478-5384, Fax: 912-478-0740, E-mail: gradadmissions@georgiasouthern.edu.

GRADUATE UNITS

Jack N. Averitt College of Graduate Studies Students: 1,112 full-time (704 women), 1,491 part-time (1,036 women); includes 805 minority (585 Black or African American, non-Hispanic/Latino; 4 American Indian or Alaska Native, non-Hispanic/Latino; 59 Asian, non-Hispanic/Latino; 102 Hispanic/Latino; 55 Two or more races, non-Hispanic/Latino), 166 international. Average age 31. 1,576 applicants, 71% accepted, 757 enrolled. *Faculty:* 723 full-time (304 women), 24 part-time/adjunct (12 women). Expenses: Contact institution. *Financial support:* In 2017–18, 805 students received support, including 40 research assistantships with partial tuition reimbursements available (averaging $7,750 per year), 215 teaching assistantships with partial tuition reimbursements available (averaging $7,750 per year); career-related internships or fieldwork, Federal Work-Study, scholarships/grants, traineeships, tuition waivers (partial), unspecified assistantships, and doctoral stipends also available. Support available to part-time students. Financial award application deadline: 4/15; financial award applicants required to submit FAFSA. In 2017, 837 master's, 66 doctorates, 79 other advanced degrees awarded. *Program availability:* Part-time, evening/weekend, 100% online, blended/hybrid learning. *Application deadline:* For fall admission, 4/1 priority date for domestic and international students; for spring admission, 10/1 priority date for domestic and international students; for summer admission, 4/1 for domestic students. Applications are processed on a rolling basis. *Application fee:* $50. Electronic applications accepted. *Application Contact:* Naronda C. Wright, Graduate Admissions Specialist, 912-478-5384, Fax: 912-478-0740, E-mail: gradadmissions@georgiasouthern.edu. *Director, College of Graduate Studies*, Dr. Ashley Walker Colquitt, 912-478-0851, Fax: 912-478-8642, E-mail: awalker@georgiasouthern.edu.

Allen E. Paulson College of Engineering and Information Technology Students: 80 full-time (17 women), 71 part-time (12 women); includes 40 minority (27 Black or African American, non-Hispanic/Latino; 5 Asian, non-Hispanic/Latino; 6 Hispanic/Latino; 2 Two or more races, non-Hispanic/Latino), 52 international. Average age 29. 160 applicants, 83% accepted, 51 enrolled. *Faculty:* 75 full-time (7 women). Expenses: Contact institution. *Financial support:* In 2017–18, 76 students received support, including 3 research assistantships with full tuition reimbursements available (averaging $7,750 per year), 4 teaching assistantships with full tuition reimbursements available (averaging $7,750 per year); Federal Work-Study, scholarships/grants, tuition waivers (full), and unspecified assistantships also available. Financial award applicants required to submit FAFSA. In 2017, 34 master's awarded. *Program availability:* Part-time, blended/hybrid learning. Offers civil engineering and construction management (MSAE); computer science (MS); electrical and electronic systems (MSAE); engineering and information technology (MSAE); engineering and manufacturing management (Graduate Certificate); engineering/energy science (MSAE); engineering/engineering management (MSAE); engineering/mechatronics (MSAE); information technology (MSAE); occupational safety and environmental compliance (Graduate Certificate); occupational safety and environmental science (Graduate Certificate). *Application deadline:* For fall admission, 3/1 priority date for domestic students, 6/1 for international students; for spring admission, 10/1 priority date for domestic students, 10/1 for international students. Applications are processed on a rolling basis. *Application fee:* $50. Electronic applications accepted. *Dean*, Dr. Mohammad S. Davoud, 912-478-8046, E-mail: mdavoud@georgiasouthern.edu.

College of Business Students: 111 full-time (53 women), 248 part-time (124 women); includes 100 minority (61 Black or African American, non-Hispanic/Latino; 1 American Indian or Alaska Native, non-Hispanic/Latino; 16 Asian, non-Hispanic/Latino; 15 Hispanic/Latino; 7 Two or more races, non-Hispanic/Latino), 19 international. Average age 31. 261 applicants, 83% accepted, 139 enrolled. *Faculty:* 94 full-time (23 women), 1 part-time/adjunct (0 women). Expenses: Contact institution. *Financial support:* In 2017–18, 65 students received support. Research assistantships with partial tuition reimbursements available, teaching assistantships with partial tuition reimbursements available, career-related internships or fieldwork, Federal Work-Study, scholarships/grants, tuition waivers (partial), and unspecified assistantships available. Support available to part-time students. Financial award application deadline: 4/15; financial award applicants required to submit FAFSA. In 2017, 167 master's, 7 other advanced degrees awarded. *Program availability:* Part-time, evening/weekend, 100% online. Offers applied economics (MS); business (M Acc, MBA, MS, PhD, Graduate Certificate); business administration (MBA); enterprise resources planning (Graduate Certificate); forensic accounting (M Acc); information systems (Graduate Certificate); logistics/supply chain management (PhD). *Application deadline:* For fall admission, 3/1 priority date for domestic and international students; for spring admission, 10/1 priority date for domestic students, 10/1 for international students. Applications are processed on a rolling basis. *Application fee:* $50. Electronic applications accepted. *Dean*, Dr. Allen Amason, 912-478-2622, Fax: 912-478-0292, E-mail: aamason@georgiasouthern.edu.

College of Education Students: 351 full-time (279 women), 840 part-time (675 women); includes 357 minority (282 Black or African American, non-Hispanic/Latino; 2 American Indian or Alaska Native, non-Hispanic/Latino; 11 Asian, non-Hispanic/Latino; 39 Hispanic/Latino; 23 Two or more races, non-Hispanic/Latino), 3 international. Average age 33. 294 applicants, 89% accepted, 216 enrolled. *Faculty:* 77 full-time (52 women), 12 part-time/adjunct (5 women). Expenses: Contact institution. *Financial support:* In 2017–18, 146 students received support, including 1 teaching assistantship with full tuition reimbursement available (averaging $7,750 per year); research assistantships with partial tuition reimbursements available, career-related internships or fieldwork, scholarships/grants, and unspecified assistantships also available. Financial award application deadline: 4/15; financial award applicants required to submit FAFSA. In 2017, 378 master's, 44 doctorates, 65 other advanced degrees awarded. *Program availability:* Part-time, evening/weekend, 100% online, blended/hybrid learning. Offers counselor education (M Ed); curriculum and instruction - accomplished teaching (M Ed); curriculum studies (Ed D); early childhood (M Ed, MAT, Ed S); early childhood education (M Ed, MAT, Ed S); education (M Ed, MAT, Ed D, Ed S); educational leadership (M Ed, Ed D, Ed S); English education (MAT); evaluation, assessment, research, and learning (M Ed); higher education (M Ed, Ed D); higher education administration (M Ed); higher education leadership (Ed D); instructional technology (M Ed, Ed S); mental health counseling (M Ed); middle grades (M Ed, MAT, Ed S); middle grades education (M Ed, MAT, Ed S); P-12 leadership (M Ed, Ed D, Ed S); reading education (M Ed, Ed S); school counseling (M Ed); school library media (M Ed, Ed S); school psychology (M Ed, Ed S); secondary education (M Ed, MAT, Ed S); Spanish P-12 education (MAT); special education (M Ed, MA Ext, Ed S). *Application deadline:* For fall admission, 3/1 priority date for domestic and international students; for spring admission, 10/1 priority date for domestic students, 10/1 for international students. Applications are processed on a rolling basis. *Application fee:* $50. Electronic applications accepted. *Application Contact:* Dr. Lydia Cross, Director, Graduate Academic Services Center, 912-478-1447, E-mail: gasc@georgiasouthern.edu. *Dean*, Dr. Thomas Koballa, 912-478-5648, Fax: 912-478-5093, E-mail: tkoballa@georgiasouthern.edu.

College of Health and Human Sciences Students: 110 full-time (68 women), 154 part-time (102 women); includes 77 minority (52 Black or African American, non-Hispanic/Latino; 7 Asian, non-Hispanic/Latino; 13 Hispanic/Latino; 5 Two or more races, non-Hispanic/Latino), 5 international. Average age 31. 287 applicants, 45% accepted, 98 enrolled. *Faculty:* 78 full-time (54 women), 6 part-time/adjunct (5 women). Expenses: Contact institution. *Financial support:* In 2017–18, 134 students received support, including 24 fellowships with full tuition reimbursements available (averaging $7,750 per year), 9 research assistantships with full tuition reimbursements available (averaging $7,750 per year), 33 teaching assistantships with full tuition reimbursements available (averaging $7,750 per year); career-related internships or fieldwork, Federal Work-Study, scholarships/grants, traineeships, and unspecified assistantships also available. Support available to part-time students. Financial award application deadline: 4/15; financial award applicants required to submit FAFSA. In 2017, 88 master's, 7 other advanced degrees awarded. *Program availability:* Part-time, evening/weekend, 100% online, blended/hybrid learning. Offers dietetics (Certificate); family nurse practitioner (MSN); health and human sciences (MS, MSN, DNP, Certificate); kinesiology (MS); nurse educator (Certificate); nurse practitioner (MSN); nursing science (DNP); psychiatric mental health nurse practitioner (MSN); sport management (MS). *Application deadline:* For fall admission, 3/1 priority date for domestic students, 3/1 for international students; for spring admission, 10/1 priority date for domestic students, 10/1 for international students. Applications are processed on a rolling basis. *Application fee:* $50. Electronic applications accepted. *Dean*, Dr. Barry Joyner, 912-478-5322, Fax: 912-478-5349, E-mail: joyner@georgiasouthern.edu.

College of Liberal Arts and Social Sciences Students: 175 full-time (122 women), 89 part-time (57 women); includes 75 minority (37 Black or African American, non-Hispanic/Latino; 1 American Indian or Alaska Native, non-Hispanic/Latino; 5 Asian, non-Hispanic/Latino; 18 Hispanic/Latino; 14 Two or more races, non-Hispanic/Latino), 12 international. Average age 28. 252 applicants, 54% accepted, 105 enrolled. *Faculty:* 217 full-time (99 women), 5 part-time/adjunct (2 women). Expenses: Contact institution. *Financial support:* In 2017–18, 160 students received support, including 72 fellowships with full tuition reimbursements available (averaging $7,750 per year), 10 research assistantships with full tuition reimbursements available (averaging $7,750 per year), 26 teaching assistantships with full tuition reimbursements available (averaging $7,750 per year); career-related internships or fieldwork, Federal Work-Study, scholarships/grants, tuition waivers (full), and unspecified assistantships also available. Support available to part-time students. Financial award application deadline: 4/15; financial award applicants required to submit FAFSA. In 2017, 89 master's, 9 other advanced degrees awarded. *Program availability:* Part-time. Offers clinical psychology (Psy D); composition (MM); conducting (MM); English (MA); fine arts (MFA); history (MA); liberal arts and social sciences (MA, MFA, MM, MPA, MS, Psy D, Graduate Certificate); music education (MM); music technology (MM); performance (MM); psychology (MS); public administration (MPA); public and nonprofit management (Graduate Certificate); public history (Graduate Certificate); social science (MA); Spanish (MA). *Application deadline:* For fall admission, 3/1 priority date for domestic and international students; for spring admission, 10/1 priority date for domestic students, 10/1 for international students. Applications are processed on a rolling basis. *Application fee:* $50. Electronic applications accepted. *Dean*, Dr. Curtis Ricker, 912-478-2527, Fax: 912-478-5346, E-mail: cricker@georgiasouthern.edu.

College of Science and Mathematics Students: 90 full-time (38 women), 18 part-time (8 women); includes 19 minority (11 Black or African American, non-Hispanic/Latino; 4 Asian, non-Hispanic/Latino; 4 Hispanic/Latino), 27 international. Average age 27. 85 applicants, 75% accepted, 34 enrolled. *Faculty:* 129 full-time (42 women). Expenses: Contact institution. *Financial support:* In 2017–18, 92 students received support, including 4 fellowships with full tuition reimbursements available (averaging $7,750 per year), 22 research assistantships with full tuition reimbursements available (averaging $7,750 per year), 79 teaching assistantships with full tuition reimbursements available (averaging $7,750 per year); career-related internships or fieldwork, Federal Work-Study, scholarships/grants, tuition waivers (full), and unspecified assistantships also available. Support available to part-time students. Financial award application deadline: 4/15; financial award applicants required to submit FAFSA. In 2017, 33 master's awarded. *Program availability:* Part-time. Offers applied physical science (MS); biology (MS); mathematics (MS); science and mathematics (MS, Certificate). *Application deadline:* For fall admission, 3/1 priority date for domestic and international students; for spring admission, 10/1 priority date for domestic students, 10/1 for international students. Applications are processed on a rolling basis. *Application fee:* $50. Electronic applications accepted. *Application Contact:* Samuel T. Aldridge, Director, Graduate Admissions, 912-478-5384, Fax: 912-478-0740, E-mail: gradadmissions@georgiasouthern.edu. *Dean*, Dr. Martha Abell, 912-478-5132, Fax: 912-478-0836, E-mail: martha@georgiasouthern.edu.

Jiann-Ping Hsu College of Public Health Students: 195 full-time (127 women), 71 part-time (58 women); includes 137 minority (115 Black or African American, non-Hispanic/Latino; 11 Asian, non-Hispanic/Latino; 7 Hispanic/Latino; 4 Two or more races, non-Hispanic/Latino), 48 international. Average age 30. 261 applicants, 83% accepted, 114 enrolled. *Faculty:* 39 full-time (19 women). Expenses: Contact institution. *Financial support:* In 2017–18, 132 students received support, including 53 fellowships with full tuition reimbursements available (averaging $7,750 per year), 3 research assistantships with full tuition reimbursements available (averaging $7,750 per year), 1 teaching assistantship with full tuition reimbursement available (averaging $7,750 per year); career-related internships or fieldwork, Federal Work-Study, scholarships/grants, tuition waivers (full), and unspecified assistantships also available. Support available to part-time students. Financial award application deadline: 4/15; financial award applicants required to submit FAFSA. In 2017, 48 master's, 13 doctorates awarded. *Program availability:* Part-time. Offers biostatistics (MPH, Dr PH); community health behavior and education (Dr PH); community health education (MPH); environmental health sciences (MPH); epidemiology (MPH); health policy and management (MPH, Dr PH); healthcare administration (MHA); public health (MHA, MPH, Dr PH). *Application deadline:* For fall admission, 7/1 priority date for domestic students, 6/1 priority date for international students; for spring admission, 11/1 for domestic students, 10/1 for international students. Applications are processed on a rolling basis. *Application fee:* $135. Electronic applications accepted. *Dean*, Dr. Greg Evans, 912-478-2676, Fax: 912-478-5605, E-mail: rgevans@georgiasouthern.edu.

GEORGIA SOUTHERN UNIVERSITY–ARMSTRONG CAMPUS, Savannah, GA 31419-1997

General Information State-supported, coed, comprehensive institution. *Enrollment:* 7,041 graduate, professional, and undergraduate students; 321 full-time matriculated graduate/professional students (226 women), 434 part-time matriculated graduate/professional students (341 women). *Enrollment by degree level:* 634 master's, 107 doctoral, 14 other advanced degrees. *Graduate faculty:* 91 full-time (58 women), 16 part-time/adjunct (11 women). Tuition, state resident: part-time $211 per credit hour. Tuition, nonresident: part-time $782 per credit hour. *Required fees:* $737 per semester. Tuition and fees vary according to course load, degree level, campus/location and program. *Graduate housing:* Room and/or apartments available on a first-come, first-served basis to single students; on-campus housing not available to married students. Typical cost: $6658 per year ($10,176 including board). Room and board charges vary according to board plan, campus/location and housing facility selected. Housing application deadline: 7/1. *Student services:* Campus employment opportunities, campus safety program, career counseling, exercise/wellness program, free psychological counseling, international student services, low-cost health insurance, multicultural affairs office, services for students with disabilities, teacher training, writing training. *Library facilities:* Lane Library plus 1 other. *Collection:* Books: 207,421 (physical), 215,400 (digital/electronic); Serial titles: 500 (physical), 2,000 (digital/electronic); Databases: 300. Weekly public service hours: 108; students can reserve study rooms.

Computer facilities: 300 computers available on campus for general student use. A campuswide network can be accessed from student residence rooms. Online class registration is available.
Website: http://www.georgiasouthern.edu/

General Application Contact: Dr. Ashley Walker Colquitt, Director of Graduate Studies, 912-478-2647, Fax: 912-478-7579, E-mail: gradschool@georgiasouthern.edu.

GRADUATE UNITS

College of Graduate Studies Students: 321 full-time (226 women), 434 part-time (341 women); includes 257 minority (195 Black or African American, non-Hispanic/Latino; 14 Asian, non-Hispanic/Latino; 27 Hispanic/Latino; 1 Native Hawaiian or other Pacific Islander, non-Hispanic/Latino; 20 Two or more races, non-Hispanic/Latino), 8 international. Average age 31. 586 applicants, 45% accepted, 222 enrolled. *Faculty:* 91 full-time (58 women), 16 part-time/adjunct (11 women). Expenses: Contact institution. *Financial support:* In 2017–18, 65 research assistantships with full tuition reimbursements (averaging $5,000 per year) were awarded; Federal Work-Study, scholarships/grants, and unspecified assistantships also available. Financial award application deadline: 3/15; financial award applicants required to submit FAFSA. In 2017, 239 master's, 32 doctorates, 7 other advanced degrees awarded. *Program availability:* Part-time, evening/weekend, 100% online. Offers adolescent and adult education (Certificate); adult education and community leadership (M Ed); adult-gerontological acute care nurse practitioner (Certificate); adult-gerontological clinical nurse specialist (Certificate); adult-gerontological primary care nurse practitioner (Certificate); American and European history (MA); communication sciences and disorders (MS); computer and information science (MSCIS); criminal justice (MS); curriculum and instruction (M Ed); cyber crime (Certificate); early childhood education (M Ed, MAT); family nurse practitioner (MSN); health services administration (MHSA); physical therapy (DPT); professional communication and leadership (MA, Certificate); public health (MPH); public history (MA); reading (Certificate); secondary education

(MAT); special education (M Ed, MAT); special education transition specialist (Certificate); sports medicine (MSSM); strength and conditioning (Certificate). *Application deadline:* For fall admission, 7/1 priority date for domestic students, 5/1 priority date for international students; for spring admission, 11/15 priority date for domestic students, 9/15 priority date for international students; for summer admission, 4/15 priority date for domestic students, 9/15 priority date for international students. Applications are processed on a rolling basis. *Application fee:* $30. Electronic applications accepted. *Application Contact:* McKenzie Peterman, Graduate Admissions Specialist, 912-478-5678, Fax: 912-478-0740, E-mail: mpeterman@georgiasouthern.edu. *Director of Graduate Studies*, Dr. Ashley Walker Colquitt, 912-478-2647, Fax: 912-478-0605, E-mail: gradschool@georgiasouthern.edu.

GEORGIA SOUTHWESTERN STATE UNIVERSITY, Americus, GA 31709-4693

General Information State-supported, coed, comprehensive institution. *Enrollment:* 3,052 graduate, professional, and undergraduate students; 257 full-time matriculated graduate/professional students (234 women), 188 part-time matriculated graduate/professional students (145 women). *Enrollment by degree level:* 327 master's, 118 other advanced degrees. *Graduate faculty:* 43 full-time (23 women), 14 part-time/adjunct (13 women). Tuition, state resident: full-time $3420; part-time $190 per credit hour. Tuition, nonresident: full-time $13,590; part-time $755 per credit hour. *Required fees:* $1340. Tuition and fees vary according to course load, campus/location and program. *Graduate housing:* Room and/or apartments available on a first-come, first-served basis to single students; on-campus housing not available to married students. Typical cost: $5290 per year ($9230 including board). Room and board charges vary according to board plan and housing facility selected. *Student services:* Campus employment opportunities, campus safety program, career counseling, exercise/wellness program, international student services, low-cost health insurance, services for students with disabilities. *Library facilities:* James Earl Carter Library. *Collection:* Books: 207,635 (physical), 68,397 (digital/electronic); Serial titles: 76 (physical), 81 (digital/electronic); Databases: 277. Weekly public service hours: 72; students can reserve study rooms.

Computer facilities: 260 computers available on campus for general student use. A campuswide network can be accessed from student residence rooms and from off campus. Online class registration is available.
Website: http://www.gsw.edu/

General Application Contact: Whitney Ford, Admissions Specialist, Office of Graduate Admissions, 800-338-0082, Fax: 229-931-2983, E-mail: graduateadmissions@gsw.edu.

GRADUATE UNITS

College of Nursing and Health Sciences Students: 23 full-time (22 women), 106 part-time (92 women); includes 41 minority (all Black or African American, non-Hispanic/Latino). Average age 35. 95 applicants, 63% accepted, 30 enrolled. *Faculty:* 10 full-time, 5 part-time/adjunct. Expenses: Contact institution. *Financial support:* Application deadline: 6/1; applicants required to submit FAFSA. In 2017, 17 master's awarded. *Program availability:* Part-time, online only, all theory courses are offered online. Offers family nurse practitioner (MSN); health informatics (Postbaccalaureate Certificate); nurse educator (Post Master's Certificate); nursing educator (MSN); nursing informatics (MSN); nursing leadership (MSN). MSN program offered by the Georgia Intercollegiate Consortium for Graduate Nursing Education, a partnership with Columbus State University. *Application deadline:* For fall admission, 1/15 for domestic students; for spring admission, 10/15 for domestic students. *Application fee:* $25. Electronic applications accepted. *Application Contact:* Whitney Ford, Admissions Specialist, Office of Graduate Admissions, 800-338-0082, Fax: 229-931-2983, E-mail: graduateadmissions@gsw.edu. *Dean*, Dr. Sandra Daniel, 229-931-2275.

School of Business Administration Students: 5 full-time (4 women), 62 part-time (41 women); includes 14 minority (all Black or African American, non-Hispanic/Latino). Average age 33. 43 applicants, 35% accepted, 9 enrolled. *Faculty:* 12 full-time (5 women), 2 part-time/adjunct (both women). Expenses: Contact institution. *Financial support:* Application deadline: 6/1; applicants required to submit FAFSA. In 2017, 15 master's awarded. *Program availability:* Part-time, online only, 100% online. Offers business administration (MBA). *Application deadline:* For fall admission, 6/30 for domestic students; for spring admission, 11/30 for domestic students; for summer admission, 4/30 for domestic students. Applications are processed on a rolling basis. *Application fee:* $25. Electronic applications accepted. *Application Contact:* Whitney Ford, Admissions Specialist, Office of Graduate Admissions, 800-338-0082, Fax: 229-931-2983, E-mail: graduateadmissions@gsw.edu. *Dean*, Dr. Liz Wilson, 229-931-2090.

School of Computing and Mathematics Students: 8 full-time (2 women), 10 part-time (3 women); includes 6 minority (3 Black or African American, non-Hispanic/Latino; 3 Asian, non-Hispanic/Latino), 7 international. Average age 35. 10 applicants, 50% accepted, 4 enrolled. *Faculty:* 3 full-time (0 women), 1 part-time/adjunct (0 women). Expenses: Contact institution. *Financial support:* Application deadline: 6/1; applicants required to submit FAFSA. In 2017, 10 master's awarded. *Program availability:* Part-time, 100% online, blended/hybrid learning. Offers computer information systems (Graduate Certificate); computer science (MS). *Application deadline:* For fall admission, 5/31 for domestic students; for spring admission, 10/15 for domestic students; for summer admission, 3/15 for domestic students. Applications are processed on a rolling basis. *Application fee:* $25. Electronic applications accepted. *Application Contact:* Whitney Ford, Admissions Specialist, Office of Graduate Admission, 800-338-0082, Fax: 229-931-2983. *Dean*, Dr. Boris V. Peltsverger, 229-931-2100.

School of Education Students: 221 full-time (206 women), 5 part-time (all women); includes 70 minority (all Black or African American, non-Hispanic/Latino). Average age 35. *Faculty:* 17 full-time (7 women), 7 part-time/adjunct (all women). Expenses: Contact institution. *Financial support:* Application deadline: 6/1; applicants required to submit FAFSA. In 2017, 89 master's, 94 Ed Ss awarded. Offers early childhood education (M Ed, Ed S); middle grades education (Ed S); middle grades language arts (M Ed); middle grades mathematics (M Ed); special education (M Ed). *Application deadline:* For summer admission, 4/15 for domestic students. *Application fee:* $25. Electronic applications accepted. *Application Contact:* Whitney Ford, Admissions Specialist, Office of Graduate Admissions, 800-338-0082, Fax: 229-931-2983. *Dean*, Dr. Rachel Abbott, 229-931-2145.

GEORGIA STATE UNIVERSITY, Atlanta, GA 30302-3083

General Information State-supported, coed, university. CGS member. *Enrollment:* 32,848 graduate, professional, and undergraduate students; 5,071 full-time matriculated graduate/professional students (3,028 women), 1,676 part-time matriculated graduate/professional students (1,075 women). *Enrollment by degree level:* 4,201 master's, 2,514 doctoral, 32 other advanced degrees. *Graduate faculty:* 744 full-time (309 women). Tuition, state resident: full-time $7020. Tuition, nonresident: full-time $22,518. *Required fees:* $2128. Tuition and fees vary according to degree level and program. *Graduate housing:* Rooms and/or apartments available on a first-come, first-served basis to single and married students. Typical cost: $10,560 per year ($14,392 including board) for single students. Room and board charges vary according to board plan, campus/location and housing facility selected. *Student services:* Campus safety program, career counseling, child daycare facilities, exercise/wellness program, international student services, services for students with disabilities. *Library facilities:* University Library plus 6 others. *Collection:* Books: 2 million (physical), 645,924 (digital/electronic); Serial titles: 11,156 (digital/electronic). Students can reserve study rooms. *Research affiliation:* Cerro Tololo Interamerican Observatory (astronomy), Research Atlanta, Inc. (policy studies), Oak Ridge National Laboratory (environmental policy), Lowell Observatory (astronomy), Brookhaven National Laboratory (physics), Argonne National Laboratory, Advanced Photon Source (crystallography).

Computer facilities: 2,040 computers available on campus for general student use. A campuswide network can be accessed from student residence rooms and from off campus. Online class registration is available.
Website: http://www.gsu.edu/

GRADUATE UNITS

Andrew Young School of Policy Studies Students: 385 full-time (249 women), 111 part-time (66 women); includes 213 minority (155 Black or African American, non-Hispanic/Latino; 13 Asian, non-Hispanic/Latino; 24 Hispanic/Latino; 21 Two or more races, non-Hispanic/Latino), 96 international. Average age 29. 702 applicants, 51% accepted, 183 enrolled. *Faculty:* 72 full-time (28 women). Expenses: Contact institution. *Financial support:* Unspecified assistantships available. Financial award application deadline: 2/15; financial award applicants required to submit FAFSA. In 2017, 161 master's, 22 doctorates, 12 other advanced degrees awarded. *Program availability:* Part-time, evening/weekend. Offers criminal justice (MPA, MS); criminal justice and criminology (PhD); disaster management (Certificate); disaster policy (MPA); economics (MA); environmental economics (PhD); environmental policy (PhD); experimental economics (PhD); health policy (PhD); labor economics (PhD); management and finance (MPA); nonprofit management (MPA, Certificate); nonprofit policy (MPA); planning and economic development (MPP, Certificate); policy (MA); policy analysis and evaluation (MPA); policy studies (MA, MPA, MPP, MS, MSW, PhD, Certificate); public and nonprofit management (PhD); public finance (PhD); public finance and budgeting (PhD); public finance policy (MPA); public health (MPA); urban and regional economics (PhD). *Application deadline:* For fall admission, 1/15 for domestic and international students. *Application fee:* $50. Electronic applications accepted. *Dean*, Dr. Sally Wallace, 404-413-0000, Fax: 404-413-0004.

School of Social Work Students: 117 full-time (107 women), 8 part-time (6 women); includes 77 minority (63 Black or African American, non-Hispanic/Latino; 2 Asian, non-Hispanic/Latino; 7 Hispanic/Latino; 5 Two or more races, non-Hispanic/Latino), 1 international. Average age 30. 168 applicants, 42% accepted, 47 enrolled. *Faculty:* 17 full-time (12 women). Expenses: Contact institution. *Financial support:* In 2017–18, research assistantships with tuition reimbursements (averaging $4,000 per year), teaching assistantships with tuition reimbursements (averaging $4,000 per year) were awarded; career-related internships or fieldwork, institutionally sponsored loans, scholarships/grants, tuition waivers, and unspecified assistantships also available. Financial award application deadline: 2/1; financial award applicants required to submit FAFSA. In 2017, 59 master's awarded. *Program availability:* Part-time. Offers child welfare leadership (Certificate); community partnerships (MSW); forensic social work (Certificate). *Application deadline:* For fall admission, 2/1 priority date for domestic and international students. *Application fee:* $50. Electronic applications accepted. *Director of School of Social Work*, Brian Bride, 404-413-1052, Fax: 404-413-1075, E-mail: bbride@gsu.edu.

Byrdine F. Lewis School of Nursing Students: 322 full-time (248 women), 481 part-time (466 women); includes 186 minority (112 Black or African American, non-Hispanic/Latino; 44 Asian, non-Hispanic/Latino; 20 Hispanic/Latino; 10 Two or more races, non-Hispanic/Latino), 18 international. Average age 31. 370 applicants, 56% accepted, 148 enrolled. *Faculty:* 69 full-time (52 women). Expenses: Contact institution. *Financial support:* In 2017–18, research assistantships with tuition reimbursements (averaging $1,666 per year), teaching assistantships with tuition reimbursements (averaging $1,920 per year) were awarded; scholarships/grants, tuition waivers (full and partial), and unspecified assistantships also available. Support available to part-time students. Financial award application deadline: 8/1; financial award applicants required to submit FAFSA. In 2017, 131 master's, 49 doctorates, 11 other advanced degrees awarded. *Program availability:* Part-time, blended/hybrid learning. Offers adult health clinical nurse specialist/nurse practitioner (MS, Certificate); child health clinical nurse specialist/pediatric nurse practitioner (MS, Certificate); family nurse practitioner (MS, Certificate); family psychiatric mental health nurse practitioner (MS, Certificate); nursing (PhD); nursing leadership in healthcare innovations (MS); nutrition (MS); perinatal clinical nurse specialist/women's health nurse practitioner (MS, Certificate); physical therapy (DPT); respiratory therapy (MS). *Application deadline:* For fall admission, 2/1 priority date for domestic and international students; for spring admission, 9/15 for domestic and international students. Applications are processed on a rolling basis. *Application fee:* $50. Electronic applications accepted. *Dean of Nursing*, Nancy Kropf, 404-413-1101, Fax: 404-413-1090, E-mail: nkropf@gsu.edu.

Division of Nutrition Students: 35 full-time (all women), 8 part-time (4 women); includes 8 minority (1 Black or African American, non-Hispanic/Latino; 2 Asian, non-Hispanic/Latino; 4 Hispanic/Latino; 1 Two or more races, non-Hispanic/Latino), 1 international. Average age 28. 53 applicants, 60% accepted, 25 enrolled. *Faculty:* 9 full-time (6 women). Expenses: Contact institution. *Financial support:* In 2017–18, research assistantships with tuition reimbursements (averaging $1,647 per year), teaching assistantships with full tuition reimbursements (averaging $2,666 per year) were awarded. Financial award application deadline: 4/1. In 2017, 22 master's awarded. *Program availability:* Part-time. Offers nutrition (MS). *Application deadline:* For fall admission, 5/15 for domestic and international students; for spring admission, 10/1 for domestic and international students. *Application fee:* $50. Electronic applications accepted. *Department Head*, Dr. Anita Nucci, 404-413-1234, Fax: 404-413-1228.

Division of Physical Therapy Students: 120 full-time (70 women); includes 23 minority (7 Black or African American, non-Hispanic/Latino; 5 Asian, non-Hispanic/Latino; 6 Hispanic/Latino; 5 Two or more races, non-Hispanic/Latino). Average age 25. *Faculty:* 10 full-time (5 women). Expenses: Contact institution. *Financial support:* In 2017–18, research assistantships with full tuition reimbursements (averaging $2,000 per year), teaching assistantships with full tuition reimbursements (averaging $2,000 per year) were awarded; scholarships/grants, tuition waivers (partial), and unspecified assistantships also available. Financial award application deadline: 4/1; financial award applicants required to submit FAFSA. In 2017, 36 doctorates awarded. Offers physical therapy (DPT). *Application deadline:* For fall admission, 11/15 for domestic and international students. *Application fee:* $50. Electronic applications accepted. *Department Head*, Dr. Andrew Butler, 404-413-1415, Fax: 404-413-1230, E-mail: andrewbutler@gsu.edu.

Division of Respiratory Therapy Students: 39 full-time (28 women), 6 part-time (5 women); includes 15 minority (10 Black or African American, non-Hispanic/Latino; 4 Asian, non-Hispanic/Latino; 1 Hispanic/Latino), 14 international. Average age 30. 34 applicants, 85% accepted, 16 enrolled. *Faculty:* 3 full-time (2 women). Expenses: Contact institution. *Financial support:* In 2017–18, research assistantships with full tuition reimbursements (averaging $2,000 per year), teaching assistantships with full tuition reimbursements (averaging $2,000 per year) were awarded; scholarships/grants and unspecified assistantships also available. Financial award application deadline: 6/1; financial award applicants required to submit FAFSA. In 2017, 20 master's awarded. Offers respiratory therapy (MS). *Application deadline:* For fall admission, 5/1 for domestic and international students; for spring admission, 9/15 for domestic and international students. *Application fee:* $50. Electronic applications accepted. *Department Head*, Dr. Douglas Gardenhire, 404-413-1270, Fax: 404-413-1230, E-mail: dgardenhire@gsu.edu.

College of Arts and Sciences Students: 1,527 full-time (851 women), 375 part-time (216 women); includes 573 minority (311 Black or African American, non-Hispanic/Latino; 1 American Indian or Alaska Native, non-Hispanic/Latino; 110 Asian, non-Hispanic/Latino; 81 Hispanic/Latino; 2 Native Hawaiian or other Pacific Islander, non-Hispanic/Latino; 68 Two or more races, non-Hispanic/Latino), 494 international. Average age 31. 2,072 applicants, 45% accepted, 469 enrolled. *Faculty:* 487 full-time (227 women). Expenses: Contact institution. *Financial support:* Fellowships with tuition reimbursements, research assistantships with tuition reimbursements, teaching assistantships with tuition reimbursements, career-related internships or fieldwork, scholarships/grants, health care benefits, tuition waivers (partial), and unspecified assistantships available. Support available to part-time students. Financial award application deadline: 4/15; financial award applicants required to submit FAFSA. In 2017, 524 master's, 154 doctorates, 34 other advanced degrees awarded. *Program availability:* Part-time, evening/weekend. Offers African-American studies (MA); analytical chemistry (MS, PhD); anthropology (MA); applied and environmental microbiology (MS, PhD); applied linguistics (MA, PhD); applied linguistics and pedagogy (MA); arts and sciences (MA, MA Ed, MFA, MHP, MM, MS, PhD, Certificate, Graduate Certificate); astronomy (PhD); biochemistry (MS, PhD); bioinformatics (MS, PhD); biophysical chemistry (PhD); biostatistics (MS, PhD); cellular and molecular biology and physiology (MS, PhD); clinical psychology (PhD); cognitive sciences (PhD); community psychology (PhD); computational chemistry (MS, PhD); computer science (MS, PhD); creative writing (MA, MFA, PhD); developmental psychology (PhD); discrete mathematics (MS); English (MA, PhD); fiction (MA, MFA); film, video, and digital imaging (MA); French (MA); French studies (MA); geochemistry (PhD); geographic information systems (Certificate); geography (MS); geology (MS); heritage preservation (MHP); historic preservation (MA); history (MA, PhD); human communication and social influence (MA); interpretation (Certificate); Latin American studies (Certificate); literary studies (MA, PhD); literature and culture (MA); mass communication (MA); mathematics (MS, PhD); media and society (PhD); molecular genetics and biochemistry (MS, PhD); moving image studies (PhD); neurobiology and behavior (MS, PhD); neuropsychology and behavioral neuroscience (PhD); organic/medicinal chemistry (MS, PhD); philosophy (MA); physical chemistry (MS); physics (MS, PhD); poetry (MA, MFA); political science (MA, PhD); public communication (PhD); public history (MA); religious studies (MA); rhetoric and composition (MA, PhD); rhetoric and politics (PhD); scientific computing (MS); sociology (MA, PhD); Spanish (MA); statistics (MS); translation (Certificate); translation and interpretation (Certificate); world history (MA). *Application deadline:* For fall admission, 7/1 for domestic and international students; for spring admission, 11/15 for domestic and international students. *Application fee:* $50. Electronic applications accepted. *Application Contact:* Amber Amari, Director, Graduate and Scheduling Services, 404-413-5037, E-mail: aamari@gsu.edu. *Dean*, Dr. William J. Long, 404-413-5114, Fax: 404-413-5117, E-mail: long@gsu.edu.

Gerontology Institute Students: 13 full-time (11 women), 17 part-time (15 women); includes 20 minority (14 Black or African American, non-Hispanic/Latino; 3 Asian, non-Hispanic/Latino; 1 Hispanic/Latino; 2 Two or more races, non-Hispanic/Latino), 4 international. Average age 45. 29 applicants, 93% accepted, 17 enrolled. *Faculty:* 4 full-time (all women). Expenses: Contact institution. *Financial support:* In 2017–18, research assistantships with full tuition reimbursements (averaging $6,000 per year) were awarded; career-related internships or fieldwork, scholarships/grants, and unspecified assistantships also available. Financial award application deadline: 4/15; financial award applicants required to submit FAFSA. In 2017, 10 master's, 6 other advanced degrees awarded. *Program availability:* Part-time. Offers gerontology (MA, Certificate). *Application deadline:* For fall admission, 4/15 for domestic and international students; for spring admission, 10/15 for domestic and international students. Applications are processed on a rolling basis. *Application fee:* $50. Electronic applications accepted. *Application Contact:* Dr. Candace L. Kemp, Director of Graduate Studies, 404-413-5210, Fax: 404-413-5219, E-mail: ckemp@gsu.edu. *Director*, Dr. Elizabeth O. Burgess, 404-413-5210, Fax: 404-413-5219, E-mail: eburgess@gsu.edu.

Institute for Women's, Gender, and Sexuality Studies Students: 14 full-time (all women), 2 part-time (both women); includes 11 minority (6 Black or African American, non-Hispanic/Latino; 1 Asian, non-Hispanic/Latino; 4 Two or more races, non-Hispanic/Latino), 2 international. Average age 29. 18 applicants, 89% accepted, 10 enrolled. *Faculty:* 6 full-time (5 women). Expenses: Contact institution. *Financial support:* In 2017–18, research assistantships with full tuition reimbursements (averaging $7,000 per year), teaching assistantships with full tuition reimbursements (averaging $7,500 per year) were awarded; career-related internships or fieldwork, health care benefits, and unspecified assistantships also available. Financial award application deadline: 2/15. In 2017, 5 master's, 5 other advanced degrees awarded. *Program availability:* Part-time. Offers women's, gender, and sexuality studies (MA, Graduate Certificate). *Application deadline:* For fall admission, 2/15 for domestic and international students. *Application fee:* $50. Electronic applications accepted. *Application Contact:* Dr. Amira Jarmakani, Director of Graduate Studies, 404-413-6583, Fax: 404-413-6585, E-mail: amira@gsu.edu. *Director*, Dr. Susan Talburt, 404-413-6581, Fax: 404-413-6585, E-mail: stalburt@gsu.edu.

Neuroscience Institute Students: 55 full-time (31 women), 2 part-time (1 woman); includes 12 minority (2 Black or African American, non-Hispanic/Latino; 4 Asian, non-Hispanic/Latino; 4 Hispanic/Latino; 2 Two or more races, non-Hispanic/Latino), 12 international. Average age 28. 48 applicants, 42% accepted, 12 enrolled. *Faculty:* 20 full-time (8 women). Expenses: Contact institution. *Financial support:* In 2017–18, fellowships (averaging $22,000 per year), research assistantships (averaging $22,000 per year) were awarded. Financial award applicants required to submit FAFSA. In 2017, 6 doctorates awarded. Offers neuroscience (PhD). *Application deadline:* For fall admission, 12/10 for domestic and international students. *Application fee:* $50. Electronic applications accepted. *Application Contact:* Dr. Laura L. Carruth, Director of Graduate Studies, 404-413-5340, E-mail: lcarruth@gsu.edu. *Director*, Prof. Walter Wilczynski, 404-413-6307, E-mail: wwilczynski@gsu.edu.

College of Education and Human Development Students: 874 full-time (662 women), 472 part-time (324 women); includes 656 minority (460 Black or African American, non-Hispanic/Latino; 1 American Indian or Alaska Native, non-Hispanic/Latino; 52 Asian, non-Hispanic/Latino; 92 Hispanic/Latino; 1 Native Hawaiian or other Pacific Islander, non-Hispanic/Latino; 50 Two or more races, non-Hispanic/Latino), 36 international. Average age 31. 1,084 applicants, 43% accepted, 333 enrolled. *Faculty:* 103 full-time (64 women). Expenses: Contact institution. *Financial support:* In 2017–18, fellowships with full tuition reimbursements (averaging $25,000 per year), research assistantships with tuition reimbursements (averaging $4,867 per year), teaching assistantships with tuition reimbursements (averaging $4,683 per year) were awarded; career-related internships or fieldwork, Federal Work-Study, scholarships/grants, tuition waivers (partial), and unspecified assistantships also available. Support available to part-time students. Financial award applicants required to submit FAFSA. In 2017, 333 master's, 64 doctorates, 36 other advanced degrees awarded. *Program availability:* Part-time, evening/weekend, online learning. Offers autism spectrum disorders (PhD); behavior and learning disabilities (M Ed); behavior disorders (PhD); communication disorders (M Ed, PhD); counseling psychology (PhD); counselor education and practice (PhD); curriculum and instruction (Ed D); early childhood and elementary education (PhD); early childhood education (M Ed, Ed S); early childhood special education (M Ed, PhD); education and human development (M Ed, MAT, MS, Ed D, PhD, Ed S); education of students with exceptionalities (PhD); educational leadership (M Ed, Ed D, Ed S); educational psychology (MS, PhD); educational research (MS, PhD); English education (MAT); exercise science (MS); health and physical education (M Ed); kinesiology (PhD); learning disabilities (PhD); mathematics education (M Ed, MAT); mental health counseling (MS, Ed S); mental retardation (PhD); middle level education (MAT); multiple and severe disabilities (M Ed); orthopedic impairments (PhD); reading, language and literacy education (M Ed, MAT); rehabilitation counseling (MS); school counseling (M Ed, Ed S); school psychology (M Ed, PhD, Ed S); science education (M Ed, MAT); sensory impairments (PhD); social foundations of education (MS, PhD); social studies education (M Ed, MAT); special education adapted curriculum (intellectual disabilities) (M Ed); special education deaf education (M Ed); special education general and adapted curriculum (autism spectrum disorders) (M Ed); special education physical and health disabilities (orthopedic impairments) (M Ed); sports administration (MS); sports medicine (MS); teaching and learning (PhD); urban education (M Ed); urban teacher leadership (M Ed). *Application fee:* $50. Electronic applications accepted. *Application Contact:* Nancy Keita, Director, Office of Academic Assistance and Graduate Admissions, 404-413-8001, E-mail: nkeita@gsu.edu. *Interim Dean*, Dr. Paul A. Alberto, 404-413-8100, Fax: 404-413-8103, E-mail: palberto@gsu.edu.

Learning Technologies Division Students: 17 full-time (12 women), 55 part-time (37 women); includes 40 minority (30 Black or African American, non-Hispanic/Latino; 3 Asian, non-Hispanic/Latino; 2 Hispanic/Latino; 5 Two or more races, non-Hispanic/Latino), 2 international. Average age 36. 41 applicants, 78% accepted, 22 enrolled. *Faculty:* 7 full-time (3 women). Expenses: Contact institution. *Financial support:* Federal Work-Study and institutionally sponsored loans available. In 2017, 10 master's, 3 doctorates awarded. *Program availability:* Part-time, evening/weekend. Offers instructional design and technology (MS); instructional technology (PhD). *Application fee:* $50. Electronic applications accepted. *Application Contact:* Nancy Keita, Director, Office of Academic Assistance and Graduate Admissions, 404-413-8001, E-mail: nkeita@gsu.edu. *Interim Dean*, Dr. Paul A. Alberto, 404-413-8100, Fax: 404-413-8103, E-mail: palberto@gsu.edu.

College of Law Students: 617 full-time (310 women), 23 part-time (9 women); includes 199 minority (78 Black or African American, non-Hispanic/Latino; 3 American Indian or Alaska Native, non-Hispanic/Latino; 53 Asian, non-Hispanic/Latino; 51 Hispanic/Latino; 14 Two or more races, non-Hispanic/Latino), 17 international. Average age 28. 1,493 applicants, 37% accepted, 204 enrolled. *Faculty:* 39 full-time (16 women). Expenses: Contact institution. *Financial support:* In 2017–18, research assistantships with tuition reimbursements (averaging $2,500 per year), teaching assistantships (averaging $2,500 per year) were awarded; scholarships/grants, tuition waivers, and unspecified assistantships also available. Financial award application deadline: 4/1; financial award applicants required to submit FAFSA. In 2017, 184 doctorates awarded. *Program availability:* Part-time, evening/weekend. Offers law (JD). *Application deadline:* For fall admission, 3/15 for domestic students, 3/15 priority date for international students. Applications are processed on a rolling basis. *Application fee:* $50. Electronic applications accepted. *Application Contact:* Dr. Cheryl Jester-George, Senior Director of Admissions, 404-413-9004, Fax: 404-413-9203, E-mail: cjgeorge@gsu.edu. *Dean, College of Law*, Dr. Steven J. Kaminshine, 404-413-9035, Fax: 404-413-9227, E-mail: skaminshine@gsu.edu.

Ernest G. Welch School of Art and Design Students: 52 full-time (35 women), 8 part-time (5 women); includes 17 minority (5 Black or African American, non-Hispanic/Latino; 3 Asian, non-Hispanic/Latino; 4 Hispanic/Latino; 5 Two or more races, non-Hispanic/Latino), 7 international. Average age 32. 116 applicants, 30% accepted, 23 enrolled. *Faculty:* 35 full-time (17 women). Expenses: Contact institution. *Financial support:* In 2017–18, fellowships with full tuition reimbursements (averaging $11,000 per year), research assistantships with full tuition reimbursements (averaging $6,000 per year), teaching assistantships with full tuition reimbursements (averaging $7,000 per year) were awarded; scholarships/grants and unspecified assistantships also available. Financial award application deadline: 4/15; financial award applicants required to submit FAFSA. In 2017, 21 master's awarded. Offers art and design (MA, MA Ed, MFA); art education (MA Ed); art history (MA); ceramics (MFA); drawing and painting (MFA); graphic design (MFA); interior design (MFA); photography (MFA); printmaking (MFA); sculpture (MFA); textiles (MFA). *Application deadline:* For fall admission, 1/6 for domestic and international students; for spring admission, 1/15 priority date for domestic and international students. *Application fee:* $50. Electronic applications accepted. *Application Contact:* Hubert Stanley Anderson, Director of Graduate Studies, 404-413-5229, Fax: 404-413-5261, E-mail: artgrad@gsu.edu. *Director, Welch School of Art and Design*, Michael White, 404-413-5228, E-mail: mwhite@gsu.edu.

J. Mack Robinson College of Business Students: 947 full-time (448 women), 334 part-time (156 women); includes 448 minority (222 Black or African American, non-Hispanic/Latino; 4 American Indian or Alaska Native, non-Hispanic/Latino; 150 Asian, non-Hispanic/Latino; 45 Hispanic/Latino; 27 Two or more races, non-Hispanic/Latino), 437 international. Average age 30. 1,907 applicants, 53% accepted, 472 enrolled. *Faculty:* 153 full-time (48 women). Expenses: Contact institution. *Financial support:* Research assistantships, teaching assistantships, scholarships/grants, tuition waivers, and unspecified assistantships available. Financial award applicants required to submit FAFSA. In 2017, 774 master's, 22 doctorates, 29 other advanced degrees awarded. *Program availability:* Part-time, evening/weekend. Offers actuarial science (MAS); business (EMBA, Exec MS, GMBA, M Tax, MAS, MBA, MIB, MPA, MPA, MS, MSCIS, MSHA, MSIS, MSRE, PMBA, EDB, PhD, Certificate); business administration (MBA); business analysis (MBA, MS); computer information systems (PhD); enterprise risk management (MBA, Certificate); entrepreneurship (MBA); executive business administration (EMBA); finance (MBA, MS, PhD); financial risk management (MBA); global business administration (GMBA); health informatics (MBA, MS); hotel real estate (MBA); human resources management (MBA, MS); information systems (MSIS, Certificate); information systems development and project management (MBA); information systems management (MBA); managing information technology (Exec MS); marketing (MBA, MS, PhD); mathematical risk management (MS); operations management (MBA, MS); organization behavior/human resource management (PhD); organization management (MBA); organizational change (MS); professional business administration (PMBA); real estate (MBA, MS, PhD, Certificate); risk and insurance (MS); risk management and insurance (MBA, MS, PhD, Certificate); strategic management (PhD); the wireless organization (MBA). *Application deadline:* For fall admission, 5/1 priority date for domestic students, 2/1 priority date for international students; for spring admission, 9/15 priority date for domestic students, 4/1 priority date for international students. Applications are processed on a rolling basis. *Application fee:* $50. Electronic applications accepted. *Application Contact:* Toby McChesney, Assistant Dean for Graduate Recruiting and Student Services, 404-413-7167, Fax: 404-413-7162, E-mail: rcbgradadmissions@gsu.edu. *Dean of the J. Mack Robinson College of Business*, Dr. Richard D. Phillips, 404-413-7000, Fax: 404-413-7035.

Institute of Health Administration Students: 40 full-time (20 women), 14 part-time (6 women); includes 22 minority (8 Black or African American, non-Hispanic/Latino; 8 Asian, non-Hispanic/Latino; 3 Hispanic/Latino; 3 Two or more races, non-Hispanic/Latino), 1 international. Average age 28. 52 applicants, 25% accepted, 7 enrolled. *Faculty:* 8 full-time (2 women). Expenses: Contact institution. *Financial support:* Research assistantships, teaching assistantships, scholarships/grants, tuition waivers, and unspecified assistantships available. In 2017, 64 master's awarded. *Program availability:* Part-time, evening/weekend. Offers health administration (MBA, MSHA); health informatics (MBA, MSCIS). *Application deadline:* For fall admission, 5/1 priority date for domestic students, 2/1 priority date for international students; for spring admission, 9/15 priority date for domestic students, 4/1 priority date for international students. Applications are processed on a rolling basis. *Application fee:* $50. Electronic applications accepted. *Application Contact:* Toby McChesney, Assistant Dean for Graduate Recruiting and Student Services, 404-413-7167, Fax: 404-413-7162, E-mail: rcbgradadmissions@gsu.edu. *Chair in Health Administration/Director of the Institute of Health*, Dr. Andrew T. Sumner, 404-413-7630, Fax: 404-413-7631.

Institute of International Business Students: 37 full-time (21 women); includes 19 minority (16 Black or African American, non-Hispanic/Latino; 1 Asian, non-Hispanic/Latino; 1 Hispanic/Latino; 1 Two or more races, non-Hispanic/Latino), 10 international. Average age 27. 44 applicants, 86% accepted, 18 enrolled. *Faculty:* 11 full-time (4 women). Expenses: Contact institution. *Financial support:* Research assistantships, teaching assistantships, scholarships/grants, tuition waivers (partial), and unspecified assistantships available. Financial award application deadline: 5/1. In 2017, 33 master's awarded. *Program availability:* Part-time, evening/weekend. Offers international business (GMBA, MBA, MIB); international business and information technology (MBA); international entrepreneurship (MBA). *Application deadline:* For fall admission, 5/1 priority date for domestic students, 2/1 priority date for international students; for spring admission, 9/15 priority date for domestic students, 5/1 priority date for international students. Applications are processed on a rolling basis. *Application fee:* $50. Electronic applications accepted. *Application Contact:* Toby McChesney, Assistant Dean for Graduate Recruiting and Student Services, 404-413-7167, Fax: 404-413-7162, E-mail: rcbgradadmissions@gsu.edu. *Professor/Director of the Institute of International Business*, Dr. Daniel Bello, 404-413-7275, Fax: 404-413-7276.

School of Accountancy Students: 150 full-time (97 women), 139 part-time (82 women); includes 145 minority (70 Black or African American, non-Hispanic/Latino; 57 Asian, non-Hispanic/Latino; 14 Hispanic/Latino; 4 Two or more races, non-Hispanic/Latino), 55 international. Average age 29. 239 applicants, 65% accepted, 108 enrolled. *Faculty:* 16 full-time (5 women). Expenses: Contact institution. *Financial support:* Research assistantships, teaching assistantships, scholarships/grants, tuition waivers, and unspecified assistantships available. Financial award applicants required to submit FAFSA. In 2017, 128 master's, 1 doctorate awarded. *Program availability:* Part-time, evening/weekend. Offers accounting (MBA, PhD); information systems audit and control (MS); professional accountancy (MPA); taxation (M Tax). *Application deadline:* For fall admission, 5/1 priority date for domestic students, 2/1 priority date for international students; for spring admission, 9/15 priority date for domestic students, 4/1 priority date for international students. Applications are processed on a rolling basis. *Application fee:* $50. Electronic applications accepted. *Application Contact:* Toby McChesney, Assistant Dean for Graduate Recruiting and Student Services, 404-413-7167, Fax: 404-413-7162, E-mail: rcbgradadmissions@gsu.edu. *Director of the School of Accountancy*, Dr. Galen R. Sevcik, 404-413-7200, Fax: 404-413-7203.

School of Music Students: 80 full-time (36 women), 10 part-time (4 women); includes 32 minority (19 Black or African American, non-Hispanic/Latino; 5 Asian, non-Hispanic/Latino; 8 Hispanic/Latino), 13 international. Average age 30. 84 applicants, 69% accepted, 42 enrolled. *Faculty:* 40 full-time (13 women). Expenses: Contact institution. *Financial support:* In 2017–18, research assistantships with full tuition reimbursements (averaging $4,000 per year) were awarded; Federal Work-Study, scholarships/grants, health care benefits, tuition waivers (partial), and unspecified assistantships also available. Financial award application deadline: 3/1; financial award applicants required to submit FAFSA. In 2017, 25 master's, 2 other advanced degrees awarded. *Program availability:* Part-time, evening/weekend. Offers choral conducting (MM); jazz studies (MM); music (Certificate); music composition (MM); music education (PhD); orchestral conducting (MM); performance (MM); piano pedagogy (MM); wind band conducting (MM). *Application deadline:* For fall admission, 3/1 priority date for domestic and international students; for spring admission, 10/1 priority date for domestic and international students. Applications are processed on a rolling basis. *Application fee:* $50. Electronic applications accepted. *Application Contact:* Dr. Steven Andrew Harper, Graduate Director, 404-413-5943, Fax: 404-413-5910, E-mail: sharper@gsu.edu. *Director, School of Music*, William Dwight Coleman, 404-413-5953, Fax: 404-413-5910, E-mail: wcoleman@gsu.edu.

School of Public Health Students: 224 full-time (166 women), 121 part-time (97 women); includes 192 minority (141 Black or African American, non-Hispanic/Latino; 1 American Indian or Alaska Native, non-Hispanic/Latino; 35 Asian, non-Hispanic/Latino; 8 Hispanic/Latino; 7 Two or more races, non-Hispanic/Latino), 36 international. Average age 29. 509 applicants, 59% accepted, 96 enrolled. *Faculty:* 21 full-time (12 women). Expenses: Contact institution. *Financial support:* In 2017–18, fellowships (averaging $2,500 per year), research assistantships with full tuition reimbursements (averaging $22,000 per year), teaching assistantships with full tuition reimbursements (averaging $22,000 per year) were awarded; career-related internships or fieldwork, scholarships/grants, health care benefits, unspecified assistantships, and out-of-state tuition waivers also available. In 2017, 104 master's, 5 doctorates, 8 other advanced degrees awarded. *Program availability:* Part-time. Offers public health (MPH, PhD, Certificate). *Application deadline:* For fall admission, 2/1 for domestic and international students; for spring admission, 10/1 for domestic and international students. *Application fee:* $50. Electronic applications accepted. *Application Contact:* Courtney M. Burton, Graduate Coordinator, 404-413-1143, E-mail: cmburton@gsu.edu. *Dean*, Dr. Michael P. Eriksen, 404-413-1132, Fax: 404-413-1140, E-mail: meriksen@gsu.edu.

GERSTNER SLOAN KETTERING GRADUATE SCHOOL OF BIOMEDICAL SCIENCES, New York, NY 10021

General Information Independent, coed, graduate-only institution. *Enrollment by degree level:* 70 doctoral. *Graduate faculty:* 126 full-time (25 women). *Graduate housing:* Rooms and/or apartments available on a first-come, first-served basis to single and married students. Typical cost: $13,764 per year for single students; $20,928 per year for married students. Room charges vary according to housing facility selected. Housing application deadline: 5/5. *Student services:* Campus safety program, career counseling, child daycare facilities, grant writing training, international student services, low-cost health insurance, multicultural affairs office, services for students with disabilities, writing training. *Library facilities:* Memorial Sloan Kettering Cancer Center Library. *Collection:* Books: 4,270 (physical), 20,056 (digital/electronic); Serial titles: 567 (physical), 6,885 (digital/electronic). Weekly public service hours: 53; students can reserve study rooms. *Research affiliation:* Memorial Sloan-Kettering Cancer Center (biomedical sciences).

Computer facilities: Online class registration is available.
Website: https://www.sloankettering.edu/gerstner

General Application Contact: Main Office, 646-888-6639, Fax: 646-422-2351, E-mail: gradstudies@sloankettering.edu.

GRADUATE UNITS

Program in Cancer Biology Students: 70 full-time (28 women); includes 11 minority (1 Black or African American, non-Hispanic/Latino; 5 Asian, non-Hispanic/Latino; 5 Hispanic/Latino), 29 international. 228 applicants, 17% accepted, 14 enrolled. *Faculty:* 126 full-time (25 women). Expenses: Contact institution. *Financial support:* In 2017–18, 70 students received support. Teaching assistantships and fellowship package including stipend ($38,655), full-tuition scholarship, first-year allowance, and comprehensive medical and dental insurance available. In 2017, 7 doctorates awarded. Offers cancer biology (PhD). *Application deadline:* For fall admission, 12/1 for domestic and international students. Electronic applications accepted. *Application Contact:* Main Office, 646-888-6639, Fax: 646-422-2351, E-mail: gradstudies@sloankettering.edu. *Associate Dean*, Linda Burnley, 646-888-6639, E-mail: burnleyl@sloankettering.edu.

GLION INSTITUTE OF HIGHER EDUCATION, CH-1823 Glion-sur-Montreux, Switzerland

General Information Proprietary, coed, comprehensive institution.

GRADUATE UNITS

Graduate Programs *Program availability:* Evening/weekend.

GLOBAL UNIVERSITY, Springfield, MO 65804

General Information Independent-religious, coed, comprehensive institution. *Graduate housing:* On-campus housing not available.

GRADUATE UNITS

Graduate School of Theology *Program availability:* Part-time, evening/weekend, online learning. Offers bible and theology (D Min); biblical language (M Div); biblical studies (MA); Christian ministry (M Div, D Min); ministerial studies (MA). Electronic applications accepted.

GODDARD COLLEGE, Plainfield, VT 05667-9432

General Information Independent, coed, comprehensive institution. *Graduate housing:* On-campus housing not available.

GRADUATE UNITS

Graduate Division *Program availability:* Part-time, online learning. Offers clinical mental health counseling (MA); community education (MA); consciousness studies (MA); creative writing (MFA); expressive arts therapy (MA); health arts and sciences (MA); interdisciplinary arts (MFA); psychology (MA); sexual orientation (MA); social innovation and sustainability (MA); teacher licensure (MA); transformative language arts (MA). Electronic applications accepted.

GOLDEN GATE UNIVERSITY, San Francisco, CA 94105-2968

General Information Independent, coed, university. *Enrollment:* 2,685 graduate, professional, and undergraduate students; 897 full-time matriculated graduate/professional students (528 women), 1,566 part-time matriculated graduate/professional students (822 women). *Enrollment by degree level:* 1,899 master's, 502 doctoral, 62 other advanced degrees. *Graduate faculty:* 55 full-time (19 women), 240 part-time/adjunct (116 women). *Graduate housing:* On-campus housing not available. *Student services:* Campus employment opportunities, career counseling, international student services, low-cost health insurance, services for students with disabilities. *Library facilities:* Golden Gate University Library plus 1 other. *Collection:* Books: 43,127 (physical), 15,700 (digital/electronic); Serial titles: 55,000 (digital/electronic); Databases: 116. Weekly public service hours: 90; students can reserve study rooms.

Computer facilities: Computer purchase and lease plans are available. 40 computers available on campus for general student use. A campuswide network can be accessed. Online class registration is available.
Website: http://www.ggu.edu/

General Application Contact: Angela Melero, Enrollment Services, 415-442-7800, Fax: 415-442-7807, E-mail: info@ggu.edu.

GRADUATE UNITS

Ageno School of Business Students: 309 full-time (147 women), 527 part-time (266 women); includes 286 minority (56 Black or African American, non-Hispanic/Latino; 1 American Indian or Alaska Native, non-Hispanic/Latino; 131 Asian, non-Hispanic/Latino; 83 Hispanic/Latino; 4 Native Hawaiian or other Pacific Islander, non-Hispanic/Latino; 11 Two or more races, non-Hispanic/Latino), 209 international. Average age 35. 549 applicants, 66% accepted, 185 enrolled. *Faculty:* 17 full-time (7 women), 280 part-time/adjunct (95 women). Expenses: Contact institution. *Financial support:* Career-related internships or fieldwork, Federal Work-Study, institutionally sponsored loans, and scholarships/grants available. Support available to part-time students. Financial award applicants required to submit FAFSA. *Program availability:* Part-time, evening/weekend. Offers accounting (MBA); adaptive leadership (MBA); advanced financial planning (MS); business administration (EMBA, MBA, DBA); business analytics (MBA, MS); entrepreneurship (MBA); finance (MBA, MS, Certificate); financial life planning

(Certificate); financial planning (MS, Certificate); global supply chain management (MBA, Certificate); human resource management (MBA, MS, Certificate); information technology management (MBA, MS, Certificate); international business (MBA); marketing (MBA, MS, Certificate); project management (MBA, MS, Certificate); psychology (MA, Certificate); public administration (EMPA, MBA); public administration leadership (Certificate). *Application deadline:* For fall admission, 5/15 for domestic and international students; for winter admission, 1/15 for domestic and international students; for spring admission, 9/15 for domestic and international students. Applications are processed on a rolling basis. *Application fee:* $65 ($105 for international students). Electronic applications accepted. *Application Contact:* Angela Melero, Enrollment Services, 415-442-7800, Fax: 415-442-7807, E-mail: info@ggu.edu. *Associate Dean*, Marianne Koch, 415-442-6542, Fax: 415-442-6579, E-mail: mkoch@ggu.edu.

School of Accounting Students: 76 full-time (51 women), 136 part-time (87 women); includes 63 minority (7 Black or African American, non-Hispanic/Latino; 35 Asian, non-Hispanic/Latino; 18 Hispanic/Latino; 1 Native Hawaiian or other Pacific Islander, non-Hispanic/Latino; 2 Two or more races, non-Hispanic/Latino), 76 international. Average age 32. 94 applicants, 69% accepted, 38 enrolled. *Faculty:* 3 full-time (1 woman), 64 part-time/adjunct (21 women). Expenses: Contact institution. *Financial support:* Career-related internships or fieldwork, Federal Work-Study, institutionally sponsored loans, and scholarships/grants available. Support available to part-time students. Financial award applicants required to submit FAFSA. *Program availability:* Part-time, evening/weekend. Offers financial accounting and reporting (M Ac, MSA, Graduate Certificate); forensic accounting (M Ac, MSA, Graduate Certificate); internal auditing (M Ac, MSA, Certificate); management accounting (M Ac, MSA); taxation (M Ac, MSA). *Application deadline:* For fall admission, 5/15 for international students; for winter admission, 1/15 for international students; for spring admission, 9/15 for international students. Applications are processed on a rolling basis. *Application fee:* $65 ($95 for international students). Electronic applications accepted. *Application Contact:* Angela Melero, Enrollment Services, 415-442-7800, Fax: 415-442-7807, E-mail: info@ggu.edu. *Dean*, Fred Sroka, 415-369-5285, Fax: 415-543-2607.

School of Law Students: 286 full-time (184 women), 245 part-time (134 women); includes 242 minority (48 Black or African American, non-Hispanic/Latino; 4 American Indian or Alaska Native, non-Hispanic/Latino; 69 Asian, non-Hispanic/Latino; 95 Hispanic/Latino; 7 Native Hawaiian or other Pacific Islander, non-Hispanic/Latino; 19 Two or more races, non-Hispanic/Latino), 71 international. Average age 31. 1,354 applicants, 66% accepted, 227 enrolled. *Faculty:* 31 full-time (19 women), 160 part-time/adjunct (77 women). Expenses: Contact institution. *Financial support:* Fellowships, research assistantships, teaching assistantships, career-related internships or fieldwork, Federal Work-Study, institutionally sponsored loans, scholarships/grants, tuition waivers (full and partial), and unspecified assistantships available. Support available to part-time students. Financial award applicants required to submit FAFSA. *Program availability:* Part-time, evening/weekend. Offers environmental law (LL M); estate planning (LL M); intellectual property law (LL M); international legal studies (LL M, SJD); law (JD); taxation law (LL M); U.S. legal studies (LL M). *Application deadline:* For fall admission, 6/30 for domestic students. Applications are processed on a rolling basis. Electronic applications accepted. *Application Contact:* Greg Egertson, Associate Dean and Director of Admissions, 415-442-6636, Fax: 415-442-6609, E-mail: lawadmit@ggu.edu. *Dean*, Anthony Niedwiecki, 415-442-6601, Fax: 415-442-6609.

School of Taxation Students: 72 full-time (44 women), 539 part-time (281 women); includes 156 minority (17 Black or African American, non-Hispanic/Latino; 3 American Indian or Alaska Native, non-Hispanic/Latino; 100 Asian, non-Hispanic/Latino; 23 Hispanic/Latino; 7 Native Hawaiian or other Pacific Islander, non-Hispanic/Latino; 6 Two or more races, non-Hispanic/Latino), 82 international. Average age 36. 252 applicants, 84% accepted, 105 enrolled. *Faculty:* 7 full-time (1 woman), 65 part-time/adjunct (19 women). Expenses: Contact institution. *Financial support:* In 2017–18, 66 students received support. Career-related internships or fieldwork, Federal Work-Study, institutionally sponsored loans, and scholarships/grants available. Support available to part-time students. Financial award applicants required to submit FAFSA. In 2017, 193 master's awarded. *Program availability:* Part-time, evening/weekend. Offers advanced studies in taxation (Certificate); estate planning (Certificate); financial planning and taxation (MS); international taxation (Certificate); state and local taxation (Certificate); taxation (MS, Certificate). *Application deadline:* For fall admission, 5/15 for international students; for winter admission, 1/15 for international students; for spring admission, 9/15 for international students. Applications are processed on a rolling basis. *Application fee:* $70 ($100 for international students). Electronic applications accepted. *Application Contact:* Angela Melero, Enrollment Services, 415-442-7800, Fax: 415-442-7807, E-mail: info@ggu.edu. *Dean*, Fred Sroka, 415-369-5285, Fax: 415-442-7807.

GOLDEY-BEACOM COLLEGE, Wilmington, DE 19808-1999

General Information Independent, coed, comprehensive institution. *Graduate housing:* Room and/or apartments available on a first-come, first-served basis to single students; on-campus housing not available to married students.

GRADUATE UNITS

Graduate Program *Program availability:* Part-time, evening/weekend. Offers business administration (MBA); finance (MS); financial management (MBA); health care management (MBA); human resource management (MBA); information technology (MBA); international business management (MBA); major finance (MBA); major taxation (MBA); management (MM); marketing management (MBA); taxation (MBA, MS). Electronic applications accepted.

GOLDFARB SCHOOL OF NURSING AT BARNES-JEWISH COLLEGE, St. Louis, MO 63110

General Information Independent, coed, primarily women, comprehensive institution. *Enrollment:* 695 graduate, professional, and undergraduate students; 61 full-time matriculated graduate/professional students (49 women), 3 part-time matriculated graduate/professional students (2 women). *Enrollment by degree level:* 61 master's, 3 doctoral. *Graduate faculty:* 42 full-time (39 women), 6 part-time/adjunct (all women). *Tuition:* Full-time $11,910; part-time $794 per credit hour. *Required fees:* $30; $15 per term. Full-time tuition and fees vary according to program. *Graduate housing:* On-campus housing not available. *Student services:* Campus employment opportunities, campus safety program, international student services, services for students with disabilities. *Library facilities:* Goldfarb School of Nursing Library plus 2 others. *Collection:* Books: 1,100 (physical), 20,000 (digital/electronic); Serial titles: 62 (digital/electronic); Databases: 14.

Computer facilities: 160 computers available on campus for general student use. A campuswide network can be accessed from off campus. Software, research databases available.
Website: http://www.barnesjewishcollege.edu/

General Application Contact: Karen Sartorius, Admission Specialist, 314-454-7057, Fax: 314-362-9250, E-mail: karen.sartorius@bjc.org.

GRADUATE UNITS

Graduate Programs Students: 61 full-time (49 women), 3 part-time (2 women); includes 13 minority (8 Black or African American, non-Hispanic/Latino; 2 Asian, non-Hispanic/Latino; 1 Hispanic/Latino; 2 Two or more races, non-Hispanic/Latino). *Faculty:* 42 full-time (39 women), 6 part-time/adjunct (all women). Expenses: Contact institution. *Financial support:* Research assistantships, Federal Work-Study, institutionally sponsored loans, scholarships/grants, and traineeships available. Support available to part-time students. Financial award applicants required to submit FAFSA. *Program availability:* Part-time, online learning. Offers adult-gerontology (MSN); adult-gerontology (MSN); health systems and population health leadership (MSN); nurse anesthesia (MSN). *Application deadline:* Applications are processed on a rolling basis. *Application fee:* $50. *Application Contact:* Karen Sartorius, Admission Specialist, 314-454-7057, Fax: 314-362-9250, E-mail: karen.sartorius@bjc.org. *Associate Dean for Academic Affairs*, Dr. Gretchen Drinkard, 314-454-7540, Fax: 314-362-9222, E-mail: gdrinkard@bjc.org.

GONZAGA UNIVERSITY, Spokane, WA 99258

General Information Independent-religious, coed, university. *Enrollment:* 7,506 graduate, professional, and undergraduate students; 592 full-time matriculated graduate/professional students (318 women), 1,665 part-time matriculated graduate/professional students (1,153 women). *Enrollment by degree level:* 1,665 master's, 592 doctoral. *Graduate faculty:* 72 full-time (43 women), 148 part-time/adjunct (85 women). *Tuition:* Part-time $984 per credit. *Required fees:* $215 per semester. Tuition and fees vary according to course load, degree level, campus/location and program. *Graduate housing:* Rooms and/or apartments available on a first-come, first-served basis to single and married students. Typical cost: $5780 per year ($11,560 including board) for single students; $5000 per year for married students. Room and board charges vary according to board plan and housing facility selected. Housing application deadline: 5/1. *Student services:* Campus employment opportunities, campus safety program, career counseling, exercise/wellness program, free psychological counseling, grant writing training, international student services, low-cost health insurance, multicultural affairs office, services for students with disabilities, writing training. *Library facilities:* Ralph E. and Helen Higgins Foley Center plus 1 other. *Collection:* Books: 266,244 (physical), 33,682 (digital/electronic); Serial titles: 6,301 (physical), 60,559 (digital/electronic); Databases: 328. Weekly public service hours: 112; study areas open 24 hours, 5–7 days a week; students can reserve study rooms.

Computer facilities: Computer purchase and lease plans are available. 500 computers available on campus for general student use. A campuswide network can be accessed from student residence rooms and from off campus. Online class registration is available.
Website: http://www.gonzaga.edu/

General Application Contact: Julie McCulloh, Dean of Admissions, 509-313-6591, Fax: 509-313-5780, E-mail: admissions@gonzaga.edu.

GRADUATE UNITS

College of Arts and Sciences Students: 1 full-time (0 women), 43 part-time (21 women); includes 9 minority (4 Black or African American, non-Hispanic/Latino; 1 American Indian or Alaska Native, non-Hispanic/Latino; 3 Asian, non-Hispanic/Latino; 1 Hispanic/Latino), 2 international. Average age 37. 47 applicants, 79% accepted, 22 enrolled. *Faculty:* 9 full-time (3 women). Expenses: Contact institution. *Financial support:* In 2017–18, 38 students received support. Scholarships/grants and unspecified assistantships available. Support available to part-time students. Financial award applicants required to submit FAFSA. In 2017, 4 master's awarded. *Program availability:* Part-time, blended/hybrid learning. Offers philosophy (MA); theology and leadership (MA). *Application deadline:* For fall admission, 7/15 for domestic students; for spring admission, 11/1 for domestic students; for summer admission, 4/9 for domestic students. Applications are processed on a rolling basis. *Application fee:* $50. Electronic applications accepted. *Application Contact:* Carolyn Von Muller, Assistant to the Dean, 509-313-5522, E-mail: vonmuller@gonzaga.edu. *Interim Dean of the College of Arts and Sciences*, Dr. Patricia Terry, 509-313-5522, Fax: 509-313-6684, E-mail: terry@gonzaga.edu.

English Language Center Students: 3 part-time (2 women); includes 1 minority (Hispanic/Latino). Average age 29. *Faculty:* 9 full-time (8 women), 3 part-time/adjunct (all women). Expenses: Contact institution. *Financial support:* In 2017–18, 5 students received support. Scholarships/grants available. Support available to part-time students. Financial award applicants required to submit FAFSA. In 2017, 15 master's awarded. *Program availability:* Part-time. Offers teaching English as a second language (MA). *Application deadline:* Applications are processed on a rolling basis. *Application fee:* $50. Electronic applications accepted. *Manager, Center for Global Engagement*, Melissa Heid, 509-313-6560, E-mail: heid@gonzaga.edu.

School of Business Administration Students: 94 full-time (32 women), 118 part-time (64 women); includes 41 minority (2 Black or African American, non-Hispanic/Latino; 9 American Indian or Alaska Native, non-Hispanic/Latino; 8 Asian, non-Hispanic/Latino; 10 Hispanic/Latino; 1 Native Hawaiian or other Pacific Islander, non-Hispanic/Latino; 11 Two or more races, non-Hispanic/Latino), 11 international. Average age 29. 218 applicants, 75% accepted, 101 enrolled. *Faculty:* 17 full-time (3 women), 11 part-time/adjunct (3 women). Expenses: Contact institution. *Financial support:* In 2017–18, 117 students received support. Scholarships/grants, tuition waivers, and unspecified assistantships available. Support available to part-time students. Financial award applicants required to submit FAFSA. In 2017, 96 master's awarded. *Program availability:* Part-time, evening/weekend. Offers accountancy (M Acc); American Indian entrepreneurship (MBA); business administration (MBA); taxation (MS). *Application deadline:* Applications are processed on a rolling basis. *Application fee:* $50. Electronic applications accepted. *Application Contact:* Stacey Chatman, Assistant Director for Admissions, 509-313-4622, E-mail: chatman@gonzaga.edu. *Dean*, Dr. Ken Anderson, 509-313-5991, E-mail: anderson@gonzaga.edu.

School of Education Students: 108 full-time (90 women), 225 part-time (140 women); includes 34 minority (4 Black or African American, non-Hispanic/Latino; 2 American Indian or Alaska Native, non-Hispanic/Latino; 5 Asian, non-Hispanic/Latino; 18 Hispanic/Latino; 5 Two or more races, non-Hispanic/Latino), 114 international. Average age 31. 367 applicants, 74% accepted, 160 enrolled. *Faculty:* 16 full-time (11 women), 31 part-time/adjunct (19 women). Expenses: Contact institution. *Financial support:* In 2017–18, 51 students received support. Scholarships/grants and unspecified assistantships available. Support available to part-time students. Financial award applicants required to submit FAFSA. In 2017, 175 master's awarded. *Program availability:* Part-time, evening/weekend, 100% online, blended/hybrid learning. Offers clinical mental health counseling (MA); educational leadership (M Ed, Ed D); elementary education (MIT); marriage and family counseling (MA); school counseling (MA);

secondary education (MIT); special education (M Ed, MIT); sport and athletic administration (MA). *Application deadline:* Applications are processed on a rolling basis. *Application fee:* $50. Electronic applications accepted. *Application Contact:* Meg Martens, Graduate Admissions Program Specialist, 509-313-4314, E-mail: martens@gonzaga.edu. *Dean*, Dr. Vincent Alfonso, 509-313-3594, Fax: 509-313-5821, E-mail: alfonso@gonzaga.edu.

School of Engineering and Applied Science Students: 1 full-time (0 women), 14 part-time (0 women); includes 3 minority (all Hispanic/Latino), 2 international. Average age 40. 7 applicants, 71% accepted, 4 enrolled. *Faculty:* 4 part-time/adjunct (0 women). Expenses: Contact institution. *Financial support:* Available to part-time students. Applicants required to submit FAFSA. In 2017, 8 master's awarded. *Program availability:* Part-time-only, evening/weekend, online only, 100% online. Offers transmission and distribution engineering (M Eng, Certificate). *Application deadline:* Applications are processed on a rolling basis. *Application fee:* $50. Electronic applications accepted. *Application Contact:* Jilliene McKinstry, Assistant Director, Transmission and Distribution, 509-313-5701, E-mail: mckinstry@gonzaga.edu. *Dean*, Dr. Stephen E. Silliman, 509-313-6117, E-mail: silliman@gonzaga.edu.

School of Law Students: 312 full-time (146 women), 1 part-time (0 women); includes 48 minority (5 Black or African American, non-Hispanic/Latino; 3 American Indian or Alaska Native, non-Hispanic/Latino; 6 Asian, non-Hispanic/Latino; 20 Hispanic/Latino; 14 Two or more races, non-Hispanic/Latino), 2 international. Average age 26. 905 applicants, 59% accepted, 122 enrolled. *Faculty:* 15 full-time (10 women), 19 part-time/adjunct (4 women). Expenses: Contact institution. *Financial support:* In 2017–18, 281 students received support. Federal Work-Study and scholarships/grants available. Support available to part-time students. Financial award applicants required to submit FAFSA. In 2017, 105 doctorates awarded. *Program availability:* Part-time. Offers law (JD). *Application deadline:* For fall admission, 4/15 priority date for domestic students. *Application fee:* $50. Electronic applications accepted. *Application Contact:* Susan Lee, Director of Admissions, 509-313-3734, E-mail: lee@gonzaga.edu. *Dean*, Jane Korn, 509-313-3700.

School of Leadership Studies Students: 46 full-time (29 women), 600 part-time (368 women); includes 125 minority (31 Black or African American, non-Hispanic/Latino; 11 American Indian or Alaska Native, non-Hispanic/Latino; 16 Asian, non-Hispanic/Latino; 43 Hispanic/Latino; 3 Native Hawaiian or other Pacific Islander, non-Hispanic/Latino; 21 Two or more races, non-Hispanic/Latino), 24 international. Average age 38. 298 applicants, 91% accepted, 199 enrolled. *Faculty:* 17 full-time (6 women), 22 part-time/adjunct (8 women). Expenses: Contact institution. *Financial support:* In 2017–18, 70 students received support. Scholarships/grants and unspecified assistantships available. Support available to part-time students. Financial award applicants required to submit FAFSA. In 2017, 405 master's, 11 doctorates awarded. *Program availability:* Part-time, evening/weekend, 100% online, blended/hybrid learning, immersion weekends. Offers communication and leadership (MA); leadership studies (PhD); organizational leadership (MA). *Application deadline:* For fall admission, 7/16 for domestic students; for spring admission, 11/16 for domestic students; for summer admission, 4/16 for domestic students. Applications are processed on a rolling basis. *Application fee:* $50. Electronic applications accepted. *Application Contact:* Teresa Crane, Assistant to the Dean, 509-313-6645, E-mail: guonlinestudentservices@gonzaga.edu. *Interim Dean*, Dr. Jolanta Weber, 509-313-6595, E-mail: weberj@gonzaga.edu.

School of Nursing and Human Physiology Students: 34 full-time (22 women), 673 part-time (566 women); includes 106 minority (18 Black or African American, non-Hispanic/Latino; 4 American Indian or Alaska Native, non-Hispanic/Latino; 29 Asian, non-Hispanic/Latino; 28 Hispanic/Latino; 1 Native Hawaiian or other Pacific Islander, non-Hispanic/Latino; 26 Two or more races, non-Hispanic/Latino), 3 international. Average age 38. 454 applicants, 38% accepted, 130 enrolled. *Faculty:* 10 full-time (all women), 57 part-time/adjunct (48 women). Expenses: Contact institution. *Financial support:* In 2017–18, 28 students received support. Scholarships/grants, traineeships, and unspecified assistantships available. Support available to part-time students. Financial award applicants required to submit FAFSA. In 2017, 180 master's, 4 doctorates awarded. *Program availability:* Part-time, evening/weekend, 100% online, immersion weekends. Offers nursing and human physiology (MSN, DNP, DNP-A). *Application deadline:* For spring admission, 9/1 for domestic students; for summer admission, 3/28 for domestic students. Applications are processed on a rolling basis. *Application fee:* $50. Electronic applications accepted. *Application Contact:* Shannon Zaranski, Assistant to the Dean, 509-313-3569, E-mail: zaranski@gonzaga.edu. *Interim Dean*, Dr. Lin Murphy, 509-313-3569, E-mail: murpheyl1@gonzaga.edu.

GORDON COLLEGE, Wenham, MA 01984-1899

General Information Independent-religious, coed, comprehensive institution. *Enrollment:* 1,963 graduate, professional, and undergraduate students; 118 full-time matriculated graduate/professional students (82 women), 143 part-time matriculated graduate/professional students (122 women). *Enrollment by degree level:* 261 master's. *Graduate faculty:* 26 full-time (18 women), 55 part-time/adjunct (29 women). *Tuition:* Full-time $6075; part-time $325 per credit. *Required fees:* $150; $75 per semester. Tuition and fees vary according to program. *Graduate housing:* Room and/or apartments available on a first-come, first-served basis to single students; on-campus housing not available to married students. Housing application deadline: 6/15. *Student services:* Campus safety program, career counseling, exercise/wellness program, international student services, low-cost health insurance, multicultural affairs office, services for students with disabilities, teacher training, writing training. *Library facilities:* Jenks Learning Resource Center. *Collection:* Books: 130,608 (physical), 178,400 (digital/electronic); Serial titles: 1,603 (physical). Weekly public service hours: 103; students can reserve study rooms. *Research affiliation:* National Association for Music Education (music education), Feierabend Association for Music Education (early childhood music education), American Choral Directors Association (choral music education), Embracing the New Music Educators Association (mentoring for new music teaching professionals).

Computer facilities: Computer purchase and lease plans are available. 100 computers available on campus for general student use. A campuswide network can be accessed from student residence rooms and from off campus. Online class registration is available.
Website: http://www.gordon.edu/

General Application Contact: Julie Lenocker, Program Administrator, 978-867-4322, Fax: 978-867-4663, E-mail: graduate-education@gordon.edu.

GRADUATE UNITS

Graduate Education Program Students: 68 full-time (50 women), 114 part-time (99 women); includes 24 minority (2 Black or African American, non-Hispanic/Latino; 8 Asian, non-Hispanic/Latino; 13 Hispanic/Latino; 1 Two or more races, non-Hispanic/Latino), 10 international. Average age 34. 248 applicants, 100% accepted, 182 enrolled. *Faculty:* 23 full-time (17 women), 32 part-time/adjunct (23 women). Expenses: Contact institution. *Financial support:* Applicants required to submit FAFSA. In 2017, 99 master's, 16 Ed Ss awarded. *Program availability:* Part-time, evening/weekend. Offers early childhood (M Ed); educational leadership (M Ed, Ed S); elementary education (M Ed); English as a second language (M Ed, Ed S); math specialist (M Ed); mathematics specialist (Ed S); middle school education (M Ed); moderate disabilities (M Ed); Montessori education (M Ed); reading (M Ed, Ed S); secondary education (M Ed). *Application deadline:* Applications are processed on a rolling basis. *Application fee:* $75. *Application Contact:* Julie Lenocker, Program Administrator, 978-867-4322, Fax: 978-867-4663, E-mail: graduate-education@gordon.edu. *Director of Graduate Studies*, Dr. Janet Arndt, 978-867-4355, Fax: 978-867-4663.

Graduate Financial Analysis Program Students: 9 part-time (3 women); includes 2 minority (both Black or African American, non-Hispanic/Latino), 2 international. Average age 23. *Faculty:* 1 full-time (0 women), 9 part-time/adjunct (1 woman). Expenses: Contact institution. *Financial support:* Applicants required to submit FAFSA. *Program availability:* Part-time, evening/weekend. Offers financial analysis (MS). *Application deadline:* For fall admission, 4/30 for domestic and international students; for spring admission, 12/10 for domestic and international students. Applications are processed on a rolling basis. *Application fee:* $75. Electronic applications accepted. *Executive Director*, Alexander Lowry, E-mail: alexander.lowry@gordon.edu.

Graduate Leadership Program Students: 34 full-time (23 women), 14 part-time (11 women); includes 1 minority (Black or African American, non-Hispanic/Latino), 2 international. Average age 40. 9 applicants, 100% accepted, 8 enrolled. *Faculty:* 8 part-time/adjunct (2 women). Expenses: Contact institution. Offers leadership (MA, Ed S). *Application deadline:* For summer admission, 4/7 for domestic students. *Application fee:* $75. *Application Contact:* Julie Lenocker, Program Administrator, 978-867-4322, Fax: 978-867-4663, E-mail: graduate-education@gordon.edu. *Director of Graduate Studies*, Dr. Janet Arndt, 978-867-4663.

Graduate Music Education Program Students: 13 full-time (7 women), 11 part-time (10 women); includes 5 minority (3 Asian, non-Hispanic/Latino; 1 Hispanic/Latino; 1 Two or more races, non-Hispanic/Latino). Average age 34. 9 applicants, 100% accepted, 9 enrolled. *Faculty:* 2 full-time (1 woman), 6 part-time/adjunct (3 women). Expenses: Contact institution. *Financial support:* Applicants required to submit FAFSA. In 2017, 10 master's awarded. *Program availability:* Part-time. Offers music education (MM Ed). *Application deadline:* For summer admission, 4/1 for domestic and international students. Applications are processed on a rolling basis. *Application fee:* $50. *Application Contact:* Kristen Harrington, Program Administrator, 978-867-4429, Fax: 978-867-4663, E-mail: kristen.harrington@gordon.edu. *Associate Professor*, Dr. Sandra Doneski, 978-867-4818, E-mail: sandra.doneski@gordon.edu.

GORDON-CONWELL THEOLOGICAL SEMINARY, South Hamilton, MA 01982-2395

General Information Independent-religious, coed, graduate-only institution. *Graduate housing:* Rooms and/or apartments available to single and married students. Housing application deadline: 4/1.

GRADUATE UNITS

Graduate and Professional Programs *Program availability:* Part-time, evening/weekend. Offers Biblical languages (MABL); church history (MACH); counseling (MACO); ministry (D Min); missions/evangelism (MAME); New Testament (MANT); Old Testament (MAOT); religion (MAR); theology (M Div, MATH, Th M, Th D).

GOSHEN COLLEGE, Goshen, IN 46526-4794

General Information Independent-religious, coed, comprehensive institution. *Enrollment:* 950 graduate, professional, and undergraduate students; 66 full-time matriculated graduate/professional students (54 women), 1 (woman) part-time matriculated graduate/professional student. *Enrollment by degree level:* 67 master's. *Graduate faculty:* 14 full-time (5 women), 2 part-time/adjunct (1 woman). *Tuition:* Full-time $13,356; part-time $742 per credit hour. Tuition and fees vary according to degree level, campus/location and program. *Graduate housing:* On-campus housing not available. *Student services:* Child daycare facilities, exercise/wellness program, international student services, multicultural affairs office, services for students with disabilities, writing training. *Library facilities:* The Harold and Wilma Good Library plus 1 other. *Collection:* Books: 106,274 (physical), 157,167 (digital/electronic); Serial titles: 2,769 (physical), 30,977 (digital/electronic); Databases: 69. Weekly public service hours: 81; students can reserve study rooms.

Computer facilities: 160 computers available on campus for general student use. A campuswide network can be accessed. Online class registration is available.
Website: http://www.goshen.edu/

General Application Contact: Natalie Shields, Admissions Counselor for Graduate and Continuing Studies, 574-535-7458, Fax: 574-535-7245, E-mail: nshields@goshen.edu.

GRADUATE UNITS

Merry Lea Environmental Learning Center Students: 11 full-time (6 women). *Faculty:* 9 full-time (1 woman), 1 part-time/adjunct (0 women). Expenses: Contact institution. *Financial support:* Application deadline: 9/10. Offers environmental education (MA). *Application deadline:* For fall admission, 3/30 for domestic students. Applications are processed on a rolling basis. *Application fee:* $25. Electronic applications accepted. *Application Contact:* Dr. David Ostergren, Director of the Graduate Program in Environmental Education, 260-799-5869, E-mail: daveo@goshen.edu. *Executive Director*, Dr. Luke Gascho, 260-799-5869, E-mail: lukeag@goshen.edu.

Program in Nursing Students: 55 full-time (48 women), 1 (woman) part-time; includes 10 minority (3 Black or African American, non-Hispanic/Latino; 2 Asian, non-Hispanic/Latino; 4 Hispanic/Latino; 1 Two or more races, non-Hispanic/Latino), 1 international. Average age 35. *Faculty:* 5 full-time (4 women), 1 (woman) part-time/adjunct. Expenses: Contact institution. *Financial support:* Scholarships/grants available. *Program availability:* Part-time, evening/weekend. Offers family nurse practitioner (MSN). *Application deadline:* For fall admission, 3/15 priority date for domestic students. Electronic applications accepted. *Application Contact:* Natalie Shields, Admissions Counselor for Graduate and Continuing Studies, 574-535-7458, E-mail: nshields@goshen.edu. *Director*, Ruth Stoltzfus, 574-535-7973, E-mail: ruthas@goshen.edu.

GOUCHER COLLEGE, Baltimore, MD 21204-2794

General Information Independent, coed, comprehensive institution. *Enrollment:* 118 full-time matriculated graduate/professional students (86 women), 603 part-time matriculated graduate/professional students (487 women). *Enrollment by degree level:* 603 master's, 88 other advanced degrees. *Graduate faculty:* 251 part-time/adjunct (166 women). *Graduate housing:* On-campus housing not available. *Student services:* Campus employment opportunities, campus safety program, career counseling, exercise/wellness program, international student services, services for students with disabilities, teacher training. *Library facilities:* Goucher College Library plus 1 other. *Collection:* Books: 250,000 (physical), 300,000 (digital/electronic); Serial titles: 96,000 (digital/electronic); Databases: 120. Weekly public service hours: 168; study areas open 24 hours, 5–7 days a week. *Research affiliation:* Sheppard-Pratt Hospital (education).

Computer facilities: Computer purchase and lease plans are available. 130 computers available on campus for general student use. A campuswide network can be accessed from student residence rooms and from off campus. Online class registration, transcripts, financial aid information, billing, ePortfolios, academic progress reports, study abroad plans are available.
Website: http://www.goucher.edu/

General Application Contact: Shelby Hillers, Assistant Director of Admissions, 410-337-6200, Fax: 410-337-6085, E-mail: shelby.hillers@goucher.edu.

GRADUATE UNITS

Graduate Programs in Education Expenses: Contact institution. *Financial support:* Career-related internships or fieldwork and unspecified assistantships available. Support available to part-time students. Financial award application deadline: 4/15; financial award applicants required to submit FAFSA. *Program availability:* Part-time, evening/weekend. Offers at-risk and diverse learners (M Ed, Certificate); athletic program leadership and administration (M Ed, Certificate); elementary education (MAT); literacy strategies for content learning (M Ed); middle school (M Ed, Certificate); Montessori studies (M Ed); reading instruction (M Ed, Certificate); reducing student, classroom, and school disruption (M Ed); school improvement leadership (M Ed); secondary education (MAT); special education (MAT); special education for certified elementary and secondary teachers (M Ed); teacher as leader in technology (M Ed). *Application deadline:* For fall admission, 9/1 for domestic students; for spring admission, 1/15 for domestic students. Applications are processed on a rolling basis. *Application fee:* $75. Electronic applications accepted. *Application Contact:* Carlton E. Surbeck, III, Director of Admissions, 410-337-6100, Fax: 410-337-6085, E-mail: admissions@goucher.edu. *Assistant Provost,* Dr. Phyllis Sunshine, 410-337-6047, Fax: 410-337-6394, E-mail: psunshin@goucher.edu.

MA and MFA Programs Expenses: Contact institution. *Financial support:* Scholarships/grants and unspecified assistantships available. Financial award application deadline: 4/15; financial award applicants required to submit FAFSA. *Program availability:* Part-time, evening/weekend, blended/hybrid learning. Offers art and technology (MFA); arts administration (MA); cultural sustainability (MA); digital arts (MA); historic preservation (MA); nonfiction (MFA). *Application deadline:* Applications are processed on a rolling basis. *Application fee:* $75. Electronic applications accepted. *Application Contact:* Carlton E. Surbeck, III, Director of Admissions, 410-337-6100, Fax: 410-337-6200, E-mail: admissions@goucher.edu. *Acting Assistant Provost for Limited Residency Graduate Programs,* Leslie Rubinkowski, 410-337-6200, E-mail: leslie.rubinkowski@goucher.edu.

Post-Baccalaureate Premedical Program Expenses: Contact institution. *Financial support:* Fellowships, institutionally sponsored loans, and scholarships/grants available. Financial award application deadline: 3/1; financial award applicants required to submit FAFSA. Offers premedical studies (Certificate). *Application deadline:* Applications are processed on a rolling basis. *Application fee:* $60. Electronic applications accepted. *Application Contact:* Theresa Reifsnider, Program Assistant, 800-414-3437, Fax: 410-337-6461, E-mail: pbpm@goucher.edu. *Director,* Betsy Merideth, 800-414-3437, Fax: 410-337-6461, E-mail: bmerideth@goucher.edu.

GOVERNORS STATE UNIVERSITY, University Park, IL 60484

General Information State-supported, coed, university. CGS member. *Enrollment:* 5,185 graduate, professional, and undergraduate students; 743 full-time matriculated graduate/professional students (512 women), 1,116 part-time matriculated graduate/professional students (831 women). *Enrollment by degree level:* 1,533 master's, 196 doctoral. *Graduate faculty:* 231 full-time (139 women), 355 part-time/adjunct (204 women). Tuition, state resident: full-time $8472; part-time $353 per credit hour. Tuition, nonresident: full-time $16,944; part-time $706 per credit hour. *Required fees:* $1824; $76 per credit hour. $38 per term. Tuition and fees vary according to course load, degree level and program. *Graduate housing:* Rooms and/or apartments available on a first-come, first-served basis to single and married students. Typical cost: $8104 per year ($10,104 including board) for single students; $8104 per year ($10,104 including board) for married students. Room and board charges vary according to board plan and housing facility selected. Housing application deadline: 6/1. *Student services:* Campus employment opportunities, career counseling, child daycare facilities, exercise/wellness program, free psychological counseling, international student services, multicultural affairs office, services for students with disabilities, writing training. *Library facilities:* University Library. *Collection:* Books: 284,377 (physical), 339,176 (digital/electronic); Serial titles: 2,438 (physical), 11,484 (digital/electronic); Databases: 176. Weekly public service hours: 75; students can reserve study rooms.

Computer facilities: A campuswide network can be accessed from student residence rooms. Online class registration, student portal are available.
Website: http://www.govst.edu/

General Application Contact: Paul McGuinness, Executive Director, Enrollment Management/Director, Admissions, 708-534-5000 Ext. 7308, E-mail: pmcguinness@govst.edu.

GRADUATE UNITS

College of Arts and Sciences Students: 157 full-time (55 women), 265 part-time (142 women); includes 164 minority (140 Black or African American, non-Hispanic/Latino; 6 Asian, non-Hispanic/Latino; 13 Hispanic/Latino; 5 Two or more races, non-Hispanic/Latino), 133 international. Average age 34. 314 applicants, 66% accepted, 62 enrolled. *Faculty:* 101 full-time (48 women), 160 part-time/adjunct (76 women). Expenses: Contact institution. *Financial support:* Federal Work-Study and unspecified assistantships available. Financial award application deadline: 5/1; financial award applicants required to submit FAFSA. In 2017, 331 master's awarded. *Program availability:* Part-time. Offers actuarial science (MS); analytical chemistry (MS); art (MA, MSN, PSM); arts and sciences (MA, MFA, MPA, MS); communication studies (MA); computer science (MS); criminal justice (MA); English (MA); environmental biology (MS); independent film and digital imaging (MFA); political and justice studies (MA); public administration (MPA). *Application deadline:* For fall admission, 4/1 for domestic students. Applications are processed on a rolling basis. *Application fee:* $50. Electronic applications accepted. *Application Contact:* Paul McGuinness, Executive Director, Enrollment Management/Director, Admissions, 708-534-5000 Ext. 7308, E-mail: pmcguinness@govst.edu. *Dean, College of Arts and Sciences/Dean, Graduate Studies,* Andrae Marak, 708-534-5000 Ext. 4589, E-mail: amarak@govst.edu.

College of Business Students: 47 full-time (27 women), 103 part-time (61 women); includes 64 minority (50 Black or African American, non-Hispanic/Latino; 3 Asian, non-Hispanic/Latino; 6 Hispanic/Latino; 5 Two or more races, non-Hispanic/Latino), 3 international. Average age 38. 118 applicants, 46% accepted, 40 enrolled. *Faculty:* 26 full-time (9 women), 34 part-time/adjunct (10 women). Expenses: Contact institution. *Financial support:* Federal Work-Study and unspecified assistantships available. Financial award application deadline: 5/1; financial award applicants required to submit FAFSA. In 2017, 74 master's awarded. *Program availability:* Part-time. Offers accounting (MS); business (MBA, MS); business administration (MBA); management information systems (MS). *Application deadline:* For fall admission, 4/1 for domestic students. Applications are processed on a rolling basis. *Application fee:* $50. Electronic applications accepted. *Application Contact:* Paul McGuinness, Executive Director, Enrollment Management/Director, Admissions, 708-534-5000 Ext. 7308, E-mail: pmcguinness@govst.edu. *Dean, College of Business,* Jun Zhao, 708-534-5000 Ext. 4953, E-mail: jzhao@govst.edu.

College of Education Students: 124 full-time (109 women), 300 part-time (244 women); includes 220 minority (169 Black or African American, non-Hispanic/Latino; 7 Asian, non-Hispanic/Latino; 36 Hispanic/Latino; 8 Two or more races, non-Hispanic/Latino), 4 international. Average age 37. 172 applicants, 38% accepted, 53 enrolled. *Faculty:* 48 full-time (33 women), 69 part-time/adjunct (51 women). Expenses: Contact institution. *Financial support:* Federal Work-Study and unspecified assistantships available. Financial award application deadline: 5/1; financial award applicants required to submit FAFSA. In 2017, 121 master's, 7 doctorates awarded. *Program availability:* Part-time. Offers counseling (MA); early childhood education (MA); education (MA, Ed D); educational administration and supervision (MA); higher education administration (Ed D); multi-categorical special education (MA); psychology (MA); reading (MA). *Application deadline:* For fall admission, 4/1 for domestic students. Applications are processed on a rolling basis. *Application fee:* $50. Electronic applications accepted. *Application Contact:* Paul McGuinness, Executive Director, Enrollment Management/Director, Admissions, 708-534-5000 Ext. 7308, E-mail: pmcguinness@govst.edu. *Interim Dean, College of Education,* Shannon Dermer, 708-534-5000 Ext. 8396, E-mail: sdermer@govst.edu.

College of Health and Human Services Students: 406 full-time (317 women), 356 part-time (311 women); includes 404 minority (270 Black or African American, non-Hispanic/Latino; 1 American Indian or Alaska Native, non-Hispanic/Latino; 27 Asian, non-Hispanic/Latino; 98 Hispanic/Latino; 1 Native Hawaiian or other Pacific Islander, non-Hispanic/Latino; 7 Two or more races, non-Hispanic/Latino), 9 international. Average age 33. 399 applicants, 54% accepted, 160 enrolled. *Faculty:* 54 full-time (47 women), 85 part-time/adjunct (63 women). Expenses: Contact institution. *Financial support:* Federal Work-Study and unspecified assistantships available. Financial award application deadline: 5/1; financial award applicants required to submit FAFSA. In 2017, 203 master's, 57 doctorates awarded. *Program availability:* Part-time. Offers addiction studies and behavioral health (MHS); communication disorders (MHS); health administration (MHA); health and human services (MHA, MHS, MOT, MSN, MSW, DPT); nursing (MSN); occupational therapy (MOT); physical therapy (DPT); social work (MSW). *Application deadline:* For fall admission, 4/1 for domestic students. Applications are processed on a rolling basis. *Application fee:* $50. Electronic applications accepted. *Application Contact:* Paul McGuinness, Executive Director, Enrollment Management/Director, Admissions, 708-534-5000 Ext. 7308, E-mail: pmcguinness@govst.edu. *Interim Dean, College of Health and Human Services,* Catherine Balthazar, 708-534-5000 Ext. 4592, E-mail: cbalthazar@govst.edu.

GRACE COLLEGE, Winona Lake, IN 46590-1294

General Information Independent-religious, coed, comprehensive institution. *Enrollment:* 109 full-time matriculated graduate/professional students (64 women), 285 part-time matriculated graduate/professional students (132 women). *Enrollment by degree level:* 338 master's, 56 doctoral. *Graduate faculty:* 5 full-time (2 women), 5 part-time/adjunct (1 woman). *Graduate housing:* On-campus housing not available. *Student services:* Campus employment opportunities, campus safety program, career counseling, exercise/wellness program, free psychological counseling. *Library facilities:* Morgan Library.

Computer facilities: 150 computers available on campus for general student use. A campuswide network can be accessed from student residence rooms and from off campus. Online class registration is available.
Website: http://www.grace.edu/

General Application Contact: Zachary Parrott, Graduate Admissions Counselor, 800-823-8533, E-mail: graceonline@grace.edu.

GRADUATE UNITS

Department of Graduate Counseling Students: 68 full-time (46 women), 23 part-time (16 women); includes 9 minority (6 Black or African American, non-Hispanic/Latino; 2 Hispanic/Latino; 1 Native Hawaiian or other Pacific Islander, non-Hispanic/Latino). Average age 32. *Faculty:* 5 full-time (2 women), 5 part-time/adjunct (1 woman). Expenses: Contact institution. *Financial support:* Teaching assistantships with partial tuition reimbursements, career-related internships or fieldwork, and unspecified assistantships available. Financial award application deadline: 3/10; financial award applicants required to submit FAFSA. In 2017, 23 master's awarded. *Program availability:* Part-time. Offers clinical mental health counseling (MA). *Application deadline:* For fall admission, 8/1 priority date for domestic students; for spring admission, 12/1 priority date for domestic students. Applications are processed on a rolling basis. *Application fee:* $250. Electronic applications accepted. *Application Contact:* Zachary Parrott, Graduate Admissions Counselor, 800-823.8533, E-mail: graceonline@grace.edu. *Chair, Department of Graduate Counseling,* Amy Gilbert, 574-322-5100 Ext. 6064, Fax: 574-372-5143, E-mail: gilberal@grace.edu.

GRACE COLLEGE OF DIVINITY, Fayetteville, NC 28314

General Information Independent-religious, coed, comprehensive institution.

GRADUATE UNITS

Graduate Program Offers theology (MCL).

GRACELAND UNIVERSITY, Lamoni, IA 50140

General Information Independent-religious, coed, comprehensive institution. *Enrollment:* 2,262 graduate, professional, and undergraduate students; 457 full-time matriculated graduate/professional students (396 women), 365 part-time matriculated graduate/professional students (325 women). *Enrollment by degree level:* 721 master's, 26 doctoral, 75 other advanced degrees. *Graduate faculty:* 16 full-time (13 women), 38 part-time/adjunct (34 women). *Tuition:* Part-time $775 per credit hour. Part-time tuition and fees vary according to degree level, campus/location and program. *Graduate housing:* On-campus housing not available. *Student services:* Campus safety program, career counseling, free psychological counseling, services for students with disabilities, teacher training, writing training. *Library facilities:* F. M. Smith Library. *Collection:* Books: 80,000 (physical), 350,000 (digital/electronic); Serial titles: 153 (physical), 60 (digital/electronic); Databases: 50. Weekly public service hours: 80; students can reserve study rooms.

Computer facilities: 179 computers available on campus for general student use. A campuswide network can be accessed from student residence rooms and from off campus. Online class registration is available.
Website: http://www.graceland.edu/

General Application Contact: Lisa Libich, Director of Retention Operations for College of Graduate and Continuing Studies, 816-423-4730, Fax: 816-833-2990, E-mail: libich@graceland.edu.

GRADUATE UNITS

Community of Christ Seminary Students: 14 full-time (10 women), 17 part-time (9 women); includes 2 minority (1 Asian, non-Hispanic/Latino; 1 Native Hawaiian or other Pacific Islander, non-Hispanic/Latino), 2 international. Average age 41. 16 applicants, 100% accepted, 11 enrolled. *Faculty:* 1 full-time (0 women), 1 part-time/adjunct (0 women). Expenses: Contact institution. *Financial support:* In 2017–18, 1 student received support. Scholarships/grants available. Financial award application deadline: 12/15; financial award applicants required to submit FAFSA. In 2017, 12 master's awarded. *Program availability:* Part-time. Offers theology (MAR). *Application deadline:* For fall admission, 8/15 priority date for domestic students. Applications are processed on a rolling basis. *Application fee:* $50. Electronic applications accepted. *Application Contact:* Sharon Ward, Administrative Assistant, 816-423-4676, Fax: 816-423-4753, E-mail: ward@graceland.edu. *Dean,* Dr. Matthew Frizzell, 641-784-5276, E-mail: mfrizzel@graceland.edu.

Gleazer School of Education Students: 117 full-time (102 women), 62 part-time (54 women); includes 8 minority (3 Black or African American, non-Hispanic/Latino; 1 Asian, non-Hispanic/Latino; 2 Hispanic/Latino; 1 Native Hawaiian or other Pacific Islander, non-Hispanic/Latino; 1 Two or more races, non-Hispanic/Latino), 1 international. Average age 35. 28 applicants, 100% accepted, 19 enrolled. *Faculty:* 2 full-time (both women), 13 part-time/adjunct (10 women). Expenses: Contact institution. *Financial support:* In 2017–18, 3 students received support. Tuition waivers available. Financial award applicants required to submit FAFSA. In 2017, 64 master's awarded. *Program availability:* Part-time, 100% online. Offers curriculum and instruction: collaborative learning and teaching (M Ed); differentiated instruction (M Ed); instructional leadership (M Ed); literacy instruction (M Ed); management in a quality classroom (M Ed); special education (M Ed); technology integration (M Ed). *Application deadline:* For fall admission, 10/1 for domestic students; for winter admission, 11/15 for domestic students; for spring admission, 2/15 priority date for domestic students; for summer admission, 6/1 for domestic students. *Application fee:* $50. Electronic applications accepted. *Application Contact:* Jeanette Calipetro, Admissions Representative, 816-423-4716, Fax: 816-833-2990, E-mail: jcali1@graceland.edu. *Interim Dean,* Dr. Lee Bash, 641-784-5072, E-mail: bash@graceland.edu.

School of Nursing Students: 338 full-time (294 women), 311 part-time (282 women); includes 102 minority (33 Black or African American, non-Hispanic/Latino; 8 American Indian or Alaska Native, non-Hispanic/Latino; 18 Asian, non-Hispanic/Latino; 29 Hispanic/Latino; 1 Native Hawaiian or other Pacific Islander, non-Hispanic/Latino; 13 Two or more races, non-Hispanic/Latino), 2 international. Average age 36. 119 applicants, 86% accepted, 95 enrolled. *Faculty:* 13 full-time (11 women), 24 part-time/adjunct (all women). Expenses: Contact institution. *Financial support:* In 2017–18, 14 students received support. Institutionally sponsored loans available. Support available to part-time students. Financial award application deadline: 6/1; financial award applicants required to submit FAFSA. In 2017, 158 master's, 2 doctorates awarded. *Program availability:* Part-time, online learning. Offers adult and gerontology acute care (MSN, PMC); family nurse practitioner (MSN, PMC); nurse educator (MSN, PMC); organizational leadership (DNP). *Application deadline:* For fall admission, 6/1 priority date for domestic students; for winter admission, 10/1 priority date for domestic students; for spring admission, 10/1 priority date for domestic students; for summer admission, 2/1 for domestic students. *Application fee:* $50. Electronic applications accepted. *Application Contact:* Admissions Representative, 816-423-4717, Fax: 816-833-2990, E-mail: distancelearning@graceland.edu. *Interim Vice President for Independence Campus/Dean,* Dr. Claudia D. Horton, 816-423-4670, Fax: 816-423-4753, E-mail: horton@graceland.edu.

GRACE MISSION UNIVERSITY, Fullerton, CA 92833

General Information Independent, coed, comprehensive institution.

GRADUATE UNITS

Graduate School Offers missions (M Div, MACE, MAICS, D Miss).

GRACE SCHOOL OF THEOLOGY, Conroe, TX 77384-4894

General Information Independent, coed, comprehensive institution.

GRADUATE UNITS

Graduate Programs Offers theology (M Div, MABS, MM, Th M).

GRACE THEOLOGICAL SEMINARY, Winona Lake, IN 46590-9907

General Information Independent-religious, coed, primarily men, graduate-only institution. *Graduate housing:* On-campus housing not available.

GRADUATE UNITS

Graduate and Professional Programs *Program availability:* Part-time, online learning. Offers biblical studies (Certificate); chaplaincy (M Div); exegetical studies (M Div); intercultural studies (M Div, MA, D Min); local church ministry (MA); pastoral counseling (M Div); pastoral studies (M Div, D Min); theology (Diploma). Electronic applications accepted.

THE GRADUATE CENTER, CITY UNIVERSITY OF NEW YORK, New York, NY 10016-4039

General Information State and locally supported, coed, graduate-only institution. CGS member. *Enrollment by degree level:* 506 master's, 3,211 doctoral. *Graduate faculty:* 1,471 full-time (318 women), 21 part-time/adjunct (5 women). *Graduate housing:* Rooms and/or apartments available to single and married students. Housing application deadline: 5/1. *Student services:* Career counseling, free psychological counseling, low-cost health insurance. *Library facilities:* Mina Rees Library. *Research affiliation:* American Museum of Natural History (anthropology), Roche Institute of Molecular Biology (biological sciences), New York Botanical Gardens (biological sciences).
Website: http://www.gc.cuny.edu/

General Application Contact: Les Gribben, Director of Admissions, 212-817-7470, Fax: 212-817-1624, E-mail: lgribben@gc.cuny.edu.

GRADUATE UNITS

Graduate Studies Students: 3,238 full-time (1,791 women), 489 part-time (312 women); includes 871 minority (210 Black or African American, non-Hispanic/Latino; 2 American Indian or Alaska Native, non-Hispanic/Latino; 219 Asian, non-Hispanic/Latino; 371 Hispanic/Latino; 3 Native Hawaiian or other Pacific Islander, non-Hispanic/Latino; 66 Two or more races, non-Hispanic/Latino), 870 international. 4,270 applicants, 25% accepted, 593 enrolled. *Faculty:* 1,471 full-time (318 women). Expenses: Contact institution. *Financial support:* In 2017–18, 2,460 fellowships, 156 research assistantships, 224 teaching assistantships were awarded; career-related internships or fieldwork, Federal Work-Study, institutionally sponsored loans, and tuition waivers (full and partial) also available. Financial award application deadline: 2/1; financial award applicants required to submit FAFSA. In 2017, 371 master's, 430 doctorates awarded. Offers accounting (PhD); anthropological linguistics (PhD); archaeology (PhD); architecture (PhD); audiology (Au D); basic applied neurocognition (PhD); behavioral science (PhD); biochemistry (PhD); biology (PhD); biopsychology (PhD); chemistry (PhD); classics (MA, PhD); clinical psychology (PhD); comparative literature (MA, PhD); computer science (PhD); criminal justice (PhD); cultural anthropology (PhD); developmental psychology (PhD); earth and environmental sciences (PhD); economics (PhD); educational psychology (PhD); English (PhD); environmental psychology (PhD); experimental psychology (PhD); finance (PhD); French (PhD); graphic arts (PhD); history (PhD); industrial psychology (PhD); Latin American, Iberian and Latino cultures (PhD); learning processes (PhD); liberal studies (MA); linguistics (MA, PhD); management planning systems (PhD); mathematics (PhD); music (DMA, PhD); neuropsychology (PhD); nursing (PhD); painting (PhD); philosophy (MA, PhD); photography (PhD); physical anthropology (PhD); physics (PhD); political science (MA, PhD); psychology (PhD); sculpture (PhD); social personality (PhD); social welfare (DSW, PhD); sociology (PhD); speech and hearing sciences (PhD); theatre (PhD); urban education (PhD). *Application fee:* $125. Electronic applications accepted. *Application Contact:* Les Gribben, Director of Admissions, 212-817-7470, Fax: 212-817-1624, E-mail: lgribben@gc.cuny.edu. *Provost and Senior Vice President for Academic Affairs,* Dr. Joy Connolly, 212-817-7200, Fax: 212-817-1612, E-mail: provost@gc.cuny.edu.

GRADUATE INSTITUTE OF APPLIED LINGUISTICS, Dallas, TX 75236

General Information Independent, coed, graduate-only institution.

GRADUATE UNITS

Graduate Programs *Program availability:* Part-time. Offers applied linguistics (MA, Certificate); language development (MA). Electronic applications accepted.

GRADUATE THEOLOGICAL UNION, Berkeley, CA 94709-1212

General Information Independent-religious, coed, graduate-only institution. *Graduate housing:* Rooms and/or apartments available on a first-come, first-served basis to single and married students. Housing application deadline: 6/1.

GRADUATE UNITS

Graduate Programs Offers art and religion (MA, PhD, Th D); biblical languages (MA); biblical studies (MA); Biblical studies (PhD, Th D); Buddhist studies (MA); Christian spirituality (MA, PhD, Th D); cultural and historical studies of religions (MA, PhD, Th D); ethics and social theory (PhD, Th D); history (MA, PhD, Th D); homiletics (MA, PhD, Th D); interdisciplinary studies (PhD, Th D); Jewish studies (MA, PhD, Th D, Certificate); liturgical studies (MA, PhD, Th D); Near Eastern religions (PhD, Th D); Orthodox Christian studies (MA); religion and psychology (MA, PhD, Th D); religion and society/ethics and social theory (MA); systematic and philosophical theology (MA, PhD, Th D). PhD programs in Jewish studies and Near Eastern religions offered jointly with University of California, Berkeley. Electronic applications accepted.

GRAMBLING STATE UNIVERSITY, Grambling, LA 71245

General Information State-supported, coed, university. CGS member. *Graduate housing:* On-campus housing not available. *Research affiliation:* U.S. Department of Defense (cyberspace technology, materials and manufacturing), National Institutes of Justice (technology and equipment in forensic science), U.S. Department of Housing and Urban Development (HUD) (housing preservation in low-income areas), National Science Foundation (science and engineering), NASA (aeronautics research), National Institutes of Health (biomedical sciences).

GRADUATE UNITS

School of Graduate Studies and Research *Program availability:* Part-time, evening/weekend. Electronic applications accepted.

College of Arts and Sciences *Program availability:* Part-time. Offers arts and sciences (MA, MPA); health services administration (MPA); human resource management (MPA); public management (MPA); social sciences (MA); state and local government (MPA). Electronic applications accepted.

College of Education *Program availability:* Part-time, evening/weekend. Offers curriculum and instruction (MS); developmental education (MS, Ed D, PMC); education (M Ed, MAT, MS, Ed D, PMC); educational leadership (M Ed); special education (M Ed); sports administration (MS). Electronic applications accepted.

College of Professional Studies *Program availability:* Part-time. Offers criminal justice (MS); family nurse practitioner (PMC); mass communication (MA); nursing (MSN); social work (MSW). Electronic applications accepted.

GRAND CANYON UNIVERSITY, Phoenix, AZ 85017-1097

General Information Independent-religious, coed, comprehensive institution. *Graduate housing:* Rooms and/or apartments available on a first-come, first-served basis to single and married students.

GRADUATE UNITS

Colangelo College of Business *Program availability:* Part-time, evening/weekend, online learning. Offers accounting (MBA, MS); business analytics (MS); disaster preparedness and executive fire service leadership (MS); finance (MBA); general management (MBA); health systems management (MBA); information technology management (MS); leadership (MBA, MS); marketing (MBA); organizational leadership and entrepreneurship (MS); project management (MBA); sports business (MBA); strategic human resource management (MBA). Electronic applications accepted.

College of Doctoral Studies Offers data analytics (DBA); general psychology (PhD); management (DBA); marketing (DBA); organizational leadership (Ed D).

College of Education *Program availability:* Part-time, evening/weekend, online learning. Offers autism spectrum disorders (MA); curriculum and instruction (MA); early childhood education (M Ed); educational administration (M Ed); educational leadership (M Ed); elementary education (M Ed); gifted education (MA); instructional technology (MS); K-12 leadership (Ed S); reading (MA); secondary education (M Ed); secondary humanities education (M Ed); secondary STEM education (M Ed); special education (M Ed); teaching and learning (Ed D); teaching English to speakers of other languages (MA). Electronic applications accepted.

College of Nursing and Health Care Professions *Program availability:* Part-time, evening/weekend, online learning. Offers acute care nurse practitioner (MSN, PMC); family nurse practitioner (MSN, PMC); health care administration (MS); health care informatics (MS, MSN); leadership in health care systems (MSN); nursing (DNP); nursing education (MSN, PMC); public health (MPH, MSN).

GRAND RAPIDS THEOLOGICAL SEMINARY OF CORNERSTONE UNIVERSITY, Grand Rapids, MI 49525-5897

General Information Independent-religious, coed, graduate-only institution. *Enrollment by degree level:* 311 master's. *Graduate faculty:* 9 full-time (2 women), 14 part-time/adjunct (5 women). *Tuition:* Full-time $9720; part-time $540 per credit hour. *Required fees:* $832; $374 per semester. Tuition and fees vary according to course load and program. *Graduate housing:* Rooms and/or apartments available on a first-come, first-served basis to single and married students. Housing application deadline: 6/1. *Student services:* Campus employment opportunities, campus safety program, career counseling, exercise/wellness program, international student services, services for students with disabilities, writing training. *Library facilities:* Miller Library. *Collection:* Weekly public service hours: 51; students can reserve study rooms.

Computer facilities: 20 computers available on campus for general student use. A campuswide network can be accessed from student residence rooms. Online class registration is available.
Website: https://www.cornerstone.edu/grts

General Application Contact: Ashley VanBemmelen, Director of Admissions, 800-697-1133, E-mail: seminary@cornerstone.edu.

GRADUATE UNITS

Graduate Programs Students: 100 full-time (53 women), 211 part-time (102 women); includes 71 minority (54 Black or African American, non-Hispanic/Latino; 1 American Indian or Alaska Native, non-Hispanic/Latino; 3 Asian, non-Hispanic/Latino; 12 Hispanic/Latino; 1 Two or more races, non-Hispanic/Latino), 3 international. Average age 36. 165 applicants, 76% accepted, 99 enrolled. *Faculty:* 9 full-time (2 women), 14 part-time/adjunct (5 women). Expenses: Contact institution. *Financial support:* In 2017–18, 96 students received support, including 8 fellowships with partial tuition reimbursements available; career-related internships or fieldwork and scholarships/grants also available. Support available to part-time students. Financial award application deadline: 8/15; financial award applicants required to submit FAFSA. In 2017, 75 master's awarded. *Program availability:* Part-time, evening/weekend, 100% online, blended/hybrid learning. Offers academic (M Div); chaplaincy ministries (M Div); Christian formation (MA); counseling (MA); formation and soul care ministries (M Div); intercultural ministries (M Div); interdisciplinary studies (MA); New Testament (Th M); Old Testament (Th M); pastoral ministries (M Div); small group and discipleship ministries (M Div); student and family ministries (M Div). *Application deadline:* For fall admission, 8/15 for domestic students, 6/15 for international students; for spring admission, 1/10 for domestic students, 11/10 for international students; for summer admission, 4/30 for domestic students. Applications are processed on a rolling basis. Electronic applications accepted. *Application Contact:* Ashley VanBemmelen, Director of Admissions, 800-697-1133, E-mail: ashley.vanbemmelen@cornerstone.edu. *Executive Vice President and Academic Dean,* Dr. John F. VerBerkmoes, 616-222-1422, E-mail: john.verberkmoes@cornerstone.edu.

GRAND VALLEY STATE UNIVERSITY, Allendale, MI 49401-9403

General Information State-supported, coed, comprehensive institution. CGS member. *Enrollment:* 25,049 graduate, professional, and undergraduate students; 1,398 full-time matriculated graduate/professional students (997 women), 4,548 part-time matriculated graduate/professional students (4,069 women). *Enrollment by degree level:* 2,634 master's, 286 doctoral, 26 other advanced degrees. *Graduate faculty:* 302 full-time (161 women), 93 part-time/adjunct (63 women). Tuition and fees vary according to degree level and program. *Graduate housing:* Rooms and/or apartments available on a first-come, first-served basis to single and married students. Typical cost: $7534 per year for single students; $8300 per year for married students. Room charges vary according to campus/location and housing facility selected. Housing application deadline: 2/1. *Student services:* Campus employment opportunities, campus safety program, career counseling, child daycare facilities, exercise/wellness program, free psychological counseling, grant writing training, international student services, low-cost health insurance, multicultural affairs office, services for students with disabilities, teacher training, writing training. *Library facilities:* Mary Idema Pew Library Learning and Information Commons plus 5 others. *Collection:* Books: 567,197 (physical), 1 million (digital/electronic). Students can reserve study rooms. *Research affiliation:* Van Andel Institute (life sciences/medical research), Spectrum Health (medical research), Elkins Innovations (life sciences), Progressive AE (water quality).

Computer facilities: 2,600 computers available on campus for general student use. A campuswide network can be accessed from student residence rooms and from off campus. Online class registration, transcript, degree audit, credit card payments are available.
Website: http://www.gvsu.edu/

General Application Contact: Tracey James-Heer, Associate Director of Admissions, 616-331-2025, Fax: 616-331-2000, E-mail: james-ht@gvsu.edu.

GRADUATE UNITS

College of Community and Public Service Students: 250 full-time (195 women), 283 part-time (229 women); includes 111 minority (47 Black or African American, non-Hispanic/Latino; 4 American Indian or Alaska Native, non-Hispanic/Latino; 11 Asian, non-Hispanic/Latino; 31 Hispanic/Latino; 18 Two or more races, non-Hispanic/Latino), 16 international. Average age 29. 290 applicants, 85% accepted, 132 enrolled. *Faculty:* 31 full-time (18 women), 24 part-time/adjunct (16 women). Expenses: Contact institution. *Financial support:* In 2017–18, 89 students received support, including 48 fellowships, 50 research assistantships with full and partial tuition reimbursements available (averaging $8,000 per year); teaching assistantships, career-related internships or fieldwork, Federal Work-Study, institutionally sponsored loans, scholarships/grants, and unspecified assistantships also available. Financial award application deadline: 5/1. In 2017, 233 master's awarded. *Program availability:* Part-time, evening/weekend. Offers community and public service (MHA, MPA, MPNL, MS, MSW). *Application deadline:* For fall admission, 5/1 priority date for domestic students; for winter admission, 11/1 priority date for domestic students; for spring admission, 4/10 priority date for domestic students. Applications are processed on a rolling basis. *Application fee:* $30. Electronic applications accepted. *Application Contact:* Tracey James-Heer, Associate Director of Admissions, 616-331-2025, Fax: 616-331-2000, E-mail: james-ht@gvsu.edu. *Dean,* George Grant, 616-331-6850.

School of Criminal Justice Students: 5 full-time (4 women), 17 part-time (7 women); includes 8 minority (2 Black or African American, non-Hispanic/Latino; 6 Hispanic/Latino). Average age 29. 11 applicants, 91% accepted, 5 enrolled. *Faculty:* 4 full-time (3 women). Expenses: Contact institution. *Financial support:* In 2017–18, 9 students received support, including 1 fellowship, 10 research assistantships with full and partial tuition reimbursements available (averaging $4,000 per year); career-related internships or fieldwork, Federal Work-Study, scholarships/grants, and unspecified assistantships also available. Financial award application deadline: 5/1. In 2017, 11 master's awarded. *Program availability:* Part-time, evening/weekend. Offers criminal justice (MS). *Application deadline:* For fall admission, 5/1 priority date for domestic students; for winter admission, 11/1 priority date for domestic students; for spring admission, 4/1 priority date for domestic students. Applications are processed on a rolling basis. *Application fee:* $30. Electronic applications accepted. *Application Contact:* Tonisha Jones, Graduate Program Director/Recruiting Contact, 616-331-7187, Fax: 616-331-7155, E-mail: jontonis@gvsu.edu. *Director,* Dr. Kathleen Bailey, 616-331-7148, Fax: 616-331-7155, E-mail: baileyk@gvsu.edu.

School of Public, Nonprofit and Health Administration Students: 33 full-time (18 women), 88 part-time (65 women); includes 22 minority (10 Black or African American, non-Hispanic/Latino; 1 American Indian or Alaska Native, non-Hispanic/Latino; 2 Asian, non-Hispanic/Latino; 6 Hispanic/Latino; 3 Two or more races, non-Hispanic/Latino), 6 international. Average age 30. 67 applicants, 79% accepted, 22 enrolled. *Faculty:* 13 full-time (6 women), 6 part-time/adjunct (3 women). Expenses: Contact institution. *Financial support:* In 2017–18, 17 students received support, including 9 fellowships, 9 research assistantships with full and partial tuition reimbursements available (averaging $4,000 per year); career-related internships or fieldwork, Federal Work-Study, scholarships/grants, and unspecified assistantships also available. Financial award application deadline: 5/1. In 2017, 44 master's awarded. *Program availability:* Part-time, evening/weekend. Offers health administration (MHA); philanthropy and nonprofit leadership (MPNL); public, nonprofit and health administration (MHA, MPA, MPNL). *Application deadline:* For fall admission, 5/1 priority date for domestic students; for winter admission, 11/1 priority date for domestic students. Applications are processed on a rolling basis. *Application fee:* $30. Electronic applications accepted. *Application Contact:* Davia Downey, Graduate Program Director/Recruiting Contact, 616-331-6681, Fax: 616-331-7120, E-mail: downeyd@gvsu.edu. *Director,* Dr. Richard Jelier, 616-331-6575, Fax: 616-331-7120, E-mail: jelierr@gvsu.edu.

School of Social Work Students: 175 full-time (146 women), 122 part-time (111 women); includes 66 minority (32 Black or African American, non-Hispanic/Latino; 3 American Indian or Alaska Native, non-Hispanic/Latino; 2 Asian, non-Hispanic/Latino; 18 Hispanic/Latino; 11 Two or more races, non-Hispanic/Latino), 2 international. Average age 28. 158 applicants, 90% accepted, 83 enrolled. *Faculty:* 14 full-time (9 women), 18 part-time/adjunct (13 women). Expenses: Contact institution. *Financial support:* In 2017–18, 46 students received support, including 29 fellowships, 18 research assistantships with full and partial tuition reimbursements available (averaging $4,000 per year); career-related internships or fieldwork, Federal Work-Study, institutionally sponsored loans, and unspecified assistantships also available. In 2017, 153 master's awarded. *Program availability:* Part-time. Offers social work (MSW). *Application deadline:* For fall admission, 5/1 priority date for domestic students; for winter admission, 10/1 priority date for domestic students; for spring admission, 3/15 priority date for domestic students. Applications are processed on a rolling basis. *Application fee:* $30. Electronic applications accepted. *Application Contact:* Dr. Cray Mulder, Graduate Program Director/Recruiting Contact, 616-331-6596, Fax: 616-331-6570, E-mail: muldercra@gvsu.edu. *Chair,* Dr. Scott Berlin, 616-331-6556, Fax: 616-331-6570, E-mail: berlins@gvsu.edu.

College of Education Students: 159 full-time (110 women), 726 part-time (575 women); includes 125 minority (61 Black or African American, non-Hispanic/Latino; 6 American Indian or Alaska Native, non-Hispanic/Latino; 8 Asian, non-Hispanic/Latino; 34 Hispanic/Latino; 16 Two or more races, non-Hispanic/Latino), 18 international. Average age 33. 316 applicants, 96% accepted, 147 enrolled. *Faculty:* 45 full-time (29 women), 17 part-time/adjunct (11 women). Expenses: Contact institution. *Financial support:* In 2017–18, 226 students received support, including 164 fellowships, 4 research assistantships with full and partial tuition reimbursements available (averaging $8,000 per year); career-related internships or fieldwork, Federal Work-Study, scholarships/grants, and unspecified assistantships also available. In 2017, 282 master's, 15 Ed Ss awarded. *Program availability:* Part-time, evening/weekend, 100% online. Offers adult and higher education (M Ed); cognitive impairment (M Ed); college student affairs leadership (M Ed); early childhood developmental delay (M Ed); early childhood education (M Ed); education (M Ed, Ed S); educational differentiation (M Ed); educational leadership (M Ed); educational technology (M Ed); educational technology integration (M Ed); elementary education (M Ed); emotional impairment (M Ed); higher education (M Ed); instruction and curriculum (M Ed); leadership (Ed S); learning disabilities (M Ed); literacy studies (M Ed); middle level education (M Ed); reading and language arts (M Ed); school counseling (M Ed); school library media services (M Ed); secondary level education (M Ed); special education (M Ed); teaching English to speakers of other languages (M Ed). *Application deadline:* Applications are processed on a rolling basis. *Application fee:* $30. Electronic applications accepted. *Application Contact:* Thomas Owens, Director, Student Information and Services Center, 616-331-6650, Fax: 616-331-6217, E-mail: owenst@gvsu.edu. *Dean,* Dr. Barry Kanpol, 616-331-6821, Fax: 616-331-6515, E-mail: kanpolb@gvsu.edu.

College of Health Professions Students: 644 full-time (503 women), 48 part-time (34 women); includes 63 minority (13 Black or African American, non-Hispanic/Latino; 1 American Indian or Alaska Native, non-Hispanic/Latino; 14 Asian, non-Hispanic/Latino; 20 Hispanic/Latino; 15 Two or more races, non-Hispanic/Latino), 7 international. Average age 25. 1,181 applicants, 29% accepted, 273 enrolled. *Faculty:* 59 full-time (45 women), 13 part-time/adjunct (all women). Expenses: Contact institution. *Financial support:* In 2017–18, 104 students received support, including 75 fellowships, 37 research assistantships with full and partial tuition reimbursements available (averaging $8,000 per year); career-related internships or fieldwork, Federal Work-Study, institutionally sponsored loans, and scholarships/grants also available. Financial award application deadline: 2/15. In 2017, 207 master's, 58 doctorates awarded. Offers clinical dietetics (MS); health professions (MPAS, MPH, MS, DPT); medical dosimetry (MS); occupational therapy (MS); physical therapy (DPT); physician assistant studies (MPAS); public health (MPH); speech-language pathology (MS). *Application deadline:* For winter admission, 1/15 priority date for domestic and international students. Applications are processed on a rolling basis. Electronic applications accepted. *Application Contact:* Darlene Zwart, Student Services Coordinator, 616-331-3958, E-mail: zwartda@gvsu.edu. *Dean,* Dr. Roy Olsson, 616-331-3356, Fax: 616-331-3350, E-mail: olssonr@gvsu.edu.

College of Liberal Arts and Sciences Students: 130 full-time (81 women), 141 part-time (88 women); includes 32 minority (12 Black or African American, non-Hispanic/Latino; 2 American Indian or Alaska Native, non-Hispanic/Latino; 3 Asian, non-Hispanic/Latino; 8 Hispanic/Latino; 7 Two or more races, non-Hispanic/Latino), 39 international. Average age 28. 185 applicants, 77% accepted, 86 enrolled. *Faculty:* 91 full-time (36 women), 2 part-time/adjunct (0 women). Expenses: Contact institution. *Financial support:* In 2017–18, 104 students received support, including 21 fellowships, 90 research assistantships; career-related internships or fieldwork, Federal Work-Study, institutionally sponsored loans, scholarships/grants, and unspecified assistantships also available. In 2017, 92 master's, 10 other advanced degrees awarded. *Program availability:* Part-time, evening/weekend. Offers applied linguistics (MA); biology (MS);

biomedical sciences (MHS); biostatistics (MS); cell and molecular biology (MS); English (MA); liberal arts and sciences (MA, MHS, MS, Psy S); school psychology (MS, Psy S). *Application deadline:* Applications are processed on a rolling basis. *Application fee:* $30. Electronic applications accepted. *Application Contact:* Betty Schaner, Assistant Dean of Advising and Student Services, 616-331-2495, Fax: 616-331-3675, E-mail: schanerb@gvsu.edu. *Dean*, Dr. Frederick Antczak, 616-331-2495, Fax: 616-331-3675, E-mail: antczakf@gvsu.edu.

School of Communications Students: 18 full-time (9 women), 35 part-time (21 women); includes 11 minority (4 Black or African American, non-Hispanic/Latino; 1 Asian, non-Hispanic/Latino; 4 Hispanic/Latino; 2 Two or more races, non-Hispanic/Latino), 11 international. Average age 29. 34 applicants, 97% accepted, 17 enrolled. *Faculty:* 2 full-time (0 women), 1 part-time/adjunct (0 women). Expenses: Contact institution. *Financial support:* In 2017–18, 12 students received support, including 8 fellowships; research assistantships, career-related internships or fieldwork, Federal Work-Study, and institutionally sponsored loans also available. Support available to part-time students. Financial award application deadline: 4/15. In 2017, 24 master's awarded. *Program availability:* Part-time, evening/weekend. Offers communications (MS). *Application deadline:* For fall admission, 8/15 priority date for domestic students; for winter admission, 12/15 priority date for domestic students; for spring admission, 4/15 priority date for domestic students. Applications are processed on a rolling basis. *Application fee:* $30. Electronic applications accepted. *Application Contact:* Dr. Alex Nesterenko, Graduate Program Director, 616-331-3667, Fax: 616-331-2700, E-mail: nesterea@gvsu.edu. *Department Director*, Dr. Jonathan Hodge, 616-331-3668, Fax: 616-895-2700, E-mail: hodgejo@gvsu.edu.

Kirkhof College of Nursing Students: 44 full-time (40 women), 74 part-time (63 women); includes 15 minority (7 Black or African American, non-Hispanic/Latino; 4 Asian, non-Hispanic/Latino; 3 Hispanic/Latino; 1 Two or more races, non-Hispanic/Latino), 4 international. Average age 33. 34 applicants, 100% accepted, 23 enrolled. *Faculty:* 17 full-time (all women), 5 part-time/adjunct (4 women). Expenses: Contact institution. *Financial support:* In 2017–18, 34 students received support, including 10 fellowships, 30 research assistantships with partial tuition reimbursements available (averaging $4,000 per year); career-related internships or fieldwork, Federal Work-Study, institutionally sponsored loans, and traineeships also available. Financial award application deadline: 2/15. In 2017, 8 master's, 22 doctorates awarded. *Program availability:* Part-time. Offers advanced practice (MSN); case management (MSN); nursing administration (MSN); nursing education (MSN); nursing practice (DNP). *Application deadline:* For fall admission, 3/15 priority date for domestic students. Applications are processed on a rolling basis. *Application fee:* $30. Electronic applications accepted. *Application Contact:* Dr. Karen Burritt, Associate Dean for Graduate Programs, 616-331-5585, Fax: 616-331-2510, E-mail: burritka@gvsu.edu. *Dean*, Dr. Cynthia McCurren, 616-331-3558, Fax: 616-331-2510, E-mail: mccurrec@gvsu.edu.

Padnos College of Engineering and Computing Students: 66 full-time (18 women), 111 part-time (20 women); includes 21 minority (4 Black or African American, non-Hispanic/Latino; 9 Asian, non-Hispanic/Latino; 5 Hispanic/Latino; 3 Two or more races, non-Hispanic/Latino), 74 international. Average age 28. 154 applicants, 78% accepted, 44 enrolled. *Faculty:* 32 full-time (5 women). Expenses: Contact institution. *Financial support:* In 2017–18, 50 students received support, including 7 fellowships, 2 research assistantships with full and partial tuition reimbursements available (averaging $8,000 per year); unspecified assistantships also available. In 2017, 50 master's awarded. *Program availability:* Part-time. Offers engineering and computing (MS, MSE); medical and bioinformatics (MS). *Application deadline:* For fall admission, 2/1 for domestic students. Applications are processed on a rolling basis. *Application fee:* $30. Electronic applications accepted. *Application Contact:* Sara Wheeler, Director, Advising Center, 616-331-6025, Fax: 616-331-6770, E-mail: wheelesa@gvsu.edu. *Dean*, Dr. Paul Plotkowski, 616-331-6260, Fax: 616-331-6770, E-mail: plotkowp@gvsu.edu.

School of Computing and Information Systems Students: 26 full-time (4 women), 59 part-time (13 women); includes 11 minority (2 Black or African American, non-Hispanic/Latino; 5 Asian, non-Hispanic/Latino; 3 Hispanic/Latino; 1 Two or more races, non-Hispanic/Latino), 27 international. Average age 30. 69 applicants, 83% accepted, 24 enrolled. *Faculty:* 10 full-time (0 women). Expenses: Contact institution. *Financial support:* In 2017–18, 11 students received support, including 3 fellowships, 6 research assistantships with full and partial tuition reimbursements available (averaging $8,000 per year). In 2017, 20 master's awarded. *Program availability:* Part-time, evening/weekend. Offers computer information systems (MS); data science and analytics (MS). *Application deadline:* For fall admission, 6/1 for international students; for winter admission, 9/1 for international students. Applications are processed on a rolling basis. *Application fee:* $30. Electronic applications accepted. *Application Contact:* Dr. D. Robert Adams, Graduate Program Director, 616-331-3885, Fax: 616-331-2144, E-mail: adamsr@gvsu.edu. *Director*, Dr. Paul Leidig, 616-331-2060, Fax: 616-331-2144, E-mail: leidigp@gvsu.edu.

School of Engineering Students: 30 full-time (9 women), 40 part-time (2 women); includes 6 minority (1 Black or African American, non-Hispanic/Latino; 2 Asian, non-Hispanic/Latino; 2 Hispanic/Latino; 1 Two or more races, non-Hispanic/Latino), 35 international. Average age 26. 71 applicants, 70% accepted, 13 enrolled. *Faculty:* 21 full-time (5 women). Expenses: Contact institution. *Financial support:* In 2017–18, 35 students received support, including 4 fellowships, 28 research assistantships with full and partial tuition reimbursements available (averaging $4,000 per year); career-related internships or fieldwork, Federal Work-Study, institutionally sponsored loans, scholarships/grants, and unspecified assistantships also available. In 2017, 20 master's awarded. *Program availability:* Part-time, evening/weekend. Offers electrical and computer engineering (MSE); manufacturing operations (MSE); mechanical engineering (MSE); product design and manufacturing engineering (MSE). *Application deadline:* Applications are processed on a rolling basis. *Application fee:* $30. Electronic applications accepted. *Application Contact:* Dr. Shabbir Choudhuri, Graduate Program Director, 616-331-6845, Fax: 616-331-7215, E-mail: choudhus@gvsu.edu. *Director*, Dr. Wael Mokhtar, 616-331-6015, Fax: 616-331-7215, E-mail: mokhtarw@gvsu.edu.

Seidman College of Business Students: 105 full-time (50 women), 165 part-time (60 women); includes 28 minority (3 Black or African American, non-Hispanic/Latino; 9 Asian, non-Hispanic/Latino; 9 Hispanic/Latino; 7 Two or more races, non-Hispanic/Latino), 14 international. Average age 30. 83 applicants, 88% accepted, 42 enrolled. *Faculty:* 22 full-time (9 women), 10 part-time/adjunct (2 women). Expenses: Contact institution. *Financial support:* In 2017–18, 57 students received support, including 37 fellowships, 24 research assistantships; Federal Work-Study, institutionally sponsored loans, and unspecified assistantships also available. Support available to part-time students. Financial award application deadline: 2/15; financial award applicants required to submit FAFSA. In 2017, 131 master's awarded. *Program availability:* Part-time, evening/weekend. Offers accounting (MSA); business (MBA, MSA, MST); business administration (MBA); taxation (MST). *Application deadline:* For fall admission, 8/1 priority date for domestic students, 5/1 priority date for international students; for winter admission, 12/1 priority date for domestic students, 11/1 priority date for international students; for spring admission, 4/1 priority date for domestic students, 3/1 priority date for international students. Applications are processed on a rolling basis. *Application fee:* $30. Electronic applications accepted. *Application Contact:* Koleta Moore, Assistant Dean of Student Engagement, Graduate Program Operations, 616-331-7400, Fax: 616-331-7389, E-mail: moorekol@gvsu.edu. *Dean*, Dr. Diana Lawson, 616-331-7385, Fax: 616-331-7380, E-mail: lawsond1@gvsu.edu.

GRAND VIEW UNIVERSITY, Des Moines, IA 50316-1599

General Information Independent-religious, coed, comprehensive institution.

GRADUATE UNITS

Graduate Studies *Program availability:* Part-time, evening/weekend. Offers athletic training (MS); clinical nurse leader (MSN, Post Master's Certificate); nursing education (MSN, Post Master's Certificate); organizational leadership (MS); sport management (MS); teacher leadership (M Ed); urban education (M Ed). Electronic applications accepted.

GRANITE STATE COLLEGE, Concord, NH 03301

General Information State and locally supported, coed, comprehensive institution. *Enrollment:* 2,019 graduate, professional, and undergraduate students; 28 full-time matriculated graduate/professional students (15 women), 96 part-time matriculated graduate/professional students (68 women). *Enrollment by degree level:* 124 master's. *Graduate faculty:* 3 full-time (all women), 36 part-time/adjunct (18 women). Tuition, state resident: full-time $9450; part-time $525 per credit. Tuition, nonresident: full-time $10,080; part-time $560 per credit. *Graduate housing:* On-campus housing not available. *Student services:* Campus employment opportunities, campus safety program, career counseling, free psychological counseling, services for students with disabilities, writing training. *Library facilities:* GSC Library and Information Commons. *Collection:* Books: 200,000 (digital/electronic); Serial titles: 23,000 (digital/electronic); Databases: 20. Weekly public service hours: 126.

Computer facilities: 120 computers available on campus for general student use. A campuswide network can be accessed. Online class registration is available.
Website: http://www.granite.edu/

General Application Contact: Ana Gonzalez, Administrative Assistant, Office of Graduate Studies, 603-513-1334, Fax: 603-513-1387, E-mail: gsc.graduatestudies@granite.edu.

GRADUATE UNITS

MS in Leadership Program Students: 14 full-time (6 women), 30 part-time (27 women); includes 2 minority (1 American Indian or Alaska Native, non-Hispanic/Latino; 1 Hispanic/Latino). Average age 36. 10 applicants, 90% accepted, 9 enrolled. *Faculty:* 1 (woman) full-time, 10 part-time/adjunct (4 women). Expenses: Contact institution. *Financial support:* Federal Work-Study and National Guard course waivers available. Financial award applicants required to submit FAFSA. In 2017, 32 master's awarded. *Program availability:* Part-time, evening/weekend, 100% online, blended/hybrid learning. Offers leadership (MS). *Application deadline:* Applications are processed on a rolling basis. *Application fee:* $0. Electronic applications accepted. *Application Contact:* Ana Gonzalez, Administrative Assistant, Office of Graduate Studies, 603-822-5433, Fax: 603-513-1387, E-mail: gsc.graduatestudies@granite.edu. *Vice Provost of Academic Affairs*, Dr. Johnna Herrick-Phelps, 603-228-3000, E-mail: johnna.herrick-phelps@granite.edu.

MS in Management Program Students: 1 full-time (0 women), 18 part-time (11 women); includes 2 minority (1 Hispanic/Latino; 1 Two or more races, non-Hispanic/Latino). Average age 38. 5 applicants, 60% accepted, 3 enrolled. *Faculty:* 1 (woman) full-time, 13 part-time/adjunct (3 women). Expenses: Contact institution. *Financial support:* Federal Work-Study and National Guard course waivers available. Financial award applicants required to submit FAFSA. In 2017, 4 master's awarded. *Program availability:* Part-time, 100% online, blended/hybrid learning. Offers management (MS). *Application deadline:* Applications are processed on a rolling basis. *Application fee:* $0. Electronic applications accepted. *Application Contact:* Ana Gonzalez, Administrative Assistant, Office of Graduate Studies, 603-822-5433, Fax: 603-513-1387, E-mail: gsc.graduatestudies@granite.edu. *Vice Provost of Academic Affairs*, Dr. Johnna Herrick-Phelps, 855-228-3000, E-mail: johnna.herrick-phelps@granite.edu.

MS in Project Management Program Students: 9 full-time (5 women), 22 part-time (10 women); includes 2 minority (1 Black or African American, non-Hispanic/Latino; 1 American Indian or Alaska Native, non-Hispanic/Latino). Average age 38. 9 applicants, 100% accepted, 9 enrolled. *Faculty:* 1 (woman) full-time, 7 part-time/adjunct (4 women). Expenses: Contact institution. *Financial support:* Federal Work-Study and National Guard course waivers available. Financial award applicants required to submit FAFSA. In 2017, 23 master's awarded. *Program availability:* Part-time, 100% online, blended/hybrid learning. Offers project management (MS). *Application deadline:* Applications are processed on a rolling basis. *Application fee:* $0. Electronic applications accepted. *Application Contact:* Ana Gonzalez, Administrative Assistant, Office of Graduate Studies, 603-513-1334, Fax: 603-513-1387, E-mail: gsc.graduatestudies@granite.edu. *Vice Provost for Academic Affairs*, Dr. Johnna Herrick-Phelps, 855-228-3000, E-mail: johnna.herrick-phelps@granite.edu.

GRANTHAM UNIVERSITY, Lenexa, KS 66219

General Information Proprietary, coed, comprehensive institution. *Enrollment:* 960 full-time matriculated graduate/professional students (421 women), 527 part-time matriculated graduate/professional students (226 women). *Enrollment by degree level:* 1,455 master's, 32 other advanced degrees. *Graduate faculty:* 2 full-time, 57 part-time/adjunct. *Tuition:* Full-time $3900; part-time $325 per credit hour. *Required fees:* $45 per term. *Student services:* Career counseling, services for students with disabilities, writing training. *Library facilities:* Grantham Online Library.

Computer facilities: Online class registration is available.
Website: http://www.grantham.edu/

General Application Contact: Jared Parlette, Vice President of Student Enrollment, 800-955-2527 Ext. 803, Fax: 866-914-4557, E-mail: admissions@grantham.edu.

GRADUATE UNITS

College of Engineering and Computer Science Students: 167 full-time (52 women), 80 part-time (15 women); includes 131 minority (94 Black or African American, non-Hispanic/Latino; 2 American Indian or Alaska Native, non-Hispanic/Latino; 8 Asian, non-Hispanic/Latino; 16 Hispanic/Latino; 11 Two or more races, non-Hispanic/Latino). Average age 41. 56 applicants, 86% accepted, 42 enrolled. *Faculty:* 1 full-time, 23 part-time/adjunct. Expenses: Contact institution. *Financial support:* Scholarships/grants available. Financial award applicants required to submit FAFSA. In 2017, 71 master's awarded. *Program availability:* Part-time, evening/weekend, online only, 100% online.

Offers information management (MS); information management technology (MS); information technology (MS). *Application deadline:* Applications are processed on a rolling basis. *Application fee:* $0. Electronic applications accepted. *Application Contact:* Jared Parlette, Vice President of Student Enrollment, 800-955-2527 Ext. 803, Fax: 866-914-4557, E-mail: admissions@grantham.edu. *Dean of the College of Engineering and Computer Science*, Dr. Nancy Miller, 913-309-4738, Fax: 855-681-5201, E-mail: nmiller@grantham.edu.

College of Nursing and Allied Health Students: 198 full-time (144 women), 113 part-time (83 women); includes 170 minority (118 Black or African American, non-Hispanic/Latino; 3 American Indian or Alaska Native, non-Hispanic/Latino; 27 Asian, non-Hispanic/Latino; 11 Hispanic/Latino; 2 Native Hawaiian or other Pacific Islander, non-Hispanic/Latino; 9 Two or more races, non-Hispanic/Latino). Average age 41. 95 applicants, 89% accepted, 72 enrolled. *Faculty:* 2 full-time, 34 part-time/adjunct. Expenses: Contact institution. *Financial support:* Scholarships/grants available. Financial award applicants required to submit FAFSA. In 2017, 123 master's awarded. *Program availability:* Part-time, evening/weekend, online only, 100% online. Offers case management (MSN); health systems management (MS); healthcare administration (MHA); nursing education (MSN); nursing informatics (MSN); nursing management and organizational leadership (MSN). *Application deadline:* Applications are processed on a rolling basis. *Application fee:* $0. Electronic applications accepted. *Application Contact:* Jared Parlette, Vice President of Student Enrollment, 800-955-2527 Ext. 803, Fax: 866-914-4557, E-mail: admissions@grantham.edu. *Dean of the College of Nursing and Allied Health*, Dr. Cheryl Rules, 913-309-4783, Fax: 844-897-6490, E-mail: crules@grantham.edu.

Mark Skousen School of Business Students: 610 full-time (231 women), 333 part-time (128 women); includes 466 minority (321 Black or African American, non-Hispanic/Latino; 12 American Indian or Alaska Native, non-Hispanic/Latino; 29 Asian, non-Hispanic/Latino; 71 Hispanic/Latino; 4 Native Hawaiian or other Pacific Islander, non-Hispanic/Latino; 29 Two or more races, non-Hispanic/Latino). Average age 40. 273 applicants, 87% accepted, 202 enrolled. *Faculty:* 1 full-time, 34 part-time/adjunct. Expenses: Contact institution. *Financial support:* Scholarships/grants available. Financial award applicants required to submit FAFSA. In 2017, 362 master's awarded. *Program availability:* Part-time, evening/weekend, online only, 100% online. Offers business administration (MBA); business intelligence (MS); human resources (Certificate); information management (MBA); performance improvement (MS); project management (MBA, Certificate). *Application deadline:* Applications are processed on a rolling basis. *Application fee:* $0. Electronic applications accepted. *Application Contact:* Jared Parlette, Vice President of Student Enrollment, 800-955-2527 Ext. 803, Fax: 866-914-4557, E-mail: admissions@grantham.edu. *Dean of the Mark Skousen School of Business*, Dr. David Marker, 913-309-4747, Fax: 844-260-6287, E-mail: dmarker@grantham.edu.

GRATZ COLLEGE, Melrose Park, PA 19027

General Information Independent-religious, coed, graduate-only institution. *Graduate housing:* On-campus housing not available.

GRADUATE UNITS

Graduate Programs *Program availability:* Part-time, evening/weekend, online learning. Offers education (MA); education leadership (Ed D); Holocaust and genocide studies (MA, PhD); Jewish Christian studies (Graduate Certificate); Jewish communal service (MA, Certificate); Jewish instructional education (MA); Jewish studies (MA); nonprofit management (MS).

GREEN MOUNTAIN COLLEGE, Poultney, VT 05764-1199

General Information Independent, coed, comprehensive institution.

GRADUATE UNITS

Program in Business Administration *Program availability:* Online learning. Offers business administration (MBA). Distance learning only. Electronic applications accepted.

Program in Environmental Studies *Program availability:* Part-time, evening/weekend, online learning. Offers environmental studies (MS). Distance learning only. Electronic applications accepted.

GREENSBORO COLLEGE, Greensboro, NC 27401-1875

General Information Independent-religious, coed, comprehensive institution. *Graduate housing:* Rooms and/or apartments guaranteed to single students and available on a first-come, first-served basis to married students. Housing application deadline: 6/1.

GRADUATE UNITS

Program in Education *Program availability:* Part-time, evening/weekend. Offers elementary education (M Ed); special education (M Ed). Electronic applications accepted.

Program in Teaching English to Speakers of Other Languages *Program availability:* Part-time, evening/weekend. Offers teaching English to speakers of other languages (MA). Electronic applications accepted.

GREENVILLE UNIVERSITY, Greenville, IL 62246-0159

General Information Independent-religious, coed, comprehensive institution. *Graduate housing:* On-campus housing not available.

GRADUATE UNITS

Program in Education Offers education (MAT); elementary education (MAE); secondary education (MAE). Electronic applications accepted.

Program in Leadership and Ministry *Program availability:* Part-time. Offers leadership and ministry (MA). Electronic applications accepted.

GWYNEDD MERCY UNIVERSITY, Gwynedd Valley, PA 19437-0901

General Information Independent-religious, coed, comprehensive institution. *Enrollment:* 2,807 graduate, professional, and undergraduate students; 670 full-time matriculated graduate/professional students (492 women), 56 part-time matriculated graduate/professional students (47 women). *Enrollment by degree level:* 506 master's, 170 doctoral, 50 other advanced degrees. *Graduate faculty:* 7 full-time (5 women), 93 part-time/adjunct (62 women). *Tuition:* Part-time $550 per credit hour. *Required fees:* $17 per credit hour. One-time fee: $165 part-time. Tuition and fees vary according to degree level and program. *Graduate housing:* On-campus housing not available. *Student services:* Campus employment opportunities, campus safety program, career counseling, exercise/wellness program, free psychological counseling, international student services, low-cost health insurance, services for students with disabilities, teacher training, writing training. *Library facilities:* Keiss Library plus 1 other. *Collection:* Books: 84,372 (physical), 150,948 (digital/electronic); Serial titles: 172 (physical), 32,373 (digital/electronic); Databases: 45. Weekly public service hours: 76; students can reserve study rooms.

Computer facilities: 250 computers available on campus for general student use. A campuswide network can be accessed from student residence rooms and from off campus. Online class registration is available.
Website: http://www.gmercyu.edu/

General Application Contact: Admission Counselor, 844-707-9060, E-mail: accelerate@gmercyu.edu.

GRADUATE UNITS

Frances M. Maguire School of Nursing and Health Professions Students: 28 full-time (25 women), 48 part-time (43 women); includes 28 minority (15 Black or African American, non-Hispanic/Latino; 11 Asian, non-Hispanic/Latino; 1 Hispanic/Latino; 1 Two or more races, non-Hispanic/Latino). Average age 37. 72 applicants, 25% accepted, 16 enrolled. *Faculty:* 4 full-time (all women), 1 (woman) part-time/adjunct. Expenses: Contact institution. *Financial support:* In 2017–18, 5 students received support. Scholarships/grants, traineeships, and unspecified assistantships available. Financial award application deadline: 8/30. In 2017, 7 master's awarded. *Program availability:* Part-time, blended/hybrid learning. Offers clinical nurse specialist (MSN); nurse educator (MSN); nurse practitioner (MSN); nursing (DNP). *Application deadline:* For fall admission, 8/1 priority date for domestic students; for winter admission, 12/1 priority date for domestic students. Applications are processed on a rolling basis. Electronic applications accepted. *Application Contact:* Dr. Barbara A. Jones, Director, 215-646-7300 Ext. 407, Fax: 215-641-5564, E-mail: jones.b@gmc.edu. *Dean*, Dr. Andrea D. Hollingsworth, 215-646-7300 Ext. 539, Fax: 215-641-5517, E-mail: hollingsworth.a@gmc.edu.

School of Education Students: 579 full-time (430 women); includes 130 minority (90 Black or African American, non-Hispanic/Latino; 11 Asian, non-Hispanic/Latino; 26 Hispanic/Latino; 3 Two or more races, non-Hispanic/Latino). Average age 36. 127 applicants, 18% accepted, 9 enrolled. *Faculty:* 8 full-time (5 women), 38 part-time/adjunct (24 women). Expenses: Contact institution. *Financial support:* In 2017–18, 2 research assistantships were awarded; career-related internships or fieldwork, Federal Work-Study, institutionally sponsored loans, tuition waivers (full and partial), and unspecified assistantships also available. Financial award applicants required to submit FAFSA. In 2017, 106 master's awarded. *Program availability:* Part-time, evening/weekend, 100% online. Offers education (Ed D); educational administration (MS); master teacher (MS); school counseling (MS); special education (MS). *Application deadline:* Applications are processed on a rolling basis. *Application Contact:* Graduate Program Coordinator, 877-499-6333, E-mail: graduate@gmercyu.edu. *Dean*, Dr. Heather Pfleger, 215-646-7300 Ext. 21581, E-mail: pfleger.h@gmercyu.edu.

School of Graduate and Professional Studies Students: 63 full-time (37 women); includes 20 minority (16 Black or African American, non-Hispanic/Latino; 2 Asian, non-Hispanic/Latino; 2 Hispanic/Latino). Average age 39. *Faculty:* 5 full-time (all women), 22 part-time/adjunct (8 women). Expenses: Contact institution. *Financial support:* Career-related internships or fieldwork, Federal Work-Study, tuition waivers (full and partial), and unspecified assistantships available. Financial award application deadline: 8/31; financial award applicants required to submit FAFSA. In 2017, 56 master's awarded. *Program availability:* Part-time, evening/weekend. Offers health care administration (MBA); management (MSM); strategic management and leadership (MBA). *Application deadline:* Applications are processed on a rolling basis. *Application Contact:* Information Contact, 800-342-5462, Fax: 215-641-5556. *Dean*, Dr. Mary Sortino, 215-646-7300, E-mail: sortino.m@gmercyu.edu.

HALLMARK UNIVERSITY, San Antonio, TX 78230

General Information Independent, coed, comprehensive institution. *Graduate housing:* On-campus housing not available.

GRADUATE UNITS

School of Business Offers global management (MBA).

HAMLINE UNIVERSITY, St. Paul, MN 55104-1284

General Information Independent-religious, coed, comprehensive institution. *Enrollment:* 3,734 graduate, professional, and undergraduate students; 100 full-time matriculated graduate/professional students (70 women), 1,131 part-time matriculated graduate/professional students (781 women). *Enrollment by degree level:* 979 master's, 60 doctoral, 192 other advanced degrees. *Graduate faculty:* 60 full-time (33 women), 132 part-time/adjunct (77 women). *Tuition:* Part-time $466 per credit. *Required fees:* $14 per credit. One-time fee: $150 part-time. Tuition and fees vary according to course level, degree level and program. *Graduate housing:* Rooms and/or apartments available on a first-come, first-served basis to single and married students. Typical cost: $5100 per year ($8988 including board) for single students; $9266 per year ($13,154 including board) for married students. Room and board charges vary according to board plan and housing facility selected. *Student services:* Campus employment opportunities, campus safety program, career counseling, exercise/wellness program, free psychological counseling, international student services, low-cost health insurance, multicultural affairs office, services for students with disabilities, teacher training, writing training. *Library facilities:* Bush Library. *Collection:* Books: 126,680 (physical), 345,792 (digital/electronic); Serial titles: 1,455 (physical), 61,526 (digital/electronic); Databases: 110. Students can reserve study rooms. *Research affiliation:* Minnesota Women Elected Officials.

Computer facilities: 300 computers available on campus for general student use. A campuswide network can be accessed from student residence rooms and from off campus. Online class registration is available.
Website: http://www.hamline.edu/

General Application Contact: Shawn Skoog, Director of Graduate Recruitment and Admission, 651-523-2900, Fax: 651-523-3058, E-mail: sskoog03@hamline.edu.

GRADUATE UNITS

College of Liberal Arts Students: 7 full-time (5 women), 157 part-time (112 women); includes 29 minority (6 Black or African American, non-Hispanic/Latino; 1 American Indian or Alaska Native, non-Hispanic/Latino; 9 Asian, non-Hispanic/Latino; 7 Hispanic/Latino; 6 Two or more races, non-Hispanic/Latino), 1 international. Average age 38. 46 applicants, 65% accepted, 16 enrolled. *Faculty:* 6 full-time (5 women), 6 part-time/adjunct (3 women). Expenses: Contact institution. *Financial support:* Federal Work-Study and scholarships/grants available. Support available to part-time students. Financial award application deadline: 4/20; financial award applicants required to submit FAFSA. In 2017, 44 master's awarded. *Program availability:* Part-time, evening/weekend. Offers creative writing (MFA); creative writing for children and young adults (MFA); law (MSL). *Application deadline:* For fall admission, 6/1 priority date for domestic and international students; for spring admission, 11/1 priority date for domestic students, 10/1 priority date for international students; for summer admission, 3/1 priority date for domestic students, 2/1 priority date for international students. Applications are processed on a rolling basis. *Application fee:* $0 ($100 for international students). Electronic applications accepted. *Application Contact:* Shawn Skoog, Director of Graduate Recruitment and Admission, 651-523-2900, Fax: 651-523-3058, E-mail: gradprog@hamline.edu. *Dean*, Dr. Marcela Kostihova, 651-523-2206, Fax: 651-523-3055, E-mail: cladean@hamline.edu.

School of Business Students: 18 full-time (8 women), 309 part-time (165 women); includes 89 minority (43 Black or African American, non-Hispanic/Latino; 3 American Indian or Alaska Native, non-Hispanic/Latino; 22 Asian, non-Hispanic/Latino; 12 Hispanic/Latino; 9 Two or more races, non-Hispanic/Latino), 15 international. Average age 34. 174 applicants, 61% accepted, 68 enrolled. *Faculty:* 16 full-time (6 women), 15 part-time/adjunct (4 women). Expenses: Contact institution. *Financial support:* Career-related internships or fieldwork, Federal Work-Study, scholarships/grants, and unspecified assistantships available. Support available to part-time students. Financial award application deadline: 4/20; financial award applicants required to submit FAFSA. In 2017, 152 master's, 4 doctorates awarded. *Program availability:* Part-time, evening/weekend, blended/hybrid learning. Offers business administration (MBA); nonprofit management (MNM); public administration (MPA, DPA). *Application deadline:* For fall admission, 6/1 for domestic and international students; for spring admission, 11/1 for domestic students, 10/1 for international students; for summer admission, 3/1 for domestic students, 2/1 for international students. Applications are processed on a rolling basis. *Application fee:* $0 ($100 for international students). Electronic applications accepted. *Application Contact:* Shawn Skoog, Director of Graduate Recruitment and Admission, 651-523-2900, Fax: 651-523-3058, E-mail: gradprog@hamline.edu. *Dean*, Dr. Anne McCarthy, 651-523-2284, Fax: 651-523-3098, E-mail: hsb@hamline.edu.

School of Education Students: 79 full-time (60 women), 898 part-time (692 women); includes 139 minority (31 Black or African American, non-Hispanic/Latino; 1 American Indian or Alaska Native, non-Hispanic/Latino; 58 Asian, non-Hispanic/Latino; 33 Hispanic/Latino; 16 Two or more races, non-Hispanic/Latino), 8 international. Average age 35. 366 applicants, 78% accepted, 193 enrolled. *Faculty:* 23 full-time (15 women), 43 part-time/adjunct (30 women). Expenses: Contact institution. *Financial support:* Career-related internships or fieldwork, Federal Work-Study, and scholarships/grants available. Support available to part-time students. Financial award application deadline: 4/20; financial award applicants required to submit FAFSA. In 2017, 236 master's, 7 doctorates awarded. *Program availability:* Part-time, evening/weekend, 100% online, blended/hybrid learning. Offers education (MA Ed, Ed D); English as a second language (MA); literacy education (MA); natural science and environmental education (MA Ed); teaching (MAT); teaching English to speakers of other languages (MA). *Application deadline:* For fall admission, 6/1 for domestic and international students; for spring admission, 11/1 for domestic and international students; for summer admission, 3/1 for domestic and international students. Applications are processed on a rolling basis. *Application fee:* $0 ($100 for international students). Electronic applications accepted. *Application Contact:* Shawn Skoog, Director of Graduate Recruitment and Admission, 651-523-2900, Fax: 651-523-3058, E-mail: gradprog@hamline.edu. *Dean*, Dr. Marcela Kostihova, 651-523-2206, Fax: 651-523-2489, E-mail: cladean@hamline.edu.

HAMPTON UNIVERSITY, Hampton, VA 23668

General Information Independent, coed, comprehensive institution. CGS member. *Enrollment:* 4,619 graduate, professional, and undergraduate students; 352 full-time matriculated graduate/professional students (239 women), 149 part-time matriculated graduate/professional students (112 women). *Enrollment by degree level:* 284 master's, 217 doctoral. *Tuition:* Full-time $22,630; part-time $575 per semester hour. *Required fees:* $70. Tuition and fees vary according to program. *Graduate housing:* Rooms and/or apartments available on a first-come, first-served basis to single and married students. Housing application deadline: 6/1. *Student services:* Campus employment opportunities, campus safety program, career counseling, child daycare facilities, exercise/wellness program, free psychological counseling, international student services, services for students with disabilities, teacher training, writing training. *Library facilities:* William R. and Norma B. Harvey Library plus 4 others. *Collection:* Books: 307,143 (physical), 91,991 (digital/electronic); Serial titles: 8,240 (physical); Databases: 115. Study areas open 24 hours, 5–7 days a week; students can reserve study rooms. *Research affiliation:* NASA Langley Research Center (physical sciences), Southeastern Universities Research Association (science), Continuous Electron Beam Accelerator Facility (science).

Computer facilities: Computer purchase and lease plans are available. 1,500 computers available on campus for general student use. A campuswide network can be accessed from student residence rooms and from off campus. Online class registration, learning management system are available.
Website: http://www.hamptonu.edu/

General Application Contact: Dr. Michelle Penn-Marshall, Dean, Graduate College, 757-727-5454, E-mail: hugrad@hamptonu.edu.

GRADUATE UNITS

Program in Business Administration Students: 25 full-time (17 women), 18 part-time (15 women); includes 40 minority (39 Black or African American, non-Hispanic/Latino; 1 Hispanic/Latino), 1 international. Average age 30. 29 applicants, 21% accepted, 1 enrolled. Expenses: Contact institution. *Financial support:* Teaching assistantships, career-related internships or fieldwork, Federal Work-Study, institutionally sponsored loans, scholarships/grants, unspecified assistantships, and stipends available. Support available to part-time students. Financial award application deadline: 6/30; financial award applicants required to submit FAFSA. In 2017, 29 master's, 4 doctorates awarded. *Program availability:* Part-time, online learning. Offers business administration (MBA, PhD). *Application deadline:* For fall admission, 6/1 priority date for domestic students, 4/1 priority date for international students; for spring admission, 11/1 priority date for domestic students, 9/1 priority date for international students; for summer admission, 4/1 priority date for domestic students, 2/1 priority date for international students. Applications are processed on a rolling basis. *Application fee:* $35. Electronic applications accepted. *Dean, School of Business*, Dr. Ziette Hayes, 757-727-5361.

School of Liberal Arts and Education Students: 85 full-time (52 women), 75 part-time (52 women); includes 144 minority (all Black or African American, non-Hispanic/Latino), 1 international. Average age 33. 79 applicants, 41% accepted, 4 enrolled. Expenses: Contact institution. *Financial support:* Fellowships, research assistantships, teaching assistantships, career-related internships or fieldwork, Federal Work-Study, institutionally sponsored loans, and scholarships/grants available. Support available to part-time students. Financial award application deadline: 5/1; financial award applicants required to submit FAFSA. In 2017, 37 master's, 10 doctorates awarded. *Program availability:* Part-time, evening/weekend. Offers biology education 6-12 (MT); college student development (MA); community agency counseling (MA); counseling (Ed S); counselor education and supervision (PhD); educational leadership (MA); educational management (PhD); English education 6-12 (MT); intercollegiate athletics (MS); international sports (MS); liberal arts and education (MA, MS, MT, PhD, Ed S); marriage and family studies (MS); mathematics education 6-12 (MT); music education PreK-12 (MT); organizational behavior and sport business leadership (MS); pastoral counseling (MA); psychology (MS); school counseling (MA). *Application deadline:* For fall admission, 6/1 priority date for domestic students, 4/1 priority date for international students; for winter admission, 9/1 priority date for international students; for spring admission, 11/1 for domestic students; for summer admission, 4/15 for domestic students, 2/1 priority date for international students. Applications are processed on a rolling basis. *Application fee:* $35. Electronic applications accepted. *Application Contact:* Dr. Michelle Penn-Marshall, Dean, Graduate College, 757-727-5454, E-mail: hugrad@hamptonu.edu. *Dean*, Dr. Linda Malone-Colon, 757-727-5400.

School of Nursing Students: 6 full-time (all women), 28 part-time (25 women); includes 31 minority (29 Black or African American, non-Hispanic/Latino; 2 Hispanic/Latino). Average age 48. 7 applicants, 14% accepted. Expenses: Contact institution. *Financial support:* In 2017–18, 2 students received support. Fellowships, research assistantships, teaching assistantships, career-related internships or fieldwork, Federal Work-Study, institutionally sponsored loans, and scholarships/grants available. Support available to part-time students. Financial award application deadline: 6/30; financial award applicants required to submit FAFSA. In 2017, 3 master's, 4 doctorates awarded. *Program availability:* Part-time, online learning. Offers community health nursing (MS); family nurse practitioner (MS); family research (PhD); nursing administration (MS); nursing education (MS). *Application deadline:* For fall admission, 6/1 priority date for domestic students, 4/1 priority date for international students; for spring admission, 11/1 priority date for domestic students, 9/1 priority date for international students; for summer admission, 4/1 priority date for domestic students, 2/1 priority date for international students. Applications are processed on a rolling basis. *Application fee:* $35. Electronic applications accepted. *Dean*, Dr. Shevallanie Lott, 757-727-5654, E-mail: shevellanie.lott@hamptonu.edu.

School of Science Students: 236 full-time (164 women), 28 part-time (20 women); includes 185 minority (157 Black or African American, non-Hispanic/Latino; 3 American Indian or Alaska Native, non-Hispanic/Latino; 15 Asian, non-Hispanic/Latino; 10 Hispanic/Latino), 11 international. Average age 26. 823 applicants, 12% accepted, 49 enrolled. Expenses: Contact institution. *Financial support:* Fellowships, research assistantships, teaching assistantships, career-related internships or fieldwork, Federal Work-Study, institutionally sponsored loans, scholarships/grants, and stipends available. Support available to part-time students. Financial award application deadline: 6/30; financial award applicants required to submit FAFSA. In 2017, 50 master's, 23 doctorates awarded. *Program availability:* Part-time, evening/weekend, online learning. Offers atmospheric science (MS, PhD); biology (MS); chemistry (MS); computational mathematics (MS); computer science (MS); environmental science (MS); information assurance (MS); medical physics (MS, PhD); medical science (MS); nonlinear science (MS); nuclear physics (MS, PhD); optical physics (MS, PhD); physical therapy (DPT); planetary science (MS, PhD); science (MA, MS, DPT, PhD); speech-language pathology (MA); statistics and probability (MS). *Application deadline:* For fall admission, 6/1 for domestic students, 4/1 for international students; for winter admission, 11/1 for domestic students, 9/1 for international students; for spring admission, 11/1 for domestic students; for summer admission, 4/1 for domestic students, 2/1 for international students. Applications are processed on a rolling basis. *Application fee:* $35. Electronic applications accepted. *Dean*, Dr. Calvin Lowe, 757-722-5239.

HANNIBAL-LAGRANGE UNIVERSITY, Hannibal, MO 63401-1999

General Information Independent-religious, coed, comprehensive institution.

GRADUATE UNITS

Program in Education *Program availability:* Part-time, evening/weekend. Offers literacy (MS Ed); teaching and learning (MS Ed).

HARDING SCHOOL OF THEOLOGY, Memphis, TN 38117-5499

General Information Independent-religious, coed, primarily men, graduate-only institution. *Enrollment by degree level:* 101 master's, 13 doctoral, 13 other advanced degrees. *Graduate faculty:* 6 full-time (0 women), 2 part-time/adjunct (1 woman). *Tuition:* Full-time $14,000. *Required fees:* $525. One-time fee: $40 full-time. *Graduate housing:* Rooms and/or apartments available on a first-come, first-served basis to single and married students. Typical cost: $7000 per year for married students. *Student services:* Career counseling, low-cost health insurance. *Library facilities:* Harding School of Theology Library. *Collection:* Books: 121,000 (physical); Serial titles: 23,000 (physical); Databases: 62. Weekly public service hours: 63; students can reserve study rooms.

Computer facilities: 20 computers available on campus for general student use. A campuswide network can be accessed from student residence rooms and from off campus. Online class registration, X are available.
Website: http://hst.edu/

General Application Contact: Dr. Matt R. Carter, Director of Admissions, 901-761-1356, Fax: 901-761-1358, E-mail: mrcarter@harding.edu.

GRADUATE UNITS

Graduate Programs Students: 28 full-time (7 women), 99 part-time (7 women); includes 26 minority (23 Black or African American, non-Hispanic/Latino; 2 Asian, non-Hispanic/Latino; 1 Hispanic/Latino), 2 international. *Faculty:* 6 full-time (0 women), 2 part-time/adjunct (1 woman). Expenses: Contact institution. *Financial support:* Research assistantships with partial tuition reimbursements, career-related internships or fieldwork, institutionally sponsored loans, scholarships/grants, tuition waivers (partial), and unspecified assistantships available. Support available to part-time students. Financial award application deadline: 3/1; financial award applicants required to submit FAFSA. *Program availability:* Part-time, online learning. Offers Christian ministry (MA); historical theology (MA); ministry (M Div); New Testament (MA); Old Testament (MA); systematic theology (MA); transforming leadership (D Min). *Application deadline:* For fall admission, 12/7 priority date for domestic students; for spring admission, 5/3 priority date for domestic students. Applications are processed on a rolling basis. *Application fee:* $40. Electronic applications accepted. *Application Contact:* Dr. Matt R. Carter, Director of Admissions, 901-761-1356, Fax: 901-761-1358, E-mail: mrcarter@harding.edu. *Dean*, Dr. Allen Black, 901-761-1352, Fax: 901-761-1358, E-mail: ablack@hst.edu.

HARDING UNIVERSITY, Searcy, AR 72149-0001

General Information Independent-religious, coed, university. *Enrollment:* 5,539 graduate, professional, and undergraduate students; 660 full-time matriculated graduate/professional students (438 women), 697 part-time matriculated graduate/professional students (452 women). *Enrollment by degree level:* 986 master's, 354 doctoral, 17 other advanced degrees. *Graduate faculty:* 88 full-time (44 women), 96 part-time/adjunct (46 women). Tuition and fees vary according to course load, degree level, campus/location and program. *Graduate housing:* Rooms and/or apartments available on a first-come, first-served basis to single and married students. *Student services:* Campus employment opportunities, campus safety program, career counseling, exercise/wellness program, free psychological counseling, international student services, services for students with disabilities, writing training. *Library facilities:* Brackett Library plus 1 other. *Collection:* Books: 187,048 (physical), 286,079 (digital/electronic); Serial titles: 959 (physical), 78,392 (digital/electronic); Databases: 178. Students can reserve study rooms.

Computer facilities: 512 computers available on campus for general student use. A campuswide network can be accessed from student residence rooms and from off campus. Online class registration is available.
Website: http://www.harding.edu/

GRADUATE UNITS

Cannon-Clary College of Education Students: 135 full-time (95 women), 316 part-time (231 women); includes 77 minority (46 Black or African American, non-Hispanic/Latino; 7 American Indian or Alaska Native, non-Hispanic/Latino; 4 Asian, non-Hispanic/Latino; 9 Hispanic/Latino; 11 Two or more races, non-Hispanic/Latino), 11 international. Average age 34. 128 applicants, 87% accepted, 111 enrolled. *Faculty:* 22 full-time (9 women), 51 part-time/adjunct (37 women). Expenses: Contact institution. *Financial support:* In 2017–18, 33 students received support. Unspecified assistantships available. In 2017, 153 master's, 24 other advanced degrees awarded. *Program availability:* Part-time, evening/weekend. Offers advanced studies in teaching and learning (M Ed); art (MSE); behavioral science (MSE); counseling (MS, Ed S); early childhood special education (M Ed, MSE); education (MSE); educational leadership (M Ed, Ed S); elementary education (M Ed); English (MSE); French (MSE); history/social science (MSE); kinesiology (MSE); math (MSE); reading (M Ed); secondary education (M Ed); Spanish (MSE); teaching (MAT); teaching English as a second language (MSE). *Application deadline:* For fall admission, 8/1 for domestic and international students; for spring admission, 1/1 for domestic and international students. Applications are processed on a rolling basis. *Application fee:* $35. *Application Contact:* Information Contact, 501-279-4315, E-mail: gradstudiesedu@harding.edu. *Chair,* Dr. Clara Carroll, 501-279-4501, Fax: 501-279-4083, E-mail: ccarroll@harding.edu.

College of Allied Health Students: 245 full-time (170 women), 78 part-time (2 women); includes 30 minority (8 Black or African American, non-Hispanic/Latino; 3 American Indian or Alaska Native, non-Hispanic/Latino; 9 Asian, non-Hispanic/Latino; 9 Hispanic/Latino; 1 Two or more races, non-Hispanic/Latino). Average age 26. 1,084 applicants, 16% accepted, 90 enrolled. *Faculty:* 27 full-time (16 women), 4 part-time/adjunct (2 women). Expenses: Contact institution. *Financial support:* In 2017–18, 6 students received support. In 2017, 53 master's, 28 doctorates awarded. Offers allied health (MS, DPT); communication sciences and disorders (MS); physical therapy (DPT); physician assistant (MS). *Application Contact:* Dr. Julie Hixson-Wallace, Vice Provost, 501-279-5205, Fax: 501-279-5192, E-mail: jahixson@harding.edu.

College of Bible and Ministry Students: 13 part-time (1 woman); includes 1 minority (Black or African American, non-Hispanic/Latino). Average age 48. *Faculty:* 3 full-time (1 woman). Expenses: Contact institution. *Financial support:* In 2017–18, 12 students received support. Scholarships/grants and unspecified assistantships available. Financial award applicants required to submit FAFSA. In 2017, 6 master's awarded. *Program availability:* Part-time, online learning. Offers Bible and ministry (M Min). *Application Contact:* 501-279-4448, Fax: 501-279-5192, E-mail: bible@harding.edu. *Dean,* Dr. Monte Cox, 501-279-4448, Fax: 501-279-4042, E-mail: mcox@harding.edu.

College of Pharmacy Students: 209 full-time (138 women), 4 part-time (3 women); includes 54 minority (21 Black or African American, non-Hispanic/Latino; 3 American Indian or Alaska Native, non-Hispanic/Latino; 25 Asian, non-Hispanic/Latino; 4 Hispanic/Latino; 1 Two or more races, non-Hispanic/Latino), 8 international. Average age 27. 293 applicants, 19% accepted, 36 enrolled. *Faculty:* 34 full-time (18 women), 1 part-time/adjunct (0 women). Expenses: Contact institution. *Financial support:* In 2017–18, 35 students received support. Scholarships/grants available. Financial award applicants required to submit FAFSA. In 2017, 55 doctorates awarded. Offers pharmacy (Pharm D). *Application deadline:* For fall admission, 3/1 priority date for domestic and international students. Applications are processed on a rolling basis. *Application fee:* $50. Electronic applications accepted. *Application Contact:* Carol Jones, Director of Admissions, 501-279-5523, Fax: 501-279-5525, E-mail: ccjones@harding.edu. *Dean,* Dr. Jeff Mercer, 501-279-5205, Fax: 501-279-5525, E-mail: jmercer@harding.edu.

Paul R. Carter College of Business Administration Students: 15 full-time (8 women), 90 part-time (36 women); includes 12 minority (8 Black or African American, non-Hispanic/Latino; 2 Asian, non-Hispanic/Latino; 2 Hispanic/Latino), 2 international. Average age 34. 15 applicants, 100% accepted, 15 enrolled. *Faculty:* 26 part-time/adjunct (6 women). Expenses: Contact institution. *Financial support:* Unspecified assistantships available. Financial award application deadline: 7/30; financial award applicants required to submit FAFSA. In 2017, 66 master's awarded. *Program availability:* Part-time, evening/weekend, 100% online. Offers international business (MBA); leadership and organizational management (MBA). *Application deadline:* For fall admission, 8/1 priority date for domestic and international students; for spring admission, 12/1 priority date for domestic and international students. Applications are processed on a rolling basis. *Application fee:* $40.

HARDIN-SIMMONS UNIVERSITY, Abilene, TX 79698-0001

General Information Independent-religious, coed, comprehensive institution. *Enrollment:* 2,252 graduate, professional, and undergraduate students; 253 full-time matriculated graduate/professional students (136 women), 252 part-time matriculated graduate/professional students (123 women). *Enrollment by degree level:* 141 master's, 34 doctoral, 2 other advanced degrees. *Graduate faculty:* 81 full-time (33 women), 34 part-time/adjunct (8 women). *Tuition:* Full-time $13,500; part-time $750 per semester hour. *Required fees:* $220 per term. One-time fee: $50. Tuition and fees vary according to course load, campus/location and program. *Graduate housing:* Rooms and/or apartments available on a first-come, first-served basis to single and married students. Typical cost: $2200 per year for married students. Room charges vary according to campus/location and housing facility selected. *Student services:* Campus employment opportunities, career counseling, free psychological counseling, international student services, services for students with disabilities. *Library facilities:* Richardson Library plus 1 other. *Collection:* Books: 254,854 (physical), 120,497 (digital/electronic); Serial titles: 212 (physical), 48,069 (digital/electronic); Databases: 141. Weekly public service hours: 89.

Computer facilities: 115 computers available on campus for general student use. A campuswide network can be accessed from student residence rooms and from off campus. Online class registration is available.
Website: http://www.hsutx.edu/

General Application Contact: Joel Templeton, Graduate Admissions Counselor, 325-670-1682, Fax: 325-671-2115, E-mail: gradoff@hsutx.edu.

GRADUATE UNITS

Graduate School Students: 253 full-time (136 women), 252 part-time (123 women); includes 124 minority (42 Black or African American, non-Hispanic/Latino; 9 Asian, non-Hispanic/Latino; 68 Hispanic/Latino; 5 Two or more races, non-Hispanic/Latino), 16 international. Average age 35. *Faculty:* 66 full-time (29 women), 30 part-time/adjunct (9 women). Expenses: Contact institution. *Financial support:* In 2017–18, 346 students received support. Fellowships, career-related internships or fieldwork, scholarships/grants, and recreation assistantships, coaching assistantships available. Support available to part-time students. Financial award application deadline: 6/30; financial award applicants required to submit FAFSA. In 2017, 121 master's, 33 doctorates awarded. *Program availability:* Part-time. *Application deadline:* For fall admission, 8/15 priority date for domestic students, 4/1 for international students; for spring admission, 1/5 priority date for domestic students, 9/1 for international students. Applications are processed on a rolling basis. *Application fee:* $50. Electronic applications accepted. *Application Contact:* Joel Templeton, Graduate Admissions Counselor, 325-670-1682, E-mail: gradoff@hsutx.edu. *Dean of Graduate Studies,* Dr. Nancy Kucinski, 325-670-1298, Fax: 325-670-1564, E-mail: gradoff@hsutx.edu.

College of Fine Arts Students: 4 full-time (2 women), 2 part-time (0 women); includes 3 minority (1 Hispanic/Latino; 2 Two or more races, non-Hispanic/Latino). Average age 29. 2 applicants, 50% accepted, 1 enrolled. *Faculty:* 14 full-time (4 women), 1 part-time/adjunct (0 women). Expenses: Contact institution. *Financial support:* In 2017–18, 6 students received support, including 3 fellowships (averaging $1,213 per year); career-related internships or fieldwork and scholarships/grants also available. Support available to part-time students. Financial award application deadline: 6/30; financial award applicants required to submit FAFSA. In 2017, 3 master's awarded. *Program availability:* Part-time. Offers church music (MM); music education (MM); music performance (MM); theory and composition (MM). *Application deadline:* For fall admission, 8/15 priority date for domestic students, 4/1 for international students; for spring admission, 1/5 priority date for domestic students, 9/1 for international students. Applications are processed on a rolling basis. *Application fee:* $50 ($150 for international students). Electronic applications accepted. *Application Contact:* Dr. Nancy Kucinski, Dean of Graduate Studies, 325-670-1298, Fax: 325-670-1564, E-mail: gradoff@hsutx.edu. *Program Director,* Dr. Lynnette Chambers, 325-670-1430, Fax: 325-670-5873, E-mail: lchambers@hsutx.edu.

College of Human Sciences and Educational Studies Students: 26 full-time (14 women), 99 part-time (69 women); includes 33 minority (16 Black or African American, non-Hispanic/Latino; 1 Asian, non-Hispanic/Latino; 13 Hispanic/Latino; 3 Two or more races, non-Hispanic/Latino), 4 international. Average age 33. 57 applicants, 98% accepted, 40 enrolled. *Faculty:* 13 full-time (8 women), 5 part-time/adjunct (3 women). Expenses: Contact institution. *Financial support:* In 2017–18, 50 students received support. Fellowships, career-related internships or fieldwork, scholarships/grants, and coaching assistantships available. Support available to part-time students. Financial award application deadline: 6/30; financial award applicants required to submit FAFSA. In 2017, 34 master's, 1 doctorate awarded. *Program availability:* Part-time. Offers counseling and human development (M Ed); educational leadership in superintendency (Ed D); gifted education (M Ed); higher education leadership (Ed D); human sciences and educational studies (M Ed, Ed D); kinesiology, sport, and recreation (M Ed); reading education (M Ed); reading specialist education (M Ed). *Application deadline:* For fall admission, 8/15 priority date for domestic students, 4/1 for international students; for spring admission, 1/5 priority date for domestic students, 9/1 for international students. Applications are processed on a rolling basis. *Application fee:* $50. Electronic applications accepted. *Application Contact:* Dr. Nancy Kucinski, Dean of Graduate Studies, 325-670-1298, Fax: 325-670-1564, E-mail: gradoff@hsutx.edu. *Dean,* Dr. Perry Kay Brown, 325-670-1021, Fax: 325-670-5859, E-mail: pkbrown@hsutx.edu.

Cynthia Ann Parker College of Liberal Arts Students: 25 full-time (19 women), 7 part-time (4 women); includes 3 minority (1 Black or African American, non-Hispanic/Latino; 1 Hispanic/Latino; 1 Two or more races, non-Hispanic/Latino), 1 international. Average age 31. *Faculty:* 15 full-time (7 women), 1 part-time/adjunct (0 women). Expenses: Contact institution. *Financial support:* In 2017–18, 25 students received support, including 18 fellowships (averaging $550 per year); scholarships/grants also available. Support available to part-time students. Financial award application deadline: 6/30; financial award applicants required to submit FAFSA. In 2017, 14 master's awarded. *Program availability:* Part-time. Offers clinical counseling and marriage and family therapy (MA); English (MA); history (MA); liberal arts (MA). *Application deadline:* For fall admission, 8/15 priority date for domestic students, 4/1 for international students; for spring admission, 1/5 priority date for domestic students, 9/1 for international students. Applications are processed on a rolling basis. *Application fee:* $50. Electronic applications accepted. *Application Contact:* Dr. Nancy Kucinski, Dean of Graduate Studies, 325-670-1298, Fax: 325-670-1564, E-mail: gradoff@hsutx.edu. *Dean,* Dr. Stephen Cook, 325-670-1487, E-mail: stephen.cook@hsutx.edu.

Holland School of Sciences and Mathematics Students: 115 full-time (77 women), 8 part-time (6 women); includes 25 minority (6 Black or African American, non-Hispanic/Latino; 2 Asian, non-Hispanic/Latino; 17 Hispanic/Latino), 1 international. Average age 25. 1,156 applicants, 7% accepted, 62 enrolled. *Faculty:* 29 full-time (15 women), 6 part-time/adjunct (4 women). Expenses: Contact institution. *Financial support:* In 2017–18, 108 students received support. Fellowships, career-related internships or fieldwork, and scholarships/grants available. Support available to part-time students. Financial award application deadline: 6/30; financial award applicants required to submit FAFSA. In 2017, 10 master's, 29 doctorates awarded. *Program availability:* Part-time. Offers environmental management (MS); mathematics (MS); physical therapy (DPT); physician assistant studies (MPAS). *Application deadline:* For fall admission, 8/15 priority date for domestic students, 4/1 for international students; for spring admission, 1/5 priority date for domestic students, 9/1 for international students. Applications are processed on a rolling basis. *Application fee:* $50 ($150 for international students). Electronic applications accepted. *Application Contact:* Dr. Nancy Kucinski, Dean of Graduate Studies, 325-670-1298, Fax: 325-670-1564, E-mail: gradoff@hsutx.edu. *Dean,* Dr. Christopher McNair, 325-670-1401, Fax: 325-670-1385, E-mail: cmcnair@hsutx.edu.

Kelley College of Business Students: 17 full-time (7 women), 14 part-time (5 women); includes 5 minority (1 Black or African American, non-Hispanic/Latino; 4 Hispanic/Latino), 2 international. Average age 26. 25 applicants, 100% accepted, 15 enrolled. *Faculty:* 6 full-time (3 women). Expenses: Contact institution. *Financial support:* In 2017–18, 22 students received support. Fellowships and scholarships/grants available. Support available to part-time students. Financial award application deadline: 6/30; financial award applicants required to submit FAFSA. In 2017, 14 master's awarded. *Program availability:* Part-time. Offers business administration (MBA); information science (MS); sports management (MBA). *Application deadline:* For fall admission, 8/15 priority date for domestic students, 4/1 for international students; for spring admission, 1/5 priority date for domestic students, 9/1 for international students. Applications are processed on a rolling basis. *Application fee:* $50. Electronic applications accepted. *Application Contact:* Dr. Nancy Kucinski, Dean of Graduate Studies, 325-670-1298, Fax: 325-670-1564, E-mail: gradoff@hsutx.edu. *Program Director,* Dr. Jennifer Plantier, 325-671-2166, Fax: 325-670-1523, E-mail: jplantier@hsutx.edu.

Logsdon Seminary Students: 52 full-time (13 women), 98 part-time (30 women); includes 41 minority (14 Black or African American, non-Hispanic/Latino; 5 Asian, non-Hispanic/Latino; 22 Hispanic/Latino), 1 international. Average age 41. *Faculty:* 13 full-time (3 women), 27 part-time/adjunct (2 women). Expenses: Contact institution. *Financial support:* In 2017–18, 145 students received support. Fellowships and scholarships/grants available. Support available to part-time students. Financial award application deadline: 6/30; financial award applicants required to submit FAFSA. In 2017, 4 master's, 3 doctorates awarded. *Program availability:* Part-time, evening/weekend. Offers family ministry (MA); ministry (D Min); religion (MA); theology (M Div, MA, D Min). *Application deadline:* For fall admission, 8/15 priority date for domestic students, 4/1 for international students; for spring admission, 1/5 priority date for domestic students, 9/1 for international students. Applications are processed on a rolling basis. *Application fee:* $50 ($150 for international students). Electronic applications accepted. *Application Contact:* Dr. Nancy Kucinski, Dean of Graduate Studies, 325-670-1298, Fax: 325-670-1564, E-mail: gradoff@hsutx.edu. *Dean*, Dr. Don Williford, 325-670-1491, Fax: 325-671-2157, E-mail: willifrd@hsutx.edu.

Patty Hanks Shelton School of Nursing Students: 17 part-time (8 women); includes 5 minority (1 Black or African American, non-Hispanic/Latino; 1 Asian, non-Hispanic/Latino; 3 Hispanic/Latino), 1 international. Average age 36. *Faculty:* 2 full-time (both women), 1 (woman) part-time/adjunct. Expenses: Contact institution. *Financial support:* In 2017–18, 10 students received support. Career-related internships or fieldwork and scholarships/grants available. Support available to part-time students. Financial award application deadline: 6/30; financial award applicants required to submit FAFSA. In 2017, 7 master's awarded. *Program availability:* Part-time. Offers education (MSN); family nurse practitioner (MSN). Programs offered jointly with McMurry University. *Application deadline:* For fall admission, 8/15 priority date for domestic students, 4/1 for international students; for spring admission, 1/5 priority date for domestic students, 9/1 for international students. Applications are processed on a rolling basis. *Application fee:* $50 ($150 for international students). Electronic applications accepted. *Application Contact:* Dr. Nancy Kucinski, Dean of Graduate Studies, 325-670-1298, Fax: 325-670-1564, E-mail: gradoff@hsutx.edu. *Dean*, Dr. Nina Ouimette, 325-671-2357, Fax: 325-671-2386, E-mail: nouimette@phssn.edu.

HARRISBURG UNIVERSITY OF SCIENCE AND TECHNOLOGY, Harrisburg, PA 17101

General Information Independent, coed, comprehensive institution. *Graduate housing:* On-campus housing not available. *Research affiliation:* MistIQ Technologies (data analytics), WildFig Data Company (data analytics).

GRADUATE UNITS

Learning Technologies and Media Systems Program *Program availability:* Part-time, evening/weekend. Offers games and simulations (MS); instructional design (MS); instructional development (MS); instructional technology (MS); integration and leadership (MS). Electronic applications accepted.

Program in Human-Centered Interaction Design Offers human-centered interaction design (MS).

Program in Information Systems Engineering and Management *Program availability:* Part-time, evening/weekend. Offers analytics (MS); digital government (MS); digital health (MS); entrepreneurship (MS); information security (MS); software engineering and systems development (MS). Electronic applications accepted.

Program in Project Management *Program availability:* Part-time, evening/weekend. Offers information technology (MS). Electronic applications accepted.

Program in Techpreneurship Offers techpreneurship (MS).

HARRISON MIDDLETON UNIVERSITY, Tempe, AZ 85282

General Information Independent, coed, graduate-only institution.

GRADUATE UNITS

Graduate Program *Program availability:* Part-time, evening/weekend, online learning. Offers education (MA, Ed D); humanities (MA); imaginative literature (MA); interdisciplinary studies (DA); jurisprudence (MA); natural science (MA); philosophy and religion (MA); social science (MA). Electronic applications accepted.

HARTFORD SEMINARY, Hartford, CT 06105-2279

General Information Independent-religious, coed, graduate-only institution. *Graduate housing:* Rooms and/or apartments available on a first-come, first-served basis to single and married students. Housing application deadline: 7/15.

GRADUATE UNITS

Graduate Programs *Program availability:* Part-time, evening/weekend, online learning. Offers Islamic studies (MA); ministry (D Min); religious studies (MA); spirituality (Certificate).

HARVARD UNIVERSITY, Cambridge, MA 02138

General Information Independent, coed, university. CGS member. *Graduate housing:* Rooms and/or apartments available on a first-come, first-served basis to single and married students. *Research affiliation:* Woods Hole Oceanographic Institution (biology).

GRADUATE UNITS

Cyprus International Institute for the Environment and Public Health in Association with Harvard School of Public Health Offers environmental health (MS); environmental/public health (PhD); epidemiology and biostatistics (MS). Electronic applications accepted.

Extension School *Program availability:* Part-time, evening/weekend. Offers applied sciences (CAS); biotechnology (ALM); educational technologies (ALM); educational technology (CET); English for graduate and professional studies (DGP); environmental management (ALM, CEM); information technology (ALM); journalism (ALM); liberal arts (ALM); management (ALM, CM); mathematics for teaching (ALM); museum studies (ALM); premedical studies (Diploma); publication and communication (CPC).

Graduate School of Arts and Sciences Offers African and African American studies (PhD); African history (PhD); Akkadian and Sumerian (AM, PhD); American history (PhD); ancient art (PhD); ancient Near Eastern art (PhD); ancient, medieval, early modern, and modern Europe (PhD); anthropology and Middle Eastern studies (PhD); Arabic (AM, PhD); archaeology (PhD); architecture (PhD); Armenian (AM, PhD); arts and sciences (AM, MDE, ME, MFS, SM, PhD); astronomy (PhD); astrophysics (PhD); Baroque art (PhD); biblical history (AM, PhD); biochemical chemistry (PhD); biological anthropology (PhD); biological sciences in dental medicine (PhD); biology (PhD); biophysics (PhD); biostatistics (PhD); business economics (PhD); Byzantine art (PhD); Byzantine Greek (PhD); chemical biology (PhD); chemical physics (PhD); Chinese (PhD); Chinese studies (AM); classical archaeology (PhD); classical art (PhD); classical philology (PhD); classical philosophy (PhD); comparative literature (PhD); composition (AM, PhD); critical theory (PhD); descriptive linguistics (PhD); diplomatic history (PhD); earth and planetary sciences (AM, PhD); East Asian history (PhD); economic and social history (PhD); economics (PhD); economics and Middle Eastern studies (PhD); eighteenth-century literature (PhD); experimental physics (PhD); fine arts and Middle Eastern studies (PhD); forest science (MFS); French (AM, PhD); German (PhD); health policy (PhD); Hebrew (AM, PhD); historical linguistics (PhD); history and Middle Eastern studies (PhD); history of American civilization (PhD); history of science (AM, PhD); Indian art (PhD); Indian philosophy (AM, PhD); Indo-Muslim culture (AM, PhD); information, technology and management (PhD); Inner Asian and Altaic studies (PhD); inorganic chemistry (PhD); intellectual history (PhD); Iranian (AM, PhD); Irish (PhD); Islamic art (PhD); Italian (AM, PhD); Japanese (PhD); Japanese and Chinese art (PhD); Japanese studies (AM); Jewish history and literature (AM, PhD); Korean (PhD); Korean studies (AM); landscape architecture (PhD); Latin American history (PhD); legal anthropology (AM); literature: nineteenth-century to the present (PhD); mathematics (PhD); medical anthropology (AM); medical engineering/medical physics (PhD); medieval art (PhD); medieval Latin (PhD); medieval literature and language (PhD); modern art (PhD); modern British and American literature (PhD); molecular and cellular biology (PhD); Mongolian (PhD); Mongolian studies (AM); musicology (AM); musicology and ethnomusicology (PhD); Near Eastern history (PhD); neurobiology (PhD); oceanic history (PhD); oral literature (PhD); organic chemistry (PhD); organizational behavior (PhD); Pali (AM, PhD); Persian (AM, PhD); philosophy (PhD); physical chemistry (PhD); Polish (PhD); political economy and government (PhD); political science (PhD); Portuguese (AM, PhD); psychology (PhD); public policy (PhD); regional studies–Middle East (AM); regional studies-Russia, Eastern Europe, and Central Asia (AM); Renaissance and modern architecture (PhD); Renaissance art (PhD); Renaissance literature (PhD); Russian (PhD); Sanskrit (AM, PhD); Scandinavian (PhD); Semitic philology (AM, PhD); Serbo-Croatian (PhD); Slavic philology (PhD); social anthropology (AM, PhD); social change and development (AM); social policy (PhD); social psychology (PhD); sociology (PhD); Spanish (AM, PhD); statistics (AM, PhD); study of religion (PhD); Syro-Palestinian archaeology (AM, PhD); systems biology (PhD); theoretical linguistics (PhD); theoretical physics (PhD); theory (AM, PhD); Tibetan (AM, PhD); Turkish (AM, PhD); Ukrainian (PhD); urban planning (PhD); Urdu (AM, PhD); Vietnamese (PhD); Vietnamese studies (AM); Welsh (PhD). Electronic applications accepted.

Division of Medical Sciences Offers biological chemistry and molecular pharmacology (PhD); cell biology (PhD); genetics (PhD); microbiology and molecular genetics (PhD); pathology (PhD).

Harvard John A. Paulson School of Engineering and Applied Sciences Students: 502 full-time (156 women), 22 part-time (15 women); includes 90 minority (1 Black or African American, non-Hispanic/Latino; 61 Asian, non-Hispanic/Latino; 17 Hispanic/Latino; 1 Native Hawaiian or other Pacific Islander, non-Hispanic/Latino; 10 Two or more races, non-Hispanic/Latino), 277 international. Average age 27. 2,707 applicants, 10% accepted, 142 enrolled. *Faculty:* 86 full-time (16 women), 51 part-time/adjunct (13 women). Expenses: Contact institution. *Financial support:* In 2017–18, 413 students received support, including 122 fellowships with full tuition reimbursements available (averaging $26,424 per year), 277 research assistantships with tuition reimbursements available (averaging $35,232 per year), 76 teaching assistantships with tuition reimbursements available (averaging $6,313 per year); health care benefits also available. In 2017, 34 master's, 64 doctorates awarded. *Program availability:* Part-time. Offers applied mathematics (PhD); applied physics (PhD); computational science and engineering (ME, SM); computer science (PhD); data science (SM); design engineering (MDE); engineering science (ME); engineering sciences (SM, PhD). MDE offered in collaboration with Graduate School of Design. *Application deadline:* For fall admission, 12/15 priority date for domestic and international students. *Application fee:* $105. Electronic applications accepted. *Application Contact:* Office of Admissions and Financial Aid, 617-495-5315, E-mail: admissions@seas.harvard.edu. *Dean*, Francis J. Doyle, III, 617-495-5829, Fax: 617-495-5264, E-mail: dean@seas.harvard.edu.

Graduate School of Design Offers architecture (M Arch); design (M Arch, M Des S, MAUD, MLA, MLAUD, MUP, Dr DES); design studies (M Des S); landscape architecture (MLA); urban planning (MUP); urban planning and design (MAUD, MLAUD). Electronic applications accepted.

Harvard Business School Offers accounting and management (DBA); business (MBA, DBA, PhD); business administration (MBA); business economics (PhD); health policy management (PhD); management (DBA); marketing (DBA); organizational behavior (PhD); science, technology and management (PhD); strategy (DBA); technology and operations management (DBA).

Harvard Divinity School Offers divinity (M Div, MTS, Th M). Electronic applications accepted.

Harvard Graduate School of Education *Program availability:* Part-time. Offers arts in education (Ed M); education (Ed M, Ed L D, PhD); education leadership (Ed L D); education policy and management (Ed M); higher education (Ed M); human development and psychology (Ed M); international education policy (Ed M); language and literacy (Ed M); learning and teaching (Ed M); mind, brain, and education (Ed M); prevention science and practice (Ed M); school leadership (Ed M); special studies (Ed M); teacher education (Ed M); technology, innovation, and education (Ed M). Electronic applications accepted.

Harvard Medical School Offers medicine (M Eng, SM, MD, PhD, Sc D). Electronic applications accepted.

Harvard T.H. Chan School of Public Health Students: 1,104 full-time (689 women), 298 part-time (140 women); includes 398 minority (66 Black or African American, non-Hispanic/Latino; 1 American Indian or Alaska Native, non-Hispanic/Latino; 217 Asian, non-Hispanic/Latino; 74 Hispanic/Latino; 40 Two or more races, non-Hispanic/Latino), 492 international. Average age 29. 2,970 applicants, 32% accepted, 662 enrolled. *Faculty:* 333 full-time (127 women), 143 part-time/adjunct (51 women). Expenses: Contact institution. *Financial support:* Fellowships, research assistantships, teaching assistantships, career-related internships or fieldwork, Federal Work-Study, scholarships/grants, traineeships, and unspecified assistantships available. Support available to part-time students. Financial award application deadline: 2/15; financial award applicants required to submit FAFSA. In 2017, 530 master's, 100 doctorates awarded. *Program availability:* Part-time. Offers biological sciences in public health (PhD); biostatistics (SM, PhD); cancer epidemiology (SM); cardiovascular epidemiology (SM); clinical effectiveness (MPH); clinical epidemiology (SM); computational biology and quantitative genetics (SM); environmental and occupational epidemiology (SM); environmental epidemiology (SM); environmental exposure assessment (SM); environmental health (PhD); epidemiologic methods (SM); epidemiology (PhD); epidemiology of aging (SM); ergonomics and safety (SM); genetic epidemiology and statistical genetics (SM); global health (MPH); global health and population (SM, PhD); health and social behavior (MPH); health data science (SM); health management (MPH); health policy (MPH); health policy and management (MHCM, SM, PhD); infectious disease epidemiology (SM); neuro-psychiatric epidemiology (SM); nutrition (PhD); nutritional epidemiology (SM); occupational and environmental health (MPH);

occupational health (SM); occupational hygiene (SM); pharmacoepidemiology (SM); population health sciences (PhD); public health (MHCM, MPH, SM, Dr PH, PhD); quantitative methods (MPH); reproductive epidemiology (SM); risk and decision science (SM); social and behavioral sciences (PhD). SM program offered jointly with Simmons College. *Application deadline:* For fall admission, 12/1 for domestic and international students. *Application fee:* $120. Electronic applications accepted. *Application Contact:* Vincent W. James, Director of Admissions, 617-432-1031, Fax: 617-432-7080, E-mail: admissions@hsph.harvard.edu. *Dean of the Faculty,* Dr. Michelle Williams, 617-432-1025, Fax: 617-277-5320, E-mail: deansoff@hsph.harvard.edu.

John F. Kennedy School of Government Students: 927 full-time (512 women), 6 part-time (2 women); includes 159 minority (34 Black or African American, non-Hispanic/Latino; 1 American Indian or Alaska Native, non-Hispanic/Latino; 69 Asian, non-Hispanic/Latino; 37 Hispanic/Latino; 1 Native Hawaiian or other Pacific Islander, non-Hispanic/Latino; 17 Two or more races, non-Hispanic/Latino), 430 international. Average age 31. 2,722 applicants, 33% accepted, 628 enrolled. Expenses: Contact institution. *Financial support:* Fellowships, research assistantships, teaching assistantships, career-related internships or fieldwork, Federal Work-Study, institutionally sponsored loans, scholarships/grants, and unspecified assistantships available. Support available to part-time students. Financial award application deadline: 2/24; financial award applicants required to submit CSS PROFILE or FAFSA. In 2017, 540 master's awarded. Offers government (MPA, MPAID, MPP, PhD); political economy and government (PhD); public administration (MPA); public administration in international development (MPAID); public policy (MPP). *Application deadline:* For fall admission, 12/1 for domestic students. *Application fee:* $100. Electronic applications accepted. *Application Contact:* 617-495-1155, Fax: 617-496-1165, E-mail: hks_admissions@harvard.edu. *Dean,* Douglas W. Elmendorf, 617-495-1122.

Law School Offers international and comparative law (JD); law (LL M, JD, SJD); law and business (JD); law and government (JD); law and social change (JD); law, science and technology (JD).

School of Dental Medicine Students: 240 full-time (136 women); includes 115 minority (12 Black or African American, non-Hispanic/Latino; 1 American Indian or Alaska Native, non-Hispanic/Latino; 77 Asian, non-Hispanic/Latino; 6 Hispanic/Latino; 1 Native Hawaiian or other Pacific Islander, non-Hispanic/Latino; 18 Two or more races, non-Hispanic/Latino), 40 international. Average age 25. 1,013 applicants, 35 enrolled. Expenses: Contact institution. *Financial support:* Federal Work-Study, institutionally sponsored loans, and scholarships/grants available. Financial award applicants required to submit CSS PROFILE or FAFSA. In 2017, 9 master's, 35 doctorates awarded. Offers advanced general dentistry (Certificate); dental medicine (M Med Sc, D Med Sc, DMD, Certificate); dental public health (Certificate); endodontics (Certificate); general practice residency (Certificate); oral biology (M Med Sc, D Med Sc); oral implantology (Certificate); oral medicine (Certificate); oral pathology (Certificate); oral surgery (Certificate); orthodontics (Certificate); pediatric dentistry (Certificate); periodontics (Certificate); prosthodontics (Certificate). *Application deadline:* For winter admission, 12/15 priority date for domestic and international students. Applications are processed on a rolling basis. *Application fee:* $80. Electronic applications accepted. *Application Contact:* Sarah M. Troy-Petrakos, Director of Admissions, 617-432-1443, Fax: 617-432-3881, E-mail: sarah_petrakos@hsdm.harvard.edu. *Dean,* Dr. R. Bruce Donoff, 617-432-1401, Fax: 617-432-4266, E-mail: bruce_donoff@hsdm.harvard.edu.

HASTINGS COLLEGE, Hastings, NE 68901

General Information Independent-religious, coed, comprehensive institution. *Graduate housing:* On-campus housing not available.

GRADUATE UNITS

Department of Teacher Education *Program availability:* Part-time. Offers teacher education (MAT). Electronic applications accepted.

HAWAI'I PACIFIC UNIVERSITY, Honolulu, HI 96813

General Information Independent, coed, comprehensive institution. *Enrollment:* 4,146 graduate, professional, and undergraduate students; 412 full-time matriculated graduate/professional students (224 women), 168 part-time matriculated graduate/professional students (98 women). *Enrollment by degree level:* 551 master's, 6 doctoral, 23 other advanced degrees. *Graduate faculty:* 67 full-time (29 women), 27 part-time/adjunct (12 women). *Tuition:* Full-time $18,000; part-time $1000 per credit. *Required fees:* $200; $26 per credit. Tuition and fees vary according to course load and program. *Graduate housing:* Rooms and/or apartments available on a first-come, first-served basis to single and married students. Typical cost: $14,204 (including board) for single students. Room and board charges vary according to board plan, campus/location and housing facility selected. *Student services:* Campus employment opportunities, campus safety program, career counseling, exercise/wellness program, free psychological counseling, international student services, low-cost health insurance, multicultural affairs office, services for students with disabilities, writing training. *Library facilities:* Meader Library plus 2 others. *Collection:* Books: 103,021 (physical), 191,075 (digital/electronic); Serial titles: 64 (physical), 4,520 (digital/electronic); Databases: 101. Students can reserve study rooms. *Research affiliation:* Oceanic Institute (marine science).

Computer facilities: 200 computers available on campus for general student use. A campuswide network can be accessed from student residence rooms and from off campus. Online class registration is available.
Website: http://www.hpu.edu/

General Application Contact: Danny Lam, Assistant Director of Graduate Admissions, 808-544-1135, E-mail: graduate@hpu.edu.

GRADUATE UNITS

College of Business Students: 121 full-time (47 women), 51 part-time (27 women); includes 96 minority (10 Black or African American, non-Hispanic/Latino; 26 Asian, non-Hispanic/Latino; 22 Hispanic/Latino; 3 Native Hawaiian or other Pacific Islander, non-Hispanic/Latino; 35 Two or more races, non-Hispanic/Latino), 33 international. Average age 33. 118 applicants, 77% accepted, 61 enrolled. *Faculty:* 16 full-time (6 women), 6 part-time/adjunct (0 women). Expenses: Contact institution. *Financial support:* In 2017–18, 29 students received support. Research assistantships, teaching assistantships, career-related internships or fieldwork, Federal Work-Study, scholarships/grants, tuition waivers (partial), and unspecified assistantships available. Financial award application deadline: 3/1; financial award applicants required to submit FAFSA. In 2017, 116 master's awarded. *Program availability:* Part-time, evening/weekend, 100% online, blended/hybrid learning. Offers business (MA, MBA, MSIS); finance (MBA); human resource management (MBA); information systems (MSIS); international business (MBA); management (MBA); marketing (MBA); organizational change (MA); organizational change and development (MBA). *Application deadline:* For fall admission, 1/15 priority date for domestic students; for spring admission, 10/15 priority date for domestic students. Applications are processed on a rolling basis. *Application fee:* $50. Electronic applications accepted. *Application Contact:* Danny Lam, Assistant Director of Graduate Admissions, 808-544-1135, E-mail: graduate@hpu.edu. *Dean,* Dr. William Rhey, 808-544-0275, E-mail: wrhey@hpu.edu.

College of Health and Society Students: 98 full-time (64 women), 34 part-time (28 women); includes 85 minority (10 Black or African American, non-Hispanic/Latino; 28 Asian, non-Hispanic/Latino; 14 Hispanic/Latino; 33 Two or more races, non-Hispanic/Latino), 7 international. Average age 35. 85 applicants, 87% accepted, 49 enrolled. *Faculty:* 7 full-time (5 women), 6 part-time/adjunct (4 women). Expenses: Contact institution. *Financial support:* In 2017–18, 17 students received support. Career-related internships or fieldwork, Federal Work-Study, scholarships/grants, traineeships, tuition waivers (partial), and unspecified assistantships available. Financial award application deadline: 3/1; financial award applicants required to submit FAFSA. In 2017, 41 master's awarded. *Program availability:* Part-time, evening/weekend, 100% online, blended/hybrid learning. Offers health and society (MPH, MSN, MSW, DNP); nursing (MSN, DNP); public health (MPH); social work (MSW). *Application deadline:* For fall admission, 1/15 priority date for domestic students; for spring admission, 10/15 priority date for domestic students. Applications are processed on a rolling basis. *Application fee:* $50. Electronic applications accepted. *Application Contact:* Danny Lam, Assistant Director of Graduate Admissions, 808-544-1135, E-mail: graduate@hpu.edu. *Acting Dean,* Dr. Jayne Smitten, 808-236-5811, E-mail: jsmitten@hpu.edu.

College of Liberal Arts Students: 110 full-time (62 women), 69 part-time (35 women); includes 82 minority (13 Black or African American, non-Hispanic/Latino; 22 Asian, non-Hispanic/Latino; 19 Hispanic/Latino; 28 Two or more races, non-Hispanic/Latino), 27 international. Average age 32. 134 applicants, 72% accepted, 69 enrolled. *Faculty:* 24 full-time (9 women), 7 part-time/adjunct (3 women). Expenses: Contact institution. *Financial support:* In 2017–18, 33 students received support. Career-related internships or fieldwork, Federal Work-Study, scholarships/grants, tuition waivers (partial), and unspecified assistantships available. Financial award application deadline: 3/1; financial award applicants required to submit FAFSA. In 2017, 61 master's awarded. *Program availability:* Part-time, evening/weekend. Offers clinical mental health counseling (MA); communication (MA); diplomacy and military studies (MA); global leadership and sustainable development (MA); liberal arts (MA); teaching English to speakers of other languages (MA). *Application deadline:* For fall admission, 1/15 priority date for domestic students; for spring admission, 10/15 priority date for domestic students. Applications are processed on a rolling basis. *Application fee:* $50. Electronic applications accepted. *Application Contact:* Danny Lam, Assistant Director of Graduate Admissions, 808-544-1135, E-mail: graduate@hpu.edu. *Dean,* Dr. Allison Gough, 808-544-1109, E-mail: agough@hpu.edu.

College of Natural and Computational Sciences Students: 29 full-time (19 women), 8 part-time (5 women); includes 6 minority (1 Asian, non-Hispanic/Latino; 5 Two or more races, non-Hispanic/Latino), 4 international. Average age 27. 39 applicants, 79% accepted, 14 enrolled. *Faculty:* 13 full-time (5 women). Expenses: Contact institution. *Financial support:* In 2017–18, 31 students received support. Career-related internships or fieldwork, Federal Work-Study, scholarships/grants, tuition waivers (partial), and unspecified assistantships available. Financial award application deadline: 3/1; financial award applicants required to submit FAFSA. In 2017, 8 master's awarded. *Program availability:* Part-time. Offers marine science (MS); natural and computational sciences (MS). *Application deadline:* For fall admission, 1/15 priority date for domestic students. *Application fee:* $50. Electronic applications accepted. *Application Contact:* Danny Lam, Assistant Director of Graduate Admissions, 808-544-1135, E-mail: graduate@hpu.edu. *Dean,* Dr. Brenda Jensen, 808-236-3533, E-mail: bjensen@hpu.edu.

College of Professional Studies Students: 35 full-time (21 women), 6 part-time (3 women); includes 27 minority (3 Black or African American, non-Hispanic/Latino; 1 American Indian or Alaska Native, non-Hispanic/Latino; 8 Asian, non-Hispanic/Latino; 5 Hispanic/Latino; 1 Native Hawaiian or other Pacific Islander, non-Hispanic/Latino; 9 Two or more races, non-Hispanic/Latino). Average age 34. 38 applicants, 82% accepted, 24 enrolled. *Faculty:* 7 full-time (4 women), 8 part-time/adjunct (5 women). Expenses: Contact institution. *Financial support:* In 2017–18, 6 students received support. Career-related internships or fieldwork, Federal Work-Study, scholarships/grants, tuition waivers (partial), and unspecified assistantships available. Financial award application deadline: 3/1; financial award applicants required to submit FAFSA. In 2017, 27 master's awarded. *Program availability:* Part-time, evening/weekend, 100% online, blended/hybrid learning. Offers educational leadership (M Ed); elementary education (M Ed); public administration (MPA); secondary education (M Ed). *Application deadline:* For fall admission, 1/15 priority date for domestic students; for spring admission, 10/15 priority date for domestic students. Applications are processed on a rolling basis. *Application fee:* $50. Electronic applications accepted. *Application Contact:* Danny Lam, Assistant Director of Graduate Admissions, 808-544-1135, E-mail: graduate@hpu.edu. *Dean,* Mani Sehgal, 808-543-8046, E-mail: msehgal@hpu.edu.

HAZELDEN BETTY FORD GRADUATE SCHOOL OF ADDICTION STUDIES, Center City, MN 55012

General Information Independent, coed, graduate-only institution. CGS member. *Graduate housing:* On-campus housing not available.

GRADUATE UNITS

Graduate Programs *Program availability:* Part-time. Offers addiction counseling (MA, Certificate).

HEBREW COLLEGE, Newton Centre, MA 02459

General Information Independent-religious, coed, graduate-only institution. *Graduate housing:* On-campus housing not available.

GRADUATE UNITS

Cantor Educator Program Offers cantor educator (MJ Ed).

Program in Jewish Studies *Program availability:* Part-time, evening/weekend, online learning. Offers Jewish liturgical music (Certificate); Jewish music education (Certificate); Jewish studies (MA).

Rabbinical School Offers rabbinics (MA).

Shoolman Graduate School of Jewish Education *Program availability:* Part-time, evening/weekend, online learning. Offers early childhood Jewish education (Certificate); Jewish day school education (Certificate); Jewish education (MJ Ed); Jewish family education (Certificate); Jewish special education (Certificate); Jewish youth education, informal education and camping (Certificate).

HEBREW UNION COLLEGE–JEWISH INSTITUTE OF RELIGION, New York, NY 10012-1186

General Information Independent-religious, coed, graduate-only institution. *Graduate housing:* On-campus housing not available.

GRADUATE UNITS

Rabbinical School Offers rabbinical studies (MAHL).

School of Education *Program availability:* Part-time. Offers education (MARE).

School of Graduate Studies *Program availability:* Part-time. Offers Hebrew letters (DHL); Judaic studies (MAJS); pastoral counseling (D Min).

School of Jewish Nonprofit Management Offers Jewish nonprofit management (MA).
School of Sacred Music Offers sacred music (MSM).

HEC MONTREAL, Montréal, QC H3T 2A7, Canada

General Information Province-supported, coed, comprehensive institution. *Enrollment:* 13,797 graduate, professional, and undergraduate students; 1,584 full-time matriculated graduate/professional students (766 women), 1,279 part-time matriculated graduate/professional students (725 women). *Enrollment by degree level:* 1,550 master's, 114 doctoral, 1,199 other advanced degrees. *Graduate faculty:* 295 full-time (105 women), 346 part-time/adjunct (120 women). *International tuition:* $19,648 Canadian dollars full-time. Tuition, province resident: full-time $2869 Canadian dollars; part-time $79.70 Canadian dollars per credit. Tuition, Canadian resident: full-time $8883 Canadian dollars; part-time $246.76 Canadian dollars per credit. *Required fees:* $41.20 Canadian dollars per credit. $67.94 Canadian dollars per term. Tuition and fees vary according to degree level and program. *Graduate housing:* Rooms and/or apartments available on a first-come, first-served basis to single and married students. Typical cost: $3930 Canadian dollars per year for single students; $6390 Canadian dollars per year for married students. *Student services:* Campus employment opportunities, campus safety program, career counseling, child daycare facilities, exercise/wellness program, free psychological counseling, grant writing training, international student services, low-cost health insurance, multicultural affairs office, services for students with disabilities. *Library facilities:* HEC Montreal Library plus 1 other. *Collection:* Books: 116,690 (physical), 206,337 (digital/electronic); Serial titles: 952 (physical), 111,941 (digital/electronic); Databases: 161. Weekly public service hours: 100; students can reserve study rooms. *Research affiliation:* CIRANO (Centre for Interuniversity Research and Analysis of Organizations) (research and transfer), ACFAS (Association Francophone Pour Le Savoir), PROMPT (Financement de la RD en TIC), CRIAQ (Consortium of Synergetic Research and Innovation in Aerospace) (aerospace), UNIVALOR (Valorisation de la recherche universitaire et le transfert technologique).

Computer facilities: 159 computers available on campus for general student use. A campuswide network can be accessed from student residence rooms. Online class registration, learning management system, corporate calendar and Web sites for resources available for classes are available.
Website: http://www.hec.ca/

General Application Contact: Louise Champagne, Registrar, 514-340-6151, Fax: 514-340-6411, E-mail: aide@hec.ca.

GRADUATE UNITS

School of Business Administration Students: 1,584 full-time (766 women), 1,279 part-time (725 women). Average age 29. 2,399 applicants, 67% accepted, 1220 enrolled. *Faculty:* 295 full-time (105 women), 346 part-time/adjunct (120 women). Expenses: Contact institution. *Financial support:* Research assistantships, teaching assistantships, and scholarships/grants available. Financial award application deadline: 9/2. In 2017, 678 master's, 23 doctorates, 629 other advanced degrees awarded. Offers accounting (PhD); accounting, management, control, and audit (M Sc); applied economics (M Sc, PhD); applied financial economics (M Sc); business administration (Graduate Diploma); business administration and management (MBA); business analysis - information technology (Graduate Diploma); business analysis and information technologies (M Sc); business analytics (M Sc); business intelligence (M Sc); data science (PhD); e-business (Graduate Diploma); electronic commerce (M Sc); entrepreneurship (Graduate Diploma); entrepreneurship-intrapreneurship-innovation (M Sc); finance (M Sc); financial engineering (M Sc, PhD); financial professions (Graduate Diploma); global supply chain management (M Sc); human resources (Graduate Diploma); human resources management (M Sc); information technology (PhD); international business (M Sc, PhD); international logistics (M Sc); logistics and operations management (PhD); management (M Sc, Graduate Diploma); management and social innovations (M Sc); management and sustainable development (Graduate Diploma); management control (M Sc); management in cultural enterprises (MM); management of cultural organizations (Graduate Diploma); management science (PhD); management, strategy and organizations (PhD); marketing (M Sc, PhD); marketing communication (Graduate Diploma); operations management (M Sc); organizational behaviour and human resources (PhD); organizational development (M Sc, Graduate Diploma); professional accounting (Graduate Diploma); strategy (M Sc); supply chain management (Graduate Diploma); taxation (Graduate Diploma); user exprerience in business context (M Sc). Most courses are given in French. *Application fee:* $88 Canadian dollars ($184 Canadian dollars for international students). Electronic applications accepted. *Application Contact:* Louise Champagne, Registrar, 514-340-6151, Fax: 514-340-6411, E-mail: aide@hec.ca. *Director*, Dr. Michel Patry, 514-340-6301, Fax: 514-340-6411, E-mail: michel.patry@hec.ca.

HEIDELBERG UNIVERSITY, Tiffin, OH 44883-2462

General Information Independent-religious, coed, comprehensive institution. *Enrollment:* 1,209 graduate, professional, and undergraduate students; 53 full-time matriculated graduate/professional students (28 women), 49 part-time matriculated graduate/professional students (29 women). *Enrollment by degree level:* 102 master's. *Graduate faculty:* 12 full-time (9 women), 15 part-time/adjunct (8 women). *Tuition:* Full-time $30,282; part-time $793 per semester hour. Full-time tuition and fees vary according to course load and program. *Graduate housing:* Room and/or apartments available on a first-come, first-served basis to single students; on-campus housing not available to married students. Typical cost: $5300 per year ($10,200 including board). *Student services:* Campus employment opportunities, campus safety program, career counseling, exercise/wellness program, free psychological counseling, international student services, multicultural affairs office, services for students with disabilities, teacher training, writing training. *Library facilities:* Beeghly Library plus 1 other. *Collection:* Books: 86,891 (physical), 279,499 (digital/electronic); Serial titles: 1,293 (physical), 61,058 (digital/electronic); Databases: 198. Weekly public service hours: 83.

Computer facilities: 125 computers available on campus for general student use. A campuswide network can be accessed from student residence rooms and from off campus. Online class registration is available.
Website: http://www.heidelberg.edu/

General Application Contact: Katie Zeyen, Graduate Admissions Coordinator, 419-448-2602, Fax: 419-448-2565, E-mail: kzeyen@heidelberg.edu.

GRADUATE UNITS

Master of Arts in Counseling Program Students: 19 full-time (15 women), 25 part-time (19 women). Expenses: Contact institution. *Financial support:* Scholarships/grants and unspecified assistantships available. Financial award applicants required to submit FAFSA. In 2017, 10 master's awarded. *Program availability:* Part-time, evening/weekend. Offers clinical mental health counseling (MA); school counseling (MA). *Application deadline:* Applications are processed on a rolling basis. *Application fee:* $0. Electronic applications accepted. *Application Contact:* Katie Zeyen, Graduate Admissions Coordinator, 419-448-2602, Fax: 419-448-2565, E-mail: kzeyen@heidelberg.edu. *Director of Graduate Studies in Counseling*, Dr. Marjorie Shavers, 419-448-2308, E-mail: mshavers@heidelberg.edu.

Master of Arts in Education Program Students: 14 part-time (4 women). Expenses: Contact institution. *Financial support:* Unspecified assistantships available. Financial award applicants required to submit FAFSA. In 2017, 15 master's awarded. *Program availability:* Part-time, evening/weekend. Offers education (MAE). *Application deadline:* Applications are processed on a rolling basis. *Application fee:* $0. Electronic applications accepted. *Application Contact:* Katie Zeyen, Graduate Admissions Coordinator, 419-448-2602, Fax: 419-448-2565, E-mail: kzeyen@heidelberg.edu. *Director of the School of Education*, Dr. Karen Jones, 419-448-2130, E-mail: kjones9@heidelberg.edu.

Master of Business Administration Program Students: 34 full-time (13 women), 10 part-time (6 women). Expenses: Contact institution. *Financial support:* Scholarships/grants and unspecified assistantships available. Financial award applicants required to submit FAFSA. In 2017, 17 master's awarded. *Program availability:* Part-time. Offers business administration (MBA). *Application deadline:* Applications are processed on a rolling basis. *Application fee:* $0. Electronic applications accepted. *Application Contact:* Katie Zeyen, Graduate Admissions Coordinator, 419-448-2602, Fax: 419-448-2565, E-mail: kzeyen@heidelberg.edu. *Dean of the School of Business*, Dr. Haseeb Ahmed, 419-448-2284, E-mail: hahmed@heidelberg.edu.

Master of Music Education Program Expenses: Contact institution. *Financial support:* Unspecified assistantships available. Financial award applicants required to submit FAFSA. In 2017, 2 master's awarded. *Program availability:* Part-time. Offers music education (MME). Program offered in summer only. *Application deadline:* For fall admission, 6/1 for domestic students. Applications are processed on a rolling basis. *Application fee:* $0. Electronic applications accepted. *Application Contact:* Katie Zeyen, Graduate Studies Coordinator, 419-448-2602, Fax: 419-448-2565, E-mail: kzeyen@heidelberg.edu. *Director*, Dr. Carol Dusdieker, 419-448-2080, E-mail: cdusdiek@heidelberg.edu.

HENDERSON STATE UNIVERSITY, Arkadelphia, AR 71999-0001

General Information State-supported, coed, comprehensive institution. CGS member. *Graduate housing:* Room and/or apartments available on a first-come, first-served basis to single students; on-campus housing not available to married students. Housing application deadline: 8/1.

GRADUATE UNITS

Graduate Studies *Program availability:* Part-time, 100% online.

Ellis College of Arts and Sciences *Program availability:* Part-time. Offers arts and sciences (MLA).

School of Business *Program availability:* Part-time, 100% online. Offers business (MBA).

Teachers College *Program availability:* Part-time, 100% online. Offers clinical mental health counseling (MS); curriculum leadership (Ed S); developmental therapy (MS, MSE, Graduate Certificate); dyslexia therapy (Graduate Certificate); education (MAT); educational leadership (MSE, Ed S, Graduate Certificate); educational technology leadership (Graduate Certificate); English as a second language (MSE, Graduate Certificate); instructional facilitator (MSE, Graduate Certificate); middle level education (MAT); secondary school counseling (MSE); special education (K-12) (MAT, MSE); special education/early childhood (MAT); sports administration (MS).

HENDRIX COLLEGE, Conway, AR 72032-3080

General Information Independent-religious, coed, comprehensive institution. *Graduate housing:* Room and/or apartments available on a first-come, first-served basis to single students. Housing application deadline: 6/1.

GRADUATE UNITS

Program in Accounting *Program availability:* Part-time. Offers accounting (MA).

HENLEY-PUTNAM SCHOOL OF STRATEGIC SECURITY, Rapid City, SD 57701

General Information Proprietary, coed, comprehensive institution.

GRADUATE UNITS

Doctorate Program in Strategic Security *Program availability:* Part-time, online learning. Offers strategic security (DSS).

Master of Science Program in Intelligence Management *Program availability:* Part-time, online learning. Offers intelligence management (MS).

Master of Science Program in Strategic Security and Protection Management *Program availability:* Part-time, online learning. Offers extremist organizations (MS).

Master of Science Program in Terrorism and Counterterrorism Studies *Program availability:* Part-time, online learning. Offers intelligence operations (MS); protective intelligence (MS).

HERITAGE CHRISTIAN UNIVERSITY, Florence, AL 35630

General Information Independent-religious, coed, primarily men, comprehensive institution.

GRADUATE UNITS

Graduate Programs Offers counseling (MM); Greek (MA); ministry (MM); New Testament (MA).

HERITAGE COLLEGE AND SEMINARY, Cambridge, ON N3C 3T2, Canada

General Information Independent-religious, coed, comprehensive institution. *Graduate housing:* Room and/or apartments available on a first-come, first-served basis to single students; on-campus housing not available to married students. Housing application deadline: 5/31.

GRADUATE UNITS

Graduate and Professional Programs Offers general (M Div); intercultural studies (M Div); pastoral (M Div); research (M Div); theological studies (MTS, CTS).

HERITAGE UNIVERSITY, Toppenish, WA 98948-9599

General Information Independent, coed, comprehensive institution. *Graduate housing:* On-campus housing not available.

GRADUATE UNITS

Graduate Programs in Education *Program availability:* Part-time, evening/weekend. Offers bilingual education/ESL (M Ed); biology (M Ed); counseling (M Ed); educational administration (M Ed); English and literature (M Ed); professional studies (M Ed); reading/literacy (M Ed); special education (M Ed); teaching (MIT).

HERZING UNIVERSITY ONLINE, Menomonee Falls, WI 53051

General Information Independent, coed, comprehensive institution. CGS member.

GRADUATE UNITS

Program in Business Administration *Program availability:* Online learning. Offers accounting (MBA); business administration (MBA); business management (MBA); healthcare management (MBA); human resources (MBA); marketing (MBA); project management (MBA); technology management (MBA).

Program in Nursing *Program availability:* Online learning. Offers nursing (MSN); nursing education (MSN); nursing management (MSN).

HIGH POINT UNIVERSITY, High Point, NC 27268

General Information Independent-religious, coed, university. *Graduate housing:* On-campus housing not available.

GRADUATE UNITS

Norcross Graduate School *Program availability:* Part-time, evening/weekend. Offers athletic training (MSAT); business administration (MBA); educational leadership (M Ed, Ed D); elementary education (M Ed, MAT); pharmacy (Pharm D); physical therapy (DPT); physician assistant studies (MPAS); secondary mathematics (M Ed, MAT); special education (M Ed); strategic communication (MA). Electronic applications accepted.

HIGH TECH HIGH GRADUATE SCHOOL OF EDUCATION, San Diego, CA 92106

General Information Private, coed, graduate-only institution.

GRADUATE UNITS

Program in Educational Leadership *Program availability:* Part-time. Offers educational leadership (M Ed).

HILBERT COLLEGE, Hamburg, NY 14075-1597

General Information Independent-religious, coed, comprehensive institution. *Enrollment:* 792 graduate, professional, and undergraduate students; 42 full-time matriculated graduate/professional students (31 women), 2 part-time matriculated graduate/professional students (both women). *Enrollment by degree level:* 44 master's. *Graduate faculty:* 6 full-time (3 women), 13 part-time/adjunct (6 women). *Tuition:* Full-time $19,200; part-time $800 per credit hour. *Required fees:* $500. *Graduate housing:* On-campus housing not available. *Student services:* Campus safety program, career counseling, exercise/wellness program, free psychological counseling, multicultural affairs office, services for students with disabilities, writing training. *Library facilities:* McGrath Library. *Collection:* Books: 36,902 (physical), 9,442 (digital/electronic); Serial titles: 172 (physical), 100,109 (digital/electronic); Databases: 49. Weekly public service hours: 77; students can reserve study rooms.

Computer facilities: 146 computers available on campus for general student use. A campuswide network can be accessed from student residence rooms. Online class registration is available.
Website: http://www.hilbert.edu/

General Application Contact: Kim Chiarmonte, Director of Adult and Graduate Recruitment, 716-926-8949, Fax: 716-649-0702, E-mail: graduatestudies@hilbert.edu.

GRADUATE UNITS

Program in Criminal Justice Administration Students: 15 full-time (6 women), 3 part-time (1 woman); includes 3 minority (1 Black or African American, non-Hispanic/Latino; 2 Two or more races, non-Hispanic/Latino). Average age 31. *Faculty:* 6 full-time (3 women), 5 part-time/adjunct (2 women). Expenses: Contact institution. *Financial support:* Scholarships/grants and tuition waivers (partial) available. Financial award application deadline: 7/1; financial award applicants required to submit FAFSA. In 2017, 13 master's awarded. *Program availability:* Evening/weekend. Offers criminal justice administration (MS). *Application deadline:* Applications are processed on a rolling basis. *Application fee:* $25. Electronic applications accepted. *Application Contact:* Kim Chiarmonte, Director for Adult and Graduate Recruitment, 716-926-8948, Fax: 716-649-0702, E-mail: kchiarmonte@hilbert.edu. *Director for Adult and Graduate Studies,* Kathryn Eskew, 716-649-7900 Ext. 305, Fax: 716-649-0702, E-mail: keskew@hilbert.edu.

Program in Public Administration Students: 27 full-time (22 women), 1 part-time (0 women); includes 8 minority (3 Black or African American, non-Hispanic/Latino; 1 American Indian or Alaska Native, non-Hispanic/Latino; 1 Hispanic/Latino; 3 Two or more races, non-Hispanic/Latino), 1 international. Average age 30. *Faculty:* 1 full-time (0 women), 12 part-time/adjunct (6 women). Expenses: Contact institution. *Financial support:* Scholarships/grants and tuition waivers (partial) available. Financial award application deadline: 7/1; financial award applicants required to submit FAFSA. In 2017, 14 master's awarded. *Program availability:* Evening/weekend. Offers health administration (MPA); public administration (MPA). *Application deadline:* Applications are processed on a rolling basis. *Application fee:* $25. Electronic applications accepted. *Application Contact:* Kim Chiarmonte, Director for Adult and Graduate Recruitment, 716-926-8948, Fax: 716-649-0702, E-mail: kchiarmonte@hilbert.edu. *Director of Adult and Graduate Studies,* Kathryn Eskew, 716-649-7900 Ext. 305, Fax: 716-649-0702, E-mail: keskew@hilbert.edu.

HILLSDALE COLLEGE, Hillsdale, MI 49242-1298

General Information Independent, coed, comprehensive institution. *Enrollment:* 1,556 graduate, professional, and undergraduate students; 48 full-time matriculated graduate/professional students. *Graduate faculty:* 11 full-time, 1 part-time/adjunct. *Tuition:* Full-time $23,420; part-time $1280 per credit hour. *Library facilities:* Michael Alex Mossey Library. *Collection:* Books: 252,517 (physical), 2 million (digital/electronic); Serial titles: 570 (physical), 30,000 (digital/electronic); Databases: 235.

Computer facilities: 312 computers available on campus for general student use. A campuswide network can be accessed from student residence rooms and from off campus. Online class registration is available.
Website: http://www.hillsdale.edu/

General Application Contact: Mariel Stauff, Graduate Program Coordinator, 517-607-2483, E-mail: gradschool@hillsdale.edu.

GRADUATE UNITS

Van Andel Graduate School of Statesmanship Students: 48 full-time. Average age 27. *Faculty:* 11 full-time, 1 part-time/adjunct. Expenses: Contact institution. *Financial support:* In 2017–18, 48 students received support, including 23 fellowships with full tuition reimbursements available (averaging $20,000 per year), 28 research assistantships with full tuition reimbursements available (averaging $4,000 per year); institutionally sponsored loans, scholarships/grants, and unspecified assistantships also available. Financial award application deadline: 12/15. In 2017, 10 master's awarded. Offers politics (MA, PhD). *Application deadline:* For fall admission, 12/15 priority date for domestic and international students; for spring admission, 10/15 for domestic and international students. *Application fee:* $25. Electronic applications accepted. *Application Contact:* Mariel Stauff, Graduate Program Coordinator, 517-607-2483, E-mail: gradschool@hillsdale.edu. *Dean,* Dr. Ronald J. Pestritto, 517-607-2483, E-mail: gradschool@hillsdale.edu.

HIRAM COLLEGE, Hiram, OH 44234

General Information Independent, coed, comprehensive institution.

GRADUATE UNITS

Graduate Studies *Program availability:* Part-time, evening/weekend. Offers interdisciplinary studies (MAIS).

HODGES UNIVERSITY, Naples, FL 34119

General Information Independent, coed, comprehensive institution. *Graduate housing:* On-campus housing not available.

GRADUATE UNITS

Graduate Programs *Program availability:* Part-time, evening/weekend, 100% online, blended/hybrid learning. Offers accounting (M Acc); business administration (MBA); clinical mental health counseling (MS); health services administration (MS); information systems management (MIS); legal studies (MS); management (MSM). Electronic applications accepted.

HOFSTRA UNIVERSITY, Hempstead, NY 11549

General Information Independent, coed, university. CGS member. *Enrollment:* 11,131 graduate, professional, and undergraduate students; 2,953 full-time matriculated graduate/professional students (1,746 women), 1,217 part-time matriculated graduate/professional students (808 women). *Enrollment by degree level:* 2,678 master's, 1,433 doctoral, 59 other advanced degrees. *Graduate faculty:* 260 full-time (131 women), 311 part-time/adjunct (150 women). *Tuition:* Full-time $1292. *Required fees:* $970. Tuition and fees vary according to program. *Graduate housing:* Room and/or apartments available on a first-come, first-served basis to single students; on-campus housing not available to married students. Typical cost: $16,720 per year ($20,950 including board). Housing application deadline: 5/1. *Student services:* Campus employment opportunities, campus safety program, career counseling, child daycare facilities, exercise/wellness program, free psychological counseling, grant writing training, international student services, multicultural affairs office, services for students with disabilities, teacher training, writing training. *Library facilities:* Axinn Library plus 3 others. *Collection:* Books: 1.1 million (physical), 199,044 (digital/electronic); Serial titles: 1,761 (physical), 17,415 (digital/electronic); Databases: 241. Weekly public service hours: 110; study areas open 24 hours, 5–7 days a week; students can reserve study rooms.

Computer facilities: Computer purchase and lease plans are available. 1,536 computers available on campus for general student use. A campuswide network can be accessed from student residence rooms and from off campus. Online class registration, Emergency alert system, online course management system, online card services balance update, online e-portfolio, software tutoring, support for specific tech-enhanced assignments, repair and rebuilding-after-virus services, and printing services are available.
Website: http://www.hofstra.edu/

General Application Contact: Sunil Samuel, Assistant Vice President of Admissions, 516-463-4723, Fax: 516-463-4664, E-mail: graduateadmission@hofstra.edu.

GRADUATE UNITS

College of Liberal Arts and Sciences Students: 266 full-time (170 women), 62 part-time (44 women); includes 90 minority (20 Black or African American, non-Hispanic/Latino; 1 American Indian or Alaska Native, non-Hispanic/Latino; 21 Asian, non-Hispanic/Latino; 43 Hispanic/Latino; 1 Native Hawaiian or other Pacific Islander, non-Hispanic/Latino; 4 Two or more races, non-Hispanic/Latino), 23 international. Average age 27. 430 applicants, 56% accepted, 103 enrolled. *Faculty:* 60 full-time (25 women), 52 part-time/adjunct (25 women). Expenses: Contact institution. *Financial support:* In 2017–18, 238 students received support, including 189 fellowships with full and partial tuition reimbursements available (averaging $6,598 per year), 9 research assistantships with full and partial tuition reimbursements available (averaging $5,597 per year); career-related internships or fieldwork, Federal Work-Study, institutionally sponsored loans, scholarships/grants, traineeships, tuition waivers (full and partial), and unspecified assistantships also available. Support available to part-time students. Financial award applicants required to submit FAFSA. In 2017, 103 master's, 25 doctorates awarded. *Program availability:* Part-time, evening/weekend, online learning. Offers applied linguistics (TESOL) (MA); applied organizational psychology (PhD); biology (MA, MS); clinical psychology (PhD); creative writing (MFA); industrial/organizational psychology (MA); liberal arts and sciences (MA, MFA, MS, PhD, Psy D); linguistics (MA); medical physics (MS); school-community psychology (Psy D); sustainability studies (MA); urban ecology (MA, MS). *Application deadline:* Applications are processed on a rolling basis. *Application fee:* $75. Electronic applications accepted. *Application Contact:* Sunil Samuel, Assistant Vice President of Admissions, 516-463-4723, Fax: 516-463-4664, E-mail: graduateadmission@hofstra.edu. *Dean,* Dr. Benjamin Rifkin, 516-463-5411, Fax: 516-463-4861, E-mail: benjamin.rifkin@hofstra.edu.

Donald and Barbara Zucker School of Medicine at Hofstra/Northwell Students: 417 full-time (196 women); includes 181 minority (20 Black or African American, non-Hispanic/Latino; 90 Asian, non-Hispanic/Latino; 56 Hispanic/Latino; 5 Native Hawaiian or other Pacific Islander, non-Hispanic/Latino; 10 Two or more races, non-Hispanic/Latino), 1 international. Average age 25. 6,088 applicants, 6% accepted, 100 enrolled. *Faculty:* 19 full-time (13 women), 15 part-time/adjunct (7 women). Expenses: Contact institution. *Financial support:* In 2017–18, 298 students received support, including 288 fellowships with full and partial tuition reimbursements available (averaging $24,461 per year), research assistantships with full and partial tuition reimbursements available (averaging $6,075 per year); career-related internships or fieldwork, Federal Work-Study, institutionally sponsored loans, scholarships/grants, tuition waivers (full and partial), and unspecified assistantships also available. Support available to part-time students. Financial award applicants required to submit FAFSA. In 2017, 75 doctorates awarded. Offers medicine (MD); molecular basis of medicine (PhD). *Application deadline:* For fall admission, 12/1 priority date for domestic students. *Application fee:* $100. Electronic applications accepted. *Application Contact:* Sunil Samuel, Assistant Vice President of Admissions, 516-463-4723, Fax: 516-463-4664. *Dean,* Dr. Lawrence Smith, 516-463-7517, Fax: 516-463-7543, E-mail: lawrence.smith@hofstra.edu.

Frank G. Zarb School of Business Students: 621 full-time (289 women), 289 part-time (122 women); includes 194 minority (42 Black or African American, non-Hispanic/Latino; 3 American Indian or Alaska Native, non-Hispanic/Latino; 76 Asian, non-Hispanic/Latino; 64 Hispanic/Latino; 2 Native Hawaiian or other Pacific Islander, non-Hispanic/Latino; 7 Two or more races, non-Hispanic/Latino), 385 international. Average age 28. 1,640 applicants, 72% accepted, 348 enrolled. *Faculty:* 49 full-time (16 women), 33 part-time/adjunct (9 women). Expenses: Contact institution. *Financial support:* In

2017–18, 279 students received support, including 255 fellowships with full and partial tuition reimbursements available (averaging $5,207 per year), 4 research assistantships with full and partial tuition reimbursements available (averaging $6,436 per year); career-related internships or fieldwork, Federal Work-Study, institutionally sponsored loans, scholarships/grants, tuition waivers (full and partial), and unspecified assistantships also available. Support available to part-time students. Financial award applicants required to submit FAFSA. In 2017, 448 master's awarded. *Program availability:* Part-time, evening/weekend, blended/hybrid learning. Offers accounting (MS, Advanced Certificate); business (EMBA, MBA, MS, Advanced Certificate); business administration (MBA); business analytics (MS); corporate finance (Advanced Certificate); finance (MS); general management (Advanced Certificate); human resource management (MS, Advanced Certificate); information systems (MS, Advanced Certificate); international business (Advanced Certificate); investment management (Advanced Certificate); marketing (MS, Advanced Certificate); marketing research (MS); quantitative finance (MS); taxation (MS, Advanced Certificate). *Application deadline:* Applications are processed on a rolling basis. *Application fee:* $75. Electronic applications accepted. *Application Contact:* Sunil Samuel, Assistant Vice President of Admissions, 516-463-4723, Fax: 516-463-4664, E-mail: graduateadmission@hofstra.edu. *Dean,* Dr. Herman Berliner, 516-463-5676, Fax: 516-463-5268, E-mail: herman.a.berliner@hofstra.edu.

Fred DeMatteis School of Engineering and Applied Sciences Students: 21 full-time (4 women), 25 part-time (6 women); includes 12 minority (1 Black or African American, non-Hispanic/Latino; 9 Asian, non-Hispanic/Latino; 1 Hispanic/Latino; 1 Native Hawaiian or other Pacific Islander, non-Hispanic/Latino), 17 international. Average age 29. 60 applicants, 77% accepted, 18 enrolled. *Faculty:* 9 full-time (3 women), 6 part-time/adjunct (1 woman). Expenses: Contact institution. *Financial support:* In 2017–18, 28 students received support, including 15 fellowships with full and partial tuition reimbursements available (averaging $3,335 per year); research assistantships with full and partial tuition reimbursements available, career-related internships or fieldwork, Federal Work-Study, institutionally sponsored loans, scholarships/grants, tuition waivers (full and partial), and unspecified assistantships also available. Support available to part-time students. Financial award applicants required to submit FAFSA. In 2017, 21 master's awarded. *Program availability:* Part-time, evening/weekend, blended/hybrid learning. Offers computer science (MS). *Application deadline:* Applications are processed on a rolling basis. *Application fee:* $75. Electronic applications accepted. *Application Contact:* Sunil Samuel, Assistant Vice President of Admissions, 516-463-4723, Fax: 516-463-4664, E-mail: graduateadmission@hofstra.edu. *Dean,* Dr. Sina Rabbany, 516-463-6672, E-mail: sina.y.rabbany@hofstra.edu.

Hofstra Northwell School of Graduate Nursing and Physician Assistant Studies Students: 152 full-time (116 women), 111 part-time (92 women); includes 79 minority (16 Black or African American, non-Hispanic/Latino; 1 American Indian or Alaska Native, non-Hispanic/Latino; 28 Asian, non-Hispanic/Latino; 31 Hispanic/Latino; 1 Native Hawaiian or other Pacific Islander, non-Hispanic/Latino; 2 Two or more races, non-Hispanic/Latino), 2 international. Average age 30. 1,738 applicants, 7% accepted, 105 enrolled. *Faculty:* 11 full-time (10 women), 11 part-time/adjunct (8 women). Expenses: Contact institution. *Financial support:* In 2017–18, 19 students received support, including 19 fellowships with full and partial tuition reimbursements available (averaging $7,300 per year); research assistantships with full and partial tuition reimbursements available, career-related internships or fieldwork, Federal Work-Study, institutionally sponsored loans, scholarships/grants, traineeships, tuition waivers (full and partial), and unspecified assistantships also available. Support available to part-time students. Financial award applicants required to submit FAFSA. In 2017, 48 master's awarded. Offers adult-gerontology acute care nurse practitioner (MS); family nurse practitioner (MS); nursing and physician assistant studies (MS); physician assistant studies (MS); psychiatric-mental health nurse practitioner (MS). *Application deadline:* For fall admission, 11/1 for domestic students. *Application fee:* $75. Electronic applications accepted. *Application Contact:* Sunil Samuel, Assistant Vice President of Admissions, 516-463-4723, Fax: 516-463-4664, E-mail: graduateadmission@hofstra.edu. *Dean,* Dr. Kathleen Gallo, 516-463-7475, Fax: 516-463-7495, E-mail: kathleen.gallo@hofstra.edu.

Lawrence Herbert School of Communication Students: 46 full-time (29 women), 20 part-time (14 women); includes 38 minority (20 Black or African American, non-Hispanic/Latino; 2 Asian, non-Hispanic/Latino; 14 Hispanic/Latino; 1 Native Hawaiian or other Pacific Islander, non-Hispanic/Latino; 1 Two or more races, non-Hispanic/Latino), 3 international. Average age 27. 61 applicants, 85% accepted, 25 enrolled. *Faculty:* 12 full-time (5 women), 8 part-time/adjunct (4 women). Expenses: Contact institution. *Financial support:* In 2017–18, 43 students received support, including 32 fellowships with full and partial tuition reimbursements available (averaging $3,199 per year), 2 research assistantships with full and partial tuition reimbursements available (averaging $7,045 per year); career-related internships or fieldwork, Federal Work-Study, institutionally sponsored loans, scholarships/grants, tuition waivers (full and partial), and unspecified assistantships also available. Support available to part-time students. Financial award applicants required to submit FAFSA. In 2017, 48 master's awarded. *Program availability:* Part-time, evening/weekend. Offers communication (MA); journalism (MA); public relations (MA). *Application deadline:* Applications are processed on a rolling basis. *Application fee:* $75. Electronic applications accepted. *Application Contact:* Sunil Samuel, Assistant Vice President of Admissions, 516-463-4723, Fax: 516-463-4664, E-mail: graduateadmission@hofstra.edu. *Dean,* Dr. Evan W. Cornog, 516-463-5215, Fax: 516-463-4866, E-mail: evan.w.cornog@hofstra.edu.

Maurice A. Deane School of Law Students: 698 full-time (382 women), 136 part-time (91 women); includes 201 minority (66 Black or African American, non-Hispanic/Latino; 3 American Indian or Alaska Native, non-Hispanic/Latino; 31 Asian, non-Hispanic/Latino; 90 Hispanic/Latino; 8 Native Hawaiian or other Pacific Islander, non-Hispanic/Latino; 3 Two or more races, non-Hispanic/Latino), 28 international. Average age 28. 3,212 applicants, 50% accepted, 317 enrolled. *Faculty:* 41 full-time (23 women), 69 part-time/adjunct (20 women). Expenses: Contact institution. *Financial support:* In 2017–18, 506 students received support, including 493 fellowships with full and partial tuition reimbursements available (averaging $33,296 per year); research assistantships with full and partial tuition reimbursements available, career-related internships or fieldwork, Federal Work-Study, institutionally sponsored loans, scholarships/grants, tuition waivers (full and partial), and unspecified assistantships also available. Support available to part-time students. Financial award applicants required to submit FAFSA. In 2017, 9 master's, 234 doctorates awarded. *Program availability:* Part-time, 100% online. Offers alternative dispute resolution (JD); American legal studies (LL M); business law honors (JD); clinical bioethics (Certificate); corporate compliance (JD); criminal law and procedure (JD); family law (LL M, JD); health law (JD); health law and policy (LL M, MA); intellectual property law honors (JD); international law honors (JD). *Application deadline:* For fall admission, 4/15 priority date for domestic and international students. Applications are processed on a rolling basis. *Application fee:* $75. Electronic applications accepted. *Application Contact:* Sunil Samuel, Assistant Vice President of Admissions, 516-463-4723, Fax: 516-463-4664. *Dean,* Gail Prudenti, 516-463-4068, E-mail: gail.prudenti@hofstra.edu.

School of Education Students: 267 full-time (193 women), 373 part-time (278 women); includes 159 minority (69 Black or African American, non-Hispanic/Latino; 1 American Indian or Alaska Native, non-Hispanic/Latino; 22 Asian, non-Hispanic/Latino; 64 Hispanic/Latino; 2 Native Hawaiian or other Pacific Islander, non-Hispanic/Latino; 1 Two or more races, non-Hispanic/Latino), 13 international. Average age 31. 433 applicants, 90% accepted, 225 enrolled. *Faculty:* 26 full-time (16 women), 60 part-time/adjunct (41 women). Expenses: Contact institution. *Financial support:* In 2017–18, 315 students received support, including 164 fellowships with full and partial tuition reimbursements available (averaging $4,332 per year), 14 research assistantships with full and partial tuition reimbursements available (averaging $7,435 per year); career-related internships or fieldwork, Federal Work-Study, institutionally sponsored loans, scholarships/grants, traineeships, tuition waivers (full and partial), and unspecified assistantships also available. Support available to part-time students. Financial award applicants required to submit FAFSA. In 2017, 200 master's, 26 doctorates, 63 other advanced degrees awarded. *Program availability:* Part-time, evening/weekend, blended/hybrid learning. Offers applied behavior analysis (Advanced Certificate); bilingual education (MA); bilingual extension (Advanced Certificate); business education (MS Ed); childhood special education (MS Ed); curriculum studies (MS Ed); early childhood and childhood education (MS Ed); early childhood education (MA, MS Ed); early childhood special education (MS Ed, Advanced Certificate); education (MA, MS, MS Ed, Ed D, Advanced Certificate); educational and policy leadership (Ed D); educational leadership (Advanced Certificate); educational leadership and policy studies (MS Ed); educational technology (Advanced Certificate); elementary education (MA, MS Ed); elementary special education (MS Ed); English education (MS Ed); family and consumer science (MS Ed); fine arts and music education (Advanced Certificate); fine arts education (MS Ed); foreign language and TESOL (MS Ed); foreign language education (MA, MS Ed); foundations of education (Advanced Certificate); gifted education (Advanced Certificate); health education (MS); health professions pedagogy and leadership (MS); higher education leadership and policy studies (MS Ed); inclusive early childhood special education (MS Ed); inclusive elementary special education (MS Ed); inclusive secondary special education (MS Ed); languages other than English and teaching English as a second language (MA); learning and teaching (Ed D); literacy studies (MA, MS Ed, Ed D, Advanced Certificate); mathematics education (MA, MS Ed); music education (MA, MS Ed); pedagogy for health professions (Advanced Certificate); physical education (MS); school district business leader (Advanced Certificate); science education (MA); secondary education (Advanced Certificate); secondary education generalist - students with disabilities 7-12 (MS Ed); secondary special education generalist (MS Ed); social studies education (MA, MS Ed); special education (MS Ed, Advanced Certificate); special education assessment and diagnosis (Advanced Certificate); special education early childhood intervention (MS Ed); special education: international perspectives (MS Ed); teaching languages other than English and TESOL (MS Ed); teaching students with severe or multiple disabilities (Advanced Certificate); technology for learning (MA); TESOL (MS Ed, Advanced Certificate); TESOL with specialization in STEM (MA); work based learning extension (Advanced Certificate). *Application deadline:* Applications are processed on a rolling basis. *Application fee:* $75. Electronic applications accepted. *Application Contact:* Sunil Samuel, Assistant Vice President of Admissions, 516-463-4723, Fax: 516-463-4664, E-mail: graduateadmission@hofstra.edu. *Dean,* Dr. Benjamin Rifkin, 516-463-5411, Fax: 516-463-4861, E-mail: benjamin.rifkin@hofstra.edu.

School of Health Professions and Human Services Students: 465 full-time (367 women), 201 part-time (161 women); includes 264 minority (98 Black or African American, non-Hispanic/Latino; 2 American Indian or Alaska Native, non-Hispanic/Latino; 84 Asian, non-Hispanic/Latino; 69 Hispanic/Latino; 8 Native Hawaiian or other Pacific Islander, non-Hispanic/Latino; 3 Two or more races, non-Hispanic/Latino), 31 international. Average age 28. 1,161 applicants, 51% accepted, 249 enrolled. *Faculty:* 33 full-time (20 women), 57 part-time/adjunct (35 women). Expenses: Contact institution. *Financial support:* In 2017–18, 265 students received support, including 169 fellowships with full and partial tuition reimbursements available (averaging $3,407 per year), 12 research assistantships with full and partial tuition reimbursements available (averaging $6,328 per year); career-related internships or fieldwork, Federal Work-Study, institutionally sponsored loans, scholarships/grants, traineeships, tuition waivers (full and partial), and unspecified assistantships also available. Support available to part-time students. Financial award applicants required to submit FAFSA. In 2017, 203 master's, 5 doctorates, 8 other advanced degrees awarded. *Program availability:* Part-time, evening/weekend. Offers audiology (Au D); counseling (MS Ed, PD); creative arts therapy (MA); foundations of public health (Advanced Certificate); health administration (MHA); health informatics (MS); health professions and human services (MA, MHA, MPH, MS, MS Ed, Au D, Advanced Certificate, PD); interdisciplinary transition specialist (Advanced Certificate); marriage and family therapy (MA); mental health counseling (MA, Advanced Certificate); occupational therapy (MS); public health (MPH); rehabilitation administration (PD); rehabilitation counseling (MS Ed, Advanced Certificate); rehabilitation counseling in mental health (MS Ed, Advanced Certificate); security and privacy in health information systems (Advanced Certificate); speech-language pathology (MA); sports science (MS); teacher of students with speech-language disabilities (Advanced Certificate). *Application deadline:* Applications are processed on a rolling basis. *Application fee:* $75. Electronic applications accepted. *Application Contact:* Sunil Samuel, Assistant Vice President of Admissions, 516-463-4723, Fax: 516-463-4664, E-mail: graduateadmission@hofstra.edu. *Dean,* Dr. Holly Seirup, 516-463-5301, Fax: 516-463-5317, E-mail: holly.j.seirup@hofstra.edu.

HOLLINS UNIVERSITY, Roanoke, VA 24020

General Information Independent, Undergraduate: women only; graduate: coed, comprehensive institution. *Enrollment:* 790 graduate, professional, and undergraduate students; 55 full-time matriculated graduate/professional students (42 women), 91 part-time matriculated graduate/professional students (81 women). *Enrollment by degree level:* 145 master's, 1 other advanced degree. *Graduate housing:* Room and/or apartments available on a first-come, first-served basis to single students; on-campus housing not available to married students. Typical cost: $8735 per year. Housing application deadline: 8/1. *Student services:* Campus safety program, career counseling, services for students with disabilities, teacher training, writing training. *Library facilities:* Wyndham Robertson Library plus 1 other. *Collection:* Books: 246,065 (physical), 122,121 (digital/electronic); Serial titles: 1,160 (physical), 51,262 (digital/electronic); Databases: 130. Weekly public service hours: 94.

Computer facilities: Computer purchase and lease plans are available. 102 computers available on campus for general student use. A campuswide network can be accessed from student residence rooms. Online class registration is available.
Website: http://www.hollins.edu/

General Application Contact: Cathy S. Koon, Manager of Graduate Services, 540-362-6326, Fax: 540-362-6288, E-mail: ckoon@hollins.edu.

GRADUATE UNITS

Graduate Programs 162 applicants, 27% accepted, 27 enrolled. Expenses: Contact institution. *Financial support:* Fellowships, teaching assistantships, Federal Work-Study, and scholarships/grants available. Financial award application deadline: 7/15; financial award applicants required to submit FAFSA. In 2017, 78 master's awarded. *Program availability:* Part-time, evening/weekend, 100% online, blended/hybrid learning. Offers children's book illustration (Certificate); children's book writing and illustrating (MFA); children's literature (MA, MFA); creative writing (MFA); dance (MFA); humanities (MALS); interdisciplinary studies (MALS); leadership (MALS); new play directing (Certificate); new play performance (Certificate); playwriting (MFA); screenwriting (MFA); screenwriting and film studies (MA); social sciences (MALS); teaching (MAT); teaching and learning (MA); visual and performing arts (MALS). *Application deadline:* For fall admission, 1/6 priority date for domestic and international students. Applications are processed on a rolling basis. *Application fee:* $40. Electronic applications accepted. *Application Contact:* Cathy S. Koon, Manager of Graduate Services, 540-362-6326, Fax: 540-362-6288, E-mail: hugrad@hollins.edu. *Vice President for Academic Affairs*, Dr. Patricia Hammer, 540-3626326, Fax: 540-362-6288, E-mail: hugrad@hollins.edu.

HOLMES INSTITUTE, Golden, CO 80401

General Information Independent-religious, coed, graduate-only institution. *Graduate housing:* On-campus housing not available.

GRADUATE UNITS

Graduate Program *Program availability:* Online learning. Offers consciousness studies (MS).

HOLY APOSTLES COLLEGE AND SEMINARY, Cromwell, CT 06416-2005

General Information Independent-religious, coed, comprehensive institution. *Graduate housing:* On-campus housing not available.

GRADUATE UNITS

Department of Theology *Program availability:* Part-time, evening/weekend, online learning. Offers bioethics (MA, Certificate, Post Master's Certificate); church history (MA, Certificate, Post Master's Certificate); dogmatic theology (MA, Certificate, Post Master's Certificate); liturgical music (MA, Certificate, Post Master's Certificate); liturgy (MA, Certificate, Post Master's Certificate); moral theology (MA, Certificate, Post Master's Certificate); philosophical theology (MA, Certificate, Post Master's Certificate); religious education (MA, Certificate, Post Master's Certificate); sacred scripture (MA, Post Master's Certificate); sacred scriptures (Certificate); theology (M Div). Electronic applications accepted.

HOLY CROSS GREEK ORTHODOX SCHOOL OF THEOLOGY, Brookline, MA 02445-7496

General Information Independent-religious, coed, primarily men, graduate-only institution. *Graduate housing:* Rooms and/or apartments available on a first-come, first-served basis to single and married students.

GRADUATE UNITS

Theological Programs *Program availability:* Part-time. Offers theology (M Div, MTS, Th M).

HOLY FAMILY UNIVERSITY, Philadelphia, PA 19114

General Information Independent-religious, coed, comprehensive institution. *Enrollment:* 3,081 graduate, professional, and undergraduate students; 249 full-time matriculated graduate/professional students (204 women), 722 part-time matriculated graduate/professional students (564 women). *Enrollment by degree level:* 862 master's, 35 doctoral, 74 other advanced degrees. *Graduate faculty:* 30 full-time (22 women), 73 part-time/adjunct (42 women). *Tuition:* Full-time $13,518; part-time $9012 per credit hour. Tuition and fees vary according to degree level and program. *Graduate housing:* On-campus housing not available. *Student services:* Campus employment opportunities, campus safety program, career counseling, child daycare facilities, exercise/wellness program, free psychological counseling, multicultural affairs office, services for students with disabilities, teacher training, writing training. *Library facilities:* Holy Family University Library plus 1 other. *Collection:* Books: 75,943 (physical), 27,681 (digital/electronic); Serial titles: 1,106 (physical), 22,214 (digital/electronic); Databases: 42. Weekly public service hours: 116; students can reserve study rooms.

Computer facilities: 300 computers available on campus for general student use. A campuswide network can be accessed from student residence rooms and from off campus. Online class registration, online course syllabi, online course evaluations are available.
Website: http://www.holyfamily.edu/

General Application Contact: Robert McIntyre, Associate Director of Graduate Admissions, 267-341-3555, Fax: 215-637-1478, E-mail: rmcintyre01@holyfamily.edu.

GRADUATE UNITS

Graduate and Professional Programs *Program availability:* Part-time, evening/weekend. Electronic applications accepted.

School of Arts and Sciences *Program availability:* Part-time, evening/weekend. Offers counseling psychology (MS); criminal justice (MA). Electronic applications accepted.

School of Business Administration *Program availability:* Part-time, evening/weekend. Offers accountancy (MS); finance (MBA); health care administration (MBA); human resource management (MBA); information systems management (MBA). Electronic applications accepted.

School of Education *Program availability:* Part-time, evening/weekend. Offers early elementary education (PreK-Grade 4) (M Ed); education (M Ed, Ed D); education leadership (M Ed); educational leadership and professional studies (Ed D); general education (M Ed); reading specialist (M Ed); special education (M Ed); TESOL and literacy (M Ed). Electronic applications accepted.

School of Nursing and Allied Health Professions *Program availability:* Part-time, evening/weekend. Offers nursing administration (MSN); nursing education (MSN). Electronic applications accepted.

HOLY NAMES UNIVERSITY, Oakland, CA 94619-1699

General Information Independent-religious, coed, comprehensive institution. *Graduate housing:* Room and/or apartments available on a first-come, first-served basis to single students; on-campus housing not available to married students. Housing application deadline: 8/15.

GRADUATE UNITS

Graduate Division *Program availability:* Part-time, evening/weekend. Offers administration/management (MSN, PMC); care transition management (MSN); counseling and forensic counseling (MA); counseling psychology (MA); creative writing (MA); educational therapy (Certificate); family nurse practitioner (MSN, PMC); finance (MBA); forensic psychology (MA); informatics (MSN); Kodaly (Certificate); management and leadership (MBA); marketing (MBA); mild/moderate disabilities (Ed S); multiple subject teaching (Credential); music education with Kodaly emphasis (MM); nurse educator (PMC); piano pedagogy (MM); single subject teaching (Credential); urban education: educational therapy (M Ed); urban education: K-12 education (M Ed); urban education: special education (M Ed); vocal pedagogy (MM). Electronic applications accepted.

HOOD COLLEGE, Frederick, MD 21701-8575

General Information Independent, coed, comprehensive institution. CGS member. *Enrollment:* 2,112 graduate, professional, and undergraduate students; 187 full-time matriculated graduate/professional students (102 women), 751 part-time matriculated graduate/professional students (511 women). *Enrollment by degree level:* 769 master's, 35 doctoral, 134 other advanced degrees. *Graduate faculty:* 36 full-time (19 women), 63 part-time/adjunct (37 women). *Tuition:* Part-time $465 per credit. *Required fees:* $110 per semester. Tuition and fees vary according to degree level and program. *Graduate housing:* On-campus housing not available. *Student services:* Campus employment opportunities, campus safety program, career counseling, international student services, multicultural affairs office, services for students with disabilities, teacher training. *Library facilities:* Beneficial-Hodson Library and Information Technology Center plus 1 other. *Collection:* Books: 172,311 (physical), 295,531 (digital/electronic); Serial titles: 235 (physical), 42,000 (digital/electronic); Databases: 96. Students can reserve study rooms. *Research affiliation:* U.S. Department of Agriculture (USDA) (biomedical science and environmental biology), United States Army Medical Research Institute of Infectious Diseases (USAMRIID) (biomedical science), National Cancer Institute (biomedical science).

Computer facilities: Computer purchase and lease plans are available. 470 computers available on campus for general student use. A campuswide network can be accessed from student residence rooms and from off campus. Online class registration, Virtual Computer Lab (VCL) are available.
Website: http://www.hood.edu/

General Application Contact: Dr. April Boulton, Dean of Graduate School, 301-696-3600, Fax: 301-696-3597, E-mail: gofurther@hood.edu.

GRADUATE UNITS

Graduate School Students: 187 full-time (102 women), 751 part-time (511 women); includes 164 minority (79 Black or African American, non-Hispanic/Latino; 2 American Indian or Alaska Native, non-Hispanic/Latino; 26 Asian, non-Hispanic/Latino; 37 Hispanic/Latino; 20 Two or more races, non-Hispanic/Latino), 131 international. Average age 33. 299 applicants, 94% accepted, 199 enrolled. *Faculty:* 36 full-time (19 women), 63 part-time/adjunct (37 women). Expenses: Contact institution. *Financial support:* Research assistantships with full tuition reimbursements, tuition waivers (partial), and unspecified assistantships available. Financial award applicants required to submit FAFSA. In 2017, 231 master's, 99 other advanced degrees awarded. *Program availability:* Part-time, evening/weekend. Offers accounting (MBA, Certificate); bioinformatics (MS, Certificate); biomedical science (MS); ceramic arts (Certificate); ceramics (MA, MFA); clinical mental health counseling (MS); computer science (MS); curriculum and instruction (MS); cybersecurity (MS, Certificate); education, multidisciplinary studies (MS); educational leadership (MS, Certificate); environmental biology (MS); finance (MBA); financial management (Certificate); geographic information systems (Certificate); high school (MS); human resource management (MBA); humanities (MA); information systems (MBA); information technology (MS); interdisciplinary studies in human behavior (MA); management information systems (MS); marketing (MBA); middle school (MS); organizational leadership (DBA, DOL); organizational management (Certificate); public management (MBA); reading specialization (MS); school counseling (MS); secondary mathematics education (Certificate); STEM education (Certificate); thanatology (Certificate). *Application deadline:* For fall admission, 8/15 priority date for domestic students, 8/5 for international students; for spring admission, 12/1 priority date for domestic students, 12/1 for international students; for summer admission, 5/1 priority date for domestic students, 4/15 for international students. Applications are processed on a rolling basis. *Application fee:* $35. Electronic applications accepted. *Dean of the Graduate School*, Dr. April M Boulton, 301-696-3600, E-mail: gofurther@hood.edu.

HOOD THEOLOGICAL SEMINARY, Salisbury, NC 28144

General Information Independent-religious, coed, graduate-only institution. *Graduate housing:* Rooms and/or apartments guaranteed to single students and available on a first-come, first-served basis to married students. Housing application deadline: 8/15.

GRADUATE UNITS

Graduate and Professional Programs *Program availability:* Part-time, evening/weekend, online learning. Offers theology (M Div, MTS, D Min).

HOPE INTERNATIONAL UNIVERSITY, Fullerton, CA 92831-3138

General Information Independent-religious, coed, comprehensive institution. *Graduate housing:* Room and/or apartments available on a first-come, first-served basis to single students; on-campus housing not available to married students. Housing application deadline: 7/1.

GRADUATE UNITS

School of Graduate and Professional Studies *Program availability:* Part-time, evening/weekend, online learning. Offers Christian leadership (MCM); church music (MA); church music (Korean track) (MCM); church planting (MCM); education administration (MA); elementary education (ME); general management (MBA, MSM); intercultural studies (MCM); international development (MBA, MSM); marketing management (MBA, MSM); marriage and family therapy (MA, MFT); non-profit management (MBA, MSM); secondary education (ME); worship (MCM). Electronic applications accepted.

HOUGHTON COLLEGE, Houghton, NY 14744

General Information Independent-religious, coed, comprehensive institution. *Graduate housing:* On-campus housing not available.

GRADUATE UNITS

Greatbatch School of Music Offers collaborative performance (MMus); composition (MMus); conducting (MMus); music (MA); performance (MMus); world music with theology and intercultural studies (MA). Electronic applications accepted.

HOUSTON BAPTIST UNIVERSITY, Houston, TX 77074-3298

General Information Independent-religious, coed, comprehensive institution. *Enrollment:* 3,325 graduate, professional, and undergraduate students; 374 full-time matriculated graduate/professional students (257 women), 600 part-time matriculated graduate/professional students (435 women). *Enrollment by degree level:* 936 master's,

38 doctoral. *Graduate faculty:* 70 full-time (30 women), 42 part-time/adjunct (19 women). *Tuition:* Full-time $9900; part-time $6600 per year. *Required fees:* $2550; $2550 per unit. Tuition and fees vary according to campus/location, program and reciprocity agreements. *Graduate housing:* Rooms and/or apartments available on a first-come, first-served basis to single and married students. Typical cost: $2932 (including board) for single students; $2932 (including board) for married students. Room and board charges vary according to campus/location and housing facility selected. Housing application deadline: 4/1. *Student services:* Campus employment opportunities, career counseling, exercise/wellness program, free psychological counseling, international student services, low-cost health insurance, services for students with disabilities, teacher training, writing training. *Library facilities:* Moody Library. *Collection:* Books: 109,715 (physical); Serial titles: 252 (physical), 57,209 (digital/electronic); Databases: 111. Students can reserve study rooms.

Computer facilities: 100 computers available on campus for general student use. A campuswide network can be accessed from student residence rooms. Online class registration, office software for 5 devices for each student are available.
Website: http://www.hbu.edu/

General Application Contact: Allyson Cates, Director of Admissions, Graduate School, 281-649-3099, Fax: 281-649-3390, E-mail: acates@hbu.edu.

GRADUATE UNITS

Archie W. Dunham College of Business Students: 124 full-time (74 women), 98 part-time (71 women); includes 125 minority (68 Black or African American, non-Hispanic/Latino; 13 Asian, non-Hispanic/Latino; 36 Hispanic/Latino; 1 Native Hawaiian or other Pacific Islander, non-Hispanic/Latino; 7 Two or more races, non-Hispanic/Latino), 51 international. Average age 29. 405 applicants, 33% accepted, 61 enrolled. *Faculty:* 13 full-time (3 women), 10 part-time/adjunct (2 women). Expenses: Contact institution. *Financial support:* In 2017–18, 40 students received support. Federal Work-Study and scholarships/grants available. Support available to part-time students. Financial award application deadline: 4/1; financial award applicants required to submit FAFSA. In 2017, 114 master's awarded. *Program availability:* Part-time, evening/weekend, 100% online. Offers business (MBA, MIB, MSHRM); business administration (MBA); human resources management (MSHRM); international business (MIB). *Application deadline:* For fall admission, 8/1 for domestic students, 6/1 for international students; for spring admission, 1/1 for domestic students, 11/1 for international students; for summer admission, 5/1 for domestic students, 3/1 for international students. Applications are processed on a rolling basis. *Application fee:* $0 ($100 for international students). Electronic applications accepted. *Application Contact:* Laurel Motal, Graduate Student Services Coordinator, 281-649-3306, E-mail: lmotal@hbu.edu. *Dean*, Dr. Michael Weeks, 281-649-3014, E-mail: mweeks@hbu.edu.

College of Education and Behavioral Sciences Students: 171 full-time (141 women), 343 part-time (293 women); includes 339 minority (181 Black or African American, non-Hispanic/Latino; 2 American Indian or Alaska Native, non-Hispanic/Latino; 29 Asian, non-Hispanic/Latino; 117 Hispanic/Latino; 10 Two or more races, non-Hispanic/Latino), 15 international. Average age 33. *Faculty:* 26 full-time (18 women), 23 part-time/adjunct (15 women). Expenses: Contact institution. *Financial support:* In 2017–18, 79 students received support. Career-related internships or fieldwork, Federal Work-Study, and scholarships/grants available. Support available to part-time students. Financial award application deadline: 4/1; financial award applicants required to submit FAFSA. In 2017, 137 master's awarded. *Program availability:* Part-time, evening/weekend, 100% online. Offers bilingual education (M Ed); Christian counseling (MACC); counseling (MAC); counselor education (M Ed); curriculum and instruction (M Ed); curriculum and instruction (EC-6 bilingual) (M Ed); curriculum and instruction in all-level art, Spanish, music, or physical education (M Ed); curriculum and instruction in EC-6 and special education (EC-12) (M Ed); curriculum and instruction in instructional technology (M Ed); curriculum and instruction in mathematics, science, or social studies (4-8) (M Ed); curriculum and instruction with EC-6 generalist (M Ed); curriculum and instruction with English language arts and reading (4-8) (M Ed); education and behavioral sciences (M Ed, MA, MAC, MACC, MAP, Ed D); educational administration (M Ed); educational diagnostician (M Ed); executive educational leadership (Ed D); higher education in business management (M Ed); higher education in Christian studies (M Ed); higher education in counseling (M Ed); higher education in educational technology (M Ed); marriage and family therapy (MA); pastoral counseling (MA); reading (M Ed); school psychology (MAP); special educational leadership (Ed D). *Application deadline:* For fall admission, 8/1 for domestic students, 6/1 for international students; for spring admission, 1/1 for domestic students, 11/1 for international students; for summer admission, 5/1 for domestic students, 3/1 for international students. Applications are processed on a rolling basis. *Application fee:* $0 ($100 for international students). Electronic applications accepted. *Application Contact:* Kristy Wright, Administrative Assistant for Graduate Programs, 281-649-3094, Fax: 281-649-3361, E-mail: kwright@hbu.edu. *Dean*, Dr. Theresa McIntyre, 281-649-3127, Fax: 281-649-3361, E-mail: mmcintyre@hbu.edu.

School of Christian Thought Students: 31 full-time (13 women), 119 part-time (49 women); includes 43 minority (26 Black or African American, non-Hispanic/Latino; 2 Asian, non-Hispanic/Latino; 12 Hispanic/Latino; 3 Two or more races, non-Hispanic/Latino), 8 international. Average age 37. 153 applicants, 52% accepted, 46 enrolled. *Faculty:* 16 full-time (3 women), 5 part-time/adjunct (1 woman). Expenses: Contact institution. *Financial support:* In 2017–18, 42 students received support. Federal Work-Study and scholarships/grants available. Support available to part-time students. Financial award application deadline: 4/1; financial award applicants required to submit FAFSA. In 2017, 32 master's awarded. *Program availability:* Part-time, evening/weekend. Offers Biblical languages (M Div); Christian leadership (MA); Christian thought (M Div, MA); cultural apologetics (MA); English languages (M Div); philosophical apologetics (MA); theological studies (MA). *Application deadline:* For fall admission, 8/1 for domestic students, 6/1 for international students; for spring admission, 1/1 for domestic students, 11/1 for international students; for summer admission, 5/1 for domestic students, 3/1 for international students. Applications are processed on a rolling basis. *Application fee:* $0 ($100 for international students). Electronic applications accepted. *Application Contact:* Celeste Risteski, Administrative Assistant to the Dean, 281-649-3383, Fax: 281-649-3012, E-mail: cristeski@hbu.edu. *Interim Dean*, Dr. Jeffrey Green, 281-649-3197, Fax: 281-649-3012, E-mail: jgreen@hbu.edu.

School of Fine Arts Students: 21 full-time (13 women), 2 part-time (both women); includes 5 minority (2 Black or African American, non-Hispanic/Latino; 3 Hispanic/Latino), 2 international. Average age 34. 40 applicants, 43% accepted, 12 enrolled. *Faculty:* 7 full-time (1 woman), 2 part-time/adjunct (1 woman). Expenses: Contact institution. *Financial support:* In 2017–18, 19 students received support. Federal Work-Study and scholarships/grants available. Support available to part-time students. Financial award application deadline: 4/1; financial award applicants required to submit FAFSA. In 2017, 10 master's awarded. *Program availability:* Part-time, evening/weekend. Offers studio art (MFA). *Application deadline:* For fall admission, 4/1 for domestic students, 2/1 for international students. Applications are processed on a rolling basis. *Application fee:* $0 ($100 for international students). Electronic applications accepted. *Application Contact:* Dr. Michael Collins, Program Director, 281-649-3624, E-mail: mcollins@hbu.edu. *Dean*, Dr. Jason Lester, 281-649-3339, E-mail: jlester@hbu.edu.

School of Humanities Students: 18 full-time (9 women), 26 part-time (11 women); includes 22 minority (8 Black or African American, non-Hispanic/Latino; 1 American Indian or Alaska Native, non-Hispanic/Latino; 4 Asian, non-Hispanic/Latino; 7 Hispanic/Latino; 2 Two or more races, non-Hispanic/Latino). Average age 32. 52 applicants, 71% accepted, 21 enrolled. *Faculty:* 8 full-time (2 women), 2 part-time/adjunct (0 women). Expenses: Contact institution. *Financial support:* In 2017–18, 19 students received support. Federal Work-Study and scholarships/grants available. Financial award application deadline: 4/1; financial award applicants required to submit FAFSA. In 2017, 20 master's awarded. *Program availability:* Part-time, evening/weekend. Offers education (EC-12 art, music, physical education, or Spanish) (MLA); education (EC-6 generalist) (MLA); general liberal arts (MLA); humanities (MA, MLA); philosophy (MA); specialization in education (4-8 or 7-12) (MLA). *Application deadline:* For fall admission, 8/1 for domestic students, 6/1 for international students; for spring admission, 1/1 for domestic students, 11/1 for international students; for summer admission, 5/1 for domestic students, 3/1 for international students. Applications are processed on a rolling basis. *Application fee:* $0 ($100 for international students). Electronic applications accepted. *Application Contact:* Allyson Cates, Director of Admissions, Graduate School, 281-649-3099, Fax: 281-649-3390, E-mail: acates@hbu.edu. *Dean, School of Humanities*, Dr. Jodey Hinze, 281-649-3130, E-mail: jhinze@hbu.edu.

HOUSTON GRADUATE SCHOOL OF THEOLOGY, Houston, TX 77092

General Information Independent-religious, coed, graduate-only institution. *Graduate housing:* On-campus housing not available.

GRADUATE UNITS

Graduate Programs *Program availability:* Part-time, evening/weekend. Offers counseling (MA); pastoral ministry (M Div, D Min); theology (MA).

HOWARD PAYNE UNIVERSITY, Brownwood, TX 76801-2715

General Information Independent-religious, coed, comprehensive institution. *Graduate housing:* Room and/or apartments available on a first-come, first-served basis to single students; on-campus housing not available to married students.

GRADUATE UNITS

Program in Business Administration *Program availability:* Part-time, evening/weekend. Offers business administration (MBA). Electronic applications accepted.

Program in Criminal Justice *Program availability:* Part-time, evening/weekend, online only, 100% online. Offers criminal justice (MS). Electronic applications accepted.

Program in Instructional Leadership *Program availability:* Part-time, evening/weekend, online only. Offers instructional leadership (M Ed). Electronic applications accepted.

Program in Sport and Wellness Leadership *Program availability:* Part-time. Offers sport and wellness leadership (M Ed). Electronic applications accepted.

Program in Theology and Ministry *Program availability:* Part-time. Offers theology and ministry (MA). Electronic applications accepted.

Program in Youth Ministry *Program availability:* Part-time. Offers youth ministry (MA). Electronic applications accepted.

HOWARD UNIVERSITY, Washington, DC 20059-0002

General Information Independent, coed, university. CGS member. *Graduate housing:* Rooms and/or apartments available on a first-come, first-served basis to single and married students. Housing application deadline: 4/1. *Research affiliation:* Ewing Marion Kauffman Foundation (science education), The Tokyo Foundation (women's studies, international affairs), National Oceanic and Atmospheric Administration (NOAA) (atmospheric science and nanotechnology), National Institute of Mental Health (NIMH) (genomics), Akilu Lamma Institute of Pathobiology (HIV/AIDS infection, water resources development, population movement), Labor Research Laboratories and Medical Center in Benin City, Nigeria (infectious diseases).

GRADUATE UNITS

Cathy Hughes School of Communications *Program availability:* Part-time, evening/weekend. Offers communication sciences (PhD); communications (MA, MFA, MS, PhD); film (MFA); intercultural communication (MA, PhD); organizational communication (MA, PhD); speech pathology (MS). Electronic applications accepted.

Department of Communication, Culture and Media Studies *Program availability:* Part-time, evening/weekend. Offers mass communication (MA, PhD); media studies (MA, PhD). Electronic applications accepted.

College of Dentistry Offers advanced education in general dentistry (Certificate); dentistry (DDS); general dentistry practice (Certificate); oral and maxillofacial surgery (Certificate); orthodontics (Certificate); pediatric dentistry (Certificate).

College of Engineering, Architecture, and Computer Sciences *Program availability:* Part-time. Offers engineering, architecture, and computer sciences (M Eng, MCS, MS, PhD). Electronic applications accepted.

School of Engineering and Computer Science *Program availability:* Part-time. Offers chemical engineering (MS); civil engineering (M Eng); electrical engineering (M Eng, PhD); engineering and computer science (M Eng, MCS, MS, PhD); mechanical engineering (M Eng, PhD); systems and computer science (MCS). Electronic applications accepted.

College of Medicine Offers biochemistry and molecular biology (PhD); biotechnology (MS); medicine (MPH, MS, MD, PhD); microbiology (PhD); pharmacology (MS, PhD); public health (MPH).

College of Nursing and Allied Health Sciences *Program availability:* Part-time. Offers nursing and allied health sciences (MPA, MSN, MSOT, DPT, Certificate). Electronic applications accepted.

Division of Allied Health Sciences Offers occupational therapy (MSOT); physical therapy (DPT); physician assistant (MPA).

Division of Nursing *Program availability:* Part-time. Offers family nurse practitioner (MSN); nurse educator (MSN).

College of Pharmacy *Program availability:* Online learning. Offers pharmacy (Pharm D). Electronic applications accepted.

Graduate School *Program availability:* Part-time, evening/weekend. Offers African diaspora (MA, PhD); African history (MA, PhD); African studies (MA, PhD); analytical chemistry (MS, PhD); anatomy (MS, PhD); applied mathematics (MS, PhD); atmospheric (MS, PhD); atmospheric sciences (MS, PhD); biochemistry (MS, PhD); biology (MS, PhD); biophysics (PhD); clinical psychology (PhD); developmental psychology (PhD); economics (MA, PhD); English (MA, PhD); environmental (MS, PhD); exercise physiology (MS); experimental psychology (PhD); French (MA); health education (MS); inorganic chemistry (MS, PhD); Latin America and the Caribbean (MA, PhD); mathematics (MS, PhD); neuropsychology (PhD); nutrition (MS, PhD); organic chemistry (MS, PhD); personality psychology (PhD); philosophy (MA); physical chemistry (MS, PhD); physics (MS, PhD); physiology (PhD); political science (MA, MAPA, PhD); psychology (MS); public administration (MAPA); public history (MA); social psychology (PhD); sociology (MA, PhD); Spanish (MA); sports studies (MS); United States history (MA, PhD); urban recreation (MS). Electronic applications accepted.

Division of Fine Arts *Program availability:* Part-time. Offers 3D reality (sculpture and ceramics) (MFA); applied music (MM); art history (MA); design (MFA); electronic studio (MFA); fine arts (MFA); history of art and visual culture (MA); instrument (MM Ed); jazz studies (MM); organ (MM Ed); painting (MFA); photography (MFA); piano (MM Ed); voice (MM Ed).

School of Business *Program availability:* Part-time, evening/weekend, online learning. Offers accounting (MBA); business (MBA); entrepreneurship (MBA); finance (MBA); general management (MBA); human resources management (MBA); information systems (MBA); international business (MBA); marketing (MBA); supply chain management (MBA).

School of Divinity *Program availability:* Part-time, evening/weekend. Offers theology (M Div, MARS, D Min). Electronic applications accepted.

School of Education Students: 115 full-time (85 women), 86 part-time (57 women); includes 163 minority (159 Black or African American, non-Hispanic/Latino; 3 Asian, non-Hispanic/Latino; 1 Hispanic/Latino), 28 international. Average age 32. 167 applicants, 63% accepted, 67 enrolled. *Faculty:* 39 full-time (27 women), 9 part-time/adjunct (4 women). Expenses: Contact institution. *Financial support:* In 2017–18, 69 students received support, including 5 fellowships (averaging $49,000 per year), 17 research assistantships (averaging $24,500 per year); career-related internships or fieldwork, Federal Work-Study, institutionally sponsored loans, scholarships/grants, tuition waivers (full and partial), and unspecified assistantships also available. Financial award application deadline: 2/15; financial award applicants required to submit FAFSA. In 2017, 8 master's, 35 doctorates awarded. Offers counseling psychology (PhD); education (M Ed, Ed D, PhD, CAGS); educational administration (Ed D); educational administration and supervision (M Ed, CAGS); educational psychology (PhD); elementary education (M Ed); school psychology (PhD); school psychology and counseling services (M Ed); secondary education (M Ed); special education (M Ed). *Application deadline:* For fall admission, 1/15 for domestic and international students. Applications are processed on a rolling basis. *Application fee:* $75. Electronic applications accepted. *Application Contact:* Dr. Kenneth A. Anderson, Interim Associate Dean for Academic Programs and Student Affairs, 202-806-7340, Fax: 202-806-7018, E-mail: kenneth.anderson@howard.edu. *Dean, School of Education,* Dr. Dawn G. Williams, 202-806-7340, Fax: 202-806-7018, E-mail: dgwilliams@howard.edu.

School of Law Offers law (LL M, JD). Electronic applications accepted.

School of Social Work *Program availability:* Part-time. Offers social work (MSW, PhD). Electronic applications accepted.

HULT INTERNATIONAL BUSINESS SCHOOL, Cambridge, MA 02141

General Information Independent, coed, comprehensive institution. *Graduate housing:* On-campus housing not available.

GRADUATE UNITS

Graduate Programs Offers business administration (EMBA); business analytics (MBA, MIB); business statistics (MBS); disruptive innovation (MDI); entrepreneurship (MBA, MIB); family business (MBA, MIB); finance (MBA, MF, MIB); international marketing (MIM); marketing (MBA, MIB); project management (MBA, MIB). MDI and MBS offered in San Francisco; MBA also offered in Boston, San Francisco, Dubai, Shanghai, and New York. Electronic applications accepted.

HUMBOLDT STATE UNIVERSITY, Arcata, CA 95521-8299

General Information State-supported, coed, comprehensive institution. *Graduate housing:* Room and/or apartments available on a first-come, first-served basis to single students; on-campus housing not available to married students. Housing application deadline: 2/1. *Research affiliation:* McIntire-Stennis (forestry), National Sea Grant, U.S. Fish and Wildlife Service-Wildlife Field Station, Redwood Sciences Laboratory of the Pacific Southwest Forest and Range Experiment Station, California Cooperative Fisheries Research Unit.

GRADUATE UNITS

Academic Programs *Program availability:* Part-time, evening/weekend. Electronic applications accepted.

College of Arts, Humanities, and Social Sciences *Program availability:* Part-time. Offers applied anthropology (MA); arts, humanities, and social sciences (MA); English (MA); environment and community (MA); sociology (MA). Electronic applications accepted.

College of Natural Resources and Sciences *Program availability:* Part-time. Offers biological sciences (MS); environmental systems (MS); natural resources (MS); natural resources and sciences (MA, MS, Certificate).

College of Professional Studies *Program availability:* Part-time, evening/weekend. Offers business (MBA); education (MA); kinesiology (MS); psychology (MA); social work (MSW).

HUMPHREYS UNIVERSITY, Stockton, CA 95207-3896

General Information Independent, coed, comprehensive institution. *Graduate housing:* On-campus housing not available.

GRADUATE UNITS

Drivon School of Law *Program availability:* Part-time, evening/weekend. Offers law (JD). Electronic applications accepted.

HUNTER COLLEGE OF THE CITY UNIVERSITY OF NEW YORK, New York, NY 10065-5085

General Information State and locally supported, coed, comprehensive institution. *Graduate housing:* Room and/or apartments available on a first-come, first-served basis to single students; on-campus housing not available to married students. *Research affiliation:* Mount Sinai Medical Center, Bellevue Hospital Center, Cornell University Medical Center, New York Hospital.

GRADUATE UNITS

Graduate School *Program availability:* Part-time, evening/weekend.

Hunter-Bellevue School of Nursing *Program availability:* Part-time. Offers adult-gerontology clinical nurse specialist (MS); adult-gerontology nurse practitioner (DNP); community/public health nursing (MS); family nurse practitioner (DNP); gerontological/adult nurse practitioner (MS); nursing (MS, DNP, AC); psychiatric-mental health nurse practitioner (MS, AC).

School of Arts and Sciences *Program availability:* Part-time, evening/weekend. Offers accounting (MS); adolescent mathematics education (MA); animal behavior and conservation (MA, Certificate); anthropology (MA); applied mathematics (MA); applied social research (MS); art history (MA); arts and sciences (MA, MFA, MS, MUP, PhD, Certificate); biochemistry (MA, PhD); bioinformatics (MA); biological sciences (MA, PhD); chemistry (MA, PhD); composition (MA); creative writing (MFA); economics (MA); ethnomusicology (MA); fiction (MFA); French (MA); general psychology (MA); geographic information science (Certificate); geography (MA); geoinformatics (MS); history (MA); integrated media arts (MFA); Italian (MA); literature, language, and theory (MA); memoir (MFA); music history (MA); music theory (MA); performance (MA); physics and astronomy (MA, PhD); playwriting (MFA); poetry (MFA); pure mathematics (MA); Spanish (MA); statistics (MA); studio art (MFA); teaching Chinese (MA); teaching Latin (MA); theatre (MA, MFA); urban affairs (MS); urban planning (MUP); urban policy and leadership (MS).

School of Education *Program availability:* Part-time, evening/weekend. Offers administration and supervision (AC); bilingual education (MS); biology education (MA); blind and visually impaired (MS Ed); chemistry education (MA); early childhood education (MS); earth science (MA); education (MA, MS, MS Ed, Ed D, AC); educational supervision and administration (Ed D, AC); elementary education (MS); English education (MA); French education (MA); instructional leadership (Ed D); Italian education (MA); mathematics education (MA); music education (MA); physics education (MA); rehabilitation counseling (MS Ed); school counseling (MS Ed); severe/multiple disabilities (MS Ed); social studies education (MA); Spanish education (MA); teaching English as a second language (MA). Electronic applications accepted.

School of Health Professions *Program availability:* Part-time, evening/weekend. Offers health professions (MS, DPT, AC); physical therapy (DPT); speech-language pathology (MS).

School of Urban Public Health *Program availability:* Part-time. Offers nutrition (MS).

Silberman School of Social Work Offers social work (MSW).

HUNTINGTON UNIVERSITY, Huntington, IN 46750-1299

General Information Independent-religious, coed, comprehensive institution. *Enrollment:* 221 full-time matriculated graduate/professional students (163 women), 22 part-time matriculated graduate/professional students (13 women). *Enrollment by degree level:* 143 master's, 100 doctoral. *Graduate faculty:* 17 full-time (10 women), 14 part-time/adjunct (4 women). *Graduate housing:* On-campus housing not available. *Student services:* Campus employment opportunities, campus safety program, career counseling, exercise/wellness program, low-cost health insurance, services for students with disabilities, teacher training. *Library facilities:* RichLyn Library. *Research affiliation:* Link Institute (youth ministry).

Computer facilities: 209 computers available on campus for general student use. A campuswide network can be accessed from student residence rooms and from off campus. Online class registration is available.
Website: http://www.huntington.edu/

General Application Contact: Evan Bennett, Assistant Director for Graduate Admissions, 260-359-4111, Fax: 260-359-4126, E-mail: graduate@huntington.edu.

GRADUATE UNITS

Graduate School Students: 221 full-time (163 women), 22 part-time (13 women). *Faculty:* 17 full-time (10 women), 14 part-time/adjunct (4 women). Expenses: Contact institution. *Financial support:* Scholarships/grants and unspecified assistantships available. Support available to part-time students. Financial award application deadline: 8/1; financial award applicants required to submit FAFSA. *Program availability:* Part-time, online learning. Offers adolescent and young adult education (M Ed); business administration (MBA); counseling (MA); early adolescent education (M Ed); elementary education (M Ed); global youth ministry (MA); occupational therapy (OTD); organizational leadership (MA); pastoral leadership (MA); TESOL education (M Ed). *Application deadline:* For fall admission, 7/1 for domestic students, 5/1 for international students; for winter admission, 10/1 for domestic students, 9/1 for international students; for spring admission, 11/30 for domestic students, 10/30 for international students. Applications are processed on a rolling basis. *Application fee:* $30. Electronic applications accepted. *Application Contact:* Evan Bennett, Assistant Director of Graduate Admissions, 260-359-4111, Fax: 260-359-4126, E-mail: graduate@huntington.edu. *Vice President for Academic Affairs,* Michael Wanous, 260-359-4008, Fax: 260-359-4126, E-mail: mwanous@huntington.edu.

HUNTINGTON UNIVERSITY OF HEALTH SCIENCES, Knoxville, TN 37918

General Information Proprietary, coed, comprehensive institution.

GRADUATE UNITS

Program in Nutrition *Program availability:* Part-time, evening/weekend, online learning. Offers clinical nutrition (DHS); nutrition (MS); personalized option (DHS). Electronic applications accepted.

HUNTSVILLE BIBLE COLLEGE, Huntsville, AL 35811-1632

General Information Independent, coed, comprehensive institution.

GRADUATE UNITS

Program in Ministry Offers biblical leadership (MM); pastoral studies (MM).

HUSSON UNIVERSITY, Bangor, ME 04401-2999

General Information Independent, coed, comprehensive institution. *Enrollment:* 3,640 graduate, professional, and undergraduate students; 450 full-time matriculated graduate/professional students (279 women), 412 part-time matriculated graduate/professional students (277 women). *Enrollment by degree level:* 585 master's, 277 doctoral. *Graduate faculty:* 58 full-time (31 women), 36 part-time/adjunct (15 women). *Tuition:* Full-time $17,310; part-time $577 per credit. *Required fees:* $480; $110 per credit. $55 per semester. One-time fee: $100 full-time. Tuition and fees vary according to degree level and program. *Graduate housing:* Room and/or apartments available on a first-come, first-served basis to single students; on-campus housing not available to married students. Typical cost: $10,300 (including board). Room and board charges vary according to housing facility selected. Housing application deadline: 6/1. *Student services:* Campus employment opportunities, campus safety program, career counseling, exercise/wellness program, free psychological counseling, international student services, writing training. *Library facilities:* Sawyer Library. *Collection:* Books: 41,659 (physical), 5,539 (digital/electronic); Serial titles: 74 (physical), 151 (digital/electronic); Databases: 91. Weekly public service hours: 98; study areas open 24 hours, 5–7 days a week; students can reserve study rooms.

Computer facilities: 131 computers available on campus for general student use. A campuswide network can be accessed from student residence rooms and from off campus. Online class registration is available.
Website: http://www.husson.edu/

General Application Contact: Melissa Rosenberg, Director of Graduate Admissions, 207-404-5660, Fax: 207-941-7850, E-mail: rosenbergm@husson.edu.

GRADUATE UNITS

Doctorate in Physical Therapy Program Students: 87 full-time (51 women), 1 (woman) part-time; includes 2 minority (1 Asian, non-Hispanic/Latino; 1 Two or more races, non-Hispanic/Latino), 2 international. Average age 25. 236 applicants, 17% accepted, 15 enrolled. *Faculty:* 10 full-time (5 women), 2 part-time/adjunct (both women). Expenses: Contact institution. *Financial support:* In 2017–18, 20 students received support. Federal Work-Study, scholarships/grants, and unspecified assistantships available. Financial award application deadline: 4/15; financial award applicants required to submit FAFSA. In 2017, 32 doctorates awarded. Offers physical therapy (DPT). *Application deadline:* For fall admission, 4/15 for domestic and international students. *Application fee:* $50. Electronic applications accepted. *Application Contact:* Cecile Ferguson, Administrative Assistant, 207-941-7101, E-mail: fergusonc@husson.edu. *Director,* Dr. Karen Huhn, 207-941-7620, E-mail: huhnk@husson.edu.

Graduate Nursing Program Students: 1 full-time (0 women), 62 part-time (54 women); includes 3 minority (2 Black or African American, non-Hispanic/Latino; 1 Hispanic/Latino), 1 international. Average age 36. 62 applicants, 55% accepted, 26 enrolled. *Faculty:* 4 full-time (all women), 4 part-time/adjunct (all women). Expenses: Contact institution. *Financial support:* In 2017–18, 1 student received support. Federal Work-Study, institutionally sponsored loans, traineeships, and unspecified assistantships available. Financial award application deadline: 3/31; financial award applicants required to submit FAFSA. In 2017, 9 master's awarded. *Program availability:* Part-time, evening/weekend. Offers educational leadership (MSN); family and community nurse practitioner (MSN, PMC); psychiatric mental health nurse practitioner (MSN, PMC). *Application deadline:* For fall admission, 7/15 for domestic students; for spring admission, 10/30 for domestic students. *Application fee:* $50. Electronic applications accepted. *Application Contact:* Kristen Card, Director of Graduate Admissions, 207-404-5660, Fax: 207-941-7935, E-mail: cardk@husson.edu. *Director, Graduate Nursing,* Prof. Mary Jude, 207-941-7769, Fax: 207-941-7198, E-mail: judem@husson.edu.

Graduate Programs in Counseling and Human Relations Students: 21 full-time (18 women), 44 part-time (39 women); includes 2 minority (1 Black or African American, non-Hispanic/Latino; 1 Hispanic/Latino), 1 international. Average age 31. 49 applicants, 41% accepted, 13 enrolled. *Faculty:* 3 full-time (2 women), 5 part-time/adjunct (all women). Expenses: Contact institution. *Financial support:* In 2017–18, 2 students received support. Federal Work-Study, scholarships/grants, and unspecified assistantships available. Financial award application deadline: 4/15; financial award applicants required to submit FAFSA. In 2017, 17 master's awarded. *Program availability:* Part-time, evening/weekend. Offers clinical mental health counseling (MS); human relations (MS); school counseling (MS). *Application deadline:* For fall admission, 2/1 for domestic students. *Application fee:* $50. Electronic applications accepted. *Application Contact:* Kristen Card, Director of Graduate Admissions, 207-404-5660, Fax: 207-941-7935, E-mail: cardk@husson.edu. *Director, Graduate Counseling Programs,* Dr. Deborah Drew, 207-992-4912, Fax: 207-992-4952, E-mail: drewd@husson.edu.

Master of Business Administration Program Students: 83 full-time (44 women), 287 part-time (176 women); includes 25 minority (7 Black or African American, non-Hispanic/Latino; 11 Asian, non-Hispanic/Latino; 4 Hispanic/Latino; 3 Two or more races, non-Hispanic/Latino), 16 international. Average age 35. 158 applicants, 77% accepted, 49 enrolled. *Faculty:* 11 full-time (5 women), 19 part-time/adjunct (4 women). Expenses: Contact institution. *Financial support:* In 2017–18, 13 students received support. Career-related internships or fieldwork, Federal Work-Study, scholarships/grants, and unspecified assistantships available. Financial award application deadline: 4/15; financial award applicants required to submit FAFSA. In 2017, 120 master's awarded. *Program availability:* Part-time, evening/weekend, 100% online, blended/hybrid learning. Offers athletic administration (MBA); biotechnology and innovation (MBA); general business administration (MBA); healthcare management (MBA); hospitality and tourism management (MBA); organizational management (MBA); risk management (MBA). *Application deadline:* Applications are processed on a rolling basis. *Application fee:* $50. Electronic applications accepted. *Application Contact:* Kristen Card, Director of Graduate Admissions, 207-404-5660, Fax: 207-941-7935, E-mail: cardk@husson.edu. *Director, Graduate and Online Programs,* Prof. Stephanie Shayne, 207-404-5632, Fax: 207-992-4987, E-mail: shaynes@husson.edu.

Master of Science in Criminal Justice Administration Program Students: 6 full-time (2 women), 11 part-time (3 women); includes 1 minority (American Indian or Alaska Native, non-Hispanic/Latino). Average age 34. 12 applicants, 100% accepted, 6 enrolled. *Faculty:* 5 full-time (2 women), 2 part-time/adjunct (0 women). Expenses: Contact institution. *Financial support:* Career-related internships or fieldwork, scholarships/grants, and unspecified assistantships available. Financial award application deadline: 4/15; financial award applicants required to submit FAFSA. In 2017, 17 master's awarded. *Program availability:* Part-time, evening/weekend. Offers criminal justice administration (MS). *Application deadline:* For fall admission, 8/1 for domestic students. Applications are processed on a rolling basis. *Application fee:* $50 ($0 for international students). Electronic applications accepted. *Application Contact:* Kristen Card, Director of Graduate Admissions, 207-404-5660, E-mail: cardk@husson.edu. *Director, School of Legal Studies,* John Michaud, 207-941-7037, E-mail: michaudj@husson.edu.

School of Pharmacy Students: 189 full-time (109 women); includes 55 minority (26 Black or African American, non-Hispanic/Latino; 2 American Indian or Alaska Native, non-Hispanic/Latino; 20 Asian, non-Hispanic/Latino; 6 Hispanic/Latino; 1 Two or more races, non-Hispanic/Latino), 7 international. Average age 26. 158 applicants, 48% accepted, 46 enrolled. *Faculty:* 24 full-time (7 women), 1 part-time/adjunct (0 women). Expenses: Contact institution. *Financial support:* In 2017–18, 112 students received support. Federal Work-Study, scholarships/grants, and unspecified assistantships available. Financial award application deadline: 3/1; financial award applicants required to submit FAFSA. In 2017, 56 doctorates awarded. Offers pharmacology (MS); pharmacy (Pharm D). *Application deadline:* For fall admission, 3/1 for domestic students. *Application fee:* $50 ($0 for international students). Electronic applications accepted. *Application Contact:* Kristen Card, Director of Graduate Admissions, 207-404-5660, E-mail: cardk@husson.edu. *Dean,* Dr. Rodney A. Larson, 207-941-7122, E-mail: larsonr@husson.edu.

HUSTON-TILLOTSON UNIVERSITY, Austin, TX 78702-2795

General Information Independent-religious, coed, comprehensive institution. *Enrollment:* 1,103 graduate, professional, and undergraduate students; 6 full-time matriculated graduate/professional students (2 women), 44 part-time matriculated graduate/professional students (31 women). *Enrollment by degree level:* 50 master's. *Library facilities:* Downs-Jones Library. **Computer facilities:** A campuswide network can be accessed from student residence rooms and from off campus. Online class registration is available.
Website: http://www.htu.edu/

GRADUATE UNITS

Graduate Programs Students: 6 full-time (2 women), 44 part-time (31 women); includes 45 minority (34 Black or African American, non-Hispanic/Latino; 11 Hispanic/Latino). Expenses: Contact institution. In 2017, 4 master's awarded. Offers educational leadership (M Ed). *Application fee:* $100. *Interim Chair, Educator Preparation Program,* Dr. Jan Seiter, 512-505-3091, E-mail: jpseiter@htu.edu.

ICAHN SCHOOL OF MEDICINE AT MOUNT SINAI, New York, NY 10029-6504

General Information Independent, coed, graduate-only institution. *Graduate housing:* Rooms and/or apartments guaranteed to single and married students. Housing application deadline: 6/1.

GRADUATE UNITS

The Bioethics Program Offers bioethics (MS). Program offered jointly with Union Graduate College.

Department of Medical Education Offers medical education (MD). Electronic applications accepted.

Graduate School of Biomedical Sciences Offers biomedical sciences (MS, PhD); clinical research education (MS, PhD); community medicine (MPH); genetic counseling (MS); neurosciences (PhD). Electronic applications accepted.

IDAHO STATE UNIVERSITY, Pocatello, ID 83209

General Information State-supported, coed, university. CGS member. *Graduate housing:* Rooms and/or apartments available on a first-come, first-served basis to single and married students. Housing application deadline: 5/1. *Research affiliation:* S.M. Stoller Corporation (ecology, waste management), ON Semiconductor (computer sciences, environmental management), Inland Northwest Research Alliance (INRA) (science), J.R. Simplot Company (plant sciences, environmental studies), Bechtel BWXT Idaho, LLC (environmental management, nuclear sciences), Environmental Science and Research Foundation (waste management, ecology).

GRADUATE UNITS

Office of Graduate Studies *Program availability:* Part-time. Electronic applications accepted.

College of Arts and Letters *Program availability:* Part-time. Offers anthropology (MA, MS); art (MFA); arts and letters (MA, MFA, MNS, MPA, MS, DA, PhD, Post-Master's Certificate, Postbaccalaureate Certificate); clinical psychology (PhD); communication (MA); English (MA); English and the teaching of English (PhD); experimental psychology (PhD); historical resources management (MA); political science (MA, DA); public administration (MPA); sociology (MA); TESOL (Post-Master's Certificate); theatre (MA). Electronic applications accepted.

College of Business *Program availability:* Part-time. Offers business administration (MBA, Postbaccalaureate Certificate); computer information systems (MS, Postbaccalaureate Certificate). Electronic applications accepted.

College of Education *Program availability:* Part-time. Offers athletic administration (MPE); athletic training (MSAT); deaf education (M Ed); education (M Ed, MPE, Ed D, PhD, 5th Year Certificate, 6th Year Certificate, Ed S); educational administration (M Ed, 6th Year Certificate, Ed S); educational leadership (Ed D); elementary education (M Ed); human exceptionality (M Ed); human resource development (MS); instructional design (PhD); instructional technology (M Ed); literacy (M Ed); music education (M Ed); school psychology (M Ed, Ed S); secondary education (M Ed). Electronic applications accepted.

College of Pharmacy *Program availability:* Part-time. Offers biopharmaceutical analysis (PhD); drug delivery (PhD); medicinal chemistry (PhD); pharmaceutical sciences (MS); pharmacology (PhD); pharmacy (MS, PhD, Pharm D); pharmacy administration (MS, PhD). Electronic applications accepted.

College of Science and Engineering *Program availability:* Part-time. Offers applied physics (PhD); biology (MNS, MS, DA, PhD); chemistry (MNS, MS); civil engineering (MS); clinical laboratory science (MS); environmental engineering (MS); environmental science and management (MS); geographic information science (MS); geology (MNS, MS); geology with emphasis in environmental geoscience (MS); geophysics/hydrology/geology (MS); geotechnology (Postbaccalaureate Certificate); health physics (MS); mathematics (MS, DA); mathematics for secondary teachers (MA); measurement and control engineering (MS); mechanical engineering (MS); microbiology (MS); nuclear science and engineering (MS, PhD); physics (MNS); science and engineering (MA, MNS, MS, DA, PhD, Postbaccalaureate Certificate). Electronic applications accepted.

Office of Medical and Oral Health Offers advanced general dentistry (Post-Doctoral Certificate); dental hygiene (MS); family medicine (Post-Master's Certificate); medical and oral health (MPAS, MS, Post-Doctoral Certificate, Post-Master's Certificate); physician assistant studies (MPAS).

School of Health Professions *Program availability:* Part-time. Offers counseling (M Coun, Ed S); counselor education and counseling (PhD); health education (MHE); health professions (M Coun, MHE, MPH, MS, PhD, Ed S); public health (MPH). Electronic applications accepted.

School of Nursing *Program availability:* Part-time. Offers nursing (MS, DNP, PhD). Electronic applications accepted.

School of Rehabilitation and Communication Sciences Offers audiology (Au D); occupational therapy (MOT); physical therapy (DPT); rehabilitation and communication sciences (MOT, MS, Au D, DPT); speech language pathology (MS).

IGLOBAL UNIVERSITY, Vienna, VA 22182

General Information Proprietary, coed, comprehensive institution.

GRADUATE UNITS

Graduate Programs

ILIFF SCHOOL OF THEOLOGY, Denver, CO 80210-4798

General Information Independent-religious, coed, graduate-only institution. *Graduate housing:* Rooms and/or apartments available on a first-come, first-served basis to single and married students.

GRADUATE UNITS

Graduate and Professional Programs *Program availability:* Part-time, evening/weekend. Offers biblical studies (MA); church history (MA); religion (MA); religion and social change (MA); specialized ministry (MASM); theology (M Div, MTS, D Min, PhD); theology/ethics (MA). PhD offered jointly with University of Denver. Electronic applications accepted.

ILLINOIS COLLEGE, Jacksonville, IL 62650-2299

General Information Independent-religious, coed, comprehensive institution. *Graduate housing:* On-campus housing not available.

GRADUATE UNITS

Program in Education *Program availability:* Part-time-only, evening/weekend. Offers education (MA Ed). Electronic applications accepted.

ILLINOIS COLLEGE OF OPTOMETRY, Chicago, IL 60616-3878

General Information Independent, coed, graduate-only institution. *Enrollment by degree level:* 599 doctoral. *Graduate faculty:* 47 full-time (34 women), 40 part-time/adjunct (24 women). *Tuition:* Full-time $40,410; part-time $842 per credit hour. *Required fees:* $355. *Graduate housing:* Rooms and/or apartments available on a first-come, first-served basis to single and married students. Typical cost: $4107 (including board) for single students; $4856 per year for married students. Room and board charges vary according to housing facility selected. Housing application deadline: 6/1. *Student services:* Campus employment opportunities, campus safety program, career counseling, exercise/wellness program, free psychological counseling, international student services, low-cost health insurance, services for students with disabilities. *Library facilities:* ICO Library. *Collection:* Students can reserve study rooms. *Research affiliation:* Rush University (cataract development), University of Chicago (vision science), University of Illinois at Chicago (neuropharmacology), Vision Service Plan (pediatric optometry), Ciba Vision (contact lenses).

Computer facilities: 44 computers available on campus for general student use. A campuswide network can be accessed from student residence rooms and from off campus.
Website: http://www.ico.edu/

General Application Contact: Teisha Johnson, Director of Admissions, 312-949-7400, Fax: 312-949-7680, E-mail: tjohnson@ico.edu.

GRADUATE UNITS

Professional Program Students: 599 full-time (426 women); includes 170 minority (12 Black or African American, non-Hispanic/Latino; 5 American Indian or Alaska Native, non-Hispanic/Latino; 140 Asian, non-Hispanic/Latino; 13 Hispanic/Latino), 94 international. *Faculty:* 47 full-time (34 women), 40 part-time/adjunct (24 women). Expenses: Contact institution. *Financial support:* Federal Work-Study and scholarships/grants available. Support available to part-time students. Financial award application deadline: 4/15; financial award applicants required to submit FAFSA. Offers optometry (OD). *Application deadline:* For fall admission, 2/15 for domestic and international students. Applications are processed on a rolling basis. *Application fee:* $75. Electronic applications accepted. *Application Contact:* Teisha Johnson, Director of Admissions, 312-949-7400, Fax: 312-949-7680, E-mail: tjohnson@ico.edu. *President,* Dr. Arol Augsburger, 312-949-7705, Fax: 312-949-7670, E-mail: aaugsburger@eyecare.ico.edu.

ILLINOIS INSTITUTE OF TECHNOLOGY, Chicago, IL 60616

General Information Independent, coed, university. CGS member. *Graduate housing:* Rooms and/or apartments available on a first-come, first-served basis to single and married students. Housing application deadline: 6/1.

GRADUATE UNITS

Chicago-Kent College of Law *Program availability:* Part-time, evening/weekend. Offers family law (LL M); financial services law (LL M); international intellectual property law (LL M); law (JD); legal studies (JSD); taxation (LL M); U.S., international, and transnational law (LL M). Electronic applications accepted.

Graduate College *Program availability:* Part-time, evening/weekend, online learning. Electronic applications accepted.

Armour College of Engineering *Program availability:* Part-time, evening/weekend, online learning. Offers architectural engineering (M Arch E); biological engineering (MAS); biomedical engineering (MAS, MS, PhD); biomedical imaging and signals (MAS); chemical engineering (MAS, MS, PhD); civil engineering (MS, PhD); computer engineering (MS, PhD); construction engineering and management (MCEM); electrical engineering (MS, PhD); electricity markets (MAS); engineering (M Arch E, M Env E, M Geoenv E, M Trans E, MAS, MCEM, MGE, MPW, MS, MSE, PhD); environmental engineering (M Env E, MS, PhD); geoenvironmental engineering (M Geoenv E); geotechnical engineering (MGE); infrastructure engineering and management (MPW); manufacturing engineering (MAS, MS); materials science and engineering (MAS, MS, PhD); mechanical and aerospace engineering (MAS, MS, PhD); network engineering (MAS); power engineering (MAS); structural engineering (MSE); telecommunications and software engineering (MAS); transportation engineering (M Trans E); VLSI and microelectronics (MAS). Electronic applications accepted.

College of Architecture *Program availability:* Part-time. Offers architecture (M Arch, MLA, MS Arch, PhD). Electronic applications accepted.

College of Science *Program availability:* Part-time, evening/weekend, online learning. Offers analytical chemistry (MAS); applied life sciences (MS); applied mathematics (MS, PhD); applied physics (MS); biochemistry (MS); biology (MS, PhD); business (MCS); cell and molecular biology (MS); chemistry (MAS, MS, PhD); computational intelligence (MCS); computer science (MCS, MS, PhD); cyber-physical systems (MCS); data analytics (MCS); data science (MAS); database systems (MCS); distributed and cloud computing (MCS); education (MCS); finance (MCS); health physics (MAS); information security and assurance (MCS); materials chemistry (MAS); mathematical finance (MAS); mathematics education (MAS, PhD); microbiology (MS); molecular biochemistry and biophysics (MS, PhD); networking and communications (MCS); physics (MS, PhD); science (MAS, MCS, MS, PhD); science education (MAS, PhD); software engineering (MCS); telecommunications and software engineering (MAS). Electronic applications accepted.

Institute of Design *Program availability:* Part-time. Offers design (M Des, MDM, PhD). Electronic applications accepted.

Lewis College of Human Sciences Offers clinical psychology (PhD); human sciences (MS, PhD); industrial and organizational psychology (PhD); information architecture (MS); personnel and human resource development (MS); rehabilitation and mental health counseling (MS); rehabilitation counseling education (PhD); technical communication (PhD); technical communication and information design (MS).

School of Applied Technology *Program availability:* Part-time, evening/weekend, online learning. Offers applied technology (MAS, MFPE, MFST, MS); cyber forensics and security (MAS); food process engineering (MFPE, MS); food safety and technology (MFST, MS); industrial technology and management (MAS); information technology and management (MAS). Electronic applications accepted.

Stuart School of Business *Program availability:* Part-time, evening/weekend. Offers business (MBA, MMF, MPA, MS, PhD); environmental management and sustainability (MS); finance (MS); management science (PhD); marketing analytics and communication (MS); mathematical finance (MMF); public administration (MPA); sustainability (MBA); technological entrepreneurship (MTE). Electronic applications accepted.

ILLINOIS STATE UNIVERSITY, Normal, IL 61790

General Information State-supported, coed, university. CGS member. *Graduate housing:* Rooms and/or apartments available to single and married students. Housing application deadline: 4/1.

GRADUATE UNITS

Graduate School *Program availability:* Part-time.

College of Applied Science and Technology *Program availability:* Part-time. Offers agribusiness (MS); applied science and technology (MA, MS, Certificate, Graduate Certificate); criminal justice sciences (MA, MS); family and consumer sciences (MA, MS); health education (MS); information technology (MS); technology (MS).

College of Arts and Sciences *Program availability:* Part-time. Offers animal behavior (MS); arts and sciences (MA, MS, MSW, PhD, SSP); bacteriology (MS); biochemistry (MS); biological sciences (MS); biology (PhD); biophysics (MS); biotechnology (MS); botany (MS, PhD); cell biology (MS); chemistry (MCE, MS, MSCE); communication (MA, MS); communication sciences and disorders (MA, MS); conservation biology (MS); developmental biology (MS); ecology (MS, PhD); economics (MA, MS); English (MA, MS, PhD); English studies (PhD); entomology (MS); evolutionary biology (MS); French (MA); French and German (MA); French and Spanish (MA); genetics (MS, PhD); geography-geology (Graduate Certificate); German (MA); German and Spanish (MA); historical archaeology (MA, MS); history (MA, MS); immunology (MS); mathematics (MA, MS); mathematics education (MA, PhD); microbiology (MS, PhD); molecular biology (MS); molecular genetics (MS); neurobiology (MS); neuroscience (MS); parasitology (MS); physiology (MS, PhD); plant biology (MS); plant molecular biology (MS); plant sciences (MS); politics and government (MA, MS); psychology (MA, MS); school psychology (PhD, SSP); social work (MSW); sociology (MA, MS); Spanish (MA); structural biology (MS); writing (MA, MS); zoology (MS, PhD).

College of Business *Program availability:* Part-time. Offers accounting (MPA, MS); business (MBA, MPA, MS); business administration (MBA).

College of Education *Program availability:* Part-time. Offers college student personnel administration (MS); curriculum and instruction (MS, MS Ed, Ed D); education (MS, MS Ed, Ed D, PhD, Certificate); educational administration (MS, MS Ed, Ed D, PhD); educational policies (Ed D); postsecondary education (Ed D); reading (MS Ed); special education (MS, MS Ed, Ed D, Certificate); supervision (Ed D).

College of Fine Arts *Program availability:* Part-time. Offers art history (MA, MS); arts technology (MS); ceramics (MFA, MS); drawing (MFA, MS); fibers (MFA, MS); fine arts (MA, MFA, MM, MM Ed, MS); glass (MFA, MS); graphic design (MFA, MS); metals (MFA, MS); music (MM, MM Ed); painting (MFA, MS); photography (MFA, MS); printmaking (MFA, MS); sculpture (MFA, MS); theatre (MA, MFA, MS).

Mennonite College of Nursing Offers family nurse practitioner (PMC); nursing (MSN, PhD).

IMCA–INTERNATIONAL MANAGEMENT CENTRES ASSOCIATION, Buckingham MK18 1BP, United Kingdom

General Information Independent, coed, graduate-only institution.

GRADUATE UNITS

Programs in Business Administration *Program availability:* Online learning. Offers business administration (M Mgt, M Phil, MBA, MS).

IMMACULATA UNIVERSITY, Immaculata, PA 19345

General Information Independent-religious, coed, university. CGS member. *Graduate housing:* Rooms and/or apartments available on a first-come, first-served basis to single and married students.

GRADUATE UNITS

College of Graduate Studies *Program availability:* Part-time, evening/weekend. Offers bilingual studies (MA); clinical mental health counseling (MA); clinical psychology (Psy D); educational leadership (MA, Ed D); forensic psychology (Graduate Certificate); integrative psychotherapy (Graduate Certificate); music therapy (MA); neuropsychology (Graduate Certificate); nutrition education for the registered dietitian (MA); nutrition education with dietetic internship (MA); nutrition education with wellness promotion (MA); organization leadership (MA); principal (Certificate); psychodynamic psychotherapy (Graduate Certificate); psychological testing (Graduate Certificate); school counseling (MA, Graduate Certificate); school psychology (MA); secondary education (Certificate); supervisor of special education (Certificate); TESOL (MA). Electronic applications accepted.

Division of Nursing *Program availability:* Part-time, evening/weekend. Offers nursing administration (MSN); nursing education (MSN).

INDEPENDENCE UNIVERSITY, Salt Lake City, UT 84107

General Information Proprietary, coed, comprehensive institution. *Graduate housing:* On-campus housing not available.

GRADUATE UNITS

Program in Business Administration Offers business administration (MBA).

Program in Business Administration in Health Care *Program availability:* Part-time, evening/weekend, online learning. Offers health care administration (MBA).

Program in Health Care Administration *Program availability:* Part-time, evening/weekend, online learning. Offers health care administration (MSHCA).

Program in Health Services *Program availability:* Part-time, evening/weekend, online learning. Offers community health (MSHS); wellness promotion (MSHS).

Program in Nursing Offers community health (MSN); gerontology (MSN); nursing administration (MSN); wellness promotion (MSN).

Program in Public Health *Program availability:* Part-time, evening/weekend, online learning. Offers public health (MPH).

INDIANA STATE UNIVERSITY, Terre Haute, IN 47809

General Information State-supported, coed, university. CGS member. *Graduate housing:* Rooms and/or apartments available on a first-come, first-served basis to single and married students. Housing application deadline: 4/18. *Research affiliation:* Indiana Space Grant (remote sensing), Indiana University School of Medicine (cancer and Lupus research), Cranberry Lake Biological Station (psychosocial impacts of cancer), Boston Museum of Science (remote sensing, biology), Great Lakes Northern Forest Cooperative Ecosystem Study Unit (biology, life sciences).

GRADUATE UNITS

College of Graduate and Professional Studies *Program availability:* Part-time, evening/weekend, online learning. Offers technology management (PhD). Electronic applications accepted.

Bayh College of Education *Program availability:* Part-time, evening/weekend. Offers clinical mental health counseling (MS); communication disorders (MS); curriculum and instruction (M Ed, PhD); education (M Ed, MS, PhD, Ed S); educational administration (PhD); educational technology (MS); higher education leadership (PhD); K-12 district leadership (PhD); school administration (Ed S); school administration and supervision (M Ed); school counseling (M Ed); school psychology (PhD, Ed S); student affairs and higher education (MS). Electronic applications accepted.

College of Arts and Sciences *Program availability:* Part-time, evening/weekend. Offers applied linguistics/teaching English as a second language (MA); arts and sciences (MA, MFA, MM, MPA, MS, PhD, Psy D, CAS); British and American literature (MA); cellular and molecular biology (PhD); ceramics (MA, MFA); clinical psychology (Psy D); communication studies (MA); computer science (MS); conducting (MM); criminology and criminal justice (MA, MS); drawing (MA, MFA); ecology, systematics and evolution (PhD); English (MA); general psychology (MA, MS); graphic design (MA, MFA); history (MA, MS); language education (PhD); life sciences (MS); mathematics (MA, MS); music education (MM); music performance (MM); painting (MA, MFA); photography (MA, MFA); physiology (PhD); printmaking (MA, MFA); public administration (MPA); radio, television and film (MA); science education (MS); sculpture (MA, MFA); Spanish/teaching english as a second language (MA); TESL/TEFL (CAS); writing (MA). Electronic applications accepted.

College of Health and Human Services Offers advanced practice nursing (DNP); applied health sciences (MS, DHS); athletic training (MS, DAT); family nurse practitioner (MS); health and human services (MA, MS, MSW, DAT, DNP, DPT, PhD); nursing administration (MS); nursing education (MS); occupational therapy (MS); physical education (MS); physical therapy (DPT); physician assistant (MS); recreation and sport management (MS); social work (MSW); sport management (PhD). Electronic applications accepted.

College of Technology Offers career and technical education (MS); electronics and computer technology (MS); human resource development (MS); occupational safety management (MS); technology (MS); technology management (MS). Electronic applications accepted.

Scott College of Business *Program availability:* Part-time, evening/weekend. Offers business (MBA). Electronic applications accepted.

INDIANA TECH, Fort Wayne, IN 46803-1297

General Information Independent, coed, comprehensive institution. *Graduate housing:* Room and/or apartments available on a first-come, first-served basis to single students; on-campus housing not available to married students. Housing application deadline: 8/15.

GRADUATE UNITS

Program in Business Administration *Program availability:* Part-time, evening/weekend, online learning. Offers accounting (MBA); health care management (MBA); human resources (MBA); management (MBA); marketing (MBA). Electronic applications accepted.

Program in Engineering Management *Program availability:* Part-time, evening/weekend, online only, 100% online. Offers engineering management (MSE). Electronic applications accepted.

Program in Global Leadership *Program availability:* Part-time, evening/weekend, online only, 100% online. Offers global leadership (PhD). Electronic applications accepted.

Program in Management *Program availability:* Part-time, evening/weekend, 100% online. Offers management (MSM). Electronic applications accepted.

Program in Organizational Leadership *Program availability:* Part-time, evening/weekend, online only, 100% online. Offers organizational leadership (MS). Electronic applications accepted.

Program in Psychology Offers psychology (MS).

INDIANA UNIVERSITY BLOOMINGTON, Bloomington, IN 47405-7000

General Information State-supported, coed, university. CGS member. *Graduate housing:* Rooms and/or apartments available to single and married students. Housing application deadline: 5/11.

GRADUATE UNITS

Jacobs School of Music Offers music (MA, MM, MME, MS, DM, DME, PhD, Artist Diploma, Performance Diploma, Spec). Electronic applications accepted.

Kelley School of Business Offers business (MBA, MPA, MS, DBA, PhD). PhD offered through University Graduate School. Electronic applications accepted.

Maurer School of Law Offers comparative law (MCL); juridical science (SJD); law (LL M, JD); law and social sciences (PhD); legal studies (Certificate). PhD offered through University Graduate School. Electronic applications accepted.

School of Education *Program availability:* Part-time, 100% online, blended/hybrid learning. Offers art education (MS, Ed D, PhD); counseling (MS, PhD, Ed S); counselor education (MS, Ed S); curriculum studies (Ed D, PhD); education (MS, Ed D, PhD, Ed S, Graduate Certificate); educational leadership (MS, Ed D, Ed S); educational psychology (MS, PhD); elementary education (MS, Ed D, PhD, Ed S); higher education (Ed D, PhD); higher education and student affairs (MS); history and philosophy of education (MS); history, philosophy, and policy in education (PhD); inquiry methodology (PhD); instructional systems technology (MS, PhD); international and comparative education (MS); learning and developmental sciences (MS, PhD); literacy, culture, and language education (MS, Ed D, PhD, Ed S); mathematics education (MS, Ed D, PhD); school psychology (PhD, Ed S); science education (MS, Ed D, PhD); secondary education (MS, Ed D, PhD); social studies education (MS, PhD); special education (PhD, Ed S). Electronic applications accepted.

School of Informatics and Computing *Program availability:* Part-time, online learning. Offers bioinformatics (MS); computer science (MS, PhD); cybersecurity risk management (MS); data science (MS, Graduate Certificate); informatics (MS, PhD); informatics and computing (MIS, MLS, MS, PhD, Graduate Certificate, Sp LIS); information architecture (Graduate Certificate); information science (MIS, PhD); intelligent systems engineering (PhD); library and information science (Sp LIS); library science (MLS); secure computing (MS, Graduate Certificate); visual heritage (PhD). PhD offered through University Graduate School. Electronic applications accepted.

School of Optometry Offers optometry (MS, OD, PhD). Electronic applications accepted.

School of Public and Environmental Affairs Students: 491 full-time (289 women). Average age 27. 519 applicants, 86% accepted, 219 enrolled. *Faculty:* 133 full-time (40 women), 125 part-time/adjunct (49 women). Expenses: Contact institution. *Financial support:* Fellowships with partial tuition reimbursements, research assistantships with partial tuition reimbursements, teaching assistantships with partial tuition reimbursements, career-related internships or fieldwork, Federal Work-Study, scholarships/grants, health care benefits, tuition waivers (partial), unspecified assistantships, and Service Corps Fellowship Program; Educational Opportunity Fellowships available. Financial award application deadline: 2/1; financial award applicants required to submit FAFSA. *Program availability:* Part-time, 100% online, blended/hybrid learning. Offers applied ecology (MSES); arts administration (MAAA); economic development (MPA); energy (MPA, MSES); environmental chemistry, toxicology, and risk assessment (MSES); environmental policy (PhD); environmental policy and natural resource management (MPA); environmental science (PhD); hazardous materials management (Certificate); information systems (MPA); international development (MPA); local government management (MPA); nonprofit management (MPA, Certificate); policy analysis (MPA); public and environmental affairs (MAAA, MES, MPA, MSES, PhD, Certificate); public budgeting and financial management (Certificate); public finance (PhD); public financial administration (MPA); public management (MPA, PhD, Certificate); public policy analysis (PhD); social entrepreneurship (Certificate); specialized environmental science (MSES); specialized public affairs (MPA); sustainability and sustainable development (MPA); water resources (MSES). *Application deadline:* For fall admission, 2/1 priority date for domestic and international students; for spring admission, 12/1 for domestic students, 10/1 for international students. Applications are processed on a rolling basis. *Application fee:* $55 ($65 for international students). Electronic applications accepted. *Application Contact:* Emily Miller, Assistant Director, Graduate Student Recruitment, 812-855-2840, E-mail: speainfo@indiana.edu. *Director, Master's Program Office*, Megan Siehl, 812-855-2840, Fax: 812-856-3665, E-mail: speampo@indiana.edu.

School of Public Health *Program availability:* Part-time, online learning. Offers applied sport science (MS); athletic administration/sport management (MS); athletic training (MS); behavioral, social, and community health (MPH); biomechanics (MS); biostatistics (MPH); environmental health (MPH, PhD); epidemiology (MPH, PhD); ergonomics (MS); exercise physiology (MS); family health (MPH); health behavior (PhD); human performance (PhD); leisure behavior (PhD); motor learning/control (MS); nutrition science (MS); outdoor recreation (MS); park and public lands management (MS); physical activity (MPH); physical activity, fitness and wellness (MS); professional health education (MPH); public health (MPH, MS, PhD); public health administration (MPH); recreation administration (MS); recreational sports administration (MS); recreational therapy (MS); safety management (MS); school and college health education (MS); tourism management (MS). Electronic applications accepted.

University Graduate School *Program availability:* Part-time. Electronic applications accepted.

College of Arts and Sciences *Program availability:* Part-time. Offers acting (MFA); African American and African diaspora studies (MA, PhD); African languages and linguistics (PhD); African studies (MA); analytical chemistry (PhD); anthropology (MA, PhD); apparel merchandising (MS); applied mathematics (MA); applied statistics (MS); arts and sciences (MA, MAT, MFA, MS, Au D, PhD, Certificate); astronomy (MA, PhD); astrophysics (PhD); audiology (Au D); auditory sciences (Au D, PhD); biochemistry (PhD); biogeochemistry (MS, PhD); biology teaching (MAT); biotechnology (MA); Central Eurasian studies (MA, PhD); chemical biology (PhD); chemistry (MAT); Chinese (MA, PhD); Chinese language pedagogy (MA); classical studies (MA, MAT, PhD); clinical science (PhD); cognitive neuroscience (PhD); cognitive psychology (PhD); cognitive science (PhD); comparative literature (MA, MAT, PhD); computational linguistics (MA, MS, PhD); creative writing (MA, MFA); crime and youth development (MA, PhD); crime, law and psychology (MA, PhD); criminal justice (MA, PhD); criminal justice institutions and practices (MA, PhD); criminology (MA, PhD); design and technology (MFA); developmental criminology (MA, PhD); developmental psychology (PhD); directing (MFA); East Asian studies (MA); economic geology (MS, PhD); economics (MS, PhD); ethnomusicology (MA, PhD); European studies (MA); evolution, ecology, and behavior (MA, PhD); French (MA, PhD); gender studies (PhD); genetics (PhD); geobiology (MS, PhD); geography (PhD); geophysics, structural geology and tectonics (MS, PhD); German philology and linguistics (PhD); German studies (MA, PhD); global and international studies (MA, MS, PhD, Certificate); history (MA, MAT, PhD); history and philosophy of science (MA, PhD); hydrogeology (MS, PhD); inorganic chemistry (PhD); interdisciplinary studies in crime and punishment (PhD); interdisciplinary studies of crime and punishment (MA); international studies (MA, MS); Italian (MA, PhD); Japanese (MA, PhD); Japanese language pedagogy (MA); Jewish studies (MA); Jewish studies and history (MA); language sciences (PhD); Latin American and Caribbean studies (MA); linguistics (MA, PhD); literature (PhD); materials chemistry (PhD); mathematical physics (PhD); mathematics education (MAT); media (MS); media arts and sciences (MA, PhD); medical physics (MS); medieval German studies (PhD); methods of behavior (PhD); microbiology (MA, PhD); mineralogy (MS, PhD); molecular systems neuroscience (PhD); molecular, cellular, and developmental biology (PhD); Near Eastern languages and cultures (MA, PhD); neuroscience (PhD); organic chemistry (PhD); philosophy (MA, PhD); physical chemistry (PhD); physics (MAT, MS, PhD); plant sciences (MA, PhD); playwriting (MFA); political science (MA, PhD); Portuguese (MA, PhD); pure mathematics (MA, PhD); religious studies (MA, PhD); rhetoric (PhD); Russian and East European studies (MA, Certificate); second language studies (MA, PhD); Slavic languages and literatures (MA, MAT, PhD); social psychology (PhD); sociology (MA, PhD); Spanish (MA, PhD); speech and hearing sciences (MA, Au D, PhD); speech and voice sciences (PhD); speech-language pathology (MA); statistical science (MS, PhD); stratigraphy and sedimentology (MS, PhD); studio art (MFA); teaching German (MAT); TESOL and applied linguistics (MA); the relationship between crime and gender, race and ethnicity (MA, PhD); theatre history, theory, and literature (MA, PhD); theoretical analyses of criminology (MA, PhD); zoology (MA, PhD). Electronic applications accepted.

INDIANA UNIVERSITY EAST, Richmond, IN 47374-1289

General Information State-supported, coed, comprehensive institution.

GRADUATE UNITS

School of Education Offers education (MS Ed).

School of Nursing Offers nursing (MSN).

School of Social Work Offers social work (MSW).

INDIANA UNIVERSITY KOKOMO, Kokomo, IN 46902-9003

General Information State-supported, coed, comprehensive institution. *Graduate housing:* On-campus housing not available.

GRADUATE UNITS

Department of Public Administration and Health Management *Program availability:* Part-time, evening/weekend. Offers health management (MPM, Graduate Certificate); public management (Graduate Certificate); public management and policy (MPM). Electronic applications accepted.

School of Business *Program availability:* Part-time, evening/weekend. Offers accounting (Postbaccalaureate Certificate); business administration (MBA); business fundamentals (Postbaccalaureate Certificate). Electronic applications accepted.

School of Nursing Offers family nurse practitioner (MSN); nurse administrator (MSN); nurse educator (MSN). Electronic applications accepted.

INDIANA UNIVERSITY NORTHWEST, Gary, IN 46408-1197

General Information State-supported, coed, comprehensive institution. *Graduate housing:* On-campus housing not available.

GRADUATE UNITS

College of Arts and Sciences *Program availability:* Part-time, evening/weekend. Offers clinical counseling (MS); community development/urban studies (Graduate Certificate); computer information systems (Graduate Certificate); liberal studies (MLS); race-ethnic studies (Graduate Certificate); women's and gender studies (Graduate Certificate). Electronic applications accepted.

School of Business and Economics *Program availability:* Part-time, evening/weekend. Offers accounting (Graduate Certificate); management (Certificate); management and administrative studies (MBA). Electronic applications accepted.

School of Education *Program availability:* Part-time, evening/weekend. Offers educational leadership (MS Ed); elementary education (MS Ed); K-12 online teaching (Graduate Certificate); secondary education (MS Ed). Electronic applications accepted.

School of Public and Environmental Affairs *Program availability:* Part-time. Offers criminal justice (MPA); environmental affairs (Graduate Certificate); health services (MPA); nonprofit management (Certificate); public management (MPA, Graduate Certificate). Electronic applications accepted.

School of Social Work *Program availability:* Part-time, evening/weekend. Offers health (MSW); mental health and addictions (MSW). Electronic applications accepted.

INDIANA UNIVERSITY OF PENNSYLVANIA, Indiana, PA 15705

General Information State-supported, coed, university. CGS member. *Enrollment:* 12,316 graduate, professional, and undergraduate students; 919 full-time matriculated graduate/professional students (536 women), 1,254 part-time matriculated graduate/professional students (786 women). *Enrollment by degree level:* 1,246 master's, 808 doctoral, 119 other advanced degrees. *Graduate faculty:* 277 full-time (124 women), 13 part-time/adjunct (10 women). Tuition, state resident: full-time $12,000; part-time $500 per credit. Tuition, nonresident: full-time $18,000; part-time $750 per credit. *Required fees:* $4073; $165.55 per credit. $64 per term. *Graduate housing:* Room and/or apartments available on a first-come, first-served basis to single students; on-campus housing not available to married students. Housing application deadline: 4/15. *Student services:* Campus employment opportunities, campus safety program, career counseling, free psychological counseling, international student services, low-cost health insurance, multicultural affairs office, services for students with disabilities. *Library facilities:* Stapleton Library. *Collection:* Books: 508,667 (physical), 79,230 (digital/electronic); Serial titles: 130,318 (physical). Weekly public service hours: 101; study areas open 24 hours, 5–7 days a week; students can reserve study rooms.

Computer facilities: Computer purchase and lease plans are available. 2,363 computers available on campus for general student use. A campuswide network can be accessed from student residence rooms and from off campus. Online class registration is available.
Website: http://www.iup.edu/

General Application Contact: Paula Stossel, Assistant Dean for Administration, 724-357-2222, Fax: 724-357-4862, E-mail: graduate-admissions@iup.edu.

GRADUATE UNITS

School of Graduate Studies and Research Students: 919 full-time (536 women), 1,254 part-time (786 women); includes 246 minority (120 Black or African American, non-Hispanic/Latino; 5 American Indian or Alaska Native, non-Hispanic/Latino; 32 Asian, non-Hispanic/Latino; 50 Hispanic/Latino; 39 Two or more races, non-Hispanic/Latino), 428 international. Average age 32. 2,140 applicants, 66% accepted, 857 enrolled. *Faculty:* 277 full-time (124 women), 13 part-time/adjunct (10 women). Expenses: Contact institution. *Financial support:* In 2017–18, 42 fellowships with full tuition reimbursements (averaging $954 per year), 426 research assistantships with tuition reimbursements (averaging $3,978 per year), 27 teaching assistantships with partial tuition reimbursements (averaging $17,551 per year) were awarded; career-related internships or fieldwork, Federal Work-Study, scholarships/grants, tuition waivers (full and partial), and unspecified assistantships also available. Support available to part-time students. Financial award application deadline: 3/15; financial award applicants required to submit FAFSA. In 2017, 673 master's, 127 doctorates, 20 other advanced degrees awarded. *Program availability:* Part-time, evening/weekend, blended/hybrid learning. *Application deadline:* Applications are processed on a rolling basis. *Application fee:* $50. Electronic applications accepted. *Application Contact:* Paula Stossel, Assistant Dean for Administration, 724-357-4511, Fax: 724-357-4862, E-mail: graduate-admissions@iup.edu. *Director of Graduate Marketing*, Simon Stuchlik, 724-357-2127, Fax: 724-357-4862, E-mail: stuchlik@iup.edu.

College of Education and Communications Students: 264 full-time (202 women), 411 part-time (272 women); includes 85 minority (52 Black or African American, non-Hispanic/Latino; 1 American Indian or Alaska Native, non-Hispanic/Latino; 3 Asian, non-Hispanic/Latino; 14 Hispanic/Latino; 15 Two or more races, non-Hispanic/Latino), 29 international. Average age 33. 622 applicants, 66% accepted, 182 enrolled. *Faculty:* 55 full-time (39 women), 12 part-time/adjunct (9 women). Expenses: Contact institution. *Financial support:* In 2017–18, 22 fellowships (averaging $919 per year), 135 research assistantships with tuition reimbursements (averaging $4,373 per year), 8 teaching assistantships with tuition reimbursements (averaging $18,450 per year) were awarded; career-related internships or fieldwork, Federal Work-Study, scholarships/grants, and unspecified assistantships also available. Support available to part-time students. Financial award application deadline: 4/15; financial award applicants required to submit FAFSA. In 2017, 159 master's, 58 doctorates, 19 other advanced degrees awarded. *Program availability:* Part-time, evening/weekend. Offers administration and leadership studies (D Ed); adult and community education (MA); adult and community education/communications technology (MA); business/administrative (M Ed); business/business specialist (M Ed); business/workforce development (M Ed); clinical mental health counseling (MA); communications media and instructional technology (PhD); community counseling (MA); curriculum and instruction (D Ed); education (M Ed); education and communications (M Ed, MA, MS, D Ed, PhD, Certificate); educational psychology (Certificate); literacy (M Ed, Certificate); principal (Certificate); reading (Certificate); school counseling (M Ed); school psychology (Certificate); special education (M Ed); speech-language pathology (MS); student affairs in higher education (MA). *Application deadline:* Applications are processed on a rolling basis. *Application fee:* $50. Electronic applications accepted. *Application Contact:* Paula Stossel, Assistant Dean for Administration, 724-357-4511, Fax: 724-357-4862, E-mail: graduate-admissions@iup.edu. *Dean*, Dr. Lara Luetkehans, 724-357-2480, Fax: 724-357-5595.

College of Fine Arts Students: 24 full-time (12 women), 29 part-time (21 women); includes 7 minority (1 Black or African American, non-Hispanic/Latino; 3 Asian, non-Hispanic/Latino; 2 Hispanic/Latino; 1 Two or more races, non-Hispanic/Latino), 4 international. Average age 27. 43 applicants, 93% accepted, 24 enrolled. *Faculty:* 21 full-time (8 women), 2 part-time/adjunct (1 woman). Expenses: Contact institution. *Financial support:* In 2017–18, 24 research assistantships with tuition reimbursements (averaging $2,955 per year) were awarded; fellowships with full tuition reimbursements, career-related internships or fieldwork, Federal Work-Study, scholarships/grants, and unspecified assistantships also available. Support available to part-time students. Financial award application deadline: 4/15; financial award applicants required to submit FAFSA. In 2017, 26 master's awarded. *Program availability:* Part-time. Offers art (MA, MFA); fine arts (MA, MFA); music education (MA); music performance (MA). *Application deadline:* Applications are processed on a rolling basis. *Application fee:* $50. Electronic applications accepted. *Application Contact:* Dr. Susan Palmisano, Graduate Coordinator, 724-357-2536, E-mail: palmisan@iup.edu. *Dean*, Michael Hood, 724-357-2397, E-mail: mhood@iup.edu.

College of Health and Human Services Students: 207 full-time (116 women), 304 part-time (209 women); includes 54 minority (28 Black or African American, non-Hispanic/Latino; 3 American Indian or Alaska Native, non-Hispanic/Latino; 4 Asian, non-Hispanic/Latino; 12 Hispanic/Latino; 7 Two or more races, non-Hispanic/Latino), 45 international. Average age 31. 477 applicants, 75% accepted, 183 enrolled. *Faculty:* 48 full-time (28 women), 2 part-time/adjunct (1 woman). Expenses: Contact institution. *Financial support:* In 2017–18, 3 fellowships with full tuition reimbursements (averaging $2,018 per year), 89 research assistantships with tuition reimbursements (averaging $4,163 per year), 6 teaching assistantships with partial tuition reimbursements (averaging $23,305 per year) were awarded; career-related internships or fieldwork, Federal Work-Study, scholarships/grants, and unspecified assistantships also available. Support available to part-time students. Financial award application deadline: 4/15; financial award applicants required to submit FAFSA. In 2017, 194 master's, 10 doctorates awarded. *Program availability:* Part-time, evening/weekend, online learning. Offers criminology (MA, PhD); employment and labor relations (MA); food and nutrition (MS); health and human services (M Ed, MA, MS, PhD, Certificate); health and physical education (M Ed); health service administration (MS); health services administration (MS); nursing (MS, PhD); nursing administration (MS); nursing education (MS); safety sciences (MS, PhD); sport science/exercise science (MS); sport science/sport management (MS); sport science/sport studies (MS). *Application deadline:* Applications are processed on a rolling basis. *Application fee:* $50. Electronic applications accepted. *Application Contact:* Paula Stossel, Assistant Dean, 724-357-4511, Fax: 724-357-4862, E-mail: graduate-admissions@iup.edu. *Acting Dean*, Dr. Mary Williams, 724-357-2560, Fax: 724-357-6205, E-mail: mary.e.williams@iup.edu.

College of Humanities and Social Sciences Students: 139 full-time (78 women), 314 part-time (190 women); includes 51 minority (23 Black or African American, non-Hispanic/Latino; 1 American Indian or Alaska Native, non-Hispanic/Latino; 9 Asian, non-Hispanic/Latino; 9 Hispanic/Latino; 9 Two or more races, non-Hispanic/Latino), 105 international. Average age 36. 331 applicants, 69% accepted, 74 enrolled. *Faculty:* 64 full-time (32 women), 1 part-time/adjunct (0 women). Expenses: Contact institution. *Financial support:* In 2017–18, 4 fellowships with full tuition reimbursements (averaging $1,760 per year), 87 research assistantships with tuition reimbursements (averaging $4,785 per year), 11 teaching assistantships with partial tuition reimbursements (averaging $12,712 per year) were awarded; career-related internships or fieldwork, Federal Work-Study, scholarships/grants, and unspecified assistantships also available. Support available to part-time students. Financial award application deadline: 4/15; financial award applicants required to submit FAFSA. In 2017, 62 master's, 44 doctorates, 1 other advanced degree awarded. *Program availability:* Part-time, evening/weekend. Offers administration and leadership studies (PhD); applied archaeology (MA); composition and literature (MA); composition and teaching English to speakers of other languages (PhD); English: generalist (MA); English: literature (MA); English: TESOL (MA); environmental planning (MS); geographic information science and geospatial techniques (Certificate); geographic information science/cartography (MS); geography (MA); history (MA); humanities and social sciences (MA, MS, PhD, Certificate); literature and criticism (PhD); public affairs (MA); public history (MA); regional planning (MS); sociology (MA, PhD); Spanish/applied linguistics and teaching methodology (MA); Spanish/Hispanic literatures and cultures (MA); teaching English (MA). *Application deadline:* Applications are processed on a rolling basis. *Application fee:* $50. Electronic applications accepted. *Application Contact:* Paula Stossel, Assistant Dean, 724-357-4511, E-mail: graduate-admissions@iup.edu. *Dean*, Dr. Yaw Asamoah, 724-357-5764, E-mail: osebo@iup.edu.

College of Natural Sciences and Mathematics Students: 82 full-time (53 women), 66 part-time (39 women); includes 22 minority (5 Black or African American, non-Hispanic/Latino; 8 Hispanic/Latino; 7 Native Hawaiian or other Pacific Islander, non-Hispanic/Latino; 2 Two or more races, non-Hispanic/Latino), 20 international. Average age 29. 335 applicants, 32% accepted, 41 enrolled. *Faculty:* 48 full-time (16 women). Expenses: Contact institution. *Financial support:* In 2017–18, 13 fellowships with full tuition reimbursements (averaging $522 per year), 67 research assistantships with tuition reimbursements (averaging $3,115 per year), 2 teaching assistantships (averaging $23,305 per year) were awarded; career-related internships or fieldwork, Federal Work-Study, scholarships/grants, and unspecified assistantships also available. Support available to part-time students. Financial award application deadline: 4/15; financial award applicants required to submit FAFSA. In 2017, 53 master's, 15 doctorates awarded. *Program availability:* Part-time. Offers applied and industrial chemistry (PSM); applied mathematics (MS); biology (MS); clinical psychology (Psy D); elementary and middle school mathematics education (M Ed); nanoscience/industrial materials (PSM); natural sciences and mathematics (M Ed, MA, MS, PSM, Psy D); physics (MA, PSM); psychology (MA); secondary mathematics education (M Ed). *Application deadline:* Applications are processed on a rolling basis. *Application fee:* $50. Electronic applications accepted. *Application Contact:* Paula Stossel, Assistant Dean of Administration, 724-357-4511, Fax: 724-357-4862, E-mail: graduate-admissions@iup.edu. *Dean*, Dr. Deanne Snavely, 724-357-2609, Fax: 724-357-5700, E-mail: snavely@iup.edu.

Eberly College of Business and Information Technology Students: 151 full-time (52 women), 122 part-time (50 women); includes 25 minority (10 Black or African

American, non-Hispanic/Latino; 6 Asian, non-Hispanic/Latino; 5 Hispanic/Latino; 4 Two or more races, non-Hispanic/Latino), 173 international. Average age 28. 243 applicants, 78% accepted, 131 enrolled. *Faculty:* 32 full-time (4 women), 1 part-time/adjunct (0 women). Expenses: Contact institution. *Financial support:* Fellowships, research assistantships, career-related internships or fieldwork, Federal Work-Study, scholarships/grants, and unspecified assistantships available. Support available to part-time students. Financial award application deadline: 4/15; financial award applicants required to submit FAFSA. In 2017, 179 master's awarded. *Program availability:* Part-time, evening/weekend. Offers business administration (MBA); business and information technology (M Ed, MBA). *Application deadline:* Applications are processed on a rolling basis. *Application fee:* $50. Electronic applications accepted. *Application Contact:* Paula Stossel, Assistant Dean, 724-357-4511, Fax: 724-357-4862, E-mail: graduate-admissions@iup.edu. *Dean,* Dr. Robert Camp, 724-357-7889, E-mail: bobcamp@iup.edu.

INDIANA UNIVERSITY–PURDUE UNIVERSITY FORT WAYNE, Fort Wayne, IN 46805-1499

General Information State-supported, coed, comprehensive institution. *Graduate housing:* Room and/or apartments available on a first-come, first-served basis to single students; on-campus housing not available to married students. *Research affiliation:* Regenstrief Institute, Inc. (nursing), Earthwatch (biology), PHD, Inc. (engineering), Bendix Commercial Vehicle Systems, LLC (engineering, technology, and computer science), Northeast Indiana Fund (education and public policy), Fort Wayne Metals (geosciences).

GRADUATE UNITS

College of Arts and Sciences *Program availability:* Part-time, evening/weekend. Offers applied mathematics (MS); applied statistics (Certificate); arts and sciences (MA, MAT, MS, Certificate); biology (MS); English (MA, MAT); mathematics (MS); operations research (MS); professional communication (MA, MS); teaching (MAT); TENL (teaching English as a new language) (Certificate).

College of Education and Public Policy *Program availability:* Part-time. Offers couple and family counseling (MS Ed); education and public policy (MPM, MS Ed, Certificate); educational leadership (MS Ed); elementary education (MS Ed); public management (MPM, Certificate); school counseling (MS Ed); secondary education (MS Ed); special education (MS Ed, Certificate).

College of Engineering, Technology, and Computer Science *Program availability:* Part-time. Offers applied computer science (MS); civil engineering (MSE); computer engineering (MSE); electrical engineering (MSE); engineering, technology, and computer science (MS, MSE, Certificate); facilities/construction management (MS); human resources (MS); industrial technology/manufacturing (MS); information technology/advanced computer applications (MS); leadership (MS); mechanical engineering (MSE); organizational leadership and supervision (Certificate); systems engineering (MSE). Electronic applications accepted.

College of Health and Human Services *Program availability:* Part-time. Offers adult-gerontology primary care nurse practitioner (MS); family nurse practitioner (MS); health and human services (MS, DNP, Certificate); nurse executive (MS); nursing administration (Certificate); nursing education (MS). Electronic applications accepted.

Doermer School of Business *Program availability:* Part-time. Offers business (MBA).

INDIANA UNIVERSITY–PURDUE UNIVERSITY INDIANAPOLIS, Indianapolis, IN 46202

General Information State-supported, coed, university. *Graduate housing:* Rooms and/or apartments available on a first-come, first-served basis to single and married students. Housing application deadline: 3/15.

GRADUATE UNITS

Herron School of Art and Design Offers art therapy (MA); visual art (MFA); visual communication design (MFA). Electronic applications accepted.

Indiana University School of Medicine Offers anatomy and cell biology (MS, PhD); biochemistry and molecular biology (MS, PhD); genetic counseling (MS); medical and molecular genetics (MS, PhD); medicine (MS, MD, PhD); microbiology and immunology (MS, PhD); pathology and laboratory medicine (MS, PhD); pharmacology (MS, PhD); toxicology (MS, PhD).

Stark Neurosciences Research Institute Offers medical neuroscience (PhD).

Kelley School of Business Offers accounting (MBA); business (MBA, MSA); business of medicine (MBA); entrepreneurship (MBA); finance (MBA); general administration (MBA); marketing (MBA); supply chain management (MBA).

Lilly Family School of Philanthropy Offers philanthropy (MA, XMA, PhD).

Richard M. Fairbanks School of Public Health Offers biostatistics (MS, PhD); environmental health (MPH); epidemiology (MPH, PhD); global health leadership (Dr PH); health administration (MHA); health policy (Graduate Certificate); health policy and management (MPH, PhD); health systems management (Graduate Certificate); product stewardship (MS); public health (Graduate Certificate); social and behavioral sciences (MPH).

Robert H. McKinney School of Law *Program availability:* Part-time. Offers advocacy skills (Certificate); American law for foreign lawyers (LL M); civil and human rights (Certificate); corporate and commercial law (LL M, Certificate); criminal law (Certificate); environmental and natural resources (Certificate); health law (Certificate); health law, policy and bioethics (LL M); intellectual property law (LL M, Certificate); international and comparative law (LL M, Certificate); international human rights law (LL M); law (MJ, JD, SJD). Electronic applications accepted.

School of Dentistry Offers cariology and operative dentistry (MSD); dental materials (MS, MSD); dental sciences (PhD); dentistry (DDS, Certificate); endodontics (MSD); oral and maxillofacial surgery (MSD); orthodontics (MSD); pediatric dentistry (MSD); periodontics (MSD); prosthodontics (MSD). Electronic applications accepted.

School of Education *Program availability:* Part-time, evening/weekend. Offers curriculum and instruction (MS); early childhood (MS); educational leadership (MS, Certificate); English as a second language (Certificate); kindergarten (Certificate); language education (MS); reading (Certificate); school counseling (MS); special education (MS, Certificate). Electronic applications accepted.

School of Engineering and Technology *Program availability:* Part-time, evening/weekend. Offers applied data management and analytics (MS); biomedical engineering (MS, PhD); electrical and computer engineering (MS, PhD); engineering (MSE); engineering and technology (MS, MS Bm E, MSE, MSME, PhD); facilities management (MS); information security and assurance (MS); mechanical engineering (MSME, PhD); motorsports (MS); music technology (MS, PhD); music therapy (MS); organizational leadership (MS); technical communication (MS). Electronic applications accepted.

School of Health and Rehabilitation Sciences *Program availability:* Part-time, evening/weekend. Offers health and rehabilitation sciences (PhD); health sciences (MS); nutrition and dietetics (MS); occupational therapy (OTD); physical therapy (DPT); physician assistant (MPAS). Electronic applications accepted.

School of Informatics and Computing *Program availability:* Part-time, evening/weekend. Offers bioinformatics (MS, PhD); health informatics (MS, PhD); human-computer interaction (MS, PhD); informatics (MS); informatics and computing (MLS, MS, PhD, Certificate); library and information science (MLS); media arts and science (MS). Electronic applications accepted.

School of Liberal Arts Offers American philosophy (Certificate); American studies (PhD); applied communication (MA); bioethics (Certificate); economics (MA); English (MA); European history (MA); general sociology (MA); geographic information systems (MS, Certificate); health communication (PhD); liberal arts (MA, MS, PhD, Certificate); medical sociology (MA); museum studies (MA, Certificate); philosophy (MA); philosophy/bioethics (MA); political science (MA); public history (MA); teaching English to speakers of other languages (TESOL) (MA, Certificate); teaching literature (Certificate); teaching writing (Certificate); United States history (MA).

School of Nursing *Program availability:* Part-time, blended/hybrid learning. Offers adult/gerontology acute care nurse practitioner (MSN); adult/gerontology clinical nurse specialist (MSN); adult/gerontology primary care nurse practitioner (MSN); clinical nursing science (PhD); executive leadership (DNP); family nurse practitioner (MSN); health systems (PhD); nursing (MSN, DNP, PhD); nursing education (MSN); nursing leadership in health systems (MSN); pediatric clinical nurse specialist (MSN); pediatric nurse practitioner (MSN). Electronic applications accepted.

School of Physical Education and Tourism Management Offers event tourism (MS); kinesiology (MS); public health (Graduate Certificate). Electronic applications accepted.

School of Public and Environmental Affairs *Program availability:* Part-time, evening/weekend, online learning. Offers criminal justice and public safety (MS); homeland security and emergency management (Graduate Certificate); library management (Graduate Certificate); nonprofit management (Graduate Certificate); public affairs (MPA); public management (Graduate Certificate); social entrepreneurship: nonprofit and public benefit organizations (Graduate Certificate). Electronic applications accepted.

School of Science *Program availability:* Part-time, evening/weekend. Offers addiction neuroscience (PhD); applied earth sciences (PhD); applied social and organizational psychology (PhD); biocomputing (Graduate Certificate); biology (MS, PhD); biometrics (Graduate Certificate); chemistry and chemical biology (MS, PhD); clinical psychology (PhD); computer science (MS, PhD); computer security (Graduate Certificate); databases and data mining (Graduate Certificate); forensic and investigative sciences (MS); geology (MS); industrial/organizational psychology (MS); mathematics (MS, PhD); physics (MS, PhD); science (MS, PhD, Graduate Certificate); software engineering (Graduate Certificate). Electronic applications accepted.

School of Social Work *Program availability:* Part-time, evening/weekend. Offers social work (MSW, PhD, Certificate).

INDIANA UNIVERSITY SOUTH BEND, South Bend, IN 46615

General Information State-supported, coed, comprehensive institution. *Graduate housing:* On-campus housing not available.

GRADUATE UNITS

College of Liberal Arts and Sciences *Program availability:* Part-time, evening/weekend. Offers advanced computer programming (Graduate Certificate); applied informatics (Graduate Certificate); applied mathematics and computer science (MS); behavior modification (Graduate Certificate); computer applications (Graduate Certificate); computer programming (Graduate Certificate); correctional management and supervision (Graduate Certificate); English (MA); health systems management (Graduate Certificate); international studies (Graduate Certificate); liberal studies (MLS); nonprofit management (Graduate Certificate); paralegal studies (Graduate Certificate); professional writing (Graduate Certificate); public affairs (MPA); public management (Graduate Certificate); social and cultural diversity (Graduate Certificate); strategic sustainability leadership (Graduate Certificate); technology for administration (Graduate Certificate).

Ernestine M. Raclin School of the Arts *Program availability:* Part-time. Offers communication studies (MA); music (MM); music performance (AD). Electronic applications accepted.

Judd Leighton School of Business and Economics *Program availability:* Part-time, evening/weekend. Offers accounting (MSA); business (Graduate Certificate); business administration (MBA). Electronic applications accepted.

School of Education *Program availability:* Part-time, evening/weekend. Offers addiction counseling (MS Ed); alcohol and drug counseling (Graduate Certificate); clinical mental health counseling (MS Ed); educational leadership (MS Ed); elementary education (MS Ed); marriage, couple, and family counseling (MS Ed); school counseling (MS Ed); secondary education (MS Ed); special education (MAT, MS Ed). Electronic applications accepted.

School of Social Work *Program availability:* Part-time, evening/weekend. Offers social work (MSW).

Vera Z. Dwyer College of Health Sciences Offers health sciences (MSN).

School of Nursing *Program availability:* Part-time, evening/weekend. Offers family nurse practitioner (MSN).

INDIANA UNIVERSITY SOUTHEAST, New Albany, IN 47150-6405

General Information State-supported, coed, comprehensive institution. *Graduate housing:* On-campus housing not available.

GRADUATE UNITS

Master of Interdisciplinary Studies Program *Program availability:* Part-time. Offers interdisciplinary studies (MIS, Graduate Certificate). Electronic applications accepted.

School of Business *Program availability:* Part-time. Offers business administration (MBA); strategic finance (MS). Electronic applications accepted.

School of Education *Program availability:* Part-time, evening/weekend. Offers counselor education (MS Ed); elementary education (MS Ed); secondary education (MS Ed). Electronic applications accepted.

INDIANA WESLEYAN UNIVERSITY, Marion, IN 46953-4974

General Information Independent-religious, coed, comprehensive institution. *Graduate housing:* On-campus housing not available. *Research affiliation:* Eli Lilly and Company.

GRADUATE UNITS

College of Adult and Professional Studies *Program availability:* Part-time, evening/weekend, online learning. Offers accounting (MBA, Graduate Certificate); applied management (MBA); business administration (MBA); health care (MBA, Graduate Certificate); human resources (MBA, Graduate Certificate); management (MS); organizational leadership (Ed D). Electronic applications accepted.

School of Educational Leadership *Program availability:* Part-time, evening/weekend, online learning. Offers educational leadership (M Ed, Ed S). Electronic applications accepted.

Graduate School *Program availability:* Part-time, evening/weekend, online learning. Electronic applications accepted.

College of Arts and Sciences *Program availability:* Part-time. Offers addictions counseling (MS); clinical mental health counseling (MS); community counseling (MS); marriage and family therapy (MS); school counseling (MS); student development counseling and administration (MS). Electronic applications accepted.

School of Nursing *Program availability:* Part-time, online learning. Offers nursing administration (MS); nursing education (MS); primary care nursing (MS).

Wesley Seminary Offers children, youth and family ministry (MA); divinity (M Div); ministerial leadership (MA); ministry (MA).

INSTITUTE FOR CHRISTIAN STUDIES, Toronto, ON M5T 1R4, Canada

General Information Independent-religious, coed, graduate-only institution. *Graduate housing:* On-campus housing not available.

GRADUATE UNITS

Graduate Programs *Program availability:* Part-time, online learning. Offers education (M Phil F, PhD); history of philosophy (M Phil F, PhD); philosophical aesthetics (M Phil F, PhD); philosophy of religion (M Phil F, PhD); political theory (M Phil F, PhD); systematic philosophy (M Phil F, PhD); theology (M Phil F, PhD); worldview studies (MWS).

INSTITUTE FOR CLINICAL SOCIAL WORK, Chicago, IL 60601

General Information Independent, coed, primarily women, graduate-only institution. *Graduate housing:* On-campus housing not available.

GRADUATE UNITS

Graduate Programs *Program availability:* Part-time. Offers clinical social work (PhD).

INSTITUTE FOR DOCTORAL STUDIES IN THE VISUAL ARTS, Portland, ME 04102

General Information Independent, coed, graduate-only institution. *Enrollment by degree level:* 60 doctoral. *Graduate faculty:* 3 full-time, 7 part-time/adjunct.
Website: http://www.idsva.org/

General Application Contact: Molly M. Davis, Director of Administration/Co-Director of Admissions, 207-771-8887, E-mail: info@idsva.edu.

GRADUATE UNITS

PhD Program in Visual Art: Philosophy, Aesthetics, and Art Theory Students: 60 full-time. *Faculty:* 3 full-time, 7 part-time/adjunct. Expenses: Contact institution. *Financial support:* Fellowships, teaching assistantships, and scholarships/grants available. Financial award applicants required to submit FAFSA. *Program availability:* Online learning. Offers aesthetics (PhD); art theory (PhD); philosophy (PhD). *Application deadline:* Applications are processed on a rolling basis. *Application fee:* $60. Electronic applications accepted. *Application Contact:* Molly M. Davis, Director of Administration/Co-Director of Admissions, 207-771-8887, E-mail: info@idsva.edu.

INSTITUTE OF AMERICAN INDIAN ARTS, Santa Fe, NM 87508

General Information Federally supported, coed, comprehensive institution. *Enrollment:* 657 graduate, professional, and undergraduate students; 46 full-time matriculated graduate/professional students (25 women), 4 part-time matriculated graduate/professional students (all women). *Enrollment by degree level:* 50 master's. Tuition, state resident: full-time $12,000; part-time $500 per credit. Tuition, nonresident: full-time $12,000; part-time $500 per credit. *Required fees:* $680. *Graduate housing:* On-campus housing not available. *Student services:* Campus safety program, career counseling, exercise/wellness program, services for students with disabilities. *Library facilities:* IAIA Library plus 1 other. *Collection:* Students can reserve study rooms.

Computer facilities: 100 computers available on campus for general student use. A campuswide network can be accessed from student residence rooms. Online class registration is available.
Website: http://www.iaia.edu/

General Application Contact: Jon Davis, Director, Low Residency MFA in Creative Writing, 505-424-2365, Fax: 505-424-3030, E-mail: jdavis@iaia.edu.

GRADUATE UNITS

Low Residency MFA in Creative Writing Program Students: 46 full-time (25 women), 4 part-time (all women); includes 34 minority (24 American Indian or Alaska Native, non-Hispanic/Latino; 7 Hispanic/Latino; 1 Native Hawaiian or other Pacific Islander, non-Hispanic/Latino; 2 Two or more races, non-Hispanic/Latino). Expenses: Contact institution. *Financial support:* Scholarships/grants available. Financial award application deadline: 2/15; financial award applicants required to submit FAFSA. In 2017, 25 master's awarded. *Program availability:* Low-residency. Offers creative writing (MFA). *Application deadline:* For fall admission, 2/15 priority date for domestic and international students. Applications are processed on a rolling basis. *Application fee:* $25. Electronic applications accepted. *Director,* Jon Davis, 505-424-2365, Fax: 505-424-3030, E-mail: mfa@iaia.edu.

INSTITUTE OF CLINICAL ACUPUNCTURE AND ORIENTAL MEDICINE, Honolulu, HI 96817

General Information Proprietary, coed, graduate-only institution.

GRADUATE UNITS

Program in Oriental Medicine Offers Oriental medicine (MSOM).

INSTITUTE OF PUBLIC ADMINISTRATION, Dublin 4, Ireland

General Information Proprietary, coed, comprehensive institution.

GRADUATE UNITS

Programs in Public Administration Offers healthcare management (MA); local government management (MA); public management (MA, Diploma).

INSTITUTE OF TAOIST EDUCATION AND ACUPUNCTURE, Louisville, CO 80027

General Information Independent, coed, graduate-only institution.

GRADUATE UNITS

Graduate Program Offers classical five-element acupuncture (M Ac).

THE INSTITUTE OF WORLD POLITICS, Washington, DC 20036

General Information Independent, coed, graduate-only institution. *Graduate housing:* On-campus housing not available.

GRADUATE UNITS

Graduate Programs in National Security, Intelligence, and International Affairs *Program availability:* Part-time, evening/weekend. Offers American foreign policy (Certificate); comparative political culture (Certificate); counterintelligence (Certificate); democracy building (Certificate); intelligence (Certificate); international politics (Certificate); national security affairs (Certificate); public diplomacy and political warfare (Certificate); statecraft and national security affairs (MA); statecraft and world politics (MA); strategic intelligence studies (MA). Electronic applications accepted.

INSTITUT FRANCO-EUROPÉEN DE CHIROPRAXIE, 94200, France

General Information Independent, coed, graduate-only institution.

GRADUATE UNITS

Professional Program Offers chiropractic (DC).

INSTITUTO CENTROAMERICANO DE ADMINISTRACIÓN DE EMPRESAS, La Garita, Alajuela, Costa Rica

General Information Independent, coed, graduate-only institution. *Graduate housing:* Rooms and/or apartments guaranteed to single students and available to married students. *Research affiliation:* Tropical Agricultural Research and Higher Education Center (agribusiness), Harvard Institute for International Development (macroeconomics and environment), Earth University (agribusiness), Inter-American Institute for Cooperation on Agriculture (agribusiness), David Rockefeller Center for Latin American Studies (competitiveness), Zamarano (agribusiness).

GRADUATE UNITS

Graduate Programs Offers agribusiness management (MIAM); business administration (EMBA); finance (MBA); real estate management (MGREM); sustainable development (MBA); technology (MBA). Electronic applications accepted.

INSTITUTO TECNOLÓGICO Y DE ESTUDIOS SUPERIORES DE MONTERREY, CAMPUS CENTRAL DE VERACRUZ, 94500 Córdoba, Veracruz, Mexico

General Information Independent, coed, comprehensive institution.

GRADUATE UNITS

Graduate Programs *Program availability:* Part-time, evening/weekend, online learning. Electronic applications accepted.

INSTITUTO TECNOLÓGICO Y DE ESTUDIOS SUPERIORES DE MONTERREY, CAMPUS CHIAPAS, 29000 Tuxtla Gutiérrez, Chiapas, Mexico

General Information Independent, coed, comprehensive institution.

INSTITUTO TECNOLÓGICO Y DE ESTUDIOS SUPERIORES DE MONTERREY, CAMPUS CHIHUAHUA, 31300 Chihuahua, Chihuahua, Mexico

General Information Independent, coed, comprehensive institution.

GRADUATE UNITS

Graduate Programs Offers computer systems engineering (Ingeniero); electrical engineering (Ingeniero); electromechanical engineering (Ingeniero); electronic engineering (Ingeniero); engineering administration (MEA); industrial engineering (MIE, Ingeniero); international trade (MIT); mechanical engineering (Ingeniero).

INSTITUTO TECNOLÓGICO Y DE ESTUDIOS SUPERIORES DE MONTERREY, CAMPUS CIUDAD DE MÉXICO, 14380 Ciudad de Mexico, DF, Mexico

General Information Independent, coed, comprehensive institution. *Graduate housing:* On-campus housing not available. *Research affiliation:* McGill University (management), Concordia University (business and management), Eli Lilly S. A. de C. U. (technological development), Ford Motor Company (industrial organizations), German Research Center on Artificial Intelligence (informatics), Brent University (telecommunications).

GRADUATE UNITS

School of Business Administration *Program availability:* Part-time, evening/weekend, online learning. Offers business administration (EMBA, MBA, PhD); economy (MBA); finance (MBA). EMBA program offered jointly with The University of Texas at Austin.

School of Design, Engineering and Architecture *Program availability:* Part-time, evening/weekend, online learning. Offers management (MA); telecommunications (MA).

School of Humanities and Social Sciences *Program availability:* Part-time, evening/weekend. Offers humanities and social sciences (LL B).

Virtual University Division *Program availability:* Part-time, evening/weekend, online learning.

INSTITUTO TECNOLÓGICO Y DE ESTUDIOS SUPERIORES DE MONTERREY, CAMPUS CIUDAD JUÁREZ, 32320 Ciudad Juárez, Chihuahua, Mexico

General Information Independent, coed, comprehensive institution.

GRADUATE UNITS

Program in Administration of Information Technology Offers administration of information technology (MAIT).

Program in Applied Public Management Offers applied public management (MPM).

Program in Business Administration *Program availability:* Part-time, online learning. Offers business administration (MBA).

Program in Education Offers education (M Ed).

Program in Educational Administration Offers educational administration (MEA).

Program in Educational Innovation Offers educational innovation (DE).

Program in Educational Technology Offers educational technology (MTE).

Program in Electronic Commerce Offers electronic commerce (MEC).

Program in Humanistic Studies Offers humanistic studies (MEH).

Program in Quality Management Offers quality management (MQM).

INSTITUTO TECNOLÓGICO Y DE ESTUDIOS SUPERIORES DE MONTERREY, CAMPUS CIUDAD OBREGÓN, 85000 Ciudad Obregón, Sonora, Mexico

General Information Independent, coed, comprehensive institution.

GRADUATE UNITS

Program in Administration Offers administration (MA).

Program in Administration of Information Technology Offers administration of information technology (MATI).
Program in Administration of Telecommunications Offers administration of telecommunications (MAT).
Program in Engineering Offers engineering (ME).
Program in Finance Offers finance (MF).
Program in International Relations Offers international relations (MIR).
Program in Marketing Technology Offers marketing technology (MMT).
Programs in Education Offers cognitive development (ME); communications (ME); mathematics (ME).

INSTITUTO TECNOLÓGICO Y DE ESTUDIOS SUPERIORES DE MONTERREY, CAMPUS COLIMA, 28010 Colima, Colima, Mexico

General Information Independent, coed, comprehensive institution.

INSTITUTO TECNOLÓGICO Y DE ESTUDIOS SUPERIORES DE MONTERREY, CAMPUS CUERNAVACA, 62000 Temixco, Morelos, Mexico

General Information Independent, coed, comprehensive institution.

GRADUATE UNITS

Programs in Business Administration Offers finance (MA); human resources management (MA); international business (MA); marketing (MA).
Programs in Information Science Offers administration of information technology (MATI); computer science (MCC, DCC); information technology (MTI).

INSTITUTO TECNOLÓGICO Y DE ESTUDIOS SUPERIORES DE MONTERREY, CAMPUS ESTADO DE MÉXICO, Estado de Mexico 52926, Mexico

General Information Independent, coed, comprehensive institution. *Graduate housing:* On-campus housing not available. *Research affiliation:* Transportadora San Marcos, S. A. de C. V. (quality control), Microsoft Visual Studio (computer science), Sony Electronics (new products), Kaltex (quality control), Texas Instruments (semiconductors).

GRADUATE UNITS

Professional and Graduate Division *Program availability:* Part-time, online learning. Offers administration of information technologies (MITA); architecture (M Arch); business administration (GMBA, MBA); computer sciences (MCS, PhD); education (M Ed); educational institution administration (MAD); educational technology and innovation (PhD); electronic commerce (MEC); environmental systems (MS); finance (MAF); humanistic studies (MHS); information sciences and knowledge management (MISKM); information systems (MS); manufacturing systems (MS); marketing (MEM); quality systems and productivity (MS); science and materials engineering (PhD); telecommunications management (MTM).

INSTITUTO TECNOLÓGICO Y DE ESTUDIOS SUPERIORES DE MONTERREY, CAMPUS GUADALAJARA, 45140 Zapopan, Jalisco, Mexico

General Information Independent, coed, comprehensive institution. *Graduate housing:* Rooms and/or apartments available to single and married students. Housing application deadline: 8/30.

GRADUATE UNITS

Program in Business Administration *Program availability:* Part-time, evening/weekend, online learning. Offers business administration (IEMBA, M Ad).
Program in Finance Offers finance (MF).

INSTITUTO TECNOLÓGICO Y DE ESTUDIOS SUPERIORES DE MONTERREY, CAMPUS HIDALGO, 42090 Pachuca, Hidalgo, Mexico

General Information Independent, coed, comprehensive institution.

INSTITUTO TECNOLÓGICO Y DE ESTUDIOS SUPERIORES DE MONTERREY, CAMPUS IRAPUATO, 36660 Irapuato, Guanajuato, Mexico

General Information Independent, coed, comprehensive institution.

GRADUATE UNITS

Graduate Programs Offers administration (MBA); administration of information technology (MAIT); administration of telecommunications (MAT); architecture (M Arch); computer science (MCS); education (M Ed); educational administration (MEA); educational innovation and technology (DEIT); educational technology (MET); electronic commerce (MBA); environmental administration and planning (MEAP); environmental systems (MES); finances (MBA); humanistic studies (MHS); international management for Latin American executives (MIMLAE); library and information science (MLIS); manufacturing quality management (MMQM); marketing research (MBA).

INSTITUTO TECNOLÓGICO Y DE ESTUDIOS SUPERIORES DE MONTERREY, CAMPUS LAGUNA, 27250 Torreón, Coahuila, Mexico

General Information Independent, coed, comprehensive institution. *Graduate housing:* On-campus housing not available.

GRADUATE UNITS

Graduate School *Program availability:* Part-time. Offers business administration (MBA); industrial engineering (MIE); management information systems (MS).

INSTITUTO TECNOLÓGICO Y DE ESTUDIOS SUPERIORES DE MONTERREY, CAMPUS LEÓN, 37120 León, Guanajuato, Mexico

General Information Independent, coed, comprehensive institution.

GRADUATE UNITS

Program in Business Administration *Program availability:* Part-time. Offers business administration (MBA).

INSTITUTO TECNOLÓGICO Y DE ESTUDIOS SUPERIORES DE MONTERREY, CAMPUS MONTERREY, 64849 Monterrey, Nuevo León, Mexico

General Information Independent, coed, comprehensive institution. *Graduate housing:* Room and/or apartments available to single students; on-campus housing not available to married students. *Research affiliation:* IBM de Mexico (computer science), Southwest Research Institute (environment), Hylsa (steel), Vitro (glass products), Cydsa (petrochemicals), Cemex (cement).

GRADUATE UNITS

Graduate and Research Division *Program availability:* Part-time, evening/weekend. Offers agricultural parasitology (PhD); agricultural sciences (MS); applied statistics (M Eng); artificial intelligence (PhD); automation engineering (M Eng); biotechnology (MS); chemical engineering (M Eng); chemistry (MS, PhD); civil engineering (M Eng); communications (MS); computer science (MS); education (MA); electrical engineering (M Eng); electronic engineering (M Eng); environmental engineering (M Eng); farming productivity (MS); food processing engineering (MS); industrial engineering (M Eng, PhD); informatics (PhD); information systems (MS); information technology (MS); manufacturing engineering (M Eng); mechanical engineering (M Eng); phytopathology (MS); systems and quality engineering (M Eng).
Graduate School of Business Administration and Leadership *Program availability:* Part-time. Offers business administration (MA, MBA); finance (M Sc); international business (M Sc); management (PhD); management and leadership (M Sc, MA, MBA, PhD); marketing (M Sc).

INSTITUTO TECNOLÓGICO Y DE ESTUDIOS SUPERIORES DE MONTERREY, CAMPUS QUERÉTARO, 76130 Querétaro, Querétaro, Mexico

General Information Independent, coed, comprehensive institution. *Graduate housing:* Room and/or apartments guaranteed to single students; on-campus housing not available to married students. Housing application deadline: 6/15. *Research affiliation:* Transmisiones y Equipos Mecanicos (manufacturing design).

GRADUATE UNITS

School of Business Offers business (MBA).

INSTITUTO TECNOLÓGICO Y DE ESTUDIOS SUPERIORES DE MONTERREY, CAMPUS SALTILLO, 25270 Saltillo, Coahuila, Mexico

General Information Independent, coed, comprehensive institution.

INSTITUTO TECNOLÓGICO Y DE ESTUDIOS SUPERIORES DE MONTERREY, CAMPUS SAN LUIS POTOSÍ, 78140 San Luis Potosí, SLP, Mexico

General Information Independent, coed, comprehensive institution.

INSTITUTO TECNOLÓGICO Y DE ESTUDIOS SUPERIORES DE MONTERREY, CAMPUS SINALOA, 80800 Culiacán, Sinaloa, Mexico

General Information Independent, coed, comprehensive institution.

INSTITUTO TECNOLÓGICO Y DE ESTUDIOS SUPERIORES DE MONTERREY, CAMPUS SONORA NORTE, 83000 Hermosillo, Sonora, Mexico

General Information Independent, coed, comprehensive institution. *Graduate housing:* On-campus housing not available. *Research affiliation:* National Council for Science and Technology (engineering).

GRADUATE UNITS

Program in Business Offers business (MA).
Program in Education Offers education (MA).
Program in Technological Information Management Offers technological information management (MA).

INSTITUTO TECNOLÓGICO Y DE ESTUDIOS SUPERIORES DE MONTERREY, CAMPUS TAMPICO, 89120 Altimira, Tamaulipas, Mexico

General Information Independent, coed, comprehensive institution.

INSTITUTO TECNOLÓGICO Y DE ESTUDIOS SUPERIORES DE MONTERREY, CAMPUS TOLUCA, 50252 Toluca, Estado de Mexico, Mexico

General Information Independent, coed, comprehensive institution.

GRADUATE UNITS

Graduate Programs *Program availability:* Part-time, evening/weekend.

INSTITUTO TECNOLÓGICO Y DE ESTUDIOS SUPERIORES DE MONTERREY, CAMPUS ZACATECAS, 98000 Zacatecas, Zacatecas, Mexico

General Information Independent, coed, comprehensive institution.

INTER AMERICAN UNIVERSITY OF PUERTO RICO, AGUADILLA CAMPUS, Aguadilla, PR 00605

General Information Independent, coed, comprehensive institution.

GRADUATE UNITS

Graduate School *Program availability:* Part-time, evening/weekend. Electronic applications accepted.

INTER AMERICAN UNIVERSITY OF PUERTO RICO, ARECIBO CAMPUS, Arecibo, PR 00614-4050

General Information Independent, coed, comprehensive institution.

GRADUATE UNITS

Program in Anesthesia Offers anesthesia (MS).
Program in Business Administration Offers accounting (MBA); finance (MBA); human resources (MBA).
Program in Nursing Offers critical care nursing (MSN); surgical nursing (MSN).
Programs in Education Offers administration and educational supervision (MA Ed); counseling and guidance (MA Ed); curriculum and teaching (MA Ed); elementary education (MA Ed).

INTER AMERICAN UNIVERSITY OF PUERTO RICO, BARRANQUITAS CAMPUS, Barranquitas, PR 00794

General Information Independent, coed, comprehensive institution. *Enrollment:* 1,884 graduate, professional, and undergraduate students; 79 full-time matriculated graduate/professional students (54 women), 46 part-time matriculated graduate/professional students (34 women). *Enrollment by degree level:* 95 master's. *Graduate faculty:* 7 full-time (2 women), 8 part-time/adjunct (5 women). *Tuition:* Full-time $3392; part-time $1696 per year. *Required fees:* $652; $652 per unit. Tuition and fees vary according to course load. *Graduate housing:* On-campus housing not available. *Student services:* Career counseling, services for students with disabilities. *Library facilities:* Centro de Accoso a la Informacio, Recinto de Barranquitas. *Collection:* Books: 34,547 (physical), 266,052 (digital/electronic); Serial titles: 187 (physical), 60,000 (digital/electronic); Databases: 84. Weekly public service hours: 71; students can reserve study rooms.

Computer facilities: 403 computers available on campus for general student use. A campuswide network can be accessed. Online class registration is available.
Website: http://www.br.inter.edu/

General Application Contact: Aramilda Cartagena-Santiago, Dean of Students, 787-857-3600 Ext. 2109, Fax: 787-857-2125, E-mail: aramildacartagena@br.inter.edu.

GRADUATE UNITS

Business Administration Program Students: 11 full-time (9 women), 1 (woman) part-time; all minorities (all Hispanic/Latino). Average age 31. 6 applicants, 83% accepted, 5 enrolled. *Faculty:* 2 full-time (1 woman), 2 part-time/adjunct (both women). Expenses: Contact institution. *Financial support:* Applicants required to submit FAFSA. In 2017, 3 master's awarded. *Program availability:* Part-time, evening/weekend. Offers accounting (MBA); human resources (MBA); managerial information systems (MBA). *Application deadline:* Applications are processed on a rolling basis. *Application fee:* $31. Electronic applications accepted. *Application Contact:* Aramilda Cartagena-Santiago, Dean of Students, 787-857-3600 Ext. 2009, Fax: 787-857-2125, E-mail: aramildacartagena@br.inter.edu. *Chancellor,* Juan A. Negron-Berrios, PhD, 787-857-3600 Ext. 2002, Fax: 787-857-2125, E-mail: janegron@br.inter.edu.

Program in Biotechnology Students: 20 full-time (12 women), 11 part-time (5 women); all minorities (all Hispanic/Latino). Average age 25. 16 applicants, 94% accepted, 15 enrolled. *Faculty:* 2 full-time (1 woman), 3 part-time/adjunct (1 woman). Expenses: Contact institution. *Financial support:* Applicants required to submit FAFSA. In 2017, 9 master's awarded. *Program availability:* Part-time, evening/weekend. Offers general biotechnology (MSB); plants biotechnology (MSB). *Application deadline:* Applications are processed on a rolling basis. *Application fee:* $31. Electronic applications accepted. *Application Contact:* Aramilda Cartagena-Santiago, Dean of Students, 787-857-3600 Ext. 2009, Fax: 787-857-2125, E-mail: aramildacartagena@br.inter.edu. *Chancellor,* Juan A. Negron-Berrios, PhD, 787-857-3600 Ext. 2002, Fax: 787-857-2125, E-mail: janegron@br.inter.edu.

Program in Criminal Justice Students: 31 full-time (17 women), 2 part-time (both women); all minorities (all Hispanic/Latino). Average age 33. 14 applicants, 86% accepted, 12 enrolled. *Faculty:* 2 full-time (0 women). Expenses: Contact institution. *Financial support:* Applicants required to submit FAFSA. In 2017, 3 master's awarded. *Program availability:* Evening/weekend. Offers criminal justice (MA). *Application deadline:* Applications are processed on a rolling basis. *Application fee:* $31. Electronic applications accepted. *Application Contact:* Aramilda Cartagena-Santiago, Dean of Students, 787-857-3600 Ext. 2009, Fax: 787-857-2125, E-mail: aramildacartagena@br.inter.edu. *Chancellor,* Juan A. Negron-Berrios, PhD, 787-857-3600 Ext. 2002, Fax: 787-857-2125, E-mail: janegron@br.inter.edu.

Program in Education Students: 17 full-time (16 women), 2 part-time (both women); all minorities (all Hispanic/Latino). Average age 34. 9 applicants, 89% accepted, 8 enrolled. *Faculty:* 1 full-time (0 women), 3 part-time/adjunct (2 women). Expenses: Contact institution. *Financial support:* Applicants required to submit FAFSA. In 2017, 5 master's awarded. *Program availability:* Part-time, evening/weekend. Offers curriculum and teaching (M Ed); educational leadership and management (MA); elementary education (M Ed); information and library service technology (M Ed); special education (MA). *Application deadline:* Applications are processed on a rolling basis. *Application fee:* $31. Electronic applications accepted. *Application Contact:* Aramilda Cartagena-Santiago, Dean of Students, 787-857-3600 Ext. 2009, Fax: 787-857-2125, E-mail: aramildacartagena@br.inter.edu. *Chancellor,* Juan A. Negron-Berrios, PhD, 787-857-3600 Ext. 2002, Fax: 787-857-2125, E-mail: janegron@br.inter.edu.

Program in Nursing Students: 30 part-time (24 women); all minorities (all Hispanic/Latino). Average age 31. 30 applicants, 97% accepted, 29 enrolled. *Faculty:* 2 full-time (both women). Expenses: Contact institution. *Financial support:* Applicants required to submit FAFSA. *Program availability:* Part-time, evening/weekend. Offers critical care nursing (MSN); medical surgical nursing (MSN). *Application deadline:* Applications are processed on a rolling basis. *Application fee:* $31. Electronic applications accepted. *Application Contact:* Aramilda Cartagena-Santiago, Dean of Students, 787-857-3600 Ext. 2009, Fax: 787-857-2125, E-mail: aramildacartagena@br.inter.edu. *Chancellor,* Juan A. Negron-Berrios, PhD, 787-857-3600 Ext. 2002, Fax: 787-857-2125, E-mail: janegron@br.inter.edu.

INTER AMERICAN UNIVERSITY OF PUERTO RICO, BAYAMÓN CAMPUS, Bayamón, PR 00957

General Information Independent, coed, comprehensive institution. *Enrollment:* 4,612 graduate, professional, and undergraduate students; 6 full-time matriculated graduate/professional students (5 women), 99 part-time matriculated graduate/professional students (62 women). *Enrollment by degree level:* 105 master's. *Graduate faculty:* 12 full-time (2 women), 3 part-time/adjunct (2 women). *Graduate housing:* Room and/or apartments available on a first-come, first-served basis to single students; on-campus housing not available to married students. *Student services:* Career counseling, free psychological counseling, international student services, services for students with disabilities. *Library facilities:* Centro de Acceso a la Informacion plus 1 other. *Collection:* Books: 28,990 (physical), 242,686 (digital/electronic); Serial titles: 148 (physical); Databases: 75. Weekly public service hours: 75; students can reserve study rooms. *Research affiliation:* Bayamon Central University.

Computer facilities: 730 computers available on campus for general student use. A campuswide network can be accessed from student residence rooms. Online class registration is available.
Website: http://bayamon.inter.edu/

General Application Contact: Director of Admissions, 787-279-1912 Ext. 2017, Fax: 787-279-2205.

GRADUATE UNITS

Graduate School Students: 6 full-time (5 women), 99 part-time (62 women); includes 104 minority (1 Black or African American, non-Hispanic/Latino; 103 Hispanic/Latino). Average age 29. 46 applicants, 98% accepted, 34 enrolled. *Faculty:* 12 full-time (2 women), 3 part-time/adjunct (2 women). Expenses: Contact institution. In 2017, 29 master's awarded. *Program availability:* Part-time, evening/weekend. Offers biology (MS); electrical engineering (ME); human resources (MBA); mechanical engineering (ME, MS). *Application deadline:* For fall admission, 7/1 for domestic students, 5/1 priority date for international students; for winter admission, 11/15 priority date for domestic and international students; for spring admission, 2/15 priority date for domestic and international students. *Application fee:* $31. *Application Contact:* Aurelis Báez, Director of Student Services, 787-279-1912 Ext. 2017, Fax: 787-279-2205, E-mail: abaez@bayamon.inter.edu. *Acting Chancellor,* Dr. Carlos J. Olivares, 787-279-1200 Ext. 2295, Fax: 787-279-2205, E-mail: colivares@bayamon.inter.edu.

INTER AMERICAN UNIVERSITY OF PUERTO RICO, FAJARDO CAMPUS, Fajardo, PR 00738-7003

General Information Independent, coed, comprehensive institution. *Enrollment:* 2,115 graduate, professional, and undergraduate students; 1 (woman) full-time matriculated graduate/professional student, 126 part-time matriculated graduate/professional students (81 women). *Enrollment by degree level:* 127 master's. *Graduate faculty:* 1 full-time (0 women), 25 part-time/adjunct (13 women). *Graduate housing:* On-campus housing not available. *Library facilities:* Antonio S. Belaval Library plus 1 other. *Collection:* Books: 46,756 (physical), 185,479 (digital/electronic); Serial titles: 22,085 (physical), 49,284 (digital/electronic); Databases: 26. Weekly public service hours: 79; students can reserve study rooms.

Computer facilities: 280 computers available on campus for general student use. A campuswide network can be accessed from off campus. Online class registration is available.
Website: http://www.fajardo.inter.edu/

General Application Contact: Ada Caraballo, Admissions Office Director, 787-863-2390 Ext. 2224, Fax: 787-860-3470, E-mail: ada.caraballo@fajardo.inter.edu.

GRADUATE UNITS

Graduate Programs Students: 1 (woman) full-time, 126 part-time (81 women). *Faculty:* 1 full-time (0 women), 25 part-time/adjunct (13 women). Expenses: Contact institution. *Program availability:* Online learning. Offers computer science (MS); educational management and leadership (MA Ed); general business (MBA); human resources (MBA); management information systems (MBA); marketing (MBA); special education (MA Ed).

INTER AMERICAN UNIVERSITY OF PUERTO RICO, GUAYAMA CAMPUS, Guayama, PR 00785

General Information Independent, coed, comprehensive institution.

GRADUATE UNITS

Department of Business Administration Offers marketing (MBA).

Department of Education and Social Sciences *Program availability:* Part-time. Offers early childhood education (0-4 years) (M Ed); elementary education (M Ed). Electronic applications accepted.

Department of Natural and Applied Sciences Offers computer security and networks (MS); networking and security (MCS).

INTER AMERICAN UNIVERSITY OF PUERTO RICO, METROPOLITAN CAMPUS, San Juan, PR 00919-1293

General Information Independent, coed, comprehensive institution. CGS member. *Graduate housing:* On-campus housing not available. *Research affiliation:* Innovation Technology (electronics).

GRADUATE UNITS

Graduate Programs *Program availability:* Part-time, evening/weekend. Offers accounting (MBA); administration of clinical laboratories (MS); advanced clinical services (MSW); advanced social work administration (MSW); American history (PhD); Christian education (PhD); clinical services (MSW); commercial education (MA); counseling psychology (MA, PhD); criminal justice (MA); curriculum and instruction (Ed D); educational administration (Ed D); educational computing (MA); elementary education (MA); English (MA); environmental evaluation and protection (MS); finance (MBA); general business (MBA); guidance and counseling (MA, Ed D); higher education administration (MA); history (MA, PhD); history education (MA); human resources (MBA); industrial management (MBA); industrial/organizational psychology (MA, PhD); international business (MIB); interregional and international business (PhD); labor relations (MA); management information systems (MBA); marketing (MBA); molecular microbiology (MS); music education (MM); occupational education (MA); open information systems (MS); pastoral theology (PhD); school psychology (MA, PhD); social work administration (MSW); Spanish (MA); Spanish education (MA); special education (MA); special education administration (Ed D); teaching English as a second language (MA); teaching of math (MA); teaching of physical education (MA); teaching of science (MA); theological studies (PhD); training and sport performance (MA); women's and gender studies (MA). Electronic applications accepted.

INTER AMERICAN UNIVERSITY OF PUERTO RICO, PONCE CAMPUS, Mercedita, PR 00715-1602

General Information Independent, coed, comprehensive institution.

GRADUATE UNITS

Graduate School

INTER AMERICAN UNIVERSITY OF PUERTO RICO, SAN GERMÁN CAMPUS, San Germán, PR 00683-5008

General Information Independent, coed, university. *Graduate housing:* Room and/or apartments available on a first-come, first-served basis to single students; on-campus housing not available to married students. Housing application deadline: 6/15.

GRADUATE UNITS

Graduate Studies Center *Program availability:* Part-time, evening/weekend. Offers accounting (MBA); applied mathematics (MA); business education (MA); counseling psychology (MA, PhD); curriculum and instruction (Ed D); drawing (MFA); education: counseling (MA, PhD); elementary education (MA); environmental sciences (MS); finance (MBA); general business administration (MBA); graphic design (MFA); health and physical education (MA); human resources (MBA, PhD); industrial relations (MBA); information systems (MBA); international and interregional business (PhD); library sciences (MLS); management (MBA); marketing (MBA); music (MA); music teacher education (MA); painting (MFA); photography (MFA); printmaking (MFA); school psychology (MA, PhD); science education (MA); sculpture (MFA); special education (MA); teaching English as a second language (MA).

INTER AMERICAN UNIVERSITY OF PUERTO RICO SCHOOL OF LAW, San Juan, PR 00936-8351

General Information Independent, coed, graduate-only institution.

GRADUATE UNITS

Professional Program *Program availability:* Part-time, evening/weekend. Offers law (JD).

INTER AMERICAN UNIVERSITY OF PUERTO RICO SCHOOL OF OPTOMETRY, Bayamón, PR 00957

General Information Independent, coed, graduate-only institution. *Graduate housing:* Room and/or apartments available on a first-come, first-served basis to single students; on-campus housing not available to married students.

GRADUATE UNITS

Professional Program Offers optometry (OD). Electronic applications accepted.

INTERDENOMINATIONAL THEOLOGICAL CENTER, Atlanta, GA 30314-4112

General Information Independent-religious, coed, graduate-only institution. *Graduate housing:* Room and/or apartments available on a first-come, first-served basis to single students; on-campus housing not available to married students. Housing application deadline: 8/1. *Research affiliation:* Atlanta University Center, Inc., Columbia Theological Seminary Library, Candler School of Theology Library, Emory University Library.

GRADUATE UNITS

Graduate and Professional Programs *Program availability:* Part-time, evening/weekend, blended/hybrid learning. Offers Christian education (MACE); ministry (D Min); pastoral counseling (Th D); theology (M Div). D Min and Th D programs offered in collaboration with the Atlanta Theological Association. Electronic applications accepted.

INTERIOR DESIGNERS INSTITUTE, Newport Beach, CA 92660

General Information Proprietary, coed, comprehensive institution.

GRADUATE UNITS

Graduate Program Offers interior design (MA).

INTERNATIONAL BAPTIST COLLEGE AND SEMINARY, Chandler, AZ 85286

General Information Independent-religious, coed, comprehensive institution. *Graduate housing:* Room and/or apartments available on a first-come, first-served basis to single students; on-campus housing not available to married students.

GRADUATE UNITS

Program in Biblical Studies Offers Biblical studies (MA).

Program in Education Offers education (M Ed).

Program in Ministry Offers ministry (M Min, D Min).

INTERNATIONAL INSTITUTE FOR RESTORATIVE PRACTICES, Bethlehem, PA 18018

General Information Independent, coed, graduate-only institution.

GRADUATE UNITS

Graduate Programs *Program availability:* Online learning. Offers restorative practices (MS, Certificate).

INTERNATIONAL TECHNOLOGICAL UNIVERSITY, San Jose, CA 95134

General Information Independent, coed, graduate-only institution. CGS member. *Research affiliation:* Linux Works, Inc. (software), @Channel (software), New Trends Technology, Inc. (hardware), Pico Turbo, Inc. (hardware).

GRADUATE UNITS

Program in Business Administration *Program availability:* Part-time, evening/weekend. Offers business administration (MBA, DBA). Electronic applications accepted.

Program in Computer Engineering *Program availability:* Part-time, evening/weekend. Offers computer engineering (MSCE). Electronic applications accepted.

Program in Digital Arts *Program availability:* Part-time. Offers digital arts (MA). Electronic applications accepted.

Program in Electrical Engineering *Program availability:* Part-time, evening/weekend. Offers electrical engineering (MSEE, PhD). Electronic applications accepted.

Program in Engineering Management *Program availability:* Part-time, evening/weekend. Offers engineering management (MSEM). Electronic applications accepted.

Program in Software Engineering *Program availability:* Part-time, evening/weekend. Offers software engineering (MSSE). Electronic applications accepted.

INTERNATIONAL UNIVERSITY IN GENEVA, CH-1215 Geneva 15, Switzerland

General Information Private, coed, comprehensive institution. *Graduate housing:* Room and/or apartments available on a first-come, first-served basis to single students; on-campus housing not available to married students. Housing application deadline: 7/31.

GRADUATE UNITS

Business Programs *Program availability:* Part-time, evening/weekend. Offers business administration (MBA, DBA); entrepreneurship (MBA); international business (MIB); international trade (MIT); sales and marketing (MBA). Electronic applications accepted.

Leadership Programs Offers international relations and diplomacy (MIRD); media and communication (MA); public administration (DPA). Electronic applications accepted.

THE INTERNATIONAL UNIVERSITY OF MONACO, MC-98000 Principality of Monaco, Monaco

General Information Independent, coed, comprehensive institution. *Graduate housing:* Rooms and/or apartments guaranteed to single and married students. *Research affiliation:* Alpstar (hedge funds).

GRADUATE UNITS

Graduate Programs *Program availability:* Part-time. Offers entrepreneurship (EMBA, MBA); financial engineering (M Sc); hedge fund and private equity (M Sc); international marketing (EMBA, MBA); international wealth management (M Sc); luxury goods and services (EMBA, M Sc, MBA); wealth and asset management (EMBA, MBA). Electronic applications accepted.

IONA COLLEGE, New Rochelle, NY 10801-1890

General Information Independent-religious, coed, comprehensive institution. *Enrollment:* 3,792 graduate, professional, and undergraduate students; 341 full-time matriculated graduate/professional students (231 women), 273 part-time matriculated graduate/professional students (148 women). *Enrollment by degree level:* 614 master's. *Graduate faculty:* 83 full-time (30 women), 42 part-time/adjunct (16 women). Tuition and fees vary according to program. *Graduate housing:* On-campus housing not available. *Student services:* Campus employment opportunities, campus safety program, career counseling, exercise/wellness program, free psychological counseling, international student services, multicultural affairs office, services for students with disabilities, writing training. *Library facilities:* Ryan Library plus 1 other. *Collection:* Books: 268,290 (physical), 330,337 (digital/electronic); Serial titles: 112 (physical), 369 (digital/electronic); Databases: 160. Weekly public service hours: 101; students can reserve study rooms. *Research affiliation:* IBM (teacher preparation).

Computer facilities: Computer purchase and lease plans are available. A campuswide network can be accessed from student residence rooms and from off campus. Online class registration, bill payment are available.
Website: http://www.iona.edu/

General Application Contact: Katelyn Brunck, Associate Director of Graduate Admissions, 914-633-2451, Fax: 914-633-2277, E-mail: kbrunck@iona.edu.

GRADUATE UNITS

School of Arts and Science Students: 227 full-time (175 women), 110 part-time (65 women); includes 124 minority (42 Black or African American, non-Hispanic/Latino; 9 Asian, non-Hispanic/Latino; 70 Hispanic/Latino; 2 Native Hawaiian or other Pacific Islander, non-Hispanic/Latino; 1 Two or more races, non-Hispanic/Latino), 15 international. Average age 26. 360 applicants, 78% accepted, 129 enrolled. *Faculty:* 50 full-time (24 women), 24 part-time/adjunct (10 women). Expenses: Contact institution. *Financial support:* In 2017–18, 79 students received support. Tuition waivers (partial) and unspecified assistantships available. Support available to part-time students. Financial award application deadline: 4/15; financial award applicants required to submit FAFSA. In 2017, 144 master's, 11 other advanced degrees awarded. *Program availability:* Part-time, evening/weekend. Offers adolescence education: biology (MS Ed, MST); adolescence education: English (MS Ed); adolescence education: mathematics (MST); adolescence education: social studies (MS Ed, MST); adolescence education: Spanish (MS Ed); adolescence special education 5-12 (MST); arts and science (MA, MS, MS Ed, MST, AC, Certificate); childhood and special education (MST); communication sciences and disorders (MA); computer science (MS); criminal justice (MS); cyber security (MS); cybercrime and security (AC); early childhood and childhood (MST); educational leadership (MS Ed); English (MA); forensic criminology and criminal justice systems (Certificate); game development (MS); general-experimental psychology (MA); history (MA); human resources (Certificate); industrial-organizational psychology (MA); marriage and family therapy (MS); mental health counseling (MA); non-profit public relations (Certificate); organizational behavior (Certificate); psychology (MA); public relations (MA); school psychology (MA); sports communication and media (MA). *Application deadline:* For fall admission, 8/1 priority date for domestic students, 5/1 priority date for international students; for winter admission, 12/1 priority date for domestic students, 8/1 priority date for international students; for spring admission, 1/1 priority date for domestic students, 9/1 priority date for international students; for summer admission, 5/1 priority date for domestic students, 1/1 priority date for international students. Applications are processed on a rolling basis. Electronic applications accepted. *Application Contact:* Dr. Katherine Zaromatidis, Director of Graduate Studies, School of Arts and Science, 914-633-2375, E-mail: kzaromatidis@iona.edu. *Interim Dean, School of Arts and Science*, Joseph Stabile, PhD, 914-633-2253, Fax: 914-633-2023, E-mail: jstabile@iona.edu.

School of Business Students: 163 full-time (83 women), 114 part-time (56 women); includes 93 minority (33 Black or African American, non-Hispanic/Latino; 2 American Indian or Alaska Native, non-Hispanic/Latino; 11 Asian, non-Hispanic/Latino; 45 Hispanic/Latino; 1 Native Hawaiian or other Pacific Islander, non-Hispanic/Latino; 1 Two or more races, non-Hispanic/Latino), 19 international. Average age 28. 115 applicants, 97% accepted, 65 enrolled. *Faculty:* 33 full-time (6 women), 18 part-time/adjunct (6 women). Expenses: Contact institution. *Financial support:* Scholarships/grants, tuition waivers (partial), and unspecified assistantships available. Support available to part-time students. Financial award application deadline: 4/15; financial award applicants required to submit FAFSA. In 2017, 249 master's, 169 other advanced degrees awarded. *Program availability:* Part-time, evening/weekend, 100% online, blended/hybrid learning. Offers accounting and information systems (MS); business (MBA, MS, AC, PMC); business administration (MBA); business continuity and risk management (AC); finance (MS); financial management (MBA, PMC); financial services (MS); general accounting (MBA, AC); health care analytics (AC); health care management (MBA, AC); human resource management (MBA, PMC); information systems (MBA, MS, PMC); international business (AC, PMC); international finance (MS); long term care services management (AC); management (MBA, PMC); marketing (MBA); project management (MS); public accounting (MBA, MS, AC); sports and entertainment management (AC). *Application deadline:* For fall admission, 8/15 priority date for domestic students, 8/1 priority date for international students; for winter admission, 11/15 priority date for domestic students, 11/1 priority date for international students; for spring admission, 2/15 priority date for domestic students, 2/1 priority date for international students; for summer admission, 5/15 priority date for domestic students, 5/1 priority date for international students. Applications are processed on a rolling basis. *Application fee:* $0. Electronic applications accepted. *Application Contact:* Katelyn Brunck, Director of Graduate Admissions, 914-633-2451, Fax: 914-633-2277, E-mail: kbrunck@iona.edu. *Dean of the School of Business*, Dr. William B. Lamb, 914-633-2254, E-mail: wlamb@iona.edu.

IOWA STATE UNIVERSITY OF SCIENCE AND TECHNOLOGY, Ames, IA 50011

General Information State-supported, coed, university. CGS member. *Graduate housing:* Rooms and/or apartments available on a first-come, first-served basis to single and married students. Housing application deadline: 6/15. *Research affiliation:* National Veterinary Services Laboratories, National Animal Disease Center, National Soil Tilth Laboratory, North Central Regional Center for Rural Development, U.S. Department of Energy-Ames Laboratory.

GRADUATE UNITS

Bioinformatics and Computational Biology Program Offers bioinformatics and computational biology (MS, PhD). Electronic applications accepted.

Department of Accounting Offers accounting (M Acc). Electronic applications accepted.

Department of Aerospace Engineering and Engineering Mechanics Offers aerospace engineering (M Eng, MS, PhD); engineering mechanics (M Eng, MS, PhD). Electronic applications accepted.

Department of Agricultural Education and Studies Offers agricultural education and studies (MS, PhD). Electronic applications accepted.

Department of Agronomy Offers agricultural meteorology (MS, PhD); agronomy (MS); crop production and physiology (MS, PhD); plant breeding (MS, PhD); soil science (MS, PhD). Electronic applications accepted.

Department of Animal Science Offers animal breeding and genetics (MS, PhD); animal physiology (MS); animal psychology (PhD); animal science (MS, PhD); meat science (MS, PhD). Electronic applications accepted.

Department of Anthropology Offers anthropology (MA). Electronic applications accepted.

Department of Apparel, Events, and Hospitality Management *Program availability:* Online learning. Offers apparel, merchandising, and design (MS, PhD); hospitality management (MS, PhD). Electronic applications accepted.

Department of Architecture Offers architectural studies (MSAS); architecture (M Arch, MS). Electronic applications accepted.

Department of Biomedical Sciences Offers biomedical sciences (MS, PhD). Electronic applications accepted.

Department of Chemical and Biological Engineering Offers chemical and biological engineering (M Eng, MS, PhD). Electronic applications accepted.

Department of Chemistry Offers chemistry (MS, PhD). Electronic applications accepted.

Department of Civil and Construction Engineering Offers civil engineering (MS, PhD). Electronic applications accepted.

Department of Community and Regional Planning Offers community and regional planning (MCRP); transportation (MS). Electronic applications accepted.

Department of Computer Science Offers computer science (MS, PhD). Electronic applications accepted.

Department of Economics Offers agricultural economics (MS, PhD); economics (MS, PhD). JD/MS and JD/PhD offered jointly with Drake University and The University of Iowa. Electronic applications accepted.

Department of Education Offers curriculum and instructional technology (M Ed, MS, PhD); elementary education (M Ed, MS); historical, philosophical, and comparative studies in education (M Ed, MS); special education (M Ed, MS, PhD). Electronic applications accepted.

Department of Educational Leadership and Policy Studies Offers counselor education (M Ed, MS); educational administration (M Ed, MS); educational leadership (PhD); higher education (M Ed, MS); organizational learning and human resource development (M Ed, MS); research and evaluation (MS); student affairs (MS). Electronic applications accepted.

Department of Electrical and Computer Engineering Offers computer engineering (M Eng, MS, PhD); electrical engineering (M Eng, MS, PhD). Electronic applications accepted.

Department of English Offers creative writing (MFA); English (MA); rhetoric and professional communication (PhD). Electronic applications accepted.

Department of Entomology Offers entomology (MS, PhD). Electronic applications accepted.

Department of Food Science and Human Nutrition Offers food science and technology (MS, PhD); nutrition (MS, PhD). Electronic applications accepted.

Department of Geological and Atmospheric Sciences Offers earth science (MS, PhD); environmental science (MS, PhD); geology (MS, PhD); meteorology (MS, PhD). Electronic applications accepted.

Department of History Offers history (MA); rural, agricultural, technological, and environmental history (PhD). Electronic applications accepted.

Department of Horticulture Offers horticulture (MS, PhD). Electronic applications accepted.

Department of Human Development and Family Studies Offers human development and family studies (MFCS, MS, PhD). Electronic applications accepted.

Department of Industrial and Manufacturing Systems Engineering Offers industrial engineering (M Eng, MS, PhD); operations research (MS); systems engineering (M Eng). Electronic applications accepted.

Department of Kinesiology Offers kinesiology (MS, PhD). Electronic applications accepted.

Department of Landscape Architecture *Program availability:* Part-time. Offers landscape architecture (MLA, MS). Electronic applications accepted.

Department of Materials Science and Engineering Offers materials science and engineering (M Eng, MS, PhD). Electronic applications accepted.

Department of Mathematics Offers applied mathematics (MS, PhD); mathematics (MS, PhD); school mathematics (MSM). Electronic applications accepted.

Department of Mechanical Engineering Offers mechanical engineering (M Eng, MS, PhD); systems engineering (M Eng). Electronic applications accepted.

Department of Natural Resource Ecology and Management Offers forestry (MS, PhD); wildlife ecology (MS, PhD). Electronic applications accepted.

Department of Physics and Astronomy Offers applied physics (MS, PhD); astrophysics (MS, PhD); condensed matter physics (MS, PhD); high energy physics (MS, PhD); nuclear physics (MS, PhD); physics (MS, PhD). Electronic applications accepted.

Department of Plant Pathology Offers plant pathology (MS, PhD). Electronic applications accepted.

Department of Political Science Offers political science (MA); public administration (MPA). JD/MA offered jointly with Drake University. Electronic applications accepted.

Department of Psychology Offers cognitive psychology (PhD); counseling psychology (PhD); psychology (MS, PhD); social psychology (PhD). Electronic applications accepted.

Department of Sociology Offers rural sociology (MS, PhD); sociology (MS, PhD). Electronic applications accepted.

Department of Statistics Offers statistics (MS, PhD). Electronic applications accepted.

Department of Veterinary Clinical Sciences Offers veterinary clinical sciences (MS). Electronic applications accepted.

Department of Veterinary Diagnostic and Production Animal Medicine Offers veterinary preventative medicine (MS). Electronic applications accepted.

Department of Veterinary Microbiology and Preventive Medicine Offers veterinary microbiology (MS, PhD). Electronic applications accepted.

Department of Veterinary Pathology Offers veterinary pathology (MS, PhD). Electronic applications accepted.

Greenlee School of Journalism and Communication Offers journalism and mass communication (MS). Electronic applications accepted.

Program in Agricultural and Biosystems Engineering Offers agricultural and biosystems engineering (M En, MS, PhD). Electronic applications accepted.

Program in Agricultural Economics Offers agricultural economics (MS, PhD). Electronic applications accepted.

Program in Agricultural Meteorology Offers agricultural meteorology (MS, PhD). Electronic applications accepted.

Program in Analytical Chemistry Offers analytical chemistry (MS, PhD). Electronic applications accepted.

Program in Animal Breeding and Genetics Offers animal breeding and genetics (MS); immunogenetics (PhD); molecular genetics (PhD); quantitative genetics (PhD). Electronic applications accepted.

Program in Animal Physiology Offers animal physiology (MS, PhD). Electronic applications accepted.

Program in Apparel, Merchandising, and Design Offers apparel, merchandising, and design (MS, PhD). Electronic applications accepted.

Program in Applied Linguistics and Technology Offers applied linguistics and technology (PhD). Electronic applications accepted.

Program in Applied Mathematics Offers applied mathematics (MS, PhD). Electronic applications accepted.

Program in Applied Physics Offers applied physics (MS, PhD). Electronic applications accepted.

Program in Astrophysics Offers astrophysics (MS, PhD).

Program in Biophysics Offers biophysics (MS, PhD). Electronic applications accepted.

Program in Biorenewable Resources and Technology Offers biorenewable resources and technology (MS, PhD). Electronic applications accepted.

Program in Business Administration Offers business administration (MBA). Electronic applications accepted.

Program in Business Analytics *Program availability:* Online learning. Offers business analytics (MS).

Program in Business and Technology Offers business and technology (PhD). Electronic applications accepted.

Program in Computer Engineering Offers computer engineering (M Eng, MS, PhD). Electronic applications accepted.

Program in Condensed Matter Physics Offers condensed matter physics (MS, PhD). Electronic applications accepted.

Program in Creative Writing and Environment Offers creative writing and environment (MFA). Electronic applications accepted.

Program in Crop Production and Physiology Offers crop production and physiology (MS, PhD). Electronic applications accepted.

Program in Diet and Exercise Offers diet and exercise (MS). Electronic applications accepted.

Program in Earth Science Offers earth science (MS, PhD). Electronic applications accepted.

Program in Ecology and Evolutionary Biology Offers ecology and evolutionary biology (MS, PhD). Electronic applications accepted.

Program in Engineering Mechanics Offers engineering mechanics (M Eng, MS, PhD). Electronic applications accepted.

Program in Environmental Sciences Offers environmental sciences (MS, PhD). Electronic applications accepted.

Program in Family and Consumer Sciences Offers family and consumer sciences (MFCS). Electronic applications accepted.

Program in Finance Offers finance (M Fin).

Program in Fisheries Biology Offers fisheries biology (MS, PhD). Electronic applications accepted.

Program in Forestry Offers forestry (MS, PhD). Electronic applications accepted.

Program in Genetics Offers genetics (MS, PhD). Electronic applications accepted.

Program in Graphic Design Offers graphic design (MA, MFA). Electronic applications accepted.

Program in High Energy Physics Offers high energy physics (MS, PhD). Electronic applications accepted.

Program in Human-Computer Interaction Offers human-computer interaction (MS, PhD). Electronic applications accepted.

Program in Immunobiology Offers immunobiology (MS, PhD). Electronic applications accepted.

Program in Industrial Agriculture and Technology Offers industrial agriculture and technology (MS, PhD). Electronic applications accepted.

Program in Industrial Design Offers industrial design (MID). Electronic applications accepted.

Program in Information Assurance Offers information assurance (M Eng, MS). Electronic applications accepted.

Program in Information Systems Offers information systems (MS). Electronic applications accepted.

Program in Inorganic Chemistry Offers inorganic chemistry (MS, PhD). Electronic applications accepted.

Program in Integrated Visual Arts Offers integrated visual arts (MFA).

Program in Interdisciplinary Graduate Studies Offers interdisciplinary graduate studies (MA, MS). Electronic applications accepted.

Program in Interior Design Offers interior design (MA, MFA). Electronic applications accepted.

Program in Meat Science Offers meat science (MS, PhD). Electronic applications accepted.

Program in Meteorology Offers meteorology (MS, PhD). Electronic applications accepted.

Program in Microbiology Offers microbiology (MS, PhD). Electronic applications accepted.

Program in Molecular, Cellular, and Developmental Biology Offers molecular, cellular, and developmental biology (MS, PhD). Electronic applications accepted.

Program in Neuroscience Offers neuroscience (MS, PhD). Electronic applications accepted.

Program in Nuclear Physics Offers nuclear physics (MS, PhD). Electronic applications accepted.

Program in Nutritional Sciences Offers nutritional sciences (MS, PhD). Electronic applications accepted.

Program in Organic Chemistry Offers organic chemistry (MS, PhD). Electronic applications accepted.

Program in Physical Chemistry Offers physical chemistry (MS, PhD). Electronic applications accepted.

Program in Plant Biology Offers plant biology (MS, PhD). Electronic applications accepted.

Program in Plant Breeding Offers plant breeding (MS, PhD). Electronic applications accepted.

Program in Rhetoric and Professional Communication Offers rhetoric and professional communication (PhD). Electronic applications accepted.

Program in Rhetoric, Composition, and Professional Communication Offers rhetoric, composition, and professional communication (MA). Electronic applications accepted.

Program in Rural Sociology Offers rural sociology (MS, PhD). Electronic applications accepted.

Program in School Mathematics Offers school mathematics (MSM). Electronic applications accepted.

Program in Science Education Offers science education (MAT). Electronic applications accepted.

Program in Seed Technology and Business Offers seed technology and business (MS). Electronic applications accepted.

Program in Soil Science Offers soil science (MS, PhD). Electronic applications accepted.

Program in Sustainable Agriculture Offers sustainable agriculture (MS, PhD). Electronic applications accepted.

Program in Systems Engineering Offers systems engineering (M Eng). Electronic applications accepted.

Program in Teaching English as a Second Language/Applied Linguistics Offers teaching English as a second language/applied linguistics (MA). Electronic applications accepted.

Program in Toxicology Offers toxicology (MS, PhD). Electronic applications accepted.

Program in Transportation Offers transportation (MS). Electronic applications accepted.

Rural, Agricultural, Technological, and Environmental History Program Offers rural, agricultural, technological, and environmental history (PhD). Electronic applications accepted.

IRELL & MANELLA GRADUATE SCHOOL OF BIOLOGICAL SCIENCES, Duarte, CA 91010

General Information Independent, coed, graduate-only institution. *Graduate housing:* Room and/or apartments available on a first-come, first-served basis to single students; on-campus housing not available to married students. Housing application deadline: 7/31.

GRADUATE UNITS

Graduate Program Offers brain metastatic cancer (PhD); cancer and stem cell metabolism (PhD); cancer biology (PhD); cancer biology and developmental therapeutics (PhD); cell biology (PhD); chemical biology (PhD); chromosomal break repair (PhD); diabetes and pancreatic progenitor cell biology (PhD); DNA repair and cancer biology (PhD); germline epigenetic remodeling and endocrine disruptors (PhD); hematology and hematopoietic cell transplantation (PhD); hematology and immunology (PhD); inflammation and cancer (PhD); micrornas and gene regulation in cardiovascular disease (PhD); mixed chimrism for reversal of autoimmunity (PhD); molecular and cellular biology (PhD); molecular biology and genetics (PhD); nanoparticle mediated twist1 silencing in metastatic cancer (PhD); neuro-oncology and stem cell biology (PhD); neuroscience (PhD); RNA directed therapies for HIV-1 (PhD); small RNA-induced transcriptional gene activation (PhD); stem cell regulation by the microenvironment (PhD); translational oncology and pharmaceutical sciences (PhD); tumor biology (PhD). Electronic applications accepted.

ITHACA COLLEGE, Ithaca, NY 14850

General Information Independent, coed, comprehensive institution. *Enrollment:* 6,516 graduate, professional, and undergraduate students; 385 full-time matriculated graduate/professional students (272 women), 69 part-time matriculated graduate/professional students (31 women). *Enrollment by degree level:* 280 master's, 174 doctoral. *Graduate faculty:* 156 full-time (77 women), 14 part-time/adjunct (8 women). *Graduate housing:* On-campus housing not available. *Student services:* Campus employment opportunities, campus safety program, career counseling, exercise/wellness program, free psychological counseling, international student services, low-cost health insurance, multicultural affairs office, services for students with disabilities, teacher training, writing training. *Library facilities:* Ithaca College Library. *Collection:* Books: 315,000 (physical), 165,000 (digital/electronic); Serial titles: 640 (physical), 68,858 (digital/electronic); Databases: 155. Weekly public service hours: 148; study areas open 24 hours, 5–7 days a week. *Research affiliation:* NASA (physics and astronomy), National Science Foundation (mathematics), National Institutes of Health (exercise and sport sciences), U.S. Department of Health and Human Services/National Institutes of Health (biology).

Computer facilities: Computer purchase and lease plans are available. 640 computers available on campus for general student use. A campuswide network can be accessed. Online class registration is available.
Website: http://www.ithaca.edu/

General Application Contact: Nicole Eversley Bradwell, Director, Office of Admission, 607-274-3124, Fax: 607-274-1263, E-mail: admission@ithaca.edu.

GRADUATE UNITS

Roy H. Park School of Communications Students: 23 part-time (11 women); includes 5 minority (3 Hispanic/Latino; 2 Two or more races, non-Hispanic/Latino), 1 international. Average age 30. 26 applicants, 65% accepted, 10 enrolled. *Faculty:* 9 full-time (2 women). Expenses: Contact institution. *Financial support:* In 2017–18, 23 students received support, including 21 fellowships (averaging $5,482 per year); career-related internships or fieldwork, Federal Work-Study, and scholarships/grants also available. Support available to part-time students. Financial award applicants required to submit FAFSA. In 2017, 6 master's awarded. *Program availability:* Part-time. Offers communications innovation (MS); image text (MFA). *Application deadline:* For fall admission, 3/15 for domestic and international students; for spring admission, 12/1 for domestic and international students. Applications are processed on a rolling basis. *Application fee:* $40. Electronic applications accepted. *Application Contact:* Nicole Eversley Bradwell, Director, Office of Admission, 607-274-3124, Fax: 607-274-1263, E-mail: admission@ithaca.edu. *Dean,* Dr. Diane Gayeski, 607-274-3895, E-mail: gayeski@ithaca.edu.

School of Business Students: 36 full-time (10 women), 2 part-time (1 woman); includes 3 minority (1 Asian, non-Hispanic/Latino; 2 Hispanic/Latino), 1 international. Average age 22. 50 applicants, 78% accepted, 36 enrolled. *Faculty:* 11 full-time (6 women), 1 (woman) part-time/adjunct. Expenses: Contact institution. *Financial support:* In 2017–18, 30 students received support, including 28 fellowships (averaging $7,750 per year); career-related internships or fieldwork, Federal Work-Study, and scholarships/grants also available. Support available to part-time students. Financial award application deadline: 3/1; financial award applicants required to submit FAFSA. In 2017, 42 master's awarded. *Program availability:* Part-time. Offers accounting (MS); business (MBA, MS); sport management (MBA). *Application deadline:* For fall admission, 5/15 for domestic and international students; for spring admission, 11/1 for domestic and international students. Applications are processed on a rolling basis. *Application fee:* $40. Electronic applications accepted. *Application Contact:* Nicole Eversley Bradwell, Director, Office of Admission, 607-274-3124, Fax: 607-274-1263, E-mail: admission@ithaca.edu. *Dean,* Dr. Sean Reid, 607-274-3341, E-mail: sreid@ithaca.edu.

School of Health Sciences and Human Performance Students: 311 full-time (238 women), 15 part-time (8 women); includes 48 minority (9 Black or African American, non-Hispanic/Latino; 15 Asian, non-Hispanic/Latino; 11 Hispanic/Latino; 13 Two or more races, non-Hispanic/Latino), 3 international. Average age 23. 371 applicants, 50% accepted, 184 enrolled. *Faculty:* 59 full-time (40 women), 3 part-time/adjunct (all women). Expenses: Contact institution. *Financial support:* In 2017–18, 214 students received support, including 69 research assistantships (averaging $12,462 per year); career-related internships or fieldwork, Federal Work-Study, scholarships/grants, and unspecified assistantships also available. Support available to part-time students. Financial award applicants required to submit FAFSA. In 2017, 99 master's, 78 doctorates awarded. *Program availability:* Part-time. Offers exercise and sport sciences (MS); health education (MS); health sciences and human performance (MS, DPT); occupational therapy (MS); physical education (MS); physical therapy (DPT); speech-language pathology (MS); speech-language pathology with teacher certification (MS). *Application deadline:* Applications are processed on a rolling basis. *Application fee:* $40. Electronic applications accepted. *Application Contact:* Nicole Eversley Bradwell, Director, Office of Admission, 607-274-3124, Fax: 607-274-1263, E-mail: admission@ithaca.edu. *Interim Dean,* Dr. John Sigg, 607-274-3237, Fax: 607-274-1263, E-mail: sigg@ithaca.edu.

School of Humanities and Sciences Students: 20 full-time (14 women); includes 3 minority (2 Hispanic/Latino; 1 Two or more races, non-Hispanic/Latino), 1 international. Average age 25. 35 applicants, 66% accepted, 18 enrolled. *Faculty:* 11 full-time (7 women), 1 part-time/adjunct (0 women). Expenses: Contact institution. *Financial support:* In 2017–18, 19 students received support, including 19 research assistantships (averaging $8,866 per year); career-related internships or fieldwork, Federal Work-Study, scholarships/grants, and unspecified assistantships also available. Support available to part-time students. Financial award application deadline: 3/1; financial award applicants required to submit FAFSA. In 2017, 36 master's awarded. *Program availability:* Part-time. Offers agriculture education (MAT); childhood education (MS); English (MAT); humanities and sciences (MAT, MS). *Application deadline:* For fall admission, 3/19 for domestic and international students. Applications are processed on a rolling basis. *Application fee:* $40. Electronic applications accepted. *Application Contact:* Nicole Eversley Bradwell, Director, Office of Admission, 607-274-3124, Fax: 607-274-1263, E-mail: admission@ithaca.edu. *Dean,* Dr. Vincent Wang, 607-274-3102, E-mail: vwang@ithaca.edu.

School of Music Students: 18 full-time (10 women), 29 part-time (11 women); includes 12 minority (3 Black or African American, non-Hispanic/Latino; 4 Asian, non-Hispanic/Latino; 4 Hispanic/Latino; 1 Two or more races, non-Hispanic/Latino), 5 international. Average age 25. 147 applicants, 44% accepted, 23 enrolled. *Faculty:* 66 full-time (22 women), 9 part-time/adjunct (4 women). Expenses: Contact institution. *Financial support:* In 2017–18, 44 students received support, including 43 teaching assistantships (averaging $10,191 per year); career-related internships or fieldwork, Federal Work-Study, scholarships/grants, and unspecified assistantships also available. Support available to part-time students. Financial award application deadline: 12/1; financial award applicants required to submit FAFSA. In 2017, 31 master's awarded. *Program availability:* Part-time. Offers composition (MM); conducting (MM); music (MM, MS); music education (MM, MS); performance (MM); Suzuki pedagogy (MM). *Application deadline:* For fall admission, 12/1 for domestic and international students. Applications are processed on a rolling basis. *Application fee:* $40. Electronic applications accepted. *Application Contact:* Nicole Eversley Bradwell, Director, Office of Admission, 607-274-3124, Fax: 607-274-1263, E-mail: admission@ithaca.edu. *Dean, School of Music,* Dr. Karl Paulnack, 607-274-3343, E-mail: kpaulnack@ithaca.edu.

JACKSON STATE UNIVERSITY, Jackson, MS 39217

General Information State-supported, coed, university. CGS member. *Graduate housing:* Room and/or apartments available on a first-come, first-served basis to single students; on-campus housing not available to married students. Housing application deadline: 7/15. *Research affiliation:* Lawrence A. Berkeley Laboratories (biology, chemistry), U.S. Department of Energy (biology), National Science Foundation (biology, chemistry), Environmental Protection Agency, Oak Ridge Associated Universities (science), Raytheon Systems Company (computer science).

GRADUATE UNITS

Graduate School *Program availability:* Part-time, evening/weekend, online only, 100% online, blended/hybrid learning. Electronic applications accepted.

College of Business *Program availability:* Part-time, evening/weekend. Offers accounting (MPA); business (MBA, MPA, PhD); business administration (MBA, PhD). Electronic applications accepted.

College of Education and Human Development *Program availability:* Part-time, evening/weekend, 100% online, blended/hybrid learning. Offers clinical mental health (MS); early childhood education (MS Ed, Ed D); education administration and supervision (Ed S); education and human development (MS, MS Ed, Ed D, PhD, Ed S); educational administration and supervision (MS Ed, PhD); elementary education (MS Ed, Ed S); higher education (Ed S); physical education (MS Ed); reading education (MS Ed); rehabilitation counseling (MS); school counseling (MS Ed); special education (MS Ed, Ed S); sport science (MS). Electronic applications accepted.

College of Liberal Arts *Program availability:* Part-time, evening/weekend. Offers clinical psychology (PhD); criminology and justice services (MA); English (MA); history (MA); liberal arts (MA, MAT, MM Ed, PhD); music education (MM Ed); political science (MA); sociology (MA); teaching English (MAT). Electronic applications accepted.

College of Public Service Offers public administration (PhD); public policy and administration (MPPA); public service (MA, MPPA, MSW, PhD); social work (MSW, PhD); urban and regional planning (MA, PhD).

College of Science, Engineering and Technology *Program availability:* Part-time, evening/weekend. Offers applied mathematics (MS); biology (MS); chemistry and biochemistry (MS, PhD); civil engineering (MS, PhD); coastal engineering (MS, PhD); computer science (MS); environmental engineering (MS, PhD); environmental science (MS); hazardous materials management (MS); mathematics education (MST); physical science (MS, PhD); pure mathematics (MS); science education (MST); science, engineering and technology (MS, MS Ed, MST, PhD); technology education (MS Ed).

School of Public Health Offers communicative disorders (MS); public health (MPH, MS, Dr PH).

JACKSONVILLE STATE UNIVERSITY, Jacksonville, AL 36265-1602

General Information State-supported, coed, comprehensive institution. *Graduate housing:* Rooms and/or apartments available on a first-come, first-served basis to single and married students.

GRADUATE UNITS

College of Graduate Studies and Continuing Education *Program availability:* Part-time, evening/weekend, 100% online, blended/hybrid learning. Electronic applications accepted.

College of Arts and Sciences *Program availability:* Part-time, evening/weekend, 100% online, blended/hybrid learning. Offers arts and sciences (MA, MPA, MS, D Sc); biology (MS); computer systems and software design (MS); criminal justice (MS); emergency management (MS, D Sc); English (MA); history (MA); liberal studies (MA); mathematics (MS); music (MA); political science (MPA); psychology (MS).

College of Commerce and Business Administration *Program availability:* Part-time, evening/weekend, 100% online, blended/hybrid learning. Offers commerce and business administration (MBA). Electronic applications accepted.

College of Education and Professional Studies *Program availability:* Part-time, evening/weekend, 100% online, blended/hybrid learning. Offers early childhood education (MS Ed); education (Ed S); education and professional studies (MS, MS Ed, Ed S); elementary education (MS Ed); guidance and counseling (MS); instructional leadership (MS Ed, Ed S); library media (MS Ed); physical education (MS Ed, Ed S); reading specialist (MS Ed); secondary education (MS Ed); special education (MS Ed). Electronic applications accepted.

College of Nursing *Program availability:* Part-time, evening/weekend. Offers nursing (MSN). Electronic applications accepted.

JACKSONVILLE UNIVERSITY, Jacksonville, FL 32211

General Information Independent, coed, comprehensive institution. *Enrollment:* 4,222 graduate, professional, and undergraduate students; 435 full-time matriculated graduate/professional students (265 women), 903 part-time matriculated graduate/professional students (708 women). *Enrollment by degree level:* 1,146 master's, 167 doctoral, 25 other advanced degrees. *Graduate faculty:* 69 full-time (35 women), 78 part-time/adjunct (43 women). *Tuition:* Full-time $13,860; part-time $7700 per credit hour. Tuition and fees vary according to program. *Graduate housing:* Room and/or apartments available on a first-come, first-served basis to single students; on-campus housing not available to married students. Typical cost: $8600 per year. Room charges vary according to housing facility selected. Housing application deadline: 8/1. *Student services:* Campus employment opportunities, campus safety program, career counseling, exercise/wellness program, free psychological counseling, international student services, low-cost health insurance, multicultural affairs office, services for students with disabilities, teacher training, writing training. *Library facilities:* Carl S. Swisher Library. *Collection:* Books: 213,571 (physical), 251,492 (digital/electronic); Serial titles: 5,833 (physical); Databases: 67. Weekly public service hours: 88; students can reserve study rooms.

Computer facilities: Computer purchase and lease plans are available. 400 computers available on campus for general student use. A campuswide network can be accessed from student residence rooms and from off campus. Online class registration, learning management systems are available.
Website: http://www.ju.edu/

General Application Contact: Allana Forte, Director of Admissions and Recruitment, 904-256-7000, E-mail: admissions@ju.edu.

GRADUATE UNITS

Brooks Rehabilitation College of Healthcare Sciences Students: 285 full-time (195 women), 661 part-time (570 women); includes 334 minority (182 Black or African American, non-Hispanic/Latino; 6 American Indian or Alaska Native, non-Hispanic/Latino; 52 Asian, non-Hispanic/Latino; 78 Hispanic/Latino; 2 Native Hawaiian or other Pacific Islander, non-Hispanic/Latino; 14 Two or more races, non-Hispanic/Latino), 24 international. Average age 35. 618 applicants, 50% accepted, 207 enrolled. *Faculty:* 48 full-time (32 women), 30 part-time/adjunct (18 women). Expenses: Contact institution. *Financial support:* In 2017–18, 5 fellowships were awarded; Federal Work-Study, institutionally sponsored loans, scholarships/grants, and health care benefits also available. Support available to part-time students. Financial award application deadline: 3/15; financial award applicants required to submit FAFSA. In 2017, 338 master's, 9 doctorates, 17 other advanced degrees awarded. *Program availability:* Part-time, 100% online, blended/hybrid learning. Offers healthcare sciences (MS, MSN, DNP, OTD, Certificate). *Application deadline:* For fall admission, 2/1 for domestic and international students. Applications are processed on a rolling basis. *Application fee:* $50. Electronic applications accepted. *Application Contact:* Tonya Alford, Assistant Director of Graduate Admissions, 904-256-7026, E-mail: talford1@ju.edu. *Interim Dean of the Brooks Rehabilitation College of Healthcare Sciences*, Dr. Cheryl Bergman, E-mail: cbergma@ju.edu.

Keigwin School of Nursing Students: 61 full-time (53 women), 549 part-time (497 women); includes 202 minority (120 Black or African American, non-Hispanic/Latino; 4 American Indian or Alaska Native, non-Hispanic/Latino; 29 Asian, non-Hispanic/Latino; 39 Hispanic/Latino; 2 Native Hawaiian or other Pacific Islander, non-Hispanic/Latino; 8 Two or more races, non-Hispanic/Latino), 1 international. Average age 40. 272 applicants, 58% accepted, 126 enrolled. *Faculty:* 18 full-time (all women), 11 part-time/adjunct (9 women). Expenses: Contact institution. *Financial support:* Federal Work-Study, institutionally sponsored loans, scholarships/grants, and health care benefits available. Support available to part-time students. Financial award application deadline: 3/15; financial award applicants required to submit FAFSA. In 2017, 293 master's, 9 doctorates awarded. *Program availability:* Part-time, 100% online, blended/hybrid learning. Offers adult gerontology acute care nurse practitioner (MSN); adult-gerontology acute care nurse practitioner (Certificate); clinical nurse educator (MSN, Certificate); emergency nurse practitioner (Certificate); family nurse practitioner (MSN, Certificate); family nurse practitioner/emergency nurse practitioner (MSN, Certificate); leadership in healthcare systems (Certificate); leadership in the healthcare system (MSN); nursing informatics (MSN, Certificate); nursing practice (DNP); psychiatric mental health nurse practitioner (Certificate); psychiatric nurse practitioner (MSN). *Application deadline:* For fall admission, 2/1 for domestic and international students. Applications are processed on a rolling basis. *Application fee:* $50. Electronic applications accepted. *Application Contact:* Stephanie Bloom, Assistant Director, Enrollment and Advanced Graduate Nursing, 904-256-7286, E-mail: sstrick4@ju.edu. *Director, Graduate Nursing Programs/Associate Professor*, Dr. Hilary Morgan, 904-256-7601, E-mail: hmorgan@ju.edu.

School of Applied Health Sciences Students: 150 full-time (118 women), 100 part-time (69 women); includes 108 minority (62 Black or African American, non-Hispanic/Latino; 2 American Indian or Alaska Native, non-Hispanic/Latino; 11 Asian, non-Hispanic/Latino; 29 Hispanic/Latino; 4 Two or more races, non-Hispanic/Latino), 3 international. Average age 31. 145 applicants, 91% accepted, 93 enrolled. *Faculty:* 18 full-time (10 women), 19 part-time/adjunct (9 women). Expenses: Contact institution. *Financial support:* Federal Work-Study, institutionally sponsored loans, scholarships/grants, and health care benefits available. Support available to part-time students. Financial award application deadline: 3/15; financial award applicants required to submit FAFSA. In 2017, 43 master's awarded. *Program availability:* Part-time, 100% online, blended/hybrid learning. Offers clinical mental health counseling (MS); health informatics (MS); kinesiological sciences (MS); occupational therapy (OTD); speech-language pathology (MS); sport management (MS). *Application deadline:* For fall admission, 2/1 for domestic and international students. Applications are processed on a rolling basis. *Application fee:* $50. Electronic applications accepted. *Application Contact:* Ashlea Rieser, Assistant Director of Enrollment and Advising, 904-256-8934, E-mail: arieser0@ju.edu. *Associate Dean, School of Applied Health Sciences*, Dr. Heather Hausenblas, 904-256-7975, E-mail: hhausen@ju.edu.

School of Orthodontics Students: 37 full-time (12 women), 6 part-time (2 women); includes 12 minority (6 Asian, non-Hispanic/Latino; 5 Hispanic/Latino; 1 Two or more races, non-Hispanic/Latino), 10 international. Average age 30. 201 applicants, 10% accepted, 20 enrolled. *Faculty:* 15 full-time (5 women), 2 part-time/adjunct (both women). Expenses: Contact institution. *Financial support:* In 2017–18, 5 fellowships (averaging $35,000 per year) were awarded; scholarships/grants and health care benefits also available. Financial award application deadline: 3/15; financial award applicants required to submit FAFSA. In 2017, 15 other advanced degrees awarded. Offers dentistry (MS); orthodontics (Certificate). *Application deadline:* For fall admission, 9/14 priority date for domestic students, 9/14 for international students. Applications are processed on a rolling basis. *Application fee:* $175. Electronic applications accepted. *Application Contact:* Sharon Frazier, Executive Operations Coordinator, 904-256-7847, Fax: 904-256-7847, E-mail: juorthoadmissions@ju.edu. *Interim Department Chair, Clinical Assistant Professor, and Director of Fellowship in Clinical Research*, Dr. Eman Othman, 904-256-7803, E-mail: eothman1@ju.edu.

College of Arts and Sciences Students: 11 full-time (10 women), 50 part-time (39 women); includes 12 minority (10 Black or African American, non-Hispanic/Latino; 1 American Indian or Alaska Native, non-Hispanic/Latino; 1 Asian, non-Hispanic/Latino), 1 international. Average age 31. 18 applicants, 56% accepted, 7 enrolled. *Faculty:* 13 full-time (4 women), 16 part-time/adjunct (9 women). Expenses: Contact institution. *Financial support:* Research assistantships, teaching assistantships, institutionally sponsored loans, scholarships/grants, and health care benefits available. Support available to part-time students. Financial award application deadline: 3/15; financial award applicants required to submit FAFSA. In 2017, 35 master's awarded. *Program availability:* Evening/weekend. Offers arts and sciences (MA, MS); leadership and learning (MS); mathematics (MA). *Application deadline:* For fall admission, 2/15 priority date for domestic and international students. Applications are processed on a rolling basis. *Application fee:* $50. Electronic applications accepted. *Application Contact:* Rakia Naze, Assistant Director of Graduate Admissions, 904-256-7004, E-mail: rnaze@ju.edu. *Interim Dean for the College of Arts and Sciences/Professor of English*, Dr. Sandra Coyle, 904-256-7100, E-mail: scoyle@ju.edu.

Marine Science Research Institute Students: 8 full-time (7 women), 19 part-time (17 women); includes 1 minority (American Indian or Alaska Native, non-Hispanic/Latino). Average age 25. 10 applicants, 80% accepted, 6 enrolled. *Faculty:* 2 full-time (0 women), 3 part-time/adjunct (0 women). Expenses: Contact institution. *Financial support:* In 2017–18, 2 teaching assistantships with partial tuition reimbursements (averaging $2,000 per year) were awarded; career-related internships or fieldwork, scholarships/grants, tuition waivers, and unspecified assistantships also available. Support available to part-time students. Financial award application deadline: 3/1. In 2017, 1 master's awarded. *Program availability:* Part-time. Offers marine science (MA, MS). MPP/MS offered jointly with JU's Public Policy Institute. *Application deadline:* For fall admission, 3/1 priority date for domestic students, 3/1 for international students. Applications are processed on a rolling basis. *Application fee:* $50. Electronic applications accepted. *Application Contact:* Rakia Naze, Assistant Director of Graduate Admissions, 904-256-7004, E-mail: rnaze@ju.edu. *Executive Director*, Dr. A. Quinton White, Jr., 904-256-7100, E-mail: qwhite@ju.edu.

College of Fine Arts Students: 24 full-time (17 women), 12 part-time (11 women); includes 14 minority (4 Black or African American, non-Hispanic/Latino; 1 Asian, non-Hispanic/Latino; 8 Hispanic/Latino; 1 Two or more races, non-Hispanic/Latino), 4 international. Average age 36. 12 applicants, 58% accepted, 4 enrolled. *Faculty:* 2 full-time (1 woman), 6 part-time/adjunct (2 women). Expenses: Contact institution. *Financial support:* In 2017–18, 2 fellowships (averaging $35,700 per year) were awarded; institutionally sponsored loans, scholarships/grants, and health care benefits also available. Support available to part-time students. Financial award application deadline: 3/1; financial award applicants required to submit FAFSA. In 2017, 12 master's awarded. *Program availability:* Blended/hybrid learning. Offers choreography (MFA); fine arts (MFA); visual arts (MFA). *Application deadline:* For spring admission, 5/1 priority date for domestic students, 2/1 priority date for international students. Applications are processed on a rolling basis. *Application fee:* $50. Electronic applications accepted. *Application Contact:* Rakia Naze, Assistant Director of Graduate Admissions, 904-256-7004, E-mail: rnaze@ju.edu. *Interim Dean of Fine Arts/Associate Professor of Music*, Dr. Timothy Snyder, 904-256-7377, E-mail: tsnyder2@ju.edu.

Davis College of Business Students: 141 full-time (50 women), 167 part-time (81 women); includes 98 minority (57 Black or African American, non-Hispanic/Latino; 1 American Indian or Alaska Native, non-Hispanic/Latino; 9 Asian, non-Hispanic/Latino; 27 Hispanic/Latino; 4 Two or more races, non-Hispanic/Latino), 25 international. Average age 35. 308 applicants, 44% accepted, 87 enrolled. *Faculty:* 24 full-time (8 women), 9 part-time/adjunct (4 women). Expenses: Contact institution. *Financial support:* In 2017–18, 4 students received support. Scholarships/grants, health care benefits, and unspecified assistantships available. Financial award application deadline: 6/30; financial award applicants required to submit FAFSA. In 2017, 120 master's, 1 doctorate awarded. *Program availability:* Part-time, evening/weekend, 100% online. Offers accounting and finance (MBA); business (MBA, MS, DBA); business administration (MBA, DBA); business management (MBA); consumer goods and services marketing (MBA); leadership development (MBA); management (MBA); management accounting (MBA); organizational leadership (MS). MBA/JD offered jointly with Florida School of Law; MSN/MBA offered jointly with JU's Keigwin School of Nursing; MBA/MPP offered jointly with JU's Public Policy Institute. *Application deadline:* For fall admission, 7/1 priority date for domestic students, 6/15 priority date for international students; for spring admission, 12/1 priority date for domestic students, 11/15 priority date for international students; for summer admission, 4/1 priority date for domestic students, 3/15 priority date for international students. Applications are processed on a rolling basis. *Application fee:* $50. Electronic applications accepted. *Application Contact:* AnnaMaria Murphy, Assistant Director of Graduate Admissions, 904-256-7426, Fax: 904-256-7012, E-mail: mba@ju.edu. *Dean,* Dr. Don Capener, 904-256-7431, Fax: 904-256-7467, E-mail: dcapene@ju.edu.

Public Policy Institute Students: 10 full-time (4 women), 19 part-time (10 women); includes 7 minority (3 Black or African American, non-Hispanic/Latino; 3 Hispanic/Latino; 1 Two or more races, non-Hispanic/Latino). Average age 34. 39 applicants, 54% accepted, 15 enrolled. *Faculty:* 3 full-time (1 woman), 3 part-time/adjunct (2 women). Expenses: Contact institution. *Financial support:* In 2017–18, 11 students received support, including 2 fellowships (averaging $40,000 per year); career-related internships or fieldwork, Federal Work-Study, scholarships/grants, and unspecified assistantships also available. Support available to part-time students. Financial award application deadline: 4/1. In 2017, 4 master's awarded. *Program availability:* Part-time, evening/weekend. Offers public policy (MPP). MPP/JD offered in partnership with Florida Coastal School of Law; MPP/MBA with JU's Davis College of Business; MPP/MS with JU's Marine Science Research Institute. *Application deadline:* For fall admission, 2/15 priority date for domestic students, 2/15 for international students. Applications are processed on a rolling basis. *Application fee:* $50. Electronic applications accepted. *Application Contact:* Rakia Naze, Assistant Director of Graduate Admissions, 904-256-7004, E-mail: rnaze@ju.edu. *Director of Public Policy Institute,* Dr. Richard A. Mullaney, 904-256-7342, E-mail: rmullan1@ju.edu.

JAMES MADISON UNIVERSITY, Harrisonburg, VA 22807

General Information State-supported, coed, comprehensive institution. CGS member. *Enrollment:* 21,836 graduate, professional, and undergraduate students; 1,011 full-time matriculated graduate/professional students (730 women), 668 part-time matriculated graduate/professional students (435 women). *Enrollment by degree level:* 1,413 master's, 190 doctoral, 59 other advanced degrees. *Graduate faculty:* 722. Tuition, state resident: full-time $10,512; part-time $438 per credit hour. Tuition, nonresident: full-time $28,358; part-time $1162 per credit hour. *Required fees:* $1128. *Graduate housing:* On-campus housing not available. *Student services:* Campus employment opportunities, campus safety program, career counseling, exercise/wellness program, free psychological counseling, international student services, multicultural affairs office, services for students with disabilities, teacher training, writing training. *Library facilities:* Carrier Library plus 2 others. *Collection:* Students can reserve study rooms. *Research affiliation:* National Institute of Standards and Technology (NIST) through George Mason University (network risk assessment), National Oceanic and Atmospheric Administration (NOAA) (applied meteorological research), National Science Foundation (development of a detector array for Compton Scattering using polarized beams and targets; quantitative skills in biology).

Computer facilities: Computer purchase and lease plans are available. A campuswide network can be accessed from student residence rooms and from off campus. Online class registration is available.
Website: http://www.jmu.edu/

General Application Contact: Dr. Jie Chen, Dean, The Graduate School, 540-568-4213, Fax: 540-568-7860, E-mail: grad@jmu.edu.

GRADUATE UNITS

The Graduate School Students: 1,011 full-time (730 women), 668 part-time (435 women); includes 238 minority (81 Black or African American, non-Hispanic/Latino; 47 Asian, non-Hispanic/Latino; 73 Hispanic/Latino; 1 Native Hawaiian or other Pacific Islander, non-Hispanic/Latino; 36 Two or more races, non-Hispanic/Latino), 45 international. Average age 30. 2,661 applicants, 47% accepted, 859 enrolled. *Faculty:* 722. Expenses: Contact institution. *Financial support:* In 2017–18, 393 students received support, including 273 fellowships with full tuition reimbursements available (averaging $7,911 per year), 40 teaching assistantships with full tuition reimbursements available (averaging $9,284 per year); research assistantships, career-related internships or fieldwork, Federal Work-Study, tuition waivers, unspecified assistantships, and 9 athletic assistantships (averaging $9284), 5 service assistantships (averaging $7911), 66 doctoral assistantships (stipend varies) also available. Financial award application deadline: 3/1; financial award applicants required to submit FAFSA. In 2017, 698 master's, 36 doctorates, 24 other advanced degrees awarded. *Program availability:* Part-time, evening/weekend, 100% online, blended/hybrid learning. *Application fee:* $55. Electronic applications accepted. *Application Contact:* Lynette D. Michael, Director of Graduate Admissions, 540-568-6131 Ext. 6395, Fax: 540-568-7860, E-mail: michaeld@jmu.edu. *Dean, The Graduate School,* Dr. Jie Chen, 540-568-4213, Fax: 540-568-7860, E-mail: grad@jmu.edu.

College of Arts and Letters Students: 97 full-time (56 women), 33 part-time (18 women); includes 23 minority (11 Black or African American, non-Hispanic/Latino; 3 Asian, non-Hispanic/Latino; 3 Hispanic/Latino; 6 Two or more races, non-Hispanic/Latino), 4 international. Average age 30. *Faculty:* 129. Expenses: Contact institution. *Financial support:* In 2017–18, 58 students received support, including 40 fellowships, 18 teaching assistantships with full tuition reimbursements available (averaging $9,284 per year); Federal Work-Study also available. Financial award application deadline: 3/1; financial award applicants required to submit FAFSA. In 2017, 67 master's awarded. *Program availability:* Part-time. Offers arts and letters (MA, MPA, MS); English (MA); environmental communication (MA); health communication (MA); individualized (MPA); political science (MA); public history (MA); public management (MPA); strategic communication (MA); U.S. history (MA); world history (MA); writing, rhetoric, and technical communication (MA, MS). *Application fee:* $55. Electronic applications accepted. *Application Contact:* Lynette D. Michael, Director of Graduate Admissions, 540-568-6131 Ext. 6395, Fax: 540-568-7860, E-mail: michaeld@jmu.edu. *Dean,* Dr. David K. Jeffrey, 540-568-7044.

College of Business Students: 113 full-time (43 women), 131 part-time (50 women); includes 43 minority (14 Black or African American, non-Hispanic/Latino; 15 Asian, non-Hispanic/Latino; 12 Hispanic/Latino; 2 Two or more races, non-Hispanic/Latino), 8 international. Average age 30. *Faculty:* 65. Expenses: Contact institution. *Financial support:* In 2017–18, 31 students received support, including 24 fellowships; career-related internships or fieldwork, Federal Work-Study, and assistantships (averaging $7911), 6 doctoral assistantships, 1 service assistantship also available. Financial award application deadline: 3/1; financial award applicants required to submit FAFSA. In 2017, 63 master's, 3 doctorates awarded. *Program availability:* Part-time, evening/weekend, blended/hybrid learning. Offers accounting information systems (MS); business (MBA, MS, PhD); postsecondary analysis and leadership (PhD); taxation (MS). *Application fee:* $55. Electronic applications accepted. *Application Contact:* Lynette D. Michael, Director of Graduate Admissions, 540-568-6395, Fax: 540-568-7860, E-mail: michaeld@jmu.edu. *Dean,* Dr. Mary A. Gowan, 540-568-3254, E-mail: gowanma@jmu.edu.

College of Education Students: 298 full-time (266 women), 181 part-time (115 women); includes 57 minority (15 Black or African American, non-Hispanic/Latino; 4 Asian, non-Hispanic/Latino; 27 Hispanic/Latino; 1 Native Hawaiian or other Pacific Islander, non-Hispanic/Latino; 10 Two or more races, non-Hispanic/Latino), 3 international. Average age 30. *Faculty:* 100. Expenses: Contact institution. *Financial support:* In 2017–18, 39 students received support, including 1 teaching assistantship; career-related internships or fieldwork, Federal Work-Study, and 38 assistantships (averaging $7911) also available. Financial award application deadline: 3/1; financial award applicants required to submit FAFSA. In 2017, 292 master's awarded. *Program availability:* Part-time, evening/weekend, 100% online, blended/hybrid learning. Offers adapted curriculum (MAT); autism (M Ed); behavior specialist (M Ed); early childhood education (MAT); early childhood education (preK-3) (MAT); early childhood special education (MAT); education (M Ed, MAT, MS Ed); educational leadership (M Ed); educational technology (M Ed); elementary education (MAT); equity and cultural diversity (M Ed); general curriculum K-12 special education (MAT); gifted education (M Ed); higher education (MS Ed); human resource management (MS Ed); inclusive early childhood education (MAT); inclusive early childhood special education (MAT); individualized (MS Ed); instructional design (MS Ed); instructional specialist (M Ed); K-12 special education (MAT); K-8 math specialist (M Ed); K-8 mathematics specialist (M Ed); leadership and facilitation (MS Ed); mathematics (M Ed); middle education (MAT); program evaluation and measurement (MS Ed); reading education (M Ed); secondary education (MAT); Spanish language and culture for educators (M Ed); TESOL (MAT); visual impairments (MAT). *Application fee:* $55. Electronic applications accepted. *Application Contact:* Lynette D. Michael, Director of Graduate Admissions, 540-568-6131 Ext. 6395, Fax: 540-568-7860, E-mail: michaeld@jmu.edu. *Dean,* Dr. Phillip M. Wishon, 540-568-6572, E-mail: wishonpm@jmu.edu.

College of Health and Behavioral Studies Students: 395 full-time (310 women), 195 part-time (172 women); includes 87 minority (31 Black or African American, non-Hispanic/Latino; 21 Asian, non-Hispanic/Latino; 20 Hispanic/Latino; 15 Two or more races, non-Hispanic/Latino), 6 international. Average age 30. *Faculty:* 193. Expenses: Contact institution. *Financial support:* In 2017–18, 196 students received support, including 15 teaching assistantships with full tuition reimbursements available (averaging $9,284 per year); career-related internships or fieldwork, Federal Work-Study, unspecified assistantships, and athletic assistantships (averaging $8837), service assistantships (averaging $7530), doctoral assistantships also available. Financial award application deadline: 3/1; financial award applicants required to submit FAFSA. In 2017, 218 master's, 19 doctorates, 17 other advanced degrees awarded. *Program availability:* Part-time, evening/weekend, 100% online, blended/hybrid learning. Offers adult/gerontology primary care nurse practitioner (MSN); applied research (MA); assessment and measurement (PhD); audiology (Au D); behavior analysis (MA); clinical and school psychology (Psy D); clinical exercise physiology (MS); clinical mental health counselingclinical nurse leader (MSN); communication sciences and disorders (PhD); counseling and supervision (PhD); exercise physiology (MS); experimental psychology (MA); family nurse practitioner (MSN); health and behavioral studies (M Ed, MA, MAT, MOT, MPAS, MS, MSN, Au D, DNP, PhD, Psy D, Ed S); kinesiology (MAT, MS); nurse administrator (MSN); nurse midwifery (MSN); nursing (MSN, DNP); nutrition and exercise (MS); nutrition and physical activity (MS); occupational therapy (MOT); physical and health education (MAT); physician assistant studies (MPAS); psychiatric mental health nurse practitioner (MSN); quantitative psychology (MA); school psychology (MA, Ed S); speech-language pathology (MS); sport and recreation leadership (MS). *Application fee:* $55. Electronic applications accepted. *Application Contact:* Lynette D. Michael, Director of Graduate Admissions, 540-568-6131 Ext. 6395, Fax: 540-568-7860, E-mail: michaeld@jmu.edu. *Dean,* Dr. Sharon E. Lovell, 540-568-2705, Fax: 540-568-2747, E-mail: lovellse@jmu.edu.

College of Integrated Science and Engineering Students: 24 full-time (10 women), 39 part-time (14 women); includes 7 minority (3 Black or African American, non-Hispanic/Latino; 1 Asian, non-Hispanic/Latino; 2 Hispanic/Latino; 1 Two or more races, non-Hispanic/Latino), 7 international. Average age 30. *Faculty:* 78. Expenses: Contact institution. *Financial support:* In 2017–18, 4 students received support. Career-related internships or fieldwork, Federal Work-Study, and 4 assistantships (averaging $7911) available. Financial award application deadline: 3/1; financial award applicants required to submit FAFSA. In 2017, 30 master's awarded. *Program availability:* Part-time, evening/weekend, 100% online, blended/hybrid learning, study abroad. Offers digital forensics (MS); environmental management and sustainability (MS); information security (MS); integrated science and engineering (MS). *Application fee:* $55. Electronic applications accepted. *Application Contact:* Lynette D. Michael, Director of Graduate Admissions, 540-568-6395, Fax: 540-568-7860, E-mail: michaeld@jmu.edu. *Dean,* Dr. Robert A. Kolvoord, 540-568-2752, E-mail: kolvoora@jmu.edu.

College of Science and Mathematics Students: 20 full-time (11 women), 21 part-time (14 women); includes 5 minority (2 Black or African American, non-Hispanic/Latino; 1 Asian, non-Hispanic/Latino; 2 Hispanic/Latino). Average age 30. *Faculty:* 71. Expenses: Contact institution. *Financial support:* In 2017–18, 16 students received support. Fellowships, Federal Work-Study, and 16 assistantships (averaging $7911) available. Financial award application deadline: 3/1; financial award applicants required to submit FAFSA. In 2017, 12 master's awarded. *Program availability:* Part-time. Offers biology (MS); mathematics (M Ed); science and mathematics (M Ed, MS). *Application fee:* $55. Electronic applications accepted. *Application Contact:* Lynette D. Michael, Director of Graduate Admissions, 540-568-6131 Ext. 6395, Fax: 540-568-7860, E-mail: michaeld@jmu.edu. *Dean,* Dr. David F. Brakke, 540-568-3508, E-mail: brakkedf@jmu.edu.

College of Visual and Performing Arts Students: 46 full-time (24 women), 15 part-time (8 women); includes 7 minority (2 Black or African American, non-Hispanic/Latino; 4 Hispanic/Latino; 1 Two or more races, non-Hispanic/Latino), 16 international. Average age 30. *Faculty:* 85. Expenses: Contact institution. *Financial support:* In 2017–18, 37 students received support, including 6 teaching assistantships with full tuition reimbursements available (averaging $9,284 per year); fellowships, Federal Work-Study, and 14 assistantships (averaging $7911), 17 doctoral assistantships (stipend varies) also available. Financial award application deadline: 3/1; financial award applicants required to submit FAFSA. In 2017, 16 master's, 8 doctorates awarded.

Program availability: Part-time. Offers art education (MA); composition (MM); conducting (MM, DMA); music education (MM); performance (MM, DMA); studio art (MA, MFA); visual and performing arts (MA, MFA, MM, DMA). *Application fee:* $55. Electronic applications accepted. *Application Contact:* Lynette D. Michael, Director of Graduate Admissions and Student Records, 540-568-6131 Ext. 6395, Fax: 540-568-7860, E-mail: michaeld@jmu.edu. *Dean,* Dr. George Sparks, 540-568-6247, E-mail: sparksge@jmu.edu.

JEFFERSON COLLEGE OF HEALTH SCIENCES, Roanoke, VA 24013

General Information Independent, coed, comprehensive institution. *Graduate housing:* Room and/or apartments available on a first-come, first-served basis to single students; on-campus housing not available to married students. *Research affiliation:* Carilion Clinic (hospital and medical services), Virginia Polytechnic Institute and State University/Carilion Medical School (medicine).

GRADUATE UNITS

Program in Nursing *Program availability:* Part-time. Offers nursing education (MSN); nursing management (MSN). Electronic applications accepted.

Program in Occupational Therapy *Program availability:* Part-time. Offers occupational therapy (MS). Electronic applications accepted.

Program in Physician Assistant Offers physician assistant (MS). Electronic applications accepted.

THE JEWISH THEOLOGICAL SEMINARY, New York, NY 10027-4649

General Information Independent-religious, coed, university. *Graduate housing:* Rooms and/or apartments available on a first-come, first-served basis to single and married students. Housing application deadline: 5/15.

GRADUATE UNITS

The Graduate School *Program availability:* Part-time. Offers ancient Judaism (MA, DHL, PhD); Bible and ancient Semitic languages (MA, DHL, PhD); interdepartmental studies (MA); Jewish art and visual culture (MA); Jewish gender and women's studies (MA); Jewish history (MA, DHL, PhD); Jewish literature (MA, DHL, PhD); Jewish philosophy (DHL); Jewish thought (MA, PhD); liturgy (MA, DHL, PhD); medieval Jewish studies (MA, DHL, PhD); Midrash (DHL); Midrash and scriptural interpretation (MA, PhD); modern Jewish studies (MA, DHL, PhD); Talmud and rabbinics (MA, DHL, PhD). MA/MSW offered jointly with Columbia University.

H. L. Miller Cantorial School and College of Jewish Music Offers Jewish music (MSM).

The Rabbinical School Offers theology (MA, Rabbi).

William Davidson Graduate School of Jewish Education *Program availability:* Part-time, online learning. Offers Jewish education (MA, Ed D). Offered in conjunction with The Rabbinical School; H. L. Miller Cantorial School and College of Jewish Music; Teacher's College, Columbia University; and Union Theological Seminary.

JOHN BROWN UNIVERSITY, Siloam Springs, AR 72761-2121

General Information Independent-religious, coed, comprehensive institution. *Graduate housing:* Rooms and/or apartments available on a first-come, first-served basis to single and married students.

GRADUATE UNITS

Graduate Counseling Programs *Program availability:* Part-time, evening/weekend. Offers clinical mental health counseling (MS); marriage and family therapy (MS); play therapy (Graduate Certificate); school counseling (MS). Electronic applications accepted.

Graduate Education Programs *Program availability:* Part-time, evening/weekend. Offers curriculum and instruction (M Ed); secondary education (MAT). Electronic applications accepted.

Soderquist College of Business *Program availability:* Part-time, evening/weekend, online only, 100% online, blended/hybrid learning. Offers international business (MBA); leadership and ethics (MBA, MS). Electronic applications accepted.

JOHN CARROLL UNIVERSITY, University Heights, OH 44118

General Information Independent-religious, coed, comprehensive institution. CGS member. *Enrollment:* 3,523 graduate, professional, and undergraduate students; 211 full-time matriculated graduate/professional students (131 women), 254 part-time matriculated graduate/professional students (144 women). *Enrollment by degree level:* 426 master's, 39 other advanced degrees. *Graduate faculty:* 45 full-time (17 women), 25 part-time/adjunct (11 women). *Tuition:* Full-time $16,238; part-time $788 per credit hour. One-time fee: $200. Part-time tuition and fees vary according to course load and program. *Graduate housing:* On-campus housing not available. *Student services:* Career counseling, exercise/wellness program, free psychological counseling, international student services, multicultural affairs office, services for students with disabilities, writing training. *Library facilities:* Grasselli Library. *Collection:* Books: 456,260 (physical), 91,554 (digital/electronic); Serial titles: 459,633 (physical), 115,548 (digital/electronic); Databases: 279. Weekly public service hours: 111; students can reserve study rooms.

Computer facilities: Computer purchase and lease plans are available. 396 computers available on campus for general student use. A campuswide network can be accessed from student residence rooms and from off campus. Online class registration, campus student online registration, billing, advising system, JCU mobile app, course management site (BlackBoard), online financial aid and billing; online course sites; online housing selection are available.
Website: http://www.jcu.edu/

General Application Contact: Dr. Anne Kugler, Associate Dean, 216-397-4770, E-mail: akugler@jcu.edu.

GRADUATE UNITS

Graduate Studies Expenses: Contact institution. *Financial support:* Research assistantships, teaching assistantships, career-related internships or fieldwork, institutionally sponsored loans, scholarships/grants, tuition waivers (partial), and unspecified assistantships available. Support available to part-time students. Financial award applicants required to submit FAFSA. *Program availability:* Part-time, evening/weekend. Offers biology (MA, MS); clinical counseling (Certificate); community counseling (MA); educational psychology (M Ed, Ed S); English (MA); humanities (MA); mathematics (MA); nonprofit administration (MA); professional teacher education (M Ed, MA); school counseling (M Ed); school psychology (Ed S); theology and religious studies (MA). *Application deadline:* Applications are processed on a rolling basis. *Application fee:* $25 ($35 for international students). Electronic applications accepted. *Application Contact:* Terry Bradley, Records Management Assistant, 216-397-1925, Fax: 216-397-1835, E-mail: tbradley@jcu.edu. *Coordinator,* Dr. Anne Kugler, 216-397-4770, Fax: 216-397-1835, E-mail: akugler@jcu.edu.

John M. and Mary Jo Boler School of Business Students: 63 full-time (21 women), 67 part-time (22 women); includes 18 minority (10 Black or African American, non-Hispanic/Latino; 4 Asian, non-Hispanic/Latino; 3 Hispanic/Latino; 1 Two or more races, non-Hispanic/Latino), 10 international. Average age 26. *Faculty:* 11 full-time (1 woman), 9 part-time/adjunct (3 women). Expenses: Contact institution. *Financial support:* Research assistantships with full tuition reimbursements, scholarships/grants, and unspecified assistantships available. Financial award application deadline: 3/15; financial award applicants required to submit FAFSA. In 2017, 50 master's awarded. *Program availability:* Part-time, evening/weekend. Offers accountancy (MS); business (MBA); laboratory administration (MS). *Application deadline:* Applications are processed on a rolling basis. *Application fee:* $25 ($35 for international students). Electronic applications accepted. *Application Contact:* Gayle T. Bruno-Gannon, Assistant to the Dean, 216-397-1970, Fax: 216-397-1728, E-mail: ggannon@jcu.edu. *Dean,* Dr. Alan R. Miciak, 216-397-4391, Fax: 216-397-1833.

JOHN F. KENNEDY UNIVERSITY, Pleasant Hill, CA 94523-4817

General Information Independent, coed, primarily women, upper-level institution. *Graduate housing:* On-campus housing not available.

GRADUATE UNITS

Graduate School of Holistic Studies *Program availability:* Part-time, evening/weekend. Offers consciousness and transformative studies (MA); counseling psychology (MA); dream studies (Certificate); holistic health education (MA); holistic studies (MA, MFA, Certificate); integral psychology (MA, Certificate); life coaching (Certificate); somatic psychology (MA); studio arts (MFA); transformative arts (MA); transpersonal psychology (MA).

Graduate School of Professional Psychology *Program availability:* Part-time, evening/weekend. Offers counseling psychology (MA); organizational psychology (MA, Certificate); professional psychology (MA, Psy D, Certificate); psychology (Psy D); sport psychology (MA).

School of Education and Liberal Arts *Program availability:* Part-time, evening/weekend. Offers education (MAT); education and liberal arts (MA, MAT, Certificate); museum studies (MA, Certificate).

School of Law *Program availability:* Part-time, evening/weekend. Offers law (JD).

School of Management *Program availability:* Part-time, evening/weekend. Offers business administration (MBA); career coaching (Certificate); career development (MA, Certificate); management (MA, MBA, Certificate); organizational leadership (Certificate).

JOHN JAY COLLEGE OF CRIMINAL JUSTICE OF THE CITY UNIVERSITY OF NEW YORK, New York, NY 10019

General Information State and locally supported, coed, comprehensive institution. CGS member. *Graduate housing:* On-campus housing not available. *Research affiliation:* Criminal Justice Center, Criminal Justice Research and Evaluation Center, Center on Violence and Human Survival, Center for Dispute Resolution, The Fire Science Institute, The Institute For Criminal Justice Ethics.

GRADUATE UNITS

Graduate Studies *Program availability:* Part-time, evening/weekend. Offers criminal justice (MA, PhD); criminology and deviance (PhD); forensic computing (MS); forensic psychology (PhD); forensic science (PhD); international crime and justice (MA); law and philosophy (PhD); organizational behavior (PhD); protection management (MS); public administration (MPA); public policy (PhD).

THE JOHN MARSHALL LAW SCHOOL, Chicago, IL 60604-3968

General Information Independent, coed, graduate-only institution. *Enrollment by degree level:* 105 master's, 900 doctoral. *Graduate faculty:* 55 full-time (23 women), 202 part-time/adjunct (72 women). *Tuition:* Full-time $46,950; part-time $32,865 per year. *Required fees:* $1650; $1650 per unit. *Graduate housing:* On-campus housing not available. *Student services:* Campus employment opportunities, campus safety program, career counseling, exercise/wellness program, free psychological counseling, international student services, low-cost health insurance, multicultural affairs office, services for students with disabilities, writing training. *Library facilities:* Louis L. Biro Law Library. *Collection:* Books: 46,081 (physical), 25,836 (digital/electronic); Serial titles: 1,187 (physical), 74,679 (digital/electronic); Databases: 71. Weekly public service hours: 96; students can reserve study rooms.

Computer facilities: 26 computers available on campus for general student use. A campuswide network can be accessed from off campus. Online class registration is available.
Website: http://www.jmls.edu/

General Application Contact: Chante Spann, Assistant Dean for Admissions, 800-537-4280, Fax: 312-427-5136, E-mail: admissions@jmls.edu.

GRADUATE UNITS

Graduate and Professional Programs Students: 688 full-time (364 women), 317 part-time (159 women); includes 379 minority (147 Black or African American, non-Hispanic/Latino; 3 American Indian or Alaska Native, non-Hispanic/Latino; 64 Asian, non-Hispanic/Latino; 140 Hispanic/Latino; 25 Two or more races, non-Hispanic/Latino), 54 international. Average age 28. 1,681 applicants, 69% accepted, 287 enrolled. *Faculty:* 55 full-time (23 women), 202 part-time/adjunct (72 women). Expenses: Contact institution. *Financial support:* In 2017–18, 538 students received support. Federal Work-Study, scholarships/grants, and tuition waivers (full and partial) available. Support available to part-time students. Financial award application deadline: 4/1; financial award applicants required to submit FAFSA. In 2017, 99 master's, 352 doctorates awarded. *Program availability:* Part-time, evening/weekend, 100% online, blended/hybrid learning. Offers law (LL M, MJ, JD). *Application deadline:* For fall admission, 4/1 priority date for domestic and international students; for spring admission, 11/15 priority date for domestic and international students. Applications are processed on a rolling basis. *Application fee:* $0. Electronic applications accepted. *Application Contact:* Chante Spann, Assistant Dean for Admissions, 800-537-4280, Fax: 312-427-5136, E-mail: admissions@jmls.edu. *Dean,* Darby Dickerson, 312-427-2737 Ext. 828, E-mail: ddickerson@jmls.edu.

JOHN PAUL THE GREAT CATHOLIC UNIVERSITY, Escondido, CA 92025

General Information Independent-religious, coed, comprehensive institution.

GRADUATE UNITS

School of Theology Offers biblical theology (MA).

JOHNS HOPKINS UNIVERSITY, Baltimore, MD 21218

General Information Independent, coed, university. CGS member. *Enrollment:* 8,155 full-time matriculated graduate/professional students (4,310 women), 9,213 part-time matriculated graduate/professional students (4,836 women). *Enrollment by degree level:* 13,068 master's, 3,778 doctoral, 522 other advanced degrees. *Graduate faculty:* 4,542 full-time (1,969 women), 226 part-time/adjunct (105 women). *Graduate housing:* On-campus housing not available. *Student services:* Campus employment opportunities, campus safety program, career counseling, exercise/wellness program, free psychological counseling, grant writing training, international student services, low-cost health insurance, multicultural affairs office, services for students with disabilities, teacher training, writing training. *Library facilities:* The Sheridan Libraries plus 2 others. *Collection:* Books: 4.1 million (physical); Serial titles: 52,351 (physical), 132,176 (digital/electronic); Databases: 648. Study areas open 24 hours, 5–7 days a week; students can reserve study rooms. *Research affiliation:* Carnegie Institution of Washington (biological sciences), SmithKline Beecham (asthma and allergy), Bristol-Myers Squibb (human nutrition), Howard Hughes Medical Institute (biomedical sciences), Space Telescope Science Institute (astronomy), General Electric Company (GE) (medical technology).

Computer facilities: Computer purchase and lease plans are available. 175 computers available on campus for general student use. A campuswide network can be accessed from student residence rooms and from off campus. Online class registration is available.
Website: http://www.jhu.edu/

GRADUATE UNITS

Bloomberg School of Public Health Students: 1,340 full-time (946 women), 932 part-time (605 women); includes 649 minority (134 Black or African American, non-Hispanic/Latino; 4 American Indian or Alaska Native, non-Hispanic/Latino; 319 Asian, non-Hispanic/Latino; 128 Hispanic/Latino; 64 Two or more races, non-Hispanic/Latino), 636 international. Average age 30. 4,234 applicants, 49% accepted, 1085 enrolled. *Faculty:* 670 full-time, 709 part-time/adjunct. Expenses: Contact institution. *Financial support:* In 2017–18, 1,605 students received support. Fellowships, research assistantships, teaching assistantships, career-related internships or fieldwork, Federal Work-Study, scholarships/grants, traineeships, health care benefits, and unspecified assistantships available. Support available to part-time students. Financial award application deadline: 3/15; financial award applicants required to submit FAFSA. In 2017, 712 master's, 123 doctorates awarded. *Program availability:* Part-time, 100% online, blended/hybrid learning. Offers biochemistry and molecular biology (MHS, Sc M, PhD); bioethics and policy (PhD); biostatistics (MHS, Sc M, PhD); cancer epidemiology (MHS, Sc M, PhD, Sc D); cardiovascular disease and clinical epidemiology (MHS, Sc M, PhD, Sc D); children's mental health services (PhD); clinical investigation (MHS, PhD); clinical trials (PhD, Sc D); clinical trials and evidence synthesis (MHS, Sc M, PhD, Sc D); demography (MHS); environmental epidemiology (MHS, Sc M, PhD, Sc D); environmental health (MHS, Sc M, Dr PH, PhD); epidemiology of aging (MHS, Sc M, PhD, Sc D); general epidemiology and methodology (MHS, Sc M); genetic counseling (Sc M); genetic epidemiology (MHS, Sc M, PhD, Sc D); global disease epidemiology and control (MSPH, PhD); global health economics (MHS); health administration (MHA); health and public policy (PhD); health economics (MHS); health economics and policy (PhD); health education and health communication (MSPH); health finance and management (MHS); health policy (MSPH); health policy and management (Dr PH); health services research and policy (PhD); health systems (MSPH, PhD); human nutrition (MSPH, PhD); infectious disease epidemiology (MHS, Sc M, PhD, Sc D); mental health (MHS); molecular microbiology and immunology (MHS, Sc M, PhD); occupational and environmental hygiene (MSPH); population, family and reproductive health (MHS, MSPH, PhD); public health (MBE, MHA, MHS, MHS, MPH, MPP, MSPH, Sc M, Dr PH, PhD, Sc D); public policy (MPP); social and behavioral interventions (MSPH, PhD); social and behavioral sciences (PhD); social factors in health (MHS); toxicity testing and human health risk assessment of environmental agents (MSPH). *Application fee:* $135. Electronic applications accepted. *Application Contact:* Office of Admissions, 410-955-3543, Fax: 410-955-0464, E-mail: jhsph.admiss@jhu.edu. *Dean,* Dr. Ellen J. MacKenzie, 410-955-3540, Fax: 410-955-0121, E-mail: jhsph.deansoffice@jhu.edu.

Berman Institute of Bioethics 20 applicants, 70% accepted, 8 enrolled. Expenses: Contact institution. Offers bioethics (MBE). *Application deadline:* For fall admission, 7/1 for domestic students. Applications are processed on a rolling basis. *Application fee:* $135. Electronic applications accepted. *Application Contact:* Office of Admissions, 410-955-3543, Fax: 410-955-0464, E-mail: jhsph.admiss@jhu.edu. *Director of the Johns Hopkins Berman Institute of Bioethics*, Dr. Jeffrey Kahn, 410-614-5679, E-mail: jeffkahn@jhu.edu.

Carey Business School Students: 1,000 full-time (542 women), 1,260 part-time (510 women); includes 526 minority (151 Black or African American, non-Hispanic/Latino; 237 Asian, non-Hispanic/Latino; 101 Hispanic/Latino; 1 Native Hawaiian or other Pacific Islander, non-Hispanic/Latino; 36 Two or more races, non-Hispanic/Latino), 973 international. Average age 27. 4,216 applicants, 70% accepted, 1160 enrolled. *Faculty:* 93 full-time (33 women), 45 part-time/adjunct (11 women). Expenses: Contact institution. *Financial support:* In 2017–18, 217 students received support. Scholarships/grants available. Support available to part-time students. Financial award application deadline: 4/15; financial award applicants required to submit FAFSA. In 2017, 1,080 master's, 31 other advanced degrees awarded. *Program availability:* Part-time, evening/weekend, blended/hybrid learning, on-site residency requirement. Offers business (MBA, MS, Certificate); business administration (MBA); business analytics and risk management (MS); finance (MS); financial management (Certificate); health care management (MS); information systems (MS); investments (Certificate); marketing (MS); real estate and infrastructure (MS). *Application deadline:* For fall admission, 5/1 for domestic and international students. Applications are processed on a rolling basis. *Application fee:* $100. Electronic applications accepted. *Application Contact:* Office of Admissions, 410-234-9220, Fax: 443-529-1554, E-mail: carey.admissions@jhu.edu. *Dean*, Dr. Bernard T. Ferrari, 410-234-9210, E-mail: bferrari@jhu.edu.

Engineering Program for Professionals *Program availability:* Part-time, evening/weekend, 100% online, blended/hybrid learning. Offers applied and computational mathematics (MS, Post-Master's Certificate); applied biomedical engineering (MS, Post-Master's Certificate); applied physics (MS, Post-Master's Certificate); chemical and biomolecular engineering (M Ch E); civil engineering (MCE, Graduate Certificate); communications and networking (MS); computer science (Post-Master's Certificate); cybersecurity (MS, Post-Master's Certificate); electrical and computer engineering (Graduate Certificate, Post-Master's Certificate); engineering (M Ch E, M Mat SE, MCE, MEE, MEM, MME, MS, MSE, Graduate Certificate, Post Master's Certificate, Post-Master's Certificate); engineering management (MEM); environmental engineering (MS, Graduate Certificate, Post-Master's Certificate); environmental engineering and science (MEE, MS, Graduate Certificate, Post-Master's Certificate); environmental planning and management (MS, Graduate Certificate, Post-Master's Certificate); financial mathematics (MS); financial risk management (Graduate Certificate); information systems engineering (MS, Graduate Certificate, Post-Master's Certificate); mechanical engineering (MME, Post Master's Certificate); nanotechnology (M Mat SE); photonics (MS); quantitative portfolio management (Graduate Certificate); securitization (Graduate Certificate); space systems engineering (MS); systems engineering (MS, MSE, Graduate Certificate, Post-Master's Certificate); technical management (MS, Graduate Certificate, Post-Master's Certificate). Electronic applications accepted.

G. W. C. Whiting School of Engineering Offers bioengineering innovation and design (MSE); biomaterials (MSEM); biomedical engineering (MSE, PhD); chemical and biomolecular engineering (MSE, PhD); civil engineering (MSEM); communications science (MSEM); computational medicine (PhD); computer science (MSE, MSSI, PhD); discrete mathematics (MA, MSE, PhD); electrical and computer engineering (MSE, PhD); engineering (M Ch E, M Mat SE, MA, MEE, MME, MS, MSE, MSEM, MSSI, PhD, Certificate, Post-Master's Certificate); environmental health and engineering (MA, MS, MSE, PhD); environmental systems analysis, economics and public policy (MSEM); financial mathematics (MSE); fluid mechanics (MSEM); materials science and engineering (MSEM); mechanical engineering (MSEM); mechanics and materials (MSEM); nano-biotechnology (MSEM); nanomaterials and nanotechnology (MSEM); operations research (MSEM); operations research/optimization (MA, MSE, PhD); probability and statistics (MSEM); robotics (MSE); security informatics (MSSI); smart product and device design (MSEM); statistics/probability (MA, MSE, PhD). Electronic applications accepted.

National Institutes of Health Sponsored Programs Offers biology (PhD); cell, molecular, and developmental biology and biophysics (PhD). Electronic applications accepted.

Peabody Conservatory Offers music (MA, MM, DMA, AD, GPD). Electronic applications accepted.

School of Advanced International Studies Offers global risk (MA); international development (MA, Certificate); international economics (Certificate); international economics and finance (MA); international public policy (MIPP); international relations (PhD); international studies (Certificate); Japan studies (MA); Korea studies (MA); South Asia studies (MA); Southeast Asia studies (MA). Electronic applications accepted.

School of Education *Program availability:* Part-time, evening/weekend, 100% online, blended/hybrid learning. Offers advanced methods for differentiated instruction and inclusive education (Graduate Certificate); applied behavior analysis (Post-Master's Certificate); clinical mental health counseling (Post-Master's Certificate); counseling (MS, Advanced Certificate); data-based decision making and organizational improvement (Graduate Certificate); early intervention/preschool special education specialist (Graduate Certificate); education (M Ed, MAT, MS, Ed D, PhD, Advanced Certificate, Graduate Certificate, Post-Master's Certificate); education of students with autism and other pervasive developmental disorders (Graduate Certificate); educational leadership for independent schools (Graduate Certificate); elementary education (MAT); evidence-based teaching in the health professions (Post-Master's Certificate); gifted education (Graduate Certificate); health professions (M Ed); intelligence analysis (MS); leadership in technology integration (Graduate Certificate); mind, brain and teaching (Graduate Certificate); organizational leadership (MS); school administration and supervision (Graduate Certificate); secondary education (MAT); special education (MS); urban education (Graduate Certificate). Electronic applications accepted.

School of Medicine Offers medicine (MA, MS, MD, PhD, Certificate). Electronic applications accepted.

Division of Health Sciences Informatics Offers applied health sciences informatics (MS); clinical informatics (Certificate); health sciences informatics (PhD); health sciences informatics research (MS). Electronic applications accepted.

Graduate Programs in Medicine Offers biochemistry, cellular and molecular biology (PhD); biological chemistry (PhD); cellular and molecular medicine (PhD); cellular and molecular physiology (PhD); functional anatomy and evolution (PhD); immunology (PhD); medical and biological illustration (MA); medicine (MA, PhD); neuroscience (PhD); pathobiology (PhD); pharmacology and molecular sciences (PhD); physiology (PhD). Electronic applications accepted.

School of Nursing Students: 508 full-time (444 women), 281 part-time (257 women); includes 293 minority (113 Black or African American, non-Hispanic/Latino; 1 American Indian or Alaska Native, non-Hispanic/Latino; 86 Asian, non-Hispanic/Latino; 67 Hispanic/Latino; 1 Native Hawaiian or other Pacific Islander, non-Hispanic/Latino; 25 Two or more races, non-Hispanic/Latino), 17 international. Average age 31. 783 applicants, 58% accepted, 279 enrolled. *Faculty:* 68 full-time (63 women), 41 part-time/adjunct (27 women). Expenses: Contact institution. *Financial support:* In 2017–18, 424 students received support, including 18 research assistantships with full tuition reimbursements available, 18 teaching assistantships with full tuition reimbursements available; fellowships with partial tuition reimbursements available, Federal Work-Study, scholarships/grants, and tuition waivers (partial) also available. Support available to part-time students. Financial award application deadline: 3/1; financial award applicants required to submit FAFSA. In 2017, 215 master's, 23 doctorates, 18 other advanced degrees awarded. *Program availability:* Part-time, 100% online, blended/hybrid learning. Offers adult/gerontological acute care nurse practitioner (DNP); adult/gerontological critical care clinical nurse specialist (DNP); adult/gerontological health clinical nurse specialist (DNP); adult/gerontological primary care nurse practitioner (DNP, PhD); family primary care nurse practitioner (DNP); health systems management (MSN); nursing (MSN, DNP, PhD, Certificate); nursing education (Certificate); nursing practice (MSN); pediatric acute care nurse practitioner (Certificate); pediatric critical care clinical nurse specialist (DNP); pediatric primary care nurse practitioner (DNP); psychiatric mental health nurse practitioner (Certificate). *Application deadline:* For fall admission, 11/1 priority date for domestic and international students; for spring admission, 7/1 priority date for domestic and international students; for summer admission, 11/1 priority date for domestic and international students. *Application fee:* $70. Electronic applications accepted. *Application Contact:* Cathy Wilson, Director of Admissions, 410-955-7548, Fax: 410-614-7086, E-mail: jhuson@jhu.edu. *Dean*, Dr. Patricia M. Davidson, 410-955-7544, Fax: 410-955-4890, E-mail: sondeansoffice@jhu.edu.

Zanvyl Krieger School of Arts and Sciences Offers anthropology (PhD); archaeology (PhD); arts and sciences (MA, MBEE, MFA, MS, PhD, Certificate); Assyriology (PhD); astronomy (PhD); biophysics (PhD); cell, molecular, developmental biology, and biophysics (PhD); chemical biology (MS, PhD); chemistry (MA, PhD); classics (PhD); cognitive science (MA, PhD); comparative literature (PhD); earth and planetary sciences (MA, PhD); economics (PhD); Egyptology (PhD); English and American literature (PhD); fiction writing (MFA); German (MA, PhD); Hebrew Bible/Northwest Semitics (PhD); history (PhD); history of art (MA, PhD); history of science and technology (MA, PhD); intellectual history (PhD); mathematics (PhD); philosophy (MA, PhD); physics (PhD); poetry (MFA); political science (MA, PhD); psychological and brain sciences (PhD); romance languages (PhD); sociology (PhD). Electronic applications accepted.

Advanced Academic Programs *Program availability:* Part-time, evening/weekend, online learning. Offers applied economics (MA); bioinformatics (MS); biotechnology (MS); biotechnology enterprise and entrepreneurship (MBEE); communication (MA); digital curation (Certificate); energy policy and climate (MS); environmental sciences (MS); film and media (MA); geographic information systems (MS, Certificate); global security studies (MA); government (MA); liberal arts (MA, Certificate); museum studies (MA); national securities study (Certificate); nonprofit management (Certificate); public management (MA); regulatory science (MS); research administration (MS); science writing (MA, Certificate); writing (MA). Electronic applications accepted.

JOHNSON & WALES UNIVERSITY, Providence, RI 02903-3703

General Information Independent, coed, comprehensive institution. *Enrollment:* 747 full-time matriculated graduate/professional students (463 women), 107 part-time matriculated graduate/professional students (64 women). *Enrollment by degree level:* 794 master's, 58 doctoral. *Tuition:* Full-time $12,636; part-time $702 per credit hour. *Graduate housing:* On-campus housing not available. *Student services:* Campus employment opportunities, campus safety program, career counseling, free psychological counseling, international student services, low-cost health insurance. *Library facilities:* Johnson & Wales University Library. *Research affiliation:* Consortium of Rhode Island Academic and Research Libraries, Association of Institutional Research.

Computer facilities: A campuswide network can be accessed from student residence rooms and from off campus. Online class registration is available.
Website: http://www.jwu.edu/providence/

GRADUATE UNITS

Graduate Studies Expenses: Contact institution. *Financial support:* Career-related internships or fieldwork, institutionally sponsored loans, tuition waivers (partial), and unspecified assistantships available. Support available to part-time students. Financial award application deadline: 5/1. *Program availability:* Part-time, evening/weekend. Offers accounting (MBA); addiction counseling (MS); business administration (MBA); business education and secondary special education (MAT); clinical mental health counseling (MS); criminal justice (MS); culinary arts education (MAT); data analytics (MS); educational leadership (Ed D); elementary education and elementary special education (MAT); finance (MBA); global fashion merchandising and management (MBA); global tourism and sustainable economic development (MS); hospitality (MBA); human resource management (MS); information security/assurance (MS); information technology (MBA); nonprofit management (MBA); occupational therapy (OTD); operations and supply chain management (MBA); organizational leadership (MBA); organizational psychology (MBA); physician assistant studies (MS); sport leadership (MBA); teaching and learning (M Ed). *Application deadline:* Applications are processed on a rolling basis. *Application fee:* $0. *Application Contact:* Graduate School Admissions, 401-598-1015, Fax: 401-598-1286, E-mail: pvdgrad@admissions.jwu.edu.

JOHNSON C. SMITH UNIVERSITY, Charlotte, NC 28216-5398

General Information Independent, coed, comprehensive institution. *Graduate housing:* Room and/or apartments available on a first-come, first-served basis to single students; on-campus housing not available to married students.

GRADUATE UNITS

Program in Social Work *Program availability:* Part-time, evening/weekend. Offers social work (MSW).

JOHNSON UNIVERSITY, Knoxville, TN 37998-1001

General Information Independent-religious, coed, comprehensive institution. *Graduate housing:* Rooms and/or apartments available on a first-come, first-served basis to single and married students. Housing application deadline: 8/1.

GRADUATE UNITS

Graduate and Professional Programs *Program availability:* Part-time, evening/weekend, 100% online, blended/hybrid learning. Offers biblical interpretation (Graduate Certificate); business administration (MBA); Christian ministries (Graduate Certificate); clinical mental health counseling (MA); educational technology (MA); intercultural studies (MA); leadership (MBA); leadership studies (PhD); New Testament (MA); nonprofit management (MBA); school counseling (MA); spiritual formation and leadership (Graduate Certificate); strategic ministry (MA); teacher education (MA). Electronic applications accepted.

JOHNSON UNIVERSITY FLORIDA, Kissimmee, FL 34744-5301

General Information Independent-religious, coed, comprehensive institution.

GRADUATE UNITS

Program in Strategic Ministry *Program availability:* Online learning. Offers children and family (MSM); church administration (MSM); church planting (MSM); intercultural studies (MSM); pastoral ministry (MSM); special needs (MSM); sports ministry (MSM); worship (MSM); youth ministry (MSM).

JOSE MARIA VARGAS UNIVERSITY, Pembroke Pines, FL 33026

General Information Proprietary, coed, comprehensive institution.

GRADUATE UNITS

Program in Preschool Education Offers preschool education (MS).

THE JUDGE ADVOCATE GENERAL'S SCHOOL, U.S. ARMY, Charlottesville, VA 22903-1781

General Information Federally supported, coed, primarily men, graduate-only institution. *Graduate housing:* On-campus housing not available.

GRADUATE UNITS

Graduate Programs Offers military law (LL M). Program available only to active duty military lawyers.

JUDSON UNIVERSITY, Elgin, IL 60123-1498

General Information Independent-religious, coed, comprehensive institution. *Enrollment:* 1,283 graduate, professional, and undergraduate students; 101 full-time matriculated graduate/professional students (61 women), 54 part-time matriculated graduate/professional students (40 women). *Enrollment by degree level:* 132 master's, 22 doctoral, 1 other advanced degree. *Graduate faculty:* 25 full-time (13 women), 48 part-time/adjunct (22 women). Tuition and fees vary according to course load, degree level and program. *Graduate housing:* Rooms and/or apartments available on a first-come, first-served basis to single and married students. Typical cost: $9840 (including board) for single students. Room and board charges vary according to board plan, campus/location and housing facility selected. Housing application deadline: 8/1. *Student services:* Campus employment opportunities, campus safety program, career counseling, exercise/wellness program, free psychological counseling, international student services, low-cost health insurance, multicultural affairs office, services for students with disabilities, writing training. *Library facilities:* Benjamin P. Browne Library. *Collection:* Books: 141,240 (physical), 2,243 (digital/electronic); Serial titles: 158 (physical), 48,401 (digital/electronic); Databases: 53. Weekly public service hours: 83; students can reserve study rooms.

Computer facilities: 140 computers available on campus for general student use. A campuswide network can be accessed from student residence rooms and from off campus. Online class registration is available.
Website: http://www.judsonu.edu/

General Application Contact: Maria Aguirre, Student Academic Advisor, 847-628-1160, E-mail: maguirre@judsonu.edu.

GRADUATE UNITS

Doctor of Education in Literacy Program Students: 15 full-time (12 women), 21 part-time (18 women); includes 2 minority (1 Black or African American, non-Hispanic/Latino; 1 Hispanic/Latino). Average age 40. 9 applicants, 100% accepted, 9 enrolled. *Faculty:* 5 full-time (3 women), 10 part-time/adjunct (all women). Expenses: Contact institution. *Financial support:* Teaching assistantships available. Financial award application deadline: 11/15; financial award applicants required to submit FAFSA. In 2017, 9 doctorates awarded. Offers literacy (Ed D). *Application deadline:* For fall admission, 11/15 for domestic and international students. *Application fee:* $200. *Application Contact:* Maria Aguirre, Student Academic Advisor, 847-628-1160, E-mail: maguirre@judsonu.edu. *Director,* Dr. Steven L. Layne, 847-628-1093, E-mail: slayne@judsonu.edu.

Master of Architecture Program Students: 11 full-time (4 women). Average age 23. 24 applicants, 83% accepted, 11 enrolled. *Faculty:* 9 full-time (3 women), 3 part-time/adjunct (1 woman). Expenses: Contact institution. *Financial support:* In 2017–18, 9 students received support. Fellowships, research assistantships, teaching assistantships, scholarships/grants, and 8 assistantships available. Financial award application deadline: 5/1; financial award applicants required to submit FAFSA. In 2017, 6 master's awarded. *Program availability:* Part-time. Offers architecture (M Arch); sustainable design (M Arch); traditional architecture and urbanism (M Arch). *Application deadline:* For fall admission, 2/15 priority date for domestic and international students; for winter admission, 11/15 for domestic students; for spring admission, 11/15 for domestic and international students. Applications are processed on a rolling basis. *Application fee:* $100. Electronic applications accepted. *Application Contact:* Molly Smith, Director of Admissions, 847-628-2521, E-mail: molly.smith@judsonu.edu. *Chair,* Dr. David M. Ogoli, 847-628-1018, E-mail: dogoli@judsonu.edu.

Master of Arts in Clinical Mental Health Counseling Program Students: 26 full-time (24 women), 3 part-time (1 woman); includes 7 minority (6 Black or African American, non-Hispanic/Latino; 1 Asian, non-Hispanic/Latino). Average age 44. 16 applicants, 100% accepted, 15 enrolled. *Faculty:* 2 full-time (1 woman), 7 part-time/adjunct (5 women). Expenses: Contact institution. *Financial support:* Unspecified assistantships available. *Program availability:* Evening/weekend. Offers clinical mental health counseling (MA). *Application deadline:* Applications are processed on a rolling basis. *Application fee:* $35. Electronic applications accepted. *Application Contact:* Maria Aguirre, Student Academic Advisor, 847-628-1160, E-mail: maguirre@judsonu.edu. *Program Director,* Dr. Amber Randolph, 847-628-1544, E-mail: amber.randolph@judsonu.edu.

Master of Arts in Human Services Administration Program Students: 10 full-time (9 women), 12 part-time (9 women); includes 13 minority (10 Black or African American, non-Hispanic/Latino; 3 Hispanic/Latino). Average age 41. 9 applicants, 89% accepted, 7 enrolled. *Faculty:* 6 full-time (3 women), 6 part-time/adjunct (3 women). Expenses: Contact institution. *Financial support:* Unspecified assistantships available. *Program availability:* Evening/weekend. Offers human services administration (MA). *Application deadline:* Applications are processed on a rolling basis. *Application fee:* $35. Electronic applications accepted. *Application Contact:* Maria Aguirre, Student Academic Advisor, 847-628-1160, E-mail: maguirre@judsonu.edu.

Master of Arts in Organizational Leadership Program Students: 13 full-time (7 women), 9 part-time (6 women); includes 9 minority (3 Black or African American, non-Hispanic/Latino; 5 Hispanic/Latino; 1 Two or more races, non-Hispanic/Latino), 1 international. Average age 34. 12 applicants, 58% accepted, 7 enrolled. *Faculty:* 4 full-time (2 women), 7 part-time/adjunct (1 woman). Expenses: Contact institution. *Financial support:* Institutionally sponsored loans and unspecified assistantships available. Financial award applicants required to submit FAFSA. In 2017, 21 master's awarded. *Program availability:* Part-time, evening/weekend, 100% online, blended/hybrid learning. Offers organizational leadership (MA). *Application deadline:* Applications are processed on a rolling basis. *Application fee:* $35. Electronic applications accepted. *Chair,* Dr. Teri Stein, 847-628-1524, E-mail: tstein@judsonu.edu.

Master of Business Administration Program Students: 41 full-time (17 women), 9 part-time (6 women); includes 19 minority (5 Black or African American, non-Hispanic/Latino; 1 Asian, non-Hispanic/Latino; 13 Hispanic/Latino). Average age 34. 20 applicants, 75% accepted, 14 enrolled. *Faculty:* 8 full-time (3 women), 33 part-time/adjunct (13 women). Expenses: Contact institution. *Financial support:* In 2017–18, 6 teaching assistantships were awarded; tuition waivers (partial) also available. Financial award applicants required to submit FAFSA. In 2017, 38 master's awarded. *Program availability:* Evening/weekend, 100% online. Offers business administration (MBA). *Application deadline:* Applications are processed on a rolling basis. *Application fee:* $35. Electronic applications accepted. *Application Contact:* Maria Aguirre, Student Academic Advisor, 847-628-1160, E-mail: maguirre@judsonu.edu. *Chair,* John C. Boggs, 847-628-1041, E-mail: john.boggs@judsonu.edu.

Master of Education in Literacy Program Students: 14 part-time (all women). Average age 42. 12 applicants, 100% accepted, 12 enrolled. *Faculty:* 4 full-time (2 women), 10 part-time/adjunct (9 women). Expenses: Contact institution. *Financial support:* Tuition discounts available. Financial award application deadline: 4/15; financial award applicants required to submit FAFSA. In 2017, 16 master's awarded. Offers literacy (M Ed). *Application deadline:* For fall admission, 4/15 for domestic and international students. Applications are processed on a rolling basis. *Application fee:* $55. *Application Contact:* Maria Aguirre, Student Academic Advisor, 847-628-1160, E-mail: maguirre@judsonu.edu. *Director,* Dr. Steven L. Layne, 847-628-1093, E-mail: slayne@judsonu.edu.

Master of Leadership in Ministry Program Students: 7 part-time (4 women); includes 3 minority (all Black or African American, non-Hispanic/Latino). Average age 39. 14 applicants, 93% accepted, 11 enrolled. *Faculty:* 4 full-time (2 women), 5 part-time/adjunct (1 woman). Expenses: Contact institution. *Financial support:* In 2017–18, 5 students received support. Scholarships/grants and tuition waivers available. Financial award application deadline: 8/15; financial award applicants required to submit FAFSA. In 2017, 1 master's awarded. *Program availability:* Evening/weekend, online only, blended/hybrid learning. Offers leadership in ministry (MLM). *Application deadline:* Applications are processed on a rolling basis. *Application fee:* $35. Electronic applications accepted. *Director,* Dr. David Sanders, 847-628-1052, E-mail: dsanders@judsonu.edu.

THE JUILLIARD SCHOOL, New York, NY 10023-6588

General Information Independent, coed, comprehensive institution. *Graduate housing:* Room and/or apartments available on a first-come, first-served basis to single students; on-campus housing not available to married students. Housing application deadline: 5/15.

GRADUATE UNITS

Graduate Programs Offers acting (MFA); jazz studies (Artist Diploma); music (MM, DMA, Diploma); music performance (Artist Diploma); opera studies (Artist Diploma); string quartet (Artist Diploma). Electronic applications accepted.

JUNIATA COLLEGE, Huntingdon, PA 16652-2119

General Information Independent-religious, coed, comprehensive institution. *Enrollment:* 1,495 graduate, professional, and undergraduate students; 8 full-time matriculated graduate/professional students (2 women), 1 part-time matriculated graduate/professional student. *Enrollment by degree level:* 9 master's. *Graduate housing:* On-campus housing not available. *Library facilities:* Beeghly Library. *Collection:* Books: 170,000 (physical); Serial titles: 241 (physical). Weekly public service hours: 107.

Computer facilities: 150 computers available on campus for general student use. A campuswide network can be accessed from student residence rooms and from off campus. Online class registration, access to bills are available.
Website: http://www.juniata.edu/

General Application Contact: Michele Bartol, Dean of Enrollment, 814-641-3432, E-mail: bartolm@juniata.edu.

GRADUATE UNITS

Department of Accounting, Business, and Economics Students: 8 full-time (2 women), 1 part-time (0 women). Average age 22. 9 applicants, 100% accepted, 7 enrolled. Expenses: Contact institution. In 2017, 5 master's awarded. Offers accounting (M Acc). *Application deadline:* Applications are processed on a rolling basis. *Chair,* Dr. Dominick Peruso, 814-641-3661, E-mail: peruso@juniata.edu.

KANSAS CITY UNIVERSITY OF MEDICINE AND BIOSCIENCES, Kansas City, MO 64106-1453

General Information Independent, coed, graduate-only institution. CGS member. *Graduate housing:* On-campus housing not available. *Research affiliation:* Boehringer Ingelheim (HIV/AIDS), Mylanta-Bertek (hypertension), Covance (hypertension), Novartis Pharmaceuticals (Chronic Obstructive Pulmonary Disease (COPD)).

GRADUATE UNITS

College of Biosciences *Program availability:* Part-time. Offers bioethics (MA); biomedical sciences (MS).

College of Osteopathic Medicine Offers osteopathic medicine (DO).

KANSAS STATE UNIVERSITY, Manhattan, KS 66506

General Information State-supported, coed, university. CGS member. *Graduate housing:* Rooms and/or apartments available on a first-come, first-served basis to single and married students. Housing application deadline: 2/1. *Research affiliation:* Visteon Corporation, Midwest Research Institute, NASA-Research Center, U.S. Grain Marketing Research Laboratory.

GRADUATE UNITS

Graduate School *Program availability:* Part-time, evening/weekend, online learning. Electronic applications accepted.

College of Agriculture *Program availability:* Part-time, online learning. Offers agricultural economics (MAB, MS, PhD); agricultural education and communication (MS); agriculture (MAB, MS, PhD, Certificate); crop science (MS, PhD); entomology (MS, PhD); food science (MS, PhD); genetics (MS, PhD); grain science and industry (MS, PhD); grassland management (Certificate); horticulture and natural resources (MS, PhD); meat science (MS, PhD); monogastric nutrition (MS, PhD); physiology (MS, PhD); plant breeding and genetics (MS, PhD); plant pathology (MS, PhD); range and forage science (MS, PhD); ruminant nutrition (MS, PhD); soil and environmental science (MS, PhD); weed science (MS, PhD). Electronic applications accepted.

College of Architecture, Planning and Design *Program availability:* Part-time. Offers architecture (M Arch, MS Arch); architecture, planning and design (M Arch, MIAPD, MLA, MRCP, MS, MS Arch, PhD); community development (MS); environmental design and planning (PhD); interior architecture and product design (MIAPD); landscape architecture (MLA); regional and community planning (MRCP). Electronic applications accepted.

College of Arts and Sciences *Program availability:* Part-time, online learning. Offers advertising (MS); art (MFA); arts and sciences (MA, MFA, MM, MPA, MS, PhD, Graduate Certificate); biochemistry and molecular biophysics (MS, PhD); biology (MS); chemistry (MS, PhD); communication studies (MA); community journalism (MS); economics (MA, PhD); English (MA); gender, women and sexuality studies (Graduate Certificate); geographic information science (Graduate Certificate); geography (MA, PhD); geology (MS); global communication (MS); health communication (MS); history (MA, PhD); literature (MA); mathematics (MS, PhD, Graduate Certificate); media management (MS); music, theatre and dance (MA, MM); physics (MS, PhD); political science (MA); psychological sciences (MS, PhD); public administration (MPA); public relations (MS); second language acquisition (MA); security studies (MA, PhD); sociology (MA, PhD); statistics (MS, PhD, Graduate Certificate); technical writing and professional communication (Graduate Certificate). Electronic applications accepted.

College of Business *Program availability:* Part-time. Offers accounting (M Acc); business (M Acc, MBA, Certificate); data analytics (MBA); finance (MBA); management (MBA); marketing (MBA); technology entrepreneurship (MBA). Electronic applications accepted.

College of Education *Program availability:* Part-time, evening/weekend, online learning. Offers academic advising (MS, Certificate); adult learning (Certificate); counseling and student development (MS); curriculum and instruction (Ed D, PhD); digital teaching and learning (MS); education (MS, Ed D, PhD, Certificate); educational computing, design and online learning (MS); educational leadership (MS, Ed D, PhD); elementary/middle level curriculum and instruction (MS); leadership dynamics for adult learners (Certificate); online learning (Certificate); qualitative research (Certificate); reading specialist endorsement (MS); reading/language arts (MS); social justice education (Certificate); special education (MS, Ed D); special education, counseling, and student affairs (PhD); teacher leader/school improvement (MS); teaching and learning (Certificate); teaching English as a second language for adult learners (Certificate). Electronic applications accepted.

College of Engineering *Program availability:* Part-time, online learning. Offers architectural engineering and construction science (MS); biological and agricultural engineering (MS, PhD); chemical engineering (MS, PhD, Graduate Certificate); civil engineering (MS, PhD); computer science (MS, MSE, PhD); electrical engineering (MS); engineering (MEM, MS, MSE, PhD, Graduate Certificate); engineering management (MEM); environmental engineering (MS, PhD); geotechnical engineering (MS, PhD); industrial engineering (MS); mechanical engineering (MS); nuclear engineering (PhD); operations research (MS); structural engineering (MS, PhD); transportation engineering (MS, PhD); water resources engineering (MS, PhD). Electronic applications accepted.

College of Human Ecology *Program availability:* Part-time, online learning. Offers apparel and textiles (MS, PhD); applied family sciences (MS, PhD); communication sciences and disorders (MS); conflict resolution (Graduate Certificate); couple and family therapy (MS, PhD); dietetics (MS); early childhood education (MS); family and community service (MS); gerontology (MS, Graduate Certificate); hospitality administration (PhD); hospitality and dietetics administration (MS); human ecology (MS, PhD, Graduate Certificate); human nutrition (PhD); kinesiology (MS, PhD); life-span human development (MS, PhD); nutrition, dietetics and sensory sciences (MS); nutritional sciences (PhD); personal financial planning (MS, PhD, Graduate Certificate); public health nutrition (PhD); public health physical activity (PhD); sensory analysis and consumer behavior (PhD); youth development (MS, Graduate Certificate). Electronic applications accepted.

College of Technology and Aviation *Program availability:* Part-time, evening/weekend, 100% online. Offers technology and aviation (MT). Electronic applications accepted.

College of Veterinary Medicine Offers biomedical science (MS); clinical sciences (MPH, Graduate Certificate); diagnostic medicine/pathobiology (PhD); physiology (PhD); veterinary medicine (MPH, MS, DVM, PhD, Graduate Certificate). Electronic applications accepted.

School of Applied and Interdisciplinary Studies *Program availability:* Part-time, 100% online, blended/hybrid learning. Offers applied science and technology (PSM); professional interdisciplinary sciences (Graduate Certificate); professional skills for STEM practitioners (Graduate Certificate). Electronic applications accepted.

KANSAS WESLEYAN UNIVERSITY, Salina, KS 67401-6196

General Information Independent-religious, coed, comprehensive institution. *Graduate housing:* Rooms and/or apartments available to single and married students.

GRADUATE UNITS

Program in Business Administration *Program availability:* Part-time, evening/weekend. Offers business administration (MBA); sports management (MBA).

KEAN UNIVERSITY, Union, NJ 07083

General Information State-supported, coed, university. *Enrollment:* 14,226 graduate, professional, and undergraduate students; 977 full-time matriculated graduate/professional students (759 women), 774 part-time matriculated graduate/professional students (593 women). *Enrollment by degree level:* 1,571 master's, 149 doctoral, 31 other advanced degrees. *Graduate faculty:* 260 full-time (137 women). Tuition, state resident: full-time $13,419; part-time $653 per credit. Tuition, nonresident: full-time $18,188; part-time $801 per credit. *Required fees:* $3382; $154 per credit. Tuition and fees vary according to course level, course load, degree level and program. *Graduate housing:* Room and/or apartments available on a first-come, first-served basis to single students; on-campus housing not available to married students. Housing application deadline: 5/1. *Student services:* Campus employment opportunities, campus safety program, career counseling, child daycare facilities, exercise/wellness program, free psychological counseling, grant writing training, international student services, low-cost health insurance, multicultural affairs office, services for students with disabilities, teacher training, writing training. *Library facilities:* Nancy Thompson Library. *Collection:* Books: 208,670 (physical), 11,430 (digital/electronic); Serial titles: 58,034 (digital/electronic); Databases: 249. Weekly public service hours: 102. *Research affiliation:* Robert Wood Johnson Foundation (the effect of tobacco control policy), Institute of Vertebrate Paleontology and Paleoanthropology (paleoanthropology), Shodor Foundation (intelligent Internet search engines for science research and education), New Jersey Institute of Technology (partitioning to support auditing and extending the UMLS), National Bureau of Economic Research (alcoholic advertising and youth).

Computer facilities: 1,700 computers available on campus for general student use. A campuswide network can be accessed from student residence rooms and from off campus. Online class registration is available.
Website: http://www.kean.edu/

General Application Contact: Helen Ramirez, Associate Director, 908-737-7137, E-mail: hramirez@kean.edu.

GRADUATE UNITS

College of Business and Public Management Students: 137 full-time (92 women), 91 part-time (61 women); includes 151 minority (76 Black or African American, non-Hispanic/Latino; 21 Asian, non-Hispanic/Latino; 49 Hispanic/Latino; 1 Native Hawaiian or other Pacific Islander, non-Hispanic/Latino; 4 Two or more races, non-Hispanic/Latino), 28 international. Average age 31. 115 applicants, 95% accepted, 65 enrolled. *Faculty:* 27 full-time (6 women). Expenses: Contact institution. *Financial support:* Federal Work-Study, scholarships/grants, and unspecified assistantships available. Financial award applicants required to submit FAFSA. In 2017, 114 master's awarded. *Program availability:* Part-time. Offers accounting (MS); business and public management (MA, MBA, MPA, MS); criminal justice (MA); executive management (MBA); global management (MBA); health services administration (MPA); non-profit management (MPA); public administration (MPA). *Application deadline:* For fall admission, 6/30 for domestic and international students; for spring admission, 12/1 for domestic and international students. Applications are processed on a rolling basis. *Application fee:* $75. Electronic applications accepted. *Application Contact:* Pedro Lopes, Admissions Counselor, 908-737-7100, E-mail: gradadmissions@kean.edu. *Acting Dean,* Dr. Geofrey Mills, 908-737-4704, Fax: 908-737-4765, E-mail: gmills@kean.edu.

College of Education Students: 27 full-time (13 women), 127 part-time (107 women); includes 60 minority (12 Black or African American, non-Hispanic/Latino; 14 Asian, non-Hispanic/Latino; 34 Hispanic/Latino), 2 international. Average age 33. 55 applicants, 98% accepted, 41 enrolled. *Faculty:* 43 full-time (26 women). Expenses: Contact institution. *Financial support:* Scholarships/grants and unspecified assistantships available. Financial award applicants required to submit FAFSA. In 2017, 66 master's awarded. *Program availability:* Part-time. Offers administration in early childhood and family studies (MA); advanced curriculum and teaching (MA); autism and developmental disabilities (MA); bilingual/bicultural education (MA); classroom instruction - P-3 certification (MA); education (MA, MS); exercise science (MS); Hindi and Urdu language pedagogy (MA); learning and behavioral disabilities (MA); teaching English as a second language (MA). *Application deadline:* For fall admission, 6/30 for domestic and international students; for spring admission, 12/1 for domestic and international students. Applications are processed on a rolling basis. *Application fee:* $75. Electronic applications accepted. *Application Contact:* Brittany Gerstenhaber, Admissions Counselor, 908-737-7100, E-mail: gradadmissions@kean.edu. *Acting Dean*, Dr. Anthony Pitmann, 908-737-3750, Fax: 908-737-3760, E-mail: polirsts@kean.edu.

College of Liberal Arts Students: 152 full-time (122 women), 118 part-time (85 women); includes 140 minority (61 Black or African American, non-Hispanic/Latino; 17 Asian, non-Hispanic/Latino; 54 Hispanic/Latino; 2 Native Hawaiian or other Pacific Islander, non-Hispanic/Latino; 6 Two or more races, non-Hispanic/Latino), 5 international. Average age 30. 180 applicants, 89% accepted, 109 enrolled. *Faculty:* 84 full-time (44 women). Expenses: Contact institution. *Financial support:* Scholarships/grants and unspecified assistantships available. Financial award applicants required to submit FAFSA. In 2017, 75 master's awarded. *Program availability:* Part-time. Offers communication studies (MA); English writing studies (MA); forensic psychology (MA); Holocaust and genocide studies (MA); human behavior and organizational psychology (MA); initial teaching certification (MA); liberal arts (MA); marriage and family therapy (MA); psychological services (MA); studio (MA); supervision (MA). *Application deadline:* For fall admission, 6/30 for domestic and international students; for spring admission, 12/1 for domestic and international students. Applications are processed on a rolling basis. *Application fee:* $75. Electronic applications accepted. *Application Contact:* Amy Clark, Program Assistant, 908-737-7100, E-mail: gradadmissions@kean.edu. *Acting Dean*, Dr. Jonathan Mercantini, 908-737-0430, Fax: 908-737-0435, E-mail: jmercant@kean.edu.

College of Natural, Applied and Health Sciences Students: 29 full-time (17 women), 75 part-time (64 women); includes 48 minority (32 Black or African American, non-Hispanic/Latino; 13 Asian, non-Hispanic/Latino; 2 Hispanic/Latino; 1 Two or more races, non-Hispanic/Latino), 17 international. Average age 43. 38 applicants, 71% accepted, 15 enrolled. *Faculty:* 36 full-time (20 women). Expenses: Contact institution. *Financial support:* Scholarships/grants and unspecified assistantships available. Financial award applicants required to submit FAFSA. In 2017, 65 master's awarded. *Program availability:* Part-time. Offers clinical management (MSN); community health nursing (MSN); computer information systems (MS); educational leadership (PhD); natural, applied and health sciences (MS, MSN, PhD). *Application deadline:* For fall admission, 6/30 for domestic and international students; for spring admission, 12/1 for domestic and international students. Applications are processed on a rolling basis. *Application fee:* $75. Electronic applications accepted. *Application Contact:* Pedro Lopes, Admissions Counselor, 908-737-7100, E-mail: gradadmissions@kean.edu. *Dean*, Dr. George Chang, 908-737-3600, Fax: 908-737-3606, E-mail: gchang@kean.edu.

Nathan Weiss Graduate College Students: 596 full-time (489 women), 350 part-time (270 women); includes 409 minority (180 Black or African American, non-Hispanic/Latino; 2 American Indian or Alaska Native, non-Hispanic/Latino; 34 Asian, non-Hispanic/Latino; 174 Hispanic/Latino; 19 Two or more races, non-Hispanic/Latino), 5 international. Average age 31. 1,544 applicants, 31% accepted, 288 enrolled. *Faculty:* 49 full-time (33 women). Expenses: Contact institution. *Financial support:* Scholarships/grants and unspecified assistantships available. Financial award applicants required to submit FAFSA. In 2017, 246 master's, 17 doctorates, 11 other advanced degrees awarded. *Program availability:* Part-time. Offers alcohol and drug abuse counseling (MA); clinical mental health counseling (MA); combined school and clinical psychology (Psy D); educational leadership (Ed D); occupational therapy (MS); physical therapy (DPT); school business administrator (MA); school counseling (MA); school psychology (Diploma); social work (MSW); speech-language pathology (MA, SLPD); supervisor and principal (MA); supervisors, principals, and school business administrators (MA). *Application deadline:* For fall admission, 6/1 for domestic and international students; for spring admission, 12/1 for domestic and international students. Applications are processed on a rolling basis. *Application fee:* $75. Electronic applications accepted. *Application Contact:* Ann-Marie Kay, Associate Director, Graduate Admissions, 908-737-7100, E-mail: grad-adm@kean.edu. *Dean*, Dr. Jeffrey Beck, 908-737-5902, Fax: 908-737-5905, E-mail: jbeck@kean.edu.

New Jersey Center for Science, Technology and Mathematics Students: 36 full-time (26 women), 13 part-time (6 women); includes 26 minority (8 Black or African American, non-Hispanic/Latino; 8 Asian, non-Hispanic/Latino; 10 Hispanic/Latino), 5 international. Average age 26. 18 applicants, 100% accepted, 12 enrolled. *Faculty:* 8 full-time (2 women). Expenses: Contact institution. *Financial support:* Scholarships/grants and unspecified assistantships available. Financial award applicants required to submit FAFSA. In 2017, 24 master's awarded. Offers biotechnology science (MS); instruction and curriculum (MA). *Application deadline:* For fall admission, 6/30 for domestic and international students; for spring admission, 12/1 for domestic and international students. Applications are processed on a rolling basis. *Application fee:* $75. Electronic applications accepted. *Application Contact:* Pedro Lopes, Admissions Counselor, 908-737-7100, E-mail: gradcoordinatorcdd@kean.edu. *Dean*, Dr. Keith Bostian, 908-737-7200, E-mail: kbostian@kean.edu.

KECK GRADUATE INSTITUTE, Claremont, CA 91711

General Information Independent, coed, graduate-only institution. CGS member.

GRADUATE UNITS

School of Applied Life Sciences Offers applied life sciences (PhD); bioscience (MBS); bioscience management (Certificate). Electronic applications accepted.

School of Pharmacy Offers pharmacy (Pharm D).

KEENE STATE COLLEGE, Keene, NH 03435

General Information State-supported, coed, comprehensive institution. *Enrollment:* 3,866 graduate, professional, and undergraduate students; 20 full-time matriculated graduate/professional students (14 women), 42 part-time matriculated graduate/professional students (20 women). *Enrollment by degree level:* 58 master's, 4 other advanced degrees. *Graduate faculty:* 6 full-time (3 women), 7 part-time/adjunct (2 women). Tuition, state resident: full-time $9360; part-time $520 per credit. Tuition, nonresident: full-time $10,260; part-time $570 per credit. *Required fees:* $1908; $106 per credit. Tuition and fees vary according to course load. *Graduate housing:* Room and/or apartments available on a first-come, first-served basis to single students; on-campus housing not available to married students. Typical cost: $7158 per year ($10,736 including board). Room and board charges vary according to board plan and housing facility selected. Housing application deadline: 5/1. *Student services:* Campus employment opportunities, campus safety program, career counseling, exercise/wellness program, free psychological counseling, grant writing training, international student services, multicultural affairs office, services for students with disabilities, teacher training, writing training. *Library facilities:* Mason Library. *Collection:* Books: 247,720 (physical), 319,081 (digital/electronic); Serial titles: 142 (physical), 73,114 (digital/electronic); Databases: 92. Weekly public service hours: 102; students can reserve study rooms.

Computer facilities: Computer purchase and lease plans are available. 600 computers available on campus for general student use. A campuswide network can be accessed from student residence rooms and from off campus. Online class registration is available. Website: http://www.keene.edu/

General Application Contact: Carl Ditkoff, Graduate Program Assistant, 603-358-2497, E-mail: kscgraduatestudies@keene.edu.

GRADUATE UNITS

School of Professional and Graduate Studies Students: 20 full-time (14 women), 42 part-time (20 women); includes 2 minority (1 Black or African American, non-Hispanic/Latino; 1 Asian, non-Hispanic/Latino), 1 international. Average age 31. 33 applicants, 58% accepted, 17 enrolled. *Faculty:* 6 full-time (3 women), 7 part-time/adjunct (2 women). Expenses: Contact institution. *Financial support:* In 2017–18, 19 students received support. Career-related internships or fieldwork, Federal Work-Study, institutionally sponsored loans, scholarships/grants, and unspecified assistantships available. Support available to part-time students. Financial award application deadline: 3/1; financial award applicants required to submit FAFSA. In 2017, 39 master's awarded. *Program availability:* Part-time, evening/weekend. Offers curriculum and instruction (M Ed); education leadership (PMC); educational leadership (M Ed); school counselor (M Ed, PMC); special education (M Ed). *Application deadline:* For fall admission, 4/1 for domestic and international students; for spring admission, 11/1 for domestic and international students; for summer admission, 3/1 for domestic and international students. Applications are processed on a rolling basis. *Application fee:* $50. Electronic applications accepted. *Application Contact:* Carl Ditkoff, Graduate Program Assistant, 603-358-2497, E-mail: kscgraduatestudies@keene.edu. *Dean of Professional and Graduate Studies*, Dr. Karrie Kalich, 603-358-2885, E-mail: kkalich@keene.edu.

KEHILATH YAKOV RABBINICAL SEMINARY, Ossining, NY 10562

General Information Independent-religious, men only, comprehensive institution.

GRADUATE UNITS

Graduate Programs

KEISER UNIVERSITY, Fort Lauderdale, FL 33309

General Information Independent, coed, university. *Student services:* Campus employment opportunities, campus safety program, career counseling, writing training. *Library facilities:* Keiser University Library. *Collection:* Books: 150,394 (physical), 145,000 (digital/electronic); Serial titles: 188 (physical), 29 (digital/electronic); Databases: 257.

Computer facilities: A campuswide network can be accessed from off campus. Online class registration is available.
Website: http://www.keiseruniversity.edu/

General Application Contact: Graduate School, 888-753-4737, E-mail: graduateschool@keiseruniversity.edu.

GRADUATE UNITS

Doctor of Business Administration Program Expenses: Contact institution. Offers global business (DBA); global management (DBA); marketing (DBA).

Ed S in Educational Leadership Program Expenses: Contact institution. Offers educational leadership (Ed S).

Ed S in Instructional Design and Technology Program Expenses: Contact institution. Offers instructional design and technology (Ed S).

Joint MS Ed/MBA Program Expenses: Contact institution.

MA in Criminal Justice Program Expenses: Contact institution. *Program availability:* Part-time, online learning. Offers criminal justice (MA).

MA in Homeland Security Program Expenses: Contact institution. Offers homeland security (MA).

Master of Accountancy Program Expenses: Contact institution. Offers forensic accounting (M Acc).

Master of Business Administration Program Expenses: Contact institution. *Program availability:* Part-time, online learning. Offers accounting (MBA); health services administration (MBA); international business (MBA); management (MBA); marketing (MBA); technology management (MBA). All concentrations except technology management also offered in Mandarin. *Department Chair*, Yan Luo-Beitler.

Master of Science in Education Program Expenses: Contact institution. *Program availability:* Part-time, online learning. Offers allied health teaching and leadership (MS Ed); career college administration (MS Ed); leadership (MS Ed); online teaching and learning (MS Ed); teaching and learning (MS Ed). *Chair of Graduate Programs*, Brian Keintz.

Master of Science in Nursing Program Expenses: Contact institution. Offers family nurse practitioner (MSN); nursing (MSN).

MS in Information Security Program Expenses: Contact institution. Offers information security (MS).

MS in Information Technology Leadership Program Expenses: Contact institution. Offers information technology leadership (MS).

MS in Occupational Therapy Program Expenses: Contact institution. Offers occupational therapy (MS). *Program Chair*, Dr. Tamara Pinchevsky-Font.

MS in Organizational Leadership Program Offers organizational leadership (MSOL).

MS in Organizational Psychology Program Expenses: Contact institution. Offers organizational psychology (MS).

MS in Physician Assistant Program Expenses: Contact institution. Offers physician assistant (MS). *Program Director*, Christine Kessler, 888-753-4737.

MS in Psychology Program Expenses: Contact institution. Offers psychology (MS).

PhD in Educational Leadership Program Expenses: Contact institution. Offers educational leadership (PhD).

PhD in Industrial and Organizational Psychology Program Expenses: Contact institution. Offers industrial and organizational psychology (PhD). *Chair*, Craig D. Marker.

PhD in Instructional Design and Technology Program Expenses: Contact institution. Offers instructional design and technology (PhD).

PhD in Psychology Program Expenses: Contact institution. Offers psychology (PhD).

KENNESAW STATE UNIVERSITY, Kennesaw, GA 30144

General Information State-supported, coed, comprehensive institution. CGS member. *Graduate housing:* Room and/or apartments available on a first-come, first-served basis to single students; on-campus housing not available to married students. *Student services:* Campus employment opportunities, campus safety program, career counseling, exercise/wellness program, free psychological counseling, international student services, low-cost health insurance, multicultural affairs office, services for students with disabilities, teacher training, writing training. *Library facilities:* KSU Library System plus 1 other. *Collection:* Books: 439,577 (physical), 667,799 (digital/electronic); Serial titles: 1,281 (physical), 114,983 (digital/electronic); Databases: 408. Weekly public service hours: 95; students can reserve study rooms.

Computer facilities: Computer purchase and lease plans are available. 4,500 computers available on campus for general student use. A campuswide network can be accessed from student residence rooms and from off campus. Online class registration is available.
Website: http://www.kennesaw.edu/

General Application Contact: Admissions Counselor, 770-420-4377, Fax: 770-423-6885, E-mail: ksugrad@kennesaw.edu.

GRADUATE UNITS

Analytics and Data Science Institute Expenses: Contact institution. Offers analytics and data science (PhD). *Application fee:* $60. *Application Contact:* Admissions Counselor, 770-420-4377, Fax: 770-423-6885, E-mail: ksugrad@kennesaw.edu. *Program Director,* Sherrill Hayes, 470-578-6499, E-mail: shayes32@kennesaw.edu.

Bagwell College of Education Expenses: Contact institution. *Financial support:* Research assistantships with tuition reimbursements, Federal Work-Study, and unspecified assistantships available. Support available to part-time students. Financial award application deadline: 4/1; financial award applicants required to submit FAFSA. *Program availability:* Part-time. Offers art education (MAT); curriculum and instruction (Ed S); early childhood education (M Ed); education (M Ed, MAT, Ed D, Ed S); educational leadership (M Ed); instructional technology (M Ed, Ed D, Ed S); leadership for learning (Ed D, Ed S); middle grades and secondary education (Ed D, Ed S); reading (M Ed); secondary English (MAT); secondary mathematics (MAT); secondary science (MAT); special education (M Ed, Ed D, Ed S); teacher leadership (M Ed, Ed D, Ed S); teaching English to speakers of other languages (MAT). *Application deadline:* For fall admission, 6/1 for domestic and international students; for spring admission, 10/1 for domestic and international students; for summer admission, 4/15 for domestic and international students. Applications are processed on a rolling basis. *Application fee:* $60. Electronic applications accepted. *Application Contact:* Cynthia Reed, Dean, 470-578-6117, Fax: 470-578-6567. *Dean,* Cynthia Reed, 470-578-6117, Fax: 470-578-6567.

Coles College of Business Expenses: Contact institution. *Financial support:* Research assistantships with tuition reimbursements, Federal Work-Study, and unspecified assistantships available. Support available to part-time students. Financial award application deadline: 4/1; financial award applicants required to submit FAFSA. *Program availability:* Part-time, evening/weekend. Offers accounting (M Acc); business (EMBA, M Acc, MBA, MS, MSIS, DBA); business administration (EMBA, MBA, DBA); health management and informatics (MS); information systems (MSIS). *Application deadline:* For fall admission, 6/1 for domestic and international students; for spring admission, 12/1 for domestic and international students; for summer admission, 5/1 for domestic and international students. Applications are processed on a rolling basis. *Application fee:* $60. Electronic applications accepted. *Application Contact:* Timothy Isles, Admissions Counselor, 470-578-4470, Fax: 470-578-9172, E-mail: ksugrad@kennesaw.edu. *Dean,* Dr. Kathryn Schwaig, 470-578-6425, E-mail: kschwaig@kennesaw.edu.

College of Architecture and Construction Management Expenses: Contact institution. *Financial support:* Research assistantships with tuition reimbursements, career-related internships or fieldwork, scholarships/grants, and unspecified assistantships available. Support available to part-time students. Financial award application deadline: 5/1; financial award applicants required to submit FAFSA. *Program availability:* Part-time, evening/weekend. Offers architecture (MS Arch); architecture and construction management (MS, MS Arch); construction management (MS). *Application deadline:* For fall admission, 7/1 priority date for domestic students, 5/1 priority date for international students; for spring admission, 11/1 priority date for domestic students, 9/1 priority date for international students. Applications are processed on a rolling basis. *Application fee:* $60. Electronic applications accepted. *Application Contact:* Richard Cole, Dean, 470-578-5481, E-mail: rcole@kennesaw.edu. *Dean,* Richard Cole, 470-578-5481, E-mail: rcole@kennesaw.edu.

College of Computing and Software Engineering Expenses: Contact institution. *Financial support:* Research assistantships with full and partial tuition reimbursements, teaching assistantships with full tuition reimbursements, career-related internships or fieldwork, scholarships/grants, and unspecified assistantships available. Support available to part-time students. Financial award application deadline: 5/1; financial award applicants required to submit FAFSA. *Program availability:* Part-time, evening/weekend, online learning. Offers computer science (MS); computing and software engineering (MS, MSIT, MSSWE, Graduate Certificate, Postbaccalaureate Certificate); data management and analytics (Graduate Certificate); health information technology (Postbaccalaureate Certificate); information technology (MSIT); information technology foundations (Postbaccalaureate Certificate); information technology security (Graduate Certificate); software engineering (MSSWE, Graduate Certificate); software engineering foundations (Graduate Certificate). *Application deadline:* For fall admission, 7/1 priority date for domestic students, 5/1 priority date for international students; for spring admission, 11/1 priority date for domestic students, 9/1 priority date for international students. Applications are processed on a rolling basis. *Application fee:* $60. Electronic applications accepted. *Application Contact:* Dr. Jon Preston, Dean, 470-578-5572, E-mail: jprest20@kennesaw.edu. *Dean,* Dr. Jon Preston, 470-578-5572, E-mail: jprest20@kennesaw.edu.

College of Humanities and Social Sciences Expenses: Contact institution. *Financial support:* Research assistantships with full tuition reimbursements, teaching assistantships with full tuition reimbursements, Federal Work-Study, and unspecified assistantships available. Support available to part-time students. Financial award application deadline: 4/1; financial award applicants required to submit FAFSA. *Program availability:* Part-time, evening/weekend. Offers American studies (MA); conflict management (MSCM); criminal justice (MS); humanities and social sciences (MA, MAPW, MPA, MS, MSCM, PhD); integrated global communication (MA); international conflict management (PhD); international policy management (MS); professional writing (MAPW); public administration (MPA). *Application deadline:* For fall admission, 6/1 priority date for domestic and international students; for spring admission, 10/1 priority date for domestic and international students. Applications are processed on a rolling basis. *Application fee:* $60. Electronic applications accepted. *Application Contact:* Admissions Counselor, 470-578-4377, Fax: 470-578-9172, E-mail: ksugrad@kennesaw.edu. *Interim Dean,* Dr. Kerwin Swint, 470-578-6124, E-mail: kswint@kennesaw.edu.

College of Science and Mathematics Expenses: Contact institution. *Financial support:* Research assistantships with full tuition reimbursements, Federal Work-Study, and unspecified assistantships available. Support available to part-time students. Financial award application deadline: 4/1; financial award applicants required to submit FAFSA. *Program availability:* Part-time, online learning. Offers applied statistics (MSAS); biochemistry (MS); chemistry (MS); integrative biology (MS); science and mathematics (MS, MSAS). *Application deadline:* For fall admission, 6/1 for domestic and international students; for spring admission, 10/1 for domestic and international students. Applications are processed on a rolling basis. *Application fee:* $60. Electronic applications accepted. *Application Contact:* Admissions Counselor, 470-578-4377, Fax: 470-578-9172, E-mail: ksugrad@kennesaw.edu. *Dean,* Dr. Mark Anderson, 470-578-6160, E-mail: mande126@kennesaw.edu.

Southern Polytechnic College of Engineering and Engineering Technology Expenses: Contact institution. *Financial support:* Research assistantships with tuition reimbursements, teaching assistantships with partial tuition reimbursements, career-related internships or fieldwork, scholarships/grants, and unspecified assistantships available. Support available to part-time students. Financial award application deadline: 5/1; financial award applicants required to submit FAFSA. *Program availability:* Part-time, evening/weekend, online learning. Offers electrical engineering (MS); engineering and engineering technology (MS); engineering management (MS); environmental engineering (MS); geotechnical engineering (MS); mechanical engineering (MS); quality assurance (MS); structural engineering (MS); systems engineering (MS); transportation and pavement engineering (MS); water resources engineering (MS). *Application deadline:* For fall admission, 7/1 priority date for domestic students, 5/1 priority date for international students; for spring admission, 11/1 priority date for domestic students, 9/1 priority date for international students. Applications are processed on a rolling basis. *Application fee:* $60. Electronic applications accepted. *Application Contact:* Dr. Renee Butler, Interim Dean, 678-915-7205, Fax: 678-915-7134. *Interim Dean,* Dr. Renee Butler, 678-915-7205, Fax: 678-915-7134.

University College Expenses: Contact institution. Offers first-year studies (MS). *Application Contact:* Admissions Counselor, 770-420-4377, Fax: 770-423-6885, E-mail: ksugrad@kennesaw.edu. *Program Director,* Dr. Richard S. Mosholder, 470-578-7866, E-mail: msfys@kennesaw.edu.

WellStar College of Health and Human Services Expenses: Contact institution. *Financial support:* Research assistantships with full tuition reimbursements and Federal Work-Study available. Support available to part-time students. Financial award application deadline: 4/1; financial award applicants required to submit FAFSA. *Program availability:* Part-time, evening/weekend, online learning. Offers exercise physiology (MS); health and human services (MS, MSN, MSW, DNS); nursing administration (MSN); nursing education (MSN); nursing science (DNS); primary care nurse practitioner (MSN); social work (MSW); sport management (MS). *Application deadline:* For fall admission, 6/1 for domestic and international students. *Application fee:* $60. Electronic applications accepted. *Application Contact:* Jerryl Morris, Admissions Counselor, 470-578-2030, Fax: 470-578-9172, E-mail: ksugrad@kennesaw.edu. *Dean,* Dr. Mark Tillman, 470-578-6565, E-mail: mtillm13@kennesaw.edu.

KENRICK-GLENNON SEMINARY, St. Louis, MO 63119-4330

General Information Independent-religious, men only, graduate-only institution. *Graduate housing:* Room and/or apartments available to single students; on-campus housing not available to married students.

GRADUATE UNITS

Graduate and Professional Programs Offers theology (M Div, MA).

KENT STATE UNIVERSITY, Kent, OH 44242-0001

General Information State-supported, coed, university. CGS member. *Enrollment:* 28,972 graduate, professional, and undergraduate students; 3,122 full-time matriculated graduate/professional students (1,848 women), 2,413 part-time matriculated graduate/professional students (1,727 women). *Enrollment by degree level:* 3,742 master's, 1,643 doctoral, 150 other advanced degrees. *Graduate faculty:* 955. *International tuition:* $18,544 full-time. Tuition, state resident: full-time $11,310; part-time $515 per credit hour. Tuition, nonresident: full-time $20,396; part-time $928 per credit hour. *Graduate housing:* Room and/or apartments available on a first-come, first-served basis to single students; on-campus housing not available to married students. *Student services:* Campus employment opportunities, campus safety program, career counseling, child daycare facilities, exercise/wellness program, free psychological counseling, grant writing training, international student services, low-cost health insurance, multicultural affairs office, services for students with disabilities, teacher training, writing training. *Library facilities:* Kent State University Main Library plus 4 others. *Collection:* Books: 3 million (physical), 1.2 million (digital/electronic); Serial titles: 35,857 (physical), 14,996 (digital/electronic); Databases: 355. Weekly public service hours: 146; study areas open 24 hours, 5–7 days a week; students can reserve study rooms.

Computer facilities: Computer purchase and lease plans are available. A campuswide network can be accessed from student residence rooms and from off campus. Online class registration is available.
Website: http://www.kent.edu/

General Application Contact: Lana Whitehead, Director of Graduate Admissions, 330-672-6336, E-mail: lwhiteh2@kent.edu.

GRADUATE UNITS

College of Aeronautics and Engineering Students: 73 full-time (23 women), 33 part-time (6 women); includes 2 minority (both Hispanic/Latino), 81 international. Average age 26. 161 applicants, 79% accepted, 21 enrolled. *Faculty:* 14 full-time (0 women), 5 part-time/adjunct (1 woman). Expenses: Contact institution. *Financial support:* Research assistantships, teaching assistantships, career-related internships or fieldwork, Federal Work-Study, scholarships/grants, and unspecified assistantships available. Financial award application deadline: 2/1; financial award applicants required to submit FAFSA. In 2017, 117 master's awarded. *Program availability:* Part-time. Offers technology (MTC). *Application deadline:* For fall admission, 7/23 for domestic and international students; for spring admission, 12/14 for domestic and international students; for summer admission, 4/30 for domestic and international students. Applications are processed on a rolling basis. *Application fee:* $45 ($70 for international students). Electronic applications accepted. *Application Contact:* Richard Mangrum, Coordinator, Graduate Program, 330-672-1933, E-mail: rmangum@kent.edu. *Dean,* Robert G. Sines, Jr., 330-672-9780, E-mail: rsines@kent.edu.

College of Architecture and Environmental Design Students: 70 full-time (27 women), 13 part-time (7 women); includes 8 minority (1 Black or African American, non-Hispanic/Latino; 1 Asian, non-Hispanic/Latino; 4 Hispanic/Latino; 2 Two or more races, non-Hispanic/Latino), 13 international. Average age 26. 100 applicants, 82% accepted, 57 enrolled. *Faculty:* 19 full-time (2 women), 15 part-time/adjunct (6 women). Expenses: Contact institution. *Financial support:* Research assistantships with full tuition reimbursements, teaching assistantships with full tuition reimbursements, Federal Work-Study, scholarships/grants, and unspecified assistantships available. Financial award application deadline: 2/1; financial award applicants required to submit FAFSA. In 2017, 59 master's awarded. *Program availability:* Part-time. Offers architecture (M Arch); architecture and environmental design (MS); health care design (MHCD); landscape architecture (MLA); urban design (MUD). *Application deadline:* Applications are processed on a rolling basis. *Application fee:* $45 ($70 for international students). Electronic applications accepted. *Application Contact:* Johnathan Fleming, Assistant Professor and Director, Master of Architecture, 330-672-0934, E-mail: jpflemi1@kent.edu. *Dean,* Mark Mistur, E-mail: mmistur1@kent.edu.

College of Arts and Sciences Students: 895 full-time (461 women), 281 part-time (159 women); includes 127 minority (55 Black or African American, non-Hispanic/Latino; 1 American Indian or Alaska Native, non-Hispanic/Latino; 26 Asian, non-Hispanic/Latino; 22 Hispanic/Latino; 23 Two or more races, non-Hispanic/Latino), 398 international. Average age 31. 1,252 applicants, 44% accepted, 261 enrolled. *Faculty:* 306 full-time (113 women), 47 part-time/adjunct (17 women). Expenses: Contact institution. *Financial support:* Fellowships with full tuition reimbursements, research assistantships with full tuition reimbursements, teaching assistantships with full tuition reimbursements, career-related internships or fieldwork, Federal Work-Study, scholarships/grants, and unspecified assistantships available. Financial award application deadline: 2/1; financial award applicants required to submit FAFSA. In 2017, 298 master's, 95 doctorates awarded. *Program availability:* Part-time, online learning. Offers anthropology (MA); applied geology (PhD); applied mathematics (MA, MS, PhD); arts and sciences (MA, MFA, MGIS, MLS, MPA, MS, PhD); biological sciences (MA, MS, PhD); chemical physics (MS, PhD); chemistry (MA, MS, PhD); clinical psychology (MA, PhD); computer science (MA, MS, PhD); creative writing (MFA); criminology and criminal justice (MA); English (MA, PhD); English for teachers (MA); experimental psychology (MA, PhD); French (MA); geographic information science (MGIS); geography (MA, PhD); geology (MS); German (MA); history (MA, PhD); Latin (MA); literature and writing (MA); mathematics for secondary teachers (MA); philosophy (MA); physics (MA, MS, PhD); political science (MA, PhD); public administration (MPA); pure mathematics (MA, MS, PhD); rhetoric and composition (PhD); sociology (MA, PhD); Spanish (MA); teaching English as a second language (MA); translation (MA); translation studies (PhD). *Application deadline:* Applications are processed on a rolling basis. *Application fee:* $45 ($70 for international students). Electronic applications accepted. *Application Contact:* Dr. Manfred Van Dulman, Associate Dean, Graduate Studies, 330-672-8973, E-mail: mvandul@kent.edu. *Dean,* Dr. James L. Blank, 330-672-2650, E-mail: jblank@kent.edu.

Center for Comparative and Integrative Programs Students: 3 part-time (all women); includes 1 minority (Black or African American, non-Hispanic/Latino). Average age 37. 6 applicants, 83% accepted, 1 enrolled. *Faculty:* 1 full-time (0 women), 1 part-time/adjunct (0 women). Expenses: Contact institution. *Financial support:* Career-related internships or fieldwork and Federal Work-Study available. Financial award application deadline: 2/1; financial award applicants required to submit FAFSA. *Program availability:* Part-time, online learning. Offers comparative and integrative programs (MLS). *Application deadline:* For fall admission, 6/15 for domestic and international students; for spring admission, 11/29 for domestic and international students. Applications are processed on a rolling basis. *Application fee:* $45 ($70 for international students). Electronic applications accepted. *Director of Center for Comparative and Integrative Programs,* Dr. David W. Odell-Scott, 330-672-0271, E-mail: dodellsc@kent.edu.

School of Biomedical Sciences Students: 75 full-time (46 women); includes 8 minority (1 Black or African American, non-Hispanic/Latino; 3 Asian, non-Hispanic/Latino; 2 Hispanic/Latino; 2 Two or more races, non-Hispanic/Latino), 25 international. Average age 28. 70 applicants, 23% accepted, 13 enrolled. *Faculty:* 22 full-time (9 women), 3 part-time/adjunct (1 woman). Expenses: Contact institution. *Financial support:* Research assistantships with full tuition reimbursements, teaching assistantships, and unspecified assistantships available. Financial award application deadline: 1/1. In 2017, 23 master's, 5 doctorates awarded. Offers biological anthropology (PhD); biomedical mathematics (MS, PhD); cellular and molecular biology (MS, PhD); neurosciences (MS, PhD); pharmacology (MS, PhD); physiology (MS, PhD). *Application deadline:* For fall admission, 1/1 for domestic and international students. Applications are processed on a rolling basis. *Application fee:* $45 ($70 for international students). Electronic applications accepted. *Director, School of Biomedical Sciences,* Dr. Ernest J. Freeman, 330-672-2363, E-mail: efreema2@kent.edu.

College of Business Administration Students: 156 full-time (69 women), 68 part-time (27 women); includes 10 minority (2 Black or African American, non-Hispanic/Latino; 2 Asian, non-Hispanic/Latino; 6 Two or more races, non-Hispanic/Latino), 73 international. Average age 30. 254 applicants, 67% accepted, 83 enrolled. *Faculty:* 168 full-time (68 women). Expenses: Contact institution. *Financial support:* In 2017–18, 13 research assistantships with full tuition reimbursements (averaging $4,500 per year), 47 teaching assistantships with full tuition reimbursements (averaging $23,000 per year) were awarded; fellowships with full tuition reimbursements, career-related internships or fieldwork, Federal Work-Study, and unspecified assistantships also available. Financial award applicants required to submit FAFSA. In 2017, 72 master's, 2 doctorates awarded. *Program availability:* Part-time, evening/weekend. Offers accounting (MS, PhD); business administration (MA, MBA, MS, MSBA, PhD); business analytics (MS); economics (MA); finance (PhD); management systems (PhD); marketing (PhD). *Application fee:* $45 ($70 for international students). Electronic applications accepted. *Application Contact:* Louise M. Ditchey, Administrative Director, 330-672-2282, Fax: 330-672-7303, E-mail: gradbus@kent.edu. *Associate Dean for Graduate and International Programs,* Dr. Robert D. Hisrich, 330-672-2772, Fax: 330-672-1231, E-mail: rhisric1@kent.edu.

College of Communication and Information Students: 319 full-time (224 women), 733 part-time (517 women); includes 118 minority (60 Black or African American, non-Hispanic/Latino; 1 American Indian or Alaska Native, non-Hispanic/Latino; 11 Asian, non-Hispanic/Latino; 31 Hispanic/Latino; 1 Native Hawaiian or other Pacific Islander, non-Hispanic/Latino; 14 Two or more races, non-Hispanic/Latino), 168 international. Average age 32. 563 applicants, 82% accepted, 232 enrolled. *Faculty:* 67 full-time (41 women), 61 part-time/adjunct (32 women). Expenses: Contact institution. *Financial support:* Fellowships with full tuition reimbursements, research assistantships with full tuition reimbursements, teaching assistantships with full tuition reimbursements, career-related internships or fieldwork, Federal Work-Study, scholarships/grants, and unspecified assistantships available. Financial award application deadline: 1/15. In 2017, 879 master's awarded. *Program availability:* Part-time, online learning. Offers communication and information (MA, MDS, MFA, MLIS, MS). *Application deadline:* For fall admission, 1/15 for domestic students, 12/15 for international students; for spring admission, 11/25 for domestic students, 10/25 for international students. Applications are processed on a rolling basis. *Application fee:* $45 ($70 for international students). Electronic applications accepted. *Application Contact:* Nzinga Hart, Graduate Academic Program Coordinator, 330-672-2502, E-mail: nbodden@kent.edu. *Professor and Dean,* Amy Reynolds, 330-672-2950, E-mail: areyno24@kent.edu.

School of Communication Studies Students: 27 full-time (22 women), 4 part-time (2 women); includes 1 minority (Black or African American, non-Hispanic/Latino), 10 international. Average age 27. 26 applicants, 92% accepted, 12 enrolled. *Faculty:* 9 full-time (5 women). Expenses: Contact institution. *Financial support:* Research assistantships with full tuition reimbursements, teaching assistantships with full tuition reimbursements, career-related internships or fieldwork, and unspecified assistantships available. Financial award application deadline: 1/15. In 2017, 11 master's awarded. *Program availability:* Part-time. Offers communication studies (MA). *Application deadline:* For fall admission, 1/15 for domestic students, 12/25 for international students; for spring admission, 11/15 for domestic students, 10/25 for international students. Applications are processed on a rolling basis. *Application fee:* $45 ($70 for international students). Electronic applications accepted. *Application Contact:* Dr. Suzy D'Enbeau, Associate Professor and Graduate Coordinator, 330-672-3802, E-mail: sdenbeau@kent.edu. *Director,* Dr. Elizabeth E. Graham, 330-672-3087, E-mail: egraha18@kent.edu.

School of Digital Sciences Students: 85 full-time (42 women), 76 part-time (30 women); includes 2 minority (both Black or African American, non-Hispanic/Latino), 133 international. Average age 26. 248 applicants, 69% accepted, 15 enrolled. *Faculty:* 3 full-time (1 woman), 9 part-time/adjunct (1 woman). Expenses: Contact institution. *Financial support:* Career-related internships or fieldwork available. In 2017, 472 master's awarded. *Program availability:* Part-time. Offers digital sciences (MDS); digital systems management (MDS); digital systems software development (MDS); digital systems telecommunication network (MDS); digital systems training technology (MDS); enterprise architecture (MDS). *Application deadline:* For fall admission, 7/1 for domestic students, 5/15 for international students; for spring admission, 11/15 for domestic students, 10/15 for international students; for summer admission, 4/15 for domestic students, 3/15 for international students. Applications are processed on a rolling basis. *Application fee:* $45 ($70 for international students). Electronic applications accepted. *Application Contact:* Amy Copus, Academic Advisor II for Graduate Students, 330-672-9105, E-mail: acopus@kent.edu. *Interim Director,* Jeff Fruit, 330-672-9105, E-mail: jfruit@kent.edu.

School of Information Students: 162 full-time (132 women), 561 part-time (422 women); includes 93 minority (41 Black or African American, non-Hispanic/Latino; 1 American Indian or Alaska Native, non-Hispanic/Latino; 10 Asian, non-Hispanic/Latino; 28 Hispanic/Latino; 1 Native Hawaiian or other Pacific Islander, non-Hispanic/Latino; 12 Two or more races, non-Hispanic/Latino), 7 international. Average age 33. 212 applicants, 98% accepted, 162 enrolled. *Faculty:* 20 full-time (16 women), 30 part-time/adjunct (19 women). Expenses: Contact institution. *Financial support:* Fellowships with full tuition reimbursements, research assistantships with full tuition reimbursements, teaching assistantships with full tuition reimbursements, scholarships/grants, and unspecified assistantships available. Financial award application deadline: 3/1. In 2017, 321 master's awarded. *Program availability:* Part-time, online learning. Offers health informatics (MS); library and information science (MLIS). *Application deadline:* For fall admission, 3/15 for domestic and international students; for spring admission, 9/15 for domestic and international students; for summer admission, 1/15 for domestic and international students. Applications are processed on a rolling basis. *Application fee:* $45 ($70 for international students). Electronic applications accepted. *Application Contact:* Dr. Karen Gracy, Graduate Co-Coordinator/Associate Professor, 330-672-2782, E-mail: kgracy@kent.edu. *Director and Professor,* Dr. Kendra Albright, 330-672-8535, E-mail: kalbrig7@kent.edu.

School of Journalism and Mass Communication Students: 13 full-time (8 women), 74 part-time (51 women); includes 14 minority (11 Black or African American, non-Hispanic/Latino; 2 Hispanic/Latino; 1 Two or more races, non-Hispanic/Latino), 4 international. Average age 35. 24 applicants, 71% accepted, 13 enrolled. *Faculty:* 15 full-time (8 women), 14 part-time/adjunct (7 women). Expenses: Contact institution. *Financial support:* Research assistantships with full tuition reimbursements, teaching assistantships with full tuition reimbursements, scholarships/grants, and unspecified assistantships available. Financial award application deadline: 2/16. In 2017, 58 master's awarded. *Program availability:* Part-time, online learning. Offers journalism and mass communication (MA). *Application deadline:* For fall admission, 7/1 for domestic and international students. Applications are processed on a rolling basis. *Application fee:* $45 ($70 for international students). Electronic applications accepted. *Application Contact:* Mark Goodman, Graduate Coordinator/Professor, 330-672-6239, E-mail: mgoodm10@kent.edu. *Interim Director and Professor,* Jeff Fruit, 330-672-2572, E-mail: jmc@kent.edu.

School of Visual Communication Design Students: 18 full-time (13 women), 9 part-time (6 women); includes 4 minority (3 Black or African American, non-Hispanic/Latino; 1 Two or more races, non-Hispanic/Latino), 9 international. Average age 29. 16 applicants, 81% accepted, 7 enrolled. *Faculty:* 10 full-time (5 women), 6 part-time/adjunct (1 woman). Expenses: Contact institution. *Financial support:* Scholarships/grants and unspecified assistantships available. Financial award application deadline: 4/9. In 2017, 17 master's awarded. *Program availability:* Part-time. Offers visual communication design (MA, MFA). *Application deadline:* For fall admission, 3/1 for domestic and international students; for spring admission, 10/1 for domestic and international students. Applications are processed on a rolling basis. *Application fee:* $45 ($70 for international students). Electronic applications accepted. *Application Contact:* Ken Visocky O'Grady, Graduate Coordinator and Associate Professor, 330-672-1353, E-mail: kogrady@kent.edu. *Interim Director,* Dr. David Robins, 330-672-2782, E-mail: drobins@kent.edu.

College of Education, Health and Human Services *Program availability:* Part-time, evening/weekend, online learning. Offers education, health and human services (M Ed, MA, MAT, MS, Au D, PhD, Ed S). Electronic applications accepted.

School of Foundations, Leadership and Administration Offers cultural foundations (M Ed, MA, PhD); evaluation and measurement (M Ed, PhD); higher education (PhD, Ed S); higher education and student personnel (M Ed); hospitality and tourism management (MS); K-12 leadership (M Ed, PhD, Ed S); sport and recreation management (MA); sports recreation and management (MA); sports studies (MA). Electronic applications accepted.

School of Health Sciences *Program availability:* Part-time, evening/weekend. Offers athletic training (MS); audiology (Au D, PhD); exercise physiology (MS, PhD); health education and promotion (M Ed, PhD); nutrition (MS); speech language pathology (MA, PhD). Electronic applications accepted.

School of Lifespan Development and Educational Sciences *Program availability:* Part-time, evening/weekend. Offers clinical mental health counseling (M Ed); computer technology (M Ed); counseling (Ed S); counseling and human development services (PhD); deaf education (M Ed); early childhood education (M Ed); educational interpreter K-12 (M Ed); educational psychology (M Ed, MA, PhD); general instructional technology (M Ed); general special education (M Ed); human development and family studies (MA); instructional technology (M Ed, PhD); mild/moderate intervention (M Ed); rehabilitation counseling (M Ed); school counseling (M Ed); school psychology (PhD, Ed S); special education (M Ed, PhD, Ed S); transition to work (M Ed). Electronic applications accepted.

School of Teaching, Learning and Curriculum Studies *Program availability:* Part-time, evening/weekend. Offers career technical teacher education (M Ed); curriculum and instruction (M Ed, PhD, Ed S); early childhood education (M Ed, MA, MAT); junior high/middle school (M Ed, MA); math specialization (M Ed, MA); reading specialization (M Ed, MA); secondary education (MAT). Electronic applications accepted.

College of Nursing Students: 167 full-time (142 women), 405 part-time (359 women); includes 70 minority (39 Black or African American, non-Hispanic/Latino; 11 Asian, non-Hispanic/Latino; 18 Hispanic/Latino; 2 Two or more races, non-Hispanic/Latino), 13 international. Average age 35. 272 applicants, 74% accepted, 166 enrolled. *Faculty:* 29 full-time (28 women), 15 part-time/adjunct (12 women). Expenses: Contact institution. *Financial support:* Scholarships/grants available. Financial award application deadline: 5/4. In 2017, 144 master's, 8 doctorates awarded. *Program availability:* Part-time, online learning. Offers advanced nursing practice (DNP); nursing (MSN, PhD). PhD program offered jointly with The University of Akron. *Application deadline:* For fall admission, 3/1 for domestic and international students; for spring admission, 10/1 for domestic and international students. Applications are processed on a rolling basis. *Application fee:* $45 ($70 for international students). Electronic applications accepted. *Application Contact:* Dr. Wendy A. Umberger, Associate Dean for Graduate Programs/Professor, 330-672-8813, E-mail: wlewando@kent.edu. *Dean*, Dr. Barbara Broome, 330-672-3777, E-mail: bbroome1@kent.edu.

College of Podiatric Medicine Offers podiatric medicine (DPM). Electronic applications accepted.

College of Public Health Students: 123 full-time (87 women), 152 part-time (120 women); includes 57 minority (37 Black or African American, non-Hispanic/Latino; 1 American Indian or Alaska Native, non-Hispanic/Latino; 8 Asian, non-Hispanic/Latino; 6 Hispanic/Latino; 5 Two or more races, non-Hispanic/Latino), 40 international. Average age 31. 176 applicants, 76% accepted, 81 enrolled. *Faculty:* 23 full-time (14 women), 12 part-time/adjunct (3 women). Expenses: Contact institution. *Financial support:* Unspecified assistantships available. In 2017, 79 master's, 5 doctorates awarded. *Program availability:* Part-time, online learning. Offers public health (MPH, PhD). *Application deadline:* For fall admission, 6/15 for domestic and international students; for spring admission, 10/15 for domestic and international students; for summer admission, 3/15 for domestic and international students. Applications are processed on a rolling basis. *Application fee:* $45 ($70 for international students). Electronic applications accepted. *Application Contact:* Dr. Mark A. James, Professor/Chair/Graduate Advisor, 330-672-6506, E-mail: mjames22@kent.edu. *Dean and Professor of Health Policy and Management*, Dr. Sonia Alemagno, 330-672-6500, E-mail: salemagn@kent.edu.

College of the Arts Students: 120 full-time (72 women), 200 part-time (144 women); includes 28 minority (10 Black or African American, non-Hispanic/Latino; 1 American Indian or Alaska Native, non-Hispanic/Latino; 3 Asian, non-Hispanic/Latino; 6 Hispanic/Latino; 1 Native Hawaiian or other Pacific Islander, non-Hispanic/Latino; 7 Two or more races, non-Hispanic/Latino), 33 international. Average age 31. 157 applicants, 89% accepted, 109 enrolled. *Faculty:* 67 full-time (30 women), 30 part-time/adjunct (20 women). Expenses: Contact institution. *Financial support:* Research assistantships with full tuition reimbursements, teaching assistantships with full tuition reimbursements, and unspecified assistantships available. Financial award application deadline: 2/2. In 2017, 102 master's, 2 doctorates awarded. *Program availability:* Part-time, online learning. Offers arts (MA, MFA, MM, PhD). *Application deadline:* For fall admission, 2/2 for domestic and international students; for spring admission, 10/15 for domestic and international students. Applications are processed on a rolling basis. *Application fee:* $45 ($70 for international students). Electronic applications accepted. *Application Contact:* 330-672-2760, E-mail: collegeofthearts@kent.edu. *Dean*, Dr. John R. Crawford-Spinelli, 330-672-2760, E-mail: jcrawfo1@kent.edu.

Hugh A. Glauser School of Music Students: 64 full-time (36 women), 178 part-time (125 women); includes 22 minority (8 Black or African American, non-Hispanic/Latino; 2 Asian, non-Hispanic/Latino; 6 Hispanic/Latino; 6 Two or more races, non-Hispanic/Latino), 31 international. Average age 31. 106 applicants, 92% accepted, 79 enrolled. *Faculty:* 34 full-time (11 women), 22 part-time/adjunct (15 women). Expenses: Contact institution. *Financial support:* Unspecified assistantships available. Financial award application deadline: 4/1. In 2017, 78 master's, 2 doctorates awarded. *Program availability:* Part-time, online learning. Offers conducting (MM); ethnomusicology (MA); music composition (MA); music education (MM, PhD); music theory (MA); music theory-composition (PhD); performance (MM). *Application deadline:* Applications are processed on a rolling basis. *Application fee:* $45 ($70 for international students). Electronic applications accepted. *Application Contact:* Michael Chunn, Graduate Coordinator/Trumpet Professor, 330-672-9234, Fax: 330-672-7837, E-mail: mchunn@kent.edu. *Interim Director*, Jane Dressler, 330-672-2172, E-mail: jdressle@kent.edu.

School of Art Students: 40 full-time (27 women), 22 part-time (19 women); includes 3 minority (2 Black or African American, non-Hispanic/Latino; 1 Two or more races, non-Hispanic/Latino). Average age 31. 40 applicants, 75% accepted, 23 enrolled. *Faculty:* 24 full-time (13 women), 3 part-time/adjunct (all women). Expenses: Contact institution. *Financial support:* Career-related internships or fieldwork, scholarships/grants, and unspecified assistantships available. Financial award application deadline: 3/16. In 2017, 22 master's awarded. *Program availability:* Part-time, online learning. Offers art education (MA); art history (MA); crafts (MA); fine arts (MA); studio art (MFA). *Application deadline:* For fall admission, 2/2 for domestic and international students; for spring admission, 10/15 for domestic and international students. Applications are processed on a rolling basis. *Application fee:* $45 ($70 for international students). Electronic applications accepted. *Application Contact:* Linda Hoeptner Poling, Graduate Coordinator and Associate Professor of Art Education, 330-672-7895, E-mail: lhoeptne@kent.edu. *Director*, Marie Bukowski, 330-672-2192, E-mail: mbukows1@kent.edu.

School of Theatre and Dance Students: 16 full-time (9 women); includes 1 minority (Asian, non-Hispanic/Latino), 2 international. Average age 34. 3 applicants, 100% accepted, 2 enrolled. *Faculty:* 9 full-time (6 women), 5 part-time/adjunct (2 women). Expenses: Contact institution. *Financial support:* Teaching assistantships with full tuition reimbursements, career-related internships or fieldwork, Federal Work-Study, scholarships/grants, and unspecified assistantships available. Financial award application deadline: 5/1. In 2017, 2 master's awarded. *Program availability:* Part-time. Offers theatre studies (MFA). *Application deadline:* Applications are processed on a rolling basis. *Application fee:* $45 ($70 for international students). Electronic applications accepted. *Application Contact:* Yuko Kurahashi, Graduate Coordinator and Associate Professor of Theatre, 330-672-9483, E-mail: ykurahas@kent.edu. *Director and Associate Professor*, Eric van Baars, 330-672-0102, E-mail: fvanbaar@kent.edu.

KENT STATE UNIVERSITY AT STARK, Canton, OH 44720-7599

General Information State-supported, coed, comprehensive institution.

GRADUATE UNITS

Graduate School of Education, Health and Human Services Offers curriculum and instruction studies (M Ed, MA).

Professional MBA Program Offers business administration (MBA).

KENTUCKY CHRISTIAN UNIVERSITY, Grayson, KY 41143-2205

General Information Independent-religious, coed, comprehensive institution. *Graduate housing:* Rooms and/or apartments available on a first-come, first-served basis to single and married students.

GRADUATE UNITS

Graduate School *Program availability:* Part-time. Offers Biblical studies (MA); Christian leadership (MA). Electronic applications accepted.

KENTUCKY STATE UNIVERSITY, Frankfort, KY 40601

General Information State-related, coed, comprehensive institution. *Enrollment:* 1,925 graduate, professional, and undergraduate students; 97 full-time matriculated graduate/professional students (45 women), 67 part-time matriculated graduate/professional students (41 women). *Enrollment by degree level:* 149 master's, 15 doctoral. *Graduate faculty:* 34 full-time (11 women), 3 part-time/adjunct (all women). Tuition, state resident: full-time $7902; part-time $439 per credit hour. Tuition, nonresident: full-time $11,898; part-time $661 per credit hour. Tuition and fees vary according to course load. *Graduate housing:* Room and/or apartments available on a first-come, first-served basis to single students; on-campus housing not available to married students. Typical cost: $3340 per year ($6690 including board). Room and board charges vary according to board plan and housing facility selected. Housing application deadline: 6/30. *Student services:* Campus employment opportunities, campus safety program, career counseling, child daycare facilities, exercise/wellness program, international student services. *Library facilities:* Paul G. Blazer Library. *Collection:* Books: 170,726 (physical), 23,417 (digital/electronic); Serial titles: 1,894 (physical), 38,647 (digital/electronic); Databases: 56. Weekly public service hours: 101; study areas open 24 hours, 5–7 days a week. *Research affiliation:* Alltech (aquaculture nutrition).

Computer facilities: 142 computers available on campus for general student use. A campuswide network can be accessed from student residence rooms and from off campus. Online class registration, student bill-pay, address verification, ability to accept financial aid awards are available.
Website: http://www.kysu.edu/

General Application Contact: Dr. James Obielodan, Director of Graduate Studies, 502-597-4723, E-mail: james.obielodan@kysu.edu.

GRADUATE UNITS

College of Agriculture, Food Science and Sustainable Systems Students: 36 full-time (14 women), 13 part-time (8 women); includes 6 minority (5 Black or African American, non-Hispanic/Latino; 1 Asian, non-Hispanic/Latino), 14 international. Average age 30. 23 applicants, 78% accepted, 15 enrolled. *Faculty:* 10 full-time (1 woman). Expenses: Contact institution. *Financial support:* In 2017–18, 48 students received support, including 21 research assistantships (averaging $24,944 per year); scholarships/grants, tuition waivers (partial), and unspecified assistantships also available. Financial award application deadline: 6/30; financial award applicants required to submit FAFSA. In 2017, 5 master's awarded. *Program availability:* Part-time, evening/weekend. Offers aquaculture (MS); environmental studies (MS). *Application deadline:* For fall admission, 7/1 for domestic students, 4/1 for international students; for spring admission, 11/15 for domestic students, 8/15 for international students; for summer admission, 5/1 for domestic students, 2/1 for international students. Applications are processed on a rolling basis. *Application fee:* $30 ($100 for international students). Electronic applications accepted. *Application Contact:* Dr. James Obielodan, Director of Graduate Studies, 502-597-4723, E-mail: james.obielodan@kysu.edu. *Interim Director of Land Grant Programs*, Dr. Kirk Pomper, 502-597-5942, E-mail: kirk.pomper@kysu.edu.

College of Arts and Sciences Students: 6 full-time (3 women), 3 part-time (1 woman); includes 7 minority (all Black or African American, non-Hispanic/Latino). Average age 31. 8 applicants, 75% accepted, 5 enrolled. *Faculty:* 3 full-time (2 women). Expenses: Contact institution. *Financial support:* In 2017–18, 9 students received support, including 1 research assistantship (averaging $12,955 per year); scholarships/grants, tuition waivers (partial), and unspecified assistantships also available. Financial award application deadline: 4/15; financial award applicants required to submit FAFSA. In 2017, 4 master's awarded. *Program availability:* Part-time, evening/weekend. Offers interdisciplinary behavioral sciences (MA). *Application deadline:* For fall admission, 7/1 for domestic students, 4/1 for international students; for spring admission, 11/15 for domestic students, 8/15 for international students; for summer admission, 5/1 for domestic students, 2/1 for international students. Applications are processed on a rolling basis. *Application fee:* $30 ($100 for international students). Electronic applications accepted. *Application Contact:* Dr. James Obielodan, Director of Graduate Studies, 502-597-4723, E-mail: james.obielodan@kysu.edu. *Acting Chair of Behavioral and Social Sciences*, Dr. Arthur Hayden, 502-597-6893, E-mail: arthur.hayden@kysu.edu.

College of Business and Computer Science Students: 26 full-time (10 women), 22 part-time (8 women); includes 25 minority (16 Black or African American, non-Hispanic/Latino; 8 Asian, non-Hispanic/Latino; 1 Two or more races, non-Hispanic/Latino), 13 international. Average age 30. 28 applicants, 79% accepted, 18 enrolled. *Faculty:* 12 full-time (1 woman). Expenses: Contact institution. *Financial support:* In 2017–18, 40 students received support, including 2 research assistantships (averaging $11,970 per year); scholarships/grants, tuition waivers (partial), and unspecified assistantships also available. Financial award application deadline: 4/15; financial award applicants required to submit FAFSA. In 2017, 16 master's awarded. *Program availability:* Part-time, evening/weekend. Offers business administration (MBA); computer science technology (MS). *Application deadline:* For fall admission, 7/1 for domestic students, 4/1 for international students; for spring admission, 11/15 for domestic students, 8/15 for international students; for summer admission, 5/1 for domestic students, 2/1 for international students. Applications are processed on a rolling basis. *Application fee:* $30 ($100 for international students). Electronic applications accepted. *Application Contact:* Dr. James Obielodan, Director of Graduate Studies, 502-597-4723, E-mail: james.obielodan@kysu.edu. *Assistant Vice President and Dean of Graduate Programs*, Dr. Kristen Broady, 502-597-6386, E-mail: kristen.broady@kysu.edu.

College of Professional Studies Students: 29 full-time (18 women), 29 part-time (24 women); includes 42 minority (40 Black or African American, non-Hispanic/Latino; 1 Asian, non-Hispanic/Latino; 1 Two or more races, non-Hispanic/Latino). Average age 35. 17 applicants, 53% accepted, 7 enrolled. *Faculty:* 9 full-time (7 women), 3 part-time/adjunct (all women). Expenses: Contact institution. *Financial support:* In 2017–18, 54 students received support, including 1 research assistantship (averaging $1,350 per year); scholarships/grants, tuition waivers (partial), and unspecified assistantships also available. Financial award application deadline: 4/15; financial award applicants required to submit FAFSA. In 2017, 11 master's, 4 doctorates awarded. *Program availability:* Part-time, evening/weekend, 100% online, blended/hybrid learning. Offers nursing (DNP); public administration (MPA); special education (MA). *Application deadline:* For fall admission, 7/1 for domestic students, 4/1 for international students; for spring admission, 11/15 for domestic students, 8/15 for international students; for summer admission, 5/1 for domestic students, 2/1 for international students. Applications are processed on a rolling basis. *Application fee:* $30 ($100 for international students). Electronic applications accepted. *Application Contact:* Dr. James Obielodan, Director of Graduate Studies, 502-597-4723, E-mail: james.obielodan@kysu.edu. *Assistant Vice President and Dean of Graduate Programs*, Dr. Kristen Broady, 502-597-6386, E-mail: kristen.broady@kysu.edu.

KETTERING COLLEGE, Kettering, OH 45429-1299

General Information Independent-religious, coed, primarily women, comprehensive institution.

GRADUATE UNITS

Program in Physician Assistant Studies Offers physician assistant studies (MPAS).

KETTERING UNIVERSITY, Flint, MI 48504

General Information Independent, coed, comprehensive institution. CGS member. *Graduate housing:* Rooms and/or apartments available on a first-come, first-served basis to single students and available to married students. Housing application deadline: 7/15. *Research affiliation:* McLaren Foundation (orthopedic surgery biomechanics), Shin-Estu Chemical Company (atmospheric plasma technology), Broad-Ocean Technologies (electric vehicle battery systems), Landaal Packaging Systems (space utilization and process flow of operations), Mahindra Tractor Assembly, dba Mahindra GenZe (electric power and control boards), TRW (crash safety).

GRADUATE UNITS

Graduate School *Program availability:* Part-time, evening/weekend, online learning. Offers business (MBA, MS); engineering (MS). Electronic applications accepted.

KEUKA COLLEGE, Keuka Park, NY 14478

General Information Independent-religious, coed, comprehensive institution. *Graduate housing:* Room and/or apartments available on a first-come, first-served basis to single students; on-campus housing not available to married students. Housing application deadline: 5/1.

GRADUATE UNITS

Program in Childhood Education/Literacy Offers literacy 5-12 (MS); literacy B-6 (MS). Electronic applications accepted.

Program in Criminal Justice Administration *Program availability:* Part-time, evening/weekend. Offers criminal justice administration (MS). Electronic applications accepted.

Program in Management *Program availability:* Part-time, evening/weekend, 100% online, blended/hybrid learning. Offers management (MS).

Program in Nursing Offers adult gerontology (MS); nursing education (MS). Electronic applications accepted.

Program in Occupational Therapy Offers occupational therapy (MS). Electronic applications accepted.

Program in Social Work Offers social work (MSW). Electronic applications accepted.

KEYSTONE COLLEGE, La Plume, PA 18440

General Information Independent, coed, comprehensive institution. *Enrollment:* 5 full-time matriculated graduate/professional students (3 women), 60 part-time matriculated graduate/professional students (55 women). *Enrollment by degree level:* 65 master's. *Graduate faculty:* 4 full-time (3 women), 5 part-time/adjunct (all women). *Tuition:* Part-time $650 per credit. One-time fee: $125 part-time. *Graduate housing:* On-campus housing not available. *Student services:* Campus employment opportunities, campus safety program, career counseling, exercise/wellness program, free psychological counseling, grant writing training, international student services, multicultural affairs office, services for students with disabilities, writing training. *Library facilities:* Miller Library.

Computer facilities: 100 computers available on campus for general student use. A campuswide network can be accessed from student residence rooms and from off campus. Online class registration is available.
Website: http://www.keystone.edu/

General Application Contact: Jennifer Sekol, Director of Admissions, 570-945-8117, Fax: 570-945-7916, E-mail: jennifer.sekol@keystone.edu.

GRADUATE UNITS

Program in Accountancy Students: 10 part-time (5 women); includes 1 minority (Hispanic/Latino). 5 applicants, 80% accepted, 3 enrolled. *Faculty:* 1 (woman) full-time, 2 part-time/adjunct (both women). Expenses: Contact institution. *Financial support:* Unspecified assistantships available. Financial award application deadline: 5/1; financial award applicants required to submit FAFSA. In 2017, 5 master's awarded. *Program availability:* Part-time, online only, 100% online. Offers accountancy (M Acc). *Application deadline:* For fall admission, 8/1 for domestic students; for spring admission, 12/1 for domestic students; for summer admission, 5/1 for domestic students. Applications are processed on a rolling basis. *Application fee:* $0. Electronic applications accepted. *Application Contact:* Jennifer Sekol, Director of Admissions, 570-945-8117, Fax: 570-945-7916, E-mail: jennifer.sekol@keystone.edu. *Professor*, Patricia Davis, PhD, 570-945-8424, E-mail: patricia.davis@keystone.edu.

Program in Business Administration Students: 5 full-time (2 women). 10 applicants, 100% accepted, 5 enrolled. Expenses: Contact institution. *Financial support:* Unspecified assistantships available. Financial award applicants required to submit FAFSA. *Program availability:* Part-time, online only, 100% online. Offers business administration (MBA). *Application deadline:* For fall admission, 8/1 for domestic students; for spring admission, 1/1 for domestic students; for summer admission, 5/1 for domestic students. Applications are processed on a rolling basis. *Application fee:* $0. Electronic applications accepted. *Application Contact:* Sarah Louzon, Admissions Counselor, 570-945-8126, Fax: 570-945-7916, E-mail: sarah.louzon@keystone.edu. *Associate Professor/Coordinator of MBA Program*, Dr. Dana Harris, 570-945-8421, E-mail: dana.harris@keystone.edu.

Program in Early Childhood Education Leadership Students: 49 part-time (all women); includes 24 minority (6 Black or African American, non-Hispanic/Latino; 1 American Indian or Alaska Native, non-Hispanic/Latino; 17 Hispanic/Latino). 23 applicants, 83% accepted, 18 enrolled. *Faculty:* 1 (woman) full-time, 4 part-time/adjunct (all women). Expenses: Contact institution. *Financial support:* Unspecified assistantships available. Financial award application deadline: 5/1; financial award applicants required to submit FAFSA. In 2017, 19 master's awarded. *Program availability:* Part-time, blended/hybrid learning. Offers early childhood education leadership (M Ed). *Application deadline:* For fall admission, 8/1 for domestic students; for spring admission, 12/1 for domestic students; for summer admission, 5/1 for domestic students. Applications are processed on a rolling basis. *Application fee:* $0. Electronic applications accepted. *Application Contact:* Jennifer Sekol, Director of Admissions, 570-945-8117, Fax: 570-945-7916, E-mail: jennifer.sekol@keystone.edu. *Dean, School of Professional Studies*, Fran Langan, PhD, 570-945-8472, E-mail: fran.langan@keystone.edu.

Program in Sport Leadership and Management Students: 5 full-time (4 women), 1 part-time (0 women). 2 applicants, 100% accepted, 1 enrolled. *Faculty:* 2 full-time (0 women). Expenses: Contact institution. *Financial support:* In 2017–18, 1 student received support. Unspecified assistantships available. Financial award application deadline: 5/1; financial award applicants required to submit FAFSA. In 2017, 9 master's awarded. *Program availability:* Part-time, online only, 100% online. Offers sport leadership and management (MS). *Application deadline:* For fall admission, 8/1 for domestic students; for spring admission, 12/1 for domestic students; for summer admission, 5/1 for domestic students. Applications are processed on a rolling basis. *Application fee:* $0. Electronic applications accepted. *Application Contact:* Jennifer Sekol, Director of Admissions, 570-945-8117, Fax: 570-945-7916, E-mail: jennifer.sekol@keystone.edu.

KING'S COLLEGE, Wilkes-Barre, PA 18711-0801

General Information Independent-religious, coed, comprehensive institution. *Graduate housing:* On-campus housing not available.

GRADUATE UNITS

Program in Education *Program availability:* Part-time, evening/weekend. Offers education (M Ed).

Program in Physician Assistant Studies Offers physician assistant studies (MSPAS). Electronic applications accepted.

William G. McGowan School of Business *Program availability:* Part-time. Offers health care administration (MS).

THE KING'S UNIVERSITY, Southlake, TX 76092

General Information Independent-religious, coed, comprehensive institution.

GRADUATE UNITS

Graduate and Professional Programs Offers Biblical studies (Graduate Certificate); Christian ministry (Graduate Certificate); ministry (M Div, MPT, D Min).

KINGSWOOD UNIVERSITY, Sussex, NB E4E 5L2, Canada

General Information Independent-religious, coed, comprehensive institution. *Enrollment:* 8 full-time matriculated graduate/professional students (4 women), 1 part-time matriculated graduate/professional student. *Enrollment by degree level:* 9 master's. *Graduate faculty:* 1 full-time (0 women), 1 part-time/adjunct (0 women). *Tuition:* Part-time $355 Canadian dollars per credit hour. One-time fee: $150 Canadian dollars part-time. *Graduate housing:* On-campus housing not available. *Student services:* Exercise/wellness program, low-cost health insurance. *Library facilities:* The Earle and Marion Trouten Library.

Computer facilities: 8 computers available on campus for general student use. A campuswide network can be accessed from student residence rooms and from off campus.
Website: http://www.kingswood.edu/

General Application Contact: Enrolment Office, 506-432-4422, Fax: 506-432-4442, E-mail: enrolment@kingswood.edu.

GRADUATE UNITS

Program in Pastoral Theology Students: 8 full-time (4 women), 1 part-time (0 women). Average age 34. *Faculty:* 1 full-time (0 women), 1 part-time/adjunct (0 women). Expenses: Contact institution. Offers pastoral theology (MA). *Application Contact:* Enrolment Office, 506-432-4422, Fax: 506-432-4442, E-mail: enrolment@kingswood.edu.

KING UNIVERSITY, Bristol, TN 37620-2699

General Information Independent-religious, coed, comprehensive institution. *Graduate housing:* Room and/or apartments available on a first-come, first-served basis to single students; on-campus housing not available to married students.

GRADUATE UNITS

School of Business and Economics *Program availability:* Part-time, evening/weekend, online learning. Offers accounting (MBA); finance (MBA); healthcare management (MBA); human resources management (MBA); leadership (MBA); management (MBA); marketing (MBA); project management (MBA). Electronic applications accepted.

School of Nursing Offers family nurse practitioner (MSN); nurse educator (MSN); nursing (DNP); nursing administration (MSN); pediatric nurse practitioner (MSN).

KNOX COLLEGE, Toronto, ON M5S 2E6, Canada

General Information Independent-religious, coed, graduate-only institution. *Graduate housing:* Room and/or apartments available on a first-come, first-served basis to single students; on-campus housing not available to married students. Housing application deadline: 5/31.

GRADUATE UNITS

College of Theology *Program availability:* Part-time. Offers theology (M Div, MRE, MTS, Th M, D Min, Th D). Applicants for D Min, Th M, and Th D must apply to Toronto School of Theology; MRE, M Div, MTS, Th D, and Th M programs offered jointly with University of Toronto.

KNOX THEOLOGICAL SEMINARY, Fort Lauderdale, FL 33308

General Information Independent-religious, coed, primarily men, graduate-only institution. *Graduate housing:* On-campus housing not available.

GRADUATE UNITS

Graduate Programs *Program availability:* Part-time, blended/hybrid learning. Offers Biblical and theological studies (MA); Christian and classical studies (MA); divinity (M Div); ministry (D Min).

KUTZTOWN UNIVERSITY OF PENNSYLVANIA, Kutztown, PA 19530-0730

General Information State-supported, coed, comprehensive institution. CGS member. *Enrollment:* 8,329 graduate, professional, and undergraduate students; 291 full-time matriculated graduate/professional students (217 women), 530 part-time matriculated graduate/professional students (407 women). *Enrollment by degree level:* 718 master's, 32 doctoral, 71 other advanced degrees. *Graduate faculty:* 98 full-time (63 women), 5 part-time/adjunct (2 women). Tuition, state resident: part-time $500 per credit. Tuition, nonresident: part-time $750 per credit. *Required fees:* $115 per credit. One-time fee: $50 part-time. Tuition and fees vary according to degree level. *Graduate housing:*

Rooms and/or apartments available on a first-come, first-served basis to single and married students. Housing application deadline: 5/1. *Student services:* Campus employment opportunities, campus safety program, career counseling, exercise/wellness program, free psychological counseling, international student services, low-cost health insurance, multicultural affairs office, services for students with disabilities. *Library facilities:* Rohrbach Library. *Collection:* Books: 317,044 (physical), 299,170 (digital/electronic); Serial titles: 88,613 (digital/electronic); Databases: 134. Weekly public service hours: 92; students can reserve study rooms.

Computer facilities: Computer purchase and lease plans are available. 1,075 computers available on campus for general student use. A campuswide network can be accessed from student residence rooms. Online class registration is available. Website: http://www.kutztown.edu/

General Application Contact: Kelly Hish, Admissions Clerk, 610-683-4190, Fax: 610-683-1375, E-mail: graduate@kutztown.edu.

GRADUATE UNITS

College of Business Students: 14 full-time (5 women), 17 part-time (6 women); includes 5 minority (1 Black or African American, non-Hispanic/Latino; 1 Asian, non-Hispanic/Latino; 1 Hispanic/Latino; 2 Two or more races, non-Hispanic/Latino), 4 international. Average age 28. 38 applicants, 74% accepted, 11 enrolled. *Faculty:* 6 full-time (3 women). Expenses: Contact institution. *Financial support:* Career-related internships or fieldwork, Federal Work-Study, scholarships/grants, and unspecified assistantships available. Financial award application deadline: 3/1; financial award applicants required to submit FAFSA. In 2017, 11 master's awarded. *Program availability:* Part-time, evening/weekend, 100% online, blended/hybrid learning. Offers business (MBA); business administration (MBA). *Application deadline:* For fall admission, 8/1 priority date for domestic and international students; for spring admission, 12/1 priority date for domestic and international students. *Application fee:* $35. Electronic applications accepted. *Dean*, Dr. Anne Carroll, 610-683-4575, Fax: 610-683-4573, E-mail: acarroll@kutztown.edu.

College of Education Students: 172 full-time (134 women), 366 part-time (293 women); includes 78 minority (30 Black or African American, non-Hispanic/Latino; 5 Asian, non-Hispanic/Latino; 35 Hispanic/Latino; 8 Two or more races, non-Hispanic/Latino), 2 international. Average age 30. 413 applicants, 85% accepted, 172 enrolled. *Faculty:* 33 full-time (28 women), 3 part-time/adjunct (0 women). Expenses: Contact institution. *Financial support:* Career-related internships or fieldwork, Federal Work-Study, and unspecified assistantships available. Financial award application deadline: 3/1; financial award applicants required to submit FAFSA. In 2017, 147 master's awarded. *Program availability:* Part-time, evening/weekend, 100% online, blended/hybrid learning. Offers biology (M Ed); clinical mental health counseling (MA); curriculum and instruction (M Ed); education (M Ed, MA, MLS, MS, Ed D); elementary education (M Ed); English (M Ed); instructional technology (M Ed); library science (MLS); marriage, couple and family counseling (MA); mathematics (M Ed); middle level (M Ed); reading (M Ed); school counseling (MS); social studies (M Ed); student affairs in higher education (M Ed); teaching (M Ed); transformational teaching and learning (Ed D). *Application deadline:* For fall admission, 8/1 for domestic and international students; for spring admission, 12/1 for domestic and international students. *Application fee:* $35. Electronic applications accepted. *Dean*, Dr. Kenneth Teitelbaum, 610-683-4253, Fax: 610-683-4255, E-mail: teitelba@kutztown.edu.

College of Liberal Arts and Sciences Students: 89 full-time (67 women), 84 part-time (54 women); includes 37 minority (19 Black or African American, non-Hispanic/Latino; 1 American Indian or Alaska Native, non-Hispanic/Latino; 1 Asian, non-Hispanic/Latino; 11 Hispanic/Latino; 5 Two or more races, non-Hispanic/Latino), 4 international. Average age 31. 143 applicants, 89% accepted, 75 enrolled. *Faculty:* 44 full-time (22 women). Expenses: Contact institution. *Financial support:* Career-related internships or fieldwork, Federal Work-Study, and unspecified assistantships available. Financial award application deadline: 3/1; financial award applicants required to submit FAFSA. In 2017, 46 master's awarded. *Program availability:* Part-time, evening/weekend. Offers computer science (MS); English (MA); liberal arts and sciences (MA, MPA, MS, MSW, DSW); public administration (MPA); social work (MSW, DSW). *Application deadline:* For fall admission, 8/1 for domestic and international students; for spring admission, 12/1 for domestic and international students. *Application fee:* $35. Electronic applications accepted. *Dean*, Dr. David Beougher, 610-683-4305, Fax: 610-683-4633, E-mail: clas@kutztown.edu.

College of Visual and Performing Arts Students: 16 full-time (11 women), 63 part-time (54 women); includes 3 minority (1 Black or African American, non-Hispanic/Latino; 1 Hispanic/Latino; 1 Two or more races, non-Hispanic/Latino), 1 international. Average age 32. 69 applicants, 93% accepted, 42 enrolled. *Faculty:* 15 full-time (10 women), 2 part-time/adjunct (both women). Expenses: Contact institution. *Financial support:* Career-related internships or fieldwork, Federal Work-Study, institutionally sponsored loans, and unspecified assistantships available. Financial award application deadline: 3/1; financial award applicants required to submit FAFSA. In 2017, 10 master's awarded. *Program availability:* Part-time. Offers art education (M Ed); arts administration (MA); communication design (MFA); music education (M Ed); visual and performing arts (M Ed, MA, MFA). *Application deadline:* For fall admission, 8/1 for domestic and international students; for spring admission, 12/1 for domestic and international students. *Application fee:* $35. Electronic applications accepted. *Dean*, Dr. Michelle Kiec, 610-683-4500, Fax: 610-683-4547, E-mail: kiec@kutztown.edu.

LAGRANGE COLLEGE, LaGrange, GA 30240-2999

General Information Independent-religious, coed, comprehensive institution. *Graduate housing:* Room and/or apartments available on a first-come, first-served basis to single students; on-campus housing not available to married students. Housing application deadline: 5/1.

GRADUATE UNITS

Graduate Programs *Program availability:* Part-time, evening/weekend. Offers clinical mental health counseling (MS); curriculum and instruction (M Ed, Ed S); middle grades (MAT); organizational leadership (MA); secondary education (MAT). Electronic applications accepted.

LAGUNA COLLEGE OF ART & DESIGN, Laguna Beach, CA 92651-1136

General Information Independent, coed, comprehensive institution.

GRADUATE UNITS

Graduate Program Electronic applications accepted.

LAKE ERIE COLLEGE, Painesville, OH 44077-3389

General Information Independent, coed, comprehensive institution. *Graduate housing:* On-campus housing not available.

GRADUATE UNITS

School of Business *Program availability:* Part-time, evening/weekend. Offers general management (MBA); health care administration (MBA); information technology management (MBA). Electronic applications accepted.

School of Education and Professional Studies *Program availability:* Part-time, evening/weekend. Offers education and professional studies (M Ed). Electronic applications accepted.

LAKE ERIE COLLEGE OF OSTEOPATHIC MEDICINE, Erie, PA 16509-1025

General Information Independent, coed, graduate-only institution. *Graduate housing:* On-campus housing not available. *Research affiliation:* West Virginia University (neurology), Neuro Structural Research Laboratories (neurology), Cornelli Consulting (CORCON) (neurology), University of Maryland (neurology), Duke University (neurology).

GRADUATE UNITS

Professional Programs Offers biomedical sciences (Postbaccalaureate Certificate); medical education (MS); osteopathic medicine (DO); pharmacy (Pharm D). Electronic applications accepted.

LAKE FOREST COLLEGE, Lake Forest, IL 60045

General Information Independent, coed, comprehensive institution. *Graduate housing:* On-campus housing not available. *Research affiliation:* Argonne National Laboratory (physics), Merck & Company, Inc., Chicago History Museum (Chicago history), Lake Forest Hospital (genomes), The Art Institute of Chicago (Asian art), Newberry Library (medieval and Renaissance history, American West).

GRADUATE UNITS

Graduate Program in Liberal Studies Students: 34 part-time (19 women); includes 3 minority (1 Asian, non-Hispanic/Latino; 2 Hispanic/Latino). Average age 36. 20 applicants, 55% accepted, 8 enrolled. *Faculty:* 11 full-time (3 women). Expenses: Contact institution. *Financial support:* In 2017–18, 2 students received support. Partial tuition grants (for full-time teachers) available. In 2017, 5 master's awarded. *Program availability:* Part-time, evening/weekend. Offers American studies (MLS); cinema in East Asia (MLS); environmental studies (MLS); history (MLS); Medieval and Renaissance art (MLS); philosophy (MLS); Spanish (MLS); writing (MLS). *Application deadline:* For fall admission, 7/15 priority date for domestic students, 6/1 priority date for international students; for spring admission, 12/1 priority date for domestic students, 10/1 priority date for international students. Applications are processed on a rolling basis. *Application fee:* $30. Electronic applications accepted. *Application Contact:* Prof. Carol Gayle, Associate Director, 847-735-5083, Fax: 847-735-6291, E-mail: gayle@lakeforest.edu. *Director*, Prof. D. L. LeMahieu, 847-735-5133, Fax: 847-735-6291, E-mail: lemahieu@lakeforest.edu.

Master of Arts in Teaching Program Offers elementary education (MAT); K-12 French (MAT); K-12 music (MAT); K-12 Spanish (MAT); K-12 visual art (MAT); secondary biology (MAT); secondary chemistry (MAT); secondary English (MAT); secondary history (MAT); secondary mathematics (MAT).

LAKE FOREST GRADUATE SCHOOL OF MANAGEMENT, Lake Forest, IL 60045

General Information Independent, coed, graduate-only institution. *Graduate housing:* On-campus housing not available.

GRADUATE UNITS

The Immersion MBA Program (iMBA) *Program availability:* Online learning. Offers global business (MBA).

The Leadership MBA Program *Program availability:* Part-time, evening/weekend. Offers finance (MBA); global business (MBA); healthcare management (MBA); management (MBA); marketing (MBA); organizational behavior (MBA). Electronic applications accepted.

LAKEHEAD UNIVERSITY, Thunder Bay, ON P7B 5E1, Canada

General Information Province-supported, coed, comprehensive institution. *Graduate housing:* Rooms and/or apartments available to single students and available on a first-come, first-served basis to married students. Housing application deadline: 3/10. *Research affiliation:* Falcon Bridge (biology), Placer Dome (biology), Centre for Northern Forest Ecosystem Research (biology, forestry, tourism), Thunder Bay Regional Cancer Centre (psychosocial oncology), Bowater Inc. (chemistry, engineering).

GRADUATE UNITS

Graduate Studies *Program availability:* Part-time, evening/weekend. Offers clinical psychology (PhD); experimental psychology (MA); geology (M Sc); gerontology (M Ed, M Sc, MA, MSW); history (MA); physics (M Sc); women's studies (MA).

Faculty of Education *Program availability:* Part-time, evening/weekend. Offers educational studies (PhD); gerontology (M Ed); women's studies (M Ed).

Faculty of Engineering *Program availability:* Part-time. Offers control engineering (M Sc Engr); electrical/computer engineering (M Sc Engr); environmental engineering (M Sc Engr).

Faculty of Natural Resources Management *Program availability:* Part-time. Offers forest sciences (PhD); forestry (M Sc F).

Faculty of Social Sciences and Humanities *Program availability:* Part-time, evening/weekend. Offers biology (M Sc); chemistry (M Sc); economics (MA); English (MA); gerontology (MA); health services and policy research (MA); social sciences and humanities (M Sc, MA, MSW, PhD); sociology (MA); women's studies (MA).

School of Kinesiology *Program availability:* Part-time. Offers kinesiology (M Sc); kinesiology and gerontology (M Sc).

School of Mathematical Sciences *Program availability:* Part-time, evening/weekend. Offers computer science (M Sc); mathematical science (MA).

School of Social Work *Program availability:* Part-time. Offers gerontology (MSW); social work (MSW); women's studies (MSW).

LAKELAND UNIVERSITY, Plymouth, WI 53073

General Information Independent-religious, coed, comprehensive institution. *Graduate housing:* On-campus housing not available.

GRADUATE UNITS

Graduate Studies Division *Program availability:* Part-time, evening/weekend. Offers accounting (MBA); counseling (MA); education (M Ed); finance (MBA); healthcare management (MBA); project management (MBA); theology (MAT).

LAMAR UNIVERSITY, Beaumont, TX 77710

General Information State-supported, coed, university. CGS member. *Enrollment:* 14,506 graduate, professional, and undergraduate students; 553 full-time matriculated graduate/professional students (234 women), 3,900 part-time matriculated graduate/professional students (2,873 women). *Enrollment by degree level:* 3,598 master's, 279 doctoral, 576 other advanced degrees. *Graduate faculty:* 391 full-time (185 women), 96 part-time/adjunct (58 women). *Graduate housing:* Rooms and/or apartments available to single students and available on a first-come, first-served basis to married students. Housing application deadline: 6/30. *Student services:* Campus employment opportunities, campus safety program, career counseling, exercise/wellness program, free psychological counseling, grant writing training, international student services, low-cost health insurance, multicultural affairs office, services for students with disabilities, teacher training, writing training. *Library facilities:* Mary and John Gray Library plus 1 other. *Collection:* Books: 496,121 (physical), 91,469 (digital/electronic); Serial titles: 42,694 (physical), 47,629 (digital/electronic); Databases: 142. Weekly public service hours: 87; students can reserve study rooms. *Research affiliation:* Grants Resource Center, National Council of Research Administrators, BASF.

Computer facilities: 1,104 computers available on campus for general student use. A campuswide network can be accessed from student residence rooms and from off campus. Online class registration is available.
Website: http://www.lamar.edu/

General Application Contact: Deidra Mayer, Executive Director, Admissions and Recruitment, 409-880-7870, Fax: 409-880-8180, E-mail: deidra.mayer@lamar.edu.

GRADUATE UNITS

College of Graduate Studies Students: 553 full-time (234 women), 3,900 part-time (2,873 women); includes 1,739 minority (842 Black or African American, non-Hispanic/Latino; 17 American Indian or Alaska Native, non-Hispanic/Latino; 78 Asian, non-Hispanic/Latino; 763 Hispanic/Latino; 2 Native Hawaiian or other Pacific Islander, non-Hispanic/Latino; 37 Two or more races, non-Hispanic/Latino), 506 international. Average age 35. 4,660 applicants, 79% accepted, 893 enrolled. *Faculty:* 391 full-time (185 women), 96 part-time/adjunct (58 women). Expenses: Contact institution. *Financial support:* Fellowships with partial tuition reimbursements, research assistantships, teaching assistantships, career-related internships or fieldwork, Federal Work-Study, institutionally sponsored loans, scholarships/grants, and tuition waivers (partial) available. Support available to part-time students. Financial award applicants required to submit FAFSA. In 2017, 1,940 master's, 91 doctorates, 52 other advanced degrees awarded. *Program availability:* Part-time, evening/weekend. *Application deadline:* Applications are processed on a rolling basis. *Application fee:* $25 ($50 for international students). Electronic applications accepted. *Application Contact:* Celeste Contreras, Director, Admissions, 409-880-8888, Fax: 409-880-7419, E-mail: gradmissions@lamar.edu. *Dean*, Dr. William E. Harn, 409-880-8229, Fax: 409-880-1723, E-mail: lugradstudies@lamar.edu.

College of Arts and Sciences Students: 128 full-time (51 women), 308 part-time (194 women); includes 174 minority (103 Black or African American, non-Hispanic/Latino; 12 Asian, non-Hispanic/Latino; 56 Hispanic/Latino; 3 Two or more races, non-Hispanic/Latino), 123 international. Average age 32. 365 applicants, 80% accepted, 119 enrolled. *Faculty:* 162 full-time (88 women), 35 part-time/adjunct (20 women). Expenses: Contact institution. *Financial support:* Fellowships, research assistantships, teaching assistantships with tuition reimbursements, career-related internships or fieldwork, Federal Work-Study, institutionally sponsored loans, scholarships/grants, and tuition waivers (partial) available. Support available to part-time students. Financial award applicants required to submit FAFSA. In 2017, 230 master's awarded. *Program availability:* Part-time, evening/weekend. Offers arts and sciences (MA, MPA, MS, MSN); biology (MS); chemistry (MS); clinical psychology (MS); computer science (MS); criminal justice (MS); English (MA); history (MA); industrial/organizational psychology (MS); mathematics (MS); nursing administration (MSN); nursing education (MSN); public administration (MPA); teaching Spanish (MA). *Application deadline:* Applications are processed on a rolling basis. *Application fee:* $25 ($50 for international students). Electronic applications accepted. *Application Contact:* Celeste Contreras, Director, Admissions, 409-880-8888, E-mail: gradmissions@lamar.edu. *Interim Dean*, Dr. Paul Bernazzani, 409-880-8508, Fax: 409-880-8007.

College of Business Students: 20 full-time (11 women), 228 part-time (118 women); includes 98 minority (58 Black or African American, non-Hispanic/Latino; 10 Asian, non-Hispanic/Latino; 26 Hispanic/Latino; 4 Two or more races, non-Hispanic/Latino), 32 international. Average age 32. 205 applicants, 92% accepted, 78 enrolled. *Faculty:* 50 full-time (14 women), 6 part-time/adjunct (2 women). Expenses: Contact institution. *Financial support:* Fellowships with tuition reimbursements, research assistantships with partial tuition reimbursements, career-related internships or fieldwork, Federal Work-Study, institutionally sponsored loans, scholarships/grants, and tuition waivers (partial) available. Support available to part-time students. Financial award application deadline: 4/1; financial award applicants required to submit FAFSA. In 2017, 69 master's awarded. *Program availability:* Part-time, evening/weekend. Offers accounting (MBA); experiential business and entrepreneurship (MBA); healthcare administration (MBA). *Application deadline:* For fall admission, 8/10 for domestic students, 7/1 for international students; for spring admission, 1/5 for domestic students, 12/1 for international students. Applications are processed on a rolling basis. *Application fee:* $25 ($50 for international students). Electronic applications accepted. *Application Contact:* Deidre Mayer, Interim Director, Admissions and Academic Services, 409-880-8888, Fax: 409-880-7419, E-mail: gradmissions@lamar.edu. *Dean*, Dr. Enrique R. Venta, 409-880-8603, Fax: 409-880-8088, E-mail: henry.venta@lamar.edu.

College of Education and Human Development Students: 74 full-time (46 women), 3,195 part-time (2,526 women); includes 1,404 minority (662 Black or African American, non-Hispanic/Latino; 16 American Indian or Alaska Native, non-Hispanic/Latino; 43 Asian, non-Hispanic/Latino; 653 Hispanic/Latino; 2 Native Hawaiian or other Pacific Islander, non-Hispanic/Latino; 28 Two or more races, non-Hispanic/Latino), 18 international. Average age 37. 3,498 applicants, 80% accepted, 564 enrolled. *Faculty:* 76 full-time (54 women), 45 part-time/adjunct (33 women). Expenses: Contact institution. *Financial support:* Fellowships, research assistantships, teaching assistantships, career-related internships or fieldwork, Federal Work-Study, institutionally sponsored loans, and scholarships/grants available. Support available to part-time students. Financial award application deadline: 4/1; financial award applicants required to submit FAFSA. In 2017, 1,484 master's, 82 doctorates, 68 other advanced degrees awarded. *Program availability:* Part-time, evening/weekend, online learning. Offers clinical mental health counseling (M Ed); digital learning and leading (M Ed); education administration (M Ed); education and human development (M Ed, MS, Ed D, Certificate); educational leadership (Ed D); educational technology (M Ed); family and consumer sciences (MS); public health (MS); school counseling (M Ed); science of kinesiology promotion (MS); special education (M Ed); teacher leadership (M Ed). *Application deadline:* For fall admission, 8/10 for domestic students, 7/1 for international students; for spring admission, 1/5 for domestic students, 12/1 for international students. Applications are processed on a rolling basis. *Application fee:* $25 ($50 for international students). Electronic applications accepted. *Application Contact:* Deidre Mayer, Interim Director, Admissions and Academic Services, 409-880-8888, Fax: 409-880-7419, E-mail: gradmissions@lamar.edu. *Dean*, Dr. Robert Spina, 409-880-8661.

College of Engineering Students: 224 full-time (34 women), 140 part-time (15 women); includes 16 minority (4 Black or African American, non-Hispanic/Latino; 1 American Indian or Alaska Native, non-Hispanic/Latino; 8 Asian, non-Hispanic/Latino; 3 Hispanic/Latino), 327 international. Average age 27. 504 applicants, 63% accepted, 76 enrolled. *Faculty:* 59 full-time (7 women), 2 part-time/adjunct (0 women). Expenses: Contact institution. *Financial support:* Fellowships with partial tuition reimbursements, research assistantships with partial tuition reimbursements, teaching assistantships with partial tuition reimbursements, career-related internships or fieldwork, Federal Work-Study, institutionally sponsored loans, scholarships/grants, tuition waivers (full and partial), and laboratory assistantships available. Support available to part-time students. Financial award application deadline: 4/1; financial award applicants required to submit FAFSA. In 2017, 120 master's, 13 doctorates awarded. *Program availability:* Part-time, evening/weekend. Offers chemical engineering (ME, PhD); civil engineering (ME, MES); electrical engineering (ME, MES, DE); engineering (ME, MEM, MES, MS, DE, PhD); engineering management (MEM); environmental engineering (MS); environmental studies (MS, DE); industrial engineering (ME, MES, DE); mechanical engineering (ME, MES, DE). *Application deadline:* For fall admission, 8/1 for domestic students, 7/1 for international students; for spring admission, 1/5 for domestic students, 12/1 for international students. Applications are processed on a rolling basis. *Application fee:* $25 ($50 for international students). Electronic applications accepted. *Application Contact:* Deidre Mayer, Interim Director, Admissions and Academic Services, 409-880-8888, Fax: 409-880-7419, E-mail: gradmissions@lamar.edu. *Dean*, Dr. Srinivas Palanki, 409-880-8784, Fax: 409-880-2197.

College of Fine Arts and Communication Students: 107 full-time (92 women), 29 part-time (20 women); includes 47 minority (15 Black or African American, non-Hispanic/Latino; 5 Asian, non-Hispanic/Latino; 25 Hispanic/Latino; 2 Two or more races, non-Hispanic/Latino), 6 international. Average age 27. 88 applicants, 84% accepted, 56 enrolled. *Faculty:* 44 full-time (22 women), 8 part-time/adjunct (3 women). Expenses: Contact institution. *Financial support:* Fellowships, research assistantships, teaching assistantships, career-related internships or fieldwork, Federal Work-Study, institutionally sponsored loans, and tuition waivers (partial) available. Support available to part-time students. Financial award application deadline: 4/1; financial award applicants required to submit FAFSA. In 2017, 37 master's, 10 doctorates awarded. *Program availability:* Part-time, evening/weekend. Offers audiology (Au D); deaf studies and deaf education (MS, Ed D); fine arts and communication (MM, MS, Au D, Ed D); music (MM); speech language pathology (MS). *Application deadline:* For fall admission, 8/10 for domestic students, 7/1 for international students; for spring admission, 1/5 for domestic students, 12/1 for international students. Applications are processed on a rolling basis. *Application fee:* $25 ($50 for international students). Electronic applications accepted. *Application Contact:* Deidre Mayer, Interim Director, Admissions and Academic Services, 409-880-8888, Fax: 409-880-7419, E-mail: gradmissions@lamar.edu. *Dean*, Dr. Derina Holtzhausen, 409-880-8137, Fax: 409-880-2286.

LANCASTER BIBLE COLLEGE, Lancaster, PA 17601

General Information Independent-religious, coed, comprehensive institution. *Graduate housing:* On-campus housing not available.

GRADUATE UNITS

Capital Bible Seminary *Program availability:* Part-time, evening/weekend. Offers biblical studies (MA, Certificate); Christian counseling and discipleship (MA, Certificate); ministry (MA); theology (M Div).

Graduate School *Program availability:* Part-time, evening/weekend. Offers adult ministries (MA); Bible (MA); children and family ministry (MA); church planting (MA); consulting resource teacher (M Ed); elementary school counseling (M Ed); leadership (PhD); leadership studies (MA); marriage and family counseling (MA); mental health counseling (MA); pastoral studies (MA); secondary school counseling (M Ed); sports ministry (MA); student ministry (MA); town and country ministry (MA).

LANCASTER THEOLOGICAL SEMINARY, Lancaster, PA 17603-2812

General Information Independent-religious, coed, graduate-only institution. *Graduate housing:* Rooms and/or apartments available on a first-come, first-served basis to single and married students. Housing application deadline: 8/1.

GRADUATE UNITS

Graduate and Professional Programs Offers biblical studies (MAR); Christian education (MAR); Christianity and the arts (MAR); church history (MAR); congregational life (MAR); lay leadership (Certificate); theological studies (M Div); theology (D Min); theology and ethics (MAR).

LANDER UNIVERSITY, Greenwood, SC 29649-2099

General Information State-supported, coed, comprehensive institution. *Graduate housing:* Room and/or apartments available on a first-come, first-served basis to single students; on-campus housing not available to married students.

GRADUATE UNITS

Graduate Studies *Program availability:* Part-time, online learning. Offers clinical nurse leader (MSN); emergency management (MS); Montessori education (M Ed); teaching and learning (M Ed). Electronic applications accepted.

LANGSTON UNIVERSITY, Langston, OK 73050

General Information State-supported, coed, comprehensive institution. CGS member. *Graduate housing:* Rooms and/or apartments available on a first-come, first-served basis to single and married students.

GRADUATE UNITS

School of Education and Behavioral Sciences *Program availability:* Part-time. Offers bilingual/multicultural (M Ed); elementary education (M Ed); English as a second language (M Ed); rehabilitation counseling (M Sc); urban education (M Ed).

School of Physical Therapy Offers physical therapy (DPT).

LA ROCHE COLLEGE, Pittsburgh, PA 15237-5898

General Information Independent-religious, coed, comprehensive institution. *Enrollment:* 1,535 graduate, professional, and undergraduate students; 79 full-time matriculated graduate/professional students (54 women), 78 part-time matriculated graduate/professional students (56 women). *Enrollment by degree level:* 146 master's, 5 doctoral, 6 other advanced degrees. *Graduate faculty:* 10 full-time (9 women), 16 part-time/adjunct (4 women). *Tuition:* Part-time $715 per credit hour. *Required fees:* $80 per credit hour. *Graduate housing:* On-campus housing not available. *Student services:* Campus employment opportunities, career counseling, free psychological counseling, international student services, low-cost health insurance, multicultural affairs office, services for students with disabilities. *Library facilities:* John J. Wright Library plus 1 other. *Collection:* Books: 75,803 (physical), 221,000 (digital/electronic); Databases: 1,248.

Computer facilities: Computer purchase and lease plans are available. A campuswide network can be accessed. Online class registration is available.
Website: http://www.laroche.edu/

General Application Contact: Hope Schiffgens, Director of Graduate Studies and Adult Education, 412-536-1266, Fax: 412-536-1283, E-mail: schombh1@laroche.edu.

GRADUATE UNITS

School of Graduate Studies and Adult Education Students: 79 full-time (54 women), 78 part-time (56 women); includes 7 minority (2 Black or African American, non-Hispanic/Latino; 1 Asian, non-Hispanic/Latino; 2 Hispanic/Latino; 2 Two or more races, non-Hispanic/Latino), 25 international. Average age 32. *Faculty:* 10 full-time (9 women), 16 part-time/adjunct (4 women). Expenses: Contact institution. *Financial support:* Unspecified assistantships available. Financial award application deadline: 3/31; financial award applicants required to submit FAFSA. In 2017, 50 master's, 5 doctorates awarded. *Program availability:* Part-time, evening/weekend, 100% online. Offers accounting (MS); clinical nurse leader (MSN); human resources management (MS, Certificate); nurse anesthesia (MS, DNAP); nursing education (MSN); nursing management (MSN). *Application deadline:* For fall admission, 8/15 for domestic and international students; for spring admission, 12/15 for domestic and international students. Applications are processed on a rolling basis. *Application fee:* $50. Electronic applications accepted. *Application Contact:* Hope Schiffgens, Director of Graduate Studies and Adult Education, 412-536-1266, Fax: 412-536-1283, E-mail: schombh1@laroche.edu. *Dean*, Dr. Rosemary McCarthy, 412-536-1193, Fax: 412-536-1763, E-mail: rosemary.mccarthy@laroche.edu.

LA SALLE UNIVERSITY, Philadelphia, PA 19141-1199

General Information Independent-religious, coed, comprehensive institution. CGS member. *Enrollment:* 5,197 graduate, professional, and undergraduate students; 270 full-time matriculated graduate/professional students (202 women), 1,079 part-time matriculated graduate/professional students (745 women). *Enrollment by degree level:* 1,126 master's, 158 doctoral, 65 other advanced degrees. *Graduate faculty:* 74 full-time (46 women), 91 part-time/adjunct (49 women). *Tuition:* Part-time $1000 per credit. *Required fees:* $285 per semester. Tuition and fees vary according to course load, degree level, program and reciprocity agreements. *Graduate housing:* Room and/or apartments available on a first-come, first-served basis to single students; on-campus housing not available to married students. Typical cost: $8890 per year ($11,390 including board). *Student services:* Campus employment opportunities, campus safety program, career counseling, exercise/wellness program, free psychological counseling, international student services, multicultural affairs office, services for students with disabilities, teacher training, writing training. *Library facilities:* Connelly Library. *Collection:* Books: 274,998 (physical), 172,068 (digital/electronic); Serial titles: 1,470 (physical), 127,163 (digital/electronic); Databases: 88. Weekly public service hours: 96; students can reserve study rooms.

Computer facilities: 1,100 computers available on campus for general student use. A campuswide network can be accessed from student residence rooms and from off campus. Online class registration, course management system are available.
Website: http://www.lasalle.edu/

General Application Contact: Elizabeth Heenan, Director, Graduate and Adult Enrollment, 215-951-1100, Fax: 215-951-1462, E-mail: heenan@lasalle.edu.

GRADUATE UNITS

School of Arts and Sciences Students: 147 full-time (114 women), 497 part-time (331 women); includes 188 minority (96 Black or African American, non-Hispanic/Latino; 3 American Indian or Alaska Native, non-Hispanic/Latino; 15 Asian, non-Hispanic/Latino; 53 Hispanic/Latino; 21 Two or more races, non-Hispanic/Latino), 18 international. Average age 32. 770 applicants, 45% accepted, 250 enrolled. *Faculty:* 34 full-time (20 women), 55 part-time/adjunct (26 women). Expenses: Contact institution. *Financial support:* In 2017–18, 139 students received support. Career-related internships or fieldwork, Federal Work-Study, scholarships/grants, and unspecified assistantships available. Support available to part-time students. Financial award application deadline: 8/31; financial award applicants required to submit FAFSA. In 2017, 296 master's, 19 doctorates, 6 other advanced degrees awarded. *Program availability:* Part-time, evening/weekend, 100% online, blended/hybrid learning. Offers American history (Certificate); application development (Certificate); arts and sciences (MA, MS, Psy D, Certificate); autism spectrum disorders (MA, Certificate); bilingual/bicultural studies (MA); child clinical psychology (Psy D); classroom management (MA); clinical health psychology (Psy D); clinical psychology (MA); communication consulting and development (MA); communication management (MA); computer information science (MS); corporate fraud (MS); dual early childhood and special education (MA); dual middle-level science and math and special education (MA); education (MA); English (MA); English as a second language (Certificate); European history (Certificate); fraud and forensic accounting (Certificate); general practice psychology (Psy D); general professional communication (MA); history (MA); history for educators (MA); industrial/organizational psychology (MA); information technology leadership (MS); instructional coach (Certificate); instructional leadership (MA); instructional technology management (MS, Certificate); marriage and family therapy (MA); network security (MS); professional and business communication (Certificate); professional clinical counseling (MA); public history (MA); public relations (MA); reading specialist (MA, Certificate); secondary education (MA); social and new media (Certificate); software project leadership (Certificate); special education (MA, Certificate); teaching advanced placement history (Certificate); world history (Certificate). *Application deadline:* Applications are processed on a rolling basis. *Application fee:* $35. Electronic applications accepted. *Application Contact:* Elizabeth Heenan, Director, Graduate and Adult Enrollment, 215-951-1100, Fax: 215-951-1886, E-mail: heenan@lasalle.edu. *Interim Dean*, Dr. Lynne A. Texter, 215-951-1043, E-mail: texter@lasalle.edu.

Hispanic Institute Students: 1 (woman) full-time, 37 part-time (26 women); includes 21 minority (7 Black or African American, non-Hispanic/Latino; 1 American Indian or Alaska Native, non-Hispanic/Latino; 1 Asian, non-Hispanic/Latino; 10 Hispanic/Latino; 2 Two or more races, non-Hispanic/Latino), 2 international. Average age 33. 24 applicants, 79% accepted, 11 enrolled. *Faculty:* 2 full-time (1 woman), 5 part-time/adjunct (1 woman). Expenses: Contact institution. *Financial support:* In 2017–18, 10 students received support. Scholarships/grants available. Support available to part-time students. Financial award application deadline: 8/31; financial award applicants required to submit FAFSA. In 2017, 4 master's, 1 other advanced degree awarded. *Program availability:* Part-time, evening/weekend. Offers bilingual/bicultural studies (MA); ESL program specialist (Certificate); interpretation: English/Spanish-Spanish/English (Certificate); teaching English to speakers of other languages (MA); translation and interpretation (MA); translation: English/Spanish-Spanish/English (Certificate). *Application deadline:* For fall admission, 8/15 priority date for domestic students, 7/15 for international students; for spring admission, 12/15 priority date for domestic students, 11/15 for international students; for summer admission, 4/15 priority date for domestic students, 3/15 for international students. Applications are processed on a rolling basis. *Application fee:* $35. Electronic applications accepted. *Application Contact:* Elizabeth Heenan, Director, Graduate and Adult Enrollment, 215-951-1100, Fax: 215-951-1462, E-mail: heenan@lasalle.edu. *Director*, Guadalupe Da Costa Montesinos, 215-951-1209, Fax: 215-991-3506, E-mail: montesin@lasalle.edu.

School of Business Students: 63 full-time (29 women), 282 part-time (172 women); includes 92 minority (58 Black or African American, non-Hispanic/Latino; 21 Asian, non-Hispanic/Latino; 10 Hispanic/Latino; 3 Two or more races, non-Hispanic/Latino), 23 international. Average age 33. 216 applicants, 57% accepted, 74 enrolled. *Faculty:* 21 full-time (10 women), 19 part-time/adjunct (8 women). Expenses: Contact institution. *Financial support:* In 2017–18, 61 students received support. Scholarships/grants and unspecified assistantships available. Support available to part-time students. Financial award application deadline: 8/31; financial award applicants required to submit FAFSA. In 2017, 146 master's awarded. *Program availability:* Part-time, evening/weekend, 100% online, blended/hybrid learning. Offers accounting (MBA, Post-MBA Certificate); business administration (MBA, Post-MBA Certificate); business systems and analytics (MBA, Post-MBA Certificate); finance (MBA, Post-MBA Certificate); general business administration (MBA, Post-MBA Certificate); human capital development (MS, Certificate); human resource management (MBA, Post-MBA Certificate); international business (Post-MBA Certificate); management (MBA, Post-MBA Certificate); marketing (Post-MBA Certificate); nonprofit leadership (MS). *Application deadline:* For fall admission, 8/15 priority date for domestic students, 7/15 for international students; for spring admission, 12/15 priority date for domestic students, 11/15 for international students; for summer admission, 4/15 priority date for domestic students, 3/15 for international students. Applications are processed on a rolling basis. *Application fee:* $35. Electronic applications accepted. *Application Contact:* Elizabeth Heenan, Director, Graduate and Adult Enrollment, 215-951-1100, Fax: 215-951-1462, E-mail: heenan@lasalle.edu. *Dean*, Dr. MarySheila McDonald, 215-951-1040, Fax: 215-951-1886, E-mail: mcdonaldms@lasalle.edu.

School of Nursing and Health Sciences Students: 60 full-time (59 women), 300 part-time (242 women); includes 95 minority (51 Black or African American, non-Hispanic/Latino; 1 American Indian or Alaska Native, non-Hispanic/Latino; 22 Asian, non-Hispanic/Latino; 13 Hispanic/Latino; 1 Native Hawaiian or other Pacific Islander, non-Hispanic/Latino; 7 Two or more races, non-Hispanic/Latino), 2 international. Average age 34. 449 applicants, 35% accepted, 55 enrolled. *Faculty:* 19 full-time (16 women), 20 part-time/adjunct (17 women). Expenses: Contact institution. *Financial support:* In 2017–18, 21 students received support. Scholarships/grants, tuition waivers (partial), and unspecified assistantships available. Support available to part-time students. Financial award application deadline: 8/31; financial award applicants required to submit FAFSA. In 2017, 131 master's, 4 doctorates, 13 other advanced degrees awarded. *Program availability:* Part-time, evening/weekend. Offers adult gerontology primary care nurse practitioner (MSN, Certificate); adult health and illness clinical nurse specialist (MSN); adult-gerontology clinical nurse specialist (MSN, Certificate); clinical nurse leader (MSN); family primary care nurse practitioner (MSN, Certificate); gerontology (Certificate); nurse anesthetist (MSN, Certificate); nursing (MSN, Certificate); nursing administration (MSN, Certificate); nursing and health sciences (MPH, MS, MSN, DNP, Certificate); nursing education (Certificate); nursing practice (DNP); nursing service administration (MSN); public health (MPH); public health nursing (MSN, Certificate); school nursing (Certificate); speech-language pathology (MS). *Application deadline:* Applications are processed on a rolling basis. *Application fee:* $35. Electronic applications accepted. *Application Contact:* Elizabeth Heenan, Director, Graduate and Adult Enrollment, 215-951-1100, Fax: 215-951-1462, E-mail: heenan@lasalle.edu. *Dean*, Dr. Kathleen Czekanski, 215-951-1430, Fax: 215-951-1896, E-mail: czekanski@lasalle.edu.

LASELL COLLEGE, Newton, MA 02466-2709

General Information Independent, coed, comprehensive institution. *Enrollment:* 2,100 graduate, professional, and undergraduate students; 123 full-time matriculated graduate/professional students (80 women), 244 part-time matriculated graduate/professional students (167 women). *Enrollment by degree level:* 364 master's, 3 other advanced degrees. *Graduate faculty:* 19 full-time (10 women), 33 part-time/adjunct (23 women). *Tuition:* Full-time $10,800; part-time $600 per credit hour. *Required fees:* $160; $160 per credit hour. One-time fee: $40. *Graduate housing:* On-campus housing not available. *Student services:* Campus employment opportunities, career counseling, exercise/wellness program, international student services, multicultural affairs office, services for students with disabilities. *Library facilities:* Brennan Library. *Collection:* Books: 41,761 (physical), 117,808 (digital/electronic); Serial titles: 67 (physical), 45,258 (digital/electronic); Databases: 86. Weekly public service hours: 83; students can reserve study rooms. *Research affiliation:* Lasell Village (education).

Computer facilities: Computer purchase and lease plans are available. 219 computers available on campus for general student use. A campuswide network can be accessed from student residence rooms and from off campus. Online class registration, online tutoring are available.
Website: http://www.lasell.edu/

General Application Contact: Adrienne Franciosi, Director of Graduate Enrollment, 617-243-2400, Fax: 617-243-2450, E-mail: gradinfo@lasell.edu.

GRADUATE UNITS

Graduate and Professional Studies in Communication Students: 25 full-time (16 women), 35 part-time (28 women); includes 12 minority (6 Black or African American, non-Hispanic/Latino; 1 Asian, non-Hispanic/Latino; 4 Hispanic/Latino; 1 Two or more races, non-Hispanic/Latino), 16 international. Average age 30. 53 applicants, 45% accepted, 22 enrolled. *Faculty:* 3 full-time (2 women), 7 part-time/adjunct (5 women). Expenses: Contact institution. *Financial support:* Federal Work-Study, scholarships/grants, and tuition discounts available. Support available to part-time students. Financial award application deadline: 8/31; financial award applicants required to submit FAFSA. In 2017, 28 master's awarded. *Program availability:* Part-time, evening/weekend, 100% online, blended/hybrid learning. Offers health communication (MSC, Graduate Certificate); integrated marketing communication (MSC, Graduate Certificate); public relations (MSC, Graduate Certificate). *Application deadline:* For fall admission, 8/31 priority date for domestic students, 6/30 priority date for international students; for spring admission, 12/31 priority date for domestic students, 10/31 priority date for international students. Applications are processed on a rolling basis. Electronic applications accepted. *Application Contact:* Adrienne Franciosi, Director of Graduate Enrollment, 617-243-2214, Fax: 617-243-2450, E-mail: gradinfo@lasell.edu. *Vice President of Graduate and Professional Studies*, Eric Turner, 617-243-2071, Fax: 617-243-2450, E-mail: gradinfo@lasell.edu.

Graduate and Professional Studies in Criminal Justice Students: 20 full-time (9 women), 31 part-time (16 women); includes 11 minority (3 Black or African American, non-Hispanic/Latino; 1 Asian, non-Hispanic/Latino; 5 Hispanic/Latino; 2 Two or more races, non-Hispanic/Latino). Average age 31. 33 applicants, 73% accepted, 23 enrolled. *Faculty:* 2 full-time (1 woman), 2 part-time/adjunct (0 women). Expenses: Contact institution. *Financial support:* Federal Work-Study, scholarships/grants, and tuition discounts available. Support available to part-time students. Financial award application deadline: 8/31; financial award applicants required to submit FAFSA. In 2017, 2 master's awarded. *Program availability:* Part-time, evening/weekend, online only, 100% online. Offers emergency and crisis management (MS, Certificate); homeland security and global justice (MS, Certificate); violence prevention and advocacy (MS, Certificate). *Application deadline:* For fall admission, 8/31 priority date for domestic students, 6/30 priority date for international students; for spring admission, 12/31 priority date for domestic students, 10/31 priority date for international students. Applications are processed on a rolling basis. Electronic applications accepted. *Application Contact:* Adrienne Franciosi, Director of Graduate Enrollment, 617-243-2214, Fax: 617-243-2450, E-mail: gradinfo@lasell.edu. *Vice President of Graduate and Professional Studies*, Eric Turner, 617-243-2071, Fax: 617-243-2450, E-mail: gradinfo@lasell.edu.

Graduate and Professional Studies in Education Students: 8 full-time (7 women), 43 part-time (38 women); includes 4 minority (2 Asian, non-Hispanic/Latino; 1 Hispanic/Latino; 1 Two or more races, non-Hispanic/Latino), 1 international. Average age 28. 23 applicants, 74% accepted, 10 enrolled. *Faculty:* 3 full-time (all women), 5 part-time/adjunct (4 women). Expenses: Contact institution. *Financial support:* Federal Work-Study, scholarships/grants, and tuition discounts available. Support available to part-time students. Financial award application deadline: 8/31; financial award applicants required to submit FAFSA. In 2017, 15 master's awarded. *Program availability:* Part-time-only, evening/weekend, blended/hybrid learning. Offers curriculum, leadership, and inclusion (M Ed); elementary education (M Ed); special education (M Ed); teaching bilingual/English learners with disabilities (Graduate Certificate). *Application deadline:* For fall admission, 8/31 priority date for domestic students, 6/30 priority date for international students; for spring admission, 12/31 priority date for domestic students, 10/31 priority date for international students. Applications are processed on a rolling basis. Electronic applications accepted. *Application Contact:* Adrienne Franciosi, Director of Graduate Enrollment, 617-243-2214, Fax: 617-243-2450, E-mail: gradinfo@lasell.edu. *Vice President of Graduate and Professional Studies*, Eric Turner, 617-243-2071, Fax: 617-243-2450, E-mail: gradinfo@lasell.edu.

Graduate and Professional Studies in Management Students: 41 full-time (25 women), 102 part-time (70 women); includes 34 minority (19 Black or African American, non-Hispanic/Latino; 5 Asian, non-Hispanic/Latino; 8 Hispanic/Latino; 2 Two or more races, non-Hispanic/Latino), 29 international. Average age 32. 128 applicants, 46% accepted, 38 enrolled. *Faculty:* 1 full-time (0 women), 15 part-time/adjunct (11 women). Expenses: Contact institution. *Financial support:* Federal Work-Study, scholarships/grants, and tuition discounts available. Support available to part-time students. Financial award application deadline: 8/31; financial award applicants required to submit FAFSA. In 2017, 66 master's, 3 other advanced degrees awarded. *Program availability:* Part-time, evening/weekend, 100% online, blended/hybrid learning. Offers business administration (MBA); elder care management (MSM); hospitality and event management (MSM); human resources management (MSM, Graduate Certificate); management (MSM, Graduate Certificate); marketing (MS, Graduate Certificate); project management (MSM, Graduate Certificate). *Application deadline:* For fall admission, 8/31 priority date for domestic students, 6/30 priority date for international students; for spring admission, 12/31 priority date for domestic students, 10/31 priority date for international students. Applications are processed on a rolling basis. Electronic applications accepted. *Application Contact:* Adrienne Franciosi, Director of Graduate Enrollment, 617-243-2214, Fax: 617-243-2450, E-mail: gradinfo@lasell.edu. *Vice President of Graduate and Professional Studies*, Eric Turner, 617-243-2071, Fax: 617-243-2450, E-mail: gradinfo@lasell.edu.

Graduate and Professional Studies in Rehabilitation Science Students: 14 full-time (12 women), 7 part-time (6 women); includes 3 minority (2 Black or African American, non-Hispanic/Latino; 1 Two or more races, non-Hispanic/Latino). Average age 26. 21 applicants, 43% accepted, 8 enrolled. *Faculty:* 4 full-time (2 women), 1 (woman) part-time/adjunct. Expenses: Contact institution. *Financial support:* Federal Work-Study, scholarships/grants, and tuition discounts available. Support available to part-time students. Financial award application deadline: 8/31; financial award applicants required to submit FAFSA. *Program availability:* Part-time, evening/weekend, online only, 100% online. Offers rehabilitation science (MS). *Application deadline:* For fall admission, 8/31 priority date for domestic students, 6/30 priority date for international students; for spring admission, 12/31 priority date for domestic students, 10/31 priority date for international students. Applications are processed on a rolling basis. Electronic applications accepted. *Application Contact:* Adrienne Franciosi, Director of Graduate Enrollment, 617-243-2214, Fax: 617-243-2450, E-mail: gradinfo@lasell.edu. *Dean of Graduate and Professional Studies*, Eric Turner, 617-243-2071, Fax: 617-243-2450, E-mail: gradinfo@lasell.edu.

Graduate and Professional Studies in Sport Management Students: 10 full-time (6 women), 25 part-time (8 women); includes 12 minority (9 Black or African American, non-Hispanic/Latino; 3 Hispanic/Latino). Average age 29. 35 applicants, 46% accepted, 11 enrolled. *Faculty:* 5 full-time (1 woman), 2 part-time/adjunct (1 woman). Expenses: Contact institution. *Financial support:* Federal Work-Study, scholarships/grants, and tuition discounts available. Support available to part-time students. Financial award application deadline: 8/31; financial award applicants required to submit FAFSA. In 2017, 26 master's awarded. *Program availability:* Part-time, evening/weekend, online only, 100% online. Offers athletic administration (MS); parks and recreation (MS); sport leadership (MS, Graduate Certificate); sport tourism and hospitality (MS). *Application deadline:* For fall admission, 8/31 priority date for domestic students, 6/30 priority date for international students; for spring admission, 12/31 priority date for domestic students, 10/31 priority date for international students. Applications are processed on a rolling basis. Electronic applications accepted. *Application Contact:* Adrienne Franciosi, Director of Graduate Enrollment, 617-243-2214, Fax: 617-243-2450, E-mail: gradinfo@lasell.edu. *Vice President of Graduate and Professional Studies*, Eric Turner, 617-243-2071, Fax: 617-243-2450, E-mail: gradinfo@lasell.edu.

LA SIERRA UNIVERSITY, Riverside, CA 92505

General Information Independent-religious, coed, comprehensive institution. CGS member. *Graduate housing:* Rooms and/or apartments available on a first-come, first-served basis to single students and available to married students.

GRADUATE UNITS

College of Arts and Sciences *Program availability:* Part-time. Offers arts and sciences (MA); communication (MA); English (MA).

School of Business and Management Offers accounting (MBA); finance (MBA); general management (MBA); human resources management (MBA); leadership, values, and ethics for business and management (Certificate); marketing (MBA).

School of Education *Program availability:* Part-time, evening/weekend. Offers administration and leadership (MA, Ed D, Ed S); counseling (MA); curriculum and instruction (MA, Ed D, Ed S); education (MA, MAT, Ed D, Ed S); educational psychology (Ed S); school psychology (Ed S); teaching (MAT).

School of Religion *Program availability:* Part-time. Offers pastoral ministry (M Div); religion (MA); religious education (MA); religious studies (MA).

LAURENTIAN UNIVERSITY, Sudbury, ON P3E 2C6, Canada

General Information Province-supported, coed, comprehensive institution. *Graduate housing:* Rooms and/or apartments available on a first-come, first-served basis to single and married students.

GRADUATE UNITS

School of Graduate Studies and Research *Program availability:* Part-time, evening/weekend. Offers analytical chemistry (M Sc); applied psychology (MA); applied social research (MA); biochemistry (M Sc); biology (M Sc); boreal ecology (PhD); environmental chemistry (M Sc); European history (MA); experimental psychology (MA); geology (M Sc); history of Northern Ontario (MA); human development (M Sc, MA); humanities: interpretation and values (MA); mineral deposits and precambrian geology (PhD); mineral exploration (M Sc); North American history (MA); nursing (M Sc N); organic chemistry (M Sc); physical/theoretical chemistry (M Sc); physics (M Sc); rural and Northern health (PhD); science communication (G Dip).

School of Commerce and Administration *Program availability:* Part-time, evening/weekend. Offers commerce and administration (MBA).

School of Engineering *Program availability:* Part-time. Offers mineral resources engineering (M Eng, MA Sc); natural resources engineering (PhD).

School of Social Work *Program availability:* Part-time. Offers social work (MSW). Open only to French-speaking students.

LAWRENCE TECHNOLOGICAL UNIVERSITY, Southfield, MI 48075-1058

General Information Independent, coed, university. *Enrollment:* 3,069 graduate, professional, and undergraduate students; 34 full-time matriculated graduate/professional students (13 women), 844 part-time matriculated graduate/professional students (217 women). *Enrollment by degree level:* 818 master's, 36 doctoral, 24 other advanced degrees. *Graduate faculty:* 62 full-time (17 women), 36 part-time/adjunct (6 women). *Tuition:* Full-time $15,274; part-time $1091 per credit. One-time fee: $150. *Graduate housing:* Rooms and/or apartments available on a first-come, first-served basis to single and married students. Typical cost: $6700 per year ($9500 including board) for single students; $6700 per year ($9500 including board) for married students. Room and board charges vary according to board plan, campus/location and housing facility selected. Housing application deadline: 5/1. *Student services:* Campus employment opportunities, campus safety program, career counseling, exercise/wellness program, free psychological counseling, international student services, low-cost health insurance, multicultural affairs office, services for students with disabilities, writing training. *Library facilities:* Lawrence Technological University Library plus 1 other. *Collection:* Books: 43,864 (physical), 298,126 (digital/electronic); Serial titles: 941 (physical), 44,608 (digital/electronic); Databases: 171. Weekly public service hours: 73; students can reserve study rooms. *Research affiliation:* Ford Motor Company (engineering), Clinton River Watershed Council (storm water analysis), Detroit Economic Growth Association (Great Lakes Shoreline Cities Green Infrastructure Project), Hyundai-KIA America Technical Center, Inc. (improvement of built-in hands-free cell phone performance), Johnson Controls Battery Group, Inc. (vehicle system power management testing), Meijer Foundation (engineering).

Computer facilities: Computer purchase and lease plans are available. 2,203 computers available on campus for general student use. A campuswide network can be accessed from student residence rooms and from off campus. Online class registration, degree audit, Canvas/Blackboard, Banner (student information), personal websites, document collection, Handshake, Placement, Mapworks advising are available.
Website: http://www.ltu.edu/

General Application Contact: Jane Rohrback, Director of Admissions, 248-204-3160, Fax: 248-204-2228, E-mail: admissions@ltu.edu.

GRADUATE UNITS

College of Architecture and Design Students: 6 full-time (2 women), 115 part-time (50 women); includes 11 minority (3 Black or African American, non-Hispanic/Latino; 1 Asian, non-Hispanic/Latino; 6 Hispanic/Latino; 1 Two or more races, non-Hispanic/Latino), 32 international. Average age 30. 150 applicants, 55% accepted, 50 enrolled. *Faculty:* 14 full-time (1 woman), 3 part-time/adjunct (1 woman). Expenses: Contact institution. *Financial support:* In 2017–18, 45 students received support, including 8 research assistantships with partial tuition reimbursements available (averaging $6,000 per year); career-related internships or fieldwork, scholarships/grants, and unspecified assistantships also available. Financial award application deadline: 4/1; financial award applicants required to submit FAFSA. In 2017, 82 master's, 3 other advanced degrees awarded. *Program availability:* Part-time, evening/weekend. Offers architecture (M Arch, MA); build information modeling (Graduate Certificate); interior design (MID); social practice (MFA); transportation design (Graduate Certificate); urban design (MUD). *Application deadline:* For fall admission, 5/27 for international students; for spring admission, 10/8 for international students; for summer admission, 2/14 for international students. Applications are processed on a rolling basis. *Application fee:* $50. Electronic applications accepted. *Application Contact:* Jane Rohrback, Director of Admissions, 248-204-3160, Fax: 248-204-2228, E-mail: admissions@ltu.edu. *Dean/Professor*, Prof. Karl Daubmann, 248-204-2805, E-mail: archdean@ltu.edu.

College of Arts and Sciences Students: 34 part-time (15 women); includes 4 minority (1 Black or African American, non-Hispanic/Latino; 2 Asian, non-Hispanic/Latino; 1 Hispanic/Latino), 7 international. Average age 31. 84 applicants, 15% accepted, 10 enrolled. *Faculty:* 6 full-time (2 women), 7 part-time/adjunct (3 women). Expenses: Contact institution. *Financial support:* In 2017–18, 8 students received support. Scholarships/grants and tuition reduction available. Financial award application deadline: 4/1; financial award applicants required to submit FAFSA. In 2017, 14 master's awarded. *Program availability:* Part-time, evening/weekend. Offers bioinformatics (Graduate Certificate); computer science (MS); educational technology (MA); instructional design, communication, and presentation (Graduate Certificate); integrated science (MA); science education (MA); technical and professional communication (MS, Graduate Certificate); writing for the digital age (Graduate Certificate). *Application deadline:* For fall admission, 5/27 for international students; for spring admission, 10/8 for international students; for summer admission, 2/14 for international students. Applications are processed on a rolling basis. *Application fee:* $50. Electronic applications accepted. *Application Contact:* Jane Rohrback, Director of Admissions, 248-204-3160, Fax: 248-204-2228, E-mail: admissions@ltu.edu. *Interim Dean*, Glen Bauer, 248-204-3532, Fax: 248-204-3518, E-mail: scidean@ltu.edu.

College of Engineering Students: 20 full-time (8 women), 415 part-time (50 women); includes 24 minority (7 Black or African American, non-Hispanic/Latino; 8 Asian, non-Hispanic/Latino; 9 Hispanic/Latino), 299 international. Average age 27. 550 applicants, 24% accepted, 77 enrolled. *Faculty:* 27 full-time (5 women), 22 part-time/adjunct (2 women). Expenses: Contact institution. *Financial support:* In 2017–18, 29 students received support, including 5 research assistantships with full tuition reimbursements available; unspecified assistantships also available. Financial award application deadline: 4/1; financial award applicants required to submit FAFSA. In 2017, 269 master's, 10 doctorates awarded. *Program availability:* Part-time, evening/weekend. Offers architectural engineering (MS); automotive engineering (MS); biomedical engineering (MS); civil engineering (MA, MS, PhD); construction engineering management (MA); electrical and computer engineering (MS); engineering management (MEM); engineering technology (MS); fire engineering (MS); industrial engineering (MS); manufacturing systems (ME); mechanical engineering (MS, DE, PhD); mechatronic systems engineering (MS). *Application deadline:* For fall admission, 5/27 for international students; for spring admission, 10/8 for international students; for summer admission, 2/14 for international students. Applications are processed on a rolling basis. *Application fee:* $50. Electronic applications accepted. *Application Contact:* Jane Rohrback, Director of Admissions, 248-204-3160, Fax: 248-204-2228, E-mail: admissions@ltu.edu. *Dean*, Dr. Nabil Grace, 248-204-2500, Fax: 248-204-2509, E-mail: engrdean@ltu.edu.

College of Management Students: 8 full-time (3 women), 280 part-time (102 women); includes 70 minority (34 Black or African American, non-Hispanic/Latino; 2 American Indian or Alaska Native, non-Hispanic/Latino; 18 Asian, non-Hispanic/Latino; 11 Hispanic/Latino; 5 Two or more races, non-Hispanic/Latino), 73 international. Average age 34. 143 applicants, 50% accepted, 68 enrolled. *Faculty:* 13 full-time (6 women), 7 part-time/adjunct (1 woman). Expenses: Contact institution. *Financial support:* In 2017–18, 35 students received support, including 8 research assistantships with partial tuition reimbursements available (averaging $3,360 per year); career-related internships or fieldwork, unspecified assistantships, and corporate tuition incentives also available. Financial award application deadline: 4/1; financial award applicants required to submit FAFSA. In 2017, 114 master's, 7 doctorates, 10 other advanced degrees awarded. *Program availability:* Part-time, evening/weekend, 100% online. Offers business administration (MBA, DBA); cybersecurity (Graduate Certificate); health IT management (Graduate Certificate); information assurance mangement (Graduate Certificate); information systems (MS); information technology (MS, DM); management (PhD); nonprofit management and leadership (Graduate Certificate); operations management (MS); project management (Graduate Certificate). *Application deadline:* For fall admission, 5/27 for international students; for spring admission, 10/8 for international students; for summer admission, 2/14 for international students. Applications are processed on a rolling basis. *Application fee:* $50. Electronic applications accepted. *Application Contact:* Jane Rohrback, Director of Admissions, 248-204-3160, Fax: 248-204-2228, E-mail: admissions@ltu.edu. *Dean*, Dr. Bahman Mirshab, 248-204-3050, E-mail: mgtdean@ltu.edu.

LEBANESE AMERICAN UNIVERSITY, Beirut, Lebanon

General Information Private, coed, comprehensive institution.

GRADUATE UNITS

School of Arts and Sciences Offers computer science (MS); international affairs (MA).

School of Business Offers business (MBA).

School of Pharmacy Offers pharmacy (Pharm D).

LEBANON VALLEY COLLEGE, Annville, PA 17003-1400

General Information Independent-religious, coed, comprehensive institution. *Enrollment:* 1,910 graduate, professional, and undergraduate students; 80 full-time matriculated graduate/professional students (50 women), 74 part-time matriculated graduate/professional students (45 women). *Enrollment by degree level:* 70 master's, 82 doctoral, 2 other advanced degrees. *Graduate faculty:* 15 full-time (6 women), 34 part-time/adjunct (13 women). *Tuition:* Full-time $46,630; part-time $660 per credit hour. *Required fees:* $1100. Tuition and fees vary according to program. *Graduate housing:* Room and/or apartments available on a first-come, first-served basis to single students; on-campus housing not available to married students. Housing application deadline: 3/3. *Student services:* Campus employment opportunities, campus safety program, career counseling, exercise/wellness program, free psychological counseling, international student services, multicultural affairs office, services for students with disabilities, teacher training, writing training. *Library facilities:* Vernon and Doris Bishop Library. *Collection:* Books: 152,349 (physical), 204,880 (digital/electronic); Serial titles: 3,047 (physical), 59,331 (digital/electronic); Databases: 256. Weekly public service hours: 101; students can reserve study rooms.

Computer facilities: Computer purchase and lease plans are available. 202 computers available on campus for general student use. A campuswide network can be accessed from student residence rooms and from off campus. Online class registration is available.
Website: http://www.lvc.edu/

General Application Contact: Edwin Wright, Vice President of Enrollment Management, 717-867-6100, E-mail: admission@lvc.edu.

GRADUATE UNITS

Program in Athletic Training 103 applicants, 54% accepted, 20 enrolled. *Faculty:* 4 full-time (2 women), 4 part-time/adjunct (2 women). Expenses: Contact institution. *Financial support:* Federal Work-Study and scholarships/grants available. Financial award applicants required to submit FAFSA. Offers athletic training (MAT). *Application deadline:* For fall admission, 3/1 priority date for domestic and international students. Applications are processed on a rolling basis. Electronic applications accepted. *Assistant Professor/Director*, Dr. Joseph M. Murphy, 717-867-6845, Fax: 717-867-6849, E-mail: jmurphy@lvc.edu.

Program in Business Administration Students: 11 full-time (5 women), 66 part-time (28 women); includes 11 minority (3 Black or African American, non-Hispanic/Latino; 4 Asian, non-Hispanic/Latino; 4 Hispanic/Latino), 3 international. Average age 34. 21 applicants, 81% accepted, 16 enrolled. *Faculty:* 7 full-time (1 woman), 8 part-time/adjunct (1 woman). Expenses: Contact institution. *Financial support:* Career-related internships or fieldwork and scholarships/grants available. Financial award application deadline: 3/1; financial award applicants required to submit FAFSA. In 2017, 32 master's awarded. *Program availability:* Part-time, evening/weekend. Offers business administration (MBA); healthcare management (MBA); human resources (MBA); leadership and ethics (MBA); project management (MBA). *Application deadline:* Applications are processed on a rolling basis. *Application fee:* $0. Electronic applications accepted. *Application Contact:* Christine M. Martin, Enrollment and Operations Specialist, 717-867-6486, Fax: 717-867-6013, E-mail: cmartin@lvc.edu. *Associate Professor/Chair of Business Administration/Director of the MBA Program*, Dr. David Setley, 717-867-6104, Fax: 717-867-6018, E-mail: setley@lvc.edu.

Program in Music Education Students: 2 part-time (1 woman). Average age 40. 1 applicant, 100% accepted, 1 enrolled. *Faculty:* 11 part-time/adjunct (3 women). Expenses: Contact institution. *Financial support:* Career-related internships or fieldwork and scholarships/grants available. Financial award application deadline: 3/1; financial award applicants required to submit FAFSA. In 2017, 9 master's awarded. *Program availability:* Part-time-only, evening/weekend. Offers music education (MME). *Application deadline:* Applications are processed on a rolling basis. *Application fee:* $0. Electronic applications accepted. *Application Contact:* Cherie VanZant, Graduate and Community Programs Administrator, 717-867-6383, E-mail: vanzant@lvc.edu. *Graduate and Community Programs Administrator*, Cherie Van Zant, 717-867-6383, E-mail: vanzant@lvc.edu.

Program in Physical Therapy Students: 70 full-time (47 women); includes 3 minority (1 Black or African American, non-Hispanic/Latino; 1 Asian, non-Hispanic/Latino; 1 Native Hawaiian or other Pacific Islander, non-Hispanic/Latino). Average age 23. 252 applicants, 51% accepted, 66 enrolled. *Faculty:* 9 full-time (4 women), 32 part-time/adjunct (13 women). Expenses: Contact institution. *Financial support:* In 2017–18, 100 students received support. Federal Work-Study and scholarships/grants available. Financial award application deadline: 3/1; financial award applicants required to submit FAFSA. In 2017, 38 doctorates awarded. Offers physical therapy (DPT). *Application deadline:* For fall admission, 2/1 for domestic and international students. Applications are processed on a rolling basis. *Application fee:* $50. Electronic applications accepted. *Application Contact:* EJ Smith, Assistant Director of Admission, 717-867-6183, E-mail: ejsmith@lvc.edu. *Co-Chair/Professor of Physical Therapy*, Dr. Katie Oriel, 717-867-6852, E-mail: oriel@lvc.edu.

Program in Science Education Students: 3 part-time (all women). Average age 42. 4 applicants, 100% accepted, 3 enrolled. *Faculty:* 14 part-time/adjunct (7 women). Expenses: Contact institution. *Financial support:* Scholarships/grants available. Financial award application deadline: 3/1; financial award applicants required to submit FAFSA. In 2017, 10 master's awarded. *Program availability:* Part-time-only, evening/weekend, 100% online, blended/hybrid learning. Offers integrative STEM education (Certificate); STEM education (MSE). *Application deadline:* Applications are processed on a rolling basis. *Application fee:* $0. Electronic applications accepted. *Director of MSE and STEM-based programs*, Carrie Coryer, 717-867-6190, Fax: 717-867-6018, E-mail: coryer@lvc.edu.

Program in Speech-Language Pathology 47 applicants, 81% accepted, 23 enrolled. *Faculty:* 2 full-time (both women). Expenses: Contact institution. *Financial support:* Federal Work-Study and scholarships/grants available. Financial award applicants required to submit FAFSA. Offers speech-language pathology (MSLP). *Application Contact:* EJ Smith, Associate Director of Admissions and Recruitment, 717-867-6183, E-mail: ejsmith@lvc.edu. *Chair/Assistant Professor of Speech Language Pathology*, Dr. Michelle Scesa, 717-867-6710, E-mail: scesa@lvc.edu.

LEE UNIVERSITY, Cleveland, TN 37320-3450

General Information Independent-religious, coed, comprehensive institution. *Enrollment:* 5,370 graduate, professional, and undergraduate students; 224 full-time matriculated graduate/professional students (123 women), 263 part-time matriculated graduate/professional students (129 women). *Enrollment by degree level:* 482 master's, 5 other advanced degrees. *Graduate faculty:* 60 full-time (21 women), 21 part-time/adjunct (7 women). *Tuition:* Full-time $12,780; part-time $710 per credit hour. *Required fees:* $60; $60 per term. Tuition and fees vary according to program. *Graduate housing:* Rooms and/or apartments available on a first-come, first-served basis to single and married students. Typical cost: $4530 per year ($8300 including board) for single students; $7200 per year ($11,200 including board) for married students. Room and board charges vary according to board plan and housing facility selected. Housing application deadline: 9/1. *Student services:* Campus employment opportunities, campus safety program, career counseling, exercise/wellness program, free psychological counseling, international student services, services for students with disabilities, teacher training, writing training. *Library facilities:* William G. Squires Library plus 2 others. *Collection:* Books: 159,161 (physical), 279,837 (digital/electronic); Serial titles: 244 (physical), 93,815 (digital/electronic); Databases: 137. Weekly public service hours: 91; students can reserve study rooms.

Computer facilities: 348 computers available on campus for general student use. A campuswide network can be accessed from student residence rooms and from off campus. Online class registration is available.
Website: http://www.leeuniversity.edu/

General Application Contact: Jeffery McGirt, Director of Graduate Enrollment, 423-614-8691, Fax: 423-614-8317, E-mail: jmcgirt@leeuniversity.edu.

GRADUATE UNITS

Graduate Studies in Counseling Students: 95 full-time (71 women), 24 part-time (18 women); includes 27 minority (5 Black or African American, non-Hispanic/Latino; 19 Hispanic/Latino; 3 Two or more races, non-Hispanic/Latino), 7 international. Average age 30. 47 applicants, 87% accepted, 33 enrolled. *Faculty:* 7 full-time (3 women), 3 part-time/adjunct (0 women). Expenses: Contact institution. *Financial support:* In 2017–18, 36 students received support. Career-related internships or fieldwork, Federal Work-Study, institutionally sponsored loans, scholarships/grants, and unspecified assistantships available. Financial award application deadline: 3/1; financial award applicants required to submit FAFSA. In 2017, 32 master's awarded. *Program availability:* Part-time, 100% online. Offers holistic child development (MS); marriage and family studies (MS); marriage and family therapy (MS); school counseling (MS). *Application deadline:* For fall admission, 4/1 priority date for domestic and international students; for spring admission, 11/1 priority date for domestic and international students. Applications are processed on a rolling basis. *Application fee:* $25. Electronic applications accepted. *Director*, Dr. Trevor Milliron, 423-614-8126, Fax: 423-614-8124, E-mail: tmilliron@leeuniversity.edu.

MBA Program Students: 15 full-time (5 women), 54 part-time (21 women); includes 10 minority (4 Black or African American, non-Hispanic/Latino; 2 American Indian or Alaska Native, non-Hispanic/Latino; 1 Asian, non-Hispanic/Latino; 3 Hispanic/Latino), 7 international. Average age 29. 35 applicants, 77% accepted, 23 enrolled. *Faculty:* 6 full-time (2 women), 1 (woman) part-time/adjunct. Expenses: Contact institution. *Financial support:* In 2017–18, 36 students received support. Scholarships/grants available. Financial award application deadline: 3/1; financial award applicants required to submit FAFSA. In 2017, 26 master's awarded. *Program availability:* Part-time, evening/weekend, 100% online. Offers business administration (MBA). *Application deadline:* For fall admission, 4/1 priority date for domestic and international students; for spring admission, 10/1 priority date for domestic and international students. Applications are processed on a rolling basis. *Application fee:* $25. Electronic applications accepted. *Director*, Dr. Shane Griffith, 423-614-8694, E-mail: mba@leeuniversity.edu.

Program in Education Students: 28 full-time (21 women), 77 part-time (48 women); includes 12 minority (7 Black or African American, non-Hispanic/Latino; 2 Hispanic/Latino; 3 Two or more races, non-Hispanic/Latino), 1 international. Average age 31. 35 applicants, 83% accepted, 22 enrolled. *Faculty:* 15 full-time (7 women), 8 part-time/adjunct (3 women). Expenses: Contact institution. *Financial support:* In 2017–18, 32 students received support. Career-related internships or fieldwork, Federal Work-Study, institutionally sponsored loans, scholarships/grants, and unspecified assistantships available. Financial award application deadline: 3/1; financial award applicants required to submit FAFSA. In 2017, 54 master's, 4 other advanced degrees awarded. *Program availability:* Part-time. Offers art (MAT); curriculum and instruction (M Ed, Ed S); early childhood (MAT); educational leadership (M Ed, Ed S); elementary education (MAT); English and math (MAT); English and science (MAT); English and social studies (MAT); higher education administration (MS); history (MAT); history and economics (MAT); math and science (MAT); math and social studies (MAT); middle grades (MAT); science and social studies (MASW); secondary education (MAT); Spanish (MAT); special education (M Ed, MAT); TESOL (MAT). *Application deadline:* For fall admission, 6/1 priority date for domestic and international students; for spring admission, 11/1 priority date for domestic and international students; for summer admission, 4/1 priority date for domestic and international students. Applications are processed on a rolling basis. *Application fee:* $25. Electronic applications accepted. *Application Contact:* Crystal Keeter, Graduate Education Secretary, 423-614-8544, E-mail: ckeeter@leeuniversity.edu. *Director*, Dr. William Kamm, 423-614-8544, E-mail: wkamm@leeuniversity.edu.

Program in Music Students: 24 full-time (10 women), 9 part-time (6 women); includes 3 minority (2 Black or African American, non-Hispanic/Latino; 1 Asian, non-Hispanic/Latino), 5 international. Average age 27. 19 applicants, 89% accepted, 12 enrolled. *Faculty:* 23 full-time (6 women), 6 part-time/adjunct (3 women). Expenses: Contact institution. *Financial support:* In 2017–18, 31 students received support. Career-related internships or fieldwork, Federal Work-Study, institutionally sponsored loans, scholarships/grants, and unspecified assistantships available. Financial award application deadline: 3/1; financial award applicants required to submit FAFSA. In 2017, 9 master's awarded. *Program availability:* Part-time. Offers conducting (MM); music education (MM); music performance (MM); religious studies (MCM); sacred music (MCM). *Application deadline:* For fall admission, 4/1 priority date for domestic and international students; for spring admission, 10/1 priority date for domestic and international students. Applications are processed on a rolling basis. *Application fee:* $25. Electronic applications accepted. *Director*, Dr. Brad J. Moffett, 423-614-8240, Fax: 423-614-8245, E-mail: gradmusic@leeuniversity.edu.

Programs in Religion Students: 62 full-time (16 women), 99 part-time (36 women); includes 68 minority (9 Black or African American, non-Hispanic/Latino; 1 Asian, non-Hispanic/Latino; 57 Hispanic/Latino; 1 Two or more races, non-Hispanic/Latino), 6 international. Average age 37. 21 applicants, 86% accepted, 8 enrolled. *Faculty:* 9 full-time (3 women), 3 part-time/adjunct (0 women). Expenses: Contact institution. *Financial support:* In 2017–18, 34 students received support, including 12 teaching assistantships (averaging $1,886 per year); career-related internships or fieldwork, Federal Work-Study, institutionally sponsored loans, scholarships/grants, and unspecified assistantships also available. Financial award application deadline: 3/1; financial award applicants required to submit FAFSA. In 2017, 13 master's awarded. *Program availability:* Part-time, 100% online. Offers biblical studies (MA); ministry studies/leadership (MA); ministry studies/worship (MA); ministry studies/youth and family (MA); theological studies (MA). *Application deadline:* For fall admission, 4/1 priority date for domestic and international students; for spring admission, 10/1 priority date for domestic and international students. Applications are processed on a rolling basis. *Application fee:* $25. Electronic applications accepted. *Director*, Dr. Lisa Long, 423-303-5100, E-mail: llong@leeuniversity.edu.

LEHIGH UNIVERSITY, Bethlehem, PA 18015

General Information Independent, coed, university. CGS member. *Enrollment:* 7,017 graduate, professional, and undergraduate students; 1,220 full-time matriculated graduate/professional students (513 women), 638 part-time matriculated graduate/professional students (306 women). *Enrollment by degree level:* 1,152 master's, 695 doctoral, 11 other advanced degrees. *Graduate faculty:* 379 full-time (116 women), 43 part-time/adjunct (21 women). *Graduate housing:* Rooms and/or apartments available on a first-come, first-served basis to single and married students. *Student services:* Campus employment opportunities, campus safety program, career counseling, child daycare facilities, exercise/wellness program, free psychological counseling, international student services, low-cost health insurance, multicultural affairs office, services for students with disabilities, teacher training, writing training. *Library facilities:* E. W. Fairchild-Martindale Library plus 1 other. *Collection:* Books: 798,207 (physical), 402,504 (digital/electronic); Serial titles: 2,050 (physical), 61,205 (digital/electronic); Databases: 191. Weekly public service hours: 83; students can reserve study rooms.

Computer facilities: Computer purchase and lease plans are available. 597 computers available on campus for general student use. A campuswide network can be accessed from student residence rooms and from off campus. Online class registration is available.
Website: http://www.lehigh.edu/

GRADUATE UNITS

College of Arts and Sciences Students: 279 full-time (135 women), 56 part-time (30 women); includes 37 minority (11 Black or African American, non-Hispanic/Latino; 1 American Indian or Alaska Native, non-Hispanic/Latino; 7 Asian, non-Hispanic/Latino; 12 Hispanic/Latino; 1 Native Hawaiian or other Pacific Islander, non-Hispanic/Latino; 5 Two or more races, non-Hispanic/Latino), 86 international. Average age 28. 551 applicants, 40% accepted, 80 enrolled. *Faculty:* 163 full-time (62 women), 8 part-time/adjunct (3 women). Expenses: Contact institution. *Financial support:* In 2017–18, fellowships with full tuition reimbursements (averaging $25,000 per year) were awarded; research assistantships, teaching assistantships, scholarships/grants, tuition waivers (full and partial), and unspecified assistantships also available. Financial award application deadline: 1/1. In 2017, 80 master's, 33 doctorates awarded. *Program availability:* Part-time, online learning. Offers Africana studies (Graduate Certificate); American studies (MA); applied mathematics (MS, PhD); arts and sciences (MA, MS, PhD, Graduate Certificate); Atlantic world (PhD); biochemistry (PhD); British history (PhD); cell and molecular biology (PhD); chemistry (MS, PhD); documentary film (Graduate Certificate); earth and environmental sciences (MS, PhD); English (MA, PhD); environmental health (Graduate Certificate); environmental justice (Graduate Certificate); environmental policy and law (Graduate Certificate); environmental policy design (MA); history (MA); industrial and modern America (PhD); integrative biology (PhD); mathematics (MS, PhD); molecular biology (MS); photonics (MS); physics (MS, PhD); politics and policy (MA); psychology (MS, PhD); public history (MA); sociology (MA); statistics (MS); sustainable development (Graduate Certificate); urban environmental policy (Graduate Certificate). *Application deadline:* For fall admission, 7/1 for domestic students, 7/15 for international students; for spring admission, 12/1 for domestic and international students. *Application fee:* $75. Electronic applications accepted. *Application Contact:* Gary Burgess, Administrative Clerk, 610-758-4281, Fax: 610-758-6232, E-mail: glb215@lehigh.edu. *Associate Dean of Graduate Studies*, Dr. Dominic Packer, 610-758-4282, Fax: 610-758-6232, E-mail: dlp208@lehigh.edu.

College of Business and Economics Students: 165 full-time (87 women), 165 part-time (45 women); includes 41 minority (6 Black or African American, non-Hispanic/Latino; 18 Asian, non-Hispanic/Latino; 13 Hispanic/Latino; 4 Two or more races, non-Hispanic/Latino), 127 international. Average age 29. 614 applicants, 54% accepted, 94 enrolled. *Faculty:* 37 full-time (5 women), 6 part-time/adjunct (2 women). Expenses: Contact institution. *Financial support:* In 2017–18, 10 fellowships with partial tuition reimbursements, 1 research assistantship with full tuition reimbursement (averaging $18,000 per year), 15 teaching assistantships with full tuition reimbursements (averaging $18,000 per year) were awarded; scholarships/grants, health care benefits, tuition waivers, and unspecified assistantships also available. Support available to part-time students. Financial award application deadline: 1/15. In 2017, 139 master's, 4 doctorates awarded. *Program availability:* Part-time, evening/weekend, synchronous with live class. Offers accounting and information analysis (MS); analytical finance (MS); business administration (MBA); business and economics (MBA, MS, PhD); economics (MS, PhD); project management (MBA). *Application deadline:* For fall admission, 7/15 for domestic students, 5/1 for international students; for spring admission, 12/1 for domestic and international students. Applications are processed on a rolling basis. *Application fee:* $75. Electronic applications accepted. *Application Contact:* Mary Theresa Taglang, Director of Recruitment and Admissions, 610-758-4386, Fax: 610-758-5283, E-mail: mtt4@lehigh.edu. *Dean*, Georgette Chapman-Phillips, 610-758-6725, Fax: 610-758-4499, E-mail: gcp214@lehigh.edu.

College of Education Students: 181 full-time (155 women), 267 part-time (186 women); includes 54 minority (12 Black or African American, non-Hispanic/Latino; 13 Asian, non-Hispanic/Latino; 27 Hispanic/Latino; 1 Native Hawaiian or other Pacific Islander, non-Hispanic/Latino; 1 Two or more races, non-Hispanic/Latino), 48 international. Average age 31. 468 applicants, 52% accepted, 79 enrolled. *Faculty:* 34 full-time (24 women), 27 part-time/adjunct (17 women). Expenses: Contact institution. *Financial support:* In 2017–18, 133 students received support, including 4 fellowships with tuition reimbursements available (averaging $24,238 per year), 57 research assistantships with full and partial tuition reimbursements available (averaging $13,229 per year); unspecified assistantships also available. Financial award application deadline: 3/1. In 2017, 148 master's, 15 doctorates, 9 other advanced degrees awarded. *Program availability:* Part-time, evening/weekend, online only, 100% online, blended/hybrid learning. Offers counseling and human services (M Ed); counseling psychology (PhD); curriculum and instruction (Certificate); education (M Ed, MA, MS, Ed D, PhD, Certificate, Ed S, Graduate Certificate); educational leadership (M Ed, Ed D); elementary education (M Ed); instructional technology (MS); international counseling (M Ed, Certificate); K-12 principal (Certificate); school counseling (M Ed); school psychology (PhD, Ed S); special education (M Ed, PhD); superintendent letter (Certificate); teaching, learning and technology (PhD). *Application deadline:* For fall admission, 1/1 for domestic and international students; for spring admission, 11/1 for domestic and international students; for summer admission, 5/1 for domestic and international students. Applications are processed on a rolling basis. *Application fee:* $65. Electronic applications accepted. *Application Contact:* Donna M. Johnson, Manager of Admissions and Recruitment, 610-758-3231, Fax: 610-758-6223, E-mail: dmj4@lehigh.edu. *Dean*, Dr. Gary M. Sasso, 610-758-3221, Fax: 610-758-6223, E-mail: gary.sasso@lehigh.edu.

P.C. Rossin College of Engineering and Applied Science Students: 595 full-time (136 women), 150 part-time (45 women); includes 60 minority (11 Black or African American, non-Hispanic/Latino; 24 Asian, non-Hispanic/Latino; 17 Hispanic/Latino; 2 Native Hawaiian or other Pacific Islander, non-Hispanic/Latino; 6 Two or more races, non-Hispanic/Latino), 446 international. Average age 26. 2,211 applicants, 33% accepted, 196 enrolled. *Faculty:* 152 full-time (25 women), 8 part-time/adjunct (0 women). Expenses: Contact institution. *Financial support:* In 2017–18, 226 students received support, including 24 fellowships with tuition reimbursements available (averaging $22,050 per year), 142 research assistantships with tuition reimbursements available (averaging $29,400 per year), 60 teaching assistantships with tuition reimbursements available (averaging $22,050 per year); scholarships/grants, tuition waivers (full and partial), and unspecified assistantships also available. Financial award application deadline: 1/15. In 2017, 219 master's, 40 doctorates awarded. *Program availability:* Part-time, 100% online, blended/hybrid learning. Offers analytical finance (MS); bioengineering (MS, PhD); biological chemical engineering (M Eng); chemical energy engineering (M Eng); chemical engineering (M Eng, MS, PhD); civil and environmental engineering (M Eng, MS, PhD); computer engineering (M Eng, MS, PhD); computer science (M Eng, MS, PhD); electrical engineering (M Eng, MS, PhD); energy systems engineering (M Eng); engineering and applied science (M Eng, MS, PhD, Certificate); healthcare systems engineering (M Eng, Certificate); industrial and systems engineering (M Eng, MS, PhD); management science and engineering (M Eng, MS); materials science and engineering (M Eng, MS, PhD); mechanical engineering (M Eng, MS, PhD); photonics (MS); polymer science/engineering (M Eng, MS, PhD); technical entrepreneurship (M Eng). *Application deadline:* For fall admission, 7/15 for domestic and international students; for spring admission, 12/1 for domestic and international students. *Application fee:* $75. Electronic applications accepted. *Application Contact:* Brianne Lisk, Manager of Graduate Programs, 610-758-6310, Fax: 610-758-5623, E-mail: brie.lisk@lehigh.edu. *Dean*, Dr. Stephen P. DeWeerth, 610-758-5308, Fax: 610-758-5623, E-mail: steve.deweerth@lehigh.edu.

Center for Polymer Science and Engineering Students: 7 full-time (4 women), 26 part-time (8 women); includes 7 minority (1 Black or African American, non-Hispanic/Latino; 5 Asian, non-Hispanic/Latino; 1 Native Hawaiian or other Pacific Islander, non-Hispanic/Latino), 6 international. Average age 30. 50 applicants, 26% accepted, 12 enrolled. *Faculty:* 21 full-time (2 women), 1 part-time/adjunct (0 women). Expenses: Contact institution. *Financial support:* In 2017–18, research assistantships with full tuition reimbursements (averaging $28,707 per year), teaching assistantships with full tuition reimbursements (averaging $22,050 per year) were awarded; health care benefits also available. Financial award application deadline: 1/15. In 2017, 6 master's, 1 doctorate awarded. *Program availability:* Part-time, evening/weekend, 100% online, blended/hybrid learning. Offers polymer science and engineering (M Eng, MS, PhD). *Application deadline:* For fall admission, 7/15 for domestic students, 1/15 for international students; for spring admission, 12/1 for domestic and international students; for summer admission, 4/30 for domestic and international students. Applications are processed on a rolling basis. *Application fee:* $75. Electronic applications accepted. *Application Contact:* James E. Roberts, Chair, Polymer Education Committee, 610-758-4841, Fax: 610-758-6536, E-mail: jer1@lehigh.edu. *Director,* Dr. Raymond A. Pearson, 610-758-3857, Fax: 610-758-3526, E-mail: rp02@lehigh.edu.

LEHMAN COLLEGE OF THE CITY UNIVERSITY OF NEW YORK, Bronx, NY 10468-1589

General Information State and locally supported, coed, comprehensive institution. *Graduate housing:* On-campus housing not available. *Research affiliation:* New York Botanical Gardens, Montefiore Hospital and Medical Center.

GRADUATE UNITS

School of Arts and Humanities *Program availability:* Part-time, evening/weekend. Offers art (MA, MFA); arts and humanities (MA, MAT, MFA); English (MA); history (MA); music (MAT); Spanish (MA).

School of Education *Program availability:* Part-time, evening/weekend. Offers bilingual special education (MS Ed); business education (MS Ed); early childhood education (MS Ed); early special education (MS Ed); education (MA, MS Ed); elementary education (MS Ed); emotional handicaps (MS Ed); English education (MS Ed); guidance and counseling (MS Ed); learning disabilities (MS Ed); mathematics 7–12 (MS Ed); mental retardation (MS Ed); music education (MS Ed); reading teacher (MS Ed); science education (MS Ed); social studies 7–12 (MA); teachers of special education (MS Ed); teaching English to speakers of other languages (MS Ed).

School of Health Sciences, Human Services and Nursing Offers adult health nursing (MS); clinical nutrition (MS); community nutrition (MS); dietetic internship (MS); health education and promotion (MA); health N–12 teacher (MS Ed); health sciences, human services and nursing (MA, MS, MS Ed, MSN, MSW); nursing of older adults (MS); nutrition (MS); parent-child nursing (MS); pediatric nurse practitioner (MS); recreation (MA, MS Ed); recreation education (MA, MS Ed); speech-language pathology (MA).

School of Natural and Social Sciences *Program availability:* Part-time, evening/weekend. Offers accounting (MS); biology (MA); businesscomputer science (MS); mathematics (MA); natural and social sciences (MA, MS, MS Ed, PhD); plant sciences (PhD).

LE MOYNE COLLEGE, Syracuse, NY 13214

General Information Independent-religious, coed, comprehensive institution. *Enrollment:* 3,431 graduate, professional, and undergraduate students; 328 full-time matriculated graduate/professional students (234 women), 257 part-time matriculated graduate/professional students (180 women). *Enrollment by degree level:* 552 master's, 33 other advanced degrees. *Graduate faculty:* 32 full-time (19 women), 52 part-time/adjunct (35 women). *Tuition:* Full-time $14,346; part-time $797 per credit hour. Tuition and fees vary according to program. *Graduate housing:* On-campus housing not available. *Student services:* Campus employment opportunities, campus safety program, career counseling, exercise/wellness program, free psychological counseling, international student services, low-cost health insurance, multicultural affairs office, services for students with disabilities, writing training. *Library facilities:* Noreen Reale Falcone Library. *Collection:* Books: 261,183 (physical), 206,330 (digital/electronic); Serial titles: 1,391 (physical), 508 (digital/electronic); Databases: 270. Weekly public service hours: 109; study areas open 24 hours, 5–7 days a week; students can reserve study rooms. *Research affiliation:* Blue Highway, Inc. (medical technology).

Computer facilities: 330 computers available on campus for general student use. A campuswide network can be accessed from student residence rooms and from off campus. Online class registration, ECHO (campus-wide portal), some virtual access from off campus are available.
Website: http://www.lemoyne.edu/

General Application Contact: Kristen P. Richards, Senior Director of Enrollment Management, 315-445-5444, Fax: 315-445-6092, E-mail: trapaskp@lemoyne.edu.

GRADUATE UNITS

Department of Education Students: 30 full-time (19 women), 126 part-time (93 women); includes 15 minority (7 Black or African American, non-Hispanic/Latino; 1 American Indian or Alaska Native, non-Hispanic/Latino; 1 Asian, non-Hispanic/Latino; 6 Hispanic/Latino), 4 international. Average age 29. 139 applicants, 65% accepted, 76 enrolled. *Faculty:* 7 full-time (5 women), 20 part-time/adjunct (12 women). Expenses: Contact institution. *Financial support:* In 2017–18, 30 students received support. Career-related internships or fieldwork, scholarships/grants, and health care benefits available. Support available to part-time students. Financial award applicants required to submit FAFSA. In 2017, 82 master's, 43 CASs awarded. *Program availability:* Part-time, evening/weekend. Offers adolescent education (MS Ed, MST); adolescent education/special education (MS Ed, MST); adolescent English (MST); adolescent English/special education (MST); adolescent foreign language (MST); adolescent history (MST); childhood education (MS Ed); childhood education/special education (MS Ed); elementary education (MS Ed); general education (MS Ed); inclusive childhood education (MST); literacy education (MS Ed); school building leader (MS Ed); school building leadership (CAS); school district business leader (MS Ed, CAS); school district leader (MS Ed); school district leadership (CAS); secondary education (MS Ed); special education (MS Ed); teaching English to speakers of other languages (MS Ed); urban studies (MS Ed). *Application deadline:* For fall admission, 4/1 priority date for domestic and international students; for spring admission, 10/1 priority date for domestic and international students; for summer admission, 3/1 priority date for domestic and international students. Applications are processed on a rolling basis. *Application fee:* $50. Electronic applications accepted. *Application Contact:* Kristen P. Richards, Senior Director of Enrollment Management, 315-445-5444, Fax: 315-445-6092, E-mail: trapaskp@lemoyne.edu. *Chair, Department of Education,* Dr. Stephen C. Fleury, 315-445-4376, Fax: 315-445-4744, E-mail: fleurysc@lemoyne.edu.

Department of Nursing Students: 27 full-time (20 women), 51 part-time (47 women); includes 10 minority (4 Black or African American, non-Hispanic/Latino; 1 Asian, non-Hispanic/Latino; 4 Hispanic/Latino; 1 Two or more races, non-Hispanic/Latino). Average age 32. 39 applicants, 95% accepted, 31 enrolled. *Faculty:* 3 full-time (all women), 5 part-time/adjunct (all women). Expenses: Contact institution. *Financial support:* In 2017–18, 2 students received support. Career-related internships or fieldwork, scholarships/grants, health care benefits, and unspecified assistantships available. Support available to part-time students. Financial award applicants required to submit FAFSA. In 2017, 20 master's, 2 other advanced degrees awarded. *Program availability:* Part-time, evening/weekend. Offers family nurse practitioner (MS, CAS); informatics (MS, CAS); nursing administration (MS, CAS); nursing education (MS, CAS). *Application deadline:* For fall admission, 8/1 priority date for domestic students, 8/1 for international students; for spring admission, 12/15 priority date for domestic students, 12/15 for international students; for summer admission, 5/1 priority date for domestic students, 5/1 for international students. Applications are processed on a rolling basis. *Application fee:* $50. Electronic applications accepted. *Application Contact:* Kristen P. Richards, Senior Director of Enrollment Management, 315-445-5444, Fax: 315-445-6092, E-mail: trapaskp@lemoyne.edu. *Professor/Chair of Nursing,* Dr. Margaret M. Wells, 315-445-5435, Fax: 315-445-6024, E-mail: wellsmm@lemoyne.edu.

Department of Occupational Therapy Students: 81 full-time (72 women); includes 9 minority (1 Black or African American, non-Hispanic/Latino; 6 Asian, non-Hispanic/Latino; 1 Hispanic/Latino; 1 Native Hawaiian or other Pacific Islander, non-Hispanic/Latino), 1 international. Average age 25. 99 applicants, 85% accepted, 43 enrolled. *Faculty:* 3 full-time (all women), 6 part-time/adjunct (4 women). Expenses: Contact institution. *Financial support:* Career-related internships or fieldwork, scholarships/grants, and health care benefits available. Financial award applicants required to submit FAFSA. In 2017, 29 master's awarded. Offers occupational therapy (MS). *Application deadline:* For fall admission, 3/30 for domestic and international students. Applications are processed on a rolling basis. *Application fee:* $125. Electronic applications accepted. *Application Contact:* Kristen P. Richards, Senior Director of Enrollment Management, 315-445-5444, Fax: 315-445-6092, E-mail: trapaskp@lemoyne.edu. *Interim Chair,* Dr. Deborah Marr, 315-445-5432, E-mail: occupationaltherapy@lemoyne.edu.

Department of Physician Assistant Studies Students: 131 full-time (100 women), 3 part-time (all women); includes 14 minority (5 Black or African American, non-Hispanic/Latino; 5 Asian, non-Hispanic/Latino; 2 Hispanic/Latino; 2 Two or more races, non-Hispanic/Latino), 1 international. Average age 26. 1,292 applicants, 7% accepted, 73 enrolled. *Faculty:* 6 full-time (4 women), 14 part-time/adjunct (10 women). Expenses: Contact institution. *Financial support:* In 2017–18, 20 students received support. Career-related internships or fieldwork, scholarships/grants, and health care benefits available. Financial award applicants required to submit FAFSA. In 2017, 74 master's awarded. Offers physician assistant studies (MS). *Application deadline:* For fall admission, 10/1 priority date for domestic and international students. *Application fee:* $177. Electronic applications accepted. *Application Contact:* Kristen P. Richards, Senior Director of Enrollment Management, 315-445-5444, Fax: 315-445-6092, E-mail: trapaskp@lemoyne.edu. *Clinical Assistant Professor/Director of Department of Physician Assistant Studies,* Mary E. Springston, 315-445-4163, Fax: 315-445-4602, E-mail: springme@lemoyne.edu.

Madden School of Business Students: 55 full-time (19 women), 65 part-time (27 women); includes 11 minority (3 Black or African American, non-Hispanic/Latino; 1 American Indian or Alaska Native, non-Hispanic/Latino; 3 Asian, non-Hispanic/Latino; 4 Hispanic/Latino), 2 international. Average age 28. 75 applicants, 92% accepted, 66 enrolled. *Faculty:* 13 full-time (4 women), 4 part-time/adjunct (2 women). Expenses: Contact institution. *Financial support:* In 2017–18, 41 students received support. Career-related internships or fieldwork, scholarships/grants, health care benefits, and unspecified assistantships available. Support available to part-time students. Financial award applicants required to submit FAFSA. In 2017, 57 master's awarded. *Program availability:* Part-time, evening/weekend. Offers business administration (MBA); information systems (MS). *Application deadline:* For fall admission, 7/1 priority date for domestic and international students; for spring admission, 11/1 priority date for domestic and international students; for summer admission, 4/1 priority date for domestic and international students. Applications are processed on a rolling basis. *Application fee:* $0. Electronic applications accepted. *Application Contact:* Kristen P. Richards, Senior Director of Enrollment Management, 315-445-5444, Fax: 315-445-6092, E-mail: trapaskp@lemoyne.edu. *Dean of Madden School of Business,* James Joseph, 315-445-4280, Fax: 315-445-4787, E-mail: josepjae@lemoyne.edu.

Program in Arts Administration Students: 4 full-time (all women), 12 part-time (10 women); includes 1 minority (Black or African American, non-Hispanic/Latino). Average age 29. 16 applicants, 81% accepted, 10 enrolled. *Faculty:* 3 part-time/adjunct (2 women). Expenses: Contact institution. *Financial support:* In 2017–18, 3 students received support. Career-related internships or fieldwork, scholarships/grants, and health care benefits available. Financial award applicants required to submit FAFSA. In 2017, 9 master's awarded. *Program availability:* Part-time, evening/weekend. Offers arts administration (MS). *Application deadline:* For fall admission, 7/1 priority date for domestic and international students; for spring admission, 11/1 priority date for domestic and international students; for summer admission, 4/1 priority date for domestic and international students. Applications are processed on a rolling basis. *Application fee:* $50. Electronic applications accepted. *Application Contact:* Kristen P. Richards, Senior Director of Enrollment Management, 315-445-5444, Fax: 315-445-6092, E-mail: trapaskp@lemoyne.edu. *Assistant Professor and Director of Arts Administration,* Travis Newton, 315-445-4201, E-mail: newtontm@lemoyne.edu.

LENOIR-RHYNE UNIVERSITY, Hickory, NC 28601

General Information Independent-religious, coed, comprehensive institution. *Graduate housing:* Room and/or apartments available on a first-come, first-served basis to single students; on-campus housing not available to married students. Housing application deadline: 5/1.

GRADUATE UNITS

Graduate Programs *Program availability:* Part-time, evening/weekend, online learning. Electronic applications accepted.

Charles M. Snipes School of Business *Program availability:* Part-time, evening/weekend, online learning. Offers accounting (MBA); business analytics and information technology (MBA); entrepreneurship (MBA); global business (MBA); healthcare administration (MBA); innovation and change management (MBA); leadership development (MBA). Electronic applications accepted.

Lutheran Theological Southern Seminary *Program availability:* Part-time. Offers theology (M Div, MACM, MAR, STM).

School of Arts and Letters Offers arts and letters (MA); writing (MA). Electronic applications accepted.

School of Counseling and Human Services *Program availability:* Part-time, evening/weekend. Offers clinical mental health counseling (MA); counseling and human services (MA); school counseling (MA). Electronic applications accepted.

School of Education *Program availability:* Part-time, evening/weekend, online learning. Offers community and nonprofit leadership (MA); community college administration (MA); education (MA, MAT, MS); general management (MA); higher education leadership (MA); management (MA); online teaching and instructional design (MS); second language community services (MA); secondary education (MAT); substance abuse (MA); vocational strategies (MA). Electronic applications accepted.

School of Health, Exercise and Sport Science *Program availability:* Part-time. Offers athletic training (MS); public health (MPH).

School of Natural Sciences *Program availability:* Part-time, evening/weekend, online learning. Offers natural sciences (MS); sustainability studies (MS). Electronic applications accepted.

School of Nursing *Program availability:* Online only. Offers nursing (MSN); nursing administration (MSN); nursing education (MSN). Electronic applications accepted.

School of Occupational Therapy Offers occupational therapy (MS).

School of Physician Assistant Studies Offers physician assistant studies (MS).

LESLEY UNIVERSITY, Cambridge, MA 02138-2790

General Information Independent, coed, primarily women, comprehensive institution. *Graduate housing:* Room and/or apartments available to single students; on-campus housing not available to married students. *Research affiliation:* TERC (education research and development).

GRADUATE UNITS

College of Art and Design *Program availability:* Part-time. Offers photography (MFA); visual arts (MFA). Electronic applications accepted.

Graduate School of Arts and Social Sciences *Program availability:* Part-time, online learning. Offers clinical mental health counseling (MA); counseling psychology (MA, CAGS); creative writing (MFA); expressive therapies (MA, PhD, CAGS); independent studies (CAGS); independent study (MA); intercultural relations (MA, CAGS); interdisciplinary studies (MA); urban environmental leadership (MA). Electronic applications accepted.

Graduate School of Education *Program availability:* Part-time, evening/weekend, online learning. Offers arts, community, and education (M Ed); autism studies (Certificate); curriculum and instruction (M Ed, CAGS); early childhood education (M Ed); ecological teaching and learning (MS); educational studies (PhD); elementary education (M Ed); emergent technologies for educators (Certificate); ESLArts: language learning through the arts (M Ed); high school education (M Ed); individually designed (M Ed); integrated teaching through the arts (M Ed); literacy for K-8 classroom teachers (M Ed); mathematics education (M Ed); middle school education (M Ed); moderate disabilities (M Ed); online learning (Certificate); reading (CAGS); science in education (M Ed); severe disabilities (M Ed); special needs (CAGS); specialist teacher of reading (M Ed); teacher of visual art (M Ed); technology in education (M Ed, CAGS). Electronic applications accepted.

LES ROCHES INTERNATIONAL SCHOOL OF HOTEL MANAGEMENT, CH-3975 Bluche, Switzerland

General Information Private, coed, comprehensive institution.

GRADUATE UNITS

Program in Hospitality Management Offers hospitality management (MBA). Available only at Switzerland campus.

LETOURNEAU UNIVERSITY, Longview, TX 75607-7001

General Information Independent-religious, coed, comprehensive institution. *Enrollment:* 3,003 graduate, professional, and undergraduate students; 55 full-time matriculated graduate/professional students (35 women), 337 part-time matriculated graduate/professional students (266 women). *Enrollment by degree level:* 392 master's. *Graduate housing:* Rooms and/or apartments available on a first-come, first-served basis to single and married students. *Student services:* Campus employment opportunities, campus safety program, career counseling, exercise/wellness program, free psychological counseling, international student services, low-cost health insurance, multicultural affairs office, services for students with disabilities, writing training. *Library facilities:* Margaret Estes Library plus 1 other. *Collection:* Books: 36,383 (physical), 233,450 (digital/electronic); Serial titles: 200 (physical), 29,839 (digital/electronic); Databases: 98.

Computer facilities: Computer purchase and lease plans are available. A campuswide network can be accessed from student residence rooms and from off campus. Online class registration is available.
Website: http://www.letu.edu/

General Application Contact: 233-4312.

GRADUATE UNITS

Graduate Programs Students: 55 full-time (35 women), 337 part-time (266 women); includes 218 minority (140 Black or African American, non-Hispanic/Latino; 2 American Indian or Alaska Native, non-Hispanic/Latino; 5 Asian, non-Hispanic/Latino; 32 Hispanic/Latino; 39 Two or more races, non-Hispanic/Latino), 3 international. Average age 37. Expenses: Contact institution. *Financial support:* Research assistantships, institutionally sponsored loans, and unspecified assistantships available. Financial award applicants required to submit FAFSA. *Program availability:* Part-time, 100% online, blended/hybrid learning. Offers business (MBA); counseling (MA); curriculum and instruction (M Ed); educational administration (M Ed); engineering (ME, MS); engineering management (MEM); health care administration (MS); marriage and family therapy (MA); psychology (MA); strategic leadership (MSL); teacher leadership (M Ed); teaching and learning (M Ed). *Application deadline:* For fall admission, 8/22 for domestic students, 8/29 for international students; for winter admission, 10/10 for domestic students; for spring admission, 1/2 for domestic students, 1/10 for international students; for summer admission, 5/1 for domestic and international students. Applications are processed on a rolling basis. Electronic applications accepted.

LEWIS & CLARK COLLEGE, Portland, OR 97219-7899

General Information Independent, coed, comprehensive institution. *Graduate housing:* On-campus housing not available.

GRADUATE UNITS

Graduate School of Education and Counseling *Program availability:* Part-time, evening/weekend. Offers curriculum and instruction (M Ed); education and counseling (M Ed, MA, MAT, MS, Ed D, Ed S); educational administration (M Ed, Ed S); educational leadership (M Ed, MA, Ed D, Ed S); elementary education (MAT); marriage, couple, and family therapy (MA, MS); professional mental health counseling (MA, MS); professional mental health counseling - addictions (MA, MS); school counseling (M Ed); school psychology (Ed S); secondary education (MAT); special education (M Ed); student affairs administration (MA). Electronic applications accepted.

Lewis & Clark Law School *Program availability:* Part-time, evening/weekend. Offers animal law (LL M); environmental, natural resources, and energy law (LL M, MSL); law (JD). Electronic applications accepted.

LEWIS UNIVERSITY, Romeoville, IL 60446

General Information Independent-religious, coed, comprehensive institution. CGS member. *Enrollment:* 6,506 graduate, professional, and undergraduate students; 458 full-time matriculated graduate/professional students (273 women), 1,439 part-time matriculated graduate/professional students (954 women). *Enrollment by degree level:* 1,809 master's, 88 doctoral. Tuition and fees vary according to program. *Graduate housing:* Room and/or apartments available on a first-come, first-served basis to single students; on-campus housing not available to married students. Housing application deadline: 7/1. *Student services:* Campus employment opportunities, campus safety program, career counseling, exercise/wellness program, free psychological counseling, international student services, low-cost health insurance, multicultural affairs office, services for students with disabilities, teacher training, writing training. *Library facilities:* Lewis University Library. *Collection:* Books: 120,468 (physical), 527,534 (digital/electronic); Serial titles: 1,622 (physical), 151,185 (digital/electronic); Databases: 115. Weekly public service hours: 102; students can reserve study rooms.

Computer facilities: 350 computers available on campus for general student use. A campuswide network can be accessed from student residence rooms and from off campus. Online class registration, online help desk, online billing, online financial aid, online payments, online admission application, online housing application, online application for graduation, online Blackboard course management system, online tutoring are available.
Website: http://www.lewisu.edu/

General Application Contact: Dr. Leslie Jacobson, Assistant Director, Graduate and Adult Admission, 815-836-5610, E-mail: grad@lewisu.edu.

GRADUATE UNITS

College of Arts and Sciences Students: 215 full-time (125 women), 580 part-time (305 women); includes 225 minority (81 Black or African American, non-Hispanic/Latino; 1 American Indian or Alaska Native, non-Hispanic/Latino; 29 Asian, non-Hispanic/Latino; 83 Hispanic/Latino; 2 Native Hawaiian or other Pacific Islander, non-Hispanic/Latino; 29 Two or more races, non-Hispanic/Latino), 28 international. Average age 33. Expenses: Contact institution. *Financial support:* Federal Work-Study, scholarships/grants, tuition waivers (partial), and unspecified assistantships available. Financial award application deadline: 5/1; financial award applicants required to submit FAFSA. *Program availability:* Part-time, evening/weekend, 100% online, blended/hybrid learning. Offers administration (MS); adult mental health counseling (MA); arts and sciences (MA, MS, MSW); chemical physics (MS); chemistry (MS); child and adolescent counseling (MA); computational biology and bioinformatics (MS); computer science (MS); criminal justice (MS); cyber security (MS); higher education/student services (MA); intelligent systems (MS); non-profit management (MA); organizational and leadership coaching (MA); organizational management (MA); physics (MS); public safety administration (MS); safety and security (MS); school counseling (MA); social work (MSW); software engineering (MS); technical (MS); training and development (MA). *Application deadline:* For fall admission, 5/1 priority date for international students; for spring admission, 11/15 priority date for international students. Applications are processed on a rolling basis. *Application fee:* $40. Electronic applications accepted. *Application Contact:* Dr. Leslie Jacobson, Director, Graduate and Adult Admission, 815-836-5610, E-mail: grad@lewisu.edu. *Dean,* Dr. Bonnie Bondavalli, 815-838-0500 Ext. 5240, Fax: 815-836-5240, E-mail: bondavbo@lewisu.edu.

College of Business Students: 167 full-time (93 women), 275 part-time (155 women); includes 116 minority (42 Black or African American, non-Hispanic/Latino; 3 American Indian or Alaska Native, non-Hispanic/Latino; 9 Asian, non-Hispanic/Latino; 53 Hispanic/Latino; 1 Native Hawaiian or other Pacific Islander, non-Hispanic/Latino; 8 Two or more races, non-Hispanic/Latino), 43 international. Average age 32. Expenses: Contact institution. *Financial support:* Career-related internships or fieldwork, Federal Work-Study, scholarships/grants, and unspecified assistantships available. Financial award application deadline: 5/1; financial award applicants required to submit FAFSA. *Program availability:* Part-time, evening/weekend, 100% online, blended/hybrid learning. Offers accounting (MBA); business (MBA, MS); custom elective option (MBA); e-business (MBA); finance (MS); financial analytics (MS); healthcare analytics (MS); healthcare management (MBA); human resources management (MBA); information security - management (MS); international business (MBA); management information systems (MBA); marketing (MBA); marketing analytics (MS); operations analytics (MS); project management (MBA); technology and operations management (MBA). *Application deadline:* For fall admission, 5/1 priority date for international students; for spring admission, 11/15 priority date for international students. Applications are processed on a rolling basis. *Application fee:* $40. Electronic applications accepted. *Application Contact:* Michele Ryan, Director of Admission, 815-836-5384, E-mail: ryanml@lewisu.edu. *Dean,* Dr. Ryan Butt, 800-838-0500, E-mail: buttry@lewisu.edu.

College of Education Students: 59 full-time (41 women), 196 part-time (135 women); includes 70 minority (29 Black or African American, non-Hispanic/Latino; 4 Asian, non-Hispanic/Latino; 34 Hispanic/Latino; 3 Two or more races, non-Hispanic/Latino), 10 international. Average age 34. Expenses: Contact institution. *Financial support:* Career-related internships or fieldwork, Federal Work-Study, scholarships/grants, and unspecified assistantships available. Financial award application deadline: 5/1; financial award applicants required to submit FAFSA. *Program availability:* Part-time, evening/weekend. Offers biology (MA); chemistry (MA); curriculum and instruction: literacy and English language learning (M Ed); curriculum and instruction: technology learning and design (M Ed); early childhood special education (MA); education (M Ed, MA, Ed D); educational leadership for teaching and learning (Ed D); educational leadership with principal preparation endorsement (M Ed, MA); educational leadership with teacher leader endorsement (M Ed); elementary education (MA); English (MA); English as a second language (M Ed); foreign language instruction (MA); history (MA); math (MA); middle level education (MA); physics (MA); psychology and social science (MA); reading and literacy (M Ed, MA); special education (MA). *Application deadline:* For fall admission, 5/1 priority date for international students; for spring admission, 11/15 priority date for international students. Applications are processed on a rolling basis. *Application fee:* $40. Electronic applications accepted. *Application Contact:* Linda Campbell, Graduate Admission Counselor, 815-836-5704, Fax: 815-836-5578, E-mail: campbeli@lewisu.edu. *Dean,* Dr. Pamela Jessee, 815-836-5316, E-mail: jesseepa@lewisu.edu.

College of Nursing and Health Professions Students: 17 full-time (14 women), 388 part-time (359 women); includes 110 minority (31 Black or African American, non-Hispanic/Latino; 35 Asian, non-Hispanic/Latino; 39 Hispanic/Latino; 5 Two or more races, non-Hispanic/Latino), 1 international. Average age 37. Expenses: Contact institution. *Financial support:* Federal Work-Study, scholarships/grants, and unspecified assistantships available. Financial award application deadline: 5/1; financial award applicants required to submit FAFSA. *Program availability:* Part-time, evening/weekend, 100% online, blended/hybrid learning. Offers adult gerontology acute care nurse practitioner (MSN); adult gerontology clinical nurse specialist (MSN); adult gerontology primary care nurse practitioner (MSN); family nurse practitioner (MSN); healthcare systems leadership (MSN); nursing (DNP); nursing and health professions (MSN, DNP); nursing education (MSN); school nurse (MSN). *Application deadline:* For fall admission, 5/1 priority date for international students; for spring admission, 11/15 priority date for international students. Applications are processed on a rolling basis. *Application fee:* $40. Electronic applications accepted. *Application Contact:* Nancy Wiksten, Graduate Admission Counselor, 815-836-5610, E-mail: wikstena@lewisu.edu. *Dean*, Dr. Peggy Rice, 815-838-0500 Ext. 5245, E-mail: ricema@lewisu.edu.

LEXINGTON THEOLOGICAL SEMINARY, Lexington, KY 40508-3218

General Information Independent-religious, coed, graduate-only institution. *Graduate housing:* Rooms and/or apartments available on a first-come, first-served basis to single and married students. Housing application deadline: 6/15.

GRADUATE UNITS

Graduate and Professional Programs *Program availability:* Part-time, evening/weekend. Offers theology (M Div, MA, MAPS, D Min). M Div/MSW offered jointly with University of Kentucky.

LIBERTY UNIVERSITY, Lynchburg, VA 24515

General Information Independent-religious, coed, comprehensive institution. *Enrollment:* 10,893 full-time matriculated graduate/professional students (6,451 women), 18,128 part-time matriculated graduate/professional students (10,939 women). *Enrollment by degree level:* 23,897 master's, 3,957 doctoral, 1,167 other advanced degrees. *Graduate housing:* Room and/or apartments available on a first-come, first-served basis to single students; on-campus housing not available to married students. *Student services:* Campus employment opportunities, career counseling, exercise/wellness program, free psychological counseling, international student services, multicultural affairs office, services for students with disabilities, writing training. *Library facilities:* Jerry Falwell Library plus 1 other. *Collection:* Books: 313,657 (physical), 377,967 (digital/electronic); Serial titles: 4,323 (physical), 118,877 (digital/electronic); Databases: 512. Students can reserve study rooms.

Computer facilities: 1,640 computers available on campus for general student use. A campuswide network can be accessed from student residence rooms and from off campus. Online class registration is available.
Website: http://www.liberty.edu/

General Application Contact: Dr. Nina Shenkle, Dean of Admissions, 877-298-9617, Fax: 434-522-0430, E-mail: residentgraduate@liberty.edu.

GRADUATE UNITS

College of Arts and Sciences Students: 176 full-time (110 women), 302 part-time (170 women); includes 101 minority (67 Black or African American, non-Hispanic/Latino; 5 American Indian or Alaska Native, non-Hispanic/Latino; 1 Asian, non-Hispanic/Latino; 14 Hispanic/Latino; 14 Two or more races, non-Hispanic/Latino), 10 international. Average age 38. 476 applicants, 57% accepted, 150 enrolled. Expenses: Contact institution. *Financial support:* Teaching assistantships with tuition reimbursements and Federal Work-Study available. In 2017, 82 master's awarded. *Program availability:* Part-time, online learning. Offers English (MA); history (MA); professional writing (MA). *Application deadline:* For fall admission, 6/1 for domestic students; for spring admission, 11/1 for domestic students. Applications are processed on a rolling basis. *Application fee:* $50. Electronic applications accepted. *Application Contact:* Dr. Terry Elam, Director of Graduate Admissions, 434-592-3966, Fax: 434-522-0430, E-mail: gradadmissions@liberty.edu. *Dean*, Dr. Roger Schultz, 434-592-4031, Fax: 434-522-0430, E-mail: rschultz@liberty.edu.

College of Osteopathic Medicine Students: 593 full-time (276 women), 6 part-time (3 women); includes 67 minority (8 Black or African American, non-Hispanic/Latino; 39 Asian, non-Hispanic/Latino; 11 Hispanic/Latino; 9 Two or more races, non-Hispanic/Latino), 20 international. Average age 27. 1,428 applicants, 11% accepted, 153 enrolled. Expenses: Contact institution. Offers osteopathic medicine (DO). *Application deadline:* Applications are processed on a rolling basis. Electronic applications accepted. *Application Contact:* Jay Bridge, Director of Admissions, 800-424-9595, Fax: 800-628-7977, E-mail: gradadmissions@liberty.edu. *Dean*, Dr. Ronnie B. Martin, 434-592-6400.

Helms School of Government Students: 287 full-time (148 women), 639 part-time (248 women); includes 231 minority (173 Black or African American, non-Hispanic/Latino; 4 American Indian or Alaska Native, non-Hispanic/Latino; 8 Asian, non-Hispanic/Latino; 20 Hispanic/Latino; 1 Native Hawaiian or other Pacific Islander, non-Hispanic/Latino; 25 Two or more races, non-Hispanic/Latino), 7 international. Average age 35. 876 applicants, 64% accepted, 277 enrolled. Expenses: Contact institution. In 2017, 211 master's awarded. *Program availability:* Part-time, online learning. Offers criminal justice (MS); international relations (MS); political science (MS); public administration (MPA); public policy (MA). *Application deadline:* Applications are processed on a rolling basis. *Application fee:* $50. Electronic applications accepted. *Application Contact:* Jay Bridge, Director of Admissions, 800-424-9595, Fax: 800-628-7977, E-mail: gradadmissions@liberty.edu. *Dean*, Shawn D. Akers, 434-592-4986.

School of Behavioral Sciences Students: 2,649 full-time (2,085 women), 5,086 part-time (4,015 women); includes 2,275 minority (1,784 Black or African American, non-Hispanic/Latino; 44 American Indian or Alaska Native, non-Hispanic/Latino; 67 Asian, non-Hispanic/Latino; 200 Hispanic/Latino; 11 Native Hawaiian or other Pacific Islander, non-Hispanic/Latino; 169 Two or more races, non-Hispanic/Latino), 145 international. Average age 39. 5,839 applicants, 51% accepted, 1710 enrolled. Expenses: Contact institution. *Financial support:* Applicants required to submit FAFSA. In 2017, 1,626 master's, 7 doctorates, 61 other advanced degrees awarded. *Program availability:* Part-time, online learning. Offers applied psychology (MA); clinical mental health counseling (MA); community care and counseling (Ed D); counselor education and supervision (PhD); human services counseling (MA); marriage and family counseling (MA); marriage and family therapy (MA); military resilience (Certificate); pastoral counseling (MA); professional counseling (MA); psychology (MS); school counseling (M Ed). *Application deadline:* Applications are processed on a rolling basis. *Application fee:* $50. Electronic applications accepted. *Application Contact:* Jay Bridge, Director of Admissions, 800-424-9595, Fax: 800-628-7977, E-mail: gradadmissions@liberty.edu. *Founding Dean, School of Behavioral Sciences*, Dr. Ronald Hawkins.

School of Business Students: 1,887 full-time (1,003 women), 4,223 part-time (1,950 women); includes 1,570 minority (1,133 Black or African American, non-Hispanic/Latino; 30 American Indian or Alaska Native, non-Hispanic/Latino; 118 Asian, non-Hispanic/Latino; 149 Hispanic/Latino; 13 Native Hawaiian or other Pacific Islander, non-Hispanic/Latino; 127 Two or more races, non-Hispanic/Latino), 109 international. Average age 35. 5,680 applicants, 51% accepted, 1510 enrolled. Expenses: Contact institution. *Financial support:* Applicants required to submit FAFSA. In 2017, 1,290 master's, 17 doctorates awarded. *Program availability:* Part-time, online learning. Offers accounting (MBA, MS); criminal justice (MBA); cyber security (MS); executive leadership (MA); information systems (MS); international business (MBA, DBA); leadership (DBA); marketing (MBA, MS, DBA); project management (MBA, DBA); public administration (MBA); public relations (MBA). *Application deadline:* Applications are processed on a rolling basis. *Application fee:* $50. Electronic applications accepted. *Application Contact:* Jay Bridge, Director of Graduate Admissions, 800-424-9595, Fax: 800-628-7977, E-mail: gradadmissions@liberty.edu. *Dean*, Dr. Scott Hicks, 434-592-4808, Fax: 434-582-2366, E-mail: smhicks@liberty.edu.

School of Communication and Digital Content Students: 118 full-time (90 women), 137 part-time (95 women); includes 60 minority (37 Black or African American, non-Hispanic/Latino; 1 American Indian or Alaska Native, non-Hispanic/Latino; 1 Asian, non-Hispanic/Latino; 11 Hispanic/Latino; 10 Two or more races, non-Hispanic/Latino), 7 international. Average age 31. 329 applicants, 50% accepted, 95 enrolled. Expenses: Contact institution. *Financial support:* Federal Work-Study and unspecified assistantships available. Financial award applicants required to submit FAFSA. In 2017, 38 master's awarded. *Program availability:* Part-time. Offers communication (MA); promotion and video content (MA); social media management (MS); strategic communication (MA). *Application deadline:* For fall admission, 6/1 for domestic students; for spring admission, 11/1 for domestic students. Applications are processed on a rolling basis. *Application fee:* $50. Electronic applications accepted. *Application Contact:* Dr. Terry Elam, Director of Graduate Admissions, 434-582-2111, Fax: 434-582-7836, E-mail: gradadmissions@liberty.edu. *Dean*, Dr. Norman Mintle, 434-582-2077, E-mail: cvkramer@liberty.edu.

School of Divinity Students: 2,140 full-time (615 women), 3,020 part-time (906 women); includes 1,312 minority (1,016 Black or African American, non-Hispanic/Latino; 9 American Indian or Alaska Native, non-Hispanic/Latino; 100 Asian, non-Hispanic/Latino; 90 Hispanic/Latino; 7 Native Hawaiian or other Pacific Islander, non-Hispanic/Latino; 90 Two or more races, non-Hispanic/Latino), 158 international. Average age 42. 4,673 applicants, 33% accepted, 977 enrolled. Expenses: Contact institution. *Financial support:* Teaching assistantships with tuition reimbursements, career-related internships or fieldwork, and Federal Work-Study available. Financial award applicants required to submit FAFSA. In 2017, 904 master's, 54 doctorates awarded. *Program availability:* Part-time, online learning. Offers Biblical exposition (MA); Biblical languages (M Div); Biblical studies (M Div, MA, MAR, Th M, D Min); chaplaincy (M Div, D Min); Christian apologetics (M Div, MA, MAR, Th M); Christian leadership and church ministries (M Div); Christian ministries (M Div); Christian ministry (MA); Christian thought (M Div); church history (M Div, MAR, Th M); community chaplaincy (M Div, MAR); discipleship (D Min); discipleship and church ministry (M Div, MAR, MCM); evangelism and church planting (MAR, MCM, D Min); expository preaching (D Min); global ministry (MA); global studies (M Div, MAR, MCM, MGS, Th M); healthcare chaplaincy (M Div); homiletics (M Div, MAR, Th M); leadership (M Div, MAR); marketplace chaplaincy (M Div, MCM); ministry leadership (Ed D); pastoral counseling (M Div, MA, MAR, D Min); pastoral leadership (D Min); pastoral ministries (M Div, M Serv Soc, MCM); religious education (MRE); sports chaplaincy (MA); theology (M Div, MAR, MTS, Th M); theology and apologetics (D Min, PhD); worship (M Div, MAR, MCM, D Min); youth and family ministries (M Div). *Application deadline:* For fall admission, 6/1 for domestic students; for spring admission, 11/1 for domestic students. Applications are processed on a rolling basis. *Application fee:* $50. Electronic applications accepted. *Application Contact:* Jay Bridge, Director of Graduate Admissions, 800-424-9595, Fax: 800-628-7977, E-mail: gradadmissions@liberty.edu. *Dean*, Dr. Ed Hindson, 434-592-4140, Fax: 434-522-0415, E-mail: ehindson@liberty.edu.

School of Education Students: 1,966 full-time (1,428 women), 3,484 part-time (2,528 women); includes 1,323 minority (1,026 Black or African American, non-Hispanic/Latino; 29 American Indian or Alaska Native, non-Hispanic/Latino; 49 Asian, non-Hispanic/Latino; 100 Hispanic/Latino; 9 Native Hawaiian or other Pacific Islander, non-Hispanic/Latino; 110 Two or more races, non-Hispanic/Latino), 58 international. Average age 37. 3,748 applicants, 58% accepted, 1167 enrolled. Expenses: Contact institution. *Financial support:* Federal Work-Study and tuition waivers (partial) available. In 2017, 656 master's, 110 doctorates, 316 other advanced degrees awarded. *Program availability:* Part-time, online learning. Offers curriculum and instruction (Ed D, Ed S); educational leadership (Ed D); gifted education (Certificate); math specialist (M Ed); middle grades (MAT, Certificate); reading specialist (M Ed); school leadership (Certificate); secondary education (MAT); sport management (MS). *Application deadline:* For fall admission, 6/1 for domestic students; for spring admission, 11/1 for domestic students. Applications are processed on a rolling basis. *Application fee:* $50. Electronic applications accepted. *Application Contact:* Jay Bridge, Director of Graduate Admissions, 800-424-9595, Fax: 800-628-7977, E-mail: gradadmissions@liberty.edu. *Dean*, Dr. Heather Schoffstall, 434-582-2445, Fax: 434-582-2468, E-mail: awgunter@liberty.edu.

School of Health Sciences Students: 542 full-time (394 women), 696 part-time (541 women); includes 402 minority (286 Black or African American, non-Hispanic/Latino; 10 American Indian or Alaska Native, non-Hispanic/Latino; 34 Asian, non-Hispanic/Latino; 46 Hispanic/Latino; 1 Native Hawaiian or other Pacific Islander, non-Hispanic/Latino; 25 Two or more races, non-Hispanic/Latino), 59 international. Average age 32. 1,592 applicants, 40% accepted, 297 enrolled. Expenses: Contact institution. *Financial support:* Applicants required to submit FAFSA. In 2017, 204 master's awarded. *Program availability:* Part-time, online learning. Offers anatomy and cell biology (PhD); biomedical sciences (MS); epidemiology (MPH); exercise science (MS); global health (MPH); health promotion (MPH); medical sciences (MA); nutrition (MPH). *Application fee:* $50. *Application Contact:* Jay Bridge, Director of Admissions, 800-424-9595, Fax: 800-628-7977, E-mail: gradadmissions@liberty.edu. *Dean*, Dr. Ralph Linstra.

School of Law Students: 251 full-time (123 women), 116 part-time (57 women); includes 84 minority (46 Black or African American, non-Hispanic/Latino; 4 American Indian or Alaska Native, non-Hispanic/Latino; 7 Asian, non-Hispanic/Latino; 17 Hispanic/Latino; 10 Two or more races, non-Hispanic/Latino), 6 international. Average age 33. 294 applicants, 67% accepted, 136 enrolled. Expenses: Contact institution. *Financial support:* Applicants required to submit FAFSA. *Program availability:* Online learning. Offers American legal studies (JM); international legal studies (JM, LL M). *Application deadline:* For fall admission, 6/1 for domestic students. *Application Contact:* Joleen Thaxton, Assistant Director of Admissions, 434-592-5300, Fax: 434-592-5400, E-mail: lawadmissions@liberty.edu. *Dean*, B. Keith Faulkner, 434-592-5300, Fax: 434-592-5400, E-mail: law@liberty.edu.

School of Music Students: 93 full-time (43 women), 181 part-time (89 women); includes 69 minority (44 Black or African American, non-Hispanic/Latino; 1 American Indian or Alaska Native, non-Hispanic/Latino; 6 Asian, non-Hispanic/Latino; 12 Hispanic/Latino; 6 Two or more races, non-Hispanic/Latino), 9 international. Average age 37. 307 applicants, 43% accepted, 69 enrolled. Expenses: Contact institution. *Financial support:* Applicants required to submit FAFSA. In 2017, 26 master's, 2 doctorates awarded. *Program availability:* Part-time, online learning. Offers ethnomusicology (MA); music and worship (MA); music education (MA); worship studies (MA, DWS). *Application deadline:*

Applications are processed on a rolling basis. *Application fee:* $50. Electronic applications accepted. *Application Contact:* Jay Bridge, Director of Admissions, 800-424-9595, Fax: 800-628-7977, E-mail: gradadmissions@liberty.edu. *Dean*, Dr. Vernon Whaley, 434-592-3463, E-mail: vwhaley@liberty.edu.

School of Nursing Students: 148 full-time (131 women), 461 part-time (421 women); includes 103 minority (58 Black or African American, non-Hispanic/Latino; 4 American Indian or Alaska Native, non-Hispanic/Latino; 15 Asian, non-Hispanic/Latino; 11 Hispanic/Latino; 3 Native Hawaiian or other Pacific Islander, non-Hispanic/Latino; 12 Two or more races, non-Hispanic/Latino), 8 international. Average age 39. 536 applicants, 30% accepted, 105 enrolled. Expenses: Contact institution. *Financial support:* Applicants required to submit FAFSA. In 2017, 100 master's, 13 doctorates awarded. *Program availability:* Part-time, online learning. Offers family nurse practitioner (DNP); nurse educator (MSN); nursing administration (MSN); nursing informatics (MSN). *Application deadline:* Applications are processed on a rolling basis. *Application fee:* $50. Electronic applications accepted. *Application Contact:* Jay Bridge, Director of Admissions, 800-424-9595, Fax: 800-628-7977, E-mail: gradadmissions@liberty.edu. *Dean*, Dr. Deanna Britt, 434-582-2519, E-mail: dbritt@liberty.edu.

School of Visual and Performing Arts Students: 37 full-time (19 women), 24 part-time (17 women); includes 9 minority (3 Black or African American, non-Hispanic/Latino; 1 Asian, non-Hispanic/Latino; 1 Hispanic/Latino; 4 Two or more races, non-Hispanic/Latino), 2 international. Average age 31. 109 applicants, 23% accepted, 12 enrolled. Expenses: Contact institution. In 2017, 12 master's awarded. Offers graphic design (MFA); studio art (MFA); visual communication design (MA). *Application fee:* $50. Electronic applications accepted. *Application Contact:* Jay Bridge, Director of Admissions, 800-424-9595, Fax: 800-628-7977, E-mail: gradadmissions@liberty.edu. *Dean*, Scott Hayes, E-mail: smhayes@liberty.edu.

LIFE CHIROPRACTIC COLLEGE WEST, Hayward, CA 94545

General Information Independent, coed, graduate-only institution. *Graduate housing:* On-campus housing not available. *Research affiliation:* National Center for Complimentary Medicine, National Center for Complementary and Alternative Medicine/University Cancer Research Fund, Advanced Orthogonality, San Jose State University, University of Calgary.

GRADUATE UNITS

Professional Program Offers chiropractic (DC). Electronic applications accepted.

LIFE UNIVERSITY, Marietta, GA 30060-2903

General Information Independent, coed, comprehensive institution. *Enrollment:* 2,619 graduate, professional, and undergraduate students; 1,634 full-time matriculated graduate/professional students (770 women), 230 part-time matriculated graduate/professional students (136 women). *Enrollment by degree level:* 213 master's, 1,651 doctoral. *Graduate faculty:* 92 full-time (36 women), 31 part-time/adjunct (12 women). *Tuition:* Full-time $30,181. *Required fees:* $1050. *Graduate housing:* Rooms and/or apartments available on a first-come, first-served basis to single and married students. Typical cost: $14,400 per year for single students. *Student services:* Campus employment opportunities, campus safety program, career counseling, exercise/wellness program, free psychological counseling, international student services, services for students with disabilities. *Library facilities:* Library & Learning Services. *Collection:* Books: 35,643 (physical), 363,658 (digital/electronic); Serial titles: 61 (physical), 31,104 (digital/electronic); Databases: 25. Weekly public service hours: 98; students can reserve study rooms.

Computer facilities: A campuswide network can be accessed from student residence rooms and from off campus. Online class registration is available.
Website: http://www.life.edu/

General Application Contact: Robyn Stanley, Director of Enrollment Services, 800-543-3202, Fax: 770-426-2741, E-mail: robyn.stanley@life.edu.

GRADUATE UNITS

College of Chiropractic Students: 1,552 full-time (712 women), 99 part-time (50 women); includes 576 minority (207 Black or African American, non-Hispanic/Latino; 17 American Indian or Alaska Native, non-Hispanic/Latino; 62 Asian, non-Hispanic/Latino; 290 Hispanic/Latino), 66 international. Average age 28. *Faculty:* 83 full-time (32 women), 22 part-time/adjunct (6 women). Expenses: Contact institution. *Financial support:* Research assistantships, Federal Work-Study, institutionally sponsored loans, scholarships/grants, and tuition waivers (partial) available. Support available to part-time students. Financial award application deadline: 9/1; financial award applicants required to submit FAFSA. In 2017, 353 doctorates awarded. Offers chiropractic (DC). *Application deadline:* For fall admission, 8/1 for domestic students; for winter admission, 11/1 for domestic students; for spring admission, 3/1 for domestic students; for summer admission, 7/1 for domestic students. Applications are processed on a rolling basis. *Application fee:* $50. Electronic applications accepted. *Application Contact:* Robyn Stanley, Director of Enrollment, 770-426-2877, Fax: 770-426-2895, E-mail: roby.stanley@life.edu. *Dean*, Dr. Leslie King, 770-426-2713, E-mail: lesliek@life.edu.

College of Graduate and Undergraduate Studies Students: 82 full-time (58 women), 131 part-time (86 women); includes 116 minority (85 Black or African American, non-Hispanic/Latino; 2 American Indian or Alaska Native, non-Hispanic/Latino; 3 Asian, non-Hispanic/Latino; 26 Hispanic/Latino), 25 international. Average age 30. *Faculty:* 11 full-time (6 women), 12 part-time/adjunct (10 women). Expenses: Contact institution. *Financial support:* Career-related internships or fieldwork, Federal Work-Study, and tuition waivers (full and partial) available. Support available to part-time students. Financial award application deadline: 9/1; financial award applicants required to submit FAFSA. In 2017, 53 master's awarded. *Program availability:* Part-time, 100% online, blended/hybrid learning. Offers athletic training (MAT); chiropractic sport science (MS); nutrition and sport science (MS); positive psychology (MS); sport coaching (MS); sport injury management (MS); sports health science (MS). *Application deadline:* For fall admission, 4/1 priority date for domestic and international students; for winter admission, 12/1 priority date for domestic and international students; for spring admission, 3/1 priority date for domestic and international students. Applications are processed on a rolling basis. *Application fee:* $50. Electronic applications accepted. *Application Contact:* Robyn Stanley, Director of Enrollment, 770-426-2889, E-mail: robin.stanley@life.edu. *Dean of Graduate and Undergraduate Studies*, Dr. Jana Holwick, 678-331-4407, Fax: 770-426-2699, E-mail: jana.holwick@life.edu.

LIM COLLEGE, New York, NY 10022-5268

General Information Proprietary, coed, primarily women, comprehensive institution. *Enrollment:* 1,563 graduate, professional, and undergraduate students; 113 full-time matriculated graduate/professional students (111 women), 48 part-time matriculated graduate/professional students (44 women). *Enrollment by degree level:* 161 master's. *Graduate faculty:* 1 full-time, 28 part-time/adjunct. *Tuition:* Full-time $27,750; part-time $925 per credit. *Required fees:* $100 per term. *Graduate housing:* Room and/or apartments available on a first-come, first-served basis to single students; on-campus housing not available to married students. Typical cost: $16,350 per year ($20,350 including board). *Student services:* Campus employment opportunities, career counseling, exercise/wellness program, free psychological counseling, international student services, low-cost health insurance, services for students with disabilities. *Library facilities:* Adrian G. Marcuse Library. *Collection:* Books: 15,000 (physical), 700 (digital/electronic); Serial titles: 172 (physical); Databases: 55. Students can reserve study rooms.

Computer facilities: Computer purchase and lease plans are available. 352 computers available on campus for general student use. A campuswide network can be accessed from student residence rooms and from off campus. Online class registration is available.
Website: http://www.limcollege.edu/

General Application Contact: Haley Drogus, Assistant Director of Graduate Admissions, 212-310-0639, E-mail: graduateadmissions@limcollege.edu.

GRADUATE UNITS

MPS Program Students: 113 full-time (111 women), 48 part-time (44 women). Average age 24. 285 applicants, 71% accepted, 114 enrolled. *Faculty:* 1 full-time, 28 part-time/adjunct. Expenses: Contact institution. *Program availability:* Part-time, 100% online. Offers business of fashion (MPS); fashion marketing (MPS); fashion merchandising and retail management (MPS); global fashion supply chain management (MPS). *Application deadline:* Applications are processed on a rolling basis. *Application fee:* $40. Electronic applications accepted. *Application Contact:* Haley Drogus, Assistant Director of Graduate Admissions, 212-310-0639, E-mail: graduateadmissions@limcollege.edu. *Dean of Graduate Studies*, Dr. Susan Baxter, E-mail: graduatestudies@limcollege.edu.

LIMESTONE COLLEGE, Gaffney, SC 29340-3799

General Information Independent, coed, comprehensive institution. *Enrollment:* 1,189 graduate, professional, and undergraduate students; 52 full-time matriculated graduate/professional students (39 women), 12 part-time matriculated graduate/professional students. *Enrollment by degree level:* 64 master's. *Graduate faculty:* 10 full-time (2 women), 1 (woman) part-time/adjunct. *Tuition:* Full-time $1950; part-time $1950 per course. *Graduate housing:* On-campus housing not available. *Student services:* Career counseling, free psychological counseling, services for students with disabilities. *Library facilities:* A. J. Eastwood Library plus 1 other. *Collection:* Books: 67,000 (physical), 239,537 (digital/electronic); Serial titles: 111 (physical), 482,082 (digital/electronic); Databases: 156. Weekly public service hours: 70.

Computer facilities: 137 computers available on campus for general student use. A campuswide network can be accessed from student residence rooms and from off campus. Online class registration is available.
Website: http://www.limestone.edu/

General Application Contact: Adair Haynes, Administrative Assistant, MBA Program, 800-795-7151 Ext. 4370, Fax: 864-487-8706, E-mail: ahaynes@limestone.edu.

GRADUATE UNITS

MBA Program Students: 52 full-time (39 women), 12 part-time (0 women); includes 23 minority (21 Black or African American, non-Hispanic/Latino; 2 Asian, non-Hispanic/Latino), 1 international. Average age 40. 74 applicants, 33 enrolled. *Faculty:* 10 full-time (2 women), 1 (woman) part-time/adjunct. Expenses: Contact institution. *Financial support:* Scholarships/grants available. Financial award application deadline: 6/15; financial award applicants required to submit FAFSA. In 2017, 25 master's awarded. *Program availability:* Part-time, evening/weekend, 100% online, but there are three 1-hour group dynamics classes offered during weekends between semesters. Offers business administration (MBA). *Application deadline:* For fall admission, 8/1 priority date for domestic and international students; for winter admission, 12/12 priority date for domestic and international students; for spring admission, 4/1 priority date for domestic and international students. Applications are processed on a rolling basis. *Application fee:* $25. Electronic applications accepted. *Application Contact:* Adair Haynes, Administrative Assistant, MBA Program, 800-795-7151 Ext. 4370, Fax: 864-487-8706, E-mail: ahaynes@limestone.edu. *Director, MBA Program*, Shannon Creighton, 864-488-4371, Fax: 864-487-8706, E-mail: screighton@limestone.edu.

LINCOLN CHRISTIAN SEMINARY, Lincoln, IL 62656-2167

General Information Independent-religious, coed, graduate-only institution. *Graduate housing:* Rooms and/or apartments available on a first-come, first-served basis to single and married students.

GRADUATE UNITS

Graduate and Professional Programs *Program availability:* Part-time. Offers Bible and theology (MA); Christian ministries (MA); counseling (MA); divinity (M Div); leadership ministry (D Min); religious education (MRE). Electronic applications accepted.

LINCOLN CHRISTIAN UNIVERSITY, Lincoln, IL 62656-2167

General Information Independent-religious, coed, comprehensive institution. *Enrollment:* 787 graduate, professional, and undergraduate students; 97 full-time matriculated graduate/professional students (42 women), 226 part-time matriculated graduate/professional students (81 women). *Enrollment by degree level:* 304 master's, 19 doctoral. *Graduate faculty:* 21 full-time (3 women), 29 part-time/adjunct (7 women). *Tuition:* Full-time $7920; part-time $5280 per credit hour. *Required fees:* $150; $150 per course. *Graduate housing:* Rooms and/or apartments available on a first-come, first-served basis to single and married students. Typical cost: $4722 per year ($6296 including board) for single students; $4722 per year ($6296 including board) for married students. Room and board charges vary according to housing facility selected. *Student services:* Campus employment opportunities, campus safety program, free psychological counseling, international student services, services for students with disabilities, writing training. *Library facilities:* Jessie Eury Library. *Collection:* Books: 92,813 (physical), 55,082 (digital/electronic); Serial titles: 719 (physical), 15,442 (digital/electronic); Databases: 52. Weekly public service hours: 82; students can reserve study rooms.

Computer facilities: 51 computers available on campus for general student use. A campuswide network can be accessed from student residence rooms and from off campus. Online class registration is available.
Website: http://www.lincolnchristian.edu/

General Application Contact: Lindsey Clark, Associate Director of Graduate Enrollment, 217-732-3168 Ext. 2398, E-mail: lclark@lincolnchristian.edu.

GRADUATE UNITS

Graduate Programs Students: 97 full-time (42 women), 226 part-time (81 women). Average age 39. *Faculty:* 21 full-time (3 women), 29 part-time/adjunct (7 women). Expenses: Contact institution. *Financial support:* Applicants required to submit FAFSA. *Program availability:* Online learning. Offers Bible and theology (MA); Biblical studies (MA); church history/historical theology (MA); counseling (MA); formative worship (MA);

intercultural studies (MA); ministry (MA); organizational leadership (MA); philosophy and apologetics (MA); spiritual formation (MA); theology (MA). MA in spiritual formation offered in Normal, IL. *Application deadline:* For fall admission, 8/1 for domestic students, 3/1 for international students; for spring admission, 11/15 for domestic students, 11/1 for international students. *Application fee:* $25 ($50 for international students). *Application Contact:* Lindsey Clark, Associate Director of Graduate Enrollment, 217-732-3168 Ext. 2398, E-mail: lclark@lincolnchristian.edu.

LINCOLN MEMORIAL UNIVERSITY, Harrogate, TN 37752-1901

General Information Independent, coed, comprehensive institution. *Graduate housing:* Rooms and/or apartments available on a first-come, first-served basis to single and married students.

GRADUATE UNITS

Carter and Moyers School of Education *Program availability:* Part-time, evening/weekend, online learning. Offers administration and supervision (M Ed, Ed S); counseling and guidance (M Ed); curriculum and instruction (M Ed, Ed D, Ed S); English (M Ed); executive leadership (Ed D); higher education administration (Ed D); human resource development (Ed D); leadership and administration (Ed D).

Caylor School of Nursing *Program availability:* Part-time. Offers family nurse practitioner (MSN); nurse anesthesia (MSN); psychiatric mental health nurse practitioner (MSN).

DeBusk College of Osteopathic Medicine Offers osteopathic medicine (DO).

Duncan School of Law *Program availability:* Part-time. Offers law (JD). Electronic applications accepted.

School of Business *Program availability:* Part-time, evening/weekend. Offers business (MBA).

LINCOLN UNIVERSITY, Oakland, CA 94612

General Information Independent, coed, comprehensive institution. *Enrollment:* 1,048 graduate, professional, and undergraduate students; 606 full-time matriculated graduate/professional students (222 women), 31 part-time matriculated graduate/professional students (14 women). *Enrollment by degree level:* 619 master's, 18 doctoral. *Graduate faculty:* 14 full-time (2 women), 20 part-time/adjunct (6 women). *Tuition:* Full-time $8100; part-time $450 per unit. *Required fees:* $360; $180 per semester. Tuition and fees vary according to course level, course load, degree level and program. *Student services:* Campus employment opportunities, career counseling, international student services, writing training. *Library facilities:* Lincoln University Library. *Collection:* Books: 14,400 (physical), 128,000 (digital/electronic); Serial titles: 350 (physical), 5,050 (digital/electronic); Databases: 19.

Computer facilities: 39 computers available on campus for general student use. A campuswide network can be accessed.
Website: http://www.lincolnuca.edu/

General Application Contact: Peggy Au, Director of Admissions and Records, 510-628-8010, Fax: 510-628-8012, E-mail: admissions@lincolnuca.edu.

GRADUATE UNITS

Graduate Studies Students: 606 full-time (222 women), 31 part-time (14 women); includes 10 minority (8 Asian, non-Hispanic/Latino; 1 Hispanic/Latino; 1 Two or more races, non-Hispanic/Latino), 623 international. Average age 26. *Faculty:* 14 full-time (2 women), 20 part-time/adjunct (6 women). Expenses: Contact institution. *Financial support:* Teaching assistantships, career-related internships or fieldwork, and scholarships/grants available. Financial award applicants required to submit FAFSA. *Program availability:* Part-time. Offers finance and investments (DBA); finance management (MS); finance management and investments (MBA); general business (MBA); human resource management (MBA, DBA); international business (MBA, MS); management information systems (MBA). *Application deadline:* For fall admission, 8/7 for domestic students, 7/14 for international students; for spring admission, 11/30 for domestic students, 10/31 for international students; for summer admission, 5/29 for domestic students, 5/5 for international students. Applications are processed on a rolling basis. *Application fee:* $75. Electronic applications accepted. *Application Contact:* Reenu Shrestha, Assistant to the President, 510-628-8017, Fax: 510-208-2826, E-mail: sreenu@lincolnuca.edu. *Provost*, Dr. Marshall Burak, 510-628-8016, Fax: 510-628-8012, E-mail: mburak@lincolnuca.edu.

LINCOLN UNIVERSITY, Jefferson City, MO 65101

General Information State-supported, coed, comprehensive institution. *Enrollment:* 2,619 graduate, professional, and undergraduate students; 40 full-time matriculated graduate/professional students (23 women), 54 part-time matriculated graduate/professional students (25 women). *Enrollment by degree level:* 94 master's. Tuition, state resident: part-time $291 per credit hour. Tuition, nonresident: part-time $541.50 per credit hour. *Graduate housing:* Room and/or apartments available on a first-come, first-served basis to single students; on-campus housing not available to married students. Housing application deadline: 7/1. *Student services:* Campus employment opportunities, career counseling, international student services, services for students with disabilities. *Library facilities:* Inman E. Page Library. *Collection:* Books: 99,126 (physical), 197,476 (digital/electronic); Serial titles: 1,194 (physical), 19,000 (digital/electronic); Databases: 39. Weekly public service hours: 88. *Research affiliation:* National Science Foundation (STEM research), Ceres Trust (agriculture), Missouri Department of Agriculture (agriculture), Center for Rural Affairs (sustainable agriculture), U.S. Department of Education (DOE) (defense, government), U.S. Department of Agriculture (USDA) (agriculture, government).

Computer facilities: Computer purchase and lease plans are available. 365 computers available on campus for general student use. A campuswide network can be accessed from student residence rooms and from off campus. Online class registration is available.
Website: http://www.lincolnu.edu/

General Application Contact: Dr. Rolundus Rice, Dean, 573-681-5247, Fax: 573-681-5106, E-mail: gradschool@lincolnu.edu.

GRADUATE UNITS

Graduate Studies Students: 40 full-time (23 women), 64 part-time (32 women); includes 33 minority (30 Black or African American, non-Hispanic/Latino; 2 Hispanic/Latino; 1 Two or more races, non-Hispanic/Latino), 12 international. Average age 33. 48 applicants, 81% accepted, 22 enrolled. Expenses: Contact institution. *Financial support:* In 2017–18, 2 fellowships with tuition reimbursements, 3 research assistantships with tuition reimbursements were awarded; Federal Work-Study, scholarships/grants, and unspecified assistantships also available. Support available to part-time students. Financial award application deadline: 3/1; financial award applicants required to submit FAFSA. In 2017, 46 master's awarded. *Program availability:* Part-time, evening/weekend, 100% online, blended/hybrid learning. Offers business administration (MBA); elementary teaching (M Ed); environmental science (MS); guidance and counseling (M Ed); higher education (MA); history (MA); integrated agricultural systems (MS); middle school (M Ed); natural sciences (MS); secondary teaching (M Ed); sociology (MA); sociology/criminal justice (MA). *Application deadline:* For fall admission, 7/1 priority date for domestic students, 5/1 priority date for international students; for spring admission, 11/1 priority date for domestic students, 10/1 priority date for international students; for summer admission, 6/1 priority date for domestic students. Applications are processed on a rolling basis. *Application fee:* $30. Electronic applications accepted. *Application Contact:* Irasema Steck, Administrative Assistant, 573-681-5247, Fax: 573-681-5106, E-mail: gradschool@lincolnu.edu. *Interim Provost*, Dr. Debra F. Greene, 573-681-5247, Fax: 573-681-5106, E-mail: gradschool@lincolnu.edu.

LINCOLN UNIVERSITY, Lincoln University, PA 19352

General Information State-related, coed, comprehensive institution. *Enrollment:* 2,266 graduate, professional, and undergraduate students; 196 full-time matriculated graduate/professional students (138 women), 68 part-time matriculated graduate/professional students (46 women). *Enrollment by degree level:* 264 master's. *Graduate faculty:* 9 full-time (3 women), 25 part-time/adjunct (15 women). Tuition, state resident: full-time $10,106; part-time $511 per credit. Tuition, nonresident: full-time $17,636; part-time $886 per credit. *Required fees:* $1314; $56 per credit. One-time fee: $195 full-time. Tuition and fees vary according to course load. *Graduate housing:* On-campus housing not available. *Student services:* Campus employment opportunities, campus safety program, career counseling, free psychological counseling, international student services, low-cost health insurance, services for students with disabilities, teacher training, writing training. *Library facilities:* Langston Hughes Memorial Library. *Collection:* Weekly public service hours: 80; study areas open 24 hours, 5–7 days a week; students can reserve study rooms. *Research affiliation:* The Treatment Research Institute (addictive disorders).

Computer facilities: 280 computers available on campus for general student use. A campuswide network can be accessed from student residence rooms and from off campus. Online class registration is available.
Website: http://www.lincoln.edu/

General Application Contact: Jernice Lea, Director, University City Student Services and Admissions, 215-590-8231, Fax: 215-387-3859, E-mail: jlea@lincoln.edu.

GRADUATE UNITS

Graduate Programs Students: 196 full-time (138 women), 68 part-time (46 women); includes 236 minority (227 Black or African American, non-Hispanic/Latino; 1 American Indian or Alaska Native, non-Hispanic/Latino; 7 Hispanic/Latino; 1 Two or more races, non-Hispanic/Latino), 3 international. Average age 34. 120 applicants, 100% accepted, 95 enrolled. *Faculty:* 9 full-time (3 women), 25 part-time/adjunct (15 women). Expenses: Contact institution. *Financial support:* Scholarships/grants available. Financial award application deadline: 6/30; financial award applicants required to submit FAFSA. In 2017, 126 master's awarded. *Program availability:* Part-time, evening/weekend. Offers counseling (MSC); early childhood education (M Ed); early childhood education and special education (M Ed); educational leadership (M Ed); finance (MBA); human resources management (MBA); human services delivery (MAHS). *Application deadline:* For fall admission, 8/1 priority date for domestic students, 7/1 priority date for international students; for spring admission, 12/1 priority date for domestic students, 10/1 for international students. Applications are processed on a rolling basis. *Application fee:* $50. Electronic applications accepted. *Application Contact:* Jernice Lea, Director, University City Student Services and Admissions, 215-590-8231, Fax: 215-387-3859, E-mail: jlea@lincoln.edu. *Provost*, Dr. Patricia Pierce Ramsey, 484-365-7437, Fax: 484-365-8108, E-mail: provost@lincoln.edu.

LINDENWOOD UNIVERSITY, St. Charles, MO 63301-1695

General Information Independent-religious, coed, comprehensive institution. *Enrollment:* 10,045 graduate, professional, and undergraduate students; 1,282 full-time matriculated graduate/professional students (843 women), 1,815 part-time matriculated graduate/professional students (1,339 women). *Enrollment by degree level:* 2,666 master's, 305 doctoral, 126 other advanced degrees. *Graduate faculty:* 106 full-time (54 women), 341 part-time/adjunct (188 women). *Tuition:* Full-time $16,300; part-time $460 per credit. *Required fees:* $660; $330 per credit. Tuition and fees vary according to degree level and program. *Graduate housing:* Rooms and/or apartments available on a first-come, first-served basis to single and married students. Typical cost: $8800 (including board) for single students. Housing application deadline: 8/27. *Student services:* Campus employment opportunities, campus safety program, career counseling, exercise/wellness program, free psychological counseling, international student services, services for students with disabilities, teacher training, writing training. *Library facilities:* Library and Academic Resource Center plus 1 other. *Collection:* Books: 82,506 (physical), 225,902 (digital/electronic); Serial titles: 197 (physical), 87 (digital/electronic); Databases: 140. Students can reserve study rooms.

Computer facilities: A campuswide network can be accessed from student residence rooms and from off campus. Online class registration is available.
Website: http://www.lindenwood.edu/

General Application Contact: Kara Schilli, Director, Evening and Graduate Admissions, 636-949-4349, Fax: 636-949-4109, E-mail: adultadmissions@lindenwood.edu.

GRADUATE UNITS

Graduate Programs Students: 1,282 full-time (843 women), 1,815 part-time (1,339 women); includes 753 minority (606 Black or African American, non-Hispanic/Latino; 15 American Indian or Alaska Native, non-Hispanic/Latino; 25 Asian, non-Hispanic/Latino; 72 Hispanic/Latino; 2 Native Hawaiian or other Pacific Islander, non-Hispanic/Latino; 33 Two or more races, non-Hispanic/Latino), 161 international. Average age 35. 1,773 applicants, 53% accepted, 754 enrolled. *Faculty:* 106 full-time (54 women), 341 part-time/adjunct (188 women). Expenses: Contact institution. *Financial support:* In 2017–18, 2,905 students received support. Career-related internships or fieldwork, Federal Work-Study, institutionally sponsored loans, scholarships/grants, tuition waivers (full), and unspecified assistantships available. Financial award application deadline: 6/30; financial award applicants required to submit FAFSA. In 2017, 1,181 master's, 63 doctorates, 94 other advanced degrees awarded. *Program availability:* Part-time, evening/weekend, 100% online. *Application deadline:* For fall admission, 8/27 priority date for domestic and international students; for spring admission, 1/14 priority date for domestic and international students; for summer admission, 6/4 priority date for domestic and international students. Applications are processed on a rolling basis. *Application fee:* $30 ($100 for international students). Electronic applications accepted. *Application Contact:* Kara Schilli, Director, Evening and Graduate Admissions, 636-949-4349, Fax: 636-949-4109, E-mail: adultadmissions@lindenwood.edu. *Provost and Vice President of Academic Affairs*, Dr. Marilyn Abbott, 636-949-4846, Fax: 636-949-4912, E-mail: mabbott@lindenwood.edu.

Plaster School of Business and Entrepreneurship Students: 201 full-time (116 women), 253 part-time (153 women); includes 102 minority (80 Black or African American, non-Hispanic/Latino; 2 American Indian or Alaska Native, non-Hispanic/Latino; 6 Asian, non-Hispanic/Latino; 7 Hispanic/Latino; 7 Two or more races, non-Hispanic/Latino), 61 international. Average age 32. 370 applicants, 42% accepted, 134 enrolled. *Faculty:* 15 full-time (8 women), 26 part-time/adjunct (9 women). Expenses: Contact institution. *Financial support:* In 2017–18, 439 students received support. Career-related internships or fieldwork, Federal Work-Study, institutionally sponsored loans, scholarships/grants, tuition waivers (partial), and unspecified assistantships available. Financial award application deadline: 6/30; financial award applicants required to submit FAFSA. In 2017, 178 master's awarded. *Program availability:* Part-time, evening/weekend, 100% online. Offers accountancy (M Acc); accounting (MBA); business administration (MBA); entrepreneurial studies (MBA); finance (MBA, MS); human resource management (MBA); international business (MBA); leadership (MA); management (MBA); marketing (MBA, MS); nonprofit administration (MA); public administration (MBA); sport management (MA); supply chain management (MBA). *Application deadline:* For fall admission, 8/27 priority date for domestic and international students; for winter admission, 1/14 priority date for domestic and international students; for spring admission, 3/18 for domestic students, 3/18 priority date for international students; for summer admission, 6/3 priority date for domestic and international students. Applications are processed on a rolling basis. *Application fee:* $30 ($100 for international students). Electronic applications accepted. *Application Contact:* Kara Schilli, Director, Evening and Graduate Admissions, 636-949-4349, Fax: 636-949-4109, E-mail: adultadmissions@lindenwood.edu. *Dean, School of Business and Entrepreneurship*, Roger Ellis, 636-949-4839, E-mail: rellis@lindenwood.edu.

School of Accelerated Degree Programs Students: 597 full-time (383 women), 202 part-time (138 women); includes 248 minority (206 Black or African American, non-Hispanic/Latino; 3 American Indian or Alaska Native, non-Hispanic/Latino; 6 Asian, non-Hispanic/Latino; 21 Hispanic/Latino; 1 Native Hawaiian or other Pacific Islander, non-Hispanic/Latino; 11 Two or more races, non-Hispanic/Latino), 69 international. Average age 36. 526 applicants, 46% accepted, 204 enrolled. *Faculty:* 12 full-time (5 women), 90 part-time/adjunct (37 women). Expenses: Contact institution. *Financial support:* In 2017–18, 738 students received support. Career-related internships or fieldwork, institutionally sponsored loans, scholarships/grants, tuition waivers (partial), and unspecified assistantships available. Financial award application deadline: 6/30; financial award applicants required to submit FAFSA. In 2017, 537 master's awarded. *Program availability:* Part-time, evening/weekend, 100% online. Offers administration (MSA); business administration (MBA); communications (MA); criminal justice and administration (MS); healthcare administration (MS); human resource management (MS); information technology (Certificate); managing information security (MS); managing information technology (MS); managing virtualization and cloud computing (MS); writing (MFA). *Application deadline:* For fall admission, 9/24 priority date for domestic and international students; for winter admission, 1/7 priority date for domestic and international students; for spring admission, 4/8 priority date for domestic and international students; for summer admission, 7/8 priority date for domestic and international students. Applications are processed on a rolling basis. *Application fee:* $30 ($100 for international students). Electronic applications accepted. *Application Contact:* Kara Schilli, Director, Evening and Graduate Admissions, 636-949-4349, Fax: 636-949-4109, E-mail: adultadmissions@lindenwood.edu. *Dean, Accelerated Degree Programs*, Dr. Gina Ganahl, 636-949-4501, Fax: 636-949-4505, E-mail: gganahl@lindenwood.edu.

School of Arts, Media, and Communications Students: 26 full-time (13 women), 11 part-time (8 women); includes 3 minority (1 American Indian or Alaska Native, non-Hispanic/Latino; 2 Hispanic/Latino), 7 international. Average age 33. 60 applicants, 45% accepted, 16 enrolled. *Faculty:* 23 full-time (6 women), 8 part-time/adjunct (4 women). Expenses: Contact institution. *Financial support:* In 2017–18, 34 students received support. Career-related internships or fieldwork, institutionally sponsored loans, scholarships/grants, tuition waivers (partial), and unspecified assistantships available. Financial award application deadline: 6/30; financial award applicants required to submit FAFSA. In 2017, 11 master's awarded. *Program availability:* Part-time. Offers advertising (MA); art history (MA); cinema and media arts (MFA); communications (MA); digital and Web design (MA); fashion and business design (MS); journalism (MA); mass communications (MA); social media and digital content (MS). *Application deadline:* For fall admission, 8/27 priority date for domestic and international students; for spring admission, 1/14 for domestic students, 1/14 priority date for international students; for summer admission, 6/4 priority date for domestic and international students. Applications are processed on a rolling basis. *Application fee:* $30 ($100 for international students). Electronic applications accepted. *Application Contact:* Kara Schilli, Director, Evening and Graduate Admissions, 636-949-4349, Fax: 636-949-4109, E-mail: adultadmissions@lindenwood.edu. *Dean, School of Arts, Media, and Communications*, Dr. Joseph Alsobrook, 636-949-4164, Fax: 636-949-4910, E-mail: jalsobrook@lindenwood.edu.

School of Education Students: 434 full-time (319 women), 1,292 part-time (989 women); includes 387 minority (313 Black or African American, non-Hispanic/Latino; 9 American Indian or Alaska Native, non-Hispanic/Latino; 13 Asian, non-Hispanic/Latino; 37 Hispanic/Latino; 1 Native Hawaiian or other Pacific Islander, non-Hispanic/Latino; 14 Two or more races, non-Hispanic/Latino), 20 international. Average age 36. 828 applicants, 61% accepted, 378 enrolled. *Faculty:* 47 full-time (31 women), 213 part-time/adjunct (135 women). Expenses: Contact institution. *Financial support:* In 2017–18, 1,615 students received support. Career-related internships or fieldwork, Federal Work-Study, institutionally sponsored loans, scholarships/grants, tuition waivers (partial), and unspecified assistantships available. Financial award application deadline: 6/30; financial award applicants required to submit FAFSA. In 2017, 431 master's, 63 doctorates, 94 other advanced degrees awarded. *Program availability:* Part-time, evening/weekend, 100% online, blended/hybrid learning. Offers behavioral analysis (MA); education (MA); educational administration (MA, Ed D, Ed S); English to speakers of other languages (MA); instructional leadership (Ed D, Ed S); library media (MA); professional counseling (MA); school administration (MA, Ed S); school counseling (MA); teaching (MA). *Application deadline:* For fall admission, 8/27 priority date for domestic and international students; for spring admission, 1/14 priority date for domestic and international students; for summer admission, 6/4 priority date for domestic and international students. Applications are processed on a rolling basis. *Application fee:* $30 ($100 for international students). Electronic applications accepted. *Application Contact:* Kara Schilli, Director, Evening and Graduate Admissions, 636-949-4349, Fax: 636-949-4109, E-mail: adultadmissions@lindenwood.edu. *Dean, School of Education*, Dr. Anthony Scheffler, 636-949-4618, Fax: 636-949-4197, E-mail: ascheffler@lindenwood.edu.

School of Health Sciences Students: 24 full-time (12 women), 57 part-time (51 women); includes 13 minority (7 Black or African American, non-Hispanic/Latino; 5 Hispanic/Latino; 1 Two or more races, non-Hispanic/Latino), 4 international. Average age 35. 65 applicants, 49% accepted, 22 enrolled. *Faculty:* 9 full-time (4 women), 4 part-time/adjunct (3 women). Expenses: Contact institution. *Financial support:* In 2017–18, 79 students received support. Career-related internships or fieldwork, Federal Work-Study, institutionally sponsored loans, scholarships/grants, tuition waivers (partial), and unspecified assistantships available. Financial award application deadline: 6/30; financial award applicants required to submit FAFSA. In 2017, 24 master's awarded. *Program availability:* Part-time, blended/hybrid learning. Offers human performance (MS); nursing (MS). *Application deadline:* For fall admission, 8/27 priority date for domestic and international students; for spring admission, 1/14 priority date for domestic and international students; for summer admission, 6/4 priority date for domestic and international students. Applications are processed on a rolling basis. *Application fee:* $30 ($100 for international students). Electronic applications accepted. *Application Contact:* Kara Schilli, Director, Evening and Graduate Admissions, 636-949-4349, Fax: 636-949-4109, E-mail: adultadmissions@lindenwood.edu. *Dean, School of Health Sciences*, Dr. Cynthia Schroeder, 636-949-4318, E-mail: cschroeder@lindenwood.edu.

LINDENWOOD UNIVERSITY–BELLEVILLE, Belleville, IL 62226

General Information Independent-religious, coed, comprehensive institution.

GRADUATE UNITS

Graduate Programs

LINDSEY WILSON COLLEGE, Columbia, KY 42728

General Information Independent-religious, coed, comprehensive institution. *Graduate housing:* Rooms and/or apartments available on a first-come, first-served basis to single and married students.

GRADUATE UNITS

Division of Education *Program availability:* Online learning. Offers teacher as leader (M Ed).

Louisville Center for Design *Program availability:* Online learning. Offers interactive design (MA).

School of Professional Counseling *Program availability:* Part-time, evening/weekend, online learning. Offers counseling and human development (M Ed); counselor education and supervision (PhD).

LIPSCOMB UNIVERSITY, Nashville, TN 37204-3951

General Information Independent-religious, coed, comprehensive institution. CGS member. *Enrollment:* 4,642 graduate, professional, and undergraduate students; 857 full-time matriculated graduate/professional students (507 women), 642 part-time matriculated graduate/professional students (442 women). *Enrollment by degree level:* 967 master's, 428 doctoral, 104 other advanced degrees. *Graduate faculty:* 106 full-time (37 women), 92 part-time/adjunct (47 women). *Graduate housing:* Room and/or apartments available on a first-come, first-served basis to single students; on-campus housing not available to married students. Housing application deadline: 7/15. *Student services:* Campus employment opportunities, campus safety program, career counseling, exercise/wellness program, free psychological counseling, international student services, multicultural affairs office, services for students with disabilities, teacher training. *Library facilities:* Beaman Library plus 1 other. *Collection:* Books: 157,824 (physical), 167,520 (digital/electronic); Serial titles: 253 (physical), 489 (digital/electronic); Databases: 100. Students can reserve study rooms.

Computer facilities: 150 computers available on campus for general student use. A campuswide network can be accessed from student residence rooms and from off campus. Online class registration is available.
Website: http://www.lipscomb.edu/

General Application Contact: Barbara Blackman, Coordinator of Graduate Studies, 615-966-6287, Fax: 615-966-7619, E-mail: graduatestudies@lipscomb.edu.

GRADUATE UNITS

College of Business Students: 157 full-time (68 women), 9 part-time (6 women); includes 26 minority (9 Black or African American, non-Hispanic/Latino; 7 Asian, non-Hispanic/Latino; 8 Hispanic/Latino; 2 Two or more races, non-Hispanic/Latino), 9 international. Average age 30. 249 applicants, 49% accepted, 52 enrolled. *Faculty:* 14 full-time (2 women), 8 part-time/adjunct (1 woman). Expenses: Contact institution. *Financial support:* Career-related internships or fieldwork, scholarships/grants, tuition waivers (partial), and unspecified assistantships available. Support available to part-time students. Financial award application deadline: 7/1; financial award applicants required to submit FAFSA. In 2017, 130 master's awarded. *Program availability:* Part-time, evening/weekend. Offers accounting and finance (MBA); audit/accounting (M Acc); business (Certificate); business administration (MM); healthcare management (MBA); leadership (MBA); tax (M Acc). *Application deadline:* For fall admission, 6/15 for domestic students, 2/1 for international students; for winter admission, 6/1 for international students; for spring admission, 11/15 for domestic students. Applications are processed on a rolling basis. *Application fee:* $50 ($75 for international students). Electronic applications accepted. *Application Contact:* Karen Risley, Manager, Graduate Business Recruiting, 615-966-5145, E-mail: karen.risley@lipscomb.edu. *Associate Dean of Graduate Business Programs*, Allison Duke, 615-966-5732, Fax: 615-966-1818, E-mail: allison.duke@lipscomb.edu.

College of Computing and Technology Students: 44 full-time (16 women), 10 part-time (1 woman); includes 18 minority (7 Black or African American, non-Hispanic/Latino; 1 American Indian or Alaska Native, non-Hispanic/Latino; 8 Asian, non-Hispanic/Latino; 2 Hispanic/Latino), 5 international. Average age 35. 54 applicants, 57% accepted, 24 enrolled. *Faculty:* 6 full-time (0 women), 6 part-time/adjunct (1 woman). Expenses: Contact institution. *Financial support:* Scholarships/grants and employer agreements available. Financial award applicants required to submit FAFSA. In 2017, 28 master's, 2 other advanced degrees awarded. *Program availability:* Part-time, evening/weekend. Offers data science (MS, Certificate); information technology (MS, Certificate); software engineering (MS, Certificate). *Application deadline:* Applications are processed on a rolling basis. *Application fee:* $50 ($75 for international students). Electronic applications accepted. *Application Contact:* Brett Ramsey, Enrollment Management Specialist, 615-966-1193, E-mail: brett.ramsey@lipscomb.edu. *Dean*, Dr. Fortune S. Mhlanga, 615-966-5073, E-mail: fortune.mhlanga@lipscomb.edu.

College of Education Students: 565 full-time (452 women), 59 part-time (45 women); includes 154 minority (102 Black or African American, non-Hispanic/Latino; 2 American Indian or Alaska Native, non-Hispanic/Latino; 8 Asian, non-Hispanic/Latino; 26 Hispanic/Latino; 16 Two or more races, non-Hispanic/Latino). Average age 32. 395 applicants, 54% accepted, 196 enrolled. *Faculty:* 21 full-time (14 women), 42 part-time/adjunct (29 women). Expenses: Contact institution. *Financial support:* Scholarships/grants, unspecified assistantships, and partnerships with local school districts available. Financial award applicants required to submit FAFSA. In 2017, 162 master's, 30 doctorates, 54 other advanced degrees awarded. *Program availability:* Part-time, evening/weekend, 100% online. Offers applied behavior analysis (MS, Certificate); coaching for learning (M Ed, Certificate, Ed S); educational leadership (M Ed, Ed S); English language learning (M Ed, Ed S); instructional coaching (M Ed, Certificate, Ed S); instructional practice (M Ed); learning organizations and strategic change (Ed D); literacy coaching (Certificate, Ed S); reading specialty (M Ed, Ed S); school counseling (M Ed, Ed S); special education (M Ed); teaching, learning, and leading (M Ed); technology integration (M Ed, Ed S); technology integration specialist (Certificate). *Application deadline:* For fall admission, 8/29 priority date for domestic students; for spring admission, 1/15 priority date for domestic students. Applications are processed on a rolling basis. *Application fee:* $50 ($75 for international students). Electronic applications accepted. *Application Contact:* Amanda Logsdon, Director of Enrollment and Outreach, 615-966-7199, E-mail: amanda.logsdon@lipscomb.edu. *Director of Graduate Studies*, Dr. Deborah Boyd, 615-966-6263, E-mail: deborah.boyd@lipscomb.edu.

College of Pharmacy Students: 349 full-time (227 women), 20 part-time (15 women); includes 100 minority (42 Black or African American, non-Hispanic/Latino; 4 American Indian or Alaska Native, non-Hispanic/Latino; 34 Asian, non-Hispanic/Latino; 13 Hispanic/Latino; 7 Two or more races, non-Hispanic/Latino), 3 international. Average age 26. 550 applicants, 33% accepted, 99 enrolled. *Faculty:* 36 full-time (17 women), 1 (woman) part-time/adjunct. Expenses: Contact institution. *Financial support:* Application deadline: 2/15; applicants required to submit FAFSA. In 2017, 22 master's, 72 doctorates awarded. Offers healthcare informatics (MS); pharmacy (Pharm D). *Application deadline:* For fall admission, 2/7 for domestic students. Applications are processed on a rolling basis. *Application fee:* $50 ($75 for international students). Electronic applications accepted. *Application Contact:* Laura Ward, Director of Admissions and Student Affairs, 615-966-7173, E-mail: laura.ward@lipscomb.edu. *Dean/Professor of Pharmacy Practice*, Dr. Roger Davis, 615-966-7161.

Department of Psychology, Counseling, and Family Science Students: 120 full-time (92 women), 30 part-time (27 women); includes 38 minority (22 Black or African American, non-Hispanic/Latino; 1 American Indian or Alaska Native, non-Hispanic/Latino; 1 Asian, non-Hispanic/Latino; 11 Hispanic/Latino; 3 Two or more races, non-Hispanic/Latino), 2 international. Average age 28. 144 applicants, 44% accepted, 42 enrolled. *Faculty:* 10 full-time (3 women), 10 part-time/adjunct (4 women). Expenses: Contact institution. *Financial support:* Scholarships/grants and unspecified assistantships available. Financial award applicants required to submit FAFSA. In 2017, 68 master's, 1 other advanced degree awarded. *Program availability:* Part-time, evening/weekend. Offers clinical mental health counseling (MS); counseling psychology (Certificate); marriage and family therapy (MMFT); psychology (MS). *Application deadline:* For fall admission, 7/1 for domestic students; for spring admission, 11/1 for domestic students. Applications are processed on a rolling basis. *Application fee:* $50 ($75 for international students). Electronic applications accepted. *Application Contact:* Kathi Johnson, Recruiting and Marketing Coordinator, 615-966-5237, E-mail: kathi.johnson@lipscomb.edu. *Director/Professor of Psychology*, Dr. Shanna Ray, 615-966-5833, E-mail: shanna.ray@lipscomb.edu.

Hazelip School of Theology Students: 89 full-time (24 women), 38 part-time (10 women); includes 20 minority (12 Black or African American, non-Hispanic/Latino; 2 Asian, non-Hispanic/Latino; 3 Hispanic/Latino; 3 Two or more races, non-Hispanic/Latino), 2 international. Average age 36. 89 applicants, 51% accepted, 33 enrolled. *Faculty:* 13 full-time (0 women), 4 part-time/adjunct (2 women). Expenses: Contact institution. *Financial support:* Scholarships/grants and unspecified assistantships available. Financial award application deadline: 3/1; financial award applicants required to submit FAFSA. In 2017, 24 master's, 10 doctorates awarded. *Program availability:* Part-time, evening/weekend, online learning. Offers missional and spiritual formation (D Min); theology (M Div). *Application deadline:* For fall admission, 8/1 priority date for domestic students; for spring admission, 12/15 for domestic students. Applications are processed on a rolling basis. *Application fee:* $50 ($75 for international students). Electronic applications accepted. *Application Contact:* Kellye McCool, Coordinator of Student Services, 615-966-5458, Fax: 615-966-6052, E-mail: kellye.mccool@lipscomb.edu. *Director*, Frank Guertin, 615-966-5709, Fax: 615-966-5352, E-mail: frank.guertin@lipscomb.edu.

Institute for Conflict Management Students: 24 full-time (18 women), 16 part-time (11 women); includes 12 minority (7 Black or African American, non-Hispanic/Latino; 1 Hispanic/Latino; 4 Two or more races, non-Hispanic/Latino), 1 international. Average age 41. 27 applicants, 70% accepted, 15 enrolled. *Faculty:* 3 full-time (1 woman), 4 part-time/adjunct (3 women). Expenses: Contact institution. *Financial support:* Tuition waivers (full) available. Financial award applicants required to submit FAFSA. In 2017, 12 master's, 8 other advanced degrees awarded. *Program availability:* Part-time, evening/weekend. Offers conflict management (MA, Certificate). *Application deadline:* For fall admission, 7/15 for domestic students; for spring admission, 12/15 for domestic students. Applications are processed on a rolling basis. *Application fee:* $50 ($75 for international students). Electronic applications accepted. *Application Contact:* Dr. Phyllis Hildreth, Academic Director, 615-966-5695, Fax: 615-966-7143, E-mail: phyllis.hildreth@lipscomb.edu. *Director*, Dr. Steve Joiner, 615-966-7141, Fax: 615-966-7143, E-mail: phyllis.hildreth@lipscomb.edu.

Institute for Sustainable Practice Students: 21 full-time (11 women), 5 part-time (4 women); includes 2 minority (1 Black or African American, non-Hispanic/Latino; 1 Hispanic/Latino). Average age 31. 24 applicants, 71% accepted, 6 enrolled. *Faculty:* 3 full-time (1 woman), 3 part-time/adjunct (1 woman). Expenses: Contact institution. *Financial support:* Unspecified assistantships available. Financial award applicants required to submit FAFSA. In 2017, 8 master's awarded. *Program availability:* Part-time, evening/weekend, online learning. Offers sustainable practice (MS, Certificate). *Application deadline:* For fall admission, 7/15 for domestic students; for spring admission, 12/15 for domestic students. Applications are processed on a rolling basis. *Application fee:* $50 ($75 for international students). Electronic applications accepted. *Application Contact:* Emily Stutzman Jones, Academic Director, 615-966-5076, E-mail: emily.jones@lipscomb.edu. *Executive Director*, G. Dodd Galbreath, 615-966-1771, E-mail: dodd.galbreath@lipscomb.edu.

Nelson and Sue Andrews Institute for Civic Leadership Students: 18 full-time (13 women); includes 11 minority (9 Black or African American, non-Hispanic/Latino; 1 Hispanic/Latino; 1 Two or more races, non-Hispanic/Latino). Average age 33. 30 applicants, 37% accepted, 7 enrolled. *Faculty:* 3 full-time (2 women). Expenses: Contact institution. *Financial support:* Applicants required to submit FAFSA. In 2017, 11 master's awarded. *Program availability:* Part-time, evening/weekend. Offers civic leadership (MA, Graduate Certificate); cross sector collaboration (MA); non-profit leadership (MA). *Application deadline:* Applications are processed on a rolling basis. *Application fee:* $50 ($75 for international students). Electronic applications accepted. *Application Contact:* Dr. Michelle Steele, Academic Director, 615-966-5181, E-mail: michelle.steele@lipscomb.edu. *Executive Director*, Linda Peek Schacht, 615-966-1341, E-mail: linda.schacht@lipscomb.edu.

Program in Biomolecular Science Students: 31 full-time (15 women); includes 10 minority (6 Black or African American, non-Hispanic/Latino; 2 Asian, non-Hispanic/Latino; 2 Hispanic/Latino). Average age 26. 67 applicants, 51% accepted, 11 enrolled. *Faculty:* 6 full-time (4 women). Expenses: Contact institution. *Financial support:* Unspecified assistantships available. Financial award applicants required to submit FAFSA. In 2017, 23 master's awarded. *Program availability:* Part-time, evening/weekend. Offers human disease (MS); laboratory research (MS). *Application deadline:* For fall admission, 8/1 for domestic students; for winter admission, 12/14 for domestic students; for spring admission, 5/14 for domestic students. Applications are processed on a rolling basis. *Application fee:* $50 ($75 for international students). Electronic applications accepted. *Application Contact:* Tina Fulford, Administrative Assistant, 615-966-5330, E-mail: tina.fulford@lipscomb.edu. *Director*, Dr. Kent Gallaher, 615-966-5721, E-mail: kent.gallaher@lipscomb.edu.

Program in Exercise and Nutrition Science Students: 40 full-time (33 women), 20 part-time (15 women); includes 12 minority (4 Black or African American, non-Hispanic/Latino; 2 Asian, non-Hispanic/Latino; 5 Hispanic/Latino; 1 Two or more races, non-Hispanic/Latino), 1 international. Average age 25. 59 applicants, 44% accepted, 12 enrolled. *Faculty:* 6 full-time (3 women). Expenses: Contact institution. *Financial support:* Unspecified assistantships available. Financial award applicants required to submit FAFSA. In 2017, 14 master's awarded. *Program availability:* Part-time, evening/weekend. Offers exercise and nutrition science (MS). *Application deadline:* For fall admission, 6/1 for domestic students; for spring admission, 12/1 for domestic students. Applications are processed on a rolling basis. *Application fee:* $50 ($75 for international students). Electronic applications accepted. *Application Contact:* Julie Lillicrap, Administrative Assistant, 615-966-5700, E-mail: julie.lillicrap@lipscomb.edu. *Director*, Dr. Karen Robichaud, 615-966-5602, E-mail: karen.robichaud@lipscomb.edu.

Program in Film and Creative Media Students: 23 full-time (12 women); includes 10 minority (all Black or African American, non-Hispanic/Latino). Average age 32. 26 applicants, 46% accepted, 9 enrolled. *Faculty:* 7 full-time (1 woman), 1 part-time/adjunct (0 women). Expenses: Contact institution. *Financial support:* Unspecified assistantships available. Financial award applicants required to submit FAFSA. In 2017, 12 master's awarded. *Program availability:* Part-time, evening/weekend. Offers writer/director (MFA). *Application deadline:* Applications are processed on a rolling basis. *Application fee:* $50 ($75 for international students). Electronic applications accepted. *Application Contact:* Josh Link, Recruiting and Marketing Coordinator, 615-966-6005, E-mail: josh.link@lipscomb.edu. *Director*, David DeBorde, 615-966-7111, E-mail: david.deborde@lipscomb.edu.

Program in Organizational Leadership Students: 27 full-time (14 women), 6 part-time (4 women); includes 8 minority (4 Black or African American, non-Hispanic/Latino; 4 Hispanic/Latino), 1 international. Average age 43. 34 applicants, 68% accepted, 15 enrolled. *Faculty:* 1 (woman) full-time, 3 part-time/adjunct (1 woman). Expenses: Contact institution. In 2017, 7 master's, 17 Certificates awarded. *Program availability:* Part-time, online only, blended/hybrid learning. Offers aging services leadership (Certificate); global leadership (Certificate); organizational leadership (MPS); performance coaching (Certificate); strategic leadership (Certificate). *Application deadline:* For fall admission, 8/1 for domestic students. Applications are processed on a rolling basis. *Application fee:* $50 ($75 for international students). Electronic applications accepted. *Application Contact:* Barbara Blackman, Coordinator of Graduate Studies, 615-966-6287, Fax: 615-966-7619, E-mail: graduatestudies@lipscomb.edu. *Director*, Dr. Hope Nordstrom, 615-966-1107, E-mail: hope.nordstrom@lipscomb.edu.

School of Public Policy Students: 12 full-time (9 women); includes 6 minority (all Black or African American, non-Hispanic/Latino). Average age 27. 33 applicants, 48% accepted, 12 enrolled. *Faculty:* 2 full-time (1 woman). Expenses: Contact institution. In 2017, 15 master's awarded. Offers leadership and public service (MA). *Application deadline:* Applications are processed on a rolling basis. *Application fee:* $50 ($75 for international students). Electronic applications accepted. *Application Contact:* Amy Goode, New Student Enrollment Manager, 615-966-6691, E-mail: amy.goode@lipscomb.edu. *Academic Director*, Dr. Kristine LaLonde, 615-966-6692, E-mail: kristine.lalonde@lipscomb.edu.

LOCK HAVEN UNIVERSITY OF PENNSYLVANIA, Lock Haven, PA 17745-2390

General Information State-supported, coed, comprehensive institution. *Graduate housing:* Room and/or apartments available on a first-come, first-served basis to single students; on-campus housing not available to married students. Housing application deadline: 6/1.

GRADUATE UNITS

College of Liberal Arts and Education *Program availability:* Part-time, evening/weekend, online learning. Offers alternative education (M Ed); educational leadership (M Ed); teaching and learning (M Ed). Electronic applications accepted.

College of Natural, Behavioral and Health Sciences Offers actuarial science (PSM); athletic training (MS); health promotion/education (MHS); healthcare management (MHS); physician assistant (MHS). Program also offered at the Clearfield, Coudersport, and Harrisburg campuses. Electronic applications accepted.

The Stephen Poorman College of Business, Information Systems, and Human Services *Program availability:* Online learning. Offers clinical mental health counseling (MS); sport science (MS). Electronic applications accepted.

LOGAN UNIVERSITY, Chesterfield, MO 63017

General Information Independent, coed, upper-level institution. *Enrollment:* 1,371 graduate, professional, and undergraduate students; 828 full-time matriculated graduate/professional students (365 women), 417 part-time matriculated graduate/professional students (314 women). *Enrollment by degree level:* 476 master's, 769 doctoral. *Graduate faculty:* 39 full-time (15 women), 7 part-time/adjunct (4 women). *Graduate housing:* On-campus housing not available. *Student services:* Campus employment opportunities, campus safety program, career counseling, free psychological counseling, services for students with disabilities. *Library facilities:* Learning Resources Center. *Collection:* Books: 11,773 (physical), 3,679 (digital/electronic); Serial titles: 23 (physical), 64 (digital/electronic); Databases: 94. Weekly public service hours: 84. *Research affiliation:* BTE-Multi-Cervical Unit (cervical spine analysis), Cadwell (electrophysiological diagnosis), Standard Process (nutrition and lipid management), Biofreeze (topical analgesics), Foot Levelers, Inc. (orthotics).

Computer facilities: 100 computers available on campus for general student use. A campuswide network can be accessed. Online class registration, student portal, learning management system, online storage, specialty health care software, high-speed printing are available.
Website: http://www.logan.edu/

General Application Contact: Natacha Douglas, Executive Director of Admissions, 636-227-2100 Ext. 1718, Fax: 636-207-2431, E-mail: admissions@logan.edu.

GRADUATE UNITS

College of Chiropractic Students: 744 full-time (302 women); includes 90 minority (29 Black or African American, non-Hispanic/Latino; 4 American Indian or Alaska Native, non-Hispanic/Latino; 19 Asian, non-Hispanic/Latino; 23 Hispanic/Latino; 1 Native Hawaiian or other Pacific Islander, non-Hispanic/Latino; 14 Two or more races, non-Hispanic/Latino), 13 international. Average age 26. 267 applicants, 58% accepted, 141 enrolled. *Faculty:* 39 full-time (15 women), 7 part-time/adjunct (4 women). Expenses: Contact institution. *Financial support:* In 2017–18, 129 students received support. Federal Work-Study and scholarships/grants available. Support available to part-time students. Financial award applicants required to submit FAFSA. In 2017, 81 doctorates awarded. Offers chiropractic (DC). *Application deadline:* Applications are processed on a rolling basis. *Application fee:* $50. Electronic applications accepted. *Application Contact:* Natacha Douglas, Executive Director of Admissions, 636-227-2100 Ext. 1718, Fax: 636-207-2425, E-mail: admissions@logan.edu. *Dean of the College of Chiropractic*, Dr. Vincent DeBono, 636-227-2100 Ext. 2701, Fax: 636-207-2431, E-mail: vincent.debono@logan.edu.

College of Health Sciences Students: 84 full-time (63 women), 417 part-time (314 women); includes 75 minority (36 Black or African American, non-Hispanic/Latino; 3 American Indian or Alaska Native, non-Hispanic/Latino; 15 Asian, non-Hispanic/Latino; 17 Hispanic/Latino; 4 Two or more races, non-Hispanic/Latino), 1 international. Average age 36. 238 applicants, 72% accepted, 134 enrolled. *Faculty:* 4 full-time (1 woman), 25 part-time/adjunct (13 women). Expenses: Contact institution. *Financial support:* In 2017–18, 4 students received support. Federal Work-Study available. Support available to part-time students. Financial award applicants required to submit FAFSA. In 2017, 61 master's awarded. *Program availability:* Part-time, online only, 100% online. Offers health informatics (MS); health professionals education (DHPE); nutrition and human performance (MS); sports science and rehabilitation (MS). *Application deadline:* Applications are processed on a rolling basis. *Application fee:* $50. Electronic applications accepted. *Application Contact:* Natacha Douglas, Executive Director of Admissions, 636-227-2100 Ext. 1718, Fax: 636-207-2425, E-mail: admissions@logan.edu. *Dean, College of Health Sciences*, Dr. Sherri Cole, 636-227-2100 Ext. 2702, Fax: 636-207-2418, E-mail: sherri.cole@logan.edu.

LOGOS EVANGELICAL SEMINARY, El Monte, CA 91731

General Information Independent-religious, coed, graduate-only institution. *Enrollment by degree level:* 151 master's, 37 doctoral, 7 other advanced degrees. *Graduate faculty:* 15 full-time (6 women), 10 part-time/adjunct (3 women). *Tuition:* Full-time $10,110; part-time $5055 per year. *Required fees:* $250; $150 per unit. *Graduate housing:* Rooms and/or apartments available on a first-come, first-served basis to single and married students. Typical cost: $8400 per year for single students; $9600 per year for married students. Housing application deadline: 7/15. *Student services:* Campus employment opportunities, campus safety program, career counseling, international student services, low-cost health insurance. *Library facilities:* Logos Library plus 1 other. *Collection:* Books: 58,235 (physical), 37,342 (digital/electronic); Serial titles: 157 (physical), 6 (digital/electronic); Databases: 11. Weekly public service hours: 65; students can reserve study rooms.

Computer facilities: 17 computers available on campus for general student use. A campuswide network can be accessed from off campus. Online class registration is available.
Website: http://www.les.edu/language/en/

General Application Contact: Becky Perng, Admission Specialist, 626-571-5110 Ext. 112, Fax: 626-571-5119, E-mail: admission@les.edu.

GRADUATE UNITS

Graduate Programs Students: 64 full-time (31 women), 131 part-time (62 women); includes 99 minority (all Asian, non-Hispanic/Latino), 96 international. Average age 48. 55 applicants, 93% accepted, 48 enrolled. *Faculty:* 15 full-time (6 women), 10 part-time/adjunct (3 women). Expenses: Contact institution. In 2017, 27 master's, 11 doctorates awarded. *Program availability:* Part-time, 100% online, blended/hybrid learning. Offers theology (M Div, MA, MAFM, MAICS, Th M, D Min, PhD, Diploma). *Application deadline:* For fall admission, 6/15 for domestic students, 5/15 for international students; for spring admission, 11/15 for domestic students, 10/15 for international students. Applications are processed on a rolling basis. *Application fee:* $75. Electronic applications accepted. *Application Contact:* Becky Perng, Admission Specialist, 626-571-5110 Ext. 112, Fax: 626-571-5119, E-mail: admission@les.edu. *Academic Dean*, Rev. Ekron Chen, PhD, 626-571-5110 Ext. 120, Fax: 626-571-5119, E-mail: ekron@les.edu.

LOMA LINDA UNIVERSITY, Loma Linda, CA 92350

General Information Independent-religious, coed, university. CGS member. *Graduate housing:* Room and/or apartments available on a first-come, first-served basis to single students; on-campus housing not available to married students. *Research affiliation:* City of Hope Hospital (cancer research), Children's Hospital Los Angeles (cancer research), Children's Hospital Orange County (cancer research).

GRADUATE UNITS

School of Allied Health Professions Offers allied health professions (MOT, MPA, MS, DPT, OTD, PhD, SLPD); occupational therapy (MOT, OTD); physical therapy (DPT, PhD); physician assistant sciences (MPA); rehabilitation (MS); speech-language pathology (MS, SLPD). Electronic applications accepted.

School of Behavioral Health Offers behavioral health (MS, MSW, DMFT, PhD, Psy D, Certificate); child life specialist (MS); clinical mediation (Certificate); clinical psychology (PhD, Psy D); counseling (MS); criminal justice (MS); drug and alcohol counseling (Certificate); family life education (Certificate); gerontology (MS); marital and family therapy (DMFT); school counseling (Certificate); social policy and social research (PhD); social work (MSW). Electronic applications accepted.

School of Dentistry Offers dentistry (MS, DDS, Certificate); endodontics (MS, Certificate); implant dentistry (MS, Certificate); oral and maxillofacial surgery (MS, Certificate); orthodontics and dentofacial orthopedics (MS, Certificate); periodontics (MS).

School of Medicine Offers biochemistry (MS, PhD); human anatomy (PhD); medicine (MS, MD, PhD); microbiology (PhD); pathology (PhD); pharmacology (PhD); physiology (PhD).

School of Nursing *Program availability:* Part-time. Offers adult/gerontology (MS); nursing (MS, DNP, PhD); nursing administration (MS); obstetrics-pediatrics (MS). Electronic applications accepted.

School of Pharmacy Offers pharmacy (Pharm D).

School of Public Health *Program availability:* Part-time. Offers biostatistics (MPH); environmental and occupational health (MPH); epidemiology (MPH, Dr PH, PhD); global health (MPH); health education (MPH, Dr PH); healthcare administration (MBA); public health (MBA, MPH, MS, Dr PH, PhD); public health nutrition (MPH, Dr PH). Electronic applications accepted.

School of Religion Offers bioethics (MA, Certificate); chaplaincy (MS); religion (MA, MS, Certificate); religion and society (MA). Electronic applications accepted.

LONDON METROPOLITAN UNIVERSITY, London N7 8DB, United Kingdom

General Information Private, coed, university.

GRADUATE UNITS

Graduate Programs

LONG ISLAND UNIVERSITY–BRENTWOOD CAMPUS, Brentwood, NY 11717

General Information Independent, coed, upper-level institution. *Enrollment:* 111 full-time matriculated graduate/professional students (89 women), 47 part-time matriculated graduate/professional students (34 women). *Enrollment by degree level:* 149 master's, 9 other advanced degrees. *Graduate faculty:* 14 full-time (9 women), 22 part-time/adjunct (11 women). *Tuition:* Full-time $21,168; part-time $1201 per credit. *Required fees:* $1840; $920 per term. Tuition and fees vary according to course load. *Graduate housing:* On-campus housing not available. *Student services:* Career counseling, services for students with disabilities, teacher training. *Library facilities:* Brentwood Campus Library.

Computer facilities: Computer purchase and lease plans are available. 50 computers available on campus for general student use. A campuswide network can be accessed from off campus. Online class registration is available.
Website: http://www.liu.edu/

General Application Contact: Jean Conroy, Associate Dean, 631-287-8500, Fax: 631-287-8575, E-mail: jean.conroy@liu.edu.

GRADUATE UNITS

Graduate Programs Students: 111 full-time (89 women), 47 part-time (34 women); includes 35 minority (8 Black or African American, non-Hispanic/Latino; 1 American Indian or Alaska Native, non-Hispanic/Latino; 3 Asian, non-Hispanic/Latino; 22 Hispanic/Latino; 1 Two or more races, non-Hispanic/Latino), 1 international. Average age 30. 110 applicants, 82% accepted, 63 enrolled. *Faculty:* 14 full-time (9 women), 22 part-time/adjunct (11 women). Expenses: Contact institution. *Financial support:* In 2017–18, 121 students received support. Scholarships/grants available. Support available to part-time students. Financial award application deadline: 2/15; financial award applicants required to submit FAFSA. In 2017, 58 master's, 5 other advanced degrees awarded. *Program availability:* Part-time. Offers childhood education (MS); childhood education/literacy B-6 (MS); childhood education/special education (grades 1-6) (MS); clinical mental health counseling (MS, Advanced Certificate); criminal justice (MS); early childhood education (MS); educational leadership (MS Ed); family nurse practitioner (MS, Advanced Certificate); health administration (MPA); library and information science (MS); literacy (B-6) (MS Ed); school counselor (MS, Advanced Certificate); social work (MSW); special education (MS Ed); students with disabilities generalist (grades 7-12) (Advanced Certificate). *Application deadline:* Applications are processed on a rolling basis. *Application fee:* $50. Electronic applications accepted. *Application Contact:* Scott Aug, Associate Director of Enrollment Management, 631-287-8506, E-mail: scott.aug@liu.edu. *Dean and Chief Operating Officer*, Dr. Abby Van Vlerah, 631-299-3831, E-mail: abagail.vanvlerah@liu.edu.

LONG ISLAND UNIVERSITY–HUDSON, Purchase, NY 10577

General Information Independent, coed, graduate-only institution. *Enrollment by degree level:* 256 master's, 62 other advanced degrees. *Graduate faculty:* 8 full-time (6 women), 41 part-time/adjunct (24 women). *Tuition:* Full-time $21,618; part-time $1201 per credit. *Required fees:* $1840; $920 per term. Tuition and fees vary according to course load. *Graduate housing:* On-campus housing not available. *Student services:* Career counseling, services for students with disabilities, teacher training. *Library facilities:* Long Island University Library System.

Computer facilities: A campuswide network can be accessed from off campus. Online class registration is available.
Website: http://liu.edu/Hudson

General Application Contact: Dr. Sylvia Blake, Dean/Chief Operating Officer, 914-831-2700, E-mail: westchester@liu.edu.

GRADUATE UNITS

Graduate School Students: 69 full-time (54 women), 249 part-time (200 women); includes 102 minority (29 Black or African American, non-Hispanic/Latino; 1 American Indian or Alaska Native, non-Hispanic/Latino; 9 Asian, non-Hispanic/Latino; 62 Hispanic/Latino; 1 Native Hawaiian or other Pacific Islander, non-Hispanic/Latino). Average age 33. 153 applicants, 96% accepted, 103 enrolled. *Faculty:* 8 full-time (6 women), 41 part-time/adjunct (24 women). Expenses: Contact institution. *Financial support:* In 2017–18, 32 students received support. Scholarships/grants available. Support available to part-time students. Financial award application deadline: 2/15; financial award applicants required to submit FAFSA. In 2017, 138 master's, 36 other advanced degrees awarded. *Program availability:* Part-time, evening/weekend. Offers autism (Advanced Certificate); bilingual education (Advanced Certificate); childhood education (MS Ed); crisis management (Advanced Certificate); early childhood education (MS Ed); educational leadership (MS Ed); health administration (MPA); literacy (MS Ed); marriage and family therapy (MS); mental health counseling (MS, Advanced Certificate); middle childhood and adolescence education (MS Ed); pharmaceutics (MS); public administration (MPA); school counseling (MS Ed, Advanced Certificate); school psychology (MS Ed); special education (MS Ed); TESOL (MS Ed); TESOL (all grades) (Advanced Certificate). *Application deadline:* Applications are processed on a rolling basis. *Application fee:* $50. Electronic applications accepted. *Dean and Chief Operating Officer*, Dr. Sylvia Blake, 914-831-2700, E-mail: westchester@liu.edu.

LONG ISLAND UNIVERSITY–LIU BROOKLYN, Brooklyn, NY 11201-8423

General Information Independent, coed, university. *Enrollment:* 6,982 graduate, professional, and undergraduate students; 1,749 full-time matriculated graduate/professional students (1,211 women), 1,298 part-time matriculated graduate/professional students (952 women). *Enrollment by degree level:* 2,347 master's, 639 doctoral, 61 other advanced degrees. *Graduate faculty:* 161 full-time (92 women), 214 part-time/adjunct (122 women). *Tuition:* Full-time $21,618; part-time $1201 per credit. *Required fees:* $1840; $920 per term. Tuition and fees vary according to course load. *Graduate housing:* Room and/or apartments available on a first-come, first-served basis to single students; on-campus housing not available to married students. Typical cost: $8532 per year ($13,720 including board). Room and board charges vary according to board plan and housing facility selected. Housing application deadline: 5/1. *Student services:* Campus employment opportunities, campus safety program, career counseling, exercise/wellness program, international student services, low-cost health insurance, services for students with disabilities, teacher training, writing training. *Library facilities:* Salena Library. *Collection:* Books: 257,706 (physical), 406,939 (digital/electronic); Serial titles: 27 (physical), 466,233 (digital/electronic); Databases: 495. *Research affiliation:* California Table Grape Commission (pharmacy), Latitude Pharmaceuticals, Inc. (pharmacy), National Institute for Pharmaceutical Technology and Education (pharmacy), Natoli Engineering Company (pharmacy), Onconova Therapeutics, Inc. (pharmacy), Simcyp Limited (pharmacy).

Computer facilities: 600 computers available on campus for general student use. A campuswide network can be accessed from student residence rooms and from off campus. Online class registration is available.
Website: http://www.liu.edu/

General Application Contact: Luis Santiago, Dean of Enrollment, 718-488-1011, Fax: 718-780-6110, E-mail: bkln-admissions@liu.edu.

GRADUATE UNITS

Arnold and Marie Schwartz College of Pharmacy and Health Sciences Students: 497 full-time (296 women), 77 part-time (42 women); includes 228 minority (26 Black or African American, non-Hispanic/Latino; 143 Asian, non-Hispanic/Latino; 31 Hispanic/Latino; 28 Two or more races, non-Hispanic/Latino), 137 international. Average age 25. 241 applicants, 62% accepted, 38 enrolled. *Faculty:* 51 full-time (29 women), 33 part-time/adjunct (14 women). Expenses: Contact institution. *Financial support:* In 2017–18, 200 students received support. Research assistantships, teaching assistantships, career-related internships or fieldwork, Federal Work-Study, scholarships/grants, tuition waivers (full and partial), and unspecified assistantships available. Support available to part-time students. Financial award application deadline: 2/15; financial award applicants required to submit FAFSA. In 2017, 57 master's, 183 doctorates awarded. *Program availability:* Part-time. Offers drug regulatory affairs (MS); pharmaceutics (MS, PhD); pharmacology and toxicology (MS); pharmacy (Pharm D). *Application deadline:* Applications are processed on a rolling basis. *Application fee:* $50. Electronic applications accepted. *Application Contact:* Michael Young, Senior Assistant Director of Admissions, 718-488-1000, E-mail: michael.young@liu.edu. *Dean*, Dr. John M. Pezzuto, 718-488-1004, Fax: 718-488-0628, E-mail: john.pezzuto@liu.edu.

Harriet Rothkopf Heilbrunn School of Nursing Students: 5 full-time (all women), 195 part-time (174 women); includes 117 minority (70 Black or African American, non-Hispanic/Latino; 28 Asian, non-Hispanic/Latino; 17 Hispanic/Latino; 2 Two or more races, non-Hispanic/Latino), 1 international. Average age 37. 168 applicants, 60% accepted, 73 enrolled. *Faculty:* 9 full-time (7 women), 6 part-time/adjunct (4 women). Expenses: Contact institution. *Financial support:* In 2017–18, 15 students received support. Career-related internships or fieldwork, Federal Work-Study, scholarships/grants, and unspecified assistantships available. Support available to part-time students. Financial award application deadline: 2/15; financial award applicants required to submit FAFSA. In 2017, 69 master's, 2 other advanced degrees awarded. *Program availability:* Part-time, evening/weekend, blended/hybrid learning. Offers adult nurse practitioner (MS, Advanced Certificate); family nurse practitioner (MS, Advanced Certificate); nurse educator (MS). *Application deadline:* Applications are processed on a rolling basis. *Application fee:* $50. Electronic applications accepted. *Application Contact:* Luis Santiago, Dean of Admissions, 718-488-1011, Fax: 718-780-6110, E-mail: bkln-admissions@liu.edu. *Interim Dean*, Peggy Tallier, 718-780-3367, E-mail: peggy.tallier@liu.edu.

Richard L. Conolly College of Liberal Arts and Sciences Students: 178 full-time (123 women), 143 part-time (96 women); includes 128 minority (65 Black or African American, non-Hispanic/Latino; 22 Asian, non-Hispanic/Latino; 31 Hispanic/Latino; 10 Two or more races, non-Hispanic/Latino), 54 international. Average age 30. 629 applicants, 38% accepted, 74 enrolled. *Faculty:* 32 full-time (13 women), 17 part-time/adjunct (6 women). Expenses: Contact institution. *Financial support:* In 2017–18, 214 students received support, including 120 fellowships with full and partial tuition reimbursements available (averaging $915 per year), 5 research assistantships with full and partial tuition reimbursements available (averaging $2,300 per year), 136 teaching assistantships with full and partial tuition reimbursements available (averaging $2,300 per year); career-related internships or fieldwork, Federal Work-Study, institutionally sponsored loans, scholarships/grants, and unspecified assistantships also available. Support available to part-time students. Financial award application deadline: 2/15; financial award applicants required to submit FAFSA. In 2017, 147 master's, 9 doctorates, 8 other advanced degrees awarded. *Program availability:* Part-time. Offers biology (MS); chemistry (MS); clinical psychology (PhD); creative writing (MFA); English (MA); media arts (MA, MFA); political science (MA); psychology (MA); social science (MS); United Nations (Advanced Certificate); urban studies (MA); writing and production for television (MFA). *Application deadline:* Applications are processed on a rolling basis. *Application fee:* $50. Electronic applications accepted. *Application Contact:* Bayu Sutrisno, Graduate Admissions Counselor, 718-488-1564, Fax: 718-780-6110, E-mail: bayu.sutrisno@liu.edu. *Dean*, Dr. Scott Krawczyk, 718-488-1003, E-mail: scott.krawczyk@liu.edu.

School of Business, Public Administration and Information Sciences Students: 226 full-time (140 women), 232 part-time (150 women); includes 272 minority (192 Black or African American, non-Hispanic/Latino; 2 American Indian or Alaska Native, non-Hispanic/Latino; 35 Asian, non-Hispanic/Latino; 40 Hispanic/Latino; 3 Two or more races, non-Hispanic/Latino), 88 international. Average age 32. 495 applicants, 64% accepted, 149 enrolled. *Faculty:* 18 full-time (7 women), 28 part-time/adjunct (8 women). Expenses: Contact institution. *Financial support:* In 2017–18, 78 students received support. Career-related internships or fieldwork, Federal Work-Study, scholarships/grants, and unspecified assistantships available. Support available to part-time students. Financial award application deadline: 2/15; financial award applicants required to submit FAFSA. In 2017, 189 master's, 13 other advanced degrees awarded. *Program availability:* Part-time, evening/weekend. Offers accounting (MBA); accounting (MS); business administration (MBA); computer science (MS); gerontology (Advanced Certificate); health administration (MPA); human resources management (MS); not-for-profit management (Advanced Certificate); public administration (MPA); taxation (MS). *Application deadline:* Applications are processed on a rolling basis. *Application fee:* $50. Electronic applications accepted. *Application Contact:* Luis Santiago, Dean of Enrollment, 718-488-1011, Fax: 718-780-6110, E-mail: bkln-admissions@liu.edu. *Dean*, Dr. Edward Rogoff, 718-488-1159, E-mail: edward.rogoff@liu.edu.

School of Education Students: 140 full-time (130 women), 563 part-time (414 women); includes 417 minority (183 Black or African American, non-Hispanic/Latino; 1 American Indian or Alaska Native, non-Hispanic/Latino; 32 Asian, non-Hispanic/Latino; 187 Hispanic/Latino; 14 Two or more races, non-Hispanic/Latino), 10 international. Average age 31. 449 applicants, 82% accepted, 264 enrolled. *Faculty:* 14 full-time (12 women), 42 part-time/adjunct (32 women). Expenses: Contact institution. *Financial support:* In 2017–18, 58 students received support. Career-related internships or fieldwork, Federal Work-Study, scholarships/grants, and unspecified assistantships available. Support available to part-time students. Financial award application deadline: 2/15; financial award applicants required to submit FAFSA. In 2017, 408 master's, 31 other advanced degrees awarded. *Program availability:* Part-time, evening/weekend, 100% online. Offers adolescence urban education (MS Ed); applied behavior analysis (Advanced Certificate); bilingual education (Advanced Certificate); bilingual education in urban setting (MS Ed); bilingual school counselor (MS Ed, Advanced Certificate); childhood urban education (MS Ed); childhood/early childhood education (MS Ed); childhood/early childhood urban education (MS Ed); early childhood urban education (MS Ed, Advanced Certificate); educational leadership (Advanced Certificate); marriage and family therapy (MS, Advanced Certificate); mental health counseling (MS, Advanced Certificate); school building district leader (Advanced Certificate); school counselor (MS Ed, Advanced Certificate); school psychologist (MS Ed); teaching students with disabilities (MS Ed); teaching urban children with disabilities (MS Ed); TESOL (MS Ed, Advanced Certificate). *Application deadline:* Applications are processed on a rolling basis. *Application fee:* $50. Electronic applications accepted. *Application Contact:* Bayu Sutrisno, Graduate Admissions Counselor, 718-488-1011, Fax: 718-780-6110, E-mail: bkln-admissions@liu.edu. *Dean*, 718-488-1055, E-mail: bkln-admissions@liu.edu.

School of Health Professions Students: 690 full-time (508 women), 86 part-time (74 women); includes 259 minority (120 Black or African American, non-Hispanic/Latino; 1 American Indian or Alaska Native, non-Hispanic/Latino; 52 Asian, non-Hispanic/Latino; 76 Hispanic/Latino; 10 Two or more races, non-Hispanic/Latino), 65 international. Average age 27. 1,241 applicants, 45% accepted, 255 enrolled. *Faculty:* 33 full-time (23 women), 82 part-time/adjunct (55 women). Expenses: Contact institution. *Financial support:* In 2017–18, 187 students received support. Research assistantships, teaching assistantships, career-related internships or fieldwork, Federal Work-Study, scholarships/grants, and unspecified assistantships available. Support available to part-time students. Financial award application deadline: 2/15; financial award applicants required to submit FAFSA. In 2017, 249 master's, 42 doctorates, 8 other advanced degrees awarded. Offers athletic training and sport sciences (MS); community health (MS Ed); exercise science (MS); forensic social work (Advanced Certificate); occupational therapy (MS); physical therapy (DPT); physician assistant (MS); public health (MPH); social work (MSW); speech-language pathology (MS). *Application deadline:* Applications are processed on a rolling basis. *Application fee:* $50. Electronic applications accepted. *Application Contact:* Dr. Dominick Fortugno, Associate Dean, 718-488-1496, Fax: 718-780-4561, E-mail: dominick.fortugno@liu.edu. *Dean*, Dr. Barry S. Eckert, 718-780-6578, Fax: 718-780-4561, E-mail: barry.eckert@liu.edu.

LONG ISLAND UNIVERSITY–LIU POST, Brookville, NY 11548-1300

General Information Independent, coed, university. *Enrollment:* 8,499 graduate, professional, and undergraduate students; 1,092 full-time matriculated graduate/professional students (826 women), 1,062 part-time matriculated graduate/professional students (799 women). *Enrollment by degree level:* 1,578 master's, 269 doctoral, 307 other advanced degrees. *Graduate faculty:* 148 full-time (79 women), 182 part-time/adjunct (96 women). *Tuition:* Full-time $21,618; part-time $1201 per credit. *Required fees:* $1840; $920 per term. Tuition and fees vary according to course load. *Graduate housing:* Room and/or apartments available on a first-come, first-served basis to single students; on-campus housing not available to married students. Typical cost: $8532 per year ($13,720 including board). Room and board charges vary according to board plan and housing facility selected. Housing application deadline: 5/1. *Student services:* Campus employment opportunities, campus safety program, career counseling, exercise/wellness program, international student services, low-cost health insurance, services for students with disabilities, teacher training, writing training. *Library facilities:* B. Davis Schwartz Memorial Library. *Collection:* Books: 459,336 (physical), 203,430 (digital/electronic); Serial titles: 482 (physical), 466,233 (digital/electronic); Databases: 478. *Research affiliation:* Structure-ase Inc. (biology).

Computer facilities: 600 computers available on campus for general student use. A campuswide network can be accessed from student residence rooms and from off campus. Online class registration is available.
Website: http://www.liu.edu/

General Application Contact: Dr. William Martinov, Chief of Admissions and Enrollment Strategy, 516-299-2900, Fax: 516-299-2137, E-mail: post-enroll@liu.edu.

GRADUATE UNITS

College of Arts, Communications and Design Students: 99 full-time (80 women), 14 part-time (12 women); includes 22 minority (7 Black or African American, non-Hispanic/Latino; 4 Asian, non-Hispanic/Latino; 9 Hispanic/Latino; 2 Two or more races, non-Hispanic/Latino), 23 international. Average age 28. 125 applicants, 70% accepted, 42 enrolled. *Faculty:* 22 full-time (10 women), 44 part-time/adjunct (24 women). Expenses: Contact institution. *Financial support:* In 2017–18, 78 students received support. Career-related internships or fieldwork, scholarships/grants, tuition waivers (full and partial), and unspecified assistantships available. Support available to part-time students. Financial award application deadline: 2/15; financial award applicants required to submit FAFSA. In 2017, 55 master's awarded. Offers art (MA); clinical art therapy (MA); clinical art therapy and counseling (MA); digital game design and development (MA); fine arts and design (MFA); interactive multimedia arts (MA); museum studies (MA); music (MA); theatre (MFA). *Application deadline:* Applications are processed on a rolling basis. *Application fee:* $50. Electronic applications accepted. *Application Contact:* Rita Langdon, Graduate Admissions, 516-299-2334, Fax: 516-299-2137, E-mail: post-enroll@liu.edu. *Dean*, Steven Breese, 516-299-2309, E-mail: steven.breese@liu.edu.

College of Education, Information and Technology Students: 472 full-time (400 women), 696 part-time (543 women); includes 254 minority (93 Black or African American, non-Hispanic/Latino; 46 Asian, non-Hispanic/Latino; 105 Hispanic/Latino; 10 Two or more races, non-Hispanic/Latino), 33 international. Average age 33. 917 applicants, 82% accepted, 357 enrolled. *Faculty:* 40 full-time (26 women), 73 part-time/adjunct (38 women). Expenses: Contact institution. *Financial support:* In 2017–18, 376 students received support. Career-related internships or fieldwork, Federal Work-Study, institutionally sponsored loans, scholarships/grants, tuition waivers (partial), and unspecified assistantships available. Support available to part-time students. Financial award application deadline: 2/15; financial award applicants required to submit FAFSA. In 2017, 408 master's, 31 other advanced degrees awarded. *Program availability:* Part-time, 100% online, blended/hybrid learning. Offers adolescence education (MS); adolescence education 7-12 (MS); archives and records management (AC); art education (MS); childhood education (MS); childhood education/literacy B-6 (MS); childhood education/special education (MS); clinical mental health counseling (MS, AC); early childhood education (MS); early childhood education/childhood education (MS); educational leadership (AC); educational technology (MS); information studies (PhD); interdisciplinary educational studies (Ed D); middle childhood education (MS); music education (MS); public library administration (AC); school counselor (MS); special education (MS Ed); speech-language pathology (MA); students with disabilities, 7-12 generalist (AC); TESOL (MA). *Application deadline:* Applications are processed on a rolling basis. *Application fee:* $50. Electronic applications accepted. *Application Contact:* Rita Langdon, Graduate Admissions, 516-299-2900, Fax: 516-299-2137, E-mail: post-enroll@liu.edu. *Dean*, Dr. Albert Inserra, 516-299-2210, E-mail: albert.inserra@liu.edu.

College of Liberal Arts and Sciences Students: 173 full-time (124 women), 62 part-time (35 women); includes 54 minority (11 Black or African American, non-Hispanic/Latino; 13 Asian, non-Hispanic/Latino; 23 Hispanic/Latino; 7 Two or more races, non-Hispanic/Latino), 12 international. Average age 28. 368 applicants, 54% accepted, 74 enrolled. *Faculty:* 41 full-time (21 women), 24 part-time/adjunct (13 women). Expenses: Contact institution. *Financial support:* In 2017–18, 165 students received support. Fellowships, research assistantships, teaching assistantships, career-related internships or fieldwork, Federal Work-Study, scholarships/grants, tuition waivers (partial), and unspecified assistantships available. Support available to part-time students. Financial award application deadline: 2/15; financial award applicants required to submit FAFSA. In 2017, 89 master's, 15 other advanced degrees awarded. *Program availability:* Part-time, evening/weekend, blended/hybrid learning. Offers applied mathematics (MS); behavior analysis (MA); biology (MS); criminal justice (MS); earth science (MS); English (MA); environmental sustainability (MS); genetic counseling (MS); history (MA); interdisciplinary studies (MA, MS); political science (MA); psychology (MA). *Application deadline:* Applications are processed on a rolling basis. *Application fee:* $50. Electronic applications accepted. *Application Contact:* Rita Langdon, Graduate Admissions, 516-299-2900, Fax: 516-299-2137, E-mail: post-enroll@liu.edu. *Dean*, Dr. Nathaniel Bowditch, 516-299-2234, Fax: 516-299-4140, E-mail: nathaniel.bowditch@liu.edu.

College of Management Students: 119 full-time (47 women), 62 part-time (23 women); includes 33 minority (11 Black or African American, non-Hispanic/Latino; 8 Asian, non-Hispanic/Latino; 13 Hispanic/Latino; 1 Two or more races, non-Hispanic/Latino), 56 international. Average age 28. 162 applicants, 62% accepted, 41 enrolled. *Faculty:* 23 full-time (7 women), 7 part-time/adjunct (1 woman). Expenses: Contact institution. *Financial support:* In 2017–18, 47 students received support. Career-related internships or fieldwork, Federal Work-Study, and scholarships/grants available. Support available to part-time students. Financial award application deadline: 2/15; financial award applicants required to submit FAFSA. In 2017, 91 master's awarded. *Program availability:* Part-time, evening/weekend, blended/hybrid learning. Offers accountancy (MS); finance (MBA); information systems (MS); international business (MBA); management (MBA); management engineering (MS); marketing (MBA); taxation (MS); technical project management (MS). *Application deadline:* Applications are processed on a rolling basis. *Application fee:* $50. Electronic applications accepted. *Application Contact:* Rita Langdon, Graduate Admissions, 516-299-2900, Fax: 516-299-2137, E-mail: post-enroll@liu.edu. *Dean*, Dr. Robert M. Valli, 516-299-3004, E-mail: rob.valli@liu.edu.

School of Health Professions and Nursing Students: 228 full-time (174 women), 227 part-time (185 women); includes 172 minority (76 Black or African American, non-Hispanic/Latino; 1 American Indian or Alaska Native, non-Hispanic/Latino; 44 Asian, non-Hispanic/Latino; 48 Hispanic/Latino; 3 Two or more races, non-Hispanic/Latino), 60 international. Average age 31. 392 applicants, 67% accepted, 138 enrolled. *Faculty:* 23 full-time (17 women), 33 part-time/adjunct (19 women). Expenses: Contact institution. *Financial support:* In 2017–18, 102 students received support. Research assistantships, teaching assistantships, career-related internships or fieldwork, Federal Work-Study, scholarships/grants, and unspecified assistantships available. Support available to part-time students. Financial award application deadline: 2/15; financial award applicants required to submit FAFSA. In 2017, 180 master's, 26 other advanced degrees awarded. *Program availability:* Part-time, blended/hybrid learning. Offers biomedical science (MS); cardiovascular perfusion (MS); clinical lab sciences (MS); clinical laboratory management (MS); dietetic internship (Advanced Certificate); family nurse practitioner (MS, Advanced Certificate); forensic social work (Advanced Certificate); gerontology (Advanced Certificate); health administration (MPA); non-profit management (Advanced Certificate); nursing education (MS); nutrition (MS); public administration (MPA); social work (MSW). *Application deadline:* Applications are processed on a rolling basis. *Application fee:* $50. Electronic applications accepted. *Application Contact:* Kathy Riley, Associate Director of Graduate Admissions, 516-299-2900, Fax: 516-299-2137, E-mail: post-enroll@liu.edu. *Dean*, Dr. Stacy Gropack, 516-299-2485, Fax: 516-299-2527, E-mail: post-shpn@liu.edu.

LONG ISLAND UNIVERSITY–RIVERHEAD, Riverhead, NY 11901

General Information Independent, coed, graduate-only institution. *Enrollment by degree level:* 74 master's, 1 other advanced degree. *Graduate faculty:* 4 full-time (1 woman), 11 part-time/adjunct (5 women). *Tuition:* Full-time $21,618; part-time $1201 per credit. *Required fees:* $1840; $920 per term. Tuition and fees vary according to course load. *Graduate housing:* On-campus housing not available. *Student services:* Career counseling, services for students with disabilities, teacher training. *Library facilities:* Long Island University Library System.

Computer facilities: A campuswide network can be accessed from off campus. Online class registration is available.
Website: http://www.liu.edu/Riverhead/

General Application Contact: Jean Conroy, Associate Dean, 631-287-8301, Fax: 631-287-8253, E-mail: jean.conroy@liu.edu.

GRADUATE UNITS

Graduate Programs Students: 17 full-time (14 women), 58 part-time (36 women); includes 14 minority (4 Black or African American, non-Hispanic/Latino; 1 American Indian or Alaska Native, non-Hispanic/Latino; 1 Asian, non-Hispanic/Latino; 6 Hispanic/Latino; 2 Two or more races, non-Hispanic/Latino). Average age 32. 68 applicants, 79% accepted, 26 enrolled. *Faculty:* 4 full-time (1 woman), 11 part-time/adjunct (5 women). Expenses: Contact institution. *Financial support:* In 2017–18, 53 students received support. Scholarships/grants available. Support available to part-time students. Financial award application deadline: 2/15; financial award applicants required to submit FAFSA. In 2017, 30 master's, 7 other advanced degrees awarded. *Program availability:* Part-time. Offers applied behavior analysis (Advanced Certificate); childhood education (MS); cybersecurity policy (Advanced Certificate); homeland security management (MS, Advanced Certificate); literacy education (MS); literacy education B-6 (MS); teaching students with disabilities (MS); TESOL (Advanced Certificate). *Application deadline:* Applications are processed on a rolling basis. *Application fee:* $50. Electronic applications accepted. *Application Contact:* Jean Conroy, Associate Dean, 631-287-8301, E-mail: jean.conroy@liu.edu. *Dean and Chief Operating Officer*, Dr. Abagail VanVlerah, 631-299-3831, E-mail: abagail.vanvlerah@liu.edu.

LONGWOOD UNIVERSITY, Farmville, VA 23909

General Information State-supported, coed, comprehensive institution. CGS member. *Graduate housing:* On-campus housing not available.

GRADUATE UNITS

College of Graduate and Professional Studies *Program availability:* Part-time, evening/weekend. Electronic applications accepted.

College of Business and Economics *Program availability:* Part-time, online only, 100% online. Offers general business (MBA); real estate (MBA); retail management (MBA). Electronic applications accepted.

College of Education and Human Services *Program availability:* Part-time, evening/weekend. Offers communication sciences and disorders (MS); education (MS); reading, literacy and learning (M Ed); school librarianship (M Ed); social work and communication sciences and disorders (MS). Electronic applications accepted.

LORAS COLLEGE, Dubuque, IA 52004-0178

General Information Independent-religious, coed, comprehensive institution. *Graduate housing:* On-campus housing not available.

GRADUATE UNITS

Graduate Division *Program availability:* Part-time, evening/weekend. Offers applied psychology (MA); educational leadership (MA); instructional strategist I K-6 and 7-12 (MA); ministry (MA); theology (MA).

LOUISIANA COLLEGE, Pineville, LA 71359-0001

General Information Independent-religious, coed, comprehensive institution.

GRADUATE UNITS

Caskey School of Divinity Offers biblical and theological studies (MA); pastoral ministry (MA).

Graduate Programs

LOUISIANA STATE UNIVERSITY AND AGRICULTURAL & MECHANICAL COLLEGE, Baton Rouge, LA 70803

General Information State-supported, coed, university. CGS member. *Enrollment:* 30,861 graduate, professional, and undergraduate students; 3,668 full-time matriculated graduate/professional students (2,024 women), 1,228 part-time matriculated graduate/professional students (725 women). *Enrollment by degree level:* 2,582 master's, 2,281 doctoral, 33 other advanced degrees. *Graduate faculty:* 1,190 full-time (356 women), 13 part-time/adjunct (5 women). *Graduate housing:* Rooms and/or apartments available on a first-come, first-served basis to single and married students. Housing application deadline: 3/15. *Student services:* Campus employment opportunities, campus safety program, career counseling, child daycare facilities, exercise/wellness program, free psychological counseling, grant writing training, international student services, low-cost health insurance, services for students with disabilities, teacher training, writing training. *Library facilities:* Troy H. Middleton Library plus 4 others. *Collection:* Books: 3 million (physical), 583,654 (digital/electronic); Serial titles: 633,678 (physical), 332,761 (digital/electronic); Databases: 367. Study areas open 24 hours, 5–7 days a week; students can reserve study rooms. *Research affiliation:* Arctic Research Consortium of the U.S., Organization for Tropical Studies, Coalition for Academic Scientific Computing, Albert Einstein Institute, Inter-University Consortium for Political and Social Research, Laser Interferometer Gravitational Wave Observatory.

Computer facilities: 1,180 computers available on campus for general student use. A campuswide network can be accessed. Online class registration, free software for download, storage, discounts on hardware, virtual computer lab are available.
Website: http://www.lsu.edu/

General Application Contact: Dr. Renee Renegar, Director of Graduate School, 225-578-1128, Fax: 225-578-1370, E-mail: rreneg1@lsu.edu.

GRADUATE UNITS

Graduate School Students: 3,668 full-time (2,024 women), 1,228 part-time (725 women); includes 1,056 minority (620 Black or African American, non-Hispanic/Latino; 11 American Indian or Alaska Native, non-Hispanic/Latino; 112 Asian, non-Hispanic/Latino; 253 Hispanic/Latino; 3 Native Hawaiian or other Pacific Islander, non-Hispanic/Latino; 57 Two or more races, non-Hispanic/Latino), 1,080 international. Average age 29. 4,316 applicants, 44% accepted, 1199 enrolled. *Faculty:* 1,190 full-time (356 women), 13 part-time/adjunct (5 women). Expenses: Contact institution. *Financial support:* In 2017–18, 2,159 students received support, including 135 fellowships (averaging $27,283 per year), 896 research assistantships (averaging $22,152 per year), 1,263 teaching assistantships (averaging $19,442 per year); scholarships/grants, tuition waivers (full and partial), and unspecified assistantships also available. Financial award application deadline: 3/1; financial award applicants required to submit FAFSA. In 2017, 1,101 master's, 399 doctorates, 42 other advanced degrees awarded. *Program availability:* Part-time, evening/weekend. *Application deadline:* For fall admission, 5/15 for domestic students, 6/15 for international students; for spring admission, 11/1 for domestic and international students; for summer admission, 5/15 for domestic students, 4/15 for international students. Applications are processed on a rolling basis. *Application fee:* $50 ($70 for international students). Electronic applications accepted. *Application Contact:* E-mail: gradsvcs@lsu.edu.

College of Agriculture Students: 243 full-time (110 women), 56 part-time (35 women); includes 36 minority (16 Black or African American, non-Hispanic/Latino; 7 Asian, non-Hispanic/Latino; 12 Hispanic/Latino; 1 Two or more races, non-Hispanic/Latino), 133 international. Average age 30. 157 applicants, 45% accepted, 46 enrolled. *Faculty:* 157 full-time (36 women). Expenses: Contact institution. *Financial support:* In 2017–18, 3 fellowships (averaging $24,104 per year), 212 research assistantships (averaging $21,154 per year), 19 teaching assistantships (averaging $18,829 per year) were awarded. In 2017, 74 master's, 26 doctorates awarded. Offers agricultural economics and agribusiness (MS, PhD); agriculture (M App St, MS, PhD); animal sciences (MS, PhD); applied statistics (M App St); entomology (MS, PhD); fisheries (MS); forestry (MS, PhD); human ecology (MS, PhD); nutrition and food sciences (MS, PhD); plant health (MS, PhD); plant, environmental and soil sciences (MS, PhD); wildlife (MS); wildlife and fisheries science (PhD).

College of Art and Design Students: 100 full-time (60 women), 11 part-time (7 women); includes 19 minority (6 Black or African American, non-Hispanic/Latino; 7 Asian, non-Hispanic/Latino; 6 Hispanic/Latino), 36 international. Average age 29. 163 applicants, 34% accepted, 29 enrolled. *Faculty:* 51 full-time (18 women). Expenses: Contact institution. *Financial support:* In 2017–18, 10 research assistantships (averaging $10,907 per year), 68 teaching assistantships (averaging $10,996 per year) were awarded. In 2017, 36 master's awarded. Offers architecture (M Arch); art and design (M Arch, MA, MFA, MLA); art history (MA); ceramics (MFA); graphic design (MFA); landscape architecture (MLA); painting and drawing (MFA); photography (MFA); printmaking (MFA); sculpture (MFA); studio art (MFA).

College of Engineering Students: 497 full-time (130 women), 151 part-time (36 women); includes 59 minority (27 Black or African American, non-Hispanic/Latino; 1 American Indian or Alaska Native, non-Hispanic/Latino; 16 Asian, non-Hispanic/Latino; 14 Hispanic/Latino; 1 Two or more races, non-Hispanic/Latino), 413 international. Average age 30. 696 applicants, 41% accepted, 93 enrolled. *Faculty:* 142 full-time (17 women), 3 part-time/adjunct (1 woman). Expenses: Contact institution. *Financial support:* In 2017–18, 37 fellowships (averaging $16,952 per year), 267 research assistantships (averaging $21,858 per year), 167 teaching assistantships (averaging $19,859 per year) were awarded. In 2017, 94 master's, 50 doctorates awarded. Offers biological and agricultural engineering (MSBAE); chemical engineering (MS Ch E, PhD); computer science (MSSS, PhD); construction management (MS, PhD); digital media arts and engineering (M Sc); electrical and computer engineering (MSEE, PhD); engineering (M Sc, MS, MS Ch E, MS Pet E, MSBAE, MSCE, MSEE, MSES, MSME, MSSS, PhD); engineering science (MS, PhD); environmental engineering (MSCE, PhD); geotechnical engineering (MSCE, PhD); mechanical and industrial engineering (MSME, PhD); petroleum engineering (MS Pet E, PhD); structural engineering and mechanics (MSCE, PhD); systems science (MSSS); transportation engineering (MSCE, PhD); water resources (MSCE, PhD).

College of Humanities and Social Sciences Students: 493 full-time (310 women), 100 part-time (59 women); includes 142 minority (65 Black or African American, non-Hispanic/Latino; 1 American Indian or Alaska Native, non-Hispanic/Latino; 15 Asian, non-Hispanic/Latino; 49 Hispanic/Latino; 1 Native Hawaiian or other Pacific Islander, non-Hispanic/Latino; 11 Two or more races, non-Hispanic/Latino), 78 international. Average age 30. 806 applicants, 27% accepted, 105 enrolled. *Faculty:* 290 full-time (113 women), 4 part-time/adjunct (2 women). Expenses: Contact institution. *Financial support:* In 2017–18, 23 fellowships (averaging $34,168 per year), 56 research assistantships (averaging $20,154 per year), 333 teaching assistantships (averaging $20,206 per year) were awarded. In 2017, 107 master's, 55 doctorates awarded. Offers biological psychology (MA, PhD); clinical psychology (MA, PhD); cognitive psychology (MA, PhD); communication sciences and disorders (MA, PhD); communication studies (MA, PhD); comparative literature (MA, PhD); creative writing (MFA); developmental psychology (MA, PhD); English (MA, PhD); French literature and linguistics (MA, PhD); geography (MA, MS); geography and anthropology (PhD); Hispanic studies (MA); history (MA, PhD); humanities and social sciences (MA, MALA, MFA, MS, PhD); liberal arts (MALA); philosophy (MA); political science (MA, PhD); school psychology (MA, PhD); sociology (MA, PhD).

College of Human Sciences and Education Students: 767 full-time (589 women), 632 part-time (489 women); includes 488 minority (362 Black or African American, non-Hispanic/Latino; 7 American Indian or Alaska Native, non-Hispanic/Latino; 18 Asian, non-Hispanic/Latino; 76 Hispanic/Latino; 1 Native Hawaiian or other Pacific Islander, non-Hispanic/Latino; 24 Two or more races, non-Hispanic/Latino), 33 international. Average age 32. 958 applicants, 61% accepted, 401 enrolled. *Faculty:* 69 full-time (33 women). Expenses: Contact institution. *Financial support:* In 2017–18, 6 fellowships (averaging $15,183 per year), 14 research assistantships (averaging $19,155 per year), 158 teaching assistantships (averaging $16,233 per year) were awarded. In 2017, 403 master's, 50 doctorates, 28 other advanced degrees awarded. Offers agriculture and extension education and youth development (MS, PhD); career and technical education (MS, PhD); comprehensive vocational education (MS, PhD); counseling (M Ed, MA, Ed S); educational administration (M Ed, MA, PhD, Ed S); educational technology (MA); elementary education (M Ed, MAT); extension and international education (MS, PhD); higher education (PhD); human resource and leadership development (MS, PhD); human sciences and education (M Ed, MA, MAT, MLIS, MS, MSW, PhD, Ed S); industrial education (MS); kinesiology (MS, PhD); library and information science (MLIS); research methodology (PhD); secondary education (M Ed, MAT); social work (MSW, PhD); vocational agriculture education (MS, PhD); vocational business education (MS); vocational home economics education (MS).

College of Music and Dramatic Arts Students: 184 full-time (85 women), 24 part-time (10 women); includes 41 minority (16 Black or African American, non-Hispanic/Latino; 1 American Indian or Alaska Native, non-Hispanic/Latino; 7 Asian, non-Hispanic/Latino; 16 Hispanic/Latino; 1 Two or more races, non-Hispanic/Latino), 55 international. Average age 30. 217 applicants, 47% accepted, 70 enrolled. *Faculty:* 72 full-time (22 women), 1 (woman) part-time/adjunct. Expenses: Contact institution. *Financial support:* In 2017–18, 5 fellowships (averaging $21,391 per year), 3 research assistantships (averaging $24,220 per year), 126 teaching assistantships (averaging $14,450 per year) were awarded. In 2017, 42 master's, 29 doctorates awarded. Offers acting (MFA); directing (MFA); music (MM, DMA, PhD); music and dramatic arts (MFA, MM, DMA, PhD); music education (PhD); theatre (PhD); theatre design/technology (MFA).

College of Science Students: 468 full-time (176 women), 23 part-time (8 women); includes 70 minority (29 Black or African American, non-Hispanic/Latino; 19 Asian, non-Hispanic/Latino; 19 Hispanic/Latino; 3 Two or more races, non-Hispanic/Latino), 193 international. Average age 28. 551 applicants, 25% accepted, 88 enrolled. *Faculty:* 177 full-time (39 women), 1 part-time/adjunct (0 women). Expenses: Contact institution. *Financial support:* In 2017–18, 55 fellowships (averaging $31,979 per year), 138 research assistantships (averaging $24,944 per year), 274 teaching assistantships (averaging $24,534 per year) were awarded. In 2017, 44 master's, 79 doctorates awarded. Offers astronomy (PhD); astrophysics (PhD); biochemistry (MS, PhD); biological science (MS, PhD); chemistry (MS, PhD); geology and geophysics (MS, PhD); mathematics (MS, PhD); medical physics (MS); natural sciences (MNS); physics (MS, PhD); science (MNS).

E. J. Ourso College of Business Students: 393 full-time (175 women), 197 part-time (63 women); includes 129 minority (73 Black or African American, non-Hispanic/Latino; 1 American Indian or Alaska Native, non-Hispanic/Latino; 14 Asian, non-Hispanic/Latino; 30 Hispanic/Latino; 1 Native Hawaiian or other Pacific Islander, non-Hispanic/Latino; 10 Two or more races, non-Hispanic/Latino), 75 international. Average age 30. 551 applicants, 50% accepted, 198 enrolled. *Faculty:* 76 full-time (20 women), 2 part-time/adjunct (0 women). Expenses: Contact institution. *Financial support:* In 2017–18, 1 fellowship (averaging $18,238 per year), 66 research assistantships (averaging $22,969 per year), 95 teaching assistantships (averaging $18,715 per year) were awarded. In 2017, 258 master's, 8 doctorates awarded. Offers accounting (MS, PhD); business (EMBA, MBA, MPA, MS, PMBA, PhD); business administration (PhD); economics (MS, PhD); finance (MS); information systems and decision sciences (MS, PhD); public administration (MPA).

Manship School of Mass Communication Students: 50 full-time (34 women), 9 part-time (5 women); includes 17 minority (16 Black or African American, non-Hispanic/Latino; 1 Two or more races, non-Hispanic/Latino), 9 international. Average age 27. 51 applicants, 65% accepted, 22 enrolled. *Faculty:* 24 full-time (10 women). Expenses: Contact institution. *Financial support:* In 2017–18, 29 research assistantships (averaging $21,011 per year), 13 teaching assistantships (averaging $25,523 per year) were awarded. In 2017, 16 master's, 6 doctorates awarded. Offers mass communication (MMC, PhD).

School of the Coast and Environment Students: 79 full-time (40 women), 18 part-time (7 women); includes 7 minority (2 Black or African American, non-Hispanic/Latino; 5 Hispanic/Latino), 36 international. Average age 30. 42 applicants, 52% accepted, 11 enrolled. *Faculty:* 40 full-time (11 women), 1 part-time/adjunct (0 women). Expenses: Contact institution. *Financial support:* In 2017–18, 4 fellowships (averaging $43,150 per year), 57 research assistantships (averaging $21,212 per year), 10 teaching assistantships (averaging $18,616 per year) were awarded. In 2017, 22 master's, 4 doctorates awarded. Offers environmental planning and management (MS); environmental science (PhD); environmental toxicology (MS); oceanography and coastal sciences (MS, PhD); the coast and environment (MS, PhD).

Paul M. Hebert Law Center Students: 534 full-time (263 women); includes 87 minority (37 Black or African American, non-Hispanic/Latino; 1 American Indian or Alaska Native, non-Hispanic/Latino; 8 Asian, non-Hispanic/Latino; 31 Hispanic/Latino; 10 Two or more races, non-Hispanic/Latino), 11 international. Average age 26. 901 applicants, 58% accepted, 178 enrolled. *Faculty:* 35 full-time (11 women), 20 part-time/adjunct (1 woman). Expenses: Contact institution. *Financial support:* In 2017–18, 522 students received support. Scholarships/grants and tuition waivers (full and partial) available. Financial award application deadline: 7/1; financial award applicants required to submit FAFSA. In 2017, 5 master's awarded. Offers law (LL M, JD). *Application deadline:* For fall admission, 3/1 priority date for domestic and international students. Applications are processed on a rolling basis. *Application fee:* $50. Electronic applications accepted. *Application Contact:* Jake T. Henry, III, Director of Admissions, 225-578-8646, Fax: 225-578-8647, E-mail: jakeh@lsu.edu. *Dean*, Thomas Galligan, 225-578-8491, Fax: 225-578-8202, E-mail: tgalligan@lsu.edu.

School of Veterinary Medicine Students: 394 full-time (315 women), 7 part-time (6 women); includes 48 minority (8 Black or African American, non-Hispanic/Latino; 9 Asian, non-Hispanic/Latino; 26 Hispanic/Latino; 5 Two or more races, non-Hispanic/Latino), 19 international. Average age 26. 124 applicants, 87% accepted, 101 enrolled. *Faculty:* 69 full-time (23 women), 1 (woman) part-time/adjunct. Expenses: Contact institution. *Financial support:* In 2017–18, 1 fellowship (averaging $50,006 per year), 43 research assistantships (averaging $26,402 per year) were awarded. In 2017, 5 master's, 92 doctorates awarded. Offers comparative biomedical sciences (MS, PhD); pathobiological sciences (MS, PhD); veterinary clinical sciences (MS, PhD); veterinary medicine (MS, DVM, PhD).

LOUISIANA STATE UNIVERSITY HEALTH SCIENCES CENTER, New Orleans, LA 70112-2223

General Information State-supported, coed, university. CGS member. *Enrollment:* 2,777 graduate, professional, and undergraduate students; 1,779 full-time matriculated graduate/professional students (1,021 women), 73 part-time matriculated graduate/professional students (61 women). *Enrollment by degree level:* 333 master's, 1,519 doctoral. *Graduate faculty:* 906 full-time (404 women). Tuition, state resident: full-time $11,835; part-time $518 per hour. Tuition, nonresident: full-time $24,108; part-time $1079 per hour. *Required fees:* $1254; $55 per hour. *Graduate housing:* Rooms and/or apartments available on a first-come, first-served basis to single and married students. Housing application deadline: 5/1. *Student services:* Campus safety program, exercise/wellness program, free psychological counseling, grant writing training, international student services, low-cost health insurance, multicultural affairs office, services for students with disabilities, teacher training, writing training. *Library facilities:* John P. Ische Library plus 2 others. *Collection:* Books: 61,199 (physical); Serial titles: 4,968 (physical), 3,068 (digital/electronic); Databases: 204. Weekly public service hours: 97; study areas open 24 hours, 5–7 days a week.

Computer facilities: Computer purchase and lease plans are available. 120 computers available on campus for general student use. A campuswide network can be accessed from student residence rooms and from off campus. Online class registration is available.
Website: http://www.lsuhsc.edu/

General Application Contact: Leigh Smith-Vaniz, Coordinator of Student Affairs, 504-568-2211, Fax: 504-568-5588, E-mail: lsmi30@lsuhsc.edu.

GRADUATE UNITS

School of Allied Health Professions Students: 361 full-time (285 women); includes 46 minority (18 Black or African American, non-Hispanic/Latino; 2 American Indian or Alaska Native, non-Hispanic/Latino; 10 Asian, non-Hispanic/Latino; 9 Hispanic/Latino; 7 Two or more races, non-Hispanic/Latino). Average age 25. 1,032 applicants, 14% accepted, 141 enrolled. *Faculty:* 28 full-time (21 women), 9 part-time/adjunct (8 women). Expenses: Contact institution. *Financial support:* In 2017–18, 13 students received support. Work assistantships available. Financial award application deadline: 4/15; financial award applicants required to submit FAFSA. In 2017, 98 master's, 46 doctorates awarded. Offers allied health professions (MCD, MHS, MOT, MPAS, Au D, DPT); audiology (Au D); clinical rehabilitation and counseling (MHS); occupational therapy (MOT); physical therapy (DPT); physician assistant studies (MPAS); speech pathology (MCD). *Application deadline:* For fall admission, 4/15 priority date for domestic students; for spring admission, 1/15 priority date for domestic students. *Application fee:* $150. Electronic applications accepted. *Application Contact:* Yudialys Delgado Cazanas, Student Affairs Director, 504-568-4253, Fax: 504-568-3185, E-mail: ydelga@lsuhsc.edu. *Dean*, Dr. Jimmy M. Cairo, 504-556-3400, Fax: 504-568-4249, E-mail: jcairo@lsuhsc.edu.

School of Dentistry Offers dentistry (DDS).

School of Graduate Studies in New Orleans Students: 70 full-time (41 women); includes 18 minority (6 Black or African American, non-Hispanic/Latino; 10 Asian, non-Hispanic/Latino; 2 Hispanic/Latino), 6 international. Average age 26. 58 applicants, 34% accepted, 15 enrolled. *Faculty:* 159 full-time (45 women). Expenses: Contact institution. *Financial support:* In 2017–18, 61 students received support. Tuition waivers (full) and unspecified assistantships available. Financial award application deadline: 4/1. In 2017, 15 doctorates awarded. Offers cell biology and anatomy (PhD); human genetics (PhD); medicine (PhD); microbiology and immunology (PhD); neuroscience (PhD); pharmacology and experimental therapeutics (PhD); physiology (PhD). *Application deadline:* For fall admission, 4/1 for domestic and international students. Applications are processed on a rolling basis. *Application fee:* $30. *Application Contact:* Leigh Smith-Vaniz, Coordinator of Student Affairs, 504-568-2211, Fax: 504-568-5588, E-mail: lsmi30@lsuhsc.edu. *Head*, Dr. Joseph M. Moerschbaecher, III, 504-568-2211, Fax: 504-568-2361.

School of Medicine in New Orleans Offers medicine (MPH, MD). Open only to Louisiana residents. Electronic applications accepted.

School of Nursing Students: 184 full-time (132 women), 41 part-time (35 women); includes 69 minority (45 Black or African American, non-Hispanic/Latino; 11 Asian, non-Hispanic/Latino; 12 Hispanic/Latino; 1 Two or more races, non-Hispanic/Latino), 1 international. Average age 30. 162 applicants, 42% accepted, 68 enrolled. *Faculty:* 29 full-time (26 women), 20 part-time/adjunct (8 women). Expenses: Contact institution.

Financial support: Federal Work-Study, institutionally sponsored loans, scholarships/grants, and traineeships available. Financial award applicants required to submit FAFSA. In 2017, 52 master's, 46 doctorates awarded. *Program availability:* Part-time. Offers adult gerontology acute care nurse practitioner (DNP, Post-Master's Certificate); adult gerontology clinical nurse specialist (DNP, Post-Master's Certificate); adult gerontology primary care nurse practitioner (DNP, Post-Master's Certificate); clinical nurse leader (MSN); executive nurse leader (DNP, Post-Master's Certificate); neonatal nurse practitioner (DNP, Post-Master's Certificate); nurse anesthesia (DNP, Post-Master's Certificate); nurse educator (MSN); nursing (DNS); primary care family nurse practitioner (DNP, Post-Master's Certificate); public/community health nursing (DNP, Post-Master's Certificate). *Application deadline:* Applications are processed on a rolling basis. *Application fee:* $100. Electronic applications accepted. *Application Contact:* Tracie Gravolet, Director, Office of Student Affairs, 504-568-4114, Fax: 504-568-5711, E-mail: tgravo@lsuhsc.edu. *Dean*, Dr. Demetrius James Porche, 504-568-4106, Fax: 504-599-0573, E-mail: dporch@lsuhsc.edu.

School of Public Health Students: 98 full-time (77 women), 24 part-time (18 women); includes 55 minority (26 Black or African American, non-Hispanic/Latino; 1 American Indian or Alaska Native, non-Hispanic/Latino; 13 Asian, non-Hispanic/Latino; 13 Hispanic/Latino; 2 Two or more races, non-Hispanic/Latino), 16 international. Average age 24. 208 applicants, 67% accepted, 54 enrolled. *Faculty:* 51 full-time (23 women), 41 part-time/adjunct (12 women). Expenses: Contact institution. *Program availability:* Part-time. Offers behavioral and community health sciences (MPH); biostatistics (MPH, MS, PhD); community health sciences (PhD); environmental and occupational health sciences (MPH); epidemiology (MPH, PhD); health policy and systems management (MPH). *Application deadline:* Applications are processed on a rolling basis. *Application fee:* $30. Electronic applications accepted. *Application Contact:* Isabel Billiot, Director of Admissions and Student Affairs, 504-568-5773, E-mail: ibilli@lsuhsc.edu. *Dean*, Dr. Dean Smith, 504-568-5700, E-mail: dgsmith@lsuhsc.edu.

LOUISIANA STATE UNIVERSITY HEALTH SCIENCES CENTER AT SHREVEPORT, Shreveport, LA 71130-3932

General Information State-supported, coed, university. *Research affiliation:* Pennington Biomedical Research Center (metabolic disorders/obesity).

GRADUATE UNITS

Department of Biochemistry and Molecular Biology Offers biochemistry and molecular biology (MS, PhD). Electronic applications accepted.

Department of Cellular Biology and Anatomy Offers cellular biology and anatomy (MS, PhD).

Department of Microbiology and Immunology Offers microbiology and immunology (MS, PhD). Electronic applications accepted.

Department of Molecular and Cellular Physiology Offers physiology (MS, PhD).

Department of Pharmacology, Toxicology and Neuroscience Offers pharmacology (PhD).

Master of Science in Biomedical Sciences Program Offers biomedical sciences (MS).

School of Medicine Offers medicine (MD).

LOUISIANA STATE UNIVERSITY IN SHREVEPORT, Shreveport, LA 71115-2399

General Information State-supported, coed, comprehensive institution. *Enrollment:* 756 full-time matriculated graduate/professional students (468 women), 2,602 part-time matriculated graduate/professional students (1,439 women). *Enrollment by degree level:* 3,287 master's, 47 doctoral, 24 other advanced degrees. Tuition, state resident: full-time $3098; part-time $344 per credit hour. Tuition, nonresident: full-time $9923; part-time $1103 per credit hour. *Required fees:* $384 per semester. Tuition and fees vary according to program. *Student services:* Campus employment opportunities, career counseling, exercise/wellness program, free psychological counseling, multicultural affairs office, services for students with disabilities, teacher training. *Library facilities:* Noel Memorial Library. *Collection:* Databases: 142. Weekly public service hours: 71; students can reserve study rooms. *Research affiliation:* Micromanufacturing Institute (manufacturing technology), U.S. Department of Agriculture (USDA) (crop science), Louisiana Manufacturing Science Center (robotics), Biomedical Research Institute, Cotton, Incorporated (plant physiology).

Computer facilities: A campuswide network can be accessed from off campus. Online class registration is available.
Website: http://www.lsus.edu/

General Application Contact: Jolie Banks, Data Coordinator, 318-798-4112, Fax: 318-798-4120, E-mail: jolie.banks@lsus.edu.

GRADUATE UNITS

College of Arts and Sciences Students: 80 full-time (54 women), 158 part-time (115 women); includes 76 minority (54 Black or African American, non-Hispanic/Latino; 2 Asian, non-Hispanic/Latino; 8 Hispanic/Latino; 12 Two or more races, non-Hispanic/Latino), 11 international. Average age 36. 287 applicants, 91% accepted, 108 enrolled. Expenses: Contact institution. *Financial support:* Unspecified assistantships available. Financial award applicants required to submit FAFSA. In 2017, 35 master's awarded. *Program availability:* Part-time, evening/weekend, 100% online. Offers arts and sciences (MA, MS); biological sciences (MS); computer systems technology (MS); liberal arts (MA); nonprofit administration (MS). *Application deadline:* For fall admission, 6/30 for domestic and international students; for spring admission, 11/30 for domestic and international students; for summer admission, 4/30 for domestic and international students. Applications are processed on a rolling basis. *Application fee:* $20 ($30 for international students). Electronic applications accepted. *Application Contact:* Mary Catherine Harvison, Director of Admissions, 318-797-2400, Fax: 318-797-5286, E-mail: mary.harvison@lsus.edu. *Dean*, Dr. Larry Anderson, 318-797-5371, Fax: 318-797-5358, E-mail: larry.anderson@lsus.edu.

College of Business, Education, and Human Development Students: 676 full-time (414 women), 2,444 part-time (1,324 women); includes 1,069 minority (736 Black or African American, non-Hispanic/Latino; 10 American Indian or Alaska Native, non-Hispanic/Latino; 75 Asian, non-Hispanic/Latino; 168 Hispanic/Latino; 3 Native Hawaiian or other Pacific Islander, non-Hispanic/Latino; 77 Two or more races, non-Hispanic/Latino), 106 international. Average age 34. 2,508 applicants, 94% accepted, 1148 enrolled. Expenses: Contact institution. *Financial support:* Research assistantships available. Financial award applicants required to submit FAFSA. In 2017, 578 master's, 2 other advanced degrees awarded. *Program availability:* Part-time. Offers business administration (MBA); business, education, and human development (M Ed, MBA, MHA, MPH, MS, Ed D, SSP); counseling (MS); curriculum and instruction (M Ed); health administration (MHA); leadership (M Ed); leadership studies (Ed D); public health (MPH); school psychology (SSP). *Application deadline:* For fall admission, 6/30 for domestic and international students; for spring admission, 10/30 for domestic students, 11/30 for international students; for summer admission, 4/30 for domestic and international students. Applications are processed on a rolling basis. *Application fee:* $20 ($30 for international students). Electronic applications accepted. *Application Contact:* Mary Catherine Harvison, Director, Admissions, 318-797-2400, Fax: 318-797-5286, E-mail: mary.harvison@lsus.edu. *Dean*, Dr. Nancy Miller, 318-797-5383, Fax: 318-797-5176, E-mail: nancy.miller@lsus.edu.

LOUISIANA TECH UNIVERSITY, Ruston, LA 71272

General Information State-supported, coed, university. *Enrollment:* 794 full-time matriculated graduate/professional students (426 women), 393 part-time matriculated graduate/professional students (240 women). *Enrollment by degree level:* 826 master's, 320 doctoral, 41 other advanced degrees. *Graduate faculty:* 303 full-time (104 women), 54 part-time/adjunct (33 women). *International tuition:* $10,267 full-time. Tuition, state resident: full-time $5146. Tuition, nonresident: full-time $10,147. *Required fees:* $2273. *Graduate housing:* Rooms and/or apartments available on a first-come, first-served basis to single and married students. Typical cost: $2910 per year ($6360 including board) for single students; $2910 per year ($6360 including board) for married students. Room and board charges vary according to board plan and housing facility selected. Housing application deadline: 1/15. *Student services:* Campus employment opportunities, career counseling, exercise/wellness program, free psychological counseling, international student services, low-cost health insurance, multicultural affairs office, services for students with disabilities. *Library facilities:* Prescott Memorial Library.

Computer facilities: A campuswide network can be accessed from student residence rooms and from off campus.
Website: http://www.latech.edu/

General Application Contact: Dr. Ramu Ramachandran, Dean of the Graduate School, 318-257-2924, Fax: 318-257-4487, E-mail: ramu@latech.edu.

GRADUATE UNITS

Graduate School Students: 794 full-time (426 women), 393 part-time (240 women); includes 234 minority (158 Black or African American, non-Hispanic/Latino; 2 American Indian or Alaska Native, non-Hispanic/Latino; 13 Asian, non-Hispanic/Latino; 37 Hispanic/Latino; 1 Native Hawaiian or other Pacific Islander, non-Hispanic/Latino; 23 Two or more races, non-Hispanic/Latino), 233 international. Average age 31. 864 applicants, 62% accepted, 187 enrolled. *Faculty:* 303 full-time (104 women), 54 part-time/adjunct (33 women). Expenses: Contact institution. *Financial support:* Fellowships, research assistantships, teaching assistantships, career-related internships or fieldwork, Federal Work-Study, institutionally sponsored loans, and tuition waivers (partial) available. Financial award application deadline: 4/1. In 2017, 428 master's, 44 doctorates, 72 other advanced degrees awarded. *Program availability:* Part-time, evening/weekend. *Application deadline:* For fall admission, 8/1 priority date for domestic students, 6/1 for international students; for winter admission, 11/1 priority date for domestic students, 9/1 for international students; for spring admission, 2/1 priority date for domestic students, 12/1 for international students; for summer admission, 5/1 priority date for domestic students, 3/1 for international students. *Application fee:* $40. Electronic applications accepted. *Application Contact:* Samantha J. Bailey, Graduate Enrollment Management Specialist, 318-257-2924, Fax: 318-257-4487, E-mail: samantha@latech.edu. *Dean*, Dr. B. Ramu Ramachandran, 318-257-2924, Fax: 318-257-4487, E-mail: ramu@latech.edu.

College of Applied and Natural Sciences Students: 75 full-time (49 women), 32 part-time (23 women); includes 32 minority (19 Black or African American, non-Hispanic/Latino; 4 Asian, non-Hispanic/Latino; 8 Hispanic/Latino; 1 Two or more races, non-Hispanic/Latino), 9 international. Average age 29. 46 applicants, 67% accepted, 10 enrolled. *Faculty:* 56 full-time (31 women), 10 part-time/adjunct (4 women). Expenses: Contact institution. *Financial support:* In 2017–18, 19 students received support, including 19 research assistantships with partial tuition reimbursements available (averaging $8,817 per year); career-related internships or fieldwork, Federal Work-Study, scholarships/grants, and unspecified assistantships also available. Financial award application deadline: 2/1. In 2017, 36 master's, 1 doctorate, 15 other advanced degrees awarded. *Program availability:* Part-time. Offers biology (MS); dietetics (Graduate Certificate); health informatics (MHI); molecular science and nanotechnology (MS, PhD). *Application deadline:* For fall admission, 8/1 priority date for domestic students, 6/1 for international students; for winter admission, 11/1 priority date for domestic students, 9/1 for international students; for spring admission, 2/1 priority date for domestic students, 12/1 for international students; for summer admission, 5/1 priority date for domestic students, 3/1 for international students. Applications are processed on a rolling basis. *Application fee:* $40. Electronic applications accepted. *Dean*, Dr. Gary A. Kennedy, 318-257-4287, Fax: 318-257-5060, E-mail: kennedy@latech.edu.

College of Business Students: 104 full-time (43 women), 40 part-time (16 women); includes 22 minority (13 Black or African American, non-Hispanic/Latino; 2 Asian, non-Hispanic/Latino; 7 Two or more races, non-Hispanic/Latino), 32 international. Average age 29. 104 applicants, 58% accepted, 25 enrolled. *Faculty:* 36 full-time (7 women), 8 part-time/adjunct (3 women). Expenses: Contact institution. *Financial support:* In 2017–18, 24 students received support, including 17 research assistantships with partial tuition reimbursements available (averaging $12,500 per year), 7 teaching assistantships with partial tuition reimbursements available (averaging $12,500 per year); scholarships/grants and unspecified assistantships also available. Financial award application deadline: 2/1. In 2017, 71 master's, 4 doctorates awarded. *Program availability:* Part-time, evening/weekend, 100% online, blended/hybrid learning. Offers accounting (M Acc, DBA); computer information systems (DBA); finance (MBA, DBA); information assurance (MBA); innovation (MBA); management (DBA); marketing (MBA, DBA). *Application deadline:* For fall admission, 8/1 priority date for domestic students, 6/1 for international students; for winter admission, 11/1 priority date for domestic students, 9/1 for international students; for spring admission, 2/1 priority date for domestic students, 12/1 for international students; for summer admission, 5/1 priority date for domestic students, 3/1 for international students. *Application fee:* $40. Electronic applications accepted. *Application Contact:* Samantha J. Bailey, Graduate Management Admissions Specialist, 318-257-2924, Fax: 318-257-4487, E-mail: samantha@latech.edu. *Dean*, Dr. Christopher D. Martin, 318-257-4526, Fax: 318-257-4253.

College of Education Students: 269 full-time (192 women), 194 part-time (150 women); includes 127 minority (94 Black or African American, non-Hispanic/Latino; 2 American Indian or Alaska Native, non-Hispanic/Latino; 6 Asian, non-Hispanic/Latino; 16 Hispanic/Latino; 1 Native Hawaiian or other Pacific Islander, non-Hispanic/Latino; 8 Two or more races, non-Hispanic/Latino), 8 international. Average age 34. 226 applicants, 74% accepted, 60 enrolled. *Faculty:* 28 full-time (16 women), 23 part-time/adjunct (22 women). Expenses: Contact institution. *Financial support:* In 2017–18, 40 students received support, including 23 research assistantships (averaging $10,346 per year), 15 teaching assistantships (averaging $6,887 per year);

fellowships and career-related internships or fieldwork also available. Financial award application deadline: 2/1. In 2017, 5 master's, 2 doctorates, 1 other advanced degree awarded. *Program availability:* Part-time. Offers counseling and guidance (MA); counseling psychology (PhD); curriculum and instruction (M Ed); cyber education (Graduate Certificate); dynamics of domestic and family violence (Graduate Certificate); early childhood education - PreK-3 (MAT); educational leadership (M Ed, Ed D); elementary education and special education mild/moderate grades 1-5 (MAT); higher education administration (Graduate Certificate); industrial/organizational psychology (MA, PhD); kinesiology (MS); middle school education (MAT); orientation and mobility (Graduate Certificate); rehabilitation teaching for the blind (Graduate Certificate); secondary education (MAT); special education: visually impaired (MAT); teacher leader education (Graduate Certificate); visual impairments - blind education (Graduate Certificate). *Application deadline:* For fall admission, 9/1 priority date for domestic students, 6/1 for international students; for winter admission, 11/1 priority date for domestic students, 9/1 for international students; for spring admission, 2/1 priority date for domestic students, 12/1 for international students; for summer admission, 5/1 priority date for domestic students, 3/1 for international students. *Application fee:* $40. Electronic applications accepted. *Application Contact:* Dr. Dawn Basinger, Associate Dean of Academic Affairs, 318-257-2977, Fax: 318-257-2379, E-mail: dbasing@latech.edu. *Dean*, Dr. Don Schillinger, 318-257-3712, E-mail: dschill@latech.edu.

College of Engineering and Science Students: 232 full-time (57 women), 96 part-time (32 women); includes 41 minority (28 Black or African American, non-Hispanic/Latino; 10 Hispanic/Latino; 3 Two or more races, non-Hispanic/Latino), 179 international. Average age 29. 339 applicants, 55% accepted, 55 enrolled. *Faculty:* 114 full-time (22 women), 8 part-time/adjunct (0 women). Expenses: Contact institution. *Financial support:* In 2017–18, 298 students received support, including 11 fellowships with full tuition reimbursements available (averaging $25,000 per year), 329 research assistantships (averaging $3,617 per year), 172 teaching assistantships (averaging $6,246 per year); career-related internships or fieldwork, Federal Work-Study, tuition waivers (partial), and unspecified assistantships also available. Financial award application deadline: 4/1. In 2017, 87 master's, 19 doctorates, 13 other advanced degrees awarded. *Program availability:* Part-time-only. Offers applied physics (MS); biomedical engineering (PhD); computer science (MS); engineering (MS, PhD); engineering and technology management (MS); mathematics (MS); molecular science and nanotechnology (MS, PhD). *Application deadline:* For fall admission, 8/1 priority date for domestic students, 6/1 for international students; for winter admission, 11/1 priority date for domestic students, 9/1 for international students; for spring admission, 2/1 priority date for domestic students, 12/1 for international students; for summer admission, 5/1 priority date for domestic students, 3/1 for international students. *Application fee:* $40. Electronic applications accepted. *Application Contact:* Samantha J. Bailey, Graduate Management Admissions Specialist, 318-257-2924, Fax: 318-257-4487, E-mail: samantha@latech.edu. *Associate Dean of Graduate Studies*, Dr. Collin Wick, 318-257-2345, Fax: 318-257-3823, E-mail: cwick@latech.edu.

College of Liberal Arts Students: 114 full-time (29 women), 31 part-time (19 women); includes 12 minority (4 Black or African American, non-Hispanic/Latino; 1 Asian, non-Hispanic/Latino; 3 Hispanic/Latino; 4 Two or more races, non-Hispanic/Latino), 5 international. Average age 30. 146 applicants, 59% accepted, 37 enrolled. *Faculty:* 63 full-time (25 women), 5 part-time/adjunct (3 women). Expenses: Contact institution. *Financial support:* In 2017–18, 63 students received support, including 46 research assistantships (averaging $5,229 per year), 7 teaching assistantships (averaging $5,543 per year); fellowships, career-related internships or fieldwork, Federal Work-Study, institutionally sponsored loans, tuition waivers (partial), and unspecified assistantships also available. Financial award application deadline: 2/1. In 2017, 49 master's, 3 doctorates awarded. *Program availability:* Part-time. Offers architecture (M Arch); art (MFA); audiology (Au D); communication (MA); English (MA); history (MA); speech pathology (MA); technical writing and communication (Graduate Certificate). *Application deadline:* For fall admission, 8/1 priority date for domestic students, 6/1 for international students; for winter admission, 11/1 priority date for domestic students, 9/1 for international students; for spring admission, 2/1 priority date for domestic students, 12/1 for international students; for summer admission, 5/1 priority date for domestic students, 3/1 for international students. *Application fee:* $40 ($50 for international students). Electronic applications accepted. *Application Contact:* Mary Green, Administrative Assistant, 318-257-2924, Fax: 318-257-4487, E-mail: meg@latech.edu. *Dean*, Dr. Donald P. Kaczvinsky, 318-257-4805, Fax: 318-257-3935, E-mail: dkaczv@latech.edu.

LOUISVILLE PRESBYTERIAN THEOLOGICAL SEMINARY, Louisville, KY 40205-1798

General Information Independent-religious, coed, graduate-only institution. *Enrollment by degree level:* 105 master's, 47 doctoral. *Graduate faculty:* 16 full-time (6 women), 14 part-time/adjunct (5 women). *Graduate housing:* Rooms and/or apartments available on a first-come, first-served basis to single and married students. Housing application deadline: 4/15. *Student services:* Campus employment opportunities, career counseling, international student services, services for students with disabilities, writing training. *Library facilities:* E.M. White Library. *Collection:* Books: 165,449 (physical), 11,301 (digital/electronic); Serial titles: 1,276 (physical), 2,618 (digital/electronic); Databases: 45. Students can reserve study rooms. *Research affiliation:* Louisville Institute (American religion).

Computer facilities: 22 computers available on campus for general student use.
Website: http://www.lpts.edu/

General Application Contact: Rev. Emily Miller, Director of Admissions, 502-895-3411 Ext. 371, Fax: 502-895-1096, E-mail: emiller@lpts.edu.

GRADUATE UNITS

Graduate and Professional Programs Students: 115 full-time (74 women), 37 part-time (20 women); includes 51 minority (41 Black or African American, non-Hispanic/Latino; 2 Asian, non-Hispanic/Latino; 7 Hispanic/Latino; 1 Native Hawaiian or other Pacific Islander, non-Hispanic/Latino), 1 international. Average age 41. *Faculty:* 16 full-time (6 women), 14 part-time/adjunct (5 women). Expenses: Contact institution. *Financial support:* Career-related internships or fieldwork, Federal Work-Study, institutionally sponsored loans, and scholarships/grants available. Financial award application deadline: 2/1. In 2017, 32 master's, 6 doctorates awarded. *Program availability:* Part-time. Offers Bible (MAR); divinity (M Div); ministry (D Min); religious thought (MAR). JD/M Div, M Div/MBA, and M Div/MSSW offered jointly with University of Louisville. *Application deadline:* For fall admission, 6/1 priority date for domestic students, 2/1 priority date for international students; for spring admission, 11/1 priority date for domestic students. Applications are processed on a rolling basis. *Application fee:* $50. Electronic applications accepted. *Application Contact:* Rev. Emily Miller, Director of Admissions, 502-895-3411, Fax: 502-895-1096, E-mail: emiller@lpts.edu. *Dean*, Dr. Susan R. Garrett, 502-895-3411, Fax: 502-895-1096, E-mail: sgarrett@lpts.edu.

LOURDES UNIVERSITY, Sylvania, OH 43560-2898

General Information Independent-religious, coed, comprehensive institution. *Graduate housing:* Rooms and/or apartments available to single and married students. Housing application deadline: 5/1.

GRADUATE UNITS

Graduate School *Program availability:* Evening/weekend. Offers business (MBA); leadership (M Ed); nurse anesthesia (MSN); nurse educator (MSN); nurse leader (MSN); organizational leadership (MOL); reading (M Ed); teaching and curriculum (M Ed); theology (MA).

LOYOLA MARYMOUNT UNIVERSITY, Los Angeles, CA 90045-2659

General Information Independent-religious, coed, comprehensive institution. CGS member. *Enrollment:* 9,618 graduate, professional, and undergraduate students; 2,215 full-time matriculated graduate/professional students (1,354 women), 428 part-time matriculated graduate/professional students (243 women). *Enrollment by degree level:* 1,585 master's, 1,058 doctoral. *Graduate faculty:* 231 full-time (104 women), 257 part-time/adjunct (121 women). *Graduate housing:* Room and/or apartments available on a first-come, first-served basis to single students; on-campus housing not available to married students. *Student services:* Campus employment opportunities, career counseling, child daycare facilities, exercise/wellness program, free psychological counseling, international student services, low-cost health insurance, multicultural affairs office, services for students with disabilities, teacher training. *Library facilities:* William H. Hannon Library. *Collection:* Study areas open 24 hours, 5–7 days a week; students can reserve study rooms.

Computer facilities: Computer purchase and lease plans are available. 820 computers available on campus for general student use. A campuswide network can be accessed from student residence rooms and from off campus. Online class registration is available.
Website: http://www.lmu.edu/

General Application Contact: Chake H. Kouyoumjian, Associate Dean of Graduate Studies, 310-338-2721, Fax: 310-338-6086, E-mail: graduateinfo@lmu.edu.

GRADUATE UNITS

Bellarmine College of Liberal Arts Students: 140 full-time (69 women), 41 part-time (24 women); includes 86 minority (7 Black or African American, non-Hispanic/Latino; 21 Asian, non-Hispanic/Latino; 47 Hispanic/Latino; 2 Native Hawaiian or other Pacific Islander, non-Hispanic/Latino; 9 Two or more races, non-Hispanic/Latino), 26 international. Average age 37. 130 applicants, 95% accepted, 83 enrolled. *Faculty:* 43 full-time (19 women), 7 part-time/adjunct (3 women). Expenses: Contact institution. *Financial support:* Research assistantships, teaching assistantships, Federal Work-Study, scholarships/grants, and unspecified assistantships available. Support available to part-time students. Financial award applicants required to submit FAFSA. In 2017, 47 master's awarded. *Program availability:* Part-time, evening/weekend. Offers bioethics (MA); English (MA); liberal arts (MA); pastoral theology (MA); philosophy (MA); theology (MA); yoga studies (MA). *Application fee:* $50. Electronic applications accepted. *Application Contact:* Chake H. Kouyoumjian, Associate Dean of Graduate Studies, 310-338-2721, Fax: 310-338-6086, E-mail: graduateinfo@lmu.edu. *Dean, Bellarmine College of Liberal Arts*, Dr. Robbin D. Crabtree, 310-338-2716, E-mail: robbin.crabtree@lmu.edu.

College of Business Administration Students: 135 full-time (57 women), 12 part-time (4 women); includes 57 minority (15 Black or African American, non-Hispanic/Latino; 1 American Indian or Alaska Native, non-Hispanic/Latino; 18 Asian, non-Hispanic/Latino; 23 Hispanic/Latino), 30 international. Average age 31. 205 applicants, 55% accepted, 61 enrolled. *Faculty:* 33 full-time (9 women), 14 part-time/adjunct (3 women). Expenses: Contact institution. *Financial support:* Research assistantships, career-related internships or fieldwork, institutionally sponsored loans, scholarships/grants, and unspecified assistantships available. Support available to part-time students. Financial award applicants required to submit FAFSA. In 2017, 99 master's awarded. *Program availability:* Part-time. Offers accounting (MS); business administration (MBA, MS); executive business administration (MBA); systems engineering leadership. *Application fee:* $50. Electronic applications accepted. *Application Contact:* Chake H. Kouyoumjian, Associate Dean of Graduate Studies, 310-338-2721, Fax: 310-338-6086, E-mail: graduateinfo@lmu.edu. *Dean, College of Business Administration*, Dr. Dennis W. Draper, 310-338-7504, E-mail: ddraper@lmu.edu.

College of Communication and Fine Arts Students: 50 full-time (47 women); includes 24 minority (1 Black or African American, non-Hispanic/Latino; 7 Asian, non-Hispanic/Latino; 13 Hispanic/Latino; 3 Two or more races, non-Hispanic/Latino). Average age 28. 53 applicants, 53% accepted, 23 enrolled. *Faculty:* 5 full-time (4 women), 14 part-time/adjunct (13 women). Expenses: Contact institution. *Financial support:* Research assistantships, career-related internships or fieldwork, institutionally sponsored loans, scholarships/grants, and unspecified assistantships available. Financial award application deadline: 5/1; financial award applicants required to submit FAFSA. In 2017, 24 master's awarded. Offers communication and fine arts (MA); marital and family therapy (MA). *Application fee:* $50. Electronic applications accepted. *Application Contact:* Chake H. Kouyoumjian, Associate Dean of Graduate Studies, 310-338-2721, Fax: 310-338-6086, E-mail: graduateinfo@lmu.edu. *Dean, College of Communication and Fine Arts*, Dr. Bryant Keith Alexander, 310-338-7430, E-mail: bryantkeithalexander@lmu.edu.

Frank R. Seaver College of Science and Engineering Students: 71 full-time (22 women), 32 part-time (15 women); includes 53 minority (7 Black or African American, non-Hispanic/Latino; 17 Asian, non-Hispanic/Latino; 25 Hispanic/Latino; 4 Two or more races, non-Hispanic/Latino), 22 international. Average age 29. 71 applicants, 92% accepted, 35 enrolled. *Faculty:* 16 full-time (1 woman), 16 part-time/adjunct (2 women). Expenses: Contact institution. *Financial support:* Research assistantships, Federal Work-Study, scholarships/grants, unspecified assistantships, and laboratory assistantships available. Support available to part-time students. Financial award application deadline: 7/18; financial award applicants required to submit FAFSA. In 2017, 45 master's awarded. *Program availability:* Part-time. Offers civil engineering (MSE); electrical engineering (MS); environmental science (MS); healthcare systems engineering (MS); mechanical engineering (MSE); science and engineering (MAT, MS, MSE); systems engineering (MS); systems engineering leadershipteaching mathematics (MAT). *Application fee:* $50. Electronic applications accepted. *Application Contact:* Chake H. Kouyoumjian, Associate Dean of Graduate Studies, 310-338-2721, Fax: 310-338-6086, E-mail: graduateinfo@lmu.edu. *Dean, Frank R. Seaver College of Science and Engineering*, Dr. Tina Choe, 310-338-2834, E-mail: tina.choe@lmu.edu.

Loyola Law School Los Angeles Students: 883 full-time (482 women), 182 part-time (92 women); includes 416 minority (47 Black or African American, non-Hispanic/Latino; 1 American Indian or Alaska Native, non-Hispanic/Latino; 123 Asian, non-Hispanic/Latino; 204 Hispanic/Latino; 41 Two or more races, non-Hispanic/Latino), 81 international. Average age 27. 3,744 applicants, 41% accepted, 378 enrolled. *Faculty:*

66 full-time (32 women), 120 part-time/adjunct (42 women). Expenses: Contact institution. *Financial support:* In 2017–18, 40 research assistantships (averaging $1,823 per year) were awarded; career-related internships or fieldwork, Federal Work-Study, scholarships/grants, and tuition waivers (partial) also available. Support available to part-time students. Financial award application deadline: 3/15; financial award applicants required to submit FAFSA. In 2017, 44 master's, 297 doctorates awarded. *Program availability:* Part-time, evening/weekend. Offers law (LL M, MLS, JD, JSD); tax (LL M in Tax, MT). *Application deadline:* For fall admission, 2/1 priority date for domestic students, 2/1 for international students. Applications are processed on a rolling basis. *Application fee:* $0. Electronic applications accepted. *Application Contact:* Jannell Lundy Roberts, Senior Assistant Dean, Admissions and Enrollment Services, 213-736-1074, Fax: 213-736-6523, E-mail: admissions@lls.edu. *Dean,* Michael Waterstone, 213-736-2243, Fax: 213-487-6736, E-mail: michael.waterstone@lls.edu.

School of Education Students: 773 full-time (601 women), 143 part-time (96 women); includes 551 minority (86 Black or African American, non-Hispanic/Latino; 79 Asian, non-Hispanic/Latino; 356 Hispanic/Latino; 2 Native Hawaiian or other Pacific Islander, non-Hispanic/Latino; 28 Two or more races, non-Hispanic/Latino), 64 international. Average age 29. 472 applicants, 73% accepted, 272 enrolled. *Faculty:* 35 full-time (24 women), 106 part-time/adjunct (71 women). Expenses: Contact institution. *Financial support:* Research assistantships, teaching assistantships, institutionally sponsored loans, scholarships/grants, and unspecified assistantships available. Support available to part-time students. Financial award application deadline: 4/15; financial award applicants required to submit FAFSA. In 2017, 376 master's, 14 doctorates awarded. *Program availability:* Part-time, evening/weekend. Offers bilingual elementary education (MA); bilingual secondary education (MA); Catholic school administration (MA); counseling (MA); education (MA, Ed D); educational leadership for social justice (Ed D); educational studies (MA); elementary education (MA); guidance and counseling (MA); higher education administration (MA); literacy education (MA); literacy instruction for urban environments (MA); literacy/language arts (MA); reading instruction (MA); school administration (MA); school counseling (MA); school psychology (MA); secondary education (MA); special education (MA); urban education (MA). *Application fee:* $50. Electronic applications accepted. *Application Contact:* Chake H. Kouyoumjian, Associate Dean of Graduate Studies, 310-338-2721, Fax: 310-338-6086, E-mail: graduateinfo@lmu.edu. *Dean, School of Education,* Dr. Shane P. Martin, 310-338-7301, E-mail: smartin@lmu.edu.

School of Film and Television Students: 179 full-time (87 women), 6 part-time (2 women); includes 71 minority (32 Black or African American, non-Hispanic/Latino; 9 Asian, non-Hispanic/Latino; 19 Hispanic/Latino; 11 Two or more races, non-Hispanic/Latino), 44 international. Average age 26. 301 applicants, 40% accepted, 67 enrolled. *Faculty:* 29 full-time (12 women), 33 part-time/adjunct (9 women). Expenses: Contact institution. *Financial support:* Research assistantships, teaching assistantships, career-related internships or fieldwork, and scholarships/grants available. Support available to part-time students. Financial award application deadline: 5/1; financial award applicants required to submit FAFSA. In 2017, 36 master's awarded. Offers film and television (MFA); film and television production (MFA); writing and producing for television (MFA); writing for the screen (MFA). *Application fee:* $50. Electronic applications accepted. *Application Contact:* Chake H. Kouyoumjian, Associate Dean of Graduate Studies, 310-338-2721, Fax: 310-338-6086, E-mail: graduateinfo@lmu.edu. *Dean, School of Film and Television,* Stephen G. Ujlaki, 310-338-5800, E-mail: sujlaki@lmu.edu.

LOYOLA UNIVERSITY CHICAGO, Chicago, IL 60660

General Information Independent-religious, coed, university. CGS member. *Enrollment:* 16,673 graduate, professional, and undergraduate students; 3,915 full-time matriculated graduate/professional students (2,460 women), 1,300 part-time matriculated graduate/professional students (943 women). *Enrollment by degree level:* 3,045 master's, 2,022 doctoral, 148 other advanced degrees. *Graduate faculty:* 924 full-time (436 women), 750 part-time/adjunct (402 women). Tuition and fees vary according to course load, degree level and program. *Graduate housing:* Room and/or apartments available on a first-come, first-served basis to single students; on-campus housing not available to married students. Typical cost: $11,630 per year ($14,170 including board). Room and board charges vary according to board plan and housing facility selected. Housing application deadline: 5/1. *Student services:* Campus employment opportunities, campus safety program, career counseling, exercise/wellness program, free psychological counseling, international student services, low-cost health insurance, services for students with disabilities, teacher training, writing training. *Library facilities:* Cudahy Library plus 7 others. *Collection:* Books: 1.9 million (physical), 568,720 (digital/electronic); Serial titles: 2,245 (physical), 58,389 (digital/electronic); Databases: 545. Weekly public service hours: 144; study areas open 24 hours, 5–7 days a week; students can reserve study rooms. *Research affiliation:* Chicago Transformational Teacher Institutes (math and science education reform), Chicagoland Lutheran Education Foundation Literacy Program (literacy professional development program for K-8 teachers), Chicago Public Schools (evaluation of dual language education initiative), Field Museum (digital learning), Big Shoulders Foundation (internal evaluation of professional development for middle grades Catholic Archdiocese science teachers).

Computer facilities: Computer purchase and lease plans are available. 1,300 computers available on campus for general student use. A campuswide network can be accessed from student residence rooms and from off campus. Online class registration is available.
Website: http://www.luc.edu/

General Application Contact: Jill Schur, Director, Graduate Enrollment Management, 312-915-8902, E-mail: gradinfo@luc.edu.

GRADUATE UNITS

Graduate School Students: 959 full-time (545 women), 269 part-time (157 women); includes 350 minority (93 Black or African American, non-Hispanic/Latino; 1 American Indian or Alaska Native, non-Hispanic/Latino; 108 Asian, non-Hispanic/Latino; 109 Hispanic/Latino; 2 Native Hawaiian or other Pacific Islander, non-Hispanic/Latino; 37 Two or more races, non-Hispanic/Latino), 121 international. Average age 31. 1,522 applicants, 38% accepted, 253 enrolled. Expenses: Contact institution. *Financial support:* Fellowships with full tuition reimbursements, research assistantships with full tuition reimbursements, teaching assistantships with tuition reimbursements, career-related internships or fieldwork, Federal Work-Study, institutionally sponsored loans, scholarships/grants, and unspecified assistantships available. Support available to part-time students. Financial award application deadline: 2/1; financial award applicants required to submit FAFSA. In 2017, 364 master's, 108 doctorates, 17 other advanced degrees awarded. *Program availability:* Part-time, evening/weekend, 100% online, blended/hybrid learning. Offers 19th century studies (PhD); applied philosophy and philosophy (MA); applied statistics (MS); biochemistry and molecular biology (MS, PhD); bioinformatics (MS); biology (MA, MS); cell and molecular physiology (MS, PhD); chemistry and biochemistry (MS, PhD); clinical psychology (MA, PhD); clinical research methods (MS); computer science (MS); criminal justice and criminology (MA); developmental psychology (MA, PhD); digital humanities (MA); English (MA); global politics (PhD); history (MA, PhD); infectious disease and immunology (MS); information technology (MS); integrative cell biology (MS, PhD); mathematics (MS); Medieval and Renaissance literature (PhD); microbiology and immunology (MS, PhD); modern literature and culture (PhD); molecular pharmacology and therapeutics (MS, PhD); neuroscience (MS, PhD); philosophy (PhD); political science (MA); public health (MPH, Certificate); public history (MA); public policy (MPP); sociology (MA, PhD); software engineering (MS); Spanish (MA); textual studies and digital humanities (PhD); theology (MA, PhD); urban affairs (MA); women's studies and gender studies (MA). *Application deadline:* Applications are processed on a rolling basis. *Application fee:* $50. Electronic applications accepted. *Application Contact:* Jill Schur, Director of Graduate Enrollment Management, 312-915-8902, E-mail: gradinfo@luc.edu. *Dean,* Dr. Thomas Regan, 773-508-3505, Fax: 773-508-3514, E-mail: tregan1@luc.edu.

Marcella Niehoff School of Nursing Students: 188 full-time (178 women), 222 part-time (208 women); includes 105 minority (23 Black or African American, non-Hispanic/Latino; 40 Asian, non-Hispanic/Latino; 30 Hispanic/Latino; 2 Native Hawaiian or other Pacific Islander, non-Hispanic/Latino; 10 Two or more races, non-Hispanic/Latino), 4 international. Average age 36. 197 applicants, 55% accepted, 80 enrolled. *Faculty:* 24 full-time (22 women), 21 part-time/adjunct (19 women). Expenses: Contact institution. *Financial support:* In 2017–18, 10 students received support, including 3 research assistantships with full tuition reimbursements available (averaging $18,000 per year), 1 teaching assistantship with full tuition reimbursement available (averaging $18,000 per year); scholarships/grants, unspecified assistantships, and nurse faculty loan program also available. Financial award application deadline: 5/1; financial award applicants required to submit FAFSA. In 2017, 94 master's, 17 doctorates, 26 other advanced degrees awarded. *Program availability:* Part-time, blended/hybrid learning. Offers adult clinical nurse specialist (MSN, Certificate); adult nurse practitioner (Certificate); dietetics (MS); family nurse practitioner (Certificate); family, adult, and women's health nurse practitioner (MSN); health systems leadership (MSN); healthcare quality using education in safety and technology (DNP); infection prevention (MSN, DNP); nursing science (PhD); women's health clinical nurse specialist (Certificate). *Application deadline:* For fall admission, 6/1 priority date for domestic and international students; for spring admission, 11/15 priority date for domestic and international students; for summer admission, 3/15 priority date for domestic and international students. Applications are processed on a rolling basis. *Application fee:* $50. Electronic applications accepted. *Application Contact:* Toni Topalova, Enrollment Advisor, 708-216-3751, Fax: 708-216-9555, E-mail: atopalova@luc.edu. *Dean,* Dr. Vickie Keough, 708-216-5448, Fax: 708-216-9555, E-mail: vkeough@luc.edu.

Neiswanger Institute for Bioethics Students: 29 full-time (19 women), 95 part-time (58 women); includes 22 minority (5 Black or African American, non-Hispanic/Latino; 1 American Indian or Alaska Native, non-Hispanic/Latino; 5 Asian, non-Hispanic/Latino; 7 Hispanic/Latino; 1 Native Hawaiian or other Pacific Islander, non-Hispanic/Latino; 3 Two or more races, non-Hispanic/Latino). Average age 48. 42 applicants, 79% accepted, 28 enrolled. *Faculty:* 7 full-time (4 women), 6 part-time/adjunct (2 women). Expenses: Contact institution. *Financial support:* Scholarships/grants available. Financial award applicants required to submit FAFSA. In 2017, 24 master's, 9 doctorates, 6 other advanced degrees awarded. *Program availability:* Online learning. Offers bioethics (MA, D Be, Certificate). *Application Contact:* Robbin Hiller, Coordinator, Bioethics Education, 708-321-9219, Fax: 708-327-9209, E-mail: rhiller@luc.edu. *Director, Neiswanger Institute for Bioethics,* Dr. Mark Kuczewski, 708-327-9200, Fax: 708-327-9209, E-mail: mkuczew@luc.edu.

School of Communication Students: 36 full-time (24 women), 20 part-time (14 women); includes 22 minority (12 Black or African American, non-Hispanic/Latino; 1 Asian, non-Hispanic/Latino; 9 Hispanic/Latino), 9 international. Average age 29. 104 applicants, 60% accepted, 29 enrolled. Expenses: Contact institution. *Financial support:* Applicants required to submit FAFSA. In 2017, 29 master's awarded. Offers digital storytelling (MC); global strategic communication (MS). *Application Contact:* Ron Martin, Associate Director of Enrollment Management, 312-915-8950, Fax: 312-915-8905, E-mail: gradapp@luc.edu. *Dean,* Dr. Don Heider, 312-915-6548, E-mail: dheider@luc.edu.

Institute of Pastoral Studies Students: 80 full-time (51 women), 150 part-time (107 women); includes 58 minority (24 Black or African American, non-Hispanic/Latino; 7 Asian, non-Hispanic/Latino; 27 Hispanic/Latino), 29 international. Average age 45. 128 applicants, 79% accepted, 72 enrolled. *Faculty:* 11 full-time (5 women), 20 part-time/adjunct (9 women). Expenses: Contact institution. *Financial support:* In 2017–18, 111 students received support. Career-related internships or fieldwork, Federal Work-Study, scholarships/grants, and unspecified assistantships available. Support available to part-time students. Financial award application deadline: 3/15. In 2017, 53 master's, 5 other advanced degrees awarded. *Program availability:* Part-time, evening/weekend, 100% online, blended/hybrid learning. Offers Christian spirituality (MA); church management (Certificate); counseling for ministry (MA); divinity (M Div); health care ministry leadership (Certificate); health care mission leadership (MA); pastoral counseling (MA, Certificate); pastoral studies (MA); religious education (Certificate); social justice (MA, Certificate); spiritual direction (Certificate). MSW/MA offered with School of Social Work. *Application deadline:* Applications are processed on a rolling basis. *Application fee:* $50. Electronic applications accepted. *Application Contact:* Dr. M. Therese Lysaught, Associate Dean, 312-915-7485, Fax: 312-915-7410, E-mail: mlysaught@luc.edu. *Dean,* Dr. Brian J. Schmisek, 312-915-7400, Fax: 312-915-7410, E-mail: bschmisek@luc.edu.

Quinlan School of Business Students: 481 full-time (274 women), 131 part-time (57 women); includes 144 minority (43 Black or African American, non-Hispanic/Latino; 1 American Indian or Alaska Native, non-Hispanic/Latino; 46 Asian, non-Hispanic/Latino; 47 Hispanic/Latino; 7 Two or more races, non-Hispanic/Latino), 181 international. Average age 28. 999 applicants, 57% accepted, 196 enrolled. *Faculty:* 84 full-time (28 women), 12 part-time/adjunct (3 women). Expenses: Contact institution. *Financial support:* In 2017–18, 101 students received support. Research assistantships, career-related internships or fieldwork, Federal Work-Study, scholarships/grants, and health care benefits available. In 2017, 349 master's, 53 other advanced degrees awarded. *Program availability:* Part-time, evening/weekend. Offers accountancy (MSA); accounting (MBA); asset management (MSF); business (MBA, MS, MSA, MSF, MSHR, MSSCM, Certificate); business data analytics (MS, Certificate); business ethics (MBA); data warehousing (Certificate); derivative markets (MBA); economics (MBA); entrepreneurship (MBA); finance (MBA); healthcare management (MBA); human resources (MSHR); human resources management (MBA); information systems (MS, Certificate); information systems and supply chain management (MSSCM); information systems management (MBA); integrated marketing communications (MS); international business (MBA); management (MBA); marketing (MBA); risk management (MBA); supply chain management (MBA, MS, Certificate). *Application deadline:* For fall admission, 7/15 for domestic and international students; for winter admission, 10/1 for domestic and international students; for spring admission, 1/15 for domestic and international students; for summer admission, 4/1 for domestic and international students. Applications are processed on a rolling basis. *Application fee:* $50. Electronic applications accepted. *Assistant Dean for Graduate Programs*, Katherine Acles, 312-915-6124, Fax: 312-915-7207, E-mail: kacles@luc.edu.

School of Education Students: 386 full-time (297 women), 210 part-time (167 women); includes 221 minority (94 Black or African American, non-Hispanic/Latino; 1 American Indian or Alaska Native, non-Hispanic/Latino; 31 Asian, non-Hispanic/Latino; 78 Hispanic/Latino; 1 Native Hawaiian or other Pacific Islander, non-Hispanic/Latino; 16 Two or more races, non-Hispanic/Latino), 22 international. Average age 32. 842 applicants, 56% accepted, 198 enrolled. *Faculty:* 49 full-time (32 women), 69 part-time/adjunct (50 women). Expenses: Contact institution. *Financial support:* In 2017–18, 293 students received support, including 120 fellowships with partial tuition reimbursements available, 80 research assistantships with full tuition reimbursements available (averaging $14,000 per year), 93 teaching assistantships (averaging $4,000 per year); career-related internships or fieldwork, Federal Work-Study, institutionally sponsored loans, scholarships/grants, traineeships, health care benefits, and unspecified assistantships also available. Support available to part-time students. Financial award application deadline: 2/1; financial award applicants required to submit FAFSA. In 2017, 203 master's, 40 doctorates, 1 other advanced degree awarded. *Program availability:* Part-time, evening/weekend. Offers administration and supervision (M Ed, Ed D, Certificate); clinical mental health counseling (Ed S); community counseling (M Ed, MA); counseling psychology (PhD); cultural and educational policy studies (M Ed, MA, PhD); curriculum and instruction (M Ed, Ed D); education (M Ed, MA, Ed D, PhD, Certificate, Ed S); elementary education (M Ed); English language teaching and learning (M Ed); higher education (M Ed, PhD); international higher education (M Ed); research methods (MA, PhD, Certificate); school counseling (M Ed, Certificate); school psychology (Ed D, PhD, Ed S); secondary education (M Ed); special education (M Ed). *Application fee:* $50. Electronic applications accepted. *Application Contact:* Mirtza Campbell, Information Contact, 312-915-8907, E-mail: mcampbell11@luc.edu. *Interim Dean*, Dr. David Slavsky, 312-915-6992, Fax: 312-915-6980, E-mail: dslavsk@luc.edu.

School of Law Students: 823 full-time (483 women), 262 part-time (201 women); includes 334 minority (124 Black or African American, non-Hispanic/Latino; 1 American Indian or Alaska Native, non-Hispanic/Latino; 54 Asian, non-Hispanic/Latino; 114 Hispanic/Latino; 1 Native Hawaiian or other Pacific Islander, non-Hispanic/Latino; 40 Two or more races, non-Hispanic/Latino), 42 international. Average age 31. 2,670 applicants, 48% accepted, 372 enrolled. *Faculty:* 69 full-time (36 women), 306 part-time/adjunct (148 women). Expenses: Contact institution. *Financial support:* In 2017–18, 598 students received support, including 67 fellowships; research assistantships, Federal Work-Study, scholarships/grants, and health care benefits also available. Financial award application deadline: 3/1; financial award applicants required to submit FAFSA. In 2017, 187 master's, 222 doctorates, 104 Certificates awarded. *Program availability:* Part-time, evening/weekend, 100% online, blended/hybrid learning. Offers advocacy (LL M); business and compliance (MJ); business law (LL M); child and family (LL M); child and family law (MJ, Certificate); global competition (LL M, MJ); health law (LL M, MJ, Certificate); international law (LL M); law (JD); public interest law (Certificate); rule of law for development (LL M, MJ); tax (LL M); tax law (Certificate); transactional law (Certificate); trial advocacy (Certificate). *Application deadline:* For fall admission, 4/1 for domestic and international students. Applications are processed on a rolling basis. *Application fee:* $0. Electronic applications accepted. *Application Contact:* Jill Schur, Director, Graduate Enrollment Management, 312-915-8902, E-mail: gradinfo@luc.edu. *Associate Dean for Administration, Law School*, James Faught, JD, 312-915-7131, Fax: 312-915-6911, E-mail: law-admissions@luc.edu.

School of Social Work *Program availability:* Part-time. Offers social work (MSW, PhD, PGC).

LOYOLA UNIVERSITY MARYLAND, Baltimore, MD 21210-2699

General Information Independent-religious, coed, university. CGS member. *Enrollment:* 453 full-time matriculated graduate/professional students (357 women), 1,277 part-time matriculated graduate/professional students (855 women). *Enrollment by degree level:* 1,621 master's, 76 doctoral, 13 other advanced degrees. *Graduate faculty:* 123 full-time (72 women), 65 part-time/adjunct (38 women). *Graduate housing:* On-campus housing not available. *Student services:* Campus employment opportunities, campus safety program, career counseling, exercise/wellness program, free psychological counseling, international student services, low-cost health insurance, multicultural affairs office, services for students with disabilities. *Library facilities:* Loyola/Notre Dame Library plus 1 other.

Computer facilities: Computer purchase and lease plans are available. 690 computers available on campus for general student use. A campuswide network can be accessed from student residence rooms and from off campus. Online class registration is available.
Website: http://www.loyola.edu/

General Application Contact: Maureen Faux, Executive Director, Graduate Admissions, 410-617-5020, Fax: 410-617-2002, E-mail: graduate@loyola.edu.

GRADUATE UNITS

Graduate Programs Students: 453 full-time (357 women), 1,277 part-time (855 women); includes 508 minority (313 Black or African American, non-Hispanic/Latino; 3 American Indian or Alaska Native, non-Hispanic/Latino; 56 Asian, non-Hispanic/Latino; 87 Hispanic/Latino; 3 Native Hawaiian or other Pacific Islander, non-Hispanic/Latino; 46 Two or more races, non-Hispanic/Latino), 25 international. Average age 33. *Faculty:* 123 full-time (72 women), 65 part-time/adjunct (38 women). Expenses: Contact institution. *Financial support:* Scholarships/grants and unspecified assistantships available. Financial award application deadline: 4/15; financial award applicants required to submit FAFSA. In 2017, 724 master's, 20 doctorates, 6 other advanced degrees awarded. *Program availability:* Part-time, evening/weekend. *Application deadline:* For fall admission, 3/1 for domestic and international students. Applications are processed on a rolling basis. *Application fee:* $60. Electronic applications accepted. *Application Contact:* Maureen Faux, Executive Director, Graduate Admissions, 410-617-5020, Fax: 410-617-2002, E-mail: graduate@loyola.edu. *Dean for Graduate Studies*, Dr. Elissa Derrickson, 410-617-5547, E-mail: ederrickson@loyola.edu.

Loyola College of Arts and Sciences Students: 295 full-time (246 women), 253 part-time (169 women); includes 157 minority (84 Black or African American, non-Hispanic/Latino; 2 American Indian or Alaska Native, non-Hispanic/Latino; 23 Asian, non-Hispanic/Latino; 30 Hispanic/Latino; 1 Native Hawaiian or other Pacific Islander, non-Hispanic/Latino; 17 Two or more races, non-Hispanic/Latino), 16 international. Average age 32. *Faculty:* 64 full-time (37 women), 31 part-time/adjunct (20 women). Expenses: Contact institution. *Financial support:* Scholarships/grants and unspecified assistantships available. Financial award application deadline: 4/15; financial award applicants required to submit FAFSA. In 2017, 244 master's, 20 doctorates awarded. *Program availability:* Part-time, evening/weekend. Offers arts and sciences (MA, MS, MTS, PhD, Psy D, CAS, Certificate); clinical psychology (MS, Psy D, CAS); counseling psychology (MS, CAS); emerging media (MA); speech-language pathology (MS); theology (MTS). *Application deadline:* For fall admission, 8/1 for domestic students. *Application fee:* $60. Electronic applications accepted. *Application Contact:* Office of Graduate Admission, 410-617-5020, E-mail: graduate@loyola.edu. *Dean, College of Arts and Sciences*, Stephen Fowl, 410-617-2327, E-mail: sfowl@loyola.edu.

School of Education Students: 104 full-time (89 women), 653 part-time (538 women); includes 269 minority (197 Black or African American, non-Hispanic/Latino; 15 Asian, non-Hispanic/Latino; 37 Hispanic/Latino; 2 Native Hawaiian or other Pacific Islander, non-Hispanic/Latino; 18 Two or more races, non-Hispanic/Latino), 6 international. Average age 32. *Faculty:* 36 full-time (27 women), 23 part-time/adjunct (15 women). Expenses: Contact institution. *Financial support:* Research assistantships, scholarships/grants, and unspecified assistantships available. Financial award application deadline: 4/15; financial award applicants required to submit FAFSA. In 2017, 333 master's, 3 other advanced degrees awarded. *Program availability:* Part-time, evening/weekend. Offers curriculum and instruction (MA); education (M Ed, MA, MAT, CAS); educational leadership (M Ed, CAS); educational technology (M Ed, MA); elementary education (M Ed, MAT); Kodaly music education (M Ed); literacy teacher (M Ed); Montessori education (CAS); reading specialist (M Ed); school counseling (M Ed, MA, CAS); secondary education (MAT). *Application deadline:* For fall admission, 6/15 for domestic students. Applications are processed on a rolling basis. *Application fee:* $60. Electronic applications accepted. *Application Contact:* Office of Graduate Admission, 410-617-5020, E-mail: graduate@loyola.edu. *Dean, School of Education*, Dr. Joshua Smith, 410-617-5343, E-mail: jssmith2@loyola.edu.

Sellinger School of Business Students: 42 full-time (17 women), 408 part-time (149 women); includes 74 minority (23 Black or African American, non-Hispanic/Latino; 20 Asian, non-Hispanic/Latino; 19 Hispanic/Latino; 1 Native Hawaiian or other Pacific Islander, non-Hispanic/Latino; 11 Two or more races, non-Hispanic/Latino), 3 international. Average age 32. Expenses: Contact institution. *Financial support:* Scholarships/grants available. Financial award application deadline: 4/15; financial award applicants required to submit FAFSA. *Program availability:* Part-time, evening/weekend. Offers business (M Acc, MBA); business administration (MBA); finance (MBA); information systems (MBA); investments and applied portfolio management (MBA); management (MBA); marketing (MBA). *Application deadline:* For fall admission, 8/1 priority date for domestic students; for winter admission, 12/1 priority date for domestic students; for spring admission, 5/1 priority date for domestic students. *Application fee:* $60. Electronic applications accepted. *Application Contact:* Office of Graduate Business Programs, 410-617-5067. *Dean*, Kathleen A. Getz, 410-617-2301, E-mail: kgetz@loyola.edu.

LOYOLA UNIVERSITY NEW ORLEANS, New Orleans, LA 70118-6195

General Information Independent-religious, coed, comprehensive institution. *Enrollment:* 3,759 graduate, professional, and undergraduate students; 517 full-time matriculated graduate/professional students (295 women), 640 part-time matriculated graduate/professional students (493 women). *Enrollment by degree level:* 575 master's, 576 doctoral, 6 other advanced degrees. *Graduate faculty:* 91 full-time (47 women), 43 part-time/adjunct (17 women). Tuition and fees vary according to course load and program. *Graduate housing:* Room and/or apartments available on a first-come, first-served basis to single students; on-campus housing not available to married students. Typical cost: $12,658 (including board). Room and board charges vary according to housing facility selected. Housing application deadline: 8/1. *Student services:* Campus employment opportunities, campus safety program, career counseling, child daycare facilities, exercise/wellness program, free psychological counseling, international student services, low-cost health insurance, multicultural affairs office, services for students with disabilities. *Library facilities:* Monroe Library plus 1 other. *Collection:* Books: 387,652 (physical), 42,637 (digital/electronic); Serial titles: 221,718 (physical). Weekly public service hours: 114; students can reserve study rooms. *Research affiliation:* New Orleans Museum of Art (communications, history, visual arts).

Computer facilities: Computer purchase and lease plans are available. 300 computers available on campus for general student use. A campuswide network can be accessed from student residence rooms and from off campus. Online class registration is available.
Website: http://www.loyno.edu/

General Application Contact: Tharren Poplion, Assistant Director, Admissions, 504-865-3240, E-mail: poplion@loyno.edu.

GRADUATE UNITS

College of Arts and Sciences Students: 15 full-time (10 women), 19 part-time (11 women); includes 12 minority (7 Black or African American, non-Hispanic/Latino; 2 American Indian or Alaska Native, non-Hispanic/Latino; 1 Asian, non-Hispanic/Latino; 1 Hispanic/Latino; 1 Two or more races, non-Hispanic/Latino). Average age 32. 30 applicants, 80% accepted, 19 enrolled. *Faculty:* 4 full-time (1 woman), 3 part-time/adjunct (2 women). Expenses: Contact institution. *Financial support:* Research assistantships, teaching assistantships, career-related internships or fieldwork, Federal Work-Study, scholarships/grants, and tuition waivers (partial) available. Support available to part-time students. Financial award application deadline: 5/1; financial award applicants required to submit FAFSA. In 2017, 10 master's awarded. *Program availability:* Part-time, evening/weekend. Offers arts and sciences (MAT, MCJ); criminology and justice (MCJ); teaching (MAT). *Application fee:* $20. Electronic applications accepted. *Application Contact:* Tharren Poplion, Assistant Director, Admissions, 504-865-3240, E-mail: poplion@loyno.edu. *Dean*, Maria Calzada, 504-865-3244, Fax: 504-865-2059.

College of Law Students: 398 full-time (203 women), 96 part-time (49 women); includes 174 minority (77 Black or African American, non-Hispanic/Latino; 12 American Indian or Alaska Native, non-Hispanic/Latino; 16 Asian, non-Hispanic/Latino; 61 Hispanic/Latino; 8 Two or more races, non-Hispanic/Latino), 10 international. Average age 28. 809 applicants, 73% accepted, 177 enrolled. *Faculty:* 42 full-time (18 women), 14 part-time/adjunct (2 women). Expenses: Contact institution. *Financial support:* Fellowships, research assistantships, teaching assistantships, career-related internships or fieldwork, institutionally sponsored loans, scholarships/grants, traineeships, health care benefits, tuition waivers, and unspecified assistantships available. Support available to part-time students. Financial award applicants required to submit FAFSA. In 2017, 132 doctorates awarded. *Program availability:* Part-time, evening/weekend, online learning. Offers law (LL M, JD). *Application deadline:* For fall admission, 8/1 priority date for domestic and international students. Applications are processed on a rolling basis. *Application fee:* $0. Electronic applications accepted. *Application Contact:* Kimberly Jones, Director of Law Admissions, 504-861-5575, Fax: 504-861-5772, E-mail: ladmit@loyno.edu. *Dean*, Madeleine Landrieu, 504-861-5847, Fax: 504-861-5677, E-mail: lmoore@loyno.edu.

College of Music and Fine Arts Students: 20 full-time (12 women), 24 part-time (16 women); includes 18 minority (6 Black or African American, non-Hispanic/Latino; 2 Asian, non-Hispanic/Latino; 6 Hispanic/Latino; 4 Two or more races, non-Hispanic/Latino), 3 international. Average age 29. 31 applicants, 71% accepted, 13 enrolled. *Faculty:* 17 full-time (12 women), 9 part-time/adjunct (5 women). Expenses: Contact institution. *Financial support:* Career-related internships or fieldwork, Federal Work-Study, institutionally sponsored loans, scholarships/grants, unspecified assistantships, and talent-based music scholarships available. Support available to part-time students. Financial award application deadline: 5/1; financial award applicants required to submit FAFSA. In 2017, 9 master's awarded. *Program availability:* Part-time. Offers music therapy (MMT); performance (MM). *Application deadline:* For fall admission, 8/15 priority date for domestic and international students; for spring admission, 1/1 priority date for domestic and international students. Applications are processed on a rolling basis. *Application fee:* $20. Electronic applications accepted. *Dean,* Dr. Kern Maass, 504-865-3039, Fax: 504-865-2852, E-mail: kdmaass@loyno.edu.

College of Nursing and Health Students: 62 full-time (60 women), 440 part-time (381 women); includes 141 minority (87 Black or African American, non-Hispanic/Latino; 3 American Indian or Alaska Native, non-Hispanic/Latino; 14 Asian, non-Hispanic/Latino; 33 Hispanic/Latino; 2 Native Hawaiian or other Pacific Islander, non-Hispanic/Latino; 2 Two or more races, non-Hispanic/Latino), 4 international. Average age 39. 277 applicants, 65% accepted, 133 enrolled. *Faculty:* 21 full-time (13 women), 9 part-time/adjunct (7 women). Expenses: Contact institution. Offers counseling (MS); nursing and health (MPS, MRE, MS, MSN, DNP, Certificate). *Application Contact:* Tharren Poplion, Assistant Director, Admissions, 504-865-3240, E-mail: poplion@loyno.edu. *Dean,* Dr. Laurie Ann Ferguson, 504-865-2880, E-mail: ferguson@loyno.edu.

Loyola Institute for Ministry Students: 2 full-time (both women), 133 part-time (96 women); includes 28 minority (12 Black or African American, non-Hispanic/Latino; 1 American Indian or Alaska Native, non-Hispanic/Latino; 2 Asian, non-Hispanic/Latino; 13 Hispanic/Latino), 2 international. Average age 47. 36 applicants, 94% accepted, 26 enrolled. *Faculty:* 3 full-time (1 woman), 4 part-time/adjunct (2 women). Expenses: Contact institution. *Financial support:* Career-related internships or fieldwork, scholarships/grants, health care benefits, and tuition waivers (partial) available. Support available to part-time students. Financial award application deadline: 5/1; financial award applicants required to submit FAFSA. In 2017, 41 master's awarded. *Program availability:* Part-time, evening/weekend, online learning. Offers pastoral studies (MPS); religious education (MRE); theology and ministry (Certificate). *Application deadline:* For fall admission, 8/15 for domestic and international students; for spring admission, 1/1 for domestic and international students. Applications are processed on a rolling basis. *Application fee:* $20. Electronic applications accepted. *Application Contact:* Diane Blair, Manager of Admissions, 504-865-3728, Fax: 504-865-2066, E-mail: lim@loyno.edu. *Director,* Dr. Tom Ryan, 504-865-2069, Fax: 504-865-2066, E-mail: tfryan@loyno.edu.

School of Nursing Students: 35 full-time (all women), 265 part-time (245 women); includes 102 minority (69 Black or African American, non-Hispanic/Latino; 2 American Indian or Alaska Native, non-Hispanic/Latino; 12 Asian, non-Hispanic/Latino; 15 Hispanic/Latino; 2 Native Hawaiian or other Pacific Islander, non-Hispanic/Latino; 2 Two or more races, non-Hispanic/Latino). Average age 41. 191 applicants, 54% accepted, 83 enrolled. *Faculty:* 13 full-time (10 women), 5 part-time/adjunct (all women). Expenses: Contact institution. *Financial support:* Traineeships and Incumbent Workers Training Program grants available. Financial award application deadline: 5/1; financial award applicants required to submit FAFSA. In 2017, 126 master's, 20 doctorates awarded. *Program availability:* Part-time, evening/weekend, online learning. Offers family nurse practitioner (DNP); nursing (MSN). *Application deadline:* For fall admission, 8/1 priority date for domestic and international students; for winter admission, 12/15 priority date for domestic and international students; for spring admission, 5/15 priority date for domestic and international students. Applications are processed on a rolling basis. *Application fee:* $40. Electronic applications accepted. *Application Contact:* Elizabeth Wadsworth, Executive Assistant to the Director, 504-865-2307, Fax: 504-865-3254, E-mail: edwadswo@loyno.edu. *Interim Director,* Dr. Laurie Ann Ferguson, 504-865-2880, Fax: 504-865-3254, E-mail: nursing@loyno.edu.

Joseph A. Butt, S.J., College of Business Students: 22 full-time (10 women), 61 part-time (36 women); includes 23 minority (13 Black or African American, non-Hispanic/Latino; 2 Asian, non-Hispanic/Latino; 8 Hispanic/Latino), 8 international. Average age 31. 51 applicants, 92% accepted, 38 enrolled. *Faculty:* 6 full-time (3 women), 7 part-time/adjunct (0 women). Expenses: Contact institution. *Financial support:* Research assistantships, scholarships/grants, tuition waivers (partial), and unspecified assistantships available. Financial award application deadline: 5/1; financial award applicants required to submit FAFSA. In 2017, 42 master's awarded. *Program availability:* Part-time, evening/weekend, online learning. Offers business (MBA); organizational performance excellence (MBA). *Application deadline:* For fall admission, 6/15 priority date for domestic students, 5/15 priority date for international students; for spring admission, 11/15 priority date for domestic students, 10/15 priority date for international students. Applications are processed on a rolling basis. *Application fee:* $50. Electronic applications accepted. *Application Contact:* Ashley Francis, Director of Graduate Programs, 504-864-7979, Fax: 504-864-7970, E-mail: mba@loyno.edu. *Interim Dean,* Dr. J. Patrick O'Brien, 504-864-7990, Fax: 504-864-7970, E-mail: mba@loyno.edu.

LUBBOCK CHRISTIAN UNIVERSITY, Lubbock, TX 79407-2099

General Information Independent-religious, coed, comprehensive institution. *Graduate housing:* Rooms and/or apartments available to single and married students. Housing application deadline: 8/15.

GRADUATE UNITS

Graduate Biblical Studies *Program availability:* Part-time. Offers Bible and ministry (MS); biblical interpretation (MA).

LUTHERAN SCHOOL OF THEOLOGY AT CHICAGO, Chicago, IL 60615-5199

General Information Independent-religious, coed, graduate-only institution. *Graduate housing:* Rooms and/or apartments available on a first-come, first-served basis to single and married students. Housing application deadline: 5/15. *Research affiliation:* Chicago Center for Public Ministry, Zygon Center for Religion and Science.

GRADUATE UNITS

Graduate and Professional Programs *Program availability:* Part-time. Offers ministry (MAM, D Min); theological studies (MATS, PhD); theology (M Div).

LUTHERAN THEOLOGICAL SEMINARY SASKATOON, Saskatoon, SK S7N 0X3, Canada

General Information Independent-religious, coed, graduate-only institution. *Graduate housing:* Room and/or apartments available to single students; on-campus housing not available to married students. Housing application deadline: 4/30.

GRADUATE UNITS

Graduate and Professional Programs *Program availability:* Part-time. Offers Biblical studies (MTS); church history (MTS); ethics/church and society (MTS); history of Christianity (STM); New Testament (STM); Old Testament (STM); pastoral studies (STM); pastoral theology (MTS); systematic theology (MTS); systematic theology and philosophy of religion (STM); theology (M Div, D Div). STM programs offered jointly with College of Emmanuel and St. Chad and St. Andrew's College.

LUTHER RICE COLLEGE & SEMINARY, Lithonia, GA 30038-2454

General Information Independent-religious, coed, comprehensive institution. *Graduate housing:* On-campus housing not available.

GRADUATE UNITS

Graduate Programs *Program availability:* Part-time, evening/weekend, online learning. Offers apologetics (MA); Bible languages (M Div); Biblical counseling (MA); Christian ministry (M Div, D Min); Christian studies (MA); leadership (MA). Electronic applications accepted.

LUTHER SEMINARY, St. Paul, MN 55108-1445

General Information Independent-religious, coed, graduate-only institution. *Graduate housing:* Rooms and/or apartments available on a first-come, first-served basis to single and married students.

GRADUATE UNITS

Graduate and Professional Programs *Program availability:* Part-time, online learning. Offers aging and health (MA); Biblical preaching (D Min); children, youth and family (M Div, MA); congregational mission and leadership (M Th, MA, D Min); history of Christianity (M Th, MA); missions and world religions (M Th); New Testament (M Th, MA); Old Testament (M Th, MA); pastoral care: clinical pastoral theology (M Th); pastoral theology and ministry (M Th); systematic theology (M Th, MA). Electronic applications accepted.

LYNN UNIVERSITY, Boca Raton, FL 33431-5598

General Information Independent, coed, comprehensive institution. *Enrollment:* 3,010 graduate, professional, and undergraduate students; 449 full-time matriculated graduate/professional students (228 women), 355 part-time matriculated graduate/professional students (196 women). *Enrollment by degree level:* 712 master's, 60 doctoral, 32 other advanced degrees. *Graduate faculty:* 132 full-time (54 women), 72 part-time/adjunct (34 women). *Tuition:* Full-time $17,760; part-time $740 per credit. One-time fee: $100. Tuition and fees vary according to class time, course load and degree level. *Graduate housing:* Room and/or apartments available on a first-come, first-served basis to single students; on-campus housing not available to married students. Typical cost: $11,970 (including board). *Student services:* Campus employment opportunities, campus safety program, career counseling, exercise/wellness program, free psychological counseling, international student services, low-cost health insurance, multicultural affairs office, services for students with disabilities. *Library facilities:* Eugene M. and Christine E. Lynn Library. *Collection:* Books: 58,952 (physical), 239,257 (digital/electronic); Serial titles: 401 (physical), 43,029 (digital/electronic); Databases: 118. Weekly public service hours: 96.

Computer facilities: Computer purchase and lease plans are available. 150 computers available on campus for general student use. A campuswide network can be accessed from student residence rooms and from off campus. Online registration with advisor approval for juniors, seniors and MBA students available.
Website: http://www.lynn.edu/

General Application Contact: Steven Pruitt, Assistant Director of Graduate Admissions, 561-237-7834, Fax: 561-237-7100, E-mail: admission@lynn.edu.

GRADUATE UNITS

College of Arts and Sciences Students: 60 full-time (47 women), 38 part-time (24 women); includes 32 minority (15 Black or African American, non-Hispanic/Latino; 2 Asian, non-Hispanic/Latino; 15 Hispanic/Latino), 6 international. Average age 30. 73 applicants, 82% accepted, 47 enrolled. *Faculty:* 59 full-time (26 women), 22 part-time/adjunct (16 women). Expenses: Contact institution. *Financial support:* Career-related internships or fieldwork, Federal Work-Study, scholarships/grants, tuition waivers (full and partial), and unspecified assistantships available. Support available to part-time students. Financial award application deadline: 3/1; financial award applicants required to submit FAFSA. In 2017, 64 master's awarded. *Program availability:* Part-time, evening/weekend, 100% online, blended/hybrid learning. Offers criminal justice (MS); mental health counseling (MS); psychology (MS). *Application deadline:* For fall admission, 8/18 for domestic students, 8/4 for international students; for spring admission, 12/15 for domestic students, 12/1 for international students; for summer admission, 4/17 for domestic students, 4/3 for international students. Applications are processed on a rolling basis. *Application fee:* $45. Electronic applications accepted. *Application Contact:* Steven Pruitt, Director of Graduate Admission, 561-237-7834, Fax: 561-237-7100, E-mail: admissionpm@lynn.edu. *Dean,* Dr. Katrina Carter-Tellison, 561-237-7412, E-mail: kcartertellison@lynn.edu.

College of Business and Management Students: 287 full-time (124 women), 195 part-time (105 women); includes 110 minority (44 Black or African American, non-Hispanic/Latino; 2 American Indian or Alaska Native, non-Hispanic/Latino; 11 Asian, non-Hispanic/Latino; 47 Hispanic/Latino; 6 Two or more races, non-Hispanic/Latino), 135 international. Average age 28. 293 applicants, 94% accepted, 192 enrolled. *Faculty:* 29 full-time (11 women), 19 part-time/adjunct (7 women). Expenses: Contact institution. *Financial support:* Career-related internships or fieldwork, Federal Work-Study, scholarships/grants, tuition waivers (full and partial), and unspecified assistantships available. Support available to part-time students. Financial award application deadline: 3/1; financial award applicants required to submit FAFSA. In 2017, 236 master's awarded. *Program availability:* Part-time, evening/weekend, 100% online, blended/hybrid learning. Offers business administration (MBA). *Application deadline:* For fall admission, 8/18 for domestic students, 8/4 for international students; for spring admission, 12/15 for domestic students, 12/1 for international students; for summer admission, 4/17 for domestic students, 4/3 for international students. Applications are processed on a rolling basis. *Application fee:* $45. Electronic applications accepted. *Application Contact:* Steven Pruitt, Director of Graduate and Undergraduate Evening Admission, 561-237-7834, Fax: 561-237-7100, E-mail: spruitt@lynn.edu. *Dean of the College of Business and Management,* Dr. RT Good, 561-237-7458, E-mail: rgood@lynn.edu.

Conservatory of Music Students: 36 full-time (13 women), 27 part-time (12 women); includes 9 minority (1 Black or African American, non-Hispanic/Latino; 6

Hispanic/Latino; 2 Two or more races, non-Hispanic/Latino), 32 international. Average age 24. 101 applicants, 72% accepted, 35 enrolled. *Faculty:* 11 full-time (3 women), 17 part-time/adjunct (3 women). Expenses: Contact institution. *Financial support:* Federal Work-Study, scholarships/grants, and unspecified assistantships available. Support available to part-time students. Financial award application deadline: 3/1; financial award applicants required to submit FAFSA. In 2017, 8 master's, 5 Certificates awarded. *Program availability:* Part-time, evening/weekend. Offers composition (MM); instrumental collaborative piano (MM); performance (MM); professional performance (Certificate). *Application deadline:* For fall admission, 8/18 for domestic students, 8/4 for international students; for spring admission, 12/15 for domestic students, 12/1 for international students; for summer admission, 4/17 for domestic students, 4/3 for international students. Applications are processed on a rolling basis. *Application fee:* $50. Electronic applications accepted. *Application Contact:* Steven Pruitt, Director of Graduate Admissions, 561-237-7834, Fax: 561-237-7100, E-mail: admission@lynn.edu. *Dean*, Dr. Jon Robertson, 561-237-7702, Fax: 561-237-9002, E-mail: jrobertson@lynn.edu.

Donald E. and Helen L. Ross College of Education Students: 31 full-time (23 women), 62 part-time (42 women); includes 32 minority (20 Black or African American, non-Hispanic/Latino; 1 American Indian or Alaska Native, non-Hispanic/Latino; 10 Hispanic/Latino; 1 Two or more races, non-Hispanic/Latino), 3 international. Average age 36. 46 applicants, 78% accepted, 30 enrolled. *Faculty:* 6 full-time (4 women), 4 part-time/adjunct (3 women). Expenses: Contact institution. *Financial support:* Career-related internships or fieldwork, Federal Work-Study, scholarships/grants, tuition waivers (partial), and unspecified assistantships available. Support available to part-time students. Financial award application deadline: 3/1; financial award applicants required to submit FAFSA. In 2017, 24 master's, 22 doctorates awarded. *Program availability:* Part-time, evening/weekend, online learning. Offers educational leadership (M Ed, Ed D); exceptional student education (M Ed). *Application deadline:* For fall admission, 8/18 for domestic students, 8/4 for international students; for spring admission, 12/15 for domestic students, 12/1 for international students; for summer admission, 4/17 for domestic students, 4/3 for international students. Applications are processed on a rolling basis. *Application fee:* $45. Electronic applications accepted. *Application Contact:* Steven Pruitt, Director of Graduate and Undergraduate Evening Admission, 561-237-7834, Fax: 561-237-7100, E-mail: spruitt@lynn.edu. *Dean, College of Education*, Dr. Kathleen Weigel, 561-237-7441, E-mail: kweigel@lynn.edu.

Eugene M. and Christine E. Lynn College of Communication and Design Students: 35 full-time (21 women), 33 part-time (13 women); includes 31 minority (12 Black or African American, non-Hispanic/Latino; 2 American Indian or Alaska Native, non-Hispanic/Latino; 2 Asian, non-Hispanic/Latino; 14 Hispanic/Latino; 1 Two or more races, non-Hispanic/Latino), 12 international. Average age 27. 59 applicants, 92% accepted, 44 enrolled. *Faculty:* 14 full-time (9 women), 7 part-time/adjunct (1 woman). Expenses: Contact institution. *Financial support:* Career-related internships or fieldwork, Federal Work-Study, institutionally sponsored loans, scholarships/grants, tuition waivers (partial), and unspecified assistantships available. Support available to part-time students. Financial award application deadline: 8/1; financial award applicants required to submit FAFSA. In 2017, 17 master's awarded. *Program availability:* Part-time, evening/weekend. Offers communication and media (MS); digital media (Certificate); graphic and Web design (MFA); visual effects animation (MFA); Web design and technology (MS). *Application deadline:* For fall admission, 8/18 for domestic students, 8/4 for international students; for spring admission, 12/15 for domestic students, 12/1 for international students; for summer admission, 4/17 for domestic students, 4/3 for international students. Applications are processed on a rolling basis. *Application fee:* $45. Electronic applications accepted. *Application Contact:* Steven Pruitt, Director of Graduate Admission, 561-237-7834, Fax: 561-237-7100, E-mail: admission@lynn.edu. *Dean*, Dr. David L. Jaffe, 561-237-7099, Fax: 561-237-7097, E-mail: djaffe@lynn.edu.

MAASTRICHT SCHOOL OF MANAGEMENT, 6201 BE Maastricht, Netherlands

General Information Private, coed, graduate-only institution.

GRADUATE UNITS

Graduate Programs Offers business administration (MBA, DBA, PhD); facility management (Exec MBA); management (M Sc); sustainability (Exec MBA).

MACHZIKEI HADATH RABBINICAL COLLEGE, Brooklyn, NY 11204-1805

General Information Independent-religious, men only, comprehensive institution. *Graduate housing:* Room and/or apartments available to single students; on-campus housing not available to married students.

GRADUATE UNITS

Graduate Programs

MADONNA UNIVERSITY, Livonia, MI 48150-1173

General Information Independent-religious, coed, comprehensive institution. *Graduate housing:* Room and/or apartments available on a first-come, first-served basis to single students; on-campus housing not available to married students. Housing application deadline: 4/29.

GRADUATE UNITS

Department of Psychology *Program availability:* Part-time, evening/weekend. Offers clinical psychology (MSCP). Electronic applications accepted.

Program in Health Services *Program availability:* Part-time. Offers health services (MSHS). Electronic applications accepted.

Program in Hospice *Program availability:* Part-time, evening/weekend. Offers hospice (MSH). Electronic applications accepted.

Program in Liberal Studies Offers liberal studies (MALS).

Program in Nursing *Program availability:* Part-time. Offers adult health: chronic health conditions (MSN); adult nurse practitioner (MSN); nursing administration (MSN). Electronic applications accepted.

Program in Religious Studies Offers pastoral ministry (MA).

Program in Teaching English to Speakers of Other Languages *Program availability:* Part-time, evening/weekend. Offers teaching English to speakers of other languages (MATESOL). Electronic applications accepted.

Programs in Education *Program availability:* Part-time, evening/weekend. Offers Catholic school leadership (MSA); educational leadership (MSA); learning disabilities (MAT); literacy education (MAT); teaching and learning (MAT). Electronic applications accepted.

School of Business *Program availability:* Part-time, evening/weekend, online learning. Offers business administration (MBA); international business (MSBA); leadership studies (MSBA); leadership studies in criminal justice (MSBA); quality and operations management (MSBA). Electronic applications accepted.

MAHARISHI UNIVERSITY OF MANAGEMENT, Fairfield, IA 52557

General Information Independent, coed, university. *Graduate housing:* Room and/or apartments guaranteed to single students; on-campus housing not available to married students. Housing application deadline: 8/1. *Research affiliation:* National Institutes of Health (stress reduction/disease prevention), U.S. Department of Defense (therapy/education/PTSD in veterans), Columbia University Medical Center (natural medicine and prevention), Institute of Noetic Sciences (psychophysiological correlates of consciousness), San Diego VA Healthcare System (veterans' health/PTSD stress reduction), Howard University Medical Center (stress reduction/hypertension prevention).

GRADUATE UNITS

Graduate Studies *Program availability:* Evening/weekend, online learning. Offers accounting (MBA); computer science (MS); Maharishi Vedic science (MA, PhD); management (PhD); physiology (PhD); screenwriting (MFA); sustainability (MBA). Electronic applications accepted.

MAINE COLLEGE OF ART, Portland, ME 04101

General Information Independent, coed, comprehensive institution.

GRADUATE UNITS

Program in Studio Art Offers studio art (MA, MFA). Electronic applications accepted.

MAINE MARITIME ACADEMY, Castine, ME 04420

General Information State-supported, coed, primarily men, comprehensive institution. *Enrollment:* 8 full-time matriculated graduate/professional students (2 women), 12 part-time matriculated graduate/professional students (7 women). *Enrollment by degree level:* 11 master's. *Graduate faculty:* 6 full-time (1 woman), 6 part-time/adjunct (2 women). *Graduate housing:* Rooms and/or apartments available on a first-come, first-served basis to single and married students. Housing application deadline: 4/15. *Student services:* Campus employment opportunities, campus safety program, career counseling, exercise/wellness program, free psychological counseling, international student services, low-cost health insurance, services for students with disabilities, writing training. *Library facilities:* Nutting Memorial Library.

Computer facilities: Computer purchase and lease plans are available. A campuswide network can be accessed from student residence rooms and from off campus. Online class registration is available.
Website: http://www.mainemaritime.edu/

General Application Contact: Debra Kingston, Coordinator, 207-326-2212, Fax: 207-326-2411, E-mail: debra.kingston@mma.edu.

GRADUATE UNITS

Loeb-Sullivan School of International Business and Logistics Students: 8 full-time (2 women), 13 part-time (7 women). Average age 30. 26 applicants. *Faculty:* 6 full-time (1 woman), 5 part-time/adjunct (1 woman). Expenses: Contact institution. *Financial support:* In 2017–18, 2 students received support, including teaching assistantships with full tuition reimbursements available (averaging $5,000 per year); career-related internships or fieldwork, Federal Work-Study, and institutionally sponsored loans also available. Support available to part-time students. Financial award application deadline: 4/15; financial award applicants required to submit FAFSA. In 2017, 17 master's awarded. *Program availability:* Part-time, 100% online. Offers global logistics and maritime management (MS); international logistics management (MS). *Application deadline:* For fall admission, 6/1 for domestic and international students; for spring admission, 3/15 for domestic and international students. Applications are processed on a rolling basis. *Application fee:* $40. Electronic applications accepted. *Application Contact:* Debra Kingston, Program Coordinator, 207-326-2212, Fax: 207-326-2411, E-mail: debra.kingston@mma.edu. *Dean*, Dr. Donald Maier, 207-326-2488, E-mail: donald.maier@mma.edu.

MALONE UNIVERSITY, Canton, OH 44709

General Information Independent-religious, coed, comprehensive institution. *Graduate housing:* On-campus housing not available.

GRADUATE UNITS

Graduate Program in Business *Program availability:* Part-time, evening/weekend, online learning. Offers business (MBA).

Graduate Program in Counseling and Human Development *Program availability:* Part-time, evening/weekend. Offers clinical counseling (MA); school counseling (MA).

Graduate Program in Education *Program availability:* Part-time, evening/weekend. Offers curriculum and instruction (MA); curriculum, instruction, and professional development (MA); educational leadership (principal license) (MA); intervention specialist (MA).

Graduate Program in Nursing *Program availability:* Part-time, evening/weekend. Offers family nurse practitioner (MSN).

Graduate Program in Organizational Leadership *Program availability:* Part-time, evening/weekend. Offers organizational leadership (MAOL).

Graduate Program in Theological Studies *Program availability:* Part-time, evening/weekend. Offers theological studies (MA).

MANCHESTER UNIVERSITY, North Manchester, IN 46962-1225

General Information Independent-religious, coed, comprehensive institution. *Enrollment:* 1,572 graduate, professional, and undergraduate students; 297 full-time matriculated graduate/professional students (180 women), 9 part-time matriculated graduate/professional students (4 women). *Enrollment by degree level:* 17 master's, 289 doctoral. *Graduate faculty:* 37 full-time (18 women), 1 part-time/adjunct (0 women). Tuition and fees vary according to program. *Graduate housing:* On-campus housing not available. *Student services:* Campus safety program, career counseling, multicultural affairs office. *Library facilities:* Funderburg Library. *Collection:* Study areas open 24 hours, 5–7 days a week.

Computer facilities: Computer purchase and lease plans are available. 226 computers available on campus for general student use. A campuswide network can be accessed from student residence rooms and from off campus. Online class registration is available.
Website: http://www.manchester.edu/

General Application Contact: Dr. Mark Huntington, Graduate Program Director, 260-982-5033, E-mail: mwhuntington@manchester.edu.

GRADUATE UNITS

Doctor of Pharmacy Program Students: 281 full-time (168 women), 8 part-time (3 women); includes 95 minority (36 Black or African American, non-Hispanic/Latino; 1 American Indian or Alaska Native, non-Hispanic/Latino; 47 Asian, non-Hispanic/Latino; 9 Hispanic/Latino; 1 Native Hawaiian or other Pacific Islander, non-Hispanic/Latino; 1 Two or more races, non-Hispanic/Latino). Average age 24. 610 applicants, 18%

accepted, 74 enrolled. *Faculty:* 33 full-time (17 women). Expenses: Contact institution. Offers pharmacy (Pharm D). *Application deadline:* For fall admission, 3/1 for domestic students. *Application fee:* $175. Electronic applications accepted. *Application Contact:* Greg Hetrick, Director of Enrollment and Student Services, 260-470-2656, E-mail: gbhetrick@manchester.edu. *Dean of Pharmacy Programs/Professor of Pharmaceutical Sciences*, W. Thomas Smith, 260-470-2668, E-mail: wtsmith@manchester.edu.

Master of Athletic Training Program Students: 21 full-time (16 women); includes 4 minority (3 Black or African American, non-Hispanic/Latino; 1 Hispanic/Latino). Average age 23. 31 applicants, 74% accepted, 15 enrolled. *Faculty:* 6 full-time (2 women), 1 part-time/adjunct (0 women). Expenses: Contact institution. *Financial support:* In 2017–18, 21 students received support, including 21 fellowships (averaging $7,850 per year). Financial award application deadline: 5/1; financial award applicants required to submit FAFSA. In 2017, 7 master's awarded. Offers athletic training (MAT). *Application deadline:* For fall admission, 1/1 priority date for domestic students. Applications are processed on a rolling basis. *Application fee:* $60. Electronic applications accepted. *Program Director, Graduate Athletic Training Education*, Mark Huntington, 260-982-5033, E-mail: mwhuntington@manchester.edu.

Master of Science in Pharmacogenomics Program Students: 2 full-time (both women), 1 (woman) part-time; includes 1 minority (Asian, non-Hispanic/Latino). Average age 23. 18 applicants, 22% accepted, 3 enrolled. *Faculty:* 9 full-time (4 women). Expenses: Contact institution. *Program availability:* Part-time, 100% online, blended/hybrid learning. Offers pharmacogenomics (MS). *Application deadline:* Applications are processed on a rolling basis. *Application fee:* $25. Electronic applications accepted. *Application Contact:* Greg Hetrick, Director of Student Services, 260-470-2656, E-mail: gbhetrick@manchester.edu. *Director*, Dr. Dave F. Kisor, 260-470-2747, E-mail: dfkisor@manchester.edu.

MANHATTAN COLLEGE, Riverdale, NY 10471

General Information Independent-religious, coed, comprehensive institution. *Enrollment:* 4,242 graduate, professional, and undergraduate students; 472 full-time matriculated graduate/professional students (241 women), 106 part-time matriculated graduate/professional students (49 women). *Graduate faculty:* 53 full-time (14 women), 41 part-time/adjunct (26 women). *Tuition:* Part-time $1034 per credit. *Required fees:* $280 per term. One-time fee: $590 part-time. Tuition and fees vary according to program. *Graduate housing:* Rooms and/or apartments available on a first-come, first-served basis to single and married students. Typical cost: $15,600 (including board) for single students. *Student services:* Career counseling, free psychological counseling, low-cost health insurance, services for students with disabilities. *Library facilities:* Mary Alice and Tom OMalley Library. *Collection:* Books: 259,987 (physical), 191,706 (digital/electronic); Serial titles: 379 (physical), 186,500 (digital/electronic). Weekly public service hours: 168; study areas open 24 hours, 5–7 days a week.

Computer facilities: 450 computers available on campus for general student use. A campuswide network can be accessed from student residence rooms and from off campus. Online class registration, course management system, degree audit/planning tool, campus card access are available.
Website: http://www.manhattan.edu/

General Application Contact: William Bisset, Vice President for Enrollment Management, 718-862-7199, Fax: 718-862-8019, E-mail: william.bisset@manhattan.edu.

GRADUATE UNITS

Graduate Programs *Program availability:* Part-time, evening/weekend.

School of Business Students: 43 full-time (23 women), 26 part-time (12 women). Average age 25. *Faculty:* 35 full-time (19 women), 2 part-time/adjunct (1 woman). Expenses: Contact institution. *Financial support:* Research assistantships, career-related internships or fieldwork, scholarships/grants, and unspecified assistantships available. In 2017, 42 master's awarded. *Program availability:* Part-time, 100% online, blended/hybrid learning. Offers business (MBA). *Application deadline:* For fall admission, 8/1 for domestic and international students; for spring admission, 1/1 for domestic and international students; for summer admission, 4/1 for domestic and international students. Applications are processed on a rolling basis. *Application fee:* $75. Electronic applications accepted. *Application Contact:* Dr. Marc Waldman, MBA Program Director, 718-862-3856, E-mail: marc.waldman@manhattan.edu. *Interim Dean*, Dr. Janet Rovenpor, 718-862-7440, Fax: 718-862-8032, E-mail: janet.rovenpor@manhattan.edu.

School of Continuing and Professional Studies Students: 64 full-time, 22 part-time; includes 41 minority (17 Black or African American, non-Hispanic/Latino; 4 Asian, non-Hispanic/Latino; 18 Hispanic/Latino; 2 Two or more races, non-Hispanic/Latino). Average age 33. *Faculty:* 13 part-time/adjunct (10 women). Expenses: Contact institution. In 2017, 46 master's awarded. *Program availability:* Part-time, evening/weekend. Offers organizational leadership (MS). *Application deadline:* For fall admission, 8/1 for domestic students; for spring admission, 11/15 for domestic students. Applications are processed on a rolling basis. *Application fee:* $75. Electronic applications accepted. *Application Contact:* William Bisset, Vice President for Enrollment Management, 718-862-7199, Fax: 718-862-8019, E-mail: william.bisset@manhattan.edu. *Dean*, Cheryl Harrison, 718-862-7862, Fax: 718-862-8049, E-mail: cheryl.harrison@manhattan.edu.

School of Education and Health *Program availability:* Part-time, evening/weekend, online learning. Offers adolescence education students with disabilities generalist extension in English or math or social studies - grades 7-12 (MS Ed); advanced leadership studies (MS Ed, Advanced Certificate); bilingual education (Advanced Certificate); bilingual pupil personnel services (Professional Diploma); dual childhood/students with disabilities - grades 1-6 (MS Ed); education and health (MA, MS, MS Ed, Advanced Certificate, Certificate, Professional Diploma); instructional design and delivery (MS); marriage and family therapy (MS); mental health counseling (MS, Advanced Certificate); school building leadership (MS Ed, Advanced Certificate); school counseling (MA, Professional Diploma); students with disabilities - grades 1-6 (MS Ed).

School of Engineering *Program availability:* Part-time, evening/weekend. Offers chemical engineering (MS); civil engineering (MS); computer engineering (MS); construction management (MS); electrical engineering (MS); environmental engineering (ME, MS); mechanical engineering (MS).

School of Science Offers applied mathematics - data analytics (MS); mathematics (MS).

MANHATTAN SCHOOL OF MUSIC, New York, NY 10027-4698

General Information Independent, coed, comprehensive institution. *Graduate housing:* Room and/or apartments available on a first-come, first-served basis to single students; on-campus housing not available to married students. Housing application deadline: 6/15.

GRADUATE UNITS

Graduate Programs Offers composition (MM, DMA); jazz (MM, DMA); music performance (MM, DMA); orchestral performance (MM). Electronic applications accepted.

Professional Studies Certificate Program Offers instrumental music (CPS); vocal music (CPS). Electronic applications accepted.

MANHATTANVILLE COLLEGE, Purchase, NY 10577-2132

General Information Independent, coed, comprehensive institution. *Enrollment:* 2,682 graduate, professional, and undergraduate students; 338 full-time matriculated graduate/professional students (212 women), 487 part-time matriculated graduate/professional students (346 women). *Enrollment by degree level:* 675 master's, 96 doctoral, 54 other advanced degrees. *Graduate faculty:* 27 full-time (18 women), 147 part-time/adjunct (80 women). *Tuition:* Full-time $16,470; part-time $915 per credit. *Required fees:* $210; $105 per semester. Tuition and fees vary according to course load, degree level and program. *Graduate housing:* Room and/or apartments available on a first-come, first-served basis to single students; on-campus housing not available to married students. Typical cost: $10,850 per year. Room charges vary according to board plan. Housing application deadline: 7/1. *Student services:* Campus employment opportunities, campus safety program, career counseling, exercise/wellness program, free psychological counseling, grant writing training, international student services, low-cost health insurance, multicultural affairs office, services for students with disabilities, teacher training, writing training. *Library facilities:* Manhattanville College Library. *Collection:* Books: 229,036 (physical), 177,644 (digital/electronic); Serial titles: 927 (physical), 59,881 (digital/electronic); Databases: 118. Weekly public service hours: 108; study areas open 24 hours, 5–7 days a week.

Computer facilities: 125 computers available on campus for general student use. A campuswide network can be accessed from student residence rooms and from off campus. Online class registration, Mobile Apps are available.
Website: http://www.mville.edu/

GRADUATE UNITS

Master of Fine Arts in Creative Writing Program Students: 5 full-time (4 women), 10 part-time (7 women). Average age 35. *Faculty:* 5 part-time/adjunct (3 women). Expenses: Contact institution. *Financial support:* Fellowships, Federal Work-Study, scholarships/grants, tuition waivers (partial), and unspecified assistantships available. Financial award application deadline: 3/15; financial award applicants required to submit FAFSA. In 2017, 11 master's awarded. *Program availability:* Part-time, evening/weekend. Offers creative writing (MFA). *Application deadline:* Applications are processed on a rolling basis. *Application fee:* $75. Electronic applications accepted. *Application Contact:* Alissa Wilson, Director, Graduate Admissions, 914-323-3150, E-mail: mfa@mville.edu. *Program Director*, Lori Soderlind, 914-323-5239, E-mail: lori.soderlind@mville.edu.

School of Business Students: 94 full-time (41 women), 30 part-time (19 women); includes 40 minority (7 Black or African American, non-Hispanic/Latino; 1 American Indian or Alaska Native, non-Hispanic/Latino; 4 Asian, non-Hispanic/Latino; 27 Hispanic/Latino; 1 Two or more races, non-Hispanic/Latino), 14 international. Average age 30. 130 applicants, 40% accepted, 36 enrolled. *Faculty:* 28 part-time/adjunct (7 women). Expenses: Contact institution. *Financial support:* Federal Work-Study, institutionally sponsored loans, scholarships/grants, and unspecified assistantships available. Financial award application deadline: 3/15; financial award applicants required to submit FAFSA. In 2017, 61 master's awarded. *Program availability:* Part-time, evening/weekend. Offers business (MS, Advanced Certificate); business leadership (MS, Advanced Certificate); finance (MS, Advanced Certificate); human resource management (Advanced Certificate); human resource management and organizational effectiveness (MS); international management (MS, Advanced Certificate); marketing communication management (MS, Advanced Certificate); sport business and entertainment management (MS, Advanced Certificate). *Application deadline:* Applications are processed on a rolling basis. *Application fee:* $75. Electronic applications accepted. *Application Contact:* Monika Pottgen, Assistant Director, Recruitment and Admissions, 914-323-5150, E-mail: business@mville.edu. *Dean*, Steve Albanese, 914-323-5469, E-mail: steve.albanese@mville.edu.

School of Education Students: 239 full-time (167 women), 574 part-time (428 women); includes 123 minority (35 Black or African American, non-Hispanic/Latino; 8 Asian, non-Hispanic/Latino; 75 Hispanic/Latino; 2 Native Hawaiian or other Pacific Islander, non-Hispanic/Latino; 3 Two or more races, non-Hispanic/Latino), 4 international. Average age 34. 192 applicants, 77% accepted, 128 enrolled. *Faculty:* 24 full-time (15 women), 76 part-time/adjunct (49 women). Expenses: Contact institution. *Financial support:* Teaching assistantships, career-related internships or fieldwork, Federal Work-Study, institutionally sponsored loans, scholarships/grants, and unspecified assistantships available. Financial award application deadline: 3/15; financial award applicants required to submit FAFSA. In 2017, 228 master's, 17 doctorates, 30 other advanced degrees awarded. *Program availability:* Part-time, evening/weekend. Offers adolescence education (grades 7-12) foreign language (MAT, Advanced Certificate); adult and international settings (MPS); bilingual education (childhood/Spanish) (Advanced Certificate); biology (MAT, Advanced Certificate); biology and special education (MPS); chemistry (MAT, Advanced Certificate); chemistry and special education (MPS); childhood (grades 1-6) (MPS); childhood education (grades 1-6) (MAT, MPS); childhood education (grades 1-6) and special education (MPS); childhood education and special education (grades 1-6) (MPS); early childhood (birth - grade 2) (MAT); early childhood (birth-grade 2) (MPS); early childhood (birth-grade 2) and special education (MPS); early childhood and childhood (birth-grade 6) (MPS); early childhood and special education (birth-grade 2) (MPS); early childhood education (birth-grade 2) (MAT); earth science (Advanced Certificate); education (Advanced Certificate); education entrepreneurship (M Ed); education for sustainability (Advanced Certificate); education leadership (Ed D); educational leadership (MPS); educational leadership - school building leader (PD); educational leadership - school district leader (PD); educational studies (M Ed); English (MAT, Advanced Certificate); English (5-9 and 7-12) (MPS); English and special education (MPS); English and special education (grades 5-12) (MPS); grades 7-12 generalist (MPS); health and wellness specialist (Advanced Certificate); higher education leadership (Ed D); literacy (birth-grade 6) and special education childhood (grades 1-6) (MPS); literacy 5-12 (MPS); literacy and special education (MPS); literacy specialist (MPS); literacy specialist (birth-grade 6) (MPS); literacy specialist (grades 5-12) (MPS); math and special education (MPS); mathematics (MAT, Advanced Certificate); mathematics (5-9 and 7-12) (MPS); mathematics and special education (grades 5-12) (MPS); music education (MAT, Advanced Certificate); physical education and sport pedagogy (MAT); physics (MAT, Advanced Certificate); school district leader (Advanced Certificate); science (biology or chemistry 5-9 and 7-12) (MPS); science and special education (grades 5-12) (MPS); science of reading: multisensory instruction (Advanced Certificate); social studies (MAT); social studies (5-9 and 7-12) (MPS); social studies and special education (MPS); social studies and special education (grades 5-12) (MPS); Spanish (grades 7-12) (MAT); special education (birth-grade 2) (MPS); special education (birth-grade 6) (MPS); special education generalist (MPS); special education: childhood (grades 1-6) (MPS, Certificate); special education: early childhood (birth - grade 2) and childhood (grades 1-6) (Certificate); special education: early childhood (birth-grade 2) (Certificate); special education: early childhood (birth-grade 2) and childhood (grades 1-6) (Certificate); special education: early childhood and childhood (birth - grade 6) (MPS); special education: grades 7-12 generalist (Certificate); teaching English as a second language (all grades) (MPS, Certificate); TESOL (all grades) (MPS); visual arts (MAT, Certificate). *Application deadline:* For summer admission, 1/1 for domestic students. Applications are processed on a rolling basis. *Application fee:* $75. Electronic applications accepted. *Application Contact:* Alissa Wilson, Director, Graduate Admissions, 914-323-3150, E-mail: edschool@mville.edu. *Dean*, Dr. Shelley Wepner, 914-323-3153, Fax: 914-323-5493, E-mail: shelly.wepner@mville.edu.

MANSFIELD UNIVERSITY OF PENNSYLVANIA, Mansfield, PA 16933

General Information State-supported, coed, comprehensive institution. *Graduate housing:* Room and/or apartments available on a first-come, first-served basis to single students; on-campus housing not available to married students.

GRADUATE UNITS

Graduate Studies *Program availability:* Part-time, evening/weekend, online learning. Offers art education (M Ed); band conducting (MA); choral conducting (MA); elementary education (M Ed); library science (M Ed); nursing (MSN); organizational leadership (MA); performance (MA); secondary education (MS); special education (M Ed). Electronic applications accepted.

MAPLE SPRINGS BAPTIST BIBLE COLLEGE AND SEMINARY, Capitol Heights, MD 20743

General Information Independent-religious, coed, comprehensive institution. *Graduate housing:* On-campus housing not available.

GRADUATE UNITS

Graduate and Professional Programs Offers biblical studies (MA, Certificate); Christian counseling (MA); church administration (MA); divinity (M Div); ministry (D Min); religious education (MRE).

MARANATHA BAPTIST UNIVERSITY, Watertown, WI 53094

General Information Independent-religious, coed, comprehensive institution. *Graduate housing:* Room and/or apartments available to single students; on-campus housing not available to married students.

GRADUATE UNITS

Chaplaincy Program Offers chaplaincy (M Div).

Doctor of Ministry Program Offers ministry (D Min).

Master of Arts in English Bible Program *Program availability:* Part-time, 100% online. Offers English Bible (MA).

Master of Arts in Intercultural Studies Program *Program availability:* Part-time. Offers intercultural studies (MA).

Master of Divinity Program *Program availability:* Part-time. Offers divinity (M Div).

Program in Biblical Counseling *Program availability:* Part-time. Offers Biblical counseling (MA).

Program in Biblical Studies *Program availability:* Part-time. Offers Biblical studies (MA).

Program in Organizational Leadership Offers organizational leadership (MOL).

Program in Teaching and Learning *Program availability:* Part-time, evening/weekend, 100% online. Offers teaching and learning (M Ed).

MARCONI INTERNATIONAL UNIVERSITY, Pembroke Pines, FL 33028

General Information Proprietary, coed, comprehensive institution.

GRADUATE UNITS

Graduate Programs

MARIAN UNIVERSITY, Indianapolis, IN 46222-1997

General Information Independent-religious, coed, comprehensive institution. *Enrollment:* 3,429 graduate, professional, and undergraduate students; 782 full-time matriculated graduate/professional students (390 women), 273 part-time matriculated graduate/professional students (189 women). *Enrollment by degree level:* 385 master's, 670 doctoral. *Graduate faculty:* 50 full-time (27 women), 26 part-time/adjunct (21 women). *Tuition:* Full-time $27,855; part-time $858 per credit hour. *Required fees:* $1500. Tuition and fees vary according to degree level and program. *Graduate housing:* Rooms and/or apartments available on a first-come, first-served basis to single and married students. Typical cost: $10,596 per year for single students; $16,308 per year for married students. Housing application deadline: 3/1. *Student services:* Campus safety program, career counseling, exercise/wellness program, free psychological counseling, international student services, low-cost health insurance, multicultural affairs office, services for students with disabilities, teacher training, writing training. *Library facilities:* Mother Theresa Hackelmeier Memorial Library. *Collection:* Books: 80,118 (physical); Serial titles: 150 (physical), 44,749 (digital/electronic). Weekly public service hours: 95.

Computer facilities: Computer purchase and lease plans are available. 118 computers available on campus for general student use. A campuswide network can be accessed from student residence rooms. Online class registration is available.
Website: http://www.marian.edu/

General Application Contact: Bryan Moody, Executive Director of Graduate Admission, 317-955-6284, E-mail: bmoody@marian.edu.

GRADUATE UNITS

College of Osteopathic Medicine Students: 715 full-time (334 women), 3 part-time (all women); includes 156 minority (19 Black or African American, non-Hispanic/Latino; 1 American Indian or Alaska Native, non-Hispanic/Latino; 88 Asian, non-Hispanic/Latino; 30 Hispanic/Latino; 1 Native Hawaiian or other Pacific Islander, non-Hispanic/Latino; 17 Two or more races, non-Hispanic/Latino), 27 international. Average age 25. 4,470 applicants, 10% accepted, 227 enrolled. *Faculty:* 33 full-time (15 women), 2 part-time/adjunct (1 woman). Expenses: Contact institution. *Financial support:* Application deadline: 4/15; applicants required to submit FAFSA. In 2017, 134 doctorates awarded. Offers osteopathic medicine (MS, DO). *Application deadline:* For fall admission, 3/1 for domestic and international students. Applications are processed on a rolling basis. *Application fee:* $100. Electronic applications accepted. *Application Contact:* Bryan Moody, Executive Director of Graduate Admission, 317-955-6284, E-mail: bmoody@marian.edu. *Vice President of Health Professions/Dean of the College of Osteopathic Medicine*, Dr. Donald Sefcik, 317-955-6289, E-mail: dsefcik@marian.edu.

Educators College Students: 36 full-time (29 women), 269 part-time (185 women); includes 92 minority (61 Black or African American, non-Hispanic/Latino; 8 Asian, non-Hispanic/Latino; 11 Hispanic/Latino; 12 Two or more races, non-Hispanic/Latino). Average age 30. 333 applicants, 59% accepted, 165 enrolled. *Faculty:* 10 full-time (6 women), 22 part-time/adjunct (18 women). Expenses: Contact institution. *Financial support:* Application deadline: 4/15; applicants required to submit FAFSA. In 2017, 105 master's awarded. *Program availability:* Part-time, evening/weekend, 100% online. Offers education (MA, MAT). *Application deadline:* For fall admission, 3/1 priority date for domestic students. Applications are processed on a rolling basis. *Application fee:* $40. Electronic applications accepted. *Senior Vice President of Teacher Learning Excellence/Dean*, Dr. Kenith Britt, 317-955-6209, Fax: 317-955-6406, E-mail: kbritt@marian.edu.

Leighton School of Nursing Students: 23 full-time (20 women), 1 (woman) part-time; includes 7 minority (5 Black or African American, non-Hispanic/Latino; 1 Asian, non-Hispanic/Latino; 1 Hispanic/Latino). Average age 36. 69 applicants, 35% accepted, 5 enrolled. *Faculty:* 6 full-time (all women), 2 part-time/adjunct (both women). Expenses: Contact institution. *Financial support:* Application deadline: 4/15; applicants required to submit FAFSA. *Program availability:* Part-time. Offers family nurse practitioner (DNP); nurse anesthesia (DNP); nursing education (MSN). *Application deadline:* For fall admission, 2/15 for domestic and international students. Applications are processed on a rolling basis. *Application fee:* $40. Electronic applications accepted. *Application Contact:* Bryan Moody, Executive Director of Graduate Admission, 317-955-6284, E-mail: bmoody@marian.edu. *Dean*, Dr. Dorothy A. Gomez, RN, 317-955-6159, E-mail: dgomez@marian.edu.

Master of Science in Counseling Program Students: 8 full-time (7 women); includes 2 minority (both Two or more races, non-Hispanic/Latino). Average age 26. 18 applicants, 44% accepted, 8 enrolled. *Faculty:* 2 full-time (1 woman). Expenses: Contact institution. *Financial support:* Application deadline: 4/15; applicants required to submit FAFSA. *Program availability:* Part-time. Offers clinical mental health counseling (MS); school counseling (MS). *Application deadline:* For fall admission, 4/13 for domestic students; for spring admission, 11/1 for international students. Applications are processed on a rolling basis. *Application fee:* $40. Electronic applications accepted. *Application Contact:* Bryan Moody, Executive Director of Graduate Admission, 317-955-6284, E-mail: bmoody@marian.edu.

MARIAN UNIVERSITY, Fond du Lac, WI 54935-4699

General Information Independent-religious, coed, comprehensive institution. CGS member. *Graduate housing:* On-campus housing not available.

GRADUATE UNITS

School of Business and Public Safety *Program availability:* Part-time, evening/weekend. Offers organizational leadership (MS). Electronic applications accepted.

School of Education *Program availability:* Part-time, evening/weekend, online learning. Offers curriculum and instruction leadership (PhD); educational administration (PhD); educational leadership (MAE); educational technology (MAE); leadership studies (PhD); special education (MAE); teacher education (MAE).

School of Nursing and Health Professions *Program availability:* Part-time, evening/weekend. Offers adult nurse practitioner (MSN); nurse educator (MSN); thanatology (MS). Electronic applications accepted.

MARIETTA COLLEGE, Marietta, OH 45750-4000

General Information Independent, coed, comprehensive institution. *Enrollment:* 1,145 graduate, professional, and undergraduate students; 79 full-time matriculated graduate/professional students (60 women), 1 part-time matriculated graduate/professional student. *Enrollment by degree level:* 80 master's. *Graduate faculty:* 11 full-time (5 women), 2 part-time/adjunct (1 woman). *Tuition:* Part-time $775 per credit hour. *Graduate housing:* On-campus housing not available. *Student services:* Campus safety program, career counseling, free psychological counseling, international student services, services for students with disabilities, teacher training, writing training. *Library facilities:* Legacy Library. *Collection:* Books: 183,103 (physical), 137,587 (digital/electronic); Serial titles: 230 (physical), 15,786 (digital/electronic); Databases: 186. Weekly public service hours: 95; students can reserve study rooms.

Computer facilities: 475 computers available on campus for general student use. A campuswide network can be accessed from student residence rooms and from off campus. Online class registration is available.
Website: http://www.marietta.edu/

General Application Contact: Scott McVicar, Director of Admissions, 740-376-4606, E-mail: scott.mcvicar@marietta.edu.

GRADUATE UNITS

Program in Physician Assistant Studies Students: 72 full-time (56 women); includes 11 minority (1 Black or African American, non-Hispanic/Latino; 4 Asian, non-Hispanic/Latino; 3 Hispanic/Latino; 3 Two or more races, non-Hispanic/Latino). Average age 25. 963 applicants, 5% accepted, 36 enrolled. *Faculty:* 5 full-time (2 women), 2 part-time/adjunct (0 women). Expenses: Contact institution. *Financial support:* Scholarships/grants available. In 2017, 36 master's awarded. Offers physician assistant studies (MS). *Application deadline:* For fall admission, 11/1 for domestic students. *Application fee:* $100. Electronic applications accepted. *Application Contact:* Lori Hart, Administrative Coordinator, 740-376-4458, E-mail: lori.hart@marietta.edu. *Director*, Miranda Collins, 740-376-4953, E-mail: miranda.collins@marietta.edu.

Program in Psychology Students: 7 full-time (4 women), 1 part-time (0 women); includes 1 minority (Two or more races, non-Hispanic/Latino). Average age 24. 12 applicants, 83% accepted, 7 enrolled. *Faculty:* 5 full-time (2 women). Expenses: Contact institution. *Financial support:* Unspecified assistantships available. In 2017, 5 master's awarded. *Program availability:* Part-time. Offers psychology (MAP). *Application deadline:* Applications are processed on a rolling basis. *Application fee:* $25. *Director*, Dr. Chris Klein, 740-376-4795, E-mail: clk002@marietta.edu.

MARIST COLLEGE, Poughkeepsie, NY 12601-1387

General Information Independent, coed, comprehensive institution. *Graduate housing:* On-campus housing not available. *Research affiliation:* Center for Advanced Brain Imaging Psychology (psychology), New York State Office of Technology and Academic Research (NYSTAR) (technology), Hudson Valley Technology Development Corporation (HVTDC) (technology), Hudson River Psychiatric Center (psychology), St. Francis Hospital, Dutchess County Community Mental Health Center (mental health).

GRADUATE UNITS

Graduate Programs *Program availability:* Part-time, evening/weekend, online learning. Electronic applications accepted.

School of Communication and the Arts *Program availability:* Part-time, online learning. Offers communication (MA); integrated marketing communication (MA); museum studies (MA). Electronic applications accepted.

School of Computer Science and Mathematics *Program availability:* Part-time, evening/weekend, online learning. Offers computer science/software development (MS); information systems (MS, Adv C); technology management (MS). Electronic applications accepted.

School of Management *Program availability:* Part-time, evening/weekend, online learning. Offers business administration (MBA, Adv C); executive leadership (Adv C); public administration (MPA); technology management (MS). Electronic applications accepted.

School of Science Offers physical therapy (DPT).

School of Social and Behavioral Sciences *Program availability:* Part-time, evening/weekend. Offers education (M Ed, MA); mental health counseling (MA); school psychology (MA, Adv C). Electronic applications accepted.

MARLBORO COLLEGE, Marlboro, VT 05344

General Information Independent, coed, comprehensive institution. *Enrollment:* 241 graduate, professional, and undergraduate students; 14 full-time matriculated graduate/professional students (8 women), 35 part-time matriculated graduate/professional students (27 women). *Enrollment by degree level:* 48 master's, 1 other advanced degree. *Graduate faculty:* 3 full-time (2 women), 42 part-time/adjunct (27 women). *Tuition:* Full-time $5502; part-time $3144 per credit. *Graduate housing:* On-campus housing not available. *Student services:* Career counseling, international student services, services for students with disabilities, teacher training, writing training. *Library facilities:* Rice-Aron Library. *Collection:* Books: 88,500 (physical), 137,548 (digital/electronic); Serial titles: 5,400 (physical), 150 (digital/electronic); Databases: 75. Study areas open 24 hours, 5–7 days a week.

Computer facilities: Computer purchase and lease plans are available. 47 computers available on campus for general student use. A campuswide network can be accessed. Online class registration is available.
Website: http://www.marlboro.edu/

General Application Contact: Amanda Mehegan, Admissions Assistant, 802-451-7505, Fax: 802-258-9201, E-mail: graduateadmissions@marlboro.edu.

GRADUATE UNITS

Graduate and Professional Studies Expenses: Contact institution. *Financial support:* Scholarships/grants available. Financial award applicants required to submit FAFSA. *Program availability:* Part-time, evening/weekend, blended/hybrid learning. Offers educational technology (Certificate); mission-driven organizations (MBA, MS); project management (MBA, MS); social innovation (MBA, MS); teaching English to speakers of other languages (MAT); teaching for social justice (MAT); teaching with technology (MAT). *Application deadline:* For fall admission, 8/5 for domestic and international students; for winter admission, 12/5 for domestic and international students; for spring admission, 4/5 for domestic and international students. Applications are processed on a rolling basis. *Application fee:* $0. Electronic applications accepted. *Application Contact:* Amanda Mehegan, Assistant Director of Graduate Admissions, 802-451-7505, Fax: 802-258-9201, E-mail: graduateadmissions@marlboro.edu. *Associate Dean*, Kate Jellema, 802-258-9203, Fax: 802-258-9201, E-mail: katej@gradschool.marlboro.edu.

MARQUETTE UNIVERSITY, Milwaukee, WI 53201-1881

General Information Independent-religious, coed, university. CGS member. *Graduate housing:* Rooms and/or apartments available on a first-come, first-served basis to single and married students. *Research affiliation:* Shriners Hospital for Children in Chicago, Rehabilitation Institute of Chicago, Froedtert Memorial Lutheran Hospital, Children's Hospital of Wisconsin, Blood Center of Wisconsin, Department of Orthopedic Surgery, Medical College of Wisconsin.

GRADUATE UNITS

Graduate School *Program availability:* Part-time, evening/weekend, online learning. Offers interdisciplinary studies (PhD); transfusion medicine (MSTM). Electronic applications accepted.

College of Arts and Sciences *Program availability:* Part-time. Offers American literature (PhD); analytical chemistry (MS, PhD); ancient philosophy (PhD); arts and sciences (MA, MACD, MS, PhD); bioanalytical chemistry (MS, PhD); bioinformatics (MS); biophysical chemistry (MS, PhD); British and American literature (MA); British empiricism and analytic philosophy (PhD); British literature (PhD); cell biology (MS, PhD); chemical physics (MS, PhD); Christian philosophy (PhD); computational sciences (MS, PhD); computing (MS); developmental biology (MS, PhD); early modern European philosophy (PhD); ecology (MS, PhD); epithelial physiology (MS, PhD); ethics (PhD); European history (MA, PhD); genetics (MS, PhD); German philosophy (PhD); global studies (MA); history of philosophy (MA); inorganic chemistry (MS, PhD); international affairs (MA); mathematics education (MS); medieval philosophy (PhD); microbiology (MS, PhD); molecular biology (MS, PhD); muscle and exercise physiology (MS, PhD); neuroscience (PhD); organic chemistry (MS, PhD); phenomenology and existentialism (PhD); philosophy of religion (PhD); physical chemistry (MS, PhD); political science (MA); psychology (PhD); public service (MA); social and applied philosophy (MA); Spanish (MA); theology (MA, PhD); United States history (MA, PhD). Electronic applications accepted.

College of Communication *Program availability:* Part-time, evening/weekend. Offers advertising and public relations (MA); communication studies (MA); digital storytelling (Certificate); journalism (MA); mass communication (MA); science, health and environmental communication (MA). Electronic applications accepted.

College of Education *Program availability:* Part-time. Offers clinical mental health counseling (MS); college student personnel administration (M Ed); community counseling (MA); counseling psychology (PhD); curriculum and instruction (MA); education (M Ed, MA, MS, PhD, Certificate); educational administration (M Ed); educational policy and foundations (MA); elementary education (Certificate); literacy (MA); principal (Certificate); reading specialist (Certificate); reading teacher (Certificate); school counseling (MA); secondary education (Certificate); superintendent (Certificate).

College of Engineering *Program availability:* Part-time, evening/weekend. Offers biocomputing (ME); bioimaging (ME); bioinstrumentation (ME); bioinstrumentation/computers (MS, PhD); biomechanics (ME); biomechanics/biomaterials (MS, PhD); biorehabilitation (ME); construction engineering and management (MS, PhD, Certificate); digital signal processing (Certificate); electric machines, drives, and controls (Certificate); electrical and computer engineering (MS, PhD); engineering (ME, MS, MSEM, PhD, Certificate); engineering innovation (Certificate); engineering management (MSEM); environmental engineering (MS, PhD); functional imaging (PhD); healthcare technologies management (MS); mechanical engineering (MS, PhD); microwaves and antennas (Certificate); new product and process development (Certificate); rehabilitation bioengineering (PhD); sensors and smart systems (Certificate); structural design (Certificate); structural engineering and structural mechanics (MS, PhD); systems physiology (MS, PhD); transportation (Certificate); transportation engineering and materials (MS, PhD); waste and wastewater treatment processes (Certificate); water resources engineering (Certificate). Electronic applications accepted.

College of Health Sciences Offers bilingual English/Spanish (Certificate); clinical and translational rehabilitation science (MS, PhD); health sciences (MPAS, MS, DPT, PhD, Certificate); physical therapy (DPT); physician assistant studies (MPAS); speech-language pathology (MS). Electronic applications accepted.

College of Nursing Offers acute care nurse practitioner (Certificate); adult clinical nurse specialist (Certificate); adult nurse practitioner (Certificate); advanced practice nursing (MSN, DNP); family nurse practitioner (Certificate); nurse-midwifery (Certificate); nursing (PhD); pediatric acute care (Certificate); pediatric primary care (Certificate); systems leadership and healthcare quality (Certificate). Electronic applications accepted.

Graduate School of Management *Program availability:* Part-time, evening/weekend. Offers accounting (MSA); business administration (MBA); business economics (MSAE); economics (MBA); entrepreneurship (Certificate); finance (MBA); financial economics (MSAE); human resources (MBA); international business (MBA); international economics (MSAE); management (MBA, MSA, MSAE, MSHR, Certificate); management information systems (MBA); marketing (MBA); marketing research (MSAE); operations and supply chain management (MBA); real estate economics (MSAE); sports business (MBA). Electronic applications accepted.

Law School *Program availability:* Part-time, evening/weekend. Offers law (JD). Electronic applications accepted.

School of Dentistry Offers advanced training in general dentistry (MS, Certificate); dental biomaterials (MS); dentistry (MS, DDS, Certificate); endodontics (MS, Certificate); orthodontics (MS, Certificate); periodontics (MS, Certificate); prosthodontics (MS, Certificate).

MARSHALL B. KETCHUM UNIVERSITY, Fullerton, CA 92831-1615

General Information Independent, coed, graduate-only institution. *Graduate housing:* On-campus housing not available. *Research affiliation:* Alcon Laboratories (ophthalmic products), Essilor (spectacle lenses), Allergan (ophthalmic products).

GRADUATE UNITS

Graduate and Professional Programs Offers optometry (OD); pharmacy (Pharm D); vision science (MS). Electronic applications accepted.

MARSHALL UNIVERSITY, Huntington, WV 25755

General Information State-supported, coed, university. *Enrollment:* 13,246 graduate, professional, and undergraduate students; 1,222 full-time matriculated graduate/professional students (706 women), 1,591 part-time matriculated graduate/professional students (940 women). *Graduate faculty:* 249 full-time (98 women), 23 part-time/adjunct (11 women). *Graduate housing:* Rooms and/or apartments available on a first-come, first-served basis to single and married students. *Student services:* Campus employment opportunities, campus safety program, career counseling, child daycare facilities, exercise/wellness program, free psychological counseling, grant writing training, international student services, low-cost health insurance, multicultural affairs office, services for students with disabilities, teacher training, writing training. *Library facilities:* John Deaver Drinko Library plus 1 other. *Collection:* Books: 399,125 (physical), 128,967 (digital/electronic); Serial titles: 2,014 (physical), 51,061 (digital/electronic); Databases: 256. Weekly public service hours: 133; study areas open 24 hours, 5–7 days a week; students can reserve study rooms. *Research affiliation:* Bayer Corporation, Kanawha Valley Local Port District, Greenbrier County Commission, Dominion Power, Wyeth-Ayerst (clinical pharmaceutical study).

Computer facilities: Computer purchase and lease plans are available. 1,200 computers available on campus for general student use. A campuswide network can be accessed from student residence rooms and from off campus. Online class registration, virtual computer lab: remote and Web conferencing are available.
Website: http://www.marshall.edu/

General Application Contact: Dr. Tammy Johnson, Graduate Admissions, 304-746-1900, Fax: 304-746-1902, E-mail: services@marshall.edu.

GRADUATE UNITS

Academic Affairs Division Students: 1,112 full-time (661 women), 1,542 part-time (946 women); includes 429 minority (103 Black or African American, non-Hispanic/Latino; 5 American Indian or Alaska Native, non-Hispanic/Latino; 231 Asian, non-Hispanic/Latino; 50 Hispanic/Latino; 6 Native Hawaiian or other Pacific Islander, non-Hispanic/Latino; 34 Two or more races, non-Hispanic/Latino), 3 international. Average age 29. *Faculty:* 249 full-time (98 women), 23 part-time/adjunct (11 women). Expenses: Contact institution. *Financial support:* Fellowships, research assistantships, teaching assistantships, career-related internships or fieldwork, Federal Work-Study, tuition waivers (full and partial), and unspecified assistantships available. Support available to part-time students. In 2017, 866 master's, 149 doctorates, 20 other advanced degrees awarded. *Program availability:* Part-time, evening/weekend. *Application deadline:* Applications are processed on a rolling basis. *Application fee:* $40 ($100 for international students). *Application Contact:* Information Contact, Graduate Admissions, 304-746-1900, Fax: 304-746-1902, E-mail: services@marshall.edu. *Provost/Senior Vice President*, Dr. Gayle Ormiston, 304-696-3716, E-mail: ormiston@marshall.edu.

College of Arts and Media Students: 22 full-time (4 women), 5 part-time (0 women); includes 4 minority (2 Asian, non-Hispanic/Latino; 1 Hispanic/Latino; 1 Two or more races, non-Hispanic/Latino). Average age 27. *Faculty:* 21 full-time (6 women), 1 (woman) part-time/adjunct. Expenses: Contact institution. In 2017, 11 master's awarded. *Program availability:* Evening/weekend. Offers arts and media (MA, MAJ, Certificate); journalism (MAJ, Certificate); music (MA). *Application fee:* $40. *Application Contact:* Information Contact, 304-746-1900, Fax: 304-746-1902, E-mail: services@marshall.edu. *Dean*, Dr. Donald Van Horn, 304-696-2964, E-mail: vanhorn@marshall.edu.

College of Business Students: 303 full-time (154 women), 98 part-time (55 women); includes 56 minority (22 Black or African American, non-Hispanic/Latino; 22 Asian, non-Hispanic/Latino; 5 Hispanic/Latino; 1 Native Hawaiian or other Pacific Islander, non-Hispanic/Latino; 6 Two or more races, non-Hispanic/Latino). Average age 29. *Faculty:* 26 full-time (7 women), 2 part-time/adjunct (1 woman). Expenses: Contact institution. *Financial support:* Career-related internships or fieldwork and tuition waivers (full) available. Support available to part-time students. Financial award applicants required to submit FAFSA. In 2017, 122 master's, 26 doctorates awarded. *Program availability:* Part-time, evening/weekend. Offers accountancy (MS); business (MBA, MS, DMPNA, Certificate, Graduate Certificate); business administration

(MBA); health care administration (MS); human resource management (MS); management foundations (Certificate); nurse anesthesia (DMPNA). *Application deadline:* Applications are processed on a rolling basis. *Application fee:* $40. *Application Contact:* Wesley Spradlin, Information Contact, 304-746-8964, Fax: 304-746-1902, E-mail: spradlin2@marshall.edu. *Interim Dean*, Dr. Deanna Mader, 304-696-2862, Fax: 304-696-4344, E-mail: maderd@marshall.edu.

College of Education and Professional Development Students: 259 full-time (202 women), 735 part-time (519 women); includes 77 minority (33 Black or African American, non-Hispanic/Latino; 1 American Indian or Alaska Native, non-Hispanic/Latino; 6 Asian, non-Hispanic/Latino; 25 Hispanic/Latino; 2 Native Hawaiian or other Pacific Islander, non-Hispanic/Latino; 10 Two or more races, non-Hispanic/Latino). Average age 35. *Faculty:* 42 full-time (20 women), 10 part-time/adjunct (7 women). Expenses: Contact institution. *Financial support:* Career-related internships or fieldwork, Federal Work-Study, tuition waivers (full and partial), and unspecified assistantships available. Support available to part-time students. Financial award applicants required to submit FAFSA. In 2017, 367 master's, 18 doctorates, 20 other advanced degrees awarded. *Program availability:* Part-time, evening/weekend. Offers adult and continuing education (MS); counseling (MA); education (MA, MS, Ed D, Certificate, Ed S); education and professional development (MA, MAT, MS, Ed D, Certificate, Ed S); leadership studies (MA); literacy education (MA); school psychology (Ed S); special education (MA); teaching (MAT). *Application deadline:* For fall admission, 5/1 for domestic students; for spring admission, 12/1 for domestic students. Applications are processed on a rolling basis. *Application fee:* $40. Electronic applications accepted. *Application Contact:* Information Contact, 304-746-1900, Fax: 304-746-1902, E-mail: services@marshall.edu. *Dean*, Dr. Teresa Eagle, 304-746-8924, E-mail: thardman@marshall.edu.

College of Health Professions Students: 161 full-time (112 women), 243 part-time (162 women); includes 39 minority (15 Black or African American, non-Hispanic/Latino; 1 American Indian or Alaska Native, non-Hispanic/Latino; 13 Asian, non-Hispanic/Latino; 4 Hispanic/Latino; 2 Native Hawaiian or other Pacific Islander, non-Hispanic/Latino; 4 Two or more races, non-Hispanic/Latino). Average age 28. *Faculty:* 22 full-time (11 women), 1 part-time/adjunct (0 women). Expenses: Contact institution. In 2017, 119 master's, 38 doctorates awarded. Offers athletic training (MS); biomechanics (MS); communication disorders (MS); dietetics (MS, Certificate); exercise science (MS); health informatics (MS); health professions (MPH, MS, MSN, MSW, DPT, Certificate); kinesiology (MS); nursing (MSN, Certificate); physical therapy (DPT); public health (MPH); social work (MSW); sport administration (MS). *Application fee:* $40. *Application Contact:* Information Contact, 304-746-1900, Fax: 304-746-1902, E-mail: services@marshall.edu. *Dean*, Dr. Michael Prewitt, 304-696-3765, E-mail: prewittm@marshall.edu.

College of Information Technology and Engineering Students: 114 full-time (23 women), 112 part-time (27 women); includes 23 minority (8 Black or African American, non-Hispanic/Latino; 11 Asian, non-Hispanic/Latino; 2 Hispanic/Latino; 2 Two or more races, non-Hispanic/Latino), 3 international. Average age 27. *Faculty:* 12 full-time (1 woman), 7 part-time/adjunct (1 woman). Expenses: Contact institution. *Financial support:* Fellowships and tuition waivers (full) available. Support available to part-time students. Financial award application deadline: 8/1; financial award applicants required to submit FAFSA. In 2017, 162 master's awarded. *Program availability:* Part-time, evening/weekend. Offers computer science (MS); electrical and computer engineering (MSEE); engineering management (MSE); environmental engineering (MSE); environmental science (MS); information systems (MS); information technology and engineering (MS, MSE, MSEE, MSME, Certificate); mechanical engineering (MSME); safety (MS); technology management (MS, Certificate); transportation and infrastructure engineering (MSE). *Application fee:* $40. *Application Contact:* Information Contact, 304-746-1900, Fax: 304-746-1902, E-mail: services@marshall.edu. *Interim Dean*, Dr. Wael Zatar, 304-696-6043, E-mail: zatar@marshall.edu.

College of Liberal Arts Students: 159 full-time (111 women), 30 part-time (15 women); includes 18 minority (6 Black or African American, non-Hispanic/Latino; 1 American Indian or Alaska Native, non-Hispanic/Latino; 2 Asian, non-Hispanic/Latino; 3 Hispanic/Latino; 1 Native Hawaiian or other Pacific Islander, non-Hispanic/Latino; 5 Two or more races, non-Hispanic/Latino). Average age 29. *Faculty:* 69 full-time (32 women), 2 part-time/adjunct (1 woman). Expenses: Contact institution. *Financial support:* Fellowships and teaching assistantships with tuition reimbursements available. In 2017, 87 master's, 13 doctorates awarded. *Program availability:* Evening/weekend. Offers clinical psychology (Certificate); communication studies (MA); English (MA, Graduate Certificate); geography (MA, MS, Certificate); history (MA, Certificate); humanities (MA, Certificate); liberal arts (MA, MPA, MS, Psy D, Certificate, Graduate Certificate); political science (MA, MPA); psychology (MA, Psy D); sociology (MA). *Application fee:* $40. *Application Contact:* Graduate Admissions, 304-746-1900, Fax: 304-746-1902, E-mail: services@marshall.edu. *Interim Dean*, Dr. Robert Bookwalter, 304-696-2731, E-mail: bookwalt@marshall.edu.

College of Science Students: 61 full-time (27 women), 11 part-time (6 women); includes 7 minority (3 Black or African American, non-Hispanic/Latino; 3 Asian, non-Hispanic/Latino; 1 Hispanic/Latino). Average age 30. *Faculty:* 47 full-time (16 women). Expenses: Contact institution. *Financial support:* Career-related internships or fieldwork available. In 2017, 32 master's awarded. Offers biological science (MA, MS); chemistry (MS); criminal justice (MS); mathematics (MA); physical and applied science (MS); science (MA, MS). *Application fee:* $40. *Application Contact:* Information Contact, Graduate Admissions, 304-746-1900, Fax: 304-746-1902, E-mail: services@marshall.edu. *Dean*, Dr. Charles Somerville, 304-696-2424, E-mail: somervil@marshall.edu.

Forensic Science Center Students: 33 full-time (28 women), 1 part-time (0 women); includes 5 minority (1 American Indian or Alaska Native, non-Hispanic/Latino; 2 Asian, non-Hispanic/Latino; 1 Hispanic/Latino; 1 Two or more races, non-Hispanic/Latino). Average age 23. Expenses: Contact institution. *Financial support:* In 2017–18, 12 research assistantships with full tuition reimbursements (averaging $4,000 per year), teaching assistantships with full tuition reimbursements (averaging $6,000 per year) were awarded; career-related internships or fieldwork, Federal Work-Study, institutionally sponsored loans, tuition waivers (partial), and unspecified assistantships also available. Financial award application deadline: 8/27; financial award applicants required to submit FAFSA. In 2017, 16 master's awarded. Offers forensic science (MS, Graduate Certificate). *Application deadline:* For fall admission, 3/1 for domestic and international students. *Application fee:* $40. *Application Contact:* Kelly Preston, Senior Administrative Secretary, 304-690-4363 Ext. 248, Fax: 304-690-4371, E-mail: forensics@marshall.edu. *Director*, Dr. Terry W. Fenger, 304-690-4373, Fax: 304-690-4360, E-mail: fenger@marshall.edu.

School of Pharmacy Students: 307 part-time (162 women); includes 50 minority (16 Black or African American, non-Hispanic/Latino; 1 American Indian or Alaska Native, non-Hispanic/Latino; 19 Asian, non-Hispanic/Latino; 8 Hispanic/Latino; 6 Two or more races, non-Hispanic/Latino). Average age 26. *Faculty:* 10 full-time (5 women). Expenses: Contact institution. In 2017, 65 doctorates awarded. Offers pharmacy (Pharm D). *Application Contact:* Dr. Tammy Johnson, Graduate Admissions, 304-746-1900, Fax: 304-746-1902, E-mail: services@marshall.edu. *Founding Dean*, Dr. Kevin W. Yingling, 304-696-7302, E-mail: pharmacy@marshall.edu.

Joan C. Edwards School of Medicine Students: 297 full-time (132 women), 2 part-time (1 woman); includes 40 minority (7 Black or African American, non-Hispanic/Latino; 1 American Indian or Alaska Native, non-Hispanic/Latino; 29 Asian, non-Hispanic/Latino; 3 Hispanic/Latino), 11 international. Average age 26. 2,009 applicants, 8% accepted, 95 enrolled. *Faculty:* 238 full-time (67 women), 43 part-time/adjunct (15 women). Expenses: Contact institution. *Financial support:* Research assistantships with tuition reimbursements, career-related internships or fieldwork, Federal Work-Study, institutionally sponsored loans, scholarships/grants, and unspecified assistantships available. Support available to part-time students. Financial award application deadline: 5/1; financial award applicants required to submit FAFSA. Offers biomedical sciences (MS, PhD); medicine (MS, MD, PhD). *Application deadline:* For fall admission, 11/15 for domestic students. Applications are processed on a rolling basis. *Application fee:* $40 for international students. Electronic applications accepted. *Application Contact:* Cynthia A. Warren, Assistant Dean for Admissions and Student Affairs, 304-691-1738, Fax: 304-691-1744, E-mail: warren@marshall.edu. *Dean*, Dr. Joseph I. Shapiro, 304-691-1700, Fax: 304-691-1726.

MARS HILL UNIVERSITY, Mars Hill, NC 28754

General Information Independent-religious, coed, comprehensive institution.

GRADUATE UNITS

Adult and Graduate Studies

MARTIN LUTHER COLLEGE, New Ulm, MN 56073

General Information Independent-religious, coed, comprehensive institution. *Enrollment:* 937 graduate, professional, and undergraduate students; 1 (woman) full-time matriculated graduate/professional student, 81 part-time matriculated graduate/professional students (28 women). *Enrollment by degree level:* 82 master's. *Graduate faculty:* 7 full-time (1 woman), 23 part-time/adjunct (10 women). *Tuition:* Part-time $315 per credit. *Graduate housing:* On-campus housing not available. *Library facilities:* Martin Luther College Library.

Computer facilities: A campuswide network can be accessed from student residence rooms.
Website: http://www.mlc-wels.edu/

General Application Contact: John E. Meyer, Director of Graduate Studies, 507-354-8221 Ext. 398, Fax: 507-354-8225, E-mail: meyerjd@mlc-wels.edu.

GRADUATE UNITS

Graduate Studies Students: 1 (woman) full-time, 81 part-time (28 women); includes 2 minority (1 Asian, non-Hispanic/Latino; 1 Two or more races, non-Hispanic/Latino), 2 international. Average age 37. 23 applicants, 100% accepted, 23 enrolled. *Faculty:* 8 full-time (1 woman), 21 part-time/adjunct (10 women). Expenses: Contact institution. *Financial support:* In 2017–18, 4 students received support. Scholarships/grants available. Financial award application deadline: 9/1. In 2017, 25 master's awarded. *Program availability:* Part-time, evening/weekend, online learning. Offers early childhood director (MS Ed Admin); educational technology (MS Ed); instruction (MS Ed); leadership (MS Ed); principal (MS Ed Admin); special education (MS Ed). *Application deadline:* Applications are processed on a rolling basis. *Application fee:* $35. Electronic applications accepted. *Director of Graduate Studies*, John E. Meyer, 507-354-8221 Ext. 398, E-mail: meyerjd@mlc-wels.edu.

MARTIN UNIVERSITY, Indianapolis, IN 46218-3867

General Information Independent, coed, comprehensive institution. *Graduate housing:* On-campus housing not available.

GRADUATE UNITS

Division of Psychology *Program availability:* Part-time, evening/weekend. Offers community psychology (MS).

Graduate School of Urban Ministry *Program availability:* Part-time, evening/weekend. Offers urban ministry studies (MA).

MARY BALDWIN UNIVERSITY, Staunton, VA 24401-3610

General Information Independent, coed, primarily women, comprehensive institution. *Graduate housing:* On-campus housing not available.

GRADUATE UNITS

Graduate Studies *Program availability:* Part-time, evening/weekend, online learning. Offers acting (M Litt); directing (M Litt); elementary education (MAT); middle grades education (MAT); occupational therapy (OTD); Shakespeare and Renaissance literature in performance (M Litt, MFA); teaching (M Litt, MAT).

MARYGROVE COLLEGE, Detroit, MI 48221-2599

General Information Independent-religious, coed, primarily women, graduate-only institution. *Enrollment:* 264 full-time matriculated graduate/professional students (186 women), 163 part-time matriculated graduate/professional students (123 women). *Tuition:* Part-time $590 per credit hour. *Required fees:* $120 per semester. One-time fee: $25 part-time. *Graduate housing:* On-campus housing not available. *Student services:* International student services, services for students with disabilities. *Library facilities:* Nancy A. McDonough Geschke Library. *Collection:* Books: 88,689 (physical), 155,430 (digital/electronic); Serial titles: 466 (physical), 89,000 (digital/electronic); Databases: 27. Students can reserve study rooms.

Computer facilities: A campuswide network can be accessed from off campus. Online class registration is available.
Website: http://www.marygrove.edu/

General Application Contact: Marygrove College Admissions, 313-927-1240, E-mail: info@marygrove.edu.

GRADUATE UNITS

Graduate Studies Students: 163 full-time (123 women), 264 part-time (186 women). Average age 34. Expenses: Contact institution. *Financial support:* Applicants required to submit FAFSA. *Program availability:* Part-time, evening/weekend, 100% online, blended/hybrid learning. Offers autism spectrum disorders (M Ed, Certificate); curriculum instruction and assessment (MAT); educational leadership (MA); educational technology (M Ed); effective teaching in the 21st century-classroom focus (MAT); effective teaching in the 21st century-technology focus (MAT); human resource management (MA, Certificate); mathematics 6-8 (MAT); mathematics K-5 (MAT); reading and literacy K-6 (MAT); reading specialist (M Ed); school administrator (Certificate); social justice (MA); special education (MAT); special education - learning disabilities (M Ed); teaching - pre-elementary education (M Ed); teaching - pre-secondary education (M Ed). *Application deadline:* Applications are processed on a rolling basis. Electronic applications accepted. *Application Contact:* Marygrove College Admissions, 313-927-1240, E-mail: info@marygrove.edu. *Marygrove College Admissions*, 313-927-1240, E-mail: info@marygrove.edu.

MARYLAND INSTITUTE COLLEGE OF ART, Baltimore, MD 21217

General Information Independent, coed, comprehensive institution. *Graduate housing:* Room and/or apartments available on a first-come, first-served basis to single students; on-campus housing not available to married students. Housing application deadline: 5/15.

GRADUATE UNITS

Graduate Studies *Program availability:* Part-time, online learning. Offers art education (MA); business of art and design (MPS); community arts (MFA); curatorial practice (MFA); filmmaking (MFA); fine arts (Postbaccalaureate Certificate); graphic design (MA, MFA); illustration practice (MFA); information visualization (MPS); photographic and electronic media (MFA); social design (MA); studio art (MFA); teaching (MAT). Electronic applications accepted.

LeRoy E. Hoffberger School of Painting Offers painting (MFA). Electronic applications accepted.

Mount Royal School of Art Offers painting (MFA). Electronic applications accepted.

Rinehart School of Sculpture Offers sculpture (MFA). Electronic applications accepted.

MARYLAND UNIVERSITY OF INTEGRATIVE HEALTH, Laurel, MD 20723

General Information Independent, coed, primarily women, graduate-only institution. *Graduate housing:* On-campus housing not available. *Research affiliation:* Food as Medicine, Georgetown University School of Complementary and Alternative Medicine, Natural Gourmet Institute, Institute for Integrative Nutrition.

GRADUATE UNITS

Program in Herbal Medicine Offers clinical herbalism (Certificate); herbal studies (Certificate); therapeutic herbalism (MS).

Program in Naturopathic Medicine Offers naturopathic medicine (ND).

Programs in Acupuncture and Oriental Medicine Offers acupuncture (M Ac, D Ac); Chinese herbs (Certificate); Oriental medicine (MOM, DOM).

Programs in Health and Wellness Coaching Offers health and wellness coaching (MA, Postbaccalaureate Certificate).

Programs in Health Promotion and Yoga Therapy Offers health promotion (MS); yoga therapy (MS).

Programs in Nutrition Offers clinical nutrition (DCN); nutrition and integrative health (MS, Post Master's Certificate).

MARYMOUNT CALIFORNIA UNIVERSITY, Rancho Palos Verdes, CA 90275-6299

General Information Independent-religious, coed, comprehensive institution.

GRADUATE UNITS

Program in Business Administration Offers business administration (MBA).

Program in Community Psychology Offers community psychology (MS).

Program in Leadership and Global Development Offers leadership and global development (MS).

MARYMOUNT UNIVERSITY, Arlington, VA 22207-4299

General Information Independent-religious, coed, comprehensive institution. *Enrollment:* 3,375 graduate, professional, and undergraduate students; 588 full-time matriculated graduate/professional students (459 women), 442 part-time matriculated graduate/professional students (312 women). *Enrollment by degree level:* 870 master's, 146 doctoral, 14 other advanced degrees. *Graduate faculty:* 76 full-time (55 women), 71 part-time/adjunct (43 women). *Tuition:* Full-time $17,550; part-time $975 per credit hour. *Required fees:* $198; $11 per credit hour. One-time fee: $250. Tuition and fees vary according to program. *Graduate housing:* Room and/or apartments available on a first-come, first-served basis to single students; on-campus housing not available to married students. Housing application deadline: 5/1. *Student services:* Campus employment opportunities, campus safety program, career counseling, free psychological counseling, international student services, low-cost health insurance, services for students with disabilities, teacher training. *Library facilities:* Emerson C. Reinsch Library plus 1 other. *Collection:* Weekly public service hours: 104; students can reserve study rooms.

Computer facilities: 250 computers available on campus for general student use. A campuswide network can be accessed from student residence rooms and from off campus. Online class registration, Online drive space are available.
Website: http://www.marymount.edu/

General Application Contact: Francesca Reed, Director, Graduate Admissions, 703-284-5901, Fax: 703-527-3815, E-mail: grad.admissions@marymount.edu.

GRADUATE UNITS

Malek School of Health Professions Students: 146 full-time (105 women), 50 part-time (46 women); includes 65 minority (26 Black or African American, non-Hispanic/Latino; 14 Asian, non-Hispanic/Latino; 17 Hispanic/Latino; 8 Two or more races, non-Hispanic/Latino), 7 international. Average age 30. 322 applicants, 53% accepted, 63 enrolled. *Faculty:* 18 full-time (16 women), 21 part-time/adjunct (17 women). Expenses: Contact institution. *Financial support:* In 2017–18, 22 students received support, including 11 teaching assistantships with full and partial tuition reimbursements available (averaging $13,199 per year); research assistantships with full and partial tuition reimbursements available, career-related internships or fieldwork, Federal Work-Study, scholarships/grants, and unspecified assistantships also available. Support available to part-time students. Financial award application deadline: 3/1; financial award applicants required to submit FAFSA. In 2017, 25 master's, 38 doctorates, 3 other advanced degrees awarded. *Program availability:* Part-time, evening/weekend. Offers family nurse practitioner (MSN, Certificate); health education and promotion (MS); health professions (MS, MSN, DNP, DPT, Certificate); nursing (DNP); physical therapy (DPT). *Application deadline:* For fall admission, 3/1 priority date for domestic and international students; for spring admission, 11/1 priority date for domestic and international students. Applications are processed on a rolling basis. *Application fee:* $40. Electronic applications accepted. *Application Contact:* Francesca Reed, Director, Graduate Admissions, 703-284-5901, Fax: 703-527-3815, E-mail: grad.admissions@marymount.edu. *Dean*, Dr. Jeanne Matthews, 703-284-1580, Fax: 703-284-3819, E-mail: jeanne.matthews@marymount.edu.

School of Arts and Sciences Students: 48 full-time (47 women), 38 part-time (31 women); includes 29 minority (15 Black or African American, non-Hispanic/Latino; 4 Asian, non-Hispanic/Latino; 7 Hispanic/Latino; 1 Native Hawaiian or other Pacific Islander, non-Hispanic/Latino; 2 Two or more races, non-Hispanic/Latino), 10 international. Average age 34. 40 applicants, 98% accepted, 25 enrolled. *Faculty:* 10 full-time (4 women), 4 part-time/adjunct (3 women). Expenses: Contact institution. *Financial support:* In 2017–18, 8 students received support, including 2 research assistantships with full and partial tuition reimbursements available (averaging $8,775 per year), 2 teaching assistantships with full and partial tuition reimbursements available (averaging $5,850 per year); career-related internships or fieldwork, Federal Work-Study, scholarships/grants, and unspecified assistantships also available. Support available to part-time students. Financial award application deadline: 3/1; financial award applicants required to submit FAFSA. In 2017, 17 master's, 1 other advanced degree awarded. *Program availability:* Part-time, evening/weekend. Offers arts and sciences (MA, Certificate); English and humanities (MA); interior design (MA); teaching English at the community college (Certificate). *Application deadline:* For fall admission, 7/15 priority date for domestic and international students; for spring admission, 11/1 priority date for domestic and international students; for summer admission, 4/15 priority date for domestic and international students. Applications are processed on a rolling basis. *Application fee:* $40. Electronic applications accepted. *Application Contact:* Francesca Reed, Director, Graduate Admissions, 703-284-5901, Fax: 703-527-3815, E-mail: grad.admissions@marymount.edu. *Dean*, Dr. Christina Clark, 703-284-1560, Fax: 703-284-3859, E-mail: christina.clark@marymount.edu.

School of Business Administration Students: 121 full-time (64 women), 179 part-time (102 women); includes 139 minority (68 Black or African American, non-Hispanic/Latino; 25 Asian, non-Hispanic/Latino; 39 Hispanic/Latino; 1 Native Hawaiian or other Pacific Islander, non-Hispanic/Latino; 6 Two or more races, non-Hispanic/Latino), 57 international. Average age 32. 182 applicants, 97% accepted, 72 enrolled. *Faculty:* 27 full-time (17 women), 21 part-time/adjunct (4 women). Expenses: Contact institution. *Financial support:* In 2017–18, 16 students received support, including 7 research assistantships with full and partial tuition reimbursements available (averaging $9,334 per year), 4 teaching assistantships with full and partial tuition reimbursements available (averaging $17,753 per year); career-related internships or fieldwork, Federal Work-Study, scholarships/grants, and unspecified assistantships also available. Support available to part-time students. Financial award application deadline: 3/1; financial award applicants required to submit FAFSA. In 2017, 114 master's, 19 other advanced degrees awarded. *Program availability:* Part-time, evening/weekend. Offers association and nonprofit management (Certificate); business administration (MBA, MS, D Sc, Certificate); cybersecurity (MS, D Sc, Certificate); health care informatics (Certificate); health care management (MS); human resource management (Certificate); information technology (MS, Certificate); information technology project management and technology leadership (Certificate); leadership and management (MS); management studies (Certificate); organization development (Certificate). *Application deadline:* For fall admission, 7/16 priority date for domestic and international students; for spring admission, 11/16 priority date for domestic and international students; for summer admission, 4/16 for domestic and international students. Applications are processed on a rolling basis. *Application fee:* $40. Electronic applications accepted. *Application Contact:* Francesca Reed, Director, Graduate Admissions, 703-284-5901, Fax: 703-527-3815, E-mail: grad.admissions@marymount.edu. *Dean*, James Ryerson, 703-284-5910, Fax: 703-527-3830, E-mail: james.ryerson@marymount.edu.

School of Education and Human Services Students: 273 full-time (243 women), 175 part-time (133 women); includes 122 minority (42 Black or African American, non-Hispanic/Latino; 2 American Indian or Alaska Native, non-Hispanic/Latino; 17 Asian, non-Hispanic/Latino; 43 Hispanic/Latino; 18 Two or more races, non-Hispanic/Latino), 13 international. Average age 29. 275 applicants, 86% accepted, 172 enrolled. *Faculty:* 21 full-time (18 women), 25 part-time/adjunct (19 women). Expenses: Contact institution. *Financial support:* In 2017–18, 38 students received support, including 11 research assistantships with full and partial tuition reimbursements available (averaging $9,791 per year), 15 teaching assistantships with full and partial tuition reimbursements available (averaging $9,693 per year); career-related internships or fieldwork, Federal Work-Study, scholarships/grants, and unspecified assistantships also available. Support available to part-time students. Financial award application deadline: 3/1; financial award applicants required to submit FAFSA. In 2017, 188 master's awarded. *Program availability:* Part-time, evening/weekend. Offers clinical mental health counseling (MA); curriculum and instruction (M Ed); education and human services (M Ed, MA); elementary education (M Ed); forensic and legal psychology (MA); intelligence studies (MA); pastoral counseling (MA); professional studies (M Ed); school counseling (MA); secondary education (M Ed); special education: general curriculum (M Ed). *Application deadline:* For fall admission, 1/15 priority date for domestic and international students; for spring admission, 10/5 for domestic and international students. Applications are processed on a rolling basis. *Application fee:* $40. Electronic applications accepted. *Application Contact:* Francesca Reed, Director, Graduate Admissions, 703-284-5901, Fax: 703-527-3815, E-mail: grad.admissions@marymount.edu. *Dean*, Dr. Lois Stover, 703-284-1620, Fax: 703-284-1631, E-mail: lois.stover@marymount.edu.

MARYVILLE UNIVERSITY OF SAINT LOUIS, St. Louis, MO 63141-7299

General Information Independent, coed, university. *Enrollment:* 7,689 graduate, professional, and undergraduate students; 552 full-time matriculated graduate/professional students (358 women), 3,946 part-time matriculated graduate/professional students (3,205 women). *Enrollment by degree level:* 3,935 master's, 563 doctoral. *Graduate faculty:* 84 full-time (64 women), 234 part-time/adjunct (165 women). *Tuition:* Part-time $675 per credit hour. One-time fee: $350 part-time. Tuition and fees vary according to program. *Graduate housing:* Room and/or apartments available on a first-come, first-served basis to single students; on-campus housing not available to married students. Typical cost: $7800 per year. Room charges vary according to board plan and housing facility selected. Housing application deadline: 5/1. *Student services:* Campus employment opportunities, campus safety program, career counseling, exercise/wellness program, free psychological counseling, international student services, low-cost health insurance, multicultural affairs office, services for students with disabilities, teacher training, writing training. *Library facilities:* University Library. *Collection:* Books: 59,580 (physical), 231,310 (digital/electronic); Serial titles: 60,067 (digital/electronic); Databases: 129. Weekly public service hours: 101; study areas open 24 hours, 5–7 days a week. *Research affiliation:* Monsanto Fund (STEM, computer coding), Southwestern Bell Foundation (secondary education curriculum and teacher education).

Computer facilities: 563 computers available on campus for general student use. A campuswide network can be accessed from student residence rooms and from off campus. Online class registration, specialized software, university catalog are available.
Website: http://www.maryville.edu/

General Application Contact: Jeannie DeLuca, Director of Admissions and Advising for Online Programs, 314-529-9355, Fax: 314-529-9927, E-mail: jdeluca@maryville.edu.

GRADUATE UNITS

College of Arts and Sciences Students: 57 full-time (30 women), 25 part-time (17 women); includes 10 minority (1 Black or African American, non-Hispanic/Latino; 1 American Indian or Alaska Native, non-Hispanic/Latino; 7 Asian, non-Hispanic/Latino; 1 Two or more races, non-Hispanic/Latino), 45 international. Average age 28. *Faculty:* 7 full-time (4 women), 10 part-time/adjunct (4 women). Expenses: Contact institution. *Financial support:* Application deadline: 4/1; applicants required to submit FAFSA. In 2017, 26 master's awarded. *Program availability:* Part-time. Offers actuarial science (MS); data science (MS); strategic communication and leadership (MA). *Application deadline:* Applications are processed on a rolling basis. Electronic applications accepted. *Application Contact:* Shani Lenore-Jenkins, Associate Vice President of Enrollment, 314-529-9359, E-mail: slenore@maryville.edu. *Dean*, Cherie Fister, 314-529-9563, Fax: 314-529-9965, E-mail: cfister@maryville.edu.

The John E. Simon School of Business Students: 222 full-time (96 women), 498 part-time (222 women); includes 185 minority (104 Black or African American, non-Hispanic/Latino; 5 American Indian or Alaska Native, non-Hispanic/Latino; 30 Asian, non-Hispanic/Latino; 37 Hispanic/Latino; 9 Two or more races, non-Hispanic/Latino), 26 international. Average age 33. *Faculty:* 5 full-time (3 women), 51 part-time/adjunct (16 women). Expenses: Contact institution. *Financial support:* Career-related internships or fieldwork, Federal Work-Study, tuition waivers (partial), and campus employment available. Financial award application deadline: 4/1; financial award applicants required to submit FAFSA. In 2017, 106 master's awarded. *Program availability:* Part-time, 100% online, blended/hybrid learning. Offers accounting (MBA, MS, Certificate); business studies (Certificate); cybersecurity (MBA, MS, Certificate); financial services (MBA, Certificate); healthcare practice management (MBA, Certificate); human resource management (MBA, Certificate); information technology (MBA, Certificate); management (MBA, Certificate); management and leadership (MA); marketing (MBA, Certificate); project management (MBA, Certificate); sport business management (MBA); supply chain management (Certificate); supply chain management/logistics (MBA). *Application deadline:* Applications are processed on a rolling basis. Electronic applications accepted. *Application Contact:* Dustin Loeffler, Director for Graduate Studies in Business, 314-529-9571, Fax: 314-529-9975, E-mail: dloeffler@maryville.edu. *Interim Dean*, Pam Horwitz, 314-529-9680, Fax: 314-529-9975.

Myrtle E. and Earl E. Walker College of Health Professions Students: 269 full-time (229 women), 3,090 part-time (2,719 women); includes 795 minority (385 Black or African American, non-Hispanic/Latino; 51 American Indian or Alaska Native, non-Hispanic/Latino; 136 Asian, non-Hispanic/Latino; 158 Hispanic/Latino; 65 Two or more races, non-Hispanic/Latino), 23 international. Average age 35. *Faculty:* 52 full-time (43 women), 152 part-time/adjunct (132 women). Expenses: Contact institution. *Financial support:* Career-related internships or fieldwork, Federal Work-Study, and campus employment available. Financial award application deadline: 4/1; financial award applicants required to submit FAFSA. In 2017, 895 master's, 80 doctorates awarded. *Program availability:* Part-time, 100% online, blended/hybrid learning. Offers health professions (MARC, MMT, MOT, MS, MSN, DNP, DPT, Post-MSN Certificate); marriage and family therapy (MARC); music therapy (MARC); occupational therapy (MOT); physical therapy (DPT); speech-language pathology (MS); substance abuse (MARC). *Application deadline:* Applications are processed on a rolling basis. Electronic applications accepted. *Application Contact:* Jeannie DeLuca, Director of Admissions and Advising, 314-529-9355, Fax: 314-529-9927, E-mail: jdeluca@maryville.edu. *Dean*, Dr. Charles Gulas, 314-529-9625, Fax: 314-529-9495, E-mail: hlthprofessions@maryville.edu.

The Catherine McAuley School of Nursing Students: 49 full-time (42 women), 2,999 part-time (2,645 women); includes 773 minority (375 Black or African American, non-Hispanic/Latino; 51 American Indian or Alaska Native, non-Hispanic/Latino; 135 Asian, non-Hispanic/Latino; 149 Hispanic/Latino; 63 Two or more races, non-Hispanic/Latino), 21 international. Average age 36. *Faculty:* 15 full-time (all women), 142 part-time/adjunct (123 women). Expenses: Contact institution. *Financial support:* Federal Work-Study and campus employment available. Support available to part-time students. Financial award application deadline: 4/1; financial award applicants required to submit FAFSA. In 2017, 843 master's, 42 doctorates awarded. *Program availability:* 100% online, blended/hybrid learning. Offers acute care nurse practitioner (MSN); adult gerontology nurse practitioner (MSN); advanced practice nursing (DNP); family nurse practitioner (MSN); pediatric nurse practitioner (MSN). *Application deadline:* Applications are processed on a rolling basis. Electronic applications accepted. *Application Contact:* Jeannie DeLuca, Director of Admissions and Advising, 314-929-9355, Fax: 314-529-9927, E-mail: cjacobsmeyer@maryville.edu. *Assistant Dean/Director of Online Nursing*, Dr. Elizabeth Buck, 314-529-9453, Fax: 314-529-9139, E-mail: ebuck@maryville.edu.

School of Education Students: 6 full-time (4 women), 337 part-time (250 women); includes 101 minority (85 Black or African American, non-Hispanic/Latino; 4 Asian, non-Hispanic/Latino; 8 Hispanic/Latino; 4 Two or more races, non-Hispanic/Latino), 3 international. Average age 38. *Faculty:* 20 full-time (14 women), 19 part-time/adjunct (13 women). Expenses: Contact institution. *Financial support:* Career-related internships or fieldwork, Federal Work-Study, tuition waivers (partial), and professional educator discounts available. Financial award application deadline: 4/1; financial award applicants required to submit FAFSA. In 2017, 34 master's, 67 doctorates awarded. *Program availability:* Part-time, 100% online, blended/hybrid learning. Offers early childhood education (MA Ed); educational leadership (Ed D); elementary education (MA Ed); higher education leadership (Ed D); literacy specialist (MA Ed); middle grades education (MA Ed); secondary teaching and inquiry (MA Ed); teacher as leader (MA Ed, Ed D). *Application deadline:* Applications are processed on a rolling basis. Electronic applications accepted. *Application Contact:* Stacey Ruffin, Coordinator of Clinical Experiences and Graduate Programs, 314-529-9542, Fax: 314-529-9921, E-mail: teachered@maryville.edu. *Dean*, Dr. Cathy Bear, 314-529-9692, Fax: 314-529-9921, E-mail: cbear@maryville.edu.

MARYWOOD UNIVERSITY, Scranton, PA 18509-1598

General Information Independent-religious, coed, comprehensive institution. *Graduate housing:* Room and/or apartments available on a first-come, first-served basis to single students; on-campus housing not available to married students.

GRADUATE UNITS

Academic Affairs *Program availability:* Part-time, evening/weekend, online learning. Electronic applications accepted.

Center for Interdisciplinary Studies *Program availability:* Part-time. Offers human development (PhD). Electronic applications accepted.

College of Health and Human Services *Program availability:* Part-time, online learning. Offers dietetic internship (Certificate); gerontology (MS); health and human services (MHSA, MPA, MS, MSW, Certificate); health services administration (MHSA); nutrition (MS); physician assistant studies (MS); public administration (MPA); social work (MHSA, MPA, MS, MSW); sports nutrition and exercise science (MS). Electronic applications accepted.

Insalaco College of Creative and Performing Arts *Program availability:* Part-time. Offers art (Graduate Certificate); art education (MA); art therapy (MA, Graduate Certificate); clay (MA, MFA); communication arts (MA); creative and performing arts (MA, MFA, MMT, Graduate Certificate); graphic design (MFA); illustration (MFA); music education (MA); painting (MA, MFA); photography (MA, MFA); printmaking (MA, MFA); sculpture (MA, MFA); studio art (MA); visual arts (MFA). Electronic applications accepted.

Munley College of Liberal Arts and Sciences *Program availability:* Part-time, online learning. Offers biotechnology (MS); criminal justice (MS); finance/investment (MBA); general management (MBA); information security (MS); liberal arts and sciences (MBA, MS); management information systems (MBA, MS). Electronic applications accepted.

Reap College of Education and Human Development *Program availability:* Part-time. Offers clinical psychology (Psy D); clinical services (MA); counselor education (MS); early childhood intervention (MS); education and human development (M Ed, MA, MAT, MS, Psy D, Certificate, Post-Master's Certificate); general theoretical psychology (MA); higher education administration (MS); instructional leadership (M Ed); mental health counseling (MA); PK-4 education (MAT); psychology (MA); reading education (MS); school leadership (MS); secondary/K-12 education (MAT); special education (MS); special education administration and supervision (MS); speech-language pathology (MS).

School of Architecture *Program availability:* Part-time. Offers architecture (M Arch, MA); interior architecture/design (MA). Electronic applications accepted.

MASSACHUSETTS COLLEGE OF ART AND DESIGN, Boston, MA 02115-5882

General Information State-supported, coed, comprehensive institution. *Enrollment:* 2,065 graduate, professional, and undergraduate students; 97 full-time matriculated graduate/professional students (52 women), 35 part-time matriculated graduate/professional students (23 women). *Enrollment by degree level:* 127 master's, 5 other advanced degrees. *Graduate faculty:* 35 full-time (13 women), 49 part-time/adjunct (23 women). Tuition, state resident: part-time $780 per credit. Tuition, nonresident: part-time $780 per credit. Tuition and fees vary according to course load and program. *Graduate housing:* Room and/or apartments available on a first-come, first-served basis to single students; on-campus housing not available to married students. Typical cost: $13,360 per year ($16,732 including board). Room and board charges vary according to board plan. Housing application deadline: 5/1. *Student services:* Campus employment opportunities, campus safety program, career counseling, exercise/wellness program, free psychological counseling, international student services, low-cost health insurance, multicultural affairs office, services for students with disabilities, teacher training, writing training. *Library facilities:* Morton R. Godine Library. *Collection:* Books: 106,885 (physical), 173,498 (digital/electronic); Databases: 75.

Computer facilities: Computer purchase and lease plans are available. 370 computers available on campus for general student use. A campuswide network can be accessed from student residence rooms and from off campus. Online class registration is available.

Website: http://www.massart.edu/

General Application Contact: Lauren O'Neill, Assistant Director of Graduate Admissions, 617-879-7222, E-mail: gradadmissions@massart.edu.

GRADUATE UNITS

Graduate Programs Students: 97 full-time (52 women), 35 part-time (23 women); includes 24 minority (3 Black or African American, non-Hispanic/Latino; 13 Asian, non-Hispanic/Latino; 7 Hispanic/Latino; 1 Two or more races, non-Hispanic/Latino), 28 international. 358 applicants, 57% accepted, 77 enrolled. *Faculty:* 35 full-time (13 women), 49 part-time/adjunct (23 women). Expenses: Contact institution. *Financial support:* In 2017–18, 88 students received support, including 1 research assistantship (averaging $2,160 per year), 53 teaching assistantships (averaging $2,160 per year); fellowships, career-related internships or fieldwork, scholarships/grants, traineeships, tuition waivers (partial), unspecified assistantships, and adjunct co-teaching positions also available. Support available to part-time students. Financial award application deadline: 1/4; financial award applicants required to submit FAFSA. In 2017, 55 master's, 5 other advanced degrees awarded. Offers 2D fine arts (MFA); 3D fine arts (MFA); architecture (M Arch); art education (M Ed, MAT); art teacher preparation (Postbaccalaureate Certificate); design (MFA, Postbaccalaureate Certificate); design innovation (M Des); fine arts (MFA); media arts (MFA, Postbaccalaureate Certificate). *Application deadline:* For fall admission, 1/4 priority date for domestic and international students; for summer admission, 1/4 priority date for domestic and international students. *Application fee:* $90. Electronic applications accepted. *Application Contact:* Lauren O'Neill, Assistant Director of Graduate Admissions, 617-879-7203, E-mail: gradadmissions@massart.edu. *Dean of Graduate Studies*, Paul Paturzo, 617-879-7166, E-mail: pjpaturzo@massart.edu.

MASSACHUSETTS COLLEGE OF LIBERAL ARTS, North Adams, MA 01247-4100

General Information State-supported, coed, comprehensive institution. *Graduate housing:* On-campus housing not available.

GRADUATE UNITS

Graduate Programs *Program availability:* Part-time, evening/weekend. Offers business (MBA); educational administration (M Ed); educational leadership (CAGS); instruction and curriculum (M Ed); instructional technology (M Ed); physical education and health (M Ed); reading (M Ed); special education (M Ed).

MASSACHUSETTS INSTITUTE OF TECHNOLOGY, Cambridge, MA 02139-4307

General Information Independent, coed, university. CGS member. *Graduate housing:* Rooms and/or apartments available to single and married students. Housing application deadline: 5/15. *Research affiliation:* Novartis Pharmaceuticals (pharmaceutical manufacturing), Singapore National Research Foundation (infectious diseases, environmental sensing, biosystems, urban transportation, low power electronics), Woods Hole Oceanographic Institution (applied ocean science and engineering), Broad Institute (genomics and biomedical research), Whitehead Institute for Biomedical Research (developmental biology), Eni S.p.A (renewable energy).

GRADUATE UNITS

MIT Sloan School of Management Expenses: Contact institution. *Financial support:* Fellowships with tuition reimbursements, research assistantships with tuition reimbursements, teaching assistantships with tuition reimbursements, Federal Work-Study, institutionally sponsored loans, scholarships/grants, health care benefits, and unspecified assistantships available. Support available to part-time students. Offers management (M Fin, MBA, MS, SM, PhD). Electronic applications accepted. *Application Contact:* Rod Garcia, Director of Admissions, 617-253-5434, Fax: 617-253-6405, E-mail: mbaadmissions@sloan.mit.edu. *Dean,* David C. Schmittlein, 617-253-2804, Fax: 617-258-6617, E-mail: dschmitt@mit.edu.

Operations Research Center Offers operations research (SM, PhD). Electronic applications accepted.

School of Architecture and Planning Offers architecture (M Arch, PhD); architecture and planning (M Arch, MCP, MSRED, SM, SM Arch S, SMACT, SMBT, PhD); architecture studies (SM Arch S); art, culture and technology (SMACT); building technology (SMBT); city planning (MCP); media arts and sciences (SM, PhD); media technology (SM); urban and regional planning (PhD); urban and regional studies (PhD); urban studies and planning (SM). Electronic applications accepted.

Center for Real Estate Offers real estate development (MSRED). Electronic applications accepted.

School of Engineering Offers aeronautics and astronautics (SM, PhD, Sc D, EAA); aerospace computational engineering (PhD, Sc D); air transportation systems (PhD, Sc D); air-breathing propulsion (PhD, Sc D); aircraft systems engineering (PhD, Sc D); applied biosciences (PhD, Sc D); archaeological materials (PhD, Sc D); autonomous systems (PhD, Sc D); bioengineering (PhD, Sc D); biological engineering (PhD, Sc D); biological oceanography (PhD, Sc D); biomedical engineering (M Eng); chemical engineering (PhD, Sc D); chemical engineering practice (SM, PhD); chemical oceanography (PhD, Sc D); civil and environmental engineering (M Eng, SM, PhD, Sc D); civil and environmental systems (PhD, Sc D); civil engineering (PhD, Sc D, CE); civil engineering and computation (PhD); coastal engineering (PhD, Sc D); communications and networks (PhD, Sc D); computation for design and optimization (SM); computational and systems biology (PhD); computer science (PhD, Sc D, ECS); computer science and engineering (PhD, Sc D); computer science and molecular biology (M Eng); construction engineering and management (PhD, Sc D); controls (PhD, Sc D); electrical engineering (PhD, Sc D, EE); electrical engineering and computer science (M Eng, SM, PhD, Sc D); engineering (M Eng, SM, PhD, Sc D, CE, EAA, ECS, EE, Mat E, Mech E, NE, Naval E); engineering and management (SM); environmental biology (PhD, Sc D); environmental chemistry (PhD, Sc D); environmental engineering (PhD, Sc D); environmental engineering and computation (PhD); environmental fluid mechanics (PhD, Sc D); geotechnical and geoenvironmental engineering (PhD, Sc D); health sciences and technology (SM, PhD, Sc D); humans in aerospace (PhD, Sc D); hydrology (PhD, Sc D); information technology (PhD, Sc D); logistics (M Eng); manufacturing (M Eng); materials and structures (PhD, Sc D); materials engineering (Mat E); materials science and engineering (SM, PhD, Sc D); mechanical engineering (SM, PhD, Sc D, Mech E); naval architecture and marine engineering (SM, PhD, Sc D); naval engineering (Naval E); nuclear science and engineering (SM, PhD, Sc D, NE); ocean engineering (SM, PhD, Sc D); oceanographic engineering (SM, PhD, Sc D); space propulsion (PhD, Sc D); space systems (PhD, Sc D); structures and materials (PhD, Sc D); toxicology (SM); transportation (PhD, Sc D). Electronic applications accepted.

Institute for Data, Systems, and Society Offers social and engineering systems (PhD); technology and policy (SM). Electronic applications accepted.

School of Humanities, Arts, and Social Sciences Offers comparative media studies (SM); economics (SM, PhD); history, anthropology, and science, technology and society (PhD); humanities, arts, and social sciences (SM, PhD); linguistics (PhD); philosophy (PhD); political science (SM, PhD); science writing (SM). Electronic applications accepted.

School of Science Offers atmospheric chemistry (PhD, Sc D); atmospheric science (SM, PhD, Sc D); biochemistry (PhD); biological chemistry (PhD); biological oceanography (PhD); biology (PhD); biophysical chemistry and molecular structure (PhD); cell biology (PhD); chemical oceanography (SM, PhD, Sc D); climate physics and chemistry (SM, PhD, Sc D); cognitive science (PhD); computational and systems biology (PhD); developmental biology (PhD); earth and planetary sciences (SM); genetics (PhD); geochemistry (PhD, Sc D); geology (PhD, Sc D); geophysics (PhD, Sc D); immunology (PhD); inorganic chemistry (PhD); marine geology and geophysics (SM, PhD, Sc D); mathematics (PhD); microbiology (PhD); molecular biology (PhD); neurobiology (PhD); neuroscience (PhD); organic chemistry (PhD); physical chemistry (PhD); physical oceanography (SM, PhD, Sc D); physics (SM, PhD); planetary sciences (PhD, Sc D); science (SM, PhD, Sc D). Electronic applications accepted.

MASSACHUSETTS MARITIME ACADEMY, Buzzards Bay, MA 02532-1803

General Information State-supported, coed, comprehensive institution.

GRADUATE UNITS

Program in Emergency Management *Program availability:* Part-time-only, evening/weekend. Offers emergency management (MS). Electronic applications accepted.

Program in Facilities Management *Program availability:* Part-time-only, evening/weekend. Offers facilities management (MS). Electronic applications accepted.

MASSACHUSETTS SCHOOL OF LAW AT ANDOVER, Andover, MA 01810

General Information Independent, coed, graduate-only institution. *Graduate housing:* On-campus housing not available.

GRADUATE UNITS

Professional Program *Program availability:* Part-time, evening/weekend. Offers law (JD). Electronic applications accepted.

THE MASTER'S UNIVERSITY, Santa Clarita, CA 91321-1200

General Information Independent-religious, coed, comprehensive institution. *Graduate housing:* On-campus housing not available.

GRADUATE UNITS

The Master's Seminary *Program availability:* Part-time. Offers biblical counseling (MABC); New Testament (Th D); Old Testament (Th D); preaching (D Min); theology (M Div, M Th, Th D).

MAYO CLINIC GRADUATE SCHOOL OF BIOMEDICAL SCIENCES, Rochester, MN 55905

General Information Independent, coed, graduate-only institution. *Enrollment by degree level:* 149 doctoral. *Graduate faculty:* 394 full-time (130 women). *Graduate housing:* On-campus housing not available. *Student services:* Campus safety program, career counseling, exercise/wellness program, free psychological counseling, grant writing training, international student services, low-cost health insurance, services for students with disabilities, writing training. *Library facilities:* Mayo Clinic Libraries plus 11 others. *Collection:* Books: 400,000 (digital/electronic); Databases: 4,300. Study areas open 24 hours, 5–7 days a week; students can reserve study rooms.

Computer facilities: A campuswide network can be accessed from off campus. Online class registration is available.
Website: http://www.mayo.edu/mayo-clinic-school-of-medicine

General Application Contact: Sarah E. Giese, PhD Admissions Coordinator, 507-538-1160, Fax: 507-293-0838, E-mail: phd.training@mayo.edu.

GRADUATE UNITS

Program in Biochemistry and Molecular Biology Students: 42 full-time (21 women); includes 20 minority (2 Black or African American, non-Hispanic/Latino; 11 Asian, non-Hispanic/Latino; 6 Hispanic/Latino; 1 Native Hawaiian or other Pacific Islander, non-Hispanic/Latino). 51 applicants, 18% accepted, 7 enrolled. *Faculty:* 104 full-time (16 women). Expenses: Contact institution. *Financial support:* Fellowships with full tuition reimbursements available. Offers biochemistry and molecular biology (MS, PhD). *Application deadline:* For fall admission, 12/1 for domestic and international students. *Application fee:* $50. Electronic applications accepted. *Application Contact:* Sarah E Giese, Admissions Coordinator, 507-538-1160, E-mail: phd.training@mayo.edu. *Director,* Dr. David J. Katzmann, 507-284-3320, E-mail: katzmann.david@mayo.edu.

Program in Biomedical Engineering and Physiology Students: 28 full-time (11 women); includes 3 minority (1 American Indian or Alaska Native, non-Hispanic/Latino; 2 Asian, non-Hispanic/Latino). 38 applicants, 32% accepted, 6 enrolled. *Faculty:* 77 full-time (10 women). Expenses: Contact institution. *Financial support:* Fellowships with full tuition reimbursements available. Offers biomedical engineering and physiology (MS, PhD). *Application deadline:* For fall admission, 12/1 for domestic and international students. *Application fee:* $50. Electronic applications accepted. *Application Contact:* Sarah E. Giese, Admissions Coordinator, 507-538-1160, E-mail: phd.training@mayo.edu. *Director,* Dr. Carlos B. Mantilla, 507-255-8544, E-mail: mantilla.carlos@mayo.edu.

Program in Clinical and Translational Science Students: 28 full-time (20 women); includes 15 minority (4 Black or African American, non-Hispanic/Latino; 6 Asian, non-Hispanic/Latino; 4 Hispanic/Latino; 1 Native Hawaiian or other Pacific Islander, non-Hispanic/Latino). 14 applicants, 36% accepted, 4 enrolled. *Faculty:* 69 full-time (16 women). Expenses: Contact institution. *Financial support:* Fellowships with full tuition reimbursements available. Offers clinical and translational science (MS); laboratory-based translational science (PhD); patient-based translational science (PhD); population-based translational science (PhD). *Application deadline:* For fall admission, 12/1 for domestic and international students. *Application fee:* $50. Electronic applications accepted. *Application Contact:* Sarah E. Giese, PhD Admissions Coordinator, 507-538-1160, E-mail: phd.training@mayo.edu. *Director,* Anthony J. Windebank, MD, 507-293-7602, E-mail: windebank.anthony@mayo.edu.

Program in Immunology Students: 31 full-time (16 women); includes 6 minority (1 American Indian or Alaska Native, non-Hispanic/Latino; 3 Asian, non-Hispanic/Latino; 2 Hispanic/Latino). 38 applicants, 45% accepted, 8 enrolled. *Faculty:* 27 full-time (7 women). Expenses: Contact institution. *Financial support:* Fellowships with full tuition reimbursements available. Offers immunology (PhD). *Application deadline:* For fall admission, 12/1 for domestic and international students. *Application fee:* $50. Electronic applications accepted. *Application Contact:* Sarah E Giese, Admissions Coordinator, 507-538-1160, E-mail: phd.training@mayo.edu. *Director,* Dr. Karen Hedin, 507-284-2713, E-mail: hedin.karen@mayo.edu.

Program in Molecular Pharmacology and Experimental Therapeutics Students: 38 full-time (24 women); includes 13 minority (2 Black or African American, non-Hispanic/Latino; 1 American Indian or Alaska Native, non-Hispanic/Latino; 8 Asian, non-Hispanic/Latino; 2 Hispanic/Latino). 30 applicants, 23% accepted, 6 enrolled. *Faculty:* 19 full-time (1 woman). Expenses: Contact institution. *Financial support:* Fellowships with full tuition reimbursements available. Offers molecular pharmacology and experimental therapeutics (MS, PhD). *Application deadline:* For fall admission, 12/1 for domestic and international students. *Application fee:* $50. Electronic applications accepted. *Application Contact:* Sarah E Giese, Admissions Coordinator, 507-538-1160, E-mail: phd.training@mayo.edu. *Director,* Dr. Richard Weinshilboum, 507-284-4308, E-mail: weinshilboum.richard@mayo.edu.

Program in Neuroscience Students: 19 full-time (11 women); includes 6 minority (5 Asian, non-Hispanic/Latino; 1 Hispanic/Latino). 37 applicants, 19% accepted, 3 enrolled. *Faculty:* 32 full-time (7 women). Expenses: Contact institution. *Financial support:* Fellowships with full tuition reimbursements available. Offers neuroscience (MS, PhD). *Application deadline:* For fall admission, 12/1 priority date for domestic students, 12/1 for international students. *Application fee:* $50. Electronic applications accepted. *Application Contact:* Sarah E. Giese, Admissions Coordinator, 507-538-1160, E-mail: phd.training@mayo.edu. *Director,* Pamela J. McLean, 904-953-6692, E-mail: mclean.pamela@mayo.edu.

Program in Virology and Gene Therapy Students: 17 full-time (6 women); includes 4 minority (3 Asian, non-Hispanic/Latino; 1 Hispanic/Latino). 24 applicants, 25% accepted, 3 enrolled. *Faculty:* 12 full-time (4 women). Expenses: Contact institution. *Financial support:* Fellowships available. Offers virology and gene therapy (PhD). *Application deadline:* For fall admission, 12/1 for domestic and international students. *Application fee:* $50. Electronic applications accepted. *Application Contact:* Sarah E. Giese, Admissions Coordinator, 507-538-1160, E-mail: phd.training@mayo.edu. *Director,* Dr. Michael Barry, 507-538-1188, E-mail: barry.michael@mayo.edu.

MAYO CLINIC SCHOOL OF HEALTH SCIENCES, Rochester, MN 55905

General Information Independent, coed, graduate-only institution. *Enrollment:* 207 full-time matriculated graduate/professional students (136 women). *Enrollment by degree level:* 207 doctoral. *Graduate faculty:* 20 full-time (11 women). *Student services:* Campus employment opportunities, campus safety program, career counseling, exercise/wellness program, free psychological counseling, international student services, multicultural affairs office, services for students with disabilities, teacher training. *Library facilities:* Venables Health Sciences Library plus 3 others. *Collection:* Study areas open 24 hours, 5–7 days a week; students can reserve study rooms.

Computer facilities: A campuswide network can be accessed from student residence rooms and from off campus. Online class registration is available.
Website: http://www.mayo.edu/mayo-clinic-school-of-health-sciences

General Application Contact: Kammi Englund, Education Coordinator, 507-284-3678, Fax: 507-284-0656, E-mail: englund.kammi@mayo.edu.

GRADUATE UNITS

Doctor of Nurse Anesthesia Practice Program Expenses: Contact institution. *Financial support:* Institutionally sponsored loans, scholarships/grants, health care benefits, and stipends available. Financial award applicants required to submit FAFSA. Offers nurse anesthesia practice (DNAP). *Application deadline:* For fall admission, 8/1 for domestic students. *Application fee:* $50. Electronic applications accepted. *Application Contact:* Julie Predmore, Administrative Assistant, 507-286-4163, Fax: 507-284-2818, E-mail: predmore.julie@mayo.edu. *Director,* Dr. Mary E. Marienau, 507-284-8331, Fax: 507-284-2818, E-mail: marienau.mary@mayo.edu.

Program in Physical Therapy Expenses: Contact institution. *Financial support:* Scholarships/grants available. Financial award applicants required to submit FAFSA. Offers physical therapy (DPT). *Application deadline:* For fall admission, 10/16 for domestic and international students. Applications are processed on a rolling basis. Electronic applications accepted. *Application Contact:* Carol Cooper, Administrative Assistant, 507-284-2054, Fax: 507-284-0656, E-mail: cooper.carol@mayo.edu. *Director,* Dr. John Hollman, 507-284-2054, Fax: 507-284-0656, E-mail: hollman.john@mayo.edu.

MAYO CLINIC SCHOOL OF MEDICINE, Rochester, MN 55905

General Information Independent, coed, graduate-only institution. *Graduate housing:* On-campus housing not available.

GRADUATE UNITS

Professional Program Offers medicine (MD). MD offered through the Mayo Foundation's Division of Education; MD/PhD, MD/Certificate with Mayo Graduate School. Electronic applications accepted.

MCCORMICK THEOLOGICAL SEMINARY, Chicago, IL 60615

General Information Independent-religious, coed, graduate-only institution. *Graduate housing:* Rooms and/or apartments available on a first-come, first-served basis to single and married students. Housing application deadline: 7/1.

GRADUATE UNITS

Graduate and Professional Programs *Program availability:* Part-time, evening/weekend. Offers ministry (D Min); theological studies (MATS, Certificate); theology (M Div). M Div/MSW offered jointly with Loyola University Chicago, University of Chicago, and University of Illinois at Chicago.

MCDANIEL COLLEGE, Westminster, MD 21157-4390

General Information Independent, coed, comprehensive institution. *Enrollment:* 2,845 graduate, professional, and undergraduate students; 130 full-time matriculated graduate/professional students (94 women), 1,138 part-time matriculated graduate/professional students (929 women). *Enrollment by degree level:* 799 master's, 469 other advanced degrees. *Graduate faculty:* 30 full-time (21 women), 124 part-time/adjunct (79 women). *Tuition:* Full-time $11,760; part-time $490 per credit hour. Tuition and fees vary according to course load and program. *Graduate housing:* On-campus housing not available. *Student services:* Campus safety program, career counseling, exercise/wellness program, free psychological counseling, international student services, multicultural affairs office, services for students with disabilities, teacher training, writing training. *Library facilities:* Hoover Library. *Collection:* Books: 182,835 (physical), 177,580 (digital/electronic); Serial titles: 1,420 (physical), 65,808 (digital/electronic); Databases: 81. Study areas open 24 hours, 5–7 days a week; students can reserve study rooms.

Computer facilities: 138 computers available on campus for general student use. A campuswide network can be accessed from student residence rooms and from off campus. Online class registration, online billing summaries, financial aid letter, tax information are available.
Website: http://www.mcdaniel.edu/

General Application Contact: Crystal L. Perry, Assistant Director of Graduate Enrollment Management, 410-857-2516, Fax: 410-857-2515, E-mail: cperry@mcdaniel.edu.

GRADUATE UNITS

Graduate and Professional Studies Students: 130 full-time (94 women), 1,138 part-time (929 women); includes 209 minority (134 Black or African American, non-Hispanic/Latino; 2 American Indian or Alaska Native, non-Hispanic/Latino; 21 Asian, non-Hispanic/Latino; 41 Hispanic/Latino; 1 Native Hawaiian or other Pacific Islander, non-Hispanic/Latino; 10 Two or more races, non-Hispanic/Latino), 16 international. Average age 33. 183 applicants, 95% accepted, 121 enrolled. *Faculty:* 30 full-time (21 women), 124 part-time/adjunct (79 women). Expenses: Contact institution. *Financial support:* Career-related internships or fieldwork, institutionally sponsored loans, scholarships/grants, and unspecified assistantships available. Support available to part-time students. Financial award application deadline: 3/1; financial award applicants required to submit FAFSA. In 2017, 277 master's, 189 other advanced degrees awarded. *Program availability:* Part-time, evening/weekend, 100% online, blended/hybrid learning. Offers counseling (MS); curriculum and instruction (MS); deaf education (MS); educational leadership (MS); elementary education (MS); elementary STEM instructional leader (Postbaccalaureate Certificate); equity and excellence in education (Postbaccalaureate Certificate); gerontology (MS, Postbaccalaureate Certificate); human resources development (MS); human services management (MS); kinesiology (MS); learning technology specialist (Postbaccalaureate Certificate); liberal arts (MLA); reading specialists: literacy leadership (MS); school librarianship (MS); secondary education (MS); special education (MS); teaching of English to speakers of other languages (MS); writing for children and young adults (Postbaccalaureate Certificate). *Application deadline:* For fall admission, 6/1 priority date for domestic students; for spring admission, 11/1 priority date for domestic students; for summer admission, 3/1 priority date for domestic students. Applications are processed on a rolling basis. *Application fee:* $75. Electronic applications accepted. *Application Contact:* Penny Pfeiffer, Senior Graduate Enrollment Management Specialist, 410-857-2513, Fax: 410-857-2515, E-mail: ppfeiffer@mcdaniel.edu. *Dean, Graduate and Professional Studies,* Dr. J. Michael Tyler, 410-857-2525, Fax: 410-857-2515, E-mail: mtyler@mcdaniel.edu.

MCGILL UNIVERSITY, Montréal, QC H3A 2T5, Canada

General Information Province-supported, coed, university. CGS member. *Graduate housing:* Room and/or apartments available to married students; on-campus housing not available to single students.

GRADUATE UNITS

Faculty of Graduate and Postdoctoral Studies

Desautels Faculty of Management Offers administration (PhD); entrepreneurial studies (MBA); finance (MBA); general management (Post Master's Certificate); information systems (MBA); international business (MBA); international practicing management (MM); management (MBA); management for development (MBA); manufacturing management (MMM); marketing (MBA); operations management (MBA); public accountancy (Diploma); strategic management (MBA). MMM offered jointly with Faculty of Engineering; PhD with Concordia University, HEC Montreal, Université de Montréal, Université du Québec à Montréal.

Faculty of Agricultural and Environmental Sciences Offers agricultural and environmental sciences (M Sc, M Sc A, PhD, Certificate, Graduate Diploma); agricultural economics (M Sc); animal science (M Sc, M Sc A, PhD); biotechnology (M Sc A, Certificate); computer applications (M Sc, M Sc A, PhD); dietetics (M Sc A, Graduate Diploma); entomology (M Sc, PhD); environmental assessment (M Sc); food engineering (M Sc, M Sc A, PhD); food science and agricultural chemistry (M Sc, PhD); forest science (M Sc, PhD); grain drying (M Sc, M Sc A, PhD); human nutrition (M Sc, M Sc A, PhD); irrigation and drainage (M Sc, M Sc A, PhD); machinery (M Sc, M Sc A, PhD); microbiology (M Sc, PhD); micrometeorology (M Sc, PhD); neotropical environment (M Sc, PhD); parasitology (M Sc, PhD); plant science (M Sc, M Sc A, PhD, Certificate); pollution control (M Sc, M Sc A, PhD); post-harvest technology (M Sc, M Sc A, PhD); soil dynamics (M Sc, M Sc A, PhD); soil science (M Sc, PhD); structure and environment (M Sc, M Sc A, PhD); vegetable and fruit storage (M Sc, M Sc A, PhD); wildlife biology (M Sc, PhD).

Faculty of Arts Offers anthropology (MA, PhD); art history and communication studies (MA, PhD); arts (MA, MSW, PhD, Diploma); bioethics (MA); East Asian studies (MA, PhD); economics (MA, PhD); English (MA, PhD); French language and literature (MA, PhD); German studies (MA, PhD); Hispanic studies (MA, PhD); history (MA, PhD); history of medicine (MA); Islamic studies (MA, PhD, Diploma); Italian studies (MA, PhD); Jewish studies (MA); language acquisition (PhD); linguistics (MA, PhD); medical anthropology (MA); medical sociology (MA); neo-tropical environment (MA); philosophy (PhD); political science (MA, PhD); Russian literature (MA, PhD); social statistics (MA); social work (MSW, PhD, Diploma); sociology (MA, PhD, Diploma).

Faculty of Dentistry Offers forensic dentistry (Certificate); oral and maxillofacial surgery (M Sc, PhD).

Faculty of Education Offers counseling psychology (MA, PhD); culture and values in education (MA, PhD); curriculum studies (MA); education (M Ed, M Sc, MA, MLIS, PhD, Certificate, Diploma); educational leadership (MA, Certificate); educational psychology (M Ed, MA, PhD); educational studies (PhD); information studies (MLIS, PhD, Certificate, Diploma); integrated studies in education (M Ed); kinesiology and physical education (M Sc, MA, PhD, Certificate, Diploma); school/applied child psychology and applied developmental psychology (M Ed, MA, PhD, Diploma); second language education (MA, PhD).

Faculty of Engineering Offers aerospace (M Eng); affordable homes (M Arch II, Diploma); architectural history and theory (M Arch II); architecture (PhD); chemical engineering (M Eng, PhD); domestic environment (M Arch II); domestic environments (Diploma); electrical and computer engineering (M Eng, PhD); engineering (M Arch I, M Arch II, M Eng, M Sc, MMM, MUP, PhD, Diploma); environmental engineering (M Eng, M Sc, PhD); environmental planning (MUP); fluid mechanics (M Sc); fluid mechanics and hydraulic engineering (M Eng, PhD); housing (MUP); manufacturing management (MMM); materials engineering (M Eng, PhD); mechanical engineering (M Eng, M Sc, PhD); minimum cost housing in developing countries (M Arch II, Diploma); mining engineering (M Eng, M Sc, PhD, Diploma); professional architecture (M Arch I); rehabilitation of urban infrastructure (M Eng, PhD); soil behavior (M Eng, PhD); soil mechanics and foundations (M Eng, PhD); structures and structural mechanics (M Eng, PhD); transportation (MUP); urban design (MUP); urban planning, policy and design (PhD); water resources (M Sc); water resources engineering (M Eng, PhD).

Faculty of Law Offers air and space law (LL M, DCL, Graduate Certificate); bioethics (LL M); comparative law (LL M, DCL, Graduate Certificate); law (LL M, DCL). Applications for LL M with specialization in bioethics are made initially through the Biomedical Ethics Unit in the Faculty of Medicine.

Faculty of Medicine Offers anatomy and cell biology (M Sc, PhD); assessing driving capability (PGC); biochemistry (M Sc, PhD); biomedical engineering (M Eng, PhD); communication science and disorders (M Sc); communication sciences and disorders (PhD); community health (M Sc); environmental health (M Sc); epidemiology and biostatistics (M Sc, PhD, Diploma); experimental medicine (M Sc, PhD); genetic counseling (M Sc); health care evaluation (M Sc); human genetics (M Sc, PhD); medical anthropology (MA, PhD); medical history (MA, PhD); medical physics (M Sc, PhD); medical sociology (MA, PhD); medical statistics (M Sc); medicine (M Eng, M Sc, M Sc A, MA, PhD, Diploma, Graduate Diploma, PGC); microbiology and immunology (M Sc, M Sc A, PhD); neurology and neurosurgery (M Sc, PhD); nurse practitioner (Graduate Diploma); nursing (M Sc A, PhD); occupational health (M Sc, PhD); otolaryngology (M Sc); pathology (M Sc, PhD); pharmacology and therapeutics (M Sc, PhD); physiology (M Sc, PhD); psychiatry (M Sc); rehabilitation science (M Sc, PhD); speech-language pathology (M Sc A); surgery (M Sc, PhD).

Faculty of Religious Studies Offers religious studies (MA, STM, PhD).

Faculty of Science Offers atmospheric science (M Sc, PhD); bioinformatics (M Sc, PhD); chemical biology (M Sc, PhD); chemistry (M Sc, PhD); clinical psychology (PhD); computational science and engineering (M Sc); computer science (M Sc, PhD); earth and planetary sciences (M Sc, PhD); environment (M Sc, PhD); experimental psychology (M Sc, MA, PhD); geography (M Sc, MA, PhD); mathematics and statistics (M Sc, MA, PhD); neo-tropical environment (M Sc, MA, PhD); physical oceanography (M Sc, PhD); physics (M Sc, PhD); science (M Sc, MA, PhD); social statistics (MA).

Schulich School of Music Offers composition (M Mus, D Mus, PhD); music education (MA, PhD); music technology (MA, PhD); musicology (MA, PhD); performance (M Mus); performance studies (D Mus); sound recording (M Mus, PhD); theory (MA, PhD).

Professional Program in Dentistry Offers dentistry (DMD). Electronic applications accepted.

Professional Program in Medicine Offers medicine.

MCKENDREE UNIVERSITY, Lebanon, IL 62254-1299

General Information Independent-religious, coed, university. *Graduate housing:* On-campus housing not available.

GRADUATE UNITS

Graduate Programs *Program availability:* Part-time, evening/weekend. Offers business administration (MBA); clinical mental health counseling (MA); curriculum design and instruction (Ed D, Ed S); educational administration and leadership (MA Ed); educational studies (MA Ed); higher education administrative services (MA Ed); human resource management (MBA); international business (MBA); music education (MA Ed); nursing education (MSN); nursing management/administration (MSN); reading (MA Ed); special education (MA Ed); teacher leadership (MA Ed); teaching certification (MA Ed). Electronic applications accepted.

MCMASTER UNIVERSITY, Hamilton, ON L8S 4M2, Canada

General Information Province-supported, coed, university. CGS member. *Graduate housing:* Room and/or apartments available to single students; on-campus housing not available to married students. Housing application deadline: 6/30. *Research affiliation:* Commonwealth Development (telecommunications), Canadian Centre for Inland Waters (chemical and civil engineering).

GRADUATE UNITS

Faculty of Health Sciences *Program availability:* Part-time, online learning. Offers biochemistry and biomedical sciences (M Sc, PhD); blood and vascular (M Sc, PhD); genetics and cancer (M Sc, PhD); health research methodology (M Sc, PhD); health sciences (M Sc, PhD); immunity and infection (M Sc, PhD); metabolism and nutrition (M Sc, PhD); neurosciences and behavioral sciences (M Sc, PhD); nursing (M Sc, PhD); occupational therapy (M Sc); physiology/pharmacology (M Sc, PhD); physiotherapy (M Sc); rehabilitation science (M Sc, PhD); rehabilitation science (course-based) (M Sc).

McMaster Divinity College *Program availability:* Part-time. Offers Biblical studies (MA, MTS, Diploma); biblical studies (M Div); Christian interpretation/history (M Div, MA, MTS, Diploma); Christian ministry (M Div, MA, MTS, Diploma); Christian Studies (Certificate); Christian theology (PhD). Affiliated with the Toronto School of Theology.

School of Graduate Studies *Program availability:* Part-time.

DeGroote School of Business *Program availability:* Part-time. Offers business (MBA, PhD); human resources and management (MBA, PhD); information systems (PhD).

Faculty of Engineering *Program availability:* Part-time. Offers chemical engineering (M Eng, MA Sc, PhD); civil engineering (M Eng, MA Sc, PhD); computer science (M Sc, PhD); electrical engineering (M Eng, MA Sc, PhD); engineering (M Eng, M Sc, MA Sc, PhD); engineering physics (M Eng, MA Sc, PhD); materials engineering (M Eng, MA Sc, PhD); materials science (M Eng, PhD); mechanical engineering (M Eng, MA Sc, PhD); nuclear engineering (PhD); software engineering (M Eng, MA Sc, PhD).

Faculty of Humanities *Program availability:* Part-time, evening/weekend. Offers classics (MA, PhD); cultural studies and critical theory (MA); English (MA, PhD); French (MA); globalization studies (MA); history (MA, PhD); humanities (MA, PhD); philosophy (MA, PhD).

Faculty of Science *Program availability:* Part-time, evening/weekend. Offers analytical chemistry (M Sc, PhD); applied statistics (M Sc); astrophysics (PhD); biology (M Sc, PhD); chemical physics (M Sc, PhD); chemistry (M Sc, PhD); geochemistry (PhD); geology (M Sc, PhD); health and radiation physics (M Sc); human geography (MA, PhD); inorganic chemistry (M Sc, PhD); mathematics (M Sc, PhD); medical physics (M Sc, PhD); medical statistics (M Sc); organic chemistry (M Sc, PhD); physical chemistry (M Sc, PhD); physical geography (M Sc, PhD); physics (PhD); polymer chemistry (M Sc, PhD); psychology (M Sc, PhD); science (M Sc, MA, PhD); statistical theory (M Sc); statistics (M Sc).

Faculty of Social Sciences *Program availability:* Part-time, evening/weekend. Offers analysis of social welfare policy (MSW); analysis of social work practice (MSW); anthropology (MA, PhD); economics (MA, PhD); human biodynamics (M Sc, PhD); international relations (PhD); political science (MA); public and the global economy (MA); public policy (PhD); public policy and administration (MA); religious studies (MA, PhD); social sciences (M Sc, MA, MSW, PhD); sociology (MA, PhD); work and society (MA).

MCMURRY UNIVERSITY, Abilene, TX 79697

General Information Independent-religious, coed, comprehensive institution.

GRADUATE UNITS

Graduate Studies

MCNEESE STATE UNIVERSITY, Lake Charles, LA 70609

General Information State-supported, coed, comprehensive institution. *Graduate housing:* Room and/or apartments available on a first-come, first-served basis to single students. Housing application deadline: 8/15. *Student services:* Campus employment opportunities, campus safety program, career counseling, exercise/wellness program, free psychological counseling, grant writing training, international student services, low-cost health insurance, multicultural affairs office, services for students with disabilities, teacher training, writing training. *Library facilities:* Frazar Memorial Library plus 1 other.

Computer facilities: A campuswide network can be accessed. Online class registration is available.
Website: http://www.mcneese.edu/

General Application Contact: Darlene Smith, Administrative Assistant II, Dore' School of Graduate Studies, 337-562-4078, Fax: 337-475-5397, E-mail: admissions@mcneese.edu.

GRADUATE UNITS

Doré School of Graduate Studies Expenses: Contact institution. *Financial support:* Application deadline: 5/1. *Program availability:* Part-time, evening/weekend. *Application deadline:* For fall admission, 5/15 priority date for domestic and international students; for spring admission, 10/15 priority date for domestic and international students. Applications are processed on a rolling basis. *Application fee:* $20 ($30 for international students). *Director,* Dr. Dustin M. Hebert, 337-475-5394, Fax: 337-475-5397, E-mail: dhebert@mcneese.edu.

Burton College of Education Expenses: Contact institution. *Financial support:* Application deadline: 5/1. *Program availability:* Part-time, evening/weekend. Offers academically gifted education (M Ed); applied behavior analysis (MA, Graduate Certificate); counseling psychology (MA); curriculum and instruction (M Ed); early childhood education grades PK-3 (Postbaccalaureate Certificate); education (M Ed, MA, MAT, MS, Ed S, Graduate Certificate, Postbaccalaureate Certificate); educational leadership (M Ed, Ed S); educational technology (Ed S); educational technology leadership (M Ed); elementary education (MAT); elementary education grades 1-5 (Postbaccalaureate Certificate); exercise physiology (MS); general/experimental psychology (MA); health promotion (MS); instructional technology (MS); middle school education grades 4-8 (Postbaccalaureate Certificate); multiple levels grades K-12 (Postbaccalaureate Certificate); nutrition and wellness (MS); reading (M Ed); school counseling (M Ed); school librarian (Postbaccalaureate Certificate); secondary education (MAT); secondary education grades 6-12 (Postbaccalaureate Certificate); special education (M Ed); special education - mild/moderate grades 1-12 (MAT); special education, mild/moderate for elementary education grades 1-5 (Postbaccalaureate Certificate). *Application deadline:* For fall admission, 5/15 priority date for domestic and international students; for spring admission, 10/15 priority date for domestic and international students. Applications are processed on a rolling basis. *Application fee:* $20 ($30 for international students). *Application Contact:* Dr. Dustin M. Hebert, Director of Dore' School of Graduate Studies, 337-475-5396, Fax: 337-475-5397, E-mail: admissions@mcneese.edu. *Dean,* Dr. Wayne R. Fetter, 337-475-5432, Fax: 337-475-5467, E-mail: wfetter@mcneese.edu.

College of Business Expenses: Contact institution. *Financial support:* Application deadline: 5/1. *Program availability:* Part-time, evening/weekend. Offers business (MBA); business administration (MBA). *Application deadline:* For fall admission, 5/15 priority date for domestic and international students; for spring admission, 10/15 priority date for domestic and international students. Applications are processed on a rolling basis. *Application fee:* $20 ($30 for international students). *Application Contact:* Dr. Akm Rahman, MBA Director, 337-475-5576, Fax: 337-475-5986, E-mail: mrahman@mcneese.edu. *Interim Dean,* Dr. Cynthia Cano, 337-475-5562, Fax: 337-475-5010, E-mail: ccano@mcneese.edu.

College of Engineering and Computer Science Expenses: Contact institution. *Financial support:* Application deadline: 5/1. *Program availability:* Part-time, evening/weekend. Offers chemical engineering (M Eng); civil engineering (M Eng); electrical engineering (M Eng); engineering management (M Eng); mechanical engineering (M Eng). *Application deadline:* For fall admission, 5/15 priority date for domestic and international students; for spring admission, 10/15 priority date for domestic and international students. Applications are processed on a rolling basis. *Application fee:* $20 ($30 for international students). *Application Contact:* Dr. Dustin M. Hebert, Director of Dore' School of Graduate Studies, 337-475-5396, Fax: 337-475-5397, E-mail: admissions@mcneese.edu. *Dean,* Dr. Nikos Kiritsis, 337-475-5875, Fax: 337-475-5237, E-mail: nikosk@mcneese.edu.

College of Liberal Arts Expenses: Contact institution. *Financial support:* Application deadline: 5/1. *Program availability:* Part-time, evening/weekend. Offers creative writing (MFA); criminal justice (MS); liberal arts (MA, MFA, MS, Postbaccalaureate Certificate); literature (MA). *Application deadline:* For fall admission, 5/15 priority date for domestic and international students; for spring admission, 10/15 priority date for domestic and international students. Applications are processed on a rolling basis. *Application fee:* $20 ($30 for international students). *Application Contact:* Dr. Dustin M. Hebert, Director of Dore' School of Graduate Studies, 337-475-5396, Fax: 337-475-5397, E-mail: admissions@mcneese.edu. *Interim Dean,* Dr. Michael Buckles, 337-475-5192, Fax: 337-475-5594, E-mail: mbuckles@mcneese.edu.

College of Nursing and Health Professions Expenses: Contact institution. *Financial support:* Application deadline: 5/1. Offers family nurse practitioner (MSN); nurse educator (MSN); nursing and health professions (MSN, PMC); psychiatric/mental health nurse practitioner (MSN). *Application deadline:* For fall admission, 5/15 priority date for domestic and international students; for spring admission, 10/15 priority date for domestic and international students. Applications are processed on a rolling basis. *Application fee:* $20 ($30 for international students). *Application Contact:* Dr. Ann Warner, Co-Coordinator, 337-475-5831, Fax: 337-475-5702, E-mail: awarner@mcneese.edu. *Dean,* Dr. Peggy L. Wolfe, 337-475-5820, Fax: 337-475-5924, E-mail: pwolfe@mcneese.edu.

College of Science and Agriculture Expenses: Contact institution. *Financial support:* Application deadline: 5/1. *Program availability:* Part-time, evening/weekend. Offers agricultural sciences (MS); computer science (MS); environmental and chemical sciences (MS); environmental science (MS); mathematics (MS); science and agriculture (MS); statistics (MS). *Application deadline:* For fall admission, 5/15 priority date for domestic and international students; for spring admission, 10/15 priority date for domestic and international students. Applications are processed on a rolling basis. *Application fee:* $20 ($30 for international students). *Application Contact:* Dr. Dustin M. Hebert, Director of Dore' School of Graduate Studies, 337-475-5396, Fax: 337-475-5397, E-mail: admissions@mcneese.edu. *Dean,* Dr. George F. Mead, Jr., 337-475-5785, Fax: 337-475-5249, E-mail: mead@mcneese.edu.

MCPHERSON COLLEGE, McPherson, KS 67460-1402

General Information Independent-religious, coed, comprehensive institution. *Graduate housing:* On-campus housing not available.

GRADUATE UNITS

Program in Education Offers education (M Ed).

MCPHS UNIVERSITY, Boston, MA 02115-5896

General Information Independent, coed, university. *Graduate housing:* Room and/or apartments available on a first-come, first-served basis to single students; on-campus housing not available to married students. Housing application deadline: 5/1. *Research affiliation:* Cephrim Biosciences, Inc. (pharmaceutics), Center for Analytical Science (analytical medicinal chemistry).

GRADUATE UNITS

Graduate Studies *Program availability:* Part-time. Offers drug regulatory affairs and health policy (MS); medicinal chemistry (MS, PhD); nursing (MS); pharmaceutics/industrial pharmacy (MS, PhD); pharmacology (MS, PhD); pharmacy (Pharm D); pharmacy and health sciences (MPAS, MS, PhD, Pharm D); physician assistant studies (MPAS).

New England School of Acupuncture *Program availability:* Part-time. Offers acupuncture (M Ac); acupuncture and Oriental medicine (MAOM).

School of Optometry Offers optometry (OD).

School of Pharmacy–Worcester/Manchester Offers pharmacy (Pharm D).

School of Physical Therapy Offers physical therapy (DPT).

MEADVILLE LOMBARD THEOLOGICAL SCHOOL, Chicago, IL 60637-1602

General Information Independent-religious, coed, graduate-only institution. *Graduate housing:* Rooms and/or apartments available on a first-come, first-served basis to single and married students. Housing application deadline: 3/15.

GRADUATE UNITS

Graduate and Professional Programs *Program availability:* Part-time, online learning. Offers divinity (M Div); ministry (D Min); religion (MA). M Div/MSW offered jointly with University of Chicago.

MEDAILLE COLLEGE, Buffalo, NY 14214-2695

General Information Independent, coed, comprehensive institution. *Graduate housing:* Rooms and/or apartments available on a first-come, first-served basis to single and married students. Housing application deadline: 8/15.

GRADUATE UNITS

Program in Business Administration - Amherst *Program availability:* Evening/weekend. Offers business administration (MBA); organizational leadership (MA). Electronic applications accepted.

Program in Business Administration - Rochester *Program availability:* Evening/weekend. Offers business administration (MBA); organizational leadership (MA).

Program in Education *Program availability:* Part-time, evening/weekend. Offers adolescent education (MS Ed); curriculum and instruction (MS Ed); education preparation (MS Ed); literacy (MS Ed); special education (MS). Electronic applications accepted.

Programs in Psychology *Program availability:* Part-time, evening/weekend. Offers clinical psychology (Psy D); marriage and family therapy (MA); mental health counseling (MA); psychology (MA). Electronic applications accepted.

MEDICAL COLLEGE OF WISCONSIN, Milwaukee, WI 53226-0509

General Information Independent, coed, graduate-only institution. CGS member. *Graduate housing:* On-campus housing not available. *Student services:* Campus employment opportunities, campus safety program, career counseling, exercise/wellness program, free psychological counseling, grant writing training, international student services, low-cost health insurance, multicultural affairs office, services for students with disabilities. *Library facilities:* Todd Wehr Library plus 2 others. *Research affiliation:* General Electric Medical Systems (biophysics, radiology).

Computer facilities: 250 computers available on campus for general student use. Online class registration is available.
Website: http://www.mcw.edu/

General Application Contact: Director of Enrollment, 414-955-8218, Fax: 414-955-6555.

GRADUATE UNITS

Graduate School Expenses: Contact institution. *Financial support:* Research assistantships with full tuition reimbursements, career-related internships or fieldwork, Federal Work-Study, institutionally sponsored loans, scholarships/grants, traineeships, health care benefits, unspecified assistantships, and all full time PhD seekers receive a full tuition scholarship plus cost of living stipend available. Financial award application deadline: 2/15; financial award applicants required to submit FAFSA. *Program availability:* Part-time, evening/weekend, online learning. Offers biochemistry (PhD); biomedical sciences (MA, MPH, MS, PhD, Graduate Certificate); biostatistics (PhD); clinical and translational science (MS); neuroscience (PhD); pharmacology and toxicology (PhD); physiology (PhD); public and community health (PhD); public health (MPH, Graduate Certificate). *Application deadline:* For fall admission, 1/15 priority date for domestic students, 1/15 for international students; for spring admission, 12/1 priority date for domestic students, 12/1 for international students. Applications are processed on a rolling basis. *Application fee:* $50. Electronic applications accepted. *Application Contact:* Dr. Ravindra P. Misra, Dean, 414-955-8218, Fax: 414-955-6555, E-mail: gradschool@mcw.edu. *Dean,* Dr. Ravindra P. Misra, 414-955-8218, Fax: 414-955-6555, E-mail: gradschool@mcw.edu.

Center for Bioethics and Medical Humanities Expenses: Contact institution. *Financial support:* Available to part-time students. Application deadline: 2/15; applicants required to submit FAFSA. *Program availability:* Part-time. Offers bioethics (MA); clinical bioethics (Graduate Certificate); research ethics (Graduate Certificate). *Application deadline:* For fall admission, 1/15 priority date for domestic students. Applications are processed on a rolling basis. *Application fee:* $50. *Application Contact:* Recruitment Office, 414-955-4402, Fax: 414-955-6555, E-mail: gradschoolrecruit@mcw.edu.

Medical Scientist Training Program Expenses: Contact institution. *Application deadline:* For fall admission, 12/1 for domestic and international students. *Application fee:* $50. *Application Contact:* Dr. Joseph T. Barbieri, Director, 414-456-8412, E-mail: jtb01@mcw.edu. *Director,* Dr. Joseph T. Barbieri, 414-456-8412, E-mail: jtb01@mcw.edu.

Interdisciplinary Program in Biomedical Sciences Expenses: Contact institution. Offers biomedical sciences (PhD). *Application deadline:* For fall admission, 12/15 priority date for domestic students. Applications are processed on a rolling basis. *Application Contact:* Dr. Joseph C. Besharse, Director, 414-955-8063, Fax: 414-955-6517, E-mail: biomed@mcw.edu. *Director,* Dr. Joseph C. Besharse, 414-955-8063, Fax: 414-955-6517, E-mail: biomed@mcw.edu.

Medical School Expenses: Contact institution. *Financial support:* Fellowships, career-related internships or fieldwork, and institutionally sponsored loans available. Financial award applicants required to submit FAFSA. *Program availability:* Part-time, online learning. Offers anesthesiology (MSA); medicine (MSA, MD). *Application deadline:* For fall admission, 1/15 for domestic and international students. *Application fee:* $50. *Application Contact:* Registrar, 414-456-8733. *Provost/Executive Vice President/Dean,* Joseph E. Kerschner, 414-955-8739.

Pharmacy School Expenses: Contact institution. Offers pharmacy (Pharm D). *Application deadline:* For fall admission, 5/1 for domestic students. *Application Contact:* Dr. George E. MacKinnon, III, Dean, E-mail: gmackinnon@mcw.edu. *Dean,* Dr. George E. MacKinnon, III, E-mail: gmackinnon@mcw.edu.

MEDICAL UNIVERSITY OF SOUTH CAROLINA, Charleston, SC 29425

General Information State-supported, coed, upper-level institution. CGS member. *Research affiliation:* Novartis Pharmaceuticals (cancer), Boston Scientific Corporation (cardiovascular diseases), Genentech (Alzheimer's disease), AstraZeneca (cancer/cardiovascular diseases), Merck & Company, Inc. (neuroscience), Eli Lilly and Company (substance abuse).

GRADUATE UNITS

College of Dental Medicine Offers dental medicine (DMD). Electronic applications accepted.

College of Graduate Studies Offers biochemistry and molecular biology (MS, PhD); cancer biology (PhD); cardiovascular biology (PhD); cardiovascular imaging (PhD); cell and molecular pharmacology and experimental therapeutics (MS, PhD); cell injury and repair (PhD); cell regulation (PhD); craniofacial biology (PhD); drug discovery (PhD); genetics and development (PhD); marine biomedicine (PhD); medicinal chemistry (PhD); microbiology and immunology (MS, PhD); neurosciences (MS, PhD); pathology and laboratory medicine (MS, PhD); toxicology (PhD). Electronic applications accepted.

Division of Biostatistics and Epidemiology Offers biostatistics (MS, PhD); epidemiology (MS, PhD). Electronic applications accepted.

South Carolina Clinical and Translational Research Institute *Program availability:* Online learning. Offers clinical and translational research (MS). Electronic applications accepted.

College of Health Professions *Program availability:* Part-time. Offers anesthesia for nurses (MSNA); health administration (DHA); health administration-executive (MHA); health administration-global (MHA); health administration-residential (MHA); health and rehabilitation science (PhD); health professions (MHA, MS, MSNA, MSOT, DHA, DPT, PhD); occupational therapy (MSOT); physical therapy (DPT); physician assistant studies (MS). Electronic applications accepted.

College of Medicine Offers medicine (MD). Electronic applications accepted.

College of Nursing *Program availability:* Part-time, online learning. Offers adult-gerontology health nurse practitioner (MSN, DNP); advanced practice nursing (DNP); family nurse practitioner (MSN, DNP); nurse administrator (MSN); nurse educator (MSN); nursing (MSN, DNP, PhD); pediatric nurse practitioner (MSN, DNP). Electronic applications accepted.

South Carolina College of Pharmacy Offers pharmacy (Pharm D). Electronic applications accepted.

MEHARRY MEDICAL COLLEGE, Nashville, TN 37208-9989

General Information Independent-religious, coed, graduate-only institution. CGS member. *Graduate housing:* Rooms and/or apartments available on a first-come, first-served basis to single and married students.

GRADUATE UNITS

School of Dentistry Offers dentistry (DDS, PhD).

School of Graduate Studies *Program availability:* Online learning. Offers biochemistry and cancer biology (PhD); microbiology and immunology (PhD); neuroscience (PhD); pharmacology (PhD). Electronic applications accepted.

Division of Public Health Practice *Program availability:* Part-time, evening/weekend. Offers occupational medicine (MSPH); public health administration (MSPH).

School of Medicine Offers medicine (MD). Electronic applications accepted.

MELBOURNE BUSINESS SCHOOL, Carlton, Victoria 3053, Australia

General Information Independent, coed, graduate-only institution.

GRADUATE UNITS

Graduate Programs Offers business administration (Exec MBA, MBA); management (PhD); management science (PhD); marketing (PhD); social impact (Graduate Certificate).

MEMORIAL UNIVERSITY OF NEWFOUNDLAND, St. John's, NL A1C 5S7, Canada

General Information Province-supported, coed, university. CGS member. *Graduate housing:* Rooms and/or apartments available on a first-come, first-served basis to single and married students. *Research affiliation:* Eastern Regional Health Authority (health research).

GRADUATE UNITS

Faculty of Medicine *Program availability:* Part-time, online learning. Offers medicine (M Sc, PhD, Diploma). Electronic applications accepted.

Graduate Programs in Medicine *Program availability:* Part-time. Offers applied health services research (M Sc); cancer (M Sc, PhD); cardiovascular (M Sc, PhD); clinical epidemiology (M Sc, PhD, Diploma); community health (M Sc, PhD, Diploma); human genetics (M Sc, PhD); immunology (M Sc, PhD); medicine (M Sc, PhD, Diploma); neuroscience (M Sc, PhD). Electronic applications accepted.

School of Graduate Studies *Program availability:* Part-time, evening/weekend, 100% online, blended/hybrid learning. Offers applied psychological sciences (MAPS); aquaculture (M Sc); archaeology and physical anthropology (MA, PhD); atomic and molecular physics (PhD); biochemistry (M Sc, PhD); biology (M Sc, PhD); chemistry (M Sc, PhD); classics (MA); clinical psychology (Psy D); cognitive and behavioral ecology (M Sc, PhD); computer engineering (MA Sc); computer science (M Sc, PhD); condensed matter physics (PhD); economics (MA); employment relations (MER); English (MA, PhD); environmental science (M Env Sc, M Sc, PhD); environmental systems engineering and management (MA Sc); ethnomusicology (MA, PhD); experimental psychology (M Sc, PhD); fisheries resource management (MMS, Graduate Diploma); folklore (MA, PhD); food science (M Sc, PhD); French studies (MA); gender (PhD); gender studies (MGS); geography (M Sc, MA, PhD); geology (M Sc, PhD); geophysics (M Sc, PhD); German language and literature (M Phil, MA); history (MA, PhD); humanities (M Phil); instrumental analysis (M Sc); linguistics (MA, PhD); marine spatial planning and management (MMS); maritime sociology (PhD); mathematics (M Sc, PhD); philosophy (MA, PhD); physical oceanography (M Sc, PhD); physics (M Sc); political science (MA); religious studies (MA); scientific computing (M Sc); social and cultural anthropology (MA, PhD); sociology (M Phil, MA); statistics (M Sc, MAS, PhD); work and development (PhD). Electronic applications accepted.

Faculty of Business Administration *Program availability:* Part-time. Offers business administration (MBA). Electronic applications accepted.

Faculty of Education *Program availability:* Part-time. Offers counseling psychology (M Ed); curriculum, teaching, and learning studies (M Ed); education (PhD); educational leadership studies (M Ed, Graduate Diploma); information technology (M Ed); post-secondary studies (M Ed, Diploma). Electronic applications accepted.

Faculty of Engineering and Applied Science *Program availability:* Part-time. Offers civil engineering (M Eng, PhD); electrical and computer engineering (M Eng, PhD); mechanical engineering (M Eng, PhD); ocean and naval architecture engineering (M Eng, PhD). Electronic applications accepted.

School of Human Kinetics and Recreation *Program availability:* Part-time. Offers administration, curriculum and supervision (MPE); biomechanics/ergonomics (MS Kin); exercise and work physiology (MS Kin); psychology of sport, exercise and recreation (MS Kin); socio-cultural studies of physical activity and health (MS Kin). Electronic applications accepted.

School of Music Offers conducting (MMus); performance pedagogy (MMus); performing (MMus). Electronic applications accepted.

School of Nursing *Program availability:* Part-time. Offers nursing (MN, PhD). Electronic applications accepted.

School of Pharmacy *Program availability:* Part-time. Offers pharmacy (MSCPharm, PhD). Electronic applications accepted.

School of Social Work Offers social work (MSW, PhD). Electronic applications accepted.

MEMPHIS THEOLOGICAL SEMINARY, Memphis, TN 38104-4395

General Information Independent-religious, coed, graduate-only institution. *Graduate housing:* Rooms and/or apartments available on a first-come, first-served basis to single and married students. Housing application deadline: 7/15. *Research affiliation:* Lilly Foundation (technology, religion), Wabash Center for Teaching and Learning (theology, religion).

GRADUATE UNITS

Graduate and Professional Programs *Program availability:* Part-time. Offers theology (M Div, MAR, D Min).

MERCER UNIVERSITY, Macon, GA 31207

General Information Independent-religious, coed, university. *Enrollment:* 7,130 graduate, professional, and undergraduate students; 2,801 full-time matriculated graduate/professional students (1,752 women), 1,071 part-time matriculated graduate/professional students (776 women). *Enrollment by degree level:* 1,922 master's, 1,907 doctoral, 6 other advanced degrees. *Graduate faculty:* 231 full-time (111 women), 128 part-time/adjunct (77 women). *Graduate housing:* On-campus housing not available. *Student services:* Campus employment opportunities, campus safety program, career counseling, exercise/wellness program, free psychological counseling, international student services, low-cost health insurance, services for students with disabilities. *Library facilities:* Jack Tarver Library plus 3 others. *Collection:* Books: 551,308 (physical), 775,934 (digital/electronic); Serial titles: 4,242 (physical), 172,037 (digital/electronic); Databases: 226. Study areas open 24 hours, 5–7 days a week; students can reserve study rooms. *Research affiliation:* Memorial Health Care (medical research), Piedmont (medical research), Total Therapeutic Management (pharmaceuticals), The Coca Cola Company (pharmaceutical research), Georgia Neurological Institute (medical research), Medical Center of Central Georgia (medical research).

Computer facilities: A campuswide network can be accessed from student residence rooms and from off campus. Online class registration is available.
Website: http://www.mercer.edu/

General Application Contact: Tracey M. Wofford, Director of Graduate Admissions, 678-547-6422, Fax: 678-547-6422, E-mail: wofford_tm@mercer.edu.

GRADUATE UNITS

Graduate Studies, Cecil B. Day Campus Students: 1,729 full-time (1,226 women), 854 part-time (633 women); includes 1,413 minority (947 Black or African American, non-Hispanic/Latino; 35 American Indian or Alaska Native, non-Hispanic/Latino; 299 Asian, non-Hispanic/Latino; 101 Hispanic/Latino; 31 Two or more races, non-Hispanic/Latino), 125 international. Average age 30. *Faculty:* 139 full-time (77 women), 87 part-time/adjunct (66 women). Expenses: Contact institution. *Financial support:* Teaching assistantships, career-related internships or fieldwork, Federal Work-Study, and scholarships/grants available. Support available to part-time students. Financial award applicants required to submit FAFSA. In 2017, 518 master's, 247 doctorates, 40 other advanced degrees awarded. *Program availability:* Part-time, evening/weekend, 100% online, blended/hybrid learning. *Application Contact:* Tracey M. Wofford, Director of Admissions, 678-547-6422, E-mail: wofford_tm@mercer.edu. *Provost*, Dr. Scott Davis, 478-301-2110, E-mail: davis_ds@mercer.edu.

College of Health Professions Students: 345 full-time (261 women), 67 part-time (55 women); includes 167 minority (116 Black or African American, non-Hispanic/Latino; 28 Asian, non-Hispanic/Latino; 21 Hispanic/Latino; 2 Two or more races, non-Hispanic/Latino), 2 international. Average age 26. *Faculty:* 23 full-time (14 women), 10 part-time/adjunct (7 women). Expenses: Contact institution. *Financial support:* Federal Work-Study, traineeships, and unspecified assistantships available. In 2017, 83 master's, 37 doctorates awarded. Offers athletic training (MAT); clinical medical psychology (Psy D); physical therapy (DPT); physician assistant studies (MM Sc); public health (MPH). *Application Contact:* Laura Ellison, Director of Admissions and Student Affairs, 678-547-6391, E-mail: ellison_la@mercer.edu. *Dean/Clinical Professor*, Dr. Lisa Lundquist, 678-547-6308, E-mail: lundquist_lm@mercer.edu.

College of Pharmacy Students: 635 full-time (407 women), 6 part-time (4 women); includes 397 minority (150 Black or African American, non-Hispanic/Latino; 206 Asian, non-Hispanic/Latino; 27 Hispanic/Latino; 14 Two or more races, non-Hispanic/Latino), 43 international. Average age 26. 677 applicants, 48% accepted, 152 enrolled. *Faculty:* 44 full-time (27 women), 1 part-time/adjunct (0 women). Expenses: Contact institution. *Financial support:* In 2017–18, 238 students received support, including 10 research assistantships with full tuition reimbursements available (averaging $15,000 per year), 35 teaching assistantships with full tuition reimbursements available (averaging $15,000 per year); Federal Work-Study, scholarships/grants, and tuition waivers (full) also available. Financial award application deadline: 5/1; financial award applicants required to submit FAFSA. In 2017, 166 doctorates awarded. Offers pharmaceutical sciences (PhD); pharmacy (Pharm D). PharmD/MBA offered jointly with Eugene W. Stetson School of Business and Economics; PharmD/MPH with College of Health Professions; PharmD/MSHI with Penfield College. *Application deadline:* For fall admission, 6/3 for domestic and international students. Applications are processed on a rolling basis. Electronic applications accepted. *Application Contact:* Jordana S. Berry, Director of Admissions, 678-547-6182, Fax: 678-547-6518, E-mail: berry_js@mercer.edu. *Dean*, Dr. Brian L. Crabtree, 678-547-6306, Fax: 678-547-6315, E-mail: crabtree_bl@mercer.edu.

Eugene W. Stetson School of Business and Economics (Atlanta) Students: 222 full-time (130 women), 138 part-time (72 women); includes 154 minority (114 Black or African American, non-Hispanic/Latino; 1 American Indian or Alaska Native, non-Hispanic/Latino; 27 Asian, non-Hispanic/Latino; 8 Hispanic/Latino; 4 Two or more races, non-Hispanic/Latino), 76 international. Average age 31. 207 applicants, 77% accepted, 110 enrolled. *Faculty:* 22 full-time (8 women), 7 part-time/adjunct (3 women). Expenses: Contact institution. *Financial support:* In 2017–18, 25 students received support. Federal Work-Study and tuition discounts available. Financial award application deadline: 5/1; financial award applicants required to submit FAFSA. In 2017, 124 master's awarded. *Program availability:* Part-time, evening/weekend, 100% online, blended/hybrid learning. Offers accounting (M Acc); innovation (PMBA); international business (MBA). *Application deadline:* For fall admission, 6/15 priority date for domestic and international students; for spring admission, 11/1 priority date for domestic and international students; for summer admission, 3/15 priority date for domestic and international students. Applications are processed on a rolling basis. *Application fee:* $50 ($100 for international students). Electronic applications accepted. *Application Contact:* Lael Whiteside, Director of Admissions, 678-547-6300, Fax: 678-547-6160, E-mail: whiteside_l@mercer.edu. *Dean*, Dr. Susan P. Gilbert, 678-547-6438, Fax: 678-547-6337, E-mail: gilbert_sp@mercer.edu.

Georgia Baptist College of Nursing Students: 72 full-time (70 women), 33 part-time (29 women); includes 44 minority (29 Black or African American, non-Hispanic/Latino; 9 Asian, non-Hispanic/Latino; 3 Hispanic/Latino; 3 Two or more races, non-Hispanic/Latino), 1 international. Average age 36. 65 applicants, 66% accepted, 30 enrolled. *Faculty:* 10 full-time (9 women), 4 part-time/adjunct (3 women). Expenses: Contact institution. *Financial support:* In 2017–18, 23 students received support, including 1 research assistantship (averaging $6,000 per year); scholarships/grants also available. Financial award application deadline: 6/30; financial award applicants required to submit FAFSA. In 2017, 27 master's, 9 doctorates awarded. *Program availability:* Part-time, blended/hybrid learning. Offers adult gerontology acute care nurse practitioner (MSN, Certificate); family nurse practitioner (MSN, Certificate); nursing (PhD); nursing practice (DNP). *Application deadline:* For fall admission, 5/1 for domestic students, 3/1 for international students; for winter admission, 11/1 for domestic students, 9/1 for international students; for spring admission, 11/1 for domestic students, 10/1 for international students; for summer admission, 3/1 for domestic and international students. Applications are processed on a rolling basis. *Application fee:* $50. Electronic applications accepted. *Application Contact:* Janda Anderson, Director of Admissions, 678-547-6700, Fax: 678-547-6794, E-mail: anderson_j@mercer.edu. *Dean/Professor*, Dr. Linda Streit, 678-547-6793, Fax: 678-547-6796, E-mail: streit_la@mercer.edu.

James and Carolyn McAfee School of Theology Students: 93 full-time (60 women), 63 part-time (29 women); includes 88 minority (80 Black or African American, non-Hispanic/Latino; 1 American Indian or Alaska Native, non-Hispanic/Latino; 1 Asian, non-Hispanic/Latino; 4 Hispanic/Latino; 1 Native Hawaiian or other Pacific Islander, non-Hispanic/Latino; 1 Two or more races, non-Hispanic/Latino), 1 international. Average age 37. 36 applicants, 58% accepted, 14 enrolled. *Faculty:* 14 full-time (7 women), 5 part-time/adjunct (0 women). Expenses: Contact institution. *Financial support:* In 2017–18, 70 students received support. Career-related internships or fieldwork, Federal Work-Study, institutionally sponsored loans, and scholarships/grants available. Support available to part-time students. Financial award application deadline: 10/1; financial award applicants required to submit FAFSA. In 2017, 40 master's, 9 doctorates awarded. *Program availability:* Part-time, 100% online. Offers Christian ministry (MACM); Christian spirituality (D Min); divinity (M Div); preaching (D Min). *Application deadline:* For fall admission, 7/1 for domestic and international students; for spring admission, 11/15 for domestic and international students. Applications are processed on a rolling basis. *Application fee:* $50. Electronic applications accepted. *Application Contact:* Nathan Cost, Director of Admissions, 678-547-6451, Fax: 678-547-6478, E-mail: cost_na@mercer.edu. *Dean*, Dr. Jeffrey Willetts, 678-547-6470, Fax: 678-547-6478, E-mail: willetts_jg@mercer.edu.

Penfield College Students: 199 full-time (165 women), 266 part-time (218 women); includes 268 minority (226 Black or African American, non-Hispanic/Latino; 1 American Indian or Alaska Native, non-Hispanic/Latino; 19 Asian, non-Hispanic/Latino; 19 Hispanic/Latino; 3 Two or more races, non-Hispanic/Latino). Average age 32. 300 applicants, 45% accepted, 114 enrolled. *Faculty:* 17 full-time (10 women), 27 part-time/adjunct (24 women). Expenses: Contact institution. *Financial support:* In 2017–18, 32 students received support. Federal Work-Study, scholarships/grants, and unspecified assistantships available. Financial award applicants required to submit FAFSA. In 2017, 101 master's, 5 doctorates awarded. *Program availability:* Part-time, evening/weekend, 100% online, blended/hybrid learning. Offers certified rehabilitation counseling (MS); clinical mental health (MS); counselor education and supervision (PhD); criminal justice and public safety leadership (MS); health informatics (MS); human services (MS); organizational leadership (MS); school counseling (MS). *Application deadline:* For fall admission, 7/1 priority date for domestic and international students; for spring admission, 11/1 priority date for domestic and international students; for summer admission, 4/1 priority date for domestic and international students. *Application fee:* $35. Electronic applications accepted. *Application Contact:* Dr. Melissa McCants Cruz, Director of Graduate Admissions, 678-547-6024, E-mail: penfield.admissions@mercer.edu. *Dean*, Dr. Priscilla R. Danheiser, 678-547-6028, Fax: 678-547-6008, E-mail: danheiser_p@mercer.edu.

Tift College of Education (Atlanta) Students: 159 full-time (131 women), 284 part-time (229 women); includes 264 minority (232 Black or African American, non-Hispanic/Latino; 1 American Indian or Alaska Native, non-Hispanic/Latino; 9 Asian, non-Hispanic/Latino; 18 Hispanic/Latino; 4 Two or more races, non-Hispanic/Latino), 2 international. Average age 35. *Faculty:* 30 full-time (18 women), 34 part-time/adjunct (27 women). Expenses: Contact institution. *Financial support:* Federal Work-Study and unspecified assistantships available. Support available to part-time students. Financial award application deadline: 5/1; financial award applicants required to submit FAFSA. In 2017, 137 master's, 22 doctorates, 40 other advanced degrees awarded. *Program availability:* Part-time, evening/weekend. Offers curriculum and instruction (PhD); early childhood education (M Ed, MAT, Ed S); educational leadership (PhD); educational leadership P-12 (M Ed, Ed S); higher education leadership (M Ed); independent and charter school leadership (M Ed); middle grades education (M Ed, MAT); secondary education (M Ed, MAT); teacher leadership (Ed S). *Application deadline:* For fall admission, 8/1 for domestic and international students; for spring admission, 12/1 for domestic and international students; for summer admission, 5/1 for domestic and international students. Applications are processed on a rolling basis. *Application fee:* $25 ($50 for international students). Electronic applications accepted. *Dean*, Dr. Scott Davis, 478-301-2110, Fax: 478-301-5576.

Graduate Studies, Macon Campus Students: 134 full-time (53 women), 196 part-time (125 women); includes 132 minority (111 Black or African American, non-Hispanic/Latino; 2 American Indian or Alaska Native, non-Hispanic/Latino; 8 Asian, non-Hispanic/Latino; 8 Hispanic/Latino; 3 Two or more races, non-Hispanic/Latino), 8 international. Average age 30. *Faculty:* 90 full-time (35 women), 24 part-time/adjunct (8 women). Expenses: Contact institution. *Financial support:* Career-related internships or fieldwork, Federal Work-Study, and institutionally sponsored loans available. Support available to part-time students. In 2017, 151 master's, 17 doctorates awarded. *Program availability:* Part-time, evening/weekend. *Application Contact:* Tracey M. Wofford, Director of Graduate Admissions, 678-547-6422, E-mail: wofford_tm@mercer.edu. *Interim Dean of Graduate Studies/Professor of Mathematics*, Keith Howard, 478-301-5983, E-mail: howard_ke@mercer.edu.

Eugene W. Stetson School of Business and Economics (Macon) Students: 43 full-time (16 women), 27 part-time (11 women); includes 28 minority (20 Black or African American, non-Hispanic/Latino; 1 American Indian or Alaska Native, non-Hispanic/Latino; 3 Asian, non-Hispanic/Latino; 3 Hispanic/Latino; 1 Two or more races, non-Hispanic/Latino), 2 international. Average age 29. 69 applicants, 78% accepted, 27 enrolled. *Faculty:* 4 full-time (1 woman), 4 part-time/adjunct (2 women). Expenses: Contact institution. *Financial support:* Unspecified assistantships and employee tuition waivers available. In 2017, 47 master's awarded. *Program availability:* Part-time, evening/weekend. Offers business and economics (MBA); health care (MBA); innovation (MBA). *Application deadline:* For fall admission, 8/1 for domestic students; for spring admission, 12/1 for domestic students; for summer admission, 5/1 for domestic students. Applications are processed on a rolling basis. *Application fee:* $50 ($100 for international students). Electronic applications accepted. *Application Contact:* Carl Collins, Director of Graduate Admissions and Academic Advising Services, 478-301-2835, Fax: 478-301-2635, E-mail: collins_rc@mercer.edu. *Dean*, Dr. Susan P. Gilbert, 478-301-6438, E-mail: gilbert_sp@mercer.edu.

School of Engineering Students: 49 full-time (12 women), 51 part-time (17 women); includes 10 minority (4 Black or African American, non-Hispanic/Latino; 1 American Indian or Alaska Native, non-Hispanic/Latino; 4 Asian, non-Hispanic/Latino; 1 Hispanic/Latino), 21 international. Average age 26. *Faculty:* 25 full-time (8 women), 3 part-time/adjunct (1 woman). Expenses: Contact institution. *Financial support:* Federal Work-Study available. Financial award applicants required to submit FAFSA. In 2017, 67 master's awarded. *Program availability:* Part-time-only, evening/weekend, online learning. Offers biomedical engineering (MSE); computer engineering (MSE); electrical engineering (MSE); engineering management (MSE); environmental engineering (MSE); environmental systems (MS); mechanical engineering (MSE); software engineering (MSE); software systems (MS); technical communications management (MS); technical management (MS). *Application deadline:* For fall admission, 4/1 priority date for domestic and international students; for spring admission, 11/1 priority date for domestic and international students. Applications are processed on a rolling basis. *Application fee:* $75. *Application Contact:* Dr. Sinjae Hyun, Program Director, 478-301-2214, Fax: 478-301-5593, E-mail: hyun_s@mercer.edu. *Dean*, Dr. Laura W. Lackey, 478-301-4106, Fax: 478-301-5593, E-mail: lackey_l@mercer.edu.

Tift College of Education (Macon) Students: 33 full-time (18 women), 51 part-time (37 women); includes 49 minority (44 Black or African American, non-Hispanic/Latino; 2 Asian, non-Hispanic/Latino; 2 Hispanic/Latino; 1 Two or more races, non-Hispanic/Latino), 1 international. Average age 32. *Faculty:* 13 full-time (8 women), 1 part-time/adjunct (0 women). Expenses: Contact institution. *Financial support:* Federal Work-Study, institutionally sponsored loans, and unspecified assistantships available. Support available to part-time students. Financial award application deadline: 5/1; financial award applicants required to submit FAFSA. In 2017, 22 master's, 17 doctorates awarded. *Program availability:* Part-time, evening/weekend, 100% online, blended/hybrid learning. Offers curriculum and instruction (PhD); early childhood education (M Ed, Ed S); educational leadership (M Ed, PhD, Ed S); higher education leadership (M Ed); independent and charter school leadership (M Ed); secondary education (MAT); teacher leadership (Ed S). *Application deadline:* For fall admission, 8/1 for domestic and international students; for spring admission, 12/1 for domestic and international students. Applications are processed on a rolling basis. *Application fee:* $35. Electronic applications accepted. *Dean*, Dr. Scott Davis, 478-301-2110, Fax: 478-301-5576, E-mail: davis_ds@mercer.edu.

Townsend School of Music Students: 12 full-time (6 women), 1 (woman) part-time; includes 3 minority (2 Black or African American, non-Hispanic/Latino; 1 Hispanic/Latino). Average age 25. 25 applicants, 48% accepted, 9 enrolled. *Faculty:* 9 full-time (3 women), 3 part-time/adjunct (2 women). Expenses: Contact institution. *Financial support:* In 2017–18, 14 students received support. Tuition waivers (full) and unspecified assistantships available. Financial award application deadline: 6/1; financial award applicants required to submit FAFSA. In 2017, 11 master's awarded. Offers choral conducting (MM); church music (MM); collaborative piano (MM); instrumental conducting (MM); performance (MM). *Application deadline:* For fall admission, 6/1 for domestic students, 5/1 for international students. Applications are processed on a rolling basis. *Application fee:* $100. *Application Contact:* Director, 912-301-2700. *Director of Graduate Studies*, Dr. Richard G. Kosowski, 478-301-4167, Fax: 478-301-5633, E-mail: keith_cd@mercer.edu.

School of Medicine Offers medicine (MFT, MPH, MSA, MD).

Walter F. George School of Law Students: 372 full-time (190 women); includes 83 minority (45 Black or African American, non-Hispanic/Latino; 7 Asian, non-Hispanic/Latino; 26 Hispanic/Latino; 1 Native Hawaiian or other Pacific Islander, non-Hispanic/Latino; 4 Two or more races, non-Hispanic/Latino), 2 international. Average age 25. 788 applicants, 52% accepted, 122 enrolled. *Faculty:* 29 full-time (11 women), 22 part-time/adjunct (4 women). Expenses: Contact institution. *Financial support:* In 2017–18, 325 students received support, including 14 fellowships (averaging $3,714 per year), 35 research assistantships (averaging $277 per year); career-related internships or fieldwork, Federal Work-Study, institutionally sponsored loans, scholarships/grants, and institutional work-study also available. Support available to part-time students. Financial award application deadline: 4/1; financial award applicants required to submit FAFSA. In 2017, 124 doctorates awarded. Offers law (JD). JD/MBA offered jointly with Eugene W. Stetson School of Business and Economics. *Application deadline:* For fall admission, 3/15 priority date for domestic students. Applications are processed on a rolling basis. *Application fee:* $0. Electronic applications accepted. *Application Contact:* Judie Simpson, Admissions Specialist, 478-301-2605, Fax: 478-301-2989, E-mail: simpson_j@law.mercer.edu. *Dean*, Cathy Cox, 478-301-2602, Fax: 478-301-2101, E-mail: cox_c@law.mercer.edu.

MERCY COLLEGE, Dobbs Ferry, NY 10522-1189

General Information Independent-religious, coed, comprehensive institution. CGS member. *Enrollment:* 9,506 graduate, professional, and undergraduate students; 1,254 full-time matriculated graduate/professional students (931 women), 1,158 part-time matriculated graduate/professional students (956 women). *Enrollment by degree level:* 2,262 master's, 116 doctoral, 34 other advanced degrees. *Tuition:* Full-time $15,426; part-time $857 per credit hour. *Required fees:* $630; $158 per term. Tuition and fees vary according to course load, degree level and program. *Graduate housing:* Room and/or apartments available on a first-come, first-served basis to single students; on-campus housing not available to married students. Typical cost: $9950 per year ($14,500 including board). Room and board charges vary according to board plan. Housing application deadline: 7/1. *Student services:* Campus employment opportunities, campus safety program, career counseling, exercise/wellness program, free psychological counseling, international student services, services for students with disabilities, teacher training, writing training. *Library facilities:* Mercy College Library plus 3 others. *Collection:* Books: 85,689 (digital/electronic); Serial titles: 21,126 (digital/electronic). Students can reserve study rooms.

Computer facilities: Computer purchase and lease plans are available. 1,100 computers available on campus for general student use. A campuswide network can be accessed from student residence rooms and from off campus. Online class registration is available.
Website: http://www.mercy.edu/

General Application Contact: Allison Gurdineer, Senior Director of Admissions, 877-637-2946, Fax: 914-674-7382, E-mail: admissions@mercy.edu.

GRADUATE UNITS

School of Business Students: 416 full-time (259 women), 115 part-time (80 women); includes 359 minority (155 Black or African American, non-Hispanic/Latino; 1 American Indian or Alaska Native, non-Hispanic/Latino; 42 Asian, non-Hispanic/Latino; 151 Hispanic/Latino; 1 Native Hawaiian or other Pacific Islander, non-Hispanic/Latino; 9 Two or more races, non-Hispanic/Latino), 40 international. Average age 32. 354 applicants, 68% accepted, 134 enrolled. Expenses: Contact institution. *Financial support:* Career-related internships or fieldwork, Federal Work-Study, scholarships/grants, and unspecified assistantships available. Support available to part-time students. Financial award applicants required to submit FAFSA. In 2017, 234 master's awarded. *Program availability:* Part-time, evening/weekend, 100% online, blended/hybrid learning. Offers accounting (MS); business (MBA, MS); business administration (MBA); human resource management (MS); organizational leadership (MS). *Application deadline:* For fall admission, 8/1 for international students. Applications are processed on a rolling basis. *Application fee:* $40. Electronic applications accepted. *Application Contact:* Allison Gurdineer, Senior Director of Admissions, 877-637-2946, E-mail: admissions@mercy.edu. *Dean, School of Business*, Ed Weis, 914-674-7490, E-mail: eweis@mercy.edu.

School of Education Students: 187 full-time (163 women), 502 part-time (425 women); includes 345 minority (128 Black or African American, non-Hispanic/Latino; 2 American Indian or Alaska Native, non-Hispanic/Latino; 19 Asian, non-Hispanic/Latino; 189 Hispanic/Latino; 1 Native Hawaiian or other Pacific Islander, non-Hispanic/Latino; 6 Two or more races, non-Hispanic/Latino). Average age 32. 344 applicants, 40% accepted, 76 enrolled. Expenses: Contact institution. *Financial support:* Career-related internships or fieldwork, Federal Work-Study, scholarships/grants, and unspecified assistantships available. Support available to part-time students. Financial award applicants required to submit FAFSA. In 2017, 410 master's, 38 other advanced degrees awarded. *Program availability:* Part-time, evening/weekend, 100% online, blended/hybrid learning. Offers adolescence education (MS); childhood education (MS); early childhood education (MS); education (MS, Advanced Certificate); educational leadership (Advanced Certificate); teaching English to speakers of other languages (TESOL) (MS, Advanced Certificate); teaching literacy (Advanced Certificate); teaching literacy, birth-6 (MS); teaching literacy, grades 5-12 (MS). *Application deadline:* For fall admission, 8/1 for international students. Applications are processed on a rolling basis. *Application fee:* $40. Electronic applications accepted. *Application Contact:* Allison Gurdineer, Senior Director of Admissions, 877-637-2946, Fax: 914-674-7382, E-mail: admissions@mercy.edu. *Dean for the School of Education*, 914-674-7350.

School of Health and Natural Sciences Students: 379 full-time (290 women), 205 part-time (182 women); includes 273 minority (85 Black or African American, non-Hispanic/Latino; 76 Asian, non-Hispanic/Latino; 100 Hispanic/Latino; 3 Native Hawaiian or other Pacific Islander, non-Hispanic/Latino; 9 Two or more races, non-Hispanic/Latino), 1 international. Average age 33. 1,117 applicants, 20% accepted, 151 enrolled. Expenses: Contact institution. *Financial support:* Career-related internships or fieldwork, Federal Work-Study, scholarships/grants, and unspecified assistantships available. Support available to part-time students. Financial award applicants required to submit FAFSA. In 2017, 184 master's, 25 doctorates awarded. *Program availability:* Part-time, evening/weekend, blended/hybrid learning. Offers communication disorders (MS); nursing (MS); nursing administration (MS); nursing education (MS); occupational therapy (MS); physical therapy (DPT); physician assistant studies (MS). *Application deadline:* For fall admission, 8/1 for international students. Applications are processed on a rolling basis. *Application fee:* $40. Electronic applications accepted. *Application Contact:* Allison Gurdineer, Senior Director of Admissions, 877-637-2946, Fax: 914-674-7382, E-mail: admissions@mercy.edu. *Dean, School of Health and Natural Sciences*, Dr. Joan Toglia, 914-674-7837, E-mail: jtoglia@mercy.edu.

School of Liberal Arts Students: 24 full-time (9 women), 71 part-time (48 women); includes 32 minority (15 Black or African American, non-Hispanic/Latino; 3 Asian, non-Hispanic/Latino; 14 Hispanic/Latino), 6 international. Average age 35. 79 applicants, 63% accepted, 30 enrolled. Expenses: Contact institution. *Financial support:* Career-related internships or fieldwork, Federal Work-Study, scholarships/grants, and unspecified assistantships available. Support available to part-time students. Financial award applicants required to submit FAFSA. In 2017, 44 master's awarded. *Program availability:* Part-time, evening/weekend, 100% online, blended/hybrid learning. Offers cybersecurity (MS); English literature (MA). *Application deadline:* For fall admission, 8/1 for international students. Applications are processed on a rolling basis. *Application fee:* $40. Electronic applications accepted. *Application Contact:* Allison Gurdineer, Senior Director of Admissions, 877-637-2946, Fax: 914-674-7382, E-mail: admissions@mercy.edu. *Dean, School of Liberal Arts*, 914-674-7593.

School of Social and Behavioral Sciences Students: 248 full-time (210 women), 265 part-time (221 women); includes 373 minority (150 Black or African American, non-Hispanic/Latino; 1 American Indian or Alaska Native, non-Hispanic/Latino; 13 Asian, non-Hispanic/Latino; 203 Hispanic/Latino; 1 Native Hawaiian or other Pacific Islander, non-Hispanic/Latino; 5 Two or more races, non-Hispanic/Latino), 7 international. Average age 34. 448 applicants, 48% accepted, 150 enrolled. Expenses: Contact institution. *Financial support:* Career-related internships or fieldwork, Federal Work-Study, scholarships/grants, and unspecified assistantships available. Support available to part-time students. Financial award applicants required to submit FAFSA. In 2017, 150 master's, 2 other advanced degrees awarded. *Program availability:* Part-time, evening/weekend, 100% online, blended/hybrid learning. Offers counseling (MS, Certificate); family counseling (Certificate); health services management (MPA, MS); marriage and family therapy (MS); mental health counseling (MS); psychology (MS); school counseling (Certificate); school psychology (MS). *Application deadline:* For fall admission, 8/1 for international students. Applications are processed on a rolling basis. *Application fee:* $40. Electronic applications accepted. *Application Contact:* Allison Gurdineer, Senior Director of Admissions, 877-637-2946, Fax: 914-674-7382, E-mail: admissions@mercy.edu. *Dean, School of Social and Behavioral Sciences*, Dr. Karol Dean, 914-674-7517, E-mail: kdean@mercy.edu.

MERCY COLLEGE OF OHIO, Toledo, OH 43604

General Information Independent-religious, coed, primarily women, comprehensive institution. *Enrollment:* 1,416 graduate, professional, and undergraduate students; 12 part-time matriculated graduate/professional students (11 women). *Enrollment by degree level:* 12 master's. *Tuition:* Part-time $600 per credit hour. *Required fees:* $450 per semester. One-time fee: $250 part-time. *Graduate housing:* On-campus housing not available. *Student services:* Career counseling, free psychological counseling, low-cost health insurance, multicultural affairs office, services for students with disabilities, writing training. *Library facilities:* Mercy College of Ohio Library. *Collection:* Books: 7,502 (physical), 70,294 (digital/electronic); Serial titles: 65 (physical), 40,683 (digital/electronic); Databases: 15. Students can reserve study rooms.

Computer facilities: 127 computers available on campus for general student use. A campuswide network can be accessed. Online class registration is available.
Website: http://www.mercycollege.edu/

GRADUATE UNITS

Program in Health Administration Expenses: Contact institution. *Financial support:* Applicants required to submit FAFSA. *Program availability:* Part-time-only, online only. Offers health administration (MHA). *Application fee:* $50. Electronic applications accepted. *Director of Graduate Studies*, Dr. Kimberly Watson, 419-251-1852, E-mail: kim.watson@mercycollege.edu.

Program in Nursing Students: 12 part-time (11 women). Expenses: Contact institution. *Financial support:* Applicants required to submit FAFSA. *Program availability:* Part-time-only, online only. Offers nursing (MSN). *Application fee:* $50. Electronic applications accepted. *MSN Program Director*, Deborah Karns, 419-251-1718, E-mail: deborah.karns@mercycollege.edu.

MERCYHURST UNIVERSITY, Erie, PA 16546

General Information Independent-religious, coed, comprehensive institution. *Graduate housing:* On-campus housing not available.

GRADUATE UNITS

Graduate Studies *Program availability:* Part-time, evening/weekend. Offers accounting (MS); administration of justice (MS); applied behavior analysis (MS); applied intelligence (MS, Certificate); archaeology and geological archaeology (MS); autism (MS); data science (MS); forensic and biological anthropology (MS); generalist (MS); higher education administration (MS); higher education leadership and disabilities (MS); human resources (MS); organizational leadership (MS, Certificate); physician assistant studies (MS); secondary education: pedagogy and practice (MS); sports leadership (MS); strategy and innovation (MS). Electronic applications accepted.

MEREDITH COLLEGE, Raleigh, NC 27607-5298

General Information Independent, Undergraduate: women only; graduate: coed, comprehensive institution. *Enrollment:* 1,981 graduate, professional, and undergraduate students; 116 full-time matriculated graduate/professional students (98 women), 183 part-time matriculated graduate/professional students (164 women). *Enrollment by degree level:* 219 master's, 80 other advanced degrees. *Graduate faculty:* 23 full-time (20 women), 7 part-time/adjunct (6 women). Tuition and fees vary according to course load and program. *Graduate housing:* On-campus housing not available. *Student services:* Campus safety program, career counseling, free psychological counseling, international student services, services for students with disabilities. *Library facilities:* Carlyle Campbell Library.

Computer facilities: A campuswide network can be accessed from student residence rooms. Online class registration is available.
Website: http://www.meredith.edu/

General Application Contact: Cindy Bell, Admissions Coordinator, 919-760-8787, E-mail: bellcyn@meredith.edu.

GRADUATE UNITS

School of Business Students: 5 full-time (all women), 88 part-time (73 women); includes 33 minority (24 Black or African American, non-Hispanic/Latino; 1 Asian, non-Hispanic/Latino; 6 Hispanic/Latino; 2 Two or more races, non-Hispanic/Latino), 4 international. Average age 34. 62 applicants, 63% accepted, 29 enrolled. Expenses: Contact institution. *Financial support:* Career-related internships or fieldwork, institutionally sponsored loans, scholarships/grants, and tuition waivers (partial) available. Support available to part-time students. Financial award application deadline: 2/15; financial award applicants required to submit FAFSA. In 2017, 18 master's awarded. *Program availability:* Part-time, evening/weekend. Offers entrepreneurship and family business (MBA); human resource management (MBA); project management (MBA). *Application deadline:* For fall admission, 7/1 priority date for domestic and international students; for spring admission, 11/1 priority date for domestic and international students. Applications are processed on a rolling basis. *Application fee:* $50. Electronic applications accepted. *Dean*, Kristie Ogilvie, 919-760-8432, Fax: 919-760-8470.

School of Education, Health and Human Sciences Students: 25 full-time (24 women), 22 part-time (all women); includes 13 minority (8 Black or African American, non-Hispanic/Latino; 1 American Indian or Alaska Native, non-Hispanic/Latino; 1 Asian, non-Hispanic/Latino; 3 Hispanic/Latino). Average age 31. 57 applicants, 54% accepted, 31 enrolled. Expenses: Contact institution. *Financial support:* Career-related internships or fieldwork, institutionally sponsored loans, and tuition waivers (partial) available. Support available to part-time students. Financial award application deadline: 2/15; financial award applicants required to submit FAFSA. In 2017, 14 master's awarded. *Program availability:* Part-time, evening/weekend. Offers academically and intellectually gifted (M Ed); dietetic internship (Postbaccalaureate Certificate); elementary education (M Ed, MAT); English as a second language (M Ed, MAT); health and physical education (MAT); industrial/organizational psychology (MA); nutrition (MS); nutrition, health and human performance (MS, Postbaccalaureate Certificate); psychology (MA); reading (M Ed); special education (MAT); special education (general curriculum) (M Ed). *Application deadline:* For fall admission, 7/1 priority date for domestic students; for spring admission, 11/1 priority date for domestic students. Applications are processed on a rolling basis. *Application fee:* $50. Electronic applications accepted. *Graduate Program Manager*, Dr. Monica McKinney, 919-760-8056, Fax: 919-760-2303, E-mail: mckinneym@meredith.edu.

MERRIMACK COLLEGE, North Andover, MA 01845-5800

General Information Independent-religious, coed, comprehensive institution. CGS member. *Enrollment:* 4,171 graduate, professional, and undergraduate students; 449 full-time matriculated graduate/professional students (295 women), 171 part-time matriculated graduate/professional students (118 women). *Enrollment by degree level:* 617 master's, 3 other advanced degrees. *Graduate faculty:* 58 full-time, 67 part-time/adjunct. *Graduate housing:* On-campus housing not available. *Student services:* Campus employment opportunities, campus safety program, career counseling, exercise/wellness program, free psychological counseling, international student services, low-cost health insurance, multicultural affairs office, services for students with disabilities, teacher training, writing training. *Library facilities:* McQuade Library.

Computer facilities: Computer purchase and lease plans are available. A campuswide network can be accessed from student residence rooms and from off campus. Online class registration is available.
Website: http://www.merrimack.edu/

General Application Contact: Megan Goddard, Office of Graduate Studies, 978-837-3563, E-mail: graduate@merrimack.edu.

GRADUATE UNITS

Girard School of Business Students: 86 full-time (33 women), 31 part-time (11 women); includes 10 minority (2 Black or African American, non-Hispanic/Latino; 2 Asian, non-Hispanic/Latino; 6 Hispanic/Latino), 34 international. Average age 27. 139 applicants, 78% accepted, 61 enrolled. *Faculty:* 13 full-time, 19 part-time/adjunct. Expenses: Contact institution. *Financial support:* Career-related internships or fieldwork, scholarships/grants, health care benefits, and unspecified assistantships available. Support available to part-time students. Financial award application deadline: 5/1; financial award applicants required to submit FAFSA. In 2017, 74 master's awarded. *Program availability:* Part-time, evening/weekend, 100% online. Offers accounting (MS); business analytics (MS); management (MS). *Application deadline:* For fall admission, 8/24 for domestic students, 7/30 for international students; for spring admission, 1/10 for domestic and international students; for summer admission, 5/10 for domestic students, 4/10 for international students. Applications are processed on a rolling basis. *Application fee:* $0. Electronic applications accepted. *Application Contact:* Jennifer Greenwood, Graduate Admission Counselor, 978-837-3563, E-mail: graduate@merrimack.edu.

School of Education and Social Policy Students: 212 full-time (175 women), 121 part-time (101 women); includes 42 minority (6 Black or African American, non-Hispanic/Latino; 6 Asian, non-Hispanic/Latino; 27 Hispanic/Latino; 3 Two or more races, non-Hispanic/Latino), 3 international. Average age 27. 420 applicants, 84% accepted, 250 enrolled. *Faculty:* 15 full-time, 36 part-time/adjunct. Expenses: Contact institution. *Financial support:* Fellowships with full tuition reimbursements, career-related internships or fieldwork, scholarships/grants, and health care benefits available. Support available to part-time students. Financial award application deadline: 5/1; financial award applicants required to submit FAFSA. In 2017, 177 master's awarded. *Program availability:* Part-time, evening/weekend, 100% online courses with immersion events and in-classroom practicum close to home. Offers community engagement (M Ed); criminology and criminal justice (MS); curriculum and instruction (M Ed); early childhood education (M Ed); educational leadership (CAGS); elementary education (M Ed); English as a second language (PreK-6) (M Ed); high school education (M Ed); higher education (M Ed); middle school education (M Ed); moderate disabilities (PreK-8) (M Ed); school counseling (M Ed). *Application deadline:* For fall admission, 8/24 for domestic students, 7/30 for international students; for spring admission, 1/10 for domestic students, 12/10 for international students; for summer admission, 5/10 for domestic students, 4/10 for international students. Applications are processed on a rolling basis. *Application fee:* $0. Electronic applications accepted. *Application Contact:* Alyssa Orlando, Graduate Admissions Counselor, 978-837-3563, E-mail: orlandoaf@merrimack.edu.

School of Health Sciences Students: 87 full-time (58 women), 4 part-time (all women); includes 10 minority (2 Black or African American, non-Hispanic/Latino; 7 Hispanic/Latino; 1 Two or more races, non-Hispanic/Latino), 3 international. Average age 25. 147 applicants, 90% accepted, 83 enrolled. *Faculty:* 8 full-time, 6 part-time/adjunct. Expenses: Contact institution. *Financial support:* Fellowships with partial tuition reimbursements, career-related internships or fieldwork, scholarships/grants, and health care benefits available. Support available to part-time students. Financial award application deadline: 5/1; financial award applicants required to submit FAFSA. In 2017, 47 master's awarded. *Program availability:* Part-time, evening/weekend. Offers athletic training (MS); community health education (MS); exercise and sport science (MS); health and wellness management (MS). *Application deadline:* For fall admission, 8/24 for domestic students, 7/30 for international students; for summer admission, 5/10 for domestic students, 4/10 for international students. Applications are processed on a rolling basis. Electronic applications accepted. *Application Contact:* Allison Pena, Office of Graduate Studies, 978-837-3563, E-mail: graduate@merrimack.edu. *Dean*, Kyle McInnis, 978-837-3590, E-mail: mcinnisk@merrimack.edu.

School of Liberal Arts Students: 30 full-time (23 women), 3 part-time (2 women); includes 3 minority (2 Black or African American, non-Hispanic/Latino; 1 Hispanic/Latino), 1 international. Average age 30. 40 applicants, 88% accepted, 20 enrolled. *Faculty:* 7 full-time, 4 part-time/adjunct. Expenses: Contact institution. *Financial support:* Career-related internships or fieldwork, scholarships/grants, and health care benefits available. Support available to part-time students. Financial award application deadline: 5/1; financial award applicants required to submit FAFSA. In 2017, 9 master's awarded. *Program availability:* Part-time, evening/weekend. Offers clinical mental health counseling (MS); interfaith spirituality (Certificate); public affairs (MPA); spiritual direction (MA, Certificate); spirituality (MA). *Application deadline:* For fall admission, 8/24 for domestic students, 7/30 for international students; for spring admission, 1/10 for domestic students, 12/10 for international students; for summer admission, 5/10 for domestic students, 4/10 for international students. Applications are processed on a rolling basis. Electronic applications accepted. *Application Contact:* Jennifer Greenwood, Graduate Admissions Counselor, 978-837-3563, E-mail: greenwoodjl@merrimack.edu.

School of Science and Engineering Students: 34 full-time (6 women), 12 part-time (0 women); includes 4 minority (1 Black or African American, non-Hispanic/Latino; 2 Asian, non-Hispanic/Latino; 1 Hispanic/Latino), 22 international. Average age 30. 77 applicants, 74% accepted, 30 enrolled. *Faculty:* 21 full-time, 8 part-time/adjunct. Expenses: Contact institution. *Financial support:* Career-related internships or fieldwork, scholarships/grants, health care benefits, and unspecified assistantships available. Support available to part-time students. Financial award application deadline: 5/1; financial award applicants required to submit FAFSA. In 2017, 25 master's awarded. *Program availability:* Part-time, evening/weekend, 100% online. Offers civil engineering (MS); computer science (MS); data science (MS); engineering management (MS); mechanical engineering (MS). *Application deadline:* For fall admission, 8/24 for domestic students, 7/30 for international students; for spring admission, 1/10 for domestic students, 12/10 for international students; for summer admission, 5/10 for domestic students, 4/10 for international students. Applications are processed on a rolling basis. *Application fee:* $0. Electronic applications accepted. *Application Contact:* Allison Pena, Graduate Admissions Counselor, 978-837-3563, E-mail: penaa@merrimack.edu.

MESIVTA OF EASTERN PARKWAY–YESHIVA ZICHRON MEILECH, Brooklyn, NY 11218-5559

General Information Independent-religious, men only, comprehensive institution.

GRADUATE UNITS

Graduate Programs

MESIVTA TORAH VODAATH RABBINICAL SEMINARY, Brooklyn, NY 11218-5299

General Information Independent-religious, men only, comprehensive institution.

GRADUATE UNITS

Graduate Programs Offers rabbinical studies (Certificate); theological and ministerial studies (Certificate).

MESIVTHA TIFERETH JERUSALEM OF AMERICA, New York, NY 10002-6301

General Information Independent-religious, men only, comprehensive institution.

GRADUATE UNITS

Graduate Programs

MESSIAH COLLEGE, Mechanicsburg, PA 17055

General Information Independent-religious, coed, comprehensive institution.

GRADUATE UNITS

Program in Business and Leadership *Program availability:* Online learning. Offers leadership (MBA, Certificate); management (Certificate); strategic leadership (MA).

Program in Conducting *Program availability:* Part-time, online learning. Offers choral conducting (MM); orchestral conducting (MM); wind conducting (MM). Electronic applications accepted.

Program in Counseling *Program availability:* Part-time, online learning. Offers clinical mental health counseling (MAC); counseling (CAGS); marriage, couple, and family counseling (MAC); school counseling (MAC). Electronic applications accepted.

Program in Education *Program availability:* Part-time, online learning. Offers curriculum and instruction (M Ed); special education (M Ed); teaching English to speakers of other languages (M Ed). Electronic applications accepted.

Program in Higher Education *Program availability:* Part-time. Offers college athletics management (MA); self-designed concentration (MA); student affairs (MA). Electronic applications accepted.

Program in Nursing Offers nurse educator (MSN).

METHODIST THEOLOGICAL SCHOOL IN OHIO, Delaware, OH 43015-8004

General Information Independent-religious, coed, graduate-only institution. *Graduate housing:* Rooms and/or apartments available on a first-come, first-served basis to single students and available to married students. Housing application deadline: 8/15.

GRADUATE UNITS

Graduate and Professional Programs *Program availability:* Part-time. Offers theology (M Div, MACE, MACM, MTS, D Min).

METHODIST UNIVERSITY, Fayetteville, NC 28311-1498

General Information Independent-religious, coed, comprehensive institution. *Graduate housing:* Room and/or apartments available on a first-come, first-served basis to single students; on-campus housing not available to married students. Housing application deadline: 6/1.

GRADUATE UNITS

School of Graduate Studies *Program availability:* Part-time, evening/weekend. Offers business administration (MBA); justice administration (MJA); physician assistant studies (MMS). Electronic applications accepted.

METROPOLITAN COLLEGE OF NEW YORK, New York, NY 10006

General Information Independent, coed, comprehensive institution. *Enrollment:* 1,113 graduate, professional, and undergraduate students; 288 full-time matriculated graduate/professional students (192 women), 48 part-time matriculated graduate/professional students (41 women). *Enrollment by degree level:* 336 master's. *Tuition:* Full-time $27,780. *Required fees:* $790. *Graduate housing:* On-campus housing not available. *Student services:* Career counseling, free psychological counseling, grant writing training, international student services. *Library facilities:* Main Library plus 1 other. *Collection:* Books: 26,191 (physical), 156,497 (digital/electronic); Serial titles: 29,206 (digital/electronic); Databases: 91. Weekly public service hours: 72. *Research affiliation:* U.S. Department of Homeland Security (homeland security), U.S. Federal Emergency Management Administration (higher education).

Computer facilities: 120 computers available on campus for general student use. A campuswide network can be accessed from off campus. Online class registration is available.
Website: http://www.mcny.edu/

General Application Contact: Steebo Varghese, Associate Director of Admissions, 212-343-1234 Ext. 2708, Fax: 212-343-8470, E-mail: svarghese@mcny.edu.

GRADUATE UNITS

Program in Business Administration Students: 164 full-time (106 women), 37 part-time (31 women); includes 153 minority (112 Black or African American, non-Hispanic/Latino; 3 American Indian or Alaska Native, non-Hispanic/Latino; 10 Asian, non-Hispanic/Latino; 24 Hispanic/Latino; 1 Native Hawaiian or other Pacific Islander, non-Hispanic/Latino; 3 Two or more races, non-Hispanic/Latino), 31 international. Average age 37. 133 applicants, 62% accepted, 66 enrolled. Expenses: Contact institution. *Financial support:* Scholarships/grants available. Financial award application deadline: 8/15; financial award applicants required to submit FAFSA. In 2017, 100 master's awarded. *Program availability:* Evening/weekend. Offers financial services (MBA); general management (MBA); healthcare systems and risk management (MBA); media management (MBA). *Application deadline:* For fall admission, 7/15 priority date for domestic students; for winter admission, 11/15 priority date for domestic students; for spring admission, 3/30 priority date for domestic students. Applications are processed on a rolling basis. *Application fee:* $45. Electronic applications accepted. *Application Contact:* Steebo Varghese, Assistant Director of Admissions, 212-343-1234 Ext. 2708, Fax: 212-343-8470. *Dean and Professor, School for Business*, Dr. Tilokie Depoo, 212-343-1234 Ext. 2204.

Program in Childhood/Special Education Students: 22 full-time (16 women), 1 (woman) part-time; includes 21 minority (15 Black or African American, non-Hispanic/Latino; 6 Hispanic/Latino). Average age 36. 44 applicants, 30% accepted, 10 enrolled. Expenses: Contact institution. *Financial support:* Career-related internships or fieldwork, Federal Work-Study, institutionally sponsored loans, and scholarships/grants available. Financial award application deadline: 8/15; financial award applicants required to submit FAFSA. In 2017, 16 master's awarded. Offers dual childhood 1-6 special education (MS). *Application deadline:* Applications are processed on a rolling basis. *Application fee:* $45. Electronic applications accepted. *Application Contact:* Steebo Varghese, Associate Director of Admissions, 212-343-1234 Ext. 2708, E-mail: svarghese@mcny.edu. *Director*, Dr. Patrick Ianniello, 212-343-1234 Ext. 2424, E-mail: pianniello@metropolitan.edu.

Program in Public Administration Students: 102 full-time (70 women), 10 part-time (9 women); includes 99 minority (71 Black or African American, non-Hispanic/Latino; 1 Asian, non-Hispanic/Latino; 25 Hispanic/Latino; 2 Two or more races, non-Hispanic/Latino), 3 international. Average age 39. 122 applicants, 45% accepted, 52 enrolled. Expenses: Contact institution. *Financial support:* Fellowships with tuition reimbursements, career-related internships or fieldwork, scholarships/grants, and tuition waivers (partial) available. Financial award application deadline: 8/15; financial award applicants required to submit FAFSA. In 2017, 129 master's awarded. *Program availability:* Evening/weekend. Offers emergency and disaster management (MPA); public affairs and administration (MPA). *Application deadline:* For fall admission, 7/30 priority date for domestic students, 7/1 for international students; for winter admission, 11/30 priority date for domestic students, 11/1 for international students; for spring admission, 3/30 priority date for domestic students, 3/1 for international students. Applications are processed on a rolling basis. *Application fee:* $45. Electronic applications accepted. *Application Contact:* Steebo Varghese, Assistant Director of Admissions, 212-343-1234 Ext. 2708, Fax: 212-343-8474, E-mail: svarghese@mcny.edu. *Dean, Graduate School for Public Affairs Administration*, Prof. Humphrey Crookendale, 212-343-1234 Ext. 2209, E-mail: hcrookendale@mcny.edu.

METROPOLITAN STATE UNIVERSITY, St. Paul, MN 55106-5000

General Information State-supported, coed, comprehensive institution. Tuition, state resident: part-time $388.55 per credit. Tuition, nonresident: part-time $777.11 per credit. *Required fees:* $35.11 per credit. Part-time tuition and fees vary according to campus/location and program. *Graduate housing:* On-campus housing not available. *Student services:* Campus employment opportunities, career counseling, free psychological counseling, international student services, low-cost health insurance, multicultural affairs office, services for students with disabilities, writing training. *Library facilities:* Library and Learning Center.

Computer facilities: A campuswide network can be accessed from off campus. Online class registration is available.
Website: http://www.metrostate.edu/

GRADUATE UNITS

College of Community Studies and Public Affairs Offers alcohol and drug counseling (MS); co-occurring disorders recovery counseling (MS); public administration (MPA); public and nonprofit administration (MPNA).

College of Liberal Arts Expenses: Contact institution. *Financial support:* Research assistantships available. Financial award applicants required to submit FAFSA. *Program availability:* Part-time, evening/weekend. Offers liberal studies (MA); technical communication (MS). *Application deadline:* For fall admission, 8/1 priority date for domestic students, 3/15 for international students; for winter admission, 10/15 for international students; for spring admission, 12/1 priority date for domestic students, 3/15 for international students. Applications are processed on a rolling basis. *Application fee:* $20. Electronic applications accepted. *Application Contact:* Susan Honsvall, Office and Administrative Specialist, 651-793-1445, E-mail: susan.honsvall@metrostate.edu.

College of Management Expenses: Contact institution. *Financial support:* Research assistantships with partial tuition reimbursements, career-related internships or fieldwork, and Federal Work-Study available. Support available to part-time students. Financial award applicants required to submit FAFSA. *Program availability:* Part-time, evening/weekend. Offers business administration (MBA, DBA); business analytics (Graduate Certificate); database administration (Graduate Certificate); global supply chain management (Graduate Certificate); information assurance security (Graduate Certificate); management information systems (MMIS); MIS generalist (Graduate Certificate); MIS systems analysis and design (Graduate Certificate); project management (Graduate Certificate). *Application deadline:* For fall admission, 7/15 for international students; for winter admission, 11/15 for international students; for spring admission, 3/15 for international students. Applications are processed on a rolling basis. *Application fee:* $20. Electronic applications accepted. *Application Contact:* Allen Bellas, Interim Dean, 612-659-7272, Fax: 612-659-7268, E-mail: allen.bellas@metrostate.edu. *Interim Dean*, Allen Bellas, 612-659-7272, Fax: 612-659-7268, E-mail: allen.bellas@metrostate.edu.

College of Nursing and Health Sciences Expenses: Contact institution. *Financial support:* Fellowships, career-related internships or fieldwork, Federal Work-Study, institutionally sponsored loans, and traineeships available. Financial award applicants required to submit FAFSA. *Program availability:* Part-time. Offers advanced dental therapy (MS); leadership and management (MSN); nurse educator (MSN); nursing (DNP). *Application deadline:* For fall admission, 1/15 for domestic and international students; for winter admission, 1/15 for international students. *Application fee:* $20.

College of Sciences Offers computer science (MS, PSM).

School of Law Enforcement and Criminal Justice Expenses: Contact institution. *Financial support:* Applicants required to submit FAFSA. *Program availability:* Part-time, evening/weekend. Offers criminal justice (MS). *Application deadline:* For fall admission, 8/1 priority date for domestic students; for spring admission, 12/1 priority date for domestic students. Electronic applications accepted. *Application Contact:* Everett Doolittle, Interim Dean, 763-657-3754, E-mail: everett.doolittle@metrostate.edu. *Interim Dean*, Everett Doolittle, 763-657-3754, E-mail: everett.doolittle@metrostate.edu.

School of Urban Education Offers curriculum, pedagogy and schooling (MS); English as a second language (MS); secondary education (MS); special education (MS).

METROPOLITAN STATE UNIVERSITY OF DENVER, Denver, CO 80204

General Information State-supported, coed, comprehensive institution. CGS member.

GRADUATE UNITS

College of Letters, Arts and Sciences Offers individual and families (MSW); macro practice (MSW); social work (MSW).

School of Business Offers accounting (MP Acc); fraud exam and forensic auditing (MP Acc); internal audit (MP Acc); public accounting (MP Acc); taxation (MP Acc).

School of Education Offers elementary education (MAT); special education (MAT).

MGH INSTITUTE OF HEALTH PROFESSIONS, Boston, MA 02129

General Information Independent, coed, primarily women, graduate-only institution. *Graduate housing:* On-campus housing not available. *Research affiliation:* Health and Disability Research Institute, Boston University (efficacy of a post-rehabilitation exercise intervention in patients after hip fracture), Eunice Kennedy Shriver National Institute of Child and Health Development (dyadic intervention for women at risk for postpartum depression and their infants), National Institutes of Health (postnatal parental depression, family dynamics in early parenting), Robert Wood Johnson Foundation (mother-infant intervention for the prevention of postpartum depression and associated mother-infant relationship dysfunction), U.S. Department of Defense (robotic nursing assistant to H-star technology), The American Academy of Nursing/John W. Hartford Foundation (building academic geriatric nursing capacity).

GRADUATE UNITS

School of Health and Rehabilitation Sciences *Program availability:* Part-time. Offers health and rehabilitation sciences (MPAS, MS, DPT, OTD, Certificate); occupational therapy (OTD); physical therapy (MS, DPT, Certificate); physician assistant studies (MPAS); reading (Certificate); speech-language pathology (MS). Electronic applications accepted.

School of Nursing Offers advanced practice nursing (MSN); gerontological nursing (MSN); nursing (DNP); pediatric nursing (MSN); psychiatric nursing (MSN); teaching and learning for health care education (Certificate); women's health nursing (MSN). Electronic applications accepted.

MIAMI INTERNATIONAL UNIVERSITY OF ART & DESIGN, Miami, FL 33132-1418

General Information Proprietary, coed, comprehensive institution.

GRADUATE UNITS

Program in Design and Media Management Offers design and media management (MA).

Program in Film *Program availability:* Online learning. Offers film (MFA).

MIAMI REGIONAL UNIVERSITY, Miami Springs, FL 33166

General Information Proprietary, coed, comprehensive institution.

GRADUATE UNITS

School of Nursing and Health Sciences Offers nursing (MSN); nursing education (MSN); nursing leadership (MSN).

MIAMI UNIVERSITY, Oxford, OH 45056

General Information State-related, coed, university. CGS member. *Enrollment:* 19,700 graduate, professional, and undergraduate students; 976 full-time matriculated graduate/professional students (559 women), 1,376 part-time matriculated graduate/professional students (1,035 women). *Enrollment by degree level:* 1,994 master's, 358 doctoral. *Graduate faculty:* 669 full-time (297 women). Tuition, state resident: full-time $13,812; part-time $575 per credit hour. Tuition, nonresident: full-time $30,860; part-time $1286 per credit hour. *Graduate housing:* Room and/or apartments available on a first-come, first-served basis to single students; on-campus housing not available to married students. Typical cost: $10,804 per year ($13,862 including board). *Student services:* Campus employment opportunities, campus safety program, career counseling, child daycare facilities, exercise/wellness program, free psychological counseling, grant writing training, international student services, low-cost health insurance, multicultural affairs office, services for students with disabilities, teacher training, writing training. *Library facilities:* King Library plus 3 others. *Collection:* Books: 2.4 million (physical), 727,667 (digital/electronic); Serial titles: 1,019 (physical), 25,772 (digital/electronic); Databases: 743. Weekly public service hours: 168; study areas open 24 hours, 5–7 days a week; students can reserve study rooms.

Computer facilities: Computer purchase and lease plans are available. A campuswide network can be accessed from student residence rooms and from off campus. Online class registration is available.
Website: http://miamioh.edu/

General Application Contact: Graduate Admission Coordinator, 513-529-3734, E-mail: applygrad@miamioh.edu.

GRADUATE UNITS

College of Arts and Science Expenses: Contact institution. *Program availability:* Part-time. Offers arts and science (M Env, MA, MAT, MGS, MPSG, MS, MS Stat, PhD); biology (MA, MAT, MS, PhD); chemistry and biochemistry (MS, PhD); English (MA, MAT, PhD); French (MA); geography (MA); geology (MA, MS, PhD); gerontology (MGS); history (MA); mathematics (MA, MAT, MS); microbiology (MS, PhD); philosophy (MA); physics (MS); political science (MA); population and social gerontology (MPSG); psychology (MA, PhD); social gerontology (PhD); speech pathology and audiology (MA, MS); statistics (MS Stat). *Application Contact:* Admission Coordinator, 513-529-3734, E-mail: applygrad@miamioh.edu. *Dean*, Dr. Chris Makaroff, 513-529-1234, E-mail: cas@miamioh.edu.

College of Creative Arts Expenses: Contact institution. Offers architecture and interior design (M Arch); art education (MA); creative arts (M Arch, MA, MFA, MM); music education (MM); music performance (MM); studio art (MFA); theatre (MA). *Application Contact:* Graduate Admission Coordinator, 513-529-3734, E-mail: applygrad@miamioh.edu. *Dean*, Dr. Liz Mullenix, 513-529-6010, E-mail: cca@miamioh.edu.

College of Education, Health and Society Expenses: Contact institution. Offers education, health and society (M Ed, MA, MAT, MS, Ed D, PhD, Ed S); educational leadership (Ed D, PhD); educational psychology (M Ed, MA, MS, Ed S); family studies and social work (MA); kinesiology and health (MS); school leadership (M Ed); student affairs in higher education (MS, PhD); teacher education (M Ed, MAT); transformative education (M Ed). *Application Contact:* Graduate Admission Coordinator, 513-529-3734, E-mail: applygrad@miamioh.edu. *Dean*, Dr. Michael Dantley, 513-529-6317, E-mail: ehs@miamioh.edu.

College of Engineering and Computing Expenses: Contact institution. Offers chemical, paper and biomedical engineering (MS); computer science (MCS); electrical and computer engineering (MS); engineering and computing (MCS, MS); mechanical and manufacturing engineering (MS). *Application Contact:* Graduate Admission Coordinator, 513-529-3734, E-mail: applygrad@miamioh.edu. *Dean*, Dr. Marek Dollar, 513-529-0700, E-mail: cec@miamioh.edu.

Farmer School of Business Expenses: Contact institution. Offers accountancy (M Acc); business (M Acc, MA, MBA); business administration (MBA); economics (MA). *Application Contact:* Admission Coordinator, 513-529-3734, E-mail: applygrad@miamioh.edu. *Dean/Chair in Business Leadership*, Dr. Marc Rubin, 513-529-3381, E-mail: deanofbusiness@miamioh.edu.

Institute for the Environment and Sustainability Students: 21 full-time (13 women), 26 part-time (15 women); includes 4 minority (1 Black or African American, non-Hispanic/Latino; 1 American Indian or Alaska Native, non-Hispanic/Latino; 1 Hispanic/Latino; 1 Two or more races, non-Hispanic/Latino), 3 international. Average age 27. Expenses: Contact institution. In 2017, 10 master's awarded. Offers environment and sustainability (M Env). Electronic applications accepted. *Application Contact:* 513-529-5811, E-mail: ies@miamioh.edu. *Director/Associate Professor of Geology and Environmental Earth Science*, Dr. Jonathan Levy, 513-529-1947, E-mail: levyj@miamioh.edu.

MICHIGAN SCHOOL OF PROFESSIONAL PSYCHOLOGY, Farmington Hills, MI 48334

General Information Independent, coed, graduate-only institution. *Enrollment by degree level:* 103 master's, 65 doctoral, 5 other advanced degrees. *Graduate faculty:* 11 full-time (7 women), 21 part-time/adjunct (17 women). *Tuition:* Full-time $34,200; part-time $16,000 per year. *Required fees:* $460 per semester. Tuition and fees vary according to course load, degree level and program. *Graduate housing:* On-campus housing not available. *Student services:* Campus employment opportunities, campus safety program, international student services, multicultural affairs office, services for students with disabilities, writing training. *Library facilities:* Moustakas Johnson Library plus 1 other. *Collection:* Books: 7,247 (physical), 4,299 (digital/electronic); Serial titles: 2 (physical); Databases: 70. Weekly public service hours: 47.

Computer facilities: 10 computers available on campus for general student use. A campuswide network can be accessed. Online class registration is available.
Website: http://www.mispp.edu/

General Application Contact: Carrie Hauser, Coordinator of Admissions and Student Engagement, 248-476-1122 Ext. 117, Fax: 248-476-1125, E-mail: chauser@mispp.edu.

GRADUATE UNITS

MA and Psy D Programs in Clinical Psychology Students: 109 full-time (85 women), 64 part-time (51 women); includes 46 minority (30 Black or African American, non-Hispanic/Latino; 3 Asian, non-Hispanic/Latino; 2 Hispanic/Latino; 11 Two or more races, non-Hispanic/Latino), 1 international. Average age 31. 194 applicants, 47% accepted, 80 enrolled. *Faculty:* 11 full-time (7 women), 21 part-time/adjunct (17 women). Expenses: Contact institution. *Financial support:* In 2017–18, 12 students received support, including 1 research assistantship (averaging $8,566 per year), 5 teaching assistantships (averaging $14,436 per year); institutionally sponsored loans, scholarships/grants, and unspecified assistantships also available. Financial award application deadline: 8/30; financial award applicants required to submit FAFSA. In 2017, 37 master's, 16 doctorates awarded. *Program availability:* Part-time, evening/weekend. Offers clinical psychology (MA, Psy D). *Application deadline:* For fall admission, 8/15 for domestic students. Applications are processed on a rolling basis. *Application fee:* $75. Electronic applications accepted. *Application Contact:* Carrie Hauser, Coordinator of Admissions and Student Engagement, 248-476-1122 Ext. 117, Fax: 248-476-1125, E-mail: chauser@mispp.edu. *Program Director*, Dr. Frances Brown, 248-476-1122, Fax: 248-476-1125.

MICHIGAN STATE UNIVERSITY, East Lansing, MI 48824

General Information State-supported, coed, university. CGS member. *Graduate housing:* Rooms and/or apartments available on a first-come, first-served basis to single and married students. *Research affiliation:* Argonne National Laboratory (high-energy physics and structural biology), Association of Sea Grant Programs (fresh water ecosystems), Fraunhofer Center (manufacturing), Michigan Economic Development Corporation (life sciences, homeland security, automotive technologies), Oak Ridge Associated Universities (scientific research and education), Southern Astrophysical Research (SOAR) Telescope (astronomy).

GRADUATE UNITS

College of Human Medicine Offers biochemistry and molecular biology (MS, PhD); epidemiology (MS, PhD); human medicine (MD); human medicine/medical scientist training program (MD); microbiology (MS); microbiology and molecular genetics (PhD); pharmacology and toxicology (MS, PhD); physiology (MS, PhD); public health (MPH).

College of Osteopathic Medicine Offers biochemistry and molecular biology (MS, PhD); integrative pharmacology (MS); microbiology (MS); microbiology and molecular genetics (PhD); osteopathic medicine (MS, DO, PhD); pharmacology and toxicology (MS, PhD); pharmacology and toxicology-environmental toxicology (PhD); physiology (MS, PhD).

College of Veterinary Medicine Offers animal science–environmental toxicology (PhD); biochemistry and molecular biology–environmental toxicology (PhD); chemistry–environmental toxicology (PhD); comparative medicine and integrative biology (MS, PhD); comparative medicine and integrative biology–environmental toxicology (PhD); crop and soil sciences–environmental toxicology (PhD); environmental engineering–environmental toxicology (PhD); environmental geosciences–environmental toxicology (PhD); fisheries and wildlife–environmental toxicology (PhD); food safety (MS); food safety and toxicology (MS); food science–environmental toxicology (PhD); forestry–environmental toxicology (PhD); genetics–environmental toxicology (PhD); human nutrition–environmental toxicology (PhD); industrial microbiology (MS, PhD); integrative toxicology (PhD); large animal clinical sciences (MS, PhD); microbiology (MS, PhD); microbiology and molecular genetics (MS, PhD); microbiology–environmental toxicology (PhD); pathobiology and diagnostic investigation (MS, PhD); pathology (MS, PhD); pathology–environmental toxicology (PhD); pharmacology and toxicology (MS, PhD); pharmacology and toxicology–environmental toxicology (PhD); physiology (MS, PhD); small animal clinical sciences (MS); veterinary medicine (DVM); veterinary medicine/medical scientist training program (DVM); zoology–environmental toxicology (PhD).

The Graduate School *Program availability:* Part-time, evening/weekend, online learning. Electronic applications accepted.

College of Agriculture and Natural Resources Offers agricultural economics (MS, PhD); agricultural, food, and resource economics (MS, PhD); agriculture and natural resources (MA, MIPS, MS, MURP, PhD); animal science (MS, PhD); animal science-environmental toxicology (PhD); biochemistry and molecular biology (PhD); biosystems engineering (MS, PhD); cellular and molecular biology (PhD); community, agriculture, recreation, and resource studies (MS, PhD); construction management (MS, PhD); crop and soil sciences (MS, PhD); crop and soil sciences-environmental toxicology (PhD); entomology (MS, PhD); environmental design (MA); fisheries and wildlife (MS, PhD); fisheries and wildlife - environmental toxicology (PhD); food science (MS, PhD); food science - environmental toxicology (PhD); forestry (MS, PhD); forestry-environmental toxicology (PhD); genetics (PhD); horticulture (MS, PhD); human nutrition (MS, PhD); human nutrition-environmental toxicology (PhD); integrated pest management (MS); interior design and facilities management (MA); international planning studies (MIPS); microbiology and molecular genetics (PhD); packaging (MS, PhD); plant biology (PhD); plant breeding and genetics (MS, PhD); plant breeding and genetics-crop and soil sciences (MS); plant breeding, genetics and biotechnology-crop and soil sciences (PhD); plant breeding, genetics and biotechnology-forestry (MS, PhD); plant breeding, genetics and biotechnology-horticulture (MS, PhD); plant pathology (MS, PhD); plant physiology (PhD); urban and regional planning (MURP).

College of Arts and Letters Offers African American and African studies (MA, PhD); American studies (MA, PhD); applied Spanish linguistics (MA); arts and letters (MA, MFA, PhD); critical studies in literacy and pedagogy (MA); digital rhetoric and professional writing (MA); English (PhD); French (MA); French language and literature (PhD); German studies (MA, PhD); Hispanic cultural studies (PhD); Hispanic literatures (MA); linguistics (MA, PhD); literature in English (MA); philosophy (MA, PhD); rhetoric and writing (PhD); second language studies (PhD); studio art (MFA); teaching English to speakers of other languages (MA); theatre (MA, MFA). Electronic applications accepted.

College of Communication Arts and Sciences Offers advertising (MA); communication (MA, PhD); communication arts and sciences (MA, MS, PhD); communication arts and sciences–media and information studies (PhD); communicative sciences and disorders (MA, PhD); digital media arts and technology (MA); health communication (MA); information and telecommunication management (MA); information, policy and society (MA); journalism (MA); public relations (MA); retailing (MS, PhD); serious game design (MA).

College of Education Offers counseling (MA); curriculum, instruction and teacher education (PhD, Ed S); education (MA, MS, PhD, Ed S); educational policy (PhD); educational psychology and educational technology (PhD); educational technology (MA); higher, adult and lifelong education (MA, PhD); K–12 educational administration (MA, PhD, Ed S); kinesiology (MS, PhD); literacy instruction (MA); measurement and quantitative methods (PhD); rehabilitation counseling (MA); rehabilitation counselor education (PhD); school psychology (MA, PhD, Ed S); special education (MA, PhD); student affairs administration (MA); teaching and curriculum (MA). Electronic applications accepted.

College of Engineering *Program availability:* Part-time. Offers chemical engineering (MS, PhD); civil engineering (MS, PhD); computer science (MS, PhD); electrical engineering (MS, PhD); engineering (MS, PhD); engineering mechanics (MS, PhD); environmental engineering (MS, PhD); environmental engineering-environmental toxicology (PhD); materials science and engineering (MS, PhD); mechanical engineering (MS, PhD). Electronic applications accepted.

College of Music Offers collaborative piano (M Mus); jazz studies (M Mus); music (PhD); music composition (M Mus, DMA); music conducting (M Mus, DMA); music education (M Mus); music performance (M Mus, DMA); music theory (M Mus); music therapy (M Mus); musicology (MA); piano pedagogy (M Mus). Electronic applications accepted.

College of Natural Science Offers applied mathematics (MS, PhD); applied statistics (MS); astrophysics and astronomy (MS, PhD); biochemistry and molecular biology (MS, PhD); biochemistry and molecular biology/environmental toxicology (PhD); biological, physical and general science for teachers (MAT, MS); biomedical laboratory operations (MS); cell and molecular biology (MS, PhD); cell and molecular biology/environmental toxicology (PhD); chemical physics (PhD); chemistry (MS, PhD); chemistry-environmental toxicology (PhD); clinical laboratory sciences (MS); computational chemistry (MS); ecology, evolutionary biology and behavior (PhD); environmental geosciences (MS, PhD); environmental geosciences-environmental toxicology (PhD); genetics (MS, PhD); genetics–environmental toxicology (PhD); geological sciences (MS, PhD); industrial mathematics (MS); mathematics (MAT, MS, PhD); mathematics education (MS, PhD); natural science (MAT, MS, PhD); neuroscience (MS, PhD); physics (MS, PhD); physiology (MS, PhD); plant biology (MS, PhD); plant breeding, genetics and biotechnology - plant biology (MS, PhD); quantitative biology (PhD); statistics (MS, PhD); zoo and aquarium management (MS); zoology (MS, PhD); zoology-environmental toxicology (PhD). Electronic applications accepted.

College of Nursing *Program availability:* Part-time, online learning. Offers nursing (MSN, PhD). Electronic applications accepted.

College of Social Science Offers anthropology (MA, PhD); Chicano/Latino studies (PhD); child development (MA); clinical social work (MSW); community services (MS); criminal justice (MS, PhD); economics (MA, PhD); family and child ecology (PhD); family studies (MA); forensic science (MS); geographic information science (MS); geography (MS, PhD); history (MA, PhD); history-secondary school teaching (MA); human resources and labor relations (MLRHR); industrial relations and human resources (PhD); law enforcement intelligence and analysis (MS); marriage and family therapy (MA); organizational and community practice (MSW); political science (MA, PhD); professional applications in anthropology (MA); psychology (MA, PhD); public policy (MPP); social science (MA, MIPS, MLRHR, MPP, MS, MSW, MURP, PhD); social work (PhD); sociology (MA, PhD); youth development (MA). Electronic applications accepted.

Eli Broad College of Business *Program availability:* Evening/weekend. Offers accounting (MS, PhD); business (MBA, MS, PhD); business analytics (MS); business information systems (PhD); finance (MS, PhD); foodservice business management (MS); hospitality business management (MS); human resource management (MBA); integrative management (MBA); logistics (PhD); management (PhD); management, strategy, and leadership (MS); marketing (MBA, PhD); marketing research (MS); operations and sourcing management (PhD); supply chain management (MBA, MS). Electronic applications accepted.

National Superconducting Cyclotron Laboratory Offers chemistry (PhD); physics (PhD).

MICHIGAN STATE UNIVERSITY COLLEGE OF LAW, East Lansing, MI 48824-1300

General Information Independent, coed, graduate-only institution. *Enrollment by degree level:* 71 master's, 785 doctoral. *Graduate faculty:* 55 full-time (23 women), 77 part-time/adjunct (27 women). *Tuition:* Full-time $43,400. *Graduate housing:* Rooms and/or apartments available on a first-come, first-served basis to single and married students. Housing application deadline: 4/1. *Student services:* Campus employment opportunities, campus safety program, career counseling, exercise/wellness program, international student services, low-cost health insurance, multicultural affairs office, services for students with disabilities, writing training. *Library facilities:* John F. Schaefer Law Library plus 5 others. *Collection:* Books: 38,664 (physical), 41,312 (digital/electronic); Serial titles: 4,001 (physical), 5,387 (digital/electronic); Databases: 31. Weekly public service hours: 71; students can reserve study rooms.

Computer facilities: 100 computers available on campus for general student use. A campuswide network can be accessed. Online class registration is available. Website: http://www.law.msu.edu/

General Application Contact: Melanie Jacobs, Senior Associate Dean of Admissions and International Programs/Professor of Law, 517-432-0222, Fax: 517-432-0098, E-mail: admiss@law.msu.edu.

GRADUATE UNITS

Graduate and Professional Programs Students: 779 full-time (407 women), 77 part-time (50 women); includes 173 minority (57 Black or African American, non-Hispanic/Latino; 9 American Indian or Alaska Native, non-Hispanic/Latino; 28 Asian, non-Hispanic/Latino; 40 Hispanic/Latino; 2 Native Hawaiian or other Pacific Islander, non-Hispanic/Latino; 37 Two or more races, non-Hispanic/Latino), 91 international. Average age 24. *Faculty:* 55 full-time (23 women), 77 part-time/adjunct (27 women). Expenses: Contact institution. *Financial support:* Career-related internships or fieldwork, Federal Work-Study, scholarships/grants, and tuition waivers (full and partial) available. Support available to part-time students. Financial award application deadline: 4/1; financial award applicants required to submit FAFSA. *Program availability:* Part-time. Offers American legal system (LL M, MJ); global food law (LL M, MJ); intellectual property law (LL M, MJ); law (JD); legal studies (MLS). *Application deadline:* For fall admission, 4/30 priority date for domestic students, 7/1 priority date for international students. Applications are processed on a rolling basis. *Application fee:* $60. Electronic applications accepted. *Application Contact:* Melanie Jacobs, Senior Associate Dean of Admissions and International Programs, 517-432-0222, Fax: 517-432-0098, E-mail: admiss@law.msu.edu. *Dean/Professor of Law,* Lawrence Ponoroff, 517-432-6993, Fax: 517-432-6801, E-mail: lponoroff@law.msu.edu.

MICHIGAN TECHNOLOGICAL UNIVERSITY, Houghton, MI 49931

General Information State-supported, coed, university. CGS member. *Enrollment:* 7,319 graduate, professional, and undergraduate students; 1,064 full-time matriculated graduate/professional students (270 women), 316 part-time matriculated graduate/professional students (104 women). *Enrollment by degree level:* 852 master's, 513 doctoral, 15 other advanced degrees. *Graduate faculty:* 469 full-time (118 women), 155 part-time/adjunct (29 women). Tuition, state resident: full-time $17,100; part-time $950 per credit. Tuition, nonresident: full-time $17,100; part-time $950 per credit. *Required fees:* $248; $124 per term. Tuition and fees vary according to course load and program. *Graduate housing:* Rooms and/or apartments available on a first-come, first-served basis to single and married students. Typical cost: $6375 per year ($10,665 including board) for single students. Room and board charges vary according to board plan and housing facility selected. *Student services:* Campus employment opportunities, campus safety program, career counseling, child daycare facilities, exercise/wellness program, free psychological counseling, grant writing training, international student services, low-cost health insurance, multicultural affairs office, services for students with disabilities, teacher training, writing training. *Library facilities:* J. R. Van Pelt and John and Ruanne Opie Library. *Collection:* Books: 362,342 (physical), 142,603 (digital/electronic); Serial titles: 14,050 (physical), 124,764 (digital/electronic); Databases: 347. Weekly public service hours: 105; study areas open 24 hours, 5–7 days a week; students can reserve study rooms. *Research affiliation:* Ariens Company (materials testing), Michelin North America, Inc. (materials testing), Osmose Inc. (materials testing), Faurecia Emissions Control Technologies (emissions testing), E3 Sparkplugs (automotive technology design), General Motors Holdings LLC (vehicle engine research).

Computer facilities: 1,079 computers available on campus for general student use. A campuswide network can be accessed from student residence rooms and from off campus. Online class registration is available. Website: http://www.mtu.edu/

General Application Contact: Carol T. Wingerson, Administrative Aide, 906-487-2328, Fax: 906-487-2284, E-mail: gradadms@mtu.edu.

GRADUATE UNITS

Graduate School Students: 1,064 full-time (270 women), 316 part-time (104 women); includes 54 minority (14 Black or African American, non-Hispanic/Latino; 3 American Indian or Alaska Native, non-Hispanic/Latino; 7 Asian, non-Hispanic/Latino; 10 Hispanic/Latino; 20 Two or more races, non-Hispanic/Latino), 849 international. Average age 28. 5,097 applicants, 30% accepted, 428 enrolled. *Faculty:* 469 full-time (118 women), 155 part-time/adjunct (29 women). Expenses: Contact institution. *Financial support:* In 2017–18, 964 students received support, including 89 fellowships with tuition reimbursements available (averaging $15,790 per year), 222 research assistantships with tuition reimbursements available (averaging $15,790 per year), 216 teaching assistantships with tuition reimbursements available (averaging $15,790 per year); career-related internships or fieldwork, Federal Work-Study, scholarships/grants, traineeships, health care benefits, unspecified assistantships, and cooperative program also available. Financial award applicants required to submit FAFSA. In 2017, 479 master's, 81 doctorates, 61 other advanced degrees awarded. *Program availability:* Part-time, 100% online, blended/hybrid learning. Offers atmospheric sciences (PhD); automotive systems and controls (Graduate Certificate); biochemistry and molecular biology (PhD); computational science and engineering (PhD); data science (MS, Graduate Certificate); engineering-environmental (PhD); international profile (Graduate Certificate); nanotechnology (Graduate Certificate); sustainability (Graduate Certificate); sustainable water resources systems (Graduate Certificate). *Application deadline:* Applications are processed on a rolling basis. Electronic applications accepted. *Application Contact:* Carol T. Wingerson, Administrative Aide, 906-487-2328, Fax: 906-487-2284, E-mail: gradadms@mtu.edu. *Dean of the Graduate School/Associate Provost for Graduate Education,* Dr. Pushpalatha Murthy, 906-487-2326, Fax: 906-487-2284, E-mail: ppmurthy@mtu.edu.

College of Engineering Students: 677 full-time (115 women), 172 part-time (40 women); includes 29 minority (8 Black or African American, non-Hispanic/Latino; 6 Asian, non-Hispanic/Latino; 8 Hispanic/Latino; 7 Two or more races, non-Hispanic/Latino), 597 international. Average age 27. 3,074 applicants, 32% accepted, 282 enrolled. *Faculty:* 259 full-time, 87 part-time/adjunct. Expenses: Contact institution. *Financial support:* In 2017–18, 598 students received support, including 51 fellowships with tuition reimbursements available (averaging $15,790 per year), 140 research assistantships with tuition reimbursements available (averaging $15,790 per year), 74 teaching assistantships with tuition reimbursements available (averaging $15,790 per year); career-related internships or fieldwork, Federal Work-Study, scholarships/grants, health care benefits, unspecified assistantships, and cooperative program also available. Financial award applicants required to submit FAFSA. In 2017, 371 master's, 55 doctorates, 61 other advanced degrees awarded. *Program availability:* Part-time, 100% online, blended/hybrid learning. Offers advanced electric power engineering (Graduate Certificate); biomedical engineering (MS, PhD); chemical engineering (MS, PhD); civil engineering (MS, PhD); computer engineering (MS, PhD); electrical engineering (MS, PhD); engineering (MS, PhD, Graduate Certificate); engineering mechanics (MS); environmental engineering (MS, PhD); environmental engineering science (MS); geological engineering (MS, PhD); geology (MS, PhD); geophysics (MS, PhD); hybrid electric drive vehicle engineering (Graduate Certificate); materials science and engineering (MS, PhD); mechanical engineering (MS); mechanical engineering-engineering mechanics (PhD); mining engineering (MS, PhD). *Application deadline:* Applications are processed on a rolling basis. Electronic applications accepted. *Application Contact:* Carol T. Wingerson, Administrative Aide, 906-487-2328, Fax: 906-487-2284, E-mail: gradadms@mtu.edu. *Dean,* Dr. Janet Callahan.

College of Sciences and Arts Students: 240 full-time (105 women), 74 part-time (30 women); includes 18 minority (4 Black or African American, non-Hispanic/Latino; 2 American Indian or Alaska Native, non-Hispanic/Latino; 1 Asian, non-Hispanic/Latino; 1 Hispanic/Latino; 10 Two or more races, non-Hispanic/Latino), 149 international. Average age 30. 1,155 applicants, 29% accepted, 73 enrolled. *Faculty:* 247 full-time (82 women), 49 part-time/adjunct. Expenses: Contact institution. *Financial support:* In 2017–18, 236 students received support, including 24 fellowships with tuition reimbursements available (averaging $15,790 per year), 44 research assistantships with tuition reimbursements available (averaging $15,790 per year), 126 teaching assistantships with tuition reimbursements available (averaging $15,790 per year); career-related internships or fieldwork, Federal Work-Study, scholarships/grants, traineeships, health care benefits, unspecified assistantships, and cooperative program also available. Financial award applicants required to submit FAFSA. In 2017, 51 master's, 23 doctorates awarded. *Program availability:* Part-time, blended/hybrid learning. Offers applied cognitive science and human factors (MS, PhD); applied physics (MS, PhD); applied science education (MS); biological sciences (MS, PhD); chemistry (MS, PhD); computer science (MS, PhD); cybersecurity (MS); environmental and energy policy (MS, PhD); industrial archaeology (MS); industrial heritage and archaeology (PhD); integrative physiology (PhD); kinesiology (MS); mathematical sciences (MS, PhD); physics (MS, PhD); post-secondary STEM education (Graduate Certificate); rhetoric, theory and culture (MS, PhD); sciences and arts (MS, PhD, Graduate Certificate). *Application deadline:* For fall admission, 4/1 for domestic and international students; for spring admission, 9/1 for domestic and international students. Applications are processed on a rolling basis. Electronic applications accepted. *Application Contact:* Carol T. Wingerson, Administrative Aide, 906-487-2328, Fax: 906-487-2284, E-mail: gradadms@mtu.edu. *Dean,* Dr. David Hemmer, 906-487-2156, Fax: 906-487-3347, E-mail: djhemmer@mtu.edu.

School of Business and Economics Students: 25 full-time (12 women), 21 part-time (13 women); includes 1 minority (Two or more races, non-Hispanic/Latino), 14 international. Average age 27. 165 applicants, 23% accepted, 22 enrolled. *Faculty:* 24

full-time (6 women), 1 part-time/adjunct. Expenses: Contact institution. *Financial support:* In 2017–18, 22 students received support. Health care benefits and unspecified assistantships available. Financial award application deadline: 2/1; financial award applicants required to submit FAFSA. In 2017, 24 master's awarded. *Program availability:* Part-time, evening/weekend. Offers accounting (MS); applied natural resource economics (MS); business administration (MBA). *Application deadline:* For fall admission, 7/1 for domestic and international students; for spring admission, 12/1 for domestic and international students. Applications are processed on a rolling basis. Electronic applications accepted. *Application Contact:* Carol T. Wingerson, Administrative Aide, 906-487-2328, Fax: 906-487-2284, E-mail: gradadms@mtu.edu. *Dean*, Dr. Dean Johnson, 906-487-2668, Fax: 906-487-1863, E-mail: dean@mtu.edu.

School of Forest Resources and Environmental Science Students: 44 full-time (15 women), 15 part-time (6 women); includes 3 minority (1 Black or African American, non-Hispanic/Latino; 2 Two or more races, non-Hispanic/Latino), 15 international. Average age 30. 125 applicants, 22% accepted, 19 enrolled. *Faculty:* 37 full-time (8 women), 19 part-time/adjunct (4 women). Expenses: Contact institution. *Financial support:* In 2017–18, 34 students received support, including 4 fellowships with tuition reimbursements available (averaging $15,790 per year), 17 research assistantships with tuition reimbursements available (averaging $15,790 per year), 7 teaching assistantships with tuition reimbursements available (averaging $15,790 per year); career-related internships or fieldwork, Federal Work-Study, scholarships/grants, health care benefits, unspecified assistantships, and cooperative program also available. Financial award applicants required to submit FAFSA. In 2017, 26 master's, 3 doctorates awarded. *Program availability:* Part-time. Offers applied ecology (MS); applied ecology and environment sciences (MS); forest molecular genetics and biotechnology (MS, PhD); forest resources and environmental science (MF, MGIS); forest science (PhD); forestry ecology and management (MS). *Application deadline:* Applications are processed on a rolling basis. Electronic applications accepted. *Application Contact:* Dr. Andrew J. Storer, Associate Dean, 906-487-3470, Fax: 906-487-2915, E-mail: storer@mtu.edu. *Dean*, Dr. Terry Sharik, 906-487-2352, Fax: 906-487-2915, E-mail: tlsharik@mtu.edu.

School of Technology Students: 8 full-time (4 women), 18 part-time (11 women); includes 2 minority (1 American Indian or Alaska Native, non-Hispanic/Latino; 1 Hispanic/Latino), 8 international. Average age 36. 70 applicants, 33% accepted, 5 enrolled. *Faculty:* 16 full-time, 4 part-time/adjunct. Expenses: Contact institution. *Financial support:* In 2017–18, 7 students received support, including 1 fellowship (averaging $15,790 per year), 3 research assistantships (averaging $15,790 per year); career-related internships or fieldwork, Federal Work-Study, scholarships/grants, and health care benefits also available. Financial award applicants required to submit FAFSA. In 2017, 7 master's awarded. *Program availability:* Part-time, 100% online, blended/hybrid learning. Offers integrated geospatial technology (MS); medical informatics (MS). *Application deadline:* Applications are processed on a rolling basis. Electronic applications accepted. *Application Contact:* Peggy A. Gorton, Executive Assistant, 906-487-2260, Fax: 906-487-2583, E-mail: pagorton@mtu.edu. *Dean*, Dr. James O. Frendewey, 906-487-2260, Fax: 906-487-2583, E-mail: jimf@mtu.edu.

MID-AMERICA BAPTIST THEOLOGICAL SEMINARY, Cordova, TN 38016

General Information Independent-religious, men only, comprehensive institution. *Enrollment:* 327 graduate, professional, and undergraduate students; 222 full-time matriculated graduate/professional students (16 women), 54 part-time matriculated graduate/professional students (11 women). *Enrollment by degree level:* 178 master's, 98 doctoral. *Graduate faculty:* 34 full-time (11 women), 5 part-time/adjunct (1 woman). *Tuition:* Part-time $250 per credit hour. One-time fee: $500 part-time. *Graduate housing:* Rooms and/or apartments available on a first-come, first-served basis to single and married students. Typical cost: $6720 per year for single students; $6720 per year for married students. Room charges vary according to housing facility selected. Housing application deadline: 7/31. *Student services:* Campus employment opportunities, career counseling, exercise/wellness program, services for students with disabilities. *Library facilities:* Ora Byram Allison Memorial Library. *Collection:* Students can reserve study rooms.

Computer facilities: 10 computers available on campus for general student use. A campuswide network can be accessed.
Website: http://www.mabts.edu/

General Application Contact: Tad Wingo, Senior Director of Admissions, 901-751-8453, Fax: 901-751-8454, E-mail: twingo@mabts.edu.

GRADUATE UNITS

Graduate and Professional Programs Expenses: Contact institution. Offers biblical counseling (M Div); Christian education (M Div, MACE); ministry (D Min); missiology and intercultural studies (M Div); pastoral ministry (M Div); theology (MA, PhD); worship (MA). *Application deadline:* For fall admission, 7/20 priority date for domestic students. Applications are processed on a rolling basis. *Application fee:* $35. Electronic applications accepted. *Application Contact:* Tanner Hickman, Director of Admissions, 901-751-3015, Fax: 901-751-8454, E-mail: tannerh@mabts.edu. *President*, Dr. Michael R. Spradlin, 901-751-3048.

MID-AMERICA BAPTIST THEOLOGICAL SEMINARY NORTHEAST BRANCH, Schenectady, NY 12303-3463

General Information Independent-religious, coed, primarily men, graduate-only institution. *Graduate housing:* Rooms and/or apartments available on a first-come, first-served basis to single and married students.

GRADUATE UNITS

Program in Theology *Program availability:* Part-time, evening/weekend. Offers theology (M Div). Electronic applications accepted.

MID-AMERICA CHRISTIAN UNIVERSITY, Oklahoma City, OK 73170-4504

General Information Independent-religious, coed, comprehensive institution.

GRADUATE UNITS

Program in Business Administration Offers business administration (MBA).

Program in Counseling Offers marital and family therapy (MS); pastoral/spiritual direction (MS); professional counselor (MS).

Program in Leadership Offers leadership (MA).

Program in Public Administration Offers public administration (MA).

MIDAMERICA NAZARENE UNIVERSITY, Olathe, KS 66062-1899

General Information Independent-religious, coed, comprehensive institution. *Graduate housing:* On-campus housing not available.

GRADUATE UNITS

Professional and Graduate Studies in Education *Program availability:* Part-time, evening/weekend, online only, 100% online. Offers ESOL (M Ed); reading specialist (M Ed); technology enhanced teaching (M Ed). Electronic applications accepted.

School of Behavioral Sciences and Counseling *Program availability:* Evening/weekend. Offers counseling (MA). Electronic applications accepted.

School of Business *Program availability:* Part-time, evening/weekend, 100% online, blended/hybrid learning. Offers management (MBA, MSM). Electronic applications accepted.

School of Nursing and Health Science *Program availability:* Part-time, evening/weekend, 100% online, blended/hybrid learning. Offers healthcare administration (MSN); healthcare quality management (MSN); nursing education (MSN); public health (MSN). Electronic applications accepted.

MID-AMERICA REFORMED SEMINARY, Dyer, IN 46311

General Information Independent-religious, men only, graduate-only institution.

GRADUATE UNITS

Graduate Programs Offers theology (M Div, MTS).

MIDDLEBURY COLLEGE, Middlebury, VT 05753-6002

General Information Independent, coed, comprehensive institution. *Enrollment:* 2,603 graduate, professional, and undergraduate students; 42 part-time matriculated graduate/professional students (35 women). *Enrollment by degree level:* 42 master's. *Graduate housing:* Room and/or apartments guaranteed to single students; on-campus housing not available to married students. *Student services:* Campus safety program, career counseling, free psychological counseling, international student services, services for students with disabilities, teacher training. *Library facilities:* Davis Family Library plus 2 others. *Collection:* Books: 764,667 (physical), 644,056 (digital/electronic); Databases: 695. Weekly public service hours: 112; students can reserve study rooms.

Computer facilities: Computer purchase and lease plans are available. 250 computers available on campus for general student use. A campuswide network can be accessed from student residence rooms and from off campus. Online class registration, personal Web pages, file servers are available.
Website: http://www.middlebury.edu/

General Application Contact: Admissions Office, 802-443-3000, Fax: 802-443-2056, E-mail: admissions@middlebury.edu.

GRADUATE UNITS

Language Schools Expenses: Contact institution. *Financial support:* Fellowships and scholarships/grants available. Financial award applicants required to submit FAFSA. Offers language (MA, DML). *Application deadline:* For summer admission, 5/1 for domestic and international students. Applications are processed on a rolling basis. *Application fee:* $75. Electronic applications accepted. *Application Contact:* Kara Gennarelli, Technical and Lead Coordinator, Language Schools Office, 802-443-5727, Fax: 802-443-2075, E-mail: languages@middlebury.edu. *Dean*, Dr. Stephen B. Snyder, 802-443-5979, Fax: 802-443-2075, E-mail: ssnyder@middlebury.edu.

Arabic School Expenses: Contact institution. *Financial support:* Fellowships and scholarships/grants available. Financial award application deadline: 3/14; financial award applicants required to submit FAFSA. Offers Arabic language pedagogy (MA); Arabic studies (MA). *Application deadline:* For summer admission, 5/1 for domestic and international students. Applications are processed on a rolling basis. *Application fee:* $75. Electronic applications accepted. *Application Contact:* Barbara Walter, Coordinator, 802-443-5230, Fax: 802-443-2075, E-mail: bwalter@middlebury.edu. *Director*, Dr. Mahmoud Abdalla, 802-443-5230, Fax: 802-443-2075, E-mail: mabdalla@miis.edu.

Chinese School Expenses: Contact institution. *Financial support:* Fellowships and scholarships/grants available. Financial award application deadline: 3/15; financial award applicants required to submit FAFSA. Offers Chinese (MA). *Application deadline:* Applications are processed on a rolling basis. *Application fee:* $75. Electronic applications accepted. *Application Contact:* Mimi Clark, Coordinator, 802-443-5520, Fax: 802-443-2075, E-mail: chineseschool@middlebury.edu. *Director*, Dr. Jianhua Bai, 802-443-5520, Fax: 802-443-2075, E-mail: jbai@middlebury.edu.

French School Expenses: Contact institution. *Financial support:* Fellowships and scholarships/grants available. Financial award application deadline: 3/10; financial award applicants required to submit FAFSA. Offers French (MA, DML). *Application deadline:* Applications are processed on a rolling basis. *Application fee:* $75. Electronic applications accepted. *Application Contact:* Sheila Schwaneflugel, Coordinator, 802-443-5526, Fax: 802-443-2075, E-mail: sschwaneflugel@middlebury.edu. *Director*, Dr. Philippe France, 802-443-5526, Fax: 802-443-2075.

German School Expenses: Contact institution. *Financial support:* Fellowships and scholarships/grants available. Financial award application deadline: 3/9; financial award applicants required to submit FAFSA. Offers German (MA, DML). *Application deadline:* Applications are processed on a rolling basis. *Application fee:* $75. Electronic applications accepted. *Application Contact:* Christina Ellison, Coordinator, 802-443-5203, Fax: 802-443-2075, E-mail: germanschool@middlebury.edu. *Director*, Dr. Bettina Matthias, 802-443-3527, Fax: 802-443-2075, E-mail: bmatthia@middlebury.edu.

Hebrew School Expenses: Contact institution. *Financial support:* Fellowships and scholarships/grants available. Financial award application deadline: 3/28; financial award applicants required to submit FAFSA. *Program availability:* Blended/hybrid learning. Offers Hebrew (MA). *Application deadline:* Applications are processed on a rolling basis. *Application fee:* $75. Electronic applications accepted. *Director*, Vardit Ringvald, 802-443-3574, E-mail: vringval@middlebury.edu.

Italian School Expenses: Contact institution. *Financial support:* Fellowships and scholarships/grants available. Financial award application deadline: 3/10; financial award applicants required to submit FAFSA. Offers Italian (MA, DML). *Application deadline:* Applications are processed on a rolling basis. *Application fee:* $75. Electronic applications accepted. *Application Contact:* Joseph Tamagni, Coordinator, 802-443-5727, Fax: 802-443-2075, E-mail: italianschool@middlebury.edu. *Director*, Dr. Antonio Vitti, 802-443-5727, Fax: 802-443-2075, E-mail: acvitti@middlebury.edu.

Russian School Expenses: Contact institution. *Financial support:* Fellowships and scholarships/grants available. Financial award application deadline: 3/14; financial award applicants required to submit FAFSA. Offers Russian (MA, DML). *Application deadline:* Applications are processed on a rolling basis. *Application fee:* $75. Electronic applications accepted. *Application Contact:* Oliver Carling, Coordinator, 802-443-2006, Fax: 802-443-2075, E-mail: ocarling@middlebury.edu. *Director*, Dr. Jason Merrill, 802-443-5230, Fax: 802-443-2075, E-mail: jmerrill@middlebury.edu.

Spanish School Expenses: Contact institution. *Financial support:* Fellowships and scholarships/grants available. Financial award application deadline: 3/8; financial award applicants required to submit FAFSA. Offers Spanish (MA, DML). *Application deadline:* Applications are processed on a rolling basis. *Application fee:* $75. Electronic applications accepted. *Application Contact:* Audrey LaRock, Coordinator, 802-443-5539, Fax: 802-443-2075, E-mail: larock@middlebury.edu. *Director,* Dr. Jacobo Sefami, 802-443-5539, Fax: 802-443-2075, E-mail: jsefami@middlelbury.edu.

Middlebury Bread Loaf School of English *Program availability:* Part-time. Offers English (M Litt, MA). Offered during summer only. Electronic applications accepted.

MIDDLEBURY INSTITUTE OF INTERNATIONAL STUDIES AT MONTEREY, Monterey, CA 93940-2691

General Information Independent, coed, graduate-only institution. *Graduate housing:* On-campus housing not available.

GRADUATE UNITS

Graduate School of International Policy and Management Offers international education management (MA); international environmental policy (MA); international policy and development (MA); international policy and management (MA, MPA); international trade and economic diplomacy (MA); nonproliferation and terrorism studies (MA); public administration (MPA). Electronic applications accepted.

Graduate School of Translation, Interpretation and Language Education Offers conference interpretation (MA); teaching English to speakers of other languages (MATESOL); teaching foreign language (MATFL); translation (MA); translation and interpretation (MA); translation and localization management (MA); translation, interpretation and language education (MA, MATESOL, MATFL). Electronic applications accepted.

MIDDLE GEORGIA STATE UNIVERSITY, Macon, GA 31206

General Information State-supported, coed, comprehensive institution.

GRADUATE UNITS

Office of Graduate Studies Offers adult/gerontology acute care nurse practitioner (MSN); information technology (MS).

MIDDLE TENNESSEE SCHOOL OF ANESTHESIA, Madison, TN 37116

General Information Independent-religious, coed, graduate-only institution. *Graduate housing:* On-campus housing not available.

GRADUATE UNITS

Graduate Programs Offers anesthesia (MS, DNAP).

MIDDLE TENNESSEE STATE UNIVERSITY, Murfreesboro, TN 37132

General Information State-supported, coed, university. CGS member. *Graduate housing:* Rooms and/or apartments available on a first-come, first-served basis to single and married students.

GRADUATE UNITS

College of Graduate Studies *Program availability:* Part-time, evening/weekend, online learning. Offers mathematics and science education (PhD). Electronic applications accepted.

College of Basic and Applied Sciences *Program availability:* Part-time, evening/weekend, online learning. Offers actuarial sciences (MS); aerospace education (M Ed); aviation administration (MS); basic and applied sciences (M Ed, MS, MSN, MST, PhD, Graduate Certificate); biology (MS); biostatistics (MS); biotechnology (MS); chemistry (MS); computational science (PhD); computer science (MS); engineering management (MS); engineering technology (MS); health care informatics (MS); horse science (MS); mathematics (MS, MST); molecular biosciences (PhD). Electronic applications accepted.

College of Behavioral and Health Sciences Offers behavioral and health sciences (MA, MCJ, MS, MSN, MSW, PhD, Ed S, Graduate Certificate); clinical psychology (MA); criminal justice administration (MCJ); exercise science (MS); experimental psychology (MA); family nurse practitioner (MSN, Graduate Certificate); health and human performance (MS); health, physical education and recreation (MS); human performance (PhD); industrial/organizational psychology (MA); leisure and sport management (MS); nursing (MSN, Graduate Certificate); psychology (MA, Ed S); quantitative psychology (MA); school psychology (MA); social work (MSW). Electronic applications accepted.

College of Education *Program availability:* Part-time, evening/weekend, online learning. Offers administration and supervision (M Ed, Ed S); curriculum and instruction (M Ed, Ed S); early childhood education (M Ed); education (M Ed, PhD, Ed S); elementary education (M Ed, Ed S); English as a second language (M Ed, Ed S); literacy studies (PhD); mental health counseling (M Ed); middle school education (M Ed); professional counseling (M Ed); reading (M Ed); school counseling (M Ed); secondary education (M Ed); special education (M Ed); technology and curriculum design (Ed S). Electronic applications accepted.

College of Liberal Arts *Program availability:* Part-time, evening/weekend, online learning. Offers archival management (Graduate Certificate); English (MA, PhD); foreign languages (MAT); geosciences (Graduate Certificate); gerontology (Graduate Certificate); history (MA); international affairs (MA); liberal arts (MA, MAT, MSW, PhD, Graduate Certificate); music (MA); public history (PhD); sociology (MA); women's and gender studies (Graduate Certificate). Electronic applications accepted.

College of Mass Communication *Program availability:* Part-time, evening/weekend, online learning. Offers mass communication (MFA, MS); recording arts and technologies (MFA). Electronic applications accepted.

Jennings A. Jones College of Business *Program availability:* Part-time, evening/weekend, online learning. Offers accounting (M Acc); business (M Acc, MA, MBA, MBE, MS, PhD); business administration (MBA); business education (MBE); computer information systems (MS); economics (MA, PhD); management (MS). Electronic applications accepted.

University College *Program availability:* Part-time, evening/weekend, online learning. Offers advanced studies in teaching and learning (M Ed); human resources leadership (MPS); nursing administration (MSN); nursing education (MSN); strategic leadership (MPS); training and development (MPS).

MIDWAY UNIVERSITY, Midway, KY 40347-1120

General Information Independent-religious, coed, comprehensive institution. *Graduate housing:* On-campus housing not available.

GRADUATE UNITS

Graduate Programs Offers education (MAT); leadership (MBA).

MIDWEST COLLEGE OF ORIENTAL MEDICINE, Racine, WI 53403-9747

General Information Proprietary, coed, graduate-only institution. *Graduate housing:* On-campus housing not available. *Research affiliation:* Guangzhou University of Traditional Chinese Medicine (pharmacology).

GRADUATE UNITS

Graduate Programs *Program availability:* Part-time, evening/weekend. Offers acupuncture (Certificate); Oriental medicine (MSOM).

Graduate Programs-Chicago *Program availability:* Part-time, evening/weekend.

MIDWESTERN BAPTIST THEOLOGICAL SEMINARY, Kansas City, MO 64118-4697

General Information Independent-religious, coed, graduate-only institution. *Graduate housing:* Rooms and/or apartments guaranteed to single and married students.

GRADUATE UNITS

Graduate and Professional Programs *Program availability:* Part-time, online learning. Offers Christian education (MACE); Christian foundations (Graduate Certificate); church music (MCM); counseling (MA); ministry (D Ed Min, D Min); Old or New Testament studies (PhD); theology (M Div). Electronic applications accepted.

MIDWESTERN STATE UNIVERSITY, Wichita Falls, TX 76308

General Information State-supported, coed, comprehensive institution. CGS member. *Graduate housing:* Rooms and/or apartments available on a first-come, first-served basis to single and married students.

GRADUATE UNITS

Billie Doris McAda Graduate School *Program availability:* Part-time, evening/weekend. Electronic applications accepted.

College of Science and Mathematics *Program availability:* Part-time, evening/weekend. Offers biology (MS); computer science (MS); science and mathematics (MS). Electronic applications accepted.

Dillard College of Business Administration *Program availability:* Part-time, evening/weekend. Offers business administration (MBA). Electronic applications accepted.

Prothro-Yeager College of Humanities and Social Sciences *Program availability:* Part-time, evening/weekend. Offers clinical/counseling psychology (MA); English (MA); history (MA); humanities and social sciences (MA, PhD); philosophy (PhD); political science (MA). Electronic applications accepted.

Robert D. and Carol Gunn College of Health Sciences and Human Services *Program availability:* Part-time, evening/weekend. Offers criminal justice (MA); exercise physiology (MS); family nurse practitioner (MSN); family psychiatric mental health nurse practitioner (MSN); health information management (MHA); health sciences and human services (MA, MHA, MS, MSN, Graduate Certificate); health services administration (Graduate Certificate); medical practice management (MHA); nurse educator (MSN); public and community sector health care management (MHA); radiologic sciences (MS); rural and urban hospital management (MHA). Electronic applications accepted.

West College of Education *Program availability:* Part-time, evening/weekend. Offers counseling (MA); curriculum and instruction (M Ed); education (M Ed, MA); educational leadership (M Ed); educational technology (M Ed); human resource development (MA); reading (M Ed); school counseling (M Ed); special education (M Ed); sport administration (M Ed); training and development (MA). Electronic applications accepted.

MIDWESTERN UNIVERSITY, DOWNERS GROVE CAMPUS, Downers Grove, IL 60515-1235

General Information Independent, coed, graduate-only institution. *Graduate housing:* Rooms and/or apartments available on a first-come, first-served basis to single and married students. *Student services:* Campus employment opportunities, campus safety program, career counseling, exercise/wellness program, free psychological counseling, low-cost health insurance. *Library facilities:* Alumni Memorial Library plus 2 others.

Computer facilities: 190 computers available on campus for general student use. Website: http://www.midwestern.edu/

General Application Contact: Michael Laken, Director of Admissions, 630-515-6171, Fax: 630-971-6086, E-mail: admissil@midwestern.edu.

GRADUATE UNITS

Chicago College of Optometry Expenses: Contact institution. Offers optometry (OD).

Chicago College of Osteopathic Medicine Expenses: Contact institution. *Financial support:* Fellowships with partial tuition reimbursements, career-related internships or fieldwork, Federal Work-Study, institutionally sponsored loans, and tuition waivers (full and partial) available. Financial award application deadline: 6/1; financial award applicants required to submit FAFSA. Offers osteopathic medicine (DO). *Application deadline:* For fall admission, 1/1 for domestic students. Applications are processed on a rolling basis. *Application fee:* $50.

Chicago College of Pharmacy Expenses: Contact institution. *Financial support:* Federal Work-Study and institutionally sponsored loans available. Support available to part-time students. Financial award applicants required to submit FAFSA. *Program availability:* Part-time, online learning. Offers pharmacy (Pharm D). *Application deadline:* For fall admission, 2/3 for domestic students. *Application fee:* $50.

College of Dental Medicine-Illinois Expenses: Contact institution. Offers dental medicine (DMD).

College of Graduate Studies Expenses: Contact institution. Offers biomedical sciences (MA, MBS). *Application Contact:* Michael Laken, Director of Admissions, 630-515-6171, Fax: 630-971-6086, E-mail: admissil@midwestern.edu.

College of Health Sciences, Illinois Campus Expenses: Contact institution. *Financial support:* Federal Work-Study, institutionally sponsored loans, and scholarships/grants available. Financial award applicants required to submit FAFSA. Offers clinical psychology (Psy D); health sciences (MA, MBS, MMS, MOT, DPT, Psy D); occupational therapy (MOT); physical therapy (DPT); physician assistant studies (MMS); speech-language pathology (MS). *Application deadline:* Applications are processed on a rolling basis. *Application fee:* $50.

MIDWESTERN UNIVERSITY, GLENDALE CAMPUS, Glendale, AZ 85308

General Information Independent, coed, graduate-only institution. *Graduate housing:* Rooms and/or apartments available on a first-come, first-served basis to single and married students. *Student services:* Exercise/wellness program. Website: http://www.midwestern.edu/

General Application Contact: James Walter, Director of Admissions, 888-247-9277, Fax: 623-572-3229, E-mail: admissaz@midwestern.edu.

GRADUATE UNITS

Arizona College of Optometry Expenses: Contact institution. Offers optometry (OD).

Arizona College of Osteopathic Medicine Expenses: Contact institution. *Financial support:* Fellowships with partial tuition reimbursements, career-related internships or fieldwork, Federal Work-Study, institutionally sponsored loans, and tuition waivers (full and partial) available. Financial award application deadline: 6/12; financial award applicants required to submit FAFSA. Offers osteopathic medicine (DO). *Application deadline:* For fall admission, 11/1 priority date for domestic students; for winter admission, 2/1 for domestic students. Applications are processed on a rolling basis. *Application fee:* $50. Electronic applications accepted.

College of Dental Medicine Expenses: Contact institution. Offers dental medicine (DMD).

College of Health Sciences, Arizona Campus Expenses: Contact institution. *Financial support:* Federal Work-Study available. *Program availability:* Part-time. Offers biomedical sciences (MA, MBS); cardiovascular science (MCVS); clinical psychology (Psy D); health sciences (MA, MBS, MCVS, MMS, MOT, MS, DPM, DPT, Psy D); nurse anesthesia (MS); occupational therapy (MOT); physical therapy (DPT); physician assistant studies (MMS); podiatric medicine (DPM); speech-language pathology (MS). *Application deadline:* For fall admission, 6/4 for domestic students. Applications are processed on a rolling basis. *Application fee:* $50.

College of Pharmacy-Glendale Expenses: Contact institution. *Financial support:* Applicants required to submit FAFSA. Offers pharmacy (Pharm D). *Application deadline:* For fall admission, 2/1 for domestic students. *Application fee:* $50.

MIDWEST UNIVERSITY, Wentzville, MO 63385

General Information Independent-religious, coed, university. *Graduate housing:* Rooms and/or apartments available on a first-come, first-served basis to single and married students. Housing application deadline: 1/21.

MIDWIVES COLLEGE OF UTAH, Salt Lake City, UT 84106

General Information Independent, women only, comprehensive institution. *Enrollment:* 242 graduate, professional, and undergraduate students; 5 matriculated graduate/professional students (all women). *Enrollment by degree level:* 5 master's. *Graduate faculty:* 6. *Graduate housing:* On-campus housing not available. *Library facilities:* MCU Library. *Collection:* Books: 644 (physical); Serial titles: 5 (digital/electronic). Weekly public service hours: 35.
Website: http://www.midwifery.edu/

GRADUATE UNITS

Graduate Program Students: 5 (all women); includes 1 minority (Hispanic/Latino). *Faculty:* 6. Expenses: Contact institution. *Financial support:* Applicants required to submit FAFSA. In 2017, 2 master's awarded. *Program availability:* Part-time. Offers midwifery (MS). *Application deadline:* For fall admission, 3/15 for domestic and international students; for winter admission, 7/9 for domestic and international students; for summer admission, 11/6 for domestic and international students. *Application fee:* $60. Electronic applications accepted. *Dean of Graduate Studies,* Courtney L. Everson, 801-649-5230 Ext. 806, Fax: 866-207-2024, E-mail: graduatedean@midwifery.edu.

MILLENNIA ATLANTIC UNIVERSITY, Doral, FL 33178

General Information Proprietary, coed, comprehensive institution.

GRADUATE UNITS

Graduate Programs *Program availability:* Online learning.

MILLERSVILLE UNIVERSITY OF PENNSYLVANIA, Millersville, PA 17551-0302

General Information State-supported, coed, comprehensive institution. CGS member. *Enrollment:* 7,720 graduate, professional, and undergraduate students; 184 full-time matriculated graduate/professional students (137 women), 601 part-time matriculated graduate/professional students (450 women). *Enrollment by degree level:* 728 master's, 42 doctoral, 15 other advanced degrees. *Graduate faculty:* 86 full-time (54 women), 41 part-time/adjunct (27 women). Tuition, state resident: full-time $9000; part-time $500 per credit. Tuition, nonresident: full-time $13,500; part-time $750 per credit. *Required fees:* $2552; $141.75 per credit. Tuition and fees vary according to course load, degree level and program. *Graduate housing:* Room and/or apartments available on a first-come, first-served basis to single students; on-campus housing not available to married students. Typical cost: $8440 per year ($13,440 including board). Room and board charges vary according to board plan and housing facility selected. *Student services:* Campus employment opportunities, campus safety program, career counseling, exercise/wellness program, free psychological counseling, grant writing training, international student services, low-cost health insurance, multicultural affairs office, services for students with disabilities, teacher training, writing training. *Library facilities:* The Francine G. McNairy Library and Learning Forum at Ganser Hall. *Collection:* Books: 315,441 (physical), 54,392 (digital/electronic); Serial titles: 4,191 (physical), 391,998 (digital/electronic); Databases: 179. Weekly public service hours: 94; students can reserve study rooms. *Research affiliation:* Chincoteague Bay Field Station of the Marine Science Consortium (biology).

Computer facilities: 430 computers available on campus for general student use. A campuswide network can be accessed from student residence rooms and from off campus. Online class registration is available.
Website: http://www.millersville.edu/

General Application Contact: Dr. Victor S. DeSantis, Dean of College of Graduate Studies and Adult Education/Associate Provost for Civic and Community Engagement, 717-871-5154, Fax: 717-871-7955, E-mail: victor.desantis@millersville.edu.

GRADUATE UNITS

College of Graduate Studies and Adult Learning Students: 184 full-time (137 women), 601 part-time (450 women); includes 99 minority (36 Black or African American, non-Hispanic/Latino; 4 American Indian or Alaska Native, non-Hispanic/Latino; 12 Asian, non-Hispanic/Latino; 43 Hispanic/Latino; 4 Two or more races, non-Hispanic/Latino), 13 international. Average age 32. 468 applicants, 87% accepted, 243 enrolled. *Faculty:* 85 full-time (53 women), 40 part-time/adjunct (26 women). Expenses: Contact institution. *Financial support:* In 2017–18, 107 students received support. Unspecified assistantships available. Financial award application deadline: 3/15; financial award applicants required to submit FAFSA. In 2017, 272 master's awarded. *Program availability:* Part-time, evening/weekend, coursework completed primarily online, with a weekend residency once a semester. *Application deadline:* Applications are processed on a rolling basis. *Application fee:* $40. Electronic applications accepted. *Application Contact:* Chad E. Baker, Director of Graduate Admissions and Recruitment, 717-871-7644, E-mail: chad.baker@millersville.edu. *Dean of College of Graduate Studies and Adult Learning/Associate Provost for Civic and Community Engagement,* Dr. Victor S. DeSantis, 717-871-7619, Fax: 717-871-7954, E-mail: victor.desantis@millersville.edu.

College of Arts, Humanities and Social Sciences Students: 9 full-time (4 women), 51 part-time (37 women); includes 8 minority (1 Black or African American, non-Hispanic/Latino; 3 Asian, non-Hispanic/Latino; 4 Hispanic/Latino), 6 international. Average age 34. 30 applicants, 90% accepted, 10 enrolled. *Faculty:* 20 full-time (12 women), 4 part-time/adjunct (3 women). Expenses: Contact institution. *Financial support:* In 2017–18, 7 students received support. Unspecified assistantships available. Financial award application deadline: 3/15; financial award applicants required to submit FAFSA. In 2017, 28 master's awarded. *Program availability:* Part-time. Offers art education (M Ed); arts, humanities and social sciences (M Ed, MA, Postbaccalaureate Certificate); English (M Ed, MA); history (MA); languages and cultures: French (MA); languages and cultures: German (MA); languages and cultures: Spanish (MA); writing (Postbaccalaureate Certificate). *Application deadline:* Applications are processed on a rolling basis. *Application fee:* $40. Electronic applications accepted. *Application Contact:* Dr. Victor S. DeSantis, Dean of College of Graduate Studies and Adult Learning/Associate Provost for Civic and Community Engagement, 717-871-7619, Fax: 717-871-7954, E-mail: victor.desantis@millersville.edu. *Interim Dean,* Dr. Orlando J. Perez, 717-871-5631, Fax: 717-871-7947, E-mail: orlando.perez@millersville.edu.

College of Education and Human Services Students: 150 full-time (120 women), 376 part-time (300 women); includes 74 minority (30 Black or African American, non-Hispanic/Latino; 3 American Indian or Alaska Native, non-Hispanic/Latino; 5 Asian, non-Hispanic/Latino; 32 Hispanic/Latino; 4 Two or more races, non-Hispanic/Latino), 3 international. Average age 30. 358 applicants, 87% accepted, 186 enrolled. *Faculty:* 48 full-time (33 women), 24 part-time/adjunct (17 women). Expenses: Contact institution. *Financial support:* In 2017–18, 81 students received support. Unspecified assistantships available. Financial award application deadline: 3/15; financial award applicants required to submit FAFSA. In 2017, 176 master's awarded. *Program availability:* Part-time, evening/weekend, coursework completed primarily online, with a weekend residency once a semester. Offers assessment, curriculum and teaching - online teaching (M Ed); assessment, curriculum and teaching - STEM education (M Ed); assessment, curriculum, and teaching (M Ed); clinical psychology (MS); coaching education (Post-Master's Certificate); early childhood education (M Ed); education (M Ed, MS, MSW, DSW, Ed D, Post-Master's Certificate); educational leadership (Ed D); gifted education (M Ed); language and literacy (M Ed); language and literacy education (M Ed); language and literacy: ESL (M Ed); language and literacy: reading specialist (M Ed); leadership for teaching and learning (M Ed); school counseling (M Ed); school psychology (MS); social work (MSW, DSW); special education (M Ed); special education: 7-12 (M Ed); special education: PreK-8 (M Ed); sport management (M Ed); sport management: athletic coaching (M Ed, Post-Master's Certificate); sport management: athletic management (M Ed). *Application fee:* $40. Electronic applications accepted. *Application Contact:* Dr. Victor S. DeSantis, Dean of College of Graduate Studies and Adult Learning/Associate Provost for Civic and Community Engagement, 717-871-7619, Fax: 717-871-7954, E-mail: victor.desantis@millersville.edu. *Dean,* Dr. George Drake, 717-871-7333, E-mail: george.drake@millersville.edu.

College of Science and Technology Students: 25 full-time (13 women), 174 part-time (113 women); includes 17 minority (5 Black or African American, non-Hispanic/Latino; 1 American Indian or Alaska Native, non-Hispanic/Latino; 4 Asian, non-Hispanic/Latino; 7 Hispanic/Latino), 4 international. Average age 34. 80 applicants, 88% accepted, 47 enrolled. *Faculty:* 18 full-time (9 women), 13 part-time/adjunct (7 women). Expenses: Contact institution. *Financial support:* In 2017–18, 19 students received support. Unspecified assistantships available. Financial award application deadline: 3/15; financial award applicants required to submit FAFSA. In 2017, 63 master's awarded. *Program availability:* Part-time, evening/weekend, 100% online, blended/hybrid learning. Offers emergency management (MS); family nurse practitioner (MSN, Post-Master's Certificate); integrated scientific applications: climate science applications (MS); integrated scientific applications: environmental systems management (MS); integrated scientific applications: geoinformatics (MS); integrated scientific applications: weather intelligence and risk management (MS); mathematics (M Ed); nursing education (MSN, Post-Master's Certificate); nursing practice (DNP); science and technology (M Ed, MS, MSN, DNP); technology and innovation (M Ed). *Application deadline:* Applications are processed on a rolling basis. *Application fee:* $40. Electronic applications accepted. *Application Contact:* Dr. Victor S. DeSantis, Dean of College of Graduate Studies and Adult Learning/Associate Provost for Civic and Community Engagement, 717-871-7619, Fax: 717-871-7954, E-mail: victor.desantis@millersville.edu. *Dean, College of Science and Technology,* Dr. Michael Jackson, 717-871-4292, E-mail: michael.jackson@millersville.edu.

MILLIGAN COLLEGE, Milligan College, TN 37682

General Information Independent-religious, coed, comprehensive institution. *Enrollment:* 1,171 graduate, professional, and undergraduate students; 247 full-time matriculated graduate/professional students (148 women), 85 part-time matriculated graduate/professional students (52 women). *Enrollment by degree level:* 313 master's, 18 doctoral. *Graduate faculty:* 23 full-time (15 women), 14 part-time/adjunct (10 women). *Graduate housing:* Rooms and/or apartments available on a first-come, first-served basis to single and married students. Housing application deadline: 4/1. *Student services:* Campus employment opportunities, career counseling, exercise/wellness program, free psychological counseling, international student services, multicultural affairs office, services for students with disabilities, teacher training, writing training. *Library facilities:* P. H. Welshimer Memorial Library plus 1 other. *Collection:* Books: 170,942 (physical), 263,494 (digital/electronic); Serial titles: 982 (physical), 22,049 (digital/electronic); Databases: 83. Weekly public service hours: 89; students can reserve study rooms.

Computer facilities: 97 computers available on campus for general student use. A campuswide network can be accessed from student residence rooms and from off campus. Online class registration is available.
Website: http://www.milligan.edu/

General Application Contact: Brenda Bourn, Operations Manager, 423-461-8482, Fax: 423-461-8789, E-mail: bsbourn@milligan.edu.

GRADUATE UNITS

Area of Business Administration Students: 30 full-time (16 women), 1 international. Average age 38. 30 applicants, 83% accepted, 24 enrolled. *Faculty:* 4 full-time (1 woman), 3 part-time/adjunct (2 women). Expenses: Contact institution. *Financial support:* Scholarships/grants available. Financial award application deadline: 12/1; financial award applicants required to submit FAFSA. In 2017, 27 master's awarded. *Program availability:* 100% online, blended/hybrid learning. Offers health sector management (MBA, Graduate Certificate); leadership (MBA, Graduate Certificate);

operations management (MBA, Graduate Certificate). *Application deadline:* For fall admission, 8/1 for domestic students, 6/1 for international students; for spring admission, 1/15 for domestic students, 12/1 for international students. Applications are processed on a rolling basis. *Application fee:* $30. Electronic applications accepted. *Application Contact:* Rebecca Banton, Graduate Admissions Recruiter, Business Area, 423-461-8662, Fax: 423-461-8789, E-mail: rbbanton@milligan.edu. *Area Chair of Business*, Dr. David Campbell, 423-461-8674, Fax: 423-461-8677, E-mail: dacampbell@milligan.edu.

Area of Counselor Education Programs Students: 24 full-time (17 women), 7 part-time (6 women); includes 4 minority (3 Black or African American, non-Hispanic/Latino; 1 Two or more races, non-Hispanic/Latino), 1 international. Average age 32. 30 applicants, 70% accepted, 13 enrolled. *Faculty:* 4 full-time (all women), 2 part-time/adjunct (0 women). Expenses: Contact institution. *Financial support:* Scholarships/grants available. Financial award application deadline: 12/1; financial award applicants required to submit FAFSA. In 2017, 9 master's awarded. *Program availability:* Part-time. Offers clinical mental health counseling (MSC); counseling ministry (Graduate Certificate); school counseling (MSC). *Application deadline:* For fall admission, 8/1 for domestic students, 6/1 for international students. Applications are processed on a rolling basis. *Application fee:* $30. Electronic applications accepted. *Application Contact:* Jenni Duran, Graduate Admissions Recruiter, Healthcare Programs, 423-461-8424, Fax: 423-461-8789, E-mail: jduran@milligan.edu. *Director of Master of Science in Counseling Program*, Dr. Christine Browning, 423-461-3513, Fax: 423-461-8777, E-mail: cmbrowning@milligan.edu.

Area of Education Students: 27 full-time (20 women), 20 part-time (11 women); includes 2 minority (1 Hispanic/Latino; 1 Two or more races, non-Hispanic/Latino), 1 international. Average age 34. 17 applicants, 35% accepted, 6 enrolled. *Faculty:* 6 full-time (4 women), 3 part-time/adjunct (2 women). Expenses: Contact institution. *Financial support:* Scholarships/grants available. Financial award application deadline: 12/1; financial award applicants required to submit FAFSA. In 2017, 21 master's awarded. *Program availability:* Part-time. Offers combined preK-3/K-5 education (M Ed); educational leadership (Ed D, Ed S); K-5 education (M Ed); middle grades education (M Ed); preK-3 education (M Ed); preK-3 special education (M Ed); secondary education (M Ed). *Application deadline:* For fall admission, 8/1 priority date for domestic students, 6/1 for international students; for spring admission, 11/15 priority date for domestic students, 12/1 for international students; for summer admission, 4/1 for domestic students. Applications are processed on a rolling basis. *Application fee:* $30. Electronic applications accepted. *Application Contact:* Melissa Dillow, Graduate Admissions Recruiter, Education, 423-461-8306, Fax: 423-461-8982, E-mail: msdillow@milligan.edu. *Area Chair of Education*, Dr. Angela Hilton-Prillhart, 423-461-8769, Fax: 423-461-3103, E-mail: anhilton-prillhart@milligan.edu.

Area of Physician Assistant Studies Expenses: Contact institution. *Financial support:* Scholarships/grants available. Financial award application deadline: 12/1; financial award applicants required to submit FAFSA. Offers physician assistant studies (MSPAS). *Application deadline:* For spring admission, 9/1 for domestic students. Electronic applications accepted. *Application Contact:* Rebekah Bess, Program Secretary, 423-461-1557, Fax: 423-461-1518, E-mail: rbess@milligan.edu. *Area Chair and Director*, Andrew Hull, 423-461-1558, Fax: 423-461-1518, E-mail: awhull@milligan.edu.

Emmanuel Christian Seminary at Milligan College Students: 52 full-time (23 women), 57 part-time (18 women); includes 11 minority (7 Black or African American, non-Hispanic/Latino; 1 Asian, non-Hispanic/Latino; 3 Hispanic/Latino), 7 international. Average age 35. 62 applicants, 89% accepted, 39 enrolled. *Faculty:* 10 full-time (1 woman), 8 part-time/adjunct (0 women). Expenses: Contact institution. *Financial support:* In 2017–18, 124 students received support. Scholarships/grants and unspecified assistantships available. Financial award application deadline: 12/1; financial award applicants required to submit FAFSA. In 2017, 19 master's, 3 doctorates awarded. *Program availability:* Part-time, blended/hybrid learning. Offers Christian care and counseling (M Div); Christian education (M Div); Christian ministries (MACM, Graduate Certificate); Christian ministry (M Div); Christian theology (M Div, MAR); church history (MAR); church history/historical theology (M Div); general studies (M Div); ministry (D Min); New Testament (M Div, MAR); Old Testament (M Div, MAR); urban ministry (M Div); world missions (M Div). *Application deadline:* For fall admission, 8/1 for domestic students, 6/1 for international students; for spring admission, 12/15 for domestic students, 8/1 for international students. Applications are processed on a rolling basis. *Application fee:* $30 ($0 for international students). Electronic applications accepted. *Application Contact:* Lauren Gullett, Director of Admissions and Recruitment for Emmanuel Christian Seminary, 423-461-1535, Fax: 423-926-6198, E-mail: lwgullett@milligan.edu. *Academic Dean, Emmanuel Christian Seminary*, Dr. Rollin Ramsaran, 423-461-1524, Fax: 423-926-6198, E-mail: raramsaran@milligan.edu.

Program in Occupational Therapy Offers occupational therapy (MSOT). Electronic applications accepted.

MILLIKIN UNIVERSITY, Decatur, IL 62522-2084

General Information Independent-religious, coed, comprehensive institution. *Enrollment:* 2,040 graduate, professional, and undergraduate students; 64 full-time matriculated graduate/professional students (37 women), 24 part-time matriculated graduate/professional students (19 women). *Enrollment by degree level:* 52 master's, 36 doctoral. *Graduate faculty:* 24 full-time (17 women), 13 part-time/adjunct (7 women). *Tuition:* Part-time $832 per credit hour. Tuition and fees vary according to course load, degree level and program. *Student services:* Campus employment opportunities, career counseling, exercise/wellness program, grant writing training, international student services, multicultural affairs office, services for students with disabilities, writing training. *Library facilities:* Staley Library. *Collection:* Books: 189,000 (physical), 82,000 (digital/electronic); Serial titles: 1,000 (physical), 53,000 (digital/electronic); Databases: 80. Weekly public service hours: 113; students can reserve study rooms.

Computer facilities: 255 computers available on campus for general student use. A campuswide network can be accessed from student residence rooms. Online class registration, online degree audit, online financials (view and pay bills, financial aid) are available.
Website: http://www.millikin.edu/

General Application Contact: Marianne Taylor, Director of Graduate Admission, 217-420-6771, Fax: 217-425-4669, E-mail: mgtaylor@millikin.edu.

GRADUATE UNITS

School of Nursing Students: 42 full-time (30 women), 20 part-time (17 women); includes 12 minority (8 Black or African American, non-Hispanic/Latino; 2 Asian, non-Hispanic/Latino; 2 Hispanic/Latino). Average age 30. 114 applicants, 36% accepted, 23 enrolled. *Faculty:* 19 full-time (17 women), 7 part-time/adjunct (6 women). Expenses: Contact institution. *Financial support:* Traineeships and unspecified assistantships available. Financial award applicants required to submit FAFSA. In 2017, 3 master's, 13 doctorates awarded. *Program availability:* Part-time. Offers entry into nursing practice (MSN); family nurse practitioner (DNP); nurse anesthesia (DNP); nurse educator (MSN). *Application deadline:* For spring admission, 7/1 priority date for domestic and international students; for summer admission, 11/1 priority date for domestic and international students. Applications are processed on a rolling basis. *Application fee:* $0. Electronic applications accepted. *Application Contact:* Bonnie Niemeyer, Administrative Assistant, 800-373-7733 Ext. 5034, Fax: 217-420-6731, E-mail: bniemeyer@millikin.edu. *Director*, Dr. Pamela Lindsey, 217-424-6348, Fax: 217-420-6731, E-mail: plindsey@millikin.edu.

Tabor School of Business Students: 22 full-time (7 women), 4 part-time (2 women); includes 5 minority (4 Black or African American, non-Hispanic/Latino; 1 Hispanic/Latino). Average age 34. 106 applicants, 50% accepted, 25 enrolled. *Faculty:* 7 full-time (2 women), 7 part-time/adjunct (2 women). Expenses: Contact institution. *Financial support:* In 2017–18, 10 students received support, including 1 research assistantship with partial tuition reimbursement available (averaging $6,000 per year), 3 teaching assistantships with partial tuition reimbursements available (averaging $6,000 per year); tuition waivers also available. Financial award applicants required to submit FAFSA. In 2017, 32 master's awarded. *Program availability:* Evening/weekend. Offers business (MBA). *Application deadline:* For fall admission, 6/1 priority date for domestic students, 5/1 priority date for international students; for spring admission, 11/1 priority date for domestic students, 8/1 priority date for international students. Applications are processed on a rolling basis. *Application fee:* $0. Electronic applications accepted. *MBA Director/Associate Professor*, Dr. Anthony Liberatore, 217-424-6338, E-mail: aliberatore@millikin.edu.

MILLSAPS COLLEGE, Jackson, MS 39210-0001

General Information Independent-religious, coed, comprehensive institution. *Graduate housing:* Room and/or apartments available to single students; on-campus housing not available to married students. Housing application deadline: 6/1. *Research affiliation:* Downtown Jackson Partners Group (real estate development), Oxbow Ventures (commercialization of renewable energy), Midtown Partners (economic development).

GRADUATE UNITS

Else School of Management *Program availability:* Part-time. Offers accounting (M Acc); business administration (MBA). Electronic applications accepted.

MILLS COLLEGE, Oakland, CA 94613-1000

General Information Independent, Undergraduate: women only; graduate: coed, comprehensive institution. *Enrollment:* 1,309 graduate, professional, and undergraduate students; 339 full-time matriculated graduate/professional students (247 women), 210 part-time matriculated graduate/professional students (174 women). *Enrollment by degree level:* 414 master's, 48 doctoral, 87 other advanced degrees. *Graduate faculty:* 47 full-time (33 women), 64 part-time/adjunct (46 women). *Tuition:* Full-time $33,480; part-time $1000 per credit. *Required fees:* $1479. Tuition and fees vary according to program. *Graduate housing:* Rooms and/or apartments available on a first-come, first-served basis to single and married students. Typical cost: $6926 per year ($12,791 including board) for single students; $17,778 (including board) for married students. Housing application deadline: 6/15. *Student services:* Campus employment opportunities, campus safety program, career counseling, exercise/wellness program, free psychological counseling, international student services, low-cost health insurance, multicultural affairs office, services for students with disabilities, teacher training, writing training. *Library facilities:* F. W. Olin Library. *Collection:* Books: 190,417 (physical), 156,636 (digital/electronic); Serial titles: 153 (physical), 51,607 (digital/electronic); Databases: 39. Weekly public service hours: 89; students can reserve study rooms.

Computer facilities: Computer purchase and lease plans are available. 335 computers available on campus for general student use. A campuswide network can be accessed from student residence rooms and from off campus. Online class registration, online degree audit are available.
Website: http://www.mills.edu/

General Application Contact: Robynne Lofton, Director of Admissions, 510-430-3295, Fax: 510-430-2159, E-mail: grad-studies@mills.edu.

GRADUATE UNITS

Graduate Studies Students: 339 full-time (247 women), 210 part-time (174 women); includes 238 minority (62 Black or African American, non-Hispanic/Latino; 4 American Indian or Alaska Native, non-Hispanic/Latino; 42 Asian, non-Hispanic/Latino; 91 Hispanic/Latino; 1 Native Hawaiian or other Pacific Islander, non-Hispanic/Latino; 38 Two or more races, non-Hispanic/Latino), 22 international. Average age 31. 796 applicants, 69% accepted, 256 enrolled. *Faculty:* 47 full-time (33 women), 64 part-time/adjunct (46 women). Expenses: Contact institution. *Financial support:* In 2017–18, 395 students received support, including 395 fellowships with tuition reimbursements available (averaging $7,119 per year), 128 teaching assistantships with tuition reimbursements available; research assistantships, career-related internships or fieldwork, institutionally sponsored loans, scholarships/grants, and unspecified assistantships also available. Support available to part-time students. Financial award application deadline: 2/1; financial award applicants required to submit FAFSA. In 2017, 186 master's, 17 doctorates, 85 other advanced degrees awarded. *Program availability:* Part-time, evening/weekend. Offers art (MFA); book art and creative writing (MFA); ceramics (MFA); composition (MA); computer science (Certificate); dance (MA, MFA); electronic music and recording media (MFA); infant mental health (MA); interdisciplinary computer science (MA); intermedia (MFA); literature (MA); music performance and literature (MFA); painting (MFA); photography (MFA); poetry (MFA); pre-medical studies (Certificate); prose (MFA); public policy (MPP); sculpture (MFA); Spanish creative writing (Certificate); translation (MFA). *Application deadline:* For fall admission, 12/15 priority date for domestic students, 12/15 for international students; for spring admission, 11/1 priority date for domestic students, 10/1 for international students. Applications are processed on a rolling basis. *Application fee:* $50. Electronic applications accepted. *Director of Admissions*, Robynne Lofton, 510-430-3295, Fax: 510-430-2159, E-mail: grad-admissions@mills.edu.

Lorry I. Lokey Graduate School of Business Students: 31 full-time (24 women), 23 part-time (22 women); includes 33 minority (13 Black or African American, non-Hispanic/Latino; 2 American Indian or Alaska Native, non-Hispanic/Latino; 1 Asian, non-Hispanic/Latino; 10 Hispanic/Latino; 7 Two or more races, non-Hispanic/Latino), 1 international. Average age 33. 49 applicants, 84% accepted, 20 enrolled. *Faculty:* 4 full-time (3 women), 8 part-time/adjunct (5 women). Expenses: Contact institution. *Financial support:* In 2017–18, 59 students received support, including 59 fellowships with tuition reimbursements available (averaging $6,398 per year), 19 teaching assistantships with tuition reimbursements available; scholarships/grants and unspecified assistantships also available. Support available to part-time students. Financial award application deadline: 2/1; financial award applicants required to submit FAFSA. In 2017, 31 master's awarded. *Program availability:* Part-time. Offers applied economics (MA); management (MBA, MM). *Application deadline:* For fall admission, 2/1 priority date for domestic students, 12/15 for international students; for spring admission, 10/1 for domestic students. Applications are processed on a rolling basis. *Application fee:* $50. *Application Contact:* Robynne Lofton, Director of Admissions, 510-430-3295, Fax: 510-430-2159, E-mail: grad-admission@mills.edu. *Dean, Lorry I. Lokey School of Business and Public Policy,* Dr. Kate Karniouchina, 510-430-3345, Fax: 510-430-2159, E-mail: kkarniouchina@mills.edu.

School of Education Students: 83 full-time (66 women), 115 part-time (100 women); includes 94 minority (26 Black or African American, non-Hispanic/Latino; 1 American Indian or Alaska Native, non-Hispanic/Latino; 19 Asian, non-Hispanic/Latino; 38 Hispanic/Latino; 1 Native Hawaiian or other Pacific Islander, non-Hispanic/Latino; 9 Two or more races, non-Hispanic/Latino), 7 international. Average age 32. 189 applicants, 72% accepted, 84 enrolled. *Faculty:* 11 full-time (9 women), 16 part-time/adjunct (14 women). Expenses: Contact institution. *Financial support:* In 2017–18, 122 students received support, including 122 fellowships with tuition reimbursements available (averaging $5,462 per year), 15 teaching assistantships with tuition reimbursements available; career-related internships or fieldwork and scholarships/grants also available. Support available to part-time students. Financial award application deadline: 2/1; financial award applicants required to submit FAFSA. In 2017, 60 master's, 17 doctorates, 49 other advanced degrees awarded. *Program availability:* Part-time, evening/weekend. Offers education (MA, Ed D, Certificate). *Application deadline:* For fall admission, 12/31 priority date for domestic students, 12/15 for international students; for spring admission, 11/1 priority date for domestic students, 10/1 for international students. Applications are processed on a rolling basis. *Application fee:* $50. Electronic applications accepted. *Application Contact:* Robynne Lofton, Director of Admissions, 510-430-3295, Fax: 510-430-2159, E-mail: grad-admission@mills.edu. *School of Education Dean,* Dr. Diane Ketelle, 510-430-3190, Fax: 510-430-2159, E-mail: dketelle@mills.edu.

MILWAUKEE SCHOOL OF ENGINEERING, Milwaukee, WI 53202-3109

General Information Independent, coed, primarily men, comprehensive institution. *Enrollment:* 2,823 graduate, professional, and undergraduate students; 73 full-time matriculated graduate/professional students (35 women), 153 part-time matriculated graduate/professional students (51 women). *Enrollment by degree level:* 226 master's. *Graduate faculty:* 27 full-time (21 women), 24 part-time/adjunct (16 women). *Tuition:* Part-time $814 per credit hour. *Required fees:* $12.50 per credit hour. *Graduate housing:* Rooms and/or apartments available on a first-come, first-served basis to single and married students. Housing application deadline: 7/1. *Student services:* Campus employment opportunities, campus safety program, career counseling, exercise/wellness program, international student services, multicultural affairs office, services for students with disabilities, writing training. *Library facilities:* Walter Schroeder. *Collection:* Books: 51,408 (physical), 370,802 (digital/electronic); Serial titles: 345 (physical), 114,238 (digital/electronic); Databases: 124. Weekly public service hours: 96; students can reserve study rooms. *Research affiliation:* Keen Foundation (entrepreneurship and engineering education), National Fluid Power Association (hydraulics and pneumatics), 3dMD (biomolecular modeling), National Additine Manufacturing Innovation Institute (rapid prototyping), Caterpillar, Inc. (electrohydraulics), Clinical Translational Science Institute (medical and healthcare innovation and transfer).

Computer facilities: Computer purchase and lease plans are available. 50 computers available on campus for general student use. A campuswide network can be accessed from student residence rooms and from off campus. Online class registration is available.
Website: http://www.msoe.edu/

General Application Contact: Brian Rutz, Graduate Admissions Counselor, 414-277-2223, E-mail: rutz@msoe.edu.

GRADUATE UNITS

MBA in STEM Leadership Program Students: 5 part-time (4 women). Average age 31. Expenses: Contact institution. *Financial support:* Application deadline: 3/15; applicants required to submit FAFSA. *Program availability:* Part-time, evening/weekend. Offers STEM leadership (MBA). *Application deadline:* Applications are processed on a rolling basis. *Application fee:* $0. Electronic applications accepted. *Application Contact:* Brian Rutz, Graduate Admission Counselor, 414-277-7200, E-mail: rutz@msoe.edu. *Interim Department Chair,* David Schmitz, 414-277-2487, E-mail: schmitz@msoe.edu.

MBA Program in Education Leadership Students: 28 part-time (14 women); includes 3 minority (1 Black or African American, non-Hispanic/Latino; 1 Asian, non-Hispanic/Latino; 1 Two or more races, non-Hispanic/Latino). Average age 35. 42 applicants, 86% accepted, 28 enrolled. Expenses: Contact institution. *Financial support:* In 2017–18, 15 students received support, including 15 fellowships (averaging $45,552 per year); career-related internships or fieldwork and scholarships/grants also available. Financial award application deadline: 3/15; financial award applicants required to submit FAFSA. In 2017, 14 master's awarded. *Program availability:* Part-time, evening/weekend. Offers education leadership (MBA). *Application deadline:* Applications are processed on a rolling basis. Electronic applications accepted. *Application Contact:* Brian Rutz, Graduate Admission Counselor, 414-277-7200, E-mail: rutz@msoe.edu. *Program Director,* Dr. Ruth Barratt, 414-277-2230, E-mail: barratt@msoe.edu.

MS Program in Architectural Engineering Students: 18 full-time (8 women); includes 1 minority (Asian, non-Hispanic/Latino). 22 applicants, 82% accepted, 18 enrolled. Expenses: Contact institution. *Financial support:* Research assistantships, career-related internships or fieldwork, institutionally sponsored loans, and scholarships/grants available. Financial award application deadline: 3/15; financial award applicants required to submit FAFSA. In 2017, 3 master's awarded. *Program availability:* Part-time, evening/weekend. Offers architectural engineering (MS). *Application deadline:* Applications are processed on a rolling basis. *Application fee:* $0. Electronic applications accepted. *Application Contact:* Brian Rutz, Graduate Admission Counselor, 414-277-7200, E-mail: rutz@msoe.edu. *Program Director,* Dr. Richard DeVries, 414-277-7596, E-mail: devries@msoe.edu.

MS Program in Civil Engineering Students: 3 full-time (1 woman), all international. Average age 25. 13 applicants, 23% accepted, 2 enrolled. Expenses: Contact institution. *Financial support:* Federal Work-Study and scholarships/grants available. Financial award application deadline: 3/15; financial award applicants required to submit FAFSA. In 2017, 14 master's awarded. *Program availability:* Part-time, evening/weekend. Offers civil engineering (MS). *Application deadline:* Applications are processed on a rolling basis. *Application fee:* $0. Electronic applications accepted. *Application Contact:* Brian Rutz, Graduate Admission Counselor, 414-277-7200, E-mail: rutz@msoe.edu. *Program Director,* Dr. Francis Mahuta, 414-277-7599, E-mail: mahuta@msoe.edu.

MS Program in Engineering Students: 8 full-time (0 women), 20 part-time (2 women); includes 2 minority (1 Black or African American, non-Hispanic/Latino; 1 Asian, non-Hispanic/Latino), 7 international. Average age 31. 32 applicants, 50% accepted, 13 enrolled. Expenses: Contact institution. *Financial support:* In 2017–18, 3 research assistantships (averaging $8,043 per year) were awarded; career-related internships or fieldwork, institutionally sponsored loans, scholarships/grants, and tuition waivers (partial) also available. Financial award application deadline: 3/15; financial award applicants required to submit FAFSA. In 2017, 16 master's awarded. *Program availability:* Part-time, evening/weekend. Offers engineering (MS). *Application deadline:* Applications are processed on a rolling basis. *Application fee:* $0. Electronic applications accepted. *Application Contact:* Brian Rutz, Graduate Admission Counselor, 414-277-7200, E-mail: rutz@msoe.edu. *Program Director,* Dr. Subha Kumpaty, 414-277-7466, Fax: 414-277-2222, E-mail: kumpaty@msoe.edu.

MS Program in Engineering Management Students: 6 full-time (4 women), 44 part-time (10 women); includes 7 minority (2 Black or African American, non-Hispanic/Latino; 1 Asian, non-Hispanic/Latino; 3 Hispanic/Latino; 1 Two or more races, non-Hispanic/Latino), 2 international. Average age 31. 23 applicants, 48% accepted, 11 enrolled. Expenses: Contact institution. *Financial support:* Career-related internships or fieldwork, institutionally sponsored loans, scholarships/grants, traineeships, and tuition waivers (partial) available. Financial award application deadline: 3/15; financial award applicants required to submit FAFSA. In 2017, 19 master's awarded. *Program availability:* Part-time, evening/weekend. Offers engineering management (MS). *Application deadline:* Applications are processed on a rolling basis. *Application fee:* $0. Electronic applications accepted. *Application Contact:* Brian Rutz, Graduate Admission Counselor, 414-277-7200, E-mail: rutz@msoe.edu. *Program Director,* Gene Wright, 414-277-2268, E-mail: wright@msoe.edu.

MS Program in Marketing and Export Management Students: 1 (woman) full-time, all international. 3 applicants, 33% accepted. Expenses: Contact institution. *Financial support:* Career-related internships or fieldwork, institutionally sponsored loans, scholarships/grants, and tuition waivers (full) available. Financial award application deadline: 3/15; financial award applicants required to submit FAFSA. In 2017, 2 master's awarded. *Program availability:* Part-time, evening/weekend. Offers marketing and export management (MS). *Application deadline:* Applications are processed on a rolling basis. *Application fee:* $0. Electronic applications accepted. *Application Contact:* Brian Rutz, Graduate Admission Counselor, 414-277-7200, E-mail: rutz@msoe.edu. *Program Director,* Gene Wright, 414-277-2268, Fax: 414-277-2487, E-mail: wright@msoe.edu.

MS Program in New Product Management Students: 1 full-time (0 women), 7 part-time (4 women). Average age 30. 4 applicants, 100% accepted, 3 enrolled. Expenses: Contact institution. *Financial support:* Career-related internships or fieldwork, institutionally sponsored loans, and scholarships/grants available. Financial award application deadline: 3/15; financial award applicants required to submit FAFSA. In 2017, 3 master's awarded. *Program availability:* Part-time, evening/weekend. Offers new product management (MS). *Application deadline:* Applications are processed on a rolling basis. *Application fee:* $0. Electronic applications accepted. *Application Contact:* Brian Rutz, Graduate Admission Counselor, 414-277-7200, E-mail: dahlinghaus@msoe.edu. *Program Director,* Gene Wright, 414-277-2268, Fax: 414-277-2487, E-mail: wright@msoe.edu.

MS Program in Nursing - Leadership and Management Students: 5 full-time (all women), 1 (woman) part-time; includes 2 minority (1 Asian, non-Hispanic/Latino; 1 Hispanic/Latino). Average age 31. 5 applicants, 60% accepted, 3 enrolled. Expenses: Contact institution. *Financial support:* In 2017–18, 2 students received support. Scholarships/grants available. Financial award application deadline: 3/15; financial award applicants required to submit FAFSA. In 2017, 3 master's awarded. *Program availability:* Part-time, evening/weekend, 100% online, blended/hybrid learning. Offers nursing - leadership and management (MSN). *Application deadline:* Applications are processed on a rolling basis. *Application fee:* $0. Electronic applications accepted. *Application Contact:* Brian Rutz, Graduate Admission Counselor, 414-277-7200, E-mail: rutz@msoe.edu. *Program Director,* Dr. Debra Jenks, 414-277-4516, E-mail: jenks@msoe.edu.

MS Program in Perfusion Students: 14 full-time (7 women). Average age 27. 69 applicants, 13% accepted, 7 enrolled. Expenses: Contact institution. *Financial support:* Career-related internships or fieldwork, institutionally sponsored loans, and scholarships/grants available. Financial award application deadline: 3/15; financial award applicants required to submit FAFSA. In 2017, 5 master's awarded. Offers perfusion (MS). *Application deadline:* Applications are processed on a rolling basis. *Application fee:* $0. Electronic applications accepted. *Application Contact:* Brian Rutz, Graduate Admission Counselor, 414-277-7200, E-mail: rutz@msoe.edu. *Program Director,* Dr. Ronald Gerrits, 414-277-7561, Fax: 414-277-7494, E-mail: gerrits@msoe.edu.

Program in Business Administration Students: 17 full-time (9 women), 48 part-time (16 women); includes 13 minority (4 Black or African American, non-Hispanic/Latino; 3 Asian, non-Hispanic/Latino; 3 Hispanic/Latino; 3 Two or more races, non-Hispanic/Latino), 2 international. Average age 29. 27 applicants, 81% accepted, 19 enrolled. Expenses: Contact institution. *Financial support:* In 2017–18, 30 students received support. Fellowships, career-related internships or fieldwork, scholarships/grants, and tuition waivers (partial) available. Financial award application deadline: 3/15; financial award applicants required to submit FAFSA. In 2017, 19 master's awarded. *Program availability:* Part-time, evening/weekend, 100% online, blended/hybrid learning. Offers business administration (MBA). *Application deadline:* Applications are processed on a rolling basis. *Application fee:* $0. Electronic applications accepted. *Application Contact:* Brian Rutz, Graduate Admission Counselor, 414-277-7200, E-mail: rutz@msoe.edu. *Program Director,* David Schmitz, 414-277-2487, Fax: 414-277-7479, E-mail: schmitz@msoe.edu.

MINNEAPOLIS COLLEGE OF ART AND DESIGN, Minneapolis, MN 55404-4347

General Information Independent, coed, comprehensive institution. *Enrollment:* 727 graduate, professional, and undergraduate students; 79 full-time matriculated graduate/professional students (58 women), 7 part-time matriculated graduate/professional students (all women). *Enrollment by degree level:* 52 master's, 34 other advanced degrees. *Graduate faculty:* 42 full-time (19 women). *Tuition:* Full-time $38,670. *Required fees:* $450. One-time fee: $300 full-time. *Graduate housing:* On-campus housing not available. *Student services:* Campus employment opportunities, campus safety program, career counseling, exercise/wellness program, free psychological counseling, grant writing training, international student services, low-cost health insurance, services for students with disabilities, teacher training, writing training. *Library facilities:* MCAD Library. *Collection:* Books: 50,000 (physical), 145,000 (digital/electronic); Serial titles: 329 (physical); Databases: 8.

Computer facilities: Computer purchase and lease plans are available. A campuswide network can be accessed from student residence rooms and from off campus. Online class registration is available.
Website: http://www.mcad.edu/

General Application Contact: Melissa Huybrecht, Vice President, Enrollment Management, 612-874-3764, E-mail: mhuybrecht@mcad.edu.

GRADUATE UNITS

Certificate Programs Students: 29 full-time (21 women), 5 part-time (all women); includes 6 minority (2 Black or African American, non-Hispanic/Latino; 1 Asian, non-Hispanic/Latino; 3 Hispanic/Latino), 1 international. *Faculty:* 42 full-time (29 women). Expenses: Contact institution. *Financial support:* Career-related internships or fieldwork and scholarships/grants available. Financial award application deadline: 3/15; financial award applicants required to submit FAFSA. In 2017, 15 Certificates awarded. *Program availability:* Part-time, 100% online, blended/hybrid learning. Offers graphic design (Certificate); media (Certificate); sustainable design (Certificate). *Application deadline:* For fall admission, 1/15 for domestic and international students; for spring admission, 10/15 for domestic and international students. *Application fee:* $50. Electronic applications accepted. *Senior Director of Continuing Education*, Lara Roy, 612-874-3778, E-mail: continuing_education@mcad.edu.

Program in Graphic and Web Design Offers graphic and Web design (MA).

Program in Sustainable Design Offers sustainable design (MA).

Program in Visual Studies Students: 30 full-time (23 women); includes 3 minority (2 Asian, non-Hispanic/Latino; 1 Hispanic/Latino), 13 international. 166 applicants, 28% accepted, 12 enrolled. *Faculty:* 42 full-time (13 women). Expenses: Contact institution. *Financial support:* In 2017–18, 23 students received support, including 15 teaching assistantships (averaging $6,000 per year); career-related internships or fieldwork, Federal Work-Study, scholarships/grants, and unspecified assistantships also available. Support available to part-time students. Financial award application deadline: 3/15; financial award applicants required to submit FAFSA. In 2017, 10 master's awarded. *Program availability:* Part-time. Offers animation (MFA); comic art (MFA); drawing (MFA); filmmaking (MFA); fine arts (MFA); furniture design (MFA); graphic design (MFA); illustration (MFA); interactive media (MFA); painting (MFA); photography (MFA); printmaking (MFA); sculpture (MFA). *Application deadline:* For fall admission, 1/15 for domestic and international students. *Application fee:* $50. Electronic applications accepted. *Application Contact:* Mary Kazura, Associate Director of Admissions, 612-874-3760, Fax: 612-874-3701, E-mail: mary_kazura@mcad.edu. *Graduate Director*, 612-209-1471, E-mail: admissions@mcad.edu.

MINNESOTA STATE UNIVERSITY MANKATO, Mankato, MN 56001

General Information State-supported, coed, university. CGS member. *Graduate housing:* Room and/or apartments available on a first-come, first-served basis to single students; on-campus housing not available to married students.

GRADUATE UNITS

College of Graduate Studies and Research *Program availability:* Part-time, online learning. Offers cross-disciplinary studies (MS). Electronic applications accepted.

College of Allied Health and Nursing *Program availability:* Part-time. Offers allied health and nursing (MA, MS, MSN, DNP, Postbaccalaureate Certificate); communication disorders (MS); community health education (MS); family nurse practitioner (MSN); nurse educator (MSN); nursing (DNP); physical education (MA, MS); public health education (Postbaccalaureate Certificate); rehabilitation counseling (MS); school health education (MS, Postbaccalaureate Certificate). Electronic applications accepted.

College of Arts and Humanities *Program availability:* Part-time, evening/weekend. Offers art (MA); art education (MAT); arts and humanities (MA, MAT, MFA, MM, MS, Certificate); choral conducting (MM); communication and composition (MA); communication education (Certificate); communication studies (MA, MS); creative writing (MFA); English studies (MA); forensics (MFA); French (MS); French education (MS); music education (MAT); piano performance (MM); professional communication (Certificate); Spanish (MS); Spanish education (MS); Spanish for the professions (MS); teaching English as a second language (MA, Certificate); technical communication (MA, Certificate); theatre arts (MA, MFA); wind band conducting (MM).

College of Business Offers accounting (MSA); business (MBA). Electronic applications accepted.

College of Education *Program availability:* Part-time, evening/weekend. Offers college student affairs (MS); counselor education and supervision (Ed D); education (MAT, MS, Ed D, Certificate); educational leadership (MS, Ed D); emotional and behavioral disorders (MS, Certificate); experiential education (MS); learning disabilities (MS, Certificate); mental health counseling (MS); professional school counseling (K-12) (MS). Electronic applications accepted.

College of Science, Engineering and Technology *Program availability:* Part-time. Offers applied statistics (MS); biology (MS); biology education (MS); environmental sciences (MS); information technology (MS); manufacturing engineering technology (MS); mathematics (MA, MS); mathematics education (MS); physics (MS); physics education (MS); science, engineering and technology (MA, MAT, MS, Certificate); statistics (MS). Electronic applications accepted.

College of Social and Behavioral Sciences *Program availability:* Part-time. Offers aging studies (MS); applied anthropology (MS); clinical psychology (MA); ethnic studies (MS); gender and women's studies (MS); geography (MS); history (MA, MS); industrial/organizational psychology (MA); local government management (Certificate); non-profit leadership (Certificate); public administration (MPA); school psychology (Psy D); social and behavioral sciences (MA, MAT, MPA, MS, MSW, Psy D, Certificate); social studies (MAT); social work (MSW); sociology (MA); sociology: college teaching (MA); sociology: corrections (MS); sociology: human services planning and administration (MS); urban and regional studies (MA); urban planning (MA, Certificate). Electronic applications accepted.

MINNESOTA STATE UNIVERSITY MOORHEAD, Moorhead, MN 56563

General Information State-supported, coed, comprehensive institution. *Enrollment:* 6,019 graduate, professional, and undergraduate students; 168 full-time matriculated graduate/professional students (131 women), 476 part-time matriculated graduate/professional students (362 women). *Enrollment by degree level:* 539 master's, 21 doctoral, 84 other advanced degrees. *Graduate faculty:* 78. Tuition, state resident: full-time $9000; part-time $374 per credit. Tuition, nonresident: full-time $18,000; part-time $748 per credit. *Required fees:* $1055; $43.96 per credit. Tuition and fees vary according to degree level, program and reciprocity agreements. *Graduate housing:* Room and/or apartments available on a first-come, first-served basis to single students; on-campus housing not available to married students. *Student services:* Campus employment opportunities, campus safety program, career counseling, child daycare facilities, exercise/wellness program, free psychological counseling, grant writing training, international student services, low-cost health insurance, multicultural affairs office, services for students with disabilities, teacher training, writing training. *Library facilities:* Livingston Lord Library plus 1 other. *Collection:* Books: 326,187 (physical), 20,401 (digital/electronic); Serial titles: 1,634 (physical), 18,041 (digital/electronic); Databases: 84. Weekly public service hours: 79. *Research affiliation:* West Central Minnesota Business Innovation Center.

Computer facilities: Computer purchase and lease plans are available. 1,500 computers available on campus for general student use. A campuswide network can be accessed from student residence rooms and from off campus. Online class registration is available.
Website: http://www.mnstate.edu/

General Application Contact: Karla Wenger, Graduate Studies Office, 218-477-2344, Fax: 218-477-2344, E-mail: wengerk@mnstate.edu.

GRADUATE UNITS

Graduate Studies Students: 168 full-time (131 women), 476 part-time (362 women). Average age 32. 313 applicants, 54% accepted. *Faculty:* 78. Expenses: Contact institution. *Financial support:* Federal Work-Study and unspecified assistantships available. Financial award application deadline: 10/1; financial award applicants required to submit FAFSA. In 2017, 197 master's, 27 other advanced degrees awarded. *Program availability:* Part-time, evening/weekend, 100% online, blended/hybrid learning. *Application deadline:* Applications are processed on a rolling basis. *Application fee:* $20. Electronic applications accepted. *Application Contact:* Karla Wenger, Graduate Studies Office Manager, 218-236-2344, Fax: 218-236-2482, E-mail: wengerk@mnstate.edu. *Director of Graduate Studies*, Dr. Lisa Karch, 218-477-2699, Fax: 218-236-2482, E-mail: lisa.karch@mnstate.edu.

College of Business and Innovation Students: 17 full-time (5 women), 26 part-time (17 women). Average age 29. 21 applicants, 81% accepted. *Faculty:* 13. Expenses: Contact institution. *Financial support:* Federal Work-Study and unspecified assistantships available. Financial award application deadline: 10/1; financial award applicants required to submit FAFSA. In 2017, 13 master's awarded. *Program availability:* Part-time. Offers accounting and finance (MS); business administration (MBA); health care management (MBA). *Application deadline:* For fall admission, 3/15 for domestic students; for spring admission, 10/15 for domestic students. Applications are processed on a rolling basis. *Application fee:* $20. Electronic applications accepted. *Application Contact:* Karla Wenger, Coordinator, 218-477-2344, E-mail: wengerk@mnstate.edu. *Interim Dean*, Denise Gorsline, 218-477-4623, E-mail: gorsline@mnstate.edu.

College of Education and Human Services Students: 117 full-time (101 women), 337 part-time (253 women). Average age 32. 248 applicants, 49% accepted. *Faculty:* 22. Expenses: Contact institution. *Financial support:* Federal Work-Study and unspecified assistantships available. Financial award application deadline: 10/1; financial award applicants required to submit FAFSA. In 2017, 149 master's, 16 other advanced degrees awarded. *Program availability:* Part-time, 100% online, blended/hybrid learning. Offers counseling and student affairs (MS); curriculum and instruction (MS); educational leadership (MS, Ed D, Ed S); special education (MS); speech-language pathology (MS). *Application deadline:* Applications are processed on a rolling basis. *Application fee:* $20. Electronic applications accepted. *Application Contact:* Karla Wenger, Office Manager, 218-477-2344, Fax: 218-477-2482, E-mail: wengerk@mnstate.edu. *Dean*, Dr. Ok-Hee Lee, 218-477-2095, E-mail: okheelee@mnstate.edu.

College of Humanities and Social Sciences Students: 9 part-time (8 women). Average age 33. 2 applicants, 50% accepted. *Faculty:* 7. Expenses: Contact institution. *Financial support:* Federal Work-Study and unspecified assistantships available. Financial award application deadline: 10/1; financial award applicants required to submit FAFSA. In 2017, 1 master's awarded. *Program availability:* Part-time, evening/weekend. Offers teaching English as a second language (MA). *Application deadline:* For fall admission, 4/15 for domestic students; for spring admission, 11/15 for domestic students. Applications are processed on a rolling basis. *Application fee:* $20. Electronic applications accepted. *Application Contact:* Karla Wenger, Graduate Studies Office Manager, 218-477-2344, Fax: 218-477-2482, E-mail: wengerk@mnstate.edu. *Dean*, Dr. Randy Cagle, 218-477-2477, E-mail: caglera@mnstate.edu.

College of Science, Health and the Environment Students: 34 full-time (25 women), 104 part-time (84 women). Average age 32. 42 applicants, 74% accepted. *Faculty:* 24. Expenses: Contact institution. *Financial support:* Federal Work-Study and unspecified assistantships available. Financial award application deadline: 10/1; financial award applicants required to submit FAFSA. In 2017, 34 master's, 11 other advanced degrees awarded. *Program availability:* Part-time. Offers healthcare administration (MHA); nursing (MS); school psychology (MS, Psy S). *Application deadline:* Applications are processed on a rolling basis. *Application fee:* $20. Electronic applications accepted. *Application Contact:* Karla Wenger, Graduate Studies Office Manager, 218-477-2344, Fax: 218-477-2482, E-mail: wengerk@mnstate.edu. *Dean*, Dr. Jeffrey Bodwin, 218-477-5892, E-mail: jeffrey.bodwin@mnstate.edu.

MINOT STATE UNIVERSITY, Minot, ND 58707-0002

General Information State-supported, coed, comprehensive institution. *Graduate housing:* Rooms and/or apartments available on a first-come, first-served basis to single and married students. Housing application deadline: 6/30. *Research affiliation:* Rural Crime and Justice Center (criminal justice research), North Dakota Center for Persons with Disabilities (NDCPD).

GRADUATE UNITS

Graduate School *Program availability:* Part-time, 100% online, blended/hybrid learning. Offers deaf/hard of hearing education (MS); elementary education (M Ed); information systems (MSIS); management (MSM); mathematics (MAT); school psychology (Ed Sp); science (MAT); specific learning disabilities (MS); speech-language pathology (MS). Electronic applications accepted.

MIRRER YESHIVA CENTRAL INSTITUTE, Brooklyn, NY 11223-2010

General Information Independent-religious, men only, comprehensive institution.

GRADUATE UNITS

Graduate Programs

MISERICORDIA UNIVERSITY, Dallas, PA 18612-1098

General Information Independent-religious, coed, comprehensive institution. *Graduate housing:* On-campus housing not available.

GRADUATE UNITS

College of Business *Program availability:* Part-time, evening/weekend. Offers accounting (MBA); business (MBA, MS); healthcare management (MBA, MS); human resource management (MBA, MS); management (MBA, MS); sport management (MBA). Electronic applications accepted.

College of Health Sciences and Education *Program availability:* Part-time, evening/weekend. Offers health sciences and education (MS, MSN, MSOT, MSSLP, DNP, DPT, OTD); instructional technology (MS); nursing (MSN, DNP); occupational therapy (MSOT, OTD); physical therapy (DPT); reading specialist (MS); special education (MS); speech-language pathology (MSSLP). Electronic applications accepted.

MISSISSIPPI COLLEGE, Clinton, MS 39058

General Information Independent-religious, coed, comprehensive institution. *Graduate housing:* Room and/or apartments available on a first-come, first-served basis to single students; on-campus housing not available to married students. Housing application deadline: 8/15. *Research affiliation:* Gulf Coast Research Laboratory (marine biology).

GRADUATE UNITS

Graduate School *Program availability:* Part-time, evening/weekend, online learning. Offers health services administration (MHSA); liberal studies (MLS). Electronic applications accepted.

College of Arts and Sciences *Program availability:* Part-time, evening/weekend. Offers administration of justice (MSS); applied communication (MSC); applied music performance (MM); art (M Ed, MA, MFA); arts and sciences (M Ed, MA, MCS, MFA, MM, MS, MSC, MSS, Certificate); biological science (M Ed); biology (MCS); biology-biological sciences (MS); biology-medical sciences (MS); chemistry and biochemistry (MCS, MS); Christian studies and the arts (M Ed, MA, MFA, MM, MSC); computer science (M Ed, MS); conducting (MM); English (M Ed, MA); history (M Ed, MA, MSS); humanities and social sciences (M Ed, MA, MS, MSS, Certificate); mathematics (M Ed, MCS, MS); music education (MM); music performance: organ (MM); paralegal studies (Certificate); political science (MSS); public relations and corporate communication (MSC); science and mathematics (M Ed, MCS, MS); social sciences (M Ed, MSS); teaching English to speakers of other languages (MA, MS); vocal pedagogy (MM). Electronic applications accepted.

School of Business *Program availability:* Part-time, evening/weekend. Offers accounting (Certificate); business administration (MBA); business education (M Ed); finance (MBA, Certificate). Electronic applications accepted.

School of Education *Program availability:* Part-time, evening/weekend, online learning. Offers art (M Ed); athletic administration (MS); biological science (M Ed); business education (M Ed); computer science (M Ed); counseling (Ed S); dyslexia therapy (M Ed); education (M Ed, MS, Ed D, Ed S); educational leadership (M Ed, Ed D, Ed S); elementary education (M Ed, Ed S); English (M Ed); higher education administration (MS); marriage and family counseling (MS); mathematics (M Ed); mental health counseling (MS); school counseling (M Ed); secondary education (M Ed); social studies (history) (M Ed); teaching arts (M Ed). Electronic applications accepted.

School of Law Offers civil law studies (Certificate); law (JD). Electronic applications accepted.

MISSISSIPPI STATE UNIVERSITY, Mississippi State, MS 39762

General Information State-supported, coed, university. CGS member. *Enrollment:* 21,883 graduate, professional, and undergraduate students; 1,952 full-time matriculated graduate/professional students (1,005 women), 1,502 part-time matriculated graduate/professional students (716 women). *Enrollment by degree level:* 1,916 master's, 1,499 doctoral, 39 other advanced degrees. *Graduate faculty:* 840 full-time (261 women), 22 part-time/adjunct (8 women). Tuition, state resident: full-time $8318; part-time $462.12 per credit hour. Tuition, nonresident: full-time $22,358; part-time $1242.12 per credit hour. *Required fees:* $110; $12.24 per credit hour. $6.12 per semester. *Graduate housing:* Room and/or apartments available on a first-come, first-served basis to single students; on-campus housing not available to married students. Typical cost: $6617 per year. Room charges vary according to housing facility selected. Housing application deadline: 8/1. *Student services:* Campus employment opportunities, campus safety program, career counseling, child daycare facilities, exercise/wellness program, free psychological counseling, grant writing training, international student services, low-cost health insurance, multicultural affairs office, services for students with disabilities, teacher training, writing training. *Library facilities:* Mitchell Memorial Library plus 2 others. *Collection:* Books: 257,296 (physical), 56,456 (digital/electronic); Serial titles: 1,646 (physical), 231,031 (digital/electronic); Databases: 185. Weekly public service hours: 110; students can reserve study rooms. *Research affiliation:* Southeastern Universities Research Association (interdisciplinary research), Oak Ridge Associated Universities (interdisciplinary energy-related research), Mississippi Research and Technology Park (interdisciplinary engineering), Mississippi Mineral Resources Institute (geology sciences and engineering), NASA-Stennis Space Center (interdisciplinary research), Mississippi Research Consortium (interdisciplinary research).

Computer facilities: 1,000 computers available on campus for general student use. A campuswide network can be accessed from student residence rooms and from off campus. Online class registration is available.
Website: http://www.msstate.edu/

General Application Contact: Forest Sparks, Admissions Manager, 662-325-7400, Fax: 662-325-1967, E-mail: grad@grad.msstate.edu.

GRADUATE UNITS

Bagley College of Engineering Students: 372 full-time (106 women), 334 part-time (73 women); includes 102 minority (52 Black or African American, non-Hispanic/Latino; 19 Asian, non-Hispanic/Latino; 27 Hispanic/Latino; 1 Native Hawaiian or other Pacific Islander, non-Hispanic/Latino; 3 Two or more races, non-Hispanic/Latino), 240 international. Average age 30. 540 applicants, 56% accepted, 186 enrolled. *Faculty:* 113 full-time (14 women), 8 part-time/adjunct (2 women). Expenses: Contact institution. *Financial support:* In 2017–18, 178 research assistantships with full tuition reimbursements (averaging $16,814 per year), 61 teaching assistantships with full tuition reimbursements (averaging $15,765 per year) were awarded; Federal Work-Study, institutionally sponsored loans, scholarships/grants, and unspecified assistantships also available. Financial award application deadline: 4/1; financial award applicants required to submit FAFSA. In 2017, 121 master's, 35 doctorates awarded. *Program availability:* Part-time, 100% online. Offers aerospace engineering (MS); civil and environmental engineering (MS, PhD); computer science and engineering (MS, PhD); electrical and computer engineering (MS, PhD); engineering (M Eng, MS, PhD); human factors and ergonomics (MS); industrial and systems engineering (PhD); industrial systems (MS); management systems (MS); manufacturing systems (MS); mechanical engineering (MS); operations research (MS). *Application deadline:* For fall admission, 7/1 for domestic students, 5/1 for international students; for spring admission, 11/1 for domestic students, 9/1 for international students. Applications are processed on a rolling basis. *Application fee:* $60 ($80 for international students). Electronic applications accepted. *Application Contact:* Angie Campbell, Admissions and Enrollment Assistant, 662-325-9514, E-mail: acampbell@grad.msstate.edu. *Dean*, Dr. Jason Keith, 662-325-7183, Fax: 662-325-8573, E-mail: keith@bagley.msstate.edu.

Dave C. Swalm School of Chemical Engineering Students: 13 full-time (4 women), 2 part-time (1 woman), 13 international. Average age 29. 13 applicants, 15% accepted, 2 enrolled. *Faculty:* 11 full-time (2 women). Expenses: Contact institution. *Financial support:* In 2017–18, 11 research assistantships with full tuition reimbursements (averaging $16,776 per year), 1 teaching assistantship with full tuition reimbursement (averaging $16,234 per year) were awarded; Federal Work-Study, institutionally sponsored loans, and unspecified assistantships also available. Financial award application deadline: 4/1; financial award applicants required to submit FAFSA. In 2017, 3 doctorates awarded. Offers chemical engineering (MS, PhD). *Application deadline:* For fall admission, 4/1 priority date for domestic students, 5/1 for international students; for spring admission, 8/1 priority date for domestic students, 9/1 for international students. Applications are processed on a rolling basis. *Application fee:* $60 ($80 for international students). Electronic applications accepted. *Application Contact:* Angie Campbell, Admissions and Enrollment Assistant, 662-325-9514, E-mail: acampbell@grad.msstate.edu. *Associate Professor/Director/Chair*, Dr. Bill Elmore, 662-325-2480, Fax: 662-325-2482, E-mail: elmore@che.msstate.edu.

College of Agriculture and Life Sciences Students: 244 full-time (129 women), 142 part-time (85 women); includes 55 minority (37 Black or African American, non-Hispanic/Latino; 1 American Indian or Alaska Native, non-Hispanic/Latino; 4 Asian, non-Hispanic/Latino; 9 Hispanic/Latino; 4 Two or more races, non-Hispanic/Latino), 80 international. Average age 31. 217 applicants, 45% accepted, 68 enrolled. *Faculty:* 188 full-time (49 women), 1 (woman) part-time/adjunct. Expenses: Contact institution. *Financial support:* In 2017–18, 159 research assistantships with full tuition reimbursements (averaging $15,428 per year), 13 teaching assistantships with full tuition reimbursements (averaging $12,517 per year) were awarded; career-related internships or fieldwork, Federal Work-Study, institutionally sponsored loans, scholarships/grants, tuition waivers (partial), and unspecified assistantships also available. Financial award application deadline: 4/1; financial award applicants required to submit FAFSA. In 2017, 89 master's, 25 doctorates awarded. *Program availability:* Blended/hybrid learning. Offers agricultural economics (MS); agricultural life sciences (MS); agricultural science (PhD); agricultural sciences (MS, PhD); agriculture (MS); agriculture and life sciences (MABM, MLA, MS, PhD); biochemistry (MS, PhD); biological engineering (MS, PhD); biomedical engineering (MS, PhD); entomology (MS, PhD); food science and technology (MS, PhD); health promotion (MS); landscape architecture (MLA); life sciences (PhD); nutrition (MS, PhD); plant pathology (MS, PhD); weed science (MS, PhD). *Application deadline:* For fall admission, 7/1 for domestic students, 5/1 for international students; for spring admission, 11/1 for domestic students, 9/1 for international students. Applications are processed on a rolling basis. *Application fee:* $60 ($80 for international students). Electronic applications accepted. *Application Contact:* Marina Hunt, Admissions and Enrollment Assistant, 662-325-5188, Fax: 662-325-1967, E-mail: mhunt@grad.msstate.edu. *Dean of Agriculture and Life Sciences/Director of Mississippi Agricultural and Forestry Experiment Station*, Dr. George Hopper, 662-325-2953, Fax: 662-325-8580, E-mail: dean@cfr.msstate.edu.

School of Human Sciences Students: 31 full-time (23 women), 54 part-time (38 women); includes 19 minority (15 Black or African American, non-Hispanic/Latino; 1 Hispanic/Latino; 3 Two or more races, non-Hispanic/Latino), 5 international. Average age 36. 26 applicants, 65% accepted, 15 enrolled. *Faculty:* 20 full-time (11 women). Expenses: Contact institution. *Financial support:* In 2017–18, 13 research assistantships (averaging $13,718 per year) were awarded; Federal Work-Study, institutionally sponsored loans, and unspecified assistantships also available. Financial award application deadline: 4/1; financial award applicants required to submit FAFSA. In 2017, 19 master's, 2 doctorates awarded. *Program availability:* Part-time. Offers agriculture and extension education (MS); agriculture science (PhD); fashion design and merchandising (MS); human development and family studies (MS, PhD). *Application deadline:* For fall admission, 7/1 for domestic students, 5/1 for international students; for spring admission, 11/1 for domestic students, 9/1 for international students. Applications are processed on a rolling basis. *Application fee:* $60 ($80 for international students). Electronic applications accepted. *Application Contact:* Marina Hunt, Admissions and Enrollment Assistant, 662-325-5188, E-mail: mhunt@grad.msstate.edu. *Professor and Director*, Dr. Michael Newman, 662-325-2950, E-mail: mnewman@humansci.msstate.edu.

College of Arts and Sciences Students: 432 full-time (196 women), 328 part-time (176 women); includes 126 minority (59 Black or African American, non-Hispanic/Latino; 3 American Indian or Alaska Native, non-Hispanic/Latino; 12 Asian, non-Hispanic/Latino; 37 Hispanic/Latino; 2 Native Hawaiian or other Pacific Islander, non-Hispanic/Latino; 13 Two or more races, non-Hispanic/Latino), 143 international. Average age 30. 688 applicants, 58% accepted, 262 enrolled. *Faculty:* 234 full-time (87 women), 4 part-time/adjunct (0 women). Expenses: Contact institution. *Financial support:* In 2017–18, 49 research assistantships with full tuition reimbursements (averaging $15,269 per year), 304 teaching assistantships with full tuition reimbursements (averaging $14,105 per year) were awarded; Federal Work-Study, institutionally sponsored loans, scholarships/grants, tuition waivers (partial), and unspecified assistantships also available. Financial award application deadline: 4/1; financial award applicants required to submit FAFSA. In 2017, 152 master's, 45 doctorates awarded. *Program availability:* Part-time, evening/weekend. Offers Africa (MA, PhD); anthropology and Middle Eastern cultures (MA); applied meteorology (MS); applied psychology (PhD); arts and sciences (MA, MPPA, MS, PhD); Asia (MA, PhD); biological sciences (MS, PhD); broadcast meteorology (MS); chemistry (MA, MS, PhD); classical and modern languages and literatures (MA); earth and atmospheric science (PhD); English (MA); environmental geosciences (MS); Europe (MA, PhD); general biology (MS); geography (MS); geology (MS); geospatial sciences (MS); Latin America (MA, PhD); mathematical sciences (PhD); mathematics (MS); physics (MS, PhD); political science (MA); professional meteorology/climatology (MS); psychology (MS); public policy and administration (MPPA, PhD); sociology (MS, PhD); statistics (MS); teachers in geosciences (MS); United States (MA, PhD); world history (MA, PhD). *Application deadline:* For fall admission, 7/1 for domestic students, 5/1 for international students; for spring admission, 11/1 for domestic students, 9/1 for international students. Applications are processed on a rolling basis. *Application fee:* $60 ($80 for international students). Electronic applications accepted. *Application Contact:* Lakan Drinker, Admissions and Enrollment Assistant, 662-325-8951, E-mail: ldrinker@grad.msstate.edu. *Dean and Professor*, Dr. Rick Travis, 662-325-2646, Fax: 662-325-8740, E-mail: rtravis@deanas.msstate.edu.

College of Business Students: 140 full-time (65 women), 200 part-time (45 women); includes 30 minority (11 Black or African American, non-Hispanic/Latino; 5 Asian, non-Hispanic/Latino; 11 Hispanic/Latino; 3 Two or more races, non-Hispanic/Latino), 30 international. Average age 29. 255 applicants, 46% accepted, 95 enrolled. *Faculty:* 60 full-time (13 women), 1 part-time/adjunct (0 women). Expenses: Contact institution. *Financial support:* In 2017–18, 1 research assistantship (averaging $11,452 per year), 43 teaching assistantships (averaging $12,062 per year) were awarded; career-related internships or fieldwork, Federal Work-Study, institutionally sponsored loans, scholarships/grants, and unspecified assistantships also available. Financial award application deadline: 4/1; financial award applicants required to submit FAFSA. In 2017, 148 master's, 6 doctorates awarded. *Program availability:* Part-time, evening/weekend, blended/hybrid learning. Offers applied economics (PhD); business (MA, MBA, MPA, MSIS, PhD); business administration (MBA, PhD); economics (MA); information systems (MSIS, PhD); management (PhD); project management (MBA). *Application deadline:*

For fall admission, 3/1 priority date for domestic students, 5/1 for international students; for spring admission, 11/1 for domestic students, 9/1 for international students. Applications are processed on a rolling basis. *Application fee:* $60 ($80 for international students). Electronic applications accepted. *Application Contact:* Lakan Drinker, Admissions and Enrollment Assistant, 662-325-8951, E-mail: ldrinker@grad.msstate.edu. *Dean and Professor,* Dr. Sharon Oswald, 662-325-2580, Fax: 662-325-2410, E-mail: slo49@msstate.edu.

Adkerson School of Accountancy Students: 61 full-time (38 women), 3 part-time (0 women); includes 8 minority (5 Black or African American, non-Hispanic/Latino; 1 Asian, non-Hispanic/Latino; 2 Hispanic/Latino), 3 international. Average age 23. 40 applicants, 70% accepted, 26 enrolled. *Faculty:* 10 full-time (0 women). Expenses: Contact institution. *Financial support:* Career-related internships or fieldwork, Federal Work-Study, institutionally sponsored loans, scholarships/grants, and unspecified assistantships available. Support available to part-time students. Financial award application deadline: 4/1; financial award applicants required to submit FAFSA. In 2017, 51 master's awarded. Offers accountancy (MPA); systems (MPA). *Application deadline:* For fall admission, 7/1 for domestic students, 5/1 for international students; for spring admission, 11/1 for domestic students, 9/1 for international students. Applications are processed on a rolling basis. *Application fee:* $60 ($80 for international students). Electronic applications accepted. *Application Contact:* Lakan Drinker, Admissions and Enrollment Assistant, 662-325-8951, E-mail: ldrinker@grad.msstate.edu. *Professor and Director,* Dr. Shawn Mauldin, 662-325-3710, Fax: 662-325-1646, E-mail: smauldin@business.msstate.edu.

College of Education Students: 283 full-time (169 women), 423 part-time (304 women); includes 243 minority (196 Black or African American, non-Hispanic/Latino; 10 American Indian or Alaska Native, non-Hispanic/Latino; 5 Asian, non-Hispanic/Latino; 15 Hispanic/Latino; 2 Native Hawaiian or other Pacific Islander, non-Hispanic/Latino; 15 Two or more races, non-Hispanic/Latino), 20 international. Average age 32. 413 applicants, 62% accepted, 202 enrolled. *Faculty:* 97 full-time (51 women), 4 part-time/adjunct (3 women). Expenses: Contact institution. *Financial support:* In 2017–18, 12 research assistantships (averaging $10,542 per year), 25 teaching assistantships (averaging $9,672 per year) were awarded; career-related internships or fieldwork, Federal Work-Study, institutionally sponsored loans, scholarships/grants, and unspecified assistantships also available. Financial award application deadline: 4/1; financial award applicants required to submit FAFSA. In 2017, 186 master's, 49 doctorates, 26 other advanced degrees awarded. *Program availability:* Part-time, evening/weekend, blended/hybrid learning. Offers clinical mental health (MS); college counseling (MS); community college education (MAT); community college leadership (PhD); counseling/mental health (PhD); counseling/school psychology (PhD); counselor education (Ed S); disability studies (MS); early childhood education (PhD); education (MAT, MS, MSIT, MST, PhD, Ed S); educational psychology/general educational psychology (PhD); educational psychology/school psychology (PhD); elementary education (MS, PhD, Ed S); exercise physiology (MS); exercise science (PhD); general curriculum and instruction (PhD); general educational psychology (MS); higher education leadership (PhD); instructional systems and workforce development (MSIT, PhD); P-12 school leadership (PhD); psychometry (MS); reading education (PhD); rehabilitation counseling (MS); school administration (MS, Ed S); school counseling (MS); school psychology (Ed S); secondary education (MAT, MS, PhD, Ed S); special education (MAT, MS, PhD, Ed S); sport administration (MS); sport pedagogy (MS); sport studies (PhD); student affairs (MS); student affairs and higher education (MS); technology (MST, Ed S); workforce education leadership (MS). *Application deadline:* For fall admission, 7/1 for domestic students, 5/1 for international students; for spring admission, 11/1 for domestic students, 9/1 for international students. Applications are processed on a rolling basis. *Application fee:* $60 ($80 for international students). Electronic applications accepted. *Application Contact:* Marina Hunt, Admissions and Enrollment Assistant, 662-325-5188, E-mail: mhunt@grad.msstate.edu. *Dean,* Dr. Richard Blackbourn, 662-325-3717, Fax: 662-325-8784, E-mail: rlb277@msstate.edu.

College of Forest Resources Students: 96 full-time (36 women), 40 part-time (13 women); includes 8 minority (1 Black or African American, non-Hispanic/Latino; 1 American Indian or Alaska Native, non-Hispanic/Latino; 2 Asian, non-Hispanic/Latino; 4 Hispanic/Latino), 37 international. Average age 29. 53 applicants, 49% accepted, 21 enrolled. *Faculty:* 56 full-time (9 women), 1 part-time/adjunct (0 women). Expenses: Contact institution. *Financial support:* In 2017–18, 94 research assistantships with full tuition reimbursements (averaging $15,236 per year) were awarded; career-related internships or fieldwork, Federal Work-Study, institutionally sponsored loans, and unspecified assistantships also available. Financial award application deadline: 4/1; financial award applicants required to submit FAFSA. In 2017, 23 master's, 11 doctorates awarded. *Program availability:* Part-time. Offers forest resources (PhD); forestry (MS); sustainable bioproducts (MS); wildlife, fisheries and aquaculture (MS, PhD). *Application deadline:* For fall admission, 7/1 for domestic students, 5/1 for international students; for spring admission, 11/1 for domestic students, 9/1 for international students. Applications are processed on a rolling basis. *Application fee:* $60 ($80 for international students). Electronic applications accepted. *Application Contact:* Nathan Drake, Admissions and Enrollment Assistant, 662-325-3804, E-mail: ndrake@grad.msstate.edu. *Dean,* Dr. George Hopper, 662-325-2953, Fax: 662-325-8726, E-mail: ghopper@cfr.msstate.edu.

College of Veterinary Medicine Students: 346 full-time (270 women), 36 part-time (21 women); includes 21 minority (5 Black or African American, non-Hispanic/Latino; 3 American Indian or Alaska Native, non-Hispanic/Latino; 1 Asian, non-Hispanic/Latino; 10 Hispanic/Latino; 2 Two or more races, non-Hispanic/Latino). Average age 24. 957 applicants, 10% accepted, 92 enrolled. Expenses: Contact institution. *Financial support:* In 2017–18, 33 research assistantships with full tuition reimbursements (averaging $15,933 per year) were awarded; career-related internships or fieldwork, Federal Work-Study, and institutionally sponsored loans also available. Financial award application deadline: 6/30; financial award applicants required to submit FAFSA. In 2017, 84 doctorates awarded. Offers veterinary medical science (MS, PhD); veterinary medicine (MS, DVM, PhD). *Application deadline:* For fall admission, 9/15 for domestic and international students. *Application fee:* $55. Electronic applications accepted. *Application Contact:* Missy Hadaway, Admissions and Student Affairs Coordinator, 662-325-9065, Fax: 663-325-1027, E-mail: missy.hadaway@msstate.edu. *Dean,* Dr. Kent H. Hoblet, 662-325-1131, Fax: 662-325-1498, E-mail: hoblet@cvm.msstate.edu.

MISSISSIPPI UNIVERSITY FOR WOMEN, Columbus, MS 39701-9998

General Information State-supported, coed, comprehensive institution. *Graduate housing:* Rooms and/or apartments available on a first-come, first-served basis to single and married students.

GRADUATE UNITS

Graduate School *Program availability:* Part-time.

College of Education and Human Sciences *Program availability:* Part-time. Offers differentiated instruction (M Ed); educational leadership (M Ed); gifted studies (M Ed); reading/literacy (M Ed); teaching (MAT).

College of Nursing and Health Sciences *Program availability:* Part-time. Offers nursing (MSN, DNP, PMC); public health education (MPH); speech-language pathology (MS).

MISSISSIPPI VALLEY STATE UNIVERSITY, Itta Bena, MS 38941-1400

General Information State-supported, coed, comprehensive institution. *Graduate housing:* On-campus housing not available.

GRADUATE UNITS

College of Education *Program availability:* Part-time, evening/weekend. Offers education (MAT, MS).

Department of Criminal Justice *Program availability:* Part-time, evening/weekend, 100% online. Offers criminal justice (MS). Electronic applications accepted.

Department of Natural Sciences and Environmental Health *Program availability:* Part-time, evening/weekend. Offers environmental health (MS).

MISSOURI BAPTIST UNIVERSITY, St. Louis, MO 63141-8660

General Information Independent-religious, coed, comprehensive institution.

GRADUATE UNITS

Graduate Programs

MISSOURI SOUTHERN STATE UNIVERSITY, Joplin, MO 64801-1595

General Information State-supported, coed, comprehensive institution.

GRADUATE UNITS

Program in Business Administration *Program availability:* Online learning. Offers business administration (MBA). Program offered jointly with Northwest Missouri State University.

Program in Criminal Justice Administration *Program availability:* Online learning. Offers criminal justice administration (MS). Program offered jointly with Southeast Missouri State University.

Program in Dental Hygiene *Program availability:* Part-time. Offers dental hygiene (MS). Program offered jointly with University of Missouri–Kansas City. Electronic applications accepted.

Program in Early Childhood Education Offers early childhood education (MS Ed). Program offered jointly with Northwest Missouri State University.

Program in Instructional Technology Offers instructional technology (MS Ed). Program offered jointly with Northwest Missouri State University.

Program in Nursing *Program availability:* Part-time. Offers nursing (MSN). Program offered jointly with University of Missouri–Kansas City. Electronic applications accepted.

Program in Teaching Offers teaching (MAT). Program offered jointly with Missouri State University.

★ MISSOURI STATE UNIVERSITY, Springfield, MO 65897

General Information State-supported, coed, comprehensive institution. CGS member. *Enrollment:* 23,697 graduate, professional, and undergraduate students; 1,443 full-time matriculated graduate/professional students (926 women), 1,671 part-time matriculated graduate/professional students (1,042 women). *Enrollment by degree level:* 2,521 master's, 372 doctoral, 221 other advanced degrees. *Graduate faculty:* 743 full-time (364 women), 392 part-time/adjunct (210 women). *International tuition:* $11,992 full-time. Tuition, state resident: full-time $2915; part-time $2021 per credit hour. Tuition, nonresident: full-time $5354; part-time $3647 per credit hour. *Required fees:* $173; $173 per credit hour. Tuition and fees vary according to class time, course level, course load, degree level, campus/location and program. *Graduate housing:* Rooms and/or apartments available on a first-come, first-served basis to single and married students. Typical cost: $8236 (including board) for single students; $8104 per year ($9310 including board) for married students. Room and board charges vary according to board plan, campus/location and housing facility selected. Housing application deadline: 32/1. *Student services:* Campus employment opportunities, campus safety program, career counseling, child daycare facilities, exercise/wellness program, free psychological counseling, grant writing training, international student services, multicultural affairs office, services for students with disabilities, teacher training, writing training. *Library facilities:* Meyer Library.

Computer facilities: A campuswide network can be accessed from student residence rooms and from off campus. Online class registration is available.
Website: http://www.missouristate.edu/

General Application Contact: Stephanie Praschan, Director, Graduate Enrollment Management, 417-836-5330, Fax: 417-836-6200, E-mail: graduateadmissions@missouristate.edu.

GRADUATE UNITS

Graduate College Students: 1,402 full-time (900 women), 1,603 part-time (990 women); includes 319 minority (92 Black or African American, non-Hispanic/Latino; 8 American Indian or Alaska Native, non-Hispanic/Latino; 50 Asian, non-Hispanic/Latino; 95 Hispanic/Latino; 4 Native Hawaiian or other Pacific Islander, non-Hispanic/Latino; 70 Two or more races, non-Hispanic/Latino), 393 international. Average age 23. 1,368 applicants, 75% accepted, 762 enrolled. *Faculty:* 743 full-time (364 women), 392 part-time/adjunct (210 women). Expenses: Contact institution. *Financial support:* In 2017–18, 585 students received support, including 44 research assistantships with full tuition reimbursements available (averaging $8,772 per year), 195 teaching assistantships with full tuition reimbursements available (averaging $8,772 per year); Federal Work-Study, institutionally sponsored loans, scholarships/grants, and unspecified assistantships also available. Financial award application deadline: 3/31; financial award applicants required to submit FAFSA. In 2017, 1,089 master's, 108 doctorates, 12 other advanced degrees awarded. *Program availability:* Part-time, 100% online, blended/hybrid learning. Offers administrative studies (Certificate); applied communication (MS); criminal justice (MS); environmental management (MS); homeland security (MS); individualized (MS); professional studies (MS); screenwriting and producing (MS); sports management (MS). *Application deadline:* For fall admission, 7/20 priority date for domestic students, 5/1 for international students; for spring admission, 12/20 priority date for domestic students, 9/1 for international students. Applications are processed on a rolling basis. *Application fee:* $35 ($50 for international students). Electronic applications accepted. *Application Contact:* Stephanie Praschan, Director, Graduate Enrollment Management, 417-836-5330, Fax: 417-836-6200, E-mail: stephaniepraschan@missouristate.edu. *Associate Provost/Dean,* Dr. Julie Masterson, 417-836-5335, Fax: 417-836-6888, E-mail: juliemasterson@missouristate.edu.

College of Arts and Letters Students: 79 full-time (55 women), 160 part-time (129 women); includes 29 minority (7 Black or African American, non-Hispanic/Latino; 3 Asian, non-Hispanic/Latino; 11 Hispanic/Latino; 1 Native Hawaiian or other Pacific Islander, non-Hispanic/Latino; 7 Two or more races, non-Hispanic/Latino), 34 international. Average age 27. 193 applicants, 52% accepted, 93 enrolled. *Faculty:* 74 full-time (32 women), 7 part-time/adjunct (5 women). Expenses: Contact institution. *Financial support:* In 2017–18, 61 teaching assistantships with full tuition reimbursements (averaging $8,772 per year) were awarded; Federal Work-Study, institutionally sponsored loans, scholarships/grants, and unspecified assistantships also available. Financial award application deadline: 3/31; financial award applicants required to submit FAFSA. In 2017, 125 master's awarded. *Program availability:* Part-time, evening/weekend, 100% online, blended/hybrid learning. Offers applied second language acquisition (MASLA); arts and letters (MA, MASLA, MFA, MM, MS Ed, Certificate); communication (MA); English (MA); English education (MS Ed); music (MM, MS Ed); speech and theatre education (MS Ed); teaching English to speakers of other languages (Certificate); visual studies (MFA); writing (MA). *Application deadline:* For fall admission, 7/20 priority date for domestic students, 5/1 for international students; for spring admission, 12/20 priority date for domestic students, 9/1 for international students; for summer admission, 5/20 priority date for domestic students. Applications are processed on a rolling basis. *Application fee:* $35 ($50 for international students). Electronic applications accepted. *Application Contact:* Stephanie Praschan, Director, Graduate Enrollment Management, 417-836-5330, Fax: 417-836-6200, E-mail: stephaniepraschan@missouristate.edu. *Interim Dean*, Dr. Shawn Wahl, 417-836-4366, Fax: 417-836-6940, E-mail: shawnwahl@missouristate.edu.

College of Business Students: 336 full-time (196 women), 434 part-time (171 women); includes 81 minority (25 Black or African American, non-Hispanic/Latino; 3 American Indian or Alaska Native, non-Hispanic/Latino; 18 Asian, non-Hispanic/Latino; 25 Hispanic/Latino; 10 Two or more races, non-Hispanic/Latino), 235 international. Average age 23. 503 applicants, 60% accepted, 216 enrolled. *Faculty:* 50 full-time (13 women), 8 part-time/adjunct (1 woman). Expenses: Contact institution. *Financial support:* In 2017–18, 4 teaching assistantships with full tuition reimbursements (averaging $10,672 per year) were awarded; Federal Work-Study, institutionally sponsored loans, scholarships/grants, and unspecified assistantships also available. Financial award application deadline: 3/31; financial award applicants required to submit FAFSA. In 2017, 530 master's awarded. *Program availability:* Part-time, evening/weekend, 100% online, blended/hybrid learning. Offers accountancy (M Acc); business (M Acc, MBA, MHA, MS, MS Ed); business administration (MBA); health administration (MHA); project management (MS). *Application deadline:* For fall admission, 7/20 priority date for domestic students, 5/1 for international students; for spring admission, 12/20 priority date for domestic students, 9/1 for international students; for summer admission, 5/20 priority date for domestic students. Applications are processed on a rolling basis. *Application fee:* $35 ($50 for international students). Electronic applications accepted. *Application Contact:* Stephanie Praschan, Director, Graduate Enrollment Management, 417-836-5330, Fax: 417-836-6200, E-mail: stephaniepraschan@missouristate.edu. *Interim Dean*, Dr. David Meinert, 417-836-5646, Fax: 417-836-4407, E-mail: coba@missouristate.edu.

College of Education Students: 144 full-time (112 women), 467 part-time (392 women); includes 63 minority (17 Black or African American, non-Hispanic/Latino; 1 American Indian or Alaska Native, non-Hispanic/Latino; 4 Asian, non-Hispanic/Latino; 27 Hispanic/Latino; 14 Two or more races, non-Hispanic/Latino), 15 international. Average age 28. 381 applicants, 69% accepted, 131 enrolled. *Faculty:* 43 full-time (26 women), 11 part-time/adjunct (6 women). Expenses: Contact institution. *Financial support:* Teaching assistantships, Federal Work-Study, institutionally sponsored loans, scholarships/grants, and unspecified assistantships available. Financial award application deadline: 3/31; financial award applicants required to submit FAFSA. In 2017, 246 master's, 12 other advanced degrees awarded. *Program availability:* Part-time. Offers counseling (MS); counseling and assessment (Ed S); early childhood and family development (MS); education (MAT, MS, MS Ed, Ed S); educational administration (MS Ed, Ed S); educational technology (MS Ed); elementary education (MS Ed); elementary principal (MS Ed, Ed S); literacy (MS Ed, Graduate Certificate); mental health counseling (MS); secondary principal (MS Ed, Ed S); special education (MS Ed); student affairs in higher education (MS); superintendent (Ed S); teacher leadership (Certificate, Ed S); teaching (MAT); teaching and learning (MA, Certificate). *Application deadline:* For fall admission, 7/20 for domestic students, 5/1 for international students; for spring admission, 12/20 for domestic students, 9/1 for international students; for summer admission, 5/20 for domestic students. Applications are processed on a rolling basis. *Application fee:* $35 ($50 for international students). Electronic applications accepted. *Application Contact:* Stephanie Praschan, Director, Graduate Enrollment Management, 417-836-5330, Fax: 417-836-6200, E-mail: stephaniepraschan@missouristate.edu. *Dean*, Dr. David Hough, 417-836-5254, Fax: 417-836-4884, E-mail: collegeofeducation@missouristate.edu.

College of Health and Human Services Students: 587 full-time (421 women), 213 part-time (151 women); includes 87 minority (26 Black or African American, non-Hispanic/Latino; 4 American Indian or Alaska Native, non-Hispanic/Latino; 19 Asian, non-Hispanic/Latino; 15 Hispanic/Latino; 3 Native Hawaiian or other Pacific Islander, non-Hispanic/Latino; 20 Two or more races, non-Hispanic/Latino), 24 international. Average age 23. 367 applicants, 35% accepted, 127 enrolled. *Faculty:* 89 full-time (58 women), 33 part-time/adjunct (21 women). Expenses: Contact institution. *Financial support:* In 2017–18, 9 research assistantships with full tuition reimbursements (averaging $8,772 per year), 33 teaching assistantships with full tuition reimbursements (averaging $8,772 per year) were awarded; Federal Work-Study, institutionally sponsored loans, scholarships/grants, and unspecified assistantships also available. Financial award application deadline: 3/31; financial award applicants required to submit FAFSA. In 2017, 201 master's, 108 doctorates awarded. *Program availability:* Part-time. Offers applied behavior analysis (MS); athletic training (MS); cell and molecular biology (MS); clinical psychology (MS); communication sciences and disorders (Au D); dietetic internship (Certificate); experimental psychology (MS); forensic child psychology (Certificate); health and human services (MOT, MPH, MS, MS Ed, MSN, MSW, Au D, DNAP, DNP, DPT, Certificate); health promotion and wellness management (MS); industrial/organizational psychology (MS); nurse anesthesia (DNAP); nursing (MSN); nursing practice (DNP); occupational therapy (MOT); physical therapy (DPT); physician assistant studies (MS); public health (MPH); secondary education (MS Ed); social work (MSW); speech language pathology (MS). *Application fee:* $35 ($50 for international students). Electronic applications accepted. *Application Contact:* Stephanie Praschan, Director, Graduate Enrollment Management, 417-836-5330, Fax: 417-836-6200, E-mail: stephaniepraschan@missouristate.edu. *Dean*, Dr. Helen Reid, 417-836-4176, Fax: 417-836-6905, E-mail: chhs@missouristate.edu.

College of Humanities and Public Affairs Students: 92 full-time (40 women), 135 part-time (56 women); includes 23 minority (7 Black or African American, non-Hispanic/Latino; 4 Asian, non-Hispanic/Latino; 6 Hispanic/Latino; 6 Two or more races, non-Hispanic/Latino), 13 international. Average age 24. 137 applicants, 62% accepted, 80 enrolled. *Faculty:* 66 full-time (20 women), 21 part-time/adjunct (5 women). Expenses: Contact institution. *Financial support:* In 2017–18, 3 teaching assistantships with partial tuition reimbursements (averaging $2,150 per year) were awarded; Federal Work-Study, institutionally sponsored loans, scholarships/grants, and unspecified assistantships also available. Financial award application deadline: 3/31; financial award applicants required to submit FAFSA. In 2017, 105 master's awarded. *Program availability:* Part-time. Offers community corrections (Certificate); criminology and criminal justice (MS); defense and strategic studies (Certificate); general weapons of mass destruction (MS); global studies (MGS); history (MA); history education (MS Ed); history for teachers (Certificate); homeland security and defense (Certificate); humanities and public affairs (MA, MGS, MIAA, MPA, MS, MS Ed, Certificate); public administration (MPA); public management (Certificate); religious studies (MA, Certificate). *Application deadline:* For fall admission, 7/20 priority date for domestic students, 5/1 for international students; for spring admission, 12/20 priority date for domestic students, 9/1 for international students; for summer admission, 5/20 priority date for domestic students. Applications are processed on a rolling basis. *Application fee:* $35 ($50 for international students). Electronic applications accepted. *Application Contact:* Stephanie Praschan, Director, Graduate Enrollment Management, 417-836-5330, Fax: 417-836-6200, E-mail: stephaniepraschan@missouristate.edu. *Dean*, Dr. Victor Matthews, 417-836-5529, Fax: 417-836-8472, E-mail: victormatthews@missouristate.edu.

College of Natural and Applied Sciences Students: 90 full-time (33 women), 68 part-time (35 women); includes 12 minority (1 Black or African American, non-Hispanic/Latino; 1 Asian, non-Hispanic/Latino; 4 Hispanic/Latino; 6 Two or more races, non-Hispanic/Latino), 33 international. Average age 25. 121 applicants, 58% accepted, 58 enrolled. *Faculty:* 87 full-time (14 women), 8 part-time/adjunct (2 women). Expenses: Contact institution. *Financial support:* In 2017–18, 11 research assistantships with full tuition reimbursements (averaging $10,672 per year), 81 teaching assistantships with full tuition reimbursements (averaging $9,483 per year) were awarded; Federal Work-Study, institutionally sponsored loans, scholarships/grants, and unspecified assistantships also available. Financial award application deadline: 3/31; financial award applicants required to submit FAFSA. In 2017, 86 master's awarded. *Program availability:* Part-time, evening/weekend. Offers biology (MS); chemistry (MS); geography, geology, and planning (Certificate); materials science (MS); mathematics (MS); natural and applied science (MNAS); natural and applied sciences (MNAS, MS, MS Ed, Certificate); secondary education (MS Ed). *Application deadline:* For fall admission, 7/20 priority date for domestic students, 5/1 for international students; for spring admission, 12/20 priority date for domestic students, 9/1 for international students; for summer admission, 5/20 priority date for domestic students. Applications are processed on a rolling basis. *Application fee:* $35 ($50 for international students). Electronic applications accepted. *Application Contact:* Stephanie Praschan, Director, Graduate Enrollment Management, 417-836-5330, Fax: 417-836-6200, E-mail: stephaniepraschan@missouristate.edu. *Dean*, Dr. Tamera Jahnke, 417-836-5249, Fax: 417-836-6934, E-mail: tamerajahnke@missouristate.edu.

Darr College of Agriculture Students: 23 full-time (10 women), 31 part-time (15 women); includes 3 minority (1 Black or African American, non-Hispanic/Latino; 2 Two or more races, non-Hispanic/Latino), 2 international. Average age 23. 24 applicants, 42% accepted, 10 enrolled. *Faculty:* 16 full-time (5 women), 1 part-time/adjunct (0 women). Expenses: Contact institution. *Financial support:* In 2017–18, 7 research assistantships with full tuition reimbursements (averaging $9,365 per year), 6 teaching assistantships with full tuition reimbursements (averaging $8,450 per year) were awarded; Federal Work-Study, institutionally sponsored loans, scholarships/grants, and unspecified assistantships also available. Financial award application deadline: 3/31; financial award applicants required to submit FAFSA. In 2017, 23 master's awarded. *Program availability:* Part-time. Offers plant science (MS); secondary education (MS Ed). *Application deadline:* For fall admission, 7/20 priority date for domestic students, 5/1 for international students; for spring admission, 12/20 priority date for domestic students, 9/1 for international students; for summer admission, 5/20 priority date for domestic students. Applications are processed on a rolling basis. *Application fee:* $35 ($50 for international students). Electronic applications accepted. *Application Contact:* Stephanie Praschan, Director, Graduate Enrollment Management, 417-836-5330, Fax: 417-836-6200, E-mail: stephaniepraschan@missouristate.edu. *Dean*, Dr. Ronald Del Vecchio, 417-836-5050, E-mail: darr@missouristate.edu.

See Display on the next page and Close-Up on page 867.

MISSOURI UNIVERSITY OF SCIENCE AND TECHNOLOGY, Rolla, MO 65409

General Information State-supported, coed, university. CGS member. *Enrollment:* 8,884 graduate, professional, and undergraduate students; 1,214 full-time matriculated graduate/professional students (255 women), 739 part-time matriculated graduate/professional students (157 women). *Enrollment by degree level:* 827 master's, 689 doctoral, 437 other advanced degrees. *Graduate faculty:* 365 full-time (96 women), 38 part-time/adjunct (3 women). Tuition, state resident: full-time $7391; part-time $3696 per year. Tuition, nonresident: full-time $21,712; part-time $10,857 per year. *Required fees:* $728; $564 per unit. Tuition and fees vary according to course load. *Graduate housing:* Rooms and/or apartments available on a first-come, first-served basis to single and married students. Typical cost: $9584 (including board) for single students. *Student services:* Campus employment opportunities, campus safety program, career counseling, exercise/wellness program, free psychological counseling, international student services, low-cost health insurance, multicultural affairs office, services for students with disabilities. *Library facilities:* Curtis Laws Wilson Library. *Collection:* Books: 305,834 (physical), 447,868 (digital/electronic); Serial titles: 14,178 (physical), 79,586 (digital/electronic); Databases: 180. Weekly public service hours: 112; students can reserve study rooms. *Research affiliation:* Idaho National Laboratory (material research), Hussmann Corporation (mining and nuclear engineering), Samsung (material research), Cisco (material research), Honeywell (material research and additive manufacturing), Caterpillar, Inc. (mining and nuclear engineering).

Computer facilities: Computer purchase and lease plans are available. 980 computers available on campus for general student use. A campuswide network can be accessed from student residence rooms and from off campus. Online class registration is available.

Website: http://www.mst.edu/

General Application Contact: Erica Bay, Graduate Student Admission Counselor, 573-341-7661, E-mail: baye@mst.edu.

GRADUATE UNITS

Department of Biological Sciences Students: 10 full-time (6 women), 6 part-time (5 women); includes 1 minority (Hispanic/Latino), 6 international. Average age 28. 19 applicants, 68% accepted, 7 enrolled. *Faculty:* 10 full-time (3 women). Expenses: Contact institution. *Financial support:* In 2017–18, 6 research assistantships (averaging $1,810 per year), 1 teaching assistantship (averaging $1,814 per year) were awarded; institutionally sponsored loans and unspecified assistantships also available. In 2017, 8 master's awarded. Offers applied and environmental biology (MS). *Application fee:* $50. *Application Contact:* Debbie Schwertz, Admissions Coordinator, 573-341-6013, Fax: 573-341-6271, E-mail: schwertz@mst.edu. *Chair,* Dr. David Duvernell, 573-341-6988, Fax: 573-341-4821, E-mail: duvernelld@mst.edu.

Department of Business and Information Technology Students: 65 full-time (26 women), 69 part-time (22 women); includes 17 minority (9 Black or African American, non-Hispanic/Latino; 5 Asian, non-Hispanic/Latino; 2 Hispanic/Latino; 1 Two or more races, non-Hispanic/Latino), 65 international. Average age 29. 146 applicants, 85% accepted, 41 enrolled. *Faculty:* 356 full-time (90 women), 51 part-time/adjunct (6 women). Expenses: Contact institution. *Financial support:* In 2017–18, 5 research assistantships (averaging $1,792 per year), 6 teaching assistantships (averaging $1,814 per year) were awarded. Financial award applicants required to submit FAFSA. In 2017, 18 master's awarded. Offers business administration (MBA); information science and technology (MS). *Application fee:* $55 ($75 for international students). Electronic applications accepted. *Application Contact:* Debbie Schwertz, Admissions Coordinator, 573-341-6013, Fax: 573-341-6271, E-mail: schwertz@mst.edu. *Chair,* Keng Siau, 573-341-4528, Fax: 573-341-4812, E-mail: siauk@mst.edu.

Department of Chemical and Biochemical Engineering Students: 52 full-time (10 women), 9 part-time (2 women); includes 4 minority (3 Black or African American, non-Hispanic/Latino; 1 Asian, non-Hispanic/Latino), 54 international. Average age 28. 76 applicants, 43% accepted, 33 enrolled. *Faculty:* 12 full-time (2 women). Expenses: Contact institution. *Financial support:* In 2017–18, 11 research assistantships (averaging $1,814 per year), 6 teaching assistantships (averaging $1,814 per year) were awarded; fellowships and unspecified assistantships also available. Financial award application deadline: 3/1; financial award applicants required to submit FAFSA. In 2017, 6 master's, 2 doctorates awarded. Offers chemical engineering (MS, PhD). *Application fee:* $55 ($75 for international students). Electronic applications accepted. *Application Contact:* Debbie Schwertz, Admissions Coordinator, 573-341-6013, Fax: 573-341-6271, E-mail: schwertz@mst.edu. *Chair,* Dr. Judy Raper, 573-341-7518, Fax: 573-341-4377, E-mail: raperj@mst.edu.

Department of Chemistry Students: 49 full-time (21 women), 7 part-time (1 woman), 40 international. Average age 28. 48 applicants, 31% accepted, 6 enrolled. *Faculty:* 18 full-time (3 women), 1 part-time/adjunct (0 women). Expenses: Contact institution. *Financial support:* In 2017–18, 4 fellowships, 12 research assistantships with tuition reimbursements (averaging $1,814 per year), 22 teaching assistantships with tuition reimbursements (averaging $1,814 per year) were awarded; institutionally sponsored loans also available. In 2017, 9 master's, 10 doctorates awarded. Offers chemistry (MS, MST, PhD). *Application deadline:* For fall admission, 7/1 for domestic students. Applications are processed on a rolling basis. *Application fee:* $55 ($75 for international students). Electronic applications accepted. *Application Contact:* Dr. Pericles Stavropaulos, Information Contact, 573-341-7220, Fax: 573-341-6033, E-mail: pericles@mst.edu. *Chair,* Dr. Phil Whitefield, 573-341-4420, E-mail: pwhite@mst.edu.

Department of Civil, Architectural, and Environmental Engineering Students: 72 full-time (19 women), 58 part-time (14 women); includes 9 minority (5 Black or African American, non-Hispanic/Latino; 3 Asian, non-Hispanic/Latino; 1 Two or more races, non-Hispanic/Latino), 51 international. Average age 28. 186 applicants, 44% accepted, 33 enrolled. *Faculty:* 20 full-time (0 women), 4 part-time/adjunct (0 women). Expenses: Contact institution. *Financial support:* In 2017–18, 21 fellowships with full tuition reimbursements (averaging $16,357 per year), 21 research assistantships with partial tuition reimbursements (averaging $1,811 per year), 10 teaching assistantships with partial tuition reimbursements (averaging $1,814 per year) were awarded; institutionally sponsored loans also available. Support available to part-time students. Financial award application deadline: 1/1; financial award applicants required to submit FAFSA. In 2017, 38 master's, 8 doctorates awarded. *Program availability:* Part-time, evening/weekend. Offers civil engineering (MS, DE, PhD); environmental engineering (MS). *Application deadline:* For fall admission, 7/1 for domestic students; for spring admission, 12/1 for domestic students. Applications are processed on a rolling basis. *Application fee:* $55 ($75 for international students). Electronic applications accepted. *Application Contact:* Dr. Rick Stephenson, Graduate Advisor, 573-341-6549, Fax: 573-341-4729, E-mail: stephens@mst.edu. *Chair,* Joel Burken, 573-341-6547, Fax: 573-341-4729, E-mail: burken@mst.edu.

Department of Computer Science Students: 64 full-time (12 women), 38 part-time (10 women); includes 4 minority (1 Black or African American, non-Hispanic/Latino; 3 Asian, non-Hispanic/Latino), 23 international. Average age 27. 211 applicants, 43% accepted, 31 enrolled. *Faculty:* 10 full-time (2 women), 1 part-time/adjunct (0 women). Expenses: Contact institution. *Financial support:* In 2017–18, 5 fellowships, 10 research assistantships with partial tuition reimbursements (averaging $1,812 per year), 13 teaching assistantships with partial tuition reimbursements (averaging $1,814 per year) were awarded; institutionally sponsored loans and unspecified assistantships also available. Financial award application deadline: 3/1; financial award applicants required to submit FAFSA. In 2017, 20 master's, 3 doctorates awarded. *Program availability:* Part-time. Offers computer science (MS, PhD). *Application deadline:* For fall admission, 7/1 for domestic students. Applications are processed on a rolling basis. *Application fee:* $55 ($75 for international students). Electronic applications accepted. *Application Contact:* Debbie Schwertz, Admissions Coordinator, 573-341-6013, Fax: 573-341-6271, E-mail: schwertz@mst.edu. *Chair,* Dr. George Markowsky, 573-341-6138, Fax: 573-341-4501, E-mail: csdept@mst.edu.

Department of Electrical and Computer Engineering Students: 189 full-time (34 women), 96 part-time (17 women); includes 15 minority (2 Black or African American, non-Hispanic/Latino; 12 Asian, non-Hispanic/Latino; 1 Hispanic/Latino), 219 international. Average age 26. 412 applicants, 55% accepted, 70 enrolled. *Faculty:* 33 full-time (5 women), 4 part-time/adjunct (0 women). Expenses: Contact institution. *Financial support:* In 2017–18, 29 fellowships with full tuition reimbursements, 77 research assistantships with partial tuition reimbursements (averaging $1,817 per year), 19 teaching assistantships with partial tuition reimbursements (averaging $1,811 per year) were awarded; career-related internships or fieldwork and institutionally sponsored loans also available. Support available to part-time students. Financial award application deadline: 3/1; financial award applicants required to submit FAFSA. In 2017, 40 master's, 14 doctorates awarded. *Program availability:* Part-time, evening/weekend. Offers computer engineering (MS, DE, PhD); electrical engineering (MS, DE, PhD). *Application deadline:* For fall admission, 6/1 for domestic students; for spring admission, 11/1 for domestic students. Applications are processed on a rolling basis. *Application fee:* $55 ($75 for international students). Electronic applications accepted. *Application Contact:* Dr. Richard DuBroff, Information Contact, 573-341-4719, Fax: 573-341-4532, E-mail: red@mst.edu. *Chair,* Daryl Beetner, 573-341-4503, Fax: 573-341-4532, E-mail: daryl@mst.edu.

Department of Engineering Management and Systems Engineering Students: 149 full-time (29 women), 195 part-time (40 women); includes 57 minority (16 Black or African American, non-Hispanic/Latino; 2 American Indian or Alaska Native, non-Hispanic/Latino; 17 Asian, non-Hispanic/Latino; 19 Hispanic/Latino; 3 Two or more races, non-Hispanic/Latino), 36 international. Average age 34. 230 applicants, 75% accepted, 113 enrolled. *Faculty:* 9 full-time (1 woman), 3 part-time/adjunct (1 woman). Expenses: Contact institution. *Financial support:* In 2017–18, 31 research assistantships (averaging $1,802 per year), 1 teaching assistantship (averaging $1,814 per year) were awarded; fellowships also available. Financial award application deadline: 3/1; financial award applicants required to submit FAFSA. In 2017, 113 master's, 5 doctorates awarded. Offers engineering management (MS, PhD); systems engineering (MS, PhD). *Application fee:* $55 ($75 for international students). Electronic applications accepted. *Application Contact:* Dr. Kenneth M. Ragsdell, Coordinator, 573-341-4157, Fax: 573-341-6567, E-mail: ragsdell@mst.edu. *Chair*, Dr. Suzanna Long, 573-341-7621, Fax: 573-341-6567.

Department of English and Technical Communication Offers technical communication (MS).

Department of Geosciences and Geological and Petroleum Engineering Students: 249 full-time (51 women), 93 part-time (17 women); includes 37 minority (10 Black or African American, non-Hispanic/Latino; 3 American Indian or Alaska Native, non-Hispanic/Latino; 6 Asian, non-Hispanic/Latino; 18 Hispanic/Latino), 169 international. Average age 31. 296 applicants, 58% accepted, 97 enrolled. *Faculty:* 18 full-time (4 women), 1 part-time/adjunct (0 women). Expenses: Contact institution. *Financial support:* In 2017–18, fellowships with full tuition reimbursements (averaging $11,250 per year), 9 research assistantships with partial tuition reimbursements (averaging $1,814 per year), 3 teaching assistantships with partial tuition reimbursements (averaging $1,814 per year) were awarded; Federal Work-Study and institutionally sponsored loans also available. Support available to part-time students. Financial award application deadline: 3/1; financial award applicants required to submit FAFSA. In 2017, 17 master's, 6 doctorates awarded. *Program availability:* Part-time. Offers geological engineering (MS, DE, PhD); geology and geophysics (MS, PhD); petroleum engineering (MS, DE, PhD). *Application deadline:* For fall admission, 7/1 for domestic students; for spring admission, 12/1 for domestic students. Applications are processed on a rolling basis. *Application fee:* $55 ($175 for international students). Electronic applications accepted. *Application Contact:* Debbie Schwertz, Admissions Coordinator, 573-341-6013, Fax: 573-341-6271, E-mail: schwertz@mst.edu. *Chair*, Dr. David Borrok, 573-341-6784, Fax: 573-341-6935, E-mail: borrokd@mst.edu.

Department of Materials Science and Engineering Students: 31 full-time (11 women), 6 part-time (1 woman); includes 1 minority (Two or more races, non-Hispanic/Latino), 16 international. Average age 27. 65 applicants, 31% accepted, 20 enrolled. *Faculty:* 23 full-time (1 woman), 5 part-time/adjunct (0 women). Expenses: Contact institution. *Financial support:* In 2017–18, 53 research assistantships (averaging $1,813 per year) were awarded; fellowships and teaching assistantships also available. Financial award applicants required to submit FAFSA. In 2017, 13 master's, 7 doctorates awarded. Offers ceramic engineering (MS, PhD); materials science and engineering (MS, PhD); metallurgical engineering (MS, PhD). *Application fee:* $55 ($75 for international students). Electronic applications accepted. *Application Contact:* Debbie Schwertz, Admissions Coordinator, 573-341-6013, Fax: 573-341-6271, E-mail: schwertz@mst.edu. *Chair*, Dr. Gregroy E. Hilmas, 573-341-6102, Fax: 573-341-6934, E-mail: ghilmas@mst.edu.

Department of Mathematics and Statistics Students: 38 full-time (16 women), 5 part-time (0 women), 33 international. Average age 29. 37 applicants, 68% accepted, 8 enrolled. *Faculty:* 21 full-time (9 women), 1 part-time/adjunct (0 women). Expenses: Contact institution. *Financial support:* In 2017–18, 5 fellowships, 1 research assistantship with partial tuition reimbursement (averaging $1,814 per year), 19 teaching assistantships with partial tuition reimbursements (averaging $1,813 per year) were awarded; institutionally sponsored loans also available. In 2017, 5 master's, 3 doctorates awarded. Offers applied mathematics (MS); mathematics (MST, PhD). *Application deadline:* For fall admission, 7/1 for domestic students. Applications are processed on a rolling basis. *Application fee:* $55 ($75 for international students). Electronic applications accepted. *Application Contact:* Dr. V. A. Samaranayake, Director of Graduate Studies, 573-341-4658, Fax: 573-341-4741, E-mail: vsam@mst.edu. *Chair*, Dr. Stephen L. Clark, 573-341-4912, Fax: 573-341-4741, E-mail: sclark@mst.edu.

Department of Mechanical and Aerospace Engineering Students: 132 full-time (20 women), 74 part-time (10 women); includes 19 minority (6 Black or African American, non-Hispanic/Latino; 4 Asian, non-Hispanic/Latino; 8 Hispanic/Latino; 1 Two or more races, non-Hispanic/Latino), 86 international. Average age 28. 335 applicants, 43% accepted, 50 enrolled. *Faculty:* 30 full-time (0 women), 3 part-time/adjunct (0 women). Expenses: Contact institution. *Financial support:* In 2017–18, 22 fellowships with tuition reimbursements (averaging $8,558 per year), 51 research assistantships with tuition reimbursements (averaging $1,816 per year), 15 teaching assistantships with tuition reimbursements (averaging $1,812 per year) were awarded; Federal Work-Study, institutionally sponsored loans, and traineeships also available. Support available to part-time students. Financial award application deadline: 3/1; financial award applicants required to submit FAFSA. In 2017, 43 master's, 7 doctorates awarded. *Program availability:* Part-time, evening/weekend. Offers aerospace engineering (MS, PhD); manufacturing engineering (M Eng, MS); mechanical engineering (MS, PhD). *Application deadline:* For fall admission, 7/1 for domestic students; for spring admission, 12/1 for domestic students. Applications are processed on a rolling basis. *Application fee:* $55 ($75 for international students). Electronic applications accepted. *Application Contact:* Dr. L. R. Dharani, Associate Chair for Graduate Affairs, 573-341-6504, Fax: 573-341-4607, E-mail: dharani@mst.edu. *Chairman*, Dr. Ashok Midha, 573-341-4662, Fax: 573-341-4607, E-mail: midha@mst.edu.

Department of Mining and Nuclear Engineering Students: 73 full-time (9 women), 109 part-time (16 women); includes 17 minority (2 American Indian or Alaska Native, non-Hispanic/Latino; 4 Asian, non-Hispanic/Latino; 8 Hispanic/Latino; 2 Native Hawaiian or other Pacific Islander, non-Hispanic/Latino; 1 Two or more races, non-Hispanic/Latino), 59 international. Average age 33. 86 applicants, 71% accepted, 36 enrolled. *Faculty:* 11 full-time (0 women). Expenses: Contact institution. *Financial support:* In 2017–18, 11 research assistantships (averaging $1,814 per year) were awarded; fellowships and teaching assistantships also available. Financial award application deadline: 3/1; financial award applicants required to submit FAFSA. In 2017, 4 master's, 2 doctorates awarded. Offers explosives engineering (MS, PhD); mining engineering (MS, DE, PhD); nuclear engineering (MS, DE, PhD). *Application fee:* $55 ($75 for international students). Electronic applications accepted. *Application Contact:* Debbie Schwertz, Admissions Coordinator, 573-341-6013, Fax: 573-341-6271, E-mail: schwertz@mst.edu. *Chairman*, Dr. Samuel Frimpong, 573-341-4753, Fax: 573-341-6934, E-mail: frimpong@mst.edu.

Department of Physics Students: 32 full-time (4 women), 2 part-time (1 woman); includes 1 minority (Hispanic/Latino), 25 international. Average age 30. 16 applicants, 38% accepted, 3 enrolled. *Faculty:* 19 full-time (2 women), 1 (woman) part-time/adjunct. Expenses: Contact institution. *Financial support:* In 2017–18, 13 research assistantships (averaging $1,814 per year), 8 teaching assistantships (averaging $1,814 per year) were awarded. Financial award applicants required to submit FAFSA. In 2017, 6 master's, 2 doctorates awarded. Offers physics (MS, MST, PhD). *Application fee:* $55 ($75 for international students). Electronic applications accepted. *Application Contact:* Debbie Schwertz, Admissions Coordinator, 573-341-6013, Fax: 573-341-6271, E-mail: schwertz@mst.edu. *Chairman*, Dr. Thomas Vojta, 573-341-4793, Fax: 573-341-4715, E-mail: vojtat@mst.edu.

Department of Psychological Science Offers industrial-organizational psychology (MS).

Program in Geotechnics Offers geotechnics (ME).

MISSOURI VALLEY COLLEGE, Marshall, MO 65340-3197

General Information Independent-religious, coed, comprehensive institution.

GRADUATE UNITS

Graduate Studies

MISSOURI WESTERN STATE UNIVERSITY, St. Joseph, MO 64507-2294

General Information State-supported, coed, comprehensive institution. CGS member. *Enrollment:* 5,533 graduate, professional, and undergraduate students; 81 full-time matriculated graduate/professional students (45 women), 151 part-time matriculated graduate/professional students (99 women). *Enrollment by degree level:* 221 master's, 11 other advanced degrees. *Graduate faculty:* 42 full-time (14 women), 7 part-time/adjunct (5 women). Tuition, state resident: full-time $6391; part-time $336 per credit hour. Tuition, nonresident: full-time $11,483; part-time $604 per credit hour. *Required fees:* $542; $99 per credit hour. $176 per semester. One-time fee: $45. Tuition and fees vary according to course load and program. *Graduate housing:* Room and/or apartments available on a first-come, first-served basis to single students; on-campus housing not available to married students. Typical cost: $6842 per year ($10,300 including board). Room and board charges vary according to board plan and housing facility selected. *Student services:* Campus employment opportunities, campus safety program, career counseling, child daycare facilities, exercise/wellness program, free psychological counseling, international student services, low-cost health insurance, multicultural affairs office, services for students with disabilities. *Library facilities:* Missouri Western State University Library. *Collection:* Books: 166,649 (physical), 215,083 (digital/electronic); Serial titles: 1,585 (physical), 57,298 (digital/electronic); Databases: 65.

Computer facilities: Computer purchase and lease plans are available. A campuswide network can be accessed from student residence rooms and from off campus. Online class registration, personal online storage are available.
Website: http://www.missouriwestern.edu/

General Application Contact: Dr. Benjamin D. Caldwell, Dean of the Graduate School, 816-271-4394, Fax: 816-271-4525, E-mail: graduate@missouriwestern.edu.

GRADUATE UNITS

Program in Applied Science Students: 37 full-time (16 women), 20 part-time (9 women); includes 8 minority (6 Black or African American, non-Hispanic/Latino; 1 Asian, non-Hispanic/Latino; 1 Two or more races, non-Hispanic/Latino), 10 international. Average age 27. 28 applicants, 86% accepted, 16 enrolled. Expenses: Contact institution. *Financial support:* Scholarships/grants and unspecified assistantships available. Support available to part-time students. In 2017, 32 master's awarded. *Program availability:* Part-time. Offers chemistry (MAS); engineering technology management (MAS); industrial life science (MAS); sport and fitness management (MAS). *Application deadline:* For fall admission, 7/15 for domestic and international students; for spring admission, 10/1 for domestic and international students; for summer admission, 3/15 for domestic students. Applications are processed on a rolling basis. *Application fee:* $45 ($50 for international students). Electronic applications accepted. *Dean of the Graduate School*, Dr. Benjamin D. Caldwell, 816-271-4394, Fax: 816-271-4525, E-mail: graduate@missouriwestern.edu.

Program in Assessment Students: 29 part-time (25 women); includes 1 minority (Black or African American, non-Hispanic/Latino). Average age 38. 8 applicants, 100% accepted, 4 enrolled. Expenses: Contact institution. *Financial support:* Scholarships/grants and unspecified assistantships available. Support available to part-time students. In 2017, 9 master's, 3 other advanced degrees awarded. *Program availability:* Part-time. Offers K-12 cross-categorical special education (MAS); TESOL (MAS, Graduate Certificate); writing (MAS). *Application deadline:* For fall admission, 7/15 for domestic and international students; for spring admission, 10/1 for domestic and international students; for summer admission, 3/15 for domestic students. Applications are processed on a rolling basis. *Application fee:* $45 ($50 for international students). Electronic applications accepted. *Application Contact:* Dr. Benjamin D. Caldwell, Dean of the Graduate School, 816-271-4394, Fax: 816-271-4525, E-mail: graduate@missouriwestern.edu. *Director of Graduate Programs in Education*, Dr. Susan Bashinski, 816-271-5629, E-mail: sbashinski@missouriwestern.edu.

Program in Business Administration Students: 4 full-time (3 women), 24 part-time (8 women); includes 5 minority (3 Black or African American, non-Hispanic/Latino; 1 Asian, non-Hispanic/Latino; 1 Two or more races, non-Hispanic/Latino). Average age 35. 30 applicants, 93% accepted, 18 enrolled. Expenses: Contact institution. *Financial support:* Scholarships/grants and unspecified assistantships available. Support available to part-time students. *Program availability:* Part-time. Offers animal and life sciences (MBA); enterprise resource planning (MBA); forensic accounting (MBA); general business (MBA). *Application deadline:* For fall admission, 7/15 for domestic and international students; for spring admission, 10/1 for domestic and international students; for summer admission, 3/15 for domestic students. Applications are processed on a rolling basis. *Application fee:* $45 ($50 for international students). Electronic applications accepted. *Application Contact:* Dr. Benjamin D. Caldwell, Dean of the Graduate School, 816-271-4394, Fax: 816-271-4525, E-mail: graduate@missouriwestern.edu. *Director*, Dr. Logan Jones, 816-271-4351, E-mail: jjones81@missouriwestern.edu.

Program in Digital Media Students: 5 full-time (2 women), 7 part-time (2 women), 6 international. Average age 30. 5 applicants, 40% accepted, 1 enrolled. Expenses: Contact institution. *Financial support:* Scholarships/grants and unspecified assistantships available. Support available to part-time students. In 2017, 7 master's awarded. *Program availability:* Part-time. Offers digital media (MAA, Graduate Certificate). *Application deadline:* For fall admission, 7/15 for domestic and international students; for spring admission, 10/1 for domestic and international students; for summer admission, 3/15 for domestic students. Applications are processed on a rolling basis. *Application fee:* $45 ($50 for international students). Electronic applications accepted. *Application Contact:* Dr. Benjamin D. Caldwell, Dean of the Graduate School, 816-271-4394, Fax: 816-271-4525, E-mail: graduate@missouriwestern.edu. *Professor*, Dr. Bob Bergland, 816-271-4446, E-mail: bergland@missouriwestern.edu.

Program in Forensic Investigations Students: 10 full-time (9 women), 12 part-time (10 women); includes 6 minority (4 Black or African American, non-Hispanic/Latino; 1 American Indian or Alaska Native, non-Hispanic/Latino; 1 Two or more races, non-Hispanic/Latino), 1 international. Average age 30. 6 applicants, 100% accepted, 6 enrolled. Expenses: Contact institution. *Financial support:* Scholarships/grants and unspecified assistantships available. Support available to part-time students. In 2017, 5 master's awarded. *Program availability:* Part-time. Offers forensic investigations (MAS, Graduate Certificate). *Application deadline:* For fall admission, 7/15 for domestic and international students; for spring admission, 10/1 for domestic and international students; for summer admission, 3/15 for domestic students. Applications are processed on a rolling basis. *Application fee:* $45 ($50 for international students). Electronic applications accepted. *Application Contact:* Dr. Benjamin D. Caldwell, Dean of the Graduate School, 816-271-4394, Fax: 816-271-4525, E-mail: graduate@missouriwestern.edu. *Forensics Graduate Program Director*, Dr. Monty Smith, 816-271-4434, E-mail: msmith84@missouriwestern.edu.

Program in Information Management Students: 9 full-time (6 women), 9 part-time (3 women); includes 1 minority (Black or African American, non-Hispanic/Latino), 9 international. Average age 32. 7 applicants, 100% accepted, 3 enrolled. Expenses: Contact institution. *Financial support:* Scholarships/grants and unspecified assistantships available. Support available to part-time students. In 2017, 33 master's awarded. *Program availability:* Part-time. Offers enterprise resource planning (MIM). *Application deadline:* For fall admission, 7/15 for domestic and international students; for spring admission, 10/1 for domestic and international students; for summer admission, 3/15 for domestic students. Applications are processed on a rolling basis. *Application fee:* $45 ($50 for international students). Electronic applications accepted. *Application Contact:* Dr. Benjamin D. Caldwell, Dean of the Graduate School, 816-271-4394, Fax: 816-271-4525, E-mail: graduate@missouriwestern.edu. *Assistant Professor*, Dr. Logan Jones, 816-271-4351, E-mail: jones@missouriwestern.edu.

Program in Information Technology Assurance Administration Students: 8 full-time (3 women), 6 part-time (0 women), 10 international. Average age 27. Expenses: Contact institution. *Financial support:* Scholarships/grants and unspecified assistantships available. Support available to part-time students. In 2017, 7 master's awarded. *Program availability:* Part-time. Offers information technology assurance administration (MS). *Application deadline:* For fall admission, 7/15 for domestic and international students; for spring admission, 10/1 for domestic and international students; for summer admission, 3/15 for domestic students. Applications are processed on a rolling basis. *Application fee:* $45 ($50 for international students). Electronic applications accepted. *Application Contact:* Dr. Benjamin D. Caldwell, Dean of the Graduate School, 816-271-4394, Fax: 816-271-4525, E-mail: graduate@missouriwestern.edu. *Assistant Professor*, Dr. Yipkei Kwok, 816-271-4523, E-mail: ykwok@missouriwestern.edu.

Program in Nursing Students: 1 (woman) full-time, 40 part-time (38 women); includes 2 minority (1 Black or African American, non-Hispanic/Latino; 1 Hispanic/Latino), 2 international. Average age 36. 9 applicants, 100% accepted, 9 enrolled. Expenses: Contact institution. *Financial support:* Scholarships/grants and unspecified assistantships available. Support available to part-time students. In 2017, 8 master's awarded. *Program availability:* Part-time. Offers health care leadership (MSN); nurse educator (MSN, Graduate Certificate). *Application deadline:* For fall admission, 7/15 for domestic and international students; for spring admission, 10/1 for domestic and international students; for summer admission, 3/15 for domestic students. Applications are processed on a rolling basis. *Application fee:* $45 ($50 for international students). Electronic applications accepted. *Application Contact:* Dr. Benjamin D. Caldwell, Dean of the Graduate School, 816-271-4394, Fax: 816-271-4525, E-mail: graduate@missouriwestern.edu. *Associate Professor*, Dr. Carolyn Brose, 816-271-5912, E-mail: brose@missouriwestern.edu.

Program in Written Communication Students: 6 full-time (5 women), 6 part-time (4 women), 6 international. Average age 31. 4 applicants, 100% accepted, 4 enrolled. Expenses: Contact institution. *Financial support:* Scholarships/grants and unspecified assistantships available. Support available to part-time students. In 2017, 2 master's, 2 other advanced degrees awarded. *Program availability:* Part-time. Offers teaching of writing (Graduate Certificate); technical communication (MAA); writing studies (MAA). *Application deadline:* For fall admission, 7/15 for domestic and international students; for spring admission, 10/1 for domestic and international students; for summer admission, 3/15 for domestic students. Applications are processed on a rolling basis. *Application fee:* $45 ($50 for international students). Electronic applications accepted. *Application Contact:* Dr. Benjamin D. Caldwell, Dean of the Graduate School, 816-271-4394, Fax: 816-271-4525, E-mail: graduate@missouriwestern.edu. *Associate Professor*, Dr. Michael Charlton, 816-271-4310, E-mail: mcharlton@missouriwestern.edu.

MITCHELL HAMLINE SCHOOL OF LAW, Saint Paul, MN 55105-3076

General Information Independent, coed, graduate-only institution.

GRADUATE UNITS

Graduate and Professional Programs *Program availability:* Part-time, evening/weekend, blended/hybrid learning. Offers law (LL M, JD). Electronic applications accepted.

MOLLOY COLLEGE, Rockville Centre, NY 11571-5002

General Information Independent, coed, comprehensive institution. *Enrollment:* 4,980 graduate, professional, and undergraduate students; 288 full-time matriculated graduate/professional students (230 women), 1,035 part-time matriculated graduate/professional students (828 women). *Enrollment by degree level:* 1,198 master's, 91 doctoral, 34 other advanced degrees. *Graduate faculty:* 70 full-time (61 women), 33 part-time/adjunct (23 women). *Tuition:* Full-time $19,980; part-time $1110 per credit. *Required fees:* $1040. Tuition and fees vary according to course load and degree level. *Graduate housing:* On-campus housing not available. *Student services:* Campus employment opportunities, campus safety program, career counseling, free psychological counseling, international student services, low-cost health insurance, services for students with disabilities, teacher training, writing training. *Library facilities:* James Edward Tobin Library plus 1 other. *Collection:* Books: 43,968 (physical), 262,675 (digital/electronic); Serial titles: 48 (physical), 67,340 (digital/electronic); Databases: 183.

Computer facilities: 784 computers available on campus for general student use. A campuswide network can be accessed from student residence rooms and from off campus. Online class registration is available.
Website: http://www.molloy.edu/

General Application Contact: Jaclyn Machowicz, Assistant Director for Admissions, 516-323-4010, E-mail: jmachowicz@molloy.edu.

GRADUATE UNITS

The Barbara H. Hagan School of Nursing Students: 19 full-time (14 women), 574 part-time (527 women); includes 336 minority (179 Black or African American, non-Hispanic/Latino; 2 American Indian or Alaska Native, non-Hispanic/Latino; 107 Asian, non-Hispanic/Latino; 42 Hispanic/Latino; 1 Native Hawaiian or other Pacific Islander, non-Hispanic/Latino; 5 Two or more races, non-Hispanic/Latino), 4 international. Average age 44. 292 applicants, 65% accepted, 147 enrolled. *Faculty:* 28 full-time (all women), 7 part-time/adjunct (6 women). Expenses: Contact institution. *Financial support:* Research assistantships with partial tuition reimbursements, teaching assistantships with partial tuition reimbursements, institutionally sponsored loans, scholarships/grants, and unspecified assistantships available. Support available to part-time students. Financial award application deadline: 3/1; financial award applicants required to submit FAFSA. In 2017, 135 master's, 9 doctorates, 5 other advanced degrees awarded. *Program availability:* Part-time, evening/weekend. Offers adult - gerontology nurse practitioner (MS); adult-gerontology clinical nurse specialist (DNP); adult-gerontology nurse practitioner (DNP); clinical nurse specialist: adult - gerontology (MS); family nurse practitioner (MS, DNP); family psychiatric/mental health nurse practitioner (MS, DNP); nursing (PhD, Advanced Certificate); nursing administration with informatics (MS); nursing education (MS); pediatric nurse practitioner (MS, DNP). *Application deadline:* For fall admission, 9/2 priority date for domestic students; for spring admission, 1/20 priority date for domestic students. Applications are processed on a rolling basis. *Application fee:* $60. Electronic applications accepted. *Application Contact:* Jaclyn Machowicz, Assistant Director for Admissions, 516-323-4010, E-mail: jmachowicz@molloy.edu. *Dean, The Barbara H. Hagan School of Nursing*, Dr. Marcia R. Gardner, 516-323-3651, E-mail: mgardner@molloy.edu.

Criminal Justice Program Students: 14 full-time (11 women), 18 part-time (8 women); includes 10 minority (4 Black or African American, non-Hispanic/Latino; 1 Asian, non-Hispanic/Latino; 3 Hispanic/Latino; 1 Native Hawaiian or other Pacific Islander, non-Hispanic/Latino; 1 Two or more races, non-Hispanic/Latino). Average age 36. 23 applicants, 70% accepted, 12 enrolled. *Faculty:* 3 full-time (2 women), 2 part-time/adjunct (0 women). Expenses: Contact institution. *Financial support:* Application deadline: 3/1; applicants required to submit FAFSA. In 2017, 13 master's awarded. *Program availability:* Part-time, evening/weekend. Offers criminal justice (MS). *Application deadline:* Applications are processed on a rolling basis. *Application fee:* $60. Electronic applications accepted. *Application Contact:* Jaclyn Machowicz, Assistant Director for Admissions, 516-323-4010, E-mail: jmachowicz@molloy.edu. *Associate Dean/Graduate Program Director*, Dr. John Eterno, 516-323-3804, E-mail: jeterno@molloy.edu.

Graduate Business Program Students: 53 full-time (29 women), 175 part-time (89 women); includes 88 minority (38 Black or African American, non-Hispanic/Latino; 18 Asian, non-Hispanic/Latino; 30 Hispanic/Latino; 2 Two or more races, non-Hispanic/Latino), 3 international. Average age 39. 128 applicants, 68% accepted, 81 enrolled. *Faculty:* 8 full-time (3 women), 7 part-time/adjunct (2 women). Expenses: Contact institution. *Financial support:* Application deadline: 3/1; applicants required to submit FAFSA. In 2017, 125 master's awarded. *Program availability:* Part-time, evening/weekend. Offers accounting (MBA); finance (MBA, Post-Master's Certificate, Postbaccalaureate Certificate); healthcare (MBA, Post-Master's Certificate, Postbaccalaureate Certificate); management (MBA); marketing (MBA, Post-Master's Certificate, Postbaccalaureate Certificate); personal financial planning (MBA). *Application deadline:* Applications are processed on a rolling basis. *Application fee:* $60. Electronic applications accepted. *Application Contact:* Jaclyn Machowicz, Assistant Director for Admissions, 516-323-4010, E-mail: jmachowicz@molloy.edu. *Dean, Division of Business/Director of Graduate Programs*, Dr. Maureen Mackenzie, 516-323-3080, E-mail: mmackenzie@molloy.edu.

Graduate Education Program Students: 102 full-time (80 women), 217 part-time (167 women); includes 65 minority (16 Black or African American, non-Hispanic/Latino; 7 Asian, non-Hispanic/Latino; 38 Hispanic/Latino; 4 Two or more races, non-Hispanic/Latino), 1 international. Average age 41. 153 applicants, 68% accepted, 85 enrolled. *Faculty:* 18 full-time (17 women), 11 part-time/adjunct (9 women). Expenses: Contact institution. *Financial support:* Application deadline: 3/1; applicants required to submit FAFSA. In 2017, 95 master's, 3 other advanced degrees awarded. *Program availability:* Part-time, evening/weekend. Offers adolescent education in biology (MS); adolescent special education (Advanced Certificate); bilingual extension (Advanced Certificate); childhood education (MS); childhood special education (Advanced Certificate); early childhood education (MS); educational technology (MS); English (MS); mathematics (MS); social studies (MS); Spanish (MS); special education on both childhood and adolescent levels (MS); teaching English to speakers of other languages (TESOL) in grades pre-K to 12 (MS); TESOL (Advanced Certificate). *Application deadline:* Applications are processed on a rolling basis. *Application fee:* $60. Electronic applications accepted. *Application Contact:* Jaclyn Machowicz, Assistant Director for Admissions, 516-323-4010, E-mail: jmachowicz@molloy.edu. *Associate Dean and Director of Graduate Education Programs*, Joanne O'Brien, 516-323-3116, E-mail: jobrien@molloy.edu.

Graduate Music Therapy Program Students: 6 full-time (5 women), 24 part-time (13 women); includes 4 minority (1 Asian, non-Hispanic/Latino; 2 Hispanic/Latino; 1 Two or more races, non-Hispanic/Latino), 7 international. Average age 34. 28 applicants, 46% accepted, 8 enrolled. *Faculty:* 4 full-time (3 women), 3 part-time/adjunct (all women). Expenses: Contact institution. *Financial support:* Application deadline: 3/1; applicants required to submit FAFSA. In 2017, 10 master's awarded. *Program availability:* Part-time, evening/weekend. Offers music therapy (MS). *Application deadline:* Applications are processed on a rolling basis. *Application fee:* $60. Electronic applications accepted. *Application Contact:* Jaclyn Machowicz, Assistant Director for Admissions, 516-323-4010, E-mail: jmachowicz@molloy.edu. *Associate Dean/Director of Graduate Music Therapy*, Suzanne Sorel, 516-323-3322, E-mail: ssorel@molloy.edu.

Program in Clinical Mental Health Counseling Students: 13 full-time (11 women), 27 part-time (24 women); includes 13 minority (7 Black or African American, non-Hispanic/Latino; 1 American Indian or Alaska Native, non-Hispanic/Latino; 1 Asian, non-Hispanic/Latino; 3 Hispanic/Latino; 1 Two or more races, non-Hispanic/Latino). Average age 38. 40 applicants, 53% accepted, 16 enrolled. *Faculty:* 2 full-time (both women). Expenses: Contact institution. *Financial support:* Application deadline: 3/1; applicants required to submit FAFSA. *Program availability:* Part-time-only, evening/weekend. Offers clinical mental health counseling (MS). *Application deadline:* Applications are processed on a rolling basis. *Application fee:* $60. Electronic applications accepted. *Application Contact:* Jaclyn Machowicz, Assistant Director for Admissions, 516-323-4010, E-mail: jmachowicz@molloy.edu. *Associate Dean and Director for Department of Clinical Mental Health Counseling*, Dr. Laura B. Kestemberg, 516-323-3842, E-mail: lkestemberg@molloy.edu.

Program in Speech Language Pathology Students: 81 full-time (80 women); includes 16 minority (1 Black or African American, non-Hispanic/Latino; 1 American Indian or Alaska Native, non-Hispanic/Latino; 2 Asian, non-Hispanic/Latino; 12 Hispanic/Latino). Average age 29. 270 applicants, 45% accepted, 44 enrolled. *Faculty:* 7 full-time (6 women), 3 part-time/adjunct (all women). Expenses: Contact institution. *Financial support:* Application deadline: 3/1; applicants required to submit FAFSA. In 2017, 43 master's awarded. *Program availability:* Part-time, evening/weekend. Offers speech language pathology (MS). *Application deadline:* For fall admission, 2/1 for domestic and international students. *Application fee:* $60. Electronic applications accepted. *Application Contact:* Jaclyn Machowicz, Assistant Director for Admissions, 516-323-4010, E-mail: jmachowicz@molloy.edu. *Associate Dean*, Susan Alimonti, 516-323-3517, E-mail: salimonti@molloy.edu.

MONMOUTH UNIVERSITY, West Long Branch, NJ 07764-1898

General Information Independent, coed, comprehensive institution. CGS member. *Enrollment:* 654 full-time matriculated graduate/professional students (517 women), 980 part-time matriculated graduate/professional students (746 women). *Enrollment by degree level:* 1,520 master's, 63 doctoral, 51 other advanced degrees. *Graduate faculty:* 136 full-time (82 women), 110 part-time/adjunct (68 women). *Tuition:* Full-time $21,366; part-time $7122 per credit. *Required fees:* $700; $175 per term. *Graduate housing:* Room and/or apartments available on a first-come, first-served basis to single students; on-campus housing not available to married students. *Student services:* Campus employment opportunities, campus safety program, career counseling, exercise/wellness program, free psychological counseling, international student services, low-cost health insurance, multicultural affairs office, services for students with disabilities, writing training. *Library facilities:* Monmouth University Library. *Collection:* Books: 275,000 (physical), 40,416 (digital/electronic); Serial titles: 1,622 (physical), 73,909 (digital/electronic); Databases: 189. Weekly public service hours: 111; students can reserve study rooms. *Research affiliation:* The Nature Conservancy, Ecotrust (healthy oceans and coastal communities), National Institute of Standards and Technology (NIST), National Oceanic and Atmospheric Administration (NOAA), Substance Abuse and Mental Health Services Administration (SAMHSA) (campus suicide prevention), Gordon and Betty Moore Foundation (environmental conservation, patient care).

Computer facilities: Computer purchase and lease plans are available. 1,000 computers available on campus for general student use. A campuswide network can be accessed from student residence rooms and from off campus. Online class registration is available.
Website: http://www.monmouth.edu/

General Application Contact: Lauren Vento-Cifelli, Associate Vice President of Undergraduate and Graduate Admission, 732-571-3562, Fax: 732-263-5123, E-mail: gradadm@monmouth.edu.

GRADUATE UNITS

Graduate Studies Students: 652 full-time (515 women), 926 part-time (702 women); includes 358 minority (125 Black or African American, non-Hispanic/Latino; 1 American Indian or Alaska Native, non-Hispanic/Latino; 68 Asian, non-Hispanic/Latino; 134 Hispanic/Latino; 2 Native Hawaiian or other Pacific Islander, non-Hispanic/Latino; 28 Two or more races, non-Hispanic/Latino), 55 international. Average age 32. 1,551 applicants, 58% accepted, 558 enrolled. *Faculty:* 111 full-time (65 women), 104 part-time/adjunct (61 women). Expenses: Contact institution. *Financial support:* In 2017–18, 595 students received support. Career-related internships or fieldwork, institutionally sponsored loans, scholarships/grants, and unspecified assistantships available. Support available to part-time students. Financial award applicants required to submit FAFSA. In 2017, 620 master's, 3 other advanced degrees awarded. *Program availability:* Part-time, evening/weekend, 100% online, blended/hybrid learning. Offers addiction studies (MA); anthropology (MA); clinical mental health counseling (MS); computer science (MS); corporate and public communication (MA); creative writing (MA); criminal justice (MA); criminal justice administration (Certificate); European history (MA); human resources management and communication (Certificate); literature (MA); professional counseling (PMC); public service communication specialist (Certificate); rhetoric and writing (MA); software development (Certificate); software engineering (MS); strategic public relations and new media (Certificate); United States history (MA); world history (MA). *Application deadline:* For fall admission, 7/15 priority date for domestic students, 6/1 for international students; for spring admission, 12/1 priority date for domestic students, 11/1 for international students; for summer admission, 5/1 for domestic students. Applications are processed on a rolling basis. *Application fee:* $50. Electronic applications accepted. *Application Contact:* Laurie Kuhn, Associate Director of Graduate Admission, 732-571-3452, Fax: 732-263-5123, E-mail: gradadm@monmouth.edu. *Vice Provost for Graduate Studies*, Dr. Michael A. Palladino, 732-571-7550, Fax: 732-263-5142.

Leon Hess Business School Students: 101 full-time (55 women), 107 part-time (44 women); includes 19 minority (3 Black or African American, non-Hispanic/Latino; 6 Asian, non-Hispanic/Latino; 6 Hispanic/Latino; 1 Native Hawaiian or other Pacific Islander, non-Hispanic/Latino; 3 Two or more races, non-Hispanic/Latino), 13 international. Average age 30. *Faculty:* 20 full-time (4 women), 8 part-time/adjunct (0 women). Expenses: Contact institution. *Financial support:* In 2017–18, 42 students received support. Institutionally sponsored loans, scholarships/grants, and unspecified assistantships available. Support available to part-time students. Financial award applicants required to submit FAFSA. In 2017, 61 master's, 1 other advanced degree awarded. *Program availability:* Part-time, evening/weekend. Offers accounting (MBA, Certificate); business administration (MBA); finance (MBA); management (MBA); marketing (MBA); real estate (MBA). *Application deadline:* For fall admission, 7/15 priority date for domestic students, 6/1 for international students; for spring admission, 12/1 priority date for domestic students, 11/1 for international students; for summer admission, 5/1 for domestic students. Applications are processed on a rolling basis. *Application fee:* $50. Electronic applications accepted. *Application Contact:* Laurie Kuhn, Associate Director of Graduate Admission, 732-571-3452, Fax: 732-263-5123, E-mail: gradadm@monmouth.edu. *MBA Program Director*, Dr. Susan Gupta, 732-571-3639, Fax: 732-263-5517, E-mail: sgupta@monmouth.edu.

Marjorie K. Unterberg School of Nursing and Health Studies Students: 90 full-time (66 women), 329 part-time (302 women); includes 129 minority (51 Black or African American, non-Hispanic/Latino; 43 Asian, non-Hispanic/Latino; 31 Hispanic/Latino; 1 Native Hawaiian or other Pacific Islander, non-Hispanic/Latino; 3 Two or more races, non-Hispanic/Latino), 1 international. Average age 36. *Faculty:* 12 full-time (all women), 20 part-time/adjunct (12 women). Expenses: Contact institution. *Financial support:* In 2017–18, 197 students received support. Institutionally sponsored loans, scholarships/grants, and unspecified assistantships available. Support available to part-time students. Financial award applicants required to submit FAFSA. In 2017, 85 master's, 4 other advanced degrees awarded. *Program availability:* Part-time, evening/weekend, 100% online, blended/hybrid learning. Offers adult-gerontological primary care nurse practitioner (MSN, Post-Master's Certificate); family nurse practitioner (MSN, Post-Master's Certificate); forensic nursing (MSN, Certificate); nursing (MSN); nursing administration (MSN); nursing education (MSN, Post-Master's Certificate); nursing practice (DNP); physician assistant (MS); psychiatric and mental health nurse practitioner (MSN, Post-Master's Certificate); school nursing (MSN, Certificate). *Application deadline:* For fall admission, 7/15 priority date for domestic students, 6/1 for international students; for spring admission, 12/1 priority date for domestic students, 11/1 for international students; for summer admission, 5/1 for domestic students. Applications are processed on a rolling basis. *Application fee:* $50. Electronic applications accepted. *Application Contact:* Lucia Fedele, Graduate Admission Counselor, 732-571-3452, Fax: 732-263-5123, E-mail: gradadm@monmouth.edu. *Dean*, Dr. Janet Mahoney, 732-571-3443, Fax: 732-263-5131, E-mail: jmahoney@monmouth.edu.

School of Education Students: 175 full-time (163 women), 168 part-time (142 women); includes 54 minority (10 Black or African American, non-Hispanic/Latino; 4 Asian, non-Hispanic/Latino; 32 Hispanic/Latino; 8 Two or more races, non-Hispanic/Latino). Average age 27. *Faculty:* 23 full-time (19 women), 33 part-time/adjunct (25 women). Expenses: Contact institution. *Financial support:* In 2017–18, 125 students received support. Institutionally sponsored loans, scholarships/grants, and unspecified assistantships available. Support available to part-time students. Financial award applicants required to submit FAFSA. In 2017, 160 master's, 3 other advanced degrees awarded. *Program availability:* Part-time, evening/weekend, 100% online, blended/hybrid learning. Offers applied behavior analysis (Certificate); autism (Certificate); director of school counseling services (Post-Master's Certificate); early childhood (M Ed); educational leadership (Ed D); elementary education (MAT); English as a second language (M Ed); learning disabilities teacher-consultant (Post-Master's Certificate); literacy (MS Ed); school counseling (MS Ed); special education (MS Ed); speech-language pathology (MS Ed); student affairs and college counseling (MS Ed); supervisor (Post-Master's Certificate); teaching English to speakers of other languages (Certificate). *Application deadline:* For fall admission, 7/15 priority date for domestic students, 7/1 for international students; for spring admission, 12/1 priority date for domestic students, 11/1 for international students; for summer admission, 5/1 for domestic students. Applications are processed on a rolling basis. *Application fee:* $50. Electronic applications accepted. *Application Contact:* Laurie Kuhn, Associate Director of Graduate Admission, 732-571-3452, Fax: 732-263-5123, E-mail: gradadm@monmouth.edu. *Dean*, Dr. John E. Henning, 732-263-5513, Fax: 732-263-5277.

School of Social Work Students: 102 full-time (97 women), 100 part-time (77 women); includes 73 minority (34 Black or African American, non-Hispanic/Latino; 1 American Indian or Alaska Native, non-Hispanic/Latino; 3 Asian, non-Hispanic/Latino; 28 Hispanic/Latino; 7 Two or more races, non-Hispanic/Latino). Average age 30. *Faculty:* 12 full-time (8 women), 22 part-time/adjunct (18 women). Expenses: Contact institution. *Financial support:* In 2017–18, 75 students received support. Institutionally sponsored loans, scholarships/grants, and unspecified assistantships available. Support available to part-time students. Financial award applicants required to submit FAFSA. In 2017, 119 master's awarded. *Program availability:* Part-time, evening/weekend. Offers clinical practice with families and children (MSW); international and community development (MSW); play therapy (Certificate). *Application deadline:* For fall admission, 3/15 for domestic and international students. Applications are processed on a rolling basis. *Application fee:* $50. Electronic applications accepted. *Application Contact:* Lucia Fedele, Graduate Admission Counselor, 732-571-3452, Fax: 732-263-5123, E-mail: gradm@monmouth.edu. *Program Director*, Dr. Carolyn Bradley, 732-263-5477, Fax: 732-263-5217, E-mail: cbradley@monmouth.edu.

Monmouth University (International Student Information)

MONROE COLLEGE, Bronx, NY 10468

General Information Proprietary, coed, comprehensive institution. *Enrollment:* 618 full-time matriculated graduate/professional students (328 women), 312 part-time matriculated graduate/professional students (226 women). *Enrollment by degree level:* 930 master's. *Graduate housing:* Rooms and/or apartments available on a first-come, first-served basis to single and married students. Housing application deadline: 5/1. *Student services:* Campus employment opportunities, career counseling, international student services, multicultural affairs office, services for students with disabilities, teacher training, writing training. *Library facilities:* Main library plus 1 other. *Collection:* Books: 44,109 (physical), 2,466 (digital/electronic); Serial titles: 739 (physical), 8 (digital/electronic); Databases: 73.

Computer facilities: 800 computers available on campus for general student use. A campuswide network can be accessed from student residence rooms and from off campus. Online class registration is available.
Website: http://www.monroecollege.edu/

General Application Contact: Craig Patrick, Vice President for Admissions, 718-933-6700, E-mail: cpatrick@monroecollege.edu.

GRADUATE UNITS

King Graduate School Expenses: Contact institution. *Program availability:* Online learning. Offers accounting (MS); business administration (MBA); computer science (MS); criminal justice (MS); hospitality management (MS); public health (MPH). *Application fee:* $50.

MONTANA STATE UNIVERSITY, Bozeman, MT 59717

General Information State-supported, coed, university. CGS member. *Graduate housing:* Rooms and/or apartments available on a first-come, first-served basis to single and married students. *Research affiliation:* Phillips Environmental (microbial technology), Microvision (information transmission systems), LigoCyte Pharmaceuticals, Inc. (pharmaceuticals), Eli Lilly and Company (antifungal technology), S2 Corporation (instrumentation), ILX Lightwave (laser diodes, electro-optical test equipment).

GRADUATE UNITS

The Graduate School *Program availability:* Part-time, online learning. Electronic applications accepted.

College of Agriculture *Program availability:* Part-time, online learning. Offers agricultural education (MS); agriculture (MS, PhD); animal and range sciences (MS, PhD); immunology and infectious diseases (MS, PhD); land rehabilitation (interdisciplinary) (MS); land resources and environmental sciences (MS); plant pathology (MS); plant sciences (MS, PhD). Electronic applications accepted.

College of Arts and Architecture *Program availability:* Part-time. Offers architecture (M Arch); art (MFA); art history (MA); arts and architecture (M Arch, MA, MFA); science and natural history filmmaking (MFA). Electronic applications accepted.

College of Business *Program availability:* Part-time. Offers professional accountancy (MP Ac). Electronic applications accepted.

College of Education, Health, and Human Development *Program availability:* Part-time, online learning. Offers adult and higher education (Ed D); curriculum and instruction (M Ed, Ed D); education (M Ed); education, health, and human development (M Ed, MS, Ed D, Ed S); educational leadership (Ed D, Ed S); family and consumer sciences (MS). Electronic applications accepted.

College of Engineering *Program availability:* Part-time. Offers chemical engineering (MS); civil engineering (MS); computer science (MS, PhD); construction engineering management (MCEM); electrical engineering (MS); engineering (PhD); environmental engineering (MS); industrial and management engineering (MS); mechanical engineering (MS). Electronic applications accepted.

College of Letters and Science *Program availability:* Part-time, online learning. Offers biochemistry (MS, PhD); biological sciences (PhD); chemistry (MS, PhD); earth sciences (MS, PhD); ecological and environmental statistics (MS); ecology and environmental sciences (PhD); English (MA); fish and wildlife biology (PhD); fish and wildlife management (MS); history (MA, PhD); letters and science (MA, MPA, MS, PhD); mathematics (MS, PhD); microbiology (MS, PhD); Native American studies (MA); neuroscience (MS, PhD); physics (MS, PhD); psychology (MS); public administration (MPA); statistics (MS, PhD). Electronic applications accepted.

College of Nursing *Program availability:* Part-time, online learning. Offers clinical nurse leader (MN); family and individual nurse practitioner (DNP); family nurse practitioner (MN, Post-Master's Certificate); nursing education (Certificate, Post-Master's Certificate); psychiatric mental health nurse practitioner (MN); psychiatric/mental health nurse practitioner (DNP). Electronic applications accepted.

MONTANA STATE UNIVERSITY BILLINGS, Billings, MT 59101

General Information State-supported, coed, comprehensive institution. *Enrollment:* 4,401 graduate, professional, and undergraduate students; 38 full-time matriculated graduate/professional students (25 women), 260 part-time matriculated graduate/professional students (207 women). *Graduate faculty:* 51 full-time (29 women). Tuition, state resident: full-time $11,740; part-time $7880 per year. Tuition, nonresident: full-time $32,200; part-time $24,140 per year. *Graduate housing:* Rooms and/or apartments available on a first-come, first-served basis to single and married students. Housing application deadline: 5/1. *Student services:* Campus employment opportunities, campus safety program, career counseling, child daycare facilities, exercise/wellness program, free psychological counseling, grant writing training, international student services, low-cost health insurance, multicultural affairs office, services for students with disabilities, teacher training, writing training. *Library facilities:* Montana State University Billings Library plus 2 others. *Collection:* Books: 138,650 (physical), 351,351 (digital/electronic); Serial titles: 1,368 (physical), 669,204 (digital/electronic); Databases: 170. Weekly public service hours: 82; students can reserve study rooms.

Computer facilities: Computer purchase and lease plans are available. 1,500 computers available on campus for general student use. A campuswide network can be accessed from student residence rooms and from off campus. Online class registration, online degree programs are available.
Website: http://www.msubillings.edu/

General Application Contact: David M. Sullivan, Graduate Studies Counselor, 406-657-2053, Fax: 406-657-2299, E-mail: dsullivan@msubillings.edu.

GRADUATE UNITS

College of Allied Health Professions Expenses: Contact institution. *Financial support:* Research assistantships with partial tuition reimbursements, teaching assistantships with partial tuition reimbursements, career-related internships or fieldwork, institutionally sponsored loans, scholarships/grants, and unspecified assistantships available. Support available to part-time students. Financial award application deadline: 5/1; financial award applicants required to submit FAFSA. *Program availability:* Part-time, evening/weekend, 100% online, blended/hybrid learning. Offers allied health professions (MHA, MS); athletic training (MS); clinical rehabilitation and mental health counseling (MS); health administration (MHA). *Application deadline:* For fall admission, 7/15 priority date for domestic students; for spring admission, 12/1 priority date for domestic students. Applications are processed on a rolling basis. *Application fee:* $40. Electronic applications accepted. *Application Contact:* Dr. John Dorr, Interim Dean, 406-896-5841, E-mail: john.dorr2@msubillings.edu. *Interim Dean,* Dr. John Dorr, 406-896-5841, E-mail: john.dorr2@msubillings.edu.

College of Arts and Sciences Expenses: Contact institution. *Financial support:* Research assistantships with partial tuition reimbursements, teaching assistantships with partial tuition reimbursements, career-related internships or fieldwork, Federal Work-Study, institutionally sponsored loans, scholarships/grants, tuition waivers (partial), and unspecified assistantships available. Support available to part-time students. Financial award application deadline: 5/1; financial award applicants required to submit FAFSA. *Program availability:* Part-time, 100% online, blended/hybrid learning. Offers arts and sciences (MS); psychology (MS); public relations (MS). *Application deadline:* For fall admission, 7/15 for international students; for spring admission, 12/1 for international students. Applications are processed on a rolling basis. *Application fee:* $40. Electronic applications accepted. *Application Contact:* Dr. Christine Shearer, Dean, 406-657-2177, E-mail: c.shearer@msubillings.edu. *Dean,* Dr. Christine Shearer, 406-657-2177, E-mail: c.shearer@msubillings.edu.

College of Education Expenses: Contact institution. *Financial support:* Research assistantships with partial tuition reimbursements, teaching assistantships with partial tuition reimbursements, career-related internships or fieldwork, Federal Work-Study, institutionally sponsored loans, scholarships/grants, tuition waivers (partial), and unspecified assistantships available. Support available to part-time students. Financial award application deadline: 5/1; financial award applicants required to submit FAFSA. *Program availability:* Part-time, 100% online, blended/hybrid learning. Offers advanced studies (MS Sp Ed); applied behavior analysis (MS Sp Ed); curriculum and instruction (M Ed); education (M Ed, MS Sp Ed, Certificate); generalist (MS Sp Ed); interdisciplinary studies (M Ed); K-8 elementary education (M Ed); online instructional technologies (M Ed); reading (M Ed); school counseling (M Ed); secondary education (M Ed); special education (MS Sp Ed); teaching (Certificate). *Application deadline:* For fall admission, 7/15 for international students; for spring admission, 12/1 for international students. Applications are processed on a rolling basis. *Application fee:* $40. Electronic applications accepted. *Application Contact:* Dr. Mary Susan Fishbaugh, Dean, 406-657-2286, Fax: 406-657-2299, E-mail: mfishbaugh@msubillings.edu. *Dean,* Dr. Mary Susan Fishbaugh, 406-657-2286, Fax: 406-657-2299, E-mail: mfishbaugh@msubillings.edu.

MONTANA STATE UNIVERSITY–NORTHERN, Havre, MT 59501-7751

General Information State-supported, coed, comprehensive institution. *Graduate housing:* Rooms and/or apartments available on a first-come, first-served basis to single students and available to married students. Housing application deadline: 8/22.

GRADUATE UNITS

Graduate Programs *Program availability:* Part-time, evening/weekend, online learning. Offers counselor education (M Ed); instruction and learning (MS Ed). Electronic applications accepted.

MONTANA TECH OF THE UNIVERSITY OF MONTANA, Butte, MT 59701-8997

General Information State-supported, coed, comprehensive institution. CGS member. *Graduate housing:* Rooms and/or apartments available on a first-come, first-served basis to single and married students. Housing application deadline: 7/1. *Research affiliation:* Newmont Mining (mining and mineral processing), Stillwater Mining (mineral production and training), NorthWestern Energy (electric efficiency), Edison Welding Institute (fuel cell design), Montana Resources, Inc. (mine reclamation and revegetation), QualTech, Inc. (battery monitor technology).

GRADUATE UNITS

Department of Environmental Engineering *Program availability:* Part-time. Offers environmental engineering (MS). Electronic applications accepted.

Department of General Engineering *Program availability:* Part-time. Offers general engineering (MS). Electronic applications accepted.

Department of Industrial Hygiene *Program availability:* Part-time, online learning. Offers industrial hygiene (MS). Electronic applications accepted.

Department of Metallurgical/Mineral Processing Engineering *Program availability:* Part-time. Offers metallurgical/mineral processing engineering (MS). Electronic applications accepted.

Department of Petroleum Engineering *Program availability:* Part-time, evening/weekend. Offers petroleum engineering (MS). Electronic applications accepted.

Department of Technical Communication *Program availability:* Part-time. Offers technical communication (MS). Electronic applications accepted.

Electrical Engineering Program *Program availability:* Part-time. Offers electrical engineering (MS). Electronic applications accepted.

Geosciences Programs *Program availability:* Part-time. Offers geochemistry (MS); geological engineering (MS); geology (MS); geophysical engineering (MS); hydrogeological engineering (MS); hydrogeology (MS). Electronic applications accepted.

Health Care Informatics Program *Program availability:* Part-time, evening/weekend, online learning. Offers health care informatics (Certificate). Electronic applications accepted.

Interdisciplinary Program *Program availability:* Part-time. Offers interdisciplinary studies (MS).

Mining Engineering Program *Program availability:* Part-time. Offers mining engineering (MS). Electronic applications accepted.

Program in Materials Science Offers materials science (PhD).

Project Engineering and Management Program *Program availability:* Part-time, evening/weekend, online learning. Offers project engineering and management (MPEM). Electronic applications accepted.

MONTCLAIR STATE UNIVERSITY, Montclair, NJ 07043-1624

General Information State-supported, coed, university. CGS member. *Graduate housing:* Room and/or apartments available on a first-come, first-served basis to single students; on-campus housing not available to married students. Housing application deadline: 3/1. *Research affiliation:* Spencer Foundation (education improvement), The International Society for Optical Engineering (optics and photonics), Deafness Research Foundation (heating science).

GRADUATE UNITS

The Graduate School *Program availability:* Part-time, evening/weekend. Electronic applications accepted.

College of Education and Human Services *Program availability:* Part-time, evening/weekend. Offers art (MAT); biology (MAT); certified alcohol and drug counselor (Certificate); chemistry (MAT); counseling (MA); counselor education (PhD); developmental models of autism intervention (Certificate); dietetics (Postbaccalaureate Certificate); earth science (MAT); education and human services (M Ed, MA, MAT, MPH, MS, Ed D, PhD, Certificate, Post Master's Certificate, Postbaccalaureate Certificate); educational leadership (MA); English (MAT); exercise science (MA); family and child studies (MA); family studies (PhD); French (MAT); health and physical education (MAT); health education (MAT); inclusive early childhood education (M Ed); infant and early childhood mental health (Certificate); learning disabilities (M Ed); mathematics (MAT); music (MAT); nutrition and exercise science (Certificate); nutrition and food science (MS); physical education (MAT); physical science (MAT); program evaluation (Certificate); public health (MPH); reading (MA); social studies (MAT); Spanish (MAT); sports administration and coaching (MA); teacher education and teacher development (PhD); teacher of English as a second language (MAT); teaching and supervision in physical education (MA). Electronic applications accepted.

College of Humanities and Social Sciences *Program availability:* Part-time, evening/weekend. Offers adolescent advocacy (Certificate); applied linguistics (MA); audiology (Sc D); child advocacy and policy (MA, Certificate); clinical psychology (MA); communication sciences and disorders (MA); computational linguistics (Certificate); conflict management and peace studies (MA); conflict management in the workplace (Certificate); data collection and management (Certificate); English (MA); family/civil forensic psychology (Certificate); forensic psychology (Certificate); French literature (MA); French studies (MA); governance, compliance and regulation (MA); humanities and social sciences (MA, Sc D, Certificate); industrial and organizational psychology (MA); intellectual property (MA); law and governance (MA); legal management (MA); paralegal studies (Certificate); psychology (MA); Spanish (MA); teaching English to speakers of other languages (Certificate); teaching writing (Certificate); translation and interpreting in Spanish (Certificate). Electronic applications accepted.

College of Science and Mathematics *Program availability:* Part-time, evening/weekend. Offers biological science/education (MS); biology (MS); chemistry (MS); computer networking (Certificate); computer science (MS); earth and environmental science (MS); ecology and evolution (MS); environmental education (MA); environmental forensics (Certificate); environmental management (MA); environmental science (MA); geographic information science (Certificate); geoscience (MS); information technology (MS); marine biology and coastal sciences (MS); mathematics education (Ed D); molecular biology (MS, Certificate); pharmaceutical biochemistry (MS); physiology (MS); pure and applied mathematics (MS); science and mathematics (MA, MAT, MS, Ed D, PhD, Certificate); statistics (MS); sustainability science (MS); teaching middle grades mathematics (MA, Certificate); teaching physical education (MAT); water resource management (Certificate). Electronic applications accepted.

College of the Arts *Program availability:* Part-time, evening/weekend. Offers arts (MA, MFA, AD, Performer's Certificate, Postbaccalaureate Certificate); arts management (MA); museum management (MA); music (MA, AD, Performer's Certificate); music education (MA); music therapy (MA, Postbaccalaureate Certificate); performance

(MA); production/stage management (MA); public and organizational relations (MA); studio (MA); studio art (MFA); theatre studies (MA); theory/composition (MA). Electronic applications accepted.

Feliciano School of Business *Program availability:* Part-time, evening/weekend. Offers accounting (MS, Post Master's Certificate); business (MBA, MS, Graduate Certificate, Post Master's Certificate); business analytics (MBA); digital marketing (MBA); finance (MBA); forensic accounting (Graduate Certificate); general business administration (MBA); human resources management (MBA); management (MBA); management of information and technology (MBA); marketing (MBA); project management (MBA). Electronic applications accepted.

MONTREAT COLLEGE, Montreat, NC 28757-1267

General Information Independent-religious, coed, comprehensive institution. *Graduate housing:* On-campus housing not available.

GRADUATE UNITS

School of Professional and Adult Studies *Program availability:* Part-time, evening/weekend, online learning. Electronic applications accepted.

MOODY BIBLE INSTITUTE, Chicago, IL 60610-3284

General Information Independent-religious, coed, comprehensive institution. *Graduate housing:* Rooms and/or apartments guaranteed to single students and available on a first-come, first-served basis to married students. Housing application deadline: 6/1.

GRADUATE UNITS

Graduate School *Program availability:* Part-time. Offers biblical studies (MABS, Graduate Certificate); intercultural studies (MAIS, Graduate Certificate); ministry (M Div, M Min); spiritual formation and discipleship (MASF, Graduate Certificate); urban studies (MA, Graduate Certificate).

MOODY THEOLOGICAL SEMINARY–MICHIGAN, Plymouth, MI 48170

General Information Independent-religious, coed, graduate-only institution. *Graduate housing:* On-campus housing not available.

GRADUATE UNITS

Graduate Programs *Program availability:* Part-time, evening/weekend. Offers Bible (Graduate Certificate); Christian education (MA); counseling psychology (MA); divinity (M Div); theological studies (MA).

MOORE COLLEGE OF ART & DESIGN, Philadelphia, PA 19103

General Information Independent, Undergraduate: women only; graduate: coed, comprehensive institution.

GRADUATE UNITS

Program in Art Education *Program availability:* Part-time. Offers art education (MA).

Program in Community Practice Offers community practice (MFA).

Program in Interior Design *Program availability:* Evening/weekend. Offers interior design (MFA).

Program in Social Engagement *Program availability:* Part-time. Offers social engagement (MA).

Program in Studio Art Offers studio art (MFA).

MORAVIAN COLLEGE, Bethlehem, PA 18018-6650

General Information Independent-religious, coed, comprehensive institution. *Enrollment:* 2,463 graduate, professional, and undergraduate students; 45 full-time matriculated graduate/professional students (33 women), 239 part-time matriculated graduate/professional students (179 women). *Enrollment by degree level:* 252 master's, 32 other advanced degrees. *Graduate faculty:* 17 full-time (10 women), 21 part-time/adjunct (9 women). *Tuition:* Full-time $15,714; part-time $2619 per course. *Required fees:* $45 per semester. Tuition and fees vary according to program. *Graduate housing:* On-campus housing not available. *Student services:* Campus employment opportunities, campus safety program, career counseling, exercise/wellness program, international student services, multicultural affairs office, services for students with disabilities, teacher training, writing training. *Library facilities:* Reeves Library. *Collection:* Books: 198,012 (physical), 168,981 (digital/electronic); Serial titles: 2,490 (physical), 183 (digital/electronic); Databases: 67. Weekly public service hours: 86.

Computer facilities: Computer purchase and lease plans are available. 230 computers available on campus for general student use. A campuswide network can be accessed from student residence rooms and from off campus. Online class registration is available.
Website: http://www.moravian.edu/

General Application Contact: Scott Dams, Executive Director of Graduate and Adult Admission, 610-861-1400, E-mail: graduate@moravian.edu.

GRADUATE UNITS

Graduate and Continuing Studies Students: 45 full-time (33 women), 239 part-time (179 women); includes 29 minority (9 Black or African American, non-Hispanic/Latino; 4 Asian, non-Hispanic/Latino; 14 Hispanic/Latino; 2 Two or more races, non-Hispanic/Latino), 2 international. Average age 33. 192 applicants, 71% accepted, 84 enrolled. *Faculty:* 17 full-time (10 women), 21 part-time/adjunct (9 women). Expenses: Contact institution. *Financial support:* In 2017–18, 3 students received support, including 3 teaching assistantships with full tuition reimbursements available. Financial award applicants required to submit FAFSA. In 2017, 60 master's awarded. *Program availability:* Part-time, evening/weekend. Offers accounting (MBA); athletic training (MS, DAT); business analytics (MBA); business management (MBA); curriculum and instruction (M Ed); education (MAT); health administration (MHA); healthcare management (MBA); HR leadership (MSHRM); human resource management (MBA); learning and performance management (MSHRM); supply chain management (MBA). *Application deadline:* For fall admission, 8/1 priority date for domestic and international students; for spring admission, 1/1 priority date for domestic and international students; for summer admission, 5/1 priority date for domestic and international students. Applications are processed on a rolling basis. Electronic applications accepted. *Application Contact:* Kristina Sullivan, Director of Student Recruitment Operations, 610-861-1400, Fax: 610-861-1466, E-mail: graduate@moravian.edu. *Dean of Graduate and Adult Enrollment*, Scott Dams, 610-861-1400, Fax: 610-861-1466, E-mail: graduate@moravian.edu.

Helen S. Breidegam School of Nursing Students: 4 full-time (all women), 64 part-time (60 women); includes 9 minority (3 Black or African American, non-Hispanic/Latino; 2 Asian, non-Hispanic/Latino; 4 Hispanic/Latino), 1 international. Average age 38. 34 applicants, 85% accepted, 20 enrolled. *Faculty:* 5 full-time (all women), 4 part-time/adjunct (2 women). Expenses: Contact institution. *Financial support:* Applicants required to submit FAFSA. In 2017, 24 master's awarded. *Program availability:* Part-time, evening/weekend. Offers clinical nurse leader (MS); nurse administrator (MS); nurse educator (MS); nurse practitioner - acute care (MS); nurse practitioner - primary care (MS). *Application deadline:* For fall admission, 8/1 priority date for domestic and international students; for spring admission, 1/1 priority date for domestic and international students; for summer admission, 5/1 priority date for domestic and international students. Applications are processed on a rolling basis. Electronic applications accepted. *Application Contact:* Caroline Febbo, Student Experience Mentor, 610-861-1400, Fax: 610-861-1466, E-mail: graduate@moravian.edu. *Professor/Chairperson*, Dr. Kerry Cheever, 610-861-1412, Fax: 610-861-1466, E-mail: nursing@moravian.edu.

MORAVIAN THEOLOGICAL SEMINARY, Bethlehem, PA 18018-6614

General Information Independent-religious, coed, graduate-only institution. *Enrollment by degree level:* 64 master's, 18 other advanced degrees. *Graduate faculty:* 8 full-time (3 women), 9 part-time/adjunct (5 women). *Tuition:* Full-time $13,680. *Required fees:* $430. *Graduate housing:* Rooms and/or apartments available on a first-come, first-served basis to single and married students. Housing application deadline: 7/31. *Student services:* Campus employment opportunities, campus safety program, exercise/wellness program, international student services, low-cost health insurance, multicultural affairs office, services for students with disabilities, writing training. *Library facilities:* Reeves Library. *Collection:* Books: 192,017 (physical), 137,800 (digital/electronic); Serial titles: 6,082 (physical), 2,168 (digital/electronic); Databases: 62. Weekly public service hours: 100; students can reserve study rooms.

Computer facilities: 227 computers available on campus for general student use. A campuswide network can be accessed from student residence rooms and from off campus. Online class registration is available.
Website: http://www.moravianseminary.edu/

General Application Contact: Dr. David H. DeRemer, Director of Enrollment, 610-861-1512, Fax: 610-861-1569, E-mail: deremerd@moravian.edu.

GRADUATE UNITS

Graduate and Certificate Programs Students: 26 full-time (12 women), 68 part-time (51 women); includes 17 minority (11 Black or African American, non-Hispanic/Latino; 5 Hispanic/Latino; 1 Two or more races, non-Hispanic/Latino), 1 international. Average age 48. 37 applicants, 65% accepted, 22 enrolled. *Faculty:* 8 full-time (3 women), 10 part-time/adjunct (6 women). Expenses: Contact institution. *Financial support:* In 2017–18, 52 students received support. Career-related internships or fieldwork, Federal Work-Study, and scholarships/grants available. Support available to part-time students. Financial award application deadline: 7/15; financial award applicants required to submit FAFSA. In 2017, 20 master's, 6 other advanced degrees awarded. *Program availability:* Part-time. Offers Biblical studies (Graduate Certificate); formative spirituality (M Div, Graduate Certificate); spiritual direction (MATS, Graduate Certificate). *Application deadline:* For fall admission, 7/15 for domestic students, 4/1 priority date for international students; for spring admission, 11/15 for domestic students, 9/1 priority date for international students. Applications are processed on a rolling basis. *Application fee:* $50. Electronic applications accepted. *Application Contact:* Dr. David H. DeRemer, Director of Enrollment, 610-861-1512, Fax: 610-861-1569, E-mail: deremerd@moravian.edu. *Dean and Vice President*, Rev. Dr. Frank L. Crouch, 610-861-1516, E-mail: crouchf@moravian.edu.

MOREHEAD STATE UNIVERSITY, Morehead, KY 40351

General Information State-supported, coed, comprehensive institution. *Graduate housing:* Room and/or apartments available on a first-come, first-served basis to single students; on-campus housing not available to married students. Housing application deadline: 3/12.

GRADUATE UNITS

Graduate Programs *Program availability:* Part-time, evening/weekend, online learning. Electronic applications accepted.

Caudill College of Arts, Humanities and Social Sciences *Program availability:* Part-time, evening/weekend, online learning. Offers art education (MA); arts, humanities and social sciences (MA, MM); communication (MA); criminology (MA); English (MA); general sociology (MA); gerontology (MA); graphic design (MA); music education (MM); music performance (MM); sociology regional analysis (MA); sociology/chemical dependency (MA); studio art (MA). Electronic applications accepted.

College of Business and Public Affairs *Program availability:* Part-time, evening/weekend, online learning. Offers business administration (MA, MBA, MSIS); business and public affairs (MA, MBA, MPA, MSIS); information systems (MSIS); public policy (MPA); sport management (MA). Electronic applications accepted.

College of Education *Program availability:* Part-time, evening/weekend. Offers adult and higher education (MA, Ed S); business and marketing education (MAT); certified professional counselor (Ed S); counseling P-12 (MA); curriculum and instruction (Ed S); education (MA, MA Ed, MAT, Ed S); educational technology (MA Ed); elementary education (MA Ed); English/language arts 5-9 (MAT); French (MAT); health P-12 (MAT); instructional leadership (Ed S); learning and behavioral disorders P-12 (MAT); mathematics 5-9 (MAT); moderate and severe disabilities P-12 (MAT); physical education P-12 (MAT); school administration (MA); school counseling (Ed S); science 5-9 (MAT); secondary biology (MAT); secondary chemistry (MAT); secondary earth science (MAT); secondary education (MA Ed); secondary English (MAT); secondary math (MAT); secondary physics (MAT); secondary social studies (MAT); social studies 5-9 (MAT); Spanish (MAT); special education (MA Ed); teacher leader business and marketing content (MA Ed); teacher leader business and marketing technology (MA Ed); teacher leader educational technology (MA Ed); teacher leader English (MA Ed); teacher leader gifted education (MA Ed); teacher leader IECE certification (MA Ed); teacher leader interdisciplinary education P-5 (MA Ed); teacher leader middle grades (MA Ed); teacher leader non IECE certification (MA Ed); teacher leader reading/writing - non-certification (MA Ed); teacher leader reading/writing certification (MA Ed); teacher leader school communication - certification (MA Ed); teacher leader school communication - non-certification (MA Ed); teacher leader social studies (MA Ed); teacher leader special education (MA Ed); teaching (MAT). Electronic applications accepted.

College of Science and Technology *Program availability:* Part-time, evening/weekend. Offers biology (MS); biology regional analysis (MS); career and technical agricultural education (MS); career and technical education (MS); clinical/counseling psychology (MS); engineering technology (MS); general/experimental psychology (MS); health/physical education (MA); science and technology (MA, MS). Electronic applications accepted.

Institute for Regional Analysis and Public Policy Offers public administration (MPA). Electronic applications accepted.

MOREHOUSE SCHOOL OF MEDICINE, Atlanta, GA 30310-1495

General Information Independent, coed, graduate-only institution. CGS member. *Graduate housing:* On-campus housing not available. *Research affiliation:* Merck & Company, Inc. (hypotension), CareStat (renal insufficiency), Wyeth (helicobacter pylori study), Bristol-Myers Squibb (pharmacokinetics), Parke-Davis (cardiovascular risk factors), NitroMel, Inc. (heart failure).

GRADUATE UNITS

Graduate Programs in Biomedical Sciences Offers biomedical research (MS); biomedical sciences (PhD); biomedical technology (MS); medical sciences (MS). Electronic applications accepted.

Master of Public Health Program *Program availability:* Part-time. Offers public health (MPH). Electronic applications accepted.

Master of Science in Clinical Research Program *Program availability:* Part-time. Offers clinical research (MS). Electronic applications accepted.

Professional Program Offers medicine (MD). Electronic applications accepted.

MORGAN STATE UNIVERSITY, Baltimore, MD 21251

General Information State-supported, coed, university. CGS member. Tuition, state resident: part-time $433 per credit. Tuition, nonresident: part-time $851 per credit. *Required fees:* $81.50 per credit. *Graduate housing:* Rooms and/or apartments available on a first-come, first-served basis to single and married students. *Student services:* Campus employment opportunities, campus safety program, career counseling, child daycare facilities, free psychological counseling, grant writing training, international student services, low-cost health insurance, services for students with disabilities, teacher training, writing training. *Library facilities:* Soper Library.

Computer facilities: 285 computers available on campus for general student use. A campuswide network can be accessed from student residence rooms and from off campus. Online class registration, engineering lab supercomputer are available.
Website: http://www.morgan.edu/

General Application Contact: Jahmaine Smith, Director, Graduate Admissions, 443-885-3185, Fax: 443-885-8226, E-mail: jahmaine.smith@morgan.edu.

GRADUATE UNITS

School of Graduate Studies Expenses: Contact institution. *Financial support:* Application deadline: 2/1. *Program availability:* Part-time, evening/weekend. *Application deadline:* For fall admission, 2/1 priority date for domestic and international students; for spring admission, 10/1 priority date for domestic and international students. Applications are processed on a rolling basis. *Application fee:* $0. *Application Contact:* Dr. Dean Campbell, Graduate Recruitment Specialist, 443-885-3185, Fax: 443-885-8226, E-mail: dean.campbell@morgan.edu. *Interim Dean*, Dr. Mark Garrison, 443-885-3185, Fax: 443-885-8226, E-mail: mark.garrisonr@morgan.edu.

Clarence M. Mitchell, Jr. School of Engineering Expenses: Contact institution. *Financial support:* Application deadline: 2/1. *Program availability:* Part-time, evening/weekend. Offers civil engineering (M Eng, D Eng); electrical and computer engineering (M Eng, MS, D Eng); industrial and systems engineering (M Eng, D Eng); transportation (MS, PhD, Postbaccalaureate Certificate); transportation and urban infrastructure studies (MS, PhD, Postbaccalaureate Certificate). *Application deadline:* For fall admission, 2/1 priority date for domestic students; for spring admission, 10/1 priority date for domestic students. Applications are processed on a rolling basis. *Application fee:* $0. *Application Contact:* Dr. Dean Campbell, Graduate Recruitment Specialist, 443-885-3185, Fax: 443-885-8226, E-mail: dean.campbell@morgan.edu. *Dean*, Dr. Eugene DeLoatch, 443-885-3231, E-mail: eugene.deloatch@morgan.edu.

College of Liberal Arts Expenses: Contact institution. *Financial support:* Application deadline: 2/1. *Program availability:* Part-time. Offers African-American studies (MA); economics (MA); English (MA, PhD); history (MA, PhD); international studies (MA); liberal arts (MA, MS, PhD); museum studies and historic preservation (MA); music (MA); psychometrics (MS, PhD); sociology (MA, MS). *Application deadline:* For fall admission, 2/1 priority date for domestic students; for spring admission, 10/1 priority date for domestic students. Applications are processed on a rolling basis. *Application fee:* $0. *Application Contact:* Dr. Dean Campbell, Graduate Recruitment Specialist, 443-885-3185, Fax: 443-885-8226, E-mail: dean.campbell@morgan.edu. *Interim Dean*, Dr. M'bare N'gom, 443-885-3090, E-mail: mbare.ngom@morgan.edu.

Earl G. Graves School of Business and Management Expenses: Contact institution. *Financial support:* Application deadline: 2/1. *Program availability:* Part-time, evening/weekend. Offers accounting (MS); business administration (MBA, PhD); business and management (MBA, PhD); hospitality management (MS); project management (MS). *Application deadline:* For fall admission, 2/1 priority date for domestic students; for spring admission, 10/1 priority date for domestic students. Applications are processed on a rolling basis. *Application fee:* $0. *Application Contact:* Dr. Dean Campbell, Graduate Recruitment Specialist, 443-885-3185, Fax: 443-885-8226, E-mail: dean.campbell@morgan.edu. *Dean*, Fikru Boghossian, 443-885-3609, E-mail: fikru.boghossian@morgan.edu.

School of Architecture and Planning Expenses: Contact institution. *Financial support:* Application deadline: 2/1. Offers architecture (M Arch); city and regional planning (MCRP); landscape architecture (MLA). *Application deadline:* For fall admission, 2/1 priority date for domestic students; for spring admission, 10/1 priority date for domestic students. Applications are processed on a rolling basis. *Application fee:* $0. *Application Contact:* Dr. Dean Campbell, Graduate Recruitment Specialist, 443-885-3185, Fax: 443-885-8226, E-mail: dean.campbell@morgan.edu. *Dean*, Mary Anne Akers, 443-885-3225, E-mail: maryanne.akers@morgan.edu.

School of Community Health and Policy Expenses: Contact institution. *Financial support:* Application deadline: 2/1. Offers nursing (MS, PhD); public health (MPH, Dr PH). *Application deadline:* For fall admission, 2/1 priority date for domestic students; for spring admission, 10/1 priority date for domestic students. Applications are processed on a rolling basis. *Application fee:* $0. *Application Contact:* Dr. Dean Campbell, Graduate Recruitment Specialist, 443-885-3185, Fax: 443-885-8226, E-mail: dean.campbell@morgan.edu. *Dean*, Dr. Kim Dobson Sydnor, 443-885-3560, E-mail: kim.sydnor@morgan.edu.

School of Computer, Mathematical, and Natural Sciences Expenses: Contact institution. *Financial support:* Application deadline: 2/1. Offers bioenvironmental science (PhD); bioinformatics (MS); biology (MS); chemistry (MS); computer science (MS); computer, mathematical, and natural sciences (MA, MS, PhD); industrial and computational mathematics (PhD); mathematics (MA); physics (MS). *Application deadline:* For fall admission, 2/1 priority date for domestic students; for spring admission, 10/1 priority date for domestic students. Applications are processed on a rolling basis. *Application fee:* $0. *Application Contact:* Dr. Dean Campbell, Graduate Recruitment Specialist, 443-885-3185, Fax: 443-885-8226, E-mail: dean.campbell@morgan.edu. *Interim Dean*, Dr. Alvin Kennedy, 443-885-4515, E-mail: alvin.kennedy@morgan.edu.

School of Education and Urban Studies Expenses: Contact institution. *Financial support:* Application deadline: 2/1. *Program availability:* Part-time. Offers community college leadership (Ed D); education and urban studies (MA, MAT, MS, Ed D, PhD); elementary education (MAT); higher education (PhD); higher education administration (MA, PhD); higher education and student affairs administration (MA); mathematics education (MS, Ed D); science education (MS, Ed D); urban educational leadership (Ed D). *Application deadline:* For fall admission, 2/1 priority date for domestic students; for spring admission, 10/1 priority date for domestic students. Applications are processed on a rolling basis. *Application fee:* $0. *Application Contact:* Dr. Dean Campbell, Graduate Recruitment Specialist, 443-885-3185, Fax: 443-885-8226, E-mail: dean.campbell@morgan.edu. *Dean*, Dr. Patricia L. Welch, 443-885-3385, Fax: 443-885-8240, E-mail: patricia.welch@morgan.edu.

School of Global Journalism and Communication Offers journalism (MA).

School of Social Work Expenses: Contact institution. Offers social work (MSW). *Application deadline:* Applications are processed on a rolling basis. *Application fee:* $0. *Application Contact:* Dr. Dean Campbell, Graduate Recruitment Specialist, 443-885-3185, Fax: 443-885-8226, E-mail: dean.campbell@morgan.edu. *Chairperson*, Dr. Melissa Littlefield, 443-885-4300, E-mail: melissa.littlefield@morgan.edu.

MORNINGSIDE COLLEGE, Sioux City, IA 51106

General Information Independent-religious, coed, comprehensive institution. *Enrollment:* 2,788 graduate, professional, and undergraduate students; 28 full-time matriculated graduate/professional students (20 women), 1,438 part-time matriculated graduate/professional students (1,201 women). *Enrollment by degree level:* 1,466 master's. *Graduate faculty:* 7 full-time (4 women), 87 part-time/adjunct (66 women). Tuition and fees vary according to program. *Graduate housing:* On-campus housing not available. *Student services:* Career counseling, free psychological counseling, writing training. *Library facilities:* Hickman-Johnson-Furrow Learning Center. *Collection:* Books: 44,113 (physical), 179,888 (digital/electronic); Serial titles: 110 (physical), 73 (digital/electronic); Databases: 43. Weekly public service hours: 93. *Research affiliation:* Iowa Public Service Company (biology, chemistry, physics).

Computer facilities: Computer purchase and lease plans are available. A campuswide network can be accessed from student residence rooms and from off campus. Online class registration, academic and financial records are available.
Website: http://www.morningside.edu/

General Application Contact: Tracy Sursely, Student Records Enrollment Coordinator, 712-274-5576, Fax: 712-274-5101, E-mail: surselyt@morningside.edu.

GRADUATE UNITS

Graduate Programs Students: 25 full-time (18 women), 950 part-time (802 women); includes 37 minority (4 Black or African American, non-Hispanic/Latino; 4 American Indian or Alaska Native, non-Hispanic/Latino; 4 Asian, non-Hispanic/Latino; 22 Hispanic/Latino; 1 Native Hawaiian or other Pacific Islander, non-Hispanic/Latino; 2 Two or more races, non-Hispanic/Latino), 1 international. Average age 33. 351 applicants, 75% accepted, 199 enrolled. *Faculty:* 7 full-time (4 women), 87 part-time/adjunct (66 women). Expenses: Contact institution. *Financial support:* Institutionally sponsored loans and tuition waivers (partial) available. Support available to part-time students. Financial award applicants required to submit FAFSA. *Program availability:* Part-time, evening/weekend, online only, 100% online. *Application deadline:* Applications are processed on a rolling basis. Electronic applications accepted. *Director*, Barbara Chambers, 712-274-5465, Fax: 712-274-5101, E-mail: chambersb@morningside.edu.

Nylen School of Nursing Students: 7 full-time (3 women), 86 part-time (81 women); includes 8 minority (1 American Indian or Alaska Native, non-Hispanic/Latino; 3 Asian, non-Hispanic/Latino; 4 Hispanic/Latino). Average age 32. 37 applicants, 100% accepted, 37 enrolled. *Faculty:* 3 full-time (all women), 4 part-time/adjunct (all women). Expenses: Contact institution. *Financial support:* In 2017–18, 67 students received support. Scholarships/grants and tuition waivers (partial) available. Financial award application deadline: 3/1; financial award applicants required to submit FAFSA. In 2017, 19 master's awarded. *Program availability:* Part-time, online only, 100% online. Offers adult gerontology primary care nurse practitioner (MSN); clinical nurse leader (MSN); family primary care nurse practitioner (MSN). *Application deadline:* Applications are processed on a rolling basis. *Application fee:* $65. Electronic applications accepted. *Dean of Graduate Nursing*, Dr. Jackie Barber, 712-274-5297, E-mail: barber@morningside.edu.

Sharon Walker School of Education Students: 18 full-time (15 women), 864 part-time (721 women); includes 29 minority (4 Black or African American, non-Hispanic/Latino; 3 American Indian or Alaska Native, non-Hispanic/Latino; 1 Asian, non-Hispanic/Latino; 18 Hispanic/Latino; 1 Native Hawaiian or other Pacific Islander, non-Hispanic/Latino; 2 Two or more races, non-Hispanic/Latino), 1 international. Average age 33. 314 applicants, 73% accepted, 162 enrolled. *Faculty:* 4 full-time (1 woman), 83 part-time/adjunct (62 women). Expenses: Contact institution. *Financial support:* In 2017–18, 266 students received support. Institutionally sponsored loans and tuition waivers (partial) available. Support available to part-time students. Financial award applicants required to submit FAFSA. In 2017, 375 master's awarded. *Program availability:* Part-time, online only, 100% online. Offers professional educator (MAT); special education (MAT). *Application deadline:* Applications are processed on a rolling basis. Electronic applications accepted. *Application Contact:* Tracy Sursely, Student Records Enrollment Coordinator, 712-274-5576, Fax: 712-274-5101, E-mail: surselyt@morningside.edu. *Director*, Barbara Chambers, 712-274-5465, Fax: 712-274-5488, E-mail: chambersb@morningside.edu.

MOUNT ALLISON UNIVERSITY, Sackville, NB E4L 1E4, Canada

General Information Province-supported, coed, comprehensive institution. *Enrollment:* 11 full-time matriculated graduate/professional students (5 women), 3 part-time matriculated graduate/professional students. *Enrollment by degree level:* 14 master's. *Graduate faculty:* 20 full-time (7 women). Full-time tuition and fees vary according to campus/location and student level. *Graduate housing:* Room and/or apartments guaranteed to single students; on-campus housing not available to married students. Housing application deadline: 8/31. *Student services:* Campus employment opportunities, campus safety program, child daycare facilities, exercise/wellness program, free psychological counseling, international student services, low-cost health insurance, services for students with disabilities. *Library facilities:* Ralph Pickard Bell Library plus 3 others. *Collection:* Students can reserve study rooms. *Research affiliation:* Atlantic Cancer Institute (medical research), Moncton Hospital (medical research), Huntsman Marine Science Centre (marine biology).

Computer facilities: 100 computers available on campus for general student use. A campuswide network can be accessed from student residence rooms and from off campus. Online class registration, online student account/Websis are available.
Website: http://www.mta.ca/

General Application Contact: Lois Wood, Dean's Office, 506-364-2302, E-mail: gradstudies@mta.ca.

GRADUATE UNITS

Department of Biology Expenses: Contact institution. *Financial support:* Fellowships available. Offers biology (M Sc). *Head*, Suzie Currie, 506-364-2260, E-mail: scurrie@mta.ca.

Department of Chemistry and Biochemistry Expenses: Contact institution. *Financial support:* Fellowships and research assistantships available. Offers chemistry (M Sc). *Head*, Andrew Grant, 506-364-2361, E-mail: agrant@mta.edu.

MOUNT ALOYSIUS COLLEGE, Cresson, PA 16630-1999

General Information Independent-religious, coed, comprehensive institution. *Enrollment:* 1,740 graduate, professional, and undergraduate students; 38 full-time matriculated graduate/professional students, 27 part-time matriculated graduate/professional students. *Enrollment by degree level:* 65 master's. *Graduate faculty:* 12 full-time (10 women), 18 part-time/adjunct (7 women). *Tuition:* Full-time $14,000; part-time $790 per credit hour. *Graduate housing:* On-campus housing not available. *Student services:* Campus employment opportunities, campus safety program, career counseling, child daycare facilities, exercise/wellness program, free psychological counseling, international student services, services for students with disabilities, writing training. *Library facilities:* Mount Aloysius College Library.

Computer facilities: Computer purchase and lease plans are available. A campuswide network can be accessed from student residence rooms and from off campus. Online class registration is available.
Website: http://www.mtaloy.edu/

General Application Contact: Matthew P. Bodenschatz, Director of Graduate and Continuing Education Admissions, 814-886-6556, Fax: 814-886-6441, E-mail: mbodenschatz@mtaloy.edu.

GRADUATE UNITS

Program in Business Administration Expenses: Contact institution. *Financial support:* Unspecified assistantships available. Financial award applicants required to submit FAFSA. *Program availability:* Part-time, evening/weekend. Offers accounting (MBA); health and human services administration (MBA); non-profit management (MBA); project management (MBA). *Application deadline:* For fall admission, 8/1 for domestic students; for spring admission, 12/1 for domestic students. Applications are processed on a rolling basis. *Application fee:* $30. Electronic applications accepted. *Application Contact:* Matthew P. Bodenschatz, Director of Graduate and Continuing Education Admissions, 814-886-6556, Fax: 814-886-6441, E-mail: mbodenschatz@mtaloy.edu.

Program in Community Counseling Expenses: Contact institution. *Financial support:* Unspecified assistantships available. Financial award applicants required to submit FAFSA. *Program availability:* Evening/weekend. Offers community counseling (MS). *Application deadline:* For fall admission, 8/1 for domestic students; for spring admission, 12/1 for domestic students. Applications are processed on a rolling basis. *Application fee:* $30. Electronic applications accepted. *Application Contact:* Matthew P. Bodenschatz, Director of Graduate and Continuing Education Admissions, 814-886-6556, Fax: 814-886-6441, E-mail: mbodenschatz@mtaloy.edu.

MOUNT ANGEL SEMINARY, Saint Benedict, OR 97373

General Information Independent-religious, Undergraduate: men only; graduate: coed, comprehensive institution. *Graduate housing:* Room and/or apartments guaranteed to single students; on-campus housing not available to married students.

GRADUATE UNITS

Program in Theology *Program availability:* Part-time. Offers theology (M Div, MA).

MOUNT CARMEL COLLEGE OF NURSING, Columbus, OH 43222

General Information Independent, coed, primarily women, comprehensive institution. *Enrollment:* 1,069 graduate, professional, and undergraduate students; 110 full-time matriculated graduate/professional students (91 women), 72 part-time matriculated graduate/professional students (65 women). *Enrollment by degree level:* 176 master's, 6 doctoral. *Graduate faculty:* 11 full-time (all women), 5 part-time/adjunct (4 women). *Tuition:* Full-time $11,403; part-time $543 per credit. *Required fees:* $50; $50 per year. *Graduate housing:* Rooms and/or apartments available on a first-come, first-served basis to single and married students. Typical cost: $5000 per year for single students; $5000 per year for married students. Room charges vary according to housing facility selected. Housing application deadline: 7/1. *Student services:* Free psychological counseling, grant writing training, multicultural affairs office, teacher training, writing training. *Library facilities:* The Mount Carmel Health Sciences Library plus 1 other. *Collection:* Books: 8,163 (physical), 297,441 (digital/electronic); Serial titles: 683 (physical), 48,768 (digital/electronic); Databases: 178. Weekly public service hours: 61; study areas open 24 hours, 5–7 days a week; students can reserve study rooms.

Computer facilities: 25 computers available on campus for general student use. A campuswide network can be accessed from student residence rooms. Online class registration is available.
Website: http://www.mccn.edu/

General Application Contact: Dr. Kim Campbell, Director of Recruitment and Admissions, 614-234-5144, Fax: 614-234-5427, E-mail: kcampbell@mccn.edu.

GRADUATE UNITS

Nursing Program Students: 112 full-time (93 women), 72 part-time (65 women); includes 35 minority (20 Black or African American, non-Hispanic/Latino; 4 Asian, non-Hispanic/Latino; 3 Hispanic/Latino; 8 Two or more races, non-Hispanic/Latino). Average age 35. 135 applicants, 65% accepted, 68 enrolled. *Faculty:* 11 full-time (all women), 5 part-time/adjunct (4 women). Expenses: Contact institution. *Financial support:* In 2017–18, 3 students received support. Institutionally sponsored loans and scholarships/grants available. Financial award application deadline: 3/1; financial award applicants required to submit FAFSA. In 2017, 64 master's awarded. *Program availability:* Part-time. Offers adult gerontology acute care nurse practitioner (MS); adult health clinical nurse specialist (MS); family nurse practitioner (MS); nursing (DNP); nursing administration (MS); nursing education (MS). *Application deadline:* For fall admission, 2/1 priority date for domestic students; for spring admission, 11/1 priority date for domestic students. Applications are processed on a rolling basis. *Application fee:* $30. Electronic applications accepted. *Application Contact:* Dr. Kim Campbell, Director of Recruitment and Admissions, 614-234-5144, Fax: 614-234-5427, E-mail: kcampbell@mccn.edu. *Associate Dean*, Dr. Jill Kilanowski, 614-234-5237, Fax: 614-234-2875, E-mail: jkilanowski@mccn.edu.

MOUNT HOLYOKE COLLEGE, South Hadley, MA 01075

General Information Independent, women only, comprehensive institution. *Enrollment:* 2,334 graduate, professional, and undergraduate students; 20 full-time matriculated graduate/professional students (18 women), 104 part-time matriculated graduate/professional students (88 women). *Enrollment by degree level:* 124 master's. *Graduate faculty:* 39 part-time/adjunct. *Tuition:* Full-time $24,500; part-time $766 per credit hour. *Required fees:* $100. Tuition and fees vary according to course load and program. *Graduate housing:* On-campus housing not available. *Student services:* Campus employment opportunities, career counseling, free psychological counseling, low-cost health insurance, services for students with disabilities. *Library facilities:* Williston Memorial Library plus 2 others. *Collection:* Books: 662,010 (physical), 853,290 (digital/electronic); Serial titles: 603 (physical), 8,098 (digital/electronic); Databases: 227. Weekly public service hours: 115; students can reserve study rooms.

Computer facilities: Computer purchase and lease plans are available. 392 computers available on campus for general student use. A campuswide network can be accessed from student residence rooms and from off campus. Online class registration, personal Web pages are available.
Website: http://www.mtholyoke.edu/

General Application Contact: Dr. Tiffany Espinosa, Executive Director of Professional and Graduate Education, 413-538-3478, Fax: 413-538-3098, E-mail: tespinos@mtholyoke.edu.

GRADUATE UNITS

Professional and Graduate Education (PaGE) Students: 20 full-time (18 women), 104 part-time (88 women); includes 18 minority (6 Black or African American, non-Hispanic/Latino; 2 Asian, non-Hispanic/Latino; 8 Hispanic/Latino; 2 Two or more races, non-Hispanic/Latino), 8 international. Average age 34. 100 applicants, 94% accepted, 68 enrolled. *Faculty:* 39 part-time/adjunct. Expenses: Contact institution. *Financial support:* Fellowships, research assistantships, scholarships/grants, and unspecified assistantships available. Support available to part-time students. In 2017, 32 master's awarded. *Program availability:* Part-time, 100% online, blended/hybrid learning. Offers mathematics teaching (MAMT); teacher leadership (MATL); teaching (MAT). *Application deadline:* For fall admission, 8/15 for domestic students, 8/16 for international students; for winter admission, 12/15 for domestic and international students; for spring admission, 1/8 for domestic and international students; for summer admission, 5/15 for domestic and international students. Applications are processed on a rolling basis. *Application fee:* $50. Electronic applications accepted. *Executive Director of Professional and Graduate Education*, Dr. Tiffany Espinosa, 413-538-3478, Fax: 413-538-3098, E-mail: tespinos@mtholyoke.edu.

MOUNT MARTY COLLEGE, Yankton, SD 57078-3724

General Information Independent-religious, coed, comprehensive institution. *Graduate housing:* On-campus housing not available.

GRADUATE UNITS

Graduate Studies Division Offers business administration (MBA); nurse anesthesia (MS); nursing (MSN); pastoral ministries (MPM). Electronic applications accepted.

MOUNT MARY UNIVERSITY, Milwaukee, WI 53222-4597

General Information Independent-religious, Undergraduate: women only; graduate: coed, comprehensive institution. CGS member. *Graduate housing:* Room and/or apartments available on a first-come, first-served basis to single students; on-campus housing not available to married students.

GRADUATE UNITS

Graduate Programs *Program availability:* Part-time, evening/weekend, 100% online, blended/hybrid learning. Offers art therapy (MS, DAT); clinical mental health counseling (MS, Certificate); clinical rehabilitation counseling (MS, Certificate); creative writing (MA); dietetics (MS); dietetics internship (MS); general management (MBA); health systems leadership (MBA); occupational therapy (MS, OTD); professional and new media writing (MA); professional development (MA); school counseling (MS, Certificate); vocational rehabilitation counseling (MS, Certificate). Electronic applications accepted.

MOUNT MERCY UNIVERSITY, Cedar Rapids, IA 52402-4797

General Information Independent-religious, coed, comprehensive institution.

GRADUATE UNITS

Program in Business Administration *Program availability:* Evening/weekend. Offers human resource (MBA); quality management (MBA). Electronic applications accepted.

Program in Criminal Justice *Program availability:* Evening/weekend, online learning. Offers criminal justice (MA).

Program in Education Offers reading (MA Ed); special education (MA Ed); teacher leadership (MA Ed). Electronic applications accepted.

Program in Marriage and Family Therapy *Program availability:* Evening/weekend. Offers marriage and family therapy (MA).

Program in Nursing *Program availability:* Evening/weekend. Offers health advocacy (MSN); nurse administration (MSN); nurse education (MSN).

Program in Strategic Leadership *Program availability:* Evening/weekend. Offers strategic leadership (MSL).

MOUNT ST. JOSEPH UNIVERSITY, Cincinnati, OH 45233-1670

General Information Independent-religious, coed, comprehensive institution. CGS member. *Enrollment:* 2,010 graduate, professional, and undergraduate students; 224 full-time matriculated graduate/professional students (155 women), 403 part-time matriculated graduate/professional students (330 women). *Enrollment by degree level:* 454 master's, 173 doctoral. *Graduate faculty:* 32 full-time (22 women), 42 part-time/adjunct (32 women). Tuition and fees vary according to degree level and program. *Graduate housing:* Room and/or apartments available on a first-come, first-served basis to single students; on-campus housing not available to married students. Typical cost: $6048 per year ($10,628 including board). Room and board charges vary according to board plan and campus/location. Housing application deadline: 4/1. *Student services:* Campus employment opportunities, campus safety program, career counseling, child daycare facilities, exercise/wellness program, free psychological counseling, international student services, low-cost health insurance, multicultural affairs office, services for students with disabilities, teacher training, writing training. *Library facilities:* Archbishop Alter Library. *Collection:* Books: 58,795 (physical), 132,030 (digital/electronic); Serial titles: 41 (physical), 29,902 (digital/electronic); Databases: 150. Weekly public service hours: 82.

Computer facilities: 172 computers available on campus for general student use. A campuswide network can be accessed from student residence rooms and from off campus. Online class registration, wireless printing, storage space are available.
Website: http://www.msj.edu/

General Application Contact: Mary Brigham, Assistant Director for Graduate Recruitment, 513-244-4233, Fax: 513-244-4629, E-mail: mary.brigham@msj.edu.

GRADUATE UNITS

Doctor of Nursing Practice Program Students: 53 part-time (50 women); includes 4 minority (all Black or African American, non-Hispanic/Latino). Average age 48. *Faculty:* 9 full-time (all women), 15 part-time/adjunct (all women). Expenses: Contact institution. *Financial support:* Applicants required to submit FAFSA. In 2017, 1 doctorate awarded. *Program availability:* Part-time-only. Offers health systems leadership (DNP). *Application deadline:* Applications are processed on a rolling basis. *Application fee:* $50. Electronic applications accepted. *Application Contact:* Autumn Richards, Admission Counselor for Graduate Studies, 513-244-4228, Fax: 513-244-4629, E-mail: autumn.richards@msj.edu. *Assistant Dean of Nursing*, Dr. Nancy Hinzman, 513-244-4325, Fax: 513-451-2547, E-mail: nancy.hinzman@msj.edu.

Graduate Education Program Students: 37 full-time (30 women), 91 part-time (83 women); includes 13 minority (11 Black or African American, non-Hispanic/Latino; 1 Hispanic/Latino; 1 Two or more races, non-Hispanic/Latino). Average age 34. *Faculty:* 6 full-time (5 women), 11 part-time/adjunct (8 women). Expenses: Contact institution. *Financial support:* Applicants required to submit FAFSA. In 2017, 79 master's awarded. *Program availability:* Part-time, evening/weekend, 100% online, blended/hybrid learning. Offers adolescent to young adult education (MA); dyslexia (Certificate); inclusive early childhood education (MA); middle childhood education (MA); multicultural special education (MA); reading science (MA). *Application deadline:* Applications are processed on a rolling basis. *Application fee:* $50. Electronic applications accepted. *Application Contact:* Mary Brigham, Assistant Director of Graduate Recruitment, 513-244-4233, Fax: 513-244-4629, E-mail: mary.brigham@msj.edu. *Dean*, Dr. Laura Saylor, 513-244-3263, E-mail: laura.saylor@msj.edu.

Graduate Program in Religious Studies Students: 1 (woman) full-time, 8 part-time (7 women); includes 4 minority (3 Black or African American, non-Hispanic/Latino; 1 Hispanic/Latino). Average age 45. *Faculty:* 1 (woman) full-time. Expenses: Contact institution. *Financial support:* In 2017–18, 7 students received support. Scholarships/grants available. Financial award applicants required to submit FAFSA. In 2017, 1 master's awarded. *Program availability:* Part-time, evening/weekend. Offers religious studies (MA); spirituality and wellness (Certificate). *Application deadline:* Applications are processed on a rolling basis. *Application fee:* $50. Electronic applications accepted. *Application Contact:* Mary Brigham, Assistant Director of Graduate Recruitment, 513-244-4233, Fax: 513-244-4629, E-mail: mary.brigham@msj.edu. *Associate Professor of Religious and Pastoral Studies/Director of Graduate Program*, Dr. John Trokan, 513-244-4272, Fax: 513-244-4222, E-mail: john.trokan@msj.edu.

Master of Business Administration Program Students: 22 full-time (6 women), 30 part-time (14 women); includes 7 minority (5 Black or African American, non-Hispanic/Latino; 1 Hispanic/Latino; 1 Two or more races, non-Hispanic/Latino), 1 international. Average age 32. *Faculty:* 6 full-time (2 women), 4 part-time/adjunct (1 woman). Expenses: Contact institution. *Financial support:* In 2017–18, 2 students received support. Scholarships/grants available. Financial award applicants required to submit FAFSA. In 2017, 24 master's awarded. *Program availability:* Part-time, evening/weekend. Offers business administration (MBA). *Application deadline:* Applications are processed on a rolling basis. *Application fee:* $50. Electronic applications accepted. *Application Contact:* Amy Wolf, Senior Admissions Counselor for Graduate Studies, 513-244-4204, Fax: 513-745-4629, E-mail: amy.wolf@msj.edu. *Assistant Dean/Director of Graduate Programs*, Dr. Anna Goldhahn, 513-244-4924, Fax: 513-244-4270, E-mail: anna.goldhahn@msj.edu.

Master of Science in Nursing Program Students: 122 part-time (113 women); includes 3 minority (2 Black or African American, non-Hispanic/Latino; 1 Two or more races, non-Hispanic/Latino). Average age 40. *Faculty:* 9 full-time (all women), 15 part-time/adjunct (all women). Expenses: Contact institution. *Financial support:* Applicants required to submit FAFSA. In 2017, 8 master's awarded. *Program availability:* Part-time. Offers administration (MSN); clinical nurse leader (MSN); education (MSN). *Application deadline:* Applications are processed on a rolling basis. *Application fee:* $50. Electronic applications accepted. *Application Contact:* Mary Brigham, Assistant Director for Graduate Recruitment, 513-244-4233, Fax: 513-244-4629, E-mail: mary.brigham@msj.edu. *MSN/DNP Director*, Dr. Nancy Hinzman, 513-244-4325, E-mail: nancy.hinzman@msj.edu.

Master of Science in Organizational Leadership Program Students: 59 part-time (41 women); includes 12 minority (9 Black or African American, non-Hispanic/Latino; 1 Hispanic/Latino; 2 Two or more races, non-Hispanic/Latino). Average age 41. *Faculty:* 1 (woman) full-time. Expenses: Contact institution. *Financial support:* Applicants required to submit FAFSA. In 2017, 31 master's awarded. *Program availability:* Part-time, evening/weekend. Offers organizational leadership (MS). *Application deadline:* Applications are processed on a rolling basis. *Application fee:* $50. Electronic applications accepted. *Application Contact:* Mary Brigham, Assistant Director of Graduate Recruitment, 513-244-4233, Fax: 513-244-4629, E-mail: mary.brigham@msj.edu. *Assistant Dean/Director of Graduate Programs*, Dr. Anna Goldhahn, 513-244-4924, Fax: 513-244-4270, E-mail: anna.goldhahn@msj.edu.

Master's Graduate Entry-Level into Nursing (MAGELIN) Program Students: 81 full-time (65 women), 3 part-time (2 women); includes 22 minority (16 Black or African American, non-Hispanic/Latino; 1 Asian, non-Hispanic/Latino; 2 Hispanic/Latino; 3 Two or more races, non-Hispanic/Latino), 1 international. Average age 27. *Faculty:* 9 full-time (all women), 15 part-time/adjunct (all women). Expenses: Contact institution. *Financial support:* In 2017–18, 1 student received support. Scholarships/grants available. Financial award applicants required to submit FAFSA. In 2017, 58 master's awarded. Offers nursing (MSN). *Application deadline:* Applications are processed on a rolling basis. *Application fee:* $50. Electronic applications accepted. *Application Contact:* Mary Brigham, Assistant Director of Graduate Recruitment, 513-244-4233, Fax: 513-244-4629, E-mail: mary.brigham@msj.edu. *Program Director*, Donna Glankler, 513-244-4321, Fax: 513-451-2547, E-mail: donna.glankler@msj.edu.

Physical Therapy Program Students: 83 full-time (53 women), 37 part-time (20 women); includes 1 minority (Black or African American, non-Hispanic/Latino). Average age 24. *Faculty:* 6 full-time (4 women), 12 part-time/adjunct (8 women). Expenses: Contact institution. *Financial support:* Applicants required to submit FAFSA. In 2017, 32 doctorates awarded. Offers physical therapy (DPT). *Application deadline:* For fall admission, 11/1 for domestic students. *Application fee:* $50. Electronic applications accepted. *Application Contact:* Mary Brigham, Assistant Director of Graduate Recruitment, 513-244-4233, Fax: 513-244-4629, E-mail: mary.brigham@msj.edu. *Chair*, Dr. Rosanne Thomas, 513-244-4519, Fax: 513-451-2547, E-mail: rosanne.thomas@msj.edu.

MOUNT SAINT MARY COLLEGE, Newburgh, NY 12550-3494

General Information Independent, coed, comprehensive institution. *Enrollment:* 2,365 graduate, professional, and undergraduate students; 62 full-time matriculated graduate/professional students (31 women), 266 part-time matriculated graduate/professional students (226 women). *Enrollment by degree level:* 318 master's, 10 other advanced degrees. *Graduate faculty:* 21 full-time (17 women), 16 part-time/adjunct (12 women). *Tuition:* Full-time $14,454; part-time $803 per credit. *Required fees:* $172; $86 per semester. *Graduate housing:* Room and/or apartments guaranteed to single students; on-campus housing not available to married students. Typical cost: $9776 per year ($16,132 including board). Housing application deadline: 5/1. *Student services:* Campus employment opportunities, campus safety program, career counseling, free psychological counseling, international student services, services for students with disabilities. *Library facilities:* Kaplan Family Library and Learning Center. *Collection:* Books: 87,924 (physical), 11,522 (digital/electronic); Serial titles: 202 (physical), 70,271 (digital/electronic); Databases: 87. Students can reserve study rooms.

Computer facilities: Computer purchase and lease plans are available. 470 computers available on campus for general student use. A campuswide network can be accessed from student residence rooms and from off campus. Online class registration is available.
Website: http://www.msmc.edu/

General Application Contact: Lisa Alvarez, Director of Admissions for Graduate Programs and Adult Degree Completion, 845-569-3166, Fax: 845-569-3450, E-mail: lisa.gallina@msmc.edu.

GRADUATE UNITS

Division of Education Students: 11 full-time (9 women), 83 part-time (62 women); includes 9 minority (1 American Indian or Alaska Native, non-Hispanic/Latino; 6 Hispanic/Latino; 2 Two or more races, non-Hispanic/Latino). Average age 28. 20 applicants, 100% accepted, 16 enrolled. *Faculty:* 10 full-time (9 women), 3 part-time/adjunct (all women). Expenses: Contact institution. *Financial support:* In 2017–18, 15 students received support. Unspecified assistantships available. Financial award application deadline: 4/15; financial award applicants required to submit FAFSA. In 2017, 57 master's awarded. *Program availability:* Part-time, evening/weekend. Offers adolescence and special education (MS Ed); childhood education (MS Ed); literacy education (MS Ed); middle school (7-9) (MS Ed). *Application deadline:* Applications are processed on a rolling basis. *Application fee:* $45. Electronic applications accepted. *Application Contact:* Lisa Alvarez, Director of Admissions for Graduate Programs and Adult Degree Completion, 845-569-3166, Fax: 845-569-3450, E-mail: lisa.gallina@msmc.edu. *Graduate Coordinator*, Dr. Monica Merritt, 845-569-3430, Fax: 845-569-3535, E-mail: monica.merritt@msmc.edu.

School of Business Students: 48 full-time (21 women), 30 part-time (21 women); includes 20 minority (6 Black or African American, non-Hispanic/Latino; 1 Asian, non-Hispanic/Latino; 12 Hispanic/Latino; 1 Two or more races, non-Hispanic/Latino). Average age 32. 17 applicants, 65% accepted, 6 enrolled. *Faculty:* 4 full-time (1 woman), 8 part-time/adjunct (4 women). Expenses: Contact institution. *Financial support:* In 2017–18, 18 students received support. Unspecified assistantships available. Financial award application deadline: 4/15; financial award applicants required to submit FAFSA. In 2017, 41 master's awarded. *Program availability:* Part-time, evening/weekend. Offers business (MBA); financial planning (MBA); health care management (MBA). *Application deadline:* Applications are processed on a rolling basis. *Application fee:* $45. Electronic applications accepted. *Application Contact:* Lisa Alvarez, Director of Admissions for Graduate Programs and Adult Degree Completion, 845-569-3166, Fax: 845-569-3450, E-mail: lisa.gallina@msmc.edu. *Graduate Coordinator*, Dr. Moira Tolan, 845-569-3121, Fax: 845-562-6762, E-mail: moira.tolan@msmc.edu.

School of Nursing Students: 3 full-time (1 woman), 153 part-time (143 women); includes 42 minority (22 Black or African American, non-Hispanic/Latino; 1 American Indian or Alaska Native, non-Hispanic/Latino; 6 Asian, non-Hispanic/Latino; 11 Hispanic/Latino; 1 Native Hawaiian or other Pacific Islander, non-Hispanic/Latino; 1 Two or more races, non-Hispanic/Latino). Average age 38. 34 applicants, 91% accepted, 28 enrolled. *Faculty:* 7 full-time (all women), 5 part-time/adjunct (all women). Expenses: Contact institution. *Financial support:* In 2017–18, 8 students received support. Unspecified assistantships available. Financial award application deadline: 4/15; financial award applicants required to submit FAFSA. In 2017, 30 master's, 5 other advanced degrees awarded. *Program availability:* Part-time, evening/weekend, blended/hybrid learning. Offers adult nurse practitioner (MS, Advanced Certificate); family nurse practitioner (Advanced Certificate); nursing education (Advanced Certificate). *Application deadline:* For fall admission, 6/3 priority date for domestic students; for spring admission, 10/31 priority date for domestic students. Applications are processed on a rolling basis. *Application fee:* $45. Electronic applications accepted. *Application Contact:* Lisa Alvarez, Director of Admissions for Graduate Programs and Adult Degree Completion, 845-569-3166, Fax: 845-569-3450, E-mail: lisa.gallina@msmc.edu. *Graduate Coordinator*, Christine Berte, 845-569-3141, Fax: 845-562-6762, E-mail: christine.berte@msmc.edu.

MOUNT SAINT MARY'S UNIVERSITY, Los Angeles, CA 90049

General Information Independent-religious, coed, primarily women, comprehensive institution. CGS member. *Enrollment:* 3,280 graduate, professional, and undergraduate students; 670 full-time matriculated graduate/professional students (552 women), 201 part-time matriculated graduate/professional students (153 women). *Enrollment by degree level:* 522 master's, 98 doctoral, 251 other advanced degrees. *Graduate faculty:* 78 full-time (62 women), 262 part-time/adjunct (184 women). *Tuition:* Part-time $905 per unit. One-time fee: $155 part-time. Tuition and fees vary according to degree level and program. *Graduate housing:* Room and/or apartments available on a first-come, first-served basis to single students; on-campus housing not available to married students. *Student services:* Campus employment opportunities, career counseling, exercise/wellness program, free psychological counseling, low-cost health insurance, services for students with disabilities, writing training. *Library facilities:* Charles Willard Coe Library plus 1 other. *Collection:* Books: 88,758 (physical), 396,855 (digital/electronic); Serial titles: 168 (physical), 39,316 (digital/electronic); Databases: 215. Weekly public service hours: 91; study areas open 24 hours, 5–7 days a week. *Research affiliation:* John Tracy Clinic (education - deaf and hard of hearing teacher preparation).

Computer facilities: 170 computers available on campus for general student use. A campuswide network can be accessed from student residence rooms and from off campus. Online class registration is available.
Website: http://www.msmu.edu/

General Application Contact: Albert Ramos, Director of Graduate Admissions, 213-477-2800, Fax: 213-477-2797, E-mail: gradprograms@msmu.edu.

GRADUATE UNITS

Graduate Division Students: 670 full-time (518 women), 147 part-time (116 women); includes 414 minority (73 Black or African American, non-Hispanic/Latino; 4 American Indian or Alaska Native, non-Hispanic/Latino; 60 Asian, non-Hispanic/Latino; 259 Hispanic/Latino; 7 Native Hawaiian or other Pacific Islander, non-Hispanic/Latino; 11 Two or more races, non-Hispanic/Latino), 4 international. Average age 32. 1,398 applicants, 21% accepted, 242 enrolled. *Faculty:* 50 full-time (35 women), 116 part-time/adjunct (81 women). Expenses: Contact institution. *Financial support:* Career-related internships or fieldwork, Federal Work-Study, institutionally sponsored loans, and tuition waivers (full and partial) available. Support available to part-time students. Financial award application deadline: 3/15; financial award applicants required to submit FAFSA. In 2017, 170 master's, 28 doctorates, 35 other advanced degrees awarded. *Program availability:* Part-time, evening/weekend. Offers business administration (MBA); counseling psychology (MS); creative writing (MFA); education (MS, Certificate); film and television (MFA); health policy and management (MS); humanities (MA); nursing (MSN, Certificate); physical therapy (DPT); religious studies (MA). *Application deadline:* For fall admission, 6/30 priority date for domestic and international students; for spring admission, 10/30 priority date for domestic and international students; for summer admission, 3/30 priority date for domestic and international students. Applications are processed on a rolling basis. *Application fee:* $50. Electronic applications accepted. *Application Contact:* Shawn Peters, Graduate Admission Counselor, 213-477-2676, E-mail: gradprograms@msmu.edu. *Director of Graduate Admissions*, Albert Ramos, 213-477-2800, E-mail: gradprograms@msmu.edu.

MOUNT ST. MARY'S UNIVERSITY, Emmitsburg, MD 21727-7799

General Information Independent-religious, coed, comprehensive institution. *Graduate housing:* Room and/or apartments available on a first-come, first-served basis to single students; on-campus housing not available to married students.

GRADUATE UNITS

Graduate Seminary Offers theology (M Div, MA).

Program in Biotechnology and Management *Program availability:* Part-time-only, evening/weekend. Offers biotechnology and management (MS). Electronic applications accepted.

Program in Business Administration *Program availability:* Part-time, evening/weekend. Offers business administration (MBA). Electronic applications accepted.

Program in Education Offers education (M Ed, MAT). Electronic applications accepted.

Program in Health Administration *Program availability:* Part-time, evening/weekend. Offers health administration (MHA). Electronic applications accepted.

Program in Philosophical Studies *Program availability:* Part-time. Offers philosophical studies (MA).

Program in Sport Management *Program availability:* Part-time, evening/weekend. Offers sport management (MS). Electronic applications accepted.

MOUNT SAINT VINCENT UNIVERSITY, Halifax, NS B3M 2J6, Canada

General Information Province-supported, coed, primarily women, comprehensive institution. *Graduate housing:* Room and/or apartments available on a first-come, first-served basis to single students; on-campus housing not available to married students. Housing application deadline: 5/15.

GRADUATE UNITS

Graduate Programs *Program availability:* Part-time, evening/weekend, online learning. Offers applied human nutrition (M Sc AHN, MAHN); child and youth study (MA); family studies and gerontology (MA); women's studies (MA). Electronic applications accepted.

Faculty of Education *Program availability:* Part-time, evening/weekend, online learning. Offers adult education (M Ed, MA Ed, MA-R); curriculum studies (M Ed, MA Ed, MA-R); education of the blind or visually impaired (M Ed, MA Ed); education of the deaf or hard of hearing (M Ed, MA Ed); education of young adolescents (M Ed, MA Ed, MA-R); educational foundations (M Ed, MA Ed, MA-R); educational psychology (M Ed, MA Ed, MA-R); elementary education (M Ed, MA Ed, MA-R); general studies (M Ed, MA Ed, MA-R); human relations (M Ed, MA Ed); literacy education (M Ed, MA Ed, MA-R); school psychology (MASP); teaching English as a second language (M Ed, MA Ed, MA-R). Electronic applications accepted.

MOUNT VERNON NAZARENE UNIVERSITY, Mount Vernon, OH 43050-9500

General Information Independent-religious, coed, comprehensive institution. *Graduate housing:* On-campus housing not available.

GRADUATE UNITS

Department of Education *Program availability:* Part-time, evening/weekend. Offers education (MA Ed); professional educator's license (MA Ed).

Program in Management *Program availability:* Part-time, evening/weekend. Offers management (MSM).

Program in Ministry *Program availability:* Part-time, evening/weekend. Offers ministry (M Min).

MULTNOMAH UNIVERSITY, Portland, OR 97220-5898

General Information Independent-religious, coed, comprehensive institution. *Enrollment:* 714 graduate, professional, and undergraduate students; 150 full-time matriculated graduate/professional students (77 women), 101 part-time matriculated graduate/professional students (42 women). *Enrollment by degree level:* 238 master's, 11 doctoral, 2 other advanced degrees. *Graduate faculty:* 10 full-time (6 women), 23 part-time/adjunct (9 women). *Tuition:* Full-time $8720; part-time $5450 per credit hour. *Required fees:* $110; $55 per credit hour. Tuition and fees vary according to course load, degree level and program. *Graduate housing:* Room and/or apartments available on a first-come, first-served basis to single students; on-campus housing not available to married students. Housing application deadline: 7/15. *Student services:* Campus employment opportunities, career counseling, free psychological counseling, low-cost health insurance, multicultural affairs office, writing training. *Library facilities:* John Mitchell Library. *Collection:* Books: 120,106 (physical), 152,698 (digital/electronic); Serial titles: 548 (physical), 20,000 (digital/electronic); Databases: 45. Weekly public service hours: 82; students can reserve study rooms.

Computer facilities: 36 computers available on campus for general student use. A campuswide network can be accessed from student residence rooms and from off campus. Online class registration is available.
Website: http://www.multnomah.edu/

General Application Contact: Mindy Kate Hasenkamp, Director of Admissions, 503-251-6483, Fax: 503-254-1268, E-mail: admiss@multnomah.edu.

GRADUATE UNITS

Graduate Programs Students: 69 full-time (53 women), 18 part-time (13 women); includes 22 minority (5 Black or African American, non-Hispanic/Latino; 3 Asian, non-Hispanic/Latino; 9 Hispanic/Latino; 5 Two or more races, non-Hispanic/Latino). Average age 30. 71 applicants, 58% accepted, 30 enrolled. *Faculty:* 6 full-time (5 women), 12 part-time/adjunct (7 women). Expenses: Contact institution. *Financial support:* Career-related internships or fieldwork and scholarships/grants available. Support available to part-time students. Financial award application deadline: 7/1; financial award applicants required to submit FAFSA. In 2017, 57 master's awarded. *Program availability:* Part-time, evening/weekend. Offers counseling (MA); global development and justice (MA); teaching (MA); TESOL (MA). *Application deadline:* For fall admission, 8/1 for domestic students, 12/1 for international students; for spring admission, 12/1 for domestic and international students. *Application fee:* $40. Electronic applications accepted. *Application Contact:* Mindy Kate Hasenkamp, Director of Admissions, 503-251-6483, Fax: 503-254-1268, E-mail: admiss@multnomah.edu. *Academic Dean*, Dr. Daniel Scalberg, 503-251-6441, E-mail: dscalberg@multnomah.edu.

Multnomah Biblical Seminary Students: 80 full-time (23 women), 83 part-time (29 women); includes 32 minority (8 Black or African American, non-Hispanic/Latino; 10 Asian, non-Hispanic/Latino; 8 Hispanic/Latino; 6 Two or more races, non-Hispanic/Latino). Average age 35. 71 applicants, 69% accepted, 38 enrolled. *Faculty:* 4 full-time (1 woman), 14 part-time/adjunct (1 woman). Expenses: Contact institution. *Financial support:* Career-related internships or fieldwork and scholarships/grants available. Support available to part-time students. Financial award application deadline: 7/1; financial award applicants required to submit FAFSA. In 2017, 35 master's, 6 doctorates awarded. *Program availability:* Part-time. Offers theology (M Div, MABS, MACL, MATS, Th M, D Min). *Application deadline:* For fall and spring admission, 12/1 priority date for domestic and international students. Applications are processed on a rolling basis. *Application fee:* $40. *Application Contact:* Mindy Kate Hasenkamp, Director of Admissions, 503-251-6483, Fax: 503-254-1268, E-mail: admiss@multnomah.edu. *Dean*, Dr. Derek Chinn, 503-252-6731, Fax: 503-251-6444, E-mail: dchinn@multnomah.edu.

MURRAY STATE UNIVERSITY, Murray, KY 42071

General Information State-supported, coed, university. *Enrollment:* 10,495 graduate, professional, and undergraduate students; 502 full-time matriculated graduate/professional students (291 women), 813 part-time matriculated graduate/professional students (527 women). *Enrollment by degree level:* 1,104 master's, 172 doctoral, 39 other advanced degrees. *Graduate faculty:* 236 full-time (101 women), 15 part-time/adjunct (4 women). *International tuition:* $14,400 full-time. Tuition, state resident: full-time $9504. Tuition, nonresident: full-time $26,811. Tuition and fees vary according to course load, degree level and reciprocity agreements. *Graduate housing:* Rooms and/or apartments available on a first-come, first-served basis to single and married students. Typical cost: $5246 per year ($8906 including board) for single students; $5500 per year ($12,820 including board) for married students. Room and board charges vary according to board plan and housing facility selected. *Student services:* Campus employment opportunities, campus safety program, career counseling, child daycare facilities, exercise/wellness program, free psychological counseling, international student services, low-cost health insurance, multicultural affairs office, services for students with disabilities. *Library facilities:* Waterfield Library plus 4 others. *Collection:* Books: 363,292 (physical), 193,453 (digital/electronic); Serial titles: 317 (physical), 639 (digital/electronic); Databases: 128. Weekly public service hours: 107; students can reserve study rooms.

Computer facilities: Computer purchase and lease plans are available. A campuswide network can be accessed from student residence rooms and from off campus. Online class registration, billing accounts, course evaluation forms, receive instant campus alerts, secure on-campus housing, pre-order of food or take-out are available.
Website: http://www.murraystate.edu/

General Application Contact: Matthew Jones, Coordinator of Graduate Recruitment and Retention, 270-809-5304, Fax: 270-809-3565, E-mail: mjones1@murraystate.edu.

GRADUATE UNITS

Arthur J. Bauernfeind College of Business Students: 125 full-time (50 women), 183 part-time (82 women); includes 35 minority (16 Black or African American, non-Hispanic/Latino; 1 American Indian or Alaska Native, non-Hispanic/Latino; 6 Asian, non-Hispanic/Latino; 4 Hispanic/Latino; 8 Two or more races, non-Hispanic/Latino), 102 international. Average age 29. 242 applicants, 68% accepted, 66 enrolled. *Faculty:* 61 full-time (10 women). Expenses: Contact institution. *Financial support:* In 2017–18, 4 research assistantships, 4 teaching assistantships were awarded; Federal Work-Study and unspecified assistantships also available. Financial award applicants required to submit FAFSA. In 2017, 91 master's awarded. *Program availability:* Part-time, evening/weekend, 100% online, blended/hybrid learning. Offers accounting (MBA); business (MA, MBA, MS, MSIS, Certificate); computer science and information systems (MSIS); economic development (MS); economics (MS); finance (MBA); global communications (MBA); human resource management (MBA); marketing (MBA); mass communications (MA, MS); nursing education (MA). MS in telecommunications systems management is an interdisciplinary program with the Jesse D. Jones College of Science, Engineering and Technology. *Application deadline:* Applications are processed on a rolling basis. *Application fee:* $40 ($50 for international students). Electronic applications accepted. *Application Contact:* Kaitlyn Burzynski, Interim Director for Graduate Admission and Records, 270-809-5732, Fax: 270-809-3780, E-mail: msu.graduateadmissions@murraystate.edu. *Dean*, Dr. Timothy S. Todd, 270-809-4181, Fax: 270-809-3482, E-mail: msu.cob@murraystate.edu.

College of Education and Human Services Students: 128 full-time (101 women), 374 part-time (296 women); includes 50 minority (34 Black or African American, non-Hispanic/Latino; 1 American Indian or Alaska Native, non-Hispanic/Latino; 6 Asian, non-Hispanic/Latino; 5 Hispanic/Latino; 4 Two or more races, non-Hispanic/Latino), 9 international. Average age 33. 218 applicants, 66% accepted, 96 enrolled. *Faculty:* 75 full-time (47 women), 5 part-time/adjunct (2 women). Expenses: Contact institution. *Financial support:* In 2017–18, 3 research assistantships were awarded; Federal Work-Study, scholarships/grants, and unspecified assistantships also available. Financial award applicants required to submit FAFSA. In 2017, 92 master's, 16 doctorates, 12 other advanced degrees awarded. *Program availability:* Part-time, evening/weekend, 100% online, blended/hybrid learning. Offers career and technical education (MS); college advising (Certificate); education administration (MA Ed); education and human services (MA Ed, MS, Ed D, Certificate, Ed S); elementary teacher leader (MA Ed); human development and leadership (MS, Certificate); interdisciplinary early childhood education (MA Ed); library media (MA Ed); middle school teacher leader (MA Ed); nonprofit leadership studies (MS, Certificate); P-20 and community leadership (Ed D); postsecondary education administration (MA Ed); school counseling (MA Ed); school guidance and counseling (Ed S); secondary teacher leader (MA Ed); special education (MA Ed); teacher education and professional development (Ed S). PhD, EdD offered jointly with University of Kentucky. *Application deadline:* Applications are processed on a rolling basis. *Application fee:* $40 ($50 for international students). Electronic applications accepted. *Application Contact:* Kaitlyn Burzynski, Interim Assistant Director for Graduate Admission and Records, 270-809-5732, Fax: 270-809-3780, E-mail: msu.graduateadmissions@murraystate.edu. *Dean, College of Education and Human Services*, Dr. David Whaley, 270-809-3817, Fax: 270-809-3889, E-mail: dwhaley2@murraystate.edu.

Center for Communication Disorders Students: 63 full-time (62 women); includes 2 minority (1 Asian, non-Hispanic/Latino; 1 Two or more races, non-Hispanic/Latino). Average age 23. 84 applicants, 43% accepted, 16 enrolled. *Faculty:* 4 full-time (all women). Expenses: Contact institution. *Financial support:* Federal Work-Study and unspecified assistantships available. Financial award applicants required to submit FAFSA. In 2017, 14 master's awarded. *Program availability:* Part-time. Offers interdisciplinary brain injury studies (Certificate); speech-language pathology (MS). *Application deadline:* Applications are processed on a rolling basis. *Application fee:* $40 ($50 for international students). Electronic applications accepted. *Application Contact:* Kaitlyn Burzynski, Interim Assistant Director for Graduate Admission and Records, 270-809-5732, Fax: 270-809-3780, E-mail: msu.graduateadmissions@murraystate.edu. *Interim Academic Director and Graduate Coordinator,* Dr. Robert Lyons, 270-809-3807, Fax: 809-809-3889, E-mail: rlyons@murraystate.edu.

College of Humanities and Fine Arts Students: 86 full-time (47 women), 128 part-time (85 women); includes 31 minority (20 Black or African American, non-Hispanic/Latino; 2 American Indian or Alaska Native, non-Hispanic/Latino; 3 Asian, non-Hispanic/Latino; 2 Hispanic/Latino; 4 Two or more races, non-Hispanic/Latino), 36 international. Average age 34. 203 applicants, 83% accepted, 68 enrolled. *Faculty:* 61 full-time (29 women), 3 part-time/adjunct (1 woman). Expenses: Contact institution. *Financial support:* In 2017–18, 10 research assistantships, 4 teaching assistantships were awarded; Federal Work-Study and unspecified assistantships also available. Financial award applicants required to submit FAFSA. In 2017, 44 master's awarded. *Program availability:* Part-time, evening/weekend, 100% online, blended/hybrid learning. Offers clinical psychology (MA, MS); creative writing (MFA); English (MA); English pedagogy and technology (DA); gender studies (Certificate); general experimental psychology (MA, MS); history (MA); humanities and fine arts (MA, MFA, MME, MPA, MS, DA, Certificate); music education (MME); political science and sociology (MPA); research design and analysis (Certificate); teaching English to speakers of other languages (TESOL) (MA). *Application deadline:* Applications are processed on a rolling basis. *Application fee:* $40 ($50 for international students). Electronic applications accepted. *Application Contact:* Kaitlyn Burzynski, Interim Assistant Director for Graduate Admission and Records, 270-809-5732, Fax: 270-809-3780, E-mail: msu.graduateadmissions@murraystate.edu. *Dean, College of Humanities and Fine Arts,* Dr. David Balthrop, 270-809-6937, Fax: 270-809-3424, E-mail: dbalthrop@murraystate.edu.

Hutson School of Agriculture Students: 35 full-time (23 women), 59 part-time (39 women); includes 5 minority (3 Black or African American, non-Hispanic/Latino; 1 Hispanic/Latino; 1 Two or more races, non-Hispanic/Latino), 5 international. Average age 28. 71 applicants, 77% accepted, 29 enrolled. *Faculty:* 15 full-time (7 women). Expenses: Contact institution. *Financial support:* In 2017–18, 1 research assistantship, 4 teaching assistantships were awarded; Federal Work-Study also available. In 2017, 19 master's, 3 other advanced degrees awarded. *Program availability:* Part-time, 100% online, blended/hybrid learning. Offers agriculture (MS); veterinary hospital management (Certificate). *Application deadline:* Applications are processed on a rolling basis. *Application fee:* $40 ($50 for international students). Electronic applications accepted. *Application Contact:* Kaitlyn Burzynski, Interim Assistant Director of Graduate Recruitment and Records, 270-809-5732, Fax: 270-809-3780, E-mail: msu.graduateadmissions@murraystate.edu. *Dean,* Dr. Tony L. Brannon, 270-809-6923, Fax: 270-809-5454, E-mail: tbannon@murraystate.edu.

Jesse D. Jones College of Science, Engineering and Technology Students: 57 full-time (17 women), 52 part-time (12 women); includes 5 minority (4 Black or African American, non-Hispanic/Latino; 1 Two or more races, non-Hispanic/Latino), 16 international. Average age 29. 150 applicants, 65% accepted, 38 enrolled. *Faculty:* 58 full-time (12 women), 3 part-time/adjunct (1 woman). Expenses: Contact institution. *Financial support:* In 2017–18, 19 research assistantships, 8 teaching assistantships were awarded; Federal Work-Study and unspecified assistantships also available. Financial award applicants required to submit FAFSA. In 2017, 39 master's awarded. *Program availability:* Part-time, evening/weekend, 100% online, blended/hybrid learning. Offers biology (MS); chemistry (MS); environmental science (MS); geosciences (MS); geospatial data science (Certificate); mathematics (MA, MS); mathematics teacher leader (MAT); science, engineering and technology (MA, MAT, MS, Certificate). *Application deadline:* Applications are processed on a rolling basis. *Application fee:* $40 ($50 for international students). Electronic applications accepted. *Application Contact:* Kaitlyn Burzynski, Interim Assistant Director for Graduate Admission and Records, 270-809-5732, Fax: 270-809-3780, E-mail: msu.graduateadmissions@murraystate.edu. *Dean, Jesse D. Jones College of Science, Engineering, and Technology,* Dr. Stephen Cobb, 270-809-2888, Fax: 270-809-2886, E-mail: scobb@murraystate.edu.

Institute of Engineering Students: 14 full-time (3 women), 39 part-time (4 women); includes 4 minority (2 Black or African American, non-Hispanic/Latino; 1 Asian, non-Hispanic/Latino; 1 Two or more races, non-Hispanic/Latino), 34 international. Average age 27. 64 applicants, 88% accepted, 8 enrolled. *Faculty:* 12 full-time (2 women), 1 part-time/adjunct (0 women). Expenses: Contact institution. *Financial support:* In 2017–18, 1 research assistantship was awarded; Federal Work-Study and unspecified assistantships also available. Financial award applicants required to submit FAFSA. In 2017, 38 master's awarded. *Program availability:* Part-time. Offers applied engineering and technology management (MS); telecommunications systems management (MS). *Application deadline:* Applications are processed on a rolling basis. *Application fee:* $40 ($50 for international students). Electronic applications accepted. *Application Contact:* Kaitlyn Burzynski, Interim Assistant Director for Graduate Recruitment and Records, 270-809-5732, Fax: 270-809-3780, E-mail: msu.graduateadmissions@murraystate.edu. *Chair, Institutes of Engineering,* Dr. Danny Claiborne, 270-809-6910, Fax: 270-809-6919, E-mail: dclairborne@murraystate.edu.

School of Nursing and Health Professions Students: 73 full-time (54 women), 28 part-time (23 women); includes 12 minority (8 Black or African American, non-Hispanic/Latino; 3 Asian, non-Hispanic/Latino; 1 Two or more races, non-Hispanic/Latino). Average age 32. 103 applicants, 43% accepted, 33 enrolled. *Faculty:* 11 full-time (10 women), 1 part-time/adjunct (0 women). Expenses: Contact institution. *Financial support:* Federal Work-Study, scholarships/grants, and unspecified assistantships available. Financial award applicants required to submit FAFSA. In 2017, 4 master's, 26 doctorates awarded. *Program availability:* Part-time, evening/weekend, 100% online, blended/hybrid learning. Offers family nurse practitioner (DNP); nurse anesthetist (DNP); nursing and health professions (MS, DNP, Certificate); nutrition (MS); registered dietitian (Certificate). *Application deadline:* Applications are processed on a rolling basis. *Application fee:* $40 ($50 for international students). Electronic applications accepted. *Application Contact:* Kaitlyn Burzynski, Interim Assistant Director for Graduate Admission and Records, 270-809-5732, Fax: 270-809-3780, E-mail: msu.graduateadmissions@murraystate.edu. *Dean, School of Nursing and Health Professions,* Dr. Marcia Hobbs, 270-809-2196, Fax: 270-809-6662, E-mail: mhobbs4@murraystate.edu.

MUSKINGUM UNIVERSITY, New Concord, OH 43762

General Information Independent-religious, coed, comprehensive institution. *Graduate housing:* On-campus housing not available.

GRADUATE UNITS

Graduate Programs in Education *Program availability:* Part-time. Offers education (MAE, MAT).

NAROPA UNIVERSITY, Boulder, CO 80302-6697

General Information Independent, coed, comprehensive institution. *Enrollment:* 966 graduate, professional, and undergraduate students; 396 full-time matriculated graduate/professional students (294 women), 165 part-time matriculated graduate/professional students (118 women). *Enrollment by degree level:* 561 master's. *Graduate faculty:* 37 full-time (19 women), 60 part-time/adjunct (44 women). *Tuition:* Full-time $21,890; part-time $11,940 per credit hour. *Required fees:* $670; $620 per year. $310 per semester. Tuition and fees vary according to course load and program. *Graduate housing:* Room and/or apartments available on a first-come, first-served basis to single students; on-campus housing not available to married students. Housing application deadline: 7/1. *Student services:* Campus employment opportunities, campus safety program, career counseling, free psychological counseling, international student services, low-cost health insurance, multicultural affairs office, services for students with disabilities, writing training. *Library facilities:* Allen Ginsberg Library plus 2 others. *Collection:* Books: 36,333 (physical), 177,800 (digital/electronic); Serial titles: 335 (physical), 33,467 (digital/electronic); Databases: 47. Weekly public service hours: 69.

Computer facilities: 48 computers available on campus for general student use. A campuswide network can be accessed from student residence rooms and from off campus. Online class registration is available.
Website: http://www.naropa.edu/

General Application Contact: Office of Admissions, 303-546-3572, Fax: 303-546-3583, E-mail: admissions@naropa.edu.

GRADUATE UNITS

Graduate Programs Students: 396 full-time (294 women), 165 part-time (118 women); includes 118 minority (15 Black or African American, non-Hispanic/Latino; 5 American Indian or Alaska Native, non-Hispanic/Latino; 12 Asian, non-Hispanic/Latino; 62 Hispanic/Latino; 24 Two or more races, non-Hispanic/Latino), 28 international. Average age 32. 486 applicants, 82% accepted, 232 enrolled. *Faculty:* 38 full-time (20 women), 63 part-time/adjunct (46 women). Expenses: Contact institution. *Financial support:* In 2017–18, 296 students received support, including 5 fellowships with full tuition reimbursements available (averaging $3,000 per year), 9 research assistantships with partial tuition reimbursements available (averaging $1,967 per year), 8 teaching assistantships with partial tuition reimbursements available (averaging $2,063 per year); career-related internships or fieldwork, Federal Work-Study, scholarships/grants, tuition waivers (partial), and unspecified assistantships also available. Support available to part-time students. Financial award application deadline: 3/1; financial award applicants required to submit FAFSA. In 2017, 176 master's awarded. *Program availability:* Part-time, blended/hybrid learning. Offers contemplative psychotherapy and Buddhist psychology (MA); creative writing (MFA); creative writing and poetics (MFA); divinity (M Div); ecopsychology (MA); mindfulness-based transpersonal counseling (MA); religious studies (MA); religious studies with language (MA); resilient leadership (MA); somatic counseling: body psychotherapy (MA); somatic counseling: dance/movement therapy (MA); theater: contemporary performance (MFA); transpersonal art therapy (MA); transpersonal wilderness therapy (MA). *Application deadline:* For fall admission, 1/15 priority date for domestic and international students; for spring admission, 10/15 priority date for domestic and international students. Applications are processed on a rolling basis. *Application fee:* $60. Electronic applications accepted. *Application Contact:* Office of Admissions, 303-546-3572, Fax: 303-546-3583, E-mail: admissions@naropa.edu. *Director of Marketing and Admissions,* Kelly Watt, 303-546-5285, Fax: 303-546-3583, E-mail: kwatt@naropa.edu.

NASHOTAH HOUSE THEOLOGICAL SEMINARY, Nashotah, WI 53058-9793

General Information Independent-religious, coed, primarily men, graduate-only institution. *Graduate housing:* Rooms and/or apartments available on a first-come, first-served basis to single and married students. Housing application deadline: 5/1.

GRADUATE UNITS

Graduate Programs *Program availability:* Part-time. Offers Anglican studies (Certificate); Biblical studies (STM); Christian spirituality (STM); church history (STM); liturgy (STM); ministry (M Div, MM); pastoral ministry (MPM); theological studies (MTS); theology (STM, D Min). Electronic applications accepted.

NATIONAL AMERICAN UNIVERSITY, Austin, TX 78731

General Information Proprietary, coed, graduate-only institution.

GRADUATE UNITS

Roueche Graduate Center *Program availability:* Part-time, evening/weekend, online learning. Offers accounting (MBA); aviation management (MBA, MM); care coordination (MSN); community college leadership (Ed D); criminal justice (MM); e-marketing (MBA, MM); health care administration (MBA, MM); higher education (MM); human resources management (MBA, MM); information technology management (MBA, MM); international business (MBA); leadership (EMBA); management (MBA); nursing administration (MSN); nursing education (MSN); nursing informatics (MSN); operations and configuration management (MBA, MM); project and process management (MBA, MM). Master's programs offered online through the Harold D. Buckingham Graduate School. Electronic applications accepted.

NATIONAL COLLEGE OF MIDWIFERY, Taos, NM 87571

General Information Independent, women only, comprehensive institution.

GRADUATE UNITS

Graduate Programs *Program availability:* Part-time, evening/weekend, online learning. Offers midwifery (MS, PhD). Electronic applications accepted.

NATIONAL DEFENSE UNIVERSITY, Washington, DC 20319-5066

General Information Federally supported, coed, graduate-only institution. *Graduate housing:* On-campus housing not available.

GRADUATE UNITS

College of International Security Affairs *Program availability:* Part-time, evening/weekend. Offers strategic security studies (MA).

The Dwight D. Eisenhower School for National Security and Resource Strategy Offers national resource strategy (MS). Open only to Department of Defense employees and specific federal agencies.

Joint Advanced Warfighting School Offers joint campaign planning and strategy (MS). Open only to Department of Defense employees and specific federal agencies.

National War College Offers national security strategy (MS). Open only to Department of Defense employees and specific federal agencies.

THE NATIONAL GRADUATE SCHOOL OF QUALITY MANAGEMENT, Falmouth, MA 02541

General Information Independent, coed, graduate-only institution.

GRADUATE UNITS

Graduate Programs Offers homeland security (MS); quality systems management (MS, DBA).

NATIONAL INTELLIGENCE UNIVERSITY, Washington, DC 20340-5100

General Information Federally supported, coed, upper-level institution. *Graduate housing:* On-campus housing not available.

GRADUATE UNITS

Graduate Program *Program availability:* Part-time, evening/weekend. Offers strategic intelligence (MSSI). Open only to federal government employees.

NATIONAL LOUIS UNIVERSITY, Chicago, IL 60603

General Information Independent, coed, university.

GRADUATE UNITS

College of Arts and Sciences *Program availability:* Part-time, evening/weekend, online learning. Offers adult education (Ed D); counseling and human services (MS); language and academic development (M Ed, Certificate); psychology (MA, PhD, Certificate); public policy (MA); written communication (MS, Certificate). Electronic applications accepted.

College of Management and Business *Program availability:* Part-time, evening/weekend. Offers business administration (MBA); human resource management and development (MS); management (MS).

National College of Education *Program availability:* Part-time, evening/weekend. Offers administration and supervision (M Ed, Ed D, CAS, Ed S); curriculum and instruction (M Ed, MS Ed, CAS); early childhood administration (M Ed, CAS); early childhood education (M Ed, MAT, MS Ed, CAS); education (Ed D); educational psychology/human learning and development (M Ed, MS Ed, CAS, Ed S); elementary education (MAT); interdisciplinary curriculum and instruction (M Ed); mathematics education (M Ed, MS Ed, CAS); middle grades education (MAT); reading and language (M Ed, MS Ed, CAS); school psychology (M Ed, Ed S); science education (M Ed, MS Ed, CAS); secondary education (MAT); special education (M Ed, MAT, CAS); technology in education (M Ed, CAS).

NATIONAL PARALEGAL COLLEGE, Phoenix, AZ 85014

General Information Proprietary, coed, comprehensive institution.

GRADUATE UNITS

Graduate Programs *Program availability:* Part-time. Offers compliance law (MS); legal studies (MS); taxation (MS). Electronic applications accepted.

NATIONAL TEST PILOT SCHOOL, Mojave, CA 93502-0658

General Information Independent, coed, graduate-only institution.

GRADUATE UNITS

National Flight Institute Offers flight test and evaluation (MS); flight test engineering (MS).

NATIONAL UNIVERSITY, La Jolla, CA 92037-1011

General Information Independent, coed, comprehensive institution. CGS member. *Tuition:* Part-time $430 per quarter hour. *Graduate housing:* On-campus housing not available. *Student services:* Campus employment opportunities, campus safety program, career counseling, international student services, services for students with disabilities, teacher training, writing training. *Library facilities:* National University Library. *Collection:* Books: 212,626 (physical), 319,622 (digital/electronic); Serial titles: 3,490 (physical), 92,431 (digital/electronic); Databases: 190. Weekly public service hours: 72; students can reserve study rooms.

Computer facilities: 2,800 computers available on campus for general student use. A campuswide network can be accessed from off campus. Online class registration is available.
Website: http://www.nu.edu/

General Application Contact: Brandon Jouganatos, Vice President for Enrollment Services, 800-628-8648, E-mail: advisor@nu.edu.

GRADUATE UNITS

College of Letters and Sciences Expenses: Contact institution. *Financial support:* Career-related internships or fieldwork, institutionally sponsored loans, scholarships/grants, and tuition waivers (partial) available. Support available to part-time students. Financial award application deadline: 6/30; financial award applicants required to submit FAFSA. *Program availability:* Part-time, evening/weekend, 100% online, blended/hybrid learning. Offers biology (MS); counseling psychology (MA); creative writing (MFA); English (MA); film studies (MA); forensic and crime scene investigations (Certificate); forensic sciences (MFS); human behavior (MA); mathematics for educators (MS); performance psychology (MA); strategic communications (MA). *Application deadline:* Applications are processed on a rolling basis. *Application fee:* $60 ($65 for international students). Electronic applications accepted. *Application Contact:* Brandon Jouganatos, Interim Vice President for Enrollment Services, 800-628-8648, E-mail: advisor@nu.edu. *Dean*, Dr. Carol Richardson, 858-642-8450, E-mail: cols@nu.edu.

Sanford College of Education Expenses: Contact institution. *Financial support:* Career-related internships or fieldwork, institutionally sponsored loans, scholarships/grants, and tuition waivers (partial) available. Support available to part-time students. Financial award application deadline: 6/30. *Program availability:* Part-time, evening/weekend, 100% online, blended/hybrid learning. Offers advanced teaching practices (MS); applied behavior analysis (MS); applied school leadership (MS); e-teaching and learning (Certificate); education (MA); educational administration (MS); educational and instructional technology (MS); educational counseling (MS); higher education administration (MS); inspired teaching and learning (M Ed); school psychology (MS); special education (MA, MS). *Application deadline:* Applications are processed on a rolling basis. *Application fee:* $60 ($65 for international students). Electronic applications accepted. *Application Contact:* Brandon Jouganatos, Vice President for Enrollment Services, 800-628-8648, E-mail: advisor@nu.edu. *Dean*, Dr. Judy Mantle, 858-642-8320, E-mail: soe@nu.edu.

School of Business and Management Expenses: Contact institution. *Financial support:* Career-related internships or fieldwork, scholarships/grants, and tuition waivers (partial) available. Support available to part-time students. Financial award application deadline: 6/30; financial award applicants required to submit FAFSA. *Program availability:* Part-time, evening/weekend, 100% online, blended/hybrid learning. Offers accountancy (M Acc, Certificate); business administration (GMBA, MBA); business analytics (MS); cause leadership (MA); global management (MGM); human resource management (MA); management information systems (MS); marketing (MS); organizational leadership (MS). GMBA offered in Spanish. *Application deadline:* Applications are processed on a rolling basis. *Application fee:* $60 ($65 for international students). Electronic applications accepted. *Application Contact:* Brandon Jouganatos, Vice President for Enrollment Services, 800-628-8648, E-mail: advisor@nu.edu. *Dean*, Dr. Alfred Ntoko, 858-642-8400, Fax: 858-642-8719, E-mail: sobm@nu.edu.

School of Engineering and Computing Expenses: Contact institution. *Financial support:* Career-related internships or fieldwork, institutionally sponsored loans, scholarships/grants, and tuition waivers (partial) available. Support available to part-time students. Financial award application deadline: 6/30; financial award applicants required to submit FAFSA. *Program availability:* Part-time, evening/weekend, 100% online, blended/hybrid learning. Offers computer science (MS); cyber security and information assurance (MS); data analytics (MS); electrical engineering (MS); engineering management (MS); information technology management (MS); management information systems (MS); sustainability management (MS). *Application deadline:* Applications are processed on a rolling basis. *Application fee:* $60 ($65 for international students). Electronic applications accepted. *Application Contact:* Brandon Jouganatos, Vice President for Enrollment Services, 800-628-8648, E-mail: advisor@nu.edu. *Interim Dean*, Dr. Jodi Reeves, 858-309-3426, E-mail: jreeves@nu.edu.

School of Health and Human Services Expenses: Contact institution. *Financial support:* Career-related internships or fieldwork, institutionally sponsored loans, scholarships/grants, and tuition waivers (partial) available. Support available to part-time students. Financial award application deadline: 6/30; financial award applicants required to submit FAFSA. *Program availability:* Part-time, evening/weekend, 100% online, blended/hybrid learning. Offers clinical affairs (MS); clinical regulatory affairs (MS); complementary and integrative healthcare (MS); family nurse practitioner (MSN); health and life science analytics (MS); health informatics (MS, Certificate); healthcare administration (MHA); nurse anesthesia (MSNA); nursing administration (MSN); nursing informatics (MSN); psychiatric-mental health nurse practitioner (MSN); public health (MPH). *Application deadline:* Applications are processed on a rolling basis. *Application fee:* $60 ($65 for international students). Electronic applications accepted. *Application Contact:* Brandon Jouganatos, Vice President for Enrollment Services, 800-628-8648, E-mail: advisor@nu.edu. *Dean*, Dr. Gloria J. McNeal, 858-309-3473, E-mail: shhs@nu.edu.

School of Professional Studies Expenses: Contact institution. *Financial support:* Career-related internships or fieldwork, institutionally sponsored loans, scholarships/grants, and tuition waivers (partial) available. Support available to part-time students. Financial award application deadline: 6/30; financial award applicants required to submit FAFSA. *Program availability:* Part-time, evening/weekend, 100% online, blended/hybrid learning. Offers criminal justice (MCJ); digital cinema production (MFA); digital journalism (MA); homeland security and emergency management (MS); juvenile justice (MS); professional screenwriting (MFA); public administration (MPA). *Application deadline:* Applications are processed on a rolling basis. *Application fee:* $60 ($65 for international students). Electronic applications accepted. *Application Contact:* Brandon Jouganatos, Vice President for Enrollment Services, 800-628-8648, E-mail: advisor@nu.edu. *Dean*, Dr. Daniel Donaldson, 858-642-8480, E-mail: sops@nu.edu.

NATIONAL UNIVERSITY COLLEGE, Bayamón, PR 00960

General Information Proprietary, coed, comprehensive institution.

GRADUATE UNITS

Graduate Programs

NATIONAL UNIVERSITY OF HEALTH SCIENCES, Lombard, IL 60148-4583

General Information Independent, coed, graduate-only institution. *Graduate housing:* Rooms and/or apartments available on a first-come, first-served basis to single and married students. *Research affiliation:* University of Illinois at Chicago (public health), Canadian Memorial Chiropractic College (mechanisms of CAM), Cox Technic F/D Enterprise LLC (mechanisms of CAM), Logan Chiropractic College (behavior research), Foot Levelers, Inc. (orthotics/biomechanics), Auburn University (mechanisms of CAM).

GRADUATE UNITS

Graduate Programs Offers acupuncture (MSAC); chiropractic (DC); diagnostic imaging (MS); naturopathic medicine (ND); Oriental medicine (MSOM).

NATIONAL UNIVERSITY OF NATURAL MEDICINE, Portland, OR 97201

General Information Independent, coed, primarily women, graduate-only institution. *Enrollment by degree level:* 160 master's, 426 doctoral. *Graduate faculty:* 39 full-time, 113 part-time/adjunct. *Tuition:* Full-time $23,979. *Graduate housing:* On-campus housing not available. *Student services:* Campus employment opportunities, campus safety program, career counseling, free psychological counseling, international student services, multicultural affairs office, services for students with disabilities. *Library facilities:* NUNM Library. *Collection:* Books: 21,012 (physical), 12 (digital/electronic); Serial titles: 409 (physical), 22,682 (digital/electronic); Databases: 26. Weekly public service hours: 67. *Research affiliation:* Metagenics, Inc. (effects of methylation diet, nutrition supplements), Divinia Water (product safety and tolerability, case reports, water).

Computer facilities: 29 computers available on campus for general student use. A campuswide network can be accessed from off campus. Online class registration, X are available.
Website: http://www.nunm.edu/

General Application Contact: Ryan Hollister, Associate Director of Admissions and Operations, 503-552-1665, Fax: 503-499-0027, E-mail: admissions@nunm.edu.

GRADUATE UNITS

College of Classical Chinese Medicine Students: 167 full-time (123 women). Average age 33. *Faculty:* 14 full-time (3 women), 22 part-time/adjunct (10 women). Expenses: Contact institution. *Financial support:* Federal Work-Study and scholarships/grants available. Financial award application deadline: 2/15; financial award applicants required to submit FAFSA. In 2017, 29 master's, 7 doctorates awarded. Offers classical Chinese medicine (M Ac, MSOM, DOM). *Application deadline:* For fall and winter admission, 5/1 priority date for domestic and international students. Applications are processed on a rolling basis. *Application fee:* $75. Electronic applications accepted. *Application*

Contact: Ryan Hollister, Associate Director of Admissions and Operations, 503-552-1665, Fax: 503-499-0027, E-mail: admissions@numn.edu. *Dean,* Dr. Laurie Regan, 503-552-1775, Fax: 503-499-0027, E-mail: admissions@nunm.edu.

College of Naturopathic Medicine Students: 367 full-time (285 women). Average age 30. *Faculty:* 18 full-time (10 women), 56 part-time/adjunct (33 women). Expenses: Contact institution. *Financial support:* Federal Work-Study and scholarships/grants available. Financial award application deadline: 2/15; financial award applicants required to submit FAFSA. In 2017, 71 doctorates awarded. Offers integrative medicine research (MS); naturopathic medicine (ND). *Application deadline:* For fall and winter admission, 5/1 priority date for domestic and international students. Applications are processed on a rolling basis. *Application fee:* $75. Electronic applications accepted. *Application Contact:* Ryan Hollister, Associate Director of Admissions and Operations, 503-552-1665, Fax: 503-499-0027, E-mail: admissions@numn.edu. *Dean,* Dr. Shehab El-Hashemy, 503-552-1848, Fax: 503-499-0027, E-mail: admissions@nunm.edu.

School of Graduate Studies Students: 184 (161 women). Average age 31. *Faculty:* 7 full-time (5 women), 35 part-time/adjunct (25 women). Expenses: Contact institution. *Financial support:* Federal Work-Study and scholarships/grants available. Financial award application deadline: 2/15; financial award applicants required to submit FAFSA. In 2017, 67 master's awarded. Offers Ayurveda (MS); global health (MS); integrative medicine research (MS); integrative mental health (MS); nutrition (MS). *Application deadline:* For fall and winter admission, 5/1 for domestic and international students. Applications are processed on a rolling basis. *Application fee:* $75. Electronic applications accepted. *Application Contact:* Ryan Hollister, Associate Director of Admissions and Operations, 503-552-1665, Fax: 503-499-0027, E-mail: admissions@numn.edu. *Dean,* Dr. Charles Kunert, 503-552-1742, Fax: 503-499-0027, E-mail: admission@nunm.edu.

NAVAJO TECHNICAL UNIVERSITY, Crownpoint, NM 87313

General Information Independent, coed, comprehensive institution.

GRADUATE UNITS

Program in Dine Studies Offers dine studies (MA).

NAVAL POSTGRADUATE SCHOOL, Monterey, CA 93943

General Information Federally supported, coed, graduate-only institution. *Graduate housing:* Rooms and/or apartments available to single and married students. *Research affiliation:* U.S. Department of Homeland Security, National Reconnaissance Office, National Oceanic and Atmospheric Administration (NOAA), National Security Agency, Federal Law Enforcement Training.

GRADUATE UNITS

Departments and Academic Groups *Program availability:* Part-time, online learning. Offers applied mathematics (MS); applied physics (MS, PhD); applied science (MS); astronautical engineer (AstE); astronautical engineering (MS); combat systems technology (MS); command and control (MS); communications (MS); computer engineering (MS); computer science (MS, PhD); cost estimating analysis (MS); defense analysis (MS); electrical engineer (EE); electrical engineering (MS, PhD); electronic warfare systems engineering (MS); engineering acoustics (MS, PhD); engineering science (MS); engineering systems (MS); financial management (MS); human systems integration (MS); identity management and cyber security (MA); information operations (MS); information sciences (PhD); information systems and operations (MS); information technology management (MS); information warfare systems engineering (MS); irregular warfare (MS); knowledge superiority (Certificate); mechanical and aerospace engineering (PhD); mechanical engineer (ME); mechanical engineering (MS, MSME); meteorology (MS, PhD); meteorology and physical oceanography (MS); modeling of virtual environments and simulations (MS, PhD); national security affairs (MA, MS); operations analysis (MS); operations research (MS, PhD); physical oceanography (MS, PhD); physics (MS, PhD); product development (MS); remote sensing intelligence (MS); security studies (MA); software engineering (MS, PhD); space systems (Engr); space systems operations (MS); special operations (MA, MS); stability, security, and development in complex operations (Certificate); system technology (command, control and communications) (MS); systems analysis (MS); systems engineering (MS, PhD, Certificate); systems engineering analysis (MS, PhD); systems engineering management (MS, PhD); tactile missiles (MS); terrorist operations and financing (MS). Programs only open to commissioned officers of the United States and friendly nations and selected United States federal civilian employees.

Graduate School of Business and Public Policy *Program availability:* Part-time, online learning. Offers acquisition and contract management (MBA); business administration (EMBA, MBA); contract management (MS); defense business management (MBA); defense systems analysis (MS); defense systems management (international) (MBA); financial management (MBA); information management (MBA); manpower systems analysis (MS); material logistics support management (MBA); program management (MS); resource planning and management for international defense (MBA); supply chain management (MBA); systems acquisition management (MBA); transportation management (MBA). Program only open to commissioned officers of the United States and friendly nations and selected United States federal civilian employees.

NAVAL WAR COLLEGE, Newport, RI 02841-1207

General Information Federally supported, coed, primarily men, graduate-only institution.

GRADUATE UNITS

Program in National Security and Strategic Studies Offers national security and strategic studies (MA). Program open only to full-time military personnel.

NAZARENE THEOLOGICAL SEMINARY, Kansas City, MO 64131-1263

General Information Independent-religious, coed, graduate-only institution. *Enrollment by degree level:* 175 master's, 17 doctoral, 18 other advanced degrees. *Graduate faculty:* 12 full-time (2 women), 16 part-time/adjunct (3 women). *Tuition:* Full-time $11,445; part-time $8175 per credit hour. *Required fees:* $200 per semester. *Graduate housing:* Rooms and/or apartments available on a first-come, first-served basis to single and married students. *Student services:* Campus employment opportunities, career counseling, free psychological counseling, international student services, services for students with disabilities, writing training. *Library facilities:* William Broadhurst Library. *Collection:* Books: 99,211 (physical), 9,784 (digital/electronic); Serial titles: 230 (physical); Databases: 4. Weekly public service hours: 49; students can reserve study rooms. *Research affiliation:* University of Missouri-Kansas City (religious studies).

Computer facilities: 3 computers available on campus for general student use. A campuswide network can be accessed. Online class registration is available.
Website: http://www.nts.edu/

General Application Contact: Pamala J. Asher, Registrar/Director of Admissions, 816-268-5442, Fax: 816-268-5500, E-mail: pjasher@nts.edu.

GRADUATE UNITS

Graduate and Professional Programs Students: 54 full-time (25 women), 156 part-time (55 women); includes 22 minority (7 Black or African American, non-Hispanic/Latino; 1 American Indian or Alaska Native, non-Hispanic/Latino; 1 Asian, non-Hispanic/Latino; 9 Hispanic/Latino; 4 Two or more races, non-Hispanic/Latino), 29 international. *Faculty:* 12 full-time (2 women), 16 part-time/adjunct (3 women). Expenses: Contact institution. *Financial support:* Teaching assistantships, institutionally sponsored loans, and scholarships/grants available. Support available to part-time students. Financial award application deadline: 3/1; financial award applicants required to submit FAFSA. *Program availability:* Part-time. Offers Christian formation and discipleship (MA); intercultural studies (MA); pastoral theology (Graduate Certificate); theological studies (MA); theology (M Div, D Min). *Application deadline:* For fall admission, 2/15 for domestic and international students; for spring admission, 11/1 for domestic and international students. Applications are processed on a rolling basis. *Application fee:* $50. Electronic applications accepted. *Application Contact:* Pamala J. Asher, Registrar/Director of Enrollment Services, 816-268-5442, Fax: 816-268-5500, E-mail: pjasher@nts.edu. *Dean of the Faculty,* Dr. Josh Sweeden, 816-268-5402, Fax: 816-268-5500, E-mail: jsweeden@nts.edu.

NAZARETH COLLEGE OF ROCHESTER, Rochester, NY 14618

General Information Independent, coed, comprehensive institution. CGS member. *Graduate housing:* Room and/or apartments available on a first-come, first-served basis to single students; on-campus housing not available to married students. Housing application deadline: 5/15.

GRADUATE UNITS

Graduate Studies *Program availability:* Part-time, evening/weekend. Offers art education (MS Ed); art therapy (MS); communication sciences and disorders (MS); educational technology (MS Ed); human resource management (MS); inclusive adolescence education (MS Ed); inclusive childhood education (MS Ed); inclusive early childhood education (MS Ed); literacy education (MS Ed); management (MS); music education (MS Ed); music performance and pedagogy (MM); music therapy (MS); physical therapy (DPT); social work (MSW); teaching English to speakers of other languages (MS Ed).

NEBRASKA METHODIST COLLEGE, Omaha, NE 68114

General Information Independent-religious, coed, comprehensive institution. *Graduate housing:* Rooms and/or apartments available on a first-come, first-served basis to single students and available to married students. Housing application deadline: 4/1.

GRADUATE UNITS

Program in Healthcare Operations Management *Program availability:* Part-time, evening/weekend, online learning. Offers healthcare operations management (MS).

Program in Health Promotion Management *Program availability:* Part-time, evening/weekend, online learning. Offers health promotion management (MS).

Program in Nursing *Program availability:* Evening/weekend, online learning. Offers nurse educator (MSN); nurse executive (MSN).

NEBRASKA WESLEYAN UNIVERSITY, Lincoln, NE 68504-2796

General Information Independent-religious, coed, comprehensive institution.

GRADUATE UNITS

University College *Program availability:* Part-time. Offers forensic science (MFS); historical studies (MA); nursing (MSN).

NER ISRAEL RABBINICAL COLLEGE, Baltimore, MD 21208

General Information Independent-religious, men only, comprehensive institution. *Graduate housing:* Rooms and/or apartments guaranteed to single students and available on a first-come, first-served basis to married students.

GRADUATE UNITS

Graduate Programs Offers rabbinics (MTL, DTL, Professional Certificate).

NER ISRAEL YESHIVA COLLEGE OF TORONTO, Thornhill, ON L4J 8A7, Canada

General Information Independent-religious, men only, comprehensive institution.

GRADUATE UNITS

Graduate Programs

NEUMANN UNIVERSITY, Aston, PA 19014-1298

General Information Independent-religious, coed, comprehensive institution. *Enrollment:* 2,715 graduate, professional, and undergraduate students; 172 full-time matriculated graduate/professional students (108 women), 458 part-time matriculated graduate/professional students (339 women). *Enrollment by degree level:* 488 master's, 142 doctoral. *Graduate faculty:* 25 full-time (19 women), 42 part-time/adjunct (20 women). *Tuition:* Part-time $700 per credit hour. Tuition and fees vary according to degree level, campus/location and program. *Graduate housing:* On-campus housing not available. *Student services:* Campus safety program, career counseling, child daycare facilities, exercise/wellness program, free psychological counseling, international student services, services for students with disabilities, teacher training, writing training. *Library facilities:* Neumann University Library plus 1 other. *Collection:* Books: 51,000 (physical), 161,000 (digital/electronic); Serial titles: 20 (physical), 100,000 (digital/electronic); Databases: 45. Weekly public service hours: 80; students can reserve study rooms.

Computer facilities: Computer purchase and lease plans are available. 275 computers available on campus for general student use. A campuswide network can be accessed from student residence rooms and from off campus. Online class registration is available.
Website: http://www.neumann.edu/

General Application Contact: Dr. Erika K. Davis, Director of Adult and Graduate Admissions, 800-9-NEUMANN Ext. 5208, Fax: 610-361-2548, E-mail: gradadultadmiss@neumann.edu.

GRADUATE UNITS

Graduate Program in Education Students: 68 full-time (56 women), 108 part-time (93 women); includes 36 minority (28 Black or African American, non-Hispanic/Latino; 3 Hispanic/Latino; 5 Two or more races, non-Hispanic/Latino). Average age 33. 83 applicants, 69% accepted, 36 enrolled. *Faculty:* 6 full-time (5 women), 16 part-time/adjunct (7 women). Expenses: Contact institution. *Financial support:* Scholarships/grants and health care benefits available. Support available to part-time students. Financial award application deadline: 3/15; financial award applicants required to submit FAFSA. In 2017, 114 master's awarded. *Program availability:* Part-time, evening/weekend, 100% online, blended/hybrid learning. Offers education (MS). *Application deadline:* Applications are processed on a rolling basis. *Application fee:* $0. Electronic applications accepted. *Application Contact:* Dr. Erika K. Davis, Director of Adult and Graduate Admissions, 800-9-NEUMANN Ext. 5208, Fax: 610-361-2548, E-mail: gradadultadmiss@neumann.edu. *Director of Graduate Education,* Dr. Stephanie Smith-Budhai, 610-358-4249, E-mail: budhais@neumann.edu.

Graduate Program in Nursing Students: 37 part-time (35 women); includes 11 minority (5 Black or African American, non-Hispanic/Latino; 2 Asian, non-Hispanic/Latino; 2 Hispanic/Latino; 2 Two or more races, non-Hispanic/Latino). Average age 41. 15 applicants, 47% accepted, 7 enrolled. *Faculty:* 2 full-time (both women), 4 part-time/adjunct (3 women). Expenses: Contact institution. *Financial support:* Scholarships/grants, traineeships, and health care benefits available. Support available to part-time students. Financial award application deadline: 3/15; financial award applicants required to submit FAFSA. In 2017, 11 master's awarded. *Program availability:* Part-time, evening/weekend. Offers adult-gerontology nurse practitioner (MS, Certificate). *Application deadline:* Applications are processed on a rolling basis. *Application fee:* $0. Electronic applications accepted. *Application Contact:* Dr. Erika K. Davis, Director of Adult and Graduate Admissions, 800-9-NEUMANN Ext. 5208, Fax: 610-361-2548, E-mail: gradadultadmiss@neumann.edu. *Dean, Division of Nursing and Health Sciences,* Dr. Kathleen Hoover, 610-558-5560, Fax: 610-361-5265, E-mail: hooverk@neumann.edu.

Graduate Programs in Business and Information Management Students: 7 full-time (1 woman), 29 part-time (14 women); includes 12 minority (10 Black or African American, non-Hispanic/Latino; 1 Asian, non-Hispanic/Latino; 1 Hispanic/Latino). Average age 30. 35 applicants, 37% accepted, 7 enrolled. *Faculty:* 2 full-time (both women), 4 part-time/adjunct (1 woman). Expenses: Contact institution. *Financial support:* Scholarships/grants and health care benefits available. Support available to part-time students. Financial award application deadline: 3/15; financial award applicants required to submit FAFSA. In 2017, 16 master's awarded. *Program availability:* Part-time, evening/weekend. Offers accounting (MS); sport business (MS). *Application deadline:* Applications are processed on a rolling basis. *Application fee:* $0. Electronic applications accepted. *Application Contact:* Dr. Erika K. Davis, Director of Adult and Graduate Admissions, 800-9-NEUMANN Ext. 5208, Fax: 610-361-2548, E-mail: gradadultadmiss@neumann.edu. *Dean of Business and Information Management,* Dr. Eric R. Wellington, 610-558-5596, Fax: 610-558-5574, E-mail: wellinge@neumann.edu.

Program in Educational Leadership Students: 2 full-time (1 woman), 37 part-time (19 women); includes 6 minority (5 Black or African American, non-Hispanic/Latino; 1 Two or more races, non-Hispanic/Latino). Average age 41. 25 applicants, 56% accepted, 9 enrolled. *Faculty:* 3 full-time (1 woman), 4 part-time/adjunct (1 woman). Expenses: Contact institution. *Financial support:* Scholarships/grants and health care benefits available. Support available to part-time students. Financial award application deadline: 3/15; financial award applicants required to submit FAFSA. In 2017, 11 doctorates awarded. *Program availability:* Part-time, evening/weekend. Offers educational leadership (Ed D). *Application deadline:* For fall admission, 7/1 for domestic and international students. *Application fee:* $0. Electronic applications accepted. *Application Contact:* Dr. Erika K. Davis, Director of Adult and Graduate Admissions, 800-9-NEUMANN Ext. 5208, Fax: 610-361-2548, E-mail: gradadultadmiss@neumann.edu. *Director of Ed D Program,* Dr. Cynthia Speace, 610-358-4243, E-mail: speacec@neumann.edu.

Program in Organizational and Strategic Leadership Students: 55 part-time (31 women); includes 9 minority (7 Black or African American, non-Hispanic/Latino; 1 Asian, non-Hispanic/Latino; 1 Hispanic/Latino), 2 international. Average age 38. 34 applicants, 76% accepted, 22 enrolled. *Faculty:* 7 part-time/adjunct (3 women). Expenses: Contact institution. *Financial support:* Scholarships/grants and health care benefits available. Support available to part-time students. Financial award application deadline: 3/15; financial award applicants required to submit FAFSA. In 2017, 50 master's awarded. *Program availability:* Part-time, evening/weekend, 100% online, blended/hybrid learning. Offers organizational and strategic leadership (MS). *Application deadline:* Applications are processed on a rolling basis. *Application fee:* $0. Electronic applications accepted. *Application Contact:* Janice Sackawicz, Coordinator of Student Services, Division of Continuing Adult and Professional Studies, 610-558-5629, Fax: 610-361-5235, E-mail: caps@neumann.edu. *Program Director, Master of Science in Organizational and Strategic Leadership,* Dr. Samuel M. Lemon, 610-361-5239, Fax: 610-361-5235, E-mail: lemons@neumann.edu.

Program in Pastoral Clinical Mental Health Counseling Students: 9 full-time (all women), 58 part-time (40 women); includes 17 minority (13 Black or African American, non-Hispanic/Latino; 1 Hispanic/Latino; 3 Two or more races, non-Hispanic/Latino), 1 international. Average age 47. 35 applicants, 40% accepted, 14 enrolled. *Faculty:* 8 full-time (5 women), 1 (woman) part-time/adjunct. Expenses: Contact institution. *Financial support:* Scholarships/grants and health care benefits available. Support available to part-time students. Financial award application deadline: 3/15; financial award applicants required to submit FAFSA. In 2017, 22 master's, 2 doctorates awarded. *Program availability:* Part-time, evening/weekend. Offers pastoral care specialist (Certificate); pastoral clinical mental health counseling (MS); pastoral clinical mental health counseling certificate of advanced study (Certificate); pastoral counseling (PhD); spiritual formation and direction (CSD); spiritual formation and direction supervision certificate of advanced study (Certificate). *Application deadline:* For fall admission, 8/1 for domestic students; for spring admission, 12/1 for domestic students. Applications are processed on a rolling basis. *Application fee:* $0. Electronic applications accepted. *Application Contact:* Dr. Erika K. Davis, Director of Adult and Graduate Admissions, 800-9-NEUMANN Ext. 5208, Fax: 610-361-2548, E-mail: gradadultadmiss@neumann.edu. *Director of Pastoral Clinical Mental Health Counseling Program,* Sr. Suzanne Mayer, 610-361-2292, Fax: 610-358-4525, E-mail: mayers@neumann.edu.

Program in Physical Therapy Students: 82 full-time (45 women); includes 18 minority (6 Black or African American, non-Hispanic/Latino; 1 American Indian or Alaska Native, non-Hispanic/Latino; 4 Asian, non-Hispanic/Latino; 5 Hispanic/Latino; 2 Two or more races, non-Hispanic/Latino). Average age 26. 169 applicants, 28% accepted, 32 enrolled. *Faculty:* 6 full-time (5 women), 3 part-time/adjunct (2 women). Expenses: Contact institution. *Financial support:* Scholarships/grants and health care benefits available. Support available to part-time students. Financial award application deadline: 3/15; financial award applicants required to submit FAFSA. In 2017, 25 doctorates awarded. *Program availability:* Evening/weekend. Offers physical therapy (DPT). *Application deadline:* For summer admission, 5/14 for domestic students. Applications are processed on a rolling basis. *Application fee:* $0. Electronic applications accepted. *Application Contact:* Dr. Erika K. Davis, Director of Adult and Graduate Admissions, 800-9-NEUMANN Ext. 5208, Fax: 610-361-2548, E-mail: gradadultadmiss@neumann.edu. *Program Director, Physical Therapy,* Dr. Robert E Post, 610-558-5233, Fax: 610-459-1370, E-mail: postr@neumann.edu.

NEW BRUNSWICK THEOLOGICAL SEMINARY, New Brunswick, NJ 08901-1196

General Information Independent-religious, coed, graduate-only institution. *Graduate housing:* Rooms and/or apartments available on a first-come, first-served basis to single and married students. Housing application deadline: 6/30.

GRADUATE UNITS

Graduate and Professional Programs *Program availability:* Part-time, evening/weekend. Offers pastoral care and counseling (D Min). Electronic applications accepted.

NEW CHARTER UNIVERSITY, Salt Lake City, UT 84101

General Information Proprietary, coed, comprehensive institution. *Graduate housing:* On-campus housing not available.

GRADUATE UNITS

College of Business *Program availability:* Part-time, evening/weekend, online learning. Offers finance (MBA); health care management (MBA); management (MBA). Electronic applications accepted.

College of Public Policy and Administration *Program availability:* Part-time, evening/weekend, online learning. Offers criminal justice (MS); public administration (MPA); public policy and administration (MPA, MS). Electronic applications accepted.

NEW COLLEGE OF FLORIDA, Sarasota, FL 34243

General Information State-supported, coed, comprehensive institution.

GRADUATE UNITS

Program in Data Science Offers data science (MDS).

NEW ENGLAND COLLEGE, Henniker, NH 03242-3293

General Information Independent, coed, comprehensive institution. *Graduate housing:* Room and/or apartments available on a first-come, first-served basis to single students; on-campus housing not available to married students. Housing application deadline: 5/1.

GRADUATE UNITS

Program in Community Mental Health Counseling *Program availability:* Part-time, evening/weekend. Offers human services (MS); mental health counseling (MS).

Program in Education *Program availability:* Part-time, evening/weekend. Offers higher education administration (MS, Ed D); K-12 leadership (Ed D); literacy and language arts (M Ed); meeting the needs of all learners/special education (M Ed); teacher leadership/school reform (M Ed).

Program in Management *Program availability:* Part-time, evening/weekend. Offers accounting (MSA); healthcare administration (MS); international relations (MA); marketing management (MS); nonprofit leadership (MS); project management (MS); strategic leadership (MS). Electronic applications accepted.

Program in Public Policy *Program availability:* Part-time, evening/weekend, online learning. Offers public policy (MA). Electronic applications accepted.

Program in Sports and Recreation Management: Coaching Offers sports and recreation management: coaching (MS).

Programs in Writing *Program availability:* Part-time, evening/weekend. Offers poetry (MFA); professional writing (MA). Electronic applications accepted.

NEW ENGLAND COLLEGE OF BUSINESS AND FINANCE, Boston, MA 02111-2645

General Information Independent, coed, primarily women, comprehensive institution.

GRADUATE UNITS

Program in Business Ethics and Compliance *Program availability:* Online learning. Offers business ethics and compliance (MS).

Program in Finance *Program availability:* Online learning. Offers finance (MSF).

NEW ENGLAND COLLEGE OF OPTOMETRY, Boston, MA 02115-1100

General Information Independent, coed, graduate-only institution. *Graduate housing:* On-campus housing not available. *Research affiliation:* Vistakon-Johnson & Johnson (contact lenses), Boston University School of Medicine (vision science).

GRADUATE UNITS

Graduate and Professional Programs Offers optometry (OD); vision science (MS). Electronic applications accepted.

NEW ENGLAND CONSERVATORY OF MUSIC, Boston, MA 02115-5000

General Information Independent, coed, comprehensive institution. *Graduate housing:* Room and/or apartments available on a first-come, first-served basis to single students; on-campus housing not available to married students. Housing application deadline: 6/15.

GRADUATE UNITS

Graduate Program in Music Offers music (MM, DMA, Diploma). Electronic applications accepted.

NEW ENGLAND INSTITUTE OF TECHNOLOGY, East Greenwich, RI 02818

General Information Independent, coed, comprehensive institution. *Enrollment:* 2,793 graduate, professional, and undergraduate students; 111 full-time matriculated graduate/professional students (63 women), 24 part-time matriculated graduate/professional students (15 women). *Enrollment by degree level:* 135 master's. *Graduate housing:* On-campus housing not available. *Student services:* Campus safety program, career counseling, exercise/wellness program. *Library facilities:* New England Institute of Technology Library. *Collection:* Books: 48,657 (physical), 25,463 (digital/electronic); Serial titles: 316 (physical), 92,321 (digital/electronic); Databases: 68. Weekly public service hours: 65; students can reserve study rooms.

Computer facilities: 1,300 computers available on campus for general student use. A campuswide network can be accessed from off campus. Online class registration is available.
Website: http://www.neit.edu/

General Application Contact: Michael Caruso, Director of Admissions, 800-736-7744 Ext. 3411, Fax: 401-886-0868, E-mail: mcaruso@neit.edu.

GRADUATE UNITS

Program in Applied Design Expenses: Contact institution. *Program availability:* Part-time-only, evening/weekend, 100% online, blended/hybrid learning, low-residency. Offers applied design (MAD). *Application deadline:* Applications are processed on a rolling basis. *Application fee:* $25. Electronic applications accepted. *Application Contact:* Michael Caruso, Director of Admissions, 800-736-7744 Ext. 3411, Fax: 401-886-0868, E-mail: mcaruso@neit.edu. *Senior Vice President and Provost*, Douglas H. Sherman, 401-739-5000 Ext. 3481, Fax: 401-886-0859, E-mail: dsherman@neit.edu.

Program in Construction Management Expenses: Contact institution. *Program availability:* Part-time-only, evening/weekend, 100% online, blended/hybrid learning. Offers construction management (MS). *Application deadline:* Applications are processed on a rolling basis. *Application fee:* $25. Electronic applications accepted. *Application Contact:* Michael Caruso, Director of Admissions, 800-736-7744 Ext. 3411, Fax: 401-886-0868, E-mail: mcaruso@neit.edu. *Senior Vice President and Provost*, Douglas H. Sherman, 401-739-5000 Ext. 3481, Fax: 401-886-0859, E-mail: dsherman@neit.edu.

Program in Engineering Management Expenses: Contact institution. *Program availability:* Part-time-only, evening/weekend, 100% online, blended/hybrid learning. Offers engineering management (MSEM). *Application deadline:* Applications are processed on a rolling basis. *Application fee:* $25. Electronic applications accepted. *Application Contact:* Michael Caruso, Director of Admissions, 800-736-7744 Ext. 3411, Fax: 401-886-0868, E-mail: mcaruso@neit.edu. *Senior Vice President and Provost*, Douglas H. Sherman, 401-739-5000 Ext. 3481, Fax: 401-886-0859, E-mail: dsherman@neit.edu.

Program in Information Technology Expenses: Contact institution. *Program availability:* Part-time-only, evening/weekend, 100% online, blended/hybrid learning. Offers information technology (MS). *Application deadline:* Applications are processed on a rolling basis. *Application fee:* $25. Electronic applications accepted. *Application Contact:* Michael Caruso, Director of Admissions, 800-736-7744 Ext. 3411, Fax: 401-886-0868, E-mail: mcaruso@neit.edu. *Senior Vice President and Provost*, Douglas H. Sherman, 401-739-5000 Ext. 3481, Fax: 401-886-0859, E-mail: dsherman@neit.edu.

Program in Occupational Therapy Expenses: Contact institution. *Program availability:* Part-time-only, evening/weekend, 100% online, blended/hybrid learning. Offers occupational therapy (MS). *Application deadline:* Applications are processed on a rolling basis. *Application fee:* $25. Electronic applications accepted. *Application Contact:* Michael Caruso, Director of Admissions, 800-736-7744 Ext. 3411, Fax: 401-886-0868, E-mail: mcaruso@neit.edu. *Senior Vice President and Provost*, Douglas H. Sherman, 401-739-5000 Ext. 3481, Fax: 401-886-0859, E-mail: dsherman@neit.edu.

Program in Public Health Expenses: Contact institution. *Program availability:* Part-time-only, evening/weekend, online only, 100% online. Offers public health (MPH). *Application deadline:* Applications are processed on a rolling basis. *Application fee:* $25. Electronic applications accepted. *Application Contact:* Michael Caruso, Director of Admissions, 800-736-7744 Ext. 3411, Fax: 401-886-0868, E-mail: mcaruso@neit.edu. *Senior Vice President and Provost*, Douglas H. Sherman, 401-739-5000 Ext. 3481, Fax: 401-886-0859, E-mail: dsherman@neit.edu.

NEW ENGLAND LAW–BOSTON, Boston, MA 02116-5687

General Information Independent, coed, graduate-only institution. *Enrollment by degree level:* 560 doctoral. *Graduate faculty:* 42 full-time (16 women), 85 part-time/adjunct (38 women). *Tuition:* Full-time $47,912; part-time $35,912 per year. *Required fees:* $80; $80 per unit. Tuition and fees vary according to class time and course load. *Graduate housing:* On-campus housing not available. *Student services:* Campus employment opportunities, career counseling, low-cost health insurance, services for students with disabilities, writing training. *Library facilities:* New England Law | Boston Law Library. *Collection:* Books: 97,855 (physical), 54,914 (digital/electronic); Serial titles: 2,912 (physical), 20,590 (digital/electronic); Databases: 114. Weekly public service hours: 104; students can reserve study rooms.

Computer facilities: 36 computers available on campus for general student use. A campuswide network can be accessed from off campus. Online class registration is available.
Website: http://www.nesl.edu/

General Application Contact: Michelle L'Etoile, Director of Admissions, 617-422-7210, Fax: 617-422-7201, E-mail: admit@nesl.edu.

GRADUATE UNITS

Graduate Programs Students: 380 full-time (247 women), 180 part-time (95 women); includes 195 minority (65 Black or African American, non-Hispanic/Latino; 1 American Indian or Alaska Native, non-Hispanic/Latino; 32 Asian, non-Hispanic/Latino; 69 Hispanic/Latino; 28 Two or more races, non-Hispanic/Latino), 15 international. *Faculty:* 42 full-time (16 women), 85 part-time/adjunct (38 women). Expenses: Contact institution. *Financial support:* Fellowships, Federal Work-Study, scholarships/grants, and tuition waivers (full and partial) available. Financial award application deadline: 3/18; financial award applicants required to submit FAFSA. *Program availability:* Part-time, evening/weekend. Offers American law (LL M); law (JD). *Application deadline:* For fall admission, 3/15 priority date for domestic and international students. Applications are processed on a rolling basis. *Application fee:* $65. Electronic applications accepted. *Application Contact:* Michelle L'Etoile, Director of Admissions, 617-422-7210, Fax: 617-422-7201, E-mail: admit@nesl.edu. *Dean*, John F. O'Brien, 617-422-7221, Fax: 617-422-7333.

NEW HAMPSHIRE INSTITUTE OF ART, Manchester, NH 03104

General Information Independent, coed, comprehensive institution. *Enrollment:* 402 graduate, professional, and undergraduate students; 59 full-time matriculated graduate/professional students (42 women), 6 part-time matriculated graduate/professional students (3 women). *Enrollment by degree level:* 65 master's. *Graduate faculty:* 31 part-time/adjunct (14 women). *Tuition:* Full-time $19,990. *Required fees:* $1590. One-time fee: $300 full-time. *Graduate housing:* Room and/or apartments available on a first-come, first-served basis to single students; on-campus housing not available to married students. Housing application deadline: 6/15. *Student services:* Campus employment opportunities, career counseling, free psychological counseling, services for students with disabilities, teacher training. *Library facilities:* Teti Library. *Collection:* Books: 17,000 (physical), 144,463 (digital/electronic); Serial titles: 80 (physical), 7,800 (digital/electronic); Databases: 30. Weekly public service hours: 63.

Computer facilities: 100 computers available on campus for general student use. A campuswide network can be accessed from student residence rooms and from off campus. Online class registration is available.
Website: http://www.nhia.edu/

General Application Contact: Graduate Admissions, 603-836-2122, E-mail: gradadmissions@nhia.edu.

GRADUATE UNITS

Graduate Studies Students: 59 full-time (42 women), 6 part-time (3 women); includes 2 minority (1 Asian, non-Hispanic/Latino; 1 Hispanic/Latino). Average age 43. 33 applicants, 36% accepted, 5 enrolled. *Faculty:* 31 part-time/adjunct (14 women). Expenses: Contact institution. *Financial support:* In 2017–18, 2 teaching assistantships (averaging $1,200 per year) were awarded; scholarships/grants and unspecified assistantships also available. Support available to part-time students. Financial award application deadline: 6/1; financial award applicants required to submit FAFSA. In 2017, 2 master's awarded. Offers art education (MA); creative writing (MFA); photography (MFA); teaching visual arts (MAT); visual arts (MFA). *Application deadline:* For fall admission, 5/1 priority date for domestic students; for spring admission, 11/1 priority date for domestic students. Applications are processed on a rolling basis. *Application fee:* $75. Electronic applications accepted. *Application Contact:* Moriah Billups, Graduate Admissions Coordinator, 603-836 2588, E-mail: gradadmissions@nhia.edu. *Dean of Graduate Studies*, Lucinda Bliss, 603-836-2522, E-mail: lucindabliss@nhia.edu.

NEW JERSEY CITY UNIVERSITY, Jersey City, NJ 07305-1597

General Information State-supported, coed, comprehensive institution. *Graduate housing:* On-campus housing not available.

GRADUATE UNITS

College of Professional Studies *Program availability:* Part-time, evening/weekend. Offers civil security leadership (D Sc); community health education (MS); criminal justice (MS); health administration (MS); national security studies (MS, Certificate); school health education (MS).

Debra Cannon Partridge Wolfe College of Education *Program availability:* Part-time, evening/weekend. Offers bilingual/bicultural education (MA); counselor education (MA); early childhood education (MAT); education (MA, MAT, Ed D); educational administration and supervision (MA); educational technology (MA); educational technology leadership (Ed D); elementary education (MAT); English as a second language (MA); secondary education (MAT); special education (MA); urban education (MA); urban education world language (MA).

Graduate Studies and Continuing Education *Program availability:* Part-time, evening/weekend, online learning.

School of Business *Program availability:* Part-time, evening/weekend. Offers accounting (MS, Graduate Certificate); business (MBA, MS, Graduate Certificate); finance (MBA, MS, Graduate Certificate); marketing (MBA); organizational management and leadership (MBA).

William J. Maxwell College of Arts and Sciences *Program availability:* Part-time, evening/weekend. Offers art (MFA); art education (MA); arts and sciences (MA, MFA, MM); mathematics education (MA); music education (MA); performance (MM); studio art (MFA).

NEW JERSEY INSTITUTE OF TECHNOLOGY, Newark, NJ 07102

General Information State-supported, coed, university. CGS member. *Enrollment:* 11,446 graduate, professional, and undergraduate students; 1,948 full-time matriculated graduate/professional students (561 women), 996 part-time matriculated graduate/professional students (268 women). *Enrollment by degree level:* 2,518 master's, 425 doctoral, 1 other advanced degree. *Graduate faculty:* 436 full-time (87 women), 317 part-time/adjunct (68 women). *Graduate housing:* Room and/or apartments available on a first-come, first-served basis to single students; on-campus housing not available to married students. Housing application deadline: 3/31. *Student services:* Campus employment opportunities, campus safety program, career counseling, child daycare facilities, exercise/wellness program, free psychological counseling, grant writing training, international student services, low-cost health insurance, services for students with disabilities, teacher training, writing training. *Library facilities:* Van Houten Library plus 1 other. *Collection:* Books: 137,517 (physical), 177,107 (digital/electronic); Serial titles: 55,291 (physical), 55,291 (digital/electronic); Databases: 34. Weekly public service hours: 105; students can reserve study rooms. *Research affiliation:* UT-Battele, LLC c/o ORNL, Brookhaven National Laboratory, Booz Allen Hamilton, Inc., The Wistar Institute, EPRI - Electronic Power Research Institute, ExxonMobil.

Computer facilities: Computer purchase and lease plans are available. 1,938 computers available on campus for general student use. A campuswide network can be accessed from student residence rooms and from off campus. Online class registration is available.
Website: http://www.njit.edu/

General Application Contact: Stephen Eck, Director of Admissions, 973-596-3300, Fax: 973-596-3461, E-mail: admissions@njit.edu.

GRADUATE UNITS

College of Architecture and Design Students: 40 full-time (23 women), 6 part-time (0 women); includes 10 minority (1 Black or African American, non-Hispanic/Latino; 3 Asian, non-Hispanic/Latino; 5 Hispanic/Latino; 1 Two or more races, non-Hispanic/Latino), 19 international. Average age 30. 129 applicants, 37% accepted, 10 enrolled. *Faculty:* 31 full-time (8 women), 37 part-time/adjunct (14 women). Expenses: Contact institution. *Financial support:* In 2017–18, 31 students received support, including 6 fellowships (averaging $6,825 per year), 8 teaching assistantships (averaging $24,834 per year); career-related internships or fieldwork, Federal Work-Study, institutionally sponsored loans, scholarships/grants, traineeships, unspecified assistantships, and studio assistantships (1 averaging $10,000) also available. Financial award application deadline: 1/15. In 2017, 16 master's, 4 doctorates awarded. *Program availability:* Part-time, evening/weekend. Offers architecture (M Arch, MS Arch); infrastructure planning (MIP); urban systems (PhD). *Application deadline:* For fall admission, 6/1 priority date for domestic students, 5/1 priority date for international students; for spring admission, 11/15 priority date for domestic and international students. Applications are processed on a rolling basis. *Application fee:* $75. Electronic applications accepted. *Application Contact:* Stephen Eck, Director of Admissions, 973-596-3300, Fax: 973-596-3461, E-mail: admissions@njit.edu. *Interim Dean*, Anthony W. Schuman, 973-596-6370, E-mail: anthony.w.schuman@njit.edu.

College of Science and Liberal Arts Average age 28. 504 applicants, 64% accepted, 65 enrolled. Expenses: Contact institution. *Financial support:* In 2017–18, 106 students received support, including 8 fellowships (averaging $3,436 per year), 51 research assistantships (averaging $23,452 per year), 91 teaching assistantships (averaging $25,553 per year); scholarships/grants, traineeships, and unspecified assistantships also available. Financial award application deadline: 1/15. In 2017, 81 master's, 18 doctorates, 1 other advanced degree awarded. *Program availability:* Part-time, evening/weekend. Offers applied mathematics (MS); applied physics (MS, PhD); applied statistics (MS, Certificate); biology (MS, PhD); biostatistics (MS); chemistry (MS, PhD); environmental and sustainability policy (MS); environmental science (MS, PhD); history (MA, MAT); materials science and engineering (MS, PhD); mathematical and computational finance (MS); mathematical sciences (PhD); pharmaceutical chemistry (MS); professional and technical communications (MS); technical communication essentials (Certificate). *Application deadline:* For fall admission, 6/1 priority date for domestic students, 5/1 priority date for international students; for spring admission, 11/15 priority date for domestic and international students. Applications are processed on a rolling basis. *Application fee:* $75. Electronic applications accepted. *Application*

Contact: Stephen Eck, Director of Admissions, 973-596-3300, Fax: 973-596-3461, E-mail: admissions@njit.edu. *Dean*, Dr. Kevin Belfield, 973-596-3676, Fax: 973-565-0586, E-mail: kevin.d.belfield@njit.edu.

Martin Tuchman School of Management Average age 31. 385 applicants, 52% accepted, 80 enrolled. Expenses: Contact institution. *Financial support:* In 2017–18, 7 students received support, including 1 fellowship (averaging $900 per year), 3 research assistantships (averaging $13,701 per year), 10 teaching assistantships (averaging $25,653 per year); career-related internships or fieldwork, Federal Work-Study, institutionally sponsored loans, and unspecified assistantships also available. Financial award application deadline: 1/15. In 2017, 81 master's, 11 other advanced degrees awarded. *Program availability:* Part-time, evening/weekend. Offers business administration (MBA); business data science (PhD); finance for managers (Certificate); management (MS); management essentials (Certificate); management of technology (Certificate). *Application deadline:* For fall admission, 6/1 priority date for domestic students, 5/1 priority date for international students; for spring admission, 11/15 priority date for domestic and international students. Applications are processed on a rolling basis. *Application fee:* $75. Electronic applications accepted. *Application Contact:* Stephen Eck, Director of Admissions, 973-596-3300, Fax: 973-596-3461, E-mail: admissions@njit.edu. *Interim Dean*, Dr. Reggie Caudill, 973-596-5856, Fax: 973-596-3074, E-mail: reggie.j.caudill@njit.edu.

Newark College of Engineering Average age 27. 2,959 applicants, 51% accepted, 442 enrolled. Expenses: Contact institution. *Financial support:* In 2017–18, 172 students received support, including 24 fellowships (averaging $7,124 per year), 112 research assistantships (averaging $19,407 per year), 101 teaching assistantships (averaging $24,173 per year); scholarships/grants also available. Financial award application deadline: 1/15. In 2017, 595 master's, 29 doctorates awarded. *Program availability:* Part-time, evening/weekend. Offers biomedical engineering (MS, PhD); chemical engineering (MS, PhD); computer engineering (MS, PhD); electrical engineering (MS, PhD); engineering management (MS); environmental engineering (PhD); healthcare systems management (MS); industrial engineering (MS, PhD); Internet engineering (MS); manufacturing engineering (MS); mechanical engineering (MS, PhD); occupational safety and health engineering (MS); pharmaceutical bioprocessing (MS); pharmaceutical engineering (MS); pharmaceutical systems management (MS); power and energy systems (MS); telecommunications (MS); transportation (MS, PhD). *Application deadline:* For fall admission, 6/1 priority date for domestic students, 5/1 priority date for international students; for spring admission, 11/15 priority date for domestic and international students. Applications are processed on a rolling basis. *Application fee:* $75. Electronic applications accepted. *Application Contact:* Stephen Eck, Director of Admissions, 973-596-3300, Fax: 973-596-3461, E-mail: admissions@njit.edu. *Dean*, Dr. Moshe Kam, 973-596-5534, E-mail: moshe.kam@njit.edu.

Ying Wu College of Computing Students: 818 full-time (241 women), 225 part-time (53 women); includes 162 minority (35 Black or African American, non-Hispanic/Latino; 77 Asian, non-Hispanic/Latino; 41 Hispanic/Latino; 9 Two or more races, non-Hispanic/Latino), 772 international. Average age 27. 2,666 applicants, 51% accepted, 377 enrolled. *Faculty:* 64 full-time (10 women), 38 part-time/adjunct (4 women). Expenses: Contact institution. *Financial support:* In 2017–18, 57 students received support, including 2 fellowships (averaging $23,254 per year), 47 research assistantships (averaging $24,412 per year), 44 teaching assistantships (averaging $23,528 per year); career-related internships or fieldwork, Federal Work-Study, institutionally sponsored loans, and unspecified assistantships also available. Financial award application deadline: 1/15. In 2017, 398 master's, 10 doctorates, 9 other advanced degrees awarded. *Program availability:* Part-time, evening/weekend. Offers big data management and mining (Certificate); business and information systems (Certificate); computer science (MS, PhD); data mining (Certificate); data science (MS); information security (Certificate); information systems (MS, PhD); information technology administration and security (MS); IT administration (Certificate); network security and information assurance (Certificate); software engineering analysis/design (Certificate); Web systems development (Certificate). *Application deadline:* For fall admission, 6/1 priority date for domestic students, 5/1 priority date for international students; for spring admission, 11/15 priority date for domestic and international students. Applications are processed on a rolling basis. *Application fee:* $75. Electronic applications accepted. *Application Contact:* Stephen Eck, Director of Admissions, 973-596-3300, Fax: 973-596-3461, E-mail: admissions@njit.edu. *Dean*, Dr. Craig Gotsman, 973-542-5488, Fax: 973-596-5777, E-mail: marek.rusinkiewicz@njit.edu.

NEWMAN THEOLOGICAL COLLEGE, Edmonton, AB T6V 1H3, Canada

General Information Independent-religious, coed, graduate-only institution. *Enrollment:* 26 full-time matriculated graduate/professional students (4 women), 112 part-time matriculated graduate/professional students (85 women). *Enrollment by degree level:* 134 master's, 4 other advanced degrees. *Graduate faculty:* 13 full-time (3 women), 13 part-time/adjunct (3 women). *Tuition:* Full-time $6390 Canadian dollars; part-time $639 Canadian dollars per credit. *Required fees:* $90 Canadian dollars per semester. Tuition and fees vary according to course level and campus/location. *Graduate housing:* On-campus housing not available. *Student services:* Campus employment opportunities, career counseling, free psychological counseling, services for students with disabilities. *Library facilities:* Sopchyshyn Family Library. *Collection:* Books: 70,995 (physical); Serial titles: 181 (physical); Databases: 13. Weekly public service hours: 45; students can reserve study rooms.

Computer facilities: 5 computers available on campus for general student use. A campuswide network can be accessed from student residence rooms and from off campus. X available.
Website: http://www.newman.edu/

General Application Contact: Maria Saulnier, Registrar, 780-392-2451, Fax: 780-462-4013, E-mail: registrar@newman.edu.

GRADUATE UNITS

Religious Education Programs Students: 103 part-time (81 women). Average age 40. 35 applicants, 100% accepted, 34 enrolled. *Faculty:* 5 full-time (2 women), 9 part-time/adjunct (4 women). Expenses: Contact institution. *Financial support:* In 2017–18, 9 students received support. Tuition bursaries available. Support available to part-time students. Financial award application deadline: 5/31. In 2017, 19 master's awarded. *Program availability:* Part-time, blended/hybrid learning. Offers religious education (MRE, Graduate Certificate). *Application deadline:* For fall admission, 8/21 priority date for domestic students; for winter admission, 11/22 priority date for domestic students; for spring admission, 4/18 priority date for domestic students. Applications are processed on a rolling basis. *Application fee:* $45 ($250 for international students). *Application Contact:* Maria Saulnier, Registrar, 780-392-2451, Fax: 780-462-4013, E-mail: registrar@newman.edu. *Director*, Sandra Talarico, 780-392-2450 Ext. 2214, Fax: 780-462-4013, E-mail: sandra.talarico@newman.edu.

Theology Programs Students: 26 full-time (4 women), 10 part-time (5 women). 10 applicants, 100% accepted, 8 enrolled. *Faculty:* 10 full-time (1 woman), 8 part-time/adjunct (1 woman). Expenses: Contact institution. *Financial support:* In 2017–18, 6 students received support. Tuition bursaries available. Support available to part-time students. Financial award application deadline: 5/31. In 2017, 14 master's awarded. *Program availability:* Part-time. Offers theology (M Div, M Th, MTS). *Application deadline:* For fall admission, 8/21 priority date for domestic students; for winter admission, 11/22 priority date for domestic students; for spring admission, 4/21 priority date for domestic students. Applications are processed on a rolling basis. *Application fee:* $45 ($250 for international students). *Application Contact:* Maria Saulnier, Registrar, 780-392-2451, Fax: 780-462-4013, E-mail: registrar@newman.edu. *Academic Dean/Vice President*, Dr. Ryan Topping, 780-392-2450 Ext. 2444, Fax: 780-462-4013, E-mail: ryan.topping@newman.edu.

NEWMAN UNIVERSITY, Wichita, KS 67213-2097

General Information Independent-religious, coed, comprehensive institution. *Graduate housing:* Rooms and/or apartments available on a first-come, first-served basis to single and married students. Housing application deadline: 8/1.

GRADUATE UNITS

Graduate Theology Program *Program availability:* Part-time, online learning. Offers theological studies (MTS); theology (MA).

Master of Science in Education Program *Program availability:* Part-time, evening/weekend, online learning. Offers building leadership (MS Ed); curriculum and instruction (MS Ed); organizational leadership (MS Ed). Electronic applications accepted.

MBA Program *Program availability:* Part-time. Offers finance (MBA); international business (MBA); leadership (MBA); management (MBA); management information technology (MBA). Electronic applications accepted.

School of Nursing and Allied Health Offers nurse anesthesia (MS). Electronic applications accepted.

School of Social Work *Program availability:* Online learning. Offers social work (MSW).

NEW MEXICO HIGHLANDS UNIVERSITY, Las Vegas, NM 87701

General Information State-supported, coed, comprehensive institution. CGS member. *Graduate housing:* Rooms and/or apartments guaranteed to single and married students. *Research affiliation:* Spectra Gases, Inc. (chemistry), Los Alamos National Laboratory (chemistry), Sigma Aldrich (chemistry).

GRADUATE UNITS

Graduate Studies *Program availability:* Part-time.

College of Arts and Sciences *Program availability:* Part-time. Offers arts and sciences (MA, MS); chemistry (MS); English (MA); human performance and sport (MA); media arts and computer science (MS); natural science (MS); psychology (MS); public affairs (MA); Southwest studies (MA). Electronic applications accepted.

Facundo Valdez School of Social Work *Program availability:* Part-time. Offers bilingual/bicultural clinical practice (MSW); clinical practice (MSW).

School of Business, Media and Technology Offers business administration (MBA); media arts and computer science (MA); media arts and technology (MA).

School of Education *Program availability:* Part-time. Offers curriculum and instruction (MA); educational leadership (MA); professional counseling (MA); special education (MA).

NEW MEXICO INSTITUTE OF MINING AND TECHNOLOGY, Socorro, NM 87801

General Information State-supported, coed, university. CGS member. *Enrollment:* 2,009 graduate, professional, and undergraduate students; 216 full-time matriculated graduate/professional students (66 women), 177 part-time matriculated graduate/professional students (84 women). *Enrollment by degree level:* 303 master's, 89 doctoral, 1 other advanced degree. *Graduate faculty:* 132 full-time (30 women), 38 part-time/adjunct (10 women). Tuition, state resident: full-time $6406; part-time $356 per credit. Tuition, nonresident: full-time $21,190; part-time $1177 per credit. *Required fees:* $1030. *Graduate housing:* Rooms and/or apartments available on a first-come, first-served basis to single and married students. Typical cost: $6976 (including board) for single students; $8166 (including board) for married students. Room and board charges vary according to board plan and housing facility selected. Housing application deadline: 6/1. *Student services:* Campus employment opportunities, campus safety program, career counseling, child daycare facilities, free psychological counseling, grant writing training, international student services, low-cost health insurance, multicultural affairs office, services for students with disabilities. *Library facilities:* The Skeen Library. *Collection:* Students can reserve study rooms. *Research affiliation:* Gas Technology Institute (natural gas recovery), Optical Surface Technologies LLC (custom optical components), National Center for Atmospheric Research (atmosphere research), National Radio Astronomy Observatory (astronomy), Joint Center for Materials Research (materials engineering, metallurgy).

Computer facilities: 225 computers available on campus for general student use. A campuswide network can be accessed from student residence rooms and from off campus. Online class registration is available.
Website: http://www.nmt.edu/

General Application Contact: Dr. Lorie Liebrock, Dean of Graduate Studies, 575-835-5513, Fax: 575-835-5476, E-mail: graduate@nmt.edu.

GRADUATE UNITS

Center for Graduate Studies Offers applied and industrial mathematics (PhD); astrophysics (PhD); atmospheric physics (PhD); biology (MS); chemistry (MS, PhD); computer science (MS, PhD); electrical engineering (MS); environmental engineering (MS); explosives engineering (MS); fluid and thermal sciences (MS); geobiology (PhD); geochemistry (MS, PhD); geology (MS, PhD); geophysics (MS, PhD); geotechnical engineering (MS); hydrology (MS, PhD); industrial mathematics (MS); instrumentation (MS); materials engineering (MS, PhD); mathematical physics (PhD); mathematics (MS); mechatronics systems engineering (MS); mining engineering (MS); operations research and statistics (MS); petroleum engineering (MS, PhD); physics (MS); science teaching (MST); solid mechanics (MS); STEM education (MEM). Electronic applications accepted.

NEW MEXICO STATE UNIVERSITY, Las Cruces, NM 88003-8001

General Information State-supported, coed, university. CGS member. *Enrollment:* 14,432 graduate, professional, and undergraduate students; 1,464 full-time matriculated graduate/professional students (775 women), 1,168 part-time matriculated graduate/professional students (700 women). *Enrollment by degree level:* 1,824 master's, 778 doctoral, 30 other advanced degrees. *Graduate faculty:* 508 full-time (202 women), 48 part-time/adjunct (22 women). Tuition, state resident: full-time $4390. Tuition, nonresident: full-time $15,309. *Required fees:* $853. *Graduate housing:* Rooms and/or apartments available on a first-come, first-served basis to single and married students. Typical cost: $5583 per year ($8021 including board) for single students; $9474 per year ($11,898 including board) for married students. Room and board charges vary according to board plan and housing facility selected. Housing application deadline: 7/1. *Student services:* Campus employment opportunities, campus safety program, career counseling, child daycare facilities, exercise/wellness program, free psychological counseling, grant writing training, international student services, low-cost health insurance, multicultural affairs office, services for students with disabilities, teacher training, writing training. *Library facilities:* New Mexico State University Library - Zuhl plus 1 other. *Collection:* Books: 1.2 million (physical), 160,068 (digital/electronic); Serial titles: 23,730 (physical), 135,113 (digital/electronic); Databases: 410. Weekly public service hours: 112; students can reserve study rooms. *Research affiliation:* Sandia National Laboratories (energy research, computation), NASA (STEM education research), Fred Hutchinson Cancer Research Center (cancer research), U.S. Air Force Research Laboratory (AFRL) (space weather, high energy research), U.S. Bureau of Land Management (BLM) (resource management research), Los Alamos National Laboratory (energy research, environmental sciences, information sciences).

Computer facilities: Computer purchase and lease plans are available. 708 computers available on campus for general student use. A campuswide network can be accessed from student residence rooms and from off campus. Online class registration, antivirus software; student portal online with file share/storage space, student employee clock-in, payments system, hardware rentals, short-term tablet checkout, software discounts are available.
Website: http://www.nmsu.edu/

General Application Contact: Dr. Loui Reyes, Dean, 575-646-5745, Fax: 575-646-7758, E-mail: gradinfo@nmsu.edu.

GRADUATE UNITS

College of Agricultural, Consumer and Environmental Sciences Students: 149 full-time (90 women), 45 part-time (27 women); includes 69 minority (3 Black or African American, non-Hispanic/Latino; 5 American Indian or Alaska Native, non-Hispanic/Latino; 1 Asian, non-Hispanic/Latino; 59 Hispanic/Latino; 1 Two or more races, non-Hispanic/Latino), 38 international. Average age 29. 102 applicants, 50% accepted, 38 enrolled. *Faculty:* 74 full-time (24 women), 2 part-time/adjunct (1 woman). Expenses: Contact institution. *Financial support:* In 2017–18, 153 students received support, including 2 fellowships (averaging $4,390 per year), 77 research assistantships (averaging $17,565 per year), 54 teaching assistantships (averaging $15,150 per year); career-related internships or fieldwork, Federal Work-Study, scholarships/grants, traineeships, health care benefits, and unspecified assistantships also available. Support available to part-time students. Financial award application deadline: 3/1. In 2017, 62 master's, 4 doctorates awarded. *Program availability:* Part-time. Offers agribusiness (MBA); agricultural and extension education (MA); agricultural, consumer and environmental sciences (M Ag, MA, MBA, MS, DED, PhD); agriculture (M Ag); animal science (MS, PhD); clothing, textiles, and merchandising (MS); economic development (DED); entomology, plant pathology and weed science (MS); family and child science (MS); family and consumer science education (MS); family and consumer sciences (MS); fish, wildlife and conservation ecology (MS); food science and technology (MS); horticulture (MS); hotel, restaurant, and tourism management (MS); human nutrition and dietetic sciences (MS); plant and environmental sciences (MS, PhD); range science (MS, PhD); water science management (MS). *Application deadline:* For fall admission, 8/15 for domestic and international students; for spring admission, 12/15 for domestic and international students; for summer admission, 5/20 for domestic and international students. Applications are processed on a rolling basis. *Application fee:* $40 ($50 for international students). Electronic applications accepted. *Application Contact:* Dr. Jerry Hawkes, Associate Dean/Director of Academic Programs, 575-646-1120, Fax: 575-646-5975, E-mail: jhawkes@nmsu.edu. *Dean*, Dr. Rolando A. Flores, 575-646-3748, Fax: 575-646-5975, E-mail: agdean@nmsu.edu.

College of Arts and Sciences Students: 507 full-time (231 women), 265 part-time (159 women); includes 253 minority (19 Black or African American, non-Hispanic/Latino; 7 American Indian or Alaska Native, non-Hispanic/Latino; 15 Asian, non-Hispanic/Latino; 191 Hispanic/Latino; 21 Two or more races, non-Hispanic/Latino), 183 international. Average age 32. 710 applicants, 52% accepted, 175 enrolled. *Faculty:* 219 full-time (83 women), 15 part-time/adjunct (5 women). Expenses: Contact institution. *Financial support:* In 2017–18, 489 students received support, including 32 fellowships (averaging $4,031 per year), 78 research assistantships (averaging $19,447 per year), 293 teaching assistantships (averaging $15,798 per year); career-related internships or fieldwork, Federal Work-Study, scholarships/grants, traineeships, health care benefits, and unspecified assistantships also available. Support available to part-time students. Financial award application deadline: 3/1. In 2017, 162 master's, 26 doctorates, 17 other advanced degrees awarded. *Program availability:* Part-time, online learning. Offers applied geography (MAG); art history (MA); arts and sciences (MA, MAG, MCJ, MFA, MM, MPA, MS, PhD, Graduate Certificate); astronomy (MS, PhD); bioinformatics (MS); biology (MS, PhD); biotechnology (MS); chemistry (MS, PhD); communication studies (MA); computer science (MS, PhD); conducting (MM); creative writing (MFA); criminal justice (MCJ); engineering psychology (PhD); English (MA); geological sciences (MS); government (MA); history (MA); mathematical sciences (MS, PhD); music education (MM); performance (MM); psychology (MA); public administration (MPA); public history (MA); rhetoric and professional communication (PhD); sociology (MA); space physics (MS); Spanish (MA); studio art (MFA). *Application fee:* $40 ($50 for international students). Electronic applications accepted. *Application Contact:* Dr. James Murphy, Associate Dean, 575-646-3500, Fax: 575-646-6096, E-mail: murphy@nmsu.edu. *Dean*, Dr. Enrico Pontelli, 575-646-3500, Fax: 575-646-6096, E-mail: epontell@nmsu.edu.

College of Business Students: 148 full-time (73 women), 162 part-time (92 women); includes 153 minority (6 Black or African American, non-Hispanic/Latino; 6 American Indian or Alaska Native, non-Hispanic/Latino; 9 Asian, non-Hispanic/Latino; 124 Hispanic/Latino; 1 Native Hawaiian or other Pacific Islander, non-Hispanic/Latino; 7 Two or more races, non-Hispanic/Latino), 53 international. Average age 33. 305 applicants, 78% accepted, 62 enrolled. *Faculty:* 51 full-time (13 women). Expenses: Contact institution. *Financial support:* In 2017–18, 119 students received support, including 6 fellowships (averaging $4,390 per year), 21 research assistantships (averaging $12,040 per year), 37 teaching assistantships (averaging $16,079 per year); career-related internships or fieldwork, Federal Work-Study, scholarships/grants, traineeships, health care benefits, and unspecified assistantships also available. Support available to part-time students. Financial award application deadline: 3/1. In 2017, 112 master's, 8 doctorates, 9 other advanced degrees awarded. *Program availability:* Part-time, 100% online. Offers accountancy (MACCT); agribusiness (MBA); applied statistics (MS); business (MA, MACCT, MBA, MS, DED, PhD, Graduate Certificate); business administration (PhD); economic development (DED); economics (MA); finance (MBA, Graduate Certificate); information systems (MBA); management (PhD); public utility regulation and economics (Graduate Certificate). *Application deadline:* For fall admission, 7/1 priority date for domestic students; for spring admission, 11/1 for domestic students. Applications are processed on a rolling basis. *Application fee:* $40 ($50 for international students). Electronic applications accepted. *Application Contact:* Graduate Admissions, 575-646-3121, E-mail: admissions@nmsu.edu. *Dean*, Dr. James Hoffman, 575-646-2821, Fax: 575-646-6155, E-mail: jhoffman@nmsu.edu.

College of Education Students: 254 full-time (188 women), 401 part-time (292 women); includes 397 minority (22 Black or African American, non-Hispanic/Latino; 16 American Indian or Alaska Native, non-Hispanic/Latino; 16 Asian, non-Hispanic/Latino; 331 Hispanic/Latino; 1 Native Hawaiian or other Pacific Islander, non-Hispanic/Latino; 11 Two or more races, non-Hispanic/Latino), 47 international. Average age 36. 413 applicants, 53% accepted, 135 enrolled. *Faculty:* 62 full-time (43 women), 16 part-time/adjunct (9 women). Expenses: Contact institution. *Financial support:* In 2017–18, 227 students received support, including 7 fellowships (averaging $4,390 per year), 11 research assistantships (averaging $16,015 per year), 56 teaching assistantships (averaging $13,836 per year); career-related internships or fieldwork, Federal Work-Study, scholarships/grants, traineeships, health care benefits, and unspecified assistantships also available. Support available to part-time students. Financial award application deadline: 3/1. In 2017, 167 master's, 32 doctorates, 24 other advanced degrees awarded. *Program availability:* Part-time-only, evening/weekend, blended/hybrid learning. Offers bilingual education (MA); communication disorders (MA); counseling psychology (PhD); curriculum and instruction (MA, Ed D, PhD, Ed S); early childhood education (MA); education (MA, MAT, Ed D, PhD, Ed S, Graduate Certificate); educational administration (MA); educational diagnostics (MA, Ed S); educational leadership (Ed D, PhD); kinesiology (PhD); language, literacy and culture (MA); learning design and technologies (MA); online teaching and learning (Graduate Certificate); school psychology (Ed S); special education (Ed D, PhD); teaching (MAT); teaching English to speakers of other languages (MA). *Application deadline:* For fall admission, 3/15 for international students; for spring admission, 10/15 for international students. Applications are processed on a rolling basis. *Application fee:* $40 ($50 for international students). Electronic applications accepted. *Application Contact:* Dr. David Rutledge, Graduate Education Advising, 575-646-5411, Fax: 575-646-6032, E-mail: rutledge@nmsu.edu. *Dean*, Dr. Donald Pope Davis, 575-646-5858, Fax: 575-646-6032, E-mail: dpd@nmsu.edu.

College of Engineering Students: 237 full-time (56 women), 164 part-time (32 women); includes 133 minority (14 Black or African American, non-Hispanic/Latino; 4 American Indian or Alaska Native, non-Hispanic/Latino; 11 Asian, non-Hispanic/Latino; 97 Hispanic/Latino; 7 Two or more races, non-Hispanic/Latino), 153 international. Average age 30. 311 applicants, 59% accepted, 91 enrolled. *Faculty:* 64 full-time (12 women), 3 part-time/adjunct (0 women). Expenses: Contact institution. *Financial support:* In 2017–18, 237 students received support, including 16 fellowships (averaging $3,605 per year), 83 research assistantships (averaging $14,069 per year), 70 teaching assistantships (averaging $13,146 per year); career-related internships or fieldwork, Federal Work-Study, scholarships/grants, traineeships, health care benefits, and unspecified assistantships also available. Support available to part-time students. Financial award application deadline: 3/1. In 2017, 111 master's, 27 doctorates, 8 other advanced degrees awarded. *Program availability:* Part-time. Offers aerospace engineering (MSAE); chemical and materials engineering (MS Ch E, PhD); civil and geological engineering (MSCE, PhD); engineering (MS Ch E, MS Env E, MSAE, MSCE, MSEE, MSIE, MSME, PhD, Graduate Certificate); environmental engineering (MS Env E); industrial engineering (MSIE, PhD); mechanical engineering (MSME, PhD); systems engineering (Graduate Certificate). *Application deadline:* For fall admission, 7/1 priority date for domestic students; for spring admission, 11/1 for domestic students. Applications are processed on a rolling basis. *Application fee:* $40 ($50 for international students). Electronic applications accepted. *Application Contact:* Graduate Admissions, 575-646-3121, E-mail: admissions@nmsu.edu. *Dean*, Dr. Lakshmi Reddi, 575-646-7234, Fax: 575-646-3549, E-mail: engrdean@nmsu.edu.

Klipsch School of Electrical and Computer Engineering Students: 69 full-time (16 women), 60 part-time (13 women); includes 46 minority (3 Black or African American, non-Hispanic/Latino; 6 Asian, non-Hispanic/Latino; 35 Hispanic/Latino; 2 Two or more races, non-Hispanic/Latino), 49 international. Average age 31. 90 applicants, 63% accepted, 24 enrolled. *Faculty:* 18 full-time (1 woman), 2 part-time/adjunct (0 women). Expenses: Contact institution. *Financial support:* In 2017–18, 72 students received support, including 1 fellowship (averaging $4,390 per year), 21 research assistantships (averaging $11,906 per year), 20 teaching assistantships (averaging $12,511 per year); career-related internships or fieldwork, Federal Work-Study, scholarships/grants, traineeships, health care benefits, and unspecified assistantships also available. Support available to part-time students. Financial award application deadline: 3/1. In 2017, 30 master's, 7 doctorates, 3 other advanced degrees awarded. *Program availability:* Part-time, evening/weekend, 100% online. Offers electrical and computer engineering (MSEE, PhD, Graduate Certificate). *Application deadline:* For fall admission, 3/1 priority date for domestic and international students; for spring admission, 8/1 priority date for domestic and international students. Applications are processed on a rolling basis. *Application fee:* $40 ($50 for international students). Electronic applications accepted. *Application Contact:* 575-646-3115, Fax: 575-646-1435, E-mail: eceoffice@nmsu.edu. *Department Head*, Dr. Satishkumar Ranade, 575-646-3115, Fax: 575-646-1435, E-mail: sranade@nmsu.edu.

College of Health and Social Services Students: 145 full-time (125 women), 127 part-time (98 women); includes 154 minority (15 Black or African American, non-Hispanic/Latino; 4 American Indian or Alaska Native, non-Hispanic/Latino; 9 Asian, non-Hispanic/Latino; 121 Hispanic/Latino; 5 Two or more races, non-Hispanic/Latino), 6 international. Average age 37. 175 applicants, 69% accepted, 64 enrolled. *Faculty:* 31 full-time (25 women), 12 part-time/adjunct (7 women). Expenses: Contact institution. *Financial support:* In 2017–18, 83 students received support, including 15 research assistantships (averaging $11,173 per year), 10 teaching assistantships (averaging $8,965 per year); career-related internships or fieldwork, Federal Work-Study, scholarships/grants, traineeships, health care benefits, and unspecified assistantships also available. Support available to part-time students. Financial award application deadline: 3/1. In 2017, 90 master's, 9 doctorates, 10 other advanced degrees awarded. *Program availability:* Part-time, evening/weekend, online learning. Offers health and social services (MPH, MSN, MSW, DNP, PhD, Graduate Certificate); public health (MPH, Graduate Certificate). *Application deadline:* For fall admission, 7/1 priority date for domestic students. Applications are processed on a rolling basis. *Application fee:* $40 ($50 for international students). Electronic applications accepted. *Application Contact:* Graduate Admissions, 575-646-3121, E-mail: admissions@nmsu.edu. *Dean*, Dr. Donna Wagner, 575-646-3526, Fax: 575-646-6166, E-mail: dlwagner@nmsu.edu.

School of Nursing Students: 29 full-time (26 women), 68 part-time (57 women); includes 46 minority (10 Black or African American, non-Hispanic/Latino; 6 Asian, non-Hispanic/Latino; 29 Hispanic/Latino; 1 Two or more races, non-Hispanic/Latino), 1 international. Average age 42. 47 applicants, 81% accepted, 25 enrolled. *Faculty:*

11 full-time (all women). Expenses: Contact institution. *Financial support:* In 2017–18, 22 students received support, including 5 teaching assistantships (averaging $11,249 per year); career-related internships or fieldwork, Federal Work-Study, scholarships/grants, traineeships, health care benefits, and unspecified assistantships also available. Support available to part-time students. Financial award application deadline: 3/1. In 2017, 3 master's, 9 doctorates, 5 other advanced degrees awarded. *Program availability:* Part-time, blended/hybrid learning. Offers family nurse practitioner (DNP, Graduate Certificate); nursing administration (MSN); nursing science (PhD); psychiatric/mental health nurse practitioner (DNP, Graduate Certificate). *Application deadline:* For fall admission, 2/1 priority date for domestic students, 2/1 for international students. *Application fee:* $40 ($50 for international students). Electronic applications accepted. *Application Contact:* Alyce Kolenovsky, 575-646-3812, Fax: 575-646-2167, E-mail: nursing@nmsu.edu. *Director*, Dr. Alexa Doig, 575-646-3812, Fax: 575-646-2167, E-mail: adoig@nmsu.edu.

School of Social Work Students: 96 full-time (81 women), 8 part-time (all women); includes 76 minority (3 Black or African American, non-Hispanic/Latino; 2 American Indian or Alaska Native, non-Hispanic/Latino; 1 Asian, non-Hispanic/Latino; 67 Hispanic/Latino; 3 Two or more races, non-Hispanic/Latino). Average age 32. 79 applicants, 70% accepted, 36 enrolled. *Faculty:* 10 full-time (8 women), 9 part-time/adjunct (6 women). Expenses: Contact institution. *Financial support:* In 2017–18, 46 students received support, including 7 research assistantships (averaging $8,482 per year), 1 teaching assistantship (averaging $8,482 per year); career-related internships or fieldwork, Federal Work-Study, scholarships/grants, traineeships, health care benefits, and unspecified assistantships also available. Support available to part-time students. Financial award application deadline: 3/1. In 2017, 68 master's awarded. *Program availability:* Part-time, online learning. Offers social work (MSW). *Application deadline:* For fall admission, 1/16 priority date for domestic students, 2/16 priority date for international students. Applications are processed on a rolling basis. *Application fee:* $40 ($50 for international students). Electronic applications accepted. *Application Contact:* Dr. Wanda Whittlesey-Jerome, Program Coordinator, 575-646-0322, Fax: 575-646-4116, E-mail: wkjerome@nmsu.edu. *Interim Director*, Dr. Ivan de la Rosa, 575-646-2143, Fax: 575-646-4116, E-mail: lilo@nmsu.edu.

Graduate School Students: 41 full-time (19 women), 16 part-time (8 women); includes 11 minority (all Hispanic/Latino), 24 international. Average age 35. 36 applicants, 64% accepted, 8 enrolled. *Faculty:* 7 full-time (2 women). Expenses: Contact institution. *Financial support:* In 2017–18, 43 students received support, including 5 fellowships (averaging $4,390 per year), 6 research assistantships (averaging $22,529 per year), 5 teaching assistantships (averaging $17,530 per year); career-related internships or fieldwork, Federal Work-Study, scholarships/grants, traineeships, health care benefits, and unspecified assistantships also available. Support available to part-time students. Financial award application deadline: 3/1. In 2017, 7 master's, 5 doctorates awarded. *Program availability:* Part-time, evening/weekend, online learning. Offers interdisciplinary studies (MA, MS, PhD); molecular biology (MS, PhD); water science management (MS, PhD). *Application fee:* $40 ($50 for international students). Electronic applications accepted. *Application Contact:* Graduate Admissions, 575-646-3121, E-mail: admissions@nmsu.edu. *Dean*, Dr. Loui Reyes, 575-646-5746, Fax: 575-646-7758, E-mail: gradinfo@nmsu.edu.

NEW ORLEANS BAPTIST THEOLOGICAL SEMINARY, New Orleans, LA 70126-4858

General Information Independent-religious, coed, primarily men, comprehensive institution. *Graduate housing:* Rooms and/or apartments available to single and married students.

GRADUATE UNITS

Graduate and Professional Programs *Program availability:* Evening/weekend. Offers theology (M Div, MA, MACE, MAMFC, MMCM, D Min, DEM, DMA, PhD).

Division of Biblical Studies Offers biblical studies (M Div, MA, PhD).

Division of Christian Education Ministries *Program availability:* Evening/weekend, online learning. Offers Christian education (M Div, MACE, D Min, DEM, PhD).

Division of Church Music Ministries *Program availability:* Online learning. Offers church music ministries (M Div, MMCM, DMA).

Division of Pastoral Ministries *Program availability:* Online learning. Offers pastoral ministries (M Div, MAMFC, D Min, PhD).

Division of Theological and Historical Studies *Program availability:* Online learning. Offers theological and historical studies (M Div, MA, D Min, PhD).

NEW SAINT ANDREWS COLLEGE, Moscow, ID 83843

General Information Independent-religious, coed, comprehensive institution. *Enrollment:* 158 graduate, professional, and undergraduate students; 12 full-time matriculated graduate/professional students (3 women), 8 part-time matriculated graduate/professional students (5 women). *Enrollment by degree level:* 19 master's, 1 other advanced degree. *Graduate faculty:* 12 part-time/adjunct (0 women). *Tuition:* Full-time $7600; part-time $475 per credit. *Graduate housing:* On-campus housing not available. *Student services:* Campus employment opportunities, career counseling, international student services. *Library facilities:* Tyndale Library plus 1 other. *Collection:* Students can reserve study rooms.

Computer facilities: 4 computers available on campus for general student use. A campuswide network can be accessed from off campus. Online class registration is available.
Website: http://www.nsa.edu/

General Application Contact: Brenda Schlect, Director of Admissions, 208-882-1566 Ext. 113, Fax: 208-882-4293, E-mail: admissions@nsa.edu.

GRADUATE UNITS

Graduate School Students: 12 full-time (3 women), 8 part-time (5 women), 1 international. Average age 25. 15 applicants, 53% accepted, 7 enrolled. *Faculty:* 12 part-time/adjunct (0 women). Expenses: Contact institution. In 2017, 3 master's awarded. *Program availability:* Part-time, blended/hybrid learning. Offers classical Christian studies (Graduate Certificate); creative writing (MFA); theology and letters (MA). *Application deadline:* For fall admission, 12/1 for domestic students. Applications are processed on a rolling basis. *Application fee:* $50. Electronic applications accepted. *Application Contact:* Brenda Schlect, Director of Admissions, 208-882-1566 Ext. 113, Fax: 208-882-4293, E-mail: admissions@nsa.edu. *President*, Benjamin Merkle, 208-882-1566 Ext. 104, E-mail: bmerkle@nsa.edu.

THE NEW SCHOOL, New York, NY 10011

General Information Independent, coed, university. *Enrollment by degree level:* 2,606 master's, 480 doctoral, 122 other advanced degrees. *Graduate faculty:* 285 full-time (134 women), 357 part-time/adjunct (167 women). *Tuition:* Full-time $44,247; part-time $1795 per credit. *Required fees:* $360; $360 per year. $180 per semester. Part-time tuition and fees vary according to course load and program. *Graduate housing:* Room and/or apartments available on a first-come, first-served basis to single students; on-campus housing not available to married students. Typical cost: $15,000 per year ($17,500 including board). Room and board charges vary according to board plan, campus/location and housing facility selected. Housing application deadline: 6/15. *Student services:* Campus employment opportunities, campus safety program, career counseling, exercise/wellness program, free psychological counseling, grant writing training, international student services, low-cost health insurance, multicultural affairs office, services for students with disabilities, writing training. *Research affiliation:* The Goldman Sachs Group, Inc., Siemens, Raytheon Corporation, National Geospatial-Intelligence Agency, Environmental Systems Research Institute, Dow Jones & Company, Inc.
Website: http://www.newschool.edu/

General Application Contact: Heather Fomin, Assistant Vice President of Enrollment, 212-229-5155 Ext. 3230, E-mail: fominh@newschool.edu.

GRADUATE UNITS

College of Performing Arts Students: 365 full-time (222 women), 3 part-time (2 women); includes 72 minority (16 Black or African American, non-Hispanic/Latino; 1 American Indian or Alaska Native, non-Hispanic/Latino; 18 Asian, non-Hispanic/Latino; 27 Hispanic/Latino; 1 Native Hawaiian or other Pacific Islander, non-Hispanic/Latino; 9 Two or more races, non-Hispanic/Latino), 176 international. Average age 26. 1,026 applicants, 46% accepted, 178 enrolled. *Faculty:* 12 full-time (6 women), 170 part-time/adjunct (75 women). Expenses: Contact institution. *Financial support:* In 2017–18, 319 students received support, including 2 fellowships (averaging $12,500 per year), 4 research assistantships (averaging $2,500 per year), 4 teaching assistantships (averaging $2,828 per year); career-related internships or fieldwork and scholarships/grants also available. Support available to part-time students. Financial award application deadline: 2/1; financial award applicants required to submit FAFSA. In 2017, 79 master's, 19 other advanced degrees awarded. *Program availability:* Part-time. Offers performing arts (MFA, MM, Advanced Diploma). *Application deadline:* For fall admission, 1/15 priority date for domestic and international students; for spring admission, 10/15 priority date for domestic and international students. Applications are processed on a rolling basis. *Application fee:* $50. Electronic applications accepted. *Application Contact:* Amanda Hosking, Director of Admission, College of Performing Arts, 212-229-5150, E-mail: copaadmissions@newschool.edu. *Executive Dean, College of Performing Arts*, Richard Kessler, 212-580-0210 Ext. 4848, E-mail: richardkessler@newschool.edu.

Mannes School of Music Students: 305 full-time (189 women), 2 part-time (1 woman); includes 53 minority (7 Black or African American, non-Hispanic/Latino; 1 American Indian or Alaska Native, non-Hispanic/Latino; 16 Asian, non-Hispanic/Latino; 20 Hispanic/Latino; 1 Native Hawaiian or other Pacific Islander, non-Hispanic/Latino; 8 Two or more races, non-Hispanic/Latino), 169 international. Average age 26. 845 applicants, 51% accepted, 157 enrolled. *Faculty:* 9 full-time (4 women), 128 part-time/adjunct (53 women). Expenses: Contact institution. *Financial support:* In 2017–18, 256 students received support, including 4 research assistantships (averaging $2,500 per year), 3 teaching assistantships (averaging $2,282 per year); career-related internships or fieldwork, Federal Work-Study, scholarships/grants, and unspecified assistantships also available. Support available to part-time students. Financial award application deadline: 2/1; financial award applicants required to submit FAFSA. In 2017, 60 master's, 20 Advanced Diplomas awarded. *Program availability:* Part-time. Offers composition (MM, Advanced Diploma); guitar (MM, Advanced Diploma); harpsichord (MM, Advanced Diploma); music theory (MM); orchestral conducting (MM, Advanced Diploma); orchestral instruments (MM, Advanced Diploma); piano (MM, Advanced Diploma); piano and collaborative piano (MM, Advanced Diploma); theory (Advanced Diploma); voice (MM, Advanced Diploma). *Application deadline:* For fall admission, 12/1 priority date for domestic and international students; for spring admission, 10/15 priority date for domestic and international students. Applications are processed on a rolling basis. *Application fee:* $50. Electronic applications accepted. *Application Contact:* Amanda Hosking, Director of Admission, College of Performing Arts, 212-229-5150 Ext. 4805, E-mail: performingarts@newschool.edu. *Executive Dean, College of Performing Arts*, Richard Kessler, 212-580-0210 Ext. 4848, E-mail: richardkessler@newschool.edu.

School of Drama Students: 60 full-time (33 women), 1 (woman) part-time; includes 19 minority (9 Black or African American, non-Hispanic/Latino; 2 Asian, non-Hispanic/Latino; 7 Hispanic/Latino; 1 Two or more races, non-Hispanic/Latino), 7 international. Average age 27. 181 applicants, 21% accepted, 21 enrolled. *Faculty:* 31 part-time/adjunct (19 women). Expenses: Contact institution. *Financial support:* In 2017–18, 61 students received support, including 2 fellowships (averaging $12,500 per year), 1 teaching assistantship (averaging $4,466 per year); career-related internships or fieldwork, Federal Work-Study, scholarships/grants, and unspecified assistantships also available. Support available to part-time students. Financial award application deadline: 2/1; financial award applicants required to submit FAFSA. In 2017, 19 master's awarded. *Program availability:* Part-time. Offers acting (MFA); directing (MFA); playwriting (MFA). *Application deadline:* For fall admission, 12/1 priority date for domestic and international students; for spring admission, 1/15 for domestic students, 1/15 priority date for international students. Applications are processed on a rolling basis. *Application fee:* $50. Electronic applications accepted. *Application Contact:* Marlon Meikle, Assistant Director of Admissions, College of Performing Arts, 212-229-5859 Ext. 4828, E-mail: performingarts@newschool.edu. *Dean, School of Drama*, Pippin Parker, 212-229-5859 Ext. 2636, E-mail: parkerp@newschool.edu.

The New School for Social Research Students: 648 full-time (338 women), 155 part-time (92 women); includes 124 minority (21 Black or African American, non-Hispanic/Latino; 25 Asian, non-Hispanic/Latino; 55 Hispanic/Latino; 23 Two or more races, non-Hispanic/Latino), 279 international. Average age 31. 880 applicants, 76% accepted, 190 enrolled. *Faculty:* 73 full-time (34 women), 14 part-time/adjunct (2 women). Expenses: Contact institution. *Financial support:* In 2017–18, 592 students received support, including 49 fellowships (averaging $38,451 per year), 28 research assistantships (averaging $13,911 per year), 146 teaching assistantships with full and partial tuition reimbursements available (averaging $8,625 per year); career-related internships or fieldwork, Federal Work-Study, scholarships/grants, and tuition waivers (full and partial) also available. Support available to part-time students. Financial award application deadline: 2/1; financial award applicants required to submit FAFSA. In 2017, 152 master's, 60 doctorates awarded. *Program availability:* Part-time. Offers anthropology (MA, PhD); clinical psychology (PhD); cognitive, social, and developmental psychology (PhD); economics (MA, MS, PhD); global political economy and finance (MA); historical studies (MA, PhD); liberal studies (MA); philosophy (MA); politics (M Phil, MA, PhD); psychoanalysis (PhD); psychology (MA); social research (M Phil, MA, MS, PhD); sociology (M Phil, MA, PhD). *Application deadline:* For fall admission, 6/15 priority date for domestic and international students; for spring admission, 10/15 priority date for domestic and international students. Applications are processed on a rolling basis. *Application fee:* $50. Electronic applications accepted. *Application Contact:* Dana Messinger, Director of Graduate Admission, 212-229-5150 Ext. 2300, E-mail: messingd@newschool.edu. *Dean, The New School for Social Research*, Dr. William Milberg, 212-229-5777, E-mail: milbergw@newschool.edu.

Parsons Paris Students: 35 full-time (32 women), 3 part-time (2 women); includes 9 minority (2 Black or African American, non-Hispanic/Latino; 3 Asian, non-Hispanic/Latino; 3 Hispanic/Latino; 1 Two or more races, non-Hispanic/Latino), 20 international. Average age 26. 42 applicants, 93% accepted, 24 enrolled. *Faculty:* 5 full-time (2 women), 46 part-time/adjunct (31 women). Expenses: Contact institution. *Financial support:* In 2017–18, 29 students received support. Career-related internships or fieldwork and scholarships/grants available. Financial award application deadline: 2/1; financial award applicants required to submit FAFSA. In 2017, 15 master's awarded. *Program availability:* Part-time. Offers art and design (MA); fashion studies (MA); history of design and curatorial studies (MA). *Application deadline:* For fall admission, 1/1 priority date for domestic and international students. Applications are processed on a rolling basis. *Application fee:* $50. Electronic applications accepted. *Application Contact:* Mike Fakih, Director of Admissions, Parsons Paris, 33 176 21 76 67, E-mail: thinkparsonsparis@newschool.edu. *Dean*, Florence Leclerc-Dickler, 33-176217661, E-mail: leclercf@newschool.edu.

Parsons School of Design Students: 890 full-time (643 women), 97 part-time (65 women); includes 192 minority (49 Black or African American, non-Hispanic/Latino; 4 American Indian or Alaska Native, non-Hispanic/Latino; 67 Asian, non-Hispanic/Latino; 59 Hispanic/Latino; 2 Native Hawaiian or other Pacific Islander, non-Hispanic/Latino; 11 Two or more races, non-Hispanic/Latino), 546 international. Average age 27. 2,280 applicants, 58% accepted, 489 enrolled. *Faculty:* 78 full-time (37 women), 119 part-time/adjunct (59 women). Expenses: Contact institution. *Financial support:* In 2017–18, 599 students received support, including 93 teaching assistantships (averaging $5,712 per year); career-related internships or fieldwork, Federal Work-Study, scholarships/grants, unspecified assistantships, and travel funding; tuition waivers for students who are also New School employees also available. Support available to part-time students. Financial award application deadline: 2/1; financial award applicants required to submit FAFSA. In 2017, 406 master's, 5 other advanced degrees awarded. *Program availability:* Part-time. Offers architecture (M Arch); business of design (Advanced Certificate); communication design (MPS); data visualization (MS); design (M Arch, MA, MFA, MPS, MS, Advanced Certificate); design and technology (MFA); design and urban ecologies (MS); design studies (MA); fashion design and society (MFA); fashion studies (MA); fine arts (MFA); history of design and curatorial studies (MA); industrial design (MFA); interior design (MFA); interior design/lighting design (MFA); interior/lighting design (MFA); lighting design (MFA); photography (MFA); strategic design and management (MS); theories of urban practice (MA); transdisciplinary design (MFA). *Application deadline:* For fall admission, 1/1 priority date for domestic and international students; for summer admission, 1/1 priority date for domestic and international students. Applications are processed on a rolling basis. *Application fee:* $50. Electronic applications accepted. *Application Contact:* Courtney Malenius, Director of Graduate Admission, 212-229-5150 Ext. 4011, E-mail: thinkparsonsgrad@newschool.edu. *Executive Dean, Parsons School of Design*, Joel Towers, 212-229-8950 Ext. 4393, E-mail: towersj@newschool.edu.

Schools of Public Engagement Students: 684 full-time (494 women), 366 part-time (255 women); includes 391 minority (163 Black or African American, non-Hispanic/Latino; 3 American Indian or Alaska Native, non-Hispanic/Latino; 42 Asian, non-Hispanic/Latino; 148 Hispanic/Latino; 1 Native Hawaiian or other Pacific Islander, non-Hispanic/Latino; 34 Two or more races, non-Hispanic/Latino), 215 international. Average age 30. 1,266 applicants, 84% accepted, 382 enrolled. *Faculty:* 53 full-time (27 women), 113 part-time/adjunct (48 women). Expenses: Contact institution. *Financial support:* In 2017–18, 771 students received support, including 28 teaching assistantships (averaging $5,005 per year); career-related internships or fieldwork, Federal Work-Study, scholarships/grants, and unspecified assistantships also available. Support available to part-time students. Financial award application deadline: 2/1; financial award applicants required to submit FAFSA. In 2017, 463 master's, 1 doctorate, 58 other advanced degrees awarded. *Program availability:* Part-time, 100% online. Offers cities and social justice (MA); conflict and security (MA); creative writing (MFA); development (MA); documentary media studies (Graduate Certificate); environmental policy and sustainability management (MS); governance and rights (MA); international affairs (MS); leadership and change (Graduate Certificate); media and culture (MA); media management (MS, Graduate Certificate); media studies (MA); nonprofit management (MS); organizational change management (MS); organizational development (Graduate Certificate); public and urban policy (PhD); public engagement (MA, MFA, MS, PhD, Graduate Certificate); teaching English to speakers of other languages (MA). *Application deadline:* For fall admission, 1/15 priority date for domestic and international students; for spring admission, 10/15 priority date for domestic and international students. Applications are processed on a rolling basis. *Application fee:* $50. Electronic applications accepted. *Application Contact:* Merida Gasbarro, Senior Director of Admissions, 212-229-5150 Ext. 3230, E-mail: escandom@newschool.edu. *Executive Dean, Schools of Public Engagement*, Mary Watson, 212-229-5613 Ext. 2130, E-mail: watsonm@newschool.edu.

NEWSCHOOL OF ARCHITECTURE AND DESIGN, San Diego, CA 92101-6634

General Information Proprietary, coed, primarily men, comprehensive institution. *Research affiliation:* Academy of Neuroscience for Architecture (neuroscience and architecture).

GRADUATE UNITS

Program in Architecture *Program availability:* Part-time, online learning. Offers architecture (M Arch, MS).

Program in Construction Management *Program availability:* Part-time, online learning. Offers construction management (MCM). Electronic applications accepted.

NEW YORK ACADEMY OF ART, New York, NY 10013-2911

General Information Independent, coed, graduate-only institution. *Enrollment by degree level:* 109 master's. *Graduate faculty:* 5 full-time (1 woman), 31 part-time/adjunct (13 women). *Tuition:* Full-time $37,436; part-time $1248 per credit. *Required fees:* $1500; $750 per semester. *Graduate housing:* On-campus housing not available. *Student services:* Campus employment opportunities, campus safety program, career counseling, grant writing training, international student services, services for students with disabilities, writing training. *Library facilities:* New York Academy of Art Library. *Collection:* Books: 9,937 (physical); Serial titles: 6 (digital/electronic); Databases: 37. Weekly public service hours: 65.

Computer facilities: 14 computers available on campus for general student use. A campuswide network can be accessed. Online class registration is available. Website: http://www.nyaa.edu/

General Application Contact: Jessica Augier, Admissions Officer, 212-842-5972, E-mail: admissions@nyaa.edu.

GRADUATE UNITS

Master of Fine Arts Program Students: 109 full-time (67 women); includes 19 minority (3 Black or African American, non-Hispanic/Latino; 2 American Indian or Alaska Native, non-Hispanic/Latino; 4 Asian, non-Hispanic/Latino; 8 Hispanic/Latino; 1 Native Hawaiian or other Pacific Islander, non-Hispanic/Latino; 1 Two or more races, non-Hispanic/Latino), 33 international. Average age 30. 161 applicants, 57% accepted, 60 enrolled. *Faculty:* 5 full-time (1 woman), 31 part-time/adjunct (13 women). Expenses: Contact institution. *Financial support:* In 2017–18, 88 students received support, including 3 fellowships (averaging $10,000 per year); career-related internships or fieldwork, Federal Work-Study, and scholarships/grants also available. Financial award application deadline: 4/15; financial award applicants required to submit FAFSA. In 2017, 56 master's awarded. Offers anatomy (MFA); drawing (MFA); fine arts (MFA); painting (MFA); printmaking (MFA); sculpture (MFA). *Application deadline:* For fall admission, 1/17 priority date for domestic and international students. *Application fee:* $80. Electronic applications accepted. *Application Contact:* Katie Hemmer, Director of Admissions/Registrar, 212-842-5961, E-mail: khemmer@nyaa.edu. *President*, David Kratz, 212-966-0300.

NEW YORK CHIROPRACTIC COLLEGE, Seneca Falls, NY 13148-0800

General Information Independent, coed, graduate-only institution. *Graduate housing:* Rooms and/or apartments available on a first-come, first-served basis to single and married students. *Research affiliation:* Foot Levelers, Inc. (orthotics research), Atrium Innovations (nutrition), Nimmo Education Foundation (muscle physiology).

GRADUATE UNITS

Doctor of Chiropractic Program Offers chiropractic (DC). Electronic applications accepted.

Finger Lakes School of Acupuncture and Oriental Medicine Offers acupuncture (MS); acupuncture and Oriental medicine (MS). Electronic applications accepted.

Program in Applied Clinical Nutrition *Program availability:* Part-time, evening/weekend. Offers applied clinical nutrition (MS). Electronic applications accepted.

Program in Clinical Anatomy Offers clinical anatomy (MS). Electronic applications accepted.

Program in Human Anatomy and Physiology Instruction *Program availability:* Online learning. Offers human anatomy and physiology (MS).

NEW YORK COLLEGE OF HEALTH PROFESSIONS, Syosset, NY 11791-4413

General Information Independent, coed, comprehensive institution. *Graduate housing:* On-campus housing not available. *Research affiliation:* North Shore Hospital (acupuncture).

GRADUATE UNITS

Graduate School of Oriental Medicine *Program availability:* Part-time. Offers acupuncture (MS); Oriental medicine (MS).

NEW YORK COLLEGE OF PODIATRIC MEDICINE, New York, NY 10035

General Information Independent, coed, graduate-only institution. *Graduate housing:* Rooms and/or apartments available on a first-come, first-served basis to single and married students. Housing application deadline: 8/15. *Research affiliation:* Cyberlogics (ultrasound use), Novartis Pharmaceuticals (fungal diseases of nail), Prescription Dispensing Laboratories (topical verapamil), Anodyne Corporation (light energy applications).

GRADUATE UNITS

Professional Program Offers podiatric medicine (DPM).

NEW YORK COLLEGE OF TRADITIONAL CHINESE MEDICINE, Mineola, NY 11501

General Information Independent, coed, graduate-only institution.

GRADUATE UNITS

Graduate Programs Offers Oriental medicine (MAOM).

NEW YORK FILM ACADEMY, Burbank, CA 91505

General Information Independent, coed, comprehensive institution.

GRADUATE UNITS

Program in Filmmaking–Los Angeles Offers acting for film (MFA); cinematography (MFA); documentary film (MFA); film and media production (MA); filmmaking (MFA); game design (MFA); photography (MFA); producing (MA, MFA); screenwriting (MA, MFA).

Program in Filmmaking–South Beach, Florida Offers acting for film (MFA); cinematography (MFA); documentary film (MFA); film and media production (MA); filmmaking (MFA); game design (MFA); photography (MFA); producing (MA, MFA); screenwriting (MA, MFA).

NEW YORK INSTITUTE OF TECHNOLOGY, Old Westbury, NY 11568-8000

General Information Independent, coed, comprehensive institution. *Enrollment:* 7,422 graduate, professional, and undergraduate students; 2,985 full-time matriculated graduate/professional students (1,485 women), 732 part-time matriculated graduate/professional students (363 women). *Enrollment by degree level:* 2,048 master's, 1,608 doctoral, 61 other advanced degrees. *Graduate faculty:* 124 full-time (47 women), 145 part-time/adjunct (68 women). *Tuition:* Full-time $23,130; part-time $1285 per credit. *Required fees:* $215; $175 per credit. Full-time tuition and fees vary according to degree level, campus/location and program. Part-time tuition and fees vary according to course load, campus/location and program. *Graduate housing:* Room and/or apartments available on a first-come, first-served basis to single students; on-campus housing not available to married students. Typical cost: $9320 per year ($14,290 including board). Room and board charges vary according to board plan, campus/location and housing facility selected. *Student services:* Campus employment opportunities, campus safety program, career counseling, exercise/wellness program, free psychological counseling, international student services, low-cost health insurance, services for students with disabilities, writing training. *Library facilities:* George and Gertrude Wisser Memorial Library plus 3 others. *Collection:* Books: 89,426 (physical), 70,248 (digital/electronic); Serial titles: 2,279 (physical), 23,926 (digital/electronic). Weekly public service hours: 78; students can reserve study rooms.

Computer facilities: 1,250 computers available on campus for general student use. A campuswide network can be accessed from student residence rooms and from off campus. Online class registration is available.
Website: http://www.nyit.edu/

General Application Contact: Alice Dolitsky, Director, Graduate Admissions, 516-686-7520, Fax: 516-686-1116, E-mail: nyitgrad@nyit.edu.

GRADUATE UNITS

College of Arts and Sciences Students: 119 full-time (78 women), 48 part-time (28 women); includes 29 minority (16 Black or African American, non-Hispanic/Latino; 2 Asian, non-Hispanic/Latino; 9 Hispanic/Latino; 2 Two or more races, non-Hispanic/Latino), 117 international. Average age 27. 149 applicants, 79% accepted, 46 enrolled. *Faculty:* 16 full-time (8 women), 23 part-time/adjunct (9 women). Expenses: Contact institution. *Financial support:* Career-related internships or fieldwork, Federal Work-Study, scholarships/grants, tuition waivers (full and partial), and unspecified assistantships available. Support available to part-time students. Financial award application deadline: 2/15; financial award applicants required to submit FAFSA. In 2017, 123 master's awarded. *Program availability:* Part-time, evening/weekend. Offers arts and sciences (MA, MFA); communication arts (MA); computer graphics (MFA). *Application deadline:* For fall admission, 6/1 for domestic and international students. Applications are processed on a rolling basis. *Application fee:* $50. Electronic applications accepted. *Application Contact:* Alice Dolitsky, Director, Graduate Admissions, 516-686-1316, Fax: 516-686-1116, E-mail: nyitgrad@nyit.edu. *Interim Dean*, Dr. Daniel Quigley, 516-686-7756, E-mail: dquigley@nyit.edu.

College of Osteopathic Medicine Students: 1,484 full-time (707 women); includes 649 minority (47 Black or African American, non-Hispanic/Latino; 540 Asian, non-Hispanic/Latino; 44 Hispanic/Latino; 18 Two or more races, non-Hispanic/Latino). Average age 27. 7,036 applicants, 13% accepted, 436 enrolled. *Faculty:* 91 full-time, 33 part-time/adjunct. Expenses: Contact institution. *Financial support:* Federal Work-Study and scholarships/grants available. Financial award application deadline: 2/15; financial award applicants required to submit FAFSA. In 2017, 16 Certificates awarded. Offers global health (Certificate). *Application deadline:* For fall admission, 2/1 for domestic students. *Application fee:* $80. Electronic applications accepted. *Application Contact:* Gina Moses, Director, Admissions, 516-686-3997, E-mail: gmoses@nyit.edu. *Dean*, Dr. Wolfgang Gilliar, 516-686-3722, Fax: 516-686-3830, E-mail: wgilliar@nyit.edu.

School of Architecture and Design Students: 14 full-time (11 women), all international. Average age 26. 45 applicants, 44% accepted, 8 enrolled. *Faculty:* 3 full-time (1 woman), 3 part-time/adjunct (0 women). Expenses: Contact institution. *Financial support:* Career-related internships or fieldwork, Federal Work-Study, institutionally sponsored loans, scholarships/grants, tuition waivers (full and partial), and unspecified assistantships available. Support available to part-time students. Financial award application deadline: 2/15; financial award applicants required to submit FAFSA. In 2017, 14 master's awarded. *Program availability:* Part-time. Offers architecture (M Arch); architecture, urban and regional design (MS). *Application deadline:* For fall admission, 3/1 for domestic and international students. Applications are processed on a rolling basis. *Application fee:* $50. Electronic applications accepted. *Application Contact:* Alice Dolitsky, Director, Graduate Admissions, 516-686-7520, Fax: 516-686-1116, E-mail: nyitgrad@nyit.edu. *Graduate Director*, Jeffrey Raven, 212-261-1547, E-mail: jraven@nyit.edu.

School of Engineering and Computing Sciences Students: 507 full-time (154 women), 269 part-time (68 women); includes 115 minority (33 Black or African American, non-Hispanic/Latino; 1 American Indian or Alaska Native, non-Hispanic/Latino; 48 Asian, non-Hispanic/Latino; 29 Hispanic/Latino; 1 Native Hawaiian or other Pacific Islander, non-Hispanic/Latino; 3 Two or more races, non-Hispanic/Latino), 583 international. Average age 26. 1,915 applicants, 62% accepted, 228 enrolled. *Faculty:* 36 full-time (8 women), 38 part-time/adjunct (12 women). Expenses: Contact institution. *Financial support:* Fellowships with partial tuition reimbursements, teaching assistantships with partial tuition reimbursements, career-related internships or fieldwork, Federal Work-Study, scholarships/grants, tuition waivers (full and partial), and unspecified assistantships available. Support available to part-time students. Financial award application deadline: 2/15; financial award applicants required to submit FAFSA. In 2017, 694 master's awarded. *Program availability:* Part-time, evening/weekend, 100% online, blended/hybrid learning. Offers bioengineering (MS); computer science (MS); electrical and computer engineering (MS); energy technology (Advanced Certificate); engineering and computing sciences (MS, Advanced Certificate); environmental management (Advanced Certificate); environmental technology and sustainability (MS); facilities management (Advanced Certificate); information, network, and computer security (MS); infrastructure security management (Advanced Certificate); mechanical engineering (MS). *Application deadline:* For fall admission, 7/1 for domestic students, 6/1 for international students; for spring admission, 12/1 for domestic and international students. Applications are processed on a rolling basis. *Application fee:* $50. Electronic applications accepted. *Application Contact:* Alice Dolitsky, Director, Graduate Admissions, 516-686-7520, Fax: 516-686-1116, E-mail: nyitgrad@nyit.edu. *Interim Dean*, Dr. Babek Beheshti, 516-686-7437, E-mail: bbehesht@nyit.edu.

School of Health Professions Students: 367 full-time (266 women), 44 part-time (36 women); includes 128 minority (16 Black or African American, non-Hispanic/Latino; 59 Asian, non-Hispanic/Latino; 44 Hispanic/Latino; 9 Two or more races, non-Hispanic/Latino), 1 international. Average age 25. 2,630 applicants, 10% accepted, 149 enrolled. *Faculty:* 27 full-time (18 women), 34 part-time/adjunct (26 women). Expenses: Contact institution. *Financial support:* Career-related internships or fieldwork, Federal Work-Study, scholarships/grants, tuition waivers (full and partial), and unspecified assistantships available. Support available to part-time students. Financial award application deadline: 2/15; financial award applicants required to submit FAFSA. In 2017, 89 master's, 32 doctorates awarded. *Program availability:* Part-time, evening/weekend, 100% online. Offers clinical nutrition (MS); health professions (MS, DPT); occupational therapy (MS); physical therapy (DPT); physician assistant studies (MS). *Application fee:* $50. Electronic applications accepted. *Application Contact:* Alice Dolitsky, Director, Graduate Admissions, 516-686-7520, Fax: 516-686-1116, E-mail: nyitgrad@nyit.edu. *Dean*, Dr. Sheldon Fields, 516-686-3939, E-mail: shp@nyit.edu.

School of Interdisciplinary Studies and Education Students: 80 full-time (67 women), 203 part-time (142 women); includes 72 minority (25 Black or African American, non-Hispanic/Latino; 13 Asian, non-Hispanic/Latino; 30 Hispanic/Latino; 4 Two or more races, non-Hispanic/Latino), 6 international. Average age 32. 151 applicants, 66% accepted, 65 enrolled. *Faculty:* 12 full-time (7 women), 23 part-time/adjunct (14 women). Expenses: Contact institution. *Financial support:* Career-related internships or fieldwork, Federal Work-Study, scholarships/grants, tuition waivers (full and partial), and unspecified assistantships available. Support available to part-time students. Financial award application deadline: 2/15; financial award applicants required to submit FAFSA. In 2017, 83 master's, 38 other advanced degrees awarded. *Program availability:* Part-time, evening/weekend, 100% online, blended/hybrid learning. Offers adolescence education (MS); adolescent education (MAT); bilingual school counseling (Advanced Certificate); childhood education (MS); early childhood (MS); emerging technologies for trainers (Advanced Certificate); instructional design for global e-learning (Advanced Certificate); instructional technology (MS); interdisciplinary studies and education (MA, MAT, MS, Advanced Certificate, Advanced Diploma); school counseling (MS); school leadership and technology (Advanced Diploma); STEM education (Advanced Certificate); student behavior management (Advanced Certificate). *Application deadline:* Applications are processed on a rolling basis. *Application fee:* $50. Electronic applications accepted. *Application Contact:* Alice Dolitsky, Director, Graduate Admissions, 516-686-7520, Fax: 516-686-1116, E-mail: nyitgrad@nyit.edu. *Interim Dean*, Dr. Christian Pomgratz, 516-686-1474, E-mail: soeinfo@nyit.edu.

School of Management Students: 414 full-time (202 women), 167 part-time (88 women); includes 68 minority (16 Black or African American, non-Hispanic/Latino; 1 American Indian or Alaska Native, non-Hispanic/Latino; 28 Asian, non-Hispanic/Latino; 19 Hispanic/Latino; 2 Native Hawaiian or other Pacific Islander, non-Hispanic/Latino; 2 Two or more races, non-Hispanic/Latino), 442 international. Average age 26. 692 applicants, 74% accepted, 206 enrolled. *Faculty:* 30 full-time (5 women), 24 part-time/adjunct (7 women). Expenses: Contact institution. *Financial support:* Career-related internships or fieldwork, Federal Work-Study, scholarships/grants, tuition waivers (full and partial), and unspecified assistantships available. Support available to part-time students. Financial award application deadline: 2/15; financial award applicants required to submit FAFSA. In 2017, 248 master's, 2 other advanced degrees awarded. *Program availability:* Part-time. Offers executive management (MBA); human resource management (Advanced Certificate); human resource management and labor relations (MS); management (MBA, MS, Advanced Certificate). *Application deadline:* Applications are processed on a rolling basis. *Application fee:* $50. Electronic applications accepted. *Application Contact:* Alice Dolitsky, Director, Graduate Admissions, 516-686-7520, Fax: 516-686-1116, E-mail: nyitgrad@nyit.edu. *Dean*, Dr. Jess Boronico, 516-686-7838, Fax: 516-686-7430, E-mail: jboronic@nyit.edu.

NEW YORK LAW SCHOOL, New York, NY 10013

General Information Independent, coed, graduate-only institution. *Enrollment by degree level:* 29 master's, 966 doctoral. *Graduate faculty:* 53 full-time (25 women), 76 part-time/adjunct (28 women). *Tuition:* Full-time $49,028; part-time $37,780 per year. *Required fees:* $1689; $1236 per unit. Tuition and fees vary according to course load and degree level. *Graduate housing:* Room and/or apartments available on a first-come, first-served basis to single students; on-campus housing not available to married students. Typical cost: $20,592 per year. Room charges vary according to housing facility selected. Housing application deadline: 7/1. *Student services:* Campus employment opportunities, campus safety program, career counseling, exercise/wellness program, free psychological counseling, international student services, low-cost health insurance, multicultural affairs office, services for students with disabilities, writing training. *Library facilities:* The Mendik Library. *Collection:* Books: 270,459 (physical), 246,854 (digital/electronic); Serial titles: 5,494 (physical), 247,568 (digital/electronic); Databases: 138. Weekly public service hours: 93.

Computer facilities: 70 computers available on campus for general student use. A campuswide network can be accessed from off campus. Online class registration is available.
Website: http://www.nyls.edu/

General Application Contact: Ella Mae Estrada, Associate Dean for Enrollment Management, Financial Aid and Diversity Initiatives, 212-431-2888, Fax: 212-966-1522, E-mail: admissions@nyls.edu.

GRADUATE UNITS

Graduate Programs Students: 737 full-time (447 women), 258 part-time (135 women); includes 327 minority (62 Black or African American, non-Hispanic/Latino; 1 American Indian or Alaska Native, non-Hispanic/Latino; 71 Asian, non-Hispanic/Latino; 166 Hispanic/Latino; 1 Native Hawaiian or other Pacific Islander, non-Hispanic/Latino; 26 Two or more races, non-Hispanic/Latino), 33 international. Average age 27. 2,752 applicants, 56% accepted, 386 enrolled. *Faculty:* 53 full-time (25 women), 76 part-time/adjunct (28 women). Expenses: Contact institution. *Financial support:* In 2017–18, 698 students received support, including 107 fellowships (averaging $4,110 per year), 22 research assistantships (averaging $4,663 per year), 19 teaching assistantships (averaging $4,661 per year); career-related internships or fieldwork, Federal Work-Study, and scholarships/grants also available. Support available to part-time students. Financial award application deadline: 7/1; financial award applicants required to submit FAFSA. In 2017, 12 master's, 241 doctorates awarded. *Program availability:* Part-time, evening/weekend. Offers law (LL M, JD). JD/MBA offered jointly with Baruch College of the City University of New York; JD/MA in forensic psychology offered jointly with John Jay College of Criminal Justice of the City University of New York. *Application deadline:* For fall admission, 7/1 priority date for domestic and international students; for winter admission, 11/15 priority date for domestic and international students; for spring admission, 12/1 priority date for domestic and international students. Applications are processed on a rolling basis. *Application fee:* $0. Electronic applications accepted. *Application Contact:* Ella Mae Estrada, Associate Dean for Enrollment Management, Financial Aid and Diversity Initiatives, 212-431-2888, Fax: 212-966-1522, E-mail: admissions@nyls.edu. *Dean and President*, Anthony W. Crowell, 212-431-2840, Fax: 212-219-3752, E-mail: anthony.crowell@nyls.edu.

NEW YORK MEDICAL COLLEGE, Valhalla, NY 10595

General Information Independent, coed, graduate-only institution. CGS member. *Enrollment by degree level:* 418 master's, 1,053 doctoral, 27 other advanced degrees. *Graduate faculty:* 1,099 full-time (446 women), 1,534 part-time/adjunct (575 women). *Tuition:* Full-time $45,000; part-time $1125 per credit. *Required fees:* $245 per term. Tuition and fees vary according to course load and program. *Graduate housing:* Rooms and/or apartments available on a first-come, first-served basis to single and married students. Typical cost: $8220 per year for single students; $17,220 per year for married students. Housing application deadline: 7/15. *Student services:* Campus employment opportunities, career counseling, exercise/wellness program, free psychological counseling, international student services, low-cost health insurance, multicultural affairs office, services for students with disabilities, writing training. *Library facilities:* Health Sciences Library plus 1 other. *Collection:* Books: 43,955 (physical), 118,930 (digital/electronic); Serial titles: 1,748 (physical), 21,561 (digital/electronic); Databases: 135. Weekly public service hours: 73; study areas open 24 hours, 5–7 days a week; students can reserve study rooms. *Research affiliation:* Touro University Worldwide (biomedical research), Westchester Medical Center (biomedical research), Metropolitan

Hospital (biomedical research), Westchester Institute for Human Development (biomedical research), Columbia University College of Physicians and Surgeons (neurosciences), Seattle Children's Hospital (pediatric pulmonary disease).

Computer facilities: 40 computers available on campus for general student use. A campuswide network can be accessed. Online class registration is available.
Website: http://www.nymc.edu/

General Application Contact: Robin Baum, Director of Admissions, 914-594-4882, Fax: 914-594-4613, E-mail: mdadmit@nymc.edu.

GRADUATE UNITS

Graduate School of Basic Medical Sciences Students: 116 full-time (63 women), 25 part-time (11 women); includes 65 minority (17 Black or African American, non-Hispanic/Latino; 1 American Indian or Alaska Native, non-Hispanic/Latino; 23 Asian, non-Hispanic/Latino; 21 Hispanic/Latino; 3 Two or more races, non-Hispanic/Latino), 27 international. Average age 27. 273 applicants, 56% accepted, 59 enrolled. *Faculty:* 70 full-time (17 women), 25 part-time/adjunct (9 women). Expenses: Contact institution. *Financial support:* Fellowships, research assistantships, Federal Work-Study, institutionally sponsored loans, scholarships/grants, tuition waivers, and health benefits (for PhD candidates only) available. Support available to part-time students. Financial award application deadline: 4/30; financial award applicants required to submit FAFSA. In 2017, 32 master's, 3 doctorates awarded. *Program availability:* Part-time, evening/weekend. Offers biochemistry and molecular biology (MS, PhD); cell biology (MS, PhD); microbiology and immunology (MS, PhD); pathology (MS, PhD); pharmacology (MS, PhD); physiology (MS, PhD). *Application deadline:* For fall admission, 7/1 priority date for domestic students, 5/1 priority date for international students; for spring admission, 12/1 priority date for domestic students, 9/15 priority date for international students. Applications are processed on a rolling basis. *Application fee:* $75 ($100 for international students). Electronic applications accepted. *Application Contact:* Valerie Romeo-Messana, Director of Admissions, 914-594-4110, Fax: 914-594-4944, E-mail: v_romeomessana@nymc.edu. *Dean,* Dr. Francis L. Belloni, 914-594-4110, Fax: 914-594-4944, E-mail: francis_belloni@nymc.edu.

School of Health Sciences and Practice Students: 221 full-time (153 women), 270 part-time (194 women); includes 202 minority (83 Black or African American, non-Hispanic/Latino; 2 American Indian or Alaska Native, non-Hispanic/Latino; 64 Asian, non-Hispanic/Latino; 47 Hispanic/Latino; 1 Native Hawaiian or other Pacific Islander, non-Hispanic/Latino; 5 Two or more races, non-Hispanic/Latino), 19 international. Average age 29. 1,118 applicants, 38% accepted, 169 enrolled. *Faculty:* 48 full-time (33 women), 235 part-time/adjunct (141 women). Expenses: Contact institution. *Financial support:* In 2017–18, 10,000 students received support. Scholarships/grants and unspecified assistantships available. Financial award application deadline: 4/30; financial award applicants required to submit FAFSA. In 2017, 110 master's, 41 doctorates awarded. *Program availability:* Part-time, evening/weekend, 100% online, blended/hybrid learning. Offers behavioral sciences and health promotion (MPH); biostatistics (MS); children with special health care (Graduate Certificate); emergency preparedness (Graduate Certificate); environmental health science (MPH); epidemiology (MPH, MS); global health (Graduate Certificate); health education (Graduate Certificate); health policy and management (MPH, Dr PH); industrial hygiene (Graduate Certificate); pediatric dysphagia (Post-Graduate Certificate); physical therapy (DPT); public health (Graduate Certificate); speech-language pathology (MS). *Application deadline:* For fall admission, 8/1 for domestic students, 4/15 for international students; for spring admission, 12/1 for domestic students; for summer admission, 5/1 for domestic students, 4/15 for international students. *Application fee:* $125. Electronic applications accepted. *Application Contact:* Irene Bundziak, Assistant to Director of Admissions, 914-594-4905, E-mail: irene_bundziak@nymc.edu. *Vice Dean,* Ben Watson, PhD, 914-594-4531, E-mail: ben_watson@nymc.edu.

School of Medicine Students: 865 full-time (466 women); includes 403 minority (86 Black or African American, non-Hispanic/Latino; 1 American Indian or Alaska Native, non-Hispanic/Latino; 211 Asian, non-Hispanic/Latino; 90 Hispanic/Latino; 15 Two or more races, non-Hispanic/Latino), 7 international. Average age 26. 9,527 applicants, 7% accepted, 216 enrolled. *Faculty:* 1,051 full-time (413 women), 1,299 part-time/adjunct (434 women). Expenses: Contact institution. *Financial support:* In 2017–18, 324 students received support. Federal Work-Study, scholarships/grants, and health care benefits available. Support available to part-time students. Financial award application deadline: 4/30; financial award applicants required to submit FAFSA. In 2017, 204 doctorates awarded. Offers medicine (MD). *Application deadline:* For fall admission, 1/31 for domestic and international students. Applications are processed on a rolling basis. *Application fee:* $120. Electronic applications accepted. *Application Contact:* Robin Baum, Assistant Dean of Admissions, 914-594-4882, Fax: 914-594-4613, E-mail: mdadmit@nymc.edu. *Senior Associate Dean for Medical Education,* Jennifer Koestler, MD, 914-594-4500, E-mail: jennifer_koestler@nymc.edu.

NEW YORK SCHOOL OF INTERIOR DESIGN, New York, NY 10021-5110

General Information Independent, coed, primarily women, comprehensive institution. *Graduate housing:* Room and/or apartments available on a first-come, first-served basis to single students; on-campus housing not available to married students. Housing application deadline: 5/1. *Research affiliation:* Metropolitan New York Library Council-Research Consortium.

GRADUATE UNITS

Program in Healthcare Interior Design Offers healthcare interior design (MPS). Electronic applications accepted.

Program in Interior Design (Post-Professional Level) Offers interior design (MFA). Electronic applications accepted.

Program in Interior Design (Professional-Level) Offers interior design (MFA). Electronic applications accepted.

Program in Interior Lighting Design Offers interior lighting design (MPS). Electronic applications accepted.

Program in Sustainable Interior Environments Offers sustainable interior environments (MPS). Electronic applications accepted.

NEW YORK STUDIO SCHOOL OF DRAWING, PAINTING AND SCULPTURE, New York, NY 10011

General Information Independent, coed, comprehensive institution.

GRADUATE UNITS

Certificate Program Offers studio art (Certificate).

MFA Program Offers painting (MFA); sculpture (MFA).

NEW YORK THEOLOGICAL SEMINARY, New York, NY 10115

General Information Independent-religious, coed, graduate-only institution. *Graduate housing:* On-campus housing not available. *Research affiliation:* Bellevue Hospital Center, Goldwater Memorial Hospital, Institutes of Religion and Health, Lutheran Medical Center, Postgraduate Center for Mental Health.

GRADUATE UNITS

Graduate and Professional Programs *Program availability:* Part-time. Offers theology (M Div, MPS, MSW, D Min). MSW offered jointly with Fordham University.

NEW YORK UNIVERSITY, New York, NY 10012-1019

General Information Independent, coed, university. CGS member. *Enrollment:* 51,123 graduate, professional, and undergraduate students; 16,977 full-time matriculated graduate/professional students (9,439 women), 7,729 part-time matriculated graduate/professional students (4,534 women). *Enrollment by degree level:* 18,243 master's, 5,751 doctoral, 712 other advanced degrees. *Graduate faculty:* 1,542 full-time (640 women), 1,712 part-time/adjunct (713 women). *Tuition:* Full-time $41,352; part-time $19,968 per year. *Required fees:* $2496; $1628 per unit. $814 per term. Tuition and fees vary according to course load and program. *Graduate housing:* Room and/or apartments available on a first-come, first-served basis to single students; on-campus housing not available to married students. Typical cost: $4850 per year ($17,664 including board). Room and board charges vary according to board plan, campus/location and housing facility selected. Housing application deadline: 5/1. *Student services:* Campus employment opportunities, campus safety program, career counseling, exercise/wellness program, free psychological counseling, grant writing training, international student services, low-cost health insurance, multicultural affairs office, services for students with disabilities, teacher training, writing training. *Library facilities:* Elmer H. Bobst Library plus 12 others. *Collection:* Books: 3.3 million (physical), 1.1 million (digital/electronic); Serial titles: 51,029 (physical), 166,202 (digital/electronic); Databases: 1,320. Study areas open 24 hours, 5–7 days a week; students can reserve study rooms. *Research affiliation:* Research Network on Opening Governance, MacArthur Foundation (technology management and innovation), Data Science Environments Program, Gordon and Betty Moore Foundation (data science), Center for the Study of Complex Malaria in India, National Institutes of Health (biology), Training in Systems and Integrative Neuroscience, National Institutes of Health (neural science).

Computer facilities: A campuswide network can be accessed from student residence rooms and from off campus. Online class registration is available.
Website: http://www.nyu.edu/

General Application Contact: Brendon Troy, New York University Information, 212-992-4723, E-mail: brendon.troy@nyu.edu.

GRADUATE UNITS

College of Dentistry Students: 1,646 full-time (821 women); includes 682 minority (26 Black or African American, non-Hispanic/Latino; 547 Asian, non-Hispanic/Latino; 99 Hispanic/Latino; 10 Two or more races, non-Hispanic/Latino), 308 international. Average age 27. 5,320 applicants, 15% accepted, 461 enrolled. *Faculty:* 275 full-time (118 women), 573 part-time/adjunct (204 women). Expenses: Contact institution. *Financial support:* Scholarships/grants available. Financial award application deadline: 4/1; financial award applicants required to submit FAFSA. In 2017, 14 master's, 363 doctorates, 43 other advanced degrees awarded. Offers biomaterials science (MS); clinical research (MS); dentistry (MS, DDS, Advanced Certificate); endodontics (Advanced Certificate); oral and maxillofacial surgery (Advanced Certificate); orthodontics (Advanced Certificate); pediatric dentistry (Advanced Certificate); periodontics (Advanced Certificate); prosthodontics (Advanced Certificate). *Application deadline:* For fall admission, 2/1 priority date for domestic and international students. Applications are processed on a rolling basis. *Application fee:* $80. Electronic applications accepted. *Application Contact:* Dr. Eugenia E. Mejia, Assistant Dean, Admissions and Enrollment Management, 212-998-9818, Fax: 212-995-4240, E-mail: dental.admissions@nyu.edu. *Dean,* Dr. Charles Bertolami, 212-998-9898, Fax: 212-995-4240, E-mail: charles.bertolami@nyu.edu.

College of Global Public Health Students: 161 full-time (136 women), 70 part-time (54 women); includes 74 minority (24 Black or African American, non-Hispanic/Latino; 1 American Indian or Alaska Native, non-Hispanic/Latino; 27 Asian, non-Hispanic/Latino; 11 Hispanic/Latino; 4 Native Hawaiian or other Pacific Islander, non-Hispanic/Latino; 7 Two or more races, non-Hispanic/Latino), 39 international. Average age 29. 802 applicants, 70% accepted, 97 enrolled. *Faculty:* 26 full-time (20 women), 104 part-time/adjunct (53 women). Expenses: Contact institution. *Financial support:* Federal Work-Study and scholarships/grants available. In 2017, 1 master's awarded. *Program availability:* Part-time, online learning. Offers biological basis of public health (PhD); community and international health (MPH); global health leadership (MPH); health systems and health services research (PhD); population and community health (PhD); public health nutrition (MPH); social and behavioral sciences (MPH); socio-behavioral health (PhD). *Application deadline:* For fall admission, 2/1 for domestic and international students. Applications are processed on a rolling basis. Electronic applications accepted. *Application Contact:* New York University Information, 212-998-1212. *Director,* Dr. Cheryl G. Healton, 212-992-6741.

Gallatin School of Individualized Study Students: 47 full-time (38 women), 85 part-time (61 women); includes 39 minority (18 Black or African American, non-Hispanic/Latino; 6 Asian, non-Hispanic/Latino; 10 Hispanic/Latino; 1 Native Hawaiian or other Pacific Islander, non-Hispanic/Latino; 4 Two or more races, non-Hispanic/Latino), 26 international. Average age 32. 157 applicants, 59% accepted, 40 enrolled. *Faculty:* 59 full-time (33 women), 129 part-time/adjunct (66 women). Expenses: Contact institution. *Financial support:* In 2017–18, 65 students received support. Federal Work-Study, institutionally sponsored loans, scholarships/grants, health care benefits, tuition waivers (full and partial), and unspecified assistantships available. Support available to part-time students. Financial award application deadline: 1/15; financial award applicants required to submit FAFSA. In 2017, 57 master's awarded. *Program availability:* Part-time, evening/weekend. Offers individualized study (MA). *Application deadline:* For fall admission, 1/15 priority date for domestic and international students; for spring admission, 10/1 for domestic and international students. Applications are processed on a rolling basis. *Application fee:* $50. Electronic applications accepted. *Application Contact:* Frances R. Levin, Director of Enrollment, 212-998-7349, E-mail: gallatin.gradadmissions@nyu.edu. *Dean,* Dr. Susanne L. Wofford, 212-998-7370.

Graduate School of Arts and Science Students: 3,555 full-time (1,847 women), 869 part-time (476 women); includes 725 minority (119 Black or African American, non-Hispanic/Latino; 10 American Indian or Alaska Native, non-Hispanic/Latino; 269 Asian, non-Hispanic/Latino; 245 Hispanic/Latino; 82 Two or more races, non-Hispanic/Latino), 1,727 international. Average age 29. 12,535 applicants, 29% accepted, 1396 enrolled. *Faculty:* 597 full-time (159 women). Expenses: Contact institution. *Financial support:* Fellowships with tuition reimbursements, research assistantships with tuition reimbursements, teaching assistantships with tuition reimbursements, career-related internships or fieldwork, Federal Work-Study, institutionally sponsored loans, scholarships/grants, health care benefits, tuition waivers (partial), unspecified assistantships, and instructorships available. Financial award applicants required to submit FAFSA. In 2017, 1,228 master's, 310 doctorates, 52 other advanced degrees awarded. *Program availability:* Part-time, evening/weekend. Offers African diaspora (PhD); African history (PhD); Africana studies (MA); American studies (MA, PhD); anthropology (MA, PhD); anthropology and French studies (PhD); applied economic analysis (Advanced Certificate); archival management (Advanced Certificate); arts and science (MA, MFA, MS, PhD, Advanced Certificate); Atlantic history (PhD); bioethics (MA); biology (PhD); biomedical journalism (MS); cancer and molecular biology (PhD); chemistry (MS, PhD); classics (MA, PhD); cognition and perception (PhD); comparative literature (MA, PhD); composition and theory (MA, PhD); computational biology (PhD); computers in biological research (MS); creative writing (MA, MFA); data science (MS); developmental genetics (PhD); early music performance (Advanced Certificate); East Asian studies (MA, PhD); economics (MA, PhD); English and American literature (MA, PhD); environmental health sciences (MS, PhD); ethnomusicology (MA, PhD); French studies and sociology (PhD); French studies/history (PhD); general biology (MS); general psychology (MA); German studies and critical thought (MA, PhD); Hebrew and Judaic studies (MA, PhD); Hebrew and Judaic studies/history (PhD); Hebrew and Judaic studies/museum studies (MA); historical and sustainable architecture (MA); history (MA, PhD); humanities and social thought (MA); immunology and microbiology (PhD); industrial/organizational psychology (MA); Irish and Irish American studies (MA); Italian (MA, PhD); Italian studies (MA); linguistics (MA, PhD); Middle Eastern history (MA); Middle Eastern studies/history (PhD); molecular genetics (PhD); museum studies (MA, Advanced Certificate); neurobiology (PhD); oral biology (MS); philosophy (MA, PhD); physics (MS, PhD); plant biology (PhD); poetics and theory (Advanced Certificate); political campaign management (MA); politics (MA, PhD); Portuguese (MA, PhD); psychotherapy and psychoanalysis (Advanced Certificate); public history (Advanced Certificate); recombinant DNA technology (MS); religion (Advanced Certificate); religious studies (MA); Russian literature (MA); Slavic literature (MA); social psychology (PhD); social theory (Advanced Certificate); sociology (MA, PhD); Spanish (PhD); Spanish and Latin American literatures and cultures (MA); Spanish language and translation (MA); world history (MA). *Application fee:* $100. Electronic applications accepted. *Application Contact:* Roberta Popik, Associate Dean for Graduate Enrollment Services, 212-998-8050, Fax: 212-995-4557, E-mail: gsas.admissions@nyu.edu. *Dean*, Dr. Lauren Benton, 212-998-8040.

Arthur L. Carter Journalism Institute Average age 26. 314 applicants, 70% accepted, 90 enrolled. Expenses: Contact institution. *Financial support:* Fellowships, teaching assistantships, Federal Work-Study, institutionally sponsored loans, scholarships/grants, and tuition waivers (partial) available. Financial award application deadline: 1/4; financial award applicants required to submit FAFSA. In 2017, 111 master's, 25 other advanced degrees awarded. *Program availability:* Part-time. Offers biomedical journalism (MS); cultural reporting and criticism (MA); French studies/journalism (MA); journalism (MA); Latin American and Caribbean studies/journalism (MA); Near Eastern studies/journalism (MA); science and environmental reporting (Advanced Certificate). *Application deadline:* For fall admission, 1/4 priority date for domestic students, 1/4 for international students. *Application fee:* $100. *Application Contact:* Charles Seife, Director of Graduate Studies, 212-998-7980, Fax: 212-995-4148, E-mail: graduate.journalism@nyu.edu. *Chair*, Perri Klass, 212-998-7980, Fax: 212-995-4148, E-mail: graduate.journalism@nyu.edu.

Center for European Studies Students: 10 full-time (7 women), 1 (woman) part-time; includes 2 minority (both Two or more races, non-Hispanic/Latino), 3 international. Average age 27. 14 applicants, 93% accepted, 8 enrolled. *Faculty:* 4 full-time (0 women). Expenses: Contact institution. *Financial support:* Fellowships with tuition reimbursements, teaching assistantships, career-related internships or fieldwork, Federal Work-Study, institutionally sponsored loans, and scholarships/grants available. Financial award application deadline: 2/1; financial award applicants required to submit FAFSA. In 2017, 4 master's awarded. Offers European studies (MA). *Application deadline:* For fall admission, 2/1 priority date for domestic students, 2/1 for international students. *Application fee:* $100. Electronic applications accepted. *Application Contact:* Mikhala Stein, Administrator, 212-998-3838, Fax: 212-995-4188, E-mail: european.studies@nyu.edu. *Director*, Larry Wolff, 212-998-3838, Fax: 212-995-4188, E-mail: european.studies@nyu.edu.

Center for French Civilization and Culture Average age 29. 123 applicants, 58% accepted, 39 enrolled. Expenses: Contact institution. *Financial support:* Fellowships, research assistantships, teaching assistantships, Federal Work-Study, institutionally sponsored loans, scholarships/grants, traineeships, unspecified assistantships, and instructorships available. Financial award application deadline: 1/4; financial award applicants required to submit FAFSA. In 2017, 31 master's, 17 doctorates, 1 other advanced degree awarded. *Program availability:* Part-time, evening/weekend. Offers French (PhD); French civilization (PhD); French civilization and culture (MA, PhD, Advanced Certificate); French language and civilization (MA); French literature (MA); French studies (MA, PhD, Advanced Certificate); French studies and anthropology (PhD); French studies and history (PhD); French studies and journalism (MA); French studies and sociology (PhD); Romance languages and literatures (MA). *Application deadline:* For fall admission, 1/4 for domestic and international students. *Application fee:* $100. *Application Contact:* Erin Brau, Graduate Department Administrator, 212-998-8700, Fax: 212-995-4187, E-mail: french.grad@nyu.edu. *Director of Graduate Studies*, Lucien Nouis, 212-998-8700, Fax: 212-995-4187, E-mail: french.grad@nyu.edu.

Center for Latin American and Caribbean Studies Students: 20 full-time (13 women), 5 part-time (4 women); includes 15 minority (1 Black or African American, non-Hispanic/Latino; 13 Hispanic/Latino; 1 Two or more races, non-Hispanic/Latino), 5 international. Average age 27. 41 applicants, 93% accepted, 14 enrolled. Expenses: Contact institution. *Financial support:* Fellowships with tuition reimbursements, teaching assistantships with tuition reimbursements, Federal Work-Study, institutionally sponsored loans, scholarships/grants, health care benefits, and unspecified assistantships available. Financial award application deadline: 2/1; financial award applicants required to submit FAFSA. In 2017, 12 master's awarded. *Program availability:* Part-time. Offers Latin American and Caribbean studies (MA). *Application deadline:* For fall admission, 2/1 priority date for domestic students, 2/1 for international students. *Application fee:* $100. *Application Contact:* Amalia Cordova, Program Administrator, 212-998-8686, Fax: 212-995-4163, E-mail: clacs.info@nyu.edu. *Director*, Jill Lane, 212-998-8686, Fax: 212-995-4163, E-mail: clacs.info@nyu.edu.

Center for Neural Science Students: 50 full-time (21 women); includes 8 minority (5 Asian, non-Hispanic/Latino; 2 Hispanic/Latino; 1 Two or more races, non-Hispanic/Latino), 14 international. Average age 28. 269 applicants, 9% accepted, 9 enrolled. *Faculty:* 15 full-time (3 women). Expenses: Contact institution. *Financial support:* Fellowships with tuition reimbursements, research assistantships with tuition reimbursements, career-related internships or fieldwork, Federal Work-Study, institutionally sponsored loans, scholarships/grants, health care benefits, and unspecified assistantships available. Financial award application deadline: 12/1; financial award applicants required to submit FAFSA. In 2017, 1 doctorate awarded. Offers neural science (PhD). *Application deadline:* For fall admission, 12/1 for domestic and international students. *Application fee:* $100. *Application Contact:* Michael Hawken, Director of Graduate Studies, 212-998-7780, Fax: 212-995-4011, E-mail: admissions@cns.nyu.edu. *Chair*, J. Anthony Movshon, 212-998-7780, Fax: 212-995-4011, E-mail: admissions@cns.nyu.edu.

Courant Institute of Mathematical Sciences Average age 27. 2,743 applicants, 24% accepted, 224 enrolled. Expenses: Contact institution. *Financial support:* Fellowships, research assistantships, teaching assistantships, career-related internships or fieldwork, Federal Work-Study, institutionally sponsored loans, scholarships/grants, health care benefits, tuition waivers (full and partial), and unspecified assistantships available. Financial award application deadline: 12/18; financial award applicants required to submit FAFSA. In 2017, 251 master's, 34 doctorates awarded. *Program availability:* Part-time, evening/weekend. Offers atmosphere ocean science and mathematics (PhD); computer science (MS, PhD); information systems (MS); mathematics (MS, PhD); mathematics and statistics/operations research (MS); mathematics in finance (MS); scientific computing (MS). *Application deadline:* For fall admission, 12/18 for domestic and international students. *Application fee:* $100. *Application Contact:* Tamar Arnon, Graduate Administrator, 212-998-3238, Fax: 212-995-4121, E-mail: admissions@math.nyu.edu. *Director of Graduate Studies*, Fedor Bogomolov, 212-998-3238, Fax: 212-995-4121, E-mail: admissions@math.nyu.edu.

Hagop Kevorkian Center for Near Eastern Studies Average age 28. 174 applicants, 37% accepted, 26 enrolled. Expenses: Contact institution. *Financial support:* Fellowships, teaching assistantships, Federal Work-Study, and institutionally sponsored loans available. Financial award application deadline: 12/18; financial award applicants required to submit FAFSA. In 2017, 22 master's, 9 doctorates awarded. *Program availability:* Part-time, evening/weekend. Offers Middle Eastern and Islamic studies (MA, PhD); Middle Eastern and Islamic studies/history (PhD); Near Eastern studies (MA); Near Eastern studies/journalism (MA); Near Eastern studies/museum studies (MA). *Application deadline:* For fall admission, 12/18 for domestic and international students. *Application fee:* $100. *Application Contact:* Everett Rowson, Acting Director of Graduate Studies, 212-998-8880, E-mail: kevorkian.center@nyu.edu. *Chair*, Zvi Ben-Dor Benite, 212-998-8880, Fax: 212-995-4689, E-mail: kevorkian.center@nyu.edu.

Institute for Law and Society Average age 36. Expenses: Contact institution. *Financial support:* Fellowships, teaching assistantships, career-related internships or fieldwork, Federal Work-Study, institutionally sponsored loans, scholarships/grants, health care benefits, and unspecified assistantships available. Financial award applicants required to submit FAFSA. In 2017, 2 doctorates awarded. Offers law and society (MA, PhD). *Application fee:* $100. *Application Contact:* Carly Vignogna, Graduate Administrator, 212-998-8040, Fax: 212-995-4557, E-mail: gsas.admissions@nyu.edu. *Director of Graduate Studies*, Jo Dixon, 212-998-8040, Fax: 212-995-4557, E-mail: gsas.admissions@nyu.edu.

Institute for the Study of the Ancient World Average age 31. 50 applicants, 10% accepted, 1 enrolled. Expenses: Contact institution. *Financial support:* Fellowships and stipends available. Financial award application deadline: 1/4; financial award applicants required to submit FAFSA. Offers study of the ancient world (PhD). *Application deadline:* For fall admission, 1/4 for domestic and international students. *Application fee:* $100. Electronic applications accepted. *Application Contact:* Marc Leblanc, Graduate Department Administrator, 212-992-7843, Fax: 212-992-7809, E-mail: isaw@nyu.edu. *Director*, Dr. Roger Bagnall, 212-992-7843, Fax: 212-992-7809, E-mail: isaw@nyu.edu.

Institute of Fine Arts Average age 31. 346 applicants, 43% accepted, 52 enrolled. Expenses: Contact institution. *Financial support:* Fellowships, research assistantships, teaching assistantships, career-related internships or fieldwork, Federal Work-Study, institutionally sponsored loans, and tuition waivers (partial) available. Financial award application deadline: 12/18; financial award applicants required to submit FAFSA. In 2017, 47 master's, 24 doctorates awarded. *Program availability:* Part-time. Offers architectural studies (PhD); art history and archaeology (MA, PhD); classical art and archaeology (PhD); curatorial studies (PhD); East and South Asian art (PhD); Near Eastern art and archaeology (PhD). *Application deadline:* For fall admission, 12/18 for domestic and international students. *Application fee:* $100. *Application Contact:* Alexander Nagel, Director of Graduate Studies, 212-992-5800, Fax: 212-992-5807, E-mail: ifa.program@nyu.edu. *Chair*, Patricia Rubin, 212-992-5800, Fax: 212-992-5807, E-mail: ifa.program@nyu.edu.

Leonard N. Stern School of Business *Program availability:* Part-time, evening/weekend. Offers accounting (MBA, PhD); business (MBA, PhD); economics (MBA, PhD); entertainment, media and technology (MBA); finance (MBA, PhD); general marketing (MBA); information systems (MBA, PhD); management organizations (MBA); marketing (PhD); operations management (MBA, PhD); organization theory (PhD); organizational behavior (PhD); product management (MBA); statistics (MBA, PhD); strategy (PhD). Electronic applications accepted.

Rory Meyers College of Nursing Students: 71 full-time (65 women), 619 part-time (564 women); includes 253 minority (64 Black or African American, non-Hispanic/Latino; 1 American Indian or Alaska Native, non-Hispanic/Latino; 126 Asian, non-Hispanic/Latino; 46 Hispanic/Latino; 1 Native Hawaiian or other Pacific Islander, non-Hispanic/Latino; 15 Two or more races, non-Hispanic/Latino), 27 international. Average age 32. 431 applicants, 59% accepted, 166 enrolled. *Faculty:* 74 full-time (68 women), 63 part-time/adjunct (57 women). Expenses: Contact institution. *Financial support:* In 2017–18, 157 students received support, including 9 research assistantships with full tuition reimbursements available (averaging $27,000 per year); career-related internships or fieldwork, Federal Work-Study, scholarships/grants, and unspecified assistantships also available. Support available to part-time students. Financial award application deadline: 3/1; financial award applicants required to submit FAFSA. In 2017, 187 master's, 18 doctorates, 5 other advanced degrees awarded. *Program availability:* Part-time, evening/weekend. Offers adult-gerontology acute care nurse practitioner (MS, Advanced Certificate); adult-gerontology primary care nurse practitioner (MS, Advanced Certificate); family nurse practitioner (MS, Advanced Certificate); gerontology nurse practitioner (Advanced Certificate); nurse-midwifery (MS, Advanced Certificate); nursing (MS, DNP, PhD, Advanced Certificate); nursing administration (MS, Advanced Certificate); nursing education (MS, Advanced Certificate); nursing informatics (MS, Advanced Certificate); nursing research and theory development (PhD); pediatrics nurse practitioner (MS, Advanced Certificate); psychiatric-mental health nurse practitioner (MS, Advanced Certificate). *Application deadline:* For fall admission, 6/15 for domestic and international students; for spring admission, 12/1 for domestic and international students; for summer admission, 3/1 for domestic and international students. *Application fee:* $80. Electronic applications accepted. *Application Contact:* Matthew Burke, Assistant Director, Graduate Student Affairs and Admissions, 212-998-7397, E-mail: mb6060@nyu.edu. *Senior Associate Dean for Academic Programs,* Dr. James Pace, 212-992-7343, E-mail: james.pace@nyu.edu.

School of Law Students: 1,364 full-time (728 women); includes 394 minority (72 Black or African American, non-Hispanic/Latino; 147 Asian, non-Hispanic/Latino; 124 Hispanic/Latino; 51 Two or more races, non-Hispanic/Latino), 127 international. 6,534 applicants, 427 enrolled. *Faculty:* 158 full-time (51 women), 204 part-time/adjunct (55 women). Expenses: Contact institution. *Financial support:* Fellowships, research assistantships, teaching assistantships, career-related internships or fieldwork, Federal Work-Study, scholarships/grants, and loan repayment assistance available. Financial award application deadline: 4/15; financial award applicants required to submit FAFSA. In 2017, 516 master's, 484 doctorates awarded. *Program availability:* Part-time, blended/hybrid learning. Offers law (LL M, JD, JSD); law and business (Advanced Certificate); taxation (MSL, Advanced Certificate). *Application deadline:* For fall admission, 2/15 for domestic students. Applications are processed on a rolling basis. *Application fee:* $85. Electronic applications accepted. *Application Contact:* Cassandra Williams, Assistant Dean for Admissions, 212-998-6060, Fax: 212-995-4527. *Dean,* Trevor Morrison, 212-998-6000, Fax: 212-995-3150.

School of Medicine Average age 24. 8,341 applicants, 6% accepted, 149 enrolled. Expenses: Contact institution. *Financial support:* In 2017–18, 240 students received support. Fellowships, research assistantships, teaching assistantships, Federal Work-Study, institutionally sponsored loans, scholarships/grants, and health care benefits available. Financial award application deadline: 3/1; financial award applicants required to submit FAFSA. In 2017, 11 master's awarded. Offers medicine (MS, MD, PhD). *Application deadline:* For fall admission, 10/15 for domestic students; for winter admission, 12/18 for domestic students, 12/15 for international students. Applications are processed on a rolling basis. *Application fee:* $110. Electronic applications accepted. *Application Contact:* Dr. Rafael Rivera, Associate Dean, Admissions and Financial Aid, 212-263-5290, Fax: 212-263-0720, E-mail: rafael.rivera@nyumc.org. *Dean,* Dr. Robert Grossman, 212-263-3269, Fax: 212-263-1828, E-mail: robert.grossman@nyumc.org.

Sackler Institute of Graduate Biomedical Sciences Students: 236 full-time (138 women), 1 part-time (0 women); includes 68 minority (13 Black or African American, non-Hispanic/Latino; 26 Asian, non-Hispanic/Latino; 28 Hispanic/Latino; 1 Native Hawaiian or other Pacific Islander, non-Hispanic/Latino), 79 international. Average age 27. 761 applicants, 18% accepted, 59 enrolled. *Faculty:* 207 full-time (51 women). Expenses: Contact institution. *Financial support:* Health care benefits, tuition waivers (full), and unspecified assistantships available. In 2017, 35 doctorates awarded. Offers biomedical imaging and technology (PhD); biostatistics (PhD); cellular and molecular biology (PhD); developmental genetics (PhD); epidemiology (PhD); genome integrity (PhD); immunology and inflammation (PhD); microbiology (PhD); molecular biophysics (PhD); molecular oncology and tumor immunology (PhD); molecular pharmacology (PhD); neuroscience and physiology (PhD); stem cell biology (PhD); systems and computational biomedicine (PhD). *Application deadline:* For fall admission, 12/1 for domestic and international students. Applications are processed on a rolling basis. *Application fee:* $100. Electronic applications accepted. *Application Contact:* Jessica Dong, Program Manager, 212-263-5648, E-mail: sackler-info@nyumc.org. *Associate Dean for Biomedical Sciences/Director, Sackler Institute,* Dr. Naoko Tanese, 212-263-8945, E-mail: naoko.tanese@nyumc.org.

School of Professional Studies Students: 2,095 full-time (1,410 women), 1,206 part-time (640 women); includes 520 minority (119 Black or African American, non-Hispanic/Latino; 5 American Indian or Alaska Native, non-Hispanic/Latino; 184 Asian, non-Hispanic/Latino; 174 Hispanic/Latino; 5 Native Hawaiian or other Pacific Islander, non-Hispanic/Latino; 33 Two or more races, non-Hispanic/Latino), 1,956 international. Average age 27. 4,166 applicants, 63% accepted, 1181 enrolled. *Faculty:* 16 full-time (9 women), 184 part-time/adjunct (82 women). Expenses: Contact institution. *Financial support:* In 2017–18, 744 students received support, including 800 fellowships with partial tuition reimbursements available (averaging $3,107 per year); career-related internships or fieldwork, Federal Work-Study, scholarships/grants, and health care benefits also available. Support available to part-time students. Financial award application deadline: 6/30; financial award applicants required to submit FAFSA. In 2017, 2,510 master's awarded. *Program availability:* Part-time, evening/weekend, 100% online, blended/hybrid learning. *Application deadline:* For fall admission, 2/1 priority date for domestic and international students; for spring admission, 10/15 priority date for domestic students, 8/15 priority date for international students; for summer admission, 5/1 priority date for domestic students, 1/15 priority date for international students. Applications are processed on a rolling basis. *Application fee:* $150. Electronic applications accepted. *Application Contact:* Office of Admissions, 212-998-7100, E-mail: sps.gradadmissions@nyu.edu. *Dean,* Dennis Di Lorenzo, 212-998-7100.

Center for Applied Liberal Arts Students: 4 full-time (2 women), 34 part-time (30 women); includes 11 minority (6 Black or African American, non-Hispanic/Latino; 1 American Indian or Alaska Native, non-Hispanic/Latino; 3 Hispanic/Latino; 1 Two or more races, non-Hispanic/Latino), 3 international. Average age 34. 24 applicants, 79% accepted, 13 enrolled. Expenses: Contact institution. *Financial support:* Fellowships, career-related internships or fieldwork, Federal Work-Study, scholarships/grants, and health care benefits available. Support available to part-time students. Financial award application deadline: 3/15; financial award applicants required to submit FAFSA. In 2017, 10 master's awarded. *Program availability:* Part-time, evening/weekend. Offers applied liberal arts (MS); professional writing (MS); translation (MS). *Application deadline:* For fall admission, 2/1 priority date for domestic and international students; for spring admission, 10/15 priority date for domestic students, 8/15 priority date for international students. Applications are processed on a rolling basis. *Application fee:* $150. Electronic applications accepted. *Application Contact:* Office of Admissions, 212-998-7100, E-mail: sps.gradadmissions@nyu.edu. *Academic Director and Clinical Associate Professor,* Lisa Springer, 212-998-7030.

Center for Global Affairs Students: 143 full-time (90 women), 115 part-time (65 women); includes 73 minority (18 Black or African American, non-Hispanic/Latino; 16 Asian, non-Hispanic/Latino; 32 Hispanic/Latino; 7 Two or more races, non-Hispanic/Latino), 82 international. Average age 28. 285 applicants, 73% accepted, 79 enrolled. Expenses: Contact institution. *Financial support:* Fellowships, career-related internships or fieldwork, Federal Work-Study, scholarships/grants, and health care benefits available. Support available to part-time students. Financial award application deadline: 6/30; financial award applicants required to submit FAFSA. In 2017, 238 master's awarded. *Program availability:* Part-time, evening/weekend. Offers global affairs (MS). *Application deadline:* For fall admission, 2/1 priority date for domestic and international students; for spring admission, 10/15 priority date for domestic students, 8/15 priority date for international students. Applications are processed on a rolling basis. *Application fee:* $150. Electronic applications accepted. *Application Contact:* Office of Admissions, 212-998-7100, E-mail: sps.gradadmissions@nyu.edu. *Divisional Dean and Clinical Associate Professor,* Vera Jelinek, 212-992-8380.

Center for Publishing Students: 55 full-time (48 women), 33 part-time (31 women); includes 20 minority (3 Black or African American, non-Hispanic/Latino; 3 Asian, non-Hispanic/Latino; 10 Hispanic/Latino; 4 Two or more races, non-Hispanic/Latino), 22 international. Average age 25. 84 applicants, 82% accepted, 39 enrolled. Expenses: Contact institution. *Financial support:* Fellowships, career-related internships or fieldwork, Federal Work-Study, scholarships/grants, and health care benefits available. Support available to part-time students. Financial award application deadline: 6/30; financial award applicants required to submit FAFSA. In 2017, 72 master's awarded. *Program availability:* Part-time, evening/weekend. Offers publishing: digital and print media (MS). *Application deadline:* For fall admission, 2/1 priority date for domestic and international students; for spring admission, 10/15 priority date for domestic students, 8/15 priority date for international students. Applications are processed on a rolling basis. *Application fee:* $150. Electronic applications accepted. *Application Contact:* Admissions Office, 212-998-7100, E-mail: sps.gradadmissions@nyu.edu. *Academic Director and Clinical Assistant Professor,* Andrea Chambers, 212-992-3232.

Division of Programs in Business Students: 1,467 full-time (1,080 women), 446 part-time (342 women); includes 240 minority (65 Black or African American, non-Hispanic/Latino; 3 American Indian or Alaska Native, non-Hispanic/Latino; 96 Asian, non-Hispanic/Latino; 64 Hispanic/Latino; 1 Native Hawaiian or other Pacific Islander, non-Hispanic/Latino; 11 Two or more races, non-Hispanic/Latino), 1,510 international. Average age 26. 2,989 applicants, 62% accepted, 785 enrolled. Expenses: Contact institution. *Financial support:* Fellowships, career-related internships or fieldwork, Federal Work-Study, scholarships/grants, and health care benefits available. Support available to part-time students. Financial award application deadline: 6/30; financial award applicants required to submit FAFSA. In 2017, 1,454 master's awarded. *Program availability:* Part-time, evening/weekend, 100% online, blended/hybrid learning. Offers human resource management and development (MS); integrated marketing (MS); leadership and human capital management (MS); management and systems (MS); marketing and public relations (MS); project management (MS); public relations and corporate communication (MS). *Application deadline:* For fall admission, 2/1 priority date for domestic and international students; for spring admission, 10/15 priority date for domestic students, 8/15 priority date for international students; for summer admission, 5/1 priority date for domestic students, 1/15 priority date for international students. Applications are processed on a rolling basis. *Application fee:* $150. Electronic applications accepted. *Application Contact:* Office of Admissions, 212-998-7100, E-mail: sps.gradadmissions@nyu.edu. *Associate Dean and Clinical Assistant Professor,* Martin Ihrig, 212-992-3288.

Jonathan M. Tisch Center of Hospitality Students: 56 full-time (39 women), 26 part-time (19 women); includes 12 minority (2 Black or African American, non-Hispanic/Latino; 7 Asian, non-Hispanic/Latino; 2 Hispanic/Latino; 1 Native Hawaiian or other Pacific Islander, non-Hispanic/Latino), 48 international. Average age 26. 109 applicants, 54% accepted, 31 enrolled. Expenses: Contact institution. *Financial support:* Fellowships, career-related internships or fieldwork, Federal Work-Study, scholarships/grants, and health care benefits available. Support available to part-time students. Financial award application deadline: 6/30; financial award applicants required to submit FAFSA. In 2017, 86 master's awarded. *Program availability:* Part-time, evening/weekend. Offers hospitality industry studies (MS); tourism management (MS). *Application deadline:* For fall admission, 2/1 priority date for domestic and international students; for spring admission, 10/15 priority date for domestic students, 8/15 priority date for international students; for summer admission, 5/1 priority date for domestic students, 1/15 priority date for international students. Applications are processed on a rolling basis. *Application fee:* $150. Electronic applications accepted. *Application Contact:* Office of Admissions, 212-998-7100, E-mail: sps.gradadmissions@nyu.edu. *Associate Dean/Clinical Associate Professor,* Nicolas Graf, 212-998-9100.

Preston Robert Tisch Institute for Global Sport Students: 70 full-time (21 women), 38 part-time (13 women); includes 21 minority (6 Black or African American, non-Hispanic/Latino; 7 Asian, non-Hispanic/Latino; 5 Hispanic/Latino; 1 Native Hawaiian or other Pacific Islander, non-Hispanic/Latino; 2 Two or more races, non-Hispanic/Latino), 52 international. Average age 26. 145 applicants, 67% accepted, 46 enrolled. Expenses: Contact institution. *Financial support:* Fellowships, career-related internships or fieldwork, Federal Work-Study, scholarships/grants, and health care benefits available. Support available to part-time students. Financial award application deadline: 6/30; financial award applicants required to submit FAFSA. In 2017, 78 master's awarded. *Program availability:* Part-time, evening/weekend. Offers sports business (MS). *Application deadline:* For fall admission, 2/1 priority date for domestic and international students; for spring admission, 10/15 priority date for domestic students, 8/15 priority date for international students. Applications are processed on a rolling basis. *Application fee:* $150. Electronic applications accepted. *Application Contact:* Admissions Office, 212-998-7100, E-mail: sps.gradadmissions@nyu.edu. *Associate Dean/Clinical Associate Professor,* Vince Gennaro, 212-995-4676.

Schack Institute of Real Estate Students: 269 full-time (101 women), 469 part-time (105 women); includes 115 minority (14 Black or African American, non-Hispanic/Latino; 1 American Indian or Alaska Native, non-Hispanic/Latino; 50 Asian, non-Hispanic/Latino; 41 Hispanic/Latino; 2 Native Hawaiian or other Pacific Islander, non-Hispanic/Latino; 7 Two or more races, non-Hispanic/Latino), 219 international. Average age 28. 488 applicants, 64% accepted, 172 enrolled. Expenses: Contact institution. *Financial support:* Fellowships, career-related internships or fieldwork, Federal Work-Study, scholarships/grants, and health care benefits available. Support available to part-time students. Financial award application deadline: 6/30; financial award applicants required to submit FAFSA. In 2017, 526 master's awarded. *Program availability:* Part-time, evening/weekend. Offers construction management (MS); real estate (MS); real estate development (MS). *Application deadline:* For fall admission, 2/1 priority date for domestic and international students; for spring admission, 10/15 priority date for domestic students, 8/15 priority date for international students; for summer admission, 5/1 priority date for domestic students, 1/15 priority date for international students. Applications are processed on a rolling basis. *Application fee:* $150. Electronic applications accepted. *Application Contact:* Office of Admissions, 212-998-7100, E-mail: sps.gradadmissions@nyu.edu. *Associate Dean/Chair/Clinical Professor,* Sam Chandan, 212-992-3335.

Silver School of Social Work Students: 772 full-time (668 women), 333 part-time (279 women); includes 369 minority (123 Black or African American, non-Hispanic/Latino; 1 American Indian or Alaska Native, non-Hispanic/Latino; 65 Asian, non-Hispanic/Latino; 160 Hispanic/Latino; 1 Native Hawaiian or other Pacific Islander, non-Hispanic/Latino; 19

Two or more races, non-Hispanic/Latino), 86 international. Average age 30. 1,568 applicants, 89% accepted, 498 enrolled. Expenses: Contact institution. *Financial support:* In 2017–18, 995 students received support. Career-related internships or fieldwork, Federal Work-Study, scholarships/grants, health care benefits, tuition waivers (partial), and unspecified assistantships available. Support available to part-time students. Financial award application deadline: 3/1; financial award applicants required to submit FAFSA. In 2017, 526 master's, 1 doctorate awarded. *Program availability:* Part-time, evening/weekend. Offers social work (MSW, PhD). *Application deadline:* For fall admission, 1/9 priority date for domestic and international students; for spring admission, 10/3 priority date for domestic and international students. Applications are processed on a rolling basis. *Application fee:* $60. Electronic applications accepted. *Application Contact:* Robert W. Sommo, Jr., Assistant Dean for Enrollment Services, 212-998-5910, Fax: 212-995-4171, E-mail: ssw.admissions@nyu.edu. *Dean,* Dr. Lynn Videka, 212-998-5959, Fax: 212-995-4172.

Steinhardt School of Culture, Education, and Human Development Average age 31. 6,757 applicants, 42% accepted, 1245 enrolled. Expenses: Contact institution. *Financial support:* Fellowships, research assistantships, teaching assistantships, career-related internships or fieldwork, Federal Work-Study, institutionally sponsored loans, scholarships/grants, traineeships, tuition waivers (partial), and unspecified assistantships available. Support available to part-time students. Financial award application deadline: 2/1; financial award applicants required to submit FAFSA. In 2017, 1,316 master's, 109 doctorates, 36 other advanced degrees awarded. *Program availability:* Part-time. Offers advanced occupational therapy (MA); applied statistics for social science research (MS); art education (MA); art therapy (MA); art, education, and community practice (MA); bilingual education (MA, PhD, Advanced Certificate); business and workplace education (MA, Advanced Certificate); business education (MA, Advanced Certificate); childhood (MA); childhood education (MA); clinical nutrition (MS); clinically rich integrated science (MA); clinically-based English education, grades 7-12 (MA); communication sciences and disorders (MS, PhD); costume studies (MA); counseling (MA, PhD, Advanced Certificate); counseling and guidance (MA, Advanced Certificate); counseling for mental health and wellness (MA); counseling psychology (PhD); culture, education, and human development (MA, MFA, MM, MPH, MS, DPS, DPT, Ed D, PhD, Advanced Certificate, Post Master's Certificate, Postbaccalaureate Certificate); dance education (MA, Advanced Certificate); developmental psychology (PhD); digital media design for learning (MA, Advanced Certificate); drama therapy (MA); early childhood (MA); early childhood and childhood education (MA); early childhood education (MA); early childhood education/early childhood special education (MA); education and Jewish studies (MA, PhD); education policy (MA); educational and developmental psychology (MA, PhD); educational communication and technology (MA, MS, PhD, Advanced Certificate); educational leadership (MA, Ed D, PhD, Advanced Certificate); educational leadership, politics and advocacy (MA); educational theatre (MA, Ed D, PhD); educational theatre and English 7-12 (MA); educational theatre and social studies 7-12 (MA); educational theatre in colleges and communities (MA, Ed D, PhD); educational theatre, all grades (MA); English education (MA, PhD, Advanced Certificate); English education, grades 7-12 (MA); environmental conservation education (MA); food studies (MA, PhD); foreign language education (MA); games for learning (MS); higher and postsecondary education (PhD); higher education (MA, Ed D, PhD); higher education administration (Ed D); higher education and student affairs (MA); history of education (MA, PhD); human development and social intervention (MA); instrumental performance (MM); international education (MA, PhD, Advanced Certificate); LGBT health, education, and social services (Advanced Certificate); literacy education (MA); mathematics education (MA); media, culture and communication (MA, PhD); multilingual/multicultural studies (MA, PhD, Advanced Certificate); music business (MA); music education (MA); music performance and composition (MM, PhD, Advanced Certificate); music technology (MA, MM, PhD); music theatre (MM); music theory and composition (MM); music therapy (MA); nutrition and dietetics (MS, PhD); occupational therapy (MS, DPS); orthopedic physical therapy (Advanced Certificate); performing arts administration (MA); physical therapy (MA, DPT, PhD); piano performance (MM); psychology and social intervention (PhD); rehabilitation sciences (PhD); research in occupational therapy (PhD); school building leader (MA); school district leader (Advanced Certificate); social and cultural studies of education (MA); social studies education (MA); sociology of education (MA, PhD); special education (MA); studio art (MA, MFA, Advanced Certificate); teachers of art, all grades (MA); teaching and learning (Ed D, PhD); teaching art/social studies 7-12 (MA); teaching dance in the professions (MA); teaching dance, all grades (MA, Advanced Certificate); teaching English to speakers of other languages (MA, PhD); teaching foreign languages, 7-12 (MA); teaching French as a foreign language (MA); teaching social studies 7-12 (MA); teaching Spanish as a foreign language (MA); visual arts administration (MA); visual culture (MA); vocal pedagogy (Advanced Certificate); vocal performance (MM); workplace learning (Advanced Certificate). *Application deadline:* Applications are processed on a rolling basis. *Application fee:* $75. Electronic applications accepted. *Application Contact:* John Myers, Director of Enrollment Management, 212-998-5030, Fax: 212-995-4328, E-mail: steinhardt.gradadmissions@nyu.edu. *Dean,* Dr. Dominic Brewer, 212-998-5000.

Tandon School of Engineering Students: 2,231 full-time (694 women), 484 part-time (144 women); includes 251 minority (38 Black or African American, non-Hispanic/Latino; 1 American Indian or Alaska Native, non-Hispanic/Latino; 142 Asian, non-Hispanic/Latino; 58 Hispanic/Latino; 12 Two or more races, non-Hispanic/Latino), 2,172 international. Average age 25. 9,020 applicants, 38% accepted, 1000 enrolled. *Faculty:* 168 full-time (36 women), 255 part-time/adjunct (49 women). Expenses: Contact institution. *Financial support:* Applicants required to submit FAFSA. In 2017, 1,303 master's, 51 doctorates, 10 other advanced degrees awarded. Offers applied physics (MS); bioinformatics (MS); biomedical engineering (MS, PhD); biotechnology (MS); biotechnology and entrepreneurship (MS); chemical engineering (MS, PhD); chemistry (MS); civil engineering (MS, PhD); computer engineering (MS); computer science (MS, PhD); construction management (MS); cyber security (MS); cybersecurity risk and strategy (MS); electrical engineering (MS, PhD); engineering (MS, PhD, Advanced Certificate, Graduate Certificate); environmental engineering (MS); environmental science (MS); financial engineering (MS); industrial engineering (MS); integrated digital media (MS); management (MS); management of technology (MS); manufacturing engineering (MS); materials chemistry (PhD); mathematics (MS, PhD); mechanical engineering (MS, PhD); mechatronics and robotics (MS); organizational behavior (MS); software engineering (Graduate Certificate); technology management (MBA, MS, PhD); transportation management (MS); transportation planning and engineering (MS, PhD); urban systems engineering and management (MS). *Application deadline:* For fall admission, 2/15 for domestic and international students; for spring admission, 11/1 for domestic and international students. Applications are processed on a rolling basis. *Application fee:* $75. Electronic applications accepted. *Application Contact:* Elizabeth Ensweiler, Senior Director of Graduate Enrollment and Graduate Admissions, 646-997-3182, E-mail: elizabeth.ensweiler@nyu.edu. *Dean of NYU Tandon School of Engineering,* Dr. Katepalli Sreenivasan, 646-997-3166, E-mail: katepalli.sreenivasan@nyu.edu.

Tisch School of the Arts Students: 757 full-time (368 women), 33 part-time (22 women); includes 169 minority (50 Black or African American, non-Hispanic/Latino; 49 Asian, non-Hispanic/Latino; 44 Hispanic/Latino; 4 Native Hawaiian or other Pacific Islander, non-Hispanic/Latino; 22 Two or more races, non-Hispanic/Latino), 292 international. Average age 25. 2,917 applicants, 26% accepted, 410 enrolled. *Faculty:* 265 full-time (114 women), 528 part-time/adjunct (220 women). Expenses: Contact institution. *Financial support:* In 2017–18, 695 students received support, including 241 fellowships with full and partial tuition reimbursements available (averaging $26,550 per year); career-related internships or fieldwork, Federal Work-Study, scholarships/grants, and tuition waivers also available. Support available to part-time students. Financial award application deadline: 2/15; financial award applicants required to submit FAFSA. In 2017, 367 master's, 10 doctorates awarded. Offers acting (MFA); arts (MA, MFA, MPS, PhD); arts politics (MA); cinema studies (MA, PhD); dance (MFA); design for stage and film (MFA); dramatic writing (MFA); interactive telecommunications (MPS); moving image archiving and preservation (MA); musical theatre writing (MFA); performance studies (MA, PhD). *Application fee:* $60. Electronic applications accepted. *Application Contact:* Dan Sandford, Director of Graduate Admissions, 212-998-1918, Fax: 212-995-4060, E-mail: tisch.gradadmissions@nyu.edu. *Dean,* Allyson Green, 212-998-1800.

Game Center Students: 59 full-time (31 women); includes 15 minority (4 Black or African American, non-Hispanic/Latino; 5 Asian, non-Hispanic/Latino; 6 Hispanic/Latino), 27 international. 137 applicants, 39% accepted, 34 enrolled. Expenses: Contact institution. In 2017, 28 master's awarded. Offers game design (MFA). *Application deadline:* For fall admission, 12/1 for domestic students. *Application Contact:* Dan Sandford, Director of Graduate Admissions, 212-998-1918, Fax: 212-995-4060, E-mail: tisch.gradadmissions@nyu.edu. *Director,* Frank Lantz, 646-997-0746, E-mail: frank.lantz@nyu.edu.

Kanbar Institute of Film and Television Students: 115 full-time (55 women); includes 31 minority (12 Black or African American, non-Hispanic/Latino; 9 Asian, non-Hispanic/Latino; 6 Hispanic/Latino; 4 Two or more races, non-Hispanic/Latino), 52 international. 747 applicants, 7% accepted, 38 enrolled. *Faculty:* 19 full-time, 20 part-time/adjunct. Expenses: Contact institution. *Financial support:* In 2017–18, 60 students received support. Fellowships, teaching assistantships, Federal Work-Study, institutionally sponsored loans, scholarships/grants, tuition waivers (full and partial), and unspecified assistantships available. Financial award application deadline: 2/15; financial award applicants required to submit FAFSA. In 2017, 80 master's awarded. Offers film and television (MFA). *Application deadline:* For fall admission, 12/1 for domestic and international students. *Application fee:* $60. Electronic applications accepted. *Application Contact:* Dan Sandford, Director of Graduate Admissions, 212-998-1918, Fax: 212-995-4060, E-mail: tisch.gradadmissions@nyu.edu. *Chair,* John Tintori, 212-998-1780, E-mail: jt42@nyu.edu.

Wagner Graduate School of Public Service Students: 541 full-time (388 women), 420 part-time (276 women); includes 306 minority (86 Black or African American, non-Hispanic/Latino; 2 American Indian or Alaska Native, non-Hispanic/Latino; 104 Asian, non-Hispanic/Latino; 90 Hispanic/Latino; 1 Native Hawaiian or other Pacific Islander, non-Hispanic/Latino; 23 Two or more races, non-Hispanic/Latino), 183 international. Average age 28. 1,573 applicants, 59% accepted, 382 enrolled. *Faculty:* 42 full-time (20 women), 88 part-time/adjunct (45 women). Expenses: Contact institution. *Financial support:* In 2017–18, 195 students received support, including 172 fellowships with full and partial tuition reimbursements available (averaging $17,454 per year), 4 research assistantships with full and partial tuition reimbursements available (averaging $45,000 per year); career-related internships or fieldwork, Federal Work-Study, scholarships/grants, health care benefits, and unspecified assistantships also available. Support available to part-time students. Financial award application deadline: 1/6; financial award applicants required to submit FAFSA. In 2017, 398 master's, 6 doctorates, 1 other advanced degree awarded. *Program availability:* Part-time. Offers global public policy and management (EMPA); health finance (MPA); health policy analysis (MPA); health services management (MPA); international health (MPA); public administration (PhD); public and nonprofit management and policy (MPA, Advanced Certificate); public service (EMPA, MPA, MUP, PhD, Advanced Certificate); urban planning (MUP). *Application deadline:* For fall admission, 1/5 for domestic and international students; for spring admission, 10/1 for domestic students, 1/1 for international students. *Application fee:* $85. Electronic applications accepted. *Application Contact:* Sandra Oliveira, Admissions Officer, 212-998-7414, Fax: 212-995-4611, E-mail: wagner.admissions@nyu.edu.

NIAGARA UNIVERSITY, Niagara University, NY 14109

General Information Independent-religious, coed, comprehensive institution. *Enrollment:* 3,949 graduate, professional, and undergraduate students; 476 full-time matriculated graduate/professional students (313 women), 415 part-time matriculated graduate/professional students (294 women). *Enrollment by degree level:* 756 master's, 56 doctoral, 79 other advanced degrees. *Graduate faculty:* 56 full-time, 61 part-time/adjunct. Tuition and fees vary according to program. *Graduate housing:* Room and/or apartments available to single students; on-campus housing not available to married students. Typical cost: $12,950 (including board). Room and board charges vary according to housing facility selected. Housing application deadline: 8/1. *Student services:* Campus employment opportunities, campus safety program, career counseling, exercise/wellness program, free psychological counseling, international student services, low-cost health insurance, multicultural affairs office, services for students with disabilities. *Library facilities:* Our Lady of Angels Library. *Collection:* Books: 122,720 (physical), 348,406 (digital/electronic); Serial titles: 32,000 (digital/electronic); Databases: 111. Weekly public service hours: 107; study areas open 24 hours, 5–7 days a week; students can reserve study rooms. *Research affiliation:* Roswell Park Memorial Institute.

Computer facilities: 81 computers available on campus for general student use. A campuswide network can be accessed from student residence rooms. Online class registration is available.
Website: http://www.niagara.edu/

General Application Contact: Evan Pierce, Associate Director for Academic Affairs, 716-286-8327, Fax: 716-286-8710, E-mail: epierce@niagara.edu.

GRADUATE UNITS

Graduate Division of Arts and Sciences Students: 34 full-time (14 women), 21 part-time (13 women); includes 11 minority (4 Black or African American, non-Hispanic/Latino; 3 Asian, non-Hispanic/Latino; 4 Hispanic/Latino), 16 international. Average age 29. *Faculty:* 9 full-time, 1 part-time/adjunct. Expenses: Contact institution. *Financial support:* Research assistantships with tuition reimbursements, teaching assistantships with tuition reimbursements, career-related internships or fieldwork, Federal Work-Study, scholarships/grants, and unspecified assistantships available. Support available to part-time students. Financial award application deadline: 4/15; financial award applicants required to submit FAFSA. In 2017, 21 master's awarded. *Program availability:* Part-time, evening/weekend. Offers criminal justice (MS); criminal justice administration (MS); information security and digital forensics (MS); interdisciplinary studies (MA). *Application deadline:* For fall admission, 8/1 for domestic students. Applications are processed on a rolling basis. *Application Contact:* Evan Pierce, Associate Dean for Graduate Recruitment, 716-286-8769, Fax: 716-286-8170. *Dean,* Dr. Peter Butera, 716-286-8060, Fax: 716-286-8061, E-mail: pbutera@niagara.edu.

Graduate Division of Business Administration Students: 173 full-time (92 women), 77 part-time (39 women); includes 38 minority (8 Black or African American, non-Hispanic/Latino; 3 American Indian or Alaska Native, non-Hispanic/Latino; 8 Asian, non-Hispanic/Latino; 8 Hispanic/Latino; 11 Two or more races, non-Hispanic/Latino), 46 international. Average age 27. *Faculty:* 17 full-time, 11 part-time/adjunct. Expenses: Contact institution. *Financial support:* Fellowships, research assistantships, career-related internships or fieldwork, and Federal Work-Study available. Support available to part-time students. Financial award application deadline: 4/15; financial award applicants required to submit FAFSA. In 2017, 139 master's awarded. *Program availability:* Part-time, evening/weekend. Offers accounting (MBA); business administration (MBA); finance (MBA, MS); financial planning (MBA); healthcare administration (MBA, MHA); human resources (MBA); international business (MBA); marketing (MBA); professional accountancy (MBA); strategic management (MBA); supply chain management (MBA). *Application deadline:* For fall admission, 8/1 for domestic students; for spring admission, 11/1 for domestic students. Applications are processed on a rolling basis. Electronic applications accepted. *Application Contact:* Evan Pierce, Associate Director for Graduate Recruitment, 716-286-8769, Fax: 716-286-8170, E-mail: epierce@niagara.edu. *MBA Director/Chair of the Marketing Department,* Dr. Paul Richardson, 716-286-8169, Fax: 716-286-8206, E-mail: psr@niagara.edu.

Graduate Division of Education Students: 260 full-time (203 women), 311 part-time (239 women); includes 67 minority (35 Black or African American, non-Hispanic/Latino; 3 American Indian or Alaska Native, non-Hispanic/Latino; 3 Asian, non-Hispanic/Latino; 18 Hispanic/Latino; 8 Two or more races, non-Hispanic/Latino), 102 international. Average age 31. *Faculty:* 24 full-time, 49 part-time/adjunct. Expenses: Contact institution. *Financial support:* Research assistantships with tuition reimbursements, teaching assistantships with tuition reimbursements, career-related internships or fieldwork, Federal Work-Study, scholarships/grants, and unspecified assistantships available. Financial award application deadline: 4/15; financial award applicants required to submit FAFSA. In 2017, 202 master's, 10 doctorates, 59 other advanced degrees awarded. *Program availability:* Part-time, evening/weekend. Offers applied behavior analysis (Certificate); early childhood and childhood education (MS Ed, Certificate); early childhood special education (MS); educational leadership (MS Ed, PhD, Certificate); leadership and policy (PhD); literacy instruction (MS Ed); mental health counseling (MS, Certificate); middle and adolescence education (MS Ed); school building leader (MS Ed); school counseling (MS Ed, Certificate); school district business leader (Certificate); school district leader (MS Ed, Certificate); school psychology (MS); special education (MS Ed); special education (grades 1-12) (Certificate); teacher education (MS, MS Ed, Certificate); teaching English to speakers of other languages (MS Ed, Certificate). *Application deadline:* For fall admission, 8/1 for domestic students. Applications are processed on a rolling basis. *Application fee:* $30. *Application Contact:* Evan Pierce, Associate Director for Graduate Recruitment, 716-286-8769, Fax: 716-286-8170, E-mail: epierce@niagara.edu. *Dean, College of Education,* Dr. Chandra Foote, 716-286-8549, Fax: 716-286-8561, E-mail: cjf@niagara.edu.

NICHOLLS STATE UNIVERSITY, Thibodaux, LA 70310

General Information State-supported, coed, comprehensive institution. *Graduate housing:* Rooms and/or apartments available on a first-come, first-served basis to single and married students. Housing application deadline: 4/15.

GRADUATE UNITS

Graduate Studies *Program availability:* Part-time, evening/weekend, online learning.

College of Arts and Sciences *Program availability:* Part-time, evening/weekend. Offers arts and sciences (MS); marine and environmental biology (MS). Electronic applications accepted.

College of Business Administration *Program availability:* Part-time, evening/weekend. Offers business administration (MBA). Electronic applications accepted.

College of Education *Program availability:* Part-time, evening/weekend. Offers clinical mental health counseling (MA); curriculum and instruction (M Ed); education (M Ed, MA, MAT, SSP); educational leadership (M Ed); elementary education (MAT); human performance education (MAT); middle school education (MAT); school counseling (M Ed); school psychology (SSP); secondary education (MAT). Electronic applications accepted.

College of Nursing and Allied Health Offers family nurse practitioner (MSN); nurse executive (MSN); nursing education (MSN); psychiatric/mental health nurse practitioner (MSN).

NICHOLS COLLEGE, Dudley, MA 01571-5000

General Information Independent, coed, comprehensive institution. *Graduate housing:* On-campus housing not available.

GRADUATE UNITS

Graduate and Professional Studies *Program availability:* Part-time, evening/weekend, online learning. Offers business administration (MBA); counterterrorism (MS); organizational leadership (MSOL). Electronic applications accepted.

NIPISSING UNIVERSITY, North Bay, ON P1B 8L7, Canada

General Information Province-supported, coed, comprehensive institution. *Graduate housing:* Room and/or apartments available to single students; on-campus housing not available to married students. Housing application deadline: 6/13. *Research affiliation:* Metals in the Human Environment Research Network (MITHE-RN) (assessing environmental pollutants on aquatic ecosystems), Tembec (forestry restoration), Canada Space Agency (CSA) and MacDonald, Dettwiler and Associates Ltd. (MDA–RADARSAT-2) (remote sensing), Education Quality and Accountability Office (EQAO) (assessing educational quality), Ontario Association of Deans of Education (OADE) (assessing pre-service practicum processes).

GRADUATE UNITS

Faculty of Education *Program availability:* Part-time, evening/weekend. Offers education (M Ed, Certificate).

NORFOLK STATE UNIVERSITY, Norfolk, VA 23504

General Information State-supported, coed, comprehensive institution. CGS member. *Graduate housing:* Room and/or apartments available to single students; on-campus housing not available to married students. Housing application deadline: 3/1. *Research affiliation:* U.S. Department of Energy/NASA (fundamental and applied research studies), NASA Langley Research Center (aerospace applications, lidar application), National Science Foundation (fundamental and applied research studies), U.S. Department of Education (DOE) (Title III projects, No Child Left Behind initiative), University of Virginia's Integrative Graduate Education and Research Traineeship (IGERT) (science and engineering interactions with matter), Applied Research Center (technology transfer).

GRADUATE UNITS

School of Graduate Studies *Program availability:* Part-time. Electronic applications accepted.

Ethelyn R. Strong School of Social Work *Program availability:* Part-time. Offers social work (MSW, PhD).

School of Education *Program availability:* Part-time. Offers early childhood education (MAT); education (MA, MAT); pre-elementary education (MA); principal preparation (MA); secondary education (MAT); severe disabilities (MA); teaching (MA); urban education/administration (MA).

School of Liberal Arts *Program availability:* Part-time. Offers community/clinical psychology (MA); criminal justice (MA); liberal arts (MA, MFA, MM, Psy D); media and communication (MA); music (MM); music education (MM); performance (MM); psychology (Psy D); theory and composition (MM); urban affairs (MA); visual studies (MA, MFA).

School of Science and Technology Offers computer science (MS); electronics engineering (MS); materials science (MS); optical engineering (MS); science and technology (MS).

NORTH AMERICAN UNIVERSITY, Stafford, TX 77477

General Information Independent, coed, comprehensive institution.

GRADUATE UNITS

Program in Educational Leadership Offers educational leadership (M Ed).

NORTH CAROLINA AGRICULTURAL AND TECHNICAL STATE UNIVERSITY, Greensboro, NC 27411

General Information State-supported, coed, university. CGS member. *Graduate housing:* Room and/or apartments available on a first-come, first-served basis to single students; on-campus housing not available to married students. Housing application deadline: 5/8. *Research affiliation:* North Carolina Biotechnology Research Center (biotechnology), Boeing (aerospace engineering), Northrop Grumman Corporation (high performance computing), Research Triangle Institute (environmental protection, advanced technology), Rockwell, Inc. (avionics technology, communications technology), Honeywell (industrial automation control).

GRADUATE UNITS

School of Graduate Studies *Program availability:* Part-time, evening/weekend. Electronic applications accepted.

College of Arts and Sciences *Program availability:* Part-time, evening/weekend. Offers applied mathematics (MS); arts and sciences (MA, MAT, MS, MSW); biology (MS); biology education (MAT); chemistry (MS, PhD); computational sciences (MS); English (MA); English and African-American literature (MA); English education (MAT, MS); physics (MS); sociology and social work (MSW).

College of Engineering *Program availability:* Part-time. Offers bioengineering (MS); biological engineering (MS); chemical engineering (MS); civil engineering (MSCE); computer science (MSCS); electrical engineering (MSEE, PhD); engineering (MS, MSCE, MSCS, MSE, MSEE, MSIE, MSME, PhD); industrial engineering (MSIE, PhD); mechanical engineering (MSME, PhD).

School of Agriculture and Environmental Sciences *Program availability:* Part-time, evening/weekend. Offers agricultural economics (MS); agricultural education (MS); agriculture and environmental sciences (MAT, MS); animal health science (MS); child development early education and family studies (MAT); family and consumer sciences (MAT); food and nutrition (MS); plant, soil and environmental science (MS).

School of Business and Economics Offers accounting (MBA); business education (MAT); human resources management (MBA); supply chain systems (MBA).

School of Education *Program availability:* Part-time, evening/weekend. Offers adult education (MS); counseling (MS); education (MA Ed, MAT, MS); elementary education (MA Ed); instructional technology (MS); physical education (MAT, MS); reading education (MA Ed); school administration (MS); teaching (MAT).

School of Technology *Program availability:* Part-time, evening/weekend. Offers construction management (MSTM); electronics and computer technology (MSIT, MSTM); environmental and occupational safety (MSTM); graphic communication systems (MSTM); information technology (MSIT, MSTM); manufacturing (MSTM); occupational safety and health (MSTM); technology (MAT, MSIT, MSTM); technology education (MAT).

NORTH CAROLINA CENTRAL UNIVERSITY, Durham, NC 27707-3129

General Information State-supported, coed, comprehensive institution. CGS member. *Enrollment:* 8,097 graduate, professional, and undergraduate students; 1,271 full-time matriculated graduate/professional students (880 women), 471 part-time matriculated graduate/professional students (348 women). *Enrollment by degree level:* 1,212 master's, 473 doctoral, 57 other advanced degrees. *Graduate faculty:* 27 full-time (13 women), 5 part-time/adjunct (3 women). Tuition, state resident: full-time $2770; part-time $692.50 per credit hour. Tuition, nonresident: full-time $9247; part-time $2311.75 per credit hour. *Graduate housing:* Room and/or apartments available on a first-come, first-served basis to single students; on-campus housing not available to married students. Typical cost: $4800 per year. Housing application deadline: 7/1. *Student services:* Campus employment opportunities, campus safety program, career counseling, child daycare facilities, exercise/wellness program, free psychological counseling, international student services, low-cost health insurance, services for students with disabilities, teacher training, writing training. *Library facilities:* Shepherd Library plus 2 others. *Collection:* Study areas open 24 hours, 5–7 days a week; students can reserve study rooms.

Computer facilities: Computer purchase and lease plans are available. 1,262 computers available on campus for general student use. A campuswide network can be accessed from student residence rooms and from off campus. Online class registration is available.
Website: http://www.nccu.edu/

General Application Contact: Dr. Caesar Jackson, Interim Dean of Graduate Studies, 919-530-7396, Fax: 919-530-7919, E-mail: graddean@nccu.edu.

GRADUATE UNITS

College of Arts and Sciences Expenses: Contact institution. Offers arts and sciences (MA, MM, MS); biological and biomedical sciences (MS); chemistry (MS); earth sciences (MS); English (MA); environmental and geographic sciences (MS); history (MA); jazz studies (MM); mathematics (MS); physics (MS). *Application Contact:* Veronica C. Nwosu, Interim Dean, 919-530-8082, E-mail: vcnwosu@nccu.edu. *Interim Dean*, Veronica C. Nwosu, 919-530-8082, E-mail: vcnwosu@nccu.edu.

College of Behavioral and Social Sciences Expenses: Contact institution. Offers behavioral and social sciences (MA, MPA, MS, MSW); clinical psychology (MA); criminal justice (MS); general physical education (MS); general psychology (MA); public administration (MPA); recreation administration (MS). *Application Contact:* Debra O. Parker, Dean, 919-530-5269, Fax: 919-530-7640, E-mail: dparker@nccu.edu. *Dean*, Debra O. Parker, 919-530-5269, Fax: 919-530-7640, E-mail: dparker@nccu.edu.

School of Business Expenses: Contact institution. *Financial support:* Teaching assistantships, Federal Work-Study, institutionally sponsored loans, and unspecified assistantships available. Support available to part-time students. Financial award application deadline: 5/1; financial award applicants required to submit FAFSA. *Program availability:* Part-time, evening/weekend. Offers business (MBA). *Application deadline:* For fall admission, 8/1 for domestic students. *Application fee:* $30. *Application Contact:* Sharon D. White, Graduate Program Director, 919-530-6404, Fax: 919-530-6163, E-mail: sharon.white@nccu.edu. *Graduate Program Director*, Sharon D. White, 919-530-6404, Fax: 919-530-6163, E-mail: sharon.white@nccu.edu.

School of Education Expenses: Contact institution. *Financial support:* Application deadline: 5/1. *Program availability:* Part-time, evening/weekend. Offers career counseling (MA); clinical mental health counseling (MA); communication disorders (MS); education (M Ed, MA, MAT, MS, MSA); educational technology (MA); emotional disabilities (M Ed, MAT); learning disabilities (M Ed, MAT); school administration (MSA); school counseling (MA); visual impairment (M Ed, MAT). *Application deadline:* For fall admission, 8/1 for domestic students. *Application fee:* $30. *Application Contact:* Audrey W. Beard, Dean, 919-530-6466, Fax: 919-530-7681, E-mail: awbeard@nccu.edu. *Dean*, Audrey W. Beard, 919-530-6466, Fax: 919-530-7681, E-mail: awbeard@nccu.edu.

School of Law Expenses: Contact institution. *Financial support:* Application deadline: 5/1; applicants required to submit FAFSA. *Program availability:* Part-time, evening/weekend. Offers law (JD). *Application deadline:* For fall admission, 4/15 for domestic students. *Application fee:* $30. *Application Contact:* Phyliss Craig-Taylor, Dean, 919-530-6333, E-mail: pcraigtaylor@nccu.edu. *Dean*, Phyliss Craig-Taylor, 919-530-6333, E-mail: pcraigtaylor@nccu.edu.

School of Library and Information Sciences Expenses: Contact institution. *Financial support:* Application deadline: 5/1; applicants required to submit FAFSA. *Program availability:* Part-time, evening/weekend. Offers library and information sciences (MIS, MLS). *Application deadline:* For fall admission, 8/1 for domestic students. *Application fee:* $30. *Application Contact:* Dr. Jon P. Gant, Dean, 919-530-6402, Fax: 919-530-6402, E-mail: slis-dean@nccu.edu. *Dean*, Dr. Jon P. Gant, 919-530-6402, Fax: 919-530-6402, E-mail: slis-dean@nccu.edu.

NORTH CAROLINA STATE UNIVERSITY, Raleigh, NC 27695

General Information State-supported, coed, university. CGS member. *Graduate housing:* Rooms and/or apartments available on a first-come, first-served basis to single and married students. *Research affiliation:* Triangle Universities Nuclear Laboratory, Research Triangle Institute, Highlands Biological Station, National Humanities Center, Microelectronics Center of North Carolina, North Carolina–Japan Center.

GRADUATE UNITS

College of Veterinary Medicine *Program availability:* Part-time. Offers cell biology (MS, PhD); infectious disease (MS, PhD); pathology (MS, PhD); pharmacology (MS, PhD); population medicine (MS, PhD); veterinary medicine (MS, MSpVM, MVPH, DVM, PhD); veterinary public health (MVPH). Electronic applications accepted.

Graduate School *Program availability:* Part-time, evening/weekend, online learning. Electronic applications accepted.

College of Agriculture and Life Sciences *Program availability:* Part-time. Offers agricultural and extension education (Ed D); agricultural and resource economics (MS); agricultural education (MAE, MS, Certificate); agriculture and life sciences (M Tox, MAE, MB, MBAE, MFG, MFM, MFS, MG, MMB, MN, MP, MS, MZS, Ed D, PhD, Certificate); animal and poultry science (PhD); animal science (MS); biochemistry (PhD); bioinformatics (MB, PhD); biological and agricultural engineering (MBAE, MS, PhD, Certificate); crop science (MS, PhD); entomology (MS, PhD); environmental and molecular toxicology (M Tox, MS, PhD); extension education (MS); financial mathematics (MFM); food science (MFS, MS, PhD); functional genomics (MFG, MS, PhD); genetics (MG, MS, PhD); genomic sciences (MS, PhD); horticultural science (MS, PhD, Certificate); microbial biotechnology (MMB); microbiology (MMB, MS, PhD); nutrition (MN, MS, PhD); physiology (MP, MS, PhD); plant biology (MS, PhD); plant pathology (MS, PhD); poultry science (MS); soil science (MS, PhD); zoology (MS, MZS, PhD). Electronic applications accepted.

College of Design *Program availability:* Part-time. Offers architecture (M Arch); art and design (MAD); design (M Arch, MAD, MGD, MID, MLA, PhD); graphic design (MGD); industrial design (MID); landscape architecture (MLA). Electronic applications accepted.

College of Education *Program availability:* Part-time. Offers adult and community college education (M Ed, MS, Ed D); agency counseling (M Ed, MS); business and marketing education (M Ed, MS); counselor education (M Ed, MS, PhD); curriculum and instruction (M Ed, MS, PhD); education (M Ed, MS, MS Ed, MSA, Ed D, PhD, Certificate); educational administration and supervision (Ed D); educational research and policy analysis (PhD); elementary education (M Ed); higher education administration (M Ed, MS, Ed D); human resource development (MS); instructional technology (M Ed, MS); mathematics education (M Ed, MS, PhD); middle grades education (M Ed, MS); school administration (MSA); science education (M Ed, MS, PhD); secondary English education (M Ed, MS Ed); social studies education (M Ed); special education (M Ed, MS); technology education (M Ed, MS, Ed D); training and development (M Ed, Ed D, Certificate). Electronic applications accepted.

College of Engineering *Program availability:* Part-time. Offers aerospace engineering (MS, PhD); biomedical engineering (MS, PhD); chemical engineering (M Ch E, MS, PhD); civil engineering (MCE, MS, PhD); computer engineering (MS, PhD); computer networking (MS); computer science (MC Sc, MS, PhD); electrical engineering (MS, PhD); engineering (M Ch E, M Eng, MC Sc, MCE, MIE, MIMS, MMSE, MNE, MOR, MS, PhD); industrial engineering (MIE, MS, PhD); integrated manufacturing systems engineering (MIMS); materials science and engineering (MMSE, MS, PhD); mechanical engineering (MS, PhD); nuclear engineering (MNE, MS, PhD); operations research (MOR, MS, PhD). Electronic applications accepted.

College of Humanities and Social Sciences *Program availability:* Part-time, evening/weekend. Offers anthropology (MA); bioarchaeology (MA); communication (MS); communication, rhetoric, and digital media (PhD); creative writing (MFA); cultural anthropology (MA); developmental psychology (PhD); English (MA); environmental anthropology (MA); ergonomics and experimental psychology (PhD); French language and literature (MA); history (MA); humanities and social sciences (M Soc, MA, MFA, MIS, MPA, MS, MSW, PhD, Certificate); industrial/organizational psychology (PhD); international studies (MIS); liberal studies (MA); nonprofit management (Certificate); psychology in the public interest (PhD); public administration (MPA, PhD); public history (MA); school psychology (PhD); social work (MSW); sociology (M Soc, MS, PhD); Spanish language and literature (MA); technical communication (MS). Electronic applications accepted.

College of Natural Resources *Program availability:* Part-time. Offers fisheries and wildlife sciences (MFWS, MS, PhD); forestry and environmental resources (MF, MS, PhD); natural resource management (MPRTM, MS); natural resources (MF, MFWS, MNR, MPRTM, MS, MWPS, PhD); park and recreation management (MPRTM, MS); parks, recreation and tourism management (PhD); recreational sport management (MPRTM, MS); spatial information science (MPRTM, MS); tourism policy and development (MPRTM, MS); wood and paper science (MS, MWPS, PhD). Electronic applications accepted.

College of Physical and Mathematical Sciences *Program availability:* Part-time. Offers applied mathematics (MS, PhD); biomathematics (M Biomath, MS, PhD); chemistry (MS, PhD); marine, earth, and atmospheric sciences (MS, PhD); mathematics (MS, PhD); meteorology (MS, PhD); oceanography (MS, PhD); physical and mathematical sciences (M Biomath, M Stat, MS, PhD); physics (MS, PhD); statistics (M Stat, MS, PhD). Electronic applications accepted.

College of Textiles *Program availability:* Part-time, evening/weekend, online learning. Offers fiber and polymer science (PhD); textile and apparel technology and management (MS, MT); textile chemistry (MS); textile engineering (MS); textile technology management (PhD); textiles (MS, MT, PhD). Electronic applications accepted.

Institute for Advanced Analytics Offers analytics (MS). Electronic applications accepted.

Poole College of Management *Program availability:* Part-time. Offers accounting (MAC); biosciences management (MBA); economics (M Econ, MA, PhD); entrepreneurship and technology commercialization (MBA); financial management (MBA); innovation management (MBA); management (M Econ, MA, MAC, MBA, MS, PhD); marketing management (MBA); services management (MBA); supply chain management (MBA). Electronic applications accepted.

NORTH CENTRAL COLLEGE, Naperville, IL 60566-7063

General Information Independent-religious, coed, comprehensive institution. CGS member. *Graduate housing:* Room and/or apartments available on a first-come, first-served basis to single students; on-campus housing not available to married students. Housing application deadline: 4/15.

GRADUATE UNITS

School of Graduate and Professional Studies *Program availability:* Part-time, evening/weekend. Offers change management (MBA); computer science (MS); culture and society (MALS); education (MA Ed); finance (MBA); human resource management (MBA); leadership studies (MLD); management (MBA). Electronic applications accepted.

NORTHCENTRAL UNIVERSITY, San Diego, CA 92106

General Information Proprietary, coed, upper-level institution. CGS member. *Enrollment:* 10,698 graduate, professional, and undergraduate students; 4,759 full-time matriculated graduate/professional students (2,997 women), 5,939 part-time matriculated graduate/professional students (3,987 women). *Enrollment by degree level:* 4,009 master's, 6,206 doctoral, 454 other advanced degrees. *Graduate faculty:* 119 full-time (77 women), 379 part-time/adjunct (195 women). Tuition and fees vary according to program. *Graduate housing:* On-campus housing not available. *Student services:* Services for students with disabilities, writing training. *Library facilities:* Northcentral University Library (Virtual). *Collection:* Databases: 123. Weekly public service hours: 79. *Research affiliation:* Coalition for Research to Practice (mental health services; aligning academic training with workforce demands).

Computer facilities: Online class registration is available.
Website: http://www.ncu.edu/

General Application Contact: Enrollment Advisor, 866-776-0331, Fax: 928-541-7817, E-mail: admissions@ncu.edu.

GRADUATE UNITS

Graduate Studies Students: 5,036 full-time (3,291 women), 5,747 part-time (3,977 women); includes 3,777 minority (2,550 Black or African American, non-Hispanic/Latino; 76 American Indian or Alaska Native, non-Hispanic/Latino; 192 Asian, non-Hispanic/Latino; 603 Hispanic/Latino; 39 Native Hawaiian or other Pacific Islander, non-Hispanic/Latino; 317 Two or more races, non-Hispanic/Latino). Average age 45. *Faculty:* 98 full-time (63 women), 385 part-time/adjunct (203 women). Expenses: Contact institution. *Financial support:* Scholarships/grants available. In 2017, 929 master's, 782 doctorates, 278 other advanced degrees awarded. *Program availability:* Part-time, evening/weekend, online only, 100% online. Offers business (MBA, DBA, PhD, Postbaccalaureate Certificate); education (M Ed, Ed D, PhD, Ed S, Post-Master's Certificate, Postbaccalaureate Certificate); marriage and family therapy (MA, DMFT, PhD, Post-Master's Certificate, Postbaccalaureate Certificate); psychology (MA, PhD, Post-Master's Certificate, Postbaccalaureate Certificate); technology (MS, PhD). *Application deadline:* Applications are processed on a rolling basis. *Application fee:* $0. Electronic applications accepted. *Application Contact:* Ken Boutelle, Vice President, Enrollment Services, 888-628-4979, E-mail: enrollmentservices@ncu.edu. *Acting Provost*, Dr. David Harpool, 888-327-2877 Ext. 8181, E-mail: provost@ncu.edu.

NORTH DAKOTA STATE UNIVERSITY, Fargo, ND 58102

General Information State-supported, coed, university. CGS member. Tuition, state resident: full-time $4323; part-time $360.21 per credit. Tuition, nonresident: full-time $6484; part-time $540.31 per credit. *Required fees:* $668; $55.70 per credit. Part-time tuition and fees vary according to degree level, program and reciprocity agreements. *Graduate housing:* Rooms and/or apartments available on a first-come, first-served basis to single and married students. *Student services:* Campus employment opportunities, career counseling, child daycare facilities, exercise/wellness program, free psychological counseling, international student services, low-cost health insurance, multicultural affairs office, services for students with disabilities. *Library facilities:* North Dakota State University Library plus 6 others. *Collection:* Books: 662,884 (physical), 162,977 (digital/electronic); Serial titles: 171,924 (physical), 99,565 (digital/electronic); Databases: 232. Weekly public service hours: 93; students can reserve study rooms. *Research affiliation:* U.S. Department of Agriculture (USDA), Metabolism and Radiation Laboratory.

Computer facilities: Computer purchase and lease plans are available. 601 computers available on campus for general student use. A campuswide network can be accessed from student residence rooms. Online class registration, online course content (e.g., learning management system, lecture capture video recordings) are available.
Website: http://www.ndsu.edu/

General Application Contact: Elizabeth Worth, Graduate Programs Manager, 701-231-6038, Fax: 701-231-6524, E-mail: elizabeth.worth@ndsu.edu.

GRADUATE UNITS

College of Graduate and Interdisciplinary Studies Students: 657 full-time (316 women), 1,380 part-time (680 women); includes 169 minority (38 Black or African American, non-Hispanic/Latino; 23 American Indian or Alaska Native, non-Hispanic/Latino; 49 Asian, non-Hispanic/Latino; 31 Hispanic/Latino; 3 Native Hawaiian or other Pacific Islander, non-Hispanic/Latino; 25 Two or more races, non-Hispanic/Latino), 569 international. Average age 28. 1,549 applicants, 39% accepted, 435 enrolled. *Faculty:* 445 full-time (151 women), 34 part-time/adjunct (11 women). Expenses: Contact institution. *Financial support:* Fellowships with full tuition reimbursements, research assistantships with full tuition reimbursements, teaching assistantships with full tuition reimbursements, career-related internships or fieldwork, Federal Work-Study, institutionally sponsored loans, scholarships/grants, traineeships, tuition waivers (full and partial), and unspecified assistantships available. Support available to part-time students. In 2017, 356 master's, 81 doctorates, 82 other advanced degrees awarded. *Program availability:* Part-time, evening/weekend, 100% online, blended/hybrid learning. Offers cellular and molecular biology (PhD); college teaching (Certificate); environmental and conservation sciences (MS, PhD); food safety (MS, PhD); genomics and bioinformatics (MS, PhD); managerial logistics (MML); materials and nanotechnology (MS, PhD); STEM education (PhD); transportation and logistics (PhD); transportation and urban systems (MS). *Application fee:* $35. Electronic applications accepted. *Application Contact:* Melissa Ostby, Graduate Admissions Coordinator, 701-231-7034, Fax: 701-231-6524, E-mail: melissa.j.ostby@ndsu.edu. *Dean*, Dr. Claudia Tomany, 701-231-7033, Fax: 701-231-6524.

College of Agriculture, Food Systems, and Natural Resources Expenses: Contact institution. *Program availability:* Part-time. Offers agribusiness and applied economics (MS); agriculture, food systems, and natural resources (MS, PhD); animal sciences (MS, PhD); cereal science (MS, PhD); entomology (MS, PhD); horticulture (MS); international agribusiness (MS); microbiology (MS); molecular pathogenesis (PhD); natural resources management (MS, PhD); plant pathology (MS, PhD); plant sciences (MS, PhD); soil sciences (MS, PhD). *Application deadline:* Applications are processed on a rolling basis. *Application fee:* $35. Electronic applications accepted. *Application Contact:* Elizabeth Worth, Marketing, Recruitment, and Public Relations Coordinator, 701-231-8476, Fax: 701-231-6524, E-mail: elizabeth.worth@ndsu.edu. *Dean*, Dr. Kenneth F. Grafton, 701-231-6693, Fax: 701-231-7566, E-mail: k.grafton@ndsu.edu.

College of Arts, Humanities and Social Sciences Expenses: Contact institution. *Program availability:* Part-time, evening/weekend. Offers anthropology (MA, MS); architecture (M Arch); arts, humanities and social sciences (M Arch, M Ed, MA, MLA, MM, MS, DMA, PhD); communication (PhD); community development (MA, MS); composition (MA); conducting (MM, DMA); criminal justice (PhD); criminal justice administration (MS); history (MA, MS, PhD); landscape architecture (MLA); mass communication (MA); music education (MM); performance (MM, DMA); rhetoric, writing and culture (PhD); sociology (MS); speech communication (MS). *Application deadline:* Applications are processed on a rolling basis. *Application fee:* $35. Electronic applications accepted. *Application Contact:* Elizabeth Worth, Marketing, Recruitment, and Public Relations Coordinator, 701-231-8476, Fax: 701-231-6524, E-mail: elizabeth.worth@ndsu.edu. *Dean*, Dr. David Bertolini, 701-231-5761, E-mail: david.bertolini@ndsu.edu.

College of Business Expenses: Contact institution. *Financial support:* Application deadline: 5/15; applicants required to submit FAFSA. *Program availability:* Part-time, evening/weekend. Offers accountancy (M Acc); business administration (MBA). *Application deadline:* For fall admission, 7/1 priority date for domestic students, 5/1 priority date for international students; for spring admission, 11/15 for domestic students, 8/1 priority date for international students. Applications are processed on a rolling basis. *Application fee:* $35. Electronic applications accepted. *Application Contact:* Paul Brown, Program Coordinator, 701-231-9407, E-mail: paul.brown@ndsu.edu. *Program Coordinator*, Paul Brown, 701-231-9407, E-mail: paul.brown@ndsu.edu.

College of Engineering Expenses: Contact institution. *Financial support:* Application deadline: 4/15. *Program availability:* Part-time. Offers agricultural and biosystems engineering (MS, PhD); civil engineering (MS, PhD); construction management (MCM, MS, Graduate Certificate); electrical and computer engineering (M Eng, MS, PhD); engineering (MCM, MS, PhD, Graduate Certificate); environmental and conservation science (PhD); environmental engineering (MS); industrial and manufacturing engineering (MS, PhD); manufacturing engineering (MS); materials and nanotechnology (PhD); mechanical engineering (MS, PhD); natural resource management (PhD); STEM education (PhD); transportation and logistics (PhD). *Application deadline:* For fall admission, 4/1 priority date for domestic students, 5/1 priority date for international students; for spring admission, 10/1 priority date for domestic students, 8/1 priority date for international students. Applications are processed on a rolling basis. *Application fee:* $35. Electronic applications accepted. *Application Contact:* Dr. Michael R. Kessler, Dean, 701-231-7525, E-mail: michael.r.kessler@ndsu.edu. *Dean*, Dr. Michael R. Kessler, 701-231-7525, E-mail: michael.r.kessler@ndsu.edu.

College of Health Professions Expenses: Contact institution. *Financial support:* Application deadline: 4/1. *Program availability:* Part-time. Offers American Indian public health (MPH); community health sciences (MPH); health professions (MPH, MS, DNP, PhD, Pharm D); management of infectious diseases (MPH); nursing (DNP); pharmacy (MS, PhD, Pharm D). *Application deadline:* Applications are processed on a rolling basis. *Application fee:* $35. Electronic applications accepted. *Application Contact:* Dr. Charles D. Peterson, Dean, 701-231-5383, Fax: 701-231-7606, E-mail: charles.peterson@ndsu.edu. *Dean*, Dr. Charles D. Peterson, 701-231-5383, Fax: 701-231-7606, E-mail: charles.peterson@ndsu.edu.

College of Human Development and Education Expenses: Contact institution. *Program availability:* Part-time, evening/weekend, online learning. Offers advanced athletic training (MS); agricultural education (M Ed, MS); athletic training (MAT); clinical mental health counseling (M Ed, MS); counselor education (M Ed, MS); counselor education and supervision (PhD); developmental science (PhD); dietetics (MS); educational leadership (M Ed, MS, Ed S); exercise science and nutrition (PhD); family and consumer sciences education (M Ed, MS); family financial planning (MS, Certificate); gerontology (PhD, Certificate); health, nutrition and exercise science (MS); human development and education (M Ed, MAT, MPH, MS, Ed D, PhD, Certificate, Ed S); school counseling (M Ed, MS); youth development (MS). *Application deadline:* Applications are processed on a rolling basis. *Application fee:* $35. Electronic applications accepted. *Application Contact:* Elizabeth Worth, Marketing, Recruitment, and Public Relations Coordinator, 701-231-8476, Fax: 701-231-6524, E-mail: elizabeth.worth@ndsu.edu. *Dean*, Dr. Margaret Fitzgerald, 701-231-8211, Fax: 701-231-7174, E-mail: margaret.fitzgerald@ndsu.edu.

College of Science and Mathematics Expenses: Contact institution. *Financial support:* Applicants required to submit FAFSA. *Program availability:* Part-time. Offers applied mathematics (MS, PhD); biochemistry (MS, PhD); biology (MS); botany (MS, PhD); chemistry (MS, PhD); clinical psychology (MS); coatings and polymeric materials (MS, PhD); computer science (MS, PhD); health and social psychology (PhD); mathematics (MS, PhD); physics (MS, PhD); psychological clinical science (PhD); psychology (MS); science and mathematics (MS, PhD, Certificate); software engineering (MS, MSE, PhD, Certificate); sports statistics (PhD); statistics (MS); visual and cognitive neuroscience (PhD); zoology (MS, PhD). *Application deadline:* Applications are processed on a rolling basis. *Application fee:* $35. Electronic applications accepted. *Application Contact:* Elizabeth Worth, Marketing, Recruitment, and Public Relations Coordinator, 701-231-8476, Fax: 701-231-6524, E-mail: elizabeth.worth@ndsu.edu. *Dean*, Dr. Scott A. Wood, 701-231-7411, E-mail: scott.wood@ndsu.edu.

NORTHEASTERN ILLINOIS UNIVERSITY, Chicago, IL 60625-4699

General Information State-supported, coed, comprehensive institution. Tuition, state resident: full-time $7274; part-time $404.11 per credit hour. Tuition, nonresident: full-time $14,548; part-time $808.23 per credit hour. *Required fees:* $1284. *Graduate housing:* Room and/or apartments available to single students; on-campus housing not available to married students. Typical cost: $11,020 per year ($13,020 including board). *Student services:* Campus employment opportunities, campus safety program, career counseling, child daycare facilities, exercise/wellness program, free psychological counseling, grant writing training, international student services, low-cost health insurance, multicultural affairs office, services for students with disabilities, teacher training, writing training. *Library facilities:* Ronald Williams Library plus 3 others. *Collection:* Books: 688,147 (physical), 156,705 (digital/electronic); Serial titles: 742 (physical), 86,898 (digital/electronic); Databases: 188. Weekly public service hours: 92. *Research affiliation:* Advocate Health Care Network (health care cost containment), Lutheran General Hospital (clinical cardiology), Advocate Medical Group (health care outcomes research).

Computer facilities: Computer purchase and lease plans are available. A campuswide network can be accessed from off campus. Online class registration, productivity software are available.
Website: http://www.neiu.edu/

General Application Contact: Hany E. Ramirez Mijares, Admissions and Records Specialist II, Graduate Enrollment Services, 773-442-6006, Fax: 773-442-6040, E-mail: h-ramirez5@neiu.edu.

GRADUATE UNITS

College of Graduate Studies and Research Expenses: Contact institution. *Financial support:* Applicants required to submit FAFSA. *Program availability:* Part-time, evening/weekend. *Application deadline:* For fall admission, 4/1 priority date for domestic students; for spring admission, 8/15 for domestic students. Applications are processed on a rolling basis. *Application fee:* $25. Electronic applications accepted. *Application Contact:* Ada Umeh, Admission Director, Graduate College, 773-442-6008, Fax: 773-442-6040, E-mail: a-umeh@neiu.edu. *Dean*, Dr. Janet P. Fredericks, 773-442-6010, Fax: 773-442-6020, E-mail: j-fredericks@neiu.edu.

College of Arts and Sciences Expenses: Contact institution. *Financial support:* Applicants required to submit FAFSA. *Program availability:* Part-time, evening/weekend. Offers arts and sciences (MA, MS, Graduate Certificate); biology (MS); chemistry (MS); communication, media and theatre (MA); computer science (MS); English (MA); geographic information science (Graduate Certificate); geography and environmental studies (MA); gerontology (MA); history (MA); Latin American literatures and cultures (MA); linguistics (MA); mathematics (MS); music (MA); political science (MA); secondary education mathematics (MS); teaching English to speakers of other languages (MA). *Application deadline:* For fall admission, 4/1 priority date for domestic students; for spring admission, 8/15 for domestic students. Applications are processed on a rolling basis. *Application fee:* $25. Electronic applications accepted. *Application Contact:* Ada Umeh, Admission Director, Graduate College, 773-442-6008, Fax: 773-442-6040, E-mail: a-umeh@neiu.edu. *Dean*, Dr. Wamucii Njogu, 773-442-5700.

College of Business and Management Expenses: Contact institution. *Program availability:* Part-time, evening/weekend. Offers accounting (MSA); business administration (MBA). *Application deadline:* For fall admission, 4/1 priority date for domestic students; for spring admission, 8/15 for domestic students. Applications are processed on a rolling basis. *Application fee:* $30. Electronic applications accepted. *Application Contact:* Ada Umeh, Admission Director, Graduate College, 773-442-6008, Fax: 773-442-6040, E-mail: a-umeh@neiu.edu. *Graduate Program Coordinator*, Dr. Charletta Gutierrez, 773-442-6128, E-mail: cf-gutierrez@neiu.edu.

Daniel L. Goodwin College of Education Expenses: Contact institution. *Financial support:* Applicants required to submit FAFSA. *Program availability:* Part-time, evening/weekend. Offers clinical mental health counseling (MA); early childhood education (MAT); education (MA, MAT, MS, MSI); educational administration and supervision (MA); elementary education (MAT); exercise science (MS); family counseling (MA); gifted education (MA); human resource development (MA); inner city studies (MA); language arts (MAT); language arts - secondary education (MSI); learning behavior specialist (MA, MS); literacy education (MA); mathematics (MAT); middle level education (MAT); rehabilitation counseling (MA); school counseling (MA); science (MAT); social science (MAT). *Application deadline:* For fall admission, 4/1 priority date for domestic students; for spring admission, 8/15 for domestic students. Applications are processed on a rolling basis. *Application fee:* $30. Electronic applications accepted. *Application Contact:* Ada Umeh, Admission Director, Graduate College, 773-442-6008, Fax: 773-442-6040, E-mail: a-umeh@neiu.edu. *Dean*, Dr. Maureen D. Gillette, 773-442-5500.

NORTHEASTERN SEMINARY AT ROBERTS WESLEYAN COLLEGE, Rochester, NY 14624

General Information Independent-religious, coed, graduate-only institution. *Enrollment by degree level:* 76 master's, 38 doctoral, 3 other advanced degrees. *Graduate faculty:* 7 full-time (2 women), 17 part-time/adjunct (2 women). *Tuition:* Full-time $9234; part-time $4617 per credit. *Required fees:* $500; $250 per credit. Tuition and fees vary according to course load, degree level and program. *Graduate housing:* On-campus housing not available. *Student services:* Campus safety program, career counseling, exercise/wellness program, international student services, services for students with disabilities, writing training. *Library facilities:* B. Thomas Golisano Library plus 1 other. *Collection:* Serial titles: 141 (physical), 75 (digital/electronic). Weekly public service hours: 80; study areas open 24 hours, 5–7 days a week; students can reserve study rooms.

Computer facilities: 104 computers available on campus for general student use. A campuswide network can be accessed from student residence rooms and from off campus. Online class registration is available.
Website: http://www.nes.edu/

General Application Contact: William Gibbons, Admissions Liaison, 585-594-6826, Fax: 585-594-6801, E-mail: gibbions_william@roberts.edu.

GRADUATE UNITS

Graduate and Professional Programs Students: 87 full-time (42 women), 30 part-time (12 women); includes 42 minority (33 Black or African American, non-Hispanic/Latino; 9 Hispanic/Latino), 4 international. Average age 47. *Faculty:* 7 full-time (2 women), 17 part-time/adjunct (2 women). Expenses: Contact institution. *Financial support:* Teaching assistantships with partial tuition reimbursements, career-related internships or fieldwork, institutionally sponsored loans, scholarships/grants, and tuition waivers (partial) available. Financial award applicants required to submit FAFSA. *Program availability:* Evening/weekend. Offers ministry (D Min); theological studies (MA); theology (M Div); theology and social justice (MA); transformational leadership (MA). M Div/MSW offered jointly with Roberts Wesleyan College. *Application deadline:* For fall admission, 8/1 priority date for domestic and international students; for spring admission, 12/15 priority date for domestic and international students. Applications are processed on a rolling basis. *Application fee:* $35. Electronic applications accepted. *Application Contact:* Cheryl Murray, Admission Assistant, 585-594-6802, Fax: 585-594-6801, E-mail: nesadmissions@roberts.edu. *Vice President and Dean*, Dr. Douglas Cullum, 585-594-6331, Fax: 585-594-6801, E-mail: cullumd@roberts.edu.

NORTHEASTERN STATE UNIVERSITY, Tahlequah, OK 74464-2399

General Information State-supported, coed, comprehensive institution. *Enrollment:* 7,906 graduate, professional, and undergraduate students; 465 full-time matriculated graduate/professional students (326 women), 623 part-time matriculated graduate/professional students (466 women). *Enrollment by degree level:* 978 master's, 110 doctoral. *Graduate faculty:* 133 full-time (64 women), 18 part-time/adjunct (10 women). Tuition, state resident: part-time $222 per credit hour. Tuition, nonresident: part-time $501.75 per credit hour. *Required fees:* $37.40 per credit hour. Tuition and fees vary according to degree level. *Graduate housing:* Rooms and/or apartments available on a first-come, first-served basis to single and married students. Typical cost: $4400 per year ($8320 including board) for single students; $6300 per year ($10,220 including board) for married students. Room and board charges vary according to board plan and housing facility selected. Housing application deadline: 6/1. *Student services:* Campus employment opportunities, campus safety program, career counseling, exercise/wellness program, free psychological counseling, international student services, low-cost health insurance, multicultural affairs office, services for students with disabilities, teacher training, writing training. *Library facilities:* John Vaughn Library. *Collection:* Books: 411,595 (physical), 60,775 (digital/electronic); Serial titles: 29,909 (physical), 77,542 (digital/electronic); Databases: 141. Weekly public service hours: 114.

Computer facilities: Computer purchase and lease plans are available. 1,160 computers available on campus for general student use. A campuswide network can be accessed from student residence rooms and from off campus. Online class registration is available.
Website: http://www.nsuok.edu/

General Application Contact: Josh McCollum, Graduate Coordinator, Advising and Admissions, 918-444-2093, E-mail: mccolluj@nsuok.edu.

GRADUATE UNITS

College of Business and Technology Students: 45 full-time (19 women), 107 part-time (54 women); includes 66 minority (9 Black or African American, non-Hispanic/Latino; 26 American Indian or Alaska Native, non-Hispanic/Latino; 2 Asian, non-Hispanic/Latino; 8 Hispanic/Latino; 21 Two or more races, non-Hispanic/Latino), 7 international. Average age 33. *Faculty:* 15 full-time (3 women), 1 part-time/adjunct (0 women). Expenses: Contact institution. *Financial support:* Teaching assistantships and Federal Work-Study available. Financial award application deadline: 3/1. In 2017, 72 master's awarded. *Program availability:* Part-time, evening/weekend. Offers accounting and financial analysis (MS); business administration (MBA, PMBA); business and technology (MBA, MS, PMBA). *Application deadline:* For fall admission, 6/1 priority date for domestic students. Applications are processed on a rolling basis. *Application fee:* $0 ($25 for international students). Electronic applications accepted. *Application Contact:* Josh McCollum, Graduate Coordinator, 918-444-2093, E-mail: mccolluj@nsuok.edu. *Dean*, Dr. Roger Collier, 918-444-2900, E-mail: colliere@nsuok.edu.

College of Education Students: 156 full-time (119 women), 362 part-time (300 women); includes 187 minority (20 Black or African American, non-Hispanic/Latino; 73 American Indian or Alaska Native, non-Hispanic/Latino; 6 Asian, non-Hispanic/Latino; 12 Hispanic/Latino; 76 Two or more races, non-Hispanic/Latino), 10 international. Average age 35. *Faculty:* 40 full-time (25 women), 9 part-time/adjunct (6 women). Expenses: Contact institution. *Financial support:* Teaching assistantships, career-related internships or fieldwork, and Federal Work-Study available. Financial award application deadline: 3/1. In 2017, 229 master's awarded. *Program availability:* Part-time, evening/weekend. Offers counseling (MS); early childhood education (M Ed); education (M Ed, MS); health and kinesiology (MS); higher education leadership (MS); instructional leadership (M Ed); library media and information technology (MS); reading (M Ed); school administration (M Ed); special education-autism spectrum disorders (M Ed). *Application deadline:* For fall admission, 6/1 priority date for domestic students. Applications are processed on a rolling basis. *Application fee:* $25. Electronic applications accepted. *Application Contact:* Josh McCollum, Graduate Coordinator, 918-444-2093, E-mail: mccolluj@nsuok.edu. *Interim Dean of the College of Education*, Dr. Vanessa Anton, 918-444-3700, Fax: 918-458-2351, E-mail: anton@nsuok.edu.

College of Liberal Arts Students: 32 full-time (20 women), 61 part-time (37 women); includes 35 minority (3 Black or African American, non-Hispanic/Latino; 11 American Indian or Alaska Native, non-Hispanic/Latino; 5 Hispanic/Latino; 16 Two or more races, non-Hispanic/Latino), 2 international. Average age 33. *Faculty:* 28 full-time (10 women), 1 (woman) part-time/adjunct. Expenses: Contact institution. *Financial support:* Teaching assistantships and Federal Work-Study available. Financial award application deadline: 3/1. In 2017, 24 master's awarded. *Program availability:* Part-time, evening/weekend. Offers American studies (MA); communication arts (MA); criminal justice (MS); English (MA); liberal arts (MA, MS). *Application deadline:* For fall admission, 6/1 priority date for domestic students. Applications are processed on a rolling basis. *Application fee:* $25. Electronic applications accepted. *Application Contact:* Josh McCollum, Graduate Coordinator, 918-444-2093, E-mail: mccolluj@nsuok.edu. *Interim Dean of Liberal Arts*, Dr. Robyn Pursley, 918-444-3600, Fax: 918-458-2348, E-mail: cola@nsuok.edu.

College of Science and Health Professions Students: 119 full-time (110 women), 65 part-time (54 women); includes 59 minority (2 Black or African American, non-Hispanic/Latino; 22 American Indian or Alaska Native, non-Hispanic/Latino; 5 Asian, non-Hispanic/Latino; 12 Hispanic/Latino; 18 Two or more races, non-Hispanic/Latino). Average age 30. *Faculty:* 36 full-time (22 women), 7 part-time/adjunct (3 women). Expenses: Contact institution. In 2017, 84 master's awarded. Offers mathematics education (M Ed); natural sciences (MS); nursing (MSN); nursing education (MSN); occupational therapy (MS); science and health professions (M Ed, MS, MSN); science education (M Ed); speech-language pathology (MS). *Application deadline:* Applications are processed on a rolling basis. *Application fee:* $25. Electronic applications accepted. *Application Contact:* Josh McCollum, Graduate Coordinator, 918-444-2093, E-mail: mccolluj@nsuok.edu. *Dean*, Dr. Pamela Hathorn, 918-444-3800, E-mail: hathorn@nsuok.edu.

Oklahoma College of Optometry Students: 110 full-time (58 women); includes 31 minority (3 Black or African American, non-Hispanic/Latino; 10 American Indian or Alaska Native, non-Hispanic/Latino; 7 Asian, non-Hispanic/Latino; 5 Hispanic/Latino; 6 Two or more races, non-Hispanic/Latino). Average age 26. *Faculty:* 14 full-time (4 women). Expenses: Contact institution. *Financial support:* Federal Work-Study, institutionally sponsored loans, scholarships/grants, tuition waivers (partial), and residencies available. Financial award application deadline: 5/1; financial award applicants required to submit FAFSA. In 2017, 29 doctorates awarded. Offers optometry (OD). *Application deadline:* For fall admission, 2/1 for domestic students. Applications are processed on a rolling basis. *Application fee:* $45. Electronic applications accepted. *Application Contact:* Sandy Medearis, Optometric Student and Alumni Services Director, 918-444-4006, Fax: 918-458-2104, E-mail: medearis@nsuok.edu. *Dean of Oklahoma College of Optometry*, Dr. Douglas Penisten, 918-444-4025, E-mail: penisten@nsuok.edu.

NORTHEASTERN UNIVERSITY, Boston, MA 02115-5096

General Information Independent, coed, university. CGS member. *Enrollment:* 26,660 graduate, professional, and undergraduate students; 8,689 full-time matriculated graduate/professional students (3,812 women), 7,023 part-time matriculated graduate/professional students (4,043 women). *Enrollment by degree level:* 11,576 master's, 3,734 doctoral, 372 other advanced degrees. *Graduate faculty:* 1,433 full-time (623 women), 1,396 part-time/adjunct (656 women). *Student services:* Campus employment opportunities, campus safety program, career counseling, child daycare facilities, exercise/wellness program, free psychological counseling, grant writing training, international student services, low-cost health insurance, multicultural affairs office, services for students with disabilities, teacher training. *Library facilities:* Snell Library plus 3 others. *Collection:* Books: 530,566 (physical), 589,334 (digital/electronic). Study areas open 24 hours, 5–7 days a week; students can reserve study rooms. *Research affiliation:* Jobs for America's Graduates (labor studies), Cytyc Corporation (medical technology), BBN Technologies (information technology), Analog Devices, Inc. (electronics), General Electric Company (GE) (engineering).

Computer facilities: Computer purchase and lease plans are available. A campuswide network can be accessed from student residence rooms and from off campus. Online class registration is available.
Website: http://www.northeastern.edu/

GRADUATE UNITS

Bouvé College of Health Sciences Students: 1,685. *Faculty:* 192 full-time. Expenses: Contact institution. *Financial support:* Fellowships, research assistantships, teaching assistantships, career-related internships or fieldwork, scholarships/grants, health care benefits, tuition waivers, and unspecified assistantships available. Support available to part-time students. Financial award applicants required to submit FAFSA. In 2017, 352 master's, 312 doctorates, 25 other advanced degrees awarded. *Program availability:* Part-time, evening/weekend, online learning. Offers applied behavior analysis (MS); audiology (Au D); counseling psychology (MS, PhD, CAGS); exercise science (MS); nursing (MS, PhD, CAGS); nursing practice (DNP); pharmaceutical sciences (MS, PhD); pharmacology (MS); pharmacy (Pharm D); school psychology (PhD); speech-language pathology (MS); urban health (MPH). *Application fee:* $75. Electronic applications accepted. *Application Contact:* 617-373-2708, Fax: 617-373-4701, E-mail: bouvegrad@northeastern.edu. *Dean, Bouve College of Health Sciences*, Susan L. Parish, 617-373-3321, Fax: 617-373-3030, E-mail: s.parish@northeastern.edu.

College of Arts, Media and Design Students: 259. *Faculty:* 145. Expenses: Contact institution. *Financial support:* Applicants required to submit FAFSA. In 2017, 83 master's awarded. Offers architecture (M Arch); game science and design (MS); information design and visualization (MFA); interdisciplinary arts (MFA); journalism (MA); music industry leadership (MS); studio art (MFA); sustainable building systems (MS); sustainable urban environments (M Des). *Application fee:* $75. Electronic applications accepted. *Application Contact:* Jane Amidon, Associate Dean for Graduate Programs and Research, 617-373-4614, E-mail: gscamd@northeastern.edu. *Dean*, Dr. Elizabeth Hudson, 617-373-5088, E-mail: n.elysse@northeastern.edu.

College of Computer and Information Science Students: 1,451. *Faculty:* 93. Expenses: Contact institution. *Financial support:* Research assistantships, teaching assistantships, scholarships/grants, health care benefits, and unspecified assistantships available. Financial award applicants required to submit FAFSA. In 2017, 322 master's, 8 doctorates awarded. *Program availability:* Part-time, evening/weekend. Offers computer science (MS, PhD); data science (MS); game science and design (MS); health informatics (MS); information assurance (MS); network science (PhD); personal health informatics (PhD). *Application fee:* $75. Electronic applications accepted. *Application Contact:* Dr. Rajmohan Rajaraman, Professor/Associate Dean/Director of the Graduate School, 617-373-2462, E-mail: ccis-gradschool@northeastern.edu. *Professor and Dean*, Dr. Carla E. Brodley, 617-373-5204, E-mail: c.brodley@northeastern.edu.

College of Engineering Students: 3,720. *Faculty:* 225 full-time. Expenses: Contact institution. *Financial support:* Fellowships, research assistantships, teaching assistantships, career-related internships or fieldwork, scholarships/grants, health care benefits, tuition waivers, and unspecified assistantships available. Support available to part-time students. Financial award applicants required to submit FAFSA. In 2017, 851 master's, 74 doctorates awarded. *Program availability:* Part-time, online learning. Offers bioengineering (MS, PhD); chemical engineering (MS, PhD); civil engineering (MS, PhD); computer engineering (PhD); computer systems engineering (MS); electrical and computer engineering (MS); electrical and computer engineering leadership (MS); electrical engineering (PhD); energy systems (MS); engineering and public policy (MS); engineering management (MS, Certificate); environmental engineering (MS); industrial engineering (MS, PhD); information assurance (PhD); information systems (MS); interdisciplinary engineering (PhD); mechanical engineering (PhD); operations research (MS); telecommunication systems management (MS). *Application fee:* $75. Electronic applications accepted. *Application Contact:* Jeffery Hengel, Director of Graduate Admissions, 617-373-2711, E-mail: j.hengel@northeastern.edu. *Dean, College of Engineering*, Dr. Nadine Aubry, 617-373-5847, E-mail: n.aubry@neu.edu.

College of Professional Studies Students: 5,278 part-time (3,230 women). *Faculty:* 82 full-time (51 women), 853 part-time/adjunct (366 women). Expenses: Contact institution. *Financial support:* Applicants required to submit FAFSA. In 2017, 1,586 master's awarded. *Program availability:* Part-time, evening/weekend, 100% online, blended/hybrid learning. Offers applied nutrition (MS); college athletics administration (MSL); commerce and economic development (MS); corporate and organizational communication (MS); criminal justice (MS); digital media (MPS); elearning and instructional design (M Ed); elementary education (MAT); geographic information technology (MPS); global studies and international relations (MS); higher education administration (M Ed); homeland security (MA); human services (MS); informatics (MPS); leadership (MS); learning analytics (M Ed); learning and instruction (M Ed); nonprofit management (MS); professional sports administration (MSL); project management (MS); regulatory affairs for drugs, biologics, and medical devices (MS); respiratory care leadership (MS); special education (M Ed); technical communication (MS). *Application deadline:* Applications are processed on a rolling basis. *Application fee:* $0. Electronic applications accepted. *Application Contact:* E-mail: cpsadmissions@northeastern.edu. *Dean of the College of Professional Studies,* Dr. Mary Loeffelholz.

College of Science Expenses: Contact institution. *Financial support:* Fellowships with tuition reimbursements, research assistantships with tuition reimbursements, teaching assistantships with tuition reimbursements, career-related internships or fieldwork, scholarships/grants, health care benefits, tuition waivers (full and partial), and unspecified assistantships available. Support available to part-time students. Financial award applicants required to submit FAFSA. *Program availability:* Part-time. Offers applied mathematics (MS); bioinformatics (MS); biology (PhD); biotechnology (MS); chemistry and chemical biology (MS, PhD); environmental science and policy (MS); marine and environmental sciences (PhD); marine biology (MS); mathematics (MS, PhD); operations research (MSOR); physics (MS, PhD); psychology (PhD). *Application deadline:* Applications are processed on a rolling basis. *Application fee:* $75. Electronic applications accepted. *Application Contact:* Graduate Student Services, 617-373-4275, E-mail: gradcos@northeastern.edu. *Dean,* Dr. Kenneth Henderson, 617-373-5089, E-mail: k.henderson@northeastern.edu.

College of Social Sciences and Humanities Students: 491. *Faculty:* 242. Expenses: Contact institution. *Financial support:* Teaching assistantships, career-related internships or fieldwork, scholarships/grants, health care benefits, tuition waivers (full and partial), and unspecified assistantships available. Support available to part-time students. Financial award applicants required to submit FAFSA. In 2017, 143 master's, 38 doctorates awarded. *Program availability:* Online learning. Offers criminology and criminal justice (MSCJ); criminology and justice policy (PhD); economics (MA, PhD); English (MA, PhD); international affairs (MA); law and public policy (PhD); political science (MA, PhD); public administration (MPA); public policy (MPP); security and resilience studies (MS); sociology (MA, PhD); urban and regional policy (MS); urban informatics (MS); world history (MA, PhD). *Application fee:* $75. Electronic applications accepted. *Application Contact:* 617-373-5990, E-mail: gradcssh@northeastern.edu. *Dean,* Dr. Uta Poiger, 617-373-5173, E-mail: college_of_social_sciences_and_humanities@neu.edu.

D'Amore-McKim School of Business Students: 1,489. *Faculty:* 184. Expenses: Contact institution. *Financial support:* Scholarships/grants available. Financial award applicants required to submit FAFSA. In 2017, 800 master's awarded. *Program availability:* Part-time, evening/weekend, online learning. Offers accounting (MS); business administration (EMBA, MBA); finance (MS); innovation (MS); international business (MS); international management (MS); taxation (MS); technological entrepreneurship (MS). *Application fee:* $75. Electronic applications accepted. *Application Contact:* Evelyn Tate, Director, Graduate Recruitment and Admissions, 617-373-3258, E-mail: e.tate@northeastern.edu. *Dean, D'Amore-McKim School of Business,* Dr. Raj Echambadi, 617-373-3232, Fax: 617-373-2056.

School of Law Students: 657. *Faculty:* 48. Expenses: Contact institution. *Financial support:* Scholarships/grants available. Financial award applicants required to submit FAFSA. In 2017, 32 master's, 175 doctorates awarded. *Program availability:* Online learning. Offers law (LL M, MLS, JD). JD/MPH offered jointly with Tufts University; JD/MSA/MBA with Graduate School of Professional Accounting; JD/MS with Program in Law and Public Policy; JD/MELP with Vermont Law School; and JD/MA with Brandeis University. *Application deadline:* Applications are processed on a rolling basis. *Application fee:* $75. Electronic applications accepted. *Application Contact:* 617-373-2395. *Dean and Professor of Law,* Jeremy R. Paul, 617-373-3307, Fax: 617-373-8793, E-mail: j.paul@northeastern.edu.

NORTHEAST OHIO MEDICAL UNIVERSITY, Rootstown, OH 44272-0095

General Information State-supported, coed, graduate-only institution. *Enrollment by degree level:* 21 master's, 914 doctoral, 16 other advanced degrees. *Graduate faculty:* 83 full-time (32 women), 2,569 part-time/adjunct (917 women). Tuition and fees vary according to program and student level. *Graduate housing:* On-campus housing not available. *Student services:* Campus employment opportunities, campus safety program, career counseling, free psychological counseling, low-cost health insurance, multicultural affairs office, services for students with disabilities. *Library facilities:* Aneal Mohan Kohli Academic and Information Technology Center. *Collection:* Books: 47,900 (physical), 122,231 (digital/electronic); Serial titles: 2 (physical), 11,060 (digital/electronic); Databases: 131. Weekly public service hours: 64; study areas open 24 hours, 5–7 days a week. *Research affiliation:* American Heart Association (physiology, biochemistry), National Science Foundation (anatomy), National Institutes of Health (anatomy, biochemistry, immunology, neurobiology, microbiology), Summa Health Systems (orthopedics, anatomy), Margaret Clark Morgan Foundation (schizophrenia, mental illness), Austen BioInnovation Institute in Akron (pharmacology, drug delivery, biotechnology, community health).

Computer facilities: 50 computers available on campus for general student use. A campuswide network can be accessed from student residence rooms and from off campus. Online class registration is available.
Website: http://www.neomed.edu/

General Application Contact: Heidi Terry, Director, Admissions and Student Services, 330-325-6270, E-mail: admission@neomed.edu.

GRADUATE UNITS

College of Graduate Studies Students: 22 full-time (13 women), 21 part-time (13 women); includes 10 minority (1 Black or African American, non-Hispanic/Latino; 8 Asian, non-Hispanic/Latino; 1 Two or more races, non-Hispanic/Latino). *Faculty:* 23 part-time/adjunct (14 women). Expenses: Contact institution. *Financial support:* Institutionally sponsored loans and tuition waivers available. Financial award application deadline: 3/15; financial award applicants required to submit FAFSA. In 2017, 3 master's, 1 doctorate awarded. *Program availability:* Part-time, evening/weekend. Offers bioethics (Certificate); health-system pharmacy administration (MS); integrated pharmaceutical medicine (MS, PhD); medical ethics and humanities (MS); public health (MPH). MPH offered as part of consortium with The University of Akron, Youngstown State University, Ohio University, and Cleveland State University. *Application deadline:* For fall admission, 5/1 priority date for domestic students; for winter admission, 1/5 priority date for domestic students. Applications are processed on a rolling basis. *Application fee:* $95. Electronic applications accepted. *Application Contact:* Heidi Terry, Executive Director, Enrollment Services, 330-325-6479, E-mail: hterry@neomed.edu. *Dean,* Dr. Steven Schmidt, 330-325-6290.

College of Medicine Students: 606 full-time (310 women); includes 276 minority (18 Black or African American, non-Hispanic/Latino; 1 American Indian or Alaska Native, non-Hispanic/Latino; 215 Asian, non-Hispanic/Latino; 14 Hispanic/Latino; 28 Two or more races, non-Hispanic/Latino). 3,401 applicants, 7% accepted, 153 enrolled. *Faculty:* 59 full-time (21 women), 1,977 part-time/adjunct (593 women). Expenses: Contact institution. *Financial support:* Institutionally sponsored loans and scholarships/grants available. Financial award application deadline: 3/15; financial award applicants required to submit FAFSA. In 2017, 140 doctorates awarded. Offers medicine (MD). *Application deadline:* For fall admission, 8/1 priority date for domestic students; for winter admission, 10/1 for domestic students. Applications are processed on a rolling basis. *Application fee:* $95. Electronic applications accepted. *Application Contact:* Heidi Terry, Executive Director, Enrollment Services, 330-325-6479, E-mail: hterry@neomed.edu. *Dean,* Dr. Jeffrey L. Susman, 330-325-6101.

College of Pharmacy Students: 302 full-time (168 women); includes 64 minority (21 Black or African American, non-Hispanic/Latino; 33 Asian, non-Hispanic/Latino; 7 Hispanic/Latino; 3 Two or more races, non-Hispanic/Latino). 400 applicants, 33% accepted, 75 enrolled. *Faculty:* 24 full-time (11 women), 579 part-time/adjunct (320 women). Expenses: Contact institution. *Financial support:* Institutionally sponsored loans and scholarships/grants available. Financial award application deadline: 3/15; financial award applicants required to submit FAFSA. In 2017, 77 doctorates awarded. Offers pharmacy (Pharm D). *Application deadline:* For fall admission, 3/1 priority date for domestic students; for winter admission, 1/5 for domestic students. Applications are processed on a rolling basis. *Application fee:* $0. Electronic applications accepted. *Application Contact:* Heidi Terry, Executive Director, Enrollment Services, 330-325-6479, E-mail: hterry@neomed.edu. *Dean,* Dr. Charles Taylor, 330-325-6461, Fax: 330-325-5930.

NORTHERN ARIZONA UNIVERSITY, Flagstaff, AZ 86011

General Information State-supported, coed, university. CGS member. *Enrollment:* 31,057 graduate, professional, and undergraduate students; 1,904 full-time matriculated graduate/professional students (1,255 women), 1,977 part-time matriculated graduate/professional students (1,432 women). *Enrollment by degree level:* 2,926 master's, 817 doctoral, 138 other advanced degrees. *Graduate faculty:* 1,132 full-time (571 women), 541 part-time/adjunct (340 women). Tuition, state resident: full-time $9240; part-time $458 per credit hour. Tuition, nonresident: full-time $21,588; part-time $1199 per credit hour. *Required fees:* $1021; $14 per credit hour. $646 per semester. Tuition and fees vary according to course load, campus/location and program. *Graduate housing:* Rooms and/or apartments available on a first-come, first-served basis to single and married students. Typical cost: $5408 per year ($9944 including board) for single students. Room and board charges vary according to housing facility selected. Housing application deadline: 5/1. *Student services:* Campus employment opportunities, campus safety program, career counseling, exercise/wellness program, free psychological counseling, grant writing training, international student services, low-cost health insurance, multicultural affairs office, services for students with disabilities, teacher training, writing training. *Library facilities:* Cline Library plus 1 other. *Collection:* Books: 574,711 (physical), 237,606 (digital/electronic); Serial titles: 6,264 (physical), 93,756 (digital/electronic); Databases: 146. Weekly public service hours: 117; students can reserve study rooms. *Research affiliation:* W.L. Gore and Associates, Inc. (biomedical engineering), Museum of Northern Arizona (anthropology), Lowell Observatory (physics and astronomy), Rocky Mountain Forest and Range Experiment Station (forestry), U.S. Naval Observatory (physics and astronomy), U.S. Geological Survey (USGS) (geology).

Computer facilities: Computer purchase and lease plans are available. 294 computers available on campus for general student use. A campuswide network can be accessed from student residence rooms and from off campus. Online class registration, computer repair service available on campus are available.
Website: http://www.nau.edu/

General Application Contact: Tina Sutton, Coordinator, 928-523-4348, Fax: 928-523-8950, E-mail: graduate@nau.edu.

GRADUATE UNITS

College of Arts and Letters Students: 171 full-time (102 women), 121 part-time (93 women); includes 72 minority (12 Black or African American, non-Hispanic/Latino; 3 American Indian or Alaska Native, non-Hispanic/Latino; 5 Asian, non-Hispanic/Latino; 38 Hispanic/Latino; 14 Two or more races, non-Hispanic/Latino), 26 international. Average age 34. 244 applicants, 60% accepted, 130 enrolled. *Faculty:* 221 full-time (122 women), 26 part-time/adjunct (21 women). Expenses: Contact institution. *Financial support:* In 2017–18, 116 students received support, including 4 fellowships with full and partial tuition reimbursements available (averaging $16,250 per year), 2 research assistantships with full and partial tuition reimbursements available (averaging $16,250 per year), 112 teaching assistantships with full and partial tuition reimbursements available (averaging $12,800 per year); institutionally sponsored loans, health care benefits, tuition waivers (full and partial), and unspecified assistantships also available. Financial award application deadline: 2/1; financial award applicants required to submit FAFSA. In 2017, 111 master's, 5 doctorates, 17 other advanced degrees awarded. *Program availability:* Part-time, 100% online, blended/hybrid learning. Offers applied linguistics (PhD); arts and letters (MA, MAT, MFA, MM, PhD, Graduate Certificate); creative writing (MFA); English (MA); history (MA); professional writing (Graduate Certificate); rhetoric, writing and digital media studies (Graduate Certificate); Spanish (MAT); Spanish education (MAT); teaching English as a second language (MA, Graduate Certificate). *Application deadline:* For fall admission, 3/1 for domestic and international students; for spring admission, 10/1 for domestic and international students. *Application fee:* $65. Electronic applications accepted. *Application Contact:* Tina Sutton, Coordinator, Graduate College, 928-523-4348, Fax: 928-523-8950, E-mail: graduate@nau.edu. *Dean,* Dr. Valerio Ferme, 928-523-8632, E-mail: valerio.ferme@nau.edu.

School of Music Students: 26 full-time (11 women), 1 part-time (0 women); includes 3 minority (1 Black or African American, non-Hispanic/Latino; 1 Asian, non-Hispanic/Latino; 1 Hispanic/Latino), 3 international. Average age 29. 31 applicants, 68% accepted, 21 enrolled. *Faculty:* 43 full-time (20 women), 13 part-time/adjunct (11 women). Expenses: Contact institution. *Financial support:* In 2017–18, 18 students received support, including 18 teaching assistantships with partial tuition reimbursements available (averaging $6,000 per year); institutionally sponsored loans, health care benefits, tuition waivers (partial), and unspecified assistantships also available. Financial award application deadline: 2/1; financial award applicants required to submit FAFSA. In 2017, 13 master's, 2 other advanced degrees awarded. *Program availability:* Part-time. Offers music (MM); music performance (Graduate Certificate). *Application deadline:* For fall admission, 3/1 for domestic and international students; for spring admission, 10/1 for domestic and international students. Applications are processed on a rolling basis. *Application fee:* $65. Electronic applications accepted. *Application Contact:* Tina Sutton, Coordinator, Graduate College, 928-523-4348, Fax: 928-523-8950, E-mail: graduate@nau.edu. *Director*, Dr. Todd E. Sullivan, 928-523-3731, Fax: 928-523-2562, E-mail: todd.sullivan@nau.edu.

College of Education Students: 525 full-time (390 women), 1,207 part-time (870 women); includes 617 minority (107 Black or African American, non-Hispanic/Latino; 96 American Indian or Alaska Native, non-Hispanic/Latino; 24 Asian, non-Hispanic/Latino; 333 Hispanic/Latino; 6 Native Hawaiian or other Pacific Islander, non-Hispanic/Latino; 51 Two or more races, non-Hispanic/Latino), 24 international. Average age 36. 805 applicants, 80% accepted, 646 enrolled. *Faculty:* 105 full-time (65 women), 10 part-time/adjunct (7 women). Expenses: Contact institution. *Financial support:* In 2017–18, 79 students received support, including 2 fellowships with full and partial tuition reimbursements available (averaging $13,285 per year), 3 research assistantships with full and partial tuition reimbursements available (averaging $13,714 per year), 29 teaching assistantships with full and partial tuition reimbursements available (averaging $13,371 per year); institutionally sponsored loans, health care benefits, tuition waivers (full and partial), and unspecified assistantships also available. Financial award application deadline: 2/1; financial award applicants required to submit FAFSA. In 2017, 597 master's, 21 doctorates, 74 other advanced degrees awarded. *Program availability:* Part-time, 100% online, blended/hybrid learning. Offers autism spectrum disorders (Certificate); bilingual/multicultural education (M Ed); career and technical education (M Ed, Certificate); clinical mental health counseling (MA); combined counseling/school psychology (PhD); community college teaching and learning (Graduate Certificate); counseling (M Ed); curriculum and instruction (Ed D); early childhood education (M Ed); education (M Ed, MA, Ed D, PhD, Certificate, Ed S, Graduate Certificate); educational leadership (M Ed, Ed D); educational technology (M Ed, Certificate); elementary education (M Ed); English as a second language (Certificate); human relations (M Ed); positive behavior support (Certificate); principal (Graduate Certificate); psychology of human development and learning (Graduate Certificate); school psychology (Ed S); secondary education (M Ed); special education (M Ed); superintendent (Graduate Certificate). *Application deadline:* For fall admission, 3/1 for domestic and international students; for spring admission, 10/1 for domestic and international students. *Application fee:* $65. Electronic applications accepted. *Application Contact:* Tina Sutton, Coordinator, Graduate College, 928-523-4348, Fax: 928-523-8950, E-mail: graduate@nau.edu. *Dean*, Dr. Ramona Mellott, 928-523-7139, Fax: 928-523-1929, E-mail: ramona.mellott@nau.edu.

College of Engineering, Forestry, and Natural Sciences Students: 374 full-time (186 women), 95 part-time (52 women); includes 63 minority (3 Black or African American, non-Hispanic/Latino; 7 American Indian or Alaska Native, non-Hispanic/Latino; 10 Asian, non-Hispanic/Latino; 29 Hispanic/Latino; 14 Two or more races, non-Hispanic/Latino), 81 international. Average age 29. 519 applicants, 40% accepted, 190 enrolled. *Faculty:* 303 full-time (94 women), 10 part-time/adjunct (5 women). Expenses: Contact institution. *Financial support:* In 2017–18, 340 students received support, including 12 fellowships with full and partial tuition reimbursements available (averaging $16,801 per year), 92 research assistantships with full and partial tuition reimbursements available (averaging $16,933 per year), 244 teaching assistantships with full and partial tuition reimbursements available (averaging $16,752 per year); institutionally sponsored loans, scholarships/grants, health care benefits, tuition waivers (full and partial), and unspecified assistantships also available. Financial award application deadline: 2/1; financial award applicants required to submit FAFSA. *Program availability:* Part-time, 100% online, blended/hybrid learning. Offers applied physics (MS); applied statistics (Graduate Certificate); astronomy and planetary science (PhD); bioengineering (PhD); biology (MS, PhD); chemistry (MS); engineering (M Eng); engineering, forestry, and natural sciences (M Eng, MA, MAT, MF, MS, MSF, PhD, Graduate Certificate); informatics and computing (PhD); mathematics (MS); mathematics education (MS); statistics (MS); teaching introductory community college mathematics (Graduate Certificate). *Application deadline:* For fall admission, 3/1 for domestic and international students; for spring admission, 10/1 for domestic and international students. *Application fee:* $65. Electronic applications accepted. *Application Contact:* Tina Sutton, Coordinator, Graduate College, 928-523-4348, Fax: 928-523-8950, E-mail: graduate@nau.edu. *Dean*, Dr. Paul W. Jagodzinski, 928-523-2701, Fax: 928-523-2300, E-mail: paul.jagodzinski@nau.edu.

Center for Science Teaching and Learning Students: 15 full-time (10 women), 15 part-time (10 women); includes 4 minority (1 Black or African American, non-Hispanic/Latino; 2 Hispanic/Latino; 1 Two or more races, non-Hispanic/Latino). Average age 29. 15 applicants, 100% accepted, 15 enrolled. *Faculty:* 8 full-time (4 women). Expenses: Contact institution. *Financial support:* In 2017–18, 7 students received support, including 4 research assistantships with full and partial tuition reimbursements available (averaging $17,500 per year), 3 teaching assistantships with full and partial tuition reimbursements available (averaging $17,500 per year); institutionally sponsored loans, health care benefits, tuition waivers (full and partial), and unspecified assistantships also available. Financial award application deadline: 2/1; financial award applicants required to submit FAFSA. In 2017, 21 master's awarded. *Program availability:* Part-time, 100% online, blended/hybrid learning. Offers science teaching (MA); science with certification (MAT). *Application deadline:* For fall admission, 3/1 for domestic and international students; for spring admission, 10/1 for domestic and international students. *Application fee:* $65. Electronic applications accepted. *Application Contact:* Lillie Giffen, Administrative Associate, 928-523-7187, E-mail: lillie.giffen@nau.edu. *Director*, Dr. Max Dass, 928-523-7120, E-mail: pradeep.dass@nau.edu.

Engineering Division Students: 34 full-time (10 women), 7 part-time (2 women); includes 6 minority (1 Asian, non-Hispanic/Latino; 3 Hispanic/Latino; 2 Two or more races, non-Hispanic/Latino), 16 international. Average age 27. 59 applicants, 29% accepted, 15 enrolled. Expenses: Contact institution. *Financial support:* In 2017–18, 43 students received support, including 13 research assistantships with full and partial tuition reimbursements available (averaging $21,673 per year), 30 teaching assistantships with full and partial tuition reimbursements available (averaging $21,673 per year); institutionally sponsored loans, scholarships/grants, health care benefits, tuition waivers (full and partial), and unspecified assistantships also available. Financial award application deadline: 2/1; financial award applicants required to submit FAFSA. In 2017, 16 master's awarded. *Program availability:* Part-time. Offers engineering (MS). *Application deadline:* For fall admission, 3/1 for domestic and international students; for spring admission, 9/15 for domestic and international students. Applications are processed on a rolling basis. *Application fee:* $65. Electronic applications accepted. *Application Contact:* Tina Sutton, Coordinator, Graduate College, 928-523-4348, Fax: 928-523-8950, E-mail: graduate@nau.edu. *Dean*, Dr. Paul W. Jagodzinski, 928-523-2701, Fax: 928-523-1902, E-mail: paul.jagodzinski@nau.edu.

School of Earth Sciences and Environmental Sustainability Students: 75 full-time (43 women), 25 part-time (10 women); includes 12 minority (2 American Indian or Alaska Native, non-Hispanic/Latino; 3 Asian, non-Hispanic/Latino; 3 Hispanic/Latino; 4 Two or more races, non-Hispanic/Latino), 6 international. Average age 29. 117 applicants, 30% accepted, 32 enrolled. *Faculty:* 31 full-time (12 women), 2 part-time/adjunct (1 woman). Expenses: Contact institution. *Financial support:* In 2017–18, 52 students received support, including 1 fellowship with full and partial tuition reimbursement available (averaging $15,161 per year), 15 research assistantships with full and partial tuition reimbursements available (averaging $15,161 per year), 37 teaching assistantships with full and partial tuition reimbursements available (averaging $15,161 per year); institutionally sponsored loans, health care benefits, tuition waivers (full and partial), and unspecified assistantships also available. Financial award application deadline: 2/1; financial award applicants required to submit FAFSA. In 2017, 31 master's awarded. *Program availability:* Part-time. Offers climate science and solutions (MS); conservation ecology (Graduate Certificate); earth sciences and environmental sustainability (PhD); environmental sciences and policy (MS); geology (MS). *Application deadline:* For fall admission, 1/15 for domestic and international students; for spring admission, 10/1 for domestic and international students. Applications are processed on a rolling basis. *Application fee:* $65. Electronic applications accepted. *Application Contact:* SESES Support, 928-523-9333, Fax: 928-523-7432, E-mail: seses_admin_support@nau.edu. *Director*, Dr. Nancy Johnson, 928-523-6473, E-mail: nancy.johnson@nau.edu.

School of Forestry Students: 44 full-time (21 women), 6 part-time (4 women); includes 7 minority (3 American Indian or Alaska Native, non-Hispanic/Latino; 3 Hispanic/Latino; 1 Two or more races, non-Hispanic/Latino), 15 international. Average age 30. 24 applicants, 71% accepted, 17 enrolled. *Faculty:* 22 full-time (8 women), 2 part-time/adjunct (1 woman). Expenses: Contact institution. *Financial support:* In 2017–18, 23 students received support, including 2 fellowships with full and partial tuition reimbursements available (averaging $19,815 per year), 20 research assistantships with full and partial tuition reimbursements available (averaging $19,815 per year), 2 teaching assistantships with full and partial tuition reimbursements available (averaging $19,815 per year); institutionally sponsored loans, scholarships/grants, health care benefits, tuition waivers (full and partial), and unspecified assistantships also available. Financial award application deadline: 2/1; financial award applicants required to submit FAFSA. In 2017, 8 master's, 1 doctorate awarded. *Program availability:* Part-time. Offers forest science (PhD); forestry (MF, MSF). *Application deadline:* For fall admission, 2/15 for domestic and international students; for spring admission, 10/15 for domestic and international students. Applications are processed on a rolling basis. *Application fee:* $65. Electronic applications accepted. *Application Contact:* Karen Blalock, Administrative Associate, 928-523-8810, E-mail: karen.blalock@nau.edu. *Executive Director*, Dr. James Allen, 928-523-5894, Fax: 928-523-1080, E-mail: james.allen@nau.edu.

College of Health and Human Services Students: 601 full-time (434 women), 268 part-time (240 women); includes 239 minority (17 Black or African American, non-Hispanic/Latino; 19 American Indian or Alaska Native, non-Hispanic/Latino; 33 Asian, non-Hispanic/Latino; 131 Hispanic/Latino; 1 Native Hawaiian or other Pacific Islander, non-Hispanic/Latino; 38 Two or more races, non-Hispanic/Latino), 2 international. Average age 29. 2,297 applicants, 14% accepted, 316 enrolled. *Faculty:* 137 full-time (112 women), 88 part-time/adjunct (65 women). Expenses: Contact institution. *Financial support:* In 2017–18, 10 students received support, including 3 research assistantships with partial tuition reimbursements available (averaging $5,000 per year); institutionally sponsored loans, health care benefits, tuition waivers (full and partial), and unspecified assistantships also available. Financial award application deadline: 2/1; financial award applicants required to submit FAFSA. In 2017, 158 master's, 109 doctorates, 4 other advanced degrees awarded. *Program availability:* Part-time, 100% online, blended/hybrid learning. Offers clinical speech-language pathology (MS); exercise science (MS); health and human services (MPAS, MS, DNP, DPT, OTD, Certificate); occupational therapy (OTD); physical education (MS); physical therapy (DPT); physician assistant studies (MPAS). *Application deadline:* For fall admission, 3/1 for domestic and international students; for spring admission, 10/1 for domestic and international students. *Application fee:* $65. Electronic applications accepted. *Application Contact:* Tina Sutton, Coordinator, Graduate College, 928-523-4348, Fax: 928-523-8950, E-mail: graduate@nau.edu. *Dean*, Dr. Lynda Ransdell, 928-523-4331, Fax: 928-523-4315, E-mail: lynda.ransdell@nau.edu.

School of Nursing Students: 12 full-time (10 women), 175 part-time (151 women); includes 57 minority (5 Black or African American, non-Hispanic/Latino; 9 American Indian or Alaska Native, non-Hispanic/Latino; 8 Asian, non-Hispanic/Latino; 32 Hispanic/Latino; 1 Native Hawaiian or other Pacific Islander, non-Hispanic/Latino; 2 Two or more races, non-Hispanic/Latino). Average age 39. 66 applicants, 83% accepted, 52 enrolled. *Faculty:* 50 full-time (45 women), 26 part-time/adjunct (21 women). Expenses: Contact institution. *Financial support:* Institutionally sponsored loans and tuition waivers (full and partial) available. Financial award application deadline: 2/1; financial award applicants required to submit FAFSA. In 2017, 60 master's, 5 doctorates, 4 other advanced degrees awarded. *Program availability:* Part-time, 100% online, blended/hybrid learning. Offers family nurse practitioner (Certificate); nursing (MS); nursing practice (DNP). *Application deadline:* For fall admission, 3/1 for domestic and international students; for spring admission, 10/1 for domestic and international students. Applications are processed on a rolling basis. *Application fee:* $65. Electronic applications accepted. *Application Contact:* Penny Walior, Student Academic Specialist, 928-523-6770, Fax: 928-523-9155, E-mail: graduatenursing@nau.edu. *Director*, Pamela Stetina, 928-523-2671, Fax: 928-523-7171, E-mail: pamela.stetina@nau.edu.

College of Social and Behavioral Sciences Students: 173 full-time (111 women), 90 part-time (52 women); includes 77 minority (11 Black or African American, non-Hispanic/Latino; 13 American Indian or Alaska Native, non-Hispanic/Latino; 2 Asian, non-Hispanic/Latino; 35 Hispanic/Latino; 16 Two or more races, non-Hispanic/Latino), 15 international. Average age 30. 248 applicants, 70% accepted, 161 enrolled. *Faculty:* 231 full-time (124 women), 19 part-time/adjunct (9 women). Expenses: Contact institution. *Financial support:* In 2017–18, 97 students received support, including 7 research assistantships with full and partial tuition reimbursements available (averaging $10,000 per year), 82 teaching assistantships with full and partial tuition reimbursements available (averaging $9,545 per year); institutionally sponsored loans, health care benefits, tuition waivers (full and partial), and unspecified assistantships also available. Financial award application deadline: 2/1; financial award applicants required to submit FAFSA. In 2017, 103 master's, 5 doctorates, 20 other advanced degrees awarded. *Program availability:* Part-time, 100% online, blended/hybrid learning. Offers anthropology (MA); applied criminology (MS); applied geospatial sciences (MS); applied sociology (MA); community planning (Certificate); ethnic studies (Graduate Certificate); geographic information systems (Certificate); indigenous and tribal nation-building (Graduate Certificate); parks and recreation management (MS); political science (MA,

PhD, Graduate Certificate); psychological sciences (MA); public administration (MPA); public management (Graduate Certificate); social and behavioral sciences (MA, MPA, MS, PhD, Certificate, Graduate Certificate); sustainable communities (MA); women's and gender studies (Graduate Certificate). *Application deadline:* For fall admission, 3/1 for domestic and international students; for spring admission, 10/1 for domestic and international students. *Application fee:* $65. Electronic applications accepted. *Application Contact:* Tina Sutton, Coordinator, Graduate College, 928-523-4348, Fax: 928-523-8950, E-mail: graduate@nau.edu. *Dean*, Dr. Karen Pugliesi, 928-523-2672, Fax: 928-523-6777, E-mail: karen.pugliesi@nau.edu.

Institute for Human Development Students: 4 part-time (3 women); includes 2 minority (both Hispanic/Latino). Average age 36. 3 applicants, 100% accepted, 3 enrolled. Expenses: Contact institution. *Financial support:* Institutionally sponsored loans available. Financial award application deadline: 2/1; financial award applicants required to submit FAFSA. In 2017, 8 Graduate Certificates awarded. *Program availability:* Part-time. Offers assistive technology (Graduate Certificate). *Application deadline:* For fall admission, 3/1 for domestic and international students; for spring admission, 10/1 for domestic and international students. Applications are processed on a rolling basis. *Application fee:* $65. Electronic applications accepted. *Application Contact:* Karen Applequist, Graduate Coordinator, 928-523-9276, E-mail: karen.applequist@nau.edu. *Executive Director*, Richard Carroll, 928-523-7033, Fax: 928-523-9127, E-mail: richard.carroll@nau.edu.

School of Communication Students: 15 full-time (9 women), 19 part-time (15 women); includes 9 minority (3 Black or African American, non-Hispanic/Latino; 1 American Indian or Alaska Native, non-Hispanic/Latino; 4 Hispanic/Latino; 1 Two or more races, non-Hispanic/Latino), 1 international. Average age 31. 25 applicants, 80% accepted, 18 enrolled. *Faculty:* 55 full-time (30 women), 4 part-time/adjunct (2 women). Expenses: Contact institution. *Financial support:* In 2017–18, 11 students received support, including 2 research assistantships with full and partial tuition reimbursements available (averaging $12,000 per year), 9 teaching assistantships with full and partial tuition reimbursements available (averaging $12,000 per year); institutionally sponsored loans, health care benefits, and unspecified assistantships also available. Financial award application deadline: 2/1; financial award applicants required to submit FAFSA. In 2017, 13 master's, 1 other advanced degree awarded. *Program availability:* Part-time, 100% online, blended/hybrid learning. Offers communication (MA); communication studies (Graduate Certificate); science communication (Graduate Certificate). *Application deadline:* For fall admission, 3/1 for domestic and international students; for spring admission, 10/1 for domestic and international students. Applications are processed on a rolling basis. *Application fee:* $65. Electronic applications accepted. *Application Contact:* Patricia Johnson, Administrative Associate, 928-523-0030, Fax: 928-523-1505, E-mail: comgrad@nau.edu. *Professor/Director*, Dr. Norman Medoff, 928-523-8257, Fax: 928-523-1505, E-mail: norm.medoff@nau.edu.

Office of the Provost Students: 6 full-time (1 woman), 12 part-time (9 women); includes 8 minority (1 American Indian or Alaska Native, non-Hispanic/Latino; 6 Hispanic/Latino; 1 Two or more races, non-Hispanic/Latino), 1 international. Average age 38. 64 applicants, 98% accepted, 62 enrolled. *Faculty:* 33 full-time (13 women), 11 part-time/adjunct (10 women). Expenses: Contact institution. *Financial support:* In 2017–18, 24 students received support, including 22 teaching assistantships with full and partial tuition reimbursements available (averaging $9,000 per year); institutionally sponsored loans and health care benefits also available. Financial award application deadline: 2/1; financial award applicants required to submit FAFSA. In 2017, 87 master's awarded. *Program availability:* Part-time, blended/hybrid learning. Offers executive police leadership (Graduate Certificate); global business administration (MGBA); organizational leadership (M Adm). *Application deadline:* For fall admission, 3/1 for domestic and international students; for spring admission, 10/1 for domestic and international students. *Application fee:* $65. Electronic applications accepted. *Application Contact:* Tina Sutton, Coordinator, Graduate College, 928-523-4348, Fax: 928-523-8950, E-mail: graduate@nau.edu. *Provost and Vice President for Academic Affairs*, Dr. Daniel L. Kain, 928-523-2230, Fax: 928-523-2344, E-mail: provost@nau.edu.

The W. A. Franke College of Business Students: 26 full-time (13 women), 1 (woman) part-time; includes 8 minority (1 Black or African American, non-Hispanic/Latino; 1 Asian, non-Hispanic/Latino; 2 Hispanic/Latino; 1 Native Hawaiian or other Pacific Islander, non-Hispanic/Latino; 3 Two or more races, non-Hispanic/Latino), 2 international. Average age 23. 77 applicants, 45% accepted, 35 enrolled. *Faculty:* 88 full-time (33 women), 21 part-time/adjunct (9 women). Expenses: Contact institution. *Financial support:* In 2017–18, 11 students received support, including 11 research assistantships with partial tuition reimbursements available (averaging $4,500 per year); institutionally sponsored loans and tuition waivers (partial) also available. Financial award application deadline: 2/1; financial award applicants required to submit FAFSA. In 2017, 31 master's awarded. *Program availability:* Part-time, 100% online, blended/hybrid learning. Offers business administration (MBA); business foundations (Graduate Certificate). *Application deadline:* For fall admission, 5/1 for domestic students, 3/1 for international students. *Application fee:* $65. Electronic applications accepted. *Application Contact:* Michelle Brown, Assistant to the Dean, 928-523-7345, Fax: 928-523-6559, E-mail: michelle.brown@nau.edu. *Dean*, Dr. Daniel Goebel, 928-523-3657, Fax: 928-523-7331, E-mail: daniel.goebel@nau.edu.

NORTHERN ILLINOIS UNIVERSITY, De Kalb, IL 60115-2854

General Information State-supported, coed, university. CGS member. *Enrollment:* 18,042 graduate, professional, and undergraduate students; 2,063 full-time matriculated graduate/professional students (1,024 women), 2,074 part-time matriculated graduate/professional students (1,142 women). *Enrollment by degree level:* 3,176 master's, 920 doctoral, 41 other advanced degrees. *Graduate faculty:* 672 full-time (248 women), 66 part-time/adjunct (17 women). *Graduate housing:* Rooms and/or apartments available on a first-come, first-served basis to single and married students. *Student services:* Campus employment opportunities, campus safety program, career counseling, child daycare facilities, exercise/wellness program, free psychological counseling, grant writing training, international student services, low-cost health insurance, services for students with disabilities, teacher training, writing training. *Library facilities:* Founders Memorial Library plus 4 others. *Collection:* Books: 1.8 million (physical), 589,600 (digital/electronic); Serial titles: 1,600 (physical), 81,832 (digital/electronic); Databases: 309. Weekly public service hours: 100; students can reserve study rooms. *Research affiliation:* Field Museum of Natural History, Burpee Museum of Natural History, Argonne National Laboratory, Fermi National Accelerator Laboratory.

Computer facilities: 1,500 computers available on campus for general student use. A campuswide network can be accessed from student residence rooms and from off campus. Online class registration is available.
Website: http://www.niu.edu/

General Application Contact: Dr. Bradley G. Bond, Dean, Graduate School, 815-753-0395, Fax: 815-753-6366, E-mail: gradsch@niu.edu.

GRADUATE UNITS

College of Law Students: 227 full-time (96 women), 42 part-time (26 women); includes 67 minority (28 Black or African American, non-Hispanic/Latino; 11 Asian, non-Hispanic/Latino; 24 Hispanic/Latino; 2 Native Hawaiian or other Pacific Islander, non-Hispanic/Latino; 2 Two or more races, non-Hispanic/Latino), 2 international. Average age 28. 626 applicants, 51% accepted, 95 enrolled. *Faculty:* 22 full-time (11 women). Expenses: Contact institution. *Financial support:* In 2017–18, 8 teaching assistantships were awarded; research assistantships, career-related internships or fieldwork, Federal Work-Study, tuition waivers (full and partial), and unspecified assistantships also available. Support available to part-time students. Financial award application deadline: 3/1; financial award applicants required to submit FAFSA. In 2017, 70 doctorates awarded. *Program availability:* Part-time. Offers law (JD). *Application deadline:* For fall admission, 4/1 priority date for domestic and international students. Applications are processed on a rolling basis. Electronic applications accepted. *Application Contact:* Amanda Noascono, Director of Admissions and Financial Aid, 815-753-8595, Fax: 815-753-5680, E-mail: law-admit@niu.edu. *Dean*, Mark Cordes, 815-753-5300, Fax: 815-753-8552, E-mail: edan@niu.edu.

Graduate School Students: 1,836 full-time (928 women), 2,031 part-time (1,115 women); includes 900 minority (240 Black or African American, non-Hispanic/Latino; 3 American Indian or Alaska Native, non-Hispanic/Latino; 282 Asian, non-Hispanic/Latino; 275 Hispanic/Latino; 100 Two or more races, non-Hispanic/Latino), 653 international. Average age 31. 3,384 applicants, 57% accepted, 818 enrolled. *Faculty:* 672 full-time (248 women), 66 part-time/adjunct (17 women). Expenses: Contact institution. *Financial support:* In 2017–18, 411 research assistantships with full tuition reimbursements, 896 teaching assistantships with full tuition reimbursements were awarded; fellowships with full tuition reimbursements, career-related internships or fieldwork, Federal Work-Study, scholarships/grants, tuition waivers (full), and staff assistantships also available. Support available to part-time students. Financial award applicants required to submit FAFSA. In 2017, 1,489 master's, 176 doctorates, 26 other advanced degrees awarded. *Program availability:* Part-time, evening/weekend, online learning. *Application deadline:* For fall admission, 8/1 for domestic students, 5/1 for international students; for spring admission, 12/1 for domestic students, 10/1 for international students. Applications are processed on a rolling basis. *Application fee:* $40. Electronic applications accepted. *Application Contact:* Graduate School Information, 815-753-0395, E-mail: gradsch@niu.edu. *Dean*, Dr. Bradley G. Bond, 815-753-9403, Fax: 815-753-6366, E-mail: bbond@niu.edu.

College of Business Students: 383 full-time (143 women), 435 part-time (141 women); includes 246 minority (34 Black or African American, non-Hispanic/Latino; 1 American Indian or Alaska Native, non-Hispanic/Latino; 115 Asian, non-Hispanic/Latino; 72 Hispanic/Latino; 24 Two or more races, non-Hispanic/Latino), 176 international. Average age 30. 606 applicants, 74% accepted, 196 enrolled. *Faculty:* 53 full-time (17 women), 3 part-time/adjunct (0 women). Expenses: Contact institution. *Financial support:* In 2017–18, 5 research assistantships with full tuition reimbursements, 3 teaching assistantships with full tuition reimbursements were awarded; fellowships with full tuition reimbursements, career-related internships or fieldwork, Federal Work-Study, scholarships/grants, tuition waivers (full), and unspecified assistantships also available. Support available to part-time students. Financial award applicants required to submit FAFSA. In 2017, 485 master's awarded. *Program availability:* Part-time, evening/weekend. Offers accountancy (MAC, MAS, MST); business (MAC, MAS, MBA, MS, MST); business administration (MBA); management information systems (MS). *Application deadline:* For fall admission, 6/1 for domestic students, 5/1 for international students; for spring admission, 11/1 for domestic students, 10/1 for international students. Applications are processed on a rolling basis. *Application fee:* $40. Electronic applications accepted. *Application Contact:* Office of Graduate Studies in Business, 815-753-6301. *Dean*, Balaji Rajagopalan, 815-753-6225, Fax: 815-753-5305, E-mail: brajagopalan@niu.edu.

College of Education Students: 328 full-time (199 women), 848 part-time (606 women); includes 284 minority (135 Black or African American, non-Hispanic/Latino; 2 American Indian or Alaska Native, non-Hispanic/Latino; 29 Asian, non-Hispanic/Latino; 84 Hispanic/Latino; 34 Two or more races, non-Hispanic/Latino), 59 international. Average age 35. 415 applicants, 77% accepted, 168 enrolled. *Faculty:* 110 full-time (66 women), 5 part-time/adjunct (3 women). Expenses: Contact institution. *Financial support:* In 2017–18, 1 research assistantship with full tuition reimbursement was awarded; fellowships with full tuition reimbursements, teaching assistantships with full tuition reimbursements, career-related internships or fieldwork, Federal Work-Study, scholarships/grants, tuition waivers (full), and staff assistantships also available. Support available to part-time students. Financial award applicants required to submit FAFSA. In 2017, 359 master's, 62 doctorates, 20 other advanced degrees awarded. *Program availability:* Part-time, evening/weekend, online learning. Offers adult and higher education (MS Ed, Ed D); counseling (MS Ed, Ed D); curriculum and instruction (MS Ed, Ed D); early childhood education (MS Ed); education (MS, MS Ed, Ed D, Ed S); educational administration (MS Ed, Ed D, Ed S); educational psychology (MS Ed, Ed D); educational research and evaluation (MS); elementary education (MS Ed); foundations of education (MS Ed); instructional technology (MS Ed, Ed D); kinesiology and physical education (MS, MS Ed); literacy education (MS Ed); school business management (MS Ed); special education (MS Ed). *Application deadline:* For fall admission, 6/1 for domestic students, 5/1 for international students; for spring admission, 11/1 for domestic students, 10/1 for international students. Applications are processed on a rolling basis. *Application fee:* $40. Electronic applications accepted. *Application Contact:* Graduate School Office, 815-753-0395, E-mail: gradsch@niu.edu. *Dean*, Laurie Elish-Piper, 815-753-1949, Fax: 851-753-2100.

College of Engineering and Engineering Technology Students: 136 full-time (29 women), 141 part-time (15 women); includes 74 minority (15 Black or African American, non-Hispanic/Latino; 42 Asian, non-Hispanic/Latino; 12 Hispanic/Latino; 5 Two or more races, non-Hispanic/Latino), 124 international. Average age 28. 422 applicants, 61% accepted, 62 enrolled. *Faculty:* 36 full-time (2 women), 2 part-time/adjunct (0 women). Expenses: Contact institution. *Financial support:* In 2017–18, 1 research assistantship with full tuition reimbursement was awarded; fellowships with full tuition reimbursements, teaching assistantships with full tuition reimbursements, career-related internships or fieldwork, Federal Work-Study, scholarships/grants, tuition waivers (full), and unspecified assistantships also available. Support available to part-time students. Financial award applicants required to submit FAFSA. In 2017, 163 master's awarded. *Program availability:* Part-time, evening/weekend. Offers electrical engineering (MS); engineering and engineering technology (MS); industrial engineering (MS); industrial management (MS); mechanical engineering (MS). *Application deadline:* For fall admission, 6/1 for domestic students, 5/1 for international students; for spring admission, 11/1 for domestic students, 10/1 for international students. Applications are processed on a rolling basis. *Application fee:* $40. Electronic applications accepted. *Application Contact:* Graduate School Office, 815-753-0395, E-mail: gradsch@niu.edu. *Dean*, Dr. Donald R Peterson, 815-753-1281, Fax: 815-753-1310, E-mail: oghrayeb@niu.edu.

College of Health and Human Sciences Students: 292 full-time (220 women), 197 part-time (163 women); includes 114 minority (26 Black or African American, non-Hispanic/Latino; 35 Asian, non-Hispanic/Latino; 40 Hispanic/Latino; 13 Two or more races, non-Hispanic/Latino), 7 international. Average age 30. 500 applicants, 41% accepted, 110 enrolled. *Faculty:* 46 full-time (37 women), 5 part-time/adjunct (3 women). Expenses: Contact institution. *Financial support:* In 2017–18, 5 research assistantships with full tuition reimbursements were awarded; fellowships with full tuition reimbursements, teaching assistantships with full tuition reimbursements, career-related internships or fieldwork, Federal Work-Study, scholarships/grants, tuition waivers (full), and staff assistantships also available. Support available to part-time students. Financial award applicants required to submit FAFSA. In 2017, 112 master's, 40 doctorates awarded. *Program availability:* Part-time, evening/weekend. Offers applied human development and family sciences (MS); audiology (Au D); communicative disorders (MA, Au D); health and human sciences (MA, MPH, MS, Au D, DNP, DPT); nursing (MS, DNP); nutrition and dietetics (MS); physical therapy (DPT); public health (MPH); speech-language pathology (MA). *Application deadline:* For fall admission, 6/1 for domestic students, 5/1 for international students; for spring admission, 11/1 for domestic students, 10/1 for international students. Applications are processed on a rolling basis. *Application fee:* $40. Electronic applications accepted. *Application Contact:* Graduate School Office, 815-753-0395, E-mail: gradsch@niu.edu. *Dean*, Dr. Derryl Block, 815-753-6157.

College of Liberal Arts and Sciences Students: 592 full-time (283 women), 356 part-time (154 women); includes 134 minority (57 Asian, non-Hispanic/Latino; 57 Hispanic/Latino; 20 Two or more races, non-Hispanic/Latino), 260 international. Average age 29. 1,301 applicants, 47% accepted, 224 enrolled. *Faculty:* 342 full-time (99 women), 36 part-time/adjunct (7 women). Expenses: Contact institution. *Financial support:* In 2017–18, 2 research assistantships with full tuition reimbursements were awarded; fellowships with full tuition reimbursements, teaching assistantships with full tuition reimbursements, career-related internships or fieldwork, Federal Work-Study, scholarships/grants, tuition waivers (full), and unspecified assistantships also available. Support available to part-time students. Financial award applicants required to submit FAFSA. In 2017, 328 master's, 67 doctorates awarded. *Program availability:* Part-time, evening/weekend. Offers anthropology (MA); biological sciences (MS, PhD); chemistry and biochemistry (MS, PhD); communication studies (MA); computer science (MS); economics (MA, PhD); English (MA, PhD); French (MA); geography (MS, PhD); geology and environmental geosciences (MS, PhD); history (MA, PhD); liberal arts and sciences (MA, MPA, MS, PhD); mathematical sciences (PhD); mathematics (MS); philosophy (MA); physics (MS, PhD); political science (MA, PhD); psychology (MA, PhD); public administration (MPA); sociology (MA); Spanish (MA); statistics (MS). *Application deadline:* For fall admission, 6/1 for domestic students, 5/1 for international students; for spring admission, 11/1 for domestic students, 10/1 for international students. Applications are processed on a rolling basis. *Application fee:* $40. Electronic applications accepted. *Application Contact:* Graduate School Office, 815-753-0395, E-mail: gradsch@niu.edu. *Acting Dean*, Dr. Judy K Ledgerwood, 815-753-1061, Fax: 815-753-7950, E-mail: mccord@niu.edu.

College of Visual and Performing Arts Students: 105 full-time (54 women), 54 part-time (36 women); includes 24 minority (6 Black or African American, non-Hispanic/Latino; 4 Asian, non-Hispanic/Latino; 10 Hispanic/Latino; 4 Two or more races, non-Hispanic/Latino), 27 international. Average age 30. 139 applicants, 58% accepted, 37 enrolled. *Faculty:* 85 full-time (27 women), 15 part-time/adjunct (4 women). Expenses: Contact institution. *Financial support:* Fellowships with full tuition reimbursements, research assistantships with full tuition reimbursements, teaching assistantships with full tuition reimbursements, career-related internships or fieldwork, Federal Work-Study, scholarships/grants, tuition waivers (full), and staff assistantships available. Support available to part-time students. Financial award applicants required to submit FAFSA. In 2017, 79 master's, 5 other advanced degrees awarded. *Program availability:* Part-time, evening/weekend. Offers art (MA, MFA, MS); music (MM, Performer's Certificate); theatre and dance (MFA); visual and performing arts (MA, MFA, MM, MS, Performer's Certificate). *Application deadline:* For fall admission, 5/1 for international students; for spring admission, 10/1 for international students. Applications are processed on a rolling basis. *Application fee:* $40. Electronic applications accepted. *Application Contact:* Graduate School Office, 815-753-0395, E-mail: gradsch@niu.edu. *Dean*, Dr. Paul Bauer, 815-753-1138, Fax: 815-753-8372, E-mail: paulbauer@niu.edu.

NORTHERN KENTUCKY UNIVERSITY, Highland Heights, KY 41099

General Information State-supported, coed, comprehensive institution. CGS member. *Graduate housing:* Room and/or apartments available on a first-come, first-served basis to single students; on-campus housing not available to married students. Housing application deadline: 5/1.

GRADUATE UNITS

Chase College of Law Students: 329 full-time (168 women), 125 part-time (62 women); includes 65 minority (42 Black or African American, non-Hispanic/Latino; 4 American Indian or Alaska Native, non-Hispanic/Latino; 6 Asian, non-Hispanic/Latino; 12 Hispanic/Latino; 1 Two or more races, non-Hispanic/Latino). Average age 27. 567 applicants, 69% accepted, 145 enrolled. *Faculty:* 32 full-time (12 women), 38 part-time/adjunct (11 women). Expenses: Contact institution. *Financial support:* Fellowships, research assistantships, career-related internships or fieldwork, Federal Work-Study, scholarships/grants, and unspecified assistantships available. Support available to part-time students. Financial award application deadline: 3/1; financial award applicants required to submit FAFSA. In 2017, 93 doctorates awarded. *Program availability:* Part-time, evening/weekend. Offers law (JD). *Application deadline:* For fall admission, 4/1 priority date for domestic and international students; for summer admission, 3/15 priority date for domestic students, 3/15 for international students. Applications are processed on a rolling basis. *Application fee:* $40. Electronic applications accepted. *Application Contact:* Ashley Folger Gray, Director of Admissions, 859-572-5841, E-mail: graya4@nku.edu. *Co-Acting Dean*, Michael Whiteman, 859-572-5717, E-mail: whiteman@nku.edu.

Office of Graduate Programs *Program availability:* Part-time, evening/weekend, online learning. Electronic applications accepted.

College of Arts and Sciences *Program availability:* Part-time, evening/weekend, online learning. Offers arts and sciences (MA, MPA, MS, Certificate); composition and rhetoric (Certificate); creative writing (Certificate); cultural studies and discourses (Certificate); English (MA); industrial psychology (Certificate); industrial-organizational psychology (MS); integrative studies (MA); non-profit management (Certificate); occupational health psychology (Certificate); organizational psychology (Certificate); professional writing (Certificate); public administration (MPA); public history (MA). Electronic applications accepted.

College of Business *Program availability:* Part-time, evening/weekend. Offers accountancy (M Acc); advanced taxation (Certificate); business (M Acc, MBA, MS, Certificate); business administration (MBA, Certificate); executive leadership and organizational change (MS). Electronic applications accepted.

College of Education and Human Services *Program availability:* Part-time, evening/weekend. Offers clinical mental health counseling (MS); education (MA, Certificate); education and human services (MA, MAT, MS, MSW, Ed D, Certificate, Ed S); educational leadership (Ed D, Ed S); school counseling (MA); social work (MSW); special education (Certificate); teaching (MAT). Electronic applications accepted.

College of Informatics *Program availability:* Part-time, evening/weekend. Offers business informatics (MS, Certificate); communication (MA); communication teaching (Certificate); computer information technology (MSCIT); computer science (MSCS); corporate information security (Certificate); documentary studies (Certificate); enterprise resource planning (Certificate); geographic information systems (Certificate); health informatics (MS, Certificate); informatics (MA, MS, MSCIT, MSCS, Certificate); public relations (Certificate); relationships (Certificate); secure software engineering (Certificate). Electronic applications accepted.

School of Nursing and Health Professions *Program availability:* Part-time, evening/weekend, online learning. Offers health science (MS); nursing (MSHS, MSN, DNP, Certificate, Post-Master's Certificate); nursing and health professions (MS, MSHS, MSN, DNP, Certificate, Post-Master's Certificate). Electronic applications accepted.

NORTHERN MICHIGAN UNIVERSITY, Marquette, MI 49855-5301

General Information State-supported, coed, comprehensive institution. CGS member. *Enrollment:* 7,612 graduate, professional, and undergraduate students; 183 full-time matriculated graduate/professional students (117 women), 272 part-time matriculated graduate/professional students (177 women). *Enrollment by degree level:* 423 master's, 16 doctoral, 16 other advanced degrees. *Graduate faculty:* 62 full-time (29 women), 4 part-time/adjunct (3 women). Tuition, state resident: full-time $9417; part-time $542 per credit hour. Tuition, nonresident: full-time $12,873; part-time $758 per credit hour. Tuition and fees vary according to course load, degree level and program. *Graduate housing:* Rooms and/or apartments available on a first-come, first-served basis to single and married students. Housing application deadline: 7/15. *Student services:* Campus employment opportunities, campus safety program, career counseling, free psychological counseling, international student services, low-cost health insurance, multicultural affairs office, services for students with disabilities. *Library facilities:* Lydia M. Olson Library.

Computer facilities: A campuswide network can be accessed from student residence rooms and from off campus. Online class registration is available.
Website: http://www.nmu.edu/

General Application Contact: Lisa Eckert, Interim Director of Graduate Education, 906-227-2300, Fax: 906-227-2315, E-mail: graduate@nmu.edu.

GRADUATE UNITS

Office of Graduate Education and Research Expenses: Contact institution. *Financial support:* Teaching assistantships with full tuition reimbursements, career-related internships or fieldwork, Federal Work-Study, institutionally sponsored loans, and unspecified assistantships available. Support available to part-time students. Financial award applicants required to submit FAFSA. *Program availability:* Part-time, evening/weekend, online learning. *Application deadline:* For fall admission, 7/1 for domestic students; for winter admission, 11/15 for domestic students; for spring admission, 3/17 for domestic students. Applications are processed on a rolling basis. *Application fee:* $50. Electronic applications accepted. *Application Contact:* Director of Graduate Education, 906-227-2300, E-mail: graduate@nmu.edu. *Director of Graduate Education*, 906-227-2300, E-mail: graduate@nmu.edu.

College of Arts and Sciences Expenses: Contact institution. *Financial support:* Career-related internships or fieldwork, Federal Work-Study, institutionally sponsored loans, and unspecified assistantships available. Support available to part-time students. Financial award application deadline: 3/1. *Program availability:* Part-time, online learning. Offers applied behavior analysis (MS); arts and sciences (MA, MFA, MS, Graduate Certificate); biology (MS); creative writing (MFA); integrated biosciences (MS); literature (MA); pedagogy (MA); psychological science (MS); teaching English to speakers of other languages (Graduate Certificate); theater (MA); writing (MA). *Application deadline:* For fall admission, 7/1 for domestic students; for winter admission, 11/15 for domestic students; for spring admission, 3/17 for domestic students. Applications are processed on a rolling basis. *Application fee:* $50. Electronic applications accepted. *Application Contact:* Robert Winn, Interim Dean, 906-227-2700, E-mail: rwinn@nmu.edu. *Interim Dean*, Robert Winn, 906-227-2700, E-mail: rwinn@nmu.edu.

College of Business Expenses: Contact institution. *Financial support:* Research assistantships with full tuition reimbursements, Federal Work-Study, institutionally sponsored loans, scholarships/grants, and unspecified assistantships available. Support available to part-time students. Financial award applicants required to submit FAFSA. *Program availability:* Part-time. Offers business (MBA). *Application deadline:* For fall admission, 7/1 for domestic students; for winter admission, 11/15 for domestic students. Applications are processed on a rolling basis. *Application fee:* $50. Electronic applications accepted. *Application Contact:* Carol W. Johnson, Interim Dean, 906-227-2947, E-mail: business@nmu.edu. *Interim Dean*, Carol W. Johnson, 906-227-2947, E-mail: business@nmu.edu.

College of Health Sciences and Professional Studies Expenses: Contact institution. *Financial support:* Career-related internships or fieldwork, Federal Work-Study, institutionally sponsored loans, tuition waivers (full), and unspecified assistantships available. Support available to part-time students. Financial award application deadline: 3/1. *Program availability:* Part-time. Offers administration and supervision (MAE); clinical molecular genetics (MS); exercise science (MS); health sciences and professional studies (MA, MA Ed, MAE, MS, DNP); instruction (MAE); learning disabilities (MAE); nursing (DNP); postsecondary biology education (MS); reading education (MAE). *Application deadline:* For fall admission, 7/1 priority date for domestic students; for winter admission, 11/15 for domestic students; for spring admission, 3/17 for domestic students. Applications are processed on a rolling basis. *Application fee:* $50. *Application Contact:* Dr. Charles Mesloh, Interim Dean, 906-227-2400, E-mail: cmesloh@nmu.edu. *Interim Dean*, Dr. Charles Mesloh, 906-227-2400, E-mail: cmesloh@nmu.edu.

NORTHERN SEMINARY, Lombard, IL 60148-5698

General Information Independent-religious, coed, primarily men, graduate-only institution. *Enrollment by degree level:* 141 master's, 67 doctoral. *Graduate faculty:* 6 full-time (1 woman), 33 part-time/adjunct (8 women). *Tuition:* Full-time $14,253; part-time

$9627 per credit. *Required fees:* $125 per quarter. *Graduate housing:* On-campus housing not available. *Student services:* Campus employment opportunities, low-cost health insurance. *Library facilities:* Brimsom Grow Library. *Collection:* Books: 53,200 (physical). Weekly public service hours: 30; students can reserve study rooms.

Computer facilities: 4 computers available on campus for general student use. A campuswide network can be accessed. Online class registration is available.
Website: http://www.seminary.edu/

General Application Contact: Greg Armstrong, Director of Admissions, 630-620-2175, Fax: 630-620-2190, E-mail: admissions@seminary.edu.

GRADUATE UNITS

Graduate and Professional Programs Students: 208 full-time (62 women); includes 89 minority (73 Black or African American, non-Hispanic/Latino; 6 Asian, non-Hispanic/Latino; 8 Hispanic/Latino; 2 Two or more races, non-Hispanic/Latino), 3 international. Average age 44. *Faculty:* 6 full-time (1 woman), 33 part-time/adjunct (8 women). Expenses: Contact institution. *Financial support:* Teaching assistantships with partial tuition reimbursements, Federal Work-Study, and scholarships/grants available. Support available to part-time students. Financial award application deadline: 9/1; financial award applicants required to submit FAFSA. *Program availability:* Part-time, evening/weekend. Offers Biblical studies (M Div); Christian community development (MA, D Min); Christian ministry (MACM); contextual theology (D Min); missional church ministry (M Div); New Testament (M Div, MANT); New Testament context (D Min); Old Testament (M Div); preaching (D Min); theology (M Div); theology and mission (MA); urban leadership (MA); worship (M Div, MAW). *Application deadline:* Applications are processed on a rolling basis. *Application fee:* $35. Electronic applications accepted. *Application Contact:* Greg Armstrong, Director of Admissions, 630-620-2175, Fax: 630-620-2190, E-mail: admissions@seminary.edu. *President*, Dr. William Shiell, 630-620-2101, Fax: 630-620-2190.

NORTHERN STATE UNIVERSITY, Aberdeen, SD 57401-7198

General Information State-supported, coed, comprehensive institution. *Graduate housing:* Room and/or apartments available on a first-come, first-served basis to single students; on-campus housing not available to married students. Housing application deadline: 8/1. *Research affiliation:* AASCU–Grants Resource Center.

GRADUATE UNITS

MME Program in Music Education *Program availability:* Part-time, online learning. Offers music education (MME). Electronic applications accepted.

MS Ed Program in Counseling *Program availability:* Part-time, online learning. Offers clinical mental health counseling (MS Ed); school counseling (MS Ed). Electronic applications accepted.

MS Ed Program in Educational Studies *Program availability:* Part-time, online learning. Offers educational studies (MS Ed). Electronic applications accepted.

MS Ed Program in Instructional Design in E-learning *Program availability:* Part-time, online learning. Offers instructional design in e-learning (MS Ed). Electronic applications accepted.

MS Ed Program in Leadership and Administration *Program availability:* Part-time, evening/weekend, online learning. Offers leadership and administration (MS Ed). Electronic applications accepted.

MS Ed Program in Sport Performance and Leadership *Program availability:* Part-time. Offers sport performance and leadership (MS Ed). Electronic applications accepted.

MS Ed Program in Teaching and Learning *Program availability:* Part-time, evening/weekend, online learning. Offers teaching and learning (MS Ed). Electronic applications accepted.

MS Program in Banking and Financial Services *Program availability:* Part-time, online learning. Offers banking and financial services (MS). Electronic applications accepted.

MS Program in Training and Development in E-learning *Program availability:* Part-time, online learning. Offers training and development in e-learning (MS). Electronic applications accepted.

NORTHERN VERMONT UNIVERSITY–JOHNSON, Johnson, VT 05656

General Information State-supported, coed, comprehensive institution. *Enrollment:* 20 full-time matriculated graduate/professional students (14 women), 113 part-time matriculated graduate/professional students (91 women). *Enrollment by degree level:* 133 master's. *Graduate faculty:* 10 full-time (5 women), 14 part-time/adjunct (8 women). Tuition, state resident: part-time $572 per credit hour. Tuition, nonresident: part-time $832 per credit hour. *Graduate housing:* Rooms and/or apartments available on a first-come, first-served basis to single and married students. Housing application deadline: 3/15. *Student services:* Campus employment opportunities, exercise/wellness program, international student services, low-cost health insurance, services for students with disabilities. *Library facilities:* Willey Library plus 1 other. *Collection:* Books: 111,100 (physical), 6,500 (digital/electronic). Study areas open 24 hours, 5–7 days a week.

Computer facilities: 160 computers available on campus for general student use. A campuswide network can be accessed from student residence rooms and from off campus. Online class registration is available.
Website: http://www.northernvermont.edu/

General Application Contact: Catherine H. Higley, Administrative Assistant, Office of Graduate and Professional Learning, 800-635-2356 Ext. 1244, Fax: 802-635-1230, E-mail: catherine.higley@jsc.edu.

GRADUATE UNITS

Program in Counseling Students: 2 full-time (1 woman), 15 part-time (9 women). *Faculty:* 2 full-time (1 woman), 11 part-time/adjunct (6 women). Expenses: Contact institution. *Financial support:* Career-related internships or fieldwork and unspecified assistantships available. Support available to part-time students. Financial award application deadline: 3/1; financial award applicants required to submit FAFSA. In 2017, 50 master's awarded. *Program availability:* Part-time. Offers addictions counseling (MA); clinical mental health counseling (MA); general counseling (MA); school counseling (MA). *Application deadline:* For fall admission, 7/1 for domestic students, 2/1 for international students; for spring admission, 11/1 for domestic students, 7/1 for international students; for summer admission, 4/1 for domestic students. Applications are processed on a rolling basis. Electronic applications accepted. *Application Contact:* Catherine H. Higley, Administrative Assistant, 800-635-2356 Ext. 1244, Fax: 802-635-1248, E-mail: catherine.higley@jsc.edu. *Coordinator*, Dr. Kimberly Donovan, 802-635-1453, Fax: 802-635-1465, E-mail: kimberly.donovan@northernvermont.edu.

Program in Education Students: 3 full-time (all women), 36 part-time (30 women). *Faculty:* 5 full-time (3 women), 4 part-time/adjunct (3 women). Expenses: Contact institution. *Financial support:* Scholarships/grants and unspecified assistantships available. Financial award application deadline: 3/1; financial award applicants required to submit FAFSA. In 2017, 23 master's awarded. *Program availability:* Part-time. Offers applied behavior analysis (MA Ed); curriculum and instruction (MA Ed); foundations of education (MA Ed); special education (MA Ed). *Application deadline:* For fall admission, 5/1 for domestic students, 2/1 for international students. Applications are processed on a rolling basis. Electronic applications accepted. *Application Contact:* Catherine H. Higley, Administrative Assistant, 800-635-2356 Ext. 1244, Fax: 802-635-1248, E-mail: catherine.higley@jsc.edu. *Chair, Department of Education*, Dr. Kathleen Brinegar, 802-635-1472, Fax: 802-635-1465, E-mail: kathleen.brinegar@jsc.edu.

Program in Studio Arts Students: 5 full-time (3 women), 2 part-time (1 woman). *Faculty:* 3 full-time (1 woman). Expenses: Contact institution. *Financial support:* Teaching assistantships and unspecified assistantships available. Support available to part-time students. Financial award application deadline: 3/1; financial award applicants required to submit FAFSA. In 2017, 2 master's awarded. *Program availability:* Part-time, online learning. Offers ceramics (MFA); digital media (MFA); drawing (MFA); painting (MFA); photography (MFA); printmaking (MFA); sculpture (MFA). *Application deadline:* For fall admission, 3/1 for domestic students, 2/1 for international students. Applications are processed on a rolling basis. Electronic applications accepted. *Application Contact:* Catherine H. Higley, Administrative Assistant, 800-635-2356 Ext. 1244, Fax: 802-635-1248, E-mail: catherine.higley@jsc.edu.

NORTHERN VERMONT UNIVERSITY–LYNDON, Lyndonville, VT 05851

General Information State-supported, coed, comprehensive institution. *Graduate housing:* On-campus housing not available.

GRADUATE UNITS

Graduate Programs in Education *Program availability:* Part-time, evening/weekend. Offers curriculum and instruction (M Ed); education (M Ed); natural sciences (MST); reading specialist (M Ed); science education (MST); special education (M Ed); teaching and counseling (M Ed).

NORTH GREENVILLE UNIVERSITY, Tigerville, SC 29688-1892

General Information Independent-religious, coed, comprehensive institution. *Graduate housing:* Room and/or apartments available on a first-come, first-served basis to single students; on-campus housing not available to married students. Housing application deadline: 8/1.

GRADUATE UNITS

T. Walter Brashier Graduate School *Program availability:* Part-time, evening/weekend, online learning. Offers Christian ministry (MCM, D Min); education (M Ed, MAT); financial planning (MBA); human resources (MBA). Electronic applications accepted.

NORTH PARK THEOLOGICAL SEMINARY, Chicago, IL 60625-4895

General Information Independent-religious, coed, graduate-only institution. *Graduate housing:* Rooms and/or apartments available to single and married students. Housing application deadline: 9/1. *Research affiliation:* Northside Chicago Theological Institute, Covenant Archives and Historical Society, American Theological Library Association.

GRADUATE UNITS

Graduate and Professional Programs *Program availability:* Part-time. Offers adult ministry (Certificate); camping and retreat ministry (Certificate); children and family ministry (Certificate); Christian formation (MA); Christian ministry (MACM); faith and health (Certificate); intercultural studies (Certificate); justice ministry (Certificate); leadership and administration (Certificate); preaching (D Min); spiritual direction (Certificate); theological studies (MATS); theology (M Div); youth ministry (Certificate).

NORTH PARK UNIVERSITY, Chicago, IL 60625-4895

General Information Independent-religious, coed, comprehensive institution. *Graduate housing:* Rooms and/or apartments available to single and married students.

GRADUATE UNITS

School of Business and Nonprofit Management *Program availability:* Part-time, evening/weekend, online learning. Offers business and nonprofit management (MBA, MHEA, MHRM, MM, MNA).

School of Education Offers education (MA).

School of Music Offers vocal performance (MM).

School of Nursing and Health Sciences *Program availability:* Part-time, evening/weekend. Offers advanced practice nursing (MS); leadership and management (MS).

NORTHWEST CHRISTIAN UNIVERSITY, Eugene, OR 97401-3745

General Information Independent-religious, coed, comprehensive institution. *Enrollment:* 798 graduate, professional, and undergraduate students; 95 full-time matriculated graduate/professional students (72 women), 98 part-time matriculated graduate/professional students (52 women). *Enrollment by degree level:* 193 master's. *Graduate faculty:* 19 full-time (6 women), 25 part-time/adjunct (15 women). *Tuition:* Full-time $7800; part-time $3900 per credit hour. *Required fees:* $90 per semester. Tuition and fees vary according to course load and program. *Graduate housing:* On-campus housing not available. *Student services:* Career counseling, free psychological counseling, services for students with disabilities, teacher training, writing training. *Library facilities:* Edward P. Kellenberger Library. *Collection:* Books: 59,536 (physical), 14 (digital/electronic); Serial titles: 156 (physical), 105,706 (digital/electronic); Databases: 105. Weekly public service hours: 70.

Computer facilities: 16 computers available on campus for general student use. A campuswide network can be accessed from student residence rooms and from off campus. Online class registration is available.
Website: http://www.nwcu.edu/

General Application Contact: Billy Dorsch, Admissions Counselor for Graduate Studies, 541-684-7279, Fax: 541-349-5281, E-mail: wdorsch@nwcu.edu.

GRADUATE UNITS

School of Business and Management Students: 61 full-time (30 women), 10 part-time (4 women); includes 21 minority (2 Black or African American, non-Hispanic/Latino; 1 American Indian or Alaska Native, non-Hispanic/Latino; 4 Asian, non-Hispanic/Latino; 8 Hispanic/Latino; 1 Native Hawaiian or other Pacific Islander, non-Hispanic/Latino; 5 Two or more races, non-Hispanic/Latino). Average age 33. *Faculty:* 6 full-time (1 woman), 8 part-time/adjunct (3 women). Expenses: Contact institution. In 2017, 36 master's awarded. *Program availability:* Part-time, evening/weekend, online only, 100% online. Offers accounting (MBA); management (MBA). *Application deadline:* Applications are processed on a rolling basis. Electronic applications accepted. *Application Contact:* Billy Dorsch, Admission Counselor for Graduate Studies, 541-684-7279, Fax: 541-349-5281, E-mail: wdorsch@nwcu.edu. *Assistant Dean*, Dr. Peter Diffenderfer, 541-684-7441, Fax: 541-684-7336, E-mail: pdiffenderfer@nwcu.edu.

School of Education and Counseling Students: 77 full-time (60 women), 44 part-time (30 women); includes 19 minority (4 Black or African American, non-Hispanic/Latino; 1 American Indian or Alaska Native, non-Hispanic/Latino; 3 Asian, non-Hispanic/Latino; 2 Hispanic/Latino; 1 Native Hawaiian or other Pacific Islander, non-Hispanic/Latino; 8 Two or more races, non-Hispanic/Latino). Average age 34. *Faculty:* 9 full-time (4 women), 14 part-time/adjunct (10 women). Expenses: Contact institution. *Financial support:* Applicants required to submit FAFSA. In 2017, 58 master's awarded. *Program availability:* Part-time, evening/weekend, online learning. Offers clinical mental health counseling (MA); elementary teaching (MAT); English for speakers of other languages (MAT); physical education (MAT); school counseling (MA); secondary teaching (MAT); special education (MAT). *Application deadline:* Applications are processed on a rolling basis. Electronic applications accepted. *Application Contact:* Billy Dorsch, Admission Counselor for Graduate Studies, 541-684-7279, Fax: 541-349-5281, E-mail: wdorsch@nwcu.edu. *Director,* Elizabeth Wosley-George, 541-349-7465, Fax: 541-684-7310, E-mail: ewosleygeorge@nwcu.edu.

NORTHWESTERN COLLEGE, Orange City, IA 51041-1996

General Information Independent-religious, coed, comprehensive institution.

GRADUATE UNITS

Program in Education *Program availability:* Online learning. Offers early childhood (M Ed); master teacher (M Ed); teacher leadership (M Ed, Graduate Certificate).

NORTHWESTERN HEALTH SCIENCES UNIVERSITY, Bloomington, MN 55431-1599

General Information Independent, coed, graduate-only institution. *Graduate housing:* On-campus housing not available. *Research affiliation:* University of Minnesota, Center for Spirituality and Healing (education research), University of Western States (clinical research), University of Pittsburgh (education research).

GRADUATE UNITS

College of Chiropractic Offers chiropractic (DC). Electronic applications accepted.

College of Health and Wellness Offers acupuncture (M Ac); applied clinical nutrition (MHS); Oriental medicine (MOM). Electronic applications accepted.

NORTHWESTERN OKLAHOMA STATE UNIVERSITY, Alva, OK 73717-2799

General Information State-supported, coed, comprehensive institution. *Graduate housing:* Room and/or apartments available to single students; on-campus housing not available to married students.

GRADUATE UNITS

Program in American Studies *Program availability:* Part-time. Offers American studies (MA).

School of Professional Studies *Program availability:* Part-time. Offers adult education management and administration (M Ed); counseling psychology (MCP); curriculum and instruction (M Ed); educational leadership (M Ed); elementary education (M Ed); reading specialist (M Ed); school counseling (M Ed); secondary education (M Ed).

NORTHWESTERN POLYTECHNIC UNIVERSITY, Fremont, CA 94539-7482

General Information Independent, coed, comprehensive institution. *Graduate housing:* Room and/or apartments available on a first-come, first-served basis to single students; on-campus housing not available to married students. Housing application deadline: 7/15.

GRADUATE UNITS

School of Business and Information Technology *Program availability:* Part-time, evening/weekend. Offers business and information technology (MBA, DBA).

School of Engineering *Program availability:* Part-time, evening/weekend. Offers computer engineering (DCE); computer science (MS); computer systems engineering (MS); electrical engineering (MS).

NORTHWESTERN STATE UNIVERSITY OF LOUISIANA, Natchitoches, LA 71497

General Information State-supported, coed, comprehensive institution. CGS member. *Graduate housing:* Room and/or apartments available on a first-come, first-served basis to single students; on-campus housing not available to married students. Housing application deadline: 3/1. *Research affiliation:* NASA (Strategic Defense Initiative), Central State Hospital, Federal Records and Archives Services.

GRADUATE UNITS

Graduate Studies and Research *Program availability:* Part-time, evening/weekend, online learning. Offers clinical psychology (MS); English (MA); health and human performance (MS); homeland security (MS). Electronic applications accepted.

College of Education and Human Development Offers adult and continuing education (MA); counseling (Ed S); curriculum and instruction (M Ed); early childhood education and teaching (M Ed, MAT); education and human development (M Ed, MA, MAT, Ed S); educational leadership (M Ed, Ed S); educational technology (Ed S); educational technology leadership (M Ed); elementary education (MAT); elementary teaching (Ed S); middle school education (MAT); reading (Ed S); school counseling (MA); secondary education (MAT); secondary teaching (Ed S); special education (Ed S); student affairs in higher education (MA). Electronic applications accepted.

College of Nursing and School of Allied Health *Program availability:* Part-time. Offers nursing and allied health (MS, MSN); radiologic sciences (MS). Electronic applications accepted.

School of Creative and Performing Arts Offers art (MA); fine and graphic arts (MA); music (MM). Electronic applications accepted.

NORTHWESTERN UNIVERSITY, Evanston, IL 60208

General Information Independent, coed, university. CGS member. *Graduate housing:* Rooms and/or apartments available on a first-come, first-served basis to single students and available to married students. Housing application deadline: 9/1. *Research affiliation:* Dow Chemical Company (materials science and engineering), E.I. du Pont de Nemours and Company (physics), Exxon Chemical Company (chemical engineering), Ford Motor Company (mechanical engineering), Medtronics, Inc. (cardiology), Amoco Oil Company (materials science and engineering).

GRADUATE UNITS

Feinberg School of Medicine Offers biostatistics (PhD); clinical investigation (MSCI); epidemiology (PhD); health and biomedical informatics (PhD); health services and outcomes research (PhD); healthcare quality and patient safety (PhD); medicine (MS, MSCI, DPT, MD, PhD); neuroscience (PhD); physical therapy (DPT); public health (MPH); translational outcomes in science (PhD). Electronic applications accepted.

The Graduate School *Program availability:* Part-time, evening/weekend. Offers biochemistry (PhD); bioengineering and biotechnology (PhD); biotechnology (PhD); cell and molecular biology (PhD); clinical investigation (MSCI, Certificate); clinical psychology (PhD); developmental and systems biology (PhD); gender and sexuality studies (Graduate Certificate); genetic counseling (MS); marital and family therapy (MS); nanotechnology (PhD); neurobiology (PhD); neuroscience (PhD); structural biology and biophysics (PhD). Electronic applications accepted.

Center for International and Comparative Studies Offers international and comparative studies (Certificate).

Judd A. and Marjorie Weinberg College of Arts and Sciences *Program availability:* Part-time, evening/weekend. Offers African American studies (PhD); African studies (Graduate Certificate); ancient philosophy (PhD); anthropology (PhD); applied physics (PhD); art history (PhD); arts and sciences (MA, MFA, MS, PhD, Graduate Certificate); brain, behavior and cognition (PhD); chemistry (PhD); clinical psychology (PhD); cognitive psychology (PhD); comparative literary studies (PhD); earth and planetary sciences (PhD); economics (PhD); English (MA, PhD); French/Francophone studies (PhD); German literature and critical thought (PhD); history (PhD); Italian studies (Graduate Certificate); linguistics (PhD); mathematics (PhD); neurobiology and physiology (MS); personality psychology (PhD); philosophy (PhD); physics and astronomy (PhD); plant biology and conservation (MA, PhD); political science (PhD); religious studies (PhD); Slavic languages and literature (PhD); social psychology (PhD); sociology (PhD); Spanish and Portuguese (PhD); statistics (MS, PhD); visual arts (MFA).

Kellogg School of Management *Program availability:* Part-time, evening/weekend. Offers accounting information and management (MBA, PhD); analytical finance (MBA); business administration (MBA); decision sciences (MBA); entrepreneurship and innovation (MBA); finance (PhD); health enterprise management (MBA); human resources management (MBA); international business (MBA); management (MBA, MS, PhD); management and organizations (MBA, PhD); management and organizations and sociology (PhD); management and strategy (PhD); management studies (MS); managerial analytics (MBA); managerial economics (MBA); managerial economics and decision sciences (PhD); managerial economics and strategy (PhD); marketing (MBA, PhD); marketing management (MBA); media management (MBA); operations management (MBA, PhD); real estate (MBA); social enterprise at Kellogg (MBA). PhD admissions and degree offered through The Graduate School. Electronic applications accepted.

School of Communication *Program availability:* Part-time. Offers audiology (Au D); communication (MA, MFA, MS, MSC, Au D, PhD); communication sciences and disorders (PhD); communication studies (PhD); directing (MFA); documentary media (MFA); leadership for creative enterprises (MS); managerial communication (MSC); media, technology and society (PhD); performance studies (MA, PhD); screen cultures (MA, PhD); speech, language, and learning (MS); stage design (MFA); technology and social behavior (PhD); theatre and drama (PhD); writing for the screen and stage (MFA). MA, MFA, and PhD admissions and degrees offered through The Graduate School; MSC admissions and degrees offered through the School of Communication.

School of Education and Social Policy *Program availability:* Part-time, evening/weekend. Offers education (MS); elementary teaching (MS); human development and social policy (PhD); learning and organizational change (MS); learning sciences (MA, PhD); secondary teaching (MS); teacher leadership (MS). MA and PhD admissions and degrees offered through The Graduate School. Electronic applications accepted.

Henry and Leigh Bienen School of Music Offers brass performance (MM, DMA); composition (DMA); conducting (MM, DMA); jazz studies (MM); music education (MME, PhD); music theory (MM); music theory and cognition (PhD); musicology (MM, PhD); percussion performance (MM, DMA); performance (MM); piano pedagogy (MME); piano performance (MM, DMA); piano performance and collaborative arts (MM, DMA); piano performance and pedagogy (MM, DMA); string performance (MM, DMA); theory (MM); voice and opera performance (MM, DMA); woodwind performance (MM, DMA). PhD admissions and degree offered through The Graduate School. Electronic applications accepted.

McCormick School of Engineering and Applied Science *Program availability:* Part-time, evening/weekend. Offers analytics (MS); biomedical engineering (MS, PhD); biotechnology (MS); chemical engineering (MS, PhD); computer engineering (MS, PhD); computer science (MS, PhD); design innovation (MBA, MS); electrical engineering (MS, PhD); engineering and applied science (MBA, MEM, MIT, MME, MMM, MPD, MS, PhD, Certificate); engineering management (MEM); engineering sciences and applied mathematics (MS, PhD); environmental engineering and science (MS, PhD); geotechnical engineering (MS, PhD); industrial engineering and management science (MS, PhD); information technology (MS); integrated computational materials engineering (Certificate); materials science and engineering (MS, PhD); mechanical engineering (MS, PhD); mechanics of materials and solids (MS, PhD); product design and development management (MS); project management (MS); robotics (MS); structural engineering and materials (MS, PhD); theoretical and applied mechanics (MS, PhD); transportation systems analysis and planning (MS, PhD). MS and PhD admissions and degrees offered through The Graduate School. Electronic applications accepted.

Segal Design Institute Offers engineering design and innovation (MS).

Medill School of Journalism, Media, and Integrated Marketing Communications Offers brand strategy (MSIMC); content marketing (MSIMC); direct and interactive marketing (MSIMC); integrated marketing communications (MSIMC); interactive publishing (MSJ); magazine writing/editing (MSJ); marketing analytics (MSIMC); reporting (MSJ); strategic communications (MSIMC); video/broadcast (MSJ). Electronic applications accepted.

Pritzker School of Law Offers international human rights (LL M); law (JD); law and business (LL M); science law (MSL); tax (LL M in Tax). Executive LL M programs offered in Madrid (Spain), Seoul (South Korea), and Tel Aviv (Israel). Electronic applications accepted.

School of Professional Studies Expenses: Contact institution. Offers American literature (MA); American studies (MA); analytics and business intelligence (MS); British literature (MA); clinical research (MS); comparative and world literature (MA); computer-based data mining (MS); creative writing (MA, MFA); database and Internet technologies (MS); global health (MS); global policy (MA); health informatics (MS); health services policy (MA); healthcare compliance (MS); history (MA); information design and strategy (MS); information systems (MS); information systems management (MS); information systems security (MS); marketing analytics (MS); medical informatics (MS); predictive modeling (MS); public administration (MA); public policy (MA); quality systems (MS); religious and ethical studies (MA); risk analytics (MS); software project management and development (MS); sports administration (MA); Web analytics (MS).

NORTHWEST MISSOURI STATE UNIVERSITY, Maryville, MO 64468-6001

General Information State-supported, coed, comprehensive institution. *Enrollment:* 6,338 graduate, professional, and undergraduate students; 365 full-time matriculated graduate/professional students (159 women), 499 part-time matriculated graduate/professional students (295 women). *Enrollment by degree level:* 821 master's, 15 doctoral, 28 other advanced degrees. *Graduate faculty:* 150 full-time (52 women). Tuition, state resident: full-time $4551; part-time $252.86 per credit hour. Tuition, nonresident: full-time $9103; part-time $505.72 per credit hour. *Required fees:* $2453; $136.25 per credit hour. Tuition and fees vary according to course load and program. *Graduate housing:* Rooms and/or apartments available on a first-come, first-served basis to single and married students. Typical cost: $7348 per year ($10,918 including board) for single students. Room and board charges vary according to board plan and housing facility selected. Housing application deadline: 6/1. *Student services:* Campus employment opportunities, campus safety program, career counseling, exercise/wellness program, free psychological counseling, international student services, low-cost health insurance, multicultural affairs office, services for students with disabilities, teacher training, writing training. *Library facilities:* Owens Library. *Collection:* Books: 172,234 (physical), 1,506 (digital/electronic); Serial titles: 31 (physical), 15 (digital/electronic); Databases: 103. Weekly public service hours: 95; students can reserve study rooms.

Computer facilities: Computer purchase and lease plans are available. 253 computers available on campus for general student use. A campuswide network can be accessed from student residence rooms and from off campus. Online class registration, online courses with library and databases are available.
Website: http://www.nwmissouri.edu/

General Application Contact: Dr. Gregory Haddock, Dean of Graduate School, 660-562-1145, Fax: 660-562-1096, E-mail: gradsch@nwmissouri.edu.

GRADUATE UNITS

Graduate School Students: 365 full-time (159 women), 499 part-time (295 women); includes 56 minority (20 Black or African American, non-Hispanic/Latino; 2 American Indian or Alaska Native, non-Hispanic/Latino; 3 Asian, non-Hispanic/Latino; 20 Hispanic/Latino; 11 Two or more races, non-Hispanic/Latino), 287 international. Average age 29. 815 applicants, 69% accepted, 312 enrolled. *Faculty:* 150 full-time (52 women). Expenses: Contact institution. *Financial support:* Research assistantships with full tuition reimbursements, teaching assistantships with full tuition reimbursements, career-related internships or fieldwork, Federal Work-Study, institutionally sponsored loans, scholarships/grants, unspecified assistantships, and administrative assistantships, tutorial assistantships available. Financial award application deadline: 4/1; financial award applicants required to submit FAFSA. In 2017, 460 master's, 35 other advanced degrees awarded. *Program availability:* Part-time, evening/weekend. *Application deadline:* For fall admission, 7/1 for domestic and international students; for spring admission, 11/15 for domestic and international students. Applications are processed on a rolling basis. *Application fee:* $0 ($50 for international students). Electronic applications accepted. *Application Contact:* Terry Immel, Executive Secretary, 660-562-1145, Fax: 660-562-1096, E-mail: gradsch@nwmissouri.edu. *Dean*, Dr. Gregory Haddock, 660-562-1145, Fax: 660-562-1096, E-mail: gradsch@nwmissouri.edu.

College of Arts and Sciences Students: 11 full-time (5 women), 70 part-time (39 women); includes 9 minority (2 Black or African American, non-Hispanic/Latino; 1 American Indian or Alaska Native, non-Hispanic/Latino; 3 Hispanic/Latino; 3 Two or more races, non-Hispanic/Latino). Average age 34. 33 applicants, 42% accepted, 10 enrolled. *Faculty:* 67 full-time (21 women). Expenses: Contact institution. *Financial support:* Research assistantships with full tuition reimbursements, teaching assistantships with full tuition reimbursements, and administrative assistantships, tutorial assistantships available. Financial award application deadline: 4/1; financial award applicants required to submit FAFSA. In 2017, 19 master's, 7 other advanced degrees awarded. *Program availability:* Part-time. Offers biology (MS); elementary mathematics specialist (MS Ed); English (MA); English education (MS Ed); English pedagogy (MA); geographic information science (MS, Certificate); history (MS Ed); mathematics (MS); mathematics education (MS Ed); teaching: science (MS Ed). *Application deadline:* For fall admission, 7/1 for domestic and international students; for spring admission, 11/15 for domestic and international students. Applications are processed on a rolling basis. *Application fee:* $0 ($50 for international students). Electronic applications accepted. *Dean*, Dr. Michael Steiner, 660-562-1197.

Melvin and Valorie Booth College of Business and Professional Studies Students: 40 full-time (13 women), 95 part-time (48 women); includes 16 minority (8 Black or African American, non-Hispanic/Latino; 1 American Indian or Alaska Native, non-Hispanic/Latino; 2 Asian, non-Hispanic/Latino; 3 Hispanic/Latino; 2 Two or more races, non-Hispanic/Latino), 15 international. Average age 31. 142 applicants, 66% accepted, 70 enrolled. *Faculty:* 17 full-time (6 women). Expenses: Contact institution. *Financial support:* Research assistantships with full tuition reimbursements, teaching assistantships with full tuition reimbursements, career-related internships or fieldwork, and administrative assistantships, tutorial assistantships available. Financial award application deadline: 4/1; financial award applicants required to submit FAFSA. In 2017, 53 master's awarded. *Program availability:* Part-time. Offers agricultural economics (MBA); business decision and analytics (MBA); general management (MBA); human resource management (MBA); marketing (MBA). *Application deadline:* For fall admission, 7/1 for domestic and international students; for spring admission, 11/15 for domestic and international students; for summer admission, 4/1 for domestic and international students. Applications are processed on a rolling basis. *Application fee:* $0 ($50 for international students). Electronic applications accepted. *Director of the Melvin And Valorie Booth School of Business*, Dr. Steve Ludwig, 660-562-1749, Fax: 660-562-1096, E-mail: sludwig@nwmissouri.edu.

School of Agricultural Sciences Students: 7 full-time (4 women), 4 part-time (1 woman), 3 international. Average age 26. 11 applicants, 64% accepted, 3 enrolled. *Faculty:* 7 full-time (1 woman). Expenses: Contact institution. *Financial support:* Research assistantships with full tuition reimbursements, teaching assistantships with full tuition reimbursements, and unspecified assistantships available. Financial award application deadline: 4/1; financial award applicants required to submit FAFSA. In 2017, 3 master's awarded. *Program availability:* Part-time. Offers agricultural economics (MBA); agricultural education (MS Ed); agriculture (MS); teaching: agriculture (MS Ed). *Application deadline:* For fall admission, 7/1 for domestic and international students; for spring admission, 11/15 for domestic and international students. Applications are processed on a rolling basis. *Application fee:* $0 ($50 for international students). Electronic applications accepted. *Director*, Rodney Barr, 660-562-1620.

School of Computer Science and Information Systems Students: 211 full-time (74 women), 64 part-time (20 women), 264 international. Average age 24. 395 applicants, 70% accepted, 75 enrolled. *Faculty:* 19 full-time (5 women). Expenses: Contact institution. *Financial support:* Research assistantships, teaching assistantships with full tuition reimbursements, and unspecified assistantships available. Financial award application deadline: 4/1; financial award applicants required to submit FAFSA. In 2017, 267 master's awarded. *Program availability:* Part-time. Offers applied computer science (MS); information systems (MS); instructional technology (MS). *Application deadline:* Applications are processed on a rolling basis. *Application fee:* $0 ($50 for international students). *Application Contact:* Dr. Gregory Haddock, Dean of Graduate School, 660-562-1145, Fax: 660-562-1096, E-mail: gradsch@nwmissouri.edu. *Director of School of Computer Science and Information Systems*, Dr. Carol Spradling, 660-562-1588, Fax: 660-562-1963, E-mail: c_sprad@nwmissouri.edu.

School of Education Students: 28 full-time (20 women), 170 part-time (114 women); includes 20 minority (7 Black or African American, non-Hispanic/Latino; 1 Asian, non-Hispanic/Latino; 8 Hispanic/Latino; 4 Two or more races, non-Hispanic/Latino). Average age 33. 168 applicants, 73% accepted, 114 enrolled. *Faculty:* 15 full-time (8 women). Expenses: Contact institution. *Financial support:* Research assistantships with full tuition reimbursements, teaching assistantships with full tuition reimbursements, and unspecified assistantships available. Financial award application deadline: 4/1; financial award applicants required to submit FAFSA. In 2017, 67 master's, 21 other advanced degrees awarded. *Program availability:* Part-time. Offers early childhood education (MS Ed); education leadership (MS Ed); educational leadership (Ed S); educational leadership and policy analysis (Ed D); elementary education (MS Ed); elementary mathematics (MS Ed); higher education leadership (MS); middle school education (MS Ed); reading (MS Ed); special education (MS Ed); teacher leadership (MS Ed); teaching English language learners (MS Ed). *Application deadline:* For fall admission, 7/1 for domestic and international students; for spring admission, 11/15 for domestic and international students. Applications are processed on a rolling basis. *Application fee:* $0 ($50 for international students). Electronic applications accepted. *Director*, Dr. Tim Wall, 660-562-1179, E-mail: timwall@nwmissouri.edu.

School of Health Science and Wellness Students: 68 full-time (43 women), 41 part-time (29 women); includes 9 minority (3 Black or African American, non-Hispanic/Latino; 4 Hispanic/Latino; 2 Two or more races, non-Hispanic/Latino), 5 international. Average age 27. 49 applicants, 47% accepted, 16 enrolled. *Faculty:* 23 full-time (11 women). Expenses: Contact institution. *Financial support:* Teaching assistantships with full tuition reimbursements and unspecified assistantships available. Financial award application deadline: 4/1; financial award applicants required to submit FAFSA. In 2017, 34 master's awarded. *Program availability:* Part-time. Offers applied health and sport sciences (MS); guidance and counseling (MS Ed); health and physical education (MS Ed); recreation (MS); sport and exercise psychology (MS). *Application deadline:* For fall admission, 7/1 for domestic and international students; for spring admission, 11/15 for domestic and international students. Applications are processed on a rolling basis. *Application fee:* $0 ($50 for international students). *Application Contact:* Gina Smith, Secretary, 660-562-1297, Fax: 660-562-1963, E-mail: smigina@nwmissouri.edu. *Director, School of Health Science and Wellness*, Dr. Terry Long, 660-562-1706, Fax: 660-562-1483, E-mail: tlong@nwmissouri.edu.

NORTHWEST NAZARENE UNIVERSITY, Nampa, ID 83686-5897

General Information Independent-religious, coed, comprehensive institution. *Enrollment:* 2,223 graduate, professional, and undergraduate students; 541 full-time matriculated graduate/professional students (354 women), 187 part-time matriculated graduate/professional students (97 women). *Enrollment by degree level:* 690 master's, 36 doctoral. *Graduate faculty:* 20 full-time (13 women), 117 part-time/adjunct (57 women). *Graduate housing:* On-campus housing not available. *Student services:* Career counseling, free psychological counseling, multicultural affairs office, services for students with disabilities, teacher training, writing training. *Library facilities:* John E. Riley Library.

Computer facilities: Computer purchase and lease plans are available. A campuswide network can be accessed from student residence rooms. Online class registration is available.
Website: http://www.nnu.edu/

General Application Contact: Dr. Paula Kellerer, Dean, College of Adult and Graduate Studies, 208-467-8729, Fax: 208-467-8252, E-mail: pkellerer@nnu.edu.

GRADUATE UNITS

Graduate Education Program Average age 39. 96 applicants, 72% accepted, 67 enrolled. Expenses: Contact institution. *Financial support:* Research assistantships available. Financial award application deadline: 1/15; financial award applicants required to submit FAFSA. In 2017, 59 master's, 13 doctorates, 33 other advanced degrees awarded. *Program availability:* Part-time, online only, 100% online, 2-week face-to-face residency (for doctoral programs). Offers curriculum and instruction (M Ed); educational leadership (M Ed, Ed D, PhD, Ed S). *Application deadline:* Applications are processed on a rolling basis. *Application fee:* $50. Electronic applications accepted. *Application Contact:* Charlene Brown, Admissions Counselor, 208-467-8492, Fax: 208-467-8384, E-mail: gradeducationinfo@nnu.edu. *Chair*, Dr. Heidi Curtis, 208-467-8250, E-mail: hlcurtis@nnu.edu.

Program in Business Administration Average age 34. 26 applicants, 62% accepted, 11 enrolled. Expenses: Contact institution. In 2017, 41 master's awarded. *Program availability:* Part-time, evening/weekend, 100% online, blended/hybrid learning. Offers business administration (MBA). *Application deadline:* Applications are processed on a rolling basis. *Application fee:* $50. Electronic applications accepted. *Application Contact:* Heather Beam, MBA Program Coordinator, 208-467-8100, Fax: 208-467-8440, E-mail: nnu-mba@nnu.edu. *Director*, Dr. Brenda Johnson, 208-467-8415, Fax: 208-467-8440, E-mail: mba@nnu.edu.

Program in Counselor Education Average age 35. 47 applicants, 66% accepted, 25 enrolled. Expenses: Contact institution. In 2017, 33 master's awarded. *Program availability:* Part-time. Offers clinical counseling (MS); marriage and family counseling (MS); school counseling (MS). *Application deadline:* For fall admission, 2/15 for domestic and international students; for spring admission, 9/15 for domestic and international students. *Application fee:* $50. Electronic applications accepted. *Application Contact:* Lynette Kingsmore, Graduate Admissions Counselor, 208-467-8107, E-mail: lkingsmore@nnu.edu. *Chair*, Dr. Michael Pitts, 208-467-8040, Fax: 208-467-8339.

Program in Nursing Average age 40. 24 applicants, 88% accepted, 12 enrolled. Expenses: Contact institution. In 2017, 10 master's awarded. *Program availability:* Online learning. Offers nursing (MSN). *Application fee:* $50. *Application Contact:* Sandy Blom, Graduate Nursing Coordinator, 208-467-8642, Fax: 208-467-8651, E-mail: sblom@nnu.edu. *Director*, Dr. Leonie Sutherland, 208-467-8679, E-mail: lsutherland@nnu.edu.

Program in Religion Average age 39. 37 applicants, 76% accepted, 24 enrolled. Expenses: Contact institution. *Financial support:* In 2017–18, 3 students received support. Scholarships/grants available. In 2017, 40 master's awarded. *Program availability:* Part-time, online only, 100% online. Offers missional leadership (M Div, MA); pastoral ministry (MA); spiritual formation (M Div, MA); youth, children, and family ministry (M Div, MA). *Application deadline:* For fall admission, 7/31 for domestic students, 7/1 for international students; for spring admission, 2/1 for domestic students, 1/5 for international students. Applications are processed on a rolling basis. *Application fee:* $50. Electronic applications accepted. *Application Contact:* Vicki Funk, Program Coordinator, 208-467-8432, Fax: 208-467-8252, E-mail: vlfunk@nnu.edu. *Director, Graduate Studies*, Dr. Jay Akkerman, 208-467-8437, Fax: 208-467-8252.

Program in Social Work Average age 27. 152 applicants, 54% accepted, 73 enrolled. Expenses: Contact institution. In 2017, 54 master's awarded. *Program availability:* Part-time-only, evening/weekend. Offers clinical mental health and addictions practice (MSW). *Application deadline:* Applications are processed on a rolling basis. *Application fee:* $50. Electronic applications accepted. *Application Contact:* Jodie Rodriguez-Engel, Program Coordinator, 208-467-8679, Fax: 208-467-8879, E-mail: jrodriguez-engel@nnu.edu. *Director/Department Chair*, Dr. Lawanna Lancaster, 208-467-8372, Fax: 208-467-8879, E-mail: mswinfo@nnu.edu.

NORTHWEST UNIVERSITY, Kirkland, WA 98033

General Information Independent-religious, coed, comprehensive institution. *Graduate housing:* Rooms and/or apartments available on a first-come, first-served basis to single and married students.

GRADUATE UNITS

College of Business *Program availability:* Part-time, evening/weekend. Offers business administration (MBA); international business (MBA); project management (MBA); social entrepreneurship (MBA). Electronic applications accepted.

College of Ministry *Program availability:* Part-time, evening/weekend, online learning. Offers ministry (MIM); missional leadership (MA); theology and culture (MA). Electronic applications accepted.

College of Social and Behavioral Sciences *Program availability:* Evening/weekend. Offers counseling psychology (MA, Psy D); international community development (MA).

School of Education *Program availability:* Part-time, evening/weekend. Offers education (M Ed); teaching (MIT). Electronic applications accepted.

NORTHWOOD UNIVERSITY, MICHIGAN CAMPUS, Midland, MI 48640-2398

General Information Independent, coed, comprehensive institution. *Graduate housing:* Room and/or apartments available on a first-come, first-served basis to single students. Housing application deadline: 8/30. *Research affiliation:* Motor & Equipment Manufacturers Association (automotive engineering), Specialized Equipment Manufacturers Association (automotive engineering), Automotive Aftermarket Industry Association (automotive engineering), Automotive Warehouse Distributors Association (automotive engineering).

GRADUATE UNITS

DeVos Graduate School *Program availability:* Part-time, evening/weekend, online learning. Offers management (MBA, MSOL). MBA also offered on Florida and Texas campuses; MSOL offered online only. Electronic applications accepted.

NORWICH UNIVERSITY, Northfield, VT 05663

General Information Independent, coed, comprehensive institution.

GRADUATE UNITS

College of Graduate and Continuing Studies *Program availability:* Evening/weekend, online only, mostly all online with a week-long residency requirement. Offers construction management (MBA, MCE); criminal justice (MS); criminal justice and public safety (MPA); diplomacy (MA); energy management (MBA); environmental (MCE); executive leadership (MS); finance (MBA); fiscal management (MPA); geotechnical (MCE); history (MA); information security and assurance (MS); international development and influence (MPA); international relations (MA); leadership (MS); logistics (MBA); military history (MA); municipal governance (MPA); nonprofit management (MPA); nursing administration (MSN); nursing education (MSN); organizational leadership (MBA); policy analysis and analytics (MPA); project management (MBA); public administration leadership and crisis management (MPA); public works and sustainability (MPA); structural (MCE); supply chain management (MBA). Electronic applications accepted.

NOTRE DAME COLLEGE, South Euclid, OH 44121-4293

General Information Independent-religious, coed, comprehensive institution. *Graduate housing:* On-campus housing not available.

GRADUATE UNITS

Graduate Programs *Program availability:* Part-time, evening/weekend. Offers mild/moderate needs (M Ed); reading (M Ed); security policy studies (MA, Graduate Certificate); technology (M Ed).

NOTRE DAME DE NAMUR UNIVERSITY, Belmont, CA 94002-1908

General Information Independent-religious, coed, comprehensive institution. *Enrollment:* 1,625 graduate, professional, and undergraduate students; 172 full-time matriculated graduate/professional students (146 women), 499 part-time matriculated graduate/professional students (363 women). *Enrollment by degree level:* 471 master's, 20 doctoral, 180 other advanced degrees. *Graduate faculty:* 30 full-time (18 women), 59 part-time/adjunct (39 women). *Tuition:* Full-time $16,128; part-time $8064 per credit hour. *Required fees:* $80; $80 per credit hour. $40 per semester. *Graduate housing:* On-campus housing not available. *Student services:* Campus employment opportunities, campus safety program, career counseling, free psychological counseling, international student services, low-cost health insurance, multicultural affairs office, services for students with disabilities, teacher training, writing training. *Library facilities:* The Carl Gellert and Celia Berta Gellert Library plus 1 other. *Collection:* Books: 88,990 (physical), 194,534 (digital/electronic); Databases: 50.

Computer facilities: 100 computers available on campus for general student use. A campuswide network can be accessed from student residence rooms and from off campus. Online class registration is available.
Website: http://www.ndnu.edu/

General Application Contact: Candace Hallmark, Associate Director of Admissions, 650-508-3600, Fax: 650-508-3426, E-mail: grad.admit@ndnu.edu.

GRADUATE UNITS

Division of Academic Affairs Expenses: Contact institution. *Financial support:* Career-related internships or fieldwork, scholarships/grants, and unspecified assistantships available. Support available to part-time students. Financial award applicants required to submit FAFSA. *Program availability:* Part-time, evening/weekend, online learning. *Application deadline:* For fall admission, 8/1 priority date for domestic students; for spring admission, 12/1 priority date for domestic students. Applications are processed on a rolling basis. *Application fee:* $60. Electronic applications accepted. *Associate Provost*, Greg White.

School of Business and Management Students: 30 full-time (25 women), 131 part-time (89 women). Average age 35. Expenses: Contact institution. *Financial support:* Scholarships/grants available. Support available to part-time students. Financial award applicants required to submit FAFSA. *Program availability:* Part-time, online learning. Offers business and management (MBA, MPA); finance (MBA); human resource management (MBA, MPA); marketing (MBA); media and promotion (MBA); public affairs administration (MPA). *Application deadline:* For fall admission, 8/1 for domestic students; for spring admission, 12/1 for domestic students. Applications are processed on a rolling basis. *Application fee:* $60. Electronic applications accepted. *Associate Provost*, Greg White, E-mail: gwhite@ndnu.edu.

School of Education and Psychology Students: 127 full-time (108 women), 368 part-time (268 women). Average age 34. Expenses: Contact institution. *Financial support:* Career-related internships or fieldwork available. Support available to part-time students. Financial award applicants required to submit FAFSA. *Program availability:* Part-time, evening/weekend. Offers art therapy (MA); art therapy psychology (PhD); clinical psychology (MS); clinical psychology: marital and family therapy (MS); curriculum and instruction (MA); disciplinary studies (MA); education and psychology (MA, MS, PhD); school administration (MA); special education (MA). *Application deadline:* For fall admission, 8/1 for domestic students; for spring admission, 12/1 for domestic students. Applications are processed on a rolling basis. *Application fee:* $60. Electronic applications accepted. *Dean, School of Education and Psychology*, Caryl Hodges, 650-508-3493, E-mail: chodges@ndnu.edu.

NOTRE DAME OF MARYLAND UNIVERSITY, Baltimore, MD 21210-2476

General Information Independent-religious, coed, primarily women, comprehensive institution. *Graduate housing:* On-campus housing not available.

GRADUATE UNITS

Graduate Studies *Program availability:* Part-time, evening/weekend. Offers contemporary communication (MA); instructional leadership for changing populations (PhD); leadership in teaching (MA); liberal studies (MA); management (MA); nonprofit management (MA); pharmacy (Pharm D); teaching (MA); teaching English to speakers of other languages (MA). Electronic applications accepted.

NOTRE DAME SEMINARY, New Orleans, LA 70118-4391

General Information Independent-religious, coed, primarily men, graduate-only institution. *Graduate housing:* Room and/or apartments guaranteed to single students; on-campus housing not available to married students. Housing application deadline: 7/31.

GRADUATE UNITS

Graduate School of Theology *Program availability:* Part-time. Offers theology (M Div, MA).

NOVA SOUTHEASTERN UNIVERSITY, Fort Lauderdale, FL 33314-7796

General Information Independent, coed, university. *Enrollment:* 20,793 graduate, professional, and undergraduate students; 10,518 full-time matriculated graduate/professional students (6,897 women), 6,775 part-time matriculated graduate/professional students (5,140 women). *Enrollment by degree level:* 8,499 master's, 4,597 doctoral, 483 other advanced degrees. Tuition and fees vary according to course load, degree level and program. *Graduate housing:* Rooms and/or apartments available on a first-come, first-served basis to single and married students. Typical cost: $5890 per year for single students; $7702 per year for married students. Room charges vary according to board plan and housing facility selected. *Student services:* Campus employment opportunities, campus safety program, career counseling, exercise/wellness program, free psychological counseling, international student services, low-cost health insurance, services for students with disabilities, teacher training. *Library facilities:* Alvin Sherman Library, Research, and Information Technology Center plus 4 others. *Collection:* Books: 498,823 (physical), 379,928 (digital/electronic); Serial titles: 6,035 (physical), 20,738 (digital/electronic); Databases: 577. Study areas open 24 hours, 5–7 days a week; students can reserve study rooms.

Computer facilities: 3,000 computers available on campus for general student use. A campuswide network can be accessed from student residence rooms and from off campus. Online class registration is available.
Website: http://www.nova.edu/

General Application Contact: Information Contact, 800-541-6682, E-mail: nsuinfo@nsu.nova.edu.

GRADUATE UNITS

Abraham S. Fischler College of Education Students: 1,513 full-time (1,199 women), 1,583 part-time (1,259 women); includes 2,373 minority (1,224 Black or African American, non-Hispanic/Latino; 5 American Indian or Alaska Native, non-Hispanic/Latino; 34 Asian, non-Hispanic/Latino; 1,057 Hispanic/Latino; 2 Native Hawaiian or other Pacific Islander, non-Hispanic/Latino; 51 Two or more races, non-Hispanic/Latino), 19 international. Average age 41. 1,753 applicants, 47% accepted, 581 enrolled. *Faculty:* 94 full-time (58 women), 204 part-time/adjunct (145 women). Expenses: Contact institution. *Financial support:* In 2017–18, 67 students received support. Career-related internships or fieldwork and Federal Work-Study available. Support available to part-time students. Financial award application deadline: 4/15; financial award applicants required to submit FAFSA. In 2017, 399 master's, 571 doctorates, 104 other advanced degrees awarded. *Program availability:* Part-time, evening/weekend, 100% online, blended/hybrid learning. Offers education (MS, Ed D, PhD, Ed S); instructional technology and distance education (MS); teaching and learning (MA). *Application deadline:* Applications are processed on a rolling basis. *Application fee:* $50. Electronic applications accepted. *Application Contact:* Adriana Garay, Executive Director for Marketing, Recruitment and Admissions, 800-986-3223 Ext. 8500, E-mail: fserecruit@nova.edu. *Interim Dean*, Dr. Kimberly Durham, 954-262-8731, Fax: 954-262-3894, E-mail: durham@nova.edu.

College of Allopathic Medicine Expenses: Contact institution. Offers allopathic medicine (MD). *Application Contact:* Information Contact, 800-541-6682, E-mail: nsuinfo@nsu.nova.edu. *Dean*, Dr. Johannes Vieweg, MD, 954-262-1501, E-mail: jvieweg@nova.edu.

College of Arts, Humanities, and Social Sciences Students: 303 full-time (238 women), 903 part-time (677 women); includes 689 minority (385 Black or African American, non-Hispanic/Latino; 4 American Indian or Alaska Native, non-Hispanic/Latino; 31 Asian, non-Hispanic/Latino; 234 Hispanic/Latino; 1 Native Hawaiian or other Pacific Islander, non-Hispanic/Latino; 34 Two or more races, non-Hispanic/Latino), 60 international. Average age 37. 624 applicants, 61% accepted, 285 enrolled. *Faculty:* 29 full-time (18 women), 27 part-time/adjunct (21 women). Expenses: Contact institution. *Financial support:* In 2017–18, 170 students received support. Career-related internships or fieldwork, Federal Work-Study, scholarships/grants, and unspecified assistantships available. Financial award application deadline: 4/1; financial award applicants required to submit CSS PROFILE. In 2017, 277 master's, 62 doctorates, 25 other advanced degrees awarded. *Program availability:* Part-time, evening/weekend, 100% online, blended/hybrid learning. Offers advanced conflict resolution practice (Graduate Certificate); child protection (MHS); college student affairs (MS); conflict analysis and resolution (MS, PhD); criminal justice (MS, PhD); cross-disciplinary studies (MA); developmental disabilities (MS); family studies (Graduate Certificate); family systems health care (Graduate Certificate); family therapy (MS, PhD); marriage and family therapy (DMFT); peace studies (Graduate Certificate); qualitative research (Graduate Certificate); solution focused coaching (Graduate Certificate). *Application deadline:* For fall admission, 5/17 priority date for domestic and international students; for winter admission, 12/1 priority date for domestic and international students; for spring admission, 4/1 priority date for domestic and international students. Applications are processed on a rolling basis. *Application fee:* $50. Electronic applications accepted. *Application Contact:* Marcia Arango, Student Recruitment Coordinator, 954-262-3006, Fax: 954-262-3968, E-mail: marango@nsu.nova.edu. *Dean*, Dr. Honggang Yang, 954-262-3016, Fax: 954-262-3968, E-mail: yangh@nova.edu.

College of Dental Medicine Students: 604 full-time (293 women), 7 part-time (3 women); includes 278 minority (4 Black or African American, non-Hispanic/Latino; 105 Asian, non-Hispanic/Latino; 155 Hispanic/Latino; 14 Two or more races, non-Hispanic/Latino), 77 international. Average age 28. 2,274 applicants, 11% accepted, 124 enrolled. *Faculty:* 106 full-time (38 women), 163 part-time/adjunct (31 women). Expenses: Contact institution. *Financial support:* Application deadline: 4/15; applicants required to submit FAFSA. In 2017, 16 master's, 129 doctorates awarded. Offers dental medicine (DMD); dentistry (MS). *Application deadline:* For fall admission, 12/31 for domestic students, 1/1 for international students. Applications are processed on a rolling basis. *Application fee:* $50. Electronic applications accepted. *Application Contact:* Su-Ann Zarrett, Associate Director of Admissions, 954-262-1108, Fax: 954-262-2282, E-mail: zarrett@nsu.nova.edu. *Dean*, Dr. Linda C. Niessen, 954-262-7334, Fax: 954-262-3293, E-mail: lniessen@nova.edu.

College of Engineering and Computing Students: 244 full-time (75 women), 351 part-time (104 women); includes 282 minority (119 Black or African American, non-Hispanic/Latino; 1 American Indian or Alaska Native, non-Hispanic/Latino; 49 Asian, non-Hispanic/Latino; 98 Hispanic/Latino; 1 Native Hawaiian or other Pacific Islander, non-Hispanic/Latino; 14 Two or more races, non-Hispanic/Latino), 112 international. Average age 40. 148 applicants, 65% accepted. *Faculty:* 19 full-time (5 women), 20 part-time/adjunct (3 women). Expenses: Contact institution. *Financial support:* Federal Work-Study, scholarships/grants, and corporate financial support available. Financial award application deadline: 4/15; financial award applicants required to submit FAFSA. In 2017, 176 master's, 37 doctorates awarded. *Program availability:* Part-time, evening/weekend, blended/hybrid learning. Offers computer science (MS, PhD); information assurance (PhD); information assurance and cybersecurity (MS); information systems (PhD); information technology (MS); management information systems (MS). *Application deadline:* Applications are processed on a rolling basis. *Application fee:* $50. Electronic applications accepted. *Application Contact:* Nancy Azoulay, Director, Admissions, 954-262-2026, Fax: 954-262-2752, E-mail: azoulayn@nova.edu. *Dean*, Dr. Yong X. Tao, 954-262-2063, Fax: 954-262-2752, E-mail: ytao@nova.edu.

College of Medical Sciences Students: 53 full-time (29 women); includes 31 minority (4 Black or African American, non-Hispanic/Latino; 7 Asian, non-Hispanic/Latino; 19 Hispanic/Latino; 1 Two or more races, non-Hispanic/Latino), 3 international. Average age 25. 350 applicants, 11% accepted, 40 enrolled. *Faculty:* 30 full-time (12 women), 1 part-time/adjunct (0 women). Expenses: Contact institution. *Financial support:* Application deadline: 4/15; applicants required to submit FAFSA. In 2017, 10 master's awarded. Offers biomedical sciences (MBS). *Application deadline:* Applications are processed on a rolling basis. *Application fee:* $50. *Application Contact:* Dr. Lori B. Dribin, Assistant Dean for Student Affairs, 954-262-1341, Fax: 954-262-1802, E-mail: lorib@nova.edu. *Dean*, Dr. Harold E. Laubach, 954-262-1303, Fax: 954-262-1802, E-mail: harold@nova.edu.

College of Optometry Students: 435 full-time (300 women), 10 part-time (7 women); includes 196 minority (33 Black or African American, non-Hispanic/Latino; 2 American Indian or Alaska Native, non-Hispanic/Latino; 74 Asian, non-Hispanic/Latino; 72 Hispanic/Latino; 15 Two or more races, non-Hispanic/Latino), 51 international. Average age 26. Expenses: Contact institution. *Financial support:* Federal Work-Study, institutionally sponsored loans, and scholarships/grants available. Support available to part-time students. Financial award application deadline: 4/15; financial award applicants required to submit FAFSA. In 2017, 104 doctorates awarded. *Program availability:* Online learning. Offers optometry (MS, OD). *Application deadline:* Applications are processed on a rolling basis. *Application fee:* $50. Electronic applications accepted. *Application Contact:* Juan Saavedra, Admissions Counselor, 954-262-1132, Fax: 954-262-2282, E-mail: jsaavedra@nova.edu. *Dean*, Dr. David Loshin, 954-262-1404, Fax: 954-262-1818, E-mail: loshin@nova.edu.

College of Pharmacy Students: 977 full-time (670 women), 48 part-time (28 women); includes 773 minority (71 Black or African American, non-Hispanic/Latino; 168 Asian, non-Hispanic/Latino; 518 Hispanic/Latino; 1 Native Hawaiian or other Pacific Islander, non-Hispanic/Latino; 15 Two or more races, non-Hispanic/Latino), 86 international. Average age 27. 1,047 applicants, 35% accepted, 248 enrolled. *Faculty:* 115 full-time (38 women), 3 part-time/adjunct (1 woman). Expenses: Contact institution. *Financial support:* In 2017–18, 62 students received support, including 12 teaching assistantships with full tuition reimbursements available (averaging $45,465 per year); career-related internships or fieldwork, Federal Work-Study, scholarships/grants, tuition waivers (full), and unspecified assistantships also available. Financial award application deadline: 4/15; financial award applicants required to submit FAFSA. In 2017, 242 doctorates awarded. Offers pharmaceutical affairs (MS); pharmaceutical sciences (MS, PhD); pharmacy (Pharm D). *Application deadline:* For fall admission, 3/15 for domestic and international students. Applications are processed on a rolling basis. *Application fee:* $50. Electronic applications accepted. *Application Contact:* Jennifer Gundersen, Admissions Counselor, 954-262-1112, Fax: 954-262-2282, E-mail: nsupharmacyinfo@nova.edu. *Dean*, Dr. Lisa Deziel, 954-262-1304, Fax: 954-262-2278, E-mail: copdean@nova.edu.

College of Psychology Students: 751 full-time (618 women), 821 part-time (709 women); includes 787 minority (268 Black or African American, non-Hispanic/Latino; 2 American Indian or Alaska Native, non-Hispanic/Latino; 38 Asian, non-Hispanic/Latino; 431 Hispanic/Latino; 2 Native Hawaiian or other Pacific Islander, non-Hispanic/Latino; 46 Two or more races, non-Hispanic/Latino), 45 international. Average age 31. 1,117 applicants, 38% accepted, 294 enrolled. *Faculty:* 51 full-time (21 women), 120 part-time/adjunct (70 women). Expenses: Contact institution. *Financial support:* In 2017–18, 197 students received support, including 15 research assistantships (averaging $5,600 per year), 68 teaching assistantships (averaging $2,000 per year); career-related internships or fieldwork, Federal Work-Study, institutionally sponsored loans, scholarships/grants, and unspecified assistantships also available. Support available to part-time students. Financial award application deadline: 4/15; financial award applicants required to submit FAFSA. In 2017, 459 master's, 100 doctorates, 10 other advanced degrees awarded. *Program availability:* 100% online, blended/hybrid learning. Offers clinical mental health counseling (MS); clinical psychology (PhD, Psy D); counseling (MS); experimental psychology (MS); forensic psychology (MS); general psychology (MS); school counseling (MS); school psychology (Psy D, Psy S); substance abuse counseling (MS); substance abuse counseling and education (MS). *Application deadline:* Applications are processed on a rolling basis. *Application fee:* $50. Electronic applications accepted. *Application Contact:* Carlos Perez, Senior Manager of Outreach, 954-262-5702, Fax: 954-262-3893, E-mail: gradschool@nova.edu. *Dean*, Dr. Karen Grosby, 954-262-5712, Fax: 954-262-3859, E-mail: grosby@nova.edu.

Dr. Kiran C. Patel College of Osteopathic Medicine Students: 1,032 full-time (479 women), 197 part-time (129 women); includes 656 minority (97 Black or African American, non-Hispanic/Latino; 308 Asian, non-Hispanic/Latino; 215 Hispanic/Latino; 1 Native Hawaiian or other Pacific Islander, non-Hispanic/Latino; 35 Two or more races, non-Hispanic/Latino), 67 international. Average age 26. 5,226 applicants, 9% accepted, 248 enrolled. *Faculty:* 98 full-time (58 women), 1,484 part-time/adjunct (401 women). Expenses: Contact institution. *Financial support:* In 2017–18, 83 students received support, including 24 fellowships with tuition reimbursements available; Federal Work-Study and scholarships/grants also available. Financial award application deadline: 6/1; financial award applicants required to submit FAFSA. In 2017, 110 master's, 239 doctorates, 7 other advanced degrees awarded. Offers biomedical informatics (MS, Graduate Certificate); disaster and emergency management (MS); medical education (MS); nutrition (MS, Graduate Certificate); osteopathic medicine (DO); public health (MPH, Graduate Certificate); social medicine (Graduate Certificate). *Application deadline:* For fall admission, 1/15 for domestic students. Applications are processed on a rolling basis. *Application fee:* $50. Electronic applications accepted. *Application Contact:* HPD Admissions, 877-640-0218, E-mail: hpdinfo@nova.edu. *Dean*, Elaine M. Wallace, 954-262-1457, Fax: 954-262-2250, E-mail: ewallace@nova.edu.

Dr. Pallavi Patel College of Health Care Sciences Students: 501 full-time (407 women); includes 131 minority (18 Black or African American, non-Hispanic/Latino; 2 American Indian or Alaska Native, non-Hispanic/Latino; 45 Asian, non-Hispanic/Latino; 65 Hispanic/Latino; 1 Two or more races, non-Hispanic/Latino). Average age 24. 7,600 applicants, 7% accepted, 452 enrolled. *Faculty:* 54 full-time (31 women), 15 part-time/adjunct (7 women). Expenses: Contact institution. *Financial support:* Federal Work-Study, institutionally sponsored loans, and scholarships/grants available. Financial award application deadline: 4/15; financial award applicants required to submit FAFSA. In 2017, 616 master's, 225 doctorates awarded. Offers anesthesiologist assistant (MSA); audiology (Au D); health science (MH Sc, DHSc, PhD); occupational therapy (MOT, Dr OT, PhD); physical therapy (DPT, TDPT); physician assistant (MMS); speech-language pathology (MS). *Application deadline:* For spring admission, 2/15 for domestic and international students; for summer admission, 12/1 for domestic and international students. Applications are processed on a rolling basis. *Application fee:* $50. Electronic applications accepted. *Application Contact:* Joey Jankie, Admissions Counselor, 954-262-7249, E-mail: joey@nova.edu. *Dean*, Dr. Stanley Wilson, 954-262-1203, E-mail: swilson@nova.edu.

Halmos College of Natural Sciences and Oceanography Students: 29 full-time (18 women), 149 part-time (93 women); includes 29 minority (5 Black or African American, non-Hispanic/Latino; 6 Asian, non-Hispanic/Latino; 12 Hispanic/Latino; 6 Two or more races, non-Hispanic/Latino), 5 international. Average age 30. 78 applicants, 73% accepted, 34 enrolled. *Faculty:* 17 full-time (3 women), 22 part-time/adjunct (11 women). Expenses: Contact institution. *Financial support:* In 2017–18, 101 students received support, including 6 fellowships with full and partial tuition reimbursements available (averaging $25,000 per year), 40 research assistantships with full and partial tuition reimbursements available (averaging $20,000 per year), 8 teaching assistantships with tuition reimbursements available (averaging $15,000 per year); career-related internships or fieldwork, Federal Work-Study, scholarships/grants, health care benefits, tuition waivers (full and partial), and unspecified assistantships also available. Support available to part-time students. Financial award application deadline: 4/15; financial award applicants required to submit FAFSA. In 2017, 46 master's, 1 doctorate awarded. *Program availability:* Part-time, evening/weekend, blended/hybrid learning. Offers biological sciences (MS); marine biology and oceanography (PhD). *Application deadline:* Applications are processed on a rolling basis. *Application fee:* $50. Electronic applications accepted. *Application Contact:* Dr. Bernhard Riegl, Chair, Department of Marine and Environmental Sciences, 954-262-3600, Fax: 954-262-4020, E-mail: rieglb@nova.edu. *Dean*, Dr. Richard Dodge, 954-262-3600, Fax: 954-262-4020, E-mail: dodge@nsu.nova.edu.

H. Wayne Huizenga College of Business and Entrepreneurship Students: 1,999 full-time (1,225 women), 335 part-time (210 women); includes 1,516 minority (597 Black or African American, non-Hispanic/Latino; 4 American Indian or Alaska Native, non-Hispanic/Latino; 92 Asian, non-Hispanic/Latino; 789 Hispanic/Latino; 3 Native Hawaiian or other Pacific Islander, non-Hispanic/Latino; 31 Two or more races, non-Hispanic/Latino), 291 international. Average age 34. 1,269 applicants, 59% accepted, 551 enrolled. *Faculty:* 85 full-time (37 women), 59 part-time/adjunct (19 women). Expenses: Contact institution. *Financial support:* In 2017–18, 325 students received support. Federal Work-Study and scholarships/grants available. Support available to part-time students. Financial award application deadline: 4/15; financial award applicants required to submit FAFSA. In 2017, 1,055 master's awarded. *Program availability:* Part-time, evening/weekend, 100% online, blended/hybrid learning. Offers accounting (M Acc); business (MBA); business intelligence/analytics (MBA); complex health systems (MBA); enterprise informatics (MBA); entrepreneurship (MBA); finance (MBA); human resource management (MBA); international business (MBA); management (MBA); marketing (MBA); process improvement (MBA); public administration (MPA); real estate development (MS); sport revenue generation (MBA); supply chain management (MBA). *Application deadline:* For fall admission, 8/5 priority date for domestic students, 7/29 priority date for international students; for winter admission, 12/16 priority date for domestic students, 12/9 priority date for international students; for summer admission, 4/21 priority date for domestic and international students. Applications are processed on a rolling basis. *Application fee:* $50. Electronic applications accepted. *Application Contact:* Zeida Rodriguez, Associate Director of Enrollment Services, 954-262-5163, Fax: 954-262-3822, E-mail: zeida@nova.edu. *Dean*, Dr. J. Preston Jones, 954-262-5127, E-mail: prestonj@nova.edu.

Ron and Kathy Assaf College of Nursing Students: 658 full-time (599 women); includes 414 minority (175 Black or African American, non-Hispanic/Latino; 37 Asian, non-Hispanic/Latino; 179 Hispanic/Latino; 1 Native Hawaiian or other Pacific Islander, non-Hispanic/Latino; 22 Two or more races, non-Hispanic/Latino), 3 international. Average age 38. 179 applicants, 100% accepted, 163 enrolled. *Faculty:* 9 full-time (all women), 47 part-time/adjunct (43 women). Expenses: Contact institution. *Financial support:* Application deadline: 4/15; applicants required to submit FAFSA. In 2017, 161 master's, 16 doctorates awarded. *Program availability:* Part-time, evening/weekend, 100% online, blended/hybrid learning, annual one-week summer institute delivered face-to-face on main campus. Offers advanced practice registered nurse (MSN); executive nurse leadership (MSN); nursing (PhD); nursing education (MSN); nursing informatics (MSN); nursing practice (DNP). *Application deadline:* For fall admission, 3/1 priority date for domestic students, 3/1 for international students; for winter admission, 11/1 for domestic and international students. Applications are processed on a rolling basis. *Application fee:* $50. Electronic applications accepted. *Application Contact:* Dianna Murphey, Director of Operations, 954-262-1975, E-mail: dgardner1@nova.edu. *Dean,* Dr. Marcella M. Rutherford, 954-262-1963, E-mail: rmarcell@nova.edu.

Shepard Broad College of Law Students: 566 full-time (297 women), 138 part-time (84 women); includes 365 minority (62 Black or African American, non-Hispanic/Latino; 3 American Indian or Alaska Native, non-Hispanic/Latino; 23 Asian, non-Hispanic/Latino; 264 Hispanic/Latino; 3 Native Hawaiian or other Pacific Islander, non-Hispanic/Latino; 10 Two or more races, non-Hispanic/Latino), 26 international. Average age 29. 1,070 applicants, 53% accepted, 224 enrolled. *Faculty:* 56 full-time (30 women), 41 part-time/adjunct (14 women). Expenses: Contact institution. *Financial support:* In 2017–18, 211 students received support, including 221 fellowships (averaging $12,000 per year); Federal Work-Study, institutionally sponsored loans, scholarships/grants, and unspecified assistantships also available. Support available to part-time students. Financial award application deadline: 4/15; financial award applicants required to submit FAFSA. In 2017, 45 master's, 225 doctorates awarded. *Program availability:* Part-time, evening/weekend, 100% online, blended/hybrid learning. Offers education law (MS); employment law (MS); health law (MS, JD); international law (JD); law and policy (MS). *Application deadline:* For fall admission, 5/1 priority date for domestic and international students; for winter admission, 12/12 for domestic and international students; for spring admission, 3/31 for domestic and international students; for summer admission, 4/1 for domestic and international students. Applications are processed on a rolling basis. *Application fee:* $0. Electronic applications accepted. *Application Contact:* William Daniel Perez, Assistant Dean of Admissions, 954-262-6121, Fax: 954-262-3844, E-mail: wperez1@nova.edu. *Dean,* Jon M. Garon, 954-262-6101, Fax: 954-262-2862, E-mail: garon@nova.edu.

NSCAD UNIVERSITY, Halifax, NS B3J 3J6, Canada

General Information Province-supported, coed, comprehensive institution. *Graduate housing:* On-campus housing not available.

GRADUATE UNITS

Program in Fine Arts Offers craft (MFA); design (M Des); fine and media arts (MFA).

NYACK COLLEGE, Nyack, NY 10960

General Information Independent-religious, coed, comprehensive institution. *Enrollment:* 2,455 graduate, professional, and undergraduate students; 467 full-time matriculated graduate/professional students (257 women), 584 part-time matriculated graduate/professional students (351 women). *Enrollment by degree level:* 964 master's, 87 doctoral. *Graduate faculty:* 26 full-time (10 women), 46 part-time/adjunct (16 women). *Graduate housing:* Rooms and/or apartments available on a first-come, first-served basis to single and married students. Housing application deadline: 9/1. *Student services:* Campus employment opportunities, career counseling, free psychological counseling, international student services, low-cost health insurance, services for students with disabilities, writing training. *Library facilities:* Bailey Library plus 3 others.

Computer facilities: A campuswide network can be accessed. Online class registration is available.
Website: http://www.nyack.edu/

General Application Contact: 845-770-5701, Fax: 845-348-3912, E-mail: admissions.grad@nyack.edu.

GRADUATE UNITS

Alliance Graduate School of Counseling Students: 66 full-time (50 women), 162 part-time (136 women); includes 183 minority (78 Black or African American, non-Hispanic/Latino; 45 Asian, non-Hispanic/Latino; 53 Hispanic/Latino; 7 Two or more races, non-Hispanic/Latino), 10 international. Average age 37. Expenses: Contact institution. *Financial support:* Career-related internships or fieldwork and scholarships/grants available. Financial award applicants required to submit FAFSA. In 2017, 48 master's awarded. *Program availability:* Part-time, evening/weekend, 100% online. Offers marriage and family therapy (MA); mental health counseling (MA). *Application deadline:* For fall admission, 8/1 for domestic students, 2/15 for international students; for spring admission, 12/15 for domestic students, 7/15 for international students. Applications are processed on a rolling basis. *Application fee:* $30. Electronic applications accepted. *Application Contact:* Chastity Crespo, Admissions Associate, 646-378-6199, E-mail: admissions.grad@nyack.edu. *Director,* Dr. Antoinette Gines-Rivera, 646-378-6160.

Alliance Theological Seminary Students: 265 full-time (107 women), 356 part-time (162 women); includes 490 minority (161 Black or African American, non-Hispanic/Latino; 2 American Indian or Alaska Native, non-Hispanic/Latino; 123 Asian, non-Hispanic/Latino; 198 Hispanic/Latino; 6 Two or more races, non-Hispanic/Latino), 37 international. Average age 42. Expenses: Contact institution. *Financial support:* Career-related internships or fieldwork, Federal Work-Study, and scholarships/grants available. Financial award applicants required to submit FAFSA. In 2017, 100 master's, 23 doctorates awarded. *Program availability:* Part-time, evening/weekend, 100% online, blended/hybrid learning. Offers Biblical literature (MA); Biblical studies (MA); Christian ministry (MPS); intercultural studies (MA); ministry (D Min); theology and missions (M Div); urban ministry (MPS). *Application deadline:* Applications are processed on a rolling basis. *Application fee:* $30. Electronic applications accepted. *Application Contact:* Jennifer Reimer, Associate Director of Admissions, 845-770-5709, E-mail: admissions.grad@nyack.edu. *Dean,* Dr. Ronald Walborn, 845-770-5715, Fax: 845-358-1663.

College of Bible and Christian Ministry Students: 1 (woman) full-time, 7 part-time (1 woman); includes 5 minority (2 Black or African American, non-Hispanic/Latino; 1 American Indian or Alaska Native, non-Hispanic/Latino; 2 Hispanic/Latino). Average age 46. Expenses: Contact institution. *Financial support:* Applicants required to submit FAFSA. In 2017, 2 master's awarded. *Program availability:* Part-time, evening/weekend, 100% online, blended/hybrid learning. Offers ancient Judaism and Christian origins (MA). *Application deadline:* Applications are processed on a rolling basis. *Application fee:* $30. Electronic applications accepted. *Application Contact:* 646-378-6113, E-mail: admissions.grad@nyack.edu. *Director,* Dr. Steven Notley, 646-378-6148, E-mail: steven.notley@nyack.edu.

School of Business and Leadership Students: 33 full-time (22 women), 10 part-time (7 women); includes 31 minority (23 Black or African American, non-Hispanic/Latino; 7 Hispanic/Latino; 1 Two or more races, non-Hispanic/Latino), 3 international. Average age 38. Expenses: Contact institution. *Financial support:* Scholarships/grants available. Financial award applicants required to submit FAFSA. In 2017, 33 master's awarded. *Program availability:* Part-time, evening/weekend, 100% online, blended/hybrid learning. Offers business administration (MBA); organizational leadership (MS). *Application deadline:* Applications are processed on a rolling basis. *Application fee:* $50. Electronic applications accepted. *Application Contact:* Joseph M. Williams, Graduate Admissions Associate, 845-770-5711, E-mail: admissions.grad@nyack.edu. *Dean,* Dr. Anita Underwood, 845-675-4511.

School of Education Students: 22 full-time (20 women), 27 part-time (23 women); includes 23 minority (10 Black or African American, non-Hispanic/Latino; 1 American Indian or Alaska Native, non-Hispanic/Latino; 1 Asian, non-Hispanic/Latino; 10 Hispanic/Latino; 1 Two or more races, non-Hispanic/Latino), 2 international. Average age 34. Expenses: Contact institution. *Financial support:* Scholarships/grants available. Financial award applicants required to submit FAFSA. In 2017, 25 master's awarded. *Program availability:* Part-time, evening/weekend, 100% online, blended/hybrid learning. Offers childhood education (MS); childhood special education (MS); TESOL (MAT, MS). *Application deadline:* Applications are processed on a rolling basis. *Application fee:* $30. Electronic applications accepted. *Application Contact:* Emma Chery, Admissions Associate, 845-770-5708, E-mail: admissions.grad@nyack.edu. *Dean,* Dr. JoAnn Looney, 845-675-4538.

School of Social Work Students: 58 full-time (50 women), 27 part-time (21 women); includes 77 minority (50 Black or African American, non-Hispanic/Latino; 5 Asian, non-Hispanic/Latino; 21 Hispanic/Latino; 1 Two or more races, non-Hispanic/Latino), 3 international. Average age 36. Expenses: Contact institution. *Financial support:* Scholarships/grants available. Financial award applicants required to submit FAFSA. In 2017, 15 master's awarded. *Program availability:* Part-time, evening/weekend. Offers clinical social work practice (MSW); leadership in organizations and communities (MSW). *Application deadline:* Applications are processed on a rolling basis. *Application fee:* $45. Electronic applications accepted. *Application Contact:* DeLissa Dixon, Admissions Associate, 646-378-6105, E-mail: admissions.grad@nyack.edu. *Director of MSW Program,* Dr. Janet Furness, 646-378-6169.

OAKLAND CITY UNIVERSITY, Oakland City, IN 47660-1099

General Information Independent-religious, coed, comprehensive institution. *Tuition:* Part-time $415 per credit hour. Part-time tuition and fees vary according to campus/location. *Graduate housing:* Rooms and/or apartments guaranteed to single students and available on a first-come, first-served basis to married students. Housing application deadline: 7/1. *Student services:* Campus employment opportunities, career counseling, free psychological counseling. *Library facilities:* Barger-Richardson Library. *Collection:* Books: 84,412 (physical), 17,690 (digital/electronic); Serial titles: 79 (physical), 50,255 (digital/electronic); Databases: 52.

Computer facilities: 200 computers available on campus for general student use. A campuswide network can be accessed from student residence rooms and from off campus. Online class registration is available.
Website: http://www.oak.edu/

General Application Contact: Director of Admissions, 812-749-1218.

GRADUATE UNITS

Chapman Seminary Expenses: Contact institution. *Financial support:* Career-related internships or fieldwork and Federal Work-Study available. Support available to part-time students. Financial award application deadline: 3/1; financial award applicants required to submit FAFSA. *Program availability:* Part-time. Offers ministry (M Div); pastoral care (M Div); theology (D Min). *Application deadline:* Applications are processed on a rolling basis. *Application fee:* $35. *Application Contact:* Dr. Danny Dunivan, Dean, 812-749-1386, Fax: 812-749-1308, E-mail: ddunivan@oak.edu. *Dean,* Dr. Danny Dunivan, 812-749-1386, Fax: 812-749-1308, E-mail: ddunivan@oak.edu.

School of Business Expenses: Contact institution. *Financial support:* Institutionally sponsored loans available. Financial award application deadline: 3/10; financial award applicants required to submit FAFSA. *Program availability:* Part-time, evening/weekend. Offers business administration (MBA); strategic management (MS). *Application deadline:* Applications are processed on a rolling basis. *Application fee:* $35. *Application Contact:* David McFarland, Director of Admissions, 812-749-1218, E-mail: dmcfarland@oak.edu. *Dean,* Dr. Cathy Robb, 812-749-1272, Fax: 812-749-1511, E-mail: crobb@oak.edu.

School of Education Expenses: Contact institution. *Financial support:* Unspecified assistantships available. Financial award applicants required to submit FAFSA. Offers building level administration (MS Ed); curriculum and instruction (MS Ed, Ed D); education (MS Ed); elementary education (MAT); organizational management (Ed D); secondary education (MAT); superintendency (Ed D). *Application deadline:* For spring admission, 5/1 for domestic students. Applications are processed on a rolling basis. *Application fee:* $35. *Application Contact:* David MacFarland, Director of Admissions, 812-749-1218, E-mail: dmcfarland@oak.edu. *Dean,* Dr. Rachel Yarbrough, 812-749-1399, Fax: 812-749-1511, E-mail: ryarbrough@oak.edu.

OAKLAND UNIVERSITY, Rochester, MI 48309-4401

General Information State-supported, coed, university. CGS member. *Enrollment:* 19,333 graduate, professional, and undergraduate students; 1,808 full-time matriculated graduate/professional students (1,038 women), 1,553 part-time matriculated graduate/professional students (832 women). *Enrollment by degree level:* 2,105 master's, 1,072 doctoral, 81 other advanced degrees. *Graduate faculty:* 313 full-time (135 women), 69 part-time/adjunct (27 women). Tuition, state resident: full-time $16,950; part-time $706.25 per credit. Tuition, nonresident: full-time $24,648; part-time $1027 per credit. *Graduate housing:* Rooms and/or apartments available on a first-come, first-served basis to single and married students. Typical cost: $9910 (including board) for single students. Room and board charges vary according to housing facility selected. Housing application deadline: 9/1. *Student services:* Campus employment opportunities, campus safety program, career counseling, child daycare facilities, exercise/wellness program, free psychological counseling, international student services, low-cost health insurance, multicultural affairs office, services for students with disabilities. *Library facilities:* Kresge Library plus 1 other. *Collection:* Books: 499,352 (physical), 648,059 (digital/electronic); Serial titles: 3,674 (physical), 59,485 (digital/electronic); Databases: 234. Weekly public service hours: 168; study areas open 24 hours, 5–7 days a week; students can reserve study rooms. *Research affiliation:* Beaumont Hospital Corporation (eye research, nursing), Henry Ford Health Systems (medical physics, health sciences).

Computer facilities: A campuswide network can be accessed. Online class registration is available.
Website: http://www.oakland.edu/

General Application Contact: Lynn Coughlin, Admissions Coordinator, 248-370-2653, Fax: 248-370-4114, E-mail: coughlin@oakland.edu.

GRADUATE UNITS

Graduate Study and Lifelong Learning Students: 1,808 full-time (1,038 women), 1,553 part-time (832 women); includes 619 minority (225 Black or African American, non-Hispanic/Latino; 13 American Indian or Alaska Native, non-Hispanic/Latino; 234 Asian, non-Hispanic/Latino; 83 Hispanic/Latino; 13 Native Hawaiian or other Pacific Islander, non-Hispanic/Latino; 51 Two or more races, non-Hispanic/Latino), 511 international. Average age 30. 2,894 applicants, 41% accepted, 855 enrolled. *Faculty:* 313 full-time (135 women), 69 part-time/adjunct (27 women). Expenses: Contact institution. *Financial support:* Fellowships, research assistantships, teaching assistantships, career-related internships or fieldwork, Federal Work-Study, institutionally sponsored loans, and tuition waivers available. Financial award application deadline: 3/1; financial award applicants required to submit FAFSA. In 2017, 808 master's, 177 doctorates, 97 other advanced degrees awarded. *Program availability:* Part-time. *Application deadline:* For fall admission, 5/1 for international students; for winter admission, 9/1 for international students. Applications are processed on a rolling basis. *Application fee:* $0. Electronic applications accepted. *Application Contact:* Lynn Coughlin, 248-370-2653, Fax: 248-370-4114, E-mail: coughlin@oakland.edu. *Dean of Graduate Education*, Claudia Petrescu, 248-370-3169, Fax: 248-370-4114, E-mail: cpetrescu@oakland.edu.

College of Arts and Sciences Students: 219 full-time (124 women), 124 part-time (72 women); includes 66 minority (33 Black or African American, non-Hispanic/Latino; 2 American Indian or Alaska Native, non-Hispanic/Latino; 16 Asian, non-Hispanic/Latino; 10 Hispanic/Latino; 5 Two or more races, non-Hispanic/Latino), 41 international. Average age 30. 514 applicants, 35% accepted, 121 enrolled. *Faculty:* 103 full-time (35 women), 8 part-time/adjunct (3 women). Expenses: Contact institution. *Financial support:* Fellowships, research assistantships, teaching assistantships, career-related internships or fieldwork, Federal Work-Study, institutionally sponsored loans, and tuition waivers available. Financial award application deadline: 3/1; financial award applicants required to submit FAFSA. In 2017, 88 master's, 18 doctorates, 3 other advanced degrees awarded. *Program availability:* Part-time, evening/weekend. Offers applied mathematical sciences (PhD); applied statistics (MS); arts and sciences (MA, MM, MPA, MS, PhD, Certificate, Graduate Certificate, PMC); biological and biomedical sciences (PhD); biology (MA, MS); biomedical sciences (PhD, Graduate Certificate); chemistry (MS); English (MA); history (MA); industrial applied mathematics (MS); liberal studies (MA); linguistics (MA); local government management (Graduate Certificate); mathematical statistics (MS); mathematics (MA); medical physics (PhD); music (MM); music education (PhD); non-profit and organizational management (PMC); physics (MS); public administration (MPA); statistical methods (Certificate); teaching English as a second language (Certificate). *Application deadline:* Applications are processed on a rolling basis. *Application fee:* $0. Electronic applications accepted. *Dean*, Kevin J. Corcoran, 248-370-2140, Fax: 248-370-4280, E-mail: corcoran@oakland.edu.

School of Business Administration *Program availability:* Part-time, evening/weekend. Offers accounting (M Acc, Certificate); business administration (EMBA, M Acc, MBA, MS, Certificate); economics (MBA, Certificate); entrepreneurship (Certificate); finance (Certificate); general management (Certificate); human resource management (Certificate); information technology management (MS); international business (Certificate); management and marketing (EMBA); management information systems (Certificate); marketing (Certificate); production and operations management (Certificate). Electronic applications accepted.

School of Education and Human Services *Program availability:* Part-time, evening/weekend. Offers advanced microcomputer applications (Graduate Certificate); applied behavior analysis (Graduate Certificate); autism spectrum disorder (Graduate Certificate); counseling (MA, PhD, Certificate); digital literacies and learning (Graduate Certificate); early childhood education (M Ed, PhD, Ed S); early education and intervention (Ed S); education and human services (M Ed, MA, MAT, PhD, Certificate, Ed S, Graduate Certificate, PMC); educational leadership (M Ed, PhD); educational studies (M Ed); elementary education (MAT); emotional impairment (Graduate Certificate); higher education (Certificate); microcomputer applications (Graduate Certificate); reading and language arts (MAT); reading education (PhD); reading, language arts and literature (PMC); school administration (Ed S); secondary education (MAT); special education (M Ed, Graduate Certificate); specific learning disabilities (Graduate Certificate); teaching and learning (Graduate Certificate). Electronic applications accepted.

School of Engineering and Computer Science *Program availability:* Part-time, evening/weekend. Offers computer science (MS); computer science and informatics (PhD); electrical and computer engineering (MS, PhD); embedded systems (MS); engineering and computer science (MS, PhD, Graduate Certificate); engineering management (MS); industrial and systems engineering (MS); mechanical engineering (MS, PhD); mechatronics (MS); productivity improvement (Graduate Certificate); software engineering and information technology (MS); systems engineering (PhD). Electronic applications accepted.

School of Health Sciences Offers clinical exercise science (Dr Sc PT); complementary medicine and wellness (Dr Sc PT); corporate worksite wellness (Dr Sc PT); exercise science (MS, Graduate Certificate); health sciences (MS, DPT, Dr Sc PT, TDPT, Graduate Certificate); neurological rehabilitation (Dr Sc PT, TDPT); orthopedic manual physical therapy (Dr Sc PT, TDPT, Graduate Certificate); orthopedic physical therapy (Graduate Certificate); orthopedics (Dr Sc PT, TDPT); pediatric rehabilitation (Dr Sc PT, TDPT); physical therapy (DPT); safety management (MS); teaching and learning for rehabilitation professionals (Dr Sc PT, TDPT). Electronic applications accepted.

School of Nursing *Program availability:* Part-time, evening/weekend. Offers adult gerontological nurse practitioner (MSN, PMC); family nurse practitioner (MSN, PMC); nurse anesthesia (MSN, PMC); nursing (MSN, DNP, PMC); nursing practice (DNP). Electronic applications accepted.

OAKWOOD UNIVERSITY, Huntsville, AL 35896

General Information Independent-religious, coed, comprehensive institution. *Graduate housing:* On-campus housing not available.

GRADUATE UNITS

Program in Pastoral Studies Offers pastoral studies (MA).

OBERLIN COLLEGE, Oberlin, OH 44074

General Information Independent, coed, comprehensive institution. *Enrollment:* 2,853 graduate, professional, and undergraduate students; 26 full-time matriculated graduate/professional students (8 women). *Enrollment by degree level:* 26 master's. *Graduate housing:* Rooms and/or apartments available on a first-come, first-served basis to single students and available to married students. Housing application deadline: 6/15. *Student services:* Campus employment opportunities, campus safety program, career counseling, exercise/wellness program, free psychological counseling, international student services, multicultural affairs office, services for students with disabilities, writing training. *Library facilities:* Mudd Center Library plus 3 others. *Collection:* Books: 1.4 million (physical), 676,883 (digital/electronic); Serial titles: 188,472 (physical). Students can reserve study rooms.

Computer facilities: Computer purchase and lease plans are available. 250 computers available on campus for general student use. A campuswide network can be accessed from student residence rooms and from off campus. Online class registration is available.
Website: http://www.oberlin.edu/

General Application Contact: Michael Manderen, Director of Conservatory Admissions, 440-775-8413, Fax: 440-775-6972, E-mail: conservatory.admissions@oberlin.edu.

GRADUATE UNITS

Conservatory of Music Students: 26 full-time (8 women). 88 applicants, 25% accepted, 19 enrolled. Expenses: Contact institution. *Financial support:* Career-related internships or fieldwork, Federal Work-Study, and scholarships/grants available. Financial award application deadline: 2/15; financial award applicants required to submit CSS PROFILE or FAFSA. Offers conducting (MM); contemporary chamber music (MM); historical performance (MM); performance (AD); piano technology (AD). *Application deadline:* For fall admission, 12/1 for domestic and international students. *Application fee:* $100. Electronic applications accepted. *Application Contact:* Michael Manderen, Director of Conservatory Admissions, 440-775-8413, Fax: 440-775-6972, E-mail: conservatory.admissions@oberlin.edu. *Dean*, Andrea Kalyn, 440-775-8200.

OBLATE SCHOOL OF THEOLOGY, San Antonio, TX 78216-6693

General Information Independent-religious, coed, graduate-only institution. *Enrollment by degree level:* 127 master's, 15 doctoral. *Graduate faculty:* 21 full-time (5 women), 4 part-time/adjunct (0 women). *Tuition:* Part-time $605 per credit hour. *Required fees:* $270 per semester. One-time fee: $65 part-time. Tuition and fees vary according to degree level and program. *Graduate housing:* On-campus housing not available. *Student services:* Campus employment opportunities, international student services, low-cost health insurance, services for students with disabilities, writing training. *Library facilities:* Donald E. O'Shaughnessy Library. *Collection:* Books: 79,000 (physical), 35,000 (digital/electronic); Serial titles: 300 (physical), 25 (digital/electronic); Databases: 15. Weekly public service hours: 71.

Computer facilities: 10 computers available on campus for general student use. A campuswide network can be accessed from student residence rooms and from off campus.
Website: http://www.ost.edu/

General Application Contact: Brenda Reyna, Registrar, 210-341-1366 Ext. 226, Fax: 210-341-4519, E-mail: registrar@ost.edu.

GRADUATE UNITS

Graduate and Professional Programs Students: 89 full-time (9 women), 54 part-time (31 women); includes 77 minority (11 Black or African American, non-Hispanic/Latino; 8 Asian, non-Hispanic/Latino; 57 Hispanic/Latino; 1 Two or more races, non-Hispanic/Latino), 24 international. Average age 39. *Faculty:* 21 full-time (5 women), 4 part-time/adjunct (0 women). Expenses: Contact institution. *Financial support:* In 2017–18, 25 students received support. Scholarships/grants available. Support available to part-time students. Financial award application deadline: 8/15; financial award applicants required to submit FAFSA. In 2017, 24 master's, 1 doctorate awarded. *Program availability:* Part-time, 100% online, blended/hybrid learning. Offers African-American pastoral leadership (D Min); divinity (M Div); pastoral leadership (D Min); pastoral ministry (MAP Min); pastoral studies (Certificate); spiritual formation in the local community (D Min); spirituality (MA Sp, PhD); spirituality and ministry (D Min); theology (MA Th); U.S. Hispanic/Latino ministry (D Min). *Application deadline:* For fall admission, 6/30 priority date for domestic and international students; for winter admission, 11/30 for domestic and international students; for spring admission, 11/30 for domestic and international students; for summer admission, 4/30 for domestic and international students. Applications are processed on a rolling basis. *Application fee:* $65. Electronic applications accepted. *Application Contact:* Brenda Reyna, Registrar, 210-341-1366 Ext. 226, Fax: 210-341-4519, E-mail: registrar@ost.edu. *Academic Dean*, Dr. R. Scott Woodward, 210-341-1366, Fax: 210-341-4519, E-mail: rsw@ost.edu.

OCCIDENTAL COLLEGE, Los Angeles, CA 90041-3314

General Information Independent, coed, comprehensive institution. *Enrollment:* 2,055 graduate, professional, and undergraduate students. *Graduate housing:* On-campus housing not available. *Student services:* Campus employment opportunities, campus safety program, career counseling, child daycare facilities, free psychological counseling, low-cost health insurance, multicultural affairs office. *Library facilities:* Mary Norton Clapp Library and Academic Commons plus 2 others. *Collection:* Study areas open 24 hours, 5–7 days a week; students can reserve study rooms.

Computer facilities: Computer purchase and lease plans are available. 200 computers available on campus for general student use. A campuswide network can be accessed. Online class registration is available.
Website: http://www.oxy.edu/

General Application Contact: Susan Molik, Academic Services Assistant, Graduate Office, 323-259-2921, Fax: 323-341-4988, E-mail: molik@oxy.edu.

GRADUATE UNITS

Department of Biology Expenses: Contact institution. *Financial support:* Fellowships, Federal Work-Study, institutionally sponsored loans, and scholarships/grants available. Support available to part-time students. Financial award application deadline: 3/1; financial award applicants required to submit FAFSA. *Program availability:* Part-time. Offers biology (MA). *Application deadline:* For fall admission, 3/1 for domestic students; for spring admission, 10/1 for domestic students. Applications are processed on a rolling basis. *Application fee:* $60. *Application Contact:* Susan Molik, Academic Services Assistant, Graduate Office, 323-259-2921, Fax: 323-341-4988, E-mail: molik@oxy.edu. *Department Chair*, 323-259-2697, E-mail: biology@oxy.edu.

OGLALA LAKOTA COLLEGE, Kyle, SD 57752-0490

General Information State and locally supported, coed, comprehensive institution. *Graduate housing:* On-campus housing not available.

GRADUATE UNITS

Graduate Studies *Program availability:* Part-time, evening/weekend. Offers educational administration (MA); Lakota leadership and management (MA).

OHIO CHRISTIAN UNIVERSITY, Circleville, OH 43113

General Information Independent-religious, coed, comprehensive institution.

GRADUATE UNITS

Graduate Programs

OHIO DOMINICAN UNIVERSITY, Columbus, OH 43219-2099

General Information Independent-religious, coed, comprehensive institution. *Enrollment:* 1,714 graduate, professional, and undergraduate students; 175 full-time matriculated graduate/professional students (108 women), 328 part-time matriculated graduate/professional students (204 women). *Enrollment by degree level:* 503 master's. *Graduate faculty:* 36 full-time (20 women), 33 part-time/adjunct (17 women). *Graduate housing:* Room and/or apartments available on a first-come, first-served basis to single students; on-campus housing not available to married students. Housing application deadline: 8/20. *Student services:* Campus employment opportunities, campus safety program, career counseling, exercise/wellness program, free psychological counseling, international student services, multicultural affairs office, services for students with disabilities, writing training. *Library facilities:* Ohio Dominican Library. *Collection:* Books: 76,769 (physical), 149,371 (digital/electronic); Serial titles: 5,325 (physical), 29,438 (digital/electronic); Databases: 261. Students can reserve study rooms.

Computer facilities: 350 computers available on campus for general student use. A campuswide network can be accessed from student residence rooms and from off campus. Online class registration is available.
Website: http://www.ohiodominican.edu/

General Application Contact: John W. Naughton, Associate Vice President of Graduate and Adult Enrollment, 614-251-4721, Fax: 614-251-6654, E-mail: grad@ohiodominican.edu.

GRADUATE UNITS

Division of Arts and Letters Students: 2 full-time (both women), 47 part-time (33 women); includes 1 minority (Hispanic/Latino). Average age 40. 27 applicants, 52% accepted, 11 enrolled. *Faculty:* 5 full-time (2 women), 2 part-time/adjunct (1 woman). Expenses: Contact institution. *Financial support:* Applicants required to submit FAFSA. *Program availability:* Part-time, evening/weekend, 100% online. Offers English (MA); theology (MA). *Application deadline:* For fall admission, 8/15 for domestic students, 6/10 for international students; for spring admission, 1/4 for domestic students, 11/2 for international students. Applications are processed on a rolling basis. *Application fee:* $25. Electronic applications accepted. *Application Contact:* John W. Naughton, Director for Graduate Admissions, 614-251-4721, Fax: 614-251-6654, E-mail: grad@ohiodominican.edu. *Chair,* Leo H. Madden, 614-251-4720, Fax: 614-253-3656, E-mail: maddenl@ohiodominican.edu.

Division of Business Students: 65 full-time (26 women), 130 part-time (57 women); includes 48 minority (30 Black or African American, non-Hispanic/Latino; 1 American Indian or Alaska Native, non-Hispanic/Latino; 6 Asian, non-Hispanic/Latino; 6 Hispanic/Latino; 5 Two or more races, non-Hispanic/Latino), 9 international. Average age 30. 148 applicants, 45% accepted, 53 enrolled. *Faculty:* 9 full-time (4 women), 14 part-time/adjunct (5 women). Expenses: Contact institution. *Financial support:* Applicants required to submit FAFSA. *Program availability:* Part-time, evening/weekend, 100% online, blended/hybrid learning. Offers accounting (MBA); business administration (MBA); data analytics (MBA); finance (MBA); healthcare administration (MS); leadership (MBA); risk management (MBA); sport management (MBA, MS). *Application deadline:* For fall admission, 8/15 for domestic students, 6/10 for international students; for spring admission, 1/4 for domestic students, 11/2 for international students. Applications are processed on a rolling basis. *Application fee:* $25. Electronic applications accepted. *Application Contact:* John W. Naughton, Director for Graduate Admissions, 614-251-4721, Fax: 614-251-6654, E-mail: grad@ohiodominican.edu. *Chair,* Dr. Kenneth C. Fah, 614-251-4566, E-mail: fahk@ohiodominican.edu.

Division of Education Students: 7 full-time (all women), 103 part-time (83 women); includes 11 minority (5 Black or African American, non-Hispanic/Latino; 1 Asian, non-Hispanic/Latino; 1 Hispanic/Latino; 4 Two or more races, non-Hispanic/Latino), 5 international. Average age 35. 59 applicants, 73% accepted, 41 enrolled. *Faculty:* 15 full-time (10 women), 15 part-time/adjunct (11 women). Expenses: Contact institution. *Financial support:* Tuition waivers and tuition discounts (for diocesan teachers) available. Financial award applicants required to submit FAFSA. *Program availability:* Part-time, evening/weekend, 100% online, blended/hybrid learning. Offers curriculum and instruction (M Ed); educational leadership (M Ed); teaching English to speakers of other languages (MA). *Application deadline:* For fall admission, 8/15 for domestic students, 6/10 for international students; for spring admission, 1/4 for domestic students, 11/2 for international students. Applications are processed on a rolling basis. *Application fee:* $25. Electronic applications accepted. *Application Contact:* John W. Naughton, Director for Graduate Admissions, 614-251-4721, Fax: 614-251-6654, E-mail: grad@ohiodominican.edu. *Chair,* Dr. JoAnn Hohenbrink, 614-251-4759, E-mail: hohenbrj@ohiodominican.edu.

Division of Physician Assistant Studies Students: 101 full-time (73 women), 48 part-time (31 women); includes 11 minority (1 Black or African American, non-Hispanic/Latino; 1 American Indian or Alaska Native, non-Hispanic/Latino; 4 Asian, non-Hispanic/Latino; 3 Hispanic/Latino; 2 Two or more races, non-Hispanic/Latino). Average age 25. 504 applicants, 15% accepted, 49 enrolled. *Faculty:* 7 full-time (4 women), 2 part-time/adjunct (0 women). Expenses: Contact institution. *Financial support:* Applicants required to submit FAFSA. In 2017, 48 master's awarded. Offers physician assistant studies (MS). *Application deadline:* For fall admission, 10/1 for domestic and international students. Applications are processed on a rolling basis. Electronic applications accepted. *Application Contact:* John W. Naughton, Associate Vice President for Enrollment Management, 614-251-4721, Fax: 614-251-6654, E-mail: grad@ohiodominican.edu. *Program Director,* Prof. Shonna Riedlinger, 614-251-8988, E-mail: riedlins@ohiodominican.edu.

OHIO NORTHERN UNIVERSITY, Ada, OH 45810-1599

General Information Independent-religious, coed, comprehensive institution. *Enrollment:* 3,088 graduate, professional, and undergraduate students; 745 full-time matriculated graduate/professional students (464 women), 31 part-time matriculated graduate/professional students (23 women). *Enrollment by degree level:* 47 master's, 729 doctoral. *Graduate faculty:* 44 full-time (20 women), 5 part-time/adjunct (1 woman). *Graduate housing:* Room and/or apartments available on a first-come, first-served basis to single students; on-campus housing not available to married students. *Student services:* Campus employment opportunities, campus safety program, career counseling, child daycare facilities, exercise/wellness program, free psychological counseling, international student services, multicultural affairs office, services for students with disabilities. *Library facilities:* Heterick Memorial Library plus 1 other. *Collection:* Students can reserve study rooms.

Computer facilities: A campuswide network can be accessed. Online class registration is available.
Website: http://www.onu.edu/

General Application Contact: Deborah Miller, Director of Admissions, 419-772-2464, E-mail: d-miller@onu.edu.

GRADUATE UNITS

Claude W. Pettit College of Law Students: 187 full-time (94 women), 1 part-time (0 women); includes 38 minority (17 Black or African American, non-Hispanic/Latino; 2 American Indian or Alaska Native, non-Hispanic/Latino; 6 Asian, non-Hispanic/Latino; 9 Hispanic/Latino; 4 Two or more races, non-Hispanic/Latino), 26 international. Average age 27. 471 applicants, 41% accepted, 55 enrolled. *Faculty:* 18 full-time (9 women), 3 part-time/adjunct (1 woman). Expenses: Contact institution. *Financial support:* Career-related internships or fieldwork, Federal Work-Study, institutionally sponsored loans, and scholarships/grants available. Financial award applicants required to submit FAFSA. In 2017, 24 master's, 54 doctorates awarded. Offers law (LL M, JD). *Application deadline:* Applications are processed on a rolling basis. Electronic applications accepted. *Application Contact:* Rachel Frey, Director of Law Admissions, 419-772-2213, Fax: 419-772-2758, E-mail: r-frey@onu.edu. *Dean,* Dr. David Crago, 419-772-2205, Fax: 419-772-3051, E-mail: d-crago@onu.edu.

College of Business Students: 21 part-time (15 women); includes 4 minority (3 Black or African American, non-Hispanic/Latino; 1 Two or more races, non-Hispanic/Latino), 2 international. Average age 25. Expenses: Contact institution. In 2017, 23 master's awarded. Offers business (MSA). *Application Contact:* Deborah Miller, Director of Admissions, 419-772-2464, E-mail: d-miller@onu.edu. *Dean,* Dr. John C. Navin, 419-772-2070, E-mail: j-navin@onu.edu.

Raabe College of Pharmacy Students: 558 full-time (370 women), 9 part-time (8 women); includes 64 minority (11 Black or African American, non-Hispanic/Latino; 25 Asian, non-Hispanic/Latino; 5 Hispanic/Latino; 23 Two or more races, non-Hispanic/Latino), 22 international. Average age 22. 658 applicants, 50% accepted, 172 enrolled. *Faculty:* 26 full-time (11 women), 2 part-time/adjunct (0 women). Expenses: Contact institution. *Financial support:* Federal Work-Study, institutionally sponsored loans, and scholarships/grants available. Financial award applicants required to submit FAFSA. In 2017, 153 doctorates awarded. Offers pharmacy (Pharm D). Students enter the program as undergraduates. *Application Contact:* Dr. Kelly Shields, Assistant Dean of Student Services, 419-772-2752, Fax: 419-772-2752, E-mail: k-shields@onu.edu. *Interim Dean,* Dr. Steve Martin, 419-772-2277, Fax: 419-772-2282, E-mail: s-martin.11@onu.edu.

THE OHIO STATE UNIVERSITY, Columbus, OH 43210

General Information State-supported, coed, university. CGS member. *Enrollment:* 59,837 graduate, professional, and undergraduate students; 11,684 full-time matriculated graduate/professional students (6,207 women), 1,639 part-time matriculated graduate/professional students (1,014 women). *Enrollment by degree level:* 5,195 master's, 8,092 doctoral, 26 other advanced degrees. *Graduate faculty:* 4,235. *Graduate housing:* Rooms and/or apartments available on a first-come, first-served basis to single and married students. *Student services:* Campus employment opportunities, campus safety program, career counseling, child daycare facilities, exercise/wellness program, free psychological counseling, grant writing training, international student services, low-cost health insurance, multicultural affairs office, services for students with disabilities, teacher training, writing training. *Library facilities:* William Oxley Thompson Library plus 10 others. *Collection:* Books: 5 million (physical), 1.3 million (digital/electronic); Serial titles: 664,616 (physical), 55,339 (digital/electronic); Databases: 2,046. Study areas open 24 hours, 5–7 days a week; students can reserve study rooms. *Research affiliation:* Transportation Research Center, Midwest Universities Consortium for International Activities, Children's Hospital (pediatrics), Ohio Learning Network (education).

Computer facilities: A campuswide network can be accessed. Online class registration, admission applications, fee payment are available.
Website: http://www.osu.edu/

General Application Contact: Graduate and Professional Admissions, 614-292-9444, Fax: 614-292-3895, E-mail: gpadmissions@osu.edu.

GRADUATE UNITS

College of Dentistry Students: 506 full-time (213 women), 11 part-time (8 women). Average age 26. *Faculty:* 86. Expenses: Contact institution. *Financial support:* Fellowships with tuition reimbursements, research assistantships with tuition reimbursements, teaching assistantships with tuition reimbursements, Federal Work-Study, institutionally sponsored loans, and health care benefits available. Financial award application deadline: 2/15. In 2017, 34 master's, 109 doctorates awarded. Offers dental anesthesiology (MS); dental hygiene (MDH); dentistry (DDS); endodontics (MS); oral and maxillofacial pathology (MS); oral and maxillofacial surgery (MS); oral biology (PhD); orthodontics (MS); pediatric dentistry (MS); periodontology (MS); prosthodontics (MS). *Application deadline:* For fall admission, 10/1 for domestic and international students; for summer admission, 4/11 for domestic students, 3/10 for international students. Applications are processed on a rolling basis. Electronic applications accepted. *Application Contact:* Graduate and Professional Admissions, 614-292-9444, Fax: 614-292-3895, E-mail: gpadmissions@osu.edu. *Dean,* Dr. Patrick M. Lloyd, 614-292-9755, E-mail: lloyd.256@osu.edu.

College of Medicine Students: 1,264 full-time (750 women), 74 part-time (46 women); includes 442 minority (99 Black or African American, non-Hispanic/Latino; 185 Asian, non-Hispanic/Latino; 100 Hispanic/Latino; 58 Native Hawaiian or other Pacific Islander, non-Hispanic/Latino), 10 international. Average age 25. *Faculty:* 1,799. Expenses: Contact institution. *Financial support:* Fellowships with tuition reimbursements, research assistantships with tuition reimbursements, teaching assistantships with tuition reimbursements, Federal Work-Study, institutionally sponsored loans, and scholarships/grants available. Support available to part-time students. Financial award application deadline: 2/15; financial award applicants required to submit FAFSA. In 2017, 107 master's, 239 doctorates awarded. Offers biomedical sciences (PhD); medicine (MOT, MS, DPT, MD, PhD). *Application deadline:* Applications are processed on a rolling basis. Electronic applications accepted. *Application Contact:* Graduate and Professional Admissions, 614-292-9444, Fax: 614-292-3895, E-mail: gpadmissions@osu.edu. *Dean and Vice President of Health Sciences,* Dr. K. Craig Kent, MD, 614-292-2600, Fax: 614-292-1301.

School of Health and Rehabilitation Sciences Students: 334 full-time (269 women), 21 part-time (11 women). Average age 25. *Faculty:* 46. Expenses: Contact institution. *Financial support:* Fellowships with tuition reimbursements, research assistantships with full tuition reimbursements, teaching assistantships with full tuition reimbursements, traineeships, unspecified assistantships, and administrative assistantships available. Financial award application deadline: 3/1. In 2017, 76 master's, 50 doctorates awarded. *Program availability:* Part-time. Offers allied health

(MS); anatomy (MS, PhD); health and rehabilitation sciences (MOT, MS, DPT, PhD); occupational therapy (MOT); physical therapy (DPT). *Application deadline:* Applications are processed on a rolling basis. *Application fee:* $60 ($70 for international students). Electronic applications accepted. *Application Contact:* Graduate and Professional Admissions, 614-292-9444, Fax: 614-292-3895, E-mail: gpadmissions@osu.edu. *Associate Dean and Director*, Dr. Deborah S. Larsen, 614-292-5645, Fax: 614-292-0210, E-mail: larsen.64@osu.edu.

College of Optometry Students: 276 (187 women); includes 39 minority (10 Black or African American, non-Hispanic/Latino; 17 Asian, non-Hispanic/Latino; 6 Hispanic/Latino; 6 Two or more races, non-Hispanic/Latino), 2 international. Average age 25. *Faculty:* 35. Expenses: Contact institution. *Financial support:* Research assistantships with full tuition reimbursements, teaching assistantships with full tuition reimbursements, institutionally sponsored loans, and scholarships/grants available. Financial award application deadline: 2/15; financial award applicants required to submit FAFSA. In 2017, 9 master's, 57 doctorates awarded. Offers optometry (OD); vision science (MS, PhD). *Application deadline:* For fall admission, 3/31 for domestic and international students; for spring admission, 12/1 for domestic students, 11/1 for international students. Applications are processed on a rolling basis. *Application fee:* $60 ($70 for international students). Electronic applications accepted. *Application Contact:* Office of Student Affairs, College of Optometry, 614-292-2647, Fax: 614-292-7493, E-mail: admissions@optometry.osu.edu. *Dean*, Dr. Karla Zadnik, 614-292-6603, E-mail: zadnik.4@osu.edu.

College of Pharmacy Students: 608 (331 women); includes 175 minority (42 Black or African American, non-Hispanic/Latino; 97 Asian, non-Hispanic/Latino; 22 Hispanic/Latino; 14 Two or more races, non-Hispanic/Latino), 61 international. Average age 25. *Faculty:* 53. Expenses: Contact institution. *Financial support:* Fellowships with full tuition reimbursements, research assistantships with full tuition reimbursements, teaching assistantships with full tuition reimbursements, career-related internships or fieldwork, Federal Work-Study, institutionally sponsored loans, scholarships/grants, and traineeships available. In 2017, 15 master's, 127 doctorates awarded. Offers pharmacy (MS, PhD, Pharm D). *Application deadline:* For fall admission, 12/15 for domestic and international students. *Application fee:* $60 ($70 for international students). Electronic applications accepted. *Application Contact:* E-mail: admissions@pharmacy.ohio-state.edu. *Dean and Professor*, Dr. Henry J. Mann, 614-292-5711, Fax: 614-292-2588, E-mail: mann.414@osu.edu.

College of Public Health Students: 241 full-time (177 women), 77 part-time (57 women); includes 75 minority (25 Black or African American, non-Hispanic/Latino; 25 Asian, non-Hispanic/Latino; 15 Hispanic/Latino; 10 Two or more races, non-Hispanic/Latino), 18 international. Average age 27. *Faculty:* 57. Expenses: Contact institution. *Financial support:* Fellowships with tuition reimbursements and research assistantships with tuition reimbursements available. In 2017, 123 master's, 7 doctorates awarded. *Program availability:* Part-time. Offers public health (MHA, MPH, MS, PhD). *Application deadline:* For fall admission, 12/1 priority date for domestic students, 11/1 priority date for international students. Applications are processed on a rolling basis. *Application fee:* $60 ($70 for international students). Electronic applications accepted. *Application Contact:* 614-292-8350, Fax: 614-247-1846, E-mail: cph@cph.osu.edu. *Dean and Professor*, Dr. William J. Martin, II, 614-292-8350, E-mail: martin.3047@osu.edu.

College of Veterinary Medicine Students: 687 full-time (535 women), 41 part-time (30 women). Average age 26. *Faculty:* 126. Expenses: Contact institution. In 2017, 21 master's, 175 doctorates awarded. Offers comparative and veterinary medicine (MS, PhD); veterinary medicine (MS, DVM, PhD). *Application deadline:* For fall admission, 9/15 for domestic and international students. Applications are processed on a rolling basis. *Application fee:* $60 ($70 for international students). Electronic applications accepted. *Application Contact:* Graduate and Professional Admissions, 614-292-9444, Fax: 614-292-3895, E-mail: gpadmissions@osu.edu. *Dean/Chair/Professor*, Dr. Rustin M. Moore, 614-688-8749, Fax: 614-292-3544, E-mail: moore.66@osu.edu.

Graduate School Students: 8,106 full-time (4,017 women), 1,432 part-time (870 women); includes 1,418 minority (462 Black or African American, non-Hispanic/Latino; 11 American Indian or Alaska Native, non-Hispanic/Latino; 344 Asian, non-Hispanic/Latino; 369 Hispanic/Latino; 232 Two or more races, non-Hispanic/Latino), 2,534 international. Average age 28. Expenses: Contact institution. *Financial support:* Fellowships with tuition reimbursements, research assistantships with tuition reimbursements, teaching assistantships with tuition reimbursements, career-related internships or fieldwork, Federal Work-Study, institutionally sponsored loans, and unspecified assistantships available. Support available to part-time students. In 2017, 2,519 master's, 887 doctorates, 1 other advanced degree awarded. *Program availability:* Part-time, evening/weekend. Offers biostatistics (PhD). *Application deadline:* For fall admission, 8/12 for domestic students, 7/1 for international students; for spring admission, 3/1 for domestic students, 2/1 for international students. Applications are processed on a rolling basis. *Application fee:* $60 ($70 for international students). Electronic applications accepted. *Application Contact:* Graduate and Professional Admissions, 614-292-9444, Fax: 614-292-3895, E-mail: gpadmissions@osu.edu. *Vice Provost and Dean*, Dr. Alicia L. Bertone, 614-292-6031, E-mail: bertone.1@osu.edu.

Center for Applied Plant Sciences Students: 10 full-time (7 women). Average age 28. Expenses: Contact institution. *Financial support:* Fellowships with tuition reimbursements and research assistantships with tuition reimbursements available. Offers applied plant sciences (PhD). *Application deadline:* For fall admission, 11/15 priority date for domestic and international students. Applications are processed on a rolling basis. *Application fee:* $60 ($70 for international students). Electronic applications accepted. *Application Contact:* Graduate and Professional Admissions, 614-292-9444, Fax: 614-292-3895, E-mail: gpadmissions@osu.edu. *Graduate Studies Committee Chair*, Dr. Thomas Mitchell, E-mail: mitchell.815@osu.edu.

Center for Latin American Studies Students: 1. Expenses: Contact institution. *Financial support:* Fellowships with tuition reimbursements available. Offers Latin American studies (MA). *Application deadline:* For fall admission, 12/13 priority date for domestic students, 11/30 priority date for international students; for spring admission, 12/12 for domestic students, 11/10 for international students; for summer admission, 4/10 for domestic students, 3/13 for international students. Applications are processed on a rolling basis. *Application fee:* $60 ($70 for international students). Electronic applications accepted. *Application Contact:* Graduate and Professional Admissions, 614-292-9444, Fax: 614-292-3895, E-mail: gpadmissions@osu.edu. *Director*, Dr. Terrell Morgan, 614-292-9555, E-mail: morgan.3@osu.edu.

Center for Slavic and East European Studies Students: 10 full-time (3 women). Average age 26. Expenses: Contact institution. *Financial support:* Fellowships, Federal Work-Study, and institutionally sponsored loans available. Support available to part-time students. In 2017, 4 master's awarded. Offers Slavic and East European studies (MA). *Application deadline:* For fall admission, 12/13 priority date for domestic students, 11/30 priority date for international students; for spring admission, 11/10 for domestic and international students; for summer admission, 3/13 for domestic and international students. Applications are processed on a rolling basis. *Application fee:* $60 ($70 for international students). Electronic applications accepted. *Application Contact:* Graduate and Professional Admissions, 614-292-9444, Fax: 614-292-3895, E-mail: gpadmissions@osu.edu. *Director*, Dr. Yana Hashamova, E-mail: hashamova.1@osu.edu.

College of Arts and Sciences Students: 2,610 full-time (1,277 women), 85 part-time (53 women); includes 389 minority (75 Black or African American, non-Hispanic/Latino; 92 Asian, non-Hispanic/Latino; 150 Hispanic/Latino; 72 Two or more races, non-Hispanic/Latino), 753 international. Average age 28. *Faculty:* 952. Expenses: Contact institution. *Financial support:* Fellowships, research assistantships, teaching assistantships, career-related internships or fieldwork, Federal Work-Study, institutionally sponsored loans, and unspecified assistantships available. Support available to part-time students. In 2017, 403 master's, 346 doctorates awarded. *Program availability:* Part-time. Offers acting (MFA); actuarial and quantitative risk management (MAQRM); African-American and African studies (MA, PhD); ancient Greek and Latin (MA, PhD); anthropology (MA, PhD); art (MFA); art education (MA); arts administration, education and policy (PhD); arts and humanities (MA, MFA, MM, DMA, PhD); arts and sciences (M Mus, MA, MAQRM, MFA, MMS, MS, DMA, PhD); arts policy and administration (MA); astronomy (MS, PhD); atmospheric sciences (MS, PhD); audiology (Au D); behavioral neuroscience (PhD); biochemistry (PhD); biophysics (MS, PhD); biostatistics (PhD); cell and developmental biology (MS, PhD); chemical physics (MS, PhD); chemistry (MS, PhD); Chinese (MA, PhD); choreography (MFA); clinical psychology (PhD); cognitive psychology (PhD); communication (MA, PhD); comparative studies (MA, PhD); computational sciences (MMS); dance (MFA, PhD); dance and technology (MFA); dance studies (PhD); design (MA, MFA); design research and development (MFA); developmental psychology (PhD); digital animation and interactive media (MFA); earth sciences (MS, PhD); economics (MA, PhD); English (MA, MFA, PhD); evolution, ecology, and organismal biology (MS, PhD); French (MA, PhD); genetics (MS, PhD); geodetic science (MS, PhD); geography (MA, PhD); geological sciences (MS, PhD); Germanic languages and literatures (MA, PhD); Greek studies (MA); hearing science (PhD); history (MA, PhD); history of art (MA, PhD); history, theory and literature (MFA); intellectual and developmental disabilities psychology (PhD); Italian (MA); Italian studies (PhD); Japanese (MA, PhD); Latin studies (MA, PhD); lighting and production (MFA); linguistics (MA, PhD); mathematical biosciences (MMS); mathematics (PhD); mathematics for educators (MMS); microbiology (MS, PhD); modern Greek (MA, PhD); molecular biology (MS, PhD); molecular, cellular and developmental biology (MS, PhD); movement analysis, Laban studies, notation and dance documentation (MFA); music (MA, MM, DMA, PhD); natural and mathematical sciences (M Appl Stat, MAQRM, MMS, MS, PhD); Near Eastern languages and cultures (MA, PhD); neuroscience (PhD); performance (MFA); philosophy (MA, PhD); physics (MS, PhD); political science (PhD); quantitative psychology (PhD); Slavic linguistics (MA, PhD); Slavic literature, film, and cultural studies (MA, PhD); social and behavioral sciences (MA, MS, Au D, PhD); social psychology (PhD); sociology (PhD); Spanish and Portuguese (MA, PhD); speech-language pathology (MA); speech-language science (PhD); statistics (M Appl Stat, MS, PhD); theatre (PhD); theatre studies (MA); women's, gender and sexuality studies (MA, PhD). *Application deadline:* For fall admission, 8/1 for domestic students, 7/1 for international students; for spring admission, 3/1 for domestic students, 2/1 for international students. Applications are processed on a rolling basis. *Application fee:* $60 ($70 for international students). Electronic applications accepted. *Application Contact:* Graduate and Professional Admissions, 614-292-9444, Fax: 614-292-3895, E-mail: gpadmissions@osu.edu. *Executive Dean and Vice Provost*, Dr. David C. Manderscheid, 614-292-3236, E-mail: manderscheid.1@osu.edu.

College of Education and Human Ecology Students: 770 full-time (499 women), 269 part-time (196 women). Average age 31. *Faculty:* 148. Expenses: Contact institution. *Financial support:* Fellowships with tuition reimbursements, research assistantships with tuition reimbursements, teaching assistantships with tuition reimbursements, career-related internships or fieldwork, Federal Work-Study, institutionally sponsored loans, scholarships/grants, traineeships, health care benefits, and unspecified assistantships available. Support available to part-time students. In 2017, 284 master's, 91 doctorates, 2 other advanced degrees awarded. Offers consumer sciences (MS, PhD); education and human ecology (M Ed, MA, MS, Ed D, PhD, Ed S); educational studies (M Ed, MA, PhD, Ed S); human development and family science (PhD); human nutrition (MS, PhD); kinesiology (MA, Ed D, PhD); teaching and learning (M Ed, MA, PhD, Ed S). *Application deadline:* Applications are processed on a rolling basis. *Application fee:* $60 ($70 for international students). Electronic applications accepted. *Application Contact:* Graduate and Professional Admissions, 614-292-9444, Fax: 614-292-3895, E-mail: gpadmissions@osu.edu. *Dean*, Dr. Cheryl Achterberg, 614-292-2461, Fax: 614-292-8052, E-mail: achterberg.1@osu.edu.

College of Engineering Students: 1,762 full-time (422 women), 152 part-time (25 women); includes 165 minority (38 Black or African American, non-Hispanic/Latino; 54 Asian, non-Hispanic/Latino; 51 Hispanic/Latino; 22 Two or more races, non-Hispanic/Latino), 1,083 international. Average age 26. *Faculty:* 362. Expenses: Contact institution. *Financial support:* Fellowships with tuition reimbursements, research assistantships with tuition reimbursements, teaching assistantships with tuition reimbursements, career-related internships or fieldwork, Federal Work-Study, institutionally sponsored loans, and unspecified assistantships available. Support available to part-time students. In 2017, 512 master's, 174 doctorates awarded. *Program availability:* Part-time, evening/weekend. Offers aerospace engineering (MS, PhD); architecture (M Arch); biomedical engineering (MS, PhD); chemical engineering (MS, PhD); city and regional planning (MCRP, PhD); civil engineering (MS, PhD); computer science and engineering (MS, PhD); electrical and computer engineering (MS, PhD); electrical engineering (MS, PhD); engineering (M Arch, M Land Arch, MCRP, MS, PhD); industrial and systems engineering (MS, PhD); landscape architecture (M Land Arch); materials science and engineering (MS, PhD); mechanical engineering (MS, PhD); nuclear engineering (MS, PhD); welding engineering (MS, PhD). *Application deadline:* For fall admission, 11/30 priority date for domestic and international students. Applications are processed on a rolling basis. *Application fee:* $60 ($70 for international students). Electronic applications accepted. *Application Contact:* Graduate and Professional Admissions, 614-292-9444, Fax: 614-292-3895, E-mail: gpadmissions@osu.edu. *Dean*, Dr. David B. Williams, 614-292-2836, Fax: 614-292-9615, E-mail: williams.4219@osu.edu.

College of Food, Agricultural, and Environmental Sciences Students: 455 full-time (258 women), 64 part-time (37 women); includes 60 minority (12 Black or African American, non-Hispanic/Latino; 14 Asian, non-Hispanic/Latino; 25 Hispanic/Latino; 9 Two or more races, non-Hispanic/Latino), 173 international. Average age 28. *Faculty:* 324. Expenses: Contact institution. *Financial support:* Fellowships with tuition reimbursements, research assistantships with tuition reimbursements, teaching assistantships with tuition reimbursements, career-related internships or fieldwork, Federal Work-Study, institutionally sponsored loans, and unspecified assistantships available. Support available to part-time students. In 2017, 137 master's, 73 doctorates awarded. *Program availability:* Part-time. Offers agricultural and extension education (M Ed, MS, PhD); agricultural, environmental, and development economics (MS, PhD); animal sciences (MAS, MS, PhD); ecological restoration (MS, PhD); ecosystem science (MS, PhD); entomology (MPHM, MS, PhD); environment and natural resources (MENR); environmental science (MS, PhD); environmental social sciences (MS, PhD); fisheries and wildlife science (MS, PhD); food science and technology (MS, PhD); food, agricultural, and biological engineering (MS, PhD); food, agricultural, and environmental sciences (M Ed, MAS, MENR, MPHM, MS, PhD); forest science (MS, PhD); horticulture and crop science (MS, PhD); plant pathology (MPHM, MS, PhD); rural sociology (MS, PhD); soil science (MS, PhD). *Application deadline:* Applications are processed on a rolling basis. *Application fee:* $60 ($70 for international students). Electronic applications accepted. *Application Contact:* Graduate and Professional Admissions, 614-292-9444, Fax: 614-292-3895, E-mail: gpadmissions@osu.edu. *Vice President and Dean*, Dr. Cathann A. Kress, 614-292-6164, E-mail: kress.98@osu.edu.

College of Nursing Students: 589 full-time (494 women), 280 part-time (237 women); includes 129 minority (53 Black or African American, non-Hispanic/Latino; 26 Asian, non-Hispanic/Latino; 22 Hispanic/Latino; 28 Two or more races, non-Hispanic/Latino), 4 international. Average age 32. *Faculty:* 60. Expenses: Contact institution. *Financial support:* Fellowships, research assistantships, teaching assistantships, Federal Work-Study, institutionally sponsored loans, and unspecified assistantships available. Support available to part-time students. In 2017, 232 master's, 11 doctorates awarded. *Program availability:* Part-time. Offers nursing (MHI, MS, DNP, PhD). *Application deadline:* For fall admission, 12/13 priority date for domestic students, 11/30 priority date for international students; for summer admission, 10/12 for domestic and international students. Applications are processed on a rolling basis. *Application fee:* $60 ($70 for international students). Electronic applications accepted. *Application Contact:* Graduate and Professional Admissions, 614-292-9444, Fax: 614-292-3895, E-mail: gpadmissions@osu.edu. *Dean*, Dr. Bernadette M. Melnyk, 614-292-4844, Fax: 614-292-4535, E-mail: melnyk.15@osu.edu.

College of Social Work Students: 471 full-time (395 women), 117 part-time (100 women); includes 108 minority (61 Black or African American, non-Hispanic/Latino; 7 Asian, non-Hispanic/Latino; 19 Hispanic/Latino; 21 Two or more races, non-Hispanic/Latino), 16 international. Average age 28. *Faculty:* 29. Expenses: Contact institution. *Financial support:* Fellowships, research assistantships, teaching assistantships, Federal Work-Study, institutionally sponsored loans, and unspecified assistantships available. Support available to part-time students. In 2017, 242 master's, 6 doctorates awarded. *Program availability:* Part-time. Offers social work (MSW, PhD). *Application deadline:* For fall admission, 12/13 priority date for domestic students, 11/30 priority date for international students; for summer admission, 4/1 for domestic students, 3/1 for international students. Applications are processed on a rolling basis. *Application fee:* $60 ($70 for international students). Electronic applications accepted. *Application Contact:* Graduate and Professional Admissions, 614-292-6031, Fax: 614-292-3656, E-mail: gpadmissions@osu.edu. *Dean*, Dr. Tom Gregoire, 614-292-9426, E-mail: gregoire.5@osu.edu.

East Asian Studies Center Students: 9 full-time (7 women). Average age 25. Expenses: Contact institution. In 2017, 5 master's awarded. Offers East Asian studies (MA). *Application deadline:* For fall admission, 12/13 priority date for domestic students, 11/30 priority date for international students; for spring admission, 12/1 for domestic students, 11/1 for international students; for summer admission, 4/10 for domestic students, 3/13 for international students. Applications are processed on a rolling basis. *Application fee:* $60 ($70 for international students). Electronic applications accepted. *Application Contact:* Graduate and Professional Admissions, 614-292-9444, Fax: 614-292-3895, E-mail: gpadmissions@osu.edu. *Associate Professor*, Dr. Etsuyo Yuasa, 614-292-5816, E-mail: yuasa.1@osu.edu.

John Glenn College of Public Affairs Students: 136 full-time (71 women), 37 part-time (25 women). Average age 30. *Faculty:* 21. Expenses: Contact institution. *Financial support:* Fellowships, research assistantships, teaching assistantships, Federal Work-Study, institutionally sponsored loans, and unspecified assistantships available. Support available to part-time students. In 2017, 77 master's, 4 doctorates awarded. *Program availability:* Part-time. Offers public administration (MA, MPA); public policy and management (PhD). *Application deadline:* For fall admission, 12/1 priority date for domestic students, 11/30 priority date for international students; for spring admission, 11/15 for domestic and international students; for summer admission, 4/1 for domestic and international students. Applications are processed on a rolling basis. *Application fee:* $60 ($70 for international students). Electronic applications accepted. *Application Contact:* Graduate and Professional Admissions, 614-292-6031, Fax: 614-292-3656, E-mail: gpadmissions@osu.edu. *Dean*, Dr. Trevor Brown, 614-292-4533, Fax: 614-292-4868, E-mail: brown.2296@osu.edu.

Max M. Fisher College of Business Students: 639 full-time (271 women), 344 part-time (137 women); includes 189 minority (66 Black or African American, non-Hispanic/Latino; 2 American Indian or Alaska Native, non-Hispanic/Latino; 80 Asian, non-Hispanic/Latino; 28 Hispanic/Latino; 13 Two or more races, non-Hispanic/Latino), 237 international. Average age 30. *Faculty:* 105. Expenses: Contact institution. *Financial support:* Fellowships, research assistantships, teaching assistantships, career-related internships or fieldwork, Federal Work-Study, institutionally sponsored loans, and unspecified assistantships available. Support available to part-time students. In 2017, 563 master's, 15 doctorates awarded. *Program availability:* Part-time, evening/weekend. Offers accounting (M Acc); business (M Acc, MA, MBA, MBLE, MBOE, MF, MHRM, PhD); business administration (MA, MBA, PhD); business logistics engineering (MBLE); business operational excellence (MBOE); finance (MF); human resource management (MHRM, PhD); labor and human resources (PhD); management information systems (PhD). *Application deadline:* Applications are processed on a rolling basis. *Application fee:* $60 ($70 for international students). Electronic applications accepted. *Application Contact:* Graduate and Professional Admissions, 614-292-9444, Fax: 614-292-3656, E-mail: gpadmissions@osu.edu. *Dean/Chair*, Dr. Anil K. Makhija, 614-292-2666, E-mail: makhija.1@osu.edu.

Moritz College of Law Offers law (LL M, MSL, JD). Electronic applications accepted.

THE OHIO STATE UNIVERSITY AT LIMA, Lima, OH 45804

General Information State-supported, coed, comprehensive institution. *Enrollment:* 1,026 graduate, professional, and undergraduate students; 4 matriculated graduate/professional students (3 women). *Enrollment by degree level:* 4 master's. *Graduate faculty:* 33. *Graduate housing:* On-campus housing not available. *Student services:* Campus safety program, career counseling, child daycare facilities, exercise/wellness program, free psychological counseling, grant writing training, international student services, low-cost health insurance, multicultural affairs office, services for students with disabilities, teacher training, writing training. *Library facilities:* Lima Campus Library. *Collection:* Books: 69,584 (physical), 1.3 million (digital/electronic); Serial titles: 50 (physical), 55,339 (digital/electronic); Databases: 2,046. Weekly public service hours: 57; students can reserve study rooms.

Computer facilities: A campuswide network can be accessed. Online class registration is available.
Website: http://lima.osu.edu/

General Application Contact: Graduate and Professional Admissions, 614-292-9444, Fax: 614-292-3895, E-mail: gpadmissions@osu.edu.

GRADUATE UNITS

Graduate Programs Students: 4 (3 women). *Faculty:* 33. Expenses: Contact institution. *Financial support:* Application deadline: 2/15. *Program availability:* Part-time. Offers social work (MSW). *Application deadline:* For fall admission, 4/1 for domestic students, 3/1 for international students; for spring admission, 10/15 for domestic and international students; for summer admission, 4/10 for domestic students, 3/1 for international students. Applications are processed on a rolling basis. *Application fee:* $60 ($70 for international students). Electronic applications accepted. *Application Contact:* Graduate and Professional Admissions, 614-292-9444, Fax: 614-292-3895, E-mail: gpadmissions@osu.edu. *Dean and Director*, Dr. Joseph Brandesky, 419-995-8600, E-mail: brandesky.1@osu.edu.

THE OHIO STATE UNIVERSITY AT MANSFIELD, Mansfield, OH 44906-1599

General Information State-supported, coed, comprehensive institution. *Enrollment:* 1,199 graduate, professional, and undergraduate students; 1 matriculated graduate/professional student. *Graduate faculty:* 39. *Graduate housing:* On-campus housing not available. *Student services:* Campus employment opportunities, campus safety program, career counseling, child daycare facilities, exercise/wellness program, free psychological counseling, grant writing training, international student services, low-cost health insurance, multicultural affairs office, services for students with disabilities, teacher training, writing training. *Library facilities:* Bromfield Library & Information Commons. *Collection:* Books: 43,140 (physical), 1.3 million (digital/electronic); Serial titles: 55,339 (digital/electronic); Databases: 2,046. Weekly public service hours: 63; students can reserve study rooms.

Computer facilities: Computer purchase and lease plans are available. A campuswide network can be accessed. Online class registration is available.
Website: http://www.mansfield.osu.edu/

General Application Contact: Graduate and Professional Admissions, 614-292-9444, Fax: 614-292-3895, E-mail: gpadmissions@osu.edu.

GRADUATE UNITS

Graduate Programs Students: 1. *Faculty:* 39. Expenses: Contact institution. *Financial support:* Teaching assistantships with full tuition reimbursements, Federal Work-Study, and scholarships/grants available. Support available to part-time students. Financial award application deadline: 2/15; financial award applicants required to submit FAFSA. *Program availability:* Part-time. Offers education (MA); social work (MSW). *Application deadline:* For fall admission, 4/1 for domestic students, 3/1 for international students; for spring admission, 10/15 for domestic and international students. Applications are processed on a rolling basis. *Application fee:* $60 ($70 for international students). Electronic applications accepted. *Application Contact:* Graduate and Professional Admissions, 614-292-9444, Fax: 614-292-3895, E-mail: gpadmissions@osu.edu. *Interim Dean and Director*, Dr. Norman W. Jones, E-mail: jones.2376@osu.edu.

THE OHIO STATE UNIVERSITY AT MARION, Marion, OH 43302-5695

General Information State-supported, coed, comprehensive institution. *Enrollment:* 1,198 graduate, professional, and undergraduate students; 1 matriculated graduate/professional student. *Graduate faculty:* 38. *Graduate housing:* On-campus housing not available. *Student services:* Campus employment opportunities, campus safety program, career counseling, child daycare facilities, exercise/wellness program, free psychological counseling, grant writing training, international student services, low-cost health insurance, multicultural affairs office, services for students with disabilities, teacher training, writing training. *Library facilities:* Marion Campus Library. *Collection:* Books: 46,288 (physical), 1.3 million (digital/electronic); Serial titles: 4,903 (physical), 55,339 (digital/electronic); Databases: 2,046. Weekly public service hours: 57; students can reserve study rooms.

Computer facilities: Computer purchase and lease plans are available. A campuswide network can be accessed. Online class registration is available.
Website: http://osumarion.osu.edu/

General Application Contact: Graduate and Professional Admissions, 614-292-9444, Fax: 614-292-3985, E-mail: gpadmissions@osu.edu.

GRADUATE UNITS

Graduate Programs Students: 1. *Faculty:* 38. Expenses: Contact institution. *Financial support:* Application deadline: 2/15; applicants required to submit FAFSA. *Program availability:* Part-time. Offers education (MA). *Application deadline:* Applications are processed on a rolling basis. *Application fee:* $60 ($70 for international students). Electronic applications accepted. *Application Contact:* Graduate and Professional Admissions, 614-292-9444, Fax: 614-292-3895, E-mail: gpadmissions@osu.edu. *Dean/Director*, Dr. Gregory S. Rose, 740-725-6218, E-mail: rose.9@osu.edu.

THE OHIO STATE UNIVERSITY AT NEWARK, Newark, OH 43055-1797

General Information State-supported, coed, comprehensive institution. *Enrollment:* 2,623 graduate, professional, and undergraduate students; 13 matriculated graduate/professional students (12 women). *Enrollment by degree level:* 13 master's. *Graduate faculty:* 49. *Graduate housing:* Rooms and/or apartments available on a first-come, first-served basis to single and married students. *Student services:* Campus safety program, career counseling, child daycare facilities, exercise/wellness program, free psychological counseling, grant writing training, international student services, low-cost health insurance, multicultural affairs office, services for students with disabilities, teacher training, writing training. *Library facilities:* John L. and Christine Warner Library. *Collection:* Weekly public service hours: 69; students can reserve study rooms.

Computer facilities: Computer purchase and lease plans are available. A campuswide network can be accessed. Online class registration is available.
Website: http://www.newark.osu.edu/

General Application Contact: Graduate and Professional Admissions, 614-292-9444, Fax: 614-292-3985, E-mail: gpadmissions@osu.edu.

GRADUATE UNITS

Graduate Programs Students: 13 (12 women). Average age 33. *Faculty:* 49. Expenses: Contact institution. *Financial support:* Application deadline: 2/15. *Program availability:* Part-time. Offers education - teaching and learning (MA); social work (MSW). *Application deadline:* For fall admission, 3/1 for domestic and international students. Applications are processed on a rolling basis. *Application fee:* $60 ($70 for international students). Electronic applications accepted. *Application Contact:* Graduate and Professional Admissions, 614-292-9444, Fax: 614-292-3985, E-mail: gpadmissions@osu.edu. *Dean and Director*, Dr. William L. MacDonald, 740-366-9333 Ext. 330, E-mail: macdonald.24@osu.edu.

OHIO UNIVERSITY, Athens, OH 45701-2979

General Information State-supported, coed, university. CGS member. *Graduate housing:* Rooms and/or apartments available on a first-come, first-served basis to single and married students. Housing application deadline: 5/1.

GRADUATE UNITS

Graduate College *Program availability:* Part-time, evening/weekend, online learning. Electronic applications accepted.

Center for International Studies *Program availability:* Part-time. Offers African studies (MA); Asian studies (MA); communications and development studies (MA); international development studies (MA); international studies (MA); Latin American studies (MA). Electronic applications accepted.

College of Arts and Sciences *Program availability:* Part-time, evening/weekend. Offers applied economics (MA); applied linguistics (MA); arts and sciences (MA, MFE, MS, MSS, PhD); astronomy (MS, PhD); biological sciences (MS, PhD); cell biology and physiology (MS, PhD); chemistry and biochemistry (MS, PhD); clinical psychology (PhD); ecology and evolutionary biology (MS, PhD); English language and literature (MA, PhD); environmental and plant biology (MS, PhD); environmental geochemistry (MS); exercise physiology and muscle biology (MS, PhD); experimental psychology (PhD); financial economics (MFE); French (MA); geography (MA, MS); history (MA, PhD); mathematics (MS, PhD); microbiology (MS, PhD); molecular and cellular biology (PhD); neuroscience (MS, PhD); organizational psychology (PhD); philosophy (MA); physics (MS, PhD); political science (MA); social sciences (MSS); sociology (MA); Spanish (MA). Electronic applications accepted.

College of Business *Program availability:* Part-time, evening/weekend, online learning. Offers athletic administration (MS); business (MBA, MS); executive management (MBA). Electronic applications accepted.

College of Fine Arts *Program availability:* Part-time, evening/weekend, online learning. Offers accompanying (MM); art history (MA); ceramics (MFA); composition (MM); conducting (MM); film (MFA); film studies (MA); fine arts (MA, MFA, MM, PhD, Certificate); graphic design (MFA); history/literature (MM); interdisciplinary arts (PhD); music education (MM); music therapy (MM); painting (MFA); performance (MM, Certificate); performance/pedagogy (MM); photography (MFA); printmaking (MFA); sculpture (MFA); theater (MA, MFA); theory (MM). Electronic applications accepted.

College of Health Sciences and Professions *Program availability:* Part-time, evening/weekend, online learning. Offers advanced clinical practice (DNP); athletic training (MS); clinical audiology (Au D); communication sciences and disorders (MA, Au D, PhD); early child development and family life (MS); executive practice (DNP); family nurse practitioner (MSN); family studies (MS); food and nutrition (MS); health administration (MHA); health sciences and professions (MA, MHA, MPH, MS, MSN, MSW, Au D, DNP, DPT, PhD); hearing science (PhD); human and consumer sciences (MS); nurse educator (MSN); physical therapy (DPT); physiology of exercise (MS); public health (MPH); social work (MSW); speech language pathology (MA); speech language science (PhD). Electronic applications accepted.

Gladys W. and David H. Patton College of Education and Human Services *Program availability:* Part-time, evening/weekend. Offers adolescent to young adult education (M Ed); coaching education (MS); college student personnel (M Ed); community/agency counseling (M Ed); computer education and technology (M Ed); counselor education (PhD); curriculum and instruction (M Ed, PhD); early childhood/special education (M Ed); education and human services (M Ed, MS, MSA, Ed D, PhD); educational administration (M Ed, Ed D); educational research and evaluation (M Ed, PhD); higher education (PhD); instructional technology (PhD); intervention specialist/mild-moderate needs (M Ed); intervention specialist/moderate-intensive needs (M Ed); middle childhood education (M Ed); reading education (M Ed); recreation studies (MS); rehabilitation counseling (M Ed); school counseling (M Ed). Electronic applications accepted.

Russ College of Engineering and Technology *Program availability:* Part-time. Offers biomedical engineering (MS); chemical engineering (MS, PhD); civil engineering (PhD); construction engineering and management (MS); electrical engineering (MS); electrical engineering and computer science (PhD); engineering and technology (M Eng Mgt, MS, PhD); environmental (MS); geoenvironmental (MS); geotechnical (MS); industrial and systems engineering (MS); mechanical and systems engineering (PhD); mechanical engineering (MS); mechanics (MS); structures (MS); transportation (MS); water resources (MS). Electronic applications accepted.

Scripps College of Communication *Program availability:* Part-time. Offers communication (MA, MCTP, MFA, MS, PhD); communication media arts (MFA); health communication (PhD); information and telecommunication systems (MCTP); journalism (MS); mass communication (PhD); media arts and studies (MA); organizational communication (MA); relating and organizing (PhD); rhetoric and public culture (PhD); visual communication (MA). Electronic applications accepted.

Voinovich School of Leadership and Public Affairs Offers environmental studies (MS, Certificate); public administration (MPA). Electronic applications accepted.

Heritage College of Osteopathic Medicine Students: 922 full-time; includes 225 minority (74 Black or African American, non-Hispanic/Latino; 4 American Indian or Alaska Native, non-Hispanic/Latino; 79 Asian, non-Hispanic/Latino; 38 Hispanic/Latino; 1 Native Hawaiian or other Pacific Islander, non-Hispanic/Latino; 29 Two or more races, non-Hispanic/Latino). Average age 26. 4,944 applicants, 7% accepted, 249 enrolled. *Faculty:* 107 full-time (55 women), 38 part-time/adjunct (12 women). Expenses: Contact institution. *Financial support:* In 2017–18, 284 students received support, including 20 fellowships (averaging $25,439 per year); Federal Work-Study, institutionally sponsored loans, scholarships/grants, and tuition waivers (partial) also available. Financial award applicants required to submit FAFSA. In 2017, 128 doctorates awarded. Offers osteopathic medicine (DO). Applicants must be U.S. residents to apply. *Application deadline:* For fall admission, 2/1 for domestic students. Applications are processed on a rolling basis. *Application fee:* $60. Electronic applications accepted. *Application Contact:* Jill Harman, Senior Director of Admissions and Recruitment, 740-593-2147, Fax: 740-593-2256, E-mail: harmanj@ohio.edu. *Executive Dean*, Dr. Kenneth Johnson, 740-593-9350, Fax: 740-593-0761, E-mail: wilcox@ohio.edu.

OHIO VALLEY UNIVERSITY, Vienna, WV 26105-8000

General Information Independent-religious, coed, comprehensive institution.

GRADUATE UNITS

School of Graduate Education *Program availability:* Online learning. Offers curriculum and instruction (M Ed).

OHR HAMEIR THEOLOGICAL SEMINARY, Cortlandt Manor, NY 10567

General Information Independent-religious, men only, comprehensive institution.

GRADUATE UNITS

Graduate Programs

OKLAHOMA BAPTIST UNIVERSITY, Shawnee, OK 74804

General Information Independent-religious, coed, comprehensive institution. *Graduate housing:* Rooms and/or apartments available on a first-come, first-served basis to single and married students. Housing application deadline: 4/15.

GRADUATE UNITS

Program in Business Administration *Program availability:* Online learning. Offers business administration (MBA); energy management (MBA).

Program in Marriage and Family Therapy *Program availability:* Part-time, evening/weekend. Offers marriage and family therapy (MS). Electronic applications accepted.

Program in Nursing Offers global nursing (MSN); nursing education (MSN).

OKLAHOMA CHRISTIAN UNIVERSITY, Oklahoma City, OK 73136-1100

General Information Independent-religious, coed, comprehensive institution. *Graduate housing:* Rooms and/or apartments available on a first-come, first-served basis to single and married students. Housing application deadline: 8/31.

GRADUATE UNITS

Graduate School of Business *Program availability:* Part-time, 100% online. Offers accounting (M Acc, MBA); financial services (MBA); general business (MBA); health services management (MBA); human resources (MBA); international business (MBA); leadership and organizational development (MBA); marketing (MBA); nonprofit management (MBA); project management (MBA). Electronic applications accepted.

Graduate School of Engineering and Computer Science *Program availability:* Part-time. Offers electrical and computer engineering (MSE); engineering management (MSE); mechanical engineering (MSE); software engineering (MSCS, MSE). Electronic applications accepted.

Graduate School of Theology *Program availability:* Part-time. Offers scripture (MTS); theology (M Div, MACM, MTS). Electronic applications accepted.

OKLAHOMA CITY UNIVERSITY, Oklahoma City, OK 73106-1402

General Information Independent-religious, coed, comprehensive institution. *Enrollment:* 2,821 graduate, professional, and undergraduate students; 839 full-time matriculated graduate/professional students (499 women), 289 part-time matriculated graduate/professional students (148 women). *Enrollment by degree level:* 607 master's, 521 doctoral. *Graduate faculty:* 87 full-time (36 women), 73 part-time/adjunct (37 women). Tuition and fees vary according to degree level and program. *Graduate housing:* Rooms and/or apartments available on a first-come, first-served basis to single and married students. Typical cost: $6000 per year ($10,796 including board) for single students. Room and board charges vary according to board plan and housing facility selected. Housing application deadline: 6/15. *Student services:* Campus employment opportunities, campus safety program, career counseling, exercise/wellness program, free psychological counseling, international student services, low-cost health insurance, multicultural affairs office, services for students with disabilities, teacher training, writing training. *Library facilities:* Dulaney Browne Library plus 1 other. *Collection:* Books: 279,046 (physical), 372,318 (digital/electronic); Serial titles: 5,543 (physical), 621,360 (digital/electronic); Databases: 114. Weekly public service hours: 99; students can reserve study rooms.

Computer facilities: Computer purchase and lease plans are available. 368 computers available on campus for general student use. A campuswide network can be accessed from student residence rooms and from off campus. Online class registration is available.
Website: http://www.okcu.edu/

General Application Contact: Michael Harrington, Director of Graduate Admissions, 800-633-7242, Fax: 405-208-5916, E-mail: gadmissions@okcu.edu.

GRADUATE UNITS

Kramer School of Nursing Students: 111 full-time (100 women), 25 part-time (all women); includes 48 minority (16 Black or African American, non-Hispanic/Latino; 9 American Indian or Alaska Native, non-Hispanic/Latino; 9 Asian, non-Hispanic/Latino; 4 Hispanic/Latino; 10 Two or more races, non-Hispanic/Latino), 8 international. Average age 37. 68 applicants, 72% accepted, 35 enrolled. *Faculty:* 10 full-time (all women), 8 part-time/adjunct (all women). Expenses: Contact institution. *Financial support:* In 2017–18, 89 students received support. Federal Work-Study, institutionally sponsored loans, scholarships/grants, and tuition waivers (full and partial) available. Support available to part-time students. Financial award application deadline: 3/1; financial award applicants required to submit FAFSA. In 2017, 10 master's, 34 doctorates awarded. *Program availability:* Part-time, evening/weekend, online learning. Offers clinical nurse leader (MSN); nursing (DNP, PhD); nursing education (MSN). *Application deadline:* Applications are processed on a rolling basis. *Application fee:* $50. Electronic applications accepted. *Application Contact:* Michael Harrington, Director of Graduate Admissions, 800-633-7242, Fax: 405-208-5916, E-mail: gadmissions@okcu.edu. *Dean, Kramer School of Nursing*, Dr. Lois Salmeron, 405-208-5900, Fax: 405-208-5914, E-mail: lsalmeron@okcu.edu.

Meinders School of Business Students: 121 full-time (49 women), 213 part-time (88 women); includes 85 minority (19 Black or African American, non-Hispanic/Latino; 6 American Indian or Alaska Native, non-Hispanic/Latino; 25 Asian, non-Hispanic/Latino; 21 Hispanic/Latino; 14 Two or more races, non-Hispanic/Latino), 58 international. Average age 33. 167 applicants, 79% accepted, 106 enrolled. *Faculty:* 18 full-time (4 women), 8 part-time/adjunct (3 women). Expenses: Contact institution. *Financial support:* In 2017–18, 252 students received support. Career-related internships or fieldwork, Federal Work-Study, institutionally sponsored loans, scholarships/grants, and tuition waivers (full and partial) available. Support available to part-time students. Financial award application deadline: 6/1; financial award applicants required to submit FAFSA. In 2017, 184 master's awarded. *Program availability:* Part-time, evening/weekend, 100% online. Offers business (MBA, MSA); computer science (MS); energy legal studies (MS); energy management (MS). *Application deadline:* Applications are processed on a rolling basis. *Application fee:* $50. Electronic applications accepted. *Application Contact:* Michael Harrington, Director of Graduate Admission, 800-633-7242, Fax: 405-208-5916, E-mail: gadmissions@okcu.edu. *Dean*, Dr. Steve Agee, 405-208-5275, Fax: 405-208-5008, E-mail: sagee@okcu.edu.

Petree College of Arts and Sciences Students: 84 full-time (61 women), 32 part-time (23 women); includes 31 minority (13 Black or African American, non-Hispanic/Latino; 3 American Indian or Alaska Native, non-Hispanic/Latino; 1 Asian, non-Hispanic/Latino; 9 Hispanic/Latino; 5 Two or more races, non-Hispanic/Latino), 30 international. Average age 34. 192 applicants, 67% accepted, 57 enrolled. *Faculty:* 6 full-time (2 women), 16 part-time/adjunct (10 women). Expenses: Contact institution. *Financial support:* In 2017–18, 19 students received support. Federal Work-Study, institutionally sponsored loans, scholarships/grants, and tuition waivers (full and partial) available. Support available to part-time students. Financial award application deadline: 6/1; financial award applicants required to submit FAFSA. In 2017, 65 master's awarded. *Program availability:* Part-time, evening/weekend. Offers applied behavioral studies (M Ed); applied sociology: nonprofit leadership (MA); creative writing (MFA); criminology (MS); early childhood education (M Ed); elementary education (M Ed); general studies (MLA); leadership/management (MLA); moving image arts (MFA); professional counseling (M Ed); teaching (MA); teaching English to speakers of other languages (MA). *Application deadline:* Applications are processed on a rolling basis. *Application fee:* $50. Electronic applications accepted. *Application Contact:* Michael Harrington, Director of Graduate Admissions, 800-633-7242, Fax: 405-208-5356, E-mail: gadmissions@okcu.edu. *Dean*, Dr. Amy Cataldi, 405-208-5446, Fax: 405-208-5447, E-mail: acataldi@okcu.edu.

School of Law Students: 387 full-time (208 women), 17 part-time (11 women); includes 148 minority (28 Black or African American, non-Hispanic/Latino; 29 American Indian or Alaska Native, non-Hispanic/Latino; 20 Asian, non-Hispanic/Latino; 43 Hispanic/Latino; 1 Native Hawaiian or other Pacific Islander, non-Hispanic/Latino; 27 Two or more races, non-Hispanic/Latino), 6 international. Average age 28. 560 applicants, 71% accepted, 158 enrolled. *Faculty:* 16 full-time (5 women), 21 part-time/adjunct (7 women). Expenses: Contact institution. *Financial support:* In 2017–18, 300 students received support. Career-related internships or fieldwork, Federal Work-Study, institutionally sponsored loans, scholarships/grants, and tuition waivers (full and partial) available. Support available to part-time students. Financial award application deadline: 2/1; financial award applicants required to submit FAFSA. In 2017, 131 doctorates awarded. *Program availability:* Part-time, evening/weekend. Offers law (LL M, JD). *Application deadline:* For fall admission, 8/1 for domestic and international students. *Application fee:* $50. Electronic applications accepted. *Application Contact:* Dr. Laurie W. Jones, Associate Dean of Admissions, Law School, 405-208-5354, Fax: 405-208-5814, E-mail: ljones@okcu.edu. *Interim Dean*, Lee Peoples, 405-208-5440, Fax: 405-208-6041, E-mail: lpeoples@okcu.edu.

Wanda L. Bass School of Music Students: 64 full-time (24 women), 2 part-time (1 woman); includes 17 minority (2 Black or African American, non-Hispanic/Latino; 3 Asian, non-Hispanic/Latino; 8 Hispanic/Latino; 4 Two or more races, non-Hispanic/Latino), 16 international. Average age 25. 95 applicants, 59% accepted, 32 enrolled. *Faculty:* 26 full-time (10 women), 19 part-time/adjunct (8 women). Expenses: Contact institution. *Financial support:* In 2017–18, 67 students received support. Career-related internships or fieldwork, Federal Work-Study, institutionally sponsored loans, scholarships/grants, and tuition waivers (full and partial) available. Support available to part-time students. Financial award application deadline: 6/1; financial award applicants required to submit FAFSA. In 2017, 22 master's awarded. *Program availability:* Part-time. Offers composition (MM); conducting (MM); musical theatre (MM); opera performance (MM); performance (MM); vocal coaching (MM). *Application deadline:* Applications are processed on a rolling basis. *Application fee:* $50. Electronic applications accepted. *Application Contact:* Michael Harrington, Director of Graduate Admission, 800-633-7242, Fax: 405-208-5916, E-mail: gadmissions@okcu.edu. *Dean*, Mark Parker, 405-208-5474, Fax: 405-208-5971, E-mail: mparker@okcu.edu.

OKLAHOMA STATE UNIVERSITY, Stillwater, OK 74078

General Information State-supported, coed, university. CGS member. *Enrollment:* 25,254 graduate, professional, and undergraduate students; 1,696 full-time matriculated graduate/professional students (949 women), 2,580 part-time matriculated graduate/professional students (1,174 women). *Enrollment by degree level:* 2,319 master's, 1,754 doctoral, 203 other advanced degrees. *Graduate faculty:* 1,210 full-time (455 women), 185 part-time/adjunct (100 women). Tuition, state resident: full-time $4019; part-time $2679.60 per year. Tuition, nonresident: full-time $15,286; part-time $10,190.40 per year. *Required fees:* $2129; $1419 per unit. Tuition and fees vary according to program. *Graduate housing:* Rooms and/or apartments available on a first-come, first-served basis to single and married students. Typical cost: $8558 (including board) for single students; $14,000 (including board) for married students. Room and board charges vary according to board plan and housing facility selected. *Student services:* Campus employment opportunities, campus safety program, career counseling, exercise/wellness program, free psychological counseling, grant writing training, international student services, low-cost health insurance, multicultural affairs office, services for students with disabilities, teacher training, writing training. *Library facilities:* Edmon Low Library plus 3 others. *Collection:* Weekly public service hours: 146; study areas open 24 hours, 5–7 days a week; students can reserve study rooms. *Research affiliation:* Allens, Inc. (horticulture and landscape architecture), General Motors (industrial engineering and management), Simons Foundation (mathematics), Howard Hughes Medical Institute (educational studies), Narramore Christian Foundation (human development and family science), LiteCure, LLC (veterinary clinical sciences).

Computer facilities: Computer purchase and lease plans are available. A campuswide network can be accessed from student residence rooms and from off campus. Online class registration is available.
Website: http://www.okstate.edu/

General Application Contact: Dr. Sheryl Tucker, Dean, 405-744-6368, Fax: 405-744-0355, E-mail: gradi@okstate.edu.

GRADUATE UNITS

Center for Veterinary Health Sciences *Program availability:* Online learning. Offers veterinary biomedical sciences (MS, PhD); veterinary health sciences (MS, DVM, PhD); veterinary medicine (DVM).

College of Agricultural Science and Natural Resources Students: 109 full-time (54 women), 296 part-time (155 women); includes 54 minority (8 Black or African American, non-Hispanic/Latino; 10 American Indian or Alaska Native, non-Hispanic/Latino; 6 Asian, non-Hispanic/Latino; 21 Hispanic/Latino; 9 Two or more races, non-Hispanic/Latino), 107 international. Average age 28. 211 applicants, 49% accepted, 83 enrolled. *Faculty:* 204 full-time (46 women), 8 part-time/adjunct (4 women). Expenses: Contact institution. *Financial support:* In 2017–18, 215 research assistantships (averaging $16,072 per year), 54 teaching assistantships (averaging $15,434 per year) were awarded; fellowships, career-related internships or fieldwork, Federal Work-Study, scholarships/grants, health care benefits, tuition waivers (partial), and unspecified assistantships also available. Support available to part-time students. Financial award application deadline: 3/1; financial award applicants required to submit FAFSA. In 2017, 122 master's, 34 doctorates awarded. *Program availability:* Online learning. Offers agricultural economics (M Ag, MS, PhD); agricultural education, communications and leadership (M Ag, MS, PhD); agricultural science and natural resources (M Ag, MS, PhD); animal sciences (M Ag, MS); biochemistry and molecular biology (MS, PhD); biosystems engineering (MS, PhD); crop science (PhD); entomology (PhD); entomology and plant pathology (MS); environmental and natural resources (MS, PhD); food science (PhD); horticulture (M Ag, MS); natural resource ecology and management (M Ag, MS, PhD); plant and soil sciences (MS); soil science (M Ag). *Application deadline:* For fall admission, 3/1 priority date for domestic and international students; for spring admission, 8/1 priority date for domestic and international students. Applications are processed on a rolling basis. *Application fee:* $40 ($75 for international students). Electronic applications accepted. *Vice President/Dean*, Dr. Thomas Coon, 405-744-2474, E-mail: thomas.coon@okstate.edu.

College of Arts and Sciences Students: 303 full-time (152 women), 584 part-time (244 women); includes 125 minority (20 Black or African American, non-Hispanic/Latino; 15 American Indian or Alaska Native, non-Hispanic/Latino; 11 Asian, non-Hispanic/Latino; 41 Hispanic/Latino; 1 Native Hawaiian or other Pacific Islander, non-Hispanic/Latino; 37 Two or more races, non-Hispanic/Latino), 272 international. Average age 30. 1,085 applicants, 29% accepted, 232 enrolled. *Faculty:* 470 full-time (175 women), 58 part-time/adjunct (29 women). Expenses: Contact institution. *Financial support:* In 2017–18, 127 research assistantships (averaging $13,365 per year), 545 teaching assistantships (averaging $14,048 per year) were awarded; career-related internships or fieldwork, Federal Work-Study, scholarships/grants, health care benefits, tuition waivers (partial), and unspecified assistantships also available. Support available to part-time students. Financial award application deadline: 3/1; financial award applicants required to submit FAFSA. In 2017, 167 master's, 75 doctorates awarded. Offers applied mathematics (MS, PhD); art history (MA); arts and sciences (MA, MFA, MM, MS, PhD); botany (MS); chemistry (MS, PhD); clinical psychology (PhD); communication sciences and disorders (MS); computer science (MS, PhD); creative writing (MFA); English (MA, PhD); environmental science (PhD); fire and emergency management administration (MS, PhD); general psychology (MS); geography (MS, PhD); graphic design (MA); history (MA, PhD); integrative biology (MS, PhD); microbiology and molecular genetics (MS, PhD); philosophy (MA); photonics (MS, PhD); political science (MA); sociology (MS, PhD); statistics (MS, PhD); theatre (MA). *Application deadline:* For fall admission, 3/1 priority date for domestic and international students; for spring admission, 8/1 priority date for domestic and international students. Applications are processed on a rolling basis. *Application fee:* $40 ($75 for international students). Electronic applications accepted. *Dean*, Dr. Bret Danilowicz, 405-744-5663, Fax: 405-744-1797, E-mail: bret.danilowicz@okstate.edu.

Boone Pickens School of Geology Students: 26 full-time (6 women), 55 part-time (12 women); includes 12 minority (2 Black or African American, non-Hispanic/Latino; 1 American Indian or Alaska Native, non-Hispanic/Latino; 4 Hispanic/Latino; 5 Two or more races, non-Hispanic/Latino), 22 international. Average age 30. 85 applicants, 20% accepted, 14 enrolled. *Faculty:* 14 full-time (3 women). Expenses: Contact institution. *Financial support:* Research assistantships, teaching assistantships, career-related internships or fieldwork, Federal Work-Study, scholarships/grants, health care benefits, tuition waivers (partial), and unspecified assistantships available. Support available to part-time students. Financial award application deadline: 3/1; financial award applicants required to submit FAFSA. In 2017, 18 master's, 3 doctorates awarded. Offers geology (MS, PhD). *Application deadline:* For fall admission, 3/1 priority date for international students; for spring admission, 8/1 priority date for international students. Applications are processed on a rolling basis. *Application fee:* $40 ($75 for international students). Electronic applications accepted. *Department Head*, Dr. Estella Atekwana, 405-744-6358, Fax: 405-744-7841, E-mail: estella.atekwana@okstate.edu.

Michael and Anne Greenwood School of Music Students: 15 full-time (6 women), 7 part-time (2 women); includes 4 minority (2 Black or African American, non-Hispanic/Latino; 1 Hispanic/Latino; 1 Two or more races, non-Hispanic/Latino), 3 international. Average age 26. 37 applicants, 49% accepted, 13 enrolled. *Faculty:* 33 full-time (14 women), 9 part-time/adjunct (2 women). Expenses: Contact institution. *Financial support:* Teaching assistantships, career-related internships or fieldwork, Federal Work-Study, scholarships/grants, health care benefits, tuition waivers (partial), and unspecified assistantships available. Support available to part-time students. Financial award application deadline: 3/1; financial award applicants required to submit FAFSA. In 2017, 5 master's awarded. Offers pedagogy and performance (MM). *Application deadline:* For fall admission, 3/1 priority date for international students; for spring admission, 8/1 priority date for international students. Applications are processed on a rolling basis. *Application fee:* $40 ($75 for international students). Electronic applications accepted. *Department Head*, Dr. Howard Potter, 405-744-8997, Fax: 405-744-9324, E-mail: osumusic@okstate.edu.

School of Media and Strategic Communications Students: 16 full-time (13 women), 13 part-time (7 women); includes 7 minority (1 Black or African American, non-Hispanic/Latino; 3 American Indian or Alaska Native, non-Hispanic/Latino; 1 Hispanic/Latino; 2 Two or more races, non-Hispanic/Latino), 2 international. Average age 27. 12 applicants, 83% accepted, 9 enrolled. *Faculty:* 17 full-time (6 women), 5 part-time/adjunct (1 woman). Expenses: Contact institution. *Financial support:* Research assistantships, teaching assistantships, career-related internships or fieldwork, Federal Work-Study, scholarships/grants, health care benefits, tuition waivers (partial), and unspecified assistantships available. Support available to part-time students. Financial award application deadline: 3/1; financial award applicants required to submit FAFSA. In 2017, 15 master's awarded. Offers mass communication (MS). *Application deadline:* For fall admission, 3/1 priority date for international students; for spring admission, 8/1 priority date for international students. Applications are processed on a rolling basis. *Application fee:* $40 ($75 for international students). Electronic applications accepted. *Director*, Dr. Craig Freem, 405-744-7676, Fax: 405-744-7104, E-mail: freemanc@okstate.edu.

College of Education, Health and Aviation Students: 261 full-time (181 women), 542 part-time (345 women); includes 224 minority (58 Black or African American, non-Hispanic/Latino; 41 American Indian or Alaska Native, non-Hispanic/Latino; 10 Asian, non-Hispanic/Latino; 51 Hispanic/Latino; 2 Native Hawaiian or other Pacific Islander, non-Hispanic/Latino; 62 Two or more races, non-Hispanic/Latino), 34 international. Average age 35. 281 applicants, 67% accepted, 158 enrolled. *Faculty:* 96 full-time (67 women), 69 part-time/adjunct (40 women). Expenses: Contact institution. *Financial support:* In 2017–18, 75 research assistantships (averaging $9,598 per year), 105 teaching assistantships (averaging $11,392 per year) were awarded; career-related internships or fieldwork, Federal Work-Study, scholarships/grants, health care benefits, tuition waivers (partial), and unspecified assistantships also available. Support available to part-time students. Financial award application deadline: 3/1; financial award applicants required to submit FAFSA. In 2017, 174 master's, 58 doctorates awarded. *Program availability:* Part-time, online learning. Offers education, health and aviation (MS, Ed D, PhD, Ed S). *Application deadline:* For fall admission, 3/1 priority date for domestic and international students; for spring admission, 8/1 priority date for domestic and international students. Applications are processed on a rolling basis. *Application fee:* $40 ($75 for international students). Electronic applications accepted. *Interim Dean,* Dr. Robert Davis, 405-744-6350, Fax: 405-744-6350, E-mail: robert.davis@okstate.edu.

School of Applied Health and Educational Psychology Students: 169 full-time (119 women), 158 part-time (102 women); includes 98 minority (29 Black or African American, non-Hispanic/Latino; 15 American Indian or Alaska Native, non-Hispanic/Latino; 5 Asian, non-Hispanic/Latino; 24 Hispanic/Latino; 25 Two or more races, non-Hispanic/Latino), 22 international. Average age 30. 140 applicants, 56% accepted, 69 enrolled. *Faculty:* 31 full-time (20 women), 9 part-time/adjunct (7 women). Expenses: Contact institution. *Financial support:* Research assistantships, teaching assistantships, career-related internships or fieldwork, Federal Work-Study, scholarships/grants, health care benefits, tuition waivers (partial), and unspecified assistantships available. Support available to part-time students. Financial award application deadline: 3/1; financial award applicants required to submit FAFSA. In 2017, 71 master's, 24 doctorates awarded. *Program availability:* Part-time. Offers applied behavioral studies (Ed D); applied health and educational psychology (MS, PhD, Ed S). *Application deadline:* For fall admission, 3/1 priority date for international students; for spring admission, 8/1 priority date for international students. Applications are processed on a rolling basis. *Application fee:* $40 ($75 for international students). Electronic applications accepted. *Head,* Dr. Aric Warren, 405-744-6040, Fax: 405-744-6779, E-mail: aric.warren@okstate.edu.

School of Educational Studies Students: 66 full-time (38 women), 232 part-time (120 women); includes 85 minority (20 Black or African American, non-Hispanic/Latino; 18 American Indian or Alaska Native, non-Hispanic/Latino; 3 Asian, non-Hispanic/Latino; 21 Hispanic/Latino; 2 Native Hawaiian or other Pacific Islander, non-Hispanic/Latino; 21 Two or more races, non-Hispanic/Latino), 5 international. Average age 38. 110 applicants, 83% accepted, 80 enrolled. *Faculty:* 28 full-time (15 women), 31 part-time/adjunct (8 women). Expenses: Contact institution. *Financial support:* Research assistantships, teaching assistantships, career-related internships or fieldwork, Federal Work-Study, scholarships/grants, health care benefits, tuition waivers (partial), and unspecified assistantships available. Support available to part-time students. Financial award application deadline: 3/1; financial award applicants required to submit FAFSA. In 2017, 42 master's, 25 doctorates awarded. *Program availability:* Part-time. Offers higher education (Ed D). *Application deadline:* For fall admission, 3/1 priority date for international students; for spring admission, 8/1 priority date for international students. Applications are processed on a rolling basis. *Application fee:* $40 ($75 for international students). Electronic applications accepted. *Head,* Dr. Jesse Mendez, 405-744-9447, Fax: 405-744-7758, E-mail: jesse.perez.mendez@okstate.edu.

School of Teaching and Curriculum Leadership Students: 26 full-time (24 women), 152 part-time (123 women); includes 41 minority (9 Black or African American, non-Hispanic/Latino; 8 American Indian or Alaska Native, non-Hispanic/Latino; 2 Asian, non-Hispanic/Latino; 6 Hispanic/Latino; 16 Two or more races, non-Hispanic/Latino), 7 international. Average age 38. 45 applicants, 91% accepted, 35 enrolled. *Faculty:* 37 full-time (32 women), 29 part-time/adjunct (25 women). Expenses: Contact institution. *Financial support:* Research assistantships, teaching assistantships, career-related internships or fieldwork, Federal Work-Study, scholarships/grants, health care benefits, tuition waivers (partial), and unspecified assistantships available. Support available to part-time students. Financial award application deadline: 3/1; financial award applicants required to submit FAFSA. In 2017, 61 master's, 8 doctorates awarded. *Program availability:* Part-time. Offers teaching and curriculum leadership (MS, PhD). *Application deadline:* For fall admission, 3/1 priority date for international students; for spring admission, 8/1 priority date for international students. Applications are processed on a rolling basis. *Application fee:* $40 ($75 for international students). Electronic applications accepted. *Interim Department Head,* Dr. Jennifer Sanders, 405-744-9214, Fax: 405-744-6290, E-mail: jenn.sanders10@okstate.edu.

College of Engineering, Architecture and Technology Students: 170 full-time (43 women), 383 part-time (75 women); includes 56 minority (7 Black or African American, non-Hispanic/Latino; 7 American Indian or Alaska Native, non-Hispanic/Latino; 8 Asian, non-Hispanic/Latino; 15 Hispanic/Latino; 1 Native Hawaiian or other Pacific Islander, non-Hispanic/Latino; 18 Two or more races, non-Hispanic/Latino), 270 international. Average age 29. 765 applicants, 22% accepted, 124 enrolled. *Faculty:* 120 full-time (15 women), 11 part-time/adjunct (2 women). Expenses: Contact institution. *Financial support:* In 2017–18, 181 research assistantships (averaging $9,808 per year), 151 teaching assistantships (averaging $7,074 per year) were awarded; career-related internships or fieldwork, Federal Work-Study, scholarships/grants, health care benefits, tuition waivers (partial), and unspecified assistantships also available. Support available to part-time students. Financial award application deadline: 3/1; financial award applicants required to submit FAFSA. In 2017, 162 master's, 24 doctorates awarded. *Program availability:* Online learning. Offers engineering, architecture and technology (MS, PhD). *Application deadline:* For fall admission, 3/1 priority date for domestic and international students; for spring admission, 8/1 priority date for domestic and international students. Applications are processed on a rolling basis. *Application fee:* $40 ($75 for international students). Electronic applications accepted. *Dean,* Dr. Paul Tikalsky, 405-744-5140, E-mail: paul.tikalsky@okstate.edu.

School of Chemical Engineering Students: 21 full-time (4 women), 24 part-time (5 women); includes 5 minority (1 Black or African American, non-Hispanic/Latino; 1 American Indian or Alaska Native, non-Hispanic/Latino; 2 Asian, non-Hispanic/Latino; 1 Two or more races, non-Hispanic/Latino), 26 international. Average age 29. 64 applicants, 20% accepted, 13 enrolled. *Faculty:* 12 full-time (2 women), 1 part-time/adjunct (0 women). Expenses: Contact institution. *Financial support:* Research assistantships, teaching assistantships, career-related internships or fieldwork, Federal Work-Study, scholarships/grants, health care benefits, tuition waivers (partial), and unspecified assistantships available. Support available to part-time students. Financial award application deadline: 3/1; financial award applicants required to submit FAFSA. In 2017, 6 master's, 5 doctorates awarded. Offers chemical engineering (MS, PhD). *Application deadline:* For fall admission, 3/1 priority date for international students; for spring admission, 8/1 priority date for international students. Applications are processed on a rolling basis. *Application fee:* $40 ($75 for international students). Electronic applications accepted. *Head,* Dr. Rob Whiteley, 405-744-5280, Fax: 405-744-6338, E-mail: rob.whiteley@okstate.edu.

School of Civil and Environmental Engineering Students: 21 full-time (5 women), 39 part-time (13 women); includes 1 minority (Two or more races, non-Hispanic/Latino), 37 international. Average age 29. 74 applicants, 26% accepted, 11 enrolled. *Faculty:* 21 full-time (2 women), 2 part-time/adjunct (0 women). Expenses: Contact institution. *Financial support:* Research assistantships, teaching assistantships, career-related internships or fieldwork, Federal Work-Study, scholarships/grants, health care benefits, tuition waivers (partial), and unspecified assistantships available. Support available to part-time students. Financial award application deadline: 3/1; financial award applicants required to submit FAFSA. In 2017, 22 master's, 6 doctorates awarded. Offers civil engineering (MS, PhD). *Application deadline:* For fall admission, 3/1 priority date for international students; for spring admission, 8/1 priority date for international students. Applications are processed on a rolling basis. *Application fee:* $40 ($75 for international students). Electronic applications accepted. *Department Head,* Dr. Norb Delatte, 405-744-5190, Fax: 405-744-7554, E-mail: norb.delatte@okstate.edu.

School of Electrical and Computer Engineering Students: 40 full-time (14 women), 39 part-time (6 women); includes 7 minority (2 Black or African American, non-Hispanic/Latino; 1 Asian, non-Hispanic/Latino; 2 Hispanic/Latino; 2 Two or more races, non-Hispanic/Latino), 50 international. Average age 29. 159 applicants, 23% accepted, 18 enrolled. *Faculty:* 20 full-time (2 women), 1 part-time/adjunct (0 women). Expenses: Contact institution. *Financial support:* Research assistantships, teaching assistantships, career-related internships or fieldwork, Federal Work-Study, scholarships/grants, health care benefits, tuition waivers (partial), and unspecified assistantships available. Support available to part-time students. Financial award application deadline: 3/1; financial award applicants required to submit FAFSA. In 2017, 30 master's, 5 doctorates awarded. *Program availability:* Online learning. Offers electrical and computer engineering (MS, PhD). *Application deadline:* For fall admission, 3/1 priority date for international students; for spring admission, 8/1 priority date for international students. Applications are processed on a rolling basis. *Application fee:* $40 ($75 for international students). Electronic applications accepted. *Application Contact:* Dr. R. G. Ramakumar, Graduate Coordinator, 405-744-5157, Fax: 405-744-9198, E-mail: ramakum@okstate.edu. *Department Head,* Dr. Jeffrey Young, 405-744-5151, Fax: 405-744-9198, E-mail: jl.young@okstate.edu.

School of Industrial Engineering and Management Students: 58 full-time (9 women), 147 part-time (28 women); includes 22 minority (4 Black or African American, non-Hispanic/Latino; 1 American Indian or Alaska Native, non-Hispanic/Latino; 2 Asian, non-Hispanic/Latino; 9 Hispanic/Latino; 1 Native Hawaiian or other Pacific Islander, non-Hispanic/Latino; 5 Two or more races, non-Hispanic/Latino), 80 international. Average age 30. 247 applicants, 21% accepted, 44 enrolled. *Faculty:* 13 full-time (4 women), 1 part-time/adjunct (0 women). Expenses: Contact institution. *Financial support:* Research assistantships, teaching assistantships, career-related internships or fieldwork, Federal Work-Study, scholarships/grants, health care benefits, tuition waivers (partial), and unspecified assistantships available. Support available to part-time students. Financial award application deadline: 3/1; financial award applicants required to submit FAFSA. In 2017, 70 master's, 2 doctorates awarded. *Program availability:* Online learning. Offers industrial engineering and management (MS, PhD). *Application deadline:* For fall admission, 3/1 priority date for international students; for spring admission, 8/1 priority date for international students. Applications are processed on a rolling basis. *Application fee:* $40 ($75 for international students). Electronic applications accepted. *Application Contact:* Dr. Baski Balasundaram, Director of Graduate Program, 405-744-6055, Fax: 405-744-4654, E-mail: baski@okstate.edu. *Head,* Dr. Sunderesh Heragu, 405-744-6055, Fax: 405-744-4654, E-mail: sunderesh.heragu@okstate.edu.

School of Materials Science and Engineering Students: 2 full-time (1 woman), 15 part-time (4 women); includes 3 minority (2 American Indian or Alaska Native, non-Hispanic/Latino; 1 Two or more races, non-Hispanic/Latino), 10 international. Average age 29. 14 applicants, 29% accepted, 4 enrolled. *Faculty:* 7 full-time (0 women), 2 part-time/adjunct (0 women). Expenses: Contact institution. *Financial support:* Research assistantships and teaching assistantships available. In 2017, 5 master's awarded. Offers materials science and engineering (MS, PhD). *Application deadline:* For fall admission, 3/1 for domestic students; for spring admission, 8/1 for domestic students. *Application fee:* $40 ($75 for international students). Electronic applications accepted. *Head,* Dr. Raj N. Singh, 918-594-8650, E-mail: rajns@okstate.edu.

School of Mechanical and Aerospace Engineering Students: 15 full-time (4 women), 98 part-time (15 women); includes 15 minority (3 American Indian or Alaska Native, non-Hispanic/Latino; 3 Asian, non-Hispanic/Latino; 2 Hispanic/Latino; 7 Two or more races, non-Hispanic/Latino), 50 international. Average age 26. 181 applicants, 22% accepted, 37 enrolled. *Faculty:* 31 full-time (1 woman), 3 part-time/adjunct (1 woman). Expenses: Contact institution. *Financial support:* Research assistantships, teaching assistantships, career-related internships or fieldwork, Federal Work-Study, scholarships/grants, health care benefits, tuition waivers (partial), and unspecified assistantships available. Support available to part-time students. Financial award application deadline: 3/1; financial award applicants required to submit FAFSA. In 2017, 29 master's, 6 doctorates awarded. *Program availability:* Online learning. Offers mechanical and aerospace engineering (MS, PhD). *Application deadline:* For fall admission, 3/1 priority date for international students; for spring admission, 8/1 priority date for international students. Applications are processed on a rolling basis. *Application fee:* $40 ($75 for international students). Electronic applications accepted. *Application Contact:* Dr. Charlotte Fore, Manager of Graduate Studies and Research Development, 405-744-5900, Fax: 405-744-7873, E-mail: charlotte.fore@okstate.edu. *Department Head,* Dr. Daniel E. Fisher, 405-744-5900, Fax: 405-744-7873, E-mail: maehead@okstate.edu.

College of Human Sciences Students: 85 full-time (64 women), 145 part-time (106 women); includes 45 minority (19 Black or African American, non-Hispanic/Latino; 3 American Indian or Alaska Native, non-Hispanic/Latino; 6 Asian, non-Hispanic/Latino; 12 Hispanic/Latino; 5 Two or more races, non-Hispanic/Latino), 51 international. Average age 31. 158 applicants, 47% accepted, 61 enrolled. *Faculty:* 84 full-time (58 women), 24 part-time/adjunct (16 women). Expenses: Contact institution. *Financial support:* In 2017–18, 87 research assistantships (averaging $4,023 per year), 71 teaching assistantships (averaging $3,751 per year) were awarded; career-related internships or fieldwork, Federal Work-Study, scholarships/grants, health care benefits, tuition waivers (partial), and unspecified assistantships also available. Support available to part-time students. Financial award application deadline: 3/1; financial award applicants required to submit FAFSA. In 2017, 49 master's, 7 doctorates awarded. *Program availability:* Online learning. Offers design, housing and merchandising (MS, PhD); human development and family science (MS, PhD); human sciences (MS, PhD); nutritional sciences (MS, PhD). *Application deadline:* For fall admission, 3/1 priority date for domestic and international students; for spring admission, 8/1 priority date for domestic and international students. Applications are processed on a rolling basis. *Application fee:* $40 ($75 for international students). Electronic applications accepted. *Dean,* Dr. Stephan M. Wilson, 405-744-9805, Fax: 405-744-7113, E-mail: stephan.m.wilson@okstate.edu.

School of Hospitality and Tourism Management Students: 16 full-time (11 women), 12 part-time (8 women); includes 4 minority (2 Black or African American, non-Hispanic/Latino; 2 Asian, non-Hispanic/Latino), 20 international. Average age 28. 17 applicants, 65% accepted, 8 enrolled. *Faculty:* 16 full-time (9 women), 7 part-time/adjunct (1 woman). Expenses: Contact institution. *Financial support:* Research assistantships, teaching assistantships, career-related internships or fieldwork, Federal Work-Study, scholarships/grants, health care benefits, tuition waivers (partial), and unspecified assistantships available. Support available to part-time students. Financial award application deadline: 3/1; financial award applicants required to submit FAFSA. In 2017, 3 master's, 2 doctorates awarded. Offers hospitality and tourism management (MS, PhD). *Application deadline:* For fall admission, 3/1 priority date for international students; for spring admission, 8/1 priority date for international students. Applications are processed on a rolling basis. *Application fee:* $40 ($75 for international students). Electronic applications accepted. *Application Contact:* Dr. Li Miao, Graduate Coordinator, 405-744-1277, Fax: 405-744-6299, E-mail: lm@okstate.edu. *Director,* Dr. Ben Goh, 405-744-7651, Fax: 405-744-6299, E-mail: ben.goh@okstate.edu.

Graduate College Students: 31 full-time (21 women), 55 part-time (32 women); includes 15 minority (5 Black or African American, non-Hispanic/Latino; 3 Asian, non-Hispanic/Latino; 5 Hispanic/Latino; 2 Two or more races, non-Hispanic/Latino), 44 international. Average age 29. 334 applicants, 84% accepted, 73 enrolled. Expenses: Contact institution. *Financial support:* Research assistantships, career-related internships or fieldwork, Federal Work-Study, scholarships/grants, health care benefits, tuition waivers (partial), and unspecified assistantships available. Support available to part-time students. Financial award application deadline: 3/1; financial award applicants required to submit FAFSA. In 2017, 29 master's, 5 doctorates awarded. Offers aerospace security (Graduate Certificate); bioenergy and sustainable technology (Graduate Certificate); business data mining (Graduate Certificate); business sustainability (Graduate Certificate); environmental science (MS); international studies (MS); non-profit management (Graduate Certificate); teaching English to speakers of other languages (Graduate Certificate); telecommunications management (MS). Programs are interdisciplinary. *Application deadline:* For fall admission, 3/1 priority date for domestic and international students; for spring admission, 8/1 priority date for domestic and international students. Applications are processed on a rolling basis. *Application fee:* $40 ($75 for international students). Electronic applications accepted. *Application Contact:* Dr. Susan Mathew, Assistant Director of Graduate Admissions, 405-744-6368, Fax: 405-744-0355, E-mail: gradi@okstate.edu. *Dean,* Dr. Sheryl Tucker, 405-744-6368, Fax: 405-744-0355, E-mail: gradi@okstate.edu.

Spears School of Business Students: 355 full-time (123 women), 395 part-time (107 women); includes 125 minority (24 Black or African American, non-Hispanic/Latino; 13 American Indian or Alaska Native, non-Hispanic/Latino; 18 Asian, non-Hispanic/Latino; 33 Hispanic/Latino; 3 Native Hawaiian or other Pacific Islander, non-Hispanic/Latino; 34 Two or more races, non-Hispanic/Latino), 215 international. Average age 30. 1,021 applicants, 31% accepted, 253 enrolled. *Faculty:* 123 full-time (35 women), 35 part-time/adjunct (14 women). Expenses: Contact institution. *Financial support:* In 2017–18, 62 research assistantships (averaging $13,692 per year), 119 teaching assistantships (averaging $7,890 per year) were awarded; career-related internships or fieldwork, Federal Work-Study, scholarships/grants, health care benefits, tuition waivers (partial), and unspecified assistantships also available. Support available to part-time students. Financial award application deadline: 3/1; financial award applicants required to submit FAFSA. In 2017, 340 master's, 22 doctorates awarded. *Program availability:* Part-time, online learning. Offers business (MBA, MS, PhD); economics and legal studies in business (MS, PhD); entrepreneurship (MBA, MS, PhD); finance (MS, PhD); management (MBA, MS, PhD); management information systems (MS); management science and information systems (PhD); telecommunications management (MS). *Application deadline:* For fall admission, 3/1 priority date for domestic and international students; for spring admission, 8/1 priority date for domestic and international students. Applications are processed on a rolling basis. *Application fee:* $40 ($75 for international students). Electronic applications accepted. *Dean,* Dr. Ken Eastman, 405-744-5064, Fax: 405-744-8956, E-mail: ken.eastman@okstate.edu.

School of Accounting Students: 32 full-time (20 women), 7 part-time (4 women); includes 8 minority (2 American Indian or Alaska Native, non-Hispanic/Latino; 1 Asian, non-Hispanic/Latino; 1 Hispanic/Latino; 4 Two or more races, non-Hispanic/Latino), 3 international. Average age 23. 34 applicants, 50% accepted, 12 enrolled. *Faculty:* 16 full-time (8 women), 4 part-time/adjunct (3 women). Expenses: Contact institution. *Financial support:* Research assistantships, teaching assistantships, career-related internships or fieldwork, Federal Work-Study, scholarships/grants, health care benefits, tuition waivers (partial), and unspecified assistantships available. Support available to part-time students. Financial award application deadline: 3/1; financial award applicants required to submit FAFSA. In 2017, 39 master's awarded. *Program availability:* Part-time. Offers accounting (MS, PhD). *Application deadline:* For fall admission, 3/1 priority date for international students; for spring admission, 8/1 priority date for international students. Applications are processed on a rolling basis. *Application fee:* $40 ($75 for international students). Electronic applications accepted. *Application Contact:* Dr. Alyssa Vowell, Graduate Coordinator, 405-744-6635, Fax: 405-744-1680, E-mail: alyssa.vowell@okstate.edu. *Department Head,* Dr. Rick Wilson, 405-744-3551, Fax: 405-744-1680, E-mail: rick.wilson@okstate.edu.

School of Marketing and International Business Students: 63 full-time (19 women), 19 part-time (9 women); includes 5 minority (2 Asian, non-Hispanic/Latino; 2 Hispanic/Latino; 1 Two or more races, non-Hispanic/Latino), 65 international. Average age 27. 234 applicants, 20% accepted, 42 enrolled. *Faculty:* 21 full-time (5 women), 5 part-time/adjunct (2 women). Expenses: Contact institution. *Financial support:* Research assistantships, teaching assistantships, career-related internships or fieldwork, Federal Work-Study, scholarships/grants, health care benefits, tuition waivers (partial), and unspecified assistantships available. Support available to part-time students. Financial award application deadline: 3/1; financial award applicants required to submit FAFSA. In 2017, 41 master's, 1 doctorate awarded. *Program availability:* Part-time. Offers business administration (PhD); marketing (MBA). *Application deadline:* For fall admission, 3/1 priority date for international students; for spring admission, 8/1 priority date for international students. Applications are processed on a rolling basis. *Application fee:* $40 ($75 for international students). Electronic applications accepted. *Application Contact:* Dr. Kevin Voss, PhD Coordinator, 405-744-5106, Fax: 405-744-5180, E-mail: kevin.voss@okstate.edu. *Department Head,* Dr. Joshua L. Wiener, 405-744-5192, Fax: 405-744-5180, E-mail: josh.wiener@okstate.edu.

OKLAHOMA STATE UNIVERSITY CENTER FOR HEALTH SCIENCES, Tulsa, OK 74107-1898

General Information State-supported, coed, graduate-only institution. *Graduate housing:* On-campus housing not available. *Research affiliation:* Viropharma, Inc. (pharmaceutical sciences), Ingenex (pharmaceutical sciences), The Procter & Gamble Company (pharmaceutical sciences), Glaxo-Smith Kline (pharmaceutical sciences), Sun River, Inc. (cognitive rehabilitation), Merck & Company, Inc. (pharmaceutical sciences).

GRADUATE UNITS

College of Osteopathic Medicine Offers osteopathic medicine (DO). Electronic applications accepted.

Graduate Program in Forensic Sciences *Program availability:* Part-time, evening/weekend, 100% online, blended/hybrid learning. Offers forensic sciences (MS). Electronic applications accepted.

Program in Biomedical Sciences Offers biomedical sciences (MS, PhD). Electronic applications accepted.

Program in Health Care Administration *Program availability:* Part-time, evening/weekend, 100% online. Offers health care administration (MS).

OKLAHOMA WESLEYAN UNIVERSITY, Bartlesville, OK 74006-6299

General Information Independent-religious, coed, comprehensive institution.

GRADUATE UNITS

Professional Studies Division

OLD DOMINION UNIVERSITY, Norfolk, VA 23529

General Information State-supported, coed, university. CGS member. *Enrollment:* 24,375 graduate, professional, and undergraduate students; 1,563 full-time matriculated graduate/professional students (991 women), 2,381 part-time matriculated graduate/professional students (1,280 women). *Enrollment by degree level:* 2,611 master's, 1,205 doctoral, 128 other advanced degrees. *Graduate faculty:* 655 full-time (254 women), 182 part-time/adjunct (107 women). Tuition, state resident: full-time $8928; part-time $496 per credit. Tuition, nonresident: full-time $22,482; part-time $1249 per credit. *Required fees:* $66 per semester. *Graduate housing:* Room and/or apartments available on a first-come, first-served basis to single students; on-campus housing not available to married students. Typical cost: $6278 per year ($11,268 including board). Room and board charges vary according to board plan and housing facility selected. Housing application deadline: 5/1. *Student services:* Campus employment opportunities, campus safety program, career counseling, exercise/wellness program, free psychological counseling, grant writing training, international student services, low-cost health insurance, multicultural affairs office, services for students with disabilities, teacher training, writing training. *Library facilities:* Patricia W. and Douglas Perry Library plus 3 others. *Collection:* Books: 1.1 million (physical), 1.6 million (digital/electronic); Serial titles: 14,465 (physical), 87,579 (digital/electronic); Databases: 449. Weekly public service hours: 146; study areas open 24 hours, 5–7 days a week; students can reserve study rooms. *Research affiliation:* Commonwealth Center for Advanced Manufacturing (CCAM) (advanced engineering and manufacturing), Huntington Ingalls Industries (Newport News Shipbuilding) (digital shipbuilding), Thomas Jefferson National Accelerator Facility (high energy physics and laser processing), NASA Langley Research Center (aeronautics and data analytics), Eastern Virginia Medical School (medicine), Virginia Institute of Marine Science (marine science and coastal resilience).

Computer facilities: 2,028 computers available on campus for general student use. A campuswide network can be accessed from student residence rooms and from off campus. Online class registration, online courses are available.
Website: http://www.odu.edu/

General Application Contact: William Heffelfinger, Director of Graduate Admissions, 757-683-5554, Fax: 757-683-3255, E-mail: gradadmit@odu.edu.

GRADUATE UNITS

College of Arts and Letters Students: 154 full-time (92 women), 178 part-time (108 women); includes 93 minority (43 Black or African American, non-Hispanic/Latino; 1 American Indian or Alaska Native, non-Hispanic/Latino; 6 Asian, non-Hispanic/Latino; 20 Hispanic/Latino; 1 Native Hawaiian or other Pacific Islander, non-Hispanic/Latino; 22 Two or more races, non-Hispanic/Latino), 24 international. Average age 34. 276 applicants, 66% accepted, 117 enrolled. *Faculty:* 135 full-time (61 women), 11 part-time/adjunct (4 women). Expenses: Contact institution. *Financial support:* In 2017–18, 156 students received support, including 5 fellowships with full tuition reimbursements available (averaging $15,000 per year), 54 research assistantships (averaging $10,000 per year), 60 teaching assistantships with full tuition reimbursements available (averaging $15,000 per year); institutionally sponsored loans, scholarships/grants, and unspecified assistantships also available. Financial award application deadline: 2/15; financial award applicants required to submit CSS PROFILE or FAFSA. In 2017, 72 master's, 15 doctorates awarded. *Program availability:* Part-time, evening/weekend, 100% online. Offers applied studies or conducting (MME); arts and entrepreneurship (Certificate); arts and letters (MA, MFA, MME, PhD, Certificate); conflict and cooperation (MA, PhD); creative writing (MFA); criminal justice (MA); criminology and criminal justice (PhD); cultural and human geography (MA); cultural studies (MA); English (MA, PhD); gender and sexuality studies (MA); general sociology (MA); health, communication and culture (Certificate); history (MA); interdependence and transnationalism (MA, PhD); international cultural studies (MA, PhD); international political economy and development (MA, PhD); lifespan and digital communication (MA); literature (MA); media and popular culture studies (MA); modeling and simulation (MA, PhD); pedagogy (MME); philosophy and religious studies (MA); professional writing (MA); research (MME); rhetoric and composition (MA); social justice and entrepreneurship (Certificate); sociolinguistics (MA); TESOL (MA); U.S. foreign policy and international relations (MA, PhD); visual studies (MA); women's studies (MA); world cultures (MA). *Application deadline:* For fall admission, 6/1 priority date for domestic students, 2/15 for international students; for spring admission, 11/1 priority date for domestic students, 10/1 for international students. *Application fee:* $50. Electronic applications accepted. *Application Contact:* Dr. Dale Miller, Associate Dean, 757-683-3866, Fax: 757-683-5746, E-mail: demiller@odu.edu. *Dean,* Dr. Kent Sandstrom, 757-683-3925, Fax: 757-683-5746, E-mail: ksandstr@odu.edu.

College of Health Sciences Students: 332 full-time (242 women), 112 part-time (98 women); includes 108 minority (55 Black or African American, non-Hispanic/Latino; 1 American Indian or Alaska Native, non-Hispanic/Latino; 17 Asian, non-Hispanic/Latino; 18 Hispanic/Latino; 17 Two or more races, non-Hispanic/Latino), 12 international. Average age 32. 1,047 applicants, 25% accepted, 202 enrolled. *Faculty:* 64 full-time (42 women), 2 part-time/adjunct (0 women). Expenses: Contact institution. *Financial support:* In 2017–18, 40 students received support, including 7 fellowships with full tuition reimbursements available (averaging $15,000 per year), 12 research assistantships with partial tuition reimbursements available (averaging $15,000 per year), 9 teaching assistantships with partial tuition reimbursements available (averaging $13,000 per year); career-related internships or fieldwork, institutionally sponsored loans, scholarships/grants, health care benefits, tuition waivers (full and partial), and unspecified assistantships also available. Support available to part-time students. Financial award application deadline: 2/15; financial award applicants required to submit FAFSA. In 2017, 91 master's, 79 doctorates awarded. *Program availability:* Part-time, evening/weekend, 100% online, blended/hybrid learning. Offers health sciences (MS, MSAT, MSN, DNP, DPT, PhD); health services research (PhD). *Application deadline:* Applications are processed on a rolling basis. *Application fee:* $50. Electronic applications accepted. *Application Contact:* William Heffelfinger, Director of Graduate Admissions, 757-683-5554, Fax: 757-683-3255, E-mail: gradadmit@odu.edu. *Dean*, Dr. Bonnie Van Lunen, 757-683-3516, Fax: 757-683-5674, E-mail: bvanlune@odu.edu.

School of Community and Environmental Health Students: 9 full-time (7 women), 12 part-time (5 women); includes 9 minority (7 Black or African American, non-Hispanic/Latino; 1 Hispanic/Latino; 1 Two or more races, non-Hispanic/Latino), 1 international. Average age 28. 15 applicants, 67% accepted, 8 enrolled. *Faculty:* 5 full-time (2 women), 4 part-time/adjunct (2 women). Expenses: Contact institution. *Financial support:* In 2017–18, 4 students received support, including 4 teaching assistantships with partial tuition reimbursements available (averaging $10,000 per year); scholarships/grants and tuition waivers (partial) also available. Financial award application deadline: 6/30; financial award applicants required to submit FAFSA. In 2017, 9 master's awarded. Offers general environmental health (MS); industrial hygiene (MS). *Application deadline:* For fall admission, 8/1 priority date for domestic students, 7/1 priority date for international students; for winter admission, 11/1 priority date for domestic students, 10/1 priority date for international students; for spring admission, 4/1 priority date for domestic students, 3/1 priority date for international students. Applications are processed on a rolling basis. *Application fee:* $50. Electronic applications accepted. *Application Contact:* William Heffelfinger, Director of Graduate Admissions, 757-683-5554, Fax: 757-683-3255, E-mail: gradadmit@odu.edu. *Graduate Program Director*, Dr. Anna Jeng, 757-683-4594, Fax: 757-683-4410, E-mail: hjeng@odu.edu.

School of Dental Hygiene Students: 3 full-time (1 woman), 22 part-time (21 women); includes 5 minority (3 Black or African American, non-Hispanic/Latino; 1 Asian, non-Hispanic/Latino; 1 Hispanic/Latino), 3 international. Average age 38. 12 applicants, 25% accepted, 2 enrolled. *Faculty:* 10 full-time (9 women). Expenses: Contact institution. *Financial support:* In 2017–18, 4 students received support, including 4 teaching assistantships with partial tuition reimbursements available (averaging $13,000 per year); scholarships/grants and health care benefits also available. Support available to part-time students. Financial award application deadline: 2/15; financial award applicants required to submit CSS PROFILE or FAFSA. In 2017, 8 master's awarded. *Program availability:* Part-time, evening/weekend, blended/hybrid learning. Offers dental hygiene (MS). *Application deadline:* For fall admission, 7/1 for domestic students, 4/15 for international students; for spring admission, 12/1 for domestic students, 10/1 for international students; for summer admission, 3/1 for domestic students, 2/1 for international students. Applications are processed on a rolling basis. *Application fee:* $50. Electronic applications accepted. *Application Contact:* William Heffelfinger, Director of Graduate Admissions, 757-683-5554, Fax: 757-683-3255, E-mail: gradadmit@odu.edu. *Assistant Professor/Graduate Program Director*, Dr. Denise M. Claiborne, 757-683-5949, Fax: 757-683-5239, E-mail: dclaibor@odu.edu.

School of Nursing Students: 165 full-time (145 women), 61 part-time (57 women); includes 68 minority (38 Black or African American, non-Hispanic/Latino; 1 American Indian or Alaska Native, non-Hispanic/Latino; 11 Asian, non-Hispanic/Latino; 10 Hispanic/Latino; 8 Two or more races, non-Hispanic/Latino), 3 international. Average age 39. 305 applicants, 66% accepted, 116 enrolled. *Faculty:* 17 full-time (16 women), 24 part-time/adjunct (21 women). Expenses: Contact institution. *Financial support:* In 2017–18, 3 students received support, including 3 research assistantships with partial tuition reimbursements available (averaging $13,000 per year); traineeships also available. Financial award application deadline: 2/15; financial award applicants required to submit FAFSA. In 2017, 45 master's, 30 doctorates awarded. *Program availability:* Part-time, 100% online, blended/hybrid learning. Offers adult gerontology clinical nurse specialist/administrator (MSN); adult gerontology clinical nurse specialist/educator (MSN); advanced practice (DNP); family nurse practitioner (MSN); neonatal clinical nurse specialist (MSN); neonatal nurse practitioner (MSN); nurse administrator (MSN); nurse anesthesia (DNP); nurse executive (DNP); nursing (MSN, DNP); pediatric clinical nurse specialist (MSN); pediatric nurse practitioner (MSN). MSN in nurse midwifery, MSN in psychiatric mental health offered in cooperation with Shenandoah University. *Application deadline:* For fall admission, 3/1 for domestic students, 4/15 for international students; for spring admission, 9/15 for domestic students. *Application fee:* $50. Electronic applications accepted. *Application Contact:* Sue Parker, Graduate Program Coordinator, 757-683-4298, Fax: 757-683-5253, E-mail: sparker@odu.edu. *Chair*, Dr. Karen Karlowicz, 757-683-5262, Fax: 757-683-5253, E-mail: nursgpd@odu.edu.

School of Physical Therapy and Athletic Training Students: 122 full-time (66 women); includes 15 minority (6 Black or African American, non-Hispanic/Latino; 7 Asian, non-Hispanic/Latino; 2 Hispanic/Latino). Average age 25. Expenses: Contact institution. *Financial support:* Applicants required to submit FAFSA. Offers athletic training (MSAT); kinesiology and rehabilitation (PhD); physical therapy (DPT). Electronic applications accepted. *Application Contact:* William Heffelfinger, Director of Graduate Admissions, 757-683-5554, Fax: 757-683-3255, E-mail: gradadmit@odu.edu. *Graduate Program Director*, Dr. Martha Walker, 757-683-4519, Fax: 757-683-4410, E-mail: ptgpd@odu.edu.

College of Sciences Students: 250 full-time (121 women), 214 part-time (98 women); includes 77 minority (23 Black or African American, non-Hispanic/Latino; 25 Asian, non-Hispanic/Latino; 16 Hispanic/Latino; 13 Two or more races, non-Hispanic/Latino), 141 international. Average age 29. *Faculty:* 141 full-time (34 women), 26 part-time/adjunct (2 women). Expenses: Contact institution. *Financial support:* In 2017–18, 312 students received support, including 14 fellowships with full tuition reimbursements available (averaging $18,000 per year), 190 research assistantships with full and partial tuition reimbursements available (averaging $18,000 per year), 122 teaching assistantships with full and partial tuition reimbursements available (averaging $16,000 per year); career-related internships or fieldwork, scholarships/grants, and tuition waivers (full and partial) also available. Support available to part-time students. Financial award application deadline: 2/15; financial award applicants required to submit FAFSA. In 2017, 89 master's, 36 doctorates awarded. *Program availability:* Part-time, evening/weekend, 100% online. Offers analytical chemistry (MS, PhD); applied mathematics (MS, PhD); applied psychological sciences (PhD); biochemistry (MS, PhD); biology (MS); biomedical sciences (PhD); biostatistics (MS); clinical psychology (PhD); computer information systems (MS); computer science (MS, PhD); ecological sciences (PhD); environmental chemistry (MS, PhD); human factors psychology (PhD); industrial/organizational psychology (PhD); inorganic chemistry (MS, PhD); microbiology and immunology (MS); ocean and earth sciences (MS); oceanography (PhD); organic chemistry (MS, PhD); physical chemistry (MS, PhD); physics (MS, PhD); psychology (MS, PhD); sciences (MS, PhD); statistics (MS); statistics/biostatistics (PhD). *Application fee:* $50. Electronic applications accepted. *Application Contact:* William Heffelfinger, Director of Graduate Admissions, 757-683-5554, Fax: 757-683-3255, E-mail: gradadmit@odu.edu. *Dean*, Dr. Gail Dodge, 757-683-3432, Fax: 757-683-3034, E-mail: gdodge@odu.edu.

Darden College of Education Students: 541 full-time (448 women), 869 part-time (679 women); includes 448 minority (284 Black or African American, non-Hispanic/Latino; 6 American Indian or Alaska Native, non-Hispanic/Latino; 25 Asian, non-Hispanic/Latino; 71 Hispanic/Latino; 3 Native Hawaiian or other Pacific Islander, non-Hispanic/Latino; 59 Two or more races, non-Hispanic/Latino), 22 international. Average age 34. 755 applicants, 69% accepted, 382 enrolled. *Faculty:* 94 full-time (55 women), 62 part-time/adjunct (40 women). Expenses: Contact institution. *Financial support:* In 2017–18, 141 students received support, including 4 fellowships with tuition reimbursements available (averaging $15,000 per year), 60 research assistantships with tuition reimbursements available (averaging $15,000 per year), 72 teaching assistantships with tuition reimbursements available (averaging $15,000 per year); career-related internships or fieldwork, Federal Work-Study, institutionally sponsored loans, scholarships/grants, tuition waivers (partial), and unspecified assistantships also available. Support available to part-time students. Financial award application deadline: 2/15; financial award applicants required to submit CSS PROFILE or FAFSA. In 2017, 375 master's, 56 doctorates, 40 other advanced degrees awarded. *Program availability:* Part-time, evening/weekend, 100% online, blended/hybrid learning. Offers adapted curriculum K-12 (MS Ed); adapted physical education (MS Ed); chemistry (MS Ed); clinical mental health counseling (MS Ed); coaching education (MS Ed); college counseling (MS Ed); community college leadership (PhD); community college teaching (MS); counseling (Ed S); counselor education (PhD); curriculum and instruction (MS Ed, PhD); early childhood education (MS Ed, PhD); early childhood special education (MS Ed); education (PhD); educational leadership (MS Ed, PhD, Ed S); elementary education (Postbaccalaureate Certificate); English (MS Ed); exercise science and wellness (MS Ed); general curriculum K-12 (MS Ed); higher education (MS Ed, PhD, Ed S); human movement science (PhD); human movement sciences (PhD); human resources training (PhD); instructional design and technology (PhD); instructional technology (MS Ed); library science (MS Ed); literacy leadership (PhD); park, recreation and tourism (MS); physical education (MS Ed); reading specialist (MS Ed); school counseling (MS Ed); secondary education (MS Ed); special education (PhD); speech-language pathology (MS); sport management (MS); technology education (PhD). *Application deadline:* For fall admission, 6/1 priority date for domestic and international students; for spring admission, 11/1 priority date for domestic and international students. Applications are processed on a rolling basis. *Application fee:* $50. Electronic applications accepted. *Application Contact:* William Heffelfinger, Director of Graduate Admissions, 757-683-5554, Fax: 757-683-3255, E-mail: gradadmit@odu.edu. *Dean*, Dr. Jane S. Bray, 757-683-3938, Fax: 757-683-5083, E-mail: jsbray@odu.edu.

Frank Batten College of Engineering and Technology Students: 175 full-time (37 women), 663 part-time (130 women); includes 198 minority (86 Black or African American, non-Hispanic/Latino; 1 American Indian or Alaska Native, non-Hispanic/Latino; 39 Asian, non-Hispanic/Latino; 54 Hispanic/Latino; 18 Two or more races, non-Hispanic/Latino), 172 international. Average age 32. 558 applicants, 63% accepted, 144 enrolled. *Faculty:* 93 full-time (12 women), 32 part-time/adjunct (5 women). Expenses: Contact institution. *Financial support:* In 2017–18, 168 students received support, including 8 fellowships with tuition reimbursements available (averaging $15,000 per year), 92 research assistantships with tuition reimbursements available (averaging $15,000 per year), 68 teaching assistantships with tuition reimbursements available (averaging $15,000 per year); career-related internships or fieldwork, Federal Work-Study, institutionally sponsored loans, scholarships/grants, and unspecified assistantships also available. Support available to part-time students. Financial award applicants required to submit FAFSA. In 2017, 221 master's, 33 doctorates awarded. *Program availability:* Part-time, evening/weekend, 100% online, blended/hybrid learning. Offers aerospace engineering (ME, MS, D Eng, PhD); biomedical engineering (ME, MS, PhD); civil and environmental engineering (D Eng, PhD); civil engineering (ME, MS); electrical and computer engineering (ME, MS, D Eng, PhD); engineering and technology (ME, MS, D Eng, PhD); engineering management (MEM, MS); engineering management and systems engineering (D Eng, PhD); environmental engineering (ME, MS); mechanical engineering (ME, MS, D Eng, PhD); modeling and simulation (ME, MS, D Eng, PhD); systems engineering (ME). *Application deadline:* For fall admission, 6/1 for domestic students, 2/15 priority date for international students; for spring admission, 11/1 for domestic students, 10/1 for international students. Applications are processed on a rolling basis. *Application fee:* $50. Electronic applications accepted. *Application Contact:* Dr. Rafael E. Landaeta, Associate Dean, 757-683-4478, Fax: 757-683-4898, E-mail: rlandaet@odu.edu. *Dean*, Dr. Stephanie G. Adams, 757-683-3789, Fax: 757-683-4898, E-mail: sgadams@odu.edu.

Strome College of Business Students: 111 full-time (51 women), 345 part-time (167 women); includes 125 minority (67 Black or African American, non-Hispanic/Latino; 22 Asian, non-Hispanic/Latino; 13 Hispanic/Latino; 1 Native Hawaiian or other Pacific Islander, non-Hispanic/Latino; 22 Two or more races, non-Hispanic/Latino), 71 international. Average age 34. 306 applicants, 63% accepted, 142 enrolled. *Faculty:* 80 full-time (19 women), 13 part-time/adjunct (7 women). Expenses: Contact institution. *Financial support:* In 2017–18, 94 students received support, including 4 fellowships with partial tuition reimbursements available (averaging $7,500 per year), 12 teaching assistantships with full tuition reimbursements available (averaging $15,000 per year); career-related internships or fieldwork, Federal Work-Study, scholarships/grants, tuition waivers (partial), and unspecified assistantships also available. Financial award application deadline: 2/15; financial award applicants required to submit FAFSA. In 2017, 125 master's, 11 doctorates awarded. *Program availability:* Part-time, evening/weekend, online learning. Offers accounting (MS); business (MA, MBA, MPA, MS, PhD); business administration (MBA, PhD); economics (MA); maritime trade and supply chain management (MS); multi-sector public service (MPA); public administration (MPA); public administration and policy (PhD). *Application deadline:* For fall admission, 6/1 priority date for domestic and international students; for winter admission, 11/1 priority date for domestic and international students. Applications are processed on a rolling basis. *Application fee:* $50. Electronic applications accepted. *Application Contact:* Dr. Kiran Karande, Associate Dean, 757-683-3520, Fax: 757-683-4076, E-mail: kkarande@odu.edu. *Dean*, Dr. Jeff Tanner, 757-683-3520, Fax: 757-683-4076, E-mail: jtanner@odu.edu.

OLIVET COLLEGE, Olivet, MI 49076-9701

General Information Independent-religious, coed, comprehensive institution.

GRADUATE UNITS

Master of Business Administration in Insurance Program *Program availability:* Part-time, online only, 100% online, blended/hybrid learning. Offers insurance (MBA). Electronic applications accepted.

OLIVET NAZARENE UNIVERSITY, Bourbonnais, IL 60914

General Information Independent-religious, coed, comprehensive institution. *Graduate housing:* Room and/or apartments available to single students; on-campus housing not available to married students. Housing application deadline: 8/15.

GRADUATE UNITS

Graduate School *Program availability:* Part-time, evening/weekend. Offers business administration (MBA); family nurse practitioner (MSN); nursing (MSN); practical ministries (MPM).

Division of Education *Program availability:* Evening/weekend. Offers curriculum and instruction (MAE); elementary education (MAT); library information specialist (MAE); reading specialist (MAE); school leadership (MAE); secondary education (MAT).

Division of Religion *Program availability:* Part-time. Offers biblical literature (MA); religion (MA); theology (MA).

Program in Organizational Leadership Offers organizational leadership (MOL).

OPEN UNIVERSITY, Milton Keynes MK7 6AA, United Kingdom

General Information Public, coed, comprehensive institution.

GRADUATE UNITS

Graduate Programs

ORAL ROBERTS UNIVERSITY, Tulsa, OK 74171

General Information Independent-religious, coed, comprehensive institution. *Graduate housing:* Room and/or apartments available on a first-come, first-served basis to single students; on-campus housing not available to married students. *Student services:* Campus employment opportunities, career counseling, exercise/wellness program, free psychological counseling, international student services, low-cost health insurance, services for students with disabilities, teacher training. *Library facilities:* John D. Messick Resources Center.

Computer facilities: A campuswide network can be accessed from student residence rooms and from off campus. Online class registration is available.
Website: http://www.oru.edu/

General Application Contact: Michael Thomas, 918-495-6618, E-mail: mathomas@oru.edu.

GRADUATE UNITS

School of Business 71 applicants, 94% accepted, 56 enrolled. *Faculty:* 7 full-time (0 women), 5 part-time/adjunct (4 women). Expenses: Contact institution. *Financial support:* In 2017–18, 39 students received support. Scholarships/grants and unspecified assistantships available. Financial award application deadline: 6/1. *Program availability:* Part-time, online learning. Offers accounting (MBA); entrepreneurship (MBA); finance (MBA); international business (MBA); management (MBA); marketing (MBA); not for profit management (MNM). *Application deadline:* Applications are processed on a rolling basis. *Application fee:* $35. Electronic applications accepted. *Application Contact:* Sam Park, Enrollment Counselor, 918-495-7179, E-mail: sampark@oru.edu. *Chair of the Graduate School of Business*, Dr. Marshal Wright, 918-495-6988, E-mail: mwright@oru.edu.

School of Education Students: 344 full-time (223 women); includes 117 minority (93 Black or African American, non-Hispanic/Latino; 7 American Indian or Alaska Native, non-Hispanic/Latino; 11 Asian, non-Hispanic/Latino; 6 Hispanic/Latino). 80 applicants, 94% accepted, 65 enrolled. *Faculty:* 7 full-time (2 women), 6 part-time/adjunct (2 women). Expenses: Contact institution. *Financial support:* Fellowships and scholarships/grants available. Financial award application deadline: 3/15. In 2017, 14 master's, 4 doctorates awarded. *Program availability:* Part-time, online learning. Offers Christian school administration (K-12) (MA Ed, Ed D); college and higher education administration (Ed D); curriculum and instruction (MA Ed); initial teaching with alternative licensure (MAT); initial teaching with licensure (MAT); public school administration (K-12) (MA Ed, Ed D). *Application deadline:* Applications are processed on a rolling basis. *Application fee:* $35. Electronic applications accepted. *Application Contact:* Audrey Ripley, Enrollment Counselor, 918-495-6375, E-mail: aripley@oru.edu. *Chair of Graduate School of Education*, Dr. Patrick Otto, 918-495-7087, E-mail: jotto@oru.edu.

School of Theology and Missions Students: 371 full-time (156 women), 110 part-time (65 women); includes 177 minority (127 Black or African American, non-Hispanic/Latino; 5 American Indian or Alaska Native, non-Hispanic/Latino; 20 Asian, non-Hispanic/Latino; 25 Hispanic/Latino), 82 international. Average age 36. 159 applicants, 95% accepted, 124 enrolled. *Faculty:* 17 full-time (2 women). Expenses: Contact institution. *Financial support:* Fellowships and scholarships/grants available. Financial award application deadline: 6/1. In 2017, 52 master's, 10 doctorates awarded. *Program availability:* Part-time, online learning. Offers biblical literature (MA); church ministries and leadership (D Min); clinical pastoral education (M Div); missions (MA); pastoral care and chaplaincy (M Div, D Min); practical theology (MA); professional counseling (MA); theological/historical studies (MA). *Application deadline:* Applications are processed on a rolling basis. *Application fee:* $35. Electronic applications accepted. *Application Contact:* Michael Thomas, Enrollment Counselor, 918-495-6618, E-mail: mthomas@oru.edu. *Chair*, Dr. Bill Buker, 918-495-6493, E-mail: bbuker@oru.edu.

OREGON COLLEGE OF ART AND CRAFT, Portland, OR 97225

General Information Independent, coed, comprehensive institution.

GRADUATE UNITS

MFA Program Offers craft (MFA).

OREGON COLLEGE OF ORIENTAL MEDICINE, Portland, OR 97216

General Information Independent, coed, graduate-only institution. *Graduate housing:* On-campus housing not available.

GRADUATE UNITS

Graduate Program in Acupuncture and Oriental Medicine *Program availability:* Part-time. Offers acupuncture and Oriental medicine (M Ac OM, MAcOM, DAOM).

OREGON HEALTH & SCIENCE UNIVERSITY, Portland, OR 97239-3098

General Information State-related, coed, upper-level institution. CGS member. *Graduate housing:* On-campus housing not available. *Research affiliation:* Oregon Regional Primate Research Center.

GRADUATE UNITS

School of Dentistry Offers biomaterials and biomechanics (MS); dentistry (MS, DMD, Certificate); endodontics (Certificate); oral and maxillofacial surgery (Certificate); oral molecular biology (MS); orthodontics (MS, Certificate); pediatric dentistry (Certificate); periodontology (MS, Certificate); restorative dentistry (MS). Electronic applications accepted.

School of Medicine Students: 924 full-time (516 women), 384 part-time (195 women); includes 343 minority (25 Black or African American, non-Hispanic/Latino; 8 American Indian or Alaska Native, non-Hispanic/Latino; 181 Asian, non-Hispanic/Latino; 63 Hispanic/Latino; 1 Native Hawaiian or other Pacific Islander, non-Hispanic/Latino; 65 Two or more races, non-Hispanic/Latino), 54 international. Average age 31. *Faculty:* 2,391. Expenses: Contact institution. *Financial support:* Fellowships, research assistantships, teaching assistantships, career-related internships or fieldwork, Federal Work-Study, institutionally sponsored loans, scholarships/grants, health care benefits, and full-tuition and stipends (for PhD students) available. Support available to part-time students. Financial award application deadline: 3/1; financial award applicants required to submit FAFSA. In 2017, 153 master's, 161 doctorates, 78 other advanced degrees awarded. *Program availability:* Part-time. Offers medicine (MBA, MBI, MBST, MCR, MPAS, MS, MSCNU, MD, PhD, Certificate, Graduate Certificate). *Application deadline:* Applications are processed on a rolling basis. Electronic applications accepted. *Application Contact:* Registrar's Office, 503-494-7800, E-mail: somgrad@ohsu.edu. *Dean of the School of Medicine*, Dr. Sharon Anderson, 503-494-8220, Fax: 503-494-3400.

Graduate Programs in Medicine Students: 355 full-time (206 women), 358 part-time (182 women); includes 179 minority (16 Black or African American, non-Hispanic/Latino; 5 American Indian or Alaska Native, non-Hispanic/Latino; 90 Asian, non-Hispanic/Latino; 38 Hispanic/Latino; 30 Two or more races, non-Hispanic/Latino), 54 international. Average age 33. *Faculty:* 470. Expenses: Contact institution. *Financial support:* Fellowships, research assistantships, teaching assistantships, scholarships/grants, health care benefits, and full-tuition and stipends (for PhD students) available. Financial award application deadline: 3/1; financial award applicants required to submit FAFSA. In 2017, 153 master's, 34 doctorates, 78 other advanced degrees awarded. *Program availability:* Part-time. Offers behavioral neuroscience (PhD); biochemistry and molecular biology (PhD); bioinformatics and computational biology (MS, PhD); biomedical engineering (MBI, MS, PhD); cancer biology (PhD); cell and developmental biology (PhD); clinical informatics (MBI, MS, PhD, Certificate); clinical research (MCR, Certificate); computer science and engineering (MS, PhD); dietetics (Certificate); electrical engineering (MS, PhD); environmental science and engineering (MS, PhD); health information management (Certificate); healthcare management (MBA, MS, Certificate); human nutrition (MS); medicine (MBA, MBI, MCR, MPAS, MS, MSCNU, PhD, Certificate); molecular and cellular biosciences (PhD); molecular and medical genetics (PhD); molecular microbiology and immunology (PhD); neuroscience (PhD); physician assistant studies (MPAS); physiology and pharmacology (PhD). *Application Contact:* Lorie Gookin, Admissions Coordinator, 503-494-6222, E-mail: somgrad@ohsu.edu. *Associate Dean for Graduate Studies*, Dr. Allison Fryer, 503-494-6222, E-mail: somgrad@ohsu.edu.

School of Nursing *Program availability:* Part-time, 100% online, blended/hybrid learning. Offers adult gerontology acute care nurse practitioner (MN); family nurse practitioner (MN); health systems and organizational leadership (MN); nurse anesthesia (MN); nurse midwifery (MN); nursing (MN, DNP, PhD, Post Master's Certificate); nursing education (MN, Post Master's Certificate); pediatric nurse practitioner (MN); psychiatric mental health nurse practitioner (MN). Electronic applications accepted.

OREGON INSTITUTE OF TECHNOLOGY, Klamath Falls, OR 97601-8801

General Information State-supported, coed, comprehensive institution. *Graduate housing:* Room and/or apartments available on a first-come, first-served basis to single students; on-campus housing not available to married students. Housing application deadline: 3/1.

GRADUATE UNITS

Program in Manufacturing Engineering Technology *Program availability:* Part-time, online learning. Offers manufacturing engineering technology (MS). Electronic applications accepted.

OREGON STATE UNIVERSITY, Corvallis, OR 97331

General Information State-supported, coed, university. CGS member. *Graduate housing:* Rooms and/or apartments guaranteed to single students and available on a first-come, first-served basis to married students. Typical cost: $11,505 per year ($15,465 including board) for single students. Housing application deadline: 5/1. *Student services:* Campus employment opportunities, campus safety program, career counseling, child daycare facilities, exercise/wellness program, free psychological counseling, grant writing training, international student services, low-cost health insurance, multicultural affairs office, services for students with disabilities, teacher training, writing training. *Library facilities:* Valley Library plus 2 others. *Collection:* Books: 1.7 million (physical), 481,665 (digital/electronic); Serial titles: 2,376 (physical), 74,203 (digital/electronic); Databases: 150. Weekly public service hours: 138; study areas open 24 hours, 5–7 days a week; students can reserve study rooms. *Research affiliation:* W.M. Keck Foundation (science, engineering), David and Lucille Packard Foundation (science, environmental science), William and Flora Hewlett Foundation (science, engineering), George and Betty Moore Foundation (medical research, science education), Comer Science and Educational Foundation (science).

Computer facilities: Computer purchase and lease plans are available. 2,179 computers available on campus for general student use. A campuswide network can be accessed from student residence rooms and from off campus. Online class registration is available.
Website: http://www.oregonstate.edu/

General Application Contact: Graduate School, 541-737-4881, Fax: 541-737-3313, E-mail: graduate.admissions@oregonstate.edu.

GRADUATE UNITS

College of Agricultural Sciences Expenses: Contact institution. *Program availability:* Part-time, online learning. Offers agricultural sciences (MA, MS, PSM, PhD); agroforestry (MS, PhD); animal science (MS); animal-habitat relationships (MS, PhD); applied systematics (MS); aquaculture (MS); breeding, genetics, and biotechnology (MS, PhD); brewing (MS, PhD); community and landscape horticultural systems (MS, PhD); conservation biology (MS, PhD); crop science (MS, PhD); ecology (MS, PhD); enology (MS, PhD); environmental chemistry and ecotoxicology (MS, PhD); environmental soil science (MS, PhD); fish genetics (MS, PhD); fisheries and wildlife administration (PSM); flavor chemistry (MS, PhD); food and seafood processing (MS, PhD); food chemistry/biochemistry (MS, PhD); food engineering (MS, PhD); food microbiology/biotechnology (MS, PhD); genetics (MS, PhD); genomics and computational biology (MS, PhD); ichthyology (MS, PhD); leadership and communication in agriculture (MS); limnology (MS, PhD); mechanistic toxicology (MS, PhD); molecular and cellular biology (MS, PhD); molecular and cellular toxicology (MS, PhD); mycology (MS, PhD); neurotoxicology (MS, PhD); parasites and diseases (MS, PhD); physiology and ecology of marine and freshwater fishes (MS, PhD); plant pathology (MS, PhD); plant physiology (MS, PhD); poultry science (MS); public health economics (MA, MS, PhD); sensory evaluation (MS, PhD); stream ecology (MS, PhD); sustainable crop production (MS, PhD); toxicology (MS, PhD); water pollution biology (MS, PhD). *Application fee:* $75 ($85 for international students). *Application Contact:* Dr. Daniel J. Arp, Dean/Director, 541-737-2331. *Dean/Director*, Dr. Daniel J. Arp, 541-737-2331.

College of Business Expenses: Contact institution. *Program availability:* Part-time, blended/hybrid learning. Offers business (MBA, PhD); business administration (PhD); corporate finance (MBA). *Application fee:* $75 ($85 for international students). *Application Contact:* Dr. Jim Coakley, Associate Dean for Academic Programs, 541-737-5510, E-mail: jim.coakley@bus.oregonstate.edu. *Dean,* Dr. Mitzi Montoya, 541-737-6024, E-mail: mitzi.montoya@oregonstate.edu.

College of Earth, Ocean, and Atmospheric Sciences Expenses: Contact institution. *Financial support:* Application deadline: 1/5. Offers atmospheric sciences (MA, MS, PhD); earth, ocean, and atmospheric sciences (MA, MS, PhD); geochemistry (MA, MS, PhD); geographic information science (MA, MS, PhD); geomorphology (MA, MS, PhD); geophysics (MA, MS, PhD); glacial geology (MA, MS, PhD); hydrology and hydrogeology (MA, MS, PhD); igneous petrology (MA, MS, PhD); marine resource management (MS); neotonics (MA, MS, PhD); oceanography (MA, MS, PhD); paleoclimatology (MA); physical geography (MA, MS, PhD); resource geography (MA, MS, PhD); structural geology (MA, MS, PhD). *Application deadline:* For fall admission, 1/5 for domestic students. *Application fee:* $75 ($85 for international students). *Application Contact:* Robert Allan, Director of Graduate Student Services and Development, 541-737-1340, E-mail: rallan@coas.oregonstate.edu. *Dean,* Dr. Roberta Marinelli, 541-737-5195, E-mail: roberta.marinelli@oregonstate.edu.

College of Education Expenses: Contact institution. *Program availability:* Part-time, 100% online, blended/hybrid learning. Offers adult and higher education (Ed M, Ed D, PhD); agricultural education (PhD); clinical mental health counseling (M Coun); clinically based elementary education (MAT); counseling (PhD); education (Ed M, M Coun, MAT, MS, Ed D, PhD); elementary education (MAT); language arts (MAT); language equity and education policy (PhD); mathematics (MAT); mathematics education (MS); music education (MAT); school counseling (M Coun); science (MAT); science education (MS); science/mathematics education (PhD); social studies (MAT). *Application fee:* $75 ($85 for international students). *Application Contact:* Toni Doolen, Dean, 541-737-5974. *Dean,* Toni Doolen, 541-737-5974.

College of Engineering Expenses: Contact institution. *Program availability:* Part-time, 100% online. Offers advanced manufacturing (M Eng, MS, PhD); algorithms and cryptography (M Eng, MS, PhD); application of nuclear techniques (M Eng, MHP, MS, PhD); bio-based products and fuels (M Eng, MS, PhD); biological systems analysis (M Eng, MS, PhD); biomaterials (M Eng, MS, PhD); biomedical devices and instrumentation (M Eng, MS, PhD); bioprocessing (M Eng, MS, PhD); bioremediation (M Eng, MS, PhD); chemical engineering (MS, PhD); chemistry (MS, PhD); civil engineering (M Eng, MS, PhD); coastal and ocean engineering (M Eng, MS, PhD); construction engineering management (M Eng, MS, PhD); ecosystems analysis and modeling (M Eng, MS, PhD); electrical and computer engineering (M Eng, MS, PhD); engineering (M Eng, MHP, MMP, MS, PhD); engineering education (M Eng, MS, PhD); engineering management (M Eng); forest products (MS, PhD); geomatics (M Eng, MS, PhD); geotechnical engineering (M Eng, MS, PhD); human performance engineering (M Eng, MS, PhD); human systems engineering (M Eng, MS, PhD); information systems engineering (M Eng, MS, PhD); infrastructure materials (M Eng, MS, PhD); manufacturing systems engineering (M Eng, MS, PhD); mathematics (MS, PhD); mechanical engineering (MS, PhD); medical health physics (MMP, MS); medical imaging (M Eng, MS, PhD); nuclear engineering (MS); physics (MS, PhD); robotics (M Eng, MS, PhD); structural engineering (M Eng, MS, PhD); systems and computational biology (M Eng, MS, PhD); therapeutic radiologic physics (PhD); transportation engineering (M Eng); water quality (M Eng, MS, PhD); water resources (M Eng, MS, PhD). *Application fee:* $75 ($85 for international students). *Application Contact:* Dr. Dorthe Wildenschild, Associate Dean for Graduate Programs, 541-737-8050, E-mail: info@engr.oregonstate.edu. *Dean,* Scott Ashford, 541-737-5232, E-mail: scott.ashford@oregonstate.edu.

College of Forestry Expenses: Contact institution. *Program availability:* Part-time, 100% online. Offers biodeterioration and materials protection (MS, PhD); engineering for sustainable forestry (MF, MS, PhD); fisheries management (MNR); forest biology (MF); forest, wildlife and landscape ecology (MS, PhD); forestry (MF, MNR, MS, PhD); forests and climate change (MNR); genetics and physiology (MS, PhD); geographic information science (MNR); integrated social and ecological systems (MS, PhD); science of conservation, restoration and sustainable management (MS, PhD); silviculture (MF); social science, policy, and natural resources (MS, PhD); soil-plant-atmosphere continuum (MS, PhD); sustainable natural resources (MNR); sustainable recreation and tourism (MS); urban forestry (MNR); water conflict management and transformation (MNR); wildlife management (MNR). *Application fee:* $75 ($85 for international students). *Application Contact:* Helene Serewis, College of Forestry Graduate Programs Manager, 541-737-1156, E-mail: forestry.gradprograms@oregonstate.edu. *Dean,* Anthony S. Davis, 541-737-1585, E-mail: anthony.davis@oregonstate.edu.

College of Liberal Arts Expenses: Contact institution. *Program availability:* Part-time. Offers applied anthropology (MA); applied cognition (MS, PhD); biomedical ethics (MA); college student services administration (Ed M, MS); contemporary Hispanic studies (MA); development of the physical, biological, and environmental sciences (MA, MS, PhD); energy policy (MPP, PhD); engineering psychology (MS, PhD); environmental action (MA); environmental policy (MPP, PhD); feminist leadership (PhD); fiction (MFA); film and visual studies (MA); health psychology (MS, PhD); international policy (MPP, PhD); law, crime and policy (MPP, PhD); liberal arts (Ed M, MA, MFA, MPP, MS, PhD); literature and culture (MA); rhetoric, writing and composition (MA); rural policy (MPP, PhD); science and technology policy (MPP, PhD); social policy (MPP, PhD). *Application fee:* $60. *Application Contact:* Dr. Larry Rodgers, Dean, 541-737-4581. *Dean,* Dr. Larry Rodgers, 541-737-4581.

College of Pharmacy Expenses: Contact institution. Offers biopharmaceutics (MS, PhD); pharmacy (MS, PhD, Pharm D). *Application Contact:* Angela Austin Haney, Director of Student Services/Head Advisor, 541-737-5784, E-mail: angela.austinhaney@oregonstate.edu. *Dean,* Dr. Mark Zabriskie, 541-737-5781.

College of Public Health and Human Sciences Expenses: Contact institution. Offers athletic training (MATRN); biophysical kinesiology (MS, PhD); biostatistics (MPH); environmental and occupational health (MPH, PhD); epidemiology (MPH, PhD); global health (MPH, PhD); human development and family studies (MS, PhD); nutrition (MS, PhD); psychosocial kinesiology (MS, PhD); public health and human sciences (MATRN, MPH, MS, PhD). Electronic applications accepted. *Application Contact:* Suzanna Chase, Manager of Admissions, Applications and Recruitment of Graduate Students, E-mail: suzanna.chase@oregonstate.edu. *Dean and Professor,* Dr. F. Javier Nieto, 541-737-3256.

College of Science Expenses: Contact institution. *Program availability:* Part-time. Offers analytical chemistry (MA, MS, PhD); atomic physics (MA, MS, PhD); behavioral ecology (MS, PhD); biochemistry and biophysics (MA, MS, PhD); computational physics (MA, MS, PhD); data analytics (MS); differential geometry (MA, MS, PhD); environmental microbiology (MA, MS, PhD); experimental physics (MA, MS, PhD); financial and actuarial mathematics (MA, MS, PhD); food microbiology (MA, MS, PhD); genomics (MA, MS, PhD); immunology (MA, MS, PhD); mathematical biology (MA, MS, PhD); mathematics education (MS, PhD); microbial ecology (MA, MS, PhD); microbial evolution (MA, MS, PhD); nuclear and particle physics (MA, MS, PhD); number theory (MA, MS, PhD); numerical analysis (MA, MS, PhD); optical physics (MA, MS, PhD); parasitology (MA, MS, PhD); pathogenic microbiology (MA, MS, PhD); probability (MA); science (MA, MS, PhD); solid state physics (MA, MS, PhD); statistics (MA, MS, PhD); virology (MA). *Application fee:* $75 ($85 for international students). *Application Contact:* Roy Haggerty, Dean, 541-737-3886, E-mail: roy.haggerty@oregonstate.edu. *Dean,* Roy Haggerty, 541-737-3886, E-mail: roy.haggerty@oregonstate.edu.

College of Veterinary Medicine Expenses: Contact institution. Offers veterinary medicine (DVM). DVM admissions open only to residents of Oregon and other states participating in the Western Interstate Commission for Higher Education. *Application deadline:* For fall admission, 9/15 for domestic and international students. *Application Contact:* Admissions, 541-737-2098, E-mail: cvmproginfo@oregonstate.edu. *Dean,* Dr. Susan J. Tornquist, 541-737-6943, Fax: 541-737-4245, E-mail: vetmed@oregonstate.edu.

Interdisciplinary/Institutional Programs Expenses: Contact institution. *Program availability:* Part-time. Offers biogeochemistry (MA, MS, PSM, PhD); bioinformatics (PhD); biomedical sciences (MS, PhD); biotechnology (PhD); ecology (MA, MS, PSM, PhD); environmental education (MA, MS, PhD); genome biology (PhD); interdisciplinary studies (MAIS); molecular virology (PhD); plant molecular biology (PhD); quantitative analysis (PSM); social science (MA, MS, PSM, PhD); water resources (MA, MS, PhD); water resources engineering (MS, PhD); water resources policy and management (MS); water resources science (MS, PhD). *Application fee:* $75 ($85 for international students). *Application Contact:* Dr. Jennifer Brown, Vice Provost/Dean. *Vice Provost/Dean,* Dr. Jennifer Brown.

OREGON STATE UNIVERSITY–CASCADES, Bend, OR 97701

General Information State-supported, coed, comprehensive institution.

GRADUATE UNITS

Program in Counseling Offers community counseling (MS); school counseling (MS).

Program in Education Offers education (MAT).

OTIS COLLEGE OF ART AND DESIGN, Los Angeles, CA 90045-9785

General Information Independent, coed, comprehensive institution. *Graduate housing:* On-campus housing not available.

GRADUATE UNITS

Program in Fine Arts Offers new genres (MFA); painting (MFA); photography (MFA); sculpture (MFA). Electronic applications accepted.

Program in Graphic Design Offers graphic design (MFA). Electronic applications accepted.

Program in Public Practice Offers public practice (MFA). Electronic applications accepted.

Program in Writing Offers writing (MFA). Electronic applications accepted.

OTTAWA UNIVERSITY, Ottawa, KS 66067-3399

General Information Independent-religious, coed, comprehensive institution. *Graduate housing:* On-campus housing not available.

GRADUATE UNITS

Graduate Studies-Arizona *Program availability:* Part-time, evening/weekend, online learning. Offers business administration (MBA); Christian counseling (MA); community college counseling (MA); curriculum and instruction (MA); early childhood (MA); education intervention (MA); education leadership (MA); education technology (MA); expressive arts therapy (MA); finance (MBA); human resources (MA, MBA); leadership (MBA); marketing (MBA); marriage and family therapy (MA); Montessori early childhood education (MA); Montessori elementary education (MA); professional development (MA); school guidance counseling (MA); special education - cross categorical (MA); treatment of trauma, abuse and deprivation (MA). Electronic applications accepted.

Graduate Studies-International *Program availability:* Online learning. Offers business administration (MBA). Electronic applications accepted.

Graduate Studies-Kansas City *Program availability:* Part-time, evening/weekend, online learning. Offers business administration (MBA); human resources (MA). Electronic applications accepted.

Graduate Studies-Wisconsin *Program availability:* Part-time, evening/weekend, online learning. Offers business administration (MBA). Electronic applications accepted.

OTTERBEIN UNIVERSITY, Westerville, OH 43081

General Information Independent-religious, coed, comprehensive institution. CGS member. *Graduate housing:* On-campus housing not available.

GRADUATE UNITS

Department of Business, Accounting and Economics *Program availability:* Part-time, evening/weekend. Offers business, accounting and economics (MBA).

Department of Education Offers education (MAE, MAT).

Department of Nursing *Program availability:* Part-time, evening/weekend, online learning. Offers advanced practice nurse educator (Certificate); clinical nurse leader (MSN); family nurse practitioner (MSN, Certificate); nurse anesthesia (MSN, Certificate); nursing (DNP); nursing service administration (MSN).

OUR LADY OF THE LAKE UNIVERSITY, San Antonio, TX 78207-4689

General Information Independent-religious, coed, comprehensive institution. *Enrollment:* 3,212 graduate, professional, and undergraduate students; 1,622 full-time matriculated graduate/professional students (1,292 women), 248 part-time matriculated graduate/professional students (216 women). *Enrollment by degree level:* 1,545 master's, 325 doctoral. *Graduate faculty:* 25 full-time (6 women), 151 part-time/adjunct (41 women). *Tuition:* Full-time $10,668; part-time $5334 per year. *Required fees:* $816; $816 per year. $408 per semester. *Graduate housing:* Room and/or apartments available on a first-come, first-served basis to single students; on-campus housing not available to married students. Typical cost: $4500 per year ($8289 including board). Room and board charges vary according to board plan and housing facility selected. Housing application deadline: 7/15. *Student services:* Campus employment opportunities, campus safety program, career counseling, exercise/wellness program, free psychological counseling, international student services, low-cost health insurance, services for students with disabilities, teacher training. *Library facilities:* The Sueltenfuss Library. *Collection:* Books: 82,924 (physical), 51,160 (digital/electronic); Serial titles: 16,651 (physical), 167,665 (digital/electronic); Databases: 96. Weekly public service hours: 95; study areas open 24 hours, 5–7 days a week. *Research affiliation:* Texas Higher Education Coordinating Board (teacher quality, education), Texas Regional Collaborative (education).

Computer facilities: 236 computers available on campus for general student use. A campuswide network can be accessed from student residence rooms and from off campus. Online class registration is available.
Website: http://www.ollusa.edu/

General Application Contact: Graduate Admissions Office, 210-431-3995, Fax: 210-431-3945, E-mail: gradadm@ollusa.edu.

GRADUATE UNITS

College of Arts and Sciences Students: 15 full-time (12 women), 7 part-time (all women); includes 17 minority (1 Black or African American, non-Hispanic/Latino; 16 Hispanic/Latino). Average age 33. 7 applicants, 100% accepted, 5 enrolled. *Faculty:* 2 part-time/adjunct (1 woman). Expenses: Contact institution. *Financial support:* Federal Work-Study, scholarships/grants, unspecified assistantships, and tuition discounts available. Support available to part-time students. Financial award application deadline: 5/1; financial award applicants required to submit FAFSA. In 2017, 2 master's awarded. *Program availability:* Part-time, evening/weekend. Offers arts and sciences (MA); literature, creative writing, and social justice (MA). *Application deadline:* For fall admission, 7/15 for domestic and international students; for spring admission, 11/15 for domestic and international students; for summer admission, 2/15 for domestic and international students. *Application fee:* $40 ($50 for international students). Electronic applications accepted. *Application Contact:* Graduate Admission, 210-431-3995, Fax: 210-431-3945, E-mail: gradadm@lake.ollusa.edu. *Interim Dean for the College of Arts and Science,* Dr. Rosa Rivera-Hainaj, 210-431-6564, E-mail: rhainaj@lake.ollusa.edu.

College of Professional Studies Students: 295 full-time (269 women), 59 part-time (50 women); includes 205 minority (29 Black or African American, non-Hispanic/Latino; 8 American Indian or Alaska Native, non-Hispanic/Latino; 1 Asian, non-Hispanic/Latino; 167 Hispanic/Latino), 1 international. Average age 31. 264 applicants, 44% accepted, 74 enrolled. *Faculty:* 11 full-time (10 women), 11 part-time/adjunct (5 women). Expenses: Contact institution. *Financial support:* In 2017–18, 111 students received support. Research assistantships, teaching assistantships, Federal Work-Study, scholarships/grants, unspecified assistantships, and tuition discounts available. Support available to part-time students. Financial award application deadline: 5/1; financial award applicants required to submit FAFSA. In 2017, 79 master's, 6 doctorates awarded. *Program availability:* Part-time, evening/weekend, 100% online, blended/hybrid learning. Offers communication and learning disorders (MA); counseling psychology (Psy D); integrated science teaching (M Ed); marriage and family therapy (MS); school counseling (M Ed); school psychology (MS); sociology (MA). *Application fee:* $40 ($50 for international students). Electronic applications accepted. *Application Contact:* Graduate Admissions, 210-431-3995 Ext. 2314, Fax: 210-431-3945, E-mail: gradadm@lake.ollusa.edu. *Dean,* Dr. Mo Cuevas, 210-431-6516, E-mail: mccuevas@ollusa.edu.

School of Business and Leadership Students: 569 full-time (337 women), 49 part-time (34 women); includes 437 minority (55 Black or African American, non-Hispanic/Latino; 382 Hispanic/Latino). Average age 39. 231 applicants, 87% accepted, 137 enrolled. *Faculty:* 15 full-time (all women), 42 part-time/adjunct (10 women). Expenses: Contact institution. *Financial support:* In 2017–18, 128 students received support. Teaching assistantships, Federal Work-Study, unspecified assistantships, and tuition discounts available. Support available to part-time students. Financial award application deadline: 5/1; financial award applicants required to submit FAFSA. In 2017, 144 master's, 39 doctorates awarded. *Program availability:* Part-time, evening/weekend, 100% online, blended/hybrid learning. Offers accounting (MS); finance (MBA); healthcare management (MBA); information systems and security (MS); leadership studies (PhD); management (MBA); nonprofit management (MS); organizational leadership (MS). *Application fee:* $40 ($50 for international students). Electronic applications accepted. *Associate Dean,* Kathryn Winney, 210-434-6711 Ext. 7051, E-mail: kmwinney@ollusa.edu.

Worden School of Social Service Students: 775 full-time (702 women), 131 part-time (122 women); includes 557 minority (274 Black or African American, non-Hispanic/Latino; 283 Hispanic/Latino). Average age 35. 296 applicants, 90% accepted, 188 enrolled. *Faculty:* 3 full-time (all women), 92 part-time/adjunct (77 women). Expenses: Contact institution. *Financial support:* In 2017–18, 35 students received support, including 1 research assistantship (averaging $15,300 per year); teaching assistantships, Federal Work-Study, scholarships/grants, unspecified assistantships, and tuition discounts also available. Support available to part-time students. Financial award application deadline: 5/1; financial award applicants required to submit FAFSA. In 2017, 339 master's awarded. *Program availability:* Part-time, evening/weekend, 100% online, blended/hybrid learning. Offers social work (MSW). *Application deadline:* For fall admission, 6/15 for domestic and international students; for spring admission, 11/15 for domestic and international students; for summer admission, 4/15 for domestic and international students. Applications are processed on a rolling basis. *Application fee:* $40 ($50 for international students). Electronic applications accepted. *Application Contact:* Office of Graduate Admissions, 210-431-3995, Fax: 210-431-3945, E-mail: gradadm@lake.ollusa.edu. *Program Director,* Rebecca Gomez, 210-434-6711 Ext. 5578, E-mail: rjgomez@ollusa.edu.

OXFORD GRADUATE SCHOOL, Dayton, TN 37321-6736

General Information Independent-religious, coed, graduate-only institution. *Graduate housing:* Rooms and/or apartments guaranteed to single students and available on a first-come, first-served basis to married students.

GRADUATE UNITS

Graduate Programs Offers family life education (M Litt); integration of religion and society (D Phil); organizational leadership (M Litt).

PACE UNIVERSITY, New York, NY 10038

General Information Independent, coed, university. *Enrollment:* 9,234 graduate, professional, and undergraduate students; 2,348 full-time matriculated graduate/professional students (1,304 women), 1,925 part-time matriculated graduate/professional students (1,262 women). *Enrollment by degree level:* 3,254 master's, 910 doctoral, 69 other advanced degrees. *Graduate housing:* Room and/or apartments available on a first-come, first-served basis to single students; on-campus housing not available to married students. *Student services:* Campus employment opportunities, career counseling, free psychological counseling, grant writing training, international student services, low-cost health insurance, multicultural affairs office, services for students with disabilities, teacher training, writing training. *Library facilities:* Henry Birnbaum Library. *Collection:* Books: 382,858 (physical), 224,418 (digital/electronic); Serial titles: 73 (physical), 576,860 (digital/electronic); Databases: 172. Weekly public service hours: 93; students can reserve study rooms.

Computer facilities: 209 computers available on campus for general student use. A campuswide network can be accessed. Online class registration, administrative functions (tuition, student records, financial aid, health insurance waiver) are available.
Website: http://www.pace.edu/nyc

General Application Contact: Susan Ford-Goldschein, Director of Graduate Admissions, 212-346-1531, Fax: 212-346-1585, E-mail: graduateadmission@pace.edu.

GRADUATE UNITS

College of Health Professions Students: 190 full-time (155 women), 706 part-time (614 women); includes 385 minority (153 Black or African American, non-Hispanic/Latino; 2 American Indian or Alaska Native, non-Hispanic/Latino; 144 Asian, non-Hispanic/Latino; 69 Hispanic/Latino; 17 Two or more races, non-Hispanic/Latino), 1 international. Average age 32. 1,817 applicants, 22% accepted, 245 enrolled. *Faculty:* 22 full-time (20 women), 31 part-time/adjunct (27 women). Expenses: Contact institution. *Financial support:* Research assistantships, teaching assistantships, career-related internships or fieldwork, institutionally sponsored loans, scholarships/grants, and unspecified assistantships available. Financial award application deadline: 2/15; financial award applicants required to submit FAFSA. In 2017, 847 master's, 45 doctorates, 27 other advanced degrees awarded. *Program availability:* Part-time. Offers health professions (MS, DNP, PhD, CAGS); physician assistant studies (MS). *Application deadline:* For fall admission, 3/1 for domestic students; for spring admission, 9/1 for domestic students. Applications are processed on a rolling basis. *Application fee:* $70. Electronic applications accepted. *Application Contact:* Susan Ford-Goldschein, Dean of Graduate Admissions, 212-346-1531, Fax: 212-346-1585, E-mail: graduateadmission@pace.edu. *Dean, College of Health Professions,* Dr. Harriet R. Feldman, 914-773-3341, Fax: 914-773-3341, E-mail: hfeldman@pace.edu.

Lienhard School of Nursing Students: 11 full-time (all women), 515 part-time (459 women); includes 277 minority (145 Black or African American, non-Hispanic/Latino; 1 American Indian or Alaska Native, non-Hispanic/Latino; 88 Asian, non-Hispanic/Latino; 34 Hispanic/Latino; 9 Two or more races, non-Hispanic/Latino), 1 international. Average age 35. 289 applicants, 74% accepted, 138 enrolled. *Faculty:* 11 full-time (10 women), 31 part-time/adjunct (27 women). Expenses: Contact institution. *Financial support:* Research assistantships, teaching assistantships, career-related internships or fieldwork, Federal Work-Study, institutionally sponsored loans, tuition waivers (partial), and unspecified assistantships available. Support available to part-time students. Financial award application deadline: 2/15; financial award applicants required to submit FAFSA. In 2017, 483 master's, 45 doctorates, 27 other advanced degrees awarded. *Program availability:* Part-time. Offers adult acute care nurse practitioner (MS, CAGS); family nurse practitioner (MS, CAGS); nursing (DNP, PhD); professional nursing leadership (MS, CAGS). *Application deadline:* For fall admission, 3/1 for domestic and international students. Applications are processed on a rolling basis. *Application fee:* $70. Electronic applications accepted. *Application Contact:* Susan Ford-Goldschein, Director of Graduate Admissions, 212-346-1531, Fax: 212-346-1585, E-mail: graduateadmission@pace.edu. *Dean, College of Health Professions,* Dr. Harriet R. Feldman, 914-773-3341, E-mail: hfeldman@pace.edu.

Dyson College of Arts and Sciences Students: 420 full-time (302 women), 262 part-time (200 women); includes 272 minority (106 Black or African American, non-Hispanic/Latino; 1 American Indian or Alaska Native, non-Hispanic/Latino; 44 Asian, non-Hispanic/Latino; 95 Hispanic/Latino; 1 Native Hawaiian or other Pacific Islander, non-Hispanic/Latino; 25 Two or more races, non-Hispanic/Latino), 57 international. Average age 28. Expenses: Contact institution. *Financial support:* In 2017–18, 34 research assistantships with partial tuition reimbursements (averaging $2,918 per year) were awarded; teaching assistantships, career-related internships or fieldwork, Federal Work-Study, scholarships/grants, and tuition waivers (partial) also available. Support available to part-time students. Financial award application deadline: 2/15; financial award applicants required to submit FAFSA. In 2017, 238 master's, 23 doctorates, 3 other advanced degrees awarded. *Program availability:* Part-time, evening/weekend, 100% online, blended/hybrid learning. Offers acting (MFA); arts and sciences (MA, MFA, MPA, MS, MS Ed, PhD, Psy D, Certificate); biochemistry and molecular biology (MS); book publishing (Certificate); business side of publishing (Certificate); digital publishing (Certificate); directing (MFA); environmental science (MS); forensic science (MS); government management (MPA); grief and loss (MS); health care administration (MPA); magazine publishing (Certificate); management for public safety and homeland security professionals (MA); media and communication arts (MA); mental health counseling (MS, PhD); not-for-profit management (MPA); playwriting (MFA); psychology (MA, MS, MS Ed, PhD, Psy D); publishing (MS); school psychology (MS Ed); school-clinical child psychology (MS Ed, Psy D); substance abuse (MS). *Application deadline:* For fall admission, 8/1 for domestic students, 6/1 for international students; for spring admission, 12/1 for domestic students, 10/1 for international students. Applications are processed on a rolling basis. *Application fee:* $70. Electronic applications accepted. *Application Contact:* Susan Ford-Goldschein, Director of Admissions, 212-346-1531, Fax: 212-346-1585, E-mail: graduateadmission@pace.edu. *Dean,* Dr. Nira Herrmann, 212-346-1517, Fax: 212-346-1725, E-mail: nherrmann@pace.edu.

Elisabeth Haub School of Law Students: 548 (301 women); includes 154 minority (31 Black or African American, non-Hispanic/Latino; 3 American Indian or Alaska Native, non-Hispanic/Latino; 20 Asian, non-Hispanic/Latino; 54 Hispanic/Latino; 1 Native Hawaiian or other Pacific Islander, non-Hispanic/Latino; 45 Two or more races, non-Hispanic/Latino), 9 international. Average age 26. 1,443 applicants, 53% accepted, 217 enrolled. *Faculty:* 26 full-time (11 women), 52 part-time/adjunct (19 women). Expenses: Contact institution. *Financial support:* In 2017–18, 473 students received support. Fellowships, research assistantships, career-related internships or fieldwork, Federal Work-Study, institutionally sponsored loans, scholarships/grants, and unspecified assistantships available. Support available to part-time students. Financial award application deadline: 2/1; financial award applicants required to submit FAFSA. In 2017, 20 master's, 170 doctorates awarded. *Program availability:* Part-time. Offers comparative legal studies (LL M); environmental law (LL M, SJD); law (JD). JD/MA offered jointly with Sarah Lawrence College; JD/MEM offered jointly with Yale University School of Forestry and Environmental Studies. *Application deadline:* For fall admission, 6/1 priority date for domestic students; for winter admission, 11/15 priority date for domestic students. Applications are processed on a rolling basis. *Application fee:* $65. Electronic applications accepted. *Application Contact:* Cathy Alexander, Assistant Dean, 914-422-4210, Fax: 914-989-8714, E-mail: calexander@law.pace.edu. *Dean,* David Yassky, 914-422-4407, E-mail: dyassky@law.pace.edu.

Lubin School of Business Students: 465 full-time (257 women), 351 part-time (181 women); includes 193 minority (50 Black or African American, non-Hispanic/Latino; 1 American Indian or Alaska Native, non-Hispanic/Latino; 80 Asian, non-Hispanic/Latino; 52 Hispanic/Latino; 1 Native Hawaiian or other Pacific Islander, non-Hispanic/Latino; 9 Two or more races, non-Hispanic/Latino), 368 international. Average age 30. 950 applicants, 63% accepted, 222 enrolled. Expenses: Contact institution. *Financial support:* Research assistantships, career-related internships or fieldwork, Federal Work-Study, tuition waivers (full and partial), and unspecified assistantships available. Support available to part-time students. Financial award application deadline: 2/15; financial award applicants required to submit FAFSA. In 2017, 363 master's, 4 doctorates awarded. *Program availability:* Part-time, evening/weekend, blended/hybrid learning. Offers analytics and customer intelligence (MS); business (MBA, MS, DPS,

APC); business economics (APC); e-business (APC); entrepreneurial studies (MBA); entrepreneurship (MS); finance (DPS); financial management (MBA, MS, APC); financial risk management (MS); human resource management (MBA, MS); information systems (MBA); international business (MBA); international economics (APC); international finance (MBA); investment management (MBA, MS, APC); management (DPS); marketing (DPS, APC); marketing management (MBA); public accounting (MBA, MS, APC); social media and mobile marketing (MS); strategic management (MBA, MS); taxation (MBA, MS). *Application deadline:* For fall admission, 8/1 priority date for domestic students, 6/1 for international students; for spring admission, 12/1 priority date for domestic students, 10/1 for international students; for summer admission, 5/1 priority date for domestic students, 3/1 for international students. Applications are processed on a rolling basis. *Application fee:* $70. Electronic applications accepted. *Application Contact:* Susan Ford-Goldschein, Director of Graduate Admissions, 212-346-1531, Fax: 212-346-1585, E-mail: graduateadmission@pace.edu. *Dean, Lubin School of Business,* Neil S. Braun, 212-618-6600, Fax: 212-618-6603, E-mail: nbraun@pace.edu.

School of Education Students: 91 full-time (76 women), 548 part-time (401 women); includes 247 minority (112 Black or African American, non-Hispanic/Latino; 2 American Indian or Alaska Native, non-Hispanic/Latino; 31 Asian, non-Hispanic/Latino; 93 Hispanic/Latino; 1 Native Hawaiian or other Pacific Islander, non-Hispanic/Latino; 8 Two or more races, non-Hispanic/Latino), 6 international. Average age 30. 188 applicants, 86% accepted, 114 enrolled. *Faculty:* 19 full-time (13 women), 86 part-time/adjunct (49 women). Expenses: Contact institution. *Financial support:* In 2017–18, 17 students received support, including 17 research assistantships with partial tuition reimbursements available (averaging $6,020 per year); career-related internships or fieldwork, Federal Work-Study, scholarships/grants, and unspecified assistantships also available. Financial award application deadline: 9/1; financial award applicants required to submit FAFSA. In 2017, 213 master's, 8 other advanced degrees awarded. *Program availability:* Part-time, evening/weekend, 100% online, blended/hybrid learning. Offers adolescent education (MST); childhood education (MST); early childhood development, learning and intervention (MST); educational technology studies (MS); inclusive adolescent education (MST); integrated instruction for educational technology (Certificate); integrated instruction for literacy and technology (Certificate); literacy (MS Ed); special education (MS Ed). *Application deadline:* For fall admission, 8/1 priority date for domestic students, 6/1 for international students; for spring admission, 12/1 priority date for domestic students, 10/1 for international students. Applications are processed on a rolling basis. *Application fee:* $70. Electronic applications accepted. *Application Contact:* Susan Ford-Goldschein, Director of Graduate Admissions, 212-346-1531, Fax: 212-346-1585, E-mail: graduateadmission@pace.edu. *Dean, School of Education,* Dr. Xiao-Lei Wang, 914-773-3876, E-mail: xwang@pace.edu.

Seidenberg School of Computer Science and Information Systems Students: 569 full-time (203 women), 319 part-time (95 women); includes 186 minority (73 Black or African American, non-Hispanic/Latino; 3 American Indian or Alaska Native, non-Hispanic/Latino; 56 Asian, non-Hispanic/Latino; 43 Hispanic/Latino; 11 Two or more races, non-Hispanic/Latino), 541 international. Average age 30. 871 applicants, 90% accepted, 272 enrolled. *Faculty:* 26 full-time (7 women), 7 part-time/adjunct (2 women). Expenses: Contact institution. *Financial support:* In 2017–18, 45 students received support. Research assistantships, career-related internships or fieldwork, scholarships/grants, and unspecified assistantships available. Support available to part-time students. Financial award application deadline: 2/15; financial award applicants required to submit FAFSA. In 2017, 311 master's, 10 doctorates, 2 other advanced degrees awarded. *Program availability:* Part-time, evening/weekend, online only, 100% online, blended/hybrid learning. Offers chief information security officer (APC); computer science (MS, PhD); enterprise analytics (MS); information and communication technology strategy and innovation (APC); information systems (MS, APC); Internet technology (MS); professional studies in computing (DPS); secure software and information engineering (APC); security and information assurance (Certificate); software development and engineering (MS, Certificate); telecommunications systems and networks (MS, Certificate). *Application deadline:* For fall admission, 8/1 priority date for domestic students, 6/1 for international students; for spring admission, 12/1 for domestic students, 10/1 for international students. Applications are processed on a rolling basis. *Application fee:* $70. Electronic applications accepted. *Application Contact:* Susan Ford-Goldschein, Director of Graduate Admissions, 914-422-4283, Fax: 212-346-1585, E-mail: graduateadmission@pace.edu. *Dean, Seidenberg School of Computer Science and Information Systems,* Dr. Jonathan Hill, 212-346-1864, E-mail: jhill@pace.edu.

PACIFICA GRADUATE INSTITUTE, Carpinteria, CA 93013

General Information Proprietary, coed, graduate-only institution. *Graduate housing:* Rooms and/or apartments guaranteed to single and married students. Housing application deadline: 8/15. *Research affiliation:* Elton B. Stevens Company (EBSCO) (journal management), American Psychological Association (psychology), North California Consortium of Psychology Libraries (psychology).

GRADUATE UNITS

Graduate Programs Offers clinical psychology (PhD); counseling psychology (MA); depth psychology (MA, PhD); mythological studies (MA, PhD).

PACIFIC COLLEGE OF ORIENTAL MEDICINE, San Diego, CA 92108

General Information Proprietary, coed, graduate-only institution. *Graduate housing:* On-campus housing not available. *Research affiliation:* National Institutes of Health (complimentary and alternative medicine).

GRADUATE UNITS

Graduate Program *Program availability:* Part-time, evening/weekend. Offers Oriental medicine (MSTOM, DAOM).

PACIFIC COLLEGE OF ORIENTAL MEDICINE–CHICAGO, Chicago, IL 60601

General Information Proprietary, coed, graduate-only institution. *Graduate housing:* On-campus housing not available. *Research affiliation:* Children's Memorial Hospital of Chicago (pediatric research).

GRADUATE UNITS

Graduate Program *Program availability:* Part-time, evening/weekend. Offers oriental medicine (MTOM).

PACIFIC COLLEGE OF ORIENTAL MEDICINE-NEW YORK, New York, NY 10010

General Information Proprietary, coed, graduate-only institution. *Graduate housing:* On-campus housing not available.

GRADUATE UNITS

Graduate Program *Program availability:* Part-time, evening/weekend. Offers Oriental medicine (MSTOM).

PACIFIC LUTHERAN UNIVERSITY, Tacoma, WA 98447

General Information Independent-religious, coed, comprehensive institution. *Graduate housing:* Rooms and/or apartments available on a first-come, first-served basis to single and married students. Housing application deadline: 5/1.

GRADUATE UNITS

Division of Humanities *Program availability:* Part-time, blended/hybrid learning. Offers creative writing (MFA). Electronic applications accepted.

Division of Social Sciences Offers marriage and family therapy (MA). Electronic applications accepted.

School of Business *Program availability:* Part-time, evening/weekend. Offers accounting (MSA); business (MBA, MS, MSA, MSF); business administration (MBA); finance (MSF); market research (MS). Electronic applications accepted.

School of Education and Kinesiology *Program availability:* Part-time, evening/weekend. Offers education and kinesiology (MAE); initial teaching certification (MAE). Electronic applications accepted.

School of Nursing Offers entry level nursing (MSN); nursing (MSN, DNP). Electronic applications accepted.

PACIFIC NORTHWEST COLLEGE OF ART, Portland, OR 97209

General Information Independent, coed, comprehensive institution.

GRADUATE UNITS

Program in Applied Craft and Design Offers applied craft and design (MFA). Program offered in collaboration with Oregon College of Art & Craft.

Program in Collaborative Design Offers collaborative design (MFA).

Program in Critical Theory and Creative Research Offers critical theory and creative research (MA).

Program in Visual Studies Offers visual studies (MFA).

PACIFIC NORTHWEST UNIVERSITY OF HEALTH SCIENCES, Yakima, WA 98901

General Information Independent, coed, graduate-only institution. *Enrollment by degree level:* 573 doctoral. *Graduate faculty:* 25 full-time (10 women), 28 part-time/adjunct (8 women). *Tuition:* Full-time $53,000; part-time $26,500 per degree program. *Graduate housing:* On-campus housing not available. *Student services:* Campus employment opportunities, campus safety program, career counseling, exercise/wellness program, free psychological counseling. *Library facilities:* PNWU Library. *Collection:* Books: 1,177 (physical), 19,391 (digital/electronic); Serial titles: 66 (physical), 35,432 (digital/electronic); Databases: 13. Weekly public service hours: 45; study areas open 24 hours, 5–7 days a week. *Research affiliation:* Yakima Valley Community Foundation (health care), Arnold P. Gold Foundation (health care), Health Resources and Services Administration (health care).

Computer facilities: 20 computers available on campus for general student use. A campuswide network can be accessed. Online class registration is available. Website: http://www.pnwu.edu/

General Application Contact: Mike Riggin, Assistant Director, Student Recruitment, 509-249-7740, Fax: 509-249-7907, E-mail: admission@pnwu.edu.

GRADUATE UNITS

College of Osteopathic Medicine Students: 572 full-time (277 women), 1 (woman) part-time; includes 163 minority (9 Black or African American, non-Hispanic/Latino; 2 American Indian or Alaska Native, non-Hispanic/Latino; 74 Asian, non-Hispanic/Latino; 41 Hispanic/Latino; 1 Native Hawaiian or other Pacific Islander, non-Hispanic/Latino; 36 Two or more races, non-Hispanic/Latino). Average age 29. 3,999 applicants, 7% accepted, 142 enrolled. *Faculty:* 25 full-time (10 women), 28 part-time/adjunct (8 women). Expenses: Contact institution. *Financial support:* In 2017–18, 10 students received support, including 1 research assistantship, 108 teaching assistantships; scholarships/grants, health care benefits, tuition waivers (full and partial), and unspecified assistantships also available. Financial award application deadline: 7/1; financial award applicants required to submit FAFSA. In 2017, 133 doctorates awarded. Offers osteopathic medicine (DO). *Application deadline:* For fall admission, 2/1 for domestic and international students. *Application fee:* $85. Electronic applications accepted. *Application Contact:* Hope Ennis, Assistant Director for Applications, 509-249-7888, Fax: 509-249-7909, E-mail: admission@pnwu.edu. *Dean,* Dr. Thomas Scandalis, 509-249-7803, E-mail: vkoch@pnwu.edu.

PACIFIC OAKS COLLEGE, Pasadena, CA 91103

General Information Independent, coed, primarily women, upper-level institution. *Graduate housing:* Room and/or apartments available to single students; on-campus housing not available to married students.

GRADUATE UNITS

Graduate School *Program availability:* Part-time, evening/weekend, online learning. Offers early childhood education (MA); human development (MA); marriage, family and child counseling (MA); preliminary education specialist (MA); preliminary multiple subject (MA).

PACIFIC RIM CHRISTIAN UNIVERSITY, Honolulu, HI 96819

General Information Independent-religious, coed, comprehensive institution.

GRADUATE UNITS

Program in Christian Ministry Offers Christian ministry (MA).

PACIFIC SCHOOL OF RELIGION, Berkeley, CA 94709-1323

General Information Independent, coed, graduate-only institution. *Graduate housing:* Rooms and/or apartments guaranteed to single and married students. Housing application deadline: 4/1. *Research affiliation:* Center for Women and Religion (women's studies), Center for Ethics and Social Policy (business ethics), Disciples Seminary Foundation (theology), Swedenborgean House of Studies (theology), Bay Area Faith and Health Consortium (public health).

GRADUATE UNITS

Graduate and Professional Programs *Program availability:* Part-time. Offers religion (M Div, MA, MTS, D Min, PhD, Th D, CAPS, CMS, CSS, CTS). MA, PhD, Th D offered jointly with Graduate Theological Union; D Min with Church Divinity School of the Pacific. Electronic applications accepted.

PACIFIC STATES UNIVERSITY, Los Angeles, CA 90010

General Information Independent, coed, comprehensive institution. *Tuition:* Part-time $380 per unit. *Graduate housing:* Room and/or apartments available on a first-come, first-served basis to single students; on-campus housing not available to married students. *Student services:* Campus employment opportunities, career counseling, international student services, low-cost health insurance. *Library facilities:* University Library plus 1 other. *Collection:* Students can reserve study rooms.

Computer facilities: 50 computers available on campus for general student use. A campuswide network can be accessed.
Website: http://www.psuca.edu/

General Application Contact: Maawiya Ayeva, Director of Admissions, 323-731-2383 Ext. 203, Fax: 323-731-7276, E-mail: admissions@psuca.edu.

GRADUATE UNITS

College of Business Expenses: Contact institution. *Financial support:* Scholarships/grants available. Financial award applicants required to submit FAFSA. *Program availability:* Part-time, evening/weekend, online learning. Offers accounting (MBA, Certificate); beauty management (MBA); finance (MBA); international business (MBA); management of information technology (MBA); project management (Certificate); real estate management (MBA). *Application deadline:* For fall admission, 9/1 priority date for domestic students, 8/1 priority date for international students; for winter admission, 12/1 priority date for domestic students, 11/1 priority date for international students; for spring admission, 3/1 priority date for domestic students, 2/1 priority date for international students; for summer admission, 6/1 priority date for domestic students, 5/1 priority date for international students. Applications are processed on a rolling basis. *Application fee:* $100. *Application Contact:* Maawiya Ayeva, Director of Admissions, 323-731-2383 Ext. 204, Fax: 323-731-7276, E-mail: admissions@psuca.edu. *MBA Program Administrator,* Chase C. Rhee, 323-731-2383 Ext. 208, Fax: 323-731-7276, E-mail: ccrhee@psuca.edu.

College of Computer Science and Information Systems Expenses: Contact institution. *Financial support:* Scholarships/grants available. Financial award applicants required to submit FAFSA. *Program availability:* Part-time, evening/weekend. Offers computer science (MS); information systems (MS). *Application deadline:* For fall admission, 9/1 priority date for domestic students, 8/1 priority date for international students; for winter admission, 12/1 priority date for domestic students, 11/1 priority date for international students; for spring admission, 3/1 priority date for domestic students, 2/1 priority date for international students; for summer admission, 6/1 priority date for domestic students, 5/1 priority date for international students. Applications are processed on a rolling basis. *Application fee:* $100. *Application Contact:* Maawiya Ayeva, Director of Admissions, 323-731-2383 Ext. 204, Fax: 323-731-7276, E-mail: admissions@psuca.edu.

PACIFIC UNION COLLEGE, Angwin, CA 94508-9707

General Information Independent-religious, coed, comprehensive institution. *Enrollment:* 3 full-time matriculated graduate/professional students (2 women), 4 part-time matriculated graduate/professional students (2 women). *Enrollment by degree level:* 7 master's. *Graduate faculty:* 3 full-time (1 woman), 1 (woman) part-time/adjunct. *Tuition:* Full-time $28,839; part-time $834 per credit hour. *Required fees:* $630; $630 per year. $210 per quarter. *Graduate housing:* Room and/or apartments available on a first-come, first-served basis to married students; on-campus housing not available to single students. Typical cost: $4767 per year ($8148 including board). *Student services:* Campus employment opportunities, career counseling, child daycare facilities, exercise/wellness program, free psychological counseling, international student services, services for students with disabilities, teacher training, writing training. *Library facilities:* W.E. Nelson Memorial Library.

Computer facilities: A campuswide network can be accessed from student residence rooms and from off campus. Online class registration, student financial information are available.
Website: http://www.puc.edu/

General Application Contact: Cherith Mundy, Credential Analyst, 707-965-6643, Fax: 707-965-6645, E-mail: teachingcredentials@puc.edu.

GRADUATE UNITS

Education Department Students: 3 full-time (2 women), 4 part-time (2 women); includes 1 minority (Black or African American, non-Hispanic/Latino). Average age 45. 4 applicants, 100% accepted, 4 enrolled. *Faculty:* 3 full-time (1 woman), 1 (woman) part-time/adjunct. Expenses: Contact institution. *Financial support:* Scholarships/grants available. Support available to part-time students. Financial award application deadline: 9/25. In 2017, 1 master's awarded. *Program availability:* Part-time. Offers education (M Ed); elementary teaching (MAT); secondary teaching (MAT). *Application deadline:* For fall admission, 8/30 for domestic and international students; for summer admission, 6/1 for domestic and international students. Applications are processed on a rolling basis. *Application fee:* $0. *Application Contact:* Cherith Mundy, Credential Analyst, 707-965-6643, Fax: 707-965-6645, E-mail: teachingcredentials@puc.edu. *Department Chair,* Prof. Thomas Lee, 707-965-6646, Fax: 707-965-6645, E-mail: tdlee@puc.edu.

PACIFIC UNIVERSITY, Forest Grove, OR 97116-1797

General Information Independent, coed, comprehensive institution. *Graduate housing:* On-campus housing not available. *Research affiliation:* NEI/PEDIG–JAEB Center of Health Research (amblyopia treatment), BSK, CIBA Vision (contact lenses), Cooper Vision (contact lenses), The Ohio State University/Vistakon-Johnson & Johnson (adolescent and child vision care).

GRADUATE UNITS

College of Business Offers business administration (MBA); finance (MSF).

College of Education *Program availability:* Part-time, evening/weekend. Offers early childhood education (MAT); education (MAE); elementary education (MAT); ESOL (MAT); high school education (MAT); middle school education (MAT); special education (MAT); speech-language pathology (MS); STEM education (MAT); talented and gifted (M Ed); visual function in learning (M Ed). Electronic applications accepted.

College of Optometry Offers optometry (OD); vision science (MS, PhD). Electronic applications accepted.

Healthcare Administration Program Offers healthcare administration (MHA).

Program in Social Work Offers social work (MSW).

Program in Writing *Program availability:* Part-time. Offers writing (MFA).

School of Audiology Offers audiology (Au D).

School of Occupational Therapy Offers occupational therapy (OTD). Electronic applications accepted.

School of Pharmacy Offers pharmacy (Pharm D). Electronic applications accepted.

School of Physical Therapy Offers athletic training (MSAT); physical therapy (DPT). Electronic applications accepted.

School of Physician Assistant Studies Offers physician assistant studies (MS).

School of Professional Psychology *Program availability:* Part-time. Offers applied psychological science (MA, MS); clinical psychology (PhD, Psy D). Electronic applications accepted.

PALM BEACH ATLANTIC UNIVERSITY, West Palm Beach, FL 33416-4708

General Information Independent-religious, coed, comprehensive institution. *Graduate housing:* On-campus housing not available.

GRADUATE UNITS

Gregory School of Pharmacy Offers pharmacy (Pharm D). Electronic applications accepted.

MacArthur School of Leadership *Program availability:* Part-time, evening/weekend, blended/hybrid learning. Offers leadership (MS). Electronic applications accepted.

Rinker School of Business *Program availability:* Part-time, evening/weekend. Offers business (MACC, MBA). Electronic applications accepted.

School of Education and Behavioral Studies *Program availability:* Part-time, evening/weekend. Offers counseling psychology (MS). Electronic applications accepted.

School of Ministry *Program availability:* Part-time. Offers Christian studies (MA); ministry (M Div). Electronic applications accepted.

School of Nursing *Program availability:* Part-time. Offers family nurse practitioner (DNP); health systems leadership (MSN). Electronic applications accepted.

PALMER COLLEGE OF CHIROPRACTIC, Davenport, IA 52803-5287

General Information Independent, coed, comprehensive institution.

GRADUATE UNITS

Division of Graduate Studies *Program availability:* Part-time. Offers clinical research (MS). Electronic applications accepted.

Professional Program *Program availability:* Part-time. Offers chiropractic (DC). Electronic applications accepted.

Professional Program–Florida Campus *Program availability:* Part-time. Offers chiropractic (DC).

Professional Program–West Campus *Program availability:* Part-time. Offers chiropractic (DC). Electronic applications accepted.

PALO ALTO UNIVERSITY, Palo Alto, CA 94304

General Information Independent, coed, upper-level institution. *Enrollment:* 1,070 graduate, professional, and undergraduate students; 762 full-time matriculated graduate/professional students (617 women), 187 part-time matriculated graduate/professional students (154 women). *Enrollment by degree level:* 327 master's, 622 doctoral. *Graduate faculty:* 59 full-time (40 women), 108 part-time/adjunct (73 women). *Tuition:* Full-time $46,266. *Required fees:* $5229. *Graduate housing:* On-campus housing not available. *Student services:* Campus employment opportunities, international student services, low-cost health insurance, services for students with disabilities, teacher training. *Library facilities:* Omar Seddiqui Research Library. *Collection:* Books: 1,771 (physical), 257,269 (digital/electronic); Serial titles: 2 (physical), 221,448 (digital/electronic); Databases: 53. Weekly public service hours: 71; students can reserve study rooms.

Computer facilities: 14 computers available on campus for general student use. A campuswide network can be accessed. Online class registration is available.
Website: http://www.paloaltou.edu/

General Application Contact: Eirian Williams, Director of Admissions, 800-818-6136, E-mail: admissions@paloaltou.edu.

GRADUATE UNITS

MA in Counseling Program Students: 158 full-time (130 women), 131 part-time (113 women); includes 138 minority (9 Black or African American, non-Hispanic/Latino; 35 Asian, non-Hispanic/Latino; 43 Hispanic/Latino; 51 Two or more races, non-Hispanic/Latino). Average age 34. 167 applicants, 74% accepted, 80 enrolled. *Faculty:* 6 full-time (4 women), 5 part-time/adjunct (4 women). Expenses: Contact institution. *Financial support:* In 2017–18, 12 students received support. Federal Work-Study available. Financial award applicants required to submit FAFSA. In 2017, 110 master's awarded. *Program availability:* Part-time, 100% online, blended/hybrid learning. Offers clinical mental health (MA); marriage, family and child (MA). *Application deadline:* For fall admission, 6/30 priority date for domestic and international students; for spring admission, 3/21 for domestic and international students. Applications are processed on a rolling basis. *Application fee:* $50. Electronic applications accepted. *Application Contact:* Yukti Singh, Director of Admissions, 650-417-2055, E-mail: ysingh@paloaltou.edu. *Director of Counseling,* Dr. William Snow, 831-246-2440, E-mail: wsnow@paloaltou.edu.

MS in Psychology (PhD Prep) Program Students: 2 full-time (both women), 36 part-time (25 women); includes 14 minority (1 Black or African American, non-Hispanic/Latino; 1 Asian, non-Hispanic/Latino; 7 Hispanic/Latino; 5 Two or more races, non-Hispanic/Latino). Average age 28. 51 applicants, 80% accepted, 19 enrolled. *Faculty:* 6 full-time (5 women), 4 part-time/adjunct (3 women). Expenses: Contact institution. *Financial support:* In 2017–18, 1 student received support. Federal Work-Study available. Financial award applicants required to submit FAFSA. In 2017, 13 master's awarded. *Program availability:* Part-time, online only, online program with 1-week on-campus intensive. Offers psychology (MS). *Application deadline:* For fall admission, 6/30 priority date for domestic and international students. Applications are processed on a rolling basis. *Application fee:* $50. Electronic applications accepted. *Application Contact:* Yukti Singh, Director of Admissions Marketing and Master's Enrollment, E-mail: ysingh@paloaltou.edu. *Director of MS in Psychology Program/Adjunct Professor,* Dr. Olga Rosito, E-mail: orosito@paloaltou.edu.

PGSP-Stanford Psy D Consortium Program Students: 167 full-time (140 women), 1 (woman) part-time; includes 56 minority (7 Black or African American, non-Hispanic/Latino; 1 American Indian or Alaska Native, non-Hispanic/Latino; 14 Asian, non-Hispanic/Latino; 15 Hispanic/Latino; 19 Two or more races, non-Hispanic/Latino). Average age 26. 417 applicants, 11% accepted, 30 enrolled. *Faculty:* 14 full-time (12 women), 61 part-time/adjunct (42 women). Expenses: Contact institution. *Financial support:* In 2017–18, 95 students received support, including fellowships (averaging $4,000 per year), research assistantships (averaging $1,000 per year), teaching assistantships (averaging $3,000 per year); Federal Work-Study and scholarships/grants also available. Financial award applicants required to submit FAFSA. In 2017, 28 doctorates awarded. Offers psychology (Psy D). Program offered jointly with Stanford

University. *Application deadline:* For fall admission, 12/2 priority date for domestic and international students. Applications are processed on a rolling basis. *Application fee:* $50. Electronic applications accepted. *Application Contact:* Dr. Kimberly Hill, Co-Director of Clinical Training, PGSP-Stanford Psy D Consortium, 650-725-5582, E-mail: khill@paloaltou.edu. *Co-Director of Clinical Training, PGSP-Stanford Psy D Consortium,* Dr. Steve Smith, E-mail: stevesmith@paloaltou.edu.

PhD in Clinical Psychology Program Students: 435 full-time (344 women), 18 part-time (14 women); includes 168 minority (24 Black or African American, non-Hispanic/Latino; 1 American Indian or Alaska Native, non-Hispanic/Latino; 45 Asian, non-Hispanic/Latino; 57 Hispanic/Latino; 2 Native Hawaiian or other Pacific Islander, non-Hispanic/Latino; 39 Two or more races, non-Hispanic/Latino). Average age 26. 346 applicants, 73% accepted, 82 enrolled. *Faculty:* 33 full-time (19 women), 37 part-time/adjunct (24 women). Expenses: Contact institution. *Financial support:* In 2017–18, 115 students received support, including fellowships (averaging $7,500 per year), research assistantships (averaging $4,000 per year), teaching assistantships (averaging $3,000 per year); Federal Work-Study and scholarships/grants also available. Financial award applicants required to submit FAFSA. In 2017, 64 doctorates awarded. Offers clinical psychology (PhD). *Application deadline:* For fall admission, 12/4 priority date for domestic and international students. Applications are processed on a rolling basis. *Application fee:* $50. Electronic applications accepted. *Application Contact:* Eirian Williams, Vice President of Enrollment Management, 800-818-6136, E-mail: admissions@paloaltou.edu. *Director of Clinical Training,* Dr. Rowena Gomez, 650-433-3823, E-mail: rgomez@paloaltou.edu.

PARIS COLLEGE OF ART, 75010 Paris, France

General Information Independent, coed, comprehensive institution.

GRADUATE UNITS

Graduate Programs Offers accessories design (MA); fashion design: new materials and technologies (MA); fashion film and photography (MA); interior design (MA); transdisciplinary new media (MA, MFA).

PARKER UNIVERSITY, Dallas, TX 75229-5668

General Information Independent, coed, graduate-only institution. *Graduate housing:* On-campus housing not available.

GRADUATE UNITS

Doctor of Chiropractic Program *Program availability:* Part-time. Offers chiropractic (DC). Electronic applications accepted.

PARK UNIVERSITY, Parkville, MO 64152-3795

General Information Independent, coed, comprehensive institution. CGS member.

GRADUATE UNITS

School of Graduate and Professional Studies *Program availability:* Part-time, evening/weekend, online learning. Offers adult education (M Ed); business and government leadership (Graduate Certificate); business, government, and global society (MPA); communication and leadership (MA); creative and life writing (Graduate Certificate); disaster and emergency management (MPA, Graduate Certificate); educational leadership (M Ed); finance (MBA, Graduate Certificate); general business (MBA); global business (Graduate Certificate); healthcare administration (MHA); healthcare services management and leadership (Graduate Certificate); international business (MBA); language and literacy (M Ed); leadership of international healthcare organizations (Graduate Certificate); management information systems (MBA, Graduate Certificate); music performance (ADP, Graduate Certificate); nonprofit and community services management (MPA); nonprofit leadership (Graduate Certificate); performance (MM); public management (MPA); social work (MSW); teacher leadership (M Ed). Electronic applications accepted.

PAYNE THEOLOGICAL SEMINARY, Wilberforce, OH 45384-3474

General Information Independent-religious, coed, graduate-only institution. *Graduate housing:* Rooms and/or apartments available on a first-come, first-served basis to single and married students. Housing application deadline: 8/15.

GRADUATE UNITS

Program in Theology *Program availability:* Part-time, evening/weekend, online learning. Offers theology (M Div).

PEIRCE COLLEGE, Philadelphia, PA 19102-4699

General Information Independent, coed, primarily women, comprehensive institution.

GRADUATE UNITS

Program in Organizational Leadership and Management Offers organizational leadership and management (MS).

PENN STATE ERIE, THE BEHREND COLLEGE, Erie, PA 16563

General Information State-related, coed, comprehensive institution. *Enrollment:* 4,502 graduate, professional, and undergraduate students; 31 full-time matriculated graduate/professional students (15 women), 126 part-time matriculated graduate/professional students (39 women). *Enrollment by degree level:* 157 master's. *Graduate housing:* Room and/or apartments available on a first-come, first-served basis to single students; on-campus housing not available to married students. *Student services:* Campus employment opportunities, campus safety program, career counseling, child daycare facilities, exercise/wellness program, free psychological counseling, grant writing training, international student services, low-cost health insurance, multicultural affairs office, services for students with disabilities. *Library facilities:* John M. Lilley Library.

Computer facilities: Computer purchase and lease plans are available. A campuswide network can be accessed from student residence rooms and from off campus. Online class registration is available.
Website: http://www.psbehrend.psu.edu/

General Application Contact: Ann M. Burbules, Assistant Director of Graduate Admissions, 814-898-7255, Fax: 814-898-6044, E-mail: behrend.admissions@psu.edu.

GRADUATE UNITS

Graduate School Students: 31 full-time (15 women), 126 part-time (39 women); includes 10 minority (4 Black or African American, non-Hispanic/Latino; 1 Hispanic/Latino; 5 Two or more races, non-Hispanic/Latino). Average age 31. 104 applicants, 75% accepted, 75 enrolled. Expenses: Contact institution. *Financial support:* Federal Work-Study available. Financial award application deadline: 2/15; financial award applicants required to submit FAFSA. In 2017, 72 master's awarded. *Program availability:* Part-time. Offers accounting (MPAC); applied clinical psychology (MA); business administration (MBA); quality and manufacturing management (MMM). *Application deadline:* Applications are processed on a rolling basis. *Application fee:* $65. Electronic applications accepted. *Application Contact:* Ann M. Burbules, Assistant Director, Graduate Admissions, 866-374-3378, Fax: 814-898-6044, E-mail: behrend.admissions@psu.edu. *Chancellor,* Dr. Ralph M. Ford, 814-898-6160, Fax: 814-898-6461.

PENN STATE GREAT VALLEY, Malvern, PA 19355-1488

General Information State-related, coed, graduate-only institution. *Enrollment by degree level:* 387 master's. *Graduate housing:* On-campus housing not available. *Student services:* Campus employment opportunities, campus safety program, career counseling, grant writing training, international student services, low-cost health insurance, multicultural affairs office, services for students with disabilities. *Library facilities:* Great Valley Library.

Computer facilities: Online class registration is available.
Website: http://greatvalley.psu.edu/

General Application Contact: JoAnn Kelly, Director of Admissions, 610-648-3315, Fax: 610-725-5296, E-mail: gvadmiss@psu.edu.

GRADUATE UNITS

Graduate Studies Students: 76 full-time (31 women), 311 part-time (103 women); includes 92 minority (18 Black or African American, non-Hispanic/Latino; 40 Asian, non-Hispanic/Latino; 21 Hispanic/Latino; 1 Native Hawaiian or other Pacific Islander, non-Hispanic/Latino; 12 Two or more races, non-Hispanic/Latino), 57 international. Average age 32. 338 applicants, 48% accepted, 128 enrolled. Expenses: Contact institution. *Financial support:* Fellowships, research assistantships, teaching assistantships, Federal Work-Study, scholarships/grants, health care benefits, and unspecified assistantships available. Support available to part-time students. Financial award application deadline: 2/15; financial award applicants required to submit FAFSA. In 2017, 204 master's awarded. *Program availability:* Part-time, evening/weekend. *Application deadline:* Applications are processed on a rolling basis. *Application fee:* $65. Electronic applications accepted. *Application Contact:* JoAnn Kelly, Director of Admissions, 610-648-3315, Fax: 610-725-5296, E-mail: gvadmiss@psu.edu. *Chancellor,* Dr. James A. Nemes, 610-648-3202, Fax: 610-725-5296.

Engineering Division Expenses: Contact institution. Offers engineering management (MEM); software engineering (MSE); systems engineering (M Eng, Certificate). *Application Contact:* JoAnn Kelly, Director of Admissions, 610-648-3315, Fax: 610-725-5296, E-mail: jek2@psu.edu. *Chancellor,* Dr. James A. Nemes, 610-648-3202 Ext. 610, Fax: 610-725-5296, E-mail: cse1@psu.edu.

Management Division Expenses: Contact institution. Offers business administration (MBA); cyber security (Certificate); data analytics (MPS, MS, Certificate); distributed energy and grid modernization (Certificate); finance (M Fin); health sector management (Certificate); human resource management (Certificate); information science (MSIS); leadership development (MLD); new ventures and entrepreneurship (Certificate); sustainable management practices (Certificate). *Application Contact:* JoAnn Kelly, Director of Admissions, 610-648-3315, Fax: 610-725-5296, E-mail: jek2@psu.edu. *Chancellor,* Dr. James A. Nemes, 610-648-3202, Fax: 610-725-5296.

PENN STATE HARRISBURG, Middletown, PA 17057

General Information State-related, coed, comprehensive institution. *Enrollment:* 5,077 graduate, professional, and undergraduate students; 207 full-time matriculated graduate/professional students (92 women), 584 part-time matriculated graduate/professional students (325 women). *Enrollment by degree level:* 712 master's. *Graduate housing:* Room and/or apartments available on a first-come, first-served basis to single students; on-campus housing not available to married students. *Student services:* Campus employment opportunities, campus safety program, career counseling, child daycare facilities, exercise/wellness program, free psychological counseling, grant writing training, international student services, low-cost health insurance, multicultural affairs office, services for students with disabilities, teacher training, writing training. *Library facilities:* Penn State Harrisburg Library.

Computer facilities: Computer purchase and lease plans are available. A campuswide network can be accessed from student residence rooms and from off campus. Online class registration is available.
Website: http://www.harrisburg.psu.edu/

General Application Contact: Robert W. Coffman, Jr., Director of Enrollment Management, Recruitment and Admissions, 717-948-6250, Fax: 717-948-6325, E-mail: hbgadmit@psu.edu.

GRADUATE UNITS

Graduate School Students: 207 full-time (92 women), 584 part-time (325 women); includes 116 minority (31 Black or African American, non-Hispanic/Latino; 35 Asian, non-Hispanic/Latino; 28 Hispanic/Latino; 22 Two or more races, non-Hispanic/Latino), 99 international. Average age 32. 680 applicants, 54% accepted, 263 enrolled. Expenses: Contact institution. *Financial support:* Fellowships, research assistantships, teaching assistantships, career-related internships or fieldwork, Federal Work-Study, and unspecified assistantships available. Support available to part-time students. Financial award application deadline: 2/15; financial award applicants required to submit FAFSA. In 2017, 254 master's, 14 doctorates awarded. *Program availability:* Part-time, evening/weekend. *Application deadline:* Applications are processed on a rolling basis. *Application fee:* $65. Electronic applications accepted. *Application Contact:* Robert W. Coffman, Jr., Director of Enrollment Management, Recruitment and Admissions, 717-948-6250, Fax: 717-948-6325, E-mail: hbgadmit@psu.edu. *Chancellor,* Dr. Mukund S. Kulkarni, 717-948-6105, Fax: 717-948-6452.

School of Behavioral Sciences and Education Expenses: Contact institution. *Program availability:* Part-time, evening/weekend. Offers adult education in the health and medical professions (Certificate); applied behavior analysis (MA); applied clinical psychology (MA); applied psychological research (MA); community psychology and social change (MA); English as a second language (ESL) program specialist and leadership (Certificate); health education (M Ed); lifelong learning and adult education (M Ed, D Ed); literacy education (M Ed); literacy leadership (Certificate); psychology: applications in clinical psychology (Certificate); psychology: health psychology (Certificate); teaching and curriculum (M Ed); training and development (M Ed, Certificate). *Application Contact:* Robert W. Coffman, Jr., Director of Enrollment Management, Recruitment and Admissions, 717-948-6250, Fax: 717-948-6325, E-mail: hbgadmit@psu.edu. *Chancellor,* Dr. Mukund S. Kulkarni, 717-948-6105, Fax: 717-948-6452.

School of Business Administration Expenses: Contact institution. *Program availability:* Part-time, evening/weekend. Offers accounting (MPAC, Certificate); business administration (MBA); information systems (MS); operations and supply chain management (Certificate). *Application Contact:* Robert W. Coffman, Jr., Director of Enrollment Management, Recruitment and Admissions, 717-948-6250, Fax: 717-948-6325, E-mail: hbgadmit@psu.edu. *Chancellor,* Dr. Mukund S. Kulkarni, 717-948-6105, Fax: 717-948-6452.

School of Humanities Expenses: Contact institution. *Program availability:* Evening/weekend. Offers American studies (MA, PhD); communications (MA); folklore and ethnography (Certificate); heritage and museum practice (Certificate); humanities (MA). *Application Contact:* Robert W. Coffman, Jr., Director of Enrollment

Management, Recruitment and Admissions, 717-948-6250, Fax: 717-948-6325, E-mail: hbgadmit@psu.edu. *Chancellor*, Dr. Mukund S. Kulkarni, 717-948-6105, Fax: 717-948-6452.

School of Public Affairs Expenses: Contact institution. Offers criminal justice (MA); health administration (MHA); health administration: long term care (Certificate); homeland security (MPS, Certificate); public administration (MPA, PhD); public administration: non-profit administration (Certificate); public budgeting and financial management (Certificate); public sector human resource management (Certificate). *Application Contact:* Robert W. Coffman, Jr., Director of Enrollment Management, Recruitment and Admissions, 717-948-6250, Fax: 717-948-6325, E-mail: hbgadmit@psu.edu. *Chancellor*, Dr. Mukund S. Kulkarni, 717-948-6105, Fax: 717-948-6452.

School of Science, Engineering and Technology Expenses: Contact institution. *Financial support:* Fellowships, career-related internships or fieldwork, and unspecified assistantships available. Support available to part-time students. *Program availability:* Part-time, evening/weekend. Offers civil engineering (MS); computer science (MS); electrical engineering (M Eng, MS); engineering management (MPS); engineering science (M Eng); environmental engineering (M Eng); environmental pollution control (MEPC, MS); mechanical engineering (MS); structural engineering (Certificate). *Application Contact:* Robert W. Coffman, Jr., Director of Enrollment Management, Recruitment and Admissions, 717-948-6250, Fax: 717-948-6325, E-mail: hbgadmit@psu.edu. *Chancellor*, Dr. Mukund S. Kulkarni, 717-948-6105, Fax: 717-948-6452.

PENN STATE HERSHEY MEDICAL CENTER, Hershey, PA 17033-2360

General Information State-related, coed, graduate-only institution. *Graduate housing:* Rooms and/or apartments available on a first-come, first-served basis to single and married students. *Student services:* Campus safety program, career counseling, child daycare facilities, exercise/wellness program, free psychological counseling, grant writing training, international student services, low-cost health insurance, multicultural affairs office, services for students with disabilities, teacher training, writing training. *Library facilities:* George T. Harrell Health Sciences Library.

Computer facilities: Online class registration is available.
Website: http://www.hmc.psu.edu/college/

General Application Contact: Dr. Michael F. Verderame, Associate Dean of Graduate Studies, 717-531-8892, Fax: 717-531-0786, E-mail: grad-hmc@psu.edu.

GRADUATE UNITS

College of Medicine Expenses: Contact institution. *Financial support:* In 2017–18, research assistantships with full tuition reimbursements (averaging $27,802 per year) were awarded; fellowships with full tuition reimbursements, career-related internships or fieldwork, scholarships/grants, health care benefits, and unspecified assistantships also available. Offers medicine (MPAS, MPH, MS, Dr PH, MD, PhD). *Application deadline:* Applications are processed on a rolling basis. Electronic applications accepted. *Application Contact:* Kristin E. Smith, Director of Graduate Admissions, 717-531-1045, Fax: 717-531-0786, E-mail: kec17@psu.edu. *Dean*, Dr. A. Craig Hillemeier, 717-531-8323, Fax: 717-531-0786, E-mail: grad-hmc@psu.edu.

Graduate School Programs in the Biomedical Sciences Expenses: Contact institution. *Financial support:* In 2017–18, research assistantships with full tuition reimbursements (averaging $27,802 per year) were awarded; fellowships with full tuition reimbursements, career-related internships or fieldwork, scholarships/grants, health care benefits, tuition waivers (full), and unspecified assistantships also available. Offers anatomy (MS, PhD); biochemistry and molecular genetics (MS, PhD); biomedical sciences (MS, PhD); biostatistics (PhD); cell and developmental biology (PhD); cellular and integrative physiology (MS, PhD); laboratory animal medicine (MS); life sciences (MS, PhD); molecular medicine (PhD); molecular toxicology (PhD); neurobiology (PhD); neuroscience (MS, PhD); public health (MPH, Dr PH); public health sciences (MS); translational therapeutics (MS, PhD); virology and immunology (MS, PhD). *Application deadline:* Applications are processed on a rolling basis. *Application fee:* $65. Electronic applications accepted. *Application Contact:* Kristin E. Smith, Director of Graduate Admissions, 717-531-1045, Fax: 717-531-0786, E-mail: kec17@psu.edu. *Associate Dean of Graduate Studies*, Dr. Charles Lang, 717-531-8892, Fax: 717-531-0786, E-mail: grad-hmc@psu.edu.

PENN STATE UNIVERSITY–DICKINSON LAW, Carlisle, PA 17013

General Information State-related, coed, graduate-only institution. *Enrollment by degree level:* 193 doctoral. *Graduate faculty:* 22 full-time (12 women), 24 part-time/adjunct (7 women). Tuition, state resident: full-time $48,000; part-time $2000 per credit hour. Tuition, nonresident: full-time $48,000; part-time $2000 per credit hour. *Required fees:* $686. *Graduate housing:* On-campus housing not available. *Student services:* Campus employment opportunities, career counseling, exercise/wellness program, free psychological counseling, international student services, low-cost health insurance, services for students with disabilities, writing training. *Library facilities:* H. Laddie Montague Jr. Law Library. *Collection:* Books: 43,776 (physical), 201,337 (digital/electronic); Serial titles: 7,320 (physical), 127,906 (digital/electronic); Databases: 167. Weekly public service hours: 43; study areas open 24 hours, 5–7 days a week; students can reserve study rooms.

Computer facilities: 21 computers available on campus for general student use. Online class registration is available.
Website: http://law.psu.edu/

General Application Contact: Bekah A. Saidman-Krauss, Assistant Dean of Admissions and Financial Aid, 717-240-5207, E-mail: ras1075@psu.edu.

GRADUATE UNITS

Graduate and Professional Programs Students: 193 full-time (76 women); includes 37 minority (8 Black or African American, non-Hispanic/Latino; 8 Asian, non-Hispanic/Latino; 15 Hispanic/Latino; 6 Two or more races, non-Hispanic/Latino), 9 international. 671 applicants, 39% accepted, 73 enrolled. *Faculty:* 21 full-time (12 women), 24 part-time/adjunct (7 women). Expenses: Contact institution. *Financial support:* Research assistantships, Federal Work-Study, and scholarships/grants available. Financial award application deadline: 4/15; financial award applicants required to submit FAFSA. In 2017, 61 doctorates awarded. Offers law (LL M, JD). *Application deadline:* Applications are processed on a rolling basis. *Application fee:* $0. Electronic applications accepted. *Application Contact:* Bekah A. Saidman-Krauss, Assistant Dean of Admissions and Financial Aid, 717-240-5207, E-mail: ras1075@psu.edu. *Dean*, Gary S. Gildin, 717-240-5238, Fax: 717-240-5213, E-mail: gsg2@psu.edu.

PENN STATE UNIVERSITY PARK, University Park, PA 16802

General Information State-related, coed, university. CGS member. *Enrollment:* 47,119 graduate, professional, and undergraduate students; 5,551 full-time matriculated graduate/professional students (2,458 women), 733 part-time matriculated graduate/professional students (375 women). *Enrollment by degree level:* 1,827 master's, 4,457 doctoral. *Graduate housing:* Rooms and/or apartments available on a first-come, first-served basis to single and married students. *Student services:* Campus employment opportunities, campus safety program, career counseling, child daycare facilities, exercise/wellness program, free psychological counseling, grant writing training, international student services, low-cost health insurance, multicultural affairs office, services for students with disabilities, teacher training, writing training. *Library facilities:* Pattee and Paterno Libraries plus 4 others. *Collection:* Books: 5 million (physical), 2.1 million (digital/electronic); Serial titles: 84,993 (physical), 160,000 (digital/electronic); Databases: 828. Weekly public service hours: 148; study areas open 24 hours, 5–7 days a week; students can reserve study rooms.

Computer facilities: 3,154 computers available on campus for general student use. A campuswide network can be accessed from student residence rooms and from off campus. Online class registration is available.
Website: http://www.psu.edu/

General Application Contact: Lori Hawn, Director, Graduate Student Services, 814-865-1795, Fax: 814-863-4627, E-mail: l-gswww@lists.psu.edu.

GRADUATE UNITS

Graduate School Students: 5,057 full-time (2,216 women), 718 part-time (367 women); includes 754 minority (169 Black or African American, non-Hispanic/Latino; 3 American Indian or Alaska Native, non-Hispanic/Latino; 185 Asian, non-Hispanic/Latino; 267 Hispanic/Latino; 4 Native Hawaiian or other Pacific Islander, non-Hispanic/Latino; 126 Two or more races, non-Hispanic/Latino), 2,513 international. Average age 28. 14,699 applicants, 24% accepted, 1819 enrolled. Expenses: Contact institution. *Financial support:* Fellowships, research assistantships, teaching assistantships, career-related internships or fieldwork, Federal Work-Study, scholarships/grants, traineeships, health care benefits, and unspecified assistantships available. Support available to part-time students. Financial award application deadline: 2/15; financial award applicants required to submit FAFSA. In 2017, 1,312 master's, 695 doctorates awarded. *Program availability:* Part-time, evening/weekend, online learning. *Application deadline:* Applications are processed on a rolling basis. *Application fee:* $65. Electronic applications accepted. *Application Contact:* Lori Hawn, Director, Graduate Student Services, 814-865-1795, Fax: 814-863-4627, E-mail: l-gswww@lists.psu.edu. *Vice Provost for Graduate Education/Dean, Graduate School*, Dr. Regina Vasilatos-Younken, 814-865-2516, Fax: 814-863-4627.

College of Agricultural Sciences Students: 291 full-time (167 women), 34 part-time (18 women). Average age 29. 473 applicants, 22% accepted, 70 enrolled. Expenses: Contact institution. *Financial support:* Fellowships, research assistantships, teaching assistantships, career-related internships or fieldwork, Federal Work-Study, scholarships/grants, traineeships, health care benefits, and unspecified assistantships available. Support available to part-time students. Financial award application deadline: 2/15; financial award applicants required to submit FAFSA. In 2017, 40 master's, 54 doctorates awarded. *Program availability:* Part-time. Offers agricultural and biological engineering (MS, PhD); agricultural and extension education (M Ed, MS, PhD, Certificate); agricultural sciences (M Ed, MPS, MS, PhD, Certificate); agronomy (MS, PhD); animal science (MPS, MS, PhD); applied youth, family and community education (M Ed); biorenewable systems (MS, PhD); energy, environmental, and food economics (MS, PhD); entomology (MS, PhD); food science (MS, PhD); forest resources (MS, PhD); horticulture (MS, PhD); pathobiology (MS, PhD); plant pathology (MS, PhD); rural sociology (MS, PhD); soil science (MS, PhD); wildlife and fisheries science (MS, PhD). *Application deadline:* Applications are processed on a rolling basis. *Application fee:* $65. Electronic applications accepted. *Application Contact:* Lori Hawn, Director, Graduate Student Services, 814-865-1795, Fax: 814-863-4627, E-mail: gswww@lists.psu.edu. *Dean*, Dr. Richard T. Roush, 814-865-2541, Fax: 814-865-3103.

College of Arts and Architecture Students: 204 full-time (132 women), 38 part-time (26 women). Average age 30. 515 applicants, 40% accepted, 98 enrolled. Expenses: Contact institution. *Financial support:* Fellowships, research assistantships, teaching assistantships, career-related internships or fieldwork, Federal Work-Study, scholarships/grants, traineeships, health care benefits, and unspecified assistantships available. Support available to part-time students. Financial award application deadline: 2/15; financial award applicants required to submit FAFSA. In 2017, 72 master's, 15 doctorates awarded. *Program availability:* Part-time, evening/weekend. Offers architecture (M Arch, MS, PhD); art (MFA); art education (MS, PhD, Certificate); art history (MA, PhD); arts and architecture (M Arch, M Mus, MA, MFA, MLA, MME, MS, DMA, PhD, Certificate); composition-theory (M Mus); conducting (M Mus); landscape architecture (MLA, MS); music (MA); music education (MME, PhD, Certificate); pedagogy and performance (M Mus); performance (M Mus); piano performance (DMA); theatre (MFA). *Application deadline:* Applications are processed on a rolling basis. *Application fee:* $65. Electronic applications accepted. *Application Contact:* Lori Hawn, Director, Graduate Student Services, 814-865-1795, Fax: 814-863-4627, E-mail: gswww@lists.psu.edu. *Dean*, Dr. Barbara O. Korner, 814-865-2592, Fax: 814-865-2018.

College of Earth and Mineral Sciences Students: 252 full-time (108 women), 32 part-time (11 women). Average age 28. 571 applicants, 18% accepted, 57 enrolled. Expenses: Contact institution. *Financial support:* Fellowships, research assistantships, teaching assistantships, career-related internships or fieldwork, Federal Work-Study, scholarships/grants, traineeships, health care benefits, and unspecified assistantships available. Support available to part-time students. Financial award application deadline: 2/15; financial award applicants required to submit FAFSA. In 2017, 41 master's, 47 doctorates awarded. Offers earth and mineral sciences (MS, PhD); energy and mineral engineering (MS, PhD); geography (MS, PhD); geosciences (MS, PhD); meteorology (MS, PhD). *Application deadline:* Applications are processed on a rolling basis. *Application fee:* $65. Electronic applications accepted. *Application Contact:* Lori Hawn, Director, Graduate Student Services, 814-865-1795, Fax: 814-863-4627, E-mail: l-gswww@lists.psu.edu. *Dean*, Dr. Lee R. Kump, 814-865-7482, Fax: 814-863-7708.

College of Education Students: 478 full-time (342 women), 194 part-time (118 women). Average age 33. 531 applicants, 56% accepted, 168 enrolled. Expenses: Contact institution. *Financial support:* Fellowships, research assistantships, teaching assistantships, career-related internships or fieldwork, Federal Work-Study, scholarships/grants, traineeships, health care benefits, and unspecified assistantships available. Support available to part-time students. Financial award application deadline: 2/15; financial award applicants required to submit FAFSA. In 2017, 151 master's, 104 doctorates awarded. *Program availability:* Part-time, evening/weekend. Offers counselor education (M Ed, D Ed, PhD, Certificate); curriculum and instruction (M Ed, MS, PhD, Certificate); education (M Ed, MA, MS, D Ed, PhD, Certificate); educational leadership (M Ed, D Ed, PhD, Certificate); educational psychology (MS, PhD, Certificate); educational theory and policy (MA, PhD); higher education (M Ed,

D Ed, PhD); learning, design, and technology (M Ed, MS, PhD, Certificate); lifelong learning and adult education (M Ed, D Ed, PhD, Certificate); school psychology (M Ed, MS, PhD, Certificate); special education (M Ed, MS, PhD); workforce education and development (M Ed, MS, PhD). *Application deadline:* Applications are processed on a rolling basis. *Application fee:* $65. Electronic applications accepted. *Application Contact:* Lori Hawn, Director, Graduate Student Services, 814-865-1795, Fax: 814-863-4627, E-mail: l-gswww@lists.psu.edu. *Dean*, Dr. David H. Monk, 814-865-2523, Fax: 814-865-0555.

College of Engineering Students: 1,167 full-time (239 women), 145 part-time (31 women). Average age 27. 4,412 applicants, 24% accepted, 456 enrolled. Expenses: Contact institution. *Financial support:* Fellowships, research assistantships, teaching assistantships, career-related internships or fieldwork, Federal Work-Study, scholarships/grants, traineeships, health care benefits, and unspecified assistantships available. Support available to part-time students. Financial award application deadline: 2/15; financial award applicants required to submit FAFSA. In 2017, 348 master's, 134 doctorates awarded. *Program availability:* Part-time, evening/weekend. Offers additive manufacturing and design (MS); aerospace engineering (M Eng, MS, PhD); architectural engineering (M Eng, MAE, MS, PhD); chemical engineering (MS, PhD); civil engineering (M Eng, MS, PhD); computer science and engineering (M Eng, MS, PhD); electrical engineering (MS, PhD); engineering (M Eng, MAE, MFR, MS, PhD); engineering at the nano-scale (MS); engineering design (M Eng, MS); engineering leadership and innovation management (M Eng); engineering mechanics (M Eng); engineering science and mechanics (MS, PhD); environmental engineering (M Eng, MS, PhD); facilities engineering and management (M Eng); industrial engineering (MS, PhD); mechanical engineering (MS, PhD); nuclear engineering (M Eng, MS, PhD). *Application deadline:* Applications are processed on a rolling basis. *Application fee:* $65. Electronic applications accepted. *Application Contact:* Lori Hawn, Director, Graduate Student Services, 814-865-1795, Fax: 814-863-4627, E-mail: l-gswww@lists.psu.edu. *Dean*, Dr. Justin Schwartz, 814-865-7537, Fax: 814-863-4749.

College of Health and Human Development Students: 267 full-time (189 women), 33 part-time (22 women). Average age 28. 514 applicants, 32% accepted, 76 enrolled. Expenses: Contact institution. *Financial support:* Fellowships, research assistantships, teaching assistantships, career-related internships or fieldwork, Federal Work-Study, scholarships/grants, traineeships, health care benefits, and unspecified assistantships available. Support available to part-time students. Financial award application deadline: 2/15; financial award applicants required to submit FAFSA. In 2017, 70 master's, 46 doctorates awarded. *Program availability:* Part-time, evening/weekend. Offers biobehavioral health (MS, PhD); communication sciences and disorders (MS, PhD, Certificate); health and human development (MHA, MS, PhD, Certificate); health policy and administration (MHA, MS, PhD); hospitality management (MS, PhD); human development and family studies (MS, PhD); kinesiology (MS, PhD, Certificate); nutritional sciences (MS, PhD); recreation, park and tourism management (MS, PhD). *Application deadline:* Applications are processed on a rolling basis. *Application fee:* $65. Electronic applications accepted. *Application Contact:* Lori Hawn, Director, Graduate Student Services, 814-865-1795, Fax: 814-863-4627, E-mail: l-gswww@lists.psu.edu. *Dean*, Dr. Ann C. Crouter, 814-865-1420, Fax: 814-865-3282.

College of Information Sciences and Technology Students: 108 full-time (36 women), 13 part-time (2 women). Average age 28. 203 applicants, 33% accepted, 38 enrolled. Expenses: Contact institution. *Financial support:* Fellowships, research assistantships, teaching assistantships, career-related internships or fieldwork, Federal Work-Study, scholarships/grants, traineeships, health care benefits, and unspecified assistantships available. Support available to part-time students. Financial award application deadline: 2/15; financial award applicants required to submit FAFSA. In 2017, 17 master's, 15 doctorates awarded. *Program availability:* Part-time, evening/weekend. Offers information sciences (MPS); information sciences and technology (MS, PhD). *Application deadline:* For fall admission, 12/15 for domestic and international students. Applications are processed on a rolling basis. *Application fee:* $65. Electronic applications accepted. *Application Contact:* Lori Hawn, Director, Graduate Student Services, 814-865-1795, Fax: 814-863-4627, E-mail: l-gswww@lists.psu.edu. *Dean*, Dr. Andrew L. Sears, 814-865-3528, Fax: 814-865-7485.

College of Nursing Students: 51 full-time (42 women), 53 part-time (47 women). Average age 32. 50 applicants, 56% accepted, 26 enrolled. Expenses: Contact institution. *Financial support:* Fellowships, research assistantships, teaching assistantships, career-related internships or fieldwork, Federal Work-Study, scholarships/grants, traineeships, health care benefits, and unspecified assistantships available. Support available to part-time students. Financial award application deadline: 2/15; financial award applicants required to submit FAFSA. In 2017, 41 master's, 4 doctorates awarded. *Program availability:* Part-time, evening/weekend. Offers nursing (MSN). *Application deadline:* Applications are processed on a rolling basis. *Application fee:* $65. Electronic applications accepted. *Application Contact:* Lori Hawn, Director, Graduate Student Services, 814-865-1795, Fax: 814-863-4627, E-mail: l-gswww@lists.psu.edu. *Dean*, Dr. Janice L. Penrod, 814-863-0245, Fax: 814-865-3779.

College of the Liberal Arts Students: 727 full-time (390 women), 40 part-time (24 women). Average age 28. 2,693 applicants, 15% accepted, 251 enrolled. Expenses: Contact institution. *Financial support:* Fellowships, research assistantships, teaching assistantships, career-related internships or fieldwork, Federal Work-Study, scholarships/grants, traineeships, health care benefits, and unspecified assistantships available. Support available to part-time students. Financial award application deadline: 2/15; financial award applicants required to submit FAFSA. In 2017, 156 master's, 98 doctorates awarded. *Program availability:* Part-time, evening/weekend. Offers anthropology (MA, PhD); applied linguistics (PhD); communication arts and sciences (MA, PhD); comparative literature (MA, PhD); criminology (MA, PhD); economics (MA, PhD); English (MA, MFA, PhD); French (MA, PhD); German (MA, PhD); history (MA, PhD); human resources and employment relations (MS); labor and global workers' rights (MPS); liberal arts (MA, MFA, MPS, MS, PhD); philosophy (MA, PhD); political science (MA, PhD); psychology (MS, PhD); Russian and comparative literature (MA); sociology (MA, PhD); Spanish (MA, PhD); teaching English as a second language (MA). *Application deadline:* Applications are processed on a rolling basis. *Application fee:* $65. Electronic applications accepted. *Application Contact:* Lori Hawn, Director, Graduate Student Services, 814-865-1795, Fax: 814-863-4627, E-mail: l-gswww@lists.psu.edu. *Dean*, Dr. Susan Welch, 814-865-7691, Fax: 814-863-2085.

Donald P. Bellisario College of Communications Students: 42 full-time (32 women), 7 part-time (6 women). Average age 29. 146 applicants, 18% accepted, 11 enrolled. Expenses: Contact institution. *Financial support:* Fellowships, research assistantships, teaching assistantships, career-related internships or fieldwork, Federal Work-Study, scholarships/grants, traineeships, health care benefits, and unspecified assistantships available. Support available to part-time students. Financial award application deadline: 2/15; financial award applicants required to submit FAFSA. In 2017, 4 master's, 10 doctorates awarded. *Program availability:* Part-time, evening/weekend. Offers communications (MA, PhD); mass communications (PhD); media studies (MA). *Application deadline:* Applications are processed on a rolling basis. *Application fee:* $65. Electronic applications accepted. *Application Contact:* Lori Hawn, Director, Graduate Student Services, 814-865-1795, Fax: 814-863-4627, E-mail: l-gswww@lists.psu.edu. *Dean*, Dr. Marie C. Hardin, 814-863-1484, Fax: 814-863-8044.

Eberly College of Science Students: 675 full-time (229 women), 35 part-time (16 women). Average age 26. 2,230 applicants, 19% accepted, 161 enrolled. Expenses: Contact institution. *Financial support:* Fellowships, research assistantships, teaching assistantships, career-related internships or fieldwork, Federal Work-Study, scholarships/grants, traineeships, health care benefits, and unspecified assistantships available. Support available to part-time students. Financial award application deadline: 2/15; financial award applicants required to submit FAFSA. In 2017, 50 master's, 97 doctorates awarded. *Program availability:* Part-time, evening/weekend. Offers applied statistics (MAS); astronomy and astrophysics (MS, PhD); biochemistry, microbiology, and molecular biology (MS, PhD); biology (MS, PhD); biotechnology (MBIOT); chemistry (MS, PhD); forensic science (MPS); mathematics (M Ed, MA, D Ed, PhD); physics (M Ed, MS, PhD); science (M Ed, MA, MAS, MBIOT, MPS, MS, D Ed, PhD); statistics (MA, MS, PhD). *Application deadline:* Applications are processed on a rolling basis. *Application fee:* $65. Electronic applications accepted. *Application Contact:* Lori Hawn, Director, Graduate Student Services, 814-865-1795, Fax: 814-863-4627, E-mail: l-gswww@lists.psu.edu. *Dean*, Dr. Douglas R. Cavener, 814-865-9591, Fax: 814-865-3634.

Intercollege Graduate Programs Students: 424 full-time (169 women), 20 part-time (8 women). Average age 26. 1,000 applicants, 19% accepted, 97 enrolled. Expenses: Contact institution. *Financial support:* Fellowships, research assistantships, teaching assistantships, career-related internships or fieldwork, Federal Work-Study, scholarships/grants, traineeships, health care benefits, and unspecified assistantships available. Support available to part-time students. Financial award application deadline: 2/15; financial award applicants required to submit FAFSA. *Program availability:* Part-time, evening/weekend. Offers acoustics (PhD); bioengineering (MS, PhD); ecology (MS, PhD); environmental pollution control (MEPC, MS); integrative and biomedical physiology (MS, PhD); materials science and engineering (MS, PhD); molecular, cellular, and integrative biosciences (MS, PhD); plant biology (MS, PhD); renewable energy and sustainability systems (MPS). *Application deadline:* Applications are processed on a rolling basis. *Application fee:* $65. Electronic applications accepted. *Application Contact:* Lori Hawn, Director, Graduate Student Services, 814-865-1795, Fax: 814-863-4627, E-mail: l-gswww@lists.psu.edu. *Vice Provost for Graduate Education and Dean of the Graduate School*, Dr. Regina Vasilatos-Younken, 814-865-2516, Fax: 814-863-4627.

School of International Affairs Students: 70 full-time (37 women), 4 part-time (1 woman). Average age 25. 236 applicants, 79% accepted, 74 enrolled. Expenses: Contact institution. *Financial support:* Fellowships, research assistantships, teaching assistantships, career-related internships or fieldwork, Federal Work-Study, scholarships/grants, traineeships, health care benefits, and unspecified assistantships available. Support available to part-time students. Financial award application deadline: 2/15; financial award applicants required to submit FAFSA. In 2017, 54 master's awarded. *Program availability:* Part-time, evening/weekend. Offers international affairs (MIA). *Application deadline:* Applications are processed on a rolling basis. *Application fee:* $65. Electronic applications accepted. *Application Contact:* Lori Hawn, Director, Graduate Student Services, 814-865-1795, Fax: 814-863-4627, E-mail: l-gswww@lists.psu.edu. *Dean*, Hari M. Osofsky, 814-863-1521, Fax: 814-863-7274.

Smeal College of Business Students: 290 full-time (97 women), 7 part-time (2 women). Average age 29. 1,125 applicants, 27% accepted, 236 enrolled. Expenses: Contact institution. *Financial support:* Fellowships, research assistantships, teaching assistantships, career-related internships or fieldwork, Federal Work-Study, scholarships/grants, traineeships, health care benefits, and unspecified assistantships available. Support available to part-time students. Financial award application deadline: 2/15; financial award applicants required to submit FAFSA. In 2017, 235 master's, 10 doctorates awarded. *Program availability:* Part-time, evening/weekend. Offers accounting (M Acc); business administration (MBA, MS, PhD); management and organizational leadership (MPS). *Application deadline:* Applications are processed on a rolling basis. *Application fee:* $65. Electronic applications accepted. *Application Contact:* Lori Hawn, Director, Graduate Student Services, 814-865-1795, Fax: 814-863-4627, E-mail: l-gswww@lists.psu.edu. *Dean*, Dr. Charles H. Whiteman, 814-863-0448, Fax: 814-865-7064.

Penn State Law Students: 495 full-time (240 women). 2,023 applicants, 45% accepted, 192 enrolled. *Faculty:* 45 full-time (21 women), 16 part-time/adjunct (5 women). Expenses: Contact institution. Offers law (LL M, JD, SJD). *Application deadline:* For fall admission, 3/31 for domestic students. Applications are processed on a rolling basis. *Application fee:* $60. Electronic applications accepted. *Application Contact:* Amanda DiPolvere, Assistant Dean, Admissions and Financial Aid, 800-840-1122, E-mail: admissions@pennstatelaw.psu.edu. *Dean*, Hari M. Osofsky, 814-863-1521.

PENN STATE YORK, York, PA 17403

General Information State-related, coed, comprehensive institution. *Enrollment:* 983 graduate, professional, and undergraduate students; 16 part-time matriculated graduate/professional students (13 women). *Enrollment by degree level:* 2 master's.

Computer facilities: Computer purchase and lease plans are available. A campuswide network can be accessed from off campus. Online class registration is available. Website: http://www.york.psu.edu/

GRADUATE UNITS

Graduate School Students: 16 part-time (13 women); includes 2 minority (1 Black or African American, non-Hispanic/Latino; 1 Two or more races, non-Hispanic/Latino). Average age 35. 3 applicants, 67% accepted, 2 enrolled. Expenses: Contact institution. In 2017, 2 master's awarded. Offers ESL specialist (Certificate); teaching and curriculum (M Ed). *Application fee:* $65. *Application Contact:* Lori Hawn, Director, Graduate Student Services, 814-865-1795, Fax: 814-863-4627, E-mail: l-gswww@lists.psu.edu. *Vice Provost for Graduate Education/Dean, Graduate School*, Dr. Regina Vasilatos-Younken, 814-865-2516, Fax: 814-863-4627.

PENNSYLVANIA ACADEMY OF THE FINE ARTS, Philadelphia, PA 19102

General Information Independent, coed, comprehensive institution. *Graduate housing:* On-campus housing not available.

GRADUATE UNITS

Division of Graduate Studies Offers drawing (MFA, Postbaccalaureate Certificate); painting (MFA, Postbaccalaureate Certificate); printmaking (MFA, Postbaccalaureate Certificate); sculpture (MFA, Postbaccalaureate Certificate). MFA program also available in a low-residency format. Electronic applications accepted.

PENNSYLVANIA COLLEGE OF HEALTH SCIENCES, Lancaster, PA 17601

General Information Independent, coed, comprehensive institution.

GRADUATE UNITS

Graduate Programs Offers administration (MSN); education (MSHS, MSN); healthcare administration (MHA).

PENSACOLA CHRISTIAN COLLEGE, Pensacola, FL 32503-2267

General Information Independent-religious, coed, comprehensive institution.

GRADUATE UNITS

Graduate Studies

PENTECOSTAL THEOLOGICAL SEMINARY, Cleveland, TN 37320-3330

General Information Independent-religious, coed, graduate-only institution. *Graduate housing:* Rooms and/or apartments available to single and married students.

GRADUATE UNITS

Graduate and Professional Programs *Program availability:* Part-time. Offers biblical studies (MTS); church ministries (MA); counseling (MA); discipleship and Christian formation (MA); ministry (D Min); Pentecostal theology (MTS); theology (M Div).

PEPPERDINE UNIVERSITY, Malibu, CA 90263

General Information Independent-religious, coed, university. *Enrollment:* 7,710 graduate, professional, and undergraduate students; 2,428 full-time matriculated graduate/professional students (1,446 women), 1,678 part-time matriculated graduate/professional students (1,040 women). *Enrollment by degree level:* 3,091 master's, 993 doctoral, 22 other advanced degrees. *Graduate faculty:* 175 full-time (64 women), 189 part-time/adjunct (91 women). *Graduate housing:* Rooms and/or apartments available on a first-come, first-served basis to single and married students. *Student services:* Campus employment opportunities, campus safety program, career counseling, exercise/wellness program, free psychological counseling, international student services, low-cost health insurance, multicultural affairs office, services for students with disabilities, teacher training. *Library facilities:* Payson Library plus 5 others. *Collection:* Books: 348,364 (physical), 237,133 (digital/electronic); Serial titles: 411 (physical), 61,042 (digital/electronic); Databases: 150. Weekly public service hours: 112; students can reserve study rooms.

Computer facilities: Computer purchase and lease plans are available. 218 computers available on campus for general student use. A campuswide network can be accessed from student residence rooms and from off campus. Online class registration is available.
Website: http://www.pepperdine.edu/

General Application Contact: Kristy Collins, Dean of Admission and Enrollment Management, Seaver College, 310-506-4392, Fax: 310-506-4861, E-mail: admission-seaver@pepperdine.edu.

GRADUATE UNITS

Graduate School of Education and Psychology Students: 713 full-time (556 women), 743 part-time (559 women); includes 649 minority (203 Black or African American, non-Hispanic/Latino; 6 American Indian or Alaska Native, non-Hispanic/Latino; 116 Asian, non-Hispanic/Latino; 266 Hispanic/Latino; 11 Native Hawaiian or other Pacific Islander, non-Hispanic/Latino; 47 Two or more races, non-Hispanic/Latino), 117 international. Average age 34. 984 applicants, 82% accepted, 414 enrolled. *Faculty:* 48 full-time (27 women), 122 part-time/adjunct (75 women). Expenses: Contact institution. *Financial support:* Research assistantships, teaching assistantships, career-related internships or fieldwork, Federal Work-Study, institutionally sponsored loans, scholarships/grants, and unspecified assistantships available. Support available to part-time students. Financial award applicants required to submit FAFSA. In 2017, 412 master's, 121 doctorates awarded. *Program availability:* Part-time, evening/weekend, blended/hybrid learning. Offers education and psychology (MA, MS, Ed D, PhD, Psy D). *Application deadline:* Applications are processed on a rolling basis. *Application fee:* $55. Electronic applications accepted. *Application Contact:* Chris Costa, Director of Enrollment, 310-568-2850, E-mail: chris.costa@pepperdine.edu. *Dean*, Dr. Helen Williams, 310-568-5615, E-mail: helen.williams@pepperdine.edu.

Division of Education Students: 214 full-time (139 women), 327 part-time (216 women); includes 248 minority (113 Black or African American, non-Hispanic/Latino; 2 American Indian or Alaska Native, non-Hispanic/Latino; 48 Asian, non-Hispanic/Latino; 61 Hispanic/Latino; 6 Native Hawaiian or other Pacific Islander, non-Hispanic/Latino; 18 Two or more races, non-Hispanic/Latino), 49 international. Average age 39. 410 applicants, 91% accepted, 160 enrolled. Expenses: Contact institution. *Financial support:* Research assistantships, teaching assistantships, career-related internships or fieldwork, institutionally sponsored loans, and scholarships/grants available. Support available to part-time students. Financial award application deadline: 7/1; financial award applicants required to submit FAFSA. In 2017, 151 master's, 88 doctorates awarded. *Program availability:* Part-time, evening/weekend, blended/hybrid learning. Offers administration and preliminary administrative services (MS); education (MA); educational leadership, administration, and policy (Ed D); global leadership and change (PhD); learning technologies (MA, Ed D); organizational leadership (Ed D); social entrepreneurship and change (MA); teaching (MA); teaching: TESOL (MA). *Application deadline:* Applications are processed on a rolling basis. *Application fee:* $55. Electronic applications accepted. *Application Contact:* Chris Costa, Director of Enrollment, 310-568-2850, E-mail: chris.costa@pepperdine.edu. *Associate Dean, Education Division*, Dr. Martine Jago, 310-568-2828, E-mail: martine.jago@pepperdine.edu.

Division of Psychology Students: 499 full-time (417 women), 416 part-time (343 women); includes 401 minority (90 Black or African American, non-Hispanic/Latino; 4 American Indian or Alaska Native, non-Hispanic/Latino; 68 Asian, non-Hispanic/Latino; 205 Hispanic/Latino; 5 Native Hawaiian or other Pacific Islander, non-Hispanic/Latino; 29 Two or more races, non-Hispanic/Latino), 68 international. Average age 31. 574 applicants, 75% accepted, 254 enrolled. Expenses: Contact institution. *Financial support:* Research assistantships, teaching assistantships, career-related internships or fieldwork, and scholarships/grants available. Support available to part-time students. Financial award application deadline: 7/1; financial award applicants required to submit FAFSA. In 2017, 253 master's, 34 doctorates awarded. *Program availability:* Part-time, evening/weekend. Offers behavioral psychology (MS); clinical psychology (Psy D); clinical psychology (MA); clinical psychology with Latinos (MA); psychology (MA). *Application deadline:* For fall admission, 2/1 for domestic students. Applications are processed on a rolling basis. *Application fee:* $55. Electronic applications accepted. *Application Contact:* Chris Costa, Director of Enrollment, 310-568-2850, E-mail: chris.costa@pepperdine.edu. *Associate Dean, Psychology Division*, Dr. Robert A. deMayo, 310-568-5747, E-mail: robert.demayo@pepperdine.edu.

Graziadio Business School Students: 1,070 full-time (552 women), 733 part-time (360 women); includes 428 minority (120 Black or African American, non-Hispanic/Latino; 9 American Indian or Alaska Native, non-Hispanic/Latino; 255 Asian, non-Hispanic/Latino; 42 Hispanic/Latino; 2 Two or more races, non-Hispanic/Latino), 438 international. Average age 31. 2,501 applicants, 59% accepted, 323 enrolled. *Faculty:* 89 full-time (23 women), 24 part-time/adjunct (8 women). Expenses: Contact institution. *Financial support:* Career-related internships or fieldwork, institutionally sponsored loans, scholarships/grants, and unspecified assistantships available. Support available to part-time students. Financial award applicants required to submit FAFSA. In 2017, 847 master's awarded. *Program availability:* Part-time. Offers accounting (MS); applied analytics (MS); applied finance (MS); business (MBA, MS); business administration (MBA); global business (MS); human resources (MS); international business administration (MBA); management and leadership (MS); organization development (MS); real estate investment and finance (MS). *Application fee:* $75. Electronic applications accepted. *Application Contact:* Morag Knapp, Assistant Director of Admission, Graziadio School of Business and Management, 310-568-5527, E-mail: morag.knapp@pepperdine.edu. *Dean*, Dr. Deryck J. Rensburg, 310-568-5689, Fax: 310-568-5500, E-mail: deryck.rensburg@pepperdine.edu.

School of Law Students: 534 full-time (285 women), 107 part-time (64 women); includes 191 minority (27 Black or African American, non-Hispanic/Latino; 3 American Indian or Alaska Native, non-Hispanic/Latino; 47 Asian, non-Hispanic/Latino; 84 Hispanic/Latino; 30 Two or more races, non-Hispanic/Latino), 63 international. Average age 28. 2,255 applicants, 46% accepted, 230 enrolled. *Faculty:* 35 full-time (13 women), 35 part-time/adjunct (8 women). Expenses: Contact institution. *Financial support:* Fellowships, research assistantships, teaching assistantships, career-related internships or fieldwork, Federal Work-Study, institutionally sponsored loans, and scholarships/grants available. Support available to part-time students. Financial award application deadline: 4/1; financial award applicants required to submit FAFSA. In 2017, 64 master's, 220 doctorates awarded. Offers dispute resolution (MDR); entertainment, media, and sports law (LL M); international commercial arbitration (LL M); international commercial law and arbitration (LL M); international commercial law and dispute resolution (LL M); law (LL M, MDR, JD); U.S. law and dispute resolution (LL M); United States law (LL M). *Application deadline:* For fall admission, 3/1 for domestic and international students. Applications are processed on a rolling basis. *Application fee:* $60. Electronic applications accepted. *Application Contact:* Shannon Phillips, Assistant Dean, 310-506-4631, Fax: 310-506-4266, E-mail: shannon.phillips@pepperdine.edu. *Dean/Professor of Law*, Dr. Tacha Deanell, 310-506-4611, E-mail: deanell.tacha@pepperdine.edu.

School of Public Policy Average age 25. 174 applicants, 55% accepted, 29 enrolled. Expenses: Contact institution. *Financial support:* Institutionally sponsored loans and scholarships/grants available. Financial award application deadline: 5/1; financial award applicants required to submit FAFSA. In 2017, 34 master's awarded. Offers American politics (MPP); economics (MPP); international relations (MPP); state and local policy (MPP). *Application deadline:* For fall admission, 6/15 for domestic students. Applications are processed on a rolling basis. *Application fee:* $50. Electronic applications accepted. *Application Contact:* Carson Bruno, Assistant Dean for Admission and Program Relations, 310-506-7493, E-mail: carson.bruno@pepperdine.edu. *Dean, School of Public Policy*, Dr. Pete Peterson, 310-506-7490, Fax: 310-506-7494, E-mail: pete.n.peterson@pepperdine.edu.

Seaver College Students: 22 full-time (11 women), 82 part-time (50 women); includes 25 minority (10 Black or African American, non-Hispanic/Latino; 1 American Indian or Alaska Native, non-Hispanic/Latino; 6 Asian, non-Hispanic/Latino; 6 Hispanic/Latino; 2 Two or more races, non-Hispanic/Latino), 6 international. Average age 30. 129 applicants, 31% accepted, 29 enrolled. Expenses: Contact institution. *Financial support:* Fellowships, research assistantships, teaching assistantships, career-related internships or fieldwork, Federal Work-Study, institutionally sponsored loans, scholarships/grants, and tuition waivers (partial) available. Support available to part-time students. Financial award application deadline: 2/15; financial award applicants required to submit FAFSA. In 2017, 24 master's awarded. *Program availability:* Part-time, evening/weekend. Offers business (MS); communication (MA, MFA); humanities (MA, MFA); religion (M Div, MA, MS). *Application deadline:* For fall admission, 2/1 priority date for domestic students. Applications are processed on a rolling basis. *Application fee:* $55. *Application Contact:* Joy Brown, Admission Counselor, 310-506-4392, E-mail: joy.brown@pepperdine.edu. *Assistant Dean, Special Academic and Graduate Programs for Seaver College*, Dr. Dana Dudley, 310-506-6047, Fax: 310-506-4816, E-mail: dana.dudley@pepperdine.edu.

Division of Business Expenses: Contact institution. Offers accounting (MS). *Application deadline:* For fall admission, 2/1 priority date for domestic students. *Application fee:* $55. Electronic applications accepted. *Application Contact:* Hayley Wolf, Director of Admission, 310-506-4392, E-mail: hayley.wolf@pepperdine.edu. *Divisional Dean/Professor of Economics and Finance*, Dr. Dean Baim, 310-506-4237, E-mail: dean.baim@pepperdine.edu.

Division of Communication Students: 8 full-time (3 women), 15 part-time (9 women); includes 9 minority (4 Black or African American, non-Hispanic/Latino; 1 American Indian or Alaska Native, non-Hispanic/Latino; 3 Asian, non-Hispanic/Latino; 1 Hispanic/Latino), 3 international. Average age 27. Expenses: Contact institution. *Financial support:* Research assistantships, teaching assistantships, career-related internships or fieldwork, and scholarships/grants available. Support available to part-time students. Financial award applicants required to submit FAFSA. In 2017, 6 master's awarded. *Program availability:* Part-time. Offers cinematic media production (MFA); strategic communication (MA). *Application deadline:* For fall admission, 2/1 priority date for domestic students, 2/1 for international students. Applications are processed on a rolling basis. *Application fee:* $65. Electronic applications accepted. *Application Contact:* Hayley Wolf, Director of Admission, 310-506-4392, E-mail: hayley.wolf@pepperdine.edu. *Divisional Dean/Professor of Journalism*, Dr. Kenneth E. Waters, 310-506-4245, E-mail: ken.waters@pepperdine.edu.

Division of Humanities Students: 9 full-time (7 women), 41 part-time (23 women); includes 10 minority (4 Black or African American, non-Hispanic/Latino; 1 Asian, non-Hispanic/Latino; 3 Hispanic/Latino; 2 Two or more races, non-Hispanic/Latino), 2 international. Average age 31. Expenses: Contact institution. *Financial support:* Applicants required to submit FAFSA. In 2017, 13 master's awarded. *Program availability:* Part-time. Offers American studies (MA); writing for screen and television (MFA). *Application deadline:* For fall admission, 2/1 priority date for domestic students. Applications are processed on a rolling basis. *Application fee:* $65. *Application*

Contact: Hayley Wolf, Director of Admission, 310-506-4392, E-mail: hayley.wolf@pepperdine.edu. *Chair/Professor of English*, Dr. Michael G. Ditmore, 310-506-4182, Fax: 310-506-7307, E-mail: michael.ditmore@pepperdine.edu.

Division of Religion Students: 3 full-time (1 woman), 12 part-time (3 women); includes 5 minority (2 Black or African American, non-Hispanic/Latino; 1 Asian, non-Hispanic/Latino; 2 Hispanic/Latino). Average age 33. Expenses: Contact institution. *Financial support:* Applicants required to submit FAFSA. In 2017, 7 master's awarded. *Program availability:* Part-time, evening/weekend. Offers ministry (MS); religion (M Div, MA). *Application deadline:* For fall admission, 2/1 priority date for domestic students. Applications are processed on a rolling basis. *Application fee:* $65. Electronic applications accepted. *Application Contact:* Hayley Wolf, Director of Admission, 310-506-4392, E-mail: hayley.wolf@pepperdine.edu. *Chair/Professor*, Dr. Timothy Willis, 310-506-4352, Fax: 310-506-7271, E-mail: timothy.willis@pepperdine.edu.

PERU STATE COLLEGE, Peru, NE 68421

General Information State-supported, coed, comprehensive institution. *Graduate housing:* Rooms and/or apartments available to single and married students.

GRADUATE UNITS

Graduate Programs *Program availability:* Part-time, online learning. Offers curriculum and instruction (MS Ed); organizational management (MS).

PFEIFFER UNIVERSITY, Misenheimer, NC 28109-0960

General Information Independent-religious, coed, comprehensive institution. *Graduate housing:* On-campus housing not available.

GRADUATE UNITS

Program in Business Administration *Program availability:* Part-time, evening/weekend, online learning. Offers business administration (MBA).

Program in Elementary Education Offers elementary education (MAT, MS).

Program in Health Administration Offers health administration (MHA).

Program in Leadership and Organizational Change Offers leadership and organizational change (MS).

Program in Practical Theology *Program availability:* Part-time, evening/weekend. Offers practical theology (MA).

PHILADELPHIA COLLEGE OF OSTEOPATHIC MEDICINE, Philadelphia, PA 19131-1694

General Information Independent, coed, graduate-only institution. *Enrollment by degree level:* 382 master's, 1,325 doctoral, 44 other advanced degrees. *Graduate faculty:* 152 full-time (67 women), 1,639 part-time/adjunct (435 women). *Graduate housing:* On-campus housing not available. *Student services:* Campus employment opportunities, campus safety program, career counseling, exercise/wellness program, free psychological counseling, low-cost health insurance, multicultural affairs office, services for students with disabilities, writing training. *Library facilities:* PCOM Library plus 1 other. *Collection:* Study areas open 24 hours, 5–7 days a week; students can reserve study rooms. *Research affiliation:* Intracell (biotechnology inflammation), Proteapex (biotechnology), Novartis Pharmaceuticals (drug development), Theramunex (biotechnology inflammation), Lankenau Institute for Medical Research (cell biology), Cleveland Museum Natural History (developmental biology).

Computer facilities: 142 computers available on campus for general student use. A campuswide network can be accessed. Online class registration is available. Website: http://www.pcom.edu/

General Application Contact: Kari A. Shotwell, Director of Admissions, 215-871-6700, Fax: 215-871-6719, E-mail: karis@pcom.edu.

GRADUATE UNITS

Graduate and Professional Programs Students: 1,737 full-time (1,003 women); includes 520 minority (168 Black or African American, non-Hispanic/Latino; 2 American Indian or Alaska Native, non-Hispanic/Latino; 61 Asian, non-Hispanic/Latino; 33 Hispanic/Latino; 256 Two or more races, non-Hispanic/Latino), 7 international. 18,451 applicants, 8% accepted, 828 enrolled. *Faculty:* 87 full-time (37 women), 927 part-time/adjunct (146 women). Expenses: Contact institution. *Financial support:* Fellowships, research assistantships, career-related internships or fieldwork, Federal Work-Study, institutionally sponsored loans, and scholarships/grants available. Financial award application deadline: 3/15; financial award applicants required to submit FAFSA. In 2017, 220 master's, 502 doctorates, 10 other advanced degrees awarded. Offers applied behavior analysis (Certificate); biomedical sciences (MS); clinical health psychology (Post-Doctoral Certificate); clinical neuropsychology (Post-Doctoral Certificate); clinical psychology (Psy D); educational psychology (PhD); forensic medicine (MS); health sciences (MS); mental health counseling (MS); organizational development and leadership (MS); osteopathic medicine (DO); psychology (Certificate); public health management and administration (MS); school psychology (MS, Psy D, Ed S). *Application deadline:* Applications are processed on a rolling basis. *Application fee:* $75. Electronic applications accepted. *Application Contact:* Kari A. Shotwell, Director of Admissions, 215-871-6700, Fax: 215-871-6719, E-mail: karis@pcom.edu.

PHILLIPS GRADUATE UNIVERSITY, Chatsworth, CA 91311

General Information Independent, coed, graduate-only institution. *Tuition:* Part-time $897 per unit. *Required fees:* $375 per semester. Part-time tuition and fees vary according to degree level and program. *Graduate housing:* On-campus housing not available. *Student services:* Campus employment opportunities, career counseling, services for students with disabilities, writing training. *Library facilities:* PGU Library plus 1 other.

Computer facilities: 4 computers available on campus for general student use. Website: http://www.pgu.edu/

General Application Contact: Christine Montagna, Admissions Advisor, 818-600-4945, Fax: 818-386-5699, E-mail: cmontagna@pgu.edu.

GRADUATE UNITS

Doctoral Program in Organizational Management and Consulting Expenses: Contact institution. *Financial support:* Tuition waivers (full and partial) available. *Program availability:* Evening/weekend. Offers organizational management and consulting (Psy D). *Application deadline:* For fall admission, 1/29 priority date for domestic students. Applications are processed on a rolling basis. *Application fee:* $80. Electronic applications accepted. *Application Contact:* Christine Montagna, Admissions Advisor, 818-600-4945, Fax: 818-386-5699, E-mail: cmontagna@pgu.edu.

Master's Program in Psychology Expenses: Contact institution. *Financial support:* Federal Work-Study and tuition waivers (full and partial) available. Financial award application deadline: 8/15; financial award applicants required to submit FAFSA. *Program availability:* Evening/weekend. Offers art therapy (MA); marriage and family therapy (MA); school counseling (MA); school psychology (MA). *Application deadline:* For fall admission, 4/16 priority date for domestic students; for spring admission, 11/15 for domestic students. Applications are processed on a rolling basis. *Application fee:* $80. Electronic applications accepted. *Application Contact:* Christine Montagna, Admissions Advisor, 818-600-4945, Fax: 818-386-5699, E-mail: cmontagna@pgu.edu.

PHILLIPS THEOLOGICAL SEMINARY, Tulsa, OK 74116

General Information Independent-religious, coed, graduate-only institution. *Graduate housing:* On-campus housing not available.

GRADUATE UNITS

Programs in Theology *Program availability:* Part-time, online learning. Offers administration of church agencies (M Div); campus ministry (M Div); church-related social work (M Div); college and seminary teaching (M Div); global mission work (M Div); institutional chaplaincy (M Div); ministerial vocations in Christian education (M Div); ministry (D Min); ministry and culture (MAMC); ministry of music (M Div); parish ministry (D Min); pastoral care and counseling (M Div); pastoral counseling (D Min); pastoral ministry (M Div); practices of ministry (D Min); theological studies (MTS).

PHOENIX INSTITUTE OF HERBAL MEDICINE & ACUPUNCTURE, Phoenix, AZ 85018

General Information Proprietary, coed, graduate-only institution.

GRADUATE UNITS

Graduate Programs Offers acupuncture (MSAC); Oriental medicine (MSOM).

PHOENIX SEMINARY, Phoenix, AZ 85018

General Information Independent-religious, coed, graduate-only institution.

GRADUATE UNITS

Graduate Programs *Program availability:* Part-time, evening/weekend. Offers Biblical and theological studies (Graduate Diploma); Biblical communication (M Div); Biblical leadership (MA); Christian counseling (Graduate Diploma); counseling and family (M Div); leadership development (M Div); ministry (D Min); professional counseling (MA).

PIEDMONT COLLEGE, Demorest, GA 30535

General Information Independent-religious, coed, comprehensive institution. *Enrollment:* 2,361 graduate, professional, and undergraduate students; 387 full-time matriculated graduate/professional students (293 women), 693 part-time matriculated graduate/professional students (575 women). *Enrollment by degree level:* 533 master's, 85 doctoral, 462 other advanced degrees. *Tuition:* Full-time $9360; part-time $520 per credit hour. *Required fees:* $200; $200 per year. $100 per term. *Graduate housing:* Room and/or apartments available on a first-come, first-served basis to single students; on-campus housing not available to married students. *Student services:* Campus employment opportunities, campus safety program, career counseling, exercise/wellness program, services for students with disabilities, teacher training, writing training. *Library facilities:* Arrendale Library plus 2 others. *Collection:* Books: 99,693 (physical), 416,680 (digital/electronic); Serial titles: 24,272 (digital/electronic). Students can reserve study rooms.

Computer facilities: 150 computers available on campus for general student use. A campuswide network can be accessed from student residence rooms and from off campus. Online class registration is available. Website: http://www.piedmont.edu/

General Application Contact: Kathleen Carter, Director of Graduate Enrollment Management, 706-778-8500 Ext. 1181, Fax: 706-776-0150, E-mail: kanderson@piedmont.edu.

GRADUATE UNITS

School of Business Students: 46 full-time (25 women), 11 part-time (4 women); includes 11 minority (8 Black or African American, non-Hispanic/Latino; 1 Asian, non-Hispanic/Latino; 1 Hispanic/Latino; 1 Native Hawaiian or other Pacific Islander, non-Hispanic/Latino). Average age 29. 32 applicants, 38% accepted, 10 enrolled. Expenses: Contact institution. *Financial support:* Federal Work-Study and unspecified assistantships available. Financial award applicants required to submit FAFSA. In 2017, 37 master's awarded. *Program availability:* Part-time, evening/weekend. Offers business (MBA). *Application deadline:* For fall admission, 7/15 for domestic students; for spring admission, 12/1 for domestic students. Applications are processed on a rolling basis. Electronic applications accepted. *Application Contact:* Kathleen Carter, Director of Graduate Enrollment Management, 706-778-3000, E-mail: kcarter@piedmont.edu. *Dean*, Dr. Edward Taylor, 706-778-3000, E-mail: etaylor@piedmont.edu.

School of Education Students: 341 full-time (268 women), 682 part-time (571 women); includes 182 minority (136 Black or African American, non-Hispanic/Latino; 2 American Indian or Alaska Native, non-Hispanic/Latino; 11 Asian, non-Hispanic/Latino; 32 Hispanic/Latino; 1 Two or more races, non-Hispanic/Latino). Average age 37. 333 applicants, 77% accepted, 103 enrolled. Expenses: Contact institution. *Financial support:* Career-related internships or fieldwork, Federal Work-Study, and unspecified assistantships available. Support available to part-time students. Financial award applicants required to submit FAFSA. In 2017, 292 master's, 9 doctorates, 318 other advanced degrees awarded. *Program availability:* Part-time, evening/weekend. Offers art education (MA, MAT); curriculum and instruction (Ed D, Ed S); early childhood education (MA, MAT); instructional technology (MA); middle grades education (MA, MAT); music education (MA, MAT); secondary education (MA, MAT); special education (MA, MAT). *Application deadline:* For fall admission, 7/15 for domestic students; for spring admission, 12/1 for domestic students. Applications are processed on a rolling basis. Electronic applications accepted. *Application Contact:* Kathleen Carter, Director of Graduate Enrollment Management, 706-778-8500 Ext. 1181, Fax: 706-778-0150, E-mail: kanderson@piedmont.edu. *Dean*, Dr. Don Gnecco, 706-778-3000 Ext. 1201, Fax: 706-776-9608, E-mail: dgnecco@piedmont.edu.

PIEDMONT INTERNATIONAL UNIVERSITY, Winston-Salem, NC 27101-5197

General Information Independent-religious, coed, university. *Graduate housing:* Rooms and/or apartments available on a first-come, first-served basis to single and married students. Housing application deadline: 5/1.

GRADUATE UNITS

Graduate School *Program availability:* Part-time, online learning. Offers Biblical studies (PhD); curriculum and instruction (M Ed); divinity (M Div); educational leadership (M Ed); leadership (MA, PhD); ministry (MA Min, D Min); non-language track (MABS); PhD preparation track (MABS). Electronic applications accepted.

Temple Baptist Seminary *Program availability:* Part-time, evening/weekend, online learning. Offers theology (M Div, D Min).

PILLAR COLLEGE, Newark, NJ 07102

General Information Independent-religious, coed, comprehensive institution.

GRADUATE UNITS

Program in Counseling Offers counseling (MA).

PITTSBURGH THEOLOGICAL SEMINARY, Pittsburgh, PA 15206-2596

General Information Independent-religious, coed, graduate-only institution. *Enrollment by degree level:* 115 master's, 81 doctoral, 17 other advanced degrees. *Graduate faculty:* 16 full-time (5 women), 6 part-time/adjunct (2 women). *Tuition:* Full-time $11,988; part-time $358 per credit hour. *Required fees:* $100 per term. Tuition and fees vary according to degree level. *Graduate housing:* Rooms and/or apartments available on a first-come, first-served basis to single and married students. Typical cost: $7775 (including board) for single students. Room and board charges vary according to housing facility selected. Housing application deadline: 6/1. *Student services:* Campus employment opportunities, campus safety program, career counseling, exercise/wellness program, free psychological counseling, international student services, low-cost health insurance, services for students with disabilities, writing training. *Library facilities:* Clifford E. Barbour Library. *Collection:* Books: 304,623 (physical), 71 (digital/electronic); Serial titles: 779 (physical), 156 (digital/electronic); Databases: 23. Weekly public service hours: 67.

Computer facilities: 15 computers available on campus for general student use. A campuswide network can be accessed from student residence rooms and from off campus. Online class registration is available.
Website: http://www.pts.edu/

General Application Contact: Tracy Riggle Young, Director of Enrollment and Retention, 412-924-1423, Fax: 412-924-1723, E-mail: triggleyoung@pts.edu.

GRADUATE UNITS

Graduate and Professional Programs Students: 170 full-time (70 women), 43 part-time (25 women); includes 56 minority (45 Black or African American, non-Hispanic/Latino; 5 Asian, non-Hispanic/Latino; 3 Hispanic/Latino; 1 Native Hawaiian or other Pacific Islander, non-Hispanic/Latino; 2 Two or more races, non-Hispanic/Latino), 13 international. Average age 35. 57 applicants, 93% accepted, 44 enrolled. *Faculty:* 16 full-time (5 women), 6 part-time/adjunct (2 women). Expenses: Contact institution. *Financial support:* In 2017–18, 104 students received support. Career-related internships or fieldwork, scholarships/grants, and institutional work-study available. Financial award application deadline: 5/1; financial award applicants required to submit FAFSA. In 2017, 26 master's, 9 doctorates awarded. *Program availability:* Part-time, evening/weekend. Offers divinity (M Div); theological studies (MA); theology (Th M); theology and ministry (MA, D Min). M Div/MSW offered jointly with University of Pittsburgh; JD/M Div with Duquesne University; M Div/MSPPM with Carnegie Mellon University. *Application deadline:* For fall admission, 6/30 priority date for domestic students, 12/1 for international students; for winter admission, 10/15 priority date for domestic students; for spring admission, 1/15 priority date for domestic students. Applications are processed on a rolling basis. *Application fee:* $50. Electronic applications accepted. *Application Contact:* Tracy Riggle Young, Director of Enrollment and Retention, 412-924-1423, Fax: 412-924-1723, E-mail: triggleyoung@pts.edu. *Dean of Faculty and Vice President for Academic Affairs,* Dr. Heather H. Vacek, 412-924-1374, Fax: 412-924-1774, E-mail: hvacek@pts.edu.

PITTSBURG STATE UNIVERSITY, Pittsburg, KS 66762

General Information State-supported, coed, comprehensive institution. CGS member. *Enrollment:* 6,907 graduate, professional, and undergraduate students; 301 full-time matriculated graduate/professional students (143 women), 757 part-time matriculated graduate/professional students (494 women). *Enrollment by degree level:* 980 master's, 44 doctoral, 34 other advanced degrees. *Graduate faculty:* 126 full-time (40 women), 35 part-time/adjunct (14 women). Tuition, state resident: full-time $7944; part-time $333 per credit hour. *Required fees:* $1552; $66 per credit hour. Full-time tuition and fees vary according to course load, degree level and campus/location. *Graduate housing:* Rooms and/or apartments available on a first-come, first-served basis to single and married students. Typical cost: $7700 (including board) for single students; $7700 (including board) for married students. Room and board charges vary according to board plan, campus/location and housing facility selected. Housing application deadline: 8/15. *Student services:* Campus employment opportunities, campus safety program, career counseling, exercise/wellness program, free psychological counseling, grant writing training, international student services, low-cost health insurance, multicultural affairs office, services for students with disabilities, teacher training, writing training. *Library facilities:* Leonard H. Axe Library plus 2 others. *Research affiliation:* Cargill, Inc. (vegetable oil).

Computer facilities: A campuswide network can be accessed from student residence rooms and from off campus. Online class registration is available.
Website: http://www.pittstate.edu/

General Application Contact: Lisa Allen, Assistant Director, 620-235-4218, Fax: 620-235-4219, E-mail: lallen@pittstate.edu.

GRADUATE UNITS

Graduate School Students: 309 full-time (150 women), 892 part-time (603 women); includes 138 minority (28 Black or African American, non-Hispanic/Latino; 18 American Indian or Alaska Native, non-Hispanic/Latino; 8 Asian, non-Hispanic/Latino; 38 Hispanic/Latino; 46 Two or more races, non-Hispanic/Latino), 127 international. 1,011 applicants, 50% accepted, 398 enrolled. *Faculty:* 223 full-time (74 women), 129 part-time/adjunct (68 women). Expenses: Contact institution. *Financial support:* In 2017–18, 7 fellowships with partial tuition reimbursements (averaging $1,000 per year), 6 research assistantships with partial tuition reimbursements (averaging $5,000 per year), 104 teaching assistantships with full tuition reimbursements (averaging $5,500 per year) were awarded; career-related internships or fieldwork, Federal Work-Study, scholarships/grants, and unspecified assistantships also available. Financial award application deadline: 2/1; financial award applicants required to submit FAFSA. In 2017, 447 master's, 13 doctorates, 7 other advanced degrees awarded. *Program availability:* Part-time, evening/weekend, 100% online, blended/hybrid learning. *Application deadline:* For fall admission, 7/15 for domestic students, 6/1 for international students; for spring admission, 12/15 for domestic students, 10/15 for international students; for summer admission, 5/15 for domestic students, 4/1 for international students. Applications are processed on a rolling basis. *Application fee:* $35 ($60 for international students). Electronic applications accepted. *Application Contact:* Lisa Allen, Assistant Director of Graduate and Continuing Studies, 620-235-4223, Fax: 620-235-4219, E-mail: lallen@pittstate.edu. *Dean of Graduate and Continuing Studies,* Dr. Pawan Kahol, 620-235-4222, Fax: 620-235-4219, E-mail: pkahol@pittstate.edu.

College of Arts and Sciences Students: 183 (113 women); includes 22 minority (2 American Indian or Alaska Native, non-Hispanic/Latino; 1 Asian, non-Hispanic/Latino; 6 Hispanic/Latino; 13 Two or more races, non-Hispanic/Latino), 35 international. Expenses: Contact institution. *Financial support:* In 2017–18, 6 research assistantships with partial tuition reimbursements (averaging $5,000 per year), 48 teaching assistantships with full tuition reimbursements (averaging $5,500 per year) were awarded; career-related internships or fieldwork, Federal Work-Study, and unspecified assistantships also available. Financial award application deadline: 2/1; financial award applicants required to submit FAFSA. In 2017, 71 master's, 13 doctorates awarded. *Program availability:* Part-time, 100% online, blended/hybrid learning. Offers arts and sciences (MA, MM, MS, MSN, DNP); biology (MS); chemistry (MS); communication (MA); conducting (MM); education (MM); English (MA); history (MA); mathematics (MS); nursing (DNP); nursing education (MSN); performance (MM); physics (MS); polymer chemistry (MS). *Application deadline:* For fall admission, 7/15 for domestic students, 6/1 for international students; for spring admission, 12/15 for domestic students, 10/15 for international students; for summer admission, 5/15 for domestic students, 4/1 for international students. Applications are processed on a rolling basis. *Application fee:* $35 ($60 for international students). Electronic applications accepted. *Application Contact:* Lisa Allen, Assistant Director of Graduate and Continuing Studies, 620-235-4223, Fax: 620-235-4219, E-mail: lallen@pittstate.edu. *Dean,* Dr. Mary Carol Pomatto, 620-235-4432, E-mail: mpomatto@pittstate.edu.

College of Education Students: 595 (413 women); includes 80 minority (17 Black or African American, non-Hispanic/Latino; 12 American Indian or Alaska Native, non-Hispanic/Latino; 3 Asian, non-Hispanic/Latino; 24 Hispanic/Latino; 24 Two or more races, non-Hispanic/Latino), 1 international. Expenses: Contact institution. *Financial support:* In 2017–18, 25 teaching assistantships with full tuition reimbursements (averaging $5,500 per year) were awarded; career-related internships or fieldwork, Federal Work-Study, and unspecified assistantships also available. Financial award application deadline: 2/1; financial award applicants required to submit FAFSA. In 2017, 266 master's, 13 other advanced degrees awarded. *Program availability:* Part-time, 100% online, blended/hybrid learning. Offers advanced studies in leadership (Ed S); autism spectrum disorder (Certificate); counselor education (MS); district level (Certificate); education (MS); educational leadership (MS); educational technology (MS); general school administration (Ed S); health, human performance, and recreation (MS); psychology (MS); school counseling (MS); school psychology (Ed S); secondary education (MAT); special education (MAT, MS); teaching (MS); TESOL (Certificate). *Application deadline:* For fall admission, 6/1 for international students; for spring admission, 10/15 for international students; for summer admission, 4/1 for international students. Applications are processed on a rolling basis. *Application fee:* $35 ($60 for international students). Electronic applications accepted. *Application Contact:* Lisa Allen, Assistant Director of Graduate and Continuing Studies, 620-235-4223, Fax: 620-235-4219, E-mail: lallen@pittstate.edu. *Dean,* Dr. Jim Truelove, 620-235-4518, Fax: 620-235-4520, E-mail: jtruelove@pittstate.edu.

College of Technology Students: 189 (75 women); includes 22 minority (9 Black or African American, non-Hispanic/Latino; 3 American Indian or Alaska Native, non-Hispanic/Latino; 3 Asian, non-Hispanic/Latino; 3 Hispanic/Latino; 4 Two or more races, non-Hispanic/Latino), 64 international. Expenses: Contact institution. *Financial support:* In 2017–18, 14 teaching assistantships with full tuition reimbursements (averaging $5,500 per year) were awarded; career-related internships or fieldwork, Federal Work-Study, and unspecified assistantships also available. Financial award application deadline: 2/1; financial award applicants required to submit FAFSA. In 2017, 104 master's, 2 other advanced degrees awarded. *Program availability:* Part-time, 100% online, blended/hybrid learning. Offers career and technical education (MS); construction engineering technology (MET); construction management (MS); electrical engineering technology (MET); general engineering technology (MET); human resource development (MS); manufacturing engineering technology (MET); mechanical engineering technology (MET); plastics engineering technology (MET); technology (MS); workforce development and education (Ed S). *Application deadline:* For fall admission, 7/15 for domestic students, 6/1 for international students; for spring admission, 12/15 for domestic students, 10/15 for international students; for summer admission, 5/15 for domestic students, 4/1 for international students. Applications are processed on a rolling basis. *Application fee:* $35 ($60 for international students). Electronic applications accepted. *Application Contact:* Lisa Allen, Assistant Director of Graduate and Continuing Studies, 620-235-4223, Fax: 620-235-4219, E-mail: lallen@pittstate.edu. *Dean,* Dr. Tim Dawsey, 620-235-4366.

Kelce College of Business Students: 91 (36 women); includes 6 minority (1 Black or African American, non-Hispanic/Latino; 1 Asian, non-Hispanic/Latino; 2 Hispanic/Latino; 2 Two or more races, non-Hispanic/Latino), 20 international. Expenses: Contact institution. *Financial support:* In 2017–18, 15 teaching assistantships with full tuition reimbursements (averaging $5,500 per year) were awarded; research assistantships, career-related internships or fieldwork, Federal Work-Study, and unspecified assistantships also available. Financial award application deadline: 2/1; financial award applicants required to submit FAFSA. In 2017, 40 master's awarded. Offers accounting (MBA); business (MBA); general administration (MBA); international business (MBA). *Application deadline:* For fall admission, 7/15 for domestic students, 6/1 for international students; for spring admission, 12/15 for domestic students, 10/15 for international students; for summer admission, 5/15 for domestic students, 4/1 for international students. Applications are processed on a rolling basis. *Application fee:* $35 ($60 for international students). Electronic applications accepted. *Application Contact:* Lisa Allen, Assistant Director of Graduate and Continuing Studies, 620-235-4218, Fax: 620-235-4219, E-mail: lallen@pittstate.edu. *Dean,* Dr. Paul Grimes, 620-235-4590, Fax: 620-235-4578, E-mail: pgrimes@pittstate.edu.

PLYMOUTH STATE UNIVERSITY, Plymouth, NH 03264-1595

General Information State-supported, coed, comprehensive institution. Tuition, state resident: part-time $525 per credit. Tuition, nonresident: part-time $605 per credit. *Required fees:* $38 per credit. Part-time tuition and fees vary according to course level and program. *Graduate housing:* Rooms and/or apartments available on a first-come, first-served basis to single students and guaranteed to married students. Housing application deadline: 5/1. *Student services:* Campus employment opportunities, campus safety program, career counseling, child daycare facilities, exercise/wellness program, free psychological counseling, grant writing training, services for students with disabilities, teacher training, writing training. *Library facilities:* Lamson Learning Commons. *Collection:* Books: 344,605 (physical), 155,000 (digital/electronic); Serial titles: 790 (physical), 1,500 (digital/electronic); Databases: 87. Weekly public service hours: 94. *Research affiliation:* Hubbard Brook Experimental Forest (science), New Hampshire Department of Environmental Services (science), White Mountain National Forest (science), National Oceanic and Atmospheric Administration (NOAA) (science).

Computer facilities: Computer purchase and lease plans are available. 600 computers available on campus for general student use. A campuswide network can be accessed from student residence rooms and from off campus. Online class registration, degree audit, academic history, account status are available.
Website: http://www.plymouth.edu/

General Application Contact: Cheryl B. Baker, Director of Academic Assessment and Accreditation, 603-535-2737, Fax: 603-535-2572, E-mail: cbaker@plymouth.edu.

GRADUATE UNITS

College of Graduate Studies Expenses: Contact institution. *Financial support:* Application deadline: 4/15; applicants required to submit FAFSA. *Program availability:* Part-time, evening/weekend, online learning. *Application deadline:* For fall admission, 5/15 for international students; for winter admission, 5/15 for international students; for spring admission, 10/15 for international students. Applications are processed on a rolling basis. *Application fee:* $75. *Application Contact:* Cheryl B. Baker, Director of Recruitment and Outreach, 603-535-2737, Fax: 603-535-2572, E-mail: cbaker@plymouth.edu. *Interim Associate Vice President*, George F. Tuthill, 603-535-3107, Fax: 603-535-2572, E-mail: gftuthill@plymouth.edu.

Graduate Studies in Business Expenses: Contact institution. *Financial support:* Application deadline: 4/15; applicants required to submit FAFSA. *Program availability:* Part-time, evening/weekend, online learning. Offers accounting (MS); general management (MBA). *Application deadline:* For fall admission, 5/15 for international students; for winter admission, 5/15 for international students; for spring admission, 10/15 for international students. Applications are processed on a rolling basis. *Application fee:* $75. *Application Contact:* Cheryl B. Baker, Director of Recruitment and Outreach, 603-535-2737, Fax: 603-535-2572, E-mail: cbaker@plymouth.edu. *Director of Graduate Business Programs*, Chen Wu, 603-535-3241, E-mail: cwu@plymouth.edu.

Graduate Studies in Education Expenses: Contact institution. *Financial support:* Application deadline: 4/15; applicants required to submit FAFSA. *Program availability:* Part-time, evening/weekend, online learning. Offers addictions treatment (MS); administrative leadership (Ed D); art education (MAT); athletic training (MS); clinical mental health counseling (CAGS); couples and family therapy (MS); curriculum and instruction (Ed D); eating disorders (M Ed); education (M Ed, MAT, MS, Ed D, CAGS); educational leadership (CAGS); English education (M Ed); health education (M Ed); health promotion (MS); heritage studies (M Ed); higher education (CAGS); integrated arts (M Ed); learning, leadership and community (Ed D); mathematics education (M Ed); music education (M Ed); play therapy (MS); school psychology (CAGS). *Application deadline:* For fall admission, 5/15 for international students; for winter admission, 5/15 for international students; for spring admission, 10/15 for international students. Applications are processed on a rolling basis. *Application fee:* $75. *Application Contact:* Cheryl B. Baker, Director of Recruitment and Outreach, 603-535-2737, Fax: 603-535-2572, E-mail: cbaker@plymouth.edu. *Interim Associate Vice President*, George F. Tuthill, 603-535-3107, Fax: 603-535-2572, E-mail: gftuthill@plymouth.edu.

Program in Historic Preservation Expenses: Contact institution. Offers historic preservation (MA, Graduate Certificate). *Application Contact:* Cheryl B. Baker, Director of Recruitment and Outreach, 603-535-2737, Fax: 603-535-2572, E-mail: cbaker@plymouth.edu. *Program Coordinator/Advisor*, Dr. Patrick May, 603-535-2501, E-mail: pmay@plymouth.edu.

Program in Personal and Organizational Wellness Expenses: Contact institution. Offers personal and organizational wellness (MA, Graduate Certificate). *Application Contact:* Cheryl B. Baker, Director of Recruitment and Outreach, 603-535-2737, Fax: 603-535-2572, E-mail: cbaker@plymouth.edu. *Program Coordinator/Advisor*, Dr. Nancy Puglisi, 603-862-3116, E-mail: npuglisi@plymouth.edu.

POINT LOMA NAZARENE UNIVERSITY, San Diego, CA 92106-2899

General Information Independent-religious, coed, comprehensive institution. *Enrollment:* 4,467 graduate, professional, and undergraduate students; 439 full-time matriculated graduate/professional students (299 women), 719 part-time matriculated graduate/professional students (521 women). *Enrollment by degree level:* 1,142 master's, 12 doctoral, 4 other advanced degrees. *Graduate faculty:* 35 full-time (18 women), 134 part-time/adjunct (84 women). *Graduate housing:* On-campus housing not available. *Student services:* Campus employment opportunities, campus safety program, career counseling, free psychological counseling, international student services, low-cost health insurance, services for students with disabilities, teacher training. *Library facilities:* Ryan Library.

Computer facilities: 346 computers available on campus for general student use. A campuswide network can be accessed from student residence rooms and from off campus. Online class registration is available.
Website: http://www.pointloma.edu/

General Application Contact: Joanie Joy, Senior Director of Enrollment Management, 619-329-6785, E-mail: gradinfo@pointloma.edu.

GRADUATE UNITS

College of Extended Learning Students: 50 full-time (40 women), 84 part-time (58 women); includes 64 minority (11 Black or African American, non-Hispanic/Latino; 1 American Indian or Alaska Native, non-Hispanic/Latino; 5 Asian, non-Hispanic/Latino; 41 Hispanic/Latino; 6 Two or more races, non-Hispanic/Latino), 2 international. Average age 32. 71 applicants, 99% accepted, 53 enrolled. *Faculty:* 24 part-time/adjunct (10 women). Expenses: Contact institution. *Financial support:* Scholarships/grants available. Financial award applicants required to submit FAFSA. In 2017, 34 master's awarded. Offers marriage and family therapy (MA); organizational leadership (MA); professional clinical counselor (MA). *Application Contact:* Joanie Joy, Senior Director of Enrollment Management, 619-329-6785, E-mail: gradinfo@pointloma.edu. *Dean*, Dave Phillips, 619-849-2771, E-mail: dphillips@pointloma.edu.

Department of Biology Students: 3 full-time (1 woman), 15 part-time (11 women); includes 10 minority (5 Asian, non-Hispanic/Latino; 2 Hispanic/Latino; 3 Two or more races, non-Hispanic/Latino), 1 international. Average age 31. 7 applicants, 71% accepted, 5 enrolled. *Faculty:* 5 full-time (3 women). Expenses: Contact institution. *Financial support:* Available to part-time students. Applicants required to submit FAFSA. In 2017, 7 master's awarded. *Program availability:* Part-time. Offers biology (MS). *Application deadline:* For fall admission, 7/26 priority date for domestic students; for spring admission, 11/29 priority date for domestic students; for summer admission, 5/23 priority date for domestic students. *Application fee:* $50. Electronic applications accepted. *Application Contact:* Maira Lopes, Enrollment Advisor, 619-948-2885, E-mail: mairalopes@pointloma.edu. *Director of Master's Program in Biology*, Dr. Dianne Anderson, 619-849-2705, E-mail: dianneanderson@pointloma.edu.

Department of Kinesiology Students: 55 full-time (26 women), 3 part-time (2 women); includes 20 minority (2 Black or African American, non-Hispanic/Latino; 3 Asian, non-Hispanic/Latino; 12 Hispanic/Latino; 1 Native Hawaiian or other Pacific Islander, non-Hispanic/Latino; 2 Two or more races, non-Hispanic/Latino), 3 international. Average age 29. 92 applicants, 92% accepted, 55 enrolled. *Faculty:* 5 full-time (2 women), 8 part-time/adjunct (2 women). Expenses: Contact institution. *Financial support:* Teaching assistantships, scholarships/grants, and unspecified assistantships available. In 2017, 30 master's awarded. *Program availability:* Part-time, online learning. Offers exercise science (MS); sport performance (MS). *Application fee:* $50. *Application Contact:* Joanie Joy, Senior Director of Enrollment Management, 619-329-6785, E-mail: gradinfo@pointloma.edu. *Chair*, Jeff Sullivan, 619-849-2629, E-mail: jeffsullivan@pointloma.edu.

Fermanian School of Business Students: 27 full-time (8 women), 94 part-time (45 women); includes 52 minority (6 Black or African American, non-Hispanic/Latino; 1 American Indian or Alaska Native, non-Hispanic/Latino; 7 Asian, non-Hispanic/Latino; 33 Hispanic/Latino; 5 Two or more races, non-Hispanic/Latino), 11 international. Average age 31. 74 applicants, 99% accepted, 56 enrolled. *Faculty:* 7 full-time (0 women), 5 part-time/adjunct (3 women). Expenses: Contact institution. *Financial support:* Applicants required to submit FAFSA. In 2017, 45 master's awarded. *Program availability:* Part-time, evening/weekend. Offers general business (MBA); healthcare management (MBA); innovation and entrepreneurship (MBA); organizational leadership (MBA); project management (MBA). *Application deadline:* For fall admission, 7/26 priority date for domestic students; for spring admission, 11/29 priority date for domestic students; for summer admission, 4/2 priority date for domestic students. Applications are processed on a rolling basis. *Application fee:* $50. Electronic applications accepted. *Application Contact:* Joanie Joy, Senior Director of Enrollment Management, 619-329-6785, E-mail: gradinfo@pointloma.edu. *Associate Dean, Graduate Business*, Jamie McIlwaine, 619-849-2721, E-mail: jmcilwai@pointloma.edu.

School of Education Students: 304 full-time (224 women), 433 part-time (334 women); includes 364 minority (25 Black or African American, non-Hispanic/Latino; 2 American Indian or Alaska Native, non-Hispanic/Latino; 28 Asian, non-Hispanic/Latino; 267 Hispanic/Latino; 6 Native Hawaiian or other Pacific Islander, non-Hispanic/Latino; 36 Two or more races, non-Hispanic/Latino), 2 international. Average age 32. 172 applicants, 98% accepted, 139 enrolled. *Faculty:* 12 full-time (9 women), 94 part-time/adjunct (68 women). Expenses: Contact institution. *Financial support:* Career-related internships or fieldwork and scholarships/grants available. Support available to part-time students. Financial award application deadline: 4/10; financial award applicants required to submit FAFSA. In 2017, 136 master's awarded. *Program availability:* Part-time, evening/weekend. Offers counseling and guidance (MA); education (MA, MAT); educational administration (MA); leadership in learning (MA); special education (MA); teaching (MAT). *Application deadline:* For fall admission, 8/4 priority date for domestic students; for spring admission, 12/8 priority date for domestic students; for summer admission, 4/13 priority date for domestic students. Applications are processed on a rolling basis. *Application fee:* $50. Electronic applications accepted. *Application Contact:* Joanie Joy, Senior Director of Enrollment Management, 619-329-6785, E-mail: gradinfo@pointloma.edu. *Dean*, Dr. Deborah Erickson, 619-849-2332, Fax: 619-849-2579, E-mail: deberickson@pointloma.edu.

School of Nursing Students: 75 part-time (65 women); includes 37 minority (6 Black or African American, non-Hispanic/Latino; 1 American Indian or Alaska Native, non-Hispanic/Latino; 7 Asian, non-Hispanic/Latino; 10 Hispanic/Latino; 5 Native Hawaiian or other Pacific Islander, non-Hispanic/Latino; 8 Two or more races, non-Hispanic/Latino), 1 international. Average age 38. 39 applicants, 95% accepted, 31 enrolled. *Faculty:* 4 full-time (3 women), 2 part-time/adjunct (1 woman). Expenses: Contact institution. *Financial support:* Scholarships/grants available. Financial award applicants required to submit FAFSA. In 2017, 21 master's awarded. *Program availability:* Part-time. Offers adult-gerontology (MSN); clinical nurse specialist (Post-MSN Certificate); family individual health (MSN); nursing (MSN, DNP, Post-MSN Certificate); pediatrics (MSN). *Application deadline:* For fall admission, 7/5 priority date for domestic students; for spring admission, 11/1 priority date for domestic students; for summer admission, 3/22 priority date for domestic students. Applications are processed on a rolling basis. *Application fee:* $50. *Application Contact:* Joanie Joy, Senior Director of Enrollment Management, 619-329-6785, E-mail: gradinfo@pointloma.edu. *Dean of the School of Nursing*, Dr. Barb Taylor, 619-849-2766, E-mail: bataylor@pointloma.edu.

School of Theology and Christian Ministry Students: 15 part-time (6 women); includes 7 minority (all Hispanic/Latino). Average age 40. 4 applicants, 100% accepted, 3 enrolled. *Faculty:* 1 full-time (0 women), 1 part-time/adjunct (0 women). Expenses: Contact institution. *Financial support:* Scholarships/grants available. Financial award application deadline: 6/5; financial award applicants required to submit FAFSA. In 2017, 2 master's awarded. *Program availability:* Part-time, online only, nine-week quads with eight weeks of online coursework and a one-week intensive. Offers theology and Christian ministry (M Min). *Application deadline:* For fall admission, 8/30 priority date for domestic students; for spring admission, 4/4 priority date for domestic students; for summer admission, 6/20 priority date for domestic students. Applications are processed on a rolling basis. *Application fee:* $0. Electronic applications accepted. *Application Contact:* Joanie Joy, Senior Director of Enrollment Management, 619-329-6785, E-mail: gradinfo@pointloma.edu. *Dean*, Dr. Mark Maddix, 619-849-2234, E-mail: markmaddix@pointloma.edu.

POINT PARK UNIVERSITY, Pittsburgh, PA 15222-1984

General Information Independent, coed, university. CGS member. *Graduate housing:* Room and/or apartments available on a first-come, first-served basis to single students; on-campus housing not available to married students. Housing application deadline: 7/31.

GRADUATE UNITS

Center for Innovative Learning Offers community engagement (PhD).

Conservatory of Performing Arts *Program availability:* Blended/hybrid learning. Offers screenwriting and playwriting (MFA). Electronic applications accepted.

Rowland School of Business *Program availability:* Part-time, evening/weekend, 100% online. Offers business (MA, MBA, MS); business analytics (MBA); global management and administration (MBA); health care administration and management (MS); health systems management (MBA); international business (MBA); leadership (MA); management (MBA); management information systems (MBA); sports, arts and entertainment management (MBA). Electronic applications accepted.

School of Arts and Sciences *Program availability:* Part-time, evening/weekend, online learning. Offers adult learning and training (MA); arts and sciences (M Ed, MA, MS, Ed D, Psy D); athletic coaching (M Ed); clinical-community psychology (MA, Psy D); criminal justice administration (MS); curriculum and instruction (MA); educational administration (MA); engineering management (MS); environmental studies (MS); intelligence and global security (MA); leadership and administration (Ed D); secondary education (M Ed); special education grades 7-12 (M Ed); special education PreK-grade 8 (M Ed). Electronic applications accepted.

School of Communication *Program availability:* Part-time, evening/weekend. Offers communication technology (MA); media communication (MA). Electronic applications accepted.

POINT UNIVERSITY, West Point, GA 31833

General Information Independent-religious, coed, comprehensive institution. *Enrollment:* 1,952 graduate, professional, and undergraduate students; 24 full-time matriculated graduate/professional students (9 women), 2 part-time matriculated graduate/professional students (both women). *Enrollment by degree level:* 26 master's. Tuition and fees vary according to program. *Library facilities:* Point University Library plus 1 other.

Computer facilities: 115 computers available on campus for general student use. A campuswide network can be accessed from student residence rooms. Online class registration is available.
Website: http://point.edu/

General Application Contact: Rusty Hassell, Executive Director of Enrollment, 706-385-1503, E-mail: rusty.hassell@point.edu.

GRADUATE UNITS

Graduate Programs Students: 24 full-time (9 women), 2 part-time (both women); includes 7 minority (6 Black or African American, non-Hispanic/Latino; 1 Hispanic/Latino). Average age 36. Expenses: Contact institution. *Program availability:* Part-time, 100% online, blended/hybrid learning. Offers business transformation (MBA); transformative ministry (MTM). *Application deadline:* Applications are processed on a rolling basis. Electronic applications accepted.

POLYTECHNIC UNIVERSITY OF PUERTO RICO, Hato Rey, PR 00918

General Information Independent, coed, comprehensive institution. CGS member. *Graduate housing:* On-campus housing not available. *Research affiliation:* University of Missouri (engineering, mathematics and science), University of Puerto Rico, Mayaguez Campus (electrical engineering), Virginia Polytechnic Institute and State University (mechanical and electrical engineering), Naval Research Laboratories (mechanical and electrical engineering), U.S. Department of Energy Laboratories (electrical engineering).

GRADUATE UNITS

Graduate School *Program availability:* Part-time, evening/weekend.

POLYTECHNIC UNIVERSITY OF PUERTO RICO, MIAMI CAMPUS, Miami, FL 33166

General Information Independent, coed, comprehensive institution.

GRADUATE UNITS

Graduate School *Program availability:* Part-time, evening/weekend, online learning. Electronic applications accepted.

POLYTECHNIC UNIVERSITY OF PUERTO RICO, ORLANDO CAMPUS, Orlando, FL 32825

General Information Independent, coed, comprehensive institution. *Graduate housing:* On-campus housing not available.

GRADUATE UNITS

Graduate School *Program availability:* Part-time, evening/weekend, online learning. Electronic applications accepted.

PONCE HEALTH SCIENCES UNIVERSITY, Ponce, PR 00732-7004

General Information Independent, coed, graduate-only institution. *Research affiliation:* The University of Texas at San Antonio (health disparities, proteomics, bioinformatics), H.L. Moffitt Cancer Center (cancer biology, oncology), Oregon Health & Science University (neurosciences, cancer, inflammation), University of Puerto Rico, Mayaguez Campus (cancer biology, molecular genetics), University of Puerto Rico, Medical Sciences Campus (translational research), University of Maryland–Institute of Human Virology (HIV/AIDS research).

GRADUATE UNITS

Professional Program Offers medicine (MD).

Program in Biomedical Sciences Offers biomedical sciences (PhD).

Program in Clinical Psychology Offers clinical psychology (PhD, Psy D).

Program in Public Health Offers epidemiology (Dr PH); public health (MPH).

PONTIFICAL CATHOLIC UNIVERSITY OF PUERTO RICO, Ponce, PR 00717-0777

General Information Independent-religious, coed, university. *Graduate housing:* Room and/or apartments available to single students; on-campus housing not available to married students. Housing application deadline: 7/15.

GRADUATE UNITS

College of Arts and Humanities *Program availability:* Part-time, evening/weekend. Offers arts and humanities (MA, Professional Certificate); grammar and writing (Professional Certificate); Hispanic studies (MA); history (MA); painting and drawing (MA); theology and philosophy (M Div).

College of Business Administration *Program availability:* Part-time, evening/weekend. Offers accounting (MBA); business administration (MBA, DBA, PhD, Professional Certificate); finance (MBA); general business (MBA, Professional Certificate); human resources (MBA, Professional Certificate); international business (MBA); management (MBA); management and accounting (Professional Certificate); management information systems (MBA, Professional Certificate); maritime logistics and transportation (Professional Certificate); marketing (MBA); office administration (MBA, MS).

College of Education *Program availability:* Part-time, evening/weekend. Offers business teacher education (M Ed, PhD); counselor education (M Ed); curriculum and instruction (M Ed, PhD); education (M Ed, MA Ed, MRE, PhD); education-general (M Ed, MA Ed); educational leadership and administration (PhD); educational psychology (M Ed); English as a second language (M Ed).

College of Graduate Studies in Behavioral Science and Community Affairs *Program availability:* Part-time, evening/weekend. Offers clinical psychology (PhD, Psy D); clinical social work (MSW); criminology (MA); industrial psychology (PhD); psychology (PhD); public administration (MSS); rehabilitation counseling (MA).

College of Sciences *Program availability:* Part-time, evening/weekend. Offers chemistry (MS); environmental sciences (MS); medical-surgical nursing (MSN); mental health and psychiatric nursing (MSN); sciences (MS, Certificate).

School of Medical Technology Offers medical technology (Certificate).

School of Law *Program availability:* Part-time, evening/weekend. Offers law (JD).

PONTIFICAL COLLEGE JOSEPHINUM, Columbus, OH 43235

General Information Independent-religious, men only, comprehensive institution. *Graduate housing:* Room and/or apartments guaranteed to single students; on-campus housing not available to married students. Housing application deadline: 8/15.

GRADUATE UNITS

School of Theology *Program availability:* Part-time. Offers theology (M Div, MA). All students are sponsored/selected by their diocese.

PONTIFICAL JOHN PAUL II INSTITUTE FOR STUDIES ON MARRIAGE AND FAMILY, Washington, DC 20064

General Information Independent-religious, coed, graduate-only institution.

GRADUATE UNITS

Graduate Programs Offers biotechnology and ethics (MTS); marriage and family (MTS, STD, STL); theology (PhD).

POPE ST. JOHN XXIII NATIONAL SEMINARY, Weston, MA 02493-2618

General Information Independent-religious, men only, graduate-only institution. *Graduate housing:* Room and/or apartments available to single students; on-campus housing not available to married students. Housing application deadline: 8/1.

GRADUATE UNITS

Graduate Program Offers theology (M Div).

PORTLAND STATE UNIVERSITY, Portland, OR 97207-0751

General Information State-supported, coed, university. CGS member. *Enrollment:* 27,305 graduate, professional, and undergraduate students; 2,548 full-time matriculated graduate/professional students (1,516 women), 2,594 part-time matriculated graduate/professional students (1,613 women). *Enrollment by degree level:* 3,955 master's, 685 doctoral, 502 other advanced degrees. *Graduate faculty:* 768 full-time (364 women), 586 part-time/adjunct (310 women). Tuition, state resident: full-time $14,436; part-time $401 per credit. Tuition, nonresident: full-time $21,780; part-time $605 per credit. *Required fees:* $1380; $22 per credit. $119 per quarter. One-time fee: $325. Tuition and fees vary according to program. *Graduate housing:* Rooms and/or apartments available on a first-come, first-served basis to single and married students. Typical cost: $7654 per year ($11,779 including board) for single students; $11,663 per year for married students. Room and board charges vary according to board plan and housing facility selected. Housing application deadline: 5/1. *Student services:* Campus employment opportunities, campus safety program, career counseling, child daycare facilities, exercise/wellness program, free psychological counseling, international student services, low-cost health insurance, multicultural affairs office, services for students with disabilities, teacher training, writing training. *Library facilities:* Branford P. Millar Library plus 1 other. *Collection:* Students can reserve study rooms. *Research affiliation:* DesignMedix Inc (chemistry, drug development for infectious diseases), Metron Inc. (computer engineering, advanced mathematical methods), Portland General Electric (electrical engineering), Semiconductor Research Corporation (computer science), Oregon Nanoscience and Microtechnologies Institute (electrical and computer engineering), Tektronix (electrical engineering).

Computer facilities: A campuswide network can be accessed from student residence rooms and from off campus. Online class registration is available.
Website: http://www.pdx.edu/

General Application Contact: Kelly Doherty, Director of Graduate Admissions, 503-725-5391, Fax: 503-725-3416, E-mail: askogs@pdx.edu.

GRADUATE UNITS

Graduate Studies Students: 2,548 full-time (1,516 women), 2,594 part-time (1,613 women); includes 1,110 minority (133 Black or African American, non-Hispanic/Latino; 48 American Indian or Alaska Native, non-Hispanic/Latino; 267 Asian, non-Hispanic/Latino; 435 Hispanic/Latino; 12 Native Hawaiian or other Pacific Islander, non-Hispanic/Latino; 215 Two or more races, non-Hispanic/Latino), 644 international. Average age 33. 3,829 applicants, 54% accepted, 1397 enrolled. *Faculty:* 768 full-time (364 women), 586 part-time/adjunct (310 women). Expenses: Contact institution. *Financial support:* In 2017–18, 1,071 students received support, including 220 research assistantships with full and partial tuition reimbursements available (averaging $12,267 per year), 472 teaching assistantships with full and partial tuition reimbursements available (averaging $10,397 per year); fellowships, career-related internships or fieldwork, Federal Work-Study, scholarships/grants, tuition waivers (full and partial), and unspecified assistantships also available. Support available to part-time students. Financial award application deadline: 3/1; financial award applicants required to submit FAFSA. In 2017, 1,593 master's, 78 doctorates awarded. *Program availability:* Part-time, evening/weekend, online learning. *Application deadline:* For fall admission, 6/1 for domestic students, 3/1 for international students; for winter admission, 10/1 for domestic students, 7/1 for international students; for spring admission, 2/1 for domestic students, 11/1 for international students. Applications are processed on a rolling basis. *Application fee:* $65. *Application Contact:* Kelly Doherty, Director of Graduate Admissions, 503-725-5391, Fax: 503-725-3416, E-mail: dohertyk@pdx.edu. *Dean of Graduate Studies*, Dr. Margaret Everett, 503-725-5258, Fax: 503-725-3416, E-mail: everettm@pdx.edu.

College of Liberal Arts and Sciences Students: 623 full-time (392 women), 388 part-time (209 women); includes 175 minority (13 Black or African American, non-Hispanic/Latino; 4 American Indian or Alaska Native, non-Hispanic/Latino; 35 Asian, non-Hispanic/Latino; 81 Hispanic/Latino; 4 Native Hawaiian or other Pacific Islander, non-Hispanic/Latino; 38 Two or more races, non-Hispanic/Latino), 67 international. Average age 32. 983 applicants, 40% accepted, 267 enrolled. *Faculty:* 337 full-time (158 women), 163 part-time/adjunct (85 women). Expenses: Contact institution. *Financial support:* In 2017–18, 393 students received support, including 64 research assistantships with full and partial tuition reimbursements available (averaging $14,776 per year), 245 teaching assistantships with full and partial tuition reimbursements available (averaging $12,274 per year); career-related internships or fieldwork, Federal Work-Study, scholarships/grants, and tuition waivers (full and partial) also available. Support available to part-time students. Financial award application deadline: 3/1; financial award applicants required to submit FAFSA. In 2017, 288 master's, 34 doctorates awarded. *Program availability:* Part-time, evening/weekend. Offers anthropology (MA, MS); applied physics (PhD); applied statistics (Certificate); biology (MA, MS, PhD); chemistry (MA, MS, PhD); computational intelligence (Certificate); computer modeling and simulation (Certificate); conflict resolution (MA, MS); creative writing (MFA); English (MA); environmental management (MEM); environmental science and management (PSM); environmental sciences and resources (PhD); environmental sciences/biology (PhD); environmental sciences/chemistry (PhD); environmental sciences/civil engineering (PhD); environmental sciences/geography (PhD); environmental sciences/geology

(PhD); environmental sciences/physics (PhD); environmental studies (MS); French (MA); general arts and letters education (MAT, MST); general science education (MAT, MST); general social science education (MAT, MST); general speech communication (MA, MS, Certificate); geography (MA, MAT, MS, MST, PhD); geology (MA, MS, Certificate); German (MA); history (MA); hydrology (Certificate); Japanese (MA); liberal arts and sciences (MA, MAT, MEM, MFA, MS, MST, PSM, PhD, Certificate); mathematical sciences (PhD); mathematics education (PhD); mathematics for middle school (Certificate); mathematics for teachers (MS); physics (MA, MS); psychology (MA, MS, PhD); science/geology (MAT, MST); sociology (MA, MS, PhD); Spanish (MA); speech-language pathology (MA, MS); statistics (MS); systems science (MS); systems science/anthropology (PhD); systems science/business administration (PhD); systems science/civil engineering (PhD); systems science/economics (PhD); systems science/engineering management (PhD); systems science/general (PhD); systems science/mathematical sciences (PhD); systems science/mechanical engineering (PhD); systems science/psychology (PhD); systems science/sociology (PhD); teaching English as a second language (Certificate); teaching English to speakers of other languages (MA); world literature and language (MA). *Application deadline:* Applications are processed on a rolling basis. *Application fee:* $65. *Application Contact:* Dr. Todd Rosenstiel, Associate Dean for Research and Graduate Programs, 503-725-8503, Fax: 503-725-3693. *Dean*, Dr. Karen Marrongelle, 503-725-5061, Fax: 503-725-3693.

College of the Arts Students: 92 full-time (52 women), 18 part-time (6 women); includes 21 minority (2 Black or African American, non-Hispanic/Latino; 7 Asian, non-Hispanic/Latino; 7 Hispanic/Latino; 5 Two or more races, non-Hispanic/Latino), 15 international. Average age 32. 110 applicants, 58% accepted, 27 enrolled. *Faculty:* 89 full-time (44 women), 123 part-time/adjunct (61 women). Expenses: Contact institution. *Financial support:* In 2017–18, 62 students received support, including 12 research assistantships with full and partial tuition reimbursements available (averaging $3,799 per year), 25 teaching assistantships with full and partial tuition reimbursements available (averaging $5,464 per year); career-related internships or fieldwork, Federal Work-Study, scholarships/grants, and unspecified assistantships also available. Support available to part-time students. Financial award application deadline: 3/1; financial award applicants required to submit FAFSA. In 2017, 44 master's awarded. *Program availability:* Part-time. Offers architecture (M Arch); conducting (Mus M); contemporary art practice: art and social practice (MFA); contemporary art practice: studio practice (MFA); jazz studies (Mus M); music (Mus M); performance (Mus M); the arts (M Arch, MFA, Mus M). *Application deadline:* For fall admission, 3/1 for domestic and international students. Applications are processed on a rolling basis. *Application fee:* $65. *Dean*, Leroy Bynum, Jr., 503-725-3105, E-mail: lbynumjr@pdx.edu.

College of Urban and Public Affairs Students: 231 full-time (129 women), 184 part-time (107 women); includes 85 minority (15 Black or African American, non-Hispanic/Latino; 7 American Indian or Alaska Native, non-Hispanic/Latino; 17 Asian, non-Hispanic/Latino; 27 Hispanic/Latino; 1 Native Hawaiian or other Pacific Islander, non-Hispanic/Latino; 18 Two or more races, non-Hispanic/Latino), 40 international. Average age 34. 347 applicants, 72% accepted, 147 enrolled. *Faculty:* 69 full-time (29 women), 44 part-time/adjunct (16 women). Expenses: Contact institution. *Financial support:* In 2017–18, 112 students received support, including 46 research assistantships with full and partial tuition reimbursements available (averaging $6,032 per year), 29 teaching assistantships with full and partial tuition reimbursements available (averaging $6,666 per year); fellowships, career-related internships or fieldwork, Federal Work-Study, scholarships/grants, and unspecified assistantships also available. Support available to part-time students. Financial award application deadline: 3/1; financial award applicants required to submit FAFSA. In 2017, 109 master's, 8 doctorates awarded. *Program availability:* Part-time, evening/weekend. Offers applied social demography (Certificate); collaborative governance (Certificate); criminology and criminal justice (MS); economics (MA, MS); energy policy and management (Certificate); environmental and resource economics (Certificate); global management and leadership (MPA); government (EMPA, MA, MPA, MS, PhD, Certificate); health administration (MPA); human resource management (MPA); local government (MPA); natural resource policy and administration (MPA); nonprofit and public management (Certificate); nonprofit management (MPA); political science (MA); public administration (EMPA); public affairs and policy (PhD); real estate development (Certificate); sustainable food systems (Certificate); transportation (Certificate); urban and public affairs (EMPA, MA, MPA, MRED, MS, MURP, MUS, PhD, Certificate); urban design (Certificate); urban studies (PhD); urban studies and planning (MRED, MURP, MUS); urban studies: regional science (PhD). *Application fee:* $65. *Dean*, Dr. Stephen Percy, 503-725-5143, Fax: 503-725-5199, E-mail: spercy@pdx.edu.

Maseeh College of Engineering and Computer Science Students: 428 full-time (126 women), 378 part-time (95 women); includes 118 minority (11 Black or African American, non-Hispanic/Latino; 58 Asian, non-Hispanic/Latino; 24 Hispanic/Latino; 25 Two or more races, non-Hispanic/Latino), 395 international. Average age 31. 717 applicants, 57% accepted, 219 enrolled. *Faculty:* 84 full-time (14 women), 27 part-time/adjunct (6 women). Expenses: Contact institution. *Financial support:* In 2017–18, 181 students received support, including 46 research assistantships (averaging $15,325 per year), 77 teaching assistantships (averaging $10,912 per year); career-related internships or fieldwork, Federal Work-Study, scholarships/grants, and unspecified assistantships also available. Support available to part-time students. Financial award application deadline: 3/1; financial award applicants required to submit FAFSA. In 2017, 266 master's, 14 doctorates awarded. *Program availability:* Part-time, evening/weekend. Offers civil and environmental engineering (M Eng, MS, PhD); computer science (MS, PhD); computer security (Certificate); electrical and computer engineering (MS, PhD); engineering and computer science (M Eng, MS, MSME, MSMSE, PhD, Certificate); engineering and technology management (MS); mechanical engineering (PhD); technology management (PhD). *Application deadline:* For fall admission, 4/1 for domestic students, 3/1 for international students; for winter admission, 9/1 for domestic and international students; for spring admission, 2/1 for domestic and international students. *Application fee:* $65. *Dean*, Dr. Renjeng Su, 503-725-2825, Fax: 503-725-2825, E-mail: renjengs@pdx.edu.

OHSU-PSU School of Public Health Students: 18 full-time (16 women), 183 part-time (150 women); includes 51 minority (6 Black or African American, non-Hispanic/Latino; 4 American Indian or Alaska Native, non-Hispanic/Latino; 10 Asian, non-Hispanic/Latino; 18 Hispanic/Latino; 13 Two or more races, non-Hispanic/Latino), 2 international. Average age 32. *Faculty:* 20 full-time (16 women), 4 part-time/adjunct (2 women). Expenses: Contact institution. *Financial support:* In 2017–18, 15 students received support, including 9 research assistantships with full and partial tuition reimbursements available (averaging $7,038 per year), 2 teaching assistantships with full and partial tuition reimbursements available (averaging $10,584 per year); Federal Work-Study and unspecified assistantships also available. Financial award applicants required to submit FAFSA. In 2017, 41 master's, 1 doctorate awarded. *Program availability:* Part-time. Offers community health (PhD); health management and policy (MPH); health promotion (MPH); health studies (MA); health systems and policy (PhD); public health (MA, MPH, PhD). *Application deadline:* For fall admission, 4/1 for domestic students. *Application fee:* $165. *Application Contact:* Kelly Doherty, Director of Graduate Admissions, 503-725-5391, Fax: 503-725-3416, E-mail: dohertyk@pdx.edu. *Dean*, Dr. David Bangsberg, 503-494-8257.

The School of Business Students: 246 full-time (124 women), 185 part-time (85 women); includes 102 minority (14 Black or African American, non-Hispanic/Latino; 42 Asian, non-Hispanic/Latino; 30 Hispanic/Latino; 1 Native Hawaiian or other Pacific Islander, non-Hispanic/Latino; 15 Two or more races, non-Hispanic/Latino), 84 international. Average age 33. 277 applicants, 71% accepted, 79 enrolled. *Faculty:* 67 full-time (29 women), 70 part-time/adjunct (28 women). Expenses: Contact institution. *Financial support:* In 2017–18, 64 students received support, including 15 research assistantships with full and partial tuition reimbursements available (averaging $7,988 per year), 1 teaching assistantship (averaging $3,538 per year); career-related internships or fieldwork, Federal Work-Study, scholarships/grants, and unspecified assistantships also available. Support available to part-time students. Financial award application deadline: 3/1; financial award applicants required to submit FAFSA. In 2017, 184 master's awarded. *Program availability:* Part-time, evening/weekend. Offers business (MBA, MIM, MRED, MS, MSF, MSFA, PhD); business administration (MBA); financial analysis (MSF); global supply chain management (MS); international management (MIM); real estate development (MRED). *Application deadline:* For fall admission, 4/1 for domestic students, 3/1 for international students. *Application fee:* $65. Electronic applications accepted. *Application Contact:* Pam Mitchell, Director, 503-725-4733, E-mail: mitchep@pdx.edu. *Dean*, Dr. Cliff Allen, 503-725-5053, Fax: 503-725-5850, E-mail: cliffa@pdx.edu.

School of Education Students: 469 full-time (347 women), 841 part-time (661 women); includes 333 minority (38 Black or African American, non-Hispanic/Latino; 16 American Indian or Alaska Native, non-Hispanic/Latino; 55 Asian, non-Hispanic/Latino; 162 Hispanic/Latino; 4 Native Hawaiian or other Pacific Islander, non-Hispanic/Latino; 58 Two or more races, non-Hispanic/Latino), 28 international. Average age 36. 669 applicants, 45% accepted, 241 enrolled. *Faculty:* 68 full-time (47 women), 108 part-time/adjunct (79 women). Expenses: Contact institution. *Financial support:* In 2017–18, 156 students received support, including 5 research assistantships with full and partial tuition reimbursements available (averaging $9,145 per year), 3 teaching assistantships with full and partial tuition reimbursements available (averaging $6,390 per year); career-related internships or fieldwork, Federal Work-Study, institutionally sponsored loans, scholarships/grants, and unspecified assistantships also available. Support available to part-time students. Financial award application deadline: 3/1; financial award applicants required to submit FAFSA. In 2017, 456 master's, 17 doctorates awarded. *Program availability:* Part-time, evening/weekend. Offers education (M Ed, MA, MAT, MS, MST, Ed D). *Application deadline:* For fall admission, 4/1 for domestic and international students; for winter admission, 9/1 for domestic and international students; for spring admission, 11/1 for domestic and international students. *Application fee:* $65. Electronic applications accepted. *Application Contact:* Information Contact, 503-725-4619, Fax: 503-725-5599, E-mail: gseinfo@pdx.edu. *Dean*, Dr. Marvin Lynn, 503-725-4697, Fax: 503-725-5399, E-mail: mlynn@pdx.edu.

School of Social Work Students: 382 full-time (304 women), 232 part-time (197 women); includes 160 minority (29 Black or African American, non-Hispanic/Latino; 14 American Indian or Alaska Native, non-Hispanic/Latino; 23 Asian, non-Hispanic/Latino; 64 Hispanic/Latino; 1 Native Hawaiian or other Pacific Islander, non-Hispanic/Latino; 29 Two or more races, non-Hispanic/Latino), 4 international. Average age 34. 624 applicants, 42% accepted, 195 enrolled. *Faculty:* 33 full-time (26 women), 46 part-time/adjunct (33 women). Expenses: Contact institution. *Financial support:* In 2017–18, 88 students received support, including 12 research assistantships with full and partial tuition reimbursements available (averaging $11,761 per year), 3 teaching assistantships with full and partial tuition reimbursements available (averaging $12,720 per year); career-related internships or fieldwork, Federal Work-Study, scholarships/grants, tuition waivers (full and partial), and unspecified assistantships also available. Support available to part-time students. Financial award application deadline: 3/1; financial award applicants required to submit FAFSA. In 2017, 205 master's, 4 doctorates awarded. *Program availability:* Part-time. Offers social work (MSW); social work and social research (PhD). *Application deadline:* For fall admission, 2/1 for domestic and international students. *Application fee:* $65. *Application Contact:* William Donlan, Director of MSW Program, 503-725-8977, E-mail: donlan@pdx.edu. *Dean*, Dr. Laura B. Nissen, 503-725-3997, Fax: 503-725-5545, E-mail: nissen@pdx.edu.

POST UNIVERSITY, Waterbury, CT 06723-2540

General Information Independent, coed, comprehensive institution. *Tuition:* Part-time $730 per credit hour. Part-time tuition and fees vary according to degree level and program. *Library facilities:* Trauriq Library and Resource Center. *Collection:* Books: 10,320 (physical), 160,000 (digital/electronic); Serial titles: 250 (physical), 36,199 (digital/electronic); Databases: 43. Weekly public service hours: 75; students can reserve study rooms.

Computer facilities: Computer purchase and lease plans are available. 150 computers available on campus for general student use. A campuswide network can be accessed. Online class registration, software applications are available.
Website: http://www.post.edu/

General Application Contact: Veronica Montalvo, Vice President, Online Education Enrollment Management and Admissions, 203-596-6164, E-mail: vmontalvo@post.edu.

GRADUATE UNITS

Program in Business Administration Expenses: Contact institution. *Program availability:* Online learning. Offers accounting (MSA); business administration (MBA); corporate finance (MBA); corporate innovation (MBA); healthcare systems leadership (MBA); leadership (MBA); marketing (MBA); project management (MBA, MS). *Application Contact:* Veronica Montalvo, Vice President, Online Education Enrollment Management and Admissions, 203-596-6164, E-mail: vmontalvo@post.edu.

Program in Counseling and Human Services Expenses: Contact institution. *Program availability:* Part-time, evening/weekend, online learning. Offers counseling and human services (MS); counseling and human services/alcohol and drug counseling (MS); counseling and human services/clinical mental health counseling (MS); counseling and human services/forensic mental health counseling (MS); counseling and human services/non-profit management (MS). *Application Contact:* Veronica Montalvo, Vice President, Online Education Enrollment Management and Admissions, 203-596-6164, E-mail: vmontalvo@post.edu.

Program in Education Expenses: Contact institution. *Program availability:* Online learning. Offers curriculum and instruction (M Ed); education (M Ed); educational technology (M Ed); higher education administration (MS); learning design and technology (M Ed); online teaching (M Ed); teaching English to speakers of other languages (TESOL) (M Ed). *Application Contact:* Veronica Montalvo, Vice President, Online Education Enrollment Management and Admissions, 203-596-6164, E-mail: vmontalvo@post.edu.

Program in Public Administration Expenses: Contact institution. *Program availability:* Online learning. Offers emergency management and homeland security (MPA). *Application Contact:* Veronica Montalvo, Vice President, Online Education Enrollment Management and Admissions, 203-596-6164, E-mail: vmontalvo@post.edu.

PRAIRIE VIEW A&M UNIVERSITY, Prairie View, TX 77446

General Information State-supported, coed, university. *Enrollment:* 9,125 graduate, professional, and undergraduate students; 539 full-time matriculated graduate/professional students (312 women), 612 part-time matriculated graduate/professional students (412 women). *Enrollment by degree level:* 1,014 master's, 123 doctoral, 14 other advanced degrees. *Graduate faculty:* 108 full-time (48 women), 17 part-time/adjunct (11 women). Tuition, state resident: part-time $242 per credit. Tuition, nonresident: part-time $695 per credit. *Required fees:* $149 per credit. *Graduate housing:* Room and/or apartments available on a first-come, first-served basis to single students; on-campus housing not available to married students. Typical cost: $8402 (including board). Room and board charges vary according to board plan. Housing application deadline: 4/16. *Student services:* Campus employment opportunities, campus safety program, career counseling, exercise/wellness program, free psychological counseling, grant writing training, international student services, low-cost health insurance, multicultural affairs office, services for students with disabilities, teacher training, writing training. *Library facilities:* John B. Coleman Library plus 3 others. *Collection:* Books: 257,702 (physical), 16,626 (digital/electronic); Serial titles: 199 (physical); Databases: 23. Weekly public service hours: 97; students can reserve study rooms. *Research affiliation:* Sandia National Laboratories (engineering and chemistry), Lawrence Livermore National Laboratory (engineering and sciences), U.S. Department of Education (DOE) (engineering), U.S. Department of Energy (engineering and sciences), Science and Engineering Alliance, NASA (space radiation on material systems and devices).

Computer facilities: 2,500 computers available on campus for general student use. A campuswide network can be accessed from student residence rooms and from off campus. Online class registration is available.
Website: http://www.pvamu.edu/

General Application Contact: Pauline Walker, Office of Graduate Admissions, 936-261-3521, Fax: 936-261-3529, E-mail: gradadmissions@pvamu.edu.

GRADUATE UNITS

College of Agriculture and Human Sciences Students: 56 full-time (52 women), 28 part-time (19 women); includes 78 minority (70 Black or African American, non-Hispanic/Latino; 2 Asian, non-Hispanic/Latino; 6 Hispanic/Latino), 2 international. Average age 31. 57 applicants, 88% accepted, 36 enrolled. *Faculty:* 6 full-time (3 women). Expenses: Contact institution. *Financial support:* Research assistantships, career-related internships or fieldwork, Federal Work-Study, institutionally sponsored loans, scholarships/grants, tuition waivers (full and partial), and unspecified assistantships available. Support available to part-time students. Financial award application deadline: 4/1; financial award applicants required to submit FAFSA. In 2017, 24 master's awarded. *Program availability:* Part-time, evening/weekend. Offers agriculture and human sciences (MS). *Application deadline:* For fall admission, 5/1 priority date for domestic and international students; for spring admission, 10/11 priority date for domestic students, 9/1 priority date for international students; for summer admission, 3/1 priority date for domestic students, 2/1 priority date for international students. Applications are processed on a rolling basis. *Application fee:* $50. Electronic applications accepted. *Application Contact:* Pauline Walker, Administrative Assistant II, 936-261-3521, Fax: 936-261-3529, E-mail: gradadmissions@pvamu.edu. *Interim Dean and Director of Land-Grant Programs*, Dr. Ali Fares, 936-261-5019, E-mail: alfares@pvamu.edu.

College of Arts and Sciences Students: 23 full-time (16 women), 7 part-time (4 women); includes 26 minority (25 Black or African American, non-Hispanic/Latino; 1 Hispanic/Latino), 3 international. Average age 28. 33 applicants, 94% accepted, 22 enrolled. *Faculty:* 9 full-time (2 women), 1 (woman) part-time/adjunct. Expenses: Contact institution. *Financial support:* In 2017–18, 8 students received support. Fellowships, research assistantships, teaching assistantships, career-related internships or fieldwork, Federal Work-Study, institutionally sponsored loans, and tuition waivers (full and partial) available. Support available to part-time students. Financial award application deadline: 4/1; financial award applicants required to submit FAFSA. In 2017, 8 master's awarded. *Program availability:* Part-time, evening/weekend. Offers arts and sciences (MA, MS); chemistry (MS). *Application deadline:* For fall admission, 5/1 priority date for domestic and international students; for spring admission, 10/11 priority date for domestic students, 9/1 priority date for international students; for summer admission, 3/1 priority date for domestic students, 2/1 priority date for international students. Applications are processed on a rolling basis. *Application fee:* $50. Electronic applications accepted. *Application Contact:* Pauline Walker, Administrative Assistant II, Research and Graduate Studies, 936-261-3521, Fax: 936-261-3529, E-mail: gradadmissions@pvamu.edu. *Dean*, Dr. Danny R. Kelley, 936-261-3180, Fax: 936-261-3188, E-mail: drkelley@pvamu.edu.

Division of Social Work, Behavioral and Political Sciences Students: 14 full-time (9 women), 6 part-time (4 women); all minorities (all Black or African American, non-Hispanic/Latino). Average age 29. 23 applicants, 96% accepted, 15 enrolled. *Faculty:* 3 full-time (0 women), 1 (woman) part-time/adjunct. Expenses: Contact institution. *Financial support:* Career-related internships or fieldwork, Federal Work-Study, institutionally sponsored loans, and tuition waivers available. Financial award application deadline: 4/1; financial award applicants required to submit FAFSA. In 2017, 1 master's awarded. *Program availability:* Part-time, evening/weekend. Offers sociology (MA). *Application deadline:* For fall admission, 5/1 priority date for domestic and international students; for spring admission, 10/1 priority date for domestic students, 9/1 priority date for international students; for summer admission, 3/1 priority date for domestic students, 2/1 priority date for international students. Applications are processed on a rolling basis. *Application fee:* $50. Electronic applications accepted. *Application Contact:* Pauline Walker, Administrative Assistant II, Research and Graduate Studies, 936-261-3521, Fax: 936-261-3529, E-mail: gradadmissions@pvamu.edu. *Division Head*, Dr. Walle Engedayehu, 936-261-3202, Fax: 936-261-3229, E-mail: waengedayehu@pvamu.edu.

College of Business Students: 82 full-time (48 women), 143 part-time (81 women); includes 192 minority (174 Black or African American, non-Hispanic/Latino; 10 Asian, non-Hispanic/Latino; 8 Hispanic/Latino), 17 international. Average age 29. 180 applicants, 84% accepted, 106 enrolled. *Faculty:* 18 full-time (3 women). Expenses: Contact institution. *Financial support:* Research assistantships, teaching assistantships, scholarships/grants, and unspecified assistantships available. Financial award application deadline: 4/1; financial award applicants required to submit FAFSA. In 2017, 98 master's awarded. *Program availability:* Part-time, evening/weekend. Offers accounting (MS); business administration (MBA). *Application deadline:* For fall admission, 5/1 for domestic students, 5/1 priority date for international students; for spring admission, 10/1 for domestic students, 9/1 priority date for international students; for summer admission, 3/1 for domestic students, 2/1 for international students. Applications are processed on a rolling basis. *Application fee:* $50. Electronic applications accepted. *Application Contact:* Gabriel Crosby, Director, Graduate Programs in Business, 936-261-9217, Fax: 936-261-9232, E-mail: mba@pvamu.edu. *Dean*, Dr. Munir Quddus, 936-261-9200, Fax: 936-261-9241, E-mail: cob@pvamu.edu.

College of Education Students: 111 full-time (81 women), 256 part-time (204 women); includes 347 minority (327 Black or African American, non-Hispanic/Latino; 1 Asian, non-Hispanic/Latino; 17 Hispanic/Latino; 1 Native Hawaiian or other Pacific Islander, non-Hispanic/Latino; 1 Two or more races, non-Hispanic/Latino), 6 international. Average age 35. 181 applicants, 88% accepted, 104 enrolled. *Faculty:* 23 full-time (13 women), 6 part-time/adjunct (5 women). Expenses: Contact institution. *Financial support:* Career-related internships or fieldwork, institutionally sponsored loans, scholarships/grants, and unspecified assistantships available. Support available to part-time students. Financial award application deadline: 4/1; financial award applicants required to submit FAFSA. In 2017, 150 master's, 11 doctorates awarded. *Program availability:* Part-time, evening/weekend, blended/hybrid learning. Offers curriculum and instruction (M Ed, MA Ed, MS Ed); education (M Ed, MA, MA Ed, MS, MS Ed, PhD); educational leadership and counseling (M Ed, MA, MS Ed, PhD); health and kinesiology (M Ed, MS). *Application deadline:* For fall admission, 5/1 priority date for domestic and international students; for spring admission, 10/1 priority date for domestic students, 9/1 priority date for international students; for summer admission, 3/1 priority date for domestic students, 2/1 priority date for international students. Applications are processed on a rolling basis. *Application fee:* $50. Electronic applications accepted. *Application Contact:* Pauline Walker, Administrative Assistant II, Research and Graduate Studies, 936-261-3521, Fax: 936-261-3529, E-mail: gradadmissions@pvamu.edu. *Dean*, Dr. Phyllis Metcalf-Turner, 936-261-3600, Fax: 936-261-3621, E-mail: pmmetcalf@pvamu.edu.

College of Engineering Students: 165 full-time (45 women), 72 part-time (19 women); includes 87 minority (70 Black or African American, non-Hispanic/Latino; 14 Asian, non-Hispanic/Latino; 3 Hispanic/Latino), 128 international. Average age 31. 122 applicants, 86% accepted, 67 enrolled. *Faculty:* 27 full-time (7 women), 1 (woman) part-time/adjunct. Expenses: Contact institution. *Financial support:* Fellowships, research assistantships, teaching assistantships, career-related internships or fieldwork, institutionally sponsored loans, scholarships/grants, health care benefits, tuition waivers (full), and unspecified assistantships available. Financial award application deadline: 4/1; financial award applicants required to submit FAFSA. In 2017, 66 master's awarded. *Program availability:* Part-time, evening/weekend. Offers computer information systems (MSCIS); computer science (MSCS); electrical engineering (MSEE, PhDEE); general engineering (MS Engr). *Application deadline:* For fall admission, 5/1 priority date for domestic and international students; for spring admission, 10/1 priority date for domestic students, 9/1 priority date for international students; for summer admission, 3/1 priority date for domestic students, 2/1 priority date for international students. Applications are processed on a rolling basis. *Application fee:* $50. Electronic applications accepted. *Application Contact:* Pauline Walker, Administrative Assistant II, Research and Graduate Studies, 936-261-3521, Fax: 936-261-3529, E-mail: gradadmissions@pvamu.edu. *Dean*, Dr. Shield Lin, 936-261-9958, Fax: 936-261-9868, E-mail: shlin@pvamu.edu.

College of Juvenile Justice and Psychology Students: 23 full-time (18 women), 30 part-time (25 women); includes 50 minority (41 Black or African American, non-Hispanic/Latino; 8 Hispanic/Latino; 1 Two or more races, non-Hispanic/Latino), 2 international. Average age 31. 39 applicants, 82% accepted, 24 enrolled. *Faculty:* 7 full-time (5 women), 3 part-time/adjunct (1 woman). Expenses: Contact institution. *Financial support:* Research assistantships, teaching assistantships, scholarships/grants, and unspecified assistantships available. Financial award application deadline: 4/1; financial award applicants required to submit FAFSA. In 2017, 19 master's, 3 doctorates awarded. *Program availability:* Part-time, evening/weekend, online only, 100% online. Offers clinical adolescent psychology (PhD); juvenile forensic psychology (MSJFP); juvenile justice (MSJJ, PhD). *Application deadline:* For fall admission, 5/1 priority date for domestic and international students; for spring admission, 10/1 priority date for domestic students, 9/1 priority date for international students; for summer admission, 3/1 priority date for domestic students, 2/1 priority date for international students. Applications are processed on a rolling basis. *Application fee:* $50. Electronic applications accepted. *Application Contact:* Pauline Walker, Executive Secretary, Graduate Program, 936-261-3521, Fax: 936-261-3529, E-mail: gradadmissions@pvamu.edu. *Dean*, Dr. Tamara L. Brown, 936-261-5206, Fax: 936-261-5253, E-mail: tlbrown@pvamu.edu.

College of Nursing Students: 37 full-time (30 women), 60 part-time (53 women); includes 92 minority (70 Black or African American, non-Hispanic/Latino; 17 Asian, non-Hispanic/Latino; 5 Hispanic/Latino), 2 international. Average age 35. 39 applicants, 95% accepted, 34 enrolled. *Faculty:* 11 full-time (all women), 2 part-time/adjunct (1 woman). Expenses: Contact institution. *Financial support:* Career-related internships or fieldwork, Federal Work-Study, institutionally sponsored loans, scholarships/grants, and traineeships available. Support available to part-time students. Financial award application deadline: 4/1; financial award applicants required to submit FAFSA. In 2017, 74 master's, 1 doctorate awarded. *Program availability:* Part-time, evening/weekend. Offers nursing (MSN, DNP). *Application deadline:* For fall admission, 5/1 priority date for domestic and international students; for spring admission, 10/1 priority date for domestic students, 9/1 priority date for international students; for summer admission, 3/1 priority date for domestic students, 2/1 priority date for international students. Applications are processed on a rolling basis. *Application fee:* $50. Electronic applications accepted. *Application Contact:* Dr. Forest Smith, Director of Student Services and Admissions, 713-797-7031, Fax: 713-797-7012, E-mail: fdsmith@pvamu.edu. *Dean*, Dr. Betty N. Adams, 713-797-7009, Fax: 713-797-7013, E-mail: bnadams@pvamu.edu.

School of Architecture Students: 42 full-time (22 women), 16 part-time (7 women); includes 50 minority (42 Black or African American, non-Hispanic/Latino; 7 Hispanic/Latino; 1 Native Hawaiian or other Pacific Islander, non-Hispanic/Latino), 7 international. Average age 29. 51 applicants, 88% accepted, 34 enrolled. *Faculty:* 3 full-time (0 women), 3 part-time/adjunct (2 women). Expenses: Contact institution. *Financial support:* Career-related internships or fieldwork, Federal Work-Study, institutionally sponsored loans, scholarships/grants, tuition waivers (full and partial), and unspecified assistantships available. Support available to part-time students. Financial award application deadline: 4/1; financial award applicants required to submit FAFSA. In 2017, 39 master's awarded. *Program availability:* Part-time, evening/weekend. Offers architecture (M Arch, MCD). *Application deadline:* For fall admission, 5/1 priority date for domestic and international students; for spring admission, 10/1 priority date for domestic students, 9/1 priority date for international students; for summer admission, 3/1 priority date for domestic students, 2/1 priority date for international students. Applications are processed on a rolling basis. *Application fee:* $50. Electronic applications accepted. *Application Contact:* Pauline Walker, Administrative Assistant II, Research and Graduate Studies, 936-261-3521, Fax: 936-261-3529, E-mail: pmwalker@pvamu.edu. *Dean*, Dr. Ikhlas Sabouni, 936-261-9800, Fax: 936-261-2350, E-mail: isabouni@pvamu.edu.

PRATT INSTITUTE, Brooklyn, NY 11205-3899

General Information Independent, coed, comprehensive institution. *Enrollment:* 4,829 graduate, professional, and undergraduate students; 1,155 full-time matriculated graduate/professional students (833 women), 222 part-time matriculated graduate/professional students (179 women). *Enrollment by degree level:* 1,376 master's, 1 other advanced degree. *Graduate faculty:* 157 full-time (75 women), 991 part-time/adjunct (439 women). *Tuition:* Full-time $30,834. *Required fees:* $1974. *Graduate housing:* Room and/or apartments available on a first-come, first-served basis to single students; on-campus housing not available to married students. Typical cost: $18,880 per year ($22,500 including board). Housing application deadline: 5/1. *Student services:* Campus employment opportunities, campus safety program, career counseling, exercise/wellness program, free psychological counseling, grant writing training, international student services, low-cost health insurance, multicultural affairs office, services for students with disabilities, teacher training, writing training. *Library facilities:* Pratt Institute Library. *Research affiliation:* The Procter & Gamble Company (product design), General Motors (transportation), Ford Motor Company (transportation).

Computer facilities: A campuswide network can be accessed from student residence rooms and from off campus. Online class registration is available.
Website: http://www.pratt.edu/

General Application Contact: Natalie Capannelli, Director of Graduate Admissions, 718-636-3551, Fax: 718-636-3670, E-mail: ncapanne@pratt.edu.

GRADUATE UNITS

School of Architecture Students: 318 full-time (190 women), 50 part-time (26 women); includes 83 minority (19 Black or African American, non-Hispanic/Latino; 1 American Indian or Alaska Native, non-Hispanic/Latino; 21 Asian, non-Hispanic/Latino; 36 Hispanic/Latino; 6 Two or more races, non-Hispanic/Latino), 180 international. Average age 27. 730 applicants, 83% accepted, 118 enrolled. Expenses: Contact institution. *Financial support:* Career-related internships or fieldwork, Federal Work-Study, institutionally sponsored loans, scholarships/grants, health care benefits, and unspecified assistantships available. Support available to part-time students. Financial award application deadline: 2/1; financial award applicants required to submit FAFSA. In 2017, 149 master's awarded. Offers architecture (M Arch, MS, MS Arch, MSCRP); architecture (first-professional) (M Arch); architecture (post-professional) (MS Arch); architecture and urban design (MS); city and regional planning (MSCRP); facilities management (MS); historic preservation (MS); real estate practice (MS); sustainable environmental systems (MS); urban placemaking and management (MS). *Application deadline:* For fall admission, 1/5 for domestic and international students; for spring admission, 10/1 for domestic and international students. *Application fee:* $50 ($90 for international students). Electronic applications accepted. *Application Contact:* Natalie Capannelli, Director of Graduate Admissions, 718-636-3551, Fax: 718-399-4242, E-mail: ncapanne@pratt.edu. *Dean*, Thomas Hanrahan, 718-399-4308, Fax: 718-399-4315, E-mail: hanrahan@pratt.edu.

School of Art Students: 251 full-time (187 women), 95 part-time (92 women); includes 89 minority (33 Black or African American, non-Hispanic/Latino; 1 American Indian or Alaska Native, non-Hispanic/Latino; 14 Asian, non-Hispanic/Latino; 32 Hispanic/Latino; 9 Two or more races, non-Hispanic/Latino), 135 international. Average age 28. 906 applicants, 50% accepted, 147 enrolled. Expenses: Contact institution. *Financial support:* Career-related internships or fieldwork, Federal Work-Study, institutionally sponsored loans, scholarships/grants, health care benefits, and unspecified assistantships available. Support available to part-time students. Financial award application deadline: 2/1; financial award applicants required to submit FAFSA. In 2017, 211 master's awarded. *Program availability:* Part-time. Offers art (MA, MFA, MPS, MS, Adv C); art and design education (MA, MS, Adv C); art therapy and creativity development (MPS); arts and cultural management (MPS); dance/movement therapy (MS); design management (MPS); digital arts (MFA); fine arts (MFA). *Application deadline:* For fall admission, 1/5 for domestic and international students; for spring admission, 10/1 for domestic and international students. *Application fee:* $50 ($90 for international students). Electronic applications accepted. *Application Contact:* Natalie Capannelli, Director of Graduate Admissions, 718-636-3551, Fax: 718-399-4242, E-mail: ncapanne@pratt.edu. *Dean*, Gerry Snyder, 718-636-3619, E-mail: gsnyder@pratt.edu.

School of Design Students: 376 full-time (288 women), 14 part-time (10 women); includes 50 minority (8 Black or African American, non-Hispanic/Latino; 23 Asian, non-Hispanic/Latino; 17 Hispanic/Latino; 2 Two or more races, non-Hispanic/Latino), 267 international. Average age 26. 905 applicants, 56% accepted, 183 enrolled. Expenses: Contact institution. *Financial support:* Career-related internships or fieldwork, Federal Work-Study, institutionally sponsored loans, scholarships/grants, health care benefits, and unspecified assistantships available. Support available to part-time students. Financial award application deadline: 2/1; financial award applicants required to submit FAFSA. In 2017, 121 master's awarded. *Program availability:* Part-time. Offers communications design (MFA); design (MFA, MID, MS); industrial design (MID); interior design (MFA); package design (MS). *Application deadline:* For fall admission, 1/5 for domestic and international students; for spring admission, 10/1 for domestic and international students. *Application fee:* $50 ($90 for international students). Electronic applications accepted. *Application Contact:* Natalie Capannelli, Director of Graduate Admissions, 718-636-3551, Fax: 718-636-3670, E-mail: ncapanne@pratt.edu. *Dean, School of Design*, Anita Cooney, 718-687-5744, Fax: 718-636-3410, E-mail: acooney@pratt.edu.

School of Information Students: 134 full-time (109 women), 52 part-time (43 women); includes 44 minority (10 Black or African American, non-Hispanic/Latino; 10 Asian, non-Hispanic/Latino; 19 Hispanic/Latino; 5 Two or more races, non-Hispanic/Latino), 31 international. Average age 30. 303 applicants, 75% accepted, 67 enrolled. Expenses: Contact institution. *Financial support:* Career-related internships or fieldwork, Federal Work-Study, institutionally sponsored loans, scholarships/grants, health care benefits, and unspecified assistantships available. Support available to part-time students. Financial award application deadline: 2/1; financial award applicants required to submit FAFSA. In 2017, 59 master's, 1 other advanced degree awarded. *Program availability:* Part-time. Offers information (MS, Adv C). *Application deadline:* For fall admission, 1/5 for domestic and international students; for spring admission, 10/1 for domestic and international students. Applications are processed on a rolling basis. *Application fee:* $50 ($90 for international students). Electronic applications accepted. *Application Contact:* Natalie Capannelli, Director of Graduate Admissions, 718-636-3551, Fax: 718-399-4242, E-mail: ncapanne@pratt.edu. *Interim Dean*, Anthony Cocciolo, 212-647-7702, Fax: 212-367-2492, E-mail: acocciol@pratt.edu.

School of Liberal Arts and Sciences Students: 76 full-time (59 women), 11 part-time (8 women); includes 38 minority (17 Black or African American, non-Hispanic/Latino; 1 American Indian or Alaska Native, non-Hispanic/Latino; 4 Asian, non-Hispanic/Latino; 11 Hispanic/Latino; 5 Two or more races, non-Hispanic/Latino), 13 international. Average age 29. 216 applicants, 75% accepted, 37 enrolled. Expenses: Contact institution. *Financial support:* Career-related internships or fieldwork, Federal Work-Study, institutionally sponsored loans, scholarships/grants, health care benefits, and unspecified assistantships available. Support available to part-time students. Financial award application deadline: 2/1; financial award applicants required to submit FAFSA. In 2017, 27 master's awarded. Offers history of art and design (MA); liberal arts and sciences (MA, MFA); media studies (MA); performance and performance studies (MFA); writing (MFA). *Application deadline:* For fall admission, 1/5 for domestic and international students; for spring admission, 10/1 for domestic and international students. *Application fee:* $50 ($90 for international students). Electronic applications accepted. *Application Contact:* Natalie Capannelli, Director of Graduate Admissions, 718-636-3551, Fax: 718-399-4242, E-mail: ncapanne@pratt.edu. *Dean*, Andrew W. Barnes, 718-636-3570, Fax: 718-399-4586, E-mail: awbarnes@pratt.edu.

PRESBYTERIAN COLLEGE, Clinton, SC 29325

General Information Independent-religious, coed, comprehensive institution.

GRADUATE UNITS

School of Pharmacy Offers pharmacy (Pharm D).

PRESCOTT COLLEGE, Prescott, AZ 86301

General Information Independent, coed, comprehensive institution. *Graduate housing:* Room and/or apartments available on a first-come, first-served basis to single students; on-campus housing not available to married students. Housing application deadline: 5/1. *Research affiliation:* Marshall Foundation (youth and wilderness), U.S. Department of Agriculture (USDA) (agro-ecology), National Park Service (forest health), Packard Foundation (Kino Bay research).

GRADUATE UNITS

Graduate Programs *Program availability:* Part-time, online learning. Offers adventure education (MA); adventure-based environmental education (MA); adventure-based psychotherapy (MA); counseling psychology (MA); early childhood education (MA); early childhood special education (MA); ecopsychology (MA); ecotherapy (MA); education (MA); elementary education (MA); environmental education leadership and administration (MA); environmental studies (MA); equine-assisted learning (MA); equine-assisted mental health (MA); expressive arts therapy (MA); humanities (MA); school guidance counseling (MA); secondary education (MA); social justice and human rights (MA); somatic psychology (MA); special education: learning disabilities (MA); special education: mental retardation (MA); special education: serious emotional disabilities (MA); student-directed concentration (MA); student-directed independent study (MA); sustainability education (PhD). Electronic applications accepted.

PRESIDIO GRADUATE SCHOOL, San Francisco, CA 94129

General Information Independent, coed, graduate-only institution. *Student services:* Campus employment opportunities, campus safety program, career counseling, free psychological counseling, grant writing training, international student services, low-cost health insurance, multicultural affairs office, services for students with disabilities, writing training.
Website: https://www.presidio.edu/

General Application Contact: Neha Hora, Senior Manager of Admissions and Community Engagement, 206-780 6212, E-mail: neha.hora@presidio.edu.

GRADUATE UNITS

Graduate Programs - San Francisco Expenses: Contact institution. Offers sustainable energy management (Certificate); sustainable management (MBA, MPA, Certificate). MBA/JD offered in conjunction with the University of California, Hastings College of the Law. *Application fee:* $75.

MBA Programs - Seattle Expenses: Contact institution. *Financial support:* Scholarships/grants available. Financial award application deadline: 6/15; financial award applicants required to submit FAFSA. *Program availability:* Part-time, evening/weekend, blended/hybrid learning. Offers cooperative management (Certificate); sustainable business (MBA); sustainable systems (MBA). *Application deadline:* For fall admission, 6/1 priority date for domestic and international students. Applications are processed on a rolling basis. *Application fee:* $75. Electronic applications accepted. *Application Contact:* Kari Dorth, Director of Admissions, 415-655-8912, E-mail: admissions@presidio.edu. *Provost*, Dariush Rafinejad, 415-651-6555, E-mail: info@presidio.edu.

PRINCETON THEOLOGICAL SEMINARY, Princeton, NJ 08542-0803

General Information Independent-religious, coed, graduate-only institution. *Graduate housing:* Rooms and/or apartments available on a first-come, first-served basis to single and married students. *Research affiliation:* Center of Theological Inquiry.

GRADUATE UNITS

Graduate and Professional Programs *Program availability:* Part-time. Offers theology (M Div, MA, Th M, D Min, PhD). Electronic applications accepted.

PRINCETON UNIVERSITY, Princeton, NJ 08544-1019

General Information Independent, coed, university. CGS member. *Graduate housing:* Rooms and/or apartments available to single and married students. Housing application deadline: 4/15. *Research affiliation:* Institute for Advanced Study (physics and mathematics), Brookhaven National Laboratory (experimental physics), Textile Research Institute (polymer research), National Oceanic and Atmospheric Administration (NOAA)–GFD Laboratory (weather prediction).

GRADUATE UNITS

Graduate School Offers anthropology (PhD); applied and computational mathematics (PhD); astronomy (PhD); atmospheric and oceanic sciences (PhD); chemistry (PhD); classical and hellenic studies (PhD); classical art and archaeology (PhD); classical philosophy (PhD); comparative literature (PhD); composition (PhD); demography (PhD, Certificate); East Asian art and archaeology (PhD); East Asian studies (PhD); ecology and evolutionary biology (PhD); economics (PhD); economics and demography (PhD); English (PhD); French language and literature (PhD); geosciences (PhD); German (PhD); history (PhD); history (the ancient world) (PhD); history of science (PhD); industrial chemistry (MS); literature and philology (PhD); mathematics (PhD); molecular biology (PhD); musicology (PhD); Near Eastern studies (MA, PhD); neuroscience (PhD); ocean sciences and marine biology (PhD); philosophy (PhD); philosophy of science

(PhD); physics (PhD); plasma physics (PhD); political philosophy (PhD); politics (PhD); psychology (PhD); public affairs and demography (PhD); religion (PhD); Russian and Slavic linguistics (PhD); Russian literature (PhD); sociology (PhD); sociology and demography (PhD); Spanish and Portuguese (PhD). Electronic applications accepted.

Bendheim Center for Finance Offers finance (M Fin). Electronic applications accepted.

School of Architecture Offers architecture (M Arch, PhD). Electronic applications accepted.

School of Engineering and Applied Science Expenses: Contact institution. *Financial support:* Fellowships with full tuition reimbursements, research assistantships with full tuition reimbursements, teaching assistantships with full tuition reimbursements, institutionally sponsored loans, and health care benefits available. Offers chemical and biological engineering (M Eng, MSE, PhD); civil and environmental engineering (M Eng, MSE, PhD); computer science (MSE, PhD); electrical engineering (M Eng, PhD); engineering and applied science (M Eng, MSE, PhD); mechanical and aerospace engineering (M Eng, MSE, PhD); operations research and financial engineering (M Eng, MSE, PhD). Electronic applications accepted. *Application Contact:* Michelle Carman, Director of Graduate Admission, 609-258-3034, Fax: 609-258-6180, E-mail: gsadmit@princeton.edu. *Vice Dean, School of Engineering and Applied Science*, Antoine Kahn, E-mail: gradaffairs@princeton.edu.

Woodrow Wilson School of Public and International Affairs Offers public affairs (MPA, PhD); public policy (MPP). JD/MPA offered jointly with Columbia University, New York University, Stanford University. Electronic applications accepted.

Princeton Institute for the Science and Technology of Materials (PRISM) Offers materials (PhD).

Princeton Neuroscience Institute Offers neuroscience (PhD). Electronic applications accepted.

PROVIDENCE COLLEGE, Providence, RI 02918

General Information Independent-religious, coed, comprehensive institution. *Graduate housing:* On-campus housing not available.

GRADUATE UNITS

Department of History *Program availability:* Part-time, evening/weekend. Offers American history (MA); modern European history (MA).

Department of Theology *Program availability:* Part-time, evening/weekend. Offers Biblical studies (MA); theology (MA, MTS).

Program in Counseling *Program availability:* Part-time, evening/weekend. Offers counseling (M Ed).

Program in Literacy *Program availability:* Part-time, evening/weekend. Offers literacy (M Ed).

Program in Special Education *Program availability:* Part-time, evening/weekend. Offers special education (M Ed).

Program in Teaching Mathematics *Program availability:* Part-time, evening/weekend. Offers teaching mathematics (MA).

Program in Urban Teaching *Program availability:* Part-time, evening/weekend. Offers urban teaching (M Ed).

Programs in Administration *Program availability:* Part-time, evening/weekend. Offers elementary administration (M Ed); secondary administration (M Ed).

Providence Alliance for Catholic Teachers (PACT) Program Offers secondary education (M Ed).

School of Business *Program availability:* Part-time, evening/weekend. Offers accounting (MBA); finance (MBA); international business (MBA); management (MBA); marketing (MBA).

PROVIDENCE UNIVERSITY COLLEGE & THEOLOGICAL SEMINARY, Otterburne, MB R0A 1G0, Canada

General Information Independent-religious, coed, comprehensive institution. *Graduate housing:* Rooms and/or apartments guaranteed to single students and available on a first-come, first-served basis to married students. Housing application deadline: 8/15.

GRADUATE UNITS

Theological Seminary *Program availability:* Part-time. Offers children's ministry (Certificate); Christian studies (MA, Certificate); counseling (MA); cross-cultural discipleship (Certificate); divinity (M Div); educational studies (MA); global studies (MA); lay counseling (Diploma); ministry (D Min); teaching English to speakers of other languages (Certificate); theological studies (MA); training teacher of English to speakers of other languages (Certificate); youth ministry (Certificate).

PURCHASE COLLEGE, STATE UNIVERSITY OF NEW YORK, Purchase, NY 10577-1400

General Information State-supported, coed, comprehensive institution. *Enrollment:* 4,224 graduate, professional, and undergraduate students; 97 full-time matriculated graduate/professional students (52 women), 7 part-time matriculated graduate/professional students (6 women). *Enrollment by degree level:* 104 master's. *Graduate housing:* Rooms and/or apartments available on a first-come, first-served basis to single and married students. *Student services:* Campus employment opportunities, campus safety program, career counseling, child daycare facilities, exercise/wellness program, free psychological counseling, international student services, low-cost health insurance, services for students with disabilities. *Library facilities:* Purchase College Library. *Collection:* Books: 237,710 (physical), 11,422 (digital/electronic); Serial titles: 107 (physical), 65,714 (digital/electronic); Databases: 176.

Computer facilities: 600 computers available on campus for general student use. A campuswide network can be accessed from student residence rooms and from off campus. Online class registration is available.
Website: http://www.purchase.edu/

General Application Contact: Garrett Marino, Admissions Counselor, 914-250-6316, Fax: 914-251-6314, E-mail: admissn@purchase.edu.

GRADUATE UNITS

Conservatory of Music Expenses: Contact institution. *Financial support:* Fellowships, teaching assistantships, career-related internships or fieldwork, Federal Work-Study, scholarships/grants, and tuition waivers (partial) available. Support available to part-time students. Financial award application deadline: 3/15; financial award applicants required to submit FAFSA. Offers classical composition (MM); instrumental performance (MM); jazz studies (MM); studio composition (MM); voice and opera studies (MM). *Application deadline:* For fall admission, 1/15 for domestic students; for spring admission, 10/15 for domestic students. *Application fee:* $85. Electronic applications accepted. *Application Contact:* Garrett Marino, Associate Director of Admissions, 914-251-6479, Fax: 914-251-6316, E-mail: admissn@purchase.edu. *Director*, Jennifer Undercofler, 914-251-6700, Fax: 914-251-6739, E-mail: jennifer.undercofler@purchase.edu.

School of Art and Design Expenses: Contact institution. *Financial support:* Fellowships, teaching assistantships, Federal Work-Study, scholarships/grants, and tuition waivers (partial) available. Support available to part-time students. Financial award application deadline: 3/15; financial award applicants required to submit FAFSA. Offers art history/visual arts (MA); visual arts (MFA). *Application deadline:* For fall admission, 2/15 for domestic students. Applications are processed on a rolling basis. *Application fee:* $85. Electronic applications accepted. *Application Contact:* Garrett Marino, Associate Director of Admissions, 914-251-6316, Fax: 914-251-6314, E-mail: admissn@purchase.edu. *Director*, Steven Lam, 914-251-6750, Fax: 914-251-6793, E-mail: steven.lam@purchase.edu.

School of Film and Media Studies Expenses: Contact institution. Offers media arts and culture (MFA). *Application Contact:* Sabrina Johnston, Admissions Counselor, 914-251-6479, Fax: 914-251-6314, E-mail: admissn@purchase.edu. *Chair*, Agustin Zarzosa, 914-251-6860, E-mail: fms@purchase.edu.

School of Humanities Expenses: Contact institution. *Financial support:* Fellowships, Federal Work-Study, scholarships/grants, and tuition waivers (partial) available. Support available to part-time students. Financial award application deadline: 3/15; financial award applicants required to submit FAFSA. Offers art history (MA). *Application deadline:* For fall admission, 3/1 for domestic students. *Application fee:* $80. Electronic applications accepted. *Application Contact:* Garrett Marino, Associate Director of Admissions, 914-251-6316, Fax: 914-251-6314, E-mail: admissn@purchase.edu. *Chair*, Ross Daly, 914-251-6550.

School of the Arts Expenses: Contact institution. *Program availability:* Part-time. Offers entrepreneurship in the arts (MA). *Acting Dean*, Dr. Peggy De Cooke, 914-251-4455, Fax: 914-251-4457, E-mail: peggy.decooke@purchase.edu.

PURDUE UNIVERSITY, West Lafayette, IN 47907

General Information State-supported, coed, university. CGS member. *Enrollment:* 41,573 graduate, professional, and undergraduate students; 6,046 full-time matriculated graduate/professional students (2,350 women), 3,415 part-time matriculated graduate/professional students (1,468 women). *Enrollment by degree level:* 4,373 master's, 4,722 doctoral, 59 other advanced degrees. *Graduate faculty:* 2,168 full-time (675 women), 114 part-time/adjunct (45 women). *Graduate housing:* Rooms and/or apartments available on a first-come, first-served basis to single and married students. Housing application deadline: 3/1. *Student services:* Campus employment opportunities, campus safety program, career counseling, child daycare facilities, exercise/wellness program, free psychological counseling, grant writing training, international student services, low-cost health insurance, multicultural affairs office, services for students with disabilities, teacher training, writing training. *Library facilities:* Purdue University Libraries plus 9 others. *Collection:* Books: 968,500 (physical), 2.2 million (digital/electronic); Serial titles: 34,790 (physical), 123,000 (digital/electronic); Databases: 575. Weekly public service hours: 168; study areas open 24 hours, 5–7 days a week; students can reserve study rooms.

Computer facilities: Computer purchase and lease plans are available. 5,237 computers available on campus for general student use. A campuswide network can be accessed from student residence rooms and from off campus.
Website: http://www.purdue.edu/

General Application Contact: Marcia Fritzlen, Graduate School Admissions, 765-494-2600, Fax: 765-494-0136, E-mail: gradinfo@purdue.edu.

GRADUATE UNITS

College of Engineering Students: 3,463. *Faculty:* 636. Expenses: Contact institution. *Financial support:* Fellowships with full and partial tuition reimbursements, research assistantships with full and partial tuition reimbursements, teaching assistantships with full and partial tuition reimbursements, career-related internships or fieldwork, scholarships/grants, health care benefits, and unspecified assistantships available. In 2017, 672 master's, 284 doctorates awarded. *Program availability:* Part-time, 100% online, blended/hybrid learning. Offers biomedical engineering (MSBME, PhD); engineering (MS, MSABE, MSBME, MSCE, MSChE, MSE, MSECE, MSIE, MSME, MSMSE, MSNE, PhD, Certificate); interdisciplinary engineering (MS, MSE). *Application deadline:* Applications are processed on a rolling basis. *Application fee:* $60 ($75 for international students). Electronic applications accepted. *Application Contact:* Dr. Janet Beagle, Director of Graduate Programs, E-mail: engrgrad@purdue.edu. *Associate Dean*, Dr. Audeen Fentiman, 765-494-1870, E-mail: engrgrad@purdue.edu.

Davidson School of Chemical Engineering Students: 159. *Faculty:* 28. Expenses: Contact institution. *Financial support:* Fellowships with full and partial tuition reimbursements, research assistantships with full and partial tuition reimbursements, teaching assistantships with full and partial tuition reimbursements, career-related internships or fieldwork, scholarships/grants, health care benefits, and unspecified assistantships available. Financial award applicants required to submit FAFSA. In 2017, 19 master's, 20 doctorates awarded. Offers chemical engineering (MSChE, PhD). *Application deadline:* For fall admission, 12/15 for domestic and international students; for spring admission, 10/15 for domestic and international students. Applications are processed on a rolling basis. *Application fee:* $60 ($75 for international students). Electronic applications accepted. *Application Contact:* Beverly Johnson, Graduate Program Administrator, 765-494-4057, E-mail: bevjohnson@purdue.edu. *Head of Chemical Engineering/Professor*, Dr. Sangtae Kim, 765-494-3492, E-mail: kim55@purdue.edu.

Division of Environmental and Ecological Engineering Students: 41. *Faculty:* 59. Expenses: Contact institution. *Financial support:* Fellowships with full and partial tuition reimbursements, research assistantships with full and partial tuition reimbursements, teaching assistantships with full and partial tuition reimbursements, career-related internships or fieldwork, scholarships/grants, health care benefits, and unspecified assistantships available. Financial award applicants required to submit FAFSA. In 2017, 3 master's awarded. Offers environmental and ecological engineering (MS, PhD). *Application deadline:* For fall admission, 12/15 for domestic and international students. *Application fee:* $60 ($75 for international students). *Application Contact:* Patricia Finney, Graduate Administrative Assistant, 765-496-0545, E-mail: eee@purdue.edu. *Professor/Head of Environmental and Ecological Engineering*, Dr. John W. Sutherland, 765-496-9697, E-mail: jwsuther@purdue.edu.

Lyles School of Civil Engineering Students: 341. *Faculty:* 74. Expenses: Contact institution. *Financial support:* Fellowships with full and partial tuition reimbursements, research assistantships with full and partial tuition reimbursements, teaching assistantships with full and partial tuition reimbursements, scholarships/grants, health care benefits, and unspecified assistantships available. Support available to part-time students. Financial award applicants required to submit FAFSA. In 2017, 84 master's, 44 doctorates awarded. *Program availability:* Part-time. Offers civil engineering (MS, MSCE, MSE, PhD). *Application deadline:* For fall admission, 1/1 priority date for domestic and international students; for spring admission, 9/15 for domestic and international students. Applications are processed on a rolling basis. *Application fee:*

$60 ($75 for international students). Electronic applications accepted. *Application Contact:* Jenny Ricksy, Graduate Program Coordinator, 765-494-2436, E-mail: jricksy@purdue.edu. *Head/Professor,* Dr. Rao Govindaraju, 765-494-2256, E-mail: govind@purdue.edu.

School of Aeronautics and Astronautics Students: 509. *Faculty:* 63. Expenses: Contact institution. *Financial support:* Fellowships with full and partial tuition reimbursements, research assistantships with full and partial tuition reimbursements, teaching assistantships with full and partial tuition reimbursements, career-related internships or fieldwork, scholarships/grants, health care benefits, and unspecified assistantships available. In 2017, 117 master's, 30 doctorates awarded. *Program availability:* Part-time, 100% online. Offers aeronautics and astronautics (MS, PhD). *Application deadline:* For fall admission, 1/1 priority date for domestic and international students; for spring admission, 9/15 priority date for domestic and international students. Applications are processed on a rolling basis. *Application fee:* $60 ($75 for international students). Electronic applications accepted. *Application Contact:* Xiaomin Qian, Graduate Program Coordinator, 765-494-5152, E-mail: xiaomin@purdue.edu. *Head/Professor of Aeronautics and Astronautics,* Dr. Tom Shih, 765-494-3006, E-mail: tomshih@purdue.edu.

School of Agricultural and Biological Engineering Students: 102. *Faculty:* 51. Expenses: Contact institution. *Financial support:* Fellowships with full and partial tuition reimbursements, research assistantships with full and partial tuition reimbursements, teaching assistantships with full and partial tuition reimbursements, career-related internships or fieldwork, scholarships/grants, health care benefits, unspecified assistantships, and instructorships available. Financial award applicants required to submit FAFSA. In 2017, 19 master's, 15 doctorates awarded. *Program availability:* Part-time. Offers agricultural and biological engineering (MS, MSABE, MSE, PhD). *Application deadline:* For fall admission, 12/1 for domestic and international students; for spring admission, 10/1 for domestic and international students; for summer admission, 12/1 for domestic and international students. Applications are processed on a rolling basis. *Application fee:* $60 ($75 for international students). Electronic applications accepted. *Application Contact:* Daniel Taylor, Assistant to Department Head, 765-494-1181, E-mail: taylordc@purdue.edu. *Department Head/Professor, Agricultural and Biological Engineering,* Dr. Bernard Engel, 765-494-1162, E-mail: engelb@purdue.edu.

School of Electrical and Computer Engineering Students: 627. *Faculty:* 130. Expenses: Contact institution. *Financial support:* Fellowships with full and partial tuition reimbursements, research assistantships with full and partial tuition reimbursements, teaching assistantships with full and partial tuition reimbursements, scholarships/grants, health care benefits, and unspecified assistantships available. Financial award application deadline: 12/15. In 2017, 115 master's, 71 doctorates awarded. *Program availability:* Part-time, online learning. Offers electrical and computer engineering (MSECE, PhD). MS and PhD degree programs in biomedical engineering offered jointly with School of Mechanical Engineering and School of Chemical Engineering. *Application deadline:* For fall admission, 12/15 priority date for domestic and international students; for spring admission, 5/1 for domestic and international students. *Application fee:* $60 ($75 for international students). Electronic applications accepted. *Application Contact:* Debra Bowman, Graduate Admissions, 765-494-3392, E-mail: dbowman1@purdue.edu. *Head/Professor,* Ragu Balakrishnan, 765-494-3539, E-mail: ragu@ecn.purdue.edu.

School of Engineering Education Students: 67. *Faculty:* 34. Expenses: Contact institution. *Financial support:* Fellowships with full and partial tuition reimbursements, research assistantships with full and partial tuition reimbursements, teaching assistantships with full and partial tuition reimbursements, health care benefits, and unspecified assistantships available. Financial award applicants required to submit FAFSA. In 2017, 15 doctorates awarded. Offers engineering education (PhD). *Application deadline:* For fall admission, 12/15 for domestic and international students; for spring admission, 9/15 for domestic and international students; for summer admission, 12/15 for domestic and international students. Applications are processed on a rolling basis. *Application fee:* $60 ($75 for international students). Electronic applications accepted. *Application Contact:* Loretta McKinniss, Secretary V, 765-494-3331, E-mail: lmckinni@purdue.edu. *Head of the School of Engineering Education,* Dr. Donna Riley, E-mail: riley@purdue.edu.

School of Industrial Engineering Students: 298. *Faculty:* 39. Expenses: Contact institution. *Financial support:* Fellowships with full and partial tuition reimbursements, research assistantships with full and partial tuition reimbursements, teaching assistantships with full and partial tuition reimbursements, scholarships/grants, health care benefits, and unspecified assistantships available. Financial award applicants required to submit FAFSA. In 2017, 69 master's, 12 doctorates awarded. *Program availability:* Part-time, online learning. Offers industrial engineering (MS, MSIE, PhD). *Application deadline:* For fall admission, 1/5 for domestic and international students; for spring admission, 9/1 for domestic and international students. Applications are processed on a rolling basis. *Application fee:* $60 ($75 for international students). Electronic applications accepted. *Application Contact:* Cheryl Barnhart, Graduate Program Administrator, 765-494-5434, E-mail: cbarnhar@purdue.edu. *Head/Professor of Industrial Engineering,* Dr. Abhijit Deshmukh, 765-496-6007, E-mail: abhi@purdue.edu.

School of Materials Engineering Students: 155. *Faculty:* 55. Expenses: Contact institution. *Financial support:* Fellowships with full and partial tuition reimbursements, research assistantships with full and partial tuition reimbursements, teaching assistantships with full and partial tuition reimbursements, career-related internships or fieldwork, scholarships/grants, health care benefits, and unspecified assistantships available. Support available to part-time students. Financial award applicants required to submit FAFSA. In 2017, 5 master's, 15 doctorates awarded. *Program availability:* Part-time. Offers materials engineering (MSMSE, PhD). *Application deadline:* For fall admission, 12/15 for domestic and international students. Applications are processed on a rolling basis. *Application fee:* $60 ($75 for international students). Electronic applications accepted. *Application Contact:* Vicki Cline, Academic Program Administrator, 765-494-4103, E-mail: vicline@purdue.edu. *Head and Professor of Materials Engineering,* Dr. David Bahr, 765-494-4100, E-mail: dfbahr@purdue.edu.

School of Mechanical Engineering Students: 629. *Faculty:* 119. Expenses: Contact institution. *Financial support:* Fellowships with full and partial tuition reimbursements, research assistantships with full and partial tuition reimbursements, teaching assistantships with full and partial tuition reimbursements, career-related internships or fieldwork, scholarships/grants, health care benefits, and unspecified assistantships available. In 2017, 126 master's, 51 doctorates awarded. *Program availability:* Part-time, online learning. Offers mechanical engineering (MS, MSE, MSME, PhD, Certificate). MS and PhD degree programs in biomedical engineering offered jointly with School of Electrical and Computer Engineering and School of Chemical Engineering. *Application deadline:* For fall admission, 12/15 for domestic and international students; for spring admission, 9/15 for domestic and international students. Applications are processed on a rolling basis. *Application fee:* $60 ($75 for international students). Electronic applications accepted. *Application Contact:* Julayne Moser, Director of Graduate Programs, 765-494-5729, E-mail: moser@purdue.edu. *Head/Professor,* Anil K. Bajaj, 765-494-5688, E-mail: bajaj@purdue.edu.

School of Nuclear Engineering Students: 48. *Faculty:* 25. Expenses: Contact institution. *Financial support:* Fellowships with full and partial tuition reimbursements, research assistantships with full and partial tuition reimbursements, teaching assistantships with full and partial tuition reimbursements, career-related internships or fieldwork, scholarships/grants, and unspecified assistantships available. Support available to part-time students. Financial award applicants required to submit FAFSA. In 2017, 6 master's, 4 doctorates awarded. *Program availability:* Part-time. Offers nuclear engineering (MS, MSNE, PhD). *Application deadline:* For fall admission, 1/15 priority date for domestic and international students; for spring admission, 9/30 for domestic and international students. Applications are processed on a rolling basis. *Application fee:* $60 ($75 for international students). Electronic applications accepted. *Application Contact:* Nancy Vestal, Academic Program Coordinator, 765-494-5749, E-mail: nvestal@purdue.edu. *Head of the School of Nuclear Engineering,* Dr. Seungjin Kim, 765-494-5742, E-mail: seungjin@purdue.edu.

College of Pharmacy Students: 709 full-time (462 women), 10 part-time (6 women); includes 157 minority (29 Black or African American, non-Hispanic/Latino; 1 American Indian or Alaska Native, non-Hispanic/Latino; 90 Asian, non-Hispanic/Latino; 22 Hispanic/Latino; 15 Two or more races, non-Hispanic/Latino), 88 international. Average age 24. 748 applicants, 28% accepted, 173 enrolled. *Faculty:* 72 full-time (29 women), 5 part-time/adjunct (3 women). Expenses: Contact institution. *Financial support:* Fellowships, research assistantships, teaching assistantships, career-related internships or fieldwork, Federal Work-Study, scholarships/grants, and traineeships available. Support available to part-time students. Financial award applicants required to submit FAFSA. In 2017, 10 master's, 29 doctorates, 142 other advanced degrees awarded. *Program availability:* Part-time. Offers biophysical and computational chemistry (PhD); cancer research (PhD); clinical pharmacy (MS, PhD); immunology and infectious disease (PhD); industrial and physical pharmacy (MS, PhD, Certificate); medicinal biochemistry and molecular biology (PhD); medicinal chemistry and chemical biology (PhD); medicinal chemistry and molecular pharmacology (MS, PhD); molecular pharmacology (PhD); neuropharmacology, neurodegeneration, and neurotoxicity (PhD); pharmaceutics (PhD); pharmacy (MS, PhD, Pharm D, Certificate); pharmacy administration (MS, PhD); pharmacy and pharmacal sciences (MS, PhD, Pharm D, Certificate); pharmacy practice (MS, PhD); regulatory quality compliance (MS, Certificate); systems biology and functional genomics (PhD). *Application deadline:* Applications are processed on a rolling basis. *Application fee:* $60 ($75 for international students). Electronic applications accepted. *Application Contact:* Danzhou Yang, Associate Dean for Research and Graduate Programs, 765-494-1362, E-mail: yangdz@purdue.edu. *Dean,* Eric L. Barker, 765-494-1368, E-mail: barkerel@purdue.edu.

Graduate School Students: 5,925 full-time (2,291 women), 3,120 part-time (1,315 women); includes 1,144 minority (277 Black or African American, non-Hispanic/Latino; 20 American Indian or Alaska Native, non-Hispanic/Latino; 358 Asian, non-Hispanic/Latino; 333 Hispanic/Latino; 9 Native Hawaiian or other Pacific Islander, non-Hispanic/Latino; 147 Two or more races, non-Hispanic/Latino), 4,026 international. Average age 29. 16,245 applicants, 31% accepted, 2381 enrolled. *Faculty:* 2,096 full-time (646 women), 109 part-time/adjunct (42 women). Expenses: Contact institution. *Financial support:* Fellowships with tuition reimbursements, research assistantships with tuition reimbursements, teaching assistantships with tuition reimbursements, career-related internships or fieldwork, scholarships/grants, tuition waivers (full and partial), and instructorships available. Support available to part-time students. Financial award applicants required to submit FAFSA. In 2017, 1,859 master's, 698 doctorates, 160 other advanced degrees awarded. *Program availability:* Part-time, evening/weekend, online learning. Offers biomedical sciences (PhD); biomolecular structure and biophysics (PhD); biotechnology (PhD); chemical biology (PhD); chromatin and regulation of gene expression (PhD); ecological sciences and engineering (MS, PhD); food science (MS, PhD); information security (MS); integrative neuroscience (PhD); integrative plant sciences (PhD); membrane biology (PhD); microbiology (PhD); molecular evolutionary and cancer biology (PhD); molecular evolutionary genetics (PhD); molecular virology (PhD); philosophy and literature (PhD). MD/PhD offered jointly with Indiana University–Purdue University Indianapolis. *Application deadline:* Applications are processed on a rolling basis. *Application fee:* $60 ($75 for international students). Electronic applications accepted. *Application Contact:* Graduate School Admissions, 765-494-2600, Fax: 765-494-0136, E-mail: gradinfo@purdue.edu. *Interim Dean,* Dr. Linda J. Mason, 765-494-0245, E-mail: lmason@purdue.edu.

College of Agriculture Students: 542 full-time (262 women), 124 part-time (48 women); includes 72 minority (21 Black or African American, non-Hispanic/Latino; 5 American Indian or Alaska Native, non-Hispanic/Latino; 15 Asian, non-Hispanic/Latino; 19 Hispanic/Latino; 12 Two or more races, non-Hispanic/Latino), 288 international. Average age 28. 529 applicants, 38% accepted, 139 enrolled. *Faculty:* 310 full-time (69 women), 11 part-time/adjunct (3 women). Expenses: Contact institution. *Financial support:* Fellowships with tuition reimbursements, research assistantships with tuition reimbursements, teaching assistantships with tuition reimbursements, career-related internships or fieldwork, and tuition waivers (partial) available. Support available to part-time students. Financial award applicants required to submit FAFSA. In 2017, 107 master's, 68 doctorates awarded. *Program availability:* Part-time. Offers agricultural economics (EMBA, MS, PhD); agriculture (EMBA, M Agr, MA, MS, MSF, PhD); agronomy (MS, PhD); animal sciences (MS, PhD); biochemistry (MS, PhD); botany and plant pathology (MS, PhD); entomology (MS, PhD); fisheries and aquatic sciences (MS, MSF, PhD); food science (MS, PhD); forest biology (MS, MSF, PhD); horticulture (M Agr, MS, PhD); natural resource social science (MS, PhD); natural resources social science (MSF); quantitative ecology (MS, MSF, PhD); wildlife science (MS, MSF, PhD); wood products and wood products manufacturing (MS, MSF, PhD); youth development and agricultural education (MA, PhD). *Application deadline:* Applications are processed on a rolling basis. *Application fee:* $60 ($75 for international students). Electronic applications accepted. *Application Contact:* Graduate School Admissions, 765-494-2600, Fax: 765-494-0136, E-mail: gradinfo@purdue.edu. *Interim Dean,* Karen Plaut, 765-494-8391, E-mail: kplaut@purdue.edu.

College of Education Students: 156 full-time (110 women), 530 part-time (370 women); includes 114 minority (41 Black or African American, non-Hispanic/Latino; 3 American Indian or Alaska Native, non-Hispanic/Latino; 18 Asian, non-Hispanic/Latino; 38 Hispanic/Latino; 1 Native Hawaiian or other Pacific Islander, non-Hispanic/Latino; 13 Two or more races, non-Hispanic/Latino), 97 international. Average age 34. 377 applicants, 64% accepted, 151 enrolled. *Faculty:* 70 full-time (51 women), 2 part-time/adjunct (1 woman). Expenses: Contact institution. *Financial support:* Fellowships with full tuition reimbursements, research assistantships with full tuition reimbursements, teaching assistantships with full tuition reimbursements, career-related internships or fieldwork, and tuition waivers (full) available. Support available to part-time students. Financial award application deadline: 3/1; financial award applicants required to submit FAFSA. In 2017, 40 master's, 145 doctorates, 6 other advanced degrees awarded. *Program availability:* Part-time, evening/weekend. Offers administration (MS Ed, PhD, Ed S); agricultural and extension education (MS, MS Ed, PhD, Ed S); art education (PhD); career and technical education (MS Ed, PhD, Ed S); counseling and development (MS Ed, PhD); curriculum studies (MS Ed, PhD, Ed S); education (MS, MS Ed, PhD, Ed S); education of the gifted (MS Ed); educational psychology (MS Ed, PhD); educational technology (MS Ed, PhD, Ed S); elementary education (MS Ed); family and consumer sciences education (MS Ed, PhD, Ed S); foreign language education (MS Ed, PhD, Ed S); foundations of education (MS Ed, PhD); higher education administration (MS Ed, PhD); industrial technology (PhD, Ed S); language arts (MS Ed, PhD, Ed S); literacy (MS Ed, PhD, Ed S); mathematics education (MS, MS Ed, PhD, Ed S); science education (MS, MS Ed, PhD, Ed S); social studies education (MS Ed, PhD, Ed S); special education (MS Ed, PhD). *Application deadline:* For fall admission, 12/15 for domestic students, 3/1 for international students; for spring admission, 9/15 for domestic students, 8/1 for international students. *Application fee:* $60 ($75 for international students). Electronic applications accepted. *Application Contact:* Graduate School Admissions, 765-494-2600, Fax: 765-494-0136, E-mail: gradinfo@purdue.edu. *Dean, College of Education,* Maryann Santos, 765-494-2336, E-mail: msdb@purdue.edu.

College of Health and Human Sciences Students: 417 full-time (312 women), 97 part-time (71 women); includes 64 minority (16 Black or African American, non-Hispanic/Latino; 1 American Indian or Alaska Native, non-Hispanic/Latino; 17 Asian, non-Hispanic/Latino; 17 Hispanic/Latino; 13 Two or more races, non-Hispanic/Latino), 121 international. Average age 28. 1,035 applicants, 34% accepted, 168 enrolled. *Faculty:* 212 full-time (119 women), 16 part-time/adjunct (11 women). Expenses: Contact institution. *Financial support:* Fellowships, research assistantships, teaching assistantships, and career-related internships or fieldwork available. Support available to part-time students. Financial award applicants required to submit FAFSA. In 2017, 53 master's, 118 doctorates, 8 other advanced degrees awarded. *Program availability:* Part-time. Offers adult gerontology primary care nurse practitioner (MS, Post Master's Certificate); animal health (MS, PhD); athletic training education administration (MS, PhD); audiology clinic (MS, Au D, PhD); behavioral neuroscience (PhD); biochemical and molecular nutrition (MS, PhD); biomechanics (MS, PhD); clinical psychology (PhD); cognitive psychology (PhD); consumer behavior (MS, PhD); developmental studies (MS, PhD); exercise physiology (MS, PhD); family and consumer economics (MS, PhD); family studies (MS, PhD); growth and development (MS, PhD); health and human sciences (MS, Au D, DNP, PhD, Post Master's Certificate); health education (MS, PhD); health physics (MS, PhD); history/philosophy of sport (MS, PhD); hospitality and tourism management (MS, PhD); human and clinical nutrition (MS, PhD); industrial/organizational psychology (PhD); linguistics (MS, PhD); marriage and family therapy (MS, PhD); mathematical and computational cognitive science (PhD); medical physics (MS, PhD); motor control and development (MS, PhD); nursing (DNP, PhD); occupational and environmental health science (MS, PhD); physical education pedagogy (PhD); physical education teacher education (MS); primary care family nurse practitioner (MS, Post Master's Certificate); primary care pediatric nurse practitioner (MS, Post Master's Certificate); public health and education (MS, PhD); radiation biology (PhD); recreation and sport management (MS, PhD); speech and hearing science (MS, PhD); speech-language pathology (MS, PhD); sport and exercise psychology (MS, PhD); toxicology (PhD). *Application deadline:* Applications are processed on a rolling basis. *Application fee:* $60 ($75 for international students). Electronic applications accepted. *Application Contact:* Graduate School Admissions, 765-494-2600, Fax: 765-494-0136, E-mail: gradinfo@purdue.edu. *Dean,* Dr. Christine M. Ladisch, 765-494-8210.

College of Liberal Arts Students: 487 full-time (286 women), 601 part-time (410 women); includes 201 minority (75 Black or African American, non-Hispanic/Latino; 2 American Indian or Alaska Native, non-Hispanic/Latino; 25 Asian, non-Hispanic/Latino; 72 Hispanic/Latino; 3 Native Hawaiian or other Pacific Islander, non-Hispanic/Latino; 24 Two or more races, non-Hispanic/Latino), 196 international. Average age 32. 1,107 applicants, 35% accepted, 284 enrolled. *Faculty:* 291 full-time (134 women), 20 part-time/adjunct (13 women). Expenses: Contact institution. *Financial support:* Fellowships, research assistantships, teaching assistantships, career-related internships or fieldwork, scholarships/grants, and tuition waivers (full) available. Support available to part-time students. Financial award applicants required to submit FAFSA. In 2017, 148 master's, 74 doctorates awarded. *Program availability:* Part-time, evening/weekend. Offers American studies (MA, PhD); anthropology (MS, PhD); art education (MA, PhD); communication (MA, MS, PhD); comparative literature (MA, PhD); creative writing (MFA); French (MA, MAT, PhD); German (MA, MAT, PhD); history (MA, PhD); industrial design (MFA); integrated studio arts (MFA); interior design (MFA); Japanese pedagogy (MA); liberal arts (MA, MAT, MFA, MS, Au D, PhD); linguistics (MS, PhD); literature (MA, PhD); philosophy (MA, PhD); photography (MFA); political science (MA, PhD); sociology (MS, PhD); Spanish (MA, MAT, PhD); theatre (MFA); visual communications design (MFA). *Application deadline:* Applications are processed on a rolling basis. *Application fee:* $60 ($75 for international students). Electronic applications accepted. *Application Contact:* Graduate School Admissions, 765-494-2600, Fax: 765-494-0136, E-mail: gradinfo@purdue.edu. *Dean,* David A. Reingold, 765-494-3661, E-mail: reingold@purdue.edu.

College of Science Students: 1,066 full-time (359 women), 173 part-time (36 women); includes 142 minority (27 Black or African American, non-Hispanic/Latino; 3 American Indian or Alaska Native, non-Hispanic/Latino; 43 Asian, non-Hispanic/Latino; 51 Hispanic/Latino; 2 Native Hawaiian or other Pacific Islander, non-Hispanic/Latino; 16 Two or more races, non-Hispanic/Latino), 678 international. Average age 27. 3,411 applicants, 19% accepted, 246 enrolled. *Faculty:* 340 full-time (60 women), 14 part-time/adjunct (3 women). Expenses: Contact institution. *Financial support:* Fellowships with tuition reimbursements, research assistantships with tuition reimbursements, teaching assistantships with tuition reimbursements, career-related internships or fieldwork, and tuition waivers (partial) available. Support available to part-time students. Financial award applicants required to submit FAFSA. In 2017, 127 master's, 156 doctorates, 3 other advanced degrees awarded. *Program availability:* Part-time. Offers analytical chemistry (MS, PhD); biochemistry (MS, PhD); biophysics (PhD); cell and developmental biology (PhD); chemical education (MS, PhD); computer sciences (MS, PhD); earth and atmospheric sciences (MS, PhD); ecology, evolutionary and population biology (MS, PhD); genetics (MS, PhD); inorganic chemistry (MS, PhD); mathematics (MS, PhD); microbiology (MS, PhD); molecular biology (PhD); neurobiology (MS, PhD); organic chemistry (MS, PhD); physical chemistry (MS, PhD); physics (MS, PhD); plant physiology (PhD); science (MS, PhD, Certificate); statistics (MS, PhD). *Application fee:* $60 ($75 for international students). Electronic applications accepted. *Application Contact:* Graduate School Admissions, 765-494-2600, Fax: 765-494-0136, E-mail: gradinfo@purdue.edu. *Dean,* Patrick Wolfe, 765-494-1730, E-mail: patrick@purdue.edu.

College of Technology Students: 301 full-time (116 women), 287 part-time (101 women); includes 84 minority (23 Black or African American, non-Hispanic/Latino; 2 American Indian or Alaska Native, non-Hispanic/Latino; 25 Asian, non-Hispanic/Latino; 24 Hispanic/Latino; 2 Native Hawaiian or other Pacific Islander, non-Hispanic/Latino; 8 Two or more races, non-Hispanic/Latino), 233 international. Average age 31. 490 applicants, 57% accepted, 171 enrolled. *Faculty:* 201 full-time (46 women), 3 part-time/adjunct (1 woman). Expenses: Contact institution. *Financial support:* In 2017–18, 37 teaching assistantships were awarded; fellowships also available. Support available to part-time students. Financial award applicants required to submit FAFSA. In 2017, 144 master's, 21 doctorates awarded. *Program availability:* Online learning. Offers aviation and aerospace management (MS); building construction management (MS); computer and information technology (MS); computer graphics technology (MS, PhD); leadership (MS, PhD); organizational leadership (MS); technology (MS, PhD); technology innovation (MS). *Application deadline:* Applications are processed on a rolling basis. *Application fee:* $60 ($75 for international students). Electronic applications accepted. *Application Contact:* Graduate School Admissions, 765-494-2600, Fax: 765-494-0136, E-mail: gradinfo@purdue.edu. *Dean,* Dr. Gary R. Bertoline, 765-494-2552, E-mail: bertoline@purdue.edu.

Krannert School of Management Students: 312 full-time (121 women), 196 part-time (55 women); includes 73 minority (21 Black or African American, non-Hispanic/Latino; 33 Asian, non-Hispanic/Latino; 10 Hispanic/Latino; 1 Native Hawaiian or other Pacific Islander, non-Hispanic/Latino; 8 Two or more races, non-Hispanic/Latino), 202 international. Average age 31. 1,546 applicants, 32% accepted, 239 enrolled. *Faculty:* 182 full-time (40 women), 23 part-time/adjunct (3 women). Expenses: Contact institution. *Financial support:* Fellowships, research assistantships, and teaching assistantships available. Offers business administration (MBA); economics (PhD); finance (MSF); global executive business administration (MBA); human resource management (MSHRM); management (MBA, MSF, MSHRM, MSIA, PhD); organizational behavior and human resource management (PhD). *Application deadline:* Applications are processed on a rolling basis. *Application fee:* $60 ($75 for international students). Electronic applications accepted. *Application Contact:* 765-494-2600, Fax: 765-494-0136, E-mail: gradinfo@purdue.edu. *Dean,* Dr. David Hummels, 765-494-9700, Fax: 765-494-4360.

School of Veterinary Medicine *Program availability:* Part-time, evening/weekend. Offers anatomy (MS, PhD); basic medical sciences (MS, PhD); comparative epidemiology and public health (MS); comparative epidemiology and public heath (PhD); comparative microbiology and immunology (MS, PhD); comparative pathobiology (MS, PhD); interdisciplinary studies (PhD); lab animal medicine (MS); pharmacology (MS, PhD); physiology (MS, PhD); veterinary anatomic pathology (MS); veterinary clinical pathology (MS); veterinary clinical sciences (MS, PhD); veterinary medicine (MS, DVM, PhD).

PURDUE UNIVERSITY GLOBAL, Davenport, IA 52807

General Information Independent, coed, comprehensive institution.

GRADUATE UNITS

School of Business *Program availability:* Part-time, evening/weekend, online learning. Offers business administration (MBA); change leadership (MS); entrepreneurship (MBA); finance (MBA); health care management (MBA, MS); human resource (MBA); international business (MBA); management (MS); marketing (MBA); project management (MBA, MS); supply chain management and logistics (MBA, MS). Electronic applications accepted.

School of Criminal Justice *Program availability:* Part-time, evening/weekend, online learning. Offers corrections (MSCJ); global issues in criminal justice (MSCJ); law (MSCJ); leadership and executive management (MSCJ); policing (MSCJ). Electronic applications accepted.

School of Higher Education Studies *Program availability:* Part-time, evening/weekend, online learning. Offers college administration and leadership (MS); college teaching and learning (MS); student services (MS).

School of Information Technology *Program availability:* Part-time, evening/weekend, online learning. Offers decision support systems (MS); information security and assurance (MS).

School of Legal Studies *Program availability:* Part-time, evening/weekend, online learning. Offers health care delivery (MS); pathway to paralegal (Postbaccalaureate Certificate); state and local government (MS).

School of Nursing *Program availability:* Part-time, evening/weekend, online learning. Offers nurse administrator (MS); nurse educator (MS).

School of Teacher Education *Program availability:* Part-time, evening/weekend, online learning. Offers education (M Ed); secondary education (M Ed); teaching and learning (MA); teaching literacy and language: grades 6-12 (MA); teaching literacy and language: grades K-6 (MA); teaching mathematics: grades 6-8 (MA); teaching mathematics: grades 9-12 (MA); teaching mathematics: grades K-5 (MA); teaching science: grades 6-12 (MA); teaching science: grades K-6 (MA); teaching students with special needs (MA); teaching with technology (MA).

PURDUE UNIVERSITY NORTHWEST, Hammond, IN 46323-2094

General Information State-supported, coed, comprehensive institution. *Graduate housing:* Room and/or apartments available on a first-come, first-served basis to single students; on-campus housing not available to married students.

GRADUATE UNITS

Graduate Studies Office *Program availability:* Part-time, evening/weekend, online learning. Electronic applications accepted.

School of Education Offers counseling (MS Ed); educational administration (MS Ed); human services (MS Ed); instructional technology (MS Ed); mental health counseling (MS Ed); school counseling (MS Ed); special education (MS Ed).

School of Engineering, Mathematics, and Science *Program availability:* Part-time, evening/weekend, online learning. Offers biology (MS); biology teaching (MS); biotechnology (MS); computer engineering (MSE); computer science (MS); electrical engineering (MSE); engineering (MS); engineering, mathematics, and science (MAT, MS, MSE); mathematics (MAT, MS); mechanical engineering (MSE). Electronic applications accepted.

School of Liberal Arts and Social Sciences *Program availability:* Part-time. Offers child development and family studies (MS); communication (MA); English (MA); history (MA); liberal arts and social sciences (MA, MS); marriage and family therapy (MS).

School of Management *Program availability:* Part-time, evening/weekend. Offers accountancy (M Acc); business administration (MBA); business administration for executives (EMBA). Electronic applications accepted.

School of Nursing *Program availability:* Part-time, online learning. Offers adult health clinical nurse specialist (MS); critical care clinical nurse specialist (MS); family nurse practitioner (MS); nurse executive (MS). Electronic applications accepted.

School of Technology Offers technology (MS).

QUEENS COLLEGE OF THE CITY UNIVERSITY OF NEW YORK, Queens, NY 11367-1597

General Information State and locally supported, coed, comprehensive institution. *Enrollment:* 19,866 graduate, professional, and undergraduate students; 443 full-time matriculated graduate/professional students (320 women), 2,743 part-time matriculated graduate/professional students (1,866 women). *Enrollment by degree level:* 2,693 master's, 352 other advanced degrees. *Graduate faculty:* 527 full-time (240 women), 854 part-time/adjunct (443 women). *Graduate housing:* Room and/or apartments available on a first-come, first-served basis to single students; on-campus housing not available to married students. *Student services:* Campus employment opportunities, career counseling, child daycare facilities, free psychological counseling, international student services, low-cost health insurance, services for students with disabilities, teacher training, writing training. *Library facilities:* The Benjamin S. Rosenthal Library plus 1 other. *Collection:* Books: 1.1 million (physical), 404,708 (digital/electronic); Serial titles: 198 (physical), 125,145 (digital/electronic); Databases: 266. Weekly public service hours: 94; students can reserve study rooms. *Research affiliation:* Hudson River Foundation (earth and environmental sciences), Consortium for Ocean Leadership (earth and environmental sciences), Institute for New Economic Thinking (economics), Social Explorer (sociology), Wildlife Conservation Society (biology), IBM (computer science).

Computer facilities: 2,480 computers available on campus for general student use. A campuswide network can be accessed from student residence rooms and from off campus. Online class registration is available.
Website: http://www.qc.cuny.edu/

General Application Contact: Richard Alvarez, Vice President for Enrollment and Student Retention, 718-997-5929, Fax: 718-997-5193, E-mail: graduate_admissions@qc.cuny.edu.

GRADUATE UNITS

Arts and Humanities Division Students: 80 full-time (50 women), 417 part-time (266 women); includes 177 minority (33 Black or African American, non-Hispanic/Latino; 50 Asian, non-Hispanic/Latino; 79 Hispanic/Latino; 15 Two or more races, non-Hispanic/Latino), 59 international. Average age 31. 795 applicants, 40% accepted, 203 enrolled. *Faculty:* 154 full-time (76 women), 266 part-time/adjunct (159 women). Expenses: Contact institution. *Financial support:* Career-related internships or fieldwork available. Financial award application deadline: 4/1; financial award applicants required to submit FAFSA. *Program availability:* Part-time. Offers applied linguistics (MA); art history (MA); arts and humanities (MA, MFA, MM, MS Ed, AC, Advanced Certificate, Advanced Diploma, Post-Master's Certificate); creative writing and literary translation (MFA); English (MA); French (MA); Italian (MA); media studies (MA); Spanish (MA); speech-language pathology (MA); studio art (MFA); TESOL (MS Ed, Post-Master's Certificate); TESOL and bilingual education (Post-Master's Certificate). *Application deadline:* For fall admission, 4/1 for domestic students; for spring admission, 11/1 for domestic students. Applications are processed on a rolling basis. *Application fee:* $125. Electronic applications accepted. *Application Contact:* Elizabeth D'Amico-Ramirez, Assistant Director of Graduate Admissions, 718-997-5203, E-mail: elizabeth.damicoramirez@qc.cuny.edu. *Acting Dean*, Dr. Janice Smith, 718-997-5790, E-mail: janice.smith@qc.cuny.edu.

Aaron Copland School of Music Students: 23 full-time (5 women), 162 part-time (72 women); includes 49 minority (8 Black or African American, non-Hispanic/Latino; 16 Asian, non-Hispanic/Latino; 17 Hispanic/Latino; 8 Two or more races, non-Hispanic/Latino), 46 international. Average age 30. Expenses: Contact institution. *Financial support:* Career-related internships or fieldwork, Federal Work-Study, institutionally sponsored loans, and tuition waivers (partial) available. Support available to part-time students. Financial award application deadline: 4/1; financial award applicants required to submit FAFSA. *Program availability:* Part-time. Offers classical performance (MM, Advanced Diploma); jazz studies (MM); music (MA); music education (MS Ed, Advanced Certificate). *Application deadline:* For fall admission, 4/1 for domestic students; for spring admission, 11/1 for domestic students. Applications are processed on a rolling basis. *Application fee:* $125. Electronic applications accepted. *Application Contact:* Elizabeth D'Amico-Ramirez, Assistant Director of Graduate Admissions, 718-997-5203, E-mail: elizabeth.damicoramirez@qc.cuny.edu. *Chair*, Dr. David Schober, 718-997-3800, E-mail: david.schober@qc.cuny.edu.

Division of Education Students: 245 full-time (208 women), 1,114 part-time (864 women); includes 649 minority (97 Black or African American, non-Hispanic/Latino; 2 American Indian or Alaska Native, non-Hispanic/Latino; 193 Asian, non-Hispanic/Latino; 335 Hispanic/Latino; 1 Native Hawaiian or other Pacific Islander, non-Hispanic/Latino; 21 Two or more races, non-Hispanic/Latino), 31 international. Average age 29. Expenses: Contact institution. *Financial support:* Career-related internships or fieldwork available. Financial award application deadline: 4/1; financial award applicants required to submit FAFSA. *Program availability:* Part-time, evening/weekend. Offers adolescent biology (MAT); art (MS Ed); bilingual education (MAT, MS Ed, AC); bilingual pupil personnel (AC); biology (MS Ed, AC); chemistry (MS Ed, AC); childhood education (MAT, MS Ed); counselor education (MS Ed); early childhood education birth-2 (MAT, MS Ed, AC); earth sciences (MS Ed, AC); education (MA, MAT, MS Ed, AC); English (MS Ed, AC); French (MS Ed); Italian (MS Ed, AC); literacy education (MS Ed); literacy education birth-grade 6 (MS Ed, AC); mathematics (MS Ed, AC); mental health counseling (MS); music (MS Ed, AC); physics (MS Ed, AC); school building leader (AC); school district leader (AC); school psychologist (MS Ed); social studies (MS Ed, AC); Spanish (MS Ed, AC); special education-childhood education (AC); special education-early childhood (MS Ed); teacher of special education 1-6 (MS Ed); teacher of special education birth-2 (MS Ed); teaching students with disabilities, grades 7-12 (MS Ed, AC). *Application deadline:* For fall admission, 4/1 for domestic students; for spring admission, 11/1 for domestic students. Applications are processed on a rolling basis. *Application fee:* $125. Electronic applications accepted. *Application Contact:* Elizabeth D'Amico-Ramirez, Assistant Director of Graduate Admissions, 718-997-5203, E-mail: elizabeth.damicoramirez@qc.cuny.edu. *Dean*, Dr. Craig Michaels, 718-997-5220, E-mail: craig.michaels@qc.cuny.edu.

Division of Social Sciences Students: 74 full-time (39 women), 663 part-time (425 women); includes 380 minority (88 Black or African American, non-Hispanic/Latino; 1 American Indian or Alaska Native, non-Hispanic/Latino; 133 Asian, non-Hispanic/Latino; 139 Hispanic/Latino; 1 Native Hawaiian or other Pacific Islander, non-Hispanic/Latino; 18 Two or more races, non-Hispanic/Latino), 45 international. Average age 32. Expenses: Contact institution. *Financial support:* Career-related internships or fieldwork available. Financial award application deadline: 4/1; financial award applicants required to submit FAFSA. *Program availability:* Part-time, evening/weekend. Offers accounting (MS); data analytics and applied social research (MA); history (MA); liberal studies (MA); risk management: accounting (MS); risk management: dynamic financial analysis (MS); risk management: finance (MS); social sciences (MA, MLS, MS, AC); urban affairs (MA). *Application deadline:* For fall admission, 4/1 for domestic students; for spring admission, 11/1 for domestic students. Applications are processed on a rolling basis. *Application fee:* $125. Electronic applications accepted. *Application Contact:* Elizabeth D'Amico-Ramirez, Assistant Director of Graduate Admissions, 718-997-5203, E-mail: elizabeth.damicoramirez@qc.cuny.edu. *Dean*, Dr. Michael Wolfe, 718-997-5210, E-mail: michael.wolfe@qc.cuny.edu.

Graduate School of Library and Information Studies Students: 28 full-time (20 women), 289 part-time (205 women); includes 116 minority (37 Black or African American, non-Hispanic/Latino; 17 Asian, non-Hispanic/Latino; 53 Hispanic/Latino; 9 Two or more races, non-Hispanic/Latino), 4 international. Average age 33. Expenses: Contact institution. *Financial support:* Career-related internships or fieldwork and unspecified assistantships available. Financial award application deadline: 4/1; financial award applicants required to submit FAFSA. *Program availability:* Part-time, evening/weekend. Offers archives and preservation of cultural materials (AC); children's and young adult services in the public library (AC); librarianship (AC); library science (MLS); school library media specialist (MLS). *Application deadline:* For fall admission, 4/1 for domestic students; for spring admission, 11/1 for domestic students. Applications are processed on a rolling basis. *Application fee:* $125. Electronic applications accepted. *Application Contact:* Elizabeth D'Amico-Ramirez, Assistant Director of Graduate Admissions, 718-997-5203, E-mail: elizabeth.damicoramirez@qc.cuny.edu. *Director/Chair*, Colleen Cool, 718-997-3790, E-mail: colleen.cool@qc.cuny.edu.

Mathematics and Natural Sciences Division Students: 42 full-time (21 women), 410 part-time (228 women); includes 205 minority (44 Black or African American, non-Hispanic/Latino; 2 American Indian or Alaska Native, non-Hispanic/Latino; 72 Asian, non-Hispanic/Latino; 72 Hispanic/Latino; 1 Native Hawaiian or other Pacific Islander, non-Hispanic/Latino; 14 Two or more races, non-Hispanic/Latino), 50 international. Average age 29. Expenses: Contact institution. *Financial support:* Career-related internships or fieldwork available. Financial award application deadline: 4/1; financial award applicants required to submit FAFSA. *Program availability:* Part-time. Offers applied behavior analysis (MA); applied mathematics (MA); behavioral neuroscience (MA); biology (MA); chemistry (MA); computer science (MA); exercise science specialist (MS); family and consumer science (K-12) (AC); family and consumer science/teaching curriculum (K-12) (MS Ed); general psychology (MA); mathematics and natural sciences (MA, MAT, MS, MS Ed, AC); nutrition and exercise science (MS); nutrition specialist (MS); photonics (MS); physical education (K-12) (AC); physical education/teaching curriculum (pre K-12) (MS Ed); physics (MA); pure mathematics (MA). *Application deadline:* For fall admission, 4/1 for domestic students; for spring admission, 11/1 for domestic students. Applications are processed on a rolling basis. *Application fee:* $125. Electronic applications accepted. *Application Contact:* Elizabeth D'Amico-Ramirez, Assistant Director of Graduate Admissions, 718-997-5203, E-mail: elizabeth.damicoramirez@qc.cuny.edu. *Interim Dean*, Dr. Susan A. Rotenberg, 718-997-4105, E-mail: susan.rotenberg@qc.cuny.edu.

School of Earth and Environmental Sciences Students: 4 full-time (all women), 18 part-time (8 women); includes 5 minority (1 Black or African American, non-Hispanic/Latino; 3 Hispanic/Latino; 1 Two or more races, non-Hispanic/Latino), 3 international. Average age 27. Expenses: Contact institution. *Financial support:* Career-related internships or fieldwork and unspecified assistantships available. Financial award application deadline: 4/1; financial award applicants required to submit FAFSA. *Program availability:* Part-time, evening/weekend. Offers applied environmental geosciences (MS); geological and environmental sciences (MA). *Application deadline:* For fall admission, 4/1 for domestic students; for spring admission, 11/1 for domestic students. Applications are processed on a rolling basis. *Application fee:* $125. Electronic applications accepted. *Application Contact:* Elizabeth D'Amico-Ramirez, Assistant Director of Graduate Admissions, 718-997-5203, E-mail: elizabeth.damicoramirez@qc.cuny.edu. *Chair*, Gregory O'Mullan, 718-997-3300, E-mail: gregory.omullan@qc.cuny.edu.

QUEEN'S UNIVERSITY AT KINGSTON, Kingston, ON K7L 3N6, Canada

General Information Province-supported, coed, university. CGS member. *Graduate housing:* Rooms and/or apartments available to single students and available on a first-come, first-served basis to married students. Housing application deadline: 6/15.

GRADUATE UNITS

Faculty of Law *Program availability:* Part-time. Offers law (LL M, JD).

Queens School of Business Offers business (M Sc, MBA, PhD); consulting and project management (MBA); finance (MBA); innovation and entrepreneurship (MBA); marketing (MBA).

Queen's School of Religion *Program availability:* Part-time. Offers religion (M Div, MTS, Certificate).

School of Graduate Studies *Program availability:* Part-time.

Faculty of Applied Science *Program availability:* Part-time. Offers applied science (M Eng, M Sc, M Sc Eng, PhD); chemical engineering (M Sc, PhD); civil engineering (M Eng, M Sc Eng, PhD); electrical and computer engineering (M Eng, M Sc, M Sc Eng, PhD); mechanical and materials engineering (M Eng, M Sc, M Sc Eng, PhD); mining engineering (M Eng, M Sc, M Sc Eng, PhD). Electronic applications accepted.

Faculty of Arts and Sciences *Program availability:* Part-time. Offers arts and sciences (M Sc, M Sc Eng, MA, PhD); biology (M Sc, PhD); brain behavior and cognitive science (MA, PhD); Canadian politics (PhD); chemistry (M Sc, PhD); classics, Greek, Latin (MA); clinical psychology (MA, PhD); communication and Information technology (MA, PhD); comparative politics (PhD); computing (M Sc, PhD); developmental psychology (MA, PhD); English language and literature (MA, PhD); feminist sociology (MA, PhD); French studies (MA, PhD); gender and politics (PhD); geography (M Sc, MA, PhD); geological sciences and geological engineering (M Sc, M Sc Eng, PhD); German (MA, PhD); international relations (PhD); mathematics (M Sc, M Sc Eng, PhD); philosophy (MA, PhD); physics (M Sc, M Sc Eng, PhD); political theory (PhD); religious studies (MA); social personality psychology (MA, PhD); socio-legal studies (MA, PhD); sociological theory (MA, PhD); Spanish language and literature (MA); statistics (M Sc, M Sc Eng, PhD). Electronic applications accepted.

Faculty of Education *Program availability:* Part-time. Offers education (M Ed, PhD).

Faculty of Health Sciences *Program availability:* Part-time. Offers biochemistry (M Sc, PhD); biology of reproduction (M Sc, PhD); cancer (M Sc, PhD); cardiovascular pathophysiology (M Sc, PhD); cell and molecular biology (M Sc, PhD); drug metabolism (M Sc, PhD); endocrinology (M Sc, PhD); epidemiology (PhD); epidemiology and population health (M Sc); health and chronic illness (M Sc); health sciences (M Sc, M Sc OT, M Sc PT, MPH, PhD, Certificate); health services (M Sc); microbiology and immunology (M Sc, PhD); motor control (M Sc, PhD); neural regeneration (M Sc, PhD); neurophysiology (M Sc, PhD); nurse scientist (PhD); occupational therapy (M Sc OT); pathology and molecular medicine (M Sc, PhD); pharmacology and toxicology (M Sc, PhD); physical therapy (M Sc PT); physiology (M Sc, PhD); policy research and clinical epidemiology (M Sc); primary health care nurse practitioner (Certificate); public health (MPH); rehabilitation science (M Sc, PhD); women's and children's health (M Sc). Electronic applications accepted.

School of Industrial Relations *Program availability:* Part-time. Offers industrial relations (MIR).

School of Kinesiology and Health Studies *Program availability:* Part-time. Offers applied exercise science (PhD); biomechanics/ergonomics (M Sc); exercise physiology (M Sc); social psychology of sport and exercise rehabilitation (MA); sociology of sport (MA). Electronic applications accepted.

School of Policy Studies *Program availability:* Part-time. Offers policy studies (MIR, MPA).

School of Urban and Regional Planning *Program availability:* Part-time. Offers urban and regional planning (M Pl).

School of Medicine Offers medicine (MD). Electronic applications accepted.

QUEENS UNIVERSITY OF CHARLOTTE, Charlotte, NC 28274-0002

General Information Independent-religious, coed, comprehensive institution. *Graduate housing:* On-campus housing not available.

GRADUATE UNITS

College of Arts and Sciences *Program availability:* Part-time, online learning. Offers creative writing (MFA); interior design (MA). Electronic applications accepted.

Knight School of Communication *Program availability:* Part-time, evening/weekend, online learning. Offers organizational and strategic communication (MA).

McColl School of Business *Program availability:* Part-time, evening/weekend, online learning. Offers business administration (EMBA, MBA, PMBA); organization development (MSOD). Electronic applications accepted.

Presbyterian School of Nursing Offers clinical nurse leader (MSN); nurse educator (MSN); nursing administrator (MSN). Electronic applications accepted.

Wayland H. Cato, Jr. School of Education *Program availability:* Part-time, evening/weekend, online learning. Offers educational leadership (MA); K-6 (MAT); literacy K-12 (M Ed).

QUINCY UNIVERSITY, Quincy, IL 62301-2699

General Information Independent-religious, coed, comprehensive institution. *Tuition:* Part-time $450 per credit hour. *Graduate housing:* Room and/or apartments available to single students; on-campus housing not available to married students. *Student services:* Campus employment opportunities, campus safety program, career counseling, exercise/wellness program, free psychological counseling, international student services, low-cost health insurance, multicultural affairs office, services for students with disabilities, teacher training, writing training. *Library facilities:* Brenner Library.

Computer facilities: 221 computers available on campus for general student use. A campuswide network can be accessed from student residence rooms and from off campus. Online class registration is available.
Website: http://www.quincy.edu/

General Application Contact: Office of Admissions, 217-228-5210, Fax: 217-228-5479, E-mail: admissions@quincy.edu.

GRADUATE UNITS

Master of Science in Education Counseling Program Expenses: Contact institution. *Financial support:* Applicants required to submit FAFSA. *Program availability:* Part-time, evening/weekend. Offers clinical mental health counseling (MS Ed); college student personnel (MS Ed); school counseling (MS Ed). *Application deadline:* Applications are processed on a rolling basis. *Application fee:* $25. Electronic applications accepted. *Application Contact:* Office of Admissions, 217-228-5210, Fax: 217-228-5479, E-mail: admissions@quincy.edu. *Director*, Dr. Kenneth Oliver, 217-228-5432 Ext. 3113, E-mail: oliveke@quincy.edu.

Master of Science in Education Programs Expenses: Contact institution. *Financial support:* Applicants required to submit FAFSA. *Program availability:* Part-time, evening/weekend, online learning. Offers curriculum and instruction (MS Ed); education studies (MS Ed); leadership (MS Ed); reading education (MS Ed); teacher leader (MS Ed). *Application deadline:* Applications are processed on a rolling basis. *Application fee:* $25. Electronic applications accepted. *Application Contact:* Office of Admissions, 217-228-5210, Fax: 217-228-5479, E-mail: admissions@quincy.edu. *Director*, Dr. Bruce Alan Spitzer, 217-228-5432 Ext. 3106, E-mail: spitzbr@quincy.edu.

MBA Program Expenses: Contact institution. *Financial support:* Applicants required to submit FAFSA. *Program availability:* Part-time, evening/weekend, online learning. Offers business administration (MBA). *Application deadline:* Applications are processed on a rolling basis. *Application fee:* $25. Electronic applications accepted. *Application Contact:* Office of Admissions, 217-228-5210, Fax: 217-228-5479, E-mail: admissions@quincy.edu. *Director*, Dr. Cynthia Haliemun, 217-228-5432 Ext. 3067, E-mail: haliecy@quincy.edu.

QUINNIPIAC UNIVERSITY, Hamden, CT 06518-1940

General Information Independent, coed, comprehensive institution. *Enrollment:* 10,200 graduate, professional, and undergraduate students; 670 full-time matriculated graduate/professional students (429 women), 967 part-time matriculated graduate/professional students (654 women). *Enrollment by degree level:* 1,366 master's, 211 doctoral, 60 other advanced degrees. *Graduate faculty:* 152 full-time (99 women), 170 part-time/adjunct (96 women). *Graduate housing:* Room and/or apartments available on a first-come, first-served basis to married students; on-campus housing not available to single students. *Student services:* Campus employment opportunities, campus safety program, career counseling, exercise/wellness program, free psychological counseling, international student services, low-cost health insurance, multicultural affairs office, services for students with disabilities. *Library facilities:* Arnold Bernhard Library plus 3 others. *Collection:* Books: 135,000 (physical), 500,000 (digital/electronic); Databases: 190. Weekly public service hours: 93; study areas open 24 hours, 5–7 days a week; students can reserve study rooms.

Computer facilities: Computer purchase and lease plans are available. 600 computers available on campus for general student use. A campuswide network can be accessed from student residence rooms and from off campus. Online class registration, e-commerce and Q card for local merchants, food service, dorm card access are available.
Website: http://www.qu.edu/

General Application Contact: Graduate Admissions, 800-462-1944, Fax: 203-582-3443, E-mail: graduate@qu.edu.

GRADUATE UNITS

College of Arts and Sciences Students: 17 full-time (11 women), 9 part-time (5 women); includes 7 minority (1 Black or African American, non-Hispanic/Latino; 2 Asian, non-Hispanic/Latino; 4 Hispanic/Latino), 4 international. 52 applicants, 58% accepted, 10 enrolled. *Faculty:* 9 full-time (5 women), 1 part-time/adjunct (0 women). Expenses: Contact institution. *Financial support:* Federal Work-Study, scholarships/grants, and unspecified assistantships available. Financial award application deadline: 6/1; financial award applicants required to submit FAFSA. In 2017, 14 master's awarded. *Program availability:* Part-time, evening/weekend. Offers arts and sciences (MS); molecular and cell biology (MS). *Application deadline:* For fall admission, 7/30 priority date for domestic students, 4/30 for international students; for spring admission, 12/15 priority date for domestic students, 9/15 for international students. Applications are processed on a rolling basis. *Application fee:* $45. Electronic applications accepted. *Application Contact:* The Office of Graduate Admissions, 800-462-1944, Fax: 203-582-3443, E-mail: graduate@qu.edu.

Frank H. Netter MD School of Medicine Offers anesthesiologist assistant (MMS); medicine (MMS, MD). Electronic applications accepted.

School of Business Students: 212 full-time (102 women), 525 part-time (284 women); includes 132 minority (55 Black or African American, non-Hispanic/Latino; 29 Asian, non-Hispanic/Latino; 28 Hispanic/Latino; 20 Two or more races, non-Hispanic/Latino), 40 international. 403 applicants, 83% accepted, 298 enrolled. *Faculty:* 41 full-time (15 women), 8 part-time/adjunct (3 women). Expenses: Contact institution. *Financial support:* Career-related internships or fieldwork, Federal Work-Study, scholarships/grants, and unspecified assistantships available. Financial award application deadline: 6/1; financial award applicants required to submit FAFSA. In 2017, 384 master's awarded. *Program availability:* Part-time, evening/weekend, 100% online, blended/hybrid learning. Offers accounting (MS); business (MBA, MS); finance (MBA); health care management (MBA); organizational leadership (MS); supply chain management (MBA). *Application deadline:* For fall admission, 7/30 priority date for domestic students, 4/30 priority date for international students; for spring admission, 12/15 priority date for domestic students, 9/30 priority date for international students. Applications are processed on a rolling basis. *Application fee:* $45. Electronic applications accepted. *Application Contact:* Office of Graduate Admissions, 800-462-1944, Fax: 203-582-3443, E-mail: graduate@qu.edu.

School of Communications Students: 41 full-time (24 women), 84 part-time (59 women); includes 30 minority (14 Black or African American, non-Hispanic/Latino; 3 Asian, non-Hispanic/Latino; 10 Hispanic/Latino; 3 Two or more races, non-Hispanic/Latino), 4 international. 112 applicants, 84% accepted, 65 enrolled. *Faculty:* 12 full-time (9 women), 15 part-time/adjunct (6 women). Expenses: Contact institution. *Financial support:* Career-related internships or fieldwork, Federal Work-Study, scholarships/grants, and unspecified assistantships available. Financial award application deadline: 6/1; financial award applicants required to submit FAFSA. In 2017, 55 master's awarded. *Program availability:* Part-time, evening/weekend, online learning. Offers communications (MS); interactive media (MS); journalism (MS); media design (MS); public relations (MS); social media (MS); sports journalism (MS); UX design (MS). *Application deadline:* For fall admission, 7/30 priority date for domestic students, 4/30 priority date for international students; for spring admission, 12/15 priority date for domestic students, 9/30 priority date for international students. Applications are processed on a rolling basis. *Application fee:* $45. Electronic applications accepted. *Program Director*, Phillip Simon, 203-582-8274.

School of Education Students: 107 full-time (97 women), 189 part-time (162 women); includes 41 minority (13 Black or African American, non-Hispanic/Latino; 3 Asian, non-Hispanic/Latino; 14 Hispanic/Latino; 11 Two or more races, non-Hispanic/Latino), 2 international. 149 applicants, 93% accepted, 123 enrolled. *Faculty:* 15 full-time (12 women), 44 part-time/adjunct (30 women). Expenses: Contact institution. *Financial support:* Career-related internships or fieldwork, Federal Work-Study, and unspecified assistantships available. Financial award application deadline: 6/1; financial award applicants required to submit FAFSA. In 2017, 116 master's, 32 other advanced degrees awarded. Offers biology (MAT); education (MAT, MS, Diploma); educational leadership (Diploma); elementary education (MAT); English (MAT); history (MAT); instructional design (MS); mathematics (MAT); Spanish (MAT); teacher leadership (MS). *Application deadline:* Applications are processed on a rolling basis. *Application fee:* $45. Electronic applications accepted.

School of Health Sciences Students: 529 full-time (385 women), 206 part-time (170 women); includes 138 minority (36 Black or African American, non-Hispanic/Latino; 39 Asian, non-Hispanic/Latino; 54 Hispanic/Latino; 9 Two or more races, non-Hispanic/Latino), 23 international. 1,453 applicants, 18% accepted, 152 enrolled. *Faculty:* 58 full-time (41 women), 89 part-time/adjunct (48 women). Expenses: Contact institution. *Financial support:* Federal Work-Study, scholarships/grants, and unspecified assistantships available. Financial award applicants required to submit FAFSA. In 2017, 303 master's awarded. Offers biomedical sciences (MHS); cardiovascular perfusion (MHS); health sciences (MHS, MSW); pathologists' assistant (MHS); physician assistant (MHS); radiologist assistant (MHS); social work (MSW). *Application deadline:* Applications are processed on a rolling basis. *Application fee:* $45. Electronic applications accepted. *Application Contact:* Office of Graduate Admissions, 800-462-1944, Fax: 203-582-3443, E-mail: graduate@qu.edu.

School of Law *Program availability:* Part-time, evening/weekend. Offers law (LL M, JD). Electronic applications accepted.

School of Nursing Students: 57 full-time (47 women), 231 part-time (205 women); includes 84 minority (40 Black or African American, non-Hispanic/Latino; 1 American Indian or Alaska Native, non-Hispanic/Latino; 23 Asian, non-Hispanic/Latino; 17 Hispanic/Latino; 3 Two or more races, non-Hispanic/Latino), 3 international. 225 applicants, 64% accepted, 104 enrolled. *Faculty:* 18 full-time (17 women), 11 part-time/adjunct (8 women). Expenses: Contact institution. *Financial support:* Federal Work-Study, scholarships/grants, and unspecified assistantships available. Financial award application deadline: 6/1; financial award applicants required to submit FAFSA. In 2017, 71 doctorates awarded. Offers adult nurse practitioner (DNP); care of populations (DNP); family nurse practitioner (DNP); nurse anesthesia (DNP); nursing (DNP); nursing leadership (DNP). *Application deadline:* Applications are processed on a rolling basis. *Application fee:* $45. Electronic applications accepted.

See Display on the next page and Close-Up on page 869.

RABBINICAL ACADEMY MESIVTA RABBI CHAIM BERLIN, Brooklyn, NY 11230-4715

General Information Independent-religious, men only, comprehensive institution. *Graduate housing:* Room and/or apartments available to single students; on-campus housing not available to married students. Housing application deadline: 9/30.

GRADUATE UNITS

Graduate Program Offers Talmudic law and rabbinics (Advanced Talmudic Degree, Second Talmudic Degree).

RABBINICAL COLLEGE BETH SHRAGA, Monsey, NY 10952-3035

General Information Independent-religious, men only, comprehensive institution.

GRADUATE UNITS

Graduate Programs Offers theology.

RABBINICAL COLLEGE BOBOVER YESHIVA B'NEI ZION, Brooklyn, NY 11219

General Information Independent-religious, men only, comprehensive institution. *Graduate housing:* Room and/or apartments available to single students; on-campus housing not available to married students.

GRADUATE UNITS

Graduate Programs Offers theology (First Talmudic Degree, Rabbi).

RABBINICAL COLLEGE OF LONG ISLAND, Long Beach, NY 11561-3305

General Information Independent-religious, men only, comprehensive institution.

GRADUATE UNITS

Graduate Programs Offers theology.

RABBINICAL SEMINARY OF AMERICA, Flushing, NY 11367

General Information Independent-religious, men only, comprehensive institution. *Graduate housing:* Room and/or apartments available to single students; on-campus housing not available to married students. Housing application deadline: 6/15.

GRADUATE UNITS

Graduate Programs School offers a master's and first professional degree.

RADFORD UNIVERSITY, Radford, VA 24142

General Information State-supported, coed, university. CGS member. *Enrollment:* 9,418 graduate, professional, and undergraduate students; 552 full-time matriculated graduate/professional students (430 women), 399 part-time matriculated graduate/professional students (303 women). *Enrollment by degree level:* 748 master's, 152 doctoral, 51 other advanced degrees. *Graduate faculty:* 148 full-time (85 women), 43 part-time/adjunct (33 women). Tuition, state resident: full-time $8336; part-time $347 per credit hour. Tuition, nonresident: full-time $16,862; part-time $702 per credit hour. *Required fees:* $3220; $135 per credit hour. Tuition and fees vary according to course load and program. *Graduate housing:* On-campus housing not available. *Student services:* Campus employment opportunities, campus safety program, career counseling, exercise/wellness program, free psychological counseling, international student services, multicultural affairs office, services for students with disabilities, teacher training, writing training. *Library facilities:* McConnell Library. *Collection:* Books: 271,383 (physical), 332,165 (digital/electronic); Serial titles: 558 (physical), 28,298 (digital/electronic); Databases: 535. Students can reserve study rooms. *Research affiliation:* U.S. Department of Health and Human Services (nursing, psychology), Virginia Department of Social Services (social work), Virginia Department of Education (teacher education and leadership), Verizon Foundation (communication sciences and disorders), National Science Foundation (communication sciences and disorders, nursing, criminal justice, psychology, mathematics, biology, computer science), U.S. Department of Education (DOE) (teacher education and leadership).

Computer facilities: Computer purchase and lease plans are available. 900 computers available on campus for general student use. A campuswide network can be accessed from student residence rooms and from off campus. Online class registration, online financial aid status and student accounts payable are available.
Website: http://www.radford.edu/

General Application Contact: Rebecca Conner, Director of Graduate Enrollment, 540-831-5431, Fax: 540-831-6061, E-mail: gradcollege@radford.edu.

GRADUATE UNITS

College of Graduate Studies and Research Students: 552 full-time (430 women), 369 part-time (278 women); includes 139 minority (70 Black or African American, non-Hispanic/Latino; 12 Asian, non-Hispanic/Latino; 34 Hispanic/Latino; 1 Native Hawaiian or other Pacific Islander, non-Hispanic/Latino; 22 Two or more races, non-Hispanic/Latino), 17 international. Average age 29. 1,150 applicants, 56% accepted, 363 enrolled. *Faculty:* 148 full-time (85 women), 43 part-time/adjunct (33 women). Expenses: Contact institution. *Financial support:* In 2017–18, 186 students received support, including 21 research assistantships (averaging $7,867 per year), 73 teaching assistantships (averaging $10,003 per year); career-related internships or fieldwork, scholarships/grants, and unspecified assistantships also available. Support available to part-time students. Financial award application deadline: 3/1; financial award applicants required to submit FAFSA. In 2017, 286 master's, 33 doctorates, 24 other advanced degrees awarded. *Program availability:* Part-time, evening/weekend, 100% online, blended/hybrid learning. Offers art (MFA); business administration (MBA); clinical-counseling psychology (MA, MS); communication sciences and disorders (MA, MS); counseling psychology (Psy D); counselor education (MS); criminal justice (MA, MS, Certificate); early childhood education (MS); educational leadership (MS); English (MA, MS); experimental psychology (MA); industrial-organizational psychology (MA, MS); literacy education (MS); mathematics education (MS); music (MA, MS); nursing practice (DNP); occupational therapy (MOT); physical therapy (DPT); school psychology (Ed S); social work (MSW); special education (MS, Certificate); strategic communication (MS). *Application deadline:* Applications are processed on a rolling basis. *Application fee:* $50. Electronic applications accepted. *Application Contact:* Rebecca Conner, Director, Graduate Enrollment, 540-831-5431, Fax: 540-831-6061, E-mail: gradcollege@radford.edu. *Dean*, Dr. Laura Jacobsen, 540-831-5724, Fax: 540-831-6061, E-mail: gradcollege@radford.edu.

Program in Data and Information Management Students: 9 full-time (1 woman), 2 part-time (0 women); includes 3 minority (2 Asian, non-Hispanic/Latino; 1 Hispanic/Latino), 3 international. Average age 30. 9 applicants, 89% accepted, 8 enrolled. *Faculty:* 4 full-time (0 women). Expenses: Contact institution. *Financial support:* In 2017–18, 4 students received support, including 4 teaching assistantships (averaging $11,000 per year); scholarships/grants and unspecified assistantships also available. Support available to part-time students. Financial award application deadline: 3/1; financial award applicants required to submit FAFSA. *Program availability:* Part-time. Offers data and information management (MS). *Application deadline:* Applications are processed on a rolling basis. *Application fee:* $50. Electronic applications accepted.

RAMAPO COLLEGE OF NEW JERSEY, Mahwah, NJ 07430-1680

General Information State-supported, coed, comprehensive institution. *Enrollment:* 6,120 graduate, professional, and undergraduate students; 121 full-time matriculated graduate/professional students (93 women), 370 part-time matriculated graduate/professional students (280 women). *Enrollment by degree level:* 491 master's. *Graduate faculty:* 19 full-time (15 women), 31 part-time/adjunct (14 women). Tuition, state resident: part-time $690.60 per credit. Tuition, nonresident: part-time $690.60 per credit. *Required fees:* $56.95 per credit. Tuition and fees vary according to program. *Graduate housing:* Room and/or apartments available on a first-come, first-served basis to single students. Typical cost: $8800 per year. Housing application deadline: 7/1. *Student services:* Career counseling, services for students with disabilities. *Library facilities:* George T. Potter Library. *Research affiliation:* American Association of State Colleges and Universities, New Jersey Council of Magnet Organizations, Council of Public Liberal Arts Colleges.

Computer facilities: A campuswide network can be accessed from student residence rooms and from off campus. Online class registration is available.
Website: http://www.ramapo.edu/

General Application Contact: Anthony Dovi, Associate Director of Admissions, Adult Learners and Graduate Programs, 201-684-7305, Fax: 201-684-7964, E-mail: adovi@ramapo.edu.

GRADUATE UNITS

Master of Arts in Educational Leadership Program Students: 28 full-time (21 women), 30 part-time (20 women); includes 7 minority (1 Black or African American, non-Hispanic/Latino; 1 American Indian or Alaska Native, non-Hispanic/Latino; 1 Asian, non-Hispanic/Latino; 3 Hispanic/Latino; 1 Two or more races, non-Hispanic/Latino). Average age 35. 51 applicants, 86% accepted, 31 enrolled. *Faculty:* 1 full-time (0 women), 9 part-time/adjunct (1 woman). Expenses: Contact institution. *Financial support:* Career-related internships or fieldwork available. Financial award application deadline: 3/1; financial award applicants required to submit FAFSA. In 2017, 44 master's awarded. *Program availability:* Part-time. Offers educational leadership (MA). *Application deadline:* For fall admission, 5/1 for domestic and international students; for spring admission, 12/1 for domestic and international students; for summer admission, 5/1 for domestic and international students. Applications are processed on a rolling basis. *Application fee:* $65. Electronic applications accepted. *Application Contact:* M. Joyce Wilson, Secretarial Assistant, 201-684-7721, Fax: 201-684-6699, E-mail: jwilson@ramapo.edu. *Associate Professor, Educational Leadership,* Dr. Brian P. Chinni, 201-684-7613, E-mail: bchinni@ramapo.edu.

Master of Arts in Special Education Program Students: 44 part-time (40 women); includes 4 minority (3 Hispanic/Latino; 1 Two or more races, non-Hispanic/Latino). Average age 28. 43 applicants, 70% accepted, 25 enrolled. *Faculty:* 2 full-time (both women), 3 part-time/adjunct (1 woman). Expenses: Contact institution. *Financial support:* Career-related internships or fieldwork available. Financial award application deadline: 3/1; financial award applicants required to submit FAFSA. In 2017, 18 master's awarded. *Program availability:* Part-time, evening/weekend. Offers special education (MA). *Application deadline:* For fall admission, 5/1 for domestic and international students. Applications are processed on a rolling basis. *Application fee:* $65. Electronic applications accepted. *Application Contact:* M. Joyce Wilson, Secretarial Assistant, 201-684-7721, Fax: 201-684-6699, E-mail: jwilson@ramapo.edu. *Director,* Dr. Julie Norflus-Good, 201-684-7246, E-mail: jgood@ramapo.edu.

Master of Business Administration Program Students: 63 part-time (30 women); includes 14 minority (2 Asian, non-Hispanic/Latino; 12 Hispanic/Latino). Average age 33. 95 applicants, 55% accepted, 33 enrolled. *Faculty:* 3 full-time (all women). Expenses: Contact institution. *Financial support:* In 2017–18, 2 students received support. Career-related internships or fieldwork and scholarships/grants available. Financial award application deadline: 3/1; financial award applicants required to submit FAFSA. In 2017, 34 master's awarded. *Program availability:* Part-time-only, evening/weekend. Offers leadership (MBA). *Application deadline:* For fall admission, 5/1 for domestic and international students. Applications are processed on a rolling basis. *Application fee:* $65. Electronic applications accepted. *Application Contact:* Timothy Landers, Assistant Dean/Director of the MBA Program, 201-684-7771, E-mail: tlanders@ramapo.edu. *Dean of the Anisfield School of Business,* Dr. Edward Petkus, 201-684-7377, E-mail: epetkus@ramapo.edu.

Master of Science in Accounting Program Students: 12 full-time (4 women), 11 part-time (8 women); includes 7 minority (1 Asian, non-Hispanic/Latino; 6 Hispanic/Latino). Average age 31. 41 applicants, 85% accepted, 23 enrolled. *Faculty:* 3 full-time (2 women). Expenses: Contact institution. *Financial support:* Career-related internships or fieldwork available. Financial award application deadline: 3/1; financial award applicants required to submit FAFSA. *Program availability:* Part-time. Offers accounting (MS). *Application deadline:* For fall admission, 5/1 for domestic and international students; for spring admission, 12/1 for domestic and international students; for summer admission, 5/1 for domestic and international students. Applications are processed on a rolling basis. *Application fee:* $65. Electronic applications accepted. *Application Contact:* Constance Crawford, Director of the Master of Science in Accounting Program, 201-684-7396, E-mail: ccrawfor@ramapo.edu. *Dean of the Anisfield School of Business,* Dr. Edward Petkus, 201-684-7377, E-mail: epetkus@ramapo.edu.

Master of Science in Educational Technology Program Students: 2 full-time (both women), 124 part-time (95 women); includes 18 minority (3 Black or African American, non-Hispanic/Latino; 1 Asian, non-Hispanic/Latino; 14 Hispanic/Latino), 3 international. Average age 34. 50 applicants, 86% accepted, 29 enrolled. *Faculty:* 10 part-time/adjunct (4 women). Expenses: Contact institution. *Financial support:* Career-related internships or fieldwork available. Financial award application deadline: 3/1; financial award applicants required to submit FAFSA. In 2017, 49 master's awarded. *Program availability:* Part-time, evening/weekend. Offers educational technology (MS). *Application deadline:* For fall admission, 5/1 for domestic and international students; for spring admission, 12/1 for domestic and international students. Applications are processed on a rolling basis. *Application fee:* $65. Electronic applications accepted. *Application Contact:* M. Joyce Wilson, Administrative Assistant, 201-684-7721, Fax: 201-684-6699, E-mail: jwilson@ramapo.edu. *Director of the Master in Educational Technology Program,* Dr. Richard Russo, 201-684-7899, Fax: 201-684-6699, E-mail: rrusso@ramapo.edu.

Master of Science in Nursing Program Students: 79 part-time (70 women); includes 28 minority (4 Black or African American, non-Hispanic/Latino; 18 Asian, non-Hispanic/Latino; 5 Hispanic/Latino; 1 Two or more races, non-Hispanic/Latino). Average age 33. 84 applicants, 67% accepted, 37 enrolled. *Faculty:* 4 full-time (all women), 2 part-time/adjunct (1 woman). Expenses: Contact institution. *Financial support:* Career-related internships or fieldwork available. Financial award application deadline: 3/1; financial award applicants required to submit FAFSA. In 2017, 9 master's awarded. *Program availability:* Part-time. Offers family nurse practitioner (MSN); nursing administrator (MSN); nursing education (MSN). *Application deadline:* For fall admission, 5/1 for domestic and international students; for spring admission, 12/1 for domestic and international students. Applications are processed on a rolling basis. *Application fee:* $65. Electronic applications accepted. *Application Contact:* Anthony Dovi, Associate Director of Admissions, Adult Learners and Graduate Programs, 201-684-7305, Fax: 201-684-7964, E-mail: adovi@ramapo.edu. *Assistant Dean of Nursing Programs/Professor,* Dr. Kathleen M. Burke, 201-684-7737, Fax: 201-684-7954, E-mail: kmburke@ramapo.edu.

Master of Social Work Program Students: 79 full-time (66 women), 19 part-time (17 women); includes 27 minority (10 Black or African American, non-Hispanic/Latino; 2 Asian, non-Hispanic/Latino; 14 Hispanic/Latino; 1 Two or more races, non-Hispanic/Latino), 1 international. Average age 32. 205 applicants, 48% accepted, 58 enrolled. *Faculty:* 6 full-time (4 women), 7 part-time/adjunct (all women). Expenses: Contact institution. *Financial support:* Scholarships/grants available. Financial award application deadline: 3/1; financial award applicants required to submit FAFSA. In 2017, 37 master's awarded. *Program availability:* Part-time. Offers social work (MSW). *Application deadline:* For fall admission, 3/1 for domestic and international students. Applications are processed on a rolling basis. *Application fee:* $65. Electronic applications accepted. *Assistant Dean/Director,* Ann Marie Moreno, 201-684-7191, E-mail: amoreno@ramapo.edu.

RANDALL UNIVERSITY, Moore, OK 73160-1208

General Information Independent-religious, coed, comprehensive institution. *Graduate housing:* Room and/or apartments available on a first-come, first-served basis to single students.

GRADUATE UNITS

Department of Bible Studies *Program availability:* Part-time, evening/weekend. Offers ministry (MA).

RANDOLPH COLLEGE, Lynchburg, VA 24503

General Information Independent-religious, coed, comprehensive institution.

GRADUATE UNITS

Program in Creative Writing Offers creative writing (MFA).

Programs in Education Offers curriculum and instruction (MAT); special education-learning disabilities (M Ed, MAT).

RECONSTRUCTIONIST RABBINICAL COLLEGE, Wyncote, PA 19095-1898

General Information Independent-religious, coed, graduate-only institution. *Graduate housing:* On-campus housing not available.

GRADUATE UNITS

Graduate Programs *Program availability:* Part-time. Offers Jewish studies (MAJS); rabbinics (MAHL, DHL); women's studies (Certificate). Certificate offered jointly with Temple University.

REED COLLEGE, Portland, OR 97202-8199

General Information Independent, coed, comprehensive institution. *Enrollment:* 1,470 graduate, professional, and undergraduate students; 29 part-time matriculated graduate/professional students (17 women). *Enrollment by degree level:* 29 master's. *Graduate faculty:* 10 part-time/adjunct (1 woman). *Graduate housing:* On-campus housing not available. *Student services:* Campus employment opportunities, campus safety program, career counseling, exercise/wellness program, free psychological counseling, low-cost health insurance, multicultural affairs office, services for students with disabilities, writing training. *Library facilities:* Eric V. Hauser Memorial Library plus 1 other. *Collection:* Study areas open 24 hours, 5–7 days a week.

Computer facilities: Computer purchase and lease plans are available. 434 computers available on campus for general student use. A campuswide network can be accessed from student residence rooms. Online class registration is available.
Website: http://www.reed.edu/

General Application Contact: Barbara A. Amen, Director, Special Programs, 503-777-7259, Fax: 503-517-7345, E-mail: bamen@reed.edu.

GRADUATE UNITS

Graduate Program in Liberal Studies Students: 29 part-time (17 women); includes 2 minority (both Black or African American, non-Hispanic/Latino). Average age 43. 5 applicants, 80% accepted, 4 enrolled. *Faculty:* 10 part-time/adjunct (1 woman). Expenses: Contact institution. *Financial support:* In 2017–18, 7 students received support. Scholarships/grants and health care benefits available. Support available to part-time students. Financial award application deadline: 5/1; financial award applicants required to submit CSS PROFILE or FAFSA. In 2017, 1 master's awarded. *Program availability:* Part-time-only, evening/weekend. Offers liberal studies (MALS). *Application deadline:* For fall admission, 7/1 priority date for domestic students, 5/1 for international students; for spring admission, 12/1 priority date for domestic students, 9/1 for international students; for summer admission, 4/1 for domestic students, 2/1 for international students. Applications are processed on a rolling basis. *Application fee:* $75. Electronic applications accepted. *Director, Graduate Studies,* Barbara A. Amen, 503-777-7259, Fax: 503-517-7345, E-mail: bamen@reed.edu.

REFORMED EPISCOPAL SEMINARY, Blue Bell, PA 19422

General Information Independent-religious, coed, graduate-only institution. *Graduate housing:* Room and/or apartments available on a first-come, first-served basis to single students; on-campus housing not available to married students.

GRADUATE UNITS

Graduate Program Offers theology (M Div).

REFORMED PRESBYTERIAN THEOLOGICAL SEMINARY, Pittsburgh, PA 15208-2594

General Information Independent-religious, coed, primarily men, graduate-only institution. *Graduate housing:* Rooms and/or apartments available on a first-come, first-served basis to single and married students.

GRADUATE UNITS

Graduate and Professional Programs *Program availability:* Part-time, evening/weekend. Offers theology (M Div, MTS, D Min). Electronic applications accepted.

REFORMED THEOLOGICAL SEMINARY–ATLANTA CAMPUS, Marietta, GA 30067

General Information Independent-religious, coed, primarily men, graduate-only institution.

GRADUATE UNITS

Graduate Programs Offers theology (M Div, MABS, MAR, D Min, Certificate).

REFORMED THEOLOGICAL SEMINARY–CHARLOTTE CAMPUS, Charlotte, NC 28226-6318

General Information Independent-religious, coed, primarily men, graduate-only institution. *Graduate housing:* On-campus housing not available.

GRADUATE UNITS

Graduate and Professional Programs *Program availability:* Part-time. Offers biblical studies (MA); ministry (D Min); pastoral ministry (M Div); theological studies (MA). Electronic applications accepted.

REFORMED THEOLOGICAL SEMINARY–DALLAS CAMPUS, Dallas, TX 75207

General Information Independent-religious, coed, graduate-only institution.

GRADUATE UNITS

Graduate and Professional Programs Offers theological studies (MA); theology (M Div).

REFORMED THEOLOGICAL SEMINARY–HOUSTON CAMPUS, Houston, TX 77024

General Information Independent-religious, coed, primarily men, graduate-only institution. *Graduate housing:* On-campus housing not available.

GRADUATE UNITS

Graduate Program Offers Biblical studies (MA). Electronic applications accepted.

REFORMED THEOLOGICAL SEMINARY–JACKSON CAMPUS, Jackson, MS 39209-3004

General Information Independent-religious, coed, primarily men, graduate-only institution. *Graduate housing:* Rooms and/or apartments available on a first-come, first-served basis to single and married students.

GRADUATE UNITS

Graduate and Professional Programs Offers Bible, theology, and missions (Certificate); Biblical exegesis (M Div); biblical studies (MA); Christian education (MA); counseling (M Div); marriage and family therapy (MA); ministry (D Min); missions (M Div, MA, D Min); theological studies (MA).

REFORMED THEOLOGICAL SEMINARY–ORLANDO CAMPUS, Oviedo, FL 32765

General Information Independent-religious, coed, primarily men, graduate-only institution. *Enrollment by degree level:* 275 master's, 53 doctoral, 4 other advanced degrees. *Graduate faculty:* 12 full-time (0 women), 11 part-time/adjunct (2 women). *Tuition:* Full-time $18,025; part-time $8755 per semester hour. *Required fees:* $160; $160 per semester hour. $80 per semester. *Graduate housing:* Rooms and/or apartments available on a first-come, first-served basis to single and married students. *Student services:* Campus employment opportunities, career counseling, free psychological counseling, international student services, writing training. *Library facilities:* RTS Library. *Collection:* Books: 89,266 (physical); Serial titles: 146 (physical). Weekly public service hours: 69.

Computer facilities: 6 computers available on campus for general student use. A campuswide network can be accessed. Online class registration is available.
Website: http://rts.edu/orlando/

General Application Contact: Winston J. Miller, Director of Admissions, 800-752-4382, Fax: 407-366-9425, E-mail: applications.orlando@rts.edu.

GRADUATE UNITS

Graduate Programs Students: 340. *Faculty:* 12 full-time (0 women), 11 part-time/adjunct (2 women). Expenses: Contact institution. *Program availability:* Part-time, online learning. Offers Bible (Certificate); biblical studies (MA); counseling (MA); missions (Certificate); reformed expository preaching (D Min); reformed theology and ministry (D Min); theological studies (MA); theology (M Div, Certificate). *Application deadline:* Applications are processed on a rolling basis. *Application fee:* $75. Electronic applications accepted. *Application Contact:* Winston J. Miller, Director of Admissions, 800-752-4382, Fax: 407-366-9425, E-mail: applications.orlando@rts.edu. *President*, Dr. Scott R. Swain, 407-278-4406, Fax: 407-366-9425.

REFORMED THEOLOGICAL SEMINARY–WASHINGTON D.C., McLean, VA 22102

General Information Independent-religious, coed, primarily men, graduate-only institution. *Enrollment by degree level:* 120 master's, 8 other advanced degrees. *Graduate faculty:* 4 full-time (0 women), 9 part-time/adjunct (2 women). *Tuition:* Full-time $12,360; part-time $6180 per credit. *Required fees:* $80; $80 per semester. Tuition and fees vary according to course load. *Graduate housing:* On-campus housing not available. *Student services:* Campus employment opportunities, campus safety program, career counseling, international student services, writing training. *Library facilities:* RTS Library. *Collection:* Books: 5,700 (physical).

Computer facilities: 1 computer available on campus for general student use. Online class registration is available.
Website: http://www.rts.edu/washington/

General Application Contact: Timo Sazo, Director of Admissions, 703-448-3393 Ext. 5104, Fax: 571-297-8010, E-mail: tsazo@rts.edu.

GRADUATE UNITS

Graduate and Professional Programs Students: 6 full-time (0 women), 122 part-time (16 women); includes 19 minority (5 Black or African American, non-Hispanic/Latino; 14 Asian, non-Hispanic/Latino). Average age 35. 66 applicants, 95% accepted, 48 enrolled. *Faculty:* 4 full-time (0 women), 8 part-time/adjunct (2 women). Expenses: Contact institution. *Financial support:* In 2017–18, 128 students received support. Scholarships/grants and tuition waivers (partial) available. Support available to part-time students. Financial award application deadline: 7/15. In 2017, 15 master's awarded. *Program availability:* Part-time, evening/weekend. Offers Bible (M Div); biblical studies (MA); practical theology (M Div); religion (MA); theology (M Div). *Application deadline:* Applications are processed on a rolling basis. *Application fee:* $75. Electronic applications accepted. *Application Contact:* Timo Sazo, Director of Admissions, 703-448-3393 Ext. 5104, Fax: 571-297-8010, E-mail: tsazo@rts.edu. *President*, Dr. John S. Redd, Jr., 703-448-3393 Ext. 5107, E-mail: sredd@rts.edu.

REGENT COLLEGE, Vancouver, BC V6T 2E4, Canada

General Information Independent-religious, coed, graduate-only institution. *Graduate housing:* On-campus housing not available. *Research affiliation:* University of British Columbia (theology, religion).

GRADUATE UNITS

Program in Theology *Program availability:* Part-time. Offers Christian history and theology (M Div, MATS); Christian studies (MATS, G Dip); Christianity, church and culture (M Div, MATS); scripture (M Div, MATS); theology (Th M). Electronic applications accepted.

REGENT'S UNIVERSITY LONDON, London NW1 4NS, United Kingdom

General Information Independent, coed, comprehensive institution.

GRADUATE UNITS

Webster Graduate School *Program availability:* Part-time. Offers business (MBA); finance (MS); human resources (MA); information technology management (MA); international business (MA); international non-governmental organizations (MA); international relations (MA); management and leadership (MA); marketing (MA).

REGENT UNIVERSITY, Virginia Beach, VA 23464-9800

General Information Independent-religious, coed, comprehensive institution. *Enrollment:* 10,187 graduate, professional, and undergraduate students; 1,103 full-time matriculated graduate/professional students (698 women), 4,171 part-time matriculated graduate/professional students (2,570 women). *Enrollment by degree level:* 3,651 master's, 1,492 doctoral, 131 other advanced degrees. *Graduate faculty:* 115 full-time (39 women), 361 part-time/adjunct (130 women). Tuition and fees vary according to course load and degree level. *Graduate housing:* Rooms and/or apartments available on a first-come, first-served basis to single and married students. Typical cost: $7530 per year ($10,410 including board) for single students. Room and board charges vary according to board plan and housing facility selected. Housing application deadline: 5/1. *Student services:* Campus employment opportunities, campus safety program, career counseling, exercise/wellness program, free psychological counseling, international student services, low-cost health insurance, services for students with disabilities, teacher training, writing training. *Library facilities:* Regent University Library plus 1 other. *Collection:* Books: 321,395 (physical), 470,995 (digital/electronic); Serial titles: 106 (physical), 84,710 (digital/electronic); Databases: 155. Weekly public service hours: 98; students can reserve study rooms.

Computer facilities: 70 computers available on campus for general student use. A campuswide network can be accessed from student residence rooms and from off campus. Online class registration is available.
Website: http://www.regent.edu/

General Application Contact: Heidi Cece, Assistant Vice President of Enrollment Management, 800-373-5504, Fax: 757-352-4381, E-mail: admissions@regent.edu.

GRADUATE UNITS

Graduate School Students: 1,103 full-time (698 women), 4,171 part-time (2,570 women); includes 2,484 minority (1,930 Black or African American, non-Hispanic/Latino; 27 American Indian or Alaska Native, non-Hispanic/Latino; 109 Asian, non-Hispanic/Latino; 280 Hispanic/Latino; 9 Native Hawaiian or other Pacific Islander, non-Hispanic/Latino; 129 Two or more races, non-Hispanic/Latino), 185 international. Average age 38. 8,042 applicants, 36% accepted, 1957 enrolled. *Faculty:* 115 full-time (39 women), 361 part-time/adjunct (130 women). Expenses: Contact institution. *Financial support:* Career-related internships or fieldwork and scholarships/grants available. Support available to part-time students. Financial award application deadline: 3/1; financial award applicants required to submit FAFSA. In 2017, 1,014 master's, 248 doctorates awarded. *Program availability:* Part-time, evening/weekend, 100% online, blended/hybrid learning. *Application deadline:* Applications are processed on a rolling basis. *Application fee:* $50. Electronic applications accepted. *Application Contact:* Heidi Cece, Assistant Vice President of Enrollment Management, 800-373-5504, Fax: 757-352-4381, E-mail: admissions@regent.edu. *Executive Vice President for Academic Affairs*, Dr. Gerson Moreno-Riano, 757-352-4320, Fax: 757-352-4448, E-mail: gmorenoriano@regent.edu.

Robertson School of Government Students: 39 full-time (23 women), 137 part-time (78 women); includes 83 minority (49 Black or African American, non-Hispanic/Latino; 1 American Indian or Alaska Native, non-Hispanic/Latino; 7 Asian, non-Hispanic/Latino; 15 Hispanic/Latino; 11 Two or more races, non-Hispanic/Latino). Average age 35. 345 applicants, 31% accepted, 57 enrolled. *Faculty:* 8 full-time (1 woman), 20 part-time/adjunct (3 women). Expenses: Contact institution. *Financial support:* In 2017–18, 116 students received support. Career-related internships or fieldwork, scholarships/grants, and unspecified assistantships available. Support available to part-time students. In 2017, 38 master's awarded. *Program availability:* Part-time, evening/weekend, 100% online, blended/hybrid learning. Offers government (MA); national security studies (MA); public administration (MPA). *Application deadline:* For fall admission, 5/1 priority date for domestic students; for spring admission, 11/1 priority date for domestic students. Applications are processed on a rolling basis. *Application fee:* $50. Electronic applications accepted. *Application Contact:* Heidi Cece, Assistant Vice President of Enrollment Management, 800-373-5504, Fax: 757-352-4381, E-mail: admissions@regent.edu. *Dean*, Dr. Eric Patterson, 757-352-4616, Fax: 757-352-4735, E-mail: epatterson@regent.edu.

School of Business and Leadership Students: 129 full-time (80 women), 1,152 part-time (598 women); includes 685 minority (546 Black or African American, non-Hispanic/Latino; 10 American Indian or Alaska Native, non-Hispanic/Latino; 29 Asian, non-Hispanic/Latino; 65 Hispanic/Latino; 6 Native Hawaiian or other Pacific Islander, non-Hispanic/Latino; 29 Two or more races, non-Hispanic/Latino), 62 international. Average age 41. 1,721 applicants, 48% accepted, 624 enrolled. *Faculty:* 9 full-time (2 women), 38 part-time/adjunct (11 women). Expenses: Contact institution. *Financial support:* In 2017–18, 829 students received support. Career-related internships or fieldwork, scholarships/grants, and unspecified assistantships available. Support available to part-time students. In 2017, 125 master's, 69 doctorates awarded. *Program availability:* Part-time, evening/weekend, 100% online, blended/hybrid learning. Offers business administration (MBA); business analytics (MS); business and design management (MA); church leadership (MA); leadership (Certificate); organizational leadership (MA, PhD); strategic leadership (DSL). *Application deadline:* For fall admission, 5/1 priority date for domestic students; for spring admission, 10/1 priority date for domestic students. Applications are processed on a rolling basis. *Application fee:* $50. Electronic applications accepted. *Application Contact:* Heidi Cece, Assistant Vice President of Enrollment Management, 800-373-5504, Fax: 757-352-4381, E-mail: admissions@regent.edu. *Dean*, Dr. Doris Gomez, 757-352-4686, Fax: 757-352-4634, E-mail: dorigom@regent.edu.

School of Communication and the Arts Students: 101 full-time (65 women), 342 part-time (237 women); includes 177 minority (127 Black or African American, non-Hispanic/Latino; 4 American Indian or Alaska Native, non-Hispanic/Latino; 9 Asian, non-Hispanic/Latino; 25 Hispanic/Latino; 12 Two or more races, non-Hispanic/Latino), 11 international. Average age 37. 498 applicants, 36% accepted, 124 enrolled. *Faculty:* 15 full-time (2 women), 66 part-time/adjunct (23 women). Expenses: Contact institution. *Financial support:* In 2017–18, 234 students received support, including 2 fellowships (averaging $10,000 per year); career-related internships or fieldwork, scholarships/grants, and unspecified assistantships also available. Support available to part-time students. In 2017, 93 master's, 22 doctorates awarded. *Program availability:* Part-time, evening/weekend, 100% online, blended/hybrid learning. Offers acting (MFA); communication (MA, PhD); film and TV (MA); film-television (MFA); journalism (MA); theatre (MA). *Application deadline:* For fall admission, 3/1 priority date for domestic students; for spring admission, 10/1 priority date for domestic students. Applications are processed on a rolling basis. *Application fee:* $50. Electronic applications accepted. *Application Contact:* Heidi Cece, Assistant Vice President of Enrollment Management, 800-373-5504, Fax: 757-352-4381, E-mail: admissions@regent.edu. *Dean*, Dr. Robert Herron, 757-352-4500, E-mail: rherron@regent.edu.

School of Divinity Students: 146 full-time (54 women), 917 part-time (404 women); includes 563 minority (470 Black or African American, non-Hispanic/Latino; 1 American Indian or Alaska Native, non-Hispanic/Latino; 17 Asian, non-Hispanic/Latino; 56 Hispanic/Latino; 1 Native Hawaiian or other Pacific Islander, non-Hispanic/Latino; 18 Two or more races, non-Hispanic/Latino), 27 international. Average age 44. 1,321 applicants, 39% accepted, 295 enrolled. *Faculty:* 17 full-time (3 women), 66 part-time/adjunct (9 women). Expenses: Contact institution. *Financial support:* In 2017–18, 721 students received support. Career-related internships or fieldwork, scholarships/grants, and unspecified assistantships available. Support available to part-time students. In 2017, 146 master's, 25 doctorates awarded. *Program availability:* Part-time, evening/weekend, 100% online, blended/hybrid learning. Offers Christian spirituality and formation (MA); divinity (M Div); leadership and renewal (D Min); practical theology (MA); renewal theology (PhD); theological studies (MTS); theology (Th M). *Application deadline:* For fall admission, 5/1 priority date for domestic students. Applications are processed on a rolling basis. *Application fee:* $50. Electronic applications accepted. *Application Contact:* Heidi Cece, Assistant Vice President of Enrollment Management, 800-373-5504, Fax: 757-352-4381, E-mail: admissions@regent.edu. *Dean*, Dr. Cornelius Bekker, 757-352-4401, Fax: 757-352-4597, E-mail: clbekker@regent.edu.

School of Education Students: 80 full-time (59 women), 945 part-time (750 women); includes 432 minority (352 Black or African American, non-Hispanic/Latino; 4 American Indian or Alaska Native, non-Hispanic/Latino; 14 Asian, non-Hispanic/Latino; 43 Hispanic/Latino; 19 Two or more races, non-Hispanic/Latino), 12 international. Average age 40. 1,125 applicants, 49% accepted, 436 enrolled. *Faculty:* 22 full-time (10 women), 44 part-time/adjunct (32 women). Expenses: Contact institution. *Financial support:* In 2017–18, 669 students received support, including 1 fellowship (averaging $10,000 per year); career-related internships or fieldwork, scholarships/grants, and unspecified assistantships also available. Support available to part-time students. In 2017, 316 master's, 24 doctorates awarded. *Program availability:* Part-time, evening/weekend, 100% online, blended/hybrid learning. Offers education (M Ed, Ed D, PhD); educational specialist (Ed S). *Application deadline:* For fall admission, 4/1 priority date for domestic students; for spring admission, 10/15 priority date for domestic students. Applications are processed on a rolling basis. *Application fee:* $50. Electronic applications accepted. *Application Contact:* Heidi Cece, Assistant Vice President of Enrollment Management, 800-373-5504, Fax: 757-352-4381, E-mail: admissions@regent.edu. *Dean*, Dr. Donald Finn, 757-352-4278, Fax: 757-352-4318, E-mail: dfinn@regent.edu.

School of Law Students: 313 full-time (181 women), 248 part-time (175 women); includes 240 minority (155 Black or African American, non-Hispanic/Latino; 3 American Indian or Alaska Native, non-Hispanic/Latino; 15 Asian, non-Hispanic/Latino; 45 Hispanic/Latino; 2 Native Hawaiian or other Pacific Islander, non-Hispanic/Latino; 20 Two or more races, non-Hispanic/Latino), 59 international. Average age 35. 923 applicants, 36% accepted, 188 enrolled. *Faculty:* 16 full-time (5 women), 76 part-time/adjunct (22 women). Expenses: Contact institution. *Financial support:* In 2017–18, 459 students received support. Career-related internships or fieldwork, scholarships/grants, and unspecified assistantships available. Support available to part-time students. In 2017, 138 master's, 80 doctorates awarded. *Program availability:* Part-time, 100% online, blended/hybrid learning. Offers American legal studies (LL M); human rights (LL M); law (MA, JD). *Application deadline:* For fall admission, 3/1 for domestic students. Applications are processed on a rolling basis. *Application fee:* $50. Electronic applications accepted. *Application Contact:* Ernie Walton, Assistant Dean of Admissions, 757-352-4315, E-mail: lawschool@regent.edu. *Dean*, Michael Hernandez, 757-352-4040, Fax: 757-352-4595, E-mail: michher@regent.edu.

School of Psychology and Counseling Students: 294 full-time (236 women), 404 part-time (317 women); includes 286 minority (218 Black or African American, non-Hispanic/Latino; 4 American Indian or Alaska Native, non-Hispanic/Latino; 17 Asian, non-Hispanic/Latino; 30 Hispanic/Latino; 17 Two or more races, non-Hispanic/Latino), 13 international. Average age 37. 2,109 applicants, 18% accepted, 233 enrolled. *Faculty:* 28 full-time (16 women), 51 part-time/adjunct (30 women). Expenses: Contact institution. *Financial support:* In 2017–18, 557 students received support, including 5 fellowships (averaging $10,000 per year), 11 research assistantships (averaging $3,200 per year); career-related internships or fieldwork, scholarships/grants, and unspecified assistantships also available. Support available to part-time students. In 2017, 158 master's, 28 doctorates awarded. *Program availability:* Part-time, evening/weekend, 100% online, blended/hybrid learning. Offers clinical mental health counseling (MA); clinical psychology (Psy D); counseling and psychological studies - clinical (PhD); counseling and psychological studies - research (PhD); counseling studies (CAGS); counselor education and supervision (PhD); general psychology (MS); human services (MA); marriage, couple, and family counseling (MA); pastoral counseling (MA); school counseling (MA). *Application deadline:* For fall admission, 4/1 priority date for domestic students; for spring admission, 11/1 priority date for domestic students. Applications are processed on a rolling basis. *Application fee:* $50. Electronic applications accepted. *Application Contact:* Heidi Cece, Assistant Vice President of Enrollment Management, 800-373-5504, Fax: 757-352-4381, E-mail: admissions@regent.edu. *Dean*, Dr. William Hathaway, 757-352-4294, Fax: 757-352-4282, E-mail: willhat@regent.edu.

REGIS COLLEGE, Toronto, ON M5S 2Z5, Canada

General Information Independent-religious, coed, graduate-only institution. *Graduate housing:* Room and/or apartments available on a first-come, first-served basis to single students; on-campus housing not available to married students. *Research affiliation:* Lonergan Research Institute (theology/philosophy), Lupina Foundation (research and innovation related to health/society issues).

GRADUATE UNITS

Graduate and Professional Programs Offers eastern Christian studies (Certificate); Ignatian spirituality (Diploma); ministry (D Min); ministry and spirituality (MAMS); philosophical studies (Diploma); retreat direction (Certificate); sacred theology (STM, STD, STB, STL); spiritual direction (Diploma); theological studies (MTS, Diploma); theology (M Div, MA, Th M, PhD, Th D).

REGIS COLLEGE, Weston, MA 02493

General Information Independent-religious, coed, comprehensive institution. *Enrollment:* 150 full-time matriculated graduate/professional students, 800 part-time matriculated graduate/professional students. *Graduate housing:* Room and/or apartments available on a first-come, first-served basis to single students; on-campus housing not available to married students. *Student services:* Campus employment opportunities, campus safety program, career counseling, exercise/wellness program, international student services, low-cost health insurance, multicultural affairs office, services for students with disabilities, teacher training, writing training. *Library facilities:* Regis College Library. *Collection:* Books: 108,313 (physical), 421,975 (digital/electronic); Serial titles: 126 (physical), 153 (digital/electronic); Databases: 58. Weekly public service hours: 108. *Research affiliation:* Beth Israel Deaconess Medical Center (nursing), Caritas Norwood Hospital (nursing), Boston Medical Center (nursing), Lahey Clinic Medical Center (nursing).

Computer facilities: 196 computers available on campus for general student use. A campuswide network can be accessed from student residence rooms and from off campus. Online class registration, online bills, financial aid award letters and check-in requirements are available.
Website: http://www.regiscollege.edu/

General Application Contact: Shelagh Tomaino, Dean of Graduate Admission, 781-768-7330, Fax: 781-768-8218, E-mail: graduatedepartment@regiscollege.edu.

GRADUATE UNITS

Department of Education Expenses: Contact institution. *Financial support:* Federal Work-Study, scholarships/grants, and unspecified assistantships available. Financial award applicants required to submit FAFSA. *Program availability:* Part-time, evening/weekend. Offers elementary teacher (M Ed); higher education leadership (Ed D); special education (M Ed). *Application deadline:* Applications are processed on a rolling basis. *Application fee:* $65. Electronic applications accepted. *Department Chair/Graduate Program Director*, Dr. Priscilla Boerger, 781-768-7422, E-mail: priscilla.boerger@regiscollege.edu.

Nursing and Health Sciences School Expenses: Contact institution. *Financial support:* Federal Work-Study, scholarships/grants, traineeships, and unspecified assistantships available. Support available to part-time students. Financial award applicants required to submit FAFSA. *Program availability:* Part-time, evening/weekend, 100% online, blended/hybrid learning. Offers applied behavior analysis (MS); counseling psychology (MA); health administration (MS); nurse practitioner (Certificate); nursing (MS, DNP); nursing education (Certificate); occupational therapy (MS). *Application deadline:* Applications are processed on a rolling basis. *Application fee:* $75. Electronic applications accepted. *Application Contact:* Hillary Lyons, Graduate Admission Counselor, 781-768-7746, E-mail: hillary.lyons@regiscollege.edu.

Program in Regulatory and Clinical Research Management Expenses: Contact institution. *Financial support:* Career-related internships or fieldwork, scholarships/grants, and unspecified assistantships available. Financial award applicants required to submit FAFSA. *Program availability:* Part-time, evening/weekend, blended/hybrid learning. Offers regulatory and clinical research management (MS). *Application deadline:* Applications are processed on a rolling basis. *Application fee:* $65. Electronic applications accepted. *Director*, Dr. Joni Beshansky, 781-768-7008, E-mail: joni.beshansky@regiscollege.edu.

Strategic Communication Program Expenses: Contact institution. *Financial support:* Federal Work-Study and unspecified assistantships available. Financial award applicants required to submit FAFSA. *Program availability:* Part-time, evening/weekend. Offers strategic communication (MA). *Application deadline:* Applications are processed on a rolling basis. *Application fee:* $65. Electronic applications accepted. *Director*, Dr. Colleen Malachowski, 781-768-7373, E-mail: colleen.malachowski@regiscollege.edu.

REGIS UNIVERSITY, Denver, CO 80221-1099

General Information Independent-religious, coed, comprehensive institution. *Graduate housing:* Room and/or apartments available on a first-come, first-served basis to single students; on-campus housing not available to married students. Housing application deadline: 5/1. *Research affiliation:* Commission for Accelerated Programs, Learning Anytime Anywhere Partnership (Internet-based technology), Transparency by Design (online programs, best practices).

GRADUATE UNITS

College of Business and Economics *Program availability:* Part-time, evening/weekend, 100% online, blended/hybrid learning. Offers accounting (MS); executive leadership (Certificate); finance (MS); finance and accounting (MBA); health industry leadership (MBA); human resource management and leadership (MSOL); management (MBA); marketing (MBA); nonprofit leadership (Post-Graduate Certificate); nonprofit management (MNM); nonprofit organizational capacity building (Certificate); operations management (MBA); organizational leadership and management (MSOL); project leadership and management (MS, MSOL); strategic business management (Certificate); strategic human resource integration (Certificate); strategic management (MBA). Programs offered at Colorado Springs Campus, Northwest Denver Campus, Southeast Denver Campus, Fort Collins Campus, Broomfield Campus, Henderson (Nevada) Campus, and Summerlin (Nevada) Campus. Electronic applications accepted.

College of Computer and Information Sciences *Program availability:* Part-time, evening/weekend, 100% online, blended/hybrid learning. Offers agile technologies (Certificate); cybersecurity (Certificate); data science (M Sc); database administration with Oracle (Certificate); database development (Certificate); database technologies (M Sc); enterprise Java software development (Certificate); enterprise resource planning (Certificate); executive information technology (Certificate); health care informatics (Certificate); health care informatics and information management (M Sc); information assurance (M Sc); information assurance policy management (Certificate); information technology management (M Sc); mobile software development (Certificate); software engineering (M Sc, Certificate); software engineering and database technology (M Sc); storage area networks (Certificate); systems engineering (M Sc, Certificate). Electronic applications accepted.

College of Contemporary Liberal Studies *Program availability:* Part-time, evening/weekend, 100% online, blended/hybrid learning. Offers creative writing (MFA); criminology (M Sc); curriculum, instruction and assessment (M Ed); education - teacher leadership (M Ed); educational leadership (M Ed); elementary education (M Ed); literacy (Certificate); reading (M Ed); secondary education (M Ed); special education (M Ed); teacher academic leadership (Certificate); teacher leadership (MA); teacher/educational leadership (M Ed); teaching the linguistically diverse (M Ed). Electronic applications accepted.

Regis College *Program availability:* Part-time. Offers biomedical sciences (MS); developmental practice (MDP); education (MA); environmental biology (MS). Electronic applications accepted.

Rueckert-Hartman College for Health Professions *Program availability:* Part-time, evening/weekend, 100% online, blended/hybrid learning. Offers advanced practice nurse (DNP); counseling (MA); counseling children and adolescents (Post-Graduate Certificate); counseling military families (Post-Graduate Certificate); depth psychotherapy (Post-Graduate Certificate); fellowship in orthopedic manual physical therapy (Certificate); health care business management (Certificate); health care quality and patient safety (Certificate); health industry leadership (MBA); health services administration (MS); marriage and family therapy (MA, Post-Graduate Certificate); neonatal nurse practitioner (MSN); nursing education (MSN); nursing leadership (MSN); occupational therapy (OTD); pharmacy (Pharm D); physical therapy (DPT). Electronic applications accepted.

REINHARDT UNIVERSITY, Waleska, GA 30183-2981

General Information Independent-religious, coed, comprehensive institution. *Graduate housing:* Room and/or apartments available on a first-come, first-served basis to single students; on-campus housing not available to married students.

GRADUATE UNITS

McCamish School of Business *Program availability:* Part-time, evening/weekend. Offers business (MBA). Program offered at the Chattahoochee Technical College campus in downtown Woodstock, GA. Electronic applications accepted.

Price School of Education *Program availability:* Part-time, evening/weekend, online learning. Offers education (M Ed, MAT). Electronic applications accepted.

Program in Creative Writing Offers creative writing (MFA).

Program in Public Administration Offers public administration (MPA).

RELAY GRADUATE SCHOOL OF EDUCATION, New York, NY 10011

General Information Independent, coed, graduate-only institution.

GRADUATE UNITS

Graduate Programs *Program availability:* Online learning. Offers education (MAT). Program also offered at Chicago, Delaware, Houston, Memphis, New Orleans, and Newark campuses.

RENSSELAER AT HARTFORD, Hartford, CT 06120-2991

General Information Independent, coed, graduate-only institution. *Graduate housing:* On-campus housing not available.

GRADUATE UNITS

Department of Computer and Information Science *Program availability:* Part-time, evening/weekend. Offers computer science (MS); information technology (MS). Electronic applications accepted.

Department of Engineering *Program availability:* Part-time, evening/weekend. Offers computer and systems engineering (ME); electrical engineering (ME, MS); engineering (ME, MS); engineering science (MS); mechanical engineering (ME, MS). Electronic applications accepted.

Lally School of Management and Technology *Program availability:* Part-time, evening/weekend, online learning. Offers management and technology (MBA, MS). Electronic applications accepted.

RENSSELAER POLYTECHNIC INSTITUTE, Troy, NY 12180-3590

General Information Independent, coed, university. CGS member. *Enrollment:* 7,633 graduate, professional, and undergraduate students; 1,120 full-time matriculated graduate/professional students (341 women), 93 part-time matriculated graduate/professional students (40 women). *Enrollment by degree level:* 388 master's, 825 doctoral. *Graduate faculty:* 477 full-time (120 women), 50 part-time/adjunct (10 women). *Tuition:* Full-time $52,550; part-time $2125 per credit hour. *Required fees:* $2890. *Graduate housing:* Rooms and/or apartments available on a first-come, first-served basis to single and married students. *Student services:* Campus employment opportunities, campus safety program, career counseling, exercise/wellness program, free psychological counseling, grant writing training, international student services, low-cost health insurance, multicultural affairs office, services for students with disabilities, teacher training, writing training. *Library facilities:* Folsom Library plus 2 others. *Collection:* Students can reserve study rooms. *Research affiliation:* Disney (synthetic characters), General Electric Company (GE) (renewable energy, power electronic, and imaging research), IBM (high performance computing, advanced modeling and simulation research), Boeing (flow control, computational fluid dynamics), Skidmore, Owings & Merrill (SOM) (built environment (solar concentrators, phytoremediation, integrated hybrid flow control, parametric design)), Mount Sinai School of Medicine (biomedical and clinical research (healthcare analytics, orthopedic-musculoskeletal research, imaging, brain-machine interfaces)).

Computer facilities: Computer purchase and lease plans are available. A campuswide network can be accessed from student residence rooms and from off campus. Online class registration, billing, downloadable software, webpages are available.
Website: http://www.rpi.edu/

General Application Contact: Jarron Decker, Director of Graduate Admissions, 518-276-6216, Fax: 518-276-4072, E-mail: gradadmissions@rpi.edu.

GRADUATE UNITS

Graduate School Students: 1,114 full-time (339 women), 153 part-time (52 women); includes 155 minority (26 Black or African American, non-Hispanic/Latino; 60 Asian, non-Hispanic/Latino; 37 Hispanic/Latino; 32 Two or more races, non-Hispanic/Latino), 593 international. Average age 27. 3,675 applicants, 32% accepted, 301 enrolled. *Faculty:* 477 full-time (120 women), 50 part-time/adjunct (10 women). Expenses: Contact institution. *Financial support:* In 2017–18, 968 students received support, including research assistantships with full tuition reimbursements available (averaging $23,000 per year), teaching assistantships with full tuition reimbursements available (averaging $23,000 per year); fellowships with full tuition reimbursements available, scholarships/grants, health care benefits, and tuition waivers (full) also available. Financial award application deadline: 1/1. *Program availability:* Part-time, evening/weekend. *Application deadline:* For fall admission, 1/1 priority date for domestic and international students; for spring admission, 8/15 priority date for domestic and international students. Applications are processed on a rolling basis. *Application fee:* $75. Electronic applications accepted.

Lally School of Management Students: 154 full-time (64 women), 45 part-time (26 women); includes 26 minority (2 Black or African American, non-Hispanic/Latino; 10 Asian, non-Hispanic/Latino; 5 Hispanic/Latino; 9 Two or more races, non-Hispanic/Latino), 133 international. Average age 26. 1,250 applicants, 33% accepted, 79 enrolled. *Faculty:* 36 full-time (9 women), 5 part-time/adjunct (0 women). Expenses: Contact institution. *Financial support:* In 2017–18, 64 students received support. Scholarships/grants available. Financial award application deadline: 1/1; financial award applicants required to submit FAFSA. In 2017, 79 master's, 7 doctorates awarded. *Program availability:* Part-time, evening/weekend. Offers business analytics (MS); management (MBA, MS, PhD); quantitative finance and risk analytics (MS); supply chain management (MS); technology commercialization and entrepreneurship (MS). *Application deadline:* For fall admission, 1/1 priority date for domestic and international students; for spring admission, 8/15 priority date for domestic and international students. Applications are processed on a rolling basis. *Application fee:* $75. Electronic applications accepted. *Associate Dean, Lally School of Management*, Dr. Chanaka Edirisinghe, 518-276-3336, E-mail: edirin@rpi.edu.

School of Architecture Students: 47 full-time (20 women), 3 part-time (1 woman); includes 9 minority (2 Black or African American, non-Hispanic/Latino; 5 Asian, non-Hispanic/Latino; 2 Hispanic/Latino), 16 international. Average age 28. 128 applicants, 66% accepted, 21 enrolled. *Faculty:* 33 full-time (8 women), 13 part-time/adjunct (1 woman). Expenses: Contact institution. *Financial support:* In 2017–18, research assistantships (averaging $23,000 per year), teaching assistantships (averaging $23,000 per year) were awarded; fellowships and scholarships/grants also available. Financial award application deadline: 1/1. In 2017, 17 master's, 14 doctorates awarded. Offers architectural acoustics (PhD); architecture (M Arch, MS, PhD); built ecologies (PhD); lighting (PhD). *Application deadline:* For fall admission, 1/1 priority date for domestic and international students; for spring admission, 8/15 for domestic and international students; for summer admission, 1/1 for domestic and international students. Applications are processed on a rolling basis. *Application fee:* $75. Electronic applications accepted. *Dean, School of Architecture*, Evan Douglis, 518-276-6460, E-mail: douglis@rpi.edu.

School of Engineering Students: 515 full-time (126 women), 73 part-time (15 women); includes 62 minority (11 Black or African American, non-Hispanic/Latino; 24 Asian, non-Hispanic/Latino; 14 Hispanic/Latino; 13 Two or more races, non-Hispanic/Latino), 305 international. Average age 27. 1,330 applicants, 30% accepted, 108 enrolled. *Faculty:* 179 full-time (28 women), 8 part-time/adjunct (0 women). Expenses: Contact institution. *Financial support:* In 2017–18, 462 students received support, including research assistantships (averaging $23,000 per year), teaching assistantships (averaging $23,000 per year); fellowships also available. Financial award application deadline: 1/1. *Program availability:* Part-time. Offers aeronautical engineering (M Eng, MS, PhD); biomedical engineering (M Eng, MS, D Eng, PhD); chemical engineering (M Eng, MS, PhD); civil engineering (M Eng, MS, PhD); computer and systems engineering (M Eng, MS, PhD); decision sciences and engineering systems (PhD); electrical engineering (M Eng, MS, PhD); engineering (M Eng, MS, D Eng, PhD); engineering physics (MS, PhD); environmental engineering (M Eng, MS, PhD); industrial and management engineering (M Eng, MS); materials engineering (M Eng, MS, D Eng, PhD); mechanical engineering (M Eng, MS, D Eng, PhD); nuclear engineering and science (M Eng, MS, D Eng, PhD); systems engineering and technology management (M Eng); transportation engineering (M Eng, MS, PhD). *Application deadline:* For fall admission, 1/1 priority date for domestic and international students; for spring admission, 8/15 priority date for domestic and international students. Applications are processed on a rolling basis. *Application fee:* $75. Electronic applications accepted. *Dean*, Shekhar Garde, 518-276-6298, E-mail: gardes@rpi.edu.

School of Humanities, Arts, and Social Sciences Students: 63 full-time (33 women), 9 part-time (4 women); includes 10 minority (3 Asian, non-Hispanic/Latino; 5 Hispanic/Latino; 2 Two or more races, non-Hispanic/Latino), 11 international. Average age 32. 73 applicants, 37% accepted, 13 enrolled. *Faculty:* 92 full-time (36 women), 12 part-time/adjunct (5 women). Expenses: Contact institution. *Financial support:* In 2017–18, research assistantships (averaging $23,000 per year), teaching assistantships (averaging $23,000 per year) were awarded; fellowships and scholarships/grants also available. Financial award application deadline: 1/1. *Program availability:* Part-time, evening/weekend, online learning. Offers cognitive science (PhD); communication and rhetoric (MS, PhD); electronic arts (PhD); humanities, arts, and social sciences (MS, PhD); science and technology studies (MS, PhD). *Application deadline:* For fall admission, 1/1 priority date for domestic students, 1/15 priority date for international students; for spring admission, 8/15 priority date for domestic and international students. Applications are processed on a rolling basis. *Application fee:* $75. Electronic applications accepted. *Associate Dean for Research and Graduate Studies*, Dr. Curtis Bahn, 518-276-6065, E-mail: crb@rpi.edu.

School of Science Students: 332 full-time (94 women), 23 part-time (6 women); includes 48 minority (11 Black or African American, non-Hispanic/Latino; 18 Asian, non-Hispanic/Latino; 11 Hispanic/Latino; 8 Two or more races, non-Hispanic/Latino), 125 international. Average age 27. 783 applicants, 24% accepted, 67 enrolled. *Faculty:* 127 full-time (33 women), 9 part-time/adjunct (4 women). Expenses: Contact institution. *Financial support:* In 2017–18, research assistantships (averaging $23,000 per year), teaching assistantships (averaging $23,000 per year) were awarded; fellowships also available. Financial award application deadline: 1/1. In 2017, 68 master's, 41 doctorates awarded. Offers applied mathematics (MS); astronomy (MS); biochemistry and biophysics (MS, PhD); biology (MS, PhD); chemistry (MS, PhD); computer science (MS, PhD); geology (MS, PhD); information technology (MS); mathematics (MS, PhD); multi-disciplinary science (MS, PhD); physics (MS, PhD); science (MS, PhD). *Application deadline:* For fall admission, 1/1 priority date for domestic and international students; for spring admission, 8/15 priority date for domestic and international students. Applications are processed on a rolling basis. *Application fee:* $75. Electronic applications accepted. *Associate Dean, School of Science*, Dr. Christian Wetzel, 518-276-3755, E-mail: wetzel@rpi.edu.

RESEARCH COLLEGE OF NURSING, Kansas City, MO 64132

General Information Independent, coed, primarily women, comprehensive institution. *Enrollment:* 415 graduate, professional, and undergraduate students; 1 (woman) full-time matriculated graduate/professional student, 150 part-time matriculated graduate/professional students (125 women). *Enrollment by degree level:* 151 master's. *Graduate faculty:* 10 full-time (all women), 4 part-time/adjunct (2 women). *Tuition:* Part-time $550 per credit hour. *Graduate housing:* Rooms and/or apartments available on a first-come, first-served basis to single and married students. Typical cost: $7200 per year for single students. Housing application deadline: 1/15. *Student services:* Campus safety program, child daycare facilities. *Library facilities:* Greenlease Library.

Computer facilities: 125 computers available on campus for general student use. A campuswide network can be accessed from student residence rooms and from off

campus. Online class registration is available.
Website: http://www.researchcollege.edu/

General Application Contact: Leslie Burry, Director of Transfer and Graduate Recruitment, 816-995-2820, Fax: 816-995-2813, E-mail: leslie.burry@researchcollege.edu.

GRADUATE UNITS

Nursing Program Students: 1 (woman) full-time, 150 part-time (125 women); includes 14 minority (7 Black or African American, non-Hispanic/Latino; 1 American Indian or Alaska Native, non-Hispanic/Latino; 2 Asian, non-Hispanic/Latino; 2 Hispanic/Latino; 1 Native Hawaiian or other Pacific Islander, non-Hispanic/Latino; 1 Two or more races, non-Hispanic/Latino). *Faculty:* 10 full-time (all women), 4 part-time/adjunct (2 women). Expenses: Contact institution. *Financial support:* Applicants required to submit FAFSA. *Program availability:* Part-time-only, 100% online. Offers adult-gerontological nurse practitioner (MSN); executive practice and healthcare leadership (MSN); family nurse practitioner (MSN). *Application deadline:* Applications are processed on a rolling basis. *Application fee:* $65. Electronic applications accepted. *Application Contact:* Leslie Burry, Director of Transfer and Graduate Recruitment, 816-995-2820, Fax: 816-995-2813, E-mail: leslie.burry@researchcollege.edu. *President*, Dr. Thad Wilson, 816-995-2815, Fax: 816-995-2817, E-mail: thad.wilson@researchcollege.edu.

RESURRECTION UNIVERSITY, Chicago, IL 60622

General Information Independent, coed, upper-level institution.

GRADUATE UNITS

Nursing Program Offers nursing (MSN).

RHODE ISLAND COLLEGE, Providence, RI 02908-1991

General Information State-supported, coed, comprehensive institution. *Enrollment:* 8,174 graduate, professional, and undergraduate students; 189 full-time matriculated graduate/professional students (156 women), 558 part-time matriculated graduate/professional students (441 women). *Enrollment by degree level:* 655 master's, 59 doctoral, 33 other advanced degrees. *Graduate faculty:* 97 full-time (57 women), 73 part-time/adjunct (59 women). Tuition, state resident: full-time $9768; part-time $407 per credit. Tuition, nonresident: full-time $19,008; part-time $792 per credit. *Required fees:* $696; $29 per credit. One-time fee: $200 full-time; $100 part-time. Tuition and fees vary according to course load. *Graduate housing:* On-campus housing not available. *Student services:* Campus employment opportunities, career counseling, free psychological counseling, international student services, low-cost health insurance, multicultural affairs office, services for students with disabilities. *Library facilities:* Adams Library. *Collection:* Books: 306,080 (physical), 302,387 (digital/electronic); Serial titles: 3,081 (physical), 52,652 (digital/electronic); Databases: 123. Weekly public service hours: 80.

Computer facilities: Computer purchase and lease plans are available. 250 computers available on campus for general student use. A campuswide network can be accessed. Online class registration is available.
Website: http://www.ric.edu/

General Application Contact: Dr. Leslie Schuster, Interim Dean of Graduate Studies, 401-456-9723, E-mail: graduatestudies@ric.edu.

GRADUATE UNITS

School of Graduate Studies Students: 189 full-time (156 women), 558 part-time (441 women); includes 151 minority (37 Black or African American, non-Hispanic/Latino; 4 American Indian or Alaska Native, non-Hispanic/Latino; 17 Asian, non-Hispanic/Latino; 85 Hispanic/Latino; 2 Native Hawaiian or other Pacific Islander, non-Hispanic/Latino; 6 Two or more races, non-Hispanic/Latino). Average age 33. *Faculty:* 97 full-time (57 women), 73 part-time/adjunct (59 women). Expenses: Contact institution. *Financial support:* In 2017–18, 2 research assistantships with full tuition reimbursements (averaging $3,000 per year), 35 teaching assistantships with full tuition reimbursements (averaging $2,351 per year) were awarded; career-related internships or fieldwork, Federal Work-Study, traineeships, health care benefits, tuition waivers (partial), and unspecified assistantships also available. Support available to part-time students. Financial award application deadline: 5/15; financial award applicants required to submit FAFSA. In 2017, 276 master's, 9 doctorates, 47 other advanced degrees awarded. *Program availability:* Part-time, evening/weekend. *Application deadline:* For fall admission, 3/1 priority date for domestic students; for spring admission, 11/1 for domestic students. Applications are processed on a rolling basis. *Application fee:* $50. Electronic applications accepted. *Application Contact:* Graduate Studies, 401-456-8700. *Interim Dean of Graduate Studies*, Dr. Leslie Schuster, 401-456-9723, E-mail: graduatestudies@ric.edu.

Faculty of Arts and Sciences Students: 12 full-time (8 women), 40 part-time (21 women); includes 9 minority (2 Black or African American, non-Hispanic/Latino; 1 American Indian or Alaska Native, non-Hispanic/Latino; 1 Asian, non-Hispanic/Latino; 5 Hispanic/Latino). Average age 30. *Faculty:* 52 full-time (23 women), 4 part-time/adjunct (1 woman). Expenses: Contact institution. *Financial support:* In 2017–18, 15 teaching assistantships with full tuition reimbursements (averaging $2,650 per year) were awarded; research assistantships with tuition reimbursements, career-related internships or fieldwork, Federal Work-Study, scholarships/grants, health care benefits, and unspecified assistantships also available. Support available to part-time students. Financial award application deadline: 5/15; financial award applicants required to submit FAFSA. In 2017, 14 master's, 7 other advanced degrees awarded. *Program availability:* Part-time, evening/weekend. Offers art education (MA, MAT); arts and sciences (MA, MAT, MM Ed, MPA, CGS); biology (MA); creative writing (MA, CGS); English (MA); health psychology (CGS); history (MA); justice studies (MA); literature (CGS); mathematics (MA); mathematics content specialist (CGS); media studies (MA); modern biological sciences (CGS); music education (MAT, MM Ed); psychology (MA); public administration (MPA). *Application deadline:* For fall admission, 3/1 for domestic students; for spring admission, 11/1 for domestic students. Applications are processed on a rolling basis. *Application fee:* $50. Electronic applications accepted. *Application Contact:* Graduate Studies, 401-456-8700. *Dean*, Dr. Earl Simson, 401-456-8107, E-mail: esimson@ric.edu.

Feinstein School of Education and Human Development Students: 57 full-time (50 women), 291 part-time (242 women); includes 56 minority (12 Black or African American, non-Hispanic/Latino; 2 American Indian or Alaska Native, non-Hispanic/Latino; 10 Asian, non-Hispanic/Latino; 29 Hispanic/Latino; 1 Native Hawaiian or other Pacific Islander, non-Hispanic/Latino; 2 Two or more races, non-Hispanic/Latino). Average age 34. Expenses: Contact institution. *Financial support:* In 2017–18, 9 teaching assistantships with full tuition reimbursements (averaging $2,333 per year) were awarded; career-related internships or fieldwork, Federal Work-Study, scholarships/grants, health care benefits, and unspecified assistantships also available. Support available to part-time students. Financial award application deadline: 5/15; financial award applicants required to submit FAFSA. In 2017, 133 master's, 9 doctorates, 20 other advanced degrees awarded. *Program availability:* Part-time, evening/weekend. Offers advanced counseling (CGS); advanced studies in teaching and learning (M Ed); agency counseling (MA); autism education (CGS); clinical mental health counseling (MS); co-occurring disorders (MA, CGS); early childhood education (M Ed); education (PhD); education and human development (M Ed, MA, MAT, MS, PhD, CAGS, CGS); educational leadership (M Ed); elementary education (M Ed, MAT); English (MAT); French (MAT); health education (M Ed); history (MAT); math (MAT); mental health counseling (CAGS); physical education (CGS); reading (M Ed); school counseling (MA); school psychology (CAGS); secondary education (MAT); severe intellectual disabilities (CGS); Spanish (MAT); special education (M Ed); teacher leadership (CGS); teaching English as a second language (M Ed). *Application deadline:* For fall admission, 3/1 for domestic students; for spring admission, 11/1 for domestic students. Applications are processed on a rolling basis. *Application fee:* $50. Electronic applications accepted. *Application Contact:* Graduate Studies, 401-456-8700. *Interim Co-Dean*, Gerri August, 401-456-8110.

School of Business Students: 7 full-time (4 women), 20 part-time (12 women); includes 10 minority (7 Black or African American, non-Hispanic/Latino; 3 Hispanic/Latino). Average age 29. *Faculty:* 1. Expenses: Contact institution. *Financial support:* In 2017–18, 2 research assistantships with full tuition reimbursements (averaging $3,000 per year), 2 teaching assistantships (averaging $3,000 per year) were awarded; Federal Work-Study, scholarships/grants, health care benefits, and unspecified assistantships also available. Support available to part-time students. Financial award application deadline: 5/15; financial award applicants required to submit FAFSA. In 2017, 17 master's, 2 other advanced degrees awarded. *Program availability:* Part-time, evening/weekend. Offers accounting (MP Ac); business (MP Ac, MS, CGS); financial planning (CGS); health care administration (MS). *Application deadline:* For fall admission, 3/1 for domestic students. Applications are processed on a rolling basis. *Application fee:* $50. Electronic applications accepted. *Application Contact:* Graduate Studies, 401-456-8700. *Dean*, Dr. Jeffrey Mello, 401-456-9650, E-mail: jmello@ric.edu.

School of Nursing Students: 21 full-time (15 women), 69 part-time (54 women); includes 11 minority (2 Black or African American, non-Hispanic/Latino; 5 Asian, non-Hispanic/Latino; 2 Hispanic/Latino; 1 Native Hawaiian or other Pacific Islander, non-Hispanic/Latino; 1 Two or more races, non-Hispanic/Latino). Average age 37. Expenses: Contact institution. *Financial support:* In 2017–18, 9 teaching assistantships with full tuition reimbursements (averaging $1,583 per year) were awarded; Federal Work-Study, scholarships/grants, health care benefits, and unspecified assistantships also available. Support available to part-time students. Financial award application deadline: 5/15; financial award applicants required to submit FAFSA. In 2017, 28 master's awarded. *Program availability:* Part-time. Offers nursing (MSN, DNP). *Application deadline:* For fall admission, 2/15 for domestic students. Applications are processed on a rolling basis. *Application fee:* $50. Electronic applications accepted. *Interim Dean*, Dr. Debra Servello, 401-456-8013, Fax: 401-456-8206.

School of Social Work Students: 92 full-time (79 women), 138 part-time (112 women); includes 65 minority (14 Black or African American, non-Hispanic/Latino; 1 American Indian or Alaska Native, non-Hispanic/Latino; 1 Asian, non-Hispanic/Latino; 46 Hispanic/Latino; 3 Two or more races, non-Hispanic/Latino). Average age 31. Expenses: Contact institution. *Financial support:* Career-related internships or fieldwork, Federal Work-Study, scholarships/grants, health care benefits, and unspecified assistantships available. Support available to part-time students. Financial award application deadline: 5/15; financial award applicants required to submit FAFSA. In 2017, 84 master's awarded. *Program availability:* Part-time. Offers social work (MSW). *Application deadline:* For fall admission, 2/1 for domestic students. Applications are processed on a rolling basis. *Application fee:* $50. Electronic applications accepted. *Interim Dean*, Dr. Jayashree Nimmagadda, 401-456-8042.

RHODE ISLAND SCHOOL OF DESIGN, Providence, RI 02903-2784

General Information Independent, coed, comprehensive institution. *Enrollment:* 2,440 graduate, professional, and undergraduate students; 464 full-time matriculated graduate/professional students (297 women). *Enrollment by degree level:* 464 master's. *Graduate faculty:* 68 full-time (31 women), 116 part-time/adjunct (46 women). *Tuition:* Full-time $48,210. *Required fees:* $260. *Graduate housing:* Rooms and/or apartments available on a first-come, first-served basis to single and married students. Typical cost: $6300 per year ($16,870 including board) for single students; $12,850 per year ($17,230 including board) for married students. Room and board charges vary according to board plan and housing facility selected. *Student services:* Campus employment opportunities, campus safety program, career counseling, exercise/wellness program, free psychological counseling, grant writing training, international student services, low-cost health insurance, multicultural affairs office, services for students with disabilities, teacher training, writing training. *Library facilities:* Fleet Library. *Collection:* Books: 160,296 (physical), 144,887 (digital/electronic); Serial titles: 1,200 (digital/electronic); Databases: 62. Weekly public service hours: 89; students can reserve study rooms.

Computer facilities: Computer purchase and lease plans are available. 65 computers available on campus for general student use. A campuswide network can be accessed from student residence rooms and from off campus. Online class registration is available.
Website: http://www.risd.edu/

General Application Contact: Molly Pettengill, Assistant Director for Graduate Recruitment, 401-454-6312, Fax: 401-454-6309, E-mail: admissions@risd.edu.

GRADUATE UNITS

Department of Architecture Students: 85 full-time (50 women); includes 16 minority (3 Black or African American, non-Hispanic/Latino; 5 Asian, non-Hispanic/Latino; 8 Hispanic/Latino), 48 international. Average age 26. 314 applicants, 47% accepted, 37 enrolled. *Faculty:* 16 full-time (8 women), 31 part-time/adjunct (14 women). Expenses: Contact institution. *Financial support:* Fellowships, research assistantships, teaching assistantships, Federal Work-Study, scholarships/grants, and unspecified assistantships available. Financial award application deadline: 2/15; financial award applicants required to submit FAFSA. In 2017, 32 master's awarded. Offers architecture (M Arch). *Application deadline:* For fall admission, 1/10 for domestic and international students. *Application fee:* $60. Electronic applications accepted. *Application Contact:* Molly Pettengill, Assistant Director for Graduate Recruitment, 401-454-6312, Fax: 401-454-6309, E-mail: mpetteng@risd.edu. *Department Head*, Amy Kulper, 401-454-6281, Fax: 401-454-6299, E-mail: archgrad@risd.edu.

Department of Ceramics Students: 10 full-time (6 women), 4 international. Average age 27. 25 applicants, 36% accepted, 6 enrolled. *Faculty:* 2 full-time (1 woman), 5 part-time/adjunct (4 women). Expenses: Contact institution. *Financial support:* Fellowships, research assistantships, teaching assistantships, Federal Work-Study, scholarships/grants, and unspecified assistantships available. Financial award application deadline: 2/15; financial award applicants required to submit FAFSA. In 2017, 6 master's awarded. Offers ceramics (MFA). *Application deadline:* For fall admission, 1/10 for domestic and international students. *Application fee:* $60. Electronic applications accepted. *Application Contact:* Molly Pettengill, Assistant Director for Graduate Recruitment, 401-454-6312, Fax: 401-454-6309, E-mail: ceramics@risd.edu. *Department Head and Graduate Coordinator,* Katy Schimert, 401-454-6190, Fax: 401-454-6191, E-mail: ceramics@risd.edu.

Department of Digital and Media Students: 19 full-time (9 women); includes 2 minority (1 Asian, non-Hispanic/Latino; 1 Two or more races, non-Hispanic/Latino), 10 international. Average age 26. 143 applicants, 18% accepted, 11 enrolled. *Faculty:* 2 full-time (0 women), 11 part-time/adjunct (5 women). Expenses: Contact institution. *Financial support:* Fellowships, research assistantships, teaching assistantships, Federal Work-Study, scholarships/grants, and unspecified assistantships available. Financial award application deadline: 2/15; financial award applicants required to submit FAFSA. In 2017, 15 master's awarded. Offers digital and media (MFA). *Application deadline:* For fall admission, 1/10 for domestic and international students. *Application fee:* $60. Electronic applications accepted. *Application Contact:* Molly Pettengill, Assistant Director for Graduate Recruitment, 401-454-6312, Fax: 401-454-6309, E-mail: mpetteng@risd.edu. *Department Head and Graduate Program Director,* Shona Kitchen, 401-454-6139, Fax: 401-277-4966, E-mail: digital@risd.edu.

Department of Furniture Design Students: 21 full-time (10 women); includes 7 minority (4 Asian, non-Hispanic/Latino; 1 Hispanic/Latino; 2 Two or more races, non-Hispanic/Latino), 8 international. Average age 28. 35 applicants, 46% accepted, 11 enrolled. *Faculty:* 4 full-time (2 women), 11 part-time/adjunct (5 women). Expenses: Contact institution. *Financial support:* Fellowships, research assistantships, teaching assistantships, Federal Work-Study, scholarships/grants, and unspecified assistantships available. Financial award application deadline: 2/15; financial award applicants required to submit FAFSA. In 2017, 8 master's awarded. Offers furniture design (MFA). *Application deadline:* For fall admission, 1/10 for domestic and international students. *Application fee:* $60. Electronic applications accepted. *Application Contact:* Molly Pettengill, Assistant Director for Graduate Recruitment, 401-454-6312, Fax: 401-454-6309, E-mail: mpetteng@risd.edu. *Department Head,* Lothar Windels, 401-454-6102, E-mail: furniture@risd.edu.

Department of Glass Students: 7 full-time (5 women), 5 international. Average age 26. 17 applicants, 35% accepted, 5 enrolled. *Faculty:* 2 full-time (both women), 5 part-time/adjunct (2 women). Expenses: Contact institution. *Financial support:* Fellowships, research assistantships, teaching assistantships, Federal Work-Study, scholarships/grants, and unspecified assistantships available. Financial award application deadline: 2/15; financial award applicants required to submit FAFSA. In 2017, 2 master's awarded. Offers glass (MFA). *Application deadline:* For fall admission, 1/10 for domestic and international students. *Application fee:* $60. Electronic applications accepted. *Application Contact:* Molly Pettengill, Assistant Director for Graduate Recruitment, 401-454-6312, Fax: 401-454-6309, E-mail: mpetteng@risd.edu. *Department Head and Graduate Program Director,* Rachel Berwick, 401-454-6190, Fax: 401-454-6680, E-mail: rberwick@risd.edu.

Department of Graphic Design Students: 37 full-time (25 women); includes 7 minority (5 Asian, non-Hispanic/Latino; 1 Hispanic/Latino; 1 Two or more races, non-Hispanic/Latino), 8 international. Average age 29. 289 applicants, 8% accepted, 15 enrolled. *Faculty:* 11 full-time (5 women), 14 part-time/adjunct (6 women). Expenses: Contact institution. *Financial support:* Fellowships, research assistantships, teaching assistantships, Federal Work-Study, scholarships/grants, and unspecified assistantships available. Financial award application deadline: 2/15; financial award applicants required to submit FAFSA. In 2017, 14 master's awarded. Offers graphic design (MFA). *Application deadline:* For fall admission, 1/10 for domestic and international students. *Application fee:* $60. Electronic applications accepted. *Application Contact:* Molly Pettengill, Assistant Director for Graduate Recruitment, 401-454-6312, Fax: 401-454-6309, E-mail: mpetteng@risd.edu. *Department Head,* John Caserta, 401-454-6171, Fax: 401-454-6117, E-mail: gd@risd.edu.

Department of Industrial Design Students: 37 full-time (16 women); includes 6 minority (4 Asian, non-Hispanic/Latino; 1 Hispanic/Latino; 1 Two or more races, non-Hispanic/Latino), 14 international. Average age 27. 218 applicants, 24% accepted, 12 enrolled. *Faculty:* 5 full-time (2 women), 18 part-time/adjunct (8 women). Expenses: Contact institution. *Financial support:* Fellowships, research assistantships, teaching assistantships, Federal Work-Study, scholarships/grants, and unspecified assistantships available. Financial award application deadline: 2/15; financial award applicants required to submit FAFSA. In 2017, 19 master's awarded. Offers industrial design (MID). *Application deadline:* For fall admission, 1/10 for domestic and international students. *Application fee:* $60. Electronic applications accepted. *Application Contact:* Molly Pettengill, Assistant Director for Graduate Recruitment, 401-454-6312, Fax: 401-454-6309, E-mail: mpetteng@risd.edu. *Department Head,* Charlie Cannon, 401-454-6160, Fax: 401-454-6157, E-mail: idgradprogram@risd.edu.

Department of Interior Architecture Students: 74 full-time (55 women); includes 6 minority (2 Black or African American, non-Hispanic/Latino; 2 Asian, non-Hispanic/Latino; 1 Hispanic/Latino; 1 Two or more races, non-Hispanic/Latino), 55 international. Average age 26. 174 applicants, 46% accepted, 46 enrolled. *Faculty:* 9 full-time (2 women), 21 part-time/adjunct (5 women). Expenses: Contact institution. *Financial support:* Fellowships, research assistantships, teaching assistantships, Federal Work-Study, scholarships/grants, and unspecified assistantships available. Financial award application deadline: 2/15; financial award applicants required to submit FAFSA. In 2017, 37 master's awarded. Offers exhibition and narrative environments (M Des); interior studies/adaptive reuse (M Des, MA). *Application deadline:* For fall admission, 1/10 for domestic and international students. *Application fee:* $60. Electronic applications accepted. *Application Contact:* Molly Pettengill, Assistant Director for Graduate Recruitment, 401-454-6312, Fax: 401-454-6309, E-mail: mpetteng@risd.edu. *Department Head,* Liliane Wong, 401-454-6272, Fax: 401-277-4962, E-mail: lwong@risd.edu.

Department of Jewelry and Metalsmithing Students: 9 full-time (all women); includes 1 minority (Asian, non-Hispanic/Latino), 5 international. Average age 24. 56 applicants, 16% accepted, 5 enrolled. *Faculty:* 2 full-time (1 woman), 8 part-time/adjunct (4 women). Expenses: Contact institution. *Financial support:* Fellowships, research assistantships, teaching assistantships, Federal Work-Study, scholarships/grants, and unspecified assistantships available. Financial award application deadline: 2/15; financial award applicants required to submit FAFSA. In 2017, 5 master's awarded. Offers jewelry and metalsmithing (MFA). *Application deadline:* For fall admission, 1/10 for domestic and international students. *Application fee:* $60. Electronic applications accepted. *Application Contact:* Molly Pettengill, Assistant Director for Graduate Recruitment, 401-454-6312, Fax: 401-454-6309, E-mail: mpetteng@risd.edu. *Department Head and Graduate Coordinator,* Tracy Steepy, 401-454-6190, Fax: 401-454-6191, E-mail: jewelry@risd.edu.

Department of Landscape Architecture Students: 68 full-time (47 women); includes 2 minority (both Asian, non-Hispanic/Latino), 56 international. Average age 24. 116 applicants, 80% accepted, 22 enrolled. *Faculty:* 4 full-time (3 women), 23 part-time/adjunct (12 women). Expenses: Contact institution. *Financial support:* Fellowships, research assistantships, teaching assistantships, Federal Work-Study, scholarships/grants, and unspecified assistantships available. Financial award application deadline: 2/15; financial award applicants required to submit FAFSA. In 2017, 23 master's awarded. Offers landscape architecture (MLA). *Application deadline:* For fall admission, 1/10 for domestic and international students. *Application fee:* $60. Electronic applications accepted. *Application Contact:* Molly Pettengill, Assistant Director for Graduate Recruitment, 401-454-6312, Fax: 401-454-6309, E-mail: mpetteng@risd.edu. *Department Head,* Emily Vogler, 401-454-6282, Fax: 401-454-6299, E-mail: ldardept@risd.edu.

Department of Painting Students: 20 full-time (12 women); includes 3 minority (all Hispanic/Latino), 6 international. Average age 28. 209 applicants, 10% accepted, 10 enrolled. *Faculty:* 4 full-time (1 woman), 9 part-time/adjunct (6 women). Expenses: Contact institution. *Financial support:* Fellowships, research assistantships, teaching assistantships, Federal Work-Study, scholarships/grants, and unspecified assistantships available. Financial award application deadline: 2/15; financial award applicants required to submit FAFSA. In 2017, 10 master's awarded. Offers painting (MFA). *Application deadline:* For fall admission, 1/10 for domestic and international students. *Application fee:* $60. Electronic applications accepted. *Application Contact:* Molly Pettengill, Assistant Director for Graduate Recruitment, 401-454-6312, Fax: 401-454-6309, E-mail: mpetteng@risd.edu. *Department Head,* Kevin Zucker, 401-454-6158, Fax: 401-454-6681, E-mail: painting@risd.edu.

Department of Photography Students: 16 full-time (5 women); includes 5 minority (2 Black or African American, non-Hispanic/Latino; 3 Hispanic/Latino), 5 international. Average age 26. 105 applicants, 13% accepted, 9 enrolled. *Faculty:* 5 full-time (3 women), 8 part-time/adjunct (7 women). Expenses: Contact institution. *Financial support:* Fellowships, research assistantships, teaching assistantships, Federal Work-Study, scholarships/grants, and unspecified assistantships available. Financial award application deadline: 2/15; financial award applicants required to submit FAFSA. In 2017, 7 master's awarded. Offers photography (MFA). *Application deadline:* For fall admission, 1/10 for domestic and international students. *Application fee:* $60. Electronic applications accepted. *Application Contact:* Molly Pettengill, Assistant Director for Graduate Recruitment, 401-454-6312, Fax: 401-454-6309, E-mail: mpetteng@risd.edu. *Department Head,* Brian Ulrich, 401-454-6122, Fax: 401-454-6385, E-mail: photo@risd.edu.

Department of Printmaking Students: 14 full-time (12 women); includes 7 minority (2 Black or African American, non-Hispanic/Latino; 1 Asian, non-Hispanic/Latino; 3 Hispanic/Latino; 1 Two or more races, non-Hispanic/Latino), 2 international. Average age 28. 37 applicants, 32% accepted, 6 enrolled. *Faculty:* 8 full-time (7 women), 7 part-time/adjunct (4 women). Expenses: Contact institution. *Financial support:* Fellowships, research assistantships, teaching assistantships, Federal Work-Study, scholarships/grants, and unspecified assistantships available. Financial award application deadline: 2/15; financial award applicants required to submit FAFSA. In 2017, 8 master's awarded. Offers printmaking (MFA). *Application deadline:* For fall admission, 1/10 for domestic and international students. *Application fee:* $60. Electronic applications accepted. *Application Contact:* Molly Pettengill, Assistant Director for Graduate Recruitment, 401-454-6312, Fax: 401-454-6309, E-mail: mpetteng@risd.edu. *Department Head,* Cornelia McSheehy, 401-454-6224, Fax: 401-454-6707, E-mail: printmaking@risd.edu.

Department of Sculpture Students: 13 full-time (9 women); includes 3 minority (1 Asian, non-Hispanic/Latino; 1 Hispanic/Latino; 1 Two or more races, non-Hispanic/Latino), 6 international. Average age 29. 75 applicants, 20% accepted, 9 enrolled. *Faculty:* 5 full-time (2 women), 10 part-time/adjunct (4 women). Expenses: Contact institution. *Financial support:* Fellowships, research assistantships, teaching assistantships, Federal Work-Study, scholarships/grants, and unspecified assistantships available. Financial award application deadline: 2/15; financial award applicants required to submit FAFSA. In 2017, 6 master's awarded. Offers sculpture (MFA). *Application deadline:* For fall admission, 1/10 for domestic and international students. *Application fee:* $60. Electronic applications accepted. *Application Contact:* Molly Pettengill, Assistant Director for Graduate Recruitment, 401-454-6312, Fax: 401-454-6309, E-mail: mpetteng@risd.edu. *Department Head,* Lisi Raskin, 401-454-6190, Fax: 401-454-6191, E-mail: sculpture@risd.edu.

Department of Teaching and Learning in Art and Design Students: 22 full-time (18 women); includes 6 minority (3 Asian, non-Hispanic/Latino; 1 Hispanic/Latino; 2 Two or more races, non-Hispanic/Latino), 4 international. Average age 28. 38 applicants, 79% accepted, 22 enrolled. *Faculty:* 2 full-time (0 women), 7 part-time/adjunct (all women). Expenses: Contact institution. *Financial support:* Fellowships, research assistantships, teaching assistantships, Federal Work-Study, scholarships/grants, and unspecified assistantships available. Financial award application deadline: 2/15; financial award applicants required to submit FAFSA. In 2017, 17 master's awarded. Offers art and design education (MA); art education (MAT). *Application deadline:* For fall admission, 1/10 for domestic and international students. *Application fee:* $60. Electronic applications accepted. *Application Contact:* Molly Pettengill, Assistant Director for Graduate Recruitment, 401-454-6312, Fax: 401-454-6309, E-mail: mpetteng@risd.edu. *Department Head and Graduate Program Director,* Paul Sproll, 401-454-6695, Fax: 401-454-6694, E-mail: teachlearn@risd.edu.

Department of Textiles Students: 12 full-time (9 women); includes 4 minority (1 Black or African American, non-Hispanic/Latino; 1 Asian, non-Hispanic/Latino; 1 Hispanic/Latino; 1 Two or more races, non-Hispanic/Latino), 3 international. Average age 28. 55 applicants, 18% accepted, 6 enrolled. *Faculty:* 4 full-time (3 women), 5 part-time/adjunct (4 women). Expenses: Contact institution. *Financial support:* Fellowships, research assistantships, teaching assistantships, Federal Work-Study, scholarships/grants, and unspecified assistantships available. Financial award application deadline: 2/15; financial award applicants required to submit FAFSA. In 2017, 5 master's awarded. Offers textiles (MFA). *Application deadline:* For fall admission, 1/10 for domestic and international students. *Application fee:* $60. Electronic applications accepted. *Application Contact:* Molly Pettengill, Assistant Director for Graduate Recruitment, 401-454-6312, Fax: 401-454-6309, E-mail: mpetteng@risd.edu. *Department Head,* MaryAnne Friel, 401-427-6967, Fax: 401-277-4883, E-mail: textiles@risd.edu.

RHODES COLLEGE, Memphis, TN 38112-1690

General Information Independent, coed, comprehensive institution. *Graduate housing:* Room and/or apartments available on a first-come, first-served basis to single students; on-campus housing not available to married students. Housing application deadline: 3/1.

GRADUATE UNITS

Department of Commerce and Business *Program availability:* Part-time. Offers accounting (MS).

RICE UNIVERSITY, Houston, TX 77251-1892

General Information Independent, coed, university. CGS member. *Graduate housing:* Rooms and/or apartments available on a first-come, first-served basis to single and married students. Housing application deadline: 7/15. *Research affiliation:* Fermi National Accelerator Laboratory, Los Alamos National Laboratory, Brookhaven National Laboratory, Arecibo Observatory, Houston Area Research Center.

GRADUATE UNITS

Graduate Programs *Program availability:* Part-time. Offers education (MAT). Electronic applications accepted.

George R. Brown School of Engineering *Program availability:* Part-time. Offers bioengineering (MS, PhD); bioinformatics (PhD); biostatistics (PhD); chemical and biomolecular engineering (MS, PhD); chemical engineering (M Ch E); circuits, controls, and communication systems (MS, PhD); civil engineering (MCE, MS, PhD); computational and applied mathematics (MA, MCAM, PhD); computational finance (PhD); computational science and engineering (PhD); computer science (MCS, MS, PhD); computer science and engineering (MS, PhD); electrical engineering (MEE); engineering (M Ch E, M Stat, MA, MBE, MCAM, MCE, MCS, MEE, MEE, MES, MME, MMS, MS, PhD); environmental engineering (MEE, MES, MS, PhD); environmental science (MEE, MES, MS, PhD); general statistics (PhD); lasers, microwaves, and solid-state electronics (MS, PhD); materials science (MMS, MS, PhD); mechanical engineering (MME, MS, PhD); statistics (M Stat, MA). MD/PhD offered jointly with Baylor College of Medicine, The University of Texas Health Science Center at Houston. Electronic applications accepted.

Jesse H. Jones Graduate School of Business Students: 228 full-time (67 women); includes 66 minority (5 Black or African American, non-Hispanic/Latino; 3 American Indian or Alaska Native, non-Hispanic/Latino; 39 Asian, non-Hispanic/Latino; 19 Hispanic/Latino), 52 international. Average age 28. 813 applicants, 27% accepted, 118 enrolled. *Faculty:* 64 full-time, 68 part-time/adjunct. Expenses: Contact institution. *Financial support:* Fellowships, career-related internships or fieldwork, Federal Work-Study, institutionally sponsored loans, scholarships/grants, and tuition waivers (full and partial) available. Financial award applicants required to submit FAFSA. In 2017, 110 master's awarded. *Program availability:* Evening/weekend. Offers business administration (EMBA, MBA, PMBA). *Application deadline:* For fall admission, 10/5 priority date for domestic students; for winter admission, 1/9 priority date for domestic students; for spring admission, 4/7 priority date for domestic students. Applications are processed on a rolling basis. *Application fee:* $200. Electronic applications accepted. *Application Contact:* Sue Oldham, Executive Director of Recruiting and Admissions, 713-348-6153, E-mail: ricemba@rice.edu. *Dean,* Dr. Peter Rodriguez, 713-348-5928, E-mail: prod@rice.edu.

School of Architecture Offers architecture (M Arch, D Arch); urban design (M Arch). Electronic applications accepted.

School of Humanities Offers African religions (PhD); African-American religions (PhD); art history (PhD); contemplative studies (PhD); English (MA, PhD); ghosticism, esotericism, mysticism (PhD); history (MA, PhD); humanities (MA, PhD); Islam (PhD); Jewish thought and philosophy (PhD); linguistics (MA, PhD); modern Christianity in thought and popular culture (PhD); philosophy (MA, PhD); psychology of religion (PhD); the Bible and beyond (PhD).

School of Social Sciences Offers archaeology (MA, PhD); cognitive sciences (MA, PhD); economics (PhD); energy economics (MEECON); industrial-organizational/social psychology (MA, PhD); political science (PhD); psychology (MA, PhD); social sciences (MA, MEECON, PhD); social-cultural anthropology (MA, PhD); sociology (PhD).

Shepherd School of Music Offers composition (MM, DMA); conducting (MM); musicology (MM); performance (MM, DMA); theory (MM).

Susanne M. Glasscock School of Continuing Studies *Program availability:* Part-time, evening/weekend. Offers liberal studies (MLS).

Wiess School of Natural Sciences *Program availability:* Part-time. Offers biochemistry and cell biology (MA, PhD); chemistry (MA); earth science (MS, PhD); ecology and evolutionary biology (MA, MS, PhD); inorganic chemistry (PhD); mathematics (PhD); nanoscale physics (MS); natural sciences (MA, MS, MST, PhD); organic chemistry (PhD); physical chemistry (PhD); physics and astronomy (PhD); science teaching (MST). Electronic applications accepted.

Wiess School–Professional Science Master's Programs Offers bioscience research and health policy (MS); environmental analysis and decision making (MS); geophysics (MS); nanoscale physics (MS); professional science (MS).

Rice Quantum Institute Offers quantum physics (MS, PhD). Electronic applications accepted.

RICHMOND, THE AMERICAN INTERNATIONAL UNIVERSITY IN LONDON, Richmond, Surrey TW10 6JP, United Kingdom

General Information Independent, coed, comprehensive institution. *Graduate housing:* Room and/or apartments available on a first-come, first-served basis to single students; on-campus housing not available to married students. Housing application deadline: 8/1.

GRADUATE UNITS

MA in Art History Program *Program availability:* Part-time. Offers art history (MA). Electronic applications accepted.

MA in International Relations Program *Program availability:* Part-time. Offers international relations (MA). Electronic applications accepted.

RICHMONT GRADUATE UNIVERSITY, Atlanta, GA 30339

General Information Independent-religious, coed, graduate-only institution.

GRADUATE UNITS

School of Counseling *Program availability:* Part-time, evening/weekend. Offers clinical mental health counseling (MA); marriage and family therapy (MA). Electronic applications accepted.

School of Ministry *Program availability:* Part-time, evening/weekend, 100% online, blended/hybrid learning. Offers ministry (MA); spiritual direction (Graduate Certificate); spiritual formation and direction (MA). Electronic applications accepted.

RIDER UNIVERSITY, Lawrenceville, NJ 08648-3001

General Information Independent, coed, comprehensive institution. *Graduate housing:* Room and/or apartments available on a first-come, first-served basis to single students; on-campus housing not available to married students. *Student services:* Campus employment opportunities, campus safety program, career counseling, exercise/wellness program, free psychological counseling, international student services, multicultural affairs office, services for students with disabilities. *Library facilities:* Franklin F. Moore Library plus 1 other. *Collection:* Books: 311,400 (physical), 150,000 (digital/electronic); Serial titles: 882 (physical), 44,599 (digital/electronic); Databases: 148. Study areas open 24 hours, 5–7 days a week; students can reserve study rooms.

Computer facilities: Computer purchase and lease plans are available. 300 computers available on campus for general student use. A campuswide network can be accessed. Online class registration is available.

Website: http://www.rider.edu/

General Application Contact: Jamie L. Mitchell, Director of Graduate and Continuing Studies Admission, 609-896-5036, Fax: 609-895-5680, E-mail: jmitchell@rider.edu.

GRADUATE UNITS

College of Business Administration Expenses: Contact institution. *Financial support:* Applicants required to submit FAFSA. *Program availability:* Part-time, evening/weekend. Offers accountancy (M Acc); business administration (EMBA, M Acc, MBA, MS, Certificate); corporate finance (MS); forensic accounting (Certificate). *Application deadline:* For fall admission, 8/1 priority date for domestic students, 3/15 priority date for international students; for spring admission, 12/1 priority date for domestic students, 11/1 priority date for international students. Applications are processed on a rolling basis. *Application fee:* $50. Electronic applications accepted. *Application Contact:* Jamie L. Mitchell, Director of Graduate Admissions, 609-896-5036, Fax: 609-895-5680, E-mail: jmitchell@rider.edu. *Dean,* Dr. Cynthia Newman, 609-895-5152, E-mail: cnewman@rider.edu.

College of Education and Human Services Expenses: Contact institution. *Financial support:* In 2017–18, 316 students received support. Applicants required to submit FAFSA. *Program availability:* Part-time, evening/weekend. Offers bilingual education (MAT); clinical mental health counseling (MA, Ed S); counseling-related services (MA); developing people and organizations (MA); director of counseling services (Ed S); director of school counseling services (Certificate); early childhood education (MAT); education and human services (MA, MAT, Certificate, Ed S); elementary education (MAT); English as a second language (MAT); higher education (MA); life and career coaching (MA); school counseling (MA, Certificate, Ed S); school psychology (Certificate, Ed S); secondary education (MAT); special education (MA); substance awareness coordinator (Certificate); teacher of students with disabilities (Certificate); world language (MAT). *Application deadline:* For fall admission, 5/1 priority date for domestic students, 3/15 priority date for international students; for spring admission, 11/1 priority date for domestic and international students. Applications are processed on a rolling basis. *Application fee:* $50. Electronic applications accepted. *Application Contact:* Jamie L. Mitchell, Director of Graduate Admissions, 609-896-5036, Fax: 609-895-5680, E-mail: jmitchell@rider.edu. *Dean,* Dr. Sharon J. Sherman, 609-895-5048, E-mail: ssherman@rider.edu.

College of Liberal Arts and Sciences Expenses: Contact institution. *Program availability:* Part-time, evening/weekend. Offers business communication studies (MA); domestic security (MA); global security (MA); health communication (MA); liberal arts and sciences (MA). *Application deadline:* For fall admission, 5/1 priority date for domestic students, 3/15 priority date for international students; for spring admission, 11/1 priority date for domestic and international students. Applications are processed on a rolling basis. *Application fee:* $50. Electronic applications accepted. *Application Contact:* Jamie L. Mitchell, Director of Graduate Admissions, 609-896-5036, Fax: 609-895-5680, E-mail: jmitchell@rider.edu. *Dean,* Jonathan Millen, 609-895-5789, E-mail: millen@rider.edu.

Westminster Choir College Expenses: Contact institution. Offers American and public musicology (MM); choral conducting (MM); composition (MM); music (MM, MME, MVP); music education (MME); organ performance (MM); piano accompanying and coaching (MM); piano pedagogy and performance (MM); piano performance (MM); sacred music (MM); voice pedagogy and performance (MM, MVP). *Application deadline:* For fall admission, 5/1 priority date for domestic students, 3/15 priority date for international students; for spring admission, 11/1 priority date for domestic and international students. Applications are processed on a rolling basis. *Application fee:* $50. Electronic applications accepted. *Application Contact:* Kate Shields, Director of Admissions, 609-921-7100 Ext. 8103, Fax: 609-921-2538, E-mail: wccadmission@rider.edu. *Dean,* Dr. Marshall Onofrio, 609-921-7100 Ext. 8206, E-mail: monofrio@rider.edu.

RIVIER UNIVERSITY, Nashua, NH 03060

General Information Independent-religious, coed, comprehensive institution. *Graduate housing:* On-campus housing not available.

GRADUATE UNITS

School of Graduate Studies *Program availability:* Part-time. Offers business administration (MBA); clinical psychology (MS); computer information systems (MS); computer science (MS); curriculum and instruction (M Ed); early childhood education (M Ed); educational administration (M Ed); educational studies (M Ed); elementary education (M Ed); elementary education and general special education (M Ed); emotional and behavioral disorders (M Ed); English (MAT); experimental psychology (MS); general social education (M Ed); leadership and learning (Ed D, CAGS); learning disabilities (M Ed); learning disabilities and reading (M Ed); mathematics (MAT); mental health counseling (MA); reading (M Ed); school counseling (M Ed); social studies education (MAT); Spanish (MAT); writing and literature (MA). Electronic applications accepted.

Division of Nursing and Health Professions *Program availability:* Part-time, evening/weekend. Offers family nurse practitioner (MS); leadership in health systems management (MS); nursing education (MS); nursing practice (DNP); psychiatric/mental health nurse practitioner (MS); public health (MPH). Electronic applications accepted.

THE ROBERT E. WEBBER INSTITUTE FOR WORSHIP STUDIES, Jacksonville, FL 32207

General Information Independent-religious, coed, graduate-only institution.

GRADUATE UNITS

Doctor of Worship Studies Program Offers worship studies (DWS).

Master of Worship Studies Program Offers worship studies (MWS).

★ ROBERT MORRIS UNIVERSITY, Moon Township, PA 15108-1189

General Information Independent, coed, university. *Enrollment:* 5,076 graduate, professional, and undergraduate students; 833 part-time matriculated graduate/professional students (459 women). *Enrollment by degree level:* 561 master's, 272 doctoral. *Graduate faculty:* 70 full-time (36 women), 29 part-time/adjunct (14 women). *Tuition:* Part-time $955 per credit. *Required fees:* $80 per credit. *Graduate housing:* On-campus housing not available. *Student services:* Campus employment opportunities, campus safety program, career counseling, exercise/wellness program, international student services, multicultural affairs office, services for students with disabilities. *Library facilities:* Robert Morris University Library. *Collection:* Books: 97,693 (physical), 172,931 (digital/electronic); Serial titles: 244 (physical), 47,791 (digital/electronic); Databases: 104. Weekly public service hours: 101; study areas open 24 hours, 5–7 days a week; students can reserve study rooms.

Computer facilities: Computer purchase and lease plans are available. 375 computers available on campus for general student use. A campuswide network can be accessed from student residence rooms and from off campus. Online class registration, online payment are available.
Website: http://www.rmu.edu/

General Application Contact: Kellie L. Laurenzi, Associate Vice President, 412-397-5200, Fax: 412-397-2425, E-mail: graduateadmissions@rmu.edu.

GRADUATE UNITS

School of Business Students: 163 part-time (61 women); includes 13 minority (6 Black or African American, non-Hispanic/Latino; 6 Asian, non-Hispanic/Latino; 1 Two or more races, non-Hispanic/Latino), 8 international. Average age 30. 167 applicants, 40% accepted, 32 enrolled. *Faculty:* 12 full-time (4 women), 3 part-time/adjunct (2 women). Expenses: Contact institution. *Financial support:* Institutionally sponsored loans available. Support available to part-time students. Financial award application deadline: 5/1; financial award applicants required to submit FAFSA. In 2017, 87 master's awarded. *Program availability:* Part-time-only, evening/weekend, 100% online. Offers business administration (MBA); human resource management (MS); taxation (MS). *Application deadline:* For fall admission, 7/1 priority date for domestic and international students; for spring admission, 11/1 priority date for domestic and international students. Applications are processed on a rolling basis. *Application fee:* $35. Electronic applications accepted. *Application Contact:* E-mail: graduateadmissions@rmu.edu. *Dean*, Dr. Michelle L. Patrick, 412-397-5445, Fax: 412-397-2585, E-mail: patrick@rmu.edu.

School of Communications and Information Systems Students: 258 part-time (99 women); includes 46 minority (22 Black or African American, non-Hispanic/Latino; 16 Asian, non-Hispanic/Latino; 5 Hispanic/Latino; 3 Two or more races, non-Hispanic/Latino), 46 international. Average age 35. 226 applicants, 52% accepted, 79 enrolled. *Faculty:* 23 full-time (10 women), 10 part-time/adjunct (3 women). Expenses: Contact institution. *Financial support:* Institutionally sponsored loans available. Support available to part-time students. Financial award application deadline: 5/1. In 2017, 148 master's, 12 doctorates awarded. *Program availability:* Part-time, evening/weekend, online learning. Offers communication and information systems (MS); cyber security (MS); data analytics (MS); information security and assurance (MS); information systems and communications (D Sc); information systems management (MS); information technology project management (MS); Internet information systems (MS); organizational leadership (MS). *Application deadline:* For fall admission, 7/1 priority date for domestic and international students; for spring admission, 11/1 priority date for domestic and international students. Applications are processed on a rolling basis. *Application fee:* $35. Electronic applications accepted. *Application Contact:* E-mail: graduateadmissions@rmu.edu. *Dean*, Ann Marie M. Le Blanc, 412-397-6433, Fax: 412-397-6469, E-mail: leblanc@rmu.edu.

School of Education and Social Sciences Students: 151 part-time (90 women); includes 23 minority (12 Black or African American, non-Hispanic/Latino; 2 Asian, non-Hispanic/Latino; 2 Hispanic/Latino; 7 Two or more races, non-Hispanic/Latino), 4 international. Average age 34. 51 applicants, 39% accepted, 10 enrolled. *Faculty:* 18 full-time (10 women), 5 part-time/adjunct (2 women). Expenses: Contact institution. In 2017, 31 master's, 16 doctorates awarded. *Program availability:* Part-time, evening/weekend, online learning. Offers business education (MS); counseling psychology (MS); education (Postbaccalaureate Certificate); higher education (MS); instructional leadership (MS); instructional management and leadership (PhD); literacy (MS); special education (MS). *Application deadline:* For fall admission, 7/1 priority date for domestic and international students; for spring admission, 11/1 priority date for domestic and international students. Applications are processed on a rolling basis. *Application fee:* $35. Electronic applications accepted. *Application Contact:* E-mail: graduateadmissions@rmu.edu. *Acting Dean*, Dr. George Semich, 412-397-6032, Fax: 412-397-6044, E-mail: semich@rmu.edu.

School of Engineering, Mathematics and Science Students: 22 part-time (3 women); includes 2 minority (1 Asian, non-Hispanic/Latino; 1 Hispanic/Latino), 14 international. Average age 28. 48 applicants, 27% accepted, 5 enrolled. *Faculty:* 4 full-time (1 woman), 4 part-time/adjunct (0 women). Expenses: Contact institution. *Financial support:* Federal Work-Study, institutionally sponsored loans, and unspecified assistantships available. Financial award application deadline: 5/1; financial award applicants required to submit FAFSA. In 2017, 27 master's awarded. *Program availability:* Part-time, evening/weekend. Offers engineering management (MS). *Application deadline:* For fall admission, 7/1 priority date for domestic and international students; for spring admission, 11/1 priority date for domestic and international students. Applications are processed on a rolling basis. *Application fee:* $35. Electronic applications accepted. *Dean*, Dr. Maria V. Kalevitch, 412-397-4020, Fax: 412-397-2472, E-mail: kalevitch@rmu.edu.

School of Nursing and Health Sciences Students: 234 part-time (202 women); includes 25 minority (19 Black or African American, non-Hispanic/Latino; 2 Asian, non-Hispanic/Latino; 2 Hispanic/Latino; 2 Two or more races, non-Hispanic/Latino). Average age 35. 130 applicants, 72% accepted, 65 enrolled. *Faculty:* 13 full-time (11 women), 7 part-time/adjunct (all women). Expenses: Contact institution. *Financial support:* Federal Work-Study, institutionally sponsored loans, and unspecified assistantships available. Financial award application deadline: 5/1; financial award applicants required to submit FAFSA. In 2017, 46 master's, 32 doctorates awarded. *Program availability:* Part-time, evening/weekend. Offers nursing and health sciences (MSN, DNP). *Application deadline:* For fall admission, 7/1 priority date for domestic and international students; for spring admission, 11/1 priority date for domestic and international students. Applications are processed on a rolling basis. *Application fee:* $35. Electronic applications accepted. *Dean*, Dr. Valerie M. Howard, 412-397-6801, Fax: 412-397-3277, E-mail: howardv@rmu.edu.

See Close-Up on page 871.

ROBERT MORRIS UNIVERSITY ILLINOIS, Chicago, IL 60605

General Information Independent, coed, comprehensive institution. *Enrollment:* 2,307 graduate, professional, and undergraduate students; 186 full-time matriculated graduate/professional students (108 women), 114 part-time matriculated graduate/professional students (57 women). *Enrollment by degree level:* 300 master's. *Graduate faculty:* 2 full-time (0 women), 26 part-time/adjunct (8 women). *Tuition:* Full-time $17,100; part-time $2850 per course. *Graduate housing:* Room and/or apartments available to single students. *Student services:* Campus employment opportunities, career counseling, exercise/wellness program, free psychological counseling, international student services, services for students with disabilities, writing training. *Library facilities:* Information Technology Library. *Collection:* Books: 165,268 (physical), 58,182 (digital/electronic); Databases: 37. Weekly public service hours: 74; students can reserve study rooms.

Computer facilities: 1,307 computers available on campus for general student use. A campuswide network can be accessed from student residence rooms. Online class registration, online credentials, online payments, online student accounts, online degree audit are available.
Website: http://www.robertmorris.edu/

General Application Contact: Mark Daugherty, Director of Admissions, 312-935-4814, Fax: 312-935-6020, E-mail: mdaugherty@robertmorris.edu.

GRADUATE UNITS

Morris Graduate School of Management Students: 186 full-time (108 women), 114 part-time (57 women); includes 167 minority (88 Black or African American, non-Hispanic/Latino; 15 Asian, non-Hispanic/Latino; 62 Hispanic/Latino; 1 Native Hawaiian or other Pacific Islander, non-Hispanic/Latino; 1 Two or more races, non-Hispanic/Latino), 18 international. Average age 32. 157 applicants, 78% accepted, 72 enrolled. *Faculty:* 2 full-time (0 women), 26 part-time/adjunct (8 women). Expenses: Contact institution. *Financial support:* In 2017–18, 381 students received support. Federal Work-Study, scholarships/grants, and unspecified assistantships available. Support available to part-time students. Financial award applicants required to submit FAFSA. In 2017, 191 master's awarded. *Program availability:* Part-time, evening/weekend. Offers accounting (MBA); accounting/finance (MBA); business analytics (MIS); health care administration (MM); higher education administration (MM); human performance (MS); human resource management (MBA); information security (MIS); information systems management (MIS); law enforcement administration (MM); management (MBA); management/finance (MBA); management/human resource management (MBA); sports administration (MM). *Application deadline:* Applications are processed on a rolling basis. *Application fee:* $20 ($100 for international students). Electronic applications accepted. *Application Contact:* Mark Daugherty, Director of Admissions, 312-935-4814, Fax: 312-935-6020, E-mail: mdaugherty@robertmorris.edu. *Dean*, Kayed Akkawi, 312-935-6050, Fax: 312-935-6020, E-mail: kakkawi@robertmorris.edu.

ROBERTS WESLEYAN COLLEGE, Rochester, NY 14624-1997

General Information Independent-religious, coed, comprehensive institution. *Graduate housing:* Rooms and/or apartments available on a first-come, first-served basis to single and married students.

GRADUATE UNITS

Department of Nursing *Program availability:* Evening/weekend, online learning. Offers nursing education (MSN); nursing informatics (MSN); nursing leadership and administration (MSN). Electronic applications accepted.

Department of Social Work Offers child and family practice (MSW); mental health practice (MSW).

Graduate Business Programs *Program availability:* Evening/weekend. Offers strategic leadership (MS); strategic marketing (MS).

Graduate Psychology Programs *Program availability:* Part-time, evening/weekend. Offers clinical/school psychology (Psy D); school counseling (MS); school psychology (MS). Electronic applications accepted.

Graduate Teacher Education Programs *Program availability:* Part-time, evening/weekend. Offers adolescence and special education (M Ed); childhood and special education (M Ed); literacy education (M Ed); special education (M Ed). Electronic applications accepted.

Health Administration Programs *Program availability:* Evening/weekend, online learning. Offers health administration (MS); healthcare informatics administration (MS).

ROCHESTER COLLEGE, Rochester Hills, MI 48307-2764

General Information Independent-religious, coed, comprehensive institution.

GRADUATE UNITS

Center for Missional Leadership Offers missional leadership (MRE).

ROCHESTER INSTITUTE OF TECHNOLOGY, Rochester, NY 14623-5603

General Information Independent, coed, university. CGS member. *Enrollment:* 16,584 graduate, professional, and undergraduate students; 2,247 full-time matriculated graduate/professional students (862 women), 869 part-time matriculated graduate/professional students (358 women). *Enrollment by degree level:* 2,814 master's, 277 doctoral, 25 other advanced degrees. *Tuition:* Full-time $43,560; part-time $1815 per credit hour. *Required fees:* $280. Tuition and fees vary according to course load, campus/location, program and reciprocity agreements. *Graduate housing:* Rooms and/or apartments available on a first-come, first-served basis to single and married students. *Student services:* Campus employment opportunities, campus safety program, career counseling, child daycare facilities, exercise/wellness program, free psychological counseling, grant writing training, international student services, low-cost health insurance, multicultural affairs office, services for students with disabilities, teacher training, writing training. *Library facilities:* Wallace Memorial Library. *Collection:* Books: 429,176 (physical), 240,712 (digital/electronic); Serial titles: 58,293 (digital/electronic); Databases: 113. Weekly public service hours: 147; study areas open 24 hours, 5–7 days a week; students can reserve study rooms. *Research affiliation:* Corning Inc. (materials science technology), Harris Corporation (information technology, broadband communications), Toyota Materials Handling N.A. (industrial equipment performance), Hewlett Packard (enterprise information technology), Bausch & Lomb (eye health), Yamaha Corporation (audio and acoustic engineering).

Computer facilities: Computer purchase and lease plans are available. 3,500 computers available on campus for general student use. A campuswide network can be accessed from student residence rooms and from off campus. Online class registration, student account information are available.
Website: http://www.rit.edu/

General Application Contact: Diane Ellison, Senior Associate Vice President, Graduate Enrollment Services, 585-475-2229, Fax: 585-475-7164, E-mail: gradinfo@rit.edu.

GRADUATE UNITS

Graduate Enrollment Services Students: 2,259 full-time (823 women), 903 part-time (326 women); includes 215 minority (46 Black or African American, non-Hispanic/Latino; 2 American Indian or Alaska Native, non-Hispanic/Latino; 76 Asian, non-Hispanic/Latino; 57 Hispanic/Latino; 34 Two or more races, non-Hispanic/Latino), 1,790 international. Average age 27. 5,927 applicants, 46% accepted, 936 enrolled. Expenses: Contact institution. *Financial support:* In 2017–18, 2,278 students received support. Research assistantships, teaching assistantships, career-related internships or fieldwork, scholarships/grants, health care benefits, and unspecified assistantships available. Support available to part-time students. Financial award applicants required to submit FAFSA. In 2017, 944 master's, 9 doctorates, 86 other advanced degrees awarded. *Program availability:* Part-time, evening/weekend, 100% online, blended/hybrid learning. *Application deadline:* Applications are processed on a rolling basis. *Application fee:* $65. Electronic applications accepted. *Senior Associate Vice President, Graduate Enrollment Services*, Dr. Diane Ellison, 585-475-2229, Fax: 585-475-7164, E-mail: gradinfo@rit.edu.

College of Applied Science and Technology Students: 171 full-time (48 women), 69 part-time (15 women); includes 15 minority (4 Black or African American, non-Hispanic/Latino; 4 Asian, non-Hispanic/Latino; 7 Hispanic/Latino), 188 international. Average age 25. 383 applicants, 62% accepted, 82 enrolled. Expenses: Contact institution. *Financial support:* In 2017–18, 209 students received support. Research assistantships with partial tuition reimbursements available, teaching assistantships with partial tuition reimbursements available, career-related internships or fieldwork, scholarships/grants, and unspecified assistantships available. Support available to part-time students. Financial award applicants required to submit FAFSA. In 2017, 104 master's awarded. *Program availability:* Part-time, evening/weekend, 100% online, blended/hybrid learning. Offers applied science and technology (MS, Advanced Certificate); engineering technology (MS); environmental, health and safety management (MS); hospitality and tourism management (MS); human resources development (MS); international hospitality and service innovation (MS, Advanced Certificate); manufacturing and mechanical systems integration (MS); organizational learning (Advanced Certificate); packaging science (MS); service leadership and innovation (MS); telecommunications engineering technology (MS); workplace learning and instruction (Advanced Certificate). *Application deadline:* Applications are processed on a rolling basis. *Application fee:* $65. Electronic applications accepted. *Application Contact:* Diane Ellison, Senior Associate Vice President, Graduate Enrollment Services, 585-475-2229, Fax: 585-475-7164, E-mail: gradinfo@rit.edu. *Interim Dean*, Dr. S. Manian Ramkumar, 585-475-5955, E-mail: smrmet@rit.edu.

College of Health Sciences and Technology Students: 15 full-time (12 women), 24 part-time (17 women); includes 12 minority (5 Black or African American, non-Hispanic/Latino; 4 Asian, non-Hispanic/Latino; 3 Hispanic/Latino), 5 international. Average age 31. 49 applicants, 41% accepted, 11 enrolled. Expenses: Contact institution. *Financial support:* In 2017–18, 14 students received support. Research assistantships with partial tuition reimbursements available, teaching assistantships with partial tuition reimbursements available, career-related internships or fieldwork, scholarships/grants, and unspecified assistantships available. Support available to part-time students. Financial award applicants required to submit FAFSA. In 2017, 8 master's awarded. *Program availability:* Part-time, evening/weekend, 100% online. Offers health care finance (Advanced Certificate); health sciences and technology (MFA, MS, Advanced Certificate); health systems administration (MS); medical illustration (MFA). *Application deadline:* Applications are processed on a rolling basis. *Application fee:* $65. Electronic applications accepted. *Application Contact:* Diane Ellison, Senior Associate Vice President, Graduate Enrollment Services, 585-475-2229, Fax: 585-475-7164, E-mail: gradinfo@rit.edu. *Vice President and Dean, Institute and College of Health Sciences and Technology*, Dr. Daniel Ornt, 585-475-4017, Fax: 585-475-4330, E-mail: daniel.ornt@rit.edu.

College of Imaging Arts and Sciences Students: 233 full-time (153 women), 90 part-time (59 women); includes 36 minority (4 Black or African American, non-Hispanic/Latino; 13 Asian, non-Hispanic/Latino; 11 Hispanic/Latino; 8 Two or more races, non-Hispanic/Latino), 208 international. Average age 27. 683 applicants, 44% accepted, 103 enrolled. Expenses: Contact institution. *Financial support:* In 2017–18, 181 students received support. Teaching assistantships with partial tuition reimbursements available, career-related internships or fieldwork, scholarships/grants, and unspecified assistantships available. Support available to part-time students. Financial award applicants required to submit FAFSA. In 2017, 40 master's, 6 other advanced degrees awarded. *Program availability:* Part-time, 100% online. Offers American crafts (MFA); ceramics (MFA); design (MFA, Advanced Certificate); film and animation (MFA); fine arts studio (MFA); furniture design (MFA); glass (MFA); imaging arts and sciences (MFA, MS, MST, Advanced Certificate); industrial design (MFA); media arts and technology (MS); media sciences (MS); metals and jewelry design (MFA); photographic arts and sciences (MFA); photography and related media (MFA); print media (MS); user experience design and development (Advanced Certificate); visual arts-all grades (MST); visual communication design (MFA). *Application deadline:* For fall admission, 2/15 priority date for domestic and international students. Applications are processed on a rolling basis. *Application fee:* $65. Electronic applications accepted. *Application Contact:* Diane Ellison, Senior Associate Vice President, Graduate Enrollment Services, 585-475-2229, Fax: 585-475-7164, E-mail: gradinfo@rit.edu. *Interim Dean*, Dr. Robin Cass, 585-475-2683, E-mail: robin.cass@rit.edu.

College of Liberal Arts Students: 55 full-time (43 women), 29 part-time (18 women); includes 8 minority (6 Black or African American, non-Hispanic/Latino; 1 Hispanic/Latino; 1 Two or more races, non-Hispanic/Latino), 10 international. Average age 26. 113 applicants, 52% accepted, 34 enrolled. Expenses: Contact institution. *Financial support:* In 2017–18, 42 students received support. Research assistantships with partial tuition reimbursements available, teaching assistantships with partial tuition reimbursements available, career-related internships or fieldwork, scholarships/grants, and unspecified assistantships available. Support available to part-time students. Financial award applicants required to submit FAFSA. In 2017, 30 master's, 9 other advanced degrees awarded. *Program availability:* Part-time, 100% online. Offers communication and digital media (Advanced Certificate); communication and media technologies (MS); criminal justice (MS); engineering psychology (Advanced Certificate); experimental psychology (MS); liberal arts (MS, Advanced Certificate); school psychology (MS, Advanced Certificate); science, technology and public policy (MS). *Application deadline:* For fall admission, 2/15 priority date for domestic and international students; for spring admission, 12/15 priority date for domestic and international students. Applications are processed on a rolling basis. *Application fee:* $65. Electronic applications accepted. *Application Contact:* Diane Ellison, Senior Associate Vice President, Graduate Enrollment Services, 585-475-2229, Fax: 585-475-7164, E-mail: gradinfo@rit.edu. *Dean*, Dr. James Winebrake, 585-475-2929, Fax: 585-475-7120, E-mail: libarts@rit.edu.

College of Science Students: 213 full-time (92 women), 105 part-time (34 women); includes 23 minority (5 Black or African American, non-Hispanic/Latino; 5 Asian, non-Hispanic/Latino; 5 Hispanic/Latino; 8 Two or more races, non-Hispanic/Latino), 122 international. Average age 28. 497 applicants, 41% accepted, 87 enrolled. Expenses: Contact institution. *Financial support:* In 2017–18, 251 students received support. Research assistantships with tuition reimbursements available, teaching assistantships with tuition reimbursements available, career-related internships or fieldwork, institutionally sponsored loans, scholarships/grants, unspecified assistantships, and health care benefits (for PhD program only) available. Support available to part-time students. Financial award applicants required to submit FAFSA. In 2017, 47 master's, 4 doctorates, 3 other advanced degrees awarded. *Program availability:* Part-time, evening/weekend, 100% online. Offers applied and computational mathematics (MS); applied statistics (MS, Advanced Certificate); astrophysical science and technology (MS, PhD); bioinformatics (MS); chemistry (MS); color science (MS, PhD); environmental science (MS); imaging science (MS, PhD); life sciences (MS); materials science and engineering (MS); mathematical modeling (PhD); science (MS, PhD, Advanced Certificate). *Application deadline:* For fall admission, 2/15 priority date for domestic and international students; for spring admission, 12/15 priority date for domestic and international students. Applications are processed on a rolling basis. *Application fee:* $65. Electronic applications accepted. *Application Contact:* Diane Ellison, Senior Associate Vice President, Graduate Enrollment Services, 585-475-2229, Fax: 585-475-7164, E-mail: gradinfo@rit.edu. *Dean*, Dr. Sophia Maggelakis, 585-475-5221, Fax: 585-475-2398, E-mail: science@rit.edu.

Golisano College of Computing and Information Sciences Students: 724 full-time (213 women), 139 part-time (60 women); includes 39 minority (4 Black or African American, non-Hispanic/Latino; 1 American Indian or Alaska Native, non-Hispanic/Latino; 24 Asian, non-Hispanic/Latino; 5 Hispanic/Latino; 5 Two or more races, non-Hispanic/Latino), 722 international. Average age 26. 2,369 applicants, 42% accepted, 262 enrolled. Expenses: Contact institution. *Financial support:* In 2017–18, 754 students received support. Research assistantships with tuition reimbursements available, teaching assistantships with tuition reimbursements available, career-related internships or fieldwork, scholarships/grants, unspecified assistantships, and health care benefits (for PhD program only) available. Support available to part-time students. Financial award applicants required to submit FAFSA. In 2017, 236 master's, 2 doctorates, 52 other advanced degrees awarded. *Program availability:* Part-time, evening/weekend, 100% online. Offers big data analytics (Advanced Certificate); computer science (MS, Advanced Certificate); computing and information sciences (PhD); computing security (MS); cybersecurity (Advanced Certificate); game design and development (MS); health informatics (MS); human computer interaction (MS); information sciences and technologies (MS); networking and systems administration (MS); networking, planning and design (Advanced Certificate); software engineering (MS); Web development (Advanced Certificate). *Application deadline:* For fall admission, 2/15 priority date for domestic and international students; for spring admission, 12/15 priority date for domestic and international students. Applications are processed on a rolling basis. *Application fee:* $65. Electronic applications accepted. *Application Contact:* Diane Ellison, Senior Associate Vice President, Graduate Enrollment Services, 585-475-2229, Fax: 585-475-7164, E-mail: gradinfo@rit.edu. *Dean*, Dr. Anne Haake, 585-475-7203, Fax: 585-475-4775, E-mail: gccis-email@rit.edu.

Golisano Institute for Sustainability Students: 64 full-time (36 women), 20 part-time (7 women); includes 1 minority (Two or more races, non-Hispanic/Latino), 50 international. Average age 29. 164 applicants, 55% accepted, 22 enrolled. Expenses: Contact institution. *Financial support:* In 2017–18, 74 students received support. Research assistantships with tuition reimbursements available, teaching assistantships with tuition reimbursements available, career-related internships or fieldwork, scholarships/grants, unspecified assistantships, and health care benefits (for PhD program only) available. Support available to part-time students. Financial award applicants required to submit FAFSA. In 2017, 12 master's, 1 doctorate awarded. *Program availability:* Part-time. Offers architecture (M Arch); sustainability (PhD); sustainable systems (MS). *Application deadline:* For fall admission, 2/15 priority date for domestic and international students; for spring admission, 12/15 priority date for domestic and international students. Applications are processed on a rolling basis. *Application fee:* $65. Electronic applications accepted. *Application Contact:* Diane Ellison, Senior Associate Vice President, Graduate Enrollment Services, 585-475-2229, Fax: 585-475-7164, E-mail: gradinfo@rit.edu. *Associate Provost and Director*, Dr. Nabil Nasr, 585-475-5101, E-mail: info@sustainability.rit.edu.

Kate Gleason College of Engineering Students: 430 full-time (92 women), 190 part-time (35 women); includes 33 minority (5 Black or African American, non-Hispanic/Latino; 13 Asian, non-Hispanic/Latino; 11 Hispanic/Latino; 4 Two or more races, non-Hispanic/Latino), 349 international. Average age 26. 1,355 applicants, 39% accepted, 166 enrolled. Expenses: Contact institution. *Financial support:* In 2017–18, 489 students received support. Fellowships with tuition reimbursements available, research assistantships with tuition reimbursements available, teaching assistantships with tuition reimbursements available, career-related internships or fieldwork, scholarships/grants, tuition waivers (full and partial), unspecified assistantships, and health care benefits (for PhD program only) available. Support available to part-time students. Financial award applicants required to submit FAFSA. In 2017, 257 master's, 2 doctorates, 4 other advanced degrees awarded. *Program availability:* Part-time, evening/weekend, 100% online. Offers computer engineering (MS); electrical engineering (MS); engineering (ME, MS, PhD, Advanced Certificate); engineering management (ME); industrial and systems engineering (ME, MS); Lean Six Sigma (Advanced Certificate); manufacturing leadership (MS); mechanical engineering (ME, MS); microelectronic engineering (MS); microelectronic manufacturing engineering (ME); microsystems engineering (PhD); product development (MS); sustainable engineering (ME, MS). *Application deadline:* For fall admission, 2/15 priority date for domestic and international students. Applications are processed on a rolling basis. *Application fee:* $65. Electronic applications accepted. *Application Contact:* Diane Ellison, Senior Associate Vice President, Graduate Enrollment Services, 585-475-2229, Fax: 585-475-7164, E-mail: gradinfo@rit.edu. *Dean*, Dr. Doreen Edwards, 585-475-2145, Fax: 585-475-6879, E-mail: coe@rit.edu.

National Technical Institute for the Deaf Students: 23 full-time (17 women), 11 part-time (all women); includes 6 minority (1 Black or African American, non-Hispanic/Latino; 4 Hispanic/Latino; 1 Two or more races, non-Hispanic/Latino), 6 international. Average age 33. 24 applicants, 33% accepted, 5 enrolled. Expenses: Contact institution. *Financial support:* Fellowships with partial tuition reimbursements, research assistantships with partial tuition reimbursements, career-related internships or fieldwork, scholarships/grants, and unspecified assistantships available. Support available to part-time students. Financial award applicants required to submit FAFSA. In 2017, 11 master's awarded. *Program availability:* Part-time, evening/weekend, blended/hybrid learning. Offers deaf studies (MS); health care interpretation (MS); secondary education for the deaf and hard of hearing (MS). *Application deadline:* For fall admission, 2/15 priority date for domestic and international students. Applications are processed on a rolling basis. *Application fee:* $65. Electronic applications accepted. *Application Contact:* Diane Ellison, Senior Associate Vice President, Graduate Enrollment Services, 585-475-2229, Fax: 585-475-7164, E-mail: gradinfo@rit.edu. *President*, Dr. Gerard J. Buckley, 585-475-6317, Fax: 585-475-5978, E-mail: gbuckley@ntid.rit.edu.

Saunders College of Business Students: 227 full-time (99 women), 105 part-time (51 women); includes 24 minority (8 Black or African American, non-Hispanic/Latino; 1

American Indian or Alaska Native, non-Hispanic/Latino; 5 Asian, non-Hispanic/Latino; 5 Hispanic/Latino; 5 Two or more races, non-Hispanic/Latino), 94 international. Average age 30. 588 applicants, 49% accepted, 138 enrolled. Expenses: Contact institution. *Financial support:* In 2017–18, 221 students received support. Research assistantships with partial tuition reimbursements available, teaching assistantships with partial tuition reimbursements available, career-related internships or fieldwork, Federal Work-Study, scholarships/grants, and unspecified assistantships available. Support available to part-time students. Financial award applicants required to submit FAFSA. In 2017, 134 master's awarded. *Program availability:* Part-time, evening/weekend, 100% online, blended/hybrid learning. Offers accounting (MBA, MS); business (Exec MBA, MBA, MS); business administration (MBA); computational finance (MS); entrepreneurship and innovative ventures (MS); executive business administration (Exec MBA); finance (MS); management (MS); marketing (MBA). *Application deadline:* Applications are processed on a rolling basis. *Application fee:* $65. Electronic applications accepted. *Application Contact:* Diane Ellison, Senior Associate Vice President, Graduate Enrollment Services, 585-475-2229, Fax: 585-475-7164, E-mail: gradinfo@rit.edu. *Dean*, Dr. Jacqueline Mozrall, 585-475-6025, E-mail: gradbus@saunders.rit.edu.

School of Individualized Study Students: 18 full-time (8 women), 54 part-time (34 women); includes 8 minority (2 Black or African American, non-Hispanic/Latino; 4 Asian, non-Hispanic/Latino; 2 Hispanic/Latino), 13 international. Average age 33. 60 applicants, 57% accepted, 15 enrolled. Expenses: Contact institution. *Financial support:* In 2017–18, 10 students received support. Career-related internships or fieldwork, scholarships/grants, and unspecified assistantships available. Support available to part-time students. Financial award applicants required to submit FAFSA. In 2017, 24 master's, 12 other advanced degrees awarded. *Program availability:* Part-time, evening/weekend, 100% online, blended/hybrid learning. Offers individualized studies (MS, Advanced Certificate); professional studies (MS); project management (Advanced Certificate). *Application deadline:* Applications are processed on a rolling basis. *Application fee:* $65. Electronic applications accepted. *Application Contact:* Diane Ellison, Senior Associate Vice President, Graduate Enrollment Services, 585-475-2229, Fax: 585-475-7164, E-mail: gradinfo@rit.edu. *Executive Director*, Dr. James Hall, 585-475-2295, Fax: 585-475-6292, E-mail: sois@rit.edu.

THE ROCKEFELLER UNIVERSITY, New York, NY 10021-6399

General Information Independent, coed, graduate-only institution. CGS member. *Enrollment by degree level:* 19 master's, 213 doctoral. *Graduate faculty:* 79 full-time (11 women). *Graduate housing:* Rooms and/or apartments guaranteed to single and married students. Typical cost: $9720 per year for single students. Room charges vary according to housing facility selected. Housing application deadline: 6/1. *Student services:* Campus safety program, career counseling, child daycare facilities, exercise/wellness program, free psychological counseling, grant writing training, low-cost health insurance, teacher training. *Library facilities:* Rita and Frits Markus Library. *Collection:* Books: 45,492 (physical), 88,925 (digital/electronic); Serial titles: 6,251 (digital/electronic); Databases: 9. Weekly public service hours: 40; study areas open 24 hours, 5–7 days a week; students can reserve study rooms.

Computer facilities: 32 computers available on campus for general student use. A campuswide network can be accessed from student residence rooms and from off campus. Online class registration is available.
Website: http://www.rockefeller.edu/

General Application Contact: Kristen Cullen, Graduate Admissions Administrator/Registrar, 212-327-8086, Fax: 212-327-8505, E-mail: phd@rockefeller.edu.

GRADUATE UNITS

The David Rockefeller Graduate Program in Bioscience Students: 232 full-time (92 women); includes 50 minority (6 Black or African American, non-Hispanic/Latino; 23 Asian, non-Hispanic/Latino; 20 Hispanic/Latino; 1 Native Hawaiian or other Pacific Islander, non-Hispanic/Latino), 72 international. Average age 25. 786 applicants, 10% accepted, 26 enrolled. *Faculty:* 79 full-time (11 women). Expenses: Contact institution. *Financial support:* In 2017–18, 232 students received support, including 232 fellowships with full tuition reimbursements available; institutionally sponsored loans, scholarships/grants, traineeships, and health care benefits also available. In 2017, 9 master's, 23 doctorates awarded. Offers bioscience (MS, PhD). *Application deadline:* For fall and winter admission, 12/1 for domestic and international students. *Application fee:* $50. Electronic applications accepted. *Application Contact:* Kristen Cullen, Graduate Admissions Administrator/Registrar, 212-327-8086, Fax: 212-327-8505, E-mail: phd@rockefeller.edu. *Dean of Graduate and Postgraduate Studies/Vice President*, Dr. Sidney Strickland, 212-327-8086, Fax: 212-327-8505, E-mail: phd@rockefeller.edu.

ROCKFORD UNIVERSITY, Rockford, IL 61108-2393

General Information Independent, coed, comprehensive institution. *Graduate housing:* Room and/or apartments available on a first-come, first-served basis to single students; on-campus housing not available to married students.

GRADUATE UNITS

Graduate Studies *Program availability:* Part-time, evening/weekend. Offers business administration (MBA); early childhood education (MAT); elementary education (MAT); instructional strategies (MAT); reading (MAT); secondary education (MAT); special education (MAT). Electronic applications accepted.

ROCKHURST UNIVERSITY, Kansas City, MO 64110-2561

General Information Independent-religious, coed, comprehensive institution. *Enrollment:* 3,043 graduate, professional, and undergraduate students; 404 full-time matriculated graduate/professional students (278 women), 431 part-time matriculated graduate/professional students (192 women). *Enrollment by degree level:* 641 master's, 141 doctoral, 49 other advanced degrees. *Graduate faculty:* 48 full-time (32 women), 32 part-time/adjunct (20 women). *Graduate housing:* Room and/or apartments available on a first-come, first-served basis to single students; on-campus housing not available to married students. Typical cost: $6120 per year ($9360 including board). Room and board charges vary according to board plan and housing facility selected. *Student services:* Campus employment opportunities, campus safety program, career counseling, free psychological counseling, services for students with disabilities, teacher training. *Library facilities:* Greenlease Library. *Collection:* Books: 112,979 (physical), 180,624 (digital/electronic); Serial titles: 798 (physical), 103,252 (digital/electronic); Databases: 110. Weekly public service hours: 85.

Computer facilities: 235 computers available on campus for general student use. A campuswide network can be accessed from student residence rooms. Online class registration, campus portal are available.
Website: http://www.rockhurst.edu/

General Application Contact: E-mail: graduate.admission@rockhurst.edu.

GRADUATE UNITS

College of Health and Human Services Expenses: Contact institution. *Financial support:* Applicants required to submit FAFSA. *Program availability:* Part-time, evening/weekend. Offers communication sciences and disorders (MS); education (M Ed); health and human services (M Ed, MOT, MS, DPT); occupational therapy (MOT); physical therapy (DPT). *Application Contact:* Beth Harris, Graduate Admissions Coordinator and Recruiter, 816-501-4097, Fax: 816-501-4059, E-mail: beth.harris@rockhurst.edu. *Dean*, Dr. Jennifer Friend, 816-501-4109, E-mail: jennifer.friend@rockhurst.edu.

Helzberg School of Management Students: 99 full-time (30 women), 355 part-time (132 women); includes 95 minority (30 Black or African American, non-Hispanic/Latino; 29 Asian, non-Hispanic/Latino; 25 Hispanic/Latino; 11 Two or more races, non-Hispanic/Latino), 8 international. Average age 32. 249 applicants, 81% accepted, 175 enrolled. *Faculty:* 18 full-time (4 women), 20 part-time/adjunct (9 women). Expenses: Contact institution. *Financial support:* Applicants required to submit FAFSA. In 2017, 145 master's, 17 other advanced degrees awarded. *Program availability:* Part-time, evening/weekend. Offers accounting (MBA); business intelligence (MBA, Certificate); business intelligence and analytics (MS); data science (MBA, Certificate); entrepreneurship (MBA); finance (MBA); fundraising leadership (MBA, Certificate); healthcare management (MBA, Certificate); human capital (Certificate); international business (Certificate); management (MA, MBA, Certificate); nonprofit administration (Certificate); organizational development (Certificate); science leadership (Certificate). *Application deadline:* Applications are processed on a rolling basis. *Application fee:* $0. Electronic applications accepted. *Application Contact:* Jonnae Hill, Director of Graduate Business Advising, 816-501-4823, E-mail: jonnae.hill@rockhurst.edu. *Dean*, Cheryl McConnell, 816-501-4201, Fax: 816-501-4650, E-mail: cheryl.mcconnell@rockhurst.edu.

ROCKY MOUNTAIN COLLEGE, Billings, MT 59102-1796

General Information Independent-religious, coed, comprehensive institution. *Enrollment:* 992 graduate, professional, and undergraduate students; 91 full-time matriculated graduate/professional students (48 women), 2 part-time matriculated graduate/professional students (both women). *Enrollment by degree level:* 93 master's. *Graduate faculty:* 7 full-time (4 women), 4 part-time/adjunct (2 women). *Graduate housing:* Rooms and/or apartments available on a first-come, first-served basis to single and married students. Typical cost: $3539 per year for single students; $3539 per year for married students. Room charges vary according to board plan and housing facility selected. *Student services:* Campus employment opportunities, campus safety program, career counseling, free psychological counseling, international student services, services for students with disabilities, teacher training. *Library facilities:* Paul M. Adams Memorial Library. *Collection:* Books: 46,075 (physical), 41,042 (digital/electronic); Serial titles: 388 (physical), 61,207 (digital/electronic); Databases: 65. Weekly public service hours: 89.

Computer facilities: 113 computers available on campus for general student use. A campuswide network can be accessed from student residence rooms and from off campus. Online class registration is available.
Website: http://www.rocky.edu/

General Application Contact: Austin Mapston, Dean of Enrollment Services, 406-657-1026, Fax: 406-657-1189, E-mail: admissions@rocky.edu.

GRADUATE UNITS

Program in Accountancy Students: 1 (woman) part-time. Average age 32. *Faculty:* 2 full-time (0 women). Expenses: Contact institution. *Financial support:* Applicants required to submit FAFSA. In 2017, 4 master's awarded. *Program availability:* Part-time-only. Offers accountancy (M Acc). *Application deadline:* Applications are processed on a rolling basis. *Application fee:* $35 ($40 for international students). Electronic applications accepted. *Application Contact:* Austin Mapston, Dean of Enrollment Services, 406-657-1026, Fax: 406-657-1189, E-mail: admissions@rocky.edu. *Professor of Business Administration and Economics*, Anthony Piltz, 406-657-1069, E-mail: piltza@rocky.edu.

Program in Educational Leadership Students: 19 full-time (7 women). Average age 37. *Faculty:* 2 full-time (both women). Expenses: Contact institution. *Financial support:* In 2017–18, 19 students received support. Scholarships/grants available. Financial award applicants required to submit FAFSA. In 2017, 20 master's awarded. Offers educational leadership (M Ed). *Application deadline:* Applications are processed on a rolling basis. *Application fee:* $35 ($40 for international students). Electronic applications accepted. *Director of Educational Leadership and Distance Education*, Dr. Stevie Schmitz, 406-657-1134, E-mail: schmitzs@rocky.edu.

Program in Physician Assistant Studies Students: 72 full-time (41 women); includes 5 minority (3 Asian, non-Hispanic/Latino; 1 Hispanic/Latino; 1 Two or more races, non-Hispanic/Latino). Average age 27. *Faculty:* 4 full-time (3 women), 3 part-time/adjunct (1 woman). Expenses: Contact institution. *Financial support:* Applicants required to submit FAFSA. In 2017, 36 master's awarded. Offers physician assistant studies (MPAS). *Application deadline:* Applications are processed on a rolling basis. *Application fee:* $45. Electronic applications accepted. *Application Contact:* Calley Thompson, PA Admissions Counselor, 406-657-1198, E-mail: calley.thompson@rocky.edu. *Program Director*, Heather Heggem, 406-657-1190, E-mail: heather.heggem@rocky.edu.

ROCKY MOUNTAIN COLLEGE OF ART + DESIGN, Lakewood, CO 80214

General Information Proprietary, coed, comprehensive institution.

GRADUATE UNITS

Program in Education, Leadership + Emerging Technologies *Program availability:* Online learning. Offers education, leadership and emerging technologies (MA).

ROCKY MOUNTAIN UNIVERSITY OF HEALTH PROFESSIONS, Provo, UT 84606

General Information Proprietary, coed, graduate-only institution. *Research affiliation:* Aegis Corporation.

GRADUATE UNITS

Doctor of Nursing Practice Program Offers nursing practice (DNP).

Doctor of Science Program in Clinical Electrophysiology *Program availability:* Online learning. Offers clinical electrophysiology (D Sc).

Program in Occupational Therapy *Program availability:* Online learning. Offers occupational therapy (OTD). Electronic applications accepted.

Program in Physician Assistant Studies Offers physician assistant studies (MPAS).

Program in Speech-Language Pathology Offers speech-language pathology (Clin Sc D).

Programs in Physical Therapy Offers physical therapy (DPT, TDPT).

ROCKY VISTA UNIVERSITY, Parker, CO 80134

General Information Proprietary, coed, graduate-only institution. *Enrollment by degree level:* 27 master's. *Student services:* Career counseling, exercise/wellness program, free psychological counseling, services for students with disabilities.
Website: http://www.rvu.edu/

General Application Contact: Julie K. Rosenthal, Executive Director of Enrollment Management and External Relations, 720-875-2804, E-mail: jrosenthal@rvu.edu.

GRADUATE UNITS

College of Osteopathic Medicine Expenses: Contact institution. Offers osteopathic medicine (DO). *Application deadline:* For fall admission, 3/15 priority date for domestic students. *Application Contact:* Dr. Thomas N. Told, Dean. *Dean*, Dr. Thomas N. Told.

Program in Biomedical Sciences Expenses: Contact institution. Offers biomedical sciences (MS). *Application fee:* $50. *Application Contact:* Dr. Francina Deason Towne, Director, 720-875-2837, E-mail: ftowne@rvu.edu. *Director*, Dr. Francina Deason Towne, 720-875-2837, E-mail: ftowne@rvu.edu.

Program in Physician Assistant Studies Offers physician assistant studies (MPAS).

ROGERS STATE UNIVERSITY, Claremore, OK 74017-3252

General Information State-supported, coed, comprehensive institution.

GRADUATE UNITS

Program in Business Administration Offers business administration (MBA).

ROGER WILLIAMS UNIVERSITY, Bristol, RI 02809

General Information Independent, coed, comprehensive institution. *Enrollment:* 5,024 graduate, professional, and undergraduate students; 606 full-time matriculated graduate/professional students (335 women), 146 part-time matriculated graduate/professional students (81 women). *Enrollment by degree level:* 299 master's, 13 other advanced degrees. *Graduate faculty:* 45 full-time (19 women), 24 part-time/adjunct (6 women). *Tuition:* Full-time $14,936; part-time $9958 per semester. *Required fees:* $258; $258 per degree program. Tuition and fees vary according to program. *Graduate housing:* On-campus housing not available. *Student services:* Campus employment opportunities, campus safety program, career counseling, exercise/wellness program, free psychological counseling, international student services, low-cost health insurance, multicultural affairs office, services for students with disabilities, teacher training. *Library facilities:* Roger Williams University Library plus 1 other. *Collection:* Books: 219,429 (physical), 448,637 (digital/electronic); Serial titles: 493 (physical), 52,585 (digital/electronic); Databases: 189. Weekly public service hours: 111; students can reserve study rooms.

Computer facilities: 100 computers available on campus for general student use. A campuswide network can be accessed from student residence rooms and from off campus. Online class registration is available.
Website: http://www.rwu.edu/

General Application Contact: Marcus Hanscom, Director of Graduate Admissions, 401-254-3345, Fax: 401-254-3557, E-mail: mhanscom@rwu.edu.

GRADUATE UNITS

Feinstein School of Humanities, Arts and Education Students: 14 part-time (all women); includes 1 minority (Hispanic/Latino). Average age 33. 10 applicants, 100% accepted, 7 enrolled. *Faculty:* 3 full-time (all women), 5 part-time/adjunct (4 women). Expenses: Contact institution. *Financial support:* Application deadline: 4/1; applicants required to submit FAFSA. In 2017, 10 master's awarded. *Program availability:* Part-time-only, evening/weekend. Offers literacy education (MA); middle school certification (Certificate). *Application deadline:* Applications are processed on a rolling basis. *Application fee:* $50. Electronic applications accepted. *Application Contact:* Marcus Hanscom, Director of Graduate Admissions, 401-254-3345, Fax: 401-254-3557, E-mail: gradadmit@rwu.edu. *Interim Dean*, Jeffrey Meriwether, 401-254-3780, E-mail: jmeriwether@rwu.edu.

Feinstein School of Social and Natural Sciences Students: 42 full-time (36 women), 2 part-time (both women); includes 8 minority (1 Black or African American, non-Hispanic/Latino; 1 Asian, non-Hispanic/Latino; 5 Hispanic/Latino; 1 Native Hawaiian or other Pacific Islander, non-Hispanic/Latino). Average age 24. 109 applicants, 62% accepted, 24 enrolled. *Faculty:* 10 full-time (5 women), 2 part-time/adjunct (0 women). Expenses: Contact institution. *Financial support:* In 2017–18, 13 students received support, including 4 research assistantships (averaging $13,476 per year), 3 teaching assistantships (averaging $13,476 per year); scholarships/grants also available. Financial award application deadline: 2/15; financial award applicants required to submit FAFSA. In 2017, 16 master's awarded. Offers clinical psychology (MA); forensic psychology (MA). *Application deadline:* For fall admission, 2/1 priority date for domestic students. Applications are processed on a rolling basis. *Application fee:* $50. Electronic applications accepted. *Application Contact:* Marcus Hanscom, Director of Graduate Admissions, 401-254-3345, Fax: 401-254-3557, E-mail: gradadmit@rwu.edu. *Dean*, Benjamin Greenstein, 401-254-3337, E-mail: bgreenstein@rwu.edu.

Mario J. Gabelli School of Business Students: 8 full-time (6 women); includes 1 minority (Hispanic/Latino). Average age 22. 15 applicants, 87% accepted, 8 enrolled. *Faculty:* 4 full-time (1 woman), 1 part-time/adjunct (0 women). Expenses: Contact institution. *Financial support:* In 2017–18, 7 students received support. Scholarships/grants available. Financial award application deadline: 4/1; financial award applicants required to submit FAFSA. Offers business (MBA). *Application deadline:* For fall admission, 4/1 priority date for domestic students. *Application fee:* $50. Electronic applications accepted. *Application Contact:* Marcus Hanscom, Director of Graduate Admissions, 401-254-3345, Fax: 401-254-3557, E-mail: mhanscom@rwu.edu. *Dean*, Dr. Susan McTiernan, 401-254-3444, E-mail: smctiernan@rwu.edu.

School of Architecture, Art and Historic Preservation Students: 107 full-time (52 women), 9 part-time (5 women); includes 10 minority (1 Asian, non-Hispanic/Latino; 7 Hispanic/Latino; 2 Two or more races, non-Hispanic/Latino), 5 international. Average age 26. 92 applicants, 93% accepted, 58 enrolled. *Faculty:* 18 full-time (5 women), 9 part-time/adjunct (1 woman). Expenses: Contact institution. *Financial support:* In 2017–18, 116 students received support, including 116 research assistantships (averaging $2,776 per year); career-related internships or fieldwork, scholarships/grants, and unspecified assistantships also available. Financial award application deadline: 4/1; financial award applicants required to submit FAFSA. In 2017, 46 master's, 1 other advanced degree awarded. Offers architecture (M Arch); art and architectural history (MA); historical preservation (MS, Certificate); urban and regional planning (Certificate). *Application deadline:* For fall admission, 4/1 for domestic students; for spring admission, 11/15 for domestic students. *Application fee:* $50. Electronic applications accepted. *Application Contact:* Marcus Hanscom, Director of Graduate Admissions, 401-254-3345, Fax: 401-254-3557, E-mail: gradadmit@rwu.edu. *Dean*, Stephen White, 401-254-3607, E-mail: swhite@rwu.edu.

School of Justice Studies Students: 16 full-time (11 women), 114 part-time (57 women); includes 33 minority (14 Black or African American, non-Hispanic/Latino; 1 American Indian or Alaska Native, non-Hispanic/Latino; 1 Asian, non-Hispanic/Latino; 17 Hispanic/Latino), 1 international. Average age 35. 58 applicants, 83% accepted, 33 enrolled. *Faculty:* 10 full-time (5 women), 7 part-time/adjunct (1 woman). Expenses: Contact institution. *Financial support:* In 2017–18, 1 student received support, including 1 research assistantship (averaging $6,942 per year). Financial award application deadline: 4/1; financial award applicants required to submit FAFSA. In 2017, 27 master's awarded. *Program availability:* Part-time, evening/weekend, 100% online, blended/hybrid learning. Offers criminal justice (MS); cybersecurity (MS); leadership (MS); public administration (MPA). *Application deadline:* For fall admission, 8/1 for domestic students; for spring admission, 1/1 for domestic students. Applications are processed on a rolling basis. *Application fee:* $50. Electronic applications accepted. *Application Contact:* Marcus Hanscom, Director of Graduate Admissions, 401-254-3345, Fax: 401-254-3557, E-mail: gradadmit@rwu.edu. *Dean*, Dr. Eric Bronson, 401-254-3336, E-mail: ebronson@rwu.edu.

School of Law Students: 433 full-time (227 women), 7 part-time (4 women); includes 113 minority (39 Black or African American, non-Hispanic/Latino; 1 American Indian or Alaska Native, non-Hispanic/Latino; 12 Asian, non-Hispanic/Latino; 43 Hispanic/Latino; 18 Two or more races, non-Hispanic/Latino), 1 international. Average age 27. 849 applicants, 71% accepted, 161 enrolled. *Faculty:* 27 full-time (16 women), 31 part-time/adjunct (14 women). Expenses: Contact institution. *Financial support:* In 2017–18, 255 students received support, including 9 fellowships (averaging $1,739 per year), 51 research assistantships (averaging $931 per year); Federal Work-Study also available. Financial award application deadline: 3/15; financial award applicants required to submit FAFSA. In 2017, 2 master's, 121 doctorates awarded. *Program availability:* Part-time. Offers law (MSL, JD). JD/MMA and JD/MLRHR offered jointly with University of Rhode Island. *Application deadline:* For fall admission, 4/1 priority date for domestic and international students. Applications are processed on a rolling basis. *Application fee:* $60. Electronic applications accepted. *Application Contact:* Michael W. Donnelly-Boylen, Assistant Dean of Admissions, 401-254-4555, Fax: 401-254-4516, E-mail: mdonnelly-boylen@rwu.edu. *Dean*, Michael Yelnosky, 401-254-4500, Fax: 401-254-3525, E-mail: myelnosky@rwu.edu.

ROLLINS COLLEGE, Winter Park, FL 32789-4499

General Information Independent, coed, comprehensive institution. *Enrollment:* 2,650 graduate, professional, and undergraduate students; 397 full-time matriculated graduate/professional students (225 women), 269 part-time matriculated graduate/professional students (160 women). *Enrollment by degree level:* 623 master's, 43 doctoral. *Graduate faculty:* 40 full-time (15 women). *Tuition:* Full-time $15,000; part-time $2500 per credit hour. *Graduate housing:* Room and/or apartments available on a first-come, first-served basis to single students; on-campus housing not available to married students. *Student services:* Campus employment opportunities, campus safety program, career counseling, exercise/wellness program, free psychological counseling, international student services, low-cost health insurance, multicultural affairs office, services for students with disabilities, writing training. *Library facilities:* Olin Library. *Collection:* Books: 259,302 (physical), 200,491 (digital/electronic); Serial titles: 2,358 (physical), 134,353 (digital/electronic); Databases: 80. Study areas open 24 hours, 5–7 days a week; students can reserve study rooms.

Computer facilities: 254 computers available on campus for general student use. A campuswide network can be accessed from student residence rooms and from off campus. Online class registration is available.
Website: http://www.rollins.edu/

General Application Contact: Faye Tydlaska, Vice President for Enrollment Management and Marketing, 407-646-2161 Ext. 2532, E-mail: eveningadmission@rollins.edu.

GRADUATE UNITS

Crummer Graduate School of Business Students: 261 full-time (119 women), 114 part-time (45 women); includes 86 minority (24 Black or African American, non-Hispanic/Latino; 13 Asian, non-Hispanic/Latino; 44 Hispanic/Latino; 5 Two or more races, non-Hispanic/Latino), 31 international. Average age 32. *Faculty:* 20 full-time (4 women). Expenses: Contact institution. *Financial support:* Scholarships/grants available. Support available to part-time students. Financial award applicants required to submit FAFSA. In 2017, 134 master's awarded. *Program availability:* Part-time, evening/weekend, online learning. Offers entrepreneurship (MBA); finance (MBA); international business (MBA); management (MBA). *Application deadline:* Applications are processed on a rolling basis. *Application fee:* $50. Electronic applications accepted. *Application Contact:* Maralyn E. Graham, Admissions Coordinator, 407-646-2405, Fax: 407-646-1550, E-mail: mbaadmissions@rollins.edu. *Dean*, Deborah Crown, 407-646-2249, Fax: 407-646-1550, E-mail: dcrown@rollins.edu.

Hamilton Holt School Students: 136 full-time (106 women), 155 part-time (115 women); includes 100 minority (29 Black or African American, non-Hispanic/Latino; 2 American Indian or Alaska Native, non-Hispanic/Latino; 8 Asian, non-Hispanic/Latino; 53 Hispanic/Latino; 1 Native Hawaiian or other Pacific Islander, non-Hispanic/Latino; 7 Two or more races, non-Hispanic/Latino), 13 international. Average age 33. *Faculty:* 14 full-time (6 women), 12 part-time/adjunct (8 women). Expenses: Contact institution. *Financial support:* Scholarships/grants and unspecified assistantships available. Support available to part-time students. Financial award applicants required to submit FAFSA. In 2017, 58 master's awarded. *Program availability:* Part-time, evening/weekend. Offers applied behavior analysis and clinical science (MA); clinical mental health counseling (MA); elementary education (M Ed, MAT); human resources (MHR); liberal studies (MLS); public health (MPH). *Application fee:* $50. *Application Contact:* Nick Georgoudiou, Director of Admission, 407-691-1781, Fax: 407-646-1551, E-mail: ngeorgoudiou@rollins.edu. *Interim Dean*, Dr. Pat Brown, 407-646-2232, Fax: 407-646-1551, E-mail: pabrown@rollins.edu.

ROOSEVELT UNIVERSITY, Chicago, IL 60605

General Information Independent, coed, comprehensive institution. *Enrollment:* 4,457 graduate, professional, and undergraduate students; 996 full-time matriculated graduate/professional students (647 women), 861 part-time matriculated graduate/professional students (573 women). *Enrollment by degree level:* 1,514 master's, 343 doctoral. *Graduate housing:* Room and/or apartments available on a first-come, first-served basis to single students; on-campus housing not available to married students. Housing application deadline: 7/1. *Student services:* Campus employment opportunities, campus safety program, career counseling, exercise/wellness program, free psychological counseling, international student services, low-cost health insurance, multicultural affairs office, services for students with disabilities, teacher training, writing training. *Library facilities:* Murray-Green Library plus 4 others. *Collection:* Books: 152,557 (physical), 43,963 (digital/electronic); Serial titles: 174 (physical), 41,406 (digital/electronic); Databases: 198.

Computer facilities: 646 computers available on campus for general student use. A campuswide network can be accessed from student residence rooms and from off campus. Online class registration is available.
Website: http://www.roosevelt.edu/

General Application Contact: Catherine Campbell, Associate Dean, 312-341-3636, E-mail: ccampbell@roosevelt.edu.

GRADUATE UNITS

Graduate Division Students: 996 full-time (647 women), 861 part-time (573 women); includes 758 minority (370 Black or African American, non-Hispanic/Latino; 1 American Indian or Alaska Native, non-Hispanic/Latino; 148 Asian, non-Hispanic/Latino; 181 Hispanic/Latino; 1 Native Hawaiian or other Pacific Islander, non-Hispanic/Latino; 57 Two or more races, non-Hispanic/Latino), 245 international. Average age 29. 1,552 applicants, 82% accepted, 550 enrolled. Expenses: Contact institution. *Financial support:* Research assistantships with full tuition reimbursements, career-related internships or fieldwork, scholarships/grants, and unspecified assistantships available. In 2017, 646 master's, 78 doctorates, 13 other advanced degrees awarded. *Program availability:* Part-time, evening/weekend. *Application deadline:* Applications are processed on a rolling basis. *Application fee:* $40. Electronic applications accepted.

Chicago College of Performing Arts Students: 116 full-time (70 women), 7 part-time (5 women); includes 10 minority (3 Black or African American, non-Hispanic/Latino; 1 Asian, non-Hispanic/Latino; 3 Hispanic/Latino; 3 Two or more races, non-Hispanic/Latino), 31 international. Average age 25. 139 applicants, 93% accepted, 54 enrolled. Expenses: Contact institution. *Financial support:* Scholarships/grants available. In 2017, 54 master's, 13 other advanced degrees awarded. Offers brass (Diploma); brass performance (MM); classical guitar (MM, Diploma); music (MM); music composition (MM); opera (Diploma); orchestral studies (MM, Diploma); percussion (MM, Diploma); performing arts (MA, MM, Diploma); performing arts administration (MA); piano (Diploma); piano performance (MM); strings (MM, Diploma); theatre directing (MA); voice (MM); woodwinds (MM, Diploma). *Application deadline:* Applications are processed on a rolling basis. *Application fee:* $100 ($0 for international students). Electronic applications accepted. *Application Contact:* Michael Holmes, Interim Assistant Dean for Enrollment Management, 312-341-3797, E-mail: mholmes04@roosevelt.edu. *Dean*, Henry Fogel, 312-341-3782.

College of Arts and Sciences Students: 460 full-time (314 women), 253 part-time (175 women); includes 270 minority (112 Black or African American, non-Hispanic/Latino; 69 Asian, non-Hispanic/Latino; 61 Hispanic/Latino; 28 Two or more races, non-Hispanic/Latino), 115 international. Average age 28. 768 applicants, 67% accepted, 225 enrolled. Expenses: Contact institution. *Financial support:* Research assistantships, teaching assistantships, career-related internships or fieldwork, Federal Work-Study, institutionally sponsored loans, scholarships/grants, and tuition waivers (full and partial) available. Support available to part-time students. Financial award application deadline: 2/1. In 2017, 244 master's, 16 doctorates awarded. *Program availability:* Part-time, evening/weekend. Offers actuarial science (MS); arts and sciences (MA, MFA, MPA, MS, MSIMC, PhD, Psy D); biology (MS); biomedical sciences (MA); biotechnology and chemical science (MS); clinical psychology (MA, Psy D); clinical psychology - counseling practice (MA); community development and action (MA); computer science (MS); creative writing (MFA); economics (MA); history (MA); industrial/organizational psychology (MA, PhD); integrated marketing communications (MSIMC); mathematics (MS); public administration (MPA). *Application deadline:* Applications are processed on a rolling basis. *Application fee:* $40. Electronic applications accepted. *Application Contact:* Sivling Lam, Graduate Admission Counselor, 312-281-3252, E-mail: slam02@roosevelt.edu. *Dean*, Bonnie Gunzenhauser, 312-341-2074.

College of Education Students: 97 full-time (75 women), 218 part-time (159 women); includes 133 minority (68 Black or African American, non-Hispanic/Latino; 6 Asian, non-Hispanic/Latino; 51 Hispanic/Latino; 1 Native Hawaiian or other Pacific Islander, non-Hispanic/Latino; 7 Two or more races, non-Hispanic/Latino), 7 international. Average age 30. 175 applicants, 98% accepted, 103 enrolled. Expenses: Contact institution. *Financial support:* Scholarships/grants and unspecified assistantships available. In 2017, 94 master's awarded. *Program availability:* Part-time, evening/weekend. Offers clinical mental health counseling (MA); early childhood education (MA); education (MA); elementary education (MA); instructional leadership (MA); reading teacher education (MA); school counseling (MA); secondary education (MA); special education (MA); training and development (MA). *Application deadline:* Applications are processed on a rolling basis. *Application fee:* $40. Electronic applications accepted. *Application Contact:* Laura Lag, Associate Dean, 312-853-4753, E-mail: llag@roosevelt.edu. *Dean*, Tom Philion, 312-853-4780.

College of Pharmacy Students: 177 full-time (106 women), 5 part-time (4 women); includes 83 minority (20 Black or African American, non-Hispanic/Latino; 41 Asian, non-Hispanic/Latino; 15 Hispanic/Latino; 7 Two or more races, non-Hispanic/Latino), 9 international. Average age 27. 181 applicants, 100% accepted, 54 enrolled. Expenses: Contact institution. *Financial support:* Scholarships/grants available. In 2017, 59 doctorates awarded. Offers pharmacy (Pharm D). Electronic applications accepted. *Application Contact:* Angela Ryan, Associate Director of Enrollment, 847-330-4531, E-mail: aryan@roosevelt.edu. *Dean*, Melissa Hogan, 847-330-4503.

Walter E. Heller College of Business Students: 146 full-time (82 women), 378 part-time (230 women); includes 218 minority (167 Black or African American, non-Hispanic/Latino; 1 American Indian or Alaska Native, non-Hispanic/Latino; 31 Asian, non-Hispanic/Latino; 5 Hispanic/Latino; 2 Native Hawaiian or other Pacific Islander, non-Hispanic/Latino; 12 Two or more races, non-Hispanic/Latino), 83 international. Average age 30. 289 applicants, 93% accepted, 123 enrolled. Expenses: Contact institution. *Financial support:* Career-related internships or fieldwork, scholarships/grants, tuition waivers, and unspecified assistantships available. In 2017, 219 master's awarded. *Program availability:* Part-time, evening/weekend. Offers accounting (MSA); accounting forensics (MSAF); business (MA, MBA, MS, MSA, MSAF, MSHRM); business administration (MBA); hospitality and tourism management (MS); human resource management (MSHRM); organization development (MA); real estate (MS). *Application deadline:* Applications are processed on a rolling basis. *Application fee:* $40. Electronic applications accepted. *Application Contact:* Michael Conwell, Graduate Admission Counselor, 312-281-3250, E-mail: mconwell@roosevelt.edu. *Dean*, Dr. Asghar Sabbaghi, 312-281-3350.

ROSALIND FRANKLIN UNIVERSITY OF MEDICINE AND SCIENCE, North Chicago, IL 60064-3095

General Information Independent, coed, graduate-only institution. CGS member. *Graduate housing:* Rooms and/or apartments available on a first-come, first-served basis to single and married students. Housing application deadline: 3/13. *Research affiliation:* Argonne National Laboratory (medical physics), Veterans Administration Hospital (pulmonary medicine).

GRADUATE UNITS

Chicago Medical School Offers medicine (MD).

College of Health Professions *Program availability:* Part-time, online learning. Offers biomedical sciences (MS); clinical nutrition (MS); clinical psychology (MS, PhD); health professions (MS, D Sc, DNAP, DPT, PhD, TDPT, Certificate); health professions education (MS); health promotion and wellness (MS); healthcare administration and management (MS, Certificate); interprofessional studies (D Sc, PhD); nurse anesthesia (DNAP); nutrition education (MS); pathologists' assistant (MS); physical therapy (MS, DPT, TDPT); physician assistant (MS).

College of Pharmacy Offers pharmacy (Pharm D).

Dr. William M. Scholl College of Podiatric Medicine Offers podiatric medicine (DPM).

School of Graduate and Postdoctoral Studies - Interdisciplinary Graduate Program in Biomedical Sciences Offers biochemistry and molecular biology (PhD); cell biology and anatomy (PhD); cellular and molecular pharmacology (MS, PhD); microbiology and immunology (PhD); neuroscience (PhD); physiology and biophysics (MS, PhD). Electronic applications accepted.

ROSE-HULMAN INSTITUTE OF TECHNOLOGY, Terre Haute, IN 47803-3999

General Information Independent, coed, primarily men, comprehensive institution. *Enrollment:* 2,245 graduate, professional, and undergraduate students; 49 full-time matriculated graduate/professional students (15 women), 28 part-time matriculated graduate/professional students (5 women). *Enrollment by degree level:* 77 master's. *Graduate faculty:* 123 full-time (27 women), 6 part-time/adjunct (1 woman). *Tuition:* Full-time $44,847. *Required fees:* $450. *Graduate housing:* On-campus housing not available. *Student services:* Campus employment opportunities, career counseling, exercise/wellness program, free psychological counseling, international student services, low-cost health insurance, services for students with disabilities. *Library facilities:* John A. Logan Library. *Collection:* Books: 29,406 (physical), 301,291 (digital/electronic); Serial titles: 42 (physical), 41,278 (digital/electronic); Databases: 33. Weekly public service hours: 101; students can reserve study rooms.

Computer facilities: Computer purchase and lease plans are available. 48 computers available on campus for general student use. A campuswide network can be accessed from student residence rooms and from off campus. Online class registration is available.
Website: http://www.rose-hulman.edu/

General Application Contact: Dr. Craig Downing, Associate Dean of Lifelong Learning, 812-877-8822, Fax: 812-877-8061, E-mail: downing@rose-hulman.edu.

GRADUATE UNITS

Faculty of Engineering and Applied Sciences Students: 49 full-time (15 women), 28 part-time (5 women); includes 13 minority (2 Black or African American, non-Hispanic/Latino; 4 Asian, non-Hispanic/Latino; 4 Hispanic/Latino; 3 Two or more races, non-Hispanic/Latino), 33 international. Average age 24. 91 applicants, 80% accepted, 30 enrolled. *Faculty:* 123 full-time (27 women), 6 part-time/adjunct (1 woman). Expenses: Contact institution. *Financial support:* In 2017–18, 69 students received support. Fellowships with tuition reimbursements available, research assistantships with tuition reimbursements available, institutionally sponsored loans, scholarships/grants, and tuition waivers (full and partial) available. Financial award applicants required to submit FAFSA. In 2017, 41 master's awarded. *Program availability:* Part-time, evening/weekend. Offers biology and biomedical engineering (MS); chemical engineering (M Eng, MS); civil engineering (MS); electrical and computer engineering (M Eng); electrical engineering (MS); engineering and applied sciences (M Eng, MS); engineering management (M Eng, MS); environmental engineering (MS); mechanical engineering (M Eng, MS); optical engineering (MS); software engineering (MS); systems engineering and management (MS). *Application deadline:* For fall admission, 2/15 priority date for domestic and international students; for winter admission, 10/1 for domestic and international students; for spring admission, 1/15 for domestic and international students. Applications are processed on a rolling basis. *Application fee:* $0. Electronic applications accepted. *Application Contact:* Dr. Craig Downing, Associate Dean of Lifelong Learning, 812-877-8822, Fax: 812-877-8061, E-mail: downing@rose-hulman.edu.

ROSEMAN UNIVERSITY OF HEALTH SCIENCES, Henderson, NV 89014

General Information Private, coed, graduate-only institution. *Enrollment by degree level:* 18 master's, 1,027 doctoral, 30 other advanced degrees. *Graduate faculty:* 94 full-time (29 women), 64 part-time/adjunct (11 women). *Graduate housing:* On-campus housing not available. *Student services:* Campus employment opportunities, career counseling, international student services, services for students with disabilities. *Library facilities:* Roseman University Library plus 1 other. *Collection:* Books: 6,572 (physical), 1,987 (digital/electronic); Serial titles: 14 (physical), 51,469 (digital/electronic); Databases: 27. Weekly public service hours: 82.

Computer facilities: 12 computers available on campus for general student use.
Website: http://www.roseman.edu/

General Application Contact: Dr. Okeleke Nzeogwu, Director, MBA Program, 702-968-1659, E-mail: onzeogwu@roseman.edu.

GRADUATE UNITS

College of Dental Medicine - Henderson Campus Students: 30 full-time (12 women); includes 19 minority (18 Asian, non-Hispanic/Latino; 1 Hispanic/Latino). Average age 30. 92 applicants, 16% accepted, 10 enrolled. *Faculty:* 6 full-time (2 women), 6 part-time/adjunct (1 woman). Expenses: Contact institution. *Financial support:* In 2017–18, 10 students received support. Scholarships/grants available. Financial award application deadline: 6/15; financial award applicants required to submit FAFSA. In 2017, 12 other advanced degrees awarded. Offers business administration (MBA); dental medicine (Post-Doctoral Certificate). *Application deadline:* For fall admission, 1/31 for domestic and international students. *Application fee:* $50. *Application Contact:* Carol Shannon, Administrative Assistant to the Program Director, 702-968-1682, E-mail: cshannon@roseman.edu. *Program Director*, Dr. Prashanti Bollu, 702-968-5690, Fax: 702-968-5277, E-mail: pbollu@roseman.edu.

College of Dental Medicine - South Jordan, Utah Campus Students: 330 full-time (149 women); includes 109 minority (2 Black or African American, non-Hispanic/Latino; 1 American Indian or Alaska Native, non-Hispanic/Latino; 81 Asian, non-Hispanic/Latino; 17 Hispanic/Latino; 4 Native Hawaiian or other Pacific Islander, non-Hispanic/Latino; 4 Two or more races, non-Hispanic/Latino), 3 international. Average age 28. 2,270 applicants, 8% accepted, 84 enrolled. *Faculty:* 43 full-time (8 women), 41 part-time/adjunct (5 women). Expenses: Contact institution. *Financial support:* In 2017–18, 32 students received support. Federal Work-Study and tuition waivers (partial) available. Financial award application deadline: 6/15; financial award applicants required to submit FAFSA. In 2017, 77 doctorates awarded. Offers dental medicine (DMD). *Application deadline:* For fall admission, 12/1 for domestic and international students.

Applications are processed on a rolling basis. *Application fee:* $75. Electronic applications accepted. *Application Contact:* Alicia Spittle, Admissions Coordinator, 801-878-1429, E-mail: aspittle@roseman.edu. *Dean, College of Dental Medicine,* Dr. Frank W. Licari, 801-878-1400, E-mail: flicari@roseman.edu.

College of Pharmacy Students: 697 full-time (382 women); includes 414 minority (49 Black or African American, non-Hispanic/Latino; 3 American Indian or Alaska Native, non-Hispanic/Latino; 313 Asian, non-Hispanic/Latino; 29 Hispanic/Latino; 5 Native Hawaiian or other Pacific Islander, non-Hispanic/Latino; 15 Two or more races, non-Hispanic/Latino), 2 international. Average age 29. 861 applicants, 41% accepted, 241 enrolled. *Faculty:* 41 full-time (18 women), 1 part-time/adjunct (0 women). Expenses: Contact institution. *Financial support:* In 2017–18, 110 students received support. Federal Work-Study and scholarships/grants available. Financial award application deadline: 7/15; financial award applicants required to submit FAFSA. In 2017, 251 doctorates awarded. Offers pharmacy (Pharm D). *Application deadline:* For fall admission, 2/1 for domestic and international students. Applications are processed on a rolling basis. *Application fee:* $60. Electronic applications accepted. *Application Contact:* Dr. Helen Park, Assistant Dean for Admissions and Student Affairs, 702-968-5248, Fax: 702-968-1644, E-mail: hpark@roseman.edu. *Dean,* Dr. Larry Fannin, 702-968-5944, Fax: 702-990-4435, E-mail: lfannin@roseman.edu.

MBA Program Students: 18 part-time (11 women); includes 4 minority (2 Black or African American, non-Hispanic/Latino; 2 Asian, non-Hispanic/Latino). Average age 42. 5 applicants, 100% accepted, 5 enrolled. *Faculty:* 4 full-time (1 woman), 16 part-time/adjunct (5 women). Expenses: Contact institution. *Financial support:* In 2017–18, 1 student received support. Federal Work-Study and scholarships/grants available. Financial award application deadline: 5/1; financial award applicants required to submit FAFSA. In 2017, 41 master's awarded. *Program availability:* Part-time, evening/weekend. Offers business administration (MBA). *Application deadline:* For fall admission, 5/15 for domestic and international students. *Application fee:* $100. *Program Director,* Dr. Okeleke Nzeogwu, 702-968-1659, Fax: 702-968-1685, E-mail: onzeogwu@roseman.edu.

ROSEMONT COLLEGE, Rosemont, PA 19010-1699

General Information Independent-religious, coed, comprehensive institution. *Graduate housing:* Room and/or apartments available on a first-come, first-served basis to single students; on-campus housing not available to married students. Housing application deadline: 8/1.

GRADUATE UNITS

Schools of Graduate and Professional Studies *Program availability:* Part-time, evening/weekend, online learning. Offers business administration (MBA); creative writing (MFA); elementary certification (MA); human services (MA); leadership (MS); management (MS); PreK-4 (MA); publishing (MA); school counseling (MA). Electronic applications accepted.

ROWAN UNIVERSITY, Glassboro, NJ 08028-1701

General Information State-supported, coed, comprehensive institution. CGS member. *Enrollment:* 18,484 graduate, professional, and undergraduate students; 1,492 full-time matriculated graduate/professional students (770 women), 1,591 part-time matriculated graduate/professional students (1,098 women). *Enrollment by degree level:* 1,301 master's, 971 doctoral, 397 other advanced degrees. *Graduate faculty:* 238 full-time (96 women), 201 part-time/adjunct (102 women). Tuition, state resident: full-time $15,020; part-time $751 per semester hour. Tuition, nonresident: full-time $15,020; part-time $751 per semester hour. *Required fees:* $3158; $157.90 per semester hour. Tuition and fees vary according to course load, campus/location and program. *Graduate housing:* Room and/or apartments available on a first-come, first-served basis to single students; on-campus housing not available to married students. Typical cost: $7836 per year ($12,236 including board). Room and board charges vary according to board plan and housing facility selected. Housing application deadline: 5/1. *Student services:* Campus employment opportunities, campus safety program, career counseling, child daycare facilities, exercise/wellness program, free psychological counseling, international student services, low-cost health insurance, multicultural affairs office, services for students with disabilities, teacher training, writing training. *Library facilities:* Keith and Shirley Campbell Library plus 4 others. *Collection:* Books: 328,891 (physical), 494,739 (digital/electronic); Serial titles: 129,972 (digital/electronic); Databases: 846. Students can reserve study rooms.

Computer facilities: 836 computers available on campus for general student use. A campuswide network can be accessed. Online class registration is available.
Website: http://www.rowan.edu/

General Application Contact: Jeffrey Fields, College of Graduate and Continuing Education, 856-256-4747, E-mail: cgce@rowan.edu.

GRADUATE UNITS

Cooper Medical School Offers medicine (MD).

Graduate School *Program availability:* Part-time, evening/weekend. Electronic applications accepted.

College of Communication and Creative Arts *Program availability:* Part-time, evening/weekend. Offers communication and creative arts (MA, CGS); editing and publishing (CGS); integrated marketing communication and new media (CGS); public relations/advertising (MA); writing (MA); writing, composition, and rhetoric (CGS). Electronic applications accepted.

College of Education *Program availability:* Part-time, evening/weekend. Offers autism spectrum disorders (CGS); counseling in educational settings (MA); education (M Ed, MA, MST, Ed D, CAGS, CGS, Ed S, Postbaccalaureate Certificate); educational leadership (Ed D, CAGS); educational technology (CGS); ESL education (CGS); higher education administration (MA); learning disabilities (MA, CGS); principal preparation (CAGS); reading education (MA, CGS); reading/writing literacy (CGS); school administration (MA); school and public librarianship (MA); school nursing (Postbaccalaureate Certificate); school psychology (MA, Ed S); special education (MA, CGS); STEM education (MA); subject matter education (MST); supervisor (CAGS); teacher leadership (M Ed); teacher of reading (Postbaccalaureate Certificate); teacher of students with disabilities (Postbaccalaureate Certificate); teaching and learning (CGS); theatre education (MST). Electronic applications accepted.

College of Engineering *Program availability:* Part-time, evening/weekend. Offers chemical engineering (MS); civil engineering (MEM, MS); electrical engineering (MS); engineering (MEM, MS, MSE); mechanical engineering (MS). Electronic applications accepted.

College of Humanities and Social Sciences Offers criminal justice (MA); history (MA, CGS); humanities and social sciences (MA, CGS).

College of Performing Arts *Program availability:* Part-time, evening/weekend. Offers performance (MM); performing arts (MA, MM, MST); theatre arts administration (MA). Electronic applications accepted.

College of Science and Mathematics *Program availability:* Part-time, evening/weekend. Offers applied behavioral analysis (MA, CAGS); bioinformatics (MS); biological science (MS); clinical mental health counseling (MA, CAGS); computer science (MS); mathematics (MA); middle grades math education (CGS); networks (CGS); nursing (MS); pharmaceutical sciences (MS); psychology (MA, CAGS); science and mathematics (MA, MS, CAGS, CGS). Electronic applications accepted.

Rohrer College of Business *Program availability:* Part-time, evening/weekend. Offers business (MBA, CAGS, CGS); business administration (MBA). Electronic applications accepted.

School of Biomedical Science and Health Professions *Program availability:* Part-time, evening/weekend, online learning. Offers health and exercise science (MA); wellness and lifestyle management (MA). Electronic applications accepted.

School of Osteopathic Medicine Offers osteopathic medicine (DO). Electronic applications accepted.

ROYAL MILITARY COLLEGE OF CANADA, Kingston, ON K7K 7B4, Canada

General Information Federally supported, coed, university.

GRADUATE UNITS

Division of Graduate Studies and Research *Program availability:* Part-time, online learning. Electronic applications accepted.

Continuing Studies Offers business administration (MBA); defense management and policy (MA); history (PhD); war studies (MA). Electronic applications accepted.

Engineering Division Offers chemical and materials (M Eng); chemical and materials science (M Sc, PhD); chemistry (M Eng); civil engineering (M Eng, MA Sc, PhD); computer engineering (M Eng, PhD); electrical engineering (M Eng, PhD); engineering (M Eng, M Sc, MA Sc, PhD); environmental (PhD); environmental engineering (M Eng, PhD); environmental science (M Sc, PhD); mechanical engineering (M Eng, MA Sc, PhD); nuclear (PhD); nuclear engineering (M Eng, MA Sc, PhD); nuclear science (M Sc, PhD); software engineering (M Eng, PhD). Electronic applications accepted.

Science Division Offers chemical engineering (M Eng, MA Sc, PhD); chemistry (M Sc, PhD); computer science (M Sc); mathematics (M Sc); physics (M Sc); science (M Eng, M Sc, MA Sc, PhD). Electronic applications accepted.

ROYAL ROADS UNIVERSITY, Victoria, BC V9B 5Y2, Canada

General Information Province-supported, coed, upper-level institution. *Enrollment:* 3,451 full-time matriculated graduate/professional students (2,051 women). *Enrollment by degree level:* 2,891 master's, 93 doctoral, 467 other advanced degrees. *Graduate faculty:* 49 full-time, 315 part-time/adjunct. *Graduate housing:* Room and/or apartments available on a first-come, first-served basis to single students; on-campus housing not available to married students. *Student services:* Career counseling, exercise/wellness program, free psychological counseling, international student services, multicultural affairs office, services for students with disabilities. *Library facilities:* Coronel Memorial Library.

Computer facilities: A campuswide network can be accessed. Online class registration, free file storage are available.
Website: http://www.royalroads.ca/

General Application Contact: Director of Admissions/Registrar, 250-391-2511, Fax: 250-391-2522, E-mail: rruregistrar@royalroads.ca.

GRADUATE UNITS

Graduate Studies Students: 3,451 full-time (2,051 women). Average age 39. *Faculty:* 49 full-time, 315 part-time/adjunct. Expenses: Contact institution. *Financial support:* Federal Work-Study, institutionally sponsored loans, scholarships/grants, and bursaries available. Support available to part-time students. In 2017, 2,891 master's, 88 doctorates, 472 other advanced degrees awarded. *Program availability:* Blended/hybrid learning. Offers conflict analysis (G Dip); conflict analysis and management (MA); disaster and emergency management (MA, G Dip); environment and management (M Sc, MA); environment and sustainability (MAIS); environmental education and communication (MA, G Dip, Graduate Certificate); human security and peacebuilding (MA, G Dip); justice studies (G Dip); peace and conflict studies (MAIS); tourism management (MA, Graduate Certificate). *Application deadline:* Applications are processed on a rolling basis. *Application fee:* $120 ($240 for international students). Electronic applications accepted. *Application Contact:* E-mail: admissions@royalroads.ca. *Director of Admissions/Registrar,* Peter Dueck.

RUSH UNIVERSITY, Chicago, IL 60612-3832

General Information Independent, coed, upper-level institution. CGS member. *Graduate housing:* Rooms and/or apartments available on a first-come, first-served basis to single and married students.

GRADUATE UNITS

College of Health Sciences Expenses: Contact institution. *Financial support:* Career-related internships or fieldwork, Federal Work-Study, institutionally sponsored loans, and scholarships/grants available. Support available to part-time students. Financial award application deadline: 4/1; financial award applicants required to submit FAFSA. *Program availability:* Part-time. Offers audiology (Au D); clinical laboratory management (MS); clinical nutrition (MS); health sciences (MS, Au D, OTD, PhD); health systems management (MS, PhD); medical laboratory science (MS); occupational therapy (OTD); perfusion technology (MS); physician assistant studies (MS); respiratory care (MS); speech-language pathology (MS). Electronic applications accepted. *Application Contact:* 312-942-7120, E-mail: chs_admissions@rush.edu.

College of Nursing Students: 424 full-time (351 women), 710 part-time (634 women); includes 292 minority (69 Black or African American, non-Hispanic/Latino; 1 American Indian or Alaska Native, non-Hispanic/Latino; 93 Asian, non-Hispanic/Latino; 104 Hispanic/Latino; 25 Two or more races, non-Hispanic/Latino). 771 applicants, 57% accepted, 323 enrolled. *Faculty:* 73 full-time (68 women), 76 part-time/adjunct (70 women). Expenses: Contact institution. *Financial support:* Research assistantships, teaching assistantships, Federal Work-Study, scholarships/grants, traineeships, and health care benefits available. Support available to part-time students. Financial award application deadline: 3/1; financial award applicants required to submit FAFSA. In 2017, 154 master's, 190 doctorates, 13 other advanced degrees awarded. *Program availability:* 100% online, blended/hybrid learning. Offers adult gerontology acute care clinical nurse specialist (DNP); adult gerontology acute care nurse practitioner (DNP, Post-Graduate Certificate); adult gerontology primary care nurse practitioner (DNP); advanced public health nursing (DNP); clinical nurse leader (MSN); family nurse practitioner (DNP); neonatal clinical nurse specialist (DNP); neonatal nurse practitioner (DNP, Post-Graduate Certificate); nurse anesthesia (DNP); nursing (MSN, DNP, PhD, Post-Graduate Certificate); nursing science (PhD); pediatric acute care nurse practitioner (DNP, Post-Graduate Certificate); pediatric clinical nurse specialist (DNP); pediatric primary care nurse practitioner (DNP); psychiatric mental health nurse practitioner (DNP); transformative leadership: population health (DNP); transformative leadership: systems (DNP). *Application deadline:* For fall admission, 1/2 for domestic students; for spring admission, 8/1 for domestic students; for summer admission, 12/1 for domestic students. Applications are processed on a rolling basis. *Application fee:* $110. Electronic applications accepted. *Application Contact:* Jennifer Thorndyke, Director of Admissions, 312-563-7526, E-mail: jennifer_thorndyke@rush.edu. *Dean*, Dr. Marquis Foreman, 312-942-7117, E-mail: marquis_d_foreman@rush.edu.

Graduate College *Program availability:* Part-time. Offers physiology (PhD). Electronic applications accepted.

Division of Anatomy and Cell Biology Offers anatomy and cell biology (MS, PhD). Electronic applications accepted.

Division of Biochemistry Offers biochemistry (MS, PhD). Electronic applications accepted.

Division of Immunology and Microbiology Offers immunology (MS, PhD); microbiology (PhD); virology (MS, PhD).

Division of Medical Physics Offers medical physics (MS, PhD). Electronic applications accepted.

Division of Neuroscience Offers neuroscience (MS, PhD). Electronic applications accepted.

Division of Pharmacology Offers clinical research (MS); pharmacology (MS, PhD).

Rush Medical College Students: 527 full-time (250 women); includes 195 minority (28 Black or African American, non-Hispanic/Latino; 114 Asian, non-Hispanic/Latino; 37 Hispanic/Latino; 16 Two or more races, non-Hispanic/Latino). Average age 26. 5,347 applicants, 6% accepted, 136 enrolled. *Faculty:* 1,246 full-time (539 women), 239 part-time/adjunct (104 women). Expenses: Contact institution. *Financial support:* In 2017–18, 273 students received support. Federal Work-Study, institutionally sponsored loans, and scholarships/grants available. Financial award application deadline: 3/1; financial award applicants required to submit FAFSA. In 2017, 116 doctorates awarded. Offers medicine (MD). *Application deadline:* For fall admission, 11/1 for domestic students. Applications are processed on a rolling basis. *Application fee:* $100. Electronic applications accepted. *Application Contact:* E-mail: rmc_admissions@rush.edu. *Assistant Dean, Admissions and Recruitment*, Dr. Cynthia E. Boyd, 312-942-6915, E-mail: rmc_admissions@rush.edu.

RUTGERS UNIVERSITY–CAMDEN, Camden, NJ 08102-1401

General Information State-supported, coed, university. *Graduate housing:* Rooms and/or apartments available to single and married students.

GRADUATE UNITS

Graduate School of Arts and Sciences *Program availability:* Part-time, evening/weekend. Offers American and public history (MA); biology (MS); chemistry (MS); childhood studies (MA, PhD); computational and integrative biology (MS, PhD); computer science (MS); creative writing (MFA); criminal justice (MA); education policy and leadership (MPA); English (MA); industrial mathematics (MBS); industrial/applied mathematics (MS); international public service and development (MPA); liberal studies (MALS); mathematical computer science (MS); physical therapy (DPT); psychology (MA); public management (MPA); pure mathematics (MS); teaching in mathematical sciences (MS). Electronic applications accepted.

School of Business *Program availability:* Part-time, evening/weekend. Offers business (MBA). Electronic applications accepted.

School of Law *Program availability:* Part-time, evening/weekend. Offers law (JD). JD/MCRP, JD/MA, JD/MPA, JD/MSW, JD/MS offered jointly with Rutgers, The State University of New Jersey, New Brunswick; JD/MPA, JD/MD, JD/DO with University of Medicine and Dentistry of New Jersey. Electronic applications accepted.

School of Nursing–Camden Offers adult gerontology primary care nurse practitioner (DNP); family nurse practitioner (DNP).

School of Public Health *Program availability:* Part-time, evening/weekend. Offers general public health (Certificate); health systems and policy (MPH). Electronic applications accepted.

RUTGERS UNIVERSITY–NEWARK, Newark, NJ 07102

General Information State-supported, coed, university. CGS member. *Graduate housing:* Room and/or apartments available to single students; on-campus housing not available to married students. Housing application deadline: 5/15.

GRADUATE UNITS

Graduate School *Program availability:* Part-time, evening/weekend. Offers accounting (PhD); accounting information systems (PhD); American political system (MA); American studies (MA, PhD); analytical chemistry (MS, PhD); applied physics (MS, PhD); biochemistry (MS, PhD); biology (MS, PhD); cognitive neuroscience (PhD); cognitive science (PhD); computational biology (MS); computer information systems (PhD); creative writing (MFA); economics (MA); English (MA); environmental geology (MS); environmental science (MS, PhD); finance (PhD); health care administration (MPA); history (MA, MAT); human resources administration (MPA); information technology (PhD); inorganic chemistry (MS, PhD); international business (PhD); international relations (MA); jazz history and research (MA); management science (PhD); marketing (PhD); mathematical sciences (PhD); organic chemistry (MS, PhD); organization management (PhD); perception (PhD); physical chemistry (MS, PhD); psychobiology (PhD); public administration (PhD); public management (MPA); public policy analysis (MPA); social cognition (PhD); urban systems (PhD); urban systems and issues (MPA). Electronic applications accepted.

Division of Global Affairs *Program availability:* Part-time, evening/weekend. Offers global affairs (MS, PhD). Electronic applications accepted.

Graduate School of Biomedical Sciences *Program availability:* Part-time, evening/weekend. Offers biochemistry and molecular biology (MS, PhD); biodefense (Certificate); biomedical engineering (PhD); biomedical sciences (interdisciplinary) (PhD); biomedical sciences (multidisciplinary) (PhD); cell biology and molecular medicine (PhD); cellular biology, neuroscience and physiology (PhD); infection, immunity and inflammation (PhD); integrative neuroscience (PhD); microbiology and molecular genetics (PhD); molecular biology, genetics and cancer (PhD); molecular pathology and immunology (PhD); neuroscience (Certificate); pharmacological sciences (Certificate); pharmacology and physiology (PhD); stem cell (Certificate). PhD in biomedical engineering offered jointly with New Jersey Institute of Technology. Electronic applications accepted.

School of Criminal Justice Offers criminal justice (MA, PhD). Electronic applications accepted.

New Jersey Medical School Offers medicine (MD). Electronic applications accepted.

Rutgers Business School–Newark and New Brunswick *Program availability:* Part-time, evening/weekend. Offers accountancy (M Accy); accounting (PhD); accounting information systems (PhD); business (MBA, MFA, MHSM, MIT, MRE); business administration (MBA); business of fashion (MBA); economics (PhD); finance (PhD); financial analysis (MFA); healthcare services management (MHSM); individualized study (PhD); information technology (PhD); international business (PhD); management science (PhD); marketing science (PhD); organizational management (PhD); pharmaceutical management (MBA); professional accounting (MBA); quantitative finance (MQF); real estate and logistics (MRE); science, technology and management (PhD); supply chain management (PhD). Electronic applications accepted.

Rutgers School of Dental Medicine Offers dental science (MS); dentistry (DMD); endodontics (Certificate); oral medicine (Certificate); orthodontics (Certificate); pediatric dentistry (Certificate); periodontics (Certificate); prosthodontics (Certificate). DMD/MPH offered jointly with New Jersey Institute of Technology, Rutgers, The State University of New Jersey, Camden. Electronic applications accepted.

Rutgers School of Nursing *Program availability:* Part-time. Offers adult health (MSN); adult occupational health (MSN); advanced practice nursing (MSN, Post Master's Certificate); family nurse practitioner (MSN); nurse anesthesia (MSN); nursing (MSN); nursing informatics (MSN); urban health (PhD); women's health practitioner (MSN). Electronic applications accepted.

School of Health Related Professions *Program availability:* Part-time. Offers biomedical informatics (MS, PhD); clinical laboratory sciences (MS); clinical nutrition (MS, DCN); community counseling (MS); dietetic internship (Certificate); health care informatics (Certificate); health care management (MS); health related professions (MS, DCN, DPT, PhD, Certificate); health sciences (MS, PhD); nutrition (PhD); physical therapy (DPT); physician assistant (MS); psychiatric rehabilitation (MS, PhD); radiologist assistant (MS); rehabilitation counseling (MS). Electronic applications accepted.

School of Law *Program availability:* Part-time, evening/weekend. Offers law (JD). JD/MCRP, JD/PhD offered jointly with Rutgers, The State University of New Jersey, New Brunswick.

School of Public Health *Program availability:* Part-time, evening/weekend. Offers clinical epidemiology (Certificate); dental public health (MPH); general public health (Certificate); public policy and oral health services administration (Certificate); quantitative methods (MPH); urban health (MPH). Electronic applications accepted.

RUTGERS UNIVERSITY–NEW BRUNSWICK, Piscataway, NJ 08854-8097

General Information State-supported, coed, university. CGS member. *Graduate housing:* Rooms and/or apartments available to single and married students.

GRADUATE UNITS

Edward J. Bloustein School of Planning and Public Policy *Program availability:* Part-time, evening/weekend, online learning. Offers planning and public policy (MCRP, MCRS, MPAP, MPH, MPP, Dr PH, PhD); public policy (MPAP, MPP); urban planning and policy development (MCRP, MCRS). Electronic applications accepted.

Ernest Mario School of Pharmacy Offers medicinal chemistry (MS, PhD); pharmaceutical science (MS, PhD); pharmacy (Pharm D). Electronic applications accepted.

Graduate School-New Brunswick *Program availability:* Part-time, evening/weekend, online learning. Offers African-American history (PhD); air pollution and resources (MS, PhD); American politics (PhD); anthropology (MA, PhD); applied mathematics (MS, PhD); applied statistics (MS); aquatic biology (MS, PhD); aquatic chemistry (MS, PhD); art history (MA, PhD); astronomy (MS, PhD); atmospheric science (MS, PhD); behavioral neuroscience (PhD); bilingualism and second language acquisition (MA, PhD); biochemistry (PhD); biological chemistry (MS, PhD); biophysics (PhD); biostatistics (MS); cell and developmental biology (MS, PhD); chemical and biochemical engineering (MS, PhD); chemistry and physics of aerosol and hydrosol systems (MS, PhD); civil and environmental engineering (MS, PhD); classics (MA, MAT, PhD); clinical psychology (PhD); cognitive psychology (PhD); communications and solid-state electronics (MS, PhD); comparative literature (MA, PhD); comparative politics (PhD); computational biology and molecular biophysics (PhD); computer engineering (MS, PhD); computer science (MS, PhD); condensed matter physics (MS, PhD); control systems (MS, PhD); cultural heritage and preservation studies (MA); curatorial studies (Certificate); data mining (MS); design and control (MS, PhD); digital signal processing (MS, PhD); early American history (PhD); early modern European history (PhD); east Asian history (PhD); East Asian languages and cultures (MA); ecology and evolution (MS, PhD); economics (MA, PhD); elementary particle physics (MS, PhD); endocrinology and animal biosciences (MS, PhD); entomology (MS, PhD); environmental chemistry (MS, PhD); environmental microbiology (MS, PhD); environmental toxicology (MS, PhD); exposure assessment (PhD); fate and effects of pollutants (MS, PhD); fluid mechanics (MS, PhD); food and business economics (MS); food science (M Phil, MS, PhD); French (MA, PhD); French studies (MAT); geography (MA, MS, PhD); geological sciences (MS, PhD); German (MAT, PhD); German literature (MA, PhD); global and comparative history (PhD); historic preservation (Certificate); history (PhD); history of diplomacy and foreign relations (PhD); history of technology, environment and health (PhD); history of the Atlantic cultures and African diaspora (PhD); horticulture and plant technology (MS, PhD); industrial and systems engineering (MS, PhD); industrial-occupational toxicology (MS, PhD); information technology (MS); inorganic chemistry (MS, PhD); interdisciplinary classical studies and ancient history (MA, PhD); interdisciplinary health psychology (PhD); intermediate energy nuclear physics (MS); international relations (PhD); Italian (MA, PhD); Italian literature and literary criticism (MA); Jewish studies (MA, Certificate); language, literature and culture (MAT); Latin American history (PhD); linguistics (PhD); literatures in English (PhD); manufacturing systems engineering (MS); materials science and engineering (MS, PhD); mathematics (MS, PhD); mechanics (MS, PhD); medieval history (PhD); microbiology and molecular genetics (MS, PhD); modern European history (PhD); molecular and cellular biology (MS, PhD); nineteenth and twentieth century American history (PhD); nuclear physics (MS, PhD); nutritional sciences (MS, PhD); nutritional toxicology (MS, PhD); oceanography (MS, PhD); operations research (PhD); organic chemistry (MS, PhD); organismal and population biology (MS, PhD); pharmaceutical toxicology (MS, PhD); philosophy (PhD); physical chemistry (MS, PhD); physics (MST); plant pathology (MS, PhD); political theory (PhD); pollution prevention and control (MS, PhD); public law (PhD); quality and productivity management (MS); quality and reliability engineering (MS); religious studies (MA, Graduate Certificate); social psychology (PhD); sociology (MA, PhD); solid mechanics (MS, PhD); Spanish (MA, MAT, PhD); Spanish literature (MA, PhD); statistics (MS, PhD); surface science (PhD); theoretical physics (MS, PhD); thermal sciences (MS, PhD); translation (MA); United Nations and global policy studies (MA); water and wastewater treatment (MS, PhD); water resources (MS, PhD); women and politics (PhD); women's and gender history (PhD); women's and gender studies (MA, PhD).

Graduate School of Applied and Professional Psychology Offers applied and professional psychology (Psy M, Psy D); clinical psychology (Psy M, Psy D); school psychology (Psy M, Psy D). Electronic applications accepted.

Graduate School of Biomedical Sciences Offers biochemistry (MS, PhD); biochemistry and molecular biology (MS, PhD); biomedical engineering (MS, PhD); biomedical science (MS); biomedical sciences (MBS, MS, PhD); cellular and molecular pharmacology (MS, PhD); clinical and translational science (MS); environmental sciences/exposure assessment (PhD); exposure science and assessment (PhD); microbiology and molecular genetics (MS, PhD); molecular genetics, microbiology and immunology (MS, PhD); neuroscience (MS, PhD); physiology and integrative biology (MS, PhD); toxicology (PhD). Electronic applications accepted.

Graduate School of Education *Program availability:* Part-time, evening/weekend. Offers college student affairs (Ed M); early childhood/elementary education (Ed M, Ed D); education (Ed M, Ed D, PhD); educational administration and supervision (Ed M, Ed D); educational policy (PhD); educational psychology (PhD); educational statistics, measurement and evaluation (Ed M); English as a second language education (Ed M); English education (Ed M); language education (Ed M, Ed D); learning, cognition and development (Ed M); literacy education (Ed M, Ed D, PhD); mathematics education (Ed M, Ed D, PhD); reading education (Ed M); school counseling and counseling psychology (Ed M); science education (Ed M, Ed D); social and philosophical foundations of education (Ed M, Ed D); social studies education (Ed M, Ed D); special education (Ed M, Ed D). Electronic applications accepted.

Mason Gross School of the Arts *Program availability:* Part-time. Offers acting (MFA); arts (MFA, MM, DMA, AD); collaborative piano (MM, DMA); conducting: choral (MM, DMA); conducting: instrumental (MM, DMA); conducting: orchestral (MM, DMA); design (MFA); drawing (MFA); jazz studies (MM); music (DMA, AD); music education (MM, DMA); music performance (MM); painting (MFA); playwriting (MFA); sculpture (MFA); stage management (MFA); technical direction (MFA); visual arts (MFA).

Robert Wood Johnson Medical School Offers medicine (MD). Electronic applications accepted.

School of Communication and Information *Program availability:* Part-time, online learning. Offers communication and information (MCIS, MI, MLS, PhD); communication and information studies (MCIS); communication, information and library studies (PhD); information (MI). Electronic applications accepted.

School of Management and Labor Relations *Program availability:* Part-time, evening/weekend. Offers human resource management (MHRM); industrial relations and human resources (PhD); labor and employment relations (MLER). Electronic applications accepted.

School of Public Health *Program availability:* Part-time, evening/weekend. Offers biostatistics (MPH, MS, Dr PH, PhD); clinical epidemiology (Certificate); environmental and occupational health (MPH, Dr PH, PhD, Certificate); epidemiology (MPH, Dr PH, PhD); general public health (Certificate); health education and behavioral science (MPH, Dr PH, PhD); health systems and policy (MPH, PhD); public health (MPH, Dr PH, PhD); public health preparedness (Certificate). Electronic applications accepted.

School of Social Work *Program availability:* Part-time. Offers social work (MSW, PhD). Electronic applications accepted.

RYERSON UNIVERSITY, Toronto, ON M5B 2K3, Canada

General Information Province-supported, coed, comprehensive institution. CGS member.

GRADUATE UNITS

School of Graduate Studies Offers photographic preservation and collections management (MA).

Ted Rogers School of Management Offers global business administration (MBA); management (MSM); management of technology and innovation (MBA).

SACRED HEART MAJOR SEMINARY, Detroit, MI 48206-1799

General Information Independent-religious, coed, comprehensive institution. *Graduate housing:* Room and/or apartments guaranteed to single students; on-campus housing not available to married students. Housing application deadline: 8/1.

GRADUATE UNITS

School of Theology *Program availability:* Part-time, evening/weekend. Offers pastoral studies (MAPS); theology (M Div, MA).

SACRED HEART SEMINARY AND SCHOOL OF THEOLOGY, Hales Corners, WI 53130-0429

General Information Independent-religious, coed, primarily men, graduate-only institution. *Graduate housing:* Room and/or apartments guaranteed to single students; on-campus housing not available to married students.

GRADUATE UNITS

Graduate and Professional Programs *Program availability:* Part-time. Offers priestly formation (Certificate); theology (M Div, MA).

SACRED HEART UNIVERSITY, Fairfield, CT 06825

General Information Independent-religious, coed, comprehensive institution. *Enrollment:* 8,543 graduate, professional, and undergraduate students; 1,074 full-time matriculated graduate/professional students (725 women), 1,769 part-time matriculated graduate/professional students (1,352 women). *Enrollment by degree level:* 2,226 master's, 377 doctoral, 240 other advanced degrees. *Graduate faculty:* 146 full-time (81 women), 152 part-time/adjunct (86 women). *Tuition:* Full-time $28,114; part-time $739 per credit. *Graduate housing:* On-campus housing not available. *Student services:* Campus employment opportunities, campus safety program, career counseling, exercise/wellness program, free psychological counseling, international student services, low-cost health insurance, multicultural affairs office, services for students with disabilities, teacher training, writing training. *Library facilities:* Ryan Matura Library plus 1 other. *Collection:* Books: 89,498 (physical), 205,348 (digital/electronic); Serial titles: 400 (physical), 52,686 (digital/electronic); Databases: 135. Weekly public service hours: 119; students can reserve study rooms.

Computer facilities: 499 computers available on campus for general student use. A campuswide network can be accessed from student residence rooms and from off campus. Online class registration is available.
Website: http://www.sacredheart.edu/

General Application Contact: Tara Chudy, Executive Director of Graduate Admissions, 203-365-7619, E-mail: gradstudies@sacredheart.edu.

GRADUATE UNITS

Graduate Programs Students: 1,150 full-time (734 women), 1,849 part-time (1,416 women); includes 493 minority (187 Black or African American, non-Hispanic/Latino; 6 American Indian or Alaska Native, non-Hispanic/Latino; 75 Asian, non-Hispanic/Latino; 205 Hispanic/Latino; 2 Native Hawaiian or other Pacific Islander, non-Hispanic/Latino; 18 Two or more races, non-Hispanic/Latino), 473 international. Average age 32. 4,320 applicants, 48% accepted, 874 enrolled. *Faculty:* 134 full-time (74 women), 158 part-time/adjunct (92 women). Expenses: Contact institution. *Financial support:* Unspecified assistantships available. Financial award applicants required to submit FAFSA. In 2017, 1,101 master's, 74 doctorates, 92 other advanced degrees awarded. *Program availability:* Part-time, evening/weekend, online learning. *Application deadline:* Applications are processed on a rolling basis. *Application fee:* $75. Electronic applications accepted. *Application Contact:* Tara Chudy, Executive Director of Graduate Admissions. *Provost and Vice President for Academic Affairs*, Rupendra Paliwal, 203-371-7851, E-mail: paliwalr@sacredheart.edu.

College of Arts and Sciences Students: 250 full-time (110 women), 324 part-time (189 women); includes 124 minority (53 Black or African American, non-Hispanic/Latino; 1 American Indian or Alaska Native, non-Hispanic/Latino; 3 Asian, non-Hispanic/Latino; 60 Hispanic/Latino; 7 Two or more races, non-Hispanic/Latino), 175 international. Average age 28. 676 applicants, 85% accepted, 188 enrolled. *Faculty:* 44 full-time (20 women), 25 part-time/adjunct (6 women). Expenses: Contact institution. *Financial support:* Unspecified assistantships available. Financial award applicants required to submit FAFSA. In 2017, 412 master's awarded. Offers applied psychology (MS); arts and sciences (MA, MA Comm, MPA, MS, MSW); bioinformatics (MS); chemistry (MS); computer science (MS); computer science gaming (MS); corporate communications and public relations (MA Comm); criminal justice (MA); cybersecurity (MS); digital multimedia journalism (MA Comm); digital multimedia production (MA Comm); film and television production (MA); information technology (MS); media literacy and digital culture (MA); molecular biology (MS); public administration (MPA); social work (MSW); sports communication and media (MA). *Application deadline:* Applications are processed on a rolling basis. *Application fee:* $75. Electronic applications accepted. *Application Contact:* Pam Pillo, Executive Director of Graduate Admissions, 203-365-7619, E-mail: gradstudies@sacredheart.edu. *Dean of College of Arts and Sciences*, Robin Cautin, 203-396-8020, E-mail: cautinr@sacredheart.edu.

College of Health Professions Students: 435 full-time (340 women), 39 part-time (27 women); includes 83 minority (18 Black or African American, non-Hispanic/Latino; 2 American Indian or Alaska Native, non-Hispanic/Latino; 27 Asian, non-Hispanic/Latino; 29 Hispanic/Latino; 7 Two or more races, non-Hispanic/Latino), 34 international. Average age 25. 1,951 applicants, 21% accepted, 233 enrolled. *Faculty:* 39 full-time (23 women), 51 part-time/adjunct (37 women). Expenses: Contact institution. *Financial support:* Research assistantships and unspecified assistantships available. Financial award applicants required to submit FAFSA. In 2017, 120 master's, 62 doctorates awarded. *Program availability:* Part-time, evening/weekend, 100% online, blended/hybrid learning. Offers exercise science and nutrition (MS); health professions (MPAS, MPH, MS, MSOT, DPT); healthcare informatics (MS); occupational therapy (MSOT); physical therapy (DPT); physician assistant studies (MPAS); public health (MPH); speech-language pathology (MS). *Application deadline:* Applications are processed on a rolling basis. *Application fee:* $75. Electronic applications accepted. *Application Contact:* Tara Chudy, Executive Director of Graduate Admissions, 203-365-4735, Fax: 203-365-4732, E-mail: chudyt@sacredheart.edu. *Dean*, Dr. Patricia Walker, 203-396-8024, Fax: 203-396-8075, E-mail: walkerp@sacredheart.edu.

College of Nursing Students: 21 full-time (20 women), 692 part-time (650 women); includes 136 minority (52 Black or African American, non-Hispanic/Latino; 2 American Indian or Alaska Native, non-Hispanic/Latino; 29 Asian, non-Hispanic/Latino; 46 Hispanic/Latino; 7 Two or more races, non-Hispanic/Latino). Average age 37. 70 applicants, 69% accepted, 32 enrolled. *Faculty:* 17 full-time (all women), 29 part-time/adjunct (26 women). Expenses: Contact institution. *Financial support:* Unspecified assistantships available. Financial award applicants required to submit FAFSA. In 2017, 260 master's, 16 doctorates awarded. *Program availability:* Part-time, evening/weekend, 100% online, blended/hybrid learning. Offers clinical (DNP); clinical nurse leader (MSN); family nurse practitioner (MSN, Post-Master's Certificate); leadership (DNP); nursing education (MSN); nursing management and executive leadership (MSN). *Application deadline:* For fall admission, 2/15 for domestic and international students. Applications are processed on a rolling basis. *Application fee:* $75. Electronic applications accepted. *Application Contact:* Tara Chudy, Executive Director of Graduate Admissions, 203-365-4735, Fax: 203-365-4732, E-mail: chudyt@sacredheart.edu. *Dean of Nursing*, Mary Alice Donius, 203-365-4508, E-mail: doniusm@sacredheart.edu.

Isabelle Farrington College of Education Students: 217 full-time (174 women), 503 part-time (383 women); includes 105 minority (33 Black or African American, non-Hispanic/Latino; 1 American Indian or Alaska Native, non-Hispanic/Latino; 8 Asian, non-Hispanic/Latino; 54 Hispanic/Latino; 9 Two or more races, non-Hispanic/Latino), 2 international. Average age 34. 261 applicants, 97% accepted, 222 enrolled. *Faculty:* 22 full-time (13 women), 29 part-time/adjunct (12 women). Expenses: Contact institution. *Financial support:* Teaching assistantships with partial tuition reimbursements and unspecified assistantships available. Financial award applicants required to submit FAFSA. In 2017, 183 master's, 4 other advanced degrees awarded. *Program availability:* Part-time, evening/weekend. Offers advanced studies in administration (Professional Certificate); advanced studies in literacy (Professional Certificate); education (M Ed, MAT, Professional Certificate); teaching: education (MAT). *Application deadline:* Applications are processed on a rolling basis. *Application fee:* $75. Electronic applications accepted. *Application Contact:* Tara Chudy, Executive Director of Graduate Admissions, 203-365-4735, E-mail: chudyt@sacredheart.edu. *Dean*, Dr. Michael Alfano, 203-365-7621, Fax: 203-365-7513, E-mail: alfanom3@sacredheart.edu.

Jack Welch College of Business Students: 151 full-time (81 women), 211 part-time (103 women); includes 70 minority (21 Black or African American, non-Hispanic/Latino; 1 American Indian or Alaska Native, non-Hispanic/Latino; 11 Asian, non-Hispanic/Latino; 33 Hispanic/Latino; 4 Two or more races, non-Hispanic/Latino), 94 international. Average age 30. 291 applicants, 91% accepted, 143 enrolled. *Faculty:* 28 full-time (8 women), 20 part-time/adjunct (7 women). Expenses: Contact institution. *Financial support:* Unspecified assistantships available. Financial award applicants required to submit FAFSA. In 2017, 140 master's awarded. *Program availability:* Part-time, evening/weekend. Offers accounting (MBA, MS, Graduate Certificate); administration (MBA, DBA); business (MBA, MS, DBA, Graduate Certificate); digital marketing (MS); finance (MBA, Graduate Certificate); finance and investment management (MS); human resource management (MS, Graduate Certificate); management (Graduate Certificate); marketing (MBA, Graduate Certificate). *Application deadline:* Applications are processed on a rolling basis. *Application fee:* $75. Electronic applications accepted. *Application Contact:* Pam Pillo, Executive Director of Graduate Admissions, 203-365-7610, E-mail: gradstudies@sacredheart.edu. *Dean*, Dr. John Chalykoff, 203-396-8084, Fax: 203-365-7538, E-mail: chalykoffj@sacredheart.edu.

SAGE GRADUATE SCHOOL, Troy, NY 12180-4115

General Information Independent, coed, graduate-only institution. *Enrollment by degree level:* 871 master's, 229 doctoral, 94 other advanced degrees. *Graduate faculty:* 58 full-time (49 women), 55 part-time/adjunct (41 women). Tuition and fees vary according to degree level and program. *Graduate housing:* Room and/or apartments available on a first-come, first-served basis to single students; on-campus housing not available to married students. Typical cost: $6430 per year ($12,618 including board). Room and board charges vary according to board plan and housing facility selected. Housing application deadline: 5/1. *Student services:* Career counseling. *Library facilities:* James Wheelock Clark Library plus 1 other. *Collection:* Books: 194,209 (physical), 160,067 (digital/electronic); Serial titles: 245 (physical), 63,276 (digital/electronic); Databases: 105. Weekly public service hours: 65; students can reserve study rooms. *Research affiliation:* Rensselaer Polytechnic Institute (education), St. Peter's Hospital (health care services), University at Albany, State University of New York (public health, health and the environment), Albany Medical College (health care services), National Center for Adaptive Neurotechnologies (NCAN).

Computer facilities: 441 computers available on campus for general student use. Online class registration is available.
Website: http://www.sage.edu/

General Application Contact: Wendy D. Diefendorf, Director of Graduate and Adult Admission, 518-244-2443, Fax: 518-244-6880, E-mail: sgsadm@sage.edu.

GRADUATE UNITS

Esteves School of Education Students: 81 full-time (73 women), 323 part-time (252 women); includes 118 minority (51 Black or African American, non-Hispanic/Latino; 1 American Indian or Alaska Native, non-Hispanic/Latino; 19 Asian, non-Hispanic/Latino; 42 Hispanic/Latino; 1 Native Hawaiian or other Pacific Islander, non-Hispanic/Latino; 4 Two or more races, non-Hispanic/Latino). Average age 33. 432 applicants, 48% accepted, 139 enrolled. *Faculty:* 15 full-time (12 women), 22 part-time/adjunct (14 women). Expenses: Contact institution. *Financial support:* Fellowships, research assistantships, scholarships/grants, and unspecified assistantships available. Financial award application deadline: 3/1; financial award applicants required to submit FAFSA. In 2017, 131 master's, 35 doctorates, 8 other advanced degrees awarded. *Program availability:* Part-time, evening/weekend. Offers applied behavior analysis and autism (MS, Post Master's Certificate); childhood education/literacy (MS); childhood special education (MS Ed); education (MS, MS Ed, Ed D, Post Master's Certificate); educational leadership (Ed D); literacy (MS Ed); literacy/childhood special education (MS Ed); school counseling (MS, Post Master's Certificate); school health education (MS); special education (MS Ed). *Application deadline:* Applications are processed on a rolling basis. *Application fee:* $30. Electronic applications accepted. *Application Contact:* Wendy D. Diefendorf, Director of Graduate and Adult Admission, 518-244-2443, Fax: 518-244-6880, E-mail: diefew@sage.edu. *Interim Dean, Esteves School of Education,* Dr. John Pelizza, 518-244-2051, Fax: 518-244-2334, E-mail: pelizj@sage.edu.

School of Health Sciences Students: 311 full-time (262 women), 337 part-time (308 women); includes 108 minority (38 Black or African American, non-Hispanic/Latino; 4 American Indian or Alaska Native, non-Hispanic/Latino; 25 Asian, non-Hispanic/Latino; 25 Hispanic/Latino; 16 Two or more races, non-Hispanic/Latino), 4 international. Average age 31. 927 applicants, 31% accepted, 199 enrolled. *Faculty:* 39 full-time (35 women), 28 part-time/adjunct (26 women). Expenses: Contact institution. *Financial support:* Fellowships, research assistantships, scholarships/grants, and unspecified assistantships available. Financial award application deadline: 3/1; financial award applicants required to submit FAFSA. In 2017, 154 master's, 42 doctorates, 32 other advanced degrees awarded. *Program availability:* Part-time, evening/weekend. Offers adult gerontology nurse practitioner (MS, Certificate); applied nutrition (MS); community psychology (MA); counseling and community psychology (MA); dietetic internship (Certificate); education and leadership (DNS); family nurse practitioner (MS); forensic mental health (MS, Certificate); health sciences (MA, MS, DNS, DPT, Certificate, Post Master's Certificate, Postbaccalaureate Certificate); nursing (MS, DNS, Certificate, Post Master's Certificate); nutrition (Certificate); occupational therapy (MS); physical therapy (DPT); psychiatric mental health nurse practitioner (MS, Post Master's Certificate); psychology (MA, Certificate). *Application deadline:* Applications are processed on a rolling basis. *Application fee:* $30. Electronic applications accepted. *Application Contact:* Wendy D. Diefendorf, Director of Graduate and Adult Admission, 518-244-2443, Fax: 518-244-6880, E-mail: diefew@sage.edu. *Dean, School of Health Sciences,* Dr. Theresa Hand, 518-244-2264, Fax: 518-244-4571, E-mail: handt@sage.edu.

School of Management Students: 46 full-time (33 women), 96 part-time (74 women); includes 29 minority (15 Black or African American, non-Hispanic/Latino; 1 American Indian or Alaska Native, non-Hispanic/Latino; 6 Asian, non-Hispanic/Latino; 7 Hispanic/Latino), 3 international. Average age 32. 124 applicants, 49% accepted, 30 enrolled. *Faculty:* 5 full-time (3 women), 5 part-time/adjunct (1 woman). Expenses: Contact institution. *Financial support:* Fellowships, research assistantships, and unspecified assistantships available. Financial award application deadline: 3/1; financial award applicants required to submit FAFSA. In 2017, 60 master's awarded. *Program availability:* Part-time, evening/weekend. Offers business administration (MBA); gerontology (MS); management (MBA, MS); organization management (MS). *Application deadline:* Applications are processed on a rolling basis. *Application fee:* $30. Electronic applications accepted. *Application Contact:* Wendy D. Diefendorf, Director of Graduate and Adult Admission, 518-244-2443, Fax: 518-244-6880, E-mail: diefew@sage.edu. *Dean, School of Management,* Dr. Kimberly Fredericks, 518-292-1782, Fax: 518-292-1964, E-mail: fredek1@sage.edu.

SAGINAW VALLEY STATE UNIVERSITY, University Center, MI 48710

General Information State-supported, coed, comprehensive institution. *Enrollment:* 8,662 graduate, professional, and undergraduate students; 246 full-time matriculated graduate/professional students (181 women), 522 part-time matriculated graduate/professional students (388 women). *Enrollment by degree level:* 721 master's, 34 doctoral, 13 other advanced degrees. *Graduate faculty:* 60 full-time (39 women), 35 part-time/adjunct (14 women). Tuition, state resident: full-time $10,156; part-time $564.20 per credit hour. Tuition, nonresident: full-time $19,336; part-time $1074.20 per credit hour. *Required fees:* $263; $14.60 per credit hour. Tuition and fees vary according to degree level and program. *Graduate housing:* Room and/or apartments available on a first-come, first-served basis to single students; on-campus housing not available to married students. Typical cost: $9749 (including board). Room and board charges vary according to board plan and housing facility selected. *Student services:* Campus employment opportunities, career counseling, exercise/wellness program, free psychological counseling, international student services, multicultural affairs office, services for students with disabilities, writing training. *Library facilities:* Zahnow Library. *Collection:* Books: 217,900 (physical), 107,479 (digital/electronic); Serial titles: 127 (physical), 50,164 (digital/electronic); Databases: 63. Weekly public service hours: 93.

Computer facilities: Computer purchase and lease plans are available. 424 computers available on campus for general student use. A campuswide network can be accessed from student residence rooms and from off campus. Online class registration is available.
Website: http://www.svsu.edu/

General Application Contact: Jenna Briggs, Director, Graduate and International Admissions, 989-964-6096, Fax: 989-964-2788, E-mail: gradadm@svsu.edu.

GRADUATE UNITS

College of Arts and Behavioral Sciences Students: 34 full-time (19 women), 41 part-time (27 women); includes 13 minority (7 Black or African American, non-Hispanic/Latino; 2 Asian, non-Hispanic/Latino; 2 Hispanic/Latino; 2 Two or more races, non-Hispanic/Latino), 22 international. Average age 29. 41 applicants, 85% accepted, 26 enrolled. *Faculty:* 11 full-time (6 women), 3 part-time/adjunct (1 woman). Expenses: Contact institution. *Financial support:* Federal Work-Study and scholarships/grants available. Support available to part-time students. Financial award applicants required to submit FAFSA. In 2017, 35 master's awarded. *Program availability:* Part-time, evening/weekend. Offers arts and behavioral sciences (MA); communication and media administration (MA); public administration (MA). *Application deadline:* For fall admission, 7/15 for international students; for winter admission, 11/15 for international students; for spring admission, 4/15 for international students. Applications are processed on a rolling basis. *Application fee:* $30 ($90 for international students). Electronic applications accepted. *Application Contact:* Jenna Briggs, Director, Graduate and International Admissions, 989-964-6096, Fax: 989-964-2788, E-mail: gradadm@svsu.edu. *Interim Dean,* Dr. Marc Peretz, 989-964-4062, Fax: 989-964-7232, E-mail: mhp@svsu.edu.

College of Business and Management Students: 29 full-time (13 women), 32 part-time (13 women); includes 8 minority (5 Black or African American, non-Hispanic/Latino; 1 Asian, non-Hispanic/Latino; 1 Hispanic/Latino; 1 Two or more races, non-Hispanic/Latino), 30 international. Average age 28. 42 applicants, 57% accepted, 11 enrolled. *Faculty:* 12 full-time (4 women), 1 part-time/adjunct (0 women). Expenses: Contact institution. *Financial support:* Federal Work-Study and scholarships/grants available. Support available to part-time students. Financial award application deadline: 4/1; financial award applicants required to submit FAFSA. In 2017, 34 master's awarded. *Program availability:* Part-time, evening/weekend, online only, 100% online, blended/hybrid learning. Offers business administration (MBA); business and management (MBA). *Application deadline:* For fall admission, 7/15 for international students; for winter admission, 11/15 for international students; for spring admission, 4/15 for international students. Applications are processed on a rolling basis. *Application fee:* $30 ($90 for international students). Electronic applications accepted. *Application Contact:* Jenna Briggs, Director, Graduate and International Admissions, 989-964-6096, Fax: 989-964-2788, E-mail: gradadm@svsu.edu. *MBA Program Coordinator,* Dr. Mark McCartney, 989-964-4064.

College of Education Students: 20 full-time (16 women), 216 part-time (173 women); includes 17 minority (7 Black or African American, non-Hispanic/Latino; 1 American Indian or Alaska Native, non-Hispanic/Latino; 1 Asian, non-Hispanic/Latino; 4 Hispanic/Latino; 4 Two or more races, non-Hispanic/Latino), 11 international. Average age 34. 88 applicants, 95% accepted, 60 enrolled. *Faculty:* 13 full-time (11 women), 17 part-time/adjunct (2 women). Expenses: Contact institution. *Financial support:* Federal Work-Study and scholarships/grants available. Support available to part-time students. Financial award applicants required to submit FAFSA. In 2017, 114 master's, 7 other advanced degrees awarded. *Program availability:* Part-time, evening/weekend, online learning. Offers early childhood education (MAT); education (M Ed, MA, MAT, Ed S); educational leadership (M Ed, Ed S); instructional technology (MA); K-12 literacy specialist (MAT); reading education (MAT); special education (MAT); teaching Chinese as a foreign language (MAT). *Application deadline:* For fall admission, 7/15 for international students; for winter admission, 11/15 for international students; for spring admission, 4/15 for international students. Applications are processed on a rolling basis. *Application fee:* $30 ($90 for international students). Electronic applications accepted. *Application Contact:* Jenna Briggs, Director, Graduate and International Admissions, 989-964-6096, Fax: 989-964-2788, E-mail: gradadm@svsu.edu. *Dean,* Dr. Craig Douglas, 989-964-4057, Fax: 989-964-4563, E-mail: coeconnect@svsu.edu.

College of Health and Human Services Students: 159 full-time (133 women), 226 part-time (172 women); includes 46 minority (17 Black or African American, non-Hispanic/Latino; 10 Asian, non-Hispanic/Latino; 7 Hispanic/Latino; 12 Two or more races, non-Hispanic/Latino), 14 international. Average age 29. 121 applicants, 83% accepted, 78 enrolled. *Faculty:* 23 full-time (20 women), 12 part-time/adjunct (11 women). Expenses: Contact institution. *Financial support:* Federal Work-Study and scholarships/grants available. Support available to part-time students. Financial award application deadline: 4/1; financial award applicants required to submit FAFSA. In 2017, 103 master's, 7 doctorates awarded. *Program availability:* Part-time, evening/weekend. Offers clinical nurse specialist (MSN); health and human services (MS, MSN, MSOT, MSW, DNP); health leadership (MS); nurse practitioner (MSN, DNP); nursing (MSN); occupational therapy (MSOT); social work (MSW). *Application deadline:* For fall admission, 7/15 for international students; for winter admission, 11/15 for international students; for spring admission, 4/15 for international students. Applications are processed on a rolling basis. *Application fee:* $30 ($90 for international students). Electronic applications accepted. *Application Contact:* Jenna Briggs, Director, Graduate and International Admissions, 989-964-6096, Fax: 989-964-2788, E-mail: gradadm@svsu.edu. *Dean,* Dr. Judith Ruland, 989-964-4145, Fax: 989-964-4024, E-mail: jruland@svsu.edu.

College of Science, Engineering, and Technology Students: 4 full-time (0 women), 7 part-time (3 women), 4 international. Average age 28. 16 applicants, 56% accepted, 7 enrolled. *Faculty:* 3 full-time (0 women), 2 part-time/adjunct (0 women). Expenses: Contact institution. *Financial support:* Federal Work-Study and scholarships/grants available. Support available to part-time students. Financial award application deadline: 4/1; financial award applicants required to submit FAFSA. In 2017, 1 master's awarded. *Program availability:* Part-time, evening/weekend. Offers science, engineering, and technology (MS). *Application deadline:* For fall admission, 7/15 for international students; for winter admission, 11/15 for international students; for spring admission, 4/15 for international students. Applications are processed on a rolling basis. *Application fee:* $30 ($90 for international students). Electronic applications accepted. *Application Contact:* Jenna Briggs, Director, Graduate and International Admissions, 989-964-6096, Fax: 989-964-2788, E-mail: gradadm@svsu.edu. *Program Coordinator,* Dr. Robert Tuttle, 989-964-4144, Fax: 989-964-2717.

ST. AMBROSE UNIVERSITY, Davenport, IA 52803-2898

General Information Independent-religious, coed, comprehensive institution. CGS member. *Graduate housing:* Room and/or apartments available on a first-come, first-served basis to single students; on-campus housing not available to married students. Housing application deadline: 3/1.

GRADUATE UNITS

College of Arts and Sciences *Program availability:* Part-time, evening/weekend. Offers arts and sciences (MCJ, MP Th, MSITM); criminal justice (MCJ); information technology management (MSITM); juvenile justice education (MCJ); pastoral theology (MP Th). Electronic applications accepted.

College of Business *Program availability:* Part-time, evening/weekend. Offers accounting (MAC); business (MAC, MBA, MOL, DBA); business administration (DBA); health care (MBA); human resources (MBA); organizational leadership (MOL). Electronic applications accepted.

College of Health and Human Services *Program availability:* Part-time, evening/weekend, online learning. Offers exercise physiology (MS); health and human services (MPAS, MPH, MS, MSLP, MSW, DPT, OTD); occupational therapy (OTD); physical therapy (DPT); physician assistant studies (MPAS); public health (MPH); social work (MSW); speech-language pathology (MSLP). Electronic applications accepted.

School of Education *Program availability:* Part-time, evening/weekend, online learning. Offers early childhood education (M Ed); educational administration (M Ed). Electronic applications accepted.

ST. ANDREW'S COLLEGE, Saskatoon, SK S7N 0W3, Canada

General Information Independent-religious, coed, graduate-only institution.

GRADUATE UNITS

Graduate Programs in Theology Offers theology (M Div, MTS, STM, D Min, Diploma).

ST. ANDREW'S COLLEGE IN WINNIPEG, Winnipeg, MB R3T 2M7, Canada

General Information Independent-religious, coed, primarily men, graduate-only institution. *Graduate housing:* Rooms and/or apartments available to single and married students. Housing application deadline: 7/31.

GRADUATE UNITS

Graduate Programs Offers theology (M Div).

SAINT ANTHONY COLLEGE OF NURSING, Rockford, IL 61114

General Information Independent-religious, coed, primarily women, upper-level institution.

GRADUATE UNITS

Graduate Program *Program availability:* Part-time. Offers nursing (MSN).

ST. AUGUSTINE'S SEMINARY OF TORONTO, Scarborough, ON M1M 1M3, Canada

General Information Independent-religious, coed, primarily men, graduate-only institution. *Graduate housing:* On-campus housing not available.

GRADUATE UNITS

Graduate and Professional Programs *Program availability:* Part-time, evening/weekend. Offers divinity (M Div); lay ministry (Diploma); religious education (MRE); theological studies (MTS, Diploma).

ST. BERNARD'S SCHOOL OF THEOLOGY AND MINISTRY, Rochester, NY 14618

General Information Independent-religious, coed, graduate-only institution. *Graduate housing:* On-campus housing not available. *Research affiliation:* Colgate Rochester Crozer Divinity School.

GRADUATE UNITS

Graduate and Professional Programs *Program availability:* Part-time, evening/weekend. Offers pastoral studies (MA, Certificate); theological studies (MA); theology (M Div).

ST. BONAVENTURE UNIVERSITY, St. Bonaventure, NY 14778-2284

General Information Independent-religious, coed, comprehensive institution. CGS member. *Enrollment:* 2,089 graduate, professional, and undergraduate students; 181 full-time matriculated graduate/professional students (104 women), 271 part-time matriculated graduate/professional students (169 women). *Enrollment by degree level:* 409 master's, 43 other advanced degrees. *Graduate faculty:* 30 full-time (14 women), 24 part-time/adjunct (15 women). *Tuition:* Part-time $733 per credit hour. One-time fee: $100 part-time. *Graduate housing:* Room and/or apartments available on a first-come, first-served basis to single students; on-campus housing not available to married students. Typical cost: $6246 per year ($11,981 including board). Room and board charges vary according to board plan. Housing application deadline: 3/19. *Student services:* Career counseling, international student services, low-cost health insurance, multicultural affairs office. *Library facilities:* Friedsam Memorial Library. *Collection:* Books: 371,691 (physical), 1.6 million (digital/electronic); Serial titles: 253 (physical), 269,989 (digital/electronic); Databases: 64. Weekly public service hours: 109; students can reserve study rooms.

Computer facilities: 320 computers available on campus for general student use. A campuswide network can be accessed from student residence rooms and from off campus. Online class registration is available.
Website: http://www.sbu.edu/

General Application Contact: Bruce Campbell, Director of Graduate Admissions, 716-375-2429, Fax: 716-375-4015, E-mail: gradsch@sbu.edu.

GRADUATE UNITS

School of Graduate Studies Students: 181 full-time (104 women), 271 part-time (169 women); includes 54 minority (19 Black or African American, non-Hispanic/Latino; 2 American Indian or Alaska Native, non-Hispanic/Latino; 5 Asian, non-Hispanic/Latino; 20 Hispanic/Latino; 1 Native Hawaiian or other Pacific Islander, non-Hispanic/Latino; 7 Two or more races, non-Hispanic/Latino), 13 international. Average age 29. 245 applicants, 91% accepted, 147 enrolled. *Faculty:* 31 full-time (15 women), 23 part-time/adjunct (14 women). Expenses: Contact institution. *Financial support:* Scholarships/grants and unspecified assistantships available. Financial award application deadline: 4/15; financial award applicants required to submit FAFSA. In 2017, 193 master's, 23 other advanced degrees awarded. *Program availability:* Part-time, evening/weekend, 100% online, blended/hybrid learning. *Application deadline:* For fall admission, 3/15 priority date for domestic students, 2/1 priority date for international students; for spring admission, 10/15 priority date for domestic students, 7/1 priority date for international students. Applications are processed on a rolling basis. *Application fee:* $0. Electronic applications accepted. *Application Contact:* Bruce Campbell, Director of Graduate Admissions, 716-375-2429, Fax: 716-375-4015, E-mail: gradsch@sbu.edu. *Dean,* Dr. Pauline Hoffmann, 716-375-2520, Fax: 716-375-2588, E-mail: hoffmann@sbu.edu.

Jandoli School of Communication Students: 36 full-time (19 women), 75 part-time (47 women); includes 22 minority (7 Black or African American, non-Hispanic/Latino; 1 American Indian or Alaska Native, non-Hispanic/Latino; 1 Asian, non-Hispanic/Latino; 9 Hispanic/Latino; 4 Two or more races, non-Hispanic/Latino), 4 international. Average age 30. 56 applicants, 86% accepted, 26 enrolled. *Faculty:* 6 full-time (4 women), 7 part-time/adjunct (5 women). Expenses: Contact institution. *Financial support:* Federal Work-Study, scholarships/grants, health care benefits, and unspecified assistantships available. Support available to part-time students. Financial award application deadline: 4/15; financial award applicants required to submit FAFSA. In 2017, 37 master's awarded. *Program availability:* Part-time, evening/weekend, 100% online. Offers communication (MA); integrated marketing communications (MA); strategic leadership (MA). *Application deadline:* For fall admission, 6/15 priority date for domestic students, 2/1 priority date for international students; for spring admission, 10/15 priority date for domestic students, 7/1 priority date for international students. Applications are processed on a rolling basis. *Application fee:* $0. Electronic applications accepted. *Application Contact:* Bruce Campbell, Director of Graduate Admissions, 716-375-2429, Fax: 716-375-4015, E-mail: gradsch@sbu.edu. *Interim Dean,* David Kassnoff, 716-375-2059, Fax: 716-375-2588, E-mail: dkassnof@sbu.edu.

School of Business Students: 81 full-time (33 women), 92 part-time (47 women); includes 16 minority (3 Black or African American, non-Hispanic/Latino; 1 American Indian or Alaska Native, non-Hispanic/Latino; 4 Asian, non-Hispanic/Latino; 5 Hispanic/Latino; 1 Native Hawaiian or other Pacific Islander, non-Hispanic/Latino; 2 Two or more races, non-Hispanic/Latino), 7 international. Average age 28. 104 applicants, 98% accepted, 79 enrolled. *Faculty:* 14 full-time (4 women), 4 part-time/adjunct (1 woman). Expenses: Contact institution. *Financial support:* Career-related internships or fieldwork, Federal Work-Study, scholarships/grants, health care benefits, and unspecified assistantships available. Support available to part-time students. Financial award application deadline: 4/15; financial award applicants required to submit FAFSA. In 2017, 78 master's awarded. *Program availability:* Part-time, evening/weekend, 100% online. Offers general business (MBA); professional accountancy (MBA). *Application deadline:* For fall admission, 6/15 priority date for domestic students, 2/1 priority date for international students; for spring admission, 11/1 priority date for domestic students, 7/1 priority date for international students. Applications are processed on a rolling basis. *Application fee:* $0. Electronic applications accepted. *Application Contact:* Bruce Campbell, Director of Graduate Admissions, 716-375-2429, Fax: 716-375-4015, E-mail: gradsch@sbu.edu. *Dean,* Dr. Matrecia James, 716-375-2200, Fax: 716-372-2191, E-mail: mjames@sbu.edu.

School of Education Students: 67 full-time (55 women), 101 part-time (72 women); includes 14 minority (7 Black or African American, non-Hispanic/Latino; 6 Hispanic/Latino; 1 Two or more races, non-Hispanic/Latino), 2 international. Average age 30. 85 applicants, 87% accepted, 60 enrolled. *Faculty:* 11 full-time (7 women), 11 part-time/adjunct (8 women). Expenses: Contact institution. *Financial support:* Career-related internships or fieldwork, Federal Work-Study, scholarships/grants, health care benefits, and unspecified assistantships available. Support available to part-time students. Financial award application deadline: 4/15; financial award applicants required to submit FAFSA. In 2017, 71 master's, 22 Adv Cs awarded. *Program availability:* Part-time, evening/weekend, 100% online, blended/hybrid learning. Offers adolescence education (MS Ed); adolescent literacy 5-12 (MS Ed); childhood literacy B-6 (MS Ed); community mental health counseling (MS Ed); education (MS Ed, Adv C); educational leadership (MS Ed); gifted education (MS Ed, Adv C); gifted education and students with disabilities (MS Ed); rehabilitation counseling (MS Ed); school building leader (Adv C); school counseling (MS Ed); school counselor (Adv C); school district leader (Adv C). *Application deadline:* For fall admission, 6/15 priority date for domestic students, 2/1 priority date for international students; for spring admission, 11/15 priority date for domestic students, 7/1 priority date for international students. Applications are processed on a rolling basis. *Application fee:* $0. Electronic applications accepted. *Application Contact:* Bruce Campbell, Director of Graduate Admissions, 716-375-2429, Fax: 716-375-4015, E-mail: gradsch@sbu.edu. *Dean,* Dr. Lisa Buenaventura, 716-375-2394, Fax: 716-375-2360, E-mail: lbuenave@sbu.edu.

ST. CATHERINE UNIVERSITY, St. Paul, MN 55105

General Information Independent-religious, Undergraduate: women only; graduate: coed, comprehensive institution. CGS member. *Enrollment:* 4,724 graduate, professional, and undergraduate students; 693 full-time matriculated graduate/professional students (606 women), 873 part-time matriculated graduate/professional students (782 women). *Enrollment by degree level:* 1,287 master's, 229 doctoral, 50 other advanced degrees. Tuition and fees vary according to program. *Graduate housing:* Rooms and/or apartments available on a first-come, first-served basis to single and married students. Housing application deadline: 5/1. *Student services:* Campus employment opportunities, campus safety program, career counseling, child daycare facilities, exercise/wellness program, free psychological counseling, international student services, low-cost health insurance, multicultural affairs office, services for students with disabilities, teacher training. *Library facilities:* St. Catherine Library.

Computer facilities: Computer purchase and lease plans are available. A campuswide network can be accessed from student residence rooms and from off campus. Online class registration, transcript are available.
Website: http://www.stkate.edu/

General Application Contact: Kristina Sande, Director of Graduate Admissions, 651-690-6933, Fax: 651-690-6064, E-mail: graduate_study@stkate.edu.

GRADUATE UNITS

Graduate Programs Expenses: Contact institution. *Financial support:* Research assistantships with tuition reimbursements, career-related internships or fieldwork, and institutionally sponsored loans available. Support available to part-time students. Financial award application deadline: 4/1; financial award applicants required to submit FAFSA. *Program availability:* Part-time, evening/weekend, online learning. Offers adult-gerontological nurse practitioner (MS); education - initial licensure (MA, Certificate); education - Montessori education (MA); education–curriculum and instruction (MA); global health (MPH); health informatics (MHI); healthcare (MBA); holistic health studies (MA); integrated marketing communications (MBA); library and information science (MLIS); management (MBA); nurse educator (MS); nursing (DNP); nursing: entry-level (MS); occupational therapy (MA, OTD); organizational leadership (MA); pastoral ministry (Certificate); pediatric nurse practitioner (MS); physical therapy (DPT); physician assistant studies (MPAS); social work (MSW, DSW); spiritual direction (Certificate); theology (MA). *Application fee:* $35.

SAINT CHARLES BORROMEO SEMINARY, OVERBROOK, Wynnewood, PA 19096

General Information Independent-religious, coed, primarily men, comprehensive institution. *Tuition:* Part-time $1750 per course. *Graduate housing:* Room and/or apartments guaranteed to single students; on-campus housing not available to married students. Housing application deadline: 7/15. *Student services:* Campus employment opportunities, career counseling. *Library facilities:* Ryan Memorial Library.

Computer facilities: 60 computers available on campus for general student use. A campuswide network can be accessed.
Website: http://www.scs.edu/

General Application Contact: Rev. Joseph T. Shenosky, Vice Rector, 610-785-6520, Fax: 610-617-9267, E-mail: jshenosky@scs.edu.

GRADUATE UNITS

School of Theological Studies Expenses: Contact institution. *Financial support:* Federal Work-Study and scholarships/grants available. Financial award application deadline: 7/15; financial award applicants required to submit CSS PROFILE or FAFSA. *Program availability:* Part-time, evening/weekend. Offers philosophical studies (MA); theological studies (MA); theology (MA). *Application deadline:* For fall admission, 7/15 for domestic students, 3/15 priority date for international students. Applications are processed on a rolling basis. *Application fee:* $0. *Application Contact:* Rev. Joseph T. Shenosky, Vice Rector, 610-785-6520, Fax: 610-617-9267, E-mail: jshenosky@scs.edu. *Rector*, Most Rev. Timothy C. Senior, 610-785-6200, Fax: 610-667-7635, E-mail: bsenior@scs.edu.

ST. CLOUD STATE UNIVERSITY, St. Cloud, MN 56301-4498

General Information State-supported, coed, comprehensive institution. CGS member. Tuition, state resident: full-time $8220; part-time $398.75 per credit. Tuition, nonresident: full-time $11,948; part-time $605.79 per credit. Tuition and fees vary according to degree level, campus/location, program and reciprocity agreements. *Graduate housing:* Room and/or apartments available on a first-come, first-served basis to single students; on-campus housing not available to married students. Typical cost: $7620 (including board). Housing application deadline: 4/15. *Student services:* Campus employment opportunities, campus safety program, career counseling, child daycare facilities, exercise/wellness program, free psychological counseling, international student services, low-cost health insurance, multicultural affairs office, services for students with disabilities, writing training. *Library facilities:* James W. Miller Learning Resources Center.

Computer facilities: Computer purchase and lease plans are available. A campuswide network can be accessed from student residence rooms and from off campus. Online class registration is available.
Website: http://www.stcloudstate.edu/

General Application Contact: Patricia M. Paquin, Director of Graduate Admissions, 320-308-2113, Fax: 320-308-5371, E-mail: pmpaquin@stcloudstate.edu.

GRADUATE UNITS

School of Graduate Studies Expenses: Contact institution. *Financial support:* Research assistantships with partial tuition reimbursements, teaching assistantships with partial tuition reimbursements, career-related internships or fieldwork, Federal Work-Study, scholarships/grants, and unspecified assistantships available. Financial award application deadline: 3/1; financial award applicants required to submit FAFSA. *Program availability:* Part-time, evening/weekend, online learning. *Application deadline:* For fall admission, 6/1 for domestic students, 4/1 for international students; for spring admission, 10/1 for domestic students, 8/1 for international students. Applications are processed on a rolling basis. *Application fee:* $35. Electronic applications accepted.

College of Liberal Arts Expenses: Contact institution. *Financial support:* Federal Work-Study, scholarships/grants, and unspecified assistantships available. Financial award application deadline: 3/1. Offers English (MS); English studies (MA); history (MA, MS); industrial-organizational psychology (MS); liberal arts (MA, MS); mass communications (MS); rhetoric and writing (MA). *Application fee:* $35.

College of Science and Engineering Expenses: Contact institution. *Financial support:* Federal Work-Study and unspecified assistantships available. Financial award application deadline: 3/1. Offers biology (MA, MS); computer science (MS); electrical engineering (MS); information assurance (MS); instructional technology (Graduate Certificate); regulatory affairs and services (MS, Graduate Certificate); science and engineering (MA, MS, Graduate Certificate). *Application fee:* $35. Electronic applications accepted.

College of Social Sciences Expenses: Contact institution. *Financial support:* Scholarships/grants and unspecified assistantships available. Financial award application deadline: 3/1. *Program availability:* Part-time. Offers applied economics (MS); criminal justice (MS); criminal justice administration (MS); cultural resource management archeology (MS, Graduate Certificate); geography and planning (MS, Graduate Certificate); public safety executive leadership (MS); social sciences (MA, MS, Graduate Certificate). *Application deadline:* Applications are processed on a rolling basis. *Application fee:* $35. Electronic applications accepted.

School of Education Expenses: Contact institution. *Financial support:* Career-related internships or fieldwork, Federal Work-Study, scholarships/grants, and unspecified assistantships available. Financial award application deadline: 3/1. *Program availability:* Part-time, evening/weekend, online learning. Offers child and family studies (MS); college counseling and student development (MS); developmental and cognitive disabilities (MS); education (MS, Ed D, Graduate Certificate); higher education administration (Ed D); information media (MS, Graduate Dental Certificate); social responsibility (MS). *Application deadline:* Applications are processed on a rolling basis. *Application fee:* $35.

School of Health and Human Services Expenses: Contact institution. Offers applied behavior analysis (MS); communication sciences and disorders (MS); educational administration and leadership (MS); educational leadership and community psychology (Spt); gerontology (MS, Graduate Certificate); health and human services (MS, Spt); marriage and family therapy (MS).

ST. EDWARD'S UNIVERSITY, Austin, TX 78704

General Information Independent-religious, coed, comprehensive institution. *Enrollment:* 153 full-time matriculated graduate/professional students (111 women), 353 part-time matriculated graduate/professional students (233 women). *Enrollment by degree level:* 506 master's. *Tuition:* Full-time $26,406; part-time $1467 per hour. *Required fees:* $75 per trimester. Full-time tuition and fees vary according to course load and program. *Graduate housing:* On-campus housing not available. *Student services:* Campus employment opportunities, campus safety program, career counseling, exercise/wellness program, free psychological counseling, international student services, low-cost health insurance, services for students with disabilities, writing training. *Library facilities:* Munday Library. *Collection:* Books: 71,983 (physical), 273,440 (digital/electronic); Serial titles: 202 (physical), 121,477 (digital/electronic); Databases: 230. Weekly public service hours: 103; students can reserve study rooms.

Computer facilities: 928 computers available on campus for general student use. A campuswide network can be accessed from student residence rooms and from off campus. Online class registration, access to address and biographical data, transcripts, statements of account, online progress reports and degree audit, campus job postings, student timesheets, financial aid information are available.
Website: http://www.stedwards.edu/

General Application Contact: Dave Bralower, Director of Graduate Admission, 512-233-1424, Fax: 512-464-8877, E-mail: davidcb@stedwards.edu.

GRADUATE UNITS

Bill Munday School of Business Students: 52 full-time (30 women), 181 part-time (94 women); includes 104 minority (14 Black or African American, non-Hispanic/Latino; 7 Asian, non-Hispanic/Latino; 74 Hispanic/Latino; 9 Two or more races, non-Hispanic/Latino), 16 international. Average age 32. 173 applicants, 58% accepted, 62 enrolled. Expenses: Contact institution. In 2017, 132 master's awarded. *Program availability:* Part-time, evening/weekend. Offers accounting (MBA); business (M Ac, MBA, MS); digital management (MBA); leadership and change (MS). *Application deadline:* For fall admission, 6/1 priority date for domestic and international students; for spring admission, 10/1 priority date for domestic and international students. Applications are processed on a rolling basis. *Application fee:* $50. Electronic applications accepted. *Application Contact:* Mike Leveriza, Graduate Recruiter, 512-448-8745, Fax: 512-464-8877, E-mail: mleveriz@stedwards.edu. *Interim Dean*, Dr. David Altounian, 512-428-1287, Fax: 512-428-1217, E-mail: davida@stedwards.edu.

School of Behavioral and Social Sciences Students: 20 full-time (14 women); includes 8 minority (1 Asian, non-Hispanic/Latino; 6 Hispanic/Latino; 1 Native Hawaiian or other Pacific Islander, non-Hispanic/Latino). Average age 28. 71 applicants, 35% accepted, 7 enrolled. Expenses: Contact institution. In 2017, 33 master's awarded. Offers environmental management and sustainability (PSM). *Application deadline:* For fall admission, 6/1 priority date for domestic and international students; for spring admission, 10/1 priority date for domestic and international students. Applications are processed on a rolling basis. *Application fee:* $50. Electronic applications accepted. *Application Contact:* Dave Bralower, Director of Graduate Admission, 512-233-1424, Fax: 512-464-8877, E-mail: davidcb@stedwards.edu. *Program Director/Associate Professor*, Dr. Peter Beck, 512-428-1249, Fax: 512-233-1664, E-mail: peterab@stedwards.edu.

School of Education Students: 81 full-time (67 women), 172 part-time (139 women); includes 94 minority (16 Black or African American, non-Hispanic/Latino; 5 Asian, non-Hispanic/Latino; 65 Hispanic/Latino; 8 Two or more races, non-Hispanic/Latino), 2 international. Average age 35. 153 applicants, 55% accepted, 56 enrolled. Expenses: Contact institution. In 2017, 99 master's awarded. *Program availability:* Part-time, evening/weekend. Offers college student development (MA); counseling (MA); education (Certificate); humanities (MLA); liberal arts (MLA, Certificate). *Application deadline:* For fall admission, 6/1 priority date for domestic and international students; for spring admission, 10/1 priority date for domestic and international students. Applications are processed on a rolling basis. *Application fee:* $50. Electronic applications accepted. *Application Contact:* Dave Bralower, Director of Graduate Admission, 512-233-1424, Fax: 512-464-8877, E-mail: davidcb@stedwards.edu. *MAC Program Director/Associate Professor of Counseling*, Dr. Elizabeth Katz, 512-464-8833, E-mail: elizk@stedwards.edu.

ST. FRANCIS COLLEGE, Brooklyn Heights, NY 11201-4398

General Information Independent-religious, coed, comprehensive institution.

GRADUATE UNITS

Program in Professional Accountancy Offers professional accountancy (MS).

SAINT FRANCIS MEDICAL CENTER COLLEGE OF NURSING, Peoria, IL 61603-3783

General Information Independent-religious, coed, primarily women, upper-level institution. *Enrollment:* 645 graduate, professional, and undergraduate students; 4 full-time matriculated graduate/professional students (all women), 239 part-time matriculated graduate/professional students (209 women). *Enrollment by degree level:* 211 master's, 24 doctoral, 8 other advanced degrees. *Graduate faculty:* 11 full-time (all women), 7 part-time/adjunct (all women). *Graduate housing:* Room and/or apartments available on a first-come, first-served basis to single students; on-campus housing not available to married students. Housing application deadline: 3/15. *Student services:* Campus safety program, exercise/wellness program, free psychological counseling, multicultural affairs office. *Library facilities:* Sister Mary Ludgera Pieperbeck Learning and Resource Center plus 1 other. *Collection:* Books: 4,054 (physical), 298 (digital/electronic); Serial titles: 126 (physical); Databases: 57. Students can reserve study rooms.

Computer facilities: 62 computers available on campus for general student use. A campuswide network can be accessed from student residence rooms and from off campus. Online class registration is available.
Website: http://www.sfmccon.edu/

General Application Contact: Dr. Kim A. Mitchell, Dean, Graduate Program, 309-655-2201, Fax: 309-624-8973, E-mail: kim.a.mitchell@osfhealthcare.org.

GRADUATE UNITS

Graduate Programs Students: 4 full-time (all women), 239 part-time (209 women); includes 24 minority (12 Black or African American, non-Hispanic/Latino; 3 Asian, non-Hispanic/Latino; 4 Hispanic/Latino; 5 Two or more races, non-Hispanic/Latino). Average age 37. 105 applicants, 83% accepted, 60 enrolled. *Faculty:* 11 full-time (all women), 7 part-time/adjunct (all women). Expenses: Contact institution. *Financial support:* In 2017–18, 13 students received support. Scholarships/grants and tuition waivers (partial) available. Support available to part-time students. Financial award application deadline: 6/15; financial award applicants required to submit FAFSA. In 2017, 52 master's, 8 doctorates awarded. *Program availability:* Part-time, online only, 100% online, blended/hybrid learning. Offers adult gerontology (MSN); clinical nurse leader (MSN); family nurse practitioner (MSN, Post-Graduate Certificate); family psychiatric mental health nurse practitioner (MSN); neonatal nurse practitioner (MSN); nurse clinician (Post-Graduate Certificate); nurse educator (MSN, Post-Graduate Certificate); nursing (DNP); nursing management leadership (MSN). *Application deadline:* For fall admission, 6/1 priority date for domestic and international students; for spring admission, 11/15 priority date for domestic and international students. Applications are processed on a rolling basis. *Application fee:* $50. *Application Contact:* Dr. Kim A. Mitchell, Dean, Graduate Program, 309-655-2201, Fax: 309-624-8973, E-mail: kim.a.mitchell@osfhealthcare.org. *President of the College*, Dr. Patti A. Stockert, 309-655-4124, Fax: 309-624-8973, E-mail: patricia.a.stockert@osfhealthcare.org.

SAINT FRANCIS UNIVERSITY, Loretto, PA 15940-0600

General Information Independent-religious, coed, comprehensive institution. *Enrollment:* 2,209 graduate, professional, and undergraduate students; 277 full-time matriculated graduate/professional students (174 women), 256 part-time matriculated graduate/professional students (185 women). *Enrollment by degree level:* 462 master's, 71 doctoral. *Graduate faculty:* 51 full-time (27 women), 13 part-time/adjunct (8 women). *Tuition:* Full-time $12,888; part-time $2148 per semester. Tuition and fees vary according to degree level and program. *Graduate housing:* On-campus housing not available. *Student services:* Campus employment opportunities, campus safety program, career counseling, exercise/wellness program, free psychological counseling, low-cost health insurance, multicultural affairs office, services for students with disabilities, writing training. *Library facilities:* Saint Francis University Library. *Collection:* Books: 76,787 (physical), 153,616 (digital/electronic); Databases: 74.

Computer facilities: Computer purchase and lease plans are available. 75 computers available on campus for general student use. A campuswide network can be accessed from student residence rooms and from off campus. Online class registration is available.
Website: http://www.francis.edu/

General Application Contact: Dr. Peter Raymond Skoner, Associate Provost, 814-472-3085, Fax: 814-472-3365, E-mail: pskoner@francis.edu.

GRADUATE UNITS

Cancer Care Program Students: 10 full-time (2 women), 1 (woman) part-time; includes 1 minority (Asian, non-Hispanic/Latino). Average age 23. *Faculty:* 10 full-time (5 women). Expenses: Contact institution. *Financial support:* Applicants required to submit FAFSA. Offers cancer care (MS). *Application deadline:* Applications are processed on a rolling basis. *Application fee:* $35. Electronic applications accepted. *Application Contact:* Dr. Peter Raymond Skoner, Associate Provost, 814-472-3085, Fax: 814-472-3365, E-mail: pskoner@francis.edu. *Coordinator*, Dr. Stephen LoRusso, 814-472-3853, E-mail: slorusso@francis.edu.

Department of Occupational Therapy Students: 42 full-time (39 women), 1 (woman) part-time; includes 3 minority (1 Black or African American, non-Hispanic/Latino; 2 Asian, non-Hispanic/Latino). Average age 23. 5 applicants, 100% accepted, 2 enrolled. *Faculty:* 6 full-time (5 women). Expenses: Contact institution. In 2017, 35 master's awarded. Offers occupational therapy (MOT). *Application fee:* $30. Electronic applications accepted. *Application Contact:* Amy Hudkins, Instructor, 814-472-2792, E-mail: ahudkins@francis.edu. *Department Chair*, Dr. Edward Mihelcic, 814-472-2760, E-mail: emihelcic@francis.edu.

Department of Physical Therapy Students: 67 full-time (37 women), 4 part-time (3 women); includes 3 minority (2 Black or African American, non-Hispanic/Latino; 1 Asian, non-Hispanic/Latino), 1 international. Average age 24. 339 applicants, 30% accepted, 40 enrolled. *Faculty:* 9 full-time (5 women), 2 part-time/adjunct (0 women). Expenses: Contact institution. *Financial support:* Teaching assistantships with partial tuition reimbursements and unspecified assistantships available. Financial award applicants required to submit FAFSA. In 2017, 33 doctorates awarded. Offers physical therapy (DPT). *Application deadline:* For winter admission, 1/15 for domestic and international students. *Application fee:* $30. Electronic applications accepted. *Application Contact:* Dr. Peter Raymond Skoner, Associate Provost, 814-472-3085, Fax: 814-472-3365, E-mail: pskoner@francis.edu. *Chair/Associate Professor*, Dr. Ivan J. Mulligan, 814-472-3123, Fax: 814-472-3140, E-mail: imulligan@francis.edu.

Department of Physician Assistant Sciences Students: 47 full-time (38 women), 3 part-time (2 women); includes 1 minority (Asian, non-Hispanic/Latino). Average age 22. *Faculty:* 9 full-time (7 women), 3 part-time/adjunct (2 women). Expenses: Contact institution. *Financial support:* Applicants required to submit FAFSA. In 2017, 52 master's awarded. Offers physician assistant sciences (MPAS). *Application deadline:* For fall admission, 10/1 for domestic and international students. Applications are processed on a rolling basis. *Application fee:* $175. Electronic applications accepted.

Graduate Education Program Students: 13 full-time (6 women), 96 part-time (65 women); includes 3 minority (2 Black or African American, non-Hispanic/Latino; 1 Hispanic/Latino). Average age 35. 22 applicants, 100% accepted, 16 enrolled. *Faculty:* 1 full-time (0 women), 15 part-time/adjunct (9 women). Expenses: Contact institution. *Financial support:* Applicants required to submit FAFSA. In 2017, 33 master's awarded. *Program availability:* Part-time, 100% online, blended/hybrid learning. Offers education (M Ed); leadership (M Ed); reading (M Ed). *Application deadline:* Applications are processed on a rolling basis. *Application fee:* $30. Electronic applications accepted. *Application Contact:* Sherri L. Toth, Coordinator, 814-472-3058, Fax: 814-472-3864, E-mail: stoth@francis.edu. *Director*, Dr. Janette D. Kelly, 814-472-3068, Fax: 814-472-3864, E-mail: jkelly@francis.edu.

Health Science Program Students: 5 full-time (all women), 64 part-time (55 women); includes 33 minority (19 Black or African American, non-Hispanic/Latino; 5 Asian, non-Hispanic/Latino; 3 Hispanic/Latino; 1 Native Hawaiian or other Pacific Islander, non-Hispanic/Latino; 5 Two or more races, non-Hispanic/Latino). Average age 36. 14 applicants, 100% accepted, 1 enrolled. *Faculty:* 2 full-time (both women), 16 part-time/adjunct (10 women). Expenses: Contact institution. *Financial support:* Available to part-time students. Applicants required to submit FAFSA. In 2017, 42 master's awarded. *Program availability:* Part-time, evening/weekend, 100% online. Offers health science (MHS). *Application deadline:* For fall admission, 7/19 for domestic and international students; for spring admission, 11/15 for domestic and international students; for summer admission, 3/22 for domestic and international students. Applications are processed on a rolling basis. *Application fee:* $50. Electronic applications accepted. *Application Contact:* Jean A. Kline, Administrative Assistant, 814-472-3357, Fax: 814-472-3066, E-mail: jkline@francis.edu.

Medical Science Program Students: 42 full-time (29 women), 45 part-time (30 women); includes 41 minority (6 Black or African American, non-Hispanic/Latino; 5 Asian, non-Hispanic/Latino; 23 Hispanic/Latino; 1 Native Hawaiian or other Pacific Islander, non-Hispanic/Latino; 6 Two or more races, non-Hispanic/Latino). Average age 31. 59 applicants, 100% accepted, 57 enrolled. *Faculty:* 2 full-time (both women), 16 part-time/adjunct (10 women). Expenses: Contact institution. *Financial support:* Available to part-time students. Applicants required to submit FAFSA. In 2017, 107 master's awarded. *Program availability:* Part-time, evening/weekend, online learning. Offers medical science (MMS). *Application deadline:* For fall admission, 6/15 for domestic students; for spring admission, 11/15 for domestic students; for summer admission, 3/15 for domestic students. Applications are processed on a rolling basis. *Application fee:* $0. Electronic applications accepted. *Application Contact:* Jean A. Kline, Administrative Assistant, 814-472-3357, Fax: 814-472-3066, E-mail: jkline@francis.edu.

Nursing Program Students: 12 part-time (all women). Average age 37. 5 applicants, 100% accepted, 4 enrolled. *Faculty:* 2 full-time (both women), 4 part-time/adjunct (all women). Expenses: Contact institution. *Financial support:* Applicants required to submit FAFSA. *Program availability:* Part-time, online only, blended/hybrid learning. Offers leadership/education (MSN). *Application fee:* $30. Electronic applications accepted. *Application Contact:* Dr. Peter Raymond Skoner, Associate Provost, 814-472-3085, Fax: 814-472-3365, E-mail: pskoner@francis.edu. *Coordinator*, Dr. Camille Wendekier, RN, E-mail: cwendekier@francis.edu.

School of Business Students: 52 full-time (17 women), 76 part-time (44 women); includes 10 minority (8 Black or African American, non-Hispanic/Latino; 1 Native Hawaiian or other Pacific Islander, non-Hispanic/Latino; 1 Two or more races, non-Hispanic/Latino), 1 international. Average age 30. 65 applicants, 77% accepted, 45 enrolled. *Faculty:* 10 full-time (4 women), 13 part-time/adjunct (9 women). Expenses: Contact institution. *Financial support:* Fellowships with partial tuition reimbursements, career-related internships or fieldwork, and unspecified assistantships available. Financial award application deadline: 8/15; financial award applicants required to submit FAFSA. In 2017, 67 master's awarded. *Program availability:* Part-time, evening/weekend. Offers business administration (MBA); human resource management (MHRM). *Application deadline:* For fall admission, 8/15 priority date for domestic and international students; for spring admission, 12/1 priority date for domestic students, 12/1 for international students. Applications are processed on a rolling basis. *Application fee:* $30. Electronic applications accepted. *Application Contact:* Nicole Marie Bauman, Coordinator, Graduate Business Programs, 814-472-3026, Fax: 814-472-3369, E-mail: nbauman@francis.edu. *Director, Graduate Business Programs*, Dr. Randy L. Frye, 814-472-3041, Fax: 814-472-3174, E-mail: rfrye@francis.edu.

ST. FRANCIS XAVIER UNIVERSITY, Antigonish, NS B2G 2W5, Canada

General Information Independent-religious, coed, comprehensive institution. *Graduate housing:* Room and/or apartments guaranteed to single students; on-campus housing not available to married students.

GRADUATE UNITS

Graduate Studies *Program availability:* Part-time, online learning. Offers adult education (M Ad Ed); biology (M Sc); Celtic studies (MA); chemistry (M Sc); community development (M Ad Ed); computer science (M Sc); curriculum and instruction (M Ed); earth sciences (M Sc); educational administration and leadership (M Ed).

ST. JOHN FISHER COLLEGE, Rochester, NY 14618-3597

General Information Independent-religious, coed, comprehensive institution. *Enrollment:* 3,782 graduate, professional, and undergraduate students; 629 full-time matriculated graduate/professional students (392 women), 394 part-time matriculated graduate/professional students (308 women). *Enrollment by degree level:* 546 master's, 477 doctoral. *Graduate faculty:* 76 full-time (48 women), 29 part-time/adjunct (21 women). *Tuition:* Part-time $920 per credit hour. *Required fees:* $10 per credit hour. Tuition and fees vary according to degree level and program. *Graduate housing:* On-campus housing not available. *Student services:* Campus employment opportunities, campus safety program, career counseling, child daycare facilities, exercise/wellness program, free psychological counseling, international student services, low-cost health insurance, multicultural affairs office, services for students with disabilities, teacher training, writing training. *Library facilities:* Charles J. Lavery Library plus 1 other. *Collection:* Books: 162,694 (physical), 137,162 (digital/electronic); Databases: 197. Students can reserve study rooms.

Computer facilities: 550 computers available on campus for general student use. A campuswide network can be accessed from student residence rooms and from off campus. Online class registration is available.
Website: http://www.sjfc.edu/

General Application Contact: Michelle Gosier, Director of Transfer and Graduate Admissions, 585-385-8064, Fax: 585-385-8344, E-mail: mgosier@sjfc.edu.

GRADUATE UNITS

Ralph C. Wilson Jr. School of Education Students: 150 full-time (99 women), 87 part-time (71 women); includes 88 minority (61 Black or African American, non-Hispanic/Latino; 2 American Indian or Alaska Native, non-Hispanic/Latino; 2 Asian, non-Hispanic/Latino; 18 Hispanic/Latino; 5 Two or more races, non-Hispanic/Latino). Average age 38. 171 applicants, 76% accepted, 92 enrolled. *Faculty:* 22 full-time (18 women), 14 part-time/adjunct (13 women). Expenses: Contact institution. *Financial support:* Scholarships/grants available. Financial award applicants required to submit FAFSA. In 2017, 66 master's, 47 doctorates, 1 other advanced degree awarded. *Program availability:* Part-time, evening/weekend. Offers adolescence education: biology with special education (MS Ed); adolescence education: chemistry with special education (MS Ed); adolescence education: English with special education (MS Ed); adolescence education: French with special education (MS Ed); adolescence education: math with special education (MS Ed); adolescence education: physics with special education (MS Ed); adolescence education: social studies with special education (MS Ed); adolescence education: Spanish with special education (MS Ed); childhood education (MS); childhood education/special education (Certificate); education (MS, MS Ed, Ed D, Certificate); educational leadership (MS Ed); executive leadership (Ed D); library media (MS); literacy birth to grade 6 (MS); literacy grades 5 to 12 (MS). *Application deadline:* Applications are processed on a rolling basis. *Application fee:* $30. Electronic applications accepted. *Application Contact:* Michelle Gosier, Director of Transfer and Graduate Admissions, 585-385-8064, E-mail: mgosier@sjfc.edu. *Dean*, Dr. Michael Wischnowski, 585-385-7361, E-mail: mwischnowski@sjfc.edu.

School of Arts and Sciences Students: 9 part-time (6 women); includes 2 minority (1 Black or African American, non-Hispanic/Latino; 1 Asian, non-Hispanic/Latino). Average age 32. 9 applicants, 100% accepted, 9 enrolled. *Faculty:* 1 full-time (0 women). Expenses: Contact institution. *Financial support:* Scholarships/grants available. Financial award applicants required to submit FAFSA. In 2017, 6 master's awarded. *Program availability:* Part-time, evening/weekend. Offers arts and sciences (MS); math, science, and technology education (MS). *Application deadline:* Applications are processed on a rolling basis. *Application fee:* $30. Electronic applications accepted. *Application Contact:* Michelle Gosier, Director of Transfer and Graduate Admissions, 585-385-8064, E-mail: mgosier@sjfc.edu. *Dean*, Ann Marie Fallon, 585-385-8477, E-mail: afallon@sjfc.edu.

School of Business Students: 76 full-time (37 women), 76 part-time (35 women); includes 19 minority (7 Black or African American, non-Hispanic/Latino; 3 Asian, non-Hispanic/Latino; 9 Hispanic/Latino), 6 international. Average age 28. 145 applicants, 78% accepted, 75 enrolled. *Faculty:* 11 full-time (0 women), 8 part-time/adjunct (4 women). Expenses: Contact institution. *Financial support:* Scholarships/grants available. Financial award applicants required to submit FAFSA. In 2017, 69 master's awarded. *Program availability:* Part-time, evening/weekend. Offers business (MBA, MS); business administration (MBA); management (MS). *Application deadline:* Applications are processed on a rolling basis. *Application fee:* $30. Electronic applications accepted. *Application Contact:* Michelle Gosier, Director of Transfer and Graduate Admissions, 585-385-8064, E-mail: mgosier@sjfc.edu. *Dean, School of Business*, Rama Yelkur, 585-385-8446, E-mail: ryelkur@sjfc.edu.

Wegmans School of Nursing Students: 74 full-time (55 women), 220 part-time (195 women); includes 49 minority (25 Black or African American, non-Hispanic/Latino; 1 American Indian or Alaska Native, non-Hispanic/Latino; 5 Asian, non-Hispanic/Latino; 15 Hispanic/Latino; 3 Two or more races, non-Hispanic/Latino). Average age 30. 214 applicants, 57% accepted, 88 enrolled. *Faculty:* 22 full-time (18 women), 7 part-time/adjunct (4 women). Expenses: Contact institution. *Financial support:* Scholarships/grants available. Financial award applicants required to submit FAFSA. In 2017, 71 master's, 5 doctorates awarded. *Program availability:* Part-time, evening/weekend. Offers advanced practice nursing (MS, Certificate); mental health counseling (MS); nursing (MS, DNP, Certificate); nursing practice (DNP). *Application deadline:* Applications are processed on a rolling basis. Electronic applications accepted. *Application Contact:* Michelle Gosier, Director of Transfer and Graduate Admissions, 585-385-8064, E-mail: mgosier@sjfc.edu. *Dean*, Dr. Diane Cooney-Miner, 585-385-8241, Fax: 585-385-8466, E-mail: dcooney-miner@sjfc.edu.

Wegmans School of Pharmacy Students: 329 full-time (201 women), 2 part-time (1 woman); includes 66 minority (12 Black or African American, non-Hispanic/Latino; 38 Asian, non-Hispanic/Latino; 10 Hispanic/Latino; 6 Two or more races, non-Hispanic/Latino), 5 international. Average age 24. 417 applicants, 32% accepted, 81 enrolled. *Faculty:* 20 full-time (12 women). Expenses: Contact institution. *Financial support:* Scholarships/grants available. Financial award applicants required to submit FAFSA. In 2017, 80 doctorates awarded. Offers pharmacy (Pharm D). *Application deadline:* For fall admission, 3/1 for domestic students. Applications are processed on a rolling basis. Electronic applications accepted. *Application Contact:* Michelle Gosier, Director of Transfer and Graduate Admissions, 585-385-8064, E-mail: mgosier@sjfc.edu. *Dean*, Dr. Christine Birnie, 585-385-7202, E-mail: cbirnie@sjfc.edu.

ST. JOHN'S COLLEGE, Annapolis, MD 21401

General Information Independent, coed, comprehensive institution. *Graduate housing:* On-campus housing not available.

GRADUATE UNITS

Graduate Institute *Program availability:* Evening/weekend. Offers liberal arts (MALA). Electronic applications accepted.

ST. JOHN'S COLLEGE, Santa Fe, NM 87505

General Information Independent, coed, comprehensive institution. *Graduate housing:* Rooms and/or apartments available on a first-come, first-served basis to single and married students. Housing application deadline: 4/1.

GRADUATE UNITS

Graduate Institute in Liberal Education *Program availability:* Evening/weekend. Offers Eastern classics (MA); liberal arts (MA); liberal education (MA).

ST. JOHN'S SEMINARY, Camarillo, CA 93012-2598

General Information Independent-religious, coed, primarily men, graduate-only institution. *Graduate housing:* Room and/or apartments guaranteed to single students; on-campus housing not available to married students.

GRADUATE UNITS

Graduate and Professional Programs *Program availability:* Part-time. Offers divinity (M Div); pastoral ministry (MAPM); theology (MA). Electronic applications accepted.

SAINT JOHN'S SEMINARY, Brighton, MA 02135

General Information Independent-religious, coed, graduate-only institution. *Graduate housing:* Room and/or apartments available to single students; on-campus housing not available to married students. Housing application deadline: 8/1.

GRADUATE UNITS

Graduate Programs Offers theology (M Div, MA Th, MAM).

SAINT JOHN'S UNIVERSITY, Collegeville, MN 56321

General Information Independent-religious, Undergraduate: men only; graduate: coed, comprehensive institution. *Graduate housing:* Rooms and/or apartments available on a first-come, first-served basis to single and married students. *Research affiliation:* Arca Artium (visual and book arts), Hill Monastic Manuscript Library (monastic studies, liturgy, spirituality), Center for Ecumenical and Cultural Research.

GRADUATE UNITS

Saint John's School of Theology and Seminary *Program availability:* Part-time, online learning. Offers divinity (M Div); liturgical music (MA); liturgical studies (MA); pastoral ministry (MA); theology (MA). Electronic applications accepted.

ST. JOHN'S UNIVERSITY, Queens, NY 11439

General Information Independent-religious, coed, university. CGS member. *Enrollment:* 21,346 graduate, professional, and undergraduate students; 2,688 full-time matriculated graduate/professional students (1,590 women), 1,892 part-time matriculated graduate/professional students (1,226 women). *Enrollment by degree level:* 2,343 master's, 2,029 doctoral, 111 other advanced degrees. *Graduate faculty:* 655 full-time (292 women), 822 part-time/adjunct (463 women). *Tuition:* Full-time $44,280; part-time $1230 per credit. *Required fees:* $340; $340 per credit. Tuition and fees vary according to course load, degree level and program. *Graduate housing:* Room and/or apartments available on a first-come, first-served basis to single students; on-campus housing not available to married students. Typical cost: $13,930 per year ($18,230 including board). Room and board charges vary according to board plan. Housing application deadline: 5/1. *Student services:* Campus employment opportunities, campus safety program, career counseling, exercise/wellness program, free psychological counseling, international student services, low-cost health insurance, services for students with disabilities, teacher training, writing training. *Library facilities:* St. John's University Library plus 3 others. *Collection:* Books: 534,824 (physical), 608,270 (digital/electronic); Serial titles: 68,549 (physical), 88,058 (digital/electronic); Databases: 226. Weekly public service hours: 92; students can reserve study rooms. *Research affiliation:* Raybiotech (biotechnology), Amneal Pharmaceuticals (pharmaceutical research), RAND Corporation, Jewish Board of Family and Children's Services (mental health and social services), Merck & Company, Inc. (pharmaceutical research), ABITEC (specialty chemicals).

Computer facilities: Computer purchase and lease plans are available. 12,702 computers available on campus for general student use. A campuswide network can be accessed from student residence rooms and from off campus. Online class registration is available.
Website: http://www.stjohns.edu/

General Application Contact: Robert Medrano, Director of Graduate Admissions, 718-990-1601, Fax: 718-990-5686, E-mail: gradhelp@stjohns.edu.

GRADUATE UNITS

College of Pharmacy and Health Sciences Students: 627 full-time (397 women), 39 part-time (15 women); includes 384 minority (26 Black or African American, non-Hispanic/Latino; 320 Asian, non-Hispanic/Latino; 22 Hispanic/Latino; 1 Native Hawaiian or other Pacific Islander, non-Hispanic/Latino; 15 Two or more races, non-Hispanic/Latino), 142 international. Average age 24. 306 applicants, 53% accepted, 41 enrolled. *Faculty:* 100 full-time (58 women), 31 part-time/adjunct (12 women). Expenses: Contact institution. *Financial support:* In 2017–18, 87 students received support, including 34 fellowships with full tuition reimbursements available (averaging $24,000 per year), 53 teaching assistantships with full tuition reimbursements available (averaging $12,000 per year); career-related internships or fieldwork, scholarships/grants, and unspecified assistantships also available. Support available to part-time students. Financial award application deadline: 2/1; financial award applicants required to submit FAFSA. In 2017, 36 master's, 285 doctorates awarded. *Program availability:* Part-time, evening/weekend. Offers pharmaceutical sciences (MPH, MS, PhD); pharmacy administration (MS); pharmacy and health sciences (MPH, MS, PhD); public health (MPH); toxicology (MS). *Application deadline:* For fall admission, 3/1 priority date for domestic students, 5/1 priority date for international students; for spring admission, 11/1 priority date for domestic and international students. Applications are processed on a rolling basis. *Application fee:* $70. Electronic applications accepted. *Application Contact:* Robert Medrano, Director of Graduate Admission, 718-990-1601, Fax: 718-990-5686, E-mail: gradhelp@stjohns.edu. *Dean*, Dr. Russell J. DiGate, 718-990-6411, Fax: 718-990-8070, E-mail: digate@stjohns.edu.

College of Professional Studies Students: 203 full-time (93 women), 59 part-time (26 women); includes 113 minority (50 Black or African American, non-Hispanic/Latino; 14 Asian, non-Hispanic/Latino; 35 Hispanic/Latino; 1 Native Hawaiian or other Pacific Islander, non-Hispanic/Latino; 13 Two or more races, non-Hispanic/Latino), 46 international. Average age 27. 295 applicants, 75% accepted, 117 enrolled. *Faculty:* 87 full-time (31 women), 245 part-time/adjunct (161 women). Expenses: Contact institution. *Financial support:* In 2017–18, 4 students received support, including 4 research assistantships with full tuition reimbursements available (averaging $5,250 per year); teaching assistantships, scholarships/grants, and unspecified assistantships also available. Financial award application deadline: 2/1; financial award applicants required to submit FAFSA. In 2017, 99 master's awarded. Offers data mining and predictive analytics (MS); homeland security and criminal justice leadership (MPS); international communications (MS); sport management (MPS). *Application deadline:* For fall admission, 5/1 for domestic students; for spring admission, 11/1 for domestic students. Applications are processed on a rolling basis. *Application fee:* $70. Electronic applications accepted. *Application Contact:* Robert Medrano, Director of Graduate Admission, 718-990-1601, Fax: 718-990-5686, E-mail: gradhelp@stjohns.edu. *Dean*, Dr. Katia Passerini, 718-990-2773, Fax: 718-990-1882, E-mail: passerik@stjohns.edu.

Institute for Biotechnology Students: 13 full-time (8 women), 3 part-time (2 women); includes 2 minority (1 Asian, non-Hispanic/Latino; 1 Hispanic/Latino), 11 international. Average age 25. 40 applicants, 65% accepted, 6 enrolled. Expenses: Contact institution. *Financial support:* In 2017–18, 1 student received support, including 1 research assistantship with full tuition reimbursement available. Financial award application deadline: 3/1; financial award applicants required to submit FAFSA. In 2017, 5 master's awarded. Offers biological and pharmaceutical biotechnology (MS). *Application deadline:* For fall admission, 5/1 for domestic students; for spring admission, 11/1 for domestic students. Applications are processed on a rolling basis. *Application fee:* $70. Electronic applications accepted. *Application Contact:* Robert Medrano, Director of Graduate Admissions, 718-990-1601, Fax: 718-990-5686, E-mail: gradhelp@stjohns.edu. *Director*, Dr. Zhe-Sheng Chen, 718-990-1432, E-mail: chenz@stjohns.edu.

The Peter J. Tobin College of Business Students: 400 full-time (199 women), 202 part-time (87 women); includes 181 minority (55 Black or African American, non-Hispanic/Latino; 65 Asian, non-Hispanic/Latino; 48 Hispanic/Latino; 1 Native Hawaiian or other Pacific Islander, non-Hispanic/Latino; 12 Two or more races, non-Hispanic/Latino), 183 international. Average age 27. *Faculty:* 98 full-time (25 women), 38 part-time/adjunct (33 women). Expenses: Contact institution. *Financial support:* In 2017–18, 28 students received support, including 28 research assistantships with full tuition reimbursements available (averaging $6,250 per year); teaching assistantships, scholarships/grants, and unspecified assistantships also available. Support available to part-time students. Financial award application deadline: 2/1; financial award applicants required to submit FAFSA. In 2017, 337 master's awarded. Offers accounting (MS); business (MBA, MS); business administration (MBA); business analytics and information systems (MBA); finance (MBA, MS); taxation (MBA, MS). *Application deadline:* For fall admission, 11/1 for domestic students, 11/1 priority date for international students; for winter admission, 3/1 for domestic students, 3/1 priority date for international students; for spring admission, 6/1 for domestic students, 6/1 priority date for international students. Applications are processed on a rolling basis. *Application fee:* $70. Electronic applications accepted. *Application Contact:* Amber Steiger, Associate Director of Enrollment Management, 718-990-1345, E-mail: steigera@stjohns.edu. *Dean*, Dr. Norean R. Sharpe, 718-990-6800, E-mail: sharpen@stjohns.edu.

School of Risk Management, Insurance and Actuarial Science Students: 51 full-time (24 women), 28 part-time (13 women); includes 15 minority (7 Black or African American, non-Hispanic/Latino; 4 Asian, non-Hispanic/Latino; 3 Hispanic/Latino; 1 Two or more races, non-Hispanic/Latino), 40 international. Average age 27. 58 applicants, 78% accepted, 27 enrolled. *Faculty:* 11 full-time (2 women), 7 part-time/adjunct (1 woman). Expenses: Contact institution. *Financial support:* Research assistantships, teaching assistantships, scholarships/grants, and unspecified assistantships available. Support available to part-time students. Financial award application deadline: 2/1; financial award applicants required to submit FAFSA. In 2017, 32 master's awarded. Offers actuarial science (MS); business administration (MBA); enterprise risk management (MBA, MS); risk management and insurance (MS). *Application deadline:* For fall admission, 11/1 for domestic and international students; for winter admission, 3/1 for domestic and international students; for spring admission, 6/1 for domestic and international students. Applications are processed on a rolling basis. *Application fee:* $70. Electronic applications accepted. *Application Contact:* Amber Steiger, Associate Director of Enrollment Management, 718-990-1345, E-mail: steigera@stjohns.edu. *Chair*, Dr. Mark J. Browne, 212-277-5175, E-mail: brownem1@stjohns.edu.

St. John's College of Liberal Arts and Sciences Students: 508 full-time (388 women), 363 part-time (262 women); includes 288 minority (89 Black or African American, non-Hispanic/Latino; 3 American Indian or Alaska Native, non-Hispanic/Latino; 68 Asian, non-Hispanic/Latino; 103 Hispanic/Latino; 3 Native Hawaiian or other Pacific Islander, non-Hispanic/Latino; 22 Two or more races, non-Hispanic/Latino), 66 international. Average age 29. 1,406 applicants, 41% accepted, 262 enrolled. *Faculty:* 261 full-time (113 women), 373 part-time/adjunct (186 women). Expenses: Contact institution. *Financial support:* In 2017–18, 124 students received support, including 68 fellowships with full tuition reimbursements available (averaging $2,721 per year), 41 research assistantships with full tuition reimbursements available (averaging $6,250 per year), 15 teaching assistantships with full tuition reimbursements available (averaging $12,000 per year); scholarships/grants, tuition waivers (full and partial), and unspecified assistantships also available. Support available to part-time students. Financial award application deadline: 2/1; financial award applicants required to submit FAFSA. In 2017, 267 master's, 46 doctorates, 18 other advanced degrees awarded. *Program availability:* Part-time, evening/weekend, 100% online, blended/hybrid learning. Offers applied and computational mathematics (MA); audiology (Au D); biological sciences (MS, PhD); chemistry (MS); clinical psychology (MA, PhD); clinical psychology-child (PhD); clinical psychology-general (PhD); criminology and justice (MA); English (MA, PhD); global development and social justice (MA); government and politics (MA, Adv C); history (MA,

PhD); international law and diplomacy (Adv C); liberal arts and sciences (MA, MS, Au D, PhD, Psy D, Adv C); liberal studies (MA); museum administration (MA); psychology (MA, MS, PhD, Psy D); public administration (Adv C); public history (MA); school psychology (MS, Psy D); sociology (MA); Spanish (MA); speech language pathology (MA); theology (MA). *Application deadline:* For fall admission, 3/1 for domestic students; for spring admission, 11/1 for domestic students. Applications are processed on a rolling basis. *Application fee:* $70. Electronic applications accepted. *Application Contact:* Robert Medrano, Director of Graduate Admission, 718-990-1601, Fax: 718-990-5686, E-mail: gradhelp@stjohns.edu. *Dean*, Dr. Jeffrey Fagen, 718-990-6068, Fax: 718-990-6593, E-mail: fagenj@stjohns.edu.

Division of Library and Information Science Students: 25 full-time (22 women), 39 part-time (33 women); includes 19 minority (7 Black or African American, non-Hispanic/Latino; 1 American Indian or Alaska Native, non-Hispanic/Latino; 4 Asian, non-Hispanic/Latino; 6 Hispanic/Latino; 1 Two or more races, non-Hispanic/Latino). Average age 33. 63 applicants, 63% accepted, 21 enrolled. *Faculty:* 5 full-time (2 women), 1 (woman) part-time/adjunct. Expenses: Contact institution. *Financial support:* Fellowships, research assistantships, teaching assistantships, scholarships/grants, tuition waivers, and unspecified assistantships available. Support available to part-time students. Financial award application deadline: 2/1; financial award applicants required to submit FAFSA. In 2017, 30 master's awarded. *Program availability:* Part-time, online only, 100% online. Offers library science (MS); management for information professionals (Adv C). *Application deadline:* For fall admission, 5/1 for domestic students; for spring admission, 11/1 for domestic students. Applications are processed on a rolling basis. *Application fee:* $70. Electronic applications accepted. *Application Contact:* Robert Medrano, Director of Graduate Admissions, 718-990-1601, Fax: 718-990-5686, E-mail: gradhelp@stjohns.edu. *Director*, Dr. James Vorbach, 718-990-1834, Fax: 718-990-2071, E-mail: vorbachj@stjohns.edu.

Institute of Asian Studies Students: 8 full-time (4 women), 2 part-time (both women); includes 2 minority (both Asian, non-Hispanic/Latino), 8 international. Average age 29. 16 applicants, 69% accepted, 6 enrolled. *Faculty:* 1 (woman) full-time, 7 part-time/adjunct (3 women). Expenses: Contact institution. *Financial support:* Fellowships, research assistantships, teaching assistantships, scholarships/grants, tuition waivers, and unspecified assistantships available. Support available to part-time students. Financial award application deadline: 2/1; financial award applicants required to submit FAFSA. In 2017, 8 master's awarded. *Program availability:* Part-time, evening/weekend. Offers Chinese studies (MA); East Asian studies (MA). *Application deadline:* For fall admission, 5/1 for domestic students; for spring admission, 11/1 for domestic students. Applications are processed on a rolling basis. *Application fee:* $70. Electronic applications accepted. *Application Contact:* Robert Medrano, Director of Graduate Admission, 718-990-1601, Fax: 718-990-5686, E-mail: gradhelp@stjohns.edu. *Director*, Dr. Bernadette Li, 718-990-1657, E-mail: lib@stjohns.edu.

The School of Education Students: 218 full-time (169 women), 1,130 part-time (783 women); includes 565 minority (233 Black or African American, non-Hispanic/Latino; 2 American Indian or Alaska Native, non-Hispanic/Latino; 89 Asian, non-Hispanic/Latino; 211 Hispanic/Latino; 1 Native Hawaiian or other Pacific Islander, non-Hispanic/Latino; 29 Two or more races, non-Hispanic/Latino), 33 international. Average age 35. 559 applicants, 90% accepted, 479 enrolled. *Faculty:* 53 full-time (34 women), 70 part-time/adjunct (29 women). Expenses: Contact institution. *Financial support:* In 2017–18, 10 students received support, including 5 fellowships with full tuition reimbursements available (averaging $16,000 per year), 5 research assistantships with full tuition reimbursements available (averaging $4,250 per year); scholarships/grants and unspecified assistantships also available. Support available to part-time students. Financial award application deadline: 2/1; financial award applicants required to submit FAFSA. In 2017, 380 master's, 62 doctorates, 168 other advanced degrees awarded. Offers administration and supervision (Ed D); adolescent education (MS Ed); bilingual education (Adv C); childhood and childhood special education (MS Ed); childhood education (MS Ed); childhood education and teaching English to speakers of other languages (MS Ed); clinical mental health counseling (MS Ed, Adv C); curriculum and instruction (PhD); early childhood (PhD); early childhood education (MS Ed); education (MS Ed, Ed D, PhD, Adv C); gifted education (Adv C); global education (PhD); instructional leadership (Ed D, Adv C); literacy (MS Ed, PhD, Adv C); literacy leadership (Adv C); school building leadership (MS Ed, Adv C); school building leadership/school district leadership (Adv C); school counseling (MS Ed, Adv C); school district leadership (Adv C); special education (MS Ed, Adv C); STEM education (PhD); teaching children with disabilities in adolescent education (Adv C); teaching children with disabilities in adolescent education (7-12) (MS Ed); teaching children with disabilities in childhood education (Adv C); teaching children with disabilities in childhood education (1-6) (MS Ed); teaching English to speakers of other languages (MS Ed, Adv C); teaching English to speakers of other languages and bilingual education (MS Ed, Adv C); teaching literacy (MS Ed, Adv C); teaching literacy (5-12) and TESOL (K-12) (MS Ed); teaching literacy (B-6) and teaching children with disabilities in childhood education (MS Ed); teaching literacy (B-6) and TESOL (K-12) (MS Ed); teaching students with disabilities and early childhood education (B-2) (MS Ed); teaching, learning, and knowing (PhD). *Application deadline:* For fall admission, 8/17 for domestic and international students; for summer admission, 5/15 for domestic and international students. *Application fee:* $70. Electronic applications accepted. *Application Contact:* Associate Director of Graduate Admissions, E-mail: graded@stjohns.edu. *Interim Dean*, Dr. Yvonne Pratt-Johnson, 718-990-2645, E-mail: prattjoy@stjohns.edu.

School of Law Students: 719 full-time (336 women), 96 part-time (51 women); includes 199 minority (54 Black or African American, non-Hispanic/Latino; 54 Asian, non-Hispanic/Latino; 70 Hispanic/Latino; 21 Two or more races, non-Hispanic/Latino), 84 international. Average age 26. 2,809 applicants, 41% accepted, 297 enrolled. *Faculty:* 39 full-time (20 women), 61 part-time/adjunct (39 women). Expenses: Contact institution. *Financial support:* In 2017–18, 520 students received support. Research assistantships, teaching assistantships, and scholarships/grants available. Financial award application deadline: 3/1; financial award applicants required to submit FAFSA. In 2017, 52 master's, 215 doctorates awarded. *Program availability:* Part-time, evening/weekend. Offers bankruptcy (LL M); law (LL M, JD); transnational legal practice (LL M); U.S. legal studies (LL M). *Application deadline:* For fall admission, 5/15 priority date for domestic and international students; for spring admission, 10/15 priority date for domestic and international students. Applications are processed on a rolling basis. *Application fee:* $100. Electronic applications accepted. *Application Contact:* Yvette Gutierrez, Director of Graduate Admissions and Bankruptcy Programs, 718-990-1923, E-mail: lawinfo@stjohns.edu. *Dean*, Michael A. Simons, Esq., 718-990-6601, Fax: 718-990-6694, E-mail: simonsm@stjohns.edu.

ST. JOSEPH'S COLLEGE, LONG ISLAND CAMPUS, Patchogue, NY 11772-2399

General Information Independent, coed, comprehensive institution. *Enrollment:* 3,966 graduate, professional, and undergraduate students; 139 full-time matriculated graduate/professional students (104 women), 756 part-time matriculated graduate/professional students (597 women). *Enrollment by degree level:* 895 master's. *Graduate faculty:* 35 full-time (24 women), 45 part-time/adjunct (20 women). *Tuition:* Full-time $17,550; part-time $975 per credit. *Required fees:* $362. *Graduate housing:* On-campus housing not available. *Student services:* Campus employment opportunities, campus safety program, career counseling, exercise/wellness program, free psychological counseling, low-cost health insurance, multicultural affairs office, services for students with disabilities, teacher training, writing training. *Library facilities:* Callahan Library plus 1 other. *Collection:* Books: 95,272 (physical), 163,718 (digital/electronic); Serial titles: 224 (physical), 59,734 (digital/electronic); Databases: 116. Weekly public service hours: 80; students can reserve study rooms.

Computer facilities: 258 computers available on campus for general student use. A campuswide network can be accessed from off campus. Online class registration, library databases, learning management system, course evaluations, print management, virtual application labs, office 365, student suggestion box are available.
Website: http://www.sjcny.edu/

General Application Contact: Christina Seifert, Director of Graduate and Professional Studies Admissions, 631-687-4525, E-mail: cseifert@sjcny.edu.

GRADUATE UNITS

Program in Forensic Computing Students: 3 full-time (1 woman), 7 part-time (0 women); includes 2 minority (1 Black or African American, non-Hispanic/Latino; 1 Hispanic/Latino). Average age 25. 12 applicants, 100% accepted, 10 enrolled. Expenses: Contact institution. *Financial support:* In 2017–18, 2 students received support. *Program availability:* Part-time, evening/weekend, 100% online, blended/hybrid learning. Offers forensic computing (MS). *Application deadline:* Applications are processed on a rolling basis. *Application fee:* $25. Electronic applications accepted. *Chairperson/Assistant Professor/Director*, Victoria Hong, 631-687-2646, E-mail: vhong@sjcny.edu.

Program in Nursing Students: 1 (woman) full-time, 40 part-time (36 women); includes 15 minority (7 Black or African American, non-Hispanic/Latino; 3 Asian, non-Hispanic/Latino; 5 Hispanic/Latino). Average age 41. 39 applicants, 69% accepted, 21 enrolled. *Faculty:* 4 full-time (all women), 1 (woman) part-time/adjunct. Expenses: Contact institution. *Financial support:* In 2017–18, 23 students received support. In 2017, 6 master's awarded. *Program availability:* Part-time, evening/weekend. Offers adult-gerontology clinical nurse specialist (MS); adult-gerontology primary care nurse practitioner (MS); nursing education (MS). *Application deadline:* Applications are processed on a rolling basis. *Application fee:* $25. Electronic applications accepted. *Director/Associate Professor*, Dr. Maria Fletcher, RN, 631-687-5180, E-mail: mfletcher@sjcny.edu.

Programs in Business Management and Administration Students: 55 full-time (32 women), 120 part-time (62 women); includes 40 minority (12 Black or African American, non-Hispanic/Latino; 1 American Indian or Alaska Native, non-Hispanic/Latino; 5 Asian, non-Hispanic/Latino; 20 Hispanic/Latino; 1 Native Hawaiian or other Pacific Islander, non-Hispanic/Latino; 1 Two or more races, non-Hispanic/Latino). Average age 32. 105 applicants, 73% accepted, 51 enrolled. *Faculty:* 15 full-time (7 women), 22 part-time/adjunct (7 women). Expenses: Contact institution. *Financial support:* In 2017–18, 37 students received support. Federal Work-Study available. In 2017, 59 master's awarded. *Program availability:* Part-time, evening/weekend, 100% online, blended/hybrid learning. Offers accounting (MBA); business administration (MBA); business management and administration (EMBA, MBA). *Application deadline:* Applications are processed on a rolling basis. *Application fee:* $25. Electronic applications accepted. *Assistant Professor/Interim Director of Graduate Management Studies*, Mary A. Chance, 631-687-1297, E-mail: mchance@sjcny.edu.

Field of Executive Business Administration Students: 18 full-time (12 women), 72 part-time (43 women); includes 24 minority (11 Black or African American, non-Hispanic/Latino; 2 Asian, non-Hispanic/Latino; 10 Hispanic/Latino; 1 Two or more races, non-Hispanic/Latino). Average age 34. 54 applicants, 67% accepted, 24 enrolled. *Faculty:* 15 full-time (7 women), 22 part-time/adjunct (7 women). Expenses: Contact institution. *Financial support:* In 2017–18, 20 students received support. Federal Work-Study available. In 2017, 24 master's awarded. *Program availability:* Part-time, evening/weekend, 100% online, blended/hybrid learning. Offers executive business administration (EMBA). *Application deadline:* Applications are processed on a rolling basis. *Application fee:* $25. Electronic applications accepted. *Assistant Professor/Interim Director of Graduate Management Studies*, Mary A. Chance, 631-687-1297, E-mail: mchance@sjcny.edu.

Programs in Education Students: 50 full-time (48 women), 341 part-time (303 women); includes 46 minority (3 Black or African American, non-Hispanic/Latino; 1 American Indian or Alaska Native, non-Hispanic/Latino; 3 Asian, non-Hispanic/Latino; 32 Hispanic/Latino; 1 Native Hawaiian or other Pacific Islander, non-Hispanic/Latino; 6 Two or more races, non-Hispanic/Latino). Average age 26. 241 applicants, 83% accepted, 163 enrolled. *Faculty:* 25 full-time (19 women), 28 part-time/adjunct (14 women). Expenses: Contact institution. *Financial support:* In 2017–18, 135 students received support. Federal Work-Study available. In 2017, 133 master's awarded. *Program availability:* Part-time, evening/weekend. Offers education (MA); educational leadership (MA); mathematics education (MA). *Application fee:* $25. *Associate Professor and Department Chair*, Nancy Gilchriest, 631-687-1472, E-mail: ngilchriest@sjcny.edu.

Field in Special Education Students: 13 full-time (12 women), 113 part-time (93 women); includes 11 minority (1 Asian, non-Hispanic/Latino; 7 Hispanic/Latino; 3 Two or more races, non-Hispanic/Latino). Average age 25. 87 applicants, 89% accepted, 56 enrolled. *Faculty:* 9 full-time (7 women), 11 part-time/adjunct (5 women). Expenses: Contact institution. *Financial support:* In 2017–18, 41 students received support. Federal Work-Study available. In 2017, 63 master's awarded. *Program availability:* Part-time, evening/weekend. Offers special education (MA). *Application fee:* $25. *Associate Professor/Director of MA in Childhood and Adolescence Education with an annotation in Severe and Multiple Disabilities*, Joan Silver, 631-687-1219, E-mail: jsilver@sjcny.edu.

Field of Infant/Toddler Early Childhood Special Education Students: 31 full-time (30 women), 95 part-time (87 women); includes 19 minority (1 Black or African American, non-Hispanic/Latino; 1 Asian, non-Hispanic/Latino; 17 Hispanic/Latino). Average age 27. 83 applicants, 77% accepted, 53 enrolled. *Faculty:* 6 full-time (5 women), 5 part-time/adjunct (all women). Expenses: Contact institution. *Financial support:* In 2017–18, 32 students received support. Applicants required to submit FAFSA. In 2017, 7 master's awarded. *Program availability:* Part-time, evening/weekend. Offers infant/toddler early childhood special education (MA). *Application deadline:* Applications are processed on a rolling basis. *Application fee:* $25. Electronic applications accepted. *Director of MA in Infant/Toddler Early Childhood Special Education*, Katherine Granelli, 631-687-1217, E-mail: kgranelli@sjcny.edu.

Field of Literacy and Cognition Students: 5 full-time (all women), 110 part-time (106 women); includes 10 minority (1 Black or African American, non-Hispanic/Latino; 1 American Indian or Alaska Native, non-Hispanic/Latino; 1 Asian, non-Hispanic/Latino; 5 Hispanic/Latino; 2 Two or more races, non-Hispanic/Latino). Average age 24. 71 applicants, 85% accepted, 54 enrolled. *Faculty:* 8 full-time (6 women), 7 part-time/adjunct (3 women). Expenses: Contact institution. *Financial support:* In 2017–18, 53 students received support. Federal Work-Study available. In 2017, 47 master's awarded. *Program availability:* Part-time, evening/weekend. Offers literacy 5-12 (MA); literacy and cognition birth-6 (MA); literacy birth-12 (MA); literacy/cognition and special education (MA). *Application deadline:* Applications are processed on a rolling basis. *Application fee:* $25. Electronic applications accepted. *Associate Professor/Director of MA in Literacy and Cognition*, Karen Megay-Nespoli, 631-687-1212, E-mail: kmegay-nespoli@sjcny.edu.

Programs in Health Care Administration Students: 7 full-time (5 women), 22 part-time (12 women); includes 8 minority (4 Black or African American, non-Hispanic/Latino; 1 Asian, non-Hispanic/Latino; 2 Hispanic/Latino; 1 Two or more races, non-Hispanic/Latino). Average age 34. 9 applicants, 78% accepted, 6 enrolled. *Faculty:* 15 full-time (7 women), 22 part-time/adjunct (7 women). Expenses: Contact institution. *Financial support:* In 2017–18, 13 students received support. In 2017, 9 master's awarded. *Program availability:* Part-time, evening/weekend, 100% online, blended/hybrid learning. Offers health care administration (MBA); health care management (MBA); health care management - health information systems (MBA). *Application fee:* $25. *Assistant Professor/Interim Director of Graduate Management Studies*, Mary A. Chance, 631-687-1297, E-mail: mchance@sjcny.edu.

Programs in Management Students: 23 full-time (17 women), 120 part-time (94 women); includes 39 minority (19 Black or African American, non-Hispanic/Latino; 1 Asian, non-Hispanic/Latino; 17 Hispanic/Latino; 2 Two or more races, non-Hispanic/Latino). Average age 36. 133 applicants, 64% accepted, 55 enrolled. *Faculty:* 15 full-time (7 women), 22 part-time/adjunct (7 women). Expenses: Contact institution. *Financial support:* In 2017–18, 27 students received support. In 2017, 41 master's awarded. *Program availability:* Part-time, evening/weekend, 100% online, blended/hybrid learning. Offers health care management (MS); human resources management (MS); human services leadership (MS); organizational management (MS). *Application deadline:* Applications are processed on a rolling basis. *Application fee:* $25. Electronic applications accepted. *Assistant Professor/Interim Director of Graduate Management Studies*, Mary A. Chance, 631-687-1297, E-mail: mchance@sjcny.edu.

ST. JOSEPH'S COLLEGE, NEW YORK, Brooklyn, NY 11205-3688

General Information Independent, coed, comprehensive institution. *Enrollment:* 1,176 graduate, professional, and undergraduate students; 43 full-time matriculated graduate/professional students (26 women), 197 part-time matriculated graduate/professional students (160 women). *Enrollment by degree level:* 240 master's. *Graduate faculty:* 13 full-time (10 women), 14 part-time/adjunct (10 women). *Tuition:* Full-time $17,550; part-time $975 per credit. *Required fees:* $362. *Graduate housing:* On-campus housing not available. *Student services:* Campus employment opportunities, campus safety program, career counseling, exercise/wellness program, free psychological counseling, low-cost health insurance, multicultural affairs office, services for students with disabilities, teacher training, writing training. *Library facilities:* McEntegart Hall Library plus 1 other. *Collection:* Books: 84,227 (physical), 163,718 (digital/electronic); Serial titles: 36 (physical), 59,734 (digital/electronic); Databases: 116. Weekly public service hours: 83; students can reserve study rooms.

Computer facilities: 238 computers available on campus for general student use. A campuswide network can be accessed from off campus. Online class registration, library databases, learning management system, course evaluations, print management, virtual application labs, office software, student suggestion box are available.
Website: http://www.sjcny.edu/

General Application Contact: Roberto Figueroa, Director, Adult, Transfer and Graduate Admissions, 718-940-5828, E-mail: rfigueroa@sjcny.edu.

GRADUATE UNITS

Program in Creative Writing Students: 14 full-time (10 women); includes 7 minority (2 Black or African American, non-Hispanic/Latino; 1 Asian, non-Hispanic/Latino; 3 Hispanic/Latino; 1 Two or more races, non-Hispanic/Latino). Average age 31. 31 applicants, 77% accepted, 3 enrolled. *Faculty:* 1 (woman) full-time, 3 part-time/adjunct (2 women). Expenses: Contact institution. *Financial support:* In 2017–18, 14 students received support. In 2017, 11 master's awarded. *Program availability:* Part-time, evening/weekend. Offers creative writing (MFA). *Application deadline:* Applications are processed on a rolling basis. Electronic applications accepted. *Associate Professor/Chair*, Theodore Hamm, 718-940-5307, E-mail: thamm@sjcny.edu.

Program in Forensic Computing Students: 4 full-time (1 woman), 4 part-time (2 women); includes 4 minority (2 Black or African American, non-Hispanic/Latino; 2 Hispanic/Latino). Average age 27. 11 applicants, 82% accepted, 3 enrolled. *Faculty:* 2 full-time (0 women), 1 (woman) part-time/adjunct. Expenses: Contact institution. *Financial support:* In 2017–18, 3 students received support. *Program availability:* Part-time, evening/weekend, online learning. Offers forensic computing (MS). *Application deadline:* Applications are processed on a rolling basis. *Application fee:* $25. Electronic applications accepted. *Application Contact:* Roberto Figueroa, Director, Graduate and Adult Admissions, 718-940-5828, E-mail: rfigueroa@sjcny.edu. *Associate Professor*, Dr. Joseph Pascarella, 718-940-5775, E-mail: jpascarella2@sjcny.edu.

Program in Nursing Students: 47 part-time (46 women); includes 38 minority (35 Black or African American, non-Hispanic/Latino; 1 Asian, non-Hispanic/Latino; 2 Two or more races, non-Hispanic/Latino). Average age 45. 51 applicants, 71% accepted, 20 enrolled. *Faculty:* 4 full-time (all women), 1 (woman) part-time/adjunct. Expenses: Contact institution. *Financial support:* In 2017–18, 7 students received support. In 2017, 7 master's awarded. *Program availability:* Part-time, evening/weekend. Offers adult-gerontology clinical nurse specialist (MS); adult-gerontology primary care nurse practitioner (MS); nursing education (MS). *Application deadline:* Applications are processed on a rolling basis. *Application fee:* $25. Electronic applications accepted. *Associate Professor/Director*, Maria Fletcher, 718-940-5891, E-mail: mfletcher@sjcny.edu.

Programs in Business Management and Administration Students: 5 full-time (2 women), 37 part-time (24 women); includes 33 minority (18 Black or African American, non-Hispanic/Latino; 2 Asian, non-Hispanic/Latino; 9 Hispanic/Latino; 4 Two or more races, non-Hispanic/Latino). Average age 37. 28 applicants, 57% accepted, 10 enrolled. *Faculty:* 1 full-time (0 women), 6 part-time/adjunct (4 women). Expenses: Contact institution. *Financial support:* In 2017–18, 9 students received support. In 2017, 18 master's awarded. *Program availability:* Part-time, evening/weekend, 100% online, blended/hybrid learning. Offers accounting (MBA); business administration (MBA); executive business administration (EMBA); management (MS). *Application deadline:* Applications are processed on a rolling basis. *Application fee:* $25. Electronic applications accepted. *Interim Director and Assistant Professor*, Mary A. Chance, 631-687-1297, E-mail: mchance@sjcny.edu.

Field of Executive Business Administration Students: 3 full-time (1 woman), 29 part-time (20 women); includes 26 minority (12 Black or African American, non-Hispanic/Latino; 2 Asian, non-Hispanic/Latino; 8 Hispanic/Latino; 4 Two or more races, non-Hispanic/Latino). Average age 40. 11 applicants, 100% accepted, 11 enrolled. *Faculty:* 1 full-time (0 women), 6 part-time/adjunct (4 women). Expenses: Contact institution. *Financial support:* In 2017–18, 6 students received support. In 2017, 16 master's awarded. *Program availability:* Part-time, evening/weekend, 100% online, blended/hybrid learning. Offers executive business administration (EMBA). *Application deadline:* Applications are processed on a rolling basis. *Application fee:* $25. Electronic applications accepted. *Co-Director of Graduate Management Studies/Assistant Professor*, Sharon Didier, 718-940-5790, E-mail: sdidier@sjcny.edu.

Programs in Education Students: 35 part-time (28 women); includes 7 minority (1 Black or African American, non-Hispanic/Latino; 6 Hispanic/Latino). Average age 23. 24 applicants, 96% accepted, 15 enrolled. *Faculty:* 5 full-time (all women), 4 part-time/adjunct (3 women). Expenses: Contact institution. *Financial support:* In 2017–18, 27 students received support. In 2017, 18 master's awarded. *Program availability:* Part-time, evening/weekend. Offers educational leadership (MA); literacy and cognition (MA); special education (MA). *Application deadline:* Applications are processed on a rolling basis. *Application fee:* $25. Electronic applications accepted. *Professor/Department Chair*, Nancy Gilchriest, 631-687-1472, E-mail: ngilchriest@sjcny.edu.

Field of Literacy and Cognition Students: 16 part-time (all women); includes 4 minority (all Hispanic/Latino). Average age 23. 10 applicants, 90% accepted, 7 enrolled. *Faculty:* 2 full-time (both women), 2 part-time/adjunct (both women). Expenses: Contact institution. *Financial support:* In 2017–18, 12 students received support. In 2017, 9 master's awarded. *Program availability:* Part-time, evening/weekend. Offers literacy and cognition (MA). *Application deadline:* Applications are processed on a rolling basis. *Application fee:* $25. Electronic applications accepted. *Associate Professor/Director of the Literacy and Cognition Program*, Esther Berkowitz, 718-940-5692, E-mail: eberkowitz@sjcny.edu.

Field of Special Education Students: 16 part-time (10 women); includes 3 minority (1 Black or African American, non-Hispanic/Latino; 2 Hispanic/Latino). Average age 23. 14 applicants, 100% accepted, 8 enrolled. *Faculty:* 3 full-time (all women), 1 (woman) part-time/adjunct. Expenses: Contact institution. *Financial support:* In 2017–18, 13 students received support. In 2017, 21 master's awarded. *Program availability:* Part-time, evening/weekend. Offers severe and multiple disabilities (MA). *Application deadline:* Applications are processed on a rolling basis. *Application fee:* $25. Electronic applications accepted. *Professor/Associate Chair/Director of the MA in Childhood and Adolescence Special Education*, Susan Straut-Collard, 718-940-5689, E-mail: sstrautcollard@sjcny.edu.

Programs in Health Care Administration Students: 8 full-time (4 women), 10 part-time (8 women); includes 14 minority (8 Black or African American, non-Hispanic/Latino; 4 Asian, non-Hispanic/Latino; 1 Hispanic/Latino; 1 Two or more races, non-Hispanic/Latino). Average age 36. 6 applicants, 50% accepted, 2 enrolled. *Faculty:* 1 full-time (0 women), 6 part-time/adjunct (4 women). Expenses: Contact institution. *Financial support:* In 2017–18, 2 students received support. In 2017, 7 master's awarded. *Program availability:* Part-time, evening/weekend, 100% online, blended/hybrid learning. Offers health care management (MBA); health care management - health information systems (MBA). *Application deadline:* Applications are processed on a rolling basis. *Application fee:* $25. Electronic applications accepted. *Associate Professor and Chair*, Lauren Pete, 718-940-5890, E-mail: lpete@sjcny.edu.

Field in Health Care Management - Health Information Systems Students: 5 full-time (2 women), 9 part-time (7 women); includes 11 minority (6 Black or African American, non-Hispanic/Latino; 4 Asian, non-Hispanic/Latino; 1 Two or more races, non-Hispanic/Latino). Average age 36. 6 applicants, 50% accepted, 2 enrolled. *Faculty:* 1 full-time (0 women), 6 part-time/adjunct (4 women). Expenses: Contact institution. *Financial support:* In 2017–18, 2 students received support. In 2017, 5 master's awarded. *Program availability:* Part-time, evening/weekend, 100% online, blended/hybrid learning. Offers health care management - health information systems (MBA). *Application deadline:* Applications are processed on a rolling basis. *Application fee:* $25. Electronic applications accepted. *Chair*, Lauren Pete, 718-940-5890, E-mail: lpete@sjcny.edu.

Programs in Management Students: 12 full-time (9 women), 60 part-time (48 women); includes 54 minority (39 Black or African American, non-Hispanic/Latino; 3 Asian, non-Hispanic/Latino; 11 Hispanic/Latino; 1 Two or more races, non-Hispanic/Latino). Average age 37. 73 applicants, 56% accepted, 36 enrolled. *Faculty:* 1 full-time (0 women), 6 part-time/adjunct (4 women). Expenses: Contact institution. *Financial support:* In 2017–18, 8 students received support. In 2017, 31 master's awarded. *Program availability:* Part-time, evening/weekend, 100% online, blended/hybrid learning. Offers human resources management (MS); management (MBA, MS); organizational management (MS). *Application deadline:* Applications are processed on a rolling basis. *Application fee:* $25. Electronic applications accepted. *Assistant Chair/Co-Director of Graduate Management Studies/Associate Professor*, Sharon Didier, 718-940-5790, E-mail: sdidier@sjcny.edu.

Field in Health Care Management Students: 4 full-time (all women), 24 part-time (19 women); includes 20 minority (14 Black or African American, non-Hispanic/Latino; 1 Asian, non-Hispanic/Latino; 5 Hispanic/Latino). Average age 36. 34 applicants, 47% accepted, 14 enrolled. *Faculty:* 1 full-time (0 women), 6 part-time/adjunct (4 women). Expenses: Contact institution. *Financial support:* In 2017–18, 2 students received support. In 2017, 12 master's awarded. *Program availability:* Part-time, evening/weekend, 100% online, blended/hybrid learning. Offers health care management (MBA). *Application deadline:* Applications are processed on a rolling basis. *Application fee:* $25. Electronic applications accepted. *Associate Professor/Chair*, Lauren Pete, 718-940-5890, E-mail: lpete@sjcny.edu.

Field in Human Services Management and Leadership Students: 13 part-time (9 women); includes 11 minority (9 Black or African American, non-Hispanic/Latino; 1 Asian, non-Hispanic/Latino; 1 Hispanic/Latino). Average age 40. 18 applicants, 61% accepted, 10 enrolled. *Faculty:* 1 full-time (0 women), 6 part-time/adjunct (4 women). Expenses: Contact institution. *Financial support:* In 2017–18, 1 student received support. In 2017, 5 master's awarded. *Program availability:* Part-time, evening/weekend, 100% online, blended/hybrid learning. Offers human services management and leadership (MS). *Application deadline:* Applications are processed on a rolling basis. *Application fee:* $25. Electronic applications accepted. *Assistant Chair/Co-Director of Graduate Management Studies/Associate Professor*, Sharon Didier, 718-940-5790, E-mail: sdidier@sjcny.edu.

SAINT JOSEPH'S COLLEGE OF MAINE, Standish, ME 04084

General Information Independent-religious, coed, comprehensive institution. *Graduate housing:* On-campus housing not available.

GRADUATE UNITS

Master of Accountancy Program *Program availability:* Part-time, online learning. Offers accountancy (M Acc). Electronic applications accepted.

Master of Arts in Pastoral Theology Program *Program availability:* Part-time, online learning. Offers pastoral theology (MA).

Master of Business Administration in Leadership Program *Program availability:* Part-time, online learning. Offers leadership (MBA).

Master of Health Administration Program *Program availability:* Part-time, online learning. Offers health administration (MHA). Degree program is external; available only by correspondence and online. Electronic applications accepted.

Master of Science in Education Program *Program availability:* Part-time, online learning. Offers adult education and training (MS Ed); Catholic school leadership (MS Ed); health care educator (MS Ed); school educator (MS Ed). Program available by correspondence. Electronic applications accepted.

Master of Science in Nursing Program *Program availability:* Part-time, online learning. Offers administration (MSN); education (MSN); family nurse practitioner (MSN); nursing administration and leadership (Certificate); nursing and health care education (Certificate). Electronic applications accepted.

ST. JOSEPH'S SEMINARY, Yonkers, NY 10704

General Information Independent-religious, coed, graduate-only institution. *Graduate housing:* Room and/or apartments guaranteed to single students; on-campus housing not available to married students.

GRADUATE UNITS

Graduate and Professional Programs Offers Catholic philosophical studies (MA); divinity (M Div); pastoral studies (MAPS); theology (MA).

SAINT JOSEPH'S UNIVERSITY, Philadelphia, PA 19131-1395

General Information Independent-religious, coed, comprehensive institution. *Enrollment:* 8,086 graduate, professional, and undergraduate students; 423 full-time matriculated graduate/professional students (220 women), 2,478 part-time matriculated graduate/professional students (1,584 women). *Enrollment by degree level:* 2,709 master's, 80 doctoral, 112 other advanced degrees. *Graduate faculty:* 107 full-time (51 women), 190 part-time/adjunct (85 women). *Graduate housing:* On-campus housing not available. *Student services:* Campus employment opportunities, campus safety program, career counseling, exercise/wellness program, free psychological counseling, international student services, low-cost health insurance, multicultural affairs office, services for students with disabilities, teacher training, writing training. *Library facilities:* Post Learning Commons and Drexel Library. *Collection:* Books: 278,990 (physical), 557,060 (digital/electronic); Serial titles: 483 (physical), 71,735 (digital/electronic); Databases: 175. Weekly public service hours: 99; students can reserve study rooms.

Computer facilities: Computer purchase and lease plans are available. 682 computers available on campus for general student use. A campuswide network can be accessed from student residence rooms and from off campus. Online class registration is available.
Website: http://www.sju.edu/

General Application Contact: Office of Graduate Operations, 610-660-1101, E-mail: graduate@sju.edu.

GRADUATE UNITS

College of Arts and Sciences Students: 188 full-time (126 women), 1,619 part-time (1,213 women); includes 467 minority (325 Black or African American, non-Hispanic/Latino; 8 American Indian or Alaska Native, non-Hispanic/Latino; 46 Asian, non-Hispanic/Latino; 74 Hispanic/Latino; 1 Native Hawaiian or other Pacific Islander, non-Hispanic/Latino; 13 Two or more races, non-Hispanic/Latino), 66 international. Average age 33. 894 applicants, 69% accepted, 395 enrolled. *Faculty:* 61 full-time (39 women), 139 part-time/adjunct (76 women). Expenses: Contact institution. *Financial support:* Scholarships/grants and unspecified assistantships available. Financial award application deadline: 5/1; financial award applicants required to submit FAFSA. In 2017, 768 master's, 13 doctorates, 30 other advanced degrees awarded. *Program availability:* Part-time, evening/weekend, 100% online, blended/hybrid learning. Offers arts and sciences (MA, MS, Ed D, Certificate, Post-Master's Certificate); behavior analysis (MS, Post-Master's Certificate); behavior management (MS); biology (MA, MS); computer science (MS); criminal justice (MS); curriculum supervisor (Certificate); educational leadership (MS, Ed D); elementary education (MS, Certificate); elementary/middle school education (Certificate); federal law enforcement (MS); health administration (MS); health informatics (MS); intelligence and crime analysis (MS); mathematics and computer science (Post-Master's Certificate); organizational development and leadership (MS); organizations development and leadership (MS); principal (Certificate); professional education (MS); psychology (MS); reading specialist (MS, Certificate); reading supervisor (Certificate); secondary education (MS, Certificate); special education (MS); special education 7-12 (Certificate); special education PK-8 (Certificate); superintendent's letter of eligibility (Certificate); supervisor of special education (Certificate); teacher of the deaf and hard of hearing (Certificate); writing studies (MA). *Application deadline:* For fall admission, 3/15 for international students; for spring admission, 11/1 for international students. Applications are processed on a rolling basis. *Application fee:* $35. Electronic applications accepted. *Application Contact:* Marketing and Admissions, Graduate Arts and Sciences, 610-660-3131, E-mail: gradstudies@sju.edu. *Dean,* Dr. Shaily Menon, 610-660-1282, E-mail: gradstudies@sju.edu.

Erivan K. Haub School of Business Students: 235 full-time (94 women), 859 part-time (371 women); includes 235 minority (109 Black or African American, non-Hispanic/Latino; 65 Asian, non-Hispanic/Latino; 45 Hispanic/Latino; 2 Native Hawaiian or other Pacific Islander, non-Hispanic/Latino; 14 Two or more races, non-Hispanic/Latino), 156 international. Average age 33. 712 applicants, 73% accepted, 281 enrolled. *Faculty:* 46 full-time (12 women), 51 part-time/adjunct (9 women). Expenses: Contact institution. *Financial support:* Scholarships/grants and unspecified assistantships available. Financial award application deadline: 5/1; financial award applicants required to submit FAFSA. In 2017, 381 master's awarded. *Program availability:* Part-time-only, evening/weekend, 100% online. Offers accounting (MBA); business (MBA, MS, Post Master's Certificate, Postbaccalaureate Certificate); business intelligence analytics (MBA); business intelligence and analytics (MS); customer analytics and insights (MS); executive business administration (MBA); finance (MBA); financial analysis reporting (Postbaccalaureate Certificate); financial services (MS); food marketing (MBA, MS); general business (MBA); health and medical services administration (MBA); international business (MBA); international marketing (MBA, MS); leading (MBA); marketing (MBA); pharmaceutical and healthcare marketing (MBA, Post Master's Certificate); strategic human resources management (MS). *Application deadline:* For fall admission, 7/15 priority date for domestic students, 5/15 priority date for international students; for spring admission, 11/15 priority date for domestic students, 10/15 priority date for international students; for summer admission, 4/15 priority date for domestic students, 2/15 priority date for international students. Applications are processed on a rolling basis. *Application fee:* $35. Electronic applications accepted. *Application Contact:* Jeannine Lajeunesse, Director, MBA and MS Programs, 610-660-1626, Fax: 610-660-1599, E-mail: jlajeune@sju.edu. *Dean,* Dr. Joseph A. DiAngelo, 610-660-1645, Fax: 610-660-1649, E-mail: jodiange@sju.edu.

ST. LAWRENCE UNIVERSITY, Canton, NY 13617

General Information Independent, coed, comprehensive institution. *Graduate housing:* Room and/or apartments available on a first-come, first-served basis to single students; on-campus housing not available to married students. Housing application deadline: 4/1.

GRADUATE UNITS

Department of Education *Program availability:* Part-time, evening/weekend. Offers combined school building leadership/school district leadership (CAS); counseling and human development (M Ed, MS, CAS); educational leadership (M Ed, CAS); general studies in education (M Ed); mental health counseling (MS); school building leadership (M Ed); school counseling (M Ed, CAS); school district leadership (CAS).

SAINT LEO UNIVERSITY, Saint Leo, FL 33574-6665

General Information Independent-religious, coed, comprehensive institution. *Enrollment:* 5,898 graduate, professional, and undergraduate students; 144 full-time matriculated graduate/professional students (120 women), 3,274 part-time matriculated graduate/professional students (1,989 women). *Enrollment by degree level:* 3,235 master's, 143 doctoral, 40 other advanced degrees. *Graduate faculty:* 99 full-time (41 women), 134 part-time/adjunct (56 women). *Tuition:* Full-time $12,960; part-time $720 per credit hour. Tuition and fees vary according to degree level, campus/location and program. *Graduate housing:* Room and/or apartments available on a first-come, first-served basis to single students; on-campus housing not available to married students. *Student services:* Campus employment opportunities, campus safety program, career counseling, exercise/wellness program, free psychological counseling, international student services, low-cost health insurance, multicultural affairs office, services for students with disabilities, teacher training, writing training. *Library facilities:* Cannon Memorial Library plus 1 other. *Collection:* Books: 97,155 (physical), 403,383 (digital/electronic); Serial titles: 265 (physical), 170,845 (digital/electronic); Databases: 72. Weekly public service hours: 119. *Research affiliation:* American Jewish Committee (religion).

Computer facilities: Computer purchase and lease plans are available. 150 computers available on campus for general student use. A campuswide network can be accessed from student residence rooms and from off campus. Online class registration is available.
Website: http://www.saintleo.edu/

General Application Contact: Mark Russum, Assistant Vice President, Enrollment, 800-707-8846, Fax: 352-588-7873, E-mail: grad.admissions@saintleo.edu.

GRADUATE UNITS

Graduate Studies in Business Students: 9 full-time (3 women), 1,867 part-time (1,079 women); includes 861 minority (598 Black or African American, non-Hispanic/Latino; 3 American Indian or Alaska Native, non-Hispanic/Latino; 38 Asian, non-Hispanic/Latino; 186 Hispanic/Latino; 3 Native Hawaiian or other Pacific Islander, non-Hispanic/Latino; 33 Two or more races, non-Hispanic/Latino), 68 international. Average age 37. 868 applicants, 63% accepted, 537 enrolled. *Faculty:* 54 full-time (18 women), 52 part-time/adjunct (18 women). Expenses: Contact institution. *Financial support:* In 2017–18, 106 students received support. Career-related internships or fieldwork, health care benefits, and tuition remission for Saint Leo employees and their dependents available. Financial award application deadline: 3/1; financial award applicants required to submit FAFSA. In 2017, 859 master's, 3 doctorates awarded. *Program availability:* Part-time, evening/weekend, 100% online, blended/hybrid learning. Offers accounting (M Acc, MBA); cybersecurity (MS); cybersecurity management (MBA); data analytics (MBA); health care management (MBA); human resource management (MBA); international and experiential business administration (MBA); management (MBA, DBA); marketing (MBA); marketing research and social media analytics (MBA); project management (MBA); social media marketing (MBA); sport business (MBA); supply chain global integration management (MBA). *Application deadline:* For fall admission, 7/1 priority date for domestic and international students; for spring admission, 11/12 priority date for domestic students, 11/1 for international students. Applications are processed on a rolling basis. *Application fee:* $80. Electronic applications accepted. *Application Contact:* Mark Russum, Assistant Vice President, Enrollment, 800-707-8846, Fax: 352-588-7873, E-mail: grad.admissions@saintleo.edu. *Dean, School of Business,* Dr. Charles Hale, 352-588-8599, Fax: 352-588-8912, E-mail: mbaslu@saintleo.edu.

Graduate Studies in Creative Writing Students: 28 part-time (18 women); includes 5 minority (3 Black or African American, non-Hispanic/Latino; 2 Hispanic/Latino). Average age 40. 21 applicants, 57% accepted, 12 enrolled. *Faculty:* 3 full-time (1 woman), 3 part-time/adjunct (1 woman). Expenses: Contact institution. *Financial support:* In 2017–18, 6 students received support. Scholarships/grants, health care benefits, and tuition remission for Saint Leo employees and their dependents available. Financial award application deadline: 3/1; financial award applicants required to submit FAFSA. *Program availability:* Part-time. Offers creative writing (MA); war literature and writing for veterans (MA). *Application deadline:* For fall admission, 7/1 priority date for domestic and international students; for spring admission, 11/1 priority date for domestic and international students. Applications are processed on a rolling basis. *Application fee:* $80. Electronic applications accepted. *Application Contact:* Mark Russum, Assistant Vice President, Enrollment, 800-707-8846, Fax: 352-588-7873, E-mail: grad.admissions@saintleo.edu. *Director,* Dr. Steve Kistulentz, 352-588-7218, Fax: 352-588-8300, E-mail: steven.kistulentz@saintleo.edu.

Graduate Studies in Education Students: 1 (woman) full-time, 360 part-time (282 women); includes 95 minority (56 Black or African American, non-Hispanic/Latino; 1 American Indian or Alaska Native, non-Hispanic/Latino; 1 Asian, non-Hispanic/Latino; 31 Hispanic/Latino; 6 Two or more races, non-Hispanic/Latino), 1 international. Average age 37. 214 applicants, 69% accepted, 125 enrolled. *Faculty:* 8 full-time (all women), 18 part-time/adjunct (11 women). Expenses: Contact institution. *Financial support:* In 2017–18, 17 students received support. Career-related internships or fieldwork, scholarships/grants, health care benefits, and tuition remission for Saint Leo employees and their dependents available. Financial award application deadline: 3/1; financial award applicants required to submit FAFSA. In 2017, 158 master's, 5 other advanced degrees awarded. *Program availability:* Part-time, evening/weekend, online only, 100% online. Offers educational leadership (M Ed); exceptional student education (M Ed); instructional design (MS, Certificate); instructional leadership (M Ed); reading (M Ed,

Certificate); school leadership (Ed S). *Application deadline:* For fall admission, 7/1 priority date for domestic students, 7/1 for international students; for winter admission, 7/1 for international students; for spring admission, 11/1 priority date for domestic students. Applications are processed on a rolling basis. *Application fee:* $80. Electronic applications accepted. *Application Contact:* Mark Russum, Assistant Vice President, Enrollment, 800-707-8846, Fax: 352-588-7873, E-mail: grad.admissions@saintleo.edu. *Director of Graduate Studies in Education*, Dr. Fern Aefsky, 352-588-8309, Fax: 352-588-8861, E-mail: kara.winkler@saintleo.edu.

Graduate Studies in Human Services Students: 70 part-time (66 women); includes 52 minority (50 Black or African American, non-Hispanic/Latino; 2 Hispanic/Latino). Average age 40. 77 applicants, 65% accepted, 47 enrolled. *Faculty:* 4 full-time (all women), 2 part-time/adjunct (both women). Expenses: Contact institution. *Financial support:* In 2017–18, 4 students received support. Career-related internships or fieldwork, scholarships/grants, health care benefits, and tuition remission for Saint Leo employees and their dependents available. Financial award application deadline: 3/1; financial award applicants required to submit FAFSA. In 2017, 7 master's awarded. *Program availability:* Part-time, evening/weekend, 100% online. Offers human services (MS). *Application deadline:* For fall admission, 7/1 for domestic and international students; for spring admission, 11/1 for domestic and international students. Applications are processed on a rolling basis. *Application fee:* $80. Electronic applications accepted. *Application Contact:* Mary Martinez-Drovie, Graduate Enrollment Counselor, 352-588-5802, Fax: 352-588-8289, E-mail: mary.martinez-drovie@saintleo.edu. *Dean, School of Education and Social Services*, Dr. Susan Kinsella, 352-588-8272, Fax: 352-588-8289, E-mail: susan.kinsella@saintleo.edu.

Graduate Studies in Public Safety Administration Students: 7 full-time (6 women), 617 part-time (385 women); includes 313 minority (235 Black or African American, non-Hispanic/Latino; 5 American Indian or Alaska Native, non-Hispanic/Latino; 3 Asian, non-Hispanic/Latino; 54 Hispanic/Latino; 1 Native Hawaiian or other Pacific Islander, non-Hispanic/Latino; 15 Two or more races, non-Hispanic/Latino). Average age 36. 336 applicants, 63% accepted, 197 enrolled. *Faculty:* 8 full-time (3 women), 32 part-time/adjunct (7 women). Expenses: Contact institution. *Financial support:* In 2017–18, 21 students received support. Scholarships/grants, health care benefits, unspecified assistantships, and tuition remission for Saint Leo employees and their dependents available. Financial award application deadline: 3/1; financial award applicants required to submit FAFSA. In 2017, 267 master's awarded. *Program availability:* Part-time, evening/weekend, 100% online, blended/hybrid learning. Offers criminal justice (MS); emergency and disaster management (MS). *Application deadline:* For fall admission, 7/1 priority date for domestic and international students; for spring admission, 11/1 priority date for domestic and international students. Applications are processed on a rolling basis. *Application fee:* $80. Electronic applications accepted. *Application Contact:* Mark Russum, Assistant Vice President, Enrollment, 800-707-8846, Fax: 352-588-7873, E-mail: grad.admissions@saintleo.edu. *Director of Graduate Studies in Safety Administration*, Dr. Robert Diemer, 352-588-8974, Fax: 352-588-8289, E-mail: graduatepublicsafety@saintleo.edu.

Graduate Studies in Social Work Students: 127 full-time (110 women), 80 part-time (68 women); includes 100 minority (78 Black or African American, non-Hispanic/Latino; 1 Asian, non-Hispanic/Latino; 18 Hispanic/Latino; 3 Two or more races, non-Hispanic/Latino). Average age 36. 257 applicants, 49% accepted, 111 enrolled. *Faculty:* 10 full-time (8 women), 17 part-time/adjunct (15 women). Expenses: Contact institution. *Financial support:* In 2017–18, 4 students received support. Career-related internships or fieldwork, Federal Work-Study, health care benefits, and tuition remission for Saint Leo employees and their dependents available. Financial award application deadline: 3/1. In 2017, 95 master's awarded. *Program availability:* Online only, blended/hybrid learning. Offers advanced clinical practice (MSW). *Application deadline:* For fall admission, 6/1 for domestic and international students. *Application fee:* $80. Electronic applications accepted. *Application Contact:* Mark Russum, Assistant Vice President, Enrollment, 800-707-8846, Fax: 352-588-7873, E-mail: grad.admissions@saintleo.edu. *Director of Graduate Studies in Social Work*, Dr. Cindy Lee, 352-588-8869, Fax: 352-588-8289, E-mail: cindy.lee@saintleo.edu.

Graduate Studies in Theology Students: 228 part-time (73 women); includes 35 minority (18 Black or African American, non-Hispanic/Latino; 1 Asian, non-Hispanic/Latino; 13 Hispanic/Latino; 1 Native Hawaiian or other Pacific Islander, non-Hispanic/Latino; 2 Two or more races, non-Hispanic/Latino), 4 international. Average age 50. 139 applicants, 76% accepted, 89 enrolled. *Faculty:* 10 full-time (0 women), 10 part-time/adjunct (3 women). Expenses: Contact institution. *Financial support:* In 2017–18, 4 students received support. Scholarships/grants, health care benefits, and tuition remission for Saint Leo employees and their dependents available. Financial award application deadline: 3/1; financial award applicants required to submit FAFSA. In 2017, 52 master's, 2 other advanced degrees awarded. *Program availability:* Part-time, evening/weekend, 100% online, blended/hybrid learning. Offers theology (MA, Certificate). *Application deadline:* For fall admission, 7/1 priority date for domestic and international students; for spring admission, 11/1 priority date for domestic and international students. Applications are processed on a rolling basis. *Application fee:* $80. Electronic applications accepted. *Application Contact:* Mark Russum, Assistant Vice President, Enrollment, 800-707-8846, Fax: 352-588-7873, E-mail: grad.admissions@saintleo.edu. *Director, Graduate Theology*, Dr. Randall Woodard, 352-588-8239, Fax: 352-588-8404, E-mail: randall.woodard@saintleo.edu.

ST. LOUIS COLLEGE OF PHARMACY, St. Louis, MO 63110-1088

General Information Independent, coed, comprehensive institution. *Enrollment:* 1,309 graduate, professional, and undergraduate students; 855 full-time matriculated graduate/professional students (507 women), 6 part-time matriculated graduate/professional students (2 women). *Enrollment by degree level:* 861 doctoral. *Graduate faculty:* 64 full-time (43 women), 30 part-time/adjunct (20 women). *Tuition:* Full-time $34,086; part-time $1136 per hour. *Required fees:* $670; $670 per semester. *Graduate housing:* Room and/or apartments available on a first-come, first-served basis to single students; on-campus housing not available to married students. Typical cost: $6300 per year ($11,572 including board). Room and board charges vary according to housing facility selected. Housing application deadline: 6/1. *Student services:* Campus employment opportunities, campus safety program, career counseling, exercise/wellness program, free psychological counseling, international student services, low-cost health insurance, multicultural affairs office, services for students with disabilities, writing training. *Library facilities:* O. J. Cloughly Alumni Library. *Collection:* Books: 14,941 (physical), 180,979 (digital/electronic); Serial titles: 445 (physical), 43,334 (digital/electronic); Databases: 62. Weekly public service hours: 101; study areas open 24 hours, 5–7 days a week; students can reserve study rooms. *Research affiliation:* Express Scripts (pharmacy), Strategic Biomedical, Inc.

Computer facilities: Computer purchase and lease plans are available. 1,390 computers available on campus for general student use. A campuswide network can be accessed from student residence rooms and from off campus. Online class registration is available.
Website: http://www.stlcop.edu/

General Application Contact: Chase Davis, Director of Admissions, 314-446-8140, Fax: 314-446-8309, E-mail: chase.davis@stlcop.edu.

GRADUATE UNITS

School of Pharmacy Students: 855 full-time (507 women), 6 part-time (2 women); includes 283 minority (62 Black or African American, non-Hispanic/Latino; 1 American Indian or Alaska Native, non-Hispanic/Latino; 194 Asian, non-Hispanic/Latino; 11 Hispanic/Latino; 2 Native Hawaiian or other Pacific Islander, non-Hispanic/Latino; 13 Two or more races, non-Hispanic/Latino), 30 international. Average age 24. 522 applicants, 56% accepted, 250 enrolled. *Faculty:* 64 full-time (43 women), 30 part-time/adjunct (20 women). Expenses: Contact institution. *Financial support:* In 2017–18, 392 students received support. Federal Work-Study and scholarships/grants available. Financial award application deadline: 3/15; financial award applicants required to submit FAFSA. In 2017, 218 doctorates awarded. Offers pharmacy (Pharm D). *Application deadline:* For fall admission, 3/1 for domestic and international students. Applications are processed on a rolling basis. *Application fee:* $55. Electronic applications accepted. *Application Contact:* Chase Davis, Director of Admissions, 314-446-8140, Fax: 314-446-8309, E-mail: chase.davis@stlcop.edu. *Dean of Pharmacy*, Dr. Bruce Canaday, 314-446-8184.

SAINT LOUIS UNIVERSITY, St. Louis, MO 63103

General Information Independent-religious, coed, university. CGS member. *Graduate housing:* Rooms and/or apartments available to single and married students. Housing application deadline: 5/1. *Research affiliation:* National Center for Atmospheric Research (earth and atmospheric sciences), Argonne National Laboratory (energy, physics, chemistry, mathematics and computer science), Small Business Administration (business, administration and entrepreneurship), Monsanto Chemical Corporation (chemistry), Missouri Botanical Garden (biology, plant science), AT&T Foundation (communication).

GRADUATE UNITS

Graduate Programs *Program availability:* Part-time, evening/weekend, online learning. Electronic applications accepted.

Center for Advanced Dental Education Offers endodontics (MSD); orthodontics (MSD); periodontics (MSD). Electronic applications accepted.

Center for Health Care Ethics Offers clinical health care ethics (Certificate); health care ethics (PhD). Electronic applications accepted.

College for Public Health and Social Justice *Program availability:* Part-time. Offers administration of justice (MA); applied behavior analysis (MS); community health (MPH, MS, MSPH); emergency management (MA); health administration (MHA); health policy (MPH); public health and social justice (MA, MHA, MPH, MS, MSPH, MSW, PhD, Certificate); public health studies (PhD); social work (MSW, PhD); treatment and rehabilitation (MA); urban planning and development (MS).

College of Arts and Sciences *Program availability:* Part-time, evening/weekend. Offers American studies (MA, MA-R, PhD); arts and sciences (M Pr Met, MA, MA-R, MS, MS-R, PhD); bioinformatics and computational biology (MS); biology (MS, MS-R, PhD); chemistry (MS, MS-R, PhD); clinical psychology (MS-R, PhD); communication (MA, MA-R); computer science (MS); English (MA, MA-R, PhD); experimental psychology (MS-R, PhD); French (MA); geophysics (PhD); geoscience (MS); historical theology (MA, PhD); history (MA, MA-R, PhD); industrial-organizational psychology (PhD); mathematics (MA, PhD); meteorology (M Pr Met, MS-R, PhD); philosophy (MA, MA-R, PhD); political science (MA); psychology (PhD); software engineering (MS); Spanish (MA); theology (MA). Electronic applications accepted.

Doisy College of Health Sciences *Program availability:* Part-time. Offers athletic training (MAT); communication sciences and disorders (MA); health sciences (MAT, MMS, MOT, MS, DPT, PhD, Certificate); medical dietetics (MS); nutrition and physical performance (MS); occupational science and occupational therapy (MOT); physical therapy (DPT); physician assistant education (MMS).

John Cook School of Business *Program availability:* Part-time, evening/weekend. Offers accounting (M Acct, MBA); business (EMIB, M Acct, MBA, MSF, PhD); business administration (MBA); executive international business (EMIB); finance (MBA, MSF); international business (MBA). Electronic applications accepted.

Parks College of Engineering, Aviation, and Technology *Program availability:* Part-time, online learning. Offers biomedical engineering (MS, MS-R, PhD); engineering, aviation, and technology (MS, MS-R, PhD).

School of Education *Program availability:* Part-time. Offers Catholic school leadership (MA); curriculum and instruction (MA, Ed D, PhD); education (MA, MA-R, MAT, Ed D, PhD, Certificate, Ed S); educational administration (MA, Ed D, PhD, Ed S); educational foundations (MA, Ed D, PhD); higher education (MA, Ed D, PhD); special education (MA); student personnel administration (MA); teaching (MAT). Electronic applications accepted.

School of Medicine Offers anatomy (MS-R, PhD); biochemistry and molecular biology (PhD); biomedical sciences (MS-R, PhD); medicine (MS-R, MD, PhD); molecular microbiology and immunology (PhD); pathology (PhD); pharmacological and physiological science (PhD). Electronic applications accepted.

School of Nursing *Program availability:* Part-time, online learning. Offers nursing (MSN, DNP, PhD, Certificate). Electronic applications accepted.

School of Law *Program availability:* Part-time, evening/weekend. Offers law (LL M, JD). Electronic applications accepted.

SAINT LOUIS UNIVERSITY–MADRID CAMPUS, 28003 Madrid, Spain

General Information Independent-religious, coed, comprehensive institution. *Graduate housing:* Room and/or apartments guaranteed to single students. *Research affiliation:* Universidad Autonoma de Madrid (English philology), Pontificia Universidade Catolica do Rio de Janeiro, Sogang University, Korea.

GRADUATE UNITS

Graduate Programs *Program availability:* Part-time. Offers English (MA); Spanish (MA).

SAINT MARTIN'S UNIVERSITY, Lacey, WA 98503

General Information Independent-religious, coed, comprehensive institution. *Enrollment:* 1,565 graduate, professional, and undergraduate students; 68 full-time matriculated graduate/professional students (36 women), 180 part-time matriculated graduate/professional students (120 women). *Enrollment by degree level:* 233 master's, 15 other advanced degrees. *Graduate faculty:* 23 full-time (11 women), 27 part-time/adjunct (13 women). *Tuition:* Full-time $21,420; part-time $1190 per credit. *Graduate housing:* Room and/or apartments available on a first-come, first-served basis to single students; on-campus housing not available to married students. Typical cost:

$5410 per year ($11,030 including board). Housing application deadline: 3/15. *Student services:* Campus employment opportunities, campus safety program, career counseling, exercise/wellness program, free psychological counseling, international student services, low-cost health insurance, multicultural affairs office, services for students with disabilities, writing training. *Library facilities:* O'Grady Library. *Collection:* Books: 86,191 (physical), 199,723 (digital/electronic); Serial titles: 94 (physical), 47,915 (digital/electronic); Databases: 115. Weekly public service hours: 88; students can reserve study rooms.

Computer facilities: 80 computers available on campus for general student use. A campuswide network can be accessed from student residence rooms. Online class registration is available.
Website: http://www.stmartin.edu/

General Application Contact: Casey Caronna, Administrative Assistant III, 360-412-6128, E-mail: ccaronna@stmartin.edu.

GRADUATE UNITS

Office of Graduate Studies Students: 68 full-time (36 women), 180 part-time (120 women); includes 70 minority (16 Black or African American, non-Hispanic/Latino; 2 American Indian or Alaska Native, non-Hispanic/Latino; 14 Asian, non-Hispanic/Latino; 25 Hispanic/Latino; 1 Native Hawaiian or other Pacific Islander, non-Hispanic/Latino; 12 Two or more races, non-Hispanic/Latino), 12 international. Average age 35. 67 applicants, 99% accepted, 50 enrolled. *Faculty:* 23 full-time (11 women), 27 part-time/adjunct (13 women). Expenses: Contact institution. *Financial support:* Career-related internships or fieldwork, institutionally sponsored loans, and scholarships/grants available. Support available to part-time students. Financial award application deadline: 3/1; financial award applicants required to submit FAFSA. In 2017, 123 master's awarded. *Program availability:* Part-time, evening/weekend. Offers civil engineering (MCE); counseling psychology (MAC); engineering management (M Eng Mgt); mechanical engineering (MME). *Application deadline:* For fall admission, 4/1 priority date for domestic and international students; for spring admission, 11/1 for domestic students, 11/1 priority date for international students. Applications are processed on a rolling basis. *Application fee:* $50. Electronic applications accepted. *Application Contact:* Casey Caronna, Administrative Assistant, 360-412-6142, E-mail: ccaronna@stmartin.edu.

College of Education Students: 26 full-time (15 women), 45 part-time (34 women); includes 7 minority (1 Black or African American, non-Hispanic/Latino; 2 Asian, non-Hispanic/Latino; 3 Hispanic/Latino; 1 Two or more races, non-Hispanic/Latino). Average age 35. 12 applicants, 92% accepted, 8 enrolled. *Faculty:* 8 full-time (6 women), 12 part-time/adjunct (6 women). Expenses: Contact institution. *Financial support:* Career-related internships or fieldwork, Federal Work-Study, institutionally sponsored loans, and unspecified assistantships available. Support available to part-time students. Financial award application deadline: 3/1; financial award applicants required to submit FAFSA. In 2017, 28 master's awarded. *Program availability:* Part-time, evening/weekend. Offers education (M Ed, MIT). *Application deadline:* For fall admission, 4/1 priority date for domestic and international students; for spring admission, 11/1 priority date for domestic and international students. Applications are processed on a rolling basis. *Application fee:* $50. Electronic applications accepted. *Application Contact:* Casey Caronna, Administrative Assistant, 360-412-6128, E-mail: ccaronna@stmartin.edu. *College of Education and Counseling Psychology,* Dr. Kathleen M. Boyle, 360-438-4333, Fax: 360-438-4486, E-mail: kboyle@stmartin.edu.

School of Business Students: 29 full-time (14 women), 33 part-time (10 women); includes 28 minority (8 Black or African American, non-Hispanic/Latino; 7 Asian, non-Hispanic/Latino; 8 Hispanic/Latino; 1 Native Hawaiian or other Pacific Islander, non-Hispanic/Latino; 4 Two or more races, non-Hispanic/Latino), 6 international. Average age 34. 16 applicants, 100% accepted, 14 enrolled. *Faculty:* 3 full-time (1 woman), 11 part-time/adjunct (4 women). Expenses: Contact institution. *Financial support:* Career-related internships or fieldwork and scholarships/grants available. Support available to part-time students. Financial award application deadline: 3/1; financial award applicants required to submit FAFSA. In 2017, 48 master's awarded. *Program availability:* Part-time, evening/weekend. Offers business (MBA). *Application deadline:* For fall admission, 7/1 priority date for domestic and international students; for spring admission, 12/1 for domestic students, 12/1 priority date for international students. Applications are processed on a rolling basis. *Application fee:* $50. Electronic applications accepted. *Application Contact:* Casey Caronna, Administrative Assistant, 360-412-6128, E-mail: ccaronna@stmartin.edu. *Director, MBA Program,* Dr. Donald Conant, 360-556-7359, E-mail: dconant@stmartin.edu.

SAINT MARY-OF-THE-WOODS COLLEGE, Saint Mary of the Woods, IN 47876

General Information Independent-religious, coed, primarily women, comprehensive institution. *Enrollment:* 952 graduate, professional, and undergraduate students; 230 full-time matriculated graduate/professional students (216 women). *Enrollment by degree level:* 230 master's. *Graduate faculty:* 18 full-time (13 women), 8 part-time/adjunct (7 women). *Tuition:* Full-time $4260; part-time $3550 per credit hour. Tuition and fees vary according to program. *Graduate housing:* On-campus housing not available. *Student services:* Campus employment opportunities, campus safety program, career counseling, exercise/wellness program, grant writing training, international student services, services for students with disabilities, writing training. *Library facilities:* Rooney Library.

Computer facilities: Computer purchase and lease plans are available. A campuswide network can be accessed.
Website: http://www.smwc.edu/

General Application Contact: Marie Elliott, Assistant Director of Admissions, 812-535-5106, E-mail: graduate@smwc.edu.

GRADUATE UNITS

Master of Arts in Art Therapy Program Students: 144 full-time (139 women); includes 20 minority (all Two or more races, non-Hispanic/Latino). Average age 37. 88 applicants, 49% accepted, 36 enrolled. *Faculty:* 2 full-time (both women). Expenses: Contact institution. *Financial support:* In 2017–18, 92 students received support. Scholarships/grants available. Financial award applicants required to submit FAFSA. In 2017, 24 master's awarded. *Program availability:* Part-time. Offers art therapy (MA, Post-Master's Certificate). *Application deadline:* For fall admission, 4/30 for domestic and international students; for winter admission, 10/31 for domestic and international students. *Application fee:* $0. Electronic applications accepted. *Application Contact:* Marie Elliott, Assistant Director of Admissions, 812-535-5106, E-mail: graduate@smwc.edu. *Director,* Dr. Jill McNutt, 812-535-5160, E-mail: jmcnutt@smwc.edu.

Master of Arts in Music Therapy Program Students: 24 full-time (22 women). Average age 32. 20 applicants, 55% accepted, 9 enrolled. Expenses: Contact institution. *Financial support:* In 2017–18, 16 students received support. Career-related internships or fieldwork, scholarships/grants, and unspecified assistantships available. Financial award applicants required to submit FAFSA. In 2017, 7 master's awarded. *Program availability:* Part-time, blended/hybrid learning. Offers music therapy (MA). *Application deadline:* For fall admission, 4/30 for domestic and international students; for winter admission, 10/31 for domestic students, 10/30 for international students. *Application fee:* $0. Electronic applications accepted. *Application Contact:* Marie Elliott, Assistant Director of Admissions, 800-926-7692, E-mail: graduate@smwc.edu. *Director,* Dr. Tracy Richardson, 812-535-5154, E-mail: trichardson@smwc.edu.

Master of Healthcare Administration Program Offers healthcare administration (MHA).

Master of Leadership Development Program Students: 47 full-time (41 women); includes 4 minority (all Black or African American, non-Hispanic/Latino). Average age 35. 26 applicants, 81% accepted, 19 enrolled. Expenses: Contact institution. *Financial support:* In 2017–18, 28 students received support. Scholarships/grants available. Financial award applicants required to submit FAFSA. In 2017, 24 master's awarded. *Program availability:* Part-time. Offers not-for-profit leadership (MLD); organizational leadership (MLD). *Application deadline:* Applications are processed on a rolling basis. *Application fee:* $0. Electronic applications accepted. *Application Contact:* Office of Graduate Admissions, 800-926-7692, E-mail: graduate@smwc.edu.

Master of Science in Nursing Program Offers nursing (MSN).

SAINT MARY'S COLLEGE, Notre Dame, IN 46556

General Information Independent-religious, women only, comprehensive institution. *Enrollment:* 57 full-time matriculated graduate/professional students (all women), 49 part-time matriculated graduate/professional students (39 women). *Enrollment by degree level:* 58 master's, 18 doctoral. *Graduate faculty:* 18 full-time (15 women), 2 part-time/adjunct (both women). *Graduate housing:* Room and/or apartments available on a first-come, first-served basis to single students; on-campus housing not available to married students. Housing application deadline: 5/1. *Student services:* Campus employment opportunities, campus safety program, career counseling, child daycare facilities, exercise/wellness program, international student services, multicultural affairs office, services for students with disabilities, writing training. *Library facilities:* Cushwa-Leighton Library. *Collection:* Books: 260,077 (physical), 140,170 (digital/electronic); Serial titles: 4,136 (physical), 205,506 (digital/electronic); Databases: 74. Weekly public service hours: 54; study areas open 24 hours, 5–7 days a week; students can reserve study rooms.

Computer facilities: Computer purchase and lease plans are available. 291 computers available on campus for general student use. A campuswide network can be accessed from student residence rooms and from off campus. Online class registration is available.
Website: http://www.saintmarys.edu/

General Application Contact: Melissa Fruscione, Associate Director of Admission, Graduate Programs, 574-284-5098, E-mail: mfruscione@saintmarys.edu.

GRADUATE UNITS

Graduate Programs Students: 57 full-time (all women), 49 part-time (39 women); includes 24 minority (8 Black or African American, non-Hispanic/Latino; 9 Asian, non-Hispanic/Latino; 7 Hispanic/Latino), 1 international. Average age 28. 268 applicants, 47% accepted, 58 enrolled. *Faculty:* 19 full-time (16 women), 2 part-time/adjunct (both women). Expenses: Contact institution. *Financial support:* Application deadline: 3/1; applicants required to submit FAFSA. In 2017, 23 master's awarded. Offers adult - gerontology acute care (DNP); adult - gerontology primary care (DNP); data science (MS); family nurse practitioner (DNP); speech language pathology (MS). *Application deadline:* Applications are processed on a rolling basis. Electronic applications accepted. *Application Contact:* Melissa Fruscione, Director of Graduate Admissions, 574-284-5098, E-mail: graduateadmission@saintmarys.edu.

SAINT MARY'S COLLEGE OF CALIFORNIA, Moraga, CA 94575

General Information Independent-religious, coed, upper-level institution. CGS member. *Graduate housing:* Room and/or apartments available on a first-come, first-served basis to single students; on-campus housing not available to married students. Housing application deadline: 6/1.

GRADUATE UNITS

Kalmanovitz School of Education *Program availability:* Part-time, evening/weekend. Offers career counseling (MA); coaching and facilitation (MA); college student services (Credential); education (M Ed, MA, MA Ed, Ed D, Credential); educational administration (MA); educational leadership (Ed D); general counseling (MA); marriage and family therapy (MA); Montessori education (MA); organizational leadership and change (MA); peacebuilding and conflict transformation (MA); preliminary administrative services (Credential); pupil personnel services (Credential); school counseling (MA); school psychology (MA); social justice (MA); special education (M Ed); supervision and leadership (MA); teaching (MA Ed); teaching leadership (MA).

School of Economics and Business Administration *Program availability:* Part-time, evening/weekend. Offers accounting (MS); business analytics (MS); executive business administration (MBA); financial analysis and investment management (MS); management (MS); professional business administration (MBA).

School of Liberal Arts *Program availability:* Part-time. Offers creative writing (MFA); dance: creative practice (MFA); dance: design and production (MFA); fitness management (MA); liberal arts (MA, MFA); sport management (MA); sport studies (MA).

ST. MARY'S COLLEGE OF MARYLAND, St. Mary's City, MD 20686-3001

General Information State-supported, coed, comprehensive institution. *Graduate housing:* Room and/or apartments available on a first-come, first-served basis to single students; on-campus housing not available to married students. Housing application deadline: 5/1.

GRADUATE UNITS

Department of Educational Studies Offers educational studies (MAT). Electronic applications accepted.

SAINT MARY SEMINARY AND GRADUATE SCHOOL OF THEOLOGY, Wickliffe, OH 44092-2527

General Information Independent-religious, coed, primarily men, graduate-only institution. *Graduate housing:* Room and/or apartments available to single students; on-campus housing not available to married students.

GRADUATE UNITS

Graduate and Professional Programs *Program availability:* Part-time. Offers theology (M Div, MA, D Min).

ST. MARY'S SEMINARY AND UNIVERSITY, Baltimore, MD 21210-1994

General Information Independent-religious, coed, primarily men, graduate-only institution. *Graduate housing:* Room and/or apartments guaranteed to single students; on-campus housing not available to married students. Housing application deadline: 8/15.

GRADUATE UNITS

Ecumenical Institute of Theology *Program availability:* Part-time, evening/weekend. Offers church ministries (MA); theology (MA Th, Certificate).

School of Theology *Program availability:* Part-time. Offers theology (M Div, MA Th, STD, STB, STL).

SAINT MARY'S UNIVERSITY, Halifax, NS B3H 3C3, Canada

General Information Province-supported, coed, comprehensive institution. *Graduate housing:* Rooms and/or apartments available on a first-come, first-served basis to single students and available to married students.

GRADUATE UNITS

Faculty of Arts *Program availability:* Part-time, evening/weekend. Offers arts (MA, Certificate, Graduate Diploma); Atlantic Canada studies (MA, Certificate); criminology (MA); history (MA); international development studies (MA, Graduate Diploma); philosophy (MA); theology and religious studies (MA); women and gender studies (MA).

Faculty of Science *Program availability:* Part-time. Offers applied psychology (M Sc, PhD); applied science (M Sc); astronomy (M Sc, PhD); science (M Sc, PhD).

Sobey School of Business *Program availability:* Part-time, evening/weekend. Offers business (MBA, MF, PhD).

ST. MARY'S UNIVERSITY, San Antonio, TX 78228

General Information Independent-religious, coed, comprehensive institution. CGS member. *Enrollment:* 3,649 graduate, professional, and undergraduate students; 904 full-time matriculated graduate/professional students (461 women), 477 part-time matriculated graduate/professional students (249 women). *Enrollment by degree level:* 508 master's, 856 doctoral, 17 other advanced degrees. *Graduate faculty:* 71 full-time (30 women), 49 part-time/adjunct (11 women). *Tuition:* Full-time $16,200; part-time $900 per credit hour. *Required fees:* $810; $405 per semester. *Graduate housing:* Room and/or apartments available on a first-come, first-served basis to single students; on-campus housing not available to married students. Typical cost: $8856 per year ($12,456 including board). Housing application deadline: 5/1. *Student services:* Campus employment opportunities, career counseling, exercise/wellness program, free psychological counseling, international student services, low-cost health insurance, services for students with disabilities. *Library facilities:* Louis J. Blume Library plus 1 other. *Collection:* Books: 265,910 (physical), 194,058 (digital/electronic); Serial titles: 486 (physical), 76,976 (digital/electronic); Databases: 97. Weekly public service hours: 100. *Research affiliation:* Southeast Research Consortium (behavioral science, biomedical engineering, social science).

Computer facilities: Computer purchase and lease plans are available. 200 computers available on campus for general student use. A campuswide network can be accessed from student residence rooms and from off campus. Online class registration is available.
Website: http://www.stmarytx.edu/

General Application Contact: Kim Thornton, Director of Graduate Admission, 210-436-3126, E-mail: kthornton@stmarytx.edu.

GRADUATE UNITS

Graduate Studies Students: 850 full-time (435 women), 472 part-time (246 women); includes 694 minority (65 Black or African American, non-Hispanic/Latino; 10 American Indian or Alaska Native, non-Hispanic/Latino; 41 Asian, non-Hispanic/Latino; 573 Hispanic/Latino; 2 Native Hawaiian or other Pacific Islander, non-Hispanic/Latino; 3 Two or more races, non-Hispanic/Latino), 117 international. Average age 30. 694 applicants, 39% accepted, 158 enrolled. *Faculty:* 71 full-time (30 women), 49 part-time/adjunct (11 women). Expenses: Contact institution. *Financial support:* Fellowships, research assistantships, career-related internships or fieldwork, Federal Work-Study, institutionally sponsored loans, scholarships/grants, health care benefits, tuition waivers, and unspecified assistantships available. Financial award application deadline: 3/31; financial award applicants required to submit FAFSA. In 2017, 174 master's, 4 doctorates, 5 other advanced degrees awarded. *Program availability:* Part-time, evening/weekend, 100% online. Offers Catholic school leadership (MA); clinical mental health counseling (MA); communication studies (MA); conflict transformation (Certificate); counselor education and supervision (PhD); education (MA); educational leadership (MA); English literature and language (MA); industrial/organizational psychology (MA, MS); international conflict resolution (MA); international development (MA); international relations (MA); public administration (MPA); public communication, public policy and public leadership (Certificate); security policy (MA); theology (MA). *Application deadline:* For fall admission, 7/1 for domestic students; for spring admission, 11/15 for domestic students; for summer admission, 4/1 for domestic students. Applications are processed on a rolling basis. Electronic applications accepted. *Application Contact:* Kim Thornton, Director of Graduate Admission, 210-436-3101, E-mail: kthornton@stmarytx.edu. *Dean of Graduate Studies*, Dr. Christopher Frost, 210-436-3737, E-mail: cfrost2@stmarytx.edu.

Greehey School of Business Students: 78 full-time (36 women), 28 part-time (15 women); includes 49 minority (4 Black or African American, non-Hispanic/Latino; 5 Asian, non-Hispanic/Latino; 39 Hispanic/Latino; 1 Native Hawaiian or other Pacific Islander, non-Hispanic/Latino), 16 international. Average age 32. 145 applicants, 36% accepted, 40 enrolled. Expenses: Contact institution. *Financial support:* Research assistantships, institutionally sponsored loans, scholarships/grants, and unspecified assistantships available. Financial award application deadline: 3/31; financial award applicants required to submit FAFSA. In 2017, 28 master's awarded. *Program availability:* Part-time, evening/weekend. Offers business administration (MBA). *Application deadline:* For fall admission, 7/1 for domestic students; for spring admission, 11/15 for domestic students; for summer admission, 4/1 for domestic students. *Application fee:* $0. Electronic applications accepted. *Director, Master of Business Administration Programs*, Jeremy Grace, 210-431-2027, E-mail: jmgrace@stmarytx.edu.

School of Law Students: 628 full-time (310 women), 201 part-time (94 women); includes 460 minority (35 Black or African American, non-Hispanic/Latino; 8 American Indian or Alaska Native, non-Hispanic/Latino; 26 Asian, non-Hispanic/Latino; 390 Hispanic/Latino; 1 Native Hawaiian or other Pacific Islander, non-Hispanic/Latino), 9 international. Average age 29. 1,417 applicants, 64% accepted, 314 enrolled. *Faculty:* 58 full-time (25 women), 26 part-time/adjunct (6 women). Expenses: Contact institution. *Financial support:* Application deadline: 2/15; applicants required to submit FAFSA. In 2017, 39 master's, 194 doctorates awarded. *Program availability:* Part-time. Offers American legal studies (LL M); business and entrepreneurship law (MJ); commercial law (MJ); compliance, business law and risk (MJ); criminal justice (MJ); education law (MJ); environmental law (MJ); health law (MJ); healthcare compliance (MJ); international and comparative law (LL M); international comparative law (MJ); international criminal law (LL M); law (LL M, MJ, JD); military and national security law (MJ); natural resource law (MJ); tax law (MJ). *Application deadline:* For fall admission, 3/1 for domestic students. *Application fee:* $0. *Application Contact:* Kim Thornton, Director of Graduate Admission, 210-436-3101, E-mail: kthornton@stmarytx.edu. *Dean*, Stephen Sheppard, 210-436-3530, E-mail: sheppard@stmarytx.edu.

School of Science, Engineering and Technology Students: 44 full-time (10 women), 45 part-time (9 women); includes 25 minority (3 Black or African American, non-Hispanic/Latino; 2 Asian, non-Hispanic/Latino; 20 Hispanic/Latino), 52 international. Average age 29. 169 applicants, 24% accepted, 17 enrolled. Expenses: Contact institution. *Financial support:* Application deadline: 3/31; applicants required to submit FAFSA. In 2017, 41 master's awarded. *Program availability:* Part-time, evening/weekend, blended/hybrid learning. Offers computer engineering (MS); computer information systems (MS); computer science (MS); cybersecurity (MS, Certificate); electrical engineering (MS); engineering systems management (MS); industrial engineering (MS); science, engineering and technology (MS, Certificate); software engineering (MS, Certificate). *Application deadline:* For fall admission, 7/1 for domestic students; for spring admission, 11/15 for domestic students; for summer admission, 4/1 for domestic students. Applications are processed on a rolling basis. *Application fee:* $0. Electronic applications accepted. *Dean*, Dr. Winston F. Erevelles, 210-436-3996, E-mail: werevelles@stmarytx.edu.

SAINT MARY'S UNIVERSITY OF MINNESOTA, Winona, MN 55987-1399

General Information Independent-religious, coed, comprehensive institution. *Enrollment:* 5,754 graduate, professional, and undergraduate students; 2,651 full-time matriculated graduate/professional students (1,846 women), 1,372 part-time matriculated graduate/professional students (904 women). *Enrollment by degree level:* 3,493 master's, 354 doctoral, 176 other advanced degrees. *Graduate faculty:* 17 full-time (8 women), 305 part-time/adjunct (170 women). *Student services:* Campus safety program, services for students with disabilities, teacher training, writing training. *Library facilities:* Fitzgerald Library plus 1 other. *Collection:* Books: 210,639 (physical), 10,144 (digital/electronic); Serial titles: 169 (physical), 82,154 (digital/electronic); Databases: 77. Weekly public service hours: 97; students can reserve study rooms.

Computer facilities: 200 computers available on campus for general student use. A campuswide network can be accessed from student residence rooms and from off campus. Online class registration is available.
Website: http://www.smumn.edu/

General Application Contact: James Callinan, Director of Admission for Graduate and Professional Programs, 612-728-5158, Fax: 612-728-5121, E-mail: jcallina@smumn.edu.

GRADUATE UNITS

Schools of Graduate and Professional Programs Students: 2,651 full-time (1,846 women), 1,372 part-time (904 women); includes 669 minority (355 Black or African American, non-Hispanic/Latino; 19 American Indian or Alaska Native, non-Hispanic/Latino; 162 Asian, non-Hispanic/Latino; 117 Hispanic/Latino; 2 Native Hawaiian or other Pacific Islander, non-Hispanic/Latino; 14 Two or more races, non-Hispanic/Latino), 112 international. Average age 35. *Faculty:* 17 full-time (8 women), 305 part-time/adjunct (170 women). Expenses: Contact institution. *Financial support:* Applicants required to submit FAFSA. In 2017, 919 master's, 13 doctorates, 245 other advanced degrees awarded. *Program availability:* Part-time, evening/weekend, 100% online, blended/hybrid learning. *Application deadline:* Applications are processed on a rolling basis. Electronic applications accepted. *Application Contact:* James Callinan, Director of Admissions for Graduate and Professional Programs, 612-728-5158, Fax: 612-728-5121, E-mail: jcallina@smumn.edu. *Vice President and Chief Academic Officer*, Br. Robert Smith, 612-728-5201, Fax: 612-728-5169, E-mail: rsmith@smumn.edu.

Graduate School of Business and Technology Students: 890 full-time (535 women), 324 part-time (178 women); includes 297 minority (168 Black or African American, non-Hispanic/Latino; 8 American Indian or Alaska Native, non-Hispanic/Latino; 71 Asian, non-Hispanic/Latino; 44 Hispanic/Latino; 1 Native Hawaiian or other Pacific Islander, non-Hispanic/Latino; 5 Two or more races, non-Hispanic/Latino), 81 international. Average age 36. Expenses: Contact institution. *Program availability:* Part-time, evening/weekend, 100% online, blended/hybrid learning. Offers accountancy (MS); business administration (MBA, DBA); business and technology (MA, MBA, MS, DBA, Certificate); business intelligence and data analytics (MS); cybersecurity (MS); geographic information science (MS, Certificate); human development (MA); human resource management (MA); information technology management (MS); international development (MA); management (MA); organizational leadership (MA); philanthropy and development (MA); project management (MS, Certificate); public administration (MA). *Application deadline:* Applications are processed on a rolling basis. Electronic applications accepted. *Application Contact:* James Callinan, Director of Admissions for Graduate and Professional Programs, 612-728-5158, Fax: 612-728-5121, E-mail: jcallina@smumn.edu. *Dean*, Dr. Thomas Marpe, 507-457-6963, E-mail: tmarpe@smumn.edu.

Graduate School of Education Students: 951 full-time (700 women), 791 part-time (524 women); includes 162 minority (74 Black or African American, non-Hispanic/Latino; 5 American Indian or Alaska Native, non-Hispanic/Latino; 38 Asian, non-Hispanic/Latino; 42 Hispanic/Latino; 3 Two or more races, non-Hispanic/Latino), 18 international. Average age 36. Expenses: Contact institution. *Program availability:* Part-time, evening/weekend, 100% online, blended/hybrid learning. Offers behavioral disorders (Certificate); culturally responsive teaching (Certificate); education (M Ed, MA, Ed D, Certificate, Ed S); educational administration (Certificate, Ed S); educational leadership (MA, Ed D); gifted inclusive education (Certificate); instruction (MA); K-12 reading teacher (Certificate); LaSallian leadership (MA); LaSallian studies (MA); learning design and technology (M Ed); learning disabilities (Certificate); literacy education (MA); special education (MA); teaching and learning (M Ed). *Application deadline:* Applications are processed on a rolling basis. Electronic applications accepted. *Application Contact:* James Callinan, Director of Admissions for Graduate and Professional Programs, 612-728-5158, Fax: 612-728-5121, E-mail: jcallina@smumn.edu. *Dean*, Dr. Rebecca Hopkins, 507-457-6620, E-mail: rhopkins@smumn.edu.

Graduate School of Health and Human Services Students: 810 full-time (611 women), 257 part-time (202 women); includes 210 minority (113 Black or African American, non-Hispanic/Latino; 6 American Indian or Alaska Native, non-

Hispanic/Latino; 53 Asian, non-Hispanic/Latino; 31 Hispanic/Latino; 1 Native Hawaiian or other Pacific Islander, non-Hispanic/Latino; 6 Two or more races, non-Hispanic/Latino), 13 international. Average age 35. Expenses: Contact institution. *Program availability:* Part-time, evening/weekend, 100% online, blended/hybrid learning. Offers addiction studies (Certificate); counseling and psychological services (MA); counseling psychology (Psy D); health and human services (MA, MS, Psy D, Certificate); health and human services administration (MA); marriage and family therapy (MA); nurse anesthesia (MS). *Application deadline:* Applications are processed on a rolling basis. Electronic applications accepted. *Application Contact:* James Callinan, Director of Admissions for Graduate and Professional Programs, 612-728-5158, Fax: 612-728-5121, E-mail: jcallina@smumn.edu. *Dean*, Dr. Todd Reinhart, 507-457-1758, E-mail: treinhar@smumn.edu.

SAINT MEINRAD SCHOOL OF THEOLOGY, Saint Meinrad, IN 47577

General Information Independent-religious, coed, primarily men, graduate-only institution. *Enrollment by degree level:* 166 master's. *Graduate faculty:* 19 full-time (2 women), 5 part-time/adjunct (1 woman). *Tuition:* Part-time $475 per credit hour. *Required fees:* $34 per course. *Graduate housing:* On-campus housing not available. *Student services:* Campus employment opportunities, campus safety program, exercise/wellness program, free psychological counseling, low-cost health insurance, writing training. *Library facilities:* Archabbey Library. *Collection:* Students can reserve study rooms.

Computer facilities: 30 computers available on campus for general student use. A campuswide network can be accessed from student residence rooms and from off campus.
Website: http://www.saintmeinrad.edu/

General Application Contact: Dr. John Schlachter, Director of Admissions, 812-357-6142, Fax: 812-357-6462, E-mail: apply@saintmeinrad.edu.

GRADUATE UNITS

Master of Arts (Catholic Philosophical Studies) Program Students: 25 full-time (0 women), 3 international. Average age 31. *Faculty:* 6 full-time (1 woman), 4 part-time/adjunct (1 woman). Expenses: Contact institution. *Financial support:* Federal Work-Study and scholarships/grants available. Financial award applicants required to submit FAFSA. In 2017, 8 master's awarded. Offers Catholic philosophical studies (MA). *Application deadline:* For fall admission, 7/31 for domestic and international students; for winter admission, 11/15 for domestic and international students. Applications are processed on a rolling basis. Electronic applications accepted. *Application Contact:* Dr. John Schlachter, Director of Admissions, 812-357-6142, Fax: 812-357-6816, E-mail: jschlachter@saintmeinrad.edu. *Academic Dean*, Dr. Robert Alvis, 812-357-6543, Fax: 812-357-6816, E-mail: ralvis@saintmeinrad.edu.

Master of Arts (Theology) Program Students: 2 full-time (both women), 56 part-time (24 women); includes 5 minority (all Hispanic/Latino), 1 international. Average age 49. *Faculty:* 20 full-time (2 women), 6 part-time/adjunct (1 woman). Expenses: Contact institution. *Financial support:* Federal Work-Study, institutionally sponsored loans, and scholarships/grants available. Support available to part-time students. Financial award application deadline: 7/31; financial award applicants required to submit FAFSA. In 2017, 23 master's awarded. *Program availability:* Part-time, evening/weekend. Offers theology (MA). *Application deadline:* For fall admission, 7/31 for domestic and international students; for winter admission, 11/15 for domestic and international students. Applications are processed on a rolling basis. *Application fee:* $30. Electronic applications accepted. *Application Contact:* Dr. John Schlachter, Director of Admissions, 812-357-6142, Fax: 812-357-6816, E-mail: apply@saintmeinrad.edu. *Director of Graduate Theology Programs*, Sr. Jeana Visel, OSB, 812-357-6721, Fax: 812-357-6816.

Master of Divinity Program Students: 85 full-time (0 women); includes 4 minority (1 Asian, non-Hispanic/Latino; 3 Hispanic/Latino), 26 international. Average age 30. *Faculty:* 21 full-time (2 women), 6 part-time/adjunct (1 woman). Expenses: Contact institution. *Financial support:* Federal Work-Study, institutionally sponsored loans, and scholarships/grants available. Support available to part-time students. Financial award application deadline: 7/31; financial award applicants required to submit FAFSA. In 2017, 28 master's awarded. Offers divinity (M Div). *Application deadline:* For fall admission, 7/31 for domestic and international students; for winter admission, 11/15 for domestic and international students. Applications are processed on a rolling basis. *Application fee:* $0. Electronic applications accepted. *Application Contact:* Dr. John Schlachter, Director of Admissions, 812-357-6142, Fax: 812-357-6816, E-mail: apply@saintmeinrad.edu. *Academic Dean*, Dr. Robert Alvis, 812-357-6543, Fax: 812-357-6816, E-mail: ralvis@saintmeinrad.edu.

SAINT MICHAEL'S COLLEGE, Colchester, VT 05439

General Information Independent-religious, coed, comprehensive institution. *Enrollment:* 2,077 graduate, professional, and undergraduate students; 41 full-time matriculated graduate/professional students (24 women), 244 part-time matriculated graduate/professional students (202 women). *Enrollment by degree level:* 285 master's. *Tuition:* Part-time $590 per credit. *Graduate housing:* Rooms and/or apartments available on a first-come, first-served basis to single and married students. Housing application deadline: 5/1. *Student services:* Campus employment opportunities, campus safety program, career counseling, child daycare facilities, international student services, multicultural affairs office, services for students with disabilities. *Library facilities:* Durick Library. *Collection:* Books: 231,418 (physical), 231,171 (digital/electronic); Serial titles: 1,653 (physical), 128,515 (digital/electronic); Databases: 142. Weekly public service hours: 102.

Computer facilities: Computer purchase and lease plans are available. 97 computers available on campus for general student use. A campuswide network can be accessed from student residence rooms and from off campus. Online class registration is available.
Website: http://www.smcvt.edu/

General Application Contact: Lindsay A. Damici, Marketing Communications Manager, 802-654-2556.

GRADUATE UNITS

Graduate Programs Students: 41 full-time (24 women), 244 part-time (202 women); includes 18 minority (5 Black or African American, non-Hispanic/Latino; 1 American Indian or Alaska Native, non-Hispanic/Latino; 2 Asian, non-Hispanic/Latino; 5 Hispanic/Latino; 5 Two or more races, non-Hispanic/Latino), 13 international. 57 applicants, 79% accepted, 31 enrolled. Expenses: Contact institution. *Financial support:* Fellowships, research assistantships, teaching assistantships with full tuition reimbursements, career-related internships or fieldwork, Federal Work-Study, institutionally sponsored loans, scholarships/grants, tuition waivers (partial), and unspecified assistantships available. Financial award application deadline: 2/1; financial award applicants required to submit FAFSA. In 2017, 64 master's awarded. *Program availability:* Part-time, evening/weekend. Offers arts in education (CAGS); clinical psychology (MA); literacy (M Ed); school leadership (CAGS); special education (M Ed); teaching English to speakers of other languages (MATESOL, Certificate). *Application deadline:* For fall admission, 7/1 for domestic students, 6/1 for international students; for spring admission, 12/1 for domestic students, 10/1 for international students; for summer admission, 4/1 for domestic students, 2/1 for international students. Applications are processed on a rolling basis. *Application fee:* $50. Electronic applications accepted. *Application Contact:* Lindsay A. Damici, Marketing Communications Manager, 802-654-2556, Fax: 802-654-2732.

ST. NORBERT COLLEGE, De Pere, WI 54115-2099

General Information Independent-religious, coed, comprehensive institution. *Enrollment:* 2,165 graduate, professional, and undergraduate students; 112 part-time matriculated graduate/professional students (68 women). *Enrollment by degree level:* 112 master's. *Graduate faculty:* 10 full-time (3 women), 18 part-time/adjunct (6 women). *Tuition:* Part-time $675 per credit. Tuition and fees vary according to program. *Graduate housing:* On-campus housing not available. *Student services:* Campus safety program, career counseling, child daycare facilities, exercise/wellness program, free psychological counseling, international student services, multicultural affairs office, services for students with disabilities, teacher training, writing training. *Library facilities:* Miriam B. and James J. Mulva Library plus 1 other. *Collection:* Books: 249,694 (physical), 89,890 (digital/electronic); Serial titles: 100,960 (physical), 100,893 (digital/electronic). Weekly public service hours: 116; students can reserve study rooms.

Computer facilities: Computer purchase and lease plans are available. 174 computers available on campus for general student use. A campuswide network can be accessed from student residence rooms and from off campus. Online class registration is available.
Website: http://www.snc.edu/

General Application Contact: Brenda Busch, Associate Director of Graduate Recruitment, 920-403-3942, Fax: 920-403-4072, E-mail: brenda.busch@snc.edu.

GRADUATE UNITS

Master of Arts in Liberal Studies Program Students: 10 part-time (8 women); includes 1 minority (Hispanic/Latino). Average age 38. 1 applicant, 100% accepted, 1 enrolled. *Faculty:* 2 part-time/adjunct (0 women). Expenses: Contact institution. *Financial support:* Applicants required to submit FAFSA. In 2017, 3 master's awarded. *Program availability:* Part-time-only, evening/weekend. Offers liberal studies (MA). *Application deadline:* Applications are processed on a rolling basis. *Application fee:* $50. Electronic applications accepted. *Application Contact:* Dinah Grassel, Program Coordinator, 920-403-3957, E-mail: dinah.grassel@snc.edu. *Director*, Dr. Howard Ebert, 920-403-3956, E-mail: howard.ebert@snc.edu.

Master of Business Administration Program Students: 68 part-time (40 women); includes 5 minority (1 American Indian or Alaska Native, non-Hispanic/Latino; 1 Asian, non-Hispanic/Latino; 2 Hispanic/Latino; 1 Two or more races, non-Hispanic/Latino), 1 international. Average age 33. 15 applicants, 100% accepted, 14 enrolled. *Faculty:* 10 full-time (3 women), 8 part-time/adjunct (2 women). Expenses: Contact institution. *Financial support:* Federal Work-Study available. Financial award application deadline: 1/1; financial award applicants required to submit FAFSA. In 2017, 12 master's awarded. *Program availability:* Part-time-only, evening/weekend. Offers business (MBA); health care (MBA); supply chain and manufacturing (MBA). *Application deadline:* For fall admission, 8/4 for domestic students; for winter admission, 12/15 for domestic students; for spring admission, 3/2 for domestic students; for summer admission, 4/20 for domestic students. Applications are processed on a rolling basis. *Application fee:* $50. Electronic applications accepted. *Application Contact:* Brenda Busch, Associate Director of Graduate Recruitment, 920-403-3942, Fax: 920-403-4072, E-mail: brenda.busch@snc.edu. *Coordinator of MBA Program*, Lisa Gray, 920-403-3449, E-mail: lisa.gray@snc.edu.

Master of Theological Studies Program Students: 34 part-time (20 women); includes 9 minority (8 Hispanic/Latino; 1 Two or more races, non-Hispanic/Latino). Average age 50. 2 applicants, 100% accepted, 2 enrolled. *Faculty:* 8 part-time/adjunct (4 women). Expenses: Contact institution. *Financial support:* In 2017–18, 16 students received support. Scholarships/grants available. Support available to part-time students. In 2017, 4 master's awarded. *Program availability:* Part-time-only, evening/weekend, students from New Mexico site video conference in to a live class in DePere. Offers theological studies (MTS). *Application deadline:* Applications are processed on a rolling basis. *Application fee:* $50. Electronic applications accepted. *Application Contact:* Dinah Grassel, Program Coordinator, 920-403-3957, E-mail: dinah.grassel@snc.edu. *Director*, Dr. Howard Ebert, 920-403-3956, E-mail: howard.ebert@snc.edu.

ST. PATRICK'S SEMINARY & UNIVERSITY, Menlo Park, CA 94025-3596

General Information Independent-religious, coed, primarily men, graduate-only institution. *Graduate housing:* Room and/or apartments guaranteed to single students; on-campus housing not available to married students. Housing application deadline: 8/15.

GRADUATE UNITS

School of Theology *Program availability:* Part-time. Offers theology (M Div, MA, STB). STB offered jointly with St. Mary's Seminary and University.

SAINT PAUL SCHOOL OF THEOLOGY, Overland Park, KS 66211

General Information Independent-religious, coed, graduate-only institution. *Graduate housing:* Rooms and/or apartments available to single and married students. Housing application deadline: 5/31.

GRADUATE UNITS

Graduate and Professional Programs *Program availability:* Part-time. Offers theology (M Div, MA, MTS, D Min).

SAINT PAUL UNIVERSITY, Ottawa, ON K1S 1C4, Canada

General Information Province-supported, coed, university. *Graduate housing:* Room and/or apartments available to single students; on-campus housing not available to married students.

GRADUATE UNITS

Faculty of Canon Law *Program availability:* Part-time. Offers canon law (MCL, JCD, PhD, Graduate Certificate, JCL); canonical practice (Graduate Certificate); ecclesiastical administration (Graduate Certificate).

Faculty of Human Sciences Offers conflict studies (MA); counseling and spirituality (MA); individual and/or marital/couple counseling (MA Past St); individual or marital/couple counseling (MA); mission and interreligious studies (MA); pastoral care in health care services (MA Past St); spiritual care (MA). Programs offered in French and English.

Faculty of Theology Offers theology (MA Th, MP Th, MRE, D Min, D Th, PhD, L Th).

ST. PETER'S SEMINARY, London, ON N6A 3Y1, Canada

General Information Independent-religious, coed, primarily men, graduate-only institution.

GRADUATE UNITS

Department of Theology Offers theology (M Div, MTS).

SAINT PETER'S UNIVERSITY, Jersey City, NJ 07306-5997

General Information Independent-religious, coed, comprehensive institution. *Graduate housing:* On-campus housing not available.

GRADUATE UNITS

Graduate Business Programs *Program availability:* Part-time, evening/weekend. Offers accountancy (MS); business (MBA, MS); business analytics (MS); finance (MBA); health care administration (MBA); human resource management (MBA); international business (MBA); management (MBA); management information systems (MBA); marketing (MBA); mobile intelligence (MS); risk management (MBA). Electronic applications accepted.

Graduate Programs in Education *Program availability:* Part-time, evening/weekend. Offers 6-8 middle school education (MA Ed, Certificate); director of school counseling services (Certificate); educational leadership (MA Ed, Ed D); general administration (MHE); higher education (MHE, Ed D); K-12 secondary education (MA Ed, Certificate); K-5 elementary education (MA Ed, Certificate); literacy (MA Ed); middle school mathematics (Certificate); professional/associate counselor (Certificate); reading (MA Ed); school business administrator (Certificate); school counseling (MA, Certificate); special education (MA Ed, Certificate); teaching (MA Ed, Certificate). Electronic applications accepted.

Program in Criminal Justice Administration *Program availability:* Part-time, evening/weekend. Offers federal law enforcement administration (MA); police administration (MA). Electronic applications accepted.

Program in Public Administration Offers public administration (MPA).

School of Nursing *Program availability:* Part-time, evening/weekend. Offers adult nurse practitioner (MSN, Certificate); advanced practice (DNP); case management (MSN, DNP); nursing (MSN, DNP, Certificate). Electronic applications accepted.

SAINTS CYRIL AND METHODIUS SEMINARY, Orchard Lake, MI 48324

General Information Independent-religious, coed, graduate-only institution. *Graduate housing:* Room and/or apartments guaranteed to single students; on-campus housing not available to married students. Housing application deadline: 7/1.

GRADUATE UNITS

Graduate and Professional Programs *Program availability:* Part-time. Offers pastoral ministry (MAPM); religious education (MARE); theology (M Div, MA).

ST. STEPHEN'S COLLEGE, Edmonton, AB T6G 2J6, Canada

General Information Independent-religious, coed, graduate-only institution. *Graduate housing:* On-campus housing not available.

GRADUATE UNITS

Programs in Theology *Program availability:* Part-time, evening/weekend, online learning. Offers ministry (D Min); pastoral counseling (MA); social transformation ministry (MA); spirituality and liturgy (MA); theological studies (MTS); theology (M Th). Electronic applications accepted.

ST. THOMAS AQUINAS COLLEGE, Sparkill, NY 10976

General Information Independent, coed, comprehensive institution. *Graduate housing:* On-campus housing not available. *Research affiliation:* Lederle Laboratories (science education), Lamont Doherty Laboratories (science education).

GRADUATE UNITS

Division of Business Administration *Program availability:* Part-time, evening/weekend. Offers business administration (MBA); finance (MBA); management (MBA); marketing (MBA). Electronic applications accepted.

Division of Teacher Education *Program availability:* Part-time, evening/weekend. Offers adolescence education (MST); childhood and special education (MST); childhood education (MST); educational leadership (MS Ed); reading (MS Ed, PMC); special education (MS Ed, PMC); teaching (MS Ed). Electronic applications accepted.

ST. THOMAS UNIVERSITY, Miami Gardens, FL 33054-6459

General Information Independent-religious, coed, university. *Graduate housing:* Room and/or apartments available on a first-come, first-served basis to single students; on-campus housing not available to married students. Housing application deadline: 7/1.

GRADUATE UNITS

Biscayne College Offers guidance and counseling (MS, Post-Master's Certificate); marriage and family therapy (MS, Post-Master's Certificate); mental health counseling (MS).

School of Business Offers accounting (MBA); business (M Acc, MBA, MIB, MS, MSM, Certificate); business administration (M Acc, MBA, Certificate); general management (MSM, Certificate); health management (MBA, MSM, Certificate); human resource management (MBA, MSM, Certificate); international business (MBA, MIB, MSM, Certificate); justice administration (MSM, Certificate); management accounting (MSM, Certificate); public management (MSM, Certificate); sports administration (MS).

School of Law *Program availability:* Online learning. Offers international human rights (LL M); international taxation (LL M); law (JD). Electronic applications accepted.

School of Leadership Studies *Program availability:* Part-time, evening/weekend. Offers art management (MA); electronic media (MA); executive management (MPS); Hispanic media (MA, Certificate); leadership studies (MA, MPS, MS, Ed D, Certificate).

Institute for Education *Program availability:* Part-time, evening/weekend. Offers earth/space science (Certificate); educational administration (MS, Certificate); educational leadership (Ed D); elementary education (MS); ESOL (Certificate); gifted education (Certificate); instructional technology (MS, Certificate); professional/studies (Certificate); reading (MS, Certificate); special education (MS). Electronic applications accepted.

School of Theology and Ministry Offers theology and ministry (MA, PhD, Certificate).

Institute for Pastoral Ministries *Program availability:* Part-time, evening/weekend. Offers pastoral ministries (MA, Certificate); practical theology (PhD). Electronic applications accepted.

ST. TIKHON'S ORTHODOX THEOLOGICAL SEMINARY, South Canaan, PA 18459

General Information Independent-religious, men only, graduate-only institution. *Graduate housing:* Room and/or apartments guaranteed to single students; on-campus housing not available to married students.

GRADUATE UNITS

Divinity Program *Program availability:* Part-time. Offers divinity (M Div).

SAINT VINCENT COLLEGE, Latrobe, PA 15650-2690

General Information Independent-religious, coed, comprehensive institution. *Graduate housing:* Room and/or apartments available on a first-come, first-served basis to single students; on-campus housing not available to married students.

GRADUATE UNITS

Program in Business Offers business (MS).

Program in Education *Program availability:* Part-time, evening/weekend. Offers curriculum and instruction (MS); instructional design and technology (MS); school administration and supervision (MS); special education (MS).

Program in Health Science Offers nurse anesthesia (MS).

ST. VINCENT DE PAUL REGIONAL SEMINARY, Boynton Beach, FL 33436-4899

General Information Independent-religious, coed, primarily men, graduate-only institution. *Graduate housing:* Room and/or apartments guaranteed to single students; on-campus housing not available to married students.

GRADUATE UNITS

Graduate and Professional Programs *Program availability:* Part-time. Offers theology (M Div, MA Th).

SAINT VINCENT SEMINARY, Latrobe, PA 15650-2690

General Information Independent-religious, coed, primarily men, graduate-only institution. *Enrollment by degree level:* 47 master's. *Graduate faculty:* 7 full-time (2 women), 12 part-time/adjunct (1 woman). *Tuition:* Full-time $27,636; part-time $918 per credit. *Graduate housing:* Room and/or apartments guaranteed to single students; on-campus housing not available to married students. Typical cost: $6874 per year ($13,530 including board). Housing application deadline: 8/15. *Student services:* Campus safety program, exercise/wellness program, free psychological counseling, international student services, services for students with disabilities, writing training. *Library facilities:* Latimer Family Library. *Collection:* Books: 288,601 (physical), 4 (digital/electronic); Serial titles: 249 (physical); Databases: 29. Weekly public service hours: 84.

Computer facilities: 150 computers available on campus for general student use. A campuswide network can be accessed from student residence rooms. Online class registration is available.
Website: http://www.saintvincentseminary.edu/

General Application Contact: Rev. Patrick T. Cronauer, OSB, Academic Dean, 724-805-2324, Fax: 724-805-2880, E-mail: patrick.cronauer@stvincent.edu.

GRADUATE UNITS

School of Theology Students: 38 full-time (0 women), 9 part-time (0 women); includes 2 minority (both Asian, non-Hispanic/Latino), 12 international. Average age 34. 11 applicants, 100% accepted, 10 enrolled. *Faculty:* 8 full-time (2 women), 12 part-time/adjunct (1 woman). Expenses: Contact institution. *Financial support:* In 2017–18, 47 students received support. Scholarships/grants available. Support available to part-time students. Financial award application deadline: 8/15. In 2017, 12 master's awarded. *Program availability:* Part-time, evening/weekend. Offers Catholic philosophical studies (MA); ecclesial ministry (MA); ministry (M Div); monastic studies (MA); sacred scripture (MA); systematic theology (MA). Saint Vincent College provides philosophy courses for the MA in Catholic Philosophical Studies degree program only. *Application deadline:* For fall admission, 8/15 for domestic and international students. Applications are processed on a rolling basis. *Application fee:* $34. *Application Contact:* Rev. Patrick T. Cronauer, OSB, Academic Dean, 724-805-2324, Fax: 724-805-2880, E-mail: patrick.cronauer@stvincent.edu. *President/Rector,* Very Rev. Edward M. Mazich, OSB, 724-805-2845, Fax: 724-532-5052, E-mail: edward.mazich@stvincent.edu.

ST. VLADIMIR'S ORTHODOX THEOLOGICAL SEMINARY, Crestwood, NY 10707-1699

General Information Independent-religious, coed, primarily men, graduate-only institution. *Enrollment by degree level:* 66 master's, 17 doctoral. *Graduate faculty:* 8 full-time (1 woman), 21 part-time/adjunct (2 women). *Tuition:* Full-time $12,000; part-time $500 per credit. *Required fees:* $150; $150 per semester. Tuition and fees vary according to course load and reciprocity agreements. *Graduate housing:* Rooms and/or apartments available on a first-come, first-served basis to single and married students. Typical cost: $6700 (including board) for single students; $8100 (including board) for married students. Housing application deadline: 5/1. *Student services:* Exercise/wellness program, international student services, services for students with disabilities, writing training. *Library facilities:* Father Georges Florovsky Library. *Collection:* Books: 200,000 (physical); Serial titles: 330 (physical); Databases: 3. Weekly public service hours: 60.

Computer facilities: 5 computers available on campus for general student use.
Website: http://www.svots.edu/

General Application Contact: Rev. David Mezynski, Director of Admissions, 914-961-8313 Ext. 322, Fax: 914-961-4507, E-mail: admissions@svots.edu.

GRADUATE UNITS

Graduate School of Theology Students: 71 full-time (6 women), 4 part-time (0 women); includes 8 minority (2 Black or African American, non-Hispanic/Latino; 6 Asian, non-Hispanic/Latino), 15 international. Average age 29. 41 applicants, 95% accepted, 37 enrolled. *Faculty:* 8 full-time (1 woman), 21 part-time/adjunct (2 women). Expenses: Contact institution. *Financial support:* In 2017–18, 75 students received support. Fellowships, research assistantships, teaching assistantships, and scholarships/grants available. Financial award application deadline: 4/1; financial award applicants required to submit FAFSA. In 2017, 26 master's awarded. *Program availability:* Part-time. Offers general theological studies (MA); theology (M Div, M Th, D Min). MA and M Div offered jointly with St. Nersess Armenian Seminary. *Application deadline:* For fall admission, 5/1 priority date for domestic and international students. Applications are processed on a rolling basis. *Application fee:* $75. Electronic applications accepted. *Application Contact:* Gabrielle Russin, Student Affairs Administrator, 914-961-8313 Ext. 348, Fax: 914-961-4507, E-mail: grussin@svots.edu. *President,* Rev. Dr. Chad Hatfield, 914-961-8313 Ext. 323, Fax: 914-961-4507, E-mail: hatfield@svots.edu.

SAINT XAVIER UNIVERSITY, Chicago, IL 60655-3105

General Information Independent-religious, coed, comprehensive institution. CGS member. *Graduate housing:* Room and/or apartments available on a first-come, first-served basis to single students; on-campus housing not available to married students. Housing application deadline: 8/15. *Research affiliation:* Alexian Brothers Hospital, Holy Cross Hospital, Little Company of Mary Hospital, Mercy Center for Health Care Services.

GRADUATE UNITS

Graduate Studies *Program availability:* Part-time, evening/weekend. Electronic applications accepted.

College of Arts and Sciences *Program availability:* Part-time, evening/weekend. Offers arts and sciences (MA, MACS, MS); computer science (MACS); speech-language pathology (MS).

Graham School of Management *Program availability:* Part-time, evening/weekend. Offers employee health benefits (Certificate); finance (MBA); financial fraud examination and management (MBA, Certificate); financial planning (MBA, Certificate); generalist/individualized (MBA); health administration (MBA); managed care (Certificate); management (MBA); marketing (MBA); project management (MBA, Certificate). Electronic applications accepted.

School of Education *Program availability:* Part-time, evening/weekend. Offers counseling (MA); curriculum and instruction (MA); early childhood education (MA); educational administration (MA); elementary education (MA); individualized studies (MA); music education (MA); reading (MA); secondary education (MA); Spanish education (MA); special education (MA); teaching and leadership (MA).

School of Nursing *Program availability:* Part-time, evening/weekend. Offers nursing (MSN, Certificate).

SALEM COLLEGE, Winston-Salem, NC 27101

General Information Independent-religious, coed, primarily women, comprehensive institution. *Enrollment:* 180 full-time matriculated graduate/professional students (161 women). *Enrollment by degree level:* 180 master's. *Graduate faculty:* 8 full-time (all women), 11 part-time/adjunct (8 women). *Tuition:* Part-time $440 per semester hour. *Graduate housing:* On-campus housing not available. *Student services:* Career counseling, teacher training, writing training. *Library facilities:* Dale H. Gramley Library plus 2 others. *Collection:* Books: 119,591 (physical), 110,764 (digital/electronic); Databases: 123.

Computer facilities: Computer purchase and lease plans are available. 54 computers available on campus for general student use. A campuswide network can be accessed from student residence rooms and from off campus. Online class registration is available.
Website: http://www.salem.edu/

General Application Contact: Sheryl Long, Director of Teacher Education, 336-721-2658, Fax: 336-917-5384, E-mail: sheryl.long@salem.edu.

GRADUATE UNITS

Graduate Studies *Faculty:* 8 full-time (all women), 11 part-time/adjunct (8 women). Expenses: Contact institution. *Financial support:* Scholarships/grants available. Support available to part-time students. Financial award applicants required to submit FAFSA. In 2017, 17 master's awarded. *Program availability:* Part-time, evening/weekend, online learning. Offers art education (MAT); elementary education (M Ed, MAT); language and literacy (M Ed); middle school education (MAT); organ (MM); piano (MM); school counseling (M Ed); second language studies (MAT); secondary education (MAT); special education (M Ed, MAT). *Application deadline:* For fall admission, 8/1 for domestic students, 7/15 for international students; for spring admission, 1/15 for domestic students; for summer admission, 5/1 for domestic students. Applications are processed on a rolling basis. *Application fee:* $30. Electronic applications accepted. *Application Contact:* Sheryl Long, Director, 336-721-2658, Fax: 336-917-5384, E-mail: sheryl.long@salem.edu.

SALEM INTERNATIONAL UNIVERSITY, Salem, WV 26426-0500

General Information Independent, coed, comprehensive institution. *Graduate housing:* Rooms and/or apartments available on a first-come, first-served basis to single students and available to married students.

GRADUATE UNITS

School of Business *Program availability:* Part-time, online learning. Offers information security (MBA); international business (MBA). Electronic applications accepted.

School of Education *Program availability:* Part-time, evening/weekend, online learning. Offers curriculum and instruction (M Ed); educational leadership (M Ed). Electronic applications accepted.

SALEM STATE UNIVERSITY, Salem, MA 01970-5353

General Information State-supported, coed, comprehensive institution. CGS member. *Graduate housing:* On-campus housing not available.

GRADUATE UNITS

School of Graduate Studies *Program availability:* Part-time, evening/weekend. Offers adult-gerontology primary care nursing (MSN); advanced professional studies in counseling (Graduate Certificate); art (MAT); business administration (MBA); chemistry (MAT); counseling and psychological services (MS, Graduate Certificate); criminal justice (MS); early childhood education (M Ed); education (CAGS); elementary education (M Ed); English (MA, MAT); geo-information science (MS); higher education in student affairs (M Ed); history (MA, MAT); humanities (M Ed); library media studies (M Ed); math/science (MAT); mathematics (MAT, MS); middle school general science (MAT); middle school math (MAT); nursing administration (MSN); nursing education (MSN); occupational therapy (MS); physical education (M Ed); reading (M Ed); school counseling (M Ed); secondary education (M Ed); social work (MSW); Spanish (MAT); special education (M Ed); teaching English as a second language (MAT).

SALISBURY UNIVERSITY, Salisbury, MD 21801-6837

General Information State-supported, coed, comprehensive institution. CGS member. *Enrollment:* 8,714 graduate, professional, and undergraduate students; 515 full-time matriculated graduate/professional students (399 women), 328 part-time matriculated graduate/professional students (259 women). *Enrollment by degree level:* 760 master's, 79 doctoral, 4 other advanced degrees. *Graduate faculty:* 104 full-time (62 women), 58 part-time/adjunct (44 women). *Graduate housing:* On-campus housing not available. *Student services:* Campus employment opportunities, campus safety program, career counseling, exercise/wellness program, free psychological counseling, international student services, multicultural affairs office, services for students with disabilities, teacher training, writing training. *Library facilities:* SU Libraries plus 2 others. *Collection:* Books: 264,146 (physical), 269 (digital/electronic); Serial titles: 692 (physical), 150 (digital/electronic); Databases: 106. Weekly public service hours: 111; study areas open 24 hours, 5–7 days a week; students can reserve study rooms. *Research affiliation:* Talbot County Senior Center (market research for demand analysis), Maryland Association of Boards of Education (statewide economic impact analysis for K-12 public education), Trinity Sterile (expansion feasibility and scenario analysis), Town of Annapolis (mixed use development economic impact analysis), Konsyl Pharmaceuticals (compensation research), Maryland Department of Labor (program effectiveness and efficiency research).

Computer facilities: 1,000 computers available on campus for general student use. A campuswide network can be accessed from student residence rooms and from off campus. Online class registration, university accounts, student web hosting are available.
Website: http://www.salisbury.edu/

General Application Contact: Lacie Doyle, Graduate Enrollment Management Specialist, 410-548-3546, Fax: 410-677-0052, E-mail: lhdoyle@salisbury.edu.

GRADUATE UNITS

Department of Conflict Analysis and Dispute Resolution Students: 37 full-time (23 women), 3 part-time (2 women); includes 15 minority (11 Black or African American, non-Hispanic/Latino; 1 Asian, non-Hispanic/Latino; 1 Hispanic/Latino; 2 Two or more races, non-Hispanic/Latino), 1 international. Average age 31. 28 applicants, 75% accepted, 21 enrolled. *Faculty:* 5 full-time (0 women). Expenses: Contact institution. *Financial support:* In 2017–18, 12 students received support, including 8 teaching assistantships with full tuition reimbursements available (averaging $8,185 per year); career-related internships or fieldwork and scholarships/grants also available. Support available to part-time students. Financial award application deadline: 3/1; financial award applicants required to submit FAFSA. In 2017, 18 master's awarded. *Program availability:* Part-time. Offers conflict analysis and dispute resolution (MA). *Application deadline:* For fall admission, 4/14 priority date for domestic and international students. Applications are processed on a rolling basis. *Application fee:* $65. Electronic applications accepted. *Application Contact:* Dr. Vitus Ozoke, Faculty, Conflict Analysis and Dispute Resolution, 410-677-0276, E-mail: vaozoke@salisbury.edu. *Graduate Program Director, Conflict Analysis and Dispute Resolution*, Dr. Ignaciyas Soosaipillai, 410-543-6435, E-mail: iksoosaipillai@salisbury.edu.

Department of English Students: 15 full-time (12 women), 14 part-time (11 women); includes 1 minority (Black or African American, non-Hispanic/Latino), 2 international. Average age 34. 27 applicants, 37% accepted, 10 enrolled. *Faculty:* 10 full-time (6 women). Expenses: Contact institution. *Financial support:* In 2017–18, 8 students received support, including 11 teaching assistantships with full tuition reimbursements available (averaging $11,275 per year); career-related internships or fieldwork and scholarships/grants also available. Support available to part-time students. Financial award application deadline: 3/1; financial award applicants required to submit FAFSA. In 2017, 26 master's awarded. *Program availability:* Part-time. Offers English (MA). *Application deadline:* For fall admission, 8/1 for domestic and international students; for spring admission, 1/1 for domestic and international students. *Application fee:* $65. Electronic applications accepted. *Graduate Program Director, English*, Dr. Christopher Vilmar, 410-677-6511, E-mail: csvilmar@salisbury.edu.

Department of History Students: 5 full-time (2 women), 6 part-time (1 woman); includes 1 minority (Two or more races, non-Hispanic/Latino). Average age 31. 7 applicants, 86% accepted, 6 enrolled. *Faculty:* 7 full-time (3 women). Expenses: Contact institution. *Financial support:* In 2017–18, 5 students received support, including 1 teaching assistantship with full tuition reimbursement available (averaging $8,000 per year); career-related internships or fieldwork and scholarships/grants also available. Support available to part-time students. Financial award application deadline: 3/1; financial award applicants required to submit FAFSA. In 2017, 10 master's awarded. *Program availability:* Part-time, evening/weekend. Offers history (MA). *Application deadline:* For fall admission, 4/15 priority date for domestic and international students; for spring admission, 10/15 priority date for domestic and international students. Applications are processed on a rolling basis. *Application fee:* $65. Electronic applications accepted. *Graduate Program Director*, Dr. Celine Carayon, 410-677-3251, E-mail: cxcarayon@salisbury.edu.

Department of Social Work Students: 295 full-time (263 women), 82 part-time (78 women); includes 66 minority (50 Black or African American, non-Hispanic/Latino; 6 Hispanic/Latino; 2 Native Hawaiian or other Pacific Islander, non-Hispanic/Latino; 8 Two or more races, non-Hispanic/Latino). Average age 32. 270 applicants, 59% accepted, 160 enrolled. *Faculty:* 22 full-time (18 women), 47 part-time/adjunct (37 women). Expenses: Contact institution. *Financial support:* In 2017–18, 22 students received support, including 6 teaching assistantships with full tuition reimbursements available (averaging $8,160 per year); career-related internships or fieldwork and scholarships/grants also available. Support available to part-time students. Financial award application deadline: 3/1; financial award applicants required to submit FAFSA. In 2017, 126 master's awarded. *Program availability:* Part-time, 100% online, blended/hybrid learning. Offers social work (MSW). *Application deadline:* For fall admission, 2/3 for domestic and international students; for spring admission, 11/15 for domestic and international students. *Application fee:* $65. Electronic applications accepted. *Application Contact:* Susan Mareski, Administrative Assistant, 410-677-5363, E-mail: smmareski@salisbury.edu. *Graduate Program Director, Social Work*, Dr. Vicki Root, 410-543-6307, E-mail: vbroot@salisbury.edu.

DNP Program Students: 35 full-time (32 women), 4 part-time (all women); includes 8 minority (all Black or African American, non-Hispanic/Latino). Average age 33. 21 applicants, 43% accepted, 9 enrolled. *Faculty:* 10 full-time (all women). Expenses: Contact institution. *Financial support:* In 2017–18, 3 students received support. Career-related internships or fieldwork and scholarships/grants available. Support available to part-time students. Financial award application deadline: 3/1; financial award applicants required to submit FAFSA. In 2017, 1 doctorate awarded. *Program availability:* Part-time. Offers family nurse practitioner (DNP); nursing leadership (DNP). *Application deadline:* For fall admission, 3/1 priority date for domestic and international students. Applications are processed on a rolling basis. *Application fee:* $65. Electronic applications accepted. *Graduate Program Director, Nursing DNP*, Dr. Lisa Seldomridge, 410-543-6413, E-mail: laseldomridge@salisbury.edu.

MS in Nursing Program Students: 3 part-time (all women); includes 1 minority (Black or African American, non-Hispanic/Latino). Average age 40. *Faculty:* 4 full-time (3 women), 2 part-time/adjunct (both women). Expenses: Contact institution. *Financial support:* Career-related internships or fieldwork and scholarships/grants available. Support available to part-time students. Financial award application deadline: 3/1; financial award applicants required to submit FAFSA. In 2017, 1 master's awarded. *Program availability:* Part-time. Offers nursing (MS). *Application deadline:* For fall admission, 3/1 for domestic and international students. *Application fee:* $65. Electronic applications accepted. *Graduate Program Director, Nursing MS*, Dr. Lisa Seldomridge, 410-543-6413, E-mail: laseldomridge@salisbury.edu.

Perdue School of Business Students: 34 full-time (17 women), 25 part-time (12 women); includes 14 minority (7 Black or African American, non-Hispanic/Latino; 2

Asian, non-Hispanic/Latino; 5 Two or more races, non-Hispanic/Latino), 4 international. Average age 29. 72 applicants, 67% accepted, 41 enrolled. *Faculty:* 7 full-time (2 women). Expenses: Contact institution. *Financial support:* In 2017–18, 4 students received support, including 6 teaching assistantships with full tuition reimbursements available (averaging $8,500 per year); career-related internships or fieldwork and scholarships/grants also available. Support available to part-time students. Financial award application deadline: 3/1; financial award applicants required to submit FAFSA. In 2017, 40 master's awarded. *Program availability:* Part-time, evening/weekend, 100% online, blended/hybrid learning. Offers business administration (MBA). *Application deadline:* For fall admission, 3/1 priority date for domestic and international students. Applications are processed on a rolling basis. *Application fee:* $65. Electronic applications accepted. *Graduate Program Director, Business Administration*, Yvonne Downie Hanley, 410-548-3983, E-mail: yxdownie@salisbury.edu.

Program in Applied Biology Students: 8 full-time (4 women), 1 part-time (0 women); includes 1 minority (Native Hawaiian or other Pacific Islander, non-Hispanic/Latino). Average age 25. 5 applicants, 60% accepted, 3 enrolled. *Faculty:* 9 full-time (4 women). Expenses: Contact institution. *Financial support:* In 2017–18, 5 students received support, including 9 teaching assistantships with full tuition reimbursements available (averaging $13,000 per year); career-related internships or fieldwork and scholarships/grants also available. Support available to part-time students. Financial award application deadline: 3/1; financial award applicants required to submit FAFSA. In 2017, 2 master's awarded. *Program availability:* Part-time. Offers applied biology (MS). *Application deadline:* For fall admission, 3/1 for domestic and international students; for spring admission, 10/1 for domestic and international students. *Application fee:* $65. Electronic applications accepted. *Application Contact:* Sandy Ramses, Program Management Specialist, 410-543-6054, E-mail: shramses@salisbury.edu. *Graduate Program Director, Applied Biology*, Dr. Dana Price, 410-543-6498, E-mail: dlprice@salisbury.edu.

Program in Applied Health Physiology Students: 27 full-time (11 women), 3 part-time (1 woman); includes 7 minority (4 Black or African American, non-Hispanic/Latino; 2 Asian, non-Hispanic/Latino; 1 Two or more races, non-Hispanic/Latino). Average age 24. 23 applicants, 74% accepted, 11 enrolled. *Faculty:* 5 full-time (0 women). Expenses: Contact institution. *Financial support:* In 2017–18, 10 students received support, including 15 teaching assistantships with full tuition reimbursements available (averaging $8,099 per year); career-related internships or fieldwork and scholarships/grants also available. Support available to part-time students. Financial award application deadline: 3/1; financial award applicants required to submit FAFSA. In 2017, 20 master's awarded. *Program availability:* Part-time. Offers applied health physiology (MS). *Application deadline:* For fall admission, 8/1 for domestic and international students; for spring admission, 12/1 for domestic and international students. *Application fee:* $65. Electronic applications accepted. *Application Contact:* Dr. Thomas Pellinger, Faculty, Applied Health Physiology, 410-677-0144, E-mail: tkpellinger@salisbury.edu. *Graduate Program Director, Applied Health Physiology*, Dr. Carlton Insley, 410-677-0145, E-mail: rcinsley@salisbury.edu.

Program in Athletic Training Students: 5 full-time (2 women), 3 part-time (all women); includes 4 minority (2 Black or African American, non-Hispanic/Latino; 2 Hispanic/Latino). Average age 24. 10 applicants, 50% accepted, 5 enrolled. *Faculty:* 3 full-time (all women). Expenses: Contact institution. *Financial support:* In 2017–18, 1 student received support. Career-related internships or fieldwork and scholarships/grants available. Support available to part-time students. Financial award application deadline: 3/1; financial award applicants required to submit FAFSA. Offers athletic training (MSAT). *Application deadline:* For summer admission, 3/1 priority date for domestic and international students. Applications are processed on a rolling basis. *Application fee:* $65. Electronic applications accepted. *Graduate Program Director, Athletic Training*, Dr. Kelly Fiala, 410-543-6335, E-mail: kafiala@salisbury.edu.

Program in Contemporary Curriculum Theory and Instruction: Literacy Students: 22 full-time (17 women), 18 part-time (17 women); includes 2 minority (1 Black or African American, non-Hispanic/Latino; 1 Two or more races, non-Hispanic/Latino). Average age 39. 14 applicants, 86% accepted, 12 enrolled. *Faculty:* 4 full-time (2 women). Expenses: Contact institution. *Financial support:* In 2017–18, 4 students received support, including 2 teaching assistantships with full tuition reimbursements available (averaging $10,000 per year); career-related internships or fieldwork and scholarships/grants also available. Support available to part-time students. Financial award application deadline: 3/1; financial award applicants required to submit FAFSA. *Program availability:* Part-time. Offers contemporary curriculum theory and instruction: literacy (Ed D). *Application deadline:* For fall admission, 3/31 priority date for domestic and international students. Applications are processed on a rolling basis. *Application fee:* $65. Electronic applications accepted. *Application Contact:* Stefani Hoffman, Administrative Assistant II, 410-677-0236, E-mail: slhoffman@salisbury.edu. *Graduate Program Director*, Dr. Judith Franzak, 410-677-0238, E-mail: jkfranzak@salisbury.edu.

Program in Curriculum and Instruction Students: 18 full-time (10 women), 83 part-time (71 women); includes 10 minority (4 Black or African American, non-Hispanic/Latino; 1 Asian, non-Hispanic/Latino; 1 Hispanic/Latino; 1 Native Hawaiian or other Pacific Islander, non-Hispanic/Latino; 3 Two or more races, non-Hispanic/Latino), 1 international. Average age 29. 37 applicants, 59% accepted, 20 enrolled. *Faculty:* 5 full-time (4 women), 3 part-time/adjunct (2 women). Expenses: Contact institution. *Financial support:* In 2017–18, 4 students received support, including 13 teaching assistantships with full tuition reimbursements available (averaging $8,191 per year); career-related internships or fieldwork and scholarships/grants also available. Support available to part-time students. Financial award application deadline: 3/1; financial award applicants required to submit FAFSA. In 2017, 27 master's awarded. *Program availability:* Part-time, evening/weekend. Offers curriculum and instruction (M Ed). *Application deadline:* For fall admission, 3/1 priority date for domestic and international students; for spring admission, 10/1 priority date for domestic and international students; for summer admission, 3/1 priority date for domestic and international students. Applications are processed on a rolling basis. *Application fee:* $65. Electronic applications accepted. *Graduate Program Director, Curriculum and Instruction*, Dr. Diana Wagner, 410-677-5490, E-mail: dmwagner@salisbury.edu.

Program in Educational Leadership Students: 38 part-time (24 women); includes 8 minority (6 Black or African American, non-Hispanic/Latino; 2 Two or more races, non-Hispanic/Latino). Average age 32. 18 applicants, 78% accepted, 14 enrolled. *Faculty:* 1 full-time (0 women), 3 part-time/adjunct (1 woman). Expenses: Contact institution. *Financial support:* Career-related internships or fieldwork and scholarships/grants available. Support available to part-time students. Financial award application deadline: 3/1; financial award applicants required to submit FAFSA. In 2017, 13 master's awarded. *Program availability:* Part-time, evening/weekend. Offers educational leadership (M Ed). *Application deadline:* For fall admission, 3/1 priority date for domestic and international students; for spring admission, 10/1 priority date for domestic and international students; for summer admission, 3/1 priority date for domestic and international students. Applications are processed on a rolling basis. *Application fee:* $65. Electronic applications accepted. *Application Contact:* Claire Williams, Program Management Specialist, 410-677-0001, E-mail: clwilliams@salisbury.edu. *Graduate Program Director, Educational Leadership*, Dr. Douglas DeWitt, 410-543-6286, E-mail: dmdewitt@salisbury.edu.

Program in Geographic Information Systems Management Students: 4 full-time (2 women), 13 part-time (4 women); includes 1 minority (Two or more races, non-Hispanic/Latino). Average age 29. 10 applicants, 70% accepted, 7 enrolled. *Faculty:* 2 full-time (0 women). Expenses: Contact institution. *Financial support:* Career-related internships or fieldwork and scholarships/grants available. Support available to part-time students. Financial award application deadline: 3/1; financial award applicants required to submit FAFSA. In 2017, 5 master's awarded. *Program availability:* Part-time, evening/weekend, online only, 100% online. Offers geographic information systems management (MS). *Application deadline:* For fall admission, 8/1 priority date for domestic and international students; for spring admission, 12/1 priority date for domestic and international students; for summer admission, 5/1 priority date for domestic and international students. Applications are processed on a rolling basis. *Application fee:* $65. Electronic applications accepted. *Application Contact:* Jennifer Horsman, Program Management Specialist, 410-543-6460, E-mail: jlgordy@salisbury.edu. *Graduate Program Director, Geographic Information Systems Management*, Dr. Stuart Hamilton, 410-543-6456, E-mail: sehamilton@salisbury.edu.

Program in Mathematics Education Students: 1 (woman) full-time, 7 part-time (5 women). Average age 27. 5 applicants, 80% accepted, 4 enrolled. *Faculty:* 4 full-time (2 women), 2 part-time/adjunct (1 woman). Expenses: Contact institution. *Financial support:* In 2017–18, 1 teaching assistantship with full tuition reimbursement (averaging $8,000 per year) was awarded; career-related internships or fieldwork and scholarships/grants also available. Support available to part-time students. Financial award application deadline: 3/1; financial award applicants required to submit FAFSA. In 2017, 5 master's awarded. *Program availability:* Part-time. Offers mathematics (MSME). *Application deadline:* For fall admission, 8/1 priority date for domestic and international students; for spring admission, 10/1 priority date for domestic and international students. Applications are processed on a rolling basis. *Application fee:* $65. Electronic applications accepted. *Graduate Program Director, Mathematics Education*, Dr. Jennifer Bergner, 410-677-5429, E-mail: jabergner@salisbury.edu.

Program in Reading Specialist Students: 1 (woman) full-time, 23 part-time (21 women); includes 2 minority (both Asian, non-Hispanic/Latino). Average age 31. 8 applicants, 63% accepted, 5 enrolled. *Faculty:* 2 full-time (both women), 1 (woman) part-time/adjunct. Expenses: Contact institution. *Financial support:* In 2017–18, 6 students received support, including 1 teaching assistantship with full tuition reimbursement available (averaging $9,000 per year); career-related internships or fieldwork and scholarships/grants also available. Support available to part-time students. Financial award application deadline: 3/1; financial award applicants required to submit FAFSA. In 2017, 8 master's awarded. *Program availability:* Part-time, evening/weekend. Offers reading specialist (M Ed). *Application deadline:* For fall admission, 3/1 priority date for domestic and international students; for spring admission, 10/1 priority date for domestic and international students; for summer admission, 3/1 priority date for domestic and international students. Applications are processed on a rolling basis. *Application fee:* $65. Electronic applications accepted. *Graduate Program Director, Reading Specialist*, Dr. Joyce Wiencek, 410-543-6288, E-mail: bjwiencek@salisbury.edu.

Program in Teaching Students: 8 full-time (2 women), 1 (woman) part-time; includes 1 minority (Hispanic/Latino). Average age 29. *Faculty:* 4 full-time (3 women). Expenses: Contact institution. *Financial support:* In 2017–18, 2 students received support. Career-related internships or fieldwork and scholarships/grants available. Support available to part-time students. Financial award application deadline: 3/1; financial award applicants required to submit FAFSA. In 2017, 7 master's awarded. Offers secondary education (MAT). *Application deadline:* For winter admission, 12/15 priority date for domestic and international students. *Application fee:* $65. Electronic applications accepted. *Graduate Program Director, Teaching*, Dr. Starlin Weaver, 410-548-5787, E-mail: sdweaver@salisbury.edu.

See Display on the next page and Close-Up on page 873.

SALUS UNIVERSITY, Elkins Park, PA 19027-1598

General Information Independent, coed, graduate-only institution. *Graduate housing:* On-campus housing not available. *Research affiliation:* Dynamis Pharmaceuticals (diabetes research), DakDak (photobiology).

GRADUATE UNITS

College of Education and Rehabilitation *Program availability:* Part-time, online learning. Offers education of children and youth with visual and multiple impairments (M Ed, Certificate); low vision rehabilitation (MS, Certificate); occupational therapy (MS); orientation and mobility therapy (MS, Certificate); speech-language pathology (MS); vision rehabilitation therapy (MS, Certificate).

College of Health Sciences Offers physician assistant (MMS); public health (MPH). Electronic applications accepted.

Osborne College of Audiology Offers audiology (Au D). Electronic applications accepted.

Pennsylvania College of Optometry Offers optometry (OD). Electronic applications accepted.

SALVE REGINA UNIVERSITY, Newport, RI 02840-4192

General Information Independent-religious, coed, comprehensive institution. *Graduate housing:* On-campus housing not available.

GRADUATE UNITS

The Newport MFA in Creative Writing Program Offers creative writing (MFA).

Program in Administration of Justice and Homeland Security *Program availability:* Part-time, evening/weekend, online learning. Offers administration of justice and homeland security (MS); cybersecurity and intelligence (CGS); digital forensics (CGS); leadership in justice (CGS). Electronic applications accepted.

Program in Applied Behavior Analysis Offers applied behavior analysis (MA, CAGS).

Program in Business Administration *Program availability:* Part-time, evening/weekend, online learning. Offers cybersecurity issues in business (MBA); entrepreneurial enterprise (MBA); health care administration and management (MBA); nonprofit management (MBA); social ventures (MBA). Electronic applications accepted.

Program in Catholic School Leadership Offers Catholic school leadership (CGS).

Program in Healthcare Administration and Management *Program availability:* Part-time, evening/weekend, online learning. Offers healthcare administration and management (MS, CGS). Electronic applications accepted.

Program in Humanities *Program availability:* Part-time, evening/weekend, online learning. Offers humanitarian assistance (MA); humanities (PhD); public humanities (MA); religion, peace and justice (MA). Electronic applications accepted.

Program in International Relations *Program availability:* Part-time, evening/weekend, online learning. Offers international relations (MA, CGS). Electronic applications accepted.

Program in Management *Program availability:* Part-time, evening/weekend, online learning. Offers business studies (CGS); human resource management (CGS); innovation and strategic management (MS); management (CGS); nonprofit management (CGS); social entrepreneurship (CGS). Electronic applications accepted.

Program in Nursing *Program availability:* Part-time, evening/weekend. Offers nursing (DNP). Electronic applications accepted.

Program in Rehabilitation Counseling *Program availability:* Part-time, evening/weekend. Offers clinical rehabilitation and mental health counseling (MA); mental health (CAGS); rehabilitation (CAGS); rehabilitation counseling (MA); substance abuse and treatment (CAGS). Electronic applications accepted.

SAMFORD UNIVERSITY, Birmingham, AL 35229

General Information Independent-religious, coed, university. *Enrollment:* 5,509 graduate, professional, and undergraduate students; 1,895 full-time matriculated graduate/professional students (1,179 women), 192 part-time matriculated graduate/professional students (140 women). *Enrollment by degree level:* 760 master's, 1,294 doctoral, 33 other advanced degrees. *Graduate faculty:* 159 full-time (89 women), 63 part-time/adjunct (23 women). *Tuition:* Full-time $19,058; part-time $813 per credit hour. *Required fees:* $550. Tuition and fees vary according to course load, degree level, program and student level. *Graduate housing:* On-campus housing not available. *Student services:* Campus employment opportunities, campus safety program, career counseling, exercise/wellness program, free psychological counseling, grant writing training, international student services, low-cost health insurance, multicultural affairs office, services for students with disabilities, teacher training, writing training. *Library facilities:* University Library plus 2 others. *Collection:* Books: 635,009 (physical), 212,093 (digital/electronic); Serial titles: 6,055 (physical), 113,159 (digital/electronic); Databases: 307. Weekly public service hours: 99; students can reserve study rooms. *Research affiliation:* Heartland Institute, Beacon Center of Tennessee, Institute for Faith, Work, and Economics, Foundation for Economic Education, Jack Miller Center.

Computer facilities: 330 computers available on campus for general student use. A campuswide network can be accessed from student residence rooms and from off campus. Online class registration, free online storage and tech support are available. Website: http://www.samford.edu/

General Application Contact: Brian L. Kennedy, Director of Recruitment, 205-726-4176, Fax: 205-726-2171, E-mail: blkenned@samford.edu.

GRADUATE UNITS

Beeson School of Divinity Students: 146 full-time (30 women), 8 part-time (4 women); includes 24 minority (22 Black or African American, non-Hispanic/Latino; 1 Asian, non-Hispanic/Latino; 1 Two or more races, non-Hispanic/Latino), 7 international. Average age 30. 61 applicants, 93% accepted, 31 enrolled. *Faculty:* 13 full-time (1 woman), 2 part-time/adjunct (0 women). Expenses: Contact institution. *Financial support:* In 2017–18, 135 students received support, including 6 teaching assistantships (averaging $1,200 per year); Federal Work-Study, scholarships/grants, and tuition waivers (full and partial) also available. Financial award application deadline: 2/15; financial award applicants required to submit FAFSA. In 2017, 40 master's, 10 doctorates awarded. *Program availability:* Part-time. Offers divinity (M Div, MATS, D Min). *Application deadline:* For fall admission, 2/15 for domestic and international students; for spring admission, 10/1 for domestic and international students. *Application fee:* $35. Electronic applications accepted. *Application Contact:* Sherri S. Brown, Director of Admission, 205-726-2066, E-mail: sbrown5@samford.edu. *Dean*, Dr. Timothy George, 205-726-2632, E-mail: tfgeorge@samford.edu.

Brock School of Business Students: 79 full-time (31 women), 18 part-time (8 women); includes 7 minority (2 Black or African American, non-Hispanic/Latino; 1 Asian, non-Hispanic/Latino; 3 Hispanic/Latino; 1 Two or more races, non-Hispanic/Latino), 8 international. Average age 28. 46 applicants, 78% accepted, 16 enrolled. *Faculty:* 8 full-time (1 woman), 5 part-time/adjunct (0 women). Expenses: Contact institution. *Financial support:* In 2017–18, 59 students received support. Scholarships/grants available. Financial award application deadline: 2/15; financial award applicants required to submit FAFSA. In 2017, 78 master's awarded. *Program availability:* Part-time, 100% online, blended/hybrid learning. Offers accountancy (M Acc); entrepreneurship (MBA); finance (MBA); marketing (MBA). Programs offered jointly with Cumberland School of Law, Beeson School of Divinity, Howard College of Arts and Sciences, and McWhorter School of Pharmacy. *Application deadline:* For fall admission, 8/1 for domestic and international students; for spring admission, 12/1 for domestic and international students; for summer admission, 5/1 for domestic and international students. Applications are processed on a rolling basis. *Application fee:* $35. Electronic applications accepted. *Application Contact:* Elizabeth Anne Gambrell, Associate Director, 205-726-2040, Fax: 205-726-2540, E-mail: eagambre@samford.edu. *Assistant Dean*, Dr. Barbara Cartledge, 205-726-2935, Fax: 205-726-2540, E-mail: bhcartle@samford.edu.

Cumberland School of Law Students: 447 full-time (232 women), 4 part-time (1 woman); includes 80 minority (46 Black or African American, non-Hispanic/Latino; 6 American Indian or Alaska Native, non-Hispanic/Latino; 4 Asian, non-Hispanic/Latino; 17 Hispanic/Latino; 1 Native Hawaiian or other Pacific Islander, non-Hispanic/Latino; 6 Two or more races, non-Hispanic/Latino), 1 international. Average age 26. 579 applicants, 73% accepted, 150 enrolled. *Faculty:* 18 full-time (7 women), 19 part-time/adjunct (7 women). Expenses: Contact institution. *Financial support:* In 2017–18, 372 students received support. Scholarships/grants available. Financial award application deadline: 2/15; financial award applicants required to submit FAFSA. In 2017, 13 master's, 142 doctorates awarded. *Program availability:* Part-time, 100% online, blended/hybrid learning. Offers law (LL M, MCL, MSL, JD). Programs offered jointly with The University of Alabama at Birmingham and Albany Medical School. *Application deadline:* For fall admission, 6/1 for domestic students, 6/1 priority date for international students. Applications are processed on a rolling basis. Electronic applications accepted. *Application Contact:* Whitney Dachelet, Interim Director of Admissions and Student Recruiting, 205-726-2702, Fax: 205-726-2057, E-mail: wdachele@samford.edu. *Dean/Professor of Law*, Henry C. Strickland, 205-726-2704, Fax: 205-726-4457, E-mail: hcstrick@samford.edu.

Howard College of Arts and Sciences Students: 6 full-time (4 women), 1 part-time (0 women); includes 2 minority (both Black or African American, non-Hispanic/Latino), 1 international. Average age 28. 25 applicants, 80% accepted, 3 enrolled. *Faculty:* 5 full-time (3 women), 4 part-time/adjunct (1 woman). Expenses: Contact institution. In 2017, 11 master's awarded. *Program availability:* Part-time, online only, 100% online. Offers energy (MSEM); environmental management (MSEM); public health (MSEM). *Application fee:* $40. *Application Contact:* Dr. Anthony Scott Overton, Professor/Chair, Biological and Environmental Sciences, 205-726-2944, E-mail: aoverton@samford.edu. *Dean of Howard College of Arts and Sciences*, Tim Hall, E-mail: thall5@samford.edu.

Ida Moffett School of Nursing Students: 296 full-time (240 women), 41 part-time (38 women); includes 67 minority (43 Black or African American, non-Hispanic/Latino; 2 American Indian or Alaska Native, non-Hispanic/Latino; 6 Asian, non-Hispanic/Latino; 8 Hispanic/Latino; 8 Two or more races, non-Hispanic/Latino). Average age 35. 79 applicants, 71% accepted, 29 enrolled. *Faculty:* 20 full-time (19 women), 3 part-time/adjunct (0 women). Expenses: Contact institution. *Financial support:* In 2017–18, 63 students received support. Application deadline: 2/15; applicants required to submit FAFSA. In 2017, 117 master's, 39 doctorates awarded. *Program availability:* Part-time, evening/weekend, blended/hybrid learning. Offers administration (DNP); advanced practice (DNP); dual nurse practitioner (family/emergency) (DNP); family nurse practitioner (MSN, DNP); nurse anesthesia (MSN, DNP); nursing administration (DNP). *Application deadline:* For fall admission, 4/1 for domestic and international students; for spring admission, 8/1 for domestic and international students; for summer admission, 1/1 for domestic and international students. *Application fee:* $50. Electronic applications accepted. *Application Contact:* Allyson Maddox, Director of Graduate Student Services, 205-726-2047, E-mail: amaddox@samford.edu. *Vice Provost, College of Health Sciences/Ida Moffett School of Nursing Dean/Professor*, Dr. Nena F. Sanders, 205-726-2612, E-mail: nfsander@samford.edu.

McWhorter School of Pharmacy Students: 469 full-time (301 women), 9 part-time (5 women); includes 93 minority (49 Black or African American, non-Hispanic/Latino; 3 American Indian or Alaska Native, non-Hispanic/Latino; 29 Asian, non-Hispanic/Latino; 5 Hispanic/Latino; 7 Two or more races, non-Hispanic/Latino), 7 international. Average age 24. 448 applicants, 28% accepted, 122 enrolled. *Faculty:* 34 full-time (23 women), 1 part-time/adjunct (0 women). Expenses: Contact institution. *Financial support:* In 2017–18, 217 students received support. Federal Work-Study and scholarships/grants available. Financial award application deadline: 2/15; financial award applicants required to submit FAFSA. In 2017, 134 doctorates awarded. Offers pharmacy (Pharm D). *Application deadline:* For fall admission, 3/1 for domestic students. Applications are processed on a rolling basis. Electronic applications accepted. *Application Contact:* Jonathan Parker, Director of Pharmacy Admissions, 205-726-4242, Fax: 205-726-4141, E-mail: jmparker@samford.edu. *Dean/Professor*, Dr. Michael Crouch, 205-726-4475, E-mail: mcrouch@samford.edu.

Orlean Beeson School of Education Students: 206 full-time (144 women), 102 part-time (75 women); includes 124 minority (113 Black or African American, non-Hispanic/Latino; 3 American Indian or Alaska Native, non-Hispanic/Latino; 3 Asian, non-Hispanic/Latino; 2 Hispanic/Latino; 3 Two or more races, non-Hispanic/Latino), 1 international. Average age 37. 134 applicants, 84% accepted, 76 enrolled. *Faculty:* 11 full-time (7 women), 22 part-time/adjunct (12 women). Expenses: Contact institution. *Financial support:* In 2017–18, 220 students received support. Scholarships/grants and unspecified assistantships available. Financial award application deadline: 2/15; financial award applicants required to submit FAFSA. In 2017, 79 master's, 34 doctorates, 21 other advanced degrees awarded. *Program availability:* Part-time, evening/weekend, 100% online, blended/hybrid learning. Offers educational leadership (MSE, Ed D); elementary education (MS Ed, MSE); gifted (MSE); instructional design and technology (MSE); instructional leadership (MSE, Ed S); secondary education (MSE); special education (MSE). *Application deadline:* For fall admission, 7/15 for domestic and international students; for winter admission, 11/15 for domestic and international students; for spring admission, 11/15 for domestic and international students; for summer admission, 4/15 for domestic and international students. *Application fee:* $35. Electronic applications accepted. *Application Contact:* Brooke Karr, Graduate Admissions Office Coordinator, 205-729-2783, Fax: 205-726-4233, E-mail: kbgilrea@samford.edu. *Interim Dean*, Dr. Bonnie Rabe, 205-726-2565, E-mail: brabe@samford.edu.

School of Health Professions Students: 140 full-time (105 women), 2 part-time (both women); includes 14 minority (3 Black or African American, non-Hispanic/Latino; 1 Asian, non-Hispanic/Latino; 4 Hispanic/Latino; 6 Two or more races, non-Hispanic/Latino). Average age 24. 191 applicants, 60% accepted, 5 enrolled. *Faculty:* 20 full-time (12 women), 1 part-time/adjunct (0 women). Expenses: Contact institution. *Financial support:* In 2017–18, 36 students received support. Scholarships/grants available. Financial award application deadline: 2/15; financial award applicants required to submit FAFSA. In 2017, 17 master's awarded. Offers athletic training (MAT); physical therapy (DPT); respiratory care (MS); speech language pathology (MS). *Application deadline:* For fall admission, 10/1 for domestic students; for spring admission, 5/1 for domestic students. *Application fee:* $120. Electronic applications accepted. *Application Contact:* Dr. Marian Carter, Assistant Dean of Enrollment Management and Student Services, 205-726-2611, E-mail: mwcarter@samford.edu. *Dean of the School of Health Professions*, Dr. Alan Jung, 205-726-2716, E-mail: apjung@samford.edu.

School of Public Health Students: 93 full-time (87 women), 5 part-time (all women); includes 20 minority (14 Black or African American, non-Hispanic/Latino; 2 Asian, non-Hispanic/Latino; 2 Hispanic/Latino; 2 Two or more races, non-Hispanic/Latino), 1 international. Average age 27. 90 applicants, 44% accepted, 32 enrolled. *Faculty:* 17 full-time (12 women), 4 part-time/adjunct (2 women). Expenses: Contact institution. *Financial support:* In 2017–18, 32 students received support. Scholarships/grants available. Financial award application deadline: 2/15; financial award applicants required to submit FAFSA. In 2017, 34 master's awarded. *Program availability:* Part-time, 100% online. Offers health informatics (MSHI); healthcare administration (MHA); nutrition (MS); public health (MPH); social work (MSW). *Application deadline:* For fall admission, 10/1 for domestic students; for spring admission, 5/1 for domestic students. *Application fee:* $75. Electronic applications accepted. *Application Contact:* Dr. Marian Carter, Assistant Dean of Enrollment Management and Student Services, 205-726-2611, E-mail: mwcarter@samford.edu. *Dean, School of Public Health*, Dr. Keith Elder, 205-726-4655, E-mail: kelder@samford.edu.

School of the Arts Students: 13 full-time (5 women), 2 part-time (both women); includes 5 minority (all Black or African American, non-Hispanic/Latino), 1 international. Average age 29. 7 applicants, 86% accepted, 4 enrolled. *Faculty:* 13 full-time (4 women), 2 part-time/adjunct (1 woman). Expenses: Contact institution. *Financial support:* In 2017–18, 13 students received support. Scholarships/grants available. Financial award application deadline: 2/15; financial award applicants required to submit FAFSA. In 2017, 1 master's awarded. *Program availability:* Part-time. Offers church music (MM); instrumental performance (MM); piano performance and pedagogy (MM); vocal performance (MM); vocal/choral or instrumental music (MME). MME program offered in traditional, fifth-year non-traditional, and national board cohort formats. *Application deadline:* For fall admission, 2/28 priority date for domestic and international students; for winter admission, 10/1 priority date for domestic and international students; for spring admission, 2/28 priority date for domestic and international students; for summer admission, 5/1 priority date for domestic and international students. Applications are processed on a rolling basis. *Application fee:* $35. Electronic applications accepted. *Application Contact:* Dr. Mark Lackey, Assistant Professor, 205-726-4623, Fax: 205-726-2615, E-mail: mlckey@samford.edu. *Dean of the School of the Arts/Professor*, Dr. Joseph Hopkin, 205-726-2778, E-mail: jhopkins@samford.edu.

SAM HOUSTON STATE UNIVERSITY, Huntsville, TX 77341

General Information State-supported, coed, university. CGS member. *Graduate housing:* Room and/or apartments available on a first-come, first-served basis to single students; on-campus housing not available to married students. Housing application deadline: 8/20. *Research affiliation:* Texas Criminal Justice Division, Texas Department of Corrections, Research Division.

GRADUATE UNITS

College of Business Administration *Program availability:* Part-time, evening/weekend, online learning. Offers accounting (MS); banking and financial institutions (EMBA); business administration (EMBA, MBA, MS); project management (MS). Electronic applications accepted.

College of Criminal Justice *Program availability:* Part-time, evening/weekend, online learning. Offers criminal justice (MS, PhD); criminal justice and criminology (MA); criminal justice leadership and management (MS); forensic science (MS); homeland security studies (MS); victim services management (MS). Electronic applications accepted.

College of Education *Program availability:* Part-time, evening/weekend, online learning. Offers administration (M Ed); counseling (M Ed, MA, PhD); curriculum and instruction (M Ed); developmental education administration (Ed D); education (M Ed, MA, MLS, Ed D, PhD); educational leadership (Ed D); higher education administration (MA); higher education leadership (Ed D); instructional leadership (M Ed, MA); international literacy (M Ed); library science (MLS); reading (M Ed); special education (M Ed, MA). Electronic applications accepted.

College of Fine Arts and Mass Communication *Program availability:* Part-time. Offers dance (MFA); digital media (MA); fine arts and mass communication (MA, MFA, MM). Electronic applications accepted.

School of Music *Program availability:* Part-time. Offers music (MM). Electronic applications accepted.

College of Health Sciences *Program availability:* Part-time. Offers dietetics (MS); family and consumer sciences (MS); health (MA); health sciences (MA, MS); sport and human performance (MA); sport management (MA). Electronic applications accepted.

College of Humanities and Social Sciences *Program availability:* Part-time, online learning. Offers communication studies (MA); creative writing, editing, and publishing (MFA); English (MA); history (MA); humanities and social sciences (MA, MFA, MPA, PhD, SSP); political science (MA); psychology (MA, PhD, SSP); public administration (MPA); sociology (MA); Spanish (MA). Electronic applications accepted.

College of Sciences *Program availability:* Part-time, evening/weekend. Offers agriculture (MS); applied geographic information science (MS); biological sciences (MA, MS); chemistry (MS); computing and information science (MS); digital forensics (MS); geographic information science (Certificate); information assurance and security (MS); mathematics (MA, MS); sciences (MA, MS, PhD, Certificate); statistics (MS). Electronic applications accepted.

SAMUEL MERRITT UNIVERSITY, Oakland, CA 94609-3108

General Information Independent, coed, primarily women, upper-level institution. *Enrollment:* 2,141 graduate, professional, and undergraduate students; 865 full-time matriculated graduate/professional students (604 women), 357 part-time matriculated graduate/professional students (276 women). *Enrollment by degree level:* 808 master's, 396 doctoral, 18 other advanced degrees. *Graduate faculty:* 117 full-time (87 women), 147 part-time/adjunct (108 women). Tuition and fees vary according to course load, degree level, program and student level. *Graduate housing:* On-campus housing not available. *Student services:* Campus employment opportunities, campus safety program, career counseling, free psychological counseling, low-cost health insurance, multicultural affairs office, services for students with disabilities, writing training. *Library facilities:* John A. Graziano Memorial Library. *Collection:* Books: 8,453 (physical), 337 (digital/electronic); Serial titles: 714 (physical), 19,832 (digital/electronic); Databases: 22. Weekly public service hours: 86; students can reserve study rooms. *Research affiliation:* Summit Medical Center (nursing).

Computer facilities: 160 computers available on campus for general student use. A campuswide network can be accessed. Online class registration is available.
Website: http://www.samuelmerritt.edu/

General Application Contact: Timothy Cranford, Dean of Admissions, 510-869-1550, Fax: 510-869-6525, E-mail: admission@samuelmerritt.edu.

GRADUATE UNITS

California School of Podiatric Medicine Students: 176 full-time (76 women), 1 part-time (0 women); includes 98 minority (2 Black or African American, non-Hispanic/Latino; 1 American Indian or Alaska Native, non-Hispanic/Latino; 62 Asian, non-Hispanic/Latino; 20 Hispanic/Latino; 13 Two or more races, non-Hispanic/Latino). 360 applicants, 31% accepted, 46 enrolled. *Faculty:* 17 full-time (6 women), 5 part-time/adjunct (3 women). Expenses: Contact institution. *Financial support:* Federal Work-Study, institutionally sponsored loans, and scholarships/grants available. Financial award applicants required to submit FAFSA. In 2017, 51 doctorates awarded. Offers podiatric medicine (DPM). *Application deadline:* For fall admission, 4/1 priority date for domestic and international students. Applications are processed on a rolling basis. *Application fee:* $160. Electronic applications accepted. *Application Contact:* Dr. David Tran, Assistant Director of Admission, 510-869-6789, Fax: 510-869-6525, E-mail: dtran@samuelmerritt.edu. *Associate Dean for Administrative Affairs*, Irma Walker-Adame, 510-869-8742, E-mail: iadame@samuelmerritt.edu.

Department of Occupational Therapy Students: 85 full-time (71 women), 39 part-time (34 women); includes 70 minority (6 Black or African American, non-Hispanic/Latino; 1 American Indian or Alaska Native, non-Hispanic/Latino; 28 Asian, non-Hispanic/Latino; 29 Hispanic/Latino; 6 Two or more races, non-Hispanic/Latino). 246 applicants, 25% accepted, 42 enrolled. *Faculty:* 12 full-time (11 women), 10 part-time/adjunct (8 women). Expenses: Contact institution. *Financial support:* Career-related internships or fieldwork, Federal Work-Study, and scholarships/grants available. Support available to part-time students. Financial award applicants required to submit FAFSA. Offers occupational therapy (OTD). *Application deadline:* For fall admission, 10/1 priority date for domestic students. *Application fee:* $140. Electronic applications accepted. *Application Contact:* Timothy Cranford, Dean of Admission, 510-869-1550, Fax: 510-869-6525, E-mail: admission@samuelmerritt.edu. *Chair*, Kate Hayner, 510-869-4780, E-mail: khayner@samuelmerritt.edu.

Department of Physical Therapy Students: 114 full-time (73 women), 3 part-time (2 women); includes 69 minority (2 Black or African American, non-Hispanic/Latino; 34 Asian, non-Hispanic/Latino; 23 Hispanic/Latino; 2 Native Hawaiian or other Pacific Islander, non-Hispanic/Latino; 8 Two or more races, non-Hispanic/Latino). 486 applicants, 18% accepted, 40 enrolled. *Faculty:* 12 full-time (10 women), 23 part-time/adjunct (10 women). Expenses: Contact institution. *Financial support:* Career-related internships or fieldwork, Federal Work-Study, and scholarships/grants available.

Financial award applicants required to submit FAFSA. In 2017, 32 doctorates awarded. Offers physical therapy (DPT). *Application deadline:* For fall admission, 10/1 priority date for domestic students. *Application fee:* $140. Electronic applications accepted. *Application Contact:* Timothy Cranford, Dean of Admissions, 510-869-1550, Fax: 510-869-6525, E-mail: admission@samuelmerritt.edu. *Co-Chair,* Dr. Nicole Christensen, 510-869-6567, Fax: 510-869-6282, E-mail: nchristensen@samuelmerritt.edu.

Department of Physician Assistant Studies Students: 89 full-time (62 women), 47 part-time (38 women); includes 80 minority (9 Black or African American, non-Hispanic/Latino; 34 Asian, non-Hispanic/Latino; 31 Hispanic/Latino; 1 Native Hawaiian or other Pacific Islander, non-Hispanic/Latino; 5 Two or more races, non-Hispanic/Latino). 2,174 applicants, 2% accepted, 44 enrolled. *Faculty:* 10 full-time (5 women), 18 part-time/adjunct (9 women). Expenses: Contact institution. *Financial support:* Federal Work-Study, institutionally sponsored loans, and scholarships/grants available. Financial award applicants required to submit FAFSA. In 2017, 40 master's awarded. Offers physician assistant studies (MPA). *Application deadline:* For fall admission, 10/1 priority date for domestic students. *Application fee:* $175. Electronic applications accepted. *Application Contact:* Timothy Cranford, Dean of Admission, 510-869-1550, Fax: 510-869-6525, E-mail: admission@samuelmerritt.edu.

School of Nursing Students: 401 full-time (322 women), 267 part-time (202 women); includes 438 minority (52 Black or African American, non-Hispanic/Latino; 4 American Indian or Alaska Native, non-Hispanic/Latino; 224 Asian, non-Hispanic/Latino; 108 Hispanic/Latino; 9 Native Hawaiian or other Pacific Islander, non-Hispanic/Latino; 41 Two or more races, non-Hispanic/Latino). 788 applicants, 54% accepted, 306 enrolled. *Faculty:* 57 full-time (49 women), 90 part-time/adjunct (77 women). Expenses: Contact institution. *Financial support:* Career-related internships or fieldwork, Federal Work-Study, scholarships/grants, and traineeships available. Support available to part-time students. Financial award applicants required to submit FAFSA. In 2017, 176 master's, 6 doctorates, 7 other advanced degrees awarded. *Program availability:* Part-time, evening/weekend, 100% online, blended/hybrid learning. Offers case management (MSN); family nurse practitioner (MSN, DNP, Certificate); nurse anesthetist (MSN, Certificate); nursing (DNP). *Application deadline:* For fall admission, 7/1 priority date for domestic students; for spring admission, 11/1 priority date for domestic students; for summer admission, 3/1 priority date for domestic students. Applications are processed on a rolling basis. *Application fee:* $65. Electronic applications accepted. *Application Contact:* Timothy Cranford, Dean of Admission, 510-869-6576, Fax: 510-869-6525, E-mail: admission@samuelmerritt.edu. *Dean of Nursing,* Dr. Audrey Berman, 510-869-6733, Fax: 510-869-6525.

SAN DIEGO CHRISTIAN COLLEGE, Santee, CA 92071

General Information Independent-religious, coed, comprehensive institution.

GRADUATE UNITS

Graduate Programs

SAN DIEGO STATE UNIVERSITY, San Diego, CA 92182

General Information State-supported, coed, university. CGS member. *Graduate housing:* Room and/or apartments available on a first-come, first-served basis to single students; on-campus housing not available to married students. Housing application deadline: 5/1. *Research affiliation:* Children's Hospital and Research Center (children's health), Qualcomm (wireless and telecommunications), Robert Wood Johnson Foundation (public health), General Atomics (technical student services), William and Flora Hewlett Foundation (teacher education), American Heart Association (biology).

GRADUATE UNITS

Graduate and Research Affairs *Program availability:* Part-time, evening/weekend. Offers interdisciplinary studies (MA, MS). Electronic applications accepted.

College of Arts and Letters *Program availability:* Part-time, evening/weekend. Offers anthropology (MA); applied linguistics and English as a second language (CAL); arts and letters (MA, MFA, PhD, CAL); Asian studies (MA); computational linguistics (MA); creative writing (MFA); economics (MA); English (MA); English as a second language/applied linguistics (MA); European studies (MA); general linguistics (MA); geography (MA, PhD); history (MA); Latin American studies (MA); lesbian, gay, bisexual and transgender studies (Graduate Certificate); liberal arts and sciences (MA); philosophy (MA); political science (MA); rhetoric and writing studies (MA); sociology (MA); Spanish (MA); women's studies (MA). Electronic applications accepted.

College of Business Administration *Program availability:* Part-time, evening/weekend. Offers accountancy (MS); business administration (MBA, MS); entrepreneurship (MS); finance (MS); human resources management (MS); information systems (MS); management science (MS); marketing (MS); sports business management (MBA). Electronic applications accepted.

College of Education *Program availability:* Part-time, evening/weekend. Offers child development (MS); counseling and school psychology (MS); education (MA, MS, Ed D, PhD); educational leadership (MA); educational leadership in post-secondary education (MA); educational technology (MA); educational technology and teaching and learning (Ed D); elementary curriculum and instruction (MA); multi-cultural emphasis (PhD); policy studies in language and cross cultural education (MA); reading education (MA); rehabilitation counseling (MS); secondary curriculum and instruction (MA); special education (MA). Electronic applications accepted.

College of Engineering *Program availability:* Part-time, evening/weekend. Offers aerospace engineering (MS); civil engineering (MS); electrical engineering (MS); engineering (MS, PhD); engineering mechanics (MS); engineering sciences and applied mechanics (PhD); flight dynamics (MS); fluid dynamics (MS); manufacture and design (MS); mechanical engineering (MS). Electronic applications accepted.

College of Health and Human Services *Program availability:* Part-time, evening/weekend. Offers audiology (Au D); biometry (MPH); communicative disorders (MA); environmental health (MPH); epidemiology (MPH, PhD); exercise physiology (MS); gerontology (MS); global emergency preparedness and response (MS); global health (PhD); health and human services (MA, MPH, MS, MSW, Au D, DPT, PhD); health behavior (PhD); health promotion (MPH); health services administration (MPH); kinesiology (MA); language and communicative disorders (PhD); nursing (MS); nutritional sciences (MS); physical therapy (DPT); social work (MSW); toxicology (MS). Electronic applications accepted.

College of Professional Studies and Fine Arts *Program availability:* Part-time. Offers advertising and public relations (MA); art history (MA); city planning (MCP); composition (acoustic and electronic) (MM); conducting (MM); criminal justice administration (MPA); criminal justice and criminology (MS); critical-cultural studies (MA); design and technology (MFA); ethnomusicology (MA); film and television production (MFA); interaction studies (MA); intercultural and international studies (MA); jazz studies (MM); musical theatre (MFA); musicology (MA); new media studies (MA); news and information studies (MA); performance (MM); piano pedagogy (MA); professional studies and fine arts (MA, MCP, MFA, MM, MPA, MS); public administration (MPA); studio arts (MA, MFA); telecommunications and media management (MA); theatre arts (MA); theory (MA).

College of Sciences *Program availability:* Part-time. Offers applied mathematics (MS); astronomy (MS); biology (MA, MS); cell and molecular biology (PhD); chemistry and biochemistry (MA, MS, PhD); clinical psychology (MS, PhD); computational science (MS, PhD); computer science (MS); ecology (MS, PhD); geological sciences (MS); industrial and organizational psychology (MS); mathematics (MA); mathematics and science education (PhD); microbiology (MS); molecular biology (MA, MS); physics (MA, MS); program evaluation (MS); psychology (MA); radiological physics (MS); regulatory affairs (MS); sciences (MA, MS, PhD); statistics (MS). Electronic applications accepted.

SANFORD BURNHAM PREBYS MEDICAL DISCOVERY INSTITUTE, La Jolla, CA 92037

General Information Independent, coed, graduate-only institution. *Enrollment by degree level:* 31 doctoral. *Graduate faculty:* 52. *Student services:* Career counseling, grant writing training, international student services, writing training.
Website: https://www.sbpdiscovery.org/education/graduate-school

General Application Contact: E-mail: gsbs@sbp.edu.

GRADUATE UNITS

Graduate School of Biomedical Sciences Students: 31 full-time (19 women). *Faculty:* 52. Expenses: Contact institution. *Financial support:* Scholarships/grants and health care benefits available. In 2017, 5 doctorates awarded. Offers biomedical sciences (PhD). *Application deadline:* For fall admission, 12/1 for domestic students. *Application fee:* $80. *Application Contact:* Andrew Bankston, Program Manager, Graduate School, 858-646-3100, E-mail: gsbs@sbp.edu. *Dean,* Dr. Guy Salvesen, 858-646-3114.

SAN FRANCISCO ART INSTITUTE, San Francisco, CA 94133

General Information Independent, coed, comprehensive institution. *Graduate housing:* Room and/or apartments available on a first-come, first-served basis to single students; on-campus housing not available to married students. Housing application deadline: 6/1. *Research affiliation:* Headlands Center for the Arts (multidisciplinary art exhibition), Kadist Art Foundation (contemporary art exhibition), San Francisco Museum of Modern Art (art history, museum studies, contemporary art), Yerba Buena Center for the Arts (art exhibits), Tremaine Foundation (education; art, environment, and learning disabilities), Prelinger Library (library).

GRADUATE UNITS

Master of Arts Programs Offers exhibition and museum studies (MA); history and theory of contemporary art (MA). Electronic applications accepted.

Master of Fine Arts Programs Offers studio art (MFA, Certificate). Electronic applications accepted.

SAN FRANCISCO CONSERVATORY OF MUSIC, San Francisco, CA 94102

General Information Independent, coed, comprehensive institution. *Enrollment:* 414 graduate, professional, and undergraduate students; 208 full-time matriculated graduate/professional students (120 women), 1 (woman) part-time matriculated graduate/professional student. *Enrollment by degree level:* 167 master's, 42 other advanced degrees. *Graduate faculty:* 27 full-time (7 women), 107 part-time/adjunct (36 women). *Tuition:* Full-time $43,700; part-time $1924 per credit. *Required fees:* $1110; $1110 per unit. One-time fee: $50. Tuition and fees vary according to course load. *Graduate housing:* Rooms and/or apartments available on a first-come, first-served basis to single and married students. Typical cost: $14,390 per year ($21,340 including board) for single students; $24,920 per year ($38,820 including board) for married students. Room and board charges vary according to board plan, campus/location and housing facility selected. Housing application deadline: 5/31. *Student services:* Campus employment opportunities, campus safety program, career counseling, free psychological counseling, grant writing training, international student services, low-cost health insurance, services for students with disabilities, teacher training, writing training. *Library facilities:* San Francisco Conservatory of Music Library. *Collection:* Books: 24,129 (physical), 31,094 (digital/electronic); Serial titles: 64 (physical), 448 (digital/electronic); Databases: 11. Weekly public service hours: 72.

Computer facilities: 12 computers available on campus for general student use. A campuswide network can be accessed from student residence rooms. Online class registration is available.
Website: http://www.sfcm.edu/

General Application Contact: Melissa Cocco-Mitten, Director of Admissions, 415-503-6231, Fax: 415-503-6299, E-mail: admit@sfcm.edu.

GRADUATE UNITS

Graduate Division Students: 208 full-time (120 women), 1 (woman) part-time; includes 37 minority (7 Black or African American, non-Hispanic/Latino; 13 Asian, non-Hispanic/Latino; 7 Hispanic/Latino; 10 Two or more races, non-Hispanic/Latino), 82 international. Average age 25. 709 applicants, 36% accepted, 117 enrolled. *Faculty:* 27 full-time (7 women), 107 part-time/adjunct (36 women). Expenses: Contact institution. *Financial support:* In 2017–18, 214 students received support. Federal Work-Study, scholarships/grants, tuition waivers (partial), and unspecified assistantships available. Financial award application deadline: 2/15; financial award applicants required to submit FAFSA. In 2017, 74 master's, 41 Artist Diplomas awarded. Offers brass (MM); chamber music (MM, Artist Certificate); composition (MM); conducting (MM); guitar (MM); harp (MM); historical performance (MM); percussion (MM); piano (MM, MM, Artist Diploma); strings (MM, Artist Diploma); voice (MM, Postgraduate Diploma); woodwinds (MM). *Application deadline:* For fall admission, 12/1 for domestic and international students; for spring admission, 10/1 for domestic and international students. *Application fee:* $110. Electronic applications accepted. *Application Contact:* Melissa Cocco-Mitten, Director of Admission, 415-503-6231, Fax: 415-503-6299, E-mail: admit@sfcm.edu. *Provost and Dean,* Kate Sheeran, 415-503-6251, Fax: 415-503-6205, E-mail: snedel@sfcm.edu.

SAN FRANCISCO STATE UNIVERSITY, San Francisco, CA 94132-1722

General Information State-supported, coed, university. *Enrollment:* 29,607 graduate, professional, and undergraduate students; 1,719 full-time matriculated graduate/professional students (1,182 women), 1,003 part-time matriculated graduate/professional students (610 women). *Graduate housing:* Room and/or apartments available on a first-come, first-served basis to single students; on-campus housing not available to married students. *Student services:* Campus employment opportunities, campus safety program, career counseling, child daycare facilities, exercise/wellness program, free psychological counseling, international student services, low-cost health insurance, multicultural affairs office, services for students with disabilities, teacher training. *Library facilities:* J. Paul Leonard Library. *Collection:* Study areas open 24 hours, 5–7 days a week; students can reserve study rooms.

Computer facilities: Computer purchase and lease plans are available. 2,000 computers available on campus for general student use. A campuswide network can be accessed from student residence rooms and from off campus. Online class registration is available.
Website: http://www.sfsu.edu/

General Application Contact: Noah Price, Director of Graduate Admissions, 415-405-3506, Fax: 415-405-0340, E-mail: nprice@sfsu.edu.

GRADUATE UNITS

Division of Graduate Studies Expenses: Contact institution. *Financial support:* Fellowships, research assistantships, teaching assistantships, career-related internships or fieldwork, Federal Work-Study, institutionally sponsored loans, tuition waivers (partial), and unspecified assistantships available. Support available to part-time students. Financial award application deadline: 3/1; financial award applicants required to submit FAFSA. *Program availability:* Part-time, evening/weekend. *Application fee:* $55. *Application Contact:* Noah Price, Director, Graduate Admissions, 415-405-3506, Fax: 415-405-0340, E-mail: nprice@sfsu.edu. *Interim Dean*, Dr. Mi-Sook Kim, 415-338-2232, Fax: 415-405-0340, E-mail: kimms@sfsu.edu.

College of Business Expenses: Contact institution. Offers accounting (MSA); business (EMBA, MA, MBA, MSA); decision sciences/operations research (MBA); economics (MA); ethics and compliance (MBA); finance (MBA); global business and innovation (MBA); healthcare administration (MBA); hospitality and tourism management (MBA); information systems (MBA); leadership (MBA); marketing (MBA); nonprofit and social enterprise leadership (MBA); sustainable business (MBA). *Application Contact:* Dr. Yim-Yu Wong, Associate Dean, 415-338-1276, Fax: 415-338-6237, E-mail: yywong@sfsu.edu. *Dean*, Linda Oubre, 415-338-1276, Fax: 415-338-6237, E-mail: loubre@sfsu.edu.

College of Education Expenses: Contact institution. Offers adult education (MA); augmentative and alternative communication (AC); autism spectrum (AC); early childhood education (MA); early childhood special education (AC); education (MA, MS, Ed D, PhD, AC, Certificate, Credential); education specialist (Credential); educational administration (MA, Credential); educational leadership (Ed D); elementary education (MA); equity and social justice (MA); instructional technologies (MA); language and literacy education (MA, Certificate, Credential); mathematics education (MA); orientation and mobility (Credential); reading (Certificate); reading and literacy leadership (Credential); secondary education (MA, Credential); special education (MA, PhD); special interest (MA); speech-language pathology (MS). *Application Contact:* Victoria Narkewicz, Executive Assistant, 415-338-2687, Fax: 415-338-7019, E-mail: toria@sfsu.edu. *Interim Dean*, Dr. Nancy Robinson, 415-338-2687, Fax: 415-338-7019, E-mail: nancyr@sfsu.edu.

College of Ethnic Studies Expenses: Contact institution. *Program availability:* Part-time. Offers Asian American studies (MA); ethnic studies (MA). *Application Contact:* Dr. Catrióna Esquibel, Interim Associate Dean, 415-338-1693, Fax: 415-338-1739, E-mail: ktrion@sfsu.edu. *Interim Dean*, Dr. Amy H. Sueyoshi, 415-338-1693, Fax: 415-338-1739, E-mail: ethnicst@sfsu.edu.

College of Health and Social Sciences Expenses: Contact institution. *Financial support:* Fellowships, research assistantships, teaching assistantships, career-related internships or fieldwork, Federal Work-Study, institutionally sponsored loans, and unspecified assistantships available. *Program availability:* Part-time. Offers adult acute care (MS); clinical mental health counseling (MS); clinical nurse specialist (MS); community health education (MPH); community/public health nursing (MS); criminal justice administration (MPA); environmental administration and policy (MPA); family and consumer sciences (MA); family nurse practitioner (Certificate); gerontology (MA); health and social sciences (MA, MPA, MPH, MS, MSW, DPT, Certificate); kinesiology (MS); marriage, family and child counseling (MS); nonprofit administration (MPA); nursing administration (MS); pediatrics (MS); physical therapy (DPT); public management (MPA); public policy (MPA); recreation, parks, and tourism (MS); sexuality studies (MA); social work (MSW); urban administration (MPA); women's health (MS). *Application Contact:* Christina Alcantara, Assistant to the Dean, 415-338-3327, Fax: 415-338-0586, E-mail: cba@sfsu.edu. *Dean*, Dr. Alvin Alvarez, 415-338-3326, Fax: 415-338-0586, E-mail: aalvarez@sfsu.edu.

College of Liberal and Creative Arts Expenses: Contact institution. *Financial support:* Teaching assistantships, career-related internships or fieldwork, and Federal Work-Study available. *Program availability:* Part-time, evening/weekend. Offers archaeology (MA); art (MFA); biological anthropology (MA); broadcast and electronic communication arts (MA); chamber music (MM); Chinese (MA); cinema (MA, MFA); classical performance (MM); classics (MA); communication studies (MA); comparative literature (MA); composition (MA, Certificate); conducting (MM); creative writing (MA, MFA); cultural anthropology (MA); French (MA); German (MA); history (MA); humanities and liberal studies (MA); immigrant literacies (Certificate); industrial arts (MA); international relations (MA); Italian (MA); Japanese (MA); liberal and creative arts (MA, MFA, MM, Certificate); linguistics (MA); literature (MA); museum studies (MA); music education (MA); music history (MA); philosophy (MA); political science (MA); Spanish (MA); teaching English to speakers of other languages (MA); teaching post-secondary reading (Certificate); theatre arts (MA, MFA); visual anthropology (MA); women and gender studies (MA). *Application Contact:* Florence Tu, Executive Assistant to the Dean, 415-338-7692, Fax: 415-338-6159, E-mail: ftu@sfsu.edu. *Dean*, Dr. Andrew Harris, 415-338-1471, Fax: 415-338-6159, E-mail: a1harris@sfsu.edu.

College of Science and Engineering Expenses: Contact institution. *Program availability:* Part-time. Offers astronomy (MS); biochemistry (MS); biotechnology (PSM); cell and molecular biology (MS); chemistry (MS); clinical psychology (MS); computer science (MS); developmental psychology (MA); ecology, evolution, and conservation biology (MS); embedded electrical and computer systems (MS); energy systems (MS); geographic information science (MS); geography (MA); geosciences (MS); industrial/organizational psychology (MS); interdisciplinary marine and estuarine science (MS); marine biology (MS); mathematics (MA); microbiology (MS); mind, brain, and behavior (MA); physics (MS); physiology and behavioral biology (MS); resource management and environmental planning (MA); school psychology (MS, Credential); science (PSM); science and engineering (MA, MS, PSM, Credential); social psychology (MA); stem cell science (PSM); structural/earthquake engineering (MS). *Application deadline:* Applications are processed on a rolling basis. Electronic applications accepted. *Application Contact:* Nadia Chan, Executive Assistant to the Dean, 415-338-1571, Fax: 415-338-6136, E-mail: nadiach@sfsu.edu. *Interim Dean*, Dr. Carmen Domingo, 415-338-1571, Fax: 415-338-6136, E-mail: cdomingo@sfsu.edu.

SAN FRANCISCO THEOLOGICAL SEMINARY, San Anselmo, CA 94960

General Information Independent-religious, coed, graduate-only institution. *Graduate housing:* Rooms and/or apartments available on a first-come, first-served basis to single and married students. Housing application deadline: 5/1.

GRADUATE UNITS

Graduate and Professional Programs *Program availability:* Part-time. Offers theology (M Div, MA, MATS, D Min, PhD, Th D). MA, Th D, PhD, M Div/MA offered jointly with Graduate Theological Union.

SAN IGNACIO UNIVERSITY, Doral, FL 33178

General Information Proprietary, coed, comprehensive institution.

GRADUATE UNITS

Graduate Programs

SAN JOAQUIN COLLEGE OF LAW, Clovis, CA 93612-1312

General Information Independent, coed, graduate-only institution. *Graduate housing:* On-campus housing not available.

GRADUATE UNITS

Law Program *Program availability:* Part-time, evening/weekend. Offers law (JD).

SAN JOSE STATE UNIVERSITY, San Jose, CA 95192-0001

General Information State-supported, coed, comprehensive institution. *Enrollment:* 2,997 full-time matriculated graduate/professional students (1,603 women), 2,010 part-time matriculated graduate/professional students (1,028 women). *Enrollment by degree level:* 4,965 master's, 42 doctoral. *Graduate faculty:* 338 full-time (167 women), 226 part-time/adjunct (114 women). Tuition, state resident: full-time $7176. Tuition, nonresident: full-time $16,680. Tuition and fees vary according to course load and program. *Graduate housing:* Room and/or apartments available on a first-come, first-served basis to single students; on-campus housing not available to married students. Typical cost: $15,733 per year ($19,063 including board). Room and board charges vary according to board plan and housing facility selected. Housing application deadline: 5/1. *Student services:* Campus employment opportunities, campus safety program, career counseling, child daycare facilities, exercise/wellness program, free psychological counseling, international student services, low-cost health insurance, multicultural affairs office, services for students with disabilities, teacher training. *Library facilities:* Dr. Martin Luther King Jr. Library plus 1 other. *Research affiliation:* Moss Landing Marine Laboratories (oceanography/marine science).

Computer facilities: Computer purchase and lease plans are available. A campuswide network can be accessed from student residence rooms and from off campus. Online class registration is available.
Website: http://www.sjsu.edu/

General Application Contact: Tricia Ryan, Director, Graduate Admissions and Program Evaluation, 408-283-7500, E-mail: tricia.ryan@sjsu.edu.

GRADUATE UNITS

Graduate Studies and Research Students: 2,997 full-time (1,603 women), 2,010 part-time (1,028 women); includes 1,898 minority (99 Black or African American, non-Hispanic/Latino; 4 American Indian or Alaska Native, non-Hispanic/Latino; 714 Asian, non-Hispanic/Latino; 678 Hispanic/Latino; 10 Native Hawaiian or other Pacific Islander, non-Hispanic/Latino; 393 Two or more races, non-Hispanic/Latino), 2,043 international. Average age 30. 7,154 applicants, 41% accepted, 1761 enrolled. *Faculty:* 338 full-time (167 women), 226 part-time/adjunct (114 women). Expenses: Contact institution. *Financial support:* Fellowships, research assistantships, teaching assistantships, career-related internships or fieldwork, Federal Work-Study, institutionally sponsored loans, scholarships/grants, and tuition waivers (full and partial) available. Support available to part-time students. Financial award application deadline: 4/28; financial award applicants required to submit FAFSA. In 2017, 2,935 master's, 7 doctorates awarded. *Program availability:* Part-time, evening/weekend, online learning. *Application deadline:* For fall admission, 2/1 for domestic and international students. Applications are processed on a rolling basis. *Application fee:* $55. Electronic applications accepted. *Application Contact:* 408-924-2480, Fax: 408-924-2477. *Associate Vice President*, Dr. Pam Stacks, 408-924-2427, Fax: 408-924-2612.

Charles W. Davidson College of Engineering Students: 1,515 full-time (526 women), 898 part-time (304 women); includes 475 minority (20 Black or African American, non-Hispanic/Latino; 2 American Indian or Alaska Native, non-Hispanic/Latino; 286 Asian, non-Hispanic/Latino; 76 Hispanic/Latino; 3 Native Hawaiian or other Pacific Islander, non-Hispanic/Latino; 88 Two or more races, non-Hispanic/Latino), 1,776 international. Average age 26. 3,021 applicants, 45% accepted, 719 enrolled. *Faculty:* 54 full-time (12 women), 59 part-time/adjunct (9 women). Expenses: Contact institution. *Financial support:* Fellowships, research assistantships, career-related internships or fieldwork, Federal Work-Study, scholarships/grants, tuition waivers, and unspecified assistantships available. Support available to part-time students. Financial award application deadline: 4/28; financial award applicants required to submit FAFSA. In 2017, 1,264 master's awarded. *Program availability:* Part-time. Offers aerospace engineering (MS); biomedical engineering (MS); chemical engineering (MS); civil engineering (MS); computer engineering (MS); electrical engineering (MS); engineering (MS); engineering management (MS); human factors and ergonomics (MS); industrial and systems engineering (MS); materials engineering (MS); mechanical engineering (MS); software engineering (MS). *Application deadline:* For fall admission, 2/1 for domestic and international students. Applications are processed on a rolling basis. *Application fee:* $55. Electronic applications accepted. *Application Contact:* Marta Ramirez-Rodenas, International Engineering Graduate Student Advisor, 408-924-3810, E-mail: marta.ramirez-rodenas@sjsu.edu. *Dean of Engineering*, Dr. Sheryl Ehrman, 408-924-3800, Fax: 408-924-3818.

College of Health and Human Sciences Students: 517 full-time (407 women), 405 part-time (302 women); includes 523 minority (39 Black or African American, non-Hispanic/Latino; 2 American Indian or Alaska Native, non-Hispanic/Latino; 141 Asian, non-Hispanic/Latino; 226 Hispanic/Latino; 2 Native Hawaiian or other Pacific Islander, non-Hispanic/Latino; 113 Two or more races, non-Hispanic/Latino), 14 international. Average age 32. 1,250 applicants, 45% accepted, 375 enrolled. *Faculty:* 15 full-time (7 women), 6 part-time/adjunct (3 women). Expenses: Contact institution. *Financial support:* Fellowships, research assistantships, teaching assistantships, career-related internships or fieldwork, Federal Work-Study, scholarships/grants, and tuition waivers (full and partial) available. Support available to part-time students. Financial award application deadline: 4/24; financial award applicants required to submit FAFSA. In 2017, 808 master's awarded. *Program availability:* Part-time, 100% online, blended/hybrid learning. Offers criminology (MS); justice studies (MS); kinesiology (MA); library and information science (MLIS); mass communications (MS); nursing

(MS); nutritional science (MS); occupational therapy (MS); public health (MPH); social work (MSW). *Application deadline:* For fall admission, 2/1 for domestic and international students. Applications are processed on a rolling basis. *Application fee:* $55. Electronic applications accepted. *Dean, College of Health and Human Sciences,* Dr. Mary Schutten, 408-924-2900, Fax: 408-924-2901, E-mail: mary.schutten@sjsu.edu.

College of Humanities and the Arts Students: 129 full-time (79 women), 106 part-time (71 women); includes 117 minority (5 Black or African American, non-Hispanic/Latino; 29 Asian, non-Hispanic/Latino; 44 Hispanic/Latino; 39 Two or more races, non-Hispanic/Latino), 28 international. Average age 35. 204 applicants, 65% accepted, 79 enrolled. *Faculty:* 35 full-time (17 women), 19 part-time/adjunct (11 women). Expenses: Contact institution. *Financial support:* Fellowships, research assistantships, Federal Work-Study, scholarships/grants, traineeships, tuition waivers (full and partial), and unspecified assistantships available. Support available to part-time students. Financial award application deadline: 4/28; financial award applicants required to submit FAFSA. In 2017, 85 master's awarded. *Program availability:* Part-time. Offers art (MA, MFA); English (MA, MFA); linguistics (MA); music (MM); music education (MA); philosophy (MA); Spanish (MA); teaching English to speakers of other languages (MA). *Application deadline:* For fall admission, 2/1 for domestic and international students. Applications are processed on a rolling basis. *Application fee:* $55. Electronic applications accepted. *Dean,* Dr. Shannon Miller, 408-924-4300, Fax: 408-924-4365, E-mail: shannon.miller@sjsu.edu.

College of Science Students: 154 full-time (76 women), 212 part-time (102 women); includes 135 minority (4 Black or African American, non-Hispanic/Latino; 78 Asian, non-Hispanic/Latino; 27 Hispanic/Latino; 1 Native Hawaiian or other Pacific Islander, non-Hispanic/Latino; 25 Two or more races, non-Hispanic/Latino), 135 international. Average age 28. 1,156 applicants, 26% accepted, 179 enrolled. *Faculty:* 78 full-time (27 women), 25 part-time/adjunct (13 women). Expenses: Contact institution. *Financial support:* Fellowships, research assistantships, career-related internships or fieldwork, Federal Work-Study, scholarships/grants, traineeships, tuition waivers (full and partial), and unspecified assistantships available. Support available to part-time students. Financial award application deadline: 4/28; financial award applicants required to submit FAFSA. In 2017, 196 master's awarded. *Program availability:* Part-time. Offers bioinformatics (MS); biological sciences (MA, MS); biotechnology (MBT); chemistry (MA, MS); computer science (MS); geology (MS); marine science (MS); mathematics (MA, MS); medical products development management (MS); meteorology (MS); physics (MS); statistics (MS). MS in marine science offered through Moss Landing Marine Labs. *Application deadline:* For fall admission, 2/1 for domestic and international students. Applications are processed on a rolling basis. *Application fee:* $55. Electronic applications accepted. *Dean,* Dr. Michael Kaufman, 408-924-4800, Fax: 408-924-4815, E-mail: michael.kaufman@sjsu.edu.

College of Social Sciences Students: 181 full-time (126 women), 221 part-time (127 women); includes 228 minority (15 Black or African American, non-Hispanic/Latino; 48 Asian, non-Hispanic/Latino; 112 Hispanic/Latino; 3 Native Hawaiian or other Pacific Islander, non-Hispanic/Latino; 50 Two or more races, non-Hispanic/Latino), 38 international. Average age 30. 532 applicants, 44% accepted, 156 enrolled. *Faculty:* 59 full-time (29 women), 18 part-time/adjunct (5 women). Expenses: Contact institution. *Financial support:* Fellowships, research assistantships, career-related internships or fieldwork, Federal Work-Study, scholarships/grants, tuition waivers (full and partial), and unspecified assistantships available. Support available to part-time students. Financial award application deadline: 4/28; financial award applicants required to submit FAFSA. In 2017, 139 master's awarded. Offers applied anthropology (MA); communication studies (MA); economics (MA); environmental studies (MS); geography (MA); history (MA); Mexican American studies (MA); psychology (MA, MS); public administration (MPA); social sciences (MS); sociology (MA). *Application deadline:* For fall admission, 2/1 for domestic and international students. Applications are processed on a rolling basis. *Application fee:* $55. Electronic applications accepted. *Dean,* Dr. Walt Jacobs, 408-924-5300, Fax: 408-924-5303, E-mail: walter.jacobs@sjsu.edu.

Connie L. Lurie College of Education Students: 414 full-time (339 women), 115 part-time (93 women); includes 341 minority (14 Black or African American, non-Hispanic/Latino; 87 Asian, non-Hispanic/Latino; 176 Hispanic/Latino; 64 Two or more races, non-Hispanic/Latino), 9 international. Average age 30. 654 applicants, 34% accepted, 161 enrolled. *Faculty:* 29 full-time (22 women), 47 part-time/adjunct (40 women). Expenses: Contact institution. *Financial support:* In 2017–18, 4 research assistantships with partial tuition reimbursements (averaging $2,500 per year) were awarded; fellowships, career-related internships or fieldwork, Federal Work-Study, scholarships/grants, traineeships, and tuition waivers (full and partial) also available. Support available to part-time students. Financial award application deadline: 4/28; financial award applicants required to submit FAFSA. In 2017, 286 master's, 7 doctorates awarded. *Program availability:* Part-time, evening/weekend. Offers child and adolescent development (MA); education (MA); educational leadership (MA, Ed D); elementary education (MA). *Application deadline:* For fall admission, 2/1 for domestic and international students. Applications are processed on a rolling basis. *Application fee:* $55. Electronic applications accepted. *Interim Dean,* Dr. Paul Cascella, 408-924-3600, Fax: 408-924-3713, E-mail: paul.cascella@sjsu.edu.

Lucas Graduate School of Business Students: 85 full-time (49 women), 51 part-time (28 women); includes 77 minority (2 Black or African American, non-Hispanic/Latino; 44 Asian, non-Hispanic/Latino; 16 Hispanic/Latino; 1 Native Hawaiian or other Pacific Islander, non-Hispanic/Latino; 14 Two or more races, non-Hispanic/Latino), 42 international. Average age 28. 328 applicants, 43% accepted, 88 enrolled. *Faculty:* 15 full-time (7 women), 6 part-time/adjunct (3 women). Expenses: Contact institution. *Financial support:* Fellowships, research assistantships, career-related internships or fieldwork, Federal Work-Study, institutionally sponsored loans, scholarships/grants, and unspecified assistantships available. Support available to part-time students. Financial award application deadline: 4/28; financial award applicants required to submit FAFSA. In 2017, 155 master's awarded. *Program availability:* Part-time, evening/weekend, online learning. Offers accountancy (MS); business administration (MBA); taxation (MS); transportation management (MS). *Application deadline:* For fall admission, 2/1 for domestic and international students. Applications are processed on a rolling basis. *Application fee:* $55. Electronic applications accepted. *Dean,* Dr. Dan Moshavi, 408-924-3400, Fax: 408-924-3426, E-mail: dan.moshavi@sjsu.edu.

SAN JUAN BAUTISTA SCHOOL OF MEDICINE, Caguas, PR 00726-4968

General Information Independent, coed, graduate-only institution. *Graduate housing:* On-campus housing not available. *Research affiliation:* Universidad Central del Caribe (molecular biology), Fundación de Investigacion de Puerto Rico (clinical and translational research), University of Puerto Rico, Medical Sciences Campus (molecular biology, microbiology, neurosciences, pediatrics, public health), Ponce School of Medicine and Health Sciences (virology, immunology), Veteran Affairs (clinical research).

GRADUATE UNITS

Graduate and Professional Programs

THE SANS TECHNOLOGY INSTITUTE, Bethesda, MD 20814

General Information Proprietary, coed, graduate-only institution.

GRADUATE UNITS

Programs in Information Security Offers information security engineering (MS); information security management (MS).

THE SANTA BARBARA AND VENTURA COLLEGES OF LAW–SANTA BARBARA, Santa Barbara, CA 93101

General Information Independent, coed, graduate-only institution.

GRADUATE UNITS

Graduate and Professional Programs Offers law (MLS, JD).

THE SANTA BARBARA AND VENTURA COLLEGES OF LAW–VENTURA, Ventura, CA 93003

General Information Independent, coed, graduate-only institution.

GRADUATE UNITS

Graduate and Professional Programs Offers law (MLS, JD).

SANTA CLARA UNIVERSITY, Santa Clara, CA 95053

General Information Independent-religious, coed, university. *Enrollment:* 8,629 graduate, professional, and undergraduate students; 1,958 full-time matriculated graduate/professional students (1,029 women), 1,108 part-time matriculated graduate/professional students (582 women). *Enrollment by degree level:* 2,183 master's, 753 doctoral, 130 other advanced degrees. *Graduate faculty:* 269 full-time (102 women), 191 part-time/adjunct (81 women). Tuition and fees vary according to course load, degree level and program. *Graduate housing:* Rooms and/or apartments available on a first-come, first-served basis to single and married students. Housing application deadline: 3/28. *Student services:* Campus employment opportunities, campus safety program, career counseling, exercise/wellness program, free psychological counseling, international student services, low-cost health insurance, multicultural affairs office, services for students with disabilities. *Library facilities:* University Library plus 1 other. *Collection:* Books: 606,483 (physical), 658,072 (digital/electronic); Serial titles: 14,096 (physical), 84,245 (digital/electronic); Databases: 356. Weekly public service hours: 121; students can reserve study rooms.

Computer facilities: Computer purchase and lease plans are available. A campuswide network can be accessed from student residence rooms and from off campus. Online class registration is available.
Website: http://www.scu.edu/

GRADUATE UNITS

College of Arts and Sciences Students: 7 full-time (6 women), 67 part-time (44 women); includes 44 minority (3 Black or African American, non-Hispanic/Latino; 1 American Indian or Alaska Native, non-Hispanic/Latino; 8 Asian, non-Hispanic/Latino; 28 Hispanic/Latino; 1 Native Hawaiian or other Pacific Islander, non-Hispanic/Latino; 3 Two or more races, non-Hispanic/Latino). Average age 48. 31 applicants, 97% accepted, 25 enrolled. *Faculty:* 2 full-time (0 women), 5 part-time/adjunct (2 women). Expenses: Contact institution. *Financial support:* In 2017–18, 93 students received support. Fellowships, research assistantships, teaching assistantships, Federal Work-Study, scholarships/grants, tuition waivers, and unspecified assistantships available. Financial award applicants required to submit FAFSA. In 2017, 11 master's awarded. *Program availability:* Part-time. Offers pastoral ministries (MA). *Application deadline:* For fall admission, 7/1 for domestic students; for winter admission, 10/1 for domestic students; for spring admission, 2/14 for domestic students. Applications are processed on a rolling basis. *Application fee:* $50. Electronic applications accepted. *Application Contact:* Lynne Lukenbill, Senior Administrative Assistant, 408-554-4831, E-mail: llukenbill@scu.edu. *Director, Graduate Program in Pastoral Ministries,* Joseph Morris, 408-554-2357, E-mail: jamorris@scu.edu.

Jesuit School of Theology Students: 120 full-time (26 women), 15 part-time (6 women); includes 78 minority (24 Black or African American, non-Hispanic/Latino; 2 American Indian or Alaska Native, non-Hispanic/Latino; 25 Asian, non-Hispanic/Latino; 20 Hispanic/Latino; 3 Native Hawaiian or other Pacific Islander, non-Hispanic/Latino; 4 Two or more races, non-Hispanic/Latino). Average age 38. 99 applicants, 96% accepted, 54 enrolled. *Faculty:* 19 full-time (5 women), 9 part-time/adjunct (5 women). Expenses: Contact institution. *Financial support:* Scholarships/grants and unspecified assistantships available. Support available to part-time students. Financial award application deadline: 3/1; financial award applicants required to submit FAFSA. In 2017, 52 master's, 9 doctorates awarded. *Program availability:* Part-time, evening/weekend, 100% online. Offers Biblical studies (MTS); Christian spirituality (MTS); church history (MTS); cultural and historical studies of Catholicism (MTS); ethics and social theory/religion and society (MTS); history of art and religion (MTS); liturgical studies (MTS); systematic and philosophical theology (MTS); theology (M Div, Th M, STD, STB, STL). MA programs offered jointly with Graduate Theological Union. *Application deadline:* For fall admission, 3/1 priority date for domestic students; for spring admission, 10/1 priority date for domestic students. Applications are processed on a rolling basis. *Application fee:* $50 ($0 for international students). Electronic applications accepted. *Application Contact:* Drew Roborts, Assistant Dean of Enrollment Management and Marketing, 510-549-5016, E-mail: ajroberts@scu.edu. *Dean,* Rev. Kevin O'Brien, 510-549-5040, E-mail: kfobrien@scu.edu.

Leavey School of Business Students: 413 full-time (226 women), 308 part-time (131 women); includes 246 minority (10 Black or African American, non-Hispanic/Latino; 175 Asian, non-Hispanic/Latino; 40 Hispanic/Latino; 2 Native Hawaiian or other Pacific Islander, non-Hispanic/Latino; 19 Two or more races, non-Hispanic/Latino), 256 international. Average age 31. 761 applicants, 63% accepted, 271 enrolled. *Faculty:* 100 full-time (30 women), 42 part-time/adjunct (16 women). Expenses: Contact institution. *Financial support:* In 2017–18, 192 students received support. Career-related internships or fieldwork, scholarships/grants, and unspecified assistantships available. Financial award applicants required to submit FAFSA. In 2017, 267 master's awarded. *Program availability:* Part-time, evening/weekend, online curriculum with 2 on-campus intensives. Offers business administration (MBA); business analytics (MS); finance (MS); information systems (MS); supply chain management and analytics (MS). *Application fee:* $100 ($150 for international students). Electronic applications accepted. *Application Contact:* Lenore Grant, Director, Graduate Business Recruitment and Admissions, 408-551-1633, E-mail: lgrant@scu.edu. *Dean,* Caryn Beck-Dudley, 408-554-4523, E-mail: cbeckdudley@scu.edu.

School of Education and Counseling Psychology Students: 253 full-time (195 women), 350 part-time (283 women); includes 296 minority (10 Black or African American, non-Hispanic/Latino; 1 American Indian or Alaska Native, non-Hispanic/Latino; 80 Asian, non-Hispanic/Latino; 179 Hispanic/Latino; 26 Two or more races, non-Hispanic/Latino), 41 international. Average age 31. 211 applicants, 75% accepted, 142 enrolled. *Faculty:* 31 full-time (21 women), 37 part-time/adjunct (25 women). Expenses: Contact institution. *Financial support:* In 2017–18, 355 students received support. Fellowships, research assistantships, teaching assistantships, Federal Work-Study, scholarships/grants, and health care benefits available. Support available to part-time students. Financial award applicants required to submit FAFSA. In 2017, 266 master's awarded. *Program availability:* Part-time. Offers alternative and correctional education (Certificate); Catholic school teaching (MAT); counseling (MA); counseling psychology (MA); educational leadership (MA); interdisciplinary education (MA); teaching multiple subjects (MAT); teaching single subjects (MAT). *Application deadline:* For fall admission, 4/16 for international students; for summer admission, 3/12 for domestic students. Applications are processed on a rolling basis. *Application fee:* $50. Electronic applications accepted. *Application Contact:* Victoria Rodriguez, Graduate Admissions Advisor, 408-554-4723, E-mail: v1rodriguez@scu.edu. *Dean*, Dr. Sabrina Zirkel, 408-551-3074, Fax: 408-554-4367, E-mail: szirkel@scu.edu.

School of Engineering Students: 495 full-time (204 women), 311 part-time (95 women); includes 198 minority (8 Black or African American, non-Hispanic/Latino; 143 Asian, non-Hispanic/Latino; 29 Hispanic/Latino; 18 Two or more races, non-Hispanic/Latino), 457 international. Average age 28. 1,290 applicants, 47% accepted, 271 enrolled. *Faculty:* 69 full-time (23 women), 57 part-time/adjunct (10 women). Expenses: Contact institution. *Financial support:* In 2017–18, 67 students received support. Fellowships, research assistantships, teaching assistantships, Federal Work-Study, health care benefits, tuition waivers, and unspecified assistantships available. Support available to part-time students. Financial award applicants required to submit FAFSA. In 2017, 315 master's, 8 doctorates awarded. *Program availability:* Part-time. Offers applied mathematics (MS); bioengineering (MS); civil engineering (MS); computer science and engineering (MS, PhD, Engineer); electrical engineering (MS, PhD, Engineer); engineering management and leadership (MS); mechanical engineering (MS, PhD, Engineer); power systems and sustainable energy (MS); software engineering (MS). *Application deadline:* For fall admission, 4/6 for domestic and international students; for winter admission, 9/8 for domestic students, 9/1 for international students; for spring admission, 2/16 for domestic students, 12/8 for international students. *Application fee:* $60. Electronic applications accepted. *Application Contact:* Stacey Tinker, Director of Admissions and Marketing, 408-554-4313, Fax: 408-554-4323, E-mail: stinker@scu.edu. *Dean*, Dr. Alfonso Ortega, 408-554-3512, E-mail: alortega@scu.edu.

School of Law Students: 670 full-time (372 women), 57 part-time (23 women); includes 344 minority (30 Black or African American, non-Hispanic/Latino; 138 Asian, non-Hispanic/Latino; 134 Hispanic/Latino; 1 Native Hawaiian or other Pacific Islander, non-Hispanic/Latino; 41 Two or more races, non-Hispanic/Latino), 63 international. Average age 27. 2,092 applicants, 62% accepted, 248 enrolled. *Faculty:* 48 full-time (24 women), 41 part-time/adjunct (23 women). Expenses: Contact institution. *Financial support:* In 2017–18, 407 students received support. Fellowships, research assistantships, teaching assistantships, Federal Work-Study, scholarships/grants, health care benefits, and tuition waivers available. Support available to part-time students. Financial award application deadline: 3/1; financial award applicants required to submit FAFSA. In 2017, 30 master's, 134 doctorates awarded. *Program availability:* Part-time. Offers high tech law (Certificate); intellectual property (LL M); international and comparative law (LL M); international law (Certificate); law (JD); public interest and social justice law (Certificate); United States law (LL M). JD/MBA, JD/MSIS offered jointly with Leavey School of Business. *Application deadline:* For fall admission, 3/1 for domestic students. *Application fee:* $0. Electronic applications accepted. *Application Contact:* Nanette Cannon, Director of Admissions, 408-551-1846, E-mail: ncannon@scu.edu. *Dean*, Lisa Kloppenberg, 408-554-4362, E-mail: lkloppenberg@scu.edu.

SARAH LAWRENCE COLLEGE, Bronxville, NY 10708-5999

General Information Independent, coed, comprehensive institution. CGS member. *Graduate housing:* On-campus housing not available. *Research affiliation:* Westchester Medical Center/New York Medical College, New York Hospital–Cornell Medical Center, Albert Einstein College of Medicine, New York University Medical Center, Columbia University Medical Center.

GRADUATE UNITS

Graduate Studies *Program availability:* Part-time. Offers art of teaching (MS Ed); child development (MA); creative non-fiction (MFA); dance (MFA); dance/movement therapy (MS); fiction (MFA); health advocacy (MA); human genetics (MS); poetry (MFA); theater (MFA); women's history (MA). Electronic applications accepted.

SAVANNAH COLLEGE OF ART AND DESIGN, Savannah, GA 31402-3146

General Information Independent, coed, comprehensive institution. CGS member. *Enrollment:* 13,842 graduate, professional, and undergraduate students; 1,826 full-time matriculated graduate/professional students (1,147 women), 692 part-time matriculated graduate/professional students (445 women). *Enrollment by degree level:* 2,518 master's. *Graduate faculty:* 544 full-time (214 women), 150 part-time/adjunct (81 women). *Tuition:* Full-time $36,765; part-time $817 per credit hour. One-time fee: $500. *Graduate housing:* Room and/or apartments available on a first-come, first-served basis to single students; on-campus housing not available to married students. Typical cost: $9591 per year ($14,550 including board). Room and board charges vary according to board plan and housing facility selected. Housing application deadline: 4/1. *Student services:* Campus employment opportunities, campus safety program, career counseling, exercise/wellness program, free psychological counseling, international student services, multicultural affairs office, services for students with disabilities, writing training. *Library facilities:* Jen Library plus 4 others. *Collection:* Books: 260,879 (physical), 199,797 (digital/electronic); Serial titles: 949 (physical), 48,391 (digital/electronic); Databases: 89. Weekly public service hours: 105; students can reserve study rooms.

Computer facilities: Computer purchase and lease plans are available. 3,464 computers available on campus for general student use. A campuswide network can be accessed from student residence rooms and from off campus. Online class registration is available.
Website: http://www.scad.edu/

General Application Contact: Jenny Jaquillard, Executive Director of Admissions, Recruitment and Events, 912-525-5100, Fax: 912-525-5985, E-mail: admission@scad.edu.

GRADUATE UNITS

Program in Accessory Design Students: 15 full-time (14 women), 4 part-time (all women); includes 5 minority (2 Asian, non-Hispanic/Latino; 3 Hispanic/Latino), 9 international. Average age 27. 11 applicants, 36% accepted, 3 enrolled. *Faculty:* 5 full-time (4 women). Expenses: Contact institution. *Financial support:* Career-related internships or fieldwork, Federal Work-Study, and scholarships/grants available. Financial award application deadline: 4/1; financial award applicants required to submit FAFSA. In 2017, 5 master's awarded. *Program availability:* Part-time. Offers accessory design (MA, MFA). *Application deadline:* For fall admission, 4/1 for domestic and international students. Applications are processed on a rolling basis. *Application fee:* $40. Electronic applications accepted. *Application Contact:* Jenny Jaquillard, Executive Director of Admissions, Recruitment and Events, 912-525-5100, Fax: 912-525-5985, E-mail: admission@scad.edu. *Dean, School of Fashion*, Michael Fink.

Program in Advertising Students: 21 full-time (11 women), 9 part-time (4 women); includes 14 minority (9 Black or African American, non-Hispanic/Latino; 2 Asian, non-Hispanic/Latino; 3 Hispanic/Latino), 11 international. Average age 27. 59 applicants, 22% accepted, 9 enrolled. *Faculty:* 10 full-time (3 women), 5 part-time/adjunct (2 women). Expenses: Contact institution. *Financial support:* Career-related internships or fieldwork, Federal Work-Study, and scholarships/grants available. Financial award application deadline: 4/1; financial award applicants required to submit FAFSA. In 2017, 23 master's awarded. *Program availability:* Part-time. Offers advertising (MA, MFA). *Application deadline:* For fall admission, 4/1 for domestic and international students. Applications are processed on a rolling basis. *Application fee:* $40. Electronic applications accepted. *Application Contact:* Jenny Jaquillard, Executive Director of Admissions, Recruitment and Events, 912-525-5100, Fax: 912-525-5985, E-mail: admission@scad.edu. *Chair of Advertising Design*, Emily Sander.

Program in Animation Students: 207 full-time (111 women), 72 part-time (38 women); includes 49 minority (29 Black or African American, non-Hispanic/Latino; 8 Asian, non-Hispanic/Latino; 12 Hispanic/Latino), 123 international. Average age 26. 220 applicants, 53% accepted, 64 enrolled. *Faculty:* 32 full-time (6 women), 6 part-time/adjunct (3 women). Expenses: Contact institution. *Financial support:* Career-related internships or fieldwork, Federal Work-Study, and scholarships/grants available. Financial award application deadline: 4/1; financial award applicants required to submit FAFSA. In 2017, 51 master's awarded. *Program availability:* Part-time, 100% online. Offers animation (MA, MFA). *Application deadline:* For fall admission, 4/1 for domestic and international students. Applications are processed on a rolling basis. *Application fee:* $40. Electronic applications accepted. *Application Contact:* Jenny Jaquillard, Executive Director of Admissions, Recruitment and Events, 912-525-5100, Fax: 912-525-5985, E-mail: admission@scad.edu. *Chair, Animation*, Greg Araya.

Program in Architectural History Students: 2 full-time (both women), 1 (woman) part-time. Average age 25. 7 applicants, 43% accepted, 2 enrolled. *Faculty:* 9 full-time (1 woman). Expenses: Contact institution. *Financial support:* Career-related internships or fieldwork, Federal Work-Study, and scholarships/grants available. Financial award application deadline: 4/1; financial award applicants required to submit FAFSA. In 2017, 1 master's awarded. *Program availability:* Part-time. Offers architectural history (MFA). *Application deadline:* For fall admission, 4/1 for domestic and international students. Applications are processed on a rolling basis. *Application fee:* $40. Electronic applications accepted. *Application Contact:* Jenny Jaquillard, Executive Director of Admissions, Recruitment and Events, 912-525-5100, Fax: 912-525-5985, E-mail: admission@scad.edu. *Chair, Architectural History*, Dr. Robin Williams.

Program in Architecture Students: 72 full-time (32 women), 19 part-time (7 women); includes 15 minority (4 Black or African American, non-Hispanic/Latino; 1 Asian, non-Hispanic/Latino; 10 Hispanic/Latino), 44 international. Average age 26. 142 applicants, 58% accepted, 28 enrolled. *Faculty:* 19 full-time (7 women), 5 part-time/adjunct (0 women). Expenses: Contact institution. *Financial support:* Career-related internships or fieldwork, Federal Work-Study, and scholarships/grants available. Financial award application deadline: 4/1; financial award applicants required to submit FAFSA. In 2017, 46 master's awarded. *Program availability:* Part-time. Offers architecture (M Arch). *Application deadline:* For fall admission, 4/1 for domestic and international students. Applications are processed on a rolling basis. *Application fee:* $40. Electronic applications accepted. *Application Contact:* Jenny Jaquillard, Executive Director of Admissions, Recruitment and Events, 912-525-5100, Fax: 912-525-5985, E-mail: admission@scad.edu. *Dean, School of Building Arts*, Ivan Chow.

Program in Art History Students: 6 full-time (5 women), 4 part-time (3 women); includes 2 minority (1 Black or African American, non-Hispanic/Latino; 1 Hispanic/Latino). Average age 30. 21 applicants, 38% accepted, 4 enrolled. *Faculty:* 34 full-time (22 women), 6 part-time/adjunct (4 women). Expenses: Contact institution. *Financial support:* Career-related internships or fieldwork, Federal Work-Study, and scholarships/grants available. Financial award application deadline: 4/1; financial award applicants required to submit FAFSA. In 2017, 3 master's awarded. *Program availability:* Part-time. Offers art history (MA). *Application deadline:* For fall admission, 4/1 for domestic and international students. Applications are processed on a rolling basis. *Application fee:* $40. Electronic applications accepted. *Application Contact:* Jenny Jaquillard, Executive Director of Admissions, Recruitment and Events, 912-525-5100, Fax: 912-525-5985, E-mail: admission@scad.edu. *Chair, Art History*, Dr. Geoffrey Taylor.

Program in Business Design and Arts Leadership Students: 40 full-time (34 women), 53 part-time (46 women); includes 26 minority (21 Black or African American, non-Hispanic/Latino; 2 Asian, non-Hispanic/Latino; 3 Hispanic/Latino), 21 international. Average age 29. 124 applicants, 39% accepted, 27 enrolled. *Faculty:* 5 full-time (1 woman), 3 part-time/adjunct (1 woman). Expenses: Contact institution. *Financial support:* Career-related internships or fieldwork, Federal Work-Study, and scholarships/grants available. Financial award application deadline: 4/1; financial award applicants required to submit FAFSA. In 2017, 18 master's awarded. *Program availability:* Part-time, 100% online. Offers business design and arts leadership (MA). *Application deadline:* For fall admission, 4/1 for domestic and international students. Applications are processed on a rolling basis. *Application fee:* $40. Electronic applications accepted. *Application Contact:* Jenny Jaquillard, Executive Director of Admissions, Recruitment and Events, 912-525-5100, Fax: 912-525-5985, E-mail: admission@scad.edu. *Academic Program Coordinator*, Anita Akella.

Program in Cinema Studies Students: 6 full-time (3 women), 2 part-time (1 woman); includes 2 minority (both Hispanic/Latino). Average age 28. 11 applicants, 55% accepted, 3 enrolled. *Faculty:* 2 full-time (1 woman). Expenses: Contact institution. *Financial support:* Career-related internships or fieldwork, Federal Work-Study, and scholarships/grants available. Financial award application deadline: 4/1; financial award applicants required to submit FAFSA. In 2017, 3 master's awarded. *Program availability:* Part-time. Offers cinema studies (MA). *Application deadline:* For fall admission, 4/1 for domestic and international students. Applications are processed on a rolling basis. *Application fee:* $40. Electronic applications accepted. *Application Contact:* Jenny Jaquillard, Executive Director of Admissions, Recruitment and Events, 912-525-5100, Fax: 912-525-5985, E-mail: admission@scad.edu. *Chair, Art History*, Dr. Geoffrey Taylor.

Program in Design for Sustainability Students: 19 full-time (15 women); includes 2 minority (both Hispanic/Latino), 11 international. Average age 26. 30 applicants, 53% accepted, 8 enrolled. Expenses: Contact institution. *Financial support:* Career-related internships or fieldwork, Federal Work-Study, and scholarships/grants available. Financial award application deadline: 4/1; financial award applicants required to submit FAFSA. In 2017, 4 master's awarded. *Program availability:* Part-time. Offers built environment (MFA); management (MFA); packaging and print media (MFA); products (MFA). *Application deadline:* For fall admission, 4/1 for domestic and international students. Applications are processed on a rolling basis. *Application fee:* $40. Electronic applications accepted. *Application Contact:* Jenny Jaquillard, Executive Director of Admissions, Recruitment and Events, 912-525-5100, Fax: 912-525-5985, E-mail: admission@scad.edu. *Dean, School of Design*, Victor Ermoli.

Program in Design Management Students: 45 full-time (30 women), 64 part-time (45 women); includes 21 minority (7 Black or African American, non-Hispanic/Latino; 5 Asian, non-Hispanic/Latino; 9 Hispanic/Latino), 37 international. Average age 30. 108 applicants, 52% accepted, 24 enrolled. *Faculty:* 3 full-time (1 woman), 7 part-time/adjunct (4 women). Expenses: Contact institution. *Financial support:* Career-related internships or fieldwork, Federal Work-Study, and scholarships/grants available. Financial award application deadline: 4/1; financial award applicants required to submit FAFSA. In 2017, 55 master's awarded. *Program availability:* Part-time, 100% online. Offers design management (MA, MFA). *Application deadline:* For fall admission, 4/1 for domestic and international students. Applications are processed on a rolling basis. *Application fee:* $40. Electronic applications accepted. *Application Contact:* Jenny Jaquillard, Executive Director of Admissions, Recruitment and Events, 912-525-5100, Fax: 912-525-5985, E-mail: admission@scad.edu. *Chair, Design Management*, Bill Lee.

Program in Dramatic Writing Students: 18 full-time (11 women), 1 part-time (0 women); includes 7 minority (all Black or African American, non-Hispanic/Latino), 4 international. Average age 25. 28 applicants, 61% accepted, 10 enrolled. *Faculty:* 5 full-time (2 women), 1 (woman) part-time/adjunct. Expenses: Contact institution. *Financial support:* Career-related internships or fieldwork, Federal Work-Study, and scholarships/grants available. Financial award application deadline: 4/1; financial award applicants required to submit FAFSA. In 2017, 10 master's awarded. *Program availability:* Part-time. Offers dramatic writing (MFA). *Application deadline:* For fall admission, 4/1 for domestic and international students. Applications are processed on a rolling basis. *Application fee:* $40. Electronic applications accepted. *Application Contact:* Jenny Jaquillard, Executive Director of Admissions, Recruitment and Events, 912-525-5100, Fax: 912-525-5985, E-mail: admission@scad.edu. *Academic Program Coordinator*, Averie Storck.

Program in Fashion Students: 64 full-time (56 women), 25 part-time (22 women); includes 18 minority (15 Black or African American, non-Hispanic/Latino; 3 Asian, non-Hispanic/Latino), 60 international. Average age 28. 114 applicants, 41% accepted, 23 enrolled. *Faculty:* 23 full-time (13 women), 4 part-time/adjunct (all women). Expenses: Contact institution. *Financial support:* Career-related internships or fieldwork, Federal Work-Study, and scholarships/grants available. Financial award application deadline: 4/1; financial award applicants required to submit FAFSA. In 2017, 11 master's awarded. *Program availability:* Part-time, 100% online. Offers fashion (MA, MFA). *Application deadline:* For fall admission, 4/1 for domestic and international students. Applications are processed on a rolling basis. *Application fee:* $40. Electronic applications accepted. *Application Contact:* Jenny Jaquillard, Executive Director of Admissions, Recruitment and Events, 912-525-5100, Fax: 912-525-5985, E-mail: admission@scad.edu.

Program in Fibers Students: 18 full-time (17 women), 9 part-time (8 women); includes 3 minority (1 Black or African American, non-Hispanic/Latino; 1 Asian, non-Hispanic/Latino; 1 Hispanic/Latino), 12 international. Average age 26. 30 applicants, 47% accepted, 9 enrolled. *Faculty:* 8 full-time (7 women), 3 part-time/adjunct (all women). Expenses: Contact institution. *Financial support:* Career-related internships or fieldwork, Federal Work-Study, and scholarships/grants available. Financial award application deadline: 4/1; financial award applicants required to submit FAFSA. In 2017, 8 master's awarded. *Program availability:* Part-time. Offers fibers (MA, MFA). *Application deadline:* For fall admission, 4/1 for domestic and international students. Applications are processed on a rolling basis. *Application fee:* $40. Electronic applications accepted. *Application Contact:* Jenny Jaquillard, Executive Director of Admissions, Recruitment and Events, 912-525-5100, Fax: 912-525-5985, E-mail: admission@scad.edu. *Chair, Fibers*, Cayewah Easley.

Program in Film and Television Students: 170 full-time (76 women), 31 part-time (13 women); includes 70 minority (58 Black or African American, non-Hispanic/Latino; 2 American Indian or Alaska Native, non-Hispanic/Latino; 3 Asian, non-Hispanic/Latino; 7 Hispanic/Latino), 89 international. Average age 26. 266 applicants, 66% accepted, 85 enrolled. *Faculty:* 14 full-time (2 women), 5 part-time/adjunct (2 women). Expenses: Contact institution. *Financial support:* Career-related internships or fieldwork, Federal Work-Study, and scholarships/grants available. Financial award application deadline: 4/1; financial award applicants required to submit FAFSA. In 2017, 45 master's awarded. *Program availability:* Part-time. Offers film and television (MA, MFA). *Application deadline:* For fall admission, 4/1 for domestic and international students. Applications are processed on a rolling basis. *Application fee:* $40. Electronic applications accepted. *Application Contact:* Jenny Jaquillard, Executive Director of Admissions, Recruitment and Events, 912-525-5100, Fax: 912-525-5985, E-mail: admission@scad.edu. *Chair, Film and Television*, Donald Moffett.

Program in Furniture Design Students: 19 full-time (11 women), 4 part-time (2 women); includes 2 minority (1 Black or African American, non-Hispanic/Latino; 1 Hispanic/Latino), 14 international. Average age 27. 27 applicants, 67% accepted, 8 enrolled. *Faculty:* 5 full-time (1 woman). Expenses: Contact institution. *Financial support:* Career-related internships or fieldwork, Federal Work-Study, and scholarships/grants available. Financial award application deadline: 4/1; financial award applicants required to submit FAFSA. In 2017, 9 master's awarded. *Program availability:* Part-time. Offers furniture design (MA, MFA). *Application deadline:* For fall admission, 4/1 for domestic and international students. Applications are processed on a rolling basis. *Application fee:* $40. Electronic applications accepted. *Application Contact:* Jenny Jaquillard, Executive Director of Admissions, Recruitment and Events, 912-525-5100, Fax: 912-525-5985, E-mail: admission@scad.edu. *Academic Program Coordinator*, Fred Spector.

Program in Graphic Design and Visual Experience Students: 96 full-time (63 women), 47 part-time (28 women); includes 16 minority (6 Black or African American, non-Hispanic/Latino; 4 Asian, non-Hispanic/Latino; 6 Hispanic/Latino), 85 international. Average age 28. 333 applicants, 35% accepted, 49 enrolled. *Faculty:* 20 full-time (9 women), 8 part-time/adjunct (3 women). Expenses: Contact institution. *Financial support:* Career-related internships or fieldwork, Federal Work-Study, and scholarships/grants available. Financial award application deadline: 4/1; financial award applicants required to submit FAFSA. In 2017, 36 master's awarded. *Program availability:* Part-time, 100% online. Offers graphic design and visual experience (MA, MFA). *Application deadline:* For fall admission, 4/1 for domestic and international students. Applications are processed on a rolling basis. *Application fee:* $40. Electronic applications accepted. *Application Contact:* Jenny Jaquillard, Executive Director of Admissions, Recruitment and Events, 912-525-5100, Fax: 912-525-5985, E-mail: admission@scad.edu. *Chair, Graphic Design and Visual Experience*, Jason Fox.

Program in Illustration Students: 113 full-time (85 women), 48 part-time (31 women); includes 18 minority (6 Black or African American, non-Hispanic/Latino; 1 American Indian or Alaska Native, non-Hispanic/Latino; 6 Asian, non-Hispanic/Latino; 5 Hispanic/Latino), 82 international. Average age 28. 171 applicants, 45% accepted, 41 enrolled. *Faculty:* 17 full-time (3 women), 4 part-time/adjunct (2 women). Expenses: Contact institution. *Financial support:* Career-related internships or fieldwork, Federal Work-Study, and scholarships/grants available. Financial award application deadline: 4/1; financial award applicants required to submit FAFSA. In 2017, 43 master's awarded. *Program availability:* Part-time, 100% online. Offers illustration (MA, MFA). *Application deadline:* For fall admission, 4/1 for domestic and international students. Applications are processed on a rolling basis. *Application fee:* $40. Electronic applications accepted. *Application Contact:* Jenny Jaquillard, Executive Director of Admissions, Recruitment and Events, 912-525-5100, Fax: 912-525-5985, E-mail: admission@scad.edu. *Chair, Illustration and Sequential Art*, George Spears.

Program in Industrial Design Students: 118 full-time (52 women), 25 part-time (10 women); includes 8 minority (3 Black or African American, non-Hispanic/Latino; 3 Asian, non-Hispanic/Latino; 2 Hispanic/Latino), 123 international. Average age 26. 152 applicants, 74% accepted, 36 enrolled. *Faculty:* 14 full-time (1 woman), 3 part-time/adjunct (1 woman). Expenses: Contact institution. *Financial support:* Career-related internships or fieldwork, Federal Work-Study, and scholarships/grants available. Financial award application deadline: 4/1; financial award applicants required to submit FAFSA. In 2017, 36 master's awarded. *Program availability:* Part-time. Offers industrial design (MA, MFA). *Application deadline:* For fall admission, 4/1 for domestic and international students. Applications are processed on a rolling basis. *Application fee:* $40. Electronic applications accepted. *Application Contact:* Jenny Jaquillard, Executive Director of Admissions, Recruitment and Events, 912-525-5100, Fax: 912-525-5985, E-mail: admission@scad.edu. *Dean, School of Design*, Victor Ermoli.

Program in Interactive Design and Game Development Students: 74 full-time (28 women), 27 part-time (9 women); includes 11 minority (3 Black or African American, non-Hispanic/Latino; 6 Asian, non-Hispanic/Latino; 2 Hispanic/Latino), 58 international. Average age 27. 145 applicants, 41% accepted, 26 enrolled. *Faculty:* 16 full-time (4 women), 4 part-time/adjunct (1 woman). Expenses: Contact institution. *Financial support:* Career-related internships or fieldwork, Federal Work-Study, and scholarships/grants available. Financial award application deadline: 4/1; financial award applicants required to submit FAFSA. In 2017, 34 master's awarded. *Program availability:* Part-time, 100% online. Offers interactive design and game development (MA, MFA). *Application deadline:* For fall admission, 4/1 for domestic and international students. Applications are processed on a rolling basis. *Application fee:* $40. Electronic applications accepted. *Application Contact:* Jenny Jaquillard, Executive Director of Admissions, Recruitment and Events, 912-525-5100, Fax: 912-525-5985, E-mail: admission@scad.edu. *Chair, Interactive Design and Game Development*, SuAnne Fu.

Program in Interior Design Students: 96 full-time (74 women), 24 part-time (20 women); includes 6 minority (1 Black or African American, non-Hispanic/Latino; 2 Asian, non-Hispanic/Latino; 3 Hispanic/Latino), 97 international. Average age 26. 237 applicants, 39% accepted, 40 enrolled. *Faculty:* 16 full-time (8 women), 6 part-time/adjunct (4 women). Expenses: Contact institution. *Financial support:* Career-related internships or fieldwork, Federal Work-Study, and scholarships/grants available. Financial award application deadline: 4/1; financial award applicants required to submit FAFSA. In 2017, 33 master's awarded. *Program availability:* Part-time, 100% online. Offers interior design (MA, MFA). *Application deadline:* For fall admission, 4/1 for domestic and international students. Applications are processed on a rolling basis. *Application fee:* $40. Electronic applications accepted. *Application Contact:* Jenny Jaquillard, Executive Director of Admissions, Recruitment and Events, 912-525-5100, Fax: 912-525-5985, E-mail: admission@scad.edu. *Chair, Interior Design*, Khoi Vo.

Program in Jewelry Students: 25 full-time (24 women), 2 part-time (both women); includes 1 minority (Black or African American, non-Hispanic/Latino), 24 international. Average age 27. 26 applicants, 73% accepted, 6 enrolled. *Faculty:* 4 full-time (all women), 1 part-time/adjunct (0 women). Expenses: Contact institution. *Financial support:* Career-related internships or fieldwork, Federal Work-Study, and scholarships/grants available. Financial award application deadline: 4/1; financial award applicants required to submit FAFSA. In 2017, 3 master's awarded. *Program availability:* Part-time. Offers jewelry (MA, MFA). *Application deadline:* For fall admission, 4/1 for domestic and international students. Applications are processed on a rolling basis. *Application fee:* $40. Electronic applications accepted. *Application Contact:* Jenny Jaquillard, Executive Director of Admissions, Recruitment and Events, 912-525-5100, Fax: 912-525-5985, E-mail: admission@scad.edu. *Chair, Jewelry*, Jay Song.

Program in Luxury and Fashion Management Students: 125 full-time (110 women), 46 part-time (41 women); includes 47 minority (35 Black or African American, non-Hispanic/Latino; 5 Asian, non-Hispanic/Latino; 7 Hispanic/Latino), 88 international. Average age 26. 192 applicants, 40% accepted, 51 enrolled. *Faculty:* 12 full-time (5 women). Expenses: Contact institution. *Financial support:* Career-related internships or fieldwork, Federal Work-Study, and scholarships/grants available. Financial award application deadline: 4/1; financial award applicants required to submit FAFSA. In 2017, 46 master's awarded. *Program availability:* Part-time, 100% online. Offers luxury and fashion management (MA, MFA). *Application deadline:* For fall admission, 4/1 for domestic and international students. Applications are processed on a rolling basis. *Application fee:* $40. Electronic applications accepted. *Application Contact:* Jenny Jaquillard, Executive Director of Admissions, Recruitment and Events, 912-525-5100, Fax: 912-525-5985, E-mail: admission@scad.edu. *Academic Program Coordinator*, Alessandro Cannata.

Program in Motion Media Design Students: 49 full-time (29 women), 28 part-time (12 women); includes 12 minority (7 Black or African American, non-Hispanic/Latino; 1 Asian, non-Hispanic/Latino; 4 Hispanic/Latino), 38 international. Average age 30. 34 applicants, 53% accepted, 13 enrolled. *Faculty:* 16 full-time (3 women), 7 part-time/adjunct (5 women). Expenses: Contact institution. *Financial support:* Career-related internships or fieldwork, Federal Work-Study, and scholarships/grants available. Financial award application deadline: 4/1; financial award applicants required to submit FAFSA. In 2017, 23 master's awarded. *Program availability:* Part-time, 100% online. Offers motion media design (MA, MFA). *Application deadline:* For fall admission, 4/1 for domestic and international students. Applications are processed on a rolling basis. *Application fee:* $40. Electronic applications accepted. *Application Contact:* Jenny Jaquillard, Executive Director of Admissions, Recruitment and Events, 912-525-5100, Fax: 912-525-5985, E-mail: admission@scad.edu. *Chair, Motion Media Design*, Kelly Carlton.

Program in Painting Students: 61 full-time (42 women), 22 part-time (14 women); includes 12 minority (4 Black or African American, non-Hispanic/Latino; 1 American Indian or Alaska Native, non-Hispanic/Latino; 1 Asian, non-Hispanic/Latino; 6

Hispanic/Latino), 21 international. Average age 34. 93 applicants, 48% accepted, 19 enrolled. *Faculty:* 9 full-time (2 women), 1 (woman) part-time/adjunct. Expenses: Contact institution. *Financial support:* Career-related internships or fieldwork, Federal Work-Study, and scholarships/grants available. Financial award application deadline: 4/1; financial award applicants required to submit FAFSA. In 2017, 18 master's awarded. *Program availability:* Part-time, 100% online. Offers painting (MA, MFA). *Application deadline:* For fall admission, 4/1 for domestic and international students. Applications are processed on a rolling basis. *Application fee:* $40. Electronic applications accepted. *Application Contact:* Jenny Jaquillard, Executive Director of Admissions, Recruitment and Events, 912-525-5100, Fax: 912-525-5985, E-mail: admission@scad.edu. *Academic Program Coordinator,* Thomas Francis.

Program in Performing Arts Students: 45 full-time (30 women), 5 part-time (3 women); includes 25 minority (18 Black or African American, non-Hispanic/Latino; 1 American Indian or Alaska Native, non-Hispanic/Latino; 1 Asian, non-Hispanic/Latino; 5 Hispanic/Latino), 1 international. Average age 27. 97 applicants, 47% accepted, 21 enrolled. *Faculty:* 10 full-time (4 women), 7 part-time/adjunct (5 women). Expenses: Contact institution. *Financial support:* Career-related internships or fieldwork, Federal Work-Study, and scholarships/grants available. Financial award application deadline: 4/1; financial award applicants required to submit FAFSA. In 2017, 14 master's awarded. *Program availability:* Part-time. Offers performing arts (MFA). *Application deadline:* For fall admission, 4/1 for domestic and international students. Applications are processed on a rolling basis. *Application fee:* $40. Electronic applications accepted. *Application Contact:* Jenny Jaquillard, Executive Director of Admissions, Recruitment and Events, 912-525-5100, Fax: 912-525-5985, E-mail: admission@scad.edu. *Chair, Performing Arts,* Mark Tymchyshyn.

Program in Photography Students: 59 full-time (28 women), 26 part-time (16 women); includes 19 minority (8 Black or African American, non-Hispanic/Latino; 1 American Indian or Alaska Native, non-Hispanic/Latino; 3 Asian, non-Hispanic/Latino; 6 Hispanic/Latino; 1 Native Hawaiian or other Pacific Islander, non-Hispanic/Latino), 26 international. Average age 33. 116 applicants, 28% accepted, 15 enrolled. *Faculty:* 21 full-time (8 women), 6 part-time/adjunct (1 woman). Expenses: Contact institution. *Financial support:* Career-related internships or fieldwork, Federal Work-Study, and scholarships/grants available. Financial award application deadline: 4/1; financial award applicants required to submit FAFSA. In 2017, 29 master's awarded. *Program availability:* Part-time, 100% online. Offers photography (MA, MFA). *Application deadline:* For fall admission, 4/1 for domestic and international students. Applications are processed on a rolling basis. *Application fee:* $40. Electronic applications accepted. *Application Contact:* Jenny Jaquillard, Executive Director of Admissions, Recruitment and Events, 912-525-5100, Fax: 912-525-5985, E-mail: admission@scad.edu. *Chair, Photography,* Rick English.

Program in Preservation Design Students: 19 full-time (13 women), 26 part-time (24 women); includes 1 minority (Hispanic/Latino). Average age 33. 52 applicants, 37% accepted, 9 enrolled. *Faculty:* 4 full-time (1 woman). Expenses: Contact institution. *Financial support:* Career-related internships or fieldwork, Federal Work-Study, and scholarships/grants available. Financial award application deadline: 4/1; financial award applicants required to submit FAFSA. In 2017, 13 master's awarded. *Program availability:* Part-time, 100% online. Offers preservation design (MA, MFA). *Application deadline:* For fall admission, 4/1 for domestic and international students. Applications are processed on a rolling basis. *Application fee:* $40. Electronic applications accepted. *Application Contact:* Jenny Jaquillard, Executive Director of Admissions, Recruitment and Events, 912-525-5100, Fax: 912-525-5985, E-mail: admission@scad.edu. *Dean, School of Building Arts,* Ivan Chow.

Program in Printmaking Students: 1 (woman) full-time, 1 (woman) part-time. Average age 28. 11 applicants, 27% accepted, 1 enrolled. *Faculty:* 3 full-time (2 women). Expenses: Contact institution. *Financial support:* Career-related internships or fieldwork, Federal Work-Study, and scholarships/grants available. Financial award application deadline: 4/1; financial award applicants required to submit FAFSA. In 2017, 1 master's awarded. *Program availability:* Part-time. Offers printmaking (MFA). *Application deadline:* For fall admission, 4/1 for domestic and international students. Applications are processed on a rolling basis. *Application fee:* $40. Electronic applications accepted. *Application Contact:* Jenny Jaquillard, Executive Director of Admissions, Recruitment and Events, 912-525-5100, Fax: 912-525-5985, E-mail: admission@scad.edu. *Chair, Printmaking,* Robert Brown.

Program in Production Design Students: 23 full-time (20 women); includes 3 minority (1 Black or African American, non-Hispanic/Latino; 2 Hispanic/Latino), 9 international. Average age 28. 34 applicants, 44% accepted, 8 enrolled. *Faculty:* 5 full-time (3 women). Expenses: Contact institution. *Financial support:* Career-related internships or fieldwork, Federal Work-Study, and scholarships/grants available. Financial award application deadline: 4/1; financial award applicants required to submit FAFSA. In 2017, 3 master's awarded. *Program availability:* Part-time. Offers production design (MA, MFA). *Application deadline:* For fall admission, 4/1 for domestic and international students. Applications are processed on a rolling basis. *Application fee:* $40. Electronic applications accepted. *Application Contact:* Jenny Jaquillard, Executive Director of Admissions, Recruitment and Events, 912-525-5100, Fax: 912-525-5985, E-mail: admission@scad.edu. *Chair, Production Design and Themed Entertainment,* Gregory Beck.

Program in Sculpture Students: 7 full-time (4 women), 2 part-time (1 woman), 6 international. Average age 34. 17 applicants, 65% accepted, 2 enrolled. *Faculty:* 2 full-time (1 woman), 1 part-time/adjunct (0 women). Expenses: Contact institution. *Financial support:* Career-related internships or fieldwork, Federal Work-Study, and scholarships/grants available. Financial award application deadline: 4/1; financial award applicants required to submit FAFSA. In 2017, 3 master's awarded. *Program availability:* Part-time. Offers sculpture (MA, MFA). *Application deadline:* For fall admission, 4/1 for domestic and international students. Applications are processed on a rolling basis. *Application fee:* $40. Electronic applications accepted. *Application Contact:* Jenny Jaquillard, Executive Director of Admissions, Recruitment and Events, 912-525-5100, Fax: 912-525-5985, E-mail: admission@scad.edu. *Chair, Sculpture,* Susan Krause.

Program in Sequential Art Students: 42 full-time (32 women), 4 part-time (3 women); includes 11 minority (3 Black or African American, non-Hispanic/Latino; 2 Asian, non-Hispanic/Latino; 6 Hispanic/Latino), 16 international. Average age 27. 40 applicants, 50% accepted, 12 enrolled. *Faculty:* 11 full-time (0 women), 6 part-time/adjunct (3 women). Expenses: Contact institution. *Financial support:* Career-related internships or fieldwork, Federal Work-Study, and scholarships/grants available. Financial award application deadline: 4/1; financial award applicants required to submit FAFSA. In 2017, 11 master's awarded. *Program availability:* Part-time. Offers sequential art (MA, MFA). *Application deadline:* For fall admission, 4/1 for domestic and international students. Applications are processed on a rolling basis. *Application fee:* $40. Electronic applications accepted. *Application Contact:* Jenny Jaquillard, Executive Director of Admissions, Recruitment and Events, 912-525-5100, Fax: 912-525-5985, E-mail: admission@scad.edu. *Chair, Illustration and Sequential Art,* George Spears.

Program in Service Design Students: 12 full-time (6 women), 6 part-time (5 women); includes 2 minority (1 Black or African American, non-Hispanic/Latino; 1 Asian, non-Hispanic/Latino), 10 international. Average age 28. 50 applicants, 56% accepted, 3 enrolled. *Faculty:* 2 full-time (1 woman). Expenses: Contact institution. *Financial support:* Career-related internships or fieldwork, Federal Work-Study, and scholarships/grants available. Financial award application deadline: 4/1; financial award applicants required to submit FAFSA. In 2017, 2 master's awarded. *Program availability:* Part-time. Offers service design (MFA). *Application deadline:* For fall admission, 4/1 for domestic and international students. Applications are processed on a rolling basis. *Application fee:* $40. Electronic applications accepted. *Application Contact:* Jenny Jaquillard, Executive Director of Admissions, Recruitment and Events, 912-525-5100, Fax: 912-525-5985, E-mail: admission@scad.edu. *Academic Program Coordinator,* Xenia Viladas.

Program in Sound Design Students: 30 full-time (9 women), 2 part-time (1 woman); includes 9 minority (5 Black or African American, non-Hispanic/Latino; 2 Asian, non-Hispanic/Latino; 2 Hispanic/Latino), 12 international. Average age 24. 34 applicants, 62% accepted, 12 enrolled. *Faculty:* 7 full-time (0 women), 2 part-time/adjunct (0 women). Expenses: Contact institution. *Financial support:* Career-related internships or fieldwork, Federal Work-Study, and scholarships/grants available. Financial award application deadline: 4/1; financial award applicants required to submit FAFSA. In 2017, 15 master's awarded. *Program availability:* Part-time. Offers sound design (MA, MFA). *Application deadline:* For fall admission, 4/1 for domestic and international students. Applications are processed on a rolling basis. *Application fee:* $40. Electronic applications accepted. *Application Contact:* Jenny Jaquillard, Executive Director of Admissions, Recruitment and Events, 912-525-5100, Fax: 912-525-5985, E-mail: admission@scad.edu. *Chair, Sound Design,* Robin Beauchamp.

Program in Themed Entertainment Design Students: 28 full-time (18 women), 1 (woman) part-time; includes 2 minority (1 Asian, non-Hispanic/Latino; 1 Hispanic/Latino), 8 international. Average age 26. 44 applicants, 57% accepted, 14 enrolled. *Faculty:* 1 full-time (0 women). Expenses: Contact institution. *Financial support:* Career-related internships or fieldwork, Federal Work-Study, and scholarships/grants available. Financial award application deadline: 4/1; financial award applicants required to submit FAFSA. In 2017, 13 master's awarded. *Program availability:* Part-time. Offers themed entertainment design (MFA). *Application deadline:* For fall admission, 4/1 for domestic and international students. Applications are processed on a rolling basis. *Application fee:* $40. Electronic applications accepted. *Application Contact:* Jenny Jaquillard, Executive Director of Admissions, Recruitment and Events, 912-525-5100, Fax: 912-525-5985, E-mail: admission@scad.edu. *Chair, Production Design and Themed Entertainment,* Gregory Beck.

Program in Urban Design Students: 7 full-time (5 women), 4 part-time (3 women), 9 international. Average age 27. 42 applicants, 57% accepted, 5 enrolled. *Faculty:* 1 full-time (0 women). Expenses: Contact institution. *Financial support:* Career-related internships or fieldwork, Federal Work-Study, and scholarships/grants available. Financial award application deadline: 4/1; financial award applicants required to submit FAFSA. In 2017, 4 master's awarded. *Program availability:* Part-time. Offers urban design (MUD). *Application deadline:* For fall admission, 4/1 for domestic and international students. Applications are processed on a rolling basis. *Application fee:* $40. Electronic applications accepted. *Application Contact:* Jenny Jaquillard, Executive Director of Admissions, Recruitment and Events, 912-525-5100, Fax: 912-525-5985, E-mail: admission@scad.edu. *Dean, School of Building Arts,* Ivan Chow.

Program in Visual Effects Students: 37 full-time (15 women), 22 part-time (7 women); includes 8 minority (2 Asian, non-Hispanic/Latino; 6 Hispanic/Latino), 36 international. Average age 27. 31 applicants, 61% accepted, 13 enrolled. *Faculty:* 16 full-time (4 women). Expenses: Contact institution. *Financial support:* Career-related internships or fieldwork, Federal Work-Study, and scholarships/grants available. Financial award application deadline: 4/1; financial award applicants required to submit FAFSA. In 2017, 17 master's awarded. *Program availability:* Part-time. Offers visual effects (MA, MFA). *Application deadline:* For fall admission, 4/1 for domestic and international students. Applications are processed on a rolling basis. *Application fee:* $40. Electronic applications accepted. *Application Contact:* Jenny Jaquillard, Executive Director of Admissions, Recruitment and Events, 912-525-5100, Fax: 912-525-5985, E-mail: admission@scad.edu. *Dean, School of Digital Media,* Max Almy.

Program in Writing Students: 37 full-time (31 women), 22 part-time (17 women); includes 24 minority (19 Black or African American, non-Hispanic/Latino; 1 Asian, non-Hispanic/Latino; 4 Hispanic/Latino), 5 international. Average age 32. 47 applicants, 38% accepted, 10 enrolled. *Faculty:* 6 full-time (2 women), 1 (woman) part-time/adjunct. Expenses: Contact institution. *Financial support:* Career-related internships or fieldwork, Federal Work-Study, and scholarships/grants available. Financial award application deadline: 4/1; financial award applicants required to submit FAFSA. In 2017, 12 master's awarded. *Program availability:* Part-time, 100% online. Offers writing (MFA). *Application deadline:* For fall admission, 4/1 for domestic and international students. Applications are processed on a rolling basis. *Application fee:* $40. Electronic applications accepted. *Application Contact:* Jenny Jaquillard, Executive Director of Admissions, Recruitment and Events, 912-525-5100, Fax: 912-525-5985, E-mail: admission@scad.edu. *Dean, School of Liberal Arts,* Dr. Beth Concepcion.

SAVANNAH LAW SCHOOL, Savannah, GA 31401

General Information Proprietary, coed, graduate-only institution. *Enrollment by degree level:* 117 doctoral. *Graduate faculty:* 12 full-time (2 women), 7 part-time/adjunct (2 women). *Tuition:* Full-time $21,100; part-time $12,660 per semester. Tuition and fees vary according to program. *Graduate housing:* On-campus housing not available. *Student services:* Campus employment opportunities, career counseling, free psychological counseling, services for students with disabilities, writing training. *Library facilities:* Savannah Law School Law Library. *Collection:* Students can reserve study rooms.

Computer facilities: A campuswide network can be accessed. Online class registration is available.
Website: http://www.savannahlawschool.org/

General Application Contact: Jiovanna Bryant, Associate Director of Admissions, 525-912-3913, E-mail: admissions@savannahlawschool.org.

GRADUATE UNITS

JD Program Students: 76 full-time (49 women), 41 part-time (27 women). *Faculty:* 12 full-time (2 women), 7 part-time/adjunct (2 women). Expenses: Contact institution. *Financial support:* Fellowships and scholarships/grants available. Financial award application deadline: 6/1; financial award applicants required to submit FAFSA. *Program availability:* Part-time. Offers law (JD). Electronic applications accepted. *Application Contact:* Jiovanna Bryant, Associate Director of Admissions, 525-912-3913, E-mail: jbryant@savannahlawschool.org. *Dean,* Malcolm L. Morris, 678-916-2603, E-mail: mmorris@savannahlawschool.org.

SAVANNAH STATE UNIVERSITY, Savannah, GA 31404

General Information State-supported, coed, comprehensive institution. CGS member. *Graduate housing:* Room and/or apartments available on a first-come, first-served basis to single students; on-campus housing not available to married students. Housing application deadline: 5/1. *Research affiliation:* Office of Naval Research (ONR) (marine science), Living Marine Resources Cooperative Science Center (LMRCSC) (marine science), National Institute of Mental Health (NIMH) (social work), U.S. Department of Homeland Security (urban studies and planning), Skidaway Institute of Oceanography (marine science), University of Georgia Marine Education Center & Aquarium (marine science).

GRADUATE UNITS

Master of Business Administration Program *Program availability:* Part-time, evening/weekend. Offers business administration (MBA). Electronic applications accepted.

Master of Public Administration Program *Program availability:* Part-time. Offers city management (MPA); human resources (MPA). Electronic applications accepted.

Master of Science in Marine Sciences Program *Program availability:* Part-time. Offers applied marine science (MSMS); marine science research (MSMS); professional advancement (MSMS). Electronic applications accepted.

Master of Science in Urban Studies and Planning Program *Program availability:* Part-time. Offers urban studies and planning (MSUS). Electronic applications accepted.

Master of Social Work Program Offers social work (MSW).

SAYBROOK UNIVERSITY, San Francisco, CA 94612

General Information Independent, coed, graduate-only institution. *Research affiliation:* Rollo May Center for Humanistic Studies.

GRADUATE UNITS

LIOS MA Residential Programs Offers leadership and organization development (MA); psychology counseling (MA).

School of Clinical Psychology Offers clinical psychology (MA). Program offered jointly with Bastyr University.

School of Mind-Body Medicine Offers mind-body medicine (MS, PhD, Certificate). Electronic applications accepted.

School of Organizational Leadership and Transformation Offers organizational leadership and transformation (MA). Program offered jointly with Bastyr University.

School of Psychology and Interdisciplinary Inquiry *Program availability:* Online learning. Offers human science (MA, PhD); organizational systems (MA, PhD); psychology (MA, PhD). Electronic applications accepted.

SCHILLER INTERNATIONAL UNIVERSITY, 69115 Heidelberg, Germany

General Information Independent, coed, comprehensive institution. *Graduate housing:* Room and/or apartments available on a first-come, first-served basis to single students; on-campus housing not available to married students.

GRADUATE UNITS

MBA Programs, Heidelberg, Germany *Program availability:* Part-time, evening/weekend. Offers international business (MBA, MIM); management of information technology (MBA).

SCHILLER INTERNATIONAL UNIVERSITY, F-75015 Paris, France

General Information Independent, coed, comprehensive institution. *Graduate housing:* On-campus housing not available.

GRADUATE UNITS

MBA Program Paris, France *Program availability:* Part-time, evening/weekend, online learning. Offers international business (MBA). Bilingual French/English MBA available for native French speakers.

Program in International Relations and Diplomacy *Program availability:* Part-time, evening/weekend. Offers international relations and diplomacy (MA).

SCHILLER INTERNATIONAL UNIVERSITY, 28002 Madrid, Spain

General Information Independent, coed, comprehensive institution. *Graduate housing:* On-campus housing not available.

GRADUATE UNITS

MBA Program, Madrid, Spain *Program availability:* Part-time. Offers international business (MBA).

SCHILLER INTERNATIONAL UNIVERSITY, Largo, FL 33771

General Information Independent, coed, comprehensive institution. *Graduate housing:* Room and/or apartments available on a first-come, first-served basis to single students; on-campus housing not available to married students. Housing application deadline: 8/1.

GRADUATE UNITS

MBA Programs, Florida *Program availability:* Part-time, evening/weekend, online learning. Offers financial planning (MBA); information technology (MBA); international business (MBA); international hotel and tourism management (MBA).

SCHOOL OF ADVANCED AIR AND SPACE STUDIES, Maxwell AFB, AL 36112-6424

General Information Federally supported, coed, primarily men, graduate-only institution.

GRADUATE UNITS

Program in Airpower Art and Science Offers airpower art and science (MA). Available to active duty military officers only.

SCHOOL OF ARCHITECTURE AT TALIESIN, Scottsdale, AZ 85261-4430

General Information Independent, coed, graduate-only institution. *Graduate housing:* Rooms and/or apartments guaranteed to single students and available on a first-come, first-served basis to married students. Housing application deadline: 3/20.

GRADUATE UNITS

Graduate Program Offers architecture (M Arch). Summer session held in Spring Green, WI. Electronic applications accepted.

SCHOOL OF THE ART INSTITUTE OF CHICAGO, Chicago, IL 60603-3103

General Information Independent, coed, comprehensive institution. *Graduate housing:* Room and/or apartments available on a first-come, first-served basis to single students; on-campus housing not available to married students. Housing application deadline: 3/21.

GRADUATE UNITS

Graduate Division *Program availability:* Part-time. Offers architecture (M Arc); art and technology studies (MFA); art education and art teaching (MAAE, MAT); art therapy (MAAT); arts administration (MAAAP); ceramics (MFA); design for emerging technologies (MFA); designed objects (M Des); fashion, body, and garment (M Des, Certificate); fiber and material studies (MFA); film, video, and new media (MFA); historic preservation (MSHP); interior architecture (M Arc); modern art history, theory, and criticism (MA); new arts journalism (MA); painting and drawing (MFA); performance (MFA); photography (MFA); printmaking (MFA); sculpture (MFA); sound (MFA); visual and critical studies (MA); visual communication (MFA); writing (MFA, Certificate).

SCHOOL OF VISUAL ARTS, New York, NY 10010-3994

General Information Proprietary, coed, comprehensive institution. CGS member. *Graduate housing:* Room and/or apartments available on a first-come, first-served basis to single students; on-campus housing not available to married students.

GRADUATE UNITS

Graduate Programs Offers art education (MAT); art practice (MFA); art therapy (MPS); art writing (MFA); branding (MPS); computer art (MFA); critical theory and the arts (MA); curatorial practice (MA); design (MFA); design for social innovation (MFA); design research, writing and criticism (MA); digital photography (MPS); directing (MPS); fashion photography (MPS); fine arts (MFA); illustration as visual essay (MFA); interaction design (MFA); photography, video and related media (MFA); products of design (MFA); social documentary film (MFA); visual narrative (MFA). Electronic applications accepted.

SCHREINER UNIVERSITY, Kerrville, TX 78028-5697

General Information Independent-religious, coed, comprehensive institution. *Graduate housing:* Room and/or apartments available on a first-come, first-served basis to single students; on-campus housing not available to married students.

GRADUATE UNITS

Department of Education *Program availability:* Part-time, evening/weekend, online learning. Offers education (M Ed); principal (Certificate). Electronic applications accepted.

MBA Program *Program availability:* Part-time, online learning. Offers ethical leadership (MBA). Electronic applications accepted.

THE SCRIPPS RESEARCH INSTITUTE, La Jolla, CA 92037

General Information Independent, coed, graduate-only institution. *Graduate housing:* On-campus housing not available.

GRADUATE UNITS

Kellogg School of Science and Technology Offers chemical and biological sciences (PhD). Electronic applications accepted.

SEATTLE INSTITUTE OF ORIENTAL MEDICINE, Seattle, WA 98115

General Information Proprietary, coed, primarily women, graduate-only institution. *Graduate housing:* On-campus housing not available.

GRADUATE UNITS

Graduate Program Offers Oriental medicine (M Ac OM).

SEATTLE PACIFIC UNIVERSITY, Seattle, WA 98119-1997

General Information Independent-religious, coed, comprehensive institution. *Enrollment:* 3,813 graduate, professional, and undergraduate students; 327 full-time matriculated graduate/professional students (243 women), 524 part-time matriculated graduate/professional students (383 women). *Enrollment by degree level:* 672 master's, 179 doctoral. *Graduate housing:* Rooms and/or apartments available on a first-come, first-served basis to single and married students. Housing application deadline: 8/1. *Student services:* Campus employment opportunities, campus safety program, career counseling, exercise/wellness program, free psychological counseling, international student services, low-cost health insurance, multicultural affairs office, services for students with disabilities, teacher training, writing training. *Library facilities:* University Library. *Research affiliation:* Washington Research Center/Gates Foundation (education effectiveness), Fred Hutchinson Cancer Research Center (cancer and tumors), Battelle Research Center (business marketing).

Computer facilities: 150 computers available on campus for general student use. A campuswide network can be accessed from student residence rooms and from off campus. Online class registration is available.
Website: http://www.spu.edu/

General Application Contact: 206-281-2091, E-mail: gradadmissions@spu.edu.

GRADUATE UNITS

Doctoral Program in Education Students: 1 full-time (0 women), 33 part-time (23 women); includes 4 minority (3 Black or African American, non-Hispanic/Latino; 1 American Indian or Alaska Native, non-Hispanic/Latino), 2 international. Average age 44. 4 applicants, 75% accepted, 2 enrolled. Expenses: Contact institution. *Financial support:* Career-related internships or fieldwork available. Financial award applicants required to submit FAFSA. In 2017, 8 doctorates awarded. Offers education (Ed D, PhD). *Application deadline:* For fall admission, 8/15 for domestic students; for winter admission, 11/15 for domestic students; for spring admission, 2/15 for domestic students; for summer admission, 5/15 for domestic students. Applications are processed on a rolling basis. *Application fee:* $50. *Director of Doctoral Programs,* Nyaradzo Mvududu, 206-281-2551, E-mail: nyaradzo@spu.edu.

Educational Leadership Programs Students: 5 full-time (all women), 57 part-time (43 women); includes 6 minority (1 Black or African American, non-Hispanic/Latino; 3 Asian, non-Hispanic/Latino; 1 Hispanic/Latino; 1 Two or more races, non-Hispanic/Latino). Average age 42. 21 applicants, 57% accepted, 11 enrolled. Expenses: Contact institution. *Financial support:* Career-related internships or fieldwork available. Financial award applicants required to submit FAFSA. In 2017, 14 master's awarded. *Program availability:* Part-time, evening/weekend. Offers educational leadership (M Ed, Ed D); principal (Certificate); program administrator (Certificate); superintendent (Certificate). *Application deadline:* For fall admission, 8/15 priority date for domestic students; for winter admission, 11/15 for domestic students; for spring admission, 2/15 priority date for domestic students; for summer admission, 5/15 for domestic students. Applications are processed on a rolling basis. *Application fee:* $50. Electronic applications accepted. *Application Contact:* The Graduate Center, 206-281-2091. *Chair,* Dr. William Prenevost, 206-281-2370, Fax: 206-281-2756, E-mail: prenew@spu.edu.

Industrial-Organizational Psychology Program Students: 51 full-time (41 women), 33 part-time (23 women); includes 9 minority (2 Black or African American, non-Hispanic/Latino; 1 American Indian or Alaska Native, non-Hispanic/Latino; 5 Asian, non-Hispanic/Latino; 1 Two or more races, non-Hispanic/Latino), 2 international. Average age 28. 67 applicants, 72% accepted, 31 enrolled. Expenses: Contact institution. *Financial support:* Applicants required to submit FAFSA. In 2017, 33 master's, 8 doctorates awarded. Offers industrial-organizational psychology (MA, PhD). *Application deadline:* For fall admission, 12/15 for domestic and international students. *Application fee:* $50. Electronic applications accepted. *Application Contact:* The Graduate Center, 206-281-2091. *Chair,* Dr. Robert B. McKenna, 206-281-2629, E-mail: rmckenna@spu.edu.

MA in Teaching English to Speakers of Other Languages Program Students: 2 full-time (both women), 11 part-time (10 women); includes 1 minority (Hispanic/Latino), 3 international. Average age 38. 5 applicants. Expenses: Contact institution. *Financial support:* Career-related internships or fieldwork available. Financial award applicants required to submit FAFSA. In 2017, 6 master's awarded. *Program availability:* Part-time. Offers K-12 (MA). *Application deadline:* For fall admission, 8/1 priority date for domestic students; for winter admission, 12/1 for domestic students; for spring admission, 3/1 for domestic students; for summer admission, 5/1 for domestic students. Applications are processed on a rolling basis. *Application fee:* $50. Electronic applications accepted. *Application Contact:* 206-281-2091. *Program Director,* Dr. Kathryn Bartholomew, 206-281-3533, Fax: 206-281-2500, E-mail: kbarthol@spu.edu.

Master of Arts in Management Program Students: 4 full-time (all women), 12 part-time (8 women), 4 international. Average age 28. 15 applicants, 60% accepted, 7 enrolled. Expenses: Contact institution. In 2017, 18 master's awarded. Offers business intelligence and data analytics (MA); cybersecurity (MA); faith and business (MA); human resources (MA); social and sustainable management (MA). *Application deadline:* For fall admission, 8/1 for domestic students, 6/1 for international students; for winter admission, 11/1 for domestic students, 9/1 for international students; for spring admission, 2/1 for domestic students, 12/1 for international students; for summer admission, 5/1 for domestic students. *Application fee:* $50. *Application Contact:* E-mail: drj@spu.edu.

Master of Arts in Teaching Program Students: 51 full-time (45 women), 81 part-time (53 women); includes 21 minority (4 Black or African American, non-Hispanic/Latino; 1 American Indian or Alaska Native, non-Hispanic/Latino; 7 Asian, non-Hispanic/Latino; 5 Hispanic/Latino; 4 Two or more races, non-Hispanic/Latino). Average age 32. 47 applicants, 62% accepted, 23 enrolled. Expenses: Contact institution. *Financial support:* Scholarships/grants available. Financial award applicants required to submit FAFSA. In 2017, 70 master's awarded. *Program availability:* Part-time, evening/weekend. Offers teaching (MAT). *Application deadline:* For fall admission, 3/15 for domestic students. *Application fee:* $50. Electronic applications accepted. *Application Contact:* The Graduate Center, 206-281-2091.

Master of Arts in Theology Program Students: 25 full-time (13 women), 42 part-time (20 women); includes 11 minority (4 Black or African American, non-Hispanic/Latino; 4 Asian, non-Hispanic/Latino; 3 Two or more races, non-Hispanic/Latino), 2 international. Average age 34. 19 applicants, 79% accepted, 11 enrolled. Expenses: Contact institution. *Financial support:* Application deadline: 4/1; applicants required to submit FAFSA. In 2017, 4 master's awarded. Offers Asian American ministry (MA); business and applied theology (MA); Christian leadership (MA); Christian scripture (MA); Christian studies (Graduate Certificate); reconciliation and intercultural studies (MA); theology (MA). *Application deadline:* For fall admission, 7/31 for domestic students, 6/15 for international students; for winter admission, 11/15 for domestic students; for spring admission, 2/15 for domestic students; for summer admission, 5/1 for domestic students. Applications are processed on a rolling basis. *Application fee:* $50. Electronic applications accepted. *Dean,* Dr. Doug Strong, 206-281-2473, E-mail: dstrong@spu.edu.

Master of Business Administration Program Students: 3 full-time (1 woman), 25 part-time (16 women); includes 6 minority (1 Black or African American, non-Hispanic/Latino; 1 Asian, non-Hispanic/Latino; 3 Hispanic/Latino; 1 Two or more races, non-Hispanic/Latino), 4 international. Average age 34. 26 applicants, 38% accepted, 7 enrolled. Expenses: Contact institution. *Financial support:* Scholarships/grants available. Financial award applicants required to submit FAFSA. In 2017, 12 master's awarded. *Program availability:* Part-time. Offers business administration (MBA); social and sustainable enterprise (MBA). *Application deadline:* For fall admission, 8/1 for domestic and international students; for winter admission, 11/1 for domestic and international students; for spring admission, 2/1 for domestic and international students. Applications are processed on a rolling basis. *Application fee:* $50. Electronic applications accepted. *Application Contact:* 206-281-2091. *Associate Dean for Graduate Studies,* Gary Karns, 206-281-2948, Fax: 206-281-2733.

Master of Divinity Program Students: 2 full-time (1 woman), 3 part-time (0 women). Average age 32. 24 applicants, 75% accepted, 13 enrolled. Expenses: Contact institution. *Financial support:* Scholarships/grants available. Financial award applicants required to submit FAFSA. In 2017, 2 master's awarded. Offers divinity (M Div). *Application deadline:* For fall admission, 7/31 for domestic students; for winter admission, 11/15 for domestic students; for spring admission, 2/15 for domestic students; for summer admission, 5/1 for domestic students. *Application fee:* $50. *Dean,* Dr. Doug Strong, 206-281-2473, E-mail: dstrong@spu.edu.

Master of Education in Literacy Program Students: 17 part-time (all women); includes 2 minority (1 Asian, non-Hispanic/Latino; 1 Hispanic/Latino). Average age 28. 9 applicants, 100% accepted, 7 enrolled. Expenses: Contact institution. *Financial support:* Scholarships/grants available. Financial award applicants required to submit FAFSA. In 2017, 5 master's awarded. *Program availability:* Part-time. Offers literacy (M Ed). *Application deadline:* For fall admission, 8/15 for domestic students; for winter admission, 11/15 for domestic students; for spring admission, 2/15 for domestic students; for summer admission, 5/15 for domestic students. Applications are processed on a rolling basis. *Application fee:* $50. Electronic applications accepted. *Application Contact:* The Graduate Center, 206-281-2091. *Chair,* Dr. Scott F. Beers, 206-281-2707, E-mail: sbeers@spu.edu.

Master of Education in School Counseling Program Students: 42 full-time (30 women), 37 part-time (34 women); includes 20 minority (2 Black or African American, non-Hispanic/Latino; 1 American Indian or Alaska Native, non-Hispanic/Latino; 10 Asian, non-Hispanic/Latino; 5 Hispanic/Latino; 1 Native Hawaiian or other Pacific Islander, non-Hispanic/Latino; 1 Two or more races, non-Hispanic/Latino), 2 international. Average age 29. 56 applicants, 55% accepted, 19 enrolled. Expenses: Contact institution. *Financial support:* Scholarships/grants available. Financial award applicants required to submit FAFSA. In 2017, 16 master's awarded. *Program availability:* Part-time. Offers school counseling (M Ed, Certificate). *Application deadline:* For fall admission, 4/1 priority date for domestic students. *Application fee:* $50. Electronic applications accepted. *Application Contact:* 206-281-2091. *Chair,* Dr. June Hyun, 206-281-2671, Fax: 206-281-2756, E-mail: jhyun@spu.edu.

Master of Education in Teacher Leadership Program Students: 35 part-time (22 women); includes 3 minority (2 Asian, non-Hispanic/Latino; 1 Two or more races, non-Hispanic/Latino), 1 international. Average age 32. 22 applicants, 77% accepted, 13 enrolled. Expenses: Contact institution. *Financial support:* Applicants required to submit FAFSA. In 2017, 7 master's awarded. *Program availability:* Part-time, evening/weekend. Offers teacher leadership (M Ed). *Application deadline:* For fall admission, 8/15 priority date for domestic students, 7/1 for international students; for winter admission, 11/15 for domestic students; for spring admission, 2/15 for domestic students, 3/1 for international students; for summer admission, 5/15 for domestic students. Applications are processed on a rolling basis. *Application fee:* $50. Electronic applications accepted. *Application Contact:* The Graduate Center, 206-281-2091. *Chair,* Robin Henrikson, 360-461-4422, E-mail: henrir@spu.edu.

Master of Fine Arts in Creative Writing Program Students: 30 part-time (22 women), 1 international. Average age 34. Expenses: Contact institution. *Financial support:* Applicants required to submit FAFSA. In 2017, 12 master's awarded. *Program availability:* Part-time. Offers creative writing (MFA). *Application deadline:* For winter admission, 11/15 for domestic students; for summer admission, 5/15 for domestic students. *Application fee:* $50. Electronic applications accepted. *Application Contact:* The Graduate Center, 206-281-2091. *Director,* Dr. Scott Cairns, 206-281-2109, E-mail: gwolfe@spu.edu.

Master of Science in Information Systems Management Program Students: 1 (woman) full-time, 18 part-time (14 women); includes 2 minority (1 Black or African American, non-Hispanic/Latino; 1 Asian, non-Hispanic/Latino), 10 international. Average age 29. 12 applicants, 42% accepted, 2 enrolled. Expenses: Contact institution. *Financial support:* Applicants required to submit FAFSA. In 2017, 10 master's awarded. *Program availability:* Part-time. Offers information systems management (MS). *Application deadline:* For fall admission, 8/1 for domestic students, 6/1 for international students; for winter admission, 11/1 for domestic and international students; for spring admission, 2/1 for domestic students, 12/1 for international students; for summer admission, 5/1 for domestic students. Applications are processed on a rolling basis. *Application fee:* $50. Electronic applications accepted. *Application Contact:* 206-281-2091. *Associate Dean for Graduate Studies,* Gary Karns, 206-281-2948, Fax: 206-281-2733.

MS in Marriage and Family Therapy Program Students: 52 full-time (38 women), 8 part-time (all women); includes 6 minority (1 Black or African American, non-Hispanic/Latino; 1 Asian, non-Hispanic/Latino; 3 Hispanic/Latino; 1 Two or more races, non-Hispanic/Latino). Average age 28. 81 applicants, 62% accepted, 36 enrolled. Expenses: Contact institution. *Financial support:* Fellowships and Federal Work-Study available. Financial award applicants required to submit FAFSA. In 2017, 37 master's awarded. *Program availability:* Part-time. Offers marriage and family therapy (MS); medical family therapy (Certificate). *Application deadline:* For fall admission, 1/23 for domestic students, 2/1 for international students. Applications are processed on a rolling basis. *Application fee:* $50. Electronic applications accepted. *Chair,* Dr. Scott Edwards, 206-281-2681, E-mail: sedwards@spu.edu.

MS in Nursing Program Students: 22 full-time (17 women), 40 part-time (35 women); includes 13 minority (4 Black or African American, non-Hispanic/Latino; 1 American Indian or Alaska Native, non-Hispanic/Latino; 7 Asian, non-Hispanic/Latino; 1 Two or more races, non-Hispanic/Latino). Average age 36. 52 applicants, 73% accepted, 22 enrolled. Expenses: Contact institution. *Financial support:* Fellowships and scholarships/grants available. Financial award applicants required to submit FAFSA. In 2017, 23 master's awarded. *Program availability:* Part-time. Offers administration (MSN); adult/gerontology nurse practitioner (MSN); clinical nurse specialist (MSN); family nurse practitioner (MSN, Certificate); informatics (MSN); nurse educator (MSN). *Application deadline:* For fall admission, 1/15 priority date for domestic students; for spring admission, 1/15 for domestic students. Applications are processed on a rolling basis. *Application fee:* $50. Electronic applications accepted. *Associate Dean,* Dr. Christine Hoyle, 206-281-2469, E-mail: hoylec@spu.edu.

PhD in Clinical Psychology Program Students: 47 full-time (37 women), 21 part-time (19 women); includes 8 minority (1 Black or African American, non-Hispanic/Latino; 4 Asian, non-Hispanic/Latino; 2 Hispanic/Latino; 1 Two or more races, non-Hispanic/Latino), 3 international. Average age 28. 95 applicants, 19% accepted, 15 enrolled. Expenses: Contact institution. *Financial support:* Fellowships and scholarships/grants available. Financial award applicants required to submit FAFSA. In 2017, 13 doctorates awarded. Offers clinical psychology (PhD). *Application deadline:* For fall admission, 12/15 for domestic and international students. Electronic applications accepted. *Application Contact:* 206-281-2091. *Acting Chair,* Dr. Lynette Bikos, 206-281-2017, E-mail: lhbikos@spu.edu.

PhD in Counselor Education Program Students: 7 part-time (6 women); includes 4 minority (1 Black or African American, non-Hispanic/Latino; 2 Asian, non-Hispanic/Latino; 1 Two or more races, non-Hispanic/Latino). Average age 35. Expenses: Contact institution. Offers counselor education (PhD). *Application deadline:* For fall admission, 8/15 for domestic students; for winter admission, 11/15 for domestic students; for spring admission, 2/15 for domestic students; for summer admission, 5/15 for domestic students. *Application fee:* $50. *Director,* Nyaradzo Mvududu, 206-281-2551, E-mail: nyaradzo@spu.edu.

Program in Digital Education Leadership Students: 12 part-time (9 women); includes 2 minority (1 American Indian or Alaska Native, non-Hispanic/Latino; 1 Hispanic/Latino). Average age 37. 10 applicants, 80% accepted, 8 enrolled. Expenses: Contact institution. In 2017, 4 master's awarded. Offers digital education leadership (M Ed). *Application deadline:* For fall admission, 9/8 for domestic students. *Application Contact:* Graduate Center, 206-281-2091. *Dean,* Rick Eigenbrood, 206-281-2710, E-mail: eigend@spu.edu.

Program in Teaching Mathematics and Science Students: 19 full-time (8 women), 2 part-time (1 woman); includes 4 minority (1 Asian, non-Hispanic/Latino; 2 Hispanic/Latino; 1 Two or more races, non-Hispanic/Latino). Average age 32. Expenses: Contact institution. In 2017, 20 master's awarded. Offers teaching mathematics and science (MTMS). *Application deadline:* For fall admission, 8/15 for domestic students; for winter admission, 11/15 for domestic students; for spring admission, 2/15 for domestic students; for summer admission, 5/15 for domestic students. *Graduate Teacher Education Chair,* David W. Dento, 206-281-2504, E-mail: dentod@spu.edu.

THE SEATTLE SCHOOL OF THEOLOGY AND PSYCHOLOGY, Seattle, WA 98121

General Information Independent-religious, coed, graduate-only institution.

GRADUATE UNITS

Graduate Programs *Program availability:* Part-time.

SEATTLE UNIVERSITY, Seattle, WA 98122-1090

General Information Independent-religious, coed, comprehensive institution. *Enrollment:* 7,278 graduate, professional, and undergraduate students; 1,343 full-time matriculated graduate/professional students (854 women), 1,279 part-time matriculated graduate/professional students (760 women). *Enrollment by degree level:* 1,549 master's, 416 doctoral, 657 other advanced degrees. *Graduate faculty:* 277 full-time (148 women), 98 part-time/adjunct (56 women). *Tuition:* Full-time $12,960. *Required fees:* $570. Tuition and fees vary according to program. *Graduate housing:* Room and/or apartments available on a first-come, first-served basis to single students; on-campus housing not available to married students. *Student services:* Campus employment opportunities, campus safety program, career counseling, exercise/wellness program, free psychological counseling, international student services, low-cost health insurance, multicultural affairs office, services for students with disabilities, teacher training, writing training. *Library facilities:* Lemieux Library & McGoldrick Learning Commons plus 1 other. *Collection:* Books: 472,572 (physical), 257,641 (digital/electronic); Serial titles: 118,353 (physical), 8,597 (digital/electronic); Databases: 235. Students can reserve study rooms. *Research affiliation:* Swedish Medical Centers (nursing).

Computer facilities: Computer purchase and lease plans are available. 467 computers available on campus for general student use. A campuswide network can be accessed from student residence rooms and from off campus. Online class registration is available.
Website: http://www.seattleu.edu/

General Application Contact: Janet Shandley, Director of Graduate Admissions, 206-296-5900, Fax: 206-298-5656, E-mail: grad_admissions@seattleu.edu.

GRADUATE UNITS

Albers School of Business and Economics Students: 277 full-time (141 women), 298 part-time (122 women); includes 125 minority (7 Black or African American, non-Hispanic/Latino; 1 American Indian or Alaska Native, non-Hispanic/Latino; 78 Asian, non-Hispanic/Latino; 23 Hispanic/Latino; 3 Native Hawaiian or other Pacific Islander, non-Hispanic/Latino; 13 Two or more races, non-Hispanic/Latino), 168 international. Average age 31. 528 applicants, 60% accepted, 177 enrolled. *Faculty:* 45 full-time (17 women), 16 part-time/adjunct (4 women). Expenses: Contact institution. *Financial support:* In 2017–18, 153 students received support. Fellowships with partial tuition reimbursements available, research assistantships, career-related internships or fieldwork, Federal Work-Study, scholarships/grants, and unspecified assistantships available. Support available to part-time students. Financial award application deadline: 6/1; financial award applicants required to submit FAFSA. In 2017, 303 master's, 288 other advanced degrees awarded. *Program availability:* Part-time, evening/weekend. Offers business administration (MBA, Certificate); business analytics (MSBA, Certificate); business and economics (EMBA, MBA, MPAC, MSBA, MSF, Certificate); finance (MSF, Certificate); professional accounting (MPAC). *Application deadline:* For fall admission, 8/20 priority date for domestic students, 4/1 priority date for international students; for winter admission, 11/20 priority date for domestic students, 9/1 priority date for international students; for spring admission, 2/20 priority date for domestic students, 12/1 priority date for international students; for summer admission, 5/20 priority date for domestic students, 1/1 priority date for international students. Applications are processed on a rolling basis. *Application fee:* $55. Electronic applications accepted. *Application Contact:* Jeff Millard, Assistant Dean of Graduate Programs, 206-296-5700, E-mail: albersgrad@seattleu.edu. *Dean*, Dr. Joseph M. Phillips, Jr., 206-296-5700, Fax: 206-296-5795, E-mail: phillipsj@seattleu.edu.

Center for Leadership Formation Students: 62 full-time (28 women); includes 6 minority (1 Black or African American, non-Hispanic/Latino; 4 Asian, non-Hispanic/Latino; 1 Native Hawaiian or other Pacific Islander, non-Hispanic/Latino), 1 international. Average age 45. 47 applicants, 96% accepted, 38 enrolled. *Faculty:* 13 full-time (5 women), 3 part-time/adjunct (2 women). Expenses: Contact institution. *Financial support:* In 2017–18, 8 students received support. Scholarships/grants available. Financial award applicants required to submit FAFSA. In 2017, 31 master's, 42 other advanced degrees awarded. *Program availability:* Evening/weekend. Offers leadership (EMBA, Certificate). *Application deadline:* Applications are processed on a rolling basis. *Application fee:* $55. Electronic applications accepted. *Application Contact:* Sommer Harrison, Manager, Graduate Programs Outreach, 206-296-2529, E-mail: emba@seattleu.edu. *Associate Dean of Executive Education*, Dr. Marilyn Gist, 206-296-5413, E-mail: gistm@seattleu.edu.

College of Arts and Sciences Students: 126 full-time (87 women), 297 part-time (205 women); includes 126 minority (25 Black or African American, non-Hispanic/Latino; 3 American Indian or Alaska Native, non-Hispanic/Latino; 29 Asian, non-Hispanic/Latino; 39 Hispanic/Latino; 2 Native Hawaiian or other Pacific Islander, non-Hispanic/Latino; 28 Two or more races, non-Hispanic/Latino), 25 international. Average age 30. 365 applicants, 69% accepted, 159 enrolled. *Faculty:* 42 full-time (21 women), 25 part-time/adjunct (14 women). Expenses: Contact institution. *Financial support:* In 2017–18, 163 students received support. Career-related internships or fieldwork, Federal Work-Study, scholarships/grants, and unspecified assistantships available. Support available to part-time students. Financial award application deadline: 3/15; financial award applicants required to submit FAFSA. In 2017, 157 master's, 101 other advanced degrees awarded. *Program availability:* Part-time, evening/weekend. Offers arts and sciences (MA Psych, MACJ, MFA, MNPL, MPA, MSAL, MSW, Certificate); arts leadership (MFA); crime analysis (Certificate); criminal justice (MACJ); existential and phenomenological therapeutic psychology (MA Psych); social work (MSW). *Application deadline:* For fall admission, 1/15 for domestic and international students; for winter admission, 10/15 for domestic and international students; for spring admission, 2/15 for domestic and international students. Applications are processed on a rolling basis. *Application fee:* $55. Electronic applications accepted. *Application Contact:* Janet Shandley, Director of Graduate Admissions, 206-296-5900, Fax: 206-298-5656, E-mail: grad_admissions@seattleu.edu. *Dean*, Dr. David Powers, 206-296-5300, E-mail: powersda@seattleu.edu.

Center for the Study of Sport and Exercise Students: 8 full-time (2 women), 31 part-time (11 women); includes 6 minority (1 Black or African American, non-Hispanic/Latino; 5 Asian, non-Hispanic/Latino), 5 international. Average age 26. 1 applicant, 100% accepted, 1 enrolled. *Faculty:* 3 full-time (1 woman). Expenses: Contact institution. *Financial support:* In 2017–18, 20 students received support. Research assistantships and scholarships/grants available. Financial award applicants required to submit FAFSA. In 2017, 22 master's awarded. *Program availability:* Part-time, evening/weekend. Offers sport and exercise (MSAL). *Application deadline:* For fall admission, 2/15 for domestic and international students. *Application fee:* $55. Electronic applications accepted. *Application Contact:* Janet Shandley, Associate Dean of Graduate Admissions, 206-296-5900, Fax: 206-298-5656, E-mail: grad_admissions@seattleu.edu. *Director*, Dr. Dan Tripps, 206-398-4605, E-mail: trippsd@seattleu.edu.

Institute of Public Service Students: 15 full-time (8 women), 122 part-time (79 women); includes 52 minority (11 Black or African American, non-Hispanic/Latino; 2 American Indian or Alaska Native, non-Hispanic/Latino; 10 Asian, non-Hispanic/Latino; 20 Hispanic/Latino; 9 Two or more races, non-Hispanic/Latino), 8 international. Average age 31. 61 applicants, 75% accepted, 33 enrolled. *Faculty:* 11 full-time (5 women), 6 part-time/adjunct (2 women). Expenses: Contact institution. *Financial support:* In 2017–18, 15 students received support. Career-related internships or fieldwork, Federal Work-Study, and unspecified assistantships available. Support available to part-time students. Financial award applicants required to submit FAFSA. In 2017, 42 master's awarded. *Program availability:* Part-time, evening/weekend. Offers public service (MNPL, MPA). *Application deadline:* For fall admission, 7/20 priority date for domestic students, 7/20 for international students; for winter admission, 10/20 priority date for domestic students, 10/20 for international students; for spring admission, 2/20 priority date for domestic students, 2/20 for international students. Applications are processed on a rolling basis. *Application fee:* $55. Electronic applications accepted. *Application Contact:* Janet Shandley, Associate Dean of Graduate Admissions, 206-296-5900, Fax: 206-298-5656, E-mail: grad_admissions@seattleu.edu. *Interim Director, Institute of Public Service*, Dr. John Collins, 206-296-5442, Fax: 206-296-5997, E-mail: collinsj@seattleu.edu.

College of Education Students: 250 full-time (196 women), 246 part-time (180 women); includes 180 minority (19 Black or African American, non-Hispanic/Latino; 7 American Indian or Alaska Native, non-Hispanic/Latino; 57 Asian, non-Hispanic/Latino; 67 Hispanic/Latino; 1 Native Hawaiian or other Pacific Islander, non-Hispanic/Latino; 29 Two or more races, non-Hispanic/Latino), 12 international. Average age 31. 460 applicants, 62% accepted, 146 enrolled. *Faculty:* 27 full-time (15 women), 13 part-time/adjunct (9 women). Expenses: Contact institution. *Financial support:* In 2017–18, 116 students received support. Career-related internships or fieldwork, Federal Work-Study, scholarships/grants, and unspecified assistantships available. Support available to part-time students. Financial award applicants required to submit FAFSA. In 2017, 176 master's, 5 doctorates, 49 other advanced degrees awarded. *Program availability:* Part-time, evening/weekend. Offers adult education and training (M Ed, MA, Certificate); counseling and school psychology (MA, Certificate, Ed S); education (M Ed, MA, MIT, Ed D, Certificate, Ed S, Post-Master's Certificate); educational administration (M Ed, MA, Certificate, Ed S); educational leadership (Ed D); special education (M Ed, MA, Certificate); student development administration (M Ed, MA); teacher education (MIT); teaching English to speakers of other languages (M Ed, MA, Certificate). *Application deadline:* Applications are processed on a rolling basis. *Application fee:* $55. Electronic applications accepted. *Application Contact:* Janet Shandley, Director of Graduate Admissions, 206-296-5900, Fax: 206-298-5656, E-mail: grad_admissions@seattleu.edu. *Dean*, Dr. Deanna Sands, 206-296-5758, E-mail: sandsd@seattleu.edu.

College of Nursing Students: 181 full-time (148 women), 37 part-time (29 women); includes 58 minority (9 Black or African American, non-Hispanic/Latino; 1 American Indian or Alaska Native, non-Hispanic/Latino; 23 Asian, non-Hispanic/Latino; 17 Hispanic/Latino; 8 Two or more races, non-Hispanic/Latino), 2 international. Average age 34. 6 applicants, 17% accepted, 1 enrolled. *Faculty:* 29 full-time (25 women), 20 part-time/adjunct (18 women). Expenses: Contact institution. *Financial support:* In 2017–18, 74 students received support. Fellowships, research assistantships, career-related internships or fieldwork, Federal Work-Study, and scholarships/grants available. Support available to part-time students. Financial award applicants required to submit FAFSA. *Program availability:* Part-time, evening/weekend. Offers nursing (DNP). *Application deadline:* For fall admission, 7/1 for domestic students. *Application fee:* $55. *Application Contact:* Janet Shandley, Director of Graduate Admissions, 206-296-5900, Fax: 206-298-5656, E-mail: grad_admissions@seattleu.edu. *Dean*, Dr. Kristen Swanson, 206-296-5676.

College of Science and Engineering Students: 76 full-time (30 women), 63 part-time (16 women); includes 29 minority (1 Black or African American, non-Hispanic/Latino; 20 Asian, non-Hispanic/Latino; 7 Hispanic/Latino; 1 Two or more races, non-Hispanic/Latino), 41 international. Average age 28. 127 applicants, 67% accepted, 53 enrolled. *Faculty:* 14 full-time (4 women), 6 part-time/adjunct (0 women). Expenses: Contact institution. *Financial support:* In 2017–18, 6 students received support. Career-related internships or fieldwork and Federal Work-Study available. Support available to part-time students. Financial award applicants required to submit FAFSA. In 2017, 54 master's awarded. *Program availability:* Part-time, evening/weekend. Offers computer science (MSCS); science and engineering (MSCS). *Application deadline:* For fall admission, 7/1 for domestic students. *Application fee:* $55. *Application Contact:* Janet Shandley, Director of Graduate Admissions, 206-296-5900, Fax: 206-298-5656, E-mail: grad_admissions@seattleu.edu. *Dean*, Dr. Michael Quinn, 206-296-5500, Fax: 206-296-2071.

School of Law Students: 500 full-time (265 women), 130 part-time (65 women); includes 268 minority (34 Black or African American, non-Hispanic/Latino; 6 American Indian or Alaska Native, non-Hispanic/Latino; 102 Asian, non-Hispanic/Latino; 69 Hispanic/Latino; 5 Native Hawaiian or other Pacific Islander, non-Hispanic/Latino; 52 Two or more races, non-Hispanic/Latino), 7 international. Average age 27. 1,443 applicants, 67% accepted, 200 enrolled. *Faculty:* 47 full-time (25 women), 48 part-time/adjunct (16 women). Expenses: Contact institution. *Financial support:* In 2017–18, 500 students received support. Career-related internships or fieldwork, Federal Work-Study, and scholarships/grants available. Support available to part-time students. Financial award application deadline: 2/15; financial award applicants required to submit FAFSA. In 2017, 300 doctorates awarded. *Program availability:* Part-time, evening/weekend. Offers American legal studies (LL M); business development (MLS); elder law (LL M); health law (MLS); innovation and technology (LL M, MLS); tribal law and governance (LL M, MLS). *Application deadline:* For fall admission, 3/1 priority date for domestic and international students. Applications are processed on a rolling basis. *Application fee:* $65. Electronic applications accepted. *Application Contact:* Gerald Heppler, Director of Admission, 206-398-4205, Fax: 206-398-4058, E-mail: hepplerg@seattleu.edu. *Dean*, Annette E. Clark, 206-398-4300, Fax: 206-398-4310, E-mail: annclark@seattleu.edu.

School of Theology and Ministry Students: 30 full-time (24 women), 107 part-time (73 women); includes 35 minority (12 Black or African American, non-Hispanic/Latino; 1 American Indian or Alaska Native, non-Hispanic/Latino; 7 Asian, non-Hispanic/Latino; 10 Hispanic/Latino; 1 Native Hawaiian or other Pacific Islander, non-Hispanic/Latino; 4 Two or more races, non-Hispanic/Latino), 4 international. Average age 44. 55 applicants, 55% accepted, 24 enrolled. *Faculty:* 15 full-time (7 women), 18 part-time/adjunct (11 women). Expenses: Contact institution. *Financial support:* In 2017–18, 84 students received support. Career-related internships or fieldwork, Federal Work-Study, and scholarships/grants available. Support available to part-time students. Financial award application deadline: 6/1; financial award applicants required to submit FAFSA. In 2017, 51 master's awarded. *Program availability:* Part-time, online learning. Offers couples and family therapy (MA); divinity (M Div, D Min); pastoral studies (MAPS); theology and ministry (M Div, MA, MAPS, MATL, MATS, D Min, Certificate); transformational leadership (MATL); transforming spirituality (MATS, Certificate). *Application deadline:* For fall admission, 6/1 priority date for domestic students, 4/1 for international students. *Application fee:* $55. Electronic applications accepted. *Application Contact:* Colette Meda Casavant, Admissions Coordinator, 206-296-5333, Fax: 206-296-5329, E-mail: casavant@seattleu.edu. *Dean*, Dr. Mark Markuly, 206-296-5330, Fax: 206-296-5329, E-mail: stm@seattleu.edu.

SELMA UNIVERSITY, Selma, AL 36701-5299

General Information Independent-religious, coed, comprehensive institution.

GRADUATE UNITS

Graduate Programs Offers Bible and Christian education (MA); Bible and pastoral ministry (MA).

SEMINARY OF THE SOUTHWEST, Austin, TX 78768-2247

General Information Independent-religious, coed, graduate-only institution. *Enrollment by degree level:* 112 master's, 4 other advanced degrees. *Graduate faculty:* 10 full-time (5 women), 9 part-time/adjunct (2 women). *Tuition:* Full-time $14,976; part-time $624 per credit. *Required fees:* $853; $506 per credit. $243 per semester. One-time fee: $95 full-time; $50 part-time. Tuition and fees vary according to class time and program. *Graduate housing:* Rooms and/or apartments available on a first-come, first-served basis to single and married students. Housing application deadline: 8/1. *Student services:* Exercise/wellness program, writing training. *Library facilities:* Booher Library. *Collection:* Books: 153,285 (physical), 129,860 (digital/electronic); Serial titles: 667 (physical), 47 (digital/electronic); Databases: 75. Weekly public service hours: 86; students can reserve study rooms.

Computer facilities: 8 computers available on campus for general student use. A campuswide network can be accessed from student residence rooms. Online class registration is available.
Website: http://www.ssw.edu/

General Application Contact: Beth Jordan, Enrollment Manager, 512-472-4133 Ext. 357, Fax: 512-472-3098, E-mail: beth.jordan@ssw.edu.

GRADUATE UNITS

Graduate and Professional Programs Students: 60 full-time (31 women), 56 part-time (42 women); includes 22 minority (10 Black or African American, non-Hispanic/Latino; 1 American Indian or Alaska Native, non-Hispanic/Latino; 2 Asian, non-Hispanic/Latino; 6 Hispanic/Latino; 3 Two or more races, non-Hispanic/Latino). Average age 38. 49 applicants, 98% accepted, 31 enrolled. *Faculty:* 10 full-time (5 women), 12 part-time/adjunct (5 women). Expenses: Contact institution. *Financial support:* In 2017–18, 92 students received support. Career-related internships or fieldwork and scholarships/grants available. Support available to part-time students. Financial award application deadline: 6/15; financial award applicants required to submit FAFSA. In 2017, 27 master's, 3 other advanced degrees awarded. *Program availability:* Part-time, evening/weekend. Offers Anglican studies (Advanced Diploma); chaplaincy and pastoral care (MA); clinical mental health counseling (MA); Latino/Hispanic studies (M Div); ministry (M Div); religion (MAR); spiritual formation (MA). *Application deadline:* For fall admission, 6/30 priority date for domestic and international students; for spring admission, 12/1 for domestic and international students. Applications are processed on a rolling basis. *Application fee:* $50. Electronic applications accepted. *Application Contact:* Hope Benko, Director of Enrollment Management, 512-472-4133 Ext. 375, Fax: 512-472-3098, E-mail: hope.benko@ssw.edu. *Dean and President,* Rev. Dr. Cynthia Briggs Kittredge, 512-472-4133 Ext. 332, Fax: 512-472-3098, E-mail: cynthia.kittredge@ssw.edu.

SETON HALL UNIVERSITY, South Orange, NJ 07079-2697

General Information Independent-religious, coed, university. CGS member. *Graduate housing:* On-campus housing not available.

GRADUATE UNITS

College of Arts and Sciences *Program availability:* Part-time, evening/weekend, online learning. Offers analytical chemistry (MS, PhD); arts and sciences (MA, MPA, MS, PhD, Graduate Certificate); Asian studies (MA); biochemistry (MS, PhD); biology (MS); biology/business administration (MS); chemistry (MS); experimental psychology (MS); history (MA); inorganic chemistry (MS, PhD); Jewish-Christian studies (MA); literature (MA); microbiology (MS); molecular bioscience (PhD); molecular bioscience/neuroscience (PhD); nonprofit organization management (Graduate Certificate); organic chemistry (MS, PhD); physical chemistry (MS, PhD); public administration (MPA); social work (MSW). Electronic applications accepted.

College of Communication and the Arts *Program availability:* Part-time, evening/weekend, online learning. Offers exhibition development (MA); museum management (MA); museum professions (MA); museum registration (MA); public relations (MA); strategic communication (MA). Electronic applications accepted.

College of Education and Human Services *Program availability:* Part-time, evening/weekend, 100% online, blended/hybrid learning. Offers college student personnel administration (MA); counseling psychology (MA, PhD); education and human services (MA, MS, Ed D, Exec Ed D, PhD, Ed S); education research, assessment and program evaluation (PhD); higher education administration (Ed D, PhD); human resource training and development (MA); individualized (MA); instructional design and technology (MA); K–12 administration and supervision (Ed D, Exec Ed D, Ed S); K–12 leadership, management and policy (Ed D, Exec Ed D, Ed S); marriage and family therapy (MA); psychological studies (MA); school counseling (MA); school psychology (MA); special education (MA); sport and exercise psychology (MA). Electronic applications accepted.

College of Nursing *Program availability:* Part-time, online learning. Offers advanced practice in primary health care (MSN, DNP); entry into practice (MSN); health systems administration (MSN, DNP); nursing (PhD); nursing case management (MSN); nursing education (MA); school nurse (MSN). Electronic applications accepted.

Immaculate Conception Seminary School of Theology *Program availability:* Part-time, evening/weekend. Offers Christian spirituality (Certificate); great spiritual books (Certificate); pastoral ministry (M Div, MA, Certificate); scripture studies (Certificate); Seminary's Theological Education for Parish Services (STEPS) (Certificate); theology (MA). Electronic applications accepted.

School of Diplomacy and International Relations *Program availability:* Part-time, evening/weekend, 100% online, blended/hybrid learning. Offers diplomacy and international relations (MA); global health management (Graduate Certificate); post-conflict state reconstruction and sustainability (Graduate Certificate); United Nations studies (Graduate Certificate). Electronic applications accepted.

School of Health and Medical Sciences *Program availability:* Part-time, evening/weekend. Offers athletic training (MS); health and medical sciences (MS, DPT, PhD); health sciences (PhD); occupational therapy (MS); physician assistant (MS); professional physical therapy (DPT); speech-language pathology (MS). Electronic applications accepted.

School of Law *Program availability:* Part-time, evening/weekend. Offers health law (LL M, JD); intellectual property (LL M, JD); law (MSJ). MD/JD, MD/MSJ offered jointly with University of Medicine and Dentistry of New Jersey. Electronic applications accepted.

School of Medicine Offers medicine (MD).

Stillman School of Business Students: 140 full-time (58 women), 154 part-time (49 women); includes 66 minority (25 Black or African American, non-Hispanic/Latino; 14 Asian, non-Hispanic/Latino; 23 Hispanic/Latino; 4 Two or more races, non-Hispanic/Latino), 88 international. Average age 32. 416 applicants, 73% accepted, 100 enrolled. *Faculty:* 29 full-time (4 women), 18 part-time/adjunct (0 women). Expenses: Contact institution. *Financial support:* In 2017–18, 41 students received support, including 41 research assistantships with full tuition reimbursements available (averaging $3,644 per year); career-related internships or fieldwork, scholarships/grants, and unspecified assistantships also available. Financial award application deadline: 6/30; financial award applicants required to submit FAFSA. In 2017, 132 master's awarded. *Program availability:* Part-time, evening/weekend. Offers accounting (MBA, MS, Certificate); business (MBA, MS, Certificate); entrepreneurial studies (Certificate); finance (MBA); financial decision making (Certificate); information technology management (MBA); international business (Certificate); management (MBA); marketing (MBA); professional accounting (MS); sport management (MBA); supply chain management (MBA, Certificate); taxation (Certificate). *Application deadline:* For fall admission, 5/31 priority date for domestic students, 3/31 priority date for international students; for spring admission, 10/31 priority date for domestic students, 9/30 priority date for international students; for summer admission, 4/30 priority date for domestic students, 3/31 priority date for international students. Applications are processed on a rolling basis. *Application fee:* $75. Electronic applications accepted. *Application Contact:* Alfred Ayoub, Director of Graduate Admissions, 973-761-9262, Fax: 973-761-9208, E-mail: alfred.ayoub@shu.edu. *Dean,* Dr. Joyce Strawser, 973-761-9013, Fax: 973-275-2465, E-mail: joyce.strawser@shu.edu.

SETON HILL UNIVERSITY, Greensburg, PA 15601

General Information Independent-religious, coed, comprehensive institution. *Enrollment:* 2,048 graduate, professional, and undergraduate students; 262 full-time matriculated graduate/professional students (186 women), 110 part-time matriculated graduate/professional students (73 women). *Enrollment by degree level:* 369 master's, 3 other advanced degrees. *Graduate faculty:* 14 full-time, 15 part-time/adjunct. *Tuition:* Part-time $734 per credit. Tuition and fees vary according to class time, course level, course load and program. *Graduate housing:* Room and/or apartments available on a first-come, first-served basis to single students; on-campus housing not available to married students. Typical cost: $6520 per year ($11,884 including board). Room and board charges vary according to board plan, campus/location and housing facility selected. Housing application deadline: 7/1. *Student services:* Campus employment opportunities, campus safety program, career counseling, exercise/wellness program, international student services, multicultural affairs office, services for students with disabilities, teacher training, writing training. *Library facilities:* Reeves Memorial Library. *Collection:* Books: 72,274 (physical), 127,160 (digital/electronic); Serial titles: 2,919 (physical); Databases: 37. Students can reserve study rooms.

Computer facilities: Computer purchase and lease plans are available. 66 computers available on campus for general student use. A campuswide network can be accessed from student residence rooms and from off campus. Online class registration is available.
Website: http://www.setonhill.edu/

General Application Contact: Director of Graduate and Adult Studies, 724-838-4208, Fax: 724-830-1891, E-mail: gadmit@setonhill.edu.

GRADUATE UNITS

MA Program in Art Therapy Expenses: Contact institution. *Financial support:* Federal Work-Study, scholarships/grants, and tuition discounts available. Financial award application deadline: 8/15; financial award applicants required to submit FAFSA. *Program availability:* Part-time. Offers counseling (MA). *Application deadline:* For fall admission, 7/1 for domestic and international students; for spring admission, 11/30 for domestic and international students. Applications are processed on a rolling basis. *Application fee:* $0. Electronic applications accepted.

MA Program in Marriage and Family Therapy Expenses: Contact institution. *Financial support:* Federal Work-Study, scholarships/grants, and unspecified assistantships available. Financial award application deadline: 8/15; financial award applicants required to submit FAFSA. Offers marriage and family therapy (MA). *Application deadline:* For fall admission, 8/15 for domestic students; for spring admission, 12/15 for domestic students. Applications are processed on a rolling basis. Electronic applications accepted.

Master of Arts Program in Elementary/Middle Level Education Expenses: Contact institution. *Financial support:* Federal Work-Study, scholarships/grants, and tuition discounts available. Financial award application deadline: 8/15; financial award applicants required to submit FAFSA. *Program availability:* Part-time, evening/weekend, blended/hybrid learning. Offers elementary/middle level education (MA). *Application deadline:* Applications are processed on a rolling basis. *Application fee:* $0. Electronic applications accepted.

Master of Arts Program in Special Education Expenses: Contact institution. *Financial support:* Scholarships/grants and tuition discounts available. Financial award application deadline: 8/15; financial award applicants required to submit FAFSA. *Program availability:* Part-time, evening/weekend, blended/hybrid learning. Offers special education (MA). *Application deadline:* Applications are processed on a rolling basis. *Application fee:* $0. Electronic applications accepted.

Master of Science Program in Physician Assistant Expenses: Contact institution. *Financial support:* Application deadline: 8/15; applicants required to submit FAFSA. Offers physician assistant (MS). *Application deadline:* Applications are processed on a rolling basis. Electronic applications accepted.

Master's and Certificate Program in Orthodontics Expenses: Contact institution. *Financial support:* Application deadline: 5/15; applicants required to submit FAFSA. Offers orthodontics (MS, Certificate). *Application deadline:* Applications are processed on a rolling basis. Electronic applications accepted.

MBA Program Expenses: Contact institution. *Financial support:* Federal Work-Study, scholarships/grants, and tuition discounts available. Financial award application deadline: 8/15; financial award applicants required to submit FAFSA. *Program availability:* Part-time, evening/weekend. Offers entrepreneurship (MBA); forensic accounting and fraud examination (MBA); healthcare administration (MBA); management (MBA). *Application deadline:* Applications are processed on a rolling basis. *Application fee:* $0. Electronic applications accepted. *Associate Professor, Business/MBA Program Director,* Dr. Douglas Nelson, E-mail: dnelson@setonhill.edu.

MFA Program in Writing Popular Fiction Expenses: Contact institution. *Financial support:* Scholarships/grants and tuition discounts available. Financial award application deadline: 8/15; financial award applicants required to submit FAFSA. *Program availability:* Part-time. Offers writing popular fiction (MFA). *Application deadline:* For fall admission, 10/1 priority date for domestic students; for spring admission, 3/1 priority date for domestic students. Applications are processed on a rolling basis. Electronic applications accepted. *Associate Professor, English/Program Director, Writing Popular Fiction,* Dr. Nicole Peeler, E-mail: peeler@setonhill.edu.

Program in Innovative Instruction Students: 2 full-time (0 women), 18 part-time (14 women); includes 2 minority (1 Black or African American, non-Hispanic/Latino; 1

Hispanic/Latino). Average age 34. 21 applicants, 48% accepted, 9 enrolled. *Faculty:* 3 full-time (2 women), 3 part-time/adjunct (2 women). Expenses: Contact institution. *Financial support:* In 2017–18, 7 students received support. Scholarships/grants, tuition waivers (partial), and unspecified assistantships available. Support available to part-time students. Financial award application deadline: 8/15; financial award applicants required to submit FAFSA. In 2017, 5 master's awarded. *Program availability:* Part-time, evening/weekend. Offers innovative instruction (M Ed). *Application deadline:* Applications are processed on a rolling basis. *Application fee:* $35. Electronic applications accepted.

Program in Special Education: Autism Specialization Students: 2 full-time (1 woman), 7 part-time (all women). Average age 27. 7 applicants, 29% accepted, 1 enrolled. *Faculty:* 4 full-time (all women), 6 part-time/adjunct (4 women). Expenses: Contact institution. *Financial support:* Scholarships/grants and tuition discounts available. Financial award applicants required to submit FAFSA. In 2017, 1 master's awarded. *Program availability:* Part-time, evening/weekend, online only, 100% online, blended/hybrid learning. Offers special education: autism (MA). *Application deadline:* Applications are processed on a rolling basis. *Application fee:* $0. Electronic applications accepted. *Application Contact:* E-mail: gadmit@setonhill.edu. *Director,* Jennifer Suppo, 724-552-4377, E-mail: jsuppo@setonhill.edu.

SHASTA BIBLE COLLEGE, Redding, CA 96002

General Information Independent-religious, coed, comprehensive institution. *Graduate housing:* Rooms and/or apartments available on a first-come, first-served basis to single and married students.

GRADUATE UNITS

Program in Biblical Counseling *Program availability:* Part-time. Offers biblical counseling and Christian family life education (MA).

Program in Christian Ministry *Program availability:* Part-time, online learning. Offers Christian ministry (MA).

Program in School and Church Administration *Program availability:* Part-time, evening/weekend. Offers school and church administration (MS).

SHAWNEE STATE UNIVERSITY, Portsmouth, OH 45662

General Information State-supported, coed, comprehensive institution.

GRADUATE UNITS

Program in Curriculum and Instruction Offers curriculum and instruction (M Ed).

Program in Occupational Therapy Offers occupational therapy (MOT).

SHAW UNIVERSITY, Raleigh, NC 27601-2399

General Information Independent-religious, coed, comprehensive institution. *Graduate housing:* Room and/or apartments available on a first-come, first-served basis to single students; on-campus housing not available to married students. *Research affiliation:* The Louisville Institute (book writing, theology), Wabash Center (philosophy of religious education), The Society of Biblical Literature (biblical studies), The American Academy of Religion (theology, ethics, Church history, contemporary issues), Society for the Study of Black Religion (African American churches), The Association of Theological Schools (theological research).

GRADUATE UNITS

Department of Education *Program availability:* Part-time, evening/weekend. Offers curriculum and instruction (MS). Electronic applications accepted.

Divinity School *Program availability:* Part-time, evening/weekend. Offers divinity (M Div, MACE). Electronic applications accepted.

SHENANDOAH UNIVERSITY, Winchester, VA 22601-5195

General Information Independent-religious, coed, university. *Enrollment:* 3,844 graduate, professional, and undergraduate students; 951 full-time matriculated graduate/professional students (683 women), 677 part-time matriculated graduate/professional students (494 women). *Enrollment by degree level:* 714 master's, 814 doctoral, 100 other advanced degrees. *Graduate faculty:* 147 full-time (94 women), 116 part-time/adjunct (81 women). *Tuition:* Full-time $15,480; part-time $860 per credit hour. *Required fees:* $1220. Tuition and fees vary according to course load and program. *Graduate housing:* Rooms and/or apartments available on a first-come, first-served basis to single and married students. Typical cost: $10,180 (including board) for single students; $8868 per year for married students. Room and board charges vary according to board plan, campus/location and housing facility selected. Housing application deadline: 3/2. *Student services:* Campus employment opportunities, campus safety program, career counseling, child daycare facilities, exercise/wellness program, free psychological counseling, international student services, low-cost health insurance, multicultural affairs office, services for students with disabilities, teacher training, writing training. *Library facilities:* Alson H. Smith, Jr. Library plus 1 other. *Collection:* Books: 122,422 (physical), 217,000 (digital/electronic); Serial titles: 700 (physical), 86,500 (digital/electronic); Databases: 135. Weekly public service hours: 96; students can reserve study rooms. *Research affiliation:* Inova Center for Personalized Health (pharmacogenomics and precision medicine).

Computer facilities: 32 computers available on campus for general student use. A campuswide network can be accessed from student residence rooms and from off campus. Online class registration, online student account information are available. Website: http://www.su.edu/

General Application Contact: Andrew Woodall, Executive Dean of Admissions, 540-665-4581, Fax: 540-665-4627, E-mail: admit@su.edu.

GRADUATE UNITS

Bernard J. Dunn School of Pharmacy Students: 317 full-time (218 women), 142 part-time (85 women); includes 156 minority (73 Black or African American, non-Hispanic/Latino; 70 Asian, non-Hispanic/Latino; 7 Hispanic/Latino; 1 Native Hawaiian or other Pacific Islander, non-Hispanic/Latino; 5 Two or more races, non-Hispanic/Latino), 17 international. Average age 32. 481 applicants, 56% accepted, 159 enrolled. *Faculty:* 38 full-time (24 women), 7 part-time/adjunct (5 women). Expenses: Contact institution. *Financial support:* In 2017–18, 28 students received support. Scholarships/grants and unspecified assistantships available. Financial award applicants required to submit FAFSA. In 2017, 153 doctorates awarded. *Program availability:* Part-time, evening/weekend, 100% online. Offers pharmacy (Pharm D). *Application deadline:* For fall admission, 6/1 for domestic and international students. *Application fee:* $30. Electronic applications accepted. *Application Contact:* Andrew Woodall, Executive Director of Recruitment and Admissions, 540-665-4581, Fax: 540-665-4627, E-mail: admit@su.edu. *Dean,* Robert DiCenzo, PhD, 540-665-1282, Fax: 540-665-1283, E-mail: rdicenzo@su.edu.

College of Arts and Sciences Students: 19 full-time (14 women), 1 (woman) part-time; includes 4 minority (3 Black or African American, non-Hispanic/Latino; 1 Asian, non-Hispanic/Latino). Average age 27. 19 applicants, 89% accepted, 12 enrolled. *Faculty:* 1 full-time (0 women), 2 part-time/adjunct (1 woman). Expenses: Contact institution. *Financial support:* In 2017–18, 1 student received support. Scholarships/grants and unspecified assistantships available. Financial award applicants required to submit FAFSA. In 2017, 7 master's awarded. *Program availability:* Part-time, evening/weekend. Offers applied behavior analysis (MS). *Application deadline:* For fall admission, 7/15 for domestic and international students. *Application fee:* $30. Electronic applications accepted. *Application Contact:* Andrew Woodall, Executive Director of Recruitment and Admissions, 540-665-4581, Fax: 540-665-4627, E-mail: admit@su.edu. *Dean,* Jeff W. Coker, PhD, 540-665-4587, Fax: 540-665-4644, E-mail: jcoker2@su.edu.

Eleanor Wade Custer School of Nursing Students: 30 full-time (26 women), 51 part-time (48 women); includes 19 minority (13 Black or African American, non-Hispanic/Latino; 3 Asian, non-Hispanic/Latino; 2 Hispanic/Latino; 1 Two or more races, non-Hispanic/Latino), 3 international. Average age 37. 52 applicants, 88% accepted, 34 enrolled. *Faculty:* 17 full-time (all women), 6 part-time/adjunct (all women). Expenses: Contact institution. *Financial support:* In 2017–18, 32 students received support. Scholarships/grants and unspecified assistantships available. Financial award applicants required to submit FAFSA. In 2017, 18 master's, 1 doctorate, 28 other advanced degrees awarded. Offers adult gerontology primary care nurse practitioner (Graduate Certificate); adult-gerontology primary care nurse practitioner (MSN); family nurse practitioner (MSN, DNP, Graduate Certificate); general (MSN); health systems leadership (DNP); health systems management (MSN, Graduate Certificate); nurse midwifery (MSN); nurse-midwifery (Graduate Certificate); nursing education (Graduate Certificate); nursing practice (DNP); psychiatric mental health nurse practitioner (MSN, DNP, Graduate Certificate). *Application deadline:* For fall admission, 4/15 priority date for domestic and international students; for spring admission, 11/1 for domestic and international students; for summer admission, 3/1 for domestic and international students. *Application fee:* $30. Electronic applications accepted. *Application Contact:* Andrew Woodall, Executive Director of Recruitment and Admissions, 540-665-4581, Fax: 540-665-4627, E-mail: admit@su.edu. *Dean,* Dr. Kathleen LaSala, RN, 540-678-4381, Fax: 540-665-5519, E-mail: klasala@su.edu.

Harry F. Byrd, Jr. School of Business Students: 53 full-time (18 women), 59 part-time (37 women); includes 26 minority (10 Black or African American, non-Hispanic/Latino; 1 American Indian or Alaska Native, non-Hispanic/Latino; 5 Asian, non-Hispanic/Latino; 8 Hispanic/Latino; 2 Two or more races, non-Hispanic/Latino), 28 international. Average age 32. 73 applicants, 93% accepted, 46 enrolled. *Faculty:* 16 full-time (8 women), 2 part-time/adjunct (0 women). Expenses: Contact institution. *Financial support:* In 2017–18, 27 students received support. Scholarships/grants and unspecified assistantships available. Financial award applicants required to submit FAFSA. In 2017, 35 master's awarded. *Program availability:* Part-time, evening/weekend. Offers business administration (MBA); business administration essentials (Certificate); healthcare management (Certificate). *Application deadline:* For fall admission, 5/1 for domestic students, 4/15 for international students; for spring admission, 11/15 for domestic students, 10/15 for international students; for summer admission, 6/15 for domestic students, 5/1 for international students. *Application fee:* $30. Electronic applications accepted. *Application Contact:* Andrew Woodall, Executive Director of Recruitment and Admissions, 540-665-4581, Fax: 540-665-4627, E-mail: admit@su.edu. *Associate Dean, School of Business,* Bogdan Daraban, PhD, 540-542-6282, Fax: 540-665-5437, E-mail: bdaraban@su.edu.

School of Education and Leadership Students: 16 full-time (14 women), 221 part-time (167 women); includes 32 minority (17 Black or African American, non-Hispanic/Latino; 1 American Indian or Alaska Native, non-Hispanic/Latino; 6 Asian, non-Hispanic/Latino; 5 Hispanic/Latino; 1 Native Hawaiian or other Pacific Islander, non-Hispanic/Latino; 2 Two or more races, non-Hispanic/Latino), 3 international. Average age 38. 81 applicants, 99% accepted, 63 enrolled. *Faculty:* 8 full-time (7 women), 22 part-time/adjunct (16 women). Expenses: Contact institution. *Financial support:* In 2017–18, 26 students received support. Scholarships/grants and unspecified assistantships available. Financial award applicants required to submit FAFSA. In 2017, 53 master's, 11 doctorates, 49 other advanced degrees awarded. *Program availability:* Part-time, evening/weekend. Offers administration and supervision (Certificate); administrative leadership (D Ed); early childhood literacy (MS); educational administration (MSE); elementary school teacher education (Certificate); emphasis in teaching (MSE); health and physical education (Certificate); individualized focus (MS, MSE); literacy education (MS); middle school teacher education (Certificate); organizational leadership (MS, D Prof); reading licensure (MS, Certificate); reading non-licensure (MS); secondary school teacher education (Certificate); special education (MSE); writing (MS). *Application deadline:* For fall admission, 5/1 priority date for domestic students, 5/1 for international students; for spring admission, 10/15 priority date for domestic students, 10/15 for international students; for summer admission, 3/15 priority date for domestic students, 3/15 for international students. *Application fee:* $30. Electronic applications accepted. *Application Contact:* Andrew Woodall, Executive Director of Recruitment and Admissions, 540-665-4581, Fax: 540-665-4627, E-mail: admit@su.edu. *Director,* Jill Lindsey, PhD, 540-535-7324, Fax: 540-665-4726, E-mail: jlindsey@su.edu.

School of Health Professions Students: 446 full-time (355 women), 134 part-time (112 women); includes 78 minority (14 Black or African American, non-Hispanic/Latino; 28 Asian, non-Hispanic/Latino; 25 Hispanic/Latino; 11 Two or more races, non-Hispanic/Latino), 22 international. Average age 28. 839 applicants, 31% accepted, 166 enrolled. *Faculty:* 35 full-time (27 women), 18 part-time/adjunct (13 women). Expenses: Contact institution. *Financial support:* In 2017–18, 53 students received support. Scholarships/grants and unspecified assistantships available. Financial award applicants required to submit FAFSA. In 2017, 100 master's, 75 doctorates, 4 other advanced degrees awarded. *Program availability:* Part-time, all online except for two on-site weekend sessions (for DPT). Offers athletic training (MSAT); non-traditional physical therapy (MS); occupational training (MS); performing arts medicine (Certificate); physician assistant studies (MS); public health (MPH, Certificate); transitional physical therapy (DPT). *Application deadline:* For fall admission, 10/1 for domestic and international students; for summer admission, 4/1 for domestic and international students. *Application fee:* $30. Electronic applications accepted. *Application Contact:* Jon Brannon, Graduate Admissions Specialist, Office of Admissions, 540-545-7394, Fax: 540-665-4627, E-mail: jbannan09@su.edu. *Dean of School of Health Professions,* Dr. Karen Elizabeth Abraham, 540-545.6209, Fax: 540-665.5530, E-mail: kabraham@su.edu.

Shenandoah Conservatory Students: 70 full-time (38 women), 69 part-time (44 women); includes 20 minority (6 Black or African American, non-Hispanic/Latino; 1 American Indian or Alaska Native, non-Hispanic/Latino; 2 Asian, non-Hispanic/Latino; 11 Hispanic/Latino), 18 international. Average age 30. 135 applicants, 77% accepted, 49 enrolled. *Faculty:* 32 full-time (11 women), 12 part-time/adjunct (6 women). Expenses: Contact institution. *Financial support:* In 2017–18, 42 students received support. Scholarships/grants and unspecified assistantships available. Financial award applicants required to submit FAFSA. In 2017, 32 master's, 13 doctorates, 11 other advanced degrees awarded. *Program availability:* Part-time. Offers church music (MM,

Certificate); collaborative piano (MM); composition (MM); conducting (MM); music (Artist Diploma); music education (MME); music therapy (MMT, Certificate); pedagogy - voice (MM, DMA); performance (MM, DMA); performing arts leadership and management (MS). *Application deadline:* For fall and spring admission, 1/15 for domestic and international students; for summer admission, 4/15 for domestic and international students. *Application fee:* $30. Electronic applications accepted. *Application Contact:* Andrew Woodall, Executive Director of Recruitment and Advancement, 540-665-4581, Fax: 540-665-4627, E-mail: admit@su.edu. *Dean*, Dr. Michael J. Stepniak, 540-542-6201, Fax: 540-665-5402, E-mail: mstepnia@su.edu.

SHEPHERDS THEOLOGICAL SEMINARY, Cary, NC 27518

General Information Independent-religious, coed, graduate-only institution. *Graduate housing:* On-campus housing not available.

GRADUATE UNITS

Graduate Programs Offers Biblical literature and languages (MA); church ministry (MA); ministry (MTS); New Testament (M Div); Old Testament (M Div); theology (M Div).

SHEPHERD UNIVERSITY, Shepherdstown, WV 25443

General Information State-supported, coed, comprehensive institution.

GRADUATE UNITS

Program in Curriculum and Instruction Offers curriculum and instruction (MA).

SHERMAN COLLEGE OF CHIROPRACTIC, Spartanburg, SC 29304-1452

General Information Independent, coed, graduate-only institution. *Graduate housing:* Room and/or apartments available to single students. *Research affiliation:* American Public Health Service (chiropractic research), Upper Cervical Research Foundation (chiropractic).

GRADUATE UNITS

Professional Program Offers chiropractic (DC). Electronic applications accepted.

SHILOH UNIVERSITY, Kalona, IA 52247

General Information Independent, coed, comprehensive institution. *Enrollment:* 59 graduate, professional, and undergraduate students; 7 full-time matriculated graduate/professional students (3 women), 29 part-time matriculated graduate/professional students (10 women). *Enrollment by degree level:* 28 master's, 8 doctoral. *Graduate faculty:* 2 full-time (0 women), 12 part-time/adjunct (2 women). *Tuition:* Full-time $3006; part-time $1503 per credit hour. Tuition and fees vary according to course level, course load and degree level. *Graduate housing:* On-campus housing not available. *Student services:* International student services, services for students with disabilities, writing training. *Library facilities:* University e-Library. *Collection:* Databases: 2.
Website: http://www.shilohuniversity.edu/

General Application Contact: Andrew Thompson, Admissions Coordinator, 319-656-2447, Fax: 319-656-2448, E-mail: admissions@shilohuniversity.edu.

GRADUATE UNITS

Graduate Programs Students: 10 full-time (3 women), 24 part-time (12 women); includes 10 minority (9 Black or African American, non-Hispanic/Latino; 1 Asian, non-Hispanic/Latino). Average age 51. 11 applicants, 91% accepted, 8 enrolled. *Faculty:* 5 full-time (1 woman), 11 part-time/adjunct (2 women). Expenses: Contact institution. *Financial support:* In 2017–18, 2 students received support. Scholarships/grants available. Financial award application deadline: 8/1; financial award applicants required to submit FAFSA. In 2017, 3 master's awarded. *Program availability:* Part-time, evening/weekend, online only, 100% online. Offers Christian ministries (M Div); leadership of church and spiritual formation (D Min); theological studies (MA). *Application deadline:* For fall admission, 6/18 priority date for domestic and international students; for spring admission, 10/22 priority date for domestic and international students; for summer admission, 2/15 priority date for domestic and international students. Applications are processed on a rolling basis. *Application fee:* $0. Electronic applications accepted. *Application Contact:* Katie Nisly, Admissions Coordinator, 319-656-2447, Fax: 319-656-2448, E-mail: admissions@shilohuniversity.edu. *Dean of Graduate Studies*, Dr. Ana Wood, 319-656-2447, Fax: 319-656-2448, E-mail: chiqui.wood@shilohuniversity.edu.

SHIPPENSBURG UNIVERSITY OF PENNSYLVANIA, Shippensburg, PA 17257-2299

General Information State-supported, coed, comprehensive institution. CGS member. *Enrollment:* 6,581 graduate, professional, and undergraduate students; 281 full-time matriculated graduate/professional students (174 women), 601 part-time matriculated graduate/professional students (336 women). *Enrollment by degree level:* 818 master's, 45 doctoral, 19 other advanced degrees. *Graduate faculty:* 149 full-time (61 women), 19 part-time/adjunct (10 women). Tuition, state resident: part-time $500 per credit. Tuition, nonresident: part-time $750 per credit. *Required fees:* $145 per credit. *Graduate housing:* On-campus housing not available. *Student services:* Campus employment opportunities, campus safety program, career counseling, child daycare facilities, exercise/wellness program, free psychological counseling, grant writing training, international student services, low-cost health insurance, multicultural affairs office, services for students with disabilities, teacher training, writing training. *Library facilities:* Ezra Lehman Memorial Library plus 1 other. *Collection:* Books: 359,138 (physical), 189,092 (digital/electronic); Serial titles: 50 (physical), 255 (digital/electronic); Databases: 106. Weekly public service hours: 97.

Computer facilities: 1,100 computers available on campus for general student use. A campuswide network can be accessed from student residence rooms and from off campus. Online class registration, personal Web pages are available.
Website: http://www.ship.edu/

General Application Contact: Maya T. Mapp, Director of Admissions, 717-477-1231, Fax: 717-477-4016, E-mail: mtmapp@ship.edu.

GRADUATE UNITS

School of Graduate Studies Students: 281 full-time (174 women), 601 part-time (336 women); includes 111 minority (53 Black or African American, non-Hispanic/Latino; 15 Asian, non-Hispanic/Latino; 32 Hispanic/Latino; 11 Two or more races, non-Hispanic/Latino), 67 international. Average age 31. 709 applicants, 69% accepted, 314 enrolled. *Faculty:* 149 full-time (61 women), 19 part-time/adjunct (10 women). Expenses: Contact institution. *Financial support:* In 2017–18, 148 students received support. Career-related internships or fieldwork, scholarships/grants, unspecified assistantships, and resident hall director and student payroll positions available. Support available to part-time students. Financial award application deadline: 3/1; financial award applicants required to submit FAFSA. In 2017, 374 master's, 84 other advanced degrees awarded. *Program availability:* Part-time, evening/weekend, 100% online, blended/hybrid learning. *Application deadline:* For fall admission, 4/30 for international students; for spring admission, 9/30 for international students. Applications are processed on a rolling basis. *Application fee:* $45. Electronic applications accepted. *Application Contact:* Maya T. Mapp, Director of Admissions, 717-477-1231, Fax: 717-477-4016, E-mail: mtmapp@ship.edu. *Associate Provost and Dean of Graduate Studies*, Dr. Tracy A. Schoolcraft, 717-477-1148, Fax: 717-477-4038, E-mail: tascho@ship.edu.

College of Arts and Sciences Students: 90 full-time (48 women), 95 part-time (49 women); includes 16 minority (9 Black or African American, non-Hispanic/Latino; 4 Hispanic/Latino; 3 Two or more races, non-Hispanic/Latino), 24 international. Average age 28. 209 applicants, 71% accepted, 69 enrolled. *Faculty:* 77 full-time (30 women), 4 part-time/adjunct (2 women). Expenses: Contact institution. *Financial support:* In 2017–18, 62 students received support. Career-related internships or fieldwork, scholarships/grants, unspecified assistantships, and resident hall director and student payroll positions available. Support available to part-time students. Financial award application deadline: 3/1; financial award applicants required to submit FAFSA. In 2017, 132 master's awarded. *Program availability:* Part-time, evening/weekend. Offers agile software engineering (Certificate); applied history (MA); arts and sciences (MA, MPA, MS, Certificate); biology (MS); communication studies (MS); computer science (MS); geoenvironmental studies (MS); IT leadership (Certificate); organizational development and leadership (MS); psychological science (MS); public administration (MPA). *Application deadline:* For fall admission, 4/30 for international students; for spring admission, 9/30 for international students. Applications are processed on a rolling basis. *Application fee:* $45. Electronic applications accepted. *Application Contact:* Maya T. Mapp, Director of Admissions, 717-477-1231, Fax: 717-477-4016, E-mail: mtmapp@ship.edu. *Dean*, Dr. James H. Mike, 717-477-1151, Fax: 717-477-4026, E-mail: jhmike@ship.edu.

College of Education and Human Services Students: 145 full-time (112 women), 305 part-time (216 women); includes 60 minority (32 Black or African American, non-Hispanic/Latino; 5 Asian, non-Hispanic/Latino; 17 Hispanic/Latino; 6 Two or more races, non-Hispanic/Latino), 21 international. Average age 32. 331 applicants, 70% accepted, 168 enrolled. *Faculty:* 49 full-time (26 women), 15 part-time/adjunct (9 women). Expenses: Contact institution. *Financial support:* In 2017–18, 72 students received support. Career-related internships or fieldwork, scholarships/grants, unspecified assistantships, and resident hall director and student payroll positions available. Support available to part-time students. Financial award application deadline: 3/1; financial award applicants required to submit FAFSA. In 2017, 137 master's awarded. *Program availability:* Part-time, evening/weekend, blended/hybrid learning. Offers college counseling (MS); college student personnel (MS); counselor education and supervision (Ed D); criminal justice (MS); curriculum and instruction (M Ed); education and human services (M Ed, MAT, MS, MSW, Ed D); educational leadership (M Ed, Ed D); mental health counseling (MS); reading (M Ed); school counseling (M Ed); social work (MSW); special education (M Ed); STEM education (MAT). *Application deadline:* For fall admission, 4/30 for international students; for spring admission, 9/30 for international students. Applications are processed on a rolling basis. *Application fee:* $45. Electronic applications accepted. *Application Contact:* Maya T. Mapp, Director of Admissions, 717-477-1231, Fax: 717-477-4016, E-mail: mtmapp@ship.edu. *Dean of the College of Education and Human Services*, Dr. Nicole R. Hill, 717-477-1373, Fax: 717-477-4012, E-mail: nrhill@ship.edu.

John L. Grove College of Business Students: 46 full-time (14 women), 201 part-time (71 women); includes 35 minority (12 Black or African American, non-Hispanic/Latino; 10 Asian, non-Hispanic/Latino; 11 Hispanic/Latino; 2 Two or more races, non-Hispanic/Latino), 22 international. Average age 32. 169 applicants, 65% accepted, 77 enrolled. *Faculty:* 23 full-time (5 women), 1 part-time/adjunct (0 women). Expenses: Contact institution. *Financial support:* In 2017–18, 14 students received support. Career-related internships or fieldwork, scholarships/grants, unspecified assistantships, and resident hall director and student payroll positions available. Support available to part-time students. Financial award application deadline: 3/1; financial award applicants required to submit FAFSA. In 2017, 105 master's, 82 other advanced degrees awarded. *Program availability:* Part-time, evening/weekend, 100% online, blended/hybrid learning. Offers advanced studies in business (Certificate); advanced supply chain and logistics management (Certificate); business administration (MBA, DBA); finance (Certificate); health care management (Certificate); management information systems (Certificate). *Application deadline:* For fall admission, 4/30 for international students; for spring admission, 9/30 for international students. Applications are processed on a rolling basis. *Application fee:* $45. Electronic applications accepted. *Application Contact:* Maya T. Mapp, Director of Admissions, 717-477-1231, Fax: 717-477-4016, E-mail: mtmapp@ship.edu. *Dean of the College of Business*, Dr. John G. Kooti, 717-477-1435, Fax: 717-477-4003, E-mail: jgkooti@ship.edu.

SHORTER UNIVERSITY, Rome, GA 30165

General Information Independent-religious, coed, comprehensive institution. *Graduate housing:* Room and/or apartments available on a first-come, first-served basis to single students; on-campus housing not available to married students. Housing application deadline: 3/30.

GRADUATE UNITS

Professional Studies *Program availability:* Evening/weekend. Offers accountancy (MAC); business administration (MBA); management (MM). Electronic applications accepted.

SH'OR YOSHUV RABBINICAL COLLEGE, Lawrence, NY 11559-1714

General Information Independent-religious, men only, comprehensive institution.

GRADUATE UNITS

Graduate Programs

SIENA COLLEGE, Loudonville, NY 12211-1462

General Information Independent-religious, coed, comprehensive institution. *Graduate housing:* On-campus housing not available.

GRADUATE UNITS

School of Business *Program availability:* Evening/weekend. Offers accounting (MS).

SIENA HEIGHTS UNIVERSITY, Adrian, MI 49221-1796

General Information Independent-religious, coed, comprehensive institution. *Graduate housing:* Rooms and/or apartments available on a first-come, first-served basis to single and married students. Housing application deadline: 5/1.

GRADUATE UNITS

Graduate College *Program availability:* Part-time, evening/weekend. Offers clinical mental health counseling (MA); educational leadership (Specialist); leadership (MA); teacher education (MA). Electronic applications accepted.

SIERRA NEVADA COLLEGE, Incline Village, NV 89451

General Information Independent, coed, comprehensive institution. *Graduate housing:* On-campus housing not available.

GRADUATE UNITS

Teacher Education Program *Program availability:* Part-time, evening/weekend, online learning. Offers advanced teaching and leadership (M Ed); elementary education (MAT); secondary education (MAT). Electronic applications accepted.

SILVER LAKE COLLEGE OF THE HOLY FAMILY, Manitowoc, WI 54220-9319

General Information Independent-religious, coed, comprehensive institution. *Graduate housing:* Room and/or apartments guaranteed to single students; on-campus housing not available to married students. Housing application deadline: 6/1.

GRADUATE UNITS

Graduate School *Program availability:* Part-time. Offers administrative leadership (MA Ed); leadership and organizational development (MS); music education-Kodaly emphasis (MM); teacher leadership (MA Ed). Electronic applications accepted.

SIMMONS COLLEGE, Boston, MA 02115

General Information Independent, Undergraduate: women only; graduate: coed, university. CGS member. *Enrollment:* 6,402 graduate, professional, and undergraduate students; 1,618 full-time matriculated graduate/professional students (1,404 women), 2,943 part-time matriculated graduate/professional students (2,605 women). *Enrollment by degree level:* 4,212 master's, 247 doctoral, 102 other advanced degrees. *Graduate faculty:* 161 full-time (124 women), 121 part-time/adjunct (97 women). *Tuition:* Full-time $20,736. *Required fees:* $55. Tuition and fees vary according to course load and program. *Graduate housing:* Room and/or apartments available on a first-come, first-served basis to single students; on-campus housing not available to married students. Typical cost: $14,800 (including board). Housing application deadline: 3/31. *Student services:* Campus employment opportunities, campus safety program, career counseling, exercise/wellness program, free psychological counseling, grant writing training, international student services, low-cost health insurance, multicultural affairs office, services for students with disabilities, writing training. *Library facilities:* Beatley Library. *Collection:* Books: 154,852 (physical), 37,362 (digital/electronic); Serial titles: 13 (physical), 278,000 (digital/electronic); Databases: 137. Weekly public service hours: 105; students can reserve study rooms. *Research affiliation:* Carnegie Corporation of New York (gender equality in higher education in Sub-Saharan African universities), Harvard Medical School (women in academic medicine), Institute for Quantitative Social Science, Harvard University (usability), Boston Children's Hospital (scholarly communication), University College London (cultural heritage and informatics), Oxfam America (gender mainstreaming).

Computer facilities: Computer purchase and lease plans are available. 570 computers available on campus for general student use. A campuswide network can be accessed from student residence rooms and from off campus. Online class registration is available.
Website: http://www.simmons.edu/

General Application Contact: Kristen Haack, Associate Vice President, Enrollment Management, 617-521-2917, Fax: 617-521-3058, E-mail: kristen.haack@simmons.edu.

GRADUATE UNITS

College of Arts and Sciences Students: 4 full-time (3 women), 39 part-time (34 women); includes 11 minority (7 Black or African American, non-Hispanic/Latino; 1 Hispanic/Latino; 3 Two or more races, non-Hispanic/Latino). Average age 26. 99 applicants, 57% accepted, 27 enrolled. *Faculty:* 19 full-time (13 women), 2 part-time/adjunct (both women). Expenses: Contact institution. *Financial support:* In 2017–18, 4 fellowships with partial tuition reimbursements, 22 teaching assistantships with partial tuition reimbursements were awarded; scholarships/grants and unspecified assistantships also available. Support available to part-time students. Financial award applicants required to submit FAFSA. In 2017, 23 master's awarded. *Program availability:* Part-time. Offers English (MA); gender/cultural studies (MA); history (MA); public health (MPH); public policy (MPP). *Application deadline:* For fall admission, 8/1 for domestic and international students; for spring admission, 12/15 for domestic and international students; for summer admission, 5/1 for domestic and international students. Applications are processed on a rolling basis. *Application fee:* $35. Electronic applications accepted. *Application Contact:* Patricia Flaherty, Director, Graduate Studies Admission, 617-521-3902, Fax: 617-521-3058, E-mail: gsa@simmons.edu. *Dean,* Dr. Leanne Doherty, 617-521-2581, E-mail: leanne.doherty@simmons.edu.

School of Library and Information Science Students: 339 full-time (287 women), 509 part-time (415 women); includes 91 minority (15 Black or African American, non-Hispanic/Latino; 18 Asian, non-Hispanic/Latino; 35 Hispanic/Latino; 23 Two or more races, non-Hispanic/Latino), 12 international. Average age 30. 533 applicants, 98% accepted, 268 enrolled. *Faculty:* 28 full-time (21 women), 34 part-time/adjunct (25 women). Expenses: Contact institution. *Financial support:* In 2017–18, 10 fellowships with partial tuition reimbursements were awarded; scholarships/grants and unspecified assistantships also available. Support available to part-time students. Financial award application deadline: 6/1; financial award applicants required to submit FAFSA. In 2017, 300 master's, 10 doctorates, 5 other advanced degrees awarded. *Program availability:* Part-time, evening/weekend, 100% online, blended/hybrid learning. Offers children's literature (MA); library and information science (MS, PhD, Certificate); writing for children (MFA). *Application deadline:* For fall admission, 3/1 for domestic and international students; for spring admission, 9/1 for domestic and international students; for summer admission, 2/1 for domestic and international students. Applications are processed on a rolling basis. *Application fee:* $65. Electronic applications accepted. *Application Contact:* Kate Benson, Director, SLIS Admission, 617-521-2801, Fax: 617-521-3192, E-mail: slisadm@simmons.edu. *Dean,* Dr. Eileen G. Abels, 617-521-2869.

School of Management Students: 7 full-time (all women), 130 part-time (118 women); includes 34 minority (14 Black or African American, non-Hispanic/Latino; 8 Asian, non-Hispanic/Latino; 10 Hispanic/Latino; 2 Two or more races, non-Hispanic/Latino), 1 international. Average age 32. 53 applicants, 68% accepted, 19 enrolled. *Faculty:* 23 full-time (15 women), 5 part-time/adjunct (all women). Expenses: Contact institution. *Financial support:* Scholarships/grants and unspecified assistantships available. Financial award applicants required to submit FAFSA. In 2017, 77 master's awarded. *Program availability:* Part-time, evening/weekend, 100% online, blended/hybrid learning. Offers business administration (MBA); health care (MBA); management (MS, MSM). *Application deadline:* For fall admission, 7/18 priority date for domestic students; for summer admission, 4/24 priority date for domestic students. Applications are processed on a rolling basis. *Application fee:* $75. Electronic applications accepted. *Associate Dean for Graduate Programs,* Patricia Deyton, 617-521-3876.

School of Nursing and Health Sciences Students: 390 full-time (350 women), 1,286 part-time (1,169 women); includes 346 minority (131 Black or African American, non-Hispanic/Latino; 6 American Indian or Alaska Native, non-Hispanic/Latino; 75 Asian, non-Hispanic/Latino; 91 Hispanic/Latino; 3 Native Hawaiian or other Pacific Islander, non-Hispanic/Latino; 40 Two or more races, non-Hispanic/Latino), 9 international. Average age 34. 1,219 applicants, 74% accepted, 481 enrolled. *Faculty:* 34 full-time (28 women), 44 part-time/adjunct (40 women). Expenses: Contact institution. *Financial support:* In 2017–18, 15 research assistantships with partial tuition reimbursements were awarded; scholarships/grants and unspecified assistantships also available. Financial award applicants required to submit FAFSA. In 2017, 423 master's, 39 doctorates, 55 other advanced degrees awarded. *Program availability:* Part-time, 100% online, blended/hybrid learning. Offers didactic dietetics (Certificate); dietetic internship (Certificate); health professions education (PhD, CAGS); nursing (MS, MSN); nursing practice (DNP); nutrition and health promotion (MS); physical therapy (DPT); sports nutrition (Certificate). *Application deadline:* For fall admission, 6/1 for international students. *Application fee:* $50. Electronic applications accepted. *Application Contact:* Brett DiMarzo, Director of Graduate Admission, 617-521-2651, Fax: 617-521-3137, E-mail: brett.dimarzo@simmons.edu. *Dean,* Dr. Judy Beal, 617-521-2139.

School of Social Work Students: 878 full-time (757 women), 979 part-time (869 women); includes 468 minority (213 Black or African American, non-Hispanic/Latino; 1 American Indian or Alaska Native, non-Hispanic/Latino; 45 Asian, non-Hispanic/Latino; 152 Hispanic/Latino; 3 Native Hawaiian or other Pacific Islander, non-Hispanic/Latino; 54 Two or more races, non-Hispanic/Latino), 12 international. Average age 30. 1,521 applicants, 74% accepted, 545 enrolled. *Faculty:* 57 full-time (47 women), 48 part-time/adjunct (36 women). Expenses: Contact institution. *Financial support:* In 2017–18, 12 fellowships with partial tuition reimbursements were awarded; scholarships/grants and unspecified assistantships also available. Support available to part-time students. Financial award applicants required to submit FAFSA. In 2017, 611 master's, 7 doctorates, 1 other advanced degree awarded. *Program availability:* Part-time, 100% online, blended/hybrid learning. Offers behavior analysis (MS, PhD, Ed S); education (MS Ed); social work (MSW, PhD); special education (MS Ed); teaching (MAT). *Application deadline:* For fall admission, 8/1 for domestic students; for spring admission, 12/15 for domestic students; for summer admission, 5/1 for domestic students. Applications are processed on a rolling basis. *Application fee:* $35. Electronic applications accepted. *Application Contact:* Carlos D. Frontado, Director of Admissions, 617-521-3920, Fax: 617-521-3980, E-mail: ssw@simmons.edu. *Dean,* Dr. Cheryl Parks, 617-521-3293, E-mail: cheryl.parks@simmons.edu.

SIMON FRASER UNIVERSITY, Burnaby, BC V5A 1S6, Canada

General Information Province-supported, coed, university. CGS member. *Graduate housing:* Room and/or apartments available on a first-come, first-served basis to single students; on-campus housing not available to married students. Housing application deadline: 12/1. *Research affiliation:* BC Cancer Agency (health sciences, biomedical sciences, physiology, kinesiology), TRIUMF (physics), Ballard Power Systems (mechatronics), Bamfield Marine Research Station (marine biology, ecology, archaeology).

GRADUATE UNITS

Office of Graduate Studies and Postdoctoral Fellows *Program availability:* Part-time, evening/weekend, online learning. Electronic applications accepted.

Faculty of Applied Sciences Offers applied sciences (M Eng, M Sc, MA Sc, PhD, Graduate Certificate); computing science (M Sc, PhD); engineering science (M Eng, MA Sc, PhD); mechatronic systems engineering (MA Sc, PhD). Electronic applications accepted.

Faculty of Arts and Social Sciences *Program availability:* Part-time, evening/weekend. Offers anthropology (MA, PhD); applied legal studies (MA); arts and social sciences (M Pub, M Sc, M Urb, MA, MALS, MPP, PhD, Graduate Certificate, Graduate Diploma); criminology (MA, PhD); economics (MA, PhD); English (MA, PhD); French (MA); gender, sexuality and women's studies (MA, PhD); gerontology (MA, PhD); history (MA, PhD); humanities (MA); international studies (MA); Latin American studies (MA, Graduate Certificate); liberal studies (MALS); linguistics (MA, PhD); philosophy (MA, PhD); political science (MA, PhD); psychology (MA, PhD); public policy (MPP); sociology (MA, PhD); teachers of English (MA); urban studies (M Urb, Graduate Diploma). Electronic applications accepted.

Faculty of Business Administration *Program availability:* Online learning. Offers business administration (EMBA, PhD, Graduate Diploma); finance (M Sc); management of technology (MBA); management of technology/biotechnology (MBA).

Faculty of Communication, Art and Technology Offers communication (MA, PhD); communication, art and technology (M Pub, M Sc, MA, MFA, PhD); contemporary arts (MA, MFA); interactive arts and technology (M Sc, MA, PhD); publishing (M Pub).

Faculty of Education Offers arts education (M Ed, MA, Ed D, PhD); counseling psychology (M Ed, MA); curriculum and instruction (M Ed); curriculum and instruction foundations (M Ed, MA); curriculum theory and implementation (PhD); education (M Ed, M Sc, MA, Ed D, PhD, Graduate Diploma); educational leadership (M Ed, MA, Ed D); educational practice (M Ed); educational psychology (M Ed, MA, PhD); educational technology and learning design (M Ed, MA, PhD); languages, cultures, and literacies (PhD); mathematics education (PhD); philosophy of education (PhD); secondary mathematics education (M Ed, M Sc); teaching English as a second/foreign language (M Ed). Electronic applications accepted.

Faculty of Environment Offers archaeology (MA, PhD); environment (M Sc, MA, MRM, PhD, Graduate Diploma); geography (M Sc, MA, PhD); quantitative methods in fisheries management (Graduate Diploma); resource and environmental management (MRM, PhD); resource and environmental planning (MRM).

Faculty of Health Sciences Offers global health (Graduate Diploma); health sciences (M Sc, PhD); public health (MPH). Electronic applications accepted.

Faculty of Science Offers actuarial science (M Sc); applied and computational mathematics (M Sc, PhD); bioinformatics (Graduate Diploma); biological sciences (M Sc, PhD); biomedical physiology and kinesiology (M Sc, PhD); chemistry (M Sc, PhD); earth sciences (M Sc, PhD); environmental toxicology (MET); mathematics (M Sc, PhD); molecular biology and biochemistry (M Sc, PhD); operations research (M Sc, PhD); pest management (MPM); physics (M Sc, PhD); science (M Sc, MET, MPM, PhD, Graduate Diploma); statistics (M Sc, PhD). Electronic applications accepted.

SIMPSON COLLEGE, Indianola, IA 50125-1297

General Information Independent-religious, coed, comprehensive institution.

GRADUATE UNITS

Department of Education Offers secondary education (MAT).

Department of Social Sciences *Program availability:* Evening/weekend. Offers criminal justice (MACJ).

SIMPSON UNIVERSITY, Redding, CA 96003-8606

General Information Independent-religious, coed, comprehensive institution. *Graduate housing:* On-campus housing not available.

GRADUATE UNITS

A.W. Tozer Theological Seminary *Program availability:* Part-time, evening/weekend, 100% online, blended/hybrid learning. Offers ministry leadership (MA). Electronic applications accepted.

School of Education *Program availability:* Part-time, evening/weekend. Offers education (MA); education and preliminary administrative services credential (MA); education and preliminary teaching credential (MA); teaching (MA). Electronic applications accepted.

School of Graduate Studies *Program availability:* Evening/weekend, 100% online, blended/hybrid learning. Offers counseling psychology (MA); organizational leadership (MA). Electronic applications accepted.

SINTE GLESKA UNIVERSITY, Mission, SD 57555

General Information Independent, coed, comprehensive institution. *Graduate housing:* Rooms and/or apartments available on a first-come, first-served basis to single and married students.

GRADUATE UNITS

Graduate Education Program *Program availability:* Part-time, evening/weekend. Offers elementary education (M Ed).

SIOUX FALLS SEMINARY, Sioux Falls, SD 57105-1599

General Information Independent-religious, coed, graduate-only institution. *Graduate housing:* On-campus housing not available.

GRADUATE UNITS

Graduate and Professional Programs *Program availability:* Part-time. Offers Bible and theology (MA); Christian leadership (MA); counseling (MA); marriage and family therapy (M Div); ministry (D Min); pastoral care and counseling (M Div); theological studies (Certificate).

SIT GRADUATE INSTITUTE, Brattleboro, VT 05302-0676

General Information Independent, coed, graduate-only institution. *Graduate housing:* Rooms and/or apartments available on a first-come, first-served basis to single and married students. Housing application deadline: 7/1.

GRADUATE UNITS

Graduate Programs *Program availability:* Part-time, online learning. Offers climate change and global sustainability (MA); global leadership and social innovation (MA); global youth development and leadership (M Ed); intercultural service, leadership, and management (self-designed) (MA); international education (MA); peace and justice leadership (MA); sustainable development (MA); teaching English as a second language (MAT). Electronic applications accepted.

SITTING BULL COLLEGE, Fort Yates, ND 58538-9701

General Information Independent, coed, comprehensive institution. *Enrollment:* 15 full-time matriculated graduate/professional students (13 women). *Enrollment by degree level:* 15 master's. *Graduate faculty:* 7 full-time (0 women). *Tuition, area resident:* Full-time $6300; part-time $350 per credit hour. *Required fees:* $310; $310 per year. $155 per semester. Tuition and fees vary according to course load. *Graduate housing:* Rooms and/or apartments available on a first-come, first-served basis to single and married students. Typical cost: $1000 per year for single students; $2000 per year for married students. Housing application deadline: 4/30. *Student services:* Career counseling, child daycare facilities, exercise/wellness program. *Library facilities:* Sitting Bull College Library.

Computer facilities: 16 computers available on campus for general student use. Website: http://www.sittingbull.edu/

General Application Contact: Dr. Mafany Mongoh, Science Faculty, 701-854-8051, Fax: 701-854-8197, E-mail: mafany.mongoh@sittingbull.edu.

GRADUATE UNITS

Graduate Programs Students: 14 full-time (13 women). 16 applicants, 100% accepted, 14 enrolled. *Faculty:* 2 full-time (0 women). Expenses: Contact institution. *Financial support:* Fellowships and scholarships/grants available. Offers curriculum and instruction (M Ed); environmental science (MS). *Application deadline:* For fall admission, 4/30 priority date for domestic students. *Application fee:* $0. *Application Contact:* Chris Fried, Division of Education Director, 701-854-8000, Fax: 701-854-8197, E-mail: travis.frank@sittingbull.edu. *Division of Education Director,* Chris Fried, 701-854-8000, Fax: 701-854-8197, E-mail: travis.frank@sittingbull.edu.

SLIPPERY ROCK UNIVERSITY OF PENNSYLVANIA, Slippery Rock, PA 16057-1383

General Information State-supported, coed, university. *Graduate housing:* Room and/or apartments available on a first-come, first-served basis to single students; on-campus housing not available to married students.

GRADUATE UNITS

Graduate Studies (Recruitment) *Program availability:* Part-time, evening/weekend, 100% online, blended/hybrid learning. Electronic applications accepted.

College of Business *Program availability:* Part-time, evening/weekend. Offers accounting/finance (MBA); business (MBA); general (MBA); marketing/management (MBA). Electronic applications accepted.

College of Education *Program availability:* Part-time, evening/weekend, 100% online. Offers adapted physical activity (MS); autism (M Ed); clinical mental health (MA); education (M Ed, MA, MS, Ed D); instructional coach (M Ed); K-12 reading (M Ed); K-12 science and math (M Ed); master teacher (M Ed); reading specialist (M Ed); school counseling (M Ed); secondary education (M Ed); special education (Ed D); student affairs in higher education (MA); student affairs in higher education with college counseling (MA); supervision (M Ed); technology for online instruction (M Ed). Electronic applications accepted.

College of Health, Environment, and Science *Program availability:* Part-time, evening/weekend, 100% online. Offers data analytics (MS); environmental education (M Ed); health informatics (MS); health, environment, and science (M Ed, MPH, MS, DPT); park and resource management (MS); physical therapy (DPT); physician assistant studies (MS); public health (MPH). Electronic applications accepted.

College of Liberal Arts *Program availability:* Part-time, evening/weekend, online only, 100% online. Offers criminal justice (MA); English (MA); history (MA); liberal arts (MA, MMT); music therapy (MMT); teaching English to speakers of other languages (MA). Electronic applications accepted.

SMITH COLLEGE, Northampton, MA 01063

General Information Independent, Undergraduate: women only; graduate: coed, comprehensive institution. *Enrollment:* 2,918 graduate, professional, and undergraduate students; 373 full-time matriculated graduate/professional students (323 women), 24 part-time matriculated graduate/professional students (18 women). *Enrollment by degree level:* 314 master's, 60 doctoral, 22 other advanced degrees. *Graduate faculty:* 276 full-time (155 women), 12 part-time/adjunct (7 women). *Tuition:* Full-time $37,440; part-time $1560 per credit. Tuition and fees vary according to course load and program. *Graduate housing:* Room and/or apartments available on a first-come, first-served basis to single students; on-campus housing not available to married students. Typical cost: $8400 per year ($16,730 including board). Housing application deadline: 5/1. *Student services:* Campus employment opportunities, campus safety program, career counseling, child daycare facilities, exercise/wellness program, international student services, low-cost health insurance, multicultural affairs office, services for students with disabilities, teacher training, writing training. *Library facilities:* Neilson Library.

Computer facilities: Computer purchase and lease plans are available. A campuswide network can be accessed. Online class registration is available. Website: http://www.smith.edu/

General Application Contact: Patricia DiBartolo, Dean of the Faculty/Dean for Academic Development, 413-585-3000, Fax: 413-585-3054, E-mail: pdibarto@smith.edu.

GRADUATE UNITS

Graduate and Special Programs Students: 12 full-time (8 women), 54 part-time (50 women); includes 15 minority (3 Black or African American, non-Hispanic/Latino; 7 Asian, non-Hispanic/Latino; 5 Hispanic/Latino), 1 international. Average age 27. 165 applicants, 52% accepted, 57 enrolled. *Faculty:* 276 full-time (155 women), 12 part-time/adjunct (7 women). Expenses: Contact institution. *Financial support:* In 2017–18, 66 students received support, including 6 fellowships with full tuition reimbursements available, 5 research assistantships with full tuition reimbursements available (averaging $13,850 per year), 11 teaching assistantships with full tuition reimbursements available (averaging $13,850 per year); scholarships/grants and human resources employee benefit also available. Support available to part-time students. Financial award application deadline: 1/15; financial award applicants required to submit CSS PROFILE or FAFSA. In 2017, 31 master's, 10 other advanced degrees awarded. *Program availability:* Part-time. Offers biological sciences (MAT, MS); dance (MFA); elementary education (MAT); exercise and sport studies (MS); middle school education (MAT); secondary education (MAT); theatre (MFA); women in mathematics (Postbaccalaureate Certificate). *Application deadline:* For fall admission, 1/15 for domestic and international students; for spring admission, 12/1 for domestic students. *Application fee:* $60. *Application Contact:* Ruth Morgan, Program Assistant, 413-585-3050, Fax: 413-585-3054, E-mail: gradstdy@smith.edu. *Director,* Danielle Ramdath, 413-585-3050, Fax: 413-585-3054, E-mail: dramdath@smith.edu.

School for Social Work Students: 272 full-time (236 women), 53 part-time (43 women); includes 85 minority (26 Black or African American, non-Hispanic/Latino; 3 American Indian or Alaska Native, non-Hispanic/Latino; 21 Asian, non-Hispanic/Latino; 28 Hispanic/Latino; 7 Two or more races, non-Hispanic/Latino), 9 international. Average age 32. 400 applicants, 64% accepted, 128 enrolled. *Faculty:* 36 full-time (26 women), 223 part-time/adjunct (178 women). Expenses: Contact institution. *Financial support:* In 2017–18, 265 students received support. Career-related internships or fieldwork and scholarships/grants available. Financial award application deadline: 3/1; financial award applicants required to submit FAFSA. In 2017, 101 master's, 6 doctorates awarded. Offers clinical social work (MSW, PhD). *Application deadline:* For fall admission, 2/21 for domestic students, 2/15 for international students. Applications are processed on a rolling basis. *Application fee:* $60. Electronic applications accepted. *Application Contact:* Irene Rodriguez Martin, Associate Dean, Graduate Enrollment and Student Services, 413-585-7960, Fax: 413-585-7994, E-mail: imartin@smith.edu. *Dean/Professor,* Dr. Marianne Yoshioka, 413-585-7977, E-mail: myoshioka@smith.edu.

SOFIA UNIVERSITY, Palo Alto, CA 94303

General Information Independent, coed, graduate-only institution. *Graduate housing:* On-campus housing not available.

GRADUATE UNITS

Hybrid: Face-to-Face/Online Programs *Program availability:* Online learning. Offers transpersonal psychology (MA, PhD). Electronic applications accepted.

Residential Programs *Program availability:* Part-time, evening/weekend. Offers clinical psychology (Psy D); computer science (MS); counseling psychology (MA); transpersonal psychology (MA, PhD). Electronic applications accepted.

SOKA UNIVERSITY OF AMERICA, Aliso Viejo, CA 92656

General Information Independent, coed, comprehensive institution. *Graduate housing:* Room and/or apartments available to single students; on-campus housing not available to married students.

GRADUATE UNITS

Graduate School *Program availability:* Evening/weekend. Offers educational leadership and societal change (MA).

SONOMA STATE UNIVERSITY, Rohnert Park, CA 94928-3609

General Information State-supported, coed, comprehensive institution. *Enrollment:* 9,223 graduate, professional, and undergraduate students; 365 full-time matriculated graduate/professional students (270 women), 307 part-time matriculated graduate/professional students (215 women). *Graduate faculty:* 58 full-time (29 women), 31 part-time/adjunct (24 women). *Graduate housing:* Room and/or apartments available on a first-come, first-served basis to single students; on-campus housing not available to married students. Housing application deadline: 1/1. *Student services:* Campus employment opportunities, career counseling, child daycare facilities, exercise/wellness program, free psychological counseling, international student services, multicultural affairs office, services for students with disabilities. *Library facilities:* Jean and Charles Schultz Information Center plus 1 other. *Collection:* Students can reserve study rooms. *Research affiliation:* Biomimetica (bioacoustics, metabolic flux modeling), Gallo Family Vineyards (science), Kenwood Vineyards (science), Natural Industries, Inc. (Sudden Oak Death research), Clean Filtration Technologies (environmental microbiology).

Computer facilities: A campuswide network can be accessed from student residence rooms and from off campus. Online class registration is available. Website: http://www.sonoma.edu/

General Application Contact: David Hartranft, Analyst, Academic Programs, 707-664-2237, Fax: 707-664-4060, E-mail: david.hartranft@sonoma.edu.

GRADUATE UNITS

Department of English Expenses: Contact institution. *Financial support:* Fellowships, teaching assistantships, career-related internships or fieldwork, and Federal Work-Study available. Financial award application deadline: 3/2; financial award applicants required to submit FAFSA. *Program availability:* Part-time, evening/weekend. Offers American literature (MA); creative writing (MA); English literature (MA); world literature (MA). *Application deadline:* For fall admission, 11/30 priority date for domestic students. *Application fee:* $55. *Application Contact:* Dr. Stefan Kiesbye, Chair of Graduate Studies, 707-664-2403, Fax: 707-664-6040, E-mail: kiesbye@sonoma.edu. *Chair,* Brantley L. Bryant, 707-664-2164, E-mail: brantley.bryant@sonoma.edu.

School of Business and Economics Expenses: Contact institution. *Financial support:* Career-related internships or fieldwork, Federal Work-Study, institutionally sponsored loans, and scholarships/grants available. Support available to part-time students. Financial award application deadline: 3/2; financial award applicants required to submit FAFSA. *Program availability:* Part-time, evening/weekend. Offers wine business (Exec MBA, MBA). *Application deadline:* For fall admission, 1/31 priority date for domestic students; for spring admission, 8/31 for domestic students. Applications are processed on a rolling basis. *Application fee:* $55. *Application Contact:* John Stayton, Executive Director, Graduate and Executive Programs, 707-664-3954, E-mail: john.stayton@sonoma.edu. *Dean,* Karen Thompson, 707-664-2220.

School of Education Expenses: Contact institution. *Financial support:* Fellowships, research assistantships, career-related internships or fieldwork, and Federal Work-Study available. Support available to part-time students. Financial award application deadline: 3/2; financial award applicants required to submit FAFSA. *Program availability:* Part-time, evening/weekend. Offers administrative services (Credential); curriculum, teaching, and learning (MA); early childhood education (MA); education specialist (Credential); educational leadership (MA); multiple subject (Credential); reading and literacy (MA, Credential); single subject (Credential); special education (MA). *Application fee:* $55. *Application Contact:* Dr. Karen Grady, Coordinator of Graduate Studies, 707-664-3328, E-mail: karen.grady@sonoma.edu. *Dean,* Dr. Carlos Ayala, 707-664-4412, E-mail: carlos.ayala@sonoma.edu.

School of Science and Technology Expenses: Contact institution. *Financial support:* Fellowships, research assistantships, teaching assistantships, career-related internships or fieldwork, Federal Work-Study, and tuition waivers (full) available. Support available to part-time students. Financial award application deadline: 3/2; financial award applicants required to submit FAFSA. *Program availability:* Part-time. Offers biochemistry (MA); exercise science/pre-physical therapy (MA); family nurse practitioner (MSN); interdisciplinary (MA); interdisciplinary pre-occupational therapy (MA); lifetime physical activity (MA); science and technology (MA, MS, MSN). *Application deadline:* For fall admission, 11/30 for domestic students. *Application fee:* $55. *Application Contact:* Dr. Farid Farahmand, Coordinator of Graduate Studies, 707-664-3491, E-mail: farahman@sonoma.edu. *Dean,* Lynn Stauffer, 707-664-2171, E-mail: lynn.stauffer@sonoma.edu.

School of Social Sciences Expenses: Contact institution. *Financial support:* Fellowships, research assistantships, teaching assistantships, career-related internships or fieldwork, and Federal Work-Study available. Support available to part-time students. Financial award application deadline: 3/2. *Program availability:* Part-time, evening/weekend. Offers clinical mental health counseling (MA); cultural resources management (MA); history (MA); public administration (MPA); school counseling (MA); social sciences (MA, MPA, Certificate). *Application deadline:* For fall admission, 11/30 for domestic students. *Application fee:* $55. *Application Contact:* Elaine Sundberg, Associate Vice President, Academic Programs and Graduate Studies, 707-664-2215, Fax: 707-664-4060, E-mail: elaine.sundberg@sonoma.edu. *Dean,* John Wingard, 707-664-2112, E-mail: wingard@sonoma.edu.

SOTHEBY'S INSTITUTE OF ART–LONDON, WC1B 3EE London, United Kingdom

General Information Private, coed, graduate-only institution. *Graduate housing:* On-campus housing not available. *Research affiliation:* University of Manchester.

GRADUATE UNITS

Graduate Programs Offers art business (MA); contemporary art (MA); fine and decorative art and design (MA); modern and contemporary Asian art (MA). Electronic applications accepted.

SOTHEBY'S INSTITUTE OF ART–NEW YORK, New York, NY 10021

General Information Proprietary, coed, graduate-only institution. *Graduate housing:* On-campus housing not available.

GRADUATE UNITS

Graduate Programs Offers art business (MA); contemporary art (MA); fine and decorative art and design (MA). Electronic applications accepted.

SOUTH BAYLO UNIVERSITY, Anaheim, CA 92801-1701

General Information Independent, coed, graduate-only institution. *Graduate housing:* On-campus housing not available. *Research affiliation:* University of California Irvine College of Medicine (complimentary and alternative medicine), National Nutritional Foods Association (herbs and nutritional supplements), Henan College of Traditional Chinese Medicine (herbology and acupuncture), Kaiser Permanente (patient care: acupuncture and Oriental medicine), University of Illinois at Chicago (testing of herbal formulations).

GRADUATE UNITS

Program in Oriental Medicine and Acupuncture *Program availability:* Evening/weekend. Offers Oriental medicine and acupuncture (MS). Electronic applications accepted.

SOUTH CAROLINA STATE UNIVERSITY, Orangeburg, SC 29117-0001

General Information State-supported, coed, comprehensive institution. *Enrollment:* 240 full-time matriculated graduate/professional students (193 women), 153 part-time matriculated graduate/professional students (101 women). *Enrollment by degree level:* 292 master's, 61 doctoral, 40 other advanced degrees. *Graduate faculty:* 43 full-time (25 women), 19 part-time/adjunct (13 women). Tuition, state resident: full-time $9388; part-time $607 per credit hour. Tuition, nonresident: full-time $19,968; part-time $1194 per credit hour. *Required fees:* $766; $766 per credit hour. *Graduate housing:* Room and/or apartments available on a first-come, first-served basis to single students; on-campus housing not available to married students. Typical cost: $7150 per year ($10,440 including board). Room and board charges vary according to board plan and housing facility selected. Housing application deadline: 7/31. *Student services:* Campus employment opportunities, career counseling, exercise/wellness program, free psychological counseling, international student services, low-cost health insurance, multicultural affairs office, services for students with disabilities, teacher training, writing training. *Library facilities:* Miller F. Whittaker Library. *Collection:* Books: 317,233 (physical), 195,578 (digital/electronic); Serial titles: 18,334 (digital/electronic); Databases: 114. Weekly public service hours: 74; students can reserve study rooms.

Computer facilities: 600 computers available on campus for general student use. A campuswide network can be accessed from student residence rooms. Online class registration is available.
Website: http://www.scsu.edu/

General Application Contact: Dr. Frederick Evans, Dean, College of Graduate and Professional Studies, 803-536-7097, Fax: 803-536-8812, E-mail: fevans6@scsu.edu.

GRADUATE UNITS

College of Graduate and Professional Studies Students: 240 full-time (193 women), 153 part-time (101 women); includes 344 minority (343 Black or African American, non-Hispanic/Latino; 1 American Indian or Alaska Native, non-Hispanic/Latino), 2 international. Average age 33. 234 applicants, 80% accepted, 166 enrolled. *Faculty:* 43 full-time (25 women), 19 part-time/adjunct (13 women). Expenses: Contact institution. *Financial support:* Fellowships, career-related internships or fieldwork, Federal Work-Study, scholarships/grants, and unspecified assistantships available. Financial award application deadline: 6/1. In 2017, 97 master's, 7 doctorates, 10 other advanced degrees awarded. *Program availability:* Part-time, evening/weekend. Offers counselor education (M Ed); early childhood education (MAT); education (M Ed); educational leadership and administration (Ed D, Ed S); elementary education (M Ed, MAT); English (MAT); general science/biology (MAT); individual and family development (MS); mathematics (MAT); nutritional sciences (MS); rehabilitation counseling (MA); secondary education (M Ed); special education (M Ed); speech pathology and audiology (MA); transportation (MS). *Application deadline:* For fall admission, 6/15 for domestic and international students; for spring admission, 11/1 for domestic and international students. *Application fee:* $25. Electronic applications accepted. *Application Contact:* Curtis Foskey, Coordinator of Graduate Admission, 803-536-8419, Fax: 803-536-8812, E-mail: cfoskey@scsu.edu. *Dean, College of Graduate and Professional Studies,* Dr. Frederick Evans, 803-536-7097, Fax: 803-536-8812, E-mail: fevans6@scsu.edu.

School of Business Students: 20 full-time (10 women), 11 part-time (7 women); all minorities (all Black or African American, non-Hispanic/Latino). Average age 27. 12 applicants, 92% accepted, 11 enrolled. *Faculty:* 7 full-time (3 women), 2 part-time/adjunct (0 women). Expenses: Contact institution. *Financial support:* Fellowships, research assistantships, career-related internships or fieldwork, Federal Work-Study, scholarships/grants, and unspecified assistantships available. Financial award application deadline: 6/1. In 2017, 10 master's awarded. *Program availability:* Part-time, evening/weekend. Offers agribusiness (MBA); entrepreneurship (MBA); general business administration (MBA); healthcare management (MBA). *Application deadline:* For fall admission, 6/15 for domestic and international students; for spring admission, 11/1 for domestic and international students. *Application fee:* $25. Electronic applications accepted. *Application Contact:* Ellen R. Ricoma, MBA Program Director, 803-533-3777, Fax: 803-516-4651, E-mail: ericoma1@scsu.edu. *Interim Chair,* Dr. David Jamison, 803-536-8443, Fax: 803-536-8078, E-mail: djamison@scsu.edu.

SOUTH COLLEGE, Knoxville, TN 37917

General Information Proprietary, coed, primarily women, comprehensive institution.

GRADUATE UNITS

Program in Pharmacy Offers pharmacy (Pharm D).

Program in Physician Assistant Studies Offers physician assistant studies (MHS).

SOUTH DAKOTA SCHOOL OF MINES AND TECHNOLOGY, Rapid City, SD 57701-3995

General Information State-supported, coed, university. *Graduate housing:* Room and/or apartments available on a first-come, first-served basis to single students; on-campus housing not available to married students. *Research affiliation:* Raven Industries (composite and thin films), Black Hills Power (NDA-Lightning (experimental and data collection)), CalxAqua (filtration media), RESPEC, Inc. (mining and waste storage), HF Webster (cold spray applications), Nanofiber Sperations (cutting edge separation media composed of functionalized nanofibers).

GRADUATE UNITS

Graduate Division *Program availability:* Part-time. Offers atmospheric and environmental sciences (MS, PhD); biomedical engineering (MS, PhD); chemical and biological engineering (PhD); chemical engineering (MS); civil and environmental engineering (MS, PhD); computational sciences and robotics (MS); construction engineering management (MS); electrical engineering (MS); engineering management (MS); geology and geological engineering (MS, PhD); materials engineering and science (MS, PhD); mechanical engineering (MS, PhD); mining engineering (MS); nanoscience and nanoengineering (PhD); paleontology (MS); physics (MS, PhD). Electronic applications accepted.

College of Engineering *Program availability:* Part-time, online learning. Offers engineering (MS, PhD). Electronic applications accepted.

College of Science and Letters *Program availability:* Part-time. Offers science and letters (MS, PhD).

SOUTH DAKOTA STATE UNIVERSITY, Brookings, SD 57007

General Information State-supported, coed, university. CGS member. *Graduate housing:* Rooms and/or apartments available to single and married students.

GRADUATE UNITS

Graduate School *Program availability:* Part-time, evening/weekend, online learning.

College of Agriculture and Biological Sciences *Program availability:* Part-time. Offers agricultural and biosystems engineering (MS, PhD); agriculture and biological sciences (MS, PhD); agronomy (PhD); animal science (MS, PhD); animal sciences (MS, PhD); biological sciences (MS, PhD); economics (MS); plant science (MS); sociology (MS, PhD); wildlife and fisheries sciences (MS, PhD).

College of Arts and Science *Program availability:* Part-time. Offers arts and science (MA, MS, PhD); chemistry (MS, PhD); communication studies and journalism (MS); English (MA); geography (MS); industrial/organizational psychology (MS).

College of Education and Human Sciences Offers agricultural education (MS); athletic training (MS); counseling and human resource development (M Ed, MS); curriculum and instruction (M Ed); dietetics (MS); education and human sciences (M Ed, MFCS, MS, PhD); educational administration (M Ed); family financial planning (MS); human sciences (MS); merchandising (MS); nutrition and exercise sciences (MS, PhD); sport and recreation studies (MS).

College of Engineering *Program availability:* Part-time. Offers agricultural, biosystems and mechanical engineering (PhD); biological sciences (MS, PhD); computational science and statistics (PhD); electrical engineering (PhD); engineering (MS);

geospatial science and engineering (PhD); industrial management (MS); mathematics (MS); statistics (MS).

College of Nursing *Program availability:* Part-time, evening/weekend, online learning. Offers nursing (MS, PhD).

College of Pharmacy and Allied Health Professions Offers biological science (MS); pharmaceutical sciences (PhD); pharmacy (Pharm D); pharmacy and allied health professions (MS, PhD, Pharm D).

SOUTHEASTERN BAPTIST THEOLOGICAL SEMINARY, Wake Forest, NC 27587

General Information Independent-religious, coed, comprehensive institution. *Graduate housing:* Rooms and/or apartments available on a first-come, first-served basis to single and married students.

GRADUATE UNITS

Graduate and Professional Programs Offers advanced biblical studies (M Div); Christian education (M Div, MACE); Christian ethics (PhD); Christian ministry (M Div); Christian planting (M Div); church music (MACM); counseling (MACO); evangelism (PhD); language (M Div); ministry (D Min); New Testament (PhD); Old Testament (PhD); philosophy (PhD); theology (Th M, PhD); women's studies (M Div).

SOUTHEASTERN LOUISIANA UNIVERSITY, Hammond, LA 70402

General Information State-supported, coed, comprehensive institution. *Enrollment:* 14,308 graduate, professional, and undergraduate students; 361 full-time matriculated graduate/professional students (254 women), 607 part-time matriculated graduate/professional students (477 women). *Enrollment by degree level:* 750 master's, 122 doctoral, 96 other advanced degrees. *Graduate faculty:* 138 full-time (68 women), 14 part-time/adjunct (9 women). Tuition, state resident: full-time $6684. Tuition, nonresident: full-time $19,162. *Required fees:* $2088. *Graduate housing:* Room and/or apartments available on a first-come, first-served basis to single students; on-campus housing not available to married students. Typical cost: $4800 per year ($8464 including board). Room and board charges vary according to board plan, campus/location and housing facility selected. Housing application deadline: 6/15. *Student services:* Campus employment opportunities, campus safety program, career counseling, exercise/wellness program, free psychological counseling, international student services, low-cost health insurance, multicultural affairs office, services for students with disabilities, teacher training, writing training. *Library facilities:* Linus A. Sims Memorial Library plus 1 other. *Collection:* Books: 1.5 million (physical), 368,573 (digital/electronic); Serial titles: 768 (physical), 344 (digital/electronic). Students can reserve study rooms. *Research affiliation:* Bradken Manufacturing (steel), Petroleum Research Fund (chemistry), Gaylord Chemical Company (chemical manufacturing), Ochsner Medical Center (medicine), Lake Ponchartrain Basin Foundation (water quality and wetland ecology).

Computer facilities: 1,031 computers available on campus for general student use. A campuswide network can be accessed from student residence rooms and from off campus. Online class registration, campus Webmail, student newspaper, transcripts, bookstore are available.
Website: http://www.southeastern.edu/

General Application Contact: John Boulahanb, Director of Graduate Studies, 985-549-2610, Fax: 985-549-5882, E-mail: graduatestudies@southeastern.edu.

GRADUATE UNITS

College of Arts, Humanities and Social Sciences Students: 71 full-time (45 women), 74 part-time (38 women); includes 32 minority (10 Black or African American, non-Hispanic/Latino; 2 Asian, non-Hispanic/Latino; 11 Hispanic/Latino; 9 Two or more races, non-Hispanic/Latino), 9 international. Average age 27. 97 applicants, 59% accepted, 39 enrolled. *Faculty:* 46 full-time (13 women), 7 part-time/adjunct (3 women). Expenses: Contact institution. *Financial support:* In 2017–18, 73 students received support, including 30 teaching assistantships (averaging $7,782 per year); research assistantships, career-related internships or fieldwork, institutionally sponsored loans, scholarships/grants, tuition waivers (full), and unspecified assistantships also available. Support available to part-time students. Financial award application deadline: 5/1; financial award applicants required to submit FAFSA. In 2017, 55 master's awarded. *Program availability:* Part-time. Offers arts, humanities and social sciences (M Mus, MA, MS); choral conducting (M Mus); creative writing (MA); criminal justice (MS); globalization and sustainability (MS); health communications (MA); history (MA); industrial/organizational psychology (MA); instrumental conducting (M Mus); journalism (MA); language and theory (MA); marketing (MA); music performance (M Mus); music theory (M Mus); professional writing (MA); public relations (MA); publishing studies (MA); sociology (MA). *Application deadline:* For fall admission, 7/15 priority date for domestic students, 6/1 priority date for international students; for spring admission, 12/1 priority date for domestic students, 10/1 priority date for international students. Applications are processed on a rolling basis. *Application fee:* $20 ($30 for international students). Electronic applications accepted. *Application Contact:* Amanda Harper, Graduate Admissions Analyst, 985-549-5620, Fax: 985-549-5632, E-mail: admissions@southeastern.edu. *Dean,* Dr. Karen Fontenot, 985-549-2101, Fax: 985-549-5014, E-mail: kfontenot@southeastern.edu.

College of Business Students: 77 full-time (39 women), 24 part-time (16 women); includes 14 minority (3 Black or African American, non-Hispanic/Latino; 1 Asian, non-Hispanic/Latino; 7 Hispanic/Latino; 3 Two or more races, non-Hispanic/Latino), 8 international. Average age 26. 62 applicants, 66% accepted, 31 enrolled. *Faculty:* 14 full-time (1 woman). Expenses: Contact institution. *Financial support:* In 2017–18, 39 students received support, including 31 teaching assistantships (averaging $8,523 per year); career-related internships or fieldwork, Federal Work-Study, institutionally sponsored loans, scholarships/grants, and unspecified assistantships also available. Support available to part-time students. Financial award application deadline: 5/1; financial award applicants required to submit FAFSA. In 2017, 60 master's awarded. Offers business (MBA). *Application deadline:* For fall admission, 7/15 priority date for domestic students, 6/1 priority date for international students; for spring admission, 12/1 priority date for domestic students, 10/1 priority date for international students. Applications are processed on a rolling basis. *Application fee:* $20 ($30 for international students). Electronic applications accepted. *Application Contact:* Amanda Harper, Graduate Admissions Analyst, 985-549-5620, Fax: 985-549-5882, E-mail: admissions@southeastern.edu. *Dean,* Dr. Antoinette Phillips, 985-549-2258, Fax: 985-549-5038, E-mail: business@southeastern.edu.

College of Education Students: 24 full-time (20 women), 274 part-time (230 women); includes 85 minority (63 Black or African American, non-Hispanic/Latino; 11 Hispanic/Latino; 11 Two or more races, non-Hispanic/Latino), 2 international. Average age 38. 94 applicants, 55% accepted, 44 enrolled. *Faculty:* 24 full-time (18 women), 3 part-time/adjunct (2 women). Expenses: Contact institution. *Financial support:* In 2017–18, 19 students received support, including 6 teaching assistantships (averaging $8,276 per year); research assistantships, career-related internships or fieldwork, Federal Work-Study, institutionally sponsored loans, scholarships/grants, and unspecified assistantships also available. Support available to part-time students. Financial award application deadline: 5/1; financial award applicants required to submit FAFSA. In 2017, 73 master's, 2 doctorates awarded. *Program availability:* Part-time. Offers curriculum and instruction (M Ed); education (M Ed, MAT, Ed D); educational leadership (M Ed, Ed D); elementary education (MAT); special education (M Ed); special education: early interventionist (MAT). *Application deadline:* For fall admission, 7/15 priority date for domestic students, 6/1 priority date for international students; for spring admission, 12/1 priority date for domestic students, 10/1 priority date for international students. Applications are processed on a rolling basis. *Application fee:* $20 ($30 for international students). Electronic applications accepted. *Application Contact:* Amanda Harper, Graduate Admissions Analyst, 985-549-5620, Fax: 985-549-5632, E-mail: admissions@southeastern.edu. *Dean,* Dr. Paula Calderon, 985-549-2217, Fax: 985-549-2070, E-mail: paula.calderon@southeastern.edu.

College of Nursing and Health Sciences Students: 158 full-time (134 women), 190 part-time (158 women); includes 88 minority (37 Black or African American, non-Hispanic/Latino; 3 Asian, non-Hispanic/Latino; 29 Hispanic/Latino; 2 Native Hawaiian or other Pacific Islander, non-Hispanic/Latino; 17 Two or more races, non-Hispanic/Latino), 1 international. Average age 31. 68 applicants, 49% accepted, 23 enrolled. *Faculty:* 38 full-time (32 women), 5 part-time/adjunct (4 women). Expenses: Contact institution. *Financial support:* In 2017–18, 71 students received support, including 8 research assistantships (averaging $9,315 per year), 4 teaching assistantships (averaging $9,682 per year); career-related internships or fieldwork, Federal Work-Study, institutionally sponsored loans, scholarships/grants, and unspecified assistantships also available. Support available to part-time students. Financial award application deadline: 5/1; financial award applicants required to submit FAFSA. In 2017, 109 master's, 13 doctorates awarded. *Program availability:* Part-time. Offers communication sciences and disorders (MS); counseling (MS); kinesiology and health studies (MS); nursing and health sciences (MS, MSN, DNP). *Application deadline:* For fall admission, 7/15 priority date for domestic students, 6/1 priority date for international students; for spring admission, 12/1 priority date for domestic students, 10/1 priority date for international students. Applications are processed on a rolling basis. *Application fee:* $20 ($30 for international students). Electronic applications accepted. *Application Contact:* Amanda Harper, Graduate Admissions Analyst, 985-549-5620, Fax: 985-549-5632, E-mail: admissions@southeastern.edu. *Dean,* Dr. Ann Carruth, 985-549-3772, Fax: 985-549-5179, E-mail: acarruth@southeastern.edu.

School of Nursing Students: 29 full-time (26 women), 133 part-time (111 women); includes 29 minority (14 Black or African American, non-Hispanic/Latino; 2 Asian, non-Hispanic/Latino; 12 Hispanic/Latino; 1 Two or more races, non-Hispanic/Latino), 1 international. Average age 35. 68 applicants, 49% accepted, 23 enrolled. *Faculty:* 17 full-time (16 women), 2 part-time/adjunct (1 woman). Expenses: Contact institution. *Financial support:* In 2017–18, 23 students received support. Federal Work-Study, institutionally sponsored loans, scholarships/grants, traineeships, tuition waivers (full), and unspecified assistantships available. Support available to part-time students. Financial award application deadline: 5/1; financial award applicants required to submit FAFSA. In 2017, 45 master's, 13 doctorates awarded. *Program availability:* Part-time. Offers nursing (MSN); nursing practice (DNP). *Application deadline:* For fall admission, 7/15 priority date for domestic students, 6/1 priority date for international students; for spring admission, 12/1 priority date for domestic students, 10/1 priority date for international students. Applications are processed on a rolling basis. *Application fee:* $20 ($30 for international students). Electronic applications accepted. *Application Contact:* Sandra Meyers, Graduate Admissions Analyst, 985-549-5620, Fax: 985-549-5632, E-mail: admissions@southeastern.edu. *Department Head, School of Nursing,* Dr. Eileen Creel, 985-549-2156, Fax: 985-549-2869, E-mail: eileen.creel@southeastern.edu.

College of Science and Technology Students: 29 full-time (14 women), 10 part-time (4 women); includes 8 minority (1 Asian, non-Hispanic/Latino; 6 Hispanic/Latino; 1 Two or more races, non-Hispanic/Latino), 9 international. Average age 27. 45 applicants, 51% accepted, 14 enrolled. *Faculty:* 17 full-time (4 women). Expenses: Contact institution. *Financial support:* In 2017–18, 18 students received support, including 5 fellowships (averaging $10,800 per year), 5 research assistantships (averaging $10,100 per year), 9 teaching assistantships (averaging $10,100 per year); career-related internships or fieldwork, Federal Work-Study, institutionally sponsored loans, and unspecified assistantships also available. Support available to part-time students. Financial award application deadline: 5/1; financial award applicants required to submit FAFSA. In 2017, 22 master's awarded. *Program availability:* Part-time. Offers biology (MS); integrated science and technology (MS); science and technology (MS). *Application deadline:* For fall admission, 7/15 priority date for domestic students, 6/1 priority date for international students; for spring admission, 12/1 priority date for domestic students, 10/1 priority date for international students. Applications are processed on a rolling basis. *Application fee:* $20 ($30 for international students). Electronic applications accepted. *Application Contact:* Amanda Harper, Graduate Admissions Analyst, 985-549-5620, Fax: 985-549-5632, E-mail: admissions@southeastern.edu. *Dean,* Dr. Daniel McCarthy, 985-549-2055, Fax: 985-549-3396, E-mail: dmccarthy@southeastern.edu.

SOUTHEASTERN OKLAHOMA STATE UNIVERSITY, Durant, OK 74701-0609

General Information State-supported, coed, comprehensive institution. *Graduate housing:* Rooms and/or apartments available on a first-come, first-served basis to single and married students. Housing application deadline: 6/15. *Research affiliation:* U.S. Department of the Interior (biological sciences), U.S. Department of Agriculture (USDA) (biological sciences), National Science Foundation (chemistry, computer science, physical sciences), U.S. Fish and Wildlife Service (biological sciences), National Institutes of Health (biological sciences, chemistry, computer science, physical sciences).

GRADUATE UNITS

Department of Aviation Science *Program availability:* Part-time, evening/weekend. Offers aerospace administration and logistics (MS). Electronic applications accepted.

John Massey School of Business *Program availability:* Part-time, evening/weekend. Offers business (MBA). Electronic applications accepted.

School of Arts and Sciences *Program availability:* Part-time, evening/weekend. Offers biology (MT); computer information systems (MT); occupational safety and health (MT). Electronic applications accepted.

School of Behavioral Sciences *Program availability:* Part-time, evening/weekend. Offers clinical mental health counseling (MS). Electronic applications accepted.

School of Education *Program availability:* Part-time, evening/weekend. Offers math specialist (M Ed); reading specialist (M Ed); school administration (M Ed); school counseling (M Ed). Electronic applications accepted.

SOUTHEASTERN UNIVERSITY, Lakeland, FL 33801-6099

General Information Independent-religious, coed, comprehensive institution. *Enrollment:* 7,163 graduate, professional, and undergraduate students; 391 full-time matriculated graduate/professional students (249 women), 532 part-time matriculated graduate/professional students (313 women). *Enrollment by degree level:* 747 master's, 144 doctoral. *Graduate faculty:* 49 full-time (18 women), 37 part-time/adjunct (13 women). *Graduate housing:* On-campus housing not available. *Student services:* Campus employment opportunities, campus safety program, career counseling, exercise/wellness program, free psychological counseling, international student services, low-cost health insurance, services for students with disabilities, writing training. *Library facilities:* Steelman Library. *Collection:* Books: 79,844 (physical), 215,769 (digital/electronic).

Computer facilities: 220 computers available on campus for general student use. A campuswide network can be accessed from student residence rooms and from off campus. Online class registration, network programs are available.
Website: http://www.seu.edu/

GRADUATE UNITS

Barnett College of Ministry and Theology Students: 81 full-time (28 women), 131 part-time (49 women); includes 63 minority (31 Black or African American, non-Hispanic/Latino; 7 Asian, non-Hispanic/Latino; 24 Hispanic/Latino; 1 Two or more races, non-Hispanic/Latino), 4 international. Average age 38. *Faculty:* 22 full-time (5 women), 10 part-time/adjunct (9 women). Expenses: Contact institution. *Program availability:* Evening/weekend, online learning. Offers family ministry (MA); ministerial leadership (MA, D Min); theological studies (MA); theology (M Div). *Application fee:* $50. Electronic applications accepted. *Dean*, 863-667-5000.

College of Behavioral and Social Sciences Students: 72 full-time (60 women), 9 part-time (all women); includes 28 minority (12 Black or African American, non-Hispanic/Latino; 2 Asian, non-Hispanic/Latino; 13 Hispanic/Latino; 1 Native Hawaiian or other Pacific Islander, non-Hispanic/Latino), 1 international. Average age 29. *Faculty:* 9 full-time (6 women), 7 part-time/adjunct (4 women). Expenses: Contact institution. *Program availability:* Evening/weekend. Offers human services (MA); international community development (MA); marriage and family counseling (MS); professional counseling (MS); school counseling (MS); social work (MSW). *Application fee:* $50. Electronic applications accepted. *Dean*, Erica H. Sirrine, 863-667-5341, E-mail: ehsirrine@seu.edu.

College of Education Students: 139 full-time (109 women), 225 part-time (172 women); includes 107 minority (57 Black or African American, non-Hispanic/Latino; 2 Asian, non-Hispanic/Latino; 48 Hispanic/Latino), 4 international. Average age 40. *Faculty:* 8 full-time (5 women), 12 part-time/adjunct (7 women). Expenses: Contact institution. Offers curriculum and instruction (Ed D); educational leadership (M Ed); elementary education (M Ed); exceptional student education (M Ed); exceptional student education/educational therapy (M Ed); kinesiology (M Ed); organizational leadership (Ed D); reading education (M Ed); teaching English to speakers of other languages (M Ed). *Application fee:* $50. Electronic applications accepted. *Dean*, James A. Anderson, 863-667-5366, E-mail: jaanderson2@seu.edu.

Jannetides College of Business and Entrepreneurial Leadership Students: 80 full-time (38 women), 110 part-time (54 women); includes 51 minority (18 Black or African American, non-Hispanic/Latino; 5 Asian, non-Hispanic/Latino; 28 Hispanic/Latino), 7 international. Average age 31. *Faculty:* 10 full-time (2 women), 8 part-time/adjunct (1 woman). Expenses: Contact institution. *Program availability:* Evening/weekend, online learning. Offers executive leadership (MBA); global business administration (MBA); healthcare administration (MBA); missional leadership (MBA); organizational leadership (PhD); sport management (MBA); strategic leadership (DSL). *Application fee:* $50. Electronic applications accepted. *Dean*, Lyle L. Bowlin, 863-667-5118, E-mail: llbowlin@seu.edu.

SOUTHEAST MISSOURI STATE UNIVERSITY, Cape Girardeau, MO 63701-4799

General Information State-supported, coed, comprehensive institution. CGS member. *Enrollment:* 11,502 graduate, professional, and undergraduate students; 375 full-time matriculated graduate/professional students (246 women), 661 part-time matriculated graduate/professional students (437 women). *Enrollment by degree level:* 946 master's, 13 doctoral, 77 other advanced degrees. *Graduate faculty:* 220 full-time (111 women), 35 part-time/adjunct (27 women). Tuition, state resident: part-time $270.34 per credit hour. Tuition, nonresident: part-time $504 per credit hour. *Required fees:* $33.40 per credit hour. *Graduate housing:* Room and/or apartments available on a first-come, first-served basis to single students; on-campus housing not available to married students. Housing application deadline: 12/1. *Student services:* Campus employment opportunities, campus safety program, career counseling, child daycare facilities, exercise/wellness program, free psychological counseling, international student services, multicultural affairs office, services for students with disabilities, teacher training, writing training. *Library facilities:* Kent Library. *Collection:* Books: 368,983 (physical), 198,866 (digital/electronic); Serial titles: 4,166 (physical), 81,800 (digital/electronic); Databases: 152. Weekly public service hours: 92.

Computer facilities: 1,550 computers available on campus for general student use. A campuswide network can be accessed from student residence rooms. Online class registration is available.
Website: http://www.semo.edu/

General Application Contact: Dr. Charles McAllister, Dean of the School of Graduate Studies, 573-651-2062, Fax: 573-651-2001, E-mail: graduateschool@semo.edu.

GRADUATE UNITS

School of Graduate Studies Students: 377 full-time (248 women), 689 part-time (464 women); includes 77 minority (51 Black or African American, non-Hispanic/Latino; 4 American Indian or Alaska Native, non-Hispanic/Latino; 13 Asian, non-Hispanic/Latino; 6 Hispanic/Latino; 3 Two or more races, non-Hispanic/Latino), 188 international. Average age 31. 622 applicants, 77% accepted, 412 enrolled. *Faculty:* 227 full-time (111 women), 35 part-time/adjunct (27 women). Expenses: Contact institution. *Financial support:* In 2017–18, 328 students received support, including 94 teaching assistantships with full tuition reimbursements available; career-related internships or fieldwork, Federal Work-Study, scholarships/grants, traineeships, tuition waivers (full), and unspecified assistantships also available. Financial award application deadline: 6/30; financial award applicants required to submit FAFSA. In 2017, 441 master's, 47 other advanced degrees awarded. *Program availability:* Part-time, evening/weekend, 100% online, blended/hybrid learning. Offers biology (MNS); career counseling (MA); chemistry (MNS); communication disorders (MA); counseling (MA, Ed S); criminal justice (MS); educational administration (MA, Ed D, Ed S); educational leadership (Ed D); elementary education (MA); environmental science (MS); exceptional child education (MA); health, human performance and recreation (MS); heritage interpretation (Certificate); higher education administration (MA); historic preservation (Certificate); history (MA); human environmental studies (MA); mathematics (MNS); mental health counseling (MA); middle and secondary education (MA); nursing (MSN); political science, philosophy and religion (MPA); polytechnic studies (MS); public history (MA); school counseling (MA); secondary administration (MA); teacher leadership (MA, Ed S); teaching English to speakers of other languages (MA). *Application deadline:* For fall admission, 8/1 for domestic students, 6/1 for international students; for spring admission, 11/21 for domestic students, 10/1 for international students; for summer admission, 5/15 for domestic students. Applications are processed on a rolling basis. *Application fee:* $30 ($40 for international students). Electronic applications accepted. *Application Contact:* Alisa Aleen McFerron, Assistant Director of Admissions for Operations, 573-651-5937, E-mail: amcferron@semo.edu. *Dean of the School of Graduate Studies*, Dr. Charles McAllister, 573-651-2062, Fax: 573-651-2001, E-mail: graduateschool@semo.edu.

Harrison College of Business Students: 71 full-time (38 women), 68 part-time (31 women); includes 13 minority (7 Black or African American, non-Hispanic/Latino; 4 Asian, non-Hispanic/Latino; 2 Two or more races, non-Hispanic/Latino), 47 international. Average age 30. 51 applicants, 100% accepted, 51 enrolled. *Faculty:* 27 full-time (7 women), 1 (woman) part-time/adjunct. Expenses: Contact institution. *Financial support:* In 2017–18, 26 students received support. Career-related internships or fieldwork, Federal Work-Study, scholarships/grants, traineeships, tuition waivers (full), and unspecified assistantships available. Financial award application deadline: 6/30; financial award applicants required to submit FAFSA. In 2017, 95 master's awarded. *Program availability:* Part-time, evening/weekend, 100% online. Offers accounting (MBA); entrepreneurship (MBA); financial management (MBA); sport management (MBA). *Application deadline:* For fall admission, 8/1 for domestic students, 6/1 for international students; for spring admission, 11/21 for domestic students, 10/1 for international students; for summer admission, 5/15 for domestic students. Applications are processed on a rolling basis. *Application fee:* $30 ($40 for international students). Electronic applications accepted. *Interim Dean, Harrison College of Business*, Dr. Judy A. Wiles, 573-651-2913, Fax: 573-651-5032, E-mail: jwiles@semo.edu.

SOUTHERN ADVENTIST UNIVERSITY, Collegedale, TN 37315-0370

General Information Independent-religious, coed, comprehensive institution. *Tuition:* Full-time $11,430; part-time $635 per credit hour. Tuition and fees vary according to degree level and program. *Graduate housing:* Rooms and/or apartments available on a first-come, first-served basis to single and married students. Housing application deadline: 7/1. *Student services:* Campus employment opportunities, campus safety program, career counseling, exercise/wellness program, free psychological counseling, international student services, low-cost health insurance, multicultural affairs office, services for students with disabilities, teacher training, writing training. *Library facilities:* McKee Library plus 7 others. *Collection:* Books: 173,284 (physical), 107,663 (digital/electronic); Serial titles: 510 (physical), 170 (digital/electronic); Databases: 160. Weekly public service hours: 82; students can reserve study rooms.

Computer facilities: 300 computers available on campus for general student use. A campuswide network can be accessed from student residence rooms and from off campus. Online class registration is available.
Website: http://www.southern.edu/

General Application Contact: Laurie Gauthier, Director of Graduate Marketing and Enrollment Management, 423-236-2585, Fax: 423-236-1694, E-mail: graduatestudies@southern.edu.

GRADUATE UNITS

School of Business Expenses: Contact institution. *Financial support:* Scholarships/grants and unspecified assistantships available. Financial award application deadline: 9/1; financial award applicants required to submit FAFSA. *Program availability:* Part-time, evening/weekend, 100% online. Offers accounting (MBA); finance (MBA); healthcare administration (MBA); management (MBA); marketing management (MBA). *Application deadline:* For fall admission, 7/1 for domestic students, 5/1 for international students; for winter admission, 11/1 for domestic students, 9/1 for international students; for summer admission, 4/1 for domestic students, 2/1 for international students. Applications are processed on a rolling basis. *Application fee:* $40. Electronic applications accepted. *Application Contact:* Teshia Price, Graduate Studies Coordinator, 423-236-2751, Fax: 423-236-1527, E-mail: tprice@southern.edu. *Dean*, Dr. Stephanie Sheehan, 423-236-2659, Fax: 423-236-1527, E-mail: ssheehan@southern.edu.

School of Computing *Program availability:* Part-time. Offers computer science (MS). Electronic applications accepted.

School of Education and Psychology Expenses: Contact institution. *Financial support:* Research assistantships with full tuition reimbursements, teaching assistantships with full tuition reimbursements, career-related internships or fieldwork, scholarships/grants, tuition waivers (partial), and unspecified assistantships available. Support available to part-time students. Financial award application deadline: 4/1; financial award applicants required to submit FAFSA. *Program availability:* Part-time, evening/weekend. Offers clinical mental health counseling (MS); instructional leadership (MS Ed); literacy education (MS Ed); outdoor education (MS Ed); professional school counseling (MS). *Application deadline:* For fall admission, 7/1 priority date for domestic students, 6/1 priority date for international students; for winter admission, 11/1 priority date for domestic students, 10/1 priority date for international students; for spring admission, 4/1 priority date for domestic students, 3/1 priority date for international students. Applications are processed on a rolling basis. *Application fee:* $40. Electronic applications accepted. *Application Contact:* Mikhaile Spence, Graduate Enrollment Counselor, 423-236-2496, Fax: 423-236-1765, E-mail: maspence@southern.edu. *Interim Dean*, Bonnie Eder, 423-236-2759, Fax: 423-236-1765, E-mail: beder@southern.edu.

School of Nursing Expenses: Contact institution. *Financial support:* Teaching assistantships with partial tuition reimbursements available. *Program availability:* Part-time. Offers adult/gerontology acute care nurse practitioner (MSN, DNP); adult/gerontology nurse practitioner (MSN); family nurse practitioner (MSN, DNP); lifestyle therapeutics (DNP); nurse educator (MSN, DNP); psychiatric mental health nurse practitioner (MSN, DNP). *Application deadline:* For fall admission, 7/1 for domestic and international students; for winter admission, 12/1 for domestic and international students. Applications are processed on a rolling basis. *Application fee:* $40. Electronic applications accepted. *Application Contact:* Sylvia Mayer, RN, Director of Nursing Admissions, 423-236-2941, Fax: 423-236-1940, E-mail: smayer@southern.edu. *Dean*, Dr. Barbara James, 423-236-2942, Fax: 423-236-1940, E-mail: bjames@southern.edu.

School of Religion Expenses: Contact institution. *Financial support:* Tuition waivers (full) available. Support available to part-time students. Financial award application deadline: 4/1; financial award applicants required to submit FAFSA. *Program availability:* Part-time. Offers Biblical and theological studies (MA); church leadership and management (M Min); church ministry and homiletics (M Min); evangelism and world mission (M Min); religious studies (MA). *Application deadline:* For spring admission, 5/1 priority date for domestic students, 4/30 for international students. Applications are processed on a rolling basis. *Application fee:* $40. *Application Contact:* Susan L. Brown, Administrative Assistant, 423-236-2033, Fax: 423-236-1977, E-mail: sbrown@southern.edu. *Dean*, Dr. Greg A. King, 423-236-2975, Fax: 423-236-1976, E-mail: gking@southern.edu.

School of Social Work Expenses: Contact institution. *Program availability:* Online learning. Offers social work (MSW). *Application fee:* $40. *Application Contact:* Laurie Gauthier, Director of Graduate Marketing and Enrollment Management, 423-236-2585, Fax: 423-236-1694, E-mail: graduatestudies@southern.edu. *Dean*, Kristie Wilder, JD, 423-236-2206, E-mail: kwilder@southern.edu.

SOUTHERN ARKANSAS UNIVERSITY–MAGNOLIA, Magnolia, AR 71753

General Information State-supported, coed, comprehensive institution. *Enrollment:* 4,643 graduate, professional, and undergraduate students; 242 full-time matriculated graduate/professional students (89 women), 889 part-time matriculated graduate/professional students (459 women). *Enrollment by degree level:* 1,131 master's. *Graduate faculty:* 36 full-time (20 women), 31 part-time/adjunct (12 women). Tuition, state resident: full-time $6038. Tuition, nonresident: full-time $8558. *Required fees:* $804. One-time fee: $110 full-time. Tuition and fees vary according to course load. *Graduate housing:* Rooms and/or apartments available on a first-come, first-served basis to single and married students. Typical cost: $2849 (including board) for single students; $4628 (including board) for married students. Housing application deadline: 8/1. *Student services:* Campus employment opportunities, campus safety program, career counseling, exercise/wellness program, free psychological counseling, international student services, low-cost health insurance, multicultural affairs office, services for students with disabilities, writing training. *Library facilities:* Magale Library. *Collection:* Books: 143,395 (physical), 10,521 (digital/electronic); Serial titles: 145 (physical), 75 (digital/electronic); Databases: 186. Weekly public service hours: 87.

Computer facilities: 199 computers available on campus for general student use. A campuswide network can be accessed from student residence rooms and from off campus. Online class registration is available.
Website: http://www.saumag.edu/

General Application Contact: Talia Burton, Administrative Assistant, School of Graduate Studies, 870-235-4150, Fax: 870-235-5227, E-mail: taliaburton@saumag.edu.

GRADUATE UNITS

School of Graduate Studies Students: 242 full-time (89 women), 889 part-time (459 women); includes 167 minority (143 Black or African American, non-Hispanic/Latino; 7 American Indian or Alaska Native, non-Hispanic/Latino; 7 Asian, non-Hispanic/Latino; 3 Hispanic/Latino; 7 Two or more races, non-Hispanic/Latino), 562 international. Average age 28. 400 applicants, 100% accepted, 239 enrolled. *Faculty:* 36 full-time (20 women), 31 part-time/adjunct (12 women). Expenses: Contact institution. *Financial support:* Career-related internships or fieldwork, Federal Work-Study, scholarships/grants, tuition waivers (full), and unspecified assistantships available. Financial award applicants required to submit FAFSA. In 2017, 875 master's awarded. *Program availability:* Part-time, 100% online, blended/hybrid learning. Offers agriculture (MS); business administration (MBA); clinical and mental health counseling (MS); computer and information sciences (MS); gifted and talented (M Ed); higher, adult and lifelong education (M Ed); kinesiology (M Ed); library media and information specialist (M Ed); public administration (MPA); school counseling K-12 (M Ed); student affairs and college counseling (M Ed); teaching (MAT). *Application deadline:* For fall admission, 7/20 for domestic students, 7/10 for international students; for spring admission, 12/1 for domestic students, 11/15 for international students; for summer admission, 4/1 for domestic students, 5/1 for international students. Applications are processed on a rolling basis. *Application fee:* $25 ($50 for international students). Electronic applications accepted. *Application Contact:* Shrijana Malakar, Admissions Specialist, 870-235-4150, Fax: 870-235-5227, E-mail: smalakar@saumag.edu. *Dean, School of Graduate Studies*, Dr. Kim Bloss, 870-235-4150, Fax: 870-235-5227, E-mail: kkbloss@saumag.edu.

THE SOUTHERN BAPTIST THEOLOGICAL SEMINARY, Louisville, KY 40280-0004

General Information Independent-religious, coed, comprehensive institution. *Graduate housing:* Rooms and/or apartments available on a first-come, first-served basis to single and married students.

GRADUATE UNITS

Billy Graham School of Missions, Evangelism and Ministry *Program availability:* Part-time, evening/weekend, online learning. Offers ministry (D Min); missiology (MA, D Miss); missions and evangelism (M Div, Th M, PhD); theological studies (MA).

School of Theology *Program availability:* Part-time, evening/weekend, online learning. Offers applied theology (D Min); biblical and theological studies (M Div); biblical counseling (M Div, MA, D Min); biblical spirituality (D Min); Christian ministry (M Div); expository preaching (D Min); pastoral studies (M Div); theological studies (MA); theology (Th M, PhD); worldview and apologetics (M Div).

SOUTHERN CALIFORNIA INSTITUTE OF ARCHITECTURE, Los Angeles, CA 90013

General Information Independent, coed, comprehensive institution. *Graduate housing:* On-campus housing not available.

GRADUATE UNITS

Center for Advanced Studies

Graduate Program in Architecture Offers architecture (M Arch). Electronic applications accepted.

SOUTHERN CALIFORNIA SEMINARY, El Cajon, CA 92019

General Information Independent-religious, coed, comprehensive institution. *Graduate housing:* Rooms and/or apartments available on a first-come, first-served basis to single and married students.

GRADUATE UNITS

Graduate and Professional Programs *Program availability:* Part-time, evening/weekend, online learning. Offers Biblical studies (MABS); counseling psychology (MACP); marriage and family therapy (MAMFT); psychology (Psy D); religious studies (MRS); theology (M Div). Electronic applications accepted.

SOUTHERN CALIFORNIA UNIVERSITY OF HEALTH SCIENCES, Whittier, CA 90609-1166

General Information Independent, coed, graduate-only institution. *Graduate housing:* On-campus housing not available. *Research affiliation:* Samueli Institute (alternative health care), Anton B. Burg Foundation (alternative health care).

GRADUATE UNITS

College of Eastern Medicine *Program availability:* Part-time, evening/weekend. Offers Eastern medicine (MAOM, DAOM). Electronic applications accepted.

Los Angeles College of Chiropractic Offers chiropractic (DC). Electronic applications accepted.

SOUTHERN COLLEGE OF OPTOMETRY, Memphis, TN 38104-2222

General Information Independent, coed, graduate-only institution. *Graduate housing:* On-campus housing not available.

GRADUATE UNITS

Professional Program Offers optometry (OD).

SOUTHERN CONNECTICUT STATE UNIVERSITY, New Haven, CT 06515-1355

General Information State-supported, coed, comprehensive institution. CGS member. *Graduate housing:* Room and/or apartments available on a first-come, first-served basis to single students; on-campus housing not available to married students.

GRADUATE UNITS

School of Graduate Studies *Program availability:* Part-time, evening/weekend, online learning. Electronic applications accepted.

School of Arts and Sciences Offers art education (MS); arts and sciences (MA, MFA, MS, Diploma); biology (MS); chemistry (MS); computer science (MS); English (MA, MS); environmental education (MS); history (MA, MS); mathematics (MS); multicultural-bilingual education/teaching English to speakers of other languages (MS); political science (MS); psychology (MA); romance languages (MA); science education (MS, Diploma); sociology (MS); women's studies (MA). Electronic applications accepted.

School of Business *Program availability:* Part-time, evening/weekend. Offers business (MBA); business administration (MBA). Electronic applications accepted.

School of Education *Program availability:* Part-time. Offers classroom teacher specialist (Diploma); community counseling (MS); counseling (Diploma); education (MLS, MS, MS Ed, Ed D, Diploma); educational coach (Diploma); educational leadership (Ed D, Diploma); elementary education (MS); information studies (Diploma); library science (MLS); reading (MS, Diploma); research, statistics, and measurement (MS); school counseling (MS); school psychology (MS, Diploma); special education (MS Ed). Electronic applications accepted.

School of Health and Human Services *Program availability:* Part-time, evening/weekend. Offers family nurse practitioner (MSN); health and human services (MPH, MS, MSN, MSW, Ed D); human performance (MS); nursing (Ed D); nursing education (MSN); physical education (MS); public health (MPH); recreation and leisure studies (MS); school health education (MS); social work (MSW); speech pathology (MS). Electronic applications accepted.

SOUTHERN EVANGELICAL SEMINARY, Matthews, NC 28105

General Information Independent-religious, coed, primarily men, graduate-only institution. *Graduate housing:* On-campus housing not available.

GRADUATE UNITS

Graduate Programs *Program availability:* Part-time, evening/weekend, online learning. Offers apologetics (MA, D Min, Certificate); Christian education (MA); church ministry (MA, Certificate); divinity (Certificate); Islamic studies (MA, Certificate); Jewish studies (MA); philosophy (MA); philosophy of religion (PhD); religion (MA); theology (M Div); youth ministry (MA).

SOUTHERN ILLINOIS UNIVERSITY CARBONDALE, Carbondale, IL 62901-4701

General Information State-supported, coed, university. CGS member. *Graduate housing:* Rooms and/or apartments available on a first-come, first-served basis to single and married students. *Research affiliation:* NASA-Ames Research Center, Argonne National Laboratory.

GRADUATE UNITS

Graduate School *Program availability:* Part-time. Offers molecular, cellular and systemic physiology (MS, PhD); molecular, cellular, and systemic physiology (PhD); pharmacology (MS, PhD); physician assistant studies (MSPA).

College of Agriculture *Program availability:* Part-time. Offers agribusiness economics (MS); agriculture (MS); animal science (MS); food and nutrition (MS); forestry (MS); plant, soil, and general agriculture (MS).

College of Applied Science Offers applied science (M Arch, MS); architecture (M Arch); fire service and homeland security (MS); medical dosimetry (MS). Electronic applications accepted.

College of Business and Administration *Program availability:* Part-time. Offers accountancy (M Acc, PhD); business administration (MBA, PhD); business and administration (M Acc, MBA, PhD). Electronic applications accepted.

College of Education and Human Services *Program availability:* Part-time. Offers behavior analysis and therapy (MS); communication disorders and sciences (MS); community health education (MPH); curriculum and instruction (MS Ed, PhD); education (MS Ed); education and human services (MPH, MS, MS Ed, MSW, PhD); educational administration (MS Ed, PhD); educational psychology (MS Ed, PhD); health education (MS Ed, PhD); higher education (MS Ed); kinesiology (MS Ed); recreation (MS Ed); social work (MSW); special education (MS Ed, PhD); workforce education and development (MS Ed, PhD). Electronic applications accepted.

College of Engineering Offers biomedical engineering (ME, MS); civil and environmental engineering (ME); civil engineering (MS); electrical and computer engineering (MS, PhD); engineering (ME, MS, PhD); engineering science (PhD); engineering sciences (PhD); mechanical engineering (MS); mining engineering (MS); quality engineering and management (MS).

College of Liberal Arts *Program availability:* Part-time. Offers anthropology (MA, PhD); clinical psychology (PhD); communication studies (MA, MS, PhD); composition (MA, PhD); counseling psychology (PhD); creative writing (MFA); criminology and criminal justice (MA, PhD); drawing (MFA); economics (MA, MS, PhD); experimental psychology (MA, MS); fiber/weaving (MFA); foreign languages and literatures (MA); geography (MS, PhD); glass (MFA); history (MA, PhD); liberal arts (MA, MFA, MM, MPA, MS, PhD); linguistics (MA); metalsmithing/blacksmithing (MFA); music (MM);

painting (MFA); philosophy (MA, PhD); political science (MA, PhD); public administration (MPA); sociology (MA, PhD); speech/theater (PhD); teaching English to speakers of other languages (MA); theater (MFA).

College of Mass Communication and Media Arts *Program availability:* Part-time. Offers mass communication and media arts (MA, MFA, MS, PhD); media theory and research (MA); professional media and media management studies (MS).

College of Science *Program availability:* Part-time. Offers biological sciences (MS); chemistry and biochemistry (MS, PhD); computer science (MS, PhD); environmental resources and policy (PhD); geology (MS); geosciences (PhD); mathematics (MA, MS, PhD); molecular biology, microbiology, and biochemistry (MS, PhD); physics (MS, PhD); plant biology (MS, PhD); science (MA, MS, PhD); zoology (MS, PhD).

School of Law *Program availability:* Part-time. Offers general law (LL M, MLS); health law and policy (LL M, MLS); law (JD); legal studies (MLS). Electronic applications accepted.

SOUTHERN ILLINOIS UNIVERSITY EDWARDSVILLE, Edwardsville, IL 62026

General Information State-supported, coed, university. CGS member. *Graduate housing:* Rooms and/or apartments available on a first-come, first-served basis to single and married students. Housing application deadline: 5/1. *Research affiliation:* Long Island Veterinary Clinic (electrical engineering), SSM DePaul Health Center (nursing), Nurturenergy (mechanical engineering), Tulsa Dental Products (dental medicine), Mallinckrodt (pharmacy), Schlumberger (mechanical engineering).

GRADUATE UNITS

Graduate School *Program availability:* Part-time, evening/weekend, blended/hybrid learning. Offers cultural heritage and resources management (MA, MS); diversity training (MA, MS); healthcare informatics (MS); organizational design thinking (MS); sustainability (MS). Electronic applications accepted.

College of Arts and Sciences *Program availability:* Part-time, evening/weekend, online learning. Offers art studio (MFA); art therapy counseling (MA); arts and sciences (MA, MFA, MM, MPA, MS, MSW, PSM, Postbaccalaureate Certificate); biology (MA, MS); chemistry (MS); computational and applied mathematics (MS); corporate and organizational communication (MA); creative writing (MA); environmental science management (PSM); environmental sciences (MS); geography (MS); health communication (MA); history (MA); interpersonal communication (MA); literature (MA, Postbaccalaureate Certificate); mass communications (MS); media literacy (Postbaccalaureate Certificate); museum studies (Postbaccalaureate Certificate); music (MM); music education (MM); music performance (MM); piano pedagogy (Postbaccalaureate Certificate); postsecondary mathematics education (MS); public administration (MPA); public relations (MA); pure mathematics (MS); school social work (MSW); social work (MSW); sociology (MA); statistics and operations research (MS); teaching English as a second language (MA, Postbaccalaureate Certificate); teaching of writing (MA, Postbaccalaureate Certificate); vocal pedagogy (Postbaccalaureate Certificate). Electronic applications accepted.

School of Business *Program availability:* Part-time, evening/weekend. Offers accountancy (MSA); business (MA, MBA, MMR, MS, MSA); business analytics (MBA); computer management and information systems (MS); economics and finance (MA, MS); management information systems (MBA); marketing research (MMR); project management (MBA); taxation (MSA). Electronic applications accepted.

School of Education, Health, and Human Behavior *Program availability:* Part-time, evening/weekend. Offers clinical child and school psychology (MS); clinical psychology (MA); college student personnel administration (MS Ed); curriculum and instruction (MS Ed); education, health, and human behavior (MA, MS, MS Ed, Ed D, Ed S, Post-Master's Certificate, Postbaccalaureate Certificate, SD); educational administration (MS Ed, Ed S); educational leadership (MS Ed, Ed D, Ed S, Postbaccalaureate Certificate); exercise and sport psychology (MS); exercise physiology (MS); industrial-organizational psychology (MA); instructional technology (MS Ed); learning, culture, and society (MS Ed); literacy education (MS Ed); literacy specialist (Post-Master's Certificate); physical education and coaching pedagogy (MS Ed); school psychology (SD); special education (MS Ed, Post-Master's Certificate); speech-language pathology (MS); Web-based learning (Postbaccalaureate Certificate). Electronic applications accepted.

School of Engineering *Program availability:* Part-time, evening/weekend. Offers computer science (MS); electrical engineering (MS); engineering (MS); environmental engineering (MS); geotechnical engineering (MS); industrial engineering (MS); mechanical engineering (MS); structural engineering (MS); transportation engineering (MS). Electronic applications accepted.

School of Nursing *Program availability:* Part-time, evening/weekend. Offers family nurse practitioner (MS, Post-Master's Certificate); health care and nursing administration (MS, Post-Master's Certificate); nurse anesthesia (DNP); nurse educator (MS, Post-Master's Certificate); nursing (MS, DNP, Post-Master's Certificate). Electronic applications accepted.

School of Dental Medicine Offers dental medicine (DMD). Electronic applications accepted.

School of Pharmacy Offers pharmacy education (Pharm D); pharmacy pediatrics (Pharm D). Electronic applications accepted.

SOUTHERN METHODIST UNIVERSITY, Dallas, TX 75275

General Information Independent-religious, coed, university. CGS member. *Graduate housing:* Rooms and/or apartments available on a first-come, first-served basis to single and married students. Housing application deadline: 6/1. *Student services:* Campus employment opportunities, campus safety program, career counseling, child daycare facilities, exercise/wellness program, free psychological counseling, grant writing training, international student services, low-cost health insurance, multicultural affairs office, services for students with disabilities, teacher training. *Library facilities:* Fondren Library plus 7 others. *Collection:* Books: 3 million (physical), 1.2 million (digital/electronic); Serial titles: 16,580 (physical), 139,891 (digital/electronic); Databases: 667. Weekly public service hours: 150; study areas open 24 hours, 5–7 days a week; students can reserve study rooms.

Computer facilities: 758 computers available on campus for general student use. A campuswide network can be accessed from student residence rooms and from off campus. Online class registration, online billing/payment processing are available. Website: http://www.smu.edu/

General Application Contact: Dr. James E. Quick, Dean of Research and Graduate Studies, 214-768-4345.

GRADUATE UNITS

Cox School of Business Expenses: Contact institution. *Financial support:* Application deadline: 3/1; applicants required to submit FAFSA. *Program availability:* Part-time, evening/weekend. Offers accounting (MBA, MSA, PMBA); business (EMBA); business administration (MBA); business analytics (PMBA); entrepreneurship (MS); finance (MBA, MSF, PMBA); information technology and operations management (MBA, PMBA); management (MSM); marketing (MBA, PMBA); real estate (MBA, PMBA); strategy and entrepreneurship (MBA, PMBA). *Application deadline:* Applications are processed on a rolling basis. Electronic applications accepted. *Application Contact:* Dr. James E. Quick, Associate Vice President for Research and Dean of Graduate Studies, 214-768-4345. *Dean,* Dr. Matthew Myers, Jr., 214-768-3012.

Dedman College of Humanities and Sciences Expenses: Contact institution. *Financial support:* Applicants required to submit FAFSA. *Program availability:* Part-time, evening/weekend. Offers American history (MA, PhD); applied economics (MA); applied economics and predictive analytics (MS); applied geophysics (MS); applied medical anthropology (MA); applied statistics and data analytics (MS); archaeology (PhD); biostatistics (PhD); chemistry (MS); clinical psychology (PhD); computational and applied mathematics (MS, PhD); cultural anthropology (PhD); earth sciences (MS, PhD); economics (PhD); English (MA, PhD); experimental chemistry (PhD); global history (MA); Hebrew Bible/Old Testament (PhD); humanities and sciences (MA, MS, PhD); law and economics (MA); medical anthropology (PhD); medieval studies (MA); molecular and cellular biology (MA, MS, PhD); physics (MS, PhD); religious studies (MA); statistical science (PhD); theoretical and computational chemistry (PhD). *Application deadline:* For fall admission, 2/1 priority date for domestic and international students; for winter admission, 11/30 priority date for domestic and international students. Applications are processed on a rolling basis. *Application fee:* $75. Electronic applications accepted. *Application Contact:* Dr. James E. Quick, Associate Vice President for Research and Dean of Graduate Studies, 214-768-4345. *Dean,* Thomas DiPiero, 214-768-3212, E-mail: tdipiero@smu.edu.

Dedman School of Law Expenses: Contact institution. *Financial support:* Application deadline: 2/15; applicants required to submit FAFSA. *Program availability:* Part-time, evening/weekend. Offers general law (LL M); international and comparative law (LL M); law (JD, SJD); taxation (LL M). *Application deadline:* For fall admission, 2/15 priority date for domestic students. Applications are processed on a rolling basis. *Application fee:* $75. Electronic applications accepted. *Application Contact:* Dr. James E. Quick, Associate Vice President for Research and Dean of Graduate Studies, 214-768-4345. *Dean,* Jennifer Collins, 214-768-2621, Fax: 214-768-2182, E-mail: jmc@smu.edu.

Lyle School of Engineering Expenses: Contact institution. *Financial support:* Applicants required to submit FAFSA. *Program availability:* Part-time, evening/weekend, online learning. Offers civil and environmental engineering (PhD); civil engineering (MS); computer engineering (MS, PhD); computer science (MS, PhD); data science (MS); datacenter systems engineering (MS); design and innovation (MA); electrical engineering (MS, PhD); engineering (MA, MS, MSIEM, DE, PhD); engineering entrepreneurship (MS); engineering management (MS, DE); environmental engineering (MS); information engineering and management (MSIEM); manufacturing systems management (MS); mechanical engineering (MS, PhD); operations research (MS, PhD); security engineering (MS); software engineering (MS, DE); sustainability and development (MA); systems engineering (MS); telecommunications and network engineering (MS). *Application deadline:* For fall admission, 7/1 for domestic students, 5/15 for international students; for spring admission, 11/15 for domestic students, 9/1 for international students. Applications are processed on a rolling basis. *Application fee:* $75. *Application Contact:* Marc Valerin, Director of Graduate and Executive Admissions, 214-768-3042, E-mail: valerin@engr.smu.edu. *Dean,* Dr. Marc P. Christensen, 214-768-3050, Fax: 214-768-3845, E-mail: dean@lyle.smu.edu.

Meadows School of the Arts Expenses: Contact institution. *Financial support:* Application deadline: 3/1; applicants required to submit FAFSA. *Program availability:* Evening/weekend. Offers arts (MA, MFA, MM, MM, MSM, PhD, Diploma). *Application deadline:* For fall admission, 2/15 for domestic students; for spring admission, 11/1 for domestic students. *Application fee:* $75. Electronic applications accepted. *Application Contact:* Joe S. Hoselton, Graduate Admissions and Records Coordinator, 214-768-3765, Fax: 214-768-3272, E-mail: hoselton@smu.edu. *Dean,* Sam S. Holland, 214-768-4154, E-mail: sholland@smu.edu.

Division of Art Expenses: Contact institution. *Financial support:* Application deadline: 3/1; applicants required to submit FAFSA. Offers studio art (MFA). *Application deadline:* For fall admission, 2/15 for domestic and international students. *Application fee:* $75. *Application Contact:* Joe S. Hoselton, Director of Graduate Admissions, 214-768-3765, Fax: 214-768-3272, E-mail: hoselton@smu.edu.

Division of Art History Expenses: Contact institution. *Financial support:* Application deadline: 3/1; applicants required to submit FAFSA. *Program availability:* Part-time, evening/weekend. Offers art history (MA); rhetorics of art, space and culture (PhD). *Application deadline:* For fall admission, 2/15 priority date for domestic and international students; for spring admission, 11/1 for domestic and international students. *Application fee:* $75. *Application Contact:* Joe S. Hoselton, Director of Graduate Admissions, 214-768-3765, Fax: 214-768-3272, E-mail: hoselton@smu.edu. *Chair and Director of Graduate Studies,* Dr. Adam Herring, 214-768-3823, E-mail: aherring@smu.edu.

Division of Arts Management and Arts Entrepreneurship Expenses: Contact institution. Offers international arts management (MM). MM offered jointly with Bocconi University Graduate School of Management in Milan and HEC Montreal. *Application deadline:* For fall admission, 1/15 priority date for domestic and international students. Applications are processed on a rolling basis. *Application fee:* $75. Electronic applications accepted. *Application Contact:* Joe S. Hoselton, Graduate Admissions and Records Coordinator, 214-768-3765, Fax: 214-768-3272, E-mail: hoselton@smu.edu. *Director,* Dr. Zannie Voss, 214-768-3425, E-mail: zvoss@smu.edu.

Division of Music Expenses: Contact institution. *Financial support:* Application deadline: 3/1; applicants required to submit FAFSA. *Program availability:* Part-time. Offers composition (MM); conducting (MM); music education (MM); musicology (MM); performance (MM); theory pedagogy (MM). *Application deadline:* For fall admission, 3/1 priority date for domestic and international students; for spring admission, 11/1 for domestic and international students. Applications are processed on a rolling basis. *Application fee:* $75. Electronic applications accepted. *Application Contact:* Joe S. Hoselton, Director of Graduate Admissions, 214-768-3765, Fax: 214-768-3272, E-mail: hoselton@smu.edu. *Division of Music Director,* Dr. David Mancini, 214-768-1951, E-mail: dmancini@smu.edu.

Division of Theatre Expenses: Contact institution. *Financial support:* Application deadline: 3/1; applicants required to submit FAFSA. Offers acting (MFA); design (MFA). *Application deadline:* For fall admission, 2/15 priority date for domestic and international students. Applications are processed on a rolling basis. *Application fee:* $75. Electronic applications accepted. *Application Contact:* Joe S. Hoselton, Director of Graduate Admissions, 214-768-3765, Fax: 214-768-3272, E-mail: hoselton@smu.edu.

Temerlin Advertising Institute Expenses: Contact institution. *Financial support:* Application deadline: 4/1; applicants required to submit FAFSA. Offers advertising (MA). *Application deadline:* For fall admission, 3/15 for domestic students. *Application fee:* $75. Electronic applications accepted. *Application Contact:* Dr. Carrie La Ferle, Director of Graduate Studies, 214-768-3378, E-mail: laferle@smu.edu. *Director,* Dr. Steve Edwards, 214-768-3090, E-mail: steve@smu.edu.

Perkins School of Theology Expenses: Contact institution. *Financial support:* Application deadline: 3/1; applicants required to submit FAFSA. *Program availability:* Part-time. Offers ministry (M Div, D Min); sacred music (MSM); theological studies (MTS). *Application deadline:* For fall admission, 5/1 for domestic students, 12/15 for international students; for spring admission, 11/1 for domestic students. Applications are processed on a rolling basis. *Application fee:* $50. *Application Contact:* Rev. Herbert S. Coleman, II, Director, Recruitment and Admissions, 214-768-2139, Fax: 214-768-4245, E-mail: theology@smu.edu. *Coordinator for the Graduate Program in Religious Studies and D Min Program,* Pamela Hogan, 214-768-2432, E-mail: phogan@smu.edu.

Simmons School of Education and Human Development Expenses: Contact institution. *Financial support:* Application deadline: 6/1. *Program availability:* Part-time, evening/weekend. Offers applied physiology (PhD); bilingual education (MBE); counseling (MS); dispute resolution (MA, Graduate Certificate); education (M Ed, PhD); education and human development (M Ed, MA, MBE, MLS, MS, DLS, PhD, Graduate Certificate); English as a second language (M Ed); gifted and talented (M Ed); health promotion management (MS); healthcare collaboration and conflict engagement (Graduate Certificate); liberal studies (MLS, DLS); literacy studies (M Ed); special education (M Ed); sport management (MS). *Application fee:* $75. *Application Contact:* Dr. James E. Quick, Associate Vice President for Research and Dean of Graduate Studies, 214-768-4345. *Dean,* Dr. Stephanie Knight, 214-768-5465, Fax: 214-768-1797, E-mail: slknight@smu.edu.

SOUTHERN NAZARENE UNIVERSITY, Bethany, OK 73008

General Information Independent-religious, coed, comprehensive institution. *Graduate housing:* Rooms and/or apartments available on a first-come, first-served basis to single and married students. Housing application deadline: 8/1.

GRADUATE UNITS

College of Professional and Graduate Studies *Program availability:* Part-time, evening/weekend. Offers counseling psychology (MA, MSCP); marital and family therapy (MA). Electronic applications accepted.

School of Business *Program availability:* Part-time, evening/weekend, online learning. Offers business administration (MBA); health care management (MBA); management (MS Mgt). Electronic applications accepted.

School of Kinesiology Offers sports management and administration (MA).

School of Nursing *Program availability:* Part-time, evening/weekend. Offers nursing education (MS); nursing leadership (MS).

SOUTHERN NEW HAMPSHIRE UNIVERSITY, Manchester, NH 03106-1045

General Information Independent, coed, university. *Tuition:* Part-time $627 per credit hour. Part-time tuition and fees vary according to campus/location and program. *Graduate housing:* Room and/or apartments available on a first-come, first-served basis to single students; on-campus housing not available to married students. *Student services:* Campus employment opportunities, campus safety program, career counseling, exercise/wellness program, free psychological counseling, international student services, low-cost health insurance, multicultural affairs office, services for students with disabilities, teacher training, writing training. *Library facilities:* Shapiro Library and Learning Commons. *Collection:* Students can reserve study rooms.

Computer facilities: Computer purchase and lease plans are available. A campuswide network can be accessed from student residence rooms and from off campus. Online class registration is available.
Website: http://www.snhu.edu/

General Application Contact: Office of Graduate Admission, 888-327-SNHU, Fax: 603-644-3144, E-mail: enroll@snhu.edu.

GRADUATE UNITS

Program in Nursing Expenses: Contact institution. *Program availability:* Online only, 100% online. Offers clinical nurse leader (MSN); nurse educator (MSN); nursing (MSN); patient safety and quality (MSN, Post Master's Certificate). *Application deadline:* Applications are processed on a rolling basis. *Application fee:* $40. Electronic applications accepted. *Application Contact:* Office of Graduate Admission, 888-327-SNHU, Fax: 603-644-3144, E-mail: enroll@snhu.edu.

School of Arts and Sciences Expenses: Contact institution. *Financial support:* Research assistantships, career-related internships or fieldwork, and scholarships/grants available. Financial award applicants required to submit FAFSA. *Program availability:* Part-time, evening/weekend. Offers clinical mental health counseling (MS); creative writing (MA); criminal justice (MS); cyber security (MS); English (MA); fiction and nonfiction (MFA); history (MA); political science (MS); psychology (MS). *Application deadline:* For fall admission, 7/1 priority date for domestic students; for winter admission, 11/1 priority date for domestic students; for spring admission, 6/1 priority date for domestic students. Applications are processed on a rolling basis. *Application fee:* $40. Electronic applications accepted. *Application Contact:* Office of Graduate Admission, 888-327-SNHU, Fax: 603-644-3144, E-mail: enroll@snhu.edu. *Dean,* Steven K. Johnson, 603-629-4626.

School of Business Expenses: Contact institution. *Financial support:* Career-related internships or fieldwork, Federal Work-Study, institutionally sponsored loans, scholarships/grants, tuition waivers (partial), and unspecified assistantships available. Support available to part-time students. Financial award applicants required to submit FAFSA. *Program availability:* Part-time, evening/weekend, online learning. Offers accounting (MBA, Graduate Certificate); accounting finance (MS); accounting/auditing (MS); accounting/forensic accounting (MS); accounting/management accounting (MS); accounting/taxation (MS); applied economics (MS); athletic administration (MBA, Graduate Certificate); business administration (IMBA, Certificate); business analytics (MBA); business intelligence (MBA); communication (MA); community economic development (MBA); criminal justice (MBA); data analytics (MS); economics (MBA); engineering management (MBA); entrepreneurship (MBA); finance (MBA, MS, Graduate Certificate); finance/corporate finance (MS); finance/investments (MS); forensic accounting (MBA); forensic accounting and fraud examination (Graduate Certificate); healthcare informatics (MBA); healthcare management (MBA); human resource management (MS); human resources (MBA); information technology (MS); information technology management (MBA); international business (PhD); Internet marketing (MBA); leadership (MBA); leadership of nonprofit organizations (Graduate Certificate); management (MS); marketing (MBA, MS, Graduate Certificate); music business (MBA); operations and project management (MS); operations and supply chain management (MBA, Graduate Certificate); organizational leadership (MS); project management (MBA, Graduate Certificate); public administration (MBA, Graduate Certificate); quantitative analysis (MBA); Six Sigma (Graduate Certificate); Six Sigma quality (MBA); social media marketing (MBA, Graduate Certificate); sport management (MBA, MS, Graduate Certificate); sustainability and environmental compliance (MBA). *Application deadline:* Applications are processed on a rolling basis. *Application fee:* $40. Electronic applications accepted. *Application Contact:* Office of Graduate Admission, 888-327-SNHU, Fax: 603-644-3144, E-mail: enroll@snhu.edu. *Dean,* Dr. Bill Lightfoot, 603-644-3102, Fax: 603-644-3144.

School of Education Expenses: Contact institution. *Financial support:* Institutionally sponsored loans available. Financial award applicants required to submit FAFSA. *Program availability:* Part-time, evening/weekend, online learning. Offers curriculum and instruction (M Ed); dyslexia studies and language-based learning disabilities (Certificate); early childhood and special education (M Ed); educational leadership (M Ed, Ed D); educational studies (M Ed); elementary and special education (M Ed); field based education (M Ed); higher education administration (MS); teaching English as a foreign language (MS). *Application deadline:* Applications are processed on a rolling basis. *Application fee:* $40. Electronic applications accepted. *Application Contact:* Office of Graduate Admission, 888-327-SNHU, Fax: 603-644-3144, E-mail: enroll@snhu.edu. *Dean,* Raymond McNulty, 603-668-2211, Fax: 603-629-4673.

SOUTHERN OREGON UNIVERSITY, Ashland, OR 97520

General Information State-supported, coed, comprehensive institution. *Graduate housing:* Rooms and/or apartments available on a first-come, first-served basis to single and married students. Housing application deadline: 8/1. *Research affiliation:* U.S. Forest Service (biology, ecology studies), U.S. Fish and Wildlife Service (forensics), Oregon Shakespeare Festival (theatre arts), Crater Lake National Park (scientific studies), Bureau of Land Management (ecological studies), Bear Creek Corporation (environmental studies).

GRADUATE UNITS

Graduate Studies *Program availability:* Part-time, evening/weekend, online learning. Offers applied computer science (PSM); environmental education (MS); French language teaching (MA); interdisciplinary studies (MIS); performance (MM); psychology (MHC); Spanish language teaching (MA). Electronic applications accepted.

Ashland Center for Theatre Studies *Program availability:* Part-time. Offers theatre studies (MTS). Electronic applications accepted.

School of Business *Program availability:* Part-time, evening/weekend, online learning. Offers accounting (Postbaccalaureate Certificate); business administration (MBA); international management (MIM). Electronic applications accepted.

School of Education *Program availability:* Online learning. Offers elementary education (MA Ed, MS Ed); secondary education (MA Ed, MS Ed); teaching (MAT). Electronic applications accepted.

SOUTHERN UNIVERSITY AND AGRICULTURAL AND MECHANICAL COLLEGE, Baton Rouge, LA 70813

General Information State-supported, coed, university. CGS member. *Graduate housing:* Room and/or apartments available on a first-come, first-served basis to single students; on-campus housing not available to married students. Housing application deadline: 6/30. *Research affiliation:* Livingston Observatory (gravitational waves, cosmic gravity waves, black waves), Michigan State University (language screening of African-Americans), University of Georgia (substance abuse prevention), The University of Alabama (diabetes), NASA (drinking water remote sensing, mechanical engineering).

GRADUATE UNITS

College of Business Offers business (MBA).

College of Nursing and Allied Health Offers nursing and allied health (MS, MSN, DNP, PhD); speech-language pathology (MS); therapeutic recreation (MS).

School of Nursing *Program availability:* Part-time. Offers educator/administrator (PhD); family health nursing (MSN); family nurse practitioner (Post Master's Certificate); geriatric nurse practitioner/gerontology (PhD); nursing (DNP).

Graduate School *Program availability:* Part-time. Offers science/mathematics education (PhD); special education (M Ed, PhD).

College of Agricultural, Family and Consumer Sciences Offers urban forestry (MS).

College of Arts and Humanities Offers arts and humanities (MA); mass communication (MA); social sciences (MA).

College of Education Offers administration and supervision (M Ed); counselor education (MA); education (M Ed, MA, MS, PhD); educational leadership (M Ed); elementary education (M Ed); media (M Ed); mental health counseling (MA); secondary education (M Ed).

College of Engineering Offers engineering (ME).

College of Sciences *Program availability:* Part-time. Offers analytical chemistry (MS); biochemistry (MS); biology (MS); environmental sciences (MS); information systems (MS); inorganic chemistry (MS); mathematics (MS); micro/minicomputer architecture (MS); operating systems (MS); organic chemistry (MS); physical chemistry (MS); physics (MS); rehabilitation counseling (MS); sciences (MA, MS).

Nelson Mandela School of Public Policy and Urban Affairs Offers criminal justice (MS); public administration (MPA); public policy (PhD); public policy and urban affairs (MA, MPA, MS, PhD); social sciences (MA).

Southern University Law Center *Program availability:* Part-time, evening/weekend. Offers law (JD). Electronic applications accepted.

SOUTHERN UNIVERSITY AT NEW ORLEANS, New Orleans, LA 70126-1009

General Information State-supported, coed, primarily women, comprehensive institution. *Graduate housing:* Room and/or apartments available on a first-come, first-served basis to single students; on-campus housing not available to married students.

GRADUATE UNITS

School of Graduate Studies *Program availability:* Part-time, evening/weekend. Offers criminal justice (MA); management information systems (MS); museum studies (MA); social work (MSW).

SOUTHERN UTAH UNIVERSITY, Cedar City, UT 84720-2498

General Information State-supported, coed, comprehensive institution. *Enrollment:* 9,468 graduate, professional, and undergraduate students; 206 full-time matriculated graduate/professional students (87 women), 673 part-time matriculated graduate/professional students (395 women). *Enrollment by degree level:* 799 master's, 80 other advanced degrees. *Graduate faculty:* 53 full-time (15 women), 40 part-time/adjunct (13 women). *Graduate housing:* Room and/or apartments available on a first-come, first-served basis to single students; on-campus housing not available to married students. *Student services:* Campus employment opportunities, campus safety program, career counseling, exercise/wellness program, free psychological counseling, international student services, low-cost health insurance, multicultural affairs office, services for students with disabilities, teacher training. *Library facilities:* Gerald R Sherratt Library. *Collection:* Books: 241,434 (physical), 441,219 (digital/electronic); Serial titles: 676 (physical), 22,603 (digital/electronic); Databases: 218. Students can reserve study rooms.

Computer facilities: A campuswide network can be accessed from student residence rooms and from off campus. Online class registration is available.
Website: http://www.suu.edu/

General Application Contact: Dr. Mark C. Atkinson, Dean of Graduate and Continuing Studies, 435-586-1966, E-mail: markatkinson@suu.edu.

GRADUATE UNITS

Master of Accountancy/MBA Dual Degree Program Students: 3 full-time (1 woman), 1 (woman) part-time. Average age 26. 8 applicants, 75% accepted. Expenses: Contact institution. *Financial support:* Unspecified assistantships available. *Program availability:* Part-time, 100% online. *Application deadline:* For fall admission, 3/1 for domestic and international students; for spring admission, 10/1 for domestic and international students; for summer admission, 3/1 for domestic and international students. Applications are processed on a rolling basis. *Application fee:* $60 ($65 for international students). Electronic applications accepted. *Application Contact:* Patricia Palmer, Academic Advisor and Graduate Program Coordinator, 435-865-8167, Fax: 435-586-5493, E-mail: patriciapalmer@suu.edu.

Program in Accounting Students: 63 full-time (22 women), 48 part-time (14 women); includes 17 minority (2 Black or African American, non-Hispanic/Latino; 3 Asian, non-Hispanic/Latino; 12 Hispanic/Latino). Average age 29. 64 applicants, 83% accepted, 46 enrolled. *Faculty:* 5 full-time (0 women), 2 part-time/adjunct (0 women). Expenses: Contact institution. *Financial support:* Unspecified assistantships available. In 2017, 62 master's awarded. *Program availability:* Part-time, 100% online. Offers accounting (M Acc). *Application deadline:* For fall admission, 3/1 for domestic and international students; for spring admission, 10/1 for domestic and international students; for summer admission, 3/1 for domestic and international students. Applications are processed on a rolling basis. *Application fee:* $60 ($65 for international students). Electronic applications accepted. *Application Contact:* Patricia Palmer, Academic Advisor and Graduate Program Coordinator, 435-865-8167, Fax: 435-586-5493, E-mail: patriciapalmer@suu.edu. *Chair, Accounting Department,* Dr. Robin Boneck, 435-586-7773, Fax: 435-586-5493, E-mail: boneck@suu.edu.

Program in Arts Administration Students: 13 full-time (7 women), 23 part-time (21 women); includes 5 minority (1 Asian, non-Hispanic/Latino; 4 Hispanic/Latino). Average age 33. 21 applicants, 62% accepted, 13 enrolled. *Faculty:* 3 full-time (2 women), 5 part-time/adjunct (2 women). Expenses: Contact institution. *Financial support:* Tuition waivers and unspecified assistantships available. In 2017, 12 master's awarded. *Program availability:* Part-time, 100% online. Offers arts administration (MA, MFA). *Application deadline:* For fall admission, 2/15 for domestic and international students. Applications are processed on a rolling basis. *Application fee:* $60 ($65 for international students). Electronic applications accepted. *Program Director/Assistant Professor,* Rachel Bishop, 435-586-7873, Fax: 435-865-8657, E-mail: bishopr@suu.edu.

Program in Business Administration Students: 25 full-time (4 women), 51 part-time (15 women); includes 6 minority (2 Black or African American, non-Hispanic/Latino; 1 Asian, non-Hispanic/Latino; 3 Hispanic/Latino), 9 international. Average age 30. 84 applicants, 40% accepted, 22 enrolled. *Faculty:* 8 full-time (0 women), 2 part-time/adjunct (0 women). Expenses: Contact institution. *Financial support:* Unspecified assistantships available. In 2017, 22 master's awarded. *Program availability:* Part-time, evening/weekend, 100% online. Offers business administration (MBA). *Application deadline:* For fall admission, 3/1 for domestic and international students; for spring admission, 10/1 for domestic and international students; for summer admission, 3/1 for domestic students, 2/1 for international students. Applications are processed on a rolling basis. *Application fee:* $60 ($65 for international students). Electronic applications accepted. *Application Contact:* Patricia Palmer, Academic Advisor and Graduate Program Coordinator, 435-865-8167, Fax: 435-586-5493, E-mail: patriciapalmer@suu.edu. *Department Chair/MBA Program Director,* Dr. Kim Craft, 435-586-5414, Fax: 435-586-5493, E-mail: craft@suu.edu.

Program in Communication Students: 18 full-time (13 women), 36 part-time (21 women); includes 4 minority (3 Black or African American, non-Hispanic/Latino; 1 Two or more races, non-Hispanic/Latino), 1 international. Average age 31. 21 applicants, 76% accepted, 15 enrolled. *Faculty:* 6 full-time (1 woman), 1 (woman) part-time/adjunct. Expenses: Contact institution. *Financial support:* Teaching assistantships with tuition reimbursements and unspecified assistantships available. Financial award application deadline: 3/15. In 2017, 25 master's awarded. *Program availability:* Part-time, 100% online. Offers communication (MA). *Application deadline:* For fall admission, 6/15 for domestic and international students; for spring admission, 10/15 for domestic and international students. Applications are processed on a rolling basis. *Application fee:* $60 ($65 for international students). Electronic applications accepted. *Application Contact:* Dr. Matthew Barton, Graduate Coordinator, 435-586-7970, Fax: 435-865-8352, E-mail: bartonm@suu.edu. *Department Chair,* Dr. Arthur Challis, 435-586-7861, Fax: 435-865-8352, E-mail: challis@suu.edu.

Program in Cyber Security and Information Assurance Students: 4 full-time (1 woman), 23 part-time (2 women); includes 3 minority (1 Asian, non-Hispanic/Latino; 1 Hispanic/Latino; 1 Native Hawaiian or other Pacific Islander, non-Hispanic/Latino). Average age 36. 10 applicants, 80% accepted, 7 enrolled. *Faculty:* 4 full-time (2 women), 2 part-time/adjunct (0 women). Expenses: Contact institution. *Program availability:* Part-time, online only, 100% online. Offers cyber security and information assurance (MS). *Application fee:* $60 ($65 for international students). Electronic applications accepted. *Application Contact:* Mary Gillins, Administrative Assistant, 435-586-5405, Fax: 435-865-8444, E-mail: marygillins@suu.edu. *Department Chair/Graduate Director,* Dr. Rob Robertson, 435-865-8560, Fax: 435-865-8444, E-mail: robertson@suu.edu.

Program in Education Students: 5 full-time (all women), 380 part-time (273 women); includes 22 minority (1 Black or African American, non-Hispanic/Latino; 8 Asian, non-Hispanic/Latino; 10 Hispanic/Latino; 3 Native Hawaiian or other Pacific Islander, non-Hispanic/Latino), 2 international. Average age 38. 72 applicants, 86% accepted, 45 enrolled. *Faculty:* 13 full-time (6 women), 16 part-time/adjunct (6 women). Expenses: Contact institution. *Financial support:* Tuition waivers (partial) available. In 2017, 195 master's awarded. *Program availability:* Part-time, 100% online. Offers education (M Ed, MMus, Certificate). *Application deadline:* For fall admission, 7/15 for domestic and international students; for spring admission, 11/15 for domestic and international students; for summer admission, 4/15 for domestic and international students. Applications are processed on a rolling basis. *Application fee:* $60 ($65 for international students). Electronic applications accepted. *Application Contact:* Tamara Lovell, Program Specialist, 435-865-8759, Fax: 435-865-8485, E-mail: tamaralovell@suu.edu. *Department Chair,* Dr. Bart Reynolds, 435-865-8125, Fax: 435-865-8485, E-mail: reynolds@suu.edu.

Program in Interdisciplinary Studies Expenses: Contact institution. *Program availability:* 100% online. Offers interdisciplinary studies (MIS). *Application fee:* $60 ($65 for international students).

Program in Music Students: 16 full-time (5 women), 1 part-time (0 women); includes 3 minority (2 Black or African American, non-Hispanic/Latino; 1 Asian, non-Hispanic/Latino). Average age 32. 16 applicants, 94% accepted, 14 enrolled. *Faculty:* 4 full-time (1 woman), 6 part-time/adjunct (0 women). Expenses: Contact institution. *Program availability:* Part-time, online learning. Offers music technology (MMus). *Application fee:* $60 ($65 for international students). *Department Chair,* Dr. Keith Bradshaw, 435-586-7891, E-mail: bradshaw@suu.edu.

Program in Public Administration Students: 42 full-time (21 women), 73 part-time (33 women); includes 18 minority (2 Black or African American, non-Hispanic/Latino; 2 American Indian or Alaska Native, non-Hispanic/Latino; 3 Asian, non-Hispanic/Latino; 8 Hispanic/Latino; 3 Native Hawaiian or other Pacific Islander, non-Hispanic/Latino), 3 international. Average age 33. 47 applicants, 70% accepted, 30 enrolled. *Faculty:* 4 full-time (0 women), 6 part-time/adjunct (4 women). Expenses: Contact institution. *Financial support:* Tuition waivers (full and partial) and unspecified assistantships available. Financial award application deadline: 5/31. In 2017, 36 master's awarded. *Program availability:* Part-time, evening/weekend, 100% online. Offers public administration (MPA). *Application deadline:* For fall admission, 7/15 for domestic and international students; for spring admission, 11/15 for domestic and international students; for summer admission, 4/15 for domestic and international students. Applications are processed on a rolling basis. *Application fee:* $60 ($65 for international students). Electronic applications accepted. *MPA Program Director,* Dr. Angela Pool-Funai, 435-865-8153, Fax: 435-586-1925, E-mail: angelapoolfunai@suu.edu.

Program in Sports Conditioning and Performance Students: 17 full-time (8 women), 37 part-time (15 women); includes 6 minority (1 Black or African American, non-Hispanic/Latino; 1 American Indian or Alaska Native, non-Hispanic/Latino; 3 Asian, non-Hispanic/Latino; 1 Native Hawaiian or other Pacific Islander, non-Hispanic/Latino), 1 international. Average age 27. 25 applicants, 92% accepted, 17 enrolled. *Faculty:* 6 full-time (3 women). Expenses: Contact institution. In 2017, 14 master's awarded. *Program availability:* Part-time, online only, three intensive summer courses/clinical workshops on campus for 1-2 weeks. Offers sports conditioning and performance (MS). *Application deadline:* For fall admission, 7/15 for domestic and international students; for spring admission, 10/15 for domestic and international students; for summer admission, 2/15 for domestic and international students. Applications are processed on a rolling basis. *Application fee:* $60 ($65 for international students). Electronic applications accepted. *Application Contact:* Joan Anderson, Administrative Assistant, 435-586-7816, Fax: 435-865-8057, E-mail: stephanie-smith@leavitt.com. *Department Chair,* Dr. Camille Thomas, 435-586-7815, Fax: 435-865-8057, E-mail: camillethomas1@suu.edu.

SOUTHERN WESLEYAN UNIVERSITY, Central, SC 29630-1020

General Information Independent-religious, coed, comprehensive institution. *Graduate housing:* On-campus housing not available.

GRADUATE UNITS

Program in Business Administration *Program availability:* Evening/weekend. Offers business administration (MBA).

Program in Christian Ministries *Program availability:* Part-time, evening/weekend. Offers Christian ministries (M Min).

Program in Education *Program availability:* Evening/weekend. Offers education (M Ed). Program also offered at Greenville, S. C. site.

Program in Management *Program availability:* Evening/weekend. Offers management (MSM).

SOUTH FLORIDA BIBLE COLLEGE AND THEOLOGICAL SEMINARY, Deerfield Beach, FL 33442

General Information Proprietary, coed, comprehensive institution.

GRADUATE UNITS

Graduate Programs Offers biblical studies (MA); theology (M Div).

SOUTH TEXAS COLLEGE OF LAW HOUSTON, Houston, TX 77002-7000

General Information Independent, coed, graduate-only institution.

GRADUATE UNITS

Professional Program *Program availability:* Part-time, evening/weekend. Offers law (JD). Electronic applications accepted.

SOUTH UNIVERSITY, Montgomery, AL 36116-1120

General Information Independent, coed, comprehensive institution.

GRADUATE UNITS

Program in Business Administration Offers business administration (MBA).

Program in Clinical Mental Health Counseling Offers clinical mental health counseling (MA).

Program in Criminal Justice Offers criminal justice (MS).

Program in Healthcare Administration Offers healthcare administration (MBA).

Program in Information Systems and Technology Offers information systems and technology (MS).

Program in Nursing Offers nursing (MSN).

Program in Public Administration Offers public administration (MPA).

SOUTH UNIVERSITY, Royal Palm Beach, FL 33411

General Information Independent, coed, comprehensive institution.

GRADUATE UNITS

Program in Business Administration Offers business administration (MBA); healthcare administration (MBA).

Program in Clinical Mental Health Counseling Offers clinical mental health counseling (MA).

Program in Criminal Justice Offers criminal justice (MS).

Program in Information Systems and Technology Offers information systems and technology (MS).

Program in Nursing Offers family nurse practitioner (MS).

Program in Occupational Therapy Offers occupational therapy (OTD).

Program in Public Administration Offers public administration (MPA).

SOUTH UNIVERSITY, Tampa, FL 33614

General Information Independent, coed, comprehensive institution.

GRADUATE UNITS

Program in Business Administration Offers business administration (MBA).

Program in Criminal Justice Offers criminal justice (MS).

Program in Healthcare Administration Offers healthcare administration (MBA).

Program in Information Systems and Technology Offers information systems and technology (MS).

Program in Nursing Offers adult health nurse practitioner (MS); family nurse practitioner (MS); nurse educator (MS).

Program in Physician Assistant Studies Offers physician assistant studies (MS).

SOUTH UNIVERSITY, Savannah, GA 31406

General Information Independent, coed, comprehensive institution.

GRADUATE UNITS

Graduate Programs

College of Arts and Sciences Offers arts and sciences (MA, MS); clinical mental health counseling (MA); criminal justice (MS).

College of Business Offers corrections (MBA); entrepreneurship and small business (MBA); healthcare administration (MBA); hospitality management (MBA); leadership (MS); public administration (MPA); sustainability (MBA).

College of Health Professions Offers anesthesiologist assistant (MM Sc); health professions (MM Sc, MS); physician assistant studies (MS).

College of Nursing Offers nurse educator (MS).

Doctor of Ministry Program Offers ministry (D Min).

School of Pharmacy

SOUTH UNIVERSITY, Columbia, SC 29203

General Information Independent, coed, comprehensive institution.

GRADUATE UNITS

Program in Business Administration Offers business administration (MBA).

Program in Clinical Mental Health Counseling Offers clinical mental health counseling (MA).

Program in Criminal Justice Offers criminal justice (MS).

Program in Healthcare Administration Offers healthcare administration (MBA).

Program in Leadership Offers leadership (MS).

Program in Nursing Offers nursing (MSN).

Program in Pharmacy Offers pharmacy (Pharm D).

SOUTH UNIVERSITY, Round Rock, TX 78681

General Information Independent, coed, comprehensive institution.

GRADUATE UNITS

Program in Business Administration Offers business administration (MBA).

Program in Clinical Mental Health Counseling Offers clinical mental health counseling (MA).

Program in Information Systems and Technology Offers information systems and technology (MS).

SOUTH UNIVERSITY, Glen Allen, VA 23060

General Information Independent, coed, comprehensive institution.

GRADUATE UNITS

Program in Business Administration Offers business administration (MBA).

Program in Clinical Mental Health Counseling Offers clinical mental health counseling (MA).

Program in Nursing Offers nursing (MSN).

SOUTH UNIVERSITY, Virginia Beach, VA 23452

General Information Independent, coed, comprehensive institution.

GRADUATE UNITS

Program in Business Administration Offers business administration (MBA).

Program in Clinical Mental Health Counseling Offers clinical mental health counseling (MA).

Program in Information Systems and Technology Offers information systems and technology (MS).

Program in Leadership Offers leadership (MS).

Program in Nursing Offers family nurse practitioner (MSN).

SOUTHWEST ACUPUNCTURE COLLEGE, Santa Fe, NM 87505

General Information Private, coed, primarily women, graduate-only institution. *Graduate housing:* On-campus housing not available.

GRADUATE UNITS

Program in Oriental Medicine, Boulder Campus *Program availability:* Part-time. Offers Oriental medicine (MS).

Program in Oriental Medicine, Santa Fe Campus *Program availability:* Part-time. Offers Oriental medicine (MS). Electronic applications accepted.

SOUTHWEST BAPTIST UNIVERSITY, Bolivar, MO 65613-2597

General Information Independent-religious, coed, comprehensive institution. *Graduate housing:* Room and/or apartments available on a first-come, first-served basis to single students; on-campus housing not available to married students.

GRADUATE UNITS

Program in Business *Program availability:* Part-time, online learning. Offers business administration (MBA); health administration (MBA).

Program in Education *Program availability:* Part-time. Offers education (MS); educational administration (MS, Ed S).

Program in Physical Therapy Offers physical therapy (DPT).

SOUTHWEST COLLEGE OF NATUROPATHIC MEDICINE AND HEALTH SCIENCES, Tempe, AZ 85282

General Information Independent, coed, graduate-only institution. *Enrollment by degree level:* 360 doctoral. *Graduate faculty:* 16 full-time (8 women), 50 part-time/adjunct (32 women). *Tuition:* Full-time $34,680; part-time $16,490 per credit hour. *Required fees:* $1655; $1595 per credit hour. $184 per quarter. One-time fee: $860. Tuition and fees vary according to course load, program and student level. *Graduate housing:* On-campus housing not available. *Student services:* Campus employment opportunities, career counseling, exercise/wellness program, free psychological counseling, international student services, services for students with disabilities. *Library facilities:* SCNM Library plus 1 other. *Collection:* Books: 5,000 (physical), 270 (digital/electronic); Serial titles: 36 (physical), 85 (digital/electronic); Databases: 15. Weekly public service hours: 95; students can reserve study rooms. *Research affiliation:* Gaia Herbs, Arizona State University, Biodesign Institute (immune modulation, virology, genomics, herbal medicine), Emory University, Aviratek, LLC (antimicrobial botanicals).

Computer facilities: 16 computers available on campus for general student use. A campuswide network can be accessed from off campus. Online class registration is available.
Website: http://www.scnm.edu/

General Application Contact: Eve Adams, Director of Admissions, 480-858-9100 Ext. 213, Fax: 480-222-9413, E-mail: e.adams@scnm.edu.

GRADUATE UNITS

Doctor of Naturopathic Medicine Program Students: 329 full-time (258 women), 31 part-time (24 women); includes 122 minority (33 Black or African American, non-Hispanic/Latino; 2 American Indian or Alaska Native, non-Hispanic/Latino; 26 Asian, non-Hispanic/Latino; 44 Hispanic/Latino; 1 Native Hawaiian or other Pacific Islander, non-Hispanic/Latino; 16 Two or more races, non-Hispanic/Latino), 13 international. Average age 30. 190 applicants, 80% accepted, 107 enrolled. *Faculty:* 16 full-time (8 women), 50 part-time/adjunct (32 women). Expenses: Contact institution. *Financial support:* In 2017–18, 132 students received support. Federal Work-Study and scholarships/grants available. Financial award application deadline: 5/1; financial award applicants required to submit FAFSA. In 2017, 83 doctorates awarded. Offers naturopathic medicine (ND). *Application deadline:* For fall admission, 4/1 priority date for domestic and international students; for spring admission, 12/1 priority date for domestic and international students. Applications are processed on a rolling basis. *Application fee:* $115. Electronic applications accepted. *Application Contact:* Eve Adams, Director of Admissions, 480-858-9100 Ext. 213, Fax: 480-222-9413, E-mail: e.adams@scnm.edu. *Dean of Academic Affairs,* Dr. Garrett Thompson, 480-858-9100 Ext. 207, E-mail: g.thompson@scnm.edu.

SOUTHWESTERN ADVENTIST UNIVERSITY, Keene, TX 76059

General Information Independent-religious, coed, comprehensive institution. *Graduate housing:* Rooms and/or apartments available on a first-come, first-served basis to single and married students. Housing application deadline: 8/31.

GRADUATE UNITS

Business Administration Department *Program availability:* Part-time, evening/weekend. Offers accounting (MBA); finance (MBA); management/leadership (MBA).

Education Department *Program availability:* Part-time, evening/weekend. Offers curriculum and instruction with reading emphasis (M Ed); educational leadership (M Ed).

SOUTHWESTERN ASSEMBLIES OF GOD UNIVERSITY, Waxahachie, TX 75165-5735

General Information Independent-religious, coed, comprehensive institution. *Graduate housing:* Room and/or apartments guaranteed to single students.

GRADUATE UNITS

Thomas F. Harrison School of Graduate Studies *Program availability:* Part-time, evening/weekend, online learning. Offers Bible and theology (MS); Biblical studies (M Div); Christian school administration (MS); counseling (M Div); counseling psychology (clinical) (MCP); cross cultural missions (M Div); curriculum development (MS); early education administration (M Ed); history (MA); human services counseling (MS); middle and secondary education (M Ed); practical theology (M Div); theological studies (M Div). Electronic applications accepted.

SOUTHWESTERN BAPTIST THEOLOGICAL SEMINARY, Fort Worth, TX 76122-0000

General Information Independent-religious, coed, primarily men, graduate-only institution. *Graduate housing:* Rooms and/or apartments available on a first-come, first-served basis to single and married students. *Research affiliation:* Campus Crusade for Christ/Jesus Film Project (evangelical missions), DAWN: Discipling A Whole Nation (evangelical missions).

GRADUATE UNITS

Jack D. Terry School of Church and Family Ministries *Program availability:* Part-time, evening/weekend. Offers church and family ministries (MA, MACE, MACSE, DEM, PhD). Electronic applications accepted.

Roy Fish School of Evangelism and Missions Offers cross-cultural missions (MTS); evangelism (M Div); evangelism and missions (D Min); international church planting (M Div); Islamic studies (M Div, MA Islamic); missiology (MA Miss); missions (M Div); North American church planting (M Div); North American evangelism and international missions (D Min); theology (Th M); world Christian studies (PhD).

School of Church Music *Program availability:* Part-time. Offers church music (MACM, MAWSHP, MM, DMA, PhD). Electronic applications accepted.

School of Preaching Offers preaching (Th M, D Min, PhD, Certificate).

School of Theology *Program availability:* Part-time, evening/weekend. Offers ministry (D Min); theology (PhD). Electronic applications accepted.

SOUTHWESTERN CHRISTIAN UNIVERSITY, Bethany, OK 73008-0340

General Information Independent-religious, coed, comprehensive institution.

GRADUATE UNITS

Program in Ministry *Program availability:* Part-time. Offers church planting (M Min); church revitalization and renewal (M Min); intercultural studies (M Min); leadership (M Min); life coaching (M Min); pastoral ministries (M Min); work place ministries (M Min). Electronic applications accepted.

SOUTHWESTERN COLLEGE, Winfield, KS 67156-2499

General Information Independent-religious, coed, comprehensive institution. *Enrollment:* 1,306 graduate, professional, and undergraduate students; 19 full-time matriculated graduate/professional students (11 women), 141 part-time matriculated graduate/professional students (72 women). *Enrollment by degree level:* 111 master's, 48 doctoral, 1 other advanced degree. *Graduate faculty:* 9 full-time (7 women), 27 part-time/adjunct (16 women). *Tuition:* Full-time $10,962; part-time $609 per credit hour. *Required fees:* $30 per semester. Tuition and fees vary according to degree level, campus/location and program. *Graduate housing:* Rooms and/or apartments available on a first-come, first-served basis to single and married students. Typical cost: $3500 per year ($7520 including board) for single students. Room and board charges vary according to board plan and housing facility selected. *Student services:* Campus employment opportunities, campus safety program, free psychological counseling, international student services, services for students with disabilities, teacher training, writing training. *Library facilities:* Harold and Mary Ellen Deets Library. *Collection:* Books: 49,349 (physical), 479,970 (digital/electronic); Serial titles: 10 (physical), 21,560 (digital/electronic); Databases: 84. Weekly public service hours: 91; students can reserve study rooms.

Computer facilities: Computer purchase and lease plans are available. 45 computers available on campus for general student use. A campuswide network can be accessed from student residence rooms and from off campus. Online class registration, everything in Self-Service and BlackBoard are available.
Website: http://www.sckans.edu/

General Application Contact: Adam Jenkins, Vice President for Enrollment Management, 620-229-6091, Fax: 620-229-6384, E-mail: adam.jenkins@sckans.edu.

GRADUATE UNITS

Education Programs Students: 12 full-time (10 women), 77 part-time (51 women); includes 12 minority (5 Black or African American, non-Hispanic/Latino; 2 American Indian or Alaska Native, non-Hispanic/Latino; 1 Asian, non-Hispanic/Latino; 3 Hispanic/Latino; 1 Native Hawaiian or other Pacific Islander, non-Hispanic/Latino), 10 international. Average age 39. 29 applicants, 86% accepted, 18 enrolled. *Faculty:* 6 full-time (5 women), 12 part-time/adjunct (10 women). Expenses: Contact institution. *Financial support:* In 2017–18, 9 students received support. Unspecified assistantships and employee tuition waivers available. Financial award applicants required to submit FAFSA. In 2017, 52 master's, 11 doctorates awarded. *Program availability:* Part-time, evening/weekend, 100% online, blended/hybrid learning. Offers curriculum and instruction (M Ed); early childhood education (M Ed); educational leadership (Ed D); special education (M Ed); teaching (MA). *Application deadline:* Applications are processed on a rolling basis. *Application fee:* $40. Electronic applications accepted. *Application Contact:* Dennis Russell, Director of Admissions and Student Services, 888-684-5335 Ext. 3372, Fax: 888-684-5218, E-mail: dennis.russell@sckans.edu. *Director of Education Operations*, Dana Pentz, 620-229-6253, E-mail: dana.pentz@sckans.edu.

Fifth-Year Graduate Programs Students: 7 full-time (1 woman), 14 part-time (8 women); includes 6 minority (4 Black or African American, non-Hispanic/Latino; 2 Hispanic/Latino), 5 international. Average age 24. 19 applicants, 100% accepted, 9 enrolled. *Faculty:* 4 full-time (2 women), 1 (woman) part-time/adjunct. Expenses: Contact institution. *Financial support:* In 2017–18, 13 students received support, including 1 fellowship (averaging $25,128 per year); unspecified assistantships also available. Financial award applicants required to submit FAFSA. In 2017, 25 master's awarded. *Program availability:* Part-time. Offers management (MBA). *Application deadline:* For fall admission, 8/28 for domestic students; for spring admission, 1/23 for domestic students. Applications are processed on a rolling basis. *Application fee:* $25. Electronic applications accepted. *Application Contact:* Adam Jenkins, Vice President for Enrollment Management, 620-229-6091, E-mail: adam.jenkins@sckans.edu. *Professor/Division Chair*, Dr. Kurt Keiser, 620-229-6361, E-mail: kurt.keiser@sckans.edu.

Professional Studies Programs Students: 50 part-time (13 women); includes 11 minority (7 Black or African American, non-Hispanic/Latino; 1 American Indian or Alaska Native, non-Hispanic/Latino; 3 Hispanic/Latino). Average age 39. 57 applicants, 74% accepted, 11 enrolled. *Faculty:* 15 part-time/adjunct (6 women). Expenses: Contact institution. *Financial support:* In 2017–18, 13 students received support. Unspecified assistantships available. Financial award applicants required to submit FAFSA. In 2017, 43 master's awarded. *Program availability:* Part-time, evening/weekend, online only, 100% online. Offers business administration (MBA); leadership (MS); management (MS); security administration (MS); specialized ministries (MA). *Application deadline:* Applications are processed on a rolling basis. *Application fee:* $40. Electronic applications accepted. *Director of Admissions and Student Services*, Dennis Russell, 888-684-5335 Ext. 3372, Fax: 316-688-5218, E-mail: dennis.russell@sckans.edu.

SOUTHWESTERN COLLEGE, Santa Fe, NM 87502-4788

General Information Independent, coed, primarily women, graduate-only institution. *Graduate housing:* On-campus housing not available.

GRADUATE UNITS

Program in Art Therapy/Counseling *Program availability:* Part-time, evening/weekend. Offers art therapy/counseling (MA).

Program in Counseling *Program availability:* Part-time, evening/weekend. Offers counseling (MA).

Program in Grief, Loss and Trauma Counseling *Program availability:* Part-time, evening/weekend, online learning. Offers grief, loss and trauma counseling (MA, Certificate).

Program in Integral Somatic Psychology Offers integral somatic psychology (Certificate).

Program in Psychodrama and Action Methods Offers psychodrama and action methods (Certificate).

Program in Transformational Ecopsychology Offers transformational ecopsychology (Certificate).

SOUTHWESTERN LAW SCHOOL, Los Angeles, CA 90010

General Information Independent, coed, graduate-only institution. *Enrollment by degree level:* 765 doctoral. *Graduate faculty:* 59 full-time (29 women), 84 part-time/adjunct (32 women). *Tuition:* Full-time $51,890; part-time $34,610 per year. *Required fees:* $200; $200 per unit. Tuition and fees vary according to program. *Graduate housing:* Rooms and/or apartments available on a first-come, first-served basis to single and married students. Typical cost: $20,520 per year for single students; $20,520 per year for married students. Room charges vary according to housing facility selected. *Student services:* Campus employment opportunities, campus safety program, career counseling, exercise/wellness program, free psychological counseling, international student services, low-cost health insurance, multicultural affairs office, services for students with disabilities, writing training. *Library facilities:* Leigh H. Taylor Law Library. *Collection:* Books: 82,845 (physical), 44,498 (digital/electronic); Serial titles: 5,560 (physical), 5,840 (digital/electronic); Databases: 139. Weekly public service hours: 108; students can reserve study rooms.

Computer facilities: 102 computers available on campus for general student use. A campuswide network can be accessed from student residence rooms. Online class registration is available.
Website: http://www.swlaw.edu/

General Application Contact: Lisa Gear, Assistant Dean of Admissions, 213-738-6834, Fax: 213-383-1688, E-mail: admissions@swlaw.edu.

GRADUATE UNITS

Graduate and Professional Programs Students: 510 full-time (281 women), 255 part-time (159 women); includes 357 minority (51 Black or African American, non-Hispanic/Latino; 77 Asian, non-Hispanic/Latino; 190 Hispanic/Latino; 5 Native Hawaiian or other Pacific Islander, non-Hispanic/Latino; 34 Two or more races, non-Hispanic/Latino), 18 international. Average age 26. 1,749 applicants, 46% accepted, 266 enrolled. *Faculty:* 59 full-time (29 women), 84 part-time/adjunct (32 women). Expenses: Contact institution. *Financial support:* In 2017–18, 408 students received support. Federal Work-Study, institutionally sponsored loans, and scholarships/grants available. Support available to part-time students. Financial award application deadline: 6/1; financial award applicants required to submit FAFSA. In 2017, 25 master's, 287 doctorates awarded. *Program availability:* Part-time, evening/weekend. Offers entertainment and media law (LL M); individualized studies (LL M); law (JD). *Application deadline:* For fall admission, 4/1 priority date for domestic and international students. Applications are processed on a rolling basis. *Application fee:* $60. Electronic applications accepted. *Application Contact:* Lisa Gear, Assistant Dean of Admissions, 213-738-6834, Fax: 213-383-1688, E-mail: admissions@swlaw.edu. *Dean*, Susan Westerberg Prager, 213-738-6710, Fax: 213-383-1688.

SOUTHWESTERN OKLAHOMA STATE UNIVERSITY, Weatherford, OK 73096-3098

General Information State-supported, coed, comprehensive institution. *Graduate housing:* Rooms and/or apartments available on a first-come, first-served basis to single and married students. Housing application deadline: 8/19. *Research affiliation:* Gulf Coast Research Laboratory.

GRADUATE UNITS

College of Arts and Sciences *Program availability:* Part-time. Offers art education (M Ed); arts and sciences (M Ed, MM); English (M Ed); mathematics (M Ed); music education (MM); natural sciences (M Ed); performance (MM); social sciences (M Ed).

College of Pharmacy Offers pharmacy (Pharm D).

College of Professional and Graduate Studies *Program availability:* Part-time, evening/weekend, online learning.

School of Behavioral Sciences and Education *Program availability:* Part-time, evening/weekend, online learning. Offers community counseling (M Ed); early childhood education (M Ed); educational administration (M Ed); elementary education (M Ed); health sciences and microbiology (M Ed); kinesiology (M Ed); parks and recreation management (M Ed); school counseling (M Ed); school psychology (MS); school psychometry (M Ed); secondary education (M Ed); special education (M Ed).

School of Business and Technology *Program availability:* Part-time, evening/weekend, online learning. Offers business and technology (MBA). MBA distance learning degree program offered to Oklahoma residents only.

SOUTHWEST MINNESOTA STATE UNIVERSITY, Marshall, MN 56258

General Information State-supported, coed, comprehensive institution. *Graduate housing:* Room and/or apartments available to single students; on-campus housing not available to married students.

GRADUATE UNITS

Department of Business and Public Affairs *Program availability:* Part-time, evening/weekend, online learning. Offers leadership (MBA); management (MBA); marketing (MBA). Electronic applications accepted.

Department of Education *Program availability:* Part-time, evening/weekend, online learning. Offers ESL (MS); math (MS); reading (MS); special education (MS); teaching, learning and leadership (MS).

SOUTHWEST UNIVERSITY, Kenner, LA 70062

General Information Proprietary, coed, comprehensive institution.

GRADUATE UNITS

MBA Program Offers business administration (MBA); management (MBA); organizational management (MBA).

Program in Criminal Justice Offers criminal justice (MS).

Program in Management Offers management (MA).

Program in Organizational Management Offers organizational management (MA).

SOUTHWEST UNIVERSITY OF VISUAL ARTS, Tucson, AZ 85716-2505

General Information Proprietary, coed, comprehensive institution.

GRADUATE UNITS

MFA Programs Offers motion arts (MFA); painting and drawing (MFA); photography (MFA).

SPALDING UNIVERSITY, Louisville, KY 40203-2188

General Information Independent-religious, coed, comprehensive institution. CGS member. *Graduate housing:* Room and/or apartments available on a first-come, first-served basis to single students; on-campus housing not available to married students.

GRADUATE UNITS

Graduate Studies *Program availability:* Part-time, evening/weekend.

College of Education *Program availability:* Part-time, evening/weekend. Offers art teacher education (MAT); business teacher education (MAT); education (M Ed, MA, MAT, Ed D); elementary school education (MAT); executive (Ed D); foreign language (MAT); high school education (MAT); middle school education (MAT); scholar-practitioner (Ed D); secondary education (MAT); special education (learning and behavioral disorders) (MAT); student guidance counselor (MA); teacher leader (M Ed). Electronic applications accepted.

College of Social Sciences and Humanities *Program availability:* Part-time, evening/weekend, online learning. Offers business and communication (MS); social sciences and humanities (MFA, MS); writing (MFA).

Kosair College of Health and Natural Sciences *Program availability:* Part-time, evening/weekend. Offers adult nurse practitioner (MSN); athletic training (MS); clinical psychology (MA, Psy D); family nurse practitioner (MSN); health and natural sciences (MA, MS, MSN, MSW, DNP, Psy D, Post-Master's Certificate); leadership in nursing and healthcare (MSN); nurse educator (Post-Master's Certificate); nurse practitioner (Post-Master's Certificate); occupational therapy (MS); pediatric nurse practitioner (MSN); social work (MSW).

SPERTUS INSTITUTE FOR JEWISH LEARNING AND LEADERSHIP, Chicago, IL 60605-1901

General Information Independent, coed, graduate-only institution. *Graduate housing:* On-campus housing not available.

GRADUATE UNITS

Program in Jewish Studies *Program availability:* Part-time, evening/weekend, online learning. Offers Jewish studies (MAJPS, MAJS, DJS, DSJS).

SPRING ARBOR UNIVERSITY, Spring Arbor, MI 49283-9799

General Information Independent-religious, coed, comprehensive institution. *Graduate housing:* Rooms and/or apartments available on a first-come, first-served basis to single and married students. Housing application deadline: 5/1.

GRADUATE UNITS

Gainey School of Business *Program availability:* Part-time, evening/weekend, online learning. Offers business (MBA).

School of Arts and Sciences *Program availability:* Part-time, online learning. Offers communication (MA); spiritual formation and leadership (MA).

School of Education *Program availability:* Part-time, evening/weekend, online learning. Offers education (MAE); reading (MAR); special education (MSE). Electronic applications accepted.

School of Human Services *Program availability:* Part-time, evening/weekend, online learning. Offers counseling (MAC); family studies (MAFS); nursing (MSN). Electronic applications accepted.

★ SPRINGFIELD COLLEGE, Springfield, MA 01109-3797

General Information Independent, coed, comprehensive institution. *Enrollment:* 806 full-time matriculated graduate/professional students (571 women), 212 part-time matriculated graduate/professional students (147 women). *Enrollment by degree level:* 879 master's, 139 doctoral. *Graduate faculty:* 202 full-time (114 women). *Graduate housing:* Rooms and/or apartments available on a first-come, first-served basis to single and married students. *Student services:* Campus employment opportunities, campus safety program, career counseling, child daycare facilities, exercise/wellness program, free psychological counseling, international student services, low-cost health insurance, multicultural affairs office, services for students with disabilities, teacher training, writing training. *Library facilities:* Babson Library.

Computer facilities: Computer purchase and lease plans are available. A campuswide network can be accessed from student residence rooms and from off campus. Website: http://www.springfield.edu/

General Application Contact: Anne Griffin, Director of Graduate Admissions, 413-748-3225, Fax: 413-748-3694, E-mail: agriffin2@springfield.edu.

GRADUATE UNITS

Graduate Programs Students: 1,057 full-time. 1,483 applicants, 40% accepted, 348 enrolled. *Faculty:* 171 full-time (75 women), 151 part-time/adjunct (75 women). Expenses: Contact institution. *Financial support:* Fellowships with partial tuition reimbursements, teaching assistantships with partial tuition reimbursements, career-related internships or fieldwork, Federal Work-Study, institutionally sponsored loans, scholarships/grants, traineeships, and unspecified assistantships available. Financial award application deadline: 3/1; financial award applicants required to submit FAFSA. *Program availability:* Part-time, evening/weekend. Offers adapted physical education (MS); advanced-level coaching (M Ed); art therapy (M Ed, MS, CAGS); athletic administration (MS); athletic counseling (MS, CAGS); athletic training (MS); business administration (MBA); clinical exercise physiology (MS); clinical mental health counseling (M Ed, CAGS); counseling psychology (Psy D); early childhood education (M Ed); educational studies (M Ed); elementary education (M Ed); exercise physiology (MS, PhD); general counseling (M Ed); health promotion and disease prevention (MS); industrial/organizational psychology (M Ed, CAGS); mental health counseling (MS); occupational therapy (MS); organizational management and leadership (MS); physical education initial licensure (CAGS); physical therapy (DPT); physician assistant (MS); recreation management (M Ed, MS); rehabilitation counseling (M Ed, MS); school counseling (M Ed, CAGS); secondary education (M Ed); special education (M Ed, CAGS); sport and exercise psychology (MS, PhD); sport management (M Ed, MS); strength and conditioning (MS); student personnel administration in higher education (M Ed, CAGS); teaching and administration (PhD); therapeutic recreation management (M Ed, MS). *Application deadline:* For fall admission, 1/1 for domestic students, 1/15 for international students; for winter admission, 11/1 for domestic and international students; for spring admission, 11/1 for domestic and international students. Applications are processed on a rolling basis. *Application fee:* $50. Electronic applications accepted. *Application Contact:* Anne Griffin, Director of Graduate Admissions, 413-748-3225, Fax: 413-748-3694, E-mail: agriffin2@springfield.edu. *Associate Vice President for Graduate Education, Grants, and Sponsored Research*, Dr. James Harnsberger, 413-748-3959, Fax: 413-748-4826, E-mail: jharnsberger@springfield.edu.

School of Social Work Students: 252 full-time (214 women), 98 part-time (84 women); includes 150 minority (89 Black or African American, non-Hispanic/Latino; 5 Asian, non-Hispanic/Latino; 47 Hispanic/Latino; 9 Two or more races, non-Hispanic/Latino). 223 applicants, 69% accepted, 102 enrolled. *Faculty:* 14 full-time (5 women), 28 part-time/adjunct (20 women). Expenses: Contact institution. *Financial support:* Fellowships with partial tuition reimbursements, research assistantships, career-related internships or fieldwork, Federal Work-Study, institutionally sponsored loans, scholarships/grants, and unspecified assistantships available. Support available to part-time students. Financial award application deadline: 3/1; financial award applicants required to submit FAFSA. In 2017, 151 master's awarded. *Program availability:* Part-time, evening/weekend. Offers advanced practice with children and adolescents (Post-Master's Certificate); social work (MSW). *Application deadline:* For fall admission, 5/1 for domestic and international students; for summer admission, 3/1 for domestic and international students. Applications are processed on a rolling basis. *Application fee:* $50. Electronic applications accepted. *Application Contact:* Franklin Kirshner, Admissions Coordinator, 413-748-3060, Fax: 413-748-3069, E-mail: fkirschner@springfield.edu. *Dean*, Dr. Francine Vecchiola, 413-748-3065.

See Display below and Close-Up on page 875.

SPRING HILL COLLEGE, Mobile, AL 36608-1791

General Information Independent-religious, coed, comprehensive institution. *Enrollment:* 1,501 graduate, professional, and undergraduate students; 6 full-time matriculated graduate/professional students (1 woman), 102 part-time matriculated graduate/professional students (49 women). *Enrollment by degree level:* 92 master's, 16 other advanced degrees. *Graduate faculty:* 24 full-time (6 women), 3 part-time/adjunct (1 woman). *Tuition:* Full-time $9270; part-time $515 per credit hour. Tuition and fees vary according to program. *Graduate housing:* On-campus housing not available. *Student*

services: Campus safety program, career counseling, exercise/wellness program, writing training. *Library facilities:* Marnie and John Burke Memorial Library plus 1 other.

Computer facilities: A campuswide network can be accessed from student residence rooms and from off campus. Online class registration is available.
Website: http://www.shc.edu/

General Application Contact: Robert Stewart, Vice President of Enrollment, 251-380-3030, Fax: 251-460-2186, E-mail: rstewart@shc.edu.

GRADUATE UNITS

Graduate Programs Students: 6 full-time (1 woman), 102 part-time (49 women); includes 25 minority (18 Black or African American, non-Hispanic/Latino; 1 American Indian or Alaska Native, non-Hispanic/Latino; 1 Asian, non-Hispanic/Latino; 3 Hispanic/Latino; 1 Native Hawaiian or other Pacific Islander, non-Hispanic/Latino; 1 Two or more races, non-Hispanic/Latino), 8 international. Average age 35. *Faculty:* 24 full-time (6 women), 3 part-time/adjunct (1 woman). Expenses: Contact institution. *Financial support:* Applicants required to submit FAFSA. In 2017, 36 master's, 4 other advanced degrees awarded. *Program availability:* Part-time, evening/weekend. Offers business administration (MBA); early childhood education (MAT, MS Ed); educational theory (MS Ed); elementary education (MAT, MS Ed); faith companioning (Postbaccalaureate Certificate); fine arts (MLA); leadership and ethics (MLA, Postbaccalaureate Certificate); literature (MLA); nursing (MSN, Post-Master's Certificate); pastoral ministry (Postbaccalaureate Certificate); pastoral studies (MPS); secondary education (MAT, MS Ed); spiritual direction (Postbaccalaureate Certificate); theological studies (MTS); theology (MA). *Application deadline:* For fall admission, 8/1 priority date for domestic and international students; for spring admission, 12/1 priority date for domestic and international students. Applications are processed on a rolling basis. *Application fee:* $25 ($35 for international students). Electronic applications accepted. *Vice President of Enrollment*, Robert Stewart, 251-380-3030, Fax: 251-460-2186, E-mail: rstewart@shc.edu.

STANBRIDGE UNIVERSITY, Irvine, CA 92612

General Information Proprietary, coed, comprehensive institution.

GRADUATE UNITS

Program in Nursing *Program availability:* Online learning. Offers nursing (MSN).

Program in Occupational Therapy Offers occupational therapy (MS).

STANFORD UNIVERSITY, Stanford, CA 94305-2004

General Information Independent, coed, university. CGS member. *Enrollment:* 16,914 graduate, professional, and undergraduate students; 9,105 full-time matriculated graduate/professional students (3,644 women), 263 part-time matriculated graduate/professional students (82 women). *Enrollment by degree level:* 3,488 master's, 5,880 doctoral. *Graduate faculty:* 2,184 full-time (635 women), 35 part-time/adjunct (15 women). *Tuition:* Full-time $48,987; part-time $10,620 per quarter. One-time fee: $400. Tuition and fees vary according to program. *Graduate housing:* Rooms and/or apartments guaranteed to single and married students. Housing application deadline: 5/10. *Student services:* Campus employment opportunities, campus safety program, career counseling, child daycare facilities, exercise/wellness program, free psychological counseling, grant writing training, international student services, low-cost health insurance, multicultural affairs office, services for students with disabilities, teacher training, writing training. *Library facilities:* Green Library plus 20 others. *Collection:* Books: 9.5 million (physical), 1.5 million (digital/electronic); Serial titles: 77,000 (physical). Study areas open 24 hours, 5–7 days a week; students can reserve study rooms.

Computer facilities: Computer purchase and lease plans are available. 1,000 computers available on campus for general student use. A campuswide network can be accessed from student residence rooms and from off campus. Online class registration is available.
Website: http://www.stanford.edu/

General Application Contact: Graduate Admissions, 866-432-7472, Fax: 650-723-8371, E-mail: gradadmissions@stanford.edu.

GRADUATE UNITS

Graduate School of Business Offers business (MBA, PhD). Electronic applications accepted.

Graduate School of Education Offers curriculum and teacher education (MA); education (MA, MAE, PhD); elementary education (MAE); international comparative education (MA, PhD); learning, design, and technology (MA); policy, organization, and leadership studies (MA); secondary education (MAE). Electronic applications accepted.

Law School Offers corporate governance and practice (LL M); environmental law and policy (LL M); international economic law, business and policy (LL M); international legal studies (JSM); law (JD, JSD); law, science and technology (LL M); legal studies (MLS). Electronic applications accepted.

School of Earth, Energy and Environmental Sciences Offers earth system science (MS, PhD); earth, energy and environmental sciences (MS, PhD, Eng); energy resources engineering (MS, PhD, Eng); geological sciences (MS, PhD, Eng); geophysics (MS, PhD); petroleum engineering (MS, PhD). Electronic applications accepted.

School of Engineering Offers aeronautics and astronautics (MS, PhD, Eng); atmosphere and energy (MS, PhD); biomechanical engineering (MSE); chemical engineering (MS, PhD); computer science (MS, PhD); construction (MS); design impact (MSE); electrical engineering (MS, PhD); engineering (MS, MSE, PhD, Engr); environmental engineering and science (MS, PhD, Eng); environmental fluid mechanics and hydrology (PhD); geomechanics (MS); management science and engineering (MS, PhD); materials science and engineering (MS, PhD, Engr); mechanical engineering (MS, PhD, Engr); product design (MS); structural engineering (MS). Electronic applications accepted.

Institute for Computational and Mathematical Engineering Offers computational and mathematical engineering (MS, PhD). Electronic applications accepted.

School of Humanities and Sciences Offers anthropology (MA); applied and engineering physics (MS); applied physics (PhD); archaeology (PhD); art history (PhD); art practice (MFA); biology (MS, PhD); biophysics (PhD); chemistry (PhD); Chinese (MA, PhD); classics (MA, PhD); communication (MA, PhD); comparative literature (PhD); composition (DMA); computer-based music theory and acoustics (PhD); culture and society (PhD); data science (MS); design (MFA); documentary film and video (MFA); ecology and environment (PhD); economics (PhD); English (MA, PhD); financial mathematics (MS); French (MA, PhD); French and Italian (PhD); German studies (MA, PhD); history (MA, PhD); humanities and sciences (MA, MFA, MS, DMA, PhD); Italian (MA, PhD); Japanese (MA, PhD); linguistics (MA, PhD); mathematics (PhD); modern thought and literature (PhD); music, science, and technology (MA); musicology (PhD); philosophy (MA, PhD); physics (PhD); political science (MA, PhD); psychology (PhD); religious studies (PhD); Slavic languages and literatures (PhD); sociology (PhD); Spanish (MA, PhD); statistics (PhD); theater and performance studies (PhD). Electronic applications accepted.

Center for East Asian Studies Offers East Asian studies (MA). Electronic applications accepted.

Center for Russian, East European and Eurasian Studies Offers Russian, East European and Eurasian studies (MA). Electronic applications accepted.

School of Medicine Offers bioengineering (MS, PhD); medicine (MS, MD, PhD). Electronic applications accepted.

Graduate Programs in Medicine Offers biochemistry (PhD); biostatistics (PhD); chemical and systems biology (PhD); developmental biology (MS, PhD); epidemiology and clinical research (MS, PhD); genetics (PhD); health policy (MS, PhD); medicine (MS, PhD); microbiology and immunology (PhD); molecular and cellular physiology (PhD); structural biology (PhD). Electronic applications accepted.

Stanford Center for Biomedical Informatics Research Offers biomedical informatics research (MS, PhD). Electronic applications accepted.

STARR KING SCHOOL FOR THE MINISTRY, Berkeley, CA 94709-1209

General Information Independent-religious, coed, graduate-only institution. *Graduate housing:* On-campus housing not available.

GRADUATE UNITS

Professional Program Offers theology (M Div).

STATE UNIVERSITY OF NEW YORK AT FREDONIA, Fredonia, NY 14063-1136

General Information State-supported, coed, comprehensive institution. *Enrollment:* 4,631 graduate, professional, and undergraduate students; 153 full-time matriculated graduate/professional students (122 women), 86 part-time matriculated graduate/professional students (56 women). *Enrollment by degree level:* 210 master's, 29 other advanced degrees. *Graduate faculty:* 69 full-time (37 women), 25 part-time/adjunct (15 women). Tuition, state resident: full-time $8154. Tuition, nonresident: full-time $16,650. *Required fees:* $1209. *Graduate housing:* Room and/or apartments available on a first-come, first-served basis to single students; on-campus housing not available to married students. Typical cost: $5130 per year ($8000 including board). Housing application deadline: 8/24. *Student services:* Campus employment opportunities, campus safety program, career counseling, child daycare facilities, exercise/wellness program, free psychological counseling, grant writing training, international student services, low-cost health insurance, multicultural affairs office, services for students with disabilities, teacher training, writing training. *Library facilities:* Daniel A. Reed Library. *Collection:* Books: 18 million (physical); Serial titles: 48,000 (physical). Weekly public service hours: 68; students can reserve study rooms.

Computer facilities: Computer purchase and lease plans are available. 500 computers available on campus for general student use. A campuswide network can be accessed. Online class registration is available.
Website: http://www.fredonia.edu/

General Application Contact: Wendy S. Dunst, Interim Graduate Recruitment and Admissions Associate, 716-673-3808, Fax: 716-673-3712, E-mail: wendy.dunst@fredonia.edu.

GRADUATE UNITS

College of Education Average age 29. 60 applicants, 97% accepted, 39 enrolled. *Faculty:* 11 full-time (9 women), 1 part-time/adjunct (0 women). Expenses: Contact institution. *Financial support:* In 2017–18, 4 teaching assistantships with full and partial tuition reimbursements (averaging $7,075 per year) were awarded. Financial award application deadline: 3/15; financial award applicants required to submit FAFSA. In 2017, 33 master's awarded. *Program availability:* Part-time. Offers curriculum and instruction (MS Ed); literacy education (MS Ed); TESOL (MS Ed). *Application deadline:* For fall admission, 4/1 priority date for domestic and international students; for spring admission, 11/1 priority date for domestic students, 11/1 for international students. Applications are processed on a rolling basis. *Application fee:* $75. Electronic applications accepted. *Application Contact:* Wendy S. Dunst, Interim Graduate Recruitment and Admissions Associate, 716-673-3808, Fax: 716-673-3712, E-mail: wendy.dunst@fredonia.edu. *Dean*, Dr. Christine Givner, 716-673-3311, E-mail: christine.givner@fredonia.edu.

College of Liberal Arts and Sciences Students: 73 full-time (62 women), 9 part-time (6 women); includes 7 minority (1 Black or African American, non-Hispanic/Latino; 1 Asian, non-Hispanic/Latino; 2 Hispanic/Latino; 1 Native Hawaiian or other Pacific Islander, non-Hispanic/Latino; 2 Two or more races, non-Hispanic/Latino). Average age 24. 200 applicants, 25% accepted, 43 enrolled. Expenses: Contact institution. *Financial support:* In 2017–18, 5 students received support, including 14 teaching assistantships with full and partial tuition reimbursements available (averaging $5,957 per year); tuition waivers (full and partial) and unspecified assistantships also available. In 2017, 41 master's, 1 other advanced degree awarded. *Program availability:* Part-time, evening/weekend. Offers biology (MS); English (MA); English education 7-12 (MA); interdisciplinary studies (MA, MS); math education (MS Ed); professional writing (CAS); speech pathology (MS). *Application deadline:* Applications are processed on a rolling basis. *Application fee:* $75. Electronic applications accepted. *Application Contact:* Wendy S. Dunst, Interim Graduate Recruitment and Admissions Associate, 716-673-3808, Fax: 716-673-3712, E-mail: wendy.dunst@fredonia.edu. *Dean*, Dr. Andy Karafa, 716-673-3173, Fax: 716-673-3338, E-mail: andy.karafa@gmail.com.

School of Music Students: 34 full-time (17 women), 21 part-time (16 women); includes 6 minority (2 Black or African American, non-Hispanic/Latino; 2 Asian, non-Hispanic/Latino; 2 Hispanic/Latino), 12 international. Average age 25. 46 applicants, 72% accepted, 14 enrolled. *Faculty:* 36 full-time (16 women), 14 part-time/adjunct (10 women). Expenses: Contact institution. *Financial support:* In 2017–18, 14 students received support, including 4 fellowships (averaging $7,314 per year). Financial award application deadline: 3/15; financial award applicants required to submit FAFSA. In 2017, 25 master's awarded. *Program availability:* Part-time. Offers music education (MM); music performance (MM); music theory/composition (MM); music therapy (MM). *Application deadline:* For fall admission, 4/1 priority date for domestic and international students; for spring admission, 11/1 priority date for domestic students, 11/1 for international students. Applications are processed on a rolling basis. *Application fee:* $75. Electronic applications accepted. *Application Contact:* Dr. Barry Kilpatrick, Admissions Coordinator, School of Music, 716-673-4635, E-mail: barry.kilpatrick@fredonia.edu. *Director, School of Music*, Dr. Melvin Unger, 716-673-3151, E-mail: melvin.unger@fredonia.edu.

STATE UNIVERSITY OF NEW YORK AT NEW PALTZ, New Paltz, NY 12561

General Information State-supported, coed, comprehensive institution. *Enrollment:* 7,565 graduate, professional, and undergraduate students; 403 full-time matriculated graduate/professional students (266 women), 429 part-time matriculated graduate/professional students (304 women). *Enrollment by degree level:* 832 master's. *Graduate faculty:* 127 full-time (71 women), 35 part-time/adjunct (23 women). *Graduate housing:* On-campus housing not available. *Student services:* Campus employment opportunities, campus safety program, career counseling, child daycare facilities, free psychological counseling, international student services, low-cost health insurance, services for students with disabilities, teacher training, writing training. *Library facilities:* Sojourner Truth Library. *Collection:* Books: 455,728 (physical), 149,851 (digital/electronic); Serial titles: 234 (physical), 85,306 (digital/electronic); Databases: 98. Weekly public service hours: 103; students can reserve study rooms.

Computer facilities: 800 computers available on campus for general student use. A campuswide network can be accessed from student residence rooms and from off campus. Online class registration is available.
Website: http://www.newpaltz.edu/

General Application Contact: Vika Shock, Director of Graduate Admissions, 845-257-3285, Fax: 845-257-3284, E-mail: gradschool@newpaltz.edu.

GRADUATE UNITS

Graduate and Extended Learning School Students: 412 full-time (271 women), 433 part-time (306 women); includes 128 minority (25 Black or African American, non-Hispanic/Latino; 17 Asian, non-Hispanic/Latino; 74 Hispanic/Latino; 12 Two or more races, non-Hispanic/Latino), 86 international. 756 applicants, 51% accepted, 110 enrolled. *Faculty:* 127 full-time (71 women), 35 part-time/adjunct (23 women). Expenses: Contact institution. *Financial support:* In 2017–18, 15 fellowships with partial tuition reimbursements (averaging $1,360 per year), 30 research assistantships with partial tuition reimbursements (averaging $5,000 per year), 40 teaching assistantships with partial tuition reimbursements (averaging $5,000 per year) were awarded; career-related internships or fieldwork, scholarships/grants, traineeships, health care benefits, and unspecified assistantships also available. Financial award application deadline: 8/1; financial award applicants required to submit FAFSA. In 2017, 324 master's, 22 other advanced degrees awarded. *Program availability:* Part-time, evening/weekend. *Application fee:* $50. Electronic applications accepted. *Application Contact:* Vika Shock, Director of Graduate Admissions, 845-257-3285, Fax: 845-257-3284, E-mail: shockv@newpaltz.edu. *Associate Provost for Academic Affairs/Dean*, Dr. Laurel M. Garrick Duhaney, 845-257-3947, Fax: 845-257-3284, E-mail: duhaneyd@newpaltz.edu.

School of Business Students: 62 full-time (27 women), 36 part-time (24 women); includes 28 minority (8 Black or African American, non-Hispanic/Latino; 6 Asian, non-Hispanic/Latino; 11 Hispanic/Latino; 3 Two or more races, non-Hispanic/Latino), 12 international. 59 applicants, 68% accepted, 28 enrolled. *Faculty:* 15 full-time (3 women), 2 part-time/adjunct (0 women). Expenses: Contact institution. *Financial support:* In 2017–18, 6 research assistantships with partial tuition reimbursements (averaging $5,000 per year), 1 teaching assistantship with partial tuition reimbursement (averaging $5,000 per year) were awarded; scholarships/grants, traineeships, and unspecified assistantships also available. Financial award application deadline: 8/1. In 2017, 43 master's awarded. *Program availability:* Part-time, evening/weekend. Offers business administration (MBA); public accountancy (MBA). *Application deadline:* Applications are processed on a rolling basis. *Application fee:* $50. Electronic applications accepted. *Application Contact:* Aaron Hines, Director of MBA Program, 845-257-2968, E-mail: mba@newpaltz.edu. *Dean*, Dr. Kristin Backhaus, 845-257-2930, E-mail: mba@newpaltz.edu.

School of Education Students: 115 full-time (84 women), 236 part-time (184 women); includes 60 minority (11 Black or African American, non-Hispanic/Latino; 5 Asian, non-Hispanic/Latino; 39 Hispanic/Latino; 5 Two or more races, non-Hispanic/Latino). 180 applicants, 75% accepted, 113 enrolled. *Faculty:* 29 full-time (22 women), 20 part-time/adjunct (14 women). Expenses: Contact institution. *Financial support:* Scholarships/grants available. Financial award application deadline: 8/1. In 2017, 147 master's, 22 other advanced degrees awarded. *Program availability:* Part-time, evening/weekend. Offers adolescence education: biology (MAT, MS Ed); adolescence education: chemistry (MAT, MS Ed); adolescence education: earth science (MAT, MS Ed); adolescence education: English (MAT, MS Ed); adolescence education: French (MAT, MS Ed); adolescence education: social studies (MAT, MS Ed); adolescence education: Spanish (MAT, MS Ed); adolescence special education (7-12) (MS Ed); adolescence special education and literacy (MS Ed); childhood education 1-6 (MS Ed, MST); childhood special education (1-6) (MS Ed); childhood special education and literacy (MS Ed); early childhood special education (B-2) (MS Ed); education (MAT, MPS, MS Ed, MST, AC, CAS); educational leadership (MS Ed); humanistic/multicultural education (MPS, AC); multicultural education (AC); school building leader (CAS); school district business leader (CAS); school district leader (CAS); second language education (MS Ed, AC); special education (MS Ed); teaching English language learners (AC). *Application deadline:* For fall admission, 3/1 for domestic and international students; for spring admission, 10/1 for domestic and international students. *Application fee:* $50. Electronic applications accepted. *Application Contact:* Vika Shock, Director of Graduate Admissions, 845-257-3285, Fax: 845-257-3284, E-mail: gradschool@newpaltz.edu. *Dean*, Dr. Michael Rosenberg, 845-257-2800, E-mail: schoolofed@newpaltz.edu.

School of Fine and Performing Arts Students: 52 full-time (40 women), 20 part-time (15 women); includes 9 minority (1 Black or African American, non-Hispanic/Latino; 2 Asian, non-Hispanic/Latino; 6 Hispanic/Latino), 10 international. 102 applicants, 49% accepted, 27 enrolled. *Faculty:* 25 full-time (16 women), 3 part-time/adjunct (2 women). Expenses: Contact institution. *Financial support:* In 2017–18, 8 research assistantships with partial tuition reimbursements (averaging $5,000 per year), 7 teaching assistantships with partial tuition reimbursements (averaging $5,000 per year) were awarded; scholarships/grants also available. Financial award application deadline: 8/1. In 2017, 23 master's awarded. *Program availability:* Part-time, evening/weekend. Offers ceramics (MFA); fine and performing arts (MFA, MS, MS Ed); metal (MFA); music therapy (MS); painting-drawing (MFA); printmaking (MFA); sculpture (MFA); visual arts education (MS Ed). *Application deadline:* For fall admission, 2/15 priority date for domestic students, 2/15 for international students. Applications are processed on a rolling basis. *Application fee:* $50. Electronic applications accepted. *Application Contact:* Vika Shock, Director of Graduate Admissions, 845-257-3286, Fax: 845-257-3284, E-mail: gradschool@newpaltz.edu. *Dean*, Prof. Jeni Mokren, 845-257-3860, E-mail: mokrenj@newpaltz.edu.

School of Liberal Arts and Sciences Students: 124 full-time (95 women), 48 part-time (32 women); includes 24 minority (3 Black or African American, non-Hispanic/Latino; 1 Asian, non-Hispanic/Latino; 15 Hispanic/Latino; 1 Native Hawaiian or other Pacific Islander, non-Hispanic/Latino; 4 Two or more races, non-Hispanic/Latino), 1 international. 274 applicants, 41% accepted, 61 enrolled. *Faculty:* 43 full-time (26 women), 6 part-time/adjunct (all women). Expenses: Contact institution. *Financial support:* In 2017–18, 1 research assistantship with partial tuition reimbursement (averaging $5,000 per year), 28 teaching assistantships with partial tuition reimbursements (averaging $5,000 per year) were awarded. Financial award application deadline: 8/1. In 2017, 37 master's, 3 other advanced degrees awarded. *Program availability:* Part-time, evening/weekend. Offers clinical mental health counseling (MS); communication disorders (MS); English (MA); liberal arts and sciences (MA, MS, AC); mental health counseling (AC); psychological science (MS); school counseling (MS); trauma and disaster mental health (AC). *Application deadline:* For fall admission, 2/1 for domestic and international students; for spring admission, 11/15 for domestic and international students. Applications are processed on a rolling basis. *Application fee:* $50. Electronic applications accepted. *Application Contact:* Vika Shock, Director of Graduate Admissions, 845-257-3286, E-mail: gradschool@newpaltz.edu. *Dean*, Dr. Laura Barrett, 845-257-3520, E-mail: barrett@newpaltz.edu.

School of Science and Engineering Students: 53 full-time (20 women), 36 part-time (10 women); includes 3 minority (1 Black or African American, non-Hispanic/Latino; 2 Asian, non-Hispanic/Latino), 59 international. 122 applicants, 64% accepted, 22 enrolled. *Faculty:* 15 full-time (4 women), 4 part-time/adjunct (1 woman). Expenses: Contact institution. *Financial support:* In 2017–18, 15 fellowships with partial tuition reimbursements (averaging $1,360 per year), 4 teaching assistantships with partial tuition reimbursements (averaging $5,000 per year) were awarded. Financial award application deadline: 8/1. In 2017, 73 master's awarded. *Program availability:* Part-time, evening/weekend. Offers computer science (MS); electrical engineering (MS); science and engineering (MS). *Application deadline:* For fall admission, 5/15 for domestic and international students; for spring admission, 11/15 for domestic and international students. Applications are processed on a rolling basis. *Application fee:* $50. Electronic applications accepted. *Application Contact:* Vika Shock, Director of Graduate Admission, 845-257-3286, E-mail: gradschool@newpaltz.edu. *Dean*, Dr. Daniel Freedman, 845-257-3728, E-mail: freedmad@newpaltz.edu.

STATE UNIVERSITY OF NEW YORK AT OSWEGO, Oswego, NY 13126

General Information State-supported, coed, comprehensive institution. CGS member. *Graduate housing:* Room and/or apartments available on a first-come, first-served basis to single students; on-campus housing not available to married students. Housing application deadline: 4/1. *Research affiliation:* Intel Corporation (research and education), IBM (research and education), Alcan (research and education), MACTEC (research and education), Entergy (research and education).

GRADUATE UNITS

Graduate Studies *Program availability:* Part-time. Offers art (MA); graphic design and digital media (MA); health informatics professional (MS); health informatics: intelligent health systems (MS); health information management: health data science (MS).

College of Liberal Arts and Sciences *Program availability:* Part-time. Offers chemistry (MS); English (MA); history (MA); human computer interaction (MA); liberal arts and sciences (MA, MS).

School of Business *Program availability:* Part-time, evening/weekend. Offers business (MBA).

School of Communication, Media and the Arts Offers strategic communication (MA).

School of Education *Program availability:* Part-time. Offers adolescence education (MST); agriculture (MS Ed); art education (MAT); business and marketing (MS Ed); childhood education (MST); curriculum and instruction (MS Ed); education (MAT, MS, MS Ed, MST, CAS); educational administration (CAS); family and consumer sciences (MS Ed); health careers (MS Ed); literacy education (MS Ed); mental health counseling (MS); school building leadership (CAS); special education (MS Ed); technical education (MS Ed); technology (MS Ed); trade education (MS Ed).

STATE UNIVERSITY OF NEW YORK AT PLATTSBURGH, Plattsburgh, NY 12901-2681

General Information State-supported, coed, comprehensive institution. *Graduate housing:* Room and/or apartments available on a first-come, first-served basis to single students; on-campus housing not available to married students. Housing application deadline: 5/1. *Research affiliation:* New York State Sea Grant (environmental science), Miner Agricultural Research Institute (environmental science).

GRADUATE UNITS

School of Arts and Sciences *Program availability:* Part-time. Offers arts and sciences (MA, MS, PSM, CAS); natural science (MS, PSM); school psychology (MA, CAS).

School of Education, Health, and Human Services *Program availability:* Part-time. Offers adolescence education (MST); biology 7-12 (MST); birth to grade 2 (MS Ed); birth to grade 6 (MS Ed); birth-grade 6 (MS Ed); chemistry 7-12 (MST); childhood education (grades 1-6) (MST); clinical mental health counseling (MS, Advanced Certificate); early childhood birth-grade 6 (Advanced Certificate); earth science 7-12 (MST); education, health, and human services (MA, MS, MS Ed, MST, Advanced Certificate, CAS); educational leadership (CAS); English 7-12 (MST); French 7-12 (MST); grades 1 to 6 (MS Ed); grades 5-12 (MS Ed); grades 7 to 12 (MS Ed); mathematics 7-12 (MST); physics 7-12 (MST); school counselor (MS Ed, CAS); social studies 7-12 (MST); Spanish 7-12 (MST); speech-language pathology (MA); student affairs counseling (MS); teacher education: teaching and learning (MS Ed).

STATE UNIVERSITY OF NEW YORK COLLEGE AT CORTLAND, Cortland, NY 13045

General Information State-supported, coed, comprehensive institution. *Graduate housing:* Room and/or apartments available on a first-come, first-served basis to single students; on-campus housing not available to married students.

GRADUATE UNITS

Graduate Studies *Program availability:* Part-time, evening/weekend. Electronic applications accepted.

School of Arts and Sciences *Program availability:* Part-time, evening/weekend. Offers arts and sciences (MA, MAT, MS Ed); biology (MAT); chemistry (MAT); English (MA); history (MA); mathematics (MAT); mathematics and physics (MS Ed); physics (MAT, MS Ed); second language education (MS Ed).

School of Education *Program availability:* Part-time, evening/weekend. Offers childhood education (MST); education (MS Ed, MST, CAS); literacy education (MS Ed); school building leader (CAS); school building leader and school district leader (CAS); school district business leader (CAS); school district leader (CAS); teaching students with disabilities (MS Ed).

School of Professional Studies *Program availability:* Part-time, evening/weekend. Offers adapted physical education (MS Ed); coaching pedagogy (MS Ed); communication sciences and disorders (MS); community health (MS); health education (MST); international sport management (MS); outdoor education (MS, MS Ed); physical education leadership (MS Ed); recreation management (MS, MS Ed); sport management (MS); therapeutic recreation (MS, MS Ed).

STATE UNIVERSITY OF NEW YORK COLLEGE AT GENESEO, Geneseo, NY 14454-1401

General Information State-supported, coed, comprehensive institution. *Enrollment:* 5,591 graduate, professional, and undergraduate students; 46 full-time matriculated graduate/professional students (31 women), 32 part-time matriculated graduate/professional students (25 women). *Enrollment by degree level:* 78 master's. *Graduate faculty:* 10 full-time (7 women), 3 part-time/adjunct (1 woman). Tuition, state resident: full-time $10,870; part-time $453 per credit hour. Tuition, nonresident: full-time $22,210; part-time $925 per credit hour. *Required fees:* $883; $36.60 per credit hour. Tuition and fees vary according to course load. *Graduate housing:* Room and/or apartments available on a first-come, first-served basis to single students; on-campus housing not available to married students. Typical cost: $8910 per year. Room charges vary according to housing facility selected. Housing application deadline: 5/1. *Student services:* Campus employment opportunities, campus safety program, career counseling, exercise/wellness program, free psychological counseling, grant writing training, international student services, multicultural affairs office, services for students with disabilities, teacher training. *Library facilities:* Milne Library plus 1 other. *Collection:* Books: 333,883 (physical), 151,724 (digital/electronic); Serial titles: 1,420 (physical), 213,056 (digital/electronic); Databases: 430. Weekly public service hours: 109; students can reserve study rooms. *Research affiliation:* Rochester City School District/School #19 (education), Avon School District (education), The Community Place of Greater Rochester (reading literacy), Central Library of Rochester (education), The Genesee Valley Educational Partnership (education), Greater Rochester Summer Learning Association (education).

Computer facilities: 409 computers available on campus for general student use. A campuswide network can be accessed from student residence rooms and from off campus. Online class registration is available.
Website: http://www.geneseo.edu/

General Application Contact: Michael R. George, Graduate Enrollment Coordinator, 585-245-5148, Fax: 585-245-5550, E-mail: georgem@geneseo.edu.

GRADUATE UNITS

Graduate Studies Students: 46 full-time (31 women), 32 part-time (25 women); includes 5 minority (3 Asian, non-Hispanic/Latino; 2 Hispanic/Latino). Average age 24. 89 applicants, 70% accepted, 56 enrolled. *Faculty:* 10 full-time (7 women), 3 part-time/adjunct (1 woman). Expenses: Contact institution. *Financial support:* In 2017–18, 9 students received support, including 9 research assistantships with full tuition reimbursements available (averaging $8,961 per year); career-related internships or fieldwork, scholarships/grants, tuition waivers (full and partial), and unspecified assistantships also available. Support available to part-time students. Financial award application deadline: 4/1; financial award applicants required to submit FAFSA. In 2017, 73 master's awarded. *Program availability:* Part-time. *Application deadline:* For fall admission, 4/1 priority date for domestic students; for spring admission, 11/1 priority date for domestic students; for summer admission, 4/1 priority date for domestic students. Applications are processed on a rolling basis. *Application fee:* $50. Electronic applications accepted. *Application Contact:* Michael R. George, Graduate Enrollment Coordinator, 585-245-5148, E-mail: georgem@geneseo.edu. *Assistant Provost for Curriculum and Assessment*, Dr. William Harrison, 585-245-5531, Fax: 585-245-5032, E-mail: harrison@geneseo.edu.

School of Business Students: 19 full-time (7 women); includes 2 minority (both Asian, non-Hispanic/Latino). Average age 22. 39 applicants, 59% accepted, 19 enrolled. *Faculty:* 3 full-time (1 woman), 2 part-time/adjunct (0 women). Expenses: Contact institution. *Financial support:* In 2017–18, 9 students received support. Research assistantships with partial tuition reimbursements available and scholarships/grants available. Financial award application deadline: 4/1; financial award applicants required to submit FAFSA. In 2017, 17 master's awarded. Offers accounting (MS). *Application deadline:* For fall admission, 6/1 priority date for domestic students. Applications are processed on a rolling basis. *Application fee:* $50. Electronic applications accepted. *Application Contact:* Michael R. George, Director of Graduate Admissions, 585-245-5148, Fax: 585-245-5550, E-mail: georgem@geneseo.edu. *Dean of the School of Business*, Dr. Michael Schinski, 585-245-5367, Fax: 585-245-5467, E-mail: schinski@geneseo.edu.

School of Education Students: 27 full-time (24 women), 32 part-time (25 women); includes 3 minority (1 Asian, non-Hispanic/Latino; 2 Hispanic/Latino). Average age 25. 50 applicants, 78% accepted, 37 enrolled. *Faculty:* 11 full-time (9 women), 1 (woman) part-time/adjunct. Expenses: Contact institution. *Financial support:* In 2017–18, 13 students received support, including 9 research assistantships with full tuition reimbursements available (averaging $8,823 per year); fellowships, career-related internships or fieldwork, scholarships/grants, tuition waivers (full and partial), and unspecified assistantships also available. Support available to part-time students. Financial award application deadline: 4/1; financial award applicants required to submit FAFSA. In 2017, 56 master's awarded. *Program availability:* Part-time. Offers childhood multicultural education (MS Ed); education (MS Ed); English 7-12 (MS Ed); French 7-12 (MS Ed); reading and literacy B-12 (MS Ed); social studies 7-12 (MS Ed); Spanish 7-12 (MS Ed). *Application deadline:* For fall admission, 4/1 priority date for domestic students; for spring admission, 11/1 priority date for domestic students; for summer admission, 4/1 priority date for domestic students. Applications are processed on a rolling basis. *Application fee:* $50. Electronic applications accepted. *Application Contact:* Michael R. George, Director of Graduate Admissions, 585-245-5148, Fax: 585-245-5550, E-mail: georgem@geneseo.edu. *Dean of School of Education*, Dr. Anjoo Sikka, 585-245-5151, Fax: 585-245-5220, E-mail: sikka@geneseo.edu.

STATE UNIVERSITY OF NEW YORK COLLEGE AT OLD WESTBURY, Old Westbury, NY 11568-0210

General Information State-supported, coed, comprehensive institution. *Enrollment:* 4,461 graduate, professional, and undergraduate students; 233 full-time matriculated graduate/professional students (123 women), 163 part-time matriculated graduate/professional students (70 women). *Enrollment by degree level:* 187 master's, 5 other advanced degrees. *Graduate faculty:* 15 full-time (4 women), 3 part-time/adjunct (2 women). *Graduate housing:* Room and/or apartments available on a first-come, first-served basis to single students; on-campus housing not available to married students. *Student services:* Campus safety program, career counseling, child daycare facilities, exercise/wellness program, free psychological counseling, international student services, services for students with disabilities, teacher training, writing training. *Library facilities:* SUNY College at Old Westbury Library plus 1 other. *Collection:* Books: 156,872 (physical), 144,263 (digital/electronic); Databases: 138. Weekly public service hours: 99.

Computer facilities: 480 computers available on campus for general student use. A campuswide network can be accessed from student residence rooms and from off campus. Online class registration, financial aid, billing information are available.
Website: http://www.oldwestbury.edu/

General Application Contact: Philip D'Angelo, Graduate Programs Admissions Counselor, 516-876-3077, E-mail: enroll@oldwestbury.edu.

GRADUATE UNITS

Program in Liberal Studies Students: 5 full-time (1 woman), 4 part-time (3 women); includes 4 minority (1 Black or African American, non-Hispanic/Latino; 1 Asian, non-Hispanic/Latino; 2 Hispanic/Latino). Average age 38. 10 applicants, 80% accepted, 5 enrolled. *Faculty:* 2 full-time (both women). Expenses: Contact institution. *Financial support:* Applicants required to submit FAFSA. In 2017, 1 master's awarded. *Program availability:* Part-time, evening/weekend. Offers liberal studies (MA). *Application deadline:* Applications are processed on a rolling basis. *Application fee:* $50. Electronic applications accepted. *Application Contact:* Philip D'Angelo, Graduate Admissions Office, 516-876-3073, E-mail: enroll@oldwestbury.edu. *Associate Professor, American Studies*, Dr. Amanda Frisken, 516-876-4853, E-mail: friskena@oldwestbury.edu.

Program in Mental Health Counseling Students: 34 full-time (29 women); includes 11 minority (4 Black or African American, non-Hispanic/Latino; 2 Asian, non-Hispanic/Latino; 5 Hispanic/Latino). Average age 29. 39 applicants, 64% accepted, 21 enrolled. *Faculty:* 3 full-time (0 women), 2 part-time/adjunct (both women). Expenses: Contact institution. *Financial support:* Applicants required to submit FAFSA. In 2017, 14 master's awarded. Offers mental health counseling (MS). *Application fee:* $50. *Application Contact:* Philip D'Angelo, Graduate Admissions Office, 516-876-3073, E-mail: enroll@oldwestbury.edu. *Director*, Dr. Fred Millan, 516-876-3315, E-mail: millanf@oldwestbury.edu.

School of Business Students: 30 full-time (13 women), 47 part-time (15 women); includes 19 minority (3 Black or African American, non-Hispanic/Latino; 11 Asian, non-Hispanic/Latino; 5 Hispanic/Latino). Average age 31. 35 applicants, 91% accepted, 25 enrolled. *Faculty:* 10 full-time (2 women), 1 part-time/adjunct (0 women). Expenses: Contact institution. *Financial support:* Applicants required to submit FAFSA. In 2017, 25 master's awarded. *Program availability:* Part-time, evening/weekend. Offers accounting (MS); taxation (MS). *Application deadline:* For fall admission, 6/15 priority date for domestic students; for spring admission, 11/15 priority date for domestic students. Applications are processed on a rolling basis. *Application fee:* $50. Electronic applications accepted. *Application Contact:* Philip D'Angelo, Graduate Admissions Office, 516-876-3073, E-mail: enroll@oldwestbury.edu. *Director of Graduate Business Programs*, Rita Buttermilch, 516-876-3900, E-mail: langec@oldwestbury.edu.

School of Education Students: 164 full-time (80 women), 112 part-time (52 women); includes 87 minority (14 Black or African American, non-Hispanic/Latino; 38 Asian, non-Hispanic/Latino; 35 Hispanic/Latino), 2 international. Average age 30. 34 applicants, 82% accepted, 25 enrolled. Expenses: Contact institution. *Financial support:* Applicants required to submit FAFSA. In 2017, 25 master's awarded. *Program availability:* Part-time, evening/weekend. Offers biology (MAT, MS); chemistry (MAT, MS); English language arts (MAT, MS); math (MAT, MS); social studies (MAT, MS); Spanish (MAT, MS). *Application fee:* $50. *Application Contact:* Philip D'Angelo, Graduate Admissions Office, 516-876-3073, E-mail: enroll@oldwestbury.edu. *Dean, School of Education*, Dr. Nancy Brown, 516-876-3275, E-mail: brownn@oldwestbury.edu.

STATE UNIVERSITY OF NEW YORK COLLEGE AT ONEONTA, Oneonta, NY 13820-4015

General Information State-supported, coed, comprehensive institution. *Graduate housing:* Room and/or apartments available on a first-come, first-served basis to single students; on-campus housing not available to married students. Housing application deadline: 5/1. *Research affiliation:* New York State Historical Association (museum studies (history and science)).

GRADUATE UNITS

Graduate Programs *Program availability:* Part-time, evening/weekend, online learning. Offers biology (MS); history museum studies (MA); lake management (MS); nutrition and dietetics (MS); science museum studies (MA).

Division of Education *Program availability:* Part-time, evening/weekend. Offers childhood education (MS Ed); educational psychology, counseling and special education (MS Ed, CAS); elementary education and reading (MS Ed); literacy education (MS Ed); school counselor K-12 (MS Ed, CAS); special education (MS Ed).

STATE UNIVERSITY OF NEW YORK COLLEGE AT POTSDAM, Potsdam, NY 13676

General Information State-supported, coed, comprehensive institution. Tuition, state resident: full-time $11,090; part-time $462 per credit hour. Tuition, nonresident: full-time $22,650; part-time $944 per credit hour. *Required fees:* $58 per credit hour. $684 per semester. *Graduate housing:* Room and/or apartments available on a first-come, first-served basis to single students; on-campus housing not available to married students. *Student services:* Campus employment opportunities, campus safety program, career counseling, child daycare facilities, exercise/wellness program, free psychological counseling, grant writing training, international student services, low-cost health insurance, multicultural affairs office, services for students with disabilities, teacher training, writing training. *Library facilities:* F. W. Crumb Memorial Library plus 1 other. *Collection:* Books: 258,039 (physical), 45,425 (digital/electronic); Serial titles: 3,227 (physical), 100,736 (digital/electronic); Databases: 144. Weekly public service hours: 119; study areas open 24 hours, 5–7 days a week; students can reserve study rooms.

Computer facilities: Computer purchase and lease plans are available. 608 computers available on campus for general student use. A campuswide network can be accessed. Online class registration, online access to financial aid status, unofficial transcripts, billing, meal plan and housing sign-up are available.
Website: http://www.potsdam.edu/

General Application Contact: Graduate Admissions Counselor, 315-267-2165, Fax: 315-267-2544, E-mail: graduate@potsdam.edu.

GRADUATE UNITS

Crane School of Music Expenses: Contact institution. *Financial support:* Teaching assistantships with full tuition reimbursements, career-related internships or fieldwork, Federal Work-Study, scholarships/grants, and unspecified assistantships available. Support available to part-time students. Financial award application deadline: 3/1; financial award applicants required to submit FAFSA. *Program availability:* Part-time. Offers music education (MM); music performance (MM). *Application deadline:* For fall admission, 4/1 for domestic and international students; for winter admission, 10/15 for domestic and international students; for spring admission, 3/1 for domestic and international students. Applications are processed on a rolling basis. *Application fee:* $50. Electronic applications accepted. *Application Contact:* Margaret Ball, Secretary, 315-267-2812, Fax: 315-267-2413, E-mail: ballmw@potsdam.edu. *Dean*, Dr. Michael R. Sitton, 315-267-2415, Fax: 315-267-2413, E-mail: sittonmr@potsdam.edu.

School of Arts and Sciences Expenses: Contact institution. *Financial support:* Teaching assistantships with full tuition reimbursements, Federal Work-Study, and unspecified assistantships available. Support available to part-time students. Financial award application deadline: 3/1; financial award applicants required to submit FAFSA. *Program availability:* Part-time, evening/weekend. Offers arts and sciences (MA); mathematics (MA). *Application deadline:* For fall admission, 4/1 for domestic and international students; for winter admission, 10/15 for domestic and international students; for spring admission, 3/1 for domestic and international students. Applications are processed on a rolling basis. *Application fee:* $50. Electronic applications accepted. *Application Contact:* Graduate Admissions Counselor, 315-267-2165, Fax: 315-267-2544, E-mail: graduate@potsdam.edu. *Dean*, Dr. Steven J. Marqusee, 315-267-3186, Fax: 315-267-3176, E-mail: marqussj@potsdam.edu.

School of Education and Professional Studies Expenses: Contact institution. *Financial support:* Fellowships, teaching assistantships with full tuition reimbursements, career-related internships or fieldwork, Federal Work-Study, scholarships/grants, tuition waivers (full), and unspecified assistantships available. Support available to part-time students. Financial award application deadline: 3/1; financial award applicants required to submit FAFSA. *Program availability:* Online learning. Offers adolescence (grades 7-12) (MS Ed); childhood (grades 1-6) (MS Ed); childhood education (MST); community health (MS); curriculum and instruction (MS Ed); early childhood (birth-grade 2) (MS Ed); education and professional studies (MS, MS Ed, MST); educational technology specialist (MS Ed); English education (MST); literacy educator (MS Ed); literacy specialist (MS Ed); mathematics education (MST); organizational performance and technology (MS); science education (MST); social studies education (MST). *Application deadline:* For fall admission, 4/1 for domestic and international students; for winter admission, 10/15 for domestic and international students; for spring admission, 3/1 for domestic and international students. Applications are processed on a rolling basis. *Application fee:* $50. Electronic applications accepted. *Application Contact:* Graduate Admissions Counselor, 315-267-2165, Fax: 315-267-2544, E-mail: graduate@potsdam.edu. *Interim Dean*, Walter J. Conley, 315-267-2515, Fax: 315-267-4802, E-mail: conleywj@potsdam.edu.

STATE UNIVERSITY OF NEW YORK COLLEGE OF ENVIRONMENTAL SCIENCE AND FORESTRY, Syracuse, NY 13210-2779

General Information State-supported, coed, university. CGS member. *Enrollment:* 2,219 graduate, professional, and undergraduate students; 344 full-time matriculated graduate/professional students (179 women), 64 part-time matriculated graduate/professional students (29 women). *Enrollment by degree level:* 234 master's, 173 doctoral, 1 other advanced degree. *Graduate faculty:* 120 full-time (37 women), 48 part-time/adjunct (18 women). Tuition, state resident: full-time $10,870; part-time $453 per credit. Tuition, nonresident: full-time $22,210; part-time $925 per credit. *Required fees:* $1435; $70.85 per credit. One-time fee: $25 full-time. Part-time tuition and fees vary according to course load. *Graduate housing:* On-campus housing not available. *Student services:* Campus employment opportunities, campus safety program, career counseling, exercise/wellness program, free psychological counseling, grant writing training, international student services, low-cost health insurance, multicultural affairs office, writing training. *Library facilities:* F. Franklin Moon Library plus 1 other. *Collection:* Books: 137,535 (physical), 348,596 (digital/electronic); Serial titles: 1,741 (physical), 241,084 (digital/electronic); Databases: 171. Weekly public service hours: 97. *Research affiliation:* U.S. Department of Agriculture (USDA) (forest and natural resources management), NASA (remote sensing and GIS), New York State Department of Agriculture and Markets (green infrastructure and food systems), New York State Department of Environmental Conservation (environmental conservation and wildlife management), Honeywell (brownfields remediation), U.S. Department of Commerce (Great Lakes water).

Computer facilities: Computer purchase and lease plans are available. 350 computers available on campus for general student use. A campuswide network can be accessed from student residence rooms and from off campus. Online class registration is available.
Website: http://www.esf.edu/

General Application Contact: Scott Shannon, Dean, Instruction and Graduate Studies, 315-470-6599, Fax: 315-470-6978, E-mail: esfgrad@esf.edu.

GRADUATE UNITS

Department of Chemistry Students: 30 full-time (12 women), 7 part-time (5 women); includes 2 minority (1 Black or African American, non-Hispanic/Latino; 1 Asian, non-Hispanic/Latino), 13 international. Average age 27. 44 applicants, 50% accepted, 6 enrolled. *Faculty:* 15 full-time (2 women), 1 part-time/adjunct (0 women). Expenses: Contact institution. *Financial support:* In 2017–18, 8 students received support. Unspecified assistantships available. Financial award application deadline: 6/30; financial award applicants required to submit FAFSA. In 2017, 3 master's, 3 doctorates awarded. *Program availability:* Part-time. Offers biochemistry (MPS, MS, PhD); environmental chemistry (MPS, MS, PhD); organic chemistry of natural products (MPS, MS, PhD); polymer chemistry (MPS, MS, PhD). *Application deadline:* For fall admission, 2/1 priority date for domestic and international students; for spring admission, 11/1 priority date for domestic and international students. Applications are processed on a rolling basis. *Application fee:* $60. Electronic applications accepted. *Application Contact:* Scott Shannon, Associate Provost for Instruction/Dean of the Graduate School, 315-470-6599, Fax: 315-470-6978, E-mail: sshannon@esf.edu. *Chair*, Prof. Ivan Gitsov, 315-470-6851, Fax: 315-470-6856, E-mail: igivanov@syr.edu.

Department of Environmental and Forest Biology Students: 117 full-time (65 women), 18 part-time (6 women); includes 8 minority (6 American Indian or Alaska Native, non-Hispanic/Latino; 1 Asian, non-Hispanic/Latino; 1 Hispanic/Latino), 23 international. Average age 30. 84 applicants, 52% accepted, 31 enrolled. *Faculty:* 30 full-time (10 women), 4 part-time/adjunct (3 women). Expenses: Contact institution. *Financial support:* In 2017–18, 42 students received support. Unspecified assistantships available. Financial award application deadline: 6/30; financial award applicants required to submit FAFSA. In 2017, 30 master's, 3 doctorates awarded. *Program availability:* Part-time. Offers applied ecology (MPS); chemical ecology (MPS, MS, PhD); conservation biology (MPS, MS, PhD); ecology (MPS, MS, PhD); entomology (MPS, MS, PhD); environmental interpretation (MPS, MS, PhD); environmental physiology (MPS, MS, PhD); fish and wildlife biology and management (MPS, MS, PhD); forest pathology and mycology (MPS, MS, PhD); plant biotechnology (MPS); plant science and biotechnology (MPS, MS, PhD). *Application deadline:* For fall admission, 2/1 priority date for domestic and international students; for spring admission, 11/1 priority date for domestic and international students. Applications are processed on a rolling basis. *Application fee:* $60. Electronic applications accepted. *Application Contact:* Scott Shannon, Associate Provost for Instruction/Dean of the Graduate School, 315-470-6599, E-mail: esfgrad@esf.edu. *Chair*, Dr. Neil H. Ringler, 315-470-6803, Fax: 315-470-6934, E-mail: nhringle@esf.edu.

Department of Environmental Resources Engineering Students: 30 full-time (9 women), 5 part-time (2 women); includes 3 minority (1 Asian, non-Hispanic/Latino; 1 Hispanic/Latino; 1 Two or more races, non-Hispanic/Latino), 18 international. Average age 28. 45 applicants, 62% accepted, 8 enrolled. *Faculty:* 9 full-time (1 woman), 3 part-time/adjunct (0 women). Expenses: Contact institution. *Financial support:* In 2017–18, 11 students received support. Unspecified assistantships available. Financial award application deadline: 6/30; financial award applicants required to submit FAFSA. In 2017, 8 master's, 3 doctorates awarded. *Program availability:* Part-time. Offers ecological engineering (MPS, MS, PhD); environmental management (MPS); environmental resources engineering (MPS, MS, PhD); geospatial information science and engineering (MPS, MS, PhD); water resources engineering (MPS, MS, PhD). *Application deadline:* For fall admission, 1/15 priority date for domestic and international students; for spring admission, 11/1 priority date for domestic and international students. Applications are processed on a rolling basis. *Application fee:* $60. Electronic applications accepted. *Application Contact:* Scott Shannon, Associate Provost for Instruction/Dean of the Graduate School, 315-470-6599, Fax: 315-470-6978, E-mail: esfgrad@esf.edu. *Chair*, Dr. Theodore Endreny, 315-470-6565, Fax: 315-470-6958, E-mail: te@esf.edu.

Department of Environmental Studies Students: 8 full-time (4 women), 1 (woman) part-time; includes 1 minority (Black or African American, non-Hispanic/Latino), 1 international. Average age 26. 10 applicants, 60% accepted, 1 enrolled. *Faculty:* 10 full-time (7 women), 3 part-time/adjunct (2 women). Expenses: Contact institution. *Financial support:* In 2017–18, 2 students received support. Unspecified assistantships available. Financial award application deadline: 6/30; financial award applicants required to submit FAFSA. In 2017, 9 master's awarded. *Program availability:* Part-time. Offers environmental communication (MPS, MS); environmental policy (MPS, MS). *Application deadline:* Applications are processed on a rolling basis. *Application fee:* $60. Electronic applications accepted. *Application Contact:* Scott Shannon, Associate Provost for Instruction/Dean of the Graduate School, 315-470-6599, Fax: 315-470-6978, E-mail: esfgrad@esf.edu. *Chair*, Dr. Bennette Whitmore, 315-470-6636, E-mail: bwhitmor@esf.edu.

Department of Forest and Natural Resources Management Students: 48 full-time (24 women), 7 part-time (2 women); includes 4 minority (1 American Indian or Alaska Native, non-Hispanic/Latino; 1 Asian, non-Hispanic/Latino; 2 Hispanic/Latino), 18 international. Average age 31. 43 applicants, 79% accepted, 14 enrolled. *Faculty:* 33 full-time (8 women), 7 part-time/adjunct (0 women). Expenses: Contact institution. *Financial support:* In 2017–18, 20 students received support. Unspecified assistantships available. Financial award application deadline: 6/30; financial award applicants required to submit FAFSA. In 2017, 21 master's, 1 doctorate awarded. *Program availability:* Part-time. Offers ecology and ecosystems (MPS, MS, PhD); economics, governance and human dimensions (MPS, MS, PhD); forest and natural resources management (MPS, MS, PhD); forest resources management (MF); monitoring, analysis and modeling (MPS, MS, PhD). *Application deadline:* For fall admission, 2/1 priority date for domestic and international students; for spring admission, 11/1 priority date for domestic and international students. Applications are processed on a rolling basis. *Application fee:* $60. *Application Contact:* Scott Shannon, Associate Provost for Instruction/Dean of the Graduate School, 315-470-6599, Fax: 315-470-6978, E-mail: esfgrad@esf.edu. *Interim Chair*, Dr. Robert Malmsheimer, 315-470-6909, Fax: 315-470-6535, E-mail: rwmalmsh@esf.edu.

Department of Landscape Architecture Students: 27 full-time (16 women), 5 part-time (3 women); includes 5 minority (3 Black or African American, non-Hispanic/Latino; 1 Asian, non-Hispanic/Latino; 1 Hispanic/Latino), 5 international. Average age 25. 31 applicants, 65% accepted, 10 enrolled. *Faculty:* 10 full-time (4 women), 7 part-time/adjunct (5 women). Expenses: Contact institution. *Financial support:* In 2017–18, 9 students received support. Unspecified assistantships available. Financial award application deadline: 6/30; financial award applicants required to submit FAFSA. In 2017, 9 master's awarded. *Program availability:* Part-time. Offers community design and planning (MLA, MS); cultural landscape studies and conservation (MLA, MS); landscape and urban ecology (MLA, MS). *Application deadline:* For fall admission, 2/1 priority date for domestic and international students; for spring admission, 11/1 priority date for domestic and international students. Applications are processed on a rolling basis. *Application fee:* $60. Electronic applications accepted. *Application Contact:* Scott Shannon, Associate Provost for Instruction/Dean of the Graduate School, 315-470-6599, Fax: 315-470-6978, E-mail: esfgrad@esf.edu. *Chair*, Dr. Douglas Johnston, 315-470-6544, Fax: 315-470-6540, E-mail: dmjohnst@esf.edu.

Department of Paper and Bioprocess Engineering Students: 25 full-time (12 women), 2 part-time (1 woman), 17 international. Average age 28. 23 applicants, 87% accepted, 13 enrolled. *Faculty:* 13 full-time (2 women), 1 part-time/adjunct (0 women). Expenses: Contact institution. *Financial support:* In 2017–18, 12 students received support. Unspecified assistantships available. Financial award application deadline: 6/30; financial award applicants required to submit FAFSA. In 2017, 7 master's, 3 doctorates awarded. *Program availability:* Part-time. Offers biomaterials engineering (MS, PhD); bioprocess engineering (MPS, MS, PhD); bioprocessing (Advanced Certificate); paper science and engineering (MPS, MS, PhD); sustainable engineering management (MPS). *Application deadline:* For fall admission, 2/1 priority date for domestic and international students; for spring admission, 11/1 priority date for domestic and international students. Applications are processed on a rolling basis. *Application fee:* $60. Electronic applications accepted. *Application Contact:* Scott Shannon, Associate Provost and Dean, Instruction and Graduate Studies, 315-470-6599, Fax: 315-470-6978, E-mail: esfgrad@esf.edu. *Interim Chair*, Dr. Bandaru Ramarao, 315-470-6502, Fax: 315-470-6945, E-mail: bvramara@esf.edu.

Program in Environmental Science Students: 57 full-time (36 women), 13 part-time (9 women); includes 5 minority (1 Black or African American, non-Hispanic/Latino; 2 Asian, non-Hispanic/Latino; 2 Hispanic/Latino), 26 international. Average age 30. 64 applicants, 63% accepted, 15 enrolled. *Faculty:* 1 full-time (0 women), 1 (woman) part-time/adjunct. Expenses: Contact institution. *Financial support:* In 2017–18, 20 students received support. Unspecified assistantships available. Financial award application deadline: 6/30; financial award applicants required to submit FAFSA. In 2017, 15 master's, 4 doctorates awarded. *Program availability:* Part-time. Offers biophysical and ecological economics (MPS); coupled natural and human systems (MPS); ecosystem restoration (MPS); environmental and community land planning (MPS, MS); environmental and natural resources policy (PhD); environmental communication and participatory processes (PhD); environmental monitoring and modeling (MPS); water and wetland resource studies (MPS, MS). *Application deadline:* For fall admission, 2/1 priority date for domestic and international students; for spring admission, 11/1 priority date for domestic and international students. Applications are processed on a rolling basis. *Application fee:* $60. Electronic applications accepted. *Application Contact:* Scott Shannon, Associate Provost for Instruction/Dean of the Graduate School, 315-470-6599, Fax: 315-470-6978, E-mail: esfgrad@esf.edu. *Director of the Division of Environmental Science*, Dr. Russell Briggs, 315-470-6989, Fax: 315-470-6700, E-mail: rdbriggs@esf.edu.

STATE UNIVERSITY OF NEW YORK COLLEGE OF OPTOMETRY, New York, NY 10036

General Information State-supported, coed, graduate-only institution. *Graduate housing:* On-campus housing not available. *Research affiliation:* Schnurmacher Institute for Vision Research (vision science).

GRADUATE UNITS

Graduate Programs *Program availability:* Part-time. Offers vision science (PhD).

Professional Program Offers optometry (OD). Electronic applications accepted.

STATE UNIVERSITY OF NEW YORK COLLEGE OF TECHNOLOGY AT DELHI, Delhi, NY 13753

General Information State-supported, coed, comprehensive institution. *Enrollment:* 3,515 graduate, professional, and undergraduate students; 6 full-time matriculated graduate/professional students (all women), 35 part-time matriculated graduate/professional students (32 women). *Enrollment by degree level:* 41 master's. *Graduate faculty:* 6 full-time (all women), 1 (woman) part-time/adjunct. *Graduate housing:* On-campus housing not available. *Student services:* Career counseling, free psychological counseling, services for students with disabilities. *Library facilities:* Resnick Library. *Collection:* Books: 37,908 (physical), 152,584 (digital/electronic); Serial titles: 350,364 (physical), 350,364 (digital/electronic); Databases: 68. Weekly public service hours: 93; students can reserve study rooms.

Computer facilities: 102 computers available on campus for general student use. A campuswide network can be accessed from student residence rooms and from off campus. Online class registration is available.
Website: http://www.delhi.edu/

General Application Contact: Misty Fields, Assistant Director of Admissions, 607-746-4546, E-mail: fieldsmr@delhi.edu.

GRADUATE UNITS

Program in Nursing Students: 6 full-time (all women), 35 part-time (32 women). *Faculty:* 6 full-time (all women), 1 (woman) part-time/adjunct. Expenses: Contact institution. *Program availability:* Online only, 100% online. Offers nursing administration (MS); nursing education (MS). *Application Contact:* Misty Fields, Associate Director of Admission, 607-746-4546, E-mail: fieldsmr@delhi.edu.

STATE UNIVERSITY OF NEW YORK DOWNSTATE MEDICAL CENTER, Brooklyn, NY 11203-2098

General Information State-supported, coed, upper-level institution. *Graduate housing:* Rooms and/or apartments available on a first-come, first-served basis to single and married students. Housing application deadline: 5/29. *Research affiliation:* Brooklyn Veterans Administration Medical Center, Polytechnic Institute of New York University (biomedical engineering).

GRADUATE UNITS

College of Medicine Offers medicine (MPH, MD); urban and immigrant health (MPH).

College of Nursing *Program availability:* Part-time, evening/weekend. Offers clinical nurse specialist (MS, Post Master's Certificate); nurse anesthesia (MS); nurse midwifery (MS, Post Master's Certificate); nurse practitioner (MS, Post Master's Certificate); nursing (MS, Post Master's Certificate).

School of Graduate Studies Offers bioimaging and neuroengineering (PhD); biomedical engineering (MS); molecular and cellular biology (PhD); neural and behavioral science (PhD); occupational therapy (MS).

STATE UNIVERSITY OF NEW YORK EMPIRE STATE COLLEGE, Saratoga Springs, NY 12866-4391

General Information State-supported, coed, comprehensive institution. *Graduate housing:* On-campus housing not available.

GRADUATE UNITS

School for Graduate Studies *Program availability:* Part-time, evening/weekend, online learning. Offers adult learning (MA); community and economic development (MA); global leadership (MBA); labor and policy studies (MA); learning and emerging technologies (MA); liberal studies (MA); management (MBA); nursing education (MSN); social policy (MA); teaching (MAT); teaching and learning (M Ed). Electronic applications accepted.

STATE UNIVERSITY OF NEW YORK MARITIME COLLEGE, Throggs Neck, NY 10465-4198

General Information State-supported, coed, comprehensive institution. *Graduate housing:* Room and/or apartments available to single students; on-campus housing not available to married students. *Research affiliation:* Port Authority of New York and New Jersey (transportation), Transportation Infrastructure Research Consortium, Transportation Research Board (maritime transportation).

GRADUATE UNITS

Program in International Transportation Management *Program availability:* Part-time, evening/weekend. Offers international transportation management (MS).

STATE UNIVERSITY OF NEW YORK POLYTECHNIC INSTITUTE, Utica, NY 13502

General Information State-supported, coed, comprehensive institution. *Enrollment:* 2,933 graduate, professional, and undergraduate students; 250 full-time matriculated graduate/professional students (123 women), 499 part-time matriculated graduate/professional students (311 women). *Enrollment by degree level:* 694 master's, 46 doctoral, 9 other advanced degrees. *Graduate faculty:* 56 full-time (14 women), 37 part-time/adjunct (23 women). Tuition, state resident: full-time $8154; part-time $2718 per year. Tuition, nonresident: full-time $16,650; part-time $5550 per year. *Required fees:* $993; $331 per unit. Tuition and fees vary according to course load, degree level, campus/location and program. *Graduate housing:* Room and/or apartments available to single students; on-campus housing not available to married students. Typical cost: $4485 per year ($6785 including board). Room and board charges vary according to board plan. *Student services:* Campus employment opportunities, campus safety program, career counseling, exercise/wellness program, free psychological counseling, international student services, low-cost health insurance, multicultural affairs office, services for students with disabilities, writing training. *Library facilities:* Peter J. Cayan Library. *Collection:* Books: 139,500 (physical), 108,500 (digital/electronic); Serial titles: 2,175 (physical), 49,045 (digital/electronic); Databases: 50. Weekly public service hours: 87; students can reserve study rooms. *Research affiliation:* Assured Information Security, Inc. (cyber security), Masconic Research Laboratory (heart research), New West Technologies (mechanical engineering), Air Force Research Laboratory (computer science/systems and signal processing).

Computer facilities: 380 computers available on campus for general student use. A campuswide network can be accessed from student residence rooms and from off campus. Online class registration is available.
Website: http://www.sunypoly.edu/

General Application Contact: Alicia Foster, Director of Graduate Admissions, E-mail: alicia.foster@sunyit.edu.

GRADUATE UNITS

Colleges of Nanoscale Science and Engineering Students: 47 full-time (15 women), 19 part-time (6 women); includes 16 minority (9 Asian, non-Hispanic/Latino; 2 Hispanic/Latino; 5 Two or more races, non-Hispanic/Latino), 16 international. Average age 27. 105 applicants, 52% accepted, 36 enrolled. *Faculty:* 35 full-time (7 women), 13 part-time/adjunct (2 women). Expenses: Contact institution. *Financial support:* Fellowships, research assistantships, teaching assistantships, and tuition waivers available. In 2017, 1 master's awarded. *Program availability:* Online learning. Offers nanoscale engineering (MS, PhD); nanoscale science (MS, PhD). *Application deadline:* For fall admission, 7/1 for domestic and international students; for spring admission, 12/1 for domestic students, 11/1 for international students. *Application fee:* $60. *Application Contact:* Krista Thompson, Assistant Dean of Graduate Studies, 518-437-8686, E-mail: kthompson@sunypoly.edu. *Interim Dean, College of Nanoscale Sciences*, Alain Diebold, 518-956-7363, E-mail: adiebold@sunypoly.edu.

MBA Program in Technology Management Students: 29 full-time (13 women), 85 part-time (41 women); includes 18 minority (4 Black or African American, non-Hispanic/Latino; 8 Asian, non-Hispanic/Latino; 6 Hispanic/Latino). Average age 32. 83 applicants, 55% accepted, 37 enrolled. *Faculty:* 8 full-time (2 women), 2 part-time/adjunct (1 woman). Expenses: Contact institution. *Financial support:* Fellowships, research assistantships, and unspecified assistantships available. Financial award application deadline: 6/1; financial award applicants required to submit FAFSA. In 2017, 41 master's awarded. *Program availability:* Part-time, online only, 100% online. Offers accounting and finance (MBA); business management (MBA); health informatics (MBA); human resource management (MBA); marketing management (MBA). *Application deadline:* For fall admission, 7/1 priority date for domestic students, 7/1 for international students; for spring admission, 12/1 for domestic students, 11/1 for international students. Applications are processed on a rolling basis. *Application fee:* $60. Electronic applications accepted. *Application Contact:* Alicia Foster, Director of Graduate Admissions, E-mail: alicia.foster@sunyit.edu. *Program Coordinator*, Dr. Rafael Romero, 315-792-7207, E-mail: rafael.romero@sunyit.edu.

Program in Accountancy Students: 27 full-time (14 women), 48 part-time (28 women); includes 24 minority (4 Black or African American, non-Hispanic/Latino; 1 American Indian or Alaska Native, non-Hispanic/Latino; 10 Asian, non-Hispanic/Latino; 8 Hispanic/Latino; 1 Two or more races, non-Hispanic/Latino). Average age 33. 86 applicants, 51% accepted, 27 enrolled. *Faculty:* 3 full-time (1 woman). Expenses: Contact institution. *Financial support:* Fellowships, research assistantships, and unspecified assistantships available. Financial award application deadline: 6/1; financial award applicants required to submit FAFSA. In 2017, 14 master's awarded. *Program availability:* Part-time, online only, 100% online. Offers accountancy (MS). *Application deadline:* For fall admission, 7/1 priority date for domestic students, 7/1 for international students; for spring admission, 12/1 for domestic students, 11/1 for international students. Applications are processed on a rolling basis. *Application fee:* $60. Electronic applications accepted. *Application Contact:* Alicia Foster, Director of Graduate Admissions, E-mail: alicia.foster@sunyit.edu. *Program Coordinator*, Peter Karl, 315-792-7120, E-mail: pak3rd@sunyit.edu.

Program in Computer and Information Science Students: 52 full-time (12 women), 34 part-time (5 women); includes 1 minority (Hispanic/Latino), 68 international. Average age 24. 135 applicants, 64% accepted, 29 enrolled. *Faculty:* 12 full-time (1 woman). Expenses: Contact institution. *Financial support:* Research assistantships, scholarships/grants, and unspecified assistantships available. Financial award application deadline: 6/1; financial award applicants required to submit FAFSA. In 2017, 36 master's awarded. *Program availability:* Part-time. Offers computer and information science (MS). *Application deadline:* For fall admission, 7/1 for domestic and international students; for spring admission, 12/1 for domestic students, 11/1 for international students. Applications are processed on a rolling basis. *Application fee:* $60. Electronic applications accepted. *Application Contact:* Alicia Foster, Director of Graduate Admissions, E-mail: fostera3@sunyit.edu. *Program Coordinator*, Dr. Roger Cavallo, 315-792-7231, Fax: 315-792-7399, E-mail: roger.cavallo@sunyit.edu.

Program in Family Nurse Practitioner Students: 64 full-time (59 women), 117 part-time (108 women); includes 22 minority (6 Black or African American, non-Hispanic/Latino; 1 American Indian or Alaska Native, non-Hispanic/Latino; 6 Asian, non-Hispanic/Latino; 6 Hispanic/Latino; 3 Two or more races, non-Hispanic/Latino). Average age 36. 197 applicants, 58% accepted, 92 enrolled. *Faculty:* 1 (woman) full-time, 18 part-time/adjunct (17 women). Expenses: Contact institution. *Financial support:* Fellowships and scholarships/grants available. Financial award application deadline: 6/1; financial award applicants required to submit FAFSA. In 2017, 40 master's awarded. *Program availability:* Part-time. Offers family nurse practitioner (MS, CAS). *Application deadline:* For fall admission, 7/1 for domestic and international students. *Application fee:* $60. *Application Contact:* Alicia Foster, Director of Graduate Admissions, E-mail: alicia.foster@sunyit.edu. *Program Coordinator*, Kathleen Maroll, RN, E-mail: marollk@sunyit.edu.

Program in Information Design and Technology Students: 7 full-time (2 women), 60 part-time (33 women); includes 13 minority (4 Black or African American, non-Hispanic/Latino; 3 Asian, non-Hispanic/Latino; 5 Hispanic/Latino; 1 Two or more races, non-Hispanic/Latino). Average age 35. 39 applicants, 56% accepted, 19 enrolled. *Faculty:* 5 full-time (1 woman). Expenses: Contact institution. *Financial support:* Application deadline: 6/1; applicants required to submit FAFSA. In 2017, 19 master's awarded. *Program availability:* Part-time, online only, 100% online. Offers information design and technology (MS). *Application deadline:* For fall admission, 7/1 for domestic and international students; for spring admission, 12/1 for domestic students, 11/1 for international students. Applications are processed on a rolling basis. *Application fee:* $60. Electronic applications accepted. *Application Contact:* Alicia Foster, Director of Graduate Admissions, E-mail: alicia.foster@sunyit.edu. *Program Coordinator*, Dr. Steve Schneider, E-mail: steve@sunyit.edu.

Program in Network and Computer Security Students: 13 full-time (1 woman), 15 part-time (2 women); includes 3 minority (1 Black or African American, non-Hispanic/Latino; 2 Asian, non-Hispanic/Latino), 17 international. Average age 28. 58 applicants, 43% accepted, 9 enrolled. *Faculty:* 3 full-time (0 women), 3 part-time/adjunct

(0 women). Expenses: Contact institution. *Financial support:* Research assistantships and unspecified assistantships available. Financial award application deadline: 6/1; financial award applicants required to submit FAFSA. In 2017, 6 master's awarded. *Program availability:* Part-time, 100% online. Offers network and computer security (MS). *Application deadline:* For fall admission, 7/1 priority date for domestic students, 7/1 for international students; for spring admission, 12/1 for domestic students, 11/1 for international students. Applications are processed on a rolling basis. *Application fee:* $60. Electronic applications accepted. *Application Contact:* Alicia Foster, Director of Graduate Admissions, E-mail: alicia.foster@sunyit.edu. *Chairperson*, Dr. John Marsh, E-mail: john.marsh@sunyit.edu.

Program in Nursing Education Students: 4 full-time (2 women), 57 part-time (52 women); includes 7 minority (3 Black or African American, non-Hispanic/Latino; 2 Asian, non-Hispanic/Latino; 2 Hispanic/Latino). Average age 40. 25 applicants, 60% accepted, 13 enrolled. *Faculty:* 2 full-time (both women), 2 part-time/adjunct (both women). Expenses: Contact institution. *Financial support:* Scholarships/grants available. Financial award application deadline: 6/1; financial award applicants required to submit FAFSA. In 2017, 17 master's awarded. *Program availability:* Part-time, 100% online. Offers nursing education (MS, CAS). *Application deadline:* For fall admission, 7/1 for domestic and international students; for spring admission, 12/1 for domestic students, 11/1 for international students. Applications are processed on a rolling basis. *Application fee:* $60. Electronic applications accepted. *Application Contact:* Alicia Foster, Director of Graduate Admissions, E-mail: alicia.foster@sunyit.edu. *Program Coordinator*, Dr. Esther Bankert, E-mail: esther.bankert@sunyit.edu.

STATE UNIVERSITY OF NEW YORK UPSTATE MEDICAL UNIVERSITY, Syracuse, NY 13210

General Information State-supported, coed, upper-level institution. CGS member. *Graduate housing:* Rooms and/or apartments available on a first-come, first-served basis to single and married students. Housing application deadline: 8/1.

GRADUATE UNITS

College of Graduate Studies Offers anatomy (MS, PhD); biochemistry (MS); biochemistry and molecular biology (PhD); microbiology (MS); microbiology and immunology (PhD); neuroscience (PhD); pharmacology (PhD); physiology (MS, PhD). Electronic applications accepted.

College of Medicine Offers medicine (MD). Electronic applications accepted.

College of Nursing *Program availability:* Part-time, online learning. Offers nurse practitioner (Post Master's Certificate); nursing (MS). Electronic applications accepted.

Department of Physical Therapy *Program availability:* Part-time, evening/weekend, online learning. Offers physical therapy (DPT). Electronic applications accepted.

Program in Medical Technology Offers medical technology (MS).

STEPHEN F. AUSTIN STATE UNIVERSITY, Nacogdoches, TX 75962

General Information State-supported, coed, comprehensive institution. *Graduate housing:* Rooms and/or apartments available on a first-come, first-served basis to single students and available to married students. Housing application deadline: 6/1. *Research affiliation:* University Health Center at Tyler (biotechnology, environmental science).

GRADUATE UNITS

Graduate School *Program availability:* Part-time, evening/weekend, online learning. Electronic applications accepted.

College of Applied Arts and Science *Program availability:* Part-time. Offers applied arts and science (MA, MIS, MSW); communication (MA); interdisciplinary studies (MIS); mass communication (MA); social work (MSW).

College of Business *Program availability:* Part-time, evening/weekend. Offers business (MBA, MPAC, MS); computer science (MS); management and marketing (MBA); professional accountancy (MPAC).

College of Education *Program availability:* Part-time, evening/weekend. Offers athletic training (MS); counseling (MA); early childhood education (M Ed); education (M Ed, MA, MS, Ed D); educational leadership (Ed D); elementary education (M Ed); human sciences (MS); kinesiology (M Ed); school psychology (MA); secondary education (M Ed); special education (M Ed); speech-language pathology (MS).

College of Fine Arts *Program availability:* Part-time. Offers art (MA); design (MFA); drawing (MFA); fine arts (MA, MFA, MM); music (MA, MM); painting (MFA); sculpture (MFA).

College of Forestry and Agriculture Offers agriculture (MS); forestry (MF, MS, PhD); forestry and agriculture (MF, MS, PhD).

College of Liberal Arts *Program availability:* Part-time, evening/weekend. Offers English (MA); history (MA); liberal arts (MA, MPA); psychology (MA); public administration (MPA).

College of Sciences and Mathematics *Program availability:* Part-time. Offers biology (MS); biotechnology (MS); chemistry (MS); environmental science (MS); geology (MS, MSNS); mathematics (MS); mathematics education (MS); physics (MS); sciences and mathematics (MS, MSNS); statistics (MS).

STEPHENS COLLEGE, Columbia, MO 65215-0002

General Information Independent, Undergraduate: women only; graduate: coed, comprehensive institution. *Graduate housing:* On-campus housing not available.

GRADUATE UNITS

Division of Graduate and Continuing Studies *Program availability:* Part-time, evening/weekend, online learning. Offers counseling (M Ed); health information administration (Postbaccalaureate Certificate); physician assistant studies (MPAS); TV and screenwriting (MFA). Electronic applications accepted.

STETSON UNIVERSITY, DeLand, FL 32723

General Information Independent, coed, comprehensive institution. *Enrollment:* 4,268 graduate, professional, and undergraduate students; 1,029 full-time matriculated graduate/professional students (584 women), 145 part-time matriculated graduate/professional students (84 women). *Enrollment by degree level:* 318 master's, 856 doctoral. *Graduate faculty:* 74 full-time (38 women), 65 part-time/adjunct (29 women). *Graduate housing:* Rooms and/or apartments available to single and married students. *Student services:* Campus employment opportunities, campus safety program, career counseling, free psychological counseling, international student services, multicultural affairs office, services for students with disabilities, teacher training. *Library facilities:* DuPont-Ball Library plus 1 other. *Collection:* Books: 205,846 (physical), 188,390 (digital/electronic); Serial titles: 295 (physical), 115,751 (digital/electronic); Databases: 145. Weekly public service hours: 99; students can reserve study rooms. *Research affiliation:* New Teacher Center (teacher education), Teacher Prep Inspection-Us, LLC (teacher preparation), Erin Deady, PA (environmental policy and legal affairs).

Computer facilities: 500 computers available on campus for general student use. A campuswide network can be accessed from student residence rooms and from off campus. Online class registration is available.
Website: http://www.stetson.edu/

General Application Contact: Jamie Vanderlip, Senior Associate Director of Admissions, 386-822-7100, Fax: 386-822-7112, E-mail: gradadmissions@stetson.edu.

GRADUATE UNITS

College of Arts and Sciences Students: 185 full-time (145 women), 14 part-time (12 women); includes 77 minority (19 Black or African American, non-Hispanic/Latino; 7 American Indian or Alaska Native, non-Hispanic/Latino; 1 Asian, non-Hispanic/Latino; 28 Hispanic/Latino; 1 Native Hawaiian or other Pacific Islander, non-Hispanic/Latino; 21 Two or more races, non-Hispanic/Latino), 6 international. Average age 33. 103 applicants, 85% accepted, 67 enrolled. *Faculty:* 14 full-time (9 women), 11 part-time/adjunct (7 women). Expenses: Contact institution. *Financial support:* In 2017–18, 75 students received support. Career-related internships or fieldwork, Federal Work-Study, scholarships/grants, unspecified assistantships, and tuition waivers (for staff and dependents) available. Support available to part-time students. Financial award applicants required to submit FAFSA. In 2017, 81 master's awarded. *Program availability:* Part-time, evening/weekend. Offers arts and sciences (M Ed, MFA, MS); creative writing (MFA). *Application deadline:* For fall admission, 8/1 priority date for domestic students; for spring admission, 1/1 priority date for domestic students; for summer admission, 5/1 priority date for domestic students. Applications are processed on a rolling basis. *Application fee:* $50. Electronic applications accepted. *Application Contact:* Jamie Vanderlip, Director of Admissions for Graduate, Transfer and Adult Populations, 386-822-7100, Fax: 386-822-7112, E-mail: jlvander@stetson.edu. *Interim Dean*, Dr. Thomas Farrell, 386-822-7515.

Division of Education Students: 168 full-time (132 women), 14 part-time (12 women); includes 73 minority (19 Black or African American, non-Hispanic/Latino; 7 American Indian or Alaska Native, non-Hispanic/Latino; 1 Asian, non-Hispanic/Latino; 25 Hispanic/Latino; 1 Native Hawaiian or other Pacific Islander, non-Hispanic/Latino; 20 Two or more races, non-Hispanic/Latino), 5 international. Average age 32. 102 applicants, 85% accepted, 66 enrolled. *Faculty:* 13 full-time (8 women), 6 part-time/adjunct (3 women). Expenses: Contact institution. *Financial support:* In 2017–18, 74 students received support. Career-related internships or fieldwork, Federal Work-Study, institutionally sponsored loans, scholarships/grants, unspecified assistantships, and tuition waivers (for staff and dependents) available. Support available to part-time students. Financial award applicants required to submit FAFSA. In 2017, 81 master's awarded. *Program availability:* Part-time, evening/weekend. Offers counselor education (MS); educational leadership (M Ed); marriage, couple and family counseling (MS); mental health counseling (MS); school counseling (MS); teacher education (M Ed). *Application deadline:* For fall admission, 8/1 priority date for domestic students; for spring admission, 1/1 priority date for domestic students; for summer admission, 5/1 priority date for domestic students. Applications are processed on a rolling basis. *Application fee:* $50. Electronic applications accepted. *Application Contact:* Jamie Vanderlip, Director of Admissions for Graduate, Transfer and Adult Programs, 386-822-7100, Fax: 386-822-7112, E-mail: jlvander@stetson.edu. *Interim Dean*, Dr. Thomas Farrell, 386-822-7515.

College of Law Students: 687 full-time (361 women), 170 part-time (85 women); includes 239 minority (56 Black or African American, non-Hispanic/Latino; 4 American Indian or Alaska Native, non-Hispanic/Latino; 23 Asian, non-Hispanic/Latino; 128 Hispanic/Latino; 28 Two or more races, non-Hispanic/Latino), 14 international. Average age 28. 1,967 applicants, 46% accepted, 300 enrolled. *Faculty:* 53 full-time (28 women), 102 part-time/adjunct (36 women). Expenses: Contact institution. *Financial support:* In 2017–18, 612 students received support, including 67 research assistantships (averaging $857 per year), 65 teaching assistantships (averaging $664 per year); career-related internships or fieldwork, Federal Work-Study, scholarships/grants, unspecified assistantships, and tuition waivers (for staff and dependents) also available. Support available to part-time students. Financial award application deadline: 8/15; financial award applicants required to submit FAFSA. In 2017, 40 master's, 265 doctorates awarded. *Program availability:* Part-time, evening/weekend, 100% online. Offers advocacy (LL M); elder law (LL M); international law (LL M); law (M Jur, JD). *Application deadline:* For fall admission, 5/15 for domestic and international students. Applications are processed on a rolling basis. *Application fee:* $55. Electronic applications accepted. *Application Contact:* Darren Kettles, Director of Admissions, 727-562-7802, Fax: 727-343-0136, E-mail: lawadmit@law.stetson.edu. *Dean/Professor of Law*, Christopher M. Pietruszkiewicz, 727-562-7809, Fax: 727-562-6428, E-mail: cmp@law.stetson.edu.

School of Business Administration Students: 98 full-time (49 women), 21 part-time (15 women); includes 39 minority (9 Black or African American, non-Hispanic/Latino; 4 Asian, non-Hispanic/Latino; 14 Hispanic/Latino; 12 Two or more races, non-Hispanic/Latino), 9 international. Average age 31. 124 applicants, 77% accepted, 56 enrolled. *Faculty:* 16 full-time (4 women), 3 part-time/adjunct (1 woman). Expenses: Contact institution. *Financial support:* In 2017–18, 37 students received support. Career-related internships or fieldwork, Federal Work-Study, institutionally sponsored loans, scholarships/grants, unspecified assistantships, and tuition waivers (for staff and dependents) available. Support available to part-time students. Financial award applicants required to submit FAFSA. In 2017, 85 master's awarded. *Program availability:* Part-time, evening/weekend. Offers accounting (M Acc); business administration (EMBA, M Acc, MBA). *Application deadline:* For fall admission, 8/1 for domestic students; for spring admission, 1/1 for domestic students; for summer admission, 5/1 for domestic students. Applications are processed on a rolling basis. *Application fee:* $50. Electronic applications accepted. *Application Contact:* Jamie Vanderlip, Director of Admissions for Graduate, Transfer and Adult Programs, 386-822-7100, Fax: 386-822-7112, E-mail: jlvander@stetson.edu. *Dean, School of Business Administration*, Dr. Neal P. Mero, 386-822-7405.

STEVENS-HENAGER COLLEGE, Salt Lake City, UT 84123

General Information Independent, coed, comprehensive institution.

STEVENS INSTITUTE OF TECHNOLOGY, Hoboken, NJ 07030

General Information Independent, coed, university. CGS member. *Enrollment:* 6,916 graduate, professional, and undergraduate students; 2,497 full-time matriculated graduate/professional students (699 women), 1,135 part-time matriculated graduate/professional students (344 women). *Enrollment by degree level:* 3,171 master's, 371 doctoral, 90 other advanced degrees. *Graduate faculty:* 289 full-time (73 women), 156 part-time/adjunct (37 women). *Tuition:* Full-time $34,494; part-time $1554 per credit. *Required fees:* $291 per semester. *Graduate housing:* Room and/or apartments available on a first-come, first-served basis to single students; on-campus housing not available to married students. Housing application deadline: 6/1. *Student services:* Campus employment opportunities, campus safety program, career counseling, exercise/wellness program, free psychological counseling, grant writing training, international student services, low-cost health insurance, multicultural affairs office, services for students with disabilities, teacher training, writing training. *Library facilities:* Samuel C. Williams Library. *Collection:* Books: 66,492 (physical), 210,243 (digital/electronic); Serial titles: 898 (physical), 35,353 (digital/electronic); Databases: 71. Students can reserve study rooms. *Research affiliation:* U.S. Department of Homeland Security (secure maritime systems), U.S. Department of Defense (systems engineering), National Science Foundation (nanotechnology and multi-scale systems, secure systems and information assurance), AT&T (intelligent networked systems).

Computer facilities: 500 computers available on campus for general student use. A campuswide network can be accessed. Online class registration, online account information, debit dining program, laundry status are available.
Website: http://www.stevens.edu/

General Application Contact: 888-783-8367, Fax: 888-555-1306, E-mail: graduate@stevens.edu.

GRADUATE UNITS

Graduate School Students: 2,497 full-time (699 women), 1,135 part-time (344 women); includes 349 minority (78 Black or African American, non-Hispanic/Latino; 8 American Indian or Alaska Native, non-Hispanic/Latino; 244 Asian, non-Hispanic/Latino; 19 Hispanic/Latino), 2,256 international. Average age 28. 7,949 applicants, 59% accepted, 1136 enrolled. *Faculty:* 289 full-time (73 women), 156 part-time/adjunct (37 women). Expenses: Contact institution. *Financial support:* Fellowships, research assistantships, teaching assistantships, career-related internships or fieldwork, Federal Work-Study, scholarships/grants, and unspecified assistantships available. Financial award application deadline: 2/15; financial award applicants required to submit FAFSA. In 2017, 1,471 master's, 55 doctorates, 564 other advanced degrees awarded. *Program availability:* Part-time, evening/weekend, online learning. *Application deadline:* For fall admission, 7/1 for domestic students, 4/15 for international students; for spring admission, 12/1 for domestic and international students. Applications are processed on a rolling basis. *Application fee:* $60. Electronic applications accepted. *Application Contact:* 888-783-8367, Fax: 888-511-1306, E-mail: graduate@stevens.edu. *Interim Director of Graduate Admissions and Enrollment*, Paul Easterling, 201-216-3670, Fax: 555-511-1306, E-mail: paul.easterling@stevens.edu.

Charles V. Schaefer Jr. School of Engineering and Science Students: 1,352 full-time (316 women), 315 part-time (86 women); includes 115 minority (23 Black or African American, non-Hispanic/Latino; 3 American Indian or Alaska Native, non-Hispanic/Latino; 84 Asian, non-Hispanic/Latino; 5 Hispanic/Latino), 1,162 international. Average age 26. 4,351 applicants, 58% accepted, 561 enrolled. *Faculty:* 162 full-time (35 women), 92 part-time/adjunct (14 women). Expenses: Contact institution. *Financial support:* Fellowships, research assistantships, teaching assistantships, career-related internships or fieldwork, Federal Work-Study, scholarships/grants, and unspecified assistantships available. Financial award application deadline: 2/15; financial award applicants required to submit FAFSA. In 2017, 762 master's, 40 doctorates, 142 other advanced degrees awarded. *Program availability:* Part-time, evening/weekend, online learning. Offers additive manufacturing (Certificate); advanced manufacturing (Certificate); air pollution technology (Certificate); analytical chemistry (Certificate); applied mathematics (MS); applied optics (Certificate); applied statistics (Certificate); armament engineering (M Eng); atmospheric and environmental science and engineering (Certificate); autonomous robotics (Certificate); bioinformatics (Certificate); biomedical chemistry (Certificate); biomedical engineering (M Eng, PhD); chemical biology (MS, PhD, Certificate); chemical engineering (M Eng, PhD, Engr); chemical physiology (Certificate); chemistry (MS, PhD); civil engineering (M Eng, PhD, Certificate, Engr); computational fluid mechanics and heat transfer (Certificate); computer and electrical engineering (M Eng); computer engineering (M Eng, PhD, Certificate); computer graphics (Certificate); computer science (MS, PhD); computer systems (M Eng, Certificate); construction management (MS, Certificate); cybersecurity (MS); data communications and networks (M Eng); database management systems (Certificate); design and production management (Certificate); digital systems design (M Eng); distributed systems (Certificate); electrical engineering (M Eng, PhD, Certificate); elements of computer science (Certificate); engineered software systems (M Eng); engineering and science (M Eng, MS, PhD, Certificate, Engr); enterprise and cloud computing (MS); enterprise computing (Certificate); enterprise security and information assurance (Certificate); environmental engineering (M Eng, PhD, Certificate); environmental hydrology (Certificate); environmental processes (M Eng); geotechnical/geoenvironmental engineering (M Eng, Engr); health informatics (Certificate); hydraulics (Certificate); hydrologic modeling (M Eng); image processing and multimedia (M Eng); information system security (M Eng); information systems (M Eng); inland and coastal environmental hydrodynamics (M Eng); integrated product development (M Eng); manufacturing technologies (M Eng); maritime systems (MS); materials science and engineering (M Eng, PhD); mathematics (MS, PhD); mechanical engineering (M Eng, PhD); media and broadcast engineering (MS); medical devices (Certificate); microdevices and microsystems (Certificate); microelectronics (Certificate); microelectronics and photonics (M Eng, MS, PhD); modeling of environmental systems (M Eng); multi-hazard engineering (Certificate); multimedia experience and management (Certificate); nanotechnology (PhD); networked information systems (MS, Certificate); networks and systems administration (Certificate); nuclear power engineering (Certificate); ocean engineering (M Eng, PhD); ordnance engineering (Certificate); pharmaceutical manufacturing (M Eng, MS, Certificate); photonics (Certificate); physics (M Eng, MS, PhD); polymer chemistry (Certificate); power generation (Certificate); product architecture and engineering (M Eng); robotics and control (Certificate); service oriented computing (Certificate); ship hydrodynamics (Certificate); soil and groundwater pollution control (M Eng); stochastic systems (MS, Certificate); stochastic systems and optimization (MS); stormwater management (M Eng); structural analysis and design (Certificate); structural engineering (M Eng, Certificate, Engr); surface water hydrology (Certificate); systems reliability and design (M Eng); transportation engineering (M Eng); vibration and noise control (Certificate); water resources engineering (M Eng, Certificate). *Application deadline:* For fall admission, 7/1 for domestic students, 4/15 for international students; for spring admission, 12/1 for domestic and international students. Applications are processed on a rolling basis. *Application fee:* $60. Electronic applications accepted. *Application Contact:* Graduate Admissions, 888-783-8367, Fax: 888-555-1306, E-mail: graduate@stevens.edu. *Dean*, Dr. Jean Zu, 201-216-2833, E-mail: jean.zu@stevens.edu.

College of Arts and Letters Students: 1 full-time (0 women), 2 part-time (both women). Average age 28. 10 applicants, 40% accepted, 3 enrolled. *Faculty:* 39 full-time (19 women), 15 part-time/adjunct (9 women). Expenses: Contact institution. *Financial support:* Fellowships, research assistantships, teaching assistantships, career-related internships or fieldwork, Federal Work-Study, scholarships/grants, and unspecified assistantships available. Financial award application deadline: 2/15; financial award applicants required to submit FAFSA. In 2017, 1 master's awarded. *Program availability:* Part-time, evening/weekend. Offers arts and letters (MA, Graduate Certificate); policy and innovation (MA, Graduate Certificate). *Application deadline:* For fall admission, 7/1 for domestic students, 4/15 for international students; for spring admission, 12/1 for domestic and international students. Applications are processed on a rolling basis. *Application fee:* $60. Electronic applications accepted. *Application Contact:* Graduate Admission, 888-783-8367, Fax: 888-511-1306, E-mail: graduate@stevens.edu. *Dean*, Dr. Kelland Thomas.

School of Business Students: 957 full-time (333 women), 557 part-time (202 women); includes 184 minority (37 Black or African American, non-Hispanic/Latino; 5 American Indian or Alaska Native, non-Hispanic/Latino; 133 Asian, non-Hispanic/Latino; 9 Hispanic/Latino), 965 international. Average age 29. 3,027 applicants, 61% accepted, 492 enrolled. *Faculty:* 58 full-time (10 women), 31 part-time/adjunct (7 women). Expenses: Contact institution. *Financial support:* Fellowships, research assistantships, teaching assistantships, career-related internships or fieldwork, Federal Work-Study, scholarships/grants, and unspecified assistantships available. Financial award application deadline: 2/15; financial award applicants required to submit FAFSA. In 2017, 500 master's, 7 doctorates, 131 other advanced degrees awarded. *Program availability:* Part-time, evening/weekend, online learning. Offers business (MS); business administration (EMBA); business intelligence and analytics (MBA); computer science (MS); e-commerce (MS); engineering management (MBA); enterprise systems (MS); entrepreneurial information technology (MS); finance (MS); financial engineering (MS, PhD, Certificate); general management (MS); global innovation management (MS); human resource management (MS); information architecture (MS); information management (MS, PhD, Certificate); information security (MS); information systems (MBA); information technology in financial services industry (MS); information technology in the pharmaceutical industry (MS); information technology outsourcing management (MS); innovation and entrepreneurship (MBA); management of wireless networks (MS); marketing (MBA); network and communication management and services (MS); online security, technology and business (MS); pharmaceutical management (MBA); professional communications (Certificate); project management (MBA, MS, Certificate); software engineering (MS); technical management (MS); technology commercialization (MS); technology management (EMBA, MBA, MS, PhD); technology management for experienced professionals (MS, Certificate); telecommunications (MS); telecommunications management (MBA, PhD, Certificate). *Application deadline:* For fall admission, 7/1 for domestic students, 4/15 for international students; for spring admission, 12/1 for domestic and international students. Applications are processed on a rolling basis. *Application fee:* $60. Electronic applications accepted. *Application Contact:* Graduate Admissions, 888-793-8367, Fax: 888-511-1306, E-mail: graduate@stevens.edu. *Dean*, Dr. Gregory Prastacos, 201-216-8366, E-mail: gprastac@stevens.edu.

School of Systems and Enterprises Students: 187 full-time (49 women), 261 part-time (53 women); includes 50 minority (18 Black or African American, non-Hispanic/Latino; 27 Asian, non-Hispanic/Latino; 5 Hispanic/Latino), 129 international. Average age 30. 552 applicants, 64% accepted, 80 enrolled. *Faculty:* 28 full-time (8 women), 14 part-time/adjunct (3 women). Expenses: Contact institution. *Financial support:* Fellowships, research assistantships, teaching assistantships, career-related internships or fieldwork, Federal Work-Study, scholarships/grants, and unspecified assistantships available. Financial award application deadline: 2/15; financial award applicants required to submit FAFSA. In 2017, 208 master's, 8 doctorates, 291 other advanced degrees awarded. *Program availability:* Part-time, evening/weekend. Offers engineering management (M Eng, PhD, Certificate); enterprise systems (Certificate); socio-technical systems (MS, PhD); software engineering (MS, Certificate); space systems engineering (M Eng, Certificate); systems and enterprises (M Eng, MS, PhD, Certificate); systems and supportability engineering (Certificate); systems design and operational effectiveness (Certificate); systems engineering (M Eng, PhD); systems engineering and architecting (Certificate); systems engineering management (Certificate); systems engineering of embedded/cyber-physical systems (Certificate); systems engineering security (Certificate). *Application deadline:* For fall admission, 7/1 for domestic students, 4/15 for international students; for spring admission, 12/1 for domestic and international students. Applications are processed on a rolling basis. *Application fee:* $60. Electronic applications accepted. *Application Contact:* Graduate Admissions, 888-783-8367, Fax: 888-511-1306, E-mail: graduate@stevens.edu. *Dean*, Dr. Dinesh Verma, 201-216-8645, Fax: 201-216-5541, E-mail: dinesh.verma@stevens.edu.

STEVENSON UNIVERSITY, Stevenson, MD 21153

General Information Independent, coed, comprehensive institution. *Enrollment:* 3,876 graduate, professional, and undergraduate students; 76 full-time matriculated graduate/professional students (46 women), 508 part-time matriculated graduate/professional students (400 women). *Enrollment by degree level:* 584 master's. *Graduate faculty:* 8 full-time (6 women), 49 part-time/adjunct (26 women). *Tuition:* Full-time $12,060; part-time $670 per credit. *Required fees:* $250; $125 per semester. Tuition and fees vary according to program. *Graduate housing:* On-campus housing not available. *Student services:* Campus employment opportunities, campus safety program, career counseling, exercise/wellness program, multicultural affairs office, services for students with disabilities. *Library facilities:* Stevenson University Learning Resource Center-Greenspring Campus plus 2 others. *Collection:* Books: 67,987 (physical), 342,648 (digital/electronic); Serial titles: 476 (physical), 72,885 (digital/electronic); Databases: 88. Weekly public service hours: 136; students can reserve study rooms.

Computer facilities: Computer purchase and lease plans are available. 515 computers available on campus for general student use. A campuswide network can be accessed from student residence rooms and from off campus. Online class registration is available.
Website: http://www.stevenson.edu/

General Application Contact: Tonia Cristino, Assistant Director, SUO Admissions, 443-352-4058, Fax: 443-352-4440, E-mail: tcristino@stevenson.edu.

GRADUATE UNITS

Master of Arts in Teaching Program Students: 18 part-time (11 women); includes 6 minority (2 Black or African American, non-Hispanic/Latino; 2 Asian, non-Hispanic/Latino; 1 Hispanic/Latino; 1 Two or more races, non-Hispanic/Latino). Average age 31. 8 applicants, 100% accepted, 8 enrolled. *Faculty:* 5 part-time/adjunct (all women). Expenses: Contact institution. *Financial support:* Unspecified assistantships available. Financial award applicants required to submit FAFSA. *Program availability:* Part-time, blended/hybrid learning. Offers secondary biology (MAT); secondary chemistry (MAT); secondary mathematics (MAT). *Application deadline:* Applications are processed on a rolling basis. Electronic applications accepted. *Application Contact:* Amanda Courter, Senior Enrollment Counselor, 443-352-4243, Fax: 443-352-4440, E-mail: acourter@stevenson.edu. *Associate Dean of Teacher Education*, Anne P. Davis.

Program in Business and Technology Management Students: 20 full-time (6 women), 95 part-time (53 women); includes 47 minority (41 Black or African American, non-Hispanic/Latino; 1 American Indian or Alaska Native, non-Hispanic/Latino; 1 Asian, non-Hispanic/Latino; 4 Two or more races, non-Hispanic/Latino). Average age 30. 45 applicants, 100% accepted, 38 enrolled. *Faculty:* 1 full-time (0 women), 18 part-time/adjunct (3 women). Expenses: Contact institution. *Financial support:* Unspecified assistantships available. Financial award applicants required to submit FAFSA. In 2017, 51 master's awarded. *Program availability:* Part-time, online only, 100% online. Offers emerging technology (MS); innovative leadership (MS). *Application deadline:* Applications are processed on a rolling basis. *Application fee:* $0. Electronic applications accepted. *Application Contact:* Tonia Cristino, Assistant Director, Recruitment and Admissions, 443-352-4058, Fax: 443-394-0538, E-mail: tcristino@stevenson.edu. *Coordinator,* Steven Engorn, 443-352-4220, Fax: 443-394-0538, E-mail: sengorn@stevenson.edu.

Program in Communication Studies Students: 6 full-time (4 women), 22 part-time (17 women); includes 14 minority (12 Black or African American, non-Hispanic/Latino; 1 Asian, non-Hispanic/Latino; 1 Two or more races, non-Hispanic/Latino). Average age 28. 18 applicants, 94% accepted, 13 enrolled. *Faculty:* 5 part-time/adjunct (3 women). Expenses: Contact institution. *Financial support:* Unspecified assistantships available. Financial award applicants required to submit FAFSA. In 2017, 16 master's awarded. *Program availability:* Part-time, online only, 100% online, blended/hybrid learning. Offers communication studies (MS). *Application deadline:* Applications are processed on a rolling basis. Electronic applications accepted. *Application Contact:* Amanda Courter, Senior Enrollment Counselor, 443-352-4243, Fax: 443-352-4440, E-mail: acourter@stevenson.edu. *Associate Dean, Communications Studies,* Dr. Nadene Vevea, 443-394-9498, E-mail: nvevea@stevenson.edu.

Program in Community-Based Education and Leadership Students: 18 part-time (12 women); includes 8 minority (6 Black or African American, non-Hispanic/Latino; 1 Asian, non-Hispanic/Latino; 1 Two or more races, non-Hispanic/Latino). Average age 31. 27 applicants, 78% accepted, 18 enrolled. *Faculty:* 6 part-time/adjunct (5 women). Expenses: Contact institution. *Financial support:* Unspecified assistantships available. Financial award applicants required to submit FAFSA. *Program availability:* Part-time, evening/weekend. Offers community-based education and leadership (MS). *Application deadline:* Applications are processed on a rolling basis. Electronic applications accepted. *Application Contact:* Tonia Cristino, Assistant Director, SUO Admissions, 443-352-4058, Fax: 443-352-4440, E-mail: tcristino@stevenson.edu. *Associate Dean,* Anne Davis.

Program in Cyber Forensics Students: 3 full-time (all women), 22 part-time (9 women); includes 9 minority (7 Black or African American, non-Hispanic/Latino; 2 Asian, non-Hispanic/Latino). Average age 38. 3 applicants, 100% accepted, 2 enrolled. *Faculty:* 6 part-time/adjunct (1 woman). Expenses: Contact institution. *Financial support:* Unspecified assistantships available. Financial award applicants required to submit FAFSA. In 2017, 16 master's awarded. *Program availability:* Part-time, 100% online. Offers cyber forensics (MS). *Application deadline:* Applications are processed on a rolling basis. Electronic applications accepted. *Application Contact:* William Wellein, Enrollment Counselor, 443-352-5843, Fax: 443-394-0538, E-mail: wwellein@stevenson.edu. *Program Coordinator,* Thomas Byrd, E-mail: tbyrd6@stevenson.edu.

Program in Forensic Science Students: 22 full-time (16 women), 21 part-time (18 women); includes 23 minority (19 Black or African American, non-Hispanic/Latino; 1 American Indian or Alaska Native, non-Hispanic/Latino; 3 Two or more races, non-Hispanic/Latino). Average age 28. 18 applicants, 100% accepted, 18 enrolled. *Faculty:* 4 full-time (3 women), 4 part-time/adjunct (2 women). Expenses: Contact institution. *Financial support:* Unspecified assistantships available. Financial award applicants required to submit FAFSA. In 2017, 26 master's awarded. *Program availability:* Part-time. Offers biology (MS); chemistry (MS); crime scene investigation (MS). Program offered in partnership with Maryland State Police Forensic Sciences Division. *Application deadline:* Applications are processed on a rolling basis. *Application fee:* $0. Electronic applications accepted. *Application Contact:* William Wellein, Enrollment Counselor, 443-352-5843, Fax: 443-394-0538, E-mail: wwellein@stevenson.edu. *Coordinator,* John Tobin, PhD, 443-352-4142, Fax: 443-394-0538, E-mail: jtobin@stevenson.edu.

Program in Forensic Studies Students: 22 full-time (15 women), 103 part-time (85 women); includes 61 minority (51 Black or African American, non-Hispanic/Latino; 3 Asian, non-Hispanic/Latino; 7 Two or more races, non-Hispanic/Latino). Average age 30. 42 applicants, 90% accepted, 34 enrolled. *Faculty:* 3 full-time (all women), 10 part-time/adjunct (1 woman). Expenses: Contact institution. *Financial support:* Unspecified assistantships available. Financial award applicants required to submit FAFSA. In 2017, 34 master's awarded. *Program availability:* Part-time, blended/hybrid learning. Offers computer forensics (MS); criminalistics (MS); forensic accounting (MS); forensic legal professional (MS); interdisciplinary track (MS); investigations (MS). *Application deadline:* Applications are processed on a rolling basis. *Application fee:* $0. Electronic applications accepted. *Application Contact:* William Wellein, Enrollment Counselor, 443-352-5843, Fax: 443-394-0538, E-mail: wwellein@stevenson.edu. *Associate Dean,* Thomas Coogan, JD, 443-352-4075, Fax: 443-394-0538, E-mail: tcoogan@stevenson.edu.

Program in Healthcare Management Students: 4 full-time (2 women), 35 part-time (28 women); includes 11 minority (9 Black or African American, non-Hispanic/Latino; 2 Asian, non-Hispanic/Latino). Average age 30. 24 applicants, 71% accepted, 13 enrolled. *Faculty:* 2 full-time (both women), 7 part-time/adjunct (4 women). Expenses: Contact institution. *Financial support:* Unspecified assistantships available. Financial award applicants required to submit FAFSA. In 2017, 10 master's awarded. *Program availability:* Part-time, online only, 100% online. Offers project management (MS); quality management and patient safety (MS). *Application deadline:* Applications are processed on a rolling basis. Electronic applications accepted. *Application Contact:* Amanda Courter, Enrollment Counselor, 443-352-4243, Fax: 443-394-0538, E-mail: acourter@stevenson.edu. *Coordinator,* Sharon Buchbinder, PhD, 443-394-9290, Fax: 443-394-0538, E-mail: sbuchbinder@stevenson.edu.

Program in Nursing Students: 174 part-time (167 women); includes 53 minority (40 Black or African American, non-Hispanic/Latino; 5 Asian, non-Hispanic/Latino; 8 Two or more races, non-Hispanic/Latino). Average age 40. 45 applicants, 100% accepted, 38 enrolled. *Faculty:* 4 full-time (all women), 12 part-time/adjunct (all women). Expenses: Contact institution. *Financial support:* Unspecified assistantships available. Financial award applicants required to submit FAFSA. In 2017, 47 master's awarded. *Program availability:* Part-time, blended/hybrid learning. Offers nursing education (MS); nursing leadership/management (MS); population-based care coordination (MS). *Application deadline:* Applications are processed on a rolling basis. *Application fee:* $0. Electronic applications accepted. *Application Contact:* Amanda Courter, Enrollment Counselor, 443-352-4243, Fax: 443-394-0538, E-mail: acourter@stevenson.edu. *Associate Dean,* Judith Feustle, PhD, 443-352-4292, Fax: 443-394-0538, E-mail: jfeustle@stevenson.edu.

STOCKTON UNIVERSITY, Galloway, NJ 08205-9441

General Information State-supported, coed, comprehensive institution. CGS member. *Enrollment:* 9,216 graduate, professional, and undergraduate students; 366 full-time matriculated graduate/professional students (286 women), 534 part-time matriculated graduate/professional students (395 women). *Enrollment by degree level:* 738 master's, 162 doctoral. *Graduate faculty:* 63 full-time (43 women), 33 part-time/adjunct (20 women). *Graduate housing:* Room and/or apartments available on a first-come, first-served basis to single students; on-campus housing not available to married students. Housing application deadline: 6/1. *Student services:* Campus employment opportunities, campus safety program, career counseling, child daycare facilities, exercise/wellness program, free psychological counseling, grant writing training, international student services, low-cost health insurance, services for students with disabilities, teacher training, writing training. *Library facilities:* Richard E. Bjork Library. *Collection:* Books: 222,477 (physical), 142,000 (digital/electronic); Serial titles: 127 (physical), 132,055 (digital/electronic); Databases: 176. Weekly public service hours: 91. *Research affiliation:* Jewish Foundation (Holocaust studies), Wetlands Institute (marine biology), Aviation Research and Technology Park (aviation research), Nature Conservancy of New Jersey (environmental studies), Association of State Colleges (civic engagement).

Computer facilities: 1,224 computers available on campus for general student use. A campuswide network can be accessed from student residence rooms and from off campus. Online class registration is available.
Website: http://www.stockton.edu/

General Application Contact: Tara Williams, Assistant Director of Graduate Enrollment Management, 609-626-3640, E-mail: gradschool@stockton.edu.

GRADUATE UNITS

Office of Graduate Studies Students: 363 full-time (283 women), 466 part-time (361 women); includes 169 minority (55 Black or African American, non-Hispanic/Latino; 2 American Indian or Alaska Native, non-Hispanic/Latino; 29 Asian, non-Hispanic/Latino; 67 Hispanic/Latino; 1 Native Hawaiian or other Pacific Islander, non-Hispanic/Latino; 15 Two or more races, non-Hispanic/Latino), 3 international. Average age 32. 1,454 applicants, 33% accepted, 332 enrolled. *Faculty:* 63 full-time (43 women), 33 part-time/adjunct (20 women). Expenses: Contact institution. *Financial support:* Fellowships, research assistantships, career-related internships or fieldwork, Federal Work-Study, scholarships/grants, and unspecified assistantships available. Support available to part-time students. Financial award application deadline: 3/1; financial award applicants required to submit FAFSA. In 2017, 259 master's, 32 doctorates awarded. *Program availability:* Part-time, evening/weekend, 100% online, blended/hybrid learning. Offers American studies (MA, Certificate); business administration (MBA); communication disorders (MS); computational science (MS); criminal justice (MA); data science and strategic analytics (MS); education (MA); environmental science (PSM); Holocaust and genocide studies (MA); instructional technology (MA); nursing (MSN); occupational therapy (MSOT); organizational leadership (Ed D); physical therapy (DPT); social work (MSW). *Application deadline:* For fall admission, 7/1 for domestic and international students. Applications are processed on a rolling basis. *Application fee:* $50. Electronic applications accepted. *Application Contact:* Tara Williams, Assistant Director of Graduate Enrollment, 609-626-3640, Fax: 609-626-6050, E-mail: gradschool@stockton.edu. *Director of Graduate Enrollment Management,* AmyBeth Glass, 609-652-4298, E-mail: graduatestudies@stockton.edu.

STONEHILL COLLEGE, Easton, MA 02357

General Information Independent-religious, coed, comprehensive institution. *Graduate housing:* On-campus housing not available.

GRADUATE UNITS

Program in Integrated Marketing Communications Offers integrated marketing communications (MA).

Program in Special Education Offers special education (MA).

STONY BROOK UNIVERSITY, STATE UNIVERSITY OF NEW YORK, Stony Brook, NY 11794

General Information State-supported, coed, university. CGS member. *Enrollment:* 25,989 graduate, professional, and undergraduate students; 5,503 full-time matriculated graduate/professional students (2,735 women), 2,749 part-time matriculated graduate/professional students (1,997 women). *Enrollment by degree level:* 4,431 master's, 3,248 doctoral, 573 other advanced degrees. *Graduate faculty:* 1,867 full-time (747 women), 767 part-time/adjunct (390 women). Tuition, state resident: full-time $10,870; part-time $453 per credit. Tuition, nonresident: full-time $22,210; part-time $925 per credit. *Graduate housing:* Rooms and/or apartments available to single and married students. Typical cost: $8402 per year ($13,446 including board) for single students. Housing application deadline: 5/1. *Student services:* Campus employment opportunities, campus safety program, career counseling, child daycare facilities, exercise/wellness program, free psychological counseling, grant writing training, international student services, multicultural affairs office, services for students with disabilities, teacher training, writing training. *Library facilities:* Frank Melville, Jr. Memorial Library plus 7 others. *Collection:* Books: 1.9 million (physical), 348,868 (digital/electronic); Serial titles: 1,225 (physical), 190,674 (digital/electronic); Databases: 679. Weekly public service hours: 131; study areas open 24 hours, 5–7 days a week; students can reserve study rooms. *Research affiliation:* Mount Sinai Health System, Veterans Affairs Medical Center, Nassau University Medical Center, Winthrop University Hospital, Cold Spring Harbor Laboratory, Brookhaven National Laboratory.

Computer facilities: Computer purchase and lease plans are available. 1,590 computers available on campus for general student use. A campuswide network can be accessed from student residence rooms and from off campus. Online class registration is available.
Website: http://www.stonybrook.edu/

General Application Contact: Melissa Jordan, Assistant Dean for Records and Admission, 631-632-9712, Fax: 631-632-7243, E-mail: gradadmissions@stonybrook.edu.

GRADUATE UNITS

Graduate School Students: 3,473 full-time (1,415 women), 701 part-time (335 women); includes 609 minority (97 Black or African American, non-Hispanic/Latino; 4 American Indian or Alaska Native, non-Hispanic/Latino; 268 Asian, non-Hispanic/Latino; 190 Hispanic/Latino; 1 Native Hawaiian or other Pacific Islander, non-Hispanic/Latino; 49 Two or more races, non-Hispanic/Latino), 2,068 international. Average age 27. 7,845 applicants, 45% accepted, 1298 enrolled. *Faculty:* 923 full-time (316 women), 331 part-time/adjunct (152 women). Expenses: Contact institution. *Financial support:* In 2017–18, 128 fellowships, 554 research assistantships, 836 teaching assistantships were awarded; career-related internships or fieldwork, Federal Work-Study, institutionally sponsored loans, scholarships/grants, traineeships, health care benefits, tuition waivers (full), and unspecified assistantships also available. In 2017, 1,166 master's, 317 doctorates, 37 other advanced degrees awarded. *Program availability:* Part-time, evening/weekend. *Application deadline:* For fall admission, 1/15 for domestic and international students; for spring admission, 10/1 for domestic and international students. *Application fee:* $100. Electronic applications accepted. *Application Contact:* Melissa Jordan, Assistant Dean for Records and Admission, 631-632-9712, Fax: 631-632-7243, E-mail: gradadmissions@stonybrook.edu. *Vice Provost for Graduate and Professional Education*, Dr. Charles Taber, 631-632-7035, Fax: 631-632-7243, E-mail: charles.taber@sunysb.edu.

College of Arts and Sciences Students: 1,552 full-time (722 women), 143 part-time (95 women); includes 268 minority (41 Black or African American, non-Hispanic/Latino; 3 American Indian or Alaska Native, non-Hispanic/Latino; 95 Asian, non-Hispanic/Latino; 101 Hispanic/Latino; 28 Two or more races, non-Hispanic/Latino), 661 international. Average age 29. 3,252 applicants, 35% accepted, 401 enrolled. *Faculty:* 536 full-time (209 women), 142 part-time/adjunct (70 women). Expenses: Contact institution. *Financial support:* In 2017–18, 73 fellowships, 241 research assistantships, 558 teaching assistantships were awarded; career-related internships or fieldwork, Federal Work-Study, scholarships/grants, traineeships, health care benefits, and unspecified assistantships also available. Financial award applicants required to submit FAFSA. In 2017, 255 master's, 199 doctorates, 17 other advanced degrees awarded. *Program availability:* Part-time, evening/weekend. Offers Africana studies (MA, Certificate); anthropological sciences (PhD); anthropology (MA, PhD); applied ecology (MA); art history and criticism (MA, PhD); arts and sciences (MA, MAPP, MAT, MFA, MM, MS, DMA, PhD, Advanced Certificate, Certificate, Graduate Certificate); astronomy (PhD); biochemistry and cell biology (MS); biochemistry and molecular biology (PhD); biochemistry and structural biology (PhD); biological sciences (MA); chemistry (MS, PhD); clinical psychology (PhD); cognitive psychology (PhD); comparative literature (MA, PhD); contemporary Asian and Asian American studies (MA); cultural studies (PhD, Certificate); dramaturgy (MFA); earth science (MAT); ecology and evolution (PhD); economics (MA, PhD); English (MA, PhD); English education (MAT); French (MA); genetics (PhD); geosciences (MS, PhD); Hispanic languages and literature (MA, PhD); history (MA, PhD); immunology and pathology (PhD); integrative neuroscience (PhD); Italian (MA); linguistics (MA, PhD); mathematics (MA, MAT, PhD); modern research instrumentation (MS); molecular and cellular biology (MA, PhD); music history/theory (MA, PhD); music performance (MM, DMA); neuroscience (MS, PhD); philosophy (MA, PhD, Advanced Certificate); physics (MA, MAT, MS, PhD); physics education (MAT); political science (MA, PhD); psychology (MA); public policy (MAPP); public policy and urban development (MA); Romance languages (MA); social and health psychology (PhD); sociology (MA, PhD); STEM education (PhD); studio art (MFA); teaching English to speakers of other languages (MA); teaching writing (Graduate Certificate); theatre arts (MA); women's, gender, and sexuality studies (Certificate). *Application deadline:* For fall admission, 1/15 for domestic students; for spring admission, 10/1 for domestic students. *Application fee:* $100. Electronic applications accepted. *Application Contact:* Melissa Jordan, Assistant Dean for Records and Admission, 631-632-9712, Fax: 631-632-7243, E-mail: melissa.jordan@stonybrook.edu. *Dean*, Dr. Sacha Kopp, 631-632-6976, Fax: 631-632-6900, E-mail: sacha.kopp@stonybrook.edu.

College of Business Students: 218 full-time (116 women), 158 part-time (78 women); includes 82 minority (17 Black or African American, non-Hispanic/Latino; 1 American Indian or Alaska Native, non-Hispanic/Latino; 43 Asian, non-Hispanic/Latino; 15 Hispanic/Latino; 1 Native Hawaiian or other Pacific Islander, non-Hispanic/Latino; 5 Two or more races, non-Hispanic/Latino), 83 international. Average age 28. 470 applicants, 57% accepted, 127 enrolled. *Faculty:* 39 full-time (13 women), 14 part-time/adjunct (5 women). Expenses: Contact institution. *Financial support:* Research assistantships and teaching assistantships available. In 2017, 232 master's, 5 other advanced degrees awarded. Offers accounting (MS); business (MBA, MS, AGC, Certificate); business administration (MBA); finance (MS, AGC); health care management (MBA); human resources (MBA); innovation (MBA); management (MBA); marketing (MBA); operations management (MBA). *Application deadline:* For fall admission, 5/15 for domestic students, 3/15 priority date for international students; for spring admission, 11/15 for domestic students, 10/15 for international students. *Application fee:* $100. *Application Contact:* Erica Robey, Graduate Coordinator, 631-632-7722, Fax: 631-632-8181, E-mail: erica.robey@stonybrook.edu. *Dean*, Dr. Manuel London, 631-632-7159, E-mail: manuel.london@stonybrook.edu.

College of Engineering and Applied Sciences Students: 1,362 full-time (393 women), 286 part-time (83 women); includes 164 minority (18 Black or African American, non-Hispanic/Latino; 99 Asian, non-Hispanic/Latino; 36 Hispanic/Latino; 11 Two or more races, non-Hispanic/Latino), 1,260 international. Average age 26. 3,648 applicants, 52% accepted, 638 enrolled. *Faculty:* 180 full-time (34 women), 46 part-time/adjunct (12 women). Expenses: Contact institution. *Financial support:* In 2017–18, 14 fellowships, 227 research assistantships, 241 teaching assistantships were awarded; career-related internships or fieldwork also available. In 2017, 553 master's, 92 doctorates, 3 other advanced degrees awarded. *Program availability:* Part-time, evening/weekend. Offers applied mathematics and statistics (MS, PhD, Advanced Certificate); biomedical engineering (MS, PhD, Certificate); biomedical informatics (MS, PhD, AGC); civil engineering (MS, PhD, Graduate Certificate); computer engineering (MS, PhD); computer science (MS, PhD); educational technology (MS); electrical engineering (MS, PhD); energy technology and policy (MS); engineering and applied sciences (MS, PhD, AGC, Advanced Certificate, Certificate, Graduate Certificate); global technology management (MS); information systems (Certificate); information systems engineering (MS); materials science and engineering (MS, PhD); mechanical engineering (MS, PhD); medical physics (MS, PhD); networking and wireless communications (Certificate); software engineering (Certificate); technology, policy, and innovation (PhD). *Application deadline:* For fall admission, 1/15 for domestic students; for spring admission, 10/1 for domestic students. *Application fee:* $100. *Application Contact:* Melissa Jordan, Assistant Dean for Records and Admission, 631-632-9712, Fax: 631-632-7243, E-mail: gradadmissions@stonybrook.edu. *Dean*, Dr. Fotis Sotiropoulos, 631-632-8380, Fax: 631-632-8205, E-mail: fotis.sotiropoulos@stonybrook.edu.

School of Marine and Atmospheric Sciences Students: 125 full-time (63 women), 13 part-time (10 women); includes 20 minority (6 Asian, non-Hispanic/Latino; 11 Hispanic/Latino; 3 Two or more races, non-Hispanic/Latino), 33 international. Average age 28. 146 applicants, 36% accepted, 31 enrolled. *Faculty:* 53 full-time (14 women), 15 part-time/adjunct (6 women). Expenses: Contact institution. *Financial support:* In 2017–18, 12 fellowships, 57 research assistantships, 28 teaching assistantships were awarded; career-related internships or fieldwork and tuition waivers (full) also available. In 2017, 24 master's, 13 doctorates awarded. Offers atmospheric sciences (MS, PhD); geospatial sciences (Graduate Certificate); marine and atmospheric sciences (MA, MS, PhD, Graduate Certificate); marine conservation and policy (MA); marine sciences (MS, PhD). *Application deadline:* For fall admission, 1/15 for domestic students; for spring admission, 10/1 for domestic students. *Application fee:* $100. *Application Contact:* Ginny Clancy, Educational Programs Coordinator, 631-632-8681, Fax: 631-632-8200. *Interim Dean*, Dr. Larry Swanson, 631-632-8700, Fax: 631-632-8820, E-mail: larry.swanson@stonybrook.edu.

School of Journalism Students: 2 part-time (both women). Average age 30. *Faculty:* 9 full-time (3 women), 23 part-time/adjunct (8 women). Expenses: Contact institution. *Financial support:* Teaching assistantships available. In 2017, 5 master's awarded. Offers health communication (Certificate); journalism (MS). *Application deadline:* For fall admission, 1/15 for domestic students; for spring admission, 10/1 for domestic students. *Application fee:* $100. *Application Contact:* Maureen Robinson, Coordinator, 631-632-7403, Fax: 631-632-7550, E-mail: maureen.robinson@stonybrook.edu. *Dean*, Prof. Howard Schneider, 631-632-7403, E-mail: howard.schneider@stonybrook.edu.

School of Professional Development Students: 190 full-time (126 women), 974 part-time (708 women); includes 255 minority (88 Black or African American, non-Hispanic/Latino; 2 American Indian or Alaska Native, non-Hispanic/Latino; 31 Asian, non-Hispanic/Latino; 113 Hispanic/Latino; 1 Native Hawaiian or other Pacific Islander, non-Hispanic/Latino; 20 Two or more races, non-Hispanic/Latino), 6 international. Average age 33. 411 applicants, 91% accepted, 288 enrolled. *Faculty:* 3 full-time (2 women), 101 part-time/adjunct (45 women). Expenses: Contact institution. *Financial support:* Fellowships, research assistantships, teaching assistantships, and career-related internships or fieldwork available. Support available to part-time students. In 2017, 333 master's, 180 other advanced degrees awarded. *Program availability:* Part-time, evening/weekend, online learning. Offers biology (MAT); chemistry (MAT); coaching (Graduate Certificate); earth science (MAT); educational computing (Graduate Certificate); educational leadership (Advanced Certificate); English (MAT); environmental management (MPS, Graduate Certificate); French (MAT); German (MAT); higher education administration (MA, Certificate); human resource management (MS, Graduate Certificate); industrial management (Graduate Certificate); information systems management (Graduate Certificate); Italian (MAT); liberal studies (MA); mathematics (MAT); operations research (Graduate Certificate); physics (MAT); school district business leadership (Advanced Certificate); social studies (MAT); Spanish (MAT). *Application deadline:* For fall admission, 1/15 for domestic students, 6/1 for international students; for spring admission, 10/1 for domestic and international students. Applications are processed on a rolling basis. *Application fee:* $100. *Application Contact:* Melissa Jordan, Assistant Dean, 631-632-7751, E-mail: melissa.jordan@stonybrook.edu. *Dean*, Dr. Ken Lindblom, 631-632-7049, Fax: 631-632-9046, E-mail: kenneth.lindblom@stonybrook.edu.

Stony Brook Medicine Students: 2,009 full-time (1,281 women), 1,106 part-time (976 women); includes 1,103 minority (288 Black or African American, non-Hispanic/Latino; 9 American Indian or Alaska Native, non-Hispanic/Latino; 457 Asian, non-Hispanic/Latino; 304 Hispanic/Latino; 3 Native Hawaiian or other Pacific Islander, non-Hispanic/Latino; 42 Two or more races, non-Hispanic/Latino), 60 international. 10,975 applicants, 17% accepted, 1130 enrolled. Expenses: Contact institution. *Financial support:* In 2017–18, 29 fellowships, 29 research assistantships were awarded; teaching assistantships also available. In 2017, 714 master's, 288 doctorates, 74 other advanced degrees awarded. Offers medicine (MHA, MPH, MS, MSW, DDS, DNP, DPT, MD, PhD, Advanced Certificate, Certificate). *Application deadline:* For fall admission, 1/15 for domestic students; for spring admission, 10/1 for domestic students. *Application fee:* $100. Electronic applications accepted. *Application Contact:* Melissa Jordan, Assistant Dean for Records and Admission, 631-632-9712, Fax: 631-632-7243, E-mail: gradadmissions@stonybrook.edu. *Dean*, Dr. Kenneth Kaushansky, 631-444-8234, E-mail: kenneth.kaushansky@stonybrook.edu.

School of Dental Medicine Students: 200 full-time (103 women), 4 part-time (all women); includes 65 minority (2 Black or African American, non-Hispanic/Latino; 52 Asian, non-Hispanic/Latino; 8 Hispanic/Latino; 3 Two or more races, non-Hispanic/Latino), 4 international. Average age 25. 1,436 applicants, 7% accepted, 52 enrolled. *Faculty:* 32 full-time (14 women), 82 part-time/adjunct (24 women). Expenses: Contact institution. *Financial support:* Fellowships, research assistantships, teaching assistantships, and Federal Work-Study available. In 2017, 41 doctorates, 9 other advanced degrees awarded. Offers dental medicine (DDS); endodontics (Certificate); oral biology and pathology (MS, PhD); orthodontics (Certificate); periodontics (Certificate). *Application deadline:* For fall admission, 1/15 for domestic students; for spring admission, 10/1 for domestic students. *Application fee:* $100. *Application Contact:* Patricia Berry, Director of Admissions, 631-632-8871, Fax: 631-632-7130, E-mail: patricia.berry@stonybrook.edu. *Dean*, Dr. Mary R. Truhlar, 631-632-6985, Fax: 631-632-6621, E-mail: mary.truhlar@stonybrookmedicine.edu.

School of Health Technology and Management Students: 565 full-time (382 women), 67 part-time (53 women); includes 179 minority (29 Black or African American, non-Hispanic/Latino; 83 Asian, non-Hispanic/Latino; 59 Hispanic/Latino; 2 Native Hawaiian or other Pacific Islander, non-Hispanic/Latino; 6 Two or more races, non-Hispanic/Latino), 14 international. Average age 27. 2,516 applicants, 16% accepted, 266 enrolled. *Faculty:* 62 full-time (42 women), 59 part-time/adjunct (36 women). Expenses: Contact institution. *Financial support:* Fellowships, research assistantships, teaching assistantships, career-related internships or fieldwork, Federal Work-Study, and institutionally sponsored loans available. Financial award application deadline: 3/15. In 2017, 162 master's, 84 doctorates, 39 other advanced degrees awarded. Offers applied health informatics (MS); disability studies (Certificate); health administration (MHA); health and rehabilitation sciences (PhD); health care management (Advanced Certificate); health care policy and management (MS); occupational therapy (MS); physical therapy (DPT); physician assistant (MS). *Application deadline:* For fall admission, 1/15 for domestic students; for spring admission, 10/1 for domestic students. *Application fee:* $100. *Application Contact:* Frances Shaw, 631-444-3240, Fax: 631-444-7621, E-mail: frances.shaw@stonybrook.edu. *Dean*, Dr. Carlos Vidal, 631-444-1009, Fax: 631-444-7621, E-mail: carlos.vidal@stonybrook.edu.

School of Medicine Students: 712 full-time (342 women), 85 part-time (68 women); includes 325 minority (43 Black or African American, non-Hispanic/Latino; 2 American Indian or Alaska Native, non-Hispanic/Latino; 204 Asian, non-Hispanic/Latino; 66 Hispanic/Latino; 10 Two or more races, non-Hispanic/Latino), 41 international. Average age 26. 5,628 applicants, 9% accepted, 154 enrolled. *Faculty:* 820 full-time (349 women), 124 part-time/adjunct (80 women). Expenses: Contact institution. *Financial support:* In 2017–18, 29 fellowships, 29 research assistantships were awarded; teaching assistantships, career-related internships or fieldwork, Federal Work-Study, and tuition waivers (full) also available. In 2017, 101 master's, 140 doctorates, 4 other advanced degrees awarded. Offers anatomical sciences (PhD); community health (MPH); evaluation sciences (MPH); family violence (MPH); health communication (Certificate); health economics (MPH); health education and promotion (Certificate); medicine (MPH, MS, MD, PhD, Pharm D, Advanced Certificate, Certificate); molecular and cellular pharmacology (MS, PhD); molecular genetics and microbiology (PhD); nutrition (MS, Advanced Certificate); pharmacy and pharmaceutical sciences (Pharm D); physiology and biophysics (PhD); population health (MPH); population health and clinical outcomes research (PhD); substance abuse (MPH). *Application deadline:* For fall admission, 1/15 for domestic students; for spring admission, 10/1 for domestic students. *Application fee:* $100. *Application Contact:* Dr. Jack Fuhrer, Associate Dean of Admissions, 631-444-2113, Fax: 631-444-6032, E-mail: somadmissions@stonybrook.edu. *Dean*, Dr. Kenneth Kaushansky, 631-444-2121, Fax: 631-632-6621, E-mail: kenneth.kaushansky@stonybrook.edu.

School of Nursing Students: 36 full-time (33 women), 928 part-time (833 women); includes 343 minority (130 Black or African American, non-Hispanic/Latino; 6 American Indian or Alaska Native, non-Hispanic/Latino; 102 Asian, non-Hispanic/Latino; 88 Hispanic/Latino; 1 Native Hawaiian or other Pacific Islander, non-Hispanic/Latino; 16 Two or more races, non-Hispanic/Latino). Average age 36. 860 applicants, 49% accepted, 344 enrolled. *Faculty:* 36 full-time (33 women), 48 part-time/adjunct (42 women). Expenses: Contact institution. *Financial support:* Fellowships, research assistantships, teaching assistantships, career-related internships or fieldwork, Federal Work-Study, institutionally sponsored loans, and traineeships available. Financial award application deadline: 3/15. In 2017, 237 master's, 21 doctorates, 21 other advanced degrees awarded. *Program availability:* Blended/hybrid learning. Offers adult health nurse practitioner (Certificate); adult health/primary care nursing (MS, DNP); child health nurse practitioner (Certificate); child health nursing (MS, DNP); family nurse practitioner (MS, DNP, Certificate); neonatal nurse practitioner (Certificate); neonatal nursing (MS, DNP); nurse midwifery (MS, DNP, Certificate); nursing (MS, DNP, PhD, Certificate); nursing education (MS, Certificate); nursing leadership (MS, Certificate); nursing practice (DNP); perinatal women's health nursing (MS, DNP, Certificate); psychiatric-mental health nurse practitioner (MS, DNP, Certificate). *Application deadline:* For fall admission, 4/15 for domestic students, 3/15 for international students. *Application fee:* $100. Electronic applications accepted. *Application Contact:* Karen Allard, Admissions Coordinator, 631-444-6628, Fax: 631-444-3136, E-mail: karen.allard@stonybrook.edu. *Dean*, Dr. Lee Anne Xippolitos, 631-444-3200, Fax: 631-444-3136, E-mail: lee.xippolitos@stonybrook.edu.

School of Social Welfare Students: 496 full-time (421 women), 22 part-time (18 women); includes 191 minority (84 Black or African American, non-Hispanic/Latino; 1 American Indian or Alaska Native, non-Hispanic/Latino; 16 Asian, non-Hispanic/Latino; 83 Hispanic/Latino; 7 Two or more races, non-Hispanic/Latino), 1 international. Average age 29. 500 applicants, 82% accepted, 283 enrolled. *Faculty:* 19 full-time (13 women), 44 part-time/adjunct (29 women). Expenses: Contact institution. *Financial support:* Fellowships, research assistantships, teaching assistantships, career-related internships or fieldwork, Federal Work-Study, and institutionally sponsored loans available. Financial award applicants required to submit FAFSA. In 2017, 214 master's, 2 doctorates awarded. *Program availability:* Part-time. Offers social welfare (PhD); social work (MSW). *Application deadline:* For fall admission, 1/15 for domestic students; for spring admission, 10/1 for domestic students. *Application fee:* $100. *Application Contact:* Jamie Weissbach, Coordinator, 631-444-3146, Fax: 631-444-7565, E-mail: jamie.weissbach@stonybrook.edu. *Dean and Assistant Vice President for Social Determinants of Health*, Dr. Jacqueline B. Mondros, 631-444-2139, E-mail: jacqueline.mondros@stonybrook.edu.

Stony Brook Southampton Students: 47 full-time (34 women), 67 part-time (45 women); includes 13 minority (4 Black or African American, non-Hispanic/Latino; 3 Asian, non-Hispanic/Latino; 6 Hispanic/Latino), 2 international. Average age 37. 84 applicants, 71% accepted, 26 enrolled. *Faculty:* 8 full-time (4 women), 37 part-time/adjunct (19 women). Expenses: Contact institution. *Financial support:* In 2017–18, 9 teaching assistantships were awarded. In 2017, 20 master's, 11 other advanced degrees awarded. Offers fiction (MFA); film (MFA); poetry (MFA); scientific writing (MFA); scriptwriting (MFA). *Application deadline:* For fall admission, 1/15 for domestic students; for spring admission, 10/1 for domestic students. Applications are processed on a rolling basis. *Application fee:* $100. *Application Contact:* Margaret S Grigonis, Administrative Coordinator, 631-632-5028, Fax: 631-982-7318, E-mail: margaret.grigonis@stonybrook.edu. *Associate Provost*, Dr. Robert Reeves, 631-632-5030, Fax: 631-982-7318, E-mail: robert.reeves@stonybrook.edu.

STRATFORD UNIVERSITY, Baltimore, MD 21202

General Information Proprietary, coed, comprehensive institution.

GRADUATE UNITS

Program in International Hospitality Management *Program availability:* Part-time, evening/weekend, online learning. Offers international hospitality management (MS).

STRATFORD UNIVERSITY, Falls Church, VA 22043

General Information Proprietary, coed, comprehensive institution. *Enrollment:* 272 full-time matriculated graduate/professional students (110 women), 204 part-time matriculated graduate/professional students (89 women). *Enrollment by degree level:* 426 master's, 7 doctoral, 17 other advanced degrees. *Tuition:* Full-time $33,405; part-time $11,135 per credit hour. One-time fee: $385 full-time. Tuition and fees vary according to degree level and program. *Graduate housing:* On-campus housing not available. *Student services:* Campus employment opportunities, career counseling, exercise/wellness program, international student services, multicultural affairs office, services for students with disabilities, writing training. *Library facilities:* Learning Resource Center.

Computer facilities: A campuswide network can be accessed from off campus. Online class registration is available.
Website: http://www.stratford.edu/

General Application Contact: Lori Smith, Admissions, 214-649-7113, E-mail: lasmith@stratford.edu.

GRADUATE UNITS

School of Graduate Studies Students: 272 full-time (110 women), 204 part-time (89 women). Expenses: Contact institution. *Financial support:* Federal Work-Study and scholarships/grants available. Financial award applicants required to submit FAFSA. *Program availability:* Part-time, evening/weekend, 100% online, blended/hybrid learning. Offers accounting (MS); business administration (MBA, DBA); cyber security (MS); cyber security leadership and policy (MS); digital forensics (MS); healthcare administration (MS); information systems (MS); information technology (DIT); networking and telecommunications (MS); software engineering (MS). *Application deadline:* Applications are processed on a rolling basis. *Application fee:* $50. Electronic applications accepted. *Application Contact:* Lori Smith, Admissions, 214-649-7113, E-mail: lasmith@stratford.edu. *Campus President*, Dr. Valarie Trimarchi, 703-539-6890, Fax: 703-539-6960.

STRAYER UNIVERSITY, Washington, DC 20005-2603

General Information Proprietary, coed, comprehensive institution. *Graduate housing:* On-campus housing not available.

GRADUATE UNITS

Graduate Studies *Program availability:* Part-time, evening/weekend, online learning. Offers accounting (MS); acquisition (MBA); business administration (MBA); communications technology (MS); educational management (M Ed); finance (MBA); health services administration (MHSA); hospitality and tourism management (MBA); human resource management (MBA); information systems (MS); management (MBA); management information systems (MS); marketing (MBA); professional accounting (MS); public administration (MPA); supply chain management (MBA); technology in education (M Ed). Programs also offered at campus locations in Birmingham, AL; Chamblee, GA; Cobb County, GA; Morrow, GA; White Marsh, MD; Charleston, SC; Columbia, SC; Greensboro, NC; Greenville, SC; Lexington, KY; Louisville, KY; Nashville, TN; North Raleigh, NC; Washington, DC. Electronic applications accepted.

SUFFOLK UNIVERSITY, Boston, MA 02108-2770

General Information Independent, coed, comprehensive institution. *Enrollment:* 7,288 graduate, professional, and undergraduate students; 1,083 full-time matriculated graduate/professional students (637 women), 1,032 part-time matriculated graduate/professional students (613 women). *Enrollment by degree level:* 1,010 master's, 1,066 doctoral, 39 other advanced degrees. *Graduate faculty:* 153 full-time (73 women), 99 part-time/adjunct (37 women). *Tuition:* Full-time $43,980; part-time $1466 per credit hour. *Required fees:* $54; $54 per unit. Part-time tuition and fees vary according to course load and program. *Graduate housing:* On-campus housing not available. *Student services:* Campus employment opportunities, campus safety program, career counseling, exercise/wellness program, free psychological counseling, grant writing training, international student services, low-cost health insurance, multicultural affairs office, services for students with disabilities, writing training. *Library facilities:* Mildred Sawyer Library plus 3 others. *Collection:* Books: 128,945 (physical), 249,567 (digital/electronic); Serial titles: 307 (physical), 65,782 (digital/electronic); Databases: 174. Weekly public service hours: 103; students can reserve study rooms.

Computer facilities: Computer purchase and lease plans are available. 675 computers available on campus for general student use. A campuswide network can be accessed from student residence rooms and from off campus. Online class registration is available.
Website: http://www.suffolk.edu/

General Application Contact: Heather O'Leary, Director of Graduate Admissions, 617-573-8302, Fax: 617-305-1733, E-mail: grad.admission@suffolk.edu.

GRADUATE UNITS

College of Arts and Sciences Students: 153 full-time (119 women), 141 part-time (116 women); includes 73 minority (25 Black or African American, non-Hispanic/Latino; 13 Asian, non-Hispanic/Latino; 31 Hispanic/Latino; 4 Two or more races, non-Hispanic/Latino), 36 international. Average age 28. 551 applicants, 49% accepted, 106 enrolled. *Faculty:* 47 full-time (23 women), 17 part-time/adjunct (8 women). Expenses: Contact institution. *Financial support:* In 2017–18, 214 students received support, including 46 fellowships (averaging $11,120 per year); career-related internships or fieldwork, Federal Work-Study, institutionally sponsored loans, scholarships/grants, and unspecified assistantships also available. Support available to part-time students. Financial award application deadline: 4/1; financial award applicants required to submit FAFSA. In 2017, 115 master's, 12 doctorates, 11 other advanced degrees awarded. *Program availability:* Part-time, evening/weekend. Offers administration of higher education (M Ed, CAGS); arts and sciences (M Ed, MA, MAC, MS, MSCJS, MSPS, PhD, CAGS, Certificate, Graduate Certificate); clinical psychology (PhD); college admission counseling (Certificate); communication studies (MAC); disability services (Certificate); ethics and public policy (MS); integrated marketing communication (MAC); international relations (MSPS); mental health counseling (MS); political science (MSPS); professional politics (MSPS, CAGS); public relations and advertising (MAC); school counseling (MS); sociology (MSCJS). *Application deadline:* For fall admission, 3/15 priority date for domestic and international students; for spring admission, 10/15 priority date for domestic students, 10/1 priority date for international students. Applications are processed on a rolling basis. *Application fee:* $50. Electronic applications accepted. *Application Contact:* Mara Marzocchi, Associate Director of Graduate Admissions, 617-573-8302, Fax: 617-305-1733, E-mail: grad.admission@suffolk.edu. *Dean*, Maria Toyoda, 617-573-8265, Fax: 617-573-8513, E-mail: mtoyada@suffolk.edu.

Law School Students: 663 full-time (358 women), 366 part-time (181 women); includes 181 minority (36 Black or African American, non-Hispanic/Latino; 2 American Indian or Alaska Native, non-Hispanic/Latino; 48 Asian, non-Hispanic/Latino; 73 Hispanic/Latino; 22 Two or more races, non-Hispanic/Latino), 37 international. Average age 27. 1,962 applicants, 66% accepted, 340 enrolled. *Faculty:* 63 full-time (31 women), 54 part-time/adjunct (18 women). Expenses: Contact institution. *Financial support:* In 2017–18, 663 students received support, including 1 fellowship (averaging $31,390 per year); career-related internships or fieldwork, Federal Work-Study, institutionally sponsored loans, and scholarships/grants also available. Support available to part-time students. Financial award application deadline: 3/1; financial award applicants required to submit FAFSA. In 2017, 22 master's, 322 doctorates awarded. *Program availability:* Part-time, evening/weekend. Offers business law and financial services (JD); civil litigation (JD); global law and technology (LL M); health and biomedical law (JD); intellectual property law (JD); international law (JD). *Application deadline:* For fall admission, 4/1 for domestic and international students. Applications are processed on a rolling basis. *Application fee:* $60. Electronic applications accepted. *Application Contact:* Matthew Gavin, Assistant Dean for Admissions and Financial Aid, 617-573-8144, Fax: 617-994-6838, E-mail: lawadm@suffolk.edu. *Dean*, Andrew Perlman, 617-573-8144, Fax: 617-994-6838, E-mail: lawadmin@suffolk.edu.

New England School of Art and Design Students: 33 full-time (28 women), 25 part-time (23 women); includes 12 minority (1 Black or African American, non-Hispanic/Latino; 7 Asian, non-Hispanic/Latino; 4 Hispanic/Latino), 16 international. Average age 28. 58 applicants, 57% accepted, 10 enrolled. *Faculty:* 13 full-time (8 women), 10 part-time/adjunct (5 women). Expenses: Contact institution. *Financial support:* In 2017–18, 46 students received support, including 4 fellowships (averaging $6,062 per year); career-related internships or fieldwork, Federal Work-Study, institutionally sponsored loans, scholarships/grants, and unspecified assistantships also available. Financial award application deadline: 4/1; financial award applicants required to submit FAFSA. In 2017, 37 master's awarded. *Program availability:* Part-time, evening/weekend. Offers graphic design (MA); interior architecture (MA). *Application deadline:* For fall admission, 3/15 priority date for domestic and international students; for spring admission, 10/15 priority date for domestic and international students. Applications are processed on a rolling basis. *Application fee:* $50. Electronic applications accepted. *Application Contact:* Mara Marzocchi, Associate Director of

Graduate Admissions, 617-573-8302, Fax: 617-305-1733, E-mail: grad.admission@suffolk.edu. *Department Chair,* Audrey Goldstein, 617-997-4290, E-mail: agoldstein@suffolk.edu.

Sawyer Business School Students: 267 full-time (160 women), 525 part-time (316 women); includes 216 minority (78 Black or African American, non-Hispanic/Latino; 67 Asian, non-Hispanic/Latino; 62 Hispanic/Latino; 9 Two or more races, non-Hispanic/Latino), 129 international. Average age 30. 862 applicants, 58% accepted, 108 enrolled. *Faculty:* 46 full-time (21 women), 30 part-time/adjunct (12 women). Expenses: Contact institution. *Financial support:* In 2017–18, 475 students received support, including 5 fellowships (averaging $4,805 per year); career-related internships or fieldwork, Federal Work-Study, institutionally sponsored loans, scholarships/grants, and unspecified assistantships also available. Support available to part-time students. Financial award application deadline: 4/1; financial award applicants required to submit FAFSA. In 2017, 388 master's awarded. *Program availability:* Part-time, evening/weekend, 100% online, blended/hybrid learning. Offers accounting (MBA, MSA, Graduate Certificate); business (EMBA, GMBA, MBA, MBAH, MHA, MPA, MS, MSA, MSBA, MSF, MSFSB, MST, Graduate Certificate); business analytics (MS, MSBA); community health (MPA); entrepreneurship (MBA); executive business administration (EMBA); finance (MBA); global business administration (GMBA); health (MBAH); health administration (MBA); healthcare administration (MHA); information systems, performance management, and big data analytics (MPA); international business (MBA); marketing (MBA); nonprofit management (MBA, MPA); organizational behavior (MBA); state and local government (MPA); strategic management (MBA); supply chain management (MBA); taxation (MBA, MST). *Application deadline:* For fall admission, 3/15 priority date for domestic and international students; for spring admission, 10/15 for domestic students, 3/15 priority date for international students. Applications are processed on a rolling basis. *Application fee:* $50. Electronic applications accepted. *Application Contact:* Mara Marzocchi, Associate Director of Graduate Admissions, 617-573-8302, Fax: 617-305-1733, E-mail: grad.admission@suffolk.edu. *Dean,* William J. O'Neill, JD, 617-573-2665, Fax: 617-573-8704, E-mail: woneill@suffolk.edu.

SULLIVAN UNIVERSITY, Louisville, KY 40205

General Information Proprietary, coed, comprehensive institution. *Graduate housing:* On-campus housing not available.

GRADUATE UNITS

College of Pharmacy Offers pharmacy (Pharm D).

School of Business *Program availability:* Part-time, online learning. Offers business (EMBA, MBA, MPM, MSCM, MSCS, MSHRL, MSM, MSMIT, PhD, Pharm D).

SUL ROSS STATE UNIVERSITY, Alpine, TX 79832

General Information State-supported, coed, comprehensive institution. *Graduate housing:* Rooms and/or apartments available on a first-come, first-served basis to single and married students. *Research affiliation:* Chihuahuan Desert Research Institute (biology, geology), Big Bend National Park (biology, geology).

GRADUATE UNITS

College of Arts and Sciences *Program availability:* Part-time, evening/weekend. Offers art history (MA); arts and sciences (MA, MS); biology (MS); English (MA); geology (MS); history (MA); political science (MA); psychology (MA); studio art (MA).

College of Professional Studies *Program availability:* Part-time, evening/weekend. Offers business administration (EMBA, MBA); counseling (M Ed); criminal justice (MS); educational diagnostics (M Ed, Certificate); homeland security (MS); master reading teacher (Certificate); physical education (M Ed); reading specialist (M Ed, Certificate); school administration (M Ed); Texas reading specialist (M Ed). Two-year Executive MBA program in cooperation with La Universidad de Chihuahua, Mexico (UACH).

Division of Agricultural and Natural Resource Science *Program availability:* Part-time. Offers agricultural and natural resource science (M Ag, MS); animal science (M Ag, MS); range and wildlife management (M Ag, MS).

Rio Grande College of Sul Ross State University *Program availability:* Part-time, evening/weekend, online learning. Offers business administration (MBA); teacher education (M Ed).

SUM BIBLE COLLEGE & THEOLOGICAL SEMINARY, Oakland, CA 94603

General Information Independent-religious, coed, comprehensive institution.

GRADUATE UNITS

Graduate Programs Offers biblical studies (MA); Christian leadership (MA); theology (M Div).

SWEDISH INSTITUTE, COLLEGE OF HEALTH SCIENCES, New York, NY 10001-6700

General Information Proprietary, coed, comprehensive institution. *Graduate housing:* On-campus housing not available.

GRADUATE UNITS

Graduate Program *Program availability:* Part-time, evening/weekend.

SWEET BRIAR COLLEGE, Sweet Briar, VA 24595

General Information Independent, women only, comprehensive institution. *Graduate housing:* Room and/or apartments available on a first-come, first-served basis to single students; on-campus housing not available to married students.

GRADUATE UNITS

Department of Education *Program availability:* Part-time. Offers education (M Ed, MAT). Electronic applications accepted.

SYRACUSE UNIVERSITY, Syracuse, NY 13244

General Information Independent, coed, university. CGS member. *Enrollment:* 22,484 graduate, professional, and undergraduate students; 4,557 full-time matriculated graduate/professional students (2,311 women), 2,506 part-time matriculated graduate/professional students (1,160 women). *Enrollment by degree level:* 5,058 master's, 1,879 doctoral, 126 other advanced degrees. *Graduate faculty:* 1,154 full-time (489 women), 575 part-time/adjunct (265 women). *Graduate housing:* On-campus housing not available. *Student services:* Campus employment opportunities, campus safety program, career counseling, child daycare facilities, exercise/wellness program, free psychological counseling, grant writing training, international student services, low-cost health insurance, multicultural affairs office, services for students with disabilities, teacher training, writing training. *Library facilities:* E. S. Bird Library plus 4 others. *Collection:* Books: 2.2 million (physical), 508,060 (digital/electronic); Serial titles: 33,629 (physical), 112,830 (digital/electronic); Databases: 544. Weekly public service hours: 146; study areas open 24 hours, 5–7 days a week; students can reserve study rooms. *Research affiliation:* South Side Innovation Center (business incubator and entrepreneurship development), IBM Green Data Center (advanced infrastructure and smarter computing technologies), Institute for Manufacturing Enterprises (promoting learning in manufacturing enterprises through teaching, application, integration, discovery, and service), Syracuse Research Corporation (defense, environmental and intelligence systems), Center of Excellence (environmental and energy systems innovation), Say Yes to Education, Inc. (academic support and funding to high school students).

Computer facilities: Computer purchase and lease plans are available. 3,500 computers available on campus for general student use. A campuswide network can be accessed from student residence rooms and from off campus. Online class registration, web conferencing, learning management system, blogging service, personal Websites, "View My Advising Report" digital asset management system, office software, online video training are available.
Website: http://www.syracuse.edu/

General Application Contact: 315-443-4492, Fax: 315-443-3423, E-mail: grad@syr.edu.

GRADUATE UNITS

College of Arts and Sciences Students: 755 full-time (430 women), 52 part-time (28 women); includes 143 minority (28 Black or African American, non-Hispanic/Latino; 4 American Indian or Alaska Native, non-Hispanic/Latino; 31 Asian, non-Hispanic/Latino; 60 Hispanic/Latino; 2 Native Hawaiian or other Pacific Islander, non-Hispanic/Latino; 18 Two or more races, non-Hispanic/Latino), 214 international. Average age 27. 2,107 applicants, 26% accepted, 231 enrolled. *Faculty:* 367 full-time (159 women), 121 part-time/adjunct (74 women). Expenses: Contact institution. *Financial support:* Fellowships with full tuition reimbursements, research assistantships with tuition reimbursements, teaching assistantships with tuition reimbursements, career-related internships or fieldwork, Federal Work-Study, scholarships/grants, health care benefits, tuition waivers, and unspecified assistantships available. Support available to part-time students. Financial award application deadline: 1/1. In 2017, 173 master's, 64 doctorates, 54 other advanced degrees awarded. *Program availability:* Part-time. Offers advanced forensic science (MS); applied statistics (MS); art history (MA); arts and sciences (MA, MFA, MS, Au D, PhD, CAS); audiology (Au D, PhD); biology (MS, PhD); biomedical forensic science (MS); chemistry (MS, PhD); clinical psychology (PhD); cognition, brain, and behavior (PhD); college science teaching (PhD); composition and cultural rhetoric (PhD); computational linguistics (MS); creative writing (MFA); earth sciences (MS, PhD); English (MA, PhD); firearm and tool mark examination (CAS); French and Francophone studies (MA); general forensic science (MS); language teaching: TESOL/TLOTE (CAS); linguistic studies (MA); math education (PhD); mathematics (MS, PhD); mathematics education (MS); medicolegal death investigation (MS, CAS); neuroscience (PhD); nuclear forensics (MS); Pan-African studies (MA); philosophy (MA, PhD); physics (MS, PhD); religion (MA, PhD); school psychology (PhD); social psychology (PhD); Spanish literature and culture (MA); speech-language pathology (MS). *Application fee:* $75. *Application Contact:* Dennis J. Nicholson, Director of Undergraduate and Graduate Recruiting, 315-443-0257, E-mail: asadmissions@syr.edu. *Dean,* Dr. Karin Ruhlandt, 315-443-1306, E-mail: kruhland@syr.edu.

College of Engineering and Computer Science Students: 897 full-time (243 women), 253 part-time (38 women); includes 89 minority (28 Black or African American, non-Hispanic/Latino; 38 Asian, non-Hispanic/Latino; 13 Hispanic/Latino; 10 Two or more races, non-Hispanic/Latino), 858 international. Average age 26. 3,160 applicants, 41% accepted, 428 enrolled. *Faculty:* 95 full-time (24 women), 16 part-time/adjunct (1 woman). Expenses: Contact institution. *Financial support:* Fellowships with full tuition reimbursements, research assistantships with tuition reimbursements, teaching assistantships with tuition reimbursements, scholarships/grants, and tuition waivers (partial) available. Financial award application deadline: 1/1; financial award applicants required to submit FAFSA. In 2017, 409 master's, 47 doctorates, 1 other advanced degree awarded. *Program availability:* Part-time, evening/weekend. Offers bioengineering (MS, PhD); chemical engineering (MS, PhD); civil engineering (MS, PhD); computer and information science and engineering (PhD); computer engineering (MS); computer science (MS); cybersecurity (MS, CAS); electrical and computer engineering (PhD); electrical engineering (MS); engineering and computer science (MS, PhD, CAS); engineering management (MS); environmental engineering (MS); environmental engineering science (MS); environmental health (CAS); mechanical and aerospace engineering (MS, PhD); sustainable enterprise (CAS). *Application deadline:* For fall admission, 7/1 priority date for domestic students, 6/1 priority date for international students; for spring admission, 11/15 priority date for domestic students, 10/15 priority date for international students. Applications are processed on a rolling basis. *Application fee:* $75. Electronic applications accepted. *Application Contact:* Kathleen Joyce, Assistant Dean, 314-443-2219, E-mail: topgrads@syr.edu. *Dean, College of Engineering and Computer Science,* Dr. Teresa Dahlberg, 315-443-2545, E-mail: dahlberg@syr.edu.

College of Law Students: 596 full-time (303 women), 3 part-time (1 woman); includes 126 minority (39 Black or African American, non-Hispanic/Latino; 2 American Indian or Alaska Native, non-Hispanic/Latino; 21 Asian, non-Hispanic/Latino; 45 Hispanic/Latino; 19 Two or more races, non-Hispanic/Latino), 59 international. Average age 26. 1,834 applicants, 49% accepted, 238 enrolled. *Faculty:* 42 full-time (15 women), 13 part-time/adjunct (3 women). Expenses: Contact institution. *Financial support:* In 2017–18, 487 students received support. Fellowships, research assistantships, career-related internships or fieldwork, Federal Work-Study, institutionally sponsored loans, scholarships/grants, and tuition waivers (partial) available. Support available to part-time students. Financial award application deadline: 2/15. In 2017, 28 master's, 149 doctorates awarded. *Program availability:* Part-time. Offers American law (LL M); law (LL M, JD). *Application deadline:* For fall admission, 4/1 priority date for domestic and international students. Applications are processed on a rolling basis. *Application fee:* $70. Electronic applications accepted. *Application Contact:* Steve Budgar, Director of Admissions, 315-443-1962, Fax: 315-443-9568, E-mail: admissions@law.syr.edu. *Dean and Professor of Law,* Craig M. Boise, 315-443-9580, E-mail: cmboise@law.syr.edu.

College of Visual and Performing Arts Students: 192 full-time (122 women), 12 part-time (9 women); includes 28 minority (5 Black or African American, non-Hispanic/Latino; 3 Asian, non-Hispanic/Latino; 7 Hispanic/Latino; 13 Two or more races, non-Hispanic/Latino), 76 international. Average age 27. 492 applicants, 40% accepted, 89 enrolled. *Faculty:* 134 full-time (61 women), 118 part-time/adjunct (53 women). Expenses: Contact institution. *Financial support:* Fellowships with full tuition reimbursements, teaching assistantships with tuition reimbursements, institutionally sponsored loans, and unspecified assistantships available. Financial award application deadline: 1/1; financial award applicants required to submit FAFSA. In 2017, 87 master's awarded. Offers art photography (MFA); art video (MFA); audio arts (MA); communication and rhetorical studies (MA); composition (MM); computer art (MFA); conducting (MM); film (MFA); illustration (MFA); museum studies (MA); music and performance (MM); studio arts (MFA); visual and performing arts (M Mu, M Mus, MA, MFA, MM, MS); voice pedagogy (MM). *Application deadline:* For fall admission, 2/1 priority date for domestic and international students; for spring admission, 3/1 priority date for domestic and international students; for summer admission, 2/1 priority date for domestic and international students. *Application fee:* $75. Electronic applications accepted. *Application Contact:* Caitlin Jarvis, Graduate Recruitment Specialist, 315-443-2769, E-mail: admissg@syr.edu. *Dean, College of Visual and Performing Arts*, Dr. Michael S. Tick, 315-443-8070, E-mail: mtick1@syr.edu.

David B. Falk College of Sport and Human Dynamics Students: 222 full-time (187 women), 93 part-time (75 women); includes 77 minority (39 Black or African American, non-Hispanic/Latino; 3 American Indian or Alaska Native, non-Hispanic/Latino; 7 Asian, non-Hispanic/Latino; 18 Hispanic/Latino; 10 Two or more races, non-Hispanic/Latino), 30 international. Average age 29. 452 applicants, 72% accepted, 165 enrolled. *Faculty:* 70 full-time (40 women), 28 part-time/adjunct (21 women). Expenses: Contact institution. *Financial support:* Fellowships with full tuition reimbursements, research assistantships with tuition reimbursements, teaching assistantships with tuition reimbursements, and tuition waivers available. Financial award application deadline: 1/1; financial award applicants required to submit FAFSA. In 2017, 145 master's, 6 doctorates, 38 other advanced degrees awarded. *Program availability:* Part-time, evening/weekend. Offers addiction studies (MA, CAS); food studies (MS, CAS); global health (MS); human development and family science (MA, MS, PhD); marriage and family therapy (MA, PhD); nutrition science (MA, MS, PhD); social work (MSW); sport and human dynamics (MA, MS, MSW, PhD, CAS); sport venue and event management (MS); trauma-informed practice (CAS). *Application deadline:* For fall admission, 2/15 priority date for domestic and international students; for spring admission, 11/15 priority date for domestic students, 11/15 for international students; for summer admission, 3/15 priority date for domestic students, 3/15 for international students. Applications are processed on a rolling basis. *Application fee:* $75. Electronic applications accepted. *Application Contact:* Felicia Otero, Director of College Admissions, 315-443-5555, Fax: 315-443-2562, E-mail: falk@syr.edu. *Dean*, Dr. Diane Lyden Murphy, 315-443-5582, Fax: 315-443-2562.

Martin J. Whitman School of Management Students: 318 full-time (154 women), 1,099 part-time (368 women); includes 446 minority (169 Black or African American, non-Hispanic/Latino; 3 American Indian or Alaska Native, non-Hispanic/Latino; 100 Asian, non-Hispanic/Latino; 132 Hispanic/Latino; 5 Native Hawaiian or other Pacific Islander, non-Hispanic/Latino; 37 Two or more races, non-Hispanic/Latino), 202 international. Average age 33. 1,363 applicants, 60% accepted, 333 enrolled. *Faculty:* 73 full-time (27 women), 64 part-time/adjunct (19 women). Expenses: Contact institution. *Financial support:* In 2017–18, 45 students received support. Fellowships with full tuition reimbursements available, research assistantships with tuition reimbursements available, teaching assistantships with tuition reimbursements available, career-related internships or fieldwork, and scholarships/grants available. Financial award application deadline: 2/15. In 2017, 274 master's, 13 doctorates awarded. *Program availability:* Part-time, 100% online. Offers accounting (MBA); business analytics (MS); entrepreneurship (MBA); finance (PhD); management (MBA, MS, PhD); management information systems (PhD); marketing management (MBA); professional accounting (MS); real estate (MBA); supply chain management (MS). *Application deadline:* For fall admission, 11/30 for domestic and international students; for winter admission, 1/1 for domestic and international students; for spring admission, 2/15 for domestic and international students; for summer admission, 4/19 for domestic students. *Application fee:* $75. Electronic applications accepted. *Application Contact:* Shri Ramakrishnan, Assistant Director, Graduate Recruitment, 315-443-3497, Fax: 315-443-9517, E-mail: sramak01@syr.edu. *Dean*, Eugene Anderson, 315-443-9494, Fax: 315-443-9517, E-mail: genea@syr.edu.

Maxwell School of Citizenship and Public Affairs Students: 507 full-time (253 women), 125 part-time (67 women); includes 102 minority (30 Black or African American, non-Hispanic/Latino; 2 American Indian or Alaska Native, non-Hispanic/Latino; 25 Asian, non-Hispanic/Latino; 34 Hispanic/Latino; 11 Two or more races, non-Hispanic/Latino), 198 international. Average age 31. 1,293 applicants, 48% accepted, 328 enrolled. *Faculty:* 162 full-time (68 women), 30 part-time/adjunct (12 women). Expenses: Contact institution. *Financial support:* Fellowships with full tuition reimbursements, research assistantships, and teaching assistantships available. Financial award application deadline: 1/1. In 2017, 312 master's, 38 doctorates, 121 other advanced degrees awarded. *Program availability:* Part-time, online learning. Offers anthropology (MA, PhD); citizenship and public affairs (EMIR, EMPA, MA, MPA, MPH, MS Sc, PhD, CAS); conflict resolution (CAS); economics (MA, PhD); geography (MA, PhD); health services management and policy (CAS); history (MA, PhD); international relations (EMIR, MA); leadership of international and non-governmental organizations (CAS); political science (MA, PhD); public administration (EMPA, MPA, PhD); public diplomacypublic infrastructure management and leadership (CAS); social sciences (MA, PhD); sociology (MA, PhD). *Application deadline:* For fall admission, 2/1 priority date for domestic and international students. Applications are processed on a rolling basis. *Application fee:* $75. Electronic applications accepted. *Application Contact:* Megan Begert, Enrollment Manager, 315-443-4000, E-mail: msbegert@syr.edu. *Dean*, Dr. David Van Slyke, 315-443-3461, E-mail: vanslyke@maxwell.syr.edu.

School of Architecture Students: 117 full-time (54 women), 2 part-time (0 women); includes 7 minority (1 Black or African American, non-Hispanic/Latino; 1 Asian, non-Hispanic/Latino; 4 Hispanic/Latino; 1 Two or more races, non-Hispanic/Latino), 90 international. Average age 26. 294 applicants, 55% accepted, 41 enrolled. *Faculty:* 41 full-time (15 women), 13 part-time/adjunct (2 women). Expenses: Contact institution. *Financial support:* Fellowships with full tuition reimbursements, research assistantships, and teaching assistantships available. Financial award application deadline: 1/1. In 2017, 25 master's awarded. Offers architecture (M Arch, MS). *Application deadline:* For fall admission, 2/1 priority date for domestic and international students. *Application fee:* $75. Electronic applications accepted. *Application Contact:* Vittoria Buccina, Director, Graduate and Undergraduate Recruitment, 315-443-5074, E-mail: vabuccin@syr.edu. *Dean, School of Architecture*, Michael Speaks, 315-443-0790, E-mail: maspeaks@syr.edu.

School of Education Students: 298 full-time (205 women), 215 part-time (153 women); includes 122 minority (53 Black or African American, non-Hispanic/Latino; 5 American Indian or Alaska Native, non-Hispanic/Latino; 12 Asian, non-Hispanic/Latino; 36 Hispanic/Latino; 1 Native Hawaiian or other Pacific Islander, non-Hispanic/Latino; 15 Two or more races, non-Hispanic/Latino), 83 international. Average age 33. 470 applicants, 57% accepted, 144 enrolled. *Faculty:* 50 full-time (29 women), 44 part-time/adjunct (29 women). Expenses: Contact institution. *Financial support:* Fellowships with full tuition reimbursements, research assistantships, teaching assistantships, career-related internships or fieldwork, institutionally sponsored loans, scholarships/grants, health care benefits, tuition waivers (partial), and unspecified assistantships available. Financial award application deadline: 1/15; financial award applicants required to submit FAFSA. In 2017, 156 master's, 22 doctorates, 43 other advanced degrees awarded. *Program availability:* Part-time. Offers art education (MS); biology (MS); chemistry (MS, PhD); clinical mental health counseling (MS); counseling and counselor education (PhD); cultural foundations of education (MS, PhD, CAS); disability studies (CAS); early childhood special education (MS); education (M Mus, MM, MS, Ed D, PhD, CAS); educational leadership (MS, Ed D, CAS); educational technology (CAS); English education preparation (grades 7-12) (MS); exercise science (MS); higher education (MS, PhD); inclusive special education (grades 1-6) (MS); inclusive special education (grades 7-12) (MS); inclusive special education: severe/multiple disabilities (MS); instructional design foundations (CAS); instructional design, development, and evaluation (MS, PhD, CAS); instructional technology (MS); literacy education (PhD); literacy education (birth - grade 12) (MS); mathematics education (MS, PhD); music education (MM, MS); school counseling (MS, CAS); school district business leadership (CAS); social studies education preparation (grades 7-12) (MS); special education (PhD); student affairs counseling (MS); teaching and curriculum (MS, PhD); teaching English language learners (Pre-K-12) (MS). *Application deadline:* Applications are processed on a rolling basis. *Application fee:* $75. Electronic applications accepted. *Application Contact:* Speranza Migliore, Graduate Recruiter, School of Education, 315-443-2505, E-mail: gradrcrt@syr.edu. *Dean*, Dr. Joanna Masingila, 315-443-4751, E-mail: jomasing@syr.edu.

School of Information Studies Students: 403 full-time (194 women), 393 part-time (219 women); includes 123 minority (45 Black or African American, non-Hispanic/Latino; 1 American Indian or Alaska Native, non-Hispanic/Latino; 34 Asian, non-Hispanic/Latino; 22 Hispanic/Latino; 1 Native Hawaiian or other Pacific Islander, non-Hispanic/Latino; 20 Two or more races, non-Hispanic/Latino), 332 international. Average age 30. 1,587 applicants, 49% accepted, 415 enrolled. *Faculty:* 37 full-time (17 women), 51 part-time/adjunct (20 women). Expenses: Contact institution. *Financial support:* Fellowships with full tuition reimbursements, research assistantships, teaching assistantships, and scholarships/grants available. Financial award application deadline: 1/1. In 2017, 306 master's, 6 doctorates, 199 other advanced degrees awarded. *Program availability:* Part-time, evening/weekend, online learning. Offers applied data science (MS); data science (CAS); e-government management and leadership (CAS); enterprise data systems (MS); information management (MS); information science and technology (PhD); information security management (CAS); information studies (MS, PhD, CAS); library and information science (MS); library and information science: school media (MS); school media (CAS). *Application deadline:* For fall admission, 1/1 priority date for domestic students, 2/1 priority date for international students; for spring admission, 10/15 priority date for domestic and international students. Applications are processed on a rolling basis. *Application fee:* $75. Electronic applications accepted. *Application Contact:* Susan Corieri, Director of Enrollment Management, 315-443-2575, E-mail: ist@syr.edu. *Dean/Professor*, Dr. Elizabeth D. Liddy, 315-443-2736, E-mail: liddy@syr.edu.

S. I. Newhouse School of Public Communications Students: 252 full-time (166 women), 259 part-time (202 women); includes 169 minority (95 Black or African American, non-Hispanic/Latino; 4 American Indian or Alaska Native, non-Hispanic/Latino; 15 Asian, non-Hispanic/Latino; 39 Hispanic/Latino; 1 Native Hawaiian or other Pacific Islander, non-Hispanic/Latino; 15 Two or more races, non-Hispanic/Latino), 107 international. Average age 29. 796 applicants, 67% accepted, 250 enrolled. *Faculty:* 81 full-time (34 women), 56 part-time/adjunct (26 women). Expenses: Contact institution. *Financial support:* Fellowships with full tuition reimbursements, research assistantships with partial tuition reimbursements, scholarships/grants, and instructional associate positions with partial tuition reimbursements available. Financial award application deadline: 2/1. In 2017, 258 master's, 3 doctorates awarded. *Program availability:* Online learning. Offers advertising (MA); arts journalism (MA); broadcast and digital journalism (MS); communications management (MS); magazine, newspaper and online journalism (MA); mass communications (PhD); media studies (MA); new media management (MS); photography (MS); public communications (MA, MS, PhD); public diplomacypublic relations (MS); television, radio, and film (MA). *Application deadline:* For fall admission, 1/15 priority date for domestic and international students; for summer admission, 1/15 priority date for domestic and international students. *Application fee:* $45. Electronic applications accepted. *Application Contact:* Martha Coria, Graduate Records Office, 315-443-4039, Fax: 315-443-1834, E-mail: pcgrad@syr.edu. *Dean*, Lorraine Branham, 315-443-3372, E-mail: lbranham@syr.edu.

TABOR COLLEGE, Hillsboro, KS 67063

General Information Independent-religious, coed, comprehensive institution.

GRADUATE UNITS

Graduate Program Offers accounting (MBA). Program offered at the Wichita campus only.

TAFT UNIVERSITY SYSTEM, Denver, CO 80246

General Information Proprietary, coed, graduate-only institution.

GRADUATE UNITS

The Boyer Graduate School of Education Offers education (M Ed).

Taft Law School Offers American jurisprudence (LL M); law (JD); taxation (LL M).

W. Edwards Deming School of Business Offers taxation (MS).

TALMUDICAL ACADEMY OF NEW JERSEY, Adelphia, NJ 07710

General Information Independent-religious, men only, comprehensive institution.

GRADUATE UNITS

Graduate Program

TALMUDIC UNIVERSITY, Miami Beach, FL 33140

General Information Independent-religious, men only, comprehensive institution. *Graduate housing:* Rooms and/or apartments available on a first-come, first-served basis to single and married students.

GRADUATE UNITS

Program in Talmudic Law Offers Talmudic law (MRE).

TARLETON STATE UNIVERSITY, Stephenville, TX 76402

General Information State-supported, coed, comprehensive institution. *Enrollment:* 13,019 graduate, professional, and undergraduate students; 400 full-time matriculated graduate/professional students (260 women), 1,331 part-time matriculated graduate/professional students (837 women). *Enrollment by degree level:* 1,608 master's, 123 doctoral. *Graduate faculty:* 162 full-time (77 women), 53 part-time/adjunct (27 women). Tuition, state resident: full-time $3775. Tuition, nonresident: full-time $11,245. *Required fees:* $2920. *Graduate housing:* Rooms and/or apartments available on a first-come, first-served basis to single and married students. Typical cost: $3870 per year ($7620 including board) for single students. Housing application deadline: 8/1. *Student services:* Campus employment opportunities, campus safety program, career counseling, child daycare facilities, exercise/wellness program, free psychological counseling, grant writing training, international student services, low-cost health insurance, multicultural affairs office, services for students with disabilities, teacher training, writing training. *Library facilities:* Dick Smith Library plus 1 other. *Collection:* Students can reserve study rooms.

Computer facilities: 1,200 computers available on campus for general student use. A campuswide network can be accessed from student residence rooms and from off campus. Online class registration is available.
Website: http://www.tarleton.edu/

General Application Contact: Wendy Weiss, Graduate Admissions Coordinator, 254-968-9104, Fax: 254-968-9670, E-mail: weiss@tarleton.edu.

GRADUATE UNITS

College of Graduate Studies Students: 400 full-time (260 women), 1,131 part-time (837 women); includes 312 minority (6 American Indian or Alaska Native, non-Hispanic/Latino; 37 Asian, non-Hispanic/Latino; 228 Hispanic/Latino; 41 Two or more races, non-Hispanic/Latino), 18 international. Average age 36. 950 applicants, 72% accepted, 507 enrolled. *Faculty:* 157 full-time (74 women), 48 part-time/adjunct (27 women). Expenses: Contact institution. *Financial support:* Research assistantships, teaching assistantships, career-related internships or fieldwork, Federal Work-Study, institutionally sponsored loans, scholarships/grants, and tuition waivers (partial) available. Support available to part-time students. Financial award application deadline: 5/1; financial award applicants required to submit FAFSA. In 2017, 473 master's, 14 doctorates awarded. *Program availability:* Part-time, evening/weekend, 100% online, blended/hybrid learning. *Application deadline:* For fall admission, 8/15 priority date for domestic students; for spring admission, 1/7 for domestic students. *Application fee:* $45 ($130 for international students). Electronic applications accepted. *Application Contact:* Wendy Weiss, Graduate Admissions Coordinator, 254-968-9104, Fax: 254-968-9670, E-mail: weiss@tarleton.edu. *Dean,* Dr. Barry Lambert, 254-968-9463, Fax: 254-968-9670, E-mail: blambert@tarleton.edu.

College of Agricultural and Environmental Sciences Students: 55 full-time (33 women), 45 part-time (28 women); includes 20 minority (4 Black or African American, non-Hispanic/Latino; 1 American Indian or Alaska Native, non-Hispanic/Latino; 1 Asian, non-Hispanic/Latino; 9 Hispanic/Latino; 5 Two or more races, non-Hispanic/Latino). Average age 26. 41 applicants, 80% accepted, 28 enrolled. *Faculty:* 25 full-time (9 women), 4 part-time/adjunct (2 women). Expenses: Contact institution. *Financial support:* Research assistantships, teaching assistantships, career-related internships or fieldwork, Federal Work-Study, and institutionally sponsored loans available. Support available to part-time students. Financial award application deadline: 5/1; financial award applicants required to submit FAFSA. In 2017, 47 master's awarded. *Program availability:* Part-time, evening/weekend, 100% online, blended/hybrid learning. Offers agricultural and consumer resources (MS); agricultural and environmental sciences (MS); agricultural and natural resource sciences (MS). *Application deadline:* For fall admission, 8/15 priority date for domestic students; for spring admission, 1/7 for domestic students. Applications are processed on a rolling basis. *Application fee:* $45 ($130 for international students). Electronic applications accepted. *Application Contact:* Wendy Weiss, Information Contact, 254-968-9104, Fax: 254-968-9670, E-mail: gradoffice@tarleton.edu. *Dean,* Dr. Steve Damron, 254-968-9227, Fax: 254-968-9655, E-mail: sdamron@tarleton.edu.

College of Business Administration Students: 65 full-time (45 women), 455 part-time (245 women); includes 143 minority (47 Black or African American, non-Hispanic/Latino; 1 American Indian or Alaska Native, non-Hispanic/Latino; 21 Asian, non-Hispanic/Latino; 60 Hispanic/Latino; 14 Two or more races, non-Hispanic/Latino), 4 international. Average age 33. 292 applicants, 89% accepted, 179 enrolled. *Faculty:* 29 full-time (7 women), 4 part-time/adjunct (1 woman). Expenses: Contact institution. *Financial support:* Research assistantships, teaching assistantships, career-related internships or fieldwork, Federal Work-Study, and institutionally sponsored loans available. Support available to part-time students. Financial award application deadline: 5/1; financial award applicants required to submit FAFSA. In 2017, 151 master's awarded. *Program availability:* Part-time, evening/weekend, 100% online, blended/hybrid learning. Offers accounting (M Acc); business administration (M Acc, MBA, MS); human resources management (MS); information systems (MS). *Application deadline:* For fall admission, 8/15 priority date for domestic students; for spring admission, 1/7 for domestic students. Applications are processed on a rolling basis. *Application fee:* $45 ($130 for international students). Electronic applications accepted. *Application Contact:* Jodie Dearing, Graduate Program Manager, 254-968-9055, E-mail: jdearing@tarleton.edu. *Dean,* Dr. Steve Steed, 254-968-9645, E-mail: ssteed@tarleton.edu.

College of Education Students: 71 full-time (45 women), 455 part-time (326 women); includes 122 minority (56 Black or African American, non-Hispanic/Latino; 2 American Indian or Alaska Native, non-Hispanic/Latino; 2 Asian, non-Hispanic/Latino; 53 Hispanic/Latino; 9 Two or more races, non-Hispanic/Latino), 4 international. Average age 39. 123 applicants, 92% accepted, 97 enrolled. *Faculty:* 29 full-time (14 women), 11 part-time/adjunct (6 women). Expenses: Contact institution. *Financial support:* Research assistantships, teaching assistantships with partial tuition reimbursements, career-related internships or fieldwork, Federal Work-Study, institutionally sponsored loans, and tuition waivers (partial) available. Support available to part-time students. Financial award application deadline: 5/1; financial award applicants required to submit FAFSA. In 2017, 162 master's, 14 doctorates awarded. *Program availability:* Part-time, evening/weekend, 100% online, blended/hybrid learning. Offers applied psychology (MS); athletic training (MS); curriculum and instruction (M Ed); education (M Ed, MS, Ed D, Certificate); educational administration (M Ed); educational diagnostician (M Ed); educational leadership (Ed D, Certificate); elementary education (M Ed); instructional design and technology (M Ed); instructional leadership (M Ed); kinesiology (MS); secondary education (M Ed); special education (M Ed); technology applications (M Ed); technology director (M Ed). *Application deadline:* For fall admission, 8/15 priority date for domestic students; for spring admission, 1/7 for domestic students. Applications are processed on a rolling basis. *Application fee:* $45 ($130 for international students). Electronic applications accepted. *Application Contact:* Wendy Weiss, Information Contact, 254-968-9104, Fax: 254-968-9670, E-mail: weiss@tarleton.edu. *Dean,* Dr. Jordan Barkley, 254-968-9088, Fax: 254-968-9525, E-mail: jbarkley@tarleton.edu.

College of Health Sciences and Human Services Students: 72 full-time (60 women), 153 part-time (133 women); includes 89 minority (36 Black or African American, non-Hispanic/Latino; 2 American Indian or Alaska Native, non-Hispanic/Latino; 3 Asian, non-Hispanic/Latino; 43 Hispanic/Latino; 5 Two or more races, non-Hispanic/Latino), 4 international. Average age 32. 193 applicants, 90% accepted, 124 enrolled. *Faculty:* 26 full-time (21 women), 11 part-time/adjunct (all women). Expenses: Contact institution. *Financial support:* Research assistantships, teaching assistantships, career-related internships or fieldwork, Federal Work-Study, scholarships/grants, and unspecified assistantships available. Financial award application deadline: 2/15; financial award applicants required to submit FAFSA. In 2017, 14 master's awarded. *Program availability:* Part-time. Offers health sciences and human services (MS, MSN, MSW, Certificate); medical laboratory sciences (MS); nursing administration (MSN); nursing education (MSN); social work (MSW). *Application deadline:* For fall admission, 8/15 for domestic students, 6/15 for international students; for spring admission, 1/5 for domestic students, 11/15 for international students; for summer admission, 5/1 for domestic students, 4/15 for international students. Applications are processed on a rolling basis. *Application fee:* $45 ($145 for international students). Electronic applications accepted. *Application Contact:* Wendy Weiss, Graduate Admissions Coordinator, 254-968-9104, Fax: 254-968-9670, E-mail: weiss@tarleton.edu. *Associate Dean,* Sally Lewis, 254-968-1692.

College of Liberal and Fine Arts Students: 50 full-time (26 women), 268 part-time (160 women); includes 116 minority (54 Black or African American, non-Hispanic/Latino; 6 Asian, non-Hispanic/Latino; 51 Hispanic/Latino; 5 Two or more races, non-Hispanic/Latino), 1 international. Average age 35. 174 applicants, 85% accepted, 119 enrolled. *Faculty:* 24 full-time (14 women), 14 part-time/adjunct (6 women). Expenses: Contact institution. *Financial support:* Research assistantships, teaching assistantships, Federal Work-Study, scholarships/grants, and unspecified assistantships available. Financial award application deadline: 5/1; financial award applicants required to submit FAFSA. In 2017, 59 master's awarded. *Program availability:* Part-time, evening/weekend, 100% online, blended/hybrid learning. Offers communication studies (MA); criminal justice (MCJ); English (MA); history (MA); liberal and fine arts (MA, MCJ, MM, MPA); music education (MM); public administration (MPA). *Application deadline:* For fall admission, 8/15 priority date for domestic students; for spring admission, 1/7 for domestic students. Applications are processed on a rolling basis. *Application fee:* $45 ($145 for international students). Electronic applications accepted. *Application Contact:* Wendy Weiss, Information Contact, 254-968-9104, Fax: 254-968-9670, E-mail: weiss@tarleton.edu. *Dean,* Kelli Styron, 254-968-9141, Fax: 254-968-9784, E-mail: styron@tarleton.edu.

College of Science and Technology Students: 37 full-time (14 women), 50 part-time (15 women); includes 18 minority (1 Black or African American, non-Hispanic/Latino; 4 Asian, non-Hispanic/Latino; 11 Hispanic/Latino; 2 Two or more races, non-Hispanic/Latino), 5 international. Average age 32. 46 applicants, 98% accepted, 36 enrolled. *Faculty:* 23 full-time (9 women), 4 part-time/adjunct (1 woman). Expenses: Contact institution. *Financial support:* Research assistantships, teaching assistantships, career-related internships or fieldwork, Federal Work-Study, and tuition waivers (partial) available. Support available to part-time students. Financial award application deadline: 5/1; financial award applicants required to submit FAFSA. In 2017, 40 master's awarded. *Program availability:* Part-time, evening/weekend, 100% online, blended/hybrid learning. Offers biology (MS); environmental science (MS); mathematics (MS); quality and engineering management (MS); science and technology (MS). *Application deadline:* For fall admission, 8/15 priority date for domestic students; for spring admission, 1/7 for domestic students. Applications are processed on a rolling basis. *Application fee:* $45 ($145 for international students). Electronic applications accepted. *Application Contact:* Wendy Weiss, Information Contact, 254-968-9104, Fax: 254-968-9670, E-mail: weiss@tarleton.edu. *Dean,* Dr. James Pierce, 254-968-9781, Fax: 254-968-0549, E-mail: jrpierce@tarleton.edu.

TAYLOR COLLEGE AND SEMINARY, Edmonton, AB T6J 4T3, Canada

General Information Independent-religious, coed, comprehensive institution. *Graduate housing:* Room and/or apartments available on a first-come, first-served basis to single students; on-campus housing not available to married students. Housing application deadline: 8/1.

GRADUATE UNITS

Graduate and Professional Programs *Program availability:* Part-time, online learning. Offers Christian studies (Diploma); intercultural studies (MA, Diploma); theology (M Div, MTS).

TAYLOR UNIVERSITY, Upland, IN 46989-1001

General Information Independent-religious, coed, comprehensive institution. *Graduate housing:* On-campus housing not available. *Student services:* Campus employment opportunities, campus safety program, career counseling, exercise/wellness program, free psychological counseling, international student services, low-cost health insurance, multicultural affairs office, services for students with disabilities, writing training. *Library facilities:* Zondervan Library. *Collection:* Books: 170,640 (physical), 277,813 (digital/electronic); Serial titles: 279 (physical); Databases: 118. Weekly public service hours: 96; study areas open 24 hours, 5–7 days a week.

Computer facilities: Computer purchase and lease plans are available. 375 computers available on campus for general student use. A campuswide network can be accessed from student residence rooms and from off campus. Online class registration is available.
Website: http://www.taylor.edu/

General Application Contact: Pat Baird, Registrar, 765-998-4877, E-mail: ptbaird@taylor.edu.

GRADUATE UNITS

Master of Arts in Higher Education Program Expenses: Contact institution. *Financial support:* Fellowships, scholarships/grants, and unspecified assistantships available. Financial award applicants required to submit FAFSA. *Program availability:* Part-time. Offers higher education (MA). *Application deadline:* For fall admission, 1/31 for domestic students, 12/31 for international students. Applications are processed on a rolling basis. *Application fee:* $100. *Application Contact:* Dr. Tim Herrmann, Chair, 765-998-5142, E-mail: tmherrmann@taylor.edu. *Chair,* Dr. Tim Herrmann, 765-998-5142, E-mail: tmherrmann@taylor.edu.

TEACHERS COLLEGE, COLUMBIA UNIVERSITY, New York, NY 10027-6696

General Information Independent, coed, graduate-only institution. *Enrollment by degree level:* 3,362 master's, 1,281 doctoral, 58 other advanced degrees. *Graduate faculty:* 170. *Graduate housing:* Rooms and/or apartments available on a first-come, first-served basis to single and married students. Housing application deadline: 12/1. *Student services:* Campus employment opportunities, campus safety program, career counseling, exercise/wellness program, free psychological counseling, grant writing training, international student services, low-cost health insurance, multicultural affairs office, services for students with disabilities, teacher training, writing training. *Library facilities:* The Gottesman Libraries. *Collection:* Books: 370,871 (physical), 179,993 (digital/electronic); Serial titles: 27,304 (digital/electronic); Databases: 93. Students can reserve study rooms.

Computer facilities: Online class registration is available.
Website: http://www.tc.columbia.edu/

General Application Contact: David Estrella, Director of Admissions, 212-678-3305, E-mail: dpe2103@tc.columbia.edu.

GRADUATE UNITS

Department of Arts and Humanities Students: 391 full-time (305 women), 418 part-time (283 women); includes 246 minority (62 Black or African American, non-Hispanic/Latino; 3 American Indian or Alaska Native, non-Hispanic/Latino; 94 Asian, non-Hispanic/Latino; 75 Hispanic/Latino; 12 Two or more races, non-Hispanic/Latino), 209 international. Average age 30. 1,053 applicants, 60% accepted, 334 enrolled. Expenses: Contact institution. *Financial support:* Fellowships, research assistantships, teaching assistantships, career-related internships or fieldwork, Federal Work-Study, institutionally sponsored loans, tuition waivers (full and partial), and unspecified assistantships available. Support available to part-time students. *Program availability:* Part-time, evening/weekend. Offers applied linguistics (MA, Ed D); art and art education (Ed M, MA, Ed D, Ed DCT); arts administration (MA); bilingual and bicultural education (MA); global competence (Certificate); history and education (Ed D, PhD); music and music education (Ed DCT); philosophy and education (MA, Ed D, PhD); social studies education (Ed M, PhD); teaching English to speakers of other languages (Ed M); teaching of English and English education (Ed M, MA, Ed D, PhD); teaching of social studies (MA); TESOL (MA, Ed D). *Application Contact:* David Estrella, Director of Admissions, 212-678-3305, Fax: 212-678-4171, E-mail: estrella@tc.columbia.edu. *Department Chair,* Prof. William Gaudelli, E-mail: gaudelli@tc.columbia.edu.

Department of Biobehavioral Sciences Students: 180 full-time (160 women), 176 part-time (141 women); includes 149 minority (17 Black or African American, non-Hispanic/Latino; 40 Asian, non-Hispanic/Latino; 83 Hispanic/Latino; 9 Two or more races, non-Hispanic/Latino), 30 international. Average age 29. 738 applicants, 41% accepted, 164 enrolled. Expenses: Contact institution. *Financial support:* Fellowships, teaching assistantships, career-related internships or fieldwork, Federal Work-Study, institutionally sponsored loans, traineeships, and tuition waivers (full and partial) available. Support available to part-time students. *Program availability:* Part-time, evening/weekend. Offers applied exercise physiology (Ed M, MA, Ed D); communication sciences and disorders (MS, Ed D, PhD); kinesiology (PhD); motor learning and control (Ed M, MA); motor learning/movement science (Ed D); neuroscience and education (MS); physical education (MA, Ed D). *Application Contact:* David Estrella, Director of Admissions, 212-678-3305, E-mail: estrella@tc.columbia.edu. *Chair,* Prof. Carol Garber, 212-678-3891, E-mail: garber@tc.columbia.edu.

Department of Counseling and Clinical Psychology Students: 430 full-time (364 women), 237 part-time (201 women); includes 243 minority (65 Black or African American, non-Hispanic/Latino; 73 Asian, non-Hispanic/Latino; 83 Hispanic/Latino; 22 Two or more races, non-Hispanic/Latino), 142 international. Average age 28. 1,568 applicants, 38% accepted, 292 enrolled. Expenses: Contact institution. *Program availability:* Part-time. Offers clinical psychology (PhD); counseling psychology (Ed M, Ed D, PhD); mental health counseling (ME); psychological counseling (ME, ND); psychology in education (MA, ND); school counselor (ME). *Application Contact:* David Estrella, Director of Admission, 212-678-3305, E-mail: estrella@tc.columbia.edu. *Head,* Prof. George Bonanno, E-mail: gab38@tc.columbia.edu.

Department of Curriculum and Teaching Students: 196 full-time (181 women), 181 part-time (161 women); includes 141 minority (45 Black or African American, non-Hispanic/Latino; 2 American Indian or Alaska Native, non-Hispanic/Latino; 45 Asian, non-Hispanic/Latino; 35 Hispanic/Latino; 14 Two or more races, non-Hispanic/Latino), 37 international. Average age 30. 509 applicants, 72% accepted, 155 enrolled. Expenses: Contact institution. *Program availability:* Part-time, evening/weekend. Offers curriculum and teaching (Ed M, MA, Ed D); curriculum and teaching: elementary education (MA); curriculum and teaching: secondary education (MA); early childhood education (MA, Ed D); early childhood education: special education (MA); elementary education-gifted extension (MA); elementary inclusive education (MA); gifted education (MA); literacy specialist (MA); secondary inclusive education (MA); special inclusive elementary education (MA). *Application Contact:* David Estrella, Director of Admission, 212-678-3305, Fax: 212-678-4171, E-mail: estrella@tc.columbia.edu. *Chair,* Prof. Daniel Friedrich, E-mail: friedrich@exchange.tc.columbia.edu.

Department of Education Policy and Social Analysis Students: 144 full-time (109 women), 107 part-time (85 women); includes 100 minority (43 Black or African American, non-Hispanic/Latino; 17 Asian, non-Hispanic/Latino; 33 Hispanic/Latino; 7 Two or more races, non-Hispanic/Latino), 69 international. Average age 29. 524 applicants, 53% accepted, 104 enrolled. Expenses: Contact institution. Offers economics and education (Ed M, MA, PhD); education policy (Ed M, MA, Ed D, PhD); politics and education (Ed M, MA, Ed D, PhD); sociology and education (Ed M, MA, Ed D, PhD). *Application Contact:* David Estrella, Director of Admissions, 212-678-3305, E-mail: estrella@tc.columbia.edu. *Chair,* Dr. Aaron Pallas, E-mail: amp155@tc.columbia.edu.

Department of Health and Behavior Studies Students: 245 full-time (226 women), 242 part-time (219 women); includes 167 minority (52 Black or African American, non-Hispanic/Latino; 2 American Indian or Alaska Native, non-Hispanic/Latino; 55 Asian, non-Hispanic/Latino; 48 Hispanic/Latino; 1 Native Hawaiian or other Pacific Islander, non-Hispanic/Latino; 9 Two or more races, non-Hispanic/Latino), 60 international. Average age 30. 480 applicants, 59% accepted, 157 enrolled. Expenses: Contact institution. *Program availability:* Part-time, evening/weekend. Offers applied behavior analysis (MA, PhD); applied educational psychology: school psychology (Ed M, PhD); behavioral nutrition (PhD); community health education (MS); community nutrition education (Ed M); education of deaf and hard of hearing (MA, PhD); health education (MA, Ed D); hearing impairment (Ed D); intellectual disability/autism (MA, Ed D, PhD); nursing education (Ed D, Advanced Certificate); nutrition and education (MS); nutrition and exercise physiology (MS); nutrition and public health (MS); nutrition education (Ed D); physical disabilities (Ed D); reading specialist (MA); severe or multiple disabilities (MA); special education (Ed M, MA, Ed D); teaching of sign language (MA). *Application Contact:* David Estrella, Director of Admission, 212-678-3305, E-mail: estrella@tc.columbia.edu. *Chair,* Prof. Dolores Perin, E-mail: dp111@tc.columbia.edu.

Department of Human Development Students: 155 full-time (105 women), 135 part-time (106 women); includes 93 minority (26 Black or African American, non-Hispanic/Latino; 44 Asian, non-Hispanic/Latino; 21 Hispanic/Latino; 2 Two or more races, non-Hispanic/Latino), 118 international. Average age 29. 459 applicants, 53% accepted, 100 enrolled. Expenses: Contact institution. *Program availability:* Part-time. Offers applied statistics (MS); cognitive studies in education (MA, Ed D, PhD); developmental psychology (MA, Ed D, PhD); educational psychology-human cognition and learning (Ed M, MA, Ed D, PhD); learning analytics (MS); measurement and evaluation (ME, Ed D, PhD); measurement, evaluation, and statistics (MA, MS, Ed D, PhD). *Application Contact:* David Estrella, Director of Admission, 212-678-3305, E-mail: estrella@tc.columbia.edu. *Chair,* Jim Corter, E-mail: jec34@tc.columbia.edu.

Department of International and Transcultural Studies Students: 150 full-time (120 women), 143 part-time (116 women); includes 95 minority (22 Black or African American, non-Hispanic/Latino; 33 Asian, non-Hispanic/Latino; 29 Hispanic/Latino; 11 Two or more races, non-Hispanic/Latino), 116 international. Average age 29. 433 applicants, 59% accepted, 120 enrolled. Expenses: Contact institution. *Program availability:* Part-time. Offers anthropology and education (MA, Ed D, PhD); applied anthropology (PhD); comparative and international education (MA, Ed D, PhD); international educational development (Ed M, MA, Ed D, PhD). *Application Contact:* David Estrella, Director of Admission, 212-678-3305, E-mail: estrella@tc.columbia.edu. *Chair,* Prof. Herve Varenne, 212-678-3190, E-mail: varenne@tc.columbia.edu.

Department of Mathematics, Science and Technology Students: 187 full-time (129 women), 228 part-time (153 women); includes 143 minority (42 Black or African American, non-Hispanic/Latino; 64 Asian, non-Hispanic/Latino; 25 Hispanic/Latino; 12 Two or more races, non-Hispanic/Latino), 125 international. Average age 32. 484 applicants, 59% accepted, 141 enrolled. Expenses: Contact institution. *Program availability:* Part-time, evening/weekend, online learning. Offers biology 7-12 (MA); chemistry 7-12 (MA); communication and education (MA, Ed D); computing in education (MA); earth science 7-12 (MA); instructional technology and media (Ed M, MA, Ed D); mathematics education (Ed M, MA, Ed D, Ed DCT, PhD); physics 7-12 (MA); science and dental education (MA); science education (Ed M, MS, Ed DCT, PhD); supervisor/teacher of science education (MA); technology specialist (MA). *Application Contact:* David Estrella, Director of Admission, 212-678-3305, E-mail: estrella@tc.columbia.edu. *Chair,* Prof. Erica Walker, E-mail: ewalker@tc.columbia.edu.

Department of Organization and Leadership Students: 342 full-time (244 women), 378 part-time (256 women); includes 288 minority (106 Black or African American, non-Hispanic/Latino; 69 Asian, non-Hispanic/Latino; 92 Hispanic/Latino; 21 Two or more races, non-Hispanic/Latino), 86 international. Average age 33. 1,063 applicants, 59% accepted, 405 enrolled. Expenses: Contact institution. *Program availability:* Part-time, evening/weekend. Offers adult education guided intensive study (Ed D); adult learning and leadership (Ed M, MA, Ed D); educational leadership (Ed D); higher and postsecondary education (MA, Ed D); leadership, policy and politics (Ed D); nurse executive (MA, Ed D); private school leadership (Ed M, MA); public school building leadership (Ed M, MA); social and organizational psychology (MA); urban education leaders (Ed D). *Application Contact:* David Estrella, Director of Admission, 212-678-3305, E-mail: estrella@tc.columbia.edu. *Chair,* Prof. Bill Baldwin, E-mail: wjb12@tc.columbia.edu.

Interdisciplinary Programs Students: 13 full-time (7 women), 23 part-time (14 women); includes 10 minority (6 Black or African American, non-Hispanic/Latino; 1 Asian, non-Hispanic/Latino; 1 Hispanic/Latino; 1 Native Hawaiian or other Pacific Islander, non-Hispanic/Latino; 1 Two or more races, non-Hispanic/Latino), 8 international. Average age 40. 5 applicants, 60% accepted, 2 enrolled. Expenses: Contact institution. *Program availability:* Part-time. Offers interdisciplinary studies (Ed M, MA, ME, Ed D). *Application Contact:* David Estrella, Director of Admissions, 212-678-3305, E-mail: estrella@tc.columbia.edu.

TEACHERS COLLEGE OF SAN JOAQUIN, Stockton, CA 95206

General Information Public, coed, graduate-only institution.

GRADUATE UNITS

Master's Program in Education Offers early education (M Ed); educational inquiry (M Ed); educational leadership and school development (M Ed); science, technology, engineering, and mathematics (M Ed); special education (M Ed).

TÉLÉ-UNIVERSITÉ, Québec, QC G1K 9H5, Canada

General Information Province-supported, coed, comprehensive institution. *Graduate housing:* On-campus housing not available.

GRADUATE UNITS

Graduate Programs *Program availability:* Part-time. Offers computer science (PhD); corporate finance (MS); distance learning (MS).

TELSHE YESHIVA–CHICAGO, Chicago, IL 60625-5598

General Information Independent-religious, men only, comprehensive institution.

GRADUATE UNITS

Graduate Program

★ TEMPLE UNIVERSITY, Philadelphia, PA 19122-6096

General Information State-related, coed, university. CGS member. *Enrollment:* 39,948 graduate, professional, and undergraduate students; 4,566 full-time matriculated graduate/professional students (2,675 women), 1,356 part-time matriculated graduate/professional students (902 women). *Enrollment by degree level:* 2,681 master's, 3,082 doctoral, 156 other advanced degrees. *Graduate faculty:* 1,415 full-time (607 women), 767 part-time/adjunct (338 women). Tuition, state resident: full-time $16,164; part-time $898 per credit hour. Tuition, nonresident: full-time $22,158; part-time $1231 per credit hour. *Required fees:* $890; $445 per semester. Full-time tuition and fees vary according to course load, degree level, campus/location and program. *Graduate housing:* Rooms and/or apartments available on a first-come, first-served basis to single and married students. Typical cost: $7540 per year ($11,478 including board) for single students; $7540 per year ($11,478 including board) for married students. Room and board charges vary according to board plan, campus/location and housing facility selected. Housing application deadline: 5/1. *Student services:* Campus employment opportunities, campus safety program, career counseling, exercise/wellness program, free psychological counseling, grant writing training, international student services, low-cost health insurance, multicultural affairs office, services for students with disabilities, teacher training, writing training. *Library facilities:* Paley Library plus 6 others. *Collection:* Books: 4 million (physical), 1.4 million (digital/electronic); Serial titles: 37,998 (physical), 117,699 (digital/electronic); Databases: 760. Students can reserve study rooms.

Computer facilities: Computer purchase and lease plans are available. 15,100 computers available on campus for general student use. A campuswide network can be accessed from student residence rooms and from off campus. Online class registration, student accounts, Web hosting are available.
Website: http://www.temple.edu/

General Application Contact: Coordinator of Outreach, 215-204-1380, Fax: 215-204-8781, E-mail: grad@temple.edu.

GRADUATE UNITS

Beasley School of Law Students: 541 full-time (288 women), 147 part-time (62 women); includes 197 minority (65 Black or African American, non-Hispanic/Latino; 2 American Indian or Alaska Native, non-Hispanic/Latino; 52 Asian, non-Hispanic/Latino; 73 Hispanic/Latino; 5 Two or more races, non-Hispanic/Latino), 11 international. Average age 27. 2,096 applicants, 41% accepted, 223 enrolled. *Faculty:* 66 full-time (33 women), 136 part-time/adjunct (51 women). Expenses: Contact institution. *Financial support:* In 2017–18, 506 students received support, including research assistantships (averaging $5,500 per year), teaching assistantships (averaging $5,500 per year);

Federal Work-Study, scholarships/grants, tuition waivers (full and partial), and unspecified assistantships also available. Support available to part-time students. Financial award application deadline: 3/1; financial award applicants required to submit FAFSA. In 2017, 218 doctorates awarded. *Program availability:* Part-time, evening/weekend. Offers Asian law (LL M); business law (Certificate); employee benefits (Certificate); estate planning (Certificate); law (LL M, JD, SJD, Certificate); legal education (SJD); taxation (LL M); transnational law (LL M); trial advocacy (LL M); trial advocacy and litigation (Certificate). *Application deadline:* For fall admission, 3/1 for domestic and international students. Applications are processed on a rolling basis. *Application fee:* $65. Electronic applications accepted. *Application Contact:* Johanne L. Johnston, Assistant Dean for Admissions and Financial Aid, 800-560-1428, Fax: 215-204-9319, E-mail: lawadmis@temple.edu. *Dean*, Gregory N. Mandel, 215-204-7863, Fax: 215-204-1185, E-mail: law@temple.edu.

Center for the Performing and Cinematic Arts Students: 297 full-time (179 women), 75 part-time (54 women); includes 65 minority (30 Black or African American, non-Hispanic/Latino; 9 Asian, non-Hispanic/Latino; 16 Hispanic/Latino; 10 Two or more races, non-Hispanic/Latino), 120 international. 519 applicants, 50% accepted, 115 enrolled. *Faculty:* 89 full-time (40 women), 75 part-time/adjunct (34 women). Expenses: Contact institution. *Financial support:* Fellowships, research assistantships, teaching assistantships, Federal Work-Study, scholarships/grants, health care benefits, and unspecified assistantships available. Financial award applicants required to submit FAFSA. In 2017, 102 master's, 5 doctorates awarded. Offers performing and cinematic arts (Ed M, MA, MFA, MM, MMT, DMA, PhD). *Application fee:* $60. Electronic applications accepted. *Dean/Vice Provost for the Arts*, Dr. Robert Stroker, 215-777-9196, E-mail: robert.stroker@temple.edu.

Boyer College of Music and Dance Students: 244 full-time (157 women), 41 part-time (25 women); includes 46 minority (14 Black or African American, non-Hispanic/Latino; 12 Asian, non-Hispanic/Latino; 13 Hispanic/Latino; 7 Two or more races, non-Hispanic/Latino), 100 international. 426 applicants, 66% accepted, 109 enrolled. *Faculty:* 53 full-time (25 women), 35 part-time/adjunct (13 women). Expenses: Contact institution. *Financial support:* Fellowships with tuition reimbursements, research assistantships with tuition reimbursements, teaching assistantships with tuition reimbursements, career-related internships or fieldwork, Federal Work-Study, scholarships/grants, health care benefits, and unspecified assistantships available. Financial award application deadline: 3/1; financial award applicants required to submit FAFSA. In 2017, 76 master's, 5 doctorates awarded. *Program availability:* Part-time, online learning. Offers choral conducting (MM); collaborative piano/chamber music (MM); collaborative piano/opera coaching (MM); composition (MM, PhD); dance (MA, MFA, PhD); instrumental conducting (MM); music and dance (MA, MFA, MM, MMT, DMA, PhD); music education (MM, PhD); music history (MM); music performance (MM, DMA); music studies (PhD); music theory (MM, PhD); music therapy (MMT, PhD); musicology (MM, PhD); opera (MM); piano pedagogy (MM); string pedagogy (MM). *Application deadline:* For fall admission, 12/15 for international students; for spring admission, 8/1 for international students. Applications are processed on a rolling basis. *Application fee:* $60. Electronic applications accepted. *Application Contact:* James Short, Director of Undergraduate and Graduate Admissions, 215-204-8598, Fax: 215-204-4957, E-mail: jshort@temple.edu. *Dean*, Dr. Robert Stroker, 215-204-8301, Fax: 215-204-4957, E-mail: rstroker@temple.edu.

School of Theater, Film and Media Arts Students: 61 full-time (33 women), 7 part-time (4 women); includes 17 minority (11 Black or African American, non-Hispanic/Latino; 1 Asian, non-Hispanic/Latino; 3 Hispanic/Latino; 2 Two or more races, non-Hispanic/Latino), 13 international. 81 applicants, 52% accepted, 27 enrolled. *Faculty:* 36 full-time (15 women), 40 part-time/adjunct (21 women). Expenses: Contact institution. *Financial support:* Application deadline: 3/1; applicants required to submit FAFSA. In 2017, 26 master's awarded. Offers acting (MFA); design (MFA); directing (MFA); film and media arts (MA, MFA); musical theater collaboration (MFA); musical theater studies (MA); playwriting (MFA); theater, film and media arts (MA, MFA). *Application fee:* $60. Electronic applications accepted. *Application Contact:* Leah Dempsey, Assistant Director for Administration, 215-204-3859, E-mail: leahdempsey@temple.edu. *Dean/Vice Provost for the Arts*, Dr. Robert Stroker, 215-204-8598, E-mail: robert.stroker@temple.edu.

College of Education Students: 493 full-time (350 women), 554 part-time (361 women); includes 298 minority (184 Black or African American, non-Hispanic/Latino; 2 American Indian or Alaska Native, non-Hispanic/Latino; 41 Asian, non-Hispanic/Latino; 46 Hispanic/Latino; 1 Native Hawaiian or other Pacific Islander, non-Hispanic/Latino; 24 Two or more races, non-Hispanic/Latino), 43 international. 776 applicants, 53% accepted, 262 enrolled. *Faculty:* 62 full-time (34 women), 97 part-time/adjunct (62 women). Expenses: Contact institution. *Financial support:* Research assistantships, teaching assistantships, career-related internships or fieldwork, Federal Work-Study, scholarships/grants, health care benefits, and unspecified assistantships available. Financial award application deadline: 1/15; financial award applicants required to submit FAFSA. In 2017, 262 master's, 50 doctorates, 63 other advanced degrees awarded. *Program availability:* Part-time, evening/weekend. Offers applied behavior analysis (MS Ed); career and technical education (Ed M); counseling psychology (Ed M); education (Ed M, MS Ed, Ed D, PhD, Ed S); educational leadership (Ed M, Ed D); educational psychology (Ed M); middle grades education (Ed M); school psychology (PhD, Ed S); secondary education (Ed M); teaching English to speakers of other languages (MS Ed); urban education (Ed M). *Application deadline:* For fall admission, 4/1 for domestic students, 1/1 for international students; for spring admission, 10/1 for domestic students, 7/3 for international students. Applications are processed on a rolling basis. *Application fee:* $60. Electronic applications accepted. *Application Contact:* Elizabeth Jung, Enrollment Management, 215-204-5634, E-mail: educate@temple.edu. *Dean*, Dr. Gregory Anderson, 215-204-8017, Fax: 215-204-5622, E-mail: coedean@temple.edu.

College of Engineering Students: 137 full-time (40 women), 71 part-time (12 women); includes 40 minority (11 Black or African American, non-Hispanic/Latino; 1 American Indian or Alaska Native, non-Hispanic/Latino; 19 Asian, non-Hispanic/Latino; 7 Hispanic/Latino; 2 Two or more races, non-Hispanic/Latino), 86 international. 317 applicants, 50% accepted, 72 enrolled. *Faculty:* 67 full-time (11 women), 49 part-time/adjunct (5 women). Expenses: Contact institution. *Financial support:* In 2017–18, 66 students received support, including 1 fellowship with full tuition reimbursement available (averaging $30,000 per year), 28 research assistantships with full tuition reimbursements available (averaging $18,698 per year), 38 teaching assistantships with full tuition reimbursements available (averaging $18,698 per year); scholarships/grants, health care benefits, and unspecified assistantships also available. Financial award application deadline: 1/15. In 2017, 44 master's, 11 doctorates awarded. *Program availability:* Part-time, 100% online, blended/hybrid learning. Offers bioengineering (PhD); civil engineering (MSCE, PhD); electrical and computer engineering (PhD); electrical engineering (MSEE, PhD); engineering (MS, MS Env E, MSCE, MSEE, MSME, PhD, Certificate, Graduate Certificate); engineering management (MS, Certificate); environmental engineering (MS Env E, PhD); mechanical engineering (MSME); storm water management (Graduate Certificate). *Application deadline:* For fall admission, 3/1 priority date for domestic and international students; for spring admission, 11/1 priority date for domestic students, 8/1 priority date for international students. Applications are processed on a rolling basis. *Application fee:* $60. Electronic applications accepted. *Application Contact:* Colleen Baillie, Director, Enrollment, 215-204-7800, Fax: 215-204-6936, E-mail: gradengr@temple.edu. *Dean*, Dr. Keya Sadeghipour, 215-204-5285.

College of Liberal Arts Students: 590 full-time (335 women), 125 part-time (58 women); includes 175 minority (81 Black or African American, non-Hispanic/Latino; 1 American Indian or Alaska Native, non-Hispanic/Latino; 25 Asian, non-Hispanic/Latino; 48 Hispanic/Latino; 20 Two or more races, non-Hispanic/Latino), 83 international. 1,099 applicants, 29% accepted, 142 enrolled. *Faculty:* 302 full-time (131 women), 109 part-time/adjunct (47 women). Expenses: Contact institution. *Financial support:* Fellowships, research assistantships, teaching assistantships, career-related internships or fieldwork, Federal Work-Study, institutionally sponsored loans, scholarships/grants, and tuition waivers (full and partial) available. Support available to part-time students. Financial award application deadline: 1/15; financial award applicants required to submit FAFSA. In 2017, 77 master's, 71 doctorates, 5 other advanced degrees awarded. *Program availability:* Part-time. Offers African American studies (MA, PhD); anthropology (PhD); creative writing (MFA); criminal justice (MA, PhD); economics (MA, PhD); English (MA, PhD); geographic information systems (PSM, Graduate Certificate); geography and urban studies (MA, PhD); history (MA, PhD); liberal arts (MA, MFA, MS, PSM, PhD, Graduate Certificate); philosophy (MA, PhD); political science (MA, PhD); psychology (MA, MS, PhD); religion (MA, PhD); sociology (MA, PhD); Spanish (MA, PhD). *Application deadline:* For fall admission, 12/15 for international students; for spring admission, 8/1 for international students. *Application fee:* $60. Electronic applications accepted. *Application Contact:* Dr. Shawn Schurr, Vice Dean, 215-204-7743, E-mail: schurr@temple.edu. *Dean*, Richard Deeg, 215-204-7747, Fax: 215-204-5022, E-mail: rdeeg@temple.edu.

College of Public Health Students: 687 full-time (556 women), 387 part-time (296 women); includes 343 minority (173 Black or African American, non-Hispanic/Latino; 1 American Indian or Alaska Native, non-Hispanic/Latino; 56 Asian, non-Hispanic/Latino; 74 Hispanic/Latino; 39 Two or more races, non-Hispanic/Latino), 31 international. 1,222 applicants, 50% accepted, 232 enrolled. *Faculty:* 109 full-time (78 women), 18 part-time/adjunct (13 women). Expenses: Contact institution. *Financial support:* Fellowships, research assistantships, teaching assistantships, career-related internships or fieldwork, Federal Work-Study, institutionally sponsored loans, traineeships, and tuition waivers (partial) available. Support available to part-time students. Financial award application deadline: 1/15. In 2017, 333 master's, 117 doctorates awarded. *Program availability:* Part-time, evening/weekend, online learning. Offers adult-gerontology primary care (DNP); applied biostatistics (MPH); athletic training (MSAT, DAT); communication sciences and disorders (PhD); environmental health (MPH); epidemiology (MPH, MS, PhD); family-individual across the lifespan (DNP); health informatics (MS); health policy (PhD); health policy and management (MPH); kinesiology (MS, PhD); neuromotor science (MS, PhD); nursing (DNP); occupational therapy (MOT, DOT); physical therapy (DPT, TDPT); public health (MA, MOT, MPH, MS, MSAT, MSW, DAT, DNP, DOT, DPT, PhD, TDPT); social and behavioral sciences (MPH, PhD); speech-language-hearing (MA); therapeutic recreation (MS). *Application fee:* $60. *Dean*, Dr. Laura Siminoff, 215-707-8624, Fax: 215-707-7819, E-mail: laura.siminoff@temple.edu.

School of Social Work Students: 213 full-time (189 women), 136 part-time (114 women); includes 154 minority (98 Black or African American, non-Hispanic/Latino; 1 American Indian or Alaska Native, non-Hispanic/Latino; 6 Asian, non-Hispanic/Latino; 33 Hispanic/Latino; 16 Two or more races, non-Hispanic/Latino). 318 applicants, 67% accepted, 86 enrolled. *Faculty:* 27 full-time (17 women), 6 part-time/adjunct (4 women). Expenses: Contact institution. *Financial support:* Research assistantships with tuition reimbursements, career-related internships or fieldwork, Federal Work-Study, scholarships/grants, traineeships, tuition waivers (partial), unspecified assistantships, and field assistantships available. Support available to part-time students. Financial award application deadline: 1/1. In 2017, 189 master's awarded. *Program availability:* Part-time, evening/weekend. Offers social work (MSW). *Application deadline:* For fall admission, 3/15 priority date for domestic students, 2/15 for international students; for spring admission, 11/1 priority date for domestic students, 10/15 for international students; for summer admission, 3/15 for domestic students, 2/15 for international students. Applications are processed on a rolling basis. *Application fee:* $60. Electronic applications accepted. *Application Contact:* Cheryl A. Hyde, Associate Professor/MSW Program Director, 215-204-7112, E-mail: chyde@temple.edu. *Chairperson*, Bernie Newman, 215-204-1205, Fax: 215-204-9606, E-mail: bernie.newman@temple.edu.

College of Science and Technology Students: 455 full-time (174 women), 69 part-time (30 women); includes 92 minority (17 Black or African American, non-Hispanic/Latino; 42 Asian, non-Hispanic/Latino; 22 Hispanic/Latino; 11 Two or more races, non-Hispanic/Latino), 223 international. 583 applicants, 39% accepted, 117 enrolled. *Faculty:* 185 full-time (48 women), 11 part-time/adjunct (3 women). Expenses: Contact institution. *Financial support:* Fellowships, research assistantships, teaching assistantships, career-related internships or fieldwork, Federal Work-Study, institutionally sponsored loans, scholarships/grants, tuition waivers (full and partial), and laboratory assistantships available. Financial award application deadline: 1/15; financial award applicants required to submit FAFSA. In 2017, 66 master's, 48 doctorates awarded. *Program availability:* Part-time, evening/weekend. Offers applied mathematics (MS); biology (MS, PSM, PhD); biotechnology (MS); chemistry (MA, PhD); computational data science (MS); computer and information sciences (PhD); computer science (MS); cyber defense and information assurance (PSM); geology (MS); geosciences (PhD); information science and technology (MS); mathematics (MS, PhD); physics (MS, PhD); science and technology (MA, MS, PSM, PhD). *Application deadline:* For fall admission, 1/5 for domestic students, 12/15 for international students; for spring admission, 9/15 for domestic students, 8/1 for international students. Applications are processed on a rolling basis. *Application fee:* $60. Electronic applications accepted. *Application Contact:* Tara Schumacher, Coordinator of Outreach, 215-204-1380, Fax: 215-204-8781, E-mail: tara.schumacher@temple.edu. *Associate Director of Graduate Studies*, Eileen Weinberg, 215-204-2150, E-mail: eileen.weinberg@temple.edu.

Fox School of Business *Program availability:* Part-time, evening/weekend, online learning. Offers accountancy (MS); accounting (MBA, PhD); actuarial science (MS); business (EMBA, IMBA, MBA, MHM, MS, PhD); business management (MBA); entrepreneurship (PhD); finance (MS, PhD); financial engineering (MS); financial management (MBA); healthcare and life sciences innovation (MBA); human resource management (MBA, MS); innovation management and entrepreneurship (MS); international business (IMBA, PhD); IT management (MBA); management information systems (PhD); marketing (MS, PhD); marketing management (MBA); pharmaceutical management (MBA); risk management and insurance (PhD); statistics (MS, PhD);

strategic management (EMBA, MBA, PhD); tourism and sport (PhD). Electronic applications accepted.

Klein College of Media and Communication Students: 79 full-time (50 women), 44 part-time (29 women); includes 32 minority (17 Black or African American, non-Hispanic/Latino; 4 Asian, non-Hispanic/Latino; 5 Hispanic/Latino; 6 Two or more races, non-Hispanic/Latino), 32 international. 130 applicants, 57% accepted, 33 enrolled. *Faculty:* 80 full-time (42 women), 64 part-time/adjunct (29 women). Expenses: Contact institution. *Financial support:* Fellowships, teaching assistantships, career-related internships or fieldwork, Federal Work-Study, institutionally sponsored loans, tuition waivers (full and partial), and unspecified assistantships available. Financial award application deadline: 1/15; financial award applicants required to submit FAFSA. In 2017, 30 master's, 7 doctorates awarded. *Program availability:* Part-time, evening/weekend. Offers communication management (MS); globalization and development communication (MS); journalism (MJ); media and communication (MA, MJ, MS, PhD); media studies and production (MA). *Application deadline:* For fall admission, 12/15 for international students. *Application fee:* $60. Electronic applications accepted. *Application Contact:* Nicole McKenna, Director, Office of Research and Graduate Studies, 215-204-1497, Fax: 215-204-0310, E-mail: nmckenna@temple.edu. *Dean*, David Boardman, 215-204-8422, Fax: 215-204-4811, E-mail: dboardman@temple.edu.

Lewis Katz School of Medicine Students: 1,078 full-time (551 women), 25 part-time (21 women); includes 411 minority (74 Black or African American, non-Hispanic/Latino; 210 Asian, non-Hispanic/Latino; 95 Hispanic/Latino; 1 Native Hawaiian or other Pacific Islander, non-Hispanic/Latino; 31 Two or more races, non-Hispanic/Latino), 27 international. 159 applicants, 34% accepted, 36 enrolled. *Faculty:* 20 full-time (7 women). Expenses: Contact institution. *Financial support:* Fellowships, research assistantships, scholarships/grants, and health care benefits available. Financial award application deadline: 2/15; financial award applicants required to submit FAFSA. In 2017, 16 master's, 217 doctorates awarded. Offers biomedical sciences (MS); medicine (MS, MD, PhD). *Application deadline:* For fall admission, 2/15 for domestic and international students. *Application fee:* $60. Electronic applications accepted. *Application Contact:* Jacob Ufberg, Associate Dean of Admissions, 215-707-5308, E-mail: tusmgrad@temple.edu. *Dean*, Larry R. Kaiser, 215-707-8773, Fax: 215-707-5072, E-mail: sks@temple.edu.

Maurice H. Kornberg School of Dentistry Offers advanced education in general dentistry (Certificate); dentistry (MS, DMD, Certificate); endodontology (Certificate); oral biology (MS); orthodontics (Certificate); periodontology (Certificate). Electronic applications accepted.

School of Pharmacy Students: 595 full-time (329 women), 313 part-time (225 women); includes 344 minority (40 Black or African American, non-Hispanic/Latino; 136 Asian, non-Hispanic/Latino; 16 Hispanic/Latino; 152 Two or more races, non-Hispanic/Latino), 70 international. 100 applicants, 57% accepted, 41 enrolled. *Faculty:* 40 full-time (22 women), 39 part-time/adjunct (15 women). Expenses: Contact institution. *Financial support:* Fellowships, research assistantships, teaching assistantships, career-related internships or fieldwork, Federal Work-Study, and institutionally sponsored loans available. Financial award application deadline: 1/15; financial award applicants required to submit FAFSA. In 2017, 108 master's, 147 doctorates awarded. *Program availability:* Part-time, evening/weekend, online learning. Offers medicinal chemistry (MS, PhD); pharmaceutics (MS, PhD); pharmacodynamics (MS, PhD); pharmacy (MS, PhD, Pharm D); regulatory affairs and quality assurance (MS). *Application deadline:* For fall admission, 2/1 priority date for domestic and international students. *Application fee:* $60. Electronic applications accepted. *Application Contact:* E-mail: phscgrad@temple.edu. *Dean*, Dr. Peter H. Doukas, 215-707-4990, Fax: 215-707-5620, E-mail: peter.doukas@temple.edu.

School of Podiatric Medicine Offers podiatric medicine (DPM). DPM/PhD offered jointly with Drexel University, University of Pennsylvania.

School of Sport, Tourism and Hospitality Management Students: 158 full-time (72 women), 32 part-time (19 women); includes 46 minority (29 Black or African American, non-Hispanic/Latino; 4 Asian, non-Hispanic/Latino; 11 Hispanic/Latino; 2 Two or more races, non-Hispanic/Latino), 31 international. 235 applicants, 74% accepted, 96 enrolled. *Faculty:* 28 full-time (9 women), 9 part-time/adjunct (2 women). Expenses: Contact institution. *Financial support:* Fellowships, research assistantships, and teaching assistantships available. Financial award application deadline: 3/1; financial award applicants required to submit FAFSA. In 2017, 37 master's awarded. *Program availability:* Part-time, evening/weekend. Offers sport business (MS); tourism and hospitality management (MTHM); tourism and sport (PhD); travel and tourism (MS). *Application deadline:* For fall admission, 3/1 priority date for domestic students, 1/15 priority date for international students; for spring admission, 8/15 priority date for domestic students, 6/30 priority date for international students. Applications are processed on a rolling basis. *Application fee:* $60. Electronic applications accepted. *Application Contact:* James Alton, Manager of Graduate Student Services, 215-204-7140, Fax: 215-204-8705, E-mail: jim.alton@temple.edu. *Dean*, Dr. M. Moshe Porat, 215-204-1836, Fax: 215-204-8705, E-mail: porat@temple.edu.

Tyler School of Art Students: 171 full-time (108 women), 45 part-time (33 women); includes 42 minority (12 Black or African American, non-Hispanic/Latino; 7 Asian, non-Hispanic/Latino; 14 Hispanic/Latino; 9 Two or more races, non-Hispanic/Latino), 18 international. 470 applicants, 31% accepted, 55 enrolled. *Faculty:* 66 full-time (31 women), 98 part-time/adjunct (49 women). Expenses: Contact institution. *Financial support:* Fellowships with full tuition reimbursements, research assistantships with full tuition reimbursements, teaching assistantships with full tuition reimbursements, career-related internships or fieldwork, Federal Work-Study, and institutionally sponsored loans available. Support available to part-time students. Financial award application deadline: 1/15; financial award applicants required to submit FAFSA. In 2017, 54 master's, 4 doctorates awarded. *Program availability:* Part-time, evening/weekend. Offers architecture (M Arch); art (Ed M, M Arch, MA, MFA, ML Arch, MS, PhD, Graduate Certificate); art education (Ed M); art history (MA, PhD); ceramics (MFA); city and regional planning (MS); fibers and material studies (MFA); glass (MFA); graphic and interactive design (MFA); landscape architecture (ML Arch); metals/jewelry/CAD-CAM (MFA); painting (MFA); photography (MFA); printmaking (MFA); sculpture (MFA); sustainable community planning (Graduate Certificate); transportation planning (Graduate Certificate). *Application deadline:* Applications are processed on a rolling basis. *Application fee:* $60. Electronic applications accepted. *Application Contact:* Tamryn McDermott, Director of Admissions, 215-777-9090, E-mail: tylerart@temple.edu. *Dean*, Susan E. Cahan, 215-777-9000, E-mail: tyler@temple.edu.

See Display on the next page and Close-Up on page 877.

TENNESSEE STATE UNIVERSITY, Nashville, TN 37209-1561

General Information State-supported, coed, comprehensive institution. CGS member. *Graduate housing:* Rooms and/or apartments available on a first-come, first-served basis to single and married students. Housing application deadline: 8/1.

GRADUATE UNITS

The School of Graduate Studies and Research

College of Agriculture, Human and Natural Sciences *Program availability:* Part-time, evening/weekend. Offers agricultural sciences (MS); biological sciences (MS, PhD); biotechnology (PhD); chemistry (MS).

College of Business *Program availability:* Part-time, evening/weekend, online learning. Offers business (MBA). Electronic applications accepted.

College of Education *Program availability:* Part-time, evening/weekend. Offers counseling psychology (MS); curriculum and instruction (M Ed, Ed D); education (M Ed, MA Ed, MS, Ed D, PhD, Ed S); elementary education (M Ed); special education (M Ed).

College of Engineering *Program availability:* Part-time, evening/weekend. Offers biomedical engineering (ME); civil engineering (ME); computer and information systems engineering (MS, PhD); electrical engineering (ME); environmental engineering (ME); manufacturing engineering (ME); mathematical sciences (MS); mechanical engineering (ME).

College of Health Sciences *Program availability:* Part-time, evening/weekend. Offers exercise science (MA Ed); family nurse practitioner (MSN, Certificate); health sciences (MA Ed, MOT, MPH, MS, MSN, DPT, Certificate); holistic nurse practitioner (MSN); holistic nursing (Certificate); nursing education (MSN, Certificate); occupational therapy (MOT); physical therapy (DPT); public health (MPH); speech and hearing science (MS); sports administration (MA Ed). Electronic applications accepted.

College of Liberal Arts *Program availability:* Part-time, evening/weekend. Offers criminal justice (MCJ); liberal arts (MCJ). Electronic applications accepted.

College of Public Service *Program availability:* Part-time, evening/weekend. Offers human resource management (MPS); public administration (MPA, PhD); social work (MSW); strategic leadership (MPS); training and development (MPS).

TENNESSEE TECHNOLOGICAL UNIVERSITY, Cookeville, TN 38505

General Information State-supported, coed, university. CGS member. *Enrollment:* 10,504 graduate, professional, and undergraduate students; 302 full-time matriculated graduate/professional students (162 women), 819 part-time matriculated graduate/professional students (445 women). *Enrollment by degree level:* 865 master's, 173 doctoral, 83 other advanced degrees. *Graduate faculty:* 341 full-time (62 women). Tuition, state resident: full-time $9925; part-time $565 per credit hour. Tuition, nonresident: full-time $22,993; part-time $1291 per credit hour. *Graduate housing:* Rooms and/or apartments available on a first-come, first-served basis to single and married students. Typical cost: $3080 per year for single students; $3080 per year for married students. Housing application deadline: 6/1. *Student services:* Campus employment opportunities, campus safety program, career counseling, child daycare facilities, exercise/wellness program, free psychological counseling, international student services, low-cost health insurance, multicultural affairs office, services for students with disabilities, teacher training. *Library facilities:* Angelo and Jennette Volpe Library and Media Center. *Collection:* Books: 235,249 (physical), 267,168 (digital/electronic); Serial titles: 120,118 (physical); Databases: 193. *Research affiliation:* Center for Excellence in Teacher Evaluation, Appalachian Center for Crafts, Center of Excellence in Water Resources, Center of Excellence in Manufacturing Resources, Center of Excellence in Energy Systems Research.

Computer facilities: 227 computers available on campus for general student use. A campuswide network can be accessed. Online class registration, 590 additional computers are available for student use in individual departmental labs are available. Website: http://www.tntech.edu/

General Application Contact: Shelia K. Kendrick, Coordinator of Graduate Studies, 931-372-3808, Fax: 931-372-3497, E-mail: skendrick@tntech.edu.

GRADUATE UNITS

College of Graduate Studies Students: 302 full-time (162 women), 819 part-time (445 women); includes 100 minority (47 Black or African American, non-Hispanic/Latino; 1 American Indian or Alaska Native, non-Hispanic/Latino; 11 Asian, non-Hispanic/Latino; 18 Hispanic/Latino; 1 Native Hawaiian or other Pacific Islander, non-Hispanic/Latino; 22 Two or more races, non-Hispanic/Latino), 140 international. 873 applicants, 66% accepted, 348 enrolled. *Faculty:* 341 full-time (62 women). Expenses: Contact institution. *Financial support:* In 2017–18, 354 students received support, including 50 fellowships (averaging $8,000 per year), 143 research assistantships (averaging $6,973 per year), 156 teaching assistantships (averaging $6,213 per year); career-related internships or fieldwork and Federal Work-Study also available. Support available to part-time students. Financial award application deadline: 4/1; financial award applicants required to submit FAFSA. In 2017, 367 master's, 23 doctorates, 43 other advanced degrees awarded. *Program availability:* Part-time, evening/weekend, 100% online, blended/hybrid learning. *Application deadline:* For fall admission, 7/1 for domestic students, 5/1 for international students; for spring admission, 12/1 for domestic students, 10/1 for international students; for summer admission, 5/1 for domestic students, 2/1 for international students. Applications are processed on a rolling basis. *Application fee:* $35 ($40 for international students). Electronic applications accepted. *Application Contact:* Shelia K. Kendrick, Coordinator of Graduate Studies, 931-372-3808, Fax: 931-372-3497, E-mail: skendrick@tntech.edu. *Senior Associate Provost and Dean of Graduate Studies*, Dr. Mark A. Stephens, 931-372-3233, Fax: 931-372-3497, E-mail: mstephens@tntech.edu.

College of Arts and Sciences Students: 16 full-time (8 women), 32 part-time (18 women); includes 3 minority (all Hispanic/Latino), 7 international. 54 applicants, 69% accepted, 17 enrolled. *Faculty:* 78 full-time (15 women). Expenses: Contact institution. *Financial support:* In 2017–18, 8 research assistantships (averaging $7,600 per year), 45 teaching assistantships (averaging $6,630 per year) were awarded; fellowships and career-related internships or fieldwork also available. Support available to part-time students. Financial award application deadline: 4/1. In 2017, 29 master's awarded. *Program availability:* Part-time. Offers arts and sciences (MA, MS); chemistry (MS); English (MA); fish, game, and wildlife management (MS); mathematics (MS). *Application deadline:* For fall admission, 8/1 for domestic students, 5/1 for international students; for spring admission, 12/1 for domestic students, 10/1 for international students; for summer admission, 5/1 for domestic students, 2/1 for international students. Applications are processed on a rolling basis. *Application fee:* $35 ($40 for international students). Electronic applications accepted. *Application Contact:* Shelia K. Kendrick, Coordinator of Graduate Studies, 931-372-3808, Fax: 931-372-3497, E-mail: skendrick@tntech.edu. *Dean*, Dr. Paul Semmes, 931-372-3118, Fax: 931-372-6142, E-mail: psemmes@tntech.edu.

College of Business Students: 54 full-time (23 women), 191 part-time (75 women); includes 27 minority (10 Black or African American, non-Hispanic/Latino; 1 American Indian or Alaska Native, non-Hispanic/Latino; 6 Asian, non-Hispanic/Latino; 6

Hispanic/Latino; 4 Two or more races, non-Hispanic/Latino), 16 international. 171 applicants, 75% accepted, 89 enrolled. *Faculty:* 28 full-time (5 women). Expenses: Contact institution. *Financial support:* In 2017–18, 2 research assistantships (averaging $4,400 per year), 4 teaching assistantships (averaging $4,400 per year) were awarded; fellowships also available. Support available to part-time students. Financial award application deadline: 4/1. In 2017, 77 master's awarded. *Program availability:* Part-time, evening/weekend, online learning. Offers accountancy (M Acc); business (M Acc, MBA); finance (MBA); human resource management (MBA); international business (MBA); management information systems (MBA). *Application deadline:* For fall admission, 8/1 for domestic students, 5/1 for international students; for spring admission, 12/1 for domestic students, 10/1 for international students; for summer admission, 5/1 for domestic students, 2/1 for international students. Applications are processed on a rolling basis. *Application fee:* $35 ($40 for international students). Electronic applications accepted. *Application Contact:* Shelia K. Kendrick, Coordinator of Graduate Studies, 931-372-3808, Fax: 931-372-3497, E-mail: skendrick@tntech.edu. *Director,* Kate Nicewicz, 931-372-3600, Fax: 931-372-6249, E-mail: knicewicz@tntech.edu.

College of Education Students: 115 full-time (88 women), 273 part-time (202 women); includes 34 minority (20 Black or African American, non-Hispanic/Latino; 1 Asian, non-Hispanic/Latino; 4 Hispanic/Latino; 9 Two or more races, non-Hispanic/Latino), 8 international. 222 applicants, 70% accepted, 117 enrolled. *Faculty:* 58 full-time (16 women). Expenses: Contact institution. *Financial support:* Fellowships, research assistantships, teaching assistantships, and career-related internships or fieldwork available. Support available to part-time students. Financial award application deadline: 4/1. In 2017, 137 master's, 10 doctorates, 31 other advanced degrees awarded. *Program availability:* Part-time, evening/weekend. Offers adapted physical education (MA); applied behavior analysis (PhD); counseling and psychology (MA, Ed S); curriculum (MA, Ed S); early childhood education (MA, Ed S); education (MA, PhD, Ed S); educational technology (MA, Ed S); elementary education (MA, Ed S); elementary/middle school physical education (MA); exceptional learning (PhD); instructional leadership (MA, Ed S); library science (MA, Ed S); lifetime wellness (MA); literacy (PhD); music (MA); program planning and evaluation (PhD); reading (MA, Ed S); secondary education (Ed S); special education (Ed S); sport management (MA); STEM education (MA, PhD, Ed S). *Application deadline:* For fall admission, 8/1 for domestic students, 5/1 for international students; for spring admission, 12/1 for domestic students, 10/1 for international students; for summer admission, 5/1 for domestic students, 2/1 for international students. Applications are processed on a rolling basis. *Application fee:* $35 ($40 for international students). Electronic applications accepted. *Application Contact:* Shelia K. Kendrick, Coordinator of Graduate Studies, 931-372-3808, Fax: 931-372-3497, E-mail: skendrick@tntech.edu. *Dean,* Dr. Lisa Zagumny, 931-372-3124, Fax: 931-372-6319, E-mail: lzagumny@tntech.edu.

College of Engineering Students: 67 full-time (12 women), 144 part-time (25 women); includes 15 minority (4 Black or African American, non-Hispanic/Latino; 5 Asian, non-Hispanic/Latino; 3 Hispanic/Latino; 3 Two or more races, non-Hispanic/Latino), 98 international. 293 applicants, 57% accepted, 53 enrolled. *Faculty:* 76 full-time (2 women). Expenses: Contact institution. *Financial support:* Fellowships, research assistantships, teaching assistantships, and career-related internships or fieldwork available. Support available to part-time students. Financial award application deadline: 4/1. In 2017, 55 master's, 11 doctorates awarded. *Program availability:* Part-time. Offers chemical engineering (MS); civil and environmental engineering (MS); electrical and computer engineering (MS); engineering (MS, PhD); Internet-based computing (MS); mechanical engineering (MS). *Application deadline:* For fall admission, 8/1 for domestic students, 5/1 for international students; for spring admission, 12/1 for domestic students, 10/1 for international students. Applications are processed on a rolling basis. *Application fee:* $35 ($40 for international students). Electronic applications accepted. *Application Contact:* Shelia K. Kendrick, Coordinator of Graduate Studies, 931-372-3808, Fax: 931-372-3497, E-mail: skendrick@tntech.edu. *Dean,* Dr. Darrell Hoy, 931-372-3172, Fax: 931-372-6172, E-mail: dhoy@tntech.edu.

College of Interdisciplinary Studies Students: 28 full-time (14 women), 91 part-time (51 women); includes 20 minority (12 Black or African American, non-Hispanic/Latino; 1 Asian, non-Hispanic/Latino; 1 Hispanic/Latino; 1 Native Hawaiian or other Pacific Islander, non-Hispanic/Latino; 5 Two or more races, non-Hispanic/Latino), 5 international. 71 applicants, 72% accepted, 38 enrolled. Expenses: Contact institution. *Financial support:* Research assistantships and teaching assistantships available. In 2017, 28 master's, 2 doctorates awarded. *Program availability:* Part-time. Offers agriculture (PhD); biology (PhD); chemistry (PhD); environmental informatics (PSM); environmental studies (PSM, PhD); geosciences (PhD); health care administration (MPS); human resources leadership (MPS); integrated research (PhD); interdisciplinary studies (MPS, PSM, PhD); manufacturing sustainability (PSM); public safety (MPS); strategic leadership (MPS); teaching English to speakers of other languages (MPS); training and development (MPS). *Application deadline:* For fall admission, 7/1 for domestic students, 5/1 for international students; for spring admission, 11/1 for domestic students, 10/1 for international students; for summer admission, 5/1 for domestic students, 2/1 for international students. Applications are processed on a rolling basis. *Application fee:* $35 ($40 for international students). Electronic applications accepted. *Application Contact:* Shelia K. Kendrick, Coordinator of Graduate Studies, 931-372-3808, Fax: 931-372-3497, E-mail: skendrick@tntech.edu. *Dean,* Dr. Mike Gotcher, 931-372-6238, E-mail: mgotcher@tntech.edu.

Whitson-Hester School of Nursing Students: 22 full-time (17 women), 88 part-time (74 women); includes 5 minority (2 Black or African American, non-Hispanic/Latino; 2 Hispanic/Latino; 1 Two or more races, non-Hispanic/Latino). 62 applicants, 58% accepted, 30 enrolled. Expenses: Contact institution. *Financial support:* Teaching assistantships available. Financial award application deadline: 4/1. In 2017, 41 master's awarded. *Program availability:* Part-time, evening/weekend, online learning. Offers adult-gerontology acute care nurse practitioner (DNP); executive leadership in nursing (DNP); family nurse practitioner (MSN, DNP); nursing (MSN, DNP); nursing administration (MSN); nursing education (MSN); pediatric nurse practitioner-primary care (DNP); psychiatric/mental health nurse practitioner (DNP); women's health care nurse practitioner (DNP). *Application deadline:* For fall admission, 7/1 for domestic students, 5/1 for international students; for spring admission, 11/1 for domestic students, 10/1 for international students; for summer admission, 5/1 for domestic students, 2/1 for international students. Applications are processed on a rolling basis. *Application fee:* $35 ($40 for international students). Electronic applications accepted. *Application Contact:* Shelia K. Kendrick, Coordinator of Graduate Studies, 931-372-3808, Fax: 931-372-3497, E-mail: skendrick@tntech.edu. *Dean,* Dr. Kim Hanna, 931-372-3547, Fax: 931-372-6244, E-mail: khanna@tntech.edu.

TENNESSEE WESLEYAN UNIVERSITY, Athens, TN 37303

General Information Independent-religious, coed, comprehensive institution. *Enrollment:* 951 graduate, professional, and undergraduate students; 2 full-time matriculated graduate/professional students (1 woman), 14 part-time matriculated graduate/professional students (10 women). *Enrollment by degree level:* 16 master's. *Graduate faculty:* 4 full-time (1 woman), 1 (woman) part-time/adjunct. *Tuition:* Part-time $500 per semester hour. *Graduate housing:* Room and/or apartments available on a first-come, first-served basis to single students; on-campus housing not available to married students. Housing application deadline: 8/5. *Student services:* Career counseling, international student services, multicultural affairs office, services for students with disabilities. *Library facilities:* Merner-Pfeiffer Library plus 1 other. *Collection:* Books: 52,465 (physical), 356,697 (digital/electronic); Serial titles: 82 (physical); Databases: 76. Weekly public service hours: 69.

Computer facilities: 205 computers available on campus for general student use. A campuswide network can be accessed from student residence rooms. Online class registration is available.
Website: http://www.tnwesleyan.edu/

General Application Contact: Mark Bucco, Adult and Graduate Admissions Counselor, 423-252-1114, Fax: 423-745-9335, E-mail: mbucco@tnwesleyan.edu.

GRADUATE UNITS

Graduate Programs Students: 2 full-time (1 woman), 14 part-time (10 women). *Faculty:* 4 full-time (1 woman), 1 (woman) part-time/adjunct. Expenses: Contact institution. *Program availability:* Evening/weekend. Offers accounting (MBA); management (MBA). *Application Contact:* Mark Bucco, Adult and Graduate Admissions Counselor, 423-252-1114, Fax: 423-745-9335, E-mail: mbucco@tnwesleyan.edu.

TEXAS A&M INTERNATIONAL UNIVERSITY, Laredo, TX 78041

General Information State-supported, coed, comprehensive institution. CGS member. *Graduate housing:* Rooms and/or apartments available on a first-come, first-served basis to single and married students.

GRADUATE UNITS

Office of Graduate Studies and Research *Program availability:* Part-time.

A.R. Sanchez, Jr. School of Business *Program availability:* Part-time, evening/weekend. Offers accounting (MP Acc); business (MBA, MP Acc, MSIS, PhD); information systems (MSIS); international banking and finance (MBA); international business management (MBA, PhD).

College of Arts and Sciences *Program availability:* Part-time, online learning. Offers arts and sciences (MA, MACP, MPA, MS, PhD); biology (MS); counseling psychology (MACP); criminal justice (MS); English (MA); history and political thought (MA); language, literature and translation (MA); mathematics (MS); psychology (MS); public administration (MPA); sociology (MA).

College of Education *Program availability:* Part-time, evening/weekend. Offers curriculum and pedagogy (MS); education (MS, MS Ed); educational administration (MS Ed); generic special education (MS Ed); school counseling (MS).

College of Nursing and Health Sciences Offers family nurse practitioner (MSN).

TEXAS A&M UNIVERSITY, College Station, TX 77843

General Information State-supported, coed, university. CGS member. *Enrollment:* 67,580 graduate, professional, and undergraduate students; 11,894 full-time matriculated graduate/professional students (5,201 women), 2,896 part-time matriculated graduate/professional students (1,426 women). *Enrollment by degree level:* 6,987 master's, 7,708 doctoral, 95 other advanced degrees. *Graduate faculty:* 2,860. *Graduate housing:* Rooms and/or apartments available on a first-come, first-served basis to single and married students. *Student services:* Campus employment opportunities, campus safety program, career counseling, child daycare facilities, exercise/wellness program, free psychological counseling, grant writing training, international student services, low-cost health insurance, multicultural affairs office, services for students with disabilities, teacher training, writing training. *Library facilities:* Sterling C. Evans Library plus 9 others. *Collection:* Books: 4.3 million (physical), 1.9 million (digital/electronic); Serial titles: 10,083 (physical), 199,378 (digital/electronic); Databases: 1,162. Weekly public service hours: 144; study areas open 24 hours, 5–7 days a week; students can reserve study rooms. *Research affiliation:* U.S. Department of Agriculture (USDA) (agriculture), National Science Foundation (geosciences), Joint Oceanographic Institutions, Inc. (geosciences), Texas Department of Transportation (transportation).

Computer facilities: 2,776 computers available on campus for general student use. A campuswide network can be accessed from student residence rooms and from off campus. Online class registration is available.
Website: http://www.tamu.edu/

General Application Contact: Graduate Admissions, 979-458-0427, E-mail: admissions@tamu.edu.

GRADUATE UNITS

Bush School of Government and Public Service Students: 332 full-time (182 women), 54 part-time (16 women); includes 94 minority (19 Black or African American, non-Hispanic/Latino; 10 Asian, non-Hispanic/Latino; 56 Hispanic/Latino; 9 Two or more races, non-Hispanic/Latino), 41 international. Average age 28. 297 applicants, 94% accepted, 164 enrolled. *Faculty:* 66. Expenses: Contact institution. *Financial support:* In 2017–18, 417 students received support, including 29 fellowships with tuition reimbursements available (averaging $20,966 per year), 71 research assistantships with tuition reimbursements available (averaging $9,778 per year); teaching assistantships, career-related internships or fieldwork, institutionally sponsored loans, scholarships/grants, traineeships, health care benefits, tuition waivers (full and partial), and unspecified assistantships also available. Support available to part-time students. Financial award application deadline: 3/15; financial award applicants required to submit FAFSA. In 2017, 154 master's awarded. Offers homeland security (Certificate); international affairs (MIA, Certificate); national security affairs (Certificate); non-profit management (Certificate); public service and administration (MPSA). *Application deadline:* For fall admission, 1/15 for domestic and international students. *Application fee:* $50 ($90 for international students). Electronic applications accepted. *Application Contact:* Kathryn Meyer, Director of Recruitment and Admissions, 979-458-4767, Fax: 979-845-4155, E-mail: bushschooladmissions@tamu.edu. *Dean,* Dr. Mark Welsh, 979-862-8007, E-mail: mwelsh@tamu.edu.

College of Agriculture and Life Sciences Students: 998 full-time (501 women), 281 part-time (146 women); includes 215 minority (35 Black or African American, non-Hispanic/Latino; 3 American Indian or Alaska Native, non-Hispanic/Latino; 35 Asian, non-Hispanic/Latino; 125 Hispanic/Latino; 1 Native Hawaiian or other Pacific Islander, non-Hispanic/Latino; 16 Two or more races, non-Hispanic/Latino), 413 international. Average age 29. 588 applicants, 53% accepted, 241 enrolled. *Faculty:* 346. Expenses: Contact institution. *Financial support:* In 2017–18, 1,020 students received support, including 144 fellowships with tuition reimbursements available (averaging $19,821 per year), 480 research assistantships with tuition reimbursements available (averaging $10,298 per year), 352 teaching assistantships with tuition reimbursements available (averaging $9,554 per year); career-related internships or fieldwork, institutionally sponsored loans, scholarships/grants, traineeships, health care benefits, tuition waivers (full and partial), and unspecified assistantships also available. Support available to part-time students. Financial award application deadline: 3/15; financial award applicants required to submit FAFSA. In 2017, 248 master's, 126 doctorates awarded. *Program availability:* Part-time, blended/hybrid learning. Offers agricultural development (M Agr); agricultural economics (M Agr, MS, PhD); agricultural education (Ed D); agricultural leadership, education and communication (M Ed, MS, PhD); agricultural systems management (M Agr, MS); agriculture and life sciences (M Agr, M Ed, M Engr, MEIM, MNRD, MRRD, MS, MWSc, Ed D, PhD); agronomy (MS, PhD); animal breeding (MS, PhD); animal science (M Agr, MS, PhD); biochemistry (MS, PhD); biological and agricultural engineering (M Engr, MS, PhD); ecosystem science and management (M Agr, MNRD); entomology (MS, PhD); equine industry management (MEIM); food science and technology (M Agr, MS); forestry (MS, PhD); horticulture (M Agr, MS, PhD); nutrition (MS, PhD); physiology of reproduction (MS, PhD); plant pathology (MS, PhD); poultry science (M Agr, MS, PhD); recreation and resources development (MRRD); recreation, park, and tourism sciences (MS, PhD); soil science (MS, PhD); wildlife and fisheries sciences (MS, PhD); wildlife science (MWSc). *Application deadline:* For fall admission, 7/21 priority date for domestic students, 6/1 priority date for international students; for spring admission, 12/1 priority date for domestic students, 10/1 priority date for international students. Applications are processed on a rolling basis. *Application fee:* $50 ($90 for international students). Electronic applications accepted. *Application Contact:* Graduate Admissions, 979-845-1044, E-mail: graduate-admissions@tamu.edu. *Vice Chancellor and Dean for Agriculture and Life Sciences,* Dr. Mark A. Hussey, 979-845-4747, Fax: 979-845-9938, E-mail: mhussey@tamu.edu.

College of Architecture Students: 431 full-time (235 women), 55 part-time (18 women); includes 76 minority (10 Black or African American, non-Hispanic/Latino; 19 Asian, non-Hispanic/Latino; 45 Hispanic/Latino; 2 Two or more races, non-Hispanic/Latino), 227 international. Average age 28. 500 applicants, 70% accepted, 162 enrolled. *Faculty:* 108. Expenses: Contact institution. *Financial support:* In 2017–18, 349 students received support, including 11 fellowships with tuition reimbursements available (averaging $14,846 per year), 112 research assistantships with tuition reimbursements available (averaging $6,442 per year), 136 teaching assistantships with tuition reimbursements available (averaging $6,099 per year); career-related internships or fieldwork, institutionally sponsored loans, scholarships/grants, traineeships, health care benefits, tuition waivers (full and partial), and unspecified assistantships also available. Support available to part-time students. Financial award application deadline: 3/15; financial award applicants required to submit FAFSA. In 2017, 138 master's, 18 doctorates awarded. Offers architecture (M Arch, MS, PhD); construction management (MS); land and property development (MLPD); landscape architecture (MLA); urban and regional planning (MUP); urban and regional science (PhD); visualization (MFA, MS). *Application deadline:* For fall admission, 1/15 priority date for domestic and international students. Applications are processed on a rolling basis. *Application fee:* $50 ($90 for international students). Electronic applications accepted. *Application Contact:* Graduate Admissions, 979-458-0427, E-mail: admissions@tamu.edu. *Dean,* Dr. Jorge Vanegas, 979-845-1223, Fax: 979-845-4491, E-mail: jvanegas@arch.tamu.edu.

College of Dentistry Students: 499 full-time (251 women), 37 part-time (12 women); includes 275 minority (54 Black or African American, non-Hispanic/Latino; 2 American Indian or Alaska Native, non-Hispanic/Latino; 100 Asian, non-Hispanic/Latino; 109 Hispanic/Latino; 10 Two or more races, non-Hispanic/Latino), 30 international. Average age 27. *Faculty:* 44. Expenses: Contact institution. *Financial support:* In 2017–18, 235 students received support, including 32 research assistantships with tuition reimbursements available (averaging $8,712 per year), 43 teaching assistantships with tuition reimbursements available (averaging $14,231 per year); career-related internships or fieldwork, institutionally sponsored loans, scholarships/grants, traineeships, health care benefits, tuition waivers (full and partial), and unspecified assistantships also available. Support available to part-time students. Financial award applicants required to submit FAFSA. In 2017, 18 master's, 2 doctorates, 101 other advanced degrees awarded. Offers advanced education in general dentistry (Certificate); biomedical sciences (MS); dental hygiene (MS); dental public health (Certificate); endodontics (Certificate); maxillofacial surgery (Certificate); oral and maxillofacial pathology (Certificate); oral and maxillofacial radiology (Certificate); oral and maxillofacial surgery (Certificate); oral biology (MS, PhD); orthodontics (Certificate); pediatric dentistry (Certificate); periodontics (Certificate); prosthodontics (Certificate). *Application fee:* $35. Electronic applications accepted. *Application Contact:* Ernestine S. Lacy, Associate Dean for Student Affairs and Student Diversity, 214-828-8374, Fax: 214-874-4572, E-mail: eslacy@tamhsc.edu. *Dean,* Dr. Lawrence E. Wolinsky, 214-828-8300, E-mail: wolinsky@tamhsc.edu.

College of Education and Human Development Students: 671 full-time (470 women), 921 part-time (683 women); includes 532 minority (162 Black or African American, non-Hispanic/Latino; 5 American Indian or Alaska Native, non-Hispanic/Latino; 49 Asian, non-Hispanic/Latino; 282 Hispanic/Latino; 4 Native Hawaiian or other Pacific Islander, non-Hispanic/Latino; 30 Two or more races, non-Hispanic/Latino), 163 international. Average age 33. 580 applicants, 68% accepted, 282 enrolled. *Faculty:* 170. Expenses: Contact institution. *Financial support:* In 2017–18, 802 students received support, including 13 fellowships with tuition reimbursements available (averaging $22,861 per year), 221 research assistantships with tuition reimbursements available (averaging $10,462 per year), 132 teaching assistantships with tuition reimbursements available (averaging $9,872 per year); career-related internships or fieldwork, institutionally sponsored loans, scholarships/grants, traineeships, health care benefits, tuition waivers (full and partial), and unspecified assistantships also available. Support available to part-time students. Financial award application deadline: 3/15; financial award applicants required to submit FAFSA. In 2017, 526 master's, 76 doctorates awarded. *Program availability:* Part-time, evening/weekend, blended/hybrid learning. Offers athletic training (MS); bilingual education (M Ed, MS); counseling psychology (PhD); curriculum and instruction (M Ed, MS, Ed D, PhD); education and human development (M Ed, MS, Ed D, PhD); educational administration (M Ed, MS, Ed D, PhD); educational human resource development (MS, PhD); educational psychology (M Ed, MS, PhD); educational technology (M Ed); health education (MS, PhD); kinesiology (MS, PhD); school psychology (PhD); special education (M Ed, MS); sports management (MS). *Application deadline:* Applications are processed on a rolling basis. *Application fee:* $50 ($90 for international students). Electronic applications accepted. *Application Contact:* Dr. Beverly Irby, Professor and Associate Dean for Academic Affairs, 979-845-5311, E-mail: beverly.irby@tamu.edu. *Professor and Dean,* Dr. Joyce Alexander, 979-862-6649, E-mail: joycemalexander@tamu.edu.

College of Engineering Students: 3,080 full-time (655 women), 603 part-time (118 women); includes 447 minority (56 Black or African American, non-Hispanic/Latino; 1 American Indian or Alaska Native, non-Hispanic/Latino; 151 Asian, non-Hispanic/Latino; 197 Hispanic/Latino; 2 Native Hawaiian or other Pacific Islander, non-Hispanic/Latino; 40 Two or more races, non-Hispanic/Latino), 2,413 international. Average age 28. 9,253 applicants, 27% accepted, 1094 enrolled. *Faculty:* 479. Expenses: Contact institution. *Financial support:* In 2017–18, 2,605 students received support, including 277 fellowships with tuition reimbursements available (averaging $20,883 per year), 1,362 research assistantships with tuition reimbursements available (averaging $11,651 per year), 582 teaching assistantships with tuition reimbursements available (averaging $9,894 per year); career-related internships or fieldwork, institutionally sponsored loans, scholarships/grants, traineeships, health care benefits, tuition waivers (full and partial), and unspecified assistantships also available. Support available to part-time students. Financial award applicants required to submit FAFSA. In 2017, 849 master's, 260 doctorates awarded. *Program availability:* Part-time, online learning. Offers aerospace engineering (M Eng, MS, PhD); biomedical engineering (M Eng, MS, PhD); chemical engineering (M Eng, MS, PhD); civil engineering (M Eng, MS, PhD); computer engineering (M Eng, MS, PhD); computer science (MCS, MS, PhD); electrical engineering (M Eng, MS, PhD); engineering (M Eng, MCS, METM, MID, MS, PhD); engineering systems management (MS); industrial distribution (MID); industrial engineering (M Eng, MS, PhD); materials science and engineering (M Eng, MS, PhD); mechanical engineering (M Eng, MS, PhD); nuclear engineering (M Eng, MS, PhD); petroleum engineering (M Eng, MS, PhD); technical management (METM). *Application fee:* $50 ($90 for international students). Electronic applications accepted. *Application Contact:* Dr. John C. Criscione, Assistant Dean for Graduate Programs, 979-845-5428, E-mail: jccriscione@tamu.edu. *Dean and Vice Chancellor*, Dr. M. Katherine Banks, 979-845-1306, E-mail: k-banks@tamu.edu.

College of Geosciences Students: 261 full-time (106 women), 76 part-time (36 women); includes 47 minority (5 Black or African American, non-Hispanic/Latino; 10 Asian, non-Hispanic/Latino; 26 Hispanic/Latino; 6 Two or more races, non-Hispanic/Latino), 126 international. Average age 29. 352 applicants, 36% accepted, 78 enrolled. *Faculty:* 98. Expenses: Contact institution. *Financial support:* In 2017–18, 256 students received support, including 55 fellowships with tuition reimbursements available (averaging $16,014 per year), 123 research assistantships with tuition reimbursements available (averaging $11,493 per year), 94 teaching assistantships with tuition reimbursements available (averaging $10,522 per year); career-related internships or fieldwork, institutionally sponsored loans, traineeships, health care benefits, tuition waivers (full and partial), and unspecified assistantships also available. Support available to part-time students. Financial award application deadline: 3/15; financial award applicants required to submit FAFSA. In 2017, 56 master's, 32 doctorates awarded. *Program availability:* Part-time. Offers atmospheric sciences (MS, PhD); geography (MS, PhD); geology (MS, PhD); geophysics (MS, PhD); geosciences (MS, PhD); oceanography (MS, PhD). *Application deadline:* For fall admission, 1/1 priority date for domestic students; for spring admission, 8/15 for domestic students. Applications are processed on a rolling basis. *Application fee:* $50 ($90 for international students). Electronic applications accepted. *Application Contact:* Dr. Eric A. Riggs, Associate Professor/Associate Dean, 979-845-3651, E-mail: emriggs@geos.tamu.edu. *Dean*, Dr. Kate C. Miller, 979-845-3651, E-mail: dean@geosciences.tamu.edu.

College of Liberal Arts Students: 692 full-time (356 women), 143 part-time (78 women); includes 173 minority (33 Black or African American, non-Hispanic/Latino; 3 American Indian or Alaska Native, non-Hispanic/Latino; 26 Asian, non-Hispanic/Latino; 102 Hispanic/Latino; 9 Two or more races, non-Hispanic/Latino), 312 international. Average age 29. 955 applicants, 42% accepted, 221 enrolled. *Faculty:* 325. Expenses: Contact institution. *Financial support:* In 2017–18, 609 students received support, including 61 fellowships with tuition reimbursements available (averaging $28,229 per year), 130 research assistantships with tuition reimbursements available (averaging $11,188 per year), 365 teaching assistantships with tuition reimbursements available (averaging $11,270 per year); career-related internships or fieldwork, institutionally sponsored loans, scholarships/grants, traineeships, health care benefits, tuition waivers (full and partial), unspecified assistantships, and assistant lecturer positions also available. Support available to part-time students. Financial award application deadline: 3/15; financial award applicants required to submit FAFSA. In 2017, 133 master's, 97 doctorates awarded. *Program availability:* Part-time. Offers anthropology (MA, PhD); clinical psychology (PhD); communication (MA, PhD); economics (MS, PhD); English (MA, PhD); Hispanic studies (MA, PhD); history (MA, PhD); industrial/organizational psychology (PhD); liberal arts (MA, MS, PhD); maritime archaeology and conservation (MS); performance studies (MA); philosophy (MA, PhD); political science (MA, PhD); psychology (MS, PhD); sociology (MS, PhD). *Application fee:* $50 ($90 for international students). Electronic applications accepted. *Application Contact:* Dr. Patricia A. Hurley, Associate Dean for Faculty and Graduate Programs, 979-845-8541, Fax: 979-845-5164, E-mail: pat-hurley@tamu.edu. *Dean*, Dr. Pamela R. Matthews, 979-862-6797, Fax: 979-845-5164, E-mail: p-matthews@tamu.edu.

College of Medicine Students: 854 full-time (404 women), 15 part-time (13 women); includes 410 minority (28 Black or African American, non-Hispanic/Latino; 2 American Indian or Alaska Native, non-Hispanic/Latino; 268 Asian, non-Hispanic/Latino; 94 Hispanic/Latino; 1 Native Hawaiian or other Pacific Islander, non-Hispanic/Latino; 17 Two or more races, non-Hispanic/Latino), 67 international. Average age 27. 304 applicants, 82% accepted, 222 enrolled. *Faculty:* 92. Expenses: Contact institution. *Financial support:* In 2017–18, 329 students received support, including 124 research assistantships with tuition reimbursements available (averaging $15,092 per year), 2 teaching assistantships (averaging $9,721 per year); career-related internships or fieldwork, institutionally sponsored loans, scholarships/grants, traineeships, health care benefits, tuition waivers (full and partial), and unspecified assistantships also available. Support available to part-time students. Financial award applicants required to submit FAFSA. In 2017, 4 master's, 11 doctorates awarded. Offers education for healthcare professionals (MS); medical sciences (MS, PhD); medicine (MD). *Application deadline:* For fall admission, 9/30 for domestic students. *Application fee:* $200. Electronic applications accepted. *Application Contact:* Filomeno G. Maldonado, Associate Dean of Admissions, 979-436-0231, Fax: 979-436-0097, E-mail: fgmaldonado@medicine.tamhsc.edu. *Interim Senior Vice President and Chief Operating Officer*, Dr. Paul E. Ogden, MD, 979-436-0202, Fax: 979-436-0092, E-mail: ogden@medicine.tamhsc.edu.

College of Nursing Students: 9 full-time (all women), 47 part-time (all women); includes 14 minority (2 Asian, non-Hispanic/Latino; 12 Hispanic/Latino). Average age 34. *Faculty:* 19. Expenses: Contact institution. *Financial support:* In 2017–18, 8 students received support, including 2 fellowships (averaging $4,300 per year); career-related internships or fieldwork, institutionally sponsored loans, scholarships/grants, traineeships, health care benefits, tuition waivers (full and partial), and unspecified assistantships also available. Support available to part-time students. Financial award applicants required to submit FAFSA. In 2017, 27 master's awarded. Offers family nurse practitioner (MSN); forensic nursing (MSN); nursing education (MSN). *Application Contact:* Jennifer Frank, Program Coordinator for Recruitment and Admission, 979-436-0110, E-mail: conadmissions@tamhsc.edu. *Founding Dean*, Dr. Sharon A. Wilkerson, 979-436-0111, Fax: 979-436-0098, E-mail: wilkerson@tamhsc.edu.

College of Science Students: 872 full-time (239 women), 426 part-time (137 women); includes 216 minority (24 Black or African American, non-Hispanic/Latino; 1 American Indian or Alaska Native, non-Hispanic/Latino; 83 Asian, non-Hispanic/Latino; 83 Hispanic/Latino; 25 Two or more races, non-Hispanic/Latino), 478 international. Average age 30. 872 applicants, 58% accepted, 291 enrolled. *Faculty:* 304. Expenses: Contact institution. *Financial support:* In 2017–18, 778 students received support, including 109 fellowships with tuition reimbursements available (averaging $19,569 per year), 273 research assistantships with tuition reimbursements available (averaging $12,501 per year), 402 teaching assistantships with tuition reimbursements available (averaging $12,840 per year); career-related internships or fieldwork, institutionally sponsored loans, scholarships/grants, traineeships, health care benefits, tuition waivers (full and partial), and unspecified assistantships also available. Support available to part-time students. Financial award applicants required to submit FAFSA. In 2017, 143 master's, 128 doctorates awarded. *Program availability:* Part-time. Offers analytics (MS); applied physics (PhD); astronomy (MS, PhD); biology (MS, PhD); chemistry (MS, PhD); mathematics (MS, PhD); microbiology (MS, PhD); physics (MS, PhD); quantitative finance (MS); science (MS, PhD); statistics (MS, PhD). *Application fee:* $50 ($90 for international students). *Application Contact:* Mark Zoran, Associate Dean for Graduate Studies, 979-458-8001, Fax: 979-845-6077, E-mail: zoran@science.tamu.edu. *Dean*, Dr. Meigan Aronson, 979-845-8817, Fax: 979-845-6077, E-mail: maronson@science.tamu.edu.

College of Veterinary Medicine and Biomedical Sciences Students: 789 full-time (598 women), 44 part-time (33 women); includes 199 minority (24 Black or African American, non-Hispanic/Latino; 48 Asian, non-Hispanic/Latino; 108 Hispanic/Latino; 19 Two or more races, non-Hispanic/Latino), 57 international. Average age 26. 268 applicants, 84% accepted, 203 enrolled. *Faculty:* 137. Expenses: Contact institution. *Financial support:* In 2017–18, 706 students received support, including 18 fellowships with tuition reimbursements available (averaging $22,465 per year), 108 research assistantships with tuition reimbursements available (averaging $12,596 per year), 31 teaching assistantships with tuition reimbursements available (averaging $10,235 per year); career-related internships or fieldwork, institutionally sponsored loans, scholarships/grants, traineeships, health care benefits, tuition waivers (full and partial), unspecified assistantships, and clinical associateships also available. Support available to part-time students. Financial award application deadline: 3/15; financial award applicants required to submit FAFSA. In 2017, 90 master's, 24 doctorates awarded. *Program availability:* Part-time. Offers biomedical sciences (MS, PhD); science and technology journalism (MS); veterinary medicine (DVM); veterinary pathobiology (MS); veterinary public health-epidemiology (MS). *Application deadline:* For fall admission, 6/1 for domestic students, 3/1 for international students; for spring admission, 11/1 for domestic students, 8/1 for international students; for summer admission, 3/1 for domestic students, 12/1 for international students. *Application fee:* $50 ($90 for international students). *Application Contact:* Graduate Admissions, 979-845-1044, E-mail: admissions@tamu.edu. *Dean*, Dr. Eleanor M. Green, 979-845-5053, Fax: 979-845-5088, E-mail: emgreen@tamu.edu.

Galveston Campus Students: 124 full-time (57 women), 26 part-time (7 women); includes 29 minority (3 Black or African American, non-Hispanic/Latino; 5 Asian, non-Hispanic/Latino; 17 Hispanic/Latino; 4 Two or more races, non-Hispanic/Latino), 9 international. Average age 29. 52 applicants, 77% accepted, 27 enrolled. *Faculty:* 62. Expenses: Contact institution. *Financial support:* In 2017–18, 117 students received support, including 1 fellowship with tuition reimbursement available (averaging $51,000 per year), 40 research assistantships with tuition reimbursements available (averaging $8,445 per year), 66 teaching assistantships with tuition reimbursements available (averaging $10,807 per year). In 2017, 50 master's, 2 doctorates awarded. Offers marine biology (MS, PhD); marine resources management (MMRM); maritime administration and logistics (MMAL). *Application Contact:* Nicole Kinslow, Director of Graduate Studies, 409-740-4937, Fax: 409-740-4754, E-mail: kinslown@tamug.edu.

Irma Lerma Rangel College of Pharmacy Students: 453 full-time (267 women), 2 part-time (1 woman); includes 343 minority (35 Black or African American, non-Hispanic/Latino; 155 Asian, non-Hispanic/Latino; 144 Hispanic/Latino; 1 Native Hawaiian or other Pacific Islander, non-Hispanic/Latino; 8 Two or more races, non-Hispanic/Latino), 7 international. Average age 27. *Faculty:* 37. Expenses: Contact institution. *Financial support:* In 2017–18, 145 students received support. Career-related internships or fieldwork, institutionally sponsored loans, scholarships/grants, traineeships, health care benefits, tuition waivers (full and partial), and unspecified assistantships available. Support available to part-time students. Financial award applicants required to submit FAFSA. Offers pharmacy (Pharm D). *Application deadline:* For fall admission, 11/1 for domestic students. *Application fee:* $100. Electronic applications accepted. *Application Contact:* Maria de Leon, Director of Admission, 361-221-0642, E-mail: mdeleon@tamhsc.edu. *Dean*, Dr. Indra K. Reddy, 361-593-4273, Fax: 361-593-4929, E-mail: ireddy@pharmacy.tamhsc.edu.

Mays Business School Students: 1,146 full-time (469 women), 17 part-time (6 women); includes 213 minority (27 Black or African American, non-Hispanic/Latino; 5 American Indian or Alaska Native, non-Hispanic/Latino; 64 Asian, non-Hispanic/Latino; 101 Hispanic/Latino; 16 Two or more races, non-Hispanic/Latino), 274 international. Average age 27. 1,849 applicants, 27% accepted, 328 enrolled. *Faculty:* 113. Expenses: Contact institution. *Financial support:* In 2017–18, 792 students received support, including 51 fellowships with tuition reimbursements available (averaging $5,758 per year), 133 research assistantships with tuition reimbursements available (averaging $8,455 per year), 111 teaching assistantships with tuition reimbursements available (averaging $4,755 per year); career-related internships or fieldwork, institutionally sponsored loans, scholarships/grants, traineeships, health care benefits, tuition waivers, and unspecified assistantships also available. Support available to part-time students. Financial award application deadline: 3/15; financial award applicants required to submit FAFSA. In 2017, 752 master's awarded. Offers accounting (MS); business (MBA, MFM, MRE, MS); entrepreneurial leadership (MS); finance (MS); financial management (MFM); human resource management (MS); land economics and real estate (MRE); management information systems (MS); marketing (MS). *Application deadline:* Applications are processed on a rolling basis. *Application fee:* $50 ($90 for international students). Electronic applications accepted. *Application Contact:* Director, MBA Program, 979-845-4714, Fax: 979-862-2393, E-mail: msprogram@mays.tamu.edu. *Dean*, Dr. Eli Jones, 979-845-4711, Fax: 979-845-6639, E-mail: elijones@tamu.edu.

School of Law Students: 404 full-time (206 women), 58 part-time (19 women); includes 120 minority (33 Black or African American, non-Hispanic/Latino; 2 American Indian or Alaska Native, non-Hispanic/Latino; 9 Asian, non-Hispanic/Latino; 73 Hispanic/Latino; 3 Two or more races, non-Hispanic/Latino), 4 international. Average age 29. 541 applicants, 100% accepted, 178 enrolled. *Faculty:* 79. Expenses: Contact institution.

Financial support: In 2017–18, 403 students received support, including 6 fellowships with tuition reimbursements available (averaging $29,510 per year); career-related internships or fieldwork, institutionally sponsored loans, scholarships/grants, traineeships, health care benefits, and tuition waivers (full and partial) also available. Support available to part-time students. Financial award applicants required to submit FAFSA. Offers intellectual property (M Jur); jurisprudence (M Jur); law (JD). *Application deadline:* For fall admission, 7/1 for domestic students. Applications are processed on a rolling basis. *Application fee:* $55. *Application Contact:* Law School Admissions, 817-212-4040, E-mail: law-admissions@law.tamu.edu. *Dean*, Dr. Andrew P. Morriss, 817-212-4139, Fax: 817-212-4139, E-mail: amorriss@law.tamu.edu.

School of Public Health Students: 279 full-time (196 women), 86 part-time (56 women); includes 153 minority (48 Black or African American, non-Hispanic/Latino; 36 Asian, non-Hispanic/Latino; 62 Hispanic/Latino; 7 Two or more races, non-Hispanic/Latino), 77 international. Average age 29. 179 applicants, 96% accepted, 148 enrolled. *Faculty:* 56. Expenses: Contact institution. *Financial support:* In 2017–18, 203 students received support, including 62 research assistantships with tuition reimbursements available (averaging $10,041 per year), 25 teaching assistantships with tuition reimbursements available (averaging $12,913 per year); career-related internships or fieldwork, institutionally sponsored loans, scholarships/grants, traineeships, health care benefits, tuition waivers (full and partial), and unspecified assistantships also available. Support available to part-time students. Financial award applicants required to submit FAFSA. In 2017, 124 master's, 8 doctorates awarded. *Program availability:* Part-time, blended/hybrid learning. Offers biostatistics (MPH, MSPH); environmental health (MPH, MSPH); epidemiology (MPH, MSPH); executive health administration (MHA); health administration (MHA); health policy and management (MPH, MSPH); health promotion and community health sciences (MPH); health services research (PhD); occupational safety and health (MPH). *Application fee:* $120. Electronic applications accepted. *Application Contact:* Erin E. Schneider, Associate Director of Admissions and Recruitment, 979-436-9380, E-mail: eschneider@sph.tamhsc.edu. *Dean*, Dr. Jay Maddock, 979-436-9322, Fax: 979-458-1878, E-mail: maddock@tamhsc.edu.

TEXAS A&M UNIVERSITY–CENTRAL TEXAS, Killeen, TX 76549

General Information State-supported, coed, upper-level institution. CGS member.

GRADUATE UNITS

Graduate Studies and Research

TEXAS A&M UNIVERSITY–COMMERCE, Commerce, TX 75429

General Information State-supported, coed, university. CGS member. *Enrollment:* 12,490 graduate, professional, and undergraduate students; 1,285 full-time matriculated graduate/professional students (754 women), 3,174 part-time matriculated graduate/professional students (2,103 women). *Enrollment by degree level:* 3,755 master's, 609 doctoral, 95 other advanced degrees. *Graduate faculty:* 253 full-time (104 women), 71 part-time/adjunct (39 women). Tuition, state resident: full-time $3630. Tuition, nonresident: full-time $11,100. *Required fees:* $2564. Tuition and fees vary according to course load, degree level and program. *Graduate housing:* Rooms and/or apartments available on a first-come, first-served basis to single and married students. Typical cost: $8326 (including board) for single students; $8326 (including board) for married students. Room and board charges vary according to board plan and housing facility selected. *Student services:* Campus employment opportunities, campus safety program, career counseling, child daycare facilities, exercise/wellness program, free psychological counseling, international student services, multicultural affairs office, services for students with disabilities, teacher training, writing training. *Library facilities:* Gee Library.

Computer facilities: A campuswide network can be accessed from student residence rooms and from off campus. Online class registration is available.
Website: http://www.tamuc.edu/

General Application Contact: Kimberly Stringer, Graduate Liaison, 903-468-3066, E-mail: kimberly.stringer@tamuc.edu.

GRADUATE UNITS

College of Agricultural Sciences and Natural Resources Students: 16 full-time (8 women), 28 part-time (20 women); includes 7 minority (2 Black or African American, non-Hispanic/Latino; 2 Asian, non-Hispanic/Latino; 1 Hispanic/Latino; 2 Two or more races, non-Hispanic/Latino), 4 international. Average age 27. 27 applicants, 59% accepted, 13 enrolled. *Faculty:* 6 full-time (0 women), 2 part-time/adjunct (both women). Expenses: Contact institution. *Financial support:* In 2017–18, 4 students received support, including 6 research assistantships with partial tuition reimbursements available (averaging $8,000 per year), 6 teaching assistantships with partial tuition reimbursements available (averaging $8,000 per year); career-related internships or fieldwork, Federal Work-Study, institutionally sponsored loans, scholarships/grants, health care benefits, and unspecified assistantships also available. Financial award application deadline: 5/1; financial award applicants required to submit FAFSA. In 2017, 25 master's awarded. *Program availability:* Part-time, evening/weekend, 100% online, blended/hybrid learning. Offers agricultural sciences (MS). *Application deadline:* For fall admission, 6/1 priority date for international students; for spring admission, 10/15 priority date for international students; for summer admission, 10/15 priority date for international students. Applications are processed on a rolling basis. *Application fee:* $50 ($75 for international students). Electronic applications accepted. *Application Contact:* Vicky Turner, Doctoral Degree and Special Programs Coordinator, 903-886-5167, E-mail: vicky.turner@tamuc.edu. *Dean*, Dr. Randy Harp, 903-886-5351, Fax: 903-886-5990, E-mail: randy.harp@tamuc.edu.

College of Business Students: 479 full-time (248 women), 1,056 part-time (556 women); includes 660 minority (281 Black or African American, non-Hispanic/Latino; 4 American Indian or Alaska Native, non-Hispanic/Latino; 120 Asian, non-Hispanic/Latino; 222 Hispanic/Latino; 33 Two or more races, non-Hispanic/Latino), 224 international. Average age 33. 930 applicants, 61% accepted, 363 enrolled. *Faculty:* 50 full-time (19 women), 7 part-time/adjunct (0 women). Expenses: Contact institution. *Financial support:* In 2017–18, 46 students received support, including 20 research assistantships with partial tuition reimbursements available (averaging $8,000 per year); Federal Work-Study, institutionally sponsored loans, scholarships/grants, health care benefits, and unspecified assistantships also available. Financial award application deadline: 5/1; financial award applicants required to submit FAFSA. In 2017, 686 master's awarded. *Program availability:* Part-time, evening/weekend, 100% online, blended/hybrid learning. Offers accounting (MSA); business administration (MBA); business analytics (MS); finance (MSF); management (MS); marketing (MS). *Application deadline:* For fall admission, 6/1 priority date for international students; for spring admission, 10/15 priority date for international students; for summer admission, 3/15 priority date for international students. Applications are processed on a rolling basis. *Application fee:* $50 ($75 for international students). Electronic applications accepted. *Application Contact:* Vicky Turner, Doctoral Degree and Special Programs Coordinator, 903-886-5167, E-mail: vicky.turner@tamuc.edu. *Dean of College of Business*, Dr. Shanan Gwaltney Gibson, 903-886-5191, Fax: 903-886-5650, E-mail: shanan.gibson@tamuc.edu.

College of Education and Human Services Students: 400 full-time (310 women), 1,400 part-time (1,117 women); includes 724 minority (412 Black or African American, non-Hispanic/Latino; 8 American Indian or Alaska Native, non-Hispanic/Latino; 24 Asian, non-Hispanic/Latino; 220 Hispanic/Latino; 60 Two or more races, non-Hispanic/Latino), 18 international. Average age 37. 951 applicants, 46% accepted, 331 enrolled. *Faculty:* 91 full-time (51 women), 38 part-time/adjunct (31 women). Expenses: Contact institution. *Financial support:* In 2017–18, 84 students received support, including 40 research assistantships with partial tuition reimbursements available (averaging $10,800 per year), 12 teaching assistantships with partial tuition reimbursements available (averaging $13,000 per year); career-related internships or fieldwork, Federal Work-Study, institutionally sponsored loans, scholarships/grants, health care benefits, and unspecified assistantships also available. Financial award application deadline: 6/15; financial award applicants required to submit FAFSA. In 2017, 564 master's, 24 doctorates awarded. *Program availability:* Part-time, evening/weekend, 100% online, blended/hybrid learning. Offers counseling (M Ed, MS, PhD); early childhood education (M Ed, MS); educational administration (M Ed, MS, Ed D); educational psychology (PhD); educational technology leadership (M Ed, MS); educational technology library science (M Ed, MS); elementary education (M Ed); health, kinesiology and sports studies (MS); higher education (MS, Ed D); psychology (MS); reading (M Ed, MS); secondary education (M Ed, MS); social work (MSW); special education (M Ed, MS); supervision, curriculum and instruction-elementary education (Ed D); training and development (MS). *Application deadline:* For fall admission, 6/1 priority date for international students; for spring admission, 10/15 priority date for international students; for summer admission, 3/15 priority date for international students. Applications are processed on a rolling basis. *Application fee:* $50. Electronic applications accepted. *Application Contact:* Vicky Turner, Doctoral Degree and Special Programs Coordinator, 903-886-5167, E-mail: vicky.turner@tamuc.edu. *Dean*, Dr. Timothy Letzring, 903-886-5181, Fax: 903-886-5905, E-mail: tim.letzring@tamuc.edu.

College of Humanities, Social Sciences and Arts Students: 133 full-time (85 women), 439 part-time (311 women); includes 204 minority (79 Black or African American, non-Hispanic/Latino; 4 American Indian or Alaska Native, non-Hispanic/Latino; 9 Asian, non-Hispanic/Latino; 98 Hispanic/Latino; 14 Two or more races, non-Hispanic/Latino), 26 international. Average age 36. 261 applicants, 50% accepted, 113 enrolled. *Faculty:* 56 full-time (26 women), 10 part-time/adjunct (5 women). Expenses: Contact institution. *Financial support:* In 2017–18, 43 students received support, including 9 research assistantships with partial tuition reimbursements available (averaging $9,000 per year), 68 teaching assistantships with partial tuition reimbursements available (averaging $9,000 per year); Federal Work-Study, institutionally sponsored loans, scholarships/grants, health care benefits, and unspecified assistantships also available. Financial award application deadline: 5/1; financial award applicants required to submit FAFSA. In 2017, 105 master's, 5 doctorates awarded. *Program availability:* Part-time. Offers applied criminology (MS); applied linguistics (MA, MS); art (MA, MFA); computational linguistics (Graduate Certificate); creative writing (Graduate Certificate); criminal justice management (Graduate Certificate); criminal justice studies (Graduate Certificate); English (MA, MS, PhD); film studies (Graduate Certificate); history (MA, MS); history of Christianity (Graduate Certificate); Holocaust studies (Graduate Certificate); homeland security (Graduate Certificate); music education (MM); music performance (MM); political science (MA, MS); public history (Graduate Certificate); sociology (MS); Spanish (MA); studies in children's and adolescent literature and culture (Graduate Certificate); teaching English to speakers of other languages (Graduate Certificate); theater (MA, MS); world history (Graduate Certificate). *Application deadline:* Applications are processed on a rolling basis. *Application fee:* $50. Electronic applications accepted. *Application Contact:* Vicky Turner, Doctoral Degree and Special Programs Coordinator, 903-886-5167, E-mail: vicky.turner@tamuc.edu. *Interim Dean*, Dr. William F. Kuracina, 903-886-5166, Fax: 903-886-5774, E-mail: william.kuracina@tamuc.edu.

College of Science and Engineering Students: 257 full-time (103 women), 251 part-time (99 women); includes 77 minority (23 Black or African American, non-Hispanic/Latino; 1 American Indian or Alaska Native, non-Hispanic/Latino; 12 Asian, non-Hispanic/Latino; 31 Hispanic/Latino; 10 Two or more races, non-Hispanic/Latino), 289 international. Average age 29. 481 applicants, 52% accepted, 105 enrolled. *Faculty:* 46 full-time (5 women), 14 part-time/adjunct (1 woman). Expenses: Contact institution. *Financial support:* In 2017–18, 66 students received support, including 11 research assistantships with partial tuition reimbursements available (averaging $8,000 per year), 41 teaching assistantships with partial tuition reimbursements available (averaging $8,000 per year); scholarships/grants, health care benefits, and unspecified assistantships also available. Financial award application deadline: 5/1; financial award applicants required to submit FAFSA. In 2017, 341 master's awarded. *Program availability:* Part-time, 100% online, blended/hybrid learning. Offers biological sciences (MS); broadfield science biology (MS); broadfield science chemistry (MS); broadfield science physics (MS); chemistry (MS); computational linguistics (Graduate Certificate); computational science (MS); computer science (MS); environmental science (Graduate Certificate); mathematics (MS); physics (MS); technology management (MS). *Application deadline:* For fall admission, 6/1 priority date for international students; for spring admission, 10/15 priority date for international students; for summer admission, 3/15 priority date for international students. Applications are processed on a rolling basis. *Application fee:* $50 ($75 for international students). Electronic applications accepted. *Application Contact:* Dayla Burgin, Graduate Student Services Coordinator, 903-886-5134, E-mail: dayla.burgin@tamuc.edu. *Dean*, Dr. Brent L. Donham, 903-886-5390, Fax: 903-886-5199, E-mail: brent.donham@tamuc.edu.

TEXAS A&M UNIVERSITY–CORPUS CHRISTI, Corpus Christi, TX 78412

General Information State-supported, coed, university. CGS member. *Enrollment:* 12,236 graduate, professional, and undergraduate students; 558 full-time matriculated graduate/professional students (342 women), 1,479 part-time matriculated graduate/professional students (990 women). *Enrollment by degree level:* 1,759 master's, 233 doctoral, 45 other advanced degrees. *Graduate faculty:* 268 full-time (112 women), 124 part-time/adjunct (58 women). Tuition, state resident: full-time $3568; part-time $198.24 per credit hour. Tuition, nonresident: full-time $11,038; part-time $613.24 per credit hour. *Required fees:* $2129; $1422.58 per semester. Tuition and fees vary according to program. *Graduate housing:* Room and/or apartments available on a first-come, first-served basis to single students; on-campus housing not available to married students. Housing application deadline: 5/1. *Student services:* Campus employment opportunities, campus safety program, career counseling, exercise/wellness program, free psychological counseling, grant writing training, international student services, low-cost health insurance, multicultural affairs office, services for students with disabilities, teacher training, writing training. *Library facilities:* Mary and Jeff Bell Library. *Collection:*

Books: 329,340 (physical), 145,756 (digital/electronic); Serial titles: 10,348 (physical), 80,843 (digital/electronic); Databases: 271. Weekly public service hours: 106; students can reserve study rooms.

Computer facilities: 1,236 computers available on campus for general student use. A campuswide network can be accessed from student residence rooms and from off campus. Online class registration is available.
Website: http://www.tamucc.edu/

General Application Contact: Maria Fonseca, Graduate Admissions Coordinator, 361-825-2177, Fax: 361-825-2755, E-mail: gradweb@tamucc.edu.

GRADUATE UNITS

College of Graduate Studies Students: 558 full-time (342 women), 1,479 part-time (990 women); includes 1,104 minority (157 Black or African American, non-Hispanic/Latino; 3 American Indian or Alaska Native, non-Hispanic/Latino; 119 Asian, non-Hispanic/Latino; 792 Hispanic/Latino; 33 Two or more races, non-Hispanic/Latino), 194 international. Average age 34. 1,505 applicants, 53% accepted, 650 enrolled. *Faculty:* 268 full-time (112 women), 124 part-time/adjunct (58 women). Expenses: Contact institution. *Financial support:* Research assistantships, teaching assistantships, career-related internships or fieldwork, institutionally sponsored loans, scholarships/grants, health care benefits, and unspecified assistantships available. Support available to part-time students. Financial award application deadline: 3/15; financial award applicants required to submit FAFSA. In 2017, 649 master's, 32 doctorates awarded. *Program availability:* Part-time, evening/weekend, 100% online, blended/hybrid learning. *Application deadline:* For fall admission, 7/15 priority date for domestic students, 5/1 priority date for international students; for spring admission, 11/15 priority date for domestic students, 9/1 priority date for international students. Applications are processed on a rolling basis. *Application fee:* $50 ($70 for international students). Electronic applications accepted. *Application Contact:* Sandra Kureska, Director, Graduate Studies, 361-825-3883, Fax: 361-825-2755, E-mail: gradweb@tamucc.edu. *Dean, College of Graduate Studies*, Dr. JoAnn Canales, 361-825-3847, Fax: 361-825-2755, E-mail: joann.canales@tamucc.edu.

College of Business Students: 107 full-time (50 women), 583 part-time (283 women); includes 259 minority (80 Black or African American, non-Hispanic/Latino; 85 Asian, non-Hispanic/Latino; 83 Hispanic/Latino; 11 Two or more races, non-Hispanic/Latino), 77 international. Average age 34. 485 applicants, 57% accepted, 236 enrolled. *Faculty:* 31 full-time (11 women), 2 part-time/adjunct (0 women). Expenses: Contact institution. *Financial support:* Research assistantships, teaching assistantships, career-related internships or fieldwork, Federal Work-Study, institutionally sponsored loans, scholarships/grants, health care benefits, and unspecified assistantships available. Support available to part-time students. Financial award application deadline: 3/15; financial award applicants required to submit FAFSA. In 2017, 310 master's awarded. *Program availability:* Part-time, evening/weekend, 100% online, blended/hybrid learning. Offers accounting (M Acc); business (MBA); finance (MBA); health care administration (MBA); international business (MBA). *Application deadline:* For fall admission, 7/15 priority date for domestic students, 5/1 priority date for international students; for spring admission, 11/15 priority date for domestic students, 9/1 priority date for international students; for summer admission, 4/15 priority date for domestic and international students. Applications are processed on a rolling basis. *Application fee:* $50 ($70 for international students). Electronic applications accepted. *Application Contact:* Sharon Polansky, Director of Master's Programs, 361-825-3448, Fax: 361-825-2755, E-mail: gradweb@tamucc.edu. *Dean*, Dr. John Gamble, 361-825-6045, Fax: 361-825-2725, E-mail: john.gamble@tamucc.edu.

College of Education and Human Development Students: 160 full-time (127 women), 366 part-time (293 women); includes 279 minority (40 Black or African American, non-Hispanic/Latino; 3 Asian, non-Hispanic/Latino; 228 Hispanic/Latino; 8 Two or more races, non-Hispanic/Latino), 18 international. Average age 35. 296 applicants, 65% accepted, 155 enrolled. *Faculty:* 50 full-time (29 women), 29 part-time/adjunct (18 women). Expenses: Contact institution. *Financial support:* Research assistantships, teaching assistantships, career-related internships or fieldwork, Federal Work-Study, institutionally sponsored loans, scholarships/grants, health care benefits, and unspecified assistantships available. Support available to part-time students. Financial award application deadline: 3/15; financial award applicants required to submit FAFSA. In 2017, 103 master's, 27 doctorates awarded. *Program availability:* Part-time, evening/weekend, blended/hybrid learning. Offers counseling (MS); counselor education (PhD); curriculum and instruction (MS, PhD); early childhood education (MS); educational administration (MS); educational leadership (Ed D); elementary education (MS); instructional design and educational technology (MS); kinesiology (MS); reading (MS); secondary education (MS); special education (MS). *Application deadline:* For fall admission, 7/15 priority date for domestic students, 5/1 priority date for international students; for spring admission, 11/15 priority date for domestic students, 9/1 priority date for international students. Applications are processed on a rolling basis. *Application fee:* $50 ($70 for international students). Electronic applications accepted. *Application Contact:* Graduate Admissions Coordinator, 361-825-2177, Fax: 361-825-2755, E-mail: gradweb@tamucc.edu. *Dean*, Dr. David Scott, 361-825-2660, E-mail: david.scott@tamucc.edu.

College of Liberal Arts Students: 83 full-time (56 women), 109 part-time (78 women); includes 112 minority (9 Black or African American, non-Hispanic/Latino; 100 Hispanic/Latino; 3 Two or more races, non-Hispanic/Latino). Average age 32. 119 applicants, 67% accepted, 65 enrolled. *Faculty:* 76 full-time (39 women), 9 part-time/adjunct (4 women). Expenses: Contact institution. *Financial support:* Research assistantships, teaching assistantships, career-related internships or fieldwork, Federal Work-Study, institutionally sponsored loans, scholarships/grants, health care benefits, and unspecified assistantships available. Support available to part-time students. Financial award application deadline: 3/15; financial award applicants required to submit FAFSA. In 2017, 65 master's awarded. *Program availability:* Part-time, evening/weekend. Offers clinical psychology (MA); communication (MA); English (MA); general psychology (MA); history (MA); psychology (MA); public administration (MPA); studio art (MFA). *Application deadline:* For fall admission, 7/15 for domestic students, 5/1 for international students; for spring admission, 11/15 priority date for domestic students, 9/1 priority date for international students. Applications are processed on a rolling basis. *Application fee:* $50 ($70 for international students). Electronic applications accepted. *Application Contact:* Graduate Admissions Coordinator, 361-825-2177, Fax: 361-825-2755, E-mail: gradweb@tamucc.edu. *Dean*, Dr. Mark Hartlaub, 361-825-2659, Fax: 361-825-5844, E-mail: mark.hartlaub@tamucc.edu.

College of Nursing and Health Sciences Students: 7 full-time (all women), 364 part-time (307 women); includes 194 minority (25 Black or African American, non-Hispanic/Latino; 26 Asian, non-Hispanic/Latino; 134 Hispanic/Latino; 9 Two or more races, non-Hispanic/Latino). Average age 38. 360 applicants, 33% accepted, 112 enrolled. *Faculty:* 17 full-time (16 women), 21 part-time/adjunct (15 women). Expenses: Contact institution. *Financial support:* Research assistantships, teaching assistantships, career-related internships or fieldwork, Federal Work-Study, institutionally sponsored loans, scholarships/grants, health care benefits, and unspecified assistantships available. Support available to part-time students. Financial award application deadline: 3/15; financial award applicants required to submit FAFSA. In 2017, 98 master's awarded. *Program availability:* Part-time, evening/weekend, online only, 100% online. Offers family nurse practitioner (MSN); leadership in nursing systems (MSN); nurse educator (MSN); nursing practice (DNP). *Application deadline:* For fall admission, 4/15 for domestic and international students; for spring admission, 1/7 for domestic and international students; for summer admission, 5/27 for domestic and international students. Applications are processed on a rolling basis. *Application fee:* $50 ($70 for international students). Electronic applications accepted. *Application Contact:* Graduate Admissions Coordinator, 361-825-2177, Fax: 361-825-2755, E-mail: gradweb@tamucc.edu. *Dean*, Dr. Julie Anne Hoff, 361-825-2275, E-mail: julie.hoff@tamucc.edu.

College of Science and Engineering Students: 201 full-time (102 women), 56 part-time (28 women); includes 33 minority (3 Black or African American, non-Hispanic/Latino; 3 American Indian or Alaska Native, non-Hispanic/Latino; 5 Asian, non-Hispanic/Latino; 20 Hispanic/Latino; 2 Two or more races, non-Hispanic/Latino), 84 international. Average age 29. 245 applicants, 56% accepted, 82 enrolled. *Faculty:* 94 full-time (17 women), 63 part-time/adjunct (21 women). Expenses: Contact institution. *Financial support:* Research assistantships, teaching assistantships, career-related internships or fieldwork, Federal Work-Study, institutionally sponsored loans, scholarships/grants, health care benefits, and unspecified assistantships available. Support available to part-time students. Financial award application deadline: 3/15; financial award applicants required to submit FAFSA. In 2017, 73 master's, 5 doctorates awarded. *Program availability:* Part-time, evening/weekend. Offers biology (MS, PhD); chemistry (MS); coastal and marine system science (MS, PhD); computer science (MS); environmental science (MS); fisheries and mariculture (MS); geospatial computing sciences (PhD); geospatial surveying engineering (MS); marine biology (MS, PhD); mathematics (MS). *Application deadline:* For fall admission, 7/15 priority date for domestic students, 5/1 priority date for international students; for spring admission, 11/15 priority date for domestic students, 9/1 priority date for international students. Applications are processed on a rolling basis. *Application fee:* $50 ($70 for international students). Electronic applications accepted. *Application Contact:* Graduate Admissions Coordinator, 361-825-2177, Fax: 361-825-2755, E-mail: gradweb@tamucc.edu. *Dean*, Dr. Frank Pezold, 361-825-2349, E-mail: frank.pezold@tamucc.edu.

TEXAS A&M UNIVERSITY–KINGSVILLE, Kingsville, TX 78363

General Information State-supported, coed, university. *Graduate housing:* Room and/or apartments available on a first-come, first-served basis to single students; on-campus housing not available to married students. Housing application deadline: 8/1. *Research affiliation:* American Chemical Society (chemistry: the use of terminally-functionalized atactic-polypropylene oligomers as supports for catalysis), Texas Citrus Producers Board (agriculture: citrus center grapefruit research), ExxonMobil, East Wildlife Foundation (agriculture: bird populations, deer research), The Brown Foundation (agriculture: invasive grass research), Wildlife Pharmaceuticals, Inc. (agriculture: deer).

GRADUATE UNITS

College of Graduate Studies *Program availability:* Part-time, online learning. Electronic applications accepted.

College of Arts and Sciences Offers arts and sciences (MA, MM, MS); biology (MS); chemistry (MS); communication sciences and disorders (MS); criminology (MS); cultural studies (MA); elementary music (MM); English (MA, MS); Hispanic culture (PhD); instrumental (MM); instrumental performance (MM); mathematics (MS); music (MM); music education (MM); psychology (MA, MS); sociology (MA, MS); Spanish (MA); statistical analytics, computing and modeling (MS); vocal (MM); vocal performance (MM). Electronic applications accepted.

College of Business Administration *Program availability:* Online only, 100% online, blended/hybrid learning. Offers business administration (MBA). Electronic applications accepted.

College of Education and Human Performance *Program availability:* 100% online, blended/hybrid learning. Offers adult education (M Ed); bilingual education (M Ed, Ed D); counseling and guidance (MA, MS); early childhood education (M Ed); education and human performance (M Ed, MA, MS, Ed D, Certificate); educational administration (MA, MS); educational leadership (Ed D); health and kinesiology (MA, MS); instructional technology (MS); reading specialization (MS); science in education (MS); special education (M Ed). Electronic applications accepted.

Dick and Mary Lewis Kleberg College of Agriculture, Natural Resources and Human Sciences Offers agribusiness (MS); agricultural science (MS); agriculture, natural resources and human sciences (MS, PhD); animal science (MS); horticulture (PhD); human sciences (MS); plant and soil science (MS); ranch management (MS); range and wildlife management (MS); wildlife science (PhD). Electronic applications accepted.

Frank H. Dotterweich College of Engineering Offers chemical engineering (ME, MS); civil engineering (ME, MS); computer science (MS); electrical engineering (ME, MS); engineering (ME, MS, PhD); environmental engineering (ME, MS, PhD); industrial engineering (ME, MS); industrial management (MS); mechanical engineering (ME, MS); natural gas engineering (ME, MS); sustainable energy systems engineering (PhD). Electronic applications accepted.

TEXAS A&M UNIVERSITY–SAN ANTONIO, San Antonio, TX 78224

General Information State-supported, coed, comprehensive institution. *Enrollment by degree level:* 920 master's. *Graduate faculty:* 58 full-time (30 women), 17 part-time/adjunct (7 women). Tuition, state resident: full-time $3475; part-time $1930 per semester. Tuition, nonresident: full-time $10,945; part-time $6080 per semester. *Required fees:* $2148; $1412 per year. $706 per semester. Tuition and fees vary according to course load. *Graduate housing:* On-campus housing not available.
Website: http://www.tamusa.edu/

General Application Contact: Caitie Garza, Graduate Admissions Coordinator, 210-784-1300, E-mail: beajaguar@tamusa.edu.

GRADUATE UNITS

Department of Counseling, Health and Kinesiology Students: 48 full-time (35 women), 146 part-time (118 women); includes 135 minority (24 Black or African American, non-Hispanic/Latino; 3 Asian, non-Hispanic/Latino; 103 Hispanic/Latino; 5 Two or more races, non-Hispanic/Latino), 2 international. Average age 34. 201 applicants, 56% accepted, 62 enrolled. *Faculty:* 12 full-time (5 women), 6 part-time/adjunct (4 women). Expenses: Contact institution. *Financial support:* In 2017–18,

10 students received support. Federal Work-Study, scholarships/grants, and tuition waivers available. Financial award application deadline: 3/15; financial award applicants required to submit FAFSA. In 2017, 68 master's awarded. *Program availability:* Part-time, evening/weekend, online learning. Offers clinical mental health counseling (MA); counseling and guidance (MA); kinesiology (MS); marriage and family counseling (MA). *Application deadline:* For fall admission, 3/15 priority date for domestic and international students; for spring admission, 11/1 priority date for domestic and international students; for summer admission, 4/1 priority date for domestic and international students. Applications are processed on a rolling basis. *Application fee:* $35 ($50 for international students). Electronic applications accepted. *Application Contact:* Caitie Garza, Graduate Admissions Coordinator, 210-784-1300, E-mail: beajaguar@tamusa.edu. *Department Chair*, Dr. Suzanne Mudge.

Department of Educator and Leadership Preparation Students: 24 full-time (21 women), 188 part-time (143 women); includes 163 minority (7 Black or African American, non-Hispanic/Latino; 1 Asian, non-Hispanic/Latino; 149 Hispanic/Latino; 6 Two or more races, non-Hispanic/Latino), 1 international. Average age 36. 191 applicants, 62% accepted, 67 enrolled. *Faculty:* 19 full-time (14 women), 8 part-time/adjunct (2 women). Expenses: Contact institution. *Financial support:* In 2017–18, 16 students received support. Research assistantships, Federal Work-Study, scholarships/grants, and tuition waivers available. Financial award application deadline: 3/15; financial award applicants required to submit FAFSA. In 2017, 70 master's awarded. *Program availability:* Part-time, evening/weekend, online learning. Offers bilingual education (MS); early childhood education (M Ed); educational administration (MA); reading specialization (MS); special education (M Ed). *Application deadline:* For fall admission, 3/15 priority date for domestic and international students; for spring admission, 11/1 priority date for domestic and international students; for summer admission, 4/1 priority date for domestic and international students. Applications are processed on a rolling basis. *Application fee:* $35 ($50 for international students). Electronic applications accepted. *Application Contact:* Caitie Garza, Graduate Admissions Coordinator, 210-784-1300, E-mail: beajaguar@tamusa.edu. *Department Chair*, Dr. Debbie Vera.

School of Arts and Sciences Students: 6 full-time (all women), 13 part-time (9 women); includes 13 minority (1 Black or African American, non-Hispanic/Latino; 11 Hispanic/Latino; 1 Two or more races, non-Hispanic/Latino). Average age 31. 20 applicants, 40% accepted, 4 enrolled. *Faculty:* 6 full-time (4 women). Expenses: Contact institution. *Financial support:* Federal Work-Study, scholarships/grants, and tuition waivers available. Financial award application deadline: 3/15; financial award applicants required to submit FAFSA. In 2017, 5 master's awarded. *Program availability:* Part-time, evening/weekend, online learning. Offers English (MA). *Application deadline:* For fall admission, 3/15 priority date for domestic and international students; for spring admission, 11/1 priority date for domestic and international students; for summer admission, 4/1 priority date for domestic and international students. Applications are processed on a rolling basis. *Application fee:* $35 ($50 for international students). Electronic applications accepted. *Application Contact:* Caitie Garza, Graduate Admissions Coordinator, 210-784-1300, E-mail: beajaguar@tamusa.edu. *Graduate Coordinator*, Dr. Katherine Gillen.

School of Business Students: 104 full-time (54 women), 391 part-time (200 women); includes 355 minority (43 Black or African American, non-Hispanic/Latino; 21 Asian, non-Hispanic/Latino; 280 Hispanic/Latino; 2 Native Hawaiian or other Pacific Islander, non-Hispanic/Latino; 9 Two or more races, non-Hispanic/Latino), 11 international. Average age 32. 365 applicants, 71% accepted, 160 enrolled. *Faculty:* 19 full-time (7 women), 2 part-time/adjunct (1 woman). Expenses: Contact institution. *Financial support:* In 2017–18, 29 students received support. Federal Work-Study, scholarships/grants, and tuition waivers available. Financial award application deadline: 3/15; financial award applicants required to submit FAFSA. In 2017, 128 master's awarded. *Program availability:* Part-time, evening/weekend, online learning. Offers business administration (MBA); professional accounting (MPA). *Application deadline:* For fall admission, 3/15 priority date for domestic and international students; for spring admission, 11/1 priority date for domestic and international students; for summer admission, 4/1 priority date for domestic and international students. Applications are processed on a rolling basis. *Application fee:* $35 ($50 for international students). Electronic applications accepted. *Application Contact:* Caitie Garza, Graduate Admissions Coordinator, 210-784-1300, E-mail: beajaguar@tamusa.edu. *Dean of the College of Business*, Dr. Tracy Hurley.

TEXAS A&M UNIVERSITY–TEXARKANA, Texarkana, TX 75503

General Information State-supported, coed, upper-level institution. *Graduate housing:* On-campus housing not available.

GRADUATE UNITS

Graduate Studies and Research *Program availability:* Part-time, evening/weekend. Electronic applications accepted.

College of Business *Program availability:* Part-time, evening/weekend. Offers accounting (MSA); business administration (MBA, MS). Electronic applications accepted.

College of Education and Liberal Arts *Program availability:* Part-time, evening/weekend. Offers adult education (MS); curriculum and instruction (M Ed); education (MS); educational administration (M Ed); English (MA); instructional technology (MS); interdisciplinary studies (MA, MS); special education (MS). Electronic applications accepted.

College of Health and Behavioral Sciences *Program availability:* Part-time, evening/weekend. Offers counseling psychology (MS). Electronic applications accepted.

TEXAS CHIROPRACTIC COLLEGE, Pasadena, TX 77505-1699

General Information Independent, coed, graduate-only institution. *Graduate housing:* On-campus housing not available.

GRADUATE UNITS

Professional Program Offers chiropractic (DC).

TEXAS CHRISTIAN UNIVERSITY, Fort Worth, TX 76129-0002

General Information Independent-religious, coed, university. CGS member. *Enrollment:* 10,489 graduate, professional, and undergraduate students; 1,351 full-time matriculated graduate/professional students (744 women), 122 part-time matriculated graduate/professional students (75 women). *Enrollment by degree level:* 940 master's, 513 doctoral, 20 other advanced degrees. *Graduate faculty:* 409 full-time (178 women), 52 part-time/adjunct (22 women). *Graduate housing:* Rooms and/or apartments available on a first-come, first-served basis to single and married students. Housing application deadline: 5/1. *Student services:* Campus employment opportunities, campus safety program, career counseling, exercise/wellness program, free psychological counseling, international student services, low-cost health insurance, multicultural affairs office, services for students with disabilities, teacher training, writing training. *Library facilities:* Mary Couts Burnett Library. *Collection:* Books: 1.4 million (physical), 1.2 million (digital/electronic); Serial titles: 10,520 (physical), 129,287 (digital/electronic); Databases: 523. Study areas open 24 hours, 5–7 days a week; students can reserve study rooms. *Research affiliation:* Lockheed Martin Corporation (business), Botanical Research Institute of Texas, Inc. (biology, environmental science, ranch management), The University of Texas Southwestern Medical School (health sciences), NextEra (environmental science, wind energy), University of North Texas Health Science Center at Fort Worth (physics, biology), Bell Helicopter (engineering).

Computer facilities: 1,400 computers available on campus for general student use. A campuswide network can be accessed from student residence rooms and from off campus. Online class registration is available.
Website: http://www.tcu.edu/

General Application Contact: Anita Unger, Admissions, TCU Graduate Studies Office, 817-257-7515, Fax: 817-257-7484, E-mail: frogmail@tcu.edu.

GRADUATE UNITS

AddRan College of Liberal Arts Students: 147 full-time (86 women); includes 33 minority (6 Black or African American, non-Hispanic/Latino; 1 Asian, non-Hispanic/Latino; 19 Hispanic/Latino; 1 Native Hawaiian or other Pacific Islander, non-Hispanic/Latino; 6 Two or more races, non-Hispanic/Latino), 4 international. Average age 32. 75 applicants, 61% accepted, 40 enrolled. *Faculty:* 58 full-time (25 women), 2 part-time/adjunct (1 woman). Expenses: Contact institution. *Financial support:* Fellowships, research assistantships, teaching assistantships, career-related internships or fieldwork, Federal Work-Study, institutionally sponsored loans, traineeships, health care benefits, tuition waivers, and unspecified assistantships available. Support available to part-time students. In 2017, 11 master's, 11 doctorates awarded. Offers criminal justice and criminology (MS); English (MA, PhD); Latin America (MA, PhD); liberal arts (MA, MS, PhD); rhetoric and composition (PhD); United States (MA, PhD). *Application Contact:* Admissions, TCU Graduate Studies Office, 817-257-7515, Fax: 817-257-7484, E-mail: frogmail@tcu.edu. *Associate Dean*, Dr. Don M. Coerver, 817-257-6290, Fax: 817-257-7709, E-mail: d.coerver@tcu.edu.

Bob Schieffer College of Communication Students: 21 full-time (18 women), 2 part-time (1 woman); includes 5 minority (1 Asian, non-Hispanic/Latino; 4 Hispanic/Latino). Average age 25. 24 applicants, 71% accepted, 12 enrolled. *Faculty:* 26 full-time (12 women). Expenses: Contact institution. *Financial support:* In 2017–18, 25 students received support, including 18 teaching assistantships with full tuition reimbursements available (averaging $10,000 per year); research assistantships, health care benefits, tuition waivers (full and partial), and unspecified assistantships also available. Financial award application deadline: 2/15. In 2017, 16 master's awarded. *Program availability:* Part-time. Offers communication studies (MS); strategic communication (MS). *Application deadline:* For fall admission, 2/15 for domestic and international students; for spring admission, 10/15 for domestic and international students. *Application fee:* $60. Electronic applications accepted. *Application Contact:* Alicia E. Craff, Academic Program Specialist, 817-257-5917, Fax: 817-257-5921, E-mail: a.e.craff@tcu.edu. *Associate Dean*, Dr. Daxton Stewart, 817-257-5911, Fax: 817-257-5921, E-mail: d.stewart@tcu.edu.

College of Education Students: 204 full-time (151 women), 40 part-time (25 women); includes 93 minority (29 Black or African American, non-Hispanic/Latino; 2 American Indian or Alaska Native, non-Hispanic/Latino; 9 Asian, non-Hispanic/Latino; 45 Hispanic/Latino; 8 Two or more races, non-Hispanic/Latino), 7 international. Average age 33. 195 applicants, 72% accepted, 109 enrolled. *Faculty:* 29 full-time (21 women), 3 part-time/adjunct (1 woman). Expenses: Contact institution. *Financial support:* In 2017–18, 193 students received support, including 1 fellowship with full tuition reimbursement available (averaging $18,500 per year), 9 research assistantships with full tuition reimbursements available (averaging $18,500 per year), 36 teaching assistantships with full tuition reimbursements available (averaging $15,000 per year); career-related internships or fieldwork, scholarships/grants, health care benefits, and unspecified assistantships also available. Support available to part-time students. Financial award application deadline: 2/1. In 2017, 62 master's, 12 doctorates awarded. *Program availability:* Part-time, evening/weekend. Offers counseling (M Ed); counseling and counselor education (PhD); curriculum and instruction (M Ed); curriculum studies (PhD); education (MAT); educational leadership (M Ed, Ed D); higher educational leadership (Ed D); science education (PhD); special education (M Ed). *Application deadline:* For fall admission, 2/1 for domestic and international students; for spring admission, 11/16 for domestic and international students; for summer admission, 2/1 for domestic and international students. *Application fee:* $60. Electronic applications accepted. *Application Contact:* Lori Kimball, Administrative Program Specialist, 817-257-7661, Fax: 817-257-7466, E-mail: l.kimball@tcu.edu. *Associate Dean*, Dr. Jan Lacina, 817-257-6786, Fax: 817-257-7466, E-mail: j.lacina@tcu.edu.

College of Fine Arts Students: 71 full-time (35 women), 4 part-time (1 woman); includes 10 minority (7 Hispanic/Latino; 3 Two or more races, non-Hispanic/Latino), 21 international. Average age 27. 95 applicants, 44% accepted, 31 enrolled. *Faculty:* 60 full-time (19 women), 15 part-time/adjunct (7 women). Expenses: Contact institution. *Financial support:* In 2017–18, 66 students received support, including 88 teaching assistantships with full tuition reimbursements available (averaging $34,120 per year); career-related internships or fieldwork, scholarships/grants, health care benefits, tuition waivers (full and partial), and unspecified assistantships also available. Financial award application deadline: 2/15. In 2017, 25 master's, 3 doctorates awarded. Offers fine arts (M Mus, MA, MFA, MM Ed, DMA, Artist Diploma). *Application deadline:* For fall admission, 2/1 for domestic and international students; for spring admission, 10/1 for domestic and international students. *Application fee:* $60. Electronic applications accepted. *Application Contact:* Donna Smolik, TCU College of Fine Arts Graduate Office, 817-257-7603, Fax: 817-257-5672, E-mail: cfagradinfo@tcu.edu. *Associate Dean, College of Fine Arts*, Dr. H. Joseph Butler, 817-257-7603, Fax: 817-257-5672, E-mail: cfagradinfo@tcu.edu.

School of Art Students: 22 full-time (17 women); includes 3 minority (all Hispanic/Latino), 5 international. Average age 28. 31 applicants, 35% accepted, 9 enrolled. *Faculty:* 11 full-time (5 women). Expenses: Contact institution. *Financial support:* In 2017–18, 18 students received support, including 17 teaching assistantships (averaging $10,000 per year); institutionally sponsored loans, scholarships/grants, health care benefits, tuition waivers (full and partial), and unspecified assistantships also available. Financial award application deadline: 2/15. In 2017, 3 master's awarded. Offers art history (MA); studio art (MFA). *Application deadline:* For fall admission, 2/1 for domestic and international students. *Application fee:* $60. Electronic applications accepted. *Application Contact:* Donna Smolik, TCU College of Fine Arts Graduate Office, 817-257-7603, Fax: 817-257-5672, E-mail: cfagradinfo@tcu.edu. *Director*, Richard Lane, 817-257-7643, E-mail: r.lane@tcu.edu.

School of Music Students: 49 full-time (18 women), 4 part-time (1 woman); includes 7 minority (4 Hispanic/Latino; 3 Two or more races, non-Hispanic/Latino), 16 international. Average age 26. 64 applicants, 48% accepted, 22 enrolled. *Faculty:* 43 full-time (10 women), 15 part-time/adjunct (7 women). Expenses: Contact institution. *Financial support:* In 2017–18, 84 students received support, including 54 research assistantships with full tuition reimbursements available (averaging $9,000 per year); career-related internships or fieldwork, institutionally sponsored loans, scholarships/grants, tuition waivers (full and partial), and unspecified assistantships also available. Financial award application deadline: 12/1; financial award applicants required to submit CSS PROFILE or FAFSA. In 2017, 21 master's, 3 doctorates awarded. Offers composition (DMA); conducting (M Mus, DMA); music (M Mus, MM Ed, DMA); music education (MM Ed); percussion (Artist Diploma); performance (DMA); piano (Artist Diploma); piano pedagogy (DMA); voice (Artist Diploma); winds (Artist Diploma). *Application deadline:* For fall admission, 12/1 for domestic and international students; for spring admission, 9/1 for domestic and international students. *Application fee:* $60. Electronic applications accepted. *Application Contact:* Dr. Joseph Butler, Associate Dean, College of Fine Arts, 817-257-6629, E-mail: h.j.butler@tcu.edu. *Director*, Dr. Richard C. Gipson, 817-257-7602, E-mail: r.gipson@tcu.edu.

College of Science and Engineering Students: 132 full-time (73 women), 3 part-time (1 woman); includes 23 minority (3 Black or African American, non-Hispanic/Latino; 1 American Indian or Alaska Native, non-Hispanic/Latino; 3 Asian, non-Hispanic/Latino; 10 Hispanic/Latino; 6 Two or more races, non-Hispanic/Latino), 20 international. Average age 27. 179 applicants, 40% accepted, 49 enrolled. *Faculty:* 87 full-time (26 women), 2 part-time/adjunct (both women). Expenses: Contact institution. *Financial support:* In 2017–18, 135 students received support, including 4 fellowships with full tuition reimbursements available (averaging $21,000 per year), 4 research assistantships with full tuition reimbursements available (averaging $21,000 per year), 92 teaching assistantships with full tuition reimbursements available (averaging $20,000 per year); health care benefits, tuition waivers (partial), and unspecified assistantships also available. Support available to part-time students. Financial award application deadline: 2/1. In 2017, 40 master's, 9 doctorates awarded. *Program availability:* Part-time. Offers applied mathematics (MS); biology (MA, MS, PhD); chemistry and biochemistry (MA, MS, PhD); developmental trauma (MS); experimental psychology (PhD); mathematics (MAT, PhD); physics (MA, MS, PhD); pure mathematics (MS); science and engineering (MA, MAT, MEM, MS, PhD). *Application deadline:* For fall admission, 2/1 for domestic and international students; for spring admission, 9/15 for domestic and international students. *Application fee:* $60. Electronic applications accepted. *Application Contact:* Sue Dolce, Director of Degree Certification, 817-257-7734, Fax: 817-257-7736, E-mail: s.dolce@tcu.edu. *Senior Associate Dean for Administration and Graduate Programs*, Dr. Magnus Rittby, 817-257-7729, Fax: 817-257-7736, E-mail: m.rittby@tcu.edu.

School of Geology, Energy and the Environment Students: 33 full-time (15 women); includes 5 minority (1 American Indian or Alaska Native, non-Hispanic/Latino; 2 Hispanic/Latino; 2 Two or more races, non-Hispanic/Latino). Average age 26. 32 applicants, 38% accepted, 6 enrolled. *Faculty:* 13 full-time (4 women). Expenses: Contact institution. *Financial support:* In 2017–18, 15 students received support, including 15 teaching assistantships with full tuition reimbursements available (averaging $16,500 per year); unspecified assistantships also available. Financial award application deadline: 2/1. In 2017, 14 master's awarded. *Program availability:* Part-time. Offers environmental science (MA, MEM, MS); geology (MS). *Application deadline:* For fall admission, 2/1 for domestic and international students; for spring admission, 9/1 for domestic and international students. *Application fee:* $60. Electronic applications accepted. *Chair*, Dr. Helge Alsleben, 817-257-7270, Fax: 817-257-7789, E-mail: h.alsleben@tcu.edu.

Harris College of Nursing and Health Sciences Students: 341 full-time (245 women), 20 part-time (19 women); includes 75 minority (17 Black or African American, non-Hispanic/Latino; 15 Asian, non-Hispanic/Latino; 32 Hispanic/Latino; 1 Native Hawaiian or other Pacific Islander, non-Hispanic/Latino; 10 Two or more races, non-Hispanic/Latino), 7 international. Average age 31. 582 applicants, 35% accepted, 166 enrolled. *Faculty:* 62 full-time (48 women), 9 part-time/adjunct (5 women). Expenses: Contact institution. *Financial support:* Application deadline: 5/1; applicants required to submit FAFSA. In 2017, 101 master's, 89 doctorates, 4 other advanced degrees awarded. *Program availability:* Part-time, 100% online, blended/hybrid learning. Offers administration (MSN); clinical nurse leader (MSN, Certificate); clinical nurse specialist (MSN); clinical nurse specialist - adult/gerontology nursing (DNP); clinical nurse specialist - pediatrics (DNP); family nurse practitioner (DNP); general (DNP); kinesiology (MS); nursing administration (DNP); nursing and health sciences (MS, MSN, MSW, DNP, DNP-A, Certificate); nursing education (MSN); social work (MSW). *Application fee:* $60. Electronic applications accepted. *Application Contact:* Debbie Rhea, Associate Dean, 817-257-5263, E-mail: d.rhea@tcu.edu. *Interim Dean*, Dr. Suzy Lockwood, 817-257-6749, E-mail: s.lockwood@tcu.edu.

Davies School of Communication Sciences and Disorders Students: 40 full-time (38 women); includes 9 minority (1 Asian, non-Hispanic/Latino; 8 Hispanic/Latino), 2 international. Average age 23. 220 applicants, 9% accepted, 20 enrolled. *Faculty:* 11 full-time (9 women). Expenses: Contact institution. *Financial support:* In 2017–18, 40 students received support, including 40 research assistantships (averaging $35,000 per year); tuition waivers (partial) and unspecified assistantships also available. Financial award application deadline: 1/15; financial award applicants required to submit FAFSA. In 2017, 20 master's awarded. Offers speech-language pathology (MS). *Application deadline:* For fall admission, 1/15 for domestic and international students. *Application fee:* $60. Electronic applications accepted. *Application Contact:* Janet Schwartz, Administrative Assistant, 817-257-7620, E-mail: janet.schwartz@tcu.edu. *Director*, Dr. Christopher Watts, 817-257-7620, E-mail: c.watts@tcu.edu.

School of Nurse Anesthesia Students: 164 full-time (99 women); includes 25 minority (4 Black or African American, non-Hispanic/Latino; 7 Asian, non-Hispanic/Latino; 8 Hispanic/Latino; 1 Native Hawaiian or other Pacific Islander, non-Hispanic/Latino; 5 Two or more races, non-Hispanic/Latino). Average age 30. 201 applicants, 36% accepted, 66 enrolled. *Faculty:* 10 full-time (5 women), 3 part-time/adjunct (2 women). Expenses: Contact institution. *Financial support:* In 2017–18, 3 students received support. Scholarships/grants available. Financial award application deadline: 7/1; financial award applicants required to submit FAFSA. In 2017, 58 doctorates awarded. Offers nurse anesthesia (DNP-A). *Application deadline:* For fall and spring admission, 7/1 for domestic and international students. Applications are processed on a rolling basis. *Application fee:* $60. Electronic applications accepted. *Application Contact:* Stephanie Morton Dwight, Administrative Assistant, 817-257-7887, Fax: 817-257-5472, E-mail: s.m.dwight@tcu.edu. *Director*, Dr. Kay K. Sanders, 817-257-7887, Fax: 817-257-5472, E-mail: k.sanders@tcu.edu.

Master of Liberal Arts Program Students: 81 full-time (33 women), 30 part-time (22 women); includes 37 minority (21 Black or African American, non-Hispanic/Latino; 2 American Indian or Alaska Native, non-Hispanic/Latino; 8 Hispanic/Latino; 1 Native Hawaiian or other Pacific Islander, non-Hispanic/Latino; 5 Two or more races, non-Hispanic/Latino), 3 international. Average age 32. 85 applicants, 93% accepted, 57 enrolled. *Faculty:* 5 part-time/adjunct (0 women). Expenses: Contact institution. *Financial support:* In 2017–18, 60 students received support. Scholarships/grants, unspecified assistantships, and employee tuition benefits available. Financial award applicants required to submit FAFSA. In 2017, 33 master's awarded. *Program availability:* Part-time, evening/weekend, 100% online. Offers liberal arts (MLA). *Application deadline:* For fall admission, 8/15 for domestic students, 6/1 for international students; for spring admission, 1/15 for domestic students, 11/1 for international students. Applications are processed on a rolling basis. *Application fee:* $60. Electronic applications accepted. *Application Contact:* Anita Unger, Graduate Program Coordinator, 817-257-7515, Fax: 817-257-7484, E-mail: a.unger@tcu.edu. *Interim Associate Provost/Dean of University Programs*, Dr. Tim Barth, 817-257-7104, Fax: 817-257-7484, E-mail: t.barth@tcu.edu.

Neeley School of Business Students: 351 full-time (100 women), 23 part-time (6 women); includes 49 minority (12 Black or African American, non-Hispanic/Latino; 2 American Indian or Alaska Native, non-Hispanic/Latino; 7 Asian, non-Hispanic/Latino; 27 Hispanic/Latino; 1 Two or more races, non-Hispanic/Latino), 34 international. Average age 30. 394 applicants, 78% accepted, 214 enrolled. *Faculty:* 83 full-time (26 women), 14 part-time/adjunct (5 women). Expenses: Contact institution. *Financial support:* Career-related internships or fieldwork, scholarships/grants, and unspecified assistantships available. Financial award application deadline: 4/1; financial award applicants required to submit FAFSA. In 2017, 208 master's awarded. *Program availability:* Part-time, evening/weekend. Offers audit (M Ac); business (M Ac, MBA); business administration (MBA); taxation (M Ac); valuation and reporting (M Ac). *Application deadline:* For fall admission, 3/1 for domestic and international students; for winter admission, 1/15 for domestic and international students; for spring admission, 11/1 for domestic and international students; for summer admission, 1/15 for domestic and international students. Applications are processed on a rolling basis. *Application fee:* $100. Electronic applications accepted. *Application Contact:* Graduate Programs Admissions Office, 817-257-7531, E-mail: mbainfo@tcu.edu. *Dean*, Dr. Homer Erekson, 817-257-7511, E-mail: neeleynews@tcu.edu.

TEXAS HEALTH AND SCIENCE UNIVERSITY, Austin, TX 78704

General Information Private, coed, graduate-only institution. *Enrollment by degree level:* 85 master's, 9 doctoral. *Graduate faculty:* 7 full-time (3 women), 8 part-time/adjunct (5 women). *Tuition:* Full-time $11,460. *Required fees:* $600. Tuition and fees vary according to course load, degree level and program. *Graduate housing:* On-campus housing not available. *Student services:* Campus employment opportunities, campus safety program, career counseling, exercise/wellness program, international student services, multicultural affairs office, services for students with disabilities. *Library facilities:* General Shu-Ping Tsao Library. *Collection:* Books: 5,996 (physical), 50 (digital/electronic); Serial titles: 58 (physical), 9,000 (digital/electronic); Databases: 4.

Computer facilities: 7 computers available on campus for general student use. Online class registration, X are available.
Website: http://www.thsu.edu/

General Application Contact: Lois Chan, Admissions Coordinator, 512-444-8082, Fax: 512-444-6345, E-mail: admissions@thsu.edu.

GRADUATE UNITS

Graduate Programs Students: 102 full-time (64 women), 9 part-time (8 women); includes 43 minority (1 Black or African American, non-Hispanic/Latino; 1 American Indian or Alaska Native, non-Hispanic/Latino; 35 Asian, non-Hispanic/Latino; 6 Hispanic/Latino). Average age 34. *Faculty:* 8 full-time (3 women), 7 part-time/adjunct (5 women). Expenses: Contact institution. *Financial support:* Teaching assistantships with partial tuition reimbursements, career-related internships or fieldwork, Federal Work-Study, institutionally sponsored loans, scholarships/grants, and tuition waivers (partial) available. Financial award applicants required to submit FAFSA. Offers acupuncture and Oriental medicine (MS, DAOM); business administration (MBA); healthcare management (MBA). *Application deadline:* For fall admission, 8/25 priority date for domestic and international students; for spring admission, 12/22 priority date for domestic and international students. Applications are processed on a rolling basis. *Application fee:* $75 ($300 for international students). Electronic applications accepted. *Application Contact:* Caleb Li, Admissions Coordinator, 512-444-8082, Fax: 512-444-6345, E-mail: admissions@thsu.edu. *Vice President of Academic Affairs*, Dr. David G. Vequist, IV, 512-444-8082.

TEXAS LUTHERAN UNIVERSITY, Seguin, TX 78155-5999

General Information Independent-religious, coed, comprehensive institution.

GRADUATE UNITS

Program in Accounting Offers accounting (M Acy).

TEXAS SOUTHERN UNIVERSITY, Houston, TX 77004-4584

General Information State-supported, coed, university. CGS member. *Graduate housing:* Room and/or apartments available on a first-come, first-served basis to single students; on-campus housing not available to married students. Housing application deadline: 7/15. *Research affiliation:* Environmental Research and Technology Transfer Center (chemistry and environmental toxicology), Institute for International and Immigration Law/Center on Legal Pedagogy (law), Innovative Transportation Research Institute (transportation planning and management), NASA University Research Biotechnology & Environmental Health (biology), Economic Development Center/JP Chase Center for Financial Education (business), Gerald B. Smith Center for Entrepreneurship and Executive Development (business, urban planning and environmental policy).

GRADUATE UNITS

Barbara Jordan-Mickey Leland School of Public Affairs *Program availability:* Part-time. Offers administration of justice (MS, PhD); public administration (MPA); public affairs (MPA, MS, PhD); urban planning and environmental policy (MS, PhD). Electronic applications accepted.

College of Education *Program availability:* Part-time, evening/weekend. Offers bilingual education (M Ed); counseling (M Ed); counselor education (Ed D); curriculum and instruction (Ed D); education (M Ed, MS, Ed D); educational administration (M Ed, Ed D); health education (MS); human performance (MS); secondary education (M Ed). Electronic applications accepted.

College of Liberal Arts and Behavioral Sciences *Program availability:* Part-time, evening/weekend. Offers English (MA); fine arts (MA); history (MA); human services and consumer sciences (MS); liberal arts and behavioral sciences (MA, MS); music (MA); psychology (MA); sociology (MA). Electronic applications accepted.

College of Pharmacy and Health Sciences *Program availability:* Online learning. Offers health care administration (MS); pharmaceutical sciences (MS, PhD); pharmacy and health sciences (MS, PhD, Pharm D); pharmacy practice (Pharm D). Electronic applications accepted.

Jesse H. Jones School of Business *Program availability:* Part-time, evening/weekend. Offers business (MBA, MS); business administration (MBA); management information systems (MS). Electronic applications accepted.

School of Science and Technology *Program availability:* Part-time, evening/weekend. Offers biology (MS); chemistry (MS); computer science (MS); environmental toxicology (MS, PhD); industrial technology (MS); mathematics (MS); science and technology (MS, PhD); transportation, planning and management (MS). Electronic applications accepted.

Tavis Smiley School of Communication *Program availability:* Part-time. Offers communication (MA). Electronic applications accepted.

Thurgood Marshall School of Law Offers law (JD). Electronic applications accepted.

TEXAS STATE UNIVERSITY, San Marcos, TX 78666

General Information State-supported, coed, university. CGS member. *Enrollment:* 38,666 graduate, professional, and undergraduate students; 2,284 full-time matriculated graduate/professional students (1,510 women), 1,653 part-time matriculated graduate/professional students (1,106 women). *Enrollment by degree level:* 3,446 master's, 366 doctoral, 125 other advanced degrees. *Graduate faculty:* 929 full-time (440 women), 207 part-time/adjunct (119 women). Tuition, state resident: full-time $7868; part-time $3934 per semester. Tuition, nonresident: full-time $17,828; part-time $8914 per semester. *Required fees:* $2092; $1435 per semester. Tuition and fees vary according to course load. *Graduate housing:* Room and/or apartments available on a first-come, first-served basis to single students; on-campus housing not available to married students. Typical cost: $3343 (including board). Room and board charges vary according to board plan and housing facility selected. Housing application deadline: 7/1. *Student services:* Campus employment opportunities, campus safety program, career counseling, exercise/wellness program, free psychological counseling, grant writing training, international student services, low-cost health insurance, multicultural affairs office, services for students with disabilities, teacher training, writing training. *Library facilities:* Alkek Library plus 1 other. *Collection:* Books: 1.5 million (physical), 664,569 (digital/electronic); Serial titles: 32,501 (physical), 129,479 (digital/electronic); Databases: 503. Weekly public service hours: 103; students can reserve study rooms. *Research affiliation:* MicroPower Global Corporation (chip prototype development), Quantum Materials Corporation (material physics), Magellan Pipeline and Bridge (environmental conservation), National Fish and Wildlife Foundation (environmental conservation), The Ewing Halsell Foundation (education: improving STEM learning), NEC Corporation of America (high-speed data analysis).

Computer facilities: Computer purchase and lease plans are available. 3,233 computers available on campus for general student use. A campuswide network can be accessed from student residence rooms and from off campus. Online class registration is available.
Website: http://www.txstate.edu/

General Application Contact: Dr. Andrea Golato, Dean of Graduate School, 512-245-2581, Fax: 512-245-8365, E-mail: gradcollege@txstate.edu.

GRADUATE UNITS

The Graduate College Students: 2,284 full-time (1,510 women), 1,653 part-time (1,106 women); includes 1,505 minority (314 Black or African American, non-Hispanic/Latino; 6 American Indian or Alaska Native, non-Hispanic/Latino; 123 Asian, non-Hispanic/Latino; 967 Hispanic/Latino; 95 Two or more races, non-Hispanic/Latino), 332 international. Average age 30. 4,101 applicants, 51% accepted, 1051 enrolled. *Faculty:* 929 full-time (440 women), 207 part-time/adjunct (119 women). Expenses: Contact institution. *Financial support:* In 2017–18, 2,341 students received support, including 210 research assistantships (averaging $16,610 per year), 719 teaching assistantships (averaging $14,524 per year); fellowships, career-related internships or fieldwork, Federal Work-Study, institutionally sponsored loans, scholarships/grants, unspecified assistantships, and laboratory instructorships, stipends also available. Support available to part-time students. Financial award application deadline: 3/1; financial award applicants required to submit FAFSA. In 2017, 1,382 master's, 50 doctorates, 38 other advanced degrees awarded. *Program availability:* Part-time, evening/weekend, blended/hybrid learning. *Application deadline:* For fall admission, 1/15 for domestic students, 1/1 for international students; for spring admission, 10/15 for domestic students, 10/1 for international students. Applications are processed on a rolling basis. *Application fee:* $40 ($90 for international students). Electronic applications accepted. *Dean,* Dr. Andrea Golato, 512-245-2581, Fax: 512-245-8365, E-mail: gradcollege@txstate.edu.

College of Applied Arts Students: 288 full-time (233 women), 306 part-time (250 women); includes 296 minority (85 Black or African American, non-Hispanic/Latino; 1 American Indian or Alaska Native, non-Hispanic/Latino; 8 Asian, non-Hispanic/Latino; 186 Hispanic/Latino; 16 Two or more races, non-Hispanic/Latino), 9 international. Average age 31. 672 applicants, 48% accepted, 163 enrolled. *Faculty:* 92 full-time (48 women), 29 part-time/adjunct (25 women). Expenses: Contact institution. *Financial support:* In 2017–18, 378 students received support, including 40 research assistantships (averaging $13,065 per year), 34 teaching assistantships (averaging $15,183 per year); career-related internships or fieldwork, Federal Work-Study, scholarships/grants, and unspecified assistantships also available. Support available to part-time students. Financial award application deadline: 3/1; financial award applicants required to submit FAFSA. In 2017, 226 master's, 6 doctorates awarded. *Program availability:* Part-time, evening/weekend, blended/hybrid learning. Offers agricultural education (M Ed); applied arts (M Ed, MAIS, MS, MSCJ, MSIS, MSW, PhD); criminal justice (MSCJ, PhD); family and child studies (MS); human nutrition (MS); management of technical education (M Ed); merchandising and consumer studies (MS); occupational education (MAIS, MSIS); social work (MSW). *Application deadline:* For fall admission, 2/1 priority date for domestic and international students; for spring admission, 10/15 priority date for domestic students, 10/1 for international students. Applications are processed on a rolling basis. *Application fee:* $40 ($90 for international students). Electronic applications accepted. *Application Contact:* Dr. Andrea Golato, Dean of Graduate School, 512-245-2581, Fax: 512-245-8365, E-mail: gradcollege@txstate.edu. *Dean,* Dr. T. Jaime Chahin, 512-245-3333, Fax: 512-245-3338, E-mail: tc03@txstate.edu.

College of Education Students: 543 full-time (411 women), 536 part-time (422 women); includes 474 minority (102 Black or African American, non-Hispanic/Latino; 35 Asian, non-Hispanic/Latino; 314 Hispanic/Latino; 23 Two or more races, non-Hispanic/Latino), 22 international. Average age 32. 921 applicants, 56% accepted, 247 enrolled. *Faculty:* 136 full-time (86 women), 72 part-time/adjunct (50 women). Expenses: Contact institution. *Financial support:* In 2017–18, 627 students received support, including 62 research assistantships (averaging $17,396 per year), 70 teaching assistantships (averaging $14,811 per year); fellowships, career-related internships or fieldwork, Federal Work-Study, institutionally sponsored loans, and scholarships/grants also available. Support available to part-time students. Financial award application deadline: 3/1; financial award applicants required to submit FAFSA. In 2017, 393 master's, 20 doctorates awarded. *Program availability:* Part-time, evening/weekend. Offers adult education (MA); adult, professional and community education (PhD); athletic training (MS); clinical mental health counseling (MA); developmental education (MA, PhD); early childhood-12 reading specialist (M Ed); educational leadership (M Ed); educational technology (M Ed); elementary education (M Ed, MA); elementary education - bilingual/bicultural (M Ed, MA); health education (M Ed); instructional leadership (MA); marriage and family counseling (MA); physical education (M Ed); recreation management (MSRLS); school counseling (MA); school improvement (PhD); school psychology (SSP); secondary education (M Ed, MA); special education (M Ed); student affairs in higher education (M Ed). *Application deadline:* For fall admission, 1/15 priority date for domestic and international students; for spring admission, 10/1 priority date for domestic and international students. Applications are processed on a rolling basis. *Application fee:* $40 ($90 for international students). Electronic applications accepted. *Application Contact:* Dr. Andrea Golato, Dean of Graduate School, 512-245-2581, Fax: 512-245-8365, E-mail: gradcollege@txstate.edu. *Dean,* Dr. Stan Carpenter, 512-245-2150, Fax: 512-245-3158, E-mail: sc33@txstate.edu.

College of Fine Arts and Communication Students: 139 full-time (89 women), 66 part-time (40 women); includes 72 minority (17 Black or African American, non-Hispanic/Latino; 1 American Indian or Alaska Native, non-Hispanic/Latino; 1 Asian, non-Hispanic/Latino; 48 Hispanic/Latino; 5 Two or more races, non-Hispanic/Latino), 17 international. Average age 29. 181 applicants, 50% accepted, 50 enrolled. *Faculty:* 131 full-time (66 women), 22 part-time/adjunct (11 women). Expenses: Contact institution. *Financial support:* In 2017–18, 144 students received support, including 102 teaching assistantships (averaging $11,371 per year); research assistantships, career-related internships or fieldwork, Federal Work-Study, institutionally sponsored loans, scholarships/grants, and unspecified assistantships also available. Support available to part-time students. Financial award application deadline: 3/1; financial award applicants required to submit FAFSA. In 2017, 90 master's awarded. *Program availability:* Part-time, evening/weekend. Offers communication design (MFA); communication studies (MA); design (MFA); directing (MFA); dramatic writing (MFA); fine arts and communication (MA, MFA, MM); mass communication (MA); music (MM); music education (MM); theatre history, dramatic criticism and dramaturgy (MA). *Application deadline:* For fall admission, 2/1 priority date for domestic and international students; for spring admission, 10/15 for domestic students, 10/1 for international students; for summer admission, 4/15 for domestic students, 3/15 for international students. Applications are processed on a rolling basis. *Application fee:* $40 ($90 for international students). Electronic applications accepted. *Application Contact:* Dr. Andrea Golato, Dean of Graduate School, 512-245-2581, Fax: 512-245-8365, E-mail: gradcollege@txstate.edu. *Dean of the College of Fine Arts and Communication,* Dr. John Fleming, 512-245-2308, Fax: 512-245-8386, E-mail: jf18@txstate.edu.

College of Health Professions Students: 348 full-time (270 women), 31 part-time (20 women); includes 162 minority (27 Black or African American, non-Hispanic/Latino; 2 American Indian or Alaska Native, non-Hispanic/Latino; 18 Asian, non-Hispanic/Latino; 102 Hispanic/Latino; 13 Two or more races, non-Hispanic/Latino), 19 international. Average age 28. 694 applicants, 32% accepted, 120 enrolled. *Faculty:* 63 full-time (43 women), 25 part-time/adjunct (14 women). Expenses: Contact institution. *Financial support:* In 2017–18, 249 students received support, including 3 research assistantships (averaging $5,752 per year), 34 teaching assistantships (averaging $9,794 per year); fellowships, career-related internships or fieldwork, Federal Work-Study, institutionally sponsored loans, scholarships/grants, unspecified assistantships, and stipends also available. Support available to part-time students. Financial award application deadline: 3/1; financial award applicants required to submit FAFSA. In 2017, 109 master's awarded. *Program availability:* Part-time, evening/weekend, blended/hybrid learning. Offers communication disorders (MA, MSCD); family nurse practitioner (MSN); health information management (MHIIM); health professions (MA, MHA, MHIIM, MSCD, MSN, DPT); healthcare administration (MHA); physical therapy (DPT). *Application deadline:* For fall admission, 1/15 priority date for domestic and international students; for spring admission, 10/1 for domestic and international students. Applications are processed on a rolling basis. *Application fee:* $40 ($90 for international students). Electronic applications accepted. *Application Contact:* Dr. Andrea Golato, Dean of Graduate School, 512-245-2581, Fax: 512-245-8365, E-mail: gradcollege@txstate.edu. *Dean,* Dr. Ruth Welborn, 512-245-3300, Fax: 512-245-3791, E-mail: mw01@txstate.edu.

College of Liberal Arts Students: 463 full-time (287 women), 344 part-time (211 women); includes 276 minority (59 Black or African American, non-Hispanic/Latino; 1 American Indian or Alaska Native, non-Hispanic/Latino; 21 Asian, non-Hispanic/Latino; 174 Hispanic/Latino; 21 Two or more races, non-Hispanic/Latino), 37 international. Average age 30. 753 applicants, 65% accepted, 251 enrolled. *Faculty:* 245 full-time (109 women), 34 part-time/adjunct (16 women). Expenses: Contact institution. *Financial support:* In 2017–18, 510 students received support, including 34 research assistantships (averaging $14,445 per year), 238 teaching assistantships (averaging $14,098 per year); fellowships, career-related internships or fieldwork, Federal Work-Study, institutionally sponsored loans, scholarships/grants, and unspecified assistantships also available. Support available to part-time students. Financial award application deadline: 3/1; financial award applicants required to submit FAFSA. In 2017, 252 master's, 9 doctorates awarded. *Program availability:* Part-time, evening/weekend. Offers anthropology (MA); applied philosophy and ethics (MA); applied sociology (MS); creative writing (MFA); dementia and aging studies (MS); geographic education (PhD); geographic information science (PhD); geography (PhD); history (M Ed, MA); international relations (MPA); international studies (MA); legal and judicial administration (MPA); legal studies (MA); liberal arts (M Ed, MA, MAG, MFA, MPA, MS, PhD); literature (MA); political science (MA); psychological research (MA); rhetoric and composition (MA); sociology (MA); Spanish (MA); sustainability (MA, MS); technical communication (MA). *Application deadline:* For fall admission, 1/15 priority date for domestic students, 1/1 priority date for international students; for spring admission, 10/15 for domestic students, 10/1 for international students; for summer admission, 4/15 for domestic students, 3/15 for international students. Applications are processed on a rolling basis. *Application fee:* $40 ($90 for international students). Electronic applications accepted. *Application Contact:* Dr. Andrea Golato, Dean of Graduate School, 512-245-2581, Fax: 512-245-8365, E-mail: gradcollege@txstate.edu. *Dean,* Dr. Michael Hennessy, 512-245-2317, Fax: 512-245-8291, E-mail: liberalarts@txstate.edu.

College of Science and Engineering Students: 351 full-time (143 women), 161 part-time (69 women); includes 109 minority (12 Black or African American, non-Hispanic/Latino; 20 Asian, non-Hispanic/Latino; 69 Hispanic/Latino; 8 Two or more races, non-Hispanic/Latino), 209 international. Average age 29. 577 applicants, 59% accepted, 137 enrolled. *Faculty:* 176 full-time (54 women), 16 part-time/adjunct (2 women). Expenses: Contact institution. *Financial support:* In 2017–18, 259 students received support, including 70 research assistantships (averaging $19,634 per year), 230 teaching assistantships (averaging $17,426 per year); career-related internships or fieldwork, Federal Work-Study, institutionally sponsored loans, scholarships/grants, health care benefits, unspecified assistantships, and laboratory instructorships also available. Support available to part-time students. Financial award application deadline: 3/1; financial award applicants required to submit FAFSA. In 2017, 133 master's, 15 doctorates awarded. *Program availability:* Part-time, evening/weekend. Offers applied mathematics (MS); aquatic resources (MS, PhD); biochemistry (MS); chemistry (MA, MS); civil engineering (MS); computer science (MA, MS, PhD); electrical engineering (MS); industrial engineering (MS); material physics (MS); materials science, engineering, and commercialization (PhD); mathematics (M Ed, MS); mathematics education (PhD); mechanical and manufacturing engineering (MS); middle school mathematics teaching (M Ed); physics (MS); population and conservation biology (MS); software engineering (MS); technology management (MS). *Application deadline:* For fall admission, 1/15 priority date for domestic and international students; for spring admission, 10/15 for domestic students, 10/1 for international students. Applications are processed on a rolling basis. *Application fee:* $40 ($90 for international students). Electronic applications accepted. *Application Contact:* Dr. Andrea Golato, Dean of Graduate School, 512-245-2581, Fax: 512-245-8365, E-mail: gradcollege@txstate.edu. *Dean,* Dr. Christine Hailey, 512-245-2119, Fax: 512-245-8095, E-mail: ceh138@txstate.edu.

Emmett and Miriam McCoy College of Business Administration Students: 152 full-time (77 women), 209 part-time (94 women); includes 116 minority (12 Black or African American, non-Hispanic/Latino; 1 American Indian or Alaska Native, non-Hispanic/Latino; 20 Asian, non-Hispanic/Latino; 74 Hispanic/Latino; 9 Two or more races, non-Hispanic/Latino), 19 international. Average age 29. 356 applicants, 46% accepted, 83 enrolled. *Faculty:* 69 full-time (26 women), 9 part-time/adjunct (1 woman). Expenses: Contact institution. *Financial support:* In 2017–18, 174 students received support, including 1 research assistantship (averaging $12,152 per year), 28 teaching assistantships (averaging $12,348 per year); Federal Work-Study, institutionally sponsored loans, scholarships/grants, health care benefits, and unspecified assistantships also available. Support available to part-time students. Financial award application deadline: 3/1; financial award applicants required to submit FAFSA. In 2017, 179 master's awarded. *Program availability:* Part-time. Offers accounting (M Acy); accounting and information technology (MS); business administration (M Acy, MBA, MS); human resource management (MS). *Application deadline:* For fall admission, 2/1 priority date for domestic and international students; for spring admission, 10/1 for domestic and international students; for summer admission, 4/1 for domestic students, 3/15 for international students. Applications are processed on a rolling basis. *Application fee:* $40 ($90 for international students). Electronic applications accepted. *Application Contact:* Dr. Andrea Golato, Dean of Graduate School, 512-245-2581, Fax: 512-245-8365, E-mail: gradcollege@txstate.edu. *Dean of the College of Business Administration,* Dr. Denise Smart, 512-245-2311, Fax: 512-245-8375, E-mail: ds37@txstate.edu.

TEXAS TECH UNIVERSITY, Lubbock, TX 79409

General Information State-supported, coed, university. CGS member. *Enrollment:* 36,996 graduate, professional, and undergraduate students; 3,879 full-time matriculated graduate/professional students (1,795 women), 2,088 part-time matriculated graduate/professional students (1,282 women). *Enrollment by degree level:* 3,055 master's, 2,912 doctoral. *Graduate faculty:* 1,563 full-time (630 women), 199 part-time/adjunct (104 women). Tuition, state resident: full-time $7632; part-time $318 per credit hour. Tuition, nonresident: full-time $17,424; part-time $726 per credit hour. *Required fees:* $2428; $50.50 per credit hour. $608 per semester. Tuition and fees vary according to program. *Graduate housing:* Room and/or apartments available on a first-come, first-served basis to single students; on-campus housing not available to married students. Typical cost: $6194 per year ($9759 including board). Room and board charges vary according to board plan and housing facility selected. Housing application deadline: 5/1. *Student services:* Campus employment opportunities, campus safety program, career counseling, exercise/wellness program, free psychological counseling, grant writing training, international student services, low-cost health insurance, multicultural affairs office, services for students with disabilities, teacher training, writing training. *Library facilities:* Texas Tech Library plus 3 others. *Collection:* Books: 2.9 million (physical), 158,677 (digital/electronic); Serial titles: 3,323 (physical), 155,124 (digital/electronic); Databases: 399. Weekly public service hours: 146; study areas open 24 hours, 5–7 days a week; students can reserve study rooms. *Research affiliation:* U.S. Department of Education (DOE) (student achievement and preparation for global competitiveness), U.S. Department of Health and Human Services (advances in medicine, public health, and social sciences), U.S. Department of Defense (pulsed power and nanotechnology for defense applications), U.S. Department of Agriculture (USDA) (food safety, development and production in agriculture), U.S. Department of Energy (research and development in wind energy), Bill and Melinda Gates Foundation (education through innovation).

Computer facilities: Computer purchase and lease plans are available. 2,597 computers available on campus for general student use. A campuswide network can be accessed from student residence rooms and from off campus. Online class registration, online degree plans, accounts, transcripts, financial aid, course and instructor evaluations, scholarship applications and submissions are available.
Website: http://www.ttu.edu/

General Application Contact: Shelby L. Cearley, Director of Graduate and International Admissions, 806-742-2787, Fax: 806-742-4038, E-mail: graduate.admissions@ttu.edu.

GRADUATE UNITS

Graduate School Students: 3,446 full-time (1,613 women), 2,083 part-time (1,281 women); includes 1,235 minority (264 Black or African American, non-Hispanic/Latino; 13 American Indian or Alaska Native, non-Hispanic/Latino; 90 Asian, non-Hispanic/Latino; 743 Hispanic/Latino; 1 Native Hawaiian or other Pacific Islander, non-Hispanic/Latino; 124 Two or more races, non-Hispanic/Latino), 1,442 international. Average age 31. 5,223 applicants, 47% accepted, 1380 enrolled. *Faculty:* 1,524 full-time (615 women), 191 part-time/adjunct (101 women). Expenses: Contact institution. *Financial support:* In 2017–18, 3,828 students received support, including 3,410 fellowships (averaging $3,352 per year), 1,068 research assistantships (averaging $14,747 per year), 1,565 teaching assistantships (averaging $13,850 per year); career-related internships or fieldwork, Federal Work-Study, scholarships/grants, traineeships, health care benefits, and unspecified assistantships also available. Support available to part-time students. Financial award application deadline: 4/15; financial award applicants required to submit FAFSA. In 2017, 1,590 master's, 346 doctorates awarded. *Program availability:* Part-time, evening/weekend, online learning. Offers arid land studies (MS); biotechnology (MS); heritage and museum sciences (MA); interdisciplinary studies (MA, MS); wind science and engineering (PhD). *Application deadline:* For fall admission, 6/1 priority date for domestic students, 1/15 priority date for international students; for spring admission, 9/1 priority date for domestic students, 6/15 priority date for international students. Applications are processed on a rolling basis. *Application fee:* $60. Electronic applications accepted. *Application Contact:* Shelby L. Cearley, Director of Graduate Admissions, 806-742-2787, Fax: 806-742-4038, E-mail: graduate.admissions@ttu.edu. *Vice Provost for Graduate and Postdoctoral Affairs/Dean of the Graduate School,* Dr. Mark Sheridan, 806-834-5537, Fax: 806-742-1746, E-mail: mark.sheridan@ttu.edu.

College of Agricultural Sciences and Natural Resources Students: 285 full-time (157 women), 115 part-time (57 women); includes 43 minority (2 Black or African American, non-Hispanic/Latino; 2 Asian, non-Hispanic/Latino; 29 Hispanic/Latino; 10 Two or more races, non-Hispanic/Latino), 107 international. Average age 30. 247 applicants, 52% accepted, 84 enrolled. *Faculty:* 123 full-time (44 women), 17 part-time/adjunct (5 women). Expenses: Contact institution. *Financial support:* In 2017–18, 355 students received support, including 273 fellowships (averaging $3,170 per year), 270 research assistantships (averaging $14,478 per year), 50 teaching assistantships (averaging $9,420 per year); scholarships/grants, health care benefits, and unspecified assistantships also available. Support available to part-time students. Financial award application deadline: 12/1; financial award applicants required to submit FAFSA. In 2017, 78 master's, 30 doctorates awarded. *Program availability:* Part-time, 100% online, blended/hybrid learning. Offers agribusiness (MAB); agricultural and applied economics (MS, PhD); agricultural communications (MS); agricultural communications and education (PhD); agricultural education (MS, Ed D); agricultural sciences and natural resources (MAB, MLA, MS, Ed D, PhD); animal science (MS, PhD); food science (MS); horticulture science (MS); landscape architecture (MLA); plant and soil science (MS, PhD); wildlife, aquatic, and wildlands science and management (MS, PhD). *Application deadline:* For fall admission, 6/1 priority date for domestic students, 1/15 priority date for international students; for spring admission, 9/1 priority date for domestic students, 6/15 priority date for international students. Applications are processed on a rolling basis. *Application fee:* $60. Electronic applications accepted. *Application Contact:* Dr. Michael Ballou, Associate Dean for Research, 806-834-6513, Fax: 806-742-2836, E-mail: michael.ballou@ttu.edu. *Professor and Interim Dean,* Dr. Steve D. Fraze, 806-834-7115, Fax: 806-742-2836, E-mail: steven.fraze@ttu.edu.

College of Architecture Students: 62 full-time (19 women), 26 part-time (10 women); includes 33 minority (4 Black or African American, non-Hispanic/Latino; 29 Hispanic/Latino), 19 international. Average age 27. 55 applicants, 56% accepted, 15 enrolled. *Faculty:* 32 full-time (8 women), 15 part-time/adjunct (3 women). Expenses: Contact institution. *Financial support:* In 2017–18, 69 students received support, including 69 fellowships (averaging $4,740 per year); research assistantships, teaching assistantships, career-related internships or fieldwork, Federal Work-Study, institutionally sponsored loans, scholarships/grants, traineeships, health care benefits, and unspecified assistantships also available. Support available to part-time students. Financial award application deadline: 2/1; financial award applicants required to submit FAFSA. In 2017, 56 master's awarded. *Program availability:* Part-time. Offers architecture (M Arch, MS); land-use planning, management, and design (PhD). *Application deadline:* For fall admission, 6/1 priority date for domestic students, 1/15 priority date for international students; for spring admission, 9/1 priority date for domestic students, 6/15 priority date for international students. Applications are processed on a rolling basis. *Application fee:* $60. Electronic applications accepted. *Application Contact:* Jeff Rammage, Graduate Advisor, 806-742-3169, Fax: 806-742-1400, E-mail: jeffrey.rammage@ttu.edu. *Dean,* Prof. James Williamson, 806-742-3136, Fax: 806-742-1400, E-mail: james.p.williamson@ttu.edu.

College of Arts and Sciences Students: 1,024 full-time (507 women), 225 part-time (122 women); includes 234 minority (42 Black or African American, non-Hispanic/Latino; 4 American Indian or Alaska Native, non-Hispanic/Latino; 30 Asian, non-Hispanic/Latino; 128 Hispanic/Latino; 1 Native Hawaiian or other Pacific Islander, non-Hispanic/Latino; 29 Two or more races, non-Hispanic/Latino), 412 international. Average age 30. 1,243 applicants, 37% accepted, 278 enrolled. *Faculty:* 528 full-time (198 women), 38 part-time/adjunct (17 women). Expenses: Contact institution. *Financial support:* In 2017–18, 1,066 students received support, including 897 fellowships (averaging $2,532 per year), 285 research assistantships (averaging $11,553 per year), 823 teaching assistantships (averaging $14,160 per year); career-related internships or fieldwork, Federal Work-Study, institutionally sponsored loans, scholarships/grants, traineeships, health care benefits, and unspecified assistantships also available. Support available to part-time students. Financial award application deadline: 2/1; financial award applicants required to submit FAFSA. In 2017, 298 master's, 91 doctorates awarded. *Program availability:* Part-time, evening/weekend, 100% online, blended/hybrid learning. Offers anthropology (MA); arts and sciences (MA, MPA, MS, MSW, PSM, PhD); atmospheric science (MS); biology (MS, PhD); chemical biology (MS); chemistry (MS, PhD); clinical psychology (PhD); counseling psychology (MA, PhD); economics (MA, PhD); English (MA, PhD); environmental sustainability and natural resource management (PSM); environmental toxicology (MS, PhD); forensic science (MS); general experimental psychology (MA, PhD); geography (MS); geosciences (MS, PhD); history (MA, PhD); kinesiology (MS); languages and cultures (MA); mathematics (MA, MS, PhD); microbiology (MS); philosophy (MA); physics (MS, PhD); political science (MA, PhD); psychology (MA); public administration (MPA); Romance languages (MA); social work (MSW); sociology (MA); Spanish (PhD); sport management (MS); statistics (MS); technical communication (MA); technical communication and rhetoric (PhD); zoology (MS, PhD). *Application deadline:* For fall admission, 6/1 priority date for domestic students, 1/15 priority date for international students; for spring admission, 9/1 priority date for domestic students, 6/15 priority date for international students. Applications are processed on a rolling basis. *Application fee:* $60. Electronic applications accepted. *Application Contact:* Dr. Jorge Iber, Associate Dean, 806-834-5511, E-mail: jorge.iber@ttu.edu. *Dean,* Dr. W. Brent Lindquist, 806-742-3831, Fax: 806-742-3893, E-mail: brent.lindquist@ttu.edu.

College of Education Students: 327 full-time (243 women), 884 part-time (695 women); includes 407 minority (110 Black or African American, non-Hispanic/Latino; 4 American Indian or Alaska Native, non-Hispanic/Latino; 15 Asian, non-Hispanic/Latino; 247 Hispanic/Latino; 31 Two or more races, non-Hispanic/Latino), 87 international. Average age 36. 667 applicants, 49% accepted, 256 enrolled. *Faculty:* 160 full-time (109 women), 12 part-time/adjunct (11 women). Expenses: Contact institution. *Financial support:* In 2017–18, 462 students received support, including 452 fellowships (averaging $3,250 per year), 100 research assistantships (averaging $12,061 per year), 7 teaching assistantships (averaging $10,995 per year); career-related internships or fieldwork, Federal Work-Study, institutionally sponsored loans, scholarships/grants, traineeships, health care benefits, and unspecified assistantships also available. Support available to part-time students. Financial award application deadline: 2/1; financial award applicants required to submit FAFSA. In 2017, 229 master's, 85 doctorates awarded. *Program availability:* Part-time, evening/weekend. Offers bilingual education (M Ed); counselor education (M Ed, PhD); curriculum and instruction (M Ed); education (M Ed, MS, Ed D, PhD); educational leadership (M Ed, Ed D, PhD); educational psychology (M Ed, PhD); elementary education (M Ed); higher education (M Ed); higher education administration (Ed D); higher education research (PhD); instructional technology (M Ed, Ed D); language/literacy education (M Ed); multidisciplinary science (MS); secondary education (M Ed); special education (M Ed, Ed D, PhD). *Application deadline:* For fall admission, 6/1 priority date for domestic students, 1/15 priority date for international students; for spring admission, 9/1 priority date for domestic students, 6/15 priority date for international students. Applications are processed on a rolling basis. *Application fee:* $60. Electronic applications accepted. *Application Contact:* Brianna Sanchez, Coordinator, 806-834-2353, Fax: 806-742-2179, E-mail: brianna.sanchez@ttu.edu. *Dean*, Dr. D. Scott Ridley, 806-834-1431, Fax: 806-742-2179, E-mail: scott.ridley@ttu.edu.

College of Human Sciences Students: 282 full-time (173 women), 177 part-time (107 women); includes 107 minority (21 Black or African American, non-Hispanic/Latino; 5 Asian, non-Hispanic/Latino; 72 Hispanic/Latino; 9 Two or more races, non-Hispanic/Latino), 100 international. Average age 30. 315 applicants, 61% accepted, 141 enrolled. *Faculty:* 109 full-time (67 women), 22 part-time/adjunct (20 women). Expenses: Contact institution. *Financial support:* In 2017–18, 306 students received support, including 293 fellowships (averaging $4,487 per year), 80 research assistantships (averaging $12,185 per year), 111 teaching assistantships (averaging $12,677 per year); institutionally sponsored loans, scholarships/grants, and unspecified assistantships also available. Financial award application deadline: 1/15; financial award applicants required to submit FAFSA. In 2017, 106 master's, 36 doctorates awarded. *Program availability:* Part-time, 100% online, blended/hybrid learning. Offers environmental design (MS); family and consumer sciences education (MS, PhD); hospitality administration (PhD); hospitality and retail management (MS); human development and family studies (MS, PhD); human sciences (MS, PhD); interior and environmental design (PhD); marriage and family therapy (MS, PhD); nutrition and dietetics (MS); nutritional sciences (MS, PhD); personal financial planning (MS, PhD). *Application deadline:* For fall admission, 6/1 priority date for domestic students, 1/15 priority date for international students; for spring admission, 9/1 priority date for domestic students, 6/15 priority date for international students. Applications are processed on a rolling basis. *Application fee:* $60. Electronic applications accepted. *Application Contact:* Prof. Mitzi Lauderdale, Associate Dean for Students, 806-834-0529, Fax: 806-742-1849, E-mail: mitzi.lauderdale@ttu.edu. *Chair in Human Sciences*, Dr. Linda C. Hoover, 806-742-3031, Fax: 806-742-1849, E-mail: linda.hoover@ttu.edu.

College of Media and Communication Students: 102 full-time (53 women), 129 part-time (92 women); includes 66 minority (10 Black or African American, non-Hispanic/Latino; 2 Asian, non-Hispanic/Latino; 46 Hispanic/Latino; 8 Two or more races, non-Hispanic/Latino), 12 international. Average age 30. 189 applicants, 62% accepted, 94 enrolled. *Faculty:* 63 full-time (24 women), 13 part-time/adjunct (10 women). Expenses: Contact institution. *Financial support:* In 2017–18, 140 students received support, including 105 fellowships (averaging $4,027 per year), 35 research assistantships (averaging $8,745 per year), 92 teaching assistantships (averaging $8,573 per year); career-related internships or fieldwork, scholarships/grants, and unspecified assistantships also available. Support available to part-time students. Financial award application deadline: 4/15; financial award applicants required to submit FAFSA. In 2017, 70 master's, 5 doctorates awarded. *Program availability:* Part-time, evening/weekend, 100% online, blended/hybrid learning. Offers communication studies (MA); mass communications (MA); media and communication (PhD); strategic communication and innovation (MA). *Application deadline:* For fall admission, 6/1 priority date for domestic students, 1/15 priority date for international students; for spring admission, 9/1 priority date for domestic students, 6/15 priority date for international students. Applications are processed on a rolling basis. *Application fee:* $60. Electronic applications accepted. *Application Contact:* Bridget Christopherson, Graduate Program Administrative, 806-834-1619, Fax: 806-742-1746, E-mail: bridget.christopherson@ttu.edu. *Associate Dean for Graduate Studies*, Dr. Coy Callison, 806-834-5344, E-mail: coy.callison@ttu.edu.

Edward E. Whitacre Jr. College of Engineering Students: 618 full-time (140 women), 207 part-time (34 women); includes 96 minority (21 Black or African American, non-Hispanic/Latino; 1 American Indian or Alaska Native, non-Hispanic/Latino; 16 Asian, non-Hispanic/Latino; 47 Hispanic/Latino; 11 Two or more races, non-Hispanic/Latino), 528 international. Average age 29. 1,455 applicants, 38% accepted, 146 enrolled. *Faculty:* 170 full-time (27 women), 19 part-time/adjunct (3 women). Expenses: Contact institution. *Financial support:* In 2017–18, 600 students received support, including 535 fellowships (averaging $3,492 per year), 262 research assistantships (averaging $21,020 per year), 187 teaching assistantships (averaging $19,039 per year); scholarships/grants, health care benefits, and unspecified assistantships also available. Financial award application deadline: 4/15; financial award applicants required to submit FAFSA. In 2017, 201 master's, 69 doctorates awarded. *Program availability:* Part-time, evening/weekend, 100% online, blended/hybrid learning. Offers bioengineering (MS); chemical engineering (MS Ch E, PhD); civil engineering (MSCE, PhD); computer science (MS, PhD); electrical engineering (MSEE, PhD); engineering (M Engr, MENVEGR, MS, MS Ch E, MSCE, MSEE, MSIE, MSME, MSPE, MSSEM, PhD); environmental engineering (MENVEGR); industrial engineering (MSIE, PhD); mechanical engineering (MSME, PhD); petroleum engineering (MSPE, PhD); software engineering (MS); systems and engineering management (MSSEM). *Application deadline:* For fall admission, 6/1 priority date for domestic students, 1/15 priority date for international students; for spring admission, 9/1 priority date for domestic students, 6/15 priority date for international students. Applications are processed on a rolling basis. *Application fee:* $60. Electronic applications accepted. *Application Contact:* Dr. Brandon Weeks, Associate Dean of Research and Graduate Programs, Edward E. Whitacre Jr. College of Engineering, 806-834-7450, Fax: 806-742-3493, E-mail: brandon.weeks@ttu.edu. *Dean, Edward E. Whitacre Jr. College of Engineering*, Dr. Albert Sacco, Jr., 806-742-3451, Fax: 806-742-3493, E-mail: al.sacco-jr@ttu.edu.

J.T. and Margaret Talkington College of Visual and Performing Arts Students: 224 full-time (113 women), 91 part-time (54 women); includes 46 minority (9 Black or African American, non-Hispanic/Latino; 2 Asian, non-Hispanic/Latino; 28 Hispanic/Latino; 7 Two or more races, non-Hispanic/Latino), 67 international. Average age 32. 193 applicants, 59% accepted, 67 enrolled. *Faculty:* 115 full-time (47 women), 19 part-time/adjunct (12 women). Expenses: Contact institution. *Financial support:* In 2017–18, 288 students received support, including 269 fellowships (averaging $3,263 per year), 207 teaching assistantships (averaging $10,542 per year); research assistantships, Federal Work-Study, institutionally sponsored loans, scholarships/grants, health care benefits, tuition waivers (partial), unspecified assistantships, and competitive grants to support graduate research also available. Financial award application deadline: 2/1; financial award applicants required to submit FAFSA. In 2017, 56 master's, 23 doctorates awarded. *Program availability:* Part-time. Offers art (MFA); art education (MAE); art history (MA); dance studies (MA); fine arts (PhD); music (MM, DMA); music education (MM Ed); theatre arts (MA, MFA); visual and performing arts (MA, MAE, MFA, MM, MM Ed, DMA, PhD). *Application deadline:* For fall admission, 6/1 priority date for domestic students, 1/15 priority date for international students; for spring admission, 9/1 priority date for domestic students, 6/15 priority date for international students. Applications are processed on a rolling basis. *Application fee:* $60. Electronic applications accepted. *Application Contact:* Shannon Samson, Coordinator of Graduate School Recruitment, 806-834-5201, Fax: 806-742-1746, E-mail: gradschool@ttu.edu. *Dean*, Dr. Noel Zahler, 806-742-0700, Fax: 806-742-0695, E-mail: noel.zahler@ttu.edu.

Rawls College of Business Administration Students: 660 full-time (252 women); includes 174 minority (30 Black or African American, non-Hispanic/Latino; 3 American Indian or Alaska Native, non-Hispanic/Latino; 20 Asian, non-Hispanic/Latino; 104 Hispanic/Latino; 17 Two or more races, non-Hispanic/Latino), 99 international. Average age 29. 492 applicants, 51% accepted, 148 enrolled. *Faculty:* 89 full-time (22 women). Expenses: Contact institution. *Financial support:* In 2017–18, 81 students received support, including 1 research assistantship with full tuition reimbursement available (averaging $22,725 per year), 63 teaching assistantships with full tuition reimbursements available (averaging $22,725 per year); career-related internships or fieldwork, Federal Work-Study, scholarships/grants, health care benefits, and unspecified assistantships also available. Financial award application deadline: 3/1; financial award applicants required to submit FAFSA. In 2017, 439 master's, 6 doctorates awarded. *Program availability:* Evening/weekend, 100% online, blended/hybrid learning. Offers accounting (MSA, PhD); data science (MS); finance (PhD); general business (MBA); healthcare management (MS); information systems and operations management (PhD); management (PhD); marketing (PhD); STEM (MBA). *Application deadline:* For fall admission, 7/1 priority date for domestic students, 1/15 for international students; for spring admission, 12/1 priority date for domestic students, 6/15 for international students; for summer admission, 5/1 for domestic students. Applications are processed on a rolling basis. *Application fee:* $60. Electronic applications accepted. *Application Contact:* Jennifer Yack, Applications Manager, Graduate and Professional Programs, 806-742-3184, E-mail: rawlsgrad@ttu.edu. *Dean*, Dr. Margaret Williams, 806-834-2839, Fax: 806-742-1092, E-mail: margaret.l.williams@ttu.edu.

School of Law Students: 434 full-time (183 women), 6 part-time (2 women); includes 113 minority (8 Black or African American, non-Hispanic/Latino; 3 American Indian or Alaska Native, non-Hispanic/Latino; 9 Asian, non-Hispanic/Latino; 68 Hispanic/Latino; 25 Two or more races, non-Hispanic/Latino), 6 international. Average age 26. 1,157 applicants, 45% accepted, 139 enrolled. *Faculty:* 39 full-time (15 women), 8 part-time/adjunct (3 women). Expenses: Contact institution. *Financial support:* In 2017–18, 42 students received support, including 42 teaching assistantships (averaging $1,027 per year); research assistantships, Federal Work-Study, tuition waivers, and tutorships also available. Financial award application deadline: 5/1; financial award applicants required to submit FAFSA. In 2017, 5 master's, 197 doctorates awarded. Offers law (JD); United States legal studies (LL M). *Application deadline:* For fall admission, 3/1 priority date for domestic and international students. Applications are processed on a rolling basis. *Application fee:* $60. Electronic applications accepted. *Application Contact:* Wendy A. Humphrey, Interim Associate Dean for Admissions and Financial Aid, 806-834-4446, Fax: 806-742-4617, E-mail: admissions.law@ttu.edu. *Dean/Professor of Law*, Jack Wade Nowlin, 806-834-1504, Fax: 806-742-4014, E-mail: jack.nowlin@ttu.edu.

TEXAS TECH UNIVERSITY HEALTH SCIENCES CENTER, Lubbock, TX 79430

General Information State-supported, coed, graduate-only institution. *Graduate housing:* On-campus housing not available.

GRADUATE UNITS

Graduate School of Biomedical Sciences Offers biomedical sciences (MS, PhD); biotechnology (MS); pharmaceutical sciences (MS, PhD). Electronic applications accepted.

School of Health Professions Students: 675 full-time (502 women), 409 part-time (260 women); includes 367 minority (65 Black or African American, non-Hispanic/Latino; 2 American Indian or Alaska Native, non-Hispanic/Latino; 74 Asian, non-Hispanic/Latino; 206 Hispanic/Latino; 6 Native Hawaiian or other Pacific Islander, non-Hispanic/Latino; 14 Two or more races, non-Hispanic/Latino). Average age 30. 3,771 applicants, 22% accepted, 529 enrolled. *Faculty:* 74 full-time (42 women), 31 part-time/adjunct (15 women). Expenses: Contact institution. *Financial support:* Research assistantships, teaching assistantships, career-related internships or fieldwork, institutionally sponsored loans, scholarships/grants, and unspecified assistantships available. Financial award application deadline: 9/1; financial award applicants required to submit FAFSA. In 2017, 283 master's, 114 doctorates awarded. *Program availability:* Part-time, 100% online, blended/hybrid learning. Offers addiction counseling (MS); athletic training (MAT); audiology (Au D); clinical mental health counseling (MS); clinical rehabilitation counseling (MRC); health professions (MAT, MOT, MPAS, MRC, MS, Au D, DPT, PhD, Sc D, TDPT); healthcare administration (MS); molecular pathology (MS); occupational therapy (MOT); physical therapy (DPT, Sc D, TDPT); physician assistant studies (MPAS); rehabilitation science (PhD); speech-language pathology (MS). *Application deadline:* Applications are processed on a rolling basis. *Application fee:* $75. Electronic applications accepted. *Application Contact:* Lindsay Johnson, Associate Dean for Admissions and Student Affairs, 806-743-3220, Fax: 806-743-2994, E-mail: lindsay.johnson@ttuhsc.edu. *Associate Dean for Admissions and Student Affairs*, Lindsay R. Johnson, 806-743-3220, Fax: 806-743-2994, E-mail: lindsay.johnson@ttuhsc.edu.

School of Medicine Offers medicine (MD). Open only to residents of Texas, eastern New Mexico, and southwestern Oklahoma; MD/PhD offered jointly with Texas Tech University; JD/MD with School of Law. Electronic applications accepted.

School of Nursing *Program availability:* Part-time, online learning. Offers acute care nurse practitioner (MSN, Certificate); administration (MSN); advanced practice (DNP); education (MSN); executive leadership (DNP); family nurse practitioner (MSN, Certificate); geriatric nurse practitioner (MSN, Certificate); pediatric nurse practitioner (MSN, Certificate).

TEXAS TECH UNIVERSITY HEALTH SCIENCES CENTER EL PASO, El Paso, TX 79905

General Information State-supported, coed, comprehensive institution.

GRADUATE UNITS

Gayle Greve Hunt School of Nursing Offers nursing (MSN).

Graduate School of Biomedical Sciences Offers biomedical sciences (MS).

Paul L. Foster School of Medicine Offers medicine (MD).

TEXAS WESLEYAN UNIVERSITY, Fort Worth, TX 76105

General Information Independent-religious, coed, university. *Enrollment:* 448 full-time matriculated graduate/professional students (246 women), 311 part-time matriculated graduate/professional students (249 women). *Enrollment by degree level:* 609 master's, 150 doctoral. *Graduate faculty:* 25 full-time (14 women), 14 part-time/adjunct (10 women). *Graduate housing:* Room and/or apartments available on a first-come, first-served basis to single students; on-campus housing not available to married students. Typical cost: $9538 (including board). *Student services:* Campus employment opportunities, campus safety program, career counseling, exercise/wellness program, free psychological counseling, international student services, low-cost health insurance, multicultural affairs office, services for students with disabilities, teacher training, writing training. *Library facilities:* Eunice and James L. West Library plus 1 other. *Collection:* Books: 185,461 (physical), 171,492 (digital/electronic); Serial titles: 1,500 (physical), 150,836 (digital/electronic); Databases: 104. Weekly public service hours: 101.

Computer facilities: 507 computers available on campus for general student use. A campuswide network can be accessed from student residence rooms and from off campus. Online class registration is available.
Website: http://www.txwes.edu/

General Application Contact: Amy Orcutt, Interim Director of Graduate Admissions, 817-531-4930, Fax: 817-531-4261, E-mail: arorcutt@txwes.edu.

GRADUATE UNITS

Graduate Programs Students: 448 full-time (246 women), 275 part-time (222 women); includes 262 minority (116 Black or African American, non-Hispanic/Latino; 6 American Indian or Alaska Native, non-Hispanic/Latino; 34 Asian, non-Hispanic/Latino; 90 Hispanic/Latino; 2 Native Hawaiian or other Pacific Islander, non-Hispanic/Latino; 14 Two or more races, non-Hispanic/Latino), 21 international. Average age 34. 650 applicants, 46% accepted, 232 enrolled. *Faculty:* 47 full-time (26 women), 18 part-time/adjunct (13 women). Expenses: Contact institution. *Financial support:* Fellowships with tuition reimbursements, career-related internships or fieldwork, Federal Work-Study, institutionally sponsored loans, scholarships/grants, and tuition waivers (full and partial) available. Support available to part-time students. Financial award application deadline: 3/15; financial award applicants required to submit FAFSA. *Program availability:* Part-time, evening/weekend, 100% online. Offers business (MBA); education (M Ed, Ed D); nurse anesthesia (MHS, MSNA, DNAP). *Application deadline:* Applications are processed on a rolling basis. *Application fee:* $64. Electronic applications accepted. *Application Contact:* Amy Orcutt, Interim Director of Graduate Admissions, 817-531-4288, E-mail: arorcutt@txwes.edu. *Provost*, Dr. Allen Henderson, 817-531-4405, Fax: 817-531-4499, E-mail: ahenderson@txwes.edu.

TEXAS WOMAN'S UNIVERSITY, Denton, TX 76204

General Information State-supported, coed, primarily women, university. CGS member. *Enrollment:* 15,472 graduate, professional, and undergraduate students; 2,080 full-time matriculated graduate/professional students (1,812 women), 2,992 part-time matriculated graduate/professional students (2,646 women). *Enrollment by degree level:* 3,940 master's, 687 doctoral, 445 other advanced degrees. *Graduate faculty:* 338 full-time (243 women), 156 part-time/adjunct (116 women). Tuition, state resident: full-time $5020; part-time $259.56 per semester hour. Tuition, nonresident: full-time $14,320; part-time $674.56 per semester hour. *Required fees:* $2500; $125 per semester hour. $290 per semester. Tuition and fees vary according to course level, course load, degree level and program. *Graduate housing:* Rooms and/or apartments available on a first-come, first-served basis to single and married students. Typical cost: $6710 per year for single students; $8000 per year for married students. Room charges vary according to board plan and housing facility selected. Housing application deadline: 2/18. *Student services:* Campus employment opportunities, campus safety program, career counseling, child daycare facilities, exercise/wellness program, free psychological counseling, grant writing training, international student services, low-cost health insurance, multicultural affairs office, services for students with disabilities, teacher training, writing training. *Library facilities:* Blagg-Huey Library. *Collection:* Books: 383,183 (physical), 407,446 (digital/electronic); Serial titles: 155,452 (physical), 595,316 (digital/electronic); Databases: 227. Weekly public service hours: 116; students can reserve study rooms.

Computer facilities: Computer purchase and lease plans are available. 285 computers available on campus for general student use. A campuswide network can be accessed from student residence rooms and from off campus. Online class registration is available.
Website: http://www.twu.edu/

General Application Contact: Korie Hawkins, Associate Director of Admissions, Graduate Recruitment, 940-898-3188, Fax: 940-898-3081, E-mail: admissions@twu.edu.

GRADUATE UNITS

Graduate School Students: 2,080 full-time (1,812 women), 2,992 part-time (2,646 women); includes 2,385 minority (885 Black or African American, non-Hispanic/Latino; 13 American Indian or Alaska Native, non-Hispanic/Latino; 508 Asian, non-Hispanic/Latino; 834 Hispanic/Latino; 6 Native Hawaiian or other Pacific Islander, non-Hispanic/Latino; 139 Two or more races, non-Hispanic/Latino), 149 international. Average age 33. 2,712 applicants, 53% accepted, 1090 enrolled. *Faculty:* 338 full-time (243 women), 156 part-time/adjunct (116 women). Expenses: Contact institution. *Financial support:* In 2017–18, 1,521 students received support, including 43 research assistantships (averaging $16,852 per year), 125 teaching assistantships (averaging $21,830 per year); career-related internships or fieldwork, Federal Work-Study, institutionally sponsored loans, scholarships/grants, traineeships, health care benefits, unspecified assistantships, and research associateships also available. Support available to part-time students. Financial award application deadline: 3/1; financial award applicants required to submit FAFSA. In 2017, 1,453 master's, 247 doctorates awarded. *Program availability:* Part-time, evening/weekend, 100% online, blended/hybrid learning. MSW offered in cooperation with The University of North Texas. *Application deadline:* For fall admission, 3/1 priority date for domestic students, 9/1 priority date for international students; for spring admission, 11/1 priority date for domestic students, 5/1 priority date for international students. Applications are processed on a rolling basis. *Application fee:* $50 ($75 for international students). Electronic applications accepted. *Application Contact:* Korie Hawkins, Associate Director of Admissions, Graduate Recruitment, 940-898-3188, Fax: 940-898-3081, E-mail: admissions@twu.edu. *Dean of Graduate School*, Dr. Carolyn Kapinus, 940-898-3415, Fax: 940-898-3412, E-mail: gradschool@twu.edu.

College of Arts and Sciences Students: 199 full-time (162 women), 372 part-time (293 women); includes 211 minority (73 Black or African American, non-Hispanic/Latino; 2 American Indian or Alaska Native, non-Hispanic/Latino; 39 Asian, non-Hispanic/Latino; 82 Hispanic/Latino; 15 Two or more races, non-Hispanic/Latino), 44 international. Average age 33. 285 applicants, 56% accepted, 115 enrolled. *Faculty:* 102 full-time (58 women), 18 part-time/adjunct (8 women). Expenses: Contact institution. *Financial support:* In 2017–18, 246 students received support, including 4 research assistantships (averaging $27,070 per year), 84 teaching assistantships (averaging $21,861 per year); career-related internships or fieldwork, Federal Work-Study, institutionally sponsored loans, scholarships/grants, traineeships, health care benefits, and unspecified assistantships also available. Support available to part-time students. Financial award application deadline: 3/1; financial award applicants required to submit FAFSA. In 2017, 78 master's, 38 doctorates, 4 other advanced degrees awarded. *Program availability:* Part-time, evening/weekend, 100% online, blended/hybrid learning. Offers art (MA, MAT, MFA); arts (MA, MAT, MFA, PhD); arts and sciences (MA, MAT, MFA, MS, PhD, SSP); biology (MS); chemistry (MS); counseling psychology (MA, PhD); dance (MA, MFA, PhD); drama (MA); emphasis in mathematics or computer science (MAT); English (MA, MAT); government (MA); history (MA); informatics (MS); mathematics (MS); mathematics teaching (MS); molecular biology (PhD); multicultural women's and gender studies (MA, PhD); music (MA); psychological science (MS); rhetoric (PhD); school psychology (PhD, SSP); social work (MS); sociology (MA, PhD). MSW offered in cooperation with The University of North Texas. *Application deadline:* For fall admission, 3/1 priority date for domestic and international students; for spring admission, 11/1 priority date for domestic students, 7/1 priority date for international students; for summer admission, 5/1 priority date for domestic students, 2/1 priority date for international students. Applications are processed on a rolling basis. *Application fee:* $50 ($75 for international students). Electronic applications accepted. *Application Contact:* Korie Hawkins, Associate Director of Admissions, Graduate Recruitment, 940-898-3188, Fax: 940-898-3081, E-mail: admissions@twu.edu. *Dean*, Dr. Abigail Tilton, 940-898-3326, Fax: 940-898-3366, E-mail: cas@twu.edu.

College of Business Students: 373 full-time (312 women), 432 part-time (368 women); includes 569 minority (312 Black or African American, non-Hispanic/Latino; 1 American Indian or Alaska Native, non-Hispanic/Latino; 116 Asian, non-Hispanic/Latino; 118 Hispanic/Latino; 3 Native Hawaiian or other Pacific Islander, non-Hispanic/Latino; 19 Two or more races, non-Hispanic/Latino), 35 international. Average age 35. 314 applicants, 82% accepted, 184 enrolled. *Faculty:* 32 full-time (12 women), 13 part-time/adjunct (9 women). Expenses: Contact institution. *Financial support:* In 2017–18, 198 students received support. Career-related internships or fieldwork, Federal Work-Study, institutionally sponsored loans, scholarships/grants, traineeships, health care benefits, and unspecified assistantships available. Support available to part-time students. Financial award application deadline: 3/1; financial award applicants required to submit FAFSA. In 2017, 443 master's awarded. *Program availability:* Part-time. Offers business administration (MBA); health systems management (MHSM); healthcare administration (MHA). *Application deadline:* For fall admission, 3/1 priority date for domestic students, 3/1 for international students; for spring admission, 11/1 priority date for domestic students, 7/1 for international students. Applications are processed on a rolling basis. *Application fee:* $50 ($75 for international students). Electronic applications accepted. *Application Contact:* Korie Hawkins, Associate Director of Admissions, Graduate Recruitment, 940-898-3188, Fax: 940-898-3081, E-mail: admissions@twu.edu. *Director*, Dr. Margaret A. Young, 940-898-2458, Fax: 940-898-2120, E-mail: mba@twu.edu.

College of Health Sciences Students: 1,167 full-time (1,015 women), 476 part-time (393 women); includes 615 minority (166 Black or African American, non-Hispanic/Latino; 4 American Indian or Alaska Native, non-Hispanic/Latino; 156 Asian, non-Hispanic/Latino; 248 Hispanic/Latino; 41 Two or more races, non-Hispanic/Latino), 45 international. Average age 29. 1,393 applicants, 37% accepted, 409 enrolled. *Faculty:* 99 full-time (76 women), 27 part-time/adjunct (21 women). Expenses: Contact institution. *Financial support:* In 2017–18, 619 students received support, including 59 research assistantships (averaging $11,499 per year), 15 teaching assistantships (averaging $11,499 per year); career-related internships or fieldwork, Federal Work-Study, institutionally sponsored loans, scholarships/grants, traineeships, health care benefits, and unspecified assistantships also available. Support available to part-time students. Financial award application deadline: 3/1; financial award applicants required to submit FAFSA. In 2017, 395 master's, 154 doctorates awarded. *Program availability:* Part-time, evening/weekend, 100% online, blended/hybrid learning. Offers education of the deaf (MS); exercise and sports nutrition (MS); food science and flavor chemistry (MS); food systems administration (MS); health sciences (MA, MOT, MS, DPT, OTD, PhD); health studies (MS, PhD); kinesiology (MS, PhD); nutrition (MS, PhD); occupational therapy (MOT, OTD, PhD); physical therapy (DPT, PhD); speech-language pathology (MS). *Application deadline:* For fall admission, 7/1 priority date for domestic students, 3/1 priority date for international students; for spring admission, 12/1 priority date for domestic students, 7/1 priority date for international students. Applications are processed on a rolling basis. *Application fee:* $50 ($75 for international students). Electronic applications accepted. *Application Contact:* Korie Hawkins, Associate Director of Admissions, Graduate Recruitment, 940-898-3188, Fax: 940-898-3081, E-mail: admissions@twu.edu. *Dean*, Dr. Christopher T. Ray, 940-898-2852, Fax: 940-898-2853.

College of Nursing Students: 23 full-time (22 women), 816 part-time (750 women); includes 475 minority (188 Black or African American, non-Hispanic/Latino; 4 American Indian or Alaska Native, non-Hispanic/Latino; 171 Asian, non-Hispanic/Latino; 83 Hispanic/Latino; 3 Native Hawaiian or other Pacific Islander, non-Hispanic/Latino; 26 Two or more races, non-Hispanic/Latino), 12 international. Average age 37. 201 applicants, 88% accepted, 123 enrolled. *Faculty:* 48 full-time (47 women), 44 part-time/adjunct (37 women). Expenses: Contact institution. *Financial support:* In 2017–18, 146 students received support, including 7 teaching assistantships (averaging $28,195 per year); research assistantships, career-related internships or fieldwork, Federal Work-Study, institutionally sponsored loans, scholarships/grants, traineeships, health care benefits, and unspecified assistantships also available. Support available to part-time students. Financial award application deadline: 3/1; financial award applicants required to submit FAFSA. In 2017, 232 master's, 17 doctorates awarded. *Program availability:* Part-time, 100% online, blended/hybrid learning. Offers adult health clinical nurse specialist (MS); adult health nurse practitioner (MS); adult/gerontology acute care nurse practitioner (MS); child health clinical nurse specialist (MS); clinical nurse leader (MS); family nurse practitioner (MS); health systems management (MS); nursing education (MS); nursing practice (DNP); nursing science (PhD); pediatric nurse practitioner (MS); women's health clinical nurse specialist (MS); women's health nurse practitioner (MS). *Application deadline:* For fall admission, 5/1 for domestic students, 3/1 priority date for international students; for spring admission, 9/15 for domestic students, 7/1 priority date for international students; for summer admission, 2/1 for domestic and international students. Applications are processed on a rolling basis. *Application fee:* $50 ($75 for international students). Electronic applications accepted. *Application Contact:* Korie Hawkins, Associate Director of Admissions, Graduate Recruitment,

940-898-3188, Fax: 940-898-3081, E-mail: admissions@twu.edu. *Dean*, Dr. Anita G. Hufft, 940-898-2401, Fax: 940-898-2437, E-mail: nursing@twu.edu.

College of Professional Education Students: 318 full-time (301 women), 896 part-time (842 women); includes 448 minority (146 Black or African American, non-Hispanic/Latino; 2 American Indian or Alaska Native, non-Hispanic/Latino; 26 Asian, non-Hispanic/Latino; 246 Hispanic/Latino; 28 Two or more races, non-Hispanic/Latino), 13 international. Average age 35. 519 applicants, 65% accepted, 259 enrolled. *Faculty:* 69 full-time (56 women), 56 part-time/adjunct (42 women). Expenses: Contact institution. *Financial support:* In 2017–18, 264 students received support, including 40 research assistantships (averaging $12,164 per year), 8 teaching assistantships (averaging $12,164 per year); career-related internships or fieldwork, Federal Work-Study, institutionally sponsored loans, scholarships/grants, traineeships, health care benefits, and unspecified assistantships also available. Support available to part-time students. Financial award application deadline: 3/1; financial award applicants required to submit FAFSA. In 2017, 301 master's, 25 doctorates awarded. *Program availability:* Part-time, evening/weekend. Offers child development (MS); child life (MS); counseling and development (MS); early childhood development and education (PhD); early childhood education (M Ed); educational administration (M Ed, MA); family studies (MS, PhD); family therapy (MS, PhD); library science (MA, MLS); professional education (M Ed, MA, MAT, MLS, MS, PhD, Certificate); reading education (M Ed, MA, PhD); special education (M Ed, PhD); teaching (MAT); teaching, learning, and curriculum (M Ed, MA); Texas all-level (K-12) reading specialist (Certificate); Texas master reading teacher (Certificate). *Application deadline:* For fall admission, 3/1 priority date for domestic and international students; for spring admission, 11/1 priority date for domestic students, 7/1 priority date for international students. Applications are processed on a rolling basis. *Application fee:* $50 ($75 for international students). Electronic applications accepted. *Application Contact:* Korie Hawkins, Associate Director of Admissions, Graduate Recruitment, 940-898-3188, Fax: 940-898-3081, E-mail: admissions@twu.edu. *Dean*, Dr. Lisa Huffman, 940-898-2202, Fax: 940-898-2209, E-mail: cope@twu.edu.

THEOLOGICAL UNIVERSITY OF THE CARIBBEAN, Saint Just, PR 00978-0901

General Information Independent-religious, coed, comprehensive institution.

GRADUATE UNITS

Graduate Programs Offers childhood and adolescent education (MA); counseling and pastoral care (MA); ministry (D Min); missions (MA).

THOMAS COLLEGE, Waterville, ME 04901-5097

General Information Independent, coed, comprehensive institution. *Graduate housing:* On-campus housing not available.

GRADUATE UNITS

Graduate School *Program availability:* Part-time, evening/weekend. Offers business (MBA); computer technology education (MS); education (MS); human resource management (MBA). Electronic applications accepted.

THOMAS EDISON STATE UNIVERSITY, Trenton, NJ 08608

General Information State-supported, coed, comprehensive institution. *Graduate housing:* On-campus housing not available.

GRADUATE UNITS

Heavin School of Arts and Sciences *Program availability:* Part-time, online learning. Offers arts and sciences (MA, MAEL, MALS, Graduate Certificate); digital humanities (MALS, Graduate Certificate); educational leadership (MAEL, Graduate Certificate); educational technology and online learning (MA); geropsychology (MALS, Graduate Certificate); industrial-organizational psychology (MALS, Graduate Certificate); learner-designed area of study (MALS); online learning and teaching (Graduate Certificate); professional communications (MALS, Graduate Certificate). Electronic applications accepted.

John S. Watson School of Public Service and Continuing Studies *Program availability:* Part-time, online learning. Offers community and economic development (MSM); environmental policy/environmental justice (MSM); homeland security (MSHS, MSM); information and technology for public service (MSM); nonprofit management (MSM); public and municipal finance (MSM); public health (MSM); public service administration and leadership (MSM); public service leadership (MPSL). Electronic applications accepted.

School of Applied Science and Technology *Program availability:* Part-time, online learning. Offers clinical trials management (MS); cybersecurity (Graduate Certificate); information technology (MS); nuclear energy technology management (MS); technical studies (MS). Electronic applications accepted.

School of Business and Management *Program availability:* Part-time, online learning. Offers accounting (MSM); business administration (MBA); business and management (MBA, MS, MSHRM, MSM); hospitality management (MS); human resources management (MSHRM); international business finance (MS); organizational leadership (MSM); project management (MSM). Electronic applications accepted.

W. Cary Edwards School of Nursing *Program availability:* Part-time, online learning. Offers nurse educator (MSN); nursing (MSN, DNP); nursing administration (MSN); nursing informatics (MSN); systems-level leadership (DNP). Electronic applications accepted.

THOMAS JEFFERSON SCHOOL OF LAW, San Diego, CA 92110-2905

General Information Independent, coed, graduate-only institution. *Graduate housing:* Rooms and/or apartments available on a first-come, first-served basis to single and married students. Housing application deadline: 5/1.

GRADUATE UNITS

Graduate and Professional Programs *Program availability:* Part-time, evening/weekend. Offers law (JD). JD/MBA offered in partnership with San Diego State University. Electronic applications accepted.

THOMAS JEFFERSON UNIVERSITY, Philadelphia, PA 19107

General Information Independent, coed, university. CGS member. *Enrollment:* 3,326 graduate, professional, and undergraduate students; 1,173 full-time matriculated graduate/professional students (592 women), 115 part-time matriculated graduate/professional students (63 women). *Graduate housing:* Rooms and/or apartments available to single and married students. *Student services:* Campus employment opportunities, campus safety program, career counseling, child daycare facilities, exercise/wellness program, free psychological counseling, grant writing training, international student services, low-cost health insurance, multicultural affairs office, services for students with disabilities, writing training. *Library facilities:* Scott Memorial Library plus 1 other. *Collection:* Study areas open 24 hours, 5–7 days a week; students can reserve study rooms. *Research affiliation:* Christiana Care Health Services (biomedical research), Lankenau Institute for Medical Research (biomedical research), A.I. du Pont for Children Nemours (biomedical research), University of Delaware (biomedical research).

Computer facilities: A campuswide network can be accessed from off campus. Online class registration is available.
Website: http://www.jefferson.edu/university.html

General Application Contact: Marc E. Stearns, Senior Associate Director of Admissions, 215-503-0155, Fax: 215-503-9920, E-mail: jcgs-info@jefferson.edu.

GRADUATE UNITS

College of Architecture and the Built Environment Offers architecture (M Arch, MS); architecture and the built environment (MS); construction management (MS); geospatial technology for geodesign (MS); interior architecture (MS); real estate development (MS); sustainable design (MS).

College of Science, Health and the Liberal Arts *Program availability:* Part-time, evening/weekend, online learning. Offers athletic training (MS); community and trauma counseling (MS); disaster medicine and management (MS); midwifery (MS); occupational therapy (MS); physician assistant studies (MS); science, health and the liberal arts (MS, Postbaccalaureate Certificate). Electronic applications accepted.

Jefferson College of Biomedical Sciences Students: 125 full-time (67 women), 144 part-time (88 women); includes 44 minority (16 Black or African American, non-Hispanic/Latino; 1 American Indian or Alaska Native, non-Hispanic/Latino; 15 Asian, non-Hispanic/Latino; 10 Hispanic/Latino; 2 Two or more races, non-Hispanic/Latino), 35 international. 356 applicants, 43% accepted, 78 enrolled. *Faculty:* 169 full-time (52 women), 39 part-time/adjunct (18 women). Expenses: Contact institution. *Financial support:* Fellowships, Federal Work-Study, institutionally sponsored loans, scholarships/grants, and traineeships available. Support available to part-time students. Financial award application deadline: 5/1; financial award applicants required to submit FAFSA. In 2017, 26 master's, 26 doctorates awarded. *Program availability:* Part-time, evening/weekend. Offers biochemistry and molecular pharmacology (PhD); biomedical sciences (MS, PhD, Certificate); cell and developmental biology (MS); cell biology and regenerative medicine (PhD); clinical research (MS); clinical research and trials: implementation (Certificate); clinical research: operations (Certificate); forensic toxicology (MS); genetics, genomics and cancer biology (PhD); human clinical investigation: theory (Certificate); human genetics and genetic counseling (MS); immunology and microbial pathogenesis (PhD); infectious disease control (Certificate); microbiology (MS); neuroscience (PhD); patient-centered research (Certificate); pharmacology (MS). *Application deadline:* Applications are processed on a rolling basis. *Application fee:* $50. Electronic applications accepted. *Application Contact:* Marc E. Stearns, Senior Associate Director of Admissions, 215-503-0155, Fax: 215-503-3433, E-mail: jgsbs-info@jefferson.edu. *Dean*, Dr. Gerald B. Grunwald, 215-503-4191, Fax: 215-503-6690, E-mail: gerald.grunwald@jefferson.edu.

Jefferson College of Health Professions Offers biotechnology (MS); couple and family therapy (MFT); cytotechnology (MS); health professions (MFT, MS, DPT, OTD); medical laboratory science (MS); occupational therapy (MS, OTD); physical therapy (DPT); physician assistant studies (MS); radiologic and imaging sciences (MS). Electronic applications accepted.

Jefferson College of Nursing *Program availability:* Part-time, online only, 100% online, blended/hybrid learning. Offers nursing (MS, DNP). Electronic applications accepted.

Jefferson College of Pharmacy Offers pharmacy (Pharm D). Electronic applications accepted.

Jefferson College of Population Health *Program availability:* Part-time, evening/weekend, online learning. Offers applied health economics and outcomes research (MS, PhD, Certificate); behavioral health science (PhD); health policy (MS, PhD, Certificate); healthcare quality and safety (MS, PhD, Certificate); population health (Certificate); public health (MPH, Certificate). Electronic applications accepted.

Kanbar College of Design, Engineering and Commerce *Program availability:* Part-time. Offers business analytics (MBA); design, engineering and commerce (MS, PhD); fashion design management (MS); general business (MBA); global fashion enterprise (MS); industrial design (MS); management (MBA); marketing (MBA); strategy and design thinking (MBA); surface imaging (MS); taxation (MS); textile design (MS); textile engineering (MS); textile engineering and sciences (PhD); user experience and interaction design (MS). Electronic applications accepted.

School of Continuing and Professional Studies

Sidney Kimmel Medical College Students: 1,086 full-time (539 women); includes 354 minority (24 Black or African American, non-Hispanic/Latino; 4 American Indian or Alaska Native, non-Hispanic/Latino; 257 Asian, non-Hispanic/Latino; 69 Hispanic/Latino), 38 international. Average age 23. 10,052 applicants, 5% accepted, 272 enrolled. *Faculty:* 1,219 full-time (449 women), 84 part-time/adjunct (41 women). Expenses: Contact institution. *Financial support:* In 2017–18, 553 students received support. Federal Work-Study, institutionally sponsored loans, and scholarships/grants available. Financial award application deadline: 3/1; financial award applicants required to submit FAFSA. In 2017, 251 doctorates awarded. Offers medicine (MD). *Application deadline:* For fall admission, 11/15 for domestic and international students. Applications are processed on a rolling basis. *Application fee:* $80. Electronic applications accepted. *Application Contact:* Dr. Clara Callahan, Dean for Students and Admissions, 215-955-4077, Fax: 215-955-5151, E-mail: clara.callahan@jefferson.edu. *Dean*, Dr. Mark Tykowcinski, 215-955-6980, Fax: 215-923-6939, E-mail: mark.tykowcinski@jefferson.edu.

THOMAS MORE COLLEGE, Crestview Hills, KY 41017-3495

General Information Independent-religious, coed, comprehensive institution. *Graduate housing:* On-campus housing not available.

GRADUATE UNITS

Program in Business Administration *Program availability:* Evening/weekend, 100% online. Offers business administration (MBA). Electronic applications accepted.

Program in Teacher Leader *Program availability:* Part-time, evening/weekend. Offers teacher leader (M Ed). Electronic applications accepted.

Program in Teaching *Program availability:* Part-time. Offers teaching (MAT). Electronic applications accepted.

THOMAS UNIVERSITY, Thomasville, GA 31792-7499

General Information Independent, coed, comprehensive institution. *Graduate housing:* Room and/or apartments available on a first-come, first-served basis to single students; on-campus housing not available to married students. Housing application deadline: 8/1.

GRADUATE UNITS

Department of Business Administration *Program availability:* Part-time. Offers business administration (MBA). Electronic applications accepted.

Department of Education *Program availability:* Part-time. Offers education (M Ed). Electronic applications accepted.

Department of Human Services *Program availability:* Part-time. Offers community counseling (MSCC); rehabilitation counseling (MRC). Electronic applications accepted.

Department of Nursing *Program availability:* Part-time. Offers nursing (MSN). Electronic applications accepted.

THOMPSON RIVERS UNIVERSITY, Kamloops, BC V2C 0C8, Canada

General Information Province-supported, coed, comprehensive institution. CGS member.

GRADUATE UNITS

Program in Business Administration *Program availability:* Part-time. Offers business administration (MBA).

Program in Education *Program availability:* Part-time. Offers education (M Ed).

Program in Environmental Science Offers environmental science (MS).

Program in Social Work Offers social work (MSW).

TIFFIN UNIVERSITY, Tiffin, OH 44883-2161

General Information Independent, coed, comprehensive institution. *Graduate housing:* Room and/or apartments available on a first-come, first-served basis to single students; on-campus housing not available to married students. Housing application deadline: 8/1.

GRADUATE UNITS

Program in Business Administration *Program availability:* Part-time, evening/weekend, online learning. Offers finance (MBA); general management (MBA); healthcare administration (MBA); human resource management (MBA); international business (MBA); leadership (MBA); marketing (MBA); non-profit management (MBA); sports management (MBA). Electronic applications accepted.

Program in Criminal Justice *Program availability:* Part-time, evening/weekend, 100% online, blended/hybrid learning. Offers criminal justice (MS). Electronic applications accepted.

Program in Education *Program availability:* Part-time, evening/weekend, online only, 100% online, blended/hybrid learning. Offers educational technology management (M Ed); higher education administration (M Ed). Electronic applications accepted.

Program in Humanities *Program availability:* Part-time, evening/weekend, online only, 100% online, blended/hybrid learning. Offers art and visual media (MH); communication (MH); creative writing (MH); English (MH); film studies (MH); humanities (MH); individualized studies (MH). Electronic applications accepted.

Program in Psychology *Program availability:* Part-time, evening/weekend, online only, 100% online. Offers psychology (MS). Electronic applications accepted.

TORONTO SCHOOL OF THEOLOGY, Toronto, ON M5S 2C3, Canada

General Information Independent-religious, coed, graduate-only institution.

GRADUATE UNITS

Graduate Programs *Program availability:* Online learning. Offers theology (M Div, MA, MAMS, MPS, MRE, MSM, MTS, Th M, D Min, PhD, Th D). Electronic applications accepted.

TOURO COLLEGE, New York, NY 10010

General Information Independent, coed, comprehensive institution. *Enrollment:* 2,419 full-time matriculated graduate/professional students (1,826 women), 4,259 part-time matriculated graduate/professional students (3,825 women). *Enrollment by degree level:* 6,474 master's. *Graduate faculty:* 181 full-time (114 women), 383 part-time/adjunct (229 women). *Student services:* Career counseling, free psychological counseling, low-cost health insurance. *Library facilities:* Touro College Library plus 14 others.

Computer facilities: A campuswide network can be accessed from off campus. Online class registration is available.
Website: http://www.touro.edu/

General Application Contact: Dr. Benjamin Enoma, Director, Graduate Admissions, 212-463-0400.

GRADUATE UNITS

Graduate School of Education Students: 756 full-time (686 women), 3,833 part-time (3,492 women). Average age 33. 1,422 applicants, 50% accepted, 675 enrolled. *Faculty:* 52 full-time (34 women), 199 part-time/adjunct (136 women). Expenses: Contact institution. *Financial support:* Federal Work-Study available. Financial award applicants required to submit FAFSA. In 2017, 6 master's awarded. *Program availability:* Part-time, evening/weekend, online learning. Offers education and special education (MS); instructional technology (MS); mathematics education (MS); school leadership (MS); teaching English to speakers of other languages (MS); teaching literacy (MS). *Application deadline:* For fall admission, 8/26 for domestic students, 7/15 for international students; for spring admission, 12/31 for domestic students, 12/15 for international students. Applications are processed on a rolling basis. *Application fee:* $50. *Application Contact:* Sharmilee Hoopnarine, Admissions, 212-463-0400. *Dean*, Dr. Jacob Easley, III, 212-463-0400 Ext. 5561, Fax: 212-462-4889, E-mail: jeasley@touro.edu.

Graduate School of Jewish Studies Students: 23 full-time (22 women), 28 part-time (26 women); includes 1 minority (Hispanic/Latino), 4 international. Average age 38. *Faculty:* 4 full-time (2 women), 5 part-time/adjunct (2 women). Expenses: Contact institution. *Financial support:* Tuition waivers (full and partial) available. Support available to part-time students. *Program availability:* Part-time. Offers Jewish studies (MA). *Application fee:* $50. *Application Contact:* Karen Rubin, Executive Assistant to the Dean, 212-463-0400 Ext. 5581, E-mail: karen.rubin@touro.edu. *Dean*, Dr. Michael Shmidman, 212-213-2230.

Graduate School of Social Work Students: 442 full-time (281 women), 86 part-time (56 women); includes 227 minority (134 Black or African American, non-Hispanic/Latino; 1 American Indian or Alaska Native, non-Hispanic/Latino; 6 Asian, non-Hispanic/Latino; 73 Hispanic/Latino; 13 Two or more races, non-Hispanic/Latino), 12 international. Average age 34. *Faculty:* 9 full-time (6 women), 54 part-time/adjunct (32 women). Expenses: Contact institution. *Financial support:* Scholarships/grants available. Offers social work (MSW). *Application Contact:* Peter Stewart, Director of Recruitment, Admissions and Enrollment Management, 212-463-0400 Ext. 5630, Fax: 212-627-3693, E-mail: peter.stewart@touro.edu. *Dean*, Dr. Steven Huberman, 212-463-0400 Ext. 5269, E-mail: msw@touro.edu.

Graduate School of Technology Students: 125 full-time (122 women), 177 part-time (163 women); includes 79 minority (39 Black or African American, non-Hispanic/Latino; 23 Asian, non-Hispanic/Latino; 14 Hispanic/Latino; 3 Two or more races, non-Hispanic/Latino), 150 international. Average age 34. *Faculty:* 18 part-time/adjunct (6 women). Expenses: Contact institution. Offers information systems (MS); instructional technology (MS); Web and multimedia design (MA). *Application fee:* $50. *Application Contact:* Jack Romano, Program Director, 212-463-0400 Ext. 5462. *Dean of the Graduate School of Technology*, Dr. Issac Herskowitz, 202-463-0400 Ext. 5231, E-mail: issac.herskowitz@touro.edu.

Jacob D. Fuchsberg Law Center Students: 445 full-time (245 women), 22 part-time (15 women); includes 166 minority (47 Black or African American, non-Hispanic/Latino; 2 American Indian or Alaska Native, non-Hispanic/Latino; 41 Asian, non-Hispanic/Latino; 72 Hispanic/Latino; 4 Two or more races, non-Hispanic/Latino), 9 international. Average age 30. *Faculty:* 35 full-time (17 women), 30 part-time/adjunct (7 women). Expenses: Contact institution. *Financial support:* Fellowships, career-related internships or fieldwork, and Federal Work-Study available. Support available to part-time students. Financial award application deadline: 5/1. *Program availability:* Part-time, evening/weekend. Offers general law (LL M); law (JD); U.S. legal studies (LL M). JD/MBA and JD/MPA offered with Long Island University-LIU Post; JD/MSW offered with Stony Brook University, State University of New York. *Application deadline:* Applications are processed on a rolling basis. *Application fee:* $60. *Application Contact:* Dr. Susan Thompson, Office of Admissions, 631-761-7010, E-mail: admissions@tourolaw.edu. *Dean*, Dr. Harry Ballan, 631-761-7100.

School of Health Sciences Students: 628 full-time (470 women), 113 part-time (73 women); includes 143 minority (31 Black or African American, non-Hispanic/Latino; 1 American Indian or Alaska Native, non-Hispanic/Latino; 61 Asian, non-Hispanic/Latino; 42 Hispanic/Latino; 1 Native Hawaiian or other Pacific Islander, non-Hispanic/Latino; 7 Two or more races, non-Hispanic/Latino), 63 international. Average age 28. *Faculty:* 81 full-time (55 women), 77 part-time/adjunct (46 women). Expenses: Contact institution. *Financial support:* Fellowships available. Offers industrial-organizational psychology (MS); mental health counseling (MS); occupational therapy (MS); physical therapy (DPT); physician assistant (MS); speech-language pathology (MS). *Application Contact:* Brian J. Diele, Director of Student Administrative Services, 631-665-1600 Ext. 6311, E-mail: brian.diele@touro.edu. *Dean, School of Health Sciences*, Dr. Louis Primavera, 516-673-3200, E-mail: louis.primavera@touro.edu.

TOURO UNIVERSITY CALIFORNIA, Vallejo, CA 94592

General Information Independent, coed, graduate-only institution. *Graduate housing:* On-campus housing not available. *Research affiliation:* University of California San Francisco (cancer, HIV/AIDS), Genetech (cancer), National Institutes of Health (diabetes, cardiac arrest in teens).

GRADUATE UNITS

Graduate Programs *Program availability:* Part-time, evening/weekend. Offers education (MA); medical health sciences (MS); osteopathic medicine (DO); pharmacy (Pharm D); public health (MPH). Electronic applications accepted.

TOWSON UNIVERSITY, Towson, MD 21252-0001

General Information State-supported, coed, university. CGS member. *Enrollment:* 22,705 graduate, professional, and undergraduate students; 1,062 full-time matriculated graduate/professional students (754 women), 1,961 part-time matriculated graduate/professional students (1,475 women). *Enrollment by degree level:* 2,600 master's, 158 doctoral, 265 other advanced degrees. *Graduate faculty:* 286 full-time (168 women), 117 part-time/adjunct (65 women). Tuition, state resident: full-time $7960; part-time $398 per unit. Tuition, nonresident: full-time $16,480; part-time $824 per unit. *Required fees:* $2600; $130 per year. $390 per term. *Graduate housing:* On-campus housing not available. *Student services:* Campus employment opportunities, campus safety program, career counseling, child daycare facilities, exercise/wellness program, free psychological counseling, international student services, low-cost health insurance, multicultural affairs office, services for students with disabilities, writing training. *Library facilities:* Cook Library. *Collection:* Books: 402,034 (physical), 245,801 (digital/electronic); Serial titles: 326 (physical), 29,155 (digital/electronic); Databases: 196. Weekly public service hours: 109; study areas open 24 hours, 5–7 days a week; students can reserve study rooms. *Research affiliation:* Exelon Generation Company (biology, mathematics), Prometheus Computing (computer science), Coracias Advance Technology, LLC (computer science), Vesperix Corporation (physics, astronomy and geosciences), Brekford Corporation (computer science), RTR Technologies (computer science).

Computer facilities: 2,500 computers available on campus for general student use. A campuswide network can be accessed from student residence rooms and from off campus. Online class registration is available.
Website: http://www.towson.edu/

General Application Contact: Coverley Beidleman, Assistant Director of Graduate Admissions, 410-704-2113, Fax: 410-704-5630, E-mail: grads@towson.edu.

GRADUATE UNITS

College of Business and Economics Students: 48 full-time (28 women), 57 part-time (32 women); includes 29 minority (12 Black or African American, non-Hispanic/Latino; 8 Asian, non-Hispanic/Latino; 4 Hispanic/Latino; 5 Two or more races, non-Hispanic/Latino), 22 international. Expenses: Contact institution. Offers accounting (MS); business and economics (MS, Postbaccalaureate Certificate); marketing intelligence (MS, Postbaccalaureate Certificate); project, program and portfolio management (Postbaccalaureate Certificate); supply chain management (MS). *Application deadline:* For fall admission, 1/17 for domestic students, 5/15 for international students; for spring admission, 10/15 for domestic students, 12/1 for international students. Applications are processed on a rolling basis. *Application fee:* $45. Electronic applications accepted. *Application Contact:* Coverley Beidleman, Assistant Director of Graduate Admissions, 410-704-5630, Fax: 410-704-3030, E-mail: cbeidleman@towson.edu. *Dean*, Shohreh Kaynama, 410-704-3342, E-mail: skaynama@towson.edu.

College of Education Students: 98 full-time (70 women), 879 part-time (786 women); includes 130 minority (71 Black or African American, non-Hispanic/Latino; 15 Asian, non-Hispanic/Latino; 29 Hispanic/Latino; 15 Two or more races, non-Hispanic/Latino), 5 international. Expenses: Contact institution. Offers early childhood education (MAT); education (M Ed, MAT, MS, Ed D, CAS, Postbaccalaureate Certificate); educational technology (MS); elementary education (M Ed); instructional design and development (MS); instructional leadership and professional development (CAS, Postbaccalaureate Certificate); reading (M Ed); reading education (CAS); school library media (MS); secondary education (MAT); special education (M Ed, MAT); teacher as leader in autism spectrum disorder (M Ed). *Application deadline:* For fall admission, 1/17 for domestic students, 5/15 for international students; for spring admission, 10/15 for domestic students, 12/1 for international students. Applications are processed on a rolling basis.

Application fee: $45. Electronic applications accepted. *Application Contact:* Coverley Beidleman, Assistant Director of Graduate Admissions, 410-704-5630, Fax: 410-704-3030, E-mail: cbeidleman@towson.edu. *Dean*, Dr. Laurie Mullen, 410-704-2570, Fax: 410-704-2733, E-mail: lmullen@towson.edu.

College of Fine Arts and Communication Students: 37 full-time (25 women), 137 part-time (105 women). Expenses: Contact institution. Offers art education (M Ed); arts integration (Postbaccalaureate Certificate); communication management (MS); fine arts and communication (M Ed, MA, MFA, MM, MS, Postbaccalaureate Certificate); interactive media design (Postbaccalaureate Certificate); interdisciplinary arts infusion (MA); music education (MS); music performance and composition (MM); studio art (MFA); theatre (MFA). *Application deadline:* For fall admission, 1/17 for domestic students, 5/15 for international students; for spring admission, 10/15 for domestic students, 12/1 for international students. Applications are processed on a rolling basis. *Application fee:* $45. Electronic applications accepted. *Application Contact:* Coverley Beidleman, Assistant Director of Graduate Admissions, 410-704-5630, Fax: 410-704-3030, E-mail: cbeidleman@towson.edu. *Dean*, Dr. Susan E. Picinich, 410-704-3288 Ext. 410, E-mail: spicinich@towson.edu.

College of Health Professions Students: 380 full-time (336 women), 132 part-time (110 women); includes 126 minority (78 Black or African American, non-Hispanic/Latino; 23 Asian, non-Hispanic/Latino; 17 Hispanic/Latino; 8 Two or more races, non-Hispanic/Latino), 8 international. Expenses: Contact institution. Offers audiology (Au D); autism studies (Postbaccalaureate Certificate); clinician to administrator transition (MS, Postbaccalaureate Certificate); health professions (MS, Au D, Sc D, Postbaccalaureate Certificate); health science (MS); nursing education (Postbaccalaureate Certificate); occupational science (Sc D); occupational therapy (MS); physician assistant studies (MS); speech-language pathology (MS). *Application deadline:* For fall admission, 1/17 for domestic students, 5/15 for international students; for spring admission, 10/15 for domestic students, 12/1 for international students. Applications are processed on a rolling basis. *Application fee:* $45. Electronic applications accepted. *Application Contact:* Coverley Beidleman, Assistant Director of Graduate Admissions, 410-704-5630, Fax: 410-704-3030, E-mail: cbeidleman@towson.edu. *Dean*, Dr. Lisa Plowfield, 410-704-2132, Fax: 410-704-3479, E-mail: lplowfield@towson.edu.

College of Liberal Arts Students: 217 full-time (170 women), 402 part-time (282 women); includes 154 minority (88 Black or African American, non-Hispanic/Latino; 1 American Indian or Alaska Native, non-Hispanic/Latino; 17 Asian, non-Hispanic/Latino; 27 Hispanic/Latino; 21 Two or more races, non-Hispanic/Latino), 6 international. Expenses: Contact institution. Offers art history (MA); child life, administration and family collaboration (MS); clinical psychology (MA); counseling psychology (MA); education leadership (MS); experimental psychology (MA); family-professional collaboration (Postbaccalaureate Certificate); general human resource management (MS); geography and environmental planning (MA); global humanities (MA); individualized plan of study (MA); integrated homeland security management (MS); liberal arts (MA, MS, CAS, Postbaccalaureate Certificate); professional writing (MS); school psychology (MA); security assessment and management (Postbaccalaureate Certificate); social science (MS); women's studies (MS, Postbaccalaureate Certificate). *Application deadline:* For fall admission, 1/17 for domestic students, 5/15 for international students; for spring admission, 10/15 for domestic students, 12/1 for international students. Applications are processed on a rolling basis. *Application fee:* $45. Electronic applications accepted. *Application Contact:* Coverley Beidleman, Assistant Director of Graduate Admissions, 410-704-5630, Fax: 410-704-3030, E-mail: cbeidleman@towson.edu. *Dean*, Terry Cooney, 410-704-2129.

Program in Leadership and Jewish Studies Students: 3 full-time (1 woman), 14 part-time (7 women); includes 3 minority (1 Black or African American, non-Hispanic/Latino; 1 Hispanic/Latino; 1 Two or more races, non-Hispanic/Latino), 1 international. Expenses: Contact institution. Offers Jewish communal service (Postbaccalaureate Certificate). *Application deadline:* For fall admission, 1/17 for domestic students, 5/15 for international students; for spring admission, 10/15 for domestic students, 12/1 for international students. Applications are processed on a rolling basis. *Application fee:* $45. Electronic applications accepted. *Application Contact:* Coverley Beidleman, Assistant Director of Graduate Admissions, 410-704-5630, Fax: 410-704-3030, E-mail: grads@towson.edu. *Program Director*, Jill Max, 410-704-7120, E-mail: jmax@towson.edu.

Jess and Mildred Fisher College of Science and Mathematics Students: 282 full-time (125 women), 354 part-time (160 women); includes 232 minority (137 Black or African American, non-Hispanic/Latino; 1 American Indian or Alaska Native, non-Hispanic/Latino; 60 Asian, non-Hispanic/Latino; 13 Hispanic/Latino; 21 Two or more races, non-Hispanic/Latino), 118 international. Expenses: Contact institution. Offers applied and industrial mathematics (MS); applied information technology (MS); applied physics (MS); biology (MS); computer science (MS); environmental science (MS, Postbaccalaureate Certificate); forensic science (MS); information technology (D Sc); integrated STEM instructional leadership (Postbaccalaureate Certificate); Internet applications development (Postbaccalaureate Certificate); mathematics education (MS); science and mathematics (MS, D Sc, Postbaccalaureate Certificate). *Application deadline:* For fall admission, 1/17 for domestic students, 5/15 for international students; for spring admission, 10/15 for domestic students, 12/1 for international students. Applications are processed on a rolling basis. *Application fee:* $45. Electronic applications accepted. *Application Contact:* Coverley Beidleman, Assistant Director of Graduate Admissions, 410-704-2113, Fax: 410-704-3030, E-mail: grads@towson.edu. *Dean*, Dr. David A. Vanko, 410-704-2121, Fax: 410-704-2604, E-mail: dvanko@towson.edu.

TOYOTA TECHNOLOGICAL INSTITUTE AT CHICAGO, Chicago, IL 60637

General Information Proprietary, coed, graduate-only institution.

GRADUATE UNITS

Program in Computer Science Offers computer science (PhD).

TRENT UNIVERSITY, Peterborough, ON K9J 7B8, Canada

General Information Province-supported, coed, university. *Graduate housing:* Room and/or apartments available to single students; on-campus housing not available to married students. Housing application deadline: 7/10. *Research affiliation:* Watershed Science Centre (watershed studies), Ontario Power Generation, Inc. (acid rain deposition), Enbridge Consumers Gas (ozone depletion), Forensics Laboratory (DNA testing).

GRADUATE UNITS

Graduate Studies *Program availability:* Part-time. Offers anthropology (MA); applications of modeling in the natural and social sciences (MA); biology (M Sc, PhD); chemistry (M Sc); computer studies (M Sc); cultural studies (PhD); environmental and resource studies (M Sc, PhD); geography (M Sc, PhD); indigenous studies (PhD); materials science (M Sc); physics (M Sc).

The Frost Centre for Canadian Studies and Indigenous Studies *Program availability:* Part-time. Offers Canadian studies (PhD); Canadian studies and indigenous studies (MA).

TREVECCA NAZARENE UNIVERSITY, Nashville, TN 37210-2877

General Information Independent-religious, coed, comprehensive institution. *Enrollment:* 3,620 graduate, professional, and undergraduate students; 1,002 full-time matriculated graduate/professional students (712 women), 378 part-time matriculated graduate/professional students (244 women). *Enrollment by degree level:* 935 master's, 387 doctoral, 58 other advanced degrees. *Graduate faculty:* 43 full-time (17 women), 87 part-time/adjunct (49 women). *Tuition:* Full-time $9281. Tuition and fees vary according to degree level and program. *Graduate housing:* On-campus housing not available. *Student services:* Services for students with disabilities, teacher training. *Library facilities:* Waggoner Library. *Collection:* Books: 85,560 (physical), 49,113 (digital/electronic); Serial titles: 299 (physical), 60,127 (digital/electronic); Databases: 44. Weekly public service hours: 91; students can reserve study rooms.

Computer facilities: 200 computers available on campus for general student use. A campuswide network can be accessed from student residence rooms and from off campus. Online class registration, Non-traditional and graduate students are registered through Academic Records are available.
Website: http://www.trevecca.edu/

General Application Contact: School of Graduate and Continuing Studies, 844-TNU-GRAD, E-mail: sgcsadmissions@trevecca.edu.

GRADUATE UNITS

Graduate Business Programs Students: 236 full-time (145 women), 50 part-time (29 women); includes 154 minority (128 Black or African American, non-Hispanic/Latino; 1 American Indian or Alaska Native, non-Hispanic/Latino; 4 Asian, non-Hispanic/Latino; 18 Hispanic/Latino; 3 Two or more races, non-Hispanic/Latino), 4 international. Average age 33. *Faculty:* 12 full-time (1 woman), 15 part-time/adjunct (8 women). Expenses: Contact institution. *Financial support:* Applicants required to submit FAFSA. In 2017, 55 master's awarded. *Program availability:* Evening/weekend, online learning. Offers business administration (MBA); health care leadership and innovation (MS); management (MSM). *Application deadline:* Applications are processed on a rolling basis. *Application fee:* $0. Electronic applications accepted. *Application Contact:* 615-248-1529, E-mail: sgcsadmissions@trevecca.edu. *Director of Graduate and Professional Programs for School of Business*, Dr. Rick Mann, 615-248-1529, E-mail: management@trevecca.edu.

Graduate Counseling Program Students: 157 full-time (129 women), 73 part-time (50 women); includes 49 minority (38 Black or African American, non-Hispanic/Latino; 5 Hispanic/Latino; 6 Two or more races, non-Hispanic/Latino). Average age 35. *Faculty:* 7 full-time (3 women), 11 part-time/adjunct (8 women). Expenses: Contact institution. *Financial support:* Applicants required to submit FAFSA. In 2017, 47 master's, 3 doctorates awarded. *Program availability:* Part-time, evening/weekend. Offers clinical counseling: teaching and supervision (PhD); clinical mental health counseling (MA); marriage and family counseling/therapy (MMFC/T). *Application deadline:* Applications are processed on a rolling basis. *Application fee:* $0. Electronic applications accepted. *Application Contact:* 615-248-1384, Fax: 615-248-1662, E-mail: admissions_gradcouns@trevecca.edu. *Director*, Dr. Susan Lahey, 615-248-1384, Fax: 615-248-1662, E-mail: admissions_gradcouns@trevecca.edu.

Graduate Education Program Students: 150 full-time (114 women), 3 part-time (1 woman); includes 54 minority (49 Black or African American, non-Hispanic/Latino; 4 Hispanic/Latino; 1 Two or more races, non-Hispanic/Latino). Average age 36. *Faculty:* 8 full-time (6 women), 22 part-time/adjunct (18 women). Expenses: Contact institution. *Financial support:* Applicants required to submit FAFSA. In 2017, 57 master's, 4 other advanced degrees awarded. *Program availability:* Part-time, evening/weekend, online learning. Offers accountability and instructional leadership (Ed S); curriculum and instruction for Christian school educators (M Ed); curriculum and instruction K-12 (M Ed); educational leadership (M Ed); English second language (M Ed); library and information science (MLI Sc); special education: visual impairments (M Ed); teaching (MAT). *Application deadline:* Applications are processed on a rolling basis. Electronic applications accepted. *Application Contact:* 844-TNU-GRAD, E-mail: sgcsadmissions@trevecca.edu. *Dean, School of Education*, Dr. Suzie Harris, 615-248-1201, Fax: 615-248-1597, E-mail: admissions_ged@trevecca.edu.

Graduate Instructional Design and Technology Program Students: 10 full-time (9 women), 15 part-time (10 women); includes 8 minority (all Black or African American, non-Hispanic/Latino). Average age 39. *Faculty:* 3 part-time/adjunct (2 women). Expenses: Contact institution. *Financial support:* Applicants required to submit FAFSA. *Program availability:* Online only. Offers instructional design and technology (MS). *Application deadline:* Applications are processed on a rolling basis. *Application fee:* $0. Electronic applications accepted. *Application Contact:* 844-TNU-GRAD, E-mail: sgcsadmissions@trevecca.edu.

Graduate Leadership Programs Students: 282 full-time (205 women), 214 part-time (141 women); includes 302 minority (254 Black or African American, non-Hispanic/Latino; 4 American Indian or Alaska Native, non-Hispanic/Latino; 1 Asian, non-Hispanic/Latino; 25 Hispanic/Latino; 1 Native Hawaiian or other Pacific Islander, non-Hispanic/Latino; 17 Two or more races, non-Hispanic/Latino), 1 international. Average age 40. *Faculty:* 9 full-time (5 women), 27 part-time/adjunct (12 women). Expenses: Contact institution. *Financial support:* Applicants required to submit FAFSA. In 2017, 68 master's, 75 doctorates awarded. *Program availability:* Online learning. Offers leadership and professional practice (Ed D); organizational leadership (MOL). *Application deadline:* Applications are processed on a rolling basis. *Application fee:* $0. Electronic applications accepted. *Application Contact:* 844-TNU-GRAD, E-mail: sgcsadmissions@trevecca.edu. *Associate Vice President and Dean, Graduate and Continuing Studies/Director of Master of Organizational Leadership*, Dr. Ricky Christman, 615-248-1529, E-mail: sgcsadmissions@trevecca.edu.

Graduate Physician Assistant Program Students: 93 full-time (70 women), 1 part-time (0 women); includes 8 minority (1 Black or African American, non-Hispanic/Latino; 5 Asian, non-Hispanic/Latino; 2 Hispanic/Latino). Average age 25. *Faculty:* 5 full-time (all women), 4 part-time/adjunct (3 women). Expenses: Contact institution. *Financial support:* Applicants required to submit FAFSA. In 2017, 45 master's awarded. Offers physician assistant (MS). *Application deadline:* For fall admission, 10/1 for domestic students. *Application Contact:* 615-248-1225, E-mail: admissions_pa@trevecca.edu. *Director*, Bret Reeves, 615-248-1225, E-mail: admissions_pa@trevecca.edu.

Graduate Religion Programs Students: 74 full-time (40 women), 22 part-time (13 women); includes 38 minority (26 Black or African American, non-Hispanic/Latino; 1 American Indian or Alaska Native, non-Hispanic/Latino; 1 Asian, non-Hispanic/Latino; 7 Hispanic/Latino; 3 Two or more races, non-Hispanic/Latino), 1 international. Average age 41. *Faculty:* 10 full-time (2 women), 7 part-time/adjunct (0 women). Expenses: Contact institution. *Financial support:* Applicants required to submit FAFSA. In 2017, 22 master's awarded. *Program availability:* Part-time, online learning. Offers biblical and theological studies (MA); Christian ministry (MA); pastoral counseling (MA). *Application deadline:* Applications are processed on a rolling basis. *Application fee:* $0. Electronic applications accepted. *Application Contact:* 844-TNU-GRAD, E-mail: sgcsadmissions@trevecca.edu. *Dean, School of Theology and Christian Ministry/Director, Graduate Religion Program*, Dr. Tim Green, 615-248-1378, Fax: 615-248-7417.

TRIDENT UNIVERSITY INTERNATIONAL, Cypress, CA 90630

General Information Independent, coed, university.

GRADUATE UNITS

College of Business Administration *Program availability:* Part-time, evening/weekend, online learning. Offers business administration (MBA, PhD); conflict and negotiation management (MBA); criminal justice administration (MBA); entrepreneurship (MBA); finance (MBA); general management (MBA); government accounting (MBA); human resource management (MBA); information security and digital assurance management (MBA); information technology management (MBA); international business (MBA); logistics management (MBA); marketing (MBA); project management (MBA); public management (MBA); quality management (MBA); strategic leadership (MBA). Electronic applications accepted.

College of Education *Program availability:* Part-time, evening/weekend, online learning. Offers adult education (MA Ed); aviation education (MA Ed); children's literacy development (MA Ed); e-learning (MA Ed); e-learning leadership (MA Ed, PhD); early childhood education (MA Ed); education (MA Ed, PhD); educational leadership (MA Ed); enrollment management (MA Ed); higher education (MA Ed); higher education leadership (PhD); K-12 leadership (PhD); teaching and instruction (MA Ed); training and development (MA Ed). Electronic applications accepted.

College of Health Sciences *Program availability:* Part-time, evening/weekend, online learning. Offers clinical research administration (MS, Certificate); emergency and disaster management (MS, Certificate); environmental health science (Certificate); health care administration (PhD); health care management (MS); health education (MS, Certificate); health informatics (Certificate); health sciences (MS, PhD, Certificate); international health (MS); international health: educator or researcher option (PhD); international health: practitioner option (PhD); law and expert witness studies (MS, Certificate); public health (MS); quality assurance (Certificate). Electronic applications accepted.

College of Information Systems *Program availability:* Part-time, evening/weekend, online learning. Offers business intelligence (Certificate); information technology management (MS). Electronic applications accepted.

TRINE UNIVERSITY, Angola, IN 46703-1764

General Information Independent, coed, comprehensive institution. *Enrollment:* 4,302 graduate, professional, and undergraduate students; 541 matriculated graduate/professional students (198 women). *Enrollment by degree level:* 444 master's, 97 doctoral. *Graduate faculty:* 23 full-time (9 women), 29 part-time/adjunct (15 women). *Tuition:* Part-time $515 per credit hour. Tuition and fees vary according to degree level and program. *Graduate housing:* On-campus housing not available. *Student services:* Campus employment opportunities, career counseling, exercise/wellness program, free psychological counseling, writing training. *Library facilities:* Sponsel Library plus 1 other. *Collection:* Books: 23,523 (physical), 225,584 (digital/electronic); Serial titles: 19 (physical), 21,141 (digital/electronic); Databases: 87.

Computer facilities: Computer purchase and lease plans are available. 400 computers available on campus for general student use. A campuswide network can be accessed from student residence rooms. Online class registration, online campus billing accounts, course management system are available.
Website: http://www.trine.edu/

General Application Contact: Scott Goplin, Vice President for Enrollment Management, 260-665-4149, E-mail: goplins@trine.edu.

GRADUATE UNITS

Lou Holtz Program in Leadership Offers leadership (MS).

Program in Business Administration Offers business administration (MBA).

Program in Criminal Justice Students: 42 (31 women). *Faculty:* 8. Expenses: Contact institution. *Financial support:* Application deadline: 3/1; applicants required to submit FAFSA. In 2017, 23 master's awarded. *Program availability:* Part-time, evening/weekend, online only, 100% online, blended/hybrid learning. Offers emergency management (MS). *Application deadline:* Applications are processed on a rolling basis. Electronic applications accepted. *Application Contact:* Jacqueline Delagrange, Director, Master of Science in Criminal Justice, 260-203-2693, E-mail: delagrangej@trine.edu. *Dean, College of Graduate and Professional Studies/Associate Professor*, Ryan Dombkowski, 260-203-2695, E-mail: dombkowskir@trine.edu.

Program in Engineering Management Offers engineering management (MS).

Program in Information Studies Offers information studies (MS).

Program in Physical Therapy Students: 97 full-time (60 women). *Faculty:* 9. Expenses: Contact institution. Offers physical therapy (DPT). *Application deadline:* Applications are processed on a rolling basis. *Application Contact:* Dr. Thomas Ruediger, Director, 260-203-2901, E-mail: ruedigert@trine.edu. *Director*, Dr. Thomas Ruediger, 260-203-2901, E-mail: ruedigert@trine.edu.

Program in Physician Assistant Studies Expenses: Contact institution. Offers physician assistant studies (MPAS). *Application Contact:* Kristina Brewer, Admissions Coordinator, 260-665-4161, E-mail: brewerk@trine.edu. *Interim Director*, Dr. Emilio de Jesus Vazquez, 260-702-3597, E-mail: vazqueze@trine.edu.

TRINITY BAPTIST COLLEGE, Jacksonville, FL 32221

General Information Independent-religious, coed, comprehensive institution. *Enrollment:* 13 part-time matriculated graduate/professional students (5 women). *Enrollment by degree level:* 13 master's. *Graduate faculty:* 6 full-time (1 woman), 5 part-time/adjunct (1 woman). *Tuition:* Part-time $295 per hour. *Required fees:* $50 per term. One-time fee: $45 part-time. *Graduate housing:* On-campus housing not available. *Student services:* Writing training.

Computer facilities: 21 computers available on campus for general student use. A campuswide network can be accessed from student residence rooms. Online class registration is available.
Website: http://www.tbc.edu/

General Application Contact: Dr. Matthew Beemer, Senior Vice President, 904-596-2400, Fax: 904-596-2531, E-mail: mbeemer@tbc.edu.

GRADUATE UNITS

Graduate Programs Students: 13 part-time (5 women). *Faculty:* 6 full-time (1 woman), 5 part-time/adjunct (1 woman). Expenses: Contact institution. *Program availability:* Online learning. Offers Bible (MA); curriculum and instruction (M Ed); educational leadership (M Ed); special education (M Ed). *Application fee:* $45. *Senior Vice President*, Dr. Matthew Beemer, 904-596-2400, Fax: 904-596-2531, E-mail: mbeemer@tbc.edu.

TRINITY BIBLE COLLEGE AND GRADUATE SCHOOL, Ellendale, ND 58436

General Information Independent-religious, coed, comprehensive institution.

GRADUATE UNITS

Graduate School Offers global theology (MA); missional leadership (MA); rural ministries (MA).

TRINITY CHRISTIAN COLLEGE, Palos Heights, IL 60463-0929

General Information Independent-religious, coed, comprehensive institution.

GRADUATE UNITS

Program in Counseling Psychology *Program availability:* Evening/weekend, online learning. Offers counseling psychology (MA).

Program in Special Education *Program availability:* Evening/weekend. Offers special education (MA). Electronic applications accepted.

TRINITY COLLEGE, Toronto, ON M5S 1H8, Canada

General Information Independent-religious, coed, graduate-only institution. *Graduate housing:* Room and/or apartments available on a first-come, first-served basis to single students; on-campus housing not available to married students. Housing application deadline: 7/15.

GRADUATE UNITS

Faculty of Divinity *Program availability:* Part-time. Offers ministry (Diploma); ministry for church musicians (Diploma); theology (M Div, MA, MTS, Th M, D Min, PhD, Th D, Diploma, L Th).

TRINITY COLLEGE, Hartford, CT 06106-3100

General Information Independent, coed, comprehensive institution. *Graduate housing:* On-campus housing not available.

GRADUATE UNITS

Graduate Programs *Program availability:* Part-time, evening/weekend. Offers American culture studies (MA); health care policy (MA); literary studies (MA); museums and communities (MA); public policy studies (MA); writing, rhetoric, and media arts (MA). Electronic applications accepted.

TRINITY INTERNATIONAL UNIVERSITY, Deerfield, IL 60015-1284

General Information Independent-religious, coed, university. *Graduate housing:* Rooms and/or apartments available on a first-come, first-served basis to single and married students.

GRADUATE UNITS

Trinity Evangelical Divinity School *Program availability:* Part-time, online learning. Offers academic ministry (M Div); Biblical and Near Eastern archaeology and languages (MA); chaplaincy and ministry care (MA); Christian studies (Certificate); church and parachurch ministry (M Div); church history (MA, Th M); counseling (Th M); educational ministries (MA); educational ministry (Th M); educational studies (PhD); intercultural studies (MA, PhD); leadership and management (D Min); mental health counseling (MA); military chaplaincy (D Min); ministry (MA); missions (Th M); missions and evangelism (D Min); New Testament (MA, Th M); Old Testament (Th M); Old Testament and Semitic languages (MA); pastoral ministry and care (D Min); pastoral theology (Th M); preaching and teaching (D Min); spiritual formation and education (D Min); systematic theology (MA, Th M); theological studies (MA, PhD); urban ministry (MA). Electronic applications accepted.

Trinity Graduate School *Program availability:* Part-time, evening/weekend, online learning. Offers athletic training (MA); bioethics (MA); counseling psychology (MA); diverse learning (M Ed); leadership (MA); teaching (MA). Electronic applications accepted.

Trinity Law School *Program availability:* Part-time, evening/weekend. Offers bioethics (MLS); church and ministry management (MLS); general legal studies (MLS); human resources management (MLS); human rights (MLS); law (JD); nonprofit organizations (MLS).

TRINITY INTERNATIONAL UNIVERSITY FLORIDA, Davie, FL 33324

General Information Independent-religious, coed, graduate-only institution. *Graduate housing:* On-campus housing not available.

GRADUATE UNITS

Divinity School Offers Christian studies (MA, Certificate).

Graduate School Offers counseling psychology (MA).

TRINITY LUTHERAN SEMINARY, Columbus, OH 43209-2334

General Information Independent-religious, coed, graduate-only institution. *Graduate housing:* Rooms and/or apartments available on a first-come, first-served basis to single and married students. Housing application deadline: 5/15.

GRADUATE UNITS

Graduate and Professional Programs *Program availability:* Part-time. Offers African American studies (MTS); Biblical studies (MTS, STM); Christian education (MA); Christian spirituality (STM); church in the world (MTS); church music (MA); divinity (M Div); general theological studies (MTS); mission and evangelism (STM); pastoral leadership and practice (STM); youth and family ministry (MA). Electronic applications accepted.

TRINITY SCHOOL FOR MINISTRY, Ambridge, PA 15003-2397

General Information Independent-religious, coed, graduate-only institution. *Graduate housing:* On-campus housing not available.

GRADUATE UNITS

Graduate Programs *Program availability:* Part-time. Offers Anglican studies (Diploma); basic Christian studies (Diploma); divinity (M Div); ministry (D Min); mission and evangelism (MAME, Diploma); religion (MAR); youth ministry (Diploma).

TRINITY UNIVERSITY, San Antonio, TX 78212-7200

General Information Independent-religious, coed, comprehensive institution. *Enrollment:* 2,604 graduate, professional, and undergraduate students; 116 full-time matriculated graduate/professional students (68 women), 60 part-time matriculated graduate/professional students (26 women). *Enrollment by degree level:* 176 master's. *Graduate faculty:* 18 full-time (12 women), 23 part-time/adjunct (10 women). *Graduate housing:* On-campus housing not available. *Student services:* Campus employment opportunities, campus safety program, career counseling, exercise/wellness program, free psychological counseling, grant writing training, international student services, services for students with disabilities, teacher training, writing training. *Library facilities:* Elizabeth Huth Coates Library plus 1 other. *Collection:* Books: 716,500 (physical); Serial titles: 1,907 (physical), 95,000 (digital/electronic); Databases: 297. Weekly public service hours: 96; students can reserve study rooms.

Computer facilities: Computer purchase and lease plans are available. 500 computers available on campus for general student use. A campuswide network can be accessed from student residence rooms and from off campus. Online class registration is available.
Website: http://www.trinity.edu/

GRADUATE UNITS

Department of Education Students: 59 full-time (42 women), 11 part-time (8 women); includes 38 minority (7 Black or African American, non-Hispanic/Latino; 1 Asian, non-Hispanic/Latino; 27 Hispanic/Latino; 3 Two or more races, non-Hispanic/Latino), 3 international. Average age 29. *Faculty:* 9 full-time (all women), 14 part-time/adjunct (10 women). Expenses: Contact institution. *Financial support:* Application deadline: 5/1; applicants required to submit FAFSA. *Program availability:* Part-time, evening/weekend. Offers school leadership (M Ed); school psychology (MA); teaching (MAT). *Application Contact:* Office of the Registrar, 210-999-7201, Fax: 210-999-7202, E-mail: roffice@trinity.edu. *Interim Chair,* Norvella Carter, 210-999-7506, Fax: 210-999-7592, E-mail: ncarter1@trinity.edu.

Department of Health Care Administration Expenses: Contact institution. *Financial support:* Fellowships, institutionally sponsored loans, scholarships/grants, and unspecified assistantships available. Support available to part-time students. Financial award application deadline: 5/1; financial award applicants required to submit FAFSA. *Program availability:* Part-time, online learning. Offers health care administration (MS). *Application deadline:* For fall admission, 6/1 for domestic students. Applications are processed on a rolling basis. *Application fee:* $50. Electronic applications accepted. *Application Contact:* Dr. Ed Schumacher, Professor/Chair, 210-999-8137, E-mail: hca@trinity.edu. *Professor/Chair,* Dr. Ed Schumacher, 210-999-8137, E-mail: hca@trinity.edu.

School of Business Expenses: Contact institution. *Financial support:* Institutionally sponsored loans and scholarships/grants available. Financial award application deadline: 5/1; financial award applicants required to submit FAFSA. Offers accounting (MS). *Application deadline:* For fall admission, 2/1 for domestic and international students. Electronic applications accepted. *Application Contact:* Dr. Julie Persellin, Chair, Department of Accounting, 210-999-7230, E-mail: jpersell@trinity.edu. *Chair, Department of Accounting,* Dr. Julie Persellin, 210-999-7230, E-mail: jpersell@trinity.edu.

TRINITY WASHINGTON UNIVERSITY, Washington, DC 20017-1094

General Information Independent-religious, women only, comprehensive institution. *Graduate housing:* Room and/or apartments available on a first-come, first-served basis to single students; on-campus housing not available to married students.

GRADUATE UNITS

School of Business and Graduate Studies *Program availability:* Part-time, evening/weekend. Offers business administration (MBA); communication (MA); international security studies (MA); organizational management (MSA).

School of Education *Program availability:* Part-time, evening/weekend. Offers clinical mental health counseling (MA); early childhood education (MAT); educating for change (M Ed); educational administration (MSA); elementary education (MAT); reading (M Ed); school counseling (MA); secondary education (MAT); special education (MAT).

TRINITY WESTERN UNIVERSITY, Langley, BC V2Y 1Y1, Canada

General Information Independent-religious, coed, comprehensive institution. *Graduate housing:* On-campus housing not available.

GRADUATE UNITS

ACTS Seminaries *Program availability:* Part-time. Offers Christian studies (MA); cross cultural ministry (MA); theology (M Div, M Th, MAMFT, MLE, MTS, D Min).

School of Graduate Studies Offers biblical studies (MA); business (MA, Certificate); Christian ministry (MA); counseling psychology (MA); education (MA, Certificate); general humanities (MAIH); healthcare (MA, Certificate); international business (MBA); linguistics (MA); management of the growing enterprise (MBA); non-profit (MA, Certificate); non-profit and charitable organization management (MBA); specialized (MAIH); teaching English to speakers of other languages (TESOL) (MA).

School of Nursing Offers nursing (MSN).

TRI-STATE BIBLE COLLEGE, South Point, OH 45680-8402

General Information Independent-religious, coed, comprehensive institution.

GRADUATE UNITS

Graduate Program Offers Biblical studies (MA). Electronic applications accepted.

TRI-STATE COLLEGE OF ACUPUNCTURE, New York, NY 10011

General Information Independent, coed, graduate-only institution. *Graduate housing:* On-campus housing not available.

GRADUATE UNITS

Graduate Programs *Program availability:* Evening/weekend. Offers acupuncture (MS); Chinese herbology (Certificate); Oriental medicine (MS). Electronic applications accepted.

TROY UNIVERSITY, Troy, AL 36082

General Information State-supported, coed, comprehensive institution. *Enrollment:* 17,521 graduate, professional, and undergraduate students; 1,132 full-time matriculated graduate/professional students (801 women), 2,290 part-time matriculated graduate/professional students (1,460 women). *Enrollment by degree level:* 3,310 master's, 87 doctoral, 25 other advanced degrees. *Graduate faculty:* 196 full-time (94 women), 82 part-time/adjunct (46 women). Tuition, state resident: part-time $417 per credit hour. Tuition, nonresident: part-time $834 per credit hour. *Required fees:* $42 per credit hour. $50 per semester. Tuition and fees vary according to campus/location. *Graduate housing:* Rooms and/or apartments available on a first-come, first-served basis to single students and available to married students. Housing application deadline: 7/31. *Student services:* Campus employment opportunities, campus safety program, career counseling, child daycare facilities, exercise/wellness program, free psychological counseling, grant writing training, international student services, low-cost health insurance, services for students with disabilities, teacher training, writing training. *Library facilities:* Lurleen B. Wallace Library (Troy Campus) plus 2 others. *Collection:* Books: 603,904 (physical), 277,690 (digital/electronic); Serial titles: 213 (physical), 134,396 (digital/electronic); Databases: 261. *Research affiliation:* Systemics Research Fund (protozoan symbionts), Birmingham Audubon Society (Alabama flora and fauna).

Computer facilities: 1,935 computers available on campus for general student use. A campuswide network can be accessed from student residence rooms and from off campus. Online class registration is available.
Website: http://www.troy.edu/

General Application Contact: Jessica A Kimbro, Director of Graduate Admissions, 334-670-3178, Fax: 334-670-3733, E-mail: jacord@troy.edu.

GRADUATE UNITS

Graduate School Students: 1,132 full-time (801 women), 2,290 part-time (1,460 women); includes 1,061 minority (879 Black or African American, non-Hispanic/Latino; 14 American Indian or Alaska Native, non-Hispanic/Latino; 44 Asian, non-Hispanic/Latino; 74 Hispanic/Latino; 3 Native Hawaiian or other Pacific Islander, non-Hispanic/Latino; 47 Two or more races, non-Hispanic/Latino). Average age 31. 1,744 applicants, 89% accepted, 886 enrolled. *Faculty:* 196 full-time (94 women), 82 part-time/adjunct (46 women). Expenses: Contact institution. *Financial support:* Fellowships, career-related internships or fieldwork, and scholarships/grants available. Support available to part-time students. Financial award application deadline: 5/1; financial award applicants required to submit FAFSA. In 2017, 1,231 master's, 16 doctorates, 44 other advanced degrees awarded. *Program availability:* Part-time, evening/weekend, 100% online, blended/hybrid learning. *Application deadline:* Applications are processed on a rolling basis. *Application fee:* $50. Electronic applications accepted. *Application Contact:* Jessica A. Kimbro, Director of Graduate Admissions, 334-670-3178, E-mail: jacord@troy.edu. *Associate Provost/Dean,* Dr. Mary Anne C. Templeton, 334-670-3189, Fax: 334-670-3912, E-mail: mtempleton@troy.edu.

College of Arts and Sciences Students: 204 full-time (91 women), 603 part-time (245 women); includes 215 minority (103 Black or African American, non-Hispanic/Latino; 4 American Indian or Alaska Native, non-Hispanic/Latino; 23 Asian, non-Hispanic/Latino; 22 Hispanic/Latino; 63 Two or more races, non-Hispanic/Latino). Average age 33. 543 applicants, 83% accepted, 233 enrolled. *Faculty:* 68 full-time (23 women), 22 part-time/adjunct (11 women). Expenses: Contact institution. *Financial support:* Fellowships, career-related internships or fieldwork, and scholarships/grants available. Support available to part-time students. Financial award applicants required to submit FAFSA. In 2017, 201 master's awarded. *Program availability:* Part-time, evening/weekend. Offers American history (MA); arts and sciences (MA, MPA, MS, MS Sc, Certificate); biomedical sciences (MS, Certificate); computer science (MS); criminal justice (MS); environmental and biological sciences (MS); European history (MA); government contracting (MPA); international relations (MS); social science (MS Sc). *Application deadline:* Applications are processed on a rolling basis. *Application fee:* $50. Electronic applications accepted. *Application Contact:* Jessica A. Kimbro, Director of Graduate Admissions, 334-670-3178, E-mail: jacord@troy.edu. *Dean,* Dr. Steven Taylor, 334-670-3673, Fax: 334-670-3399, E-mail: rinehart@troy.edu.

College of Business Students: 149 full-time (76 women), 677 part-time (391 women); includes 261 minority (212 Black or African American, non-Hispanic/Latino; 5 American Indian or Alaska Native, non-Hispanic/Latino; 14 Asian, non-Hispanic/Latino; 18 Hispanic/Latino; 1 Native Hawaiian or other Pacific Islander, non-Hispanic/Latino; 11 Two or more races, non-Hispanic/Latino). Average age 29. 474 applicants, 89% accepted, 243 enrolled. *Faculty:* 42 full-time (14 women), 2 part-time/adjunct (0 women). Expenses: Contact institution. *Financial support:* In 2017–18, 5 research assistantships were awarded; career-related internships or fieldwork and scholarships/grants also available. Support available to part-time students. Financial award applicants required to submit FAFSA. In 2017, 396 master's awarded. *Program availability:* Part-time, evening/weekend, 100% online, blended/hybrid learning. Offers accountancy (M Acc); accounting (EMBA, MBA); business (EMBA, M Acc, MA, MBA, MBAi, MS, MSM); criminal justice (EMBA); economics (MA); finance (MBA); general management (EMBA, MBA); healthcare management (EMBA); human resources management (MS); information systems (EMBA, MBA); international economic development (MBA); management (MS, MSM). *Application deadline:* Applications are processed on a rolling basis. *Application fee:* $50. Electronic applications accepted. *Application Contact:* Jessica A. Kimbro, Director of Graduate Admissions, 334-670-3178, Fax: 334-670-3733, E-mail: bcamp@troy.edu. *Dean,* Dr. Judson Edwards, 334-670-3989, Fax: 334-670-3708, E-mail: jcedwards@troy.edu.

College of Communication and Fine Arts Students: 47 full-time (33 women), 76 part-time (60 women); includes 29 minority (26 Black or African American, non-Hispanic/Latino; 1 Hispanic/Latino; 1 Native Hawaiian or other Pacific Islander, non-Hispanic/Latino; 1 Two or more races, non-Hispanic/Latino). Average age 27. 52 applicants, 100% accepted, 42 enrolled. *Faculty:* 5 full-time (3 women). Expenses: Contact institution. *Financial support:* Fellowships, career-related internships or fieldwork, and scholarships/grants available. Support available to part-time students. Financial award applicants required to submit FAFSA. In 2017, 44 master's awarded. *Program availability:* Part-time, evening/weekend. Offers strategic communication (MS). *Application deadline:* For fall admission, 6/1 for international students; for spring admission, 10/15 for international students. Applications are processed on a rolling basis. *Application fee:* $50. Electronic applications accepted. *Application Contact:* Jessica A. Kimbro, Director of Graduate Admissions, 334-670-3178, E-mail: jacord@troy.edu. *Dean,* Dr. Larry Blocher, 334-670-3869, Fax: 334-670-3858, E-mail: lblocher@troy.edu.

College of Education Students: 424 full-time (349 women), 188 part-time (93 women); includes 305 minority (261 Black or African American, non-Hispanic/Latino; 5 American Indian or Alaska Native, non-Hispanic/Latino; 2 Asian, non-Hispanic/Latino; 23 Hispanic/Latino; 1 Native Hawaiian or other Pacific Islander, non-Hispanic/Latino; 13 Two or more races, non-Hispanic/Latino). Average age 35. 319 applicants, 93% accepted, 229 enrolled. *Faculty:* 75 full-time (45 women), 26 part-time/adjunct (19 women). Expenses: Contact institution. *Financial support:* Fellowships, career-related internships or fieldwork, and scholarships/grants available. Support available to part-time students. Financial award applicants required to submit FAFSA. In 2017, 109 master's, 22 other advanced degrees awarded. *Program availability:* Part-time, evening/weekend. Offers adult education (MS); community counseling (MS); early childhood education (MS, Ed S); education (MS, MS Ed, Ed S); educational administration/leadership (MS, Ed S); K-6 elementary and collaborative education (MS, Ed S); postsecondary education (MS Ed); school counseling (MS, Ed S); second language instruction (MS); secondary education (MS); teacher education-multiple levels (MS). *Application deadline:* For fall admission, 1/1 for domestic students, 6/1 for international students; for spring admission, 10/15 for international students. Applications are processed on a rolling basis. *Application fee:* $50. Electronic applications accepted. *Application Contact:* Jessica A. Kimbro, Director of Graduate Admissions, 334-670-3178, E-mail: jacord@troy.edu. *Dean,* Dr. Royce Dasinger, 334-670-3365, Fax: 334-670-3474, E-mail: rdasinger@troy.edu.

College of Health and Human Services Students: 115 full-time (75 women), 292 part-time (218 women); includes 83 minority (64 Black or African American, non-

Hispanic/Latino; 1 American Indian or Alaska Native, non-Hispanic/Latino; 3 Asian, non-Hispanic/Latino; 7 Hispanic/Latino; 8 Two or more races, non-Hispanic/Latino). Average age 32. 149 applicants, 87% accepted, 90 enrolled. *Faculty:* 32 full-time (19 women), 14 part-time/adjunct (12 women). Expenses: Contact institution. *Financial support:* Tuition waivers and unspecified assistantships available. Support available to part-time students. Financial award application deadline: 4/5; financial award applicants required to submit FAFSA. In 2017, 243 master's, 16 doctorates, 9 other advanced degrees awarded. *Program availability:* Part-time, evening/weekend. Offers adult health (MSN); family nurse practitioner (DNP); health and human services (MS, MS Sc, MSN, MSW, DNP, DPH, PMC); maternal infant (MSN); nursing informatics specialist (MSN); social work (MSW); sport and fitness management (MS, DPH). *Application deadline:* Applications are processed on a rolling basis. *Application fee:* $50. Electronic applications accepted. *Application Contact:* Jessica A. Kimbro, Director of Graduate Admissions, 334-670-3178, E-mail: jacord@troy.edu. *Dean*, Dr. Denise Green, 334-670-3712, Fax: 334-670-3743, E-mail: dmgreen@troy.edu.

TRUETT MCCONNELL UNIVERSITY, Cleveland, GA 30528

General Information Independent-religious, coed, comprehensive institution. *Enrollment:* 2,187 graduate, professional, and undergraduate students; 26 full-time matriculated graduate/professional students (3 women), 23 part-time matriculated graduate/professional students (9 women). *Enrollment by degree level:* 49 master's. *Tuition:* Part-time $325 per credit hour. *Required fees:* $910 per year. $455 per semester. *Graduate housing:* Rooms and/or apartments available on a first-come, first-served basis to single and married students. Typical cost: $5000 per year for single students; $10,000 per year for married students. Room charges vary according to housing facility selected. Housing application deadline: 7/1. *Student services:* Career counseling, services for students with disabilities. *Library facilities:* Cofer Library.

Computer facilities: 40 computers available on campus for general student use. A campuswide network can be accessed from student residence rooms. Online class registration is available.
Website: http://www.truett.edu/

General Application Contact: Jim Dunnington, Coordinator of Online and Graduate Admissions, 706-865-2134 Ext. 2131, E-mail: jdunnington@truett.edu.

GRADUATE UNITS

Balthasar Hubmaier School of Theology and Missions Students: 18 full-time (1 woman), 10 part-time (2 women). Expenses: Contact institution. *Financial support:* Application deadline: 8/1; applicants required to submit FAFSA. In 2017, 4 master's awarded. *Program availability:* Part-time, 100% online. Offers theology (MA). *Application deadline:* Applications are processed on a rolling basis. Electronic applications accepted. *Application Contact:* Jim Dunnington, Coordinator of Online and Graduate Admissions, 706-865-2134 Ext. 2131, E-mail: jdunnington@truett.edu. *Dean*, Dr. Jason Graffagnino, 706-865-2134 Ext. 3002, E-mail: jgraffagnino@truett.edu.

Hans Hut School of Business Students: 6 full-time (1 woman), 3 part-time (0 women). *Faculty:* 2 full-time (both women). Expenses: Contact institution. *Financial support:* Applicants required to submit FAFSA. *Program availability:* Part-time, evening/weekend, 100% online. Offers business (MBA). *Application deadline:* For fall admission, 8/1 for domestic students; for spring admission, 12/1 for domestic students; for summer admission, 5/1 for domestic students. Applications are processed on a rolling basis. Electronic applications accepted. *Application Contact:* Jim Dunnington, Coordinator of Online and Graduate Admissions, 706-865-2134 Ext. 2131, E-mail: jdunnington@truett.edu. *Dean*, Dr. Janet Forney, 706-865-2134 Ext. 6501, E-mail: jforney@truett.edu.

The Leonhard Schiemer School of Psychology and Biblical Counseling Students: 2 full-time (1 woman), 9 part-time (6 women). *Faculty:* 2 full-time (1 woman). Expenses: Contact institution. *Financial support:* Applicants required to submit FAFSA. *Program availability:* Part-time. Offers professional counseling (MA). *Application deadline:* For fall admission, 8/1 for domestic students; for spring admission, 12/1 for domestic students; for summer admission, 5/1 for domestic students. Applications are processed on a rolling basis. Electronic applications accepted. *Application Contact:* Jim Dunnington, Coordinator of Online and Graduate Admissions, 706-865-2134 Ext. 2131, E-mail: jdunnington@truett.edu. *Dean*, Dr. Holly Haynes, 706-865-2134 Ext. 1604, E-mail: hhaynes@truett.edu.

Pilgram Marpeck School of Science, Technology, Engineering and Mathematics Students: 1 (woman) full-time. *Faculty:* 2 full-time (0 women). Expenses: Contact institution. *Financial support:* Teaching assistantships available. Financial award applicants required to submit FAFSA. *Program availability:* Part-time. Offers biology (MS). *Application deadline:* For fall admission, 8/1 for domestic students; for spring admission, 12/1 for domestic students; for summer admission, 5/1 for domestic students. Applications are processed on a rolling basis. Electronic applications accepted. *Application Contact:* Jim Dunnington, Coordinator of Online and Graduate Admissions, 706-865-2134 Ext. 2131, E-mail: jdunnington@truett.edu. *Dean*, Dr. Robert Bowen, 706-865-2134 Ext. 6400, E-mail: rbowen@truett.edu.

TRUMAN STATE UNIVERSITY, Kirksville, MO 63501-4221

General Information State-supported, coed, comprehensive institution. CGS member. *Graduate housing:* Rooms and/or apartments available on a first-come, first-served basis to single and married students. Housing application deadline: 5/1. *Research affiliation:* Gulf Coast Research Laboratory (marine science), Kirksville College of Osteopathic Medicine (biology).

GRADUATE UNITS

Graduate School Electronic applications accepted.

School of Arts and Letters Offers arts and letters (MA, MS); biology (MS); English (MA); music (MA). Electronic applications accepted.

School of Business Offers accounting (M Ac); business (M Ac). Electronic applications accepted.

School of Health Sciences and Education Offers communication disorders (MA); education (MAE); health sciences and education (MA, MAE). Electronic applications accepted.

★ TUFTS UNIVERSITY, Medford, MA 02155

General Information Independent, coed, university. CGS member. *Enrollment:* 11,449 graduate, professional, and undergraduate students; 5,106 full-time matriculated graduate/professional students (3,043 women), 622 part-time matriculated graduate/professional students (369 women). *Enrollment by degree level:* 2,332 master's, 3,037 doctoral, 359 other advanced degrees. *Graduate faculty:* 998 full-time (452 women), 556 part-time/adjunct (274 women). *Tuition:* Full-time $49,892. *Required fees:* $874. Full-time tuition and fees vary according to degree level, program and student level. Part-time tuition and fees vary according to course load. *Graduate housing:* Room and/or apartments available on a first-come, first-served basis to single students; on-campus housing not available to married students. Housing application deadline: 4/15. *Student services:* Campus employment opportunities, campus safety program, career counseling, child daycare facilities, exercise/wellness program, free psychological counseling, international student services, low-cost health insurance, multicultural affairs office, services for students with disabilities, teacher training, writing training. *Library facilities:* Tisch Library plus 3 others. *Collection:* Books: 1.3 million (physical), 432,877 (digital/electronic); Serial titles: 1,012 (physical); Databases: 83,216. Weekly public service hours: 110; students can reserve study rooms. *Research affiliation:* Maine Medical Center (medicine), The Stockholm Environmental Institute (environmental science and policy), Caritas St. Elizabeth's Medical Center (medicine), Tufts Medical Center (medicine), Lahey Clinic Medical Center (medicine), Baystate Medical Center (medicine).

Computer facilities: Computer purchase and lease plans are available. 1,039 computers available on campus for general student use. A campuswide network can be accessed from student residence rooms and from off campus. Online class registration, Cloud storage for all students, staff, and faculty are available.
Website: http://www.tufts.edu/

General Application Contact: Information Contact, 617-628-5000.

GRADUATE UNITS

Cummings School of Veterinary Medicine Offers animals and public policy (MS); biomedical sciences (PhD); conservation medicine (MS); veterinary medicine (DVM). Electronic applications accepted.

The Fletcher School of Law and Diplomacy *Program availability:* Online learning. Offers economics and public policy (PhD); international affairs (PhD); international business (MIB); international law (LL M); law and diplomacy (MA, MALD); transatlantic affairs (MA). MA in transatlantic affairs offered jointly with The College of Europe; PhD in economics and public policy with Tufts' Graduate School of Arts and Sciences. Electronic applications accepted.

The Gerald J. and Dorothy R. Friedman School of Nutrition Science and Policy *Program availability:* Part-time. Offers agriculture, food and environment (MS, PhD); biochemical and molecular nutrition (PhD); dietetic internship (MS); food policy and applied nutrition (MS, PhD); humanitarian assistance (MAHA); nutrition (MS, PhD); nutrition communication (MS); nutritional epidemiology (MS, PhD). Electronic applications accepted.

Graduate School of Arts and Sciences Students: 906 full-time (604 women), 76 part-time (57 women); includes 181 minority (42 Black or African American, non-Hispanic/Latino; 64 Asian, non-Hispanic/Latino; 50 Hispanic/Latino; 25 Two or more races, non-Hispanic/Latino), 182 international. Average age 28. 2,148 applicants, 41% accepted, 391 enrolled. Expenses: Contact institution. *Financial support:* In 2017–18, 860 students received support. Fellowships, research assistantships, teaching assistantships, Federal Work-Study, scholarships/grants, health care benefits, tuition waivers (full and partial), and unspecified assistantships available. Support available to part-time students. Financial award application deadline: 1/15. In 2017, 301 master's, 67 doctorates, 14 other advanced degrees awarded. *Program availability:* Part-time. Offers art education (MAT); art history (MA); art history and museum studies (MA); arts and sciences (MA, MAT, MPP, MS, OTD, PhD, Certificate, Ed S); astrophysics (MS, PhD); bioengineering (Certificate); biology (MS, PhD); biotechnology (Certificate); biotechnology engineering (Certificate); chemical physics (PhD); chemistry (MS, PhD); chemistry/biotechnology (PhD); child study and human development (MA, PhD); classics (MA); classics with teaching licensure (MA); cognitive science (PhD); community development (MA); community environmental studies (Certificate); composition (MA); computer science (Certificate); computer science minor (Certificate); digital tools for premodern studies (MA); diversity and inclusion leadership (MA); economics (MS); economics and public policy (PhD); education (MA, MAT, MS, PhD); educational studies (MA); elementary education (MAT); English (MA, PhD); environmental management (Certificate); environmental policy (MA); epidemiology (Certificate); ethnomusicology (MA); French (MA); German (MA); German with teaching licensure (MA); health and human welfare (MA); history (MA, PhD); history and museum studies (MA); housing policy (MA); human-computer interaction (Certificate); interdisciplinary studies (PhD); international environment/development policy (MA); management of community organizations (Certificate); manufacturing engineering (Certificate); mathematics (MS, PhD); microwave and wireless engineering (Certificate); middle and secondary education (MAT); museum education (MA); museum studies (Certificate); music theory (MA); occupational therapy (Certificate); philosophy (MA); physics (MS, PhD); physics education (PhD); program evaluation (Certificate); psychology (MS, PhD); public policy (MPP); school psychology (MA, Ed S); secondary education (MA); soft materials robotics (PhD); STEM education (MS, PhD); theatre and performance studies (MA, PhD). *Application deadline:* For fall admission, 1/15 priority date for domestic and international students; for spring admission, 10/15 priority date for domestic and international students. Applications are processed on a rolling basis. *Application fee:* $85. Electronic applications accepted. *Application Contact:* Office of Graduate Admissions, 617-627-3395, E-mail: gradadmissions@tufts.edu. *Dean*, Dr. Robert Cook, 617-627-2546.

Sackler School of Graduate Biomedical Sciences Offers biomedical sciences (MS, PhD, Certificate); cancer biology (PhD); clinical and translational science (MS, PhD, Certificate); developmental and regenerative biology (PhD); genetics (PhD); immunology (PhD); mammalian genetics (PhD); medically-oriented research in graduate education (PhD); molecular and cellular medicine (PhD); molecular microbiology (PhD); neuroscience (PhD); structural and chemical biology (PhD). Electronic applications accepted.

School of Dental Medicine Offers dental medicine (MS, DMD, Certificate); dentistry (Certificate). DMD/MPH offered with School of Medicine.

School of Engineering Students: 648 full-time (228 women), 120 part-time (57 women); includes 120 minority (15 Black or African American, non-Hispanic/Latino; 66 Asian, non-Hispanic/Latino; 28 Hispanic/Latino; 11 Two or more races, non-Hispanic/Latino), 271 international. Average age 29. 1,435 applicants, 46% accepted, 264 enrolled. *Faculty:* 105 full-time (26 women), 79 part-time/adjunct (25 women). Expenses: Contact institution. *Financial support:* Fellowships with full tuition reimbursements, research assistantships with full and partial tuition reimbursements, teaching assistantships with full and partial tuition reimbursements, Federal Work-Study, scholarships/grants, tuition waivers (partial), and unspecified assistantships available. Financial award application deadline: 5/15; financial award applicants required to submit FAFSA. In 2017, 160 master's, 26 doctorates awarded. *Program availability:* Part-time. Offers bioengineering (MS); biomedical engineering (MS, PhD); biotechnology (PhD); chemical engineering (MS, PhD); civil and environmental engineering (MS, PhD); cognitive science/computer science (PhD); computer science (MS, PhD); electrical engineering (MS, PhD); engineering (MS, MSEM, PhD); human factors (MS); mechanical engineering (MS, PhD); soft material robotics (PhD). *Application deadline:* For fall admission, 12/15 priority date for domestic students, 12/15 for international students; for spring admission, 9/15 for domestic and international students. Applications are processed on a rolling basis. *Application fee:* $85. Electronic applications accepted. *Application Contact:* Office of Graduate Admissions, 617-627-3395, Fax: 617-627-4079, E-mail: gradadmissions@tufts.edu. *Dean of Graduate Education*, Dr. Karen Panetta, E-mail: enggradstudies@tufts.edu.

The Gordon Institute Students: 204 full-time (68 women), 20 part-time (2 women); includes 54 minority (9 Black or African American, non-Hispanic/Latino; 28 Asian, non-Hispanic/Latino; 14 Hispanic/Latino; 3 Two or more races, non-Hispanic/Latino), 35 international. Average age 31. 118 applicants, 62% accepted, 62 enrolled. *Faculty:* 7 full-time, 25 part-time/adjunct. Expenses: Contact institution. In 2017, 65 master's awarded. *Program availability:* Part-time. Offers engineering management (MS); innovation and management (MS). *Application deadline:* For fall admission, 3/15 for domestic students, 1/15 for international students. Applications are processed on a rolling basis. *Application fee:* $85. Electronic applications accepted. *Application Contact:* Carla Eberle, Admissions Manager, 617-627-3395, E-mail: tgi@tufts.edu. *Graduate Program Director*, Nancy Buczko.

School of Medicine Expenses: Contact institution. Offers biomedical sciences (MS); health communication (MS, Certificate); medicine (MPH, MS, Dr PH, MD, Certificate); pain research, education and policy (MS, Certificate); physician assistant (MS); public health (MPH, Dr PH). *Dean*, Dr. Harris Berman, 617-636-6565.

School of the Museum of Fine Arts at Tufts University Students: 55 full-time. Average age 25. *Faculty:* 31 full-time (19 women), 23 part-time/adjunct (16 women). Expenses: Contact institution. *Financial support:* Fellowships, teaching assistantships, Federal Work-Study, and scholarships/grants available. Financial award application deadline: 1/15. In 2017, 44 master's, 15 other advanced degrees awarded. Offers art education (MAT); studio art (MFA, Postbaccalaureate Certificate). *Application deadline:* For fall admission, 1/15 priority date for domestic and international students. Applications are processed on a rolling basis. *Application fee:* $85. Electronic applications accepted. *Application Contact:* Office of Graduate Admissions, 617-627-3395, E-mail: gradadmissions@tufts.edu. *Associate Director of Graduate Programs*, Lisa Bynoe, 617-627-0031, E-mail: lisa.bynoe@tufts.edu.

See Display below and Close-Up on page 879.

TULANE UNIVERSITY, New Orleans, LA 70118-5669

General Information Independent, coed, university. CGS member. *Enrollment:* 11,248 graduate, professional, and undergraduate students; 4,373 full-time matriculated graduate/professional students (2,371 women), 794 part-time matriculated graduate/professional students (488 women). *Enrollment by degree level:* 2,230 master's, 2,773 doctoral, 164 other advanced degrees. *Graduate faculty:* 67 full-time (32 women), 30 part-time/adjunct (17 women). *Tuition:* Full-time $50,920; part-time $2829 per credit hour. *Required fees:* $2040; $44.50 per credit hour. $580 per term. Tuition and fees vary according to course load, degree level and program. *Graduate housing:* Rooms and/or apartments available on a first-come, first-served basis to single and married students. Typical cost: $9660 per year for single students; $19,200 per year for married students. Room charges vary according to board plan, campus/location and housing facility selected. *Student services:* Campus employment opportunities, campus safety program, career counseling, child daycare facilities, exercise/wellness program, free psychological counseling, grant writing training, international student services, low-cost health insurance, multicultural affairs office, services for students with disabilities, teacher training, writing training. *Library facilities:* Howard Tilton Memorial Library plus 8 others. *Collection:* Books: 4.6 million (physical); Serial titles: 72,300 (physical). Study areas open 24 hours, 5–7 days a week. *Research affiliation:* Louisiana Cancer Research Consortium (treatment and prevention of cancer), Boehringer-Ingelheim (clinical research in coronary and pulmonary diseases, diabetes, and stroke), Blue Cross and Blue Shield of Louisiana (BCBSLA) (healthcare innovation including access, delivery, and outcomes), AbbVie (hepatitis and diabetes), Genentech (antiviral treatment and pulmonary disease), New Orleans BioInnovation Center (NOBIC) (business consulting and start-up support, including educational events).

Computer facilities: 556 computers available on campus for general student use. A campuswide network can be accessed from student residence rooms and from off campus. Online class registration is available.
Website: http://www.tulane.edu/

General Application Contact: Jennifer O'Brien, Program Manager, 504-247-1213, Fax: 504-865-6723, E-mail: ogps@tulane.edu.

GRADUATE UNITS

A. B. Freeman School of Business Students: 561 full-time (287 women), 297 part-time (151 women); includes 112 minority (43 Black or African American, non-Hispanic/Latino; 2 American Indian or Alaska Native, non-Hispanic/Latino; 24 Asian, non-Hispanic/Latino; 38 Hispanic/Latino; 5 Two or more races, non-Hispanic/Latino), 515 international. Average age 27. 2,021 applicants, 74% accepted, 476 enrolled. *Faculty:* 51 full-time (15 women), 38 part-time/adjunct (3 women). Expenses: Contact institution. *Financial support:* In 2017–18, 176 students received support. Fellowships with tuition reimbursements available, research assistantships, teaching assistantships, career-related internships or fieldwork, Federal Work-Study, tuition waivers (full and partial), and unspecified assistantships available. Support available to part-time students. Financial award application deadline: 4/15; financial award applicants required to submit FAFSA. In 2017, 632 master's, 9 doctorates awarded. *Program availability:* Part-time, evening/weekend. Offers accounting (M Acct); analytics (MBA); banking and financial services (M Fin); energy (M Fin, MBA); entrepreneurship (MBA); finance (MBA, PhD); financial accounting (PhD); international business (MBA); international management (MBA); strategic management and leadership (MBA). *Application deadline:* For fall admission, 11/1 priority date for domestic and international students; for winter admission, 1/6 for domestic and international students; for spring admission, 3/1 priority date for domestic and international students; for summer admission, 5/5 for domestic students. Applications are processed on a rolling basis. *Application fee:* $125. Electronic applications accepted. *Application Contact:* Melissa Booth, Assistant Dean for Graduate Admissions, 800-223-5402, E-mail: freeman.admissions@tulane.edu. *Dean*, Ira Solomon, PhD, 504-865-5407, Fax: 504-865-5491, E-mail: businessdean@tulane.edu.

School of Architecture *Program availability:* Part-time. Offers architecture (M Arch, M Arch II, MPS, MSRED).

School of Law Offers American business law (LL M); international development (MS, PhD); law (JD, SJD). Electronic applications accepted.

The Payson Center for International Development *Program availability:* Part-time. Offers international development (MS, PhD); law and development (LL M). Electronic applications accepted.

School of Liberal Arts *Program availability:* Part-time. Offers anthropology (PhD); classical studies (MA); design and technical production (MFA); economics (MA, PhD); English (MA); French (MA, PhD); history (MA, PhD); history of art (MA); liberal arts (MA, MFA, PhD); music (MA, MFA); philosophy (MA, PhD); political science (PhD);

Portuguese (MA); sociology (MA); Spanish and Portuguese (PhD); studio art (MFA). Electronic applications accepted.

Roger Thayer Stone Center for Latin American Studies Offers Latin American studies (MA, PhD). Electronic applications accepted.

School of Medicine Offers medicine (MS, MD, PhD).

Graduate Programs in Biomedical Sciences Offers biochemistry and molecular biology (MS); biomedical sciences (MS, PhD); human genetics (MS); microbiology and immunology (MS); molecular and cellular biology (PhD); neuroscience (MS, PhD); pharmacology (MS); physiology (MS); structural and cellular biology (MS, PhD).

School of Professional Advancement *Program availability:* Part-time. Offers health and wellness management (MPS); homeland security studies (MPS); information technology management (MPS); liberal arts (MLA).

School of Public Health and Tropical Medicine Students: 487 full-time (352 women), 134 part-time (97 women); includes 183 minority (73 Black or African American, non-Hispanic/Latino; 2 American Indian or Alaska Native, non-Hispanic/Latino; 48 Asian, non-Hispanic/Latino; 42 Hispanic/Latino; 18 Two or more races, non-Hispanic/Latino), 127 international. Average age 24. 1,341 applicants, 74% accepted, 240 enrolled. *Faculty:* 117 full-time (61 women), 25 part-time/adjunct (16 women). Expenses: Contact institution. *Financial support:* In 2017–18, 188 students received support, including 10 fellowships with full and partial tuition reimbursements available (averaging $25,000 per year), 149 research assistantships (averaging $1,870 per year), 39 teaching assistantships (averaging $1,612 per year); Federal Work-Study, scholarships/grants, traineeships, and unspecified assistantships also available. Financial award application deadline: 4/15; financial award applicants required to submit FAFSA. *Program availability:* Part-time, evening/weekend, 100% online, synchronous sessions. Offers biostatistics and bioinformatics (MS, MSPH, PhD); clinical tropical medicine and travelers health (Diploma); community health sciences (MPH); epidemiology (MPH, MS, Dr PH, PhD); global community health and behavioral sciences (Dr PH, PhD); global environmental health sciences (MPH, MSPH, PhD); global health management and policy (MHA, MPH, PhD, Sc D); parasitology (PhD); public health (MSPH); public health and tropical medicine (MPHTM). *Application deadline:* For fall admission, 7/15 priority date for domestic students, 6/15 priority date for international students; for winter admission, 11/15 priority date for domestic students, 10/15 priority date for international students; for spring admission, 11/15 for domestic students, 10/15 for international students; for summer admission, 5/15 for domestic students, 4/15 for international students. Applications are processed on a rolling basis. *Application fee:* $135. Electronic applications accepted. *Application Contact:* Ian Shirt, Admissions Counselor, 504-988-0908, E-mail: sphtmadmissions@tulane.edu. *Dean*, Pierre Buekens, 504-988-5388, Fax: 504-988-5718, E-mail: sphtmdo@tulane.edu.

School of Science and Engineering *Program availability:* Part-time. Offers biomedical engineering (MS, PhD); cell and molecular biology (MS, PhD); chemical and biomolecular engineering (MS, PhD); chemistry (MS, PhD); ecology and evolutionary biology (MS, PhD); interdisciplinary studies (PhD); mathematics (MS, PhD); neuroscience (MS, PhD); physics (PhD); psychology (MS, PhD); science and engineering (MS, PhD). MS and PhD offered through the Graduate School. Electronic applications accepted.

School of Social Work *Program availability:* Part-time. Offers city, culture and community (PhD); disaster resilience leadership (MS); social work (MSW, DSW). Electronic applications accepted.

TUSCULUM COLLEGE, Greeneville, TN 37743-9997

General Information Independent-religious, coed, comprehensive institution. *Enrollment:* 1,767 graduate, professional, and undergraduate students; 226 full-time matriculated graduate/professional students (157 women), 53 part-time matriculated graduate/professional students (33 women). *Enrollment by degree level:* 279 master's. *Graduate housing:* On-campus housing not available. *Library facilities:* Thomas J. Garland Library plus 2 others. *Collection:* Students can reserve study rooms.

Computer facilities: A campuswide network can be accessed from student residence rooms and from off campus. Online class registration is available.
Website: http://www.tusculum.edu/

General Application Contact: Lindsey Seal, Director of Enrollment, 423-636-7300 Ext. 5006, E-mail: lseal@tusculum.edu.

GRADUATE UNITS

Program in Business Administration Expenses: Contact institution. *Program availability:* Evening/weekend. Offers general management (MBA). *Application Contact:* Lindsey Seal, Director of Enrollment, 423-636-7300 Ext. 5006, E-mail: lseal@tusculum.edu. *Dean of the School of Business*, Dr. Jacob Fait, 423-636-7300 Ext. 5022, E-mail: jfait@tusculum.edu.

Program in Curriculum and Instruction Expenses: Contact institution. *Program availability:* Evening/weekend. Offers special education (MA Ed). *Application deadline:* Applications are processed on a rolling basis. *Application fee:* $0. *Application Contact:* Lindsey Seal, Director of Enrollment, 423-636-7300 Ext. 5006, E-mail: lseal@tusculum.edu. *Dean, School of Education*, Dr. Tricia Hunsader, 423-636-7300 Ext. 5693, E-mail: thunsader@tusculum.edu.

Program in Nursing Expenses: Contact institution. *Program availability:* Part-time. Offers family nurse practitioner (MSN). *Application deadline:* For spring admission, 12/10 for domestic students. *Application fee:* $25. *Application Contact:* Lindsey Seal, Director of Enrollment, 423-636-7300 Ext. 5006, E-mail: lseal@tusculum.edu.

Program in Talent Development Expenses: Contact institution. *Program availability:* Online learning. Offers talent development (MA). *Application Contact:* Lindsey Seal, Director of Enrollment, 423-636-7300 Ext. 5006, E-mail: lseal@tusculum.edu.

Program in Teaching Expenses: Contact institution. *Program availability:* Evening/weekend. Offers teaching (MAT). *Application Contact:* Lindsey Seal, Director of Enrollment, 423-636-7300 Ext. 5006, E-mail: lseal@tusculum.edu. *Dean, School of Education*, Dr. Tricia Hunsader, 423-636-7300 Ext. 5693, E-mail: thunsader@tusculum.edu.

TUSKEGEE UNIVERSITY, Tuskegee, AL 36088

General Information Independent, coed, comprehensive institution. *Graduate housing:* Rooms and/or apartments available to single students and available on a first-come, first-served basis to married students. Housing application deadline: 5/1. *Research affiliation:* Boeing (engineering), Chevron (engineering), 3M Corporation (engineering), U.S. Department of Education (DOE) (agriculture), U.S. Department of Defense (agriculture).

GRADUATE UNITS

Graduate Programs *Program availability:* Part-time. Offers integrative biosciences (PhD).

Andrew F. Brimmer College of Business and Information Science Offers information systems and security management (MS).

College of Agriculture, Environment and Nutrition Sciences Offers agricultural and resource economics (MS); agriculture, environment and nutrition sciences (MS); animal and poultry breeding (MS); animal and poultry nutrition (MS); animal and poultry physiology (MS); animal and poultry sciences (MS); environmental sciences (MS); food and nutritional sciences (MS); plant and soil sciences (MS).

College of Arts and Sciences Offers arts and sciences (MS); biology (MS); chemistry (MS).

College of Engineering Offers electrical engineering (MSEE); engineering (MSEE, MSME, PhD); materials science and engineering (PhD); mechanical engineering (MSME).

College of Veterinary Medicine, Nursing and Allied Health Offers occupational therapy (MS); veterinary medicine (MS, DVM); veterinary medicine, nursing and allied health (MS, DVM).

TYNDALE UNIVERSITY COLLEGE & SEMINARY, Toronto, ON M2M 3S4, Canada

General Information Independent-religious, coed, comprehensive institution. *Graduate housing:* Room and/or apartments available on a first-come, first-served basis to single students; on-campus housing not available to married students.

GRADUATE UNITS

Graduate Programs *Program availability:* Part-time, online learning. Offers Biblical studies (M Div); Christian foundations (MTS); Christian studies (Diploma); counseling (M Div); educational ministry (M Div); missions (M Div, Diploma); pastoral and Chinese ministry (M Div); pastoral ministry (M Div); Pentecostal studies (MTS); spiritual formation (M Div, Diploma); theological studies (M Div); theology (Th M); worship and liturgy (M Div, MTS); youth and family ministry (M Div). Electronic applications accepted.

UNIFICATION THEOLOGICAL SEMINARY, Barrytown, NY 12507

General Information Independent-religious, coed, graduate-only institution. *Enrollment by degree level:* 95 master's, 38 doctoral. *Graduate faculty:* 4 full-time (1 woman), 12 part-time/adjunct (1 woman). *Tuition:* Full-time $12,000; part-time $500 per credit. *Required fees:* $260; $210 per year. $105 per semester. Tuition and fees vary according to campus/location. *Graduate housing:* Rooms and/or apartments available on a first-come, first-served basis to single and married students. Typical cost: $5400 per year for single students; $9600 per year for married students. Room charges vary according to campus/location and housing facility selected. *Student services:* Campus employment opportunities, career counseling, free psychological counseling, international student services, writing training. *Library facilities:* Seminary Library plus 1 other. *Collection:* Books: 58,264 (physical), 69,025 (digital/electronic); Databases: 26. Weekly public service hours: 44.

Computer facilities: 10 computers available on campus for general student use. A campuswide network can be accessed. Online class registration is available.
Website: http://www.uts.edu/

General Application Contact: Henry Christopher, Director of Admissions, 212-563-6647 Ext. 105, Fax: 212-563-6431, E-mail: h.christopher@uts.edu.

GRADUATE UNITS

Graduate Programs Expenses: Contact institution. *Financial support:* Scholarships/grants available. Financial award application deadline: 6/15; financial award applicants required to submit FAFSA. *Program availability:* Part-time, evening/weekend, online learning. Offers family and educational ministry (D Min); interfaith peacebuilding (MRE); peace and justice ministry (D Min); religious education (MRE); religious studies (MA); theology (M Div). *Application deadline:* For fall admission, 3/15 priority date for domestic and international students; for spring admission, 9/15 priority date for domestic and international students. Applications are processed on a rolling basis. *Application fee:* $30. Electronic applications accepted. *Application Contact:* Henry Christopher, Director of Admissions and Financial Aid, 212-563-6647 Ext. 105, Fax: 845-752-3014, E-mail: admissions@uts.edu. *Vice-President for Administration*, Michael Mickler, 845-752-3235, Fax: 845-752-3014, E-mail: mm@uts.edu.

UNIFORMED SERVICES UNIVERSITY OF THE HEALTH SCIENCES, Bethesda, MD 20814-4799

General Information Federally supported, coed, graduate-only institution. *Graduate housing:* On-campus housing not available. *Research affiliation:* National Library of Medicine, National Institutes of Health, Walter Reed Army Institute of Research, Armed Forces Institute of Pathology, U.S. Armed Forces Radiobiology Research Institute.

GRADUATE UNITS

Daniel K. Inouye Graduate School of Nursing Students: 170 full-time (98 women); includes 51 minority (21 Black or African American, non-Hispanic/Latino; 17 Asian, non-Hispanic/Latino; 11 Hispanic/Latino; 2 Native Hawaiian or other Pacific Islander, non-Hispanic/Latino). Average age 34. 88 applicants, 75% accepted, 66 enrolled. *Faculty:* 42 full-time (28 women), 2 part-time/adjunct (1 woman). Expenses: Contact institution. In 2017, 55 doctorates awarded. Offers adult-gerontology clinical nurse specialist (MSN, DNP); family nurse practitioner (DNP); nurse anesthesia (DNP); nursing science (PhD); psychiatric mental health nurse practitioner (DNP); women's health nurse practitioner (DNP). *Application deadline:* For winter admission, 2/15 for domestic students; for summer admission, 8/15 for domestic students. *Application fee:* $0. Electronic applications accepted. *Application Contact:* Maureen Jackson, Registrar, 301-295-1055, Fax: 301-295-1707, E-mail: maureen.jackson.ctr@usuhs.edu. *Associate Dean for Academic Affairs*, Dr. Diane C. Seibert, 301-295-1080, Fax: 301-295-1707, E-mail: diane.seibert@usuhs.edu.

F. Edward Hebert School of Medicine Offers medicine (MPH, MS, MSPH, MTMH, Dr PH, MD, PhD).

Graduate Programs in the Biomedical Sciences and Public Health Average age 25. 598 applicants, 17% accepted, 77 enrolled. Expenses: Contact institution. *Financial support:* In 2017–18, 50 fellowships (averaging $43,000 per year) were awarded; research assistantships, career-related internships or fieldwork, scholarships/grants, and health care benefits also available. In 2017, 19 master's, 50 doctorates awarded. Offers clinical psychology (PhD); emerging infectious diseases (PhD); environmental health sciences (PhD); healthcare administration and policy (MS); medical and clinical psychology (PhD); medical psychology (PhD); medical zoology (PhD); medicine (MS, PhD); molecular and cell biology (MS, PhD); neuroscience (PhD); preventive medicine and biometrics (MPH, MS, MSPH, MTMH, PhD); public health (MPH, MSPH); tropical medicine and hygiene (MTMH). *Application deadline:* For fall admission, 12/1 priority date for domestic students. *Application fee:* $0. Electronic applications accepted. *Application Contact:* Tina Finley, Administrative Officer, 301-

295-3642, Fax: 301-295-6772, E-mail: netina.finley@usuhs.edu. *Associate Dean*, Dr. Gregory Mueller, 301-295-3507, E-mail: gregory.mueller@usuhs.edu.

UNION COLLEGE, Barbourville, KY 40906-1499

General Information Independent-religious, coed, comprehensive institution. *Graduate housing:* Rooms and/or apartments available to single and married students.

GRADUATE UNITS

Graduate Programs *Program availability:* Part-time, evening/weekend. Offers clinical psychology (MA); counseling psychology (MA); elementary education (MA); health (MA Ed); health and physical education (MA); middle grades (MA); music education (MA); principalship (MA); reading specialist (MA); school psychology (MA); secondary education (MA); special education (MA).

UNION COLLEGE, Lincoln, NE 68506-4300

General Information Independent-religious, coed, comprehensive institution. *Enrollment:* 868 graduate, professional, and undergraduate students; 87 full-time matriculated graduate/professional students (65 women). *Enrollment by degree level:* 87 master's. *Graduate faculty:* 5 full-time (3 women), 8 part-time/adjunct (2 women). *Graduate housing:* Rooms and/or apartments available on a first-come, first-served basis to single and married students. *Student services:* Career counseling, exercise/wellness program, free psychological counseling, international student services, low-cost health insurance, services for students with disabilities. *Library facilities:* Ella Johnson Crandall Library. *Collection:* Books: 143,808 (physical), 187,159 (digital/electronic); Serial titles: 136 (physical), 136 (digital/electronic); Databases: 61. Students can reserve study rooms.

Computer facilities: A campuswide network can be accessed from student residence rooms and from off campus. Online class registration is available.
Website: http://www.ucollege.edu/

General Application Contact: Jan Lemon, Physician Assistant Program, 402-486-2527, Fax: 402-486-2559, E-mail: jan.lemon@ucollege.edu.

GRADUATE UNITS

Physician Assistant Program Students: 87 full-time (65 women); includes 12 minority (2 Black or African American, non-Hispanic/Latino; 2 Asian, non-Hispanic/Latino; 8 Hispanic/Latino). Average age 28. *Faculty:* 5 full-time (3 women), 8 part-time/adjunct (2 women). Expenses: Contact institution. *Financial support:* Applicants required to submit FAFSA. Offers physician assistant (MPAS). *Application deadline:* For fall admission, 11/1 for domestic and international students. Applications are processed on a rolling basis. Electronic applications accepted. *Application Contact:* Jan Lemon, Admissions Coordinator/Office Manager, 402-486-2527, Fax: 402-486-2559, E-mail: jan.lemon@ucollege.edu. *Director*, Megan Heidtbrink, 402-486-2527, Fax: 402-486-2559.

UNION INSTITUTE & UNIVERSITY, Cincinnati, OH 45206-1925

General Information Independent, coed, university. *Enrollment:* 313 full-time matriculated graduate/professional students (228 women), 134 part-time matriculated graduate/professional students (101 women). *Enrollment by degree level:* 172 master's, 179 doctoral, 11 other advanced degrees. *Graduate faculty:* 26 full-time (14 women), 31 part-time/adjunct (20 women). *Student services:* Campus employment opportunities, career counseling, international student services, low-cost health insurance, services for students with disabilities, writing training. *Library facilities:* Union Institute & University Library. *Collection:* Books: 3 million (digital/electronic); Serial titles: 77,317 (digital/electronic); Databases: 171. Weekly public service hours: 50.

Computer facilities: Computer purchase and lease plans are available. 65 computers available on campus for general student use. A campuswide network can be accessed from off campus. Online class registration, CampusWeb: access to basic information are available.
Website: http://www.myunion.edu/

General Application Contact: Admissions Office, 513-861-6400, E-mail: admissions@myunion.edu.

GRADUATE UNITS

Master of Arts Program Students: 9 full-time (7 women), 70 part-time (56 women); includes 33 minority (22 Black or African American, non-Hispanic/Latino; 1 American Indian or Alaska Native, non-Hispanic/Latino; 6 Hispanic/Latino; 4 Two or more races, non-Hispanic/Latino). Average age 40. Expenses: Contact institution. *Financial support:* Career-related internships or fieldwork and tuition waivers available. Financial award applicants required to submit FAFSA. *Program availability:* Part-time, online only, 100% online. Offers creativity studies (MA); health and wellness (MA); history and culture (MA); leadership, public policy, and social issues (MA); literature and writing (MA). *Application deadline:* For spring admission, 3/13 for domestic students. Applications are processed on a rolling basis. *Application fee:* $50. Electronic applications accepted. *Application Contact:* Director of Admissions, 800-861-6400. *Director*, Elden Golden, 513-487-1153, E-mail: elden.golden@myunion.edu.

Master of Arts Program in Clinical Mental Health Counseling Expenses: Contact institution. *Financial support:* Federal Work-Study available. Financial award applicants required to submit FAFSA. *Program availability:* Part-time, online only, blended/hybrid learning. Offers clinical mental health counseling (MA). *Application deadline:* Applications are processed on a rolling basis. *Application fee:* $50. Electronic applications accepted. *Application Contact:* Director of Admissions, 888-828-8575. *Director*, Dr. Rosalyn Y. Brown Beatty, 802-254-0152.

Master of Science Program in Healthcare Leadership Offers healthcare leadership (MS).

Master of Science Program in Organizational Leadership Expenses: Contact institution. *Financial support:* Federal Work-Study available. *Program availability:* Part-time, online only, 100% online. Offers organizational leadership (MS). *Application deadline:* Applications are processed on a rolling basis. *Application fee:* $50. Electronic applications accepted. *Application Contact:* Admissions Office, 513-861-6400, E-mail: admissions@myunion.edu.

PhD Program in Interdisciplinary Studies Expenses: Contact institution. *Financial support:* Federal Work-Study and scholarships/grants available. Financial award application deadline: 5/1; financial award applicants required to submit FAFSA. *Program availability:* Part-time, online only, blended/hybrid learning. Offers educational studies (PhD); ethical and creative leadership (PhD); humanities and culture (PhD); public policy and social change (PhD). Program requires participation in brief on-campus residencies twice each year (January and July). *Application deadline:* Applications are processed on a rolling basis. *Application fee:* $50. Electronic applications accepted. *Application Contact:* Admissions Counselor, 800-486-3116. *Dean of Graduate College*, Dr. Michael Raffanti, 800-641-6400 Ext. 1237, E-mail: michael.raffanti@myunion.edu.

UNION PRESBYTERIAN SEMINARY, Richmond, VA 23227-4597

General Information Independent-religious, coed, graduate-only institution. *Graduate housing:* Rooms and/or apartments available on a first-come, first-served basis to single and married students. Housing application deadline: 6/30.

GRADUATE UNITS

Graduate and Professional Programs *Program availability:* Part-time, evening/weekend, online learning. Electronic applications accepted.

UNION THEOLOGICAL SEMINARY IN THE CITY OF NEW YORK, New York, NY 10027-5710

General Information Independent-religious, coed, graduate-only institution. *Graduate housing:* Rooms and/or apartments available on a first-come, first-served basis to single and married students. Housing application deadline: 5/15.

GRADUATE UNITS

Graduate and Professional Programs *Program availability:* Part-time. Offers theology (M Div, MA, STM, D Min, PhD). M Div/MSSW with Columbia University.

UNION UNIVERSITY, Jackson, TN 38305-3697

General Information Independent-religious, coed, comprehensive institution. *Graduate housing:* Rooms and/or apartments available on a first-come, first-served basis to single and married students. Housing application deadline: 8/1.

GRADUATE UNITS

College of Pharmacy Students: 192 full-time (118 women); includes 46 minority (22 Black or African American, non-Hispanic/Latino; 1 American Indian or Alaska Native, non-Hispanic/Latino; 15 Asian, non-Hispanic/Latino; 6 Hispanic/Latino; 2 Two or more races, non-Hispanic/Latino). Average age 25. 218 applicants, 38% accepted, 46 enrolled. *Faculty:* 25 full-time (11 women), 3 part-time/adjunct (0 women). Expenses: Contact institution. *Financial support:* In 2017–18, 4 fellowships (averaging $45,000 per year) were awarded. Financial award application deadline: 8/1; financial award applicants required to submit FAFSA. In 2017, 56 doctorates awarded. Offers pharmacy (Pharm D). *Application deadline:* For spring admission, 3/1 for domestic and international students. Applications are processed on a rolling basis. Electronic applications accepted. *Application Contact:* Stephen Hauss, Director of Admissions and Recruitment, 731-661-5979, E-mail: shauss@uu.edu. *Dean*, Sheila Mitchell, 731-661-5953, E-mail: smitchell@uu.edu.

Institute for International and Intercultural Studies *Program availability:* Part-time, evening/weekend. Offers international and intercultural studies (MAIS). Electronic applications accepted.

McAfee School of Business Administration *Program availability:* Evening/weekend, online learning. Offers accountancy (M Acc). Program also available at Germantown campus. Electronic applications accepted.

School of Education *Program availability:* Part-time, evening/weekend, online learning. Offers education (M Ed, MA Ed); education administration generalist (Ed S); educational leadership (Ed D); educational supervision (Ed S); higher education (Ed D). M Ed also available at Germantown campus. Electronic applications accepted.

School of Nursing Offers executive leadership (DNP); nurse anesthesia (DNP); nurse practitioner (DNP); nursing education (MSN, PMC). Electronic applications accepted.

School of Social Work Offers social work (MSW).

School of Theology and Missions *Program availability:* Part-time, evening/weekend, online learning. Offers Christian studies (MCS); expository preaching (D Min). Electronic applications accepted.

UNITED LUTHERAN SEMINARY, Gettysburg, PA 17325-1795

General Information Independent-religious, coed, graduate-only institution. *Graduate housing:* Rooms and/or apartments available on a first-come, first-served basis to single and married students. Housing application deadline: 4/1.

GRADUATE UNITS

Graduate and Professional Programs *Program availability:* Part-time, online learning. Offers divinity (M Div); ministerial studies (MAMS); outdoor ministry (MAR); parish ministry (D Min); theology (STM). Electronic applications accepted.

UNITED LUTHERAN SEMINARY, Philadelphia, PA 19119-1794

General Information Independent-religious, coed, graduate-only institution. *Graduate housing:* Rooms and/or apartments available on a first-come, first-served basis to single and married students. Housing application deadline: 5/15.

GRADUATE UNITS

Graduate School *Program availability:* Part-time, evening/weekend. Offers divinity (M Div); ministry (D Min); public leadership (MA); religion (MAR); social ministry and church (Certificate); theology (STM, PhD). Electronic applications accepted.

UNITED STATES ARMY COMMAND AND GENERAL STAFF COLLEGE, Fort Leavenworth, KS 66027-2301

General Information Federally supported, coed, primarily men, graduate-only institution. *Graduate housing:* Rooms and/or apartments available to single and married students.

GRADUATE UNITS

Graduate Program Offers military art and science (MMAS). Only career military officers are selected to attend United States Army Command and General Staff College; Graduate Program is voluntary for first-year students, but mandatory for second-year students.

UNITED STATES INTERNATIONAL UNIVERSITY–AFRICA, Nairobi 00800, Kenya

General Information Independent, coed, comprehensive institution. *Graduate housing:* Room and/or apartments available on a first-come, first-served basis to single students; on-campus housing not available to married students. Housing application deadline: 7/31.

GRADUATE UNITS

School of Arts and Sciences *Program availability:* Part-time, evening/weekend. Offers counseling psychology (MA); international relations (MA).

School of Business Administration *Program availability:* Part-time, evening/weekend. Offers business administration (GEMBA); entrepreneurship (MBA); finance (MBA); human resource management (MBA); information technology management (MBA); integrated studies (MBA); international business administration (MBA); management and organizational development (MS); marketing (MBA); organizational development (EMS); strategic management (MBA).

UNITED STATES MERCHANT MARINE ACADEMY, Kings Point, NY 11024-1699

General Information Federally supported, coed, comprehensive institution.

GRADUATE UNITS

Graduate Program Offers marine engineering (MS).

UNITED STATES SPORTS ACADEMY, Daphne, AL 36526-7055

General Information Independent, coed, upper-level institution. *Enrollment:* 291 graduate, professional, and undergraduate students; 63 full-time matriculated graduate/professional students (29 women), 104 part-time matriculated graduate/professional students (30 women). *Graduate housing:* On-campus housing not available. *Student services:* Campus employment opportunities, campus safety program, career counseling, exercise/wellness program, free psychological counseling, international student services, low-cost health insurance. *Library facilities:* United States Sports Academy Library plus 1 other. *Collection:* Weekly public service hours: 5.

Computer facilities: A campuswide network can be accessed from off campus. Online class registration is available.
Website: http://www.ussa.edu/

General Application Contact: Dr. Taffy Sithole, Student Services Coordinator, 251-626-3303 Ext. 7147, Fax: 251-625-1035, E-mail: tsithole@ussa.edu.

GRADUATE UNITS

Graduate Programs Students: 63 full-time (29 women), 104 part-time (30 women). Expenses: Contact institution. *Financial support:* Research assistantships with full tuition reimbursements, career-related internships or fieldwork, Federal Work-Study, scholarships/grants, and service assistantships available. Support available to part-time students. Financial award application deadline: 8/15; financial award applicants required to submit FAFSA. In 2017, 51 master's, 24 doctorates awarded. *Program availability:* Part-time, 100% online. Offers recreation management (MSS); sports coaching (MSS); sports health and fitness (MSS); sports management (MSS, Ed D); sports studies (MSS). *Application deadline:* Applications are processed on a rolling basis. *Application fee:* $50 ($125 for international students). Electronic applications accepted. *Application Contact:* Dr. Taffy Sithole, Student Services Coordinator, 251-626-3303 Ext. 7147, Fax: 251-625-1035, E-mail: tsithole@ussa.edu. *Vice President of Academic Affairs,* Dr. Tomi Wahlstrom, 251-626-3303, Fax: 251-626-1149, E-mail: vicepresident@ussa.edu.

UNITED STATES UNIVERSITY, San Diego, CA 92108

General Information Proprietary, coed, comprehensive institution.

GRADUATE UNITS

Family Nurse Practitioner Program Offers family nurse practitioner (MSN).

UNITED TALMUDICAL SEMINARY, Brooklyn, NY 11211

General Information Independent-religious, men only, comprehensive institution.

GRADUATE UNITS

Graduate Programs

UNITED THEOLOGICAL SEMINARY, Dayton, OH 45426

General Information Independent-religious, coed, graduate-only institution.

GRADUATE UNITS

Graduate and Professional Programs *Program availability:* Part-time, evening/weekend, online learning. Offers Christian ministries (MA); ministry (M Div, D Min); theological studies (MTS). Electronic applications accepted.

UNITED THEOLOGICAL SEMINARY OF THE TWIN CITIES, New Brighton, MN 55112-2598

General Information Independent-religious, coed, graduate-only institution. *Graduate housing:* Rooms and/or apartments available on a first-come, first-served basis to single and married students.

GRADUATE UNITS

Graduate Programs *Program availability:* Part-time, evening/weekend. Offers advanced theological studies (Diploma); justice and peace studies (M Div, MA); leadership toward racial justice (M Div, MA, Certificate); Methodist studies (M Div, MA, Certificate); ministry (D Min); ministry renewal and professional development (Certificate); pastoral care and counseling (M Div, MA, MARL); religion and theology (MA); theological and religious studies (Certificate); theology and the arts (M Div, MA); urban ministry (M Div, MA, MARL); women's studies: religion, theology and ministry (M Div, MA).

UNITY COLLEGE, Unity, ME 04988

General Information Independent, coed, comprehensive institution.

GRADUATE UNITS

Program in Professional Science *Program availability:* Online learning. Offers sustainability science (MS); sustainable natural resource management (MS).

UNIVERSIDAD ADVENTISTA DE LAS ANTILLAS, Mayagüez, PR 00681-0118

General Information Independent-religious, coed, comprehensive institution. *Graduate housing:* Rooms and/or apartments available on a first-come, first-served basis to single and married students.

GRADUATE UNITS

EGECED Department Offers curriculum and instruction (M Ed); medical surgical nursing (MN); school administration and supervision (M Ed). Electronic applications accepted.

UNIVERSIDAD CENTRAL DEL CARIBE, Bayamón, PR 00960-6032

General Information Independent, coed, comprehensive institution. *Graduate housing:* On-campus housing not available.

GRADUATE UNITS

Program in Substance Abuse Counseling Offers substance abuse counseling (MHS).

School of Medicine Offers anatomy and cell biology (MA, MS); biochemistry (MS); biomedical sciences (MA); cellular and molecular biology (PhD); medicine (MA, MS, MD, PhD); microbiology and immunology (MA, MS); pharmacology (MS); physiology (MS).

UNIVERSIDAD DE LAS AMERICAS, A.C., 06700 Mexico City, Mexico

General Information Independent, coed, comprehensive institution.

GRADUATE UNITS

Program in Business Administration Offers finance (MBA); marketing research (MBA); production and quality (MBA).

Program in Education Offers education (M Ed).

Program in International Organizations and Institutions Offers international organizations and institutions (MA).

Program in Psychology Offers family therapy (MA).

UNIVERSIDAD DE LAS AMÉRICAS PUEBLA, Puebla CP 72810, Mexico

General Information Independent, coed, university. CGS member. *Graduate housing:* On-campus housing not available. *Research affiliation:* Empacadora San Marcos S. A. de C. U. (food service), Volkswagen de Mexico S. A. de C. U. (mechanical engineering), Institute Mexicano del Tecnologa del agua (electronic engineering), Frugosa S. A. de C. U. (chemical engineering).

GRADUATE UNITS

Division of Graduate Studies *Program availability:* Part-time, evening/weekend.

School of Business and Economics *Program availability:* Part-time, evening/weekend. Offers business administration (MBA); finance (M Adm).

School of Engineering *Program availability:* Part-time, evening/weekend. Offers chemical engineering (MS); computer science (PhD); construction management (M Adm); electronic engineering (MS); engineering (M Adm, MS, PhD); food sciences (MS); food technology (MS); industrial engineering (MS); manufacturing administration (MS); production management (M Adm).

School of Humanities *Program availability:* Part-time, evening/weekend. Offers humanities (MA); information design (MA); linguistics (MA); literature (MA).

School of Sciences *Program availability:* Part-time, evening/weekend. Offers biotechnology (MS); clinical analysis (biomedicine) (MS); sciences (MS).

School of Social Sciences *Program availability:* Part-time, evening/weekend. Offers American studies (MA); anthropology (MA); archaeology (MA); economics (MA); education (MA); finance (M Adm); psychology (MA); social sciences (M Adm, MA).

UNIVERSIDAD DEL ESTE, Carolina, PR 00984

General Information Independent, coed, comprehensive institution.

GRADUATE UNITS

Graduate School Offers accounting (MBA); adult education (M Ed); agribusiness (MBA); criminal justice and criminology (MA); curriculum and instruction - early education (M Ed); curriculum and instruction - elementary (M Ed); curriculum and instruction - English (M Ed); curriculum and instruction - Spanish (M Ed); human resources (MBA); information security management (MBA); information technology and Web business development (MBA); management (MBA); public policy (MPA); social work (MA); special education (M Ed); strategic leadership (MBA).

UNIVERSIDAD DEL TURABO, Gurabo, PR 00778-3030

General Information Independent, coed, university. CGS member. *Graduate housing:* On-campus housing not available.

GRADUATE UNITS

Graduate Programs *Program availability:* Part-time, evening/weekend, 100% online, blended/hybrid learning. Offers athletic therapeutic (MPHE); coaching (MPHE); counseling (M Ed); curriculum and instruction and appropriate environment (D Ed); curriculum and teaching (M Ed); education (M Ed, MPHE, D Ed); educational administration (M Ed); educational leadership (D Ed); environmental analysis (MSE); environmental management (MSE); environmental science (D Sc); library service and information technology (M Ed); special education (M Ed); teaching at primary level (M Ed); teaching English as a second language (M Ed); teaching of fine arts (M Ed); wellness (MPHE). Electronic applications accepted.

School of Business and Entrepreneurship *Program availability:* Part-time, evening/weekend. Offers accounting (MBA); business and entrepreneurship (MBA, DBA); human resources (MBA); logistics and materials management (MBA); management (MBA, DBA); management of information systems (DBA); marketing (MBA); project management (MBA); quality management (MBA). Electronic applications accepted.

School of Engineering Offers computer engineering (M Eng); electrical engineering (M Eng); mechanical engineering (M Eng); telecommunications and network systems administration (M Eng). Electronic applications accepted.

School of Health Sciences Offers family nurse practitioner (MSN, Certificate); family nurse practitioner - adult nursing (MSN, Certificate); health sciences (MS, MSN, ND, Certificate); naturopathy (ND); speech and language pathology (MS). Electronic applications accepted.

School of Social Sciences and Humanities Offers arts administration (MPA); conflict and mediation studies (MPA); counseling psychology (M Psych, Psy D, Certificate); criminal justice studies (MPA); forensic psychology (Certificate); forensic science (MPA); human services administration (MPA); psychology (M Psych); social sciences and humanities (M Psych, MPA, Psy D, Certificate). Electronic applications accepted.

UNIVERSIDAD DE MONTERREY, 66238 San Pedro Garza Garcia, NL, Mexico

General Information Independent-religious, coed, comprehensive institution.

GRADUATE UNITS

Graduate Programs

UNIVERSIDAD METROPOLITANA, San Juan, PR 00928-1150

General Information Independent, coed, comprehensive institution. *Graduate housing:* On-campus housing not available. *Research affiliation:* Berkeley National Laboratories (bioremediation), University Corporation for Atmospheric Research (computer science, atmospheric science), University of Colorado Boulder (computer science, biology), University of Puerto Rico (physics, chemistry), University of Utah (computational chemistry), Howard University (computational chemistry).

GRADUATE UNITS

School of Business Administration *Program availability:* Part-time, evening/weekend. Offers accounting (MBA); finance (MBA); human resources management (MBA); international business (MBA); management (MBA); management information systems (MBA); marketing (MBA). Electronic applications accepted.

School of Education *Program availability:* Part-time, evening/weekend. Offers administration and supervision (M Ed); curriculum and teaching (M Ed); education (M Ed, Ed D); educational administration and supervision (M Ed); managing recreation and sports services (M Ed); pedagogy (PhD); pre-school centers administration (M Ed); special education (M Ed); teaching of adult physical education (M Ed); teaching of elementary physical education (M Ed); teaching of physical education (M Ed); teaching of secondary physical education (M Ed). Electronic applications accepted.

School of Environmental Affairs *Program availability:* Part-time. Offers environmental management (MSEM); environmental planning (MP); environmental studies (MAES). Electronic applications accepted.

School of Health Sciences Offers case management (Certificate); health sciences (MSN, Certificate); nursing (MSN); oncology nursing (Certificate).

School of Social Sciences, Humanities and Communications Offers counseling psychology (MA).

UNIVERSITÉ DE MONCTON, Moncton, NB E1A 3E9, Canada

General Information Province-supported, coed, comprehensive institution. *Graduate housing:* Rooms and/or apartments available on a first-come, first-served basis to single and married students.

GRADUATE UNITS

Faculty of Administration Students: 27 full-time (11 women), 16 international. Average age 26. 125 applicants, 41% accepted, 17 enrolled. *Faculty:* 23 full-time (9 women), 24 part-time/adjunct (9 women). Expenses: Contact institution. *Financial support:* In 2017–18, 7 fellowships (averaging $2,500 per year) were awarded; teaching assistantships and institutionally sponsored loans also available. Support available to part-time students. Financial award application deadline: 5/30. In 2017, 20 master's awarded. *Program availability:* Part-time, evening/weekend, 100% online. Offers administration (MBA). *Application deadline:* For fall admission, 6/1 for domestic students, 2/1 for international students; for winter admission, 11/15 for domestic students, 9/1 for international students; for spring admission, 3/31 for domestic students, 1/1 for international students; for summer admission, 3/31 for domestic students, 1/1 for international students. Applications are processed on a rolling basis. *Application fee:* $60. Electronic applications accepted. *Application Contact:* Natalie Allain, Admission Counselor, 506-858-4273, Fax: 506-858-4093, E-mail: natalie.allain@umoncton.ca. *Director,* Jean-Pierre Booto Ekionea, 506-858-4174, Fax: 506-858-4093, E-mail: jean-pierre.booto.ekionea@umoncton.ca.

Faculty of Arts and Social Sciences *Program availability:* Part-time. Offers arts and social sciences (MA, MPA, MSW, PhD); economics (MA); French studies (MA, PhD); history (MA); public administration (MPA). Electronic applications accepted.

School of Social Work Offers social work (MSW).

Faculty of Education *Program availability:* Part-time. Offers education (M Ed, MA Ed).

Graduate Studies in Education *Program availability:* Part-time. Offers educational psychology (M Ed, MA Ed); guidance (M Ed, MA Ed); school administration (M Ed, MA Ed); teaching (M Ed, MA Ed).

Faculty of Engineering Offers civil engineering (M Sc A); electrical engineering (M Sc A); industrial engineering (M Sc A); mechanical engineering (M Sc A).

Faculty of Sciences *Program availability:* Part-time. Offers biochemistry (M Sc); biology (M Sc); chemistry (M Sc); information technology (M Sc, Certificate, Diploma); mathematics (M Sc); physics and astronomy (M Sc); sciences (M Sc, Certificate, Diploma). Electronic applications accepted.

School of Food Science, Nutrition and Family Studies *Program availability:* Part-time. Offers foods/nutrition (M Sc). Electronic applications accepted.

UNIVERSITÉ DE MONTRÉAL, Montréal, QC H3C 3J7, Canada

General Information Province-supported, coed, university. *Graduate housing:* Room and/or apartments available on a first-come, first-served basis to single students; on-campus housing not available to married students. Housing application deadline: 2/1. *Research affiliation:* Centre Hospitalier Universitaire Mere-Enfant de l'Hopital Sainte-Justine, Centre de Recherche de L'Hopital Sacre-Coeur, Institut de Recherches Cliniques de Montreal, Institut de Cardiologie de Montreal, Institut Universitaire de geriatric de Montreal.

GRADUATE UNITS

Department of Kinesiology Offers kinesiology (M Sc, DESS); physical activity (M Sc, PhD). Electronic applications accepted.

Faculty of Arts and Sciences *Program availability:* Part-time. Offers anthropology (M Sc, PhD); applied human sciences (PhD); art history (MA, PhD); arts and sciences (M Sc, MA, MIS, PhD, DESS); biological sciences (M Sc, PhD); chemistry (M Sc, PhD); classical studies (MA); communication (PhD); communication sciences (M Sc); comparative literature (MA); computer systems (M Sc, PhD); demography (M Sc, PhD); economics (M Sc, PhD); electronic commerce (M Sc); English studies (MA, PhD); environment and durable development (DESS); film studies (MA, PhD); French literature (MA, PhD); geography (M Sc, PhD, DESS); German literature (PhD); German studies (MA); Hispanic literature (PhD); Hispanic studies (MA); history (MA, PhD); international studies (M Sc, DESS); linguistics (MA, PhD); literature (PhD); mathematical and computational finance (M Sc, DESS); mathematics (M Sc, PhD); museology (MA); philosophy (MA, PhD); physics (M Sc, PhD); political science (M Sc, PhD); psychology (M Sc, PhD); societies, public policies and health (DESS); sociology (M Sc, PhD); statistics (M Sc, PhD); translation (MA, PhD, DESS). Electronic applications accepted.

School of Criminology Offers criminology (M Sc, PhD). Electronic applications accepted.

School of Industrial Relations *Program availability:* Part-time. Offers industrial relations (M Sc, PhD, DESS). Electronic applications accepted.

School of Library and Information Sciences Offers information sciences (MIS, PhD). Electronic applications accepted.

School of Psychoeducation *Program availability:* Part-time. Offers psychoeducation (M Sc, PhD). Electronic applications accepted.

School of Social Service *Program availability:* Part-time. Offers social administration (DESS); social work (M Sc, PhD). M Sc and PhD offered jointly with McGill University. Electronic applications accepted.

Faculty of Dental Medicine Offers dental medicine (M Sc, Certificate); multidisciplinary residency (Certificate); oral and dental sciences (M Sc); orthodontics (M Sc); pediatric dentistry (M Sc); prosthodontics rehabilitation (M Sc); stomatology residency (Certificate). Electronic applications accepted.

Faculty of Education *Program availability:* Part-time, evening/weekend. Offers administration and foundations of education (M Ed, MA, PhD, DESS); didactics (M Ed, MA, PhD, DESS); education (M Ed, MA, PhD, DESS); psychopedagogy and andragogy (M Ed, MA, PhD, DESS). Electronic applications accepted.

Faculty of Environmental Design and Planning Offers environmental design and planning (M Sc A, PhD); environmental planning and design projects (DESS); game design (DESS); urban management for developing countries (DESS); urban planning (M Urb). DESS programs offered jointly with HEC Montreal and École Polytechnique de Montréal. Electronic applications accepted.

Faculty of Law *Program availability:* Part-time. Offers business law (DESS); common law (North America) (JD); international law (DESS); law (LL M, LL D, DDN, DESS, LL B); tax law (LL M). Electronic applications accepted.

Faculty of Medicine Offers biochemistry (M Sc, PhD, DEPD); bioethics (MA, DESS); bioinformatics (M Sc, PhD); biomedical sciences (M Sc, PhD); clinical biochemistry (DEPD); community health (M Sc, DESS); echography transoephagian perioperatoryenvironment, health and disaster management (DESS); environmental and occupational health (M Sc); genetic counseling (DESS); health administration (M Sc, DESS); health sciencesinsurance medicine and expertise (English) (DESS); insurance medicine and expertise in health sciences (DESS); medical genetics (DESS); medicine (M Sc, M Sc A, MA, PMS, DES, MD, PhD, DEPD, DESS); microbiology and immunology (M Sc, PhD); mobility and posture (DESS); molecular biology (M Sc, PhD); neurological sciences (M Sc, PhD); nutrition (M Sc, PhD, DESS); occupational therapy (DESS); pathology and cellular biology (M Sc, PhD); pharmacology (M Sc, PhD); physiology (M Sc, PhD); public health (PhD); toxicology and risk analysis (DESS). Electronic applications accepted.

Institute of Biomedical Engineering Offers biomedical engineering (M Sc A, PhD, DESS). M Sc A and PhD programs offered jointly with École Polytechnique de Montréal. Electronic applications accepted.

School of Speech Therapy and Audiology Offers audiology (PMS); speech therapy (PMS, DESS). Electronic applications accepted.

Faculty of Music Offers composition (M Mus, D Mus); interpretation (M Mus, D Mus, DESS); music (MA, PhD); orchestral repertoire (DESS). Electronic applications accepted.

Faculty of Nursing *Program availability:* Part-time. Offers nursing (M Sc, PhD, Certificate, DESS). PhD offered jointly with McGill University. Electronic applications accepted.

Faculty of Pharmacy *Program availability:* Part-time. Offers drugs development (DESS); pharmaceutical care (DESS); pharmaceutical practice (M Sc); pharmaceutical sciences (M Sc, PhD); pharmacist-supervisor teacher (DESS). Electronic applications accepted.

Faculty of Theology and Sciences of Religions Offers health, spirituality and bioethics (DESS); practical theology (MA, PhD); religious sciences (MA, PhD); theology (MA, D Th, PhD, L Th); theology-Biblical studies (PhD). Electronic applications accepted.

Faculty of Veterinary Medicine Offers veterinary medicine (M Sc, DES, PhD); veterinary sciences (M Sc, PhD); virology and immunology (PhD). Electronic applications accepted.

School of Optometry *Program availability:* Part-time. Offers optometry (M Sc, OD, DESS); vision sciences (M Sc); visual impairment intervention-orientation and mobility (DESS); visual impairment intervention-readaptation (DESS). Electronic applications accepted.

UNIVERSITÉ DE SAINT-BONIFACE, Saint-Boniface, MB R2H 0H7, Canada

General Information Independent-religious, coed, comprehensive institution.

GRADUATE UNITS

Department of Education Offers education (M Ed).

Program in Canadian Studies Offers Canadian studies (MA).

UNIVERSITÉ DE SHERBROOKE, Sherbrooke, QC J1K 2R1, Canada

General Information Independent, coed, university. *Graduate housing:* Room and/or apartments available to single students; on-campus housing not available to married students. Housing application deadline: 6/1. *Research affiliation:* Societe de Microelectronique Industrielle.

GRADUATE UNITS

Faculty of Administration *Program availability:* Part-time, evening/weekend. Offers accounting (M Sc); administration (EMBA, M Adm, M Sc, M Tax, MBA, DBA, PhD, Diploma); business administration (EMBA, MBA, DBA); e-commerce (M Sc); economic development (PhD); economics (M Sc); executive business administration (EMBA); finance (M Sc); general management (MBA); governance, audit and security of information technology (M Adm); international business (M Sc); management and governance of cooperatives and mutuals (M Adm); management information systems (M Sc); marketing (M Sc); marketing communications (M Adm); organizational change and intervention (M Sc); public management (M Adm); taxation (M Tax, Diploma).

Faculty of Education *Program availability:* Part-time, evening/weekend. Offers education (M Ed, MA, Diploma); elementary education (M Ed, Diploma); postsecondary education training (M Ed, Diploma); school administration (M Ed); sciences of education (MA); special education (M Ed, Diploma).

Faculty of Engineering *Program availability:* Part-time. Offers chemical engineering (M Sc A, PhD); civil engineering (M Sc A, PhD); electrical engineering (M Sc A, PhD); engineering (M Eng, M Env, M Sc A, PhD, Diploma); engineering management (M Eng, Diploma); environment (M Env); mechanical engineering (M Sc A, PhD). Electronic applications accepted.

Faculty of Law *Program availability:* Part-time, evening/weekend. Offers alternative dispute resolution (LL M, Diploma); business law (Diploma); common law (JD); criminal and penal law (Diploma); health law (LL M, Diploma); international law (LL M); law (LL D); legal management (Diploma); notarial law (Diploma); transnational law (Diploma). Electronic applications accepted.

Faculty of Letters and Human Sciences *Program availability:* Part-time. Offers comparative Canadian literature (MA, PhD); economics (MA); French literature (MA, PhD); geography and remote sensing (M Sc, PhD); gerontology (MA); history (MA); letters and human sciences (M Psych, M Sc, MA, MSS, PhD, Diploma); linguistics (MA); philosophy (MA); social service (MSS); theatre (MA).

Institute of Management and Development of Cooperatives Offers management and development of cooperatives (MA, Diploma).

Faculty of Medicine and Health Sciences *Program availability:* Part-time. Offers medicine (MD); medicine and health sciences (M Sc, MD, PhD). Electronic applications accepted.

Graduate Programs in Medicine *Program availability:* Part-time. Offers biochemistry (M Sc, PhD); cell biology (M Sc, PhD); clinical sciences (M Sc, PhD); immunology (M Sc, PhD); medicine (M Sc, PhD); microbiology (M Sc, PhD); pharmacology (M Sc, PhD); physiology and biophysics (M Sc, PhD); radiobiology (M Sc, PhD). Electronic applications accepted.

Faculty of Physical Education and Sports *Program availability:* Part-time. Offers kinanthropology (M Sc); physical activity (Diploma); physical education (M Sc, Diploma).

Faculty of Sciences Offers biology (M Sc, PhD, Diploma); chemistry (M Sc, PhD, Diploma); informatics (M Sc, PhD); mathematics (M Sc, PhD); physics (M Sc, PhD); sciences (M Sc, PhD, Diploma).

Centre de Formation en Technologies de L'information Offers information technologies (M Sc, Diploma). Electronic applications accepted.

Centre Universitaire de Formation en Environnement *Program availability:* Online learning. Offers environment (M Sc, Diploma). Electronic applications accepted.

Faculty of Theology and Religious Studies *Program availability:* Part-time, evening/weekend, online learning. Offers applied ethics (Diploma); human science of religions (MA); intercultural training (Diploma); philosophy (MA, PhD); spiritual anthropology (Diploma); theology (MA, PhD, Diploma).

UNIVERSITÉ DU QUÉBEC À CHICOUTIMI, Chicoutimi, QC G7H 2B1, Canada

General Information Province-supported, coed, university. CGS member. *Graduate housing:* Room and/or apartments available to single students; on-campus housing not available to married students.

GRADUATE UNITS

Graduate Programs *Program availability:* Part-time. Offers didactics of French-mother tongue (Diploma); earth sciences (M Sc A); education (M Ed, MA, PhD); engineering (M Sc A, PhD); ethics (Diploma); fine arts (MA); genetics (M Sc); linguistics (MA); literary studies (MA); mineral resources (PhD); project management (M Sc); regional studies (MA); renewable resources (M Sc); small and medium-sized organization management (M Sc); theology (pastoral studies) (MA, PhD).

UNIVERSITÉ DU QUÉBEC À MONTRÉAL, Montréal, QC H3C 3P8, Canada

General Information Province-supported, coed, university. CGS member. *Graduate housing:* Room and/or apartments available to single students; on-campus housing not available to married students. *Research affiliation:* Labopharm, Inc. (pharmacology), Hydro-Quebec (environmental sciences), Bell (computer sciences), Microcreatif (computer sciences), University Corporation for Atmospheric Research.

GRADUATE UNITS

Graduate Programs *Program availability:* Part-time. Offers accounting (M Sc, MPA, Diploma); actuarial sciences (Diploma); art history (PhD); art studies (MA); atmospheric sciences (M Sc); biology (M Sc, PhD); business administration (PhD); business administration (research) (MBA); chemistry (M Sc, PhD); communications (MA, PhD); dance (MA); death (Diploma); Earth and atmospheric sciences (PhD); Earth science (M Sc); earth sciences (M Sc); economics (M Sc, PhD); education (M Ed, MA, PhD); education of the environmental sciences (Diploma); environmental sciences (M Sc, PhD, Certificate); ergonomics in occupational health and safety (Diploma); finance (Diploma); fine arts (MA); geographical information systems (Diploma); geography (M Sc); history (MA, PhD); human movement studies (M Sc); linguistics (MA, PhD); literary studies (MA, PhD); management consultant (Diploma); management information systems (M Sc, M Sc A); mathematics (M Sc, PhD); meteorology (PhD, Diploma); mineral resources (PhD); museology (MA); non-renewable resources (DESS); philosophy (MA, PhD); political science (MA, PhD); project management (MGP, Diploma); psychology (D Ps, PhD); religious sciences (MA, PhD); semiology (PhD); sexology (MA); social and labor law (Certificate); social intervention (MA); sociology (MA, PhD); study and practices of the arts (PhD); urban analysis and management (MA); urban studies (MA, PhD).

UNIVERSITÉ DU QUÉBEC À RIMOUSKI, Rimouski, QC G5L 3A1, Canada

General Information Province-supported, coed, comprehensive institution. CGS member. *Graduate housing:* Rooms and/or apartments available on a first-come, first-served basis to single students. *Research affiliation:* Institut des Sciences de la Mer de Rimouski (ISMER) (marine sciences), CRDT (territory development), Centre d'Etudes Nordiques (Nordicity), Quebec Ocean (oceans), Centre Recherche en Forestene (forestry).

GRADUATE UNITS

Graduate Programs *Program availability:* Part-time. Offers biology (PhD); business administration (MBA); education (M Ed, MA, PhD, Diploma); engineering (M Sc A); ethics (MA, Diploma); literary studies (MA, PhD); management of marine resources (M Sc, Diploma); management of people in working situation (M Sc, Diploma); nursing studies (M Sc, Diploma); oceanography (M Sc, PhD); project management (M Sc, Diploma); psychosocial studies (MA); regional development (MA, PhD, Diploma); wildlife resources management (M Sc, Diploma).

UNIVERSITÉ DU QUÉBEC À TROIS-RIVIÈRES, Trois-Rivières, QC G9A 5H7, Canada

General Information Province-supported, coed, university. CGS member. *Graduate housing:* Room and/or apartments available to single students; on-campus housing not available to married students. Housing application deadline: 2/1.

GRADUATE UNITS

Graduate Programs *Program availability:* Part-time. Offers accounting science (MBA); biophysics and cellular biology (M Sc, PhD); business administration (MBA, DBA); chemistry (M Sc); chiropractic (DC); education (M Ed, PhD); educational administration (DESS); electrical engineering (M Sc A, PhD); environmental sciences (M Sc, PhD); finance (DESS); industrial engineering (M Sc, DESS); labor relations (DESS); leisure, culture and tourism sciences (MA, DESS); literary studies (MA); mathematics and computer science (M Sc); matter and energy (MS, PhD); nursing sciences (M Sc, DESS); philosophy (MA, PhD); physical education (M Sc); psychoeducation (M Ed, PhD); psychology (PhD, Certificate); social communication (MA, DESS).

UNIVERSITÉ DU QUÉBEC, ÉCOLE DE TECHNOLOGIE SUPÉRIEURE, Montréal, QC H3C 1K3, Canada

General Information Province-supported, coed, primarily men, comprehensive institution. CGS member. *Graduate housing:* Rooms and/or apartments available on a first-come, first-served basis to single and married students.

GRADUATE UNITS

Graduate Programs *Program availability:* Online learning. Offers engineering (M Eng, PhD, Diploma).

UNIVERSITÉ DU QUÉBEC, ÉCOLE NATIONALE D'ADMINISTRATION PUBLIQUE, Quebec, QC G1K 9E5, Canada

General Information Province-supported, coed, graduate-only institution. CGS member. *Graduate housing:* On-campus housing not available.

GRADUATE UNITS

Graduate Programs in Public Administration *Program availability:* Part-time. Offers international administration (MAP, Diploma); public administration (MAGU, MAP, PhD, Diploma); urban analysis and management (MAGU).

UNIVERSITÉ DU QUÉBEC EN ABITIBI-TÉMISCAMINGUE, Rouyn-Noranda, QC J9X 5E4, Canada

General Information Province-supported, coed, comprehensive institution. CGS member. *Graduate housing:* Room and/or apartments available on a first-come, first-served basis to single students; on-campus housing not available to married students. Housing application deadline: 3/1.

GRADUATE UNITS

Graduate Programs *Program availability:* Part-time. Offers biology (MS); business administration (MBA); education (M Ed, MA, PhD, DESS); engineering (ME); environmental sciences (PhD); mineral engineering (ME); mining engineering (DESS); organization management (M Sc); project management (M Sc, DESS); social work (MSW); sustainable forest ecosystem management (MS).

UNIVERSITÉ DU QUÉBEC EN OUTAOUAIS, Gatineau, QC J8X 3X7, Canada

General Information Province-supported, coed, university. CGS member. *Graduate housing:* Rooms and/or apartments available on a first-come, first-served basis to single and married students.

GRADUATE UNITS

Graduate Programs *Program availability:* Part-time, evening/weekend. Offers accounting (MA, DESS, Diploma); computer science (M Sc, PhD, DESS); education (M Ed, MA, PhD, DESS, Diploma); executive certified management accounting (MA, MBA, DESS); financial services (MBA, DESS, Diploma); industrial relations (M Sc, MA, PhD, Diploma); nursing (M Sc, DESS, Diploma); project management (M Sc, MA, DESS, Diploma); psychoeducation (M Ed, MA); regional development (MA); second and foreign language teaching (Diploma); social work (MA). Electronic applications accepted.

UNIVERSITÉ DU QUÉBEC, INSTITUT NATIONAL DE LA RECHERCHE SCIENTIFIQUE, Québec, QC G1K 9A9, Canada

General Information Province-supported, coed, graduate-only institution. CGS member. *Enrollment by degree level:* 239 master's, 429 doctoral, 1 other advanced degree. *Graduate faculty:* 148 full-time. *Graduate housing:* On-campus housing not available. *Student services:* Exercise/wellness program, free psychological counseling, international student services, low-cost health insurance, services for students with disabilities. *Library facilities:* Service de documentation et d'information specialisees (SDIS) plus 3 others. *Research affiliation:* Sigma Devtech Inc. (green technologies), MPB Technologies Inc. (communications, space, fusion technology, electromagnetics), Biosecur Lab. Inc. (creation and development of active antimicrobial ingredients).

Computer facilities: 500 computers available on campus for general student use. A campuswide network can be accessed from student residence rooms and from off campus. Online class registration is available.
Website: http://www.inrs.ca/

General Application Contact: Sylvie Richard, Registrar, 418-654-2518, Fax: 418-654-3858, E-mail: sylvie.richard@inrs.ca.

GRADUATE UNITS

Graduate Programs Students: 608 full-time (274 women), 61 part-time (33 women), 407 international. Average age 31. 177 applicants, 89% accepted, 126 enrolled. *Faculty:* 148 full-time. Expenses: Contact institution. *Financial support:* In 2017–18, fellowships (averaging $16,500 per year) were awarded; research assistantships and scholarships/grants also available. In 2017, 62 master's, 71 doctorates awarded. *Program availability:* Part-time. *Application deadline:* For fall admission, 3/30 for domestic and international students; for winter admission, 11/1 for domestic and international students; for spring admission, 3/1 for domestic and international students. *Application fee:* $45. Electronic applications accepted. *Application Contact:* Sylvie Richard, Registrar, 418-654-2518, Fax: 418-654-3858, E-mail: sylvie.richard@adm.inrs.ca. *Acting Director of Research and Academic Affairs,* Jean-François Blais Begin, 418-654-2575, E-mail: jean-françois.blais@inrs.ca.

Centre for Energie Materiaux Telecommunications Students: 203 full-time (54 women), 13 part-time (2 women), 180 international. Average age 31. 63 applicants, 90% accepted, 38 enrolled. *Faculty:* 37 full-time. Expenses: Contact institution. *Financial support:* In 2017–18, fellowships (averaging $16,500 per year) were awarded; research assistantships and scholarships/grants also available. In 2017, 15 master's, 27 doctorates awarded. *Program availability:* Part-time. Offers energy and materials science (M Sc, PhD); telecommunications (M Sc, PhD). *Application deadline:* For fall admission, 3/30 for domestic and international students; for winter admission, 11/1 for domestic and international students; for spring admission, 3/1 for domestic and international students. *Application fee:* $45. Electronic applications accepted. *Application Contact:* Sylvie Richard, Registrar, 418-654-2518, Fax: 418-654-3858, E-mail: sylvie.richard@adm.inrs.ca. *Director,* Federico Rosei, 450-228-6905, E-mail: rosei@emt.inrs.ca.

Centre for Urbanisation Culture Societe Students: 82 full-time (42 women), 12 part-time (10 women), 13 international. Average age 32. 35 applicants, 83% accepted, 23 enrolled. *Faculty:* 29 full-time. Expenses: Contact institution. *Financial support:* In 2017–18, fellowships (averaging $16,500 per year) were awarded; research assistantships also available. In 2017, 10 master's, 3 doctorates awarded. *Program availability:* Part-time. Offers demography (M Sc, PhD); research practices and public action (MA, DESS); urban studies (M Sc, PhD). *Application deadline:* For fall admission, 3/30 for domestic and international students; for winter admission, 11/1 for domestic and international students; for spring admission, 3/1 for domestic and international students. *Application fee:* $45. Electronic applications accepted. *Application Contact:* Sylvie Richard, Registrar, 418-654-2518, Fax: 418-654-3858, E-mail: sylvie.richard@adm.inrs.ca. *Director,* Hélène Belleau, 514-499-4001, Fax: 514-499-4065, E-mail: helene.belleau@ucs.inrs.ca.

INRS - Institut Armand-Frappier Students: 149 full-time (89 women), 18 part-time (11 women), 86 international. Average age 30. 29 applicants, 93% accepted, 25 enrolled. *Faculty:* 48 full-time. Expenses: Contact institution. *Financial support:* In 2017–18, fellowships (averaging $16,500 per year) were awarded; research assistantships also available. In 2017, 16 master's, 13 doctorates awarded. *Program availability:* Part-time. Offers applied microbiology (M Sc); biology (PhD); experimental health sciences (M Sc); virology and immunology (M Sc, PhD). *Application deadline:* For fall admission, 3/30 for domestic and international students; for winter admission, 11/1 for domestic and international students; for spring admission, 3/1 for domestic and international students. *Application fee:* $45 Canadian dollars. Electronic applications accepted. *Application Contact:* Sylvie Richard, Registrar, 418-654-2518, Fax: 418-654-3858, E-mail: sylvie.richard@adm.inrs.ca. *Director,* Pierre Talbot, 450-687-5010 Ext. 4300, Fax: 450-686-5501, E-mail: pierre.talbot@iaf.inrs.ca.

Research Center–Water Earth Environment Students: 174 full-time (89 women), 18 part-time (10 women), 128 international. Average age 29. 54 applicants, 81%

accepted, 40 enrolled. *Faculty:* 34 full-time. Expenses: Contact institution. *Financial support:* In 2017–18, fellowships (averaging $16,500 per year) were awarded; research assistantships also available. In 2017, 21 master's, 28 doctorates awarded. *Program availability:* Part-time. Offers earth sciences (M Sc, PhD); earth sciences - environmental technologies (M Sc); water sciences (M Sc, PhD). *Application deadline:* For fall admission, 3/30 for domestic and international students; for winter admission, 11/1 for domestic and international students; for spring admission, 3/1 for domestic and international students. *Application fee:* $45. Electronic applications accepted. *Application Contact:* Sylvie Richard, Registrar, 418-654-2518, Fax: 418-654-3858, E-mail: sylvie.richard@adm.inrs.ca. *Director,* Claude Fortin, 418-654-3770, Fax: 418-654-2600, E-mail: claude.fortin@ete.inrs.ca.

UNIVERSITÉ LAVAL, Québec, QC G1K 7P4, Canada

General Information Independent, coed, university. *Graduate housing:* Room and/or apartments available on a first-come, first-served basis to single students; on-campus housing not available to married students. *Research affiliation:* Centre Hospitalier Universitaire de Quebec (biomedical research), Institut National d'optique (optics and photonics), Centre de Developpement de la Geomatique (applied geomatics), Institut Maurice-Lamontagne (oceanography), Forintek Canada (forestry and wood processing), Societe des pades de Sciences Naturelles du Quebec (biology).

GRADUATE UNITS

Faculty of Administrative Sciences *Program availability:* Part-time, online learning. Offers accounting (MBA); administrative sciences (M Sc, MBA, PhD, Diploma); administrative studies (M Sc, PhD); agri-food management (MBA); electronic business (MBA, Diploma); factory management and logistics (MBA); finance (MBA); financial engineering (M Sc); firm management (MBA); geomatic management (MBA); information technology management (MBA); international management (MBA); management (MBA); management accounting (MBA, Diploma); marketing (MBA); modeling and organizational decision (MBA); occupational health and safety management (MBA); organizations management and development (Diploma); pharmacy management (MBA); public accountancy (MBA, Diploma); social and environmental responsibility (MBA); technological entrepreneurship (Diploma). Electronic applications accepted.

Faculty of Agricultural and Food Sciences *Program availability:* Part-time. Offers agri-food engineering (M Sc); agricultural and food sciences (M Sc, PhD, Diploma); agricultural economics (M Sc); agricultural microbiology (M Sc); agro-food microbiology (PhD); animal sciences (M Sc, PhD); consumer sciences (Diploma); environmental technology (M Sc); food sciences and technology (M Sc, PhD); integrated rural development (Diploma); nutrition (M Sc, PhD); plant biology (M Sc, PhD); soils and environment science (M Sc, PhD). Electronic applications accepted.

Faculty of Architecture, Planning and Visual Arts Offers architecture, planning and visual arts (M Arch, M Sc, MA, MATDR, PhD); planning and regional development (MATDR, PhD). Electronic applications accepted.

School of Architecture *Program availability:* Part-time. Offers architecture (M Arch, M Sc). Electronic applications accepted.

School of Visual Arts Offers graphic design and multimedia (MA); visual arts (MA). Electronic applications accepted.

Faculty of Dentistry Offers buccal and maxillofacial surgery (DESS); dentistry (M Sc, DMD, DESS); gerodontology (DESS); multidisciplinary dentistry (DESS); periodontics (DESS). Electronic applications accepted.

Faculty of Education *Program availability:* Part-time. Offers didactics (MA, PhD); education (MA, PhD, Diploma); educational administration and evaluation (MA, PhD); educational pedagogy (Diploma); educational practice (Diploma); educational psychology (MA, PhD); orientation sciences (MA, PhD); pedagogy management and development (Diploma); school adaptation (Diploma); teaching technology (MA, PhD). Electronic applications accepted.

Faculty of Forestry, Geography and Geomatics Offers agroforestry (M Sc); forestry sciences (M Sc, PhD); forestry, geography and geomatics (M Sc, M Sc Geogr, PhD); geographical sciences (M Sc Geogr, PhD); geography (M Sc Geogr, PhD); geomatics sciences (M Sc, PhD); wood sciences (M Sc, PhD). Electronic applications accepted.

Faculty of Law *Program availability:* Part-time. Offers environment, sustainable development and food safety (LL M); international and transnational law (LL M, Diploma); law (LL M, LL D, Diploma); law of business (LL M, Diploma); notarial law (Diploma). Electronic applications accepted.

Faculty of Letters *Program availability:* Part-time. Offers ancient civilization (MA, PhD); archaeology (MA, PhD); art history (MA, PhD); English literatures (MA, PhD); ethnology of French-speaking people in North America (MA, PhD); history (MA, PhD, Diploma); international journalism (Diploma); letters (MA, PhD, Diploma); linguistics (MA, PhD); literary studies (MA, PhD); literature and arts of the screen and stage (PhD); literature and arts of the screen and stage (MA); museology (Diploma); public communication (MA, PhD); public relations (Diploma); Spanish literature (MA, PhD); terminology and translation (MA, Diploma). Electronic applications accepted.

Faculty of Medicine *Program availability:* Part-time. Offers accident prevention and occupational health and safety management (Diploma); anatomy–pathology (DESS); anesthesiology (DESS); cardiology (DESS); care of older people (Diploma); cellular and molecular biology (M Sc, PhD); clinical research (DESS); community health (M Sc, PhD); dermatology (DESS); diagnostic radiology (DESS); emergency medicine (Diploma); epidemiology (M Sc, PhD); experimental medicine (M Sc, PhD); family medicine (DESS); general surgery (DESS); geriatrics (DESS); hematology (DESS); internal medicine (DESS); kinesiology (M Sc, PhD); maternal and fetal medicine (Diploma); medical biochemistry (DESS); medical microbiology and infectious diseases (DESS); medical oncology (DESS); medicine (M Sc, MD, PhD, DESS, Diploma); microbiology-immunology (M Sc, PhD); nephrology (DESS); neurobiology (M Sc, PhD); neurology (DESS); neurosurgery (DESS); obstetrics and gynecology (DESS); ophthalmology (DESS); orthopedic surgery (DESS); oto-rhino-laryngology (DESS); palliative medicine (Diploma); pediatrics (DESS); physiology-endocrinology (M Sc, PhD); plastic surgery (DESS); psychiatry (DESS); pulmonary medicine (DESS); radiology–oncology (DESS); speech therapy (M Sc); thoracic surgery (DESS); urology (DESS). Electronic applications accepted.

Faculty of Music Offers composition (M Mus); instrumental didactics (M Mus); interpretation (M Mus); music (M Mus, PhD); music education (M Mus, PhD); musicology (M Mus, PhD). Electronic applications accepted.

Faculty of Nursing Offers nursing (M Sc, PhD, DESS, Diploma). Electronic applications accepted.

Faculty of Pharmacy *Program availability:* Part-time. Offers community pharmacy (DESS); hospital pharmacy (M Sc); pharmacy (M Sc, PhD, DESS). Electronic applications accepted.

Faculty of Philosophy Offers philosophy (MA, PhD). Electronic applications accepted.

Faculty of Sciences and Engineering *Program availability:* Part-time. Offers aerospace engineering (M Sc); biochemistry (M Sc, PhD); biology (M Sc, PhD); chemical engineering (M Sc, PhD); chemistry (M Sc, PhD); civil engineering (M Sc, PhD); computer science (M Sc, PhD); earth sciences (M Sc, PhD); electrical engineering (M Sc, PhD); environmental technologies (M Sc); environmental technology (M Sc); geology (M Sc, PhD); industrial engineering (Diploma); mathematics (M Sc, PhD); mechanical engineering (M Sc, PhD); metallurgical engineering (M Sc, PhD); microbiology (M Sc, PhD); mining engineering (M Sc, PhD); oceanography (PhD); physics (M Sc, PhD); sciences and engineering (M Sc, PhD, Diploma); software engineering (Diploma); statistics (M Sc); urban infrastructure engineering (Diploma). Electronic applications accepted.

Faculty of Social Sciences *Program availability:* Part-time. Offers anthropology (MA, PhD); economics (MA, PhD); feminist studies (Diploma); industrial relations (MA, PhD); policy analysis (MA); political science (MA, PhD); social sciences (M Serv Soc, MA, PhD, Psy D, Diploma); sociology (MA, PhD). Electronic applications accepted.

School of Psychology Offers clinical psychology (PhD); community psychology (PhD); psychology (PhD, Psy D). Electronic applications accepted.

School of Social Work Offers social work (M Serv Soc, PhD). Electronic applications accepted.

Faculty of Theology and Religious Sciences Offers applied ethics (DESS); human sciences of religion (MA, PhD); practical theology (D Th P); theology (MA, PhD); theology and religious sciences (MA, D Th P, PhD, DESS). Electronic applications accepted.

Québec Institute for Advanced International Studies Offers advanced international studies (MA, PhD); international relations (MA, PhD). Electronic applications accepted.

UNIVERSITÉ SAINTE-ANNE, Church Point, NS B0W 1M0, Canada

General Information Province-supported, coed, comprehensive institution.

GRADUATE UNITS

Program in Education *Program availability:* Part-time. Offers education (M Ed).

UNIVERSITY AT ALBANY, STATE UNIVERSITY OF NEW YORK, Albany, NY 12222-0001

General Information State-supported, coed, university. CGS member. *Enrollment:* 17,743 graduate, professional, and undergraduate students; 2,108 full-time matriculated graduate/professional students (1,257 women), 1,951 part-time matriculated graduate/professional students (1,195 women). *Enrollment by degree level:* 2,419 master's, 1,421 doctoral, 219 other advanced degrees. *Graduate faculty:* 518 full-time (214 women), 240 part-time/adjunct (136 women). Tuition, state resident: full-time $10,870; part-time $453 per credit hour. Tuition, nonresident: full-time $22,210; part-time $925 per credit hour. *Required fees:* $84.68 per credit hour. $508.06 per semester. Part-time tuition and fees vary according to course load and program. *Graduate housing:* On-campus housing not available. *Student services:* Campus employment opportunities, campus safety program, career counseling, child daycare facilities, exercise/wellness program, free psychological counseling, grant writing training, international student services, low-cost health insurance, multicultural affairs office, services for students with disabilities, teacher training, writing training. *Library facilities:* University Library plus 2 others. *Collection:* Books: 2.3 million (physical), 342,263 (digital/electronic); Serial titles: 97,614 (digital/electronic). Weekly public service hours: 113; students can reserve study rooms. *Research affiliation:* Naval Research Laboratories (organizational structures (public administration)), General Electric Corporate Research and Development Center (engineering), Whiteface Mountain Observatory (earth and atmospheric sciences), Woods Hole Oceanographic Institution (marine science and engineering), Wadsworth Laboratories, New York State Department of Health (biomedical sciences, epidemiology, environmental health).

Computer facilities: Computer purchase and lease plans are available. 500 computers available on campus for general student use. A campuswide network can be accessed from student residence rooms and from off campus. Online class registration is available.
Website: http://www.albany.edu/

General Application Contact: Michael DeRensis, Director, Graduate Admissions, 518-442-3980, Fax: 518-442-3922, E-mail: graduate@albany.edu.

GRADUATE UNITS

College of Arts and Sciences Students: 584 full-time (291 women), 568 part-time (317 women); includes 209 minority (48 Black or African American, non-Hispanic/Latino; 3 American Indian or Alaska Native, non-Hispanic/Latino; 50 Asian, non-Hispanic/Latino; 84 Hispanic/Latino; 1 Native Hawaiian or other Pacific Islander, non-Hispanic/Latino; 23 Two or more races, non-Hispanic/Latino), 258 international. 1,381 applicants, 43% accepted, 285 enrolled. *Faculty:* 205 full-time (65 women), 19 part-time/adjunct (7 women). Expenses: Contact institution. *Financial support:* Fellowships, research assistantships, teaching assistantships, career-related internships or fieldwork, Federal Work-Study, institutionally sponsored loans, traineeships, and unspecified assistantships available. Financial award applicants required to submit FAFSA. In 2017, 153 master's, 62 doctorates, 14 other advanced degrees awarded. *Program availability:* Part-time, evening/weekend, 100% online, blended/hybrid learning. Offers African studies (MA); Afro-American studies (MA); anthropology (MA, PhD); art (MA, MFA); arts and sciences (MA, MALS, MFA, MRP, MS, PhD, Certificate); atmospheric science (MS, PhD); behavioral neuroscience (PhD); chemistry (MS, PhD); clinical psychology (PhD); cognitive psychology (PhD); communication (MA); demography (Certificate); economic forecasting (MA); economics (MA, PhD); English (MA, PhD); forensic biology (MS); geographic information science (Certificate); geography (MA); history (MA, PhD); industrial/organizational psychology (MA, PhD); Latin American, Caribbean, and U.S. Latino studies (MA, PhD, Certificate); liberal studies (MALS); mathematics (MA, PhD); philosophy (MA, PhD); physics (MS, PhD); public history (Certificate); regional planning (MRP); social-personality psychology (PhD); sociology (MA, PhD); sociology and communication (PhD); Spanish (MA, PhD); urban policy (Certificate); women's, gender and sexuality studies (MA). *Application deadline:* Applications are processed on a rolling basis. *Application fee:* $75. Electronic applications accepted. *Application Contact:* Michael DeRensis, Director, Graduate Admissions, 518-442-3980, Fax: 518-442-3922, E-mail: graduate@albany.edu. *Dean,* Edelgard Wulfert, 518-442-4654, Fax: 518-442-4651.

College of Emergency Preparedness, Homeland Security and Cybersecurity Students: 59 full-time (40 women), 77 part-time (49 women); includes 23 minority (4 Black or African American, non-Hispanic/Latino; 6 Asian, non-Hispanic/Latino; 10 Hispanic/Latino; 3 Two or more races, non-Hispanic/Latino), 14 international. 90 applicants, 67% accepted, 36 enrolled. *Faculty:* 10 full-time (4 women), 14 part-time/adjunct (5 women). Expenses: Contact institution. In 2017, 30 master's, 1 doctorate, 24 other advanced degrees awarded. Offers cybersecurity (Certificate); emergency preparedness (Certificate); homeland security (Certificate); information science (MS, PhD). *Application Contact:* Michael DeRensis, Director, Graduate Admissions, 518-442-3980, Fax: 518-442-3922, E-mail: graduate@albany.edu. *Dean*, Dr. Robert Griffin, 518-442-5258.

College of Engineering and Applied Sciences Students: 237 full-time (69 women), 80 part-time (22 women); includes 10 minority (1 Black or African American, non-Hispanic/Latino; 6 Asian, non-Hispanic/Latino; 2 Hispanic/Latino; 1 Two or more races, non-Hispanic/Latino), 282 international. Average age 27. 552 applicants, 51% accepted, 193 enrolled. *Faculty:* 33 full-time (11 women), 20 part-time/adjunct (3 women). Expenses: Contact institution. *Financial support:* Fellowships and Federal Work-Study available. Financial award application deadline: 4/1. In 2017, 84 master's, 3 doctorates awarded. *Program availability:* Part-time. Offers computer science (MS, PhD); engineering and applied sciences (MS, PhD, CAS). *Application deadline:* For fall admission, 3/1 for domestic students. Applications are processed on a rolling basis. *Application fee:* $75. Electronic applications accepted. *Dean*, Kim L. Boyer, 518-956-8240, Fax: 518-442-5367, E-mail: ceasinfo@albany.edu.

Nelson A. Rockefeller College of Public Affairs and Policy Students: 138 full-time (69 women), 115 part-time (62 women); includes 45 minority (12 Black or African American, non-Hispanic/Latino; 9 Asian, non-Hispanic/Latino; 21 Hispanic/Latino; 3 Two or more races, non-Hispanic/Latino), 45 international. Average age 33. 288 applicants, 68% accepted, 94 enrolled. *Faculty:* 43 full-time (16 women), 23 part-time/adjunct (10 women). Expenses: Contact institution. *Financial support:* Fellowships, research assistantships, teaching assistantships, career-related internships or fieldwork, Federal Work-Study, and institutionally sponsored loans available. Financial award application deadline: 2/1. In 2017, 62 master's, 4 doctorates, 14 other advanced degrees awarded. *Program availability:* Part-time. Offers financial management and public economics (MPA); financial market regulation (MPA); health policy (MPA); healthcare management (MPA); homeland security (MPA); human resources management (MPA); information strategy and management (MPA); local government management (MPA); nonprofit management (MPA); nonprofit management and leadership (Certificate); organizational behavior and theory (MPA, PhD); planning and policy analysis (CAS); policy analysis (MPA); political science (MA, PhD); politics and administration (PhD); public affairs and policy (MA, MPA, PhD, CAS, Certificate); public finance (PhD); public management (PhD); public policy (PhD); public sector management (Certificate); women and public policy (Certificate). *Application deadline:* For fall admission, 2/1 priority date for domestic students, 5/1 for international students. Applications are processed on a rolling basis. *Application fee:* $75. Electronic applications accepted. *Dean*, Karl R. Rethemeyer, 518-442-5283, E-mail: kretheme@albany.edu.

School of Business Students: 265 full-time (105 women), 172 part-time (64 women); includes 101 minority (22 Black or African American, non-Hispanic/Latino; 1 American Indian or Alaska Native, non-Hispanic/Latino; 47 Asian, non-Hispanic/Latino; 22 Hispanic/Latino; 9 Two or more races, non-Hispanic/Latino), 45 international. 485 applicants, 63% accepted, 236 enrolled. *Faculty:* 45 full-time (17 women), 20 part-time/adjunct (7 women). Expenses: Contact institution. *Financial support:* Fellowships, research assistantships, career-related internships or fieldwork, and Federal Work-Study available. In 2017, 221 master's awarded. *Program availability:* Part-time, evening/weekend. Offers business (MBA, MS); business administration (MBA); cyber security (MBA); entrepreneurship (MBA); finance (MBA); human resource information systems (MBA); information systems and business analytics (MBA); marketing (MBA). *Application deadline:* For fall admission, 3/1 for domestic students, 5/1 for international students. Applications are processed on a rolling basis. *Application fee:* $75. Electronic applications accepted. *Application Contact:* Michael DeRensis, Director, Graduate Admissions, 518-442-3980, Fax: 518-442-3922, E-mail: graduate@albany.edu. *Dean*, Hany Shawky, 518-956-8370, E-mail: hshawky@albany.edu.

School of Criminal Justice Students: 68 full-time (44 women), 22 part-time (16 women); includes 39 minority (13 Black or African American, non-Hispanic/Latino; 2 Asian, non-Hispanic/Latino; 21 Hispanic/Latino; 3 Two or more races, non-Hispanic/Latino), 7 international. 121 applicants, 55% accepted, 31 enrolled. *Faculty:* 16 full-time (6 women). Expenses: Contact institution. *Financial support:* Fellowships, research assistantships, teaching assistantships, career-related internships or fieldwork, Federal Work-Study, and institutionally sponsored loans available. Financial award application deadline: 4/1. In 2017, 44 master's, 1 doctorate awarded. *Program availability:* Part-time. Offers criminal justice (MA, PhD). *Application deadline:* For fall admission, 7/1 for domestic students, 5/1 for international students. Applications are processed on a rolling basis. *Application fee:* $75. Electronic applications accepted. *Application Contact:* Jane Champagne, Director, Graduate Admissions, 518-442-3980, Fax: 518-442-3922, E-mail: graduate@albany.edu. *Dean*, William Alex Pridemore, 518-442-5210, E-mail: pridemore@albany.edu.

School of Education Students: 329 full-time (255 women), 505 part-time (383 women); includes 119 minority (37 Black or African American, non-Hispanic/Latino; 1 American Indian or Alaska Native, non-Hispanic/Latino; 25 Asian, non-Hispanic/Latino; 42 Hispanic/Latino; 14 Two or more races, non-Hispanic/Latino), 72 international. Average age 31. 588 applicants, 64% accepted, 310 enrolled. *Faculty:* 67 full-time (36 women), 75 part-time/adjunct (56 women). Expenses: Contact institution. *Financial support:* Fellowships, career-related internships or fieldwork, and Federal Work-Study available. In 2017, 192 master's, 18 doctorates, 24 other advanced degrees awarded. *Program availability:* Part-time, evening/weekend, 100% online, blended/hybrid learning. Offers counseling psychology (PhD, CAS); curriculum and instruction (PhD, CAS); curriculum development and instructional technology (MS); education (MS, PhD, Psy D, CAS); educational policy and leadership (MS, PhD); general education studies (MS); higher education (MS); international education management (CAS); literacy teaching and learning (MS, PhD, CAS); mental health counseling (MS). *Application fee:* $75. Electronic applications accepted. *Dean*, Robert Bangert-Drowns, 518-442-4988, E-mail: rbangert-drowns@albany.edu.

School of Public Health Students: 177 full-time (141 women), 272 part-time (194 women); includes 130 minority (53 Black or African American, non-Hispanic/Latino; 1 American Indian or Alaska Native, non-Hispanic/Latino; 36 Asian, non-Hispanic/Latino; 29 Hispanic/Latino; 11 Two or more races, non-Hispanic/Latino), 42 international. 375 applicants, 69% accepted, 181 enrolled. *Faculty:* 69 full-time (36 women), 32 part-time/adjunct (17 women). Expenses: Contact institution. *Financial support:* Fellowships and research assistantships available. In 2017, 81 master's, 12 doctorates, 47 other advanced degrees awarded. *Program availability:* Part-time, evening/weekend, 100% online, blended/hybrid learning. Offers biomedical sciences (MS, PhD); environmental and occupational health (MS, PhD); environmental chemistry (MS, PhD); epidemiology and biostatistics (MS, PhD); health policy, management, and behavior (MPH, MS, Dr PH, PhD); public health (MPH, MS, Dr PH, PhD, Certificate); toxicology (MS, PhD). *Application deadline:* For fall admission, 1/1 for domestic students. Applications are processed on a rolling basis. *Application fee:* $75. Electronic applications accepted. *Application Contact:* Michael DeRensis, Director, Graduate Admissions, 518-442-3980, Fax: 518-442-3922, E-mail: graduate@albany.edu. *Dean*, Dr. David Holtgrave, 518-485-5500, E-mail: dholtgrave@albany.edu.

School of Social Welfare Students: 281 full-time (235 women), 110 part-time (93 women); includes 102 minority (43 Black or African American, non-Hispanic/Latino; 1 American Indian or Alaska Native, non-Hispanic/Latino; 8 Asian, non-Hispanic/Latino; 42 Hispanic/Latino; 8 Two or more races, non-Hispanic/Latino), 13 international. 435 applicants, 63% accepted, 192 enrolled. *Faculty:* 30 full-time (23 women), 37 part-time/adjunct (31 women). Expenses: Contact institution. *Financial support:* Fellowships, career-related internships or fieldwork, and Federal Work-Study available. Financial award application deadline: 2/15. In 2017, 144 master's, 7 doctorates awarded. *Program availability:* Part-time, evening/weekend. Offers social welfare (MSW, PhD). *Application deadline:* For fall admission, 2/15 for domestic and international students. *Application fee:* $75. Electronic applications accepted. *Dean*, Lynn Warner, 518-442-5324, E-mail: lwarner@albany.edu.

UNIVERSITY AT BUFFALO, THE STATE UNIVERSITY OF NEW YORK, Buffalo, NY 14260

General Information State-supported, coed, university. CGS member. *Enrollment:* 30,648 graduate, professional, and undergraduate students; 6,186 full-time matriculated graduate/professional students (3,182 women), 3,295 part-time matriculated graduate/professional students (1,634 women). *Enrollment by degree level:* 4,436 master's, 4,830 doctoral, 215 other advanced degrees. *Graduate faculty:* 1,675 full-time (624 women), 179 part-time/adjunct (64 women). *Graduate housing:* Rooms and/or apartments available on a first-come, first-served basis to single and married students. Housing application deadline: 5/1. *Student services:* Campus employment opportunities, campus safety program, career counseling, child daycare facilities, exercise/wellness program, free psychological counseling, international student services, low-cost health insurance, multicultural affairs office, services for students with disabilities, teacher training, writing training. *Library facilities:* Lockwood Memorial Library plus 11 others. *Collection:* Books: 3.4 million (physical), 826,650 (digital/electronic); Serial titles: 2,352 (physical), 175,278 (digital/electronic); Databases: 383. Weekly public service hours: 168; study areas open 24 hours, 5–7 days a week; students can reserve study rooms. *Research affiliation:* Hauptman-Woodward Medical Research Institute, Roswell Park Cancer Institute, Veterans Administration Medical Center, Calspan-University of Buffalo Research Center.

Computer facilities: 3,061 computers available on campus for general student use. A campuswide network can be accessed from student residence rooms and from off campus. Online class registration is available.
Website: http://www.buffalo.edu/

General Application Contact: Danielle D. Ianni, Director of Enrollment Operations, 716-645-3482, Fax: 716-645-6998, E-mail: ddianni@buffalo.edu.

GRADUATE UNITS

Graduate School Students: 6,186 full-time (3,182 women), 3,295 part-time (1,634 women); includes 1,553 minority (387 Black or African American, non-Hispanic/Latino; 27 American Indian or Alaska Native, non-Hispanic/Latino; 722 Asian, non-Hispanic/Latino; 276 Hispanic/Latino; 141 Two or more races, non-Hispanic/Latino), 2,918 international. 22,831 applicants, 35% accepted, 3397 enrolled. *Faculty:* 1,675 full-time (624 women), 179 part-time/adjunct (64 women). Expenses: Contact institution. *Financial support:* Fellowships with tuition reimbursements, research assistantships with tuition reimbursements, teaching assistantships with tuition reimbursements, career-related internships or fieldwork, Federal Work-Study, institutionally sponsored loans, scholarships/grants, traineeships, tuition waivers (full and partial), unspecified assistantships, and stipends available. Support available to part-time students. Financial award applicants required to submit FAFSA. In 2017, 2,340 master's, 426 doctorates, 638 other advanced degrees awarded. *Program availability:* Part-time, evening/weekend, 100% online. *Application deadline:* Applications are processed on a rolling basis. *Application fee:* $75. Electronic applications accepted. *Application Contact:* Lisa C. Coia, Associate Director, 716-645-3482, Fax: 716-645-6998, E-mail: grad@buffalo.edu. *Vice Provost for Graduate Education/Dean of the Graduate School*, Dr. Graham Hammill, 716-645-2939, Fax: 716-645-6142, E-mail: grad@buffalo.edu.

College of Arts and Sciences *Program availability:* Part-time. Offers American studies (MA, PhD); anthropology (MA, PhD); arts and sciences (MA, MAH, MFA, MM, MS, Au D, PhD, Advanced Certificate, Certificate); arts management (MA); audiology (Au D); biological sciences (MA, MS, PhD); Canadian studies (MA); chemistry (MA, PhD); classics (MA, PhD); communication (MA, PhD); communicative disorders and sciences (MA, PhD); comparative literature (MA, PhD); computational science (Advanced Certificate); contemporary performance (Advanced Certificate); critical museum studies (MA); dance (MFA); earth systems science (MA, MS); econometrics and quantitative economics (MS); economic geography and business geographics (MS); economics (MA, PhD); English (MA, PhD); environmental modeling and analysis (MA); evolution, ecology and behavior (MS, PhD, Certificate); film and media study (MAH); financial economics (Certificate); French (MA, PhD); geographic information science (MA, MS); geography (MA, PhD); geology (MA, MS, PhD); global gender studies (MA, PhD); health geography (MS); health services (Certificate); historical musicology and music theory (PhD); history (MA, PhD, Advanced Certificate); humanities (MA); information and Internet economics (Certificate); interdisciplinary computational linguistics (MS); international economics (Certificate); international trade (MA); Latin (MA); law and regulation (Certificate); linguistics (MA, PhD); mathematics (MA, PhD); media arts production (MFA); media study (PhD); medicinal chemistry (MS, PhD); music composition (MA, PhD); music history (MA); music performance (MM); music theory (MA); natural sciences (MS); new media design (Certificate); philosophy (MA, PhD); physics (MS, PhD); political science (MA, PhD); psychology (MA, PhD); public history (MA); social media (MAH); social sciences (MS); sociology (MA, PhD); Spanish (MA, PhD); studio art (MFA); theatre and performance (MA, PhD); urban and regional analysis (MA); urban and regional economics (Certificate); visual studies (MA, PhD). Electronic applications accepted.

Graduate Programs in Cancer Research and Biomedical Sciences at Roswell Park Cancer Institute Students: 15 full-time (10 women); includes 1 minority (Two or more races, non-Hispanic/Latino), 6 international. 186 applicants, 25% accepted, 28 enrolled. *Faculty:* 128 full-time (35 women). Expenses: Contact institution. *Financial support:* In 2017–18, 91 students received support, including 91 research assistantships with full tuition reimbursements available (averaging $27,000 per year); scholarships/grants, health care benefits, and unspecified assistantships also available. Financial award application deadline: 1/5. In 2017, 15 master's, 11 doctorates awarded. Offers cancer pathology and prevention (PhD); cellular and molecular biology (PhD); immunology (PhD); interdisciplinary natural sciences (MS); molecular and cellular biophysics and biochemistry (PhD); molecular pharmacology and cancer therapeutics (PhD). *Application deadline:* For fall admission, 1/5 priority date for domestic and international students. *Application fee:* $75. Electronic applications accepted. *Application Contact:* Dr. Norman J. Karin, Associate Dean, 716-845-2339, Fax: 716-845-8178, E-mail: norman.karin@roswellpark.edu.

Graduate School of Education Students: 452 full-time (338 women), 748 part-time (554 women); includes 116 minority (78 Black or African American, non-Hispanic/Latino; 9 American Indian or Alaska Native, non-Hispanic/Latino; 22 Asian, non-Hispanic/Latino; 7 Hispanic/Latino), 94 international. Average age 33. 914 applicants, 72% accepted, 449 enrolled. *Faculty:* 72 full-time (46 women), 144 part-time/adjunct (105 women). Expenses: Contact institution. *Financial support:* In 2017–18, 98 fellowships (averaging $5,401 per year), 125 research assistantships with tuition reimbursements (averaging $11,177 per year) were awarded; teaching assistantships, Federal Work-Study, institutionally sponsored loans, scholarships/grants, tuition waivers (full and partial), and unspecified assistantships also available. Support available to part-time students. Financial award applicants required to submit FAFSA. In 2017, 290 master's, 50 doctorates, 78 other advanced degrees awarded. *Program availability:* Part-time, 100% online. Offers applied statistical analysis (Advanced Certificate); biology education (Ed M, Certificate); chemistry education (Ed M, Certificate); childhood education (Ed M); childhood education with bilingual extension (Ed M); college teaching (Advanced Certificate); counseling/school psychology (PhD); counselor education (PhD); curriculum, instruction and the science of learning (PhD); early childhood education (Ed M); early childhood education with bilingual extension (Ed M); earth science education (Ed M, Certificate); economics and education policy analysis (MA); education (Ed M, MA, MS, Ed D, PhD, Advanced Certificate, Certificate); education and technology (Ed M); education studies (Ed M); educational administration (Ed M, Ed D, PhD); educational culture, policy and society (PhD); educational psychology (MA, PhD); educational technology and new literacies (Certificate); educational technology and new literacies (Advanced Certificate); elementary education (Ed D); English education (Ed M, Certificate); English education studies (Ed M); English for speakers of other languages (Ed M); foreign and second language education (PhD); French education (Ed M, Certificate); German education (Ed M, Certificate); gifted education (Certificate); higher education administration (Ed M, PhD); information and library science (MS); Latin education (Ed M, Certificate); library and information studies (Certificate); literacy education studies (Ed M); literacy specialist (Ed M); literacy teaching and learning (Certificate); mathematics education (Ed M, Certificate); mental health counseling (MS, Certificate); mindful counseling for wellness and engagement (Advanced Certificate); music education (Ed M, Certificate); music education studies (Ed M); music learning theory (Advanced Certificate); online education (Advanced Certificate); physics education (Ed M, Certificate); rehabilitation counseling (MS, Advanced Certificate); school building leadership (Certificate); school business and human resource administration (Certificate); school counseling (Ed M, Certificate); school district business leadership (Certificate); school district leadership (Certificate); school librarianship (MS); science and the public (Ed M); social studies education (Ed M, Certificate); Spanish education (Ed M, Certificate); special education (PhD); teaching English to speakers of other languages (Ed M). *Application deadline:* Applications are processed on a rolling basis. *Application fee:* $50. Electronic applications accepted. *Application Contact:* Cory Meyers, Assistant Dean for Enrollment Management, 716-645-2110, Fax: 716-645-7937, E-mail: gse-info@buffalo.edu. *Dean,* Dr. Suzanne Rosenblith, 716-645-1354, Fax: 716-645-2479, E-mail: gse-info@buffalo.edu.

Jacobs School of Medicine and Biomedical Sciences Students: 816 full-time (393 women), 14 part-time (6 women); includes 280 minority (28 Black or African American, non-Hispanic/Latino; 5 American Indian or Alaska Native, non-Hispanic/Latino; 151 Asian, non-Hispanic/Latino; 63 Hispanic/Latino; 33 Two or more races, non-Hispanic/Latino), 26 international. Average age 26. 4,446 applicants, 13% accepted, 255 enrolled. *Faculty:* 269 full-time (69 women), 11 part-time/adjunct (2 women). Expenses: Contact institution. *Financial support:* In 2017–18, 142 students received support, including 112 fellowships with full tuition reimbursements available (averaging $13,083 per year), 85 research assistantships with full tuition reimbursements available (averaging $24,843 per year), 8 teaching assistantships with full tuition reimbursements available (averaging $19,967 per year); career-related internships or fieldwork, Federal Work-Study, institutionally sponsored loans, scholarships/grants, traineeships, health care benefits, and unspecified assistantships also available. Financial award applicants required to submit FAFSA. In 2017, 33 master's, 160 doctorates awarded. Offers anatomical sciences (MA, PhD); bioinformatics (PhD); biochemistry (MA, PhD); biomedical informatics (MS); biomedical ontology (PhD); biomedical sciences (PhD); biophysics (MS, PhD); biotechnology (MS); clinical informatics (PhD); computational cell biology, anatomy, and pathology (PhD); genetics, genomics and bioinformatics (MS, PhD); medical physics (MS, PhD); medicine (MD); medicine and biomedical sciences (MA, MS, MD, PhD); microbiology and immunology (MS, PhD); neuroscience (MS, PhD); pathology (MA, PhD); pharmacology (MS, PhD); physiology (MA, PhD); structural biology (MS, PhD). *Application deadline:* Applications are processed on a rolling basis. *Application fee:* $0. Electronic applications accepted. *Application Contact:* Elizabeth A. White, Administrative Director, 716-829-3399, Fax: 716-829-2437, E-mail: bethw@buffalo.edu. *Dean,* Dr. Michael E. Cain, 716-829-3955, Fax: 716-829-3395, E-mail: mcain@buffalo.edu.

School of Architecture and Planning Students: 180 full-time (73 women), 30 part-time (13 women); includes 43 minority (21 Black or African American, non-Hispanic/Latino; 3 Asian, non-Hispanic/Latino; 13 Hispanic/Latino; 6 Two or more races, non-Hispanic/Latino), 41 international. Average age 26. 411 applicants, 24% accepted, 64 enrolled. *Faculty:* 47 full-time (17 women), 23 part-time/adjunct (8 women). Expenses: Contact institution. *Financial support:* In 2017–18, 120 students received support, including 9 fellowships with full tuition reimbursements available (averaging $26,550 per year), 5 research assistantships with partial tuition reimbursements available (averaging $14,336 per year), 60 teaching assistantships with partial tuition reimbursements available (averaging $8,405 per year); career-related internships or fieldwork, Federal Work-Study, institutionally sponsored loans, scholarships/grants, health care benefits, tuition waivers (partial), and unspecified assistantships also available. Support available to part-time students. Financial award application deadline: 3/1; financial award applicants required to submit FAFSA. In 2017, 96 master's, 1 doctorate, 5 other advanced degrees awarded. *Program availability:* Part-time. Offers architecture (M Arch); architecture and planning (M Arch, MS Arch, MSRED, MUP, PhD, Certificate); community health and food systems (MUP); ecological practices (MS Arch); economic development (MUP); environment/land use (MUP); historic preservation (MUP, Certificate); neighborhood/community development (MUP); real estate development (MSRED); urban and regional planning (PhD); urban design (MUP). *Application deadline:* Applications are processed on a rolling basis. *Application fee:* $75. Electronic applications accepted. *Application Contact:* Shannon Phillips, Assistant Dean for Graduate Education, 716-829-5224, Fax: 716-829-3256, E-mail: smp2@buffalo.edu. *Dean,* Robert G. Shibley, 716-829-3981, Fax: 716-829-2297, E-mail: dean@ap.buffalo.edu.

School of Dental Medicine Offers biomaterials (MS); dental medicine (MS, DDS, PhD, Certificate); oral biology (PhD); oral sciences (MS); orthodontics (MS, Certificate). Electronic applications accepted.

School of Engineering and Applied Sciences *Program availability:* Part-time, evening/weekend, online learning. Offers advanced manufacturing (Certificate); aerospace engineering (MS, PhD); bioengineering nanotechnology (Certificate); biomedical engineering (MS, PhD); chemical and biological engineering (ME, MS, PhD); civil engineering (MS, PhD); computational and data enabled sciences (PhD); computer science and engineering (MS, PhD); electrical engineering (ME, MS, PhD); engineering and applied sciences (ME, MS, PhD, Certificate); engineering science (MS); environmental and water resources engineering (MS); industrial engineering (ME, MS, PhD); information assurance (Certificate); materials design and innovation (MS, PhD); mechanical engineering (MS, PhD); nanomaterials and materials informatics (Certificate); sustainable transportation and logistics (MS). Electronic applications accepted.

School of Law Students: 453 full-time (238 women), 2 part-time (both women); includes 85 minority (29 Black or African American, non-Hispanic/Latino; 1 American Indian or Alaska Native, non-Hispanic/Latino; 20 Asian, non-Hispanic/Latino; 22 Hispanic/Latino; 13 Two or more races, non-Hispanic/Latino), 17 international. Average age 27. 903 applicants, 54% accepted, 167 enrolled. *Faculty:* 49 full-time (23 women), 68 part-time/adjunct (25 women). Expenses: Contact institution. *Financial support:* In 2017–18, 338 students received support. Federal Work-Study, institutionally sponsored loans, scholarships/grants, tuition waivers (full and partial), and unspecified assistantships available. Financial award application deadline: 3/1; financial award applicants required to submit FAFSA. In 2017, 2 master's, 151 doctorates awarded. Offers criminal law (LL M); cross-border legal studies (LL M); environmental law (LL M); general law (LL M); law (JD). *Application deadline:* Applications are processed on a rolling basis. *Application fee:* $85. Electronic applications accepted. *Application Contact:* Lindsay Gladney, Vice Dean for Admissions, 716-645-2907, Fax: 716-645-6676, E-mail: law-admissions@buffalo.edu. *Dean,* Aviva Abramovsky, 716-645-2052, E-mail: aabramov@buffalo.edu.

School of Management Students: 597 full-time (251 women); includes 83 minority (19 Black or African American, non-Hispanic/Latino; 59 Asian, non-Hispanic/Latino; 5 Hispanic/Latino), 306 international. Average age 25. 2,109 applicants, 46% accepted, 376 enrolled. *Faculty:* 80 full-time (26 women), 45 part-time/adjunct (12 women). Expenses: Contact institution. *Financial support:* Fellowships with full and partial tuition reimbursements, research assistantships with full and partial tuition reimbursements, teaching assistantships with full and partial tuition reimbursements, career-related internships or fieldwork, Federal Work-Study, institutionally sponsored loans, scholarships/grants, health care benefits, and unspecified assistantships available. Financial award application deadline: 2/15. In 2017, 371 master's, 13 doctorates awarded. *Program availability:* Part-time, evening/weekend. Offers accounting (MS); analytics (MBA); business administration (PMBA); consulting (MBA); finance (MBA, MS); healthcare (MBA); information assurance (MBA); information systems (MBA); international management (MBA); management (EMBA, PhD); management information systems (MS); marketing (MBA); supply chain and operations (MBA); supply chains and operations management (MS). *Application deadline:* For fall admission, 10/15 priority date for domestic and international students; for winter admission, 2/1 priority date for domestic and international students; for spring admission, 4/15 for domestic students; for summer admission, 5/15 for domestic students. *Application fee:* $100. Electronic applications accepted. *Application Contact:* Meghan Felser, Director of Admissions and Recruiting, 716-645-3204, Fax: 716-645-2341, E-mail: mpwood@buffalo.edu. *Assistant Dean and Director of Graduate Programs,* Erin K. O'Brien, 716-645-3204, Fax: 716-645-2341, E-mail: ekobrien@buffalo.edu.

School of Nursing Students: 64 full-time (39 women), 136 part-time (120 women); includes 32 minority (13 Black or African American, non-Hispanic/Latino; 1 American Indian or Alaska Native, non-Hispanic/Latino; 18 Asian, non-Hispanic/Latino). Average age 34. 182 applicants, 39% accepted, 50 enrolled. *Faculty:* 41 full-time (36 women), 15 part-time/adjunct (all women). Expenses: Contact institution. *Financial support:* In 2017–18, 80 students received support, including 2 fellowships with tuition reimbursements available (averaging $17,000 per year), 4 research assistantships with tuition reimbursements available (averaging $10,600 per year), 7 teaching assistantships with tuition reimbursements available (averaging $10,600 per year); scholarships/grants, traineeships, health care benefits, and unspecified assistantships also available. Financial award application deadline: 4/1; financial award applicants required to submit FAFSA. In 2017, 3 master's, 32 doctorates, 2 other advanced degrees awarded. *Program availability:* Part-time, 100% online. Offers adult gerontology nurse practitioner (DNP); family nurse practitioner (DNP); health care systems and leadership (MS); nurse anesthetist (DNP); nursing (PhD); nursing education (Certificate); psychiatric/mental health nurse practitioner (DNP). *Application deadline:* For fall admission, 4/1 for domestic students, 2/1 for international students; for spring admission, 1/15 for domestic students, 10/1 for international students; for summer admission, 4/1 for domestic students. Applications are processed on a rolling basis. *Application fee:* $75. Electronic applications accepted. *Application Contact:* Jennifer H. Schreier, Director of Graduate Student Services, 716-829-3311, Fax: 716-829-2067, E-mail: jhv2@buffalo.edu. *Dean and Professor,* Dr. Marsha L. Lewis, 716-829-2533, Fax: 716-829-2566, E-mail: ubnursingdean@buffalo.edu.

School of Pharmacy and Pharmaceutical Sciences Students: 639 full-time (366 women), 22 part-time (15 women); includes 251 minority (28 Black or African American, non-Hispanic/Latino; 219 Asian, non-Hispanic/Latino; 4 Hispanic/Latino), 58 international. Average age 24. 955 applicants, 22% accepted, 148 enrolled. *Faculty:* 38 full-time (12 women), 10 part-time/adjunct (5 women). Expenses: Contact institution. *Financial support:* In 2017–18, 367 students received support, including 43 research assistantships with full tuition reimbursements available (averaging $23,994 per year); scholarships/grants also available. Financial award application deadline: 3/1; financial award applicants required to submit FAFSA. In 2017, 13 master's, 125 doctorates awarded. Offers pharmaceutical sciences (MS, PhD); pharmacy (Pharm D); pharmacy and pharmaceutical sciences (MS, PhD, Pharm D). *Application deadline:* For fall admission, 2/1 priority date for domestic and international students. Applications are processed on a rolling basis. *Application fee:* $50. Electronic applications accepted. *Application Contact:* Dr. Jennifer M. Rosenberg, Associate Dean, 716-645-2825 Ext. 1, Fax: 716-829-6568, E-mail: prepharm@buffalo.edu. *Dean,* Dr. James M. O'Donnell, 716-645-2823, Fax: 716-829-6568.

School of Public Health and Health Professions Students: 475 full-time (343 women), 45 part-time (25 women); includes 74 minority (13 Black or African American, non-Hispanic/Latino; 1 American Indian or Alaska Native, non-Hispanic/Latino; 59 Asian, non-Hispanic/Latino; 1 Hispanic/Latino), 80 international. Average age 25. 597 applicants, 48% accepted, 229 enrolled. *Faculty:* 73 full-time (42 women), 28 part-time/adjunct (14 women). Expenses: Contact institution. *Financial support:* In 2017–18, 47 students received support, including 8 fellowships with full tuition reimbursements available (averaging $2,500 per year), 15 research assistantships with full tuition reimbursements available (averaging $15,000 per year), 16 teaching assistantships with full tuition reimbursements available (averaging $8,500 per year); career-related internships or fieldwork, Federal Work-Study, institutionally sponsored loans, scholarships/grants, tuition waivers (full and partial), and unspecified assistantships also available. Financial award application deadline: 3/15; financial award applicants required to submit FAFSA. In 2017, 151 master's, 53 doctorates, 21 other advanced degrees awarded. *Program availability:* Part-time. Offers assistive and rehabilitation technology (Certificate); biostatistics (MA, MPH, MS, PhD); community health and health behavior (MPH, PhD); epidemiology (MS, PhD); exercise science (MS, PhD); nutrition (MS, Advanced Certificate); occupational therapy (MS); physical therapy (DPT); public health (MPH); public health and health professions (MA, MPH, MS, DPT, PhD, Advanced Certificate, Certificate); rehabilitation science (PhD). *Application deadline:* For fall admission, 2/1 priority date for domestic and international students. *Application fee:* $50. Electronic applications accepted. *Dean*, Dr. Lynn Kozlowski, 716-829-6951, Fax: 716-829-6040, E-mail: lk22@buffalo.edu.

School of Social Work Students: 272 full-time (265 women), 228 part-time (163 women); includes 81 minority (51 Black or African American, non-Hispanic/Latino; 3 American Indian or Alaska Native, non-Hispanic/Latino; 17 Asian, non-Hispanic/Latino; 10 Hispanic/Latino). Average age 30. 445 applicants, 74% accepted, 222 enrolled. *Faculty:* 32 full-time (24 women), 53 part-time/adjunct (42 women). Expenses: Contact institution. *Financial support:* In 2017–18, 10 fellowships with full tuition reimbursements (averaging $10,800 per year), 2 research assistantships with full tuition reimbursements (averaging $16,500 per year), 13 teaching assistantships with full tuition reimbursements (averaging $5,000 per year) were awarded; Federal Work-Study, scholarships/grants, health care benefits, tuition waivers (full and partial), unspecified assistantships, and instructorships and research grants (for PhD students) also available. Financial award application deadline: 4/30; financial award applicants required to submit FAFSA. In 2017, 240 master's, 1 doctorate awarded. *Program availability:* Part-time, 100% online, blended/hybrid learning. Offers social welfare (PhD); social work (MSW). *Application deadline:* For fall admission, 3/1 priority date for domestic and international students; for spring admission, 9/15 for domestic and international students; for summer admission, 2/1 for domestic and international students. *Application fee:* $75. Electronic applications accepted. *Application Contact:* Maria Carey, Admissions Processor, 716-645-3381, Fax: 716-645-3456, E-mail: sw-info@buffalo.edu. *Dean*, Dr. Nancy J. Smyth, 716-645-3381, Fax: 716-645-3883, E-mail: sw-dean@buffalo.edu.

UNIVERSITY OF ADVANCING TECHNOLOGY, Tempe, AZ 85283-1042

General Information Proprietary, coed, primarily men, comprehensive institution. *Graduate housing:* Room and/or apartments available on a first-come, first-served basis to single students; on-campus housing not available to married students.

GRADUATE UNITS

Master of Science Program in Technology Offers advancing computer science (MS); emerging technologies (MS); game production and management (MS); information assurance (MS); technology leadership (MS). Electronic applications accepted.

THE UNIVERSITY OF AKRON, Akron, OH 44325

General Information State-supported, coed, university. CGS member. *Enrollment:* 20,169 graduate, professional, and undergraduate students; 2,000 full-time matriculated graduate/professional students (933 women), 1,151 part-time matriculated graduate/professional students (707 women). *Enrollment by degree level:* 2,340 master's, 763 doctoral, 48 other advanced degrees. *Graduate faculty:* 440 full-time (155 women), 146 part-time/adjunct (82 women). *Graduate housing:* Room and/or apartments available on a first-come, first-served basis to single students; on-campus housing not available to married students. Housing application deadline: 3/1. *Student services:* Campus employment opportunities, campus safety program, career counseling, exercise/wellness program, free psychological counseling, international student services, low-cost health insurance, multicultural affairs office, services for students with disabilities. *Library facilities:* Bierce Library plus 2 others. *Collection:* Books: 1.1 million (physical); Serial titles: 25,089 (physical). Study areas open 24 hours, 5–7 days a week; students can reserve study rooms.

Computer facilities: Computer purchase and lease plans are available. 3,150 computers available on campus for general student use. A campuswide network can be accessed from student residence rooms and from off campus. Online class registration, library laptops for student checkout are available.
Website: http://www.uakron.edu/

General Application Contact: Lauri Thorpe, Associate Dean, Enrollment, 330-972-6367, Fax: 330-972-6475, E-mail: lauri@uakron.edu.

GRADUATE UNITS

Graduate School Students: 2,060 full-time (993 women), 1,151 part-time (707 women); includes 445 minority (219 Black or African American, non-Hispanic/Latino; 1 American Indian or Alaska Native, non-Hispanic/Latino; 76 Asian, non-Hispanic/Latino; 81 Hispanic/Latino; 68 Two or more races, non-Hispanic/Latino), 756 international. Average age 28. 2,033 applicants, 67% accepted, 596 enrolled. *Faculty:* 440 full-time (155 women), 146 part-time/adjunct (82 women). Expenses: Contact institution. *Financial support:* In 2017–18, 17 fellowships with full and partial tuition reimbursements, 355 research assistantships with full and partial tuition reimbursements, 536 teaching assistantships with full and partial tuition reimbursements were awarded. Financial award application deadline: 12/1; financial award applicants required to submit FAFSA. In 2017, 1,114 master's, 165 doctorates awarded. *Program availability:* Part-time, evening/weekend. *Application deadline:* For fall admission, 12/1 priority date for domestic and international students. Applications are processed on a rolling basis. *Application fee:* $45 ($70 for international students). Electronic applications accepted. *Application Contact:* Marnie Saunders, Associate Dean, 330-972-6590, Fax: 330-972-6475, E-mail: mms129@uakron.edu. *Executive Dean*, Dr. Chand Midha, 330-972-7664, Fax: 330-972-6475, E-mail: cmidha@uakron.edu.

Buchtel College of Arts and Sciences Students: 427 full-time (208 women), 156 part-time (98 women); includes 93 minority (44 Black or African American, non-Hispanic/Latino; 19 Asian, non-Hispanic/Latino; 19 Hispanic/Latino; 11 Two or more races, non-Hispanic/Latino), 130 international. Average age 29. 664 applicants, 65% accepted, 241 enrolled. *Faculty:* 193 full-time (65 women), 53 part-time/adjunct (21 women). Expenses: Contact institution. *Financial support:* In 2017–18, 4 fellowships with full and partial tuition reimbursements, 50 research assistantships with full and partial tuition reimbursements, 283 teaching assistantships with full and partial tuition reimbursements were awarded; career-related internships or fieldwork, Federal Work-Study, institutionally sponsored loans, scholarships/grants, and unspecified assistantships also available. Support available to part-time students. Financial award application deadline: 12/1; financial award applicants required to submit FAFSA. In 2017, 234 master's, 29 doctorates awarded. *Program availability:* Part-time, evening/weekend. Offers accompanying (MM); adult development and aging (PhD); applied mathematics (MS); applied politics (MAP); arts administration (MA); arts and sciences (MA, MAP, MFA, MM, MPA, MS, PhD); biology (MS); chemistry (MS, PhD); child development (MA); clothing, textiles and interiors (MA); communication (MA); composition (MA, MM); computer science (MS); counseling psychology (MA, PhD); creative writing (MFA); earth science (MS); engineering geology (MS); environmental geology (MS); geology (MS); history (MA, PhD); industrial/organizational psychology (MA, PhD); integrated bioscience (PhD); literature (MA); mathematics (MS); music education (MM); music technology (MM); performance (MM); political science (MA, MAP); psychology (MA); public administration (MPA); statistics (MS); theatre arts (MA); theory (MM). *Application deadline:* For fall admission, 1/15 for domestic and international students. Applications are processed on a rolling basis. *Application fee:* $45 ($70 for international students). Electronic applications accepted. *Dean*, Dr. John Green, 330-972-7857, E-mail: green@uakron.edu.

College of Business Administration Students: 138 full-time (54 women), 155 part-time (54 women); includes 33 minority (10 Black or African American, non-Hispanic/Latino; 12 Asian, non-Hispanic/Latino; 5 Hispanic/Latino; 6 Two or more races, non-Hispanic/Latino), 62 international. Average age 28. 187 applicants, 86% accepted, 115 enrolled. *Faculty:* 49 full-time (15 women), 13 part-time/adjunct (5 women). Expenses: Contact institution. *Financial support:* In 2017–18, 3 research assistantships with full and partial tuition reimbursements, 37 teaching assistantships with full and partial tuition reimbursements were awarded; Federal Work-Study also available. In 2017, 254 master's awarded. *Program availability:* Part-time, evening/weekend. Offers accounting (MSA); business administration (MA, MBA, MS, MSA, MSM, MT); economics (MA); finance (MBA); global technological innovation (MBA); information systems management (MSM); management (MBA); marketing (MBA); supply chain management (MBA); taxation (MT). *Application deadline:* For fall admission, 7/15 for domestic and international students; for spring admission, 11/15 for domestic and international students; for summer admission, 4/15 for domestic students, 3/15 for international students. *Application fee:* $45 ($70 for international students). Electronic applications accepted. *Application Contact:* Dr. William Hauser, Director of Graduate Business Programs, 330-972-7043, E-mail: whauser@uakron.edu. *Dean*, Dr. Ravi Krovi, 330-972-7442, E-mail: cbadean@uakron.edu.

College of Education Students: 67 full-time (40 women), 158 part-time (119 women); includes 38 minority (28 Black or African American, non-Hispanic/Latino; 3 Asian, non-Hispanic/Latino; 3 Hispanic/Latino; 4 Two or more races, non-Hispanic/Latino), 12 international. Average age 34. 79 applicants, 94% accepted, 74 enrolled. *Faculty:* 26 full-time (18 women), 7 part-time/adjunct (6 women). Expenses: Contact institution. *Financial support:* In 2017–18, 2 teaching assistantships with full tuition reimbursements were awarded; scholarships/grants and administrative assistantships also available. In 2017, 98 master's awarded. *Program availability:* Part-time. Offers adolescent to young adult education (MS); art education (MS); chemistry (MS); chemistry and physics (MS); curriculum and instruction (MS); drama/theatre (MS); earth science (MS); earth science and chemistry (MS); earth science and physics (MS); education (MA, MS); elementary education - literacy (MA); integrated language arts (MS); integrated mathematics (MS); integrated social studies (MS); life science (MS); life science and chemistry (MS); life science and earth science (MS); life science and physics (MS); P-12 multi-age education (MS); physics (MS); principalship (MA, MS). *Application deadline:* Applications are processed on a rolling basis. *Application fee:* $45 ($70 for international students). Electronic applications accepted. *Application Contact:* Kelly Chaff, College Program Specialist, 330-972-7028, E-mail: klchaff@uakron.edu. *Acting Dean*, Dr. Jarrod Tudor, 330-972-7750, E-mail: grt2@uakron.edu.

College of Engineering Students: 298 full-time (73 women), 73 part-time (14 women); includes 20 minority (7 Black or African American, non-Hispanic/Latino; 5 Asian, non-Hispanic/Latino; 5 Hispanic/Latino; 3 Two or more races, non-Hispanic/Latino), 267 international. Average age 28. 305 applicants, 71% accepted, 68 enrolled. *Faculty:* 86 full-time (15 women), 5 part-time/adjunct (0 women). Expenses: Contact institution. *Financial support:* In 2017–18, 140 research assistantships with full tuition reimbursements, 113 teaching assistantships with full tuition reimbursements were awarded; career-related internships or fieldwork and Federal Work-Study also available. In 2017, 86 master's, 49 doctorates awarded. *Program availability:* Part-time, evening/weekend. Offers biomedical engineering (MS); chemical engineering (MS); civil engineering (MS); computer engineering (MS, PhD); electrical engineering (MS); engineering (PhD); mechanical engineering (MS). *Application deadline:* Applications are processed on a rolling basis. *Application fee:* $45 ($70 for international students). Electronic applications accepted. *Application Contact:* Dr. Craig Menzemer, Associate Dean for Graduate Studies and Administration, 330-972-5536, E-mail: ccmenze@uakron.edu. *Dean*, Dr. Donald Visco, 330-972-6978, E-mail: dviscoj@uakron.edu.

College of Health Professions Students: 467 full-time (370 women), 468 part-time (348 women); includes 172 minority (95 Black or African American, non-Hispanic/Latino; 1 American Indian or Alaska Native, non-Hispanic/Latino; 20 Asian, non-Hispanic/Latino; 25 Hispanic/Latino; 31 Two or more races, non-Hispanic/Latino), 16 international. Average age 29. 716 applicants, 48% accepted, 262 enrolled. *Faculty:* 55 full-time (38 women), 66 part-time/adjunct (50 women). Expenses: Contact institution. *Financial support:* In 2017–18, 12 fellowships with full and partial tuition reimbursements, 2 research assistantships with full and partial tuition reimbursements, 62 teaching assistantships with full and partial tuition reimbursements were awarded. In 2017, 376 master's, 36 doctorates awarded. Offers audiology (Au D); clinical mental health counseling (MA); counselor education and supervision (PhD); exercise physiology/adult fitness (MA, MS); health professions (MA, MS, MSN, MSW, Au D, DNP, PhD); marriage and family counseling/therapy (MA, MS); nursing (MSN, DNP); school counseling (MA, MS); social work (MSW); speech-language pathology (MA); speech-language pathology and audiology (MA, Au D); sport science/coaching (MA, MS). *Application deadline:* For fall admission, 1/1 for domestic and international students. Applications are processed on a rolling basis. *Application fee:* $45 ($70 for international students). Electronic applications accepted. *Application Contact:* Timothy McCarragher, Interim Associate Dean of Strategic Operations and Graduate Studies, 330-972-5976, E-mail: mccarra@uakron.edu. *Acting Dean*, Elizabeth Kennedy, 330-972-7552, E-mail: eak2@uakron.edu.

College of Polymer Science and Polymer Engineering Students: 314 full-time (96 women), 30 part-time (11 women); includes 20 minority (5 Black or African American, non-Hispanic/Latino; 9 Asian, non-Hispanic/Latino; 4 Hispanic/Latino; 2 Two or more races, non-Hispanic/Latino), 262 international. Average age 24. 251 applicants, 54% accepted, 99 enrolled. *Faculty:* 31 full-time (4 women), 2 part-time/adjunct (0 women).

Expenses: Contact institution. *Financial support:* In 2017–18, 1 fellowship with tuition reimbursement, 160 research assistantships with full tuition reimbursements, 39 teaching assistantships with full tuition reimbursements were awarded. In 2017, 66 master's, 45 doctorates awarded. *Program availability:* Part-time, evening/weekend. Offers polymer engineering (MS, PhD); polymer science (MS, PhD). *Application deadline:* For fall admission, 12/1 priority date for domestic and international students. *Application fee:* $45 ($70 for international students). Electronic applications accepted. *Application Contact:* Dr. Kevin Cavicchi, Associate Dean of Academic Affairs, 330-972-8368, E-mail: kac58@uakron.edu. *Dean*, Dr. Eric Amis, 330-972-7500, E-mail: amis@uakron.edu.

School of Law Students: 349 full-time (152 women), 111 part-time (63 women); includes 69 minority (30 Black or African American, non-Hispanic/Latino; 8 Asian, non-Hispanic/Latino; 20 Hispanic/Latino; 11 Two or more races, non-Hispanic/Latino), 7 international. Average age 27. 816 applicants, 56% accepted, 161 enrolled. *Faculty:* 38 full-time (16 women), 16 part-time/adjunct (2 women). Expenses: Contact institution. *Financial support:* In 2017–18, 264 students received support. Career-related internships or fieldwork, scholarships/grants, and tuition waivers (full and partial) available. Support available to part-time students. Financial award applicants required to submit FAFSA. In 2017, 2 master's, 122 doctorates awarded. *Program availability:* Part-time, evening/weekend. Offers law (LL M, JD). *Application deadline:* For fall admission, 3/1 priority date for domestic and international students. Applications are processed on a rolling basis. *Application fee:* $45 ($70 for international students). Electronic applications accepted. *Application Contact:* Lauri S. File, Assistant Dean of Admission and Financial Aid, 330-972-7331, Fax: 330-258-2343, E-mail: lfile@uakron.edu. *Dean*, Martin H. Belsky, 330-972-6359, Fax: 330-258-2343, E-mail: belsky@uakron.edu.

THE UNIVERSITY OF ALABAMA, Tuscaloosa, AL 35487

General Information State-supported, coed, university. CGS member. *Enrollment:* 38,563 graduate, professional, and undergraduate students; 3,294 full-time matriculated graduate/professional students (1,807 women), 1,783 part-time matriculated graduate/professional students (1,177 women). *Enrollment by degree level:* 3,015 master's, 2,011 doctoral, 51 other advanced degrees. *Graduate faculty:* 1,049 full-time (427 women), 95 part-time/adjunct (46 women). *Graduate housing:* On-campus housing not available. *Student services:* Campus employment opportunities, campus safety program, career counseling, child daycare facilities, exercise/wellness program, free psychological counseling, grant writing training, international student services, low-cost health insurance, multicultural affairs office, services for students with disabilities, teacher training, writing training. *Library facilities:* Amelia Gayle Gorgas Library plus 8 others. *Collection:* Books: 3.3 million (physical), 1.5 million (digital/electronic); Serial titles: 419 (physical), 199,096 (digital/electronic); Databases: 589. Weekly public service hours: 146; study areas open 24 hours, 5–7 days a week; students can reserve study rooms. *Research affiliation:* Mercedes-Benz (automotive engineering), Alabama Power (utilities), TDK Corp. (materials science), Nucor Steel (materials science), Boeing (aerospace, manufacturing), Lockheed Martin Corporation (business analytics).

Computer facilities: 2,500 computers available on campus for general student use. A campuswide network can be accessed from student residence rooms and from off campus. Online class registration is available.
Website: http://www.ua.edu/

General Application Contact: Patrick D. Fuller, Senior Graduate Admissions Counselor, 205-348-5923, Fax: 205-348-0400, E-mail: patrick.d.fuller@ua.edu.

GRADUATE UNITS

Graduate School Students: 3,294 full-time (1,807 women), 1,783 part-time (1,177 women); includes 1,053 minority (675 Black or African American, non-Hispanic/Latino; 20 American Indian or Alaska Native, non-Hispanic/Latino; 66 Asian, non-Hispanic/Latino; 173 Hispanic/Latino; 8 Native Hawaiian or other Pacific Islander, non-Hispanic/Latino; 111 Two or more races, non-Hispanic/Latino), 550 international. Average age 31. 6,273 applicants, 44% accepted, 1759 enrolled. *Faculty:* 1,009 full-time (410 women), 62 part-time/adjunct (39 women). Expenses: Contact institution. *Financial support:* Fellowships with tuition reimbursements, research assistantships with tuition reimbursements, teaching assistantships with tuition reimbursements, career-related internships or fieldwork, Federal Work-Study, institutionally sponsored loans, scholarships/grants, traineeships, health care benefits, tuition waivers (full and partial), and unspecified assistantships available. Support available to part-time students. Financial award application deadline: 2/15; financial award applicants required to submit FAFSA. In 2017, 1,571 master's, 438 doctorates, 38 other advanced degrees awarded. *Program availability:* Part-time, evening/weekend, online learning. *Application deadline:* For fall admission, 7/1 priority date for domestic students, 3/15 for international students; for spring admission, 11/1 priority date for domestic students, 7/1 for international students. Applications are processed on a rolling basis. *Application fee:* $50 ($60 for international students). Electronic applications accepted. *Application Contact:* Lesley Campbell, Director of Graduate Recruitment, 205-348-0051, Fax: 205-348-0400, E-mail: lesley.campbell@ua.edu. *Dean*, Dr. Susan Carvalho, 205-348-5921, Fax: 205-348-0400, E-mail: scarvalho@ua.edu.

Capstone College of Nursing Students: 151 full-time (131 women), 197 part-time (170 women); includes 124 minority (98 Black or African American, non-Hispanic/Latino; 3 American Indian or Alaska Native, non-Hispanic/Latino; 3 Asian, non-Hispanic/Latino; 15 Hispanic/Latino; 1 Native Hawaiian or other Pacific Islander, non-Hispanic/Latino; 4 Two or more races, non-Hispanic/Latino), 1 international. Average age 40. 352 applicants, 55% accepted, 150 enrolled. *Faculty:* 29 full-time (26 women), 6 part-time/adjunct (5 women). Expenses: Contact institution. *Financial support:* Scholarships/grants available. Financial award application deadline: 6/15; financial award applicants required to submit FAFSA. In 2017, 53 master's, 61 doctorates awarded. *Program availability:* Part-time, online learning. Offers nursing (MSN, DNP). *Application deadline:* For fall admission, 3/1 priority date for domestic students. Applications are processed on a rolling basis. *Application fee:* $50 ($60 for international students). Electronic applications accepted. *Application Contact:* Vickie L. Samuel, Graduate Recruitment and Retention Liaison, 205-348-8163, Fax: 205-348-6674, E-mail: vsamuel@ua.edu. *Dean*, Dr. Suzanne Prevost, 205-348-1040, Fax: 205-348-5559, E-mail: sprevost@ua.edu.

College of Arts and Sciences Students: 888 full-time (481 women), 109 part-time (47 women); includes 160 minority (78 Black or African American, non-Hispanic/Latino; 3 American Indian or Alaska Native, non-Hispanic/Latino; 14 Asian, non-Hispanic/Latino; 42 Hispanic/Latino; 23 Two or more races, non-Hispanic/Latino), 182 international. Average age 28. 1,578 applicants, 33% accepted, 290 enrolled. *Faculty:* 432 full-time (174 women), 13 part-time/adjunct (6 women). Expenses: Contact institution. *Financial support:* Career-related internships or fieldwork, Federal Work-Study, institutionally sponsored loans, scholarships/grants, and unspecified assistantships available. Support available to part-time students. Financial award applicants required to submit FAFSA. In 2017, 235 master's, 67 doctorates awarded. *Program availability:* Part-time, online learning. Offers acting (MFA); American studies (MA); anthropology (MA, PhD); applied mathematics (PhD); arranging (MM); art history (MA); arts and sciences (MA, MATESOL, MFA, MM, MPA, MS, DMA, PhD); biological sciences (MS, PhD); chemistry (MS, PhD); choral conducting (MM, DMA); church music (MM); clinical psychology (PhD); composition (MM, DMA); composition and rhetoric (PhD); costume design (MFA); creative writing (MFA); criminal justice (MS); directing (MFA); earth system science (MS, PhD); environment and natural resources (MS, PhD); environment and society (MS, PhD); experimental psychology (PhD); French (MA, PhD); French and Spanish (PhD); geographic information science (MS, PhD); geological sciences (MS, PhD); German (MA); history (MA, PhD); literature (MA, PhD); mathematics (MA, PhD); music education (MA, PhD); musicology (MM); performance (MM, DMA); physics and astronomy (MS, PhD); political science (MA, PhD); public administration (MPA); pure mathematics (PhD); rhetoric and composition (MA); Romance languages (MA, PhD); scene design/technical production (MFA); Spanish (MA, PhD); speech language pathology (MS); stage management (MFA); studio art (MA, MFA); teaching English as a second language (MATESOL); theatre (MFA); theatre management/administration (MFA); theory (MM); wind conducting (MM, DMA); women's studies (MA). *Application fee:* $50 ($60 for international students). Electronic applications accepted. *Application Contact:* Patrick D. Fuller, Senior Graduate Admissions Counselor, 205-348-5923, Fax: 205-348-0400, E-mail: patrick.d.fuller@ua.edu. *Dean*, Dr. Robert F. Olin, 205-348-7007, Fax: 205-348-0272, E-mail: olin@as.ua.edu.

College of Communication and Information Sciences Students: 137 full-time (94 women), 234 part-time (182 women); includes 53 minority (25 Black or African American, non-Hispanic/Latino; 1 American Indian or Alaska Native, non-Hispanic/Latino; 2 Asian, non-Hispanic/Latino; 11 Hispanic/Latino; 14 Two or more races, non-Hispanic/Latino), 31 international. Average age 32. 279 applicants, 70% accepted, 137 enrolled. *Faculty:* 68 full-time (33 women), 2 part-time/adjunct (both women). Expenses: Contact institution. *Financial support:* In 2017–18, 70 students received support. Fellowships with tuition reimbursements available, research assistantships with tuition reimbursements available, teaching assistantships with tuition reimbursements available, institutionally sponsored loans, health care benefits, and unspecified assistantships available. Financial award application deadline: 2/15. In 2017, 117 master's, 15 doctorates awarded. Offers book arts (MFA); communication and information sciences (MA, MFA, MLIS, PhD); communication studies (MA); journalism and creative media (MA); library and information studies (MLIS, PhD). *Application deadline:* For fall admission, 2/15 priority date for domestic and international students; for winter admission, 11/1 priority date for international students; for spring admission, 11/1 priority date for domestic students. Applications are processed on a rolling basis. *Application fee:* $50 ($60 for international students). Electronic applications accepted. *Application Contact:* Marylou Cox, Information Contact, 205-348-8593, Fax: 205-348-6774, E-mail: mcox@ua.edu. *Dean*, Dr. Mark Nelson, 205-348-4787, E-mail: mnelson@ua.edu.

College of Education Students: 338 full-time (239 women), 471 part-time (337 women); includes 227 minority (160 Black or African American, non-Hispanic/Latino; 4 American Indian or Alaska Native, non-Hispanic/Latino; 13 Asian, non-Hispanic/Latino; 26 Hispanic/Latino; 2 Native Hawaiian or other Pacific Islander, non-Hispanic/Latino; 22 Two or more races, non-Hispanic/Latino), 48 international. Average age 36. 465 applicants, 61% accepted, 214 enrolled. *Faculty:* 111 full-time (59 women), 9 part-time/adjunct (6 women). Expenses: Contact institution. *Financial support:* In 2017–18, 119 students received support. Research assistantships with tuition reimbursements available, teaching assistantships with tuition reimbursements available, career-related internships or fieldwork, Federal Work-Study, institutionally sponsored loans, scholarships/grants, and unspecified assistantships available. Financial award applicants required to submit FAFSA. In 2017, 165 master's, 90 doctorates, 38 other advanced degrees awarded. *Program availability:* Part-time, online learning. Offers alternative sport pedagogy (MA); choral music education (MA); collaborative special education (M Ed, Ed S); early intervention (M Ed, Ed S); education (M Ed, MA, Ed D, PhD, Ed S); educational administration (Ed D, PhD); educational leadership (MA, Ed S); educational studies in psychology, research methodology and counseling (MA, Ed D, PhD, Ed S); elementary education (MA, Ed D, PhD, Ed S); exercise science (PhD); gifted and talented education (M Ed, Ed S); higher education administration (MA, Ed D, PhD); instructional leadership (Ed D, PhD); instrumental music education (MA); multiple abilities (M Ed); music education (Ed D, PhD, Ed S); secondary education (MA, Ed D, PhD, Ed S); special education (Ed D, PhD). *Application deadline:* For fall admission, 7/1 for domestic and international students; for spring admission, 11/15 for domestic students, 11/17 for international students. Applications are processed on a rolling basis. *Application fee:* $50 ($60 for international students). *Application Contact:* Dr. Kathy S. Wetzel, Assistant Dean for Student Services, 205-348-1154, Fax: 205-348-0080, E-mail: kwetzel@bamaed.ua.edu. *Dean*, Dr. Peter Hlebowitsh, 205-348-6052, E-mail: peter.hleb@ua.edu.

College of Engineering Students: 254 full-time (46 women), 50 part-time (5 women); includes 21 minority (11 Black or African American, non-Hispanic/Latino; 3 Asian, non-Hispanic/Latino; 4 Hispanic/Latino; 3 Two or more races, non-Hispanic/Latino), 152 international. Average age 27. 327 applicants, 39% accepted, 65 enrolled. *Faculty:* 123 full-time (15 women). Expenses: Contact institution. *Financial support:* In 2017–18, 229 students received support, including fellowships with full tuition reimbursements available (averaging $16,022 per year), research assistantships with full tuition reimbursements available (averaging $16,022 per year), teaching assistantships with full tuition reimbursements available (averaging $16,022 per year); career-related internships or fieldwork, Federal Work-Study, and institutionally sponsored loans also available. Financial award application deadline: 2/15. In 2017, 57 master's, 36 doctorates awarded. *Program availability:* Part-time, online learning. Offers aerospace engineering (MSAEM); chemical and biological engineering (MS Ch E, PhD); civil engineering (MSCE, PhD); computer science (MS, PhD); electrical engineering (MS, PhD); engineering (MS, MS Ch E, MS Met E, MSAEM, MSCE, PhD); engineering science and mechanics (PhD); environmental engineering (MS); materials science (PhD); mechanical engineering (MS, PhD); metallurgical and materials engineering (MS Met E, PhD). *Application deadline:* For fall admission, 7/1 for domestic students, 4/15 for international students; for spring admission, 11/15 for domestic students, 9/1 for international students. Applications are processed on a rolling basis. *Application fee:* $50 ($60 for international students). Electronic applications accepted. *Application Contact:* Dr. David A. Francko, Dean, 205-348-8280, Fax: 205-348-0400, E-mail: dfrancko@ua.edu. *Dean*, Dr. Charles Karr, 205-348-6405, Fax: 205-348-8573.

College of Human Environmental Sciences Students: 209 full-time (139 women), 425 part-time (308 women); includes 147 minority (95 Black or African American, non-Hispanic/Latino; 3 American Indian or Alaska Native, non-Hispanic/Latino; 7 Asian, non-Hispanic/Latino; 21 Hispanic/Latino; 4 Native Hawaiian or other Pacific Islander, non-Hispanic/Latino; 17 Two or more races, non-Hispanic/Latino), 2 international.

Average age 33. 147 applicants, 82% accepted, 112 enrolled. *Faculty:* 57 full-time (40 women), 8 part-time/adjunct (6 women). Expenses: Contact institution. *Financial support:* In 2017–18, 44 students received support, including research assistantships with full tuition reimbursements available (averaging $9,000 per year); fellowships with tuition reimbursements available, teaching assistantships with full tuition reimbursements available, career-related internships or fieldwork, Federal Work-Study, institutionally sponsored loans, and scholarships/grants also available. In 2017, 275 master's, 8 doctorates awarded. *Program availability:* Part-time, evening/weekend, online learning. Offers apparel and textiles (MSHES); consumer sciences (MS); health education and promotion (PhD); health studies (MA); human development and family studies (MSHES); human environmental sciences (MA, MS, MSHES, PhD); human nutrition and hospitality management (MSHES); interactive technology (MS); marriage and family therapy (MSHES); parent and family life education (MSHES); quality management (MS); restaurant and meeting management (MS); rural community health (MS); sport management (MS). *Application deadline:* For fall admission, 7/6 for domestic students. Applications are processed on a rolling basis. *Application fee:* $50 ($60 for international students). Electronic applications accepted. *Application Contact:* Patrick D. Fuller, Admissions Officer, 205-348-5923, Fax: 205-348-0400, E-mail: patrick.d.fuller@ua.edu. *Dean,* Dr. Milla D. Boschung, 205-348-6250, Fax: 205-348-1786, E-mail: mboschun@ches.ua.edu.

Manderson Graduate School of Business Students: 507 full-time (189 women), 125 part-time (43 women); includes 85 minority (38 Black or African American, non-Hispanic/Latino; 2 American Indian or Alaska Native, non-Hispanic/Latino; 15 Asian, non-Hispanic/Latino; 15 Hispanic/Latino; 15 Two or more races, non-Hispanic/Latino), 78 international. Average age 28. 847 applicants, 59% accepted, 273 enrolled. *Faculty:* 136 full-time (30 women), 3 part-time/adjunct (0 women). Expenses: Contact institution. *Financial support:* In 2017–18, 183 students received support, including research assistantships with tuition reimbursements available (averaging $14,500 per year), teaching assistantships with tuition reimbursements available (averaging $16,500 per year); fellowships with tuition reimbursements available, career-related internships or fieldwork, Federal Work-Study, institutionally sponsored loans, and scholarships/grants also available. Support available to part-time students. Financial award application deadline: 2/5. In 2017, 409 master's, 13 doctorates awarded. *Program availability:* Part-time, evening/weekend, online learning. Offers accounting (M Acc, PhD); applied statistics (MS, PhD); business (EMBA, M Acc, MA, MBA, MS, MTA, PhD); economics (MA, PhD); finance (MS, PhD); general commerce and business (EMBA, MBA); management (MA, MS, PhD); marketing (MS, PhD); operations management (MS, PhD); tax accounting (MTA). *Application deadline:* For fall admission, 4/15 priority date for domestic and international students. Applications are processed on a rolling basis. *Application fee:* $60 ($75 for international students). Electronic applications accepted. *Application Contact:* Patricia Wilson, Director of MBA Recruiting and Admissions, 205-348-9122, Fax: 205-348-4504, E-mail: pewilson@cba.ua.edu. *Associate Dean,* Dr. J. Brian Gray, 205-348-8912, Fax: 205-348-4504, E-mail: bgray@cba.ua.edu.

School of Social Work Students: 344 full-time (295 women), 66 part-time (55 women); includes 130 minority (111 Black or African American, non-Hispanic/Latino; 1 Asian, non-Hispanic/Latino; 9 Hispanic/Latino; 1 Native Hawaiian or other Pacific Islander, non-Hispanic/Latino; 8 Two or more races, non-Hispanic/Latino), 13 international. Average age 31. 450 applicants, 55% accepted, 186 enrolled. *Faculty:* 27 full-time (21 women), 18 part-time/adjunct (15 women). Expenses: Contact institution. *Financial support:* In 2017–18, 21 students received support, including research assistantships with full tuition reimbursements available (averaging $12,744 per year), teaching assistantships with full tuition reimbursements available (averaging $12,744 per year); career-related internships or fieldwork, scholarships/grants, traineeships, health care benefits, and unspecified assistantships also available. Financial award application deadline: 2/1; financial award applicants required to submit FAFSA. In 2017, 190 master's, 3 doctorates awarded. *Program availability:* Part-time, blended/hybrid learning. Offers social work (MSW, PhD). *Application deadline:* For fall admission, 2/1 priority date for domestic and international students; for spring admission, 9/1 priority date for domestic and international students; for summer admission, 2/1 priority date for domestic and international students. *Application fee:* $50 ($60 for international students). Electronic applications accepted. *Application Contact:* Amanda Moore, Coordinator of Student Services, 205-348-5272, Fax: 205-348-9419, E-mail: almoore2@ua.edu. *Professor and Dean,* Dr. Vikki L. Vandiver, 205-348-3924, Fax: 205-348-9419, E-mail: vlvandiver@sw.ua.edu.

Interdisciplinary Programs Students: 6 full-time (4 women), 8 part-time (5 women); includes 2 minority (both Black or African American, non-Hispanic/Latino). Average age 41. 2 applicants, 100% accepted, 2 enrolled. Expenses: Contact institution. In 2017, 2 doctorates awarded. *Program availability:* Part-time, evening/weekend. Offers interdisciplinary studies (PhD). *Application deadline:* For fall admission, 5/1 for international students; for winter admission, 9/15 for international students. Applications are processed on a rolling basis. Electronic applications accepted. *Application Contact:* Patrick D. Fuller, Senior Graduate Admissions Counselor, 205-348-5923, Fax: 205-348-0400, E-mail: patrick.d.fuller@ua.edu. *Assistant Dean of the Graduate School,* Dr. Andrew Mark Goodliffe, 205-348-8283, Fax: 205-348-0400, E-mail: amg@ua.edu.

School of Law Students: 412 full-time (175 women), 56 part-time (17 women); includes 94 minority (53 Black or African American, non-Hispanic/Latino; 4 American Indian or Alaska Native, non-Hispanic/Latino; 9 Asian, non-Hispanic/Latino; 22 Hispanic/Latino; 6 Two or more races, non-Hispanic/Latino), 6 international. Average age 27. 1,532 applicants, 25% accepted, 165 enrolled. *Faculty:* 40 full-time (17 women), 33 part-time/adjunct (7 women). Expenses: Contact institution. *Financial support:* Applicants required to submit FAFSA. In 2017, 45 master's, 132 doctorates awarded. Offers business transactions (LL M); comparative law (LL M, JSD); law (JD, JSD); taxation (LL M). *Application deadline:* Applications are processed on a rolling basis. *Application fee:* $40. Electronic applications accepted. *Application Contact:* Martha Griffith, Assistant Director for Admissions, 205-348-7945, Fax: 205-348-3917, E-mail: mgriffith@law.ua.edu. *Associate Dean for Admissions,* Claude R. Arrington, 205-348-6557, Fax: 205-348-3077, E-mail: carrington@law.ua.edu.

THE UNIVERSITY OF ALABAMA AT BIRMINGHAM, Birmingham, AL 35294

General Information State-supported, coed, university. CGS member. *Enrollment:* 20,902 graduate, professional, and undergraduate students; 3,957 full-time matriculated graduate/professional students (2,362 women), 3,530 part-time matriculated graduate/professional students (2,461 women). *Enrollment by degree level:* 4,924 master's, 2,521 doctoral, 42 other advanced degrees. *Graduate faculty:* 1,791 full-time (649 women), 142 part-time/adjunct (60 women). *Graduate housing:* Room and/or apartments available on a first-come, first-served basis to single students; on-campus housing not available to married students. Typical cost: $7532 per year ($11,682 including board). Housing application deadline: 5/1. *Student services:* Campus employment opportunities, campus safety program, career counseling, exercise/wellness program, free psychological counseling, grant writing training, international student services, low-cost health insurance, multicultural affairs office, services for students with disabilities, teacher training, writing training. *Library facilities:* Mervyn Sterne Library plus 2 others. *Collection:* Books: 1.3 million (physical). Students can reserve study rooms. *Research affiliation:* Southern Research Institute (cancer therapeutics, biodefense).

Computer facilities: A campuswide network can be accessed from student residence rooms and from off campus. Online class registration, transcript requests are available. Website: http://www.uab.edu/

General Application Contact: Holly Hebard, Director of Graduate School Operations, 205-934-8227, Fax: 205-934-8413, E-mail: gradschool@uab.edu.

GRADUATE UNITS

Collat School of Business Students: 136 full-time (50 women), 508 part-time (227 women); includes 174 minority (110 Black or African American, non-Hispanic/Latino; 2 American Indian or Alaska Native, non-Hispanic/Latino; 32 Asian, non-Hispanic/Latino; 17 Hispanic/Latino; 13 Two or more races, non-Hispanic/Latino), 55 international. Average age 34. *Faculty:* 44 full-time (8 women), 11 part-time/adjunct (4 women). Expenses: Contact institution. *Financial support:* In 2017–18, 2 research assistantships (averaging $5,000 per year), 4 teaching assistantships (averaging $5,000 per year) were awarded; career-related internships or fieldwork and unspecified assistantships also available. Financial award applicants required to submit FAFSA. In 2017, 232 master's awarded. *Program availability:* Part-time, evening/weekend, blended/hybrid learning. Offers accounting (M Acct); business (M Acct, MBA, MS); business administration (MBA); management information systems (MS). MD/MBA program offered in partnership with the School of Medicine. *Application deadline:* For fall admission, 8/1 for domestic and international students; for spring admission, 12/1 for domestic and international students; for summer admission, 5/1 for domestic and international students. Applications are processed on a rolling basis. *Application fee:* $60 ($75 for international students). Electronic applications accepted. *Application Contact:* Susan Noblitt Banks, Director of Graduate School Operations, 205-934-8227, Fax: 205-934-8413, E-mail: gradschool@uab.edu. *Dean,* Dr. Eric Jack, 205-934-8800, Fax: 205-934-8886, E-mail: ejack@uab.edu.

College of Arts and Sciences *Program availability:* Part-time, evening/weekend, online learning. Offers anthropology (MA); applied mathematics (PhD); art history (MA); arts and sciences (MA, MPA, MS, MSCJ, MSFS, PhD); behavioral neuroscience (PhD); biology (MS, PhD); chemistry (MS, PhD); communication management (MA); computer and information sciences (MS, PhD); computer forensics and security management (MS); creative writing (MA); criminal justice (MSCJ); forensic science (MSFS); history (MA); lifespan developmental psychology (PhD); literature (MA); mathematics (MS); medical sociology (PhD); medical/clinical psychology (PhD); physics (MS, PhD); psychology (MA); public administration (MPA); rhetoric and composition (MA). Electronic applications accepted.

Joint Health Sciences Students: 326 full-time (185 women); includes 125 minority (33 Black or African American, non-Hispanic/Latino; 2 American Indian or Alaska Native, non-Hispanic/Latino; 64 Asian, non-Hispanic/Latino; 18 Hispanic/Latino; 8 Two or more races, non-Hispanic/Latino). Average age 27. 314 applicants, 26% accepted, 41 enrolled. *Faculty:* 370. Expenses: Contact institution. *Financial support:* In 2017–18, fellowships with full tuition reimbursements (averaging $29,000 per year), research assistantships with full tuition reimbursements (averaging $30,000 per year) were awarded; health care benefits also available. In 2017, 49 doctorates awarded. Offers basic medical sciences (MSBMS); biochemistry, structural, and stem cell biology (PhD); cancer biology (PhD); cell, molecular, and developmental biology (PhD); genetics, genomics, and bioinformatics (PhD); health sciences (MSBMS, PhD); immunology (PhD); microbiology (PhD); neuroscience (PhD); pathobiology and molecular medicine (PhD). *Application deadline:* For fall admission, 12/31 for domestic and international students. Applications are processed on a rolling basis. Electronic applications accepted. *Application Contact:* Alyssa Zasada, Admissions Manager for Graduate Biomedical Sciences, 205-934-3857, E-mail: grad-gbs@uab.edu. *Associate Dean for Graduate Biomedical Sciences,* Dr. David A. Schneider, 205-934-2845, E-mail: dschneid@uab.edu.

School of Dentistry Offers dentistry (MS, DMD).

School of Education *Program availability:* Part-time, evening/weekend, online learning. Offers arts education (MA Ed); community health and human services (MA Ed); counseling (MA); curriculum education (Ed S); early childhood education (MA Ed, PhD); education (MA, MA Ed, Ed D, PhD, Ed S); educational leadership (MA Ed, Ed D, Ed S); elementary education (MA Ed); English as a second language (MA Ed, Ed S); high school education (MA Ed); reading (MA Ed); special education (MA Ed). Electronic applications accepted.

School of Engineering Students: 170 full-time (37 women), 357 part-time (63 women); includes 139 minority (80 Black or African American, non-Hispanic/Latino; 26 Asian, non-Hispanic/Latino; 18 Hispanic/Latino; 3 Native Hawaiian or other Pacific Islander, non-Hispanic/Latino; 12 Two or more races, non-Hispanic/Latino), 125 international. Average age 34. 365 applicants, 69% accepted, 137 enrolled. *Faculty:* 31 full-time (5 women), 23 part-time/adjunct (3 women). Expenses: Contact institution. *Financial support:* In 2017–18, 141 students received support, including 23 fellowships with full tuition reimbursements available (averaging $25,000 per year), 78 research assistantships with full tuition reimbursements available, 32 teaching assistantships; institutionally sponsored loans also available. Support available to part-time students. In 2017, 146 master's, 9 doctorates awarded. *Program availability:* Part-time, evening/weekend, 100% online, blended/hybrid learning. Offers advanced safety engineering and management (M Eng); biomedical engineering (MSBME, PhD); civil engineering (MSCE, PhD); computational engineering (PhD); computer engineering (PhD); construction engineering management (M Eng); design and commercialization (M Eng); electrical engineering (MSEE); engineering (M Eng, MS Mt E, MSBME, MSCE, MSEE, MSME, PhD); information engineering management (M Eng); materials engineering (MS Mt E, PhD); mechanical engineering (MSME); structural engineering (M Eng); sustainable smart cities (M Eng). *Application deadline:* For fall admission, 8/1 for domestic and international students; for spring admission, 12/1 for domestic and international students; for summer admission, 5/1 for domestic and international students. Applications are processed on a rolling basis. *Application fee:* $50 ($60 for international students). Electronic applications accepted. *Application Contact:* Holly Hebard, Director of Graduate School Operations, 205-934-8227, Fax: 205-934-8413, E-mail: gradschool@uab.edu. *Dean,* Dr. J. Iwan Alexander, 205-975-5890, Fax: 205-934-8437, E-mail: ialex@uab.edu.

School of Health Professions *Program availability:* Part-time, online learning. Offers administration/health services (D Sc, PhD); biotechnology (MS); clinical laboratory science (MS); genetic counseling (MS); health administration (MSHA); health informatics (MSHI); health professions (MS, MSHA, MSHI, MSPAS, D Sc, DPT, PhD,

Certificate); low vision rehabilitation (Certificate); nutrition sciences (MS, PhD); occupational therapy (MS); physical therapy (DPT); physician assistant studies (MSPAS); rehabilitation science (PhD). Electronic applications accepted.

School of Medicine Offers medicine (MD). Electronic applications accepted.

School of Nursing *Program availability:* Part-time, online only, blended/hybrid learning. Offers clinical nurse leader (MSN); nurse anesthesia (DNP); nurse practitioner (MSN, DNP); nursing (MSN, DNP, PhD); nursing health systems administration (MSN); nursing informatics (MSN). Electronic applications accepted.

School of Optometry Offers optometry (MS, OD, PhD); sensory impairment (PhD); vision science (MS, PhD). Electronic applications accepted.

School of Public Health *Program availability:* Part-time. Offers applied epidemiology and pharmacoepidemiology (MSPH); biostatistics (MPH, MS, MSPH, PhD); clinical and translational science (MSPH); environmental health (MPH); environmental health and toxicology (MSPH); environmental health sciences research (PhD); epidemiology (PhD); general theory and practice (MPH); health behavior (MPH); health care organization (MPH); health education and health promotion (PhD); health policy quantitative policy analysis (MPH); industrial hygiene (MPH, MSPH, PhD); maternal and child health policy (Dr PH); maternal and child health policy and leadership (MPH); occupational health and safety (MPH); outcomes research (MSPH, Dr PH); public health (PhD); public health management (Dr PH); public health preparedness management (MPH). Electronic applications accepted.

THE UNIVERSITY OF ALABAMA IN HUNTSVILLE, Huntsville, AL 35899

General Information State-supported, coed, university. CGS member. *Graduate housing:* Rooms and/or apartments available on a first-come, first-served basis to single and married students. Housing application deadline: 6/1. *Research affiliation:* Oak Ridge, Lawrence Livermore and Savannah River National Labs - Y12National Security Complex (neutron science, energy technologies, high-performance computing, systems biology, materials science at the nanoscale, national security), Cummings Research Park/Boeing/ADTRAN/SAIC/Teledyne Brown Engineering/Lockheed Martin/Dynetics, Inc. (computer science, aerospace engineering, information systems, space systems, defense systems, informatics), National Oceanic and Atmospheric Administration (NOAA) (climate modeling, weather and air quality research, oceans, satellites), Hudson Alpha Institute for Biotechnology (medical research, biotechnology, genomic research, molecular biology), U.S. Department of Defense/U.S. Army Aviation and Missile Command (missile research, development and engineering and manufacturing technology), NASA/Marshall Space Flight Center/Goddard Space Flight Center (space science, earth science, information technology, materials science, optical science).

GRADUATE UNITS

School of Graduate Studies *Program availability:* Part-time, evening/weekend, 100% online, blended/hybrid learning. Electronic applications accepted.

College of Arts, Humanities, and Social Sciences *Program availability:* Part-time, evening/weekend. Offers arts, humanities, and social sciences (MA, Certificate); education (MA); English (MA); history (MA); industrial/organizational psychology (MA); psychology (MA); public affairs (MA); technical writing (Certificate); TESOL (Certificate). Electronic applications accepted.

College of Business Administration *Program availability:* Part-time, evening/weekend. Offers accounting (M Acc); business administration (M Acc, MBA, MS, MSIS, MSM, MSMS, Certificate); business analytics (MSMS); cybersecurity (MS, Certificate); enterprise resource planning (Certificate); federal contracting and procurement management (Certificate); human resource management (MSM); information systems (MSIS); management (MBA); supply chain and logistics management (MS); supply chain management (Certificate); technology and innovation management (Certificate). Electronic applications accepted.

College of Education Offers autism spectrum disorders (M Ed, Graduate Certificate); biology (MAT); chemistry (MAT); differentiated instruction in elementary education (M Ed); English language arts (MAT); English speakers of other languages (M Ed, MAT); history (MAT); mathematics (MAT); physics (MAT); reading education (M Ed); secondary education (M Ed).

College of Engineering *Program availability:* Part-time, evening/weekend, online learning. Offers aerospace systems engineering (MS, PhD); biotechnology science and engineering (PhD); chemical and materials engineering (MSE); civil and environmental engineering (PhD); civil engineering (MSE); computer engineering (MSE, PhD); electrical engineering (MSE, PhD); engineering (MS, MSE, MSOR, MSSE, PhD); engineering management (MSE, PhD); industrial engineering (MSE, PhD); materials science (PhD); mechanical engineering (PhD); operations research (MSOR); optical science and engineering (PhD); software engineering (MSSE); systems engineering (MSE, PhD). Electronic applications accepted.

College of Nursing *Program availability:* Part-time, evening/weekend, online learning. Offers family nurse practitioner (Certificate); nursing (MSN, DNP); nursing education (Certificate). DNP offered jointly with The University of Alabama at Birmingham. Electronic applications accepted.

College of Science *Program availability:* Part-time, evening/weekend. Offers applied mathematics (PhD); atmospheric science (MS, PhD); biology (MS); biotechnology science and engineering (PhD); chemistry (MS); computer science (MS, PhD); cybersecurity (MS); earth system science (MS); education (MA, MS); materials science (MS, PhD); mathematics (MA, MS); modeling and simulation (MS, PhD, Certificate); optics and photonics technology (MS); physics (MS, PhD); science (MA, MS, MSSE, PhD, Certificate); software engineering (MSSE, Certificate); space science (MS, PhD). Electronic applications accepted.

UNIVERSITY OF ALASKA ANCHORAGE, Anchorage, AK 99508

General Information State-supported, coed, comprehensive institution. Tuition, state resident: part-time $489 per credit hour. Tuition, nonresident: part-time $1028 per credit hour. *Graduate housing:* Rooms and/or apartments available on a first-come, first-served basis to single and married students. Housing application deadline: 7/1. *Student services:* Campus employment opportunities, campus safety program, career counseling, child daycare facilities, exercise/wellness program, free psychological counseling, grant writing training, international student services, low-cost health insurance, multicultural affairs office, services for students with disabilities, teacher training, writing training. *Library facilities:* Consortium Library. *Research affiliation:* Conoco Phillips (energy), Habitat for Humanity (project management), BP Alaska (energy), Municipality of Anchorage (government), Providence Hospital (health care).

Computer facilities: Computer purchase and lease plans are available. A campuswide network can be accessed from student residence rooms and from off campus. Online class registration is available.
Website: http://www.uaa.alaska.edu/

General Application Contact: Elisa Mattison, Director, Graduate School, 907-786-1096, Fax: 907-786-1791, E-mail: uaa_gradschool@uaa.alaska.edu.

GRADUATE UNITS

College of Arts and Sciences Expenses: Contact institution. *Financial support:* Research assistantships with full tuition reimbursements, teaching assistantships with full tuition reimbursements, career-related internships or fieldwork, Federal Work-Study, scholarships/grants, traineeships, tuition waivers, and unspecified assistantships available. Support available to part-time students. Financial award application deadline: 4/1; financial award applicants required to submit FAFSA. *Program availability:* Part-time. Offers anthropology (MA); arts and sciences (MA, MFA, MS, PhD); biological sciences (MS); clinical psychology (MS); clinical-community psychology with rural-indigenous emphasis (PhD); creative writing and literary arts (MFA); English (MA). *Application deadline:* For fall admission, 7/1 for domestic and international students; for spring admission, 11/1 for domestic and international students. *Application fee:* $45. *Application Contact:* Dr. John Stalvey, Dean, 907-786-1707, E-mail: jstalvey@uaa.alaska.edu. *Dean,* Dr. John Stalvey, 907-786-1707, E-mail: jstalvey@uaa.alaska.edu.

College of Business and Public Policy Expenses: Contact institution. *Financial support:* Research assistantships with full tuition reimbursements, career-related internships or fieldwork, Federal Work-Study, scholarships/grants, health care benefits, and unspecified assistantships available. Support available to part-time students. Financial award application deadline: 4/1; financial award applicants required to submit FAFSA. *Program availability:* Part-time, evening/weekend. Offers business administration (MBA); business and public policy (MBA, MPA, MS); global supply chain management (MS); public administration (MPA). *Application deadline:* For fall admission, 7/1 priority date for domestic and international students; for spring admission, 11/1 for domestic and international students. Applications are processed on a rolling basis. *Application fee:* $45. *Application Contact:* Karen Markel, Dean, 907-786-4121, Fax: 907-786-4131. *Dean,* Karen Markel, 907-786-4121, Fax: 907-786-4131.

College of Health Expenses: Contact institution. *Financial support:* Career-related internships or fieldwork, Federal Work-Study, and traineeships available. Support available to part-time students. Financial award application deadline: 4/1; financial award applicants required to submit FAFSA. *Program availability:* Part-time, evening/weekend. Offers health (MPA, MPH, MS, MSW, Certificate, Graduate Certificate); health administration (MPA); physicians assistant (MS); public health practice (MPH). *Application fee:* $45. *Application Contact:* Elisa Mattison, Director, Graduate School, 907-786-1096, Fax: 907-786-1791, E-mail: emattison@uaa.alaska.edu. *Dean,* William H. Hogan, 907-786-4407, Fax: 907-786-4440, E-mail: whhogan@uaa.alaska.edu.

School of Nursing Expenses: Contact institution. *Financial support:* Teaching assistantships, career-related internships or fieldwork, Federal Work-Study, and health care benefits available. Support available to part-time students. Financial award application deadline: 4/1; financial award applicants required to submit FAFSA. *Program availability:* Part-time, evening/weekend. Offers nursing (MS, DNP, Graduate Certificate). *Application deadline:* For fall admission, 3/1 for domestic students; for spring admission, 11/1 for domestic students. *Application fee:* $45. *Application Contact:* Jeffrey Jessee, Dean, 907-786-4406, Fax: 907-786-4440. *Dean,* Jeffrey Jessee, 907-786-4406, Fax: 907-786-4440.

School of Social Work Expenses: Contact institution. *Financial support:* Application deadline: 4/1; applicants required to submit FAFSA. *Program availability:* Part-time, evening/weekend, online learning. Offers children's mental health (Graduate Certificate); social work (MSW). *Application deadline:* For fall admission, 1/15 for domestic and international students. *Application fee:* $45. Electronic applications accepted. *Application Contact:* Jeffrey Jessee, Dean, 907-786-4406, Fax: 907-786-4440. *Dean,* Jeffrey Jessee, 907-786-4406, Fax: 907-786-4440.

School of Education Expenses: Contact institution. *Financial support:* Research assistantships, teaching assistantships, career-related internships or fieldwork, Federal Work-Study, scholarships/grants, traineeships, and unspecified assistantships available. Support available to part-time students. Financial award application deadline: 4/1; financial award applicants required to submit FAFSA. *Program availability:* Part-time. Offers early childhood special education (M Ed); education (M Ed, Certificate); educational leadership (M Ed); master teacher (M Ed); principal licensure (Certificate); special education (M Ed, Certificate); teaching (M Ed). *Application deadline:* For fall admission, 3/5 for domestic and international students; for spring admission, 10/15 for domestic and international students. *Application fee:* $45. *Application Contact:* Dr. Claudia Dybdahl, Interim Director, 907-786-4613. *Interim Director,* Dr. Claudia Dybdahl, 907-786-4613.

UNIVERSITY OF ALASKA FAIRBANKS, Fairbanks, AK 99775-7520

General Information State-supported, coed, university. *Graduate housing:* Rooms and/or apartments available on a first-come, first-served basis to single and married students. Housing application deadline: 8/1. *Research affiliation:* Institute of Northern Forestry, Alaska Cooperative Fishery and Wildlife Research Unit.

GRADUATE UNITS

College of Engineering and Mines *Program availability:* Part-time. Offers civil engineering (MS); computer science (MS); design and construction management (Graduate Certificate); electrical engineering (MEE, MS); engineering (PhD); engineering and mines (MCE, MEE, MS, PhD, Graduate Certificate); environmental engineering (PhD); geological engineering (MS); mechanical engineering (MS); mineral preparation engineering (MS); mining engineering (MS); petroleum engineering (MS). Electronic applications accepted.

College of Fisheries and Ocean Sciences *Program availability:* Part-time. Offers fisheries (MS, PhD); fisheries and ocean sciences (MS, PhD); marine biology (MS, PhD); oceanography (MS, PhD). Electronic applications accepted.

College of Liberal Arts *Program availability:* Part-time, 100% online, blended/hybrid learning. Offers anthropology (MA, PhD); applied linguistics (MA); Arctic policy (MA); art (MFA); ceramics (MFA); clinical-community psychology (PhD); computer art (MFA); creative writing (MFA); cross-cultural studies (MA); drawing (MFA); environmental politics and policy (MA); justice (MA); liberal arts (MA, MFA, MM, PhD); literature (MA); music (MM); Northern history (MA); painting (MFA); photography (MFA); printmaking (MFA); professional communication (MA); sculpture (MFA). Electronic applications accepted.

College of Natural Sciences and Mathematics *Program availability:* Part-time. Offers atmospheric science (MS, PhD); biochemistry and neuroscience (PhD); biological sciences (MS, PhD); chemistry (MA, MS); computational physics (MS); environmental chemistry (PhD); geophysics (MS); mathematics (PhD); natural sciences and mathematics (MA, MS, PhD, Graduate Certificate); physics (MS, PhD); space physics (MS); statistics (MS, Graduate Certificate); wildlife biology and conservation (MS). Electronic applications accepted.

College of Rural and Community Development *Program availability:* Part-time, 100% online, blended/hybrid learning. Offers rural and community development (MA); rural development (MA). Electronic applications accepted.

Graduate School for Interdisciplinary Studies *Program availability:* Part-time. Offers indigenous studies (PhD); interdisciplinary studies (MA, MS, PhD). Electronic applications accepted.

School of Education *Program availability:* 100% online, blended/hybrid learning. Offers community counseling (M Ed); education (M Ed, Graduate Certificate); special education (M Ed). Electronic applications accepted.

School of Management *Program availability:* Part-time, 100% online, blended/hybrid learning. Offers capital markets (MBA); general management (MBA); management (MBA, MS, MSDM); resource and applied economics (MS); security and disaster management (MSDM). Electronic applications accepted.

School of Natural Resources and Extension *Program availability:* Part-time. Offers natural resources and sustainability (PhD); natural resources management (MS). Electronic applications accepted.

UNIVERSITY OF ALASKA SOUTHEAST, Juneau, AK 99801

General Information State-supported, coed, comprehensive institution. *Graduate housing:* Rooms and/or apartments available on a first-come, first-served basis to single and married students. Housing application deadline: 5/1. *Research affiliation:* National Park Service (environmental resources, cultural studies), North Pacific Research Board (marine biology, oceanography), U.S. Department of Education (DOE) (teaching, early childhood education), National Science Foundation (marine biology), U.S. Department of Agriculture (USDA) (forest service), Alaska Department of Education (teaching).

GRADUATE UNITS

Graduate Programs *Program availability:* Part-time, evening/weekend, online learning. Offers educational leadership (M Ed); elementary education (MAT); learning design and technology (M Ed); mathematics education (M Ed); public administration (MPA); reading specialist (M Ed); secondary education (MAT); special education (M Ed, MAT). Electronic applications accepted.

UNIVERSITY OF ALBERTA, Edmonton, AB T6G 2E1, Canada

General Information Province-supported, coed, university. CGS member. *Graduate housing:* Rooms and/or apartments available on a first-come, first-served basis to single and married students.

GRADUATE UNITS

Faculty of Extension Offers communications and technology (MA).

Faculty of Graduate Studies and Research *Program availability:* Part-time, evening/weekend. Offers accounting (PhD); adult education (M Ed, Ed D, PhD); agricultural economics (M Ag, M Sc, PhD); agricultural, food and nutritional science (M Ag, M Eng, M Sc, PhD); agroforestry (M Ag, M Sc, MF); ancient history (PhD); anthropology (MA, PhD); applied linguistics (Germanic, Romance, Slavic) (MA); applied mathematics (M Sc, PhD); applied music (M Mus); astrophysics (M Sc, PhD); biostatistics (M Sc); business administration (Exec MBA, MBA); chemical engineering (M Eng, M Sc, PhD); chemistry (M Sc, PhD); Chinese literature (MA); choral conducting (M Mus); classical archaeology (MA, PhD); classical literature (PhD); classics (MA); communications (M Eng, M Sc, PhD); communications and technology (MACT); composition (M Mus); computer engineering (M Eng, M Sc, PhD); computing science (M Sc, PhD); condensed matter (M Sc, PhD); conservation biology (M Sc, PhD); construction engineering and management (M Eng, M Sc, PhD); counseling psychology (M Ed, PhD); criminal justice (MA); demography (MA, PhD); design (MFA); directing (MFA); drama (MA); drawing (MFA); earth and atmospheric sciences (M Sc, MA, PhD); East Asian interdisciplinary studies (MA); economics (MA, PhD); economics and finance (MA); educational administration and leadership (M Ed, Ed D, PhD, Postgraduate Diploma); educational psychology (M Ed, PhD); electromagnetics (M Eng, M Sc, PhD); elementary education (M Ed, Ed D, PhD); engineering management (M Eng); English (MA, PhD); environmental and natural resource economics (PhD); environmental biology and ecology (M Sc, PhD); environmental engineering (M Eng, M Sc, PhD); environmental science (M Sc, PhD); experimental linguistics (M Sc, PhD); family ecology and practice (M Sc, PhD); finance (PhD); First Nations education (M Ed, Ed D, PhD); forest biology and management (M Sc, PhD); forest economics (M Ag, M Sc, PhD); French language, literatures and linguistics (PhD); French language, literatures, and linguistics (MA); geoenvironmental engineering (M Eng, M Sc, PhD); geophysics (M Sc, PhD); geotechnical engineering (M Eng, M Sc, PhD); Germanic languages, literatures and linguistics (PhD); Germanic languages, literatures, and linguistics (MA); history (MA, PhD); history of art, design, and visual culture (MA); human resources/industrial relations (PhD); industrial design (M Des); instructional technology (M Ed); international business (MBA); Italian studies (MA); Japanese literature (MA); land reclamation and remediation (M Sc, PhD); leisure and sport management (MBA); management science (PhD); marketing (PhD); materials engineering (M Eng, M Sc, PhD); mathematical finance (M Sc, PhD); mathematical physics (M Sc, PhD); mathematics (M Sc, PhD); mechanical engineering (M Eng, M Sc, PhD); medical physics (M Sc, PhD); microbiology and biotechnology (M Sc, PhD); mining engineering (M Eng, M Sc, PhD); molecular biology and genetics (M Sc, PhD); music (PhD); nanotechnology and microdevices (M Eng, M Sc, PhD); natural resources and energy (MBA); occupational therapy (M Sc, PhD); organ and choral conductors (D Mus); organizational analysis (PhD); painting (MFA); petroleum engineering (M Eng, M Sc, PhD); pharmacology (M Sc, PhD); pharmacy and pharmaceutical sciences (M Sc, PhD); philosophy (MA, PhD); physical education (M Sc); physical therapy (M Sc, PhD); physiology and cell biology (M Sc, PhD); piano (D Mus); plant biology (M Sc, PhD); political science (MA, PhD); power/power electronics (M Eng, M Sc, PhD); printmaking (MFA); process control (M Eng, M Sc, PhD); protected areas and wildlands management (M Sc, PhD); psychology (M Sc, MA, PhD); recreation and physical education (MA, PhD); rural sociology (M Ag, M Sc); school counseling (M Ed); school psychology (M Ed, PhD); sculpture (MFA); secondary education (M Ed, Ed D, PhD); Slavic languages and literatures (Russian, Ukrainian) (MA, PhD); Slavic linguistics (Russian, Ukrainian) (MA, PhD); sociology (MA, PhD); soil science (M Ag, M Sc, PhD); Spanish and Latin American studies (MA, PhD); special education (M Ed, PhD); special education-deafness studies (M Ed); speech pathology and audiology (PhD); speech-language pathology (M Sc); statistics (M Sc, PhD, Postgraduate Diploma); structural engineering (M Eng, M Sc, PhD); subatomic physics (M Sc, PhD); systematics and evolution (M Sc, PhD); systems (M Eng, M Sc, PhD); teaching English as a second language (M Ed); technology commercialization (MBA); textiles and clothing (M Sc, MA, PhD); theoretical, cultural and international studies in education (M Ed, Ed D, PhD); Ukrainian folklore (MA, PhD); visual communication design (M Des); water and land resources (M Ag, M Sc, PhD); water resources (M Eng, M Sc, PhD); welding (M Eng); wildlife ecology and management (M Sc, PhD). Electronic applications accepted.

Facultè Saint Jean *Program availability:* Part-time, evening/weekend, online learning. Offers education (M Ed).

Faculty of Nursing *Program availability:* Part-time. Offers nursing (MN, PhD).

Faculty of Rehabilitation Medicine Offers rehabilitation medicine (PhD). Electronic applications accepted.

School of Library and Information Studies Offers library and information studies (MLIS). Electronic applications accepted.

Faculty of Law *Program availability:* Part-time. Offers law (LL M, PhD). Electronic applications accepted.

Faculty of Medicine and Dentistry Offers dental hygiene (Diploma); dentistry (DDS); medicine and dentistry (M Sc, DDS, MD, PhD, Diploma); orthodontics (M Sc, PhD); TMD/orofacial pain (M Sc). Electronic applications accepted.

Graduate Programs in Medicine *Program availability:* Part-time. Offers biochemistry (M Sc, PhD); biomedical engineering (M Sc); cell and molecular biology (M Sc, PhD); medical genetics (M Sc, PhD); medical microbiology and immunology (M Sc, PhD); medical sciences (M Sc, PhD); medicine (M Sc, MD, PhD); neuroscience (M Sc, PhD); obstetrics and gynecology (MD); oncology (M Sc, PhD); ophthalmology (M Sc, PhD); pediatrics (M Sc, PhD); physiology (M Sc, PhD); psychiatry (M Sc, PhD); radiology and diagnostic imaging (M Sc); surgery (M Sc, PhD).

School of Public Health Offers clinical epidemiology (M Sc, MPH); environmental and occupational health (MPH); environmental health sciences (M Sc); epidemiology (M Sc); global health (M Sc, MPH); health policy and management (MPH); health policy research (M Sc); health technology assessment (MPH); occupational health (M Sc); population health (M Sc); public health (M Sc, MPH, PhD, Postgraduate Diploma); public health leadership (MPH); public health sciences (PhD); quantitative methods (MPH).

Centre for Health Promotion Studies *Program availability:* Part-time, online learning. Offers health promotion (M Sc, Postgraduate Diploma).

UNIVERSITY OF ANTELOPE VALLEY, Lancaster, CA 93534

General Information Proprietary, coed, comprehensive institution.

GRADUATE UNITS

Program in Business Management Offers business management (MS).

Program in Criminal Justice Offers criminal justice (MS).

THE UNIVERSITY OF ARIZONA, Tucson, AZ 85721

General Information State-supported, coed, university. CGS member. *Graduate housing:* Rooms and/or apartments available on a first-come, first-served basis to single students and available to married students. Housing application deadline: 5/1. *Research affiliation:* Smithsonian Astrophysical Observatory (astronomy), Research Corporation (astronomy), National Center for Atmospheric Research (atmospheric physics), Kitt Peak National Observatory (astronomy), Argonne National Laboratory (physics).

GRADUATE UNITS

College of Agriculture and Life Sciences *Program availability:* Part-time. Offers agricultural and biosystems engineering (MS, PhD); agricultural education (MAE, MS, Graduate Certificate); agriculture and life sciences (MAE, MHE Ed, MS, PhD, Graduate Certificate); animal sciences (MS, PhD); applied econometrics and data analytics (MS); applied economics and policy analysis (MS); arid lands resource sciences (PhD); nutritional sciences (MS, PhD); soil, water and environmental science (MS, PhD, Graduate Certificate). Electronic applications accepted.

School of Animal and Comparative Biomedical Sciences Offers animal and comparative biomedical sciences (MS, PhD). Electronic applications accepted.

School of Family and Consumer Sciences *Program availability:* Part-time. Offers family and consumer sciences (PhD). Electronic applications accepted.

School of Natural Resources and the Environment Offers ecology and management of rangelands (MS, PhD); natural resources (MS, PhD); water, society, and policy (MS); watershed management (MS, PhD). Electronic applications accepted.

School of Plant Sciences *Program availability:* Part-time. Offers plant pathology (MS, PhD); plant sciences (MS, PhD). Electronic applications accepted.

College of Architecture, Planning, and Landscape Architecture *Program availability:* Part-time. Offers architecture, planning, and landscape architecture (M Ar, M Arch, ML Arch, MRED, MS, PhD, Graduate Certificate); landscape architecture (ML Arch); planning (MS). Electronic applications accepted.

School of Architecture Offers architecture (M Arch, MS). Electronic applications accepted.

College of Education *Program availability:* Part-time, online learning. Offers counseling and mental health (MA); cross-categorical special education (MA); deaf and hard of hearing (MA); education (M Ed, MA, MS, Ed D, PhD, Certificate, Ed S); educational leadership (M Ed, Ed D, Ed S); educational psychology (MA, PhD); educational research methodology (Certificate); family studies and human development (M Ed); higher education (MA, PhD); language, reading and culture (MA, Ed D, PhD, Ed S); learning disabilities (MA); motivating learning environments (Certificate); reading instruction (Graduate Certificate); rehabilitation counseling (MA, PhD); school counseling (MA); school psychology (PhD, Ed S); severe and multiple disabilities (MA); special education (MA, PhD); teaching and teacher education (M Ed, MA, PhD); visual impairment (MA). Electronic applications accepted.

College of Engineering *Program availability:* Part-time, online learning. Offers aerospace engineering (MS, PhD); chemical engineering (MS, PhD); civil engineering and engineering mechanics (MS, PhD); electrical and computer engineering (MS, PhD); engineering (ME, MS, PhD, Certificate); engineering management (Graduate Certificate); environmental engineering (MS, PhD); industrial engineering (MS); materials science and engineering (MS, PhD); mechanical engineering (MS, PhD); mining and geological engineering (MS, PhD); mining engineering (Certificate); systems and industrial engineering (MS, PhD); systems engineering (MS, PhD, Graduate Certificate). Electronic applications accepted.

College of Fine Arts *Program availability:* Part-time. Offers fine arts (MA, MFA, MM, PhD, Graduate Certificate). Electronic applications accepted.

School of Art *Program availability:* Part-time. Offers art (MA, MFA, PhD); art education (MA); art history (MA); art history and education (PhD); history and theory of art (PhD). Electronic applications accepted.

School of Dance Offers dance (MFA). Electronic applications accepted.

School of Music *Program availability:* Part-time. Offers composition (MM, DMA); conducting (MM, DMA); ethnomusicology (MM); music (MM, PhD); music education (MM, PhD); music theory (MM, PhD); musical arts (DMA); musicology (MM); performance (MM, DMA). Electronic applications accepted.

School of Theatre, Film and Television Offers theatre, film and television (MFA). Electronic applications accepted.

College of Humanities *Program availability:* Part-time. Offers classics (MA); creative writing (MFA); East Asian studies (MA, PhD); English (MA, PhD); English language/linguistics (MA, PhD); ESL (MA); French (MA); German (MA); humanities (MA,

MFA, PhD); rhetoric, composition and the teaching of English (MA, PhD); Russian (MA); Spanish (MA, PhD); teaching English as a second language (Graduate Certificate); transcultural German (PhD). Electronic applications accepted.

College of Medicine *Program availability:* Part-time. Offers cellular and molecular medicine (MS, PhD); immunobiology (PhD); medical sciences (MS, PhD); medicine (MS, MD, PhD, Graduate Certificate). MD program open only to state residents.

College of Nursing *Program availability:* Part-time, online learning. Offers health care informatics (Certificate); nurse practitioner (MS); nursing (DNP, PhD). Electronic applications accepted.

College of Optical Sciences *Program availability:* Part-time. Offers optical sciences (MS, PhD, Graduate Certificate). Electronic applications accepted.

College of Pharmacy Offers medical pharmacology (MS, PhD); medicinal and natural products chemistry (MS, PhD); perfusion science (MS); pharmaceutical economics (MS, PhD); pharmaceutics and pharmacokinetics (MS, PhD); pharmacy (MS, PhD, Pharm D).

College of Science *Program availability:* Part-time. Offers applied biosciences (PSM); astronomy (PhD); atmospheric sciences (MS, PhD); biochemistry (PhD); biochemistry and molecular and cellular biology (PhD); chemistry (MA, MS, PhD); computer science (MS, PhD); ecology and evolutionary biology (MS, PhD); geosciences (MS, PSM, PhD); hydrology (PhD); mathematics (MA, MS, PhD); medical physics (PSM); physics (PhD); planetary sciences (MS, PhD); psychology (MA, PhD); science (MS, PSM, PhD, Certificate, Graduate Certificate); secondary mathematics education (MA); speech, language, and hearing sciences (MS, PhD, Certificate). Electronic applications accepted.

College of Social and Behavioral Sciences *Program availability:* Part-time, evening/weekend. Offers communication (MA, PhD); gender and women's studies (MA, PhD, Certificate); history (MA, PhD, Graduate Certificate); human language technology (MS); linguistics and anthropology (PhD); Native American linguistics (MA); philosophy (MA, PhD); political science (MA, PhD); public administration (MPA); public administration and policy (PhD); social and behavioral sciences (MA, MPA, MS, PhD, Certificate, Graduate Certificate); sociology (MA, PhD). Electronic applications accepted.

Center for Latin American Studies *Program availability:* Part-time. Offers Latin American studies (MA). Electronic applications accepted.

School of Anthropology *Program availability:* Part-time. Offers anthropology (MA, MS, PhD, Graduate Certificate). Electronic applications accepted.

School of Geography and Development *Program availability:* Part-time. Offers geographic information systems technology (MA); geography (PhD). Electronic applications accepted.

School of Information Resources and Library Science *Program availability:* Part-time. Offers information resources and library science (MA, PhD). Electronic applications accepted.

School of Journalism *Program availability:* Part-time. Offers international journalism studies (MA); professional journalism (MA). Electronic applications accepted.

School of Middle Eastern and North African Studies *Program availability:* Part-time, evening/weekend. Offers Middle Eastern and North African studies (MA, PhD, Graduate Certificate). Electronic applications accepted.

Eller College of Management *Program availability:* Evening/weekend. Offers accounting (M Ac, MS); business administration (MBA); economics (MA, PhD); finance (MS); management (M Ac, MA, MBA, MS, PhD, Graduate Certificate); management and organization (MS, PhD); management information systems (MS, Graduate Certificate); marketing (MBA, MS, PhD). Electronic applications accepted.

Graduate Interdisciplinary Programs *Program availability:* Part-time. Offers American Indian studies (MA, PhD); applied mathematics (MS, PMS, PhD); biomedical engineering (MS, PhD); cancer biology (PhD); entomology (MA); entomology and insect science (MS, PhD); genetics (MS, PhD); mathematical sciences (PMS); neuroscience (PhD); physiological sciences (MS, PhD); second language acquisition and teaching (PhD); statistics (MS, PhD).

James E. Rogers College of Law Offers indigenous peoples law and policy (LL M); international trade and business law (LL M); law (JD). Electronic applications accepted.

Mel and Enid Zuckerman College of Public Health Offers biostatistics (MS, PhD); epidemiology (MS, PhD); public health (MPH, MS, MSPH, Dr PH, PhD, Graduate Certificate). Electronic applications accepted.

★ UNIVERSITY OF ARKANSAS, Fayetteville, AR 72701

General Information State-supported, coed, university. CGS member. *Enrollment:* 27,558 graduate, professional, and undergraduate students; 2,060 full-time matriculated graduate/professional students (1,040 women), 2,101 part-time matriculated graduate/professional students (1,046 women). *Graduate faculty:* 685 full-time (216 women), 47 part-time/adjunct (32 women). Tuition, state resident: full-time $3782. Tuition, nonresident: full-time $10,238. *Graduate housing:* Room and/or apartments available on a first-come, first-served basis to single students; on-campus housing not available to married students. *Student services:* Campus employment opportunities, campus safety program, career counseling, exercise/wellness program, free psychological counseling, international student services, low-cost health insurance, multicultural affairs office, services for students with disabilities, teacher training, writing training. *Library facilities:* David W. Mullins Library plus 4 others. *Collection:* Books: 1.7 million (physical), 659,516 (digital/electronic); Serial titles: 3,154 (physical), 92,699 (digital/electronic); Databases: 332. Weekly public service hours: 109; students can reserve study rooms. *Research affiliation:* Southern Regional Education Board, Southeastern Universities Research Association, Southern Regional Education Board Uncommon Facilities Program, Oak Ridge Associated Universities, Science Coalition, National Minority Graduate Feeder Project.

Computer facilities: Computer purchase and lease plans are available. 675 computers available on campus for general student use. A campuswide network can be accessed from student residence rooms and from off campus. Online class registration is available.

Website: http://www.uark.edu/

GRADUATE UNITS

Graduate School Students: 2,060 full-time (1,040 women), 2,101 part-time (1,046 women); includes 627 minority (227 Black or African American, non-Hispanic/Latino; 54 American Indian or Alaska Native, non-Hispanic/Latino; 74 Asian, non-Hispanic/Latino; 189 Hispanic/Latino; 5 Native Hawaiian or other Pacific Islander, non-Hispanic/Latino; 78 Two or more races, non-Hispanic/Latino), 726 international. Average age 33. 4,608 applicants, 46% accepted, 1318 enrolled. *Faculty:* 685 full-time (216 women), 47 part-time/adjunct (32 women). Expenses: Contact institution. *Financial support:* In 2017–18, 761 research assistantships, 484 teaching assistantships with full tuition reimbursements were awarded; fellowships with tuition reimbursements, career-related internships or fieldwork, Federal Work-Study, institutionally sponsored loans, scholarships/grants, traineeships, and unspecified assistantships also available. Support available to part-time students. Financial award application deadline: 4/1; financial award applicants required to submit FAFSA. In 2017, 657 master's, 131 doctorates, 20 other advanced degrees awarded. *Program availability:* Part-time, online learning. Offers cell and molecular biology (MS, PhD); comparative literature and cultural studies (MA, PhD); environmental dynamics (PhD); microelectronics and photonics (MS, PhD); public policy (PhD); space and planetary sciences (MS, PhD). *Application deadline:* For fall admission, 8/1 for domestic students, 4/1 for international students; for spring admission, 12/1 for domestic students, 10/1 for international students; for summer admission, 4/15 for domestic students, 3/1 for international students. Applications are processed on a rolling basis. *Application fee:* $60. Electronic applications accepted. *Application Contact:* Lynn Mosesso, Director, Graduate and International Recruitment and Admissions, 479-575-6247, Fax: 479-575-5908, E-mail: mosesso@uark.edu. *Dean,* Dr. Kim L. Needy, 479-575-4401, Fax: 479-575-5908, E-mail: kneedy@uark.edu.

College of Education and Health Professions Expenses: Contact institution. *Financial support:* In 2017–18, 110 research assistantships, 15 teaching assistantships were awarded; fellowships with tuition reimbursements, career-related internships or fieldwork, and Federal Work-Study also available. Support available to part-time students. Financial award application deadline: 4/1; financial award applicants required to submit FAFSA. In 2017, 399 master's, 43 doctorates awarded. Offers adult and lifelong learning (M Ed, Ed D); athletic training (MAT); childhood education (MAT); communication disorders (MS); community health promotion (MS, PhD); counselor education (MS, PhD); curriculum and instruction (M Ed, MAT, MS, Ed D, PhD, Ed S); education and health professions (M Ed, MAT, MAT, MS, MSN, Ed D, PhD, Ed S); education policy (PhD); educational leadership (M Ed, Ed D, Ed S); educational statistics and research methods (MS, PhD); educational technology (M Ed); health science (MS, PhD); higher education (M Ed, Ed D, Ed S); human resource and workforce development education (M Ed, Ed D); kinesiology (MS, PhD); middle-level education (MAT); nursing (MSN); physical education (M Ed, MAT); recreation and sports management (M Ed, Ed D); rehabilitation (MS, PhD); secondary education (M Ed, MAT, Ed S); special education (M Ed, MAT); vocational education (M Ed, Ed D). *Application deadline:* For fall admission, 8/1 for domestic students, 4/1 for international students; for spring admission, 12/1 for domestic students, 10/1 for international students; for summer admission, 4/15 for domestic students, 3/1 for international students. Applications are processed on a rolling basis. *Application fee:* $60. Electronic applications accepted. *Dean,* Dr. Michael T. Miller, 479-575-3582, Fax: 479-575-3119, E-mail: mtmille@uark.edu.

College of Engineering Expenses: Contact institution. *Financial support:* In 2017–18, 198 research assistantships, 21 teaching assistantships were awarded; fellowships with tuition reimbursements, career-related internships or fieldwork, and Federal Work-Study also available. Support available to part-time students. Financial award application deadline: 4/1; financial award applicants required to submit FAFSA. In 2017, 296 master's, 22 doctorates awarded. Offers biological and agricultural engineering (MSE, PhD); biological engineering (MSBE); biomedical engineering (MSBME); chemical engineering (MS Ch E, MSE, PhD); civil engineering (MSCE, MSE, PhD); computer engineering (MS Cmp E, MSE, PhD); computer science (MS, PhD); electrical engineering (MSEE, PhD); engineering (MS, MS Cmp E, MS Ch E, MS En E, MS Tc E, MSBE, MSBME, MSCE, MSE, MSEE, MSIE, MSME, MSOR, MSTE, PhD); environmental engineering (MS En E, MSE); industrial engineering (MSE, MSIE, PhD); mechanical engineering (MSE, MSME, PhD); operations management (MS); operations research (MSE, MSOR); telecommunications engineering (MS Tc E); transportation engineering (MSE, MSTE). *Application deadline:* For fall admission, 8/1 for domestic students, 4/1 for international students; for spring admission, 12/1 for domestic students, 10/1 for international students; for summer admission, 4/15 for domestic students, 3/1 for international students. Applications are processed on a rolling basis. *Application fee:* $60. Electronic applications accepted. *Application Contact:* Dr. Norman Dennis, Associate Dean, 479-575-3052, E-mail: ndennis@uark.edu. *Dean,* Dr. John R. English, 479-575-3054, Fax: 479-575-4346, E-mail: jre@uark.edu.

Dale Bumpers College of Agricultural, Food and Life Sciences 164 applicants, 59% accepted. Expenses: Contact institution. *Financial support:* In 2017–18, 167 research assistantships, 7 teaching assistantships were awarded; fellowships with tuition reimbursements, career-related internships or fieldwork, Federal Work-Study, scholarships/grants, and unspecified assistantships also available. Support available to part-time students. Financial award application deadline: 4/1; financial award applicants required to submit FAFSA. In 2017, 97 master's, 24 doctorates awarded. Offers agricultural and extension education (MS); agricultural economics and agribusiness (MS); agricultural, food and life sciences (MS, PhD); agronomy (MS, PhD); animal science (MS, PhD); entomology (MS, PhD); food safety (MS); food science (MS, PhD); horticulture (MS); human environmental sciences (MS); plant pathology (MS); plant science (PhD); poultry science (MS, PhD). *Application deadline:* For fall admission, 8/1 for domestic students, 4/1 for international students; for spring admission, 12/1 for domestic students, 10/1 for international students; for summer admission, 4/15 for domestic students, 3/1 for international students. Applications are processed on a rolling basis. *Application fee:* $60. Electronic applications accepted. *Interim Dean,* Dr. Lona J. Robertson, 479-575-2252, Fax: 479-575-7273, E-mail: ljrobert@uark.edu.

J. William Fulbright College of Arts and Sciences Expenses: Contact institution. *Financial support:* In 2017–18, 143 research assistantships, 373 teaching assistantships with full tuition reimbursements were awarded; fellowships, career-related internships or fieldwork, Federal Work-Study, institutionally sponsored loans, and traineeships also available. Support available to part-time students. Financial award application deadline: 4/1; financial award applicants required to submit FAFSA. In 2017, 206 master's, 47 doctorates awarded. Offers anthropology (MA, PhD); applied physics (MS); art (MFA); arts and sciences (MA, MFA, MM, MPA, MS, MSW, PhD); biological sciences (MA, MS, PhD); chemistry (MS, PhD); communication (MA); creative writing (MFA); English (MA, MFA, PhD); French (MA); geography (MA); geology (MS); German (MA); history (MA, PhD); journalism (MA); mathematics (MS, PhD); music (MM); philosophy (MA, PhD); physics (MS, PhD); physics education (MA); political science (MA); psychology (MA, PhD); public administration (MPA); secondary mathematics (MA); social work (MSW); sociology (MA); Spanish (MA); statistics (MS); theatre (MA, MFA). *Application deadline:* For fall admission, 8/1 for domestic students, 4/1 for international students; for spring admission, 12/1 for domestic students, 10/1 for international students; for summer admission, 4/15 for domestic students, 3/1 for international students. Applications are processed on a rolling basis. *Application fee:* $60. Electronic applications accepted. *Application Contact:* Dr. Steven Beaupre, Associate Dean, 479-575-7561, E-mail: sbeaupre@uark.edu. *Dean,* Dr. Todd G. Shields, 479-575-4804, Fax: 479-575-2642, E-mail: tshield@uark.edu.

Sam M. Walton College of Business Administration Expenses: Contact institution. *Financial support:* In 2017–18, 64 research assistantships, 17 teaching assistantships were awarded; fellowships, career-related internships or fieldwork, and

Federal Work-Study also available. Support available to part-time students. Financial award application deadline: 4/1; financial award applicants required to submit FAFSA. In 2017, 185 master's, 8 doctorates awarded. Offers accounting (M Acc); business administration (M Acc, MA, MBA, MIS, PhD); economics (MA, PhD); information systems (MIS). *Application deadline:* For fall admission, 8/1 for domestic students, 4/1 for international students; for spring admission, 12/1 for domestic students, 10/1 for international students; for summer admission, 4/15 for domestic students, 3/1 for international students. *Application fee:* $60. Electronic applications accepted. *Application Contact:* Rebel Smith, Assistant Director of Marketing and Recruiting, 479-575-6123, E-mail: gsb@walton.uark.edu. *Dean*, Dr. Matt Waller, 479-575-5949, Fax: 479-575-4435, E-mail: mwaller@walton.uark.edu.

School of Law Expenses: Contact institution. *Financial support:* In 2017–18, fellowships with full tuition reimbursements (averaging $6,000 per year), 8 research assistantships (averaging $2,500 per year) were awarded; teaching assistantships, career-related internships or fieldwork, Federal Work-Study, and scholarships/grants also available. Support available to part-time students. Financial award application deadline: 4/1; financial award applicants required to submit FAFSA. In 2017, 104 doctorates awarded. Offers agricultural law (LL M); law (JD). *Application deadline:* For fall admission, 8/1 for domestic students, 4/1 for international students; for spring admission, 12/1 for domestic students, 10/1 for international students; for summer admission, 4/15 for domestic students, 3/1 for international students. Applications are processed on a rolling basis. *Application fee:* $60. Electronic applications accepted. *Dean*, Stacy L. Leeds, 479-575-5601, Fax: 479-575-3320, E-mail: sleeds@uark.edu.

See Display below and Close-Up on page 881.

UNIVERSITY OF ARKANSAS AT LITTLE ROCK, Little Rock, AR 72204-1099

General Information State-supported, coed, university. CGS member. *Graduate housing:* Room and/or apartments available on a first-come, first-served basis to single students; on-campus housing not available to married students. Housing application deadline: 9/1.

GRADUATE UNITS

Graduate School *Program availability:* Part-time, evening/weekend, online learning. Electronic applications accepted.

Clinton School of Public Service Offers public service (MPS, Graduate Certificate).

College of Arts, Letters, and Sciences *Program availability:* Part-time, evening/weekend. Offers applied statistics (Graduate Certificate); art education (MA); art history (MA); arts, letters, and sciences (MA, MS, Graduate Certificate); biology (MS); chemistry (MA, MS); mathematical sciences (MS); philosophy and interdisciplinary studies (MA); public history (MA); second languages (MA); studio art (MA).

College of Business *Program availability:* Part-time, evening/weekend. Offers business administration (MBA); business information systems (MS, Graduate Certificate); management (Graduate Certificate).

College of Education and Health Professions *Program availability:* Part-time, evening/weekend. Offers administration (MA); adult education (M Ed); clinical social work (MSW); college student affairs (MA); counselor education (M Ed); curriculum and instruction (M Ed); education and health professions (M Ed, MA, MS, MSW, Ed D, Ed S, Graduate Certificate); educational administration and supervision (M Ed, Ed D, Ed S); exercise science (MS); gerontology (Graduate Certificate); gifted and talented education (M Ed, Graduate Certificate); health education and promotion (MS); health professions teaching and learning (MA); higher education (MA, Ed D); learning systems technology education (M Ed); management and community practice (MSW); middle childhood education (M Ed); reading education (M Ed, PhD, Ed S); rehabilitation counseling (MA, Graduate Certificate); rehabilitation for the blind: orientation and mobility (MA); secondary education (M Ed); social work (MSW, Graduate Certificate); special education (M Ed); sport management (MS); two-year college teaching (MA).

College of Social Sciences and Communication *Program availability:* Part-time, evening/weekend. Offers applied communication studies (MA); applied psychology (MAP); conflict mediation (Graduate Certificate); criminal justice (MA, MS, PhD); mass communication (MA); nonprofit management (Graduate Certificate); professional and technical writing (MA); public administration (MPA); social sciences and communication (MA, MAP, MPA, MS, PhD, Graduate Certificate).

George W. Donaghey College of Engineering and Information Technology *Program availability:* Part-time, evening/weekend. Offers applied science (MS, PhD); bioinformatics (MS, PhD); computer science (MS, PhD); construction management (MS); engineering and information technology (MS, PhD, Graduate Certificate); geospatial technology (Graduate Certificate); information quality (MS, PhD, Graduate Certificate); systems engineering (MS, PhD, Graduate Certificate); technology innovation (Graduate Certificate).

William H. Bowen School of Law *Program availability:* Part-time, evening/weekend. Offers law (JD). Electronic applications accepted.

UNIVERSITY OF ARKANSAS AT MONTICELLO, Monticello, AR 71656

General Information State-supported, coed, comprehensive institution. *Graduate housing:* Rooms and/or apartments guaranteed to single students and available on a first-come, first-served basis to married students. Housing application deadline: 8/15.

GRADUATE UNITS

School of Education *Program availability:* Part-time, evening/weekend, online learning. Offers education (M Ed, MAT); educational leadership (M Ed). Electronic applications accepted.

School of Forest Resources *Program availability:* Part-time. Offers forest resources (MS). Electronic applications accepted.

UNIVERSITY OF ARKANSAS AT PINE BLUFF, Pine Bluff, AR 71601-2799

General Information State-supported, coed, comprehensive institution. *Graduate housing:* Room and/or apartments available on a first-come, first-served basis to single students; on-campus housing not available to married students. Housing application deadline: 8/1.

GRADUATE UNITS

Division of Graduate Studies and Continuing Education Offers addiction studies (MS).

School of Agriculture, Fisheries and Human Sciences Offers agricultural regulations (MS); aquaculture and fisheries (MS, PhD).

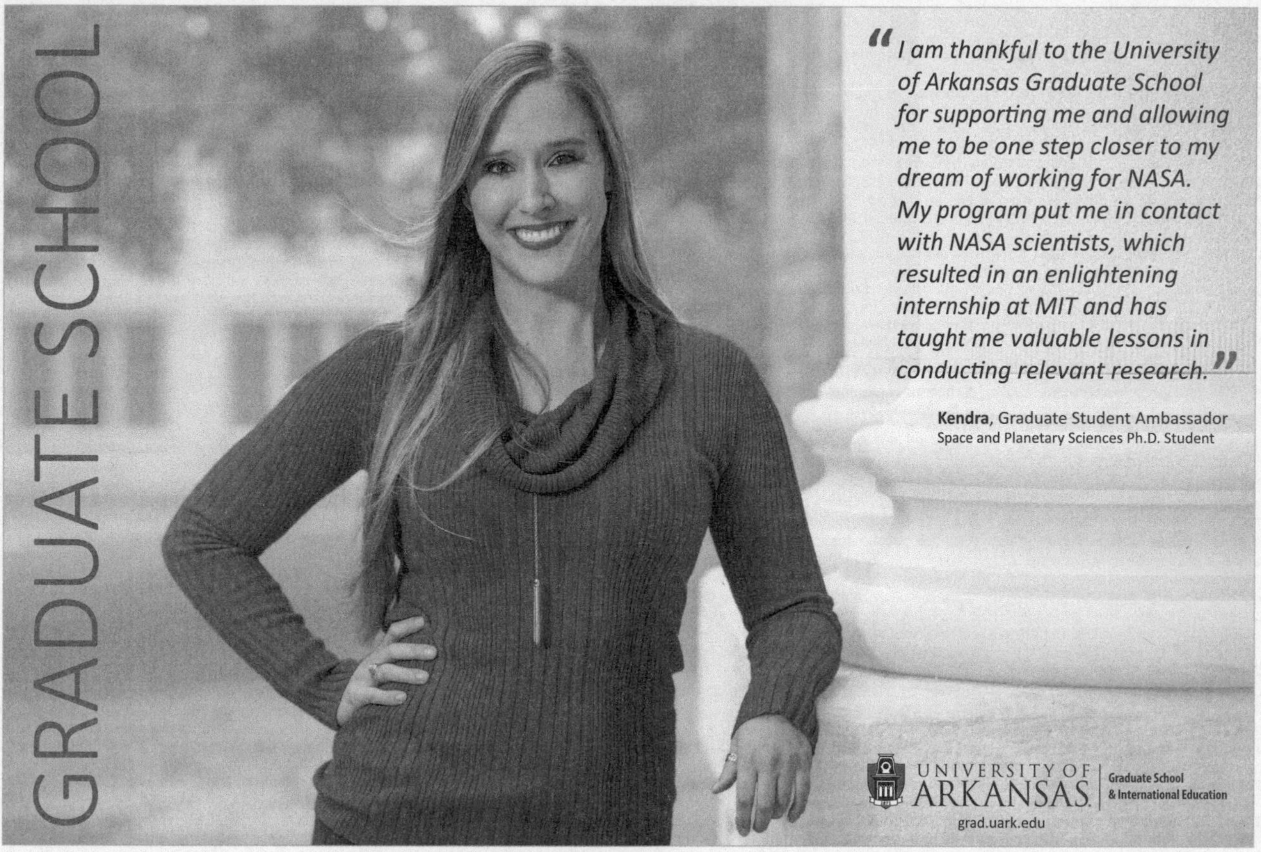
GRADUATE SCHOOL
"I am thankful to the University of Arkansas Graduate School for supporting me and allowing me to be one step closer to my dream of working for NASA. My program put me in contact with NASA scientists, which resulted in an enlightening internship at MIT and has taught me valuable lessons in conducting relevant research."
Kendra, Graduate Student Ambassador
Space and Planetary Sciences Ph.D. Student
UNIVERSITY OF ARKANSAS
Graduate School & International Education
grad.uark.edu

School of Education *Program availability:* Part-time, evening/weekend. Offers elementary education (M Ed); secondary education (M Ed); teaching (MAT).

UNIVERSITY OF ARKANSAS FOR MEDICAL SCIENCES, Little Rock, AR 72205-7199

General Information State-supported, coed, university. *Graduate housing:* Rooms and/or apartments available on a first-come, first-served basis to single and married students. Housing application deadline: 7/15. *Research affiliation:* National Center for Toxicological Research, Veterans Administration Hospital, Oak Ridge Associated Universities, Arkansas Children's Hospital.

GRADUATE UNITS

College of Health Professions *Program availability:* Part-time, online learning. Offers audiology (Au D); communication sciences and disorders (MS, PhD); genetic counseling (MS); nuclear medicine advanced associate (MIS); physician assistant studies (MPAS); radiologist assistant (MIS). PhD offered through consortium with University of Arkansas at Little Rock and University of Central Arkansas. Electronic applications accepted.

College of Medicine Offers medicine (MD). Electronic applications accepted.

College of Nursing *Program availability:* Part-time. Offers nursing (PhD).

College of Pharmacy Offers pharmacy (MS, Pharm D). Electronic applications accepted.

College of Public Health *Program availability:* Part-time. Offers biostatistics (MPH); environmental and occupational health (MPH, Certificate); epidemiology (MPH, PhD); health behavior and health education (MPH); health policy and management (MPH); health promotion and prevention research (PhD); health services administration (MHSA); health systems research (PhD); public health (Certificate); public health leadership (Dr PH). Electronic applications accepted.

Graduate School *Program availability:* Part-time. Offers biochemistry and molecular biology (MS, PhD); bioinformatics (MS, PhD); cellular physiology and molecular biophysics (MS, PhD); clinical nutrition (MS); interdisciplinary biomedical sciences (MS, PhD, Certificate); interdisciplinary toxicology (MS); microbiology and immunology (PhD); neurobiology and developmental sciences (PhD); pharmacology (PhD). Bioinformatics programs hosted jointly with the University of Arkansas at Little Rock. Electronic applications accepted.

UNIVERSITY OF ARKANSAS–FORT SMITH, Fort Smith, AR 72913-3649

General Information State and locally supported, coed, comprehensive institution.

GRADUATE UNITS

Program in Healthcare Administration *Program availability:* Online learning. Offers healthcare administration (MS).

UNIVERSITY OF BALTIMORE, Baltimore, MD 21201-5779

General Information State-supported, coed, comprehensive institution. *Graduate housing:* On-campus housing not available.

GRADUATE UNITS

Graduate School *Program availability:* Part-time, evening/weekend, online learning. Electronic applications accepted.

College of Public Affairs Offers criminal justice (MS); health systems management (MS); human services administration (MS); negotiations and conflict management (MS); public administration (MPA, DPA); public affairs (MPA, MS, DPA).

Merrick School of Business *Program availability:* Part-time, evening/weekend, online learning. Offers accounting and business advisory services (MS); accounting fundamentals (Graduate Certificate); business (MBA, MS, Graduate Certificate); business/finance (MS); forensic accounting (Graduate Certificate); global leadership (MS); innovation management and technology commercialization (MS); taxation (MS). Electronic applications accepted.

Yale Gordon College of Arts and Sciences *Program availability:* Part-time, evening/weekend. Offers arts and sciences (MA, MFA, MS, DS); counseling psychology (MS); creative writing and publishing arts (MFA); information and interaction design (DS); integrated design (MA, MFA); interaction design and information architecture (MS); legal studies (MA). Electronic applications accepted.

Joint University of Baltimore/Towson University (UB/Towson) MBA Program *Program availability:* Part-time, evening/weekend, online learning. Offers business administration (MBA). MBA/MSN, MBA/Pharm D offered jointly with University of Maryland, Baltimore.

School of Law *Program availability:* Part-time, evening/weekend. Offers business law (JD); criminal practice (JD); estate planning (JD); family law (JD); intellectual property (JD); international law (JD); law (JD); law of the United States (LL M); litigation and advocacy (JD); public service (JD); real estate practice (JD); taxation (LL M). JD/MS offered jointly with Division of Criminology, Criminal Justice, and Social Policy; JD/PhD with University of Maryland, Baltimore. Electronic applications accepted.

UNIVERSITY OF BRIDGEPORT, Bridgeport, CT 06604

General Information Independent, coed, comprehensive institution. CGS member. *Graduate housing:* Rooms and/or apartments guaranteed to single students and available on a first-come, first-served basis to married students. Housing application deadline: 8/15. *Research affiliation:* Connecticut Medicine Research Consortia, Marine Biology Station, Burndy Library.

GRADUATE UNITS

Acupuncture Institute *Program availability:* Part-time. Offers acupuncture (MS). Electronic applications accepted.

College of Chiropractic Offers chiropractic (DC). Electronic applications accepted.

College of Naturopathic Medicine Offers naturopathic medicine (ND). Electronic applications accepted.

College of Public and International Affairs *Program availability:* Part-time, evening/weekend. Offers East Asian and Pacific Rim studies (MA); global development and peace (MA); global media and communication studies (MA).

Fones School of Dental Hygiene *Program availability:* Part-time, evening/weekend, online learning. Offers dental hygiene (MS).

Nutrition Institute *Program availability:* Part-time, evening/weekend, online learning. Offers human nutrition (MS). Electronic applications accepted.

Physician Assistant Institute Offers physician assistant (MS).

School of Arts and Sciences *Program availability:* Part-time, evening/weekend. Offers arts and sciences (MS); clinical mental health counseling (MS); college student personnel (MS); community counseling (MS); human resource development (MS); human service (MS). Electronic applications accepted.

School of Business *Program availability:* Part-time, evening/weekend. Offers accounting (MBA); finance (MBA); general business (MBA); global financial services (MBA); human resource management (MBA); information systems and knowledge management (MBA); international business (MBA); management (MBA); marketing (MBA); operations management (MBA); small business and entrepreneurship (MBA); specialized business (MBA). Electronic applications accepted.

School of Education *Program availability:* Part-time, evening/weekend. Offers education (MS, Ed D, Diploma); educational management (Ed D, Diploma); elementary education (MS, Diploma); intermediate administrator or supervisor (Diploma); leadership (Ed D); middle school education (MS); music education (MS); remedial reading and language arts (Diploma); secondary education (MS, Diploma). Electronic applications accepted.

School of Engineering *Program availability:* Part-time, evening/weekend, online learning. Offers biomedical engineering (MS); computer engineering (MS); computer science (MS); computer science and engineering (PhD); electrical engineering (MS); engineering (MS, PhD); mechanical engineering (MS); technology management (MS, PhD). Electronic applications accepted.

Shintaro Akatsu School of Design *Program availability:* Part-time, evening/weekend. Offers design management (MPS). Electronic applications accepted.

THE UNIVERSITY OF BRITISH COLUMBIA, Vancouver, BC V6T 1Z1, Canada

General Information Province-supported, coed, university. CGS member. *Graduate housing:* Rooms and/or apartments available on a first-come, first-served basis to single and married students. Housing application deadline: 3/1. *Research affiliation:* British Columbia Research (chemical and biological science technology), Forintek Canada (forest technology), National Research Council of Canada Institute of Machinery Research (machinery research), Pulp and Paper Research Institute of Canada, Pacific Environment Institute, Pacific Biological Station (fisheries and oceanography).

GRADUATE UNITS

Faculty of Applied Science *Program availability:* Part-time. Offers applied science (M Arch, M Eng, M Sc, M Sc P, MA Sc, MAP, MASA, MASLA, MCRP, MEL, MLA, MN, MSN, MUD, PhD); chemical and biological engineering (M Eng, M Sc, MA Sc, PhD); civil engineering (M Eng, MA Sc, PhD); electrical and computer engineering (M Eng, MA Sc, PhD); materials engineering (M Sc, MA Sc, PhD); mechanical engineering (M Eng, MA Sc, PhD); mining engineering (M Eng, MA Sc, PhD). Electronic applications accepted.

Clean Energy Research Center Offers clean energy engineering (MEL).

School of Architecture and Landscape Architecture Offers advanced studies in landscape architecture (MASLA); architecture (M Arch, MASA); landscape architecture (MASLA, MLA, MUD); urban design (MUD). Electronic applications accepted.

School of Biomedical Engineering Offers biomedical engineering (M Eng, MA Sc, PhD).

School of Community and Regional Planning Offers community and regional planning (M Sc P, MAP, MCRP, PhD). Electronic applications accepted.

School of Nursing *Program availability:* Part-time. Offers nurse practitioner (MN); nursing (MSN, PhD). Electronic applications accepted.

Faculty of Arts Offers ancient culture, religion and ethnicity (MA); ancient culture, religion, and ethnicity (MA); anthropology (MA, PhD); art history (MA, PhD); arts (M Mus, M Sc, MA, MAS, MDM, MFA, MJ, MLIS, MSW, DMA, PhD, CAS, Diploma); Asian studies (MA, PhD); behavioral neuroscience (MA, PhD); classical and Near Eastern archaeology (MA); classical and Near eastern archaeology (MA); classics (MA, PhD); clinical psychology (MA, PhD); cognitive science (MA, PhD); creative writing (MFA); creative writing and theatre (MFA); critical and curatorial studies (MA); developmental psychology (MA, PhD); English (MA, PhD); film (MA, MFA); film production (MFA); film production and creative writing (MFA); film studies (MA); finance (MA); French (MA, PhD); geography (M Sc, MA, PhD); Germanic studies (MA, PhD); health psychology (MA, PhD); Hispanic studies (MA, PhD); linguistics (MA, PhD); philosophy (MA, PhD); political science (MA, PhD); quantitative methods (MA, PhD); religious studies (MA); social/personality psychology (MA, PhD); sociology (MA, PhD); theatre (MA, MFA, PhD); theatre design (MFA); theatre directing (MFA); visual art (MFA). Electronic applications accepted.

Center for Digital Media Offers digital media (MDM).

Institute for Gender, Race, Sexuality, and Social Justice Offers gender, race, sexuality, and social justice (MA, PhD).

School of Journalism Offers journalism (MJ). Electronic applications accepted.

School of Library, Archival and Information Studies *Program availability:* Part-time. Offers archival studies (MAS); children's literature (MA); library and information studies (MLIS); library, archival and information studies (PhD). Electronic applications accepted.

School of Music *Program availability:* Part-time. Offers music (M Mus, MA, DMA, PhD). Electronic applications accepted.

School of Social Work Offers social work (MSW, PhD). Electronic applications accepted.

Vancouver School of Economics Offers economics (MA, PhD). Electronic applications accepted.

Faculty of Dentistry *Program availability:* Part-time. Offers craniofacial science (M Sc, PhD); dentistry (M Sc, DMD, PhD). Electronic applications accepted.

Faculty of Education *Program availability:* Part-time, evening/weekend, online learning. Offers adult learning and education (M Ed); adult learning and global change (M Ed); art education (M Ed, MA); counseling psychology (M Ed, MA, PhD); curriculum and leadership (M Ed); curriculum studies (M Ed, MA, PhD); education (M Ed, M Kin, M Sc, MA, MET, MHPCTL, Ed D, PhD, Diploma); educational administration and leadership (M Ed); educational leadership and policy (Ed D); educational studies (M Ed, MA, PhD); guidance studies (Diploma); higher education (M Ed); home economics education (M Ed, MA); human development, learning and culture (M Ed, MA, PhD); literacy education (M Ed, MA, PhD); mathematics education (M Ed, MA); measurement, evaluation, and research methodology (M Ed, MA, PhD); media and technology studies education (M Ed, MA); modern languages education (M Ed, MA); music education (M Ed, MA); physical education (M Ed, MA); school psychology (M Ed, MA, PhD); science education (M Ed, MA); social studies education (M Ed, MA); society, culture and politics in education (M Ed); special education (M Ed, MA, PhD, Diploma); teaching English as a second language (M Ed, MA, PhD). Electronic applications accepted.

School of Kinesiology *Program availability:* Part-time. Offers high performance coaching and technical leadership (MHPCTL); kinesiology (M Kin, M Sc, MA, PhD). Electronic applications accepted.

Faculty of Forestry Offers forestry (M Sc, MA Sc, MF, MGEM, MIF, MSFM, PhD); geomatics for environmental management (MGEM); international forestry (MIF); sustainable forest management (MSFM). Electronic applications accepted.

Faculty of Land and Food Systems *Program availability:* Part-time. Offers applied animal biology (M Sc, PhD); food and resource economics (MFRE); food science (M Sc, MFS, PhD); human nutrition (M Sc, PhD); integrated studies in land and food systems (M Sc, PhD); land and food systems (M Sc, MFRE, MFS, MLWS, PhD); land and water systems (MLWS); plant science (M Sc, PhD); soil science (M Sc, PhD). Electronic applications accepted.

Faculty of Medicine *Program availability:* Part-time. Offers biochemistry and molecular biology (M Sc, PhD); bioinformatics (M Sc, PhD); cell and developmental biology (M Sc, PhD); experimental medicine (M Sc, PhD); genetic counselling (M Sc); genome science and technology (M Sc, PhD); medical genetics (M Sc, PhD); medicine (M Sc, MH Sc, MHA, MOT, MPH, MPT, MRSc, MD, PhD); neuroscience (M Sc, PhD); occupational therapy (MOT); pathology (M Sc, PhD); pharmacology (M Sc, PhD); physical therapy (MPT); reproductive and developmental sciences (M Sc, PhD); surgery (M Sc).

School of Audiology and Speech Sciences Offers audiology and speech sciences (M Sc, PhD). Electronic applications accepted.

School of Population and Public Health *Program availability:* Online learning. Offers health administration (MHA); health sciences (MH Sc); occupational and environmental hygiene (M Sc); population and public health (M Sc, MPH, PhD). Electronic applications accepted.

School of Rehabilitation Sciences Offers rehabilitation sciences (M Sc, MRSc, PhD). Electronic applications accepted.

Faculty of Pharmaceutical Sciences Offers pharmaceutical sciences (M Sc, PhD, Pharm D). Electronic applications accepted.

Faculty of Science *Program availability:* Part-time. Offers astronomy (M Sc, PhD); atmospheric science (M Sc, PhD); botany (M Sc, PhD); chemistry (M Sc, PhD); computer science (M Sc, PhD); data science (MDS); geological engineering (M Eng, MA Sc, PhD); geological sciences (M Sc, PhD); geophysics (M Sc, MA Sc, PhD); mathematics (M Sc, PhD); microbiology and immunology (M Sc, PhD); oceanography (M Sc, PhD); physics (M Sc, PhD); science (M Eng, M Sc, MA, MA Sc, MDS, PhD); statistics (M Sc, PhD); zoology (M Sc, PhD). Electronic applications accepted.

Institute for Resources, Environment and Sustainability Offers resources, environment and sustainability (M Sc, MA, PhD). Electronic applications accepted.

Institute of Asian Research Offers Asia Pacific policy studies (MAAPPS); public policy and global affairs (MPPGA). Electronic applications accepted.

Peter A. Allard School of Law *Program availability:* Part-time. Offers common law (LL M CL); law (LL M, PhD); taxation (LL M). Electronic applications accepted.

Sauder School of Business *Program availability:* Part-time, evening/weekend. Offers accounting (PhD); business (IMBA, M Sc, MBA, MM, MSBA, PhD); business administration (IMBA, MBA, PhD); business analytics (MSBA); finance (PhD); management information systems (PhD); management science (PhD); marketing (PhD); organizational behavior (PhD); strategy and business economics (PhD); transportation and logistics (PhD); urban land economics (PhD). Electronic applications accepted.

UNIVERSITY OF CALGARY, Calgary, AB T2N 1N4, Canada

General Information Province-supported, coed, university. CGS member. *Graduate housing:* Rooms and/or apartments available on a first-come, first-served basis to single and married students. Housing application deadline: 3/31. *Research affiliation:* Alta Telecommunications Research Centre, Alberta Sulphur Research, Calgary Society for Students with Learning Difficulties, Canadian Institute of Resources Law, Canadian Music Centre, Canadian Energy Research Institute.

GRADUATE UNITS

Cumming School of Medicine *Program availability:* Part-time. Offers biochemistry and molecular biology (M Sc, PhD); biomedical technology (MBT); cancer biology (M Sc, PhD); cardiovascular and respiratory sciences (M Sc, PhD); community health sciences (M Sc, PhD); critical care medicine (M Sc, PhD); gastrointestinal sciences (M Sc, PhD); joint injury and arthritis (M Sc, PhD); medicine (M Sc, MBT, MCM, MD, PhD); microbiology, immunology and infectious diseases (M Sc, PhD); molecular and medical genetics (M Sc, PhD); mountain medicine and high altitude physiology (M Sc, PhD); neuroscience (M Sc, PhD); pathologists' assistant (M Sc, PhD). Electronic applications accepted.

Faculty of Graduate Studies *Program availability:* Part-time, evening/weekend, blended/hybrid learning. Offers interdisciplinary research (M Sc, MA, PhD); resources and the environment (M Sc, MA, PhD). Electronic applications accepted.

Centre for Military and Strategic Studies *Program availability:* Part-time. Offers military and strategic studies (MSS, PhD). PhD offered in special cases only.

Faculty of Arts *Program availability:* Part-time, evening/weekend. Offers anthropology (MA, PhD); archaeology (MA); art (MA, MFA); arts (MA, PhD); clinical psychology (M Sc, PhD); communication and culture (MA, MCS, PhD); design and technical theatre (MFA); directing (MFA); economics (MA, PhD); English (MA, PhD); French (MA, PhD); geography (M Sc, MA, MGIS, PhD); German (MA); Greek and Roman studies (MA, PhD); history (MA, PhD); linguistics (MA, PhD); music (M Mus, MA, PhD); philosophy (MA, PhD); playwriting (MFA); political science (MA, PhD); psychology (M Sc, PhD); religious studies (MA, PhD); sociology (MA, PhD); Spanish (MA, PhD); theatre studies (MFA). Electronic applications accepted.

Faculty of Environmental Design Offers architecture (M Arch); environmental design (M Env Des, PhD); landscape architecture (MLA); planning (M Plan).

Faculty of Kinesiology Offers kinesiology (M Kin, M Sc, PhD). Electronic applications accepted.

Faculty of Law Offers law (LL M, JD, Postbaccalaureate Certificate); natural resources, energy and environmental law (LL M, Postbaccalaureate Certificate).

Faculty of Nursing *Program availability:* Part-time. Offers nursing (MN, PhD, PMD). Electronic applications accepted.

Faculty of Science *Program availability:* Part-time. Offers analytical chemistry (M Sc, PhD); applied chemistry (M Sc, PhD); biological sciences (M Sc, PhD); computer science (M Sc, PhD); geology (M Sc, PhD); geophysics (M Sc, PhD); hydrology (M Sc, PhD); inorganic chemistry (M Sc, PhD); mathematics and statistics (M Sc, PhD); organic chemistry (M Sc, PhD); physical chemistry (M Sc, PhD); physics and astronomy (M Sc, PhD); polymer chemistry (M Sc, PhD); science (M Sc, PhD); software engineering (M Sc); theoretical chemistry (M Sc, PhD).

Faculty of Social Work Offers social work (MSW, PhD, Postgraduate Diploma). Electronic applications accepted.

Haskayne School of Business *Program availability:* Part-time, evening/weekend. Offers business (EMBA, GEMBA, MBA, PhD); business administration (EMBA, MBA); management (MBA, PhD).

The School of Public Policy *Program availability:* Part-time. Offers public policy (MPP).

Schulich School of Engineering *Program availability:* Part-time, evening/weekend. Offers avalanche mechanics (M Sc, PhD); biomedical engineering (M Sc, PhD); chemical engineering (M Eng, M Sc, PhD); civil engineering (M Eng, M Sc, PhD); electrical and computer engineering (M Eng, M Sc, PhD); energy and environment engineering (M Eng, M Sc, PhD); energy and environmental systems (M Eng, M Sc, PhD); engineering (M Eng, M Sc, MPM, PhD); environmental engineering (M Eng, M Sc, PhD); geomatics engineering (M Eng, M Sc, PhD); geotechnical engineering (M Eng, M Sc, PhD); materials science (M Eng, M Sc, PhD); mechanical and manufacturing engineering (M Eng, M Sc, PhD); petroleum engineering (M Eng, M Sc, PhD); project management (M Eng, M Sc, PhD); reservoir characterization (M Eng, M Sc); structures and solid mechanics (M Eng, M Sc, PhD); transportation engineering (M Eng, M Sc, PhD); water resources (M Eng, M Sc, PhD). Electronic applications accepted.

Werklund School of Education *Program availability:* Part-time, evening/weekend, online learning. Offers adult learning (M Ed, MA, Ed D, PhD); counseling psychology (M Sc, MC, PhD); curriculum and learning (M Ed, MA, Ed D, PhD); education (M Ed, M Sc, MA, MC, Ed D, PhD); educational leadership (M Ed, MA, Ed D, PhD); languages and diversity (M Ed, MA, Ed D, PhD); learning sciences (M Ed, MA, Ed D, PhD); school and applied child psychology (M Ed, M Sc, PhD). Electronic applications accepted.

UNIVERSITY OF CALIFORNIA, BERKELEY, Berkeley, CA 94720-1500

General Information State-supported, coed, university. CGS member. *Graduate housing:* Rooms and/or apartments available to single and married students.

GRADUATE UNITS

Graduate Division *Program availability:* Part-time, blended/hybrid learning. Offers bioengineering (PhD); comparative biochemistry (PhD); East Asian studies (MA); global studies (MA); neuroscience (PhD); Northeast Asian studies (MA); South Asian studies (MA); Southeast Asian studies (MA); vision science (MS, PhD).

College of Chemistry Offers chemical engineering (PhD); chemistry (MS, PhD); product development (MS). Electronic applications accepted.

College of Engineering *Program availability:* Part-time, 100% online, blended/hybrid learning. Offers applied science and technology (PhD); bioengineering (M Eng, MTM); computer science (MS, PhD); decision analytics (M Eng); electrical engineering (M Eng, MS, PhD); engineering (M Eng, MS, MTM, PhD); engineering and project management (M Eng, MS, PhD); engineering science (M Eng, MS, PhD); environmental engineering (M Eng, MS, PhD); geoengineering (M Eng, MS, PhD); industrial engineering and operations research (M Eng, MS, PhD); mechanical engineering (M Eng, MS, PhD); nuclear engineering (M Eng, MS, PhD); structural engineering, mechanics and materials (M Eng, MS, PhD); transportation engineering (M Eng, MS, PhD). Electronic applications accepted.

College of Environmental Design Offers architecture (M Arch); building science (MS, PhD); building structures, construction and materials (MS, PhD); city and regional planning (MCP, PhD); design theories, methods, and practices (MS, PhD); environmental design (M Arch, MA, MCP, MLA, MS, MUD, PhD); environmental design in developing countries (MS, PhD); history of architecture and urbanism (MS, PhD); landscape architecture (MLA); landscape architecture and environmental planning (PhD); social and cultural processes in architecture and urbanism (MS, PhD); urban design (MUD). Electronic applications accepted.

College of Letters and Science Offers African American studies (PhD); ancient history and Mediterranean archaeology (MA, PhD); anthropology (MA, PhD); applied mathematics (PhD); art practice (MFA); astrophysics (PhD); biophysics (PhD); Buddhist studies (PhD); Chinese language (PhD); classical archaeology (MA, PhD); classics (MA, PhD); comparative literature (PhD); composition (PhD); Czech (PhD); demography (PhD); economics (PhD); endocrinology (MA, PhD); English (PhD); ethnic studies (PhD); ethnomusicology (PhD); film and media (PhD); folklore (MA); French (PhD); geography (PhD); geology (MA, MS, PhD); geophysics (MA, MS, PhD); German (PhD); Greek (MA); Hindi (MA, PhD); Hispanic languages and literatures (PhD); history (PhD); history of art (PhD); Indonesian (MA, PhD); integrative biology (PhD); Italian (PhD); Italian studies (PhD); Japanese language (PhD); Latin (MA); letters and science (MA, MFA, MS, PhD); linguistics (PhD); logic and the methodology of science (PhD); mathematics (MA, PhD); medical anthropology (PhD); molecular and cell biology (PhD); musicology (PhD); Near Eastern studies (MA, PhD); performance studies (PhD); philosophy (PhD); physics (PhD); Polish (PhD); political science (PhD); psychology (PhD); rhetoric (PhD); Russian (PhD); Sanskrit (MA, PhD); Scandinavian languages and literatures (PhD); Serbo-Croatian (PhD); sociology (PhD); sociology and demography (MA, PhD); Spanish (PhD); statistics (MA, PhD); Tamil (MA, PhD). Electronic applications accepted.

College of Natural Resources Offers agricultural and resource economics (PhD); development practice (MDP); energy and resources (MA, MS, PhD); environmental science, policy, and management (MS, PhD); forestry (MF); metabolic biology (MS, PhD); microbiology (PhD); molecular toxicology (PhD); natural resources (MA, MDP, MF, MS, PhD); plant biology (PhD); range management (MS).

Graduate School of Journalism Offers journalism (MJ). Electronic applications accepted.

Graduate School of Public Policy Offers public affairs (MPA); public policy (MPA, MPP, PhD). Electronic applications accepted.

Haas School of Business Students: 683 full-time (256 women), 933 part-time (275 women); includes 628 minority (46 Black or African American, non-Hispanic/Latino; 1 American Indian or Alaska Native, non-Hispanic/Latino; 484 Asian, non-Hispanic/Latino; 57 Hispanic/Latino; 3 Native Hawaiian or other Pacific Islander, non-Hispanic/Latino; 37 Two or more races, non-Hispanic/Latino), 238 international. *Faculty:* 90 full-time (21 women), 166 part-time/adjunct (41 women). Expenses: Contact institution. *Program availability:* Part-time, evening/weekend. Offers accounting (PhD); business (EMBA, MBA, MFE, PhD); business administration (EMBA, MBA, PhD); business and public policy (PhD); finance (PhD); financial engineering (MFE); management of organizations (PhD); marketing (PhD); real estate (PhD). *Dean,* Richard K. Lyons, 510-643-2027, Fax: 510-642-9128, E-mail: lyons@haas.berkeley.edu.

School of Education Offers development in mathematics and science (MA); education (MA, PhD); education in mathematics, science, and technology (MA, PhD); human development and education (MA, PhD); leadership education (MA); science and mathematics education (PhD); special education (PhD); teacher education (MA). Electronic applications accepted.

School of Information Offers information (MIDS, MIMS, PhD); information and data science (MIDS); information management and systems (MIMS, PhD). Electronic applications accepted.

School of Public Health *Program availability:* Blended/hybrid learning. Offers biostatistics (MA, PhD); environmental health sciences (MS, PhD); epidemiology (MS, PhD); health policy (PhD); infectious diseases (PhD); infectious diseases and immunity (PhD); public health (MA, MPH, MS, Dr PH, PhD). Electronic applications accepted.

School of Social Welfare Offers social welfare (MSW, PhD). Electronic applications accepted.

School of Law Offers jurisprudence and social policy (PhD); law (LL M, JD, JSD).

School of Optometry Offers optometry (OD, Certificate). Electronic applications accepted.

UC Berkeley Extension *Program availability:* Part-time, evening/weekend, online learning. Offers accounting (Certificate); alcohol and drug abuse studies (Certificate); business administration (Certificate); clinical research conduct and management (Certificate); college admissions and career planning (Certificate); construction management (Certificate); finance (Certificate); global business management (Certificate); human resource management (Certificate); HVAC (Certificate); information systems and management (Postbaccalaureate Certificate); integrated circuit design and techniques (online) (Certificate); interior design and interior architecture (Certificate); landscape architecture (Certificate); leadership in sustainability and environmental management (Professional Certificate); management (Certificate); marketing (Certificate); project management (Certificate); solar energy and green building (Professional Certificate); sustainable design (Professional Certificate); teaching English as a second language (Certificate); UNIX/LINUX system administration (Certificate); visual arts (Postbaccalaureate Certificate); writing (Postbaccalaureate Certificate).

UNIVERSITY OF CALIFORNIA, DAVIS, Davis, CA 95616

General Information State-supported, coed, university. CGS member. *Graduate housing:* Rooms and/or apartments available to single and married students. Housing application deadline: 4/1.

GRADUATE UNITS

College of Engineering *Program availability:* Part-time. Offers aeronautical engineering (M Engr, MS, D Engr, PhD, Certificate); applied science (MS, PhD); biological systems engineering (M Engr, MS, D Engr, PhD); biomedical engineering (MS, PhD); chemical engineering (MS, PhD); civil and environmental engineering (M Engr, MS, D Engr, PhD, Certificate); computer science (MS, PhD); electrical and computer engineering (MS, PhD); engineering (M Engr, MS, D Engr, PhD, Certificate); materials science and engineering (MS, PhD); mechanical engineering (M Engr, MS, D Engr, PhD, Certificate); transportation, technology and policy (MS, PhD). Electronic applications accepted.

Graduate School of Management Students: 189 full-time (103 women), 323 part-time (133 women); includes 198 minority (10 Black or African American, non-Hispanic/Latino; 127 Asian, non-Hispanic/Latino; 35 Hispanic/Latino; 26 Two or more races, non-Hispanic/Latino), 124 international. Average age 28. 1,549 applicants, 29% accepted, 249 enrolled. *Faculty:* 28 full-time (9 women), 51 part-time/adjunct (14 women). Expenses: Contact institution. *Financial support:* In 2017–18, 230 students received support, including 230 fellowships with full and partial tuition reimbursements available; teaching assistantships with partial tuition reimbursements available, institutionally sponsored loans, scholarships/grants, health care benefits, tuition waivers (partial), and unspecified assistantships also available. Support available to part-time students. Financial award application deadline: 3/1; financial award applicants required to submit FAFSA. In 2017, 211 master's awarded. *Program availability:* Part-time, evening/weekend. Offers audit analytics (MP Ac); business analytics (MSBA); business analytics and technologies (MBA); entrepreneurship and innovation (MBA); finance and accounting (MBA); financial accounting (MP Ac); general management (MBA); management (MBA, MP Ac, MSBA); marketing (MBA); organizational behavior (MBA); public health management (MBA); strategy (MBA); technology management (MBA). *Application deadline:* For fall admission, 5/18 priority date for domestic and international students. *Application fee:* $125. Electronic applications accepted. *Application Contact:* Kristy MaKieve, Interim Director of Admissions, 530-752-7658, Fax: 530-754-9355, E-mail: admissions@gsm.ucdavis.edu. *Senior Assistant Dean of Student Affairs*, James Stevens, 530-752-7658, Fax: 530-754-9355, E-mail: admissions@gsm.ucdavis.edu.

Graduate Studies Offers acting (MFA); agricultural and environmental chemistry (MS, PhD); agricultural and resource economics (MS, PhD); animal behavior (PhD); animal biology (MAM, MS, PhD); anthropology (MA, PhD); applied linguistics (MA, PhD); applied mathematics (MS, PhD); art (MFA); art history (MA); atmospheric sciences (MS, PhD); avian sciences (MS); biochemistry and molecular biology (MS, PhD); biophysics (MS, PhD); biostatistics (MS, PhD); cell and developmental biology (MS, PhD); chemistry (MS, PhD); child development (MS); clinical research (MAS); communication (MA); community development (MS); comparative literature (PhD); comparative pathology (MS, PhD); composition (MA, PhD); conducting (MA, PhD); creative writing (MA); cultural studies (MA, PhD); dramatic art (PhD); ecology (MS, PhD); economics (MA, PhD); education (MA, Ed D); English (MA, PhD); entomology (MS, PhD); epidemiology (MS, PhD); exercise science (MS); food science (MS, PhD); forensic science (MS); French (PhD); genetics (MS, PhD); geography (MA, PhD); geology (MS, PhD); German (MA, PhD); health informatics (MS); history (MA, PhD); horticulture and agronomy (MS); human development (PhD); hydrologic sciences (MS, PhD); immunology (MS, PhD); instructional studies (PhD); integrated pest management (MS); international agricultural development (MS); linguistics (MA); mathematics (MA, MAT, PhD); microbiology (MS, PhD); molecular, cellular and integrative physiology (MS, PhD); musicology (MA, PhD); Native American studies (MA, PhD); neuroscience (PhD); nutrition (MS, PhD); pharmacology/toxicology (MS, PhD); philosophy (MA, PhD); physics (MS, PhD); plant biology (MS, PhD); plant pathology (MS, PhD); political science (MA, PhD); population biology (PhD); psychological studies (PhD); psychology (PhD); sociocultural studies (PhD); sociology (MA, PhD); soils and biogeochemistry (MS, PhD); Spanish (MA, PhD); statistics (MS, PhD); textile arts and costume design (MFA); textiles (MS); viticulture and enology (MS, PhD). Electronic applications accepted.

School of Law Students: 500 full-time (267 women); includes 220 minority (15 Black or African American, non-Hispanic/Latino; 1 American Indian or Alaska Native, non-Hispanic/Latino; 75 Asian, non-Hispanic/Latino; 83 Hispanic/Latino; 1 Native Hawaiian or other Pacific Islander, non-Hispanic/Latino; 45 Two or more races, non-Hispanic/Latino), 38 international. Average age 24. 2,988 applicants, 30% accepted, 150 enrolled. *Faculty:* 51 full-time (26 women), 60 part-time/adjunct (21 women). Expenses: Contact institution. *Financial support:* In 2017–18, 445 students received support, including 35 research assistantships, 27 teaching assistantships with partial tuition reimbursements available; Federal Work-Study, institutionally sponsored loans, scholarships/grants, and health care benefits also available. Financial award application deadline: 3/2; financial award applicants required to submit FAFSA. In 2017, 167 doctorates awarded. Offers law (LL M, JD). *Application deadline:* For fall admission, 3/15 priority date for domestic students, 3/15 for international students. Applications are processed on a rolling basis. *Application fee:* $0. Electronic applications accepted. *Application Contact:* Kristen Mercado, JD, Director, Admissions, 530-752-6477, Fax: 530-754-8371, E-mail: admissions@law.ucdavis.edu. *Dean*, Kevin R. Johnson, 530-752-0243, Fax: 530-752-7279, E-mail: krjohnson@ucdavis.edu.

School of Medicine Offers medicine (MD). Electronic applications accepted.

School of Veterinary Medicine Offers preventive veterinary medicine (MPVM); veterinary medicine (MPVM, DVM, Certificate).

UNIVERSITY OF CALIFORNIA, HASTINGS COLLEGE OF THE LAW, San Francisco, CA 94102-4978

General Information State-supported, coed, graduate-only institution. *Graduate housing:* Rooms and/or apartments available on a first-come, first-served basis to single and married students.

GRADUATE UNITS

Graduate Programs Offers law (LL M, MS, MSL, JD). MSL and MS offered jointly with University of California, San Francisco. Electronic applications accepted.

UNIVERSITY OF CALIFORNIA, IRVINE, Irvine, CA 92697

General Information State-supported, coed, university. CGS member. *Enrollment:* 35,242 graduate, professional, and undergraduate students; 5,366 full-time matriculated graduate/professional students (2,499 women), 473 part-time matriculated graduate/professional students (206 women). *Graduate housing:* Rooms and/or apartments available on a first-come, first-served basis to single and married students. *Student services:* Campus employment opportunities, campus safety program, career counseling, child daycare facilities, exercise/wellness program, free psychological counseling, grant writing training, international student services, low-cost health insurance, multicultural affairs office, services for students with disabilities, teacher training, writing training. *Library facilities:* Langson Library plus 4 others. *Collection:* Books: 2.3 million (physical), 1.3 million (digital/electronic); Serial titles: 4,559 (physical), 146,177 (digital/electronic); Databases: 1,486. Study areas open 24 hours, 5–7 days a week; students can reserve study rooms.

Computer facilities: 1,500 computers available on campus for general student use. A campuswide network can be accessed from student residence rooms and from off campus. Online class registration is available.
Website: http://www.uci.edu/

General Application Contact: Sheree McPeak, Student Affairs Officer, Graduate Division, 949-824-4611, Fax: 949-824-9096, E-mail: ymcpeak@uci.edu.

GRADUATE UNITS

Claire Trevor School of the Arts Students: 144 full-time (76 women), 8 part-time (6 women); includes 54 minority (15 Asian, non-Hispanic/Latino; 22 Hispanic/Latino; 17 Two or more races, non-Hispanic/Latino), 12 international. Average age 29. 432 applicants, 21% accepted, 64 enrolled. Expenses: Contact institution. *Financial support:* Fellowships, teaching assistantships, institutionally sponsored loans, traineeships, health care benefits, and unspecified assistantships available. Financial award application deadline: 3/1; financial award applicants required to submit FAFSA. In 2017, 45 master's, 1 doctorate awarded. Offers accompanying (MFA); acting (MFA); art (MFA); arts (MFA, PhD); choral conducting (MFA); composition and technology (MFA); dance (MFA); design and stage management (MFA); directing (MFA); drama (MFA); drama and theatre (PhD); guitar/lute performance (MFA); instrumental performance (MFA); piano performance (MFA); vocal performance (MFA). *Application deadline:* For fall admission, 1/15 for domestic and international students. Applications are processed on a rolling basis. *Application fee:* $105 ($125 for international students). Electronic applications accepted. *Application Contact:* Prof. Vincent Olivieri, Associate Dean, 949-824-5684, Fax: 949-824-2450, E-mail: olivieri@uci.edu. *Dean*, Dr. Stephen Barker, 949-824-8792, Fax: 949-824-2450, E-mail: barker@uci.edu.

Donald Bren School of Information and Computer Sciences Students: 491 full-time (159 women), 19 part-time (6 women); includes 58 minority (4 Black or African American, non-Hispanic/Latino; 37 Asian, non-Hispanic/Latino; 8 Hispanic/Latino; 9 Two or more races, non-Hispanic/Latino), 348 international. Average age 27. 3,994 applicants, 11% accepted, 201 enrolled. Expenses: Contact institution. *Financial support:* Fellowships, research assistantships with full tuition reimbursements, teaching assistantships, institutionally sponsored loans, traineeships, health care benefits, and unspecified assistantships available. Financial award applicants required to submit FAFSA. In 2017, 140 master's, 28 doctorates awarded. Offers computer science (MS, PhD); informatics (MS, PhD); information and computer science (MS, PhD); networked systems (MS, PhD); statistics (MS, PhD). *Application deadline:* For fall admission, 12/15 for domestic and international students. *Application fee:* $105 ($125 for international students). Electronic applications accepted. *Application Contact:* Kris Bolcer, Director of Student Affairs, 949-824-5156, Fax: 949-824-4163, E-mail: kbolcer@uci.edu. *Dean*, Marios C. Papaefthymiou, 949-824-7427, E-mail: marios@uci.edu.

Francisco J. Ayala School of Biological Sciences Students: 302 full-time (160 women), 3 part-time (1 woman); includes 125 minority (4 Black or African American, non-Hispanic/Latino; 1 American Indian or Alaska Native, non-Hispanic/Latino; 53 Asian, non-Hispanic/Latino; 54 Hispanic/Latino; 13 Two or more races, non-Hispanic/Latino), 45 international. Average age 26. 913 applicants, 23% accepted, 102 enrolled. Expenses: Contact institution. *Financial support:* Fellowships with full tuition reimbursements, research assistantships with full tuition reimbursements, teaching assistantships with full tuition reimbursements, career-related internships or fieldwork, institutionally sponsored loans, scholarships/grants, traineeships, health care benefits, and unspecified assistantships available. Financial award application deadline: 3/1; financial award applicants required to submit FAFSA. In 2017, 54 master's, 44 doctorates awarded. Offers biological science (MS); biological sciences (MS, PhD); biotechnology (MS); biotechnology management (MS); interdisciplinary cellular and molecular biosciences (PhD); mathematical, computational and systems biology (PhD); neuroscience (PhD). *Application deadline:* For fall admission, 12/15 for domestic and international students. Applications are processed on a rolling basis. *Application fee:* $105 ($125 for international students). Electronic applications accepted. *Application Contact:* Prof. R. Michael Mulligan, Associate Dean, 949-824-8433, Fax: 949-824-4709, E-mail: rmmullig@uci.edu. *Dean*, Prof. Frank Laferla, 949-824-5315, Fax: 949-824-3035, E-mail: laferla@uci.edu.

Henry Samueli School of Engineering Students: 882 full-time (279 women), 67 part-time (20 women); includes 157 minority (12 Black or African American, non-Hispanic/Latino; 106 Asian, non-Hispanic/Latino; 30 Hispanic/Latino; 9 Two or more races, non-Hispanic/Latino), 596 international. Average age 26. 3,732 applicants, 27% accepted, 294 enrolled. Expenses: Contact institution. *Financial support:* Fellowships with tuition reimbursements, research assistantships with full tuition reimbursements, teaching assistantships with tuition reimbursements, institutionally sponsored loans, traineeships, health care benefits, and unspecified assistantships available. Financial award application deadline: 3/1; financial award applicants required to submit FAFSA. In 2017, 283 master's, 87 doctorates awarded. *Program availability:* Part-time. Offers biomedical engineering (MS, PhD); chemical and biochemical engineering (MS, PhD); civil and environmental engineering (MS, PhD); electrical engineering and computer science (MS, PhD); engineering (MS, PhD); engineering management (MS); materials science and engineering (MS, PhD); mechanical and aerospace engineering (MS, PhD);

networked systems (MS, PhD). *Application deadline:* For fall admission, 1/15 priority date for domestic students, 1/15 for international students. Applications are processed on a rolling basis. *Application fee:* $105 ($125 for international students). Electronic applications accepted. *Application Contact:* Jean Bennett, Director of Graduate Student Affairs, 949-824-6475, Fax: 949-824-8200, E-mail: jean.bennett@uci.edu. *Dean*, Gregory N. Washington, 949-824-4333, Fax: 949-824-8200, E-mail: engineering@uci.edu.

Institute of Transportation Studies Students: 9 full-time (5 women), 2 part-time (0 women); includes 2 minority (both Asian, non-Hispanic/Latino), 9 international. Average age 30. 20 applicants, 45% accepted, 3 enrolled. Expenses: Contact institution. *Financial support:* Fellowships, research assistantships with full tuition reimbursements, teaching assistantships, institutionally sponsored loans, traineeships, health care benefits, and unspecified assistantships available. Financial award application deadline: 3/1. In 2017, 1 master's, 3 doctorates awarded. Offers transportation studies (MA, PhD). *Application deadline:* For fall admission, 1/15 for domestic and international students. *Application fee:* $105 ($125 for international students). *Application Contact:* Amelia Regan, Director, Transportation Science Program, 949-824-2611, E-mail: aregan@uci.edu. *Director*, Stephen G. Ritchie, 949-824-4214, E-mail: sritchie@uci.edu.

The Paul Merage School of Business Students: 691 full-time (325 women), 216 part-time (79 women); includes 356 minority (13 Black or African American, non-Hispanic/Latino; 30 American Indian or Alaska Native, non-Hispanic/Latino; 300 Asian, non-Hispanic/Latino; 12 Hispanic/Latino; 1 Native Hawaiian or other Pacific Islander, non-Hispanic/Latino), 241 international. Average age 31. 2,524 applicants, 34% accepted, 497 enrolled. Expenses: Contact institution. *Financial support:* Career-related internships or fieldwork, Federal Work-Study, institutionally sponsored loans, scholarships/grants, traineeships, health care benefits, and unspecified assistantships available. Support available to part-time students. Financial award application deadline: 3/1; financial award applicants required to submit FAFSA. In 2017, 383 master's, 9 doctorates awarded. *Program availability:* Part-time, evening/weekend. Offers business (EMBA, MBA, MPA, MS, PhD); business administration (EMBA, MBA); business analytics (MS); health care administration (MBA); management (PhD); professional accountancy (MPA). *Application deadline:* For fall admission, 1/2 priority date for domestic and international students. Applications are processed on a rolling basis. *Application fee:* $105 ($125 for international students). Electronic applications accepted. *Dean*, Eric Spangenberg, 949-824-8470, E-mail: ers@uci.edu.

Programs in Health Sciences Students: 117 full-time (96 women), 13 part-time (10 women); includes 80 minority (4 Black or African American, non-Hispanic/Latino; 41 Asian, non-Hispanic/Latino; 23 Hispanic/Latino; 12 Two or more races, non-Hispanic/Latino), 7 international. Average age 30. 519 applicants, 32% accepted, 61 enrolled. Expenses: Contact institution. In 2017, 38 master's, 1 doctorate awarded. Offers health sciences (MPH, MSN, PhD); medicinal chemistry and pharmacology (PhD); nursing science (MSN); public health (MPH, PhD). *Application fee:* $105 ($125 for international students). *Application Contact:* Sheree McPeak, Graduate Division, 949-824-4611, Fax: 949-824-9096, E-mail: ogsfront@uci.edu.

School of Education Students: 210 full-time (157 women), 1 (woman) part-time; includes 104 minority (1 Black or African American, non-Hispanic/Latino; 46 Asian, non-Hispanic/Latino; 39 Hispanic/Latino; 1 Native Hawaiian or other Pacific Islander, non-Hispanic/Latino; 17 Two or more races, non-Hispanic/Latino), 20 international. Average age 27. 451 applicants, 46% accepted, 147 enrolled. Expenses: Contact institution. *Financial support:* Fellowships, research assistantships with full tuition reimbursements, institutionally sponsored loans, traineeships, health care benefits, and unspecified assistantships available. Financial award application deadline: 3/1; financial award applicants required to submit FAFSA. In 2017, 130 master's, 7 doctorates awarded. *Program availability:* Part-time, evening/weekend. Offers educational administration (Ed D); educational administration and leadership (Ed D); elementary and secondary education (MAT). *Application deadline:* For fall admission, 1/2 priority date for domestic students, 1/2 for international students. *Application fee:* $105 ($125 for international students). Electronic applications accepted. *Application Contact:* Denise Earley, Assistant Director of Student Affairs, 949-824-4022, E-mail: denise.earley@uci.edu. *Dean*, Richard Arum, 949-824-2534, E-mail: richard.arum@uci.edu.

School of Humanities Students: 287 full-time (152 women), 13 part-time (7 women); includes 103 minority (8 Black or African American, non-Hispanic/Latino; 24 Asian, non-Hispanic/Latino; 44 Hispanic/Latino; 27 Two or more races, non-Hispanic/Latino), 38 international. Average age 32. 872 applicants, 16% accepted, 77 enrolled. Expenses: Contact institution. *Financial support:* Fellowships with tuition reimbursements, research assistantships with full tuition reimbursements, teaching assistantships with tuition reimbursements, institutionally sponsored loans, traineeships, health care benefits, and unspecified assistantships available. Financial award application deadline: 3/1; financial award applicants required to submit FAFSA. In 2017, 63 master's, 29 doctorates awarded. Offers Chinese (MA, PhD); classics (MA, PhD); comparative literature (MA, PhD); creative writing (MFA); culture and theory (PhD); East Asian languages and literatures (MA, PhD); English (MA, PhD); English and American literature (PhD); French (MA, PhD); German (MA, PhD); history (MA, PhD); humanities (MA, MAT, MFA, PhD); Japanese (MA, PhD); philosophy (MA, PhD); Spanish (MA, MAT, PhD); visual studies (MA, PhD); writing (MFA). *Application deadline:* For fall admission, 1/15 for domestic and international students. Applications are processed on a rolling basis. *Application fee:* $105 ($125 for international students). Electronic applications accepted. *Application Contact:* Amy Fujitani, Director of Graduate Student Affairs, 949-824-4303, Fax: 949-824-1360, E-mail: amy.fujitani@uci.edu. *Dean*, Georges Van Den Abbeele, 949-824-5133, E-mail: gvandena@uci.edu.

School of Law Students: 417 full-time (232 women); includes 191 minority (18 Black or African American, non-Hispanic/Latino; 1 American Indian or Alaska Native, non-Hispanic/Latino; 90 Asian, non-Hispanic/Latino; 64 Hispanic/Latino; 18 Two or more races, non-Hispanic/Latino), 17 international. 2,314 applicants, 166 enrolled. Expenses: Contact institution. In 2017, 94 doctorates awarded. Offers law (JD). *Application deadline:* For fall admission, 3/1 for domestic students. *Application fee:* $0. Electronic applications accepted. *Application Contact:* Estuardo Ponciano, Director of Admissions, 949-824-9926, E-mail: eponciano@law.uci.edu. *Dean*, L. Song Richardson, 949-824-7722, E-mail: srichardson@law.uci.edu.

School of Medicine Students: 570 full-time (308 women), 53 part-time (25 women); includes 112 minority (12 Black or African American, non-Hispanic/Latino; 2 American Indian or Alaska Native, non-Hispanic/Latino; 64 Asian, non-Hispanic/Latino; 32 Hispanic/Latino; 2 Two or more races, non-Hispanic/Latino), 29 international. Average age 28. 313 applicants, 21% accepted, 37 enrolled. Expenses: Contact institution. *Financial support:* Fellowships, research assistantships with full tuition reimbursements, teaching assistantships, career-related internships or fieldwork, institutionally sponsored loans, traineeships, health care benefits, and unspecified assistantships available. Financial award application deadline: 3/1; financial award applicants required to submit FAFSA. In 2017, 23 master's, 124 doctorates awarded. Offers biological sciences (MS, PhD); biomedical and translational science (MS); environmental health sciences (MS); environmental toxicology (PhD); epidemiology (MS, PhD); experimental pathology (PhD); exposure sciences and risk assessment (PhD); genetic counseling (MS); medicine (MS, MD, PhD); pharmacological sciences (PhD). *Application deadline:* For fall admission, 1/15 for domestic and international students. *Application fee:* $105 ($125 for international students). Electronic applications accepted. *Application Contact:* Leora Fellus, Graduate Studies Director, 949-824-1028, E-mail: lfellus@uci.edu. *Dean*, Dr. Michael Stamos, 949-824-1046, E-mail: mstamos@uci.edu.

School of Physical Sciences Students: 505 full-time (159 women), 4 part-time (3 women); includes 136 minority (4 Black or African American, non-Hispanic/Latino; 1 American Indian or Alaska Native, non-Hispanic/Latino; 63 Asian, non-Hispanic/Latino; 42 Hispanic/Latino; 1 Native Hawaiian or other Pacific Islander, non-Hispanic/Latino; 25 Two or more races, non-Hispanic/Latino), 111 international. Average age 27. 1,011 applicants, 31% accepted, 111 enrolled. Expenses: Contact institution. *Financial support:* Fellowships, research assistantships with full tuition reimbursements, teaching assistantships, career-related internships or fieldwork, institutionally sponsored loans, traineeships, health care benefits, and unspecified assistantships available. Financial award application deadline: 3/1; financial award applicants required to submit FAFSA. In 2017, 62 master's, 82 doctorates awarded. Offers chemical and materials physics (MS, PhD); chemistry (MS, PhD); earth system science (MS, PhD); mathematics (MS, PhD); physical sciences (MS, PhD); physics (MS, PhD). *Application deadline:* For fall admission, 1/15 priority date for domestic and international students. Applications are processed on a rolling basis. *Application fee:* $105 ($125 for international students). Electronic applications accepted. *Application Contact:* Prof. Roger McWilliams, Associate Dean, 949-824-6228, Fax: 949-824-2174, E-mail: mcw@uci.edu. *Dean*, Kenneth C. Janda, 949-824-6022, Fax: 949-824-2261, E-mail: kcjanda@uci.edu.

School of Social Ecology Students: 339 full-time (212 women), 67 part-time (44 women); includes 184 minority (22 Black or African American, non-Hispanic/Latino; 50 Asian, non-Hispanic/Latino; 75 Hispanic/Latino; 1 Native Hawaiian or other Pacific Islander, non-Hispanic/Latino; 36 Two or more races, non-Hispanic/Latino), 52 international. Average age 29. 775 applicants, 46% accepted, 173 enrolled. Expenses: Contact institution. *Financial support:* Fellowships, research assistantships with full tuition reimbursements, teaching assistantships, institutionally sponsored loans, traineeships, health care benefits, and unspecified assistantships available. Financial award application deadline: 3/1; financial award applicants required to submit FAFSA. In 2017, 115 master's, 28 doctorates awarded. Offers criminology, law and society (MAS, PhD); environmental analysis and design (PhD); epidemiology and public health (PhD); planning, policy and design (PhD); psychology and social behavior (PhD); social ecology (PhD); urban and regional planning (MURP). *Application deadline:* For fall admission, 1/15 priority date for domestic students, 1/15 for international students. Applications are processed on a rolling basis. *Application fee:* $105 ($125 for international students). Electronic applications accepted. *Application Contact:* Jennifer Craig, Director of Graduate Student Services, 949-824-5918, E-mail: craigj@uci.edu. *Dean*, Nancy Guerra, 949-824-5466, Fax: 949-824-1845, E-mail: nguerra1@uci.edu.

School of Social Sciences Students: 402 full-time (179 women), 7 part-time (4 women); includes 133 minority (11 Black or African American, non-Hispanic/Latino; 2 American Indian or Alaska Native, non-Hispanic/Latino; 42 Asian, non-Hispanic/Latino; 49 Hispanic/Latino; 29 Two or more races, non-Hispanic/Latino), 81 international. Average age 29. 708 applicants, 30% accepted, 110 enrolled. Expenses: Contact institution. *Financial support:* Fellowships, research assistantships with full tuition reimbursements, teaching assistantships, institutionally sponsored loans, traineeships, health care benefits, and unspecified assistantships available. Financial award application deadline: 3/1; financial award applicants required to submit FAFSA. In 2017, 91 master's, 52 doctorates awarded. Offers anthropology (MA, PhD); demographic and social analysis (MA); economics (MA, PhD); philosophy (PhD); political psychology (PhD); political sciences (PhD); psychology (PhD); public choice (MA, PhD); social networks (PhD); social science (PhD); social sciences (MA, PhD); sociology and social relations (PhD); transportation economics (MA, PhD). *Application deadline:* For fall admission, 1/15 priority date for domestic students, 1/15 for international students. Applications are processed on a rolling basis. *Application fee:* $105 ($125 for international students). Electronic applications accepted. *Application Contact:* John Sommerhauser, Director of Graduate Affairs, 949-824-4074, E-mail: john.sommerhauser@uci.edu. *Dean*, William M. Maurer, 949-824-6802, E-mail: wmmaurer@uci.edu.

Institute for Mathematical Behavioral Sciences Students: 8 full-time (4 women), 2 part-time (0 women); includes 3 minority (1 Asian, non-Hispanic/Latino; 2 Two or more races, non-Hispanic/Latino), 2 international. Average age 35. 11 applicants, 18% accepted, 2 enrolled. Expenses: Contact institution. *Financial support:* Fellowships, research assistantships with full tuition reimbursements, teaching assistantships, institutionally sponsored loans, traineeships, health care benefits, and unspecified assistantships available. Financial award application deadline: 3/1; financial award applicants required to submit FAFSA. In 2017, 4 master's, 1 doctorate awarded. Offers games, decisions, and dynamical systems (PhD); mathematical behavioral sciences (MA). *Application deadline:* For fall admission, 1/15 priority date for domestic students, 1/15 for international students. Applications are processed on a rolling basis. *Application fee:* $105 ($125 for international students). Electronic applications accepted. *Application Contact:* John Sommerhauser, Director of Graduate Affairs, 949-824-4074, E-mail: john.sommerhauser@uci.edu. *Graduate Program Director*, Louis Narens, 949-824-5360, E-mail: lnarens@uci.edu.

UNIVERSITY OF CALIFORNIA, LOS ANGELES, Los Angeles, CA 90095

General Information State-supported, coed, university. CGS member. *Graduate housing:* Rooms and/or apartments available on a first-come, first-served basis to single and married students.

GRADUATE UNITS

David Geffen School of Medicine Offers biological chemistry (MS, PhD); biomathematics (MS, PhD); biomedical physics (MS, PhD); cellular and molecular pathology (MS, PhD); clinical research (MS); experimental pathology (MS, PhD); human genetics (MS, PhD); medicine (MS, MD, PhD); microbiology, immunology and molecular genetics (MS, PhD); molecular and medical pharmacology (MS, PhD); neurobiology (MS, PhD); neuroscience (PhD); physiology (PhD). Electronic applications accepted.

Graduate Division Electronic applications accepted.

College of Letters and Science Offers Afro-American studies (MA); American Indian studies (MA); anthropology (MA, PhD); applied economics (MAE); applied linguistics (PhD); applied linguistics and teaching English as a second language (MA); archaeology (MA, PhD); art history (MA, PhD); Asian languages and cultures (MA, PhD); Asian-American studies (MA); astronomy (MAT, MS, PhD); atmospheric and oceanic sciences (MS, PhD); biochemistry and molecular biology (MS, PhD); bioinformatics (MS, PhD); biological chemistry (PhD); cellular and molecular pathology (PhD); chemistry (MS, PhD); classics (MA, PhD); comparative literature

(MA, PhD); conservation of archaeological and ethnographic materials (MA); ecology and evolutionary biology (MA, PhD); economics (MAE, PhD); English (MA, PhD); French and Francophone studies (MA, PhD); gender studies (MA, PhD); geochemistry (MS, PhD); geography (MA, PhD); geology (MS, PhD); geophysics and space physics (MS, PhD); Germanic languages (MA, PhD); Greek (MA); Hispanic languages and literature (PhD); history (MA, PhD); human genetics (PhD); Indo-European studies (PhD); Italian (MA, PhD); Latin (MA); letters and science (MA, MAT, MS, PhD, Certificate); linguistics (MA, PhD); mathematics (MA, MAT, PhD); microbiology, immunology, and molecular genetics (PhD); molecular biology (PhD); molecular toxicology (PhD); molecular, cell and developmental biology (MA, PhD); molecular, cellular and integrative physiology (PhD); musicology (MA, PhD); Near Eastern languages and cultures (MA, PhD); neurobiology (PhD); oral biology (PhD); philosophy (MA, PhD); physics (MS, PhD); physiological science (MS); physiology (PhD); political science (MA, PhD); Portuguese (MA); psychology (MA, PhD); Scandinavian (MA); Slavic languages and literatures (MA, PhD); sociology (MA, PhD); Spanish (MA); statistics (MS, PhD); teaching English as a second language (Certificate). Electronic applications accepted.

Graduate School of Education and Information Studies *Program availability:* Part-time, evening/weekend. Offers archival studies (MLIS); education (M Ed, MA, Ed D, PhD); education and information studies (M Ed, MA, MLIS, Ed D, PhD, Certificate); educational leadership (Ed D); informatics (MLIS); information studies (PhD); library and information science (Certificate); library studies (MLIS); moving image archive studies (MA); rare books, print and visual culture (MLIS); special education (PhD). Electronic applications accepted.

Henry Samueli School of Engineering and Applied Science Students: 2,265 full-time (506 women); includes 554 minority (17 Black or African American, non-Hispanic/Latino; 3 American Indian or Alaska Native, non-Hispanic/Latino; 367 Asian, non-Hispanic/Latino; 110 Hispanic/Latino; 2 Native Hawaiian or other Pacific Islander, non-Hispanic/Latino; 55 Two or more races, non-Hispanic/Latino), 1,280 international. 6,868 applicants, 28% accepted, 874 enrolled. *Faculty:* 173 full-time (27 women), 28 part-time/adjunct (1 woman). Expenses: Contact institution. *Financial support:* In 2017–18, 749 fellowships, 1,382 research assistantships, 772 teaching assistantships were awarded; career-related internships or fieldwork, Federal Work-Study, institutionally sponsored loans, and tuition waivers (full and partial) also available. Financial award application deadline: 3/2; financial award applicants required to submit FAFSA. In 2017, 716 master's, 156 doctorates awarded. *Program availability:* Evening/weekend, blended/hybrid learning. Offers aerospace engineering (MS, PhD); bioengineering (MS, PhD); chemical and biomolecular engineering (MS, PhD); civil and environmental engineering (MS, PhD); computer science (MS, PhD); electrical and computer engineering (MS, PhD); engineering (MS); engineering and applied science (MS, PhD); manufacturing engineering (MS); materials science and engineering (MS, PhD); mechanical engineering (MS, PhD). *Application deadline:* For fall admission, 12/1 for domestic and international students. *Application fee:* $105 ($125 for international students). Electronic applications accepted. *Application Contact:* Jan LaBuda, Director, Office of Academic and Student Affairs, 310-825-2514, Fax: 310-825-2473, E-mail: jan@seas.ucla.edu. *Associate Dean, Academic and Student Affairs,* Dr. Richard D. Wesel, 310-825-2942, E-mail: wesel@ee.ucla.edu.

Institute of the Environment and Sustainability Offers environmental science and engineering (D Env).

International Institute Offers African studies (MA); East Asian studies (MA); Islamic studies (MA, PhD); Latin American studies (MA). Electronic applications accepted.

Luskin School of Public Affairs Offers public affairs (MA, MPP, MSW, PhD); public policy (MPP); social welfare (MSW, PhD); urban planning (MA, PhD). Electronic applications accepted.

School of Nursing Offers nursing (MSN, PhD). Electronic applications accepted.

School of Public Health Offers biostatistics (MPH, MS, Dr PH, PhD); environmental health sciences (MS, PhD); environmental science and engineering (D Env); epidemiology (MPH, MS, Dr PH, PhD); health services (MPH, MS, Dr PH, PhD); molecular toxicology (PhD); public health (MPH, MS, D Env, Dr PH, PhD). Electronic applications accepted.

School of the Arts and Architecture Offers architecture and urban design (M Arch, MA, PhD); art (MFA); arts and architecture (M Arch, MA, MFA, MM, DMA, PhD); composition (MA, PhD); culture and performance (MA, PhD); dance (MFA); design media arts (MFA); ethnomusicology (MA, PhD); performance (MM, DMA). Electronic applications accepted.

School of Theater, Film and Television Offers animation (MFA); cinema and media studies (MA, PhD); cinematography (MFA); film and television (MA, MFA, PhD); moving image archive studies (MA); production (MFA); screenwriting (MFA); theater (MA, MFA); theater and performance studies (PhD); theater, film and television (MA, MFA, PhD). Electronic applications accepted.

UCLA Anderson School of Management Students: 918 full-time (314 women), 1,269 part-time (399 women); includes 743 minority (38 Black or African American, non-Hispanic/Latino; 3 American Indian or Alaska Native, non-Hispanic/Latino; 531 Asian, non-Hispanic/Latino; 115 Hispanic/Latino; 4 Native Hawaiian or other Pacific Islander, non-Hispanic/Latino; 52 Two or more races, non-Hispanic/Latino), 544 international. Average age 31. 5,842 applicants, 29% accepted, 1015 enrolled. *Faculty:* 88 full-time (20 women), 107 part-time/adjunct (21 women). Expenses: Contact institution. *Financial support:* In 2017–18, 649 students received support, including 440 fellowships (averaging $29,273 per year); research assistantships with partial tuition reimbursements available, teaching assistantships with partial tuition reimbursements available, career-related internships or fieldwork, institutionally sponsored loans, and scholarships/grants also available. Support available to part-time students. In 2017, 855 master's, 14 doctorates awarded. *Program availability:* Part-time, evening/weekend. Offers accounting (PhD); behavioral decision making (PhD); business administration (EMBA, MBA); business analytics (MSBA); decisions, operations, and technology management (PhD); finance (PhD); financial engineering (MFE); global economics and management (PhD); management and organizations (PhD); marketing (PhD); strategy and policy (PhD). *Application deadline:* For fall admission, 10/2 for domestic and international students; for winter admission, 1/8 for domestic and international students; for spring admission, 4/16 for domestic and international students. Applications are processed on a rolling basis. *Application fee:* $200. Electronic applications accepted. *Application Contact:* Alex Lawrence, Assistant Dean and Director of MBA Admissions, 310-825-6944, Fax: 310-825-8582, E-mail: mba.admissions@anderson.ucla.edu. *Dean,* 310-825-7982, Fax: 310-206-2073.

School of Dentistry Offers dentistry (MS, DDS, PhD, Certificate); oral biology (MS, PhD). Electronic applications accepted.

School of Law Offers law (LL M, JD, SJD). Electronic applications accepted.

UNIVERSITY OF CALIFORNIA, MERCED, Merced, CA 95343

General Information State-supported, coed, university. CGS member. *Enrollment:* 587 full-time matriculated graduate/professional students (265 women), 5 part-time matriculated graduate/professional students (2 women). *Enrollment by degree level:* 53 master's, 539 doctoral. *Graduate faculty:* 227 full-time (89 women), 5 part-time/adjunct (2 women). Tuition, state resident: full-time $11,502; part-time $5751 per semester. Tuition, nonresident: full-time $26,604; part-time $13,302 per semester. *Required fees:* $564 per semester. *Graduate housing:* On-campus housing not available. *Student services:* Campus employment opportunities, campus safety program, career counseling, child daycare facilities, exercise/wellness program, free psychological counseling, grant writing training, international student services, low-cost health insurance, multicultural affairs office, services for students with disabilities, teacher training, writing training. *Library facilities:* Kolligian Library. *Collection:* Students can reserve study rooms. *Research affiliation:* NASA (nanotechnology and engineering), National Science Foundation (STEM), National Institutes of Health (health and behavioral sciences), DARPA (STEM), Department of Defense (physics and engineering), Keck (bioengineering and nanotechnology).

Computer facilities: 230 computers available on campus for general student use. A campuswide network can be accessed from student residence rooms and from off campus. Online class registration, student calendar, 10Gb online cloud storage, free office software are available.
Website: http://www.ucmerced.edu/

General Application Contact: Tsu Ya, Director of Admissions and Academic Services, 209-228-4521, Fax: 209-228-6906, E-mail: tya@ucmerced.edu.

GRADUATE UNITS

Graduate Division Students: 589 full-time (266 women), 3 part-time (1 woman); includes 198 minority (14 Black or African American, non-Hispanic/Latino; 57 Asian, non-Hispanic/Latino; 106 Hispanic/Latino; 3 Native Hawaiian or other Pacific Islander, non-Hispanic/Latino; 18 Two or more races, non-Hispanic/Latino), 197 international. Average age 29. 820 applicants, 36% accepted, 176 enrolled. *Faculty:* 227 full-time (89 women), 5 part-time/adjunct (2 women). Expenses: Contact institution. *Financial support:* In 2017–18, 487 students received support, including 50 fellowships with full tuition reimbursements available (averaging $23,241 per year), 90 research assistantships with full tuition reimbursements available (averaging $15,463 per year), 413 teaching assistantships with full tuition reimbursements available; scholarships/grants, traineeships, and health care benefits also available. Financial award application deadline: 1/15. In 2017, 29 master's, 43 doctorates awarded. *Application deadline:* For fall admission, 1/15 for domestic and international students. *Application fee:* $105 ($125 for international students). Electronic applications accepted. *Application Contact:* Tsu Ya, Director of Admissions and Academic Services, 209-228-4521, Fax: 209-228-6906, E-mail: tya@ucmerced.edu. *Vice Provost and Graduate Dean,* Dr. Marjorie S. Zatz, 209-228-2408, Fax: 209-228-6906, E-mail: mzatz@ucmerced.edu.

School of Engineering Students: 184 full-time (60 women), 1 part-time (0 women); includes 41 minority (2 Black or African American, non-Hispanic/Latino; 16 Asian, non-Hispanic/Latino; 18 Hispanic/Latino; 1 Native Hawaiian or other Pacific Islander, non-Hispanic/Latino; 4 Two or more races, non-Hispanic/Latino), 112 international. Average age 28. 348 applicants, 35% accepted, 55 enrolled. *Faculty:* 55 full-time (13 women), 2 part-time/adjunct (1 woman). Expenses: Contact institution. *Financial support:* In 2017–18, 150 students received support, including 16 fellowships with full tuition reimbursements available (averaging $19,088 per year), 45 research assistantships with full tuition reimbursements available (averaging $18,389 per year), 89 teaching assistantships with full tuition reimbursements available (averaging $19,249 per year); scholarships/grants, traineeships, and health care benefits also available. Financial award application deadline: 1/15. In 2017, 13 master's, 15 doctorates awarded. Offers biological engineering and small scale technologies (MS, PhD); electrical engineering and computer science (MS, PhD); environmental systems (MS, PhD); management of innovation, sustainability, and technology (MM); mechanical engineering (MS); mechanical engineering and applied mechanics (PhD). *Application deadline:* For fall admission, 1/15 priority date for domestic and international students. Applications are processed on a rolling basis. *Application fee:* $90 ($110 for international students). Electronic applications accepted. *Application Contact:* Tsu Ya, Director of Admissions and Academic Services, 209-228-4521, Fax: 209-228-6906, E-mail: tya@ucmerced.edu. *Dean,* Dr. Mark Matsumoto, 209-228-4047, Fax: 209-228-4047, E-mail: mmatsumoto@ucmerced.edu.

School of Natural Sciences Students: 208 full-time (75 women); includes 71 minority (5 Black or African American, non-Hispanic/Latino; 24 Asian, non-Hispanic/Latino; 33 Hispanic/Latino; 1 Native Hawaiian or other Pacific Islander, non-Hispanic/Latino; 8 Two or more races, non-Hispanic/Latino), 52 international. Average age 28. 293 applicants, 45% accepted, 51 enrolled. *Faculty:* 71 full-time (27 women). Expenses: Contact institution. *Financial support:* In 2017–18, 170 students received support, including 19 fellowships with full tuition reimbursements available (averaging $23,832 per year), 32 research assistantships with full tuition reimbursements available (averaging $16,429 per year), 148 teaching assistantships with full tuition reimbursements available (averaging $16,038 per year); scholarships/grants, traineeships, and health care benefits also available. Financial award application deadline: 1/15. In 2017, 9 master's, 18 doctorates awarded. Offers applied mathematics (MS, PhD); chemistry and chemical biology (MS, PhD); physics (MS, PhD); quantitative and systems biology (MS, PhD). *Application deadline:* For fall admission, 1/15 for domestic and international students. *Application fee:* $90 ($110 for international students). Electronic applications accepted. *Application Contact:* Tsu Ya, Director of Graduate Admissions and Academic Services, 209-228-4521, Fax: 209-228-6906, E-mail: tya@ucmerced.edu. *Dean,* Dr. Elizabeth Dumont, 209-228-4487, Fax: 209-228-4060, E-mail: edumont@ucmerced.edu.

School of Social Sciences, Humanities and Arts Students: 197 full-time (131 women), 2 part-time (1 woman); includes 86 minority (7 Black or African American, non-Hispanic/Latino; 17 Asian, non-Hispanic/Latino; 55 Hispanic/Latino; 1 Native Hawaiian or other Pacific Islander, non-Hispanic/Latino; 6 Two or more races, non-Hispanic/Latino), 33 international. Average age 31. 190 applicants, 41% accepted, 49 enrolled. *Faculty:* 101 full-time (49 women), 3 part-time/adjunct (1 woman). Expenses: Contact institution. *Financial support:* In 2017–18, 167 students received support, including 17 fellowships with full tuition reimbursements available (averaging $23,250 per year), 13 research assistantships with full tuition reimbursements available (averaging $15,387 per year), 162 teaching assistantships with full tuition reimbursements available (averaging $16,103 per year); scholarships/grants, traineeships, and health care benefits also available. Financial award application deadline: 1/15. In 2017, 7 master's, 10 doctorates awarded. Offers cognitive and information sciences (PhD); interdisciplinary humanities (MA, PhD); psychological sciences (MA, PhD); social sciences (MA, PhD); sociology (MA, PhD). *Application* *deadline:* For fall admission, 1/15 for domestic and international students. *Application fee:* $90 ($110 for international students). Electronic applications accepted. *Application Contact:* Tsu Ya, Director of Admissions and Academic Services, 209-228-4521, Fax: 209-228-6906, E-mail: tya@ucmerced.edu. *Dean*, Dr. Jill Robbins, 209-228-7843, E-mail: jillrobbins@ucmerced.edu.

UNIVERSITY OF CALIFORNIA, RIVERSIDE, Riverside, CA 92521-0102

General Information State-supported, coed, university. CGS member. *Enrollment:* 23,278 graduate, professional, and undergraduate students; 3,084 full-time matriculated graduate/professional students (1,376 women), 14 part-time matriculated graduate/professional students (5 women). *Enrollment by degree level:* 909 master's, 2,008 doctoral, 181 other advanced degrees. *Graduate faculty:* 689 full-time (221 women). Tuition, state resident: full-time $5746. Tuition, nonresident: full-time $10,780. Tuition and fees vary according to campus/location and program. *Graduate housing:* Rooms and/or apartments available on a first-come, first-served basis to single and married students. Housing application deadline: 6/1. *Student services:* Campus employment opportunities, campus safety program, career counseling, child daycare facilities, exercise/wellness program, free psychological counseling, grant writing training, international student services, low-cost health insurance, multicultural affairs office, services for students with disabilities, teacher training, writing training. *Library facilities:* Tomas Rivera Library plus 4 others. *Collection:* Books: 3 million (physical), 938,175 (digital/electronic); Serial titles: 71,249 (physical); Databases: 1,713. Weekly public service hours: 96; study areas open 24 hours, 5–7 days a week; students can reserve study rooms. *Research affiliation:* Los Alamos National Laboratory (botany and plant sciences, chemistry, earth sciences, physics), Brookhaven National Laboratory (chemistry, physics), U.S. Salinity Laboratory (environmental sciences, biochemistry), J. Paul Getty Museum (art history), Lawrence Livermore National Laboratory (anthropology), Fermi National Accelerator Laboratory (physics).

Computer facilities: Computer purchase and lease plans are available. 556 computers available on campus for general student use. A campuswide network can be accessed from student residence rooms and from off campus. Online class registration, online viewing of financial information are available.
Website: http://www.ucr.edu/

General Application Contact: Graduate Admissions, 951-8273313, E-mail: grdadmis@ucr.edu.

GRADUATE UNITS

Graduate Division *Program availability:* Part-time, evening/weekend. Offers anthropology (MA, MS, PhD); archival management (MA); art history (MA, PhD); biochemistry and molecular biology (MS, PhD); bioengineering (MS, PhD); biomedical sciences (PhD); cell, molecular, and developmental biology (MS, PhD); chemical and environmental engineering (MS, PhD); chemistry (MS, PhD); classics (PhD); comparative literature (MA, PhD); composition (PhD); computer engineering (MS); computer science (MS, PhD); creative writing and writing for the performing arts (MFA); cultural politics and production (PhD); economics (MA, PhD); electrical engineering (MS, PhD); English (MA, PhD); entomology (MS, PhD); environmental sciences (MS, PhD); environmental toxicology (MS, PhD); ethnomusicology (MA); evolution, ecology and organismal biology (MS, PhD); experimental choreography (MFA); genetics, genomics, and bioinformatics (PhD); geological sciences (MS, PhD); history (PhD); materials science and engineering (MS); mathematics (MS, PhD); mechanical engineering (MS, PhD); microbiology (MS, PhD); neuroscience (PhD); philosophy (MA, PhD); physics (MS, PhD); plant biology (MS, PhD); plant pathology (MS, PhD); political science (MA, PhD); psychology (PhD); religious studies (MA, PhD); sociology (MA, PhD); Southeast Asian studies (MA); Spanish (MA, PhD); statistics (MS); visual arts (MFA). Electronic applications accepted.

The A. Gary Anderson Graduate School of Management Students: 180 full-time (92 women), 114 part-time (48 women); includes 75 minority (13 Black or African American, non-Hispanic/Latino; 1 American Indian or Alaska Native, non-Hispanic/Latino; 33 Asian, non-Hispanic/Latino; 28 Hispanic/Latino), 187 international. Average age 27. 722 applicants, 63% accepted, 169 enrolled. *Faculty:* 32 full-time (8 women), 38 part-time/adjunct (7 women). Expenses: Contact institution. *Financial support:* Fellowships with partial tuition reimbursements, research assistantships with full tuition reimbursements, teaching assistantships with partial tuition reimbursements, career-related internships or fieldwork, institutionally sponsored loans, scholarships/grants, and tuition waivers (full) available. Financial award application deadline: 5/1; financial award applicants required to submit FAFSA. In 2017, 133 master's, 1 doctorate awarded. *Program availability:* Part-time, evening/weekend. Offers accounting (MPAC); business administration (MBA, PhD); finance (M Fin). *Application deadline:* For fall admission, 9/1 for domestic students, 5/1 for international students; for winter admission, 12/1 for domestic students, 9/1 for international students; for spring admission, 3/1 for domestic students, 10/1 for international students. Applications are processed on a rolling basis. *Application fee:* $100 ($125 for international students). Electronic applications accepted. *Application Contact:* Mark Estrada, Director of Graduate Admissions, 951-827-2915, E-mail: mark.estrada@ucr.edu. *Dean, School of Business*, Yunzeng Wang, 951-827-3704, E-mail: yunzeng.wang@ucr.edu.

Graduate School of Education Students: 241 full-time (188 women). 396 applicants, 42% accepted, 166 enrolled. *Faculty:* 29 full-time (16 women), 2 part-time/adjunct (1 woman). Expenses: Contact institution. *Financial support:* In 2017–18, 105 students received support, including 16 fellowships with full tuition reimbursements available (averaging $31,000 per year), 25 research assistantships with full tuition reimbursements available (averaging $31,000 per year), 10 teaching assistantships with full tuition reimbursements available (averaging $31,000 per year); career-related internships or fieldwork, Federal Work-Study, institutionally sponsored loans, scholarships/grants, and unspecified assistantships also available. Financial award application deadline: 12/15. In 2017, 130 master's, 15 doctorates, 14 other advanced degrees awarded. Offers applied behavior analysis (M Ed); diversity and equity (M Ed); education policy analysis and leadership (PhD); education specialist (Credential); education, society, and culture (MA, PhD); educational psychology (MA, PhD); general education (M Ed); higher education administration and policy (M Ed, PhD); multiple subject (Credential); research, evaluation, measurement and statistics (MA); school psychology (PhD); single subject (Credential); special education (M Ed, PhD); special education and autism (MA); TESOL (M Ed). *Application deadline:* For fall admission, 9/1 for domestic students, 6/1 for international students; for winter admission, 11/15 for domestic students, 9/1 for international students; for spring admission, 3/1 for domestic students, 12/1 for international students. Applications are processed on a rolling basis. *Application fee:* $80 ($100 for international students). Electronic applications accepted. *Application Contact:* Heather Killeen, Graduate Program Coordinator, 951-827-6362, E-mail: heather.killeen@ucr.edu. *Dean*, Thomas Smith, 951-827-4633, E-mail: thomas.smith@ucr.edu.

School of Public Policy Offers global health (MS); public policy (MPP, PhD). MD/MPP offered in partnership with School of Medicine.

School of Medicine Offers medicine (MD).

UNIVERSITY OF CALIFORNIA, SAN DIEGO, La Jolla, CA 92093

General Information State-supported, coed, university. CGS member. *Enrollment:* 35,772 graduate, professional, and undergraduate students; 5,692 full-time matriculated graduate/professional students (2,143 women), 715 part-time matriculated graduate/professional students (274 women). *Enrollment by degree level:* 3,147 master's, 3,255 doctoral. *Graduate housing:* Rooms and/or apartments available on a first-come, first-served basis to single and married students. *Student services:* Campus employment opportunities, campus safety program, career counseling, child daycare facilities, exercise/wellness program, free psychological counseling, grant writing training, international student services, low-cost health insurance, multicultural affairs office, services for students with disabilities, teacher training, writing training. *Library facilities:* Geisel Library plus 1 other. *Collection:* Books: 3.5 million (physical), 958,000 (digital/electronic). Study areas open 24 hours, 5–7 days a week; students can reserve study rooms. *Research affiliation:* Sanford Burnham Institute, National Oceanic and Atmospheric Administration (NOAA) Fisheries, Veterans Administration Medical Center, Scripps Research Institute, La Jolla Institute for Allergy and Immunology, Salk Institute for Biological Studies.

Computer facilities: A campuswide network can be accessed from student residence rooms and from off campus. Online class registration is available.
Website: http://www.ucsd.edu/

General Application Contact: Graduate Admissions Office, 858-534-3554, E-mail: gradadmissions@ucsd.edu.

GRADUATE UNITS

Graduate Division Students: 5,692 full-time (2,143 women), 715 part-time (274 women); includes 1,486 minority (148 Black or African American, non-Hispanic/Latino; 28 American Indian or Alaska Native, non-Hispanic/Latino; 827 Asian, non-Hispanic/Latino; 478 Hispanic/Latino; 5 Native Hawaiian or other Pacific Islander, non-Hispanic/Latino), 2,928 international. 21,710 applicants, 29% accepted, 2397 enrolled. Expenses: Contact institution. *Financial support:* Fellowships with tuition reimbursements, research assistantships with tuition reimbursements, teaching assistantships with partial tuition reimbursements, career-related internships or fieldwork, institutionally sponsored loans, scholarships/grants, traineeships, health care benefits, and unspecified assistantships available. Support available to part-time students. Financial award applicants required to submit FAFSA. In 2017, 1,619 master's, 542 doctorates awarded. Offers acting (MFA); aerospace engineering (MS, PhD); anthropology (PhD); applied mathematics (MA); applied mechanics (MS, PhD); applied ocean science (MS, PhD); applied physics (MS, PhD); architecture-based enterprise systems engineering (MAS); art history, theory, and criticism (PhD); bioengineering (M Eng, MS, PhD); bioinformatics and systems biology (PhD); biophysics (PhD); chemical engineering (MS, PhD); chemistry (MS, PhD); climate science and policy (MAS); clinical psychology (PhD); cognitive science (PhD); communication (PhD); communication of science (PhD); communication theory and systems (MS, PhD); computational neuroscience (PhD); computational science (PhD); computational science, mathematics and engineering (MS); computer engineering (MS, PhD); computer science (MS, PhD); contemporary music performance (DMA); dance theatre (MFA); data science and engineering (MAS); design (MFA); directing (MFA); drama and theatre (PhD); earth sciences (PhD); economics (PhD); education (M Ed, PhD); educational leadership (Ed D); electronic circuits and systems (MS, PhD); engineering physics (MS, PhD); engineering sciences (PhD); epidemiology (PhD); ethnic studies (PhD); geophysics (PhD); global health (PhD); health behavior (PhD); history (MA, PhD); history of science (PhD); intelligent systems, robotics and control (MS, PhD); Judaic studies (MA); language and communicative disorders (PhD); Latin American studies (MA); linguistics (PhD); literature (PhD); marine biodiversity and conservation (MAS); materials science and engineering (MS, PhD); mathematics (MA, PhD); mathematics and science education (PhD); mechanical engineering (MS, PhD); medical device engineering (MAS); medical devices and systems (MS, PhD); multi-scale biology (PhD); music (MA, PhD); nanoengineering (MS, PhD); nanoscale devices and systems (MS, PhD); oceanography (MS, PhD); philosophy (PhD); philosophy of science (PhD); photonics (MS, PhD); physics (MS, PhD); playwriting (MFA); political science (PhD); political science and international affairs (PhD); psychology (PhD); quantitative biology (PhD); signal and image processing (MS, PhD); sociology (PhD); sociology of science (PhD); stage management (MFA); statistics (MS, PhD); structural engineering (MS, PhD); structural health monitoring, prognosis, and validated simulations (MS); teaching and learning (MA, Ed D); visual arts (MFA); wireless embedded systems (MAS); writing (MFA). *Application fee:* $105 ($125 for international students). Electronic applications accepted. *Application Contact:* Graduate Admissions, 858-534-3554, E-mail: gradadmissions@ucsd.edu. *Dean*, Dr. Kit Pogliano, 858-534-6655, E-mail: graduatedean@ucsd.edu.

Division of Biological Sciences Students: 335 full-time (191 women), 6 part-time (1 woman). 728 applicants, 28% accepted, 139 enrolled. Expenses: Contact institution. *Financial support:* Fellowships, research assistantships, teaching assistantships, scholarships/grants, traineeships, and unspecified assistantships available. Financial award applicants required to submit FAFSA. In 2017, 35 doctorates awarded. Offers anthropogeny (PhD); bioinformatics (PhD); biology (PhD); interdisciplinary environmental research (PhD); multi-scale biology (PhD); quantitative biology (PhD). PhD in biology offered jointly with San Diego State University. *Application deadline:* For fall admission, 11/28 for domestic students. *Application fee:* $105 ($125 for international students). Electronic applications accepted. *Application Contact:* Brandon Keith, Program Coordinator, 858-534-8983, E-mail: biogradprog@ucsd.edu. *Chair*, Jens Lykke-Andersen, 858-822-3659.

Rady School of Management Students: 436 full-time (201 women), 119 part-time (60 women). 2,265 applicants, 33% accepted, 307 enrolled. *Faculty:* 28 full-time (5 women), 5 part-time/adjunct (1 woman). Expenses: Contact institution. *Financial support:* Fellowships, teaching assistantships, and scholarships/grants available. Financial award applicants required to submit FAFSA. In 2017, 193 master's, 2 doctorates awarded. *Program availability:* Part-time, evening/weekend. Offers business administration (MBA); business analytics (MS); finance (MF); management (PhD). *Application deadline:* Applications are processed on a rolling basis. *Application fee:* $200. Electronic applications accepted. *Application Contact:* Jay Bryant, Director of Graduate Recruitment and Admissions, 858-534-0864, E-mail: radygradadmissions@ucsd.edu. *Dean*, Robert Sullivan, 858-822-0830, E-mail: rssullivan@ucsd.edu.

School of Global Policy and Strategy *Program availability:* Part-time. Offers American policy in global context (MPP); business, government and regulation (MPP); Chinese economic and political affairs (MCEPA); energy and environmental policy (MPP); health policy (MPP); international affairs (MAS, MIA); international development and nonprofit management (MIA); international economics (MIA); international environmental policy (MIA); international management (MIA); international politics (MIA); political science and international affairs (PhD); program design and evaluation (MPP); public policy (MPP); security policy (MPP). Electronic applications accepted.

School of Medicine Students: 502. Expenses: Contact institution. Offers anthropogeny (PhD); audiology (Au D); bioinformatics (PhD); biomedical science (PhD); biostatistics (PhD); clinical research (MAS); leadership of healthcare organizations (MAS); medicine (MAS, Au D, MD, PhD); multi-scale biology (PhD); neurosciences (PhD). *Application Contact:* 858-534-3880, E-mail: somadmissions@ucsd.edu. *Associate Dean for Admissions*, Dr. Carolyn J. Kelly, MD.

Skaggs School of Pharmacy and Pharmaceutical Sciences Students: 251. Expenses: Contact institution. Offers pharmacy and pharmaceutical sciences (Pharm D). *Application Contact:* 858-822-4900, Fax: 858-822-5591, E-mail: sppsadmissions@ucsd.edu. *Dean*, Dr. James McKerrow.

UNIVERSITY OF CALIFORNIA, SAN FRANCISCO, San Francisco, CA 94143

General Information State-supported, coed, graduate-only institution. CGS member. *Graduate housing:* Rooms and/or apartments available to single and married students.

GRADUATE UNITS

Graduate Division *Program availability:* Part-time. Offers biochemistry and molecular biology (PhD); bioengineering (PhD); biomedical imaging (MS); biomedical sciences (PhD); cell biology (PhD); developmental biology (PhD); genetics (PhD); health policy and law (MS); history of health sciences (MA, PhD); medical anthropology (PhD); neuroscience (PhD); oral and craniofacial sciences (MS, PhD); physical therapy (DPT, DPTSc).

School of Nursing Offers nursing (MS, PhD); sociology (PhD).

School of Dentistry Offers dentistry (DDS).

School of Medicine Offers medicine (MD, PhD). Electronic applications accepted.

School of Pharmacy Offers bioinformatics (PhD); biophysics (PhD); chemistry and chemical biology (PhD); pharmaceutical sciences and pharmacogenomics (PhD); pharmacy (MS, PhD, Pharm D). Electronic applications accepted.

UNIVERSITY OF CALIFORNIA, SANTA BARBARA, Santa Barbara, CA 93106-2014

General Information State-supported, coed, university. CGS member. *Graduate housing:* Rooms and/or apartments guaranteed to single students and available on a first-come, first-served basis to married students. Housing application deadline: 6/1. *Research affiliation:* California NanoSystems Institute, The Institute for Social, Behavioral and Economic Research, National Center for Ecological Analysis and Synthesis, The Institute for Collaborative Biotechnologies, Institute for Polymers and Organic Solids, Mitsubishi Chemical Center for Advanced Materials.

GRADUATE UNITS

Graduate Division Electronic applications accepted.

College of Engineering Offers bioengineering (PhD); chemical engineering (MS, PhD); communications, control and signal processing (MS, PhD); computer engineering (MS, PhD); computer science (MS, PhD); electronics and photonics (MS, PhD); engineering (MS, MTM, PhD); materials (MS, PhD); mechanical engineering (MS); technology management (MTM). Electronic applications accepted.

College of Letters and Sciences Offers ancient history (PhD); ancient Mediterranean studies (PhD); applied linguistics (PhD); applied mathematics (MA); art (MFA); art history (PhD); astrophysics (PhD); biochemistry and molecular biology (PhD); bioengineering (PhD); brass (MM); chemistry (MA, MS, PhD); classics (MA, PhD); cognitive science (PhD); communication (PhD); comparative literature (PhD); composition (MA, PhD); conducting (MM, DMA); dynamical neuroscience (PhD); earth science (MS, PhD); East Asian languages and cultural studies (MA); East Asian literatures (PhD); ecology, evolution, and marine biology (MA, PhD); economics (MA); English (PhD); ethnomusicology (MA, PhD); European medieval studies (PhD); feminist studies (MA, PhD); film and media studies (PhD); financial mathematics and statistics (PhD); French (PhD); geography (MA, PhD); global culture, ideology, and religion (MA, PhD); global government, human rights, and civil society (MA, PhD); global studies (PhD); Hispanic languages and literatures (PhD); Hispanic linguistics (MA); humanities and fine arts (MA, MFA, MM, MS, DMA, PhD); interdisciplinary emphasis: Black studies (PhD); interdisciplinary emphasis: environment and society (PhD); interdisciplinary emphasis: feminist studies (PhD); interdisciplinary emphasis: global studies (PhD); interdisciplinary emphasis: language, interaction and social organization (PhD); interdisciplinary emphasis: quantitative methods in the social sciences (PhD); interdisciplinary emphasis: technology and society (PhD); keyboard (MM, DMA); language, interaction and social organization (PhD); Latin American and Iberian studies (MA); letters and sciences (MA, MFA, MM, MS, DMA, PhD); linguistics (PhD); literature and theory (MA); Luso-Brazilian literature (MA); marine science (MS, PhD); mathematical economics (PhD); mathematics (MA, PhD); mathematics, life, and physical sciences (MA, MS, PhD); media arts and technology (MS, PhD); molecular, cellular, and developmental biology (MA, PhD); musicology (MA, PhD); philosophy (PhD); physics (PhD); piano accompanying (MM); political economy, sustainable development, and the environment (MA, PhD); political science (PhD); psychology (PhD); public finance (PhD); public historical studies (PhD); quantitative methods in the social sciences (PhD); religious studies (MA, PhD); social sciences (MA, PhD); society and technology (PhD); sociocultural anthropology (PhD); sociology (PhD); Spanish or Spanish-American literature (MA); statistics (MA); statistics and applied probability (PhD); strings (MM, DMA); technology and society (PhD); theater studies (MA, PhD); theory (MA, PhD); translation studies (PhD); transportation (PhD); voice (MM, DMA); women's studies (PhD); woodwinds (MM). Electronic applications accepted.

Donald Bren School of Environmental Science and Management Offers economics and environmental science (PhD); environmental science and management (MESM, PhD); technology and society (PhD). Electronic applications accepted.

Gevirtz Graduate School of Education Offers counseling, clinical and school psychology (MA, PhD, Credential); education (MA, PhD); teacher education (M Ed, Credential). Electronic applications accepted.

UNIVERSITY OF CALIFORNIA, SANTA CRUZ, Santa Cruz, CA 95064

General Information State-supported, coed, university. CGS member. *Graduate housing:* Rooms and/or apartments available on a first-come, first-served basis to single and married students. Housing application deadline: 5/20. *Research affiliation:* Center for Biomimetic MicroElectronic Systems (science and engineering), Center for Information Technology Research in the Interest of Society (science and engineering), Institute for Regenerative Medicine (science and engineering), Center for Adaptive Optics (science and engineering), Center for Biomolecular Science and Engineering (science and engineering), Institute for Quantitative Biology (science and engineering).

GRADUATE UNITS

Division of Graduate Studies Electronic applications accepted.

Division of Humanities Offers history (MA, PhD); history of consciousness (PhD); humanities (MA, PhD); linguistics (MA, PhD); literature (MA, PhD); philosophy (MA, PhD). Electronic applications accepted.

Division of Physical and Biological Sciences Offers astronomy and astrophysics (PhD); chemistry and biochemistry (MS, PhD); earth and planetary sciences (MS, PhD); ecology and evolutionary biology (MA, PhD); environmental toxicology (MS, PhD); mathematics (MA, PhD); molecular, cellular, and developmental biology (MA, PhD); ocean sciences (MS, PhD); physical and biological sciences (MA, MS, PhD, Certificate); physics (MS, PhD); science communication (Certificate). Electronic applications accepted.

Division of Social Sciences Offers applied economics and finance (MS); cultural anthropology (PhD); education (MA, PhD); environmental studies (PhD); international economics (PhD); politics (PhD); psychology (PhD); social documentation (MA); social sciences (MA, MS, PhD); sociology (PhD). Electronic applications accepted.

Division of the Arts Offers arts (MA, MFA, DMA, PhD, Certificate); digital arts and new media (MFA); ethnomusicology (MA); film and digital media (PhD); music (PhD); music composition (MA, DMA); music composition (DMA); performance practice (MA); theater arts (Certificate); visual studies (PhD). Electronic applications accepted.

Jack Baskin School of Engineering Students: 537 full-time (134 women), 53 part-time (11 women); includes 87 minority (6 Black or African American, non-Hispanic/Latino; 3 American Indian or Alaska Native, non-Hispanic/Latino; 45 Asian, non-Hispanic/Latino; 25 Hispanic/Latino; 8 Native Hawaiian or other Pacific Islander, non-Hispanic/Latino), 318 international. 2,109 applicants, 30% accepted, 196 enrolled. *Faculty:* 102 full-time (20 women), 24 part-time/adjunct (4 women). Expenses: Contact institution. *Financial support:* Fellowships, research assistantships, teaching assistantships, institutionally sponsored loans, traineeships, health care benefits, and tuition waivers (full and partial) available. Financial award applicants required to submit FAFSA. In 2017, 120 master's, 43 doctorates awarded. *Program availability:* Part-time. Offers biomolecular engineering and bioinformatics (MS, PhD); computational media (MS, PhD); computer engineering (MS, PhD); computer science (MS, PhD); electrical engineering (MS, PhD); engineering (MS, PhD); games and playable media (MS); scientific computing and applied mathematics (MS); statistics and applied mathematics (MS, PhD); technology management (PhD). *Application fee:* $105 ($125 for international students). Electronic applications accepted. *Application Contact:* BSOE Graduate Student Affairs Office, 831-459-3531, E-mail: bsoe-ga@rt.ucsc.edu. *Associate Dean of Graduate Studies*, Dr. Abel Rodriguez, 831-459-1047, E-mail: abel.rod@ucsc.edu.

UNIVERSITY OF CENTRAL ARKANSAS, Conway, AR 72035-0001

General Information State-supported, coed, university. CGS member. *Graduate housing:* Rooms and/or apartments available on a first-come, first-served basis to single and married students. Housing application deadline: 7/1. *Student services:* Campus employment opportunities, campus safety program, career counseling, exercise/wellness program, free psychological counseling, grant writing training, international student services, low-cost health insurance, multicultural affairs office, services for students with disabilities, teacher training, writing training. *Library facilities:* Torreyson Library plus 1 other. *Collection:* Books: 334,487 (physical), 16,056 (digital/electronic); Serial titles: 2,979 (physical), 55,507 (digital/electronic); Databases: 125. Study areas open 24 hours, 5–7 days a week; students can reserve study rooms. *Research affiliation:* 3M Corporation, State Farm Foundation (insurance), Arkansas Game and Fish Commission, Acxiom (math, computers), Arkansas Educational Television Network.

Computer facilities: 610 computers available on campus for general student use. A campuswide network can be accessed from student residence rooms and from off campus. Online class registration is available.
Website: http://www.uca.edu/

General Application Contact: Colleen Elliott, Admission Specialist, 501-450-5065, Fax: 501-450-5678, E-mail: colleene@uca.edu.

GRADUATE UNITS

Graduate School Expenses: Contact institution. *Financial support:* Research assistantships with partial tuition reimbursements, teaching assistantships with partial tuition reimbursements, career-related internships or fieldwork, Federal Work-Study, scholarships/grants, traineeships, tuition waivers (partial), and unspecified assistantships available. Support available to part-time students. Financial award application deadline: 2/15; financial award applicants required to submit FAFSA. *Program availability:* Part-time, evening/weekend, online learning. Offers leadership studies (PhD). *Application deadline:* For fall admission, 3/1 priority date for domestic and international students; for spring admission, 10/1 priority date for domestic and international students. Applications are processed on a rolling basis. *Application fee:* $25 ($50 for international students).

College of Business Administration Expenses: Contact institution. *Financial support:* Research assistantships with full tuition reimbursements, career-related internships or fieldwork, Federal Work-Study, scholarships/grants, and unspecified assistantships available. Support available to part-time students. Financial award application deadline: 2/15; financial award applicants required to submit FAFSA. *Program availability:* Part-time, evening/weekend. Offers accounting (M Acc); business administration (M Acc, MBA). *Application deadline:* For fall admission, 3/1 priority date for domestic and international students; for spring admission, 10/1 priority date for domestic and international students. Applications are processed on a rolling basis. *Application fee:* $25 ($50 for international students).

College of Education Expenses: Contact institution. *Financial support:* Career-related internships or fieldwork, Federal Work-Study, scholarships/grants, tuition waivers (partial), and unspecified assistantships available. Financial award application deadline: 2/15; financial award applicants required to submit FAFSA. *Program availability:* Part-time, evening/weekend, online learning. Offers collaborative instructional specialist (ages 0-8) (MSE); collaborative instructional specialist (grades 4-12) (MSE); college student personnel (MS); district-level administration (PMC); education (MAT, MS, MSE, Ed S, Graduate Certificate, PMC); educational leadership - district level (Ed S); gifted and talented education (Graduate Certificate); instructional facilitator (Graduate Certificate); instructional technology (MS); library media and information technology (MS); reading education (MSE); school counseling (MS); school leadership (MS); school-based leadership adult education program administration (PMC); school-based leadership building administration (PMC); school-based leadership curriculum administration (PMC); school-based leadership gifted and talented program administration (PMC); school-based leadership special education program administration (PMC); special education (MSE, Graduate

Certificate); special education instructional specialist grades 4-12 (Graduate Certificate); special education instructional specialist P-4 (Graduate Certificate); teaching (MAT); teaching and learning (MSE). *Application deadline:* For fall admission, 3/1 priority date for domestic and international students; for spring admission, 10/1 priority date for domestic and international students. Applications are processed on a rolling basis. *Application fee:* $25 ($50 for international students). Electronic applications accepted.

College of Fine Arts and Communication Expenses: Contact institution. *Financial support:* Federal Work-Study, scholarships/grants, tuition waivers (partial), and unspecified assistantships available. Financial award application deadline: 2/15; financial award applicants required to submit FAFSA. *Program availability:* Part-time. Offers choral conducting (MM); creative writing (MFA); digital filmmaking (MFA); fine arts and communication (MFA, MM, PC); instrumental conducting (MM); music (PC); music education (MM); music theory (MM); performance (MM). *Application deadline:* For fall admission, 3/1 priority date for domestic students; for spring admission, 10/1 priority date for domestic students. Applications are processed on a rolling basis. *Application fee:* $25 ($50 for international students). Electronic applications accepted. *Application Contact:* Terry Wright, Dean, 501-450-3293, E-mail: terryw@uca.edu. *Dean*, Terry Wright, 501-450-3293, E-mail: terryw@uca.edu.

College of Health and Behavioral Sciences Expenses: Contact institution. *Financial support:* Career-related internships or fieldwork, Federal Work-Study, scholarships/grants, traineeships, tuition waivers (partial), and unspecified assistantships available. Support available to part-time students. Financial award application deadline: 2/15; financial award applicants required to submit FAFSA. *Program availability:* Part-time, evening/weekend, online learning. Offers adult nurse practitioner (PMC); clinical nurse leader (PMC); clinical nurse specialist (MSN); communication sciences and disorders (PhD); community counseling (MS); counseling psychology (MS); family and consumer sciences (MS); family nurse practitioner (PMC); health and behavioral sciences (MS, MSN, DPT, PhD, PMC); health education (MS); kinesiology (MS); nurse educator (PMC); nurse practitioner (MSN); nutrition (MS); occupational therapy (MS); physical therapy (DPT, PhD); school psychology (MS, PhD, PMC); speech-language pathology (MS). *Application deadline:* For fall admission, 3/1 priority date for domestic and international students; for spring admission, 10/1 for domestic and international students. Applications are processed on a rolling basis. *Application fee:* $25 ($50 for international students). Electronic applications accepted. *Application Contact:* Sandy Burks, Administrative Assistant, 501-450-3124, Fax: 501-450-5678, E-mail: slburks@uca.edu. *Dean*, Dr. Neil Hattlestad, 501-450-3122, Fax: 501-450-5503, E-mail: neilh@uca.edu.

College of Liberal Arts Expenses: Contact institution. *Financial support:* Teaching assistantships with partial tuition reimbursements, Federal Work-Study, scholarships/grants, and unspecified assistantships available. Financial award application deadline: 2/15; financial award applicants required to submit FAFSA. *Program availability:* Part-time. Offers community and economic development (MS); English (MA); geographic information systems (MGIS, Certificate); history (MA); liberal arts (MA); Spanish (MA). *Application deadline:* For fall admission, 3/1 priority date for domestic students; for spring admission, 10/1 priority date for domestic students. Applications are processed on a rolling basis. *Application fee:* $25 ($50 for international students). Electronic applications accepted.

College of Natural Sciences and Math Expenses: Contact institution. *Financial support:* Research assistantships, career-related internships or fieldwork, Federal Work-Study, and unspecified assistantships available. Financial award application deadline: 2/15; financial award applicants required to submit FAFSA. *Program availability:* Part-time. Offers applied computing (MS); applied mathematics (MS); biological science (MS); math education (MA); natural sciences and math (MA, MS). *Application deadline:* For fall admission, 3/1 priority date for domestic and international students; for spring admission, 10/1 priority date for domestic and international students. Applications are processed on a rolling basis. *Application fee:* $25 ($50 for international students). Electronic applications accepted.

UNIVERSITY OF CENTRAL FLORIDA, Orlando, FL 32816

General Information State-supported, coed, university. CGS member. *Enrollment:* 66,183 graduate, professional, and undergraduate students; 4,111 full-time matriculated graduate/professional students (2,219 women), 4,254 part-time matriculated graduate/professional students (2,721 women). *Graduate faculty:* 1,623 full-time (692 women), 620 part-time/adjunct (335 women). Tuition, state resident: part-time $288.16 per credit hour. Tuition, nonresident: part-time $1073.31 per credit hour. Tuition and fees vary according to program. *Graduate housing:* Room and/or apartments available on a first-come, first-served basis to single students; on-campus housing not available to married students. Housing application deadline: 3/1. *Student services:* Campus employment opportunities, campus safety program, career counseling, child daycare facilities, exercise/wellness program, free psychological counseling, grant writing training, international student services, low-cost health insurance, multicultural affairs office, services for students with disabilities, teacher training, writing training. *Library facilities:* University Library plus 1 other. *Collection:* Books: 1.6 million (physical), 157,535 (digital/electronic); Serial titles: 737 (physical), 68,194 (digital/electronic); Databases: 481. Weekly public service hours: 106; students can reserve study rooms.

Computer facilities: Computer purchase and lease plans are available. 4,113 computers available on campus for general student use. A campuswide network can be accessed from student residence rooms and from off campus. Online class registration is available.
Website: http://www.ucf.edu/

General Application Contact: Associate Director, Graduate Admissions, 407-823-2766, Fax: 407-823-6442, E-mail: gradadmissions@ucf.edu.

GRADUATE UNITS

College of Arts and Humanities Students: 265 full-time (119 women), 256 part-time (135 women); includes 148 minority (23 Black or African American, non-Hispanic/Latino; 15 Asian, non-Hispanic/Latino; 96 Hispanic/Latino; 14 Two or more races, non-Hispanic/Latino), 43 international. Average age 30. 471 applicants, 67% accepted, 214 enrolled. *Faculty:* 320 full-time (158 women), 107 part-time/adjunct (46 women). Expenses: Contact institution. *Financial support:* In 2017–18, 122 students received support, including 40 fellowships with partial tuition reimbursements available (averaging $6,840 per year), 34 research assistantships with partial tuition reimbursements available (averaging $6,794 per year), 89 teaching assistantships with partial tuition reimbursements available (averaging $8,679 per year); career-related internships or fieldwork, Federal Work-Study, institutionally sponsored loans, scholarships/grants, health care benefits, tuition waivers (partial), and unspecified assistantships also available. Financial award application deadline: 3/1; financial award applicants required to submit FAFSA. In 2017, 148 master's, 6 doctorates, 29 other advanced degrees awarded. *Program availability:* Part-time, evening/weekend. Offers arts and humanities (MA, MFA, MS, PhD, Certificate); creative writing (MFA); English (MA, Certificate); history (MA); Spanish (MA); teaching English as a foreign language (Certificate); teaching English to speakers of other languages (MA, Certificate); texts and technology (PhD). *Application fee:* $30. Electronic applications accepted. *Application Contact:* Associate Director, Graduate Admissions, 407-823-2766, Fax: 407-823-6442, E-mail: gradadmissions@ucf.edu. *Dean*, Jeffrey Moore, 407-823-2573, E-mail: jeffrey.moore@ucf.edu.

Florida Interactive Entertainment Academy Students: 73 full-time (19 women), 68 part-time (17 women); includes 39 minority (8 Black or African American, non-Hispanic/Latino; 7 Asian, non-Hispanic/Latino; 18 Hispanic/Latino; 6 Two or more races, non-Hispanic/Latino), 25 international. Average age 25. 150 applicants, 62% accepted, 70 enrolled. Expenses: Contact institution. *Financial support:* Application deadline: 3/1; applicants required to submit FAFSA. In 2017, 53 master's awarded. Offers interactive entertainment (MS). *Application deadline:* For fall admission, 7/15 for domestic students. *Application fee:* $30. Electronic applications accepted. *Application Contact:* Associate Director, Graduate Admissions, 407-823-2766, Fax: 407-823-6442, E-mail: gradadmissions@ucf.edu. *Executive Director*, Ben Noel, 407-235-3580, Fax: 407-317-7094, E-mail: bnoel@fiea.ucf.edu.

School of Performing Arts Students: 32 full-time (14 women), 18 part-time (8 women); includes 11 minority (1 Black or African American, non-Hispanic/Latino; 8 Hispanic/Latino; 2 Two or more races, non-Hispanic/Latino), 4 international. Average age 33. 51 applicants, 59% accepted, 18 enrolled. Expenses: Contact institution. *Financial support:* In 2017–18, 26 students received support, including 7 fellowships with partial tuition reimbursements available (averaging $7,857 per year), 5 research assistantships with partial tuition reimbursements available (averaging $5,539 per year), 21 teaching assistantships with partial tuition reimbursements available (averaging $7,179 per year); career-related internships or fieldwork, Federal Work-Study, institutionally sponsored loans, health care benefits, tuition waivers (partial), and unspecified assistantships also available. Financial award application deadline: 3/1; financial award applicants required to submit FAFSA. In 2017, 17 master's awarded. *Program availability:* Part-time. Offers music (MA); theatre (MA, MFA). *Application deadline:* For fall admission, 7/15 for domestic students; for spring admission, 12/1 for domestic students. *Application fee:* $30. Electronic applications accepted. *Application Contact:* Associate Director, Graduate Admissions, 407-823-2766, Fax: 407-823-6442, E-mail: gradadmissions@ucf.edu. *Director*, Dr. Michael Wainstein, 407-823-2519, Fax: 407-823-3378, E-mail: michael.wainstein@ucf.edu.

School of Visual Arts and Design Students: 38 full-time (13 women), 9 part-time (3 women); includes 16 minority (6 Black or African American, non-Hispanic/Latino; 2 Asian, non-Hispanic/Latino; 8 Hispanic/Latino), 3 international. Average age 30. 61 applicants, 54% accepted, 20 enrolled. Expenses: Contact institution. *Financial support:* In 2017–18, 17 students received support, including 7 fellowships with partial tuition reimbursements available (averaging $10,000 per year), 3 research assistantships with partial tuition reimbursements available (averaging $6,355 per year), 15 teaching assistantships with partial tuition reimbursements available (averaging $8,208 per year); scholarships/grants, health care benefits, and unspecified assistantships also available. Financial award application deadline: 3/1; financial award applicants required to submit FAFSA. In 2017, 8 master's awarded. *Program availability:* Part-time. Offers digital media (MA); emerging media (MFA). *Application deadline:* For fall admission, 7/1 for domestic students. *Application fee:* $30. Electronic applications accepted. *Application Contact:* Associate Director, Graduate Admissions, 407-823-2766, Fax: 407-823-6442, E-mail: gradadmissions@ucf.edu. *Director*, Dr. Rudy McDaniel, 407-823-3145, E-mail: rudy@ucf.edu.

College of Business Administration Students: 260 full-time (116 women), 648 part-time (315 women); includes 334 minority (79 Black or African American, non-Hispanic/Latino; 65 Asian, non-Hispanic/Latino; 172 Hispanic/Latino; 18 Two or more races, non-Hispanic/Latino), 36 international. Average age 30. 788 applicants, 58% accepted, 363 enrolled. *Faculty:* 134 full-time (38 women), 26 part-time/adjunct (4 women). Expenses: Contact institution. *Financial support:* In 2017–18, 103 students received support, including 10 fellowships with partial tuition reimbursements available (averaging $4,540 per year), 51 research assistantships with partial tuition reimbursements available (averaging $7,552 per year), 63 teaching assistantships with partial tuition reimbursements available (averaging $11,666 per year); career-related internships or fieldwork, Federal Work-Study, institutionally sponsored loans, health care benefits, and tuition waivers (partial) also available. Financial award application deadline: 3/1; financial award applicants required to submit FAFSA. In 2017, 347 master's, 10 doctorates, 29 other advanced degrees awarded. *Program availability:* Part-time, evening/weekend. Offers business administration (MBA, MSA, MSBM, MSM, MSRE, PhD, Graduate Certificate); entrepreneurship (Graduate Certificate); management (MSM); sport business management (MSBM); technology ventures (Graduate Certificate). *Application fee:* $30. Electronic applications accepted. *Application Contact:* Associate Director, Graduate Admissions, 407-823-2766, Fax: 407-823-6442, E-mail: gradadmissions@ucf.edu. *Dean*, Dr. Paul Jarley, 407-823-5133, E-mail: pjarley@bus.ucf.edu.

Dr. P. Phillips School of Real Estate Students: 13 part-time (3 women); includes 8 minority (2 Black or African American, non-Hispanic/Latino; 3 Asian, non-Hispanic/Latino; 2 Hispanic/Latino; 1 Two or more races, non-Hispanic/Latino). Average age 31. 25 applicants, 84% accepted, 13 enrolled. Expenses: Contact institution. *Financial support:* Application deadline: 3/1; applicants required to submit FAFSA. In 2017, 19 master's awarded. *Program availability:* Part-time. Offers real estate (MSRE). *Application deadline:* For fall admission, 7/1 for domestic students. *Application fee:* $30. Electronic applications accepted. *Application Contact:* Associate Director, Graduate Admissions, 407-823-2766, Fax: 407-823-6442, E-mail: gradadmissions@ucf.edu. *Chair and Director*, Dr. Ajai Singh, 407-823-5756, Fax: 407-823-6676, E-mail: ajai.singh@ucf.edu.

Kenneth G. Dixon School of Accounting Students: 91 full-time (43 women), 60 part-time (32 women); includes 47 minority (4 Black or African American, non-Hispanic/Latino; 20 Asian, non-Hispanic/Latino; 17 Hispanic/Latino; 6 Two or more races, non-Hispanic/Latino), 3 international. Average age 28. 119 applicants, 56% accepted, 49 enrolled. Expenses: Contact institution. *Financial support:* In 2017–18, 20 students received support, including 1 research assistantship with partial tuition reimbursement available (averaging $180 per year), 20 teaching assistantships with partial tuition reimbursements available (averaging $9,445 per year); fellowships, career-related internships or fieldwork, Federal Work-Study, institutionally sponsored loans, health care benefits, tuition waivers (partial), and unspecified assistantships also available. Financial award application deadline: 3/1; financial award applicants required to submit FAFSA. In 2017, 79 master's awarded. *Program availability:* Part-time, evening/weekend. Offers accounting (MSA). *Application deadline:* For fall admission, 7/15 for domestic students; for spring admission, 12/1 for domestic students; for summer admission, 4/15 for domestic students. *Application fee:* $30. Electronic applications accepted. *Application Contact:* Associate Director, Graduate Admissions, 407-823-2766, Fax: 407-823-6442, E-mail: gradadmissions@ucf.edu.

Director, Dr. Gregory Trompeter, 407-823-2876, Fax: 407-823-3881, E-mail: trompete@ucf.edu.

College of Community Innovation and Education Students: 616 full-time (479 women), 988 part-time (803 women); includes 570 minority (220 Black or African American, non-Hispanic/Latino; 6 American Indian or Alaska Native, non-Hispanic/Latino; 43 Asian, non-Hispanic/Latino; 276 Hispanic/Latino; 25 Two or more races, non-Hispanic/Latino), 43 international. Average age 32. 1,274 applicants, 67% accepted, 576 enrolled. *Faculty:* 131 full-time (88 women), 123 part-time/adjunct (88 women). Expenses: Contact institution. *Financial support:* In 2017–18, 136 students received support, including 39 fellowships with partial tuition reimbursements available (averaging $5,202 per year), 72 research assistantships with partial tuition reimbursements available (averaging $8,810 per year), 68 teaching assistantships with partial tuition reimbursements available (averaging $11,197 per year); career-related internships or fieldwork, Federal Work-Study, institutionally sponsored loans, health care benefits, tuition waivers (partial), and unspecified assistantships also available. Financial award application deadline: 3/1; financial award applicants required to submit FAFSA. In 2017, 470 master's, 89 doctorates, 162 other advanced degrees awarded. *Program availability:* Part-time, evening/weekend. Offers applied exercise physiology (MS); applied learning and instruction (MA); career and technical education (MA); career counseling (Certificate); community innovation and education (M Ed, MA, MAT, MHA, MNM, MPA, MRA, MS, Ed D, PhD, Certificate, Ed S); corrections leadership (Certificate); counselor education (M Ed, MA, Certificate, Ed S); criminal justice (MS, PhD); curriculum and instruction (M Ed, Ed D); e-learning (Certificate); education (PhD); educational leadership (M Ed, MA, Ed D, Ed S); educational technology (Certificate); gifted education (M Ed, Graduate Certificate); health administration (MHA); health care informatics (MS); health information administration (Certificate); higher education/college teaching and leadership (MA); higher education/student personnel (MA); instructional design (Certificate); instructional design and technology (MA, Certificate); instructional design for simulations (Certificate); juvenile justice leadership (Certificate); marriage, couple, and family therapy (MA, Certificate); methodology, measurement and analysis (Graduate Certificate); play therapy (Certificate); police leadership (Certificate); public affairs (PhD); school psychology (Ed S); sport and exercise science (MS). *Application fee:* $30. Electronic applications accepted. *Application Contact:* Associate Director, Graduate Admissions, 407-823-2766, Fax: 407-823-6442, E-mail: gradadmissions@ucf.edu. *Dean*, Dr. Pamela S. Carroll, 407-823-1463, E-mail: pamela.carroll@ucf.edu.

School of Public Administration Students: 110 full-time (76 women), 290 part-time (215 women); includes 193 minority (96 Black or African American, non-Hispanic/Latino; 2 American Indian or Alaska Native, non-Hispanic/Latino; 13 Asian, non-Hispanic/Latino; 74 Hispanic/Latino; 8 Two or more races, non-Hispanic/Latino), 6 international. Average age 32. 255 applicants, 78% accepted, 152 enrolled. Expenses: Contact institution. *Financial support:* In 2017–18, 11 students received support, including 2 fellowships with partial tuition reimbursements available (averaging $5,300 per year), 6 research assistantships with partial tuition reimbursements available (averaging $9,637 per year), 3 teaching assistantships with partial tuition reimbursements available (averaging $9,390 per year); career-related internships or fieldwork, Federal Work-Study, institutionally sponsored loans, health care benefits, tuition waivers (partial), and unspecified assistantships also available. Financial award application deadline: 3/1; financial award applicants required to submit FAFSA. In 2017, 95 master's, 34 other advanced degrees awarded. *Program availability:* Part-time, evening/weekend. Offers emergency management and homeland security (Certificate); fundraising (Certificate); nonprofit management (MNM, Certificate); public administration (MPA); research administration (MRA); urban and regional planning (MS). *Application deadline:* For fall admission, 6/15 for domestic students; for spring admission, 11/1 for domestic students. *Application fee:* $30. Electronic applications accepted. *Application Contact:* Associate Director, Graduate Admissions, 407-823-2766, Fax: 407-823-6442, E-mail: gradadmissions@ucf.edu. *Director*, Dr. Naim Kapucu, 407-823-6096, Fax: 407-823-5651, E-mail: kapucu@ucf.edu.

School of Teacher Education Students: 63 full-time (59 women), 218 part-time (190 women); includes 104 minority (34 Black or African American, non-Hispanic/Latino; 1 American Indian or Alaska Native, non-Hispanic/Latino; 13 Asian, non-Hispanic/Latino; 52 Hispanic/Latino; 4 Two or more races, non-Hispanic/Latino), 5 international. Average age 31. 189 applicants, 78% accepted, 98 enrolled. Expenses: Contact institution. *Financial support:* In 2017–18, 5 students received support, including 1 fellowship with partial tuition reimbursement available (averaging $1,000 per year), 4 research assistantships with partial tuition reimbursements available (averaging $5,617 per year), 1 teaching assistantship with partial tuition reimbursement available (averaging $9,086 per year); career-related internships or fieldwork, Federal Work-Study, institutionally sponsored loans, health care benefits, tuition waivers (partial), and unspecified assistantships also available. Financial award application deadline: 3/1; financial award applicants required to submit FAFSA. In 2017, 124 master's, 16 other advanced degrees awarded. *Program availability:* Part-time, evening/weekend. Offers applied learning and instruction (MA); art education (MAT); autism spectrum disorders (Certificate); curriculum and instruction (M Ed); elementary education (M Ed, MA); English language (MAT); exceptional student education (M Ed, MA, Certificate); exceptional student education K-12 (MA); intervention specialist (Certificate); K-8 mathematics and science education (M Ed, Certificate); mathematics education (MAT); middle school mathematics (MAT); middle school science (MAT); pre-kindergarten disabilities (Certificate); reading education (M Ed, Certificate); science education (MAT); severe or profound disabilities (Certificate); social science education (MAT); special education (Certificate); teacher education (MAT); world languages education - English for speakers of other languages (ESOL) (Certificate); world languages education - languages other than English (LOTE) (Certificate). *Application deadline:* For fall admission, 7/15 for domestic students; for spring admission, 12/15 for domestic students. *Application fee:* $30. Electronic applications accepted. *Application Contact:* Associate Director, Graduate Admissions, 407-823-2766, Fax: 407-823-6442, E-mail: gradadmissions@ucf.edu. *Director*, Dr. Michael Hynes, 407-823-1768, E-mail: michael.hynes@ucf.edu.

College of Engineering and Computer Science Students: 927 full-time (202 women), 649 part-time (166 women); includes 428 minority (83 Black or African American, non-Hispanic/Latino; 2 American Indian or Alaska Native, non-Hispanic/Latino; 92 Asian, non-Hispanic/Latino; 231 Hispanic/Latino; 20 Two or more races, non-Hispanic/Latino), 634 international. Average age 30. 1,680 applicants, 64% accepted, 489 enrolled. *Faculty:* 181 full-time (28 women), 46 part-time/adjunct (6 women). Expenses: Contact institution. *Financial support:* In 2017–18, 566 students received support, including 181 fellowships with partial tuition reimbursements available (averaging $11,128 per year), 376 research assistantships with partial tuition reimbursements available (averaging $11,618 per year), 205 teaching assistantships with partial tuition reimbursements available (averaging $12,393 per year); career-related internships or fieldwork, Federal Work-Study, institutionally sponsored loans, tuition waivers (partial), and unspecified assistantships also available. Financial award application deadline: 3/1; financial award applicants required to submit FAFSA. In 2017, 322 master's, 81 doctorates, 22 other advanced degrees awarded. *Program availability:* Part-time, evening/weekend. Offers aerospace engineering (MSAE); civil engineering (MS, MSCE, PhD, Certificate); computer engineering (MS Cp E, PhD); computer science (MS, PhD); digital forensics (MS); electrical engineering (MSEE, PhD); engineering and computer science (MS, MS Cp E, MS Env E, MSAE, MSCE, MSEE, MSEM, MSIE, MSME, MSMSE, PhD, Certificate); engineering management (MSEM); environmental engineering (MS, MS Env E, PhD); industrial engineering (MS, MSIE, PhD); materials science and engineering (MSMSE, PhD); mechanical engineering (MSME, PhD); project engineering (Certificate); quality assurance (Certificate); structural engineering (Certificate); systems engineering (Certificate); training simulation (Certificate); transportation engineering (Certificate). *Application deadline:* For fall admission, 7/15 for domestic students; for spring admission, 12/1 for domestic students. *Application fee:* $30. Electronic applications accepted. *Application Contact:* Associate Director, Graduate Admissions, 407-823-2766, Fax: 407-823-6442, E-mail: gradadmissions@ucf.edu. *Dean*, Dr. Michael Georgiopoulos, 407-823-2156, E-mail: michaelg@ucf.edu.

College of Graduate Studies Students: 53 full-time (30 women), 65 part-time (33 women); includes 43 minority (13 Black or African American, non-Hispanic/Latino; 8 Asian, non-Hispanic/Latino; 21 Hispanic/Latino; 1 Two or more races, non-Hispanic/Latino), 6 international. Average age 32. 130 applicants, 68% accepted, 64 enrolled. *Faculty:* 3 full-time (1 woman), 2 part-time/adjunct (1 woman). Expenses: Contact institution. *Financial support:* In 2017–18, 18 students received support, including 6 fellowships with partial tuition reimbursements available (averaging $6,757 per year), 15 research assistantships with partial tuition reimbursements available (averaging $14,540 per year), 3 teaching assistantships with partial tuition reimbursements available (averaging $16,694 per year); health care benefits also available. Financial award application deadline: 3/1; financial award applicants required to submit FAFSA. In 2017, 18 master's, 14 other advanced degrees awarded. Offers geographic information systems (Certificate); interdisciplinary studies (MA, MS); modeling and simulation (MS, PhD); modeling and simulation of behavioral cybersecurity (Certificate); modeling and simulation of technical systems (Certificate); nanotechnology (MS, PSM). *Application deadline:* For fall admission, 7/15 for domestic students; for spring admission, 12/1 for domestic students. *Application fee:* $30. Electronic applications accepted. *Application Contact:* Associate Director, Graduate Admissions, 407-823-2766, Fax: 407-823-6442, E-mail: gradadmissions@ucf.edu. *Vice President for Research/Dean, College of Graduate Studies*, Dr. Elizabeth Klonoff, 407-823-6432, Fax: 407-823-6442, E-mail: elizabeth.klonoff@ucf.edu.

College of Health Professions and Sciences Students: 941 full-time (725 women), 980 part-time (760 women); includes 912 minority (375 Black or African American, non-Hispanic/Latino; 8 American Indian or Alaska Native, non-Hispanic/Latino; 87 Asian, non-Hispanic/Latino; 394 Hispanic/Latino; 5 Native Hawaiian or other Pacific Islander, non-Hispanic/Latino; 43 Two or more races, non-Hispanic/Latino), 27 international. Average age 30. 1,497 applicants, 60% accepted, 602 enrolled. *Faculty:* 190 full-time (106 women), 127 part-time/adjunct (79 women). Expenses: Contact institution. *Financial support:* In 2017–18, 77 students received support, including 27 fellowships with partial tuition reimbursements available (averaging $5,905 per year), 45 research assistantships with partial tuition reimbursements available (averaging $9,280 per year), 31 teaching assistantships with partial tuition reimbursements available (averaging $8,443 per year); career-related internships or fieldwork, Federal Work-Study, institutionally sponsored loans, traineeships, health care benefits, tuition waivers (partial), and unspecified assistantships also available. Financial award application deadline: 3/1; financial award applicants required to submit FAFSA. In 2017, 526 master's, 45 doctorates, 87 other advanced degrees awarded. *Program availability:* Part-time, evening/weekend. Offers athletic training (MAT); health professions and sciences (MA, MAT, MHA, MNM, MRA, MS, MSW, DPT, PhD, Certificate); kinesiology (MS); physical therapy (DPT). *Application fee:* $30. Electronic applications accepted. *Application Contact:* Associate Director, Graduate Admissions, 407-823-2766, Fax: 407-823-6442, E-mail: gradadmissions@ucf.edu. *Interim Dean*, Dr. Jose Fernandez, 407-823-0171, E-mail: jose.fernandez@ucf.edu.

School of Communication Sciences and Disorders Students: 204 full-time (192 women), 6 part-time (5 women); includes 62 minority (7 Black or African American, non-Hispanic/Latino; 1 American Indian or Alaska Native, non-Hispanic/Latino; 8 Asian, non-Hispanic/Latino; 41 Hispanic/Latino; 5 Two or more races, non-Hispanic/Latino), 1 international. Average age 26. 332 applicants, 36% accepted, 31 enrolled. Expenses: Contact institution. *Financial support:* In 2017–18, 15 students received support, including 6 fellowships with partial tuition reimbursements available (averaging $3,833 per year), 4 research assistantships with partial tuition reimbursements available (averaging $6,020 per year), 7 teaching assistantships with partial tuition reimbursements available (averaging $7,138 per year); career-related internships or fieldwork, Federal Work-Study, institutionally sponsored loans, and unspecified assistantships also available. Financial award application deadline: 3/1; financial award applicants required to submit FAFSA. In 2017, 94 master's awarded. *Program availability:* Part-time, evening/weekend. Offers communication sciences and disorders (MA); medical speech-language pathology (Certificate). *Application deadline:* For fall admission, 2/1 for domestic students; for spring admission, 10/1 for domestic students. *Application fee:* $30. Electronic applications accepted. *Application Contact:* Associate Director, Graduate Admissions, 407-823-2766, Fax: 407-823-6442, E-mail: gradadmissions@ucf.edu. *Program Coordinator*, Dr. Linda Rosa-Lugo, 407-823-4798, E-mail: csdgraduate@ucf.edu.

School of Social Work Students: 215 full-time (190 women), 267 part-time (236 women); includes 241 minority (106 Black or African American, non-Hispanic/Latino; 2 American Indian or Alaska Native, non-Hispanic/Latino; 7 Asian, non-Hispanic/Latino; 113 Hispanic/Latino; 2 Native Hawaiian or other Pacific Islander, non-Hispanic/Latino; 11 Two or more races, non-Hispanic/Latino), 1 international. Average age 31. 336 applicants, 53% accepted, 135 enrolled. Expenses: Contact institution. *Financial support:* In 2017–18, 2 students received support, including 2 research assistantships with partial tuition reimbursements available (averaging $5,068 per year); fellowships, career-related internships or fieldwork, institutionally sponsored loans, and unspecified assistantships also available. Financial award application deadline: 3/1; financial award applicants required to submit FAFSA. In 2017, 131 master's, 17 other advanced degrees awarded. *Program availability:* Part-time, evening/weekend. Offers military social work (Certificate); social work (MSW). *Application deadline:* For fall admission, 4/1 for domestic students. *Application fee:* $30. Electronic applications accepted. *Application Contact:* Associate Director, Graduate Admissions, 407-823-2766, Fax: 407-823-6442, E-mail: gradadmissions@ucf.edu. *Director*, Dr. Bonnie Yegidis, 407-823-2114, E-mail: bonnie.yegidis@ucf.edu.

College of Medicine Expenses: Contact institution. *Financial support:* Fellowships, research assistantships, and teaching assistantships available. Offers medicine (MS,

MD, PhD). *Application Contact:* Associate Director, Graduate Admissions, 407-823-2766, Fax: 407-823-6442, E-mail: gradadmissions@ucf.edu. *Vice President for Medical Affairs/Dean*, Dr. Deborah C. German, 407-266-1000, E-mail: deb@ucf.edu.

Burnett School of Biomedical Sciences Students: 91 full-time (56 women), 11 part-time (5 women); includes 37 minority (10 Black or African American, non-Hispanic/Latino; 5 Asian, non-Hispanic/Latino; 19 Hispanic/Latino; 3 Two or more races, non-Hispanic/Latino), 26 international. Average age 27. 196 applicants, 36% accepted, 44 enrolled. *Faculty:* 69 full-time (30 women), 5 part-time/adjunct (2 women). Expenses: Contact institution. *Financial support:* In 2017–18, 53 students received support, including 20 fellowships with partial tuition reimbursements available (averaging $13,780 per year), 52 research assistantships with partial tuition reimbursements available (averaging $10,670 per year), 12 teaching assistantships with partial tuition reimbursements available (averaging $12,067 per year); scholarships/grants and health care benefits also available. Financial award application deadline: 3/1; financial award applicants required to submit FAFSA. In 2017, 20 master's, 8 doctorates awarded. Offers biomedical sciences (MS, PhD); biotechnology (MS). *Application deadline:* For fall admission, 1/15 for domestic students. *Application fee:* $30. Electronic applications accepted. *Application Contact:* Associate Director, Graduate Admissions, 407-823-2766, Fax: 407-823-6442, E-mail: gradadmissions@ucf.edu. *Director*, Dr. Griffith Parks, 407-226-7001, E-mail: griffith.parks@ucf.edu.

College of Nursing Students: 63 full-time (58 women), 327 part-time (297 women); includes 131 minority (40 Black or African American, non-Hispanic/Latino; 1 American Indian or Alaska Native, non-Hispanic/Latino; 16 Asian, non-Hispanic/Latino; 62 Hispanic/Latino; 12 Two or more races, non-Hispanic/Latino), 1 international. Average age 38. 303 applicants, 64% accepted, 129 enrolled. *Faculty:* 57 full-time (49 women), 70 part-time/adjunct (68 women). Expenses: Contact institution. *Financial support:* In 2017–18, 3 students received support, including 2 fellowships with partial tuition reimbursements available (averaging $7,377 per year), 1 research assistantship with partial tuition reimbursement available (averaging $11,952 per year); career-related internships or fieldwork, Federal Work-Study, institutionally sponsored loans, traineeships, and unspecified assistantships also available. Financial award application deadline: 3/1; financial award applicants required to submit FAFSA. In 2017, 87 master's, 5 doctorates, 4 other advanced degrees awarded. *Program availability:* Part-time, evening/weekend. Offers adult-gerontology acute care nurse practitioner (Certificate); adult-gerontology primary care nurse practitioner (Certificate); family nurse practitioner (Certificate); nursing (MSN, PhD); nursing education (Post-Master's Certificate); nursing practice (DNP). *Application deadline:* For fall admission, 3/15 for domestic students; for spring admission, 10/15 for domestic students. *Application fee:* $30. Electronic applications accepted. *Application Contact:* Associate Director, Graduate Admissions, 407-823-2766, Fax: 407-823-6442, E-mail: gradadmissions@ucf.edu. *Dean*, Dr. Mary Lou Sole, 407-823-5496, Fax: 407-823-5675, E-mail: mary.sole@ucf.edu.

College of Optics and Photonics Students: 128 full-time (24 women), 4 part-time (0 women); includes 11 minority (1 Black or African American, non-Hispanic/Latino; 4 Asian, non-Hispanic/Latino; 4 Hispanic/Latino; 2 Two or more races, non-Hispanic/Latino), 91 international. Average age 27. 184 applicants, 34% accepted, 26 enrolled. *Faculty:* 46 full-time (4 women), 8 part-time/adjunct (1 woman). Expenses: Contact institution. *Financial support:* In 2017–18, 116 students received support, including 31 fellowships with partial tuition reimbursements available (averaging $19,619 per year), 98 research assistantships with partial tuition reimbursements available (averaging $15,342 per year), 16 teaching assistantships with partial tuition reimbursements available (averaging $7,686 per year); career-related internships or fieldwork, Federal Work-Study, institutionally sponsored loans, health care benefits, tuition waivers (partial), and unspecified assistantships also available. Financial award application deadline: 3/1; financial award applicants required to submit FAFSA. In 2017, 19 master's, 8 doctorates awarded. *Program availability:* Part-time, evening/weekend. Offers optics and photonics (MS, PhD). *Application deadline:* For fall admission, 7/15 for domestic students; for spring admission, 12/1 for domestic students. *Application fee:* $30. Electronic applications accepted. *Application Contact:* Associate Director, Graduate Admissions, 407-823-2766, Fax: 407-823-6442, E-mail: gradadmissions@ucf.edu. *Dean and Director*, Dr. Bahaa E. Saleh, 407-823-6817, E-mail: besaleh@creol.ucf.edu.

College of Sciences Students: 653 full-time (343 women), 159 part-time (93 women); includes 209 minority (46 Black or African American, non-Hispanic/Latino; 1 American Indian or Alaska Native, non-Hispanic/Latino; 49 Asian, non-Hispanic/Latino; 95 Hispanic/Latino; 18 Two or more races, non-Hispanic/Latino), 155 international. Average age 29. 1,130 applicants, 38% accepted, 250 enrolled. *Faculty:* 360 full-time (127 women), 52 part-time/adjunct (20 women). Expenses: Contact institution. *Financial support:* In 2017–18, 502 students received support, including 131 fellowships with partial tuition reimbursements available (averaging $9,207 per year), 158 research assistantships with partial tuition reimbursements available (averaging $11,247 per year), 376 teaching assistantships with partial tuition reimbursements available (averaging $12,982 per year); health care benefits also available. Financial award application deadline: 3/1; financial award applicants required to submit FAFSA. In 2017, 200 master's, 54 doctorates, 37 other advanced degrees awarded. Offers anthropology (MA); applied sociology (MA); biology (MS); chemistry (MS, PhD); clinical psychology (MA, PhD); computer forensics (Certificate); conservation biology (PhD); data mining (MS); human factors and cognitive psychology (PhD); industrial/organizational psychology (MS, PhD); intelligence and national security (Certificate); mathematical science (MS, Certificate); mathematics (PhD); physics (MS, PhD); political science (MA); SAS data mining (Certificate); sciences (MA, MS, PhD, Certificate); security studies (PhD); sociology (PhD); statistical computing (MS). *Application fee:* $30. Electronic applications accepted. *Application Contact:* Associate Director, Graduate Admissions, 407-823-2766, Fax: 407-823-6442, E-mail: gradadmissions@ucf.edu. *Dean*, Dr. Michael Johnson, 407-823-1911, E-mail: michael.johnson@ucf.edu.

Nicholson School of Communication Students: 32 full-time (23 women), 25 part-time (20 women); includes 14 minority (5 Black or African American, non-Hispanic/Latino; 1 Asian, non-Hispanic/Latino; 5 Hispanic/Latino; 3 Two or more races, non-Hispanic/Latino), 8 international. Average age 28. 52 applicants, 75% accepted, 27 enrolled. Expenses: Contact institution. *Financial support:* In 2017–18, 21 students received support, including 4 fellowships with partial tuition reimbursements available (averaging $2,000 per year), 4 research assistantships with partial tuition reimbursements available (averaging $5,339 per year), 18 teaching assistantships with partial tuition reimbursements available (averaging $9,407 per year); career-related internships or fieldwork, Federal Work-Study, institutionally sponsored loans, health care benefits, tuition waivers (partial), and unspecified assistantships also available. Financial award application deadline: 3/1; financial award applicants required to submit FAFSA. In 2017, 27 master's, 17 other advanced degrees awarded. *Program availability:* Part-time, evening/weekend. Offers communication (MA); corporate communication (Certificate). *Application deadline:* For fall admission, 6/1 for domestic students; for spring admission, 11/1 for domestic students. *Application fee:* $30. Electronic applications accepted. *Application Contact:* Associate Director, Graduate Admissions, 407-823-2766, Fax: 407-823-6442, E-mail: gradadmissions@ucf.edu. *Director*, Dr. Robert Littlefield, 407-823-1708, E-mail: robert.littlefield@ucf.edu.

Rosen College of Hospitality Management Students: 76 full-time (50 women), 161 part-time (111 women); includes 72 minority (28 Black or African American, non-Hispanic/Latino; 1 American Indian or Alaska Native, non-Hispanic/Latino; 7 Asian, non-Hispanic/Latino; 31 Hispanic/Latino; 5 Two or more races, non-Hispanic/Latino), 24 international. Average age 30. 195 applicants, 65% accepted, 82 enrolled. *Faculty:* 71 full-time (29 women), 30 part-time/adjunct (8 women). Expenses: Contact institution. *Financial support:* In 2017–18, 24 students received support, including 7 fellowships with partial tuition reimbursements available (averaging $1,971 per year), 2 research assistantships with partial tuition reimbursements available (averaging $9,323 per year), 22 teaching assistantships with partial tuition reimbursements available (averaging $12,876 per year); health care benefits also available. Financial award application deadline: 3/1; financial award applicants required to submit FAFSA. In 2017, 31 master's, 5 doctorates, 32 other advanced degrees awarded. *Program availability:* Part-time. Offers destination marketing and management (Certificate); event management (Certificate); hospitality and tourism management (MS); hospitality management (PhD). *Application deadline:* For fall admission, 7/15 for domestic students; for spring admission, 12/1 for domestic students. *Application fee:* $30. Electronic applications accepted. *Application Contact:* Associate Director, Graduate Admissions, 407-823-2766, Fax: 407-823-6442, E-mail: gradadmissions@ucf.edu. *Dean*, Dr. Abraham C. Pizam, 407-903-8010, E-mail: abraham.pizam@ucf.edu.

UNIVERSITY OF CENTRAL MISSOURI, Warrensburg, MO 64093

General Information State-supported, coed, comprehensive institution. CGS member. *Enrollment:* 12,333 graduate, professional, and undergraduate students; 785 full-time matriculated graduate/professional students (398 women), 1,633 part-time matriculated graduate/professional students (1,063 women). *Enrollment by degree level:* 2,206 master's, 21 doctoral, 191 other advanced degrees. *Graduate faculty:* 337 full-time (145 women), 41 part-time/adjunct (28 women). Tuition, state resident: full-time $8771; part-time $292.35 per credit hour. Tuition, nonresident: full-time $17,541; part-time $584.70 per credit hour. *Required fees:* $372; $24.78 per credit hour. *Graduate housing:* Rooms and/or apartments available on a first-come, first-served basis to single and married students. Typical cost: $5394 per year ($8536 including board) for single students. Housing application deadline: 5/1. *Student services:* Campus employment opportunities, campus safety program, career counseling, child daycare facilities, exercise/wellness program, free psychological counseling, grant writing training, international student services, low-cost health insurance, multicultural affairs office, services for students with disabilities, teacher training, writing training. *Library facilities:* James C. Kirkpatrick Library plus 1 other. *Collection:* Books: 499,982 (physical), 268,431 (digital/electronic); Serial titles: 1,579 (physical), 89,008 (digital/electronic); Databases: 97. Weekly public service hours: 96; students can reserve study rooms.

Computer facilities: 6,395 computers available on campus for general student use. A campuswide network can be accessed from student residence rooms and from off campus. Online class registration is available.
Website: http://www.ucmo.edu/

General Application Contact: Shellie Hewitt, Director, Graduate Student Services, 660-543-4621, E-mail: giss@ucmo.edu.

GRADUATE UNITS

The Graduate School Students: 785 full-time (398 women), 1,633 part-time (1,063 women); includes 231 minority (102 Black or African American, non-Hispanic/Latino; 4 American Indian or Alaska Native, non-Hispanic/Latino; 16 Asian, non-Hispanic/Latino; 52 Hispanic/Latino; 57 Two or more races, non-Hispanic/Latino), 692 international. Average age 30. *Faculty:* 337 full-time (145 women), 41 part-time/adjunct (28 women). Expenses: Contact institution. *Financial support:* In 2017–18, 99 students received support. Research assistantships, teaching assistantships, career-related internships or fieldwork, Federal Work-Study, scholarships/grants, and administrative and laboratory assistantships available. Support available to part-time students. Financial award application deadline: 3/1; financial award applicants required to submit FAFSA. In 2017, 2,605 master's, 122 other advanced degrees awarded. *Program availability:* Part-time, 100% online, blended/hybrid learning. Offers accountancy (MA); accounting (MBA); applied mathematics (MS); aviation safety (MA); biology (MS); business administration (MBA); career and technical education leadership (MS); college student personnel administration (MS); communication (MA); computer science (MS); counseling (MS); criminal justice (MS); educational leadership (Ed D); educational technology (MS); elementary and early childhood education (MSE); English (MA); environmental studies (MA); finance (MBA); history (MA); human services/educational technology (Ed S); human services/learning resources (Ed S); human services/professional counseling (Ed S); industrial hygiene (MS); industrial management (MS); information systems (MBA); information technology (MS); kinesiology (MS); library science and information services (MS); literacy education (MSE); marketing (MBA); mathematics (MS); music (MA); occupational safety management (MS); psychology (MS); rural family nursing (MS); school administration (MSE); social gerontology (MS); sociology (MA); special education (MSE); speech language pathology (MS); superintendency (Ed S); teaching (MAT); teaching English as a second language (MA); technology (MS); technology management (PhD); theatre (MA). *Application deadline:* For fall admission, 6/1 priority date for domestic and international students; for spring admission, 10/1 priority date for domestic and international students; for summer admission, 4/1 priority date for domestic and international students. Applications are processed on a rolling basis. *Application fee:* $30 ($75 for international students). Electronic applications accepted. *Application Contact:* 660-543-4621, E-mail: admit_intl@ucmo.edu. *Director of Graduate and International Student Services*, Shellie Hewitt, 660-543-4621, Fax: 660-543-4778, E-mail: hewitt@ucmo.edu.

UNIVERSITY OF CENTRAL OKLAHOMA, Edmond, OK 73034-5209

General Information State-supported, coed, comprehensive institution. CGS member. *Enrollment:* 15,973 graduate, professional, and undergraduate students; 630 full-time matriculated graduate/professional students (401 women), 922 part-time matriculated graduate/professional students (682 women). *Enrollment by degree level:* 1,552 master's. *Graduate faculty:* 242 full-time (125 women), 66 part-time/adjunct (32 women). Tuition, state resident: full-time $5375; part-time $268.75 per credit hour. Tuition, nonresident: full-time $13,295; part-time $664.75 per credit hour. *Required fees:* $626; $31.30 per credit hour. One-time fee: $50. Tuition and fees vary according to program. *Graduate housing:* Rooms and/or apartments available on a first-come, first-served basis to single and married students. Typical cost: $8050 (including board) for single students. Room and board charges vary according to board plan and housing facility selected. *Student services:* Campus employment opportunities, campus safety program, career counseling, exercise/wellness program, free psychological counseling, international student services, multicultural affairs office, services for students with disabilities. *Library facilities:* Max Chambers Library plus 1 other. *Collection:* Books: 555,825 (physical), 296,818 (digital/electronic); Serial titles: 23,218 (physical), 124,803 (digital/electronic); Databases: 239. Weekly public service hours: 107; students can reserve study rooms. *Research affiliation:* National Science Foundation, U.S. Department of Education (DOE), U.S. Department of Veteran Affairs, Oklahoma Department of Human Services, Oklahoma Idea Network of Biomedical Research Excellence, Oklahoma Small Business Administration.

Computer facilities: 650 computers available on campus for general student use. A campuswide network can be accessed from student residence rooms and from off campus. Online class registration is available.
Website: http://www.uco.edu/

General Application Contact: Dr. Richard Bernard, Dean, Jackson College of Graduate Studies, 405-974-3341, Fax: 405-974-3852, E-mail: gradcoll@uco.edu.

GRADUATE UNITS

The Jackson College of Graduate Studies Students: 630 full-time (401 women), 922 part-time (682 women); includes 442 minority (172 Black or African American, non-Hispanic/Latino; 54 American Indian or Alaska Native, non-Hispanic/Latino; 30 Asian, non-Hispanic/Latino; 106 Hispanic/Latino; 2 Native Hawaiian or other Pacific Islander, non-Hispanic/Latino; 78 Two or more races, non-Hispanic/Latino), 156 international. Average age 32. 1,157 applicants, 74% accepted, 514 enrolled. *Faculty:* 242 full-time (125 women), 66 part-time/adjunct (32 women). Expenses: Contact institution. *Financial support:* In 2017–18, 348 students received support, including 53 research assistantships with partial tuition reimbursements available (averaging $4,977 per year), 77 teaching assistantships with partial tuition reimbursements available (averaging $7,958 per year); career-related internships or fieldwork, Federal Work-Study, scholarships/grants, tuition waivers (partial), and unspecified assistantships also available. Financial award application deadline: 3/31; financial award applicants required to submit FAFSA. In 2017, 526 master's awarded. *Program availability:* Part-time, evening/weekend. *Application deadline:* For fall admission, 7/15 for international students; for spring admission, 11/15 for international students. Applications are processed on a rolling basis. *Application fee:* $60. Electronic applications accepted. *Application Contact:* Elise Ellis, Admissions Counselor, 405-974-2523, Fax: 405-974-3852, E-mail: eellis5@uco.edu. *Dean, Graduate College*, Dr. Richard Bernard, 405-974-3341, Fax: 405-974-3852, E-mail: gradcoll@uco.edu.

College of Business Students: 76 full-time (32 women), 29 part-time (16 women); includes 28 minority (8 Black or African American, non-Hispanic/Latino; 7 American Indian or Alaska Native, non-Hispanic/Latino; 5 Asian, non-Hispanic/Latino; 2 Hispanic/Latino; 6 Two or more races, non-Hispanic/Latino), 13 international. Average age 30. 161 applicants, 58% accepted, 66 enrolled. *Faculty:* 17 full-time (6 women), 2 part-time/adjunct (0 women). Expenses: Contact institution. *Financial support:* In 2017–18, 12 students received support, including 2 teaching assistantships (averaging $8,873 per year); research assistantships, career-related internships or fieldwork, Federal Work-Study, scholarships/grants, tuition waivers (partial), and unspecified assistantships also available. Financial award application deadline: 3/31; financial award applicants required to submit FAFSA. In 2017, 45 master's awarded. *Program availability:* Part-time. Offers business administration (MBA); business analytics (MS). *Application deadline:* For fall admission, 7/15 for international students; for spring admission, 11/15 for international students. Applications are processed on a rolling basis. *Application fee:* $60. Electronic applications accepted. *Application Contact:* Jeffrey Hicks, Director of MBA Enrollment, 405-974-5445, E-mail: mba@uco.edu. *Interim Dean*, Dr. Randal Ice, 405-974-2810.

College of Education and Professional Studies Students: 280 full-time (220 women), 615 part-time (501 women); includes 280 minority (115 Black or African American, non-Hispanic/Latino; 26 American Indian or Alaska Native, non-Hispanic/Latino; 15 Asian, non-Hispanic/Latino; 73 Hispanic/Latino; 51 Two or more races, non-Hispanic/Latino), 44 international. Average age 33. 486 applicants, 81% accepted, 255 enrolled. *Faculty:* 72 full-time (48 women), 30 part-time/adjunct (18 women). Expenses: Contact institution. *Financial support:* In 2017–18, 179 students received support, including 19 research assistantships with partial tuition reimbursements available (averaging $4,047 per year), 2 teaching assistantships with partial tuition reimbursements available (averaging $4,436 per year); career-related internships or fieldwork, scholarships/grants, tuition waivers (partial), and unspecified assistantships also available. Financial award application deadline: 3/31; financial award applicants required to submit FAFSA. In 2017, 310 master's awarded. *Program availability:* Part-time. Offers adult and higher education (M Ed); athletic training (MS); bilingual education/teaching English as a second language (M Ed); early childhood education (M Ed); education and professional studies (M Ed, MA, MS); educational leadership (M Ed); elementary education (M Ed); family and child studies (MS); library media education (M Ed); nutrition-food science (MS); psychology (MA); reading (M Ed); school counseling (M Ed); secondary education (M Ed); special education (M Ed); speech-language pathology (MS); wellness management (MS). *Application deadline:* For fall admission, 7/15 for international students; for spring admission, 11/15 for international students. Applications are processed on a rolling basis. *Application fee:* $60. Electronic applications accepted. *Application Contact:* Carlie Wellington, Assistant Director, CEPS Graduate Enrollment, 405-974-5105, Fax: 405-974-3851, E-mail: gradcoll@uco.edu. *Dean*, Dr. James Machell, 405-974-5701, Fax: 405-974-3851.

College of Fine Arts and Design Students: 57 full-time (26 women), 17 part-time (10 women); includes 11 minority (4 Black or African American, non-Hispanic/Latino; 2 American Indian or Alaska Native, non-Hispanic/Latino; 4 Hispanic/Latino; 1 Two or more races, non-Hispanic/Latino), 25 international. Average age 29. 52 applicants, 71% accepted, 25 enrolled. *Faculty:* 32 full-time (16 women), 16 part-time/adjunct (6 women). Expenses: Contact institution. *Financial support:* In 2017–18, 30 students received support, including 2 research assistantships with partial tuition reimbursements available (averaging $7,394 per year), 18 teaching assistantships with partial tuition reimbursements available (averaging $6,671 per year); career-related internships or fieldwork, Federal Work-Study, scholarships/grants, tuition waivers (partial), and unspecified assistantships also available. Financial award application deadline: 3/31; financial award applicants required to submit FAFSA. In 2017, 23 master's awarded. *Program availability:* Part-time, evening/weekend. Offers design (MFA); fine arts and design (MFA, MM); jazz studies (MM); music (MM). *Application deadline:* For fall admission, 4/1 for domestic students, 7/15 for international students; for spring admission, 10/1 for domestic students, 11/15 for international students. Applications are processed on a rolling basis. *Application fee:* $60. Electronic applications accepted. *Dean of the College of Fine Arts and Design*, Steven Hansen, 405-974-3771, Fax: 405-974-3775, E-mail: gradcoll@uco.edu.

College of Liberal Arts Students: 147 full-time (87 women), 180 part-time (101 women); includes 104 minority (39 Black or African American, non-Hispanic/Latino; 18 American Indian or Alaska Native, non-Hispanic/Latino; 4 Asian, non-Hispanic/Latino; 23 Hispanic/Latino; 2 Native Hawaiian or other Pacific Islander, non-Hispanic/Latino; 18 Two or more races, non-Hispanic/Latino), 36 international. Average age 34. 248 applicants, 78% accepted, 88 enrolled. *Faculty:* 68 full-time (39 women), 13 part-time/adjunct (5 women). Expenses: Contact institution. *Financial support:* In 2017–18, 78 students received support, including 16 research assistantships with partial tuition reimbursements available (averaging $7,024 per year), 22 teaching assistantships with partial tuition reimbursements available (averaging $9,358 per year); career-related internships or fieldwork, Federal Work-Study, scholarships/grants, tuition waivers (partial), and unspecified assistantships also available. Financial award application deadline: 3/31; financial award applicants required to submit FAFSA. In 2017, 103 master's awarded. *Program availability:* Part-time. Offers composition and rhetoric (MA); creative writing (MA); crime and intelligence analysis (MA); criminal justice management and administration (MA); gerontology (MA); liberal arts (MA, MPA); liberal studies (MA); literature (MA); museum studies (MA); political science (MA); public administration (MPA); substance abuse studies (MA); teaching English as a second language (MA). *Application deadline:* For fall admission, 7/15 for international students; for spring admission, 11/15 for international students. Applications are processed on a rolling basis. *Application fee:* $60. Electronic applications accepted. *Dean of the College of Liberal Arts*, Dr. Catherine Webster, 405-974-5540, Fax: 405-974-3823, E-mail: gradcoll@uco.edu.

College of Mathematics and Science Students: 56 full-time (23 women), 63 part-time (39 women); includes 16 minority (6 Black or African American, non-Hispanic/Latino; 1 American Indian or Alaska Native, non-Hispanic/Latino; 5 Asian, non-Hispanic/Latino; 3 Hispanic/Latino; 1 Two or more races, non-Hispanic/Latino), 37 international. Average age 31. 191 applicants, 67% accepted, 75 enrolled. *Faculty:* 49 full-time (16 women), 2 part-time/adjunct (1 woman). Expenses: Contact institution. *Financial support:* In 2017–18, 43 students received support, including 15 research assistantships with partial tuition reimbursements available (averaging $3,783 per year), 33 teaching assistantships with partial tuition reimbursements available (averaging $7,886 per year); career-related internships or fieldwork, Federal Work-Study, scholarships/grants, tuition waivers (partial), and unspecified assistantships also available. Financial award application deadline: 3/31; financial award applicants required to submit FAFSA. In 2017, 40 master's awarded. *Program availability:* Part-time. Offers applied mathematical science (MS); applied mathematics and computer science (MS); biology (MS); computational science (PSM); engineering physics (MS); mathematics and science (MS, PSM); nursing (MS). *Application deadline:* For fall admission, 7/15 for international students; for spring admission, 11/15 for international students. Applications are processed on a rolling basis. *Application fee:* $60. Electronic applications accepted. *Dean*, Dr. Wei Chen, 405-974-2461, Fax: 405-974-3824, E-mail: gradcoll@uco.edu.

Forensic Science Institute Students: 14 full-time (13 women), 17 part-time (14 women); includes 3 minority (1 Asian, non-Hispanic/Latino; 1 Hispanic/Latino; 1 Two or more races, non-Hispanic/Latino), 1 international. Average age 28. 19 applicants, 37% accepted, 6 enrolled. *Faculty:* 8 full-time (2 women), 3 part-time/adjunct (2 women). Expenses: Contact institution. *Financial support:* In 2017–18, 6 students received support, including 1 research assistantship with partial tuition reimbursement available (averaging $2,958 per year); teaching assistantships and scholarships/grants also available. Financial award application deadline: 3/31; financial award applicants required to submit FAFSA. In 2017, 5 master's awarded. Offers biology/chemistry (MS); forensic science (MS). *Application deadline:* For fall admission, 4/15 for domestic and international students; for spring admission, 11/15 for international students. *Application fee:* $60. Electronic applications accepted. *Application Contact:* Dr. John Mabry, Graduate Advisor, 405-974-6913, Fax: 405-974-3804, E-mail: gradcoll@uco.edu. *Director*, Dr. Dwight Adams, 405-974-6911, Fax: 405-974-3804.

UNIVERSITY OF CHARLESTON, Charleston, WV 25304-1099

General Information Independent, coed, comprehensive institution. *Graduate housing:* Rooms and/or apartments available on a first-come, first-served basis to single and married students. *Research affiliation:* Walmart (pharmacy).

GRADUATE UNITS

Doctor of Executive Leadership Program Offers leadership (DEL). Electronic applications accepted.

Master of Business Administration Program *Program availability:* Part-time, evening/weekend. Offers business administration (MBA). Electronic applications accepted.

Master of Forensic Accounting Program *Program availability:* Part-time, blended/hybrid learning. Offers forensic accounting (EMFA). Electronic applications accepted.

Master of Science in Strategic Leadership Program Offers strategic leadership (MS). Electronic applications accepted.

Physician Assistant Program Offers physician assistant (MPAS). Electronic applications accepted.

School of Pharmacy Offers pharmacy (Pharm D). Electronic applications accepted.

UNIVERSITY OF CHICAGO, Chicago, IL 60637-1513

General Information Independent, coed, university. CGS member. *Enrollment:* 13,736 graduate, professional, and undergraduate students; 7,364 full-time matriculated graduate/professional students (3,323 women), 2,172 part-time matriculated graduate/professional students (623 women). *Enrollment by degree level:* 5,439 master's, 4,097 doctoral. *Graduate faculty:* 2,219 full-time (775 women), 445 part-time/adjunct (150 women). *Graduate housing:* Rooms and/or apartments available on a first-come, first-served basis to single and married students. *Student services:* Campus employment opportunities, campus safety program, career counseling, exercise/wellness program, free psychological counseling, grant writing training, international student services, low-cost health insurance, multicultural affairs office, services for students with disabilities, teacher training, writing training. *Library facilities:* Joseph Regenstein Library plus 5 others. *Collection:* Students can reserve study rooms. *Research affiliation:* National Opinion Research Center (social science), Argonne National Laboratory (energy, materials), Marine Biological Laboratory (molecular biology), Fermilab (high-energy physics).

Computer facilities: Computer purchase and lease plans are available. A campuswide network can be accessed from student residence rooms and from off campus. Online class registration is available.
Website: http://www.uchicago.edu/

General Application Contact: Program Coordinator, Graduate Enrollment and Initiatives, 773-702-3760, Fax: 773-702-4199, E-mail: gradadmissions@uchicago.edu.

GRADUATE UNITS

Booth School of Business Students: 1,313 full-time (519 women), 1,874 part-time (465 women). *Faculty:* 154 full-time (26 women), 61 part-time/adjunct (12 women). Expenses: Contact institution. *Financial support:* Applicants required to submit FAFSA. In 2017, 1,255 master's, 22 doctorates awarded. *Program availability:* Part-time, evening/weekend. Offers accounting (MBA); analytic finance (MBA); analytic management (MBA); business (MBA, PhD, Certificate); business administration (MBA, Certificate); econometrics and statistics (MBA); economics (MBA); entrepreneurship (MBA); executive business administration (MBA); finance (MBA); general management (MBA); health administration and policy (Certificate); international business (MBA); managerial and organizational behavior (MBA); marketing analytics (MBA); marketing management (MBA); operations management (MBA); strategic management (MBA). Electronic applications accepted. *Application Contact:* Admissions, 773-702-7369, E-mail: admissions@chicagobooth.edu. *Dean*, Madhav V. Rajan.

Divinity School Students: 263 full-time (100 women), 14 part-time (5 women); includes 40 minority (13 Black or African American, non-Hispanic/Latino; 15 Asian, non-Hispanic/Latino; 6 Hispanic/Latino; 6 Two or more races, non-Hispanic/Latino), 35 international. Average age 31. 386 applicants, 44% accepted, 76 enrolled. *Faculty:* 31 full-time (11 women), 10 part-time/adjunct (1 woman). Expenses: Contact institution. *Financial support:* In 2017–18, 305 students received support, including 21 fellowships with tuition reimbursements available (averaging $24,000 per year); research assistantships, teaching assistantships, career-related internships or fieldwork, Federal Work-Study, institutionally sponsored loans, scholarships/grants, health care benefits, and tuition waivers (full and partial) also available. Support available to part-time students. Financial award application deadline: 12/15. In 2017, 61 master's, 12 doctorates awarded. Offers anthropology and sociology of religions (PhD); Bible (PhD); divinity (M Div, MA, PhD); history of Christianity (PhD); history of Judaism (PhD); history of religions (PhD); Islamic studies (PhD); ministry (M Div); philosophy of religions (PhD); religion (MA, PhD); religion, literature, and visual culture (PhD); religions in America (PhD); religious ethics (PhD); religious studies (MA); theology (PhD). *Application deadline:* For fall admission, 12/15 for domestic and international students. *Application fee:* $75. Electronic applications accepted. *Application Contact:* Anita Lumpkin, Associate Dean of Students, 773-702-8249, E-mail: divinityadmissions@uchicago.edu. *Interim Dean/Executive Vice Provost*, Dr. David Nirenberg, 773-702-8200, E-mail: divinityadmissions@uchicago.edu.

Division of the Biological Sciences Students: 408 full-time (195 women), 11 part-time (5 women); includes 111 minority (13 Black or African American, non-Hispanic/Latino; 1 American Indian or Alaska Native, non-Hispanic/Latino; 50 Asian, non-Hispanic/Latino; 33 Hispanic/Latino; 1 Native Hawaiian or other Pacific Islander, non-Hispanic/Latino; 13 Two or more races, non-Hispanic/Latino), 86 international. Average age 27. 1,152 applicants, 18% accepted, 86 enrolled. *Faculty:* 1,111 full-time (447 women), 178 part-time/adjunct (76 women). Expenses: Contact institution. *Financial support:* In 2017–18, 86 students received support, including 86 research assistantships with full tuition reimbursements available (averaging $31,000 per year); fellowships, institutionally sponsored loans, scholarships/grants, traineeships, and health care benefits also available. Financial award application deadline: 12/1. In 2017, 34 master's, 73 doctorates awarded. Offers biochemistry and molecular biology (PhD); biological sciences (MS, PhD); cancer biology (PhD); cell and molecular biology (PhD); computational neuroscience (PhD); development, regeneration, and stem cell biology (PhD); ecology and evolution (PhD); evolutionary biology (PhD); genetics, genomics and systems biology (PhD); human genetics (PhD); immunology (PhD); integrative biology (PhD); medical physics (PhD); microbiology (PhD); molecular metabolism and nutrition (PhD); neurobiology (PhD); public health sciences (MS, PhD). *Application deadline:* For fall admission, 12/1 for domestic and international students. *Application fee:* $90. Electronic applications accepted. *Application Contact:* E-mail: bsdadmissions@uchicago.edu. *Dean and Executive Vice President for Medical Affairs*, Kenneth Polonsky, MD, 773-702-3004, E-mail: bsdadmissions@uchicago.edu.

Division of the Humanities Students: 713 full-time (355 women), 6 part-time (4 women); includes 129 minority (17 Black or African American, non-Hispanic/Latino; 1 American Indian or Alaska Native, non-Hispanic/Latino; 42 Asian, non-Hispanic/Latino; 51 Hispanic/Latino; 18 Two or more races, non-Hispanic/Latino), 221 international. Average age 29. 2,487 applicants, 28% accepted, 190 enrolled. *Faculty:* 244 full-time (103 women), 52 part-time/adjunct (23 women). Expenses: Contact institution. *Financial support:* Fellowships, teaching assistantships, career-related internships or fieldwork, Federal Work-Study, institutionally sponsored loans, scholarships/grants, health care benefits, and tuition waivers (full and partial) available. Financial award application deadline: 12/15. In 2017, 144 master's, 81 doctorates awarded. Offers ancient Greek and Roman philosophy (PhD); ancient Mediterranean world (PhD); ancient philosophy (PhD); anthropology and linguistics (PhD); art history (MA); cinema and media studies (MA); classic languages (MA); classical languages and literatures (PhD); comparative literature (MA); composition (PhD); creative writing (MA); cultural policy studies (MA); digital humanities (MA); digital studies of language, culture, and history (MA); East Asian languages and civilizations (MA); English language and literature (PhD); ethnomusicology (PhD); French and Francophone studies (PhD); gender and sexuality studies (MA); Germanic studies (PhD); Hispanic and Luso-Brazilian studies (PhD); humanities (MA, MFA, PhD); Italian studies (PhD); linguistics (MA, PhD); music (MA); music history and theory (PhD); Near Eastern languages and civilizations (PhD); near Eastern languages and civilizations (MA); philosophy (MA, PhD); poetics (MA); race, politics and culture (MA); Renaissance and early modern studies (PhD); Romance languages and literatures (MA); Slavic languages and literatures (MA); South Asian languages and civilizations (MA, PhD); theater and performance studies (MA); transformations in the classical tradition (PhD); visual arts (MFA). *Application deadline:* For fall admission, 12/15 for domestic and international students. *Application fee:* $90. Electronic applications accepted. *Application Contact:* Michael Beetley, Assistant Dean of Students, 773-702-1552, Fax: 773-834-9148, E-mail: humanitiesadmissions@uchicago.edu. *Dean of Students*, Martina Munsters, 773-702-8512, E-mail: humanitiesadmissions@uchicago.edu.

Division of the Physical Sciences Students: 1,032 full-time (276 women), 196 part-time (58 women); includes 154 minority (8 Black or African American, non-Hispanic/Latino; 103 Asian, non-Hispanic/Latino; 32 Hispanic/Latino; 11 Two or more races, non-Hispanic/Latino), 678 international. Average age 25. 5,659 applicants, 20% accepted, 414 enrolled. *Faculty:* 272 full-time (47 women), 57 part-time/adjunct (5 women). Expenses: Contact institution. *Financial support:* Fellowships, research assistantships, teaching assistantships, career-related internships or fieldwork, Federal Work-Study, institutionally sponsored loans, scholarships/grants, traineeships, health care benefits, and unspecified assistantships available. Support available to part-time students. In 2017, 359 master's, 85 doctorates awarded. Offers astronomy and astrophysics (PhD); atmospheric sciences (PhD); biophysical sciences (PhD); chemistry (PhD); computational and applied mathematics (PhD); computer science (MS, PhD); earth sciences (PhD); financial mathematics (MS); mathematics (PhD); paleobiology (PhD); physical sciences (MS, PhD); physics (PhD); planetary and space sciences (PhD); statistics (MS, PhD). *Application fee:* $90. Electronic applications accepted. *Application Contact:* Emily Easton, Associate Dean of Students, 773-702-9708, E-mail: psd-admissions@lists.uchicago.edu.

Division of the Social Sciences Students: 1,272 full-time (593 women), 3 part-time (all women); includes 251 minority (51 Black or African American, non-Hispanic/Latino; 3 American Indian or Alaska Native, non-Hispanic/Latino; 74 Asian, non-Hispanic/Latino; 88 Hispanic/Latino; 35 Two or more races, non-Hispanic/Latino), 496 international. Average age 28. 3,775 applicants, 38% accepted, 475 enrolled. *Faculty:* 226 full-time (71 women), 27 part-time/adjunct (7 women). Expenses: Contact institution. *Financial support:* In 2017–18, 275 students received support, including 99 fellowships with full tuition reimbursements available (averaging $27,000 per year); research assistantships, teaching assistantships, career-related internships or fieldwork, Federal Work-Study, institutionally sponsored loans, scholarships/grants, and health care benefits also available. In 2017, 382 master's, 103 doctorates awarded. Offers archaeology (PhD); comparative human development (PhD); computational social science (MA); conceptual and historical studies of science (PhD); economics (PhD); history (PhD); international relations (MA); political science (PhD); psychology (PhD); social sciences (MA, PhD); social thought (PhD); sociocultural and linguistic anthropology (PhD); sociology (PhD). *Application deadline:* For fall admission, 12/1 priority date for domestic students, 12/1 for international students. *Application fee:* $90. Electronic applications accepted. *Application Contact:* Cathy Mican, Office of the Dean of Students, E-mail: ssd-admissions@uchicago.edu. *Dean*, Prof. Amanda Woodward, E-mail: ssd-admissions@uchicago.edu.

Center for Latin American Studies Students: 6 full-time (0 women). 20 applicants, 85% accepted, 6 enrolled. *Faculty:* 54. Expenses: Contact institution. *Financial support:* In 2017–18, 6 students received support. Federal Work-Study, institutionally sponsored loans, and scholarships/grants available. Financial award application deadline: 1/4. In 2017, 3 master's awarded. Offers Latin American studies (MA). *Application deadline:* For fall admission, 1/4 priority date for domestic and international students. *Application fee:* $90. Electronic applications accepted. *Application Contact:* Office of the Dean of Students, 773-702-8415, E-mail: ssd-admissions@uchicago.edu. *Director*, Prof. Brodwyn Fischer, E-mail: clas@uchicago.edu.

Center for Middle Eastern Studies Students: 61 full-time (30 women), 1 (woman) part-time; includes 7 minority (1 Black or African American, non-Hispanic/Latino; 3 Asian, non-Hispanic/Latino; 2 Hispanic/Latino; 1 Two or more races, non-Hispanic/Latino), 6 international. Average age 25. 91 applicants, 96% accepted, 30 enrolled. *Faculty:* 18. Expenses: Contact institution. *Financial support:* In 2017–18, 8 students received support. Federal Work-Study, institutionally sponsored loans, and scholarships/grants available. Financial award application deadline: 1/4. In 2017, 29 master's awarded. Offers Middle Eastern studies (MA). *Application deadline:* For fall admission, 1/4 priority date for domestic and international students. *Application fee:* $90. Electronic applications accepted. *Application Contact:* Office of the Dean of Students, 773-702-8415, E-mail: ssd-admissions@uchicago.edu. *Director*, Prof. Orit Bashkin, E-mail: oritb@uchicago.edu.

Graham School of Continuing Liberal and Professional Studies Students: 147 full-time (79 women), 239 part-time (87 women); includes 106 minority (24 Black or African American, non-Hispanic/Latino; 43 Asian, non-Hispanic/Latino; 33 Hispanic/Latino; 6 Two or more races, non-Hispanic/Latino), 83 international. Average age 32. 824 applicants, 34% accepted, 196 enrolled. *Faculty:* 14 part-time/adjunct (1 woman). Expenses: Contact institution. *Financial support:* Applicants required to submit FAFSA. In 2017, 117 master's awarded. *Program availability:* Part-time, evening/weekend. Offers analytics (M Sc); biomedical informatics (M Sc); liberal arts (MLA); threat and response management (M Sc); urban teacher education (MAT). *Application deadline:* Applications are processed on a rolling basis. *Application fee:* $75. Electronic applications accepted. *Application Contact:* 773-702-1722, E-mail: grahamschool@uchicago.edu. *Interim Dean*, Christopher Guymon, 773-702-1730, E-mail: cguymon@uchicago.edu.

Harris School of Public Policy Students: 490 full-time (269 women), 10 part-time (6 women); includes 83 minority (16 Black or African American, non-Hispanic/Latino; 3 American Indian or Alaska Native, non-Hispanic/Latino; 36 Asian, non-Hispanic/Latino; 21 Hispanic/Latino; 7 Two or more races, non-Hispanic/Latino), 281 international. Average age 26. 1,803 applicants, 51% accepted, 333 enrolled. *Faculty:* 46 full-time (15 women), 16 part-time/adjunct (7 women). Expenses: Contact institution. *Financial support:* In 2017–18, 149 fellowships with full and partial tuition reimbursements (averaging $11,000 per year) were awarded; research assistantships, teaching assistantships, career-related internships or fieldwork, Federal Work-Study, institutionally sponsored loans, scholarships/grants, and health care benefits also available. Support available to part-time students. Financial award application deadline: 1/10. In 2017, 167 master's, 10 doctorates awarded. *Program availability:* Part-time, evening/weekend. Offers computational analysis and public policy (MS); environmental science and policy (MS); public policy (AM, MPP, MS, PhD); public policy studies (AM). *Application deadline:* For fall admission, 1/10 priority date for domestic and international students. *Application fee:* $50. Electronic applications accepted. *Application Contact:* Ranjan Daniels, Associate Dean of Student Recruitment and Global Outreach, 773-702-8401, E-mail: harrisadmissions@uchicago.edu. *Dean*, Katherine Baicker, 773-702-8400, E-mail: harrisadmissions@uchicago.edu.

Institute for Molecular Engineering Students: 99 full-time (36 women); includes 14 minority (1 Black or African American, non-Hispanic/Latino; 5 Asian, non-Hispanic/Latino; 2 Hispanic/Latino; 6 Two or more races, non-Hispanic/Latino), 44 international. Average age 24. 246 applicants, 29% accepted, 28 enrolled. *Faculty:* 26 full-time (5 women). Expenses: Contact institution. *Financial support:* In 2017–18, 36 students received support, including 45 research assistantships with full tuition reimbursements available (averaging $31,362 per year); fellowships, career-related internships or fieldwork, scholarships/grants, traineeships, health care benefits, and unspecified assistantships also available. Financial award application deadline: 1/5. In 2017, 4 doctorates awarded. Offers molecular engineering (PhD). *Application deadline:* For fall admission, 1/5 for domestic and international students. *Application fee:* $90. Electronic applications accepted. *Application Contact:* David Taylor, Associate Dean of Students, 773-834-2057, E-mail: ime-admissions@uchicago.edu. *Dean*, Dr. Matthew Tirrell, E-mail: ime@uchicago.edu.

The Law School Offers law (LL M, MCL, DCL, JD, JSD). Electronic applications accepted.

Pritzker School of Medicine Students: 364 full-time (183 women); includes 172 minority (54 Black or African American, non-Hispanic/Latino; 3 American Indian or Alaska Native, non-Hispanic/Latino; 73 Asian, non-Hispanic/Latino; 27 Hispanic/Latino; 2 Native Hawaiian or other Pacific Islander, non-Hispanic/Latino; 13 Two or more races, non-Hispanic/Latino), 1 international. Average age 26. 5,549 applicants, 5% accepted,

90 enrolled. *Faculty:* 911 full-time (366 women), 124 part-time/adjunct (67 women). Expenses: Contact institution. *Financial support:* In 2017–18, 354 students received support. Career-related internships or fieldwork, Federal Work-Study, institutionally sponsored loans, and scholarships/grants available. Financial award application deadline: 8/2. In 2017, 89 doctorates awarded. Offers medicine (MD). *Application deadline:* For fall admission, 10/15 for domestic and international students. Applications are processed on a rolling basis. *Application fee:* $85. Electronic applications accepted. *Application Contact:* Dr. Keme Carter, Assistant Dean for Admissions, 773-702-1937, Fax: 773-834-5412, E-mail: pritzkeradmissions@bsd.uchicago.edu. *Dean for Medical Education*, Dr. Holly J. Humphrey, 773-834-2138, E-mail: dean-for-meded@bsd.uchicago.edu.

School of Social Service Administration Students: 414 full-time (344 women), 61 part-time (53 women); includes 167 minority (53 Black or African American, non-Hispanic/Latino; 39 Asian, non-Hispanic/Latino; 64 Hispanic/Latino; 1 Native Hawaiian or other Pacific Islander, non-Hispanic/Latino; 10 Two or more races, non-Hispanic/Latino), 39 international. Average age 28. 737 applicants, 58% accepted, 214 enrolled. *Faculty:* 38 full-time (25 women), 29 part-time/adjunct (17 women). Expenses: Contact institution. *Financial support:* In 2017–18, 415 students received support. Fellowships, research assistantships, teaching assistantships, Federal Work-Study, institutionally sponsored loans, scholarships/grants, and health care benefits available. In 2017, 205 master's, 7 doctorates awarded. *Program availability:* Part-time, evening/weekend. Offers social service administration (AM, MA, PhD). AM/M Div offered jointly with the Divinity School, MBA/AM offered jointly with Booth School of Business, MPP/AM offered jointly with Harris School of Public Policy. *Application deadline:* For fall admission, 12/15 priority date for domestic and international students. *Application fee:* $75. Electronic applications accepted. *Application Contact:* Ronald Martin, Director of Admissions, 773-702-1250, E-mail: admissions@ssa.uchicago.edu. *Interim Dean/Professor*, Dr. Deborah Gorman-Smith, 773-702-1250, E-mail: admissions@ssa.uchicago.edu.

UNIVERSITY OF CINCINNATI, Cincinnati, OH 45221

General Information State-supported, coed, university. CGS member. *Enrollment:* 37,204 graduate, professional, and undergraduate students; 5,455 full-time matriculated graduate/professional students (2,884 women), 4,955 part-time matriculated graduate/professional students (3,293 women). *Enrollment by degree level:* 6,321 master's, 3,438 doctoral, 651 other advanced degrees. *Graduate faculty:* 1,345 full-time (521 women), 454 part-time/adjunct (253 women). *International tuition:* $26,460 full-time. *Tuition, area resident:* Full-time $14,468. Tuition, state resident: full-time $14,968; part-time $754 per credit hour. Tuition, nonresident: full-time $24,210; part-time $1311 per credit hour. *Required fees:* $3958; $84 per credit hour. One-time fee: $85 full-time. Tuition and fees vary according to course load, degree level and program. *Graduate housing:* Rooms and/or apartments available on a first-come, first-served basis to single and married students. Typical cost: $10,400 per year for single students; $10,400 per year for married students. *Student services:* Campus employment opportunities, campus safety program, career counseling, child daycare facilities, exercise/wellness program, free psychological counseling, grant writing training, international student services, low-cost health insurance, multicultural affairs office, services for students with disabilities, teacher training. *Library facilities:* Walter C. Langsam Library plus 13 others. *Collection:* Books: 2.7 million (physical), 1.6 million (digital/electronic); Serial titles: 98,491 (physical), 2.1 million (digital/electronic); Databases: 1,270. Study areas open 24 hours, 5–7 days a week; students can reserve study rooms. *Research affiliation:* Cincinnati Children's Hospital Medical Center, Cincinnati Department of Veterans Affairs Medical Center, Shriners Hospitals for Children-Cincinnati.

Computer facilities: 499 computers available on campus for general student use. A campuswide network can be accessed from student residence rooms and from off campus. Online class registration is available.
Website: http://www.uc.edu/

General Application Contact: Dr. Marshall Montrose, Vice Provost and Dean, The Graduate School, 513-556-4336, E-mail: marshall.montrose@uc.edu.

GRADUATE UNITS

Carl H. Lindner College of Business Students: 537 full-time (214 women), 575 part-time (241 women); includes 153 minority (55 Black or African American, non-Hispanic/Latino; 50 Asian, non-Hispanic/Latino; 27 Hispanic/Latino; 2 Native Hawaiian or other Pacific Islander, non-Hispanic/Latino; 19 Two or more races, non-Hispanic/Latino), 363 international. Average age 30. 2,268 applicants, 28% accepted, 511 enrolled. *Faculty:* 102 full-time (20 women), 29 part-time/adjunct (6 women). Expenses: Contact institution. *Financial support:* In 2017–18, 395 students received support, including 25 research assistantships with full and partial tuition reimbursements available (averaging $23,250 per year), 25 teaching assistantships with full and partial tuition reimbursements available (averaging $3,000 per year); scholarships/grants, tuition waivers (full and partial), and unspecified assistantships also available. Financial award application deadline: 3/15; financial award applicants required to submit FAFSA. In 2017, 584 master's, 5 doctorates awarded. *Program availability:* Part-time, evening/weekend, 100% online, blended/hybrid learning. Offers accounting (MS, PhD); applied economics (MS); business (MA, MBA, MS, PhD); business administration (MBA); business analytics (MS, PhD); economics (PhD); finance (MS, PhD); human resources (MA); information systems (MS, PhD); management (PhD); marketing (MS, PhD); operations and business analytics (PhD); operations research (PhD); taxation (MS). *Application deadline:* For fall admission, 6/30 priority date for domestic students, 3/15 for international students; for spring admission, 12/15 for domestic students, 9/15 for international students; for summer admission, 4/15 for domestic and international students. Applications are processed on a rolling basis. *Application fee:* $65 ($70 for international students). Electronic applications accepted. *Application Contact:* Dona Clary, Executive Director, Graduate Programs, 513-556-3546, Fax: 513-558-7006, E-mail: dona.clary@uc.edu. *Dean*, Dr. David Szymanski, 513-556-7001, Fax: 513-556-4891, E-mail: david.szymanski@uc.edu.

College of Law Offers law (LL M, JD). Electronic applications accepted.

Graduate School *Program availability:* Part-time, evening/weekend, online learning. Offers neuroscience (PhD). Electronic applications accepted.

College-Conservatory of Music Offers arts administration (MA); choral conducting (MM, DMA); composition (MM, DMA); directing (MFA); keyboard studies (MM, DMA, AD); music (MA, MFA, MM, DMA, PhD, AD); music education (MM); music history (MM); music theory (MM, PhD); musicology (PhD); orchestral conducting (MM, DMA); performance (MM, DMA, AD); theater design and production (MFA); voice and opera (MM, DMA); wind conducting (MM, DMA). Electronic applications accepted.

College of Allied Health Sciences *Program availability:* Part-time. Offers allied health sciences (MA, MS, MSW, Au D, DPT, PhD); communication sciences and disorders (MA, Au D, PhD); health informatics (MHI); medical genetics (MS); nutritional sciences (MS); physical therapy (DPT); social work (MSW).

College of Design, Architecture, Art, and Planning *Program availability:* Part-time. Offers architecture (M Arch); art history (MA); community planning (MCP); design, architecture, art, and planning (M Arch, M Des, MA, MCP, MFA, PhD); fashion design (M Des); fine arts (MFA); graphic design (M Des); industrial design (M Des); interaction design (M Des); product development (M Des); regional development planning (PhD); visual arts education (MA). Electronic applications accepted.

College of Education, Criminal Justice, and Human Services *Program availability:* Part-time, online learning. Offers counselor education (Ed D); criminal justice (MS, PhD); curriculum and instruction (M Ed, Ed D); education (M Ed, Ed D, PhD, Ed S); education, criminal justice, and human services (M Ed, MA, MS, Ed D, PhD, CAGS, Certificate, Ed S, Graduate Certificate); educational leadership (M Ed, Ed S); educational studies (M Ed, PhD); exercise and fitness (MS); health education (PhD); human services (M Ed, MA, MPH, MS, Ed D, PhD, Ed S, Graduate Certificate); information technology (MS, Graduate Certificate); literacy and second language studies (M Ed, Ed D); mental health (MA); public and community health (MS); public health (MPH); school counseling (M Ed); school psychology (PhD, Ed S); special education (M Ed, Ed D); sport administration (MS); substance abuse prevention (Graduate Certificate); urban educational leadership (Ed D). Electronic applications accepted.

College of Engineering and Applied Science Students: 615 full-time (141 women), 308 part-time (59 women); includes 41 minority (15 Black or African American, non-Hispanic/Latino; 18 Asian, non-Hispanic/Latino; 8 Hispanic/Latino), 626 international. Average age 27. 2,366 applicants, 22% accepted, 250 enrolled. *Faculty:* 149 full-time (11 women), 8 part-time/adjunct (0 women). Expenses: Contact institution. *Financial support:* In 2017–18, 486 students received support, including 24 fellowships with tuition reimbursements available (averaging $18,000 per year), 327 research assistantships with tuition reimbursements available (averaging $18,000 per year), 135 teaching assistantships with tuition reimbursements available (averaging $10,400 per year); career-related internships or fieldwork, tuition waivers (full and partial), and unspecified assistantships also available. Support available to part-time students. Financial award application deadline: 1/31. In 2017, 194 master's, 73 doctorates awarded. *Program availability:* Part-time, 100% online. Offers aerospace engineering and engineering mechanics (M Eng, MS, PhD); biomechanics (PhD); chemical engineering (MS, PhD); civil engineering (M Eng, MS, PhD); computer engineering (MS); computer science (MS); computer science and engineering (PhD); electrical engineering (MS, PhD); engineering and applied science (M Eng, MS, PhD); environmental engineering (MS, PhD); environmental sciences (MS, PhD); industrial engineering (PhD); materials science and engineering (MS, PhD); mechanical engineering (MS, PhD); medical imaging (PhD); nuclear engineering (PhD); tissue engineering (PhD). *Application deadline:* For fall admission, 1/31 priority date for domestic and international students. Applications are processed on a rolling basis. *Application fee:* $50. Electronic applications accepted. *Application Contact:* Julie Muenchen, Director, Academics, 513-556-3647, E-mail: julie.muenchen@uc.edu. *Senior Associate Dean*, Dr. Frank M. Gerner, 513-556-3647, E-mail: frank.gerner@uc.edu.

College of Medicine Offers biomedical informatics (PhD, Graduate Certificate); biomedical research (MS); biomedical sciences (MS, PhD, Graduate Certificate); cancer and cell biology (PhD); cell biophysics (PhD); environmental and industrial hygiene (MS, PhD); environmental and occupational medicine (MS); environmental genetics and molecular toxicology (MS, PhD); epidemiology and biostatistics (MS, PhD); immunobiology (PhD); immunology (MS, PhD); medical physics (MS); medicine (MS, MD, PhD, Graduate Certificate); molecular and developmental biology (PhD); molecular genetics, biochemistry and microbiology (MS, PhD); occupational safety and ergonomics (MS, PhD); pathology (PhD); pharmacology (PhD); systems biology and physiology (PhD). Electronic applications accepted.

College of Nursing Students: 323 full-time (261 women), 1,084 part-time (949 women); includes 311 minority (113 Black or African American, non-Hispanic/Latino; 4 American Indian or Alaska Native, non-Hispanic/Latino; 56 Asian, non-Hispanic/Latino; 108 Hispanic/Latino; 1 Native Hawaiian or other Pacific Islander, non-Hispanic/Latino; 29 Two or more races, non-Hispanic/Latino), 12 international. Average age 34. 582 applicants, 64% accepted, 314 enrolled. *Faculty:* 74 full-time (69 women), 112 part-time/adjunct (105 women). Expenses: Contact institution. *Financial support:* In 2017–18, 123 students received support, including 8 fellowships with full tuition reimbursements available (averaging $30,423 per year), 7 research assistantships with full tuition reimbursements available (averaging $17,971 per year), 5 teaching assistantships with full tuition reimbursements available (averaging $17,971 per year); Federal Work-Study, institutionally sponsored loans, scholarships/grants, traineeships, health care benefits, tuition waivers (partial), and unspecified assistantships also available. Support available to part-time students. Financial award application deadline: 5/1; financial award applicants required to submit FAFSA. In 2017, 579 master's, 18 doctorates awarded. *Program availability:* Part-time, 100% online, blended/hybrid learning. Offers nurse midwifery (MSN); nurse practitioner (MSN, DNP); nursing (MSN, PhD). *Application deadline:* For fall admission, 5/1 priority date for domestic students, 5/1 for international students; for spring admission, 10/1 for domestic students; for summer admission, 3/1 priority date for domestic students. Applications are processed on a rolling basis. *Application fee:* $130 ($70 for international students). Electronic applications accepted. *Application Contact:* Office of Student Recruitment, 513-558-8400, Fax: 513-558-5012, E-mail: nursingbearcats@uc.edu. *Dean*, Dr. Greer Glazer, 513-558-5330, Fax: 513-558-9030, E-mail: greer.glazer@uc.edu.

McMicken College of Arts and Sciences *Program availability:* Part-time, evening/weekend. Offers analytical chemistry (MS, PhD); anthropology (MA); applied mathematics (MS, PhD); arts and sciences (MA, MALER, MAT, MS, PhD, Certificate); biochemistry (MS, PhD); biological sciences (MS, PhD); classics (MA, PhD); clinical psychology (PhD); communication (MA); English and comparative literature (MA, MAT, PhD); experimental psychology (PhD); French (MA, PhD); geography (MA, PhD); geology (MS, PhD); German studies (MA, PhD); history (MA, PhD); inorganic chemistry (MS, PhD); interdisciplinary studies (PhD); labor and employment relations (MALER); mathematics education (MAT); organic chemistry (MS, PhD); organizational leadership (MALER); philosophy (MA, PhD); physical chemistry (MS, PhD); physics (MS, PhD); political science (MA, PhD); polymer chemistry (MS, PhD); pure mathematics (MS, PhD); Romance languages and literatures (PhD); sensors (PhD); sociology (MA, PhD); Spanish (MA, PhD); statistics (MS, PhD); women's, gender, and sexuality studies (MA, Certificate).

James L. Winkle College of Pharmacy *Program availability:* Part-time. Offers pharmacy (MS, PhD, Pharm D).

Division of Pharmaceutical Sciences Students: 36 full-time (18 women), 28 part-time (12 women); includes 9 minority (all Asian, non-Hispanic/Latino), 24 international. Average age 27. 197 applicants. *Faculty:* 15 full-time (2 women), 8 part-time/adjunct (3 women). Expenses: Contact institution. *Financial support:* In 2017–18, 29 students received support, including 29 fellowships with tuition reimbursements available (averaging $23,000 per year); research assistantships, tuition waivers (full), and unspecified assistantships also available. Support available to part-time students. Financial award application deadline: 3/1. In 2017, 3 master's, 5 doctorates awarded. *Program availability:* Part-time, evening/weekend, 100% online, blended/hybrid learning. Offers biomembrane science (MS); biomembrane sciences (PhD); experiential therapeutics (MS). *Application deadline:* For fall admission, 3/1 priority date for domestic students, 3/1 for international students. *Application fee:* $75. Electronic applications accepted. *Application Contact:* Karen Henry, Associate to the Director, 513-558-6172, Fax: 513-558-3233, E-mail: karen.henry@uc.edu. *Associate Dean of Research and Innovation*, Dr. Bingfang Yan, 513-558-6297, Fax: 513-558-3233, E-mail: bingfang.yan@uc.edu.

Division of Pharmacy Practice Offers pharmacy practice (Pharm D).

UNIVERSITY OF COLORADO BOULDER, Boulder, CO 80309

General Information State-supported, coed, university. CGS member. *Enrollment:* 35,230 graduate, professional, and undergraduate students; 5,528 full-time matriculated graduate/professional students (2,325 women), 521 part-time matriculated graduate/professional students (245 women). *Graduate faculty:* 1,214 full-time (416 women). *Graduate housing:* Rooms and/or apartments available to single and married students. *Student services:* Campus employment opportunities, campus safety program, career counseling, child daycare facilities, free psychological counseling, international student services, low-cost health insurance. *Library facilities:* Norlin Library plus 5 others. *Collection:* Books: 664,601 (physical), 984,952 (digital/electronic); Databases: 594. Students can reserve study rooms. *Research affiliation:* National Institute of Standards and Technology (NIST), National Oceanic and Atmospheric Administration (NOAA), U.S. West Advanced Technologies, NASA, National Center for Atmospheric Research.

Computer facilities: Computer purchase and lease plans are available. 1,689 computers available on campus for general student use. A campuswide network can be accessed from student residence rooms and from off campus. Online class registration, training, tutorials, workshops, seminars, standard and academic software, student government voting are available.
Website: http://www.colorado.edu/

GRADUATE UNITS

Graduate School Students: 4,401 full-time (1,827 women), 509 part-time (235 women); includes 705 minority (60 Black or African American, non-Hispanic/Latino; 13 American Indian or Alaska Native, non-Hispanic/Latino; 162 Asian, non-Hispanic/Latino; 321 Hispanic/Latino; 2 Native Hawaiian or other Pacific Islander, non-Hispanic/Latino; 147 Two or more races, non-Hispanic/Latino), 1,106 international. Average age 28. 10,845 applicants, 34% accepted, 1317 enrolled. *Faculty:* 1,115 full-time (390 women). Expenses: Contact institution. *Financial support:* In 2017–18, 9,754 students received support, including 2,640 fellowships (averaging $6,114 per year), 1,274 research assistantships with full and partial tuition reimbursements available (averaging $36,842 per year), 1,547 teaching assistantships with full and partial tuition reimbursements available (averaging $24,364 per year); institutionally sponsored loans, scholarships/grants, health care benefits, and unspecified assistantships also available. Financial award applicants required to submit FAFSA. In 2017, 1,049 master's, 415 doctorates awarded. Offers materials science and engineering (MS, PhD); museum and field studies (MS); organizational leadership. *Application fee:* $60 ($80 for international students). Electronic applications accepted. *Application Contact:* E-mail: gradinfo@colorado.edu.

College of Arts and Sciences Students: 2,078 full-time (999 women), 67 part-time (36 women); includes 318 minority (21 Black or African American, non-Hispanic/Latino; 6 American Indian or Alaska Native, non-Hispanic/Latino; 73 Asian, non-Hispanic/Latino; 140 Hispanic/Latino; 78 Two or more races, non-Hispanic/Latino), 306 international. Average age 28. 5,627 applicants, 24% accepted, 511 enrolled. *Faculty:* 728 full-time (265 women). Expenses: Contact institution. *Financial support:* In 2017–18, 5,060 students received support, including 1,123 fellowships (averaging $7,291 per year), 582 research assistantships with full and partial tuition reimbursements available (averaging $34,311 per year), 1,083 teaching assistantships with full and partial tuition reimbursements available (averaging $24,230 per year); institutionally sponsored loans, scholarships/grants, health care benefits, and unspecified assistantships also available. Financial award applicants required to submit FAFSA. In 2017, 298 master's, 250 doctorates awarded. Offers anthropology (MA, PhD); applied mathematics (MS, PhD); art history (MA); arts and sciences (MA, MFA, MS, Au D, PhD); Asian languages and civilizations (MA, PhD); astrophysics (MS, PhD); atmospheric and oceanic sciences (MS, PhD); cellular structure and function (MA, PhD); ceramics (MFA); chemistry and biochemistry (MS, PhD); classics (MA, PhD); dance (MFA); developmental biology (PhD); economics (MA, PhD); environmental studies (MS, PhD); ethnic studies (PhD); French and Italian (MA, PhD); geography (MA, PhD); geology (MS, PhD); geophysics (PhD); Germanic and Slavic languages and literatures (MA); Hispanic linguistics (MA); history (MA, PhD); integrative physiology (MS, PhD); linguistics (MA, PhD); literature (MA, PhD); mathematical physics (PhD); mathematics (MA, MS, PhD); medieval and early modern Hispanic literatures (PhD); molecular biology (PhD); peninsular and Latin American literature (MA); philosophy (MA, PhD); photography and media arts (MFA); planetary science (PhD); political science (MA, PhD); population biology (MA); printmaking (MFA); psychology and neuroscience (MA, PhD); religious studies (MA); Russian studies (MA); sculpture (MFA); sociology (PhD); speech, language and hearing sciences (MA, Au D, PhD); theatre (MA, PhD). *Application fee:* $60 ($80 for international students). Electronic applications accepted.

College of Engineering and Applied Science Students: 1,783 full-time (500 women), 244 part-time (53 women); includes 244 minority (20 Black or African American, non-Hispanic/Latino; 5 American Indian or Alaska Native, non-Hispanic/Latino; 77 Asian, non-Hispanic/Latino; 89 Hispanic/Latino; 1 Native Hawaiian or other Pacific Islander, non-Hispanic/Latino; 52 Two or more races, non-Hispanic/Latino), 758 international. Average age 27. 3,960 applicants, 44% accepted, 596 enrolled. *Faculty:* 218 full-time (46 women). Expenses: Contact institution. *Financial support:* In 2017–18, 3,301 students received support, including 1,030 fellowships (averaging $6,375 per year), 601 research assistantships with full and partial tuition reimbursements available (averaging $40,330 per year), 208 teaching assistantships with full and partial tuition reimbursements available (averaging $27,448 per year); institutionally sponsored loans, scholarships/grants, health care benefits, and unspecified assistantships also available. Financial award applicants required to submit FAFSA. In 2017, 534 master's, 122 doctorates awarded. Offers aerospace engineering sciences (MS, PhD); chemical and biological engineering (ME, MS, PhD); civil, environmental, and architectural engineering (MS, PhD); computer science (ME, MS, PhD); electrical, computer and energy engineering (ME, MS, PhD); engineering and applied science (ME, MS, PhD); engineering management (ME); mechanical engineering (ME, MS, PhD); technology, learning, and society (MS, PhD); telecommunications (MS). *Application fee:* $60 ($80 for international students). Electronic applications accepted.

College of Media, Communication and Information Students: 139 full-time (85 women), 7 part-time (5 women); includes 19 minority (3 Black or African American, non-Hispanic/Latino; 4 Asian, non-Hispanic/Latino; 10 Hispanic/Latino; 2 Two or more races, non-Hispanic/Latino), 16 international. Average age 31. 279 applicants, 44% accepted, 55 enrolled. *Faculty:* 67 full-time (36 women). Expenses: Contact institution. *Financial support:* In 2017–18, 393 students received support, including 125 fellowships (averaging $1,542 per year), 23 research assistantships with full and partial tuition reimbursements available (averaging $23,508 per year), 90 teaching assistantships with full and partial tuition reimbursements available (averaging $30,255 per year); institutionally sponsored loans, scholarships/grants, health care benefits, and unspecified assistantships also available. Financial award application deadline: 3/1; financial award applicants required to submit FAFSA. In 2017, 35 master's, 10 doctorates awarded. Offers communication (MA, PhD); information science (PhD); interdisciplinary documentary media practices (MFA); intermedia art, writing and performance (PhD); journalism (MA); media research and practice (PhD); media studies (PhD); media, communication and information (MA, MFA, PhD); strategic communication design (MA). *Application deadline:* Applications are processed on a rolling basis. *Application fee:* $60 ($80 for international students). Electronic applications accepted. *Application Contact:* E-mail: cmcigrad@colorado.edu.

College of Music Students: 165 full-time (79 women), 35 part-time (12 women); includes 22 minority (3 Black or African American, non-Hispanic/Latino; 3 Asian, non-Hispanic/Latino; 10 Hispanic/Latino; 6 Two or more races, non-Hispanic/Latino), 19 international. Average age 29. 459 applicants, 41% accepted, 65 enrolled. *Faculty:* 64 full-time (19 women). Expenses: Contact institution. *Financial support:* In 2017–18, 546 students received support, including 250 fellowships (averaging $2,731 per year), 116 teaching assistantships with full and partial tuition reimbursements available (averaging $19,272 per year); research assistantships, institutionally sponsored loans, scholarships/grants, health care benefits, and unspecified assistantships also available. Financial award application deadline: 2/15; financial award applicants required to submit FAFSA. In 2017, 46 master's, 22 doctorates awarded. Offers composition (M Mus, D Mus A); conducting (M Mus); instrumental conducting and literature (D Mus A); literature and performance of choral music (D Mus A); music education (M Mus Ed, PhD); music theory (M Mus); performance (M Mus, D Mus A); performance and pedagogy (M Mus, D Mus A). *Application deadline:* For fall admission, 12/1 for domestic and international students; for spring admission, 10/1 for domestic and international students. Applications are processed on a rolling basis. *Application fee:* $60 ($80 for international students). Electronic applications accepted. *Application Contact:* E-mail: gradmusc@colorado.edu.

School of Education Students: 176 full-time (119 women), 153 part-time (126 women); includes 89 minority (11 Black or African American, non-Hispanic/Latino; 1 American Indian or Alaska Native, non-Hispanic/Latino; 3 Asian, non-Hispanic/Latino; 67 Hispanic/Latino; 1 Native Hawaiian or other Pacific Islander, non-Hispanic/Latino; 6 Two or more races, non-Hispanic/Latino), 5 international. Average age 33. 401 applicants, 52% accepted, 82 enrolled. *Faculty:* 38 full-time (24 women). Expenses: Contact institution. *Financial support:* In 2017–18, 381 students received support, including 92 fellowships (averaging $4,091 per year), 66 research assistantships with full and partial tuition reimbursements available (averaging $32,538 per year), 35 teaching assistantships with full and partial tuition reimbursements available (averaging $10,002 per year); scholarships/grants, health care benefits, and unspecified assistantships also available. Financial award application deadline: 2/15; financial award applicants required to submit FAFSA. In 2017, 133 master's, 11 doctorates awarded. Offers curriculum and instruction (MA, PhD); education (MA, PhD); educational and psychological studies (MA, PhD); educational equity and cultural diversity (PhD); educational foundations, policy, and practice (MA, PhD); multicultural education (MA); research and evaluation methodology (PhD). *Application deadline:* For fall admission, 12/1 for domestic and international students; for spring admission, 9/1 for domestic and international students. *Application fee:* $60 ($80 for international students). Electronic applications accepted.

Leeds School of Business Students: 574 full-time (221 women), 2 part-time (1 woman); includes 83 minority (8 Black or African American, non-Hispanic/Latino; 28 Asian, non-Hispanic/Latino; 37 Hispanic/Latino; 10 Two or more races, non-Hispanic/Latino), 82 international. Average age 28. 797 applicants, 57% accepted, 170 enrolled. *Faculty:* 59 full-time (11 women). Expenses: Contact institution. *Financial support:* In 2017–18, 594 students received support, including 402 fellowships (averaging $7,741 per year), 37 teaching assistantships with full and partial tuition reimbursements available (averaging $23,813 per year); research assistantships, institutionally sponsored loans, scholarships/grants, health care benefits, and unspecified assistantships also available. Financial award application deadline: 2/15; financial award applicants required to submit FAFSA. In 2017, 237 master's, 3 doctorates awarded. Offers business (MBA, MS, PhD); business administration (MS, PhD). *Application deadline:* For fall admission, 12/1 for domestic students; for spring admission, 12/1 for domestic students. Applications are processed on a rolling basis. *Application fee:* $60 ($80 for international students). Electronic applications accepted.

MBA Program Students: 351 full-time (122 women), 2 part-time (1 woman); includes 45 minority (5 Black or African American, non-Hispanic/Latino; 15 Asian, non-Hispanic/Latino; 22 Hispanic/Latino; 3 Two or more races, non-Hispanic/Latino), 43 international. Average age 30. 438 applicants, 73% accepted, 107 enrolled. Expenses: Contact institution. *Financial support:* In 2017–18, 357 students received support, including 273 fellowships (averaging $8,866 per year), 2 teaching assistantships with full and partial tuition reimbursements available (averaging $9,804 per year); institutionally sponsored loans, scholarships/grants, health care benefits, and unspecified assistantships also available. Financial award application deadline: 2/15; financial award applicants required to submit FAFSA. In 2017, 150 master's awarded. Offers business administration (MBA). *Application deadline:* For fall admission, 12/1 for domestic students; for spring admission, 12/1 for domestic students. Applications are processed on a rolling basis. *Application fee:* $60 ($80 for international students). Electronic applications accepted. *Application Contact:* E-mail: leedsmba@colorado.edu.

School of Law Students: 553 full-time (277 women), 10 part-time (9 women); includes 124 minority (10 Black or African American, non-Hispanic/Latino; 13 American Indian or Alaska Native, non-Hispanic/Latino; 29 Asian, non-Hispanic/Latino; 67 Hispanic/Latino; 5 Two or more races, non-Hispanic/Latino), 4 international. Average age 27. 1,071 applicants, 100% accepted, 202 enrolled. *Faculty:* 40 full-time (15 women). Expenses: Contact institution. *Financial support:* In 2017–18, 1,056 students received support, including 768 fellowships (averaging $8,286 per year); institutionally sponsored loans, scholarships/grants, health care benefits, and unspecified assistantships also available. Financial award application deadline: 2/15; financial award applicants required to submit FAFSA. In 2017, 169 doctorates awarded. Offers law (JD). *Application deadline:* For fall admission, 2/15 for domestic students. Applications are processed on a rolling basis.

Application fee: $60 ($80 for international students). Electronic applications accepted. *Application Contact:* E-mail: lawadmin@colorado.edu.

UNIVERSITY OF COLORADO COLORADO SPRINGS, Colorado Springs, CO 80918

General Information State-supported, coed, university. CGS member. *Enrollment:* 12,932 graduate, professional, and undergraduate students; 418 full-time matriculated graduate/professional students (247 women), 1,418 part-time matriculated graduate/professional students (773 women). *Enrollment by degree level:* 1,512 master's, 226 doctoral, 98 other advanced degrees. *Graduate faculty:* 444 full-time (232 women), 330 part-time/adjunct (195 women). Tuition, state resident: full-time $10,351. Tuition, nonresident: full-time $20,934. Tuition and fees vary according to class time, course load and program. *Graduate housing:* Room and/or apartments available on a first-come, first-served basis to single students; on-campus housing not available to married students. Typical cost: $8850 per year. Room charges vary according to board plan and housing facility selected. *Student services:* Campus safety program, career counseling, child daycare facilities, exercise/wellness program, free psychological counseling, grant writing training, international student services, low-cost health insurance, multicultural affairs office, services for students with disabilities, teacher training, writing training. *Library facilities:* Kraemer Family Library. *Collection:* Books: 337,790 (physical), 168,770 (digital/electronic); Serial titles: 3,020 (physical); Databases: 154. Students can reserve study rooms. *Research affiliation:* Georgia Institute of Technology (education), University of North Texas Health Science Center (psychology), National Institute of Arthritis and Musculoskeletal and Skin Diseases (NIAMS) (mechanical and aerospace engineering), National Geographic Society (geography and environmental studies), i-CORE (physics), Structured Material Industries, NJ (electrical and computer engineering).

Computer facilities: Computer purchase and lease plans are available. A campuswide network can be accessed from student residence rooms and from off campus. Online class registration, student portal, learning management system are available.
Website: http://www.uccs.edu/

General Application Contact: KrisAnn McBroom, Graduate School Administrator, 719-255-3417, Fax: 719-255-3045, E-mail: gradinfo@uccs.edu.

GRADUATE UNITS

College of Business Students: 65 full-time (18 women), 267 part-time (126 women); includes 73 minority (9 Black or African American, non-Hispanic/Latino; 17 Asian, non-Hispanic/Latino; 29 Hispanic/Latino; 18 Two or more races, non-Hispanic/Latino), 11 international. Average age 34. 161 applicants, 81% accepted, 92 enrolled. *Faculty:* 40 full-time (14 women), 57 part-time/adjunct (19 women). Expenses: Contact institution. *Financial support:* In 2017–18, 35 students received support. Career-related internships or fieldwork, Federal Work-Study, and scholarships/grants available. Support available to part-time students. Financial award application deadline: 3/1; financial award applicants required to submit FAFSA. In 2017, 106 master's awarded. *Program availability:* Part-time, evening/weekend, 100% online, blended/hybrid learning. Offers business (MBA, MSA). *Application deadline:* For fall admission, 6/1 priority date for domestic students, 6/1 for international students; for spring admission, 11/1 priority date for domestic students, 11/1 for international students; for summer admission, 4/1 priority date for domestic students, 4/1 for international students. Applications are processed on a rolling basis. *Application fee:* $60 ($100 for international students). Electronic applications accepted. *Application Contact:* Janice Dowsett, Director of Graduate Programs, 719-255-3070, E-mail: cobgrad@uccs.edu. *Interim Dean*, Dr. Eric Olson, 719-255-3113, Fax: 719-255-3100, E-mail: eolson@uccs.edu.

College of Education Students: 190 full-time (132 women), 286 part-time (202 women); includes 117 minority (20 Black or African American, non-Hispanic/Latino; 2 American Indian or Alaska Native, non-Hispanic/Latino; 12 Asian, non-Hispanic/Latino; 59 Hispanic/Latino; 24 Two or more races, non-Hispanic/Latino), 6 international. Average age 36. 169 applicants, 85% accepted, 113 enrolled. *Faculty:* 30 full-time (21 women), 61 part-time/adjunct (38 women). Expenses: Contact institution. *Financial support:* In 2017–18, 81 students received support. Career-related internships or fieldwork, Federal Work-Study, scholarships/grants, and unspecified assistantships available. Support available to part-time students. Financial award application deadline: 3/1; financial award applicants required to submit FAFSA. In 2017, 160 master's, 16 doctorates awarded. *Program availability:* Part-time, evening/weekend, 100% online, blended/hybrid learning. Offers counseling and human services (MA); curriculum and instruction (MA); educational leadership (MA); educational leadership, research and policy (PhD); special education (MA); teaching English to speakers of other languages (MA). *Application deadline:* For fall admission, 1/28 priority date for domestic and international students; for spring admission, 11/1 priority date for domestic and international students. Applications are processed on a rolling basis. *Application fee:* $60 ($100 for international students). Electronic applications accepted. *Application Contact:* The College of Education Student Resource Office, 719-255-4996, E-mail: education@uccs.edu. *Dean*, Dr. Valerie Martin Conley, 719-255-4133, E-mail: vmconley@uccs.edu.

College of Engineering and Applied Science Students: 31 full-time (4 women), 288 part-time (58 women); includes 57 minority (12 Black or African American, non-Hispanic/Latino; 13 Asian, non-Hispanic/Latino; 19 Hispanic/Latino; 13 Two or more races, non-Hispanic/Latino), 85 international. Average age 33. 162 applicants, 86% accepted, 79 enrolled. *Faculty:* 43 full-time (11 women), 36 part-time/adjunct (9 women). Expenses: Contact institution. *Financial support:* In 2017–18, 57 students received support. Career-related internships or fieldwork, Federal Work-Study, and scholarships/grants available. Support available to part-time students. Financial award application deadline: 3/1; financial award applicants required to submit FAFSA. In 2017, 58 master's, 11 doctorates awarded. *Program availability:* Part-time, evening/weekend. Offers computer science (MS, PhD); electrical engineering (MS, PhD); energy engineering (ME); engineering and applied science (ME, MS, PhD); engineering management (ME); information assurance (ME); mechanical engineering (MS, PhD); software engineering (ME); space operations (ME); systems engineering (ME). *Application deadline:* For fall admission, 6/1 for domestic students, 4/1 for international students; for spring admission, 11/1 for domestic students, 10/1 for international students. Applications are processed on a rolling basis. *Application fee:* $60 ($100 for international students). *Application Contact:* Ali Langfels, Office of Student Support, 719-255-3544, E-mail: alangfel@uccs.edu. *Interim Dean*, Dr. Xiaobo Charles Zhou, 719-255-3543, E-mail: xzhou@uccs.edu.

College of Letters, Arts and Sciences Students: 59 full-time (39 women), 189 part-time (102 women); includes 53 minority (8 Black or African American, non-Hispanic/Latino; 3 American Indian or Alaska Native, non-Hispanic/Latino; 4 Asian, non-Hispanic/Latino; 23 Hispanic/Latino; 15 Two or more races, non-Hispanic/Latino), 9 international. Average age 32. 467 applicants, 33% accepted, 76 enrolled. *Faculty:* 145 full-time (65 women), 100 part-time/adjunct (56 women). Expenses: Contact institution. *Financial support:* In 2017–18, 122 students received support. Career-related internships or fieldwork, Federal Work-Study, scholarships/grants, and unspecified assistantships available. Support available to part-time students. Financial award application deadline: 3/1; financial award applicants required to submit FAFSA. In 2017, 72 master's, 3 doctorates awarded. *Program availability:* Part-time, evening/weekend, 100% online, blended/hybrid learning. Offers applied mathematics (MS); applied sciences (PhD); communication (MA); geography and environmental studies (MA); history (MA); interdisciplinary sciences (M Sc); letters, arts and sciences (M Sc, MA, MS, PhD); psychology (MA, PhD); sociology (MA). *Application deadline:* Applications are processed on a rolling basis. *Application fee:* $60 ($100 for international students). Electronic applications accepted. *Application Contact:* Sarah Elsey, Graduate Recruitment and Retention Specialist, 719-255-3072, E-mail: gradinfo@uccs.edu. *Dean of the Graduate School*, Dr. Kelli Klebe, 719-255-3779, Fax: 719-255-3045, E-mail: kklebe@uccs.edu.

Helen and Arthur E. Johnson Beth-El College of Nursing and Health Sciences Students: 7 full-time (6 women), 213 part-time (192 women); includes 50 minority (8 Black or African American, non-Hispanic/Latino; 1 American Indian or Alaska Native, non-Hispanic/Latino; 11 Asian, non-Hispanic/Latino; 23 Hispanic/Latino; 1 Native Hawaiian or other Pacific Islander, non-Hispanic/Latino; 6 Two or more races, non-Hispanic/Latino). Average age 37. 125 applicants, 66% accepted, 57 enrolled. *Faculty:* 11 full-time (10 women), 13 part-time/adjunct (12 women). Expenses: Contact institution. *Financial support:* In 2017–18, 28 students received support. Research assistantships, career-related internships or fieldwork, Federal Work-Study, and scholarships/grants available. Support available to part-time students. Financial award application deadline: 3/1; financial award applicants required to submit FAFSA. In 2017, 47 master's, 10 doctorates awarded. *Program availability:* Part-time, 100% online, blended/hybrid learning. Offers nursing practice (DNP); primary care nurse practitioner (MSN). *Application deadline:* For fall admission, 3/15 priority date for domestic students, 3/15 for international students; for spring admission, 8/15 for domestic and international students. Applications are processed on a rolling basis. *Application fee:* $60 ($100 for international students). Electronic applications accepted. *Application Contact:* Diane Busch, Program Assistant II, 719-255-4424, Fax: 719-255-4416, E-mail: dbusch@uccs.edu. *Nursing Department Chair*, Dr. Deborah Pollard, 719-255-3577, Fax: 719-255-4416, E-mail: dpollard@uccs.edu.

School of Public Affairs Students: 19 full-time (11 women), 164 part-time (101 women); includes 57 minority (6 Black or African American, non-Hispanic/Latino; 1 American Indian or Alaska Native, non-Hispanic/Latino; 5 Asian, non-Hispanic/Latino; 37 Hispanic/Latino; 8 Two or more races, non-Hispanic/Latino). Average age 35. 61 applicants, 95% accepted, 40 enrolled. *Faculty:* 13 full-time (6 women), 16 part-time/adjunct (3 women). Expenses: Contact institution. *Financial support:* In 2017–18, 25 students received support. Career-related internships or fieldwork, scholarships/grants, and tuition waivers available. Support available to part-time students. Financial award application deadline: 3/1; financial award applicants required to submit FAFSA. In 2017, 44 master's awarded. *Program availability:* Part-time, evening/weekend, 100% online, blended/hybrid learning. Offers criminal justice (MCJ); public administration (MPA). *Application deadline:* Applications are processed on a rolling basis. *Application fee:* $60 ($100 for international students). Electronic applications accepted. *Application Contact:* Crista Hill, Outreach Student Services Specialist, 719-255-4993, Fax: 719-255-4183, E-mail: chill12@uccs.edu. *Dean*, Dr. George Reed, 719-255-4109, E-mail: george.reed@uccs.edu.

UNIVERSITY OF COLORADO DENVER, Denver, CO 80217-3364

General Information State-supported, coed, university. CGS member. *Graduate housing:* Room and/or apartments available on a first-come, first-served basis to single students; on-campus housing not available to married students. *Student services:* Campus employment opportunities, campus safety program, career counseling, child daycare facilities, exercise/wellness program, free psychological counseling, international student services, low-cost health insurance, multicultural affairs office, services for students with disabilities, teacher training, writing training. *Library facilities:* Auraria Library plus 1 other. *Collection:* Books: 573,818 (physical), 325,936 (digital/electronic); Serial titles: 5,780 (physical), 92,591 (digital/electronic); Databases: 308. Weekly public service hours: 85; students can reserve study rooms. *Research affiliation:* The Children's Hospital (pediatrics), National Jewish Health (pediatrics, immunology, respiratory disease), Denver Health (trauma, primary care, under-served populations).

Computer facilities: 750 computers available on campus for general student use. A campuswide network can be accessed from student residence rooms and from off campus. Online class registration is available.
Website: http://www.ucdenver.edu/

General Application Contact: Graduate School Admissions, 303-556-2704, E-mail: admissions@ucdenver.edu.

GRADUATE UNITS

Business School Expenses: Contact institution. *Financial support:* Fellowships, research assistantships, teaching assistantships, Federal Work-Study, institutionally sponsored loans, scholarships/grants, and traineeships available. Financial award application deadline: 4/1; financial award applicants required to submit FAFSA. *Program availability:* Part-time, evening/weekend, online learning. Offers accounting and information systems audit and control (MS); accounting and information systems audit control (MS); advanced market analytics in a big data world (MS); auditing (MS); brand communication in the digital era (MS); business (MBA, MS, PhD); business administration (MBA); business intelligence systems (MS); business strategy (MS); change and innovation (MS); computer science and information systems (PhD); controllership and financial leadership (MS); digital health entrepreneurship (MS); economics (MS); enterprise risk management (MS); enterprise technology management (MS); entrepreneurship and innovation (MS); finance (MS); financial analysis and management (MS); financial and commodities risk management (MS); geographic information systems (MS); global energy management (MS); global management (MS); global marketing (MS); health administration (MBA); health information technology (MS); high-tech and entrepreneurial marketing (MS); international business (MS); leadership (MS); managing for sustainability (MS); managing human resources (MS); marketing and global sustainability (MS); marketing intelligence and strategy in the 21st century (MS); risk management and insurance (MS); sports and entertainment (MS); sports and entertainment business (MS); strategic management (MS); taxation (MS); technology innovation and entrepreneurship (MS); Web and mobile computing (MS). *Application deadline:* For fall admission, 4/15 priority date for domestic students, 3/15 priority date for international students; for spring admission, 10/15 priority date for domestic students, 9/15 priority date for international students; for summer admission, 2/15 priority date for domestic students, 1/15 priority date for international students. Applications are processed on a rolling basis. *Application fee:* $0. Electronic applications accepted. *Application Contact:* Dr. Rohan Christie-David, Dean and Professor of Finance, 303-315-8000, E-mail: rohan.christie-david@ucdenver.edu. *Dean and Professor of Finance*, Dr. Rohan Christie-David, 303-315-8000, E-mail: rohan.christie-david@ucdenver.edu.

College of Architecture and Planning Expenses: Contact institution. *Financial support:* Fellowships with tuition reimbursements, research assistantships, teaching assistantships, Federal Work-Study, institutionally sponsored loans, scholarships/grants, and traineeships available. Financial award application deadline: 4/1; financial award applicants required to submit FAFSA. *Program availability:* Part-time. Offers architecture (M Arch); architecture and planning (M Arch, MLA, MS, MUD, MURP, PhD); economic and community development planning (MURP); historic preservation (MS); history of architecture, landscape and urbanism (PhD); land use and environmental planning (MURP); landscape architecture (MLA); sustainable and healthy environments (PhD); urban design (MUD); urban place making (MURP). *Application deadline:* For fall admission, 1/15 for domestic students, 1/1 for international students. Applications are processed on a rolling basis. *Application fee:* $0. Electronic applications accepted. *Application Contact:* Rachael Kuroiwa, Manager of Admissions and Outreach, 303-315-2325, E-mail: rachael.kuroiwa@ucdenver.edu. *Dean*, Dr. Nan Ellin, 303-315-1000, E-mail: mark.gelernter@ucdenver.edu.

College of Arts and Media Students: 28 full-time (6 women), 12 part-time (4 women); includes 13 minority (2 Black or African American, non-Hispanic/Latino; 1 Asian, non-Hispanic/Latino; 6 Hispanic/Latino; 4 Two or more races, non-Hispanic/Latino), 1 international. Average age 31. 25 applicants, 84% accepted, 17 enrolled. *Faculty:* 35 full-time (12 women), 2 part-time/adjunct (both women). Expenses: Contact institution. *Financial support:* In 2017–18, 4 students received support. Federal Work-Study, institutionally sponsored loans, scholarships/grants, traineeships, and unspecified assistantships available. Financial award application deadline: 4/1; financial award applicants required to submit FAFSA. In 2017, 10 master's awarded. *Program availability:* Part-time, evening/weekend. Offers recording arts (MS). *Application deadline:* For fall admission, 4/1 for domestic students, 3/1 for international students. *Application fee:* $50 ($75 for international students). Electronic applications accepted. *Application Contact:* Lisa Funderburg, Program Assistant, 303-352-3833, E-mail: lisa.funderburg@ucdenver.edu. *Dean, College of Arts and Media*, Laurence D. Kaptain, 303-556-2279, E-mail: laurence.kaptain@ucdenver.edu.

College of Engineering and Applied Science 708 applicants, 55% accepted, 98 enrolled. Expenses: Contact institution. *Program availability:* Part-time, evening/weekend. Offers basic research (MS, PhD); biomedical device design (MS); civil engineering (M Eng, EASPh D); civil engineering systems (PhD); computer science (MS); computer science and engineering (EASPh D); computer science and information systems (PhD); electrical engineering (M Eng); engineering and applied science (M Eng, MS, EASPh D, PhD); entrepreneurship (PhD); entrepreneurship and regulatory affairs (MS); environmental and sustainability engineering (MS, PhD); geographic information systems (MS); geotechnical engineering (MS, PhD); hydrology and hydraulics (MS, PhD); mechanical engineering (M Eng, MS); mechanics (MS); structural engineering (MS, PhD); thermal sciences (MS); translational bioengineering (PhD); transportation engineering (MS, PhD). *Application fee:* $50 ($75 for international students). Electronic applications accepted. *Application Contact:* Graduate School Admissions, 303-556-2704, E-mail: admissions@ucdenver.edu. *Dean*, Dr. Mark Ingber, 303-556-2870, Fax: 303-556-2511, E-mail: marc.ingber@ucdenver.edu.

College of Liberal Arts and Sciences 613 applicants, 47% accepted, 145 enrolled. *Faculty:* 211 full-time (90 women), 21 part-time/adjunct (12 women). Expenses: Contact institution. In 2017, 170 master's, 5 doctorates awarded. *Program availability:* Part-time, evening/weekend. Offers applied linguistics (MA); applied mathematics (MS, PhD); applied science (MIS); archaeological studies (MA); biological anthropology (MA); biology (MS); chemistry (MS); clinical health psychology (PhD); communication (MA); community health (MSS); computer science (MIS); economics (MA); environmental sciences (MS); ethnic studies (MH, MSS); European history (MA); global history (MA); health and behavioral sciences (PhD); humanities (MH, Graduate Certificate); integrative and systems biology (PhD); international studies (MSS); liberal arts and sciences (MA, MH, MIS, MS, MSS, PhD, Graduate Certificate); mathematics (MS); medical anthropology (MA); philosophy and theory (MH); political science (MA); public history (MA); social justice (MH, MSS); society and the environment (MSS); sociology (MA); Spanish (MA); sustainable development and political ecology (MA); U.S. history (MA); visual studies (MH); women's and gender studies (MH, MSS). *Application fee:* $50 ($75 for international students). Electronic applications accepted. *Application Contact:* College of Liberal Arts and Sciences, 303-556-2555, E-mail: clas@ucdenver.edu. *Dean*, Pamela Jansma, 303-556-2557, E-mail: pamela.jansma@ucdenver.edu.

College of Nursing 297 applicants, 55% accepted, 141 enrolled. Expenses: Contact institution. In 2017, 138 master's, 18 doctorates awarded. *Program availability:* Part-time, evening/weekend, online learning. Offers adult clinical nurse specialist (MS); adult nurse practitioner (MS); family nurse practitioner (MS); family psychiatric mental health nurse practitioner (MS); health care informatics (MS); nurse-midwifery (MS); nursing (DNP, PhD); nursing leadership and health care systems (MS); pediatric nurse practitioner (MS); women's health (MS). *Application deadline:* For fall admission, 2/15 for domestic students, 1/15 for international students; for spring admission, 7/1 for domestic students, 6/1 for international students. *Application fee:* $50 ($75 for international students). Electronic applications accepted. *Application Contact:* Judy Campbell, Graduate Programs Coordinator, 303-724-8503, E-mail: judy.campbell@ucdenver.edu. *Dean*, Dr. Sarah Thompson, 303-724-1679, E-mail: sarah.a.thompson@ucdenver.edu.

Colorado School of Public Health Students: 514 full-time (424 women), 86 part-time (69 women); includes 131 minority (18 Black or African American, non-Hispanic/Latino; 5 American Indian or Alaska Native, non-Hispanic/Latino; 36 Asian, non-Hispanic/Latino; 56 Hispanic/Latino; 1 Native Hawaiian or other Pacific Islander, non-Hispanic/Latino; 15 Two or more races, non-Hispanic/Latino), 19 international. Average age 31. 950 applicants, 27% accepted, 218 enrolled. Expenses: Contact institution. In 2017, 216 master's, 15 doctorates awarded. *Program availability:* Part-time. Offers biostatistics and informatics (MS, PhD); community and behavioral health (MPH, Dr PH); epidemiology (MS, PhD); health services research (MS, PhD); public health (MPH, MS, Dr PH, PhD). *Application deadline:* For fall admission, 1/15 for domestic and international students. *Application fee:* $50 ($75 for international students). Electronic applications accepted. *Application Contact:* Office of Student Affairs, 303-724-4613, Fax: 303-724-4620, E-mail: admissions.csph@ucdenver.edu. *Interim Dean*, Dr. Elaine Morrato, 303-724-4450, E-mail: elaine.morratof@ucdenver.edu.

School of Dental Medicine Expenses: Contact institution. In 2017, 118 doctorates awarded. Offers dental surgery (DDS); orthodontics (Certificate); periodontics (Certificate). *Application fee:* $0. *Application Contact:* Graduate Student Admissions, 303-724-7122, Fax: 303-724-7109, E-mail: ddsadmissioninquiries@ucdenver.edu. *Dean*, Dr. Denise K. Kassebaum, 303-724-7100, Fax: 303-724-7109, E-mail: denise.kassebaum@ucdenver.edu.

School of Education and Human Development Expenses: Contact institution. In 2017, 517 master's, 28 doctorates, 15 other advanced degrees awarded. *Program availability:* Part-time, evening/weekend, online learning. Offers administrative leadership and policy (PhD); administrative leadership and policy studies (MA, Ed S); assessment (MA); counseling (MA); e-learning design and implementation (MA); early childhood education (MA); early childhood special education/early childhood education (PhD); education and human development (MA, MS Ed, Ed D, PhD, Psy D, Ed S); educational studies and research (PhD); elementary linguistically diverse education (MA); elementary math and science education (MA); elementary math education (MA); elementary reading and writing (MA); elementary science education (MA); executive leadership (Ed D); family science and human development (PhD); human development and family relations (MA); instructional design and adult learning (MA); instructional leadership (Ed D); K-12 teaching (MA); learning (MA); mathematics education (MS Ed); research and evaluation methods (MA); research, assessment and evaluation (PhD); school counseling (MA); school psychology (Psy D); science education (PhD); secondary English education (MA); secondary linguistically diverse education (MA); secondary math education (MA); secondary reading and writing (MA); secondary science education (MA); special education (MA); urban ecologies (PhD). *Application fee:* $0. *Application Contact:* Student Services Center, 303-315-6300, Fax: 303-315-6311, E-mail: education@ucdenver.edu. *Dean*, Rebecca Kantor, 303-315-6343, E-mail: rebecca.kantor@ucdenver.edu.

School of Medicine Expenses: Contact institution. In 2017, 114 master's, 275 doctorates awarded. Offers anesthesiology (MS); biochemistry (PhD); biochemistry and molecular genetics (PhD); bioinformatics (PhD); biomedical sciences (MS, PhD); biomolecular structure (PhD); biophysics and genetics (MS); cancer biology (PhD); cell biology, stem cells, and developmental biology (PhD); child health associate (MPAS); clinical investigation (PhD); clinical sciences (MS); computational bioscience (PhD); health information technology (PhD); health services research (PhD); human medical genetics and genomics (PhD); immunology (PhD); medicine (MPAS, MS, DPT, MD, PhD); microbiology (PhD); microbiology and immunology (PhD); modern human anatomy (MS); neuroscience (PhD); physical therapy (DPT); rehabilitation science (PhD). *Application fee:* $0. *Application Contact:* W. Vidal Dickerson, Director of Student Life, 303-724-6407, E-mail: somadmin@ucdenver.edu. *Dean*, Dr. John Reilly, Jr., 303-724-0882, E-mail: john.reillyjr@ucdenver.edu.

School of Public Affairs 234 applicants, 79% accepted, 102 enrolled. *Faculty:* 25 full-time (14 women), 13 part-time/adjunct (6 women). Expenses: Contact institution. In 2017, 149 master's, 6 doctorates awarded. *Program availability:* Part-time, evening/weekend, online learning. Offers criminal justice (MCJ); public administration (MPA); public affairs (PhD). *Application deadline:* For fall admission, 2/1 priority date for domestic students, 1/15 priority date for international students; for spring admission, 10/15 priority date for domestic students. *Application fee:* $50 ($75 for international students). Electronic applications accepted. *Application Contact:* Antoinette Sandoval, Student Service Specialist, 303-315-2487, Fax: 303-315-2229, E-mail: antoinette.sandoval@ucdenver.edu. *Dean*, Paul Teske, 303-315-2805, Fax: 303-315-2229, E-mail: paul.teske@ucdenver.edu.

Skaggs School of Pharmacy and Pharmaceutical Sciences Expenses: Contact institution. *Program availability:* Online learning. Offers clinical pharmaceutical sciences (PhD); pharmacy (Pharm D); pharmacy and pharmaceutical sciences (PhD, Pharm D); toxicology (PhD). *Application fee:* $0. *Application Contact:* Jackie Milowski, Department of Pharmaceutical Sciences Administrative Assistant, 303-724-7263, E-mail: jackie.milowski@ucdenver.edu. *Dean*, Dr. Ralph Altiere, 303-724-2631, E-mail: ralph.altiere@ucdenver.edu.

UNIVERSITY OF CONNECTICUT, Storrs, CT 06269

General Information State-supported, coed, university. CGS member. *Graduate housing:* Rooms and/or apartments available on a first-come, first-served basis to single and married students. Housing application deadline: 4/1. *Research affiliation:* U.S. Navy–Submarine Medical Research Laboratory, Haskins Laboratories.

GRADUATE UNITS

Graduate School *Program availability:* Part-time, evening/weekend, online learning. Electronic applications accepted.

College of Agriculture, Health and Natural Resources Offers agricultural and resource economics (MS, PhD); agriculture, health and natural resources (MS, PhD); animal science (MS, PhD); exercise science (MS, PhD); natural resources management and engineering (MS, PhD); nutritional sciences (MS, PhD); pathobiology (MS, PhD); physical therapy (DPT); plant and soil sciences (MS, PhD); sport management (MS). Electronic applications accepted.

College of Liberal Arts and Sciences Offers anthropology (MA, PhD); applied financial mathematics (MS); applied genomics (PSM); audiology (Au D, PhD); behavioral neuroscience (PhD); biopsychology (PhD); botany (MS, PhD); cell and developmental biology (MS, PhD); chemistry (MS, PhD); clinical psychology (MA, PhD); cognition and instruction (PhD); communication processes (MA); comparative physiology (MS, PhD); developmental psychology (MA, PhD); ecological psychology (PhD); economics (MA, PhD); English (MA, PhD); European studies (MA); experimental psychology (PhD); general psychology (MA, PhD); genetics and genomics (MS, PhD); geography (MA, PhD); geological sciences (MS, PhD); history (MA, PhD); human development and family studies (MA, PhD); industrial/organizational psychology (PhD); international studies (MA); Italian history and culture (MA); Judaic studies (MA); language and cognition (PhD); Latino and Latin American studies (MA); liberal arts and sciences (MA, MPA, MS, Au D, PhD, Certificate, Graduate Certificate); linguistics (MA, PhD); medieval studies (MA, PhD); microbial systems analysis (PSM); microbiology (MS, PhD); neuroscience (PhD); philosophy (MA, PhD); physics (MS, PhD); political science (MA, PhD); public administration (MPA, Graduate Certificate); quantitative research methods (Graduate Certificate); social psychology (MA, PhD); sociology (MA, PhD); speech-language pathology (MA, Au D, PhD); statistics (MS, PhD); structural biology, biochemistry and biophysics (MS, PhD); survey research (MA, Graduate Certificate). Electronic applications accepted.

eCampus *Program availability:* Online learning. Offers continuing studies (MS, Certificate); human resource management (MS); occupational safety and health management (Certificate).

Neag School of Education Offers adult learning (MA, PhD); agriculture (MA); agriculture education (PhD); bilingual and bicultural education (MA, PhD); cognition and instruction (MA, PhD); cognition, instruction, and learning technology (MA, PhD); counseling psychology (PhD); education (MA, PhD); educational administration (MA); elementary education (MA, PhD); English education (MA, PhD); gifted and talented education (Graduate Certificate); higher education and student affairs (MA); history and social sciences education (MA, PhD); mathematics education (MA, PhD); music education (MA); reading education (MA, PhD); school counseling (MA); science education (MA, PhD); secondary education (MA, PhD); world languages education (MA, PhD). Electronic applications accepted.

School of Business Offers accounting (MS, PhD); business (PhD); business administration (MBA); business analytics and project management (MS); finance (PhD); financial risk management (MS); health care management and insurance studies (MBA); human resource management (MS); management (PhD);

management consulting (MBA); marketing (PhD); marketing intelligence (MBA); operations and information management (PhD). Electronic applications accepted.

School of Engineering Offers biomedical engineering (MS, PhD); chemical engineering (MS, PhD); civil engineering (MS, PhD); computer science (MS, PhD); electrical engineering (MS, PhD); engineering (M Eng, MS, PhD); environmental engineering (MS, PhD); materials science and engineering (MS, PhD); mechanical engineering (MS, PhD); metallurgy and materials engineering (M Eng). Electronic applications accepted.

School of Fine Arts Offers acting (MA, MFA); conducting (M Mus, DMA); design (MA, MFA); fine arts (M Mus, MA, MFA, DMA, PhD); historical musicology (MA); music theory (MA); music theory and history (PhD); performance (M Mus, DMA); puppetry (MA, MFA); technical direction (MA, MFA). Electronic applications accepted.

School of Nursing Offers adult gerontological acute care nurse practitioner (MS); adult gerontological primary care nurse practitioner (MS); adult gerontology acute care nurse practitioner (Post-Master's Certificate); adult gerontology primary care nurse practitioner (Post-Master's Certificate); family nurse practitioner (MS); neonatal nurse practitioner (MS, Post-Master's Certificate); nursing (MS, DNP, PhD, Post-Master's Certificate). Electronic applications accepted.

School of Pharmacy Offers medicinal chemistry (MS, PhD); pharmaceutics (MS, PhD); pharmacology (MS, PhD); pharmacology and toxicology (MS, PhD); pharmacy (MS, PhD, Pharm D); toxicology (MS, PhD). Electronic applications accepted.

School of Social Work Offers social work (MSW, PhD). Electronic applications accepted.

Institute of Materials Science Offers materials science (MS, PhD); polymer science and engineering (MS, PhD).

School of Law *Program availability:* Part-time. Offers law (JD). Electronic applications accepted.

UNIVERSITY OF CONNECTICUT HEALTH CENTER, Farmington, CT 06030

General Information State-supported, coed, graduate-only institution. *Graduate housing:* On-campus housing not available.

GRADUATE UNITS

Graduate School *Program availability:* Part-time, evening/weekend. Offers biomedical sciences (PhD); biomedical sciences - integrated (PhD); cell analysis and modeling (PhD); cell biology (PhD); clinical and translational research (MS); genetics and developmental biology (PhD); immunology (PhD); molecular biology and biochemistry (PhD); neuroscience (PhD); public health (MPH); skeletal biology and regeneration (PhD).

School of Dental Medicine Offers dental medicine (MDS, DMD, Certificate); dental science (MDS). Electronic applications accepted.

School of Medicine Offers medicine (MD). Electronic applications accepted.

UNIVERSITY OF DALLAS, Irving, TX 75062-4736

General Information Independent-religious, coed, university. *Enrollment:* 2,520 graduate, professional, and undergraduate students; 265 full-time matriculated graduate/professional students (110 women), 795 part-time matriculated graduate/professional students (339 women). *Enrollment by degree level:* 969 master's, 85 doctoral, 6 other advanced degrees. *Graduate faculty:* 52. *Tuition:* Full-time $33,750; part-time $22,500 per year. Tuition and fees vary according to program. *Graduate housing:* Room and/or apartments available on a first-come, first-served basis to single students; on-campus housing not available to married students. Typical cost: $10,530 (including board). Housing application deadline: 6/1. *Student services:* Campus employment opportunities, career counseling, exercise/wellness program, international student services, services for students with disabilities, teacher training. *Library facilities:* William A. Blakley Library.

Computer facilities: Computer purchase and lease plans are available. 125 computers available on campus for general student use. A campuswide network can be accessed from student residence rooms and from off campus. Online class registration is available.
Website: http://www.udallas.edu/

General Application Contact: Breonna Collins, Director, Graduate Admissions and College of Business Enrollment Management, 972-721-5304, E-mail: bcollins@udallas.edu.

GRADUATE UNITS

Ann and Joe O. Neuhoff School of Ministry Expenses: Contact institution. *Financial support:* Application deadline: 2/15. *Program availability:* Part-time, evening/weekend, online learning. Offers ministry (MCSL). *Application deadline:* For fall admission, 7/15 for domestic students; for spring admission, 11/15 for domestic students. *Application fee:* $50. *Coordinator of Graduate Enrollment and Student Services,* Sheri Collier, 972-721-5814, Fax: 972-721-4076, E-mail: scollier@udallas.edu.

Braniff Graduate School of Liberal Arts Expenses: Contact institution. *Financial support:* Application deadline: 2/15; applicants required to submit FAFSA. *Program availability:* Part-time. Offers American studies (MAS); ceramics (MFA); classics (MA, MC); clinical psychology (M Psych); English (MA); humanities (M Hum, MA); leadership (MA); liberal arts (M Hum, M Pol, M Psych, M Th, MA, MAS, MC, MCSL, MEL, MFA, PhD); painting (MFA); philosophy (MA); politics (M Pol, MA); printmaking (MFA); psychology (M Psych, MA); sculpture (MFA); theology (M Th, MA). *Application deadline:* For fall admission, 2/15 priority date for domestic students; for spring admission, 11/15 for domestic students. Applications are processed on a rolling basis. *Application Contact:* Angela Rojas, Graduate Coordinator, 972-721-5174, Fax: 972-721-5280, E-mail: arojas@udallas.edu. *Dean,* Dr. Joshua Parens, 972-721 5241, E-mail: parens@udallas.edu.

Institute of Philosophic Studies Expenses: Contact institution. *Financial support:* Application deadline: 2/15. Offers literature (PhD); philosophy (PhD); politics (PhD). *Application deadline:* For fall admission, 2/15 priority date for domestic students. *Application fee:* $50. *Dean,* Dr. David Sweet, 972-721-5288, Fax: 972-721-5280, E-mail: dsweet@udallas.edu.

Satish and Yasmin Gupta College of Business Expenses: Contact institution. *Financial support:* Application deadline: 2/15; applicants required to submit FAFSA. *Program availability:* Part-time, evening/weekend, online learning. Offers accounting (MBA, MS); business administration (DBA); business analytics (MS); business management (MBA); corporate finance (MBA); cybersecurity (MS); finance (MS); financial services (MBA); global business (MBA, MS); health services management (MBA); human resource management (MBA); information and technology management (MS); information assurance (MBA); information technology (MBA); information technology service management (MBA); marketing management (MBA); organization development (MBA); project management (MBA); sports and entertainment management (MBA); strategic leadership (MBA); supply chain management (MBA). *Application deadline:* Applications are processed on a rolling basis. *Application fee:* $50. Electronic applications accepted. *Application Contact:* Dr. David Sweet, Dean, Braniff Graduate School, 972-721-5288, Fax: 972-721-5280, E-mail: dsweet@udallas.edu. *Dean,* Brett J.L. Landry, 972-721-5356, E-mail: blandry@udallas.edu.

UNIVERSITY OF DAYTON, Dayton, OH 45469

General Information Independent-religious, coed, university. CGS member. *Enrollment:* 10,882 graduate, professional, and undergraduate students; 1,657 full-time matriculated graduate/professional students (821 women), 491 part-time matriculated graduate/professional students (272 women). *Enrollment by degree level:* 1,529 master's, 604 doctoral, 15 other advanced degrees. *Graduate faculty:* 315 full-time (128 women), 228 part-time/adjunct (112 women). Tuition and fees vary according to degree level and program. *Graduate housing:* Room and/or apartments available on a first-come, first-served basis to single students; on-campus housing not available to married students. *Student services:* Campus employment opportunities, campus safety program, career counseling, child daycare facilities, exercise/wellness program, free psychological counseling, grant writing training, international student services, multicultural affairs office, services for students with disabilities, teacher training, writing training. *Library facilities:* Roesch Library plus 3 others. *Collection:* Books: 881,689 (physical), 972,137 (digital/electronic); Serial titles: 2,325 (physical), 96,661 (digital/electronic); Databases: 316. Weekly public service hours: 134; students can reserve study rooms. *Research affiliation:* California Institute of Technology (materials development), Dayton Area Graduate Studies Institute (materials testing), Kern Family Foundation (curriculum development), Ohio Aerospace Institute (engine analysis), Riverside Research Institute (radar and materials research), Southwest Research Institute (engineering services).

Computer facilities: 7,675 computers available on campus for general student use. A campuswide network can be accessed from student residence rooms and from off campus. Online class registration, applications, admission/enrollment status, virtual orientation, online digital resources, online courses, assistive technology, learning management system, multimedia labs, payment, cyber cafes, centrally-licensed, downloadable software and training are available.
Website: http://www.udayton.edu/

General Application Contact: Graduate Admissions, 937-229-4411, E-mail: graduateadmission@udayton.edu.

GRADUATE UNITS

Department of Biology Students: 21 full-time (14 women); includes 3 minority (1 Black or African American, non-Hispanic/Latino; 2 Asian, non-Hispanic/Latino), 7 international. Average age 27. 30 applicants, 7% accepted. *Faculty:* 18 full-time (7 women). Expenses: Contact institution. *Financial support:* In 2017–18, 2 research assistantships with full tuition reimbursements (averaging $20,200 per year), 18 teaching assistantships with full tuition reimbursements (averaging $20,200 per year) were awarded; career-related internships or fieldwork, institutionally sponsored loans, and unspecified assistantships also available. Financial award application deadline: 3/1; financial award applicants required to submit FAFSA. In 2017, 1 master's, 1 doctorate awarded. Offers biology (MS, PhD). *Application deadline:* For fall admission, 1/31 for domestic and international students. Applications are processed on a rolling basis. *Application fee:* $50 for international students. Electronic applications accepted. *Application Contact:* Dr. Amit Singh, Director, Biology Graduate Programs, 937-229-2894, Fax: 937-229-2021, E-mail: asingh1@udayton.edu.

Department of Chemical Engineering Students: 32 full-time (8 women), 6 part-time (2 women); includes 1 minority (Black or African American, non-Hispanic/Latino), 27 international. Average age 26. 47 applicants, 45% accepted. *Faculty:* 11 full-time (2 women). Expenses: Contact institution. *Financial support:* In 2017–18, 2 research assistantships with full tuition reimbursements (averaging $13,500 per year) were awarded; teaching assistantships and institutionally sponsored loans also available. Financial award application deadline: 3/1; financial award applicants required to submit FAFSA. In 2017, 17 master's awarded. *Program availability:* Part-time, online learning. Offers bioengineering (MS); chemical engineering (MS Ch E). *Application deadline:* Applications are processed on a rolling basis. *Application fee:* $0 ($50 for international students). Electronic applications accepted. *Application Contact:* Dr. Kevin Myers, Graduate Program Director, 937-229-2627, E-mail: kmyers1@udayton.edu.

Department of Chemistry and Biochemistry Students: 5 full-time (4 women), 1 international. Average age 25. 56 applicants, 14% accepted. *Faculty:* 11 full-time (2 women). Expenses: Contact institution. *Financial support:* In 2017–18, 4 teaching assistantships with full tuition reimbursements (averaging $13,600 per year) were awarded; fellowships, research assistantships, and institutionally sponsored loans also available. Financial award application deadline: 5/15; financial award applicants required to submit FAFSA. In 2017, 3 master's awarded. *Program availability:* Part-time. Offers chemistry and biochemistry (MS). *Application deadline:* For fall admission, 5/15 priority date for domestic and international students; for winter admission, 7/1 priority date for international students; for spring admission, 11/1 priority date for international students. *Application fee:* $0 ($50 for international students). Electronic applications accepted. *Application Contact:* Dr. Kevin Church, Graduate Program Director, 937-229-2659, E-mail: kchurch1@udayton.edu. *Chair,* Dr. David Johnson, 937-229-2631, E-mail: djohnson1@udayton.edu.

Department of Civil and Environmental Engineering and Engineering Mechanics Students: 31 full-time (5 women), 5 part-time (2 women); includes 3 minority (2 Asian, non-Hispanic/Latino; 1 Hispanic/Latino), 27 international. Average age 26. 112 applicants, 34% accepted. *Faculty:* 8 full-time (2 women), 2 part-time/adjunct (0 women). Expenses: Contact institution. *Financial support:* In 2017–18, 1 research assistantship with full and partial tuition reimbursement (averaging $13,500 per year), 1 teaching assistantship with partial tuition reimbursement (averaging $13,500 per year) were awarded; institutionally sponsored loans, scholarships/grants, and department-funded awards (averaging $2448 per year) also available. Financial award application deadline: 3/1; financial award applicants required to submit FAFSA. In 2017, 24 master's awarded. *Program availability:* Part-time, blended/hybrid learning. Offers engineering mechanics (MSEM); environmental engineering (MSCE); geotechnical engineering (MSCE); structural engineering (MSCE); transportation engineering (MSCE); water resources engineering (MSCE). *Application deadline:* For fall admission, 8/1 priority date for domestic students, 5/1 priority date for international students; for spring admission, 11/1 for domestic students, 11/1 priority date for international students. Applications are processed on a rolling basis. *Application fee:* $0 ($50 for international students). Electronic applications accepted. *Application Contact:* 937-229-4462, E-mail: graduateadmission@udayton.edu. *Chair,* Dr. Robert Liang, 937-229-3847, Fax: 937-229-3491, E-mail: rliang1@udayton.edu.

Department of Communication Students: 14 full-time (13 women), 4 part-time (2 women); includes 1 minority (Black or African American, non-Hispanic/Latino), 3 international. Average age 30. 33 applicants, 30% accepted, 4 enrolled. *Faculty:* 11 full-time (5 women). Expenses: Contact institution. *Financial support:* In 2017–18, 4 research assistantships with full tuition reimbursements (averaging $11,105 per year), 7 teaching assistantships with full tuition reimbursements (averaging $11,105 per year) were awarded; institutionally sponsored loans and unspecified assistantships also available. Financial award application deadline: 3/9; financial award applicants required to submit FAFSA. In 2017, 6 master's awarded. *Program availability:* Part-time, 100% online. Offers communication (MA); interdisciplinary communication (MA). *Application deadline:* Applications are processed on a rolling basis. *Application fee:* $0 ($50 for international students). Electronic applications accepted. *Application Contact:* Dr. JeeHee Han, Graduate Program Director, 937-229-2486, E-mail: jhan01@udayton.edu. *Chair,* Dr. Joseph Valenzano, III, 937-229-2028, E-mail: jvalenzano1@udayton.edu.

Department of Computer Science Students: 92 full-time (45 women), 19 part-time (7 women); includes 2 minority (1 Asian, non-Hispanic/Latino; 1 Hispanic/Latino), 100 international. Average age 25. 198 applicants, 40% accepted. *Faculty:* 15 full-time (2 women). Expenses: Contact institution. *Financial support:* In 2017–18, 4 teaching assistantships with full and partial tuition reimbursements (averaging $10,000 per year) were awarded; fellowships, research assistantships, institutionally sponsored loans, and unspecified assistantships also available. Financial award application deadline: 3/1; financial award applicants required to submit FAFSA. In 2017, 75 master's awarded. *Program availability:* Part-time. Offers computer science (MCS). *Application deadline:* Applications are processed on a rolling basis. *Application fee:* $0 ($50 for international students). Electronic applications accepted. *Application Contact:* Dr. James Buckley, Graduate Program Director, 937-229-3831, E-mail: jbuckley1@udayton.edu. *Chair,* Dr. Mehdi Zargham, 937-229-3831, E-mail: mzargham1@udayton.edu.

Department of Counselor Education and Human Services Students: 194 full-time (153 women), 83 part-time (68 women); includes 58 minority (37 Black or African American, non-Hispanic/Latino; 2 Asian, non-Hispanic/Latino; 9 Hispanic/Latino; 10 Two or more races, non-Hispanic/Latino), 3 international. Average age 30. 426 applicants, 28% accepted. *Faculty:* 11 full-time (6 women), 34 part-time/adjunct (24 women). Expenses: Contact institution. *Financial support:* In 2017–18, 5 research assistantships with partial tuition reimbursements (averaging $9,950 per year) were awarded; career-related internships or fieldwork, institutionally sponsored loans, and unspecified assistantships also available. Financial award application deadline: 3/1; financial award applicants required to submit FAFSA. In 2017, 107 master's, 6 Ed Ss awarded. *Program availability:* Part-time. Offers clinical mental health counseling (MS Ed); college student personnel (MS Ed); higher education administration (MS Ed); human services (MS Ed); school counseling (MS Ed); school psychology (MS Ed, Ed S). *Application deadline:* For fall admission, 1/10 priority date for domestic and international students; for spring admission, 9/10 priority date for domestic and international students; for summer admission, 11/10 priority date for domestic and international students. *Application fee:* $0 ($50 for international students). Electronic applications accepted. *Application Contact:* Kathleen Brown, Administrative Assistant, 937-229-3644, Fax: 937-229-1055, E-mail: kbrown1@udayton.edu. *Chair,* Dr. Alan Demmitt, 937-229-3644, Fax: 937-229-1055, E-mail: ademmitt1@udayton.edu.

Department of Educational Administration Students: 58 full-time (37 women), 65 part-time (46 women); includes 12 minority (7 Black or African American, non-Hispanic/Latino; 2 Hispanic/Latino; 3 Two or more races, non-Hispanic/Latino), 3 international. Average age 34. 74 applicants, 31% accepted. *Faculty:* 6 full-time (3 women), 17 part-time/adjunct (3 women). Expenses: Contact institution. *Financial support:* In 2017–18, 5 research assistantships with partial tuition reimbursements (averaging $9,640 per year) were awarded; career-related internships or fieldwork and institutionally sponsored loans also available. Financial award application deadline: 3/1; financial award applicants required to submit FAFSA. In 2017, 69 master's awarded. *Program availability:* Part-time, blended/hybrid learning. Offers Catholic school leadership (MS Ed); educational leadership (MS Ed, Ed S); leadership for educational systems (MS Ed). Ed S program in educational leadership offered jointly by the Graduate Schools of the University of Dayton and Wright State University. *Application deadline:* For fall admission, 8/20 for domestic students; for spring admission, 1/10 for domestic students; for summer admission, 5/10 for domestic students. Applications are processed on a rolling basis. *Application fee:* $0 ($50 for international students). Electronic applications accepted. *Application Contact:* Janice Keivel, Administrative Associate, 937-229-3738, Fax: 937-229-1055, E-mail: jkeivel1@udayton.edu. *Chair,* Dr. David D. Dolph, 937-229-3105, Fax: 937-229-1055, E-mail: ddolph1@udayton.edu.

Department of Electrical and Computer Engineering Students: 129 full-time (21 women), 18 part-time (2 women); includes 13 minority (1 Black or African American, non-Hispanic/Latino; 7 Asian, non-Hispanic/Latino; 2 Hispanic/Latino; 3 Two or more races, non-Hispanic/Latino), 88 international. Average age 29. 82 applicants, 22% accepted. *Faculty:* 18 full-time (1 woman), 11 part-time/adjunct (1 woman). Expenses: Contact institution. *Financial support:* In 2017–18, 19 research assistantships with full tuition reimbursements (averaging $15,000 per year), 19 teaching assistantships with full and partial tuition reimbursements (averaging $12,000 per year) were awarded; institutionally sponsored loans and unspecified assistantships also available. Financial award application deadline: 3/1; financial award applicants required to submit FAFSA. In 2017, 56 master's, 9 doctorates awarded. *Program availability:* Part-time, blended/hybrid learning. Offers computer engineering (MS); electrical engineering (MSEE, PhD). *Application deadline:* For fall admission, 8/1 for domestic students, 5/1 priority date for international students; for spring admission, 11/1 priority date for international students. Applications are processed on a rolling basis. *Application fee:* $0 ($50 for international students). Electronic applications accepted. *Application Contact:* E-mail: graduateadmission@udayton.edu. *Chair,* Dr. Guru Subramanyam, 937-229-3188, Fax: 937-229-4529, E-mail: gsubramanyam1@udayton.edu.

Department of Electro-Optics and Photonics Students: 49 full-time (16 women), 8 part-time (2 women); includes 4 minority (3 Black or African American, non-Hispanic/Latino; 1 Hispanic/Latino), 32 international. Average age 29. 59 applicants, 85% accepted, 13 enrolled. *Faculty:* 5 full-time (0 women), 9 part-time/adjunct (0 women). Expenses: Contact institution. *Financial support:* In 2017–18, 15 research assistantships with full tuition reimbursements (averaging $21,000 per year), 7 teaching assistantships with full tuition reimbursements (averaging $14,000 per year) were awarded; institutionally sponsored loans also available. Financial award application deadline: 3/1; financial award applicants required to submit FAFSA. In 2017, 3 master's, 6 doctorates awarded. Offers electro-optics (MSEO, PhD). *Application deadline:* Applications are processed on a rolling basis. *Application fee:* $0 ($50 for international students). Electronic applications accepted. *Application Contact:* Meghan L. Brophy, Administrative Assistant, 937-229-2797, Fax: 937-229-2097, E-mail: graduateadmission@udayton.edu. *Chair,* Dr. Partha P. Banerjee, 937-229-2797, Fax: 937-229-2099, E-mail: pbanerjee1@udayton.edu.

Department of Engineering Management, Systems and Technology Students: 51 full-time (19 women), 20 part-time (3 women); includes 5 minority (3 Black or African American, non-Hispanic/Latino; 2 Two or more races, non-Hispanic/Latino), 32 international. Average age 29. 206 applicants, 21% accepted. *Faculty:* 4 full-time (2 women), 6 part-time/adjunct (0 women). Expenses: Contact institution. *Financial support:* In 2017–18, 2 teaching assistantships with full and partial tuition reimbursements (averaging $9,600 per year) were awarded; research assistantships, career-related internships or fieldwork, institutionally sponsored loans, and unspecified assistantships also available. Financial award application deadline: 3/1; financial award applicants required to submit FAFSA. In 2017, 40 master's awarded. *Program availability:* Part-time, 100% online, blended/hybrid learning. Offers engineering management (MSEM); management science (MSMS). *Application deadline:* Applications are processed on a rolling basis. *Application fee:* $0 ($50 for international students). Electronic applications accepted. *Application Contact:* Dr. Edward F. Mykytka, Graduate Program Director, 937-229-2620, E-mail: emykytka1@udayton.edu. *Chair,* Dr. Scott J. Schneider, 937-229-4216, E-mail: et@udayton.edu.

Department of English Students: 20 full-time (14 women), 1 (woman) part-time; includes 2 minority (both Black or African American, non-Hispanic/Latino), 7 international. Average age 26. 35 applicants, 34% accepted. *Faculty:* 22 full-time (11 women). Expenses: Contact institution. *Financial support:* In 2017–18, 9 teaching assistantships with full tuition reimbursements (averaging $11,105 per year) were awarded; institutionally sponsored loans also available. Financial award application deadline: 3/1; financial award applicants required to submit FAFSA. In 2017, 9 master's awarded. *Program availability:* Part-time. Offers literary and cultural studies (MA); teaching English to speakers of other languages (TESOL) (MA); writing and rhetoric (MA). *Application deadline:* For fall admission, 6/15 priority date for domestic and international students; for spring admission, 12/15 priority date for domestic and international students. Applications are processed on a rolling basis. *Application fee:* $0 ($50 for international students). Electronic applications accepted. *Application Contact:* Dr. Tereza Szeghi, Director of Graduate Studies, 937-229-3443, E-mail: tszeghi1@udayton.edu. *Chair,* Dr. Andrew Slade, 937-229-3434, Fax: 937-229-3563, E-mail: aslade1@udayton.edu.

Department of Health and Sport Science Students: 7 full-time (4 women), 2 part-time (1 woman); includes 3 minority (2 Black or African American, non-Hispanic/Latino; 1 Hispanic/Latino), 3 international. Average age 24. 37 applicants, 30% accepted. *Faculty:* 10 full-time (5 women), 23 part-time/adjunct (16 women). Expenses: Contact institution. *Financial support:* In 2017–18, 4 research assistantships with partial tuition reimbursements (averaging $9,640 per year) were awarded; career-related internships or fieldwork, institutionally sponsored loans, and unspecified assistantships also available. Financial award application deadline: 3/1; financial award applicants required to submit FAFSA. In 2017, 7 master's awarded. *Program availability:* Part-time, 100% online. Offers exercise science (MS Ed). *Application deadline:* Applications are processed on a rolling basis. *Application fee:* $0 ($50 for international students). Electronic applications accepted. *Application Contact:* Laura Greger, Administrative Assistant, 937-229-4225, E-mail: lgreger1@udayton.edu. *Chair,* Dr. Corinne Daprano, 937-229-4240, Fax: 937-229-4244, E-mail: cdaprano1@udayton.edu.

Department of Mathematics Students: 20 full-time (9 women), 9 part-time (4 women); includes 2 minority (both Black or African American, non-Hispanic/Latino), 20 international. Average age 26. 112 applicants, 20% accepted. *Faculty:* 22 full-time (8 women). Expenses: Contact institution. *Financial support:* In 2017–18, 6 teaching assistantships with full tuition reimbursements (averaging $15,000 per year) were awarded; fellowships and institutionally sponsored loans also available. Financial award application deadline: 3/1; financial award applicants required to submit FAFSA. In 2017, 20 master's awarded. *Program availability:* Part-time. Offers applied mathematics (MAS); financial mathematics (MFM). *Application deadline:* Applications are processed on a rolling basis. *Application fee:* $0 ($50 for international students). Electronic applications accepted. *Application Contact:* Dr. Paul W. Eloe, Graduate Program Director/Professor, 937-229-2016, E-mail: peloe1@udayton.edu. *Chair,* Dr. Wiebke Diestelkamp, 937-229-2511, Fax: 937-229-2566, E-mail: wdiestelkamp1@udayton.edu.

Department of Mechanical and Aerospace Engineering Students: 143 full-time (15 women), 31 part-time (5 women); includes 12 minority (7 Asian, non-Hispanic/Latino; 2 Hispanic/Latino; 3 Two or more races, non-Hispanic/Latino), 90 international. Average age 27. 432 applicants, 15% accepted. *Faculty:* 23 full-time (4 women), 9 part-time/adjunct (1 woman). Expenses: Contact institution. *Financial support:* In 2017–18, 27 research assistantships with full and partial tuition reimbursements, 3 teaching assistantships with partial tuition reimbursements (averaging $10,800 per year) were awarded; fellowships and institutionally sponsored loans also available. Support available to part-time students. Financial award application deadline: 3/1; financial award applicants required to submit FAFSA. In 2017, 81 master's, 9 doctorates awarded. *Program availability:* Part-time, 100% online, blended/hybrid learning. Offers aerospace engineering (MSAE, PhD); mechanical engineering (MSME, PhD); renewable and clean energy (MS). *Application deadline:* For fall admission, 6/15 for domestic and international students; for spring admission, 11/15 for domestic and international students; for summer admission, 3/15 for domestic and international students. *Application fee:* $0 ($50 for international students). Electronic applications accepted. *Application Contact:* Dr. Vinod Jain, Graduate Program Director, 937-229-2992, Fax: 937-229-4766, E-mail: vjain1@udayton.edu. *Chair,* Dr. Kelly Kissock, 937-229-2999, Fax: 937-229-4766, E-mail: jkissock1@udayton.edu.

Department of Physical Therapy Students: 109 full-time (71 women); includes 6 minority (1 Black or African American, non-Hispanic/Latino; 1 Asian, non-Hispanic/Latino; 1 Hispanic/Latino; 3 Two or more races, non-Hispanic/Latino), 1 international. Average age 24. 70 applicants, 87% accepted, 44 enrolled. *Faculty:* 10 full-time (4 women), 19 part-time/adjunct (15 women). Expenses: Contact institution. *Financial support:* In 2017–18, 7 research assistantships with partial tuition reimbursements (averaging $13,920 per year) were awarded; institutionally sponsored loans and unspecified assistantships also available. Support available to part-time students. Financial award application deadline: 3/1; financial award applicants required to submit FAFSA. In 2017, 37 doctorates awarded. Offers physical therapy (DPT). *Application deadline:* For fall admission, 10/1 priority date for domestic and international students. *Application fee:* $50 for international students. Electronic applications accepted. *Application Contact:* Trista Cathcart, Admissions Coordinator, 937-229-5611, Fax: 937-229-5601, E-mail: tcathcart1@udayton.edu. *Chair/Associate Professor,* Dr. Philip A. Anloague, 937-229-5600, Fax: 937-229-5601, E-mail: panalogue1@udayton.edu.

Department of Physician Assistant Education Students: 111 full-time (83 women), 1 (woman) part-time; includes 12 minority (4 Black or African American, non-Hispanic/Latino; 4 Asian, non-Hispanic/Latino; 3 Hispanic/Latino; 1 Two or more races, non-Hispanic/Latino). Average age 26. 48 applicants. *Faculty:* 6 full-time (all women), 2 part-time/adjunct (both women). Expenses: Contact institution. *Financial support:* In 2017–18, 9 research assistantships with partial tuition reimbursements (averaging $9,640 per year) were awarded; teaching assistantships, career-related internships or fieldwork, institutionally sponsored loans, and unspecified assistantships also available. Financial award application deadline: 3/1; financial award applicants required to submit FAFSA. In 2017, 30 master's awarded. Offers physician assistant practice (MPAP). *Application deadline:* For fall admission, 11/1 for domestic and international students.

Application fee: $0 ($50 for international students). Electronic applications accepted. *Application Contact:* Amy Kidwell, Admissions Coordinator/Senior Administrative Secretary, 937-229-2900, E-mail: akidwell1@udayton.edu. *Director/Chair,* Lindsey Hammett, 937-229-4847, E-mail: lhammett1@udayton.edu.

Department of Religious Studies Students: 48 full-time (24 women), 10 part-time (4 women); includes 7 minority (2 Black or African American, non-Hispanic/Latino; 2 Asian, non-Hispanic/Latino; 3 Hispanic/Latino), 1 international. Average age 34. 53 applicants, 57% accepted. *Faculty:* 23 full-time (7 women), 2 part-time/adjunct (1 woman). Expenses: Contact institution. *Financial support:* In 2017–18, 21 research assistantships with full tuition reimbursements (averaging $11,250 per year), 20 teaching assistantships with full tuition reimbursements (averaging $18,130 per year) were awarded; fellowships and institutionally sponsored loans also available. Financial award application deadline: 3/1; financial award applicants required to submit FAFSA. In 2017, 10 master's, 5 doctorates awarded. *Program availability:* Part-time. Offers pastoral ministry (MA); theological studies (MA); theology (PhD). *Application deadline:* For fall admission, 2/1 priority date for domestic students, 2/1 for international students. Applications are processed on a rolling basis. *Application fee:* $0 ($50 for international students). Electronic applications accepted. *Application Contact:* Amy Doorley, Coordinator of Graduate Studies, 937-229-4321, Fax: 937-229-4330, E-mail: adoorley1@udayton.edu. *Chair,* Dr. Daniel Thompson, 937-229-4321, Fax: 937-229-4330.

Department of Teacher Education Students: 45 full-time (38 women), 68 part-time (57 women); includes 7 minority (3 Black or African American, non-Hispanic/Latino; 1 Hispanic/Latino; 3 Two or more races, non-Hispanic/Latino), 6 international. Average age 31. 106 applicants, 28% accepted. *Faculty:* 23 full-time (20 women), 41 part-time/adjunct (36 women). Expenses: Contact institution. *Financial support:* In 2017–18, 5 research assistantships with partial tuition reimbursements (averaging $9,640 per year) were awarded; teaching assistantships, career-related internships or fieldwork, institutionally sponsored loans, and unspecified assistantships also available. Financial award application deadline: 3/1; financial award applicants required to submit FAFSA. In 2017, 70 master's awarded. *Program availability:* Part-time, 100% online. Offers adolescence to young adult education (MS Ed); early childhood leadership and advocacy (MS Ed); interdisciplinary education (MS Ed); interdisciplinary education studies (MS Ed); leadership in educational systems (MS Ed); literacy (MS Ed); mathematics education (MS Ed); middle childhood education (MS Ed); multi-age education (MS Ed); music education (MS Ed); teacher as leader (MS Ed); teacher education (MS Ed); technology-enhanced learning (MS Ed); trans-disciplinary early childhood education (MS Ed). *Application deadline:* Applications are processed on a rolling basis. *Application fee:* $0 ($50 for international students). Electronic applications accepted. *Application Contact:* Gina Seiter, Coordinator of Graduate Programs and Licensing, 937-229-3103, E-mail: gseiter1@udayton.edu. *Chair,* Dr. Connie L. Bowman, 937-229-3348, E-mail: cbowman1@udayton.edu.

Master of Public Administration Program Students: 20 full-time (12 women), 8 part-time (6 women); includes 4 minority (2 Black or African American, non-Hispanic/Latino; 2 Two or more races, non-Hispanic/Latino). Average age 29. 54 applicants, 19% accepted. *Faculty:* 8 full-time (2 women), 5 part-time/adjunct (3 women). Expenses: Contact institution. *Financial support:* In 2017–18, 3 research assistantships with full tuition reimbursements (averaging $11,868 per year) were awarded; unspecified assistantships also available. Financial award application deadline: 3/1; financial award applicants required to submit FAFSA. In 2017, 10 master's awarded. *Program availability:* Part-time, evening/weekend. Offers public administration (MPA). *Application deadline:* Applications are processed on a rolling basis. *Application fee:* $0 ($50 for international students). Electronic applications accepted. *Director of MPA Program,* Dr. Joshua D. Ambrosius, 937-229-3924, Fax: 937-229-1400, E-mail: jambrosius1@udayton.edu.

PhD Program in Educational Leadership Students: 50 full-time (31 women); includes 7 minority (5 Black or African American, non-Hispanic/Latino; 1 Hispanic/Latino; 1 Two or more races, non-Hispanic/Latino), 3 international. Average age 42. 36 applicants, 19% accepted. *Faculty:* 1 full-time (0 women), 5 part-time/adjunct (2 women). Expenses: Contact institution. *Financial support:* In 2017–18, 1 research assistantship with full and partial tuition reimbursement (averaging $13,920 per year) was awarded; fellowships, teaching assistantships, career-related internships or fieldwork, Federal Work-Study, and institutionally sponsored loans also available. Financial award application deadline: 3/1; financial award applicants required to submit FAFSA. In 2017, 7 doctorates awarded. *Program availability:* Part-time. Offers educational leadership (PhD). *Application deadline:* For fall admission, 8/21 for domestic students. Applications are processed on a rolling basis. *Application fee:* $0 ($50 for international students). Electronic applications accepted. *Application Contact:* Elizabeth Pearn, Publication and Doctoral Program Specialist, 937-229-4003, E-mail: epearn1@udayton.edu. *Director,* Dr. Charles Russo, 937-229-3722, E-mail: crusso1@udayton.edu.

Program in Clinical Psychology Students: 12 full-time (8 women). Average age 24. 84 applicants, 7% accepted. *Faculty:* 6 full-time (3 women), 1 part-time/adjunct (0 women). Expenses: Contact institution. *Financial support:* In 2017–18, 6 research assistantships with full tuition reimbursements (averaging $11,645 per year) were awarded; fellowships, teaching assistantships, institutionally sponsored loans, and tuition waivers (full and partial) also available. Financial award application deadline: 3/1; financial award applicants required to submit FAFSA. In 2017, 4 master's awarded. Offers clinical psychology (MA). *Application deadline:* For fall admission, 2/15 priority date for domestic and international students. *Application fee:* $0 ($50 for international students). Electronic applications accepted. *Graduate Program Director,* Dr. Catherine L. Zois, 937-229-2164, Fax: 937-229-2164, E-mail: czois1@udayton.edu.

Program in General Psychology Students: 5 full-time (0 women), 1 (woman) part-time. Average age 26. 62 applicants, 8% accepted. *Faculty:* 11 full-time (5 women). Expenses: Contact institution. *Financial support:* In 2017–18, 5 students received support, including 3 fellowships with full tuition reimbursements available (averaging $11,675 per year), 6 research assistantships with full tuition reimbursements available (averaging $11,675 per year), 6 teaching assistantships with full tuition reimbursements available (averaging $11,675 per year); institutionally sponsored loans, traineeships, and tuition waivers (partial) also available. Financial award application deadline: 3/1; financial award applicants required to submit FAFSA. In 2017, 2 master's awarded. Offers general psychology (MA). *Application deadline:* For fall admission, 3/1 for domestic and international students. *Application fee:* $0 ($50 for international students). Electronic applications accepted. *Graduate Program Director,* Dr. Erin M. O'Mara, 937-229-2161, E-mail: eomara1@udayton.edu.

Program in Materials Engineering Students: 54 full-time (14 women), 10 part-time (2 women); includes 13 minority (7 Black or African American, non-Hispanic/Latino; 3 Asian, non-Hispanic/Latino; 3 Hispanic/Latino), 18 international. Average age 28. 52 applicants, 48% accepted. *Faculty:* 4 full-time (0 women), 9 part-time/adjunct (0 women). Expenses: Contact institution. *Financial support:* In 2017–18, 4 research assistantships with full and partial tuition reimbursements (averaging $22,968 per year) were awarded; institutionally sponsored loans also available. Financial award application deadline: 3/1; financial award applicants required to submit FAFSA. In 2017, 27 master's, 2 doctorates awarded. *Program availability:* Part-time, evening/weekend, blended/hybrid learning. Offers materials engineering (MS, DE, PhD). *Application deadline:* Applications are processed on a rolling basis. *Application fee:* $0 ($50 for international students). Electronic applications accepted. *Chair/Interim Graduate Program Director,* Dr. Charles Browning, 937-229-2679, E-mail: cbrowning1@udayton.edu.

School of Business Administration Students: 57 full-time (24 women), 82 part-time (32 women); includes 10 minority (5 Black or African American, non-Hispanic/Latino; 2 Asian, non-Hispanic/Latino; 3 Hispanic/Latino), 18 international. Average age 31. 269 applicants, 31% accepted. *Faculty:* 23 full-time (8 women), 12 part-time/adjunct (2 women). Expenses: Contact institution. *Financial support:* In 2017–18, 10 research assistantships with partial tuition reimbursements (averaging $9,295 per year) were awarded; teaching assistantships, career-related internships or fieldwork, institutionally sponsored loans, scholarships/grants, traineeships, tuition waivers, and unspecified assistantships also available. Financial award application deadline: 3/1; financial award applicants required to submit FAFSA. In 2017, 88 master's awarded. *Program availability:* Part-time, evening/weekend, blended/hybrid learning. Offers accounting (MBA); cyber security (MBA); finance (MBA); marketing (MBA). *Application deadline:* For fall admission, 5/1 for international students; for spring admission, 11/1 for international students. Applications are processed on a rolling basis. *Application fee:* $0 ($50 for international students). Electronic applications accepted. *Application Contact:* Mandy Bingaman, MBA Program Manager, 937-229-3733, Fax: 937-229-3882, E-mail: mbingaman1@udayton.edu. *Director, MBA Program,* Scott MacDonald, 937-229-3733, Fax: 937-229-3882, E-mail: smacdonald1@udayton.edu.

School of Law Students: 242 full-time (126 women), 27 part-time (13 women); includes 46 minority (29 Black or African American, non-Hispanic/Latino; 1 American Indian or Alaska Native, non-Hispanic/Latino; 5 Asian, non-Hispanic/Latino; 11 Hispanic/Latino), 12 international. Average age 27. 578 applicants, 38% accepted, 118 enrolled. *Faculty:* 21 full-time (13 women), 23 part-time/adjunct (6 women). Expenses: Contact institution. *Financial support:* In 2017–18, 15 fellowships (averaging $1,000 per year), 5 research assistantships (averaging $1,000 per year), 13 teaching assistantships (averaging $400 per year) were awarded; Federal Work-Study, scholarships/grants, tuition waivers (full and partial), and bar course grants also available. Financial award application deadline: 3/1; financial award applicants required to submit FAFSA. In 2017, 4 master's, 93 doctorates awarded. *Program availability:* Part-time, 100% online. Offers American and transnational law (LL M); criminal law (JD); government contracting and procurement (MSL); intellectual property and technology (MSL). *Application deadline:* For fall admission, 7/1 priority date for domestic students; for summer admission, 4/15 for domestic students. *Application fee:* $0. *Application Contact:* Claire Schrader, Assistant Dean/Executive Director of Enrollment Management and Marketing, 937-229-3555, Fax: 937-229-4194, E-mail: lawinfo@udayton.edu. *Dean,* Andrew Strauss, 937-229-3795, Fax: 937-229-2469, E-mail: astrauss1@udayton.edu.

UNIVERSITY OF DELAWARE, Newark, DE 19716

General Information State-related, coed, university. CGS member. *Graduate housing:* Rooms and/or apartments available to single and married students. Housing application deadline: 3/15. *Research affiliation:* Hagley Museum, Winterthur Museum, Longwood Gardens, Bartol Research Foundation.

GRADUATE UNITS

Alfred Lerner College of Business and Economics *Program availability:* Part-time, evening/weekend. Offers accounting (MS); business administration (MBA); business and economics (MA, MBA, MS, PhD); economic education (PhD); economics (MA, MS, PhD); economics for entrepreneurship and educators (MA); finance (MS); financial service analytics (PhD); hospitality information management (MS); information systems and technology management (MS). Electronic applications accepted.

Center for Energy and Environmental Policy Offers energy and environmental policy (MA, MEEP, PhD); urban affairs and public policy (PhD). Electronic applications accepted.

College of Agriculture and Natural Resources *Program availability:* Part-time. Offers agricultural and resource economics (MS); agricultural education (MA); agriculture and natural resources (MA, MS, PhD); animal sciences (MS, PhD); bioresources engineering (MS); entomology and applied ecology (MS, PhD); food sciences (MS); operations research (MS); plant and soil sciences (MS, PhD); public horticulture (MS); statistics (MS). Electronic applications accepted.

College of Arts and Sciences *Program availability:* Part-time, evening/weekend. Offers acting (MFA); American material culture (MA); applied mathematics (MS, PhD); art (MA, MFA); art conservation (MS); art history (MA, PhD); arts and sciences (MA, MALS, MFA, MM, MS, DPT, PhD); behavioral neuroscience (PhD); biochemistry (MA, MS, PhD); biomechanics and movement science (MS, PhD); biotechnology (MS); cancer biology (MS, PhD); cell and extracellular matrix biology (MS, PhD); cell and systems physiology (MS, PhD); chemistry (MA, MS, PhD); clinical psychology (PhD); cognitive psychology (PhD); communication (MA); composition (MM); criminology (MA, PhD); developmental biology (MS, PhD); ecology and evolution (MS, PhD); English and American literature (MA, PhD); fashion and apparel studies (MS); foreign languages and literatures (MA); foreign languages pedagogy (MA); history (MA, PhD); history of technology and industrialization (MA, PhD); liberal studies (MALS); linguistics (PhD); linguistics and cognitive science (MA); mathematics (MS, PhD); microbiology (MS, PhD); molecular biology and genetics (MS, PhD); music education (MM); performance (MM); physics and astronomy (MS, PhD); political science and international relations (MA, PhD); preservation studies (PhD); social psychology (PhD); sociology (MA, PhD); stage management (MFA); technical Chinese translation (MA); technical production (MFA). Electronic applications accepted.

School of Public Policy and Administration *Program availability:* Part-time, evening/weekend. Offers disaster science and management (MS, PhD); governance planning and management (PhD); historic preservation (MA); public administration (MPA); public policy and administration (MA, MPA, PhD); social and urban policy (PhD); technology, environment and society (PhD); urban affairs and public policy (MA). Electronic applications accepted.

College of Earth, Ocean, and Environment Offers geography (MA, MS, PhD); geological sciences (MA, PhD); geology (MS, PhD); marine science and policy (MMP, MS, PhD); ocean engineering (MS, PhD). Electronic applications accepted.

School of Marine Science and Policy Offers marine policy (MMP); marine studies (MS, PhD); oceanography (PhD).

College of Education and Human Development *Program availability:* Part-time, evening/weekend. Offers education and human development (M Ed, MA, MEEP, MI, MPA, MS, Ed D, PhD, Ed S); human development and family studies (MS, PhD). Electronic applications accepted.

School of Education *Program availability:* Part-time, evening/weekend. Offers education (PhD); educational leadership (Ed D); higher education (M Ed); instruction (MI); reading (M Ed); school leadership (M Ed); school psychology (MA, Ed S);

teaching English as a second language (TESL) (MA). Electronic applications accepted.

College of Engineering *Program availability:* Part-time, evening/weekend, online learning. Offers chemical engineering (M Ch E, PhD); computer and information sciences (MS, PhD); electrical and computer engineering (MSECE, PhD); engineering (M Ch E, MAS, MCE, MEM, MMSE, MS, MSECE, MSME, PhD); environmental engineering (MAS, MCE, PhD); geotechnical engineering (MAS, MCE, PhD); materials science and engineering (MMSE, PhD); mechanical engineering (MEM, MSME, PhD); ocean engineering (MAS, MCE, PhD); structural engineering (MAS, MCE, PhD); transportation engineering (MAS, MCE, PhD); water resource engineering (MAS, MCE, PhD). Electronic applications accepted.

College of Health Sciences *Program availability:* Part-time, evening/weekend, online learning. Offers adult nurse practitioner (MSN, PMC); cardiopulmonary clinical nurse specialist (MSN, PMC); cardiopulmonary clinical nurse specialist/adult nurse practitioner (MSN, PMC); family nurse practitioner (MSN, PMC); gerontology clinical nurse specialist (MSN, PMC); gerontology clinical nurse specialist geriatric nurse practitioner (PMC); gerontology clinical nurse specialist/geriatric nurse practitioner (MSN); health promotion (MS); health sciences (MS, MSN, DPT, PMC); health services administration (MSN, PMC); human nutrition (MS); kinesiology and applied physiology (MS, PhD); nursing of children clinical nurse specialist (MSN, PMC); nursing of children clinical nurse specialist/pediatric nurse practitioner (MSN, PMC); oncology/immune deficiency clinical nurse specialist (MSN, PMC); oncology/immune deficiency clinical nurse specialist/adult nurse practitioner (MSN, PMC); perinatal/women's health clinical nurse specialist (MSN, PMC); perinatal/women's health clinical nurse specialist/women's health nurse practitioner (MSN, PMC); physical therapy (DPT); psychiatric nursing clinical nurse specialist (MSN, PMC); speech-language pathology (MA). Electronic applications accepted.

UNIVERSITY OF DENVER, Denver, CO 80208

General Information Independent, coed, university. CGS member. *Enrollment:* 11,434 graduate, professional, and undergraduate students; 2,955 full-time matriculated graduate/professional students (1,918 women), 2,600 part-time matriculated graduate/professional students (1,459 women). *Enrollment by degree level:* 3,705 master's, 1,439 doctoral, 411 other advanced degrees. *Graduate faculty:* 701 full-time (309 women), 585 part-time/adjunct (307 women). Tuition and fees vary according to course load, campus/location and program. *Graduate housing:* Rooms and/or apartments available on a first-come, first-served basis to single and married students. Housing application deadline: 5/1. *Student services:* Campus employment opportunities, campus safety program, career counseling, exercise/wellness program, free psychological counseling, international student services, low-cost health insurance, multicultural affairs office, services for students with disabilities, teacher training, writing training. *Library facilities:* Anderson Academic Commons plus 1 other. *Collection:* Books: 1.7 million (physical), 2.3 million (digital/electronic); Serial titles: 594,063 (physical), 218,954 (digital/electronic); Databases: 1,306. Weekly public service hours: 145; study areas open 24 hours, 5–7 days a week; students can reserve study rooms. *Research affiliation:* National Center for Atmospheric Research (infrared measurements).

Computer facilities: Computer purchase and lease plans are available. 150 computers available on campus for general student use. A campuswide network can be accessed from student residence rooms and from off campus. Online class registration is available.

Website: http://www.du.edu/

General Application Contact: Office of Graduate Studies, 303-871-2706, Fax: 303-871-4942, E-mail: gradinfo@du.edu.

GRADUATE UNITS

Daniel Felix Ritchie School of Engineering and Computer Science Students: 37 full-time (11 women), 126 part-time (26 women); includes 26 minority (6 Black or African American, non-Hispanic/Latino; 6 Asian, non-Hispanic/Latino; 9 Hispanic/Latino; 1 Native Hawaiian or other Pacific Islander, non-Hispanic/Latino; 4 Two or more races, non-Hispanic/Latino), 70 international. Average age 28. 320 applicants, 70% accepted, 84 enrolled. *Faculty:* 38 full-time (4 women), 9 part-time/adjunct (4 women). Expenses: Contact institution. *Financial support:* In 2017–18, 105 students received support, including 5 research assistantships with tuition reimbursements available (averaging $11,283 per year), 2 teaching assistantships with tuition reimbursements available (averaging $5,834 per year); Federal Work-Study, institutionally sponsored loans, scholarships/grants, health care benefits, and unspecified assistantships also available. Financial award application deadline: 2/15; financial award applicants required to submit FAFSA. In 2017, 43 master's, 7 doctorates awarded. Offers bioengineering (MS); computer engineering (MS); computer science (MS, PhD); cybersecurity (MS); data science (MS); electrical and computer engineering (PhD); electrical engineering (MS); engineering (MS, PhD); engineering and computer science (MS, PhD); materials science (MS, PhD); mechanical engineering (MS, PhD); mechatronic systems engineering (MS, PhD). *Application deadline:* Applications are processed on a rolling basis. *Application fee:* $65. Electronic applications accepted. *Application Contact:* Information Contact, 303-871-3787, E-mail: ritchieschool@du.edu. *Dean*, JB Holston, 303-871-3733, Fax: 303-871-2716, E-mail: jb.holston@du.edu.

Daniels College of Business Students: 429 full-time (190 women), 212 part-time (104 women); includes 117 minority (16 Black or African American, non-Hispanic/Latino; 1 American Indian or Alaska Native, non-Hispanic/Latino; 24 Asian, non-Hispanic/Latino; 59 Hispanic/Latino; 17 Two or more races, non-Hispanic/Latino), 124 international. Average age 30. 1,032 applicants, 53% accepted, 246 enrolled. *Faculty:* 104 full-time (36 women), 48 part-time/adjunct (12 women). Expenses: Contact institution. *Financial support:* In 2017–18, 536 students received support, including 3 teaching assistantships with tuition reimbursements available (averaging $3,217 per year); career-related internships or fieldwork, Federal Work-Study, institutionally sponsored loans, scholarships/grants, and unspecified assistantships also available. Support available to part-time students. Financial award application deadline: 2/15; financial award applicants required to submit FAFSA. In 2017, 485 master's awarded. *Program availability:* Part-time, evening/weekend. Offers business (M Acc, MBA, MS); business administration (MBA); business information and analytics (MBA, MS); general business administration (MBA); management (MS); marketing (MBA, MS). *Application deadline:* For fall admission, 11/15 priority date for domestic and international students; for spring admission, 10/1 priority date for domestic and international students. Applications are processed on a rolling basis. *Application fee:* $100. Electronic applications accepted. *Application Contact:* Information Contact, 303-871-3416, Fax: 303-871-4466, E-mail: daniels@du.edu. *Dean*, Dr. Brent Chrite, 303-871-4324, Fax: 303-871-2156, E-mail: brent.chrite@du.edu.

Franklin L. Burns School of Real Estate and Construction Management Students: 21 full-time (6 women), 54 part-time (12 women); includes 16 minority (2 Black or African American, non-Hispanic/Latino; 2 Asian, non-Hispanic/Latino; 8 Hispanic/Latino; 4 Two or more races, non-Hispanic/Latino), 4 international. Average age 33. 43 applicants, 79% accepted, 19 enrolled. *Faculty:* 7 full-time (1 woman), 7 part-time/adjunct (1 woman). Expenses: Contact institution. *Financial support:* In 2017–18, 57 students received support, including 1 teaching assistantship with tuition reimbursement available (averaging $748 per year); Federal Work-Study, institutionally sponsored loans, scholarships/grants, and unspecified assistantships also available. Support available to part-time students. Financial award application deadline: 2/15; financial award applicants required to submit FAFSA. In 2017, 39 master's awarded. *Program availability:* Part-time, evening/weekend. Offers real estate and the built environment (MBA, MS). *Application deadline:* For fall admission, 11/15 priority date for domestic and international students; for spring admission, 10/1 priority date for domestic and international students. Applications are processed on a rolling basis. *Application fee:* $100. Electronic applications accepted. *Application Contact:* Ceci Smith, Assistant to the Director, 303-871-2145, E-mail: ceci.smith@du.edu. *Associate Professor and Director*, Dr. Barbara Jackson, 303-871-3470, Fax: 303-871-2971, E-mail: barbara.jackson@du.edu.

Reiman School of Finance Students: 32 full-time (13 women), 25 part-time (10 women); includes 1 minority (Hispanic/Latino), 35 international. Average age 26. 232 applicants, 43% accepted, 25 enrolled. *Faculty:* 18 full-time (4 women), 3 part-time/adjunct (0 women). Expenses: Contact institution. *Financial support:* In 2017–18, 53 students received support. Teaching assistantships with tuition reimbursements available, career-related internships or fieldwork, Federal Work-Study, institutionally sponsored loans, scholarships/grants, tuition waivers, and unspecified assistantships available. Support available to part-time students. Financial award application deadline: 2/15; financial award applicants required to submit FAFSA. In 2017, 53 master's awarded. *Program availability:* Part-time, evening/weekend. Offers applied quantitative finance (MS); finance (MBA). *Application deadline:* For fall admission, 11/15 priority date for domestic and international students; for spring admission, 10/1 priority date for domestic and international students. Applications are processed on a rolling basis. *Application fee:* $100. Electronic applications accepted. *Application Contact:* Kay Brisch, Assistant to Director, 303-871-3222, E-mail: ebrisch@du.edu. *Director*, Dr. Conrad Ciccotello, 303-871-2282, E-mail: conrad.ciccotello@du.edu.

School of Accountancy Students: 31 full-time (19 women), 42 part-time (31 women); includes 17 minority (1 Black or African American, non-Hispanic/Latino; 1 American Indian or Alaska Native, non-Hispanic/Latino; 6 Asian, non-Hispanic/Latino; 8 Hispanic/Latino; 1 Two or more races, non-Hispanic/Latino), 31 international. Average age 26. 189 applicants, 46% accepted, 28 enrolled. *Faculty:* 19 full-time (8 women), 7 part-time/adjunct (1 woman). Expenses: Contact institution. *Financial support:* In 2017–18, 70 students received support, including 3 teaching assistantships with tuition reimbursements available (averaging $1,242 per year); career-related internships or fieldwork, Federal Work-Study, institutionally sponsored loans, scholarships/grants, and unspecified assistantships also available. Support available to part-time students. Financial award application deadline: 2/15; financial award applicants required to submit FAFSA. In 2017, 110 master's awarded. *Program availability:* Part-time, evening/weekend. Offers accounting (M Acc, MBA). *Application deadline:* For fall admission, 11/15 priority date for domestic and international students; for spring admission, 10/1 priority date for domestic and international students. Applications are processed on a rolling basis. *Application fee:* $100. Electronic applications accepted. *Application Contact:* Jacquelyn Villa, Assistant to the Director, 303-871-2032, E-mail: jacquelyn.villa@du.edu. *Professor/Director, School of Accountancy*, Dr. Sharon Lassar, 303-871-2032, Fax: 303-871-2016, E-mail: slassar@du.edu.

Division of Arts, Humanities and Social Sciences Students: 107 full-time (67 women), 181 part-time (115 women); includes 52 minority (9 Black or African American, non-Hispanic/Latino; 9 Asian, non-Hispanic/Latino; 22 Hispanic/Latino; 12 Two or more races, non-Hispanic/Latino), 31 international. Average age 29. 1,017 applicants, 31% accepted, 132 enrolled. *Faculty:* 132 full-time (61 women), 33 part-time/adjunct (16 women). Expenses: Contact institution. *Financial support:* In 2017–18, 259 students received support, including 3 research assistantships with tuition reimbursements available (averaging $15,556 per year), 31 teaching assistantships with tuition reimbursements available (averaging $14,035 per year); career-related internships or fieldwork, Federal Work-Study, institutionally sponsored loans, scholarships/grants, and unspecified assistantships also available. Support available to part-time students. Financial award application deadline: 2/15; financial award applicants required to submit FAFSA. In 2017, 89 master's, 24 doctorates, 4 other advanced degrees awarded. *Program availability:* Part-time. Offers affective/cognitive/social psychology (PhD); archaeology (MA); arts, humanities and social sciences (MA, MFA, MM, MPP, MS, PhD, Certificate); clinical child psychology (PhD); creative writing (PhD); critical theory and religion (MA); cultural anthropology (MA); culture and communication (MA, PhD); developmental psychology (PhD); economics (MA); emergent digital practices (MA, MFA); international and intercultural communication (MA); interpersonal and family communication (MA, PhD); literary studies (MA, PhD); lived religions (MA); media and public communication (MA); museum and heritage studies (MA); philosophy of religion (MA); religion and international studies (MA); rhetoric and communication ethics (MA, PhD); sacred texts (MA). *Application deadline:* Applications are processed on a rolling basis. *Application fee:* $65. Electronic applications accepted. *Application Contact:* Information Contact, 360-871-4449, Fax: 303-871-4436, E-mail: ahss@du.edu. *Dean*, Dr. Danny McIntosh, 303-871-4449, Fax: 303-871-4436, E-mail: daniel.mcintosh@du.edu.

Lamont School of Music Students: 27 full-time (9 women), 76 part-time (38 women); includes 20 minority (3 Black or African American, non-Hispanic/Latino; 3 Asian, non-Hispanic/Latino; 7 Hispanic/Latino; 7 Two or more races, non-Hispanic/Latino), 14 international. Average age 28. 149 applicants, 79% accepted, 54 enrolled. *Faculty:* 32 full-time (9 women), 33 part-time/adjunct (15 women). Expenses: Contact institution. *Financial support:* In 2017–18, 89 students received support, including 7 teaching assistantships with tuition reimbursements available (averaging $6,917 per year); career-related internships or fieldwork, Federal Work-Study, institutionally sponsored loans, scholarships/grants, tuition waivers, and unspecified assistantships also available. Support available to part-time students. Financial award application deadline: 2/15; financial award applicants required to submit FAFSA. In 2017, 37 master's, 3 other advanced degrees awarded. *Program availability:* Part-time. Offers composition (MM); composition - jazz emphasis (MM); conducting (MM, Certificate); jazz studies (Certificate); music theory (MA); musicology (MA); orchestral studies (Certificate); pedagogy (MM); performance (MM, Certificate); performance - jazz emphasis (MM); Suzuki teaching (Certificate). *Application deadline:* For fall admission, 1/15 priority date for domestic and international students. Applications are processed on a rolling basis. *Application fee:* $65. Electronic applications accepted. *Application Contact:* Stephen Campbell, Director of Admission, 303-871-6973, Fax: 303-871-3118, E-mail: stephen.l.campbell@du.edu. *Professor and Director*, Dr. Nancy Cochran, 303-871-6986, Fax: 303-871-3118, E-mail: nancy.cochran@du.edu.

School of Art and Art History Students: 5 full-time (4 women), 14 part-time (all women); includes 1 minority (Hispanic/Latino), 1 international. Average age 24. 33 applicants, 79% accepted, 13 enrolled. *Faculty:* 16 full-time (10 women), 8 part-time/adjunct (7 women). Expenses: Contact institution. *Financial support:* In 2017–18, 19 students received support. Research assistantships with tuition reimbursements available, teaching assistantships with tuition reimbursements available, career-related internships or fieldwork, Federal Work-Study, institutionally sponsored loans, scholarships/grants, and unspecified assistantships available. Support available to part-time students. Financial award application deadline: 2/15; financial award applicants required to submit FAFSA. In 2017, 7 master's awarded. *Program availability:* Part-time. Offers art history (MA); museum studies (MA). *Application deadline:* For fall admission, 1/31 priority date for domestic and international students. Applications are processed on a rolling basis. *Application fee:* $65. Electronic applications accepted. *Application Contact:* Jason Kellermeyer, Coordinator of Academic Programs, 303-871-2846, E-mail: jason.kellermeyer@du.edu. *Associate Professor and Director*, Catherine Chauvin, 303-871-2367, Fax: 303-871-4112, E-mail: catherine.chauvin@du.edu.

Division of Natural Sciences and Mathematics Students: 17 full-time (10 women), 131 part-time (60 women); includes 34 minority (3 Black or African American, non-Hispanic/Latino; 3 Asian, non-Hispanic/Latino; 17 Hispanic/Latino; 11 Two or more races, non-Hispanic/Latino), 15 international. Average age 29. 253 applicants, 51% accepted, 58 enrolled. *Faculty:* 86 full-time (28 women), 19 part-time/adjunct (8 women). Expenses: Contact institution. *Financial support:* In 2017–18, 141 students received support, including 3 research assistantships with tuition reimbursements available (averaging $17,333 per year), 21 teaching assistantships with tuition reimbursements available (averaging $18,523 per year); career-related internships or fieldwork, institutionally sponsored loans, scholarships/grants, and unspecified assistantships also available. Support available to part-time students. Financial award application deadline: 2/15; financial award applicants required to submit FAFSA. In 2017, 38 master's, 14 doctorates awarded. *Program availability:* Part-time, evening/weekend. Offers biology, ecology and evolution (MS, PhD); biomedical sciences (PSM); cell and molecular biology (MS, PhD); chemistry (MA, MS, PhD); geographic information science (MS); geography (MA, PhD); mathematics (MA, MS, PhD); natural sciences and mathematics (MA, MS, PSM, PhD); physics (MS, PhD). *Application deadline:* Applications are processed on a rolling basis. *Application fee:* $65. Electronic applications accepted. *Application Contact:* Kirsten Norwood, Executive Assistant to the Dean, 303-871-2693, Fax: 303-871-3223, E-mail: kirsten.norwood@du.edu. *Dean*, Dr. Andrei Kutateladze, 303-871-2995, Fax: 303-871-3223, E-mail: andrei.kutateladze@du.edu.

DU/Iliff Joint PhD Program in the Study of Religion Students: 29 full-time (7 women), 19 part-time (6 women); includes 10 minority (1 Black or African American, non-Hispanic/Latino; 1 Asian, non-Hispanic/Latino; 6 Hispanic/Latino; 2 Two or more races, non-Hispanic/Latino), 2 international. Average age 39. 26 applicants, 54% accepted, 7 enrolled. *Faculty:* 10 part-time/adjunct (4 women). Expenses: Contact institution. *Financial support:* In 2017–18, 30 students received support, including 11 teaching assistantships with tuition reimbursements available (averaging $2,788 per year); scholarships/grants and unspecified assistantships also available. Financial award application deadline: 1/15. In 2017, 9 doctorates awarded. *Program availability:* Part-time. Offers future faculty in religion (Certificate); Latinx studies (Certificate); study of religion (PhD). Program jointly offered with Iliff School of Theology. *Application deadline:* For fall admission, 1/15 priority date for domestic and international students. Applications are processed on a rolling basis. *Application fee:* $65. Electronic applications accepted. *Application Contact:* Information Contact, 303-765-3136, Fax: 303-871-4942, E-mail: jointphd@iliff.edu. *Director*, Annette Stott, 303-871-3278.

Graduate School of Professional Psychology Students: 233 full-time (180 women), 79 part-time (46 women); includes 81 minority (22 Black or African American, non-Hispanic/Latino; 9 Asian, non-Hispanic/Latino; 31 Hispanic/Latino; 1 Native Hawaiian or other Pacific Islander, non-Hispanic/Latino; 18 Two or more races, non-Hispanic/Latino), 7 international. Average age 26. 866 applicants, 30% accepted, 135 enrolled. *Faculty:* 23 full-time (13 women), 25 part-time/adjunct (14 women). Expenses: Contact institution. *Financial support:* In 2017–18, 235 students received support, including 2 teaching assistantships with tuition reimbursements available (averaging $1,976 per year); career-related internships or fieldwork, Federal Work-Study, institutionally sponsored loans, scholarships/grants, unspecified assistantships, and clinical assistantships also available. Support available to part-time students. Financial award application deadline: 2/15; financial award applicants required to submit FAFSA. In 2017, 106 master's, 23 doctorates awarded. Offers clinical psychology (Psy D); forensic psychology (MA); international disaster psychology (MA); sport and performance psychology (MA); sport coaching (MA); strength and conditioning and fitness coaching (Certificate). *Application deadline:* For fall admission, 1/5 for domestic and international students. *Application fee:* $65. Electronic applications accepted. *Application Contact:* Admissions Counselor, 303-871-3736, Fax: 303-871-4220, E-mail: gsppinfo@du.edu. *Dean*, Dr. Shelly Smith-Acuna, 303-871-3880, Fax: 303-871-4220, E-mail: shelly.smith-acuna@du.edu.

Graduate School of Social Work Students: 511 full-time (457 women), 11 part-time (10 women); includes 117 minority (19 Black or African American, non-Hispanic/Latino; 7 American Indian or Alaska Native, non-Hispanic/Latino; 14 Asian, non-Hispanic/Latino; 58 Hispanic/Latino; 19 Two or more races, non-Hispanic/Latino), 1 international. Average age 28. 919 applicants, 79% accepted, 302 enrolled. *Faculty:* 40 full-time (27 women), 103 part-time/adjunct (88 women). Expenses: Contact institution. *Financial support:* In 2017–18, 492 students received support, including 1 teaching assistantship with tuition reimbursement available (averaging $16,000 per year); Federal Work-Study, scholarships/grants, and unspecified assistantships also available. Support available to part-time students. Financial award application deadline: 2/15; financial award applicants required to submit FAFSA. In 2017, 278 master's, 7 doctorates, 55 other advanced degrees awarded. *Program availability:* Part-time, evening/weekend. Offers animal-assisted social work (Certificate); couples and family therapy (Certificate); social work (MSW, PhD); social work with Latinos/as (Certificate). *Application deadline:* For fall admission, 1/15 priority date for domestic and international students. Applications are processed on a rolling basis. *Application fee:* $65. Electronic applications accepted. *Application Contact:* Roberto Garcia, Director of Enrollment Management, 303-871-2602, E-mail: gssw-admission@du.edu. *Dean*, Dr. Amanda Moore McBride, 303-871-2203, Fax: 303-871-2845.

Josef Korbel School of International Studies Students: 245 full-time (132 women), 40 part-time (21 women); includes 58 minority (8 Black or African American, non-Hispanic/Latino; 2 American Indian or Alaska Native, non-Hispanic/Latino; 11 Asian, non-Hispanic/Latino; 27 Hispanic/Latino; 10 Two or more races, non-Hispanic/Latino), 22 international. Average age 27. 627 applicants, 74% accepted, 106 enrolled. *Faculty:* 46 full-time (16 women), 28 part-time/adjunct (8 women). Expenses: Contact institution. *Financial support:* In 2017–18, 225 students received support, including 1 teaching assistantship with tuition reimbursement available (averaging $2,236 per year); research assistantships with tuition reimbursements available, career-related internships or fieldwork, Federal Work-Study, institutionally sponsored loans, scholarships/grants, and unspecified assistantships also available. Support available to part-time students. Financial award application deadline: 2/15; financial award applicants required to submit FAFSA. In 2017, 218 master's, 6 doctorates, 25 other advanced degrees awarded. *Program availability:* Part-time. Offers conflict resolution (MA); global business and corporate social responsibility (Certificate); global finance, trade and economic integration (MA); global health affairs (Certificate); homeland security (Certificate); humanitarian assistance (Certificate); international administration (MA); international development (MA); international human rights (MA); international security (MA); international studies (MA, PhD); public policy studies (MPP); religion and international affairs (Certificate). *Application deadline:* For fall admission, 1/15 priority date for domestic and international students; for winter admission, 11/1 for domestic and international students. Applications are processed on a rolling basis. *Application fee:* $65. Electronic applications accepted. *Application Contact:* Admissions Contact, E-mail: korbeladm@du.edu. *Dean*, Dr. Pardis Mahdavi, 303-871-6338, E-mail: pardis.mahdavi@du.edu.

Institute for Public Policy Studies Average age 26. 21 applicants, 81% accepted, 4 enrolled. Expenses: Contact institution. *Financial support:* In 2017–18, 17 students received support, including 2 teaching assistantships with tuition reimbursements available (averaging $3,750 per year); Federal Work-Study, scholarships/grants, and unspecified assistantships also available. Financial award application deadline: 2/15; financial award applicants required to submit FAFSA. In 2017, 9 master's awarded. Offers public policy studies (MPP). *Application deadline:* For fall admission, 7/1 priority date for domestic and international students; for winter admission, 11/15 priority date for domestic and international students. Applications are processed on a rolling basis. *Application fee:* $65. Electronic applications accepted. *Co-Director*, Dr. Richard Caldwell, 303-871-2468, Fax: 303-871-3066, E-mail: richard.caldwell@du.edu.

Morgridge College of Education Students: 502 full-time (406 women), 361 part-time (267 women); includes 233 minority (54 Black or African American, non-Hispanic/Latino; 6 American Indian or Alaska Native, non-Hispanic/Latino; 25 Asian, non-Hispanic/Latino; 113 Hispanic/Latino; 35 Two or more races, non-Hispanic/Latino), 52 international. Average age 31. 1,167 applicants, 64% accepted, 415 enrolled. *Faculty:* 39 full-time (29 women), 60 part-time/adjunct (42 women). Expenses: Contact institution. *Financial support:* In 2017–18, 765 students received support, including 26 research assistantships with tuition reimbursements available (averaging $10,957 per year), 38 teaching assistantships with tuition reimbursements available (averaging $3,391 per year); career-related internships or fieldwork, Federal Work-Study, institutionally sponsored loans, scholarships/grants, and unspecified assistantships also available. Support available to part-time students. Financial award application deadline: 2/15; financial award applicants required to submit FAFSA. In 2017, 285 master's, 51 doctorates, 157 other advanced degrees awarded. *Program availability:* Part-time, evening/weekend, online learning. Offers child, family and school psychology (MA, PhD, Ed S); counseling psychology (MA, PhD); curriculum and instruction (MA, Ed D, PhD); curriculum instruction and teaching (Certificate); early childhood special education (MA, Certificate); educational leadership and policy studies (MA, Ed D, PhD, Certificate); higher education (Ed D, PhD); library and information science (MLIS); research methods and statistics (MA, PhD). *Application deadline:* Applications are processed on a rolling basis. *Application fee:* $65. Electronic applications accepted. *Application Contact:* Jodi Dye, Director of Admissions, 303-871-2510, Fax: 303-871-4456, E-mail: jodi.dye@du.edu. *Dean*, Dr. Karen Riley, 303-871-3665, Fax: 303-871-4456, E-mail: karen.riley@du.edu.

Sturm College of Law Students: 789 full-time (426 women), 153 part-time (97 women); includes 208 minority (30 Black or African American, non-Hispanic/Latino; 5 American Indian or Alaska Native, non-Hispanic/Latino; 33 Asian, non-Hispanic/Latino; 109 Hispanic/Latino; 31 Two or more races, non-Hispanic/Latino), 53 international. Average age 29. 2,616 applicants, 53% accepted, 322 enrolled. *Faculty:* 86 full-time (42 women), 70 part-time/adjunct (31 women). Expenses: Contact institution. *Financial support:* In 2017–18, 596 students received support, including 5 teaching assistantships with tuition reimbursements available (averaging $8,900 per year); career-related internships or fieldwork, Federal Work-Study, institutionally sponsored loans, scholarships/grants, unspecified assistantships, and tutorships also available. Support available to part-time students. Financial award application deadline: 2/15; financial award applicants required to submit FAFSA. In 2017, 106 master's, 251 doctorates, 91 Certificates awarded. *Program availability:* Part-time, evening/weekend. Offers environmental and natural resources law and policy (LL M, MLS); law (LL M, MLS, MRLS, MSLA, MT, JD, Certificate); legal administration (MSLA, Certificate); natural resources law and policy (Certificate); tax (LL M, MT). *Application deadline:* Applications are processed on a rolling basis. *Application fee:* $65. Electronic applications accepted. *Application Contact:* Yvonne Cherena-Pacheco, Associate Director of Admissions, 303-871-6192, Fax: 303-871-6992, E-mail: admissions@law.du.edu. *Dean*, Dr. Bruce Smith, 303-871-6103, Fax: 303-871-6992.

University College Students: 56 full-time (32 women), 1,287 part-time (707 women); includes 330 minority (99 Black or African American, non-Hispanic/Latino; 7 American Indian or Alaska Native, non-Hispanic/Latino; 43 Asian, non-Hispanic/Latino; 141 Hispanic/Latino; 3 Native Hawaiian or other Pacific Islander, non-Hispanic/Latino; 37 Two or more races, non-Hispanic/Latino), 84 international. Average age 34. 783 applicants, 86% accepted, 420 enrolled. *Faculty:* 118 part-time/adjunct (62 women). Expenses: Contact institution. *Financial support:* In 2017–18, 29 students received support. Teaching assistantships available. Financial award applicants required to submit FAFSA. In 2017, 461 master's, 173 other advanced degrees awarded. *Program availability:* Part-time, evening/weekend, online learning. Offers arts and culture (MA, Certificate); communication management (MS, Certificate); environmental policy and management (MS); geographic information systems (MS); global affairs (MA, Certificate); healthcare leadership (MS); information communications and technology (MS); leadership and organizations (MS); professional creative writing (MA, Certificate); security management (MS, Certificate); strategic human resources (Certificate). *Application deadline:* For fall admission, 6/21 priority date for domestic students, 5/1 priority date for international students; for winter admission, 9/14 priority date for domestic students, 9/19 priority date for international students; for spring admission, 1/11 priority date for domestic students, 12/12 priority date for international students; for summer admission, 3/29 priority date for domestic students, 3/6 priority date for international students. Applications are processed on a rolling basis. *Application fee:* $75. Electronic applications accepted. *Application Contact:* Information Contact, 303-871-2291, E-mail: ucoladm@du.edu. *Dean*, Dr. Michael McGuire, 303-871-3518, Fax: 303-871-3303, E-mail: mmcguire@du.edu.

UNIVERSITY OF DETROIT MERCY, Detroit, MI 48221

General Information Independent-religious, coed, university. *Graduate housing:* Room and/or apartments available on a first-come, first-served basis to single students; on-campus housing not available to married students.

GRADUATE UNITS

College of Business Administration *Program availability:* Part-time, evening/weekend, 100% online, blended/hybrid learning. Offers business administration (MBA); business fundamentals (Certificate); business turnaround management (Certificate); ethical leadership and change management (Certificate); finance (Certificate); forensic accounting (Certificate). Electronic applications accepted.

College of Engineering and Science *Program availability:* Part-time, evening/weekend. Offers chemistry (MS); civil and environmental engineering (DE); electrical and computer engineering (ME); electrical engineering (DE); engineering management (M Eng Mgt); environmental engineering (MEE); mechanical engineering (MME, DE); product development (MS); software engineering (MSSE); teaching of mathematics (MATM). Electronic applications accepted.

College of Health Professions Offers clinical nurse leader (MSN); family nurse practitioner (MSN); health services administration (MHSA); health systems management (MSN); nurse anesthesia (MS); nursing (DNP); nursing education (MSN, Certificate); nursing leadership and financial management (Certificate); outcomes performance management (Certificate); physician assistant (MS).

College of Liberal Arts and Education *Program availability:* Part-time, evening/weekend. Offers addiction counseling (MA); addiction studies (Certificate); clinical mental health counseling (MA); clinical psychology (MA, PhD); computer and information systems (MS); criminal justice (MA); curriculum and instruction (MA); economics (MA); educational administration (MA); financial economics (MA); industrial/organizational psychology (MA); information assurance (MS); intelligence analysis (MA); liberal studies (MALS); religious studies (MA); school counseling (MA, Certificate); school psychology (Spec); security administration (MS); special education: emotionally impaired/behaviorally disordered (MA); special education: learning disabilities (MA).

School of Architecture Offers architecture (M Arch); community development (MA).

School of Dentistry Offers dentistry (MS, DDS, Certificate).

School of Law *Program availability:* Part-time. Offers law (JD).

UNIVERSITY OF DUBUQUE, Dubuque, IA 52001-5099

General Information Independent-religious, coed, comprehensive institution. *Graduate housing:* Rooms and/or apartments available on a first-come, first-served basis to single students and available to married students.

GRADUATE UNITS

Program in Business Administration *Program availability:* Part-time, evening/weekend. Offers business administration (MBA). Electronic applications accepted.

Program in Communication *Program availability:* Part-time, evening/weekend. Offers information technologies communication (MAC); leadership and management (MAC); strategic and corporate communication (MAC). Electronic applications accepted.

University of Dubuque Theological Seminary *Program availability:* Part-time, 100% online, blended/hybrid learning. Offers theology (M Div, D Min). Electronic applications accepted.

UNIVERSITY OF EAST-WEST MEDICINE, Sunnyvale, CA 94085-3922

General Information Proprietary, coed, graduate-only institution. *Graduate housing:* On-campus housing not available.

GRADUATE UNITS

Graduate Programs Offers acupuncture and Oriental medicine (DAOM); Tai Chi (MS); traditional Chinese medicine (MSTCM).

UNIVERSITY OF EVANSVILLE, Evansville, IN 47722

General Information Independent-religious, coed, comprehensive institution. *Graduate housing:* Room and/or apartments available to single students; on-campus housing not available to married students. *Research affiliation:* The New American Colleges and Universities (higher education administration), Independent Colleges of Indiana (higher education administration), Council of Independent Colleges (higher education administration), Military Family Research Institute (higher education administration).

GRADUATE UNITS

Center for Adult Education *Program availability:* Part-time, evening/weekend. Offers public service administration (MS).

College of Education and Health Sciences Offers education and health sciences (MPH, MS, MSAT, DPT); physical therapy (DPT).

School of Health Sciences *Program availability:* Part-time, evening/weekend. Offers athletic training (MSAT); health policy (MPH); health services administration (MS).

THE UNIVERSITY OF FINDLAY, Findlay, OH 45840-3653

General Information Independent-religious, coed, comprehensive institution. *Enrollment:* 4,888 graduate, professional, and undergraduate students; 688 full-time matriculated graduate/professional students (430 women), 553 part-time matriculated graduate/professional students (308 women). *Graduate housing:* Room and/or apartments available on a first-come, first-served basis to single students; on-campus housing not available to married students. *Student services:* Campus employment opportunities, campus safety program, career counseling, exercise/wellness program, free psychological counseling, international student services, low-cost health insurance, multicultural affairs office, services for students with disabilities, writing training. *Library facilities:* Shafer Library plus 4 others. *Collection:* Books: 98,272 (physical), 325,566 (digital/electronic); Serial titles: 361 (physical), 78,798 (digital/electronic); Databases: 173. Weekly public service hours: 94; study areas open 24 hours, 5–7 days a week. *Research affiliation:* The Ohio State University Research Foundation (biology), Rollin M. Gerstacker Foundation (environmental research), U.S. Department of Agriculture (USDA) (wildlife research), U.S. Department of Education (DOE) (technology innovation, bilingual teaching research), U.S. Department of Health and Human Services (terrorism preparedness).

Computer facilities: Computer purchase and lease plans are available. 151 computers available on campus for general student use. A campuswide network can be accessed from student residence rooms and from off campus. Online class registration is available.

Website: http://www.findlay.edu/

General Application Contact: Milena Velez, Assistant Director for Graduate and Transfer Admissions, 419-434-6902, Fax: 419-434-4898, E-mail: velez@findlay.edu.

GRADUATE UNITS

Office of Graduate Admissions Students: 688 full-time (430 women), 553 part-time (308 women), 170 international. Average age 28. Expenses: Contact institution. *Financial support:* In 2017–18, 10 research assistantships with partial tuition reimbursements (averaging $7,200 per year), 35 teaching assistantships with partial tuition reimbursements (averaging $7,200 per year) were awarded; Federal Work-Study, institutionally sponsored loans, and unspecified assistantships also available. Financial award applicants required to submit FAFSA. In 2017, 366 master's, 137 doctorates awarded. *Program availability:* Part-time, evening/weekend, 100% online, blended/hybrid learning. Offers applied security and analytics (MSAS); athletic training (MAT); business (MBA); education (MA Ed, Ed D); environmental, safety, and health management (MSEM); health informatics (MS); occupational therapy (MOT); pharmacy (Pharm D); physical therapy (DPT); physician assistant (MPA); rhetoric and writing (MA); teaching English to speakers of other languages (TESOL) and applied linguistics (MA). *Application deadline:* Applications are processed on a rolling basis. Electronic applications accepted. *Application Contact:* Madeline Fauser Brennan, Graduate Admissions Counselor, 419-434-4636, Fax: 419-434-4898, E-mail: fauserbrennan@findlay.edu. *Director of Admissions*, Christopher M. Harris, 419-434-4347, E-mail: harrisc1@findlay.edu.

UNIVERSITY OF FLORIDA, Gainesville, FL 32611

General Information State-supported, coed, university. CGS member. *Graduate housing:* Rooms and/or apartments available on a first-come, first-served basis to single and married students. *Research affiliation:* Los Alamos National Laboratory (high magnetic field research), National Center for Automated Information Research (law and business data), Oracle Corporation (database management), IBM (information infrastructure), Association of Universities for Research in Astronomy (Gemini multinational telescope).

GRADUATE UNITS

College of Dentistry Offers dentistry (MS, DMD, PhD, Certificate); endodontics (MS, Certificate); foreign trained dentistry (Certificate); oral biology (PhD); orthodontics (MS, Certificate); periodontology (MS, Certificate); prosthodontics (MS, Certificate).

College of Medicine Offers biochemistry and molecular biology (PhD); biomedical sciences (MS, PhD); clinical investigation (MS); epidemiology (MS); genetics (PhD); immunology and microbiology (PhD); medicine (MPAS, MPH, MS, MD, PhD); molecular cell biology (PhD); molecular genetics and microbiology (MS); neuroscience (PhD); physician assistant (MPAS); physiology and pharmacology (PhD); public health (MPH). Electronic applications accepted.

College of Veterinary Medicine *Program availability:* Part-time. Offers forensic toxicology (Certificate); veterinary medical sciences (MS, PhD); veterinary medicine (MS, DVM, PhD, Certificate).

Graduate School *Program availability:* Part-time, evening/weekend, online learning. Electronic applications accepted.

College of Agricultural and Life Sciences *Program availability:* Part-time. Offers agribusiness (MS); agricultural and life sciences (MAB, MFAS, MFRC, MS, DPM, PhD, Certificate); agricultural education and communication (MS, PhD); agroecology (MS); agronomy (MS, PhD); animal molecular and cellular biology (MS, PhD); animal sciences (MS, PhD); community studies (MS); environmental education and communications (Certificate); environmental horticulture (MS, PhD); family and youth development (MS); family, youth and community sciences (MS); fisheries and aquatic sciences (MFAS, MS, PhD); food and resource economics (MAB, MS, PhD); food science (PhD); food science and human nutrition (MS); forest resources and conservation (MFRC, MS, PhD); geographic information systems (MS); horticultural sciences (MS, PhD); hydrologic sciences (MS, PhD); microbiology and cell science (MS, PhD); nonprofit organization development (MS); nutritional sciences (MS, PhD); plant medicine (DPM); plant molecular and cellular biology (MS, PhD); plant pathology (MS, PhD); soil and water science (MS, PhD); toxicology (MS, PhD); tropical conservation and development (MAB, MS, DPM, PhD); wildlife ecology and conservation (MS, PhD). Electronic applications accepted.

College of Design, Construction and Planning *Program availability:* Part-time, online learning. Offers architecture (M Arch, MSAS); construction management (MSCM, PhD); design, construction and planning (M Arch, MAURP, MFES, MICM, MID, MLA, MSAS, MSCM, MURP, PhD); fire and emergency services (MFES); geographic information systems (MAURP, MLA, PhD); historic preservation (M Arch, MAURP, MID, MLA, MSAS, MSCM, PhD); interior design (MID, PhD); international construction (MICM); landscape architecture (MLA, PhD); sustainable architecture (M Arch, MSAS); sustainable construction (MSCM); sustainable design (M Arch, MAURP, MID, MLA, MSAS, MSCM); tropical conservation and development (MAURP); urban and regional planning (MAURP, MURP, PhD); wetland sciences (MAURP, MLA). Electronic applications accepted.

College of Education *Program availability:* Part-time, evening/weekend, online learning. Offers counseling and counselor education (Ed D, PhD); curriculum and instruction (M Ed, MAE, Ed D, PhD, Ed S); early childhood education (M Ed, MAE); education (M Ed, MAE, Ed D, PhD, Ed S); educational leadership (M Ed, MAE, Ed D, PhD, Ed S); elementary education (M Ed, MAE); English education (M Ed, MAE); higher education administration (Ed D, PhD); marriage and family counseling (M Ed, MAE, Ed D, PhD, Ed S); mathematics education (M Ed, MAE); mental health counseling (M Ed, MAE, Ed D, PhD, Ed S); reading education (M Ed, MAE); research and evaluation methodology (M Ed, MAE, Ed D, PhD); school counseling and guidance (M Ed, MAE, Ed D, PhD, Ed S); school psychology (M Ed, MAE, Ed D, PhD, Ed S); science education (M Ed, MAE); social studies education (M Ed, MAE); special education (M Ed, MAE, Ed D, PhD, Ed S); student personnel in higher education (M Ed, MAE). Electronic applications accepted.

College of Health and Human Performance *Program availability:* Part-time. Offers applied physiology and kinesiology (MS); athletic training/sports medicine (MS); biobehavioral science (MS); clinical exercise physiology (MS); exercise physiology (MS); health and human performance (PhD); health communication (Graduate Certificate); health education and behavior (MS); human performance (MS); recreation, parks and tourism (MS); sport management (MS). Electronic applications accepted.

College of Journalism and Communications *Program availability:* Part-time, online learning. Offers advertising (M Adv); international/intercultural communication (MAMC); journalism (MAMC); mass communication (MAMC, PhD); public relations (MAMC); science/health communication (MAMC); telecommunication (MAMC). Electronic applications accepted.

College of Liberal Arts and Sciences *Program availability:* Part-time. Offers anthropology (MA, MAT, PhD); applications of geographic technologies (MA, MS); astronomy (MS, MST, PhD); botany (MS, MST, PhD); chemistry (MS, MST, PhD); classical studies (MA, PhD); clinical and translational science (PhD); counseling psychology (PhD); creative writing (MFA); criminology, law, and society (MA, PhD); educational policy (PhD); English (MA, PhD); French and Francophone studies (MA, PhD); gender and development (Graduate Certificate); geographic information systems (MA, MS, PhD); geography (MA, MS, PhD); geology (MS, MST, PhD); German (MA, PhD); historic preservation (MA, PhD); history (MA, PhD); hydrologic sciences (MS, PhD); imaging science and technology (PhD); international development policy and administration (MA, Certificate); international relations (MA, MAT); Jewish studies (MA); Latin (MA, MAT, ML); Latin American studies (MA, Certificate); liberal arts and sciences (M Ag, M Stat, MA, MAT, MDP, MFA, ML, MS, MS Stat, MST, MWS, PhD, Certificate, Graduate Certificate); linguistics (MA, PhD); mathematics (MAT, MS, MST, PhD); philosophy (MA, PhD); physics (MS, MST, PhD); political campaigning (MA, Certificate); political science (MA, PhD); psychology (MA, MS, PhD); public affairs (MA, Certificate); quantitative finance (PhD); religion (MA, PhD); sociology (MA, PhD); Spanish (MA, MAT, PhD); statistics (M Stat, MS Stat, PhD); sustainable development practice (MDP); teaching English as a second language (Certificate); tropical conservation and development (MA, MS, MST, PhD); wetland sciences (MA, MS, MST, PhD); women's and gender studies (MA, PhD); women's studies (MA, Graduate Certificate); zoology (MS, MST, PhD). Electronic applications accepted.

College of Nursing *Program availability:* Part-time. Offers clinical and translational science (PhD); clinical nursing (DNP); nursing (MSN); nursing sciences (PhD). Electronic applications accepted.

College of Pharmacy *Program availability:* Part-time, evening/weekend, online learning. Offers clinical and translational sciences (PhD); clinical pharmaceutical sciences (PhD); clinical pharmacy (MSP); clinical toxicology (MSP, Certificate); drug chemistry (Certificate); environmental forensics (Certificate); forensic death investigation (Certificate); forensic DNA and serology (MSP, Certificate); forensic drug chemistry (MSP); forensic science (MSP); forensic toxicology (Certificate); medicinal chemistry (MSP, PhD); pharmaceutical chemistry (MSP); pharmaceutical outcomes and policy (MSP, PhD); pharmaceutical sciences (MSP, PhD); pharmacodynamics (MSP, PhD); pharmacy (MSP, PhD). Electronic applications accepted.

College of Public Health and Health Professions *Program availability:* Part-time. Offers audiology (Au D); biostatistics (MS, PhD); clinical and translational science (PhD); communication sciences and disorders (MA, PhD); environmental health (MPH, PhD); epidemiology (MPH, MS, PhD); health administration (MHA); health management and policy (MPH); health services research (PhD); occupational therapy (MHS, MOT); one health (MHS, PhD); physical therapy (DPT); psychology (MS); public health (MPH, PhD, Certificate); public health and health professions (MA, MHA, MHS, MHS, MOT, MPH, MS, Au D, DPT, PhD, Certificate); public health practice (MPH); rehabilitation science (PhD); social and behavioral sciences (MPH). Electronic applications accepted.

College of The Arts *Program availability:* Online learning. Offers art (MA); art education (MA); art history (MA, PhD); arts (MA, MFA, MM, PhD, Graduate Certificate); choral conducting (MM); composition (MM, PhD); electronic music (MM); ethnomusicology (MM); instrumental conducting (MM); museology (MA); music (MM, PhD); music education (MM, PhD); music history and literature (MM, PhD); music theory (MM); performance (MM); sacred music (MM); theatre (MFA). Electronic applications accepted.

Herbert Wertheim College of Engineering *Program availability:* Part-time, online learning. Offers aerospace engineering (ME, MS, PhD); agricultural and biological engineering (ME, MS, PhD); biological systems modeling (Certificate); biomedical engineering (ME, MS, PhD, Certificate); chemical engineering (ME, MS, PhD, Engr); civil engineering (ME, MS, PhD); clinical and translational science (PhD); coastal and oceanographic engineering (ME, MS, PhD); computer engineering (ME, MS, PhD); computer science (MS); digital arts and sciences (MS); electrical and computer engineering (ME, MS, PhD); engineering (ME, MS, PhD, Certificate, Engr); environmental engineering sciences (ME, MS, PhD, Engr); geographic information systems (ME, MS, PhD); hydrologic sciences (ME, MS, PhD); imaging science and technology (PhD); industrial and systems engineering (ME, MS, PhD, Engr); material science and engineering (MS); materials science and engineering (ME, PhD); mechanical engineering (ME, MS, PhD); medical physics (MS, PhD); nuclear engineering (ME, PhD); nuclear engineering (MS); nuclear engineering sciences (ME, MS, PhD); quantitative finance (PhD); structural engineering (ME, MS); wetland sciences (ME, MS, PhD). Electronic applications accepted.

School of Natural Resources and Environment Offers interdisciplinary ecology (MS, PhD). Electronic applications accepted.

Warrington College of Business Administration *Program availability:* Part-time, evening/weekend, online learning. Offers accounting (M Acc, PhD); business administration (M Acc, MA, MBA, MS, PhD, Certificate); competitive strategy (MBA); economics (MA, PhD); entrepreneurship (MS); finance (MBA, MS, PhD); financial services (Certificate); global management (MBA); Graham-Buffett security analysis (MBA); health care risk management (MS); human resource management (MBA); information systems and operations management (MBA, PhD); insurance (PhD); international business (MA); international studies (MBA); management (MBA, MS, PhD); marketing (MA, MS, PhD); quantitative finance (PhD); real estate (MBA, MS); real estate and urban analysis (PhD); supply chain management (Certificate). Electronic applications accepted.

Levin College of Law Offers comparative law (LL M); environmental and land use law (LL M); international taxation (LL M); law (JD); taxation (LL M, SJD). Electronic applications accepted.

UNIVERSITY OF FORT LAUDERDALE, Lauderhill, FL 33313

General Information Independent-religious, coed, comprehensive institution.

GRADUATE UNITS

Graduate Program Offers ministry (MS).

UNIVERSITY OF GEORGIA, Athens, GA 30602

General Information State-supported, coed, university. CGS member. *Graduate housing:* Rooms and/or apartments available on a first-come, first-served basis to single and married students. *Research affiliation:* Skidaway Institute of Oceanography, Southeast Water Laboratory, Russell Research Laboratory, Organization for Tropical Studies.

GRADUATE UNITS

Biomedical and Health Sciences Institute Offers neuroscience (PhD).

College of Agricultural and Environmental Sciences Offers agricultural and environmental sciences (MAE, MS, PhD); agricultural economics (MAE, MS, PhD); animal and dairy science (PhD); animal nutrition (PhD); animal science (MS); crop and soil sciences (MS, PhD); entomology (MS, PhD); environmental economics (MS); food science (MS, PhD); horticulture (MS, PhD); plant pathology (MS, PhD); poultry science (MS, PhD). Electronic applications accepted.

Institute of Plant Breeding, Genetics and Genomics Offers plant breeding, genetics and genomics (MS, PhD).

College of Education Offers adult education (Ed D, Ed S); college student affairs administration (M Ed, PhD); communication science and disorders (M Ed, MA, PhD, Ed S); education (M Ed, MA, MA Ed, MAT, MS, Ed D, PhD, Ed S); educational psychology (Ed S); English education (M Ed); higher education (M Ed, Ed D, PhD); kinesiology (MS, PhD); language and literacy education (PhD); learning, design, and technology (M Ed, PhD, Ed S); lifelong education, administration and policy (PhD); mathematics education (M Ed, PhD, Ed S); professional school counseling (Ed S); special education (Ed D); workforce education (MAT, Ed D). Electronic applications accepted.

College of Engineering Offers engineering (MS).

College of Environment and Design Offers environmental planning and design (MEPD); historic preservation (MHP); landscape architecture (MLA).

College of Family and Consumer Sciences Offers child and family development (MS); family and consumer sciences (MS, PhD); foods and nutrition (MS, PhD); historical and cultural aspects of dress and textiles (MS); interior environments (MS); international merchandising (PhD); merchandising and international trade (MS); polymer, fiber and textile science (MS); polymer, fiber, and textile sciences (PhD). Electronic applications accepted.

College of Pharmacy Offers clinical and experimental therapeutics (PhD); pharmaceutical and biomedical sciences (MS, PhD); pharmacy (MS, PhD, Pharm D, Certificate); pharmacy care administration (PhD). Electronic applications accepted.

College of Public Health Offers environmental health science (MPH, MS, PhD); health promotion and behavior (MA, MPH, Dr PH, PhD); public health (MA, MPH, MS, Dr PH, PhD, Certificate).

Institute of Gerontology Offers gerontology (Certificate).

College of Veterinary Medicine Offers infectious diseases (PhD); pharmacology (MS, PhD); veterinary medicine (MS, DVM, PhD); veterinary pathology (MS, PhD). Electronic applications accepted.

Eugene P. Odum School of Ecology Offers conservation ecology and sustainable development (MS); ecology (PhD). Electronic applications accepted.

Franklin College of Arts and Sciences Offers analytical chemistry (MS, PhD); anthropology (MA, PhD); applied mathematical science (MAMS); arts and sciences (MA, MAMS, MAT, MFA, MM, MM Ed, MS, DMA, PhD, Certificate); biochemistry and molecular biology (MS, PhD); cellular biology (MS, PhD); classical languages (MA); comparative literature (MA, PhD); computer science (MS, PhD); English (MA, MAT, PhD); French (PhD); genetics (MS, PhD); geography (MA, MS, PhD); geology (MS, PhD); German (MA); Greek (MA); history (MA, PhD); Italian (MA, PhD); Latin (MA); linguistics (MA, PhD); marine sciences (MS, PhD); mathematics (MA, PhD); microbiology (MS, PhD); philosophy (MA, PhD); physics (MS, PhD); plant biology (MS, PhD); Portuguese (MA, PhD); psychology (PhD); religion (MA); romance linguistics (MA); sociology (MA, PhD); Spanish (PhD); statistics (MS, PhD); theatre (MFA, PhD). Electronic applications accepted.

Artificial Intelligence Center Offers artificial intelligence (MS). Electronic applications accepted.

Hugh Hodgson School of Music Offers composition (MM, DMA); conducting (MM, DMA); music (PhD); music education (MM Ed, Ed D); musicology (MA); performance (MM, DMA). Ed D offered jointly with College of Education. Electronic applications accepted.

Institute for Women's Studies Offers women's studies (Certificate).

Lamar Dodd School of Art Offers art (MFA, PhD); art history (MA). Electronic applications accepted.

Grady College of Journalism and Mass Communication Offers journalism and mass communication (MA); mass communication (PhD). Electronic applications accepted.

Institute of Bioinformatics Offers bioinformatics (MS, PhD).

School of Law Offers law (LL M, MSL, JD). Electronic applications accepted.

School of Public and International Affairs Offers international affairs (MA, MIP, PhD); political science (MA, PhD); public administration (MPA, PhD); public and international affairs (MA, MIP, MPA, PhD). Electronic applications accepted.

School of Social Work *Program availability:* Part-time, evening/weekend. Offers social work (MA, MSW, PhD, Certificate). Electronic applications accepted.

Terry College of Business Offers business (Exec MBA, M Acc, MA, MBA, MMR, PhD); business administration (Exec MBA, MBA); economics (MA, PhD). Electronic applications accepted.

J.M. Tull School of Accounting Offers accounting (M Acc). Electronic applications accepted.

Warnell School of Forestry and Natural Resources Offers forestry and natural resources (MFR, MS, PhD). Electronic applications accepted.

UNIVERSITY OF GUAM, Mangilao, GU 96923

General Information Territory-supported, coed, comprehensive institution. *Graduate housing:* Room and/or apartments available on a first-come, first-served basis to single students; on-campus housing not available to married students. Housing application deadline: 5/1. *Research affiliation:* Bernice Pauahi Bishop Museum (science, cultural preservation), Pilar Project, Inc. (salvage of artifacts, archaeology), Cancer Research Center of Hawaii (cancer research).

GRADUATE UNITS

Office of Graduate Studies *Program availability:* Part-time.

College of Liberal Arts and Social Sciences *Program availability:* Part-time. Offers ceramics (MA); English (MA); graphics (MA); liberal arts and social sciences (MA); Micronesian studies (MA); painting (MA).

College of Natural and Applied Sciences Offers environmental science (MS); natural and applied sciences (MS, MSW); social work (MSW); tropical marine biology (MS).

School of Business and Public Administration *Program availability:* Part-time. Offers business administration (PMBA); business and public administration (MPA, PMBA); public administration (MPA).

School of Education *Program availability:* Part-time. Offers administration and supervision (M Ed); counseling (MA); education (M Ed, MA); language and literacy (M Ed); secondary education (M Ed); special education (M Ed); teaching English to speakers of other languages (M Ed).

UNIVERSITY OF GUELPH, Guelph, ON N1G 2W1, Canada

General Information Province-supported, coed, university. *Graduate housing:* Rooms and/or apartments available to single and married students. Housing application deadline: 5/28.

GRADUATE UNITS

Graduate Studies *Program availability:* Part-time, evening/weekend, online learning. Offers biophysics (M Sc, PhD). Electronic applications accepted.

Collaborative International Development Studies *Program availability:* Part-time. Offers international development studies (M Eng, M Sc, MA, MBA, PhD).

College of Arts *Program availability:* Part-time. Offers arts (MA, MFA, PhD); drama (MA); English (MA); European studies (MA); French studies (MA); history (MA, PhD); literary studies/theatre studies in English (PhD); philosophy (MA, PhD); studio art (MFA).

College of Biological Science *Program availability:* Part-time. Offers biochemistry (M Sc, PhD); biological science (M Sc, PhD); biophysics (M Sc, PhD); botany (M Sc, PhD); microbiology (M Sc, PhD); molecular biology and genetics (M Sc, PhD); nutritional sciences (M Sc, PhD); zoology (M Sc, PhD). Electronic applications accepted.

College of Management and Economics Offers economics (MA, PhD); food and agribusiness management (MBA); hospitality and tourism management (MBA); leadership (MA); management and economics (M Sc, MA, MBA, PhD); marketing and consumer studies (M Sc).

College of Physical and Engineering Science *Program availability:* Part-time. Offers applied computer science (M Sc); applied mathematics (PhD); applied statistics (PhD); biological engineering (M Eng, M Sc, MA Sc, PhD); chemistry and biochemistry (M Sc, PhD); computer science (PhD); engineering systems and computing (M Eng, M Sc, MA Sc, PhD); environmental engineering (M Eng, M Sc, MA Sc, PhD); mathematics and statistics (M Sc); physical and engineering science (M Eng, M Sc, MA Sc, PhD); physics (M Sc, PhD); water resources engineering (M Eng, M Sc, MA Sc, PhD).

College of Social and Applied Human Sciences *Program availability:* Part-time. Offers anthropology (MA); applied nutrition (MAN); applied social psychology (MA, PhD); clinical psychology: applied development emphasis (PhD); clinical psychology: applied developmental emphasis (MA); comparative politics (MA); crime and criminal justice policy (MA); criminology and criminal justice policy (MA); family relations and human development (M Sc, PhD); geography (M Sc, MA, PhD); industrial/organizational psychology (MA, PhD); international development (MA); neuroscience and applied cognitive science (MA, PhD); political science (MA); public policy and public administration (MA); social and applied human sciences (M Sc, MA, MAN, PhD); sociology (MA, PhD); the Americas (Canada emphasis) (MA).

Ontario Agricultural College *Program availability:* Part-time, online learning. Offers agricultural economics (M Sc, PhD); agriculture (M Sc, MLA, PhD, Diploma); animal and poultry science (M Sc, PhD); aquaculture (M Sc); atmospheric science (M Sc, PhD); capacity development and extension (M Sc); entomology (M Sc, PhD); environmental and agricultural earth sciences (M Sc, PhD); environmental microbiology and biotechnology (M Sc, PhD); environmental toxicology (M Sc, PhD); food safety and quality assurance (M Sc); food science (M Sc, PhD); international rural planning and development (M Sc); land resources management (M Sc, PhD); landscape architecture (MLA); plant agriculture (M Sc, PhD); plant and forest systems (M Sc, PhD); plant pathology (M Sc, PhD); rural planning and development (M Sc); rural planning and development in Canada (M Sc); rural studies (PhD); soil science (M Sc, PhD).

Ontario Veterinary College Offers toxicology (M Sc, PhD); veterinary medicine (M Sc, DV Sc, PhD, Diploma).

Graduate Programs in Veterinary Sciences Offers anatomic pathology (DV Sc, Diploma); anesthesiology (M Sc, DV Sc); cardiology (DV Sc, Diploma); clinical pathology (Diploma); clinical studies (Diploma); comparative pathology (M Sc, PhD); dermatology (M Sc); diagnostic imaging (M Sc, DV Sc); emergency/critical care (M Sc, DV Sc, Diploma); epidemiology (M Sc, DV Sc, PhD); health management (DV Sc); immunology (M Sc, PhD); laboratory animal science (DV Sc); medicine (M Sc, DV Sc); morphology (M Sc, DV Sc, PhD); neurology (M Sc, DV Sc); neuroscience (M Sc, DV Sc, PhD); ophthalmology (M Sc, DV Sc); pathology (M Sc, PhD, Diploma); pharmacology (M Sc, DV Sc, PhD); physiology (M Sc, DV Sc, PhD); population medicine and health management (M Sc); surgery (M Sc, DV Sc); swine health management (M Sc); theriogenology (M Sc, DV Sc); toxicology (M Sc, DV Sc, PhD); veterinary infectious diseases (M Sc, PhD); veterinary sciences (M Sc, DV Sc, PhD, Diploma); zoo animal/wildlife medicine (DV Sc).

UNIVERSITY OF HARTFORD, West Hartford, CT 06117-1599

General Information Independent, coed, comprehensive institution. CGS member. *Graduate housing:* On-campus housing not available.

GRADUATE UNITS

Barney School of Business *Program availability:* Part-time, evening/weekend. Offers business (MBA, MSAT, Certificate); business administration (MBA); professional accounting (Certificate); taxation (MSAT). Electronic applications accepted.

College of Arts and Sciences *Program availability:* Part-time, evening/weekend. Offers arts and sciences (MA, MS, Psy D); biology (MS); clinical practices (MA, Psy D); communication (MA); general experimental psychology (MA); neuroscience (MS); organizational behavior (MS); psychology (MA); school psychology (MS). Electronic applications accepted.

College of Education, Nursing, and Health Professions *Program availability:* Part-time, evening/weekend. Offers administration and supervision (CAGS); community/public health nursing (MSN); counseling (M Ed, MS, Sixth Year Certificate); early childhood education (M Ed); education, nursing, and health professions (M Ed, MS, MSN, MSPT, DPT, Ed D, CAGS, Sixth Year Certificate); educational leadership (Ed D, CAGS); educational technology (M Ed); elementary education (M Ed); nursing education (MSN); nursing management (MSN); physical therapy (MSPT, DPT). Electronic applications accepted.

College of Engineering, Technology and Architecture *Program availability:* Part-time, evening/weekend. Offers architecture (M Arch); engineering (M Eng); engineering, technology and architecture (M Arch, M Eng). Electronic applications accepted.

Hartford Art School *Program availability:* Part-time. Offers art (MFA). Electronic applications accepted.

The Hartt School *Program availability:* Part-time. Offers choral conducting (MM Ed); composition (MM, DMA, Artist Diploma, Diploma); conducting (MM, DMA, Artist Diploma, Diploma); early childhood education (MM Ed); instrumental conducting (MM Ed); Kodály (MM Ed); music (CAGS); music education (DMA, PhD); music history (MM); music theory (MM); pedagogy (MM Ed); performance (MM, MM Ed, DMA, Artist Diploma, Diploma); research (MM Ed); technology (MM Ed). Electronic applications accepted.

UNIVERSITY OF HAWAII AT HILO, Hilo, HI 96720-4091

General Information State-supported, coed, comprehensive institution. *Graduate housing:* Rooms and/or apartments available on a first-come, first-served basis to single and married students.

GRADUATE UNITS

Program in Clinical Psychopharmacology Offers clinical psychopharmacology (MS). Electronic applications accepted.

Program in Counseling Psychology Offers counseling psychology (MA).

Program in Education *Program availability:* Part-time, evening/weekend. Offers education (M Ed). Electronic applications accepted.

Program in Hawaiian and Indigenous Language and Culture Revitalization Offers Hawaiian and indigenous language and culture revitalization (PhD). Electronic applications accepted.

Program in Hawaiian Language and Literature Offers Hawaiian language and literature (MA). Electronic applications accepted.

Program in Indigenous Language and Culture Education Offers indigenous language and culture education (MA). Electronic applications accepted.

Program in Nursing Practice Offers nursing practice (DNP). Electronic applications accepted.

Program in Pharmaceutical Sciences Offers pharmaceutical sciences (PhD). Electronic applications accepted.

Program in Pharmacy Offers pharmacy (Pharm D). Electronic applications accepted.

Program in Teaching Offers teaching (MA). Electronic applications accepted.

Program in Tropical Conservation Biology and Environmental Science Offers tropical conservation biology and environmental science (MS). Electronic applications accepted.

UNIVERSITY OF HAWAII AT MANOA, Honolulu, HI 96822

General Information State-supported, coed, university. CGS member. *Graduate housing:* Rooms and/or apartments available to single and married students. Housing application deadline: 5/1. *Research affiliation:* Hawaiian Volcano Observatory (geology, geophysics), Honolulu Academy of Arts, East-West Center (communication, geography, economics), U.S. Geological Survey (USGS), Hawaii Agriculture Research Center, Bernice Pauahi Bishop Museum (anthropology, zoology).

GRADUATE UNITS

John A. Burns School of Medicine *Program availability:* Part-time. Offers cell and molecular biology (MS, PhD); communication sciences and disorders (MS); developmental and reproductive biology (MS, PhD); epidemiology (PhD); global health and population studies (Graduate Certificate); medicine (MPH, MS, Dr PH, MD, PhD, Graduate Certificate); public health (MPH, MS, Dr PH).

Graduate Programs in Biomedical Sciences *Program availability:* Part-time. Offers biomedical sciences (MS, PhD); tropical medicine (MS, PhD).

Office of Graduate Education *Program availability:* Part-time. Offers communication and information sciences (PhD); international cultural studies (Graduate Certificate). Electronic applications accepted.

College of Arts and Humanities *Program availability:* Part-time. Offers American studies (MA, PhD); art history (MA); arts and humanities (M Mus, MA, MFA, PhD, Graduate Certificate); communicology (MA); dance (MA, MFA); historic preservation (Graduate Certificate); history (MA, PhD); museum studies (Graduate Certificate); music (M Mus, MA, PhD); philosophy (MA, PhD); religion (MA); theatre (MA, MFA, PhD); visual arts (MFA).

College of Education *Program availability:* Part-time, evening/weekend. Offers curriculum and instruction (PhD); curriculum studies (M Ed); disability and diversity studies (Graduate Certificate); early childhood education (M Ed); education (M Ed, M Ed T, MS, Ed D, PhD, Graduate Certificate); educational administration (M Ed); educational foundations (M Ed); educational policy studies (PhD); educational psychology (PhD); educational technology (M Ed); exceptionalities (PhD); kinesiology (MS, PhD); learning design and technology (PhD); professional practice (Ed D); special education (M Ed); teaching (M Ed T).

College of Engineering *Program availability:* Part-time. Offers civil and environmental engineering (MS, PhD); electrical engineering (MS, PhD); engineering (MS, PhD); mechanical engineering (MS, PhD).

College of Languages, Linguistics and Literature *Program availability:* Part-time. Offers Chinese (MA, PhD); English (MA, PhD); English as a second language (MA, Graduate Certificate); French (MA); Japanese (MA, PhD); Korean (MA, PhD); languages, linguistics and literature (MA, PhD, Graduate Certificate); linguistics (MA, PhD); second language acquisition (PhD); Spanish (MA).

College of Natural Sciences *Program availability:* Part-time. Offers advanced library and information science (Graduate Certificate); astronomy (MS, PhD); botany (MS, PhD); chemistry (MS, PhD); computer science (MS, PhD); library and information science (MLI Sc, Graduate Certificate); mathematics (MA, PhD); microbiology (MS, PhD); natural sciences (MA, MLI Sc, MS, PhD, Graduate Certificate); physics (MS, PhD); zoology (MS, PhD).

College of Social Sciences *Program availability:* Part-time, evening/weekend. Offers advanced women's studies (Graduate Certificate); anthropology (MA, PhD); clinical psychology (PhD); communication (MA); community and cultural psychology (PhD); community and culture (MA); community planning (MURP); conflict resolution (Graduate Certificate); disaster management and humanitarian assistance (Graduate Certificate); disaster preparedness and emergency management (Graduate Certificate); economics (MA, PhD); environmental planning and sustainability (MURP); geography (MA, PhD); international development planning (MURP); land use, transportation and infrastructure planning (MURP); ocean policy (Graduate Certificate); planning studies (Graduate Certificate); political science (MA, PhD); psychology (MA, PhD, Graduate Certificate); public administration (MPA, Graduate Certificate); public policy (Graduate Certificate); social sciences (MA, MPA, MURP, PhD, Graduate Certificate); sociology (MA, PhD); telecommunication and information resource management (Graduate Certificate); urban and regional planning (PhD, Graduate Certificate).

College of Tropical Agriculture and Human Resources *Program availability:* Part-time. Offers animal sciences (MS); bioengineering (MS); entomology (MS, PhD); food science (MS); molecular bioscience and bioengineering (MS); molecular biosciences and bioengineering (PhD); natural resources and environmental management (MS, PhD); nutrition (PhD); nutritional sciences (MS, PhD); tropical agriculture and human resources (MS, PhD); tropical plant and soil sciences (MS, PhD); tropical plant pathology (MS, PhD).

Hawai'inuiakea School of Hawaiian Knowledge *Program availability:* Part-time. Offers Hawaiian (MA); Hawaiian studies (MA).

School of Nursing and Dental Hygiene *Program availability:* Part-time, online learning. Offers clinical nurse specialist (MS); nurse practitioner (MS); nursing (PhD, Graduate Certificate); nursing administration (MS).

School of Ocean and Earth Science and Technology *Program availability:* Part-time. Offers high-pressure geophysics and geochemistry (MS, PhD); hydrogeology and engineering geology (MS, PhD); marine biology (MS, PhD); marine geology and geophysics (MS, PhD); meteorology (MS, PhD); ocean and earth science and technology (MS, PhD); ocean and resources engineering (MS, PhD); oceanography (MS, PhD); planetary geosciences and remote sensing (MS, PhD); seismology and solid-earth geophysics (MS, PhD); volcanology, petrology, and geochemistry (MS, PhD).

School of Pacific and Asian Studies *Program availability:* Part-time. Offers Asian studies (MA, Graduate Certificate); Chinese studies (Graduate Certificate); Japanese studies (Graduate Certificate); Korean studies (Graduate Certificate); Pacific and Asian studies (MA, Graduate Certificate); Pacific Island studies (MA, Graduate Certificate); Philippine studies (Graduate Certificate); Southeast Asian studies (Graduate Certificate).

School of Social Work *Program availability:* Part-time. Offers social welfare (PhD); social work (MSW).

School of Travel Industry Management *Program availability:* Part-time. Offers travel industry management (MS). Electronic applications accepted.

Shidler College of Business *Program availability:* Part-time, evening/weekend. Offers accounting (M Acc); accounting law (M Acc); Asian business studies (MBA); Asian finance (PhD); business (EMBA, M Acc, MBA, MHRM, MS, PhD, Graduate Certificate); Chinese business studies (MBA); decision sciences (MBA); entrepreneurship (MBA, Graduate Certificate); executive business administration (EMBA); finance (MBA); finance and banking (MBA); global information technology management (PhD); human resources management (MHRM); information management (MBA); information systems (M Acc); information technology (MBA); international accounting (PhD); international business (MBA); international marketing (PhD); international organization and strategy (PhD); Japanese business studies (MBA); marketing (MBA); organizational behavior (MBA); organizational management (MBA); real estate (MBA); student-designed track (MBA); taxation (M Acc); Vietnam focused business administration (EMBA).

School of Architecture *Program availability:* Part-time. Offers architecture (D Arch).

William S. Richardson School of Law Offers law (LL M, JD, Graduate Certificate).

UNIVERSITY OF HOLY CROSS, New Orleans, LA 70131-7399

General Information Independent-religious, coed, comprehensive institution. *Enrollment:* 180 full-time matriculated graduate/professional students (140 women), 153 part-time matriculated graduate/professional students (127 women). *Enrollment by degree level:* 242 master's, 91 doctoral. *Graduate faculty:* 22 full-time (11 women), 16 part-time/adjunct (8 women). *Tuition:* Full-time $10,890; part-time $605 per credit hour. *Required fees:* $1624; $812 per semester. One-time fee: $50. *Graduate housing:* On-campus housing not available. *Student services:* Career counseling, free psychological counseling, teacher training. *Library facilities:* Blaine Kern Library.

Computer facilities: A campuswide network can be accessed.
Website: http://www.uhcno.edu/

General Application Contact: Ashley Maxwell, Graduate Admissions Counselor, 504-398-2341, Fax: 504-391-1182, E-mail: armaxwell-admis@uhcno.edu.

GRADUATE UNITS

Graduate Programs Students: 67 full-time (55 women), 69 part-time (55 women); includes 51 minority (46 Black or African American, non-Hispanic/Latino; 2 American Indian or Alaska Native, non-Hispanic/Latino; 1 Asian, non-Hispanic/Latino; 2 Hispanic/Latino). Average age 30. 20 applicants, 50% accepted. *Faculty:* 7 full-time (4 women), 8 part-time/adjunct (3 women). Expenses: Contact institution. *Financial support:* Federal Work-Study and tuition waivers (partial) available. Support available to part-time students. Financial award application deadline: 6/1. In 2017, 28 degrees awarded. *Program availability:* Part-time, evening/weekend, online learning. Offers biomedical sciences (MS); Catholic theology (MA); counseling (MA, PhD); educational leadership (M Ed); executive leadership (Ed D); management (MS); teaching and learning (M Ed). *Application deadline:* For fall admission, 9/1 for domestic students. *Application fee:* $15. *Application Contact:* Anne-Katherine Lene, Director of Student Enrollment, 504-394-7744 Ext. 110, Fax: 504-391-2421, E-mail: aklene@olhcc.edu. *Dean of Humanities, Education, and Counseling,* Dr. Myles Seghers, 504-394-7744 Ext. 214, Fax: 504-391-2421, E-mail: mseghers@olhcc.edu.

UNIVERSITY OF HOUSTON, Houston, TX 77204

General Information State-supported, coed, university. CGS member. *Graduate housing:* Rooms and/or apartments available on a first-come, first-served basis to single and married students. *Research affiliation:* Keck Consortium.

GRADUATE UNITS

Bauer College of Business *Program availability:* Part-time, evening/weekend. Offers accountancy (MS Accy); accountancy and taxation (PhD); business (MBA, MS, MS Accy, PhD); decision and information sciences (PhD); finance (MS); management (PhD); marketing (PhD). Electronic applications accepted.

College of Education *Program availability:* Part-time. Offers administration and supervision (M Ed, Ed D); administration and supervision - higher education (M Ed); counseling (M Ed); counseling psychology (PhD); curriculum and instruction (M Ed, Ed D); education (M Ed, Ed D, PhD); educational psychology (M Ed); higher education (M Ed); historical, social, and cultural foundations of education (M Ed); professional leadership (Ed D); school psychology (PhD); school psychology and individual differences (PhD); special education (M Ed). Electronic applications accepted.

College of Liberal Arts and Social Sciences *Program availability:* Part-time, online learning. Offers anthropology (MA); applied economics (MA); applied English linguistics (MA); clinical psychology (PhD); communication sciences and disorders (MA); creative writing (MFA); creative writing and literature (MA, PhD); developmental psychology (PhD); economics (MA, PhD); English (MA, PhD); exercise science (MS); Hispanic literature and linguistics (PhD); history (MA, PhD); human nutrition (MS); human space exploration sciences (MS); industrial/organizational psychology (PhD); kinesiology (PhD); liberal arts and social sciences (M Ed, MA, MFA, MM, MPP, MS, DMA, PhD); philosophy (MA); physical education (M Ed); political science (MA, PhD); psychology (MA); public administration (MA); social psychology (PhD); sociology (MA); Spanish (MA, PhD); world cultures and literatures (MA). Electronic applications accepted.

Hobby School of Public Affairs Students: 30 full-time (18 women), 5 part-time (3 women); includes 17 minority (9 Black or African American, non-Hispanic/Latino; 1 American Indian or Alaska Native, non-Hispanic/Latino; 1 Asian, non-Hispanic/Latino; 4 Hispanic/Latino; 2 Two or more races, non-Hispanic/Latino). Average age 25. 30 applicants, 83% accepted, 21 enrolled. *Faculty:* 5 full-time (0 women), 4 part-time/adjunct (2 women). Expenses: Contact institution. *Financial support:* In 2017–18, 35 students received support. Career-related internships or fieldwork, Federal Work-Study, institutionally sponsored loans, scholarships/grants, traineeships, health care benefits, and unspecified assistantships available. Support available to part-time students. Financial award application deadline: 6/15; financial award applicants required to submit FAFSA. In 2017, 9 master's awarded. *Program availability:* Part-time. Offers public policy (MPP). *Application deadline:* For fall admission, 6/15 for domestic and international students. Applications are processed on a rolling basis. *Application fee:* $75 ($125 for international students). Electronic applications accepted. *Application Contact:* Scott Mason, Program Manager II, 713-743-5572, E-mail: smason@uh.edu. *Executive Director,* Dr. Jim Granato, 713-743-3887, Fax: 713-743-3978, E-mail: jgranato@uh.edu.

Jack J. Valenti School of Communication *Program availability:* Part-time. Offers health communication (MA); mass communication studies (MA); public relations studies (MA); speech communication (MA). Electronic applications accepted.

College of Natural Sciences and Mathematics *Program availability:* Part-time, online learning. Offers applied mathematics (MS); atmospheric science (PhD); biochemistry (MA, PhD); biology (MA); chemistry (MA, PhD); computer science (MA, PhD); geology (MA, PhD); geophysics (PhD); mathematics (MA, PhD); natural sciences and mathematics (MA, MS, PhD); physics (MA, PhD). Electronic applications accepted.

College of Nursing Students: 29 full-time (24 women); includes 15 minority (6 Black or African American, non-Hispanic/Latino; 5 Asian, non-Hispanic/Latino; 4 Hispanic/Latino), 3 international. Average age 37. 36 applicants, 61% accepted, 15 enrolled. *Faculty:* 13 full-time (12 women). Expenses: Contact institution. *Financial support:* In 2017–18, 19 students received support. Federal Work-Study, scholarships/grants, and unspecified assistantships available. Support available to part-time students. Financial award application deadline: 5/1; financial award applicants required to submit FAFSA. In 2017, 14 master's awarded. Offers family nurse practitioner (MSN); nursing administration (MSN); nursing education (MSN). *Application deadline:* For fall admission, 7/1 for domestic students, 6/1 for international students; for spring admission, 12/1 for domestic students, 10/1 for international students. *Application fee:* $75. Electronic applications accepted. *Application Contact:* Tammy N. Whatley, Student Affairs Director, 832-842-8220, E-mail: tnwhatley@uh.edu. *Dean,* Dr. Kathryn Tart, 832-842-8200, E-mail: kmtart@uh.edu.

College of Optometry *Program availability:* Part-time. Offers optometry (MS, OD, PhD); physiological optics (MS, PhD). Electronic applications accepted.

College of Pharmacy *Program availability:* Part-time. Offers pharmaceutics (MSPHR, PhD); pharmacology (MSPHR, PhD); pharmacy (Pharm D); pharmacy administration (MSPHR, PhD). Electronic applications accepted.

College of Technology *Program availability:* Part-time. Offers construction management (MS); engineering technology (MS); future studies in commerce (MS); human resources development (MS); information security (MS); network communications (M Tech); supply chain and logistics technology (MS); technology (M Tech, MS); technology project management (MS). Electronic applications accepted.

Conrad N. Hilton College of Hotel and Restaurant Management *Program availability:* Part-time. Offers hospitality management (MS). Electronic applications accepted.

Cullen College of Engineering *Program availability:* Part-time. Offers biomedical engineering (PhD); chemical engineering (MCHE, PhD); civil engineering (MCE, PhD); electrical engineering (MEE, MSEE, PhD); engineering (M Pet E, MCE, MCHE, MEE, MIE, MME, MSEE, MSME, PhD); industrial engineering (MIE, PhD); mechanical engineering (MME, MSME, PhD); petroleum engineering (M Pet E).

Gerald D. Hines College of Architecture and Design Students: 92 full-time (40 women), 6 part-time (2 women); includes 23 minority (1 Black or African American, non-Hispanic/Latino; 1 American Indian or Alaska Native, non-Hispanic/Latino; 9 Asian, non-Hispanic/Latino; 9 Hispanic/Latino; 3 Two or more races, non-Hispanic/Latino), 20 international. Average age 28. 192 applicants, 45% accepted, 47 enrolled. *Faculty:* 15 full-time (4 women), 13 part-time/adjunct (3 women). Expenses: Contact institution. *Financial support:* In 2017–18, 15 students received support, including 2 research assistantships with partial tuition reimbursements available (averaging $7,720 per year), 11 teaching assistantships with partial tuition reimbursements available (averaging $5,264 per year); career-related internships or fieldwork, Federal Work-Study, institutionally sponsored loans, scholarships/grants, health care benefits, and unspecified assistantships also available. Support available to part-time students. Financial award application deadline: 2/1. In 2017, 21 master's awarded. Offers architectural studies (MA); architecture (M Arch, MS); industrial design (MS). *Application deadline:* For fall admission, 2/1 priority date for domestic students, 2/1 for international students. Applications are processed on a rolling basis. *Application fee:* $50. Electronic applications accepted. *Application Contact:* Trang Phan, Assistant Dean, 713-743-2400, Fax: 713-743-2358, E-mail: tphan@uh.edu. *Dean,* Patricia Belton Oliver, 713-743-2400, Fax: 713-743-2358, E-mail: poliver@central.uh.edu.

Graduate College of Social Work *Program availability:* Part-time. Offers social work (MSW, PhD).

Kathrine G. McGovern College of the Arts Offers arts (MA, MFA, MM, DMA).

Moores School of Music *Program availability:* Part-time. Offers accompanying and chamber music (MM); applied music (MM); composition (MM); music education (DMA); music theory (MM); performance (DMA). Electronic applications accepted.

School of Art Offers art history (MA); interdisciplinary practice and emerging forms (MFA); painting (MFA); studio art (MFA). Electronic applications accepted.

School of Theatre and Dance *Program availability:* Part-time. Offers theatre (MA, MFA). Electronic applications accepted.

University of Houston Law Center Students: 695 full-time (331 women), 120 part-time (55 women); includes 319 minority (62 Black or African American, non-Hispanic/Latino; 10 American Indian or Alaska Native, non-Hispanic/Latino; 73 Asian, non-Hispanic/Latino; 172 Hispanic/Latino; 2 Native Hawaiian or other Pacific Islander, non-Hispanic/Latino), 33 international. Average age 26. 2,751 applicants, 33% accepted, 227 enrolled. *Faculty:* 58 full-time (23 women), 130 part-time/adjunct (36 women). Expenses: Contact institution. *Financial support:* In 2017–18, 442 students received support, including 20 fellowships (averaging $2,980 per year); research assistantships, career-related internships or fieldwork, Federal Work-Study, scholarships/grants, and tuition waivers also available. Support available to part-time students. Financial award application deadline: 3/15; financial award applicants required to submit FAFSA. In 2017, 75 master's, 231 doctorates awarded. *Program availability:* Part-time, evening/weekend. Offers energy, environment, and natural resources (LL M); health law (LL M); intellectual property and information law (LL M); international law (LL M); law (JD); tax law (LL M); U.S. law (LL M). *Application deadline:* For fall admission, 2/15 for domestic and international students. Applications are processed on a rolling basis. *Application fee:* $0. Electronic applications accepted. *Application Contact:* Pilar Mensah,

Assistant Dean for Admissions, 713-743-2280, Fax: 713-743-2194, E-mail: lpmensah@central.uh.edu. *Dean and Professor of Law,* Leonard M. Baynes, 713-743-2100, Fax: 713-743-2122, E-mail: lbaynes@central.uh.edu.

UNIVERSITY OF HOUSTON–CLEAR LAKE, Houston, TX 77058-1002

General Information State-supported, coed, comprehensive institution. CGS member. *Graduate housing:* Rooms and/or apartments available on a first-come, first-served basis to single students and available to married students. *Research affiliation:* NASA–Johnson Space Center (computer science, computer engineering), Baylor College of Medicine (life sciences), Schlumberger (ergonomic software).

GRADUATE UNITS

School of Business *Program availability:* Part-time, evening/weekend. Offers accounting (MS); business (MA, MBA, MHA, MS); business administration (MBA); environmental management (MS); finance (MS); healthcare administration (MHA); human resource management (MA); management information systems (MS); professional accounting (MS). Electronic applications accepted.

School of Education *Program availability:* Part-time, evening/weekend. Offers counseling (MS); curriculum and instruction (MS); early childhood education (MS); education (MS, Ed D); educational leadership (Ed D); educational management (MS); instructional technology (MS); multicultural studies (MS); reading (MS); school library and information science (MS). Electronic applications accepted.

School of Human Sciences and Humanities *Program availability:* Part-time, evening/weekend. Offers behavioral sciences (MA); clinical psychology (MA); criminology (MA); cross cultural studies (MA); family therapy (MA); fitness and human performance (MA); history (MA); human sciences and humanities (MA); humanities (MA); literature (MA); school psychology (MA).

School of Science and Computer Engineering *Program availability:* Part-time, evening/weekend. Offers biological sciences (MS); biotechnology (MS); chemistry (MS); computer engineering (MS); computer information systems (MS); computer science (MS); environmental science (MS); mathematical sciences (MS); physics (MS); science and computer engineering (MS); software engineering (MS); statistics (MS); system engineering (MS).

UNIVERSITY OF HOUSTON–DOWNTOWN, Houston, TX 77002

General Information State-supported, coed, comprehensive institution. *Enrollment:* 13,919 graduate, professional, and undergraduate students; 131 full-time matriculated graduate/professional students (75 women), 1,381 part-time matriculated graduate/professional students (820 women). *Enrollment by degree level:* 1,512 master's. *Graduate faculty:* 88 full-time (36 women), 18 part-time/adjunct (7 women). Tuition, state resident: full-time $6030; part-time $335 per credit hour. Tuition, nonresident: full-time $12,600; part-time $700 per credit hour. *Required fees:* $1166; $970 per credit hour. Tuition and fees vary according to program. *Graduate housing:* On-campus housing not available. *Student services:* Campus employment opportunities, campus safety program, career counseling, child daycare facilities, exercise/wellness program, free psychological counseling, international student services, low-cost health insurance, multicultural affairs office, services for students with disabilities, teacher training. *Library facilities:* W. I. Dykes Library. *Collection:* Books: 188,649 (physical), 531,458 (digital/electronic); Serial titles: 88,715 (digital/electronic). Weekly public service hours: 85; study areas open 24 hours, 5–7 days a week; students can reserve study rooms.

Computer facilities: 613 computers available on campus for general student use. A campuswide network can be accessed from off campus. Online class registration, electronic classrooms and labs - 2,229 are available.
Website: http://www.uhd.edu/

General Application Contact: Ceshia Love, Director of Admissions, 713-221-8093, Fax: 713-221-8658, E-mail: gradadmissions@uhd.edu.

GRADUATE UNITS

College of Humanities and Social Sciences Students: 37 full-time (22 women), 106 part-time (80 women); includes 95 minority (58 Black or African American, non-Hispanic/Latino; 2 American Indian or Alaska Native, non-Hispanic/Latino; 3 Asian, non-Hispanic/Latino; 32 Hispanic/Latino), 2 international. Average age 34. 61 applicants, 92% accepted, 46 enrolled. *Faculty:* 14 full-time (5 women), 3 part-time/adjunct (0 women). Expenses: Contact institution. *Financial support:* Federal Work-Study and scholarships/grants available. Financial award application deadline: 4/1; financial award applicants required to submit FAFSA. In 2017, 31 master's awarded. *Program availability:* Part-time, evening/weekend, 100% online. Offers humanities and social sciences (MA, MS); non-profit management (MA); rhetoric and composition (MA); technical communication (MS). *Application fee:* $35 ($80 for international students). Electronic applications accepted. *Application Contact:* Ceshia Love, Director, Admissions, 713-221-8093, Fax: 713-223-7408, E-mail: gradadmissions@uhd.edu. *Dean,* Dr. DoVeanna Fulton, 713-221-8009, Fax: 713-223-7465, E-mail: fultond@uhd.edu.

College of Public Service Students: 29 full-time (20 women), 88 part-time (76 women); includes 89 minority (39 Black or African American, non-Hispanic/Latino; 1 American Indian or Alaska Native, non-Hispanic/Latino; 4 Asian, non-Hispanic/Latino; 45 Hispanic/Latino), 1 international. Average age 35. 58 applicants, 76% accepted, 29 enrolled. *Faculty:* 25 full-time (14 women), 2 part-time/adjunct (0 women). Expenses: Contact institution. *Financial support:* Federal Work-Study and scholarships/grants available. Financial award application deadline: 4/1; financial award applicants required to submit FAFSA. In 2017, 26 master's awarded. *Program availability:* Part-time, evening/weekend, 100% online. Offers criminal justice and social work (MS); curriculum and instruction (MAT); public service (MAT, MS). *Application fee:* $35 ($60 for international students). Electronic applications accepted. *Application Contact:* Ceshia Love, Director of Admissions, 713-221-8093, Fax: 713-223-7408, E-mail: gradadmissions@uhd.edu. *Interim Dean,* Dr. Leigh Van Horn, 713-221-8991, Fax: 713-226-5274, E-mail: vanhornl@uhd.edu.

College of Sciences and Technology Students: 60 full-time (30 women), 55 part-time (30 women); includes 67 minority (18 Black or African American, non-Hispanic/Latino; 32 Asian, non-Hispanic/Latino; 17 Hispanic/Latino), 19 international. Average age 32. 63 applicants, 90% accepted, 47 enrolled. *Faculty:* 10 full-time (3 women). Expenses: Contact institution. *Financial support:* Federal Work-Study and scholarships/grants available. Financial award application deadline: 4/1; financial award applicants required to submit FAFSA. In 2017, 5 master's awarded. *Program availability:* Part-time, evening/weekend. Offers data analytics (MS). *Application deadline:* For fall admission, 7/15 for domestic and international students. *Application fee:* $35 ($60 for international students). Electronic applications accepted. *Application Contact:* Ceshia Love, Director of Admissions, 713-221-8093, Fax: 713-221-8658, E-mail: gradadmissions@uhd.edu. *Dean,* Dr. J. Akif Uzman, 713-221-8019, E-mail: st_dean@uhd.edu.

Marilyn Davies College of Business Students: 5 full-time (3 women), 1,128 part-time (632 women); includes 870 minority (413 Black or African American, non-Hispanic/Latino; 3 American Indian or Alaska Native, non-Hispanic/Latino; 144 Asian, non-Hispanic/Latino; 310 Hispanic/Latino), 33 international. Average age 38. 440 applicants, 88% accepted, 323 enrolled. *Faculty:* 39 full-time (14 women), 13 part-time/adjunct (7 women). Expenses: Contact institution. *Financial support:* Federal Work-Study and scholarships/grants available. Financial award application deadline: 4/1; financial award applicants required to submit FAFSA. In 2017, 322 master's awarded. *Program availability:* Part-time, evening/weekend, 100% online. Offers accounting (MBA); business (MBA, MSM); finance (MBA); human resource management (MBA); international business (MBA); investment management (MBA); leadership (MBA); project management and process improvement (MBA); sales management and business development (MBA); security management (MSM); supply chain management (MBA). *Application deadline:* For fall admission, 7/15 for domestic and international students. *Application fee:* $35 ($60 for international students). Electronic applications accepted. *Application Contact:* Ceshia Love, Director of Admissions, 713-221-8093, Fax: 713-223-7408, E-mail: gradadmissions@uhd.edu. *Dean,* Dr. Charles E. Gengler, 713-221-8179, Fax: 713-221-8675.

UNIVERSITY OF HOUSTON–VICTORIA, Victoria, TX 77901-4450

General Information State-supported, coed, upper-level institution. *Graduate housing:* On-campus housing not available.

GRADUATE UNITS

School of Arts and Sciences *Program availability:* Part-time, evening/weekend, online learning. Offers arts and sciences (MA, MAIS, MFA, MS); biological sciences (MS); biomedical sciences (MS); computer information systems (MS); computer science (MS); counseling psychology (MA); creative writing (MFA); forensic psychology (MA); forensic science (MS); interdisciplinary studies (MAIS); publishing (MS); school psychology (MA). Electronic applications accepted.

School of Business Administration *Program availability:* Part-time, evening/weekend, online learning. Offers accounting (MBA); economic development and entrepreneurship (MS); finance (GMBA, MBA); general business (MBA); international business (MBA); management (GMBA, MBA); marketing (MBA). Electronic applications accepted.

School of Education, Health Professions and Human Development *Program availability:* Part-time, evening/weekend, online learning. Offers administration and supervision (M Ed); adult and higher education (M Ed); counselor education (M Ed); curriculum and instruction (M Ed); dyslexia education (Certificate); educational technology (M Ed); special education (M Ed). Electronic applications accepted.

UNIVERSITY OF IDAHO, Moscow, ID 83844-2282

General Information State-supported, coed, university. CGS member. *Enrollment:* 12,072 graduate, professional, and undergraduate students; 1,251 full-time matriculated graduate/professional students (548 women), 708 part-time matriculated graduate/professional students (319 women). *Enrollment by degree level:* 1,204 master's, 755 doctoral. *Graduate faculty:* 443 full-time (142 women), 40 part-time/adjunct (19 women). Tuition, state resident: full-time $6722; part-time $430 per credit hour. Tuition, nonresident: full-time $23,046; part-time $1337 per credit hour. *Required fees:* $2142; $63 per credit hour. *Graduate housing:* Rooms and/or apartments available on a first-come, first-served basis to single and married students. Typical cost: $8670 (including board) for single students. *Student services:* Campus employment opportunities, campus safety program, career counseling, exercise/wellness program, free psychological counseling, grant writing training, international student services, low-cost health insurance, multicultural affairs office, services for students with disabilities, writing training. *Library facilities:* University of Idaho Library plus 1 other. *Collection:* Books: 1.5 million (physical), 876,025 (digital/electronic); Serial titles: 143,154 (physical), 189,954 (digital/electronic). *Research affiliation:* Battelle Energy Alliance LLC (energy research), Columbia River Inter-Tribal Fish Commission (fish research), J. A. and Kathryn Albertson Foundation, Inc. (education), Howard Hughes Medical Institute (undergraduate research education), M. J. Murdock Charitable Trust (equipment support), Prograno (plant sciences).

Computer facilities: Computer purchase and lease plans are available. 510 computers available on campus for general student use. A campuswide network can be accessed from student residence rooms and from off campus. Online class registration is available.
Website: http://www.uidaho.edu/

General Application Contact: Sean Scoggin, Graduate Recruitment Coordinator, 208-885-4723, Fax: 208-885-4406, E-mail: graduateadmissions@uidaho.edu.

GRADUATE UNITS

College of Graduate Studies Students: 957 full-time (421 women), 695 part-time (311 women); includes 201 minority (26 Black or African American, non-Hispanic/Latino; 20 American Indian or Alaska Native, non-Hispanic/Latino; 23 Asian, non-Hispanic/Latino; 93 Hispanic/Latino; 39 Two or more races, non-Hispanic/Latino), 266 international. Average age 33. 1,356 applicants, 59% accepted, 513 enrolled. *Faculty:* 415 full-time (124 women), 30 part-time/adjunct (16 women). Expenses: Contact institution. *Financial support:* Fellowships, research assistantships, teaching assistantships, career-related internships or fieldwork, Federal Work-Study, institutionally sponsored loans, scholarships/grants, and tuition waivers (full and partial) available. Support available to part-time students. Financial award applicants required to submit FAFSA. In 2017, 507 master's, 54 doctorates, 51 other advanced degrees awarded. *Program availability:* Online learning. Offers interdisciplinary studies (MA, MS). *Application deadline:* For fall admission, 8/1 for domestic students, 5/1 for international students; for spring admission, 12/15 for domestic students, 8/1 for international students. Applications are processed on a rolling basis. *Application fee:* $60 ($70 for international students). Electronic applications accepted. *Application Contact:* Rance Larsen, Director of Graduate Admissions, 208-885-2809, E-mail: graduateadmissions@uidaho.edu. *Dean of the College of Graduate Studies,* Dr. Jerry McMurtry, 208-885-6243, Fax: 208-885-6198, E-mail: uigrad@uidaho.edu.

College of Agricultural and Life Sciences Students: 121 full-time (66 women), 51 part-time (27 women). Average age 30. *Faculty:* 80 full-time (29 women). Expenses: Contact institution. *Financial support:* Research assistantships, teaching assistantships, career-related internships or fieldwork, and Federal Work-Study available. Support available to part-time students. Financial award application deadline: 2/15; financial award applicants required to submit FAFSA. In 2017, 30 master's, 4 doctorates awarded. Offers agricultural and life sciences (MS, PhD); agricultural economics and rural sociology (MS); animal and veterinary science (MS, PhD); engineering and science (PhD); engineering and science (MS); family and consumer sciences (MS); food science (MS, PhD); law, management and policy (MS, PhD); plant science (MS); plant sciences (MS, PhD); science and management (MS, PhD); soil and land resources (MS, PhD). *Application deadline:* For fall admission, 8/1 for domestic students; for spring admission, 12/15 for domestic students. Applications are processed on a rolling basis. *Application fee:* $60 ($70 for international students). Electronic applications accepted. *Application Contact:* Sean Scoggin, Graduate Recruitment Coordinator, 208-885-4723, Fax: 208-885-6198, E-mail: gadms@uidaho.edu. *Dean*, Dr. Michael Parrella, 208-885-6681, E-mail: ag@uidaho.edu.

College of Art and Architecture Students: 67 full-time, 7 part-time. Average age 28. *Faculty:* 20 full-time (7 women). Expenses: Contact institution. *Financial support:* Applicants required to submit FAFSA. In 2017, 43 master's awarded. Offers art and architecture (M Arch, MFA, MLA, MS); bioregional planning and community design (MS). *Application deadline:* For fall admission, 8/1 for domestic students; for spring admission, 12/15 for domestic students. Applications are processed on a rolling basis. *Application fee:* $60. Electronic applications accepted. *Application Contact:* Sean Scoggin, Graduate Recruitment Coordinator, 208-885-4001, Fax: 208-885-4406, E-mail: graduateadmissions@uidaho.edu. *Interim Dean*, Dr. Shauna Corry, 208-885-4409, E-mail: caa@uidaho.edu.

College of Business and Economics Students: 31 full-time, 5 part-time. Average age 33. *Faculty:* 10 full-time. Expenses: Contact institution. *Financial support:* Research assistantships, teaching assistantships, Federal Work-Study, and scholarships/grants available. Support available to part-time students. Financial award applicants required to submit FAFSA. In 2017, 33 master's awarded. Offers accountancy (M Acct); business and economics (M Acct, MBA); general management (MBA). *Application deadline:* For fall admission, 8/1 for domestic students; for spring admission, 12/15 for domestic students. Applications are processed on a rolling basis. *Application fee:* $60. Electronic applications accepted. *Application Contact:* Sean Scoggin, Graduate Recruitment Coordinator, 208-885-4001, Fax: 208-885-4406, E-mail: graduateadmissions@uidaho.edu. *Dean*, Dr. Marc Chopin, 208-885-6725, E-mail: cbe@uidaho.edu.

College of Education, Health and Human Sciences Students: 164 full-time (94 women), 248 part-time (150 women). Average age 35. *Faculty:* 61 full-time, 9 part-time/adjunct. Expenses: Contact institution. *Financial support:* Teaching assistantships and Federal Work-Study available. Support available to part-time students. Financial award applicants required to submit FAFSA. In 2017, 119 master's, 7 doctorates, 49 other advanced degrees awarded. Offers adult/organizational learning and leadership (Ed S); athletic training (MSAT, DAT); career and technology education (M Ed); curriculum and instruction (M Ed, Ed S); education (Ed D, PhD); education, health and human sciences (M Ed, MS, MSAT, DAT, Ed D, PhD, Ed S); educational leadership (Ed S); exercise science and health (MS); physical education teacher education (M Ed, MS); recreation, sport, and tourism management (MS); rehabilitation counseling and human services (M Ed); school counseling (M Ed, MS); special education (M Ed). *Application deadline:* For fall admission, 8/1 for domestic students; for spring admission, 12/15 for domestic students. Applications are processed on a rolling basis. *Application fee:* $60. Electronic applications accepted. *Application Contact:* Sean Scoggin, Graduate Recruitment Coordinator, 208-885-4001, Fax: 208-885-4406, E-mail: graduateadmissions@uidaho.edu. *Dean*, Dr. Alison Carr-Chellman, 208-885-6772, E-mail: coe@uidaho.edu.

College of Engineering Students: 177 full-time (33 women), 189 part-time (24 women). Average age 33. *Faculty:* 73 full-time, 9 part-time/adjunct. Expenses: Contact institution. *Financial support:* Fellowships, research assistantships, teaching assistantships, career-related internships or fieldwork, and Federal Work-Study available. Support available to part-time students. Financial award applicants required to submit FAFSA. In 2017, 101 master's, 7 doctorates awarded. Offers biological engineering (M Engr, MS, PhD); chemical engineering (M Engr, MS, PhD); civil and environmental engineering (M Engr, PhD); computer science (MS, PhD); electrical and computer engineering (MS, PhD); electrical engineering (M Engr); engineering (M Engr, MS, PhD); geological engineering (MS); materials science and engineering (PhD); mechanical engineering (M Engr, MS, PhD); nuclear engineering (M Engr, MS, PhD). *Application deadline:* For fall admission, 8/1 for domestic students; for spring admission, 12/15 for domestic students. Applications are processed on a rolling basis. *Application fee:* $60. Electronic applications accepted. *Application Contact:* Sean Scoggin, Graduate Recruitment Coordinator, 208-885-4001, Fax: 208-885-4406, E-mail: graduateadmissions@uidaho.edu. *Dean*, Dr. Larry Stauffer, 208-885-6470, E-mail: deanengr@uidaho.edu.

College of Letters, Arts and Social Sciences Students: 127 full-time (54 women), 45 part-time (31 women). Average age 32. *Faculty:* 71. Expenses: Contact institution. *Financial support:* Fellowships, research assistantships, teaching assistantships, and Federal Work-Study available. Support available to part-time students. Financial award applicants required to submit FAFSA. In 2017, 82 master's, 1 doctorate awarded. Offers anthropology (MA); creative writing (MFA); English (MA, MAT); experimental psychology (PhD); history (MA, PhD); letters, arts and social sciences (M Mus, MA, MAT, MFA, MPA, MS, PhD); music (M Mus, MA); political science (MA, PhD); psychology and communication studies (MS); public administration (MPA); theatre arts (MFA). *Application deadline:* For fall admission, 8/1 for domestic students; for spring admission, 12/15 for domestic students. Applications are processed on a rolling basis. *Application fee:* $60. Electronic applications accepted. *Application Contact:* Sean Scoggin, Graduate Recruitment Coordinator, 208-885-4001, Fax: 208-885-4406, E-mail: graduateadmissions@uidaho.edu. *Dean*, Dr. Andrew Kersten, 208-885-6426, E-mail: class@uidaho.edu.

College of Natural Resources Students: 142 full-time (78 women), 128 part-time (62 women). Average age 33. *Faculty:* 53 full-time, 5 part-time/adjunct. Expenses: Contact institution. *Financial support:* Fellowships, research assistantships, teaching assistantships, and Federal Work-Study available. Support available to part-time students. Financial award applicants required to submit FAFSA. In 2017, 70 master's, 14 doctorates awarded. Offers environmental science (MS, PhD); natural resources (MNR, MS, PSM, PhD). *Application deadline:* For fall admission, 8/1 for domestic students; for spring admission, 12/15 for domestic students. Applications are processed on a rolling basis. *Application fee:* $60. Electronic applications accepted. *Application Contact:* Sean Scoggin, Graduate Recruitment Coordinator, 208-885-4723, Fax: 208-885-4406, E-mail: graduateadmissions@uidaho.edu. *Dean*, Dr. Kurt Scott Pregitzer, 208-885-8981, Fax: 208-885-5534, E-mail: cnr@uidaho.edu.

College of Science Students: 131 full-time (50 women), 22 part-time (10 women). Average age 30. *Faculty:* 77. Expenses: Contact institution. *Financial support:* Applicants required to submit FAFSA. In 2017, 28 master's, 21 doctorates awarded. Offers bioinformatics and computational biology (MS, PhD); biology (MS, PhD); chemistry (MS, PhD); geography (MS, PhD); geology (MS, PhD); mathematics (MAT, MS, PhD); microbiology, molecular biology and biochemistry (PhD); physics (MS, PhD); science (MAT, MS, PhD); statistical science (MS). *Application deadline:* Applications are processed on a rolling basis. *Application fee:* $60. Electronic applications accepted. *Application Contact:* Sean Scoggin, Graduate Recruitment Coordinator, 208-885-4001, Fax: 208-885-4406, E-mail: graduateadmissions@uidaho.edu. *Interim Dean*, Dr. Mark Nielson, 208-885-6195, E-mail: science@uidaho.edu.

College of Law Students: 296 full-time (127 women), 12 part-time (7 women). Average age 28. *Faculty:* 30 full-time, 10 part-time/adjunct. Expenses: Contact institution. *Financial support:* Career-related internships or fieldwork, Federal Work-Study, and institutionally sponsored loans available. Financial award applicants required to submit FAFSA. Offers law (LL M, JD). *Application deadline:* For fall admission, 3/15 priority date for domestic students. Applications are processed on a rolling basis. *Application fee:* $50 ($60 for international students). Electronic applications accepted. *Application Contact:* Carole Wells, Director of Admissions, 208-885-2300, Fax: 208-885-2252, E-mail: lawadmit@uidaho.edu. *Dean*, Mark Adams, 208-885-4977, E-mail: uilaw@uidaho.edu.

UNIVERSITY OF ILLINOIS AT CHICAGO, Chicago, IL 60607-7128

General Information State-supported, coed, university. CGS member. *Graduate housing:* Room and/or apartments available on a first-come, first-served basis to single students; on-campus housing not available to married students. Housing application deadline: 3/1. *Research affiliation:* Chicago Manufacturing Technology Extension Center (manufacturing research and development, industrial research), Eastern Cooperative Oncology Group (clinical cancer research), Argonne National Laboratory (battery performance), National Surgical Adjuvant Breast and Bowel Project (prevention of breast cancer).

GRADUATE UNITS

College of Applied Health Sciences *Program availability:* Part-time. Offers applied health sciences (MS, DPT, OTD, PhD, CAS, Certificate); biomedical visualization (MS); disability and human development (MS, PhD); health informatics (MS, CAS); health information management (Certificate); kinesiology (MS, PhD); nutrition (MS, PhD); occupational therapy (MS, OTD); physical therapy (MS, DPT). Electronic applications accepted.

College of Architecture, Design and the Arts *Program availability:* Part-time, evening/weekend. Offers architecture, design and the arts (M Arch, M Des, MA, MFA, MS, MS Arch, PhD). Electronic applications accepted.

School of Architecture Offers architecture (M Arch, MA, MS, MS Arch). Electronic applications accepted.

School of Art and Art History *Program availability:* Part-time, evening/weekend. Offers art history (MA); electronic visualization (MFA); museum and exhibition studies (MA); new media arts (MFA). Electronic applications accepted.

School of Design Offers graphic design (M Des); industrial design (M Des). Electronic applications accepted.

College of Dentistry Offers dentistry (MS, DDS, DMD, PhD); oral sciences (MS, PhD). Electronic applications accepted.

College of Education *Program availability:* Part-time, evening/weekend. Offers curriculum studies (PhD); early childhood education (M Ed); education (M Ed, Ed D, PhD); educational psychology (PhD); elementary education (M Ed); measurement, evaluation, statistics, and assessment (M Ed); policy studies (M Ed); policy studies in urban education (PhD); secondary education (M Ed); special education (M Ed, PhD); urban education leadership (Ed D); youth development (M Ed). Electronic applications accepted.

College of Engineering *Program availability:* Part-time, evening/weekend. Offers bioengineering (MS, PhD); chemical engineering (MS, PhD); civil and materials engineering (MS, PhD); computer science (MS, PhD); electrical and computer engineering (MS, PhD); energy engineering (MEE); engineering (M Eng, MEE, MS, PhD); fluids engineering (MS, PhD); industrial engineering (MS, PhD); industrial engineering and operations research (PhD); mechanical analysis and design (MS, PhD); mechanical engineering (MS, PhD); thermomechanical and power engineering (MS, PhD). Electronic applications accepted.

College of Liberal Arts and Sciences *Program availability:* Part-time, evening/weekend. Offers anthropology (MA, PhD); biological sciences (MS, PhD); chemistry (MS, PhD); communication (MA, PhD); criminology, law, and justice (MA, PhD); earth and environmental sciences (MS, PhD); economics (MA, PhD); English (MA, PhD); environmental and urban geography (MA); history (MA, MAT, PhD); Latin American and Latino studies (MA); liberal arts and sciences (MA, MAT, MS, MST, DA, PhD); mathematics (DA); philosophy (MA, PhD); physics (MS, PhD); political science (MA, PhD); probability and statistics (PhD); psychology (MA, PhD); secondary school mathematics (MST); sociology (MA, PhD); statistics (MS). Electronic applications accepted.

School of Literatures, Cultural Studies and Linguistics *Program availability:* Part-time. Offers French and Francophone studies (MA); Germanic studies (MA, PhD); Hispanic and Italian studies (MAT, PhD); Hispanic linguistics (PhD); linguistics (MA); Slavic and Baltic languages and literatures (MA); Slavic and Baltic languages and literatures (PhD); Slavic studies (MA, PhD). Electronic applications accepted.

College of Medicine *Program availability:* Part-time. Offers anatomy and cell biology (MS); biochemistry and molecular genetics (PhD); medical education (MHPE); medicine (MHPE, MS, MD, PhD); microbiology and immunology (PhD); pharmacology (PhD); physiology and biophysics (MS, PhD); surgery (MS).

College of Nursing *Program availability:* Part-time. Offers acute care clinical nurse specialist (MS); administrative nursing leadership (Certificate); adult nurse practitioner (MS); adult/geriatric nurse practitioner (MS); advanced community health nurse specialist (MS); family nurse practitioner (MS); geriatric clinical nurse specialist (MS); geriatric nurse practitioner (MS); nurse midwifery (MS); nursing (MS, DNP, PhD, Certificate); nursing practice (DNP); nursing science (PhD); occupational health/advanced community health nurse specialist (MS); occupational health/family nurse practitioner (MS); pediatric nurse practitioner (MS); perinatal clinical nurse specialist (MS); school/advanced community health nurse specialist (MS); school/family nurse practitioner (MS); women's health nurse practitioner (MS). Electronic applications accepted.

College of Pharmacy Offers biopharmaceutical sciences (PhD); comparative effectiveness research (MS); forensic science (MS); forensic toxicology (MS); medicinal chemistry (MS, PhD); pharmacognosy (MS, PhD); pharmacy (PhD).

College of Urban Planning and Public Affairs *Program availability:* Part-time, evening/weekend. Offers public administration (MPA, PhD); urban planning and policy (MUPP, PhD); urban planning and public affairs (MPA, MUPP, PhD). Electronic applications accepted.

Jane Addams College of Social Work *Program availability:* Part-time. Offers social work (MSW, PhD, Certificate). Electronic applications accepted.

Liautaud Graduate School of Business *Program availability:* Part-time, evening/weekend. Offers accounting (MS); business (MA, MBA, MS, PhD); business administration (MBA, PhD); finance (MS); management information systems (PhD); real estate (MA). Electronic applications accepted.

Program in Learning Sciences Offers learning sciences (PhD).

Program in Neuroscience Offers cellular and systems neuroscience and cell biology (PhD); neuroscience (MS).

School of Public Health *Program availability:* Part-time. Offers public health (MHA, MPH, MS, Dr PH, PhD). Electronic applications accepted.

Division of Community Health Sciences *Program availability:* Part-time. Offers community health sciences (MPH, MS, Dr PH, PhD). Electronic applications accepted.

Division of Environmental and Occupational Health Sciences *Program availability:* Part-time. Offers environmental and occupational health sciences (MPH, MS, Dr PH, PhD). Electronic applications accepted.

Division of Health Policy and Administration *Program availability:* Part-time. Offers clinical and translational science (MS); health policy (PhD); health services research (PhD); healthcare administration (MHA); public health policy management (MPH). Electronic applications accepted.

Epidemiology and Biostatistics Division *Program availability:* Part-time. Offers biostatistics (MPH, MS, PhD); epidemiology (MPH, MS, PhD). Electronic applications accepted.

UNIVERSITY OF ILLINOIS AT SPRINGFIELD, Springfield, IL 62703-5407

General Information State-supported, coed, comprehensive institution. CGS member. *Enrollment:* 4,956 graduate, professional, and undergraduate students; 649 full-time matriculated graduate/professional students (328 women), 1,223 part-time matriculated graduate/professional students (564 women). *Enrollment by degree level:* 1,807 master's, 32 doctoral, 33 other advanced degrees. *Graduate faculty:* 158 full-time (68 women), 37 part-time/adjunct (22 women). Tuition, state resident: full-time $7896; part-time $329 per credit hour. Tuition, nonresident: full-time $16,200; part-time $675 per credit hour. Tuition and fees vary according to program. *Graduate housing:* Rooms and/or apartments available on a first-come, first-served basis to single and married students. Housing application deadline: 5/1. *Student services:* Campus employment opportunities, campus safety program, career counseling, child daycare facilities, exercise/wellness program, free psychological counseling, international student services, low-cost health insurance, multicultural affairs office, services for students with disabilities, teacher training, writing training. *Library facilities:* Norris L Brookens Library plus 1 other. *Collection:* Books: 460,486 (physical), 213,074 (digital/electronic); Serial titles: 9,843 (physical), 14,828 (digital/electronic); Databases: 172. Weekly public service hours: 90; students can reserve study rooms. *Research affiliation:* Council of Public Liberal Arts Colleges (COPLAC), Interuniversity Consortium for Political and Social Research, Council of Undergraduate Research, The Nature Conservancy, Illinois Flood Plan Restoration.

Computer facilities: 560 computers available on campus for general student use. A campuswide network can be accessed from student residence rooms and from off campus. Online class registration is available.
Website: http://www.uis.edu/

General Application Contact: Dr. Cecelia Cornell, Associate Vice Chancellor for Graduate Education, 888-977-4847, Fax: 217-206-7230, E-mail: ccorn1@uis.edu.

GRADUATE UNITS

Graduate Programs Students: 649 full-time (328 women), 1,223 part-time (564 women); includes 363 minority (181 Black or African American, non-Hispanic/Latino; 2 American Indian or Alaska Native, non-Hispanic/Latino; 85 Asian, non-Hispanic/Latino; 64 Hispanic/Latino; 31 Two or more races, non-Hispanic/Latino), 516 international. Average age 31. 1,860 applicants, 44% accepted, 463 enrolled. *Faculty:* 158 full-time (68 women), 37 part-time/adjunct (22 women). Expenses: Contact institution. *Financial support:* In 2017–18, 8 research assistantships with full tuition reimbursements (averaging $10,249 per year), 5 teaching assistantships with full tuition reimbursements (averaging $10,303 per year) were awarded; fellowships, career-related internships or fieldwork, Federal Work-Study, scholarships/grants, health care benefits, and unspecified assistantships also available. Support available to part-time students. Financial award application deadline: 11/15; financial award applicants required to submit FAFSA. In 2017, 1,150 master's, 29 other advanced degrees awarded. *Program availability:* Part-time, evening/weekend, 100% online, blended/hybrid learning. *Application deadline:* Applications are processed on a rolling basis. *Application fee:* $60 ($75 for international students). Electronic applications accepted. *Associate Vice Chancellor for Graduate Education*, Dr. Cecelia Cornell, 217-206-7230, Fax: 217-206-7623, E-mail: ccorn1@uis.edu.

College of Business and Management Students: 217 full-time (100 women), 224 part-time (96 women); includes 63 minority (24 Black or African American, non-Hispanic/Latino; 24 Asian, non-Hispanic/Latino; 11 Hispanic/Latino; 4 Two or more races, non-Hispanic/Latino), 188 international. Average age 30. 562 applicants, 35% accepted, 106 enrolled. *Faculty:* 33 full-time (5 women), 7 part-time/adjunct (3 women). Expenses: Contact institution. *Financial support:* In 2017–18, research assistantships with full tuition reimbursements (averaging $10,249 per year), teaching assistantships with full tuition reimbursements (averaging $10,303 per year) were awarded; fellowships, career-related internships or fieldwork, Federal Work-Study, scholarships/grants, health care benefits, and unspecified assistantships also available. Support available to part-time students. Financial award application deadline: 11/15; financial award applicants required to submit FAFSA. In 2017, 307 master's awarded. *Program availability:* Part-time, evening/weekend, 100% online, blended/hybrid learning. Offers accountancy (MA); business administration (MBA); business and management (MA, MBA, MS); management information systems (MS). *Application deadline:* Applications are processed on a rolling basis. *Application fee:* $60 ($75 for international students). Electronic applications accepted. *Interim Dean*, Dr. James Ermatinger, 217-206-6533, Fax: 217-206-7541, E-mail: cbmdean@uis.edu.

College of Education and Human Services Students: 68 full-time (58 women), 222 part-time (167 women); includes 68 minority (44 Black or African American, non-Hispanic/Latino; 1 American Indian or Alaska Native, non-Hispanic/Latino; 1 Asian, non-Hispanic/Latino; 15 Hispanic/Latino; 7 Two or more races, non-Hispanic/Latino), 2 international. Average age 33. 145 applicants, 50% accepted, 65 enrolled. *Faculty:* 15 full-time (10 women), 16 part-time/adjunct (13 women). Expenses: Contact institution. *Financial support:* In 2017–18, research assistantships with full tuition reimbursements (averaging $10,249 per year), teaching assistantships with full tuition reimbursements (averaging $10,303 per year) were awarded; fellowships, career-related internships or fieldwork, Federal Work-Study, scholarships/grants, health care benefits, and unspecified assistantships also available. Support available to part-time students. Financial award application deadline: 11/15; financial award applicants required to submit FAFSA. In 2017, 70 master's, 6 other advanced degrees awarded. *Program availability:* Part-time, evening/weekend, 100% online, blended/hybrid learning. Offers alcohol and substance abuse (Graduate Certificate); alcoholism and substance abuse (MA); chief school business official (CAS); child and family services (MA); education and human services (MA, CAS, Certificate, Graduate Certificate); educational leadership (MA, CAS); educational technology (Graduate Certificate); English as a second language (Graduate Certificate); gerontology (MA); higher education online pedagogy (Graduate Certificate); human development counseling (MA); leadership and learning (Graduate Certificate); legal aspects of education (Graduate Certificate); social services administration (MA). *Application deadline:* Applications are processed on a rolling basis. *Application fee:* $60 ($75 for international students). Electronic applications accepted. *Dean*, Dr. Hanfu Mi, 217-206-6784, Fax: 217-206-6775, E-mail: hmi2@uis.edu.

College of Liberal Arts and Sciences Students: 210 full-time (79 women), 418 part-time (109 women); includes 96 minority (33 Black or African American, non-Hispanic/Latino; 1 American Indian or Alaska Native, non-Hispanic/Latino; 38 Asian, non-Hispanic/Latino; 15 Hispanic/Latino; 9 Two or more races, non-Hispanic/Latino), 295 international. Average age 30. 791 applicants, 48% accepted, 153 enrolled. *Faculty:* 73 full-time (34 women), 5 part-time/adjunct (1 woman). Expenses: Contact institution. *Financial support:* In 2017–18, research assistantships with full tuition reimbursements (averaging $10,249 per year), teaching assistantships with full tuition reimbursements (averaging $10,303 per year) were awarded; fellowships, career-related internships or fieldwork, Federal Work-Study, scholarships/grants, health care benefits, and unspecified assistantships also available. Support available to part-time students. Financial award application deadline: 11/15; financial award applicants required to submit FAFSA. In 2017, 642 master's awarded. *Program availability:* Part-time, evening/weekend, 100% online, blended/hybrid learning. Offers biology (MS); communication (MA); computer science (MS); data analytics (MS); English (MA); history (MA); liberal and integrative studies (MA); liberal arts and sciences (MA, MS, Graduate Certificate); teaching English (Graduate Certificate). *Application deadline:* Applications are processed on a rolling basis. *Application fee:* $60 ($75 for international students). Electronic applications accepted. *Dean*, Dr. James Ermatinger, 217-206-6512, Fax: 217-206-6217, E-mail: jerma2@uis.edu.

College of Public Affairs and Administration Students: 154 full-time (91 women), 359 part-time (192 women); includes 136 minority (80 Black or African American, non-Hispanic/Latino; 22 Asian, non-Hispanic/Latino; 23 Hispanic/Latino; 11 Two or more races, non-Hispanic/Latino), 31 international. Average age 34. 362 applicants, 48% accepted, 139 enrolled. *Faculty:* 37 full-time (19 women), 9 part-time/adjunct (5 women). Expenses: Contact institution. *Financial support:* In 2017–18, research assistantships with full tuition reimbursements (averaging $10,249 per year), teaching assistantships with full tuition reimbursements (averaging $10,303 per year) were awarded; fellowships, career-related internships or fieldwork, Federal Work-Study, scholarships/grants, health care benefits, and unspecified assistantships also available. Support available to part-time students. Financial award application deadline: 11/15; financial award applicants required to submit FAFSA. In 2017, 131 master's, 23 other advanced degrees awarded. *Program availability:* Part-time, evening/weekend, 100% online, blended/hybrid learning. Offers community health education (Graduate Certificate); emergency preparedness and homeland security (Graduate Certificate); environmental health (MPH, Graduate Certificate); environmental risk assessment (Graduate Certificate); environmental science (MS); environmental studies (MA); epidemiology (Graduate Certificate); legal studies (MA); management of nonprofit organizations (Graduate Certificate); political science (MA); public administration (MPA, DPA); public affairs and administration (MA, MPA, MPH, MS, DPA, Graduate Certificate); public affairs reporting (MA); public health (MPH). *Application deadline:* Applications are processed on a rolling basis. *Application fee:* $60 ($75 for international students). Electronic applications accepted. *Dean*, Dr. Robert Smith, 217-206-6523, Fax: 217-206-7807, E-mail: cpaa@uis.edu.

UNIVERSITY OF ILLINOIS AT URBANA–CHAMPAIGN, Champaign, IL 61820

General Information State-supported, coed, university. CGS member. *Graduate housing:* Rooms and/or apartments available to single and married students. *Research affiliation:* Midwest Universities Research Association, Sandia National Laboratories, National Center for Atmospheric Research.

GRADUATE UNITS

College of Law Offers law (LL M, MCL, JD, JSD).

College of Veterinary Medicine Offers comparative biosciences (MS, PhD); pathobiology (MS, PhD); veterinary clinical medicine (MS, PhD); veterinary medical science (DVM); veterinary medicine (MS, DVM, PhD).

Graduate College Offers strategic brand communication (MS).

College of Agricultural, Consumer and Environmental Sciences Offers agricultural and applied economics (MS, PhD); agricultural and biological engineering (MS, PhD); agricultural education (MS); agricultural production (MS); agricultural, consumer and environmental sciences (MS, PSM, PhD); animal sciences (MS, PhD); bioenergy (PSM); bioinformatics: animal sciences (MS); bioinformatics: crop sciences (MS); crop sciences (MS, PhD); food science (MS); food science and human nutrition (MS, PhD); human and community development (MS, PhD); human nutrition (MS); natural resources and environmental science (MS, PhD); nutritional sciences (MS, PhD); technical systems management (MS, PSM).

College of Applied Health Sciences Offers applied health sciences (MA, MPH, MS, MSPH, Au D, PhD); audiology (Au D); community health (MS, MSPH, PhD); kinesiology (MS, PhD); public health (MPH); recreation, sport and tourism (MS, PhD); rehabilitation (MS); speech and hearing science (MA, PhD).

College of Education *Program availability:* Part-time, online learning. Offers curriculum and instruction (Ed M, MA, MS, Ed D, PhD, CAS); early childhood education (Ed M); education (Ed M, MA, MS, Ed D, PhD, CAS); educational organization and leadership (Ed M, MS, Ed D, PhD, CAS); educational policy studies (Ed M, MA, PhD); educational psychology (Ed M, MA, MS, PhD, CAS); elementary education (Ed M); human resource education (Ed M, MS, Ed D, PhD, CAS); secondary education (Ed M); special education (Ed M, MS, Ed D, PhD, CAS).

College of Engineering *Program availability:* Part-time, evening/weekend, online learning. Offers aerospace engineering (MS, PhD); bioengineering (MS, PhD); bioinformatics (MS); civil engineering (MS, PhD); computer science (MCS, MS, PhD); electrical and computer engineering (MS, PhD); energy systems (M Eng); engineering (M Eng, MCS, MS, PhD); environmental engineering in civil engineering (MS, PhD); financial engineering (MS); industrial engineering (MS, PhD); materials science and engineering (M Eng, MS, PhD); mechanical engineering (MS, PhD); nuclear, plasma, and radiological engineering (MS, PhD); physics (MS, PhD); systems and entrepreneurial engineering (MS, PhD); teaching of physics (MS); theoretical and applied mechanics (MS, PhD).

College of Fine and Applied Arts Offers architectural studies (MS); architecture (M Arch, PhD); art and design (MFA); art education (Ed M, MA, PhD); art history (MA, PhD); crafts (MFA); dance (MFA); fine and applied arts (Ed M, M Arch, M Mus, MA, MFA, MLA, MME, MS, MUP, AD, DMA, PhD); graphic design (MFA); industrial design (MFA); landscape architecture (MLA, PhD); metals (MFA); music (M Mus, AD, DMA); music education (MME, PhD); musicology (PhD); painting (MFA); photography (MFA); regional planning (PhD); sculpture (MFA); theatre (MA, MFA, PhD); urban planning (MUP).

College of Liberal Arts and Sciences *Program availability:* Online learning. Offers African studies (MA); analytics (MS); animal biology (ecology, ethology and evolution) (MS, PhD); anthropology (MA, PhD); applied mathematics (MS); applied mathematics: actuarial science (MS); applied statistics (MS); astrochemistry (PhD); astronomy (MS, PhD); atmospheric sciences (MS, PhD); biochemistry (MS, PhD); bioinformatics: chemical and biomolecular engineering (MS); biophysics and computational biology (MS, PhD); cell and developmental biology (PhD); chemical engineering (MS, PhD); chemical physics (PhD); chemical sciences (MA, MS, PhD); chemistry (MA, MS, PhD); classical philology (PhD); classics (MA); communication (MA, PhD); comparative literature (MA, PhD); creative writing (MFA); earth, society and environment (MA, MS, PhD); East Asian languages and cultures (PhD); East Asian studies (MA); ecology, evolution and conservation biology (MS, PhD); economics (MS, PhD); English (MA, PhD); entomology (MS, PhD); European Union studies (MA); French (MA, PhD); geography and geographic information science (MA, MS, PhD); geology (MS, PhD); German (MA, PhD); history (MA, PhD); integrative biology (MS, MST, PSM, PhD); Italian (MA, PhD); Latin American studies (MA); liberal arts and sciences (MA, MFA, MS, MST, PSM, PhD); linguistics (MA, PhD); literatures, cultures and linguistics (MA, MS, PhD); mathematics (MS, PhD); microbiology (MS, PhD); molecular and cellular biology (MS, PhD); molecular and integrative physiology (MS, PhD); neuroscience (PhD); philosophy (MA, PhD); plant biology (MS, PhD); plant biotechnology (PSM); policy economics (MS); political science (MA, PhD); Portuguese (MA, PhD); psychology (MA, MS, PhD); religious studies (MA); romance linguistics (PhD); Russian, East European, and Eurasian studies (MA); second language acquisition and teacher education (PhD); Slavic languages and literatures (MA, PhD); sociology (MA, PhD); south Asian and Middle Eastern studies (MA); Spanish (MA, PhD); statistics (MS, PhD); teaching of chemistry (MS); teaching of earth sciences (MS); teaching of English as a second language (MA); teaching of Latin (MA); teaching of mathematics (MS); translation and interpreting (MA).

College of Media Offers advertising (MS); communications and media (PhD); journalism (MS); media (MS, PhD).

Gies College of Business *Program availability:* Online learning. Offers accountancy (MS, PhD); accounting science (MAS); business (MAS, MBA, MS, PhD); business administration (MS, PhD); finance (MS, PhD); technology management (MS).

School of Information Sciences *Program availability:* Part-time, online learning. Offers bioinformatics (MS); digital libraries (CAS); information management (MS); library and information science (MS, PhD, CAS).

School of Labor and Employment Relations Offers human resources and industrial relations (MHRIR, PhD).

School of Social Work Offers advocacy, leadership, and social change (MSW); children, youth and family services (MSW); health care (MSW); mental health (MSW); school social work (MSW); social work (PhD).

Illinois Informatics Institute Offers informatics (PhD).

UNIVERSITY OF INDIANAPOLIS, Indianapolis, IN 46227-3697

General Information Independent-religious, coed, comprehensive institution. CGS member. *Graduate housing:* Rooms and/or apartments available on a first-come, first-served basis to single and married students.

GRADUATE UNITS

Graduate Programs *Program availability:* Part-time, evening/weekend, online learning.

Center for Aging and Community *Program availability:* Part-time, evening/weekend, online learning. Offers gerontology (MS, Certificate).

College of Arts and Sciences *Program availability:* Part-time, evening/weekend. Offers anthropology (MS); applied sociology (MA); art (MA); arts and sciences (MA, MS); English (MA); history (MA); human biology (MS); international relations (MA).

College of Health Sciences Offers health sciences (MHS, MOT, MPH, MS, DHS, DPT, OTD); occupational therapy (MOT, DHS, OTD); physical therapy (MHS, DHS, DPT); public health (MPH); sport management (MS).

School of Business *Program availability:* Part-time, evening/weekend. Offers business (EMBA, MBA, Graduate Certificate).

School of Education *Program availability:* Part-time, evening/weekend. Offers art education (MAT); biology (MAT); chemistry (MAT); curriculum and instruction (MA); earth sciences (MAT); education (MA, MAT); educational leadership (MA); elementary education (MA); English (MAT); French (MAT); math (MAT); physical education (MAT); physics (MAT); secondary education (MA); social studies (MAT); Spanish (MAT).

School of Nursing Offers advanced practice nursing (DNP); family nurse practitioner (MSN); gerontological nurse practitioner (MSN); neonatal nurse practitioner (MSN); nurse-midwifery (MSN); nursing (MSN); nursing and health systems leadership (MSN); nursing education (MSN); women's health nurse practitioner (MSN). Electronic applications accepted.

School of Psychological Sciences Offers clinical psychology (Psy D); clinical psychology/mental health counseling (MA).

THE UNIVERSITY OF IOWA, Iowa City, IA 52242-1316

General Information State-supported, coed, university. CGS member. *Graduate housing:* Rooms and/or apartments available on a first-come, first-served basis to single and married students.

GRADUATE UNITS

College of Dentistry Offers dental public health (MS); dentistry (MS, DDS, PhD, Certificate); endodontics (MS, Certificate); operative dentistry (MS, Certificate); oral and maxillofacial surgery (MS, PhD, Certificate); oral pathology, radiology and medicine (MS, PhD, Certificate); oral science (MS, PhD); orthodontics (MS, Certificate); pediatric dentistry (Certificate); periodontics (MS, Certificate); preventive and community dentistry (MS); prosthodontics (MS, Certificate).

College of Law Students: 432 full-time (188 women); includes 96 minority (23 Black or African American, non-Hispanic/Latino; 2 American Indian or Alaska Native, non-Hispanic/Latino; 17 Asian, non-Hispanic/Latino; 41 Hispanic/Latino; 13 Two or more races, non-Hispanic/Latino), 23 international. Average age 24. 1,651 applicants, 41% accepted, 143 enrolled. *Faculty:* 44 full-time (20 women), 26 part-time/adjunct (11 women). Expenses: Contact institution. *Financial support:* In 2017–18, 387 students received support, including 387 fellowships with partial tuition reimbursements available (averaging $17,909 per year), 133 research assistantships with partial tuition reimbursements available (averaging $2,175 per year); career-related internships or fieldwork, Federal Work-Study, scholarships/grants, and health care benefits also available. Financial award applicants required to submit FAFSA. In 2017, 9 master's, 137 doctorates awarded. Offers law (LL M, MSL, JD, SJD). *Application deadline:* For fall admission, 5/1 priority date for domestic and international students. Applications are processed on a rolling basis. *Application fee:* $0. Electronic applications accepted. *Application Contact:* Collins Byrd, Assistant Dean of Enrollment Management, 319-335-9095, Fax: 319-335-9646, E-mail: law-admissions@uiowa.edu. *Dean,* Gail Agrawal, 319-335-9034, Fax: 319-335-9019, E-mail: gail-agrawal@uiowa.edu.

College of Pharmacy Offers clinical pharmaceutical sciences (PhD); medicinal and natural products chemistry (PhD); pharamaceutics (PhD); pharmaceutical socioeconomics (PhD); pharmaceutics (MS); pharmacy (Pharm D). Electronic applications accepted.

Graduate College *Program availability:* Part-time, evening/weekend, online learning. Offers applied mathematical and computational sciences (PhD); bioinformatics (MS, PhD); bioinformatics and computational biology (Certificate); genetics (PhD); geoinformatics (MS, PhD, Certificate); health informatics (MS, PhD, Certificate); human toxicology (MS, PhD); immunology (PhD); information science (MS, PhD, Certificate); molecular and cellular biology (PhD); neuroscience (PhD); translational biomedicine (MS, PhD); urban and regional planning (MA, MS). Electronic applications accepted.

College of Education Offers art education (MA); counseling psychology (PhD); counselor education and supervision (PhD); couple and family therapy (PhD); developmental reading (MA); education (MA, MAT, MM, PhD); educational leadership (MA, PhD, Ed S); educational measurement and statistics (MA, PhD); educational psychology (MA, PhD); elementary education (MA); English education (MA, MAT); foreign and second language education (MAT); foreign language education (MA); foreign language/ESL education (PhD); higher education and student affairs (MA, PhD); language, literacy and culture (PhD); mathematics education (MA, MAT, PhD); music education (MM, PhD); rehabilitation and mental health counseling (MA); rehabilitation counselor education (PhD); school counseling (MA); school psychology (PhD, Ed S); schools, culture, and society (MA, PhD); science education (MA); secondary education (MA); social studies (MA, PhD); special education (MA, PhD). Electronic applications accepted.

College of Engineering Students: 212 full-time (55 women), 64 part-time (12 women); includes 27 minority (3 Black or African American, non-Hispanic/Latino; 4 Asian, non-Hispanic/Latino; 12 Hispanic/Latino; 8 Two or more races, non-Hispanic/Latino), 115 international. Average age 27. 542 applicants, 23% accepted, 65 enrolled. *Faculty:* 95 full-time (10 women), 17 part-time/adjunct (2 women). Expenses: Contact institution. *Financial support:* In 2017–18, 295 students received support, including 29 fellowships with full and partial tuition reimbursements available (averaging $26,000 per year), 200 research assistantships with full and partial tuition reimbursements available (averaging $23,234 per year), 29 teaching assistantships with full and partial tuition reimbursements available (averaging $19,016 per year); career-related internships or fieldwork, Federal Work-Study, scholarships/grants, traineeships, health care benefits, and unspecified assistantships also available. Financial award application deadline: 1/15; financial award applicants required to submit FAFSA. In 2017, 62 master's, 55 doctorates awarded. Offers biomedical engineering (MS, PhD); chemical and biochemical engineering (MS, PhD); electrical and computer engineering (MS, PhD); energy systems (MS, PhD); engineering (MS, PhD); engineering design (MS, PhD); engineering design and manufacturing (MS, PhD); environmental engineering and science (MS, PhD); fluid dynamics (MS, PhD); healthcare systems (MS, PhD); human factors (MS, PhD); hydraulics and water resources (MS, PhD); information and engineering management (MS, PhD); materials and manufacturing (MS, PhD); operations research (MS, PhD); structures, mechanics and materials (MS, PhD); sustainable water development (MS, PhD); transportation engineering (MS, PhD); wind energy (MS, PhD). *Application deadline:* For fall admission, 1/15 priority date for domestic and international students; for spring admission, 8/1 priority date for domestic and international students; for summer admission, 1/1 for domestic and international students. Applications are processed on a rolling basis. *Application fee:* $60 ($100 for international students). Electronic applications accepted. *Dean,* Dr. Alec Scranton, 319-335-5766, Fax: 319-335-6086, E-mail: alec-scranton@uiowa.edu.

College of Liberal Arts and Sciences *Program availability:* Part-time, online learning. Offers actuarial science (MS); American studies (MA, PhD); anthropology (MA, PhD); art (MA, MFA); art history (MA, PhD); astronomy (MS); athletic training (MS); biology (MS, PhD); cell and developmental biology (MS, PhD); chemistry (PhD); Chinese (MA); classics (MA, PhD); clinical exercise physiology (MS); communication sciences and disorders (MA, Au D, PhD); computer science (MCS, PhD); dance (MFA); earth and environmental science (MS, PhD); English (PhD); evolution (MS, PhD); film and video production (MFA); film studies (MA, PhD); French (MA, PhD); gender, women's and sexuality studies (Certificate); genetics (MS, PhD); geographical and sustainability sciences (MA, PhD, Certificate); Greek (MA); health and human physiology (PhD); Hindi (MA); history (MA, PhD); interpersonal communication and relationships (MA, PhD); journalism and media communication (MA); Latin (MA); leisure studies (MA, PhD); liberal arts and sciences (MA, MCS, MFA, MS, MSW, Au D, DMA, PhD, Certificate); linguistics (MA, PhD); literary studies (MA); mass communication (PhD); mathematics (MS, PhD); media studies (MA, PhD); music (MA, MFA, DMA, PhD); neurobiology (MS, PhD); nonfiction writing (MFA); philosophy (PhD); physics (MS, PhD); political science (PhD); psychology (MA, PhD); religious studies (MA, PhD); rhetoric and public advocacy (MA, PhD); Sanskrit (MA); second language acquisition (PhD); social work (MSW, PhD); sociology (MA, PhD); South Asian studies (MA); Spanish (MA, PhD); Spanish creative writing (MFA); statistics (MS, PhD); strategic communication (MA); theatre arts (MFA). Electronic applications accepted.

College of Nursing Offers nursing (MSN, DNP, PhD). Electronic applications accepted.

College of Public Health Offers agricultural safety and health (MS, PhD); biostatistics (MS, PhD, Certificate); clinical investigation (MS); community and behavioral health (MPH, MS, PhD); epidemiology (MPH, MS, PhD); ergonomics (MPH); health management and policy (MHA, PhD); industrial hygiene (MS, PhD); occupational and environmental health (MPH, MS, PhD, Certificate); public health (MHA, MPH, MS, PhD, Certificate); quantitative methods (MPH). Electronic applications accepted.

School of Library and Information Science Offers library and information science (MA, PhD). Electronic applications accepted.

Roy J. and Lucille A. Carver College of Medicine *Program availability:* Part-time. Offers medicine (MA, MPAS, MS, DPT, MD, PhD). Electronic applications accepted.

Graduate Programs in Medicine *Program availability:* Part-time. Offers anatomy and cell biology (PhD); biochemistry (MS, PhD); free radical and radiation biology (MS); general microbiology and microbial physiology (MS, PhD); immunology (MS, PhD);

medicine (MA, MPAS, MS, DPT, PhD); microbial genetics (MS, PhD); molecular physiology and biophysics (MS, PhD); pathogenic bacteriology (MS, PhD); pathology (MS); pharmacology (MS, PhD); physical rehabilitation science (MA, PhD); physical therapy (DPT); physician assistant studies and services (MPAS); virology (MS, PhD). Electronic applications accepted.

Tippie College of Business Students: 237 full-time (80 women), 1,972 part-time (691 women); includes 254 minority (44 Black or African American, non-Hispanic/Latino; 3 American Indian or Alaska Native, non-Hispanic/Latino; 133 Asian, non-Hispanic/Latino; 49 Hispanic/Latino; 1 Native Hawaiian or other Pacific Islander, non-Hispanic/Latino; 24 Two or more races, non-Hispanic/Latino), 257 international. Average age 32. 1,581 applicants, 50% accepted, 636 enrolled. *Faculty:* 133 full-time (34 women), 70 part-time/adjunct (18 women). Expenses: Contact institution. *Financial support:* Applicants required to submit FAFSA. In 2017, 412 master's, 15 doctorates awarded. Offers accounting (M Ac, PhD); business (EMBA, M Ac, MBA, MS, PhD); business administration (EMBA, MBA); business analytics (MBA); economics (PhD); finance (MBA); leadership (MBA); management and organizations (PhD); management sciences (PhD); marketing (MBA). *Application deadline:* Applications are processed on a rolling basis. Electronic applications accepted. *Dean,* Prof. Sarah Fisher Gardial, 319-335-0862, Fax: 319-335-0860, E-mail: sarah-gardial@uiowa.edu.

UNIVERSITY OF JAMESTOWN, Jamestown, ND 58405

General Information Independent-religious, coed, comprehensive institution.

GRADUATE UNITS

Program in Education Offers curriculum and instruction (M Ed).

Program in Physical Therapy Offers physical therapy (DPT).

THE UNIVERSITY OF KANSAS, Lawrence, KS 66045

General Information State-supported, coed, university. CGS member. *Enrollment:* 27,625 graduate, professional, and undergraduate students; 5,654 full-time matriculated graduate/professional students (3,074 women), 2,443 part-time matriculated graduate/professional students (1,493 women). *Enrollment by degree level:* 3,575 master's, 4,283 doctoral, 239 other advanced degrees. *Graduate housing:* Rooms and/or apartments available on a first-come, first-served basis to single and married students. Housing application deadline: 3/1. *Student services:* Campus employment opportunities, campus safety program, career counseling, child daycare facilities, exercise/wellness program, free psychological counseling, grant writing training, international student services, low-cost health insurance, multicultural affairs office, services for students with disabilities, teacher training, writing training. *Library facilities:* Watson Library plus 11 others. *Collection:* Books: 4.7 million (physical), 1 million (digital/electronic). Weekly public service hours: 168; study areas open 24 hours, 5–7 days a week; students can reserve study rooms.

Computer facilities: 1,500 computers available on campus for general student use. A campuswide network can be accessed from student residence rooms and from off campus. Online class registration, online payments are available.
Website: http://www.ku.edu/

General Application Contact: Graduate Studies, 785-864-8040, Fax: 785-864-7209, E-mail: graduate@ku.edu.

GRADUATE UNITS

Graduate Studies Students: 3,452 full-time (1,843 women), 1,878 part-time (1,142 women); includes 722 minority (213 Black or African American, non-Hispanic/Latino; 55 American Indian or Alaska Native, non-Hispanic/Latino; 128 Asian, non-Hispanic/Latino; 147 Hispanic/Latino; 1 Native Hawaiian or other Pacific Islander, non-Hispanic/Latino; 178 Two or more races, non-Hispanic/Latino), 1,009 international. Average age 30. 5,818 applicants, 52% accepted, 1798 enrolled. Expenses: Contact institution. *Financial support:* Fellowships, research assistantships, teaching assistantships, career-related internships or fieldwork, Federal Work-Study, institutionally sponsored loans, scholarships/grants, traineeships, and unspecified assistantships available. Support available to part-time students. Financial award application deadline: 4/15; financial award applicants required to submit FAFSA. In 2017, 1,638 master's, 353 doctorates, 458 other advanced degrees awarded. *Program availability:* Part-time, evening/weekend, online learning. *Application fee:* $65 ($85 for international students). Electronic applications accepted. *Application Contact:* Abby Ehling, Assistant Dean, 785-864-8040, Fax: 785-864-7209, E-mail: graduate@ku.edu. *Dean of Graduate Studies,* Michael Roberts, 785-864-8040, E-mail: mroberts@ku.edu.

College of Liberal Arts and Sciences Students: 1,478 full-time (779 women), 211 part-time (125 women); includes 216 minority (56 Black or African American, non-Hispanic/Latino; 26 American Indian or Alaska Native, non-Hispanic/Latino; 31 Asian, non-Hispanic/Latino; 51 Hispanic/Latino; 52 Two or more races, non-Hispanic/Latino), 381 international. Average age 30. 2,247 applicants, 37% accepted, 438 enrolled. Expenses: Contact institution. *Financial support:* Fellowships, research assistantships with partial tuition reimbursements, teaching assistantships with tuition reimbursements, career-related internships or fieldwork, Federal Work-Study, institutionally sponsored loans, scholarships/grants, traineeships, and unspecified assistantships available. Support available to part-time students. Financial award applicants required to submit FAFSA. In 2017, 312 master's, 153 doctorates, 32 other advanced degrees awarded. *Program availability:* Part-time, evening/weekend, online learning. Offers African and African-American studies (MA); African studies (Graduate Certificate); American studies (MA, PhD); anthropology (MA, PhD); applied behavioral science (MA); applied mathematics (Graduate Certificate); art history (MA, PhD); atmospheric science (MS); audiology (PhD); behavioral psychology (PhD); biochemistry and biophysics (PhD); Brazilian studies (Graduate Certificate); Central American and Mexican studies (Graduate Certificate); ceramics (MFA); chemistry (MS, PhD); child language (MA, PhD); city and county management (Graduate Certificate); classics (MA); clinical psychology (MA, PhD); cognitive and brain sciences (MA, PhD); communication studies (MA, PhD); community health and development (Graduate Certificate); computational biology (PhD); creative writing (MFA); developmental psychology (MA, PhD); drawing and painting (MFA); East Asian languages and cultures (MA, Graduate Certificate); ecology and evolutionary biology (MA, PhD); economics (MA, PhD); English (MA, PhD); expanded media (MFA); film and media studies (MA, PhD); foreign area officer (MA); French (MA, PhD); geographic information science (Graduate Certificate); geography (MA, PhD); geology (MS, PhD); gerontology (PhD); global and international studies (MA); history (MA, PhD); indigenous studies (MA, Graduate Certificate); Latin American and Caribbean studies (Graduate Certificate); Latin American studies (MA); liberal arts and sciences (MA, MFA, MPA, MS, MUP, PhD, Graduate Certificate); linguistics (MA, PhD); mathematics (MA, PhD); metalsmithing/jewelry (MFA); microbiology (PhD); molecular, cellular, and developmental biology (PhD); museum studies (MA, Graduate Certificate); performance management (Graduate Certificate); philosophy (MA, PhD); physics and astronomy (MS, PhD); political science (MA, PhD); professional workplace communication (Graduate Certificate); public administration (MPA, PhD); quantitative psychology (PhD); religious studies (MA, Graduate Certificate); Russian, East European and Eurasian studies (MA, Graduate Certificate); sculpture (MFA); Slavic languages and literatures (MA, PhD); social psychology (MA, PhD); sociology (PhD); Spanish and Portuguese (MA, PhD); speech-language pathology (MA, PhD); textiles/fibers (MFA); theatre (MA, PhD); theatre design (MFA); urban planning (MUP); visual art education (MA). *Application fee:* $65 ($85 for international students). Electronic applications accepted. *Application Contact:* Kristine Latta, Director of the College Office of Graduate Affairs, 785-864-1784, E-mail: klatta@ku.edu. *Dean, College of Liberal Arts and Sciences,* Carl W. Lejuez, 785-864-3661, E-mail: clejuez@ku.edu.

School of Architecture and Design Students: 93 full-time (44 women), 32 part-time (16 women); includes 18 minority (4 Black or African American, non-Hispanic/Latino; 5 Asian, non-Hispanic/Latino; 4 Hispanic/Latino; 5 Two or more races, non-Hispanic/Latino), 24 international. Average age 27. 114 applicants, 54% accepted, 23 enrolled. Expenses: Contact institution. *Financial support:* Fellowships, research assistantships, teaching assistantships, career-related internships or fieldwork, scholarships/grants, health care benefits, and unspecified assistantships available. Financial award application deadline: 1/15; financial award applicants required to submit FAFSA. In 2017, 85 master's, 7 doctorates, 5 other advanced degrees awarded. *Program availability:* Part-time. Offers architectural acoustics (Certificate); architecture (M Arch, PhD); architecture and design (M Arch, MA, PhD, Certificate, Graduate Certificate); design management (MA); health and wellness (Certificate); historic preservation (Certificate); interaction design (MA); urban design (Certificate). *Application deadline:* For fall admission, 1/15 priority date for domestic and international students; for summer admission, 1/15 priority date for domestic and international students. *Application fee:* $65 ($85 for international students). Electronic applications accepted. *Application Contact:* Gera Elliott, Admissions Coordinator, 785-864-3167, E-mail: archku@ku.edu. *Dean,* Mahesh Daas, 785-864-3114, E-mail: mahesh@ku.edu.

School of Business Students: 291 full-time (107 women), 468 part-time (163 women); includes 134 minority (35 Black or African American, non-Hispanic/Latino; 5 American Indian or Alaska Native, non-Hispanic/Latino; 28 Asian, non-Hispanic/Latino; 25 Hispanic/Latino; 41 Two or more races, non-Hispanic/Latino), 50 international. Average age 31. 683 applicants, 73% accepted, 419 enrolled. Expenses: Contact institution. *Financial support:* Fellowships, research assistantships, teaching assistantships, career-related internships or fieldwork, Federal Work-Study, and unspecified assistantships available. Financial award application deadline: 1/15; financial award applicants required to submit FAFSA. In 2017, 267 master's, 8 doctorates awarded. *Program availability:* Part-time, evening/weekend. Offers accounting (M Acc); business (M Acc, MBA, MS, PhD); business administration and management (MBA); business and organizational leadership (MS); decision sciences and supply chain management (PhD); finance (PhD); human resources management (PhD); marketing (PhD); organizational behavior (PhD); strategic management (PhD); supply chain management and logistics (MS). *Application deadline:* For fall admission, 1/15 priority date for domestic and international students. *Application fee:* $65 ($85 for international students). Electronic applications accepted. *Application Contact:* Patricia McCaffrey, MBA Coordinator, 785-864-9692, E-mail: pmccaffr@ku.edu. *Dean,* Dr. James P. Guthrie, 785-864-7546, E-mail: jguthrie@ku.edu.

School of Education Students: 503 full-time (326 women), 839 part-time (671 women); includes 212 minority (76 Black or African American, non-Hispanic/Latino; 11 American Indian or Alaska Native, non-Hispanic/Latino; 31 Asian, non-Hispanic/Latino; 43 Hispanic/Latino; 1 Native Hawaiian or other Pacific Islander, non-Hispanic/Latino; 50 Two or more races, non-Hispanic/Latino), 103 international. Average age 33. 907 applicants, 69% accepted, 450 enrolled. Expenses: Contact institution. *Financial support:* Fellowships, research assistantships, teaching assistantships, career-related internships or fieldwork, scholarships/grants, and unspecified assistantships available. Financial award application deadline: 2/1. In 2017, 388 master's, 59 doctorates, 78 other advanced degrees awarded. *Program availability:* Part-time, online learning. Offers autism spectrum disorder (Certificate); counseling psychology (MS, PhD); curriculum and teaching (MA, MS Ed, PhD); early childhood unified (MS Ed); education (MA, MS, MS Ed, MSE, Ed D, PhD, Certificate, Ed S); education leadership and policy (MSE, PhD); educational administration (MSE, Ed D, PhD); educational psychology and research (MS Ed, PhD); educational technology (MS Ed, PhD); exercise science (MS Ed); health, sport, and exercise sciences (PhD); higher education administration (MS Ed, Ed D, PhD); policy studies (PhD); school psychology (PhD, Ed S); social and cultural studies in education (MSE, PhD); special and inclusive education leadership (Certificate); special education (PhD); sport management (MS Ed). *Application fee:* $65 ($85 for international students). Electronic applications accepted. *Application Contact:* Kim Huggett, Graduate Student Services Manager, 785-864-4510, E-mail: khuggett@ku.edu. *Dean,* Dr. Rick J. Ginsberg, 785-864-3726, E-mail: ginsberg@ku.edu.

School of Engineering Students: 398 full-time (104 women), 239 part-time (50 women); includes 76 minority (23 Black or African American, non-Hispanic/Latino; 25 Asian, non-Hispanic/Latino; 12 Hispanic/Latino; 16 Two or more races, non-Hispanic/Latino), 282 international. Average age 29. 669 applicants, 56% accepted, 147 enrolled. Expenses: Contact institution. *Financial support:* Fellowships, research assistantships, teaching assistantships, career-related internships or fieldwork, Federal Work-Study, scholarships/grants, and unspecified assistantships available. In 2017, 178 master's, 31 doctorates, 5 other advanced degrees awarded. *Program availability:* Part-time, evening/weekend, online learning. Offers aerospace engineering (ME, MS, DE, PhD); architectural engineering (MS); bioengineering (MS, PhD); chemical and petroleum engineering (PhD); chemical engineering (MS); civil engineering (MCE, MS, PhD); computer engineering (MS); computer science (MS, PhD); construction management (MCM); electrical engineering (MS, PhD); engineering (MCE, MCM, ME, MS, DE, PhD, Certificate); engineering management (MS, Certificate); environmental engineering (MS, PhD); environmental science (MS, PhD); information technology (MS); mechanical engineering (MS, PhD); petroleum engineering (MS); petroleum management (Certificate); project management (ME, MS). *Application fee:* $65 ($85 for international students). Electronic applications accepted. *Application Contact:* Amy Wierman, Assistant to the Dean, 785-864-2930, E-mail: awierman@ku.edu. *Dean,* Dr. Michael S. Branicky, 785-864-2930, E-mail: msb@ku.edu.

School of Music Students: 157 full-time (77 women), 39 part-time (24 women); includes 14 minority (3 Black or African American, non-Hispanic/Latino; 6 Asian, non-Hispanic/Latino; 5 Two or more races, non-Hispanic/Latino), 53 international. Average age 30. 218 applicants, 58% accepted, 53 enrolled. Expenses: Contact institution. *Financial support:* Fellowships, research assistantships, teaching assistantships, scholarships/grants, and unspecified assistantships available. In 2017, 36 master's, 26 doctorates awarded. Offers music (MM, MME, DMA, PhD); music education (MME, PhD); music therapy (MME, PhD). *Application fee:* $65 ($85 for international students). Electronic applications accepted. *Application Contact:* Jane Gnojek, Graduate Services Coordinator, 785-864-2862, E-mail: jgnojek@ku.edu. *Dean,* Dr. Robert Walzel, 785-864-3421, E-mail: robert.walzel@ku.edu.

School of Pharmacy Students: 94 full-time (44 women), 15 part-time (8 women); includes 12 minority (1 American Indian or Alaska Native, non-Hispanic/Latino; 6 Asian, non-Hispanic/Latino; 3 Hispanic/Latino; 2 Two or more races, non-Hispanic/Latino), 43 international. Average age 28. 165 applicants, 25% accepted, 25 enrolled. Expenses: Contact institution. *Financial support:* Fellowships, research assistantships, teaching assistantships, career-related internships or fieldwork, scholarships/grants, traineeships, and unspecified assistantships available. In 2017, 23 master's, 15 doctorates awarded. Offers medicinal chemistry (MS, PhD); neurosciences (MS, PhD); pharmaceutical chemistry (MS, PhD); pharmacology and toxicology (MS, PhD); pharmacy (MS, PhD). *Application fee:* $65 ($85 for international students). Electronic applications accepted. *Application Contact:* Gina King, Senior Administrative Associate, 785-864-3592, E-mail: ginaking@ku.edu. *Dean,* Kenneth L. Audus, 785-864-3591, E-mail: audus@ku.edu.

School of Social Welfare Students: 330 full-time (290 women), 56 part-time (49 women); includes 87 minority (34 Black or African American, non-Hispanic/Latino; 7 American Indian or Alaska Native, non-Hispanic/Latino; 8 Asian, non-Hispanic/Latino; 17 Hispanic/Latino; 21 Two or more races, non-Hispanic/Latino), 5 international. Average age 30. 315 applicants, 82% accepted, 185 enrolled. Expenses: Contact institution. *Financial support:* Fellowships, research assistantships, teaching assistantships, Federal Work-Study, scholarships/grants, and tuition waivers (partial) available. Support available to part-time students. Financial award application deadline: 1/17; financial award applicants required to submit FAFSA. In 2017, 180 master's, 4 doctorates awarded. *Program availability:* Part-time, online learning. Offers social welfare (MSW, PhD). *Application deadline:* For fall admission, 1/17 for domestic and international students. *Application fee:* $65 ($85 for international students). Electronic applications accepted. *Application Contact:* Becky Hofer, Director of Graduate Admissions, 785-864-8956, E-mail: bhofer@ku.edu. *Interim Dean,* Steve Kapp, 785-864-2269, E-mail: stevek@ku.edu.

William Allen White School of Journalism and Mass Communications Students: 39 full-time (27 women), 60 part-time (44 women); includes 19 minority (9 Black or African American, non-Hispanic/Latino; 2 Asian, non-Hispanic/Latino; 1 Hispanic/Latino; 1 Native Hawaiian or other Pacific Islander, non-Hispanic/Latino; 6 Two or more races, non-Hispanic/Latino), 10 international. Average age 33. 74 applicants, 82% accepted, 42 enrolled. Expenses: Contact institution. *Financial support:* Fellowships, research assistantships, teaching assistantships, career-related internships or fieldwork, scholarships/grants, and unspecified assistantships available. Support available to part-time students. Financial award application deadline: 2/1; financial award applicants required to submit FAFSA. In 2017, 8 master's, 6 doctorates awarded. *Program availability:* Part-time. Offers journalism (MS); journalism and mass communications (PhD). *Application deadline:* For fall admission, 1/1 priority date for domestic and international students; for spring admission, 11/1 for domestic and international students. *Application fee:* $65 ($85 for international students). Electronic applications accepted. *Application Contact:* Jammie A. Johnson, Graduate Advisor/Administrative Assistant, 785-864-7649, E-mail: jamjohn@ku.edu. *Dean,* Ann Brill, 785-864-4755, E-mail: abrill@ku.edu.

School of Law Students: 334 full-time (154 women), 35 part-time (6 women); includes 64 minority (16 Black or African American, non-Hispanic/Latino; 2 American Indian or Alaska Native, non-Hispanic/Latino; 14 Asian, non-Hispanic/Latino; 26 Hispanic/Latino; 6 Two or more races, non-Hispanic/Latino), 27 international. Average age 25. 690 applicants, 54% accepted, 121 enrolled. *Faculty:* 30 full-time (16 women), 20 part-time/adjunct (8 women). Expenses: Contact institution. *Financial support:* In 2017–18, 6 fellowships (averaging $1,800 per year), 65 research assistantships (averaging $1,257 per year), 8 teaching assistantships (averaging $1,875 per year) were awarded; career-related internships or fieldwork, Federal Work-Study, institutionally sponsored loans, and scholarships/grants also available. Financial award application deadline: 2/15; financial award applicants required to submit FAFSA. In 2017, 121 doctorates awarded. Offers law (JD). *Application deadline:* For fall admission, 4/1 priority date for domestic students, 4/1 for international students. Applications are processed on a rolling basis. *Application fee:* $55. Electronic applications accepted. *Application Contact:* Steven Freedman, Assistant Dean for Admissions, 866-220-3654, E-mail: admitlaw@ku.edu. *Dean,* Stephen W. Mazza, 785-864-4550, Fax: 785-864-5054.

University of Kansas Medical Center Students: 1,572 full-time (898 women), 482 part-time (369 women); includes 388 minority (57 Black or African American, non-Hispanic/Latino; 7 American Indian or Alaska Native, non-Hispanic/Latino; 116 Asian, non-Hispanic/Latino; 96 Hispanic/Latino; 1 Native Hawaiian or other Pacific Islander, non-Hispanic/Latino; 111 Two or more races, non-Hispanic/Latino), 95 international. Average age 28. *Faculty:* 1,297. Expenses: Contact institution. In 2017, 161 master's, 349 doctorates, 25 other advanced degrees awarded. Offers health informatics (MS, Post Master's Certificate). *Executive Vice Chancellor,* Dr. Robert Simari, 913-588-1440, E-mail: rsimari@kumc.edu.

School of Health Professions Students: 451 full-time (325 women), 75 part-time (67 women); includes 60 minority (11 Black or African American, non-Hispanic/Latino; 4 American Indian or Alaska Native, non-Hispanic/Latino; 9 Asian, non-Hispanic/Latino; 19 Hispanic/Latino; 1 Native Hawaiian or other Pacific Islander, non-Hispanic/Latino; 16 Two or more races, non-Hispanic/Latino), 22 international. Average age 27. *Faculty:* 110. Expenses: Contact institution. In 2017, 60 master's, 100 doctorates, 21 other advanced degrees awarded. Offers dietetic internship (Graduate Certificate); dietetics and nutrition (MS); health professions (MOT, MS, Au D, DNAP, DPT, OTD, PhD, SLPD, Graduate Certificate); medical nutrition science (PhD); molecular biotechnology (MS); nurse anesthesia education (DNAP); occupational therapy (MOT, OTD); physical therapy (DPT); rehabilitation science (PhD); therapeutic science (PhD). *Dean,* Dr. Abiodun Akinwuntan, 913-588-5235, Fax: 913-588-5254, E-mail: aakinwuntan@kumc.edu.

School of Medicine Students: 1,073 full-time (529 women), 136 part-time (61 women); includes 273 minority (32 Black or African American, non-Hispanic/Latino; 1 American Indian or Alaska Native, non-Hispanic/Latino; 91 Asian, non-Hispanic/Latino; 69 Hispanic/Latino; 80 Two or more races, non-Hispanic/Latino), 72 international. Average age 27. *Faculty:* 1,131. Expenses: Contact institution. In 2017, 60 master's, 231 doctorates, 1 other advanced degree awarded. Offers anatomy and cell biology (MS, PhD); applied statistics and analytics (MS); biochemistry and molecular biology (PhD); biomedical sciences (PhD); biostatistics (MS, PhD, Graduate Certificate); cancer biology (MS, PhD); clinical research (MS); epidemiology (MPH); health policy and management (PhD); health services administration (MHSA); medicine (MHSA, MPH, MS, MD, PhD, Graduate Certificate); microbiology, molecular genetics and immunology (MS, PhD); molecular and integrative physiology (PhD); neuroscience (PhD); pathology and laboratory medicine (MS, PhD); pharmacology (PhD); public health management (MPH); social and behavioral health (MPH); statistical applications (Graduate Certificate); toxicology (PhD). *Executive Dean,* Dr. Robert Simari, 913-588-7201, E-mail: rsimari@kumc.edu.

School of Nursing Students: 48 full-time (44 women), 260 part-time (235 women); includes 50 minority (12 Black or African American, non-Hispanic/Latino; 2 American Indian or Alaska Native, non-Hispanic/Latino; 16 Asian, non-Hispanic/Latino; 8 Hispanic/Latino; 12 Two or more races, non-Hispanic/Latino). Average age 36. 87 applicants, 95% accepted, 61 enrolled. *Faculty:* 56. Expenses: Contact institution. *Financial support:* In 2017–18, 5 research assistantships with tuition reimbursements (averaging $20,000 per year), 30 teaching assistantships with tuition reimbursements (averaging $20,000 per year) were awarded; scholarships/grants and traineeships also available. Financial award application deadline: 3/1; financial award applicants required to submit FAFSA. In 2017, 37 master's, 18 doctorates, 3 other advanced degrees awarded. *Program availability:* Part-time, 100% online, blended/hybrid learning. Offers adult/gerontological clinical nurse specialist (PMC); adult/gerontological nurse practitioner (PMC); health care informatics (PMC); health professions educator (PMC); nurse midwife (PMC); nursing (MS, DNP, PhD); organizational leadership (PMC); psychiatric/mental health nurse practitioner (PMC); public health nursing (PMC). *Application deadline:* For fall admission, 4/1 for domestic and international students; for spring admission, 9/1 for domestic and international students. *Application fee:* $75. Electronic applications accepted. *Application Contact:* Dr. Pamela K. Barnes, Associate Dean, Student Affairs, 913-588-1619, Fax: 913-588-1615, E-mail: pbarnes2@kumc.edu. *Dean,* Dr. Sally Maliski, 913-588-1601, Fax: 913-588-1660, E-mail: smaliski@kumc.edu.

UNIVERSITY OF KENTUCKY, Lexington, KY 40506-0032

General Information State-supported, coed, university. CGS member. *Graduate housing:* Rooms and/or apartments available to single and married students. *Research affiliation:* Continuous Electron Beam Accelerator Facility (high-energy physics), Battelle–Pacific Northwest National Laboratory (environmental sciences), Oak Ridge National Laboratory (nuclear physics), National Institute of Occupational Health and Safety (environmental health), National Drug Addiction Center (drug abuse and prevention).

GRADUATE UNITS

College of Dentistry Students: 260 full-time (135 women); includes 93 minority (25 Black or African American, non-Hispanic/Latino; 1 American Indian or Alaska Native, non-Hispanic/Latino; 35 Asian, non-Hispanic/Latino; 16 Hispanic/Latino; 16 Two or more races, non-Hispanic/Latino), 3 international. Average age 27. 1,838 applicants, 7% accepted, 65 enrolled. *Faculty:* 66 full-time (20 women), 45 part-time/adjunct (13 women). Expenses: Contact institution. *Financial support:* In 2017–18, 158 students received support. Institutionally sponsored loans and scholarships/grants available. Financial award application deadline: 3/1; financial award applicants required to submit FAFSA. In 2017, 66 doctorates awarded. Offers dentistry (DMD). *Application deadline:* For fall admission, 12/1 priority date for domestic students. Applications are processed on a rolling basis. *Application fee:* $75. Electronic applications accepted. *Application Contact:* Rebekah Huff, Student Affairs Officer, 859-323-6071, Fax: 859-257-5550, E-mail: rebekah.huff@uky.edu. *Dean,* Dr. Stephanos Kyrkanides, 859-323-1884, Fax: 859-323-1042, E-mail: stephanos@uky.edu.

College of Law Offers law (JD). Electronic applications accepted.

College of Medicine Students: 543 full-time (245 women). Average age 24. Expenses: Contact institution. *Financial support:* Institutionally sponsored loans available. Financial award applicants required to submit FAFSA. Offers medicine (MD). *Application deadline:* For fall admission, 11/1 for domestic students. Applications are processed on a rolling basis. *Application fee:* $50. Electronic applications accepted. *Application Contact:* Kimberly Scott, Assistant Director of Admissions, 859-323-6161, E-mail: kymedap@uky.edu. *Associate Dean for Admissions,* Dr. Wendy L. Jackson, 859-323-6161.

Graduate School *Program availability:* Part-time, evening/weekend. Offers dentistry (MS); pharmaceutical sciences (MS, PhD); pharmacy (Pharm D). Electronic applications accepted.

College of Agriculture, Food and Environment *Program availability:* Part-time. Offers agricultural economics (MS, PhD); agriculture, food and environment (MS, MSFOR, PhD); animal and food sciences (MS, PhD); biosystems and agricultural engineering (MS, PhD); entomology (MS, PhD); family studies, human development, and resource management (MS, PhD); forestry (MSFOR); hospitality and dietetics administration (MS); integrated plant and soil sciences (MS, PhD); plant pathology (MS, PhD); veterinary science (MS, PhD). Electronic applications accepted.

College of Arts and Sciences *Program availability:* Part-time. Offers anthropology (MA, PhD); applied mathematics (MS); arts and sciences (MA, MS, PhD); biology (MS, PhD); chemistry (MS, PhD); English (MA, PhD); geography (MA, PhD); geology (MS, PhD); German (MA); Hispanic studies (MA, PhD); history (MA, PhD); mathematics (MA, MS, PhD); modern and classical languages and literatures (MA); philosophy (MA, PhD); physics and astronomy (MS, PhD); political science (MA, PhD); psychology (MA, PhD); sociology (MA, MS, PhD); statistics (MS, PhD); teaching world languages (MA). Electronic applications accepted.

College of Communication and Information *Program availability:* Part-time. Offers communication (MA, PhD); communication and information (MA, MSLS, PhD); library and information science (MA, MSLS). Electronic applications accepted.

College of Design Offers architecture (M Arch); design (M Arch, MAIDM, MHP, MSIDM); historic preservation (MHP); interior design (MA). Electronic applications accepted.

College of Education *Program availability:* Part-time, evening/weekend. Offers biomechanics (MS); counseling psychology (MS, PhD, Ed S); curriculum and instruction (Ed D, PhD); early childhood (MS Ed); education (M Ed, MA Ed, MRC, MS, MS Ed, Ed D, PhD, Ed S); educational leadership (M Ed, Ed D, PhD, Ed S); educational policy studies and evaluation (Ed D); educational psychology (MS, PhD); educational sciences (PhD); elementary education (MA Ed); exercise physiology (MS, PhD); exercise science (PhD); family resource and youth services (M Ed, Ed S); health promotion (MS, Ed D); higher education (MS Ed, PhD); instructional system design (MS Ed); literacy (MA Ed); middle school education (MA Ed, MS Ed); physical education training (Ed D); principalship (Ed D, Ed S); rehabilitation counseling (MRC, PhD); school psychology (PhD, Ed S); school technology leadership (M Ed, PhD, Ed S); secondary education (MA Ed, MS Ed); social and philosophical studies (MS Ed); special education (MS Ed, PhD); sport leadership (MS); teacher leadership (M Ed, Ed S); teaching and coaching (MS). Electronic applications accepted.

College of Engineering *Program availability:* Part-time. Offers biomedical engineering (MSBE, PBME, PhD); chemical engineering (MS, PhD); civil engineering (MSCE, PhD); computer science (MS, PhD); electrical engineering (MSEE, PhD); engineering (M Eng, MCE, MME, MS, MS Ch E, MS Min, MSCE, MSEE, MSEM, MSMAE, MSME, MSMSE, PhD); manufacturing systems engineering (MSMSE); materials science and engineering (MS, PhD); mechanical engineering (MSME, PhD); mining engineering (MME, MS Min, PhD). Electronic applications accepted.

College of Fine Arts *Program availability:* Part-time, evening/weekend. Offers art education (MA); art history (MA); art studio (MFA); arts administration (MA); composition (MM, DMA); conducting (MM, DMA); fine arts (MA, MFA, MM, DMA, PhD); music education (MM, PhD); music theory (MA, PhD); music therapy (MM); musicology (MA, PhD); performance (MM, DMA); sacred music (MM). Electronic applications accepted.

College of Health Sciences *Program availability:* Part-time. Offers athletic training (MS); communication disorders (MS); health administration (MHA); health sciences (MHA, MS, MSCD, MSHP, MSNS, MSPAS, MSPT, MSRMP, DS, PhD); nutritional sciences (MSNS, PhD); physical therapy (DPT); physician assistant studies (MSPAS); rehabilitation sciences (PhD). Electronic applications accepted.

College of Nursing Offers nursing (DNP, PhD). Electronic applications accepted.

College of Public Health Offers clinical research design (MS); epidemiology and biostatistics (PhD); gerontology (PhD, Graduate Certificate); public health (MPH, Dr PH, PhD). Electronic applications accepted.

College of Social Work Offers social work (MSW, PhD). Electronic applications accepted.

Gatton College of Business and Economics *Program availability:* Part-time, evening/weekend. Offers accounting (MSACC); business administration (MBA, PhD); business and economics (MBA, MS, MSACC, PhD); economics (MS, PhD). Electronic applications accepted.

Graduate School Programs from the College of Medicine Offers anatomy and neurobiology (PhD); medical science (MS); medicine (MS, PhD); microbiology and immunology (PhD); molecular and biomedical pharmacology (PhD); molecular and cellular biochemistry (PhD); physiology (PhD); radiation sciences (MSRMP); toxicology (MS, PhD). Electronic applications accepted.

Martin School of Public Policy and Administration *Program availability:* Part-time, evening/weekend, 100% online. Offers public administration (MPA); public financial management (MPFM, Graduate Certificate); public policy (MPP); public policy and administration (PhD). Electronic applications accepted.

Patterson School of Diplomacy and International Commerce Offers diplomacy and international commerce (MA). Electronic applications accepted.

UNIVERSITY OF KING'S COLLEGE, Halifax, NS B3H 2A1, Canada

General Information Province-supported, coed, comprehensive institution. *Graduate housing:* Room and/or apartments available on a first-come, first-served basis to single students; on-campus housing not available to married students. Housing application deadline: 4/1.

GRADUATE UNITS

Graduate and Advanced Programs Offers creative nonfiction (MFA); journalism (MJ).

UNIVERSITY OF LA VERNE, La Verne, CA 91750-4443

General Information Independent, coed, university. *Enrollment:* 4,803 graduate, professional, and undergraduate students; 1,588 full-time matriculated graduate/professional students (1,027 women), 1,519 part-time matriculated graduate/professional students (1,029 women). *Enrollment by degree level:* 1,955 master's, 536 doctoral, 316 other advanced degrees. *Graduate faculty:* 152 full-time (82 women), 237 part-time/adjunct (121 women). Tuition and fees vary according to program. *Graduate housing:* Room and/or apartments available on a first-come, first-served basis to single students; on-campus housing not available to married students. *Student services:* Campus employment opportunities, campus safety program, career counseling, exercise/wellness program, free psychological counseling, international student services, low-cost health insurance, multicultural affairs office, services for students with disabilities, teacher training, writing training. *Library facilities:* Wilson Library. *Collection:* Students can reserve study rooms. *Research affiliation:* San Antonio Community Hospital, Riverside Community Hospital, Presbyterian Intercommunity Hospital, Huntington Memorial Hospital (health services management), Southern California Healthcare Systems, Methodist Hospital of Southern California.

Computer facilities: A campuswide network can be accessed from student residence rooms and from off campus. Online class registration, MyLaVerne (online) are available. Website: http://www.laverne.edu/

General Application Contact: Graduate Admission Office, 877-GO-TO-ULV, Fax: 909-392-2761, E-mail: gradadmission@laverne.edu.

GRADUATE UNITS

College of Arts and Sciences Students: 60 full-time (55 women), 48 part-time (40 women); includes 57 minority (7 Black or African American, non-Hispanic/Latino; 1 Asian, non-Hispanic/Latino; 48 Hispanic/Latino; 1 Two or more races, non-Hispanic/Latino), 1 international. Average age 27. *Faculty:* 9 full-time (4 women), 17 part-time/adjunct (11 women). Expenses: Contact institution. *Financial support:* Career-related internships or fieldwork, institutionally sponsored loans, scholarships/grants, and unspecified assistantships available. Financial award application deadline: 3/2; financial award applicants required to submit FAFSA. *Program availability:* Part-time. Offers arts and sciences (MFT, MS, Psy D); clinical psychology (Psy D); marriage and family therapy (MFT, MS). *Application deadline:* Applications are processed on a rolling basis. *Application Contact:* Christy Ranells, Associate Director of Graduate Admissions, 909-448-4644, Fax: 909-971-2295, E-mail: cranells@laverne.edu. *Dean, College of Arts and Sciences*, Dr. Lawrence Potter, 909-448-4188, E-mail: lpotter@laverne.edu.

College of Business and Public Management Students: 642 full-time (339 women), 276 part-time (157 women); includes 286 minority (42 Black or African American, non-Hispanic/Latino; 2 American Indian or Alaska Native, non-Hispanic/Latino; 36 Asian, non-Hispanic/Latino; 197 Hispanic/Latino; 2 Native Hawaiian or other Pacific Islander, non-Hispanic/Latino; 7 Two or more races, non-Hispanic/Latino), 486 international. Average age 30. *Faculty:* 50 full-time (25 women), 38 part-time/adjunct (9 women). Expenses: Contact institution. *Financial support:* Career-related internships or fieldwork, institutionally sponsored loans, and scholarships/grants available. Financial award application deadline: 3/2; financial award applicants required to submit FAFSA. *Program availability:* Part-time, evening/weekend, online learning. Offers accounting (MBA, MBA-EP); business and public management (MBA, MBA-EP, MHA, MPA, MS, DPA, Certificate); finance (MS); financial management (MHA); gerontology (MS, Certificate); health services management (MBA); human resource management (Certificate); information technology (MBA, MBA-EP); international business (MBA, MBA-EP); leadership and management (MS); management and leadership (MBA, MBA-EP, MHA); marketing (MBA, MBA-EP); marketing and business development (MHA); nonprofit (MPA); nonprofit management (Certificate); organizational leadership (Certificate); public administration (MPA, DPA); public health (MPA); supply chain management (MBA, MBA-EP); urban management and affairs (MPA). *Application deadline:* Applications are processed on a rolling basis. *Application fee:* $50. Electronic applications accepted. *Application Contact:* Rina Lazarian-Chehab, Senior Associate Director of Graduate Admissions, 909-448-4317, Fax: 909-971-2295, E-mail: rlazarian@laverne.edu. *Dean, College of Business and Public Management*, Dr. Abe Helou, 909-448-4455, E-mail: ihelou@laverne.edu.

College of Law *Program availability:* Part-time, evening/weekend. Offers law (JD). Electronic applications accepted.

LaFetra College of Education Students: 277 full-time (218 women), 633 part-time (493 women); includes 523 minority (49 Black or African American, non-Hispanic/Latino; 3 American Indian or Alaska Native, non-Hispanic/Latino; 31 Asian, non-Hispanic/Latino; 419 Hispanic/Latino; 1 Native Hawaiian or other Pacific Islander, non-Hispanic/Latino; 20 Two or more races, non-Hispanic/Latino), 8 international. Average age 34. *Faculty:* 33 full-time (24 women), 35 part-time/adjunct (29 women). Expenses: Contact institution. *Financial support:* Federal Work-Study, institutionally sponsored loans, and scholarships/grants available. Financial award application deadline: 3/2; financial award applicants required to submit FAFSA. *Program availability:* Part-time, evening/weekend, 100% online, blended/hybrid learning. Offers advanced teaching skills (M Ed); child development (MS); child life (MS); education (M Ed, MA, MS, Ed D, Certificate, Credential); educational counseling (MS); educational leadership (M Ed); mild/moderate education specialist (Credential); multiple subject (Credential); organizational leadership (Ed D); pupil personnel services (Credential); reading (M Ed, Certificate); reading and language arts specialist (Credential); school psychology (MS); single subject (Credential); social justice higher education administration (MA); special education studies (MS); special emphasis (M Ed); teaching (MA). *Application deadline:* Applications are processed on a rolling basis. *Application fee:* $50. *Application Contact:* Christy Ranells, Associate Director of Graduate Admission, 909-448-4644, Fax: 909-971-2295, E-mail: cranells@laverne.edu. *Dean of LaFetra College of Education*, Dr. Kimberly White-Smith, 909-448-4583, E-mail: kwhite-smith@laverne.edu.

Regional and Online Campuses Students: 456 full-time (328 women), 516 part-time (334 women); includes 562 minority (68 Black or African American, non-Hispanic/Latino; 6 American Indian or Alaska Native, non-Hispanic/Latino; 55 Asian, non-Hispanic/Latino; 400 Hispanic/Latino; 5 Native Hawaiian or other Pacific Islander, non-Hispanic/Latino; 28 Two or more races, non-Hispanic/Latino). Average age 36. *Faculty:* 40 full-time (27 women), 125 part-time/adjunct (65 women). Expenses: Contact institution. *Financial support:* Application deadline: 3/2; applicants required to submit FAFSA. In 2017, 356 master's, 144 other advanced degrees awarded. *Program availability:* Part-time, evening/weekend. Offers administration services (preliminary) (Credential); business administration (MBA, MBA-EP); business administration for experienced professionals (MBA, MBA-EP, MS); child development (MS); education (special emphasis) (M Ed); education specialist: mild/moderate (Credential); educational (special emphasis) (M Ed); educational counseling (MS); educational leadership (M Ed); English (Certificate); health administration (MHA); leadership and management (MS); mild/moderate education specialist (Credential); multiple subject (elementary) (Credential); multiple subject teaching (Credential); organizational leadership (Ed D); preliminary administrative services (Credential); pupil personnel services (Credential); pupil personnel services: school counseling (Credential); single subject (secondary) (Credential); single subject teaching (Credential); special education (MS); special education studies (MS); special emphasis (M Ed). *Application deadline:* Applications are processed on a rolling basis. *Application fee:* $50. *Application Contact:* Graduate Admission Office, 877-468-6858, E-mail: gradadmission@laverne.edu. *Interim Dean*, Dr. Nelly Kazman, 909-448-4995, E-mail: nkazman@laverne.edu.

UNIVERSITY OF LETHBRIDGE, Lethbridge, AB T1K 3M4, Canada

General Information Province-supported, coed, university. CGS member. *Graduate housing:* Rooms and/or apartments available on a first-come, first-served basis to single and married students. Housing application deadline: 4/1. *Research affiliation:* Plains Midstream Canada ULC, Pacific Forestry Institution.

GRADUATE UNITS

School of Graduate Studies *Program availability:* Part-time, evening/weekend. Offers addictions counseling (M Sc); agricultural biotechnology (M Sc); agricultural studies (M Sc, MA); anthropology (MA); archaeology (M Sc, MA); art (MA, MFA); biochemistry (M Sc); biological sciences (M Sc); biomolecular science (PhD); biosystems and biodiversity (PhD); Canadian studies (MA); chemistry (M Sc); computer science (M Sc); computer science and geographical information science (M Sc); counseling (MC); counseling psychology (M Ed); dramatic arts (MA); earth, space, and physical science (PhD); economics (MA); education (MA, PhD); educational leadership (M Ed); English (MA); environmental science (M Sc); evolution and behavior (PhD); exercise science (M Sc); French (MA); French/German (MA); French/Spanish (MA); general education (M Ed); geography (M Sc, MA); German (MA); health sciences (M Sc); individualized multidisciplinary (M Sc, MA); kinesiology (M Sc, MA); management (M Sc); mathematics (M Sc); music (M Mus, MA); Native American studies (MA); neuroscience (M Sc, PhD); new media (MA, MFA); nursing (M Sc, MN); philosophy (MA); physics (M Sc); political science (MA); psychology (M Sc, MA); religious studies (MA); sociology (MA); theatre and dramatic arts (MFA); theoretical and computational science (PhD); urban and regional studies (MA); women and gender studies (MA). Electronic applications accepted.

UNIVERSITY OF LOUISIANA AT LAFAYETTE, Lafayette, LA 70504

General Information State-supported, coed, university. CGS member. *Enrollment:* 924 full-time matriculated graduate/professional students (471 women), 707 part-time matriculated graduate/professional students (454 women). *Enrollment by degree level:* 1,176 master's, 420 doctoral, 2,424 other advanced degrees. *Graduate faculty:* 319 full-time (115 women), 18 part-time/adjunct (11 women). *Graduate housing:* Rooms and/or apartments available on a first-come, first-served basis to single and married students. Housing application deadline: 66/15. *Student services:* Campus employment opportunities, campus safety program, career counseling, child daycare facilities, free psychological counseling, international student services, low-cost health insurance, services for students with disabilities. *Library facilities:* Edith Garland Dupre Library. *Collection:* Books: 1.4 million (physical); Serial titles: 20,881 (physical); Databases: 149. Students can reserve study rooms. *Research affiliation:* National Wetlands Research Center (biology, wetlands restoration), Louisiana Universities Marine Consortium (marine biology), U.S. Fish and Wildlife Service (ecology), Army Corps of Engineers (wetlands), U.S. Geological Survey (USGS), U.S. Department of Agriculture (USDA).

Computer facilities: 413 computers available on campus for general student use. A campuswide network can be accessed from off campus. Online class registration is available.
Website: http://www.louisiana.edu/

General Application Contact: Dr. Mary J. Farmer-Kaiser, Dean, 337-482-6965, Fax: 337-482-1333, E-mail: kaiser@louisiana.edu.

GRADUATE UNITS

BI Moody III College of Business Administration MBA Program Expenses: Contact institution. *Program availability:* Part-time, evening/weekend. Offers accounting (MS); business administration (MBA); entrepreneurship (MBA); finance (MBA); global management (MBA); health care administration (MBA); hospitality management (MBA); human resource management (MBA); project management (MBA); sales leadership (MBA). *Application deadline:* For fall admission, 5/15 for domestic students. *Application fee:* $25 ($30 for international students). *Application Contact:* Dr. C. E. Palmer, Dean, 337-482-6965, Fax: 337-482-1333, E-mail: palmer@louisiana.edu. *Graduate Coordinator*, P. Robert Viguerie, Jr., 337-482-5882, E-mail: MBADirector@louisiana.edu.

College of Education Expenses: Contact institution. *Financial support:* Application deadline: 5/1. *Program availability:* Part-time. Offers counselor education (MS); education (M Ed, MS, Ed D); education of the gifted (M Ed); educational curriculum and instruction (M Ed); educational foundations and leadership (M Ed, Ed D); instructional specialist (M Ed); K-8 mathematics education (M Ed); non-public schools administration (M Ed); special education diagnostics (M Ed); teacher researcher (M Ed). *Application deadline:* For fall admission, 5/15 for domestic and international students; for spring admission, 10/1 for domestic and international students. Applications are processed on a rolling basis. *Application fee:* $25 ($30 for international students). Electronic applications accepted. *Application Contact:* Dr. Nathan Roberts, Coordinator, 337-482-6747, Fax: 337-482-5842, E-mail: nmr0713@louisiana.edu. *Dean*, Dr. Nathan Roberts, 337-482-6678, E-mail: nroberts@louisiana.edu.

College of Engineering Expenses: Contact institution. *Program availability:* Part-time, evening/weekend. Offers chemical engineering (MSE); civil engineering (MSE); computer engineering (MS, PhD); electrical engineering (MSE); engineering (MS, MSE, MSTC, PhD); mechanical engineering (MSE); petroleum engineering (MSE); systems engineering (PhD); systems technology (MRE). *Application deadline:* For fall admission, 5/15 for domestic and international students; for spring admission, 10/1 for domestic and international students. Applications are processed on a rolling basis. *Application fee:* $25 ($30 for international students). Electronic applications accepted. *Application Contact:* Dr. C. E. Palmer, Dean, 337-482-6965, Fax: 337-482-1333, E-mail: palmer@louisiana.edu. *Dean*, Dr. Mark E. Zappi, 337-482-6685, Fax: 337-482-6688, E-mail: zappi@louisiana.edu.

College of Liberal Arts Expenses: Contact institution. *Financial support:* Application deadline: 5/1. *Program availability:* Part-time. Offers American culture (MA, PhD); American literature and language (PhD); applied language and speech sciences (PhD); communication (MS); creative writing (MA, PhD); folklore (MA, PhD); Francophone studies (PhD); French (MA); history (MA); liberal arts (MA, MS, PhD); linguistic studies (MA, PhD); professional writing (PhD); psychology (MS); rhetoric (MA, PhD); speech pathology and audiology (MS); TESOL studies (MA, PhD). *Application deadline:* For fall admission, 5/15 for domestic and international students; for spring admission, 10/1 for domestic and international students. Applications are processed on a rolling basis. *Application fee:* $25 ($30 for international students). Electronic applications accepted. *Application Contact:* Dr. C. E. Palmer, Dean, 337-482-6965, Fax: 337-482-1333, E-mail: palmer@louisiana.edu. *Dean*, Dr. Jordan Kellman, 337-482-6219, E-mail: kellman@louisiana.edu.

College of Nursing and Allied Health Professions Expenses: Contact institution. Offers family nurse practitioner (MSN); nurse executive curriculum (MSN); nursing and allied health professions (DNP). Program offered jointly with Southern Louisiana University, McNeese State University, Southern University and Agricultural and Mechanical College. *Application deadline:* For fall admission, 5/15 for domestic and international students; for spring admission, 10/1 for domestic students. Applications are processed on a rolling basis. *Application fee:* $25 ($30 for international students). Electronic applications accepted. *Application Contact:* Dr. Carolyn P. Delahoussaye, Graduate Coordinator, 337-482-5617, Fax: 337-482-5649, E-mail: cgp6303@louisiana.edu. *Department Head*, Dr. Lisa Broussard, 337-482-5654, E-mail: lisabroussard@louisiana.edu.

College of Sciences Expenses: Contact institution. *Program availability:* Part-time. Offers biology (MS); environmental and evolutionary biology (PhD); environmental resource science (MS); geosciences (MS); mathematics (MS, PhD); physics (MS); sciences (MS, PhD). *Application deadline:* For fall admission, 5/15 for domestic and international students; for spring admission, 10/1 for domestic and international students. Applications are processed on a rolling basis. *Application fee:* $25 ($30 for international students). Electronic applications accepted. *Application Contact:* Dr. C. E. Palmer, Dean, 337-482-6965, Fax: 337-482-1333, E-mail: palmer@louisiana.edu. *Dean*, Dr. Azmy S. Ackleh, 337-482-6986, E-mail: ackleh@louisiana.edu.

Institute of Cognitive Science Offers cognitive science (PhD). Electronic applications accepted.

College of the Arts Expenses: Contact institution. *Financial support:* Application deadline: 5/1. Offers arts (M Arch, MM). *Application deadline:* For fall admission, 5/15 for domestic and international students; for spring admission, 10/1 for domestic and international students. Applications are processed on a rolling basis. *Application fee:* $25 ($30 for international students). Electronic applications accepted. *Application Contact:* Dr. C. E. Palmer, Dean, 337-482-6965, Fax: 337-482-1333, E-mail: palmer@louisiana.edu. *Dean*, H. Gordon Brooks, II, 337-482-6224, Fax: 337-482-5907, E-mail: gbrooks@louisiana.edu.

School of Architecture Expenses: Contact institution. Offers architecture (M Arch). *Application deadline:* For fall admission, 5/15 for domestic and international students; for spring admission, 10/1 for domestic and international students. Applications are processed on a rolling basis. *Application fee:* $25 ($30 for international students). Electronic applications accepted. *Application Contact:* Michael McClure, Coordinator, 337-482-5313, Fax: 337-482-1128, E-mail: mxn9999@louisiana.edu. *Graduate Coordinator*, Kari Smith, 337-482-5315, E-mail: kjs9673@louisiana.edu.

School of Music Expenses: Contact institution. *Financial support:* Application deadline: 5/1. Offers conducting (MM); music education (MM); performance (MM); performance pedagogy (MM); theory/composition (MM). *Application deadline:* For fall admission, 5/15 for domestic and international students; for spring admission, 10/1 for domestic and international students. Applications are processed on a rolling basis. *Application fee:* $25 ($30 for international students). Electronic applications accepted. *Application Contact:* Dr. Andrea Loewy, Graduate Coordinator, 337-482-5214, Fax: 337-482-5017, E-mail: akl9749@louisiana.edu. *Graduate Coordinator*, Dr. Catherine Roche-Wallace, 337-482-5208, E-mail: roche-wallace@louisiana.edu.

UNIVERSITY OF LOUISIANA AT MONROE, Monroe, LA 71209-0001

General Information State-supported, coed, university. *Enrollment:* 9,181 graduate, professional, and undergraduate students; 802 full-time matriculated graduate/professional students (537 women), 410 part-time matriculated graduate/professional students (286 women). *Enrollment by degree level:* 648 master's, 511 doctoral, 53 other advanced degrees. *Graduate faculty:* 102 full-time (51 women), 20 part-time/adjunct (14 women). Tuition, state resident: full-time $6489; part-time $479 per hour. Tuition, nonresident: full-time $12,100; part-time $479 per hour. *Required fees:* $8860; $802 per hour. $3273 per semester. *Graduate housing:* Room and/or apartments available on a first-come, first-served basis to single students; on-campus housing not available to married students. Typical cost: $7850 (including board). Housing application deadline: 5/1. *Student services:* Campus employment opportunities, career counseling, child daycare facilities, exercise/wellness program, free psychological counseling, international student services, services for students with disabilities. *Library facilities:* University Library. *Collection:* Books: 150,255 (physical), 293,246 (digital/electronic); Serial titles: 245 (physical), 93,407 (digital/electronic); Databases: 101. Students can reserve study rooms. *Research affiliation:* Juvenile Diabetes Research Foundation (pharmacology), Philip Morris, Inc. (medicinal chemistry), Harvard Hughes Medical Institute (biology), Xenoport, Inc. (pharmaceutics), U.S. Army Corps of Engineers (toxicology, environmental science), National Center for Toxicological Research (toxicology).

Computer facilities: Computer purchase and lease plans are available. A campuswide network can be accessed from student residence rooms and from off campus. Online class registration is available.
Website: http://www.ulm.edu/

General Application Contact: Karen Higuera, Coordinator of Graduate Admissions, 318-342-1753, Fax: 318-342-1042, E-mail: gradadmissions@ulm.edu.

GRADUATE UNITS

Graduate School Students: 804 full-time (537 women), 429 part-time (303 women); includes 341 minority (219 Black or African American, non-Hispanic/Latino; 3 American Indian or Alaska Native, non-Hispanic/Latino; 48 Asian, non-Hispanic/Latino; 39 Hispanic/Latino; 1 Native Hawaiian or other Pacific Islander, non-Hispanic/Latino; 31 Two or more races, non-Hispanic/Latino), 67 international. Average age 29. 439 applicants, 64% accepted, 194 enrolled. *Faculty:* 102 full-time (51 women), 19 part-time/adjunct (14 women). Expenses: Contact institution. *Financial support:* In 2017–18, 361 students received support. Research assistantships, teaching assistantships, career-related internships or fieldwork, Federal Work-Study, institutionally sponsored loans, tuition waivers (full and partial), and unspecified assistantships available. Support available to part-time students. Financial award application deadline: 4/1; financial award applicants required to submit FAFSA. In 2017, 278 master's, 126 doctorates awarded. *Program availability:* Part-time, evening/weekend, 100% online, blended/hybrid learning. *Application deadline:* For fall admission, 3/1 priority date for domestic and international students; for winter admission, 4/1 priority date for domestic students, 4/1 for international students; for spring admission, 8/1 priority date for domestic and international students. Applications are processed on a rolling basis. *Application fee:* $20 ($30 for international students). Electronic applications accepted. *Application Contact:* Karen Higuera, Coordinator of Graduate Admissions, 318-342-1038, Fax: 318-342-1042, E-mail: higuera@ulm.edu. *Dean*, Dr. Sushma Krishnamurthy, 318-342-1036, Fax: 318-342-1042, E-mail: krishnamurthy@ulm.edu.

College of Arts, Education, and Sciences Students: 87 full-time (54 women), 142 part-time (111 women); includes 59 minority (52 Black or African American, non-Hispanic/Latino; 1 Asian, non-Hispanic/Latino; 6 Two or more races, non-Hispanic/Latino), 11 international. Average age 32. 155 applicants, 39% accepted, 42 enrolled. *Faculty:* 30 full-time (14 women), 4 part-time/adjunct (3 women). Expenses: Contact institution. *Financial support:* Research assistantships with full tuition reimbursements, teaching assistantships with full tuition reimbursements, career-related internships or fieldwork, Federal Work-Study, institutionally sponsored loans, and unspecified assistantships available. Support available to part-time students. Financial award application deadline: 4/1; financial award applicants required to submit FAFSA. In 2017, 48 master's, 8 doctorates awarded. *Program availability:* Part-time, evening/weekend. Offers arts, education, and sciences (M Ed, MA, MAT, MS, Ed D); biology (MS); communication (MA); curriculum and instruction (M Ed, Ed D); elementary education (MAT); English (MA); history (MA); secondary education (MAT); special education (MAT). *Application deadline:* For fall admission, 8/24 priority date for domestic students, 3/1 priority date for international students; for winter admission, 12/14 priority date for domestic students, 4/1 priority date for international students; for spring admission, 1/19 priority date for domestic students, 8/1 priority date for international students. Applications are processed on a rolling basis. *Application fee:* $20 ($30 for international students). Electronic applications accepted. *Application Contact:* Dr. Jeffrey Anderson, Interim Associate Dean, 318-342-1243, Fax: 318-342-1755, E-mail: jeanderson@ulm.edu. *Interim Dean*, Dr. Chris Michaelides, 318-342-1235, Fax: 318-342-1755, E-mail: cmichaelides@ulm.edu.

College of Business and Social Sciences Students: 94 full-time (63 women), 115 part-time (67 women); includes 76 minority (56 Black or African American, non-Hispanic/Latino; 3 Asian, non-Hispanic/Latino; 10 Hispanic/Latino; 7 Two or more races, non-Hispanic/Latino), 21 international. Average age 28. 173 applicants, 61% accepted, 62 enrolled. *Faculty:* 23 full-time (8 women), 4 part-time/adjunct (2 women). Expenses: Contact institution. *Financial support:* In 2017–18, 69 students received support. Research assistantships, career-related internships or fieldwork, Federal Work-Study, and unspecified assistantships available. Financial award application deadline: 4/1; financial award applicants required to submit FAFSA. In 2017, 69 master's awarded. *Program availability:* Part-time, evening/weekend, online learning. Offers business administration (MBA); business and social sciences (MA, MBA, MPA, MS); criminal justice (MA); forensic psychology (MS); general psychology (MS); psychometrics (MS); public administration (MPA). *Application deadline:* For fall admission, 8/24 for domestic students, 7/1 for international students; for winter admission, 12/14 for domestic students; for spring admission, 1/19 for domestic students, 11/1 for international students. Applications are processed on a rolling basis. *Application fee:* $20 ($30 for international students). Electronic applications accepted. *Dean*, Dr. Ronald Berry, 318-342-1103, E-mail: rberry@ulm.edu.

College of Health and Pharmaceutical Sciences Students: 591 full-time (395 women), 95 part-time (65 women); includes 178 minority (95 Black or African American, non-Hispanic/Latino; 3 American Indian or Alaska Native, non-Hispanic/Latino; 42 Asian, non-Hispanic/Latino; 20 Hispanic/Latino; 1 Native Hawaiian or other Pacific Islander, non-Hispanic/Latino; 17 Two or more races, non-Hispanic/Latino), 35 international. Average age 27. 335 applicants, 28% accepted, 81 enrolled. *Faculty:* 50 full-time (30 women), 11 part-time/adjunct (9 women). Expenses: Contact institution. *Financial support:* In 2017–18, 165 students received support. Research assistantships, career-related internships or fieldwork, Federal Work-Study, and unspecified assistantships available. Financial award application deadline: 4/1; financial award applicants required to submit FAFSA. In 2017, 90 master's, 110 doctorates awarded. Offers aging studies (MA); applied exercise science (MS); clinical exercise physiology (MS); clinical mental health counseling (MS); gerontology (CGS); grief care management (MA); health and pharmaceutical sciences (MA, MOT, MS, PhD, CGS); long-term care administration (MA); marriage and family therapy (MA, PhD); mental health (MA); occupational therapy (MOT); pharmacy (PhD); program administration (MA); school counseling (MS); small business management (MA);

speech-language pathology (MS); sports, fitness and recreation management (MS); toxicology (PhD). *Application deadline:* For fall admission, 8/24 priority date for domestic students, 7/1 for international students; for winter admission, 12/14 priority date for domestic students; for spring admission, 1/19 for domestic students, 11/1 for international students. Applications are processed on a rolling basis. *Application fee:* $20 ($30 for international students). Electronic applications accepted. *Dean*, Dr. Glenn Anderson, Jr., 318-342-1600, E-mail: ganderson@ulm.edu.

UNIVERSITY OF LOUISVILLE, Louisville, KY 40292-0001

General Information State-supported, coed, university. CGS member. *Enrollment:* 21,403 graduate, professional, and undergraduate students; 4,060 full-time matriculated graduate/professional students (2,099 women), 1,578 part-time matriculated graduate/professional students (819 women). *Enrollment by degree level:* 2,873 master's, 2,627 doctoral, 138 other advanced degrees. *Graduate faculty:* 1,814 full-time (756 women), 556 part-time/adjunct (299 women). Tuition, state resident: full-time $12,246; part-time $681 per credit hour. Tuition, nonresident: full-time $25,486; part-time $1417 per credit hour. *Required fees:* $196. Tuition and fees vary according to course load, program and reciprocity agreements. *Graduate housing:* Rooms and/or apartments available on a first-come, first-served basis to single and married students. Typical cost: $5231 per year ($8428 including board) for single students. Room and board charges vary according to board plan, campus/location and housing facility selected. *Student services:* Campus employment opportunities, campus safety program, career counseling, child daycare facilities, exercise/wellness program, free psychological counseling, grant writing training, international student services, low-cost health insurance, multicultural affairs office, services for students with disabilities, teacher training, writing training. *Library facilities:* William F. Ekstrom Library plus 6 others. *Collection:* Books: 1.6 million (physical), 367,856 (digital/electronic); Serial titles: 2,158 (physical), 90,689 (digital/electronic); Databases: 345. Weekly public service hours: 97; study areas open 24 hours, 5–7 days a week; students can reserve study rooms. *Research affiliation:* Ford Motor Company, General Electric Company (GE), Oak Ridge National Laboratory, Argonne National Laboratory.

Computer facilities: Computer purchase and lease plans are available. 400 computers available on campus for general student use. A campuswide network can be accessed from student residence rooms and from off campus. Online class registration is available.
Website: http://www.louisville.edu/

General Application Contact: Latonia Craig, Director of Graduate Recruitment and Diversity Retention, 502-852-5207, E-mail: gradadm@louisville.edu.

GRADUATE UNITS

Graduate School Students: 4,060 full-time (2,099 women), 1,578 part-time (819 women); includes 1,181 minority (508 Black or African American, non-Hispanic/Latino; 7 American Indian or Alaska Native, non-Hispanic/Latino; 252 Asian, non-Hispanic/Latino; 226 Hispanic/Latino; 3 Native Hawaiian or other Pacific Islander, non-Hispanic/Latino; 185 Two or more races, non-Hispanic/Latino), 466 international. Average age 30. 7,099 applicants, 34% accepted, 1663 enrolled. *Faculty:* 1,814 full-time (756 women), 556 part-time/adjunct (299 women). Expenses: Contact institution. *Financial support:* In 2017–18, 80 students received support, including 80 fellowships with full tuition reimbursements available (averaging $20,000 per year); diversity scholarships also available. Financial award application deadline: 1/1; financial award applicants required to submit FAFSA. In 2017, 830 master's, 398 doctorates, 73 other advanced degrees awarded. *Program availability:* Part-time. *Application deadline:* For fall admission, 12/1 priority date for domestic and international students; for winter admission, 11/1 for domestic students, 6/1 for international students; for spring admission, 11/1 for domestic students, 6/1 for international students; for summer admission, 4/1 for domestic students, 1/1 for international students. Applications are processed on a rolling basis. *Application fee:* $65. Electronic applications accepted. *Application Contact:* Dr. Paul DeMarco, Associate Dean, 502-852-6490, E-mail: gradadm@louisville.edu. *Dean and Vice Provost for Graduate Affairs*, Dr. Beth A. Boehm, 502-852-6495, Fax: 502-852-2365, E-mail: beth.boehm@louisville.edu.

College of Arts and Sciences Students: 484 full-time (247 women), 234 part-time (114 women); includes 141 minority (63 Black or African American, non-Hispanic/Latino; 1 American Indian or Alaska Native, non-Hispanic/Latino; 9 Asian, non-Hispanic/Latino; 34 Hispanic/Latino; 34 Two or more races, non-Hispanic/Latino), 94 international. Average age 33. 438 applicants, 60% accepted, 164 enrolled. *Faculty:* 403 full-time (172 women), 158 part-time/adjunct (90 women). Expenses: Contact institution. *Financial support:* In 2017–18, 10 research assistantships with full tuition reimbursements (averaging $18,000 per year), 240 teaching assistantships with full tuition reimbursements (averaging $18,000 per year) were awarded; scholarships/grants, health care benefits, and unspecified assistantships also available. In 2017, 105 master's, 29 doctorates, 33 other advanced degrees awarded. *Program availability:* Part-time, 100% online. Offers African and Diaspora studies (MA); African-American studies (MA); analytical chemistry (MS, PhD); anthropology (MA); applied and industrial mathematics (PhD); applied geography (MS); applied sociology (PhD); art history (MA, PhD); arts and sciences (MA, MFA, MPA, MS, MUP, PhD, Certificate); biochemistry (MS, PhD); biology (MS); chemical physics (PhD); civic leadership (MA); clinical psychology (PhD); communication (MA); criminal justice (MS, PhD); culture, criticism, and contemporary thought (PhD); curatorial studies (MA); design (MFA); digital politics (MA); English (MA); environmental biology (PhD); experimental psychology (PhD); French (MA); history (MA); humanities (MA, PhD); inorganic chemistry (MS, PhD); linguistics (MA); mathematics (MA); organic chemistry (MS, PhD); performance (MFA); physical chemistry (MS, PhD); physics (MS, PhD); political science (MA); public administration (MPA); public arts and letters (PhD); public history (Certificate); rhetoric and composition (PhD); sociology (MA); Spanish (MA); studio art (MFA); traditional humanities (MA); translation and interpretation (Certificate); urban and public affairs (PhD); urban planning (MUP); women's and gender studies (MA, Certificate). *Application deadline:* Applications are processed on a rolling basis. *Application fee:* $65. Electronic applications accepted. *Application Contact:* Dr. Janet Woodruff-Borden, Associate Dean for Graduate Education, 502-852-8966, Fax: 502-852-6888, E-mail: j.woodruff-borden@louisville.edu. *Dean*, Dr. Kimberly Kempf-Leonard, 502-852-6490, Fax: 502-852-6888, E-mail: kleonard@louisville.edu.

College of Business Students: 288 full-time (117 women), 51 part-time (23 women); includes 57 minority (28 Black or African American, non-Hispanic/Latino; 1 American Indian or Alaska Native, non-Hispanic/Latino; 12 Asian, non-Hispanic/Latino; 11 Hispanic/Latino; 5 Two or more races, non-Hispanic/Latino), 34 international. Average age 31. 346 applicants, 64% accepted, 180 enrolled. *Faculty:* 78 full-time (22 women), 18 part-time/adjunct (4 women). Expenses: Contact institution. *Financial support:* Fellowships with full tuition reimbursements, research assistantships with full tuition reimbursements, teaching assistantships with full tuition reimbursements, scholarships/grants, health care benefits, and unspecified assistantships available. Financial award application deadline: 3/15; financial award applicants required to submit FAFSA. In 2017, 86 master's awarded. *Program availability:* Part-time. Offers accountancy (MAC); business (MAC, MBA, PhD); entrepreneurship (PhD); global business (MBA); health sector management (MBA). *Application deadline:* For fall admission, 3/31 for domestic students, 5/1 priority date for international students; for spring admission, 12/1 for domestic students, 11/1 priority date for international students; for summer admission, 4/1 priority date for international students. Applications are processed on a rolling basis. *Application fee:* $60. *Application Contact:* Susan E. Hildebrand, Program Director, 502-852-7257, Fax: 502-852-4901, E-mail: s.hildebrand@louisville.edu. *Dean*, Dr. Todd Mooradian, 502-852-6443, Fax: 502-852-7557, E-mail: todd.mooradian@louisville.edu.

College of Education and Human Development Students: 477 full-time (250 women), 717 part-time (431 women); includes 318 minority (184 Black or African American, non-Hispanic/Latino; 2 American Indian or Alaska Native, non-Hispanic/Latino; 23 Asian, non-Hispanic/Latino; 68 Hispanic/Latino; 2 Native Hawaiian or other Pacific Islander, non-Hispanic/Latino; 39 Two or more races, non-Hispanic/Latino), 14 international. Average age 32. 588 applicants, 70% accepted, 269 enrolled. *Faculty:* 106 full-time (71 women), 71 part-time/adjunct (48 women). Expenses: Contact institution. *Financial support:* In 2017–18, 8 fellowships with full tuition reimbursements (averaging $20,694 per year), 34 research assistantships with full tuition reimbursements (averaging $20,694 per year), 13 teaching assistantships with full tuition reimbursements (averaging $20,694 per year) were awarded; Federal Work-Study, scholarships/grants, health care benefits, and unspecified assistantships also available. Financial award application deadline: 3/1; financial award applicants required to submit FAFSA. In 2017, 194 master's, 7 doctorates, 19 other advanced degrees awarded. *Program availability:* Part-time, evening/weekend, 100% online, blended/hybrid learning. Offers art education (MAT); autism and applied behavior analysis (Certificate); community health education (M Ed); counseling and personnel services (M Ed, PhD); curriculum and instruction (PhD); early elementary education (MAT); education and human development (M Ed, MA, MAT, MS, Ed D, PhD, Certificate, Ed S); educational leadership and organizational development (Ed D, PhD); exercise physiology (MS); health and physical education (MAT); health professions education (Certificate); higher education (MA); higher education administration (MA); human resources and organization development (MS); instructional technology (M Ed); interdisciplinary early childhood education (MAT); middle school education (MAT); music education (MAT); P-12 educational administration (Ed S); secondary education (MAT); special education (MAT); sport administration (MS); teacher leadership (M Ed). *Application deadline:* For fall admission, 6/1 priority date for domestic students; for spring admission, 10/1 priority date for domestic students; for summer admission, 3/1 priority date for domestic students. *Application fee:* $65. *Application Contact:* Betty Hampton, Director, Graduate Student Services, 502-852-0411, Fax: 502-852-1465, E-mail: edadvise@louisville.edu. *Dean, College of Education and Human Development*, Dr. Ann A. Larson, 502-852-6411, Fax: 502-852-1464, E-mail: cehdinfo@louisville.edu.

Kent School of Social Work Students: 402 full-time (357 women), 103 part-time (88 women); includes 119 minority (68 Black or African American, non-Hispanic/Latino; 1 American Indian or Alaska Native, non-Hispanic/Latino; 8 Asian, non-Hispanic/Latino; 16 Hispanic/Latino; 26 Two or more races, non-Hispanic/Latino), 5 international. Average age 31. 396 applicants, 78% accepted, 228 enrolled. *Faculty:* 31 full-time (22 women), 44 part-time/adjunct (35 women). Expenses: Contact institution. *Financial support:* In 2017–18, 11 research assistantships with full tuition reimbursements (averaging $21,500 per year), 1 teaching assistantship with full tuition reimbursement (averaging $19,000 per year) were awarded; scholarships/grants, health care benefits, and unspecified assistantships also available. Financial award application deadline: 5/15; financial award applicants required to submit FAFSA. In 2017, 179 master's awarded. *Program availability:* Part-time, evening/weekend, 100% online, blended/hybrid learning. Offers marriage and family therapy (PMC); social work (MSSW, PhD). *Application deadline:* For fall admission, 5/30 for domestic and international students; for spring admission, 9/30 for domestic and international students; for summer admission, 2/28 for domestic and international students. Applications are processed on a rolling basis. *Application fee:* $65. Electronic applications accepted. *Application Contact:* Misty Kupka, Program Manager for Admissions and Recruitment, 502-852-0414, Fax: 502-852-0422, E-mail: misty.kupka@louisville.edu. *Dean*, Dr. David Jenkins, 502-852-3944, Fax: 502-852-0422, E-mail: dajenk03@exchange.louisville.edu.

School of Music Students: 51 full-time (14 women), 3 part-time (2 women); includes 8 minority (3 Black or African American, non-Hispanic/Latino; 2 Asian, non-Hispanic/Latino; 2 Hispanic/Latino; 1 Two or more races, non-Hispanic/Latino), 7 international. Average age 26. 73 applicants, 53% accepted, 29 enrolled. *Faculty:* 38 full-time (11 women), 39 part-time/adjunct (16 women). Expenses: Contact institution. *Financial support:* In 2017–18, 1 fellowship with full tuition reimbursement (averaging $12,000 per year), 12 teaching assistantships with full tuition reimbursements (averaging $12,000 per year) were awarded; Federal Work-Study, scholarships/grants, health care benefits, and unspecified assistantships also available. Financial award application deadline: 3/1. In 2017, 29 master's awarded. *Program availability:* Part-time. Offers composition (MM); electronic composition (MM); music education (MME); music history and literature (MM); music performance (MM); music theory (MM). *Application fee:* $60. Electronic applications accepted. *Application Contact:* Laura Angermeier, Admissions Counselor/Senior Advising Counselor, 502-852-1623, Fax: 502-852-0520, E-mail: leange01@louisville.edu. *Dean*, Dr. Christopher P. Doane, 502-852-6907, Fax: 502-852-0520, E-mail: c0doan01@louisville.edu.

School of Nursing Students: 130 full-time (107 women), 30 part-time (25 women); includes 33 minority (16 Black or African American, non-Hispanic/Latino; 7 Asian, non-Hispanic/Latino; 5 Hispanic/Latino; 5 Two or more races, non-Hispanic/Latino), 2 international. Average age 33. 61 applicants, 67% accepted, 36 enrolled. *Faculty:* 44 full-time (40 women), 45 part-time/adjunct (41 women). Expenses: Contact institution. *Financial support:* In 2017–18, 8 research assistantships with full tuition reimbursements (averaging $20,000 per year), 4 teaching assistantships with full tuition reimbursements (averaging $15,000 per year) were awarded; fellowships with full tuition reimbursements, scholarships/grants, and unspecified assistantships also available. Financial award application deadline: 10/1; financial award applicants required to submit FAFSA. In 2017, 54 master's awarded. *Program availability:* Part-time. Offers adult gerontology nurse practitioner (MSN, DNP); education and administration (MSN); family nurse practitioner (MSN, DNP); neonatal nurse practitioner (MSN, DNP); nursing research (PhD); psychiatric/mental health nurse practitioner (MSN, DNP); women's health nurse practitioner (MSN). *Application deadline:* For fall admission, 1/15 priority date for domestic students, 1/15 for international students; for summer admission, 10/15 priority date for domestic students. *Application fee:* $65. Electronic applications accepted. *Application Contact:*

Trish Hart, Assistant Dean for Student Affairs, 502-852-5825, Fax: 502-852-8783, E-mail: trish.hart@louisville.edu. *Dean and Professor*, Dr. Marcia J. Hern, RN, 502-852-8300, Fax: 502-852-8783, E-mail: m.hern@louisville.edu.

School of Public Health and Information Sciences Students: 130 full-time (84 women), 63 part-time (40 women); includes 59 minority (32 Black or African American, non-Hispanic/Latino; 17 Asian, non-Hispanic/Latino; 6 Hispanic/Latino; 4 Two or more races, non-Hispanic/Latino), 38 international. Average age 32. 179 applicants, 75% accepted, 78 enrolled. *Faculty:* 44 full-time (17 women), 3 part-time/adjunct (1 woman). Expenses: Contact institution. *Financial support:* In 2017–18, 3 fellowships with full tuition reimbursements (averaging $20,000 per year), 8 research assistantships with full tuition reimbursements (averaging $20,000 per year), 2 teaching assistantships with full tuition reimbursements (averaging $20,000 per year) were awarded; career-related internships or fieldwork, Federal Work-Study, scholarships/grants, health care benefits, and unspecified assistantships also available. Support available to part-time students. Financial award application deadline: 5/1; financial award applicants required to submit FAFSA. In 2017, 33 master's, 5 doctorates awarded. *Program availability:* Part-time, evening/weekend. Offers biostatistics (MPH, MS, PhD); decision science (MS); epidemiology (MPH, MS); health policy (MPH); population health management (MPH); public health and information sciences (MPH, MS, PhD); public health sciences (PhD). *Application deadline:* For fall admission, 7/1 for domestic students, 3/1 for international students; for spring admission, 11/1 for domestic students, 10/1 for international students; for summer admission, 4/1 for domestic students, 3/1 for international students. Applications are processed on a rolling basis. *Application fee:* $60. Electronic applications accepted. *Application Contact:* Vicki Lewis, Administrative Assistant, 502-852-1798, Fax: 502-852-3294, E-mail: vicki.lewis@louisville.edu. *Associate Dean for Academic Affairs*, Dr. Craig Elliot Blakely, 502-852-3297, Fax: 502-852-3291, E-mail: craig.blakely@louisville.edu.

J. B. Speed School of Engineering Students: 366 full-time (87 women), 317 part-time (65 women); includes 99 minority (29 Black or African American, non-Hispanic/Latino; 1 American Indian or Alaska Native, non-Hispanic/Latino; 25 Asian, non-Hispanic/Latino; 24 Hispanic/Latino; 20 Two or more races, non-Hispanic/Latino), 214 international. Average age 29. 334 applicants, 46% accepted, 123 enrolled. *Faculty:* 111 full-time (21 women), 14 part-time/adjunct (3 women). Expenses: Contact institution. *Financial support:* In 2017–18, 9 fellowships with full tuition reimbursements (averaging $22,000 per year) were awarded; research assistantships with full tuition reimbursements, teaching assistantships with full tuition reimbursements, scholarships/grants, health care benefits, tuition waivers (full), and unspecified assistantships also available. Financial award application deadline: 2/1. In 2017, 107 master's, 11 doctorates, 5 other advanced degrees awarded. *Program availability:* 100% online, blended/hybrid learning. Offers advancing bioengineering technologies through entrepreneurship (PhD); bioengineering (M Eng, PhD); chemical engineering (M Eng, MS, PhD); civil engineering (M Eng, MS, PhD); computer engineering and computer science (M Eng, MS, PhD); data science (Certificate); engineering (M Eng, MS, PhD, Certificate); engineering management (M Eng); industrial engineering (M Eng, MS, PhD); logistics and distribution (Certificate); network and information security (Certificate). *Application deadline:* For fall admission, 5/1 priority date for domestic and international students; for spring admission, 11/1 priority date for domestic and international students; for summer admission, 3/1 priority date for domestic students, 4/1 priority date for international students. Applications are processed on a rolling basis. *Application fee:* $65. Electronic applications accepted. *Application Contact:* Dr. Michael Harris, Director, Graduate Student Affairs, 502-852-6278, Fax: 502-852-7294, E-mail: mharris@louisville.edu. *Interim Dean, J. B. Speed School of Engineering*, Dr. Gail W. Depuy, 502-852-0115, E-mail: gail.depuy@louisville.edu.

Louis D. Brandeis School of Law *Program availability:* Part-time. Offers law (JD). Electronic applications accepted.

School of Dentistry Students: 507 full-time (228 women), 15 part-time (11 women); includes 122 minority (20 Black or African American, non-Hispanic/Latino; 60 Asian, non-Hispanic/Latino; 26 Hispanic/Latino; 16 Two or more races, non-Hispanic/Latino), 16 international. Average age 26. 183 applicants, 93% accepted, 137 enrolled. *Faculty:* 77 full-time (32 women), 70 part-time/adjunct (18 women). Expenses: Contact institution. *Financial support:* In 2017–18, 1 research assistantship with full tuition reimbursement (averaging $20,000 per year) was awarded. Financial award application deadline: 3/15; financial award applicants required to submit FAFSA. In 2017, 7 master's, 113 doctorates awarded. *Program availability:* Part-time. Offers dentistry (DMD); oral biology (MS). *Application deadline:* For fall admission, 1/1 for domestic and international students. Applications are processed on a rolling basis. *Application fee:* $65. Electronic applications accepted. *Application Contact:* Robin Benningfield, Admissions Counselor, 502-852-5081, Fax: 502-852-1210, E-mail: dmdadms@louisville.edu. *Dean*, Dr. T. Gerry Bradley, 502-852-5295, E-mail: t0brad03@exchange.louisville.edu.

School of Interdisciplinary and Graduate Studies Students: 26 full-time (17 women), 12 part-time (6 women); includes 5 minority (1 Black or African American, non-Hispanic/Latino; 2 Hispanic/Latino; 2 Two or more races, non-Hispanic/Latino), 9 international. Average age 31. 29 applicants, 38% accepted, 11 enrolled. Expenses: Contact institution. *Financial support:* In 2017–18, 120 fellowships with full tuition reimbursements (averaging $20,000 per year) were awarded. Financial award application deadline: 1/15. *Program availability:* Part-time. Offers interdisciplinary studies (MA, MS, PhD). *Application deadline:* For fall admission, 12/1 priority date for domestic and international students; for winter admission, 11/1 for domestic students, 6/1 for international students; for spring admission, 11/1 for domestic students, 6/1 for international students; for summer admission, 4/1 for domestic students, 1/1 for international students. Applications are processed on a rolling basis. *Application fee:* $65. Electronic applications accepted. *Application Contact:* Dr. Paul DeMarco, Associate Dean, 502-852-6490, E-mail: gradadm@louisville.edu. *Dean and Vice Provost for Graduate Affairs*, Dr. Beth A. Boehm, 502-852-6495, E-mail: beth.boehm@louisville.edu.

School of Medicine Students: 883 full-time (448 women), 40 part-time (24 women); includes 181 minority (52 Black or African American, non-Hispanic/Latino; 75 Asian, non-Hispanic/Latino; 22 Hispanic/Latino; 32 Two or more races, non-Hispanic/Latino), 35 international. Average age 26. 3,909 applicants, 11% accepted, 264 enrolled. *Faculty:* 810 full-time (307 women), 82 part-time/adjunct (40 women). Expenses: Contact institution. *Financial support:* Scholarships/grants available. Financial award applicants required to submit FAFSA. In 2017, 32 master's, 166 doctorates awarded. Offers anatomical sciences and neurobiology (MS, PhD); audiology (Au D); biochemistry and molecular genetics (MS, PhD); medicine (MS, Au D, MD, PhD); microbiology and immunology (MS, PhD); pharmacology and toxicology (MS, PhD); physiology (MS, PhD); speech-language pathology (MS). *Application deadline:* For fall admission, 10/15 priority date for domestic students. Applications are processed on a rolling basis. *Application fee:* $75. Electronic applications accepted. *Application Contact:* Dr. Stephen F. Wheeler, Associate Professor, 502-852-5193, Fax: 502-852-0302, E-mail: sfwhee01@louisville.edu. *Dean*, Dr. Toni M. Ganzel, 502-852-1499, Fax: 502-852-1484, E-mail: toni.ganzel@louisville.edu.

UNIVERSITY OF LYNCHBURG, Lynchburg, VA 24501-3199

General Information Independent-religious, coed, comprehensive institution. *Enrollment:* 2,808 graduate, professional, and undergraduate students; 405 full-time matriculated graduate/professional students (271 women), 305 part-time matriculated graduate/professional students (208 women). *Enrollment by degree level:* 405 master's, 270 doctoral, 35 other advanced degrees. *Graduate faculty:* 54 full-time (30 women), 15 part-time/adjunct (8 women). *Graduate housing:* Room and/or apartments available on a first-come, first-served basis to single students; on-campus housing not available to married students. *Student services:* Campus employment opportunities, career counseling, exercise/wellness program, free psychological counseling, international student services, multicultural affairs office, services for students with disabilities, teacher training, writing training. *Library facilities:* Knight-Capron Library. *Collection:* Books: 109,236 (physical), 323,591 (digital/electronic); Serial titles: 109 (physical), 58,732 (digital/electronic); Databases: 98. Study areas open 24 hours, 5–7 days a week; students can reserve study rooms.

Computer facilities: 300 computers available on campus for general student use. A campuswide network can be accessed from student residence rooms and from off campus. Online class registration is available.
Website: http://www.lynchburg.edu/

General Application Contact: Ty Eccles, Director of Graduate Studies, 434-544-8913, E-mail: eccles.t@lynchburg.edu.

GRADUATE UNITS

Graduate Studies Students: 405 full-time (271 women), 305 part-time (208 women); includes 117 minority (67 Black or African American, non-Hispanic/Latino; 11 Asian, non-Hispanic/Latino; 21 Hispanic/Latino; 1 Native Hawaiian or other Pacific Islander, non-Hispanic/Latino; 17 Two or more races, non-Hispanic/Latino), 29 international. Average age 31. 1,054 applicants, 43% accepted, 311 enrolled. *Faculty:* 54 full-time (30 women), 15 part-time/adjunct (8 women). Expenses: Contact institution. *Financial support:* In 2017–18, 205 students received support, including 39 fellowships with full and partial tuition reimbursements available (averaging $8,696 per year), 5 research assistantships with full tuition reimbursements available (averaging $9,666 per year); career-related internships or fieldwork, scholarships/grants, unspecified assistantships, and room and board benefits also available. Financial award applicants required to submit FAFSA. In 2017, 169 master's, 50 doctorates, 8 other advanced degrees awarded. *Program availability:* Part-time, evening/weekend. Offers athletic training (MS); business administration (MBA); clinical mental health counseling (M Ed); criminal justice leadership (MA); educational leadership (Ed D); health informatics management (Certificate); higher education (M Ed); instructional leadership (M Ed); non profit leadership (MA); physical therapy (DPT); physician assistant medicine (MA); physician assisted medicine (D Med Sc); PK-12 administrative and supervisory (M Ed); public health (MPH); reading instruction (M Ed); reading specialist (M Ed); school counseling (M Ed); science education (M Ed); special education (M Ed); teacher licensure (M Ed). *Application deadline:* For fall admission, 7/31 for domestic students; for spring admission, 11/30 for domestic students; for summer admission, 5/1 for domestic students. Applications are processed on a rolling basis. *Application fee:* $30. Electronic applications accepted. *Application Contact:* Ellen Thompson, Graduate Admissions Counselor, 434-544-8841, E-mail: thompson_e@lynchburg.edu. *Dean of Graduate Studies*, Dr. Atul Gupta, 434-544-8651, E-mail: gupta@lynchburg.edu.

UNIVERSITY OF MAINE, Orono, ME 04469

General Information State-supported, coed, university. CGS member. *Enrollment:* 11,240 graduate, professional, and undergraduate students; 1,193 full-time matriculated graduate/professional students (698 women), 377 part-time matriculated graduate/professional students (262 women). *Enrollment by degree level:* 1,030 master's, 441 doctoral, 99 other advanced degrees. *Graduate faculty:* 652 full-time (227 women), 232 part-time/adjunct (100 women). Tuition, state resident: full-time $7722; part-time $429 per credit hour. Tuition, nonresident: full-time $25,146; part-time $1397 per credit hour. *Required fees:* $1162; $581 per credit hour. *Graduate housing:* Rooms and/or apartments available on a first-come, first-served basis to single and married students. Typical cost: $10,260 (including board) for single students. Room and board charges vary according to board plan. Housing application deadline: 8/1. *Student services:* Campus employment opportunities, campus safety program, career counseling, child daycare facilities, exercise/wellness program, free psychological counseling, grant writing training, international student services, low-cost health insurance, multicultural affairs office, services for students with disabilities, teacher training, writing training. *Library facilities:* Fogler Library. *Collection:* Books: 1.2 million (physical), 893,818 (digital/electronic); Serial titles: 65,908 (physical), 130,590 (digital/electronic); Databases: 367. Weekly public service hours: 103; students can reserve study rooms. *Research affiliation:* Mount Desert Island Biological Laboratory (marine molecular biology), Sensor Research Development Corporation (electrical sensors), Maine Medical Center Research Institute (clinical medicine), Maine Institute for Human Genetics (medical genetics), Jackson Laboratory (medical genetics), Bigelow Laboratories for Ocean Sciences (marine science).

Computer facilities: Computer purchase and lease plans are available. 600 computers available on campus for general student use. A campuswide network can be accessed from student residence rooms and from off campus. Online class registration, online housing and financial aid information are available.
Website: http://www.umaine.edu/

General Application Contact: Scott G. Delcourt, Assistant Vice President for Graduate Studies and Senior Associate Dean, 207-581-3291, Fax: 207-581-3232, E-mail: graduate@maine.edu.

GRADUATE UNITS

Graduate School Students: 1,193 full-time (698 women), 377 part-time (262 women); includes 113 minority (12 Black or African American, non-Hispanic/Latino; 26 American Indian or Alaska Native, non-Hispanic/Latino; 24 Asian, non-Hispanic/Latino; 28 Hispanic/Latino; 23 Two or more races, non-Hispanic/Latino), 221 international. Average age 32. 1,369 applicants, 61% accepted, 525 enrolled. *Faculty:* 652 full-time (227 women), 232 part-time/adjunct (100 women). Expenses: Contact institution. *Financial support:* In 2017–18, 868 students received support, including 28 fellowships with full tuition reimbursements available (averaging $22,400 per year), 305 research assistantships with full tuition reimbursements available (averaging $18,200 per year), 312 teaching assistantships with full tuition reimbursements available (averaging $16,000 per year); career-related internships or fieldwork, Federal Work-Study, institutionally sponsored loans, scholarships/grants, tuition waivers (full and partial), and unspecified assistantships also available. Support available to part-time students. Financial award application deadline: 3/1; financial award applicants required to submit

FAFSA. In 2017, 371 master's, 58 doctorates, 81 other advanced degrees awarded. *Program availability:* Part-time, evening/weekend, 100% online, blended/hybrid learning. Offers interdisciplinary studies (MA, PhD); intermedia (MFA). *Application deadline:* For fall admission, 1/15 priority date for domestic and international students; for spring admission, 11/15 priority date for domestic and international students. Applications are processed on a rolling basis. *Application fee:* $65. Electronic applications accepted. *Assistant Vice President for Graduate Studies/Senior Associate Dean,* Scott G. Delcourt, 207-581-3291, Fax: 207-581-3232, E-mail: graduate@maine.edu.

Climate Change Institute Students: 8 full-time (all women), 1 (woman) part-time. Average age 24. 20 applicants, 45% accepted, 1 enrolled. *Faculty:* 39 full-time (11 women). Expenses: Contact institution. *Financial support:* In 2017–18, 9 students received support, including 4 research assistantships with full tuition reimbursements available (averaging $15,200 per year), 1 teaching assistantship with full tuition reimbursement available (averaging $15,200 per year); institutionally sponsored loans and unspecified assistantships also available. Financial award application deadline: 3/1. In 2017, 2 master's awarded. *Program availability:* Part-time. Offers climate change (MS, CGS). *Application deadline:* For fall admission, 11/1 priority date for domestic and international students; for spring admission, 2/1 priority date for domestic and international students. Applications are processed on a rolling basis. *Application fee:* $65. Electronic applications accepted. *Application Contact:* Dr. Karl Kreutz, Graduate Coordinator, 207-581-3011, E-mail: karl.kreutz@maine.edu. *Director,* Dr. Paul Mayewski, 207-581-3019, Fax: 207-581-1203, E-mail: paul.mayewski@maine.edu.

College of Education and Human Development Students: 136 full-time (107 women), 258 part-time (214 women); includes 29 minority (3 Black or African American, non-Hispanic/Latino; 11 American Indian or Alaska Native, non-Hispanic/Latino; 3 Asian, non-Hispanic/Latino; 7 Hispanic/Latino; 5 Two or more races, non-Hispanic/Latino), 4 international. Average age 37. 230 applicants, 89% accepted, 125 enrolled. *Faculty:* 35 full-time (19 women), 47 part-time/adjunct (34 women). Expenses: Contact institution. *Financial support:* In 2017–18, 51 students received support, including 22 teaching assistantships with full tuition reimbursements available (averaging $15,200 per year); career-related internships or fieldwork, Federal Work-Study, institutionally sponsored loans, scholarships/grants, and unspecified assistantships also available. Support available to part-time students. Financial award application deadline: 3/1. In 2017, 110 master's, 7 doctorates, 52 other advanced degrees awarded. *Program availability:* Part-time, evening/weekend. Offers classroom technology integrationist (CGS); counselor education (M Ed, MA, MS, CAS); early childhood teacher (CGS); education (PhD); education and human development (M Ed, MA, MAT, MS, Ed D, PhD, CAS, CGS); education data specialist (CGS); educational leadership (M Ed, CAS); educational technology coordinator (CGS); elementary education (M Ed, CAS); higher education (CAS); human development (MS); individualized education (M Ed); kinesiology and physical education (M Ed, MS); literacy education (CAS); response to intervention for behavior (CGS); science education (M Ed, MS); secondary education (M Ed, CAS); social studies education (M Ed); special education (M Ed, CAS); STEM education (PhD). *Application deadline:* For fall admission, 1/15 priority date for domestic students. Applications are processed on a rolling basis. *Application fee:* $65. Electronic applications accepted. *Application Contact:* Scott G. Delcourt, Senior Associate Dean of the Graduate School, 207-581-3291, Fax: 207-581-3232, E-mail: graduate@maine.edu. *Dean,* Dr. Timothy Reagan, 207-581-2441, Fax: 207-581-2423.

College of Engineering Students: 97 full-time (26 women), 48 part-time (7 women); includes 10 minority (2 Black or African American, non-Hispanic/Latino; 1 American Indian or Alaska Native, non-Hispanic/Latino; 4 Asian, non-Hispanic/Latino; 2 Hispanic/Latino; 1 Two or more races, non-Hispanic/Latino), 59 international. Average age 29. 126 applicants, 69% accepted, 50 enrolled. *Faculty:* 52 full-time (8 women), 5 part-time/adjunct (0 women). Expenses: Contact institution. *Financial support:* In 2017–18, 120 students received support, including 4 fellowships (averaging $22,650 per year), 48 research assistantships (averaging $20,700 per year), 22 teaching assistantships (averaging $16,300 per year); Federal Work-Study, institutionally sponsored loans, scholarships/grants, tuition waivers (full and partial), and unspecified assistantships also available. Financial award application deadline: 3/1. In 2017, 24 master's, 8 doctorates awarded. *Program availability:* Part-time. Offers chemical engineering (MS, PhD); civil and environmental engineering (MS, PSM, PhD); computer engineering (MS); electrical engineering (MS, PhD); engineering (ME, MS, PSM, PhD); mechanical engineering (MS, PSM, PhD). *Application deadline:* For fall admission, 2/1 priority date for domestic students. Applications are processed on a rolling basis. *Application fee:* $65. Electronic applications accepted. *Application Contact:* Scott G. Delcourt, Assistant Vice President for Graduate Studies and Senior Associate Dean, 207-581-3291, Fax: 207-581-3232, E-mail: graduate@maine.edu. *Dean,* Dr. Dana Humphrey, 207-581-2217, Fax: 207-581-2220, E-mail: dana.humphrey@umit.maine.edu.

College of Liberal Arts and Sciences Students: 226 full-time (103 women), 74 part-time (32 women); includes 23 minority (3 Black or African American, non-Hispanic/Latino; 1 American Indian or Alaska Native, non-Hispanic/Latino; 4 Asian, non-Hispanic/Latino; 8 Hispanic/Latino; 7 Two or more races, non-Hispanic/Latino), 55 international. Average age 31. 310 applicants, 41% accepted, 74 enrolled. *Faculty:* 147 full-time (46 women), 42 part-time/adjunct (14 women). Expenses: Contact institution. *Financial support:* In 2017–18, 250 students received support, including 13 fellowships (averaging $19,200 per year), 35 research assistantships (averaging $17,500 per year), 160 teaching assistantships (averaging $16,200 per year); career-related internships or fieldwork, Federal Work-Study, institutionally sponsored loans, scholarships/grants, and tuition waivers (full and partial) also available. Support available to part-time students. Financial award application deadline: 3/1. In 2017, 69 master's, 16 doctorates, 6 other advanced degrees awarded. *Program availability:* Part-time, evening/weekend. Offers anthropology and environmental policy (PhD); chemistry (MS, PhD); communication and journalism (MA, PhD); computing and information science (MS, PhD, CGS); English (MA); French (MA, MAT); global policy (MA); history (MA, PhD); liberal arts and sciences (MA, MAT, ME, MM, MS, MST, PhD, CGS); mathematics (MA); performing arts (MM); physics and astronomy (ME, MS, PhD); psychological sciences (PhD); Spanish (MAT). *Application deadline:* For fall admission, 2/1 priority date for domestic students. Applications are processed on a rolling basis. *Application fee:* $65. Electronic applications accepted. *Application Contact:* Scott G. Delcourt, Assistant Vice President for Graduate Studies and Senior Associate Dean, 207-581-3291, Fax: 207-581-3232, E-mail: graduate@maine.edu. *Dean,* Dr. Emily Haddad, 207-581-1954, Fax: 207-581-1947, E-mail: emily.haddad@maine.edu.

College of Natural Sciences, Forestry, and Agriculture Students: 439 full-time (314 women), 96 part-time (61 women); includes 36 minority (4 Black or African American, non-Hispanic/Latino; 8 American Indian or Alaska Native, non-Hispanic/Latino; 10 Asian, non-Hispanic/Latino; 9 Hispanic/Latino; 5 Two or more races, non-Hispanic/Latino), 82 international. Average age 30. 545 applicants, 55% accepted, 191 enrolled. *Faculty:* 193 full-time (86 women), 122 part-time/adjunct (45 women). Expenses: Contact institution. *Financial support:* In 2017–18, 347 students received support, including 7 fellowships (averaging $23,900 per year), 190 research assistantships (averaging $19,700 per year), 93 teaching assistantships (averaging $16,000 per year); career-related internships or fieldwork, Federal Work-Study, institutionally sponsored loans, scholarships/grants, health care benefits, tuition waivers (full and partial), and unspecified assistantships also available. Support available to part-time students. Financial award application deadline: 3/1. In 2017, 132 master's, 22 doctorates, 9 other advanced degrees awarded. *Program availability:* Part-time, evening/weekend. Offers biological sciences (PhD); botany and plant pathology (MS); communication sciences and disorders (MA); earth and climate sciences (MS, PhD); economics (MA); entomology (MS); financial economics (MA); forest resources (MF, MS, PhD); horticulture (MS); individualized (MS); marine sciences (MS, PSM, PhD); microbiology (PhD); natural sciences, forestry, and agriculture (MA, MF, MPS, MS, MSW, MWC, PSM, PhD, CAS, CGS); nursing education (CGS); resource economics and policy (MS); rural health family nurse practitioner (MS, CAS); social work (MSW, CGS); wildlife ecology (PhD); zoology (MS, PhD). *Application deadline:* For fall admission, 2/1 priority date for domestic students. Applications are processed on a rolling basis. *Application fee:* $65. Electronic applications accepted. *Application Contact:* Scott G. Delcourt, Assistant Vice President for Graduate Studies and Senior Associate Dean, 207-581-3291, Fax: 207-581-3232, E-mail: graduate@maine.edu. *Interim Dean,* Dr. Fred Servello, 207-581-3206, Fax: 207-581-3207.

Graduate School of Biomedical Science and Engineering Students: 34 full-time (17 women), 16 part-time (9 women); includes 1 minority (Two or more races, non-Hispanic/Latino), 13 international. Average age 29. 39 applicants, 41% accepted, 15 enrolled. *Faculty:* 160 full-time (48 women). Expenses: Contact institution. *Financial support:* In 2017–18, 47 students received support, including 3 fellowships with full tuition reimbursements available (averaging $28,300 per year), 28 research assistantships with full tuition reimbursements available (averaging $25,000 per year), 5 teaching assistantships with full tuition reimbursements available (averaging $15,200 per year); scholarships/grants and unspecified assistantships also available. Financial award application deadline: 3/1. In 2017, 3 doctorates awarded. Offers bioinformatics (PSM); biomedical engineering (PhD); biomedical science (PhD). *Application deadline:* For fall admission, 1/1 priority date for domestic and international students. *Application fee:* $65. *Application Contact:* Scott G. Delcourt, Assistant Vice President for Graduate Studies and Senior Associate Dean, 207-581-3291, Fax: 207-581-3232, E-mail: graduate@maine.edu. *Director,* Dr. David Neivandt, 207-581-2803.

The Maine Business School Students: 42 full-time (15 women), 43 part-time (19 women); includes 4 minority (3 Asian, non-Hispanic/Latino; 1 Two or more races, non-Hispanic/Latino), 4 international. Average age 30. 69 applicants, 90% accepted, 44 enrolled. *Faculty:* 14 full-time (4 women), 6 part-time/adjunct (1 woman). Expenses: Contact institution. *Financial support:* In 2017–18, 15 students received support, including 1 research assistantship with full tuition reimbursement available (averaging $8,100 per year), 4 teaching assistantships with full tuition reimbursements available (averaging $13,600 per year); career-related internships or fieldwork, Federal Work-Study, institutionally sponsored loans, scholarships/grants, tuition waivers (full and partial), and unspecified assistantships also available. Financial award application deadline: 3/1. In 2017, 25 master's, 7 other advanced degrees awarded. *Program availability:* Part-time, evening/weekend, online learning. Offers business (MBA, CGS). *Application deadline:* For fall admission, 7/1 priority date for domestic and international students; for spring admission, 12/1 priority date for domestic and international students; for summer admission, 4/1 priority date for domestic and international students. Applications are processed on a rolling basis. *Application fee:* $65. Electronic applications accepted. *Application Contact:* Scott G. Delcourt, Assistant Vice President for Graduate Studies and Senior Associate Dean, 207-581-3291, Fax: 207-581-3232, E-mail: graduate@maine.edu. *MBA Director and Lecturer in Management,* Scott Spolan, 207-581-1973, E-mail: scott.spolan@maine.edu.

University of Maine School of Law Students: 222 full-time (114 women), 15 part-time (11 women); includes 28 minority (7 Black or African American, non-Hispanic/Latino; 5 American Indian or Alaska Native, non-Hispanic/Latino; 4 Asian, non-Hispanic/Latino; 12 Hispanic/Latino), 3 international. Average age 27. 604 applicants, 54% accepted, 82 enrolled. *Faculty:* 23 full-time (12 women), 52 part-time/adjunct (21 women). Expenses: Contact institution. *Financial support:* In 2017–18, 28 fellowships (averaging $3,300 per year), 5 research assistantships (averaging $1,000 per year), 5 teaching assistantships with partial tuition reimbursements (averaging $2,500 per year) were awarded; Federal Work-Study, scholarships/grants, and unspecified assistantships also available. Financial award application deadline: 2/15; financial award applicants required to submit FAFSA. In 2017, 83 doctorates awarded. *Program availability:* Part-time. Offers law (JD). JD/MBA offered in conjunction with the University of Maine and University of Southern Maine; JD/MPH and JD/MPPM offered with the Muskie School of Public Service. *Application deadline:* For fall admission, 7/31 for domestic students, 6/1 for international students; for spring admission, 11/15 for international students. Applications are processed on a rolling basis. *Application fee:* $0. Electronic applications accepted. *Application Contact:* Caroline Wilshusen, Director of Admissions, 207-780-4341, Fax: 207-780-4239, E-mail: lawadmissions@maine.edu. *Dean,* Danielle Conway, 207-780-4344, Fax: 207-780-4239.

UNIVERSITY OF MAINE AT FARMINGTON, Farmington, ME 04938

General Information State-supported, coed, comprehensive institution. *Enrollment:* 2,080 graduate, professional, and undergraduate students; 106 part-time matriculated graduate/professional students (92 women). *Enrollment by degree level:* 106 master's. *Graduate faculty:* 8 full-time (7 women), 2 part-time/adjunct (1 woman). *Student services:* Exercise/wellness program, low-cost health insurance, services for students with disabilities. *Library facilities:* Mantor Library plus 1 other. *Collection:* Weekly public service hours: 88; students can reserve study rooms.

Computer facilities: Computer purchase and lease plans are available. 220 computers available on campus for general student use. A campuswide network can be accessed from student residence rooms and from off campus. Online class registration is available.
Website: http://www.umf.maine.edu/

General Application Contact: Valerie Soucie, Administrative Specialist, 207-778-7502, Fax: 207-778-8134, E-mail: gradstudies@maine.edu.

GRADUATE UNITS

Graduate Programs in Education Students: 106 part-time (92 women). Average age 36. 6 applicants, 100% accepted, 6 enrolled. *Faculty:* 8 full-time (7 women), 2 part-time/adjunct (1 woman). Expenses: Contact institution. *Financial support:* Applicants required to submit FAFSA. In 2017, 29 master's awarded. *Program availability:* Part-time-only, evening/weekend, 100% online, blended/hybrid learning. Offers early childhood education (MS Ed); educational leadership (MS Ed); instructional technology (M Ed). M Ed offered in collaboration with University of Maine and University of Southern Maine. *Application deadline:* For fall admission, 8/10 for domestic students; for spring admission, 1/5 for domestic students; for summer admission, 4/10 for domestic students. Applications are processed on a rolling basis. *Application fee:* $60. Electronic applications accepted. *Application Contact:* Valerie Soucie, Administrative Specialist, 207-778-7502, Fax: 207-778-8134, E-mail: gradstudies@maine.edu. *Director of Graduate Programs in Education*, Dr. Johanna Prince, 207-778-7066, E-mail: gradstudies@maine.edu.

UNIVERSITY OF MANAGEMENT AND TECHNOLOGY, Arlington, VA 22209-1609

General Information Proprietary, coed, comprehensive institution. *Graduate housing:* On-campus housing not available.

GRADUATE UNITS

Program in Business Administration *Program availability:* Part-time, evening/weekend, online learning. Offers general management (MBA, DBA); project management (MBA). Electronic applications accepted.

Program in Computer Science *Program availability:* Part-time, evening/weekend, online learning. Offers computer science (MS); information technology (AC); project management (AC); software engineering (MS). Electronic applications accepted.

Program in Criminal Justice *Program availability:* Part-time, evening/weekend, online learning. Offers homeland security (MS).

Program in Engineering Management Offers engineering management (MS).

Program in Health Administration Offers health administration (MHA).

Program in Homeland Security Offers homeland security (MS).

Program in Information Technology Offers information technology (MS, Advanced Certificate).

Program in Management *Program availability:* Part-time, evening/weekend, online learning. Offers acquisition management (MS, AC); criminal justice administration (MS); general management (MS); project management (MS, AC). Electronic applications accepted.

Program in Public Administration Offers public administration (MPA, Advanced Certificate).

THE UNIVERSITY OF MANCHESTER, Manchester M13 9PL, United Kingdom

General Information Public, coed, comprehensive institution.

GRADUATE UNITS

Alliance Manchester Business School Offers accounting and finance (M Sc); business (M Ent); business analysis and strategic management (M Sc); business analytics: operational research and risk analysis (M Sc); business psychology (M Sc); corporate communications and reputation management (M Sc); finance (M Sc); finance and business economics (M Sc); human resource management and industrial relations (M Sc); innovation management and entrepreneurship (M Sc); international business and management (M Sc); international human resource management and comparative industrial relations (M Sc); management (M Sc); marketing (M Sc); operations, project and supply chain management (M Sc); organizational psychology (M Sc); quantitative finance (M Sc). Electronic applications accepted.

Manchester Institute of Education Offers counseling (D Couns); counseling psychology (D Couns); education (M Phil, Ed D, PhD); educational and child psychology (Ed D); educational psychology (Ed D).

School of Arts, Languages and Cultures Offers anthropology, media and performance (PhD); applied theatre (PhD); Arab world studies (PhD); archaeology (PhD); art history and visual studies (PhD); arts and cultural management (PhD); arts management and cultural policy (PhD); Chinese studies (PhD); classics and ancient history (PhD); composition (PhD); creative writing (PhD); drama (PhD); East Asian studies (PhD); electroacoustic composition (PhD); English and American studies (PhD); English language (PhD); French studies (PhD); German studies (PhD); history (PhD); humanitarianism and conflict response (PhD); interpreting studies (PhD); Japanese studies (PhD); Latin American cultural studies (PhD); linguistics (PhD); Middle Eastern studies (PhD); museology (PhD); museum practice (PhD); music (PhD); musicology (PhD); Polish studies (PhD); Portuguese studies (PhD); religions and theology (PhD); Russian studies (PhD); Spanish studies (PhD); translation and intercultural studies (PhD).

School of Biological Sciences Offers adaptive organismal biology (M Phil, PhD); animal biology (M Phil, PhD); biochemistry (M Phil, PhD); bioinformatics (M Phil, PhD); biomolecular sciences (M Phil, PhD); biotechnology (M Phil, PhD); cell biology (M Phil, PhD); cell matrix research (M Phil, PhD); channels and transporters (M Phil, PhD); developmental biology (M Phil, PhD); environmental biology (M Phil, PhD); evolutionary biology (M Phil, PhD); gene expression (M Phil, PhD); genetics (M Phil, PhD); history of science, technology and medicine (M Phil, PhD); immunology (M Phil, PhD); integrative neurobiology and behavior (M Phil, PhD); membrane trafficking (M Phil, PhD); microbiology (M Phil, PhD); molecular and cellular neuroscience (M Phil, PhD); molecular biology (M Phil, PhD); molecular cancer studies (M Phil, PhD); neuroscience (M Phil, PhD); ophthalmology (M Phil, PhD); optometry (M Phil, PhD); organelle function (M Phil, PhD); pharmacology (M Phil, PhD); physiology (M Phil, PhD); plant sciences (M Phil, PhD); stem cell research (M Phil, PhD); structural biology (M Phil, PhD); systems neuroscience (M Phil, PhD); toxicology (M Phil, PhD).

School of Chemical Engineering and Analytical Science Offers biocatalysis (M Phil, PhD); chemical engineering (M Phil, PhD); chemical engineering and analytical science (M Phil, D Eng, PhD); colloids, crystals, interfaces and materials (M Phil, PhD); environment and sustainable technology (M Phil, PhD); instrumentation (M Phil, PhD); multi-scale modeling (M Phil, PhD); process integration (M Phil, PhD); systems biology (M Phil, PhD).

School of Chemistry Offers biological chemistry (PhD); chemistry (M Ent, M Phil, M Sc, D Ent, PhD); inorganic chemistry (PhD); materials chemistry (PhD); nanoscience (PhD); nuclear fission (PhD); organic chemistry (PhD); physical chemistry (PhD); theoretical chemistry (PhD).

School of Computer Science Offers computer science (M Phil, PhD).

School of Dentistry Offers basic dental sciences (cancer studies) (M Phil, PhD); basic dental sciences (molecular genetics) (M Phil, PhD); basic dental sciences (stem cell biology) (M Phil, PhD); biomaterials sciences and dental technology (M Phil, PhD); dental public health/community dentistry (M Phil, PhD); dental science (clinical) (PhD); endodontology (M Phil, PhD); fixed and removable prosthodontics (M Phil, PhD); operative dentistry (M Phil, PhD); oral and maxillofacial surgery (M Phil, PhD); oral radiology (M Phil, PhD); orthodontics (M Phil, PhD); restorative dentistry (M Phil, PhD).

School of Earth and Environmental Sciences Offers atmospheric sciences (M Phil, M Sc, PhD); basin studies and petroleum geosciences (M Phil, M Sc, PhD); earth, atmospheric and environmental sciences (M Phil, M Sc, PhD); environmental geochemistry and cosmochemistry (M Phil, M Sc, PhD); isotope geochemistry and cosmochemistry (M Phil, M Sc, PhD); paleontology (M Phil, M Sc, PhD); physics and chemistry of minerals and fluids (M Phil, M Sc, PhD); structural and petrological geosciences (M Phil, M Sc, PhD).

School of Electrical and Electronic Engineering Offers electrical and electronic engineering (M Phil, PhD).

School of Environment, Education and Development Offers architecture (M Phil, PhD); development policy and management (M Phil, PhD); human geography (M Phil, PhD); physical geography (M Phil, PhD); planning and landscape (M Phil, PhD).

School of Law Offers bioethics and medical jurisprudence (PhD); criminology (M Phil, PhD); law (M Phil, PhD).

School of Materials Offers advanced aerospace materials engineering (M Sc); advanced metallic systems (PhD); biomedical materials (M Phil, M Sc, PhD); ceramics and glass (M Phil, M Sc, PhD); composite materials (M Sc, PhD); corrosion and protection (M Phil, M Sc, PhD); materials (M Phil, PhD); metallic materials (M Phil, M Sc, PhD); nanostructural materials (M Phil, M Sc, PhD); paper science (M Phil, M Sc, PhD); polymer science and engineering (M Phil, M Sc, PhD); technical textiles (M Sc); textile design, fashion and management (M Phil, M Sc, PhD); textile science and technology (M Phil, M Sc, PhD); textiles (M Phil, PhD); textiles and fashion (M Ent).

School of Mathematics Offers actuarial science (PhD); applied mathematics (M Phil, PhD); applied numerical computing (M Phil, PhD); financial mathematics (M Phil, PhD); mathematical logic (M Phil); probability (M Phil, PhD); pure mathematics (M Phil, PhD); statistics (M Phil, PhD).

School of Mechanical, Aerospace and Civil Engineering Offers advanced manufacturing technology (M Ent); aerospace engineering (M Phil, M Sc, PhD); civil engineering (M Phil, M Sc, PhD); environmental engineering (M Phil, PhD); management of projects (M Phil, M Sc, PhD); mechanical engineering (M Phil, M Sc, PhD); mechanical engineering design (M Ent); nuclear engineering (M Phil, D Eng, PhD).

School of Medicine Offers medicine (M Phil, PhD).

School of Nursing, Midwifery and Social Work Offers nursing (M Phil, PhD); social work (M Phil, PhD).

School of Pharmacy and Pharmaceutical Sciences Offers pharmacy and pharmaceutical sciences (M Phil, PhD).

School of Physics and Astronomy Offers astronomy and astrophysics (M Sc, PhD); biological physics (M Sc, PhD); condensed matter physics (M Sc, PhD); nonlinear and liquid crystals physics (M Sc, PhD); nuclear physics (M Sc, PhD); particle physics (M Sc, PhD); photon physics (M Sc, PhD); physics (M Sc, PhD); theoretical physics (M Sc, PhD).

School of Psychological Sciences Offers audiology (M Phil, PhD); clinical psychology (M Phil, PhD, Psy D); psychology (M Phil, PhD).

School of Social Sciences Offers ethnographic documentary (M Phil); interdisciplinary study of culture (PhD); philosophy (PhD); politics (PhD); social anthropology (PhD); social anthropology with visual media (PhD); social change (PhD); social statistics (PhD); sociology (PhD); visual anthropology (M Phil).

UNIVERSITY OF MANITOBA, Winnipeg, MB R3T 2N2, Canada

General Information Province-supported, coed, university. CGS member. *Graduate housing:* Rooms and/or apartments available to single and married students. *Research affiliation:* Canada Department of Agriculture Research Station, Freshwater Institute, Atomic Energy of Canada, Manitoba Department of Mines, Resources, and Environmental Management, Northern Scientific Training Program (Northern studies), Taiga Biological Research Trust.

GRADUATE UNITS

Dr. Gerald Niznick College of Dentistry Offers dental diagnostic and surgical sciences (M Dent); dentistry (M Dent, M Sc, DMD, PhD); oral and maxillofacial surgery (M Dent); oral biology (M Sc, PhD); orthodontics (M Sc); periodontology (M Dent); preventive dental science (M Sc); restorative dentistry (M Dent).

Faculty of Graduate Studies *Program availability:* Part-time.

Asper School of Business Offers business (M Sc, MBA, PhD).

Clayton H. Riddell Faculty of Environment, Earth, and Resources Offers environment (M Env); environment and geography (M Sc); environment, earth, and resources (M Env, M Sc, MA, MNRM, PhD); geography (MA, PhD); geology (M Sc, PhD); geophysics (M Sc, PhD); natural resources and environmental management (PhD); natural resources management (MNRM).

College of Nursing Offers cancer nursing (MN); nursing (MN).

College of Pharmacy Offers pharmacy (M Sc, PhD).

College of Rehabilitation Sciences Offers applied health sciences (PhD); occupational therapy (MOT); physical therapy (MPT); rehabilitation sciences (M Sc).

College Universitaire de Saint Boniface Offers Canadian studies (MA); education (M Ed).

Desautels Faculty of Music Offers music (M Mus).

Faculty of Agricultural and Food Sciences Offers agribusiness (M Sc, PhD); agricultural and food sciences (M Sc, PhD); agronomy and plant protection (M Sc, PhD); animal science (M Sc, PhD); entomology (M Sc, PhD); food science (M Sc, PhD); horticulture (M Sc, PhD); human nutritional sciences (M Sc, PhD); plant breeding and genetics (M Sc, PhD); plant physiology-biochemistry (M Sc, PhD); soil science (M Sc, PhD).

Faculty of Architecture Offers architecture (M Arch, M Land Arch, MCP, MID); city planning (MCP); interior design (MID); landscape architecture (M Land Arch).

Faculty of Arts Offers anthropology (MA, PhD); archival studies (MA); arts (MA, MPA, PhD); classics (MA); clinical psychology (PhD); economics (MA, PhD); English (MA, PhD); French (MA, PhD); German language and literature (MA); history (MA, PhD); Icelandic language and literature (MA); linguistics (MA, PhD); native studies (MA); philosophy (MA); political studies (MA); psychology (MA, PhD); public administration (MPA); religion (MA, PhD); school psychology (MA); Slavic languages and literatures (MA); sociology (MA, PhD).

Faculty of Education Offers adult and post-secondary education (M Ed); education (M Ed, PhD); educational administration (M Ed); guidance and counseling (M Ed); inclusive special education (M Ed); language and literacy (M Ed); second language education (M Ed); social foundations of education (M Ed); studies in curriculum, teaching and learning (M Ed).

Faculty of Engineering Offers biosystems engineering (M Eng, M Sc, PhD); civil engineering (M Eng, M Sc, PhD); electrical and computer engineering (M Eng, M Sc,

PhD); engineering (M Eng, M Sc, PhD); mechanical and manufacturing engineering (M Eng, M Sc, PhD).

Faculty of Kinesiology and Recreation Management Offers kinesiology and recreation (M Sc, MA).

Faculty of Law Offers law (LL M). Electronic applications accepted.

Faculty of Science Offers botany (M Sc, PhD); chemistry (M Sc, PhD); computer science (M Sc, PhD); ecology (M Sc, PhD); mathematical, computational and statistical sciences (MMCSS); mathematics (M Sc, PhD); microbiology (M Sc, PhD); physics and astronomy (M Sc, PhD); science (M Sc, MMCSS, PhD); statistics (M Sc, PhD); zoology (M Sc, PhD).

Faculty of Social Work Offers social work (MSW, PhD).

Interdisciplinary Programs Offers disability studies (M Sc, MA); individual interdisciplinary studies (M Sc, MA, PhD); interdisciplinary studies (M Sc, MA, PhD).

Max Rady College of Medicine *Program availability:* Part-time. Offers medicine (M Sc, PhD). Electronic applications accepted.

Graduate Programs in Medicine *Program availability:* Part-time. Offers biochemistry and medical genetics (M Sc, PhD); community health sciences (M Sc, MPH, PhD, G Dip); genetic counseling (M Sc); human anatomy and cell science (M Sc, PhD); immunology (M Sc, PhD); medical microbiology and infectious diseases (M Sc, PhD); medicine (M Sc, MPH, PhD, G Dip); pathology (M Sc); pediatrics and child health (M Sc); pharmacology and therapeutics (M Sc, PhD); physiology and pathophysiology (M Sc, PhD); psychiatry (M Sc); surgery (M Sc).

UNIVERSITY OF MARY, Bismarck, ND 58504-9652

General Information Independent-religious, coed, comprehensive institution. *Graduate housing:* Room and/or apartments available on a first-come, first-served basis to single students; on-campus housing not available to married students. Housing application deadline: 7/15.

GRADUATE UNITS

Gary Tharaldson School of Business *Program availability:* Part-time, evening/weekend. Offers business administration (MBA); energy management (MBA, MS); executive (MBA, MS); health care (MBA, MS); human resource management (MBA); project management (MBA, MPM); virtuous leadership (MBA, MPM, MS). Electronic applications accepted.

Liffrig Family School of Education and Behavioral Sciences Offers curriculum, instruction and assessment (M Ed); education (Ed D); education and behavioral sciences (M Ed, Ed D); elementary administration (M Ed); reading (M Ed); secondary administration (M Ed); special education strategist (M Ed).

School of Health Sciences Offers bioethics (MS); clinical exercise physiology (MS); health sciences (MS, MSN, MSOT, DNP, DPT); kinesiology (MS); occupational therapy (MSOT); physical therapy (DPT); respiratory therapy (MS); sports and physical education administration (MS). Electronic applications accepted.

Division of Nursing *Program availability:* Part-time, evening/weekend, online learning. Offers family nurse practitioner (DNP); nurse administrator (MSN); nursing educator (MSN). Electronic applications accepted.

UNIVERSITY OF MARY HARDIN-BAYLOR, Belton, TX 76513

General Information Independent-religious, coed, comprehensive institution. *Enrollment:* 3,914 graduate, professional, and undergraduate students; 387 full-time matriculated graduate/professional students (230 women), 194 part-time matriculated graduate/professional students (104 women). *Enrollment by degree level:* 377 master's, 204 doctoral. *Graduate faculty:* 58 full-time (33 women), 32 part-time/adjunct (18 women). *Tuition:* Full-time $15,570; part-time $10,380 per credit hour. *Required fees:* $1350; $75 per credit hour. $50 per term. Tuition and fees vary according to course load and degree level. *Graduate housing:* On-campus housing not available. *Student services:* Campus employment opportunities, career counseling, exercise/wellness program, free psychological counseling, international student services, multicultural affairs office, services for students with disabilities, teacher training. *Library facilities:* Townsend Memorial Library. *Collection:* Books: 183,109 (physical), 28,162 (digital/electronic); Serial titles: 507 (physical), 144,900 (digital/electronic); Databases: 128. Weekly public service hours: 99; students can reserve study rooms.

Computer facilities: Computer purchase and lease plans are available. 275 computers available on campus for general student use. A campuswide network can be accessed from student residence rooms and from off campus. Online class registration is available.
Website: http://www.umhb.edu/

General Application Contact: Sharon Aguilera, Assistant Director, Graduate Admissions, 254-295-4835, E-mail: saguilera@umhb.edu.

GRADUATE UNITS

Graduate Studies in Business Administration Students: 16 full-time (10 women), 39 part-time (16 women); includes 15 minority (3 Black or African American, non-Hispanic/Latino; 1 Asian, non-Hispanic/Latino; 10 Hispanic/Latino; 1 Two or more races, non-Hispanic/Latino), 10 international. Average age 30. 72 applicants, 81% accepted, 16 enrolled. *Faculty:* 12 full-time (5 women), 6 part-time/adjunct (4 women). Expenses: Contact institution. *Financial support:* In 2017–18, 32 students received support. Federal Work-Study, institutionally sponsored loans, unspecified assistantships, and scholarships for some active duty military personnel available. Support available to part-time students. Financial award applicants required to submit FAFSA. In 2017, 34 master's awarded. *Program availability:* Part-time, evening/weekend. Offers accounting (MBA); information systems management (MBA); international business (MBA); management (MBA). *Application deadline:* For fall admission, 6/1 for domestic students, 4/30 priority date for international students; for spring admission, 11/1 for domestic students, 9/30 priority date for international students. Applications are processed on a rolling basis. *Application fee:* $35 ($135 for international students). Electronic applications accepted. *Application Contact:* Sharon Aguilera, Assistant Director, Graduate Admissions, 254-295-4835, E-mail: saguilera@umhb.edu. *Assistant Dean, Graduate Programs in McLane College of Business*, Dr. Kirk Fischer, 254-295-4655, E-mail: kfischer@umhb.edu.

Graduate Studies in Counseling Students: 74 full-time (58 women), 13 part-time (8 women); includes 44 minority (23 Black or African American, non-Hispanic/Latino; 18 Hispanic/Latino; 3 Two or more races, non-Hispanic/Latino). Average age 32. 54 applicants, 65% accepted, 29 enrolled. *Faculty:* 7 full-time (4 women), 1 part-time/adjunct (0 women). Expenses: Contact institution. *Financial support:* In 2017–18, 55 students received support. Federal Work-Study, unspecified assistantships, and scholarships for some active duty military personnel available. Support available to part-time students. Financial award applicants required to submit FAFSA. In 2017, 27 master's awarded. *Program availability:* Part-time, evening/weekend. Offers clinical and mental health counseling (MA); marriage, family and child counseling (MA); non-clinical professional studies (MA). *Application deadline:* For fall admission, 6/1 for domestic students, 4/30 priority date for international students; for spring admission, 11/1 for domestic students, 9/30 priority date for international students. Applications are processed on a rolling basis. *Application fee:* $35 ($135 for international students). Electronic applications accepted. *Application Contact:* Sharon Aguilera, Assistant Director, Graduate Admissions, 254-295-4835, E-mail: saguilera@umhb.edu. *Director, Graduate Counseling*, Dr. Dan Williamson, 254-295-5018, E-mail: dwilliamson@umhb.edu.

Graduate Studies in Education Students: 29 full-time (20 women), 79 part-time (55 women); includes 53 minority (35 Black or African American, non-Hispanic/Latino; 17 Hispanic/Latino; 1 Two or more races, non-Hispanic/Latino), 1 international. Average age 39. 15 applicants, 80% accepted, 10 enrolled. *Faculty:* 12 full-time (8 women), 5 part-time/adjunct (2 women). Expenses: Contact institution. *Financial support:* In 2017–18, 90 students received support. Federal Work-Study and scholarships for some active duty military personnel available. Support available to part-time students. Financial award application deadline: 6/1; financial award applicants required to submit FAFSA. In 2017, 47 master's, 16 doctorates awarded. *Program availability:* Part-time, evening/weekend. Offers curriculum and instruction (M Ed); educational administration (M Ed, Ed D). *Application deadline:* For fall admission, 6/1 for domestic students, 4/30 priority date for international students; for spring admission, 11/1 for domestic students, 9/30 priority date for international students. Applications are processed on a rolling basis. *Application fee:* $35 ($135 for international students). Electronic applications accepted. *Application Contact:* Sharon Aguilera, Assistant Director, Graduate Admissions, 254-295-4835, E-mail: saguilera@umhb.edu. *Director, Graduate Programs in Education*, Dr. Craig Hammonds, 254-295-4189, E-mail: rhammonds@umhb.edu.

Graduate Studies in Exercise Physiology Students: 18 full-time (5 women), 30 part-time (11 women); includes 21 minority (5 Black or African American, non-Hispanic/Latino; 14 Hispanic/Latino; 2 Two or more races, non-Hispanic/Latino). Average age 26. 30 applicants, 90% accepted, 19 enrolled. *Faculty:* 6 full-time (2 women). Expenses: Contact institution. *Financial support:* In 2017–18, 37 students received support. Federal Work-Study, unspecified assistantships, and scholarships for some active duty military personnel available. Support available to part-time students. Financial award application deadline: 6/1; financial award applicants required to submit FAFSA. In 2017, 19 master's awarded. *Program availability:* Part-time, 100% online. Offers exercise physiology (MS Ed); sport administration (MS Ed). *Application deadline:* For fall admission, 6/1 for domestic students, 4/30 priority date for international students; for spring admission, 11/1 for domestic students, 9/30 priority date for international students. Applications are processed on a rolling basis. *Application fee:* $35 ($135 for international students). Electronic applications accepted. *Application Contact:* Sharon Aguilera, Assistant Director, Graduate Admissions, 254-295-4835, E-mail: saguilera@umhb.edu. *Director, MS Ed in Exercise Physiology Program*, Dr. Lem Taylor, 254-295-4895, E-mail: ltaylor@umhb.edu.

Graduate Studies in Information Systems Students: 94 full-time (26 women), 23 part-time (5 women); includes 2 minority (1 Asian, non-Hispanic/Latino; 1 Hispanic/Latino), 113 international. Average age 24. 225 applicants, 98% accepted, 11 enrolled. *Faculty:* 5 full-time (1 woman), 2 part-time/adjunct (0 women). Expenses: Contact institution. *Financial support:* In 2017–18, 106 students received support. Federal Work-Study, unspecified assistantships, and scholarships for some active duty military personnel available. Support available to part-time students. Financial award applicants required to submit FAFSA. In 2017, 131 master's awarded. *Program availability:* Part-time, evening/weekend. Offers information systems (MS). *Application deadline:* For fall admission, 6/1 for domestic students, 4/30 priority date for international students; for spring admission, 11/1 for domestic students, 9/30 priority date for international students. Applications are processed on a rolling basis. *Application fee:* $35 ($135 for international students). Electronic applications accepted. *Application Contact:* Sharon Aguilera, Assistant Director, Graduate Admissions, 254-295-4835, E-mail: saguilera@umhb.edu. *Associate Dean, Graduate Programs in McLane College of Business*, Dr. Kirk Fischer, 254-295-4655, E-mail: kfischer@umhb.edu.

Graduate Studies in Nursing Students: 44 full-time (40 women), 10 part-time (9 women); includes 19 minority (10 Black or African American, non-Hispanic/Latino; 7 Hispanic/Latino; 2 Two or more races, non-Hispanic/Latino). Average age 34. 47 applicants, 83% accepted, 31 enrolled. *Faculty:* 6 full-time (all women), 8 part-time/adjunct (7 women). Expenses: Contact institution. *Financial support:* In 2017–18, 34 students received support. Federal Work-Study, unspecified assistantships, and scholarships for some active duty military personnel available. Support available to part-time students. Financial award applicants required to submit FAFSA. In 2017, 44 master's, 2 other advanced degrees awarded. *Program availability:* Evening/weekend. Offers family nurse practitioner (MSN, Post-Master's Certificate); nursing education (MSN); nursing practice (DNP). *Application deadline:* For fall admission, 6/1 for domestic students, 4/30 priority date for international students; for spring admission, 11/1 for domestic students, 9/30 priority date for international students. Applications are processed on a rolling basis. *Application fee:* $35 ($135 for international students). Electronic applications accepted. *Application Contact:* Sharon Aguilera, Assistant Director, Graduate Admissions, 254-295-4835, E-mail: saguilera@umhb.edu. *Dean, College of Nursing/MSN and DNP Programs Director*, Dr. Sharon Souter, 254-295-4662, E-mail: ssouter@umhb.edu.

Graduate Studies in Physical Therapy Students: 112 full-time (71 women); includes 29 minority (6 Black or African American, non-Hispanic/Latino; 7 Asian, non-Hispanic/Latino; 15 Hispanic/Latino; 1 Two or more races, non-Hispanic/Latino). Average age 26. 120 applicants, 45% accepted, 40 enrolled. *Faculty:* 10 full-time (7 women), 10 part-time/adjunct (5 women). Expenses: Contact institution. *Financial support:* In 2017–18, 110 students received support. Federal Work-Study, unspecified assistantships, and scholarships for some active duty military personnel available. Financial award applicants required to submit FAFSA. Offers physical therapy (DPT). *Application deadline:* For fall admission, 6/1 for domestic students, 4/30 priority date for international students; for spring admission, 11/1 for domestic students, 9/30 priority date for international students. Applications are processed on a rolling basis. *Application fee:* $35 ($135 for international students). Electronic applications accepted. *Application Contact:* Sharon Aguilera, Assistant Director, Graduate Admissions, 254-295-4835, E-mail: saguilera@umhb.edu. *Director, Doctor of Physical Therapy Program/Associate Professor*, Dr. Barbara Gresham, 254-295-4921, E-mail: bgresham@umhb.edu.

UNIVERSITY OF MARYLAND, BALTIMORE, Baltimore, MD 21201

General Information State-supported, coed, graduate-only institution. CGS member. *Enrollment by degree level:* 2,043 master's, 3,523 doctoral, 116 other advanced degrees. *Graduate faculty:* 1,863 full-time (875 women), 976 part-time/adjunct (658 women). Tuition, state resident: full-time $13,990; part-time $661 per credit. Tuition, nonresident: full-time $30,484; part-time $1310 per credit. *Required fees:* $1894; $94 per credit. $415 per semester. Part-time tuition and fees vary according to course load, degree level and program. *Graduate housing:* Rooms and/or apartments available on a first-come, first-served basis to single and married students. *Student services:* Campus employment opportunities, campus safety program, career counseling, exercise/wellness program, free psychological counseling, grant writing training, international student services, low-cost health insurance, services for students with disabilities, writing training. *Library facilities:* Health Sciences and Human Services Library plus 1 other. *Collection:* Books: 292,010 (physical), 50,988 (digital/electronic); Serial titles: 306,853 (physical), 162,832 (digital/electronic); Databases: 206. Students can reserve study rooms. *Research affiliation:* University of Maryland Medical System (medical research), University of Maryland Biotechnology Institute (biology), University of Maryland BioPark (biology).

Computer facilities: A campuswide network can be accessed from student residence rooms. Online class registration is available.
Website: http://www.umaryland.edu/

General Application Contact: Keith T. Brooks, Director, Graduate Enrollment Affairs, 410-706-7131, Fax: 410-706-3473, E-mail: kbrooks@umaryland.edu.

GRADUATE UNITS

Francis King Carey School of Law Students: 547 full-time (292 women), 224 part-time (125 women); includes 278 minority (126 Black or African American, non-Hispanic/Latino; 2 American Indian or Alaska Native, non-Hispanic/Latino; 73 Asian, non-Hispanic/Latino; 53 Hispanic/Latino; 24 Two or more races, non-Hispanic/Latino), 28 international. Average age 27. 2,135 applicants, 53% accepted, 291 enrolled. *Faculty:* 47 full-time (24 women), 70 part-time/adjunct (26 women). Expenses: Contact institution. *Financial support:* In 2017–18, 664 students received support, including 23 fellowships (averaging $4,000 per year); Federal Work-Study, institutionally sponsored loans, and scholarships/grants also available. Support available to part-time students. Financial award application deadline: 3/1; financial award applicants required to submit FAFSA. In 2017, 45 master's, 187 doctorates awarded. *Program availability:* Part-time, evening/weekend, 100% online. Offers law (LL M, JD). *Application deadline:* For fall admission, 4/1 priority date for domestic and international students. Applications are processed on a rolling basis. *Application fee:* $70. Electronic applications accepted. *Application Contact:* Susan Krinsky, Associate Dean for Student Affairs and Communications, 410-706-3492, Fax: 410-706-1793, E-mail: admissions@law.umaryland.edu. *Dean/Professor,* Donald B. Tobin, 410-706-7214, Fax: 410-706-4045, E-mail: dtobin@law.umaryland.edu.

Graduate School Students: 665 full-time (482 women), 668 part-time (536 women); includes 487 minority (225 Black or African American, non-Hispanic/Latino; 163 Asian, non-Hispanic/Latino; 63 Hispanic/Latino; 2 Native Hawaiian or other Pacific Islander, non-Hispanic/Latino; 34 Two or more races, non-Hispanic/Latino), 151 international. Average age 32. 1,449 applicants, 45% accepted, 391 enrolled. Expenses: Contact institution. *Financial support:* Fellowships with full and partial tuition reimbursements, research assistantships with full tuition reimbursements, teaching assistantships with full tuition reimbursements, Federal Work-Study, institutionally sponsored loans, scholarships/grants, health care benefits, and unspecified assistantships available. Support available to part-time students. Financial award application deadline: 3/1; financial award applicants required to submit FAFSA. In 2017, 313 master's, 87 doctorates, 22 other advanced degrees awarded. *Program availability:* Part-time, evening/weekend, online learning. Offers biochemistry (MS, PhD); biochemistry and molecular biology (MS, PhD); biomedical sciences (MS, PhD); cancer biology (PhD); cell and molecular physiology (PhD); cellular and molecular biomedical science (MS); clinical research (Postbaccalaureate Certificate); epidemiology (MS, PhD); forensic medicine (MS); gerontology (PhD); health science (MS); human genetics and genomic medicine (PhD); marine-estuarine-environmental sciences (MS, PhD); medical and research technology (MS); molecular medicine (PhD); molecular microbiology and immunology (PhD); molecular toxicology and pharmacology (PhD); neuroscience (PhD); oral pathology (PhD); pharmaceutical health service research (MS, PhD); pharmaceutical sciences (PhD); pharmacometrics (MS); pharmacy administration (PhD); physical rehabilitation science (PhD); regulatory science (MS); research ethics (Certificate); thanatology (Certificate); toxicology (MS, PhD). *Application deadline:* For fall admission, 4/15 priority date for domestic students, 1/15 priority date for international students. Applications are processed on a rolling basis. *Application fee:* $75. Electronic applications accepted. *Application Contact:* Keith T. Brooks, Assistant Dean, 410-706-7131, Fax: 410-706-3473, E-mail: kbrooks@umaryland.edu. *Chief Academic and Research Officer/Dean of the Graduate School,* Dr. Bruce E. Jarrell, 410-706-2304, Fax: 410-706-0500, E-mail: bjarrell@som.umaryland.edu.

School of Social Work Offers social work (MSW, PhD). MSW/MA offered jointly with Baltimore Hebrew University; MBA/MSW with University of Maryland, College Park; MSW/MPH with The Johns Hopkins University. Electronic applications accepted.

Professional and Advanced Education Programs in Dentistry Students: 583 full-time (311 women), 2 part-time (1 woman); includes 255 minority (58 Black or African American, non-Hispanic/Latino; 126 Asian, non-Hispanic/Latino; 44 Hispanic/Latino; 27 Two or more races, non-Hispanic/Latino), 23 international. Average age 26. 799 applicants, 72% accepted, 133 enrolled. Expenses: Contact institution. *Financial support:* Career-related internships or fieldwork, Federal Work-Study, scholarships/grants, and traineeships available. Financial award application deadline: 3/1; financial award applicants required to submit FAFSA. In 2017, 131 doctorates, 22 Certificates awarded. Offers advanced general dentistry (Certificate); dentistry (DDS); endodontics (Certificate); oral-maxillofacial surgery (Certificate); orthodontics (Certificate); pediatric dentistry (Certificate); periodontics (Certificate); prosthodontics (Certificate). *Application deadline:* Applications are processed on a rolling basis. *Application fee:* $85. Electronic applications accepted. *Application Contact:* Dr. Judith A. Porter, Assistant Dean for Admissions and Recruitment, 410-706-7472, Fax: 410-706-0945, E-mail: ddsadmissions@umaryland.edu. *Dean,* Dr. Mark A. Reynolds, 410-706-7461.

Professional Program in Pharmacy Offers pharmacy (Pharm D). Electronic applications accepted.

School of Medicine Students: 1,134 full-time (715 women), 87 part-time (55 women); includes 428 minority (88 Black or African American, non-Hispanic/Latino; 1 American Indian or Alaska Native, non-Hispanic/Latino; 248 Asian, non-Hispanic/Latino; 60 Hispanic/Latino; 31 Two or more races, non-Hispanic/Latino), 67 international. Average age 26. 5,894 applicants, 14% accepted, 387 enrolled. Expenses: Contact institution. *Financial support:* In 2017–18, research assistantships with partial tuition reimbursements (averaging $25,000 per year) were awarded; fellowships, Federal Work-Study, scholarships/grants, health care benefits, and unspecified assistantships also available. Financial award application deadline: 3/1; financial award applicants required to submit FAFSA. In 2017, 59 master's, 270 doctorates awarded. *Program availability:* Part-time. Offers biostatistics (MS); clinical research (MS); epidemiology and preventive medicine (MPH, MS, PhD); genetic counseling (MGC); gerontology (PhD); human genetics and genomic medicine (MS, PhD); medicine (MGC, MPH, MS, DPT, MD, PhD); molecular epidemiology (MS, PhD); pathologists' assistant (MS); physical rehabilitation science (PhD); physical therapy and rehabilitation science (DPT); toxicology (MS, PhD). Electronic applications accepted. *Application Contact:* 410-706-7478, Fax: 410-706-0467, E-mail: admissions@som.umaryland.edu. *Dean and Vice President for Medical Affairs,* Dr. E. Albert Reece, 410-706-7410, Fax: 410-706-0235, E-mail: deanmed@som.umaryland.edu.

School of Nursing Students: 504 full-time (442 women), 532 part-time (482 women); includes 443 minority (249 Black or African American, non-Hispanic/Latino; 1 American Indian or Alaska Native, non-Hispanic/Latino; 115 Asian, non-Hispanic/Latino; 48 Hispanic/Latino; 2 Native Hawaiian or other Pacific Islander, non-Hispanic/Latino; 28 Two or more races, non-Hispanic/Latino), 15 international. Average age 33. 935 applicants, 62% accepted, 394 enrolled. *Faculty:* 130 full-time (117 women), 125 part-time/adjunct (114 women). Expenses: Contact institution. *Financial support:* In 2017–18, 22 research assistantships with full and partial tuition reimbursements (averaging $21,523 per year), 41 teaching assistantships with full and partial tuition reimbursements (averaging $13,439 per year) were awarded; fellowships and scholarships/grants also available. Financial award application deadline: 3/1; financial award applicants required to submit FAFSA. In 2017, 182 master's, 57 doctorates awarded. *Program availability:* Part-time. Offers adult-gerontology acute care nurse practitioner (DNP); adult-gerontology primary care nurse practitioner (DNP); clinical nurse leader (MS); community/public health nursing (MS); family nurse practitioner (DNP); global health (Postbaccalaureate Certificate); health services leadership and management (MS); neonatal nurse practitioner (DNP); nurse anesthesia (DNP); nursing (PhD); nursing informatics (MS, Postbaccalaureate Certificate); pediatric acute/primary care nurse practitioner (DNP); psychiatric mental health nurse practitioner (DNP); teaching in nursing and health professions (Postbaccalaureate Certificate). MS/MBA offered jointly with University of Baltimore. *Application deadline:* For fall admission, 11/1 for domestic and international students; for spring admission, 8/1 for domestic and international students. *Application fee:* $75. Electronic applications accepted. *Application Contact:* Larry Fillian, Associate Dean of Student and Academic Services, 410-706-6298, E-mail: lfillian@umaryland.edu. *Dean,* Dr. Jane Kirschling, 410-706-4359, E-mail: kirschling@umaryland.edu.

UNIVERSITY OF MARYLAND, BALTIMORE COUNTY, Baltimore, MD 21250

General Information State-supported, coed, university. CGS member. *Enrollment:* 13,662 graduate, professional, and undergraduate students; 1,126 full-time matriculated graduate/professional students (535 women), 1,234 part-time matriculated graduate/professional students (628 women). *Enrollment by degree level:* 1,502 master's, 728 doctoral, 130 other advanced degrees. *Graduate faculty:* 522 full-time, 197 part-time/adjunct. *Required fees:* $132. *Graduate housing:* Room and/or apartments available on a first-come, first-served basis to single students; on-campus housing not available to married students. Housing application deadline: 6/1. *Student services:* Campus employment opportunities, campus safety program, career counseling, child daycare facilities, exercise/wellness program, free psychological counseling, grant writing training, international student services, low-cost health insurance, multicultural affairs office, services for students with disabilities, teacher training, writing training. *Library facilities:* Albin O. Kuhn Library and Gallery. *Collection:* Books: 703,486 (physical), 175,156 (digital/electronic); Serial titles: 27,505 (physical), 142,969 (digital/electronic); Databases: 388. Weekly public service hours: 94; study areas open 24 hours, 5–7 days a week; students can reserve study rooms. *Research affiliation:* Sciences Applications International Corporation (information systems and technology), Halliburton Energy Services, IBM (computers and information technology), BouMatic (dairy industry), Pfizer, Inc. (pharmaceuticals), Fujitsu Laboratories of America (information technology and communications).

Computer facilities: Computer purchase and lease plans are available. 1,065 computers available on campus for general student use. A campuswide network can be accessed from student residence rooms and from off campus. Online class registration, billing, housing, parking, degree audit and advising are available.
Website: http://www.umbc.edu/

General Application Contact: Kathryn Nee, Coordinator of Domestic Admissions, 410-455-2944, E-mail: nee@umbc.edu.

GRADUATE UNITS

The Graduate School Students: 1,126 full-time (535 women), 1,234 part-time (628 women); includes 560 minority (308 Black or African American, non-Hispanic/Latino; 3 American Indian or Alaska Native, non-Hispanic/Latino; 101 Asian, non-Hispanic/Latino; 101 Hispanic/Latino; 2 Native Hawaiian or other Pacific Islander, non-Hispanic/Latino; 45 Two or more races, non-Hispanic/Latino), 562 international. Average age 32. 2,705 applicants, 55% accepted, 680 enrolled. *Faculty:* 522 full-time, 197 part-time/adjunct. Expenses: Contact institution. *Financial support:* In 2017–18, 597 students received support, including 27 fellowships with tuition reimbursements available (averaging $18,909 per year), 284 research assistantships with tuition reimbursements available (averaging $18,909 per year), 286 teaching assistantships with tuition reimbursements available (averaging $18,909 per year); career-related internships or fieldwork, Federal Work-Study, scholarships/grants, traineeships, health care benefits, and unspecified assistantships also available. Financial award applicants required to submit FAFSA. In 2017, 631 master's, 88 doctorates, 124 other advanced degrees awarded. Offers engineering management (MS, Postbaccalaureate Certificate); marine-estuarine-environmental sciences (MS, PhD); systems engineering (MS, Postbaccalaureate Certificate). *Application deadline:* For fall admission, 1/1 for international students; for spring admission, 5/1 for international students. Applications are processed on a rolling basis. *Application fee:* $50. Electronic applications accepted.

College of Arts, Humanities and Social Sciences Students: 360 full-time (243 women), 614 part-time (431 women); includes 281 minority (134 Black or African American, non-Hispanic/Latino; 2 American Indian or Alaska Native, non-Hispanic/Latino; 64 Asian, non-Hispanic/Latino; 55 Hispanic/Latino; 1 Native Hawaiian or other Pacific Islander, non-Hispanic/Latino; 25 Two or more races, non-Hispanic/Latino), 47 international. Average age 33. 763 applicants, 60% accepted, 266 enrolled. *Faculty:* 271 full-time, 111 part-time/adjunct. Expenses: Contact institution. *Financial support:* In 2017–18, 201 students received support, including 11 fellowships (averaging $19,000 per year), 106 research assistantships (averaging $19,000 per year), 84 teaching assistantships (averaging $19,000 per year); career-related internships or fieldwork, scholarships/grants, health care benefits, and unspecified assistantships also available. Financial award applicants required to submit FAFSA. In 2017, 213 master's, 20 doctorates, 88 other advanced degrees awarded. *Program availability:* Part-time, evening/weekend, online learning. Offers aging policy issues (PhD); American contemporary music (Postbaccalaureate Certificate); applied behavioral analysis (MA); applied developmental psychology (PhD); applied sociology (MA); arts, humanities and social science (MA, MAE, MAE, MAT, MFA, MPP, MPS, MS, PhD, Certificate, Graduate Certificate, Postbaccalaureate Certificate); distance education (Graduate Certificate); early childhood education

(MAT); economic policy analysis (MA); education (MAE, MAE); elementary education (MAT); emergency health services (MS); emergency management (Postbaccalaureate Certificate); English: texts, technologies, and literature (MA); epidemiology of aging (PhD); gender and women's studies (Postbaccalaureate Certificate); geographic information systems (MPS, Certificate); geography and environmental systems (MPS, MS, PhD, Certificate); historical studies (MA); human services psychology (MA, PhD); industrial/organizational psychology (MPS); instructional systems development (MA, Graduate Certificate); instructional technology (Graduate Certificate); intercultural communication (MA); intermedia and digital arts (MFA); K-8 mathematics instructional leadership (MAE); K-8 science education (MAE); K-8 STEM education (MAE); language, literacy, and culture (PhD); nonprofit sector (Postbaccalaureate Certificate); public policy (MPP, PhD); secondary mathematics education (MAE); secondary science education (MAE); secondary STEM education (MAE); social, cultural, and behavioral sciences (PhD); teaching (MAT); teaching English to speakers of other languages (MA, Postbaccalaureate Certificate). *Application deadline:* For fall admission, 1/1 for international students; for spring admission, 5/1 for international students. Applications are processed on a rolling basis. *Application fee:* $50. Electronic applications accepted. *Application Contact:* Kathryn Nee, Coordinator of Domestic Admissions, 410-455-2944, E-mail: nee@umbc.edu. *Dean*, Dr. Scot E. Casper, 410-455-2385, Fax: 410-455-1095, E-mail: casper@umbc.edu.

College of Engineering and Information Technology Students: 554 full-time (199 women), 569 part-time (170 women); includes 300 minority (148 Black or African American, non-Hispanic/Latino; 1 American Indian or Alaska Native, non-Hispanic/Latino; 98 Asian, non-Hispanic/Latino; 38 Hispanic/Latino; 15 Two or more races, non-Hispanic/Latino), 447 international. Average age 31. 1,544 applicants, 58% accepted, 336 enrolled. *Faculty:* 125 full-time (39 women), 110 part-time/adjunct (21 women). Expenses: Contact institution. *Financial support:* In 2017–18, 9 fellowships with full tuition reimbursements (averaging $21,750 per year), 121 research assistantships with full tuition reimbursements (averaging $19,250 per year), 94 teaching assistantships with full tuition reimbursements (averaging $16,750 per year) were awarded; career-related internships or fieldwork, Federal Work-Study, scholarships/grants, health care benefits, tuition waivers (partial), and unspecified assistantships also available. Support available to part-time students. Financial award application deadline: 6/30; financial award applicants required to submit FAFSA. In 2017, 367 master's, 37 doctorates, 35 other advanced degrees awarded. *Program availability:* Part-time. Offers biochemical regulatory engineering (Postbaccalaureate Certificate); chemical and biochemical engineering (MS, PhD); computational thermal fluid dynamics (Postbaccalaureate Certificate); computer engineering (MS, PhD); computer science (MS, PhD); cybersecurity (MPS, Postbaccalaureate Certificate); cybersecurity operations (Postbaccalaureate Certificate); cybersecurity strategy and policy (Postbaccalaureate Certificate); data science (MPS); electrical engineering (MS, PhD); engineering and information technology (MPS, MS, PhD, Postbaccalaureate Certificate); environmental engineering (MS, PhD); health information technology (MPS); human-centered computing (MS, PhD); information systems (MPS, MS, PhD); mechanical engineering (MS, PhD, Postbaccalaureate Certificate); mechatronics (Postbaccalaureate Certificate); technical management (MPS). *Application deadline:* For fall admission, 6/1 for domestic students, 1/1 for international students; for spring admission, 11/1 for domestic students, 6/1 for international students. Applications are processed on a rolling basis. *Application fee:* $70. Electronic applications accepted. *Dean and Professor*, Dr. Julia M. Ross, 410-455-3270, Fax: 410-455-3559, E-mail: jross@umbc.edu.

College of Natural and Mathematical Sciences Students: 199 full-time (85 women), 42 part-time (20 women); includes 53 minority (20 Black or African American, non-Hispanic/Latino; 21 Asian, non-Hispanic/Latino; 7 Hispanic/Latino; 1 Native Hawaiian or other Pacific Islander, non-Hispanic/Latino; 4 Two or more races, non-Hispanic/Latino), 67 international. Average age 29. 379 applicants, 44% accepted, 67 enrolled. *Faculty:* 111 full-time, 17 part-time/adjunct. Expenses: Contact institution. *Financial support:* In 2017–18, 171 students received support, including 7 fellowships (averaging $18,909 per year), 57 research assistantships with tuition reimbursements available (averaging $18,909 per year), 107 teaching assistantships with full tuition reimbursements available (averaging $18,909 per year). In 2017, 41 master's, 31 doctorates, 1 other advanced degree awarded. *Program availability:* Part-time. Offers applied mathematics (MS, PhD); applied molecular biology (MS); atmospheric physics (MS, PhD); biological sciences (MPS, MS, PhD, Graduate Certificate); biostatistics (PhD); biotechnology (MPS); biotechnology (Graduate Certificate); biotechnology management (Graduate Certificate); chemistry (MS, PhD); chemistry and biochemistry (Postbaccalaureate Certificate); environmental statistics (MS); molecular and cell biology (PhD); natural and mathematical sciences (MPS, MS, PhD, Graduate Certificate, Postbaccalaureate Certificate); neuroscience and cognitive sciences (PhD); physics (MS, PhD); statistics (MS, PhD). *Application deadline:* Applications are processed on a rolling basis. *Application fee:* $50. Electronic applications accepted. *Application Contact:* Kathryn Nee, Coordinator of Domestic Admissions, 410-455-2944, E-mail: nee@umbc.edu. *Dean*, Dr. William R. LaCourse, 410-455-5827, Fax: 410-455-5831, E-mail: lacourse@umbc.edu.

Erickson School of Aging Studies Students: 18 full-time (11 women); includes 9 minority (8 Black or African American, non-Hispanic/Latino; 1 Hispanic/Latino). Average age 30. 23 applicants, 91% accepted, 18 enrolled. *Faculty:* 4 full-time (1 woman), 7 part-time/adjunct (1 woman). Expenses: Contact institution. *Financial support:* In 2017–18, 15 students received support, including 1 teaching assistantship with full tuition reimbursement available (averaging $21,600 per year). Financial award applicants required to submit FAFSA. In 2017, 13 master's awarded. *Program availability:* Part-time. Offers management of aging services (MA). *Application deadline:* For fall admission, 6/1 for domestic students; for spring admission, 12/1 for domestic students. Applications are processed on a rolling basis. *Application fee:* $50. Electronic applications accepted. *Application Contact:* Michelle Howell, Administrative Assistant, 443-543-5607, E-mail: mhowell@umbc.edu. *Graduate Program Director*, Bill Holman, 443-543-5603, E-mail: holman1@umbc.edu.

UNIVERSITY OF MARYLAND, COLLEGE PARK, College Park, MD 20742

General Information State-supported, coed, university. CGS member. *Graduate housing:* On-campus housing not available. *Research affiliation:* Battelle–Pacific Northwest National Laboratory, Canon U.S. Life Sciences, Inc. (technology development and analysis), Bill and Melinda Gates Foundation (international aid and outreach), Lockheed Martin Corporation (science and technology), BAE Systems (science and technology).

GRADUATE UNITS

Academic Affairs *Program availability:* Part-time, evening/weekend, online learning. Offers history, library, and information services. Electronic applications accepted.

A. James Clark School of Engineering *Program availability:* Part-time, evening/weekend, online learning. Offers advanced engineering education (M Eng); aerospace engineering (M Eng, MS, PhD); bioengineering (MS, PhD); chemical engineering (M Eng, MS, PhD); civil and environmental engineering (M Eng, MS, PhD); electrical and computer engineering (M Eng, MS, PhD); electrical engineering (MS, PhD); electronic packaging and reliability (MS, PhD); engineering (M Eng, ME, MS, PhD, Certificate); engineering and public policy (MS); fire protection engineering (M Eng, MS); manufacturing and design (MS, PhD); materials science and engineering (MS, PhD); mechanics and materials (MS, PhD); nuclear engineering (ME, MS, PhD); reliability engineering (M Eng, MS, PhD); systems engineering (M Eng, MS); telecommunications (MS); thermal and fluid sciences (MS, PhD).

College of Agriculture and Natural Resources *Program availability:* Part-time, evening/weekend. Offers agriculture and natural resources (MS, DVM, PhD); agriculture economics (MS, PhD); animal sciences (MS, PhD); environmental science and technology (MS, PhD); food science (MS, PhD); landscape architecture (MLA); natural resource sciences (MS, PhD); nutrition (MS, PhD); plant science (MS, PhD); resource economics (MS, PhD); veterinary medical sciences (MS, PhD); veterinary medicine (MS, DVM, PhD). Electronic applications accepted.

College of Arts and Humanities *Program availability:* Part-time, evening/weekend. Offers American studies (MA, PhD); art (MFA); art history (MA, PhD); arts and humanities (M Ed, MA, MFA, MM, DMA, Ed D, PhD); classics (MA); communication (MA, PhD); comparative literature (MA, PhD); creative writing (MA, MFA, PhD); dance (MFA); English language and literature (MA, PhD); ethnomusicology (MA); French language and literature (MA); Germanic language and literature (MA, PhD); history (MA, PhD); Jewish studies (MA); languages, literatures, and cultures (MA, PhD); linguistics (MA, PhD); modern French studies (PhD); music (M Ed, MA, MM, DMA, Ed D, PhD); performance (MFA); philosophy (MA, PhD); second language instruction (PhD); second language learning (PhD); second language measurement and assessment (PhD); second language use (PhD); Spanish language and literatures (MA, PhD); theatre (MA, MFA, PhD); theatre and performance studies (MA, PhD); theatre design (MFA); women's studies (MA, PhD). Electronic applications accepted.

College of Behavioral and Social Sciences *Program availability:* Part-time, evening/weekend. Offers American politics (PhD); applied anthropology (MAA); audiology (MA, PhD); behavioral and social sciences (MA, MAA, MS, Au D, PhD); clinical psychology (PhD); comparative politics (PhD); criminology and criminal justice (MA, PhD); developmental psychology (PhD); economics (MA, PhD); experimental psychology (PhD); geography (MA, PhD); hearing and speech sciences (Au D); industrial psychology (MA, MS, PhD); international relations (PhD); language pathology (MA, PhD); neuroscience (PhD); neurosciences and cognitive sciences (PhD); political economy (PhD); political theory (PhD); social psychology (PhD); sociology (MA, PhD); speech (MA, PhD); survey methodology (MS, PhD). Electronic applications accepted.

College of Computer, Mathematical and Natural Sciences *Program availability:* Part-time, evening/weekend, online learning. Offers analytical chemistry (MS, PhD); applied mathematics (MS, PhD); astronomy (MS, PhD); atmospheric and oceanic science (MS, PMS, PhD); behavior, ecology, and systematics (PhD); behavior, ecology, evolution, and systematics (MS, PhD); biochemistry (MS, PhD); biological sciences (PhD); biology (MS, PhD); biophysics (PhD); cell biology and molecular genetics (MS, PhD); chemical physics (MS, PhD); chemistry (MS, PhD); computational biology, bioinformatics, and genomics (PhD); computer science (MS, PhD); computer, mathematical and natural sciences (MA, MLS, MS, PMS, PhD); entomology (MS, PhD); geology (MS, PhD); inorganic chemistry (MS, PhD); life sciences (MLS); marine-estuarine-environmental sciences (MS, PhD); mathematical statistics (MA, PhD); mathematics (MA, PhD); molecular and cellular biology (PhD); organic chemistry (MS, PhD); physical chemistry (MS, PhD); physics (MS, PhD); physiological systems (PhD); plant biology (MS, PhD); sustainable development and conservation biology (MS).

College of Education *Program availability:* Part-time, evening/weekend, online learning. Offers college student personnel (M Ed, MA); college student personnel administration (PhD); community counseling (CAGS); community/career counseling (M Ed, MA); counseling and personnel services (M Ed, MA, PhD); counseling psychology (PhD); counselor education (PhD); curriculum and educational communications (M Ed, MA, Ed D, PhD); education (M Ed, MA, Ed D, PhD, AGSC, CAGS); human development and quantitative methodology (MA, Ed D, PhD); reading (M Ed, MA, PhD, CAGS); rehabilitation counseling (M Ed, MA, AGSC); school counseling (M Ed, MA); school psychology (M Ed, MA, PhD); secondary education (M Ed, MA, Ed D, PhD, CAGS); social foundations of education (M Ed, MA, Ed D, PhD, CAGS); teaching English to speakers of other languages (M Ed). Electronic applications accepted.

College of Information Studies *Program availability:* Part-time, evening/weekend. Offers information studies (MIM, MLS, PhD). Electronic applications accepted.

Philip Merrill College of Journalism *Program availability:* Part-time, evening/weekend. Offers broadcast journalism (MA); journalism (MA); journalism and media studies (PhD); online news (MA); public affairs reporting (MA). Electronic applications accepted.

Robert H. Smith School of Business *Program availability:* Part-time, evening/weekend, online learning. Offers business (EMBA, MBA, MS, PhD); business administration (MBA); business and management (MS, PhD); executive business administration (EMBA). Electronic applications accepted.

School of Architecture, Planning and Preservation *Program availability:* Part-time, evening/weekend. Offers architecture (M Arch); architecture, planning and preservation (M Arch, MCP, MHP, MRED, PhD, Certificate); historic preservation (MHP, Certificate); real estate development (MRED); urban and regional planning/design (PhD); urban studies and planning (MCP). Electronic applications accepted.

School of Public Health *Program availability:* Part-time, evening/weekend. Offers biostatistics (MPH); community health education (MPH); environmental health sciences (MPH); epidemiology (MPH, PhD); family studies (PhD); health services administration (MHA, PhD); kinesiology (MA, PhD); marriage and family therapy (MS); maternal and child health (PhD); public health (MA, MHA, MPH, MS, PhD); public/community health (PhD). Electronic applications accepted.

School of Public Policy *Program availability:* Part-time, evening/weekend, online learning. Offers policy studies (PhD); public management (MPM); public policy (MPM, MPP, PhD). Electronic applications accepted.

UNIVERSITY OF MARYLAND EASTERN SHORE, Princess Anne, MD 21853

General Information State-supported, coed, university. CGS member. Tuition, state resident: part-time $325 per credit hour. Tuition, nonresident: part-time $604 per credit hour. *Required fees:* $85 per credit hour. Part-time tuition and fees vary according to campus/location, program and reciprocity agreements. *Graduate housing:* Room and/or apartments available to single students; on-campus housing not available to married students. *Student services:* Campus employment opportunities, campus safety program, career counseling, child daycare facilities, exercise/wellness program, free psychological counseling, grant writing training, international student services, services for students with disabilities, teacher training, writing training. *Library facilities:* Frederick Douglass Library. *Collection:* Books: 137,271 (physical), 27,434 (digital/electronic); Serial titles: 459 (physical), 1,019 (digital/electronic); Databases: 134. Study areas open 24 hours, 5–7 days a week; students can reserve study rooms.

Computer facilities: A campuswide network can be accessed. Online class registration is available.
Website: http://www.umes.edu/

General Application Contact: Kimberly D. Whitehead, Acting Vice President for Academic Affairs/Provost, 410-651-6508, E-mail: kdwhitehead@umes.edu.

GRADUATE UNITS

Graduate Programs Expenses: Contact institution. *Financial support:* Research assistantships, teaching assistantships, career-related internships or fieldwork, scholarships/grants, traineeships, and unspecified assistantships available. Support available to part-time students. Financial award application deadline: 3/1; financial award applicants required to submit FAFSA. *Program availability:* Part-time, evening/weekend. Offers applied computer science (MS); career and technology education (M Ed); chemistry (MS); criminal justice (MS); education leadership (Ed D); food and agricultural sciences (MS); food science and technology (PhD); guidance and counseling (M Ed); marine-estuarine-environmental sciences (MS, PhD); organizational leadership (PhD); physical therapy (DPT); quantitative fisheries and resource economics (PMS); rehabilitation counseling (MS); special education (M Ed); teaching (MAT); toxicology (MS, PhD). *Application deadline:* For fall admission, 2/1 priority date for domestic and international students; for winter admission, 10/1 for domestic and international students; for spring admission, 8/1 priority date for domestic students, 6/1 priority date for international students. Applications are processed on a rolling basis. *Application fee:* $30. Electronic applications accepted. *Associate Vice President for Academic Affairs,* Benita Sims-Tucker, 410-651-6508, E-mail: bsimstucker@umes.edu.

School of Pharmacy Expenses: Contact institution. Offers pharmaceutical sciences (MS, PhD); pharmacy (Pharm D). *Application Contact:* Dr. Mark Simmons, 410-651-8327, E-mail: masimmons1@umes.edu.

UNIVERSITY OF MARYLAND UNIVERSITY COLLEGE, Adelphi, MD 20783

General Information State-supported, coed, comprehensive institution. *Enrollment:* 59,379 graduate, professional, and undergraduate students; 3,999 full-time matriculated graduate/professional students (1,847 women), 9,631 part-time matriculated graduate/professional students (5,446 women). *Enrollment by degree level:* 12,925 master's, 170 doctoral, 535 other advanced degrees. *Graduate faculty:* 189 full-time (84 women), 3,502 part-time/adjunct (1,611 women). *Graduate housing:* On-campus housing not available. *Student services:* Campus employment opportunities, career counseling, international student services, services for students with disabilities, writing training. *Library facilities:* Information and Library Services plus 1 other. *Collection:* Books: 1,234 (physical), 110,587 (digital/electronic); Serial titles: 149,268 (physical); Databases: 102. Weekly public service hours: 95.

Computer facilities: Computer purchase and lease plans are available. 484 computers available on campus for general student use. A campuswide network can be accessed from off campus. Online class registration is available.
Website: http://www.umuc.edu/

General Application Contact: Coordinator, Graduate Admissions, 800-888-UMUC, Fax: 240-684-2151, E-mail: newgrad@umuc.edu.

GRADUATE UNITS

The Graduate School Students: 3,999 full-time (1,847 women), 9,631 part-time (5,446 women); includes 7,771 minority (5,383 Black or African American, non-Hispanic/Latino; 54 American Indian or Alaska Native, non-Hispanic/Latino; 859 Asian, non-Hispanic/Latino; 980 Hispanic/Latino; 41 Native Hawaiian or other Pacific Islander, non-Hispanic/Latino; 454 Two or more races, non-Hispanic/Latino), 300 international. Average age 36. 4,874 applicants, 100% accepted, 2803 enrolled. *Faculty:* 189 full-time (84 women), 3,502 part-time/adjunct (1,611 women). Expenses: Contact institution. *Financial support:* Federal Work-Study and scholarships/grants available. Support available to part-time students. Financial award application deadline: 6/1; financial award applicants required to submit FAFSA. In 2017, 3,780 master's, 27 doctorates, 648 other advanced degrees awarded. *Program availability:* Part-time, evening/weekend, online learning. Offers accounting and financial management (MS); biotechnology (MS, Certificate); business administration (MBA); cloud computing architecture (MS); cybersecurity management and policy (MS, Certificate); cybersecurity technology (MS, Certificate); data analytics (MS, Certificate); digital forensics and cyber investigation (MS, Certificate); distance education and e-learning (MDE); environmental management (MS); health care administration (MS); health informatics administration (MS); information technology (MS); learning design and technology (MS); management (MS, DM, Certificate); management and technology (MAT, MBA, MDE, MS, DM, Certificate); teaching (MAT). *Application deadline:* Applications are processed on a rolling basis. *Application fee:* $50. Electronic applications accepted. *Application Contact:* Coordinator, Graduate Admissions, 800-888-8682, Fax: 240-684-2151, E-mail: newgrad@umuc.edu. *Dean and Vice Provost,* Kathryn Klose, 240-684-2406, E-mail: kathryn.klose@umuc.edu.

UNIVERSITY OF MARY WASHINGTON, Fredericksburg, VA 22401-5358

General Information State-supported, coed, comprehensive institution. *Graduate housing:* Room and/or apartments available on a first-come, first-served basis to single students; on-campus housing not available to married students.

GRADUATE UNITS

College of Business *Program availability:* Part-time-only, evening/weekend. Offers business (MBA). Electronic applications accepted.

College of Education *Program availability:* Part-time, evening/weekend. Offers education (M Ed); elementary education (MS). Electronic applications accepted.

UNIVERSITY OF MASSACHUSETTS AMHERST, Amherst, MA 01003

General Information State-supported, coed, university. CGS member. *Graduate housing:* Rooms and/or apartments available on a first-come, first-served basis to single and married students. Housing application deadline: 6/15.

GRADUATE UNITS

Graduate School *Program availability:* Part-time, evening/weekend. Electronic applications accepted.

College of Education *Program availability:* Part-time, online learning. Offers bilingual, English as a second language, and multicultural education (M Ed, Ed S); child study and early education (M Ed); children, families and schools (Ed D, Ed S); early childhood and elementary teacher education (M Ed); education (M Ed, Ed D, PhD, Ed S); educational leadership (M Ed); educational policy and leadership (Ed D); higher education (M Ed); international education (M Ed); language, literacy and culture (Ed D); learning, media and technology (M Ed, Ed S); mathematics, science, and learning technologies (Ed D); reading and writing (M Ed); research, educational measurement and psychometrics (Ed D); school counselor education (M Ed, Ed S); school psychology (M Ed, PhD, Ed S); science education (Ed S); secondary teacher education (M Ed); social justice education (M Ed, Ed D, Ed S); special education (M Ed, Ed D, Ed S); teacher education and school improvement (Ed D, Ed S). Electronic applications accepted.

College of Engineering *Program availability:* Part-time. Offers chemical engineering (MSChE, PhD); civil engineering (MSCE, PhD); electrical and computer engineering (MSECE, PhD); engineering (MS, MS Env E, MSCE, MSChE, MSECE, MSEM, MSIE, MSME, PhD); environmental and water resources engineering (MSCE); geotechnical engineering (MSCE); industrial engineering and operations research (MS, PhD); mechanical engineering (MSME, PhD); structural engineering and mechanics (MSCE); transportation engineering (MSCE). Electronic applications accepted.

College of Humanities and Fine Arts *Program availability:* Part-time. Offers Afro-American studies (MA, PhD); American studies (PhD); architecture (M Arch); art (MA, MFA); Asian languages and literatures (MA); Chinese (MA); collaborative piano (MM); comparative literature (MA, PhD); composition (MM); composition and rhetoric (PhD); conducting (MM); costume design (MFA); creative writing (MFA); design (MS); design in historic preservation (MS); directing (MFA); dramaturgy (MFA); English and American literature (MA, PhD); French (MAT); French and Francophone studies (MA, MAT); German and Scandinavian studies (MA, PhD); Hispanic literatures, cultures and linguistics (MA, PhD); history (MA, PhD); history of art and architecture (MA); humanities and fine arts (M Arch, MA, MAT, MFA, MM, MS, PhD); Italian studies (MAT); Japanese (MA); jazz composition/arranging (MM); Latin and classical humanities (MAT); lighting design (MFA); linguistics (MA, PhD); music education (MM, PhD); music history (MM); music theory (PhD); performance (MM); philosophy (MA, PhD); scenic design (MFA); Spanish and Portuguese studies (MA, MAT, PhD); teaching Spanish (MAT). Electronic applications accepted.

College of Natural Sciences *Program availability:* Part-time. Offers animal biotechnology and biomedical sciences (MS, PhD); applied mathematics (MS); astronomy (MS, PhD); biochemistry and molecular biology (MS, PhD); building systems (MS, PhD); chemistry (MS, PhD); clinical psychology (MS, PhD); cognitive psychology (MS, PhD); computer science (MS, PhD); developmental science (MS, PhD); environmental policy and human dimensions (MS, PhD); food science (MS, PhD); forest resources (MS, PhD); geography (MS); geosciences (MS, PhD); mathematics (MS, PhD); microbiology (MS, PhD); natural sciences (MS, PhD); physics (MS, PhD); polymer science and engineering (MS, PhD); psychology of peace and violence (MS, PhD); social psychology (MS, PhD); statistics (MS, PhD); sustainability science (MS); water, wetlands and watersheds (MS, PhD); wildlife and fisheries conservation (MS, PhD). Electronic applications accepted.

College of Nursing *Program availability:* Part-time, online learning. Offers adult gerontology primary care nurse practitioner (DNP); clinical nurse leader (MS); family nurse practitioner (DNP); nursing (PhD); public health nurse leader (DNP). Electronic applications accepted.

College of Social and Behavioral Sciences *Program availability:* Part-time. Offers anthropology (MA, PhD); communication (MA, PhD); economics (MA, PhD); labor studies (MS); landscape architecture (MLA); political science (MA, PhD); public policy and administration (MPP, MPPA); regional planning (MRP, PhD); resource economics (MS, PhD); social and behavioral sciences (MA, MLA, MPP, MPPA, MRP, MS, PhD); sociology (MA, PhD); union leadership and administration (MS). Electronic applications accepted.

Interdisciplinary Programs *Program availability:* Part-time. Offers animal behavior and learning (PhD); biochemistry and metabolism (MS, PhD); biological chemistry and molecular biophysics (PhD); biomedicine (PhD); cell biology and physiology (MS, PhD); cellular and developmental biology (PhD); environmental, ecological and integrative biology (MS, PhD); genetics and evolution (MS, PhD); interdisciplinary studies (MS, PhD); marine science and technology (MS, PhD); molecular and cellular neuroscience (PhD); neural and behavioral development (PhD); neuroendocrinology (PhD); neuroscience and behavior (MS); organismic and evolutionary biology (MS, PhD); sensorimotor, cognitive, and computational neuroscience (PhD). Electronic applications accepted.

Isenberg School of Management *Program availability:* Part-time, evening/weekend, online learning. Offers accounting (MSA); business administration (MBA); entrepreneurship (MBA); finance (MBA, PhD); healthcare administration (MBA); hospitality and tourism management (PhD); management (MBA, MS, MSA, PhD); management science (PhD); marketing (MBA, PhD); organization studies (PhD); sport management (PhD); strategic management (PhD). Electronic applications accepted.

School of Public Health and Health Sciences *Program availability:* Part-time, evening/weekend, online learning. Offers audiology (Au D, PhD); biostatistics (MPH, MS, PhD); clinical audiology (PhD); community health education (MPH, MS, PhD); community nutrition (MS); environmental health sciences (MPH, MS, PhD); epidemiology (MPH, MS, PhD); health policy and management (MPH, MS, PhD); kinesiology (MS, PhD); nutrition (MPH, PhD); nutrition science (MS); public health and health sciences (MA, MPH, MS, Au D, PhD); public health practice (MPH); speech-language pathology (MA, PhD). Electronic applications accepted.

UNIVERSITY OF MASSACHUSETTS BOSTON, Boston, MA 02125-3393

General Information State-supported, coed, university. CGS member. *Enrollment:* 16,415 graduate, professional, and undergraduate students; 1,325 full-time matriculated graduate/professional students (852 women), 2,047 part-time matriculated graduate/professional students (1,409 women). *Enrollment by degree level:* 2,266 master's, 776 doctoral, 330 other advanced degrees. *Graduate faculty:* 700 full-time (353 women), 446 part-time/adjunct (264 women). Tuition, state resident: full-time $17,375. Tuition, nonresident: full-time $33,915. *Required fees:* $355. *Graduate housing:* On-campus housing not available. *Student services:* Campus employment opportunities, campus safety program, career counseling, child daycare facilities, exercise/wellness program, free psychological counseling, international student services, low-cost health insurance, multicultural affairs office, services for students with disabilities, teacher training, writing training. *Library facilities:* Joseph P. Healey Library. *Collection:* Books: 459,163 (physical), 547,086 (digital/electronic); Databases: 124. *Research affiliation:* New England Aquarium (environmental sciences), Dana Farber/Harvard Cancer Center (biomedical sciences), John F. Kennedy Presidential Library (history).

Computer facilities: 350 computers available on campus for general student use. A campuswide network can be accessed from off campus. Online class registration is available.
Website: http://www.umb.edu/

General Application Contact: Graduate Admissions Coordinator, 617-287-6400, Fax: 617-287-6236, E-mail: gadm@umb.edu.

GRADUATE UNITS

College of Advancing and Professional Studies Students: 17 full-time (13 women), 121 part-time (84 women); includes 2 minority (1 American Indian or Alaska Native, non-Hispanic/Latino; 1 Hispanic/Latino), 1 international. Average age 40. 61 applicants, 89% accepted, 43 enrolled. *Faculty:* 2 full-time (1 woman), 40 part-time/adjunct (22 women). Expenses: Contact institution. In 2017, 38 master's, 48 other advanced degrees awarded. *Program availability:* Online learning. Offers critical and creative thinking (MA, Certificate); instructional design (M Ed, Certificate). *Application Contact:* Graduate Admissions Coordinator, 617-287-6400, Fax: 617-287-6236, E-mail: bos.gadm@dpc.umassp.edu. *Dean,* Dr. Philip DiSalvio, 617-287-7926, Fax: 617-287-5699, E-mail: philip.disalvio@umb.edu.

College of Education and Human Development Students: 350 full-time (269 women), 425 part-time (302 women); includes 21 minority (10 Black or African American, non-Hispanic/Latino; 6 Asian, non-Hispanic/Latino; 5 Hispanic/Latino), 1 international. Average age 33. 779 applicants, 56% accepted, 300 enrolled. *Faculty:* 56 full-time (40 women), 43 part-time/adjunct (26 women). Expenses: Contact institution. *Financial support:* Research assistantships, teaching assistantships, career-related internships or fieldwork, Federal Work-Study, and unspecified assistantships available. Support available to part-time students. Financial award application deadline: 3/1; financial award applicants required to submit FAFSA. In 2017, 306 master's, 17 doctorates, 139 other advanced degrees awarded. *Program availability:* Part-time, evening/weekend. Offers counseling and school psychology (PhD); early childhood education and care (PhD); education (M Ed, Ed D, PhD); education and human development (M Ed, MS, Ed D, PhD, CAGS); educational administration (M Ed, CAGS); family therapy (MS); higher education (Ed D, PhD); mental health counseling (MS); school counseling (M Ed); school psychology (M Ed); special education (M Ed); urban education, leadership, and policy studies (Ed D, PhD). *Application deadline:* For fall admission, 3/1 for domestic students. *Application Contact:* Graduate Admissions Coordinator, 617-287-6400, Fax: 617-287-6236, E-mail: bos.gadm@dpc.umassp.edu. *Dean,* Dr. Joseph Berger, 617-287-7606.

College of Liberal Arts Students: 210 full-time (155 women), 360 part-time (227 women); includes 91 minority (27 Black or African American, non-Hispanic/Latino; 1 American Indian or Alaska Native, non-Hispanic/Latino; 35 Asian, non-Hispanic/Latino; 27 Hispanic/Latino; 1 Two or more races, non-Hispanic/Latino), 15 international. Average age 32. 761 applicants, 35% accepted, 152 enrolled. *Faculty:* 312 full-time (171 women), 154 part-time/adjunct (78 women). Expenses: Contact institution. *Financial support:* Research assistantships, teaching assistantships, career-related internships or fieldwork, Federal Work-Study, and unspecified assistantships available. Support available to part-time students. Financial award application deadline: 3/1; financial award applicants required to submit FAFSA. In 2017, 148 master's, 12 doctorates awarded. *Program availability:* Part-time, evening/weekend. Offers American studies (MA); applied economics (MA); applied linguistics (PhD); applied sociology (MA); archival methods (MA); clinical psychology (PhD); creative writing (MFA); developmental and brain sciences (MA); English (MA); historical archaeology (MA); Latin and classical humanities (MA); liberal arts (MA, MFA, MS, PhD); sociology (PhD); transnational, cultural, and community studies (MS). *Application deadline:* For fall admission, 3/1 for domestic students; for spring admission, 1/1 for domestic students. *Application Contact:* Graduate Admissions Coordinator, 617-287-6400, Fax: 617-287-6236, E-mail: bos.gadm@dpc.umassp.edu.

College of Management Students: 238 full-time (105 women), 257 part-time (129 women); includes 24 minority (3 Black or African American, non-Hispanic/Latino; 19 Asian, non-Hispanic/Latino; 2 Hispanic/Latino), 11 international. Average age 31. 450 applicants, 39% accepted, 102 enrolled. *Faculty:* 79 full-time (28 women), 26 part-time/adjunct (7 women). Expenses: Contact institution. *Financial support:* Research assistantships, teaching assistantships, career-related internships or fieldwork, Federal Work-Study, and unspecified assistantships available. Support available to part-time students. Financial award application deadline: 3/1; financial award applicants required to submit FAFSA. In 2017, 220 master's awarded. *Program availability:* Part-time, evening/weekend. Offers accounting (MS); business administration (MBA); business analytics (MS); finance (MS); information technology (MS); international management (MS); management (MBA, MS). *Application deadline:* For fall admission, 3/1 for domestic students; for spring admission, 11/1 for domestic students. *Application Contact:* Graduate Admissions Coordinator, 617-287-6400, Fax: 617-287-6236, E-mail: bos.gadm@dpc.umassp.edu.

College of Nursing and Health Sciences Students: 91 full-time (76 women), 288 part-time (264 women); includes 15 minority (6 Black or African American, non-Hispanic/Latino; 8 Asian, non-Hispanic/Latino; 1 Hispanic/Latino), 4 international. Average age 36. 251 applicants, 68% accepted, 106 enrolled. *Faculty:* 51 full-time (43 women), 87 part-time/adjunct (78 women). Expenses: Contact institution. *Financial support:* Research assistantships, teaching assistantships, career-related internships or fieldwork, Federal Work-Study, and unspecified assistantships available. Support available to part-time students. Financial award application deadline: 3/1; financial award applicants required to submit FAFSA. In 2017, 64 master's, 17 doctorates awarded. *Program availability:* Part-time, evening/weekend. Offers exercise and health sciences (MS, PhD); nursing (MS, DNP, PhD); nursing practice (DNP). *Application deadline:* For fall admission, 3/1 for domestic students; for spring admission, 11/1 for domestic students. *Application Contact:* Graduate Admissions Coordinator, 617-287-6400, Fax: 617-287-6236, E-mail: bos.gadm@dpc.umassp.edu.

College of Public and Community Service 2 applicants. *Faculty:* 3 full-time (2 women), 1 (woman) part-time/adjunct. Expenses: Contact institution. *Financial support:* Research assistantships, teaching assistantships, career-related internships or fieldwork, Federal Work-Study, and unspecified assistantships available. Support available to part-time students. Financial award application deadline: 3/1; financial award applicants required to submit FAFSA. *Program availability:* Part-time, evening/weekend. Offers human services (MS); public and community service (MS). *Application deadline:* For fall admission, 3/1 for domestic students. Applications are processed on a rolling basis. *Application Contact:* Dr. Stephanie Hartwell, Interim Dean, 617-287-6288, E-mail: stephanie.hartwell@umb.edu. *Dean,* Dr. Adenrele Awotona, 617-287-7112, Fax: 617-287-5544, E-mail: adenrele.awotona@umb.edu.

College of Science and Mathematics Students: 189 full-time (75 women), 93 part-time (38 women); includes 37 minority (5 Black or African American, non-Hispanic/Latino; 27 Asian, non-Hispanic/Latino; 5 Hispanic/Latino), 10 international. Average age 29. 449 applicants, 35% accepted, 86 enrolled. *Faculty:* 125 full-time (35 women), 33 part-time/adjunct (16 women). Expenses: Contact institution. *Financial support:* Research assistantships, teaching assistantships, career-related internships or fieldwork, Federal Work-Study, institutionally sponsored loans, and unspecified assistantships available. Support available to part-time students. Financial award application deadline: 3/1; financial award applicants required to submit FAFSA. In 2017, 79 master's, 14 doctorates awarded. *Program availability:* Part-time, evening/weekend. Offers applied physics (MS); biology (MS, PhD); biomedical engineering and biotechnology (PhD); biotechnology and biomedical sciences (MS); chemistry (MS, PhD); computational sciences (PhD); computer science (MS, PhD); integrative biosciences (PhD); science and mathematics (MS, PhD). *Application deadline:* For fall admission, 3/1 for domestic students; for spring admission, 11/1 for domestic students. Applications are processed on a rolling basis. *Application Contact:* 617-287-6400, Fax: 617-287-6236, E-mail: bos.gadm@dpc.umassp.edu. *Associate Dean,* Dr. William Hagar, 617-287-5777.

Graduate School of Global Inclusion and Social Development Students: 39 full-time (34 women), 225 part-time (188 women); includes 8 minority (1 Black or African American, non-Hispanic/Latino; 6 Asian, non-Hispanic/Latino; 1 Hispanic/Latino). Average age 38. 155 applicants, 66% accepted, 77 enrolled. *Faculty:* 9 full-time (7 women), 20 part-time/adjunct (14 women). Expenses: Contact institution. In 2017, 38 master's awarded. Offers global inclusion and social development (M Ed, MA, MS, PhD); rehabilitation counseling (MS); vision studies (M Ed). *Application Contact:* Graduate Admissions Coordinator, 617-287-6400, Fax: 617-287-6236, E-mail: bos.gadm@dpc.umassp.edu.

McCormack Graduate School of Policy and Global Studies Students: 142 full-time (97 women), 240 part-time (158 women); includes 5 minority (3 Black or African American, non-Hispanic/Latino; 2 Asian, non-Hispanic/Latino), 3 international. Average age 36. 277 applicants, 61% accepted, 116 enrolled. *Faculty:* 34 full-time (17 women), 19 part-time/adjunct (12 women). Expenses: Contact institution. *Financial support:* Research assistantships, teaching assistantships, career-related internships or fieldwork, Federal Work-Study, and unspecified assistantships available. Support available to part-time students. Financial award application deadline: 3/1; financial award applicants required to submit FAFSA. In 2017, 93 master's, 15 doctorates, 24 other advanced degrees awarded. *Program availability:* Part-time, evening/weekend. Offers conflict resolution (MA, Certificate); gerontology (PhD); global comparative public administration (MPA); global governance and human security (MA); international relations (MA); policy and global studies (MA, MPA, MS, PhD, Certificate); public administration (MPA); public policy (MS, PhD). *Application Contact:* Graduate Admissions Coordinator, 617-287-6400, Fax: 617-287-6236, E-mail: bos.gadm@dpc.umassp.edu. *Dean,* Dr. David Cash, 617-287-5551, E-mail: david.cash@umb.edu.

School for the Environment Students: 49 full-time (28 women), 38 part-time (19 women); includes 5 minority (all Asian, non-Hispanic/Latino), 6 international. Average age 31. 27 applicants, 67% accepted, 10 enrolled. *Faculty:* 19 full-time (5 women), 10 part-time/adjunct (5 women). Expenses: Contact institution. In 2017, 8 master's, 5 doctorates awarded. Offers environment (MS, PSM, PhD); environmental sciences (MS, PhD); marine science and technology (MS, PhD); urban planning and community development (MS). *Application Contact:* Graduate Admissions Coordinator, 617-287-6400, Fax: 617-287-6236, E-mail: gadm@umb.edu. *Dean,* Robyn Hannigan, 617-287-7440, E-mail: thegreendean@umb.edu.

UNIVERSITY OF MASSACHUSETTS DARTMOUTH, North Dartmouth, MA 02747-2300

General Information State-supported, coed, university. *Enrollment:* 8,406 graduate, professional, and undergraduate students; 683 full-time matriculated graduate/professional students (323 women), 842 part-time matriculated graduate/professional students (488 women). *Enrollment by degree level:* 969 master's, 465 doctoral, 91 other advanced degrees. *Graduate faculty:* 306 full-time (144 women), 128 part-time/adjunct (70 women). Tuition, state resident: full-time $15,449; part-time $643.71 per credit. Tuition, nonresident: full-time $27,880; part-time $1161.67 per credit. *Required fees:* $405; $25.88 per credit. Tuition and fees vary according to course load and reciprocity agreements. *Graduate housing:* Room and/or apartments available on a first-come, first-served basis to single students; on-campus housing not available to married students. Typical cost: $9165 per year ($13,910 including board). Room and board charges vary according to board plan and housing facility selected. Housing application deadline: 3/14. *Student services:* Campus employment opportunities, campus safety program, career counseling, exercise/wellness program, free psychological counseling, grant writing training, international student services, low-cost health insurance, multicultural affairs office, services for students with disabilities, teacher training, writing training. *Library facilities:* Claire T. Carney Library plus 1 other. *Collection:* Books: 241,507 (physical), 75,709 (digital/electronic); Serial titles: 1,407 (physical), 85,115 (digital/electronic); Databases: 142. Students can reserve study rooms. *Research affiliation:* National Oceanic and Atmospheric Administration (NOAA) (marine science and technology), National Science Foundation (biology), Health Resources Service Administration (nursing), Office of Naval Research (ONR) (engineering), Woods Hole Oceanographic Institution (marine science and technology), National Institute of Aerospace (engineering).

Computer facilities: Computer purchase and lease plans are available. 368 computers available on campus for general student use. A campuswide network can be accessed from student residence rooms and from off campus. Online class registration is available.
Website: http://www.umassd.edu/

General Application Contact: Steven Briggs, Director of Marketing and Recruitment for Graduate Studies, 508-999-8604, Fax: 508-999-8183, E-mail: graduate@umassd.edu.

GRADUATE UNITS

Graduate School Students: 683 full-time (323 women), 842 part-time (488 women); includes 277 minority (73 Black or African American, non-Hispanic/Latino; 2 American Indian or Alaska Native, non-Hispanic/Latino; 59 Asian, non-Hispanic/Latino; 96 Hispanic/Latino; 1 Native Hawaiian or other Pacific Islander, non-Hispanic/Latino; 46 Two or more races, non-Hispanic/Latino), 322 international. Average age 31. 1,855 applicants, 67% accepted, 551 enrolled. *Faculty:* 306 full-time (144 women), 128 part-time/adjunct (70 women). Expenses: Contact institution. *Financial support:* In 2017–18, 55 fellowships (averaging $14,785 per year), 87 research assistantships (averaging $16,422 per year), 89 teaching assistantships (averaging $12,594 per year) were awarded; tuition waivers (full and partial), unspecified assistantships, and instructional assistantships, dissertation writing support, doctoral support, studio assistantships also available. Support available to part-time students. Financial award application deadline: 3/1; financial award applicants required to submit FAFSA. In 2017, 403 master's, 95 doctorates, 42 other advanced degrees awarded. *Program availability:* Part-time, 100% online, blended/hybrid learning. Offers data science (MS); nursing (MS, DNP, PhD). *Application fee:* $60. Electronic applications accepted. *Application Contact:* Steven Briggs, Director of Marketing and Recruitment for Graduate Studies, 508-999-8604, Fax: 508-999-8183, E-mail: graduate@umassd.edu. *Director of Graduate Studies and Admissions*, Scott Webster, 508-999-8202, Fax: 508-999-8183, E-mail: graduate@umassd.edu.

Charlton College of Business Students: 169 full-time (77 women), 188 part-time (103 women); includes 70 minority (19 Black or African American, non-Hispanic/Latino; 1 American Indian or Alaska Native, non-Hispanic/Latino; 22 Asian, non-Hispanic/Latino; 19 Hispanic/Latino; 9 Two or more races, non-Hispanic/Latino), 105 international. Average age 32. 233 applicants, 86% accepted, 145 enrolled. *Faculty:* 46 full-time (18 women), 19 part-time/adjunct (5 women). Expenses: Contact institution. *Financial support:* In 2017–18, 2 research assistantships (averaging $8,000 per year) were awarded; teaching assistantships, tuition waivers (full and partial), and unspecified assistantships also available. Support available to part-time students. Financial award application deadline: 3/1; financial award applicants required to submit FAFSA. In 2017, 190 master's, 21 other advanced degrees awarded. *Program availability:* Part-time, 100% online, blended/hybrid learning. Offers accounting (MS, Postbaccalaureate Certificate); accounting and finance (MS, Postbaccalaureate Certificate); business administration (MBA); decision and information sciences (MS); finance (Postbaccalaureate Certificate); healthcare management (MS); technology management (MS). *Application deadline:* For fall admission, 8/1 priority date for domestic students, 7/1 priority date for international students; for spring admission, 11/15 priority date for domestic students, 10/15 priority date for international students. *Application fee:* $60. Electronic applications accepted. *Application Contact:* Steven Briggs, Director of Recruitment and Marketing for Graduate Studies, 508-999-8604, Fax: 508-999-8183, E-mail: graduate@umassd.edu. *Assistant Dean of Graduate Programs*, Melissa Pacheco, 508-999-8543, Fax: 508-999-8646, E-mail: mpacheco@umassd.edu.

College of Arts and Sciences Students: 130 full-time (87 women), 282 part-time (186 women); includes 74 minority (15 Black or African American, non-Hispanic/Latino; 1 American Indian or Alaska Native, non-Hispanic/Latino; 11 Asian, non-Hispanic/Latino; 28 Hispanic/Latino; 19 Two or more races, non-Hispanic/Latino), 25 international. Average age 32. 306 applicants, 74% accepted, 160 enrolled. *Faculty:* 114 full-time (57 women), 47 part-time/adjunct (23 women). Expenses: Contact institution. *Financial support:* In 2017–18, 27 fellowships (averaging $15,926 per year), 18 research assistantships (averaging $15,534 per year), 35 teaching assistantships (averaging $13,797 per year) were awarded; tuition waivers (full and partial), unspecified assistantships, and instructional assistantships, dissertation writing support, doctoral support also available. Support available to part-time students. Financial award application deadline: 3/1; financial award applicants required to submit FAFSA. In 2017, 95 master's, 13 doctorates, 18 other advanced degrees awarded. *Program availability:* Part-time, 100% online, blended/hybrid learning. Offers arts and sciences (MA, MAT, MPP, MS, Ed D, PhD, Graduate Certificate, Post-Master's Certificate, Postbaccalaureate Certificate); autism studies (Graduate Certificate); biology (MS); chemistry (MS, PhD); educational leadership (Ed D, PhD); educational leadership and policy studies (Ed D, PhD); educational policy (Graduate Certificate); English as a second language (Postbaccalaureate Certificate); environmental policy (Graduate Certificate); integrative biology (PhD); Luso-Afro Brazilian studies and theory (PhD); marine biology (MS); mathematics education (PhD); middle school education (MAT); Portuguese studies (MA); professional writing (MA, Postbaccalaureate Certificate); psychology - applied behavioral analysis (MA, Post-Master's Certificate); psychology - clinical (MA); psychology - research (MA); public management (Graduate Certificate); public policy (MPP); secondary school education (MAT); STEM education and teacher development (MAT, PhD, Postbaccalaureate Certificate). *Application fee:* $60. Electronic applications accepted. *Application Contact:* Steven Briggs, Director of Marketing and Recruitment for Graduate Studies, 508-999-8604, Fax: 508-999-8183, E-mail: graduate@umassd.edu. *Interim Dean, College of Arts and Sciences*, Amy Shapiro, 508-910-9101, E-mail: ashapiro@umassd.edu.

College of Engineering Students: 174 full-time (50 women), 143 part-time (27 women); includes 38 minority (7 Black or African American, non-Hispanic/Latino; 9 Asian, non-Hispanic/Latino; 15 Hispanic/Latino; 7 Two or more races, non-Hispanic/Latino), 165 international. Average age 28. 329 applicants, 58% accepted, 94 enrolled. *Faculty:* 53 full-time (10 women), 7 part-time/adjunct (1 woman). Expenses: Contact institution. *Financial support:* In 2017–18, 14 fellowships (averaging $19,613 per year), 43 research assistantships (averaging $14,491 per year), 40 teaching assistantships (averaging $12,359 per year) were awarded; tuition waivers (full and partial), unspecified assistantships, and instructional assistantships, doctoral support, dissertation writing support also available. Support available to part-time students. Financial award application deadline: 3/1; financial award applicants required to submit FAFSA. In 2017, 88 master's, 11 doctorates awarded. *Program availability:* Part-time, 100% online, blended/hybrid learning. Offers biomedical engineering/biotechnology (PhD); civil engineering (MS); communications (Postbaccalaureate Certificate); computer science (MS, Graduate Certificate); computing infrastructure security (Postbaccalaureate Certificate); digital signal processing (Postbaccalaureate Certificate); electrical engineering (MS, PhD); electrical engineering systems (Postbaccalaureate Certificate); engineering (MS, PhD, Graduate Certificate, Postbaccalaureate Certificate); engineering and applied science (PhD); industrial and systems engineering (Postbaccalaureate Certificate); mechanical engineering (MS); physics (MS); software development and design (Postbaccalaureate Certificate). *Application fee:* $60. Electronic applications accepted. *Application Contact:* Steven Briggs, Director of Marketing and Recruitment for Graduate Studies, 508-999-8604, Fax: 508-999-8183, E-mail: graduate@umassd.edu. *Interim Dean, College of Engineering*, Ramprasad Balasubramanian, 508-910-6919, Fax: 508-999-9144, E-mail: rbala@umassd.edu.

College of Visual and Performing Arts Students: 28 full-time (15 women), 37 part-time (30 women); includes 10 minority (1 Black or African American, non-Hispanic/Latino; 3 Asian, non-Hispanic/Latino; 5 Hispanic/Latino; 1 Two or more races, non-Hispanic/Latino), 8 international. Average age 33. 78 applicants, 60% accepted, 23 enrolled. *Faculty:* 34 full-time (18 women), 5 part-time/adjunct (3 women). Expenses: Contact institution. *Financial support:* In 2017–18, 12 fellowships (averaging $5,549 per year), 2 teaching assistantships (averaging $4,300 per year) were awarded; tuition waivers (full and partial), unspecified assistantships, and studio assistantships also available. Support available to part-time students. Financial award application deadline: 3/1; financial award applicants required to submit FAFSA. In 2017, 15 master's, 3 other advanced degrees awarded. *Program availability:* Part-time. Offers art education, art history and media studies (MAE); artisanry (MFA, Postbaccalaureate Certificate); fine arts (MFA, Postbaccalaureate Certificate); visual and performing arts (MAE, MFA, Postbaccalaureate Certificate); visual design (MFA). *Application fee:* $60. Electronic applications accepted. *Application Contact:* Steven Briggs, Director of Marketing and Recruitment for Graduate Studies, 508-999-8604, Fax: 508-999-8183, E-mail: graduate@umassd.edu. *Dean, College of Visual and Performing Arts*, David Klamen, 508-999-9286, E-mail: dklamen@umassd.edu.

School for Marine Science and Technology Students: 20 full-time (14 women), 29 part-time (14 women); includes 4 minority (1 Asian, non-Hispanic/Latino; 3 Two or more races, non-Hispanic/Latino), 8 international. Average age 31. 22 applicants, 55% accepted, 7 enrolled. *Faculty:* 12 full-time (1 woman). Expenses: Contact institution. *Financial support:* In 2017–18, 1 fellowship (averaging $18,000 per year), 24 research assistantships (averaging $21,251 per year), 2 teaching assistantships (averaging $18,500 per year) were awarded; tuition waivers (full), unspecified assistantships, and dissertation writing support, China scholarship council also available. Support available to part-time students. Financial award application deadline: 3/1; financial award applicants required to submit FAFSA. In 2017, 6 master's, 4 doctorates awarded. *Program availability:* Part-time. Offers coastal and ocean administration science and technology (MS); marine science and technology (MS, PhD). *Application deadline:* For fall admission, 2/15 priority date for domestic students, 1/15 priority date for international students; for spring admission, 11/15 priority date for domestic students, 10/15 priority date for international students. *Application fee:* $60. Electronic applications accepted. *Application Contact:* Steven Briggs, Director of Marketing and Recruitment for Graduate Studies, 508-999-8604, Fax: 508-999-8183, E-mail: graduate@umassd.edu. *Dean, School for Marine Science and Technology*, Steven Lohrenz, 508-910-6550, E-mail: slohrenz@umassd.edu.

University of Massachusetts School of Law –Dartmouth Students: 154 full-time (77 women), 48 part-time (27 women); includes 59 minority (19 Black or African American, non-Hispanic/Latino; 9 Asian, non-Hispanic/Latino; 24 Hispanic/Latino; 1 Native Hawaiian or other Pacific Islander, non-Hispanic/Latino; 6 Two or more races, non-Hispanic/Latino), 2 international. Average age 30. 793 applicants, 64% accepted, 82 enrolled. *Faculty:* 15 full-time (8 women), 15 part-time/adjunct (3 women). Expenses: Contact institution. *Financial support:* Fellowships, institutionally sponsored loans, and scholarships/grants available. Support available to part-time students. Financial award application deadline: 3/1; financial award applicants required to submit FAFSA. In 2017, 50 doctorates awarded. *Program availability:* Part-time, evening/weekend. Offers law (JD). *Application deadline:* For fall admission, 6/30 priority date for domestic students, 5/30 priority date for international students. *Application fee:* $60. Electronic applications accepted. *Application Contact:* Nancy Fitzsimmons-Hebert, Assistant Director of Marketing and Recruitment, 508-985-1110, Fax: 508-985-1175, E-mail: lawadmissions@umassd.edu. *Assistant Dean, University of Massachusetts School of Law - Dartmouth*, Daniel Fitzpatrick, 508-985-1110, Fax: 508-985-1175, E-mail: lawadmissions@umassd.edu.

UNIVERSITY OF MASSACHUSETTS LOWELL, Lowell, MA 01854

General Information State-supported, coed, university. CGS member. *Graduate housing:* Rooms and/or apartments available on a first-come, first-served basis to single students and available to married students. Housing application deadline: 4/1.

GRADUATE UNITS

College of Fine Arts, Humanities and Social Sciences Offers community social psychology (MA); fine arts, humanities and social sciences (MA, MM, PhD); music education (MM); peace and conflict studies (MA); regional economic and social development (MA, Graduate Certificate).

School of Criminology and Justice Studies *Program availability:* Part-time, evening/weekend. Offers criminal justice (MA). Electronic applications accepted.

College of Health Sciences *Program availability:* Part-time. Offers cleaner production and pollution prevention (Sc D); clinical laboratory sciences (MS); health sciences (MS, DNP, DPT, PhD); physical therapy (DPT).

School of Nursing Offers adult/gerontological nursing (MS); family health nursing (MS); nursing (DNP, PhD).

College of Sciences *Program availability:* Part-time, evening/weekend. Offers analytical chemistry (PhD); biochemistry (PhD); biological sciences (MS); chemistry (MS, PhD); computer science (MS, PhD); environmental studies (PhD); green chemistry (PhD); inorganic chemistry (PhD); mathematical sciences (Ed D); organic chemistry (PhD); physics (MS, PhD); polymer science (MS); radiological sciences and protection (MS, PSM); sciences (MA, MM, MS, Ed D, PhD).

Francis College of Engineering *Program availability:* Part-time, evening/weekend. Offers chemical engineering (MS Eng, PhD); computer engineering (MS Eng, PhD); electrical engineering (MS Eng, PhD); energy engineering (MS Eng, PhD); engineering (MS, MS Eng, PhD); environmental studies (PhD); mechanical engineering (MS Eng, PhD); plastics engineering (MS Eng, PhD).

Graduate School of Education *Program availability:* Part-time, evening/weekend, online learning. Offers curriculum and instruction (M Ed). Electronic applications accepted.

Manning School of Business *Program availability:* Part-time, evening/weekend. Offers business administration (MBA, PhD); healthcare innovation and entrepreneurship (MS).

UNIVERSITY OF MASSACHUSETTS MEDICAL SCHOOL, Worcester, MA 01655-0115

General Information State-supported, coed, graduate-only institution. CGS member. *Enrollment by degree level:* 7 master's, 1,063 doctoral, 2 other advanced degrees. *Graduate faculty:* 1,347 full-time (554 women), 396 part-time/adjunct (263 women). *Graduate housing:* On-campus housing not available. *Student services:* Campus employment opportunities, campus safety program, career counseling, child daycare facilities, exercise/wellness program, free psychological counseling, grant writing training, international student services, low-cost health insurance, multicultural affairs office, services for students with disabilities, teacher training, writing training. *Library facilities:* Lamar Soutter Library. *Collection:* Books: 165,090 (physical), 50,883 (digital/electronic); Serial titles: 5,187 (digital/electronic); Databases: 298. Weekly public service hours: 82; study areas open 24 hours, 5–7 days a week. *Research affiliation:* Abbott Bioresearch Center (biomedical research and training), Charles River Laboratories (pre-clinical biomedical research).

Computer facilities: 107 computers available on campus for general student use. A campuswide network can be accessed. Online class registration is available. Website: http://www.umassmed.edu/

General Application Contact: Karen Lawton, Director of Admissions, 508-856-2323, Fax: 508-856-3629, E-mail: admissions@umassmed.edu.

GRADUATE UNITS

Graduate School of Biomedical Sciences Students: 347 full-time (180 women); includes 61 minority (10 Black or African American, non-Hispanic/Latino; 1 American Indian or Alaska Native, non-Hispanic/Latino; 35 Asian, non-Hispanic/Latino; 15 Hispanic/Latino), 130 international. Average age 29. 608 applicants, 28% accepted, 54 enrolled. *Faculty:* 1,316 full-time (526 women), 357 part-time/adjunct (229 women). Expenses: Contact institution. *Financial support:* In 2017–18, 15 fellowships with partial tuition reimbursements (averaging $29,000 per year), 296 research assistantships with full tuition reimbursements (averaging $31,212 per year) were awarded; institutionally sponsored loans and scholarships/grants also available. Financial award application deadline: 5/15. In 2017, 6 master's, 51 doctorates awarded. Offers biomedical sciences (PhD); biomedical sciences (millennium program) (PhD); clinical and population health research (PhD); clinical investigation (MS). *Application deadline:* For fall admission, 12/15 for domestic and international students. Applications are processed on a rolling basis. *Application fee:* $80. Electronic applications accepted. *Application Contact:* Dr. Kendall Knight, Assistant Vice Provost for Admissions, 508-856-5628, Fax: 508-856-3659, E-mail: kendall.knight@umassmed.edu. *Dean,* Dr. Mary Ellen Lane, 508-856-4018, E-mail: maryellen.lane@umassmed.edu.

Graduate School of Nursing Students: 129 full-time (111 women), 31 part-time (30 women); includes 35 minority (17 Black or African American, non-Hispanic/Latino; 10 Asian, non-Hispanic/Latino; 7 Hispanic/Latino; 1 Native Hawaiian or other Pacific Islander, non-Hispanic/Latino), 1 international. Average age 32. 124 applicants, 55% accepted, 59 enrolled. *Faculty:* 31 full-time (28 women), 39 part-time/adjunct (34 women). Expenses: Contact institution. *Financial support:* In 2017–18, 6 students received support. Scholarships/grants available. Support available to part-time students. Financial award application deadline: 5/15; financial award applicants required to submit FAFSA. In 2017, 48 master's, 10 doctorates, 2 other advanced degrees awarded. Offers adult gerontological acute care nurse practitioner (DNP, Post Master's Certificate); adult gerontological primary care nurse practitioner (DNP, Post Master's Certificate); family nursing practitioner (DNP); nurse administrator (DNP); nurse educator (MS, Post Master's Certificate); nursing (PhD). *Application deadline:* For fall admission, 12/1 priority date for domestic students. Applications are processed on a rolling basis. *Application fee:* $60. Electronic applications accepted. *Application Contact:* Diane Brescia, Admissions Coordinator, 508-856-3488, Fax: 508-856-5851, E-mail: diane.brescia@umassmed.edu. *Dean,* Dr. Joan Vitello-Cicciu, 508-856-5081, Fax: 508-856-6552, E-mail: joan.vitello@umassmed.edu.

School of Medicine Students: 565 full-time (310 women); includes 178 minority (31 Black or African American, non-Hispanic/Latino; 3 American Indian or Alaska Native, non-Hispanic/Latino; 128 Asian, non-Hispanic/Latino; 15 Hispanic/Latino; 1 Native Hawaiian or other Pacific Islander, non-Hispanic/Latino), 1 international. Average age 26. 3,614 applicants, 9% accepted, 162 enrolled. *Faculty:* 1,316 full-time (526 women), 357 part-time/adjunct (229 women). Expenses: Contact institution. *Financial support:* In 2017–18, 485 students received support, including 4 fellowships with partial tuition reimbursements available (averaging $29,000 per year), 31 research assistantships with full tuition reimbursements available (averaging $31,212 per year); institutionally sponsored loans, scholarships/grants, and tuition waivers (partial) also available. Financial award application deadline: 3/31; financial award applicants required to submit FAFSA. In 2017, 132 doctorates awarded. Offers medicine (MD). *Application deadline:* For fall admission, 12/1 for domestic students. Applications are processed on a rolling basis. *Application fee:* $100. Electronic applications accepted. *Application Contact:* Jennifer Lee Shea, Admissions Coordinator, 508-856-2323, Fax: 508-856-3629, E-mail: admissions@umassmed.edu. *Dean/Provost/Executive Deputy Chancellor,* Dr. Terence R. Flotte, 508-856-8000, E-mail: terry.flotte@umassmed.edu.

UNIVERSITY OF MEMPHIS, Memphis, TN 38152

General Information State-supported, coed, university. CGS member. *Enrollment:* 21,521 graduate, professional, and undergraduate students; 1,870 full-time matriculated graduate/professional students (1,068 women), 2,029 part-time matriculated graduate/professional students (1,268 women). *Graduate faculty:* 513 full-time (200 women), 100 part-time/adjunct (46 women). *Graduate housing:* Rooms and/or apartments available on a first-come, first-served basis to single and married students. *Student services:* Campus employment opportunities, campus safety program, career counseling, child daycare facilities, exercise/wellness program, free psychological counseling, grant writing training, international student services, multicultural affairs office, services for students with disabilities, teacher training, writing training. *Library facilities:* McWherter Library plus 4 others. *Collection:* Books: 2.3 million (physical), 333,541 (digital/electronic); Serial titles: 519 (physical); Databases: 646. Weekly public service hours: 91; students can reserve study rooms. *Research affiliation:* Memphis Bioworks Foundation, FedEx Corp, Oak Ridge National Laboratory, St. Jude Children's Research Hospital, Medtronic Inc., Urban Child Institute.

Computer facilities: 1,255 computers available on campus for general student use. A campuswide network can be accessed from student residence rooms and from off campus. Online class registration is available.
Website: http://www.memphis.edu/

General Application Contact: Dr. Jasbir Dhaliwal, Dean of the Graduate School, 901-678-4653, Fax: 901-678-0378, E-mail: graduateschool@memphis.edu.

GRADUATE UNITS

Cecil C. Humphreys School of Law Students: 297 full-time (128 women), 14 part-time (10 women); includes 79 minority (60 Black or African American, non-Hispanic/Latino; 5 American Indian or Alaska Native, non-Hispanic/Latino; 5 Asian, non-Hispanic/Latino; 9 Hispanic/Latino). Average age 26. 647 applicants, 52% accepted, 107 enrolled. *Faculty:* 25 full-time (11 women), 23 part-time/adjunct (7 women). Expenses: Contact institution. *Financial support:* In 2017–18, 138 students received support, including 26 fellowships (averaging $12,118 per year), 20 research assistantships (averaging $5,000 per year); teaching assistantships, career-related internships or fieldwork, Federal Work-Study, scholarships/grants, and tuition waivers (partial) also available. Support available to part-time students. Financial award application deadline: 5/1; financial award applicants required to submit FAFSA. In 2017, 1 doctorate awarded. *Program availability:* Part-time. Offers law (JD). *Application deadline:* For fall admission, 3/15 priority date for domestic and international students. Applications are processed on a rolling basis. *Application fee:* $0 ($40 for international students). Electronic applications accepted. *Application Contact:* Dr. Sue Ann McClellan, Assistant Dean for Law Admissions, Recruiting and Scholarships, 901-678-5403, Fax: 901-678-0741, E-mail: smcclell@memphis.edu. *Dean,* Peter V. Letsou, 901-678-2421, Fax: 901-678-5210, E-mail: pvletsou@memphis.edu.

Graduate School Students: 1,967 full-time (1,109 women), 1,979 part-time (1,193 women); includes 1,293 minority (911 Black or African American, non-Hispanic/Latino; 6 American Indian or Alaska Native, non-Hispanic/Latino; 154 Asian, non-Hispanic/Latino; 119 Hispanic/Latino; 2 Native Hawaiian or other Pacific Islander, non-Hispanic/Latino; 101 Two or more races, non-Hispanic/Latino), 456 international. Average age 32. 2,964 applicants, 60% accepted, 560 enrolled. *Faculty:* 533 full-time (189 women), 103 part-time/adjunct (51 women). Expenses: Contact institution. *Financial support:* In 2017–18, 2,179 students received support, including 4 research assistantships with full tuition reimbursements available (averaging $23,318 per year); fellowships with full tuition reimbursements available, teaching assistantships with full tuition reimbursements available, career-related internships or fieldwork, Federal Work-Study, institutionally sponsored loans, scholarships/grants, and unspecified assistantships also available. Support available to part-time students. Financial award application deadline: 2/1; financial award applicants required to submit FAFSA. In 2017, 1,062 master's, 130 doctorates, 112 other advanced degrees awarded. *Program availability:* Part-time, evening/weekend, 100% online, blended/hybrid learning. *Application deadline:* For fall admission, 7/1 for domestic students, 5/1 for international students; for spring admission, 12/1 for domestic students, 9/15 for international students. Applications are processed on a rolling basis. *Application fee:* $35 ($60 for international students). Electronic applications accepted. *Application Contact:* Lemmie Griggs, Supervisor of Graduate Admissions, 901-678-5580, Fax: 901-678-0378, E-mail: lgriggs@memphis.edu. *Interim Vice Provost for Graduate Studies,* Dr. Jasbir Dhaliwal, 901-678-4653, Fax: 901-678-0378, E-mail: gradsch@memphis.edu.

College of Arts and Sciences Students: 637 full-time (290 women), 357 part-time (169 women); includes 293 minority (196 Black or African American, non-Hispanic/Latino; 39 Asian, non-Hispanic/Latino; 36 Hispanic/Latino; 1 Native Hawaiian or other Pacific Islander, non-Hispanic/Latino; 21 Two or more races, non-Hispanic/Latino), 167 international. Average age 30. 839 applicants, 53% accepted, 283 enrolled. *Faculty:* 208 full-time (75 women), 37 part-time/adjunct (19 women). Expenses: Contact institution. *Financial support:* In 2017–18, 467 students received support, including 10 teaching assistantships with full tuition reimbursements available (averaging $20,042 per year); fellowships with full tuition reimbursements available, research assistantships with full tuition reimbursements available, career-related internships or fieldwork, Federal Work-Study, institutionally sponsored loans, scholarships/grants, tuition waivers (full and partial), and unspecified assistantships also available. Financial award application deadline: 2/1; financial award applicants required to submit FAFSA. *Program availability:* Part-time, evening/weekend. Offers adults and families (MSW); African-American literature (Graduate Certificate); analytical chemistry (MS, PhD); ancient Egyptian history (MA, PhD); applied linguistics (PhD); applied mathematics (MS); applied statistics (PhD); arts and sciences (MA, MCRP, MFA, MPA, MS, MSW, PhD, Ed S, Graduate Certificate); bioinformatics (MS); biology (MS, PhD); children, youth, and families (MSW); city and regional planning (MCRP); clinical psychology (PhD); composition studies (PhD); computational chemistry (MS, PhD); computational physics (MS); computer science (MS, PhD); creative writing (MFA); criminology and criminal justice (MA); earth sciences (MA, MS, PhD); English as a second language (MA); experimental psychology (PhD); general physics (MS); general psychology (MS); geographic information systems (Graduate Certificate); inorganic chemistry (MS, PhD); linguistics (MA); literary and cultural studies (PhD); literature (MA); local government management (Graduate Certificate); material science (MS); mathematics (MS, PhD); medical anthropology (MA); museum studies (Graduate Certificate); organic chemistry (MS, PhD); philanthropy and nonprofit leadership (Graduate Certificate); philosophy (MA, PhD); physical chemistry (MS, PhD); political science (MA); professional writing (MA, PhD); romance languages (MA); school psychology (MA, PhD, Ed S); sociology (MA); statistics (MS); teaching English as a second/foreign language (Graduate Certificate); teaching of mathematics (MS); women's and gender studies (Graduate Certificate). *Application deadline:* Applications are processed on a rolling basis. *Application fee:* $35 ($60 for international students). Electronic applications accepted. *Dean,* Thomas J. Nenon, 901-678-3067, Fax: 901-678-4831, E-mail: tnenon@memphis.edu.

College of Communication and Fine Arts Students: 139 full-time (74 women), 99 part-time (52 women); includes 62 minority (32 Black or African American, non-Hispanic/Latino; 4 Asian, non-Hispanic/Latino; 15 Hispanic/Latino; 11 Two or more races, non-Hispanic/Latino), 15 international. Average age 33. 145 applicants, 75% accepted, 64 enrolled. *Faculty:* 85 full-time (31 women), 9 part-time/adjunct (4 women). Expenses: Contact institution. *Financial support:* Research assistantships with full tuition reimbursements, teaching assistantships with full tuition reimbursements, career-related internships or fieldwork, Federal Work-Study, institutionally sponsored loans, scholarships/grants, and unspecified assistantships available. Financial award application deadline: 2/1; financial award applicants required to submit FAFSA. *Program availability:* Part-time, online learning. Offers architecture (M Arch); art history (MA); ceramics (MFA); communication (MA); communication and fine arts (M Arch, M Mu, MA, MFA, DMA, PhD, Graduate Certificate); communication arts (PhD); composition (M Mu, DMA); conducting (M Mu, DMA); entrepreneurial journalism (Graduate Certificate); film and video production (MA); graphic design (MFA); jazz and studio music (M Mu); journalism and strategic media (MA); museum studies (Graduate Certificate); music education (M Mu, PhD); music theory (DCC); musicology (PhD); Orff-Schulwerk (M Mu); painting (MFA); pedagogy (M Mu); performance (M Mu, DMA); printmaking/photography (MFA); sculpture (MFA); theatre (MFA). *Application deadline:* Applications are processed on a rolling basis. *Application fee:* $35 ($60 for international students). Electronic applications accepted. *Dean,* Dr. Anne Hogan, 901-678-2350, Fax: 901-678-5118, E-mail: anne.hogan@memphis.edu.

College of Education Students: 2 full-time (1 woman), 22 part-time (15 women); includes 13 minority (11 Black or African American, non-Hispanic/Latino; 2 Two or more races, non-Hispanic/Latino). Average age 37. 13 applicants, 54% accepted, 6 enrolled. *Faculty:* 58 full-time (36 women), 32 part-time/adjunct (21 women). Expenses: Contact institution. *Financial support:* In 2017–18, 921 students received support, including 18 research assistantships with full tuition reimbursements available, 14 teaching assistantships with full tuition reimbursements available; career-related internships or fieldwork, Federal Work-Study, scholarships/grants, tuition waivers (partial), and unspecified assistantships also available. Financial award application deadline: 2/1; financial award applicants required to submit FAFSA. In 2017, 21 other advanced degrees awarded. *Program availability:* Part-time, evening/weekend, 100% online, blended/hybrid learning. Offers adult education (Ed D); advanced studies in teaching and learning (M Ed); applied behavior analysis (Graduate Certificate); autism studies (Graduate Certificate); community college teaching and leadership (Graduate Certificate); community education (Ed D); counseling (MS, Ed D); counseling psychology (PhD); early childhood education (MAT, MS, Ed D); education (M Ed, MAT, MS, Ed D, PhD, Graduate Certificate); educational leadership (Ed D); educational psychology and research (MS, PhD); elementary education (MAT); higher education (Ed D); instruction and curriculum (MS, Ed D); instruction design and technology (MS, Ed D); instructional design and technology (Graduate Certificate); leadership (MS); literacy, leadership, and coaching (Graduate Certificate); policy studies (Ed D); reading (MS, Ed D); school administration and supervision (MS); school library information specialist (Graduate Certificate); secondary education (MAT); special education (MAT, MS, Ed D); STEM teacher leadership (Graduate Certificate); student personnel (MS); urban education (Graduate Certificate). *Application deadline:* Applications are processed on a rolling basis. *Application fee:* $35 ($60 for international students). Electronic applications accepted. *Application Contact:* Dr. Suzanne Lease, Interim Assistant Dean of Education for Graduate Programs, 901-678-2352, Fax: 901-678-4476, E-mail: slease@memphis.edu. *Dean*, Dr. Kandi Hill-Clarke, 901-678-5495, Fax: 901-678-4778, E-mail: k.hill-clarke@memphis.edu.

Fogelman College of Business and Economics Students: 216 full-time (96 women), 396 part-time (158 women); includes 198 minority (110 Black or African American, non-Hispanic/Latino; 60 Asian, non-Hispanic/Latino; 15 Hispanic/Latino; 13 Two or more races, non-Hispanic/Latino), 84 international. Average age 30. 336 applicants, 86% accepted, 203 enrolled. *Faculty:* 15 full-time (1 woman), 2 part-time/adjunct (0 women). Expenses: Contact institution. *Financial support:* In 2017–18, 199 students received support, including 1 teaching assistantship with full tuition reimbursement available (averaging $6,000 per year); fellowships, research assistantships with full tuition reimbursements available, career-related internships or fieldwork, Federal Work-Study, scholarships/grants, and unspecified assistantships also available. Financial award application deadline: 2/1; financial award applicants required to submit FAFSA. *Program availability:* Part-time, evening/weekend, online learning. Offers accountancy (MS); accounting (MBA, MS, PhD); business administration (IMBA, MBA, MS, PhD); business information and technology (MS, PhD, Graduate Certificate); economics (MA, PhD); executive business administration (MBA); finance (PhD); management (PhD); marketing (MS); marketing and supply chain management (PhD); real estate development (MS). *Application deadline:* For fall admission, 7/1 for domestic students, 5/1 for international students; for winter admission, 9/15 for international students; for spring admission, 12/1 for domestic students. *Application fee:* $35 ($60 for international students). Electronic applications accepted. *Application Contact:* Dr. Chuck Pierce, Associate Dean for Academic Programs and Research, 901-678-4620, Fax: 901-678-3759, E-mail: chuck.pierce@memphis.edu. *Interim Dean*, Dr. Marla Royne Stafford, 901-678-3633, Fax: 901-678-4705, E-mail: mstaffrd@memphis.edu.

Herff College of Engineering Students: 37 full-time (8 women), 42 part-time (13 women); includes 14 minority (3 Black or African American, non-Hispanic/Latino; 10 Asian, non-Hispanic/Latino; 1 Hispanic/Latino), 54 international. Average age 32. 44 applicants, 91% accepted, 12 enrolled. *Faculty:* 41 full-time (4 women), 2 part-time/adjunct (0 women). Expenses: Contact institution. *Financial support:* In 2017–18, 29 students received support, including 15 research assistantships with full tuition reimbursements available (averaging $14,906 per year), 1 teaching assistantship with full tuition reimbursement available (averaging $5,504 per year); fellowships with full tuition reimbursements available, career-related internships or fieldwork, Federal Work-Study, scholarships/grants, tuition waivers (full and partial), and unspecified assistantships also available. Financial award application deadline: 2/1; financial award applicants required to submit FAFSA. In 2017, 7 doctorates awarded. *Program availability:* Part-time. Offers applied lean leadership (Graduate Certificate); biomedical engineering (MS, PhD); civil engineering (PhD); computer engineering (MS, PhD); electrical engineering (MS, PhD); engineering (MS, PhD, Graduate Certificate); engineering seismology (MS); engineering technology (MS); environmental engineering (MS); freight transportation (Graduate Certificate); geotechnical engineering (MS); imaging and signal processing (Graduate Certificate); power systems (MS); structural engineering (MS); transportation engineering (MS); water resources engineering (MS). *Application deadline:* For fall admission, 8/1 for domestic students, 5/1 for international students; for spring admission, 12/1 for domestic students, 9/15 for international students; for summer admission, 5/1 for domestic students. *Application fee:* $35 ($60 for international students). Electronic applications accepted. *Application Contact:* Dr. Russell Deaton, Associate Dean of Academic Affairs and Administration, 901-678-2175, Fax: 901-678-5030, E-mail: rjdeaton@memphis.edu. *Dean*, Dr. Richard Joseph Sweigard, 901-678-4306, Fax: 901-678-4180, E-mail: rjswgard@memphis.edu.

Kemmons Wilson School of Hospitality and Resort Management Students: 11 full-time (3 women), 27 part-time (12 women); includes 18 minority (16 Black or African American, non-Hispanic/Latino; 1 Hispanic/Latino; 1 Two or more races, non-Hispanic/Latino), 1 international. Average age 28. 24 applicants, 100% accepted, 19 enrolled. *Faculty:* 6 full-time (1 woman), 2 part-time/adjunct (0 women). Expenses: Contact institution. *Financial support:* In 2017–18, 5 research assistantships (averaging $8,400 per year), 6 teaching assistantships (averaging $9,000 per year) were awarded; career-related internships or fieldwork, Federal Work-Study, scholarships/grants, and unspecified assistantships also available. Support available to part-time students. Financial award application deadline: 2/1. In 2017, 19 master's awarded. *Program availability:* Part-time. Offers hospitality management specialist (Graduate Certificate); sports commerce (MS). *Application deadline:* For fall admission, 7/1 for domestic students, 5/1 for international students; for spring admission, 12/1 for domestic students, 9/1 for international students; for summer admission, 5/1 for domestic students, 2/1 for international students. *Application fee:* $35 ($60 for international students). Electronic applications accepted. *Application Contact:* Dr. Timothy Ryan, Coordinator of Graduate Studies, 901-678-5003, E-mail: tdryan@memphis.edu. *Director*, Dr. Radesh Palakurthi, 901-678-3430, E-mail: rplkrthi@memphis.edu.

School of Communication Sciences and Disorders Average age 28. 442 applicants, 26% accepted, 40 enrolled. Expenses: Contact institution. *Financial support:* In 2017–18, 25 research assistantships with full tuition reimbursements (averaging $8,560 per year) were awarded; Federal Work-Study, scholarships/grants, and unspecified assistantships also available. Financial award application deadline: 2/1; financial award applicants required to submit FAFSA. In 2017, 16 master's, 10 doctorates awarded. *Program availability:* Part-time. Offers audiology (Au D); communication sciences and disorders (PhD); speech-language pathology (MA). *Application deadline:* For fall admission, 2/1 priority date for domestic students. Applications are processed on a rolling basis. *Application fee:* $35 ($60 for international students). Electronic applications accepted. *Application Contact:* Dr. Lisa Mendel, Interim Associate Dean, 901-678-5800, E-mail: lmendel@memphis.edu. *Interim Dean*, Dr. Linda Jarmulowicz, 901-678-5800, Fax: 901-525-1282, E-mail: ljrmlwcz@memphis.edu.

School of Health Studies *Faculty:* 19 full-time (10 women), 2 part-time/adjunct (both women). Expenses: Contact institution. *Financial support:* In 2017–18, 33 research assistantships (averaging $11,930 per year), 4 teaching assistantships (averaging $10,000 per year) were awarded; career-related internships or fieldwork, Federal Work-Study, scholarships/grants, and unspecified assistantships also available. Financial award application deadline: 2/1; financial award applicants required to submit FAFSA. In 2017, 42 master's awarded. *Program availability:* 100% online. Offers faith and health (Graduate Certificate); health studies (MS); nutrition (MS); sport nutrition and dietary supplementation (Graduate Certificate). *Application deadline:* For fall admission, 4/15 priority date for domestic students; for spring admission, 10/15 priority date for domestic students; for summer admission, 4/15 priority date for domestic students. *Application fee:* $35 ($60 for international students). *Application Contact:* Dr. Lawrence Weiss, Director of Graduate Programs, 901-678-5037, E-mail: lweiss@memphis.edu. *Director*, Dr. Richard J. Bloomer, 901-678-4316, Fax: 901-678-3591, E-mail: rbloomer@memphis.edu.

School of Public Health Students: 111 full-time (76 women), 59 part-time (45 women); includes 77 minority (48 Black or African American, non-Hispanic/Latino; 18 Asian, non-Hispanic/Latino; 6 Hispanic/Latino; 5 Two or more races, non-Hispanic/Latino), 23 international. Average age 31. 100 applicants, 91% accepted, 60 enrolled. *Faculty:* 20 full-time (7 women), 4 part-time/adjunct (1 woman). Expenses: Contact institution. *Financial support:* In 2017–18, 46 students received support, including 8 research assistantships with full tuition reimbursements available (averaging $8,950 per year); Federal Work-Study, scholarships/grants, and unspecified assistantships also available. Financial award application deadline: 2/1; financial award applicants required to submit FAFSA. In 2017, 56 master's, 4 doctorates awarded. *Program availability:* Part-time, evening/weekend. Offers biostatistics (MPH); environmental health (MPH); epidemiology (MPH, PhD); health systems and policy (PhD); health systems management (MPH); public health (MHA); social and behavioral sciences (MPH, PhD). *Application deadline:* For fall admission, 4/1 for domestic students; for spring admission, 11/1 for domestic students. *Application fee:* $35 ($60 for international students). Electronic applications accepted. *Application Contact:* Dr. Marian Levy, Assistant Dean, 901-678-4514, Fax: 901-678-5023, E-mail: sph-admin@memphis.edu. *Dean*, Dr. Lisa M. Klesges, 901-678-4501, E-mail: lmklsges@memphis.edu.

University College Students: 27 full-time (16 women), 105 part-time (79 women); includes 86 minority (78 Black or African American, non-Hispanic/Latino; 1 Asian, non-Hispanic/Latino; 2 Hispanic/Latino; 1 Native Hawaiian or other Pacific Islander, non-Hispanic/Latino; 4 Two or more races, non-Hispanic/Latino), 4 international. Average age 38. 70 applicants, 76% accepted, 39 enrolled. *Faculty:* 3 full-time (1 woman), 1 part-time/adjunct (0 women). Expenses: Contact institution. *Financial support:* In 2017–18, 123 students received support, including 4 teaching assistantships with tuition reimbursements available (averaging $13,000 per year); research assistantships with full tuition reimbursements available, Federal Work-Study, scholarships/grants, and unspecified assistantships also available. Financial award application deadline: 2/3; financial award applicants required to submit FAFSA. *Program availability:* Part-time, evening/weekend. Offers human resources leadership (MPS); liberal studies (MALS, Graduate Certificate); strategic leadership (MPS, Graduate Certificate); training and development (MPS). *Application deadline:* For fall admission, 7/1 for domestic students, 5/1 for international students; for spring admission, 11/1 for domestic students, 9/15 for international students. Applications are processed on a rolling basis. *Application fee:* $35 ($60 for international students). Electronic applications accepted. *Application Contact:* Dr. Colin Chapell, Graduate Studies Coordinator, 901-678-3066, Fax: 901-678-2971, E-mail: cbchpell@memphis.edu. *Interim Dean*, Dr. Joanne Gikas, 901-678-2716, E-mail: jgikas@memphis.edu.

Loewenberg College of Nursing Students: 16 full-time (15 women), 225 part-time (201 women); includes 90 minority (72 Black or African American, non-Hispanic/Latino; 1 American Indian or Alaska Native, non-Hispanic/Latino; 9 Asian, non-Hispanic/Latino; 5 Hispanic/Latino; 1 Native Hawaiian or other Pacific Islander, non-Hispanic/Latino; 2 Two or more races, non-Hispanic/Latino). Average age 35. 168 applicants, 53% accepted, 55 enrolled. *Faculty:* 15 full-time (14 women), 3 part-time/adjunct (all women). Expenses: Contact institution. *Financial support:* In 2017–18, 147 students received support. Federal Work-Study and scholarships/grants available. Financial award application deadline: 2/1; financial award applicants required to submit FAFSA. In 2017, 120 master's, 6 other advanced degrees awarded. *Program availability:* Part-time, evening/weekend, online learning. Offers advanced practice nursing (Graduate Certificate); executive leadership (MSN); family nurse practitioner (MSN); nursing administration (MSN, Graduate Certificate); nursing education (MSN, Graduate Certificate). *Application deadline:* For fall admission, 2/15 for domestic and international students; for spring admission, 10/1 for domestic and international students. *Application fee:* $35 ($60 for international students). *Application Contact:* Dr. Shirleatha Lee, Associate Dean for Academic Programs, 901-678-2036, Fax: 901-678-5023, E-mail: sntaylr1@memphis.edu. *Dean*, Dr. Lin Zhan, 901-678-2003, Fax: 901-678-4907, E-mail: lzhan@memphis.edu.

UNIVERSITY OF MIAMI, Coral Gables, FL 33124

General Information Independent, coed, university. CGS member. *Graduate housing:* On-campus housing not available. *Research affiliation:* Howard Hughes Medical Institute (biology), The Buoniconti Fund: Miami Project to Cure Paralysis (paralysis research), Organization for Tropical Studies, National Center for Atmospheric Research (atmospheric science).

GRADUATE UNITS

Graduate School *Program availability:* Part-time, evening/weekend, online learning. Offers international administration (MAIA). Electronic applications accepted.

College of Arts and Sciences *Program availability:* Part-time, evening/weekend. Offers adult clinical (PhD); art history (MA); arts and sciences (MA, MAIA, MALS, MFA, MPA, MS, PhD); behavioral neuroscience (PhD); biology (MS, PhD); ceramics/glass (MFA); chemistry (MS); child clinical (PhD); computer science (MS, PhD); creative writing (MFA); developmental psychology (PhD); English (MA, PhD); genetics and evolution (MS, PhD); geography (MA); graphic design/multimedia (MFA); health clinical (PhD); history (MA, PhD); inorganic chemistry (PhD); international studies (MA, PhD); Latin American studies (MA); liberal studies (MALS); mathematical finance (MS); mathematics (MA, MS, PhD); organic chemistry (PhD); painting (MFA); philosophy (MA, PhD); photography/digital imaging (MFA); physical chemistry (PhD); physics (MS, PhD); political science (MPA); printmaking (MFA); psychology (MS); romance studies (PhD); sculpture (MFA); sociology (MA, PhD). Electronic applications accepted.

College of Engineering *Program availability:* Part-time, evening/weekend. Offers architectural engineering (MSAE); biomedical engineering (MSBE, PhD); civil engineering (MSCE, PhD); electrical and computer engineering (MSECE, PhD); engineering (MS, MSAE, MSBE, MSCE, MSECE, MSIE, MSME, MSOES, PhD); environmental health and safety (MS); ergonomics (PhD); industrial engineering (MSIE, PhD); management of technology (MS); mechanical and aerospace engineering (MSME, PhD); occupational ergonomics and safety (MS, MSOES). Electronic applications accepted.

Frost School of Music Offers accompanying and chamber music (MM, DMA); choral conducting (MM, DMA); composition (MM, DMA); electronic music (MM); instrumental conducting (MM, DMA); instrumental performance (MM, DMA, AD); jazz composition (DMA); jazz pedagogy (MM); jazz performance (MM, DMA); keyboard performance and pedagogy (MM, DMA); media writing and production (MM); multiple woodwinds (MM, DMA); music (MM, MS, DMA, PhD, AD, Spec M); music business and entertainment industries (MM); music education (MM, PhD, Spec M); music engineering (MS); music theory (MM); music therapy (MM); musicology (MM); piano performance (MM, DMA, AD); studio jazz writing (MM); vocal pedagogy (DMA); vocal performance (MM, DMA, AD). Electronic applications accepted.

Miller School of Medicine Offers biochemistry and molecular biology (PhD); cancer biology (PhD); epidemiology (PhD); medicine (MPH, MSPH, DPT, MD, PhD); microbiology and immunology (PhD); molecular and cellular pharmacology (PhD); molecular cell and developmental biology (PhD); neuroscience (PhD); physical therapy (DPT, PhD); physiology and biophysics (PhD); public health (MPH, MSPH). Electronic applications accepted.

Rosenstiel School of Marine and Atmospheric Science *Program availability:* Part-time. Offers applied marine physics (MS, PhD); marine affairs and policy (MA, MS); marine and atmospheric chemistry (MS, PhD); marine and atmospheric science (MA, MS, PhD); marine biology and fisheries (MA, MS, PhD); marine geology and geophysics (MS, PhD); meteorology (MS, PhD); physical oceanography (MS, PhD). Electronic applications accepted.

School of Architecture Offers architecture (M Arch); suburb and town design (M Arch). Electronic applications accepted.

School of Communication *Program availability:* Part-time. Offers communication (PhD); communication studies (MA); film studies (MA, PhD); motion pictures (MFA); print journalism (MA); public relations (MA); Spanish language journalism (MA); television broadcast journalism (MA). Electronic applications accepted.

School of Education and Human Development *Program availability:* 100% online. Offers athletic training (MS Ed); community and social change (MS Ed); community well-being (PhD); counseling (MS Ed, Certificate); counseling and research (MS Ed); counseling psychology (PhD); early childhood special education (MS Ed, Ed S); education and human development (MS Ed, Ed D, PhD, Certificate, Ed S); education and social change (MS Ed); enrollment management (MS Ed, Certificate); exercise physiology (MS Ed, PhD); higher education administration (MS Ed, Ed D, Certificate); higher education leadership (Ed D); language and literacy learning in multilingual settings (PhD); Latino mental health (Certificate); marriage and family therapy (MS Ed); mental health counseling (MS Ed); nutrition for health and human performance (MS Ed); research, measurement, and evaluation (MS Ed, PhD); science, technology, engineering and mathematics (PhD); special education (PhD); sport administration (MS Ed); sports medicine (MS Ed); strength and conditioning (MS Ed); student life and development (MS Ed, Certificate); teaching and learning (PhD); women's health (Certificate). Electronic applications accepted.

School of Nursing and Health Studies *Program availability:* Part-time. Offers acute care (MSN); nursing (PhD); primary care (MSN). Electronic applications accepted.

University of Miami School of Law Students: 1,099 full-time (534 women), 93 part-time (48 women); includes 455 minority (63 Black or African American, non-Hispanic/Latino; 3 American Indian or Alaska Native, non-Hispanic/Latino; 25 Asian, non-Hispanic/Latino; 330 Hispanic/Latino; 1 Native Hawaiian or other Pacific Islander, non-Hispanic/Latino; 33 Two or more races, non-Hispanic/Latino), 53 international. 2,356 applicants, 59% accepted, 316 enrolled. *Faculty:* 89 full-time (45 women), 115 part-time/adjunct (27 women). Expenses: Contact institution. *Financial support:* Fellowships, research assistantships, career-related internships or fieldwork, Federal Work-Study, institutionally sponsored loans, scholarships/grants, and unspecified assistantships available. Financial award application deadline: 3/1; financial award applicants required to submit FAFSA. *Program availability:* Part-time. Offers entertainment, arts, and sports law (LL M); estate planning (LL M); intensive English (LL M); international arbitration (LL M); international law (LL M); law (JD); maritime law (LL M); real estate/property development (LL M); taxation (LL M); taxation of cross-border investment (LL M); the business of innovation, law and technology (BILT) (JD); U.S. and transnational law for foreign-trained lawyers (LL M). *Application deadline:* For fall admission, 7/31 for domestic and international students. Applications are processed on a rolling basis. *Application fee:* $60. Electronic applications accepted. *Application Contact:* Therese Lambert, Director of Student Recruitment, 305-284-6746, Fax: 305-284-3084, E-mail: tlambert@law.miami.edu. *Associate Dean of Admissions and Enrollment Management,* Michael Goodnight, 305-284-2527, Fax: 305-284-3084, E-mail: mgoodnig@law.miami.edu.

Miami Business School Students: 987 full-time (411 women); includes 549 minority (79 Black or African American, non-Hispanic/Latino; 2 American Indian or Alaska Native, non-Hispanic/Latino; 174 Asian, non-Hispanic/Latino; 280 Hispanic/Latino; 14 Two or more races, non-Hispanic/Latino). Average age 30. 2,564 applicants, 38% accepted, 450 enrolled. *Faculty:* 155 full-time (47 women), 14 part-time/adjunct (5 women). Expenses: Contact institution. *Financial support:* In 2017–18, 184 students received support, including 2 fellowships with full tuition reimbursements available (averaging $20,000 per year), 10 research assistantships with full and partial tuition reimbursements available (averaging $20,000 per year), 5 teaching assistantships with full and partial tuition reimbursements available (averaging $20,000 per year); career-related internships or fieldwork, Federal Work-Study, institutionally sponsored loans, scholarships/grants, and unspecified assistantships also available. Support available to part-time students. Financial award application deadline: 3/26; financial award applicants required to submit FAFSA. In 2017, 476 master's, 7 doctorates awarded. *Program availability:* Part-time, evening/weekend, 100% online, blended/hybrid learning. Offers business (M Acc, MBA, MHA, MIBS, MS Tax, MSBA, MSF, PhD). *Application deadline:* For fall admission, 6/30 priority date for domestic students, 5/30 priority date for international students; for spring admission, 10/31 priority date for domestic students, 9/30 priority date for international students. Applications are processed on a rolling basis. Electronic applications accepted. *Application Contact:* Loubna Bouamane, Director of Graduate Business Recruiting and Admissions, 305-284-2510, Fax: 305-284-5905, E-mail: loubna@miami.edu. *Dean,* Dr. John Quelch, 305-284-6515, Fax: 305-284-6526, E-mail: jquelch@miami.edu.

UNIVERSITY OF MICHIGAN, Ann Arbor, MI 48109

General Information State-supported, coed, university. CGS member. *Enrollment:* 44,718 graduate, professional, and undergraduate students; 14,578 full-time matriculated graduate/professional students (7,130 women), 1,298 part-time matriculated graduate/professional students (480 women). *Enrollment by degree level:* 7,914 master's, 7,929 doctoral, 33 other advanced degrees. *Graduate faculty:* 4,721 full-time (1,901 women), 1,210 part-time/adjunct (673 women). Tuition, state resident: full-time $22,368; part-time $1201 per credit hour. Tuition, nonresident: full-time $45,156; part-time $2467 per credit hour. *Required fees:* $376 per term. Tuition and fees vary according to course load, degree level and program. *Graduate housing:* Rooms and/or apartments available on a first-come, first-served basis to single and married students. Typical cost: $6350 per year for single students; $12,170 per year for married students. Room charges vary according to housing facility selected. *Student services:* Campus employment opportunities, campus safety program, career counseling, child daycare facilities, exercise/wellness program, free psychological counseling, grant writing training, international student services, low-cost health insurance, multicultural affairs office, services for students with disabilities, teacher training, writing training. *Library facilities:* Shapiro Undergraduate Library plus 9 others. *Collection:* Books: 9 million (physical), 3.3 million (digital/electronic); Serial titles: 464,460 (physical), 163,830 (digital/electronic); Databases: 10,078. Weekly public service hours: 168; study areas open 24 hours, 5–7 days a week; students can reserve study rooms.

Computer facilities: Computer purchase and lease plans are available. 3,940 computers available on campus for general student use. A campuswide network can be accessed from student residence rooms and from off campus. Online class registration, file storage, personal Web pages, printing are available.
Website: http://www.umich.edu/

General Application Contact: Admissions Office, 734-764-8129, Fax: 734-647-7740, E-mail: rackadmis@umich.edu.

GRADUATE UNITS

College of Engineering Students: 3,325 full-time (853 women), 362 part-time (70 women). 11,743 applicants, 25% accepted, 1129 enrolled. *Faculty:* 417 full-time (82 women). Expenses: Contact institution. *Financial support:* Fellowships, research assistantships, teaching assistantships, career-related internships or fieldwork, Federal Work-Study, institutionally sponsored loans, scholarships/grants, traineeships, health care benefits, tuition waivers (full and partial), and unspecified assistantships available. Support available to part-time students. Financial award applicants required to submit FAFSA. In 2017, 1,106 master's, 265 doctorates awarded. *Program availability:* Part-time, 100% online. Offers aerospace engineering (M Eng, MS, MSE, PhD); applied climate (M Eng); atmospheric, oceanic and space sciences (MS, PhD); automotive engineering (M Eng); biomedical engineering (MS, MSE, PhD); chemical engineering (MSE, PhD, Ch E); civil engineering (MSE, PhD, CE); computer science and engineering (MS, MSE, PhD); construction engineering and management (M Eng, MSE); design science (MS, PhD); electrical and computer engineering (MS, MSE, PhD); energy systems engineering (M Eng, MS); engineering (M Eng, MS, MSE, D Eng, PhD, CE, Certificate, Ch E, Mar Eng, Nav Arch, Nuc E); environmental engineering (MSE, PhD); geoscience and remote sensing (PhD); global automotive and manufacturing engineering (M Eng); industrial and operations engineering (MS, MSE, PhD); manufacturing engineering (M Eng, D Eng); materials science and engineering (MS, MSE, PhD); mechanical engineering (MSE, PhD); naval architecture and marine engineering (MS, MSE, PhD, Mar Eng, Nav Arch); nuclear engineering (Nuc E); nuclear engineering and radiological sciences (MSE, PhD); nuclear science (MS, PhD); pharmaceutical engineering (M Eng); robotics (MS, PhD); robotics and autonomous vehicles (M Eng); space and planetary sciences (PhD); space engineering (M Eng); structural engineering (M Eng); systems engineering and design (M Eng). *Application deadline:* Applications are processed on a rolling basis. Electronic applications accepted. *Application Contact:* Jeanne Murabito, Executive Director for Student Affairs, 734-647-7118, E-mail: coe-studentaffairs@umich.edu. *Dean of Engineering,* Prof. Alec D. Gallimore, 734-647-7008, Fax: 734-647-7009, E-mail: rasta@umich.edu.

College of Pharmacy Students: 83 full-time (33 women); includes 12 minority (1 Black or African American, non-Hispanic/Latino; 5 Asian, non-Hispanic/Latino; 4 Hispanic/Latino; 2 Two or more races, non-Hispanic/Latino), 24 international. Average age 27. 179 applicants, 15% accepted, 14 enrolled. *Faculty:* 38 full-time (14 women), 10 part-time/adjunct (0 women). Expenses: Contact institution. Offers clinical pharmacy (PhD); medicinal chemistry (PhD); pharmaceutical sciences (PhD); pharmacy (PhD, Pharm D). *Application deadline:* For fall admission, 1/5 for domestic and international students. Applications are processed on a rolling basis. *Application fee:* $150. Electronic applications accepted. *Application Contact:* Admissions Office, 734-764-8129, Fax: 734-647-7740, E-mail: rackadmis@umich.edu. *Dean,* James T. Dalton, 734-764-7144, Fax: 734-763-2022, E-mail: cop.deansoffice@med.umich.edu.

Gerald R. Ford School of Public Policy Students: 272 full-time (141 women); includes 86 minority (26 Black or African American, non-Hispanic/Latino; 26 Asian, non-Hispanic/Latino; 24 Hispanic/Latino; 10 Two or more races, non-Hispanic/Latino), 52 international. Average age 28. 633 applicants, 66% accepted, 106 enrolled. *Faculty:* 36 full-time (16 women), 34 part-time/adjunct (13 women). Expenses: Contact institution. *Financial support:* In 2017–18, 213 students received support, including 181 fellowships with tuition reimbursements available, 27 teaching assistantships with tuition reimbursements available; research assistantships, career-related internships or fieldwork, traineeships, health care benefits, and unspecified assistantships also available. Financial award application deadline: 1/15; financial award applicants required to submit FAFSA. In 2017, 84 master's, 7 doctorates awarded. Offers public policy (MPA, MPP, PhD). *Application deadline:* For fall admission, 1/15 priority date for domestic students, 1/15 for international students. *Application fee:* $75 ($90 for international students). Electronic applications accepted. *Application Contact:* Beth Soboleski, Director, Admissions and Recruiting, 734-764-0453, Fax: 734-647-7486, E-mail: fspp-admissions@umich.edu. *Dean of Public Policy,* Michael S. Barr, 734-764-2258, E-mail: ford.school.dean@umich.edu.

Law School Students: 931 full-time (435 women); includes 194 minority (36 Black or African American, non-Hispanic/Latino; 7 American Indian or Alaska Native, non-Hispanic/Latino; 65 Asian, non-Hispanic/Latino; 44 Hispanic/Latino; 42 Two or more races, non-Hispanic/Latino), 52 international. 5,284 applicants, 22% accepted, 320 enrolled. *Faculty:* 113 full-time (40 women), 33 part-time/adjunct (7 women). Expenses: Contact institution. *Financial support:* In 2017–18, 777 students received support. Career-related internships or fieldwork, Federal Work-Study, institutionally sponsored loans, and scholarships/grants available. Financial award applicants required to submit FAFSA. In 2017, 41 master's, 331 doctorates awarded. Offers comparative law (MCL); international tax (LL M); law (LL M, JD, SJD). *Application deadline:* For fall admission, 2/15 for domestic students. Applications are processed on a rolling basis. *Application fee:* $75. Electronic applications accepted. *Application Contact:* Sarah C. Zearfoss, Assistant Dean and Director of Admissions, 734-764-0537, Fax: 734-647-3218, E-mail: law.jd.admissions@umich.edu. *Dean,* Mark D. West, 734-764-1358.

Medical School Students: 735 full-time (394 women); includes 224 minority (46 Black or African American, non-Hispanic/Latino; 124 Asian, non-Hispanic/Latino; 54 Hispanic/Latino). Average age 27. 5,991 applicants, 6% accepted, 170 enrolled. *Faculty:* 2,466 full-time (937 women), 1,357 part-time/adjunct (701 women). Expenses: Contact institution. *Financial support:* Institutionally sponsored loans and scholarships/grants available. Financial award application deadline: 9/30; financial award applicants required to submit FAFSA. In 2017, 174 doctorates awarded. Offers medicine (MD). *Application deadline:* For fall admission, 9/30 for domestic students. Applications are processed on a rolling basis. Electronic applications accepted. *Application Contact:* Carol Teener, Director of Admissions, 734-764-6317, Fax: 734-936-3510, E-mail: cteener@umich.edu. *Dean,* Dr. Marschall S. Runge, MD, 734-764-8175, E-mail: mrunge@umich.edu.

Rackham Graduate School Students: 7,866 full-time (3,435 women), 693 part-time (288 women); includes 1,584 minority (299 Black or African American, non-Hispanic/Latino; 19 American Indian or Alaska Native, non-Hispanic/Latino; 540 Asian, non-Hispanic/Latino; 537 Hispanic/Latino; 5 Native Hawaiian or other Pacific Islander, non-Hispanic/Latino; 184 Two or more races, non-Hispanic/Latino), 3,531 international. Average age 27. 28,127 applicants, 25% accepted, 2724 enrolled. Expenses: Contact institution. *Financial support:* Fellowships with full and partial tuition reimbursements, research assistantships with full and partial tuition reimbursements, teaching assistantships with full and partial tuition reimbursements, career-related internships or fieldwork, Federal Work-Study, scholarships/grants, traineeships, health care benefits, and unspecified assistantships available. Support available to part-time students. In 2017, 2,163 master's, 801 doctorates awarded. Offers cancer chemical biology (MS); chemical biology (PhD); data science (MS, PhD); education and psychology (PhD); English and education (PhD); social and psychological (MS, PhD); statistical (MS, PhD); survey methodology (Certificate). *Application deadline:* Applications are processed on a rolling basis. *Application fee:* $75 ($90 for international students). Electronic applications accepted. *Application Contact:* Admissions Office, 734-764-8129, E-mail: rackadmis@umich.edu. *Interim Dean/Interim Vice Provost for Academic Affairs, Graduate Studies*, Dr. Michael J. Solomon, 734-764-4400.

College of Literature, Science, and the Arts Students: 2,513 full-time (1,223 women). Expenses: Contact institution. *Financial support:* Fellowships with tuition reimbursements, research assistantships with tuition reimbursements, teaching assistantships with tuition reimbursements, Federal Work-Study, scholarships/grants, traineeships, health care benefits, tuition waivers (full and partial), and unspecified assistantships available. In 2017, 405 master's, 299 doctorates awarded. Offers American culture (AM, PhD); analytical chemistry (PhD); ancient Near Eastern studies (AM, PhD); anthropological archaeology (PhD); anthropology and history (PhD); applied and interdisciplinary mathematics (AM, MS, PhD); applied economics (AM); applied physics (PhD); applied statistics (MS); Arabic for professional purposes (AM); Arabic language and literature (AM, PhD); Armenian studies (AM, PhD); Asian languages and cultures (PhD); astronomy and astrophysics (PhD); biological anthropology (PhD); biophysics (PhD); biopsychology (PhD); chemical biology (PhD); chemical sciences (MS); Chinese studies (MA, Graduate Certificate); Christianity in late antiquity (AM, PhD); classical art and archaeology (MA, PhD); classical studies (MA, PhD); clinical science (PhD); cognition and cognitive neuroscience (PhD); communication studies (PhD); comparative literature (PhD); creative writing (MFA); data science (MS); developmental psychology (PhD); earth and environmental sciences (MS, PhD); ecology and evolutionary biology (MS, PhD); economics (AM, PhD); Egyptology (AM, PhD); English and education (PhD); English and women's studies (PhD); English language and literature (PhD); French (PhD); German (AM, PhD); German studies (Certificate); Greek and Roman history (PhD); Hebrew Bible and ancient Israel (AM, PhD); Hebrew literature (AM, PhD); history (PhD); history and women's studies (PhD); history of art (PhD); inorganic chemistry (PhD); Islamic studies (AM, PhD); Italian (PhD); Japanese studies (AM); Jewish cultural studies (AM, PhD); Jewish mysticism (AM, PhD); Judaic studies (MA, Graduate Certificate); Latin (MA); Latin with teaching certification (MAT); LGBTQ studies (Certificate); linguistic anthropology (PhD); linguistics (PhD); literature, science, and the arts (AM, MA, MAT, MFA, MS, PhD, Certificate, Graduate Certificate); materials chemistry (PhD); mathematics (AM, MS, PhD); Middle Eastern and North African studies (AM); molecular, cellular, and developmental biology (MS, PhD); organic chemistry (PhD); Persian and Iranian studies (AM, PhD); personality and social contexts (PhD); philosophy (AM, PhD); physical chemistry (PhD); physics (PhD); political science (PhD); political science and public policy (PhD); psychology and women's studies (PhD); public policy and economics (PhD); public policy and sociology (PhD); quantitative finance and risk management (MS); Rabbinic literature (AM, PhD); Russian, East European, and Eurasian studies (AM, Certificate); screen arts and cultures (PhD, Certificate); Second Temple Judaism (AM, PhD); Slavic languages and literatures (AM, PhD); social psychology (PhD); social work and economics (PhD); social work and political science (PhD); social work and sociology (PhD); sociocultural anthropology (PhD); sociology (PhD); South Asian studies (MA, Certificate); Southeast Asian studies (MA, Graduate Certificate); Spanish (PhD); statistics (AM, PhD); teaching Arabic as a foreign language (AM); Turkish studies (AM, PhD); women's studies (Certificate). *Application fee:* $75 ($90 for international students). Electronic applications accepted. *Application Contact:* Rackham Graduate School Admissions Office, 734-764-8129, E-mail: rackadmis@umich.edu. *Dean*, Dr. Andrew D. Martin, 734-764-1817.

Penny W. Stamps School of Art and Design Students: 18 (12 women). 179 applicants, 6% accepted, 10 enrolled. *Faculty:* 37. Expenses: Contact institution. *Financial support:* In 2017–18, 19 students received support. Fellowships with full tuition reimbursements available, research assistantships with full tuition reimbursements available, teaching assistantships with full tuition reimbursements available, career-related internships or fieldwork, Federal Work-Study, institutionally sponsored loans, scholarships/grants, health care benefits, tuition waivers (full and partial), and unspecified assistantships available. Support available to part-time students. Financial award application deadline: 1/1. In 2017, 9 master's awarded. Offers art and design (MFA); integrative design (M Des). *Application deadline:* For fall admission, 1/1 for domestic and international students. *Application fee:* $75 ($90 for international students). Electronic applications accepted. *Application Contact:* Meghan Jellema, Graduate Programs Coordinator, 734-763-5247, E-mail: stamps-graduate-info@umich.edu. *Dean*, Gunalan Nadarajan, 734-764-0397, E-mail: artdes-dean@umich.edu.

Program in Biomedical Sciences (PIBS) Students: 72 full-time (42 women); includes 28 minority (6 Black or African American, non-Hispanic/Latino; 7 Asian, non-Hispanic/Latino; 15 Hispanic/Latino), 6 international. Average age 24. 869 applicants, 22% accepted, 72 enrolled. *Faculty:* 548 full-time. Expenses: Contact institution. *Financial support:* In 2017–18, 73 students received support, including 73 fellowships with full tuition reimbursements available (averaging $30,600 per year); scholarships/grants, health care benefits, and unspecified assistantships also available. Financial award application deadline: 12/1. Offers bioinformatics (MS, PhD); biological chemistry (MS, PhD); biomedical sciences (MS, PhD); cancer biology (PhD); cell and developmental biology (PhD); cellular and molecular biology (PhD); genetic counseling (MS); human genetics (MS, PhD); immunology (PhD); microbiology and immunology (MS, PhD); molecular and cellular pathology (PhD); molecular and integrative physiology (MS, PhD); neuroscience (PhD); pharmacology (MS, PhD). *Application deadline:* For fall admission, 12/1 for domestic and international students. *Application fee:* $75 ($90 for international students). Electronic applications accepted. *Application Contact:* Michelle DiMondo, Academic Affairs and Student Success Coordinator, 734-647-5773, Fax: 734-647-7022, E-mail: mdimondo@umich.edu. *Associate Professor, Cell and Developmental Biology/Director of the Program in Biomedical Sciences*, Dr. Scott Barolo, 734-615-7005, Fax: 734-647-7022, E-mail: sbarolo@umich.edu.

School of Information *Program availability:* Part-time. Offers health informatics (MHI); information (MSI, PhD). Electronic applications accepted.

School of Kinesiology Students: 94 full-time (40 women); includes 22 minority (6 Black or African American, non-Hispanic/Latino; 5 Asian, non-Hispanic/Latino; 7 Hispanic/Latino; 4 Two or more races, non-Hispanic/Latino). Average age 26. 230 applicants, 48% accepted, 52 enrolled. *Faculty:* 31 full-time (16 women). Expenses: Contact institution. *Financial support:* In 2017–18, 34 students received support, including 11 fellowships with full tuition reimbursements available, 12 research assistantships with full tuition reimbursements available, 11 teaching assistantships with full tuition reimbursements available; Federal Work-Study, scholarships/grants, traineeships, health care benefits, and unspecified assistantships also available. Financial award application deadline: 12/1. In 2017, 25 master's, 7 doctorates awarded. Offers movement science (MS, PhD); sport management (MS, PhD). *Application deadline:* For fall admission, 12/1 priority date for domestic students, 12/1 for international students. Applications are processed on a rolling basis. *Application fee:* $75 ($90 for international students). Electronic applications accepted. *Application Contact:* Charlene F. Ruloff, Graduate Program Coordinator, 734-764-1343, Fax: 734-647-2808, E-mail: cruloff@umich.edu. *Associate Dean for Graduate Programs*, Dr. Ketra L. Armstrong, 734-647-3027, Fax: 734-647-2808, E-mail: ketra@umich.edu.

School of Music, Theatre, and Dance Offers composition (MA, MM, A Mus D); composition and theory (PhD); conducting (MM, A Mus D); media arts (MA); modern dance performance and choreography (MFA); music education (MM, PhD, Spec M); music theory (PhD); music, theatre, and dance (MA, MFA, MM, A Mus D, PhD, Spec M); musicology (MA, PhD); performance (MM, A Mus D, Spec M). Electronic applications accepted.

School of Nursing *Program availability:* Part-time, online learning. Offers acute care pediatric nurse practitioner (MS); nursing (DNP, PhD, Post Master's Certificate).

Ross School of Business *Program availability:* Part-time, evening/weekend. Offers accounting (M Acc); business (MBA); business administration (PhD); supply chain management (MSCM). Electronic applications accepted.

School for Environment and Sustainability Offers behavior, education and communication (MS); conservation ecology (MS); environmental informatics (MS); environmental justice (MS, Certificate); environmental policy and planning (MS); industrial ecology (Certificate); landscape architecture (MLA); natural resources and environment (MS, PhD); spatial analysis (Certificate); sustainability (Certificate); sustainable systems (MS). Electronic applications accepted.

School of Dentistry Students: 636 full-time (331 women); includes 173 minority (2 American Indian or Alaska Native, non-Hispanic/Latino; 134 Asian, non-Hispanic/Latino; 23 Hispanic/Latino; 14 Two or more races, non-Hispanic/Latino), 98 international. Average age 26. 2,776 applicants, 12% accepted, 163 enrolled. *Faculty:* 33 full-time (9 women). Expenses: Contact institution. Offers dental hygiene (MS); dentistry (MS, DDS, PhD); endodontics (MS); oral health sciences (PhD); orthodontics (MS); pediatric dentistry (MS); periodontics (MS); prosthodontics (MS); restorative dentistry (MS). *Application deadline:* Applications are processed on a rolling basis. *Application fee:* $75 ($90 for international students). Electronic applications accepted. *Application Contact:* Patricia Katcher, Admissions Associate Director, 734-763-3316, Fax: 734-764-1922, E-mail: ddsadmissions@umich.edu. *Dean*, Dr. Laurie McCauley, 734-763-3311, E-mail: mccauley@umich.edu.

School of Education Offers education (MA, MS, PhD). Electronic applications accepted.

School of Public Health *Program availability:* Evening/weekend. Offers biostatistics (MPH, MS, PhD); clinical research design and statistical analysis (MS); dietetics (MPH); environmental health policy and promotion (MPH); environmental health sciences (MS, PhD); environmental quality, sustainability and health (MPH); epidemiological science (PhD); general epidemiology (MPH); global health epidemiology (MPH); health behavior and health education (MPH, PhD); health management and policy (MHSA, MPH); health services organization and policy (PhD); hospital and molecular epidemiology (MPH); industrial hygiene (MPH, MS); nutritional sciences (MPH, MS, PhD); occupational and environmental epidemiology (MPH); public health (MHSA, MPH, MS, PhD); toxicology (MPH, MS, PhD). MS and PhD offered through the Rackham Graduate School. Electronic applications accepted.

School of Social Work Students: 755 full-time (635 women); includes 229 minority (78 Black or African American, non-Hispanic/Latino; 2 American Indian or Alaska Native, non-Hispanic/Latino; 34 Asian, non-Hispanic/Latino; 85 Hispanic/Latino; 1 Native Hawaiian or other Pacific Islander, non-Hispanic/Latino; 29 Two or more races, non-Hispanic/Latino), 30 international. Average age 23. 1,249 applicants, 74% accepted, 417 enrolled. *Faculty:* 57 full-time (36 women), 56 part-time/adjunct (42 women). Expenses: Contact institution. *Financial support:* In 2017–18, 663 students received support. Career-related internships or fieldwork, Federal Work-Study, scholarships/grants, traineeships, and unspecified assistantships available. Financial award application deadline: 3/15; financial award applicants required to submit FAFSA. In 2017, 376 master's awarded. Offers social work (MSW, PhD); social work and anthropology (PhD); social work and economics (PhD); social work and political science (PhD); social work and psychology (PhD); social work and sociology (PhD). PhD offered through the Rackham Graduate School. *Application deadline:* For fall admission, 3/1 priority date for domestic students, 2/1 priority date for international students. Applications are processed on a rolling basis. *Application fee:* $75. Electronic applications accepted. *Application Contact:* Timothy Colenback, Assistant Dean for Student Services, 734-936-0961, Fax: 734-936-1961, E-mail: timot@umich.edu. *Dean*, Lynn Videka, 734-764-5347, Fax: 734-615-5403, E-mail: lvideka@umich.edu.

Taubman College of Architecture and Urban Planning Offers architecture (M Arch); architecture and urban planning (M Arch, MS, MUD, MURP, PhD, Graduate Certificate); design and health (MS); digital technologies (MS); material systems (MS); urban and regional planning (MURP, PhD); urban design (MUD). Electronic applications accepted.

UNIVERSITY OF MICHIGAN–DEARBORN, Dearborn, MI 48128

General Information State-supported, coed, comprehensive institution. *Enrollment:* 9,339 graduate, professional, and undergraduate students; 549 full-time matriculated graduate/professional students (184 women), 1,599 part-time matriculated graduate/professional students (510 women). *Enrollment by degree level:* 2,076 master's, 60 doctoral, 12 other advanced degrees. *Graduate faculty:* 317 full-time (128 women), 234 part-time/adjunct (97 women). Tuition, state resident: full-time $13,602; part-time $788 per credit hour. Tuition, nonresident: full-time $22,234; part-time $1281 per credit hour. *Required fees:* $754; $754 per year. $377 per term. Tuition and fees vary according to course load, degree level, program and reciprocity agreements. *Student services:* Campus employment opportunities, campus safety program, career counseling, child daycare facilities, exercise/wellness program, free psychological counseling, grant writing training, international student services, low-cost health insurance, multicultural affairs office, services for students with disabilities, teacher training, writing training. *Library facilities:* Mardigian Library. *Collection:* Books: 277,320 (physical), 617,638 (digital/electronic);

Serial titles: 390 (physical), 95,980 (digital/electronic); Databases: 1,135. Weekly public service hours: 95; students can reserve study rooms. *Research affiliation:* Henry W. Patton Center for Engineering Education and Practice, Center for Lightweighting Automotive Materials and Processing, Center for Electric Drive Transportation, DTE Power Electronics and Electric Drives Lab, Cybersecurity Center (CCERO).

Computer facilities: Computer purchase and lease plans are available. 1,060 computers available on campus for general student use. A campuswide network can be accessed from off campus. Online class registration, tuition and application payments accepted online are available.
Website: http://www.umdearborn.edu/

General Application Contact: Office of Graduate Studies, 313-583-6321, E-mail: umd-graduatestudies@umich.edu.

GRADUATE UNITS

College of Arts, Sciences, and Letters Students: 37 full-time (27 women), 67 part-time (42 women); includes 31 minority (12 Black or African American, non-Hispanic/Latino; 6 Asian, non-Hispanic/Latino; 10 Hispanic/Latino; 3 Two or more races, non-Hispanic/Latino), 3 international. Average age 32. 95 applicants, 67% accepted, 37 enrolled. *Faculty:* 55 full-time (28 women), 20 part-time/adjunct (10 women). Expenses: Contact institution. *Financial support:* In 2017–18, 56 students received support. Scholarships/grants and non-resident tuition scholarships available. Financial award application deadline: 3/1; financial award applicants required to submit FAFSA. In 2017, 46 master's awarded. *Program availability:* Part-time, evening/weekend. Offers applied and computational mathematics (MS); arts, sciences, and letters (MPA, MS); clinical health psychology (MS); criminology and criminal justice (MS); environmental science (MS); health psychology (MS); public administration (MPA). *Application deadline:* For fall admission, 8/1 priority date for domestic students, 5/1 priority date for international students; for winter admission, 12/1 priority date for domestic students, 9/1 priority date for international students; for spring admission, 4/1 priority date for domestic students, 1/1 priority date for international students. Applications are processed on a rolling basis. *Application fee:* $60. Electronic applications accepted. *Application Contact:* Office of Graduate Studies, 313-583-6321, E-mail: umd-graduatestudies@umich.edu. *Dean*, Dr. Martin Hershock, 313-593-5552, E-mail: mhershoc@umich.edu.

College of Business Students: 105 full-time (55 women), 347 part-time (120 women); includes 82 minority (19 Black or African American, non-Hispanic/Latino; 43 Asian, non-Hispanic/Latino; 14 Hispanic/Latino; 6 Two or more races, non-Hispanic/Latino), 108 international. Average age 30. 523 applicants, 53% accepted, 147 enrolled. *Faculty:* 45 full-time (19 women), 4 part-time/adjunct (2 women). Expenses: Contact institution. *Financial support:* In 2017–18, 177 students received support. Scholarships/grants and non-resident tuition scholarships available. Financial award application deadline: 3/1; financial award applicants required to submit FAFSA. In 2017, 152 master's awarded. *Program availability:* Part-time, evening/weekend, 100% online. Offers accounting (MS); business (MBA, MS); business administration (MBA); business analytics (MS); finance (MS); information systems (MS); supply chain management (MS). *Application deadline:* For fall admission, 8/1 priority date for domestic students, 5/1 priority date for international students; for winter admission, 12/1 priority date for domestic students, 9/1 priority date for international students; for spring admission, 4/1 priority date for domestic students, 1/1 priority date for international students. Applications are processed on a rolling basis. *Application fee:* $60. Electronic applications accepted. *Application Contact:* Joan Doherty, Academic Advisor/Counselor, 313-593-5460, Fax: 313-271-9838, E-mail: umd-gradbusiness@umich.edu. *Dean*, Dr. Raju Balakrishnan, 313-593-5460, Fax: 313-271-9835, E-mail: umd-cob-dean@umich.edu.

College of Education, Health, and Human Services Students: 20 full-time (16 women), 199 part-time (164 women); includes 45 minority (27 Black or African American, non-Hispanic/Latino; 6 Asian, non-Hispanic/Latino; 8 Hispanic/Latino; 4 Two or more races, non-Hispanic/Latino), 5 international. Average age 34. 112 applicants, 67% accepted, 51 enrolled. *Faculty:* 22 full-time (17 women), 34 part-time/adjunct (23 women). Expenses: Contact institution. *Financial support:* In 2017–18, 53 students received support. Career-related internships or fieldwork and scholarships/grants available. Financial award application deadline: 3/1; financial award applicants required to submit FAFSA. In 2017, 86 master's, 9 doctorates awarded. *Program availability:* Part-time, evening/weekend, 100% online. Offers applied behavior analysis (MS); community based education (MA); curriculum and practice (Ed D, Ed S); early childhood education (MA); education (MA, Ed D, Ed S); education, health, and human services (M Ed, MA, MAT, MS, Ed D, Certificate, Ed S); educational leadership (Ed D, Ed S); educational technology (MA); health information technology (MS); metropolitan education (Ed D, Ed S); program evaluation and assessment (MA); science education (MS); special education (M Ed); teaching (MAT). *Application deadline:* For fall admission, 8/1 priority date for domestic students, 5/1 priority date for international students; for winter admission, 12/1 priority date for domestic students, 9/1 priority date for international students; for spring admission, 4/1 priority date for domestic students, 1/1 priority date for international students. Applications are processed on a rolling basis. *Application fee:* $60. Electronic applications accepted. *Application Contact:* Dr. Stein Brunvand, Director, Master's Programs, 313-583-6415, E-mail: sbrunvan@umich.edu. *Dean*, Dr. Ann Lampkin-Williams, 313-593-5090, E-mail: lampkin@umich.edu.

College of Engineering and Computer Science Students: 387 full-time (86 women), 986 part-time (184 women); includes 192 minority (54 Black or African American, non-Hispanic/Latino; 3 American Indian or Alaska Native, non-Hispanic/Latino; 77 Asian, non-Hispanic/Latino; 37 Hispanic/Latino; 1 Native Hawaiian or other Pacific Islander, non-Hispanic/Latino; 20 Two or more races, non-Hispanic/Latino), 573 international. Average age 27. 1,526 applicants, 51% accepted, 406 enrolled. *Faculty:* 81 full-time (10 women), 43 part-time/adjunct (3 women). Expenses: Contact institution. *Financial support:* In 2017–18, 407 students received support. Research assistantships with full tuition reimbursements available, teaching assistantships with full tuition reimbursements available, career-related internships or fieldwork, scholarships/grants, health care benefits, and non-residential student scholarships available. Financial award application deadline: 3/1; financial award applicants required to submit FAFSA. In 2017, 390 master's, 6 doctorates awarded. *Program availability:* Part-time, evening/weekend, 100% online. Offers automotive systems engineering (MSE, PhD); bioengineering (MSE); computer and information science (MS, PhD); computer engineering (MSE); data management (PhD); data science (MS); electrical and computer engineering (PhD); electrical engineering (MSE); energy systems engineering (MSE); engineering and computer science (MS, MSE, PhD); engineering management (MS); industrial and systems engineering (MSE, PhD); information systems and technology (MS); manufacturing systems engineering (MSE); mechanical engineering (MSE); mechanical sciences and engineering (PhD); program and project management (MS); software engineering (MS); systems and security (PhD). *Application deadline:* For fall admission, 8/1 priority date for domestic students, 5/1 priority date for international students; for winter admission, 12/1 priority date for domestic students, 9/1 priority date for international students; for spring admission, 4/1 priority date for domestic students, 1/1 priority date for international students. Applications are processed on a rolling basis. *Application fee:* $60. Electronic applications accepted. *Application Contact:* Office of Graduate Studies Staff, 313-583-6321, E-mail: umd-graduatestudies@umich.edu. *Dean*, Dr. Anthony England, 313-593-5290, E-mail: cecsdeansoffice@umich.edu.

UNIVERSITY OF MICHIGAN–FLINT, Flint, MI 48502-1950

General Information State-supported, coed, comprehensive institution. CGS member. *Enrollment:* 7,836 graduate, professional, and undergraduate students; 511 full-time matriculated graduate/professional students (344 women), 891 part-time matriculated graduate/professional students (551 women). *Enrollment by degree level:* 863 master's, 499 doctoral, 40 other advanced degrees. *Graduate faculty:* 326 full-time (169 women), 247 part-time/adjunct (153 women). *Graduate housing:* Room and/or apartments available on a first-come, first-served basis to single students; on-campus housing not available to married students. Typical cost: $7686 per year ($10,686 including board). Room and board charges vary according to board plan and housing facility selected. *Student services:* Campus employment opportunities, campus safety program, career counseling, child daycare facilities, exercise/wellness program, free psychological counseling, international student services, services for students with disabilities, teacher training, writing training. *Library facilities:* Frances Willson Thompson Library plus 1 other. *Collection:* Books: 251,483 (physical), 981,065 (digital/electronic); Serial titles: 1,862 (physical), 163,338 (digital/electronic); Databases: 1,387. Weekly public service hours: 96; students can reserve study rooms.

Computer facilities: Computer purchase and lease plans are available. 512 computers available on campus for general student use. A campuswide network can be accessed from student residence rooms and from off campus. Online class registration is available.
Website: http://www.umflint.edu/

General Application Contact: Bradley T. Maki, Director of Graduate Admissions, 810-762-3171, Fax: 810-766-6789, E-mail: bmaki@umflint.edu.

GRADUATE UNITS

College of Arts and Sciences Students: 48 full-time (28 women), 138 part-time (68 women); includes 43 minority (19 Black or African American, non-Hispanic/Latino; 3 Asian, non-Hispanic/Latino; 16 Hispanic/Latino; 1 Native Hawaiian or other Pacific Islander, non-Hispanic/Latino; 4 Two or more races, non-Hispanic/Latino), 46 international. Average age 33. 424 applicants, 55% accepted, 70 enrolled. *Faculty:* 101 full-time (50 women), 36 part-time/adjunct (19 women). Expenses: Contact institution. *Financial support:* Federal Work-Study, scholarships/grants, and unspecified assistantships available. Support available to part-time students. Financial award application deadline: 3/1; financial award applicants required to submit FAFSA. In 2017, 118 master's awarded. *Program availability:* Part-time. Offers applied communication (MA); arts and sciences (MA, MS, MSE); biology (MS); computer science (MS); gender studies (MA); global studies (MA); information systems (MS); literature (MA); mathematics (MA); mechanical engineering (MSE); U.S. history and politics (MA); writing and rhetoric (MA). *Application deadline:* For fall admission, 8/1 for domestic students, 5/1 for international students; for winter admission, 11/15 for domestic students, 9/1 for international students; for spring admission, 3/15 for domestic students, 1/1 for international students; for summer admission, 5/15 for domestic students. Applications are processed on a rolling basis. *Application fee:* $55. Electronic applications accepted. *Application Contact:* Bradley T. Maki, Director of Graduate Admissions, 810-762-3171, Fax: 810-766-6789, E-mail: bmaki@umflint.edu. *Dean*, Dr. Susan Gano-Phillips, 810-762-3234, Fax: 810-762-3006, E-mail: sganop@umflint.edu.

Graduate Programs Students: 20 full-time (11 women), 114 part-time (71 women); includes 46 minority (32 Black or African American, non-Hispanic/Latino; 5 American Indian or Alaska Native, non-Hispanic/Latino; 3 Asian, non-Hispanic/Latino; 1 Hispanic/Latino; 5 Two or more races, non-Hispanic/Latino), 3 international. Average age 39. 87 applicants, 77% accepted, 47 enrolled. *Faculty:* 8 full-time (4 women), 12 part-time/adjunct (7 women). Expenses: Contact institution. *Financial support:* Federal Work-Study, scholarships/grants, traineeships, and unspecified assistantships available. Support available to part-time students. Financial award application deadline: 3/1; financial award applicants required to submit FAFSA. In 2017, 61 master's awarded. *Program availability:* Part-time, evening/weekend, online learning. Offers administration of non-profit agencies (MPA); criminal justice administration (MPA); educational administration (MPA); general public administration (MPA); healthcare administration (MPA); liberal studies in American culture (MA, MLS); performance (MA). *Application deadline:* For fall admission, 8/1 for domestic students, 5/1 for international students; for winter admission, 11/15 for domestic students, 9/1 for international students; for spring admission, 3/15 for domestic students, 1/1 for international students; for summer admission, 5/15 for domestic students. Applications are processed on a rolling basis. *Application fee:* $55. Electronic applications accepted. *Application Contact:* Bradley T. Maki, Director of Graduate Admissions, 810-762-3171, Fax: 810-766-6789, E-mail: bmaki@umflint.edu. *Dean of Graduate Programs*, Dr. Vahid Lotfi, 810-762-3171, Fax: 810-766-6789, E-mail: vahid@umflint.edu.

School of Education and Human Services Students: 34 full-time (23 women), 192 part-time (137 women); includes 61 minority (46 Black or African American, non-Hispanic/Latino; 2 Asian, non-Hispanic/Latino; 5 Hispanic/Latino; 2 Native Hawaiian or other Pacific Islander, non-Hispanic/Latino; 6 Two or more races, non-Hispanic/Latino), 2 international. Average age 39. 124 applicants, 87% accepted, 81 enrolled. *Faculty:* 18 full-time (11 women), 26 part-time/adjunct (13 women). Expenses: Contact institution. *Financial support:* Federal Work-Study and unspecified assistantships available. Support available to part-time students. Financial award application deadline: 3/1; financial award applicants required to submit FAFSA. In 2017, 89 master's, 3 doctorates awarded. *Program availability:* Part-time, mixed mode format. Offers curriculum and instruction (Ed S); early childhood education (MA); education (Ed D); education and human services (MA, Ed D, Ed S); educational leadership (Ed S); educational technology (MA); literacy education (MA); secondary education with certification (MA). *Application deadline:* For fall admission, 7/1 for domestic students, 4/1 for international students; for winter admission, 11/15 for domestic students, 9/1 for international students; for spring admission, 3/15 for domestic students, 1/1 for international students. Applications are processed on a rolling basis. *Application fee:* $55. Electronic applications accepted. *Application Contact:* Bradley T. Maki, Director of Graduate Admissions, 810-762-3171, Fax: 810-766-6789, E-mail: bmaki@umflint.edu. *Dean*, Dr. Bob Barnett, 810-766-6878, Fax: 810-766-6891, E-mail: rbarnett@umflint.edu.

School of Health Professions and Studies Students: 231 full-time (131 women), 120 part-time (87 women); includes 65 minority (16 Black or African American, non-Hispanic/Latino; 4 American Indian or Alaska Native, non-Hispanic/Latino; 30 Asian, non-Hispanic/Latino; 5 Hispanic/Latino; 10 Two or more races, non-Hispanic/Latino), 23 international. Average age 29. 489 applicants, 37% accepted, 101 enrolled. *Faculty:* 32 full-time (23 women), 53 part-time/adjunct (29 women). Expenses: Contact institution. *Financial support:* Federal Work-Study, scholarships/grants, and unspecified assistantships available. Support available to part-time students. Financial award application deadline: 3/1; financial award applicants required to submit FAFSA. In 2017,

38 master's, 99 doctorates, 4 other advanced degrees awarded. *Program availability:* Part-time, 100% online. Offers adult neurology (PhD); anesthesia (DNAP); health administration (MPH); health education (MPH); health professions and studies (MPH, DNAP, DPT, PhD, Certificate); neurology (Certificate); orthopedics (PhD, Certificate); pediatrics (PhD, Certificate); physical therapy (DPT). *Application deadline:* For fall admission, 8/1 for domestic students, 5/1 for international students; for winter admission, 11/15 for domestic students, 9/1 for international students; for spring admission, 3/15 for domestic students, 1/1 for international students. Applications are processed on a rolling basis. *Application fee:* $55. Electronic applications accepted. *Application Contact:* Bradley T. Maki, Director of Graduate Admissions, 810-762-3171, Fax: 810-766-6789, E-mail: bmaki@umflint.edu. *Dean,* Dr. Donna Fry, 810-237-6503, Fax: 810-237-6532, E-mail: donnafry@umflint.edu.

School of Management Students: 19 full-time (8 women), 179 part-time (62 women); includes 39 minority (18 Black or African American, non-Hispanic/Latino; 1 American Indian or Alaska Native, non-Hispanic/Latino; 13 Asian, non-Hispanic/Latino; 5 Hispanic/Latino; 2 Two or more races, non-Hispanic/Latino), 29 international. Average age 34. 141 applicants, 59% accepted, 41 enrolled. *Faculty:* 32 full-time (5 women), 8 part-time/adjunct (2 women). Expenses: Contact institution. *Financial support:* Federal Work-Study, scholarships/grants, and unspecified assistantships available. Support available to part-time students. Financial award application deadline: 3/1; financial award applicants required to submit FAFSA. In 2017, 81 master's, 6 other advanced degrees awarded. *Program availability:* Part-time, evening/weekend, mixed mode format. Offers accounting (MBA); computer information systems (MBA); finance (MBA, Post-Master's Certificate); general business (Graduate Certificate); general business administration (MBA); health care management (MBA); international business (MBA, Post-Master's Certificate); leadership and organizational dynamics (MS); lean manufacturing (MBA); management (MBA, MS, MSA, Graduate Certificate, Post-Master's Certificate); marketing (Post-Master's Certificate); marketing and innovation management (MBA); organizational leadership (MBA, Post-Master's Certificate). *Application deadline:* For fall admission, 8/1 for domestic students, 5/1 for international students; for winter admission, 11/15 for domestic students, 9/1 for international students; for spring admission, 3/15 for domestic students, 1/1 for international students; for summer admission, 5/15 for domestic students. Applications are processed on a rolling basis. *Application fee:* $55. Electronic applications accepted. *Application Contact:* Bradley T. Maki, Director of Graduate Admissions, 810-762-3171, Fax: 810-766-6789, E-mail: bmaki@umflint.edu. *Dean, School of Management,* Dr. Scott Johnson, 810-762-6579, Fax: 810-237-6685, E-mail: scotjohn@umflint.edu.

School of Nursing Students: 159 full-time (143 women), 148 part-time (126 women); includes 80 minority (36 Black or African American, non-Hispanic/Latino; 5 American Indian or Alaska Native, non-Hispanic/Latino; 14 Asian, non-Hispanic/Latino; 14 Hispanic/Latino; 2 Native Hawaiian or other Pacific Islander, non-Hispanic/Latino; 9 Two or more races, non-Hispanic/Latino), 3 international. Average age 37. 86 applicants, 78% accepted, 41 enrolled. *Faculty:* 36 full-time (35 women), 66 part-time/adjunct (61 women). Expenses: Contact institution. *Financial support:* Federal Work-Study, scholarships/grants, and unspecified assistantships available. Support available to part-time students. Financial award application deadline: 3/1; financial award applicants required to submit FAFSA. In 2017, 12 master's, 42 doctorates, 9 other advanced degrees awarded. *Program availability:* Part-time, evening/weekend, 100% online. Offers adult-gerontology acute care (DNP); adult-gerontology primary care (DNP); family nurse practitioner (DNP); nursing (MSN); psychiatric mental health (DNP); psychiatric mental health nurse practitioner (Certificate). *Application deadline:* For fall admission, 7/1 for domestic students, 5/1 for international students; for winter admission, 11/1 for domestic students, 9/1 for international students; for spring admission, 3/15 for domestic students, 1/1 for international students. Applications are processed on a rolling basis. *Application fee:* $55. Electronic applications accepted. *Application Contact:* Bradley T. Maki, Director of Graduate Admissions, 810-762-3171, Fax: 810-766-6789, E-mail: bmaki@umflint.edu. *Director,* Dr. Constance J. Creech, 810-762-3420, Fax: 810-766-6851, E-mail: ccreech@umflint.edu.

UNIVERSITY OF MINNESOTA, DULUTH, Duluth, MN 55812-2496

General Information State-supported, coed, comprehensive institution. *Graduate housing:* Room and/or apartments available to single students; on-campus housing not available to married students. Housing application deadline: 3/1. *Research affiliation:* Environmental Protection Agency Environmental Research Laboratory (aquatic biology), Minnesota Geological Survey, Northeastern Minnesota National Historical Center (local history), U.S. Forest Service, Northcentral Forest Experiment Station.

GRADUATE UNITS

Graduate School *Program availability:* Part-time, evening/weekend, online learning. Offers toxicology (MS, PhD).

College of Education and Human Service Professions *Program availability:* Part-time, evening/weekend, online learning. Offers communication sciences and disorders (MA); education (M Ed, Ed D); education and human service professions (M Ed, MA, MSW, Ed D); social work (MSW).

College of Liberal Arts *Program availability:* Part-time. Offers criminology (MA); English (MA); liberal arts (MA, MLS); liberal studies (MLS).

Labovitz School of Business and Economics *Program availability:* Part-time, evening/weekend. Offers business administration (MBA); business and economics (MBA).

School of Fine Arts *Program availability:* Part-time. Offers fine arts (MFA, MM); graphic design (MFA); music education (MM); performance (MM).

Swenson College of Science and Engineering *Program availability:* Part-time, evening/weekend, online learning. Offers applied and computational mathematics (MS); chemistry and biochemistry (MS); computer science (MS); electrical and computer engineering (MSECE); engineering management (MSEM); environmental health and safety (MEHS); geological sciences (MS, PhD); integrated biosciences (MS, PhD); physics (MS); science and engineering (MEHS, MS, MSECE, MSEM, PhD).

Medical School *Program availability:* Part-time. Offers biochemistry, molecular biology and biophysics (MS); biology and biophysics (PhD); medicine (MS, MD, PhD); microbiology, immunology and molecular pathobiology (MS, PhD); pharmacology (MS, PhD); physiology (MS, PhD); social, administrative, and clinical pharmacy (MS, PhD); toxicology (MS, PhD).

UNIVERSITY OF MINNESOTA ROCHESTER, Rochester, MN 55904

General Information State-supported, coed, comprehensive institution.

GRADUATE UNITS

Graduate Programs

UNIVERSITY OF MINNESOTA, TWIN CITIES CAMPUS, Minneapolis, MN 55455-0213

General Information State-supported, coed, university. CGS member. *Graduate housing:* Rooms and/or apartments available on a first-come, first-served basis to single and married students. Housing application deadline: 5/1.

GRADUATE UNITS

Carlson School of Management Students: 589 full-time (254 women), 1,059 part-time (366 women); includes 213 minority (25 Black or African American, non-Hispanic/Latino; 5 American Indian or Alaska Native, non-Hispanic/Latino; 106 Asian, non-Hispanic/Latino; 51 Hispanic/Latino; 1 Native Hawaiian or other Pacific Islander, non-Hispanic/Latino; 25 Two or more races, non-Hispanic/Latino), 333 international. Average age 28. 2,219 applicants, 42% accepted, 535 enrolled. *Faculty:* 140 full-time (42 women), 46 part-time/adjunct (9 women). Expenses: Contact institution. *Financial support:* Fellowships with full and partial tuition reimbursements, research assistantships with full tuition reimbursements, teaching assistantships with full and partial tuition reimbursements, career-related internships or fieldwork, Federal Work-Study, institutionally sponsored loans, scholarships/grants, health care benefits, tuition waivers (full and partial), and unspecified assistantships available. Support available to part-time students. Financial award application deadline: 4/1; financial award applicants required to submit FAFSA. In 2017, 559 master's, 14 doctorates awarded. *Program availability:* Part-time, evening/weekend. Offers accountancy (M Acc); accounting (PhD); business analytics (MS); business taxation (MBT); finance (MBA, PhD); human resources and industrial relations (MA); information and decision sciences (PhD); information technology (MBA); management (MBA); marketing (MBA, PhD); medical industry orientation (MBA); strategic management and entrepreneurship (PhD); supply chain and operations (MBA, PhD); work and organizations (PhD). *Application fee:* $75 ($95 for international students). Electronic applications accepted. *Application Contact:* Graduate School Admissions, 612-625-3014, Fax: 612-625-6002, E-mail: gsquest@umn.edu. *Associate Dean of Faculty and Research,* Prof. Alok Gupta, 612-626-0276, Fax: 612-624-6374, E-mail: gupta037@umn.edu.

College of Pharmacy *Program availability:* Part-time. Offers experimental and clinical pharmacology (MS, PhD); medicinal chemistry (MS, PhD); pharmaceutics (PhD); pharmacy (MS, PhD, Pharm D); social and administrative pharmacy (MS, PhD).

College of Science and Engineering *Program availability:* Part-time, evening/weekend, online learning. Offers aerospace engineering and mechanics (MS, PhD); biomedical engineering (MS, PhD); chemical engineering (M Ch E, MS Ch E, PhD); chemical physics (MS, PhD); chemistry (MS, PhD); civil engineering (MCE, MS, PhD); computer science (MCS, MS, PhD); data science (MS); earth sciences (MS, PhD); electrical and computer engineering (MSEE, PhD); geological engineering (M Geo E, MS); history of science, technology and medicine (MA, PhD); industrial and systems engineering (MS, PhD); materials science and engineering (M Mat SE, MS Mat SE, PhD); mechanical engineering (MSME, PhD); science and engineering (M Ch E, M Geo E, M Mat SE, MA, MCE, MCS, MFM, MS, MS Ch E, MS Mat SE, MSEE, MSME, MSMOT, MSSE, MSST, PhD, Certificate); scientific computation (MS, PhD); software engineering (MSSE); stream restoration science and engineering (Certificate). Electronic applications accepted.

School of Mathematics *Program availability:* Part-time. Offers mathematics (MS, PhD); quantitative finance (Certificate). Electronic applications accepted.

School of Physics and Astronomy *Program availability:* Part-time. Offers astrophysics (MS, PhD); physics (MS, PhD).

Technological Leadership Institute *Program availability:* Evening/weekend. Offers management of technology (MSMOT); medical device innovation (MS); security technologies (MSST). Electronic applications accepted.

College of Veterinary Medicine *Program availability:* Part-time. Offers comparative and molecular bioscience (MS, PhD); veterinary medicine (MS, PhD). Electronic applications accepted.

Graduate School *Program availability:* Part-time, evening/weekend, online learning. Offers biophysical sciences and medical physics (MS, PhD); genetic counseling (MS); health informatics (MHI, MS, PhD); history of science, technology and medicine (MA, PhD); integrative biology and physiology (PhD); microbial engineering (MS); microbiology, immunology and cancer biology (PhD); molecular, cellular, developmental biology and genetics (PhD); neuroscience (MS, PhD); stem cell biology (MS). Electronic applications accepted.

College of Biological Sciences *Program availability:* Part-time. Offers biochemistry, molecular biology and biophysics (PhD); biological science (MBS); biological sciences (MBS, MS, PhD); ecology, evolution, and behavior (MS, PhD); plant biological sciences (MS, PhD). Electronic applications accepted.

College of Design Offers apparel (MA, MS, PhD); architecture (M Arch); design (M Arch, MA, MFA, MLA, MS, PhD, Postbaccalaureate Certificate); design communication (MA, MS, PhD); housing studies (MA, MS, PhD, Postbaccalaureate Certificate); interactive design (MFA); interior design (MA, MS, PhD); landscape architecture (MLA, MS); sustainable design (MS). Electronic applications accepted.

College of Education and Human Development Students: 1,449 full-time (1,067 women), 727 part-time (498 women); includes 465 minority (129 Black or African American, non-Hispanic/Latino; 16 American Indian or Alaska Native, non-Hispanic/Latino; 112 Asian, non-Hispanic/Latino; 119 Hispanic/Latino; 3 Native Hawaiian or other Pacific Islander, non-Hispanic/Latino; 86 Two or more races, non-Hispanic/Latino), 188 international. Average age 32. 1,926 applicants, 53% accepted, 918 enrolled. *Faculty:* 171 full-time (91 women). Expenses: Contact institution. *Financial support:* In 2017–18, 101 fellowships, 291 research assistantships with full tuition reimbursements (averaging $12,285 per year), 218 teaching assistantships with full tuition reimbursements (averaging $11,848 per year) were awarded; scholarships/grants and tuition waivers (partial) also available. Financial award applicants required to submit FAFSA. In 2017, 767 master's, 112 doctorates, 79 other advanced degrees awarded. *Program availability:* Part-time. Offers adult literacy (Certificate); applied child and adolescent development (MA); art education (M Ed, MA, PhD); autism spectrum disorder (Certificate); child psychology (PhD); comparative and international development education (MA, PhD); counseling and student personnel psychology (MA); curriculum and instruction (M Ed, MA, PhD, Certificate); disability policy and services (Certificate); early childhood education (M Ed); early childhood special education (M Ed); education and human development (M Ed, MA, MS, MSW, Ed D, PhD, Certificate, Ed S); education policy and leadership (M Ed, MA, Ed D, PhD); educational policy and leadership (MA, Ed D, PhD); elementary education (MA, PhD); English education (PhD); evaluation studies (MA, PhD); family education (M Ed); higher education (MA, Ed D, PhD); human resource development (M Ed, MA, Ed D, PhD, Certificate); kinesiology (MS, PhD); language and immersion education (Certificate); leadership in education (M Ed); learning technologies (MA, PhD); literacy education (MA, PhD); marriage and family therapy (MA, PhD); multicultural college teaching and learning (MA); PK-12 administrative licensure (Certificate); prevention science (MA); private college leadership (Certificate); professional development (Certificate); program evaluation (Certificate); psychological foundations of education (MA, PhD); quantitative methods in education (MA, PhD); school psychology (MA, PhD, Ed S); second language education (MA, PhD); social studies education (MA, PhD); social work (MSW, PhD); special education (M Ed, MA, PhD); sport and exercise science (M Ed); sport management (M Ed, MA); STEM education (MA, PhD); talent development and gifted education (Certificate); teaching (M Ed); teaching English to speakers of other languages (MA); technical education (Certificate); technology enhanced learning (Certificate); undergraduate multicultural teaching and learning (Certificate); youth development leadership (M Ed). *Application fee:* $75 ($95 for international students). *Application Contact:* Dr. Brianne Keeney, Director of Graduate Education Initiatives, 612-626-9145, E-mail: keen0113@umn.edu. *Dean,* Dr. Jean K. Quam, 612-626-9252, Fax: 612-626-7496, E-mail: jquam@umn.edu.

College of Food, Agricultural and Natural Resource Sciences *Program availability:* Part-time. Offers animal sciences (MS, PhD); applied economics (MS, PhD); applied plant sciences (MS, PhD); assessment, monitoring, and geospatial analysis (MS, PhD); bioproducts and biosystems science, engineering and management (MS, PhD); conservation biology (MS, PhD); economics, policy, management, and society (MS, PhD); entomology (MS, PhD); food science (MS, PhD); food, agricultural and natural resource sciences (MS, PhD); forest hydrology and watershed management (MS, PhD); forest products (MS, PhD); forests: biology, ecology, conservation, and management (MS, PhD); land and atmospheric science (MS, PhD); natural resources science and management (MS, PhD); nutrition (MS, PhD); paper science and engineering (MS, PhD); plant pathology (MS, PhD); recreation resources, tourism, and environmental education (MS, PhD); water resources science (MS, PhD). Electronic applications accepted.

College of Liberal Arts *Program availability:* Part-time, evening/weekend. Offers American studies (PhD); ancient and medieval art and archaeology (MA, PhD); anthropology (MA, PhD); art (MFA); art history (MA, PhD); Asian literatures, cultures, and media (PhD); audiology (Au D); biological psychopathology (PhD); classics (MA, PhD); clinical psychology (PhD); cognitive and biological psychology (PhD); communication studies (MA, PhD); comparative literature (PhD); comparative studies in discourse and society (PhD); counseling psychology (PhD); design technology (MFA); economics (MA, PhD); English (MA, PhD); English as a second language (MA); feminist studies (PhD); French (MA, PhD); geographic information science (MGIS); geography, environment and society (MA, PhD); Germanic studies (MA, PhD); Greek (MA, PhD); Hispanic and Lusophone literatures, cultures and linguistics (PhD); Hispanic linguistics (MA); Hispanic literature (MA); history (MA, PhD); industrial/organizational psychology (PhD); Latin (MA, PhD); liberal arts (MA, MFA, MGIS, MM, MS, Au D, DMA, PhD); linguistics (MA, PhD); Lusophone literature (MA); mass communication (MA, PhD); music (MA, MM, DMA, PhD); personality, individual differences, and behavior genetics (PhD); philosophy (MA, PhD); political science (PhD); quantitative/psychometric methods (PhD); religions in antiquity (MA); school psychology (PhD); social psychology (PhD); sociology (MA, PhD); speech-language pathology (MA); speech-language-hearing sciences (PhD); statistics (MS, PhD); strategic communication (professional program) (MA); theatre arts (MA, PhD). Electronic applications accepted.

Humphrey School of Public Affairs *Program availability:* Part-time, evening/weekend. Offers development practice (MDP); management and governance (PhD); public affairs (MDP, MPA, MPP, MS, MURP, PhD); public policy (PhD); science, technology, and environmental policy (PhD); urban and regional planning (MURP); urban planning (PhD). Electronic applications accepted.

School of Nursing *Program availability:* Part-time, online learning. Offers adult/gerontological clinical nurse specialist (DNP); adult/gerontological primary care nurse practitioner (DNP); family nurse practitioner (DNP); health innovation and leadership (DNP); integrative health and healing (DNP); nurse anesthesia (DNP); nurse midwifery (DNP); nursing (MN, PhD); nursing informatics (DNP); pediatric clinical nurse specialist (DNP); primary care certified pediatric nurse practitioner (DNP); psychiatric/mental health nurse practitioner (DNP); women's health nurse practitioner (DNP).

Law School Students: 566 full-time (268 women); includes 87 minority (8 Black or African American, non-Hispanic/Latino; 3 American Indian or Alaska Native, non-Hispanic/Latino; 35 Asian, non-Hispanic/Latino; 22 Hispanic/Latino; 19 Two or more races, non-Hispanic/Latino), 58 international. 1,808 applicants, 47% accepted, 191 enrolled. *Faculty:* 74 full-time (30 women), 138 part-time/adjunct (44 women). Expenses: Contact institution. *Financial support:* In 2017–18, 577 students received support. Fellowships, research assistantships, career-related internships or fieldwork, Federal Work-Study, institutionally sponsored loans, and scholarships/grants available. Financial award application deadline: 7/1; financial award applicants required to submit FAFSA. In 2017, 206 doctorates awarded. Offers law (LL M, MS, JD, SJD). *Application deadline:* For fall admission, 7/15 for domestic students. Applications are processed on a rolling basis. *Application fee:* $60. Electronic applications accepted. *Application Contact:* Robin Ingli, Director of Admissions, 612-625-3487, Fax: 612-625-2011, E-mail: jdadmissions@umn.edu. *Dean,* Garry W. Jenkins, 612-625-4841.

Medical School *Program availability:* Part-time, evening/weekend. Offers medicine (MA, MS, DPT, MD, PhD); pharmacology (MS, PhD).

School of Dentistry Offers dentistry (MS, DDS, PhD, Certificate); endodontics (MS, Certificate); oral biology (MS, PhD); oral health services for older adults (geriatrics) (MS, Certificate); orthodontics (MS); pediatric dentistry (MS); periodontology (MS); prosthodontics (MS); temporomandibular joint disorders (MS).

School of Public Health *Program availability:* Part-time, online learning. Offers biostatistics (MPH, MS, PhD); clinical research (MS); community health education (MPH); core concepts (Certificate); epidemiology (MPH, PhD); food safety and biosecurity (Certificate); health services research, policy, and administration (MS, PhD); healthcare administration (MHA); maternal and child health (MPH); occupational health and safety (Certificate); preparedness, response and recovery (Certificate); public health (MHA, MPH, MS, PhD, Certificate); public health administration and policy (MPH); public health nutrition (MPH); public health practice (MPH). Electronic applications accepted.

Division of Environmental Health Sciences *Program availability:* Part-time. Offers environmental and occupational epidemiology (MPH, MS, PhD); environmental chemistry (MS, PhD); environmental health policy (MPH, MS, PhD); environmental infectious diseases (MPH, MS, PhD); environmental toxicology (MPH, MS, PhD); exposure sciences (MS); general environmental health (MPH, MS); global environmental health (MPH, MS, PhD); industrial hygiene (MPH, MS, PhD); occupational health nursing (MPH, MS, PhD); occupational medicine (MPH). Electronic applications accepted.

UNIVERSITY OF MISSISSIPPI, University, MS 38677

General Information State-supported, coed, university. CGS member. *Enrollment:* 23,136 graduate, professional, and undergraduate students; 2,022 full-time matriculated graduate/professional students (1,079 women), 747 part-time matriculated graduate/professional students (450 women). *Enrollment by degree level:* 1,212 master's, 1,456 doctoral, 101 other advanced degrees. *Graduate faculty:* 878 full-time (386 women), 217 part-time/adjunct (118 women). *Graduate housing:* Rooms and/or apartments available to single and married students. *Student services:* Campus employment opportunities, campus safety program, career counseling, exercise/wellness program, free psychological counseling, international student services, low-cost health insurance, multicultural affairs office, services for students with disabilities, teacher training, writing training. *Library facilities:* J. D. Williams Library plus 1 other. *Collection:* Books: 3.3 million (physical), 814,143 (digital/electronic); Serial titles: 39,667 (physical), 135,210 (digital/electronic); Databases: 389. Weekly public service hours: 109. *Research affiliation:* Mississippi Geographic Alliance, Mississippi Research Consortium, Mississippi-Alabama Sea Grant Consortium, Oak Ridge Associated Universities, Southeastern Universities Research Association, Mississippi Space Grant Consortium.

Computer facilities: 259 computers available on campus for general student use. A campuswide network can be accessed from student residence rooms and from off campus. Online class registration is available.
Website: http://www.olemiss.edu/

General Application Contact: Dr. Christy M. Wyandt, Associate Dean of Graduate School, 662-915-7474, Fax: 662-915-7577, E-mail: cwyandt@olemiss.edu.

GRADUATE UNITS

Graduate School Students: 1,957 full-time (1,051 women), 689 part-time (413 women); includes 526 minority (338 Black or African American, non-Hispanic/Latino; 2 American Indian or Alaska Native, non-Hispanic/Latino; 79 Asian, non-Hispanic/Latino; 68 Hispanic/Latino; 1 Native Hawaiian or other Pacific Islander, non-Hispanic/Latino; 38 Two or more races, non-Hispanic/Latino), 331 international. Average age 28. *Faculty:* 866 full-time (379 women), 194 part-time/adjunct (87 women). Expenses: Contact institution. *Financial support:* Fellowships, research assistantships, teaching assistantships, career-related internships or fieldwork, Federal Work-Study, institutionally sponsored loans, scholarships/grants, tuition waivers (full), and unspecified assistantships available. Financial award application deadline: 3/1; financial award applicants required to submit FAFSA. *Program availability:* Part-time. *Application deadline:* For fall admission, 2/1 priority date for domestic students; for spring admission, 10/1 for domestic students. Applications are processed on a rolling basis. *Application fee:* $50. Electronic applications accepted. *Interim Dean,* Dr. Christy M. Wyandt, 662-915-7474, Fax: 662-915-7577, E-mail: gschool@olemiss.edu.

College of Liberal Arts Students: 466 full-time (229 women), 72 part-time (34 women); includes 87 minority (38 Black or African American, non-Hispanic/Latino; 18 Asian, non-Hispanic/Latino; 24 Hispanic/Latino; 7 Two or more races, non-Hispanic/Latino), 121 international. Average age 29. *Faculty:* 465 full-time (207 women), 82 part-time/adjunct (46 women). Expenses: Contact institution. *Financial support:* Fellowships, research assistantships, teaching assistantships, career-related internships or fieldwork, Federal Work-Study, institutionally sponsored loans, scholarships/grants, and unspecified assistantships available. Financial award application deadline: 3/1; financial award applicants required to submit FAFSA. *Program availability:* Part-time. Offers anthropology (MA); biology (MS, PhD); chemistry (MS, DA, PhD); creative writing (MFA); documentary expression (MFA); economics (MA, PhD); English (MA, PhD); experimental psychology (PhD); history (MA, PhD); mathematics (MS, PhD); modern languages (MA); music (MM); philosophy (MA); physics (MA, MS, PhD); political science (MA, PhD); Southern studies (MA); studio art (MFA). *Application deadline:* For fall admission, 2/1 priority date for domestic students; for spring admission, 10/1 for domestic students. Applications are processed on a rolling basis. *Application fee:* $50. Electronic applications accepted. *Application Contact:* Dr. Christy M. Wyandt, Associate Dean of Graduate School, 662-915-7474, Fax: 662-915-7577, E-mail: cwyandt@olemiss.edu. *Dean,* Dr. Lee Michael Cohen, 662-915-7177, Fax: 662-915-5792, E-mail: libarts@olemiss.edu.

Meek School of Journalism and New Media Students: 39 full-time (18 women), 7 part-time (1 woman); includes 6 minority (4 Black or African American, non-Hispanic/Latino; 1 Asian, non-Hispanic/Latino; 1 Two or more races, non-Hispanic/Latino), 5 international. Average age 26. *Faculty:* 30 full-time (15 women), 19 part-time/adjunct (11 women). Expenses: Contact institution. In 2017, 11 master's awarded. Offers integrated marketing communications (MA); journalism (MA). *Application deadline:* For fall admission, 3/31 priority date for domestic and international students. Applications are processed on a rolling basis. *Application fee:* $40. *Application Contact:* Dr. Joseph Atkins, Professor of Journalism, 662-915-5510, E-mail: jbatkins@olemiss.edu. *Dean,* Dr. Will Norton, Jr., 662-915-7146, Fax: 662-915-7765, E-mail: meekschool@olemiss.edu.

School of Accountancy Students: 116 full-time (48 women), 7 part-time (3 women); includes 10 minority (7 Black or African American, non-Hispanic/Latino; 1 Asian, non-Hispanic/Latino; 1 Native Hawaiian or other Pacific Islander, non-Hispanic/Latino; 1 Two or more races, non-Hispanic/Latino), 3 international. Average age 24. *Faculty:* 17 full-time (4 women), 5 part-time/adjunct (3 women). Expenses: Contact institution. *Financial support:* Scholarships/grants available. Financial award application deadline: 3/1; financial award applicants required to submit FAFSA. Offers accountancy (M Acc, PhD); accounting and data analytics (MA); taxation accounting (M Tax). *Application deadline:* For fall admission, 8/1 for domestic students; for spring admission, 12/1 for domestic students; for summer admission, 5/1 for domestic students. Applications are processed on a rolling basis. *Application fee:* $50. *Application Contact:* Dr. Dale Flesher, Associate Dean/Professor/Chair, 662-915-7623, E-mail: acdlf@olemiss.edu. *Dean, School of Accountancy,* Dr. W. Mark Wilder, 662-915-7468, Fax: 662-915-7483, E-mail: umaccy@olemiss.edu.

School of Applied Sciences Students: 182 full-time (139 women), 41 part-time (27 women); includes 49 minority (41 Black or African American, non-Hispanic/Latino; 1 American Indian or Alaska Native, non-Hispanic/Latino; 3 Asian, non-Hispanic/Latino; 3 Hispanic/Latino; 1 Two or more races, non-Hispanic/Latino), 13 international. Average age 26. *Faculty:* 66 full-time (38 women), 33 part-time/adjunct (14 women). Expenses: Contact institution. *Financial support:* Scholarships/grants available. Financial award application deadline: 3/1; financial award applicants required to submit FAFSA. Offers communicative disorders (MS); criminal justice (MCJ); exercise science (MS); food and nutrition services (MS); health and kinesiology (PhD); health promotion (MS); nutrition and hospitality management (PhD); park and recreation management (MA); social welfare (PhD); social work (MSW). *Application deadline:* For fall admission, 4/1 for domestic students; for spring admission, 10/1 for domestic students. Applications are processed on a rolling basis. *Application fee:* $50.

Electronic applications accepted. *Dean*, Dr. Teresa C. Carithers, 662-915-1081, Fax: 662-915-5717, E-mail: applsci@olemiss.edu.

School of Business Administration Students: 71 full-time (26 women), 112 part-time (27 women); includes 11 minority (4 Black or African American, non-Hispanic/Latino; 3 Asian, non-Hispanic/Latino; 1 Hispanic/Latino; 3 Two or more races, non-Hispanic/Latino), 17 international. Average age 29. *Faculty:* 58 full-time (15 women), 8 part-time/adjunct (3 women). Expenses: Contact institution. *Financial support:* Fellowships, career-related internships or fieldwork, scholarships/grants, tuition waivers (full), and unspecified assistantships available. Financial award application deadline: 3/1; financial award applicants required to submit FAFSA. In 2017, 83 master's, 6 doctorates awarded. Offers business administration (MBA, PhD); finance (PhD); management (PhD); management information systems (PhD); marketing (PhD). *Application deadline:* For fall admission, 2/1 priority date for domestic students; for spring admission, 11/1 for domestic students; for summer admission, 4/1 for domestic students. Applications are processed on a rolling basis. *Application fee:* $50. Electronic applications accepted. *Application Contact:* Ashley Jones McGee, Director of MBA and MHA Administration, 662-915-5483, E-mail: ajones@olemiss.edu. *Dean*, Dr. Ken Cyree, 662-915-5820, Fax: 662-915-5821, E-mail: info@bus.olemiss.edu.

School of Education Students: 185 full-time (148 women), 410 part-time (310 women); includes 193 minority (168 Black or African American, non-Hispanic/Latino; 7 Asian, non-Hispanic/Latino; 14 Hispanic/Latino; 4 Two or more races, non-Hispanic/Latino), 7 international. Average age 33. *Faculty:* 65 full-time (40 women), 25 part-time/adjunct (5 women). Expenses: Contact institution. *Financial support:* Scholarships/grants available. Financial award application deadline: 3/1; financial award applicants required to submit FAFSA. In 2017, 176 master's, 20 doctorates, 37 other advanced degrees awarded. Offers counselor education (M Ed, PhD); counselor education - play therapy (Ed S); early childhood (M Ed); educational leadership K-12 (M Ed, Ed D, PhD, Ed S); elementary education (M Ed, Ed D, Ed S); higher education/student personnel (Ed D, PhD); literacy education (M Ed); math education (Ed D); secondary education (M Ed, PhD, Ed S); special education (M Ed, PhD, Ed S); teacher corporations (MA); teacher education (MA). *Application deadline:* For fall admission, 3/1 for domestic students; for spring admission, 10/1 for domestic students; for summer admission, 3/1 for domestic students. Applications are processed on a rolling basis. *Application fee:* $50. Electronic applications accepted. *Application Contact:* Dr. Joe Sumrall, Professor of Elementary Education, 662-915-7350, E-mail: soe@olemiss.edu. *Dean*, Dr. David Rock, 662-915-7063, Fax: 662-915-7249, E-mail: soe@olemiss.edu.

School of Engineering Students: 123 full-time (26 women), 21 part-time (4 women); includes 13 minority (6 Black or African American, non-Hispanic/Latino; 5 Asian, non-Hispanic/Latino; 1 Hispanic/Latino; 1 Two or more races, non-Hispanic/Latino), 77 international. Average age 29. *Faculty:* 68 full-time (15 women), 5 part-time/adjunct (2 women). Expenses: Contact institution. *Financial support:* Scholarships/grants available. Financial award application deadline: 3/1; financial award applicants required to submit FAFSA. In 2017, 28 master's, 12 doctorates awarded. Offers aeroacoustics (MS, PhD); chemical engineering (MS, PhD); civil engineering (MS, PhD); computational hydroscience (MS, PhD); computer science (MS, PhD); electrical engineering (MS, PhD); electromagnetics (MS, PhD); environmental engineering (MS, PhD); geology and geological engineering (MS, PhD); hydrology (MS); material science (MS); mechanical engineering (MS, PhD); telecommunications (MS). *Application deadline:* For fall admission, 4/1 for domestic students; for spring admission, 10/1 for domestic students. Applications are processed on a rolling basis. *Application fee:* $50. Electronic applications accepted. *Dean*, Dr. Alexander Cheng, 662-915-7407, Fax: 662-915-1287, E-mail: engineer@olemiss.edu.

School of Pharmacy Students: 417 full-time (256 women), 16 part-time (7 women); includes 71 minority (24 Black or African American, non-Hispanic/Latino; 1 American Indian or Alaska Native, non-Hispanic/Latino; 36 Asian, non-Hispanic/Latino; 4 Hispanic/Latino; 6 Two or more races, non-Hispanic/Latino), 88 international. Average age 25. *Faculty:* 71 full-time (32 women), 17 part-time/adjunct (6 women). Expenses: Contact institution. *Financial support:* Fellowships, research assistantships, teaching assistantships, career-related internships or fieldwork, Federal Work-Study, institutionally sponsored loans, scholarships/grants, tuition waivers (full), and unspecified assistantships available. Financial award application deadline: 3/1; financial award applicants required to submit FAFSA. In 2017, 22 master's, 49 doctorates awarded. *Program availability:* Part-time. Offers environmental toxicology (MS, PhD); industrial pharmacy (MS); medicinal chemistry (MS, PhD); pharmaceutics (MS, PhD); pharmacognosy (MS, PhD); pharmacology (MS, PhD); pharmacy (Pharm D); pharmacy administration (MS, PhD). *Application deadline:* For fall admission, 2/1 priority date for domestic students; for spring admission, 10/1 priority date for domestic students. Applications are processed on a rolling basis. *Application fee:* $50. Electronic applications accepted. *Dean*, Dr. David D. Allen, II, 662-915-7265, Fax: 662-915-5118, E-mail: sopdean@olemiss.edu.

School of Law Students: 358 full-time (161 women), 3 part-time (0 women); includes 86 minority (46 Black or African American, non-Hispanic/Latino; 5 Asian, non-Hispanic/Latino; 21 Hispanic/Latino; 14 Two or more races, non-Hispanic/Latino). Average age 25. *Faculty:* 32 full-time (14 women), 9 part-time/adjunct (3 women). Expenses: Contact institution. *Financial support:* Fellowships, research assistantships, teaching assistantships, career-related internships or fieldwork, Federal Work-Study, institutionally sponsored loans, and scholarships/grants available. Support available to part-time students. Financial award application deadline: 3/1; financial award applicants required to submit FAFSA. In 2017, 179 doctorates awarded. Offers law (LL M, JD). *Application deadline:* For fall admission, 4/1 for domestic students. *Application fee:* $50. *Application Contact:* Macey Edmondson, Assistant Dean for Admissions and Scholarships, 662-915-6819, Fax: 662-915-7577, E-mail: clee@olemiss.edu. *Dean*, Dr. Susan Duncan, 662-915-6900, Fax: 662-915-6895, E-mail: lawadmin@olemiss.edu.

UNIVERSITY OF MISSISSIPPI MEDICAL CENTER, Jackson, MS 39216-4505

General Information State-supported, coed, upper-level institution. *Graduate housing:* On-campus housing not available. *Research affiliation:* NASA-Stennis Space Center (imaging technology), Catfish Genetics Research Unit (immunology), Oak Ridge National Laboratory (physiology, biomedical engineering), Gulf Coast Research Laboratory (microbiology).

GRADUATE UNITS

School of Dentistry Offers craniofacial and dental research (MS, PhD); dentistry (MS, DMD, PhD).

School of Graduate Studies in the Health Sciences *Program availability:* Part-time. Offers biochemistry (PhD); biomedical materials science (MS, PhD); biomedical sciences (MS); clinical anatomy (MS, PhD); health sciences (MS, PhD); microbiology (PhD); neuroscience (PhD); pathology (PhD); pharmacology and toxicology (PhD); physiology and biophysics (PhD).

School of Health Related Professions *Program availability:* Part-time. Offers health related professions (MOT, MPT); occupational therapy (MOT); physical therapy (MPT).

School of Medicine *Program availability:* Part-time. Offers medicine (MD). Electronic applications accepted.

School of Nursing *Program availability:* Part-time, evening/weekend, online learning. Offers nursing (MSN, DNP, PhD). Electronic applications accepted.

UNIVERSITY OF MISSOURI, Columbia, MO 65211

General Information State-supported, coed, university. CGS member. *Enrollment:* 30,870 graduate, professional, and undergraduate students; 4,489 full-time matriculated graduate/professional students (2,500 women), 2,564 part-time matriculated graduate/professional students (1,615 women). *Enrollment by degree level:* 2,917 master's, 3,685 doctoral, 275 other advanced degrees. Tuition, state resident: full-time $6480. Tuition, nonresident: full-time $17,744. *Required fees:* $1108. Tuition and fees vary according to course load, campus/location and program. *Graduate housing:* Rooms and/or apartments available on a first-come, first-served basis to single and married students. Typical cost: $7425 per year ($9975 including board) for single students. Room and board charges vary according to campus/location and housing facility selected. Housing application deadline: 12/1. *Student services:* Campus employment opportunities, campus safety program, career counseling, child daycare facilities, exercise/wellness program, free psychological counseling, grant writing training, international student services, low-cost health insurance, multicultural affairs office, services for students with disabilities, teacher training, writing training. *Library facilities:* Ellis Library plus 10 others. *Collection:* Books: 4.7 million (physical), 1.4 million (digital/electronic). Students can reserve study rooms.

Computer facilities: Computer purchase and lease plans are available. 1,200 computers available on campus for general student use. A campuswide network can be accessed from student residence rooms and from off campus. Online class registration is available. Website: http://www.missouri.edu/

General Application Contact: Terrence Grus, Director of Graduate Admissions and Student Services, 573-882-6311, E-mail: gradadmin@missouri.edu.

GRADUATE UNITS

College of Veterinary Medicine Expenses: Contact institution. Offers veterinary medicine (MS, PhD).

Graduate Programs in Veterinary Medicine Expenses: Contact institution. Offers biomedical sciences (MS, PhD); comparative medicine (MS); pathobiology (MS, PhD); veterinary medicine (MS, PhD); veterinary medicine and surgery (MS).

Office of Research and Graduate Studies Expenses: Contact institution. *Program availability:* Part-time, evening/weekend.

College of Agriculture, Food and Natural Resources Expenses: Contact institution. *Program availability:* Part-time. Offers agricultural economics (MS, PhD); agricultural education (MS, PhD); agriculture, food and natural resources (MS, PhD); animal sciences (MS, PhD); biochemistry (MS, PhD); food science (MS, PhD); rural sociology (MS, PhD).

College of Arts and Science Expenses: Contact institution. *Financial support:* Fellowships, research assistantships, teaching assistantships, career-related internships or fieldwork, institutionally sponsored loans, scholarships/grants, health care benefits, tuition waivers (full and partial), and unspecified assistantships available. Support available to part-time students. *Program availability:* Part-time. Offers analytical chemistry (PhD); anthropology (MA, PhD); applied mathematics (MS); art (MFA); arts and science (MA, MFA, MS, PhD, Certificate, Graduate Certificate); communication (MA, PhD); economics (MA, PhD); English (MA, PhD); evolutionary biology and ecology (MA, PhD); French (MA, PhD); geographic information science (Graduate Certificate); geography (MA); geological sciences (MS, PhD); German and Russian studies (MA); history (MA, PhD); mathematics (MA, PhD); music (MA, Certificate); philosophy (MA, PhD); physics and astronomy (MS, PhD); political science (MA, PhD, Certificate); psychological sciences (MA, PhD, Certificate); religious studies (MA); sociology (MA, PhD); statistics (MA, PhD); theatre (MA, PhD).

College of Education Expenses: Contact institution. *Financial support:* Fellowships, research assistantships, teaching assistantships, institutionally sponsored loans, scholarships/grants, traineeships, health care benefits, and unspecified assistantships available. Support available to part-time students. *Program availability:* Part-time, evening/weekend. Offers administration and supervision of special education (PhD); agricultural education (M Ed, PhD, Ed S); art education (M Ed, PhD, Ed S); business and office education (M Ed, PhD, Ed S); counseling psychology (M Ed, MA, PhD, Ed S); early childhood education (M Ed, PhD, Ed S); education (M Ed, MA, Ed D, PhD, Ed S); education administration (M Ed, MA, Ed D, PhD, Ed S); educational psychology (M Ed, MA, PhD, Ed S); elementary education (M Ed, PhD, Ed S); English education (M Ed, PhD, Ed S); foreign language education (M Ed, PhD, Ed S); health education and promotion (M Ed, PhD); higher and adult education (M Ed, MA, Ed D, PhD, Ed S); information science and learning technology (PhD); learning and instruction (M Ed); marketing education (M Ed, PhD, Ed S); mathematics education (M Ed, PhD, Ed S); music education (M Ed, PhD, Ed S); reading education (M Ed, PhD, Ed S); school psychology (M Ed, MA, PhD, Ed S); science education (M Ed, PhD, Ed S); social studies education (M Ed, PhD, Ed S); vocational education (M Ed, PhD, Ed S).

College of Engineering Expenses: Contact institution. *Financial support:* Fellowships, research assistantships, teaching assistantships, institutionally sponsored loans, scholarships/grants, traineeships, health care benefits, and unspecified assistantships available. Support available to part-time students. *Program availability:* Part-time. Offers agricultural engineering (MS); biological engineering (PhD); chemical engineering (MS, PhD); civil engineering (MS, PhD); electrical and computer engineering (MSCE, MSEE, PhD); engineering (ME, MS, PhD, Certificate); industrial and manufacturing systems engineering (ME, MS, PhD); mechanical and aerospace engineering (ME, MS, PhD).

College of Human Environmental Sciences Expenses: Contact institution. *Financial support:* Fellowships, research assistantships, teaching assistantships, institutionally sponsored loans, scholarships/grants, traineeships, health care benefits, and unspecified assistantships available. Support available to part-time students. *Program availability:* Part-time. Offers architectural studies (M Arch, MS, PhD); exercise physiology (MS, PhD); human development and family studies (MA, MS, PhD); human environmental sciences (MA, MS, PhD, Certificate, Graduate Certificate); nutritional sciences (MS, PhD); personal financial planning (PhD); textile and apparel management (MS, PhD). *Application deadline:* Applications are processed on a rolling basis.

Harry S Truman School of Public Affairs Expenses: Contact institution. *Financial support:* Fellowships, research assistantships, teaching assistantships, institutionally sponsored loans, scholarships/grants, traineeships, health care benefits, and unspecified assistantships available. Support available to part-time students. Offers grantsmanship (Graduate Certificate); nonprofit management (Graduate Certificate); organizational change (Graduate Certificate); public affairs (MPA, PhD); public management (Graduate Certificate); science and public policy (Graduate Certificate). *Application deadline:* For fall admission, 2/1 priority date for domestic and international students. Applications are processed on a rolling basis. Electronic applications accepted. *Application Contact:* Laer Keiser, Director, 573-882-3304, E-mail: truman@missouri.edu. *Director,* Laer Keiser, 573-882-3304, E-mail: truman@missouri.edu.

Informatics Institute Expenses: Contact institution. *Financial support:* Scholarships/grants, health care benefits, and unspecified assistantships available. Support available to part-time students. Offers informatics (MS). *Application deadline:* Applications are processed on a rolling basis. Electronic applications accepted. *Application Contact:* Dr. Chi-Ren Shyu, Director. *Director,* Dr. Chi-Ren Shyu.

Robert J. Trulaske, Sr. College of Business Expenses: Contact institution. *Financial support:* Fellowships, research assistantships, teaching assistantships, and institutionally sponsored loans available. *Program availability:* Part-time. Offers accountancy (M Acc, PhD); business (Exec MBA, M Acc, MBA, PhD, Certificate); business administration (MBA); finance (PhD); taxation (Certificate). *Application deadline:* Applications are processed on a rolling basis.

School of Journalism Expenses: Contact institution. *Financial support:* Fellowships, research assistantships, teaching assistantships, career-related internships or fieldwork, institutionally sponsored loans, scholarships/grants, health care benefits, and unspecified assistantships available. Support available to part-time students. *Program availability:* Part-time. Offers health communications (MA); journalism (PhD). *Application deadline:* Applications are processed on a rolling basis. Electronic applications accepted.

School of Social Work Expenses: Contact institution. *Financial support:* Fellowships, research assistantships, teaching assistantships, institutionally sponsored loans, scholarships/grants, health care benefits, and unspecified assistantships available. Support available to part-time students. *Program availability:* Part-time. Offers social work (MSW, PhD). *Application deadline:* For fall admission, 1/15 priority date for domestic and international students. Applications are processed on a rolling basis. Electronic applications accepted.

Sinclair School of Nursing Expenses: Contact institution. *Financial support:* Fellowships, research assistantships, teaching assistantships, career-related internships or fieldwork, institutionally sponsored loans, scholarships/grants, traineeships, health care benefits, tuition waivers (full), and unspecified assistantships available. Support available to part-time students. *Program availability:* Part-time. Offers adult-gerontology clinical nurse specialist (DNP, Certificate); family nurse practitioner (DNP); family psychiatric and mental health nurse practitioner (DNP); nursing (MS, PhD); nursing leadership and innovations in health care (DNP); pediatric clinical nurse specialist (DNP, Certificate); pediatric nurse practitioner (DNP). *Application deadline:* Applications are processed on a rolling basis. Electronic applications accepted.

School of Health Professions Expenses: Contact institution. *Financial support:* Fellowships, research assistantships, teaching assistantships, and institutionally sponsored loans available. Offers communication science and disorders (MHS, PhD); diagnostic medical ultrasound (MHS); health professions (MHS, MOT, DPT, PhD); occupational therapy (MOT); physical therapy (DPT). *Application deadline:* Applications are processed on a rolling basis.

School of Law Expenses: Contact institution. *Financial support:* Fellowships, Federal Work-Study, and institutionally sponsored loans available. Financial award applicants required to submit FAFSA. Offers dispute resolution (LL M); law (JD). *Application deadline:* Applications are processed on a rolling basis.

School of Medicine Expenses: Contact institution. *Financial support:* Fellowships, research assistantships, teaching assistantships, career-related internships or fieldwork, institutionally sponsored loans, and scholarships/grants available. Support available to part-time students. Financial award applicants required to submit FAFSA. *Program availability:* Part-time. Offers family and community medicine (MS); health administration (MS); medical pharmacology and physiology (MS, PhD); medicine (MS, MD, PhD, Graduate Certificate); molecular microbiology and immunology (PhD); pathology and anatomical sciences (MS, PhD). *Application deadline:* Applications are processed on a rolling basis.

UNIVERSITY OF MISSOURI–KANSAS CITY, Kansas City, MO 64110-2499

General Information State-supported, coed, university. CGS member. *Graduate housing:* Room and/or apartments available on a first-come, first-served basis to single students; on-campus housing not available to married students. *Research affiliation:* Children's Mercy Hospital (health sciences), Truman Medical Center (health sciences), Veterans Administration Hospital (health sciences), Midwest Research Institute (health sciences), St. Luke's Hospital (health sciences).

GRADUATE UNITS

College of Arts and Sciences *Program availability:* Part-time, evening/weekend. Offers analytical chemistry (PhD); art and art history (MA, PhD); arts and sciences (MA, MFA, MS, MSW, PhD); community psychology (PhD); criminal justice and criminology (MS); economics (MA, PhD); English (MA, PhD); geosciences (MS, PhD); history (MA, PhD); inorganic chemistry (PhD); mathematics and statistics (MA, MS, PhD); organic chemistry (PhD); physical chemistry (PhD); physics (MS, PhD); political science (MA); polymer chemistry (MS, PhD); romance languages and literatures (MA); sociology (MA); theatre (MA, MFA). Electronic applications accepted.

School of Social Work *Program availability:* Part-time, evening/weekend. Offers social work (MSW).

Conservatory of Music and Dance *Program availability:* Part-time. Offers composition (MM, DMA); conducting (MM, DMA); music (MA); music education (MME, PhD); music history and literature (MM); music theory (MM); music therapy (MA); performance (MM, DMA). PhD (interdisciplinary) offered through the School of Graduate Studies.

Henry W. Bloch School of Management *Program availability:* Part-time, evening/weekend. Offers accounting (MS); finance (MS); public affairs (MPA, PhD). PhD (interdisciplinary) offered through the School of Graduate Studies. Electronic applications accepted.

School of Biological Sciences *Program availability:* Part-time, evening/weekend. Offers biology (MA); cell biology and biophysics (PhD); cellular and molecular biology (MS); molecular biology and biochemistry (PhD). PhD (interdisciplinary) offered through the School of Graduate Studies.

School of Computing and Engineering *Program availability:* Part-time. Offers civil engineering (MS); computer and electrical engineering (PhD); computer science (MS); computer science and informatics (PhD); computing (PhD); electrical engineering (MS); engineering (PhD); engineering and construction management (Graduate Certificate); mechanical engineering (MS); telecommunications and computer networking (PhD). PhD (interdisciplinary) offered through the School of Graduate Studies.

School of Dentistry Offers advanced education in dentistry (Graduate Dental Certificate); dental hygiene education (MS); endodontics (Graduate Dental Certificate); oral and maxillofacial surgery (Graduate Dental Certificate); oral biology (MS, PhD); orthodontics and dentofacial orthopedics (Graduate Dental Certificate); periodontics (Graduate Dental Certificate). PhD (interdisciplinary) offered through the School of Graduate Studies.

School of Education *Program availability:* Part-time, evening/weekend. Offers administration (Ed D); counseling and guidance (MA, Ed S); counseling psychology (PhD); curriculum and instruction (MA, Ed S); education (PhD); educational administration (MA, Ed S); reading education (MA); special education (MA). PhD in education offered through the School of Graduate Studies.

School of Graduate Studies Offers interdisciplinary studies (PhD). Electronic applications accepted.

School of Law *Program availability:* Part-time. Offers law (LL M, JD). Electronic applications accepted.

School of Medicine Offers health professions education (MS).

School of Nursing and Health Studies *Program availability:* Part-time, online learning. Offers adult clinical nurse specialist (MSN); adult clinical nursing practice (DNP); clinical nursing practice (DNP); neonatal nurse practitioner (MSN); nurse educator (MSN); nurse executive (MSN); nursing practice (DNP); pediatric clinical nursing practice (DNP); pediatric nurse practitioner (MSN).

School of Pharmacy *Program availability:* Online learning. Offers pharmacy (PhD, Pharm D). PhD offered through School of Graduate Studies. Electronic applications accepted.

UNIVERSITY OF MISSOURI–ST. LOUIS, St. Louis, MO 63121

General Information State-supported, coed, university. CGS member. *Enrollment:* 16,740 graduate, professional, and undergraduate students; 833 full-time matriculated graduate/professional students (556 women), 1,785 part-time matriculated graduate/professional students (1,204 women). *Enrollment by degree level:* 1,814 master's, 602 doctoral, 202 other advanced degrees. *Graduate faculty:* 387 full-time (180 women), 199 part-time/adjunct (118 women). Tuition, state resident: part-time $476.50 per credit hour. Tuition, nonresident: part-time $1169.70 per credit hour. *Graduate housing:* Rooms and/or apartments available on a first-come, first-served basis to single and married students. Housing application deadline: 7/1. *Student services:* Campus employment opportunities, campus safety program, career counseling, child daycare facilities, exercise/wellness program, free psychological counseling, grant writing training, international student services, low-cost health insurance, multicultural affairs office, services for students with disabilities, teacher training. *Library facilities:* Thomas Jefferson Library plus 1 other. *Collection:* Books: 1.3 million (physical), 206,616 (digital/electronic); Serial titles: 990 (physical), 1,295 (digital/electronic); Databases: 195. Weekly public service hours: 82; students can reserve study rooms. *Research affiliation:* Express Scripts (business), St. Louis Zoo (biology), Missouri Botanical Garden (biology), Donald Danforth Plant Science Center (biology).

Computer facilities: Computer purchase and lease plans are available. 1,391 computers available on campus for general student use. A campuswide network can be accessed from student residence rooms and from off campus. Online class registration is available.
Website: http://www.umsl.edu/

General Application Contact: Graduate Admissions, 314-516-5458, Fax: 314-516-6996, E-mail: gradadm@umsl.edu.

GRADUATE UNITS

College of Arts and Sciences Students: 310 full-time (172 women), 274 part-time (129 women); includes 84 minority (37 Black or African American, non-Hispanic/Latino; 3 American Indian or Alaska Native, non-Hispanic/Latino; 21 Asian, non-Hispanic/Latino; 12 Hispanic/Latino; 3 Native Hawaiian or other Pacific Islander, non-Hispanic/Latino; 8 Two or more races, non-Hispanic/Latino), 108 international. 597 applicants, 42% accepted, 122 enrolled. *Faculty:* 215 full-time (83 women), 56 part-time/adjunct (18 women). Expenses: Contact institution. *Financial support:* Research assistantships with tuition reimbursements, teaching assistantships with tuition reimbursements, career-related internships or fieldwork, Federal Work-Study, health care benefits, and unspecified assistantships available. Support available to part-time students. Financial award applicants required to submit FAFSA. *Program availability:* Part-time, evening/weekend. Offers American politics (MA); applied physics (MS); arts and sciences (MA, MFA, MS, PhD, Certificate); astrophysics (MS); behavioral neuroscience (MA, PhD); biochemistry and biotechnology (MS); biology (MS, PhD, Certificate); chemistry (MS, PhD); clinical psychology (PhD); communication (MA); comparative politics (MA); computer science (MS); creative writing (MFA); criminology and criminal justice (MA, PhD); economics (MA); English (MA); history (MA); history education (Certificate); international politics (MA); mathematical and computational sciences (PhD); mathematics (MA); museum studies (MA, Certificate); philosophy (MA); physics (PhD); political process and behavior (MA); political science (PhD); public administration and public policy (MA); trauma studies (Certificate); urban and regional politics (MA). *Application deadline:* For fall admission, 7/1 for domestic and international students; for spring admission, 12/1 for domestic and international students. *Application fee:* $50 ($40 for international students). Electronic applications accepted. *Application Contact:* Graduate Admissions, 314-516-5458, Fax: 314-516-6996, E-mail: gradadm@umsl.edu. *Interim Dean,* Dr. Teresa Thiel, 314-516-5501, E-mail: thielt@usml.edu.

College of Business Administration Students: 146 full-time (77 women), 326 part-time (143 women); includes 82 minority (32 Black or African American, non-Hispanic/Latino; 1 American Indian or Alaska Native, non-Hispanic/Latino; 34 Asian, non-Hispanic/Latino; 11 Hispanic/Latino; 4 Two or more races, non-Hispanic/Latino), 89 international. 276 applicants, 83% accepted, 142 enrolled. *Faculty:* 51 full-time (21 women), 25 part-time/adjunct (5 women). Expenses: Contact institution. *Financial support:* Research assistantships with tuition reimbursements, teaching assistantships with tuition reimbursements, career-related internships or fieldwork, Federal Work-Study, and institutionally sponsored loans available. Support available to part-time students. Financial award application deadline: 4/1; financial award applicants required to submit FAFSA. *Program availability:* Part-time, evening/weekend. Offers accounting (M Acc); business administration (MBA, DBA, PhD, Certificate); business intelligence (Certificate); cybersecurity (Certificate); digital and social media marketing (Certificate); human resources management (Certificate); information systems (MS); logistics and supply chain management (Certificate); marketing management (Certificate). *Application deadline:* For fall admission, 7/1 priority date for domestic and international students; for spring admission, 12/1 priority date for domestic and international students. Applications are processed on a rolling basis. *Application fee:* $50 ($40 for international students). Electronic applications accepted. *Application Contact:* 314-516-5458, Fax: 314-516-6996, E-mail: gradadm@umsl.edu. *Dean*, Charles E. Hoffman, 314-516-6109, Fax: 314-516-6420.

College of Education Students: 226 full-time (179 women), 910 part-time (700 women); includes 309 minority (217 Black or African American, non-Hispanic/Latino; 5 American Indian or Alaska Native, non-Hispanic/Latino; 21 Asian, non-Hispanic/Latino; 53 Hispanic/Latino; 13 Two or more races, non-Hispanic/Latino), 12 international. 456 applicants, 88% accepted, 286 enrolled. *Faculty:* 69 full-time (41 women), 93 part-time/adjunct (76 women). Expenses: Contact institution. *Financial support:* Research assistantships with tuition reimbursements and teaching assistantships with tuition reimbursements available. Financial award application deadline: 4/1; financial award applicants required to submit FAFSA. *Program availability:* Part-time, evening/weekend. Offers adult and higher education (M Ed); counseling (PhD); education (M Ed, Ed D, PhD, Certificate, Ed S); educational leadership and policy studies (PhD); educational psychology (M Ed, PhD); elementary education (M Ed); leadership in educational practice (Ed D); program evaluation (Certificate); school psychology (Ed S); secondary education (M Ed); special education (M Ed); teaching-learning processes (PhD). *Application deadline:* For fall admission, 7/1 priority date for domestic and international students; for spring admission, 12/1 priority date for domestic and international students. Applications are processed on a rolling basis. *Application fee:* $50 ($40 for international students). Electronic applications accepted. *Application Contact:* 314-516-5458, Fax: 314-516-6996, E-mail: gradadm@umsl.edu. *Dean*, Ann Taylor, 314-516-5109, Fax: 314-516-5227, E-mail: taylorann@umsl.edu.

College of Nursing Students: 47 full-time (44 women), 162 part-time (152 women); includes 53 minority (37 Black or African American, non-Hispanic/Latino; 10 Asian, non-Hispanic/Latino; 4 Hispanic/Latino; 2 Two or more races, non-Hispanic/Latino), 3 international. 112 applicants, 93% accepted, 70 enrolled. *Faculty:* 24 full-time (22 women), 12 part-time/adjunct (11 women). Expenses: Contact institution. *Financial support:* Research assistantships with tuition reimbursements available. Financial award application deadline: 4/1; financial award applicants required to submit FAFSA. *Program availability:* Part-time. Offers adult/geriatric nurse practitioner (Post Master's Certificate); family nurse practitioner (Post Master's Certificate); nursing (DNP, PhD); pediatric acute care nurse practitioner (Post Master's Certificate); pediatric nurse practitioner (Post Master's Certificate); psychiatric-mental health nurse practitioner (Post Master's Certificate); women's health nurse practitioner (Post Master's Certificate). *Application deadline:* For fall admission, 2/15 for domestic and international students. *Application fee:* $50 ($40 for international students). Electronic applications accepted. *Application Contact:* 314-516-5458, Fax: 314-516-6996, E-mail: gradadm@umsl.edu. *Dean*, Sue Dean-Baar, 314-516-6066.

College of Optometry Students: 172 full-time (103 women); includes 18 minority (2 Black or African American, non-Hispanic/Latino; 13 Asian, non-Hispanic/Latino; 3 Hispanic/Latino), 4 international. Average age 23. 403 applicants, 26% accepted, 49 enrolled. *Faculty:* 19 full-time (12 women), 13 part-time/adjunct (5 women). Expenses: Contact institution. *Financial support:* Fellowships with full tuition reimbursements, research assistantships, Federal Work-Study, institutionally sponsored loans, and scholarships/grants available. Financial award applicants required to submit FAFSA. Offers optometry (OD). *Application deadline:* For fall admission, 2/15 for domestic and international students. Applications are processed on a rolling basis. *Application fee:* $50. Electronic applications accepted. *Application Contact:* Nick Palisch, Director, Student and Alumni Services, 314-516-6263, Fax: 314-516-6708, E-mail: optstuaff@umsl.edu. *Dean*, Dr. Larry J. Davis, 314-516-5606, Fax: 314-516-6708, E-mail: optometry@umsl.edu.

Graduate School Students: 14 full-time (6 women), 48 part-time (29 women); includes 18 minority (11 Black or African American, non-Hispanic/Latino; 4 Asian, non-Hispanic/Latino; 1 Hispanic/Latino; 2 Two or more races, non-Hispanic/Latino). 49 applicants, 82% accepted, 20 enrolled. *Faculty:* 2 full-time (1 woman), 4 part-time/adjunct (3 women). Expenses: Contact institution. *Financial support:* Research assistantships with full tuition reimbursements available. Financial award application deadline: 4/1; financial award applicants required to submit FAFSA. *Program availability:* Part-time, evening/weekend. Offers local government management (MPPA, Certificate); nonprofit management and leadership (MPPA, Certificate); policy and program evaluation (MPPA, Certificate). *Application deadline:* For fall admission, 7/1 priority date for domestic and international students; for spring admission, 12/1 priority date for domestic and international students. Applications are processed on a rolling basis. *Application fee:* $50 ($40 for international students). Electronic applications accepted. *Application Contact:* Graduate Admissions, 314-516-5458, Fax: 314-516-6996, E-mail: gradadm@umsl.edu. *Vice Provost for Graduate Studies and Research*, Christopher Spilling, 314-516-5437, Fax: 314-516-7015, E-mail: graduate@umsl.edu.

School of Social Work Students: 90 full-time (78 women), 65 part-time (51 women); includes 36 minority (27 Black or African American, non-Hispanic/Latino; 1 Asian, non-Hispanic/Latino; 4 Hispanic/Latino; 1 Native Hawaiian or other Pacific Islander, non-Hispanic/Latino; 3 Two or more races, non-Hispanic/Latino), 1 international. 118 applicants, 68% accepted, 62 enrolled. *Faculty:* 13 full-time (8 women), 3 part-time/adjunct (2 women). Expenses: Contact institution. *Financial support:* Research assistantships with tuition reimbursements, teaching assistantships with tuition reimbursements, and scholarships/grants available. Financial award applicants required to submit FAFSA. *Program availability:* Part-time. Offers social work (MSW). *Application deadline:* For fall admission, 3/1 for domestic and international students; for spring admission, 10/15 for domestic and international students. *Application fee:* $50 ($40 for international students). Electronic applications accepted. *Application Contact:* 314-516-5458, Fax: 314-516-6996, E-mail: gradadm@umsl.edu. *Dean*, Sharon Johnson, 314-516-6385, Fax: 314-516-5816, E-mail: socialwork@umsl.edu.

UNIVERSITY OF MOBILE, Mobile, AL 36613

General Information Independent-religious, coed, comprehensive institution. *Graduate housing:* Room and/or apartments available on a first-come, first-served basis to single students; on-campus housing not available to married students. Housing application deadline: 8/15. *Student services:* Campus employment opportunities, career counseling, free psychological counseling, international student services, low-cost health insurance. *Library facilities:* J. L. Bedsole Library. *Collection:* Books: 66,089 (physical), 157,420 (digital/electronic); Serial titles: 153 (physical), 151,115 (digital/electronic); Databases: 80.

Computer facilities: 100 computers available on campus for general student use. A campuswide network can be accessed. Online class registration is available.
Website: http://www.umobile.edu/

General Application Contact: Brian Boyle, Director of Recruitment, 251-442-2727, Fax: 251-442-2523.

GRADUATE UNITS

Graduate Studies Expenses: Contact institution. *Financial support:* Application deadline: 8/1; applicants required to submit FAFSA. *Program availability:* Part-time, evening/weekend, online learning. Offers biblical and theological studies (MA); business administration (MBA); education (MA); education/administration (MSN); higher education leadership and policy (M Ed); marriage and family counseling (MA); nurse practitioner (DNP); piano performance (MM); vocal performance (MM, DMA); worship leadership and theology (MA). *Application deadline:* For fall admission, 8/1 priority date for domestic and international students. Applications are processed on a rolling basis. *Application fee:* $40 ($50 for international students). Electronic applications accepted. *Application Contact:* Brian Boyle, Director of Recruitment, 251-442-2727, Fax: 251-442-2523.

UNIVERSITY OF MONTANA, Missoula, MT 59812

General Information State-supported, coed, university. CGS member. *Graduate housing:* Rooms and/or apartments available on a first-come, first-served basis to single and married students. *Research affiliation:* Arthur Carhart National Wilderness Training Center (environmental research), Nature Center at Ft. Missoula Museum (environmental research), Rocky Mountain National Laboratories (medical research), Community Hospital Medical Center (medical research), Aldo Leopold Wilderness Institute (forestry).

GRADUATE UNITS

Alexander Blewett III School of Law Offers law (JD).

Graduate School *Program availability:* Part-time. Offers individualized interdisciplinary studies (PhD); interdisciplinary studies (MIS).

College of Forestry and Conservation Offers fish and wildlife biology (PhD); forest and conservation sciences (PhD); forestry (MS); recreation management (MS); resource conservation (MS); systems ecology (MS, PhD); wildlife biology (MS).

College of Health Professions and Biomedical Sciences Offers biomedical and pharmaceutical sciences (MS, PhD); biomedical sciences (PhD); health professions and biomedical sciences (MPH, MS, MSW, DPT, PhD, Pharm D, CPH); medicinal chemistry (MS, PhD); molecular and cellular toxicology (MS, PhD); neuroscience (PhD); pharmaceutical sciences (MS); pharmacy (Pharm D); physical therapy (DPT); public health (MPH, CPH); social work (MSW).

College of Humanities and Sciences *Program availability:* Part-time. Offers anthropology (MA, PhD); applied anthropology (PhD); applied medical anthropology (MA); cellular and developmental biology (PhD); cellular, molecular and microbial biology (PhD); chemistry (MS, PhD); clinical psychology (PhD); communication studies (MA); community and environmental planning (MA); computer science (MS); creative writing (MFA); criminology (MA); cultural heritage (MA, PhD); economics (MA); environmental studies (MS); experimental psychology (PhD); fiction (MFA); forensic anthropology (MA); French (MA); geography (MA, MS); geosciences (MS, PhD); German (MA); history (MA, PhD); humanities and sciences (MA, MFA, MPA, MS, PhD, Ed S); inequality and social justice (MA); linguistic anthropology (MA); linguistics (MA); literature (MA); mathematics (MA, PhD); mathematics education (MA); microbial evolution and ecology (PhD); microbiology and immunology (PhD); molecular biology and biochemistry (PhD); non-fiction (MFA); organismal biology and ecology (MS, PhD); philosophy (MA); poetry (MFA); political science (MA); public administration (MPA); rural and environmental change (MA); school psychology (MA, PhD, Ed S); sociology (MA); Spanish (MA); systems ecology (MS, PhD); teaching (MA).

College of Visual and Performing Arts Offers design/technology (MFA); digital filmmaking (MFA); fine arts (MA); integrated arts and education (MA); integrated digital media (MFA); performance (MM); photography (MFA); theatre (MA); visual and performing arts (MA, MFA, MM).

Phyllis J. Washington College of Education and Human Sciences *Program availability:* Part-time. Offers clinical mental health counseling (MA); community health (MS); counseling and supervision (Ed D); counselor education (Ed S); curriculum and instruction (M Ed, Ed D); early childhood education (M Ed); education (MA); education and human sciences (M Ed, MA, MS, Ed D, Ed S); educational leadership (M Ed, Ed D, Ed S); exercise science (MS); health and human performance generalist (MS); intercultural youth and family development (MA); school counseling (MA); speech-language pathology (MS, Postbaccalaureate Certificate); teaching and learning (PhD).

School of Business Administration *Program availability:* Part-time, evening/weekend, online learning. Offers accounting (M Acct); business administration (M Acct, MBA).

School of Journalism Offers journalism (MA). Electronic applications accepted.

UNIVERSITY OF MONTEVALLO, Montevallo, AL 35115

General Information State-supported, coed, comprehensive institution. *Enrollment:* 2,717 graduate, professional, and undergraduate students; 157 full-time matriculated graduate/professional students (129 women), 194 part-time matriculated graduate/professional students (142 women). Tuition, state resident: full-time $9888. Tuition, nonresident: full-time $21,144. *Required fees:* $1920. *Graduate housing:* Rooms and/or apartments guaranteed to single students and available on a first-come, first-served basis to married students. Typical cost: $7612 (including board) for single students. *Student services:* Campus employment opportunities, campus safety program, career counseling, free psychological counseling, international student services, low-cost health insurance, services for students with disabilities, writing training. *Library facilities:* Carmichael Library. *Collection:* Students can reserve study rooms.

Computer facilities: 340 computers available on campus for general student use. A campuswide network can be accessed from student residence rooms and from off campus. Online class registration is available.
Website: http://www.montevallo.edu/

GRADUATE UNITS

College of Arts and Sciences Students: 51 full-time (all women), 5 part-time (4 women); includes 3 minority (2 Black or African American, non-Hispanic/Latino; 1 Hispanic/Latino). Expenses: Contact institution. *Financial support:* Federal Work-Study, scholarships/grants, and unspecified assistantships available. *Program availability:* Part-time, evening/weekend. Offers arts and sciences (MA, MS); communication science and disorders (MS); English (MA). *Application deadline:* For fall admission, 7/15 for domestic students; for spring admission, 11/15 for domestic students. *Application fee:* $30. *Application Contact:* Tonja Battle, Administrative Assistant, 205-665-6508, E-mail: battletl@montevallo.edu. *Dean*, Dr. Mary Beth Armstrong, 205-665-6508.

College of Education Students: 92 full-time (72 women), 164 part-time (121 women); includes 54 minority (41 Black or African American, non-Hispanic/Latino; 7 Hispanic/Latino; 6 Two or more races, non-Hispanic/Latino). Expenses: Contact institution. *Financial support:* Federal Work-Study, scholarships/grants, and unspecified assistantships available. *Program availability:* Part-time, evening/weekend. Offers counseling (M Ed); education (M Ed, Ed S); educational administration (M Ed, Ed S); elementary education (M Ed); secondary/high school education (M Ed). *Application deadline:* For fall admission, 7/15 for domestic students; for spring admission, 11/15 for domestic students. *Application fee:* $30. *Application Contact:* Colleen Kennedy, Graduate Program Assistant, 205-665-6350, E-mail: ckennedy@montevallo.edu. *Interim Dean*, Dr. Charlotte Daughhetee, 205-665-6360, E-mail: daughc@montevallo.edu.

Stephens College of Business Students: 14 full-time (6 women), 25 part-time (17 women); includes 7 minority (3 Black or African American, non-Hispanic/Latino; 1 Asian, non-Hispanic/Latino; 2 Hispanic/Latino; 1 Two or more races, non-Hispanic/Latino), 3 international. Expenses: Contact institution. *Program availability:* Part-time, evening/weekend. Offers business (MBA). *Application deadline:* For fall admission, 7/15 for domestic students; for spring admission, 11/15 for domestic students. *Application fee:* $30. *Application Contact:* 205-665-6540, E-mail: scob@montevallo.edu. *Dean*, Dr. Stephen H. Craft, 205-665-6540, E-mail: scob@montevallo.edu.

UNIVERSITY OF MOUNT OLIVE, Mount Olive, NC 28365

General Information Independent-religious, coed, comprehensive institution.

GRADUATE UNITS

Graduate Programs *Program availability:* Online learning.

UNIVERSITY OF MOUNT UNION, Alliance, OH 44601-3993

General Information Independent-religious, coed, comprehensive institution. *Enrollment:* 2,257 graduate, professional, and undergraduate students; 161 full-time matriculated graduate/professional students (107 women), 1 (woman) part-time matriculated graduate/professional student. *Enrollment by degree level:* 104 master's, 58 doctoral. *Graduate faculty:* 13 full-time (8 women), 4 part-time/adjunct (3 women). *Graduate housing:* Rooms and/or apartments available on a first-come, first-served basis to single and married students. Typical cost: $5000 per year for single students; $10,000 per year for married students. Room charges vary according to board plan and housing facility selected. Housing application deadline: 4/13. *Student services:* Campus safety program, career counseling, exercise/wellness program, international student services, low-cost health insurance, multicultural affairs office, services for students with disabilities, writing training. *Library facilities:* University of Mount Union Library plus 1 other. *Collection:* Books: 327,033 (physical), 423,723 (digital/electronic); Serial titles: 2,492 (physical), 60,137 (digital/electronic); Databases: 226. Study areas open 24 hours, 5–7 days a week; students can reserve study rooms.

Computer facilities: Computer purchase and lease plans are available. 265 computers available on campus for general student use. A campuswide network can be accessed from student residence rooms and from off campus. Online class registration is available.
Website: http://www.mountunion.edu/

General Application Contact: Jess Canavan, Director of Admissions, 330-823-2579, E-mail: canavajl@mountunion.edu.

GRADUATE UNITS

Program in Educational Leadership Students: 27 full-time (18 women), 1 (woman) part-time; includes 2 minority (both Hispanic/Latino). Average age 29. *Faculty:* 1 (woman) full-time, 2 part-time/adjunct (both women). Expenses: Contact institution. *Financial support:* Applicants required to submit FAFSA. In 2017, 11 master's awarded. *Program availability:* Part-time, online only, 100% online. Offers educational leadership (MA). *Application deadline:* For fall admission, 7/31 for domestic and international students; for summer admission, 4/30 for domestic and international students. Applications are processed on a rolling basis. *Application fee:* $30. Electronic applications accepted. *Application Contact:* Eric Young, Director of Admission, 330-829-8238, E-mail: younger@mountunion.edu. *Director*, Dr. Mandy Capel, 330-829-8159, E-mail: capelml@mountunion.edu.

Program in Physical Therapy Students: 58 full-time (33 women); includes 6 minority (2 Black or African American, non-Hispanic/Latino; 2 Asian, non-Hispanic/Latino; 1 Hispanic/Latino; 1 Two or more races, non-Hispanic/Latino). Average age 24. 190 applicants, 22% accepted, 30 enrolled. *Faculty:* 7 full-time (4 women), 4 part-time/adjunct (1 woman). Expenses: Contact institution. *Financial support:* Applicants required to submit FAFSA. Offers physical therapy (DPT). *Application deadline:* For fall admission, 10/2 for domestic and international students. Electronic applications accepted. *Application Contact:* Brandon Crites, Admission Representative, 330-823-2587, E-mail: critesbr@mountunion.edu. *Director*, Dr. Robert Frampton, 330-823-4786, E-mail: framptrm@mountunion.edu.

Program in Physician Assistant Studies Students: 76 full-time (56 women); includes 4 minority (2 Asian, non-Hispanic/Latino; 2 Two or more races, non-Hispanic/Latino). Average age 24. 273 applicants, 18% accepted, 40 enrolled. *Faculty:* 5 full-time (3 women), 3 part-time/adjunct (2 women). Expenses: Contact institution. *Financial support:* Applicants required to submit FAFSA. In 2017, 28 master's awarded. Offers physician assistant studies (MS). *Application deadline:* For summer admission, 10/1 for domestic and international students. Electronic applications accepted. *Application Contact:* Laurie Scarpitti, Admission Representative, 330-823-2419, E-mail: scarpill@mountunion.edu. *Director*, Betsy Ekey, 330-829-8954, E-mail: ekeybd@mountunion.edu.

UNIVERSITY OF NEBRASKA AT KEARNEY, Kearney, NE 68849-0001

General Information State-supported, coed, comprehensive institution. CGS member. *Graduate housing:* Room and/or apartments available on a first-come, first-served basis to single students; on-campus housing not available to married students. Housing application deadline: 6/15.

GRADUATE UNITS

College of Business and Technology *Program availability:* Part-time, evening/weekend. Offers accounting (MBA); business and technology (MBA); generalist (MBA); human resources (MBA); human services (MBA); marketing (MBA). Electronic applications accepted.

College of Education *Program availability:* Part-time, evening/weekend, 100% online. Offers clinical mental health counseling (MS Ed); curriculum and instruction (MA Ed); curriculum supervisor of academic area (MA Ed); education (MA Ed, MS Ed, Ed S); general physical education (MA Ed); instructional technology (MS Ed); physical education exercise science (MA Ed); physical education master teacher (MA Ed); reading PK-12 (MA Ed); school counseling (MS Ed); school principalship 7-12 (MA Ed); school principalship PK-8 (MA Ed); school psychology (Ed S); school superintendent (Ed S); special education (MA Ed); speech/language pathology (MS Ed); student affairs (MS Ed); supervisor of special education (MA Ed). Electronic applications accepted.

College of Fine Arts and Humanities *Program availability:* Part-time, evening/weekend, 100% online. Offers art education (MA Ed); creative writing (MA); fine arts and humanities (MA, MA Ed); literature (MA); music education (MA Ed); Spanish education (MA Ed); writing (MA). Electronic applications accepted.

College of Natural and Social Sciences *Program availability:* Part-time, evening/weekend, online learning. Offers biology (MS); history (MA); natural and social sciences (MA, MA Ed, MS); science/math education (MA Ed). Electronic applications accepted.

UNIVERSITY OF NEBRASKA AT OMAHA, Omaha, NE 68182

General Information State-supported, coed, university. CGS member. *Graduate housing:* Room and/or apartments available on a first-come, first-served basis to single students; on-campus housing not available to married students.

GRADUATE UNITS

Graduate Studies *Program availability:* Part-time, evening/weekend, online learning. Electronic applications accepted.

College of Arts and Sciences *Program availability:* Part-time, evening/weekend, online learning. Offers advanced writing (Certificate); American government (Certificate); applied behavior analysis (Certificate); arts and sciences (MA, MAT, MS, PhD, Certificate, Ed S); biology (MS); business for bioscientists (Certificate); critical and creative thinking (MA); English (MA); geographic information science (Certificate); geography (MA); global information operations (Certificate); history (MA); human resources and training (Certificate); industrial/organizational psychology (MS); intelligence and national security (Certificate); language teaching (MA); mathematics (MA, MAT, MS); political science (MS); psychology (MA, PhD); school psychology (MS, Ed S); sociology (MA); teaching English to speakers of other languages (Certificate); technical communication (Certificate). Electronic applications accepted.

College of Business Administration *Program availability:* Part-time, evening/weekend. Offers accounting (M Acc); business administration (MBA); business for bioscientists (Certificate); economics (MA, MS); executive business administration (EMBA); human resources and training (Certificate). Electronic applications accepted.

College of Communication, Fine Arts and Media *Program availability:* Part-time, evening/weekend. Offers arts (MA); communication (MA); communication, fine arts and media (MA, MFA, MM, Certificate); human resources and training (Certificate); music (MM); technical communication (Certificate); writing (MFA). Electronic applications accepted.

College of Education *Program availability:* Part-time, evening/weekend. Offers athletic training (MA); counseling (MA, MS); education (MA, MS, Ed D, PhD, Certificate, Ed S); educational administration and supervision (Ed D); educational leadership (MS, Ed S); elementary education (MS); exercise science (PhD); health, physical education, and recreation (MA, MS); instruction in urban schools (Certificate); secondary education (MS, Certificate); special education (MS); speech-language pathology (MS). Electronic applications accepted.

College of Information Science and Technology *Program availability:* Part-time, evening/weekend. Offers artificial intelligence (Certificate); biomedical informatics (MS, PhD); communication networks (Certificate); computer science (MA, MS); computer science education (MS, Certificate); data analytics (Certificate); information assurance (MS, Certificate); information science and technology (MA, MIT, MS, PhD, Certificate); information technology (MIT, PhD); management information systems (MS); project management (Certificate); software engineering (Certificate); system and architecture (Certificate); systems analysis and design (Certificate). Electronic applications accepted.

College of Public Affairs and Community Service *Program availability:* Part-time, evening/weekend, online learning. Offers criminology and criminal justice (MA, MS, PhD); gerontology (PhD, Certificate); managing juvenile and adult populations (Certificate); public administration (MPA, PhD); public affairs and community service (MA, MPA, MS, MSW, PhD, Certificate); public management (Certificate); social gerontology (MA); social work (MSW); urban studies (MS). Electronic applications accepted.

UNIVERSITY OF NEBRASKA–LINCOLN, Lincoln, NE 68588

General Information State-supported, coed, university. CGS member. *Graduate housing:* Rooms and/or apartments available on a first-come, first-served basis to single and married students. Housing application deadline: 7/1. *Research affiliation:* U.S. Department of Agriculture (USDA), U.S. Department of Defense, NASA, National Science Foundation, National Institutes of Health, U.S. Meat Animal Research Center.

GRADUATE UNITS

College of Law Offers law (JD); legal studies (MLS); space and telecommunications law (LL M). Electronic applications accepted.

Graduate College *Program availability:* Part-time, evening/weekend, online learning. Offers environmental health, occupational health and toxicology (MS, PhD); survey research and methodology (MS, PhD). Electronic applications accepted.

College of Agricultural Sciences and Natural Resources Offers agribusiness (MBA); agricultural economics (MS, PhD); agricultural sciences and natural resources (M Ag, MA, MBA, MS, PhD); agronomy (MS, PhD); animal science (MS, PhD); biochemistry (MS, PhD); community development (M Ag); entomology (MS, PhD); food science and technology (MS, PhD); geography (PhD); horticulture (MS, PhD); leadership development (MS); leadership education (MS); mechanized systems management (MS); natural resources (MS, PhD); nutrition (MS, PhD); statistics (MS, PhD); teaching and extension education (MS); veterinary science (MS). Electronic applications accepted.

College of Architecture Offers architecture (M Arch, MS, PhD); community and regional planning (MCRP); interior design (MS). Electronic applications accepted.

College of Arts and Sciences Offers analytical chemistry (PhD); anthropology (MA); arts and sciences (M Sc T, MA, MAT, MS, PhD, Graduate Certificate); astronomy (MS, PhD); biochemistry (PhD); bioinformatics (MS, PhD); biological sciences (MA, MS, PhD); biopsychology (PhD); chemistry (MS); classics and religious studies (MA); clinical psychology (PhD); cognitive psychology (PhD); composition and rhetoric (MA, PhD); computer engineering (MS, PhD); computer science (MS, PhD); creative writing (MA, PhD); developmental psychology (PhD); French (MA, PhD); geography (MA, PhD); geosciences (MS, PhD); German (MA, PhD); history (MA, PhD); information technology (PhD); inorganic chemistry (PhD); instructional communication (MA, PhD); interpersonal communication (MA, PhD); literature studies (MA, PhD); marketing, communication studies, and advertising (MA, PhD); materials chemistry (PhD); mathematics (MA, MAT, MS, PhD); mathematics and computer science (PhD); organic chemistry (PhD); organizational communication (MA, PhD); philosophy (MA, PhD); physical chemistry (PhD); physics (MS, PhD); political science (MA, PhD); professional archaeology (MA); psychology (MA); public policy analysis (Graduate Certificate); rhetoric and culture (MA, PhD); social/personality psychology (PhD); sociology (MA, PhD); Spanish (MA, PhD). Electronic applications accepted.

College of Business Administration *Program availability:* Part-time, evening/weekend. Offers accountancy (MPA, PhD); actuarial science (MS); business (MA, MBA, PhD); business administration (MA, MBA, MPA, MS, PhD); economics (MA, PhD); finance (MA, PhD); management (MA, PhD); marketing (MA, PhD). Electronic applications accepted.

College of Education and Human Sciences Offers administration, curriculum and instruction (Ed D, PhD); adult and continuing education (MA); audiology and hearing science (Au D); audiology research (PhD); child development/early childhood education (MS, PhD); child, youth and family studies (MS); clinical audiology (Au D); cognition, learning and development (MA); community nutrition and health promotion (MS); counseling psychology (MA); education and human sciences (M Ed, MA, MS, MST, Au D, Ed D, PhD, Certificate, Ed S); educational administration (M Ed, MA, Ed D, Certificate); educational psychology (MA, Ed S); educational studies (Ed D, PhD); family and consumer sciences education (MS, PhD); family financial planning (MS); family science (MS, PhD); gerontology (PhD); human sciences (PhD); marriage and family therapy (MS); medical family therapy (PhD); merchandising (MS); nutrition (MS, PhD); nutrition and exercise (MS); nutrition and health sciences (MS, PhD); psychological studies in education (PhD); quantitative, qualitative, and psychometric methods (MA); school psychology (MA, Ed S); special education (M Ed, MA, Ed S); speech-language pathology and audiology (MS, Au D); teaching, learning and teacher education (M Ed, MA, MST, Ed D, PhD); textile history/quilt studies (MA); textile science (MS); textile-apparel (MA); textiles, clothing and design (MA, MS); vocational and adult education (M Ed, MA); youth development (MS). Electronic applications accepted.

College of Engineering Offers agricultural and biological systems engineering (MS, PhD); architectural engineering (M Eng, MAE, MS, PhD); biological engineering (PhD); biomedical engineering (PhD); chemical and biomolecular engineering (MS, PhD); civil engineering (MS, PhD); electrical engineering (MS, PhD); engineering (M Eng, MAE, MEE, MS, PhD); engineering management (M Eng); engineering mechanics (MS, PhD); environmental engineering (MS, PhD); industrial and management systems engineering (MS, PhD); manufacturing systems engineering (MS); materials engineering (PhD); mechanical engineering (MS); mechanical engineering and applied mechanics (PhD); mechanized systems management (MS). Electronic applications accepted.

College of Fine and Performing Arts Offers acting (MFA); art history (MA); composition (MM, DMA); conducting (MM, DMA); costume (MFA); directing (MFA); fine and performing arts (MA, MFA, MM, DMA, PhD); music education (MM, PhD); music history (MM); music theory (MM); performance (MM, DMA); piano pedagogy (MM); stage design (MFA); studio art (MFA); woodwind specialties (MM). Electronic applications accepted.

College of Journalism and Mass Communications *Program availability:* Online learning. Offers marketing, communication and advertising (MA); professional journalism (MA). Electronic applications accepted.

UNIVERSITY OF NEBRASKA MEDICAL CENTER, Omaha, NE 68198

General Information State-supported, coed, upper-level institution. CGS member. *Enrollment:* 2,115 full-time matriculated graduate/professional students (1,262 women), 375 part-time matriculated graduate/professional students (280 women). *Enrollment by degree level:* 709 master's, 1,649 doctoral, 111 other advanced degrees. *Graduate faculty:* 1,323 full-time (574 women), 221 part-time/adjunct (134 women). Tuition, state resident: full-time $8451; part-time $4225 per semester. Tuition, nonresident: full-time $24,219; part-time $11,295 per semester. *Required fees:* $589; $117 per term. *Student services:* Campus safety program, child daycare facilities, exercise/wellness program, free psychological counseling, international student services, low-cost health insurance, multicultural affairs office, services for students with disabilities. *Library facilities:* McGoogan Library of Medicine. *Research affiliation:* UNeMed Corporation (biotechnology).

Computer facilities: 120 computers available on campus for general student use. A campuswide network can be accessed from off campus. Online class registration is available.
Website: http://www.unmc.edu/

General Application Contact: Cody Phillips, Graduate Studies Specialist, 402-559-4476, E-mail: cody.phillips@unmc.edu.

GRADUATE UNITS

College of Allied Health Professions Offers allied health professions (MPAS, MPS, DPT, Certificate); cytotechnology (Certificate); dietetic internship (Certificate); distance education perfusion education (MPS); perfusion science (MPS).

Division of Physical Therapy Education Offers physical therapy education (DPT).

Division of Physician Assistant Education Offers physician assistant education (MPAS). Electronic applications accepted.

College of Dentistry Offers dentistry (MS, DDS, PhD, Certificate). Electronic applications accepted.

College of Medicine Offers medicine (MD, Certificate). Electronic applications accepted.

College of Pharmacy Offers pharmacy (Pharm D). Electronic applications accepted.

College of Public Health *Program availability:* Part-time, online learning. Offers public health (MPH). Electronic applications accepted.

Department of Biostatistics Students: 6 full-time (1 woman), 4 part-time (1 woman); includes 2 minority (1 Black or African American, non-Hispanic/Latino; 1 Asian, non-Hispanic/Latino), 3 international. Average age 28. 3 applicants, 100% accepted, 2 enrolled. *Faculty:* 8 full-time (5 women). Expenses: Contact institution. *Financial support:* In 2017–18, 1 research assistantship with full tuition reimbursement (averaging $24,000 per year), 5 teaching assistantships with full tuition reimbursements (averaging $24,000 per year) were awarded; health care benefits and unspecified assistantships also available. Financial award application deadline: 4/1. *Program availability:* Part-time. Offers biostatistics (PhD). *Application deadline:* For fall admission, 6/1 for domestic students, 4/1 for international students. *Application fee:* $60. Electronic applications accepted. *Application Contact:* Dr. Gleb Haynatzki, Graduate Program Director/Professor, 402-559-3294, E-mail: ghaynatzki@unmc.edu. *Campus Director of Assessment, Assistant Dean Graduate Studies, Professor and Chair,* Dr. Kendra Schmid, 402-559-8117, E-mail: kkschmid@unmc.edu.

Department of Epidemiology *Program availability:* Part-time. Offers epidemiology (PhD). Electronic applications accepted.

Department of Health Promotion, Social and Behavioral Health *Program availability:* Part-time. Offers health promotion and disease prevention research (PhD). Electronic applications accepted.

Department of Health Services Research and Administration Students: 9 full-time (7 women), 1 part-time (0 women); includes 2 minority (both Asian, non-Hispanic/Latino), 6 international. Average age 31. 11 applicants, 55% accepted, 3 enrolled. *Faculty:* 7 full-time (4 women), 2 part-time/adjunct (0 women). Expenses: Contact institution. *Financial support:* In 2017–18, 5 students received support. Federal Work-Study, scholarships/grants, and unspecified assistantships available. Financial award application deadline: 2/15; financial award applicants required to submit FAFSA. In 2017, 5 doctorates awarded. *Program availability:* Part-time, 100% online, blended/hybrid learning. Offers health administration (MHA); health services research, administration, and policy (PhD); public health administration and policy (MPH). *Application deadline:* For fall admission, 6/1 for domestic students, 4/1 for international students. *Application fee:* $60. Electronic applications accepted. *Application Contact:* Denise Howard, Coordinator, 402-559-5260, E-mail: denise.howard@unmc.edu. *Associate Professor,* Dr. Fernando Wilson, 402-552-6948, E-mail: fernando.wilson@unmc.edu.

Department of Pharmaceutical Sciences Students: 57 full-time (24 women), 48 international. Average age 29. 72 applicants, 21% accepted, 13 enrolled. *Faculty:* 20 full-time (3 women), 1 part-time/adjunct (0 women). Expenses: Contact institution. *Financial support:* In 2017–18, 95 students received support, including 10 fellowships with full tuition reimbursements available (averaging $25,000 per year), 35 research assistantships with full tuition reimbursements available (averaging $24,500 per year); scholarships/grants and unspecified assistantships also available. Financial award application deadline: 4/1. In 2017, 9 doctorates awarded. Offers pharmaceutical sciences (MS, PhD). *Application deadline:* For fall admission, 6/1 priority date for domestic students, 4/1 priority date for international students; for spring admission, 10/1 for domestic students, 8/1 for international students. Applications are processed on a rolling basis. *Application fee:* $60. Electronic applications accepted. *Application Contact:* Renee Kaszynski, Office Associate, 402-559-5320, E-mail: renee.kaszynski@unmc.edu. *Chair, Pharmaceutical Sciences Graduate Program Committee,* Dr. Ram Mahato, 402-559-5422, E-mail: ram.mahato@unmc.edu.

Environmental Health, Occupational Health and Toxicology Graduate Program Offers environmental health, occupational health and toxicology (PhD). Electronic applications accepted.

Interdisciplinary Graduate Program in Biomedical Sciences Students: 20 full-time (8 women); includes 3 minority (1 Black or African American, non-Hispanic/Latino; 2 Asian, non-Hispanic/Latino), 6 international. Average age 24. 89 applicants, 31% accepted, 20 enrolled. *Faculty:* 222 full-time (60 women). Expenses: Contact institution. *Financial support:* In 2017–18, 20 students received support. Health care benefits, tuition waivers (full), and unspecified assistantships available. Financial award application deadline: 5/15. Offers biochemistry and molecular biology (MS); biomedical sciences (MS, PhD); cancer research (PhD); genetics, cell biology and anatomy (PhD); immunology, pathology and infectious disease (MS, PhD); integrative physiology and molecular medicine (PhD); medical anatomy (MS); molecular genetics and cell biology (MS); pharmacology and experimental neuroscience (PhD). *Application deadline:* For fall admission, 5/15 for domestic students, 3/15 for international students; for summer admission, 2/15 for domestic students, 12/15 for international students. Applications are processed on a rolling basis. Electronic applications accepted. *IGPBS Program Coordinator,* Kimberly Rothgeb, 402-559-3362, Fax: 402-559-5368, E-mail: krothgeb@unmc.edu.

Medical Sciences Interdepartmental Area Students: 48 full-time (31 women), 59 part-time (37 women); includes 34 minority (1 Black or African American, non-Hispanic/Latino; 30 Asian, non-Hispanic/Latino; 3 Hispanic/Latino). Average age 32. 68 applicants, 34% accepted, 23 enrolled. *Faculty:* 170 full-time, 20 part-time/adjunct. Expenses: Contact institution. *Financial support:* In 2017–18, 72 students received support, including 1 fellowship with full tuition reimbursement available (averaging $23,400 per year), 37 research assistantships with full tuition reimbursements available (averaging $23,400 per year), 2 teaching assistantships with full tuition reimbursements available (averaging $23,400 per year); scholarships/grants and health care benefits also available. Financial award application deadline: 2/15; financial award applicants required to submit FAFSA. In 2017, 26 master's, 915 doctorates awarded. *Program availability:* Part-time. Offers applied behavior analysis (PhD); clinical translational research (MS, PhD); health practice and medical education research (MS); oral biology (MS, PhD). *Application deadline:* For fall admission, 6/1 for domestic students, 4/1 for international students; for spring admission, 10/1 for domestic students, 9/1 for international students. Applications are processed on a rolling basis. *Application fee:* $60. Electronic applications accepted. *Application Contact:* Rhonda Sheibal-Carver, Interdisciplinary Programs Coordinator, 402-559-5141, E-mail: rhonda.sheibalcarver@unmc.edu. *Graduate Committee Chair,* Dr. Laura Bilek, 402-559-6923, E-mail: lbilek@unmc.edu.

PhD in Nursing Program Students: 15 full-time (14 women), 6 part-time (all women); includes 3 minority (1 Black or African American, non-Hispanic/Latino; 1 Asian, non-Hispanic/Latino; 1 Hispanic/Latino). Average age 42. 6 applicants, 100% accepted, 6 enrolled. *Faculty:* 19 full-time (13 women), 13 part-time/adjunct (all women). Expenses: Contact institution. *Financial support:* In 2017–18, 10 students received support. Scholarships/grants and unspecified assistantships available. Financial award application deadline: 2/1; financial award applicants required to submit FAFSA. In 2017, 5 doctorates awarded. *Program availability:* Part-time, blended/hybrid learning. Offers nursing (PhD). *Application deadline:* For spring admission, 1/15 for domestic and international students. *Application fee:* $65. Electronic applications accepted. *Application Contact:* Rolee Kelly, Graduate Coordinator, Student Services, 402-559-4120, E-mail: rolee.kelly@unmc.edu. *Professor,* Dr. Carol Pullen, 402-559-6548, E-mail: chpullen@unmc.edu.

Program in Biomedical Informatics Students: 3 full-time (1 woman), 6 part-time (2 women); includes 4 minority (all Asian, non-Hispanic/Latino). Average age 32. *Faculty:* 29 full-time (7 women). Expenses: Contact institution. *Financial support:* In 2017–18, 9 students received support, including 1 fellowship with full tuition reimbursement available (averaging $23,400 per year), 4 research assistantships with full tuition reimbursements available (averaging $23,400 per year); scholarships/grants also available. Financial award application deadline: 2/15; financial award applicants required to submit FAFSA. In 2017, 2 doctorates awarded. *Program availability:* Part-time. Offers biomedical informatics (MS, PhD). *Application deadline:* For fall admission, 6/1 for domestic students, 4/1 for international students; for spring admission, 10/1 for domestic students, 9/1 for international students. Applications are processed on a rolling basis. *Application fee:* $60. Electronic applications accepted. *Application Contact:* Rhonda Sheibal-Carver, Academic Program Coordinator, 402-559-5141, E-mail: rhonda.sheibalcarver@unmc.edu. *Director,* Dr. Jim McClay, 402-559-3587, E-mail: jmcclay@unmc.edu.

Program in Emergency Preparedness *Program availability:* Part-time, 100% online, blended/hybrid learning. Offers emergency preparedness (MS). Electronic applications accepted.

UNIVERSITY OF NEVADA, LAS VEGAS, Las Vegas, NV 89154

General Information State-supported, coed, university. CGS member. *Enrollment:* 30,471 graduate, professional, and undergraduate students; 2,368 full-time matriculated graduate/professional students (1,416 women), 1,367 part-time matriculated graduate/professional students (838 women). *Enrollment by degree level:* 2,586 master's, 1,035 doctoral, 114 other advanced degrees. *Graduate faculty:* 505 full-time

(177 women), 174 part-time/adjunct (98 women). Tuition, state resident: full-time $8904. Tuition, nonresident: full-time $23,376. *Required fees:* $2354. One-time fee: $291 full-time. Tuition and fees vary according to course load, program and reciprocity agreements. *Graduate housing:* Room and/or apartments available on a first-come, first-served basis to single students; on-campus housing not available to married students. Typical cost: $6400 per year ($8700 including board). Room and board charges vary according to board plan. Housing application deadline: 7/1. *Student services:* Campus employment opportunities, campus safety program, career counseling, child daycare facilities, exercise/wellness program, free psychological counseling, grant writing training, international student services, low-cost health insurance, multicultural affairs office, services for students with disabilities, teacher training, writing training. *Library facilities:* Lied Library. *Collection:* Books: 939,652 (physical), 1.3 million (digital/electronic); Serial titles: 20,453 (physical), 59,248 (digital/electronic); Databases: 320. Weekly public service hours: 101; students can reserve study rooms. *Research affiliation:* Tesla (effluent remediation), Teledyne Brown Engineering (aerospace engineering), Eli Lilly and Company (clinical trials), Cryolife (clinical trials), Metawater (water treatment).

Computer facilities: 2,100 computers available on campus for general student use. A campuswide network can be accessed from student residence rooms and from off campus. Online class registration is available.
Website: http://www.unlv.edu/

General Application Contact: Sebern Coleman, Graduate Recruitment and CRM Specialist, 702-895-3423, Fax: 702-895-4180, E-mail: sebern.coleman@unlv.edu.

GRADUATE UNITS

Graduate College Students: 2,368 full-time (1,416 women), 1,367 part-time (838 women); includes 1,331 minority (267 Black or African American, non-Hispanic/Latino; 14 American Indian or Alaska Native, non-Hispanic/Latino; 262 Asian, non-Hispanic/Latino; 560 Hispanic/Latino; 15 Native Hawaiian or other Pacific Islander, non-Hispanic/Latino; 213 Two or more races, non-Hispanic/Latino), 334 international. Average age 33. 2,596 applicants, 58% accepted, 1051 enrolled. *Faculty:* 505 full-time (177 women), 174 part-time/adjunct (98 women). Expenses: Contact institution. *Financial support:* In 2017–18, 1,080 students received support, including 10 fellowships with partial tuition reimbursements available (averaging $19,500 per year), 359 research assistantships with partial tuition reimbursements available (averaging $15,577 per year), 721 teaching assistantships with partial tuition reimbursements available (averaging $15,869 per year); institutionally sponsored loans, scholarships/grants, health care benefits, and unspecified assistantships also available. Financial award application deadline: 3/15; financial award applicants required to submit FAFSA. In 2017, 1,045 master's, 154 doctorates, 52 other advanced degrees awarded. *Program availability:* Part-time. *Application deadline:* For fall admission, 8/1 for domestic students, 5/1 for international students; for spring admission, 11/1 for domestic students, 10/1 for international students. *Application fee:* $60 ($95 for international students). Electronic applications accepted. *Application Contact:* Elizabeth Jost, Senior Admissions Analyst, 702-895-5412, E-mail: elizabeth.jost@unlv.edu. *Dean,* Dr. Kathryn Korgan, 702-895-0446, Fax: 702-895-4180, E-mail: kate.korgan@unlv.edu.

College of Education Students: 691 full-time (525 women), 545 part-time (384 women); includes 509 minority (131 Black or African American, non-Hispanic/Latino; 4 American Indian or Alaska Native, non-Hispanic/Latino; 61 Asian, non-Hispanic/Latino; 231 Hispanic/Latino; 6 Native Hawaiian or other Pacific Islander, non-Hispanic/Latino; 76 Two or more races, non-Hispanic/Latino), 28 international. Average age 35. 582 applicants, 79% accepted, 379 enrolled. *Faculty:* 67 full-time (37 women), 50 part-time/adjunct (38 women). Expenses: Contact institution. *Financial support:* In 2017–18, 120 students received support, including 54 research assistantships with partial tuition reimbursements available (averaging $15,952 per year), 66 teaching assistantships with partial tuition reimbursements available (averaging $18,625 per year); institutionally sponsored loans, scholarships/grants, health care benefits, and unspecified assistantships also available. Financial award application deadline: 3/15; financial award applicants required to submit FAFSA. In 2017, 390 master's, 30 doctorates, 12 other advanced degrees awarded. *Program availability:* Part-time. Offers addiction studies (Advanced Certificate); chief diversity officer in higher education (Certificate); college sport leadership (Certificate); counselor education (M Ed, MS); curriculum and instruction (M Ed, MS, Ed D, PhD, Ed S); early childhood education (M Ed); early childhood special education (Certificate); education (M Ed, MS, Ed D, PhD, Advanced Certificate, Certificate, Ed S); educational psychology (M Ed, MS, PhD, Ed S); elementary teaching (Certificate); English language learning (M Ed); higher education (M Ed, PhD, Certificate); mental health counseling (Advanced Certificate); online teaching and training (Certificate); psychology/learning and technology (PhD); secondary teaching (Certificate); social justice studies (Certificate); special education (M Ed, PhD); teaching and learning (PhD); workforce development/educational leadership (PhD). *Application fee:* $60 ($95 for international students). Electronic applications accepted. *Dean,* Dr. Kim Metcalf, 702-895-3375, Fax: 702-895-4068, E-mail: kim.metcalf@unlv.edu.

College of Fine Arts Students: 149 full-time (82 women), 36 part-time (17 women); includes 61 minority (12 Black or African American, non-Hispanic/Latino; 12 Asian, non-Hispanic/Latino; 29 Hispanic/Latino; 2 Native Hawaiian or other Pacific Islander, non-Hispanic/Latino; 6 Two or more races, non-Hispanic/Latino), 26 international. Average age 33. 144 applicants, 58% accepted, 56 enrolled. *Faculty:* 61 full-time (21 women), 34 part-time/adjunct (9 women). Expenses: Contact institution. *Financial support:* In 2017–18, 100 students received support, including 20 research assistantships with full tuition reimbursements available (averaging $14,592 per year), 80 teaching assistantships with full tuition reimbursements available (averaging $14,306 per year); institutionally sponsored loans, scholarships/grants, health care benefits, and unspecified assistantships also available. Financial award application deadline: 3/15; financial award applicants required to submit FAFSA. In 2017, 45 master's, 17 doctorates, 5 other advanced degrees awarded. *Program availability:* Part-time. Offers architecture (M Arch); art (MFA); film/writing for dramatic media (MFA); fine arts (M Arch, MA, MFA, MHID, MM, DMA, Certificate); healthcare interior design (MHID); hospitality design (Certificate); K-12 music (Certificate); music (MM); musical arts (DMA); theatre (MA, MFA); writing for dramatic media (Certificate). *Application fee:* $60 ($95 for international students). Electronic applications accepted. *Dean/Professor,* Dr. Nancy J. Uscher, 702-895-4210, Fax: 702-895-4194, E-mail: nancy.uscher@unlv.edu.

College of Liberal Arts Students: 231 full-time (129 women), 98 part-time (53 women); includes 89 minority (10 Black or African American, non-Hispanic/Latino; 2 American Indian or Alaska Native, non-Hispanic/Latino; 13 Asian, non-Hispanic/Latino; 43 Hispanic/Latino; 1 Native Hawaiian or other Pacific Islander, non-Hispanic/Latino; 20 Two or more races, non-Hispanic/Latino), 13 international. Average age 33. 394 applicants, 27% accepted, 62 enrolled. *Faculty:* 99 full-time (37 women), 8 part-time/adjunct (6 women). Expenses: Contact institution. *Financial support:* In 2017–18, 5 fellowships with partial tuition reimbursements (averaging $19,000 per year), 52 research assistantships with full tuition reimbursements (averaging $15,721 per year), 162 teaching assistantships with full tuition reimbursements (averaging $15,607 per year) were awarded; institutionally sponsored loans, scholarships/grants, health care benefits, and unspecified assistantships also available. Financial award application deadline: 3/15; financial award applicants required to submit FAFSA. In 2017, 36 master's, 23 doctorates, 3 other advanced degrees awarded. *Program availability:* Part-time. Offers anthropology (MA, PhD); creative writing (MFA); English (MA, PhD); Hispanic studies (MA); history (MA, PhD); liberal arts (MA, MFA, PhD, Certificate); political science (MA, PhD); psychology (MA, PhD, Certificate); sociology (MA, PhD); Spanish translation (Certificate). *Application fee:* $60 ($95 for international students). Electronic applications accepted. *Dean,* Dr. Chris Heavey, 702-895-3401, Fax: 702-895-4097, E-mail: chris.heavey@unlv.edu.

College of Sciences Students: 182 full-time (74 women), 50 part-time (20 women); includes 50 minority (3 Black or African American, non-Hispanic/Latino; 2 American Indian or Alaska Native, non-Hispanic/Latino; 18 Asian, non-Hispanic/Latino; 18 Hispanic/Latino; 9 Two or more races, non-Hispanic/Latino), 40 international. Average age 31. 196 applicants, 34% accepted, 39 enrolled. *Faculty:* 75 full-time (10 women), 4 part-time/adjunct (1 woman). Expenses: Contact institution. *Financial support:* In 2017–18, 188 students received support, including 2 fellowships with partial tuition reimbursements available (averaging $20,000 per year), 48 research assistantships with partial tuition reimbursements available (averaging $18,749 per year), 140 teaching assistantships with partial tuition reimbursements available (averaging $19,424 per year); institutionally sponsored loans, scholarships/grants, health care benefits, and unspecified assistantships also available. Financial award application deadline: 3/15; financial award applicants required to submit FAFSA. In 2017, 27 master's, 11 doctorates awarded. *Program availability:* Part-time. Offers astronomy (MS, PhD); biochemistry (MS); biological sciences (MS, PhD); chemistry (MS, PhD); geoscience (MS, PhD); mathematical sciences (MS, PhD); physics (MS, PhD); radio chemistry (PhD); science (MA); sciences (MA, MS, PhD); water resources management (MS). *Application fee:* $60 ($95 for international students). Electronic applications accepted. *Associate Dean,* Dr. Javier Rodriguez, 702-895-5551, E-mail: javier.rodriguez@unlv.edu.

Greenspun College of Urban Affairs Students: 345 full-time (257 women), 176 part-time (125 women); includes 239 minority (63 Black or African American, non-Hispanic/Latino; 2 American Indian or Alaska Native, non-Hispanic/Latino; 16 Asian, non-Hispanic/Latino; 120 Hispanic/Latino; 4 Native Hawaiian or other Pacific Islander, non-Hispanic/Latino; 34 Two or more races, non-Hispanic/Latino), 11 international. Average age 33. 365 applicants, 64% accepted, 172 enrolled. *Faculty:* 39 full-time (22 women), 27 part-time/adjunct (14 women). Expenses: Contact institution. *Financial support:* In 2017–18, 105 students received support, including 1 fellowship with full and partial tuition reimbursement available (averaging $20,000 per year), 30 research assistantships with full and partial tuition reimbursements available (averaging $13,680 per year), 75 teaching assistantships with full and partial tuition reimbursements available (averaging $13,360 per year); institutionally sponsored loans, scholarships/grants, health care benefits, and unspecified assistantships also available. Financial award application deadline: 3/15; financial award applicants required to submit FAFSA. In 2017, 181 master's, 6 doctorates, 14 other advanced degrees awarded. *Program availability:* Part-time. Offers communication studies (MA); couple and family therapy (MS); criminal justice (MA); criminology and criminal justice (PhD); crisis and emergency management (MS); emergency crisis management cybersecurity (Certificate); environmental science (MS, PhD); journalism and media studies (MA); non-profit management (Certificate); public administration (MPA); public affairs (PhD); public management (Certificate); social work (MSW); urban affairs (MA, MPA, MS, MSW, PhD, Certificate); urban leadership (MA). *Application fee:* $60 ($95 for international students). Electronic applications accepted. *Dean,* Dr. Robert Ulmer, 702-895-0628, E-mail: robert.ulmer@unlv.edu.

Howard R. Hughes College of Engineering Students: 169 full-time (47 women), 95 part-time (24 women); includes 61 minority (6 Black or African American, non-Hispanic/Latino; 1 American Indian or Alaska Native, non-Hispanic/Latino; 22 Asian, non-Hispanic/Latino; 20 Hispanic/Latino; 12 Two or more races, non-Hispanic/Latino), 111 international. Average age 30. 208 applicants, 68% accepted, 73 enrolled. *Faculty:* 56 full-time (9 women), 4 part-time/adjunct (1 woman). Expenses: Contact institution. *Financial support:* In 2017–18, 170 students received support, including 1 fellowship with full and partial tuition reimbursement available (averaging $20,000 per year), 65 research assistantships with full and partial tuition reimbursements available (averaging $15,596 per year), 105 teaching assistantships with full and partial tuition reimbursements available (averaging $15,356 per year); institutionally sponsored loans, scholarships/grants, health care benefits, and unspecified assistantships also available. Financial award application deadline: 3/15; financial award applicants required to submit FAFSA. In 2017, 53 master's, 14 doctorates, 3 other advanced degrees awarded. *Program availability:* Part-time. Offers aerospace engineering (MS); biomedical engineering (MS); civil and environmental engineering (PhD); civil and environmental engineering /transportation (MS); computer science (MS, PhD); construction management (MS); electrical and computer engineering (MS, PhD); engineering (MS, PhD, Certificate); materials and nuclear engineering (MS); mechanical engineering (MS, PhD); nuclear criticality safety (Certificate); nuclear safeguards and security (Certificate); solar and renewable energy (Certificate); transportation (MS). *Application fee:* $60 ($95 for international students). Electronic applications accepted. *Dean,* Dr. Rama Venkat, 702-895-3699, Fax: 702-895-4059, E-mail: rama.venkat@unlv.edu.

Lee Business School Students: 240 full-time (101 women), 141 part-time (59 women); includes 124 minority (16 Black or African American, non-Hispanic/Latino; 47 Asian, non-Hispanic/Latino; 40 Hispanic/Latino; 21 Two or more races, non-Hispanic/Latino), 57 international. Average age 31. 212 applicants, 73% accepted, 109 enrolled. *Faculty:* 40 full-time (9 women), 14 part-time/adjunct (4 women). Expenses: Contact institution. *Financial support:* In 2017–18, 57 students received support, including 23 research assistantships with full and partial tuition reimbursements available (averaging $12,335 per year), 34 teaching assistantships with full and partial tuition reimbursements available (averaging $11,875 per year); institutionally sponsored loans, scholarships/grants, health care benefits, and unspecified assistantships also available. Financial award application deadline: 3/15; financial award applicants required to submit FAFSA. In 2017, 171 master's, 11 other advanced degrees awarded. *Program availability:* Part-time. Offers accountancy (MS); accounting (Advanced Certificate, Certificate); applied economics (MA); business (Exec MBA, MA, MBA, MS, Advanced Certificate, Certificate); business administration (Certificate); data analytics (Certificate); data analytics and applied economics (MS); management (Certificate); management information systems (MS, Certificate); new venture management (Certificate). *Application fee:* $60 ($95 for international students). Electronic applications accepted. *Dean,* Dr. Brent Hathaway, 702-895-3362, Fax: 702-895-4090, E-mail: brent.hathaway@unlv.edu.

School of Allied Health Sciences Students: 173 full-time (75 women), 24 part-time (10 women); includes 57 minority (4 Black or African American, non-Hispanic/Latino; 1 American Indian or Alaska Native, non-Hispanic/Latino; 22 Asian, non-Hispanic/Latino; 19 Hispanic/Latino; 11 Two or more races, non-Hispanic/Latino), 8 international. Average age 28. 82 applicants, 54% accepted, 28 enrolled. *Faculty:* 19 full-time (7 women), 13 part-time/adjunct (8 women). Expenses: Contact institution. *Financial support:* In 2017–18, 49 students received support, including 1 fellowship with full and partial tuition reimbursement available (averaging $20,000 per year), 27 research assistantships with full and partial tuition reimbursements available (averaging $17,009 per year), 22 teaching assistantships with full and partial tuition reimbursements available (averaging $14,239 per year); institutionally sponsored loans, scholarships/grants, health care benefits, and unspecified assistantships also available. Financial award application deadline: 3/15; financial award applicants required to submit FAFSA. In 2017, 19 master's, 33 doctorates awarded. *Program availability:* Part-time. Offers allied health sciences (MS, DMP, DPT, PhD, Advanced Certificate); exercise physiology (MS); health physics (MS); interdisciplinary health sciences (PhD); kinesiology (PhD); medical physics (DMP, Advanced Certificate); nutrition sciences (MS); physical therapy (DPT). *Application fee:* $60 ($95 for international students). Electronic applications accepted. *Dean,* Dr. Ronald T. Brown, 702-895-3693, Fax: 702-895-1356, E-mail: ronald.brown@unlv.edu.

School of Community Health Sciences Students: 82 full-time (58 women), 70 part-time (48 women); includes 66 minority (12 Black or African American, non-Hispanic/Latino; 2 American Indian or Alaska Native, non-Hispanic/Latino; 19 Asian, non-Hispanic/Latino; 22 Hispanic/Latino; 1 Native Hawaiian or other Pacific Islander, non-Hispanic/Latino; 10 Two or more races, non-Hispanic/Latino), 15 international. Average age 32. 97 applicants, 81% accepted, 47 enrolled. *Faculty:* 23 full-time (10 women), 8 part-time/adjunct (6 women). Expenses: Contact institution. *Financial support:* In 2017–18, 40 students received support, including 35 research assistantships with full and partial tuition reimbursements available (averaging $13,724 per year), 5 teaching assistantships with full and partial tuition reimbursements available (averaging $12,957 per year); institutionally sponsored loans, scholarships/grants, health care benefits, and unspecified assistantships also available. Financial award application deadline: 3/15; financial award applicants required to submit FAFSA. In 2017, 39 master's, 3 doctorates, 1 other advanced degree awarded. *Program availability:* Part-time. Offers community health sciences (Exec MHA, MHA, MPH, PhD, Certificate); health care administration (Exec MHA, MHA); infection prevention (Certificate); public health (MPH, PhD, Certificate). *Application fee:* $60 ($95 for international students). Electronic applications accepted. *Dean,* Dr. Shawn Gerstenberger, 702-895-1565, Fax: 702-895-5184, E-mail: shawn.gerstenberger@unlv.edu.

School of Nursing Students: 46 full-time (40 women), 78 part-time (73 women); includes 43 minority (6 Black or African American, non-Hispanic/Latino; 16 Asian, non-Hispanic/Latino; 12 Hispanic/Latino; 9 Two or more races, non-Hispanic/Latino). Average age 37. 185 applicants, 38% accepted, 54 enrolled. *Faculty:* 11 full-time (9 women), 10 part-time/adjunct (all women). Expenses: Contact institution. *Financial support:* In 2017–18, 3 students received support, including 1 research assistantship with partial tuition reimbursement available (averaging $20,250 per year), 2 teaching assistantships with partial tuition reimbursements available (averaging $20,250 per year); institutionally sponsored loans, scholarships/grants, health care benefits, and unspecified assistantships also available. Financial award application deadline: 3/15; financial award applicants required to submit FAFSA. In 2017, 35 master's, 9 doctorates, 3 other advanced degrees awarded. *Program availability:* Part-time, 100% online, blended/hybrid learning. Offers biobehavioral nursing (Advanced Certificate); family nurse practitioner (Advanced Certificate); nursing (MS, DNP, PhD); nursing education (Advanced Certificate). *Application deadline:* For fall admission, 2/1 for domestic students. *Application fee:* $60 ($95 for international students). Electronic applications accepted. *Dean,* Dr. Carolyn Yucha, 702-895-3906, Fax: 702-895-4807, E-mail: carolyn.yucha@unlv.edu.

William F. Harrah College of Hospitality Students: 42 full-time (21 women), 54 part-time (25 women); includes 25 minority (4 Black or African American, non-Hispanic/Latino; 10 Asian, non-Hispanic/Latino; 5 Hispanic/Latino; 1 Native Hawaiian or other Pacific Islander, non-Hispanic/Latino; 5 Two or more races, non-Hispanic/Latino), 23 international. Average age 35. 131 applicants, 50% accepted, 32 enrolled. *Faculty:* 15 full-time (6 women), 2 part-time/adjunct (1 woman). Expenses: Contact institution. *Financial support:* In 2017–18, 34 students received support, including 4 research assistantships with full and partial tuition reimbursements available (averaging $13,438 per year), 30 teaching assistantships with full and partial tuition reimbursements available (averaging $12,768 per year); institutionally sponsored loans, scholarships/grants, health care benefits, and unspecified assistantships also available. Financial award application deadline: 3/15; financial award applicants required to submit FAFSA. In 2017, 44 master's, 8 doctorates awarded. *Program availability:* Part-time, evening/weekend, 100% online, blended/hybrid learning. Offers hospitality administration (MHA, PhD); hotel administration (MS). *Application deadline:* For fall admission, 8/1 for domestic students, 5/1 for international students; for spring admission, 11/15 for domestic students, 10/1 for international students. *Application fee:* $60 ($95 for international students). Electronic applications accepted. *Dean,* Dr. Stowe Shoemaker, 702-895-3308, Fax: 702-895-4109, E-mail: stowe.shoemaker@unlv.edu.

School of Dental Medicine Students: 356 full-time (152 women); includes 118 minority (3 Black or African American, non-Hispanic/Latino; 2 American Indian or Alaska Native, non-Hispanic/Latino; 71 Asian, non-Hispanic/Latino; 23 Hispanic/Latino; 2 Native Hawaiian or other Pacific Islander, non-Hispanic/Latino; 17 Two or more races, non-Hispanic/Latino), 3 international. Average age 28. 1,754 applicants, 7% accepted, 88 enrolled. *Faculty:* 67 full-time (28 women), 57 part-time/adjunct (17 women). Expenses: Contact institution. *Financial support:* In 2017–18, 28 students received support. Federal Work-Study, institutionally sponsored loans, scholarships/grants, health care benefits, and unspecified assistantships available. Support available to part-time students. Financial award application deadline: 3/15; financial award applicants required to submit FAFSA. In 2017, 5 master's, 75 doctorates, 6 other advanced degrees awarded. *Program availability:* Part-time, evening/weekend, online learning. Offers dental medicine (DMD); dental surgery (DDS); dentistry (DMD); oral biology (MS); orthodontics and dentofacial orthopedics (Certificate). *Application deadline:* For fall admission, 1/1 for domestic and international students; for summer admission, 3/1 for domestic students. Applications are processed on a rolling basis. *Application fee:* $75. Electronic applications accepted. *Application Contact:* Kamber Davoren, Admissions and Records Assistant, 702-774-2520, Fax: 702-774-2520, E-mail: kamber.davoren@unlv.edu. *Assistant Dean of Admissions and Student Affairs,* Dr. Christine C. Ancajas, 702-774-2522, Fax: 702-774-2521, E-mail: christine.ancajas@unlv.edu.

William S. Boyd School of Law Students: 315 full-time (157 women), 63 part-time (29 women); includes 140 minority (28 Black or African American, non-Hispanic/Latino; 21 Asian, non-Hispanic/Latino; 71 Hispanic/Latino; 1 Native Hawaiian or other Pacific Islander, non-Hispanic/Latino; 19 Two or more races, non-Hispanic/Latino), 4 international. Average age 30. 643 applicants, 34% accepted, 124 enrolled. *Faculty:* 38 full-time (24 women), 20 part-time/adjunct (4 women). Expenses: Contact institution. *Financial support:* In 2017–18, 252 students received support, including 18 fellowships with partial tuition reimbursements available (averaging $17,950 per year), 26 research assistantships (averaging $503 per year); career-related internships or fieldwork, scholarships/grants, and tuition waivers (full and partial) also available. Support available to part-time students. Financial award application deadline: 5/1; financial award applicants required to submit FAFSA. In 2017, 12 master's, 126 doctorates awarded. *Program availability:* Part-time, evening/weekend. Offers gaming law and regulation (LL M); law (JD). *Application deadline:* For fall admission, 3/15 for domestic students. Applications are processed on a rolling basis. *Application fee:* $50. Electronic applications accepted. *Application Contact:* Lindsey Baker, Administrative Assistant IV, 702-895-2424, Fax: 702-895-2414, E-mail: lindsey.baker@unlv.edu. *Dean,* Daniel W. Hamilton, 702-895-3671, Fax: 702-895-1095, E-mail: christine.smith@unlv.edu.

UNIVERSITY OF NEVADA, RENO, Reno, NV 89557

General Information State-supported, coed, university. CGS member. *Graduate housing:* Rooms and/or apartments available on a first-come, first-served basis to single and married students. Housing application deadline: 5/16. *Research affiliation:* National Institutes of Health (nursing), Desert Research Institute (natural resource sciences, environmental sciences).

GRADUATE UNITS

Graduate School *Program availability:* Part-time, evening/weekend, online learning. Offers atmospheric sciences (MS, PhD); Basque studies (PhD); biomedical engineering (MS, PhD); cell and molecular biology (MS, PhD); cellular and molecular pharmacology and physiology (PhD); chemical physics (PhD); ecology, evolution, and conservation biology (PhD); environmental sciences and health (MS, PhD); hydrogeology (MS, PhD); hydrology (MS, PhD); social psychology (PhD). Electronic applications accepted.

College of Agriculture, Biotechnology and Natural Resources Offers agriculture, biotechnology and natural resources (MS, PhD); animal science (MS); biochemistry (MS, PhD); biotechnology (MS); natural resources and environmental sciences (MS); nutrition (MS); resource economics (MS, PhD). Electronic applications accepted.

College of Business Administration *Program availability:* Part-time, online learning. Offers accounting and information systems (M Acc); business administration (M Acc, MA, MBA, MS); economics (MA, MS); finance (MS); information systems (MS). Electronic applications accepted.

College of Education Offers counseling and educational psychology (M Ed, MA, MS, Ed D, PhD, Ed S); curriculum and instruction (PhD); curriculum, teaching and learning (Ed D, PhD); education (M Ed, MA, MS, Ed D, PhD, Ed S); educational leadership (M Ed, MA, MS, Ed D, PhD, Ed S); educational specialties (M Ed, MS, Ed D, PhD); elementary education (M Ed, MA, MS); human development and family studies (MS); literacy studies (M Ed, MA, Ed D, PhD); secondary education (M Ed, MA, MS); special education (M Ed, MA, MS, Ed D, PhD); special education and disability studies (PhD); teaching English to speakers of other languages (MA). Electronic applications accepted.

College of Engineering Offers chemical engineering (MS, PhD); civil and environmental engineering (MS, PhD); computer science and engineering (MS, PhD); electrical engineering (MS, PhD); engineering (MS, PhD); materials science and engineering (MS, PhD); mechanical engineering (MS, PhD). Electronic applications accepted.

College of Liberal Arts *Program availability:* Part-time, evening/weekend, online learning. Offers anthropology (MA, PhD); behavior analysis (MA, PhD); clinical psychology (PhD); cognitive brain science (MA, PhD); criminal justice (MA); English (MA, MATE, PhD); fine arts (MFA); French (MA); German (MA); history (MA, PhD); judicial studies (MJS, PhD); justice management (MJM); liberal arts (MA, MATE, MFA, MJM, MJS, MM, MPA, PhD); music (MA, MM); philosophy (MA); political science (MA, PhD); public administration (MPA); public administration and policy (MPA); social research and justice studies (MA, MJM, MJS, PhD); sociology (MA); Spanish (MA); speech communications (MA). Electronic applications accepted.

College of Science Offers biology (MS); chemistry (MS, PhD); earth sciences and engineering (MS, PhD); geochemistry (MS, PhD); geography (MS, PhD); geological engineering (MS, PhD); geology (MS, PhD); geophysics (MS, PhD); land use planning (MS); mathematics (MS); mining engineering (MS); physics (MS, PhD); science (MATM, MS, PhD); teaching mathematics (MATM). Electronic applications accepted.

Division of Health Sciences Offers health sciences (MPH, MS, MSN, MSW, DNP, PhD); nursing (MSN, DNP); public health (MPH, PhD); social work (MSW); speech pathology (PhD); speech pathology and audiology (MS). Electronic applications accepted.

Donald W. Reynolds School of Journalism Offers journalism (MA). Electronic applications accepted.

School of Medicine Offers medicine (MD).

UNIVERSITY OF NEW BRUNSWICK FREDERICTON, Fredericton, NB E3B 5A3, Canada

General Information Province-supported, coed, university. *Graduate housing:* Rooms and/or apartments available on a first-come, first-served basis to single and married students. Housing application deadline: 5/31. *Research affiliation:* Huntsman Marine Science Centre (marine sciences), Petroleum Research Atlantic Canada (petroleum), Atlantic Associate for Research in the Mathematical Sciences (mathematical sciences), Atlantic Hydrogen, Inc. (hydrogen), Pulp and Paper Research Institute of Canada (pulp and paper), National Research Council Institute for Information Technology (information technology).

GRADUATE UNITS

School of Graduate Studies *Program availability:* Part-time, evening/weekend, online learning. Offers applied health services (MAHSR); citizen engagement/dispute resolution (M Phil); community development (M Phil); interdisciplinary studies (M IDST, PhD); international development (M Phil); leadership (M Phil); sustainability/environmental issues (M Phil); worldviews (M Phil).

Faculty of Arts *Program availability:* Part-time. Offers anthropology (MA); applied economics and finance (M Sc); arts (M Sc, MA, PhD); classics (MA); economics (MA); English (MA, PhD); history (MA, PhD); political science (MA); psychology (MA, PhD); sociology (MA, PhD). Electronic applications accepted.

Faculty of Business Administration *Program availability:* Part-time. Offers business administration (MBA); engineering management (MBA); entrepreneurship (MBA); sports and recreation management (MBA). Electronic applications accepted.

Faculty of Computer Science *Program availability:* Part-time. Offers computer science (M Sc CS, PhD). Electronic applications accepted.

Faculty of Education *Program availability:* Part-time, online learning. Offers education (M Ed, PhD). Electronic applications accepted.

Faculty of Engineering *Program availability:* Part-time. Offers applied mechanics (M Eng, M Sc E, PhD); chemical engineering (M Eng, M Sc E, PhD); construction engineering and management (M Eng, M Sc E, PhD); electrical and computer engineering (M Eng, M Sc E, PhD); engineering (M Eng, M Sc E, PhD, Certificate); environmental engineering (M Eng, M Sc E, PhD); environmental studies (M Eng); geodesy and geomatics engineering (M Eng, M Sc E, PhD); geotechnical engineering (M Eng, M Sc E, PhD); groundwater/hydrology (M Eng, M Sc E, PhD); materials (M Eng, M Sc E, PhD); mechanical engineering (M Eng, M Sc E, PhD); pavements (M Eng, M Sc E, PhD); structures (M Eng, M Sc E, PhD); transportation (M Eng, M Sc E, PhD). Electronic applications accepted.

Faculty of Forestry and Environmental Management *Program availability:* Part-time. Offers ecological foundations of forest management (PhD); environmental management (MEM); forest engineering (M Sc FE, MFE); forest products marketing (MBA); forest resources (M Sc F, MF, PhD). Electronic applications accepted.

Faculty of Kinesiology *Program availability:* Part-time. Offers exercise and sport science (M Sc); sport and recreation management (MBA); sport and recreation studies (MA). Electronic applications accepted.

Faculty of Nursing *Program availability:* Part-time, online learning. Offers nurse educator (MN); nurse practitioner (MN); nursing (MN). Electronic applications accepted.

Faculty of Science *Program availability:* Part-time. Offers biology (M Sc, PhD); chemistry (M Sc, PhD); earth sciences (M Sc, PhD); mathematics and statistics (M Sc, PhD); physics (M Sc, PhD); science (M Sc, PhD). Electronic applications accepted.

UNIVERSITY OF NEW BRUNSWICK SAINT JOHN, Saint John, NB E2L 4L5, Canada

General Information Province-supported, coed, comprehensive institution. *Graduate housing:* Rooms and/or apartments available on a first-come, first-served basis to single and married students. Housing application deadline: 3/31. *Research affiliation:* Cook Aquaculture (aquaculture), Horizon Health (health research), Dalhousie Medicine New Brunswick (cancer and general health), Fisheries and Oceans Canada (biology/ecology), New Brunswick Community College (health research).

GRADUATE UNITS

Department of Biology *Program availability:* Part-time. Offers biology (M Sc, PhD). Electronic applications accepted.

Department of Psychology *Program availability:* Part-time. Offers clinical psychology (PhD); experimental psychology (MA, PhD). Electronic applications accepted.

Faculty of Business *Program availability:* Part-time. Offers administration (MBA); electronic commerce (MBA); international business (MBA); natural resource management (MBA). Electronic applications accepted.

UNIVERSITY OF NEW ENGLAND, Biddeford, ME 04005-9526

General Information Independent, coed, comprehensive institution. *Enrollment:* 8,291 graduate, professional, and undergraduate students; 3,223 full-time matriculated graduate/professional students (2,208 women), 605 part-time matriculated graduate/professional students (482 women). *Enrollment by degree level:* 1,931 master's, 1,732 doctoral, 165 other advanced degrees. *Graduate faculty:* 159 full-time (73 women), 221 part-time/adjunct (82 women). Tuition and fees vary according to degree level, program and student level. *Graduate housing:* On-campus housing not available. *Student services:* Campus employment opportunities, campus safety program, career counseling, exercise/wellness program, free psychological counseling, international student services, low-cost health insurance, multicultural affairs office, services for students with disabilities, teacher training, writing training. *Library facilities:* Jack S. Ketchum Library plus 1 other. *Collection:* Books: 135,000 (physical), 1.2 million (digital/electronic); Serial titles: 140,000 (digital/electronic); Databases: 200. Weekly public service hours: 146; study areas open 24 hours, 5–7 days a week; students can reserve study rooms.

Computer facilities: Computer purchase and lease plans are available. 91 computers available on campus for general student use. A campuswide network can be accessed from student residence rooms and from off campus. Online class registration is available.
Website: http://www.une.edu/

General Application Contact: Scott Steinberg, Dean of University Admission, 207-221-4225, Fax: 207-523-1925, E-mail: ssteinberg@une.edu.

GRADUATE UNITS

College of Arts and Sciences Students: 14 full-time (11 women), 6 part-time (3 women); includes 1 minority (Asian, non-Hispanic/Latino). Average age 25. 29 applicants, 34% accepted, 8 enrolled. *Faculty:* 30 full-time (17 women), 2 part-time/adjunct (1 woman). Expenses: Contact institution. *Financial support:* Fellowships, research assistantships, teaching assistantships, career-related internships or fieldwork, scholarships/grants, traineeships, and unspecified assistantships available. Financial award application deadline: 5/1; financial award applicants required to submit FAFSA. In 2017, 4 master's awarded. *Program availability:* Part-time. Offers biological sciences (MS); marine sciences (MS). *Application deadline:* Applications are processed on a rolling basis. Electronic applications accepted. *Application Contact:* Scott Steinberg, Dean of University Admissions, 207-221-4225, Fax: 207-523-1925, E-mail: ssteinberg@une.edu. *Dean, College of Arts and Sciences*, Dr. Jeanne A.K. Hey, 207-602-2371, Fax: 207-602-5973, E-mail: jhey@une.edu.

College of Dental Medicine Students: 252 full-time (127 women); includes 50 minority (2 Black or African American, non-Hispanic/Latino; 1 American Indian or Alaska Native, non-Hispanic/Latino; 33 Asian, non-Hispanic/Latino; 9 Hispanic/Latino; 5 Two or more races, non-Hispanic/Latino), 10 international. Average age 27. 1,912 applicants, 6% accepted, 49 enrolled. *Faculty:* 23 full-time (12 women), 29 part-time/adjunct (9 women). Expenses: Contact institution. *Financial support:* Application deadline: 5/1; applicants required to submit FAFSA. In 2017, 62 doctorates awarded. Offers dental medicine (DMD). *Application deadline:* For fall admission, 11/1 for domestic and international students. Electronic applications accepted. *Application Contact:* Scott Steinberg, Dean of University Admissions, 207-221-4225, Fax: 207-523-1925, E-mail: ssteinberg@une.edu. *Dean, College of Dental Medicine*, Dr. Jon Ryder, 207-221-4707, Fax: 207-523-1915, E-mail: jryder2@une.edu.

College of Graduate and Professional Studies Students: 1,403 full-time (1,128 women), 594 part-time (475 women); includes 474 minority (332 Black or African American, non-Hispanic/Latino; 13 American Indian or Alaska Native, non-Hispanic/Latino; 83 Asian, non-Hispanic/Latino; 27 Hispanic/Latino; 11 Native Hawaiian or other Pacific Islander, non-Hispanic/Latino; 8 Two or more races, non-Hispanic/Latino). Average age 35. 3,153 applicants, 41% accepted, 990 enrolled. *Faculty:* 125 part-time/adjunct (94 women). Expenses: Contact institution. *Financial support:* Application deadline: 5/1; applicants required to submit FAFSA. In 2017, 307 master's, 59 doctorates, 124 other advanced degrees awarded. *Program availability:* Part-time, evening/weekend, online only, 100% online. Offers advanced educational leadership (CAGS); applied nutrition (MS); career and technical education (MS Ed); curriculum and instruction (MS Ed); education (CAGS, Post-Master's Certificate); educational leadership (MS Ed, Ed D); generalist (MS Ed); health informatics (MS, Graduate Certificate); inclusion education (MS Ed); literacy K-12 (MS Ed); medical education leadership (MMEL); public health (MPH); public health (Graduate Certificate); reading specialist (MS Ed); social work (MSW). *Application deadline:* Applications are processed on a rolling basis. Electronic applications accepted. *Associate Provost for Online Worldwide Learning/Dean of the College of Graduate and Professional Studies*, Dr. Martha Wilson, 207-221-4985, E-mail: mwilson13@une.edu.

College of Osteopathic Medicine Students: 710 full-time (344 women); includes 114 minority (4 Black or African American, non-Hispanic/Latino; 2 American Indian or Alaska Native, non-Hispanic/Latino; 97 Asian, non-Hispanic/Latino; 5 Hispanic/Latino; 6 Two or more races, non-Hispanic/Latino), 24 international. Average age 27. 4,586 applicants, 10% accepted, 178 enrolled. *Faculty:* 39 full-time (16 women), 36 part-time/adjunct (15 women). Expenses: Contact institution. *Financial support:* Application deadline: 5/1; applicants required to submit FAFSA. In 2017, 161 doctorates awarded. Offers osteopathic medicine (DO). *Application deadline:* For fall admission, 3/1 for domestic students. *Application Contact:* Scott Steinberg, Dean of University Admission, 207-221-4225, Fax: 207-523-1925, E-mail: ssteinberg@une.edu. *Dean, College of Osteopathic Medicine*, Dr. Jane Carreiro, 207-602-2898, E-mail: deanunecom@une.edu.

College of Pharmacy Students: 317 full-time (197 women); includes 102 minority (34 Black or African American, non-Hispanic/Latino; 2 American Indian or Alaska Native, non-Hispanic/Latino; 52 Asian, non-Hispanic/Latino; 8 Hispanic/Latino; 1 Native Hawaiian or other Pacific Islander, non-Hispanic/Latino; 5 Two or more races, non-Hispanic/Latino), 3 international. Average age 26. 351 applicants, 33% accepted, 49 enrolled. *Faculty:* 24 full-time (11 women), 3 part-time/adjunct (1 woman). Expenses: Contact institution. *Financial support:* Application deadline: 5/1; applicants required to submit FAFSA. In 2017, 87 doctorates awarded. Offers pharmacy (Pharm D). *Application deadline:* For fall admission, 3/1 for domestic students. Applications are processed on a rolling basis. Electronic applications accepted. *Application Contact:* Scott Steinberg, Dean of University Admission, 207-221-4225, Fax: 207-523-1925, E-mail: ssteinberg@une.edu. *Dean, College of Pharmacy*, Dr. Gayle A. Brazeau, 207-221-4500, Fax: 207-523-1927, E-mail: gbrazeau@une.edu.

Westbrook College of Health Professions Students: 527 full-time (401 women), 5 part-time (4 women); includes 50 minority (11 Black or African American, non-Hispanic/Latino; 1 American Indian or Alaska Native, non-Hispanic/Latino; 24 Asian, non-Hispanic/Latino; 5 Hispanic/Latino; 1 Native Hawaiian or other Pacific Islander, non-Hispanic/Latino; 8 Two or more races, non-Hispanic/Latino), 1 international. Average age 27. 2,499 applicants, 18% accepted, 226 enrolled. *Faculty:* 43 full-time (30 women), 26 part-time/adjunct (19 women). Expenses: Contact institution. *Financial support:* Application deadline: 5/1; applicants required to submit FAFSA. In 2017, 440 master's, 71 doctorates awarded. *Program availability:* Part-time. Offers nurse anesthesia (MSNA); occupational therapy (MS); physical therapy (DPT); physician assistant (MS); social work (MSW). *Application deadline:* Applications are processed on a rolling basis. Electronic applications accepted. *Application Contact:* Scott Steinberg, Dean of University Admission, 207-221-4225, Fax: 207-523-1925, E-mail: ssteinberg@une.edu. *Dean, Westbrook College of Health Professions*, Dr. Elizabeth Francis- Connolly, 207-221-4523, E-mail: efrancisconnonlly@une.edu.

UNIVERSITY OF NEW HAMPSHIRE, Durham, NH 03824

General Information State-supported, coed, university. CGS member. *Enrollment:* 15,364 graduate, professional, and undergraduate students; 1,310 full-time matriculated graduate/professional students (769 women), 909 part-time matriculated graduate/professional students (476 women). *Enrollment by degree level:* 1,591 master's, 586 doctoral, 42 other advanced degrees. *Graduate faculty:* 587. *Graduate housing:* Rooms and/or apartments available on a first-come, first-served basis to single and married students. Housing application deadline: 7/15. *Student services:* Campus employment opportunities, campus safety program, career counseling, child daycare facilities, exercise/wellness program, free psychological counseling, grant writing training, international student services, low-cost health insurance, multicultural affairs office, services for students with disabilities, teacher training, writing training. *Library facilities:* Dimond Library plus 4 others. *Collection:* Books: 1.1 million (physical), 889,664 (digital/electronic); Serial titles: 749 (physical), 90,600 (digital/electronic); Databases: 456. Weekly public service hours: 117; students can reserve study rooms.

Computer facilities: Computer purchase and lease plans are available. 320 computers available on campus for general student use. A campuswide network can be accessed from student residence rooms and from off campus. Online class registration is available.
Website: http://www.unh.edu/

General Application Contact: Dovev L. Levine, Assistant Dean, 603-862-3000, Fax: 603-862-0275, E-mail: grad.school@unh.edu.

GRADUATE UNITS

Graduate School Students: 1,310 full-time (769 women), 909 part-time (476 women); includes 167 minority (28 Black or African American, non-Hispanic/Latino; 2 American Indian or Alaska Native, non-Hispanic/Latino; 47 Asian, non-Hispanic/Latino; 64 Hispanic/Latino; 26 Two or more races, non-Hispanic/Latino), 306 international. Average age 30. *Faculty:* 587. Expenses: Contact institution. *Financial support:* In 2017–18, 26 fellowships with full and partial tuition reimbursements, 199 research assistantships with full and partial tuition reimbursements, 445 teaching assistantships with full and partial tuition reimbursements were awarded; Federal Work-Study, scholarships/grants, health care benefits, tuition waivers (full and partial), and unspecified assistantships also available. Support available to part-time students. Financial award application deadline: 3/1; financial award applicants required to submit FAFSA. *Program availability:* Part-time, evening/weekend. *Application deadline:* For fall admission, 7/1 priority date for domestic students, 4/1 priority date for international students; for spring admission, 2/1 priority date for domestic students, 11/1 priority date for international students; for summer admission, 4/1 priority date for domestic and international students. Applications are processed on a rolling basis. *Application fee:* $65. Electronic applications accepted. *Application Contact:* Dovev Levine, Assistant Dean, 603-862-2234, E-mail: dovev.levine@unh.edu. *Interim Dean*, Dr. Cari Moorhead, 603-862-3005, Fax: 603-862-0275, E-mail: cari.moorhead@unh.edu.

Carsey School of Public Policy Students: 20 full-time (10 women), 17 part-time (9 women); includes 5 minority (2 Black or African American, non-Hispanic/Latino; 1 Hispanic/Latino; 2 Two or more races, non-Hispanic/Latino), 9 international. Average age 28. 27 applicants, 70% accepted, 11 enrolled. Expenses: Contact institution.

Financial support: Fellowships, research assistantships, teaching assistantships, and scholarships/grants available. Financial award application deadline: 2/15. In 2017, 37 master's awarded. *Program availability:* Part-time. Offers community development policy and practice (MA); public administration (MPA); public policy (MA, MPA, MPP). *Application deadline:* For fall admission, 2/15 for domestic students; for spring admission, 12/15 for domestic students; for summer admission, 4/15 for domestic students. *Application fee:* $65. Electronic applications accepted. *Application Contact:* Sarah Dorner, Administrative Assistant, 603-862-2338, E-mail: sarah.dorner@unh.edu. *Director*, Michael Swack, 603-862-2821, Fax: 603-862-0275, E-mail: michael.swack@unh.edu.

College of Engineering and Physical Sciences Students: 316 full-time (92 women), 177 part-time (52 women); includes 30 minority (5 Black or African American, non-Hispanic/Latino; 2 American Indian or Alaska Native, non-Hispanic/Latino; 11 Asian, non-Hispanic/Latino; 8 Hispanic/Latino; 4 Two or more races, non-Hispanic/Latino), 199 international. Average age 27. 727 applicants, 52% accepted, 130 enrolled. Expenses: Contact institution. *Financial support:* In 2017–18, 360 students received support, including 11 fellowships, 127 research assistantships, 193 teaching assistantships; career-related internships or fieldwork, Federal Work-Study, scholarships/grants, and tuition waivers also available. Support available to part-time students. Financial award application deadline: 2/15; financial award applicants required to submit FAFSA. *Program availability:* Part-time, evening/weekend. Offers applied mathematics (PhD); chemical engineering (M Engr, MS, PhD); chemistry (MS, PhD); chemistry education (PhD); civil and environmental engineering (M Engr, MS, PhD); computer science (MS, PhD); electrical and computer engineering (MS); electrical engineering (M Engr, PhD); engineering and physical sciences (M Engr, MS, MST, PhD, Certificate, Postbaccalaureate Certificate); geochemical systems (MS); geology (MS); hydrology (MS); industrial statistics (Certificate); materials science (MS); materials science and engineering (PhD); mathematics (MS, MST, PhD); mathematics education (PhD); mathematics: applied mathematics (MS); mathematics: statistics (MS, PhD); mechanical engineering (M Engr, MS, PhD); ocean mapping (MS); oceanography (MS); physics (MS, PhD); ubiquitous computing (Certificate); wireless communication systems (Certificate). *Application deadline:* For fall admission, 7/1 priority date for domestic students, 4/1 for international students; for spring admission, 12/1 priority date for domestic students. Applications are processed on a rolling basis. *Application fee:* $65. Electronic applications accepted. *Application Contact:* 603-862-3000, Fax: 603-862-0275, E-mail: grad.school@unh.edu. *Dean*, Wayne Jones, 603-862-1781.

College of Health and Human Services Students: 435 full-time (371 women), 174 part-time (146 women); includes 47 minority (6 Black or African American, non-Hispanic/Latino; 8 Asian, non-Hispanic/Latino; 26 Hispanic/Latino; 7 Two or more races, non-Hispanic/Latino), 7 international. Average age 30. 585 applicants, 56% accepted, 206 enrolled. Expenses: Contact institution. *Financial support:* In 2017–18, 76 students received support, including 36 teaching assistantships; fellowships, research assistantships, career-related internships or fieldwork, Federal Work-Study, scholarships/grants, and tuition waivers (full and partial) also available. Support available to part-time students. Financial award application deadline: 2/15. In 2017, 234 master's, 1 doctorate, 15 other advanced degrees awarded. *Program availability:* Part-time, evening/weekend. Offers adapted physical education (Postbaccalaureate Certificate); adaptive sports (MS); adolescent development (Postbaccalaureate Certificate); adult neurogenic communication (MS); assistive technology (Postbaccalaureate Certificate); child welfare (Postbaccalaureate Certificate); communication sciences and disorders (MS); early childhood intervention (MS); family nurse practitioner (Postbaccalaureate Certificate); health and human services (MPH, MS, MSW, DNP, Postbaccalaureate Certificate); human development and family studies (MS); human development and family studies: marriage and family therapy (MS); intellectual and development disabilities (Postbaccalaureate Certificate); kinesiology (MS); kinesiology and social work (MS); language and literacy disorders (MS); nursing (MS, DNP); occupational therapy (MS); psychiatric mental health (Postbaccalaureate Certificate); public health (MPH, Postbaccalaureate Certificate); recreation administration (MS); social work (MSW); substance use disorders (Postbaccalaureate Certificate); therapeutic recreation administration (MS). *Application deadline:* For fall admission, 7/1 priority date for domestic students, 4/1 for international students; for spring admission, 12/1 for domestic students. *Application fee:* $65. Electronic applications accepted. *Application Contact:* 603-862-3000, Fax: 603-862-0275, E-mail: grad.school@unh.edu. *Dean*, Dr. Michael S. Ferrara, 603-862-1178.

College of Liberal Arts Students: 236 full-time (155 women), 247 part-time (164 women); includes 37 minority (7 Black or African American, non-Hispanic/Latino; 9 Asian, non-Hispanic/Latino; 16 Hispanic/Latino; 5 Two or more races, non-Hispanic/Latino), 19 international. Average age 32. 424 applicants, 56% accepted, 134 enrolled. Expenses: Contact institution. *Financial support:* In 2017–18, 186 students received support, including 7 fellowships, 2 research assistantships, 113 teaching assistantships; career-related internships or fieldwork, Federal Work-Study, scholarships/grants, and tuition waivers (full and partial) also available. Support available to part-time students. Financial award application deadline: 2/15; financial award applicants required to submit FAFSA. In 2017, 227 master's, 18 doctorates, 5 other advanced degrees awarded. *Program availability:* Part-time. Offers assessment evaluation and policy (Postbaccalaureate Certificate); autism spectrum disorders (Postbaccalaureate Certificate); children and youth in communities (PhD); curriculum and instruction leadership (Postbaccalaureate Certificate); early childhood education (M Ed); early childhood education: special needs (M Ed); education (PhD, Postbaccalaureate Certificate); educational administration and supervision (Ed S); educational studies (M Ed); elementary education (M Ed); English (MST, PhD); history (MA, PhD); history: museum studies (MA); justice studies (MA); language and linguistics (MA); liberal arts (M Ed, MA, MALS, MAT, MFA, MPA, MST, PhD, Ed S, Postbaccalaureate Certificate); liberal studies (MALS); literature (MA); mentoring teachers (Postbaccalaureate Certificate); music composition (MA); music conducting (MA); musicology (MA); political science (MA, Postbaccalaureate Certificate); psychology (PhD); secondary education (M Ed, MAT); sociology (MA, PhD); Spanish (MA, Postbaccalaureate Certificate); special education (M Ed, Postbaccalaureate Certificate); special education administration (Postbaccalaureate Certificate); technology integration (Postbaccalaureate Certificate); writing (MFA). *Application deadline:* For fall admission, 3/1 for domestic students, 4/1 for international students; for spring admission, 12/1 for domestic students. *Application fee:* $65. Electronic applications accepted. *Application Contact:* 603-862-3000, Fax: 603-862-0275, E-mail: grad.school@unh.edu. *Dean*, Heidi Bostic, 603-862-2062.

College of Life Sciences and Agriculture Students: 78 full-time (40 women), 87 part-time (48 women); includes 11 minority (6 Hispanic/Latino; 5 Two or more races, non-Hispanic/Latino), 19 international. Average age 28. 186 applicants, 37% accepted, 51 enrolled. Expenses: Contact institution. *Financial support:* In 2017–18, 136 students received support, including 1 fellowship, 49 research assistantships, 82 teaching assistantships; career-related internships or fieldwork, Federal Work-Study, scholarships/grants, and tuition waivers (full and partial) also available. Support available to part-time students. Financial award application deadline: 2/15; financial award applicants required to submit FAFSA. In 2017, 25 master's, 7 doctorates awarded. *Program availability:* Part-time. Offers agricultural sciences (MS, PhD); animal and nutritional sciences (MS, PhD); biochemistry (MS, PhD); environmental conservation (MS); environmental economics (MS); forestry (MS); genetics (MS, PhD); integrative and organismal biology (MS, PhD); life sciences and agriculture (MS, PhD); marine biology (MS, PhD); microbiology (MS, PhD); molecular and evolutionary systems biology (PhD); natural resources (MS); nutritional sciences (MS, PhD); resource administration and management (MS); soil and water resource management (MS); wildlife and conservation biology (MS). *Application deadline:* For fall admission, 2/15 for domestic students, 4/1 for international students. *Application fee:* $65. Electronic applications accepted. *Application Contact:* 603-862-3000, Fax: 603-862-0275, E-mail: grad.school@unh.edu. *Dean*, Jon Wraith, 603-862-1453.

Interdisciplinary Programs Students: 96 full-time (56 women), 32 part-time (14 women); includes 13 minority (4 Black or African American, non-Hispanic/Latino; 2 Asian, non-Hispanic/Latino; 4 Hispanic/Latino; 3 Two or more races, non-Hispanic/Latino), 17 international. Average age 32. 79 applicants, 43% accepted, 19 enrolled. Expenses: Contact institution. *Financial support:* In 2017–18, 53 students received support, including 7 fellowships, 16 research assistantships, 9 teaching assistantships. Financial award application deadline: 2/15. In 2017, 35 master's, 2 doctorates, 6 other advanced degrees awarded. *Program availability:* Part-time. Offers analytics (MS, Postbaccalaureate Certificate); college teaching (Postbaccalaureate Certificate); earth and environmental sciences (PhD); feminist studies (Postbaccalaureate Certificate); geospatial science (Postbaccalaureate Certificate); natural resources and environmental studies (PhD). *Application deadline:* For fall admission, 2/15 priority date for domestic students, 4/1 for international students; for winter admission, 12/1 priority date for domestic students. *Application fee:* $65. Electronic applications accepted. *Application Contact:* Dovev Levine, Assistant Dean, 603-862-3000, E-mail: grad.school@unh.edu. *Dean*, Dr. Cari Moorhead, 603-862-3000, E-mail: grad.school@unh.edu.

Graduate School Manchester Campus Students: 13 full-time (6 women), 17 part-time (0 women); includes 7 minority (1 Black or African American, non-Hispanic/Latino; 4 Asian, non-Hispanic/Latino; 1 Hispanic/Latino; 1 Two or more races, non-Hispanic/Latino), 10 international. Average age 33. 42 applicants, 71% accepted, 8 enrolled. Expenses: Contact institution. *Financial support:* Fellowships, research assistantships, teaching assistantships, Federal Work-Study, scholarships/grants, health care benefits, and unspecified assistantships available. Support available to part-time students. Financial award application deadline: 2/15; financial award applicants required to submit FAFSA. In 2017, 4 master's awarded. *Program availability:* Part-time, evening/weekend. Offers business administration (MBA); cybersecurity policy and risk management (MS); educational administration and supervision (Ed S); educational studies (M Ed); elementary education (M Ed); information technology (MS); public administration (MPA); public health (MPH, Certificate); secondary education (M Ed, MAT); social work (MSW); substance use disorders (Certificate). *Application deadline:* For fall admission, 6/1 for domestic students, 4/1 for international students; for spring admission, 12/1 for domestic students. *Application fee:* $65. Electronic applications accepted. *Educational Programs Coordinator*, Candice Morey, 603-641-4313, E-mail: unhm.gradcenter@unh.edu.

Peter T. Paul College of Business and Economics Students: 136 full-time (49 women), 175 part-time (52 women); includes 22 minority (5 Black or African American, non-Hispanic/Latino; 13 Asian, non-Hispanic/Latino; 3 Hispanic/Latino; 1 Two or more races, non-Hispanic/Latino), 35 international. Average age 32. 308 applicants, 69% accepted, 137 enrolled. Expenses: Contact institution. *Financial support:* In 2017–18, 84 students received support, including 5 research assistantships, 12 teaching assistantships; fellowships, career-related internships or fieldwork, Federal Work-Study, scholarships/grants, and tuition waivers (full and partial) also available. Support available to part-time students. Financial award application deadline: 2/15. In 2017, 142 master's, 3 doctorates awarded. *Program availability:* Part-time, evening/weekend. Offers accounting (MS); business administration (MBA); business and economics (MA, MBA, MS, PhD); economics (MA, PhD). *Application deadline:* For fall admission, 6/1 for domestic students, 4/1 for international students; for spring admission, 12/1 for domestic students. *Application fee:* $65. Electronic applications accepted. *Application Contact:* 603-862-3000, Fax: 603-862-0275, E-mail: grad.school@unh.edu. *Dean*, Deborah Merrill-Sands, 603-862-1983.

School of Marine Science and Ocean Engineering Students: 21 full-time (12 women), 4 part-time (0 women); includes 2 minority (1 Black or African American, non-Hispanic/Latino; 1 Hispanic/Latino), 10 international. Average age 29. 36 applicants, 64% accepted, 12 enrolled. Expenses: Contact institution. *Financial support:* In 2017–18, 18 students received support, including 1 fellowship, 14 research assistantships, 2 teaching assistantships; Federal Work-Study, scholarships/grants, and tuition waivers (full and partial) also available. Support available to part-time students. Financial award application deadline: 2/15. In 2017, 4 master's, 6 other advanced degrees awarded. Offers ocean engineering (MS, PhD); ocean mapping (MS, Postbaccalaureate Certificate). *Application deadline:* For fall admission, 4/1 for domestic and international students; for spring admission, 12/1 for domestic students. *Application fee:* $65. Electronic applications accepted. *Application Contact:* Lauren Foxall, Administrative Assistant, 603-862-1352, E-mail: ocean.engineering@unh.edu. *Chairperson*, Diane Foster, 603-862-3089.

School of Law *Program availability:* Part-time, 100% online, limited residential. Offers business law (JD); commerce and technology (LL M, MCT, Diploma); criminal law (JD); intellectual property (LL M, MIP, JD, Diploma); international criminal law and justice (LL M, MICLJ); litigation (JD); public interest and social justice (JD); sports and entertainment law (JD). Electronic applications accepted.

UNIVERSITY OF NEW HAVEN, West Haven, CT 06516

General Information Independent, coed, comprehensive institution. CGS member. *Enrollment:* 6,984 graduate, professional, and undergraduate students; 1,070 full-time matriculated graduate/professional students (538 women), 691 part-time matriculated graduate/professional students (306 women). *Enrollment by degree level:* 1,703 master's, 37 doctoral, 21 other advanced degrees. *Graduate faculty:* 116 full-time (35 women), 94 part-time/adjunct (22 women). *Tuition:* Full-time $16,020; part-time $890 per credit hour. *Required fees:* $220; $90 per term. *Graduate housing:* Room and/or apartments available on a first-come, first-served basis to single students; on-campus housing not available to married students. *Student services:* Campus employment opportunities, campus safety program, career counseling, free psychological counseling, international student services, low-cost health insurance, multicultural affairs office, services for students with disabilities, writing training. *Library facilities:* Marvin K. Peterson Library.

Computer facilities: Computer purchase and lease plans are available. A campuswide network can be accessed from student residence rooms. Online class registration, computer repair services are available.
Website: http://www.newhaven.edu/

General Application Contact: Shobi Sivadasan, Senior Associate Vice President, Graduate and International Admissions, E-mail: gradinfo@newhaven.edu.

GRADUATE UNITS

Graduate School Students: 1,070 full-time (538 women), 691 part-time (306 women); includes 349 minority (176 Black or African American, non-Hispanic/Latino; 3 American Indian or Alaska Native, non-Hispanic/Latino; 70 Asian, non-Hispanic/Latino; 79 Hispanic/Latino; 2 Native Hawaiian or other Pacific Islander, non-Hispanic/Latino; 19 Two or more races, non-Hispanic/Latino), 504 international. Average age 29. 2,318 applicants, 77% accepted, 641 enrolled. *Faculty:* 116 full-time (35 women), 94 part-time/adjunct (22 women). Expenses: Contact institution. *Financial support:* Research assistantships with partial tuition reimbursements, teaching assistantships with partial tuition reimbursements, Federal Work-Study, scholarships/grants, and unspecified assistantships available. Financial award applicants required to submit FAFSA. In 2017, 925 master's, 48 other advanced degrees awarded. *Program availability:* Part-time, evening/weekend. *Application deadline:* Applications are processed on a rolling basis. *Application fee:* $50. Electronic applications accepted. *Application Contact:* Shobi Sivadasan, Senior Associate Vice President, Graduate and International Enrollment, E-mail: gradinfo@newhaven.edu.

College of Arts and Sciences Students: 185 full-time (127 women), 48 part-time (29 women); includes 46 minority (23 Black or African American, non-Hispanic/Latino; 1 American Indian or Alaska Native, non-Hispanic/Latino; 8 Asian, non-Hispanic/Latino; 12 Hispanic/Latino; 2 Two or more races, non-Hispanic/Latino), 20 international. Average age 26. 281 applicants, 89% accepted, 115 enrolled. *Faculty:* 23 full-time (13 women), 15 part-time/adjunct (10 women). Expenses: Contact institution. *Financial support:* Research assistantships with partial tuition reimbursements, teaching assistantships with partial tuition reimbursements, Federal Work-Study, scholarships/grants, and unspecified assistantships available. Support available to part-time students. Financial award application deadline: 5/1; financial award applicants required to submit FAFSA. In 2017, 189 master's, 7 other advanced degrees awarded. *Program availability:* Part-time, evening/weekend. Offers applications of psychology (Graduate Certificate); arts and sciences (MA, MS, Graduate Certificate); cellular and molecular biology (MS); community clinical services (MA); community psychology (MA); conflict management (MA); environmental ecology (MS); environmental geoscience (MS); environmental health and management (MS); environmental science (MS); forensic psychology (MA); geographical information systems (MS); human nutrition (MS); industrial organizational psychology (MA); industrial-human resources psychology (MA); nutritional genomics (MS, Graduate Certificate); organizational development and consultation (MA); program development (MA); psychology of conflict management (Graduate Certificate). *Application deadline:* Applications are processed on a rolling basis. *Application fee:* $50. Electronic applications accepted. *Application Contact:* Shobi Sivadasan, Senior Associate Vice President, Graduate and International Enrollment, E-mail: gradinfo@newhaven.edu. *Acting Dean*, Dr. Stuart Sidle, 203-932-7339, E-mail: ssidle@newhaven.edu.

College of Business Students: 254 full-time (126 women), 174 part-time (103 women); includes 113 minority (65 Black or African American, non-Hispanic/Latino; 21 Asian, non-Hispanic/Latino; 20 Hispanic/Latino; 1 Native Hawaiian or other Pacific Islander, non-Hispanic/Latino; 6 Two or more races, non-Hispanic/Latino), 92 international. Average age 31. 386 applicants, 91% accepted, 169 enrolled. *Faculty:* 27 full-time (7 women), 15 part-time/adjunct (5 women). Expenses: Contact institution. *Financial support:* Research assistantships with partial tuition reimbursements, teaching assistantships with partial tuition reimbursements, Federal Work-Study, scholarships/grants, and unspecified assistantships available. Support available to part-time students. Financial award application deadline: 5/1; financial award applicants required to submit FAFSA. In 2017, 192 master's, 7 other advanced degrees awarded. *Program availability:* Part-time, evening/weekend. Offers accounting (MBA); business (EMBA, MBA, MS, Graduate Certificate); business administration (EMBA, MBA); business intelligence (MBA); business policy and strategic leadership (MBA); collegiate athletic administration (MS); facility management (MS); finance (MBA); global marketing (MBA); health care administration (MS, Graduate Certificate); health care marketing (MS); health policy and finance (MS); human resource management (MS); human resources management (MBA); long-term care (MS); long-term health care (Graduate Certificate); managed care (MS); medical group management (MS); sport analytics (MS); sport management (MBA, Graduate Certificate); taxation (MS, Graduate Certificate). *Application deadline:* Applications are processed on a rolling basis. *Application fee:* $50. Electronic applications accepted. *Application Contact:* Michelle Mason, Director of Graduate Enrollment, 203-932-7067, E-mail: mmason@newhaven.edu. *Dean*, Dr. Brian Kench, 203-932-7115, E-mail: bkench@newhaven.edu.

Henry C. Lee College of Criminal Justice and Forensic Sciences Students: 297 full-time (183 women), 256 part-time (118 women); includes 136 minority (69 Black or African American, non-Hispanic/Latino; 1 American Indian or Alaska Native, non-Hispanic/Latino; 16 Asian, non-Hispanic/Latino; 39 Hispanic/Latino; 1 Native Hawaiian or other Pacific Islander, non-Hispanic/Latino; 10 Two or more races, non-Hispanic/Latino), 39 international. Average age 31. 462 applicants, 85% accepted, 210 enrolled. *Faculty:* 37 full-time (11 women), 34 part-time/adjunct (6 women). Expenses: Contact institution. *Financial support:* Research assistantships with partial tuition reimbursements, teaching assistantships with partial tuition reimbursements, Federal Work-Study, scholarships/grants, and unspecified assistantships available. Support available to part-time students. Financial award applicants required to submit FAFSA. In 2017, 214 master's, 14 other advanced degrees awarded. *Program availability:* Part-time, evening/weekend, 100% online, blended/hybrid learning. Offers criminal investigations (MS); criminal justice (MS, PhD); criminal justice and forensic sciences (MPA, MS, PhD, Graduate Certificate); criminal justice management (Graduate Certificate); digital forensic investigations (MS); emergency management (MS, Graduate Certificate); financial crimes investigations (MS); fire and emergency medical services (MPA); fire science (MS); fire/arson investigation (MS, Graduate Certificate); forensic computer investigation (Graduate Certificate); forensic science (MS, Graduate Certificate); forensic science/fire science (Graduate Certificate); forensic technology (MS); municipal management (MPA); national security (MS, Graduate Certificate); national security administration (Graduate Certificate); nonprofit organization management (MPA); public administration (MPA, Graduate Certificate); public finance (MPA); public safety (MPA); public safety management (MS). *Application deadline:* Applications are processed on a rolling basis. *Application fee:* $50. Electronic applications accepted. *Application Contact:* Michelle Mason, Director of Graduate Enrollment, 203-932-7067, E-mail: mmason@newhaven.edu. *Dean*, Dr. Mario Gaboury, 203-932-7253, E-mail: mgaboury@newhaven.edu.

Tagliatela College of Engineering Students: 332 full-time (101 women), 213 part-time (56 women); includes 53 minority (18 Black or African American, non-Hispanic/Latino; 1 American Indian or Alaska Native, non-Hispanic/Latino; 25 Asian, non-Hispanic/Latino; 8 Hispanic/Latino; 1 Two or more races, non-Hispanic/Latino), 353 international. Average age 27. 1,186 applicants, 67% accepted, 145 enrolled. *Faculty:* 29 full-time (4 women), 30 part-time/adjunct (1 woman). Expenses: Contact institution. *Financial support:* Research assistantships with partial tuition reimbursements, teaching assistantships with partial tuition reimbursements, Federal Work-Study, scholarships/grants, and unspecified assistantships available. Support available to part-time students. Financial award applicants required to submit FAFSA. In 2017, 330 master's, 20 other advanced degrees awarded. *Program availability:* Part-time, evening/weekend. Offers biomedical engineering (MS); civil engineering (MS); computer engineering (MS); computer programming (Graduate Certificate); computer science (MS); control systems (MS); cybersecurity and networks (MS); digital signal processing and communication (MS); electrical engineering (MS); engineering (MS, MSIE, Graduate Certificate); engineering and operations management (MS); engineering management (MS); environmental engineering (MS); industrial and hazardous waste (MS); industrial engineering (MSIE); Lean Six Sigma (Graduate Certificate); mechanical engineering (MS); network systems (MS); quality engineering (Graduate Certificate); software development (MS); water and wastewater treatment (MS); water resources (MS). *Application deadline:* Applications are processed on a rolling basis. *Application fee:* $50. Electronic applications accepted. *Application Contact:* Michelle Mason, Director of Graduate Enrollment, 203-932-7440, E-mail: mmason@newhaven.edu. *Dean*, Dr. Ronald Harichandran, 203-932-7167, E-mail: rharichandran@newhaven.edu.

UNIVERSITY OF NEW MEXICO, Albuquerque, NM 87131-2039

General Information State-supported, coed, university. CGS member. *Enrollment:* 26,278 graduate, professional, and undergraduate students; 2,073 full-time matriculated graduate/professional students (1,117 women), 1,979 part-time matriculated graduate/professional students (1,117 women). *Enrollment by degree level:* 2,135 master's, 1,734 doctoral, 183 other advanced degrees. *Graduate faculty:* 758 full-time (346 women), 72 part-time/adjunct (37 women). *Graduate housing:* Rooms and/or apartments available on a first-come, first-served basis to single and married students. Housing application deadline: 7/16. *Student services:* Campus employment opportunities, campus safety program, career counseling, child daycare facilities, exercise/wellness program, free psychological counseling, grant writing training, international student services, low-cost health insurance, multicultural affairs office, services for students with disabilities, teacher training, writing training. *Library facilities:* College of University Libraries and Learning Sciences plus 7 others. *Collection:* Students can reserve study rooms. *Research affiliation:* Phillips Laboratory, Oak Ridge National Laboratory, Sandia National Laboratories, New Mexico Consortium, Los Alamos National Laboratory, Lovelace Respiratory Research Institute.

Computer facilities: Computer purchase and lease plans are available. 990 computers available on campus for general student use. A campuswide network can be accessed from student residence rooms and from off campus. Online class registration is available.
Website: http://www.unm.edu/

General Application Contact: Deborah Kieltyka, Associate Director, Admissions, 505-277-3140, Fax: 505-277-6686, E-mail: deborahk@unm.edu.

GRADUATE UNITS

Anderson School of Management Students: 288 full-time (136 women), 364 part-time (206 women); includes 314 minority (10 Black or African American, non-Hispanic/Latino; 27 American Indian or Alaska Native, non-Hispanic/Latino; 28 Asian, non-Hispanic/Latino; 229 Hispanic/Latino; 1 Native Hawaiian or other Pacific Islander, non-Hispanic/Latino; 19 Two or more races, non-Hispanic/Latino), 59 international. Average age 31. 325 applicants, 60% accepted, 166 enrolled. *Faculty:* 62 full-time (25 women), 42 part-time/adjunct (16 women). Expenses: Contact institution. *Financial support:* In 2017–18, 89 students received support, including 50 fellowships (averaging $15,746 per year), 52 research assistantships with partial tuition reimbursements available (averaging $15,400 per year); career-related internships or fieldwork, Federal Work-Study, scholarships/grants, and unspecified assistantships also available. Support available to part-time students. Financial award application deadline: 6/1; financial award applicants required to submit FAFSA. In 2017, 274 master's awarded. *Program availability:* Part-time, evening/weekend. Offers accounting (MBA); advanced accounting (M Acct); entrepreneurship (MBA); finance (MBA); information assurance (M Acct, MBA); information systems and assurance (MS); international management (MBA); international management in Latin America (MBA); management (EMBA, M Acct, MBA, MS); management information systems (MBA); management of technology (MBA); marketing management (MBA); operations management (MBA); organizational behavior and human resources management (MBA); professional accounting (M Acct); strategic management and policy (MBA); tax accounting (M Acct). *Application deadline:* For fall admission, 4/1 priority date for domestic and international students; for spring admission, 10/1 priority date for domestic and international students. Applications are processed on a rolling basis. *Application fee:* $50. Electronic applications accepted. *Application Contact:* Lisa Beauchene, Student Recruitment Specialist, 505-277-6471, E-mail: andersonadvising@unm.edu. *Dean*, Dr. Craig White, 505-277-1792, E-mail: cwhite@unm.edu.

Graduate Studies Students: 2,073 full-time (1,117 women), 1,979 part-time (1,117 women); includes 1,459 minority (82 Black or African American, non-Hispanic/Latino; 171 American Indian or Alaska Native, non-Hispanic/Latino; 105 Asian, non-Hispanic/Latino; 984 Hispanic/Latino; 5 Native Hawaiian or other Pacific Islander, non-Hispanic/Latino; 112 Two or more races, non-Hispanic/Latino), 657 international. Average age 34. 3,340 applicants, 40% accepted, 1021 enrolled. *Faculty:* 758 full-time (346 women), 72 part-time/adjunct (37 women). Expenses: Contact institution. *Financial support:* Fellowships, research assistantships, teaching assistantships, career-related internships or fieldwork, Federal Work-Study, institutionally sponsored loans, scholarships/grants, health care benefits, tuition waivers (full and partial), and project assistantships, residencies available. Support available to part-time students. Financial award application deadline: 3/1; financial award applicants required to submit FAFSA. In 2017, 975 master's, 257 doctorates, 57 other advanced degrees awarded. *Program availability:* Part-time, evening/weekend, online only, 100% online, blended/hybrid learning. Offers hydroscience (MWR); policy management (MWR). *Application fee:* $50. Electronic applications accepted. *Application Contact:* Deborah Kieltyka, Associate Director, Admissions, 505-277-3140, Fax: 505-277-6686, E-mail: deborahk@unm.edu. *Dean*, Dr. Julie A. Coonrod, 505-277-2711, Fax: 505-277-7405, E-mail: jcoonrod@unm.edu.

College of Arts and Sciences Students: 728 full-time (368 women), 530 part-time (259 women); includes 349 minority (12 Black or African American, non-Hispanic/Latino; 25 American Indian or Alaska Native, non-Hispanic/Latino; 27 Asian, non-

Hispanic/Latino; 238 Hispanic/Latino; 2 Native Hawaiian or other Pacific Islander, non-Hispanic/Latino; 45 Two or more races, non-Hispanic/Latino), 253 international. Average age 32. 1,345 applicants, 29% accepted, 303 enrolled. *Faculty:* 318 full-time (132 women), 13 part-time/adjunct (5 women). Expenses: Contact institution. *Financial support:* Scholarships/grants, health care benefits, tuition waivers (full and partial), and unspecified assistantships available. Financial award application deadline: 3/1; financial award applicants required to submit FAFSA. In 2017, 225 master's, 114 doctorates awarded. *Program availability:* Part-time. Offers American studies (MA, PhD); archaeology (MA, MS, PhD); arts and sciences (MA, MFA, MS, PhD); behavioral neuroscience (PhD); biology (MS, PhD); chemistry (MS, PhD); clinical psychology (PhD); cognitive neuroimaging (PhD); communication (MA, PhD); comparative literature and cultural studies (MA); creative writing (MFA); developmental psychology (PhD); earth and planetary sciences (MS, PhD); econometrics (MA); economic theory (MA); English (MA, PhD); environmental/natural resource economics (MA, PhD); ethnology (MA, MS, PhD); evolution (PhD); evolutionary anthropology (PhD); French (MA); French studies (PhD); geography and environmental studies (MS); German studies (MA); health psychology (PhD); history (MA, PhD); imaging science (MS, PhD); international/development and sustainability economics (MA, PhD); Latin American studies (MA, PhD); linguistics (MA, PhD); mathematics (MS, PhD); optical science and engineering (MS, PhD); philosophy (MA, PhD); photonics (MS, PhD); physics (MS, PhD); political science (MA, PhD); Portuguese (MA); public archaeology (MA, MS, PhD); public economics (MA, PhD); quantitative methodology (PhD); sociology (MA, PhD); Spanish (MA); Spanish and Portuguese (PhD); speech-language pathology (MS); statistics (MS, PhD). *Application fee:* $50. Electronic applications accepted. *Application Contact:* Vicki Hall, Academic Administrator III, 505-277-6131, Fax: 505-277-0351, E-mail: vhall@unm.edu. *Dean,* Dr. Brenda J. Claiborne, 505-277-6131, Fax: 505-277-0351, E-mail: brendac@unm.edu.

College of Education Students: 353 full-time (244 women), 570 part-time (424 women); includes 436 minority (30 Black or African American, non-Hispanic/Latino; 68 American Indian or Alaska Native, non-Hispanic/Latino; 19 Asian, non-Hispanic/Latino; 298 Hispanic/Latino; 1 Native Hawaiian or other Pacific Islander, non-Hispanic/Latino; 20 Two or more races, non-Hispanic/Latino), 77 international. Average age 37. 398 applicants, 56% accepted, 212 enrolled. *Faculty:* 110 full-time (70 women), 17 part-time/adjunct (12 women). Expenses: Contact institution. *Financial support:* Career-related internships or fieldwork, Federal Work-Study, scholarships/grants, health care benefits, and unspecified assistantships available. Support available to part-time students. Financial award application deadline: 3/1; financial award applicants required to submit FAFSA. In 2017, 288 master's, 33 doctorates, 39 other advanced degrees awarded. *Program availability:* Part-time, evening/weekend. Offers American Indian education (MA); art education (MA); bilingual education (MA, PhD); community health education (MS); counseling (MA); counselor education (PhD); curriculum and instruction (PhD); education (MA, MS, Ed D, PhD, Ed S, Graduate Certificate); educational leadership (MA, Ed D, Ed S); educational linguistics (PhD); educational psychology (MA, PhD); educational thought and sociocultural studies (MA, PhD); exercise science (PhD); family life education (MA); family relations (MA); family studies (PhD); human development in families (MA); intensive social, language and behavioral needs (Graduate Certificate); learning and behavioral exceptionalities (MA); literacy/language arts (MA, PhD); math, science, and educational technology (MA); mental retardation and severe disabilities (MA); multicultural teacher and childhood education (Ed D, PhD); nutrition (MS); social studies (MA); special education (Ed D, PhD, Ed S); sports administration (PhD); TESOL (MA, PhD). *Application deadline:* For fall admission, 3/1 for international students; for spring admission, 8/1 for international students. *Application fee:* $50. Electronic applications accepted. *Application Contact:* Academic Graduate Coordinator, 505-277-3190, E-mail: coeac@unm.edu. *Dean,* Dr. Richard Howell, 505-277-2231, Fax: 505-277-8427, E-mail: rhowell@unm.edu.

College of Fine Arts Students: 99 full-time (57 women), 73 part-time (43 women); includes 51 minority (5 Black or African American, non-Hispanic/Latino; 4 American Indian or Alaska Native, non-Hispanic/Latino; 3 Asian, non-Hispanic/Latino; 34 Hispanic/Latino; 5 Two or more races, non-Hispanic/Latino), 22 international. Average age 31. 200 applicants, 52% accepted, 63 enrolled. *Faculty:* 64 full-time (32 women), 9 part-time/adjunct (6 women). Expenses: Contact institution. *Financial support:* Unspecified assistantships available. Financial award application deadline: 3/1; financial award applicants required to submit FAFSA. In 2017, 41 master's awarded. *Program availability:* Part-time. Offers art history (MA); art of the Americas (MA); collaborative piano (M Mu); conducting (M Mu); dance (MFA); dance history (MA); dramatic writing (MFA); fine arts (M Mu, MA, MFA, PhD); history of architecture (PhD); history of graphic arts (PhD); history of photography (PhD); modern Latin American art (PhD); music education (M Mu); music history and literature (M Mu); Native American art (PhD); performance (M Mu); Pre-Columbian art and architecture (PhD); Spanish colonial art (PhD); studio art (MFA); theatre education and outreach (MA); theory and composition (M Mu). *Application fee:* $50. *Application Contact:* Deanna Sanchez-Mulcahy, Associate Director, Admissions, 505-277-4817, Fax: 505-277-0708, E-mail: dmulcahy@unm.edu. *Dean,* Dr. Jim Linnell, 505-277-2112, Fax: 505-277-0708, E-mail: jlinnell@unm.edu.

College of Pharmacy *Program availability:* Part-time. Offers pharmaceutical sciences (MS, PhD); pharmacy (MS, PhD, Pharm D). Electronic applications accepted.

College of University Libraries and Learning Sciences Average age 45. 30 applicants, 80% accepted, 21 enrolled. Expenses: Contact institution. *Financial support:* Fellowships, research assistantships, teaching assistantships, and career-related internships or fieldwork available. Financial award application deadline: 3/1; financial award applicants required to submit FAFSA. In 2017, 19 master's, 4 doctorates awarded. *Program availability:* Part-time, evening/weekend, online learning. Offers organization, information and learning sciences (MA, PhD, Ed S). *Application deadline:* For fall admission, 3/15 for domestic and international students; for spring admission, 10/15 for domestic and international students. *Application fee:* $50. Electronic applications accepted. *Application Contact:* Linda Wood, Program Coordinator, 505-277-4131, Fax: 505-277-1427, E-mail: woodl@unm.edu. *Program Director,* Dr. Charlotte Gunawardens, 505-277-5046, Fax: 505-277-1427, E-mail: lani@unm.edu.

Health Sciences Center Average age 30. 218 applicants, 47% accepted, 94 enrolled. Expenses: Contact institution. Offers biochemistry and molecular biology (MS, PhD); cell biology and physiology (MS, PhD); clinical and translational science (Certificate); community health (MPH); dental hygiene (MS); education (MS); epidemiology (MPH); health sciences (MOT, MPH, MPT, MS, MSN, DNP, DPT, MD, PhD, Pharm D, Certificate); health systems, services and policy (MPH); laboratory management (MS); molecular genetics and microbiology (MS, PhD); neuroscience (MS, PhD); nursing (MSN, DNP, PhD); occupational therapy (MOT); pathology (MS, PhD); physical therapy (DPT); physician assistant studies (MS); research and development (MS); toxicology (MS, PhD). *Application Contact:* Deborah Kieltyka, Associate Director, Admissions, 505-277-3140, Fax: 505-277-6686, E-mail: deborahk@unm.edu. *Interim Vice President,* Dr. R. Philip Eaton, 505-272-5849.

School of Architecture and Planning Students: 141 full-time (67 women), 41 part-time (22 women); includes 75 minority (1 Black or African American, non-Hispanic/Latino; 14 American Indian or Alaska Native, non-Hispanic/Latino; 3 Asian, non-Hispanic/Latino; 50 Hispanic/Latino; 7 Two or more races, non-Hispanic/Latino), 37 international. Average age 32. 148 applicants, 56% accepted, 71 enrolled. *Faculty:* 37 full-time (19 women), 13 part-time/adjunct (5 women). Expenses: Contact institution. *Financial support:* Application deadline: 3/1; applicants required to submit FAFSA. In 2017, 73 master's, 11 other advanced degrees awarded. Offers architecture (M Arch); architecture and planning (M Arch, MCRP, MLA, Graduate Certificate); community and regional planning (MCRP); historic preservation and regionalism (Graduate Certificate); landscape architecture (MLA). *Application deadline:* For fall admission, 2/1 for domestic and international students. *Application fee:* $50. Electronic applications accepted. *Application Contact:* Elizabeth M. Rowe, Senior Academic Adviser, 505-277-1303, Fax: 505-277-0076, E-mail: erowe@unm.edu. *Dean,* Geraldine Forbes Isais, 505-277-2053, E-mail: gforbes@unm.edu.

School of Engineering Students: 307 full-time (67 women), 377 part-time (88 women); includes 166 minority (7 Black or African American, non-Hispanic/Latino; 5 American Indian or Alaska Native, non-Hispanic/Latino; 26 Asian, non-Hispanic/Latino; 113 Hispanic/Latino; 15 Two or more races, non-Hispanic/Latino), 217 international. Average age 31. 651 applicants, 32% accepted, 171 enrolled. *Faculty:* 99 full-time (20 women), 10 part-time/adjunct (3 women). Expenses: Contact institution. *Financial support:* Federal Work-Study, scholarships/grants, health care benefits, and unspecified assistantships available. Financial award application deadline: 3/1; financial award applicants required to submit FAFSA. In 2017, 142 master's, 53 doctorates awarded. *Program availability:* Part-time. Offers biomedical engineering (MS, PhD); chemical engineering (MS, PhD); civil engineering (M Eng, MSCE); computer engineering (MS, PhD); computer science (MS, PhD); construction management (MCM); electrical and computer engineering (MS, PhD); engineering (M Eng, MCM, MEME, MS, MSCE, PhD); manufacturing engineering (MEME); mechanical engineering (MS, PhD); nanoscience and microsystems engineering (MS, PhD); nuclear engineering (MS, PhD). *Application deadline:* For fall admission, 1/15 priority date for domestic and international students; for spring admission, 7/14 priority date for domestic and international students. Applications are processed on a rolling basis. *Application fee:* $50. Electronic applications accepted. *Application Contact:* Deborah Kieltyka, Associate Director, Admissions, 505-277-3140, Fax: 505-277-6686, E-mail: deborahk@unm.edu. *Dean,* Christos Christodoulou, 505-277-5522, Fax: 505-277-5521, E-mail: christos@unm.edu.

School of Public Administration Students: 70 full-time (45 women), 129 part-time (93 women); includes 116 minority (10 Black or African American, non-Hispanic/Latino; 29 American Indian or Alaska Native, non-Hispanic/Latino; 4 Asian, non-Hispanic/Latino; 72 Hispanic/Latino; 1 Two or more races, non-Hispanic/Latino), 11 international. Average age 36. 94 applicants, 80% accepted, 64 enrolled. *Faculty:* 13 full-time (4 women), 2 part-time/adjunct (0 women). Expenses: Contact institution. *Financial support:* Fellowships with partial tuition reimbursements, research assistantships with partial tuition reimbursements, career-related internships or fieldwork, scholarships/grants, health care benefits, and unspecified assistantships available. Financial award application deadline: 3/31; financial award applicants required to submit FAFSA. In 2017, 95 master's awarded. *Program availability:* Part-time, evening/weekend, online learning. Offers health administration (MHA); public administration (MHA, MPA). *Application deadline:* For fall admission, 4/1 for domestic students, 3/1 for international students; for spring admission, 10/1 for domestic students, 8/1 for international students. *Application fee:* $50. Electronic applications accepted. *Application Contact:* Gene V. Henley, Associate Director and Graduate Academic Advisor, 505-277-9196, Fax: 505-277-2529, E-mail: spadvise@unm.edu. *Director,* Dr. Uday Desai, 505-277-1092, Fax: 505-277-2529, E-mail: ucdesai@unm.edu.

School of Law Offers law (JD). Electronic applications accepted.

School of Medicine Offers medicine (MOT, MPH, MS, DPT, MD, PhD, Certificate); university science teaching (Certificate). Electronic applications accepted.

UNIVERSITY OF NEW ORLEANS, New Orleans, LA 70148

General Information State-supported, coed, university. *Graduate housing:* Rooms and/or apartments available on a first-come, first-served basis to single and married students. *Student services:* Campus employment opportunities, campus safety program, career counseling, child daycare facilities, exercise/wellness program, free psychological counseling, international student services, low-cost health insurance, multicultural affairs office, services for students with disabilities. *Library facilities:* Earl K. Long Library. *Collection:* Books: 1 million (physical), 220,863 (digital/electronic); Serial titles: 25,831 (physical), 55,551 (digital/electronic); Databases: 154. Students can reserve study rooms. *Research affiliation:* John C. Stennis Space Center (acoustics, computer science), Northrop Grumman Corporation (engineering), TJ Watson Research Center-IBM (chemistry), Paratek Microwave, Inc. (nanotechnology), Applied Research Lab-Penn State University (engineering), Lockheed Martin Corporation (materials).

Computer facilities: 1,050 computers available on campus for general student use. A campuswide network can be accessed from student residence rooms and from off campus. Online class registration, learning management system are available.
Website: http://www.uno.edu/

General Application Contact: Amanda M. Athey, Director of Graduate School, 504-280-1155, Fax: 504-280-6298, E-mail: gradschool@uno.edu.

GRADUATE UNITS

Graduate School Expenses: Contact institution. *Financial support:* Fellowships, research assistantships, teaching assistantships, career-related internships or fieldwork, Federal Work-Study, institutionally sponsored loans, scholarships/grants, tuition waivers (full and partial), and unspecified assistantships available. Financial award application deadline: 2/15; financial award applicants required to submit FAFSA. *Program availability:* Part-time, evening/weekend. *Application deadline:* For fall admission, 7/1 priority date for domestic students, 6/1 for international students; for spring admission, 11/1 priority date for domestic students, 10/1 for international students. Applications are processed on a rolling basis. *Application fee:* $50. Electronic applications accepted. *Application Contact:* Amanda M. Athey, Associate Executive Director of Graduate School, 504-280-1155, Fax: 504-280-6298, E-mail: gradschool@uno.edu. *Provost/Vice President for Academic Affairs/Executive Director of Graduate School,* Dr. James E. Payne, 504-280-6237, Fax: 504-280-6298, E-mail: graddean@uno.edu.

College of Business Administration Expenses: Contact institution. *Financial support:* Fellowships, research assistantships, teaching assistantships, and Federal Work-Study available. Financial award application deadline: 3/15; financial award applicants required to submit FAFSA. *Program availability:* Part-time, evening/weekend. Offers accounting (MS); business administration (MBA, MS, PhD); finance (MS); financial economics (PhD); health care management (MS); hospitality and tourism management (MS); taxation (MS). *Application deadline:* For fall admission, 7/1 priority date for domestic students, 6/1 for international students; for spring admission, 11/1 priority date for domestic students, 10/1 for international students. Applications are processed on a rolling basis. *Application fee:* $20. Electronic applications accepted. *Application Contact:* Dr. Paul Hensel, Associate Dean, 504-280-6954, Fax: 504-280-6693, E-mail: phensel@uno.edu. *Dean*, Dr. James W. Logan, 504-280-6954, Fax: 504-280-6958.

College of Engineering Expenses: Contact institution. *Financial support:* Fellowships, research assistantships, teaching assistantships, and institutionally sponsored loans available. Financial award application deadline: 3/15; financial award applicants required to submit FAFSA. *Program availability:* Part-time. Offers civil engineering (MS); electrical engineering (MS); engineering (MS, PhD); engineering and applied science (PhD); engineering management (MS); mechanical engineering (MS); naval architecture and marine engineering (MS). *Application deadline:* For fall admission, 7/1 priority date for domestic students, 6/1 for international students; for spring admission, 11/1 priority date for domestic students, 10/1 for international students. Applications are processed on a rolling basis. *Application fee:* $20. Electronic applications accepted. *Application Contact:* Dr. Bhaskar Kura, Associate Dean for Program Development, 504-280-6572, Fax: 504-280-7413, E-mail: bkura@uno.edu. *Associate Dean for Research and Graduate Programs*, Dr. Paul Chirlian, 504-280-5504, Fax: 504-286-7413, E-mail: pchirlia@uno.edu.

College of Liberal Arts, Education and Human Development Expenses: Contact institution. *Financial support:* Fellowships, research assistantships, teaching assistantships, career-related internships or fieldwork, Federal Work-Study, institutionally sponsored loans, and tuition waivers (full and partial) available. Financial award application deadline: 3/15; financial award applicants required to submit FAFSA. *Program availability:* Part-time, evening/weekend. Offers arts administration (MA); counseling (M Ed); counselor education (M Ed, PhD); creative writing (MFA); curriculum and instruction (M Ed); design (MFA); educational administration (PhD); educational leadership (M Ed, PhD); English (MA, MFA); film production (MFA); fine arts (MFA); higher education (M Ed); history (MA); liberal arts, education and human development (MA, MFA, MM, MPA, MS, MURP, PhD); music (MM); political science (MA, PhD); public administration (MPA); Romance languages (MA); sociology (MA); teaching (MAT); theatre performance (MFA); transportation (MS); urban and regional planning (MURP); urban studies (MS, PhD). *Application deadline:* For fall admission, 7/1 priority date for domestic students, 6/1 for international students; for spring admission, 11/1 priority date for domestic students, 10/1 for international students. Applications are processed on a rolling basis. *Application fee:* $20. Electronic applications accepted. *Application Contact:* Dr. Kevin Graves, Professor and Associate Dean, 504-280-6268, Fax: 504-280-6468, E-mail: kgraves@uno.edu. *Dean*, Dr. Susan Krantz, 504-280-6267, Fax: 504-280-6468, E-mail: susan.krantz@uno.edu.

College of Sciences Expenses: Contact institution. *Financial support:* Fellowships, research assistantships, teaching assistantships, career-related internships or fieldwork, Federal Work-Study, institutionally sponsored loans, and unspecified assistantships available. Financial award application deadline: 3/15; financial award applicants required to submit FAFSA. *Program availability:* Part-time, evening/weekend. Offers biological sciences (MS); chemistry (MS, PhD); computer science (MS, PhD); earth and environmental sciences (MS, PhD); mathematics (MS); physics (MS, PhD); psychology (MS, PhD); sciences (MS, PhD). *Application deadline:* For fall admission, 7/1 priority date for domestic students, 6/1 for international students; for spring admission, 11/1 priority date for domestic students, 10/1 for international students. Applications are processed on a rolling basis. *Application fee:* $20. Electronic applications accepted. *Application Contact:* Dr. Miriam Daunis, Associate Dean, 504-280-6303, Fax: 504-280-7483, E-mail: mdaunis@uno.edu. *Dean*, Dr. Steven G. Johnson, 504-280-6303, Fax: 504-280-7483, E-mail: sgjohnso@uno.edu.

UNIVERSITY OF NORTH ALABAMA, Florence, AL 35632-0001

General Information State-supported, coed, comprehensive institution. *Enrollment:* 7,457 graduate, professional, and undergraduate students; 354 full-time matriculated graduate/professional students (199 women), 852 part-time matriculated graduate/professional students (504 women). *Enrollment by degree level:* 1,169 master's, 37 other advanced degrees. *Graduate faculty:* 105 full-time (39 women), 19 part-time/adjunct (6 women). Tuition, state resident: full-time $7824; part-time $5943 per year. Tuition, nonresident: full-time $15,648; part-time $11,736 per year. *Required fees:* $3064; $2298 per unit. Tuition and fees vary according to course load and reciprocity agreements. *Graduate housing:* Rooms and/or apartments available on a first-come, first-served basis to single and married students. Typical cost: $4500 per year for single students; $9600 per year for married students. Room charges vary according to board plan and housing facility selected. *Student services:* Campus employment opportunities, campus safety program, career counseling, exercise/wellness program, free psychological counseling, grant writing training, international student services, multicultural affairs office, services for students with disabilities, writing training. *Library facilities:* Collier Library plus 3 others. *Collection:* Books: 225,076 (physical), 469,260 (digital/electronic); Serial titles: 4,070 (physical), 55,929 (digital/electronic); Databases: 182. Weekly public service hours: 98; students can reserve study rooms.

Computer facilities: 925 computers available on campus for general student use. A campuswide network can be accessed. Online class registration is available.
Website: http://www.una.edu/

General Application Contact: Hillary N. Coats, Graduate Admissions Coordinator, 256-765-4447, E-mail: hcoats@una.edu.

GRADUATE UNITS

Anderson College of Nursing Students: 42 full-time (39 women), 56 part-time (49 women); includes 25 minority (21 Black or African American, non-Hispanic/Latino; 1 Asian, non-Hispanic/Latino; 1 Hispanic/Latino; 2 Two or more races, non-Hispanic/Latino). Average age 34. 53 applicants, 77% accepted, 32 enrolled. *Faculty:* 14 full-time (all women). Expenses: Contact institution. *Financial support:* In 2017–18, 4 students received support. Scholarships/grants available. Financial award application deadline: 2/1; financial award applicants required to submit FAFSA. In 2017, 37 master's awarded. *Program availability:* Part-time, online only, 100% online, blended/hybrid learning. Offers nursing (MSN). *Application deadline:* Applications are processed on a rolling basis. *Application fee:* $50 ($100 for international students). Electronic applications accepted. *Application Contact:* Hillary N. Coats, Graduate Admissions Coordinator, 256-465-4447, E-mail: graduate@una.edu. *Dean*, Dr. Vicky G. Pierce, 256-765-4311, E-mail: vgpierce@una.edu.

College of Arts and Sciences Students: 47 full-time (23 women), 95 part-time (63 women); includes 21 minority (14 Black or African American, non-Hispanic/Latino; 1 American Indian or Alaska Native, non-Hispanic/Latino; 2 Asian, non-Hispanic/Latino; 4 Hispanic/Latino), 15 international. Average age 32. 94 applicants, 72% accepted, 49 enrolled. *Faculty:* 53 full-time (20 women), 7 part-time/adjunct (3 women). Expenses: Contact institution. *Financial support:* In 2017–18, 44 students received support. Career-related internships or fieldwork, Federal Work-Study, scholarships/grants, and unspecified assistantships available. Financial award application deadline: 2/1; financial award applicants required to submit FAFSA. In 2017, 42 master's awarded. *Program availability:* Part-time, 100% online. Offers arts and sciences (MA, MPS, MS, MSCJ); creative writing (MA); criminal justice (MSCJ); English (MA); family studies (MS); geospatial science (MS); historic preservation (MA); historical administration (MA); history (MA); professional studies (MPS); public history (MA); rhetoric and composition (MA); technical writing (MA); writing (MA). *Application deadline:* Applications are processed on a rolling basis. *Application fee:* $50 ($100 for international students). Electronic applications accepted. *Application Contact:* Hillary N. Coats, Graduate Admissions Coordinator, 256-765-4447, E-mail: graduate@una.edu. *Dean*, Dr. Carmen L. Burkhalter, 256-765-4288, Fax: 256-765-4778, E-mail: cburkhalter@una.edu.

College of Business Students: 178 full-time (78 women), 498 part-time (237 women); includes 229 minority (92 Black or African American, non-Hispanic/Latino; 8 American Indian or Alaska Native, non-Hispanic/Latino; 104 Asian, non-Hispanic/Latino; 14 Hispanic/Latino; 11 Two or more races, non-Hispanic/Latino), 53 international. Average age 34. 354 applicants, 71% accepted, 190 enrolled. *Faculty:* 26 full-time (1 woman), 4 part-time/adjunct (0 women). Expenses: Contact institution. *Financial support:* In 2017–18, 114 students received support. Scholarships/grants available. Financial award application deadline: 2/1; financial award applicants required to submit FAFSA. In 2017, 156 master's awarded. *Program availability:* Part-time, 100% online, blended/hybrid learning. Offers business administration (MBA). *Application deadline:* Applications are processed on a rolling basis. *Application fee:* $50 ($100 for international students). Electronic applications accepted. *Application Contact:* Hillary N. Coats, Graduate Admissions Coordinator, 256-765-4447, E-mail: graduate@una.edu. *Dean*, Dr. Gregory A. Carnes, 256-765-4261, Fax: 256-765-4170, E-mail: gacarnes@una.edu.

College of Education Students: 87 full-time (59 women), 203 part-time (155 women); includes 34 minority (23 Black or African American, non-Hispanic/Latino; 3 American Indian or Alaska Native, non-Hispanic/Latino; 2 Hispanic/Latino; 6 Two or more races, non-Hispanic/Latino), 3 international. Average age 32. 161 applicants, 61% accepted, 81 enrolled. *Faculty:* 23 full-time (13 women), 8 part-time/adjunct (3 women). Expenses: Contact institution. *Financial support:* In 2017–18, 39 students received support. Federal Work-Study, scholarships/grants, and unspecified assistantships available. Financial award application deadline: 2/1; financial award applicants required to submit FAFSA. In 2017, 106 master's, 32 other advanced degrees awarded. *Program availability:* Part-time, 100% online, blended/hybrid learning. Offers clinical mental health counseling (MA); collaborative teacher special education (MA Ed); counseling (MA Ed); education (MA, MA Ed, MS, Ed S); elementary education (MA Ed, Ed S); health and human performance (MS); instructional leadership (MA Ed, Ed S); secondary education (MA Ed); special education (MA Ed); teacher leader (Ed S). *Application deadline:* Applications are processed on a rolling basis. *Application fee:* $50 ($100 for international students). Electronic applications accepted. *Application Contact:* Hillary N. Coats, Graduate Admissions Coordinator, 256-765-4447, E-mail: graduate@una.edu. *Dean*, Dr. Donna Lefort, 256-765-4252, Fax: 256-765-4664, E-mail: dpjacobs@una.edu.

UNIVERSITY OF NORTH CAROLINA AT ASHEVILLE, Asheville, NC 28804-3299

General Information State-supported, coed, comprehensive institution. *Enrollment:* 3,852 graduate, professional, and undergraduate students; 1 full-time matriculated graduate/professional student, 24 part-time matriculated graduate/professional students (12 women). *Enrollment by degree level:* 25 master's. *Graduate faculty:* 7 full-time (1 woman), 3 part-time/adjunct (1 woman). Tuition, state resident: full-time $4914. Tuition, nonresident: full-time $21,236. *Required fees:* $3023. *Graduate housing:* Room and/or apartments available on a first-come, first-served basis to single students; on-campus housing not available to married students. Typical cost: $5134 per year ($9106 including board). Housing application deadline: 5/1. *Student services:* Campus employment opportunities, career counseling, exercise/wellness program, international student services, low-cost health insurance, multicultural affairs office, services for students with disabilities, writing training. *Library facilities:* D. Hiden Ramsey Library. *Collection:* Books: 279,970 (physical), 670,018 (digital/electronic); Serial titles: 199 (physical), 76,919 (digital/electronic); Databases: 178. Students can reserve study rooms.

Computer facilities: Computer purchase and lease plans are available. 500 computers available on campus for general student use. A campuswide network can be accessed. Online class registration is available.
Website: http://www.unca.edu/

General Application Contact: Jordan Dolfi, Program Associate, Graduate Studies, 828-250-2399.

GRADUATE UNITS

Master of Liberal Arts and Sciences Program Students: 1 full-time (0 women), 24 part-time (12 women); includes 3 minority (2 Black or African American, non-Hispanic/Latino; 1 Two or more races, non-Hispanic/Latino). Average age 44. 18 applicants, 83% accepted, 8 enrolled. *Faculty:* 7 full-time (1 woman), 3 part-time/adjunct (1 woman). Expenses: Contact institution. *Financial support:* Application deadline: 5/1; applicants required to submit FAFSA. In 2017, 19 master's awarded. *Program availability:* Part-time, evening/weekend. Offers climate change and society (Graduate Certificate); environmental and cultural sustainability (Graduate Certificate). *Application deadline:* For fall admission, 4/15 priority date for domestic students; for spring admission, 11/15 priority date for domestic students. Applications are processed on a rolling basis. *Application fee:* $60. Electronic applications accepted. *Application Contact:* Jordan Dolfi, Program Coordinator, Master of Liberal Arts and Sciences Program and the Asheville Graduate Center, 828-251-6099, E-mail: jdolfi@unca.edu. *Director, Master of Liberal Arts and Sciences Program and the Asheville Graduate Center*, Gerard Voos, 828-232-5040, E-mail: gvoos@unca.edu.

THE UNIVERSITY OF NORTH CAROLINA AT CHAPEL HILL, Chapel Hill, NC 27599

General Information State-supported, coed, university. CGS member. *Graduate housing:* Rooms and/or apartments available on a first-come, first-served basis to single and married students. *Research affiliation:* Research Triangle Institute, Centers for Disease Control (CDC), Triangle Universities Nuclear Laboratory.

GRADUATE UNITS

Eshelman School of Pharmacy Students: 107 full-time (60 women); includes 27 minority (3 Black or African American, non-Hispanic/Latino; 17 Asian, non-

Hispanic/Latino; 4 Hispanic/Latino; 3 Two or more races, non-Hispanic/Latino), 16 international. Average age 26. 229 applicants, 7% accepted, 16 enrolled. *Faculty:* 115 full-time (47 women), 362 part-time/adjunct (189 women). Expenses: Contact institution. *Financial support:* In 2017–18, 107 students received support, including 18 fellowships with full tuition reimbursements available (averaging $30,000 per year), 56 research assistantships with full tuition reimbursements available (averaging $30,000 per year); career-related internships or fieldwork, Federal Work-Study, institutionally sponsored loans, scholarships/grants, traineeships, health care benefits, tuition waivers (full), and unspecified assistantships also available. Financial award application deadline: 12/12. In 2017, 8 master's, 16 doctorates awarded. Offers pharmaceutical sciences (PhD); pharmaceutical sciences - health system pharmacy administration (MS); pharmacy (Pharm D). *Application deadline:* For fall admission, 12/12 for domestic students, 12/12 priority date for international students. Applications are processed on a rolling basis. *Application fee:* $90. Electronic applications accepted. *Application Contact:* Olivia Hammill, Assistant Director of Recruitment and Admissions, 919-962-0097, Fax: 919-966-9428, E-mail: olivia_hammill@unc.edu. *Dean,* Dr. Dhiren Thakker, 919-966-1122, Fax: 919-966-6919, E-mail: dhiren_thakker@unc.edu.

Graduate School *Program availability:* Online learning. Electronic applications accepted.

College of Arts and Sciences *Program availability:* Part-time. Offers acting (MFA); anthropology (MA, PhD); art history (MA, PhD); arts and sciences (MA, MCRP, MFA, MPA, MRP, MS, MSRA, PhD, Certificate); athletic training (MA); behavioral neuroscience psychology (PhD); botany (MA, MS, PhD); cell biology, development, and physiology (MA, MS, PhD); cell motility and cytoskeleton (PhD); chemistry (MA, MS, PhD); city and regional planning (MCRP); classical archaeology (MA, PhD); classics (MA, PhD); clinical psychology (PhD); cognitive psychology (PhD); communication studies (PhD); computer science (MS, PhD); costume production (MFA); developmental psychology (PhD); ecology (MA, MS, PhD); ecology and behavior (MA, MS, PhD); economics (MS, PhD); English (MA, PhD); exercise physiology (MA); folklore (MA); French (MA, PhD); genetics and molecular biology (MA, MS, PhD); geography (MA, PhD); geological sciences (MS, PhD); German studies (PhD); global studies (MA); history (MA, PhD); Italian (MA, PhD); Latin American studies (Certificate); linguistics (MA); marine sciences (MS, PhD); mathematics (MA, MS, PhD); morphology, systematics, and evolution (MA, MS, PhD); music (MA, PhD); operations research (MS, PhD); philosophy (MA, PhD); physics (MS, PhD); planning (PhD); political science (MA, PhD); Portuguese (MA, PhD); public policy (PhD); public policy analysis (PhD); quantitative psychology (PhD); religious studies (MA, PhD); Romance languages (MA, PhD); Romance philology (MA, PhD); social psychology (PhD); sociology (MA, PhD); Spanish (MA, PhD); sport administration (MA); statistics (MS, PhD); studio art (MFA); technical production (MFA); trans-Atlantic studies (MA). Electronic applications accepted.

Gillings School of Global Public Health Students: 1,116 full-time (808 women), 132 part-time (81 women); includes 382 minority (106 Black or African American, non-Hispanic/Latino; 2 American Indian or Alaska Native, non-Hispanic/Latino; 111 Asian, non-Hispanic/Latino; 81 Hispanic/Latino; 1 Native Hawaiian or other Pacific Islander, non-Hispanic/Latino; 81 Two or more races, non-Hispanic/Latino), 163 international. Average age 30. 1,969 applicants, 41% accepted, 423 enrolled. *Faculty:* 240 full-time (139 women), 514 part-time/adjunct (257 women). Expenses: Contact institution. *Financial support:* Fellowships, research assistantships, teaching assistantships, career-related internships or fieldwork, Federal Work-Study, scholarships/grants, traineeships, health care benefits, and unspecified assistantships available. Financial award application deadline: 12/11; financial award applicants required to submit FAFSA. In 2017, 300 master's, 94 doctorates awarded. *Program availability:* Part-time, 100% online, blended/hybrid learning. Offers biostatistics (MPH, MS, Dr PH, PhD); clinical research (MSCR); environmental engineering (MPH, MS, MSEE, MSPH); environmental health sciences (MPH, MS, MSPH, PhD); epidemiology (MPH, PhD); global public health (MHA, MPH, MS, MSCR, MSEE, MSPH, Dr PH, PhD); health behavior (MPH, PhD); health care and prevention (MPH); health policy and management (MHA, MPH, MSPH, Dr PH, PhD); leadership (MPH); maternal and child health (MPH, MSPH, Dr PH, PhD); nutrition (MPH, PhD); nutrition/registered dietitian (MPH); nutritional biochemistry (MS); occupational health nursing (MPH); veterinary epidemiology (MPH). *Application deadline:* For fall admission, 1/10 for domestic and international students. Applications are processed on a rolling basis. *Application fee:* $85. Electronic applications accepted. *Application Contact:* Johnston King, Enrollment Management Coordinator, 919-962-6314, Fax: 919-966-6352, E-mail: sph-osa@unc.edu. *Dean,* Dr. Barbara K. Rimer, 919-966-3245, Fax: 919-966-7678.

School of Education *Program availability:* Part-time. Offers culture, curriculum and change (MA, PhD); early childhood intervention and family support (M Ed); early childhood, intervention and literacy (MA, PhD); education (M Ed, MA, MAT, MSA, Ed D, PhD); education for experienced teachers (K-12) (M Ed); educational leadership (Ed D); educational psychology, measurement and evaluation (MA, PhD); English (Grades 9-12) (MAT); English as a second language (MAT); French (Grades K-12) (MAT); German (Grades K-12) (MAT); Japanese (Grades K-12) (MAT); Latin (Grades 9-12) (MAT); mathematics (Grades 9-12) (MAT); music (Grades K-12) (MAT); school administration (MSA); school counseling (M Ed); school psychology (M Ed, MA, PhD); science (Grades 9-12) (MAT); social studies (Grades 9-12) (MAT); Spanish (Grades K-12) (MAT). Electronic applications accepted.

School of Government Offers government (MPA). Electronic applications accepted.

School of Information and Library Science Students: 228 full-time (169 women), 27 part-time (20 women); includes 36 minority (7 Black or African American, non-Hispanic/Latino; 10 Asian, non-Hispanic/Latino; 4 Hispanic/Latino; 15 Two or more races, non-Hispanic/Latino), 55 international. Average age 28. 304 applicants, 75% accepted, 100 enrolled. *Faculty:* 24 full-time (8 women), 46 part-time/adjunct (23 women). Expenses: Contact institution. *Financial support:* In 2017–18, 59 fellowships with full tuition reimbursements (averaging $2,565 per year), 46 research assistantships with full tuition reimbursements (averaging $3,528 per year), 7 teaching assistantships with full tuition reimbursements (averaging $22,917 per year) were awarded; career-related internships or fieldwork, Federal Work-Study, scholarships/grants, health care benefits, and unspecified assistantships also available. Financial award application deadline: 12/12. In 2017, 67 master's, 10 doctorates awarded. *Program availability:* Part-time. Offers data curation (PMC); digital curation (PSM); information and library science (PhD); information science (MSIS); library science (MSLS). *Application deadline:* For fall admission, 12/12 priority date for domestic and international students; for spring admission, 10/10 for domestic and international students. Applications are processed on a rolling basis. *Application fee:* $88. Electronic applications accepted. *Application Contact:* Lara Bailey, Student Services Coordinator, 919-962-7601, Fax: 919-962-8071, E-mail: bailey@email.unc.edu. *Dean,* Dr. Gary Marchionini, 919-962-8363, Fax: 919-962-8071, E-mail: gary@ils.unc.edu.

School of Media and Journalism Students: 75 full-time (50 women), 63 part-time (41 women); includes 44 minority (10 Black or African American, non-Hispanic/Latino; 11 Asian, non-Hispanic/Latino; 5 Hispanic/Latino; 18 Two or more races, non-Hispanic/Latino), 6 international. Average age 31. 207 applicants, 41% accepted, 63 enrolled. *Faculty:* 51 full-time (22 women), 4 part-time/adjunct (2 women). Expenses: Contact institution. *Financial support:* In 2017–18, 73 students received support, including 47 fellowships with full tuition reimbursements available (averaging $16,006 per year), 6 research assistantships with full tuition reimbursements available (averaging $17,405 per year); scholarships/grants and health care benefits also available. Financial award application deadline: 12/4; financial award applicants required to submit FAFSA. In 2017, 32 master's, 9 doctorates, 17 other advanced degrees awarded. *Program availability:* Part-time, all course instruction online, plus two on-campus experiences totaling seven days. Offers digital communication (MA, Certificate); media and communication (MA, PhD). MA/JD and JD/PhD offered jointly with School of Law. *Application fee:* $88. Electronic applications accepted. *Application Contact:* Casey Hart, Marketing and Instructional Design Coordinator, 919-843-9471, Fax: 919-962-0620, E-mail: mjgrad@unc.edu. *Dean,* Susan King, 919-962-1204, Fax: 919-962-0620, E-mail: susanking@unc.edu.

School of Social Work *Program availability:* Part-time. Offers social work (MSW, PhD). Electronic applications accepted.

Kenan-Flagler Business School *Program availability:* Evening/weekend, online learning. Offers accounting (MAC); business (MAC, MBA, PhD); business administration (MBA, PhD); finance (PhD); marketing (PhD); operations management (PhD); organizational behavior (PhD); strategy (PhD). Electronic applications accepted.

School of Dentistry Offers dental hygiene (MS); dentistry (MS, DDS, PhD); endodontics (MS); epidemiology (PhD); operative dentistry (MS); oral and maxillofacial pathology (MS); oral and maxillofacial radiology (MS); oral biology (PhD); orthodontics (MS); pediatric dentistry (MS); periodontology (MS); prosthodontics (MS). Electronic applications accepted.

School of Law Offers law (LL M, JD). Electronic applications accepted.

School of Medicine Offers audiology (Au D); biochemistry and biophysics (MS, PhD); bioinformatics and computational biology (PhD); biomedical engineering (MS, PhD); cell and developmental biology (PhD); cell and molecular physiology (PhD); clinical rehabilitation and mental health counseling (MS); experimental pathology (PhD); genetics and molecular biology (MS, PhD); human movement science (PhD); immunology (MS, PhD); medicine (MPT, MS, Au D, DPT, MD, PhD); microbiology (MS, PhD); neurobiology (PhD); occupational science (PhD); occupational science and occupational therapy (MS, PhD); occupational therapy (MS); pharmacology (PhD); physical therapy (DPT); speech and hearing sciences (MS, Au D, PhD); speech-language pathology (MS); toxicology (MS, PhD). Electronic applications accepted.

School of Nursing Students: 208 full-time (186 women), 128 part-time (116 women); includes 100 minority (49 Black or African American, non-Hispanic/Latino; 4 American Indian or Alaska Native, non-Hispanic/Latino; 23 Asian, non-Hispanic/Latino; 7 Hispanic/Latino; 17 Two or more races, non-Hispanic/Latino), 17 international. Average age 33. 624 applicants, 25% accepted, 150 enrolled. *Faculty:* 86 full-time (78 women), 44 part-time/adjunct (40 women). Expenses: Contact institution. *Financial support:* In 2017–18, 8 fellowships with full tuition reimbursements, 6 research assistantships with partial tuition reimbursements (averaging $8,000 per year), 10 teaching assistantships with partial tuition reimbursements (averaging $8,000 per year) were awarded; scholarships/grants, traineeships, health care benefits, and unspecified assistantships also available. Support available to part-time students. Financial award application deadline: 3/1; financial award applicants required to submit FAFSA. In 2017, 91 master's, 14 doctorates awarded. *Program availability:* Part-time. Offers advanced practice registered nurse (DNP); nursing (MSN, PhD, PMC). *Application deadline:* For fall admission, 12/15 for domestic and international students. *Application fee:* $88. Electronic applications accepted. *Application Contact:* Emily Sayed, Assistant Director, Graduate Admissions, 919-966-4260, Fax: 919-966-3540, E-mail: sayed@unc.edu. *Dean/Professor,* Dr. Nilda Peragallo Montano, 919-966-3731, Fax: 919-966-3540, E-mail: npm@email.unc.edu.

THE UNIVERSITY OF NORTH CAROLINA AT CHARLOTTE, Charlotte, NC 28223-0001

General Information State-supported, coed, university. CGS member. *Enrollment:* 29,317 graduate, professional, and undergraduate students; 2,501 full-time matriculated graduate/professional students (1,302 women), 2,902 part-time matriculated graduate/professional students (1,730 women). *Enrollment by degree level:* 3,439 master's, 933 doctoral, 988 other advanced degrees. *Graduate faculty:* 895 full-time (372 women), 90 part-time/adjunct (51 women). Tuition, state resident: full-time $4337. Tuition, nonresident: full-time $17,771. *Required fees:* $3211. Tuition and fees vary according to course load and program. *Graduate housing:* Room and/or apartments available on a first-come, first-served basis to single students; on-campus housing not available to married students. Housing application deadline: 6/1. *Student services:* Campus employment opportunities, campus safety program, career counseling, exercise/wellness program, free psychological counseling, international student services, low-cost health insurance, multicultural affairs office, services for students with disabilities, teacher training, writing training. *Library facilities:* J. Murrey Atkins Library plus 1 other. *Collection:* Books: 812,959 (physical), 980,416 (digital/electronic); Serial titles: 4,578 (physical), 92,904 (digital/electronic); Databases: 675. Study areas open 24 hours, 5–7 days a week; students can reserve study rooms. *Research affiliation:* McGraw Hill Education (special education and child development), SAS Institute (computer science), SURVICE Engineering Company (physics, optical sciences), Health Resources and Services Administration (public health sciences), National Science Foundation (bioinformatics, genomics), HDR Engineering, Inc. of the Carolinas (civil and environmental engineering).

Computer facilities: 1,600 computers available on campus for general student use. A campuswide network can be accessed from student residence rooms and from off campus. Online class registration is available.
Website: http://www.uncc.edu/

General Application Contact: Kathy B. Giddings, Director of Graduate Admissions, 704-687-5503, Fax: 704-687-1668, E-mail: gradadm@uncc.edu.

GRADUATE UNITS

Belk College of Business Students: 246 full-time (98 women), 428 part-time (134 women); includes 133 minority (45 Black or African American, non-Hispanic/Latino; 1 American Indian or Alaska Native, non-Hispanic/Latino; 42 Asian, non-Hispanic/Latino; 32 Hispanic/Latino; 13 Two or more races, non-Hispanic/Latino), 206 international. Average age 30. 599 applicants, 67% accepted, 253 enrolled. *Faculty:* 80 full-time (27 women), 5 part-time/adjunct (0 women). Expenses: Contact institution. *Financial support:* In 2017–18, 82 students received support, including 61 research assistantships (averaging $7,174 per year), 21 teaching assistantships (averaging $20,648 per year); career-related internships or fieldwork, institutionally sponsored loans, scholarships/grants, and unspecified assistantships also available. Support available to part-time students. Financial award application deadline: 3/1; financial award applicants required to submit FAFSA. In 2017, 265 master's, 1 doctorate, 2 other advanced degrees awarded. *Program availability:* Part-time, evening/weekend. Offers applied econometrics (Graduate Certificate); business (M Acct, MBA, MS, DBA, PhD, Graduate Certificate, Post-Master's Certificate, Postbaccalaureate Certificate); business administration (MBA, DBA, PhD); business analytics (Graduate Certificate); economics (MS); management (MS); mathematical finance (MS); real estate (MS, Graduate Certificate). *Application deadline:* Applications are processed on a rolling basis. *Application fee:* $75. Electronic applications accepted. *Application Contact:* Kathy B. Giddings, Director of Graduate Admissions, 704-687-5503, Fax: 704-687-1668, E-mail: gradadm@uncc.edu. *Dean*, Dr. Steven Ott, 704-687-7577, Fax: 704-687-1393, E-mail: cob-dean@uncc.edu.

Turner School of Accountancy Students: 63 full-time (35 women), 48 part-time (22 women); includes 22 minority (5 Black or African American, non-Hispanic/Latino; 11 Asian, non-Hispanic/Latino; 5 Hispanic/Latino; 1 Two or more races, non-Hispanic/Latino), 13 international. Average age 27. 149 applicants, 69% accepted, 76 enrolled. *Faculty:* 10 full-time (3 women), 1 part-time/adjunct (0 women). Expenses: Contact institution. *Financial support:* Research assistantships, teaching assistantships, career-related internships or fieldwork, institutionally sponsored loans, scholarships/grants, and unspecified assistantships available. Support available to part-time students. Financial award application deadline: 3/1; financial award applicants required to submit FAFSA. In 2017, 63 master's awarded. *Program availability:* Part-time, evening/weekend. Offers accountancy (M Acct). *Application deadline:* For fall admission, 3/1 priority date for domestic and international students; for spring admission, 10/1 priority date for domestic and international students; for summer admission, 4/1 priority date for domestic and international students. Applications are processed on a rolling basis. *Application fee:* $75. Electronic applications accepted. *Application Contact:* Kathy B. Giddings, Director of Graduate Admissions, 704-687-5503, Fax: 704-687-1668, E-mail: gradadm@uncc.edu. *Chair*, Dr. Hughlene Burton, 704-687-7701, Fax: 704-687-1382, E-mail: haburton@uncc.edu.

Cato College of Education Students: 294 full-time (232 women), 1,126 part-time (897 women); includes 436 minority (315 Black or African American, non-Hispanic/Latino; 3 American Indian or Alaska Native, non-Hispanic/Latino; 20 Asian, non-Hispanic/Latino; 76 Hispanic/Latino; 22 Two or more races, non-Hispanic/Latino), 27 international. Average age 34. 966 applicants, 79% accepted, 570 enrolled. *Faculty:* 108 full-time (64 women), 40 part-time/adjunct (27 women). Expenses: Contact institution. *Financial support:* In 2017–18, 44 students received support, including 38 research assistantships (averaging $12,881 per year), 4 teaching assistantships (averaging $3,500 per year); career-related internships or fieldwork, institutionally sponsored loans, scholarships/grants, unspecified assistantships, and administrative assistantships also available. Support available to part-time students. Financial award application deadline: 3/1; financial award applicants required to submit FAFSA. In 2017, 265 master's, 31 doctorates, 272 other advanced degrees awarded. *Program availability:* Part-time, evening/weekend, 100% online, blended/hybrid learning. Offers academically or intellectually gifted (Graduate Certificate); art education (Graduate Certificate); autism spectrum disorders (Graduate Certificate); child and family development: birth through kindergarten (Graduate Certificate); child and family development: early childhood education (MAT); child and family studies: early education (M Ed); counseling (MA); counselor education and supervision (PhD); curriculum and instruction (PhD); education (M Ed, MA, MAT, MSA, Ed D, PhD, Graduate Certificate, Post-Master's Certificate, Postbaccalaureate Certificate); education research, measurement, and evaluation (PhD); educational leadership (Ed D); elementary education (M Ed, MAT, Graduate Certificate); elementary mathematics education (Graduate Certificate); foreign language education (MAT); instructional systems technology (M Ed, Graduate Certificate); middle grades and secondary education (M Ed); middle grades education (MAT); play therapy (Postbaccalaureate Certificate); quantitative analysis (Graduate Certificate); reading education (M Ed); school administration (MSA, Post-Master's Certificate); school counseling (Post-Master's Certificate); secondary education (MAT); special education (M Ed, MAT, PhD, Graduate Certificate); substance abuse counseling (Postbaccalaureate Certificate); teaching (Graduate Certificate); teaching English as a second language (M Ed, MAT, Graduate Certificate); theatre education (Graduate Certificate); university and college teaching (Graduate Certificate). *Application deadline:* Applications are processed on a rolling basis. *Application fee:* $75. Electronic applications accepted. *Application Contact:* Kathy B. Giddings, Director of Graduate Admissions, 704-687-5503, Fax: 704-687-1668, E-mail: gradadm@uncc.edu. *Dean*, Dr. Ellen McIntyre, 704-687-8722, E-mail: ellen.mcintyre@uncc.edu.

College of Arts and Architecture Students: 81 full-time (45 women), 2 part-time (both women); includes 16 minority (10 Black or African American, non-Hispanic/Latino; 5 Hispanic/Latino; 1 Two or more races, non-Hispanic/Latino), 27 international. Average age 25. 120 applicants, 86% accepted, 33 enrolled. *Faculty:* 55 full-time (20 women). Expenses: Contact institution. *Financial support:* In 2017–18, 34 students received support, including 31 research assistantships (averaging $6,486 per year), 2 teaching assistantships (averaging $10,000 per year); career-related internships or fieldwork, institutionally sponsored loans, unspecified assistantships, and administrative assistantship also available. Support available to part-time students. Financial award application deadline: 3/1; financial award applicants required to submit FAFSA. In 2017, 55 master's awarded. *Program availability:* Part-time. Offers arts and architecture (M Arch I, M Arch II, MS, MUD, Graduate Certificate); vocal pedagogy (Graduate Certificate). *Application deadline:* Applications are processed on a rolling basis. *Application fee:* $75. Electronic applications accepted. *Application Contact:* Kathy B. Giddings, Director of Graduate Admissions, 704-687-5503, Fax: 704-687-1668, E-mail: gradadm@uncc.edu. *Dean*, Kenneth A. Lambla, 704-687-0090, E-mail: kalambla@uncc.edu.

School of Architecture Students: 81 full-time (45 women), 2 part-time (both women); includes 16 minority (10 Black or African American, non-Hispanic/Latino; 5 Hispanic/Latino; 1 Two or more races, non-Hispanic/Latino), 27 international. Average age 25. 120 applicants, 86% accepted, 33 enrolled. *Faculty:* 26 full-time (9 women). Expenses: Contact institution. *Financial support:* In 2017–18, 33 students received support, including 30 research assistantships (averaging $6,644 per year), 2 teaching assistantships (averaging $5,000 per year); institutionally sponsored loans, scholarships/grants, unspecified assistantships, and administrative assistantship also available. Financial award application deadline: 3/1; financial award applicants required to submit FAFSA. In 2017, 55 master's awarded. Offers architecture (M Arch I, M Arch II, MS); urban design (MUD). *Application deadline:* For fall admission, 1/15 priority date for domestic and international students. Applications are processed on a rolling basis. *Application fee:* $75. Electronic applications accepted. *Application Contact:* Kathy B. Giddings, Director of Graduate Admissions, 704-687-5503, Fax: 704-687-1668, E-mail: gradadm@uncc.edu. *Dean*, Kenneth A. Lambla, 704-687-0090, E-mail: kalambla@uncc.edu.

College of Computing and Informatics Students: 462 full-time (175 women), 269 part-time (85 women); includes 70 minority (26 Black or African American, non-Hispanic/Latino; 24 Asian, non-Hispanic/Latino; 14 Hispanic/Latino; 1 Native Hawaiian or other Pacific Islander, non-Hispanic/Latino; 5 Two or more races, non-Hispanic/Latino), 555 international. Average age 26. 1,900 applicants, 40% accepted, 217 enrolled. *Faculty:* 69 full-time (22 women), 9 part-time/adjunct (1 woman). Expenses: Contact institution. *Financial support:* In 2017–18, 201 students received support, including 11 fellowships (averaging $37,293 per year), 78 research assistantships (averaging $11,480 per year), 112 teaching assistantships (averaging $8,543 per year); career-related internships or fieldwork, institutionally sponsored loans, scholarships/grants, and unspecified assistantships also available. Support available to part-time students. Financial award application deadline: 3/1; financial award applicants required to submit FAFSA. In 2017, 318 master's, 19 doctorates, 17 other advanced degrees awarded. *Program availability:* Part-time, evening/weekend. Offers advanced databases and knowledge discovery (Graduate Certificate); bioinformatics (PSM); bioinformatics and computational biology (PhD); bioinformatics applications (Graduate Certificate); bioinformatics technology (Graduate Certificate); computer science (MS); computing and informatics (MS, PSM, PhD, Graduate Certificate); computing and information systems (PhD); game design and development (Graduate Certificate); information security and privacy (Graduate Certificate); information technology (MS); management of information technology (Graduate Certificate); network security (Graduate Certificate); secure software development (Graduate Certificate). *Application deadline:* Applications are processed on a rolling basis. *Application fee:* $75. Electronic applications accepted. *Application Contact:* Kathy B. Giddings, Director of Graduate Admissions, 704-687-5503, Fax: 704-687-1668, E-mail: gradadm@uncc.edu. *Dean*, Dr. Fatma Mili, 704-687-8450, E-mail: fmili@uncc.edu.

College of Health and Human Services Students: 418 full-time (338 women), 216 part-time (185 women); includes 210 minority (135 Black or African American, non-Hispanic/Latino; 5 American Indian or Alaska Native, non-Hispanic/Latino; 21 Asian, non-Hispanic/Latino; 29 Hispanic/Latino; 20 Two or more races, non-Hispanic/Latino), 17 international. Average age 31. 970 applicants, 45% accepted, 298 enrolled. *Faculty:* 78 full-time (53 women), 21 part-time/adjunct (16 women). Expenses: Contact institution. *Financial support:* In 2017–18, 114 students received support, including 1 fellowship (averaging $11,869 per year), 72 research assistantships (averaging $6,516 per year), 39 teaching assistantships (averaging $10,824 per year); career-related internships or fieldwork, institutionally sponsored loans, scholarships/grants, traineeships, unspecified assistantships, and administrative assistantships also available. Support available to part-time students. Financial award application deadline: 3/1; financial award applicants required to submit FAFSA. In 2017, 219 master's, 12 doctorates, 12 other advanced degrees awarded. *Program availability:* Part-time, evening/weekend, 100% online, blended/hybrid learning. Offers community health (Certificate); health administration (MHA); health and human services (MHA, MPH, MS, MSN, MSW, DNP, PhD, Certificate, Graduate Certificate, Post-Master's Certificate); health services research (PhD); kinesiology (MS); public health (MPH); public health core concepts (Graduate Certificate); public health sciences (PhD); respiratory care (MS). *Application deadline:* Applications are processed on a rolling basis. *Application fee:* $75. Electronic applications accepted. *Application Contact:* Kathy B. Giddings, Director of Graduate Admissions, 704-687-5503, Fax: 704-687-1668, E-mail: gradadm@uncc.edu. *Dean*, Dr. Nancy Fey-Yensan, 704-687-7917, E-mail: fey-yensan@uncc.edu.

School of Nursing Students: 113 full-time (84 women), 163 part-time (150 women); includes 63 minority (47 Black or African American, non-Hispanic/Latino; 2 American Indian or Alaska Native, non-Hispanic/Latino; 6 Asian, non-Hispanic/Latino; 3 Hispanic/Latino; 5 Two or more races, non-Hispanic/Latino). Average age 37. 443 applicants, 31% accepted, 113 enrolled. *Faculty:* 24 full-time (22 women), 6 part-time/adjunct (4 women). Expenses: Contact institution. *Financial support:* In 2017–18, 6 students received support, including 4 research assistantships (averaging $6,338 per year), 2 teaching assistantships (averaging $6,250 per year); career-related internships or fieldwork, institutionally sponsored loans, scholarships/grants, traineeships, and unspecified assistantships also available. Support available to part-time students. Financial award application deadline: 3/1; financial award applicants required to submit FAFSA. In 2017, 83 master's, 8 doctorates, 8 other advanced degrees awarded. *Program availability:* Part-time, blended/hybrid learning. Offers adult-gerontology acute care nurse practitioner (Post-Master's Certificate); advanced clinical nursing (MSN); family nurse practitioner across the lifespan (Post-Master's Certificate); nurse anesthesia (MSN); nurse anesthesia across the lifespan (Post-Master's Certificate); nursing (DNP); nursing administration (Graduate Certificate); nursing education (Graduate Certificate); systems/population nursing (MSN). *Application deadline:* For fall admission, 1/10 for domestic and international students; for spring admission, 9/10 for domestic and international students; for summer admission, 4/1 for domestic and international students. Applications are processed on a rolling basis. *Application fee:* $75. Electronic applications accepted. *Application Contact:* Kathy B. Giddings, Director of Graduate Admissions, 704-687-5503, Fax: 704-687-1668, E-mail: gradadm@uncc.edu. *Director*, Dr. Dena Evans, 704-687-7974, E-mail: devans37@uncc.edu.

School of Social Work Students: 168 full-time (153 women); includes 80 minority (50 Black or African American, non-Hispanic/Latino; 9 Asian, non-Hispanic/Latino; 15 Hispanic/Latino; 6 Two or more races, non-Hispanic/Latino), 4 international. Average age 28. 295 applicants, 49% accepted, 96 enrolled. *Faculty:* 14 full-time (11 women), 11 part-time/adjunct (10 women). Expenses: Contact institution. *Financial support:* In 2017–18, 16 students received support, including 16 research assistantships (averaging $4,029 per year); career-related internships or fieldwork, Federal Work-Study, institutionally sponsored loans, scholarships/grants, unspecified assistantships, and administrative assistantship also available. Support available to part-time students. Financial award application deadline: 3/1; financial award applicants required to submit FAFSA. In 2017, 73 master's awarded. *Program availability:* Part-time. Offers social work (MSW). *Application deadline:* For fall admission, 2/1 for domestic and international students. Applications are processed on a rolling basis. *Application fee:* $75. Electronic applications accepted. *Application Contact:* Kathy B. Giddings, Director of Graduate Admissions, 704-687-5503, Fax: 704-687-1668, E-mail: gradadm@uncc.edu. *Associate Professor and MSW Director*, Dr. Diana Rowan, 704-687-7934, E-mail: drowan@uncc.edu.

College of Liberal Arts and Sciences Students: 450 full-time (277 women), 351 part-time (214 women); includes 176 minority (71 Black or African American, non-Hispanic/Latino; 2 American Indian or Alaska Native, non-Hispanic/Latino; 22 Asian, non-Hispanic/Latino; 63 Hispanic/Latino; 18 Two or more races, non-Hispanic/Latino), 125 international. Average age 29. 804 applicants, 53% accepted, 239 enrolled. *Faculty:* 369 full-time (162 women), 11 part-time/adjunct (4 women). Expenses: Contact institution. *Financial support:* In 2017–18, 361 students received support, including 15 fellowships (averaging $41,389 per year), 105 research assistantships (averaging $10,426 per year), 236 teaching assistantships (averaging $11,242 per year); career-related internships or fieldwork, institutionally sponsored loans, scholarships/grants, and administrative assistantships also available. Support available to part-time students. Financial award application deadline: 3/1; financial award applicants required to submit FAFSA. In 2017, 178 master's, 46 doctorates, 32 other advanced degrees awarded. *Program availability:* Part-time, evening/weekend. Offers Africana studies (Graduate Certificate); anthropology (MA); applied linguistics (Graduate Certificate); applied mathematics (PhD); applied physics (MS); biological sciences (MS, PhD); chemistry (MS); cognitive science (Graduate Certificate); communication studies (MA); criminal justice and criminology (MS); earth sciences (MS); emergency management (Graduate Certificate); English (MA); ethics and applied philosophy (MA, Graduate Certificate); gender, sexuality, and women's studies (Graduate Certificate); geography (MA); geography and urban regional analysis (PhD); gerontology (MA, Graduate Certificate); health psychology (PhD); history (MA); industrial/organizational psychology (MA); languages and culture studies: translating (Graduate Certificate); Latin American studies (MA); liberal arts and sciences (MA, MPA, MS, PhD, Graduate Certificate); liberal studies (MA); mathematics (MS); nanoscale science (PhD); non-profit management (Graduate Certificate); optical science and engineering (MS, PhD); organizational science (PhD); psychology (MA); public administration (MPA); public budgeting and finance (Graduate Certificate); public policy (PhD); religious studies (MA); sociology (MA); Spanish (MA); technical and professional writing (Graduate Certificate); urban management and policy (Graduate Certificate). *Application deadline:* Applications are processed on a rolling basis. *Application fee:* $75. Electronic applications accepted. *Application Contact:* Kathy B. Giddings, Director of Graduate Admissions, 704-687-5503, Fax: 704-687-1668, E-mail: gradadm@uncc.edu. *Dean*, Dr. Nancy A. Gutierrez, 704-687-0081, E-mail: ngutierr@uncc.edu.

The Graduate School Students: 84 full-time (35 women), 100 part-time (42 women); includes 43 minority (16 Black or African American, non-Hispanic/Latino; 15 Asian, non-Hispanic/Latino; 7 Hispanic/Latino; 1 Native Hawaiian or other Pacific Islander, non-Hispanic/Latino; 4 Two or more races, non-Hispanic/Latino), 66 international. Average age 32. 512 applicants, 28% accepted, 73 enrolled. *Faculty:* 3 full-time (2 women), 2 part-time/adjunct (both women). Expenses: Contact institution. *Financial support:* In 2017–18, 27 students received support, including 12 research assistantships (averaging $19,833 per year), 3 teaching assistantships (averaging $6,833 per year); career-related internships or fieldwork, institutionally sponsored loans, scholarships/grants, traineeships, unspecified assistantships, and administrative assistantships also available. Support available to part-time students. Financial award application deadline: 3/1; financial award applicants required to submit FAFSA. In 2017, 63 master's, 24 other advanced degrees awarded. *Program availability:* Part-time, evening/weekend. Offers data science and business analytics (MS, PSM, Graduate Certificate); health informatics (PSM). *Application deadline:* Applications are processed on a rolling basis. *Application fee:* $75. Electronic applications accepted. *Application Contact:* Kathy B. Giddings, Director of Graduate Admissions, 704-687-5503, Fax: 704-687-1668, E-mail: gradadm@uncc.edu. *Dean and Associate Provost*, Dr. Thomas L. Reynolds, 704-687-7248, E-mail: gradadm@uncc.edu.

William States Lee College of Engineering Students: 447 full-time (93 women), 200 part-time (36 women); includes 42 minority (16 Black or African American, non-Hispanic/Latino; 1 American Indian or Alaska Native, non-Hispanic/Latino; 12 Asian, non-Hispanic/Latino; 9 Hispanic/Latino; 4 Two or more races, non-Hispanic/Latino), 417 international. Average age 27. 1,124 applicants, 69% accepted, 199 enrolled. *Faculty:* 132 full-time (21 women), 2 part-time/adjunct (1 woman). Expenses: Contact institution. *Financial support:* In 2017–18, 285 students received support, including 4 fellowships (averaging $40,450 per year), 162 research assistantships (averaging $8,256 per year), 119 teaching assistantships (averaging $7,217 per year); career-related internships or fieldwork, institutionally sponsored loans, scholarships/grants, and unspecified assistantships also available. Support available to part-time students. Financial award application deadline: 3/1; financial award applicants required to submit FAFSA. In 2017, 200 master's, 28 doctorates, 5 other advanced degrees awarded. *Program availability:* Part-time, evening/weekend, blended/hybrid learning. Offers applied energy (Graduate Certificate); applied energy and electromechanical systems (MS); civil engineering (MSCE); construction and facilities management (MS); electrical engineering (MSEE, PhD); energy analytics (Graduate Certificate); engineering (MS, MSCE, MSE, MSEE, MSEM, MSME, PhD, Graduate Certificate); engineering management (MSEM); fire protection and administration (MS); infrastructure and environmental systems (PhD); Lean Six Sigma (Graduate Certificate); logistics and supply chains (Graduate Certificate); mechanical engineering (MSME, PhD); systems analytics (Graduate Certificate). *Application deadline:* Applications are processed on a rolling basis. *Application fee:* $75. Electronic applications accepted. *Application Contact:* Kathy B. Giddings, Director of Graduate Admissions, 704-687-5503, Fax: 704-687-1668, E-mail: gradadm@uncc.edu. *Dean*, Dr. Robert E. Johnson, 704-687-8242, E-mail: robejohn@uncc.edu.

THE UNIVERSITY OF NORTH CAROLINA AT GREENSBORO, Greensboro, NC 27412-5001

General Information State-supported, coed, university. CGS member. *Graduate housing:* Room and/or apartments available to single students; on-campus housing not available to married students. Housing application deadline: 5/15. *Research affiliation:* Moses Cone Memorial Hospital, North Carolina Zoological Park, North Carolina Baptist Hospital.

GRADUATE UNITS

Graduate School *Program availability:* Part-time, evening/weekend, online learning. Offers liberal studies (MALS). Electronic applications accepted.

Bryan School of Business and Economics *Program availability:* Part-time. Offers accounting (MS); applied economics (MA); business administration (MBA, PMC, Postbaccalaureate Certificate); business and economics (MA, MBA, MS, PhD, Certificate, PMC, Postbaccalaureate Certificate); consumer, apparel, and retail studies (MS, PhD); economics (MA, PhD); financial analysis (PMC); financial economics (MA); information systems (PhD); information technology (Certificate); information technology and management (MS); supply chain management (Certificate). Electronic applications accepted.

College of Arts and Sciences *Program availability:* Part-time. Offers advanced Spanish language and Hispanic cultural studies (Certificate); American literature (PhD); applied geography (MA); arts and sciences (M Ed, MA, MFA, MPA, MS, PhD, Certificate); biochemistry (MS); biology (MS); chemistry (MS); clinical psychology (MA, PhD); cognitive psychology (MA, PhD); communication studies (MA); computer science (MS); creative writing (MFA); criminology (MA); developmental psychology (MA, PhD); English (M Ed, MA, PhD, Certificate); English literature (PhD); film and video production (MFA); French (MA); geographic information science (Certificate); geography (PhD); historic preservation (Certificate); history (MA); interior architecture (MS); Latin (M Ed); mathematics (MA, PhD); museum studies (Certificate); nonprofit management (Certificate); public affairs (MPA); rhetoric and composition (PhD); social psychology (MA, PhD); sociology (MA); Spanish (MA, Certificate); studio arts (MFA); U.S. history (PhD); urban and economic development (Certificate); women's and gender studies (MA, Certificate). Electronic applications accepted.

School of Education *Program availability:* Part-time, evening/weekend. Offers advanced school counseling (PMC); college teaching and adult learning (Certificate); counseling and counselor education (PhD); counseling and educational development (MS); couple and family counseling (PMC); cross-categorical special education (M Ed); curriculum and instruction (M Ed); curriculum and teaching (PhD); education (M Ed, MLIS, MS, MSA, Ed D, PhD, Certificate, Ed S, PMC); educational leadership (Ed D, Ed S); educational research, measurement and evaluation (PhD); English as a second language (Certificate); higher education (M Ed, PhD); interdisciplinary studies in special education (M Ed); leadership early care and education (Certificate); library and information studies (MLIS); school administration (MSA); school counseling (PMC); special education (M Ed, PhD); supervision (M Ed); teacher education and development (PhD). Electronic applications accepted.

School of Health and Human Sciences Offers athletic training (MSAT); community health education (MPH, Dr PH); community recreation management (MS); genetic counseling (MS); gerontology (MS, Certificate); health and human sciences (M Ed, MA, MFA, MPH, MS, Dr PH, Ed D, PhD); human development and family studies (M Ed, MS, PhD); kinesiology (MS, Ed D, PhD); nutrition (MS, PhD); peace and conflict studies (MA, Certificate); social work (MSW); speech language pathology (PhD); speech pathology and audiology (MA); therapeutic recreation (MS). Electronic applications accepted.

School of Music, Theatre and Dance Offers acting (MFA); composition (MM); dance (MA, MFA); design (MFA); directing (MFA); education (MM); music education (PhD); performance (MM, DMA); theater education (M Ed); theater for youth (MFA); theatre (M Ed, MFA); theory (MM). Electronic applications accepted.

School of Nursing Offers adult clinical nurse specialist (MSN, PMC); adult/gerontological nurse practitioner (MSN, PMC); nurse anesthesia (MSN, PMC); nursing (PhD); nursing administration (MSN); nursing education (MSN). Electronic applications accepted.

THE UNIVERSITY OF NORTH CAROLINA AT PEMBROKE, Pembroke, NC 28372-1510

General Information State-supported, coed, comprehensive institution. CGS member. *Graduate housing:* Room and/or apartments available to single students; on-campus housing not available to married students. Housing application deadline: 4/15. *Student services:* Campus employment opportunities, career counseling, exercise/wellness program, free psychological counseling, international student services, low-cost health insurance, multicultural affairs office, services for students with disabilities. *Library facilities:* Livermore Library. *Collection:* Books: 409,000 (physical), 172,000 (digital/electronic); Serial titles: 425 (physical), 52,000 (digital/electronic). Weekly public service hours: 92; students can reserve study rooms.

Computer facilities: 501 computers available on campus for general student use. A campuswide network can be accessed from student residence rooms and from off campus. Online class registration, commuter/off campus connection to network, discounted computer software/hardware are available.
Website: http://www.uncp.edu/

General Application Contact: Gary Locklear, Executive Assistant, 910-521-6271, Fax: 910-521-6751, E-mail: grad@uncp.edu.

GRADUATE UNITS

The Graduate School Students: 771; includes 247 minority (121 Black or African American, non-Hispanic/Latino; 107 American Indian or Alaska Native, non-Hispanic/Latino; 5 Asian, non-Hispanic/Latino; 14 Hispanic/Latino). Average age 28. *Faculty:* 157 full-time, 38 part-time/adjunct. Expenses: Contact institution. *Financial support:* In 2017–18, 30 research assistantships with partial tuition reimbursements (averaging $6,000 per year) were awarded; career-related internships or fieldwork, scholarships/grants, and unspecified assistantships also available. Support available to part-time students. Financial award application deadline: 4/15; financial award applicants required to submit FAFSA. In 2017, 226 master's awarded. *Program availability:* Part-time, evening/weekend, 100% online, blended/hybrid learning. Offers art (MAT); art education (MA); clinical nurse leader (MSN); criminal justice (MPA); emergency management (MPA); English education (MA, MAT); health administration (MPA); mathematics education (MA); nurse educator (MSN); public management (MPA); rural case manager (MSN); science education (MA, MAT); social studies education (MA, MAT); social work (MSW). *Application deadline:* For fall admission, 3/15 priority date for domestic and international students; for spring admission, 10/15 priority date for domestic and international students. Applications are processed on a rolling basis. *Application fee:* $45 ($60 for international students). Electronic applications accepted. *Application Contact:* Gary Locklear, Executive Assistant, 910-521-6271, Fax: 910-521-6751, E-mail: grad@uncp.edu. *Dean*, Dr. Irene P. Aiken, 910-521-6271, Fax: 910-521-6751, E-mail: grad@uncp.edu.

School of Business Expenses: Contact institution. *Financial support:* Application deadline: 4/15; applicants required to submit FAFSA. *Program availability:* Part-time, evening/weekend. Offers business (MBA). *Application deadline:* For fall admission, 7/15 priority date for domestic and international students; for spring admission, 12/1 priority date for domestic and international students. Applications are processed on a rolling basis. *Application fee:* $45 ($60 for international students). *Program Director*, Christine Bell, 910-521-6836, E-mail: christine.bell@uncp.edu.

School of Education Expenses: Contact institution. *Financial support:* Application deadline: 4/15. *Program availability:* Part-time, evening/weekend. Offers clinical mental health counseling (MA Ed); education (MA, MA Ed, MAT, MSA); elementary education (MA Ed, MAT); health/physical education (MAT); physical education (MA); professional school counseling (MA Ed); reading education (MA Ed); school administration (MSA). *Application deadline:* For fall admission, 7/15 priority date for domestic and international students; for spring admission, 12/1 priority date for domestic and international students. Applications are processed on a rolling basis. *Application fee:* $45 ($60 for international students). *Dean*, Dr. Alfred Bryant, Jr., 910-775-4009, Fax: 910-521-6165, E-mail: alfred.bryant@uncp.edu.

UNIVERSITY OF NORTH CAROLINA SCHOOL OF THE ARTS, Winston-Salem, NC 27127-2738

General Information State-supported, coed, comprehensive institution. *Graduate housing:* Room and/or apartments available on a first-come, first-served basis to single students. Housing application deadline: 5/1.

GRADUATE UNITS

School of Design and Production Offers costume design (MFA); costume technology (MFA); scene design (MFA); scenic art (MFA); sound design (MFA); stage automation

(MFA); stage properties (MFA); technical direction (MFA); wig and makeup design (MFA). Electronic applications accepted.

School of Filmmaking Offers creative producing (MFA); film music composition (MFA); screenwriting (MFA). Electronic applications accepted.

School of Music Offers music (Artist Certificate); music performance (MM); vocal performance (MM). Electronic applications accepted.

THE UNIVERSITY OF NORTH CAROLINA WILMINGTON, Wilmington, NC 28403-3297

General Information State-supported, coed, comprehensive institution. CGS member. *Enrollment:* 16,487 graduate, professional, and undergraduate students; 842 full-time matriculated graduate/professional students (581 women), 1,053 part-time matriculated graduate/professional students (776 women). *Enrollment by degree level:* 1,707 master's, 141 doctoral, 47 other advanced degrees. *Graduate faculty:* 398 full-time (204 women), 12 part-time/adjunct (7 women). Tuition, state resident: full-time $4626; part-time $226.76 per credit hour. Tuition, nonresident: full-time $17,834; part-time $874.22 per credit hour. *Required fees:* $2124. Tuition and fees vary according to program. *Graduate housing:* Room and/or apartments available on a first-come, first-served basis to single students; on-campus housing not available to married students. Typical cost: $11,496 (including board). Room and board charges vary according to board plan, campus/location and housing facility selected. Housing application deadline: 4/30. *Student services:* Campus employment opportunities, campus safety program, career counseling, exercise/wellness program, free psychological counseling, international student services, low-cost health insurance, multicultural affairs office, services for students with disabilities. *Library facilities:* William Madison Randall Library. *Collection:* Books: 573,457 (physical), 272,920 (digital/electronic); Serial titles: 4,761 (physical), 71,907 (digital/electronic); Databases: 305. Weekly public service hours: 110; study areas open 24 hours, 5–7 days a week; students can reserve study rooms. *Research affiliation:* Seatox Research Inc. (biotechnology research and development), CMS Technology (seafood technology and safety), A-1 Biochem Labs (pharmaceuticals development), O.TM Biotech (environmental testing), OCIS Biotechnology (pharmaceuticals development).

Computer facilities: Computer purchase and lease plans are available. 1,423 computers available on campus for general student use. A campuswide network can be accessed from student residence rooms and from off campus. Online class registration is available.
Website: http://www.uncw.edu/

General Application Contact: Kimberly Harris, Administrative Specialist, Graduate School, 910-962-7449, Fax: 910-962-3787, E-mail: harrisk@uncw.edu.

GRADUATE UNITS

Cameron School of Business Students: 161 full-time (62 women), 69 part-time (40 women); includes 34 minority (16 Black or African American, non-Hispanic/Latino; 3 Asian, non-Hispanic/Latino; 8 Hispanic/Latino; 7 Two or more races, non-Hispanic/Latino), 20 international. Average age 27. 194 applicants, 76% accepted, 134 enrolled. *Faculty:* 48 full-time (15 women). Expenses: Contact institution. *Financial support:* Scholarships/grants and unspecified assistantships available. Financial award application deadline: 1/1; financial award applicants required to submit FAFSA. In 2017, 117 master's awarded. *Program availability:* Part-time. Offers accountancy (MSA); business administration (MBA); business administration - international (MBA); business administration - professional (MBA). *Application deadline:* Applications are processed on a rolling basis. *Application fee:* $75. Electronic applications accepted. *Application Contact:* Candace Wilhelm, Graduate Programs Coordinator, 910-962-3903, Fax: 910-962-2184, E-mail: wilhelmc@uncw.edu. *Dean*, Dr. Robert Burrus, 910-962-3226, Fax: 910-962-3815, E-mail: burrusr@uncw.edu.

Center for Marine Science Students: 7 full-time (6 women), 16 part-time (7 women); includes 4 minority (1 Black or African American, non-Hispanic/Latino; 1 Hispanic/Latino; 2 Two or more races, non-Hispanic/Latino). Average age 25. 12 applicants, 42% accepted, 4 enrolled. *Faculty:* 6 full-time (1 woman). Expenses: Contact institution. *Financial support:* Scholarships/grants and unspecified assistantships available. Financial award application deadline: 1/1; financial award applicants required to submit FAFSA. In 2017, 9 master's awarded. *Program availability:* Part-time. Offers marine science (MS). *Application deadline:* For fall admission, 6/15 for domestic students; for spring admission, 11/15 for domestic students. Applications are processed on a rolling basis. *Application fee:* $75. Electronic applications accepted. *Director*, Dr. Stephen Skrabal, 910-962-7160, E-mail: skrabals@uncw.edu.

College of Arts and Sciences Students: 252 full-time (166 women), 352 part-time (223 women); includes 86 minority (29 Black or African American, non-Hispanic/Latino; 2 American Indian or Alaska Native, non-Hispanic/Latino; 9 Asian, non-Hispanic/Latino; 32 Hispanic/Latino; 14 Two or more races, non-Hispanic/Latino), 7 international. Average age 28. 557 applicants, 42% accepted, 190 enrolled. *Faculty:* 213 full-time (96 women), 4 part-time/adjunct (1 woman). Expenses: Contact institution. *Financial support:* Research assistantships, teaching assistantships, Federal Work-Study, scholarships/grants, unspecified assistantships, and tuition remission available. Support available to part-time students. Financial award application deadline: 1/1; financial award applicants required to submit FAFSA. In 2017, 243 master's, 2 doctorates awarded. *Program availability:* Part-time. Offers applied statistics (Professional Certificate); arts and sciences (MA, MFA, MPA, MS, PhD, Graduate Certificate, Postbaccalaureate Certificate, Professional Certificate); biology (MS); chemistry (MS); clinical psychology (PhD); coastal and ocean policy (MS); conflict management and resolution (MA); creative writing (MFA); English (MA); environmental studies (MS); geographic information science (Graduate Certificate); geoscience (MS); Hispanic studies (Postbaccalaureate Certificate); history (MA); liberal studies (MA); marine biology (MS, PhD); mathematics (MS); psychology (MA); public administration (MPA); sociology and criminology (MA); Spanish (MA). *Application deadline:* Applications are processed on a rolling basis. *Application fee:* $75. Electronic applications accepted. *Application Contact:* Kimberly Harris, Administrative Specialist, Graduate School, 910-962-7449, Fax: 910-962-3787, E-mail: harrisk@uncw.edu. *Dean, College of Arts and Sciences*, Dr. Aswani Volety, 910-962-3111, Fax: 910-962-3114, E-mail: voletya@uncw.edu.

Interdisciplinary Program in Computer Science and Information Systems Students: 32 full-time (15 women), 10 part-time (2 women); includes 4 minority (1 Black or African American, non-Hispanic/Latino; 3 Hispanic/Latino), 8 international. Average age 28. 45 applicants, 56% accepted, 23 enrolled. *Faculty:* 11 full-time (3 women). Expenses: Contact institution. *Financial support:* Scholarships/grants and unspecified assistantships available. Financial award application deadline: 1/1; financial award applicants required to submit FAFSA. In 2017, 4 master's awarded. Offers computer science and information systems (MS); data science (MS). *Application deadline:* For fall admission, 3/1 priority date for domestic students; for spring admission, 11/15 for domestic students. Applications are processed on a rolling basis. *Application fee:* $75. Electronic applications accepted. *Application Contact:* Candace Wilhelm, Graduate Coordinator, 910-962-3903, Fax: 910-962-7457, E-mail: wilhelmc@uncw.edu. *Program Coordinator*, Dr. Clayton Ferner, 910-962-7552, E-mail: cferner@uncw.edu.

School of Health and Applied Human Sciences Students: 2 full-time (both women), 2 part-time (both women); includes 1 minority (Black or African American, non-Hispanic/Latino). Average age 41. 4 applicants, 100% accepted, 2 enrolled. *Faculty:* 12 full-time (8 women). Expenses: Contact institution. *Financial support:* Scholarships/grants and unspecified assistantships available. Financial award application deadline: 1/1; financial award applicants required to submit FAFSA. In 2017, 4 master's awarded. *Program availability:* Part-time. Offers applied gerontology (MS). *Application deadline:* For fall admission, 6/15 for domestic students; for spring admission, 11/15 for domestic students; for summer admission, 3/15 for domestic students. Applications are processed on a rolling basis. *Application fee:* $75. Electronic applications accepted. *Application Contact:* Dr. Anne Glass, Program Coordinator, 910-962-7509, E-mail: glassa@uncw.edu. *Interim Director*, Dr. Steve Elliott, 910-962-2115, Fax: 910-962-7073, E-mail: elliotts@uncw.edu.

School of Nursing Students: 160 full-time (148 women), 237 part-time (213 women); includes 79 minority (55 Black or African American, non-Hispanic/Latino; 3 American Indian or Alaska Native, non-Hispanic/Latino; 6 Asian, non-Hispanic/Latino; 9 Hispanic/Latino; 6 Two or more races, non-Hispanic/Latino). Average age 36. 287 applicants, 71% accepted, 167 enrolled. *Faculty:* 44 full-time (38 women). Expenses: Contact institution. *Financial support:* Application deadline: 1/1; applicants required to submit FAFSA. In 2017, 40 master's awarded. *Program availability:* Part-time, 100% online. Offers clinical research and product development (MS); family nurse practitioner (Post-Master's Certificate); nurse educator (Post-Master's Certificate); nursing (MSN); nursing practice (DNP). *Application deadline:* For fall admission, 3/1 for domestic students. Applications are processed on a rolling basis. *Application fee:* $75. Electronic applications accepted. *Application Contact:* Dr. Micah Scott, MSN Graduate Coordinator, 910-962-7534, E-mail: scottmi@uncw.edu. *Director*, Dr. Laurie Badzek, 910-962-7410, Fax: 910-962-3723, E-mail: badzekl@uncw.edu.

School of Social Work Students: 69 full-time (64 women), 36 part-time (33 women); includes 19 minority (7 Black or African American, non-Hispanic/Latino; 1 Asian, non-Hispanic/Latino; 8 Hispanic/Latino; 3 Two or more races, non-Hispanic/Latino). Average age 29. 101 applicants, 52% accepted, 46 enrolled. *Faculty:* 13 full-time (8 women). Expenses: Contact institution. *Financial support:* Teaching assistantships and scholarships/grants available. Financial award application deadline: 1/1; financial award applicants required to submit FAFSA. In 2017, 41 master's awarded. *Program availability:* Part-time. Offers social work (MSW). *Application deadline:* For fall admission, 2/1 for domestic students. Applications are processed on a rolling basis. *Application fee:* $75. Electronic applications accepted. *Application Contact:* Dr. Kristin Bolton, Interim Graduate Coordinator, 910-962-2308, Fax: 910-962-7283, E-mail: boltonk@uncw.edu. *Director*, Dr. Stacey Kolomer, 910-962-2853, Fax: 910-962-7283, E-mail: kolomers@uncw.edu.

Watson College of Education Students: 159 full-time (118 women), 331 part-time (256 women); includes 136 minority (86 Black or African American, non-Hispanic/Latino; 10 American Indian or Alaska Native, non-Hispanic/Latino; 5 Asian, non-Hispanic/Latino; 22 Hispanic/Latino; 2 Native Hawaiian or other Pacific Islander, non-Hispanic/Latino; 11 Two or more races, non-Hispanic/Latino), 1 international. Average age 34. 199 applicants, 79% accepted, 125 enrolled. *Faculty:* 51 full-time (35 women), 8 part-time/adjunct (6 women). Expenses: Contact institution. *Financial support:* Scholarships/grants and unspecified assistantships available. Financial award application deadline: 1/1; financial award applicants required to submit FAFSA. In 2017, 180 master's, 20 doctorates awarded. *Program availability:* Part-time. Offers curriculum, instruction and supervision (M Ed); education (M Ed, MAT, MS, MSA, Ed D); educational leadership and administration (Ed D); educational leadership, policy, and advocacy (M Ed); elementary education (M Ed, MAT); English as a second language (M Ed, MAT); higher education (M Ed); instructional technology (MS); language and literacy (M Ed); middle grades education (MAT); school administration (MSA); secondary education (M Ed, MAT). *Application deadline:* Applications are processed on a rolling basis. *Application fee:* $75. Electronic applications accepted. *Application Contact:* Kimberly Harris, Administrative Specialist, Graduate School, 910-962-7449, Fax: 910-962-3787, E-mail: harrisk@uncw.edu. *Dean*, Dr. Van Dempsey, 910-962-3354, Fax: 910-962-4081, E-mail: dempseyv@uncw.edu.

UNIVERSITY OF NORTH DAKOTA, Grand Forks, ND 58202

General Information State-supported, coed, university. CGS member. *Graduate housing:* Rooms and/or apartments guaranteed to single students and available on a first-come, first-served basis to married students. *Research affiliation:* U.S. Department of Agriculture (USDA), Human Nutrition Research Center, Neuropsychiatric Research Institute (neurosciences), Environmental Energy Research Center.

GRADUATE UNITS

Graduate School *Program availability:* Part-time, evening/weekend, online learning. Offers clinical translation science (MS, PhD); medicine (MOT, MPAS, MS, DPT, PhD); occupational therapy (MOT); physical therapy (DPT); physician assistant (MPAS). Electronic applications accepted.

College of Arts and Sciences *Program availability:* Part-time, online learning. Offers arts and sciences (M Ed, MA, MFA, MM, MS, DA, PhD); biology (MS); chemistry (MS, PhD); clinical psychology (PhD); communication and public discourse (PhD); criminal justice (PhD); English (MA, PhD); fisheries/wildlife (PhD); forensic psychology (MA, MS); genetics (PhD); geography and geographic information science (MA, MS); history (M Ed, MA, DA, PhD); linguistics (MA); mathematics (M Ed, MS); music (MM); music education (PhD); physics and astrophysics (MA, MS, PhD); sociology (MA); speech-language pathology (MS); visual arts (MFA); zoology (PhD). Electronic applications accepted.

College of Business and Public Administration *Program availability:* Part-time, evening/weekend, online learning. Offers applied economics (MSAE); business administration (MBA); business and public administration (MBA, MPA, MSAE, MSIT); public administration (MPA). Electronic applications accepted.

College of Education and Human Development *Program availability:* Part-time, evening/weekend, online learning. Offers counseling (MA); counseling psychology (PhD); early childhood education (MS); education and human development (M Ed, MA, MS, MSW, Ed D, PhD, Ed S); education/general studies (MS); educational leadership (M Ed, Ed D, PhD, Ed S); elementary education (M Ed, MS); instructional design and technology (M Ed, MS); kinesiology (MS); reading education (M Ed, MS); special education (M Ed, MS). Electronic applications accepted.

College of Nursing and Professional Disciplines *Program availability:* Part-time, evening/weekend, online learning. Offers adult-gerontological nurse practitioner (MS); advanced public health nurse (MS); family nurse practitioner (MS); nurse anesthesia (MS); nurse educator (MS); nursing (PhD, Post-Master's Certificate); nursing and professional disciplines (MS, MSW, DNP, PhD, Post-Master's Certificate); nursing practice (DNP); psychiatric and mental health nurse practitioner (MS); social work (MSW). Electronic applications accepted.

John D. Odegard School of Aerospace Sciences *Program availability:* Part-time, evening/weekend, online learning. Offers aerospace sciences (MEM, MS, PhD); atmospheric sciences (MS, PhD); aviation (MS); computer science (MS); earth system science and policy (MEM, MS, PhD); space studies (MS). Electronic applications accepted.

School of Engineering and Mines *Program availability:* Part-time. Offers chemical engineering (M Engr, MS, PhD); civil engineering (M Engr); electrical engineering (M Engr, MS, PhD); engineering (PhD); engineering and mines (M Engr, MA, MS, PhD); environmental engineering (M Engr, MS, PhD); geological engineering (MS, PhD); geology (MA, MS, PhD); mechanical engineering (M Engr, MS, PhD). Electronic applications accepted.

School of Law Offers law (JD).

School of Medicine and Health Sciences *Program availability:* Online learning. Offers medicine and health sciences (MPH); public health (MPH).

UNIVERSITY OF NORTHERN BRITISH COLUMBIA, Prince George, BC V2N 4Z9, Canada

General Information Province-supported, coed, university. *Graduate housing:* Room and/or apartments available on a first-come, first-served basis to single students; on-campus housing not available to married students. Housing application deadline: 2/15. *Research affiliation:* Houston Forest Products (forestry–wood debris management), TRC Cedar Ltd. (forestry–cyanolicen growth rate study), Remote Law Online Systems Corporation (computer science), Canadian Natural Oils Ltd. (chemistry–oil fractionation), Stella Jones, Inc. (forestry–Douglas fir cores), Insurance Corporation of British Columbia (moose involved in highway traffic accidents).

GRADUATE UNITS

Office of Graduate Studies *Program availability:* Part-time, evening/weekend, online learning.

UNIVERSITY OF NORTHERN COLORADO, Greeley, CO 80639

General Information State-supported, coed, university. CGS member. *Graduate housing:* Rooms and/or apartments available on a first-come, first-served basis to single and married students. Housing application deadline: 5/30.

GRADUATE UNITS

Graduate School *Program availability:* Part-time, evening/weekend, online learning. Electronic applications accepted.

College of Education and Behavioral Sciences *Program availability:* Part-time, online learning. Offers applied statistics and research methods (MS, PhD); clinical counseling (MA); counseling psychology (PhD); counselor education and supervision (PhD); curriculum studies (MAT); deaf/hard of hearing (MA); early childhood special education (MA); education and behavioral sciences (MA, MAT, MS, Ed D, PhD, Ed S); educational leadership (MA, Ed S); educational leadership and policy studies (MA, Ed D, Ed S); educational psychology (MA, PhD); educational studies (Ed D); elementary education (MAT); English education (MAT); gifted and talented (MA); higher education and student affairs leadership (PhD); literacy (MA); multilingual education (MA); school counseling (MA); school psychology (Ed S); special education (MA, PhD); teaching American Sign Language (MA); teaching diverse learners (MA); visual impairment (MA).

College of Humanities and Social Sciences *Program availability:* Part-time. Offers communication (MA); criminal justice (MA); English (MA); history (MA); humanities and social sciences (MA); sociology (MA). Electronic applications accepted.

College of Natural and Health Sciences Offers adult-gerontology acute care nurse practitioner (MSN, DNP); audiology (Au D); biological sciences (MS); biology education (PhD); biomedical sciences (MBS); chemical education (MS, PhD); chemistry (MS); community health education (MPH); earth sciences (MA); educational mathematics (PhD); exercise science (MS, PhD); family nurse practitioner (MSN, DNP); gerontology (MA); global health and community health education (MPH); healthy aging and community health education (MPH); human sciences (MA, MPH, Au D, PhD); mathematical teaching (MA); mathematics (MA); natural and health sciences (MA, MAT, MBS, MPH, MS, MSN, Au D, DNP, PhD); nursing education (PhD); nursing practice (DNP); physical education and physical activity leadership (MAT); rehabilitation counseling (MA); rehabilitation sciences (PhD); speech-language pathology (MA); sport administration (MS, PhD); sport pedagogy (MS, PhD); sports coaching (MA). Electronic applications accepted.

College of Performing and Visual Arts *Program availability:* Part-time. Offers art education (MA); art history (MA); collaborative piano (MM, DA); composition (DA); conducting (MM, DA); instrumental performance (MM); jazz studies (MM, DA); music education (MM, DA); music history and literature (MM, DA); music theory and composition (MM); performance (DA); performing and visual arts (MA, MM, DA); studio art (MA); vocal performance (MM). Electronic applications accepted.

Monfort College of Business Offers accounting (MA); general business management (MBA); healthcare administration (MBA); human resources management (MBA).

UNIVERSITY OF NORTHERN IOWA, Cedar Falls, IA 50614

General Information State-supported, coed, comprehensive institution. CGS member. *Graduate housing:* Rooms and/or apartments available on a first-come, first-served basis to single and married students.

GRADUATE UNITS

Graduate College *Program availability:* Part-time, evening/weekend. Offers philanthropy and nonprofit development (MA); women's and gender studies (MA). Electronic applications accepted.

College of Business Administration *Program availability:* Part-time, evening/weekend. Offers accounting (M Acc); business administration (M Acc, MBA).

College of Education *Program availability:* Part-time, evening/weekend. Offers allied health, recreation, and community services (Ed D); athletic training (MS); career/vocational programming and transition (MAE); community health education (MA); consultant (MAE); curriculum and instruction (Ed D); early childhood education (MAE); education (MA, MAE, MS, Ed D, Ed S); educational leadership (Ed D); educational psychology: context and techniques of assessment (MAE); educational psychology: context and techniques of assessment (MAE); educational psychology: professional development for teachers (MAE); elementary education (MAE); field specialization (MAE); health education (MA); health promotion/fitness management (MA); instructional technology (MA); kinesiology (MA); leisure, youth and human services (MA); literacy education (MAE); performance and training technology (MA); physical education (MA); postsecondary education: student affairs (MA); principalship (MAE); school health education (MA); school library endorsement (MA); school library studies (MA); school psychology (Ed S); special education (MAE); teaching/coaching (MA). Electronic applications accepted.

College of Humanities, Arts and Sciences *Program availability:* Part-time, evening/weekend. Offers art education (MA); biology (MS); communication studies (MA); community college teaching (MA); composition (MM); conducting (MM); creative writing (MA); earth science education (MA); English (MA); humanities, arts and sciences (MA, MM, MS, PSM, DIT); industrial mathematics (PSM); industrial technology (DIT); jazz pedagogy (MM); literature (MA); mathematics (MA); mathematics for the middle grades (MA); music (MA, MM); music education (MM); music history (MM); percussion (MM); performance (MM); physics education (MA); piano performance and pedagogy (MM); piano/organ (MM); science education (MA); secondary teaching (MA); Spanish (MA); Spanish teaching (MA); speech-language pathology (MA); strings (MM); teaching English in secondary schools (MA); teaching English to speakers of other languages (MA); technology (MS, DIT); TESOL/Spanish (MA); voice (MM); woodwind (MM). Electronic applications accepted.

College of Social and Behavioral Sciences *Program availability:* Part-time, evening/weekend. Offers counseling (MA); geography (MA); history (MA); mental health counseling (MA); psychology (MA); public history (MA); public policy (MPP); school counseling (MA); social and behavioral sciences (MA, MPP, MSW); social science (MA); social work (MSW). Electronic applications accepted.

UNIVERSITY OF NORTH FLORIDA, Jacksonville, FL 32224

General Information State-supported, coed, comprehensive institution. CGS member. *Graduate housing:* Room and/or apartments available on a first-come, first-served basis to single students; on-campus housing not available to married students. Housing application deadline: 6/1.

GRADUATE UNITS

Brooks College of Health *Program availability:* Part-time, evening/weekend. Offers aging services (Certificate); clinical and applied movement sciences (MSH, DPT); community health (MPH); health (MHA, MPH, MS, MSH, MSN, DNP, DPT, Certificate); nutrition and dietetics (MSH). Electronic applications accepted.

School of Nursing *Program availability:* Part-time. Offers family nurse practitioner (Certificate); nurse anesthetist (MSN). Electronic applications accepted.

Coggin College of Business *Program availability:* Part-time, evening/weekend. Offers accountancy (M Acc); accounting (MBA); business (M Acc, MBA); construction management (MBA); e-commerce (MBA); economics (MBA); finance (MBA); human resource management (MBA); international business (MBA); logistics (MBA); management applications (MBA). Electronic applications accepted.

College of Arts and Sciences *Program availability:* Part-time, evening/weekend. Offers applied ethics (Graduate Certificate); arts and sciences (MA, MAC, MPA, MS, Graduate Certificate); biology (MA, MS); counseling psychology (MAC); criminal justice (MS); English (MA); European history (MA); general psychology (MA); mathematical sciences (MS); nonprofit management (Graduate Certificate); practical philosophy and applied ethics (MA); public administration (MPA); statistics (MS); U.S. history (MA). Electronic applications accepted.

College of Computing, Engineering, and Construction *Program availability:* Part-time. Offers computing, engineering, and construction (MS, MSCE, MSEE, MSME). Electronic applications accepted.

School of Computing *Program availability:* Part-time. Offers computer science (MS); information systems (MS); software engineering (MS). Electronic applications accepted.

School of Engineering *Program availability:* Part-time. Offers engineering (MSCE, MSEE, MSME).

College of Education and Human Services *Program availability:* Part-time, evening/weekend. Offers adult learning (M Ed); American Sign Language (MS); American Sign Language/English interpreting (M Ed); applied behavior analysis (M Ed); autism (M Ed); counselor education (M Ed); deaf education (M Ed); disability services (M Ed); education and human services (M Ed, MS, Ed D); educational leadership (M Ed, Ed D); exceptional student education (M Ed); literacy (M Ed); professional education (M Ed); TESOL (M Ed). Electronic applications accepted.

UNIVERSITY OF NORTH GEORGIA, Dahlonega, GA 30597

General Information State-supported, coed, comprehensive institution. *Enrollment:* 18,782 graduate, professional, and undergraduate students; 152 full-time matriculated graduate/professional students (106 women), 457 part-time matriculated graduate/professional students (303 women). *Enrollment by degree level:* 453 master's, 87 doctoral, 24 other advanced degrees. *Graduate faculty:* 79 full-time (41 women), 7 part-time/adjunct (5 women). Tuition, state resident: full-time $2025. Tuition, nonresident: full-time $8082. Tuition and fees vary according to course load, degree level and program. *Graduate housing:* Room and/or apartments available on a first-come, first-served basis to single students; on-campus housing not available to married students. Typical cost: $5520 per year ($10,800 including board). Housing application deadline: 2/1. *Student services:* Campus employment opportunities, campus safety program, career counseling, exercise/wellness program, free psychological counseling, international student services, low-cost health insurance, multicultural affairs office, services for students with disabilities, teacher training, writing training. *Library facilities:* Library Technology Center plus 4 others. *Collection:* Books: 195,525 (physical), 433,929 (digital/electronic); Serial titles: 168 (physical); Databases: 298. Weekly public service hours: 94; students can reserve study rooms. *Research affiliation:* Northeast Georgia Medical Center, Morehouse School of Medicine, St. Joseph's Hospital, Mettler Electronic Corporation.

Computer facilities: 3,500 computers available on campus for general student use. A campuswide network can be accessed from student residence rooms and from off campus. Online class registration is available.
Website: http://www.ung.edu/

General Application Contact: Melinda Maxwell, Director of Graduate Admissions, 706-864-1543, E-mail: melinda.maxwell@ung.edu.

GRADUATE UNITS

Department of Counseling Students: 29 full-time (24 women), 26 part-time (20 women); includes 13 minority (7 Black or African American, non-Hispanic/Latino; 1 Asian, non-Hispanic/Latino; 3 Hispanic/Latino; 2 Two or more races, non-Hispanic/Latino). Average age 29. 58 applicants, 55% accepted, 20 enrolled. *Faculty:* 4 full-time (3 women). Expenses: Contact institution. *Financial support:* Fellowships, research assistantships, teaching assistantships, and career-related internships or fieldwork available. Financial award application deadline: 3/17; financial award applicants required to submit FAFSA. In 2017, 13 master's awarded. *Program availability:* Part-time. Offers counseling (MS). *Application deadline:* For fall admission, 3/1 for domestic students. *Application fee:* $40. Electronic applications accepted. *Application Contact:* Melinda Maxwell, Director of Graduate Admissions, 706-864-1543,

E-mail: melinda.maxwell@ung.edu. *Department Head*, Dr. P. Clay Rowell, 706-867-2791, E-mail: clay.rowell@ung.edu.

Department of Criminal Justice Students: 1 (woman) full-time, 14 part-time (10 women); includes 4 minority (3 Black or African American, non-Hispanic/Latino; 1 Two or more races, non-Hispanic/Latino). Average age 30. 14 applicants, 100% accepted, 7 enrolled. *Faculty:* 3 full-time (1 woman). Expenses: Contact institution. *Financial support:* Fellowships and research assistantships available. Financial award application deadline: 3/17; financial award applicants required to submit FAFSA. In 2017, 12 master's awarded. *Program availability:* Part-time, evening/weekend, online only, 100% online. Offers criminal justice (MS). *Application deadline:* For fall admission, 8/10 for domestic students; for spring admission, 12/10 for domestic students; for summer admission, 5/10 for domestic students. *Application fee:* $40. Electronic applications accepted. *Application Contact:* Melinda Maxwell, Director of Graduate Admissions, 706-864-1543, E-mail: melinda.maxwell@ung.edu. *Department Head*, Dr. Brent Paterline, 706-864-1914, E-mail: brent.paterline@ung.edu.

Department of History, Anthropology and Philosophy Students: 2 full-time (0 women), 13 part-time (4 women); includes 1 minority (Hispanic/Latino). Average age 34. 9 applicants, 78% accepted, 3 enrolled. *Faculty:* 10 full-time (5 women), 1 part-time/adjunct (0 women). Expenses: Contact institution. *Financial support:* Unspecified assistantships available. Financial award application deadline: 3/17; financial award applicants required to submit FAFSA. In 2017, 2 master's awarded. *Program availability:* Part-time, evening/weekend. Offers history (MA). *Application deadline:* For fall admission, 4/1 priority date for domestic students. Applications are processed on a rolling basis. *Application fee:* $40. Electronic applications accepted. *Application Contact:* Melinda Maxwell, Director of Graduate Admissions, 706-864-1543, E-mail: melinda.maxwell@ung.edu. *Department Head*, Dr. Jeff Pardue, 678-717-3867.

Department of Physical Therapy Students: 87 full-time (62 women); includes 7 minority (2 Black or African American, non-Hispanic/Latino; 3 Hispanic/Latino; 2 Two or more races, non-Hispanic/Latino). Average age 25. *Faculty:* 8 full-time (4 women). Expenses: Contact institution. *Financial support:* Unspecified assistantships available. Financial award application deadline: 5/1; financial award applicants required to submit CSS PROFILE or FAFSA. In 2017, 30 doctorates awarded. Offers physical therapy (DPT). *Application deadline:* For summer admission, 10/3 for domestic students. Applications are processed on a rolling basis. *Application fee:* $50. Electronic applications accepted. *Application Contact:* Melinda Maxwell, Director of Graduate Admissions, 706-864-1543, E-mail: melinda.maxwell@ung.edu. *Department Head*, Dr. Mary Ellen Oesterle, 706-867-4589, E-mail: maryellen.oesterle@ung.edu.

Doctor of Education Program in Higher Education Leadership and Practice Students: 13 part-time (8 women); includes 2 minority (1 American Indian or Alaska Native, non-Hispanic/Latino; 1 Hispanic/Latino), 1 international. Average age 43. 35 applicants, 49% accepted, 13 enrolled. Expenses: Contact institution. *Financial support:* Application deadline: 3/17; applicants required to submit FAFSA. *Program availability:* Part-time, evening/weekend, online only, 100% online. Offers higher education leadership and practice (Ed D). *Application deadline:* For fall admission, 7/24 for domestic students. *Application fee:* $40. Electronic applications accepted. *Application Contact:* Melinda Maxwell, Director of Graduate Admissions, 706-867-2077, E-mail: melinda.maxwell@ung.edu. *Dean*, Dr. Susan Brandenburg-Ayres, 706-864-1998, E-mail: susan.ayres@ung.edu.

Ed S in Educational Leadership Program Students: 37 part-time (24 women); includes 1 minority (Asian, non-Hispanic/Latino). Average age 41. 30 applicants, 93% accepted, 18 enrolled. *Faculty:* 1 (woman) full-time, 2 part-time/adjunct (1 woman). Expenses: Contact institution. *Financial support:* Application deadline: 3/17; applicants required to submit FAFSA. *Program availability:* Part-time, evening/weekend, blended/hybrid learning. Offers educational leadership (Certificate, Ed S). *Application deadline:* For fall admission, 7/15 for domestic students. *Application fee:* $40. Electronic applications accepted. *Application Contact:* Melinda Maxwell, Director of Graduate Admissions, 706-867-2077, E-mail: melinda.maxwell@ung.edu. *Dean*, Dr. Susan Brandenburg-Ayres, 706-864-1998, E-mail: susan.ayres@ung.edu.

Master of Arts in Teaching Program Students: 27 part-time (20 women). Average age 29. 12 applicants, 75% accepted, 7 enrolled. Expenses: Contact institution. *Financial support:* Application deadline: 3/17; applicants required to submit FAFSA. In 2017, 15 master's awarded. Offers physical education (MAT); secondary education - English (MAT); secondary education - history (MAT); secondary education - mathematics (MAT); secondary education - middle grades (MAT). *Application deadline:* For summer admission, 2/1 for domestic students. *Application fee:* $40. Electronic applications accepted. *Application Contact:* Melinda Maxwell, Director of Graduate Admissions, 706-867-2077, E-mail: melinda.maxwell@ung.edu. *Dean*, Dr. Susan Brandenburg-Ayres, 706-864-1998, E-mail: susan.ayres@ung.edu.

Mike Cottrell College of Business Students: 1 full-time (0 women), 79 part-time (40 women); includes 17 minority (5 Black or African American, non-Hispanic/Latino; 6 Asian, non-Hispanic/Latino; 5 Hispanic/Latino; 1 Two or more races, non-Hispanic/Latino). Average age 34. 60 applicants, 77% accepted, 37 enrolled. *Faculty:* 5 full-time (3 women), 2 part-time/adjunct (1 woman). Expenses: Contact institution. *Financial support:* In 2017–18, 7 students received support. Unspecified assistantships available. Financial award application deadline: 3/17; financial award applicants required to submit CSS PROFILE or FAFSA. In 2017, 12 master's awarded. *Program availability:* Part-time-only, evening/weekend. Offers business (MBA). *Application deadline:* For fall admission, 4/1 priority date for domestic and international students. *Application fee:* $40. Electronic applications accepted. *Application Contact:* Melinda Maxwell, Director of Graduate Admissions, 706-864-1543, E-mail: melinda.maxwell@ung.edu. *Dean*, Dr. Donna Mayo, 706-864-1620, E-mail: donna.mayo@ung.edu.

Program in Athletic Training Students: 44 part-time (25 women); includes 5 minority (3 Black or African American, non-Hispanic/Latino; 1 Hispanic/Latino; 1 Two or more races, non-Hispanic/Latino). Average age 26. 45 applicants, 82% accepted, 35 enrolled. *Faculty:* 15 full-time (6 women), 3 part-time/adjunct (all women). Expenses: Contact institution. *Financial support:* Application deadline: 3/17; applicants required to submit FAFSA. In 2017, 32 master's awarded. Offers athletic training (MS). *Application deadline:* For fall admission, 5/10 for domestic students; for summer admission, 4/1 priority date for domestic students. *Application fee:* $40. Electronic applications accepted. *Application Contact:* Melinda Maxwell, Director of Graduate Admissions, 706-864-1543, E-mail: melinda.maxwell@ung.edu. *Dean*, Dr. Susan Brandenburg-Ayres, 706-864-1998, E-mail: susan.ayres@ung.edu.

Program in Curriculum and Instruction Students: 4 full-time (3 women), 27 part-time (23 women); includes 4 minority (2 Hispanic/Latino; 2 Two or more races, non-Hispanic/Latino). Average age 33. Expenses: Contact institution. *Financial support:* Application deadline: 3/17; applicants required to submit FAFSA. In 2017, 1 master's awarded. *Program availability:* Part-time. Offers curriculum and instruction (M Ed). *Application deadline:* For fall admission, 8/10 for domestic students; for spring admission, 12/10 for domestic students; for summer admission, 5/15 for domestic students. *Application fee:* $40. Electronic applications accepted. *Application Contact:* Melinda Maxwell, Director of Graduate Admissions, 706-867-2077, E-mail: melinda.maxwell@ung.edu. *Dean*, Dr. Susan Brandenburg-Ayres, 706-864-1998, E-mail: susan.ayres@ung.edu.

Program in Early Childhood Education Students: 8 part-time (all women); includes 3 minority (all Hispanic/Latino). Average age 29. *Faculty:* 13 full-time (10 women), 6 part-time/adjunct (5 women). Expenses: Contact institution. *Financial support:* Application deadline: 3/17; applicants required to submit FAFSA. In 2017, 19 master's awarded. *Program availability:* Part-time, blended/hybrid learning. Offers early childhood education (M Ed). *Application deadline:* For summer admission, 5/15 for domestic students. *Application fee:* $40. Electronic applications accepted. *Application Contact:* Melinda Maxwell, Director of Graduate Admissions, 706-867-2077, E-mail: melinda.maxwell@ung.edu. *Dean, College of Education*, Dr. Susan Brandenburg-Ayres, 706-864-1998, E-mail: susan.ayers@ung.edu.

Program in Family Nurse Practitioner Students: 50 part-time (47 women); includes 12 minority (5 Black or African American, non-Hispanic/Latino; 5 Asian, non-Hispanic/Latino; 2 Two or more races, non-Hispanic/Latino). Average age 36. 2 applicants, 100% accepted, 2 enrolled. Expenses: Contact institution. *Financial support:* Application deadline: 3/17; applicants required to submit FAFSA. In 2017, 29 master's, 1 other advanced degree awarded. *Program availability:* Part-time. Offers family nurse practitioner (MS, Certificate). *Application deadline:* For summer admission, 2/28 for domestic students. *Application fee:* $40. Electronic applications accepted. *Application Contact:* Melinda Maxwell, Director of Graduate Admissions, 706-864-1543, E-mail: melinda.maxwell@ung.edu. *Department Head*, Dr. Kim Hudson-Gallogly, 706-864-1934, E-mail: kim.hudson-gallogly@ung.edu.

Program in Human Services and Delivery Administration Students: 2 full-time (1 woman), 4 part-time (all women); includes 1 minority (Black or African American, non-Hispanic/Latino), 1 international. Average age 27. 12 applicants, 75% accepted, 6 enrolled. *Faculty:* 4 full-time (3 women). Expenses: Contact institution. *Financial support:* Application deadline: 3/17; applicants required to submit FAFSA. *Program availability:* Evening/weekend. Offers human services and delivery administration (MS). *Application deadline:* For fall admission, 4/1 for domestic students. *Application fee:* $40. Electronic applications accepted. *Application Contact:* Melinda Maxwell, Director of Graduate Admissions, 706-864-1543, E-mail: melinda.maxwell@ung.edu. *Head, Department of Sociology and Human Services*, Sara Mason, 678-717-3878, E-mail: sara.mason@ung.edu.

Program in International Affairs Students: 10 full-time (3 women), 31 part-time (12 women); includes 8 minority (5 Black or African American, non-Hispanic/Latino; 1 Hispanic/Latino; 2 Two or more races, non-Hispanic/Latino). Average age 33. 20 applicants, 80% accepted, 10 enrolled. *Faculty:* 5 full-time (1 woman). Expenses: Contact institution. *Financial support:* In 2017–18, 1 student received support. Unspecified assistantships available. Financial award application deadline: 3/17; financial award applicants required to submit CSS PROFILE or FAFSA. In 2017, 12 master's awarded. *Program availability:* Part-time, evening/weekend, 100% online. Offers international affairs (MAIA). *Application deadline:* For fall admission, 8/1 priority date for domestic students; for spring admission, 12/1 priority date for domestic students; for summer admission, 5/1 priority date for domestic students. Applications are processed on a rolling basis. *Application fee:* $40. Electronic applications accepted. *Application Contact:* Melinda Maxwell, Director of Graduate Admissions, 706-864-1543, E-mail: melinda.maxwell@ung.edu. *Program Coordinator*, Dr. Cristian Harris, 706-867-3251, E-mail: cristian.harris@ung.edu.

Program in Kinesiology Students: 1 full-time (0 women), 33 part-time (19 women); includes 8 minority (6 Black or African American, non-Hispanic/Latino; 1 Asian, non-Hispanic/Latino; 1 Hispanic/Latino). Average age 26. Expenses: Contact institution. *Financial support:* Application deadline: 3/17; applicants required to submit FAFSA. *Program availability:* Part-time, evening/weekend, online only, 100% online. Offers kinesiology (MS). *Application deadline:* For summer admission, 5/20 priority date for domestic students. *Application fee:* $40. Electronic applications accepted. *Application Contact:* Melinda Maxwell, Director of Graduate Admissions, 706-867-2077, E-mail: melinda.maxwell@ung.edu. *Coordinator*, Dr. Mitchum Parker, 706-864-1600, E-mail: coegrads@ung.edu.

Program in Middle Grades Math and Science Students: 6 full-time (all women), 12 part-time (8 women); includes 1 minority (Black or African American, non-Hispanic/Latino). Average age 29. 4 applicants, 75% accepted, 3 enrolled. Expenses: Contact institution. *Financial support:* Application deadline: 3/17; applicants required to submit FAFSA. In 2017, 8 master's awarded. *Program availability:* Part-time, evening/weekend, online only, 100% online. Offers middle grades math and science (M Ed). *Application deadline:* For fall admission, 7/24 for domestic students; for spring admission, 12/12 for domestic students; for summer admission, 4/26 for domestic students. *Application fee:* $40. Electronic applications accepted. *Application Contact:* Melinda Maxwell, Director of Graduate Studies, 706-867-2077, E-mail: melinda.maxwell@ung.edu. *Dean*, Dr. Susan Brandenburg-Ayres, 706-864-1998, E-mail: susan.ayres@ung.edu.

Program in Nursing Education Students: 3 part-time (all women). Average age 43. Expenses: Contact institution. *Financial support:* Application deadline: 3/17; applicants required to submit FAFSA. *Program availability:* Part-time, evening/weekend, online only, 100% online. Offers nursing education (MS). *Application deadline:* For summer admission, 2/28 for domestic students. *Application fee:* $40. Electronic applications accepted. *Application Contact:* Melinda Maxwell, Director of Graduate Admissions, 706-867-2077, E-mail: melinda.maxwell@ung.edu. *Department Head*, Dr. Kim Hudson-Gallogly, 706-864-1934, E-mail: kim.hudson-gallogly@ung.edu.

Program in Public Administration Students: 9 full-time (6 women), 19 part-time (14 women); includes 5 minority (3 Black or African American, non-Hispanic/Latino; 1 Hispanic/Latino; 1 Two or more races, non-Hispanic/Latino), 1 international. Average age 29. 38 applicants, 76% accepted, 24 enrolled. *Faculty:* 2 full-time (1 woman), 1 (woman) part-time/adjunct. Expenses: Contact institution. *Financial support:* Teaching assistantships available. Financial award application deadline: 3/17; financial award applicants required to submit FAFSA. In 2017, 4 master's awarded. *Program availability:* Part-time, evening/weekend, online only, 100% online. Offers public administration (MPA). *Application deadline:* For fall admission, 8/10 for domestic students; for spring admission, 12/10 for domestic students; for summer admission, 5/10 for domestic students. *Application fee:* $40. Electronic applications accepted. *Application Contact:* Melinda Maxwell, Director of Graduate Admissions, 706-864-1543, E-mail: melinda.maxwell@ung.edu. *Department Head*, Dr. Dlynn Williams, 706-864-1869, E-mail: dlynn.williams@ung.edu.

UNIVERSITY OF NORTH TEXAS, Denton, TX 76203

General Information State-supported, coed, university. CGS member. *Graduate housing:* Rooms and/or apartments available on a first-come, first-served basis to single and married students. Housing application deadline: 9/1. *Research affiliation:* Delta and Pine Land Company (natural science), Semiconductor Research Corporation (materials science), Tech America (technology transfer), National Business Incubation Association (entrepreneurship), International Economic Development Council (economic growth).

GRADUATE UNITS

Robert B. Toulouse School of Graduate Studies *Program availability:* Part-time, evening/weekend, online learning. Offers accounting (MS); applied anthropology (MA, MS); applied behavior analysis (Certificate); applied geography (MA); applied technology and performance improvement (M Ed, MS); art education (MA); art history (MA); art museum education (Certificate); arts leadership (Certificate); audiology (Au D); behavior analysis (MS); behavioral science (PhD); biochemistry and molecular biology (MS); biology (MA, MS); biomedical engineering (MS); business analysis (MS); chemistry (MS); clinical health psychology (PhD); communication studies (MA, MS); computer engineering (MS); computer science (MS); counseling (M Ed, MS); creative writing (MA); criminal justice (MS); curriculum and instruction (M Ed); decision sciences (MBA); design (MA, MFA); early childhood studies (MS); economics (MS); educational leadership (M Ed, Ed D); educational psychology (MS, PhD); electrical engineering (MS); emergency management (MPA); engineering technology (MS); English (MA); English as a second language (MA); environmental science (MS); finance (MBA, MS); financial management (MPA); French (MA); health services management (MBA); higher education (M Ed, Ed D); history (MA, MS); hospitality management (MS); human resources management (MPA); information science (MS); information systems (PhD); information technologies (MBA); interdisciplinary studies (MA, MS); international studies (MA); international sustainable tourism (MS); jazz studies (MM); journalism (MA, MJ, Graduate Certificate); kinesiology (MS); linguistics (MA); local government management (MPA); logistics (PhD); logistics and supply chain management (MBA); long-term care, senior housing, and aging services (MA); management (PhD); marketing (MBA); mathematics (MA, MS); mechanical and energy engineering (MS, PhD); music (MA); music composition (PhD); music education (MM Ed, PhD); nonprofit management (MPA); operations and supply chain management (MBA); performance (MM, DMA); philosophy (MA); political science (MA); professional and technical communication (MA); radio, television and film (MA, MFA); rehabilitation counseling (Certificate); sociology (MA); Spanish (MA); special education (M Ed); speech-language pathology (MA); strategic management (MBA); studio art (MFA); teaching (M Ed). Electronic applications accepted.

UNIVERSITY OF NORTH TEXAS AT DALLAS, Dallas, TX 75241

General Information State-supported, coed, comprehensive institution.

GRADUATE UNITS

College of Law Offers law (JD).

Graduate School

UNIVERSITY OF NORTH TEXAS HEALTH SCIENCE CENTER AT FORT WORTH, Fort Worth, TX 76107-2699

General Information State-supported, coed, graduate-only institution. CGS member. *Graduate housing:* On-campus housing not available. *Research affiliation:* Ethnobotanical Product Investigation Consortium (natural plant products), Genelink (familial DNA depository), Botanical Research Institutions of Texas, Myogen, Inc. (cardiac research), My-tech, Inc. (cardiovascular research), Novopharm, Inc. (gene control).

GRADUATE UNITS

Graduate School of Biomedical Sciences Offers biochemistry and cancer biology (MS, PhD); biotechnology (MS); cell biology, immunology and microbiology (MS, PhD); clinical research management (MS); forensic genetics (MS); genetics (MS, PhD); integrative physiology (MS, PhD); medical sciences (MS); pharmaceutical sciences and pharmacotherapy (MS, PhD); pharmacology and neuroscience (MS, PhD); structural anatomy and rehabilitation sciences (MS, PhD).

School of Health Professions Offers physical therapy (DPT); physician assistant studies (MPAS).

School of Public Health *Program availability:* Part-time, evening/weekend, 100% online. Offers biostatistics (MS); epidemiology (MPH, MS, PhD); food security and public health (Graduate Certificate); GIS in public health (Graduate Certificate); global health (Graduate Certificate); global health for medical professionals (Graduate Certificate); health administration (MHA); health behavior research (MS, PhD); maternal and child health (MPH); public health (Graduate Certificate); public health practice (MPH). Electronic applications accepted.

Texas College of Osteopathic Medicine Offers osteopathic medicine (DO). Electronic applications accepted.

UNIVERSITY OF NORTHWESTERN OHIO, Lima, OH 45805-1498

General Information Independent, coed, comprehensive institution.

GRADUATE UNITS

Graduate College *Program availability:* Evening/weekend, online learning.

UNIVERSITY OF NORTHWESTERN–ST. PAUL, St. Paul, MN 55113-1598

General Information Independent-religious, coed, comprehensive institution. *Graduate housing:* On-campus housing not available. *Student services:* Campus employment opportunities, campus safety program, career counseling, international student services, multicultural affairs office, services for students with disabilities, writing training. *Library facilities:* Berntsen Library.

Computer facilities: Computer purchase and lease plans are available. 200 computers available on campus for general student use. A campuswide network can be accessed from student residence rooms and from off campus. Online class registration, network file space, personal web site, integrated student portal, b/w and color printing, virtual labs are available.
Website: http://www.unwsp.edu/

General Application Contact: Tami Treder, Graduate Admission Counselor, 651-628-3351, E-mail: tjtreder@unwsp.edu.

GRADUATE UNITS

Master of Arts in Education Program Expenses: Contact institution. *Program availability:* Part-time, evening/weekend, online learning. Offers education (MA Ed). *Application deadline:* Applications are processed on a rolling basis. Electronic applications accepted. *Application Contact:* Graduate Studies Admissions, 651-631-5200, E-mail: gradstudies@unwsp.edu.

Master of Arts in Human Services Program Expenses: Contact institution. *Program availability:* Part-time, evening/weekend, online learning. Offers human services (MAHS). *Application deadline:* Applications are processed on a rolling basis. Electronic applications accepted. *Application Contact:* Graduate Studies Admissions, 651-631-5200, E-mail: gradstudies@unwsp.edu.

Master of Arts in Theological Studies Program Expenses: Contact institution. *Program availability:* Part-time, evening/weekend, online learning. Offers theological studies (MATS). *Application deadline:* Applications are processed on a rolling basis. Electronic applications accepted. *Application Contact:* Graduate Studies Admissions, 651-631-5200, E-mail: gradstudies@unwsp.edu.

Master of Business Administration Program Expenses: Contact institution. *Program availability:* Part-time, evening/weekend, online learning. Offers business administration (MBA). *Application deadline:* Applications are processed on a rolling basis. Electronic applications accepted. *Application Contact:* Graduate Studies Admissions, 651-631-5200, E-mail: gradstudies@unwsp.edu.

Master of Divinity Program Expenses: Contact institution. *Program availability:* Part-time, evening/weekend, online learning. Offers theology and Christian ministry (M Div). *Application deadline:* Applications are processed on a rolling basis. Electronic applications accepted. *Application Contact:* Graduate Studies Admissions, 651-631-5200, E-mail: gradstudies@unwsp.edu.

Master of Organizational Leadership Program Expenses: Contact institution. *Program availability:* Part-time, evening/weekend, online learning. Offers organizational leadership (MOL). *Application deadline:* Applications are processed on a rolling basis. Electronic applications accepted. *Application Contact:* Graduate Studies Admissions, 651-631-5200, E-mail: gradstudies@unwsp.edu.

UNIVERSITY OF NOTRE DAME, Notre Dame, IN 46556

General Information Independent-religious, coed, university. CGS member. *Graduate housing:* Rooms and/or apartments available on a first-come, first-served basis to single and married students. Housing application deadline: 5/1. *Research affiliation:* Space Telescope Science Institute, Brookhaven National Laboratory, Fermi National Accelerator Laboratory, Argonne National Laboratory.

GRADUATE UNITS

Graduate School *Program availability:* Part-time. Electronic applications accepted.

College of Arts and Letters *Program availability:* Part-time. Offers art history (MA); arts and letters (M Div, M Ed, MA, MFA, MMS, MSM, MTS, PhD); cognitive psychology (PhD); counseling psychology (PhD); creative writing (MFA); design (MFA); developmental psychology (PhD); early Christian studies (MA); economics and econometrics (MA, PhD); educational initiatives (M Ed, MA); English (MA, PhD); French and Francophone studies (MA); history (MA, PhD); history and philosophy of science (MA, PhD); humanities (M Div, MA, MFA, MMS, MSM, MTS, PhD); Iberian and Latin American studies (MA); international peace studies (MA, PhD); Italian studies (MA); literature (PhD); medieval studies (MMS, PhD); philosophy (PhD); political science (PhD); quantitative psychology (PhD); Romance literatures (MA); social science (M Ed, MA, PhD); sociology (PhD); studio art (MFA); theology (M Div, MA, MSM, MTS, PhD); theology and science (PhD). Electronic applications accepted.

College of Engineering Offers aerospace and mechanical engineering (M Eng, PhD); aerospace engineering (MS Aero E); bioengineering (MS Bio E); chemical and biomolecular engineering (MS Ch E, PhD); civil engineering (MSCE); civil engineering and geological sciences (PhD); computer science and engineering (MSCSE, PhD); electrical engineering (MSEE, PhD); engineering (M Eng, MEME, MS, MS Aero E, MS Bio E, MS Ch E, MS Env E, MSCE, MSCSE, MSEE, MSME, PhD); environmental engineering (MS Env E); geological sciences (MS); mechanical engineering (MEME, MSME). Electronic applications accepted.

College of Science Offers algebra (PhD); algebraic geometry (PhD); applied and computational mathematics and statistics (PhD); applied mathematics (MSAM); applied statistics (MS); aquatic ecology, evolution and environmental biology (MS, PhD); biochemistry (MS, PhD); cellular and molecular biology (MS, PhD); complex analysis (PhD); computational finance (MS); differential geometry (PhD); genetics (MS, PhD); inorganic chemistry (MS, PhD); logic (PhD); organic chemistry (MS, PhD); partial differential equations (PhD); physical chemistry (MS, PhD); physics (MS, PhD); physiology (MS, PhD); science (MS, MSAM, PhD); topology (PhD); vector biology and parasitology (MS, PhD). Electronic applications accepted.

Keough School of Global Affairs Offers global affairs (MGA); international peace studies (MGA); sustainable development (MGA).

School of Architecture Offers architectural design and urbanism (M ADU); architecture (M Arch). Electronic applications accepted.

Law School Offers human rights (LL M, JSD); international and comparative law (LL M); law (JD). Electronic applications accepted.

Mendoza College of Business Students: 619 full-time (171 women), 63 part-time (34 women); includes 132 minority (35 Black or African American, non-Hispanic/Latino; 6 American Indian or Alaska Native, non-Hispanic/Latino; 29 Asian, non-Hispanic/Latino; 46 Hispanic/Latino; 2 Native Hawaiian or other Pacific Islander, non-Hispanic/Latino; 14 Two or more races, non-Hispanic/Latino), 104 international. Average age 30. 1,454 applicants, 53% accepted, 461 enrolled. *Faculty:* 86 full-time (16 women), 36 part-time/adjunct (5 women). Expenses: Contact institution. *Financial support:* In 2017–18, 476 students received support, including 476 fellowships (averaging $15,066 per year); scholarships/grants and unspecified assistantships also available. Financial award applicants required to submit FAFSA. In 2017, 531 master's awarded. Offers assurance and advisory services (MSA); business (MBA, MNA, MSA, MSBA, MSF, MSM); business analytics (MSBA); business leadership (MBA); consulting (MBA); corporate finance (MBA); executive business administration (MBA); finance (MSF); innovation and entrepreneurship (MBA); investments (MBA); management (MSM); marketing (MBA); nonprofit administration (MNA); tax services (MSA). *Application deadline:* Applications are processed on a rolling basis. Electronic applications accepted. *Dean,* Dr. Roger D. Huang, 574-631-1691, Fax: 574-631-4825, E-mail: roger.huang.31@nd.edu.

UNIVERSITY OF OKLAHOMA, Norman, OK 73019-0390

General Information State-supported, coed, university. CGS member. *Enrollment:* 28,527 graduate, professional, and undergraduate students; 3,001 full-time matriculated graduate/professional students (1,532 women), 3,372 part-time matriculated graduate/professional students (1,784 women). *Enrollment by degree level:* 4,340 master's, 2,009 doctoral, 24 other advanced degrees. *Graduate faculty:* 1,181 full-time (407 women), 71 part-time/adjunct (28 women). Tuition, state resident: full-time $5119; part-time $213.30 per credit hour. Tuition, nonresident: full-time $19,778; part-time $824.10 per credit hour. *Required fees:* $3458; $133.55 per credit hour. $126.50 per semester. *Graduate housing:* Rooms and/or apartments available on a first-come, first-served basis to single and married students. Typical cost: $6948 per year ($11,344 including board) for single students; $6948 per year for married students. *Student services:* Campus employment opportunities, campus safety program, career counseling, child daycare facilities, exercise/wellness program, free psychological counseling, grant writing training, international student services, low-cost health insurance, multicultural affairs office, services for students with disabilities, teacher training, writing training. *Library facilities:* Bizzell Memorial Library plus 5 others.

Collection: Books: 4.4 million (physical), 1.4 million (digital/electronic); Serial titles: 71,289 (physical), 128,934 (digital/electronic); Databases: 311. Weekly public service hours: 114; students can reserve study rooms. *Research affiliation:* National Oceanic and Atmospheric Administration (NOAA)/National Severe Storms Laboratory (weather), Nanowave Technologies, Inc. (radar), Department of the Interior South Central Region Climate Science Center (climate science), Weathernews Americas (weather), Sandia National Laboratories (national security), U.S. Department of Transportation Southern Plains Transportation Center (transportation infrastructure).

Computer facilities: Computer purchase and lease plans are available. 4,500 computers available on campus for general student use. A campuswide network can be accessed from student residence rooms and from off campus. Online class registration is available.
Website: http://www.ou.edu/

General Application Contact: Dr. Randall S. Hewes, Dean, Graduate College, 405-325-3811, Fax: 405-325-5346, E-mail: gradinfo@ou.edu.

GRADUATE UNITS

Christopher C. Gibbs College of Architecture Students: 102 full-time (56 women), 31 part-time (14 women); includes 23 minority (5 Black or African American, non-Hispanic/Latino; 4 American Indian or Alaska Native, non-Hispanic/Latino; 2 Asian, non-Hispanic/Latino; 6 Hispanic/Latino; 6 Two or more races, non-Hispanic/Latino), 46 international. Average age 30. 94 applicants, 70% accepted, 38 enrolled. *Faculty:* 32 full-time (12 women), 2 part-time/adjunct (0 women). Expenses: Contact institution. *Financial support:* In 2017–18, 107 students received support, including 1 fellowship (averaging $5,000 per year), 42 research assistantships with partial tuition reimbursements available (averaging $12,429 per year), 5 teaching assistantships with partial tuition reimbursements available (averaging $10,997 per year); scholarships/grants and unspecified assistantships also available. Financial award application deadline: 6/1; financial award applicants required to submit FAFSA. In 2017, 37 master's, 2 doctorates awarded. *Program availability:* Part-time. Offers architecture (M Arch, MCM, MLA, MRCP, MS, PhD, Graduate Certificate); planning, design, and construction (PhD); resilient planning, design, and construction (Graduate Certificate). *Application deadline:* For fall admission, 3/1 for international students. *Application fee:* $50 ($100 for international students). Electronic applications accepted. *Application Contact:* Dr. Charlie Warnken, Associate Dean for Instructional Services, 405-325-2444, Fax: 405-325-7558, E-mail: cwarnken@ou.edu. *Dean*, Hans Butzer, 405-325-2444, Fax: 405-325-7558, E-mail: butzer@ou.edu.

Division of Architecture Students: 33 full-time (22 women), 9 part-time (2 women); includes 6 minority (2 Black or African American, non-Hispanic/Latino; 1 American Indian or Alaska Native, non-Hispanic/Latino; 1 Hispanic/Latino; 2 Two or more races, non-Hispanic/Latino), 13 international. Average age 29. 25 applicants, 72% accepted, 11 enrolled. *Faculty:* 32 full-time (12 women), 2 part-time/adjunct (0 women). Expenses: Contact institution. *Financial support:* In 2017–18, 34 students received support, including 17 research assistantships with partial tuition reimbursements available (averaging $12,585 per year), 1 teaching assistantship with partial tuition reimbursement available (averaging $10,372 per year); career-related internships or fieldwork, scholarships/grants, health care benefits, tuition waivers, and unspecified assistantships also available. Financial award application deadline: 6/1; financial award applicants required to submit FAFSA. In 2017, 7 master's awarded. *Program availability:* Part-time. Offers architecture (MS); data and digital representation (M Arch); design entrepreneurship and real estate (M Arch); planning, design and construction (PhD); resilient planning, design, and construction (M Arch). *Application deadline:* For spring admission, 5/1 for domestic students, 3/1 for international students. Applications are processed on a rolling basis. *Application fee:* $50 ($100 for international students). Electronic applications accepted. *Application Contact:* Marjorie Callahan, Graduate Liaison, Fax: 405-325-7588, E-mail: mcallahan@ou.edu. *Director*, Dr. Stephanie Pilat, 405-325-9352, Fax: 405-325-7588, E-mail: architecture.director@ou.edu.

Division of Interior Design Students: 5 full-time (4 women), 2 part-time (both women); includes 2 minority (1 American Indian or Alaska Native, non-Hispanic/Latino; 1 Hispanic/Latino), 2 international. Average age 30. 5 applicants, 60% accepted, 1 enrolled. Expenses: Contact institution. *Financial support:* In 2017–18, 5 students received support, including 1 research assistantship with partial tuition reimbursement available (averaging $10,372 per year), 3 teaching assistantships with full and partial tuition reimbursements available (averaging $10,372 per year); career-related internships or fieldwork, scholarships/grants, and unspecified assistantships also available. Financial award application deadline: 6/1; financial award applicants required to submit FAFSA. In 2017, 1 master's awarded. *Program availability:* Part-time. Offers interior design (MS); professional applications of interior design (Graduate Certificate). *Application deadline:* Applications are processed on a rolling basis. *Application fee:* $50 ($100 for international students). Electronic applications accepted. *Application Contact:* Dr. Suchismita Bhattacharjee, Assistant Professor and Graduate Liaison, 405-325-2548, Fax: 405-325-7558, E-mail: suchi@ou.edu. *Academic Director and Associate Professor*, Elizabeth Pober, 405-325-6764, Fax: 405-325-7558, E-mail: epober@ou.edu.

Division of Landscape Architecture Students: 16 full-time (10 women), 7 part-time (3 women); includes 5 minority (1 American Indian or Alaska Native, non-Hispanic/Latino; 2 Asian, non-Hispanic/Latino; 2 Two or more races, non-Hispanic/Latino), 10 international. Average age 27. 14 applicants, 71% accepted, 5 enrolled. Expenses: Contact institution. *Financial support:* In 2017–18, 21 students received support, including 7 research assistantships with full and partial tuition reimbursements available (averaging $13,334 per year); scholarships/grants and unspecified assistantships also available. Financial award application deadline: 6/1; financial award applicants required to submit FAFSA. In 2017, 4 master's awarded. Offers landscape architectural studies (MLA); landscape architecture (MLA). *Application deadline:* For fall admission, 2/15 priority date for domestic and international students. Applications are processed on a rolling basis. *Application fee:* $50 ($100 for international students). Electronic applications accepted. *Associate Dean and Director*, Leehu Loon, 405-325-1519, Fax: 405-325-7558, E-mail: lloon@ou.edu.

Division of Regional and City Planning Students: 24 full-time (12 women), 2 part-time (both women); includes 2 minority (1 American Indian or Alaska Native, non-Hispanic/Latino; 1 Hispanic/Latino), 6 international. Average age 27. 19 applicants, 89% accepted, 12 enrolled. Expenses: Contact institution. *Financial support:* In 2017–18, 20 students received support, including 1 fellowship (averaging $5,000 per year), 7 research assistantships with full tuition reimbursements available (averaging $13,502 per year); teaching assistantships with full tuition reimbursements available, career-related internships or fieldwork, Federal Work-Study, scholarships/grants, health care benefits, tuition waivers, and unspecified assistantships also available. Financial award application deadline: 6/1; financial award applicants required to submit FAFSA. In 2017, 15 master's awarded. *Program availability:* Part-time. Offers community development (MRCP); physical planning (MRCP). *Application deadline:* For fall admission, 4/1 priority date for international students. Applications are processed on a rolling basis. *Application fee:* $50 ($100 for international students). Electronic applications accepted. *Director*, Dr. Charles Warnken, 405-325-2444, Fax: 405-325-7558, E-mail: cwarnken@ou.edu.

Haskell and Irene Lemon Division of Construction Science Students: 19 full-time (5 women), 5 part-time (3 women); includes 7 minority (2 Black or African American, non-Hispanic/Latino; 3 Hispanic/Latino; 2 Two or more races, non-Hispanic/Latino), 9 international. Average age 32. 19 applicants, 74% accepted, 8 enrolled. Expenses: Contact institution. *Financial support:* In 2017–18, 19 students received support, including 8 research assistantships with full and partial tuition reimbursements available (averaging $11,219 per year), 1 teaching assistantship with full and partial tuition reimbursement available (averaging $13,500 per year); fellowships with full and partial tuition reimbursements available, career-related internships or fieldwork, and scholarships/grants also available. Financial award application deadline: 6/1; financial award applicants required to submit FAFSA. In 2017, 10 master's awarded. *Program availability:* Part-time. Offers construction management (MS); construction science (MCM); planning, design, and construction (PhD). *Application fee:* $50 ($100 for international students). Electronic applications accepted. *Application Contact:* Anthony Perrenoud, Graduate Liaison, 405-325-2674, E-mail: perrenoud@ou.edu. *Director*, Ben Bigelow, 405-325-6404, E-mail: bigelow@ou.edu.

College of Arts and Sciences Students: 1,153 full-time (710 women), 1,104 part-time (704 women); includes 743 minority (253 Black or African American, non-Hispanic/Latino; 108 American Indian or Alaska Native, non-Hispanic/Latino; 59 Asian, non-Hispanic/Latino; 189 Hispanic/Latino; 6 Native Hawaiian or other Pacific Islander, non-Hispanic/Latino; 128 Two or more races, non-Hispanic/Latino), 211 international. Average age 32. 1,132 applicants, 56% accepted, 482 enrolled. *Faculty:* 503 full-time (201 women), 28 part-time/adjunct (17 women). Expenses: Contact institution. *Financial support:* In 2017–18, 1,172 students received support, including 58 fellowships with tuition reimbursements available (averaging $3,989 per year), 190 research assistantships with tuition reimbursements available (averaging $15,144 per year), 552 teaching assistantships with tuition reimbursements available (averaging $15,275 per year); career-related internships or fieldwork, Federal Work-Study, institutionally sponsored loans, scholarships/grants, traineeships, health care benefits, and unspecified assistantships also available. Support available to part-time students. Financial award application deadline: 6/1; financial award applicants required to submit FAFSA. In 2017, 647 master's, 82 doctorates, 110 other advanced degrees awarded. *Program availability:* Part-time, evening/weekend, online learning. Offers anthropology (MA, PhD); applied linguistic anthropology (MA); archaeology (PhD); arts and sciences (MA, MHR, MLIS, MPA, MS, MSW, PhD, Graduate Certificate); biology (MS, PhD); cellular and behavioral neurobiology (PhD); chemistry (MS, PhD); clinical mental health (MHR); communication (MA); communication technology (PhD); ecology and evolutionary biology (PhD); economics (MA, PhD); engineering physics (MS); exercise physiology (MS, PhD); French (MA, PhD); general (MPA); German (MA); health and exercise science (MS); health and human biology (PhD); health communication (PhD); health promotion (MS, PhD); helping skills in human relations (Graduate Certificate); history (MA, PhD); history of science, technology and medicine (MA, PhD); human relations (MHR); human resource diversity and development (Graduate Certificate); human resource management (Graduate Certificate); human resources (MHR); intercultural/international communication (PhD); licensed professional counselor (MHR); literary and cultural studies (MA, PhD); mathematics (MA, MS, PhD); microbiology (MS, PhD); Native American studies (MA); nonprofit management (MPA); organizational communication (PhD); organizational dynamics (MA, Graduate Certificate); philosophy (MA, PhD); physics (MS, PhD); plant biology (MS, PhD); political science (MA, MPA, PhD); political/mass communication (PhD); project management (Graduate Certificate); psychology (MS, PhD); public administration (MPA); public management (MPA); public policy (MPA); social influence/interpersonal communication (PhD); socio-cultural and linguistics (PhD); socio-cultural anthropology (MA); sociology (MA, PhD); Spanish (MA, PhD); women's and gender studies (Graduate Certificate); writing and rhetoric studies (MA, PhD). *Application fee:* $50 ($100 for international students). Electronic applications accepted. *Interim Dean*, David Wrobel, 405-325-2077, Fax: 405-325-7709, E-mail: david.wrobel@ou.edu.

Anne and Henry Zarrow School of Social Work Students: 212 full-time (177 women), 194 part-time (163 women); includes 169 minority (56 Black or African American, non-Hispanic/Latino; 40 American Indian or Alaska Native, non-Hispanic/Latino; 6 Asian, non-Hispanic/Latino; 27 Hispanic/Latino; 40 Two or more races, non-Hispanic/Latino). Average age 32. 187 applicants, 74% accepted, 116 enrolled. *Faculty:* 30 full-time (21 women), 12 part-time/adjunct (9 women). Expenses: Contact institution. *Financial support:* In 2017–18, 132 students received support, including 20 research assistantships with tuition reimbursements available (averaging $10,372 per year), 1 teaching assistantship (averaging $12,750 per year); career-related internships or fieldwork, scholarships/grants, traineeships, health care benefits, tuition waivers, and unspecified assistantships also available. Support available to part-time students. Financial award application deadline: 6/1; financial award applicants required to submit FAFSA. In 2017, 153 master's awarded. *Program availability:* Part-time, evening/weekend. Offers direct practice (MSW). *Application deadline:* For fall admission, 2/1 priority date for domestic and international students; for summer admission, 2/1 priority date for domestic and international students. *Application fee:* $50 ($100 for international students). Electronic applications accepted. *Application Contact:* Amy Ann Arnold, Admissions and Enrollment Coordinator, 918-660-3385, Fax: 918-660-3383, E-mail: aarnold@ou.edu. *Director*, Dr. Julie Miller-Cribbs, 918-660-3378, Fax: 918-660-3383, E-mail: jmcribbs@ou.edu.

School of Library and Information Studies Students: 64 full-time (53 women), 117 part-time (95 women); includes 40 minority (6 Black or African American, non-Hispanic/Latino; 6 American Indian or Alaska Native, non-Hispanic/Latino; 3 Asian, non-Hispanic/Latino; 14 Hispanic/Latino; 1 Native Hawaiian or other Pacific Islander, non-Hispanic/Latino; 10 Two or more races, non-Hispanic/Latino). Average age 32. 58 applicants, 93% accepted, 48 enrolled. *Faculty:* 11 full-time (8 women), 1 (woman) part-time/adjunct. Expenses: Contact institution. *Financial support:* In 2017–18, 82 students received support, including 3 research assistantships with full tuition reimbursements available (averaging $10,579 per year), 3 teaching assistantships with full tuition reimbursements available (averaging $10,579 per year); scholarships/grants, health care benefits, and unspecified assistantships also available. Financial award application deadline: 6/1; financial award applicants required to submit FAFSA. In 2017, 53 master's awarded. *Program availability:* Part-time, evening/weekend, 100% online, blended/hybrid learning. Offers archival studies (Graduate Certificate); digital humanities (Graduate Certificate); information studies (PhD); library and information studies (MLIS). *Application deadline:* Applications are processed on a rolling basis. *Application fee:* $50 ($100 for international students).

Electronic applications accepted. *Application Contact:* Sarah Connelly, Admissions and Student Services Coordinator, 405-325-3921, E-mail: sarahee@ou.edu. *Director*, Dr. Susan K. Burke, 405-325-3921, E-mail: sburke@ou.edu.

College of Atmospheric and Geographic Sciences Students: 70 full-time (34 women), 41 part-time (15 women); includes 17 minority (3 Black or African American, non-Hispanic/Latino; 3 Asian, non-Hispanic/Latino; 8 Hispanic/Latino; 3 Two or more races, non-Hispanic/Latino), 21 international. Average age 27. 86 applicants, 36% accepted, 27 enrolled. *Faculty:* 65 full-time (16 women), 1 part-time/adjunct (0 women). Expenses: Contact institution. *Financial support:* In 2017–18, 107 students received support, including 3 fellowships with tuition reimbursements available (averaging $4,667 per year), 63 research assistantships with full tuition reimbursements available (averaging $18,592 per year), 32 teaching assistantships with full tuition reimbursements available (averaging $18,069 per year); scholarships/grants, health care benefits, and unspecified assistantships also available. Support available to part-time students. Financial award application deadline: 6/1; financial award applicants required to submit FAFSA. In 2017, 29 master's, 13 doctorates awarded. *Program availability:* Part-time. Offers atmospheric and geographic sciences (MA, MS, PhD); environmental sustainability (MS); geography (MA, MS, PhD). *Application deadline:* For fall admission, 1/15 for domestic and international students. *Application fee:* $50 ($100 for international students). Electronic applications accepted. *Application Contact:* Mary Anne Hempe, Assistant Dean for Student Services, 405-325-3095, Fax: 405-325-3148, E-mail: mahempe@ou.edu. *Dean*, Dr. Berrien Moore, 405-325-3095, Fax: 405-325-1180, E-mail: berrien@ou.edu.

School of Meteorology Students: 41 full-time (13 women), 31 part-time (10 women); includes 8 minority (1 Black or African American, non-Hispanic/Latino; 2 Asian, non-Hispanic/Latino; 4 Hispanic/Latino; 1 Two or more races, non-Hispanic/Latino), 12 international. Average age 26. 60 applicants, 22% accepted, 13 enrolled. *Faculty:* 42 full-time (8 women), 1 part-time/adjunct (0 women). Expenses: Contact institution. *Financial support:* In 2017–18, 70 students received support, including 2 fellowships with tuition reimbursements available (averaging $4,500 per year), 41 research assistantships with full tuition reimbursements available (averaging $20,415 per year), 19 teaching assistantships with full tuition reimbursements available (averaging $20,837 per year); health care benefits, tuition waivers (full and partial), and unspecified assistantships also available. Support available to part-time students. Financial award application deadline: 6/1; financial award applicants required to submit FAFSA. In 2017, 21 master's, 9 doctorates awarded. Offers meteorology (MS, PhD). *Application deadline:* For fall admission, 1/15 for domestic students, 2/1 for international students; for spring admission, 10/1 for domestic and international students. Applications are processed on a rolling basis. *Application fee:* $50 ($100 for international students). Electronic applications accepted. *Application Contact:* Christie Upchurch, Academic Coordinator, Graduate Program, 405-325-6571, Fax: 405-325-7689, E-mail: cupchurch@ou.edu. *Director*, Dr. David Parsons, 405-325-6561, Fax: 405-325-7689, E-mail: dparsons@ou.edu.

College of International Studies Students: 80 full-time (35 women), 307 part-time (97 women); includes 118 minority (33 Black or African American, non-Hispanic/Latino; 2 American Indian or Alaska Native, non-Hispanic/Latino; 15 Asian, non-Hispanic/Latino; 45 Hispanic/Latino; 1 Native Hawaiian or other Pacific Islander, non-Hispanic/Latino; 22 Two or more races, non-Hispanic/Latino), 7 international. Average age 32. 121 applicants, 89% accepted, 68 enrolled. *Faculty:* 20 full-time (7 women), 1 part-time/adjunct (0 women). Expenses: Contact institution. *Financial support:* In 2017–18, 31 students received support, including 4 research assistantships with full tuition reimbursements available (averaging $13,500 per year), 4 teaching assistantships with full tuition reimbursements available (averaging $13,500 per year); fellowships with full tuition reimbursements available, career-related internships or fieldwork, scholarships/grants, health care benefits, and unspecified assistantships also available. Financial award application deadline: 6/1; financial award applicants required to submit FAFSA. In 2017, 73 master's awarded. *Program availability:* Part-time, online courses with an 8-10 day study abroad. Offers economics and development (MAIS); global affairs (MA). *Application deadline:* For fall admission, 2/15 for domestic and international students. Applications are processed on a rolling basis. *Application fee:* $50 ($100 for international students). Electronic applications accepted. *Application Contact:* Katie Watkins, Academic Advisor, 405-325-2337, Fax: 405-325-7738, E-mail: kwatkins@ou.edu. *Professor/Associate Dean for Academic Affairs*, Dr. Mitchell Smith, 405-325-1584, Fax: 405-325-7738, E-mail: mps@ou.edu.

College of Law Students: 518 full-time (223 women), 237 part-time (165 women); includes 243 minority (36 Black or African American, non-Hispanic/Latino; 112 American Indian or Alaska Native, non-Hispanic/Latino; 14 Asian, non-Hispanic/Latino; 30 Hispanic/Latino; 51 Two or more races, non-Hispanic/Latino), 10 international. Average age 28. 960 applicants, 40% accepted, 159 enrolled. *Faculty:* 31 full-time (14 women), 21 part-time/adjunct (7 women). Expenses: Contact institution. *Financial support:* In 2017–18, 471 students received support. Career-related internships or fieldwork, Federal Work-Study, scholarships/grants, and tuition waivers (full and partial) available. Financial award application deadline: 6/1; financial award applicants required to submit FAFSA. In 2017, 24 master's, 156 doctorates awarded. *Program availability:* Part-time, 100% online, blended/hybrid learning. Offers law (LL M, JD). *Application deadline:* For fall admission, 3/15 for domestic and international students. Applications are processed on a rolling basis. *Application fee:* $50. Electronic applications accepted. *Application Contact:* Vicki Ferguson, Admissions Coordinator, 405-325-4728, Fax: 405-325-0502, E-mail: admissions@law.ou.edu. *Dean*, Joseph Harroz, Jr., 405-325-4884, Fax: 405-325-7712, E-mail: jharroz@ou.edu.

College of Professional and Continuing Studies Students: 64 full-time (39 women), 558 part-time (278 women); includes 191 minority (42 Black or African American, non-Hispanic/Latino; 42 American Indian or Alaska Native, non-Hispanic/Latino; 16 Asian, non-Hispanic/Latino; 46 Hispanic/Latino; 1 Native Hawaiian or other Pacific Islander, non-Hispanic/Latino; 44 Two or more races, non-Hispanic/Latino), 4 international. Average age 35. 151 applicants, 95% accepted, 97 enrolled. *Faculty:* 16 full-time (8 women). Expenses: Contact institution. *Financial support:* In 2017–18, 92 students received support. Career-related internships or fieldwork, institutionally sponsored loans, scholarships/grants, health care benefits, and tuition waivers available. Support available to part-time students. Financial award application deadline: 6/1; financial award applicants required to submit FAFSA. In 2017, 202 master's, 11 other advanced degrees awarded. *Program availability:* Part-time, 100% online, blended/hybrid learning. Offers administrative leadership (MA, Graduate Certificate); corrections management (Graduate Certificate); criminal justice (MS); integrated studies (MA); museum studies (MA); prevention science (MPS); restorative justice administration (Graduate Certificate). *Application deadline:* For fall admission, 7/15 for domestic and international students; for winter admission, 12/1 for domestic and international students; for spring admission, 5/1 for domestic and international students. Applications are processed on a rolling basis. *Application fee:* $50 ($100 for international students). Electronic applications accepted. *Application Contact:* Lindsey Gunderson, Graduate Academic Advisor, 405-325-5827, Fax: 405-325-7132, E-mail: lindsey.gunderson@ou.edu. *Associate Provost for Continuing Education/Interim Dean, College of Professional and Continuing Studies*, Dr. Martha L. Banz, 405-325-4414, Fax: 405-325-7132, E-mail: mlbanz@ou.edu.

Gallogly College of Engineering Students: 335 full-time (92 women), 219 part-time (42 women); includes 88 minority (15 Black or African American, non-Hispanic/Latino; 4 American Indian or Alaska Native, non-Hispanic/Latino; 25 Asian, non-Hispanic/Latino; 29 Hispanic/Latino; 15 Two or more races, non-Hispanic/Latino), 308 international. Average age 29. 583 applicants, 46% accepted, 129 enrolled. *Faculty:* 158 full-time (23 women), 4 part-time/adjunct (0 women). Expenses: Contact institution. *Financial support:* In 2017–18, 387 students received support, including 6 fellowships with full tuition reimbursements available (averaging $6,933 per year), 167 research assistantships with full and partial tuition reimbursements available (averaging $15,411 per year), 119 teaching assistantships with full and partial tuition reimbursements available (averaging $13,402 per year); career-related internships or fieldwork, institutionally sponsored loans, tuition waivers (partial), and unspecified assistantships also available. Support available to part-time students. Financial award application deadline: 6/1; financial award applicants required to submit FAFSA. In 2017, 127 master's, 33 doctorates awarded. *Program availability:* Part-time. Offers data science and analytics (MS); engineering (M Env Sc, MS, PhD); engineering physics (MS, PhD); general engineering (MS, PhD). *Application fee:* $50 ($100 for international students). Electronic applications accepted. *Application Contact:* Dr. John Antonio, Senior Associate Dean, 405-325-4397, Fax: 405-325-7508, E-mail: antonio@ou.edu. *Dean*, Dr. Thomas Landers, 405-325-2621, Fax: 405-325-7508, E-mail: landers@ou.edu.

School of Aerospace and Mechanical Engineering Students: 38 full-time (9 women), 22 part-time (2 women); includes 10 minority (1 Black or African American, non-Hispanic/Latino; 1 American Indian or Alaska Native, non-Hispanic/Latino; 1 Asian, non-Hispanic/Latino; 5 Hispanic/Latino; 2 Two or more races, non-Hispanic/Latino), 32 international. Average age 28. 60 applicants, 58% accepted, 21 enrolled. *Faculty:* 26 full-time (3 women), 1 part-time/adjunct (0 women). Expenses: Contact institution. *Financial support:* In 2017–18, 44 students received support, including 2 fellowships with full tuition reimbursements available (averaging $5,000 per year), 26 research assistantships with full tuition reimbursements available (averaging $13,458 per year), 26 teaching assistantships with full tuition reimbursements available (averaging $13,554 per year); scholarships/grants also available. Financial award application deadline: 6/1; financial award applicants required to submit FAFSA. In 2017, 10 master's, 3 doctorates awarded. *Program availability:* Part-time. Offers aerospace engineering (MS, PhD); mechanical engineering (MS, PhD). *Application deadline:* For fall admission, 1/15 for domestic and international students; for spring admission, 9/1 for domestic and international students. *Application fee:* $50 ($100 for international students). Electronic applications accepted. *Application Contact:* Bethany Burklund, AME Student Services Coordinator, 405-325-5013, Fax: 405-325-1088, E-mail: bethanyhb@ou.edu. *Director*, Zahed Siddique, 405-325-5011, Fax: 405-325-1088, E-mail: zsiddique@ou.edu.

School of Biomedical Engineering Students: 15 full-time (5 women), 6 part-time (2 women); includes 5 minority (1 Black or African American, non-Hispanic/Latino; 1 Asian, non-Hispanic/Latino; 1 Hispanic/Latino; 2 Two or more races, non-Hispanic/Latino), 10 international. Average age 27. 12 applicants, 50% accepted, 4 enrolled. *Faculty:* 19 full-time (3 women). Expenses: Contact institution. *Financial support:* In 2017–18, 16 students received support, including 8 research assistantships with full tuition reimbursements available (averaging $16,313 per year), 9 teaching assistantships with full tuition reimbursements available (averaging $18,650 per year); fellowships with full tuition reimbursements available, scholarships/grants, health care benefits, and unspecified assistantships also available. Financial award application deadline: 6/1; financial award applicants required to submit FAFSA. In 2017, 2 master's awarded. *Program availability:* Part-time. Offers biomedical engineering (MS, PhD). *Application deadline:* For fall admission, 1/15 priority date for domestic and international students; for spring admission, 9/15 priority date for domestic and international students. *Application fee:* $50 ($100 for international students). Electronic applications accepted. *Application Contact:* Shayla Palmer, Student Programs Coordinator, 405-325-3947, E-mail: chrishaylapalmer@ou.edu. *Director*, Dr. Michael Detamore, 405-325-2144, E-mail: detamore@ou.edu.

School of Chemical, Biological and Materials Engineering Students: 23 full-time (7 women), 6 part-time (2 women); includes 2 minority (1 Black or African American, non-Hispanic/Latino; 1 Hispanic/Latino), 18 international. Average age 27. 71 applicants, 8% accepted, 5 enrolled. *Faculty:* 15 full-time (1 woman). Expenses: Contact institution. *Financial support:* In 2017–18, 27 students received support, including 25 research assistantships with full tuition reimbursements available (averaging $17,454 per year), 3 teaching assistantships (averaging $20,139 per year). Financial award application deadline: 6/1; financial award applicants required to submit FAFSA. In 2017, 6 master's, 1 doctorate awarded. *Program availability:* Part-time. Offers chemical engineering (MS, PhD). *Application deadline:* For fall admission, 4/1 for international students; for spring admission, 9/1 for international students; for summer admission, 2/1 for international students. Applications are processed on a rolling basis. *Application fee:* $50 ($100 for international students). Electronic applications accepted. *Application Contact:* Donna King, Graduate Program Staff Assistant, 405-325-5812, Fax: 405-325-5813, E-mail: donnaking@ou.edu. *Director*, Dr. Brian Grady, 405-325-5814, Fax: 405-325-5813, E-mail: cbme@ou.edu.

School of Civil Engineering and Environmental Science Students: 35 full-time (12 women), 15 part-time (8 women); includes 7 minority (1 Black or African American, non-Hispanic/Latino; 1 American Indian or Alaska Native, non-Hispanic/Latino; 5 Two or more races, non-Hispanic/Latino), 26 international. Average age 28. 52 applicants, 33% accepted, 9 enrolled. *Faculty:* 23 full-time (5 women), 1 part-time/adjunct (0 women). Expenses: Contact institution. *Financial support:* In 2017–18, 49 students received support, including 2 fellowships with partial tuition reimbursements available (averaging $12,500 per year), 33 research assistantships with partial tuition reimbursements available (averaging $16,416 per year), 18 teaching assistantships with partial tuition reimbursements available (averaging $15,006 per year); scholarships/grants also available. Financial award application deadline: 6/1; financial award applicants required to submit FAFSA. In 2017, 18 master's, 7 doctorates awarded. *Program availability:* Part-time. Offers civil engineering (MS, PhD); environmental engineering (MS, PhD); environmental science (M Env Sc, PhD). *Application deadline:* For fall admission, 1/15 for domestic and international students; for spring admission, 5/15 for domestic and international students. *Application fee:* $50 ($100 for international students). Electronic applications accepted. *Application Contact:* Graduate Studies Coordinator, 405-325-2344, Fax: 405-325-4217, E-mail: ceesgradstudies@ou.edu. *Director*, Dr. Randall Kolar, 405-325-4267, Fax: 405-325-4217, E-mail: kolar@ou.edu.

School of Computer Science Students: 52 full-time (17 women), 11 part-time (3 women); includes 4 minority (2 Black or African American, non-Hispanic/Latino; 1 Asian, non-Hispanic/Latino; 1 Two or more races, non-Hispanic/Latino), 53 international. Average age 27. 96 applicants, 41% accepted, 20 enrolled. *Faculty:* 16 full-time (3 women). Expenses: Contact institution. *Financial support:* In 2017–18, 50 students received support, including 9 research assistantships with full tuition reimbursements available (averaging $16,158 per year), 28 teaching assistantships with full tuition reimbursements available (averaging $12,380 per year); fellowships with full tuition reimbursements available, scholarships/grants, and unspecified assistantships also available. Financial award application deadline: 6/1; financial award applicants required to submit FAFSA. In 2017, 24 master's, 4 doctorates awarded. *Program availability:* Part-time. Offers computer science (MS, PhD). *Application deadline:* For fall admission, 4/1 for domestic students, 3/1 for international students; for spring admission, 10/1 for domestic students, 9/1 for international students. Applications are processed on a rolling basis. *Application fee:* $50 ($100 for international students). Electronic applications accepted. *Application Contact:* Virginie Perez Woods, Academic Programs Coordinator, 405-325-0145, Fax: 405-325-4044, E-mail: vpw@cs.ou.edu. *Director*, Dr. Sridhar Radhakrishnan, 405-325-4042, Fax: 405-325-4044, E-mail: sridhar@ou.edu.

School of Electrical and Computer Engineering Students: 87 full-time (18 women), 53 part-time (9 women); includes 14 minority (1 Black or African American, non-Hispanic/Latino; 1 American Indian or Alaska Native, non-Hispanic/Latino; 4 Asian, non-Hispanic/Latino; 7 Hispanic/Latino; 1 Two or more races, non-Hispanic/Latino), 89 international. Average age 28. 137 applicants, 52% accepted, 30 enrolled. *Faculty:* 45 full-time (3 women), 2 part-time/adjunct (0 women). Expenses: Contact institution. *Financial support:* In 2017–18, 115 students received support, including 53 research assistantships with full and partial tuition reimbursements available (averaging $15,028 per year), 19 teaching assistantships with full and partial tuition reimbursements available (averaging $11,456 per year); fellowships with full and partial tuition reimbursements available, career-related internships or fieldwork, scholarships/grants, and health care benefits also available. Financial award application deadline: 6/1; financial award applicants required to submit FAFSA. In 2017, 30 master's, 15 doctorates awarded. *Program availability:* Part-time. Offers electrical and computer engineering (MS, PhD); telecommunications engineering (MS). *Application deadline:* For fall admission, 4/1 for domestic students, 3/1 for international students; for spring admission, 11/1 for domestic students, 10/1 for international students. Applications are processed on a rolling basis. *Application fee:* $50 ($100 for international students). Electronic applications accepted. *Application Contact:* Emily Benton Wilkins, Graduate Programs Coordinator, 405-325-7334, Fax: 405-325-7066, E-mail: emily.d.benton-1@ou.edu. *Director*, Dr. J.R. Cruz, 405-325-8131, Fax: 405-325-7066, E-mail: jcruz@ou.edu.

School of Industrial and Systems Engineering Students: 36 full-time (11 women), 19 part-time (6 women); includes 8 minority (1 Black or African American, non-Hispanic/Latino; 2 Asian, non-Hispanic/Latino; 3 Hispanic/Latino; 2 Two or more races, non-Hispanic/Latino), 41 international. Average age 28. 78 applicants, 53% accepted, 15 enrolled. *Faculty:* 13 full-time (4 women). Expenses: Contact institution. *Financial support:* In 2017–18, 32 students received support, including 8 research assistantships with full tuition reimbursements available (averaging $14,391 per year), 15 teaching assistantships with full tuition reimbursements available (averaging $11,607 per year); Federal Work-Study, institutionally sponsored loans, scholarships/grants, and health care benefits also available. Financial award application deadline: 6/1; financial award applicants required to submit FAFSA. In 2017, 23 master's, 3 doctorates awarded. Offers industrial and systems engineering (MS, PhD). *Application deadline:* For fall admission, 6/1 priority date for domestic students, 4/1 priority date for international students; for spring admission, 11/1 priority date for domestic students, 9/1 priority date for international students. Applications are processed on a rolling basis. *Application fee:* $50 ($100 for international students). Electronic applications accepted. *Application Contact:* Dr. Janet Allen, Chair/Graduate Liaison, 405-550-3969, Fax: 405-325-7555, E-mail: janet.allen@ou.edu. *Professor/Interim Director*, Dr. Shivakumar Raman, 405-819-3710, Fax: 405-325-7555, E-mail: raman@ou.edu.

Gaylord College of Journalism and Mass Communication Students: 28 full-time (13 women), 22 part-time (12 women); includes 8 minority (3 Black or African American, non-Hispanic/Latino; 1 Asian, non-Hispanic/Latino; 3 Hispanic/Latino; 1 Two or more races, non-Hispanic/Latino), 14 international. Average age 33. 24 applicants, 67% accepted, 8 enrolled. *Faculty:* 31 full-time (14 women), 1 part-time/adjunct (0 women). Expenses: Contact institution. *Financial support:* In 2017–18, 41 students received support, including 2 fellowships (averaging $3,000 per year), 7 research assistantships with full tuition reimbursements available (averaging $16,586 per year), 20 teaching assistantships with full tuition reimbursements available (averaging $13,752 per year); career-related internships or fieldwork, scholarships/grants, health care benefits, unspecified assistantships, and research and research travel awards also available. Financial award application deadline: 6/1; financial award applicants required to submit FAFSA. In 2017, 13 master's awarded. *Program availability:* Part-time. Offers broadcast and electronic media (MA); journalism (MA); journalism and mass communication (MA, MPW, PhD); media arts (PhD); media management (MA); news and information (PhD); professional writing (MPW); strategic communication (MA, PhD). *Application deadline:* For fall admission, 2/1 priority date for domestic students, 2/1 for international students; for spring admission, 11/1 for domestic students, 9/1 for international students; for summer admission, 3/1 for domestic students. Applications are processed on a rolling basis. *Application fee:* $50 ($100 for international students). Electronic applications accepted. *Application Contact:* Larry Laneer, Graduate Advisor, 405-325-2722, Fax: 405-325-7565, E-mail: llaneer@ou.edu. *Director of Graduate Studies/Professor of Journalism*, Dr. Peter Gade, 405-325-5528, Fax: 405-325-7565, E-mail: pgade@ou.edu.

Graduate College Students: 13 full-time (3 women), 68 part-time (31 women); includes 27 minority (5 Black or African American, non-Hispanic/Latino; 3 American Indian or Alaska Native, non-Hispanic/Latino; 4 Asian, non-Hispanic/Latino; 10 Hispanic/Latino; 1 Native Hawaiian or other Pacific Islander, non-Hispanic/Latino; 4 Two or more races, non-Hispanic/Latino), 4 international. Average age 38. 22 applicants, 73% accepted, 2 enrolled. *Faculty:* 45 full-time (19 women), 1 (woman) part-time/adjunct. Expenses: Contact institution. *Financial support:* In 2017–18, 7 students received support, including 5 research assistantships with full tuition reimbursements available (averaging $15,913 per year), 3 teaching assistantships with full tuition reimbursements available (averaging $42,600 per year); fellowships with full tuition reimbursements available, scholarships/grants, health care benefits, tuition waivers, and unspecified assistantships also available. Financial award application deadline: 6/1; financial award applicants required to submit FAFSA. In 2017, 33 master's, 6 doctorates, 4 other advanced degrees awarded. *Program availability:* Part-time, evening/weekend, blended/hybrid learning. Offers interdisciplinary studies (MA, MS, PhD). *Application deadline:* For fall admission, 4/1 for international students; for spring admission, 9/1 for international students; for summer admission, 2/1 for international students. Applications are processed on a rolling basis. *Application fee:* $50 ($100 for international students). Electronic applications accepted. *Application Contact:* Amy Shaw, Director, Office of Graduate Admissions, 405-325-6765, Fax: 405-325-5345, E-mail: ashaw@ou.edu. *Dean and Professor*, Dr. Randall S. Hewes, 405-325-3811, Fax: 405-325-5343, E-mail: hewes@ou.edu.

Jeannine Rainbolt College of Education Students: 253 full-time (178 women), 503 part-time (383 women); includes 224 minority (75 Black or African American, non-Hispanic/Latino; 36 American Indian or Alaska Native, non-Hispanic/Latino; 12 Asian, non-Hispanic/Latino; 50 Hispanic/Latino; 1 Native Hawaiian or other Pacific Islander, non-Hispanic/Latino; 50 Two or more races, non-Hispanic/Latino), 35 international. Average age 34. 359 applicants, 64% accepted, 189 enrolled. *Faculty:* 73 full-time (44 women), 5 part-time/adjunct (2 women). Expenses: Contact institution. *Financial support:* In 2017–18, 468 students received support, including 45 research assistantships with full and partial tuition reimbursements available (averaging $12,416 per year), 12 teaching assistantships with full and partial tuition reimbursements available (averaging $12,723 per year); fellowships with full and partial tuition reimbursements available, career-related internships or fieldwork, Federal Work-Study, institutionally sponsored loans, scholarships/grants, traineeships, health care benefits, and unspecified assistantships also available. Support available to part-time students. Financial award application deadline: 6/1; financial award applicants required to submit FAFSA. In 2017, 199 master's, 43 doctorates, 6 other advanced degrees awarded. *Program availability:* Part-time, evening/weekend. Offers adult and higher education (M Ed, PhD); applied behavior analysis (M Ed); communication, culture and pedagogy for Hispanic (ESL/ELL) populations in educational settings (Graduate Certificate); education (M Ed, Ed D, PhD, Graduate Certificate); educational administration, curriculum and supervision (M Ed, Ed D, PhD); educational psychology (M Ed); educational studies (M Ed, PhD); higher education and community support (PhD); higher education professor (PhD); instructional design and technology (M Ed); instructional leadership and academic curriculum (M Ed, PhD); instructional psychology and technology (M Ed, PhD); integrating technology in teaching (M Ed); professional counseling (M Ed); reading specialist (M Ed); school instruction and leadership (PhD); secondary transition education (M Ed); special education (M Ed, PhD). *Application fee:* $50 ($100 for international students). Electronic applications accepted. *Application Contact:* Anna Steele, Graduate Programs Officer, 405-325-4525, E-mail: jrcoe_gps@ou.edu. *Dean*, Dr. Gregg Garn, 405-325-1082, Fax: 405-325-7390, E-mail: garn@ou.edu.

Mewbourne College of Earth and Energy Students: 136 full-time (28 women), 94 part-time (26 women); includes 19 minority (3 Black or African American, non-Hispanic/Latino; 2 American Indian or Alaska Native, non-Hispanic/Latino; 4 Asian, non-Hispanic/Latino; 5 Hispanic/Latino; 5 Two or more races, non-Hispanic/Latino), 139 international. Average age 29. 318 applicants, 23% accepted, 49 enrolled. *Faculty:* 46 full-time (5 women), 4 part-time/adjunct (0 women). Expenses: Contact institution. *Financial support:* In 2017–18, 158 students received support, including 95 research assistantships with full and partial tuition reimbursements available (averaging $16,947 per year), 54 teaching assistantships with full and partial tuition reimbursements available (averaging $15,275 per year); scholarships/grants, health care benefits, and unspecified assistantships also available. Financial award application deadline: 6/1; financial award applicants required to submit FAFSA. In 2017, 71 master's, 7 doctorates, 1 other advanced degree awarded. *Program availability:* Part-time, evening/weekend. Offers earth and energy (MS, PhD, Graduate Certificate). *Application fee:* $50 ($100 for international students). Electronic applications accepted. *Dean*, Dr. J. Mike Stice, 405-325-3821, Fax: 405-325-3180, E-mail: mstice@ou.edu.

ConocoPhillips School of Geology and Geophysics Students: 57 full-time (14 women), 49 part-time (19 women); includes 11 minority (1 Black or African American, non-Hispanic/Latino; 1 American Indian or Alaska Native, non-Hispanic/Latino; 2 Asian, non-Hispanic/Latino; 4 Hispanic/Latino; 3 Two or more races, non-Hispanic/Latino), 45 international. Average age 27. 168 applicants, 19% accepted, 27 enrolled. *Faculty:* 27 full-time (4 women), 3 part-time/adjunct (0 women). Expenses: Contact institution. *Financial support:* In 2017–18, 70 students received support, including 28 research assistantships with full tuition reimbursements available (averaging $19,481 per year), 24 teaching assistantships with full tuition reimbursements available (averaging $17,493 per year); scholarships/grants, health care benefits, and unspecified assistantships also available. Financial award application deadline: 6/1; financial award applicants required to submit FAFSA. In 2017, 28 master's, 4 doctorates awarded. *Program availability:* Part-time. Offers geology (MS, PhD); geophysics (MS, PhD). *Application deadline:* For fall admission, 1/10 priority date for domestic and international students; for spring admission, 9/1 for domestic and international students. *Application fee:* $50 ($100 for international students). Electronic applications accepted. *Application Contact:* Rebecca Fay, Coordinator of Academic Student Services, 405-325-3253, Fax: 405-325-3140, E-mail: rfay@ou.edu. *Director*, Dr. Gerilyn S Soreghan, 405-325-3253, Fax: 405-325-3140, E-mail: lsoreg@ou.edu.

Mewbourne School of Petroleum and Geological Engineering Students: 80 full-time (14 women), 45 part-time (7 women); includes 8 minority (2 Black or African American, non-Hispanic/Latino; 1 American Indian or Alaska Native, non-Hispanic/Latino; 2 Asian, non-Hispanic/Latino; 1 Hispanic/Latino; 2 Two or more races, non-Hispanic/Latino), 95 international. Average age 30. 150 applicants, 28% accepted, 22 enrolled. *Faculty:* 19 full-time (1 woman), 1 part-time/adjunct (0 women). Expenses: Contact institution. *Financial support:* In 2017–18, 88 students received support, including 1 fellowship with partial tuition reimbursement available (averaging $2,000 per year), 57 research assistantships with partial tuition reimbursements available (averaging $15,295 per year), 30 teaching assistantships with partial tuition reimbursements available (averaging $13,500 per year); scholarships/grants also available. Financial award application deadline: 6/1; financial award applicants required to submit FAFSA. In 2017, 43 master's, 3 doctorates, 1 other advanced degree awarded. *Program availability:* Part-time, evening/weekend. Offers geological engineering (MS, PhD); natural gas engineering and management (MS, Graduate Certificate); natural gas technology (Graduate Certificate); petroleum engineering (MS, PhD). *Application deadline:* For fall admission, 3/1 for domestic and international students; for spring admission, 9/1 for domestic and international students. *Application fee:* $50 ($100 for international students). Electronic applications accepted. *Application Contact:* Danika Hines-Barnett, Graduate Student Coordinator, 405-325-2921, E-mail: danika@ou.edu. *Director/Chair*, Dr. Chandra Rai, 405-325-2921, E-mail: crai@ou.edu.

Price College of Business Students: 138 full-time (45 women), 188 part-time (46 women); includes 63 minority (9 Black or African American, non-Hispanic/Latino; 6 American Indian or Alaska Native, non-Hispanic/Latino; 16 Asian, non-Hispanic/Latino; 20 Hispanic/Latino; 12 Two or more races, non-Hispanic/Latino), 44 international. Average age 31. 320 applicants, 37% accepted, 81 enrolled. *Faculty:* 69 full-time (17 women), 3 part-time/adjunct (1 woman). Expenses: Contact institution. *Financial support:* In 2017–18, 162 students received support, including 11 fellowships with full tuition reimbursements available (averaging $3,398 per year), 33 research assistantships with partial tuition reimbursements available (averaging $14,091 per year), 26 teaching assistantships with partial tuition reimbursements available (averaging $14,370 per year); career-related internships or fieldwork, scholarships/grants, health care benefits, and unspecified assistantships also available. Support available to part-time students. Financial award application deadline: 6/1; financial award applicants required to submit FAFSA. In 2017, 151 master's, 9 doctorates, 19 other advanced degrees awarded. *Program availability:* Part-time, evening/weekend, 100% online. Offers accounting (M Acc); business administration (EMBA, MBA, PMBA, PhD); business entrepreneurship (Graduate Certificate); foundations of business (Graduate Certificate); management information systems (MS, Graduate Certificate); the business of energy (Graduate Certificate). *Application deadline:* Applications are processed on a rolling basis. *Application fee:* $50 ($100 for international students). Electronic applications accepted. *Application Contact:* Amber Hasbrook, Academic Counselor, 405-325-5815, Fax: 405-325-7753, E-mail: ahasbrook@ou.edu. *Dean*, Daniel Pullin, JD, 405-325-0100, Fax: 405-325-3421, E-mail: dpullin@ou.edu.

Division of Management Information Systems Students: 35 full-time (15 women), 13 part-time (7 women); includes 12 minority (2 Black or African American, non-Hispanic/Latino; 1 American Indian or Alaska Native, non-Hispanic/Latino; 3 Asian, non-Hispanic/Latino; 4 Hispanic/Latino; 2 Two or more races, non-Hispanic/Latino), 13 international. Average age 28. 24 applicants, 38% accepted, 8 enrolled. *Faculty:* 11 full-time (5 women). Expenses: Contact institution. *Financial support:* In 2017–18, 40 students received support, including 2 research assistantships with partial tuition reimbursements available (averaging $16,864 per year), 8 teaching assistantships with partial tuition reimbursements available (averaging $11,121 per year); career-related internships or fieldwork, scholarships/grants, and unspecified assistantships also available. Support available to part-time students. Financial award application deadline: 6/1; financial award applicants required to submit FAFSA. In 2017, 23 master's, 2 other advanced degrees awarded. *Program availability:* Part-time, evening/weekend. Offers digital technologies (Graduate Certificate); management of information technology (MS). *Application deadline:* For fall admission, 6/15 for domestic students, 3/1 for international students; for spring admission, 10/1 for domestic students, 8/1 for international students. Applications are processed on a rolling basis. *Application fee:* $50 ($100 for international students). Electronic applications accepted. *Application Contact:* Jennifer Aragon, Academic Advisor, 405-325-2074, Fax: 405-325-7118, E-mail: jhardman@ou.edu. *Chair/Division Director*, Radhika Santhanam, 405-325-0791, E-mail: radhika@ou.edu.

John T. Steed School of Accounting Students: 19 full-time (11 women), 29 part-time (12 women); includes 17 minority (5 Black or African American, non-Hispanic/Latino; 1 American Indian or Alaska Native, non-Hispanic/Latino; 4 Asian, non-Hispanic/Latino; 3 Hispanic/Latino; 4 Two or more races, non-Hispanic/Latino), 5 international. Average age 31. 49 applicants, 80% accepted, 32 enrolled. *Faculty:* 13 full-time (5 women). Expenses: Contact institution. *Financial support:* In 2017–18, 15 students received support, including 1 fellowship (averaging $5,000 per year), 5 research assistantships (averaging $14,940 per year), 9 teaching assistantships (averaging $13,701 per year); career-related internships or fieldwork, scholarships/grants, and unspecified assistantships also available. Support available to part-time students. Financial award application deadline: 6/1; financial award applicants required to submit FAFSA. In 2017, 10 master's awarded. *Program availability:* Part-time, 100% online. Offers accounting (M Acc). *Application deadline:* For fall admission, 6/15 for domestic students, 3/1 for international students; for spring admission, 11/15 for domestic students, 8/1 for international students; for summer admission, 3/15 for domestic students, 1/1 for international students. Applications are processed on a rolling basis. *Application fee:* $50 ($100 for international students). Electronic applications accepted. *Application Contact:* Jennifer Aragon, Academic Advisor, 405-325-2074, Fax: 405-325-7118, E-mail: jhardman@ou.edu. *Director/Chair*, Wayne Thomas, 405-325-5799, Fax: 405-325-7348, E-mail: wthomas@ou.edu.

Weitzenhoffer Family College of Fine Arts Students: 131 full-time (65 women), 79 part-time (38 women); includes 36 minority (3 Black or African American, non-Hispanic/Latino; 6 American Indian or Alaska Native, non-Hispanic/Latino; 6 Asian, non-Hispanic/Latino; 12 Hispanic/Latino; 9 Two or more races, non-Hispanic/Latino), 27 international. Average age 30. 211 applicants, 40% accepted, 54 enrolled. *Faculty:* 92 full-time (27 women). Expenses: Contact institution. *Financial support:* In 2017–18, 157 students received support, including 3 fellowships with full and partial tuition reimbursements available (averaging $6,000 per year), 36 research assistantships with full tuition reimbursements available (averaging $10,511 per year), 84 teaching assistantships with full tuition reimbursements available (averaging $10,758 per year); career-related internships or fieldwork, Federal Work-Study, institutionally sponsored loans, scholarships/grants, health care benefits, tuition waivers (full and partial), and unspecified assistantships also available. Support available to part-time students. Financial award application deadline: 6/1; financial award applicants required to submit FAFSA. In 2017, 49 master's, 18 doctorates awarded. Offers fine arts (M Mus, M Mus Ed, MA, MFA, DMA, PhD, Graduate Certificate). *Application fee:* $50 ($100 for international students). Electronic applications accepted. *Dean*, Dr. Mary Margaret Holt, 405-325-7370, Fax: 405-325-1667, E-mail: marymholt@ou.edu.

School of Dance Students: 5 full-time (all women); includes 1 minority (Two or more races, non-Hispanic/Latino), 1 international. Average age 41. 1 applicant. *Faculty:* 4 full-time (2 women). Expenses: Contact institution. *Financial support:* In 2017–18, 4 students received support, including 1 fellowship with full tuition reimbursement available (averaging $8,000 per year), 4 teaching assistantships (averaging $16,122 per year); health care benefits and unspecified assistantships also available. Financial award application deadline: 6/1; financial award applicants required to submit FAFSA. Offers ballet (MFA); modern dance (MFA). *Application deadline:* For fall admission, 4/15 for domestic students, 3/1 for international students. Applications are processed on a rolling basis. *Application fee:* $50 ($100 for international students). Electronic applications accepted. *Application Contact:* Jeremy Lindberg, Associate Professor, 405-325-0567 Ext. 15, Fax: 405-325-7024, E-mail: jlindberg@ou.edu. *Director*, Michael R. Bearden, 405-325-4051, Fax: 405-325-7024, E-mail: mrbearden@ou.edu.

School of Music Students: 104 full-time (43 women), 70 part-time (29 women); includes 26 minority (3 Black or African American, non-Hispanic/Latino; 5 American Indian or Alaska Native, non-Hispanic/Latino; 5 Asian, non-Hispanic/Latino; 8 Hispanic/Latino; 5 Two or more races, non-Hispanic/Latino), 26 international. Average age 29. 182 applicants, 42% accepted, 48 enrolled. *Faculty:* 56 full-time (13 women). Expenses: Contact institution. *Financial support:* In 2017–18, 123 students received support, including 2 fellowships with full tuition reimbursements available (averaging $5,000 per year), 35 research assistantships with full tuition reimbursements available (averaging $10,515 per year), 62 teaching assistantships with full tuition reimbursements available (averaging $10,452 per year); health care benefits, tuition waivers, and unspecified assistantships also available. Financial award application deadline: 6/1; financial award applicants required to submit FAFSA. In 2017, 41 master's, 15 doctorates awarded. Offers choral conducting (M Mus); composition (M Mus, DMA); conducting (M Mus Ed, DMA); general (M Mus Ed); instrumental (M Mus Ed); instrumental conducting (M Mus); music education (PhD); music performance (Graduate Certificate); music theory (M Mus); musicology (M Mus); organ (M Mus, DMA); piano (M Mus, DMA); piano pedagogy (M Mus Ed); voice (M Mus, DMA); wind/percussion/string instruments (M Mus, DMA). *Application deadline:* For fall admission, 2/1 for domestic and international students; for spring admission, 10/1 for domestic students, 9/1 for international students; for summer admission, 2/1 for domestic and international students. Applications are processed on a rolling basis. *Application fee:* $50 ($100 for international students). Electronic applications accepted. *Application Contact:* Jan Russell, Graduate Admissions and Recruiting Advisor, 405-325-5393, Fax: 405-325-7574, E-mail: jrussell@ou.edu. *Director*, Dr. Roland Barrett, 405-325-2081, Fax: 405-325-7574, E-mail: rcbarrett@ou.edu.

School of Visual Arts Students: 22 full-time (17 women), 9 part-time (all women); includes 9 minority (1 American Indian or Alaska Native, non-Hispanic/Latino; 1 Asian, non-Hispanic/Latino; 4 Hispanic/Latino; 3 Two or more races, non-Hispanic/Latino). Average age 33. 28 applicants, 25% accepted, 6 enrolled. *Faculty:* 24 full-time (8 women). Expenses: Contact institution. *Financial support:* In 2017–18, 30 students received support, including 1 research assistantship with full tuition reimbursement available (averaging $10,373 per year), 16 teaching assistantships with full tuition reimbursements available (averaging $10,377 per year); fellowships with full tuition reimbursements available, career-related internships or fieldwork, Federal Work-Study, institutionally sponsored loans, scholarships/grants, health care benefits, tuition waivers (full and partial), and unspecified assistantships also available. Support available to part-time students. Financial award application deadline: 6/1; financial award applicants required to submit FAFSA. In 2017, 6 master's, 3 doctorates awarded. Offers art (MFA); art and technology (MFA); art history (MA, PhD); art of the American West (PhD); ceramics (MFA); design (MFA); Native American art history (PhD); painting (MFA); printmaking (MFA); sculpture (MFA); visual communication (MFA). *Application deadline:* For fall admission, 2/1 for domestic and international students. *Application fee:* $50 ($100 for international students). Electronic applications accepted. *Application Contact:* Peter Froslie, MFA Coordinator, E-mail: froslie@ou.edu. *Director*, Dr. Bette Talvacchia, 405-325-2691, Fax: 405-325-1668, E-mail: bette.talvacchia-1@ou.edu.

UNIVERSITY OF OKLAHOMA HEALTH SCIENCES CENTER, Oklahoma City, OK 73190

General Information State-supported, coed, upper-level institution. CGS member. *Graduate housing:* Rooms and/or apartments available on a first-come, first-served basis to single and married students. *Research affiliation:* Peggy and Charles Stephenson Oklahoma Cancer Center (cancer research), Oklahoma Medical Research Foundation, Dean A. McGee Eye Institute (ophthalmology), Oklahoma Children's Memorial Hospital (pediatrics), Veterans Administration Medical Center (clinical and applied medicine), University of Oklahoma Medical Center.

GRADUATE UNITS

College of Dentistry Offers dentistry (MS, DDS, Certificate); general dentistry (Certificate); orthodontics (MS); periodontics (MS). Electronic applications accepted.

College of Medicine Offers biochemistry (MS, PhD); biochemistry and molecular biology (MS, PhD); biological psychology (MS, PhD); cell biology (MS, PhD); genetic counseling (MS); immunology (MS, PhD); medical radiation physics (MS, PhD); medical sciences (MS); medicine (MHS, MS, MD, PhD); microbiology (MS, PhD); microbiology and immunology (MS, PhD); molecular biology (MS, PhD); neuroscience (MS, PhD); pathology (PhD); physician associate (MHS); physiology (MS, PhD); psychiatry and behavioral sciences (MS, PhD); radiological sciences (MS, PhD). Electronic applications accepted.

College of Pharmacy Offers pharmacy (MS, PhD, Pharm D).

Graduate College *Program availability:* Part-time, evening/weekend.

College of Allied Health *Program availability:* Part-time. Offers allied health (MOT, MPT, MS, Au D, PhD, Certificate); allied health sciences (PhD); audiology (MS, Au D, PhD); communication sciences and disorders (Certificate); education of the deaf (MS); nutritional sciences (MS); occupational therapy (MOT); physical therapy (MPT); rehabilitation sciences (MS); speech-language pathology (MS, PhD).

College of Nursing *Program availability:* Part-time. Offers nursing (MS). MS/MBA offered jointly with Oklahoma State University and University of Oklahoma.

College of Public Health *Program availability:* Part-time. Offers biostatistics (MPH, MS, Dr PH, PhD); epidemiology (MPH, MS, Dr PH, PhD); general public health (MPH, Dr PH); health administration and policy (MHA, MPH, MS, Dr PH, PhD); health promotion sciences (MPH, MS, Dr PH, PhD); occupational and environmental health (MPH, MS, Dr PH, PhD); preparedness and terrorism (MPH); public health (MHA, MPH, MS, Dr PH, PhD).

UNIVERSITY OF OREGON, Eugene, OR 97403

General Information State-supported, coed, university. CGS member. *Graduate housing:* Rooms and/or apartments available to single and married students. *Research affiliation:* Oregon Research Institute, Battelle–Pacific Northwest National Laboratory, National Renewable Energy Laboratory (NREL), Stanford Linear Accelerator Center, Naval Research Laboratories.

GRADUATE UNITS

Graduate School *Program availability:* Part-time, evening/weekend. Offers applied information management (MS).

Charles H. Lundquist College of Business *Program availability:* Part-time, evening/weekend. Offers accounting (M Actg, PhD); business (M Actg, MA, MBA, MS, PhD); decision sciences (MA, MS); finance (PhD); management (PhD); management: general business (MBA); marketing (PhD); sports product management (MS).

College of Arts and Sciences *Program availability:* Part-time, evening/weekend. Offers anthropology (MA, MS, PhD); arts and sciences (MA, MFA, MS, PhD); Asian studies (MA); biochemistry (MA, MS, PhD); chemistry (MA, MS, PhD); Chinese (MA, PhD); classical civilization (MA); classics (MA); clinical psychology (PhD); cognitive psychology (MA, MS, PhD); comparative literature (MA, PhD); computer and information science (MA, MS, PhD); creative writing (MFA); developmental psychology (MA, MS, PhD); ecology and evolution (MA, MS, PhD); economics (MA, MS, PhD); English (MA, PhD); environmental science, studies, and policy (PhD); environmental studies (MA, MS); French (MA); geography (MA, MS, PhD); geological sciences (MA, MS, PhD); Germanic languages and literatures (MA, PhD); Greek (MA); history (MA, PhD); human physiology (MS, PhD); independent study: folklore (MA, MS); international studies (MA); Italian (MA); Japanese (MA, PhD); language teaching studies (MA); Latin (MA); linguistics (MA, PhD); marine biology (MA, MS, PhD); mathematics (MA, MS, PhD); molecular, cellular and genetic biology (PhD); neuroscience and development (PhD); philosophy (MA, PhD); physics (MA, MS,

PhD); physiological psychology (MA, MS, PhD); political science (MA, MS, PhD); psychology (MA, MS, PhD); Romance languages (MA, PhD); Russian and East European Studies (MA); social/personality psychology (MA, MS, PhD); sociology (MA, MS, PhD); Spanish (MA); theater arts (MA, MFA, MS, PhD).

College of Design *Program availability:* Part-time, evening/weekend. Offers architecture (M Arch); art (MFA); art history (MA, PhD); community and regional planning (MCRP); design (M Arch, MA, MCRP, MFA, MI Arch, MLA, MNM, MPA, MS, PhD, Graduate Certificate); historic preservation (MS); interior architecture (MI Arch); landscape architecture (MLA, PhD); nonprofit management (MNM, Graduate Certificate); public administration (MPA); sports product design (MS).

College of Education *Program availability:* Part-time. Offers communication disorders and sciences (MA, MS, PhD); counseling psychology (PhD); couples and family therapy (MS); critical and sociocultural studies in education (PhD); curriculum and teacher education (MA, MS); educational leadership (MS, D Ed, PhD); prevention science (M Ed, MS, PhD); school psychology (MS, PhD); special education (M Ed, MA, MS, PhD).

School of Journalism and Communication *Program availability:* Part-time. Offers journalism (MA, MS); media studies (MA, MS, PhD); multimedia journalism (MA, MS); strategic communication (MA, MS).

School of Music *Program availability:* Part-time. Offers composition (M Mus, DMA, PhD); conducting (M Mus); dance (MA, MS); jazz studies (M Mus); music (M Mus, MA, MS, DMA, PhD); music education (M Mus, DMA, PhD); music history (PhD); music theory (PhD); performance (M Mus, DMA); piano pedagogy (M Mus).

School of Law Offers law (MA, MS, JD).

UNIVERSITY OF OTTAWA, Ottawa, ON K1N 6N5, Canada

General Information Province-supported, coed, university. *Graduate housing:* Rooms and/or apartments available on a first-come, first-served basis to single and married students. Housing application deadline: 3/15. *Research affiliation:* IBM (performance analytics software, supercomputing), General Electric Company (GE) (hardware, imaging, medical devices), Rio Tinto Alcan (aluminum and aluminum products), Pratt and Whitney Canada (turbine engines, advanced materials, aerospace), Wright Medical Technology Canada (orthopedic medical devices), Air Products and Chemicals Inc. (industrial gases (hydrogen), performance materials, equipment and technology).

GRADUATE UNITS

Faculty of Graduate and Postdoctoral Studies *Program availability:* Part-time, evening/weekend. Offers biomedical engineering (MA Sc); e-business technologies (M Sc, MEBT); globalization and international development (MA); population health (PhD); systems science (M Sc, M Sys Sc, Certificate). MCL, MRE, MP Th offered jointly with Saint Paul University. Electronic applications accepted.

Faculty of Arts *Program availability:* Part-time, evening/weekend. Offers arts (M Geog, M Mus, M Sc, MA, PhD, Certificate); classical studies (MA); communication (MA); directing for theatre (MA); economics (PhD); English (MA, PhD); geography (M Geog, M Sc, MA, PhD); history (PhD); interpreting (MA); lettres Françaises (MA, PhD); linguistics (MA, PhD); music (M Mus, MA); orchestral studies (Certificate); philosophy (PhD); piano pedagogy research (Certificate); political science (PhD); psychology (PhD); religious studies (PhD); Spanish (MA, PhD); Spanish translation (MA); translation (MA); translation studies (PhD). Electronic applications accepted.

Faculty of Education *Program availability:* Online learning. Offers education (M Ed, MA Ed, PhD, Certificate). Electronic applications accepted.

Faculty of Engineering Offers chemical and biological engineering (M Eng, MA Sc, PhD); civil engineering (M Eng, MA Sc, PhD); computer science (MCS, PhD); electrical and computer engineering (M Eng, MA Sc, PhD); engineering (M Eng, MA Sc, MCS, PhD, Certificate); engineering management (M Eng); information technology (Certificate); mechanical and aerospace engineering (M Eng, MA Sc, PhD); project management (Certificate). Electronic applications accepted.

Faculty of Health Sciences *Program availability:* Part-time, evening/weekend. Offers audiology (M Sc); health sciences (M Sc, MA, PhD, Certificate); human kinetics (MA); nurse practitioner (Certificate); nursing (M Sc, PhD); nursing/primary health care (M Sc); orthophony (M Sc). Electronic applications accepted.

Faculty of Law *Program availability:* Part-time, evening/weekend. Offers law (LL M, LL D). Electronic applications accepted.

Faculty of Medicine Offers biochemistry (M Sc, PhD); cellular and molecular medicine (M Sc, PhD); epidemiology (M Sc); medicine (M Sc, MD, PhD); microbiology and immunology (M Sc, PhD). Electronic applications accepted.

Faculty of Science *Program availability:* Part-time, evening/weekend. Offers biology (M Sc, PhD); chemistry (M Sc, PhD); earth sciences (M Sc, PhD); mathematics and statistics (M Sc, PhD); physics (M Sc, PhD); science (M Sc, PhD). Electronic applications accepted.

Faculty of Social Sciences *Program availability:* Part-time, evening/weekend. Offers criminology (MA, MCA); economics (MA, PhD); education (MA); English (MA); history (MA); human kinetics (MA); law (LL M); lettres Françaises (MA); nursing (M Sc); pastoral studies (MA); political science (MA); political studies (MA, PhD); psychology (PhD); religious studies (MA); social sciences (LL M, M Sc, MA, MCA, MSS, PhD); social work (MSS); sociology (MA); sociology and anthropology (MA). Electronic applications accepted.

Telfer School of Management *Program availability:* Part-time, evening/weekend. Offers business administration (MBA); executive business administration (EMBA); health administration (MHA); management (EMBA, MBA, MHA). Electronic applications accepted.

UNIVERSITY OF PENNSYLVANIA, Philadelphia, PA 19104

General Information Independent, coed, university. CGS member. *Enrollment:* 21,907 graduate, professional, and undergraduate students; 11,053 full-time matriculated graduate/professional students (5,787 women), 1,959 part-time matriculated graduate/professional students (1,269 women). *Enrollment by degree level:* 7,003 master's, 5,843 doctoral, 166 other advanced degrees. *Graduate faculty:* 2,666 full-time (898 women), 2,453 part-time/adjunct (1,027 women). *Graduate housing:* Rooms and/or apartments available on a first-come, first-served basis to single and married students. *Student services:* Campus employment opportunities, campus safety program, career counseling, child daycare facilities, exercise/wellness program, free psychological counseling, international student services, low-cost health insurance, multicultural affairs office, services for students with disabilities, writing training. *Library facilities:* Van Pelt Library plus 14 others. *Collection:* Books: 6.4 million (physical); Serial titles: 188,604 (physical). Study areas open 24 hours, 5–7 days a week; students can reserve study rooms. *Research affiliation:* Children's Hospital of Philadelphia, The Wistar Institute (anatomy and biology), BioAdvance, Regional Nanotechnology Center.

Computer facilities: Computer purchase and lease plans are available. A campuswide network can be accessed. Online class registration, billing information, financial aid application, status, academic records, student services are available.
Website: http://www.upenn.edu/

GRADUATE UNITS

Annenberg School for Communication Students: 80 full-time (42 women), 1 part-time (0 women); includes 9 minority (2 Black or African American, non-Hispanic/Latino; 3 Asian, non-Hispanic/Latino; 2 Hispanic/Latino; 2 Two or more races, non-Hispanic/Latino), 29 international. Average age 30. 257 applicants, 7% accepted, 11 enrolled. *Faculty:* 17 full-time (7 women), 7 part-time/adjunct (2 women). Expenses: Contact institution. *Financial support:* In 2017–18, 80 students received support. In 2017, 6 doctorates awarded. Offers communication (PhD). *Application Contact:* Joanne Murray, Assistant Dean for Graduate Studies, 215-573-6349, Fax: 215-898-2024, E-mail: joanne.murray@asc.upenn.edu.

Graduate School of Education Students: 1,057 full-time (751 women), 299 part-time (203 women); includes 432 minority (208 Black or African American, non-Hispanic/Latino; 99 Asian, non-Hispanic/Latino; 81 Hispanic/Latino; 1 Native Hawaiian or other Pacific Islander, non-Hispanic/Latino; 43 Two or more races, non-Hispanic/Latino), 355 international. Average age 31. 3,105 applicants, 51% accepted, 888 enrolled. *Faculty:* 73 full-time (30 women), 45 part-time/adjunct (21 women). Expenses: Contact institution. In 2017, 559 master's, 77 doctorates awarded. *Program availability:* Part-time, evening/weekend, online learning. Offers education (M Phil, MS, MS Ed, Ed D, PhD, Certificate); educational leadership (Ed D); learning leadership (Ed D); medical education (MS Ed, Certificate); teaching (MS Ed); urban teaching (MS Ed). *Application fee:* $80. Electronic applications accepted. *Dean,* Dr. Pam Grossman, 215-898-7014, Fax: 215-746-6884, E-mail: admissions@gse.upenn.edu.

Division of Educational Linguistics Students: 157 full-time (140 women), 28 part-time (17 women); includes 16 minority (1 Black or African American, non-Hispanic/Latino; 8 Asian, non-Hispanic/Latino; 5 Hispanic/Latino; 2 Two or more races, non-Hispanic/Latino), 136 international. Average age 25. 554 applicants, 34% accepted, 98 enrolled. Expenses: Contact institution. *Financial support:* In 2017–18, 55 students received support. Fellowships, research assistantships, teaching assistantships, Federal Work-Study, scholarships/grants, health care benefits, and unspecified assistantships available. In 2017, 91 master's, 6 doctorates awarded. *Program availability:* Part-time. Offers educational linguistics (MS Ed, PhD); intercultural communication (MS Ed); teaching English to speakers of other languages (MS Ed). *Application deadline:* For fall admission, 12/8 priority date for domestic and international students. Applications are processed on a rolling basis. *Application fee:* $75. Electronic applications accepted. *Program Manager,* Kristina Lewis, 215-898-5212, E-mail: klewi@upenn.edu.

Division of Education Policy Average age 28. 250 applicants, 50% accepted, 34 enrolled. Expenses: Contact institution. *Financial support:* In 2017–18, 13 students received support. Fellowships, research assistantships, teaching assistantships, Federal Work-Study, scholarships/grants, and health care benefits available. In 2017, 16 master's, 2 doctorates awarded. *Program availability:* Part-time. Offers education policy (MS Ed, PhD). *Application deadline:* For fall admission, 12/8 priority date for domestic and international students. Applications are processed on a rolling basis. *Application fee:* $75. Electronic applications accepted. *Program Manager,* Krista Featherstone, 215-573-8075, E-mail: kfeat@upenn.edu.

Division of Higher Education Average age 35. 401 applicants, 46% accepted, 90 enrolled. Expenses: Contact institution. *Financial support:* In 2017–18, 24 students received support. Fellowships, research assistantships, teaching assistantships, Federal Work-Study, scholarships/grants, health care benefits, and unspecified assistantships available. In 2017, 45 master's, 29 doctorates awarded. *Program availability:* Part-time. Offers higher education (MS Ed, Ed D, PhD); higher education management (Ed D). *Application deadline:* For fall admission, 12/8 priority date for domestic and international students. *Application fee:* $75. Electronic applications accepted. *Program Manager,* Dr. Ross Aikins, 215-898-8398, E-mail: raikins@upenn.edu.

Division of Human Development and Quantitative Methods Average age 27. 622 applicants, 52% accepted, 192 enrolled. Expenses: Contact institution. *Financial support:* In 2017–18, 95 students received support. Fellowships, research assistantships, teaching assistantships, career-related internships or fieldwork, Federal Work-Study, scholarships/grants, health care benefits, and unspecified assistantships available. In 2017, 134 master's, 1 doctorate awarded. *Program availability:* Part-time-only, evening/weekend. Offers counseling and mental health services (M Phil, MS Ed); human development (MS Ed, PhD); quantitative methods (M Phil, MS, PhD); school and mental health counseling (MS Ed); statistics, measurement, assessment, and research technology (MS). *Application deadline:* For fall admission, 12/8 priority date for domestic and international students. Applications are processed on a rolling basis. *Application fee:* $75. Electronic applications accepted. *Application Contact:* 215-898-6415, Fax: 215-746-6884, E-mail: admissions@gse.upenn.edu. *Program Manager,* Dr. Elizabeth Mackenzie, 215-898-4176, E-mail: emackenz@upenn.edu.

Division of Literacy, Culture, and International Education Average age 30. 462 applicants, 47% accepted, 95 enrolled. Expenses: Contact institution. *Financial support:* In 2017–18, 44 students received support. Fellowships, research assistantships, teaching assistantships, Federal Work-Study, scholarships/grants, and health care benefits available. In 2017, 54 master's, 11 doctorates awarded. *Program availability:* Part-time. Offers education, culture and society (MS Ed, PhD); international educational development (MS Ed); language and literacy (MS Ed); reading/writing/literacy (MS Ed, Ed D, PhD). *Application deadline:* For fall admission, 12/8 priority date for domestic and international students. Applications are processed on a rolling basis. *Application fee:* $75. Electronic applications accepted. *Program Manager,* Dr. Alex Posecznick, 215-573-3947, E-mail: alpos@upenn.edu.

Division of Teaching, Learning, and Leadership Average age 32. 546 applicants, 56% accepted, 174 enrolled. Expenses: Contact institution. *Financial support:* In 2017–18, 13 students received support. Fellowships, research assistantships, teaching assistantships, Federal Work-Study, scholarships/grants, health care benefits, and unspecified assistantships available. In 2017, 122 master's, 3 doctorates awarded. *Program availability:* Part-time. Offers education entrepreneurship (MS Ed); educational leadership (MS Ed, Ed D, PhD); elementary education (MS Ed); learning sciences and technologies (MS Ed); school leadership (MS Ed); secondary education (MS Ed); teacher education (MS Ed); teaching and learning (MS Ed); teaching, learning, and leadership (MS Ed); teaching, learning, and teacher education (Ed D, PhD). *Application deadline:* For fall admission, 12/8 priority date for domestic and international students. Applications are processed on a rolling basis. *Application fee:* $75. Electronic applications accepted. *Application Contact:* Mercury Meulman, Administrative Coordinator, 215-898-4176, E-mail: mercury@upenn.edu. *Program Manager,* Dr. Veronica Aplenc, 215-898-2566, E-mail: vaplenc@upenn.edu.

Law School Students: 736 full-time (351 women); includes 208 minority (49 Black or African American, non-Hispanic/Latino; 2 American Indian or Alaska Native, non-Hispanic/Latino; 78 Asian, non-Hispanic/Latino; 48 Hispanic/Latino; 31 Two or more races, non-Hispanic/Latino), 47 international. Average age 27. 5,601 applicants, 18% accepted, 234 enrolled. *Faculty:* 100 full-time (36 women), 146 part-time/adjunct (52 women). Expenses: Contact institution. *Financial support:* In 2017–18, 366 students received support, including 172 research assistantships (averaging $3,112 per year), 4 teaching assistantships (averaging $1,250 per year); fellowships, career-related internships or fieldwork, Federal Work-Study, institutionally sponsored loans, and scholarships/grants also available. Financial award application deadline: 3/1; financial award applicants required to submit CSS PROFILE or FAFSA. In 2017, 256 doctorates awarded. Offers law (LL CM, LL M, ML, JD, SJD). JD/LL M offered jointly with Hong Kong University. *Application deadline:* For fall admission, 3/1 for domestic and international students. Applications are processed on a rolling basis. *Application fee:* $80. Electronic applications accepted. *Application Contact:* Renee Post, Associate Dean of Admissions and Financial Aid, 215-898-7400, Fax: 215-898-9606, E-mail: contactadmissions@law.upenn.edu. *Dean*, Theodore W. Ruger, 215-898-7463, Fax: 215-573-2025.

Perelman School of Medicine Students: 1,875 full-time (1,008 women), 87 part-time (70 women); includes 816 minority (110 Black or African American, non-Hispanic/Latino; 375 Asian, non-Hispanic/Latino; 220 Hispanic/Latino; 111 Two or more races, non-Hispanic/Latino), 124 international. 8,221 applicants, 10% accepted, 432 enrolled. *Faculty:* 3,170 full-time (1,294 women), 1,251 part-time/adjunct (576 women). Expenses: Contact institution. *Financial support:* In 2017–18, 1,101 students received support. In 2017, 152 master's, 135 doctorates awarded. Offers environmental health (MPH); generalist (MPH); global health (MPH); health policy research (MSHP); medical ethics and health policy (MBE, MSME); medicine (MBE, MPH, MRA, MS, MSCE, MSHP, MSME, MTR, MD, PhD); regulatory affairs (MRA); translational research (MTR). *Application Contact:* Gaye Sheffler, Director, Admissions, 215-898-8000, E-mail: sheffler@mail.med.upenn.edu. *Senior Vice Dean for Education*, Dr. Gail Morrison, 215-898-8034, E-mail: morrisog@mail.med.upenn.edu.

Biomedical Graduate Studies Students: 883 full-time (496 women), 23 part-time (18 women); includes 323 minority (33 Black or African American, non-Hispanic/Latino; 146 Asian, non-Hispanic/Latino; 102 Hispanic/Latino; 42 Two or more races, non-Hispanic/Latino), 94 international. 1,591 applicants, 22% accepted, 181 enrolled. *Faculty:* 1,121. Expenses: Contact institution. *Financial support:* In 2017–18, 651 students received support. In 2017, 79 master's, 135 doctorates awarded. Offers biochemistry and molecular biophysics (PhD); biomedical studies (MS, PhD); biostatistics (MS, PhD); cancer biology (PhD); cell biology, physiology, and metabolism (PhD); developmental stem cell regenerative biology (PhD); epidemiology (PhD); gene therapy and vaccines (PhD); genetics and gene regulation (PhD); genomics and computational biology (PhD); immunology (PhD); microbiology, virology, and parasitology (PhD); neuroscience (PhD); pharmacology (PhD). *Application fee:* $80. *Application Contact:* Aislinn Wallace, Admissions Coordinator, 215-746-6349, E-mail: aislinnw@mail.med.upenn.edu. *Director*, Dr. Michael Nusbaum, 215-898-1585, E-mail: nusbaum@mail.med.upenn.edu.

Center for Clinical Epidemiology and Biostatistics Students: 92 full-time (61 women), 3 part-time (2 women); includes 35 minority (11 Black or African American, non-Hispanic/Latino; 18 Asian, non-Hispanic/Latino; 6 Hispanic/Latino). Average age 35. 45 applicants, 87% accepted, 30 enrolled. *Faculty:* 102 full-time (49 women), 69 part-time/adjunct (25 women). Expenses: Contact institution. *Financial support:* In 2017–18, 50 students received support, including 50 fellowships with tuition reimbursements available (averaging $45,500 per year); research assistantships, teaching assistantships, and tuition waivers also available. Financial award application deadline: 12/1. In 2017, 23 master's awarded. *Program availability:* Part-time. Offers clinical epidemiology (MSCE). *Application deadline:* For fall admission, 12/1 priority date for domestic students, 12/1 for international students. *Application fee:* $0. Electronic applications accepted. *Application Contact:* Jennifer Kuklinski, Program Coordinator, 215-573-2382, E-mail: jkuklins@mail.med.upenn.edu. *Director*, Dr. Harold I. Feldman, 215-573-0901, E-mail: hfeldman@mail.med.upenn.edu.

School of Arts and Sciences Students: 1,626 full-time (777 women), 442 part-time (251 women); includes 362 minority (93 Black or African American, non-Hispanic/Latino; 2 American Indian or Alaska Native, non-Hispanic/Latino; 111 Asian, non-Hispanic/Latino; 100 Hispanic/Latino; 56 Two or more races, non-Hispanic/Latino), 659 international. Average age 30. 6,611 applicants, 18% accepted, 595 enrolled. *Faculty:* 488 full-time (167 women), 21 part-time/adjunct (9 women). Expenses: Contact institution. In 2017, 482 master's, 204 doctorates, 33 other advanced degrees awarded. *Program availability:* Part-time, evening/weekend. Offers Africana studies (MA, PhD); ancient history (AM, PhD); anthropology (AM, MS, PhD); applied mathematics and computational science (PhD); art and archaeology of the Mediterranean world (AM, PhD); arts and sciences (AM, MA, MBA, MES, MGA, MGA, MLA, MPA, MS, PhD, Certificate); biology (PhD); chemistry (MS, PhD); classical studies (AM, PhD); comparative literature (AM, PhD); criminology (MA, MS, PhD); demography (AM, PhD); earth and environmental science (MS, PhD); East Asian languages and civilizations (AM, PhD); economics (AM, PhD); English (AM, PhD); French (AM, PhD); Germanic languages (AM, PhD); history (AM, PhD); history and sociology of science (AM, PhD); history of art (AM, PhD); international studies (AM); Italian (AM, PhD); linguistics (AM, PhD); literary theory (AM, PhD); mathematics (AM, PhD); medical physics (MS); music (AM, PhD); Near Eastern languages and civilizations (AM, PhD); philosophy (AM, PhD); physics (PhD); political science (AM, PhD); psychology (PhD); religious studies (PhD); sociology (AM, PhD); South Asian regional studies (AM, PhD); Spanish (AM, PhD).

College of Liberal and Professional Studies Students: 191 full-time (112 women), 311 part-time (178 women); includes 99 minority (34 Black or African American, non-Hispanic/Latino; 2 American Indian or Alaska Native, non-Hispanic/Latino; 28 Asian, non-Hispanic/Latino; 24 Hispanic/Latino; 11 Two or more races, non-Hispanic/Latino), 83 international. Average age 34. 633 applicants, 52% accepted, 249 enrolled. Expenses: Contact institution. In 2017, 141 master's awarded. Offers applied geosciences (MSAG); applied positive psychology (MAP); chemical sciences (MCS); environmental studies (MES); individualized study (MLA); liberal arts (M Phil); medical physics (MMP); organization dynamics (M Phil). *Vice Dean, Professional and Liberal Education*, Nora Lewis, 215-898-7326, E-mail: nlewis@sas.upenn.edu.

Fels Institute of Government Students: 44 full-time (27 women), 78 part-time (41 women); includes 30 minority (9 Black or African American, non-Hispanic/Latino; 8 Asian, non-Hispanic/Latino; 10 Hispanic/Latino; 3 Two or more races, non-Hispanic/Latino), 10 international. Average age 31. 333 applicants, 47% accepted, 88 enrolled. Expenses: Contact institution. *Financial support:* Application deadline: 1/1. In 2017, 57 master's, 9 other advanced degrees awarded. *Program availability:* Part-time, evening/weekend. Offers economic development and growth (Certificate); government administration (MGA); nonprofit administration (Certificate); organization dynamics (MS); politics (Certificate); public administration (MPA); public finance (Certificate).

Joseph H. Lauder Institute of Management and International Studies Offers international studies (MA); management and international studies (MBA). Applications must be made concurrently and separately to the Wharton MBA program. Electronic applications accepted.

School of Dental Medicine Offers dental medicine (DMD).

School of Design Students: 700 full-time (409 women), 12 part-time (5 women); includes 98 minority (14 Black or African American, non-Hispanic/Latino; 1 American Indian or Alaska Native, non-Hispanic/Latino; 36 Asian, non-Hispanic/Latino; 35 Hispanic/Latino; 1 Native Hawaiian or other Pacific Islander, non-Hispanic/Latino; 11 Two or more races, non-Hispanic/Latino), 406 international. Average age 27. 2,191 applicants, 14% accepted, 135 enrolled. *Faculty:* 43 full-time (18 women), 16 part-time/adjunct (5 women). Expenses: Contact institution. *Financial support:* In 2017–18, 29 students received support. In 2017, 259 master's, 9 doctorates, 50 other advanced degrees awarded. *Program availability:* Part-time. Offers architecture (M Arch, PhD); city and regional planning (PhD); city planning (MCP); design (M Arch, MCP, MEBD, MFA, MLA, MS, MUSA, PhD, Advanced Certificate, Certificate); ecological architecture (Certificate); emerging design and research (Certificate); environmental building design (MEBD); fine arts (MFA); GIS and spatial analysis (Certificate); historic preservation (MS, Certificate); land preservation (Certificate); landscape architecture (MLA); landscape studies (Certificate); time-based and interactive media (Certificate); urban design (Certificate); urban redevelopment (Certificate); urban spatial analytics (MUSA).

School of Engineering and Applied Science Students: 1,149 full-time (342 women), 378 part-time (127 women); includes 207 minority (15 Black or African American, non-Hispanic/Latino; 129 Asian, non-Hispanic/Latino; 42 Hispanic/Latino; 21 Two or more races, non-Hispanic/Latino), 968 international. Average age 25. 6,844 applicants, 24% accepted, 896 enrolled. *Faculty:* 119 full-time (21 women), 29 part-time/adjunct (5 women). Expenses: Contact institution. In 2017, 516 master's, 68 doctorates awarded. *Program availability:* Part-time. Offers bioengineering (MSE, PhD); biotechnology (MBT); chemical and biomolecular engineering (MSE, PhD); computer and information science (MSE, PhD); computer and information technology (MCIT); computer graphics and game technology (MSE); data science (MSE); electrical and systems engineering (MSE, PhD); embedded systems (MSE); engineering and applied science (MBT, MCIT, MIPD, MSE, PhD); integrated product design (MIPD, MSE); materials science and engineering (MSE, PhD); mechanical engineering and applied mechanics (MSE, PhD); nanotechnology (MSE); robotics (MSE); scientific computing (MSE). *Application deadline:* For fall admission, 12/15 for domestic and international students. *Application fee:* $80. Electronic applications accepted. *Application Contact:* William Fenton, Assistant Director of Graduate Admissions, 215-898-4542, Fax: 215-573-5577, E-mail: gradstudies@seas.upenn.edu.

School of Nursing Students: 247 full-time (208 women), 452 part-time (410 women); includes 166 minority (47 Black or African American, non-Hispanic/Latino; 1 American Indian or Alaska Native, non-Hispanic/Latino; 62 Asian, non-Hispanic/Latino; 36 Hispanic/Latino; 1 Native Hawaiian or other Pacific Islander, non-Hispanic/Latino; 19 Two or more races, non-Hispanic/Latino), 11 international. Average age 32. 728 applicants, 57% accepted, 373 enrolled. *Faculty:* 52 full-time (46 women), 35 part-time/adjunct (31 women). Expenses: Contact institution. In 2017, 320 master's, 15 doctorates awarded. *Program availability:* Part-time, online learning. Offers adult and special populations (MSN); adult gerontology clinical nurse specialist (MSN); adult-gerontology acute care nurse practitioner (MSN); adult-gerontology primary care nurse practitioner (MSN); child and family (MSN); family nurse practitioner (MSN, Certificate); geropsychiatrics (MSN); health leadership (MSN); neonatal clinical nurse specialist (MSN); neonatal nurse practitioner (MSN); nurse anesthesia (MSN); nurse midwifery (MSN); nursing (MSN, PhD, Certificate); nursing and health care administration (MSN, PhD); pediatric acute care nurse practitioner (MSN); pediatric clinical nurse specialist (MSN); pediatric primary care nurse practitioner (MSN); women's health/gender related nurse practitioner (MSN). *Application Contact:* Sylvia English, Enrollment Management Coordinator, 215-898-8439, Fax: 215-573-8439, E-mail: sylviaj@nursing.upenn.edu. *Assistant Dean for Admissions and Academic Affairs*, Dr. Christina Costanzo Clark, 215-898-4271, Fax: 215-573-8439, E-mail: costanzo@nursing.upenn.edu.

School of Social Policy and Practice Students: 415 full-time (340 women), 84 part-time (72 women); includes 148 minority (68 Black or African American, non-Hispanic/Latino; 2 American Indian or Alaska Native, non-Hispanic/Latino; 16 Asian, non-Hispanic/Latino; 44 Hispanic/Latino; 18 Two or more races, non-Hispanic/Latino), 50 international. Average age 29. 919 applicants, 291 enrolled. *Faculty:* 28 full-time (16 women), 50 part-time/adjunct (38 women). Expenses: Contact institution. *Financial support:* In 2017–18, 291 students received support, including 24 fellowships (averaging $24,378 per year); career-related internships or fieldwork, Federal Work-Study, institutionally sponsored loans, scholarships/grants, tuition waivers (partial), and unspecified assistantships also available. Support available to part-time students. Financial award applicants required to submit FAFSA. In 2017, 249 master's, 13 doctorates awarded. *Program availability:* Part-time, blended/hybrid learning. Offers social policy and practice (MNPL, MSSP, MSW, DSW, PhD); social welfare (PhD); social work (MNPL, MSSP, MSW, DSW). *Application deadline:* For fall admission, 2/1 priority date for domestic and international students. Applications are processed on a rolling basis. *Application fee:* $65. Electronic applications accepted. *Application Contact:* Dr. Mary C. Mazzola, Associate Dean, Enrollment Management, 215-898-5550, Fax: 215-573-2099, E-mail: mmazzola@sp2.upenn.edu. *Dean*, John L. Jackson, Jr., 215-898-5541, Fax: 215-573-2099, E-mail: jjackson@sp2.upenn.edu.

School of Veterinary Medicine Students: 468 full-time (383 women), 8 part-time (all women); includes 61 minority (7 Black or African American, non-Hispanic/Latino; 24 Asian, non-Hispanic/Latino; 20 Hispanic/Latino; 10 Two or more races, non-Hispanic/Latino), 3 international. Average age 26. 1,093 applicants, 11% accepted, 113 enrolled. *Faculty:* 106 full-time (51 women), 63 part-time/adjunct (42 women). Expenses: Contact institution. In 2017, 119 doctorates awarded. Offers veterinary medicine (VMD).

Wharton School *Program availability:* Evening/weekend. Offers accounting (PhD); applied economics (PhD); business (MBA, PhD); business administration (MBA); business and public policy (MBA, PhD); ethics and legal studies (PhD); finance (PhD); health care management (MBA, PhD); health care management and economics (PhD); insurance and risk management (MBA, PhD); legal studies and business ethics (MBA, PhD); management (PhD); marketing (PhD); operations and information management (PhD); real estate (MBA, PhD); statistics (MBA, PhD). Electronic applications accepted.

The Wharton MBA Program for Executives *Program availability:* Evening/weekend. Offers executive business administration (MBA).

UNIVERSITY OF PHILOSOPHICAL RESEARCH, Los Angeles, CA 90027

General Information Proprietary, coed, graduate-only institution.

GRADUATE UNITS

Master's in Consciousness Studies Program Offers consciousness studies (MA). Electronic applications accepted.

Master's in Transformational Psychology Program Offers transformational psychology (MA). Electronic applications accepted.

UNIVERSITY OF PHOENIX–BAY AREA CAMPUS, San Jose, CA 95134-1805

General Information Proprietary, coed, comprehensive institution. *Graduate housing:* On-campus housing not available.

GRADUATE UNITS

College of Criminal Justice and Security Offers administration of justice and security (MS).

College of Education *Program availability:* Evening/weekend, online learning. Offers administration and supervision (MA Ed); adult education and training (MA Ed); early childhood education (MA Ed); education (Ed S); educational leadership (Ed D); elementary teacher education (MA Ed); higher education administration (PhD); secondary teacher education (MA Ed); special education (MA Ed); teacher leadership (MA Ed). Electronic applications accepted.

College of Information Systems and Technology *Program availability:* Evening/weekend. Offers information systems (MIS); organizational leadership/information systems and technology (DM). Electronic applications accepted.

College of Nursing *Program availability:* Evening/weekend, online learning. Offers education (MHA); gerontology (MHA); health administration (MHA, DHA); informatics (MHA, MSN); nursing (MSN, PhD); nursing/health care education (MSN). Electronic applications accepted.

College of Social Sciences *Program availability:* Evening/weekend. Offers marriage, family, and child therapy (MSC).

School of Business *Program availability:* Evening/weekend, online learning. Offers accountancy (MS); accounting (MBA); business administration (MBA, DBA); energy management (MBA); global management (MBA); health care management (MBA); human resource management (MBA); human resources management (MM); management (MM); marketing (MBA); organizational leadership (DM); project management (MBA); public administration (MPA); technology management (MBA). Electronic applications accepted.

UNIVERSITY OF PHOENIX–CENTRAL VALLEY CAMPUS, Fresno, CA 93720-1552

General Information Proprietary, coed, comprehensive institution.

GRADUATE UNITS

College of Education Offers curriculum and instruction (MA Ed); curriculum and instruction-computer education (MA Ed); elementary teacher education (MA Ed); secondary teacher education (MA Ed).

College of Human Services Offers marriage, family and child therapy (MSC).

College of Information Systems and Technology Offers information systems (MIS); technology management (MBA).

College of Nursing Offers education (MHA); gerontology (MHA); health administration (MHA); nursing (MSN).

School of Business Offers accounting (MBA); business administration (MBA); global management (MBA); human resources management (MBA, MM); management (MM); marketing (MBA); public administration (MBA, MM).

UNIVERSITY OF PHOENIX–DALLAS CAMPUS, Dallas, TX 75251

General Information Proprietary, coed, comprehensive institution. *Graduate housing:* On-campus housing not available.

GRADUATE UNITS

College of Criminal Justice and Security *Program availability:* Online learning. Offers administration of justice and security (MS). Electronic applications accepted.

College of Education Offers curriculum and instruction (MA Ed).

College of Information Systems and Technology *Program availability:* Evening/weekend. Offers e-business (MBA); information systems (MIS); technology management (MBA). Electronic applications accepted.

School of Business *Program availability:* Evening/weekend, online learning. Offers accounting (MBA); business administration (MBA); global management (MBA); human resources management (MBA, MM); management (MM); marketing (MBA); public administration (MBA, MM). Electronic applications accepted.

UNIVERSITY OF PHOENIX–HAWAII CAMPUS, Honolulu, HI 96813-3800

General Information Proprietary, coed, comprehensive institution. *Graduate housing:* On-campus housing not available.

GRADUATE UNITS

College of Education *Program availability:* Evening/weekend. Offers administration and supervision (MA Ed); curriculum and instruction (MA Ed); elementary education (MA Ed); secondary education (MA Ed); special education (MA Ed); teacher education for elementary licensure (MA Ed). Electronic applications accepted.

College of Information Systems and Technology *Program availability:* Evening/weekend. Offers information systems (MIS); technology management (MBA). Electronic applications accepted.

College of Nursing *Program availability:* Evening/weekend. Offers education (MHA); family nurse practitioner (MSN); gerontology (MHA); health administration (MHA); nursing (MSN); nursing/health care education (MSN). Electronic applications accepted.

School of Business *Program availability:* Evening/weekend. Offers accounting (MBA); business administration (MBA); global management (MBA); human resources management (MBA, MM); management (MM); marketing (MBA); public administration (MBA, MM). Electronic applications accepted.

UNIVERSITY OF PHOENIX–HOUSTON CAMPUS, Houston, TX 77079-2004

General Information Proprietary, coed, comprehensive institution. *Graduate housing:* On-campus housing not available.

GRADUATE UNITS

College of Education Offers curriculum and instruction (MA Ed).

College of Information Systems and Technology *Program availability:* Evening/weekend, online learning. Offers e-business (MBA); information systems (MIS); technology management (MBA). Electronic applications accepted.

College of Nursing *Program availability:* Online learning. Offers health administration (MHA). Electronic applications accepted.

School of Business *Program availability:* Evening/weekend, online learning. Offers accounting (MBA); business administration (MBA); global management (MBA); human resources management (MBA, MM); management (MM); marketing (MBA); public administration (MBA, MM). Electronic applications accepted.

UNIVERSITY OF PHOENIX–LAS VEGAS CAMPUS, Las Vegas, NV 89135

General Information Proprietary, coed, comprehensive institution. *Graduate housing:* On-campus housing not available.

GRADUATE UNITS

College of Education *Program availability:* Evening/weekend. Offers administration and supervision (MA Ed); curriculum and instruction (MA Ed); school counseling (MSC); teacher education-elementary licensure (MA Ed). Electronic applications accepted.

College of Human Services *Program availability:* Online learning. Offers marriage, family, and child therapy (MSC); mental health counseling (MSC); school counseling (MSC). Electronic applications accepted.

College of Information Systems and Technology *Program availability:* Evening/weekend. Offers information systems (MIS); technology management (MBA). Electronic applications accepted.

School of Business *Program availability:* Evening/weekend, online learning. Offers accounting (MBA); business administration (MBA); global management (MBA); human resources management (MBA, MM); management (MM); marketing (MBA); public administration (MM). Electronic applications accepted.

UNIVERSITY OF PHOENIX–ONLINE CAMPUS, Phoenix, AZ 85034-7209

General Information Proprietary, coed, comprehensive institution. *Graduate housing:* On-campus housing not available.

GRADUATE UNITS

College of Education *Program availability:* Evening/weekend, online learning. Offers administration and supervision (MAEd, Certificate); adult education and training (MAEd); curriculum and instruction (MAEd); early childhood education (MAEd); educational studies (MAEd); elementary teacher education (MAEd); principal licensure (Certificate); secondary teacher education (MAEd); special education (MAEd, Certificate); teacher education (MAEd); teacher education middle level mathematics (MAEd); teacher education middle level science (MAEd); teacher education secondary mathematics (MAEd); teacher education secondary science (MAEd); teacher leadership (MAEd); teachers of English learners (Certificate); transition to teaching (Certificate). Electronic applications accepted.

College of Health Sciences and Nursing *Program availability:* Evening/weekend, online learning. Offers family nurse practitioner (Certificate); health care (Certificate); health care education (Certificate); health care informatics (Certificate); informatics (MSN); nursing (MSN); nursing and health care education (MSN). Electronic applications accepted.

College of Information Systems and Technology *Program availability:* Evening/weekend, online learning. Offers information systems and technology (MIS). Electronic applications accepted.

College of Justice and Security *Program availability:* Evening/weekend, online learning. Offers administration of justice and security (MS); public administration (MPA). Electronic applications accepted.

College of Social Science *Program availability:* Evening/weekend, online learning. Offers mediation (Certificate); psychology (MS). Electronic applications accepted.

School of Advanced Studies *Program availability:* Evening/weekend, online learning. Offers business administration (DBA); education (Ed S); educational leadership (Ed D); health administration (DHA); higher education administration (PhD); industrial/organizational psychology (PhD); nursing (PhD); organizational leadership (DM). Electronic applications accepted.

School of Business *Program availability:* Evening/weekend, online learning. Offers accountancy (MS); accounting (MBA, Certificate); business administration (MBA); energy management (MBA); global management (MBA); health care management (MBA); human resource management (MBA, Certificate); human resources management (MM); management (MM); marketing (MBA, Certificate); project management (MBA, Certificate); public administration (MBA, MM); technology management (MBA). Electronic applications accepted.

UNIVERSITY OF PHOENIX–PHOENIX CAMPUS, Tempe, AZ 85282-2371

General Information Proprietary, coed, comprehensive institution. CGS member. *Graduate housing:* On-campus housing not available.

GRADUATE UNITS

College of Criminal Justice and Security *Program availability:* Evening/weekend, online learning. Offers administration of justice and security (MS); global and homeland security (MS); law enforcement organizations (MS); public administration (MPA). Electronic applications accepted.

College of Education *Program availability:* Evening/weekend, online learning. Offers administration and supervision (MA Ed); adult education and training (MA Ed); curriculum and instruction reading (MA Ed); early childhood education (MA Ed); education studies (MA Ed); elementary teacher education (MA Ed); secondary teacher education (MA Ed); special education (MA Ed); teacher leadership (MA Ed). Electronic applications accepted.

College of Health Sciences and Nursing *Program availability:* Evening/weekend, online learning. Offers family nurse practitioner (MSN, Certificate); gerontology health care (Certificate); health care education (MSN, Certificate); health care informatics (Certificate); informatics (MSN); nursing (MSN). Electronic applications accepted.

College of Social Sciences *Program availability:* Evening/weekend, online learning. Offers counseling (MS); psychology (MS). Electronic applications accepted.

School of Business *Program availability:* Evening/weekend, online learning. Offers accounting (MBA, MS, Certificate); business administration (MBA); energy management (MBA); global management (MBA); health care management (MBA); human resource management (MBA, Certificate); management (MM); marketing (MBA); project management (MBA); technology management (MBA). Electronic applications accepted.

UNIVERSITY OF PHOENIX–SACRAMENTO VALLEY CAMPUS, Sacramento, CA 95833-4334

General Information Proprietary, coed, comprehensive institution. *Graduate housing:* On-campus housing not available.

GRADUATE UNITS

College of Education *Program availability:* Evening/weekend. Offers adult education (MA Ed); curriculum instruction (MA Ed); elementary teacher education (MA Ed); secondary teacher education (MA Ed); teacher education (Certificate). Electronic applications accepted.

College of Information Systems and Technology *Program availability:* Evening/weekend. Offers management (MIS); technology management (MBA). Electronic applications accepted.

College of Nursing *Program availability:* Evening/weekend. Offers family nurse practitioner (MSN); health administration (MHA); health care education (MSN); nursing (MSN). Electronic applications accepted.

School of Business *Program availability:* Evening/weekend. Offers accounting (MBA); business administration (MBA); global management (MBA); human resources management (MBA, MM); management (MM); marketing (MBA); public administration (MBA, MM). Electronic applications accepted.

UNIVERSITY OF PHOENIX–SAN ANTONIO CAMPUS, San Antonio, TX 78230

General Information Proprietary, coed, comprehensive institution.

GRADUATE UNITS

College of Criminal Justice and Security Offers administration of justice and security (MS).

College of Education Offers curriculum and instruction (MA Ed).

College of Information Systems and Technology Offers information systems (MIS); technology management (MBA).

College of Nursing Offers health administration (MHA).

School of Business Offers accounting (MBA); business administration (MBA); e-business (MBA); global management (MBA); human resources management (MBA, MM); management (MM); marketing (MBA); public administration (MBA, MM).

UNIVERSITY OF PHOENIX–SAN DIEGO CAMPUS, San Diego, CA 92123

General Information Proprietary, coed, comprehensive institution. *Graduate housing:* On-campus housing not available.

GRADUATE UNITS

College of Education *Program availability:* Evening/weekend. Offers curriculum and instruction (MA Ed); elementary teacher education (MA Ed); secondary teacher education (MA Ed). Electronic applications accepted.

College of Information Systems and Technology *Program availability:* Evening/weekend. Offers management (MIS); technology management (MBA). Electronic applications accepted.

College of Nursing *Program availability:* Evening/weekend. Offers health care education (MSN); nursing (MSN). Electronic applications accepted.

School of Business *Program availability:* Evening/weekend. Offers accounting (MBA); business administration (MBA); global management (MBA); human resources management (MBA, MM); management (MM); marketing (MBA); public administration (MBA). Electronic applications accepted.

UNIVERSITY OF PIKEVILLE, Pikeville, KY 41501

General Information Independent-religious, coed, comprehensive institution. *Enrollment:* 2,335 graduate, professional, and undergraduate students; 758 full-time matriculated graduate/professional students (372 women), 18 part-time matriculated graduate/professional students (12 women). *Enrollment by degree level:* 118 master's, 658 doctoral. *Graduate faculty:* 43 full-time (18 women), 15 part-time/adjunct (8 women). *Graduate housing:* Room and/or apartments available on a first-come, first-served basis to single students; on-campus housing not available to married students. Housing application deadline: 5/1. *Student services:* Campus employment opportunities, campus safety program, career counseling, exercise/wellness program, free psychological counseling, international student services, low-cost health insurance, services for students with disabilities. *Library facilities:* Allara Library plus 2 others. *Collection:* Books: 73,924 (physical), 214,499 (digital/electronic); Serial titles: 1,437 (physical), 88,386 (digital/electronic); Databases: 73. Weekly public service hours: 105; students can reserve study rooms.

Computer facilities: 308 computers available on campus for general student use. A campuswide network can be accessed from student residence rooms and from off campus.
Website: http://www.upike.edu/

General Application Contact: John Yancey, Director of Admissions, 606-218-5251, Fax: 606-218-5255, E-mail: johnyancey@upike.edu.

GRADUATE UNITS

Coleman College of Business Students: 35 full-time (16 women), 2 part-time (both women); includes 3 minority (all Black or African American, non-Hispanic/Latino), 4 international. Average age 29. *Faculty:* 5 part-time/adjunct (2 women). Expenses: Contact institution. *Financial support:* Tuition waivers (full) and university employee grants available. Financial award application deadline: 2/15; financial award applicants required to submit FAFSA. In 2017, 18 master's awarded. *Program availability:* Part-time, evening/weekend. Offers business (MBA); entrepreneurship (MBA); healthcare (MBA). *Application deadline:* For fall admission, 8/15 for domestic students, 7/1 for international students. Applications are processed on a rolling basis. *Application fee:* $50. *Application Contact:* Cathy Maynard, Secretary, Business and Economics, 606-218-5020, Fax: 606-218-5031, E-mail: cathymaynard@upike.edu. *Dean,* Dr. Howard V. Roberts, 606-218-5019, Fax: 606-218-5031, E-mail: howardroberts@upike.edu.

Kentucky College of Optometry Students: 124 full-time (71 women); includes 20 minority (6 Black or African American, non-Hispanic/Latino; 2 American Indian or Alaska Native, non-Hispanic/Latino; 5 Asian, non-Hispanic/Latino; 7 Hispanic/Latino). Average age 24. 504 applicants, 44% accepted, 60 enrolled. *Faculty:* 15 full-time (5 women). Expenses: Contact institution. *Financial support:* Fellowships available. Financial award application deadline: 7/1; financial award applicants required to submit FAFSA. Offers optometry (OD). *Application deadline:* For fall admission, 4/15 for domestic students. *Application Contact:* Casey Price, Coordinator of Admissions, 606-218-5517, E-mail: caseyprice@upike.edu. *Acting Dean,* Dr. Donnie Akers, 606-218-5510, E-mail: andrewbuzzelli@upike.edu.

Kentucky College of Osteopathic Medicine Students: 534 full-time (227 women); includes 50 minority (3 Black or African American, non-Hispanic/Latino; 1 American Indian or Alaska Native, non-Hispanic/Latino; 22 Asian, non-Hispanic/Latino; 21 Hispanic/Latino; 3 Native Hawaiian or other Pacific Islander, non-Hispanic/Latino). Average age 25. 3,262 applicants, 7% accepted, 135 enrolled. *Faculty:* 24 full-time (9 women), 35 part-time/adjunct (13 women). Expenses: Contact institution. *Financial support:* In 2017–18, 11 students received support, including 11 fellowships with full and partial tuition reimbursements available (averaging $28,169 per year); scholarships/grants also available. Financial award application deadline: 8/1; financial award applicants required to submit FAFSA. In 2017, 128 doctorates awarded. Offers osteopathic medicine (DO). *Application deadline:* For fall admission, 5/1 for domestic students. Applications are processed on a rolling basis. *Application fee:* $75. *Application Contact:* Dr. Linda Dunatov, Associate Dean for Student Affairs, 606-218-5408, Fax: 606-218-5442, E-mail: lindadunatov@upike.edu. *Dean,* Dr. Boyd Buser, 606-218-5410, Fax: 606-218-8442, E-mail: boydbuser@upike.edu.

Patton College of Education Students: 66 full-time (56 women), 15 part-time (11 women). Average age 35. *Faculty:* 10 part-time/adjunct (6 women). Expenses: Contact institution. *Financial support:* Application deadline: 2/1; applicants required to submit FAFSA. In 2017, 25 master's awarded. *Program availability:* Part-time, evening/weekend. Offers teacher leader (MA). *Application deadline:* For fall admission, 8/15 for domestic students. Applications are processed on a rolling basis. *Application fee:* $50. *Application Contact:* Fairy Coleman, Administrative Assistant, 606-218-5314, E-mail: fairycoleman@upike.edu. *Division Chair,* Dr. Coletta Parsley, 606-218-5318, E-mail: colettaparsley@upike.edu.

UNIVERSITY OF PITTSBURGH, Pittsburgh, PA 15260

General Information State-related, coed, university. CGS member. *Enrollment:* 28,642 graduate, professional, and undergraduate students; 7,383 full-time matriculated graduate/professional students (4,091 women), 1,765 part-time matriculated graduate/professional students (1,027 women). *Enrollment by degree level:* 4,151 master's, 4,757 doctoral, 240 other advanced degrees. *Graduate faculty:* 4,318 full-time (1,821 women), 756 part-time/adjunct (359 women). *Student services:* Campus employment opportunities, campus safety program, career counseling, exercise/wellness program, free psychological counseling, international student services, low-cost health insurance, services for students with disabilities, writing training. *Library facilities:* Hillman Library plus 16 others. *Collection:* Books: 5.8 million (physical), 1.7 million (digital/electronic); Serial titles: 109,160 (physical), 228,331 (digital/electronic); Databases: 571. Weekly public service hours: 145; study areas open 24 hours, 5–7 days a week; students can reserve study rooms. *Research affiliation:* National Institutes of Health, National Science Foundation, General Electric Company (GE), Shire, Phillips.

Computer facilities: Computer purchase and lease plans are available. 1,156 computers available on campus for general student use. A campuswide network can be accessed from student residence rooms and from off campus. Online class registration, online class listings, online tuition payment are available.
Website: http://www.pitt.edu/

General Application Contact: Information Contact, 412-624-4141, E-mail: graduate@pitt.edu.

GRADUATE UNITS

Graduate School of Public and International Affairs Students: 290 full-time (179 women), 144 part-time (86 women); includes 57 minority (23 Black or African American, non-Hispanic/Latino; 14 Asian, non-Hispanic/Latino; 20 Hispanic/Latino), 100 international. Average age 32. 597 applicants, 79% accepted, 158 enrolled. *Faculty:* 30 full-time (11 women), 14 part-time/adjunct (5 women). Expenses: Contact institution. *Financial support:* In 2017–18, 147 students received support, including 10 fellowships with full tuition reimbursements available (averaging $37,000 per year), 31 research assistantships with full tuition reimbursements available (averaging $37,000 per year); teaching assistantships, career-related internships or fieldwork, and scholarships/grants also available. Financial award application deadline: 1/15. In 2017, 175 master's, 2 doctorates awarded. *Program availability:* Part-time, evening/weekend, 100% online. Offers energy and environment (MID, MPA); governance and international public management (MID, MPA); human security (MID, MPIA); international affairs (PhD); international development (PhD); international political economy (MPIA); nongovernmental organizations and civil society (MID); policy research and analysis (MPA); public administration (PhD); public and international affairs (MID, MPA, MPIA, MPPM, PhD); public and nonprofit management (MPA); public policy (PhD); public policy and management (MPPM); security and intelligence studies (MPIA); urban affairs and planning (MID, MPA). *Application deadline:* For fall admission, 2/1 priority date for domestic students, 1/15 priority date for international students; for spring admission, 11/1 priority date for domestic students, 8/1 priority date for international students; for summer admission, 3/1 priority date for domestic students, 1/15 priority date for international students. *Application fee:* $50. *Application Contact:* Dr. Michael Rizzi, Director of Student Services, 412-648-7643, Fax: 412-648-7641, E-mail: rizzim@pitt.edu. *Dean,* Dr. John Keeler, 412-648-7605, Fax: 412-648-7601, E-mail: gspia@pitt.edu.

Graduate School of Public Health Students: 486 full-time (341 women), 104 part-time (77 women); includes 121 minority (32 Black or African American, non-Hispanic/Latino; 44 Asian, non-Hispanic/Latino; 24 Hispanic/Latino; 2 Native Hawaiian or other Pacific Islander, non-Hispanic/Latino; 19 Two or more races, non-Hispanic/Latino), 134 international. Average age 28. 1,496 applicants, 54% accepted, 231 enrolled. *Faculty:* 158 full-time (75 women), 179 part-time/adjunct (92 women). Expenses: Contact institution. *Financial support:* In 2017–18, 131 students received support, including 80 fellowships (averaging $10,000 per year), 118 research assistantships (averaging $20,500 per year), 5 teaching assistantships (averaging $18,500 per year); career-related internships or fieldwork, scholarships/grants, traineeships, health care benefits, and unspecified assistantships also available. Financial award applicants required to submit FAFSA. In 2017, 163 master's, 40 doctorates awarded. *Program availability:* Part-time. Offers applied research and leadership in behavioral and community health sciences (Dr PH); applied social and behavioral concepts in public health (MPH); biostatistics (MS, PhD); community-based participatory research (Certificate); decision sciences (MS); environmental and occupational health (MPH, MS, PhD); epidemiology (MPH, MS, PhD); evaluation of public health programs (Certificate); genetic counseling (MS); global health (Certificate); health equity (Certificate); health policy and economics (MS); health policy and management (MHA, MPH, PhD); human genetics (MS, PhD); infectious diseases and microbiology (MS, PhD); LGBT health and wellness (Certificate); management, intervention, and community practice (MPH); maternal and child health (MPH); pathogenesis, eradication, and laboratory practice (MPH); public health (MHA, MPH, MS, Dr PH, PhD, Certificate); public health genetics (MPH, Certificate); theory and research methods (Dr PH). *Application deadline:* For fall admission, 1/15 for domestic and international students; for spring admission, 10/15 for domestic students, 8/1 for international students; for summer admission, 3/15 for domestic students, 12/1 for international students. Applications are processed on a rolling basis. *Application fee:* $135. Electronic applications accepted. *Application Contact:* Karrie A. Lukin, Admissions Manager, 412-624-3003, Fax: 412-624-3755, E-mail: presutti@pitt.edu. *Dean*, Dr. Donald S. Burke, MD, 412-624-3001, Fax: 412-624-3013, E-mail: bradym1@pitt.edu.

Katz Graduate School of Business Students: 434 full-time (211 women), 364 part-time (113 women); includes 95 minority (33 Black or African American, non-Hispanic/Latino; 35 Asian, non-Hispanic/Latino; 18 Hispanic/Latino; 9 Two or more races, non-Hispanic/Latino), 260 international. Average age 29. 2,062 applicants, 41% accepted, 376 enrolled. *Faculty:* 91 full-time (30 women), 14 part-time/adjunct (4 women). Expenses: Contact institution. *Financial support:* Research assistantships with full tuition reimbursements, teaching assistantships with full tuition reimbursements, Federal Work-Study, scholarships/grants, health care benefits, and unspecified assistantships available. Financial award application deadline: 6/1; financial award applicants required to submit FAFSA. In 2017, 405 master's, 7 doctorates awarded. *Program availability:* Part-time, evening/weekend, blended/hybrid learning. Offers accounting (PhD); business (EMBA, MBA, MS, PhD, Certificate); business administration (EMBA, MBA, PhD); business analytics and operations (PhD); finance (MS); information systems (MBA); information systems and technology management (PhD); international business administration (Certificate); management information systems (MS); marketing (MBA, PhD); marketing science (MS); operations (MBA); organizational behavior and human resources (MBA, PhD); public and international affairsstrategic management (PhD); strategy, environment and organizations (MBA); supply chain management (MS). *Application deadline:* For fall admission, 4/1 priority date for domestic students, 2/1 priority date for international students. *Application fee:* $50. Electronic applications accepted. *Application Contact:* Thomas Keller, Director of MBA Admissions, 412-648-1700, Fax: 412-648-1659, E-mail: mba@katz.pitt.edu. *Dean*, Dr. Arjang A. Assad, 412-648-1556, Fax: 412-648-1552, E-mail: aassad@katz.pitt.edu.

Kenneth P. Dietrich School of Arts and Sciences Students: 1,568 full-time (765 women), 29 part-time (14 women); includes 377 minority (58 Black or African American, non-Hispanic/Latino; 6 American Indian or Alaska Native, non-Hispanic/Latino; 193 Asian, non-Hispanic/Latino; 101 Hispanic/Latino; 2 Native Hawaiian or other Pacific Islander, non-Hispanic/Latino; 17 Two or more races, non-Hispanic/Latino), 378 international. Average age 29. 4,091 applicants, 18% accepted, 334 enrolled. *Faculty:* 1,045 full-time (420 women), 65 part-time/adjunct (32 women). Expenses: Contact institution. *Financial support:* Fellowships with full tuition reimbursements, research assistantships with full tuition reimbursements, teaching assistantships with full tuition reimbursements, career-related internships or fieldwork, Federal Work-Study, institutionally sponsored loans, scholarships/grants, traineeships, health care benefits, tuition waivers (full and partial), and unspecified assistantships available. Support available to part-time students. Financial award applicants required to submit FAFSA. *Program availability:* Part-time. Offers anthropology (MA, PhD); applied linguistics (MA); applied linguistics with TESOL (MA); applied mathematics (MA, MS); applied statistics (MA, MS); arts and sciences (MA, MFA, MS, Pro-MS, PhD, Certificate, Doctoral Certificate, Master's Certificate); biological and health psychology (PhD); chemistry (MS, PhD); Chinese (MA); clinical psychology (PhD); cognitive psychology (PhD); communication (MA, PhD); composition and theory (PhD); cultural studies (Certificate); developmental psychology (PhD); ecology and evolution (PhD); economics (MA, PhD); English (MA, PhD); ethnomusicology (PhD); film and media studies (PhD, Certificate); film studies (PhD); French (MA, PhD); gender, sexuality, and women's studies (Doctoral Certificate, Master's Certificate); geographical information systems and remote sensing (Pro-MS); geology and environmental science (MS, PhD); historical musicology (PhD); history (MA, PhD); history and philosophy of science (PhD); history of art and architecture (MA, PhD); Italian (MA); Japanese (MA); jazz studies (PhD); mathematics (MA, MS, PhD); medieval and Renaissance studies (Doctoral Certificate, Master's Certificate); molecular, cellular, and developmental biology (PhD); music (MA); philosophy (PhD); physics and astronomy (MS, PhD); political science (MA, PhD); Russian literature and culture (MA, PhD); social psychology (PhD); sociolinguistics (PhD); sociology (MA, PhD); statistics (MA, MS, PhD); teaching English to speakers of other languages (Certificate); TESOL (PhD); theatre arts (MA, MFA, PhD); writing (MFA). *Application deadline:* Applications are processed on a rolling basis. *Application fee:* $50. Electronic applications accepted. *Application Contact:* Katelyn White, Student Services Assistant, 412-624-6094, Fax: 412-624-6855, E-mail: kmw127@pitt.edu. *Associate Dean, Graduate Studies and Research*, Dr. Holger Hoock, 412-624-3939, Fax: 412-624-6855.

Center for Bioethics and Health Law Students: 2 full-time (1 woman), 5 part-time (all women). Average age 27. 8 applicants, 88% accepted, 6 enrolled. *Faculty:* 8 full-time (4 women), 1 (woman) part-time/adjunct. Expenses: Contact institution. *Financial support:* In 2017–18, 7 students received support. Scholarships/grants and tuition waivers (partial) available. Financial award application deadline: 3/1. *Program availability:* Part-time. Offers bioethics (MA). *Application deadline:* For fall admission, 3/1 priority date for domestic and international students. Applications are processed on a rolling basis. *Application fee:* $50. Electronic applications accepted. *Application Contact:* Beth Ann Pischke, Administrator, 412-648-7007, Fax: 412-648-2649, E-mail: pischke@pitt.edu. *Director*, Dr. Lisa S. Parker, 412-648-7007, Fax: 412-648-2649, E-mail: lisap@pitt.edu.

Center for Neuroscience Students: 46 full-time (27 women); includes 9 minority (1 Black or African American, non-Hispanic/Latino; 4 Asian, non-Hispanic/Latino; 2 Hispanic/Latino; 2 Two or more races, non-Hispanic/Latino), 2 international. Average age 26. 189 applicants, 23% accepted, 12 enrolled. *Faculty:* 110 full-time (32 women). Expenses: Contact institution. *Financial support:* In 2017–18, 42 students received support, including 19 fellowships with full tuition reimbursements available (averaging $29,500 per year), 15 research assistantships with full tuition reimbursements available (averaging $29,500 per year), 1 teaching assistantship with full tuition reimbursement available (averaging $29,500 per year); traineeships also available. Offers neuroscience (PhD). Program held jointly with School of Medicine. *Application deadline:* For fall admission, 12/1 priority date for domestic and international students. *Application fee:* $50. Electronic applications accepted. *Application Contact:* Lisa M. Summe, Graduate Program Administrator, 412-383-3260, Fax: 412-648-1441, E-mail: lms232@pitt.edu. *Co-Director*, Dr. Brian Davis, 412-645-9745, Fax: 412-648-1441, E-mail: bmd1@pitt.edu.

School of Computing and Information Students: 483 full-time (187 women), 105 part-time (56 women); includes 33 minority (8 Black or African American, non-Hispanic/Latino; 13 Asian, non-Hispanic/Latino; 6 Hispanic/Latino; 6 Two or more races, non-Hispanic/Latino), 422 international. Average age 28. 1,374 applicants, 70% accepted, 274 enrolled. *Faculty:* 64 full-time (14 women), 29 part-time/adjunct (10 women). Expenses: Contact institution. *Financial support:* Fellowships with full and partial tuition reimbursements, research assistantships with full and partial tuition reimbursements, teaching assistantships with full and partial tuition reimbursements, career-related internships or fieldwork, scholarships/grants, traineeships, health care benefits, tuition waivers, and unspecified assistantships available. Support available to part-time students. Financial award application deadline: 1/15; financial award applicants required to submit FAFSA. In 2017, 198 master's, 14 doctorates awarded. *Program availability:* Part-time, evening/weekend, 100% online. Offers big data analytics (Certificate); biological science (PhD); computer science (MS, PhD); computing and information (MLIS, MS, MSIS, MST, PhD, Certificate); information science (MSIS, PhD, Certificate); intelligent systems (MS, PhD); library and information science (MLIS, PhD); security assurance/information systems (Certificate); telecommunications (MST, Certificate). *Application deadline:* For fall admission, 1/15 priority date for domestic and international students; for winter admission, 9/15 priority date for domestic students, 6/15 priority date for international students; for spring admission, 9/15 priority date for domestic students, 6/15 priority date for international students; for summer admission, 1/15 priority date for domestic students, 12/15 priority date for international students. Applications are processed on a rolling basis. *Application fee:* $50. Electronic applications accepted. *Application Contact:* Shabana Reza, Enrollment Manager, 412-624-3988, Fax: 412-624-5231, E-mail: shabana.reza@pitt.edu. *Dean and Professor*, Dr. Paul Cohen, 412-383-3498, E-mail: prcohen@pitt.edu.

School of Dental Medicine Students: 327 full-time (175 women); includes 118 minority (6 Black or African American, non-Hispanic/Latino; 8 American Indian or Alaska Native, non-Hispanic/Latino; 79 Asian, non-Hispanic/Latino; 17 Hispanic/Latino; 1 Native Hawaiian or other Pacific Islander, non-Hispanic/Latino; 7 Two or more races, non-Hispanic/Latino). Average age 25. 1,904 applicants, 80 enrolled. Expenses: Contact institution. *Financial support:* Scholarships/grants and stipends available. Financial award application deadline: 4/30; financial award applicants required to submit FAFSA. Offers dental anesthesiology (Certificate); dental medicine (MDS, MPH, MS, DMD, PhD, Certificate); dental science (MDS); endodontics (Certificate); general dentistry (Certificate); general practice (Certificate); multidisciplinary public health (MPH); oral and maxillofacial pathology (Certificate); oral and maxillofacial surgery (Certificate); oral biology (MS, PhD); orthodontics (MDS, Certificate); pediatric cranio-maxillofacial surgery (Certificate); pediatric dentistry (Certificate); periodontics (MDS, Certificate); prosthodontics (MDS, Certificate). *Application deadline:* For fall admission, 11/1 for domestic and international students. Applications are processed on a rolling basis. *Application fee:* $50 ($75 for international students). Electronic applications accepted. *Application Contact:* Christine Wankiiri-Hale, Associate Dean for Student Affairs, 412-383-9975, Fax: 412-648-9571, E-mail: chwst11@pitt.edu. *Dean*, Bernard J. Costello, 412-692-2229, Fax: 412-648-8219, E-mail: bjc1@pitt.edu.

School of Education *Program availability:* Part-time, evening/weekend, online learning. Offers applied behavior analysis (M Ed); applied developmental psychology (M Ed, MS, PhD); developmental movement (MS); early childhood education (M Ed); early intervention (M Ed, PhD); education (M Ed, MA, MAT, MS, Ed D, PhD); elementary education (M Ed, MAT); elementary education (MAT); English and communications education (M Ed, MAT); exercise physiology (MS, PhD); foreign language education (M Ed, MAT); general special education (M Ed, Ed D); higher education management (M Ed, Ed D, PhD); language, literacy and culture education (Ed D, PhD); learning sciences and policy (PhD); mathematics education (M Ed, MAT, Ed D, PhD); reading education (PhD); research methodology (M Ed, MA, PhD); school leadership (M Ed, Ed D, PhD); science education (M Ed, MAT, Ed D, PhD); secondary education (M Ed, MAT, Ed D, PhD); social and comparative analysis in education (M Ed, MA, Ed D, PhD); social studies education (M Ed, MAT); special education (M Ed, PhD); special education (Ed D); special education teacher preparation (M Ed); STEM education (Ed D); vision studies (M Ed, PhD). Electronic applications accepted.

School of Health and Rehabilitation Sciences Students: 773 full-time (563 women), 55 part-time (43 women); includes 88 minority (17 Black or African American, non-Hispanic/Latino; 2 American Indian or Alaska Native, non-Hispanic/Latino; 29 Asian, non-Hispanic/Latino; 24 Hispanic/Latino; 1 Native Hawaiian or other Pacific Islander, non-Hispanic/Latino; 15 Two or more races, non-Hispanic/Latino), 74 international. Average age 27. 2,308 applicants, 36% accepted, 400 enrolled. *Faculty:* 111 full-time (67 women), 28 part-time/adjunct (16 women). Expenses: Contact institution. *Financial support:* Fellowships with full tuition reimbursements, research assistantships with tuition reimbursements, teaching assistantships with full tuition reimbursements, career-related internships or fieldwork, Federal Work-Study, scholarships/grants, traineeships, and unspecified assistantships available. Financial award applicants required to submit FAFSA. *Program availability:* Part-time, evening/weekend. Offers audiology (MA, MS, Au D); clinical rehabilitation and mental health counseling (MS); communication science and disorders (PhD); health and rehabilitation sciences (MS); medical speech language pathology (CScD); nutrition and dietetics (MS); occupational therapy (MS, CScD, OTD); physical therapy (MS, DPT); physician assistant studies (MS); prosthetics and orthotics (DPT); rehabilitation science (PhD); rehabilitation technology (MS); speech language pathology (MA, MS). *Application deadline:* Applications are processed on a rolling basis. Electronic applications accepted. *Application Contact:* Jessica Maguire, Director of Admissions, 412-383-6557, Fax: 412-383-6535, E-mail: maguire@pitt.edu. *Dean*, Dr. Anthony Delitto, 412-383-6560, Fax: 412-383-6535, E-mail: delitto@pitt.edu.

School of Law Students: 404 full-time (191 women), 1 part-time (0 women); includes 95 minority (31 Black or African American, non-Hispanic/Latino; 1 American Indian or Alaska Native, non-Hispanic/Latino; 21 Asian, non-Hispanic/Latino; 30 Hispanic/Latino; 12 Two or more races, non-Hispanic/Latino), 10 international. Average age 24. 1,713 applicants, 31% accepted, 140 enrolled. *Faculty:* 47 full-time (22 women), 116 part-time/adjunct (29 women). Expenses: Contact institution. *Financial support:* Scholarships/grants available. Financial award application deadline: 3/1; financial award applicants required to submit FAFSA. *Program availability:* Part-time, online learning. Offers biomedical and health services research (MSL); business law (MSL); Constitutional law (MSL); criminal law and justice (MSL); disability law (MSL); disability legal studies (Certificate); elder and estate planning law (MSL); employment and labor law (MSL); energy law (MSL); environmental and real estate law (MSL); family law (MSL); health law (MSL); intellectual property and technology law (MSL); international and human rights law (MSL); jurisprudence (MSL); law (LL M, MSL, JD, SJD, Certificate); regulatory law (MSL); self-designed (MSL); U.S. law (LL M). *Application deadline:* For fall admission, 4/1 for domestic and international students. Applications are processed on a rolling basis. *Application fee:* $65. Electronic applications accepted. *Application Contact:* Charmaine McCall, Assistant Dean for Admissions and Financial Aid, 412-648-1414, Fax: 412-648-1318, E-mail: cmccall@law.pitt.edu. *Dean*, William M. Carter, Jr., 412-648-1401, Fax: 412-648-2647, E-mail: william.carter@law.pitt.edu.

School of Medicine Students: 929 full-time (480 women), 97 part-time (64 women); includes 324 minority (76 Black or African American, non-Hispanic/Latino; 167 Asian, non-Hispanic/Latino; 49 Hispanic/Latino; 32 Two or more races, non-Hispanic/Latino), 87 international. Average age 27. 7,535 applicants, 10% accepted, 334 enrolled. *Faculty:* 3,250 full-time (1,169 women), 150 part-time/adjunct (52 women). Expenses: Contact institution. *Financial support:* In 2017–18, 623 students received support, including 70 fellowships with full tuition reimbursements available (averaging $29,500 per year), 97 research assistantships with full tuition reimbursements available (averaging $29,500 per year), 4 teaching assistantships with full tuition reimbursements available (averaging $29,500 per year); scholarships/grants, traineeships, and employee benefits also available. In 2017, 47 master's, 204 doctorates, 23 other advanced degrees awarded. *Program availability:* Part-time, blended/hybrid learning. Offers biomedical informatics (MS, PhD, Certificate); biomedical sciences (MS); cell biology and molecular physiology (PhD); cellular and molecular pathology (PhD); clinical and translational science (PhD); clinical research (MS, Certificate); computational biology (PhD); integrative systems biology (PhD); interdisciplinary biomedical sciences (PhD); medical education (MS, Certificate); medicine (MS, MD, PhD, Certificate); microbiology and immunology (PhD); molecular biophysics and structural biology (PhD); molecular genetics and developmental biology (PhD); molecular pharmacology (PhD). Electronic applications accepted. *Vice Dean,* Dr. Ann Thompson, 412-648-9000, E-mail: upsom@medschool.pitt.edu.

School of Nursing Students: 198 full-time (154 women), 126 part-time (106 women); includes 42 minority (12 Black or African American, non-Hispanic/Latino; 1 American Indian or Alaska Native, non-Hispanic/Latino; 28 Asian, non-Hispanic/Latino; 1 Hispanic/Latino), 15 international. Average age 32. 284 applicants, 41% accepted, 102 enrolled. *Faculty:* 43 full-time (35 women), 7 part-time/adjunct (6 women). Expenses: Contact institution. *Financial support:* In 2017–18, 165 students received support, including 17 fellowships (averaging $16,924 per year), 8 research assistantships (averaging $11,530 per year), 21 teaching assistantships (averaging $13,069 per year); scholarships/grants, tuition waivers, and unspecified assistantships also available. Financial award applicants required to submit FAFSA. In 2017, 65 master's, 52 doctorates awarded. *Program availability:* Part-time. Offers adult-gerontology acute care (DNP); adult-gerontology primary care (DNP); clinical nurse leader (MSN); clinical nurse specialist (DNP); family (individual across the lifespan) (DNP); health systems executive leadership (DNP); neonatal (MSN, DNP); nurse anesthesia (DNP); nurse-midwife (DNP); nursing (MSN, DNP, PhD); nursing informatics (MSN); pediatric primary care (DNP); psychiatric mental health (DNP). *Application deadline:* For fall admission, 5/1 priority date for domestic students, 2/15 priority date for international students. *Application fee:* $50. Electronic applications accepted. *Application Contact:* Laurie Lapsley, Graduate Administrator, 412-624-9670, Fax: 412-624-2409, E-mail: lapsleyl@pitt.edu. *Dean/Professor,* Dr. Jacqueline Dunbar-Jacob, 412-624-7838, Fax: 412-624-2401, E-mail: dunbar@pitt.edu.

School of Pharmacy Students: 536 full-time (343 women), 2 part-time (0 women); includes 117 minority (15 Black or African American, non-Hispanic/Latino; 1 American Indian or Alaska Native, non-Hispanic/Latino; 82 Asian, non-Hispanic/Latino; 7 Hispanic/Latino; 12 Two or more races, non-Hispanic/Latino), 69 international. Average age 28. 609 applicants, 31% accepted, 146 enrolled. *Faculty:* 140 full-time (70 women), 12 part-time/adjunct (1 woman). Expenses: Contact institution. *Financial support:* Fellowships with full tuition reimbursements, research assistantships with full tuition reimbursements, teaching assistantships with full tuition reimbursements, Federal Work-Study, institutionally sponsored loans, scholarships/grants, health care benefits, tuition waivers (full), and unspecified assistantships available. Financial award application deadline: 10/1. *Program availability:* Part-time. Offers community, leadership, innovation, and practice (Pharm D); global health (Pharm D); pediatrics (Pharm D); pharmaceutical sciences (MS, PhD); pharmacotherapy (Pharm D); pharmacy (MS, PhD, Pharm D); pharmacy business administration (MS). *Application deadline:* For fall admission, 12/1 for domestic students; for winter admission, 1/5 for domestic students. Applications are processed on a rolling basis. Electronic applications accepted. *Application Contact:* Marcia Borrelli, Director of Student Services, 412-648-1120, Fax: 412-383-9996, E-mail: borrelli@pitt.edu. *Dean,* Dr. Patricia Dowley Kroboth, 412-624-2400, Fax: 412-648-1086, E-mail: pkroboth@pitt.edu.

School of Social Work Students: 419 full-time (357 women), 54 part-time (46 women); includes 88 minority (58 Black or African American, non-Hispanic/Latino; 20 Hispanic/Latino; 10 Two or more races, non-Hispanic/Latino). Average age 28. 568 applicants, 80% accepted, 207 enrolled. *Faculty:* 24 full-time (14 women), 37 part-time/adjunct (27 women). Expenses: Contact institution. *Financial support:* In 2017–18, 40 fellowships (averaging $10,000 per year), 8 teaching assistantships with full tuition reimbursements (averaging $18,450 per year) were awarded; research assistantships with full tuition reimbursements, career-related internships or fieldwork, institutionally sponsored loans, scholarships/grants, traineeships, tuition waivers (full), and unspecified assistantships also available. Financial award application deadline: 3/31; financial award applicants required to submit FAFSA. *Program availability:* Part-time. Offers social work (MSW, PhD, Certificate). *Application deadline:* For fall admission, 12/31 priority date for domestic and international students. Applications are processed on a rolling basis. *Application fee:* $40 ($50 for international students). Electronic applications accepted. *Application Contact:* Philip Mack, Director of Admissions, 412-624-6346, Fax: 412-624-6323, E-mail: psm8@pitt.edu. *Dean,* Dr. Larry E. Davis, 412-624-6304, Fax: 412-624-6323, E-mail: ledavis@pitt.edu.

Swanson School of Engineering Students: 724 full-time (179 women), 193 part-time (47 women); includes 107 minority (20 Black or African American, non-Hispanic/Latino; 1 American Indian or Alaska Native, non-Hispanic/Latino; 41 Asian, non-Hispanic/Latino; 26 Hispanic/Latino; 1 Native Hawaiian or other Pacific Islander, non-Hispanic/Latino; 18 Two or more races, non-Hispanic/Latino), 507 international. 2,645 applicants, 39% accepted, 270 enrolled. *Faculty:* 130 full-time (19 women), 42 part-time/adjunct (6 women). Expenses: Contact institution. *Financial support:* In 2017–18, 112 fellowships with full tuition reimbursements (averaging $31,632 per year), 243 research assistantships with full tuition reimbursements (averaging $28,224 per year), 105 teaching assistantships with full tuition reimbursements (averaging $27,108 per year) were awarded; career-related internships or fieldwork, Federal Work-Study, institutionally sponsored loans, scholarships/grants, traineeships, health care benefits, tuition waivers (full), and unspecified assistantships also available. Support available to part-time students. Financial award application deadline: 3/1. In 2017, 250 master's, 63 doctorates awarded. *Program availability:* Part-time. Offers bioengineering (MSBENG, PhD); chemical engineering (MS Ch E, PhD); civil and environmental engineering (MSCEE, PhD); electrical and computer engineering (MS, PhD); engineering (MS, MS Ch E, MSBENG, MSCEE, MSIE, MSME, MSNE, MSPE, PhD); industrial engineering (MSIE, PhD); mechanical engineering and materials science (MSME, MSNE, PhD); petroleum engineering (MSPE). *Application deadline:* For fall admission, 3/1 priority date for domestic and international students; for spring admission, 7/1 priority date for domestic and international students. Applications are processed on a rolling basis. *Application fee:* $50. Electronic applications accepted. *Application Contact:* Rama Bazaz, Director, 412-624-9800, Fax: 412-624-9808, E-mail: ssoeadm@pitt.edu. *Dean,* Dr. Gerald D. Holder, 412-624-9809, Fax: 412-624-0412, E-mail: holder@engr.pitt.edu.

University Center for International Studies Students: 183 full-time (108 women), 9 part-time (all women); includes 78 minority (6 Black or African American, non-Hispanic/Latino; 23 Asian, non-Hispanic/Latino; 47 Hispanic/Latino; 2 Two or more races, non-Hispanic/Latino). Average age 29. Expenses: Contact institution. *Financial support:* In 2017–18, 25 fellowships with full tuition reimbursements (averaging $26,117 per year) were awarded; scholarships/grants, traineeships, health care benefits, and unspecified assistantships also available. *Program availability:* Part-time, evening/weekend, online learning. Offers African studies (Certificate); Asian studies (Certificate); European Union studies (Certificate); global studies (Certificate); Latin American studies (Certificate); Russian and East European studies (Certificate); West European studies (Certificate). *Director,* Dr. Ariel Armony, 412-648-7374, Fax: 412-624-4672, E-mail: armony@pitt.edu.

UNIVERSITY OF PORTLAND, Portland, OR 97203-5798

General Information Independent-religious, coed, comprehensive institution. *Graduate housing:* On-campus housing not available. *Research affiliation:* Portland Area Nursing Consortium, Kaiser Center Health Resources.

GRADUATE UNITS

Department of Communication Studies *Program availability:* Part-time, evening/weekend. Offers communication (MA); management communication (MS).

Department of Performing and Fine Arts *Program availability:* Part-time, evening/weekend. Offers directing (MFA).

Department of Theology *Program availability:* Part-time. Offers pastoral ministry (MA).

Dr. Robert B. Pamplin, Jr. School of Business *Program availability:* Part-time, evening/weekend. Offers entrepreneurship (MBA); finance (MBA, MS); health care management (MBA); marketing (MBA); nonprofit management (EMBA); operations and technology management (MBA, MS); sustainability (MBA).

School of Education *Program availability:* Part-time, evening/weekend. Offers education (MA, MAT); educational leadership (M Ed); English for speakers of other languages (M Ed); initial administrator licensure (M Ed); neuroeducation (M Ed, Ed D); organizational leadership and development (Ed D); reading (M Ed); school leadership and development (Ed D); special education (M Ed). M Ed also available through the Graduate Outreach Program for teachers residing in the Oregon and Washington state areas.

School of Engineering *Program availability:* Part-time, evening/weekend. Offers biomedical engineering (MBME); civil engineering (ME); computer science (ME); electrical engineering (ME); mechanical engineering (ME).

School of Nursing *Program availability:* Part-time, evening/weekend, online learning. Offers clinical nurse leader (MS); family nurse practitioner (DNP); nurse educator (MS).

UNIVERSITY OF PRINCE EDWARD ISLAND, Charlottetown, PE C1A 4P3, Canada

General Information Province-supported, coed, comprehensive institution. *Graduate housing:* Room and/or apartments available on a first-come, first-served basis to single students; on-campus housing not available to married students. *Research affiliation:* National Research Council of Canada Institute for Nutrisciences and Health, PEI Food Technology Centre, Agriculture Canada Research Station, Diagnostic Chemicals, Ltd., Canadian Food Inspection Agency, AquaHealth.

GRADUATE UNITS

Atlantic Veterinary College *Program availability:* Part-time. Offers anatomy (M Sc, PhD); bacteriology (M Sc, PhD); clinical pharmacology (M Sc, PhD); clinical sciences (M Sc, PhD); epidemiology (M Sc, PhD); fish health (M Sc, PhD); food animal nutrition (M Sc, PhD); immunology (M Sc, PhD); microanatomy (M Sc, PhD); parasitology (M Sc, PhD); pathology (M Sc, PhD); pharmacology (M Sc, PhD); physiology (M Sc, PhD); toxicology (M Sc, PhD); veterinary medicine (M Sc, M Vet Sc, DVM, PhD); veterinary science (M Vet Sc); virology (M Sc, PhD).

Faculty of Arts *Program availability:* Part-time. Offers island studies (MA).

Faculty of Education *Program availability:* Part-time. Offers educational studies (PhD); leadership in learning (M Ed).

Faculty of Science Offers environmental sciences (M Sc, PhD); human biology (M Sc); molecular and macromolecular sciences (M Sc, PhD); sustainable design engineering (M Sc).

UNIVERSITY OF PROVIDENCE, Great Falls, MT 59405

General Information Independent-religious, coed, comprehensive institution. *Graduate housing:* On-campus housing not available.

GRADUATE UNITS

Graduate Studies *Program availability:* Part-time, online learning. Offers counseling (MSC); criminal justice (MSM); human development (MSM); management (MSM). Electronic applications accepted.

UNIVERSITY OF PUERTO RICO–MAYAGÜEZ, Mayagüez, PR 00681-9000

General Information Commonwealth-supported, coed, university. *Graduate housing:* On-campus housing not available. *Research affiliation:* U.S. Department of Education (DOE) (STEM education), National Endowment for the Humanities, Tropical Agriculture Research Station (agriculture), Corporation for the Development and Administration of Marine Resources of Puerto Rico (marine science), National Science Foundation.

GRADUATE UNITS

Graduate Studies *Program availability:* Part-time, evening/weekend. Electronic applications accepted.

College of Agricultural Sciences *Program availability:* Part-time. Offers agricultural economics and rural sociology (MS); agricultural education (MS); agricultural extension (MS); agricultural sciences (MS); agronomy (MS); animal science (MS); crop protection (MS); food science and technology (MS); horticulture (MS); soils (MS).

College of Arts and Sciences *Program availability:* Part-time. Offers applied chemistry (MS, PhD); applied mathematics (MS); arts and sciences (MA, MS, PhD); biology (MS); English education (MA); geology (MS); Hispanic studies (MA); kinesiology (MA); marine sciences (MS, PhD); physics (MS); pre-college math education (MS); pure mathematics (MS); scientific computing (MS); statistics (MS).

College of Business Administration *Program availability:* Part-time, evening/weekend. Offers business administration (MBA); finance (MBA); human resources (MBA); industrial management (MBA). Electronic applications accepted.

College of Engineering *Program availability:* Part-time. Offers chemical engineering (ME, MS, PhD); civil engineering (ME, MS, PhD); computer engineering (ME, MS); computer science and engineering (PhD); computing and information sciences and engineering (PhD); electrical engineering (ME, MS); engineering (ME, MS, PhD); industrial engineering (ME, MS); materials science and engineering (MS); mechanical engineering (ME, MS, PhD). Electronic applications accepted.

UNIVERSITY OF PUERTO RICO–MEDICAL SCIENCES CAMPUS, San Juan, PR 00936-5067

General Information Commonwealth-supported, coed, primarily women, university. *Graduate housing:* On-campus housing not available.

GRADUATE UNITS

Graduate School of Public Health *Program availability:* Part-time. Offers biostatistics (MPH); demography (MS); developmental disabilities-early intervention (Certificate); environmental health (MS, Dr PH); epidemiology (MPH, MS); evaluative research of health systems (MS); gerontology (MPH, Certificate); health services administration (MHSA, MS); industrial hygiene (MS); maternal and child health (MPH); nurse midwifery (MPH, Certificate); nutrition (MS); public health (MHSA, MPH, MPHE, MS, Dr PH, Certificate); public health education (MPHE); school health promotion (Certificate).

School of Dental Medicine Offers dental medicine (DMD, Certificate); dentistry (DMD, Certificate); general dentistry (Certificate); oral and maxillofacial surgery (Certificate); orthodontics (Certificate); pediatric dentistry (Certificate); prosthodontics (Certificate). Electronic applications accepted.

School of Health Professions Offers audiology (Au D); clinical laboratory science (MS); clinical research (MS, Graduate Certificate); cytotechnology (Certificate); dietetics (Certificate); health information administration (MS); health professions (MS, Au D, Certificate); medical technology (Certificate); occupational therapy (MS); physical therapy (MS); speech-language pathology (MS). Electronic applications accepted.

School of Medicine Offers medicine (MS, MD, PhD). Electronic applications accepted.

Biomedical Sciences Graduate Program Offers anatomy (MS, PhD); biochemistry (MS, PhD); biomedical sciences (MS, PhD); microbiology and medical zoology (MS, PhD); pharmacology and toxicology (MS, PhD); physiology (MS, PhD). Electronic applications accepted.

School of Nursing Offers adult and elderly nursing (MSN); child and adolescent nursing (MSN); critical care nursing (MSN); family and community nursing (MSN); family nurse practitioner (MSN); maternity nursing (MSN); mental health and psychiatric nursing (MSN). Electronic applications accepted.

School of Pharmacy *Program availability:* Part-time, evening/weekend. Offers industrial pharmacy (MS); pharmaceutical sciences (MS); pharmacy (Pharm D). Electronic applications accepted.

UNIVERSITY OF PUERTO RICO–RÍO PIEDRAS, San Juan, PR 00931-3300

General Information Commonwealth-supported, coed, university. *Graduate housing:* Room and/or apartments available to single students; on-campus housing not available to married students. Housing application deadline: 6/15. *Research affiliation:* U.S. Department of Education (DOE) (social sciences, general studies, physics, biology), U.S. Department of Health and Human Services (social sciences, biology), National Science Foundation (ecology, biology), Ocean Conservancy (ecology, biology), Ford International (ecology).

GRADUATE UNITS

College of Business Administration *Program availability:* Part-time. Offers accounting (MBA); finance (MBA, PhD); general business (MBA); human resources management (MBA); international trade and business (MBA, PhD); marketing (MBA); operations management (MBA); quantitative methods (MBA).

College of Education *Program availability:* Part-time. Offers biology education (M Ed); chemistry education (M Ed); curriculum and teaching (Ed D); early child education (M Ed); education (M Ed, MS, Ed D); educational research and evaluation (M Ed); exercise sciences (MS); family ecology and nutrition (M Ed); guidance and counseling (M Ed, Ed D); history education (M Ed); mathematics education (M Ed); physics education (M Ed); school administration and supervision (M Ed, Ed D); Spanish education (M Ed); special and differentiated education (M Ed); teaching English as a second language (M Ed).

College of Humanities *Program availability:* Part-time. Offers Caribbean history (PhD); Caribbean linguistics (PhD); Caribbean literature (PhD); comparative literature (MA); English (MA); Hispanic linguistics (PhD); Hispanic studies (MA); history (MA); humanities (MA, PhD, Certificate); Latin American literature (PhD); linguistics (MA); philosophy (MA); Puerto Rican history (PhD); Puerto Rican literature (PhD); Spanish literature (PhD); translation (MA, Certificate).

College of Natural Sciences *Program availability:* Part-time. Offers chemical physics (PhD); chemistry (MS, PhD); ecology/systematics (MS, PhD); environmental sciences (MS, PhD); evolution/genetics (MS, PhD); mathematics (MS, PhD); molecular/cellular biology (MS, PhD); natural sciences (MS, PhD); neuroscience (MS, PhD); physics (MS).

College of Social Sciences *Program availability:* Part-time. Offers clinical psychology (MA); economics (MA); industrial organizational psychology (MA); investigative academic psychology (MA); psychology (PhD); social sciences (MA, MPA, MRC, MSW, PhD); social-community psychology (MA); sociology (MA).

Graduate School of Rehabilitation Counseling *Program availability:* Part-time. Offers rehabilitation counseling (MRC).

Graduate School of Social Work *Program availability:* Part-time. Offers social work (MSW, PhD).

School of Public Administration *Program availability:* Part-time. Offers public administration (MPA).

Graduate School of Information Sciences and Technologies *Program availability:* Part-time. Offers administration of academic libraries (PMC); administration of public libraries (PMC); administration of special libraries (PMC); consultant in information services (PMC); documents and files administration (Post-Graduate Certificate); electronic information resources analyst (Post-Graduate Certificate); information science (MIS); librarianship and information services (MLS); school librarian (Post-Graduate Certificate); school librarian distance education mode (Post-Graduate Certificate); specialist in legal information (PMC).

Graduate School of Planning *Program availability:* Part-time. Offers economic planning systems (MP); environmental planning (MP); social policy and planning (MP); urban and territorial planning (MP).

School of Architecture *Program availability:* Part-time. Offers architecture (M Arch).

School of Communication *Program availability:* Part-time. Offers communication (MA); communication theory and research (MA); journalism (MA).

School of Law *Program availability:* Part-time, evening/weekend. Offers law (LL M, JD).

UNIVERSITY OF PUGET SOUND, Tacoma, WA 98416

General Information Independent, coed, comprehensive institution. *Graduate housing:* On-campus housing not available.

GRADUATE UNITS

School of Education *Program availability:* Part-time. Offers education (M Ed, MAT); elementary education (MAT); mental health counseling (M Ed); school counseling (M Ed); secondary education (MAT). Electronic applications accepted.

School of Occupational Therapy Offers occupational therapy (MSOT, Dr OT). Electronic applications accepted.

School of Physical Therapy Offers physical therapy (DPT). Electronic applications accepted.

UNIVERSITY OF REDLANDS, Redlands, CA 92373-0999

General Information Independent, coed, comprehensive institution. *Graduate housing:* Rooms and/or apartments available on a first-come, first-served basis to single students and available to married students. Housing application deadline: 8/19. *Research affiliation:* Environmental Systems Research Institute (geographic information systems).

GRADUATE UNITS

College of Arts and Sciences Offers arts and sciences (MM, MS); communicative disorders (MS); geographic information systems (MS). Electronic applications accepted.

School of Music *Program availability:* Part-time. Offers music (MM).

School of Business *Program availability:* Evening/weekend. Offers business (MBA); information technology (MS); management (MA).

School of Education *Program availability:* Part-time, evening/weekend. Offers education (MA, Ed D, Certificate).

UNIVERSITY OF REGINA, Regina, SK S4S 0A2, Canada

General Information Province-supported, coed, university. CGS member. *Enrollment:* 15,276 graduate, professional, and undergraduate students; 965 full-time matriculated graduate/professional students (494 women), 657 part-time matriculated graduate/professional students (454 women). *Enrollment by degree level:* 1,304 master's, 270 doctoral, 45 other advanced degrees. *Graduate faculty:* 456 full-time (182 women), 204 part-time/adjunct (67 women). *International tuition:* $24,713 Canadian dollars full-time. Tuition, Canadian resident: full-time $21,330 Canadian dollars; part-time $18,165 Canadian dollars per year. *Required fees:* $5136 Canadian dollars; $3118 Canadian dollars per credit hour. $1008 Canadian dollars per semester. Tuition and fees vary according to program. *Graduate housing:* Room and/or apartments available on a first-come, first-served basis to single students; on-campus housing not available to married students. Typical cost: $9000 Canadian dollars per year ($12,000 Canadian dollars including board). Room and board charges vary according to board plan, campus/location and housing facility selected. *Student services:* Campus employment opportunities, campus safety program, career counseling, child daycare facilities, exercise/wellness program, free psychological counseling, grant writing training, international student services, low-cost health insurance, multicultural affairs office, services for students with disabilities, writing training. *Library facilities:* Dr. John Archer Library plus 5 others. *Collection:* Books: 832,203 (physical), 571,698 (digital/electronic); Serial titles: 133,988 (physical), 123,622 (digital/electronic); Databases: 517. Weekly public service hours: 105; students can reserve study rooms. *Research affiliation:* TR Labs (telecommunications), Regional Centre of Expertise on Education for Sustainable Development in Saskatchewan (sustainable development), Petroleum Technology Research Center (green energy technologies), Saskatchewan Population Health and Evaluation Research Unit (health research), Canadian Plains Research Centre (CPRC) (climate change adaptation), Prairie Adaptation Research Collaborative (climate change and adaptation options).

Computer facilities: 412 computers available on campus for general student use. A campuswide network can be accessed from student residence rooms and from off campus. Online class registration is available.
Website: http://www.uregina.ca/

General Application Contact: Dr. Karen Meagher, Associate Dean, Faculty of Graduate Studies and Research, 306-585-5186, Fax: 306-337-2444, E-mail: grad.studies@uregina.ca.

GRADUATE UNITS

Faculty of Graduate Studies and Research Students: 965 full-time (494 women), 657 part-time (454 women). 2,908 applicants, 23% accepted, 331 enrolled. *Faculty:* 456 full-time (182 women), 204 part-time/adjunct (67 women). Expenses: Contact institution. *Financial support:* In 2017–18, 208 fellowships (averaging $5,774 per year), 419 teaching assistantships (averaging $1,294 per year) were awarded; research assistantships, career-related internships or fieldwork, institutionally sponsored loans, scholarships/grants, unspecified assistantships, and travel awards also available. Financial award application deadline: 9/30. In 2017, 424 master's, 40 doctorates, 38 other advanced degrees awarded. *Program availability:* Part-time, evening/weekend. *Application deadline:* For fall admission, 2/15 for domestic and international students; for winter admission, 7/15 for domestic and international students; for spring admission, 10/15 for domestic and international students. Applications are processed on a rolling basis. *Application fee:* $100. Electronic applications accepted. *Application Contact:* Dr. Karen Meagher, Associate Dean, 306-585-5186, Fax: 306-337-2444, E-mail: grad.assocdean1@uregina.ca. *Dean*, Dr. Thomas Bredohl, 306-585-5185, Fax: 306-337-2444, E-mail: grad.dean@uregina.ca.

Faculty of Arts Students: 99 full-time (68 women), 32 part-time (17 women). 187 applicants, 25% accepted. *Faculty:* 141 full-time (54 women), 49 part-time/adjunct (11 women). Expenses: Contact institution. *Financial support:* In 2017–18, 117 fellowships, 236 teaching assistantships (averaging $2,562 per year) were awarded; research assistantships, career-related internships or fieldwork, scholarships/grants, and tuition waivers also available. Financial award application deadline: 6/15. In 2017, 37 master's, 8 doctorates awarded. *Program availability:* Part-time. Offers anthropology (MA); applied economics and policy analysis (MA); arts (M Sc, MA, MJ, PhD); Canadian plains studies (MA, PhD); clinical psychology (MA, PhD); creative writing (MA); English (MA, PhD); experimental and applied psychology (MA, PhD); French (MA); geography (M Sc, MA, PhD); gerontology (M Sc, MA); history (MA); journalism (MJ); justice studies (MA); linguistics (MA); philosophy (MA); police studies (MA); religious studies (MA); social and political thought (MA); social studies (MA); sociology (MA); women's and gender studies (MA). *Application deadline:* For fall admission, 2/15 for domestic and international students; for winter admission, 9/15 for domestic and international students. Applications are processed on a rolling basis. *Application fee:* $100. Electronic applications accepted. *Application Contact:* Dr. Nilgun Onder, Associate Dean, Research and Graduate Studies, 306-585-4336, Fax: 306-585-5368, E-mail: arts.assocdean-rg@uregina.ca. *Dean*, Dr. Richard Kleer, 306-585-4895, Fax: 306-585-5368, E-mail: arts.dean@uregina.ca.

Faculty of Education Students: 99 full-time (76 women), 285 part-time (223 women). 297 applicants, 41% accepted. *Faculty:* 48 full-time (33 women), 13 part-time/adjunct (6 women). Expenses: Contact institution. *Financial support:* In 2017–18, 15 fellowships (averaging $5,042 per year), 25 teaching assistantships (averaging $2,562 per year) were awarded; research assistantships, career-related internships or fieldwork, and scholarships/grants also available. Financial award application deadline: 6/15. In 2017, 119 master's, 8 doctorates, 2 other advanced degrees awarded. *Program availability:* Part-time. Offers adult education (MA Ed); curriculum and instruction (M Ed); education (M Ed, MA Ed, MHRD, PhD, Master's Certificate); educational administration (M Ed); educational psychology (M Ed); human resource development (MHRD). *Application deadline:* For fall admission, 2/15 for domestic and international students; for winter admission, 10/15 for domestic and international students; for spring admission, 2/15 for domestic and international students. *Application fee:* $100. Electronic applications accepted. *Application Contact:* Linda Jiang, Graduate Program Coordinator, 306-585-4506, Fax: 306-585-5387, E-mail: edgrad@uregina.ca. *Associate Dean, Research and Graduate Programs in Education*, Dr. Paul Clarke, 306-585-5353, Fax: 306-585-5387, E-mail: paul.clarke@uregina.ca.

Faculty of Engineering and Applied Science Students: 271 full-time (80 women), 64 part-time (14 women). 969 applicants, 11% accepted. *Faculty:* 42 full-time (6 women), 45 part-time/adjunct (10 women). Expenses: Contact institution. *Financial support:* In 2017–18, 24 fellowships (averaging $6,000 per year), 70 teaching assistantships (averaging $2,562 per year) were awarded; research assistantships, career-related internships or fieldwork, and scholarships/grants also available. Financial award application deadline: 6/15. In 2017, 65 master's, 11 doctorates awarded. *Program availability:* Part-time. Offers electronic systems (M Eng, MA Sc, PhD); electronic systems engineering (M Eng, MA Sc, PhD); environmental systems (M Eng, MA Sc, PhD); environmental systems engineering (M Eng, MA Sc, PhD); industrial systems (M Eng, MA Sc, PhD); industrial systems engineering (M Eng, MA Sc, PhD); petroleum systems (M Eng, MA Sc, PhD); petroleum systems engineering (M Eng, MA Sc, PhD); process systems (M Eng, MA Sc, PhD); process systems engineering (M Eng, MA Sc, PhD); software systems (M Eng, MA Sc, PhD); software systems engineering (M Eng, MA Sc, PhD). *Application deadline:* For fall admission, 3/31 for domestic and international students; for winter admission, 7/31 for domestic and international students; for spring admission, 11/30 for domestic and international students. *Application fee:* $100. Electronic applications accepted. *Application Contact:* Dr. Amr Henni, Associate Dean, Graduate Studies and Research, 306-585-4960, Fax: 306-585-4855, E-mail: amr.henni@uregina.ca. *Dean*, Dr. Esam Hussein, 306-585-4160, Fax: 306-585-4556, E-mail: esam.hussein@uregina.ca.

Faculty of Kinesiology and Health Studies Students: 41 full-time (18 women), 15 part-time (8 women). 30 applicants, 53% accepted. *Faculty:* 17 full-time (8 women), 29 part-time/adjunct (15 women). Expenses: Contact institution. *Financial support:* In 2017–18, fellowships (averaging $6,750 per year), teaching assistantships (averaging $2,562 per year) were awarded; research assistantships and scholarships/grants also available. Financial award application deadline: 6/15. In 2017, 3 master's, 2 doctorates awarded. Offers kinesiology and health studies (M Sc, PhD). *Application deadline:* Applications are processed on a rolling basis. *Application fee:* $100. Electronic applications accepted. *Application Contact:* Dr. Darren Candow, Associate Dean, Graduate Studies and Research, 306-585-4906, Fax: 306-585-4854, E-mail: darren.candow@uregina.ca. *Dean*, Dr. Harold Riemer, 306-585-4131, Fax: 306-585-4854, E-mail: khs.dean@uregina.ca.

Faculty of Media, Art, and Performance Students: 2 full-time (1 woman), 4 part-time (1 woman). 47 applicants, 21% accepted. *Faculty:* 30 full-time (17 women), 8 part-time/adjunct (3 women). Expenses: Contact institution. *Financial support:* In 2017–18, fellowships (averaging $7,200 per year), teaching assistantships (averaging $2,562 per year) were awarded; research assistantships and scholarships/grants also available. Financial award application deadline: 6/15. In 2017, 12 master's awarded. *Program availability:* Part-time. Offers ceramics (MFA); composition (MMus); conducting (MMus); drawing (MFA); interdisciplinary studies (MA, MFA); intermedia (MFA); media production (MFA); media studies (MA); media, art, and performance (MA, MFA, MMus); music theory (MA); musicology (MA); painting (MFA); performance (MMus); sculpture (MFA). *Application deadline:* For fall admission, 1/15 for domestic and international students. Applications are processed on a rolling basis. *Application fee:* $100. Electronic applications accepted. *Application Contact:* Dr. Kathleen Irwin, Associate Dean, Graduate and Research, 306-585-5519, Fax: 306-585-5544, E-mail: kathleen.irwin@uregina.ca. *Dean*, Dr. Rae Staseson, 306-585-5510, Fax: 306-585-5544, E-mail: map.dean@uregina.ca.

Faculty of Nursing Students: 14 full-time (13 women), 40 part-time (37 women). 44 applicants, 50% accepted. *Faculty:* 18 full-time (14 women), 9 part-time/adjunct (all women). Expenses: Contact institution. *Financial support:* In 2017–18, fellowships (averaging $6,000 per year), teaching assistantships (averaging $2,652 per year) were awarded; scholarships/grants also available. Financial award application deadline: 6/15. In 2017, 10 master's awarded. Offers nurse practictioner clinical nurse specialist (MN); nursing (M Sc, PhD). *Application deadline:* For fall admission, 3/15 for domestic and international students. *Application fee:* $100. Electronic applications accepted. *Application Contact:* Gillian Borys, Graduate Program Assistant, 306-337-3355, Fax: 306-337-8493, E-mail: gillian.borys@uregina.ca. *Associate Dean, Graduate Programs and Research*, Dr. Glenn Donnelly, 306-337-8544, Fax: 306-337-8493, E-mail: glenn.donnelly@uregina.ca.

Faculty of Science Students: 272 full-time (113 women), 51 part-time (14 women). 603 applicants, 18% accepted. *Faculty:* 82 full-time (18 women), 44 part-time/adjunct (19 women). Expenses: Contact institution. *Financial support:* In 2017–18, fellowships (averaging $6,333 per year), teaching assistantships (averaging $2,562 per year) were awarded; research assistantships, career-related internships or fieldwork, and scholarships/grants also available. Financial award application deadline: 6/15. In 2017, 54 master's, 15 doctorates awarded. *Program availability:* Part-time. Offers biology (M Sc, PhD); biophysics of biological interfaces (M Sc, PhD); computational chemistry (M Sc, PhD); computer science (M Sc, PhD); environmental analytical chemistry (M Sc, PhD); enzymology/chemical biology (M Sc, PhD); geology (M Sc, PhD); inorganic/organometallic chemistry (M Sc, PhD); mathematics (M Sc, PhD); physics (M Sc, PhD); science (M Sc, PhD); signal transduction and mechanisms of cancer cell regulation (M Sc, PhD); statistics (M Sc, PhD); supramolecular organic photochemistry and photophysics (M Sc, PhD); synthetic organic chemistry (M Sc, PhD). *Application deadline:* Applications are processed on a rolling basis. *Application fee:* $100. Electronic applications accepted. *Application Contact:* Dr. Cory Butz, Associate Dean for Research, 306-585-4201, Fax: 306-585-4291, E-mail: cory.butz@uregina.ca. *Dean*, Dr. Douglas Farenick, 306-337-2110, Fax: 306-585-4291, E-mail: douglas.farenick@uregina.ca.

Faculty of Social Work Students: 24 full-time (20 women), 83 part-time (73 women). 68 applicants, 38% accepted. *Faculty:* 24 full-time (17 women), 11 part-time/adjunct (5 women). Expenses: Contact institution. *Financial support:* In 2017–18, fellowships (averaging $6,000 per year), teaching assistantships (averaging $2,562 per year) were awarded; research assistantships, career-related internships or fieldwork, and scholarships/grants also available. Financial award application deadline: 6/15. In 2017, 25 master's awarded. *Program availability:* Part-time. Offers indigenous social work (MISW); social work (MSW, PhD). PhD offered as a special case program. *Application deadline:* For fall admission, 1/31 for domestic and international students. *Application fee:* $100. Electronic applications accepted. *Application Contact:* Dr. Nuelle Novik, Graduate Program Coordinator, 306-585-4573, Fax: 306-585-4872, E-mail: nuelle.novik@uregina.ca. *Dean*, Dr. Judy White, 306-585-4037, Fax: 306-585-5691, E-mail: sw.dean@uregina.ca.

Johnson-Shoyama Graduate School of Public Policy Students: 104 full-time (65 women), 189 part-time (123 women). 285 applicants, 52% accepted. *Faculty:* 9 full-time (4 women), 26 part-time/adjunct (10 women). Expenses: Contact institution. *Financial support:* In 2017–18, fellowships (averaging $6,059 per year), teaching assistantships (averaging $2,562 per year) were awarded; research assistantships, career-related internships or fieldwork, and scholarships/grants also available. Financial award application deadline: 6/15. In 2017, 30 master's awarded. *Program availability:* Part-time. Offers economic analysis for public policy (Master's Certificate); health administration (MHA); health systems management (Master's Certificate); public management (MPA, Master's Certificate); public policy (MPA, MPP, PhD); public policy analysis (Master's Certificate). *Application deadline:* For fall admission, 5/1 for domestic and international students; for winter admission, 11/1 for domestic and international students; for spring admission, 3/15 for domestic and international students. *Application fee:* $100. Electronic applications accepted. *Application Contact:* John Bird, Manager, Main Campus, 306-585-5469, Fax: 306-585-5461, E-mail: john.bird@uregina.ca. *Executive Director, Main Campus*, Dr. Kathleen McNutt, 306-585-4759, Fax: 306-585-5461, E-mail: kathy.mcnutt@uregina.ca.

Kenneth Levene Graduate School of Business Students: 75 full-time (41 women), 109 part-time (78 women). 357 applicants, 41% accepted. *Faculty:* 39 full-time (13 women), 12 part-time/adjunct (7 women). Expenses: Contact institution. *Financial support:* In 2017–18, fellowships (averaging $6,000 per year), teaching assistantships (averaging $2,562 per year) were awarded; research assistantships, career-related internships or fieldwork, and scholarships/grants also available. Financial award application deadline: 6/15. In 2017, 57 master's, 15 other advanced degrees awarded. *Program availability:* Part-time, evening/weekend. Offers business (EMBA, M Admin, MBA, MHRM, Master's Certificate, PGD); business foundations (PGD); engineering management (MBA); executive business administration (EMBA); human resources management (MHRM, Master's Certificate); international business (MBA); leadership (M Admin); organizational leadership (Master's Certificate); project management (Master's Certificate); public safety management (MBA). *Application deadline:* Applications are processed on a rolling basis. *Application fee:* $100. Electronic applications accepted. *Application Contact:* Dr. Gina Grandy, Associate Dean, Research and Graduate Programs/Director of Kenneth Levene Graduate School, 306-585-5647, Fax: 306-585-5361, E-mail: gina.grandy@uregina.ca. *Dean*, Dr. David Senkow, 306-585-4719, Fax: 306-585-4805, E-mail: david.senkow@uregina.ca.

UNIVERSITY OF RHODE ISLAND, Kingston, RI 02881

General Information State-supported, coed, university. CGS member. *Enrollment:* 18,098 graduate, professional, and undergraduate students; 1,829 full-time matriculated graduate/professional students (1,112 women), 948 part-time matriculated graduate/professional students (562 women). *Enrollment by degree level:* 1,331 master's, 1,401 doctoral, 45 other advanced degrees. *Graduate faculty:* 655 full-time (316 women), 5 part-time/adjunct (2 women). Tuition, state resident: full-time $12,706; part-time $786 per credit. Tuition, nonresident: full-time $25,216; part-time $1401 per credit. *Required fees:* $1598; $45 per credit. One-time fee: $30 part-time. *Graduate housing:* Rooms and/or apartments available on a first-come, first-served basis to single and married students. Housing application deadline: 5/1. *Student services:* Campus employment opportunities, campus safety program, career counseling, free psychological counseling, international student services, low-cost health insurance, multicultural affairs office, services for students with disabilities. *Library facilities:* Robert L. Carothers Library and Learning Commons plus 3 others. *Collection:* Study areas open 24 hours, 5–7 days a week; students can reserve study rooms. *Research affiliation:* Sustainable Coastal Communities and Ecosystems (SUCCESS)-Leader with Associates, Rhode Island Network for Molecular Toxicology, Rhode Island Teacher Education Renewal (RITER), U.S. Department of Agriculture (USDA) (food stamp nutrition education).

Computer facilities: Computer purchase and lease plans are available. 2,500 computers available on campus for general student use. A campuswide network can be accessed from student residence rooms and from off campus. Online class registration is available.
Website: http://www.uri.edu/

General Application Contact: 401-874-2262, E-mail: urigrad@etal.uri.edu.

GRADUATE UNITS

Graduate School Students: 1,829 full-time (1,112 women), 948 part-time (562 women); includes 352 minority (72 Black or African American, non-Hispanic/Latino; 12 American Indian or Alaska Native, non-Hispanic/Latino; 141 Asian, non-Hispanic/Latino; 88 Hispanic/Latino; 5 Native Hawaiian or other Pacific Islander, non-Hispanic/Latino; 34 Two or more races, non-Hispanic/Latino), 304 international. 2,653 applicants, 49% accepted, 752 enrolled. *Faculty:* 655 full-time (316 women), 5 part-time/adjunct (2 women). Expenses: Contact institution. *Financial support:* In 2017–18, 133 research assistantships with full tuition reimbursements (averaging $12,116 per year), 286 teaching assistantships with full tuition reimbursements (averaging $14,092 per year) were awarded; unspecified assistantships also available. Financial award application deadline: 2/1; financial award applicants required to submit FAFSA. In 2017, 547 master's, 256 doctorates, 69 other advanced degrees awarded. *Program availability:* Part-time, evening/weekend, 100% online, blended/hybrid learning. *Application deadline:* For fall admission, 7/15 for domestic students, 2/1 for international students; for spring admission, 11/15 for domestic students, 7/15 for international students. *Application fee:* $65. Electronic applications accepted. *Application Contact:* Shandra Pelagio, Graduate Admissions, 401-874-2873, E-mail: shandra@uri.edu. *Dean of the Graduate School*, Dr. Nasser H. Zawia, 401-874-5909, Fax: 401-874-5787, E-mail: nzawia@uri.edu.

Alan Shawn Feinstein College of Education and Professional Studies Students: 59 full-time (44 women), 145 part-time (114 women); includes 24 minority (6 Black or African American, non-Hispanic/Latino; 6 American Indian or Alaska Native, non-Hispanic/Latino; 7 Asian, non-Hispanic/Latino; 3 Hispanic/Latino; 2 Two or more races, non-Hispanic/Latino), 6 international. 91 applicants, 65% accepted, 53 enrolled. *Faculty:* 23 full-time (14 women), 1 (woman) part-time/adjunct. Expenses: Contact institution. *Financial support:* In 2017–18, 1 research assistantship with tuition reimbursement (averaging $8,862 per year), 6 teaching assistantships with tuition reimbursements (averaging $16,306 per year) were awarded; unspecified assistantships also available. In 2017, 50 master's, 9 doctorates awarded. Offers education (PhD); education and professional studies (MA, MM, MS, PhD); reading (MA); special education (MA). *Dean*, R. Anthony Rolle, 401-277-5489, E-mail: anthony_rolle@uri.edu.

College of Arts and Sciences Students: 215 full-time (107 women), 270 part-time (136 women); includes 56 minority (19 Black or African American, non-Hispanic/Latino; 16 Asian, non-Hispanic/Latino; 12 Hispanic/Latino; 3 Native Hawaiian or other Pacific Islander, non-Hispanic/Latino; 6 Two or more races, non-Hispanic/Latino), 54 international. 388 applicants, 66% accepted, 165 enrolled. *Faculty:* 219 full-time (98 women). Expenses: Contact institution. *Financial support:* In 2017–18, 12 research assistantships with tuition reimbursements (averaging $12,163 per year), 122 teaching assistantships with tuition reimbursements (averaging $16,191 per year) were awarded; unspecified assistantships also available. Financial award applicants required to submit FAFSA. In 2017, 107 master's, 22 doctorates, 20 other advanced degrees awarded. *Program availability:* Part-time, evening/weekend. Offers American literature and culture (PhD); applied analysis (MS); applied mathematical sciences (PhD); archaeology and anthropology (MA); arts and sciences (MA, MLIS, MM, MPA, MS, PSM, PhD, Graduate Certificate); British literature and culture (PhD); chemistry (MS, PhD); combinatorics and graph theory (MS); communication studies (MA); complex dynamical systems (MS); computer science (MS, PhD); creative writing (PhD); critical theories (PhD); cyber security (PSM, Graduate Certificate); difference equations (MS); digital forensics (Graduate Certificate); English (MA); European history (MA); film (PhD); gender and women's studies (Graduate Certificate); gender studies (PhD); international relations (MA); libraries, leadership and transforming communities (MLIS); medical physics (MS); music education (MM); music performance (MM); numerical analysis (MS); organization of digital media (MLIS); physics (MS, PhD); public policy and administration (MPA); pure mathematics (PhD); school library media (MLIS); Spanish (MA). *Application fee:* $65. Electronic applications accepted. *Dean*, Dr. Jeannette Riley, 401-874-4101, E-mail: jen_riley@uri.edu.

College of Business Students: 88 full-time (37 women), 180 part-time (94 women); includes 36 minority (9 Black or African American, non-Hispanic/Latino; 2 American Indian or Alaska Native, non-Hispanic/Latino; 13 Asian, non-Hispanic/Latino; 10 Hispanic/Latino; 2 Two or more races, non-Hispanic/Latino), 20 international. 205 applicants, 68% accepted, 97 enrolled. *Faculty:* 61 full-time (28 women), 2 part-time/adjunct (1 woman). Expenses: Contact institution. *Financial support:* In 2017–18, 19 teaching assistantships with tuition reimbursements (averaging $14,589 per year) were awarded; research assistantships also available. Financial award applicants required to submit FAFSA. In 2017, 128 master's, 1 doctorate, 20 other advanced degrees awarded. *Program availability:* Part-time, evening/weekend. Offers accounting (MS); business administration (MBA, PhD); fashion merchandising (Certificate); finance (MBA, MS, PhD); general business (MBA); health care management (MBA); labor relations and human resources (MS, Graduate Certificate); labor research (MS, Graduate Certificate); management (MBA); marketing (MBA, PhD); master seamstress (Certificate); operations and supply chain management (PhD); strategic innovation (MBA); supply chain management (MBA); textiles, fashion merchandising and design (MS, Certificate). *Application fee:* $65. Electronic applications accepted. *Application Contact:* Lisa Lancellotta, Coordinator, MBA Programs, 401-874-4241, Fax: 401-874-4312, E-mail: mba@uri.edu. *Dean*, Dr. Maling Ebrahimpour, 401-874-4348, Fax: 401-874-4312, E-mail: mebrahimpour@uri.edu.

College of Engineering Students: 123 full-time (28 women), 93 part-time (17 women); includes 25 minority (3 Black or African American, non-Hispanic/Latino; 1 American Indian or Alaska Native, non-Hispanic/Latino; 11 Asian, non-Hispanic/Latino; 9 Hispanic/Latino; 1 Two or more races, non-Hispanic/Latino), 84 international. 203 applicants, 65% accepted, 64 enrolled. *Faculty:* 71 full-time (13 women), 1 part-time/adjunct (0 women). Expenses: Contact institution. *Financial support:* In 2017–18, 29 research assistantships with tuition reimbursements (averaging $10,329 per year), 19 teaching assistantships with tuition reimbursements (averaging $11,394 per year) were awarded. Financial award applicants required to submit FAFSA. In 2017, 53 master's, 20 doctorates, 2 other advanced degrees awarded. *Program availability:* Part-time. Offers acoustics and underwater acoustics (MS, PhD); biomedical engineering (MS, PhD); chemical engineering (MS, PhD); circuits and devices (MS); civil and environmental engineering (MS, PhD); communication theory (MS, PhD); computer architectures and digital systems (MS, PhD); computer networks (MS, PhD); digital signal processing (MS); embedded systems and computer applications (MS, PhD); engineering (MS, PhD, Graduate Certificate, Postbaccalaureate Certificate); fault-tolerant computing (MS, PhD); industrial and systems engineering (MS, PhD); materials and optics (MS, PhD); ocean engineering (MS, PhD); polymer (Postbaccalaureate Certificate); systems theory (MS, PhD). *Application fee:* $65. Electronic applications accepted. *Dean*, Dr. Raymond Wright, 401-874-2186, Fax: 401-782-1066, E-mail: dean@egr.uri.edu.

College of Health Sciences Students: 272 full-time (206 women), 97 part-time (78 women); includes 44 minority (13 Black or African American, non-Hispanic/Latino; 2 American Indian or Alaska Native, non-Hispanic/Latino; 18 Asian, non-Hispanic/Latino; 9 Hispanic/Latino; 2 Two or more races, non-Hispanic/Latino), 12 international. 551 applicants, 19% accepted, 97 enrolled. *Faculty:* 80 full-time (53 women), 1 part-time/adjunct (0 women). Expenses: Contact institution. *Financial support:* In 2017–18, 12 research assistantships with tuition reimbursements (averaging $14,702 per year), 45 teaching assistantships with tuition reimbursements (averaging $11,894 per year) were awarded. Financial award applicants required to submit FAFSA. In 2017, 96 master's, 56 doctorates awarded. *Program availability:* Part-time, evening/weekend, 100% online, blended/hybrid learning. Offers behavioral science (PhD); clinical psychology (PhD); college student personnel (MS); cultural studies of sport and physical culture (MS); dietetic internship (MS); exercise science (MS); health sciences (MA, MM, MS, DPT, PhD); human development and family studies (MS); marriage and family therapy (MS); nutrition (MS); online dietetics (MS); physical therapy (DPT); psychosocial/behavioral aspects of physical activity (MS); school psychology (MS, PhD); speech-language pathology (MS). *Application fee:* $65. Electronic applications accepted. *Dean*, Dr. Gary Liguori, 401-874-9330, E-mail: gliguori@uri.edu.

College of Nursing Students: 42 full-time (36 women), 86 part-time (79 women); includes 12 minority (3 Black or African American, non-Hispanic/Latino; 3 Asian, non-Hispanic/Latino; 3 Hispanic/Latino; 1 Native Hawaiian or other Pacific Islander, non-Hispanic/Latino; 2 Two or more races, non-Hispanic/Latino), 3 international. 33 applicants, 79% accepted, 23 enrolled. *Faculty:* 31 full-time (30 women). Expenses: Contact institution. *Financial support:* In 2017–18, 1 research assistantship with tuition reimbursement (averaging $18,080 per year), 5 teaching assistantships with tuition reimbursements (averaging $10,133 per year) were awarded. Financial award application deadline: 2/1; financial award applicants required to submit FAFSA. In 2017, 25 master's, 8 doctorates, 2 other advanced degrees awarded. *Program availability:* Part-time, evening/weekend, 100% online, blended/hybrid learning. Offers acute care nurse practitioner (adult-gerontology focus) (Post Master's Certificate); adult gerontology nurse practitioner/clinical nurse specialist (Post Master's Certificate); adult-gerontological acute care nurse practitioner (MS); adult-gerontological nurse practitioner/clinical nurse specialist (MS); family nurse practitioner (MS, Post Master's Certificate); nursing (DNP, PhD); nursing education (MS, Post Master's Certificate). *Application deadline:* For fall admission, 2/15 for domestic students, 2/1 for international students; for spring admission, 10/15 for domestic students, 7/15 for international students. *Application fee:* $65. Electronic applications accepted. *Application Contact:* Dr. Denise Coppa, Associate Professor/Interim Associate Dean for Graduate Programs, 401-874-5036, E-mail: dcoppa@uri.edu. *Dean*, Dr. Barbara Wolfe, 401-874-5324, E-mail: bwolfe@uri.edu.

College of Pharmacy Students: 768 full-time (508 women), 11 part-time (5 women); includes 121 minority (7 Black or African American, non-Hispanic/Latino; 1 American Indian or Alaska Native, non-Hispanic/Latino; 59 Asian, non-Hispanic/Latino; 37 Hispanic/Latino; 17 Two or more races, non-Hispanic/Latino), 61 international. 802 applicants, 47% accepted, 151 enrolled. *Faculty:* 53 full-time (36 women). Expenses: Contact institution. *Financial support:* In 2017–18, 10 research assistantships with tuition reimbursements (averaging $13,958 per year), 10 teaching assistantships with tuition reimbursements (averaging $11,291 per year) were awarded. Financial award application deadline: 2/1; financial award applicants required to submit FAFSA. In 2017, 3 master's, 122 doctorates awarded. *Program availability:* Part-time. Offers health outcomes (MS, PhD); medicinal chemistry and pharmacognosy (MS, PhD); pharmaceutics and pharmacokinetics (MS, PhD); pharmacology and toxicology (MS, PhD); pharmacy (MS, PhD, Pharm D); pharmacy practice (Pharm D). *Application fee:* $65. Electronic applications accepted. *Dean/Professor*, Dr. E. Paul Larrat, 401-874-5003, Fax: 401-874-2181, E-mail: larrat@uri.edu.

College of the Environment and Life Sciences Students: 207 full-time (114 women), 52 part-time (34 women); includes 26 minority (6 Black or African American, non-Hispanic/Latino; 12 Asian, non-Hispanic/Latino; 5 Hispanic/Latino; 1 Native Hawaiian or other Pacific Islander, non-Hispanic/Latino; 2 Two or more races, non-Hispanic/Latino), 54 international. 276 applicants, 47% accepted, 77 enrolled. *Faculty:* 90 full-time (34 women). Expenses: Contact institution. *Financial support:* In 2017–18, 47 research assistantships with tuition reimbursements (averaging $13,374 per year), 53 teaching assistantships with tuition reimbursements (averaging $14,582 per year) were awarded. Financial award applicants required to submit FAFSA. In 2017, 75 master's, 12 doctorates, 18 other advanced degrees awarded. *Program availability:* Part-time. Offers animal health and disease (MS); animal science (MS); aquaculture (MS); aquatic pathology (MS); biochemistry (MS, PhD); cell and molecular biology (MS, PhD); clinical laboratory sciences (MS); earth and environmental sciences (MS, PhD); ecology and ecosystem sciences (MS, PhD); environment and life sciences (MA, MESM, MMA, MS, PhD, Graduate Certificate); environmental and earth sciences (MS, PhD); environmental and natural resource economics (MS, PhD); environmental science and management (MESM); environmental sciences (PhD); evolutionary and marine biology (MS, PhD); fisheries (MS); hydrology (Graduate Certificate); marine affairs (MA, MMA, PhD); microbiology (MS, PhD); molecular genetics (MS, PhD); natural resources science (MS, PhD); sustainable agriculture and food systems (MS, PhD). *Application fee:* $65. Electronic applications accepted. *Dean*, Dr. John Kirby, 401-874-2957, Fax: 401-874-4017, E-mail: jdkirby@uri.edu.

Graduate School of Oceanography Students: 55 full-time (32 women), 14 part-time (5 women); includes 2 minority (both Asian, non-Hispanic/Latino), 10 international. 104 applicants, 69% accepted, 25 enrolled. *Faculty:* 27 full-time (10 women). Expenses: Contact institution. *Financial support:* In 2017–18, 23 research assistantships with tuition reimbursements (averaging $10,636 per year), 9 teaching assistantships with tuition reimbursements (averaging $11,586 per year) were awarded. Financial award application deadline: 1/15; financial award applicants required to submit FAFSA. In 2017, 10 master's, 6 doctorates awarded. *Program availability:* Part-time. Offers biological oceanography (MS, PhD); coastal ocean management (MO); coastal systems (MO); fisheries (MO); general oceanography (MO); marine and atmospheric chemistry (MS, PhD); marine fisheries management (MO); marine geology and geophysics (MS, PhD); ocean technology and data (MO); physical oceanography (MS, PhD). *Application deadline:* For fall admission, 1/15 for domestic and international students. *Application fee:* $65. Electronic applications accepted. *Application Contact:* Dr. David Smith, Professor of Oceanography/Associate Dean for Academic Affairs, 401-874-6172, E-mail: dcsmith@uri.edu. *Dean*, Dr. Bruce Corliss, 401-874-6222, Fax: 401-874-6931, E-mail: bruce.corliss@gso.uri.edu.

UNIVERSITY OF RICHMOND, University of Richmond, VA 23173

General Information Independent, coed, comprehensive institution. *Graduate housing:* On-campus housing not available.

GRADUATE UNITS

Robins School of Business *Program availability:* Part-time, evening/weekend. Offers business (MBA). Electronic applications accepted.

School of Law Offers law (JD). JD/MSW, JD/MHA, JD/MPA offered jointly with Virginia Commonwealth University; JD/MURP with Virginia Commonwealth University; JD/MA with Department of History; JD/MS with Department of Biology. Electronic applications accepted.

UNIVERSITY OF RIO GRANDE, Rio Grande, OH 45674

General Information Independent, coed, comprehensive institution. *Graduate housing:* Room and/or apartments available on a first-come, first-served basis to single students; on-campus housing not available to married students.

GRADUATE UNITS

Graduate School *Program availability:* Part-time. Offers athletic coaching leadership (M Ed); educational leadership (M Ed); integrated arts (M Ed); intervention specialist in early childhood (M Ed); intervention specialist in mild/moderate (M Ed).

UNIVERSITY OF ROCHESTER, Rochester, NY 14627

General Information Independent, coed, university. CGS member. *Graduate housing:* Rooms and/or apartments available on a first-come, first-served basis to single and married students. *Research affiliation:* General Motors (chemical engineering, mechanical engineering, biomedical engineering), American Heart and Lung Associations (biochemistry/biophysics, cardiovascular research, environmental toxicology, oral biology, pulmonary medicine, pathology, pharmacology and physiology), Bausch & Lomb (optics, ophthalmology), Fermilab, Jet Propulsion Laboratory, and Lawrence Livermore National Laboratory (physics and astronomy, laser energetics), Johnson & Johnson (biology, neurosurgery, ophthalmology, psychiatry), IBM (computer science, electrical engineering, computer engineering).

GRADUATE UNITS

Eastman School of Music *Program availability:* Part-time. Offers conducting (MM, DMA); ethnomusicology (MA); jazz studies/contemporary media (MM); music composition (MA, MM, DMA, PhD); music education (MA, MM, DMA, PhD); music theory (PhD); music theory pedagogy (MA); musicology (PhD); performance and literature (MM, DMA); piano accompanying and chamber music (MM, DMA).

Hajim School of Engineering and Applied Sciences Students: 595 full-time (153 women), 37 part-time (11 women); includes 59 minority (12 Black or African American, non-Hispanic/Latino; 2 American Indian or Alaska Native, non-Hispanic/Latino; 19 Asian, non-Hispanic/Latino; 17 Hispanic/Latino; 9 Two or more races, non-Hispanic/Latino), 381 international. Average age 25. 2,507 applicants, 38% accepted, 227 enrolled. *Faculty:* 95 full-time (13 women). Expenses: Contact institution. *Financial support:* Fellowships, research assistantships, teaching assistantships, career-related internships or fieldwork, scholarships/grants, traineeships, health care benefits, tuition waivers, and unspecified assistantships available. Support available to part-time students. In 2017, 196 master's, 42 doctorates awarded. Offers algorithms and complexity (MS); alternative energy (MS); artificial intelligence and machine learning (MS); biomedical engineering (MS); biomedical ultrasound and biomedical engineering (MS); chemical engineering (MS, PhD); computer architecture (MS); computer science (PhD); engineering and applied sciences (MS, PhD); human computer interaction (MS); integrated electronics and computer engineering (PhD); materials science (MS, PhD); mechanical engineering (MS, PhD); musical acoustics and signal processing (MS); natural language processing (MS); physical electronics, electron magnetism, and acoustics (PhD); programming languages and computer systems (MS); signal and image processing and communications (MS); signal processing and communications (PhD). *Application fee:* $60. Electronic applications accepted. *Application Contact:* Gretchen Briscoe, Director of Graduate Enrollment, 585-275-2059, E-mail: gretchen.briscoe@rochester.edu. *Dean, Hajim School of Engineering and Applied Sciences/Professor of Electrical and Computer Engineering,* Dr. Wendi Heinzelman, 585-273-3958, E-mail: wendi.heinzelman@rochester.edu.

Institute of Optics Students: 125 full-time (29 women), 6 part-time (2 women); includes 17 minority (1 American Indian or Alaska Native, non-Hispanic/Latino; 7 Asian, non-Hispanic/Latino; 7 Hispanic/Latino; 2 Two or more races, non-Hispanic/Latino), 65 international. Average age 25. 245 applicants, 47% accepted, 39 enrolled. *Faculty:* 19 full-time (1 woman). Expenses: Contact institution. In 2017, 22 master's, 11 doctorates awarded. Offers optics (MS, PhD). Electronic applications accepted. *Application Contact:* Jackie Thomas, Graduate Program Coordinator, 585-275-7720, E-mail: jacqueline.thomas-bell@rochester.edu. *Director/Professor of Optics,* Scott Carney, 585-274-0113, E-mail: scott.carney@rochester.edu.

Margaret Warner Graduate School of Education and Human Development *Program availability:* Part-time, evening/weekend. Offers counseling (Ed D); education and human development (MS, Ed D, PhD); educational administration (Ed D); educational policy (MS); educational policy and theory (PhD); higher education (MS, PhD); higher education student affairs (MS); human development (MS); human development in educational context (PhD); school and community counseling (MS); school counseling (MS); school leadership (MS); teaching and curriculum (MS); teaching, curriculum, and change (PhD).

School of Arts and Sciences Students: 671 full-time (276 women), 26 part-time (18 women); includes 83 minority (9 Black or African American, non-Hispanic/Latino; 1 American Indian or Alaska Native, non-Hispanic/Latino; 22 Asian, non-Hispanic/Latino; 36 Hispanic/Latino; 15 Two or more races, non-Hispanic/Latino), 245 international. Average age 27. 2,335 applicants, 24% accepted, 176 enrolled. *Faculty:* 247 full-time (68 women). Expenses: Contact institution. *Financial support:* Fellowships, research assistantships, teaching assistantships, career-related internships or fieldwork, Federal Work-Study, institutionally sponsored loans, scholarships/grants, traineeships, health care benefits, tuition waivers, and unspecified assistantships available. Support available to part-time students. In 2017, 174 master's, 79 doctorates awarded. Offers arts and sciences (MA, MS, PhD, AC); biology (MS); brain and cognitive sciences (PhD); clinical psychology (PhD); comparative literature (MA); computational linguistics (MS); developmental psychology (PhD); ecology, genetics, and genomics (PhD); economics (PhD); English (MA, PhD); epistemology (PhD); ethics (PhD); geological sciences (MS); geosciences (PhD); history (MA, PhD); history of ancient philosophy (PhD); history of modern philosophy (PhD); inorganic chemistry (PhD); language documentation and description (MA); linguistics (MA); literary translation studies (MA, AC); mathematics (PhD); metaphysics (PhD); molecular, cellular, and developmental biology evolution (PhD); organic chemistry (PhD); philosophy of language (PhD); philosophy of mind (PhD); photographic preservation and collections management (MA); physical chemistry (PhD); physics and astronomy (PhD); political science (PhD); social-personality psychology (PhD); visual and cultural studies (PhD). Electronic applications accepted. *Application Contact:* Gretchen Briscoe, Director of Graduate Enrollment, 585-275-5029, E-mail: gretchen.briscoe@rochester.edu. *Dean of the School of Arts and Sciences/Professor of Biology,* Gloria Culver, 585-273-5000, E-mail: gloria.culver@rochester.edu.

Goergen Institute for Data Science Students: 25 full-time (12 women), 1 (woman) part-time; includes 2 minority (1 Black or African American, non-Hispanic/Latino; 1 Asian, non-Hispanic/Latino), 19 international. Average age 27. 357 applicants, 32% accepted, 24 enrolled. Expenses: Contact institution. *Financial support:* In 2017–18, 26 students received support, including 1 fellowship with partial tuition reimbursement available (averaging $18,900 per year); tuition waivers (partial) also available. Financial award applicants required to submit FAFSA. In 2017, 28 master's awarded. *Program availability:* Part-time. Offers business and social science (MS); computational and statistical methods (MS); health and biomedical sciences (MS). *Application deadline:* For fall admission, 4/15 priority date for domestic and international students. *Application fee:* $60. Electronic applications accepted. *Application Contact:* Lisa Altman, Education Program Coordinator, 585-275-5288, E-mail: lisa.altman@rochester.edu. *Deputy Director,* Anand Ajay, 585-276-3149, E-mail: ajay.anand@rochester.edu.

School of Medicine and Dentistry *Program availability:* Part-time. Offers medicine (MD); medicine and dentistry (MA, MPH, MS, MD, PhD, Certificate). Electronic applications accepted.

Graduate Programs in Medicine and Dentistry *Program availability:* Part-time. Offers biochemistry (PhD); biochemistry and molecular biology (PhD); biophysics (PhD); biophysics, structural and computational biology (PhD); clinical investigation (MS); clinical translational research (MS); dental science (MS); epidemiology (PhD); genetics, genomics and development (PhD); health services research and policy (PhD); marriage and family therapy (MS); medical microbiology (MS, PhD); medical statistics (MS); medicine and dentistry (MA, MPH, MS, PhD); microbiology and immunology (MS, PhD); neurobiology and anatomy (PhD); neuroscience (PhD); pathology (PhD); pharmacology (MS, PhD); physiology (MS, PhD); public health (MPH, MS); statistics (MA, PhD); toxicology (PhD); translational biomedical science (PhD). Electronic applications accepted.

School of Nursing Students: 17 full-time (12 women), 306 part-time (252 women); includes 46 minority (16 Black or African American, non-Hispanic/Latino; 1 American Indian or Alaska Native, non-Hispanic/Latino; 7 Asian, non-Hispanic/Latino; 17 Hispanic/Latino; 5 Two or more races, non-Hispanic/Latino), 3 international. Average age 34. 143 applicants, 71% accepted, 87 enrolled. *Faculty:* 62 full-time (51 women), 73 part-time/adjunct (63 women). Expenses: Contact institution. *Financial support:* In 2017–18, 63 students received support, including 2 fellowships with full and partial tuition reimbursements available (averaging $16,000 per year); scholarships/grants, traineeships, health care benefits, tuition waivers (full and partial), and unspecified assistantships also available. Support available to part-time students. Financial award application deadline: 6/30; financial award applicants required to submit CSS PROFILE or FAFSA. In 2017, 48 master's, 8 doctorates awarded. *Program availability:* Part-time, 100% online, blended/hybrid learning. Offers adult gerontological acute care nurse practitioner (MS); adult gerontological primary care nurse practitioner (MS); clinical nurse leader (MS); family nurse practitioner (MS); family psychiatric mental health nurse practitioner (MS); health care organization management and leadership (MS); nursing (DNP); nursing and health science (PhD); nursing education (MS); pediatric nurse practitioner (MS); pediatric nurse practitioner/neonatal nurse practitioner (MS). *Application deadline:* For fall admission, 4/1 for domestic and international students; for spring admission, 9/1 for domestic and international students; for summer admission, 1/2 for domestic and international students. *Application fee:* $50. Electronic applications accepted. *Application Contact:* Elaine Andolina, Director of Admissions, 585-275-2375, Fax: 585-756-8299, E-mail: elaine_andolina@urmc.rochester.edu. *Dean,* Dr. Kathy H. Rideout, 585-273-8902, Fax: 585-273-1268, E-mail: kathy_rideout@urmc.rochester.edu.

Simon Business School *Faculty:* 70 full-time (12 women), 23 part-time/adjunct (6 women). Expenses: Contact institution. *Financial support:* In 2017–18, 585 students received support. Fellowships, research assistantships, teaching assistantships, institutionally sponsored loans, scholarships/grants, tuition waivers (full and partial), and unspecified assistantships available. *Program availability:* Part-time, evening/weekend. Offers accountancy (MS); accounting (PhD); business (MBA, MS, PhD); business administration (MBA, PhD); business analytics (MS); business systems consulting (MBA); competitive and organizational strategy (MBA); computer information systems (PhD); computers and information systems (MBA); corporate accounting (MBA); entrepreneurship (MBA); finance (MS); health sciences management (MBA); marketing (MBA, PhD); marketing analytics (MS); operations management (MBA, PhD); public accounting (MBA); strategy and organizations (MBA). *Application deadline:* For fall admission, 10/15 for domestic and international students; for winter admission, 1/5 for domestic and international students; for spring admission, 3/15 for domestic and international students; for summer admission, 5/15 for domestic and international students. Applications are processed on a rolling basis. *Application fee:* $150. Electronic applications accepted. *Application Contact:* Rebekah S. Lewin, Assistant Dean for Admissions and Financial Aid, 585-275-3533, E-mail: admissions@simon.rochester.edu. *Dean,* Andrew Ainslie, 585-275-3316, E-mail: andrew.ainslie@simon.rochester.edu.

UNIVERSITY OF ST. AUGUSTINE FOR HEALTH SCIENCES, San Marcos, CA 92069

General Information Proprietary, coed, graduate-only institution. *Graduate housing:* On-campus housing not available.

GRADUATE UNITS

Graduate Programs *Program availability:* Part-time, evening/weekend, online learning. Offers athletic training (MHS); executive leadership (MHS); health administration (MHA); health science (DH Sc); health sciences education (Ed D); informatics (MHS); nurse educator (MSN); nurse executive (MSN); nurse informatics (MSN); nursing (MSN, DNP); occupational therapy (TOTD); physical therapy (DPT); teaching and learning (MHS).

UNIVERSITY OF ST. FRANCIS, Joliet, IL 60435-6169

General Information Independent-religious, coed, comprehensive institution. *Enrollment:* 2,479 graduate, professional, and undergraduate students; 385 full-time matriculated graduate/professional students (278 women), 956 part-time matriculated graduate/professional students (766 women). *Enrollment by degree level:* 1,112 master's, 164 doctoral, 65 other advanced degrees. *Graduate faculty:* 39 full-time (28 women), 88 part-time/adjunct (59 women). *Tuition:* Part-time $748 per credit hour. *Required fees:* $125 per semester. Tuition and fees vary according to degree level and program. *Graduate housing:* Room and/or apartments available on a first-come, first-served basis to single students; on-campus housing not available to married students. Housing application deadline: 8/1. *Student services:* Campus employment opportunities, campus safety program, career counseling, free psychological counseling, international student services, multicultural affairs office, services for students with disabilities, teacher training, writing training. *Library facilities:* Brown Library. *Collection:* Books: 113,077 (physical), 4,118 (digital/electronic); Serial titles: 605 (physical), 113 (digital/electronic); Databases: 76. Weekly public service hours: 74; students can reserve study rooms.

Computer facilities: 560 computers available on campus for general student use. A campuswide network can be accessed from student residence rooms and from off campus. Online class registration, billing/payment are available.
Website: http://www.stfrancis.edu/

General Application Contact: Sandra Sloka, Director of Admissions for Graduate and Degree Completion Programs, 800-735-7500, Fax: 815-740-3431, E-mail: ssloka@stfrancis.edu.

GRADUATE UNITS

College of Arts and Sciences Students: 107 full-time (82 women), 24 part-time (22 women); includes 40 minority (13 Black or African American, non-Hispanic/Latino; 3 Asian, non-Hispanic/Latino; 20 Hispanic/Latino; 2 Native Hawaiian or other Pacific Islander, non-Hispanic/Latino; 2 Two or more races, non-Hispanic/Latino), 6 international. Average age 28. 69 applicants, 48% accepted, 26 enrolled. *Faculty:* 7 full-time (5 women), 5 part-time/adjunct (4 women). Expenses: Contact institution. *Financial support:* In 2017–18, 10 students received support. Scholarships/grants and unspecified assistantships available. Support available to part-time students. Financial award applicants required to submit FAFSA. In 2017, 64 master's awarded. *Program availability:* Part-time. Offers forensic social work (Post-Master's Certificate); physician assistant practice (MS); social work (MSW). *Application deadline:* Applications are processed on a rolling basis. *Application fee:* $30. Electronic applications accepted. *Application Contact:* Sandra Sloka, Director of Admissions for Graduate and Degree Completion Programs, 800-735-7500, Fax: 815-740-3431, E-mail: ssloka@stfrancis.edu. *Dean,* Dr. Robert Kase, 815-740-3367, Fax: 815-740-6366.

College of Business and Health Administration Students: 173 full-time (103 women), 229 part-time (164 women); includes 97 minority (47 Black or African American, non-Hispanic/Latino; 15 Asian, non-Hispanic/Latino; 30 Hispanic/Latino; 1 Native Hawaiian or other Pacific Islander, non-Hispanic/Latino; 4 Two or more races, non-Hispanic/Latino), 55 international. Average age 38. 265 applicants, 54% accepted, 106 enrolled. *Faculty:* 12 full-time (6 women), 19 part-time/adjunct (8 women). Expenses: Contact institution. *Financial support:* In 2017–18, 128 students received support. Scholarships/grants and unspecified assistantships available. Support available to part-time students. Financial award applicants required to submit FAFSA. In 2017, 166 master's, 6 other advanced degrees awarded. *Program availability:* Part-time, evening/weekend, 100% online, blended/hybrid learning. Offers business and health administration (MBA, MS, MSM, Certificate). *Application deadline:* Applications are processed on a rolling basis. *Application fee:* $30. Electronic applications accepted. *Application Contact:* Sandra Sloka, Director of Admissions for Graduate and Degree Completion Programs, 800-735-7500, Fax: 815-740-3431, E-mail: ssloka@stfrancis.edu. *Dean*, Dr. Orlando Griego, 815-740-3395, Fax: 815-740-3537, E-mail: ogriego@stfrancis.edu.

College of Education Students: 39 full-time (32 women), 411 part-time (318 women); includes 106 minority (57 Black or African American, non-Hispanic/Latino; 8 Asian, non-Hispanic/Latino; 37 Hispanic/Latino; 4 Two or more races, non-Hispanic/Latino), 4 international. Average age 37. 277 applicants, 55% accepted, 137 enrolled. *Faculty:* 11 full-time (8 women), 52 part-time/adjunct (36 women). Expenses: Contact institution. *Financial support:* In 2017–18, 40 students received support. Scholarships/grants and unspecified assistantships available. Support available to part-time students. Financial award applicants required to submit FAFSA. In 2017, 199 master's, 28 doctorates awarded. *Program availability:* Part-time, evening/weekend, 100% online, blended/hybrid learning. Offers educational leadership (MS, Ed D); elementary education (M Ed); reading (MS); secondary education (M Ed); special education (M Ed); teaching and learning (MS); TESOL (Certificate). *Application deadline:* Applications are processed on a rolling basis. *Application fee:* $30. Electronic applications accepted. *Application Contact:* Sandra Sloka, Director of Admissions for Graduate and Degree Completion Programs, 800-735-7500, Fax: 815-740-3431, E-mail: ssloka@stfrancis.edu. *Dean*, Dr. John Gambro, 815-740-3829, Fax: 815-740-2264, E-mail: jgambro@stfrancis.edu.

Leach College of Nursing Students: 66 full-time (61 women), 292 part-time (262 women); includes 136 minority (67 Black or African American, non-Hispanic/Latino; 2 American Indian or Alaska Native, non-Hispanic/Latino; 25 Asian, non-Hispanic/Latino; 29 Hispanic/Latino; 3 Native Hawaiian or other Pacific Islander, non-Hispanic/Latino; 10 Two or more races, non-Hispanic/Latino). Average age 40. 280 applicants, 34% accepted, 81 enrolled. *Faculty:* 9 full-time (all women), 12 part-time/adjunct (11 women). Expenses: Contact institution. *Financial support:* In 2017–18, 115 students received support. Scholarships/grants available. Support available to part-time students. Financial award applicants required to submit FAFSA. In 2017, 117 master's, 5 doctorates, 12 other advanced degrees awarded. *Program availability:* Part-time, evening/weekend, 100% online. Offers family nurse practitioner (MSN, Post-Master's Certificate); nursing administration (MSN); nursing education (MSN); nursing practice (DNP); psychology/mental health nurse practitioner (MSN, Post-Master's Certificate); teaching in nursing (Certificate). *Application deadline:* Applications are processed on a rolling basis. *Application fee:* $30. Electronic applications accepted. *Application Contact:* Sandra Sloka, Director of Admissions for Graduate and Degree Completion Programs, 800-735-7500, Fax: 815-740-3431, E-mail: ssloka@stfrancis.edu. *Dean*, Dr. Carol Wilson, 815-740-3840, Fax: 815-740-4243, E-mail: cwilson@stfrancis.edu.

UNIVERSITY OF SAINT FRANCIS, Fort Wayne, IN 46808-3994

General Information Independent-religious, coed, comprehensive institution. *Enrollment:* 2,322 graduate, professional, and undergraduate students; 196 full-time matriculated graduate/professional students (139 women), 209 part-time matriculated graduate/professional students (147 women). *Enrollment by degree level:* 394 master's, 11 doctoral. *Graduate faculty:* 29 full-time (16 women), 28 part-time/adjunct (16 women). *Tuition:* Full-time $16,290; part-time $905 per credit hour. *Required fees:* $30 per credit hour. $145 per term. Tuition and fees vary according to degree level, campus/location and program. *Graduate housing:* Room and/or apartments available on a first-come, first-served basis to single students; on-campus housing not available to married students. Typical cost: $9840 (including board). Room and board charges vary according to housing facility selected. Housing application deadline: 7/1. *Student services:* Campus employment opportunities, campus safety program, career counseling, exercise/wellness program, multicultural affairs office, services for students with disabilities. *Library facilities:* Lee and Jim Vann Library. *Collection:* Books: 67,110 (physical), 182,832 (digital/electronic); Serial titles: 798 (physical), 39,156 (digital/electronic); Databases: 110. Weekly public service hours: 86; study areas open 24 hours, 5–7 days a week; students can reserve study rooms.

Computer facilities: Computer purchase and lease plans are available. 120 computers available on campus for general student use. A campuswide network can be accessed from student residence rooms and from off campus. Online class registration is available. Website: http://www.sf.edu/

General Application Contact: Kyle Richardson, Enrollment Services Specialist, 260-399-7700 Ext. 6310, E-mail: krichardson@sf.edu.

GRADUATE UNITS

Graduate School Students: 196 full-time (139 women), 209 part-time (147 women); includes 61 minority (32 Black or African American, non-Hispanic/Latino; 5 Asian, non-Hispanic/Latino; 16 Hispanic/Latino; 1 Native Hawaiian or other Pacific Islander, non-Hispanic/Latino; 7 Two or more races, non-Hispanic/Latino), 2 international. Average age 32. 189 applicants, 90% accepted, 135 enrolled. *Faculty:* 29 full-time (16 women), 28 part-time/adjunct (16 women). Expenses: Contact institution. *Financial support:* In 2017–18, 25 students received support. Federal Work-Study, scholarships/grants, and unspecified assistantships available. Financial award application deadline: 4/15; financial award applicants required to submit FAFSA. In 2017, 222 master's, 2 other advanced degrees awarded. *Program availability:* Part-time, evening/weekend, 100% online, blended/hybrid learning. Offers clinical mental health counseling (MS, Post Master's Certificate); family nurse practitioner (MSN, Post Master's Certificate); nurse anesthesia (DNP); nursing practice (DNP); physician assistant studies (MS); psychology (MS); school counseling (MS Ed); secondary education (MAT); special education (MS Ed); studio art (MA, MFA). *Application deadline:* For fall admission, 7/1 for international students; for spring admission, 11/1 for international students; for summer admission, 3/1 for international students. Applications are processed on a rolling basis. *Application fee:* $0. Electronic applications accepted. *Application Contact:* Kyle Richardson, Associate Director of Enrollment Services for Adult Learning, 260-399-7700 Ext. 6310, E-mail: krichardson@sf.edu. *Associate Vice President of Academic Affairs*, Joseph M. Friona, 260-399-7700 Ext. 8400, E-mail: jfriona@sf.edu.

Keith Busse School of Business and Entrepreneurial Leadership Students: 75 full-time (43 women), 108 part-time (59 women); includes 37 minority (21 Black or African American, non-Hispanic/Latino; 1 Asian, non-Hispanic/Latino; 11 Hispanic/Latino; 1 Native Hawaiian or other Pacific Islander, non-Hispanic/Latino; 3 Two or more races, non-Hispanic/Latino). Average age 34. 101 applicants, 98% accepted, 75 enrolled. *Faculty:* 4 full-time (3 women), 11 part-time/adjunct (1 woman). Expenses: Contact institution. *Financial support:* Application deadline: 4/15; applicants required to submit FAFSA. In 2017, 133 master's awarded. *Program availability:* Part-time, evening/weekend, online only, 100% online. Offers business administration (MBA); environmental health (MEH); healthcare administration (MHA); organizational leadership (MOL). *Application deadline:* For fall admission, 7/1 for international students; for spring admission, 11/1 for international students; for summer admission, 3/1 for international students. Applications are processed on a rolling basis. *Application fee:* $0. Electronic applications accepted. *Application Contact:* Kyle Richardson, Associate Director of Enrollment Services for Adult Learning, 260-399-7700 Ext. 6310, Fax: 260-399-8152, E-mail: krichardson@sf.edu. *Dean*, Dr. Robert Lee, 260-399-7700 Ext. 8304, Fax: 260-399-8174, E-mail: rlee@sf.edu.

UNIVERSITY OF SAINT JOSEPH, West Hartford, CT 06117-2700

General Information Independent-religious, coed, primarily women, comprehensive institution. *Enrollment:* 2,405 graduate, professional, and undergraduate students; 537 full-time matriculated graduate/professional students (419 women), 1,058 part-time matriculated graduate/professional students (896 women). *Enrollment by degree level:* 1,284 master's, 258 doctoral, 53 other advanced degrees. *Graduate faculty:* 72 full-time (51 women), 83 part-time/adjunct (55 women). *Graduate housing:* Room and/or apartments available on a first-come, first-served basis to single students; on-campus housing not available to married students. Housing application deadline: 6/1. *Student services:* Campus employment opportunities, campus safety program, career counseling, exercise/wellness program, free psychological counseling, multicultural affairs office, services for students with disabilities, teacher training, writing training. *Library facilities:* Pope Pius XII Library.

Computer facilities: 72 computers available on campus for general student use. A campuswide network can be accessed from student residence rooms and from off campus. Online class registration is available.
Website: http://www.usj.edu/

GRADUATE UNITS

Department of Biology Expenses: Contact institution. *Financial support:* Unspecified assistantships available. Support available to part-time students. Financial award applicants required to submit FAFSA. *Program availability:* Part-time, online learning. Offers biology (MS). *Application deadline:* Applications are processed on a rolling basis. *Application fee:* $50. Electronic applications accepted.

Department of Business Administration Expenses: Contact institution. *Financial support:* Career-related internships or fieldwork and unspecified assistantships available. Support available to part-time students. Financial award applicants required to submit FAFSA. *Program availability:* Part-time, evening/weekend. Offers management (MS). *Application deadline:* Applications are processed on a rolling basis. *Application fee:* $50. Electronic applications accepted. *Chair*, Steven B. Jarett, 860-231-5288, E-mail: sjarett@usj.edu.

Department of Chemistry Expenses: Contact institution. *Financial support:* Career-related internships or fieldwork and unspecified assistantships available. Support available to part-time students. Financial award applicants required to submit FAFSA. *Program availability:* Part-time, evening/weekend, online learning. Offers biochemistry (MS); chemistry (MS). *Application deadline:* Applications are processed on a rolling basis. *Application fee:* $50. Electronic applications accepted. *Chair*, Dr. Ellen Anderson, 860-231-5239, E-mail: eanderson@usj.edu.

Department of Counseling and Applied Behavioral Studies Expenses: Contact institution. *Financial support:* Career-related internships or fieldwork and unspecified assistantships available. Support available to part-time students. Financial award applicants required to submit FAFSA. *Program availability:* Part-time, evening/weekend. Offers clinical mental health counseling (MA); school counseling (MA). *Application deadline:* Applications are processed on a rolling basis. *Application fee:* $50. Electronic applications accepted.

Department of Education Expenses: Contact institution. *Financial support:* Career-related internships or fieldwork and unspecified assistantships available. Support available to part-time students. Financial award applicants required to submit FAFSA. *Program availability:* Part-time, evening/weekend. Offers curriculum and instruction (MA); elementary education (MAT); instructional technology (MA); literacy (MA); secondary education (MAT); TESOL (MA). *Application deadline:* Applications are processed on a rolling basis. *Application fee:* $50. Electronic applications accepted.

Department of Nursing Expenses: Contact institution. *Financial support:* Career-related internships or fieldwork and unspecified assistantships available. Support available to part-time students. Financial award applicants required to submit FAFSA. *Program availability:* Part-time, evening/weekend. Offers family nurse practitioner (MS); nurse educator (MS); nursing practice (DNP); psychiatric/mental health nurse practitioner (MS). *Application deadline:* Applications are processed on a rolling basis. *Application fee:* $50. Electronic applications accepted.

Department of Nutrition and Public Health Expenses: Contact institution. *Financial support:* Career-related internships or fieldwork and unspecified assistantships available. Support available to part-time students. Financial award applicants required to submit FAFSA. *Program availability:* Part-time, evening/weekend, online learning. Offers nutrition (MS); public health (MPH). *Application deadline:* Applications are processed on a rolling basis. *Application fee:* $50. Electronic applications accepted.

Program in Marriage and Family Therapy Expenses: Contact institution. *Financial support:* Career-related internships or fieldwork and unspecified assistantships available. Support available to part-time students. Financial award applicants required to submit FAFSA. *Program availability:* Part-time, evening/weekend. Offers marriage and family therapy (MA). *Application deadline:* Applications are processed on a rolling basis. *Application fee:* $50. Electronic applications accepted. *Director*, Dr. Rachel Diamond, E-mail: rdiamond@usj.edu.

Program in Special Education Expenses: Contact institution. *Financial support:* Career-related internships or fieldwork and unspecified assistantships available. Support available to part-time students. Financial award applicants required to submit FAFSA. *Program availability:* Part-time, evening/weekend. Offers autism spectrum disorders (Graduate Certificate); special education (MA). *Application deadline:* Applications are processed on a rolling basis. *Application fee:* $50. Electronic applications accepted.

School of Pharmacy and Physician Assistant Studies Expenses: Contact institution. *Financial support:* Career-related internships or fieldwork available. Offers pharmacy (Pharm D). *Application deadline:* Applications are processed on a rolling basis. *Application fee:* $50. Electronic applications accepted. *Dean*, Dr. Joseph Ofosu, 860-231-5451, E-mail: jofosu@usj.edu.

UNIVERSITY OF SAINT MARY, Leavenworth, KS 66048-5082

General Information Independent-religious, coed, comprehensive institution. *Enrollment:* 1,310 graduate, professional, and undergraduate students; 462 full-time matriculated graduate/professional students (284 women), 110 part-time matriculated graduate/professional students (81 women). *Enrollment by degree level:* 452 master's, 120 doctoral. *Graduate housing:* Room and/or apartments available on a first-come, first-served basis to single students; on-campus housing not available to married students. *Student services:* Career counseling, free psychological counseling. *Library* *facilities:* De Paul Library plus 1 other. *Collection:* Books: 75,000 (physical), 10,500 (digital/electronic); Serial titles: 15 (physical), 38,459 (digital/electronic); Databases: 63. Weekly public service hours: 68; students can reserve study rooms.

Computer facilities: 30 computers available on campus for general student use. A campuswide network can be accessed from student residence rooms and from off campus. Online class registration is available.
Website: http://www.stmary.edu/

General Application Contact: Dr. Ron Logan, Graduate Dean, 913-345-8288, Fax: 913-345-2802, E-mail: loganr@stmary.edu.

GRADUATE UNITS

Graduate Programs *Program availability:* Part-time, evening/weekend, online learning. Offers counseling psychology (MA); education (MA); elementary education (MA); enterprise risk management (MBA); finance (MBA); general management (MBA); health care management (MBA); human resource management (MBA); marketing and advertising management (MBA); nurse administrator (MSN); nurse educator (MSN); physical therapy (DPT); psychology (MA); special education (MA); teaching (MAT). Electronic applications accepted.

UNIVERSITY OF SAINT MARY OF THE LAKE–MUNDELEIN SEMINARY, Mundelein, IL 60060

General Information Independent-religious, men only, graduate-only institution. *Graduate housing:* Room and/or apartments guaranteed to single students; on-campus housing not available to married students. Housing application deadline: 8/1.

GRADUATE UNITS

Graduate and Professional Programs Offers liturgical studies (MA); ministry (D Min); pastoral studies (MA); theology (M Div). Electronic applications accepted.

UNIVERSITY OF ST. MICHAEL'S COLLEGE, Toronto, ON M5S 1J4, Canada

General Information Independent-religious, coed, graduate-only institution. *Graduate housing:* Rooms and/or apartments available on a first-come, first-served basis to single and married students. Housing application deadline: 8/15.

GRADUATE UNITS

Faculty of Theology *Program availability:* Part-time. Offers Catholic leadership (MA); eastern Christian studies (Diploma); religious education (Diploma); theological studies (Diploma); theology (M Div, MA, MRE, MTS, D Min, PhD, Th D); theology and Jewish studies (MA). Th D offered jointly with University of Toronto. Electronic applications accepted.

UNIVERSITY OF ST. THOMAS, St. Paul, MN 55105-1096

General Information Independent-religious, coed, university. *Enrollment:* 9,878 graduate, professional, and undergraduate students; 1,141 full-time matriculated graduate/professional students (649 women), 2,538 part-time matriculated graduate/professional students (1,315 women). *Enrollment by degree level:* 2,807 master's, 607 doctoral, 230 other advanced degrees. *Graduate faculty:* 172 full-time (68 women), 279 part-time/adjunct (137 women). Tuition and fees vary according to course load, degree level, campus/location and program. *Graduate housing:* Room and/or apartments available on a first-come, first-served basis to single students; on-campus housing not available to married students. Housing application deadline: 5/1. *Student services:* Campus employment opportunities, campus safety program, career counseling, child daycare facilities, exercise/wellness program, free psychological counseling, international student services, low-cost health insurance, multicultural affairs office, services for students with disabilities, writing training. *Library facilities:* O'Shaughnessy-Frey Library plus 7 others. *Collection:* Books: 502,033 (physical), 251,462 (digital/electronic); Serial titles: 16,463 (physical), 118,059 (digital/electronic); Databases: 406. Students can reserve study rooms.

Computer facilities: Computer purchase and lease plans are available. A campuswide network can be accessed from student residence rooms and from off campus. Online class registration is available.
Website: http://www.stthomas.edu/

General Application Contact: 651-962-8816, E-mail: gradmissions@stthomas.edu.

GRADUATE UNITS

College of Arts and Sciences Expenses: Contact institution. *Program availability:* Part-time, evening/weekend. Offers art history (MA); arts and sciences (MA, Ed D, Certificate, Graduate Certificate); Catholic studies (MA); choral (MA); creative writing and publishing (MA); English literature (MA); instrumental (MA); Kodaly (MA); leadership in music education (Ed D); museum studies (Graduate Certificate); Orff Schulwerk (MA); piano pedagogy (MA); teaching college English (Certificate). *Dean,* Dr. Yohuru Williams, 651-962-6001, Fax: 651-962-6004, E-mail: ywilliams@stthomas.edu.

College of Education, Leadership and Counseling Expenses: Contact institution. *Financial support:* Research assistantships, career-related internships or fieldwork, institutionally sponsored loans, scholarships/grants, and unspecified assistantships available. Support available to part-time students. Financial award application deadline: 8/1; financial award applicants required to submit FAFSA. *Program availability:* Part-time, evening/weekend, 100% online, blended/hybrid learning. Offers education leadership and administration (MA); education, leadership and counseling (MA, Ed D, Psy D, Certificate, Ed S); educational leadership and learning (Ed D); executive coaching (Certificate); K-12 administration (Ed S); leadership in student affairs (MA); organization development and change (Ed D); special education (MA, Certificate, Ed S); teacher education (MA). *Application deadline:* For fall admission, 7/15 priority date for domestic students, 7/15 for international students; for spring admission, 12/9 priority date for domestic students, 12/9 for international students; for summer admission, 4/3 for domestic and international students. Applications are processed on a rolling basis. Electronic applications accepted. *Dean,* Dr. Joseph L. Kreitzer, 651-962-6032, Fax: 651-962-4169, E-mail: jlkreitzer@stthomas.edu.

Graduate School of Professional Psychology Expenses: Contact institution. *Financial support:* Fellowships with partial tuition reimbursements, research assistantships, teaching assistantships, institutionally sponsored loans, and scholarships/grants available. Support available to part-time students. Financial award application deadline: 8/1; financial award applicants required to submit FAFSA. *Program availability:* Part-time, evening/weekend. Offers counseling psychology (MA, Psy D). *Application deadline:* For fall admission, 2/5 priority date for domestic students; for winter admission, 1/5 priority date for domestic students; for spring admission, 10/15 priority date for domestic students, 3/1 for international students. Electronic applications accepted. *Application Contact:* Melissa Anderson, Program Manager, 651-962-4669, Fax: 651-962-4651, E-mail: msanderson@stthomas.edu. *Chair,* Dr. Christopher S. Vye, 651-962-4666, E-mail: csvye@stthomas.edu.

Opus College of Business Expenses: Contact institution. Offers accountancy (MS); business (MBA, MS, MSBA); business administration (MBA, MSBA); executive business administration (MBA); health care business administration (MBA); health care communication (MS). *Application Contact:* Tiffany Cork, Director of Recruiting and Admissions, 651-962-8801, Fax: 651-962-4129, E-mail: ustmba@stthomas.edu. *Dean,* Dr. Stefanie Lenway, 651-962-4200, Fax: 651-962-4129, E-mail: ocbdean@stthomas.edu.

The Saint Paul Seminary School of Divinity Expenses: Contact institution. *Financial support:* Fellowships, research assistantships, institutionally sponsored loans, and scholarships/grants available. Support available to part-time students. Financial award application deadline: 4/1; financial award applicants required to submit FAFSA. *Program availability:* Part-time, evening/weekend. Offers pastoral ministry (MAPM); religious education (MARE); theology (MA). *Application deadline:* For fall admission, 6/1 priority date for domestic students. Applications are processed on a rolling basis. *Application fee:* $40. Electronic applications accepted. *Application Contact:* Ana Theisen, Recruiter/Admissions Counselor, 651-962-5069, Fax: 651-962-5790, E-mail: aztheisen@stthomas.edu. *Rector/Vice President,* Rev. Msgr. Aloysius R. Callaghan, 651-962-5052, Fax: 651-962-5790, E-mail: arcallaghan@stthomas.edu.

School of Engineering Students: 522 full-time (152 women), 360 part-time (107 women); includes 208 minority (97 Black or African American, non-Hispanic/Latino; 101 Asian, non-Hispanic/Latino; 10 Hispanic/Latino), 252 international. Average age 34. *Faculty:* 18 full-time (3 women), 34 part-time/adjunct (7 women). Expenses: Contact institution. *Financial support:* Federal Work-Study available. Financial award application deadline: 4/1; financial award applicants required to submit FAFSA. In 2017, 113 master's awarded. *Program availability:* Part-time, evening/weekend. Offers data science (MS); electrical engineering (MS); information technology (MS); manufacturing engineering (MS); manufacturing systems (Certificate); mechanical engineering (MS); medical device development (Certificate); regulatory science (MS); software engineering (MS); software management (MS); systems engineering (MS); technology leadership (Certificate); technology management (MS). *Application deadline:* For fall admission, 8/1 priority date for domestic students; for spring admission, 1/1 priority date for domestic students. Applications are processed on a rolling basis. *Application fee:* $50. Electronic applications accepted. *Application Contact:* Alison Thompson, Graduate Program Manager, 651-962-5597, Fax: 651-962-6419, E-mail: alison.thompson@stthomas.edu. *Dean,* Don Weinkauf, 651-962-5760, Fax: 651-962-6419, E-mail: dhweinkauf@stthomas.edu.

School of Law Students: 387 full-time (207 women); includes 65 minority (21 Black or African American, non-Hispanic/Latino; 1 American Indian or Alaska Native, non-Hispanic/Latino; 13 Asian, non-Hispanic/Latino; 20 Hispanic/Latino; 10 Two or more races, non-Hispanic/Latino), 9 international. Average age 25. 545 applicants, 64% accepted, 145 enrolled. *Faculty:* 29 full-time (8 women), 68 part-time/adjunct (26 women). Expenses: Contact institution. *Financial support:* In 2017–18, 364 students received support. Scholarships/grants available. Financial award application deadline: 7/1; financial award applicants required to submit FAFSA. In 2017, 5 master's, 122 doctorates awarded. *Program availability:* 100% online. Offers law (JD); organizational ethics and compliance (LL M, MSL); U.S. law (LL M). *Application deadline:* For fall admission, 8/1 priority date for domestic and international students. Applications are processed on a rolling basis. *Application fee:* $0. Electronic applications accepted. *Application Contact:* Cari Haaland, Assistant Dean for Admissions, 651-962-4872, Fax: 651-962-4876, E-mail: lawschool@stthomas.edu. *Dean,* Robert K. Vischer, 651-962-4838, Fax: 651-962-4881, E-mail: rkvischer@stthomas.edu.

School of Social Work Students: 79 full-time (75 women), 226 part-time (202 women); includes 55 minority (16 Black or African American, non-Hispanic/Latino; 1 American Indian or Alaska Native, non-Hispanic/Latino; 13 Asian, non-Hispanic/Latino; 10 Hispanic/Latino; 15 Two or more races, non-Hispanic/Latino). Average age 28. Expenses: Contact institution. *Financial support:* Fellowships, research assistantships, career-related internships or fieldwork, Federal Work-Study, institutionally sponsored loans, scholarships/grants, and unspecified assistantships available. Support available to part-time students. Financial award application deadline: 7/1; financial award applicants required to submit FAFSA. In 2017, 142 master's awarded. *Program availability:* Part-time, evening/weekend, blended/hybrid learning. Offers social work (MSW). Programs offered in collaboration with St. Catherine University. *Application deadline:* For fall admission, 1/10 for domestic and international students. *Application fee:* $0. Electronic applications accepted. *Application Contact:* Mary Palin, Graduate Admissions Counselor, 651-690-6185, Fax: 651-690-6549, E-mail: mbpalin@stkate.edu. *Interim Dean and Professor,* Dr. Corrine Carvalho, 651-962-6031, Fax: 651-962-6031, E-mail: clcarvalho@stthomas.edu.

UNIVERSITY OF ST. THOMAS, Houston, TX 77006-4696

General Information Independent-religious, coed, comprehensive institution. *Enrollment:* 3,312 graduate, professional, and undergraduate students; 360 full-time matriculated graduate/professional students (187 women), 984 part-time matriculated graduate/professional students (733 women). *Enrollment by degree level:* 1,258 master's, 75 doctoral, 11 other advanced degrees. *Graduate faculty:* 95 full-time (44 women), 72 part-time/adjunct (37 women). *Tuition:* Full-time $20,934; part-time $1163 per credit hour. *Required fees:* $250; $210 per semester. *Graduate housing:* Room and/or apartments available on a first-come, first-served basis to single students; on-campus housing not available to married students. *Student services:* Campus employment opportunities, campus safety program, career counseling, free psychological counseling, international student services, services for students with disabilities. *Library facilities:* Doherty Library. *Collection:* Books: 262,245 (physical), 2,496 (digital/electronic); Serial titles: 74,347 (physical), 74,347 (digital/electronic); Databases: 274. Weekly public service hours: 100.

Computer facilities: Computer purchase and lease plans are available. 441 computers available on campus for general student use. A campuswide network can be accessed from student residence rooms. Online class registration is available.
Website: http://www.stthom.edu/

General Application Contact: Dr. Ravi Srinivas, Associate Vice President for Academic Affairs, 713-525-3804, Fax: 713-525-6924, E-mail: srinivas@stthom.edu.

GRADUATE UNITS

Cameron School of Business Students: 136 full-time (73 women), 200 part-time (113 women); includes 155 minority (41 Black or African American, non-Hispanic/Latino; 1 American Indian or Alaska Native, non-Hispanic/Latino; 24 Asian, non-Hispanic/Latino; 81 Hispanic/Latino; 8 Two or more races, non-Hispanic/Latino), 99 international. Average age 31. 121 applicants, 97% accepted, 70 enrolled. *Faculty:* 26 full-time (10 women), 7 part-time/adjunct (1 woman). Expenses: Contact institution. *Financial support:* In 2017–18, 22 students received support, including research assistantships with partial tuition reimbursements available (averaging $3,000 per year); Federal Work-Study, scholarships/grants, unspecified assistantships, and state work-study, institutional employment also available. Support available to part-time students. Financial award application deadline: 4/15; financial award applicants required to submit FAFSA. In 2017, 186 master's awarded. *Program availability:* Part-time, evening/weekend. Offers business (MBA, MCTM, MIB, MSA, MSF). *Application deadline:* For fall admission, 7/15 for domestic and international students; for winter admission, 7/15 for domestic and international students; for spring admission, 11/15 for domestic students, 10/15 for international students. Applications are processed on a rolling basis. *Application fee:* $35. Electronic applications accepted. *Application Contact:* 713-525-2100, Fax: 713-525-2110, E-mail: cameron@stthom.edu. *Dean*, Dr. Beena George, 713-525-2100, Fax: 713-525-2110, E-mail: cameron@stthom.edu.

Center for Faith and Culture Students: 1 full-time (0 women), 10 part-time (8 women); includes 3 minority (1 Black or African American, non-Hispanic/Latino; 1 Asian, non-Hispanic/Latino; 1 Hispanic/Latino). Average age 51. 1 applicant, 100% accepted. *Faculty:* 1 full-time (0 women), 1 part-time/adjunct (0 women). Expenses: Contact institution. *Financial support:* In 2017–18, 6 students received support. Federal Work-Study, scholarships/grants, and state work-study, institutional employment available. Support available to part-time students. Financial award application deadline: 4/15; financial award applicants required to submit FAFSA. In 2017, 10 master's awarded. *Program availability:* Part-time. Offers faith and culture (MA). *Application deadline:* For fall admission, 7/1 for domestic students, 6/1 for international students; for spring admission, 11/1 for domestic students, 10/1 for international students. Applications are processed on a rolling basis. *Application fee:* $35. Electronic applications accepted. *Application Contact:* Dr. Adam Martinez, Program Director, 713-942-5066, E-mail: cfc@stthom.edu. *Director*, Fr. Donald S. Nesti, 713-942-5066, E-mail: cfc@stthom.edu.

Center for Thomistic Studies Students: 9 full-time (2 women), 22 part-time (2 women); includes 6 minority (1 Asian, non-Hispanic/Latino; 3 Hispanic/Latino; 2 Two or more races, non-Hispanic/Latino), 1 international. Average age 33. 11 applicants, 64% accepted, 7 enrolled. *Faculty:* 5 full-time (1 woman). Expenses: Contact institution. *Financial support:* In 2017–18, 18 students received support. Fellowships with tuition reimbursements available, teaching assistantships, Federal Work-Study, scholarships/grants, unspecified assistantships, and state work-study, institutional employment available. Support available to part-time students. Financial award application deadline: 2/1; financial award applicants required to submit FAFSA. In 2017, 4 master's, 4 doctorates awarded. *Program availability:* Part-time. Offers philosophy (MA, PhD). *Application deadline:* For fall admission, 2/1 priority date for domestic and international students. Applications are processed on a rolling basis. *Application fee:* $35. Electronic applications accepted. *Application Contact:* Valerie Hall, Administrative Assistant II, 713-525-3591, Fax: 713-942-3464, E-mail: hallvl@stthom.edu. *Director*, Dr. Thomas Osborne, 713-942-3483, Fax: 713-942-3464, E-mail: osborntm@stthom.edu.

Program in Liberal Arts Students: 11 full-time (9 women), 56 part-time (39 women); includes 26 minority (11 Black or African American, non-Hispanic/Latino; 1 Asian, non-Hispanic/Latino; 13 Hispanic/Latino; 1 Two or more races, non-Hispanic/Latino), 4 international. Average age 38. 27 applicants, 100% accepted, 25 enrolled. *Faculty:* 23 full-time (10 women), 13 part-time/adjunct (8 women). Expenses: Contact institution. *Financial support:* In 2017–18, 3 students received support. Federal Work-Study, scholarships/grants, and state work-study, institutional employment available. Support available to part-time students. Financial award application deadline: 4/15; financial award applicants required to submit FAFSA. In 2017, 23 master's awarded. *Program availability:* Part-time, evening/weekend. Offers liberal arts (MLA). *Application deadline:* Applications are processed on a rolling basis. *Application fee:* $35. Electronic applications accepted. *Application Contact:* Kate Henderson, Program Coordinator, 713-525-3556, Fax: 713-525-6924, E-mail: mla@stthom.edu. *Associate Vice President for Academic Affairs/Dean of Extended Programs/MLA Director*, Dr. Ravi Srinivas, 713-525-3804, Fax: 713-525-6924, E-mail: mla@stthom.edu.

School of Arts and Sciences Students: 4 full-time (3 women), 21 part-time (13 women); includes 18 minority (8 Black or African American, non-Hispanic/Latino; 10 Hispanic/Latino), 1 international. Average age 34. 8 applicants, 100% accepted, 8 enrolled. *Faculty:* 2 full-time (0 women), 5 part-time/adjunct (3 women). Expenses: Contact institution. *Financial support:* In 2017–18, 6 students received support. Federal Work-Study, scholarships/grants, and state work-study, institutional employment available. Support available to part-time students. Financial award application deadline: 4/15; financial award applicants required to submit FAFSA. In 2017, 8 master's awarded. *Program availability:* Part-time. Offers public policy administration (MPPA); sacred music (MSM). *Application deadline:* For fall admission, 7/15 priority date for domestic and international students; for spring admission, 12/1 priority date for domestic and international students; for summer admission, 5/1 priority date for domestic and international students. Applications are processed on a rolling basis. *Application fee:* $35. Electronic applications accepted. *Application Contact:* Elizabeth Kimes, 713-942-3491, E-mail: kimese@stthom.edu. *Dean, School of Arts and Sciences*, Dr. Christopher Evans, 713-525-7863, E-mail: evanscp@stthom.edu.

School of Education and Human Services Students: 119 full-time (97 women), 597 part-time (529 women); includes 478 minority (166 Black or African American, non-Hispanic/Latino; 29 Asian, non-Hispanic/Latino; 277 Hispanic/Latino; 2 Native Hawaiian or other Pacific Islander, non-Hispanic/Latino; 4 Two or more races, non-Hispanic/Latino), 19 international. Average age 36. 306 applicants, 91% accepted, 181 enrolled. *Faculty:* 33 full-time (22 women), 43 part-time/adjunct (26 women). Expenses: Contact institution. *Financial support:* In 2017–18, 27 students received support. Federal Work-Study, scholarships/grants, and state work-study, institutional employment available. Support available to part-time students. Financial award application deadline: 4/15; financial award applicants required to submit FAFSA. In 2017, 328 master's awarded. *Program availability:* Part-time, evening/weekend, online learning. Offers all level education (M Ed); bilingual/dual language (M Ed); Catholic school teaching (M Ed); Catholic/private school leadership (M Ed); counselor education (M Ed); curriculum and instruction (M Ed); education (Ed D); educational leadership (M Ed); elementary teaching (M Ed); English as a second language (M Ed); exceptionality/educational diagnostician (M Ed); exceptionality/special education (M Ed); generalist (M Ed); reading (M Ed); secondary teaching (M Ed); teaching (MAT). *Application deadline:* Applications are processed on a rolling basis. *Application fee:* $35. Electronic applications accepted. *Application Contact:* 713-525-3540, E-mail: education@stthom.edu. *Dean*, Dr. Paul C. Paese, 713-942-5999, Fax: 713-525-3871, E-mail: paesep@stthom.edu.

School of Theology Students: 80 full-time (3 women), 78 part-time (29 women); includes 64 minority (5 Black or African American, non-Hispanic/Latino; 24 Asian, non-Hispanic/Latino; 34 Hispanic/Latino; 1 Two or more races, non-Hispanic/Latino), 25 international. Average age 38. 56 applicants, 100% accepted, 18 enrolled. *Faculty:* 10 full-time (2 women), 7 part-time/adjunct (1 woman). Expenses: Contact institution. *Financial support:* In 2017–18, 9 students received support. Scholarships/grants available. Support available to part-time students. Financial award application deadline: 4/15; financial award applicants required to submit FAFSA. In 2017, 38 master's awarded. *Program availability:* Part-time. Offers divinity (M Div); pastoral studies (MAPS); theological studies (MA). *Application deadline:* Applications are processed on a rolling basis. *Application fee:* $10. Electronic applications accepted. *Application Contact:* E-mail: sms@stthom.edu. *Dean*, Dr. Sandra C. Magie, 713-686-4345 Ext. 242, Fax: 713-683-8673, E-mail: smagie@stthom.edu.

UNIVERSITY OF SAN DIEGO, San Diego, CA 92110-2492

General Information Independent-religious, coed, university. *Enrollment:* 8,905 graduate, professional, and undergraduate students; 1,624 full-time matriculated graduate/professional students (1,046 women), 1,335 part-time matriculated graduate/professional students (742 women). *Enrollment by degree level:* 2,003 master's, 955 doctoral, 1 other advanced degree. *Graduate faculty:* 165 full-time (73 women), 207 part-time/adjunct (103 women). *Graduate housing:* Room and/or apartments available on a first-come, first-served basis to single students; on-campus housing not available to married students. Typical cost: $12,980 (including board). Room and board charges vary according to board plan and housing facility selected. Housing application deadline: 5/1. *Student services:* Campus employment opportunities, campus safety program, career counseling, child daycare facilities, exercise/wellness program, free psychological counseling, international student services, low-cost health insurance, multicultural affairs office, services for students with disabilities, teacher training. *Library facilities:* Helen K. and James S. Copley Library plus 1 other. *Collection:* Books: 566,393 (physical), 834,947 (digital/electronic); Serial titles: 6,403 (physical), 75,037 (digital/electronic); Databases: 331. Weekly public service hours: 116; students can reserve study rooms. *Research affiliation:* Leon R. Hubbard Hatchery (marine science), Southwest Fisheries Science Center (marine science), Hubbs-SeaWorld Research Institute (marine science), Tijuana River National Estuarine Research Reserve (marine science), Old Globe Theater (dramatic arts).

Computer facilities: Computer purchase and lease plans are available. 951 computers available on campus for general student use. A campuswide network can be accessed from student residence rooms and from off campus. Online class registration is available.
Website: http://www.sandiego.edu/

General Application Contact: Monica Mahon, Associate Director of Graduate Admissions, 619-260-4524, Fax: 619-260-4158, E-mail: grads@sandiego.edu.

GRADUATE UNITS

College of Arts and Sciences Students: 38 full-time (16 women), 32 part-time (18 women); includes 22 minority (4 Black or African American, non-Hispanic/Latino; 4 Asian, non-Hispanic/Latino; 11 Hispanic/Latino; 3 Two or more races, non-Hispanic/Latino), 4 international. Average age 29. *Faculty:* 17 full-time (8 women), 5 part-time/adjunct (0 women). Expenses: Contact institution. *Financial support:* In 2017–18, 54 students received support. Fellowships, career-related internships or fieldwork, Federal Work-Study, institutionally sponsored loans, scholarships/grants, and unspecified assistantships available. Support available to part-time students. Financial award application deadline: 4/1; financial award applicants required to submit FAFSA. In 2017, 31 master's awarded. *Program availability:* Part-time, evening/weekend. Offers acting (MFA); arts and sciences (MA, MFA, MS); environmental and ocean sciences (MS); international relations (MA). *Application deadline:* Applications are processed on a rolling basis. *Application fee:* $45. Electronic applications accepted. *Application Contact:* Monica Mahon, Associate Director of Graduate Admissions, 619-260-4524, Fax: 619-260-4158, E-mail: grads@sandiego.edu. *Dean*, Dr. Noelle Norton, 619-260-4545.

Division of Professional and Continuing Education Students: 239 part-time (60 women); includes 88 minority (12 Black or African American, non-Hispanic/Latino; 18 Asian, non-Hispanic/Latino; 55 Hispanic/Latino; 3 Two or more races, non-Hispanic/Latino), 1 international. Average age 39. 197 applicants, 91% accepted, 118 enrolled. *Faculty:* 13 part-time/adjunct (1 woman). Expenses: Contact institution. *Financial support:* Application deadline: 4/1; applicants required to submit FAFSA. *Program availability:* Part-time-only, evening/weekend, 100% online. Offers cyber security operations and leadership (MS); law enforcement and public safety leadership (MS). *Application deadline:* For fall admission, 8/7 for domestic students; for spring admission, 12/3 for domestic students; for summer admission, 4/24 for domestic students. Applications are processed on a rolling basis. *Application fee:* $45. Electronic applications accepted. *Application Contact:* Monica Mahon, Associate Director of Graduate Admissions, 619-260-4524, Fax: 619-260-4158, E-mail: grads@sandiego.edu.

Hahn School of Nursing and Health Science Students: 238 full-time (198 women), 230 part-time (167 women); includes 230 minority (32 Black or African American, non-Hispanic/Latino; 104 Asian, non-Hispanic/Latino; 75 Hispanic/Latino; 19 Two or more races, non-Hispanic/Latino), 12 international. Average age 35. *Faculty:* 26 full-time (21 women), 36 part-time/adjunct (29 women). Expenses: Contact institution. *Financial support:* In 2017–18, 242 students received support. Scholarships/grants and traineeships available. Support available to part-time students. Financial award application deadline: 4/1; financial award applicants required to submit FAFSA. In 2017, 93 master's, 44 doctorates awarded. *Program availability:* Part-time, evening/weekend. Offers adult-gerontology clinical nurse specialist (MSN); adult-gerontology nurse practitioner/family nurse practitioner (MSN); clinical nurse leader (MSN); executive nurse leader (MSN); family nurse practitioner (MSN); healthcare informatics (MS, MSN); nursing (PhD); nursing practice (DNP); pediatric/family nurse practitioner (MSN); psychiatric-mental health nurse practitioner (MSN). *Application deadline:* Applications are processed on a rolling basis. *Application fee:* $45. Electronic applications accepted. *Application Contact:* Monica Mahon, Associate Director of Graduate Admissions, 619-260-4524, Fax: 619-260-4158, E-mail: grads@sandiego.edu. *Interim Dean*, Dr. Janes Georges, 619-260-4550, Fax: 619-260-6814, E-mail: nursing@sandiego.edu.

Joan B. Kroc School of Peace Studies Students: 71 full-time (58 women), 14 part-time (13 women); includes 33 minority (1 Black or African American, non-Hispanic/Latino; 3 Asian, non-Hispanic/Latino; 25 Hispanic/Latino; 4 Two or more races, non-Hispanic/Latino), 12 international. Average age 29. *Faculty:* 6 full-time (3 women), 3 part-time/adjunct (1 woman). Expenses: Contact institution. *Financial support:* In 2017–18, 35 students received support. Career-related internships or fieldwork, Federal Work-Study, institutionally sponsored loans, scholarships/grants, and unspecified assistantships available. Support available to part-time students. Financial award application deadline: 4/1; financial award applicants required to submit FAFSA. In 2017, 17 master's awarded. Offers conflict management and resolution (MS); peace and justice (MA); social innovation (MA). *Application fee:* $45. Electronic applications accepted. *Application Contact:* Monica Mahon, Associate Director of Graduate Admissions, 619-260-4524, Fax: 619-260-4158, E-mail: grads@sandiego.edu. *Dean*, Dr. Patricia Marquez, 619-260-7919, E-mail: krocschool@sandiego.edu.

School of Business Students: 199 full-time (86 women), 208 part-time (84 women); includes 110 minority (14 Black or African American, non-Hispanic/Latino; 25 Asian, non-Hispanic/Latino; 58 Hispanic/Latino; 4 Native Hawaiian or other Pacific Islander, non-Hispanic/Latino; 9 Two or more races, non-Hispanic/Latino), 99 international. Average age 31. *Faculty:* 38 full-time (10 women), 28 part-time/adjunct (9 women). Expenses: Contact institution. *Financial support:* In 2017–18, 168 students received support. Career-related internships or fieldwork, Federal Work-Study, institutionally sponsored loans, and scholarships/grants available. Support available to part-time students. Financial award application deadline: 4/1; financial award applicants required to submit FAFSA. In 2017, 211 master's awarded. *Program availability:* Part-time, evening/weekend. Offers accountancy (MS); business (MBA, MS, MSF, Certificate); business administration (MBA); executive leadership (MS); finance (MSF); global leadership (MS); real estate (MS); supply chain management (MS, Certificate); taxation (MS). *Application fee:* $80. Electronic applications accepted. *Application Contact:* Monica Mahon, Associate Director of Graduate Admissions, 619-260-4524, Fax: 619-260-4158, E-mail: grads@sandiego.edu. *Dean*, Dr. Jaime Alonso Gómez, 619-260-4886, E-mail: sbadean@sandiego.edu.

School of Law Students: 693 full-time (371 women), 96 part-time (40 women); includes 265 minority (31 Black or African American, non-Hispanic/Latino; 15 American Indian or Alaska Native, non-Hispanic/Latino; 97 Asian, non-Hispanic/Latino; 107 Hispanic/Latino; 4 Native Hawaiian or other Pacific Islander, non-Hispanic/Latino; 11 Two or more races, non-Hispanic/Latino), 28 international. Average age 27. 3,260 applicants, 238 enrolled. *Faculty:* 45 full-time (13 women), 46 part-time/adjunct (13 women). Expenses: Contact institution. *Financial support:* In 2017–18, 617 students received support. Career-related internships or fieldwork, Federal Work-Study, institutionally sponsored loans, and scholarships/grants available. Support available to part-time students. Financial award application deadline: 3/1; financial award applicants required to submit FAFSA. In 2017, 57 master's, 206 doctorates awarded. *Program availability:* Part-time, evening/weekend. Offers business and corporate law (LL M); comparative law (LL M); general studies (LL M); international law (LL M); law (JD); taxation (LL M, Diploma). *Application deadline:* For fall admission, 2/1 priority date for domestic students. Applications are processed on a rolling basis. Electronic applications accepted. *Application Contact:* Jorge Garcia, Assistant Dean, JD Admissions, 619-260-4528, Fax: 619-260-2218, E-mail: jdinfo@sandiego.edu. *Dean*, Dr. Stephen C. Ferruolo, 619-260-4527, E-mail: lawdean@sandiego.edu.

School of Leadership and Education Sciences Students: 385 full-time (317 women), 473 part-time (358 women); includes 355 minority (47 Black or African American, non-Hispanic/Latino; 1 American Indian or Alaska Native, non-Hispanic/Latino; 60 Asian, non-Hispanic/Latino; 209 Hispanic/Latino; 2 Native Hawaiian or other Pacific Islander, non-Hispanic/Latino; 36 Two or more races, non-Hispanic/Latino), 48 international. Average age 31. *Faculty:* 32 full-time (18 women), 74 part-time/adjunct (49 women). Expenses: Contact institution. *Financial support:* In 2017–18, 424 students received support. Career-related internships or fieldwork, Federal Work-Study, institutionally sponsored loans, unspecified assistantships, and stipends available. Support available to part-time students. Financial award application deadline: 4/1; financial award applicants required to submit FAFSA. In 2017, 273 master's, 15 doctorates awarded. *Program availability:* Part-time, evening/weekend. Offers clinical mental health counseling (MA); curriculum and instruction (M Ed); higher education leadership (MA); inclusive learning (M Ed); leadership and education sciences (M Ed, MA, PhD, Certificate); leadership studies (MA, PhD, Certificate); literacy and digital learning (M Ed); marital and family therapy (MA); nonprofit leadership and management (MA); school counseling (MA); school leadership (M Ed); special education (M Ed); STEAM (science, technology, engineering, arts, and mathematics) (M Ed); TESOL, literacy and culture (M Ed). *Application fee:* $45. *Application Contact:* Monica Mahon, Associate Director of Graduate Admissions, 619-260-4524, Fax: 619-260-4158, E-mail: grads@sandiego.edu. *Dean*, Dr. Nicholas Ladany, 619-260-4540, Fax: 619-260-6835, E-mail: nladany@sandiego.edu.

Shiley-Marcos School of Engineering Students: 43 part-time (2 women); includes 24 minority (8 Black or African American, non-Hispanic/Latino; 6 Asian, non-Hispanic/Latino; 10 Hispanic/Latino), 2 international. Average age 35. 45 applicants, 71% accepted, 21 enrolled. *Faculty:* 1 full-time (0 women), 2 part-time/adjunct (1 woman). Expenses: Contact institution. *Financial support:* In 2017–18, 2 students received support. Institutionally sponsored loans and scholarships/grants available. Financial award application deadline: 4/1; financial award applicants required to submit FAFSA. *Program availability:* Part-time, evening/weekend. Offers cyber security engineering (MS). *Application deadline:* For fall admission, 8/7 for domestic students; for spring admission, 12/3 for domestic students; for summer admission, 4/24 for domestic students. *Application fee:* $45. *Application Contact:* Monica Mahon, Associate Director of Graduate Admissions, 619-260-4524, Fax: 619-260-4158, E-mail: grads@sandiego.edu. *Dean*, Dr. Chell Roberts, 619-260-4627, E-mail: croberts@sandiego.edu.

UNIVERSITY OF SAN FRANCISCO, San Francisco, CA 94117-1080

General Information Independent-religious, coed, university. *Graduate housing:* Room and/or apartments available on a first-come, first-served basis to single students; on-campus housing not available to married students. Housing application deadline: 5/1. *Research affiliation:* NASA-Ames Research Center.

GRADUATE UNITS

College of Arts and Sciences *Program availability:* Part-time, evening/weekend. Offers arts and sciences (MA, MFA, MMS, MPA, MS, PSM); Asia Pacific studies (MA); biology (MS); biotechnology (PSM); chemistry (MS); computer science (MS); data science (MS); economics (MA, MS); energy systems management (MS); environmental management (MS); international and development economics (MA); international studies (MA); migration studies (MMS); museum studies (MA); professional communication (MA); public affairs (MPA); sport management (MA); urban and public affairs (MA); writing (MFA). Electronic applications accepted.

School of Education *Program availability:* Part-time, evening/weekend. Offers Catholic school leadership (Ed D); counseling (MA); digital media and learning (MA); digital technologies for teaching and learning (MA); education (MA, Ed D); international and multicultural education (MA, Ed D); leadership studies (MA, Ed D); learning and instruction (MA, Ed D); special education (MA, Ed D); teaching (MA); teaching reading (MA); teaching urban education and social justice (MA). Electronic applications accepted.

School of Law *Program availability:* Part-time, evening/weekend. Offers intellectual property and technology law (LL M); international transactions and comparative law (LL M); law (LL M, JD). Electronic applications accepted.

School of Management *Program availability:* Part-time, evening/weekend, online learning. Offers entrepreneurship and innovation (MBA); executive business administration (MBA); finance (MBA); financial analysis (MSFA); global entrepreneurial management (MGEM); health services administration (MPA); information systems (MS); management (MBA, MGEM, MNA, MPA, MS, MSFA, MSOD, MSRM); marketing (MBA); nonprofit administration (MNA); organization development (MSOD); public administration (MPA). Electronic applications accepted.

School of Nursing and Health Professions *Program availability:* Part-time, 100% online, blended/hybrid learning. Offers behavioral health (MS); clinical psychology (Psy D); health informatics (MS); nursing and health professions (MPH, MS, MSBH, MSN, DNP, Psy D); nursing practice (DNP); public health (MPH). Electronic applications accepted.

UNIVERSITY OF SASKATCHEWAN, Saskatoon, SK S7N 5A2, Canada

General Information Province-supported, coed, university. *Graduate housing:* Rooms and/or apartments available on a first-come, first-served basis to single and married students. *Research affiliation:* Canada Agriculture (agriculture research), Saskatchewan Research Council, University Hospital (cancer research), Innovation Place, Vaccine and Infectious Disease Organization/InterVac Laboratory (vaccinology and immunotherapeutics), Canadian Light Source.

GRADUATE UNITS

College of Dentistry Offers dentistry (DMD). Electronic applications accepted.

College of Graduate Studies and Research *Program availability:* Part-time. Electronic applications accepted.

College of Agriculture *Program availability:* Part-time. Offers agricultural economics (M Ag, M Sc, MA, PhD, PGD); agriculture (M Ag, M Sc, MA, PhD, Diploma, PGD); animal and poultry science (M Ag, M Sc, PhD); applied microbiology and food science (M Ag, M Sc, PhD); plant sciences (M Sc, PhD); soil science (M Ag, M Sc, PhD, Diploma).

College of Arts and Science *Program availability:* Part-time. Offers archaeology (MA, PhD); art and art history (MFA); arts and science (M Math, M Mus, M Sc, MA, MFA, PhD, Diploma); biology (M Sc, PhD); chemistry (M Sc, PhD); computer science (M Sc, PhD); drama (MA); economics (MA, Diploma); English (MA, PhD); geography (M Sc, MA, PhD); geological sciences (M Sc, PhD, Diploma); history (MA, PhD); languages and linguistics (MA); mathematics and statistics (M Math, MA, PhD); music (M Mus, MA); native studies (MA, PhD); philosophy (MA); physics and engineering physics (M Sc, PhD); political studies (MA); psychology (MA, PhD); religion and culture (MA); sociology (MA, PhD); women's and gender studies (MA, PhD). Electronic applications accepted.

College of Education *Program availability:* Part-time. Offers curriculum studies (M Ed, PhD, Diploma); education (M Ed, MC Ed, PhD, Diploma); educational administration (M Ed, PhD, Diploma); educational foundations (M Ed, MC Ed, PhD, Diploma); educational psychology and special education (M Ed, PhD, Diploma). Electronic applications accepted.

College of Engineering *Program availability:* Part-time. Offers biological engineering (M Eng, M Sc, PhD); biomedical engineering (M Eng, M Sc, PhD); chemical engineering (M Eng, M Sc, PhD); civil and geological engineering (M Eng, M Sc, PhD); electrical engineering (M Eng, M Sc, PhD, PGD); engineering (M Eng, M Sc, PhD, PGD); mechanical engineering (M Eng, M Sc, PhD). Electronic applications accepted.

College of Kinesiology Offers kinesiology (M Sc, PhD, Diploma).

College of Law *Program availability:* Part-time. Offers law (LL M, JD).

College of Nursing *Program availability:* Part-time. Offers nursing (MN).

College of Pharmacy and Nutrition Offers pharmacy and nutrition (M Sc, PhD).

Edwards School of Business *Program availability:* Part-time. Offers accounting (M Sc, MP Acc); agribusiness management (MBA); biotechnology management (MBA); business (M Sc, MBA, MP Acc); finance (M Sc); health services management (MBA); indigenous management (MBA); international business management (MBA); marketing (M Sc).

School of Environment and Sustainability Offers environment and sustainability (MES).

School of Public Policy Offers public policy (MIT, MPA, MPP, PhD).

Toxicology Centre Offers toxicology (M Sc, PhD, Diploma).

College of Medicine Offers anatomy and cell biology (M Sc, PhD); biochemistry (M Sc, PhD); community health and epidemiology (M Sc, PhD); medicine (M Sc, DPT, MD, PhD); microbiology and immunology (M Sc, PhD); obstetrics, gynecology and reproductive services (M Sc, PhD); pathology (M Sc, PhD); pharmacology (M Sc, PhD); physiology (M Sc, PhD); psychiatry (M Sc, PhD); surgery (M Sc).

Western College of Veterinary Medicine Offers large animal clinical sciences (M Sc, M Vet Sc, PhD); small animal clinical sciences (M Sc, M Vet Sc, PhD); veterinary anatomy (M Sc); veterinary anesthesiology, radiology and surgery (M Vet Sc); veterinary biomedical sciences (M Sc, M Vet Sc, PhD); veterinary internal medicine (M Vet Sc); veterinary medicine (M Sc, M Vet Sc, DVM, PhD); veterinary microbiology (M Sc, M Vet Sc, PhD); veterinary pathology (M Sc, M Vet Sc, PhD); veterinary physiological sciences (M Sc, PhD).

THE UNIVERSITY OF SCRANTON, Scranton, PA 18510

General Information Independent-religious, coed, comprehensive institution. CGS member. *Graduate housing:* Room and/or apartments available on a first-come, first-served basis to single students; on-campus housing not available to married students. *Research affiliation:* Allied Services (rehabilitation), Lackawanna River Corridor Association (environment), Universidad Iberoamericana (counseling and human services), Wyoming Valley Health Care System (nursing), Community Medical Center (health services), National Health Management Center (health care management).

GRADUATE UNITS

College of Arts and Sciences *Program availability:* Part-time, evening/weekend, 100% online. Offers arts and sciences (MA, MS); biochemistry (MS); chemistry (MS); clinical chemistry (MS); theology (MA). Electronic applications accepted.

Kania School of Management Offers accountancy (M Acc); accounting (MBA); finance (MBA); general business administration (MBA); health care management (MBA); international business (MBA); management (M Acc, MBA, MS); management information systems (MBA); marketing (MBA); operations management (MBA); software engineering (MS).

Panuska College of Professional Studies Offers clinical mental health counseling (MS); curriculum and instruction (MS); educational administration (MS); family nurse practitioner (MSN, PMC); health administration (MHA); human resources (MS); nurse anesthesia (MSN, PMC); nursing leadership (DNP); occupational therapy (MS); physical therapy (DPT); professional counseling (CAGS); reading education (MS); rehabilitation counseling (MS); school counseling (MS); secondary education (MS); special education (MS).

UNIVERSITY OF SIOUX FALLS, Sioux Falls, SD 57105-1699

General Information Independent-religious, coed, comprehensive institution. *Graduate housing:* Rooms and/or apartments available on a first-come, first-served basis to single and married students.

GRADUATE UNITS

Fredrikson School of Education *Program availability:* Part-time, evening/weekend. Offers educational administration (Ed S); leadership in reading (M Ed); leadership in schools (M Ed); leadership in technology (M Ed); teaching (M Ed). Admission in summer only.

Vucurevich School of Business *Program availability:* Part-time, evening/weekend. Offers entrepreneurial leadership (MBA); general management (MBA); health care management (MBA); marketing (MBA).

UNIVERSITY OF SOUTH AFRICA, Pretoria 0003, South Africa

General Information Private, coed, university.

GRADUATE UNITS

College of Agriculture and Environmental Sciences Offers agriculture (MS); consumer science (MCS); environmental management (MA, MS, PhD); environmental science (MA, MS, PhD); geography (MA, MS, PhD); horticulture (M Tech); human ecology (MHE); life sciences (MS); nature conservation (M Tech).

College of Economic and Management Sciences Offers accounting (D Admin, D Com); accounting science (DA); auditing (D Admin, D Com); business administration (M Tech); business economics (D Admin); business leadership (DBL); business management (D Admin, D Com); economic management analysis (M Tech); economics (D Admin, D Com, PhD); human resource development (M Tech); industrial psychology (D Admin, D Com, PhD); logistics (D Com); marketing (M Tech); public administration (D Admin, D Com, DPA, PhD); public management (M Tech); quantitative management (D Admin, D Com); real estate (M Tech); statistics (D Admin, PhD); tourism management (D Admin, D Com); transport economics (D Admin, D Com).

College of Human Sciences Offers adult education (M Ed); African languages (MA, PhD); African politics (MA, PhD); Afrikaans (MA, PhD); ancient history (MA, PhD); ancient Near Eastern studies (MA, PhD); anthropology (MA, PhD); applied linguistics (MA); Arabic (MA, PhD); archaeology (MA); art history (MA); Biblical archaeology (MA); Biblical studies (M Th, D Th, PhD); Christian spirituality (M Th, D Th); church history (M Th, D Th); classical studies (MA, PhD); clinical psychology (MA); communication (MA, PhD); comparative education (M Ed, Ed D); consulting psychology (D Admin, D Com, PhD); curriculum studies (M Ed, Ed D); development studies (M Admin, MA, D Admin, PhD); didactics (M Ed, Ed D); education (M Tech); education management (M Ed, Ed D); educational psychology (M Ed); English (MA); environmental education (M Ed); French (MA, PhD); German (MA, PhD); Greek (MA); guidance and counseling (M Ed); health studies (MA, PhD); history (MA, PhD); history of education (Ed D); inclusive education (M Ed, Ed D); information and communications technology policy and regulation (MA); information science (MA, MIS, PhD); international politics (MA, PhD); Islamic studies (MA, PhD); Italian (MA, PhD); Judaica (MA, PhD); linguistics (MA, PhD); mathematical education (M Ed); mathematics education (MA); missiology (M Th, D Th); modern Hebrew (MA, PhD); musicology (MA, MMus, D Mus, PhD); natural science education (M Ed); New Testament (M Th, D Th); Old Testament (D Th); pastoral therapy (M Th, D Th); philosophy (MA); philosophy of education (M Ed, Ed D); politics (MA, PhD); Portuguese (MA, PhD); practical theology (M Th, D Th); psychology (MA, MS, PhD); psychology of education (M Ed, Ed D); public health (MA); religious studies (MA, D Th, PhD); Romance languages (MA); Russian (MA, PhD); Semitic languages (MA, PhD); social behavior studies in HIV/AIDS (MA); social science (mental health) (MA); social science in development studies (MA); social science in psychology (MA); social science in social work (MA); social science in sociology (MA); social work (MSW, DSW, PhD); socio-education (M Ed, Ed D); sociolinguistics (MA); sociology (MA, PhD); Spanish (MA, PhD); systematic theology (M Th, D Th); TESOL (teaching English to speakers of other languages) (MA); theological ethics (M Th, D Th); theory of literature (MA, PhD); urban ministries (D Th); urban ministry (M Th).

College of Law Offers correctional services management (M Tech); criminology (MA, PhD); law (LL M, LL D); penology (MA, PhD); police science (MA, PhD); policing (M Tech); security risk management (M Tech); social science in criminology (MA).

College of Science, Engineering and Technology Offers chemical engineering (M Tech); information technology (M Tech).

Graduate School of Business Leadership Offers business leadership (MBA, MBL, DBL).

Institute for Science and Technology Education Offers mathematics, science and technology education (M Sc, PhD).

UNIVERSITY OF SOUTH ALABAMA, Mobile, AL 36688-0002

General Information State-supported, coed, university. CGS member. *Enrollment:* 15,569 graduate, professional, and undergraduate students; 3,619 full-time matriculated graduate/professional students (2,792 women), 962 part-time matriculated graduate/professional students (765 women). *Enrollment by degree level:* 3,402 master's, 1,075 doctoral, 104 other advanced degrees. *Graduate faculty:* 308 full-time (158 women), 143 part-time/adjunct (123 women). Tuition, state resident: full-time $10,104; part-time $421 per semester hour. Tuition, nonresident: full-time $20,208; part-time $842 per semester hour. *Graduate housing:* Room and/or apartments available on a first-come, first-served basis to single students; on-campus housing not available to married students. Typical cost: $3980 per year ($7490 including board). Room and board charges vary according to board plan and housing facility selected. Housing application deadline: 3/1. *Student services:* Campus employment opportunities, campus safety program, career counseling, exercise/wellness program, free psychological counseling, grant writing training, international student services, low-cost health insurance, multicultural affairs office, services for students with disabilities, teacher training, writing training. *Library facilities:* Marx Library plus 5 others. *Collection:* Books: 690,889 (physical), 40,397 (digital/electronic); Serial titles: 4,343 (physical), 1.2 million (digital/electronic); Databases: 669. *Research affiliation:* Radiation Therapy Oncology Group (oncology), National Institutes of Health (biomedical science), American College of Surgeons Oncology Group (oncology), Dauphin Island Marine Laboratory (marine sciences), Gynecologic Oncology Group (oncology), Eastern Cooperative Oncology Group (oncology).

Computer facilities: A campuswide network can be accessed from student residence rooms and from off campus. Online class registration is available.
Website: http://www.southalabama.edu/

General Application Contact: Dr. Harold Pardue, Dean, Graduate School, 251-460-6310, Fax: 251-461-1513, E-mail: hpardue@southalabama.edu.

GRADUATE UNITS

College of Arts and Sciences Students: 142 full-time (91 women), 41 part-time (20 women); includes 38 minority (22 Black or African American, non-Hispanic/Latino; 4 Asian, non-Hispanic/Latino; 5 Hispanic/Latino; 7 Two or more races, non-Hispanic/Latino), 1 international. Average age 28. 154 applicants, 45% accepted, 54 enrolled. *Faculty:* 81 full-time (28 women), 1 part-time/adjunct (0 women). Expenses: Contact institution. *Financial support:* Research assistantships, teaching assistantships, career-related internships or fieldwork, Federal Work-Study, institutionally sponsored loans, scholarships/grants, and unspecified assistantships available. Support available to part-time students. Financial award application deadline: 3/31; financial award applicants required to submit FAFSA. In 2017, 50 master's, 3 doctorates awarded. *Program availability:* Part-time, evening/weekend. Offers arts and sciences (MA, MFA, MM, MPA, MS, PhD); biological sciences (MS); collaborative keyboard (MM); communication (MA); creative technologies and practice (MFA); creative writing (MA); history (MA); literature (MA); marine conservation and resource management (MS); marine sciences (MS, PhD); mathematics (MS); music education (MM); performance (MM); psychology (MS); public administration (MPA); sociology (MA). *Application deadline:* For fall admission, 7/15 priority date for domestic students, 6/15 priority date for international students; for spring admission, 12/1 priority date for domestic students, 11/1 priority date for international students; for summer admission, 5/1 priority date for domestic students. Applications are processed on a rolling basis. *Application fee:* $35. Electronic applications accepted. *Application Contact:* Dr. Eric Loomis, Associate Dean, College of Arts and Sciences, 251-460-7811, Fax: 251-461-1744, E-mail: ejloomis@southalabama.edu. *Dean, College of Arts and Sciences*, Dr. Andrzej Wierzbicki, 251-460-6280, Fax: 251-460-7928, E-mail: awierzbicki@southalabama.edu.

College of Education and Professional Studies Students: 361 full-time (254 women), 142 part-time (109 women); includes 140 minority (106 Black or African American, non-Hispanic/Latino; 4 American Indian or Alaska Native, non-Hispanic/Latino; 10 Asian, non-Hispanic/Latino; 17 Hispanic/Latino; 3 Two or more races, non-Hispanic/Latino), 9 international. Average age 33. 258 applicants, 55% accepted, 112 enrolled. *Faculty:* 34 full-time (20 women), 20 part-time/adjunct (15 women). Expenses: Contact institution. *Financial support:* Fellowships, research assistantships, teaching assistantships, career-related internships or fieldwork, Federal Work-Study, institutionally sponsored loans, scholarships/grants, and unspecified assistantships available. Support available to part-time students. Financial award application deadline: 3/31; financial award applicants required to submit FAFSA. In 2017, 128 master's, 17 doctorates, 10 other advanced degrees awarded. *Program availability:* Part-time, evening/weekend. Offers art education (M Ed); clinical mental health counseling (MS); early childhood education (M Ed); education and professional studies (M Ed, MS, Ed D, PhD, Ed S); educational leadership (M Ed, Ed D); educational media (M Ed); educational media and technology (MS); elementary education (M Ed); exercise science (MS); health education (M Ed, MS); instructional design and development (MS, PhD); instructional leadership (Ed S); physical education (M Ed); reading education (M Ed); school counseling (M Ed); science education (M Ed); secondary education (M Ed); special education (M Ed); sport management (MS). *Application deadline:* For fall admission, 7/15 priority date for domestic students, 6/15 priority date for international students; for spring admission, 11/15 priority date for domestic students, 11/1 priority date for international students; for summer admission, 4/15 priority date for domestic students, 4/1 for international students. Applications are processed on a rolling basis. *Application fee:* $35. Electronic applications accepted. *Application Contact:* Dr. Susan Santoli, Director of Graduate Studies, 251-380-2738, Fax: 251-380-2758, E-mail: ssantoli@southalabama.edu. *Dean, College of Education*, Dr. Andrea M. Kent, 251-380-2738, Fax: 251-380-2748, E-mail: akent@southalabama.edu.

College of Engineering Students: 62 full-time (20 women), 23 part-time (0 women); includes 10 minority (5 Black or African American, non-Hispanic/Latino; 3 Asian, non-Hispanic/Latino; 2 Two or more races, non-Hispanic/Latino), 23 international. Average age 29. 115 applicants, 53% accepted, 22 enrolled. *Faculty:* 25 full-time (4 women), 3 part-time/adjunct (0 women). Expenses: Contact institution. *Financial support:* Fellowships, research assistantships, teaching assistantships, career-related internships or fieldwork, Federal Work-Study, institutionally sponsored loans, scholarships/grants, and unspecified assistantships available. Support available to part-time students. Financial award application deadline: 3/31; financial award applicants required to submit FAFSA. In 2017, 68 master's awarded. *Program availability:* Part-time. Offers chemical and biomolecular engineering (MS Ch E); civil, coastal, and environmental engineering (MSCE); computer engineering (MSCE); electrical engineering (MSEE); engineering (MS Ch E, MSCE, MSEE, MSME, D Sc); mechanical engineering (MSME); systems engineering (D Sc). *Application deadline:* For fall admission, 7/1 priority date for domestic students, 6/1 priority date for international students; for spring admission, 12/1 priority date for domestic students, 11/1 priority date for international students; for summer admission, 5/1 priority date for domestic students, 4/1 priority date for international students. Applications are processed on a rolling basis. *Application fee:* $35. Electronic applications accepted. *Application Contact:* Brenda Poole, Academic Records Specialist, 251-460-6140, Fax: 251-460-6343, E-mail: engineering@southalabama.edu. *Dean, College of Engineering*, Dr. John Steadman, 251-460-6140, Fax: 251-460-6343, E-mail: engineering@southalabama.edu.

College of Medicine Students: 338 full-time (151 women), 3 part-time (0 women); includes 86 minority (38 Black or African American, non-Hispanic/Latino; 2 American Indian or Alaska Native, non-Hispanic/Latino; 39 Asian, non-Hispanic/Latino; 4 Hispanic/Latino; 3 Two or more races, non-Hispanic/Latino), 8 international. Average age 25. *Faculty:* 181 full-time (54 women), 37 part-time/adjunct (11 women). Expenses: Contact institution. *Financial support:* Fellowships, research assistantships, teaching assistantships, career-related internships or fieldwork, institutionally sponsored loans, scholarships/grants, and unspecified assistantships available. Support available to part-time students. Financial award application deadline: 3/31; financial award applicants required to submit FAFSA. In 2017, 77 doctorates awarded. Offers basic medical sciences (PhD); medicine (MD). *Application deadline:* For fall admission, 11/15 for domestic and international students. *Application fee:* $75. Electronic applications accepted. *Application Contact:* Mark Scott, Director, Medical Admissions, 251-460-7176, Fax: 251-460-6278, E-mail: mscott@southalabama.edu. *Vice President of Medical Affairs/Dean of the College of Medicine*, Dr. John V. Marymont, 251-341-3030, Fax: 251-341-3994, E-mail: jmarymont@southalabama.edu.

College of Nursing Students: 2,163 full-time (1,905 women), 714 part-time (619 women); includes 882 minority (566 Black or African American, non-Hispanic/Latino; 26 American Indian or Alaska Native, non-Hispanic/Latino; 117 Asian, non-Hispanic/Latino; 102 Hispanic/Latino; 7 Native Hawaiian or other Pacific Islander, non-Hispanic/Latino; 64 Two or more races, non-Hispanic/Latino), 6 international. Average age 35. 918 applicants, 77% accepted, 522 enrolled. *Faculty:* 73 full-time (67 women), 112 part-time/adjunct (103 women). Expenses: Contact institution. *Financial support:* Fellowships, research assistantships, teaching assistantships, career-related internships or fieldwork, Federal Work-Study, institutionally sponsored loans, scholarships/grants, and unspecified assistantships available. Support available to part-time students. Financial award application deadline: 3/31; financial award applicants required to submit FAFSA. In 2017, 791 master's, 96 doctorates, 95 other advanced degrees awarded. *Program availability:* Part-time, online learning. Offers nursing (MSN, DNP); nursing administration (Certificate); nursing education (Certificate); nursing practice (Certificate). *Application deadline:* For fall admission, 2/15 for domestic students; for spring admission, 7/15 priority date for domestic students; for summer admission, 11/15 priority date for domestic students. Applications are processed on a rolling basis. *Application fee:* $100. Electronic applications accepted. *Application Contact:* Brenda Mosley, Academic Advisor II, 251-445-9400, Fax: 251-445-9416, E-mail: bmosley@southalabama.edu. *Interim Dean, College of Nursing*, Dr. Heather Hall, 251-445-9400, Fax: 251-445-9416, E-mail: heatherhall@southalabama.edu.

Graduate School Students: 33 full-time (15 women), 8 part-time (7 women); includes 5 minority (3 Black or African American, non-Hispanic/Latino; 1 Hispanic/Latino; 1 Two or more races, non-Hispanic/Latino). Average age 27. 108 applicants, 8% accepted, 9 enrolled. *Faculty:* 5 full-time (1 woman), 1 (woman) part-time/adjunct. Expenses: Contact institution. *Financial support:* Fellowships, research assistantships, teaching assistantships, career-related internships or fieldwork, Federal Work-Study, institutionally sponsored loans, scholarships/grants, and unspecified assistantships available. Support available to part-time students. Financial award application deadline: 3/31; financial award applicants required to submit FAFSA. In 2017, 3 master's, 10 doctorates awarded. *Program availability:* Part-time, evening/weekend. Offers basic medical sciences (MS); biology (MS); chemistry (MS); clinical and counseling psychology (PhD); environmental toxicology (MS); exposure route and chemical transport (MS). *Application deadline:* For fall admission, 7/1 priority date for domestic students, 6/1 priority date for international students; for spring admission, 12/1 priority date for domestic students, 11/1 priority date for international students. Applications are processed on a rolling basis. *Application fee:* $50. Electronic applications accepted. *Application Contact:* Deanna Cobb, Graduate School Services Specialist, 251-460-6310, E-mail: deannacobb@southalabama.edu. *Dean of the Graduate School*, John Harold Pardue, 251-460-6310, E-mail: hpardue@southalabama.edu.

Mitchell College of Business Students: 81 full-time (44 women), 10 part-time (2 women); includes 18 minority (9 Black or African American, non-Hispanic/Latino; 1 American Indian or Alaska Native, non-Hispanic/Latino; 5 Asian, non-Hispanic/Latino; 3 Hispanic/Latino), 10 international. Average age 33. 95 applicants, 42% accepted, 31 enrolled. *Faculty:* 14 full-time (3 women). Expenses: Contact institution. *Financial support:* Fellowships, research assistantships, teaching assistantships, career-related internships or fieldwork, Federal Work-Study, institutionally sponsored loans, scholarships/grants, and unspecified assistantships available. Support available to part-time students. Financial award application deadline: 3/31; financial award applicants required to submit FAFSA. In 2017, 28 master's, 2 doctorates awarded. *Program availability:* Part-time, evening/weekend. Offers accounting (M Acc); business administration (MBA, DBA); management (DBA); marketing (DBA). *Application deadline:* For fall admission, 7/15 for domestic students, 6/15 for international students; for spring admission, 12/1 for domestic students, 11/1 for international students; for summer admission, 1/31 for domestic students. *Application fee:* $35. Electronic applications accepted. *Application Contact:* Dr. Alex Sharland, Assistant Dean and Director of Graduate Studies, 251-460-6418, Fax: 251-460-6529, E-mail: mcobgraduate@southalabama.edu. *Dean, Business*, Dr. Bob Wood, 251-460-6419, Fax: 251-460-6529, E-mail: bgwood@southalabama.edu.

Pat Capps Covey College of Allied Health Professions Students: 365 full-time (287 women), 1 (woman) part-time; includes 14 minority (4 Black or African American, non-Hispanic/Latino; 1 American Indian or Alaska Native, non-Hispanic/Latino; 1 Asian, non-Hispanic/Latino; 2 Hispanic/Latino; 1 Native Hawaiian or other Pacific Islander, non-Hispanic/Latino; 5 Two or more races, non-Hispanic/Latino), 2 international. Average age 25. 902 applicants, 27% accepted, 96 enrolled. *Faculty:* 31 full-time (26 women), 5 part-time/adjunct (4 women). Expenses: Contact institution. *Financial support:* Fellowships, research assistantships, teaching assistantships, career-related internships or fieldwork, Federal Work-Study, institutionally sponsored loans, scholarships/grants, and unspecified assistantships available. Support available to part-time students. Financial award application deadline: 3/31; financial award applicants required to submit FAFSA. In 2017, 89 master's, 51 doctorates awarded. Offers allied health professions (MHS, MS, Au D, DPT, PhD); audiology (Au D); communication sciences and disorders (PhD); occupational therapy (MS); physical therapy (DPT); physician assistant studies (MHS); speech-language pathology (MS). *Application deadline:* For fall admission, 7/15 priority date for domestic students, 6/15 priority date for international students; for spring admission, 12/1 priority date for domestic students, 11/1 priority date for international students. Applications are processed on a rolling basis. *Application fee:* $35. Electronic applications accepted. *Application Contact:* Dr. Susan Gordon-Hickey, Associate Dean, College of Allied Health, 251-445-9250, Fax: 251-445-9259, E-mail: gordonhickey@southalabama.edu. *Dean, College of Allied Health*, Dr. Gregory Frazer, 251-445-9250, Fax: 251-445-9259, E-mail: gfrazer@southalabama.edu.

School of Computing Students: 74 full-time (25 women), 20 part-time (7 women); includes 12 minority (2 Black or African American, non-Hispanic/Latino; 1 American Indian or Alaska Native, non-Hispanic/Latino; 6 Asian, non-Hispanic/Latino; 1 Native Hawaiian or other Pacific Islander, non-Hispanic/Latino; 2 Two or more races, non-Hispanic/Latino), 43 international. Average age 29. 124 applicants, 53% accepted, 17 enrolled. *Faculty:* 18 full-time (2 women). Expenses: Contact institution. *Financial support:* Fellowships, research assistantships, teaching assistantships, Federal Work-Study, institutionally sponsored loans, scholarships/grants, and unspecified assistantships available. Support available to part-time students. Financial award application deadline: 3/31; financial award applicants required to submit FAFSA. In 2017, 89 master's awarded. *Program availability:* Part-time, evening/weekend. Offers computer science (MS); information systems (MS). *Application deadline:* For fall admission, 7/15 priority date for domestic students, 6/15 priority date for international students; for spring admission, 12/1 priority date for domestic students, 11/1 priority date for international students; for summer admission, 5/1 priority date for domestic students, 4/1 priority date for international students. Applications are processed on a rolling basis. *Application fee:* $35. Electronic applications accepted. *Application Contact:* Dr. Debra Chapman, Interim Graduate Director, 251-460-1599, Fax: 251-460-7274, E-mail: dchapman@southalabama.edu. *Dean, School of Computing*, Dr. Alec Yasinsac, 251-460-6390, Fax: 251-460-7274, E-mail: yasinsac@southalabama.edu.

UNIVERSITY OF SOUTH CAROLINA, Columbia, SC 29208

General Information State-supported, coed, university. CGS member. *Graduate housing:* Rooms and/or apartments available to single and married students. *Research affiliation:* E.I. du Pont de Nemours and Company (engineering, chemical engineering), Westinghouse/Savannah River Corporation (environmental restoration, hazardous waste remediation), Motorola Corporation–Energy Production Division (electrochemical engineering), Glaxo-Wellcome (pharmaceuticals), NCR Corporation (electrical and computer engineering).

GRADUATE UNITS

The Graduate School *Program availability:* Part-time, evening/weekend, online learning. Offers gerontology (Certificate). Electronic applications accepted.

Arnold School of Public Health *Program availability:* Part-time, online learning. Offers biostatistics (MPH, MSPH, Dr PH, PhD); communication sciences and disorders (MCD, MSP, PhD); environmental health science (MS); environmental quality (MPH, MS, MSPH, PhD); epidemiology (MPH, MSPH, Dr PH, PhD); exercise science (MS, DPT, PhD); general public health (MPH); hazardous materials management (MPH, MSPH, PhD); health education (MAT); health promotion, education, and behavior (MPH, MS, MSPH, Dr PH, PhD); health services policy and management (MHA, MPH, Dr PH, PhD); industrial hygiene (MPH, MSPH, PhD); physical activity and public health (MPH); public health (MAT, MCD, MHA, MPH, MS, MSP, MSPH, DPT, Dr PH, PhD, Certificate); school health education (Certificate). Electronic applications accepted.

College of Arts and Sciences *Program availability:* Part-time, evening/weekend. Offers anthropology (MA, PhD); applied statistics (CAS); archive management (MA); art education (IMA, MA, MAT); art history (MA); art studio (MA); arts and sciences (IMA, M Math, MA, MAT, MFA, MIS, MMA, MPA, MS, PSM, PhD, CAS, Certificate); biology (MS, PhD); biology education (IMA, MAT); chemistry and biochemistry (IMA, MAT, MS, PhD); clinical/community psychology (MA, PhD); comparative literature (MA, PhD); creative writing (MFA); criminology and criminal justice (MA, PhD); ecology, evolution and organismal biology (MS, PhD); English (MA, PhD); English education (MAT); experimental psychology (MA, PhD); foreign languages (MAT); French (MA); general psychology (MA); geography (MA, MS, PhD); geography education (IMA); geological sciences (MS, PhD); German (MA); historic preservation (MA); history (MA, PhD); industrial statistics (MIS); international studies (MA, PhD); linguistics (MA, PhD); marine science (MS, PhD); mathematics (MA, MS, PhD); mathematics education (M Math, MAT); media arts (MMA); molecular, cellular, and developmental biology (MS, PhD); museum administration (MA); museum management (Certificate); philosophy (MA, PhD); physics and astronomy (IMA, MAT, MS, PSM, PhD); political science (MA, MPA, PhD); public administration (MPA); public history (MA, Certificate); religious studies (MA); school psychology (PhD); sociology (MA, PhD); Spanish (MA); statistics (MS, PhD); studio art (MFA); teaching English to speakers of other languages (Certificate); theatre (MA, MAT, MFA); women's studies (Certificate). Electronic applications accepted.

College of Education *Program availability:* Part-time, evening/weekend, online learning. Offers art education (IMA, MAT); business education (IMA, MAT); counseling education (PhD, Ed S); curriculum and instruction (Ed D); early childhood education (M Ed, Ed D, PhD); education (IMA, M Ed, MAT, MS, MT, Ed D, PhD, Certificate, Ed S); educational administration (M Ed, PhD, Ed S); educational psychology, research (M Ed, PhD); educational technology (M Ed); elementary education (MAT, Ed D, PhD); English (MAT); foreign language (MAT); foundations in education (PhD); health education (MAT); higher education and student affairs (M Ed); higher education leadership (Certificate); language and literacy (M Ed, PhD); mathematics (MAT); physical education (IMA, MAT, MS, PhD); science (IMA, MAT); secondary (Ed D); secondary education (IMA, MAT, MT, Ed D, PhD); social studies (MAT); special education (M Ed, MAT, PhD); teaching (M Ed, Ed S); theatre and speech (MAT). Electronic applications accepted.

College of Engineering and Computing *Program availability:* Part-time, evening/weekend, online learning. Offers chemical engineering (ME, MS, PhD); civil engineering (ME, MS, PhD); computer science and engineering (ME, MS, PhD); electrical engineering (ME, MS, PhD); engineering and computing (ME, MS, PhD); mechanical engineering (ME, MS, PhD); nuclear engineering (ME, MS, PhD); software engineering (MS). Electronic applications accepted.

College of Hospitality, Retail, and Sport Management *Program availability:* Part-time, online learning. Offers hospitality, retail, and sport management (MIHTM, MR, MS); hotel, restaurant and tourism management (MIHTM); live sport and entertainment events (MS); public assembly facilities management (MS); retailing (MR). Electronic applications accepted.

College of Mass Communications and Information Studies Offers journalism and mass communications (MA, MMC, PhD); library and information science (MLIS, PhD, Certificate, Specialist); mass communications and information studies (MA, MLIS, MMC, PhD, Certificate, Specialist).

College of Nursing *Program availability:* Part-time, online learning. Offers acute care clinical specialist (MSN); acute care nurse practitioner (MSN, Certificate); adult nurse practitioner (MSN); advanced practice clinical nursing (MSN, Certificate); advanced practice nursing in primary care (MSN, Certificate); advanced practice nursing in psychiatric mental health (MSN, Certificate); clinical nursing (MSN); community mental health and psychiatric health nursing (MSN); community/public health clinical nurse specialist (MSN); family nurse practitioner (MSN); health nursing (MSN); nursing administration (MSN); nursing practice (DNP); nursing science (PhD); pediatric nurse practitioner (MSN); psychiatric/mental health nurse practitioner (MSN); psychiatric/mental health specialist (MSN); women's health nurse practitioner (MSN). Electronic applications accepted.

College of Social Work *Program availability:* Part-time. Offers social work (MSW, PhD). Electronic applications accepted.

Darla Moore School of Business *Program availability:* Part-time, evening/weekend, online learning. Offers accountancy (M Acc); business administration (MBA, PhD); business measurement and assurance (M Acc); economics (MA, PhD); human resources (MHR); international business administration (IMBA). Electronic applications accepted.

School of Music *Program availability:* Part-time. Offers composition (MM, DMA); conducting (MM, DMA); jazz studies (MM); music education (MM Ed, PhD); music history (MM); music performance (Certificate); music theory (MM); opera theater (MM); performance (MM, DMA); piano pedagogy (MM, DMA). Electronic applications accepted.

School of the Environment *Program availability:* Part-time, online learning. Offers earth and environmental resources management (MEERM); environment (MEERM). Electronic applications accepted.

School of Law Offers law (JD).

School of Medicine Offers biomedical science (MBS, PhD); genetic counseling (MS); medicine (MBS, MNA, MRC, MS, MD, PhD, Certificate); nurse anesthesia (MNA); psychiatric rehabilitation (Certificate); rehabilitation counseling (MRC, Certificate). Electronic applications accepted.

South Carolina College of Pharmacy *Program availability:* Part-time. Offers pharmaceutical sciences (MS, PhD); pharmacy (MS, PhD, Pharm D). Electronic applications accepted.

UNIVERSITY OF SOUTH CAROLINA AIKEN, Aiken, SC 29801

General Information State-supported, coed, comprehensive institution. *Enrollment:* 3,506 graduate, professional, and undergraduate students; 18 full-time matriculated graduate/professional students (15 women), 27 part-time matriculated graduate/professional students (18 women). *Enrollment by degree level:* 45 master's. *Graduate faculty:* 14 full-time (9 women). Tuition, state resident: full-time $13,254; part-time $552.25 per credit hour. Tuition, nonresident: full-time $28,368; part-time $1182.70 per credit hour. *Required fees:* $12 per credit hour. $25 per semester. Full-time tuition and fees vary according to course load. *Graduate housing:* Room and/or apartments available on a first-come, first-served basis to single students; on-campus housing not available to married students. Typical cost: $4942 per year ($7592 including board). Room and board charges vary according to board plan. Housing application deadline:

5/1. *Student services:* Campus employment opportunities, campus safety program, career counseling, child daycare facilities, exercise/wellness program, free psychological counseling, grant writing training, international student services, multicultural affairs office, services for students with disabilities, teacher training, writing training. *Library facilities:* Gregg-Graniteville Library. *Collection:* Books: 138,003 (physical), 382,370 (digital/electronic); Serial titles: 15,842 (physical), 110,572 (digital/electronic); Databases: 236. Weekly public service hours: 78; students can reserve study rooms. *Research affiliation:* VA Boston Healthcare System (Post Traumatic Stress Disorder (PTSD)), Dwight D. Eisenhower Army Medical Center (neuroscience), University of South Florida (psychology), Baruch College of the City University of New York (psychology), Illinois Institute of Technology (psychology), University of Rochester (psychology).

Computer facilities: 550 computers available on campus for general student use. A campuswide network can be accessed from student residence rooms and from off campus. Online class registration is available.
Website: http://www.usca.edu/

General Application Contact: Dan Robb, Associate Vice Chancellor for Enrollment Management, 803-641-3487, Fax: 803-641-3727, E-mail: danr@usca.edu.

GRADUATE UNITS

Program in Applied Clinical Psychology Students: 18 full-time (15 women), 13 part-time (11 women); includes 7 minority (3 Black or African American, non-Hispanic/Latino; 1 Asian, non-Hispanic/Latino; 1 Native Hawaiian or other Pacific Islander, non-Hispanic/Latino; 2 Two or more races, non-Hispanic/Latino). Average age 25. 36 applicants, 42% accepted, 8 enrolled. *Faculty:* 9 full-time (7 women). Expenses: Contact institution. *Financial support:* In 2017–18, 27 students received support, including 19 research assistantships with partial tuition reimbursements available (averaging $2,887 per year), 4 teaching assistantships with partial tuition reimbursements available (averaging $2,604 per year); career-related internships or fieldwork, Federal Work-Study, scholarships/grants, tuition waivers (partial), and unspecified assistantships also available. Financial award application deadline: 3/1; financial award applicants required to submit FAFSA. In 2017, 10 master's awarded. *Program availability:* Part-time. Offers applied clinical psychology (MS). *Application deadline:* For fall admission, 5/1 priority date for domestic and international students. Applications are processed on a rolling basis. *Application fee:* $45 ($100 for international students). Electronic applications accepted. *Application Contact:* Dan Robb, Associate Vice Chancellor for Enrollment Management, 803-641-3487, Fax: 803-641-3727, E-mail: danr@usca.edu. *Director,* Dr. Jane Stafford, 803-641-3358, Fax: 803-641-3720, E-mail: jstafford@usca.edu.

Program in Business Administration Students: 13 part-time (6 women), 1 international. Average age 37. 1 applicant. *Faculty:* 3 full-time (2 women). Expenses: Contact institution. *Financial support:* In 2017–18, 3 students received support. Scholarships/grants and tuition waivers (partial) available. Support available to part-time students. Financial award application deadline: 3/1; financial award applicants required to submit FAFSA. *Program availability:* Part-time, evening/weekend, online only, 100% online. Offers business administration (MBA). *Application deadline:* For fall admission, 8/6 for domestic and international students; for spring admission, 12/14 for domestic and international students. Applications are processed on a rolling basis. *Application fee:* $45 ($100 for international students). Electronic applications accepted. *Application Contact:* Dan Robb, Associate Vice Chancellor for Enrollment Management, 803-641-3487, Fax: 803-641-3727, E-mail: danr@usca.edu. *Dean for School of Business Administration,* Dr. Michael J. Fekula, 803-641-3340, E-mail: mickf@usca.edu.

Program in Educational Technology Students: 1 (woman) part-time. Average age 30. 5 applicants. *Faculty:* 2 full-time (0 women). Expenses: Contact institution. *Financial support:* Fellowships with partial tuition reimbursements, career-related internships or fieldwork, Federal Work-Study, scholarships/grants, tuition waivers (partial), and unspecified assistantships available. Support available to part-time students. Financial award application deadline: 3/1; financial award applicants required to submit FAFSA. In 2017, 2 master's awarded. *Program availability:* Part-time, evening/weekend, online only, 100% online. Offers educational technology (M Ed). Program offered with University of South Carolina in Columbia. *Application deadline:* Applications are processed on a rolling basis. *Application fee:* $45 ($100 for international students). Electronic applications accepted. *Application Contact:* Dan Robb, Associate Vice Chancellor for Enrollment Management, 803-641-3487, Fax: 803-641-3727, E-mail: danr@usca.edu. *Educational Technology Program Coordinator,* Dr. Erin Besser, 803-641-3712, E-mail: erinbe@usca.edu.

UNIVERSITY OF SOUTH CAROLINA UPSTATE, Spartanburg, SC 29303-4999

General Information State-supported, coed, comprehensive institution. *Graduate housing:* On-campus housing not available.

GRADUATE UNITS

Graduate Programs *Program availability:* Part-time, evening/weekend. Offers early childhood education (M Ed); elementary education (M Ed); informatics (MS); special education: visual impairment (M Ed).

UNIVERSITY OF SOUTH DAKOTA, Vermillion, SD 57069

General Information State-supported, coed, university. CGS member. *Enrollment:* 10,261 graduate, professional, and undergraduate students; 732 full-time matriculated graduate/professional students (453 women), 1,241 part-time matriculated graduate/professional students (711 women). *Enrollment by degree level:* 1,144 master's, 569 doctoral, 260 other advanced degrees. *Graduate faculty:* 364 full-time (163 women), 54 part-time/adjunct (31 women). *Graduate housing:* Rooms and/or apartments available on a first-come, first-served basis to single and married students. Housing application deadline: 5/1. *Student services:* Campus employment opportunities, campus safety program, career counseling, child daycare facilities, exercise/wellness program, free psychological counseling, grant writing training, international student services, low-cost health insurance, multicultural affairs office, services for students with disabilities, teacher training, writing training. *Library facilities:* I. D. Weeks Library plus 2 others. *Collection:* Books: 530,277 (physical), 112,215 (digital/electronic); Serial titles: 5,139 (physical), 68,439 (digital/electronic); Databases: 302. Weekly public service hours: 119; students can reserve study rooms.

Computer facilities: 975 computers available on campus for general student use. A campuswide network can be accessed from student residence rooms and from off campus. Online class registration is available.
Website: http://www.usd.edu/

General Application Contact: Brandy Durham, Graduate School Recruitment Coordinator, 605-658-6138, Fax: 605-677-6118, E-mail: grad@usd.edu.

GRADUATE UNITS

Graduate School Students: 732 full-time (453 women), 1,241 part-time (711 women); includes 240 minority (42 Black or African American, non-Hispanic/Latino; 53 American Indian or Alaska Native, non-Hispanic/Latino; 47 Asian, non-Hispanic/Latino; 47 Hispanic/Latino; 3 Native Hawaiian or other Pacific Islander, non-Hispanic/Latino; 48 Two or more races, non-Hispanic/Latino), 137 international. 1,844 applicants, 40% accepted, 515 enrolled. *Faculty:* 364 full-time (163 women), 51 part-time/adjunct (30 women). Expenses: Contact institution. *Financial support:* In 2017–18, 565 students received support. Research assistantships with partial tuition reimbursements available, teaching assistantships with partial tuition reimbursements available, career-related internships or fieldwork, Federal Work-Study, scholarships/grants, unspecified assistantships, and clinical assistantships available. Support available to part-time students. Financial award applicants required to submit FAFSA. In 2017, 570 master's, 219 doctorates, 88 other advanced degrees awarded. *Program availability:* Part-time, evening/weekend, 100% online, blended/hybrid learning. Offers interdisciplinary studies (MA). *Application deadline:* For fall admission, 7/20 for international students; for spring admission, 12/10 for international students. Applications are processed on a rolling basis. *Application fee:* $35. Electronic applications accepted. *Application Contact:* Graduate School, 605-658-6140, Fax: 605-677-6118, E-mail: grad@usd.edu. *Director of Graduate Education,* Brittany Wagner, 605-658-6140, Fax: 605-677-6118, E-mail: grad@usd.edu.

Beacom School of Business Expenses: Contact institution. *Financial support:* Research assistantships with partial tuition reimbursements, teaching assistantships with partial tuition reimbursements, career-related internships or fieldwork, Federal Work-Study, and unspecified assistantships available. Support available to part-time students. Financial award applicants required to submit FAFSA. *Program availability:* Part-time, evening/weekend, 100% online, blended/hybrid learning. Offers accounting (MP Acc); business administration (MBA, Graduate Certificate); business analytics (MBA, Graduate Certificate); health services administration (MBA); long term care management (Graduate Certificate); marketing (MBA, Graduate Certificate); operations and supply chain management (MBA, Graduate Certificate); professional accountancy (MP Acc). *Application deadline:* For fall admission, 6/1 priority date for domestic students, 5/1 priority date for international students; for spring admission, 10/1 priority date for domestic students, 9/1 priority date for international students; for summer admission, 3/1 for domestic students. Applications are processed on a rolling basis. *Application fee:* $35. Electronic applications accepted. *Application Contact:* Graduate School, 605-658-6140, Fax: 605-677-6118, E-mail: grad@usd.edu.

College of Arts and Sciences Expenses: Contact institution. *Financial support:* Research assistantships with partial tuition reimbursements, teaching assistantships with partial tuition reimbursements, career-related internships or fieldwork, Federal Work-Study, scholarships/grants, unspecified assistantships, and clinical assistantships available. Support available to part-time students. Financial award applicants required to submit FAFSA. *Program availability:* Part-time, online learning. Offers addiction studies (MSA); arts and sciences (MA, MNS, MS, MSA, Au D, PhD); audiology (Au D); biology (MS, PhD); chemistry (MS, PhD); clinical psychology (MA, PhD); communication studies (MA); computer science (MS); criminal justice studies (MSA); English (MA, PhD); health services administration (MSA); history (MA); human factors (MA, PhD); human resources (MSA); interdisciplinary studies (MSA); long term care administration (MSA); mathematics (MA, MS); organizational leadership (MSA); physics (MS, PhD); speech-language pathology (MA); sustainability (MS, PhD). *Application deadline:* Applications are processed on a rolling basis. *Application fee:* $35. Electronic applications accepted. *Application Contact:* Graduate School, 605-658-6140, Fax: 605-677-6118, E-mail: grad@usd.edu.

College of Fine Arts Expenses: Contact institution. *Financial support:* Research assistantships with partial tuition reimbursements, teaching assistantships with partial tuition reimbursements, Federal Work-Study, and unspecified assistantships available. Financial award applicants required to submit FAFSA. Offers art education (MFA); ceramics (MFA); collaborative piano (MM); conducting (MM); design/technology (MFA); directing (MFA); fine arts (MA, MFA, MM); graphic design (MFA); history of musical instruments (MM); music education (MM); music history (MM); music performance (MM); painting (MFA); photography (MFA); printmaking (MFA); sculpture (MFA); theatre (MA). *Application deadline:* Applications are processed on a rolling basis. *Application fee:* $35. Electronic applications accepted. *Application Contact:* Graduate School, 605-658-6140, Fax: 605-677-6118, E-mail: grad@usd.edu.

Sanford School of Medicine Expenses: Contact institution. *Financial support:* In 2017–18, 197 students received support. Fellowships with partial tuition reimbursements available, research assistantships with partial tuition reimbursements available, teaching assistantships with partial tuition reimbursements available, career-related internships or fieldwork, institutionally sponsored loans, scholarships/grants, traineeships, tuition waivers (partial), and unspecified assistantships available. Financial award application deadline: 5/1; financial award applicants required to submit FAFSA. *Program availability:* Part-time. Offers bioethics (Certificate); cardiovascular research (MS, PhD); cellular and molecular biology (MS, PhD); medicine (MS, MD, PhD, Certificate); molecular microbiology and immunology (MS, PhD); neuroscience (MS, PhD); physiology and pharmacology (MS, PhD). *Application deadline:* For fall admission, 4/15 for international students. Applications are processed on a rolling basis. *Application fee:* $35.

School of Education Expenses: Contact institution. *Financial support:* Research assistantships with partial tuition reimbursements, teaching assistantships with partial tuition reimbursements, career-related internships or fieldwork, Federal Work-Study, and unspecified assistantships available. Support available to part-time students. Financial award applicants required to submit FAFSA. *Program availability:* Part-time, evening/weekend, 100% online, blended/hybrid learning. Offers American Indian education (Certificate); counseling (MA, PhD, Ed S); curriculum and instruction (Ed D, Ed S); education (MA, MS, Ed D, PhD, Certificate, Ed S); educational administration (MA, Ed D, Ed S); elementary education (MA); English language learners (Certificate); exercise science (MA); human development and educational psychology (MA, PhD, Ed S); literacy leadership and coaching (Certificate); mental health counseling (Certificate); reading interventionist (Certificate); school psychology (PhD, Ed S); science, technology and math pedagogy (Certificate); secondary education (MA); special education (MA); sport management (MA); technology for education and training (MS). *Application deadline:* For summer admission, 3/1 for domestic students. Applications are processed on a rolling basis. *Application fee:* $35. Electronic applications accepted. *Application Contact:* Graduate School, 605-658-6140, Fax: 605-677-6118.

School of Health Sciences Expenses: Contact institution. *Financial support:* Research assistantships, teaching assistantships, career-related internships or fieldwork, Federal Work-Study, scholarships/grants, traineeships, and unspecified assistantships available. Financial award applicants required to submit FAFSA. *Program availability:* Part-time. Offers health sciences (MA, MPH, MS, MSW, DPT,

OTD, PhD, Graduate Certificate); occupational therapy (OTD); physical therapy (DPT); physician assistant studies (MS); post-professional clinical occupational therapy (OTD); public health (MPH); social work (MSW). *Application fee:* $35. *Application Contact:* Graduate School, 605-658-6140, Fax: 605-677-6118, E-mail: grad@usd.edu.

School of Law Expenses: Contact institution. *Financial support:* Research assistantships with partial tuition reimbursements, career-related internships or fieldwork, Federal Work-Study, scholarships/grants, and unspecified assistantships available. Financial award application deadline: 4/1; financial award applicants required to submit FAFSA. *Program availability:* Part-time. Offers law (JD). *Application deadline:* For fall admission, 3/1 priority date for domestic students. Applications are processed on a rolling basis. *Application fee:* $35. Electronic applications accepted. *Application Contact:* Admissions Officer/Registrar, 605-677-5444, E-mail: jean.henriques@usd.edu.

UNIVERSITY OF SOUTHERN CALIFORNIA, Los Angeles, CA 90089

General Information Independent, coed, university. CGS member. *Graduate housing:* Rooms and/or apartments available on a first-come, first-served basis to single and married students. *Research affiliation:* SETI Institute (astronomy/astrobiology), Rancho Los Amigos Medical Center (medicine), Children's Hospital Los Angeles (medicine), Doheny Eye Institute (medicine), House Ear Institute (medicine), Jet Propulsion Laboratory (engineering and technology).

GRADUATE UNITS

Graduate School Electronic applications accepted.

Annenberg School for Communication and Journalism *Program availability:* Part-time, evening/weekend, online learning. Offers communication (MA, MCM, MPD, MS, PhD); communication and journalism (MA, MCM, MPD, MS, PhD); communication management (MCM); culture and community (PhD); digital social media (MS); global and transnational communication (PhD); groups, organizations and networks (PhD); health communication and social dynamics (PhD); information, political economy and entertainment (PhD); journalism (MA, MS); new media and technology (PhD); public diplomacy (MPD); rhetoric, politics and public media (PhD); specialized journalism (MA); specialized journalism (the arts) (MA); strategic public relations (MA). Electronic applications accepted.

Dana and David Dornsife College of Letters, Arts and Sciences Offers American studies and ethnicity (PhD); applied mathematics (MA, MS, PhD); art history (MA, PhD); biology (MS); brain and cognitive science (PhD); chemistry (PhD); classical Chinese literature (MA, PhD); classical Japanese literature (MA, PhD); classics (MA, PhD); clinical science (PhD); comparative literature (PhD); comparative media and culture (PhD); computational biology and bioinformatics (PhD); computational molecular biology (MS); developmental psychology (PhD); earth sciences (MS, PhD); East Asian linguistics (PhD); East Asian studies (MA); economic development programming (MA, PhD); English (MA, PhD); geographic information science and technology (MS, Graduate Certificate); Hispanic linguistics (PhD); history (PhD); human behavior (MHB); integrative and evolutionary biology (PhD); letters, arts and sciences (MA, MHB, MMM, MPW, MS, PhD, Graduate Certificate); linguistics (MA, PhD); literature and creative writing (PhD); marine and environmental biology (MS); marine biology and biological oceanography (MS, PhD); mathematical finance (MS); mathematics (MA, PhD); modern Chinese literature (MA, PhD); modern Japanese literature (MA, PhD); modern Korean literature (MA, PhD); molecular and computational biology (PhD); molecular biology (PhD); neurobiology (PhD); neuroscience (MS, PhD); ocean sciences (MS, PhD); philosophy (MA, PhD); physical chemistry (PhD); physics (MA, MS, PhD); political science and international relations (PhD); professional writing (MPW); quantitative methods (PhD); Slavic languages and literatures (MA, PhD); Slavic linguistics (PhD); social psychology (PhD); sociology (PhD); Spanish and Latin American studies (PhD); statistics (MS); visual studies (Graduate Certificate). Electronic applications accepted.

Gould School of Law Offers comparative law for foreign attorneys (MCL); law (JD); law for foreign-educated attorneys (LL M).

Herman Ostrow School of Dentistry Offers biokinesiology (MS, PhD); craniofacial biology (MS, PhD, Graduate Certificate); dentistry (MA, MS, DDS, DPT, OTD, PhD, Graduate Certificate); occupational science (PhD); occupational therapy (MA, OTD); physical therapy (DPT). Electronic applications accepted.

Leonard Davis School of Gerontology *Program availability:* Part-time, online learning. Offers aging services management (MASM); biology of aging (PhD); gerontology (MA, MS, PhD, Graduate Certificate); long term care administration (MLTCA). PhD in biology of aging offered jointly with Buck Institute for Research on Aging. Electronic applications accepted.

Marshall School of Business Offers accounting (M Acc); business (M Acc, MBA, MBT, MBV, MMM, MS, PhD); business administration (MBA, MMM, MS, PhD); business taxation (MBT); entrepreneurship and innovation (MS). Electronic applications accepted.

Roski School of Fine Arts Offers art and curatorial practices in the public sphere (MA); fine arts (MA, MFA); new genres (MFA); painting/drawing (MFA); photography (MFA); sculpture (MFA). Electronic applications accepted.

Rossier School of Education Offers education (MAT, ME, MMFT, Ed D, PhD); educational counseling (ME); educational psychology (Ed D, PhD); higher education administration (Ed D); higher education administration and policy (PhD); K-12 leadership in urban school settings (Ed D); K-12 policy and practice (PhD); marriage, family and child counseling (MMFT); postsecondary administration and student affairs [PASA] (ME); school counseling (ME); teacher education in multicultural societies (Ed D); teaching (online) (MAT); teaching and teaching credential (MAT); teaching English to speakers of other languages (MAT). Electronic applications accepted.

School of Architecture Offers architecture (M Arch, MBS, MHP, MLA, PhD). Electronic applications accepted.

School of Cinematic Arts Offers animation and digital arts (MFA); cinema-television (MA); cinema-television (critical studies) (PhD); cinematic arts (MA, MFA, PhD); film and television production (MFA); interactive media (MFA); media arts and practice (PhD); motion picture producing (MFA); writing for screen and television (MFA). Electronic applications accepted.

School of Dramatic Arts Offers acting (MFA); dramatic writing (MFA). Electronic applications accepted.

School of Pharmacy Offers clinical and experimental therapeutics (PhD); clinical research design and management (Graduate Certificate); food safety (Graduate Certificate); healthcare decision analysis (MS); patient and product safety (Graduate Certificate); pharmaceutical economics and policy (MS, PhD); pharmacology and pharmaceutical sciences (MS, PhD); pharmacy (MS, DRSc, PhD, Pharm D, Graduate Certificate); preclinical drug development (Graduate Certificate); regulatory and clinical affairs (Graduate Certificate); regulatory science (MS, DRSc).

School of Social Work Offers community organization, planning and administration (MSW); families and children (MSW); health (MSW); mental health (MSW); military social work and veterans services (MSW); older adults (MSW); public child welfare (MSW); school settings (MSW); social work (MSW, PhD); systems of mental illness recovery (MSW); work and life (MSW). Electronic applications accepted.

Sol Price School of Public Policy Offers ambulatory care (Graduate Certificate); health administration (EMHA, MHA, Graduate Certificate); homeland security and public policy (Graduate Certificate); international public policy and management (MPPM); leadership (EML); long-term care (Graduate Certificate); nonprofit management and policy (Graduate Certificate); policy, planning, and development (DPPD); political management (Graduate Certificate); public administration (MPA); public management (Graduate Certificate); public policy (EMHA, EML, M Pl, MHA, MPA, MPP, MPPM, MRED, DPPD, PhD, Graduate Certificate); public policy and management (PhD); real estate development (MRED); sustainable cities (Graduate Certificate); transportation systems (Graduate Certificate); urban planning (M Pl); urban planning and development (PhD). Electronic applications accepted.

Thornton School of Music *Program availability:* Part-time, evening/weekend. Offers brass performance (MM, DMA, Graduate Certificate); choral and sacred music (MM, DMA); classical guitar (MM, DMA, Graduate Certificate); composition (MM, DMA); early music (MA, DMA); harp performance (MM, DMA, Graduate Certificate); historical musicology (PhD); jazz studies (MM, DMA, Graduate Certificate); keyboard collaborative arts (MM, DMA, Graduate Certificate); music education (MM, DMA); organ performance (MM, DMA, Graduate Certificate); percussion performance (MM, DMA, Graduate Certificate); piano performance (MM, DMA, Graduate Certificate); scoring for motion pictures and television (Graduate Certificate); strings performance (MM, DMA, Graduate Certificate); studio jazz guitar (MM, DMA, Graduate Certificate); teaching music (MA); vocal arts (classical voice/opera) (MM, DMA, Graduate Certificate); woodwind performance (MM, DMA, Graduate Certificate). Electronic applications accepted.

Viterbi School of Engineering *Program availability:* Part-time, online learning. Offers aerospace and mechanical engineering: computational fluid and solid mechanics (MS); aerospace and mechanical engineering: dynamics and control (MS); aerospace engineering (MS, PhD, Engr); applied mechanics (MS); astronautical engineering (MS, PhD, Engr, Graduate Certificate); biomedical engineering (PhD); chemical engineering (MS, PhD, Engr); civil engineering (MS, PhD); computer engineering (MS, PhD); computer networks (MS); computer science (MS, PhD); computer security (MS); computer-aided engineering (ME, Graduate Certificate); construction management (MCM); digital supply chain management (MS); electric power (MS); electrical engineering (MS, PhD, Engr); engineering (MCM, ME, MS, PhD, Engr, Graduate Certificate); engineering management (MS); engineering technology commercialization (Graduate Certificate); engineering technology communication (Graduate Certificate); environmental engineering (MS, PhD); environmental quality management (ME); game development (MS); geoscience technologies (MS); green technologies (MS); health systems operations (Graduate Certificate); high performance computing and simulations (MS); human language technology (MS); industrial and systems engineering (MS, PhD, Engr); intelligent robotics (MS); manufacturing engineering (MS); materials engineering (MS); materials science (MS, PhD, Engr); mechanical engineering (MS, PhD, Engr); medical device and diagnostic engineering (MS); medical imaging and imaging informatics (MS); multimedia and creative technologies (MS); operations research engineering (MS); optimization and supply chain management (Graduate Certificate); petroleum engineering (MS, PhD, Engr); product development engineering (MS); safety systems and security (MS); smart oilfield technologies (MS, Graduate Certificate); software engineering (MS); structural design (ME); sustainable cities (Graduate Certificate); systems architecting and engineering (MS, Graduate Certificate); systems safety and security (Graduate Certificate); telecommunications (MS); transportation systems (MS, Graduate Certificate); VLSI design (MS); water and waste management (MS); wireless health technology (MS). Electronic applications accepted.

Keck School of Medicine Students: 1,663 full-time (991 women), 82 part-time (62 women); includes 899 minority (96 Black or African American, non-Hispanic/Latino; 3 American Indian or Alaska Native, non-Hispanic/Latino; 503 Asian, non-Hispanic/Latino; 234 Hispanic/Latino; 7 Native Hawaiian or other Pacific Islander, non-Hispanic/Latino; 56 Two or more races, non-Hispanic/Latino), 178 international. Average age 25. 10,290 applicants, 11% accepted, 588 enrolled. *Faculty:* 320 full-time (114 women), 54 part-time/adjunct (28 women). Expenses: Contact institution. *Financial support:* In 2017–18, 211 students received support. Fellowships, research assistantships, teaching assistantships, career-related internships or fieldwork, Federal Work-Study, institutionally sponsored loans, scholarships/grants, traineeships, and health care benefits available. Support available to part-time students. Financial award applicants required to submit FAFSA. In 2017, 328 master's, 218 doctorates awarded. Offers cancer biology and genomics (PhD); development, stem cell and regenerative medicine (PhD); medical biology (PhD); medical biophysics (PhD); medicine (MPAP, MPH, MS, DNAP, MD, PhD, Certificate); nurse anesthesia (DNAP). *Application deadline:* Applications are processed on a rolling basis. *Application fee:* $90. Electronic applications accepted. *Application Contact:* Marisela Zuniga, Department Business Administrator, 323-442-1607, Fax: 323-442-1199, E-mail: mzuniga@usc.edu. *Dean,* Dr. Rohit Varma, 323-442-1900.

Graduate Programs in Medicine Students: 943 full-time (652 women), 82 part-time (62 women); includes 486 minority (51 Black or African American, non-Hispanic/Latino; 2 American Indian or Alaska Native, non-Hispanic/Latino; 245 Asian, non-Hispanic/Latino; 159 Hispanic/Latino; 6 Native Hawaiian or other Pacific Islander, non-Hispanic/Latino; 23 Two or more races, non-Hispanic/Latino), 177 international. Average age 26. 2,191 applicants, 32% accepted, 402 enrolled. *Faculty:* 320 full-time (114 women), 54 part-time/adjunct (28 women). Expenses: Contact institution. *Financial support:* Fellowships, research assistantships, teaching assistantships, career-related internships or fieldwork, Federal Work-Study, institutionally sponsored loans, scholarships/grants, traineeships, and health care benefits available. Support available to part-time students. Financial award applicants required to submit CSS PROFILE or FAFSA. In 2017, 328 master's, 19 doctorates awarded. Offers applied biostatistics and epidemiology (MS); biochemistry and molecular biology (MS); biomedical and biological sciences (PhD); biostatistics (MS, PhD); biostatistics and epidemiology (MPH); biotechnology (MS); child and family health (MPH); environmental health (MPH); epidemiology (PhD); experimental and molecular pathology (MS); geohealth (MPH); global health leadership (MPH); global medicine (MS, Certificate); health behavior research (PhD); health communication (MPH); health education and promotion (MPH); medicine (MPAP, MPH, MS, PhD, Certificate); molecular epidemiology (MS); molecular microbiology and immunology (MS); physiology and biophysics (MS); primary care physician assistant (MPAP); public health (MPH); public health policy (MPH); stem cell biology and regenerative medicine (MS). *Application deadline:* Applications are processed on a rolling basis. *Application fee:* $90. Electronic applications accepted. *Application Contact:* Marisela Zuniga, Administrative Coordinator, 323-442-1607, Fax:

323-442-1199, E-mail: mzuniga@usc.edu. *Associate Dean for Graduate Affairs*, Dr. Ite Offringa, 323-442-1607, Fax: 323-442-1199, E-mail: ilaird@usc.edu.

UNIVERSITY OF SOUTHERN INDIANA, Evansville, IN 47712-3590

General Information State-supported, coed, comprehensive institution. CGS member. *Enrollment:* 9,014 graduate, professional, and undergraduate students; 714 full-time matriculated graduate/professional students (464 women), 594 part-time matriculated graduate/professional students (420 women). *Enrollment by degree level:* 1,215 master's, 26 doctoral, 67 other advanced degrees. *Graduate faculty:* 118 full-time (57 women), 14 part-time/adjunct (6 women). Tuition, state resident: full-time $9394. Tuition, nonresident: full-time $17,917. *Required fees:* $510. *Graduate housing:* Room and/or apartments available on a first-come, first-served basis to single students; on-campus housing not available to married students. Housing application deadline: 3/1. *Student services:* Campus employment opportunities, campus safety program, career counseling, child daycare facilities, exercise/wellness program, free psychological counseling, international student services, low-cost health insurance, multicultural affairs office, services for students with disabilities. *Library facilities:* David L. Rice Library. *Collection:* Books: 241,710 (physical), 230,844 (digital/electronic); Serial titles: 1,075 (physical), 141,229 (digital/electronic); Databases: 168. Weekly public service hours: 114; students can reserve study rooms.

Computer facilities: 1,165 computers available on campus for general student use. A campuswide network can be accessed from student residence rooms and from off campus. Online class registration is available.
Website: http://www.usi.edu/

General Application Contact: Dr. Mayola Rowser, Director, Graduate Studies, 812-465-7015, Fax: 812-464-1956, E-mail: mrowser@usi.edu.

GRADUATE UNITS

Graduate Studies Students: 714 full-time (464 women), 594 part-time (420 women); includes 166 minority (83 Black or African American, non-Hispanic/Latino; 3 American Indian or Alaska Native, non-Hispanic/Latino; 22 Asian, non-Hispanic/Latino; 38 Hispanic/Latino; 1 Native Hawaiian or other Pacific Islander, non-Hispanic/Latino; 19 Two or more races, non-Hispanic/Latino), 34 international. Average age 33. 1,045 applicants, 54% accepted, 509 enrolled. *Faculty:* 118 full-time (57 women), 14 part-time/adjunct (6 women). Expenses: Contact institution. *Financial support:* In 2017–18, 69 students received support. Federal Work-Study, scholarships/grants, tuition waivers (full and partial), and unspecified assistantships available. Financial award application deadline: 3/1; financial award applicants required to submit FAFSA. In 2017, 285 master's, 10 doctorates, 18 other advanced degrees awarded. *Program availability:* Part-time, evening/weekend. *Application deadline:* Applications are processed on a rolling basis. *Application fee:* $40. Electronic applications accepted. *Director*, Dr. Mayola Rowser, 812-465-7015, Fax: 812-464-1956, E-mail: mrowser@usi.edu.

College of Liberal Arts Students: 153 full-time (124 women), 34 part-time (27 women); includes 24 minority (12 Black or African American, non-Hispanic/Latino; 3 Asian, non-Hispanic/Latino; 6 Hispanic/Latino; 3 Two or more races, non-Hispanic/Latino), 11 international. Average age 31. *Faculty:* 58 full-time (33 women), 7 part-time/adjunct (2 women). Expenses: Contact institution. *Financial support:* In 2017–18, 27 students received support. Federal Work-Study, scholarships/grants, tuition waivers (full and partial), and unspecified assistantships available. Financial award application deadline: 3/1; financial award applicants required to submit FAFSA. In 2017, 88 master's awarded. *Program availability:* Part-time, evening/weekend. Offers communication (MA); English (MA); liberal arts (MA, MALS, MPA, MSW); liberal studies (MALS); nonprofit administration (MPA); public sector administration (MPA); second language acquisition, policy, and culture (MA); social work (MSW). *Application deadline:* Applications are processed on a rolling basis. *Application fee:* $40. Electronic applications accepted. *Application Contact:* Dr. Mayola Rowser, Director, Graduate Studies, 812-465-7015, E-mail: mrowser@usi.edu. *Dean*, Dr. James M. Beeby, 812-464-1853, E-mail: jmbeeby@usi.edu.

College of Nursing and Health Professions Students: 193 full-time (152 women), 375 part-time (317 women); includes 57 minority (23 Black or African American, non-Hispanic/Latino; 3 American Indian or Alaska Native, non-Hispanic/Latino; 11 Asian, non-Hispanic/Latino; 14 Hispanic/Latino; 1 Native Hawaiian or other Pacific Islander, non-Hispanic/Latino; 5 Two or more races, non-Hispanic/Latino), 5 international. Average age 34. *Faculty:* 13 full-time (9 women), 2 part-time/adjunct (both women). Expenses: Contact institution. *Financial support:* In 2017–18, 10 students received support. Federal Work-Study, scholarships/grants, tuition waivers (full and partial), and unspecified assistantships available. Financial award application deadline: 3/1; financial award applicants required to submit FAFSA. In 2017, 121 master's, 10 doctorates, 18 other advanced degrees awarded. *Program availability:* Part-time, blended/hybrid learning. Offers adult-gerontology acute care nurse practitioner (MSN, PMC); adult-gerontology clinical nurse specialist (MSN, PMC); adult-gerontology primary care nurse practitioner (MSN, PMC); advanced nursing practice (DNP); family nurse practiioner (MSN); family nurse practitioner (PMC); health administration (MHA); nursing and health professions (MHA, MSN, MSOT, DNP, PMC); nursing education (MSN, PMC); nursing management and leadership (MSN, PMC); occupational therapy (MSOT); organizational and systems leadership (DNP); psychiatric mental health nurse practitioner (MSN, PMC). *Application deadline:* For fall admission, 2/1 for domestic and international students. Applications are processed on a rolling basis. *Application fee:* $40. Electronic applications accepted. *Application Contact:* Dr. Mayola Rowser, Director, Graduate Studies, 812-465-7015, Fax: 812-464-1956, E-mail: mrowser@usi.edu. *Dean*, Dr. Ann White, 812-465-1151, E-mail: awhite@usi.edu.

Pott College of Science, Engineering, and Education Students: 51 full-time (18 women), 24 part-time (14 women); includes 11 minority (5 Black or African American, non-Hispanic/Latino; 4 Hispanic/Latino; 2 Two or more races, non-Hispanic/Latino), 6 international. Average age 29. *Faculty:* 21 full-time (10 women), 3 part-time/adjunct (2 women). Expenses: Contact institution. *Financial support:* In 2017–18, 16 students received support. Federal Work-Study, scholarships/grants, tuition waivers (full and partial), and unspecified assistantships available. Financial award application deadline: 3/1; financial award applicants required to submit FAFSA. In 2017, 20 master's awarded. *Program availability:* Part-time, evening/weekend. Offers administrative leadership (Ed D); educational leadership (Ed D); elementary education (MSE); industrial management (MSIM); pedagogical leadership (Ed D); school administration and leadership (MSE); science, engineering, and education (MSE, MSIM, MSSM, Ed D); secondary education (MSE); sport management (MSSM). *Application deadline:* For fall admission, 8/15 priority date for domestic students, 3/1 priority date for international students. Applications are processed on a rolling basis. *Application fee:* $40. Electronic applications accepted. *Application Contact:* Dr. Mayola Rowser, Director, Graduate Studies, 812-465-7015, Fax: 812-464-1956, E-mail: mrowser@usi.edu. *Dean*, Dr. Zane W. Mitchell, 812-465-7137, E-mail: zwmitchell@usi.edu.

Romain College of Business Students: 312 full-time (167 women), 148 part-time (56 women); includes 72 minority (43 Black or African American, non-Hispanic/Latino; 8 Asian, non-Hispanic/Latino; 13 Hispanic/Latino; 8 Two or more races, non-Hispanic/Latino), 10 international. Average age 33. *Faculty:* 22 full-time (4 women), 2 part-time/adjunct (0 women). Expenses: Contact institution. *Financial support:* In 2017–18, 18 students received support. Career-related internships or fieldwork, Federal Work-Study, scholarships/grants, tuition waivers (full and partial), and unspecified assistantships available. Financial award application deadline: 3/1; financial award applicants required to submit FAFSA. In 2017, 34 master's awarded. *Program availability:* Part-time, evening/weekend. Offers accounting (MBA); business (MBA); data analytics (MBA); engineering management (MBA); general business administration (MBA); healthcare administration (MBA); human resource management (MBA). *Application deadline:* For fall admission, 8/1 for domestic students, 3/1 priority date for international students. Applications are processed on a rolling basis. *Application fee:* $40. Electronic applications accepted. *Application Contact:* Dr. Jack Smothers, MBA Director, 812-461-5248, Fax: 812-464-1956, E-mail: jesmothers@usi.edu. *Dean*, Dr. Mohammed F. Khayum, 812-465-1681, E-mail: mkhayum@usi.edu.

UNIVERSITY OF SOUTHERN MAINE, Portland, ME 04103

General Information State-supported, coed, comprehensive institution. CGS member. *Graduate housing:* Rooms and/or apartments available on a first-come, first-served basis to single and married students. Housing application deadline: 5/1.

GRADUATE UNITS

College of Arts, Humanities, and Social Sciences *Program availability:* Part-time, evening/weekend, online learning. Offers American and New England studies (MA, CGS); arts, humanities, and social sciences (MA, MFA, MM, CGS); creative writing (MFA). Electronic applications accepted.

School of Music Offers composition (MM); conducting (MM); jazz studies (MM); music education (MM); performance (MM).

College of Management and Human Service Offers management and human service (MBA, MCPD, MPH, MPPM, MS, MS Ed, MSW, Psy D, CAS, CGS).

Muskie School of Public Service *Program availability:* Part-time, evening/weekend, online learning. Offers community planning and development (MCPD, CGS); health policy and management (MPH, CGS); public policy and management (MPPM). Electronic applications accepted.

School of Business *Program availability:* Part-time, evening/weekend. Offers accounting (MBA); business administration (MBA); finance (MBA); health management and policy (MBA); sustainability (MBA). Electronic applications accepted.

School of Education and Human Development *Program availability:* Part-time, evening/weekend, online learning. Offers adult and higher education (MS); adult learning (CAS); applied behavior analysis (MS, CGS); applied literacy (MS Ed); assistant principal (CGS); clinical mental health counseling (MS); counseling (CAS); culturally responsive practices in education and human development (CGS); education and human development (MS, MS Ed, Psy D, CAS, CGS); educational leadership (MS Ed, CAS); English as a second language (MS Ed, CAS, CGS); gifted and talented education (CGS); literacy education (MS Ed, CAS, CGS); mental health rehabilitation technician/community (CGS); professional educator (MS Ed); professional teacher (MS Ed); rehabilitation counseling (MS); school counseling (MS); school psychology (MS, Psy D); special education (MS); substance abuse counseling (CGS); teaching all students (CGS); teaching and learning (MS Ed); youth with moderate to severe disabilities (CGS). Electronic applications accepted.

School of Social Work *Program availability:* Part-time, evening/weekend. Offers social work (MSW). Electronic applications accepted.

College of Science, Technology, and Health *Program availability:* Part-time, evening/weekend. Offers applied medical sciences (MS); biology (MS); computer science (MS); science, technology, and health (MS, DNP, CAS, CGS, PMC); software systems (CGS); statistics (MS, CGS). Electronic applications accepted.

School of Nursing *Program availability:* Part-time. Offers adult-gerontology primary care nurse practitioner (MS, PMC); education (MS); family nurse practitioner (MS, PMC); family psychiatric/mental health nurse practitioner (MS); management (MS); nursing (CAS, CGS); psychiatric-mental health nurse practitioner (PMC). Electronic applications accepted.

Lewiston-Auburn College Offers creative leadership/global strategies (CGS); leadership studies (MA); occupational therapy (MOT).

UNIVERSITY OF SOUTHERN MISSISSIPPI, Hattiesburg, MS 39406-0001

General Information State-supported, coed, university. CGS member. *Enrollment:* 14,478 graduate, professional, and undergraduate students; 1,325 full-time matriculated graduate/professional students (823 women), 408 part-time matriculated graduate/professional students (305 women). *Enrollment by degree level:* 1,127 master's, 594 doctoral, 12 other advanced degrees. Tuition, state resident: full-time $3830. *Graduate housing:* On-campus housing not available. *Student services:* Campus employment opportunities, campus safety program, career counseling, child daycare facilities, exercise/wellness program, free psychological counseling, grant writing training, international student services, low-cost health insurance, multicultural affairs office, services for students with disabilities, teacher training, writing training. *Library facilities:* Cook Memorial Library plus 4 others. *Collection:* Books: 1.4 million (physical), 331,932 (digital/electronic); Serial titles: 27,243 (physical), 118,798 (digital/electronic); Databases: 200. Weekly public service hours: 117; students can reserve study rooms. *Research affiliation:* Oak Ridge Associated Universities.

Computer facilities: Computer purchase and lease plans are available. 436 computers available on campus for general student use. A campuswide network can be accessed from student residence rooms and from off campus. Online class registration is available.
Website: http://www.usm.edu/

General Application Contact: Tracy Barnhill, Manager of Graduate Admissions, 601-266-5137, Fax: 601-266-5138, E-mail: graduateschool@usm.edu.

GRADUATE UNITS

College of Arts and Letters Students: 475 full-time (233 women); includes 92 minority (55 Black or African American, non-Hispanic/Latino; 4 American Indian or Alaska Native, non-Hispanic/Latino; 9 Asian, non-Hispanic/Latino; 21 Hispanic/Latino; 3 Two or more races, non-Hispanic/Latino), 39 international. 265 applicants, 69% accepted, 118 enrolled. Expenses: Contact institution. *Financial support:* Fellowships, research assistantships with full tuition reimbursements, teaching assistantships with full tuition reimbursements, Federal Work-Study, institutionally sponsored loans, scholarships/grants, health care benefits, and unspecified assistantships available. Financial award application deadline: 3/15; financial award applicants required to submit

FAFSA. In 2017, 102 master's, 33 doctorates awarded. *Program availability:* Part-time, evening/weekend, online learning. Offers anthropology and sociology (MA); arts and letters (MA, MATL, MFA, MM, MME, MS, DMA, PhD); communication studies (MA, PhD); costume design (MFA); creative writing (MA, PhD); directing (MFA); English education (MA); history (MA, MS, PhD); lighting and sound design (MFA); literature (MA, PhD); performance (MFA); political science, international development and international affairs (MA, PhD); scenic design (MFA); Spanish (MATL). *Application deadline:* For fall admission, 5/1 for domestic students, 3/1 for international students. Applications are processed on a rolling basis. *Application fee:* $60. Electronic applications accepted. *Application Contact:* Shonna Breland, Manager of Graduate Admissions, 601-266-4369, Fax: 601-266-5138, E-mail: shonna.breland@usm.edu. *Dean*, Dr. Maureen Ryan, 601-266-4316, Fax: 601-266-6541, E-mail: maureen.ryan@usm.edu.

School of Music Students: 37 full-time (14 women), 2 part-time (0 women). 89 applicants, 74% accepted, 39 enrolled. Expenses: Contact institution. *Financial support:* Fellowships with full tuition reimbursements, research assistantships, teaching assistantships with full tuition reimbursements, Federal Work-Study, institutionally sponsored loans, scholarships/grants, health care benefits, tuition waivers (partial), and unspecified assistantships available. Financial award application deadline: 2/1; financial award applicants required to submit FAFSA. In 2017, 3 master's, 1 doctorate awarded. *Program availability:* Blended/hybrid learning. Offers conducting (DMA); music education (MME); performance and pedagogy (DMA); piano accompanying (MM); theory (MM); woodwind performance and pedagogy (MM). *Application deadline:* For fall admission, 6/1 for domestic students; for spring admission, 11/1 for domestic students; for summer admission, 3/1 for domestic students. Applications are processed on a rolling basis. *Application fee:* $60. *Director*, Dr. Richard Kravchak, 601-266-5543, Fax: 601-266-6427.

College of Business Students: 68 full-time (36 women), 4 part-time (3 women). 117 applicants, 73% accepted, 67 enrolled. Expenses: Contact institution. *Financial support:* Research assistantships with full tuition reimbursements, teaching assistantships with full tuition reimbursements, Federal Work-Study, institutionally sponsored loans, scholarships/grants, and health care benefits available. Support available to part-time students. Financial award application deadline: 3/15; financial award applicants required to submit FAFSA. In 2017, 33 master's awarded. *Program availability:* Part-time, evening/weekend. Offers business (MBA, MPA, MS); business administration (MBA); economic development (MS); sport management (MS); sport security management (MBA). *Application deadline:* For fall admission, 7/15 priority date for domestic students, 3/1 for international students; for spring admission, 11/15 priority date for domestic students, 11/5 for international students. Applications are processed on a rolling basis. *Application fee:* $60. Electronic applications accepted. *Application Contact:* Amy Yeend, Assistant Dean, Academic and Career Services, 601-266-4663, Fax: 601-266-5814. *Dean*, Dr. Faye W. Gilbert, 601-266-4659, Fax: 601-266-5814, E-mail: faye.gilbert@usm.edu.

School of Accountancy Students: 11 full-time (7 women). 18 applicants, 67% accepted, 11 enrolled. Expenses: Contact institution. *Financial support:* Research assistantships with full tuition reimbursements, Federal Work-Study, institutionally sponsored loans, scholarships/grants, health care benefits, and unspecified assistantships available. Support available to part-time students. Financial award application deadline: 3/15; financial award applicants required to submit FAFSA. In 2017, 6 master's awarded. *Program availability:* Part-time, evening/weekend. Offers accountancy (MPA). *Application deadline:* For fall admission, 7/15 priority date for domestic students, 7/15 for international students; for spring admission, 11/15 priority date for domestic students, 11/15 for international students. Applications are processed on a rolling basis. *Application fee:* $60. Electronic applications accepted. *Application Contact:* Amy Yeend, Assistant Dean, Academic and Career Services, 601-266-4663, Fax: 601-266-5814. *Director*, Gwen Pate, 601-266-4641, Fax: 601-266-4642.

College of Education and Psychology Students: 136 full-time (104 women), 16 part-time (14 women). 387 applicants, 48% accepted, 136 enrolled. Expenses: Contact institution. *Financial support:* Research assistantships with full tuition reimbursements, teaching assistantships with full tuition reimbursements, career-related internships or fieldwork, Federal Work-Study, institutionally sponsored loans, scholarships/grants, health care benefits, and unspecified assistantships available. Financial award application deadline: 3/15; financial award applicants required to submit FAFSA. In 2017, 16 master's, 10 doctorates awarded. *Program availability:* Part-time. Offers child and family studies (M Ed, MS); education and psychology (M Ed, MA, MAT, MLIS, MS, Ed D, PhD, Ed S, Graduate Certificate); educational administration (M Ed, Ed D, PhD, Ed S); educational administration and supervision (M Ed); educational studies and research (MS); elementary education (M Ed, PhD); higher education (Ed D); higher education administration (PhD); higher education: student affairs (M Ed); instructional technology (MS); instructional technology and design (PhD); psychology (MS, PhD); research, evaluation, statistics, assessment (PhD); secondary education (MAT); special education (M Ed, PhD). *Application deadline:* For fall admission, 3/1 priority date for domestic students, 3/1 for international students; for spring admission, 11/1 priority date for domestic students, 11/1 for international students. Applications are processed on a rolling basis. *Application fee:* $60. Electronic applications accepted. *Dean*, Dr. Trent Gould, 601-266-4224, Fax: 601-266-4175, E-mail: trent.gould@usm.edu.

School of Library and Information Science Students: 17 full-time (12 women), 8 part-time (all women). 35 applicants, 100% accepted, 25 enrolled. Expenses: Contact institution. *Financial support:* Fellowships with tuition reimbursements, research assistantships with full tuition reimbursements, teaching assistantships with full tuition reimbursements, career-related internships or fieldwork, Federal Work-Study, institutionally sponsored loans, scholarships/grants, health care benefits, and unspecified assistantships available. Financial award application deadline: 3/15; financial award applicants required to submit FAFSA. *Program availability:* Part-time, evening/weekend, online learning. Offers library and information science (MLIS); youth services and literature (Graduate Certificate). *Application deadline:* For fall admission, 3/15 priority date for domestic students, 3/15 for international students; for spring admission, 1/10 priority date for domestic and international students. Applications are processed on a rolling basis. *Application fee:* $60. Electronic applications accepted. *Director*, Dr. Theresa Welsh, 601-266-4236, Fax: 601-266-5774.

College of Health Students: 84 full-time (61 women), 3 part-time (all women). 350 applicants, 60% accepted, 84 enrolled. Expenses: Contact institution. *Financial support:* Fellowships with full tuition reimbursements, research assistantships with full tuition reimbursements, teaching assistantships with full tuition reimbursements, career-related internships or fieldwork, Federal Work-Study, institutionally sponsored loans, scholarships/grants, health care benefits, and unspecified assistantships available. Financial award application deadline: 3/15; financial award applicants required to submit FAFSA. In 2017, 9 master's, 2 doctorates awarded. *Program availability:* Part-time, evening/weekend. Offers epidemiology and biostatistics (MPH); health (MA, MLS, MPH, MS, MSW, Au D, PhD); health policy and administration (MPH); medical laboratory science (MLS); nutrition and food systems (MS); speech and hearing sciences (MA, MS, Au D). *Application deadline:* For fall admission, 3/1 for domestic and international students; for spring admission, 1/10 priority date for domestic and international students. Applications are processed on a rolling basis. *Application fee:* $60. Electronic applications accepted. *Dean*, Dr. Trent Gould, 601-266-5253.

School of Kinesiology Students: 17 full-time (12 women), 1 (woman) part-time. 34 applicants, 74% accepted, 18 enrolled. Expenses: Contact institution. *Financial support:* Fellowships, research assistantships with full tuition reimbursements, teaching assistantships with full tuition reimbursements, career-related internships or fieldwork, Federal Work-Study, institutionally sponsored loans, scholarships/grants, health care benefits, and unspecified assistantships available. Financial award application deadline: 3/15; financial award applicants required to submit FAFSA. In 2017, 3 doctorates awarded. *Program availability:* Part-time, evening/weekend. Offers kinesiology (MS, PhD). *Application deadline:* For fall admission, 3/1 priority date for domestic students, 3/1 for international students; for spring admission, 1/10 priority date for domestic and international students. Applications are processed on a rolling basis. *Application fee:* $60. Electronic applications accepted. *Application Contact:* Dr. Trenton Gould, Dean, College of Health, 601-266-6339, Fax: 601-266-4445. *Director*, Dr. Scott Piland, 601-266-5386, Fax: 601-266-4445, E-mail: scott.piland@usm.edu.

School of Social Work Students: 40 full-time (32 women), 2 part-time (both women). 92 applicants, 79% accepted, 42 enrolled. Expenses: Contact institution. *Financial support:* Research assistantships with tuition reimbursements, teaching assistantships with tuition reimbursements, career-related internships or fieldwork, Federal Work-Study, scholarships/grants, health care benefits, and unspecified assistantships available. Financial award application deadline: 3/15; financial award applicants required to submit FAFSA. In 2017, 1 master's awarded. *Program availability:* Part-time. Offers social work (MSW). *Application deadline:* For fall admission, 4/1 priority date for domestic and international students; for spring admission, 1/10 priority date for domestic and international students. Applications are processed on a rolling basis. *Application fee:* $60. Electronic applications accepted. *Director*, Dr. Tim Rehner, 601-266-4171, Fax: 601-266-4165, E-mail: tim.rehner@usm.edu.

College of Nursing Students: 51 full-time (42 women), 2 part-time (both women). 134 applicants, 64% accepted, 51 enrolled. Expenses: Contact institution. *Financial support:* Research assistantships with full tuition reimbursements, teaching assistantships, Federal Work-Study, institutionally sponsored loans, scholarships/grants, traineeships, health care benefits, and unspecified assistantships available. Financial award application deadline: 3/15; financial award applicants required to submit FAFSA. In 2017, 1 master's, 1 doctorate, 2 other advanced degrees awarded. *Program availability:* Part-time, evening/weekend. Offers nursing (MSN, DNP, PhD, Graduate Certificate). *Application deadline:* For fall admission, 3/15 priority date for domestic students, 5/1 for international students; for spring admission, 1/10 priority date for domestic and international students. Applications are processed on a rolling basis. *Application fee:* $60. Electronic applications accepted. *Application Contact:* Dr. Sandra Bishop, Graduate Coordinator, 601-266-5500, Fax: 601-266-5927. *Interim Dean*, Dr. Kathleen Masters, 601-266-6485, Fax: 601-266-5927, E-mail: kathleen.masters@usm.edu.

College of Science and Technology Students: 103 full-time (33 women), 2 part-time (both women). 275 applicants, 68% accepted, 99 enrolled. Expenses: Contact institution. *Financial support:* Fellowships with full tuition reimbursements, research assistantships with full tuition reimbursements, teaching assistantships with full tuition reimbursements, career-related internships or fieldwork, Federal Work-Study, institutionally sponsored loans, scholarships/grants, health care benefits, and unspecified assistantships available. Financial award application deadline: 3/15; financial award applicants required to submit FAFSA. *Program availability:* Part-time, evening/weekend. Offers biological sciences (MS, PhD); chemistry and biochemistry (MS, PhD); computational science (PhD); geography (PhD); geography and geology (MS); mathematics (MS); physics (MS); science and technology (MA, MS, PhD). *Application deadline:* For fall admission, 3/1 priority date for domestic students, 3/1 for international students; for spring admission, 1/10 priority date for domestic and international students. Applications are processed on a rolling basis. *Application fee:* $60. *Interim Dean*, Dr. Chris Winstead, 601-266-4883, Fax: 601-266-5829.

Division of Coastal Sciences Students: 10 full-time (6 women). 21 applicants, 86% accepted, 10 enrolled. Expenses: Contact institution. *Financial support:* Fellowships with full tuition reimbursements, research assistantships with full tuition reimbursements, Federal Work-Study, scholarships/grants, health care benefits, and unspecified assistantships available. Financial award application deadline: 3/15; financial award applicants required to submit FAFSA. *Program availability:* Part-time. Offers coastal sciences (MS, PhD). *Application deadline:* For fall admission, 3/1 priority date for domestic students, 3/1 for international students. Applications are processed on a rolling basis. *Application fee:* $60. Electronic applications accepted. *Application Contact:* Kalin Buttrich, Administrative Assistant, 228-872-4201, Fax: 228-872-4295. *Chair*, Dr. Robert J. Griffitt, 228-818-8027, Fax: 228-872-4295, E-mail: joe.griffitt@usm.edu.

Division of Marine Science *Program availability:* Part-time. Offers hydrographic science (MS); marine science (MS, PhD). Electronic applications accepted.

School of Computing Students: 16 full-time (7 women). 52 applicants, 81% accepted, 16 enrolled. Expenses: Contact institution. *Financial support:* Research assistantships with full tuition reimbursements, teaching assistantships with full tuition reimbursements, Federal Work-Study, institutionally sponsored loans, scholarships/grants, health care benefits, and unspecified assistantships available. Financial award application deadline: 3/15; financial award applicants required to submit FAFSA. Offers computational science (MS, PhD); computer science (MS). *Application deadline:* For fall admission, 3/15 priority date for domestic students, 3/15 for international students; for spring admission, 1/10 priority date for domestic and international students. Applications are processed on a rolling basis. *Application fee:* $60. Electronic applications accepted. *Application Contact:* Dr. Chaoyang Zhang, Manager of Graduate Admissions, 601-266-4949, Fax: 601-266-6452. *Director*, Andrew H. Sung, 601-266-4949, Fax: 601-266-5829.

School of Construction Students: 10 full-time (0 women). 12 applicants, 100% accepted, 10 enrolled. Expenses: Contact institution. *Financial support:* Research assistantships with full tuition reimbursements, teaching assistantships with full tuition reimbursements, career-related internships or fieldwork, Federal Work-Study, scholarships/grants, health care benefits, and unspecified assistantships available. Financial award application deadline: 3/15; financial award applicants required to submit FAFSA. *Program availability:* Part-time, online learning. Offers construction (MS). *Application deadline:* For fall admission, 3/1 priority date for domestic students, 3/1 for international students. Applications are processed on a rolling basis. *Application fee:* $60. *Director*, Dr. Erich Connell, 601-266-4895.

School of Criminal Justice Students: 5 full-time (3 women), 1 (woman) part-time. 7 applicants, 57% accepted, 4 enrolled. Expenses: Contact institution. *Financial* *support:* Research assistantships with full tuition reimbursements, teaching assistantships with full tuition reimbursements, career-related internships or fieldwork, Federal Work-Study, institutionally sponsored loans, scholarships/grants, health care benefits, and unspecified assistantships available. Financial award application deadline: 3/15; financial award applicants required to submit FAFSA. *Program availability:* Part-time. Offers criminal justice (MA, MS, PhD); forensic science (MS). *Application deadline:* For fall admission, 3/15 priority date for domestic students, 3/15 for international students; for spring admission, 1/10 priority date for domestic and international students. Applications are processed on a rolling basis. *Application fee:* $60. Electronic applications accepted. *Application Contact:* Tera Wright, Manager of Graduate Admissions, 601-266-4509, Fax: 601-266-4391. *Director*, Dr. Lisa Nored, 601-266-4509, Fax: 601-266-4391.

School of Polymers and High Performance Materials Students: 12 full-time (3 women). 44 applicants, 61% accepted, 12 enrolled. Expenses: Contact institution. *Financial support:* Fellowships, research assistantships with full tuition reimbursements, teaching assistantships with full tuition reimbursements, Federal Work-Study, scholarships/grants, health care benefits, and unspecified assistantships available. Financial award application deadline: 3/15; financial award applicants required to submit FAFSA. Offers polymer science and engineering (MS, PhD). *Application deadline:* For fall admission, 3/1 priority date for domestic students, 3/1 for international students. Applications are processed on a rolling basis. *Application fee:* $60. Electronic applications accepted. *Director*, Dr. Jeffery Wiggins, 601-266-4868, Fax: 601-266-6178.

UNIVERSITY OF SOUTH FLORIDA, Tampa, FL 33620-9951

General Information State-supported, coed, university. CGS member. *Enrollment:* 6,905 full-time matriculated graduate/professional students (3,660 women), 3,894 part-time matriculated graduate/professional students (2,460 women). *Enrollment by degree level:* 6,889 master's, 3,864 doctoral, 46 other advanced degrees. *Graduate faculty:* 1,173 full-time (492 women), 52 part-time/adjunct (20 women). *Graduate housing:* Room and/or apartments available on a first-come, first-served basis to single students; on-campus housing not available to married students. Typical cost: $8200 per year ($11,980 including board). Room and board charges vary according to board plan and housing facility selected. Housing application deadline: 8/20. *Student services:* Campus employment opportunities, campus safety program, career counseling, exercise/wellness program, free psychological counseling, international student services, low-cost health insurance, multicultural affairs office, services for students with disabilities, teacher training, writing training. *Library facilities:* Tampa Campus Library plus 5 others. *Collection:* Books: 1.8 million (physical), 652,513 (digital/electronic); Serial titles: 537 (physical), 58,975 (digital/electronic); Databases: 930. Weekly public service hours: 116; study areas open 24 hours, 5–7 days a week; students can reserve study rooms. *Research affiliation:* Moffitt Cancer Center (medicine (primarily oncology)), Jaeb Center for Health Research (medicine), Florida Orthopaedic Institute (medicine), James A. Haley & Bay Pines VA Hospitals (medicine), Florida Institute of Oceanography (marine science), National Science Foundation ICORPS (engineering, marine science, physics).

Computer facilities: 825 computers available on campus for general student use. A campuswide network can be accessed from student residence rooms and from off campus. Online class registration is available.
Website: http://www.usf.edu/

General Application Contact: Dr. Dwayne Smith, Senior Vice Provost and Dean, Office of Graduate Studies, 813-974-2846, Fax: 813-974-5762, E-mail: mdsmith3@usf.edu.

GRADUATE UNITS

College of Arts and Sciences Students: 1,238 full-time (660 women), 535 part-time (345 women); includes 377 minority (91 Black or African American, non-Hispanic/Latino; 2 American Indian or Alaska Native, non-Hispanic/Latino; 55 Asian, non-Hispanic/Latino; 187 Hispanic/Latino; 2 Native Hawaiian or other Pacific Islander, non-Hispanic/Latino; 40 Two or more races, non-Hispanic/Latino), 343 international. Average age 30. 1,944 applicants, 42% accepted, 493 enrolled. *Faculty:* 366 full-time (136 women), 4 part-time/adjunct (2 women). Expenses: Contact institution. *Financial support:* In 2017–18, 309 students received support, including 2 research assistantships with tuition reimbursements available (averaging $13,650 per year); career-related internships or fieldwork, Federal Work-Study, institutionally sponsored loans, scholarships/grants, tuition waivers (full and partial), and unspecified assistantships also available. Support available to part-time students. Financial award applicants required to submit FAFSA. In 2017, 402 master's, 119 doctorates awarded. *Program availability:* Part-time, evening/weekend, online learning. Offers applied anthropology (MA, PhD); applied physics (PhD); arts and sciences (MA, MFA, MPA, MS, PhD, Graduate Certificate); biology (MS); cancer biology (PhD); cancer chemical biology (PhD); cancer immunology and immunotherapy (PhD); cell and molecular biology (PhD); chemistry (MA, MS, PhD); communication (MA, PhD); creative writing (MFA); economics (MA, PhD); English (MA, PhD); French (MA); history (MA, PhD); integrative biology (PhD); liberal arts (MA); linguistics (MA); linguistics and applied linguistics studies (PhD); linguistics: English as a second language (MA); mathematics (MA, PhD); medical anthropology (Graduate Certificate); microbiology (MS); philosophy (MA, PhD); physics (MS); psychology (PhD); religious studies (MA); sociology (MA, PhD); Spanish (MA); statistics (MA); women's and gender studies (MA). *Application fee:* $30. Electronic applications accepted. *Application Contact:* Susan Hall, Executive Assistant to the Dean, 813-974-0853, Fax: 813-974-5911, E-mail: hall@usf.edu. *Dean*, Dr. Eric Eisenberg, 813-974-2804, Fax: 813-974-5911, E-mail: eisenberg@usf.edu.

School of Geosciences Students: 106 full-time (50 women), 41 part-time (21 women); includes 21 minority (6 Black or African American, non-Hispanic/Latino; 5 Asian, non-Hispanic/Latino; 6 Hispanic/Latino; 4 Two or more races, non-Hispanic/Latino), 41 international. Average age 29. 132 applicants, 57% accepted, 38 enrolled. *Faculty:* 31 full-time (6 women). Expenses: Contact institution. *Financial support:* In 2017–18, 43 students received support, including 3 research assistantships (averaging $12,345 per year), 25 teaching assistantships with tuition reimbursements available (averaging $12,807 per year); unspecified assistantships also available. Financial award application deadline: 3/1. In 2017, 32 master's, 10 doctorates awarded. *Program availability:* Part-time, evening/weekend. Offers environmental science and policy (MS); geography (MA); geography and environmental science and policy (PhD); geology (MS, PhD). *Application deadline:* For fall admission, 2/15 priority date for domestic students, 2/15 for international students; for spring admission, 10/15 priority date for domestic students, 9/15 for international students; for summer admission, 2/15 priority date for domestic students, 1/15 for international students. *Application fee:* $30. Electronic applications accepted. *Application Contact:* Dr. Ruiliang Pu, Associate Professor and Graduate Program Coordinator, 813-974-1508, Fax: 813-974-5911, E-mail: rpu@usf.edu. *Professor and Chair*, Dr. Mark Rains, 813-974-3310, Fax: 813-974-5911, E-mail: mrains@usf.edu.

School of Information Students: 120 full-time (87 women), 187 part-time (141 women); includes 89 minority (26 Black or African American, non-Hispanic/Latino; 9 Asian, non-Hispanic/Latino; 47 Hispanic/Latino; 7 Two or more races, non-Hispanic/Latino), 1 international. Average age 32. 180 applicants, 86% accepted, 98 enrolled. *Faculty:* 16 full-time (9 women). Expenses: Contact institution. *Financial support:* In 2017–18, 25 students received support. Unspecified assistantships available. Financial award application deadline: 6/30. In 2017, 90 master's awarded. *Program availability:* Part-time, evening/weekend, online learning. Offers intelligence studies (MS); library and information science (MA). *Application deadline:* For fall admission, 6/1 priority date for domestic students, 5/1 for international students; for spring admission, 10/15 priority date for domestic students, 9/15 for international students. Applications are processed on a rolling basis. *Application fee:* $30. Electronic applications accepted. *Application Contact:* Dr. Randy Borum, Graduate Program Director, 813-974-3520, Fax: 813-974-6840, E-mail: wborum@usf.edu. *Director and Associate Professor*, Dr. Jim Andrews, 813-974-2108, Fax: 813-974-6840, E-mail: jimandrews@usf.edu.

School of Interdisciplinary Global Studies 3 applicants. *Faculty:* 14 full-time (2 women). Expenses: Contact institution. *Financial support:* In 2017–18, 3 students received support, including 18 teaching assistantships with tuition reimbursements available (averaging $12,390 per year); unspecified assistantships also available. Financial award application deadline: 4/1. In 2017, 9 master's, 1 doctorate awarded. *Program availability:* Part-time, evening/weekend. Offers government (PhD); Latin American, Caribbean and Latino studies (MA); liberal arts (MA); political science (MA). *Application deadline:* For fall admission, 1/5 for domestic and international students; for spring admission, 10/15 for domestic students, 9/15 for international students. Applications are processed on a rolling basis. *Application fee:* $30. Electronic applications accepted. *Application Contact:* Dr. Bernd Reiter, Associate Professor and Director of Graduate Studies, 813-974-3583, Fax: 813-974-0832, E-mail: breiter@usf.edu. *Associate Professor/Interim Chair*, Dr. Steven Tauber, 813-974-2278, Fax: 813-974-0832, E-mail: stauber@usf.edu.

Zimmerman School of Advertising and Mass Communications Students: 25 full-time (20 women), 25 part-time (20 women); includes 7 minority (4 Black or African American, non-Hispanic/Latino; 2 Hispanic/Latino; 1 Native Hawaiian or other Pacific Islander, non-Hispanic/Latino), 29 international. Average age 26. 28 applicants, 64% accepted, 15 enrolled. *Faculty:* 10 full-time (6 women). Expenses: Contact institution. *Financial support:* In 2017–18, 10 students received support, including 9 teaching assistantships with tuition reimbursements available (averaging $10,513 per year); unspecified assistantships also available. Financial award application deadline: 2/28. In 2017, 8 master's awarded. *Program availability:* Part-time, evening/weekend. Offers mass communications (MA). *Application deadline:* For fall admission, 2/15 priority date for domestic and international students. *Application fee:* $30. Electronic applications accepted. *Application Contact:* Dr. Artermio Ramirez, Jr., Associate Director, Fax: 813-974-2592, E-mail: aramirez2@usf.edu. *Director and Senior Instructor*, Dr. Wayne Garcia, 813-498-1925, Fax: 813-974-2592, E-mail: wgarcia@usf.edu.

College of Behavioral and Community Sciences Students: 631 full-time (552 women), 289 part-time (231 women); includes 377 minority (91 Black or African American, non-Hispanic/Latino; 2 American Indian or Alaska Native, non-Hispanic/Latino; 55 Asian, non-Hispanic/Latino; 187 Hispanic/Latino; 2 Native Hawaiian or other Pacific Islander, non-Hispanic/Latino; 40 Two or more races, non-Hispanic/Latino), 18 international. Average age 28. 1,260 applicants, 36% accepted, 300 enrolled. *Faculty:* 101 full-time (67 women), 4 part-time/adjunct (2 women). Expenses: Contact institution. *Financial support:* In 2017–18, 148 students received support. In 2017, 271 master's, 27 doctorates awarded. Offers applied behavior analysis (MA, MS, PhD); audiology (Au D); behavioral and community sciences (MA, MS, MSW, Au D, PhD, Graduate Certificate); child and adolescent behavioral health (MS); communication sciences and disorders (PhD); criminal justice administration (MA); criminology (MA, PhD); cybercrime (MS); rehabilitation and mental health counseling (MA); speech-language pathology (MS). *Application Contact:* Francisco Vera, Assistant Director for Graduate Admissions, 813-974-2829, E-mail: fvera@usf.edu. *Dean*, Dr. Julianne Serovich, 813-974-1990, Fax: 813-974-2365, E-mail: jserovich@usf.edu.

School of Aging Studies Students: 23 full-time (17 women), 6 part-time (5 women); includes 8 minority (4 Black or African American, non-Hispanic/Latino; 1 Asian, non-Hispanic/Latino; 1 Hispanic/Latino; 2 Two or more races, non-Hispanic/Latino), 1 international. Average age 29. 36 applicants, 36% accepted, 8 enrolled. *Faculty:* 9 full-time (4 women). Expenses: Contact institution. *Financial support:* In 2017–18, 4 students received support, including 2 research assistantships with tuition reimbursements available (averaging $15,690 per year), 13 teaching assistantships with tuition reimbursements available (averaging $13,503 per year). Financial award application deadline: 2/3. In 2017, 7 master's, 5 doctorates awarded. *Program availability:* Part-time, evening/weekend. Offers aging studies (PhD); gerontology (MA). *Application deadline:* For fall admission, 12/11 priority date for domestic and international students; for spring admission, 10/15 for domestic students, 9/15 for international students; for summer admission, 2/15 for domestic students, 1/15 for international students. *Application fee:* $30. Electronic applications accepted. *Application Contact:* Brent Small, Professor, 813-974-9746, Fax: 813-974-9754, E-mail: bsmall@usf.edu. *Director and Professor*, Dr. Cathy L. McEvoy, 813-974-1940, Fax: 813-974-9754, E-mail: cmcevoy@usf.edu.

School of Social Work Students: 179 full-time (161 women), 41 part-time (34 women); includes 89 minority (42 Black or African American, non-Hispanic/Latino; 1 American Indian or Alaska Native, non-Hispanic/Latino; 4 Asian, non-Hispanic/Latino; 38 Hispanic/Latino; 1 Native Hawaiian or other Pacific Islander, non-Hispanic/Latino; 3 Two or more races, non-Hispanic/Latino), 1 international. Average age 30. 228 applicants, 51% accepted, 76 enrolled. *Faculty:* 13 full-time (12 women). Expenses: Contact institution. *Financial support:* In 2017–18, 29 students received support, including 1 research assistantship with tuition reimbursement available (averaging $9,001 per year); unspecified assistantships also available. Financial award application deadline: 3/15; financial award applicants required to submit FAFSA. In 2017, 127 master's, 4 doctorates awarded. *Program availability:* Part-time, evening/weekend. Offers social work (MSW, PhD). *Application deadline:* For fall admission, 2/15 priority date for domestic students, 2/15 for international students; for spring admission, 10/15 for domestic students, 9/15 for international students; for summer admission, 2/15 for domestic students, 1/15 for international students. Applications are processed on a rolling basis. *Application fee:* $30. Electronic applications accepted. *Application Contact:* Dr. Marion Becker, MSW Chair/Professor, 813-974-7188, Fax: 813-974-4675, E-mail: mbecker2@usf.edu. *PhD Program Chair/Assistant Professor*, Dr. Nan Sook Park, 813-974-4194, Fax: 813-974-4675, E-mail: nanpark@usf.edu.

College of Education Students: 466 full-time (344 women), 687 part-time (487 women); includes 341 minority (165 Black or African American, non-Hispanic/Latino; 5 American Indian or Alaska Native, non-Hispanic/Latino; 27 Asian, non-Hispanic/Latino;

126 Hispanic/Latino; 1 Native Hawaiian or other Pacific Islander, non-Hispanic/Latino; 17 Two or more races, non-Hispanic/Latino), 104 international. Average age 35. 843 applicants, 55% accepted, 308 enrolled. *Faculty:* 89 full-time (54 women). Expenses: Contact institution. *Financial support:* In 2017–18, 206 students received support, including 9 fellowships with full tuition reimbursements available (averaging $15,000 per year), 2 research assistantships with full tuition reimbursements available (averaging $15,000 per year); career-related internships or fieldwork, Federal Work-Study, institutionally sponsored loans, scholarships/grants, health care benefits, and unspecified assistantships also available. Support available to part-time students. Financial award applicants required to submit FAFSA. In 2017, 280 master's, 68 doctorates, 17 other advanced degrees awarded. *Program availability:* Part-time, evening/weekend, online learning. Offers adult education (MA, Ed D, PhD, Ed S); career and technical education (MA); career and workforce education (PhD); college student affairs (M Ed); counselor education (MA, PhD, Ed S); early childhood education (M Ed, MA, PhD); education (M Ed, MA, MAT, Ed D, PhD, Ed S); elementary education (MA, MAT, PhD); higher education/community college teaching (MA, Ed D, PhD); interdisciplinary education (PhD, Ed S); reading/language arts (MA, PhD, Ed S); school psychology (PhD, Ed S); vocational education (Ed S). *Application deadline:* For fall admission, 2/15 for domestic students, 1/2 for international students; for spring admission, 10/15 for domestic students, 6/1 for international students. *Application fee:* $30. Electronic applications accepted. *Application Contact:* Dr. Diane Briscoe, Coordinator of Graduate Studies, 813-974-1804, Fax: 813-974-3391, E-mail: briscoe@usf.edu. *Dean,* Dr. Colleen S. Kennedy, 813-974-3400, Fax: 813-974-3826.

College of Engineering Students: 950 full-time (228 women), 334 part-time (73 women); includes 143 minority (37 Black or African American, non-Hispanic/Latino; 28 Asian, non-Hispanic/Latino; 67 Hispanic/Latino; 11 Two or more races, non-Hispanic/Latino), 901 international. Average age 27. 2,056 applicants, 48% accepted, 379 enrolled. *Faculty:* 132 full-time (21 women), 1 part-time/adjunct (0 women). Expenses: Contact institution. *Financial support:* In 2017–18, 193 students received support. Career-related internships or fieldwork, Federal Work-Study, scholarships/grants, health care benefits, and unspecified assistantships available. Financial award application deadline: 3/1. In 2017, 505 master's, 50 doctorates awarded. *Program availability:* Part-time, evening/weekend. Offers biomedical engineering (MSBE); chemical engineering (MSCH, PhD); civil engineering (MCE, MSCE, PhD); computer engineering (MSCP); computer science (MSCS); computer science and engineering (PhD); electrical engineering (MSEE, PhD); engineering (MCE, MEVE, MSBE, MSCE, MSCH, MSCP, MSCS, MSEE, MSEM, MSEV, MSIE, MSIT, MSME, MSMSE, PhD, Graduate Certificate); engineering management (MSEM); environmental engineering (MEVE, MSEV, PhD); industrial engineering (MSIE, PhD); information technology (MSIT); materials science and engineering (MSMSE); mechanical engineering (MSME, PhD). *Application deadline:* For fall admission, 2/15 for domestic students, 1/2 priority date for international students; for spring admission, 10/15 for domestic students, 6/1 priority date for international students. Applications are processed on a rolling basis. *Application fee:* $30. Electronic applications accepted. *Application Contact:* Dr. Sanjukta Bhanja, Associate Dean for Academic Affairs, 813-974-4755, Fax: 813-974-5094, E-mail: bhanja@usf.edu. *Dean,* Dr. Robert Bishop, 813-974-3864, Fax: 813-974-5094, E-mail: robertbishop@usf.edu.

College of Global Sustainability Students: 124 full-time (64 women), 77 part-time (45 women); includes 33 minority (12 Black or African American, non-Hispanic/Latino; 1 American Indian or Alaska Native, non-Hispanic/Latino; 1 Asian, non-Hispanic/Latino; 14 Hispanic/Latino; 5 Two or more races, non-Hispanic/Latino), 87 international. Average age 28. 220 applicants, 65% accepted, 101 enrolled. *Faculty:* 2 full-time (0 women). Expenses: Contact institution. *Financial support:* In 2017–18, 22 students received support. In 2017, 50 master's awarded. Offers energy, global, water and sustainable tourism (Graduate Certificate); global sustainability (MA). *Application deadline:* For fall admission, 6/1 for domestic students, 5/1 for international students; for spring admission, 10/15 for domestic students, 9/15 for international students. Electronic applications accepted. *Dean,* Dr. Govindan Parayil, 813-974-9694, E-mail: gparayil@usf.edu.

College of Graduate Studies Students: 79 full-time (12 women), 167 part-time (50 women); includes 95 minority (34 Black or African American, non-Hispanic/Latino; 1 American Indian or Alaska Native, non-Hispanic/Latino; 12 Asian, non-Hispanic/Latino; 42 Hispanic/Latino; 1 Native Hawaiian or other Pacific Islander, non-Hispanic/Latino; 5 Two or more races, non-Hispanic/Latino), 2 international. Average age 36. 117 applicants, 66% accepted, 61 enrolled. *Faculty:* 1 (woman) full-time. Expenses: Contact institution. *Financial support:* In 2017–18, 11 students received support. Teaching assistantships available. Financial award application deadline: 2/1; financial award applicants required to submit FAFSA. In 2017, 112 master's awarded. *Program availability:* Part-time, evening/weekend, online learning. Offers cybersecurity (MS). *Application deadline:* For fall admission, 2/15 for domestic and international students; for spring admission, 10/15 for domestic students, 9/15 for international students; for summer admission, 2/15 for domestic and international students. *Application fee:* $30. Electronic applications accepted. *Application Contact:* Paul Crawford, Associate Director for Graduate Admissions, 813-974-8800, E-mail: pjcrawford@usf.edu. *Senior Vice Provost and Dean of the Office of Graduate Studies,* Dr. Dwayne Smith, 813-974-7359, Fax: 813-974-5762, E-mail: mdsmith8@usf.edu.

College of Marine Science Students: 75 full-time (51 women), 23 part-time (13 women); includes 16 minority (1 Black or African American, non-Hispanic/Latino; 10 Hispanic/Latino; 5 Two or more races, non-Hispanic/Latino), 15 international. Average age 29. 72 applicants, 29% accepted, 16 enrolled. *Faculty:* 25 full-time (6 women), 1 part-time/adjunct (0 women). Expenses: Contact institution. *Financial support:* In 2017–18, 41 students received support, including 45 research assistantships with partial tuition reimbursements available (averaging $14,199 per year), 10 teaching assistantships with partial tuition reimbursements available (averaging $14,196 per year); health care benefits and unspecified assistantships also available. Financial award application deadline: 1/15. In 2017, 9 master's, 10 doctorates awarded. *Program availability:* Part-time. Offers marine science (MS, PhD). *Application deadline:* For fall admission, 1/10 for domestic and international students; for spring admission, 10/1 for domestic and international students. Applications are processed on a rolling basis. *Application fee:* $30. Electronic applications accepted. *Application Contact:* Dr. David F. Naar, Associate Professor and Director of Academic Affairs, 727-553-1637, Fax: 727-553-1189, E-mail: naar@usf.edu. *Dean,* Dr. Jacqueline E. Dixon, 727-553-3369, Fax: 727-553-1189, E-mail: jdixon@usf.edu.

College of Nursing Students: 224 full-time (178 women), 669 part-time (577 women); includes 309 minority (105 Black or African American, non-Hispanic/Latino; 2 American Indian or Alaska Native, non-Hispanic/Latino; 53 Asian, non-Hispanic/Latino; 122 Hispanic/Latino; 1 Native Hawaiian or other Pacific Islander, non-Hispanic/Latino; 26 Two or more races, non-Hispanic/Latino), 6 international. Average age 32. 949 applicants, 47% accepted, 382 enrolled. *Faculty:* 37 full-time (32 women), 2 part-time/adjunct (1 woman). Expenses: Contact institution. *Financial support:* In 2017–18, 132 students received support, including 7 research assistantships with tuition reimbursements available (averaging $18,935 per year), 29 teaching assistantships with tuition reimbursements available (averaging $30,814 per year); tuition waivers (partial) and unspecified assistantships also available. Financial award application deadline: 2/1; financial award applicants required to submit FAFSA. In 2017, 264 master's, 39 doctorates awarded. *Program availability:* Part-time. Offers nurse anesthesia (DNP); nursing (MS, DNP); nursing education (Post Master's Certificate); nursing science (PhD); simulation based academic fellowship in advanced pain management (Graduate Certificate). *Application deadline:* For fall admission, 12/15 for domestic and international students; for spring admission, 10/1 for domestic students, 9/15 for international students. *Application fee:* $30. Electronic applications accepted. *Application Contact:* Dr. Brian Graves, Assistant Professor/Assistant Dean, 813-974-8054, Fax: 813-974-5418, E-mail: bgraves1@health.usf.edu. *Dean, College of Nursing,* Dr. Victoria Rich, 813-974-8939, Fax: 813-974-5418, E-mail: victoriarich@health.usf.edu.

College of Pharmacy Students: 381 full-time (226 women), 3 part-time (1 woman); includes 172 minority (27 Black or African American, non-Hispanic/Latino; 70 Asian, non-Hispanic/Latino; 59 Hispanic/Latino; 4 Native Hawaiian or other Pacific Islander, non-Hispanic/Latino; 12 Two or more races, non-Hispanic/Latino), 4 international. Average age 25. 678 applicants, 31% accepted, 105 enrolled. *Faculty:* 39 full-time (28 women), 1 part-time/adjunct (0 women). Expenses: Contact institution. *Financial support:* In 2017–18, 91 students received support. In 2017, 111 doctorates awarded. Offers pharmaceutical nanotechnology (MS); pharmacy (Pharm D). *Application deadline:* For fall admission, 2/1 priority date for domestic students, 2/1 for international students; for spring admission, 10/15 for domestic students, 9/15 for international students; for summer admission, 2/15 for domestic and international students. Electronic applications accepted. *Application Contact:* Dr. Amy Schwartz, Associate Dean, 813-974-2251, E-mail: aschwar1@health.usf.edu. *Dean,* Dr. Kevin Sneed, 813-974-5699, E-mail: ksneed@health.usf.edu.

College of Public Health Students: 399 full-time (278 women), 399 part-time (298 women); includes 237 minority (122 Black or African American, non-Hispanic/Latino; 3 American Indian or Alaska Native, non-Hispanic/Latino; 48 Asian, non-Hispanic/Latino; 64 Hispanic/Latino), 94 international. Average age 33. 1,200 applicants, 54% accepted, 400 enrolled. *Faculty:* 60 full-time (27 women), 34 part-time/adjunct (13 women). Expenses: Contact institution. *Financial support:* In 2017–18, 46 students received support, including 18 fellowships with full tuition reimbursements available (averaging $32,033 per year), 135 research assistantships with full and partial tuition reimbursements available (averaging $19,597 per year), 66 teaching assistantships (averaging $19,296 per year); career-related internships or fieldwork, Federal Work-Study, institutionally sponsored loans, scholarships/grants, traineeships, and unspecified assistantships also available. Support available to part-time students. Financial award application deadline: 11/15; financial award applicants required to submit FAFSA. In 2017, 136 master's, 6 doctorates awarded. *Program availability:* Part-time, evening/weekend, 100% online, blended/hybrid learning. Offers community and family health (MPH, MSPH, Dr PH, PhD); environmental and occupational health (MPH, MSPH, PhD); epidemiology and biostatistics (MPH, MSPH, PhD); global health (MPH, MSPH, Dr PH, PhD); health policy and management (MHA, MPH, MSPH, PhD); public health (MHA, MPH, MSPH, Dr PH, PhD); public health practice (MPH). *Application deadline:* For fall admission, 5/1 for domestic and international students; for spring admission, 6/15 for domestic and international students; for summer admission, 11/15 for domestic and international students. Applications are processed on a rolling basis. *Application fee:* $30. Electronic applications accepted. *Application Contact:* Kamala Dontamsetti, Assistant Director of Graduate Admissions, 813-974-8874, Fax: 813-974-8121, E-mail: kamalad@health.usf.edu. *Dean,* Dr. Donna J. Petersen, 813-974-3623, Fax: 813-974-7390.

College of The Arts Students: 189 full-time (87 women), 40 part-time (13 women); includes 61 minority (9 Black or African American, non-Hispanic/Latino; 8 Asian, non-Hispanic/Latino; 37 Hispanic/Latino; 7 Two or more races, non-Hispanic/Latino), 47 international. Average age 28. 168 applicants, 46% accepted, 62 enrolled. *Faculty:* 60 full-time (21 women), 1 part-time/adjunct (0 women). Expenses: Contact institution. *Financial support:* In 2017–18, 106 students received support. Unspecified assistantships available. In 2017, 88 master's, 2 doctorates awarded. *Program availability:* Part-time, evening/weekend. Offers the arts (M Arch, MA, MFA, MM, MUCD, PhD). *Application deadline:* For fall admission, 1/15 for domestic and international students; for spring admission, 10/15 for domestic students, 9/15 for international students; for summer admission, 2/15 for domestic students, 1/15 for international students. *Application fee:* $30. Electronic applications accepted. *Application Contact:* Prof. Barton Lee, Senior Associate Dean, 813-974-2301, Fax: 813-974-2091, E-mail: blee@usf.edu. *Dean,* Dr. James S. Moy, 813-974-7380, Fax: 813-974-2091, E-mail: moy@usf.edu.

School of Architecture and Community Design Students: 92 full-time (40 women), 18 part-time (5 women); includes 38 minority (6 Black or African American, non-Hispanic/Latino; 7 Asian, non-Hispanic/Latino; 22 Hispanic/Latino; 3 Two or more races, non-Hispanic/Latino), 23 international. Average age 26. 61 applicants, 44% accepted, 22 enrolled. *Faculty:* 10 full-time (1 woman). Expenses: Contact institution. *Financial support:* In 2017–18, 34 students received support, including 3 teaching assistantships with tuition reimbursements available (averaging $9,360 per year); Federal Work-Study, scholarships/grants, and unspecified assistantships also available. In 2017, 48 master's awarded. Offers architecture (M Arch); urban and community design (MUCD). *Application deadline:* For fall admission, 2/1 priority date for domestic students, 2/1 for international students. Applications are processed on a rolling basis. *Application fee:* $30. Electronic applications accepted. *Application Contact:* Mildred Abreu, Academic Advisor, 813-974-1216, Fax: 813-974-2557, E-mail: abreu@arch.usf.edu. *Director and Professor, School of Architecture and Community Design,* Dr. Robert MacLeod, 813-974-6015, Fax: 813-974-2557, E-mail: rmacleod@arch.usf.edu.

School of Art and Art History Students: 35 full-time (19 women), 2 part-time (1 woman); includes 10 minority (8 Hispanic/Latino; 2 Two or more races, non-Hispanic/Latino), 3 international. Average age 29. 48 applicants, 29% accepted, 13 enrolled. *Faculty:* 21 full-time (11 women). Expenses: Contact institution. *Financial support:* In 2017–18, 33 students received support, including 37 teaching assistantships with partial tuition reimbursements available (averaging $9,440 per year); scholarships/grants, health care benefits, and unspecified assistantships also available. Support available to part-time students. Financial award application deadline: 2/15; financial award applicants required to submit FAFSA. In 2017, 13 master's awarded. *Program availability:* Part-time. Offers art history (MA); studio art (MFA). *Application deadline:* For fall admission, 1/15 priority date for domestic students, 2/1 for international students. *Application fee:* $30. Electronic applications accepted. *Application Contact:* Prof. Neil Bender, Associate Professor and Graduate

Program Director, 813-974-2360, Fax: 813-974-9226, E-mail: nb2@usf.edu. *Director*, Prof. Wallace Wilson, 813-974-2360, Fax: 813-974-9226, E-mail: wwilson2@usf.edu.

School of Music Students: 62 full-time (28 women), 20 part-time (7 women); includes 13 minority (3 Black or African American, non-Hispanic/Latino; 1 Asian, non-Hispanic/Latino; 7 Hispanic/Latino; 2 Two or more races, non-Hispanic/Latino), 21 international. Average age 30. 59 applicants, 61% accepted, 27 enrolled. *Faculty:* 27 full-time (8 women), 1 part-time/adjunct (0 women). Expenses: Contact institution. *Financial support:* In 2017–18, 39 students received support, including 1 research assistantship with tuition reimbursement available (averaging $15,724 per year), 46 teaching assistantships with tuition reimbursements available (averaging $10,099 per year); unspecified assistantships also available. Financial award application deadline: 2/15. In 2017, 27 master's, 2 doctorates awarded. *Program availability:* Part-time, evening/weekend. Offers music (MM, PhD); music education (MA). *Application deadline:* For fall admission, 2/15 priority date for domestic students, 2/1 for international students; for spring admission, 10/15 for domestic students, 9/15 for international students; for summer admission, 2/15 for domestic students, 1/15 for international students. *Application fee:* $30. Electronic applications accepted. *Application Contact:* Dr. David Williams, Associate Director/Associate Professor of Music Education, 813-974-9166, Fax: 813-974-8721, E-mail: davidw@usf.edu. *Director*, Dr. Karen Bryan, 813-974-2311, Fax: 813-974-8721, E-mail: kmbryan@usf.edu.

Innovative Education Expenses: Contact institution. Offers adult, career and higher education (Graduate Certificate); Africana studies (Graduate Certificate); aging studies (Graduate Certificate); art research (Graduate Certificate); business foundations (Graduate Certificate); chemical and biomedical engineering (Graduate Certificate); child and family studies (Graduate Certificate); civil and industrial engineering (Graduate Certificate); community and family health (Graduate Certificate); criminology (Graduate Certificate); data science for public administration (Graduate Certificate); digital humanities (Graduate Certificate); educational measurement and research (Graduate Certificate); English (Graduate Certificate); entrepreneurship (Graduate Certificate); environmental health (Graduate Certificate); epidemiology and biostatistics (Graduate Certificate); geography, environment and planning (Graduate Certificate); geology (Graduate Certificate); global health (Graduate Certificate); government and international affairs (Graduate Certificate); health policy and management (Graduate Certificate); hearing specialist: early intervention (Graduate Certificate); industrial and management systems engineering (Graduate Certificate); information studies (Graduate Certificate); information systems/decision sciences (Graduate Certificate); instructional technology (Graduate Certificate); internal medicine, bioethics and medical humanities (Graduate Certificate); Latin American and Caribbean studies (Graduate Certificate); leadership for coastal resiliency planning (Graduate Certificate); mass communications (Graduate Certificate); mathematics and statistics (Graduate Certificate); medicine (Graduate Certificate); national and competitive intelligence (Graduate Certificate); nursing (Graduate Certificate); psychological and social foundations (Graduate Certificate); public affairs (Graduate Certificate); public health (Graduate Certificate); public health practices (Graduate Certificate); rehabilitation and mental health counseling (Graduate Certificate); secondary education (Graduate Certificate); social work (Graduate Certificate); special education (Graduate Certificate); world languages (Graduate Certificate). *Application Contact:* Owen Hooper, Director, Summer and Alternative Calendar Programs, 813-974-6917, E-mail: hooper@usf.edu. *Associate Vice President and Assistant Vice Provost*, Dr. Cynthia DeLuca, 813-974-3077, Fax: 813-974-7061, E-mail: deluca@usf.edu.

Morsani College of Medicine Students: 1,271 full-time (650 women), 256 part-time (167 women); includes 582 minority (113 Black or African American, non-Hispanic/Latino; 8 American Indian or Alaska Native, non-Hispanic/Latino; 282 Asian, non-Hispanic/Latino; 154 Hispanic/Latino; 25 Two or more races, non-Hispanic/Latino), 66 international. Average age 26. 9,224 applicants, 10% accepted, 555 enrolled. *Faculty:* 181 full-time (73 women), 27 part-time/adjunct (12 women). Expenses: Contact institution. *Financial support:* In 2017–18, 766 students received support. In 2017, 441 master's, 268 doctorates awarded. *Program availability:* Part-time. Offers advanced athletic training (MS); athletic training (MS); bioinformatics and computational biology (MSBCB); biotechnology (MSB); health informatics (MSHI); medical sciences (MSMS, PhD); medicine (MS, MSB, MSBCB, MSHI, MSMS, DPT, MD, PhD). *Application deadline:* For fall admission, 2/1 priority date for domestic students, 2/1 for international students. *Application fee:* $30. Electronic applications accepted. *Application Contact:* Dr. Michael Barber, Associate Dean/Professor, 813-974-9702, Fax: 813-974-4990, E-mail: mbarber@health.usf.edu. *Dean*, Dr. Charles J. Lockwood, 813-974-0533, Fax: 813-974-4990, E-mail: cjlockwood@health.usf.edu.

School of Physical Therapy Students: 139 full-time (94 women); includes 28 minority (6 Black or African American, non-Hispanic/Latino; 1 American Indian or Alaska Native, non-Hispanic/Latino; 9 Asian, non-Hispanic/Latino; 11 Hispanic/Latino; 1 Two or more races, non-Hispanic/Latino). Average age 24. 1,433 applicants, 5% accepted, 50 enrolled. *Faculty:* 11 full-time (6 women). Expenses: Contact institution. *Financial support:* In 2017–18, 83 students received support. Teaching assistantships available. In 2017, 80 doctorates awarded. Offers physical therapy (DPT); rehabilitation sciences (PhD). *Application deadline:* For fall admission, 6/1 for domestic students, 1/1 for international students; for spring admission, 10/15 for domestic students, 9/15 for international students. *Application fee:* $30. Electronic applications accepted. *Application Contact:* Dr. Gina Maria Musolino, Associate Professor and Coordinator for Clinical Education, 813-974-2254, Fax: 813-974-8915, E-mail: gmusolin@health.usf.edu. *Director*, Dr. William S. Quillen, 813-974-9863, Fax: 813-974-8915, E-mail: wquillen@health.usf.edu.

Muma College of Business Students: 850 full-time (291 women), 417 part-time (163 women); includes 224 minority (65 Black or African American, non-Hispanic/Latino; 51 Asian, non-Hispanic/Latino; 94 Hispanic/Latino; 1 Native Hawaiian or other Pacific Islander, non-Hispanic/Latino; 13 Two or more races, non-Hispanic/Latino), 573 international. Average age 29. 2,020 applicants, 55% accepted, 578 enrolled. *Faculty:* 74 full-time (19 women), 1 part-time/adjunct (0 women). Expenses: Contact institution. *Financial support:* In 2017–18, 206 students received support. Career-related internships or fieldwork, scholarships/grants, health care benefits, and unspecified assistantships available. Financial award applicants required to submit FAFSA. In 2017, 510 master's, 10 doctorates awarded. *Program availability:* Part-time, evening/weekend. Offers business (M Acc, MS, MSM, MSRE, DBA, PhD); business administration (PhD); business analytics and information systems (MS); finance (MS); management (MS); marketing (MSM); real estate (MSRE); sport and entertainment management (MS). *Application deadline:* For fall admission, 1/2 for domestic and international students; for spring admission, 10/1 for domestic students, 9/15 for international students. *Application fee:* $30. Electronic applications accepted. *Application Contact:* Dr. Jacqueline Reck, Professor/Interim Associate Dean, 813-974-6721, Fax: 813-974-6528, E-mail: jreck@usf.edu. *Dean*, Dr. Moez Limayem, 813-974-4281, Fax: 813-974-3030, E-mail: mlimayem@usf.edu.

Center for Entrepreneurship Students: 51 full-time (17 women), 7 part-time (3 women). Average age 29. *Faculty:* 4 full-time (2 women). Expenses: Contact institution. In 2017, 55 master's awarded. *Program availability:* Part-time, evening/weekend. Offers entrepreneurship and applied technologies (MS). *Application deadline:* For fall admission, 6/1 for domestic students, 2/1 for international students; for spring admission, 10/15 for domestic students, 7/1 for international students. Applications are processed on a rolling basis. *Application fee:* $30. Electronic applications accepted. *Application Contact:* Dr. Tapas Das, Assistant Director/Professor, 813-974-5585, Fax: 813-974-5953, E-mail: das@usf.edu. *Director, Center for Entrepreneurship*, Dr. Michael W. Fountain, 813-974-7825, Fax: 813-974-6175, E-mail: fountain@usf.edu.

Lynn Pippenger School of Accountancy Students: 74 full-time (35 women), 26 part-time (15 women); includes 32 minority (4 Black or African American, non-Hispanic/Latino; 6 Asian, non-Hispanic/Latino; 19 Hispanic/Latino; 3 Two or more races, non-Hispanic/Latino), 10 international. Average age 25. 102 applicants, 53% accepted, 43 enrolled. *Faculty:* 13 full-time (4 women). Expenses: Contact institution. *Financial support:* In 2017–18, 43 students received support, including 18 teaching assistantships with tuition reimbursements available (averaging $12,273 per year); scholarships/grants, health care benefits, and unspecified assistantships also available. Financial award applicants required to submit FAFSA. In 2017, 58 master's, 1 doctorate awarded. *Program availability:* Part-time, evening/weekend. Offers accountancy (M Acc, PhD). *Application deadline:* For fall admission, 3/1 priority date for domestic students, 3/1 for international students; for spring admission, 10/1 for domestic students, 9/15 for international students; for summer admission, 2/15 for domestic and international students. *Application fee:* $30. Electronic applications accepted. *Application Contact:* Stacee Bender, 813-974-4516, E-mail: staceebender@usf.edu. *Interim Director, School of Accountancy*, Dr. Uday Murthy, 813-974-6516, Fax: 813-974-6528, E-mail: umurthy@usf.edu.

UNIVERSITY OF SOUTH FLORIDA, ST. PETERSBURG, St. Petersburg, FL 33701

General Information State-supported, coed, comprehensive institution. *Graduate housing:* Rooms and/or apartments available on a first-come, first-served basis to single and married students.

GRADUATE UNITS

College of Arts and Sciences *Program availability:* Part-time, online learning. Offers digital journalism and design (MA); environmental science and policy (MA, MS); Florida studies (MLA); journalism and media studies (MA); liberal studies (MLA); psychology (MA). Electronic applications accepted.

College of Education *Program availability:* Part-time. Offers educational leadership development (M Ed); elementary education (MA); English education (MA); middle grades STEM education (MS); reading education (MA). Electronic applications accepted.

Kate Tiedemann College of Business *Program availability:* Part-time. Offers business (MBA). Electronic applications accepted.

UNIVERSITY OF SOUTH FLORIDA SARASOTA-MANATEE, Sarasota, FL 34243

General Information State-supported, coed, comprehensive institution. *Enrollment:* 2,117 graduate, professional, and undergraduate students; 66 full-time matriculated graduate/professional students (31 women), 83 part-time matriculated graduate/professional students (59 women). *Enrollment by degree level:* 149 master's. *Graduate faculty:* 26 full-time (14 women), 8 part-time/adjunct (6 women). Tuition, state resident: full-time $8350; part-time $418 per credit hour. Tuition, nonresident: full-time $19,047; part-time $863 per credit hour. *Required fees:* $1689. Tuition and fees vary according to degree level and program. *Student services:* Campus employment opportunities, campus safety program, career counseling, exercise/wellness program, free psychological counseling, international student services, low-cost health insurance, services for students with disabilities, teacher training, writing training. *Library facilities:* USF Libraries. *Collection:* Books: 1,231 (physical), 676,353 (digital/electronic); Serial titles: 61,782 (digital/electronic); Databases: 959. Weekly public service hours: 96; students can reserve study rooms.

Computer facilities: Computer purchase and lease plans are available. 56 computers available on campus for general student use. A campuswide network can be accessed from off campus. Online class registration is available.
Website: http://www.usfsm.edu/

General Application Contact: Andy Telatovich, Director, Admissions, 941-359-4330, E-mail: atelatovich@sar.usf.edu.

GRADUATE UNITS

College of Business Students: 42 full-time (15 women), 38 part-time (20 women); includes 30 minority (8 Black or African American, non-Hispanic/Latino; 8 Asian, non-Hispanic/Latino; 11 Hispanic/Latino; 3 Two or more races, non-Hispanic/Latino). Average age 32. 86 applicants, 23% accepted, 19 enrolled. *Faculty:* 8 full-time (1 woman). Expenses: Contact institution. *Financial support:* In 2017–18, 2 students received support. Federal Work-Study, scholarships/grants, health care benefits, and unspecified assistantships available. Support available to part-time students. Financial award application deadline: 3/1; financial award applicants required to submit FAFSA. In 2017, 30 master's awarded. *Program availability:* Part-time, evening/weekend. Offers business (MBA). *Application deadline:* For fall admission, 3/1 priority date for domestic students, 3/1 for international students; for spring admission, 10/1 priority date for domestic students, 10/1 for international students. Applications are processed on a rolling basis. *Application fee:* $30. Electronic applications accepted. *Application Contact:* Andy Telatovich, Director, Admissions, 941-359-4330, E-mail: atelatovich@sar.usf.edu. *Dean*, Dr. James M. Curran, 941-359-4605, Fax: 941-359-4367, E-mail: jmcurran@sar.usf.edu.

College of Hospitality and Technology Leadership Students: 13 full-time (6 women), 2 part-time (both women); includes 2 minority (1 Black or African American, non-Hispanic/Latino; 1 Hispanic/Latino), 5 international. Average age 32. 17 applicants, 29% accepted, 3 enrolled. *Faculty:* 3 full-time (1 woman). Expenses: Contact institution. *Financial support:* In 2017–18, 5 research assistantships with tuition reimbursements (averaging $7,831 per year) were awarded; teaching assistantships with tuition reimbursements, career-related internships or fieldwork, institutionally sponsored loans, health care benefits, and unspecified assistantships also available. Support available to part-time students. Financial award application deadline: 3/1; financial award applicants required to submit FAFSA. In 2017, 15 master's awarded. *Program availability:* Part-time. Offers hospitality management (MS). *Application deadline:* For fall admission, 3/1 priority date for domestic students, 3/1 for international students; for spring admission, 10/1 priority date for domestic students, 10/1 for international students. Applications are processed on a rolling basis. *Application fee:* $30. Electronic applications accepted. *Application Contact:* Andy Telatovich, Director, Admissions, 941-359-4330, E-mail:

atelatovich@sar.usf.edu. *Dean,* Dr. Pat Moreo, 941-359-4327, E-mail: pmoreo@sar.usf.edu.

College of Liberal Arts and Social Sciences Students: 11 full-time (10 women), 43 part-time (37 women); includes 17 minority (7 Black or African American, non-Hispanic/Latino; 2 Asian, non-Hispanic/Latino; 8 Hispanic/Latino), 1 international. Average age 35. 62 applicants, 27% accepted, 14 enrolled. *Faculty:* 15 full-time (12 women), 8 part-time/adjunct (6 women). Expenses: Contact institution. *Financial support:* In 2017–18, 1 student received support. Career-related internships or fieldwork, institutionally sponsored loans, scholarships/grants, health care benefits, and unspecified assistantships available. Support available to part-time students. Financial award application deadline: 3/1; financial award applicants required to submit FAFSA. In 2017, 32 master's awarded. *Program availability:* Part-time, 100% online, blended/hybrid learning. Offers criminal justice (MA); education (MA); educational leadership (M Ed); elementary education (MAT); English education (MA); social work (MSW). *Application deadline:* For fall admission, 3/1 priority date for domestic students, 3/1 for international students; for spring admission, 10/1 priority date for domestic students, 10/1 for international students. Applications are processed on a rolling basis. *Application fee:* $30. Electronic applications accepted. *Application Contact:* Brandon Avery, Assistant Director, Admissions, 941-359-4331, E-mail: bavery@sar.usf.edu. *Dean,* Dr. Jane Rose, 941-359-4469, Fax: 941-359-4778, E-mail: jane.rose@sar.usf.edu.

THE UNIVERSITY OF TAMPA, Tampa, FL 33606-1490

General Information Independent, coed, comprehensive institution. *Enrollment:* 8,839 graduate, professional, and undergraduate students; 286 full-time matriculated graduate/professional students (135 women), 579 part-time matriculated graduate/professional students (366 women). *Enrollment by degree level:* 865 master's. *Graduate faculty:* 56 full-time (26 women), 23 part-time/adjunct (14 women). *Tuition:* Full-time $7428. *Required fees:* $80. *Graduate housing:* Rooms and/or apartments available on a first-come, first-served basis to single and married students. Housing application deadline: 5/1. *Student services:* Campus employment opportunities, campus safety program, career counseling, international student services, services for students with disabilities. *Library facilities:* Macdonald Kelce Library. *Collection:* Books: 195,067 (physical), 145,016 (digital/electronic); Serial titles: 1,214 (physical), 190,560 (digital/electronic); Databases: 214. Weekly public service hours: 100; students can reserve study rooms. *Research affiliation:* Tampa General Hospital (nursing).

Computer facilities: Computer purchase and lease plans are available. 802 computers available on campus for general student use. A campuswide network can be accessed from student residence rooms and from off campus. Online class registration is available.
Website: http://www.ut.edu/

General Application Contact: Dr. Joshua Stagner, Director of Graduate and Continuing Studies, 813-257-3016, Fax: 813-258-7451, E-mail: jstagner@ut.edu.

GRADUATE UNITS

Program in Creative Writing Students: 56 full-time (34 women); includes 13 minority (3 Black or African American, non-Hispanic/Latino; 1 Asian, non-Hispanic/Latino; 7 Hispanic/Latino; 2 Two or more races, non-Hispanic/Latino). Average age 39. 51 applicants, 55% accepted, 14 enrolled. *Faculty:* 3 full-time (1 woman), 11 part-time/adjunct (3 women). Expenses: Contact institution. *Financial support:* In 2017–18, 11 students received support. Career-related internships or fieldwork, scholarships/grants, and unspecified assistantships available. Financial award applicants required to submit FAFSA. In 2017, 30 master's awarded. *Program availability:* Part-time. Offers creative writing (MFA). *Application deadline:* Applications are processed on a rolling basis. *Application fee:* $40. Electronic applications accepted. *Application Contact:* Chanelle Cox, Staff Assistant, Graduate and Continuing Studies, 813-253-6249, E-mail: ccox@ut.edu. *Director,* Dr. Erica Dawson, 813-257-6311, E-mail: edawson@ut.edu.

Program in Criminology and Criminal Justice Students: 15 full-time (10 women), 2 part-time (both women); includes 2 minority (1 Black or African American, non-Hispanic/Latino; 1 Two or more races, non-Hispanic/Latino). Average age 27. *Faculty:* 3 full-time (1 woman). Expenses: Contact institution. *Financial support:* Fellowships, career-related internships or fieldwork, scholarships/grants, and unspecified assistantships available. Offers criminology and criminal justice (MS). *Application deadline:* Applications are processed on a rolling basis. *Application fee:* $40. Electronic applications accepted. *Application Contact:* Dr. Joshua Stagner, Director of Graduate and Continuing Studies, 813-257-3016, Fax: 813-258-7451, E-mail: jstagner@ut.edu. *Coordinator,* Christopher R. Capsambelis, 813-257-3348, E-mail: ccapsambelis@ut.edu.

Program in Exercise and Nutrition Science Students: 37 full-time (20 women), 7 part-time (6 women); includes 7 minority (4 Black or African American, non-Hispanic/Latino; 1 Asian, non-Hispanic/Latino; 2 Two or more races, non-Hispanic/Latino), 3 international. Average age 26. 207 applicants, 52% accepted, 33 enrolled. *Faculty:* 3 full-time (1 woman), 1 (woman) part-time/adjunct. Expenses: Contact institution. *Financial support:* In 2017–18, 1 student received support. Career-related internships or fieldwork, scholarships/grants, and unspecified assistantships available. Financial award applicants required to submit FAFSA. In 2017, 44 master's awarded. *Program availability:* Part-time, evening/weekend. Offers exercise and nutrition science (MS). *Application deadline:* Applications are processed on a rolling basis. *Application fee:* $40. Electronic applications accepted. *Application Contact:* Chanelle Cox, Staff Assistant, Admissions for Graduate and Continuing Studies, 813-253-6249, E-mail: ccox@ut.edu. *Associate Professor, Health Sciences and Human Performance,* Dr. Ronda C. Sturgill, 813-257-3445, E-mail: rsturgill@ut.edu.

Program in Nursing Students: 4 full-time (all women), 166 part-time (148 women); includes 29 minority (15 Black or African American, non-Hispanic/Latino; 8 Asian, non-Hispanic/Latino; 6 Two or more races, non-Hispanic/Latino), 2 international. Average age 33. 132 applicants, 64% accepted, 51 enrolled. *Faculty:* 7 full-time (6 women), 6 part-time/adjunct (all women). Expenses: Contact institution. *Financial support:* In 2017–18, 9 students received support. Career-related internships or fieldwork, scholarships/grants, and unspecified assistantships available. Financial award applicants required to submit FAFSA. In 2017, 45 master's awarded. *Program availability:* Part-time, evening/weekend. Offers adult nursing practitioner (MSN); family nursing practitioner (MSN); nursing (MS). *Application deadline:* Applications are processed on a rolling basis. *Application fee:* $40. Electronic applications accepted. *Application Contact:* Chanelle Cox, Staff Assistant, Admissions for Graduate and Continuing Studies, 813-253-6249, E-mail: ccox@ut.edu. *Director,* Michele Wolf, 813-257-3179, E-mail: mwolf@ut.edu.

Programs in Education Students: 41 full-time (27 women), 69 part-time (52 women); includes 20 minority (18 Black or African American, non-Hispanic/Latino; 2 Two or more races, non-Hispanic/Latino), 14 international. Average age 32. 126 applicants, 40% accepted, 29 enrolled. *Faculty:* 5 full-time (4 women), 7 part-time/adjunct (5 women). Expenses: Contact institution. *Financial support:* In 2017–18, 20 students received support. Career-related internships or fieldwork, scholarships/grants, and unspecified assistantships available. Financial award applicants required to submit FAFSA. In 2017, 47 master's awarded. *Program availability:* Part-time, evening/weekend. Offers curriculum and instruction (M Ed); educational leadership (M Ed); instructional design and technology (MS). *Application deadline:* Applications are processed on a rolling basis. *Application fee:* $40. Electronic applications accepted. *Application Contact:* Chanelle Cox, Staff Assistant, Admissions for Graduate and Continuing Studies, 813-253-6249, E-mail: ccox@ut.edu. *Chair,* Dr. Antony Erben, 813-257-3414, E-mail: terben@ut.edu.

Sykes College of Business Students: 229 full-time (1 woman), 115 part-time (51 women). Average age 28. 1,305 applicants, 39% accepted, 192 enrolled. *Faculty:* 38 full-time (14 women), 6 part-time/adjunct (1 woman). Expenses: Contact institution. *Financial support:* In 2017–18, 116 students received support. Career-related internships or fieldwork, scholarships/grants, and unspecified assistantships available. Financial award applicants required to submit FAFSA. In 2017, 266 master's awarded. *Program availability:* Part-time, evening/weekend. Offers accounting (MS); business analytics (MBA); cybersecurity (MBA, MS); entrepreneurship (MBA, MS); finance (MBA, MS); information systems management (MBA); innovation management (MBA); international business (MBA); marketing (MBA, MS); nonprofit management (MBA, Certificate). *Application deadline:* Applications are processed on a rolling basis. *Application fee:* $40. Electronic applications accepted. *Application Contact:* Chanelle Cox, Staff Assistant, Admissions for Graduate and Continuing Studies, 813-253-6249, E-mail: ccox@ut.edu. *Associate Dean,* Dr. Natasha F. Veltri, 813-253-6289, E-mail: nveltri@ut.edu.

THE UNIVERSITY OF TENNESSEE, Knoxville, TN 37996

General Information State-supported, coed, university. CGS member. *Graduate housing:* Room and/or apartments available on a first-come, first-served basis to single students; on-campus housing not available to married students. Housing application deadline: 2/1. *Research affiliation:* Intel Corporation (computational science), Boeing (mechanical and aerospace engineering), Eastman Chemical (chemical engineering, chemistry), Mars, Inc. (materials science and engineering, polymer science, food science), DuPont (biofuels), Goodyear (chemical engineering; materials science and engineering; polymer science).

GRADUATE UNITS

College of Law Offers business transactions (JD); law (JD); trial advocacy and dispute resolution (JD). Electronic applications accepted.

Graduate School *Program availability:* Part-time, evening/weekend, online learning. Offers aviation systems (MS); comparative and experimental medicine (MS, PhD). Electronic applications accepted.

College of Agricultural Sciences and Natural Resources *Program availability:* Part-time, online learning. Offers agricultural education (MS); agricultural extension education (MS); agricultural sciences and natural resources (MS, PhD); animal anatomy (PhD); biosystems engineering (MS, PhD); biosystems engineering technology (MS); breeding (MS, PhD); entomology (MS, PhD); floriculture (MS); food science and technology (MS, PhD); forestry (MS); integrated pest management and bioactive natural products (PhD); landscape design (MS); management (MS, PhD); nutrition (MS, PhD); physiology (MS, PhD); plant pathology (MS, PhD); public horticulture (MS); turfgrass (MS); wildlife and fisheries science (MS); woody ornamentals (MS). Electronic applications accepted.

College of Architecture and Design Offers architecture (professional) (M Arch); architecture (research) (M Arch); architecture and design (M Arch, MA, MLA, MS); landscape architecture (MLA); landscape architecture (research) (MA, MS). Electronic applications accepted.

College of Arts and Sciences *Program availability:* Part-time, evening/weekend. Offers accompanying (MM); acting (MFA); American history (PhD); analytical chemistry (MS, PhD); applied linguistics (PhD); applied mathematics (MS); archaeology (MA, PhD); arts and sciences (M Math, MA, MFA, MM, MPA, MS, PhD); audiology (MA); behavior (MS, PhD); biochemistry, cellular and molecular biology (MS, PhD); biological anthropology (MA, PhD); ceramics (MFA); chemical physics (PhD); choral conducting (MM); clinical psychology (PhD); composition (MM); computer science (MS, PhD); costume design (MFA); criminology (MA, PhD); cultural anthropology (MA, PhD); drawing (MFA); ecology (MS, PhD); energy, environment, and resource policy (MA, PhD); English (MA, PhD); environmental chemistry (MS, PhD); European history (PhD); evolutionary biology (MS, PhD); experimental psychology (MA, PhD); French (MA, PhD); genome science and technology (MS, PhD); geography (MS, PhD); geology (MS, PhD); German (MA); graphic design (MFA); hearing science (PhD); history (MA); inorganic chemistry (MS, PhD); instrumental conducting (MM); inter-area studies (MFA); Italian (PhD); jazz (MM); lighting design (MFA); mathematical ecology (PhD); mathematics (M Math, MS, PhD); media arts (MFA); medical ethics (MA, PhD); microbiology (MS, PhD); modern foreign languages (PhD); music education (MM); music theory (MM); musicology (MM); organic chemistry (MS, PhD); painting (MFA); performance (MM); philosophy (MA, PhD); physical chemistry (MS, PhD); physics (MS, PhD); piano pedagogy and literature (MM); plant physiology and genetics (MS, PhD); political economy (MA, PhD); political science (MA, PhD); polymer chemistry (MS, PhD); Portuguese (PhD); printmaking (MFA); psychology (MA); public administration (MPA); religious studies (MA); Russian (PhD); scene design (MFA); sculpture (MFA); Spanish (MA); speech and hearing science (PhD); speech and language pathology (PhD); speech and language science (PhD); speech pathology (MA); theoretical chemistry (PhD); watercolor (MFA); zoo-archaeology (MA, PhD). Electronic applications accepted.

College of Business Administration *Program availability:* Part-time, online learning. Offers accounting (M Acc, PhD); business administration (M Acc, MA, MBA, MS, PhD); economics (MA, PhD); finance (MBA, PhD); industrial and organizational psychology (PhD); industrial statistics (MS); logistics and transportation (MBA, PhD); management (PhD); management science (MS, PhD); marketing (MBA, PhD); operations management (MBA); professional business administration (MBA); statistics (MS, PhD); systems (M Acc); taxation (M Acc); teacher licensure (MS); training and development (MS). Electronic applications accepted.

College of Communication and Information *Program availability:* Part-time, evening/weekend, online learning. Offers advertising (MS, PhD); broadcasting (MS, PhD); communications (MS, PhD); information sciences (MS, PhD); journalism (MS, PhD); public relations (MS, PhD); speech communication (MS, PhD). Electronic applications accepted.

College of Education, Health and Human Sciences *Program availability:* Part-time, evening/weekend, online learning. Offers adult education (MS); applied educational psychology (MS); art education (MS); biomechanics/sports medicine (MS, PhD); child and family studies (MS, PhD); collaborative learning (Ed D); college student personnel (MS); community health (PhD); community health education (MPH);

consumer services management (MS); counseling education (PhD); cultural studies in education (PhD); curriculum (MS, Ed S); curriculum, educational research and evaluation (Ed D, PhD); early childhood education (MS, PhD); early childhood special education (MS); education of deaf and hard of hearing (MS); education, health and human sciences (MPH, MS, Ed D, PhD, Ed S); educational administration and policy studies (Ed D, PhD); educational administration and supervision (MS, Ed S); educational psychology (Ed D, PhD); elementary education (MS, Ed S); elementary teaching (MS); English education (MS, Ed S); exercise physiology (MS, PhD); exercise science (MS, PhD); foreign language/ESL education (MS, Ed S); gerontology (MPH); health planning/administration (MPH); health promotion and health education (MS); hospitality management (MS); hotel, restaurant, and tourism management (MS); instructional technology (MS, Ed D, PhD, Ed S); literacy, language and ESL education (PhD); literacy, language education, and ESL education (Ed D); mathematics education (MS, Ed S); mental health counseling (MS); modified and comprehensive special education (MS); nutrition (MS); nutrition science (PhD); reading education (MS, Ed S); recreation and leisure studies (MS); rehabilitation counseling (MS); retail and consumer sciences (MS); retailing and consumer sciences (PhD); safety (MS); school counseling (MS, Ed S); school psychology (PhD, Ed S); science education (MS, Ed S); secondary teaching (MS); social foundations (MS); social science education (MS, Ed S); socio-cultural foundations of sports and education (PhD); special education (Ed S); sport management (MS); sport studies (MS, PhD); teacher education (Ed D, PhD); textile science (MS, PhD); therapeutic recreation (MS); tourism (MS). Electronic applications accepted.

College of Nursing *Program availability:* Part-time. Offers nursing (MSN, PhD). Electronic applications accepted.

College of Social Work *Program availability:* Part-time, online learning. Offers clinical practice and leadership (DSW); evidenced-based interpersonal practice (MSSW); management leadership and community practice (MSSW); social work (MSSW, DSW, PhD). Electronic applications accepted.

College of Veterinary Medicine Offers veterinary medicine (DVM).

Tickle College of Engineering Students: 863 full-time (186 women), 271 part-time (60 women); includes 110 minority (24 Black or African American, non-Hispanic/Latino; 33 Asian, non-Hispanic/Latino; 38 Hispanic/Latino; 15 Two or more races, non-Hispanic/Latino), 409 international. Average age 29. 1,269 applicants, 40% accepted, 293 enrolled. *Faculty:* 255 full-time (36 women), 70 part-time/adjunct (14 women). Expenses: Contact institution. *Financial support:* In 2017–18, 721 students received support, including 111 fellowships with full tuition reimbursements available (averaging $24,411 per year), 401 research assistantships with full tuition reimbursements available (averaging $23,476 per year), 209 teaching assistantships with full tuition reimbursements available (averaging $20,367 per year); career-related internships or fieldwork, Federal Work-Study, institutionally sponsored loans, health care benefits, and unspecified assistantships also available. Financial award application deadline: 2/1; financial award applicants required to submit FAFSA. In 2017, 165 master's, 110 doctorates awarded. *Program availability:* Part-time, online learning. Offers aerospace engineering (MS, PhD); biomedical engineering (MS, PhD); chemical engineering (MS, PhD); civil engineering (MS, PhD); computer engineering (MS, PhD); computer science (MS, PhD); data science and engineering (PhD); electrical engineering (MS, PhD); energy science and engineering (PhD); engineering (MS, PhD); engineering management (MS); engineering science (MS, PhD); environmental engineering (MS); industrial engineering (MS, PhD); materials science and engineering (MS, PhD); mechanical engineering (MS, PhD); nuclear engineering (MS, PhD); reliability and maintainability engineering (MS). *Application deadline:* For fall admission, 2/1 priority date for domestic and international students; for spring admission, 6/15 for domestic and international students; for summer admission, 10/15 for domestic and international students. Applications are processed on a rolling basis. *Application fee:* $60. Electronic applications accepted. *Application Contact:* Dr. Masood Parang, Associate Dean of Student Affairs, 865-974-2454, Fax: 865-974-9871, E-mail: mparang@utk.edu. *Dean*, Dr. Wayne T. Davis, 865-974-5321, Fax: 865-974-8890, E-mail: wtdavis@utk.edu.

The University of Tennessee Space Institute *Program availability:* Part-time, blended/hybrid learning. Offers aerospace engineering (MS, PhD); biomedical engineering (MS, PhD); engineering science (MS, PhD); industrial and systems engineering/engineering management (MS, PhD); mechanical engineering (MS, PhD); physics (MS, PhD). Electronic applications accepted.

THE UNIVERSITY OF TENNESSEE AT CHATTANOOGA, Chattanooga, TN 37403-2598

General Information State-supported, coed, comprehensive institution. CGS member. *Enrollment:* 11,587 graduate, professional, and undergraduate students; 696 full-time matriculated graduate/professional students (428 women), 715 part-time matriculated graduate/professional students (392 women). *Enrollment by degree level:* 992 master's, 312 doctoral, 107 other advanced degrees. Tuition, state resident: full-time $8244; part-time $458 per credit hour. Tuition, nonresident: full-time $24,362; part-time $1353 per credit hour. *Required fees:* $1776; $487 per semester. Tuition and fees vary according to course load. *Graduate housing:* Room and/or apartments available on a first-come, first-served basis to single students; on-campus housing not available to married students. Typical cost: $5226 per year ($8556 including board). Housing application deadline: 6/1. *Student services:* Campus employment opportunities, campus safety program, career counseling, exercise/wellness program, free psychological counseling, grant writing training, international student services, low-cost health insurance, multicultural affairs office, services for students with disabilities, teacher training, writing training. *Library facilities:* UTC Library plus 1 other. *Collection:* Books: 743,490 (physical); Databases: 219. Study areas open 24 hours, 5–7 days a week; students can reserve study rooms. *Research affiliation:* UT Law Enforcement Innovation Center (criminal justice), Highland Biological Field Station (biology and environmental science), Tennessee Valley Authority (engineering), Gulf Coast Research Laboratory (biology and environmental science), Tennessee Coalition against Domestic and Sexual Violence (criminal justice).

Computer facilities: A campuswide network can be accessed from student residence rooms and from off campus. Online class registration is available.
Website: http://www.utc.edu/

General Application Contact: Dr. Joanne Romagni, Dean of the Graduate School, 423-425-4478, Fax: 423-425-5223, E-mail: joanne-romagni@utc.edu.

GRADUATE UNITS

Department of Health and Human Performance Students: 42 full-time (30 women); includes 7 minority (2 Black or African American, non-Hispanic/Latino; 3 Hispanic/Latino; 2 Two or more races, non-Hispanic/Latino). Average age 23. 24 applicants, 100% accepted, 22 enrolled. Expenses: Contact institution. *Financial support:* Research assistantships with tuition reimbursements, teaching assistantships with tuition reimbursements, career-related internships or fieldwork, scholarships/grants, and unspecified assistantships available. Support available to part-time students. Financial award application deadline: 7/1; financial award applicants required to submit FAFSA. In 2017, 21 master's awarded. Offers athletic training (MSAT); health and human performance (MS). *Application deadline:* For fall admission, 6/15 priority date for domestic students, 7/1 for international students; for spring admission, 11/1 priority date for domestic students, 11/1 for international students. Applications are processed on a rolling basis. *Application fee:* $35 ($40 for international students). Electronic applications accepted. *Application Contact:* Dr. Joanne Romagni, Dean of the Graduate School, 423-425-4478, Fax: 423-425-5223, E-mail: joanne-romagni@utc.edu. *Department Head*, Dr. Marisa Colston, 423-425-4743, E-mail: marisa-colston@utc.edu.

Department of Occupational Therapy Students: 64 full-time (62 women), 1 (woman) part-time; includes 7 minority (2 Hispanic/Latino; 5 Two or more races, non-Hispanic/Latino). Average age 24. 32 applicants, 88% accepted, 24 enrolled. *Faculty:* 4 full-time (all women), 1 (woman) part-time/adjunct. Expenses: Contact institution. *Financial support:* Fellowships, research assistantships, career-related internships or fieldwork, scholarships/grants, and unspecified assistantships available. Support available to part-time students. Financial award application deadline: 7/1; financial award applicants required to submit FAFSA. In 2017, 13 doctorates awarded. Offers occupational therapy (OTD). *Application deadline:* For fall admission, 6/15 priority date for domestic students, 7/1 for international students; for spring admission, 11/1 priority date for domestic students, 11/1 for international students. Applications are processed on a rolling basis. *Application fee:* $35 ($40 for international students). Electronic applications accepted. *Application Contact:* Dr. Joanne Romagni, Dean of the Graduate School, 423-425-4478, Fax: 423-425-5223, E-mail: joanne-romagni@utc.edu. *Department Head*, Susan McDonald, 423-425-5759, E-mail: susan-mcdonald@utc.edu.

Department of Political Science and Public Service Students: 14 full-time (7 women), 12 part-time (9 women); includes 8 minority (5 Black or African American, non-Hispanic/Latino; 2 Asian, non-Hispanic/Latino; 1 Two or more races, non-Hispanic/Latino). Average age 30. 18 applicants, 100% accepted, 11 enrolled. Expenses: Contact institution. *Financial support:* Research assistantships, career-related internships or fieldwork, scholarships/grants, and unspecified assistantships available. Support available to part-time students. Financial award application deadline: 7/1; financial award applicants required to submit FAFSA. In 2017, 7 master's, 1 other advanced degree awarded. *Program availability:* Part-time, evening/weekend. Offers local government management (MPA); non profit management (MPA); public administration (MPA); public administration and non-profit management (Postbaccalaureate Certificate). *Application deadline:* For fall admission, 6/15 priority date for domestic students, 7/1 for international students; for spring admission, 11/1 priority date for domestic students, 11/1 for international students. Applications are processed on a rolling basis. *Application fee:* $35 ($40 for international students). Electronic applications accepted. *Application Contact:* Dr. Joanne Romagni, Dean of the Graduate School, 423-425-4478, Fax: 423-425-5223, E-mail: joanne-romagni@utc.edu. *Department Head*, Dr. Michelle D. Deardorf, 423-425-4231, Fax: 423-425-2373, E-mail: michelle-deardorff@utc.edu.

Engineering Management and Technology Program Students: 14 full-time (3 women), 50 part-time (11 women); includes 17 minority (10 Black or African American, non-Hispanic/Latino; 1 Asian, non-Hispanic/Latino; 6 Hispanic/Latino), 5 international. Average age 33. 34 applicants, 94% accepted, 20 enrolled. Expenses: Contact institution. *Financial support:* Research assistantships, teaching assistantships, career-related internships or fieldwork, scholarships/grants, and unspecified assistantships available. Support available to part-time students. Financial award application deadline: 7/1; financial award applicants required to submit FAFSA. In 2017, 18 master's, 6 other advanced degrees awarded. *Program availability:* 100% online, blended/hybrid learning. Offers construction management (Graduate Certificate); engineering management (MS); fundamentals of engineering management (Graduate Certificate); leadership and ethics (Graduate Certificate); logistics and supply chain management (Graduate Certificate); power systems management (Graduate Certificate); project and technology management (Graduate Certificate); quality management (Graduate Certificate). *Application deadline:* For fall admission, 6/15 priority date for domestic students, 7/1 for international students; for spring admission, 11/1 priority date for domestic students, 11/1 for international students. Applications are processed on a rolling basis. *Application fee:* $35 ($40 for international students). Electronic applications accepted. *Application Contact:* Dr. Joanne Romagni, Dean of the Graduate School, 423-425-4478, Fax: 423-425-5223, E-mail: joanne-romagni@utc.edu. *Department Head*, Dr. Neslihan Alp, 423-425-4032, Fax: 423-425-5818, E-mail: neslihan-alp@utc.edu.

Program in Accountancy Students: 8 full-time (6 women), 20 part-time (12 women); includes 5 minority (1 Black or African American, non-Hispanic/Latino; 3 Asian, non-Hispanic/Latino; 1 Two or more races, non-Hispanic/Latino). Average age 26. 19 applicants, 63% accepted, 11 enrolled. Expenses: Contact institution. *Financial support:* Research assistantships, teaching assistantships, career-related internships or fieldwork, scholarships/grants, and unspecified assistantships available. Support available to part-time students. Financial award application deadline: 7/1; financial award applicants required to submit FAFSA. In 2017, 10 master's awarded. *Program availability:* Part-time, evening/weekend. Offers accountancy (M Acc). *Application deadline:* For fall admission, 6/15 priority date for domestic students, 7/1 for international students; for spring admission, 11/1 priority date for domestic students, 11/1 for international students. Applications are processed on a rolling basis. *Application fee:* $35 ($40 for international students). Electronic applications accepted. *Application Contact:* Dr. Joanne Romagni, Dean of the Graduate School, 413-425-4478, Fax: 423-425-5223, E-mail: randy-walker@utc.edu. *Department Head*, Dr. Dan Hollingsworth, 423-425-4664, Fax: 423-425-5255, E-mail: dan-hollingsworth@utc.edu.

Program in Business Administration Students: 63 full-time (26 women), 238 part-time (110 women); includes 60 minority (21 Black or African American, non-Hispanic/Latino; 1 American Indian or Alaska Native, non-Hispanic/Latino; 9 Asian, non-Hispanic/Latino; 14 Hispanic/Latino; 15 Two or more races, non-Hispanic/Latino), 5 international. Average age 32. 150 applicants, 90% accepted, 98 enrolled. Expenses: Contact institution. *Financial support:* Research assistantships, teaching assistantships, career-related internships or fieldwork, scholarships/grants, health care benefits, tuition waivers (partial), and unspecified assistantships available. Support available to part-time students. Financial award application deadline: 7/1. In 2017, 103 master's awarded. *Program availability:* Part-time, evening/weekend. Offers business administration (EMBA, MBA, PMBA). *Application deadline:* For fall admission, 6/15 priority date for domestic students, 7/1 for international students; for spring admission, 11/1 priority date for domestic students, 11/1 for international students. Applications are processed on a rolling basis. *Application fee:* $35 ($40 for international students). Electronic applications accepted. *Application Contact:* Dr. Joanne Romagni, Dean of the Graduate School, 423-425-4478, Fax: 423-425-5223, E-mail: joanne-romagni@utc.edu. *Director of Graduate Programs*, Elizabeth Bell, 423-425-2326, Fax: 423-425-5255, E-mail: elizabeth-bell@utc.edu.

Program in Computational Science Students: 9 full-time (1 woman), 12 part-time (3 women); includes 4 minority (2 Black or African American, non-Hispanic/Latino; 1 Asian, non-Hispanic/Latino; 1 Hispanic/Latino), 9 international. Average age 36. 7 applicants, 86% accepted, 5 enrolled. Expenses: Contact institution. *Financial support:* Research assistantships, career-related internships or fieldwork, scholarships/grants, and unspecified assistantships available. Support available to part-time students. Financial award application deadline: 7/1. In 2017, 12 doctorates awarded. Offers computational science (PhD). *Application deadline:* For fall admission, 6/15 priority date for domestic students, 7/1 for international students; for spring admission, 11/1 priority date for domestic students, 11/1 for international students. Applications are processed on a rolling basis. *Application fee:* $35 ($40 for international students). Electronic applications accepted. *Application Contact:* Dr. Joanne Romagni, Dean of the Graduate School, 423-425-4478, Fax: 423-425-5223, E-mail: joanne-romagni@utc.edu. *Department Head,* Dr. Joseph Kizza, 423-425-4043, Fax: 423-425-5311, E-mail: joseph-kizza@utc.edu.

Program in Computer Science Students: 27 full-time (6 women), 32 part-time (12 women); includes 18 minority (7 Black or African American, non-Hispanic/Latino; 1 American Indian or Alaska Native, non-Hispanic/Latino; 4 Asian, non-Hispanic/Latino; 3 Hispanic/Latino; 3 Two or more races, non-Hispanic/Latino), 5 international. Average age 31. 34 applicants, 88% accepted, 19 enrolled. Expenses: Contact institution. *Financial support:* Research assistantships, teaching assistantships, career-related internships or fieldwork, scholarships/grants, health care benefits, and unspecified assistantships available. Support available to part-time students. Financial award application deadline: 7/1; financial award applicants required to submit FAFSA. In 2017, 8 master's awarded. *Program availability:* Part-time. Offers biomedical informatics (Post Master's Certificate); computer science (MS). *Application deadline:* For fall admission, 6/15 priority date for domestic students, 7/1 for international students; for spring admission, 11/1 priority date for domestic students, 11/1 for international students. Applications are processed on a rolling basis. *Application fee:* $35 ($40 for international students). Electronic applications accepted. *Application Contact:* Dr. Joanne Romagni, Dean of the Graduate School, 423-425-4478, Fax: 423-425-5223, E-mail: joanne-romagni@utc.edu. *Department Head,* Dr. Joseph Kizza, 423-425-4043, Fax: 423-425-5442, E-mail: joseph-kizza@utc.edu.

Program in Counseling Students: 44 full-time (36 women), 11 part-time (10 women); includes 13 minority (8 Black or African American, non-Hispanic/Latino; 1 Hispanic/Latino; 4 Two or more races, non-Hispanic/Latino). Average age 26. 49 applicants, 67% accepted, 24 enrolled. Expenses: Contact institution. *Financial support:* Research assistantships, career-related internships or fieldwork, scholarships/grants, and unspecified assistantships available. Support available to part-time students. Financial award application deadline: 7/1; financial award applicants required to submit FAFSA. In 2017, 13 master's awarded. Offers mental health (M Ed); school counseling (M Ed, Post Master's Certificate). *Application deadline:* For fall admission, 6/15 priority date for domestic students, 7/1 for international students; for spring admission, 11/1 priority date for domestic students, 11/1 for international students. Applications are processed on a rolling basis. *Application fee:* $35 ($40 for international students). Electronic applications accepted. *Application Contact:* Dr. Joanne Romagni, Dean of the Graduate School, 423-425-4478, Fax: 423-425-4052, E-mail: joanne-romagni@utc.edu. *Director,* Dr. Elizabeth O'Brien, 423-425-4544, E-mail: elizabeth-o'brien@utc.edu.

Program in Criminal Justice Students: 14 full-time (8 women), 23 part-time (10 women); includes 14 minority (8 Black or African American, non-Hispanic/Latino; 2 Hispanic/Latino; 4 Two or more races, non-Hispanic/Latino). Average age 29. 15 applicants, 93% accepted, 14 enrolled. Expenses: Contact institution. *Financial support:* Research assistantships, teaching assistantships, career-related internships or fieldwork, scholarships/grants, and unspecified assistantships available. Support available to part-time students. Financial award application deadline: 7/1; financial award applicants required to submit FAFSA. In 2017, 9 master's awarded. *Program availability:* Part-time. Offers criminal justice (MSCJ). *Application deadline:* For fall admission, 6/15 priority date for domestic students, 7/1 for international students; for spring admission, 11/1 priority date for domestic students, 11/1 for international students. Applications are processed on a rolling basis. *Application fee:* $35 ($40 for international students). Electronic applications accepted. *Application Contact:* Dr. Joanne Romagni, Dean of the Graduate School, 423-425-4478, Fax: 423-425-5223, E-mail: joanne-romagni@utc.edu. *Graduate Coordinator,* Dr. Tammy Garland, 423-425-5245, Fax: 423-425-2228, E-mail: tammy-garland@utc.edu.

Program in Engineering Students: 26 full-time (2 women), 17 part-time (3 women); includes 13 minority (4 Black or African American, non-Hispanic/Latino; 5 Asian, non-Hispanic/Latino; 3 Hispanic/Latino; 1 Two or more races, non-Hispanic/Latino), 16 international. Average age 29. 22 applicants, 82% accepted, 12 enrolled. Expenses: Contact institution. *Financial support:* Research assistantships, teaching assistantships, career-related internships or fieldwork, scholarships/grants, health care benefits, and unspecified assistantships available. Support available to part-time students. Financial award application deadline: 7/1. In 2017, 20 master's awarded. *Program availability:* Part-time. Offers automotive (MS Engr); chemical (MS Engr); civil (MS Engr); electrical (MS Engr); mechanical (MS Engr). *Application deadline:* For fall admission, 6/15 priority date for domestic students, 7/1 for international students; for spring admission, 11/1 priority date for domestic students, 11/1 for international students. Applications are processed on a rolling basis. *Application fee:* $35 ($40 for international students). Electronic applications accepted. *Application Contact:* Dr. Joanne Romagni, Dean of the Graduate School, 423-425-4478, Fax: 423-425-5223, E-mail: joanne-romagni@utc.edu. *Dean,* Dr. Daniel Pack, 423-425-2256, Fax: 423-425-5311, E-mail: daniel-pack@utc.edu.

Program in English Students: 12 full-time (8 women), 14 part-time (11 women); includes 4 minority (1 Black or African American, non-Hispanic/Latino; 1 Asian, non-Hispanic/Latino; 1 Hispanic/Latino; 1 Two or more races, non-Hispanic/Latino). Average age 27. 10 applicants, 100% accepted, 7 enrolled. Expenses: Contact institution. *Financial support:* Research assistantships, teaching assistantships, career-related internships or fieldwork, scholarships/grants, health care benefits, and unspecified assistantships available. Support available to part-time students. Financial award application deadline: 7/1; financial award applicants required to submit FAFSA. In 2017, 12 master's awarded. *Program availability:* Part-time. Offers creative writing (MA); literary study (MA); rhetoric and writing (MA). *Application deadline:* For fall admission, 6/15 priority date for domestic students, 7/1 for international students; for spring admission, 11/1 priority date for domestic students, 11/1 for international students. Applications are processed on a rolling basis. *Application fee:* $35 ($40 for international students). Electronic applications accepted. *Application Contact:* Dr. Joanne Romagni, Dean of the Graduate School, 423-425-4478, Fax: 423-425-5223, E-mail: joanne-romagni@utc.edu. *Department Head,* Dr. Christopher Stuart, 423-425-2140, Fax: 423-425-2282, E-mail: chris-stuart@utc.edu.

Program in Environmental Science Students: 20 full-time (12 women), 11 part-time (8 women); includes 5 minority (1 Black or African American, non-Hispanic/Latino; 1 Asian, non-Hispanic/Latino; 1 Hispanic/Latino; 2 Two or more races, non-Hispanic/Latino). Average age 27. 15 applicants, 87% accepted, 13 enrolled. Expenses: Contact institution. *Financial support:* Research assistantships, teaching assistantships, career-related internships or fieldwork, scholarships/grants, and unspecified assistantships available. Support available to part-time students. Financial award application deadline: 7/1; financial award applicants required to submit FAFSA. In 2017, 11 master's awarded. *Program availability:* Part-time. Offers environmental science (MS). *Application deadline:* For fall admission, 6/15 priority date for domestic students, 7/1 for international students; for spring admission, 11/1 priority date for domestic students, 11/1 for international students. Applications are processed on a rolling basis. *Application fee:* $35 ($40 for international students). Electronic applications accepted. *Application Contact:* Dr. Joanne Romagni, Dean of the Graduate School, 423-425-4478, Fax: 423-425-5223, E-mail: joanne-romagni@utc.edu. *Department Head,* Dr. John Tucker, 423-425-4341, Fax: 423-425-2285, E-mail: john-tucker@utc.edu.

Program in Interior Design Students: 5 full-time (4 women), 2 part-time (both women); includes 1 minority (Two or more races, non-Hispanic/Latino). Average age 37. 3 applicants, 100% accepted, 2 enrolled. Expenses: Contact institution. *Financial support:* Career-related internships or fieldwork, scholarships/grants, and unspecified assistantships available. Support available to part-time students. Financial award application deadline: 7/1; financial award applicants required to submit FAFSA. Offers interior design (MID, MS). *Application deadline:* For fall admission, 6/15 priority date for domestic students, 7/1 for international students; for spring admission, 11/1 priority date for domestic students, 11/1 for international students. Applications are processed on a rolling basis. *Application fee:* $35 ($40 for international students). Electronic applications accepted. *Application Contact:* Dr. Joanne Romagni, Dean of the Graduate School, 423-425-4478, Fax: 423-425-5223, E-mail: joanne-romagni@utc.edu. *Graduate Program Director,* Dr. Dana Moody, 423-425-4459, Fax: 423-425-4479, E-mail: dana-moody@utc.edu.

Program in Learning and Leadership Students: 1 (woman) full-time, 86 part-time (49 women); includes 18 minority (12 Black or African American, non-Hispanic/Latino; 1 Asian, non-Hispanic/Latino; 3 Hispanic/Latino; 2 Two or more races, non-Hispanic/Latino). Average age 43. 19 applicants, 58% accepted, 11 enrolled. Expenses: Contact institution. *Financial support:* Research assistantships, career-related internships or fieldwork, scholarships/grants, and unspecified assistantships available. Support available to part-time students. Financial award application deadline: 7/1; financial award applicants required to submit FAFSA. In 2017, 7 doctorates awarded. Offers educational leadership (Ed D, PhD). *Application deadline:* For fall admission, 6/15 priority date for domestic students, 7/1 for international students; for spring admission, 11/1 priority date for domestic students, 11/1 for international students. Applications are processed on a rolling basis. *Application fee:* $35 ($40 for international students). Electronic applications accepted. *Application Contact:* Dr. Joanne Romagni, Dean of the Graduate School, 423-425-4478, Fax: 423-425-5223, E-mail: joanne-romagni@utc.edu. *Director,* Dr. David Rausch, 423-425-5270, E-mail: utclead@utc.edu.

Program in Mathematics Students: 10 full-time (2 women), 6 part-time (3 women); includes 4 minority (1 Hispanic/Latino; 3 Two or more races, non-Hispanic/Latino), 1 international. Average age 27. 6 applicants, 100% accepted, 5 enrolled. Expenses: Contact institution. *Financial support:* Research assistantships and teaching assistantships available. Financial award application deadline: 7/1; financial award applicants required to submit FAFSA. In 2017, 9 master's awarded. *Program availability:* Part-time. Offers applied mathematics (MS); applied statistics (MS); mathematics education (MS); pre-professional mathematics (MS). *Application deadline:* For fall admission, 6/15 for domestic students, 7/1 for international students; for spring admission, 11/1 for domestic and international students. Applications are processed on a rolling basis. *Application fee:* $35 ($40 for international students). Electronic applications accepted. *Application Contact:* Dr. Joanne Romagni, Dean of the Graduate School, 423-425-4478, Fax: 423-425-5223, E-mail: joanne-romagni@utc.edu. *Graduate Program Coordinator,* Dr. Francesco Barioli, 423-425-2198, E-mail: francesco-barioli@utc.edu.

Program in Music Expenses: Contact institution. *Financial support:* Research assistantships, Federal Work-Study, scholarships/grants, and unspecified assistantships available. Financial award application deadline: 7/1; financial award applicants required to submit FAFSA. In 2017, 6 master's awarded. Offers music education (MM); performance (MM). *Application deadline:* For fall admission, 6/15 priority date for domestic students, 7/1 for international students; for spring admission, 11/1 priority date for domestic students, 11/1 for international students. Applications are processed on a rolling basis. *Application fee:* $35 ($40 for international students). Electronic applications accepted. *Application Contact:* Dr. Joanne Romagni, Dean of the Graduate School, 423-425-4478, Fax: 423-425-5223, E-mail: joanne-romagni@utc.edu. *Interim Department Head,* Dr. Stuart Benkert, 423-425-4614, Fax: 423-425-4603, E-mail: stuart-benkert@utc.edu.

Program in Physical Therapy Students: 107 full-time (70 women); includes 17 minority (1 Black or African American, non-Hispanic/Latino; 1 Asian, non-Hispanic/Latino; 1 Hispanic/Latino; 14 Two or more races, non-Hispanic/Latino). Average age 24. 45 applicants, 84% accepted, 36 enrolled. *Faculty:* 10 full-time (7 women), 3 part-time/adjunct (2 women). Expenses: Contact institution. *Financial support:* Research assistantships, teaching assistantships, career-related internships or fieldwork, scholarships/grants, and unspecified assistantships available. Support available to part-time students. Financial award application deadline: 7/1; financial award applicants required to submit FAFSA. In 2017, 33 doctorates awarded. Offers physical therapy (DPT). *Application deadline:* For fall admission, 6/15 priority date for domestic students, 7/1 for international students; for spring admission, 11/1 priority date for domestic students, 11/1 for international students. Applications are processed on a rolling basis. *Application fee:* $35 ($40 for international students). Electronic applications accepted. *Application Contact:* Dr. Joanne Romagni, Dean of the Graduate School, 423-425-4478, Fax: 423-425-5223, E-mail: joanne-romagni@utc.edu. *Interim Department Head,* Dr. Debbie Ingram, 423-425-4767, Fax: 423-425-2380, E-mail: debbie-ingram@utc.edu.

Program in Psychology Students: 46 full-time (28 women), 4 part-time (3 women); includes 5 minority (2 Black or African American, non-Hispanic/Latino; 1 Asian, non-Hispanic/Latino; 2 Hispanic/Latino). Average age 25. 85 applicants, 38% accepted, 25 enrolled. Expenses: Contact institution. *Financial support:* Research assistantships, teaching assistantships, career-related internships or fieldwork, scholarships/grants, and unspecified assistantships available. Support available to part-time students. Financial award application deadline: 7/1; financial award applicants required to submit FAFSA. In 2017, 20 master's awarded. *Program availability:* Part-time. Offers industrial/organizational psychology (MS); research psychology (MS). *Application deadline:* For fall admission, 6/15 priority date for domestic students, 7/1 for international students; for spring admission, 11/1 priority date for domestic students, 11/1 for international students. Applications are processed on a rolling basis. *Application fee:* $35 ($40 for international students). Electronic applications accepted. *Application Contact:* Dr. Joanne Romagni, Dean of the Graduate School, 423-425-4478, Fax: 423-

425-5223, E-mail: joanne-romagni@utc.edu. *Department Head*, Dr. Brian O'Leary, 423-425-4283, Fax: 423-425-4284, E-mail: brian-o'leary@utc.edu.

Program in Social Work Students: 39 full-time (30 women), 2 part-time (1 woman); includes 10 minority (5 Black or African American, non-Hispanic/Latino; 4 Hispanic/Latino; 1 Two or more races, non-Hispanic/Latino). Average age 28. 41 applicants, 73% accepted, 28 enrolled. Expenses: Contact institution. *Financial support:* Career-related internships or fieldwork, scholarships/grants, and unspecified assistantships available. Support available to part-time students. Financial award application deadline: 7/1; financial award applicants required to submit FAFSA. Offers social work (MSW). *Application deadline:* For fall admission, 6/15 priority date for domestic students, 7/1 for international students; for spring admission, 11/1 priority date for domestic students, 11/1 for international students. Applications are processed on a rolling basis. *Application fee:* $35 ($40 for international students). Electronic applications accepted. *Application Contact:* Dr. Joanne Romagni, Dean of the Graduate School, 423-425-4478, Fax: 423-425-5223, E-mail: joanne-romagni@utc.edu. *Coordinator*, Dr. Amy Doolittle, 423-425-5563, E-mail: amy-doolittle@utc.edu.

School of Education Students: 43 full-time (30 women), 58 part-time (47 women); includes 18 minority (9 Black or African American, non-Hispanic/Latino; 1 Asian, non-Hispanic/Latino; 1 Hispanic/Latino; 7 Two or more races, non-Hispanic/Latino). Average age 31. 118 applicants, 75% accepted, 33 enrolled. Expenses: Contact institution. *Financial support:* Research assistantships, teaching assistantships, career-related internships or fieldwork, institutionally sponsored loans, scholarships/grants, and unspecified assistantships available. Support available to part-time students. Financial award application deadline: 7/1; financial award applicants required to submit FAFSA. In 2017, 59 master's, 7 other advanced degrees awarded. *Program availability:* Part-time. Offers counseling (M Ed); education (M Ed, Post-Master's Certificate); elementary education (M Ed); learning and leadership (Ed D); school leadership (Post-Master's Certificate); school leadership: principal licensure (Ed S); secondary education (M Ed); special education (M Ed). *Application deadline:* For fall admission, 6/15 for domestic students, 7/1 for international students; for spring admission, 11/1 for domestic and international students. Applications are processed on a rolling basis. *Application fee:* $35 ($40 for international students). Electronic applications accepted. *Application Contact:* Dr. Joanne Romagni, Dean of the Graduate School, 423-425-4478, Fax: 423-425-5223, E-mail: joanne-romagni@utc.edu. *Director*, Dr. Renee Murley, 423-425-4684, Fax: 423-425-5380, E-mail: renee-murley@utc.edu.

School of Nursing Students: 62 full-time (33 women), 69 part-time (61 women); includes 24 minority (11 Black or African American, non-Hispanic/Latino; 1 American Indian or Alaska Native, non-Hispanic/Latino; 5 Asian, non-Hispanic/Latino; 3 Hispanic/Latino; 4 Two or more races, non-Hispanic/Latino). Average age 34. 47 applicants, 100% accepted, 45 enrolled. Expenses: Contact institution. *Financial support:* Teaching assistantships, career-related internships or fieldwork, and scholarships/grants available. Support available to part-time students. Financial award application deadline: 7/1; financial award applicants required to submit FAFSA. In 2017, 33 master's, 14 doctorates, 7 other advanced degrees awarded. Offers certified nurse anesthetist (Post-Master's Certificate); family nurse practitioner (MSN, Post-Master's Certificate); gerontology acute care (MSN, Post-Master's Certificate); nurse anesthesia (MSN); nurse education (Post-Master's Certificate); nursing (DNP). *Application deadline:* For fall admission, 6/15 priority date for domestic students, 7/1 for international students; for spring admission, 11/1 priority date for domestic students, 11/1 for international students. Applications are processed on a rolling basis. *Application fee:* $35 ($40 for international students). Electronic applications accepted. *Application Contact:* Dr. Joanne Romagni, Dean of the Graduate School, 423-425-4478, Fax: 423-425-5223, E-mail: joanne-romagni@utc.edu. *Director*, Dr. Chris Smith, 423-425-1741, Fax: 423-425-4668, E-mail: chris-smith@utc.edu.

THE UNIVERSITY OF TENNESSEE AT MARTIN, Martin, TN 38238

General Information State-supported, coed, comprehensive institution. *Enrollment:* 6,800 graduate, professional, and undergraduate students; 60 full-time matriculated graduate/professional students (45 women), 309 part-time matriculated graduate/professional students (206 women). *Enrollment by degree level:* 369 master's. *Graduate faculty:* 134. *International tuition:* $22,602 full-time. Tuition, state resident: full-time $8658; part-time $481 per credit hour. Tuition, nonresident: full-time $14,418; part-time $801 per credit hour. *Required fees:* $1404; $79 per credit hour. Part-time tuition and fees vary according to course load. *Graduate housing:* Rooms and/or apartments available on a first-come, first-served basis to single and married students. Typical cost: $2730 per year ($5976 including board) for single students; $5460 per year for married students. Room and board charges vary according to board plan and housing facility selected. Housing application deadline: 3/1. *Student services:* Campus employment opportunities, campus safety program, career counseling, child daycare facilities, exercise/wellness program, free psychological counseling, international student services, low-cost health insurance, multicultural affairs office, services for students with disabilities, teacher training, writing training. *Library facilities:* Paul Meek Library. *Collection:* Books: 309,179 (physical), 90,675 (digital/electronic); Serial titles: 2,377 (physical), 335,337 (digital/electronic); Databases: 215. Weekly public service hours: 92; study areas open 24 hours, 5–7 days a week. *Research affiliation:* U.S. Department of Education (DOE) (academic extensions), National Writing Project (humanities), U.S. Department of Health and Human Services (infant health), U.S. Department of Justice (criminal justice), The University of Tennessee Research Foundation (science and technology), Oak Ridge National Laboratory (science, technology, engineering, and math (STEM)).

Computer facilities: 1,402 computers available on campus for general student use. A campuswide network can be accessed from student residence rooms and from off campus. Online class registration, online fee payments, degree progress, financial aid data, housing applications, transcripts are available.
Website: http://www.utm.edu/

General Application Contact: Jolene L. Cunningham, Student Services Specialist, 731-881-7012, Fax: 731-881-7499, E-mail: jcunningham@utm.edu.

GRADUATE UNITS

Graduate Programs Students: 60 full-time (45 women), 309 part-time (206 women); includes 52 minority (37 Black or African American, non-Hispanic/Latino; 2 Asian, non-Hispanic/Latino; 6 Hispanic/Latino; 7 Two or more races, non-Hispanic/Latino). Average age 33. 226 applicants, 61% accepted, 88 enrolled. *Faculty:* 134. Expenses: Contact institution. *Financial support:* In 2017–18, 114 students received support, including 8 research assistantships with full tuition reimbursements available (averaging $7,414 per year), 18 teaching assistantships with full tuition reimbursements available (averaging $7,178 per year); scholarships/grants and tuition waivers (full and partial) also available. Financial award application deadline: 2/1; financial award applicants required to submit FAFSA. In 2017, 94 master's awarded. *Program availability:* Part-time, 100% online, blended/hybrid learning. *Application deadline:* For fall admission, 7/27 priority date for domestic and international students; for spring admission, 12/17 priority date for domestic and international students; for summer admission, 5/10 priority date for domestic and international students. Applications are processed on a rolling basis. *Application fee:* $30 ($130 for international students). Electronic applications accepted. *Application Contact:* Jolene L. Cunningham, Student Services Specialist, 731-881-7012, Fax: 731-881-7499, E-mail: jcunningham@utm.edu. *Associate Vice Chancellor and Dean of Graduate Studies*, Dr. Victoria S. Seng, 731-881-7012, Fax: 731-881-7499, E-mail: vseng@utm.edu.

College of Agriculture and Applied Sciences Students: 11 full-time (8 women), 57 part-time (36 women); includes 11 minority (9 Black or African American, non-Hispanic/Latino; 1 Hispanic/Latino; 1 Two or more races, non-Hispanic/Latino). Average age 31. 58 applicants, 83% accepted, 25 enrolled. *Faculty:* 25. Expenses: Contact institution. *Financial support:* In 2017–18, 32 students received support, including 2 teaching assistantships with full tuition reimbursements available (averaging $7,892 per year); research assistantships, scholarships/grants, and tuition waivers (full and partial) also available. Financial award application deadline: 2/1; financial award applicants required to submit FAFSA. In 2017, 23 master's awarded. *Program availability:* Part-time, 100% online, blended/hybrid learning. Offers agricultural and natural resources management (MSANR); agriculture and applied sciences (MSANR, MSFCS); dietetics (MSFCS); general family and consumer sciences (MSFCS). *Application deadline:* For fall admission, 7/27 priority date for domestic and international students; for spring admission, 12/17 priority date for domestic and international students; for summer admission, 5/10 priority date for domestic and international students. Applications are processed on a rolling basis. *Application fee:* $30 ($130 for international students). Electronic applications accepted. *Application Contact:* Jolene L. Cunningham, Student Services Specialist, 731-881-7012, Fax: 731-881-7499, E-mail: jcunningham@utm.edu. *Dean*, Dr. Todd Winters, 731-881-7250, E-mail: winters@utm.edu.

College of Business and Global Affairs Students: 12 full-time (5 women), 73 part-time (31 women); includes 12 minority (7 Black or African American, non-Hispanic/Latino; 2 Asian, non-Hispanic/Latino; 2 Hispanic/Latino; 1 Two or more races, non-Hispanic/Latino). Average age 34. 33 applicants, 24% accepted, 6 enrolled. *Faculty:* 31. Expenses: Contact institution. *Financial support:* In 2017–18, 29 students received support, including 4 research assistantships with full tuition reimbursements available (averaging $7,226 per year), 2 teaching assistantships with full tuition reimbursements available (averaging $7,540 per year); scholarships/grants and tuition waivers (full and partial) also available. Financial award application deadline: 2/1; financial award applicants required to submit FAFSA. In 2017, 38 master's awarded. *Program availability:* Part-time, 100% online, blended/hybrid learning. Offers agricultural business (MBA); business (MBA); financial services (MBA); general business (MBA). *Application deadline:* For fall admission, 7/27 priority date for domestic and international students; for spring admission, 12/17 priority date for domestic and international students; for summer admission, 5/10 priority date for domestic and international students. Applications are processed on a rolling basis. *Application fee:* $30 ($130 for international students). Electronic applications accepted. *Application Contact:* Jolene L. Cunningham, Student Services Specialist, 731-881-7012, Fax: 731-881-7499, E-mail: jcunningham@utm.edu. *Dean*, Dr. Ross Dickens, 731-881-7227, Fax: 731-881-7241, E-mail: rdicken2@utm.edu.

College of Education, Health and Behavioral Sciences Students: 37 full-time (32 women), 164 part-time (127 women); includes 26 minority (21 Black or African American, non-Hispanic/Latino; 3 Hispanic/Latino; 2 Two or more races, non-Hispanic/Latino). Average age 33. 125 applicants, 61% accepted, 52 enrolled. *Faculty:* 47. Expenses: Contact institution. *Financial support:* In 2017–18, 42 students received support, including 2 research assistantships with full tuition reimbursements available (averaging $6,912 per year), 7 teaching assistantships with full tuition reimbursements available (averaging $6,796 per year); scholarships/grants and tuition waivers (full and partial) also available. Financial award application deadline: 2/1; financial award applicants required to submit FAFSA. In 2017, 33 master's awarded. *Program availability:* Part-time, online only, 100% online. Offers addictions counseling (MS Ed); community counseling (MS Ed); curriculum and instruction (MS Ed); education, health and behavioral sciences (MS Ed); educational leadership (MS Ed); initial licensure (MS Ed); initial licensure K-12 (MS Ed); interdisciplinary (MS Ed); school counseling (MS Ed); student affairs and college counseling (MS Ed). *Application deadline:* For fall admission, 7/27 priority date for domestic and international students; for spring admission, 12/17 priority date for domestic and international students; for summer admission, 5/10 priority date for domestic and international students. Applications are processed on a rolling basis. *Application fee:* $30 ($130 for international students). Electronic applications accepted. *Application Contact:* Jolene L. Cunningham, Student Services Specialist, 731-881-7012, Fax: 731-881-7499, E-mail: jcunningham@utm.edu. *Dean*, Cynthia West, 731-881-7127, Fax: 731-881-7975, E-mail: cwest@utm.edu.

College of Humanities and Fine Arts Students: 15 part-time (12 women). Average age 34. 10 applicants, 50% accepted, 5 enrolled. *Faculty:* 20 full-time (7 women). Expenses: Contact institution. *Financial support:* In 2017–18, 11 students received support, including 1 research assistantship with full tuition reimbursement available (averaging $9,048 per year); teaching assistantships, scholarships/grants, and tuition waivers (full and partial) also available. Financial award application deadline: 2/1; financial award applicants required to submit FAFSA. *Program availability:* Part-time, blended/hybrid learning. Offers strategic communication (MASC). *Application deadline:* For fall admission, 7/27 priority date for domestic and international students; for spring admission, 12/15 priority date for domestic and international students; for summer admission, 5/10 priority date for domestic and international students. Applications are processed on a rolling basis. *Application fee:* $30 ($130 for international students). Electronic applications accepted. *Application Contact:* Jolene L. Cunningham, Student Services Specialist, 731-881-7012, Fax: 731-881-7499, E-mail: jcunningham@utm.edu. *Dean*, Dr. Lynn Alexander, 731-881-7490, Fax: 731-881-7276, E-mail: lalexand@utm.edu.

THE UNIVERSITY OF TENNESSEE HEALTH SCIENCE CENTER, Memphis, TN 38163-0002

General Information State-supported, coed, upper-level institution. CGS member. *Graduate housing:* On-campus housing not available. *Research affiliation:* Saint Jude's Children's Research Hospital, Veterans Administration Medical Center, University of Memphis, LeBonheur Children's Medical Center.

GRADUATE UNITS

College of Dentistry Offers dentistry (DDS). Electronic applications accepted.

College of Graduate Health Sciences Students: 258 full-time (130 women); includes 87 minority (14 Black or African American, non-Hispanic/Latino; 68 Asian, non-Hispanic/Latino; 5 Hispanic/Latino). Average age 28. 673 applicants, 17% accepted, 102 enrolled. *Faculty:* 528 full-time (176 women). Expenses: Contact institution. *Financial support:* In 2017–18, 150 students received support, including 150 research assistantships (averaging $25,000 per year); fellowships, institutionally sponsored loans, scholarships/grants, health care benefits, and tuition waivers (full and partial) also available. Support available to part-time students. In 2017, 23 master's, 30 doctorates awarded. Offers biomedical engineering (MS, PhD); biomedical sciences (PhD); dental sciences (MDS); epidemiology (MS); health outcomes and policy research (PhD); laboratory research and management (MS); nursing science (PhD); pharmaceutical sciences (PhD); pharmacology (MS); speech and hearing science (PhD). MS and PhD programs in biomedical engineering offered jointly with University of Memphis. *Application deadline:* For winter admission, 1/1 for domestic and international students; for spring admission, 3/1 for domestic and international students. Applications are processed on a rolling basis. *Application fee:* $0. Electronic applications accepted. *Application Contact:* Dr. Isaac O. Donkor, Associate Dean for Student Affairs, 901-448-5538, E-mail: idonkor@uthsc.edu. *Dean,* Dr. Donald B. Thomason, 901-448-5538, E-mail: dthomaso@uthsc.edu.

College of Health Professions *Program availability:* Part-time, evening/weekend, online learning. Offers audiology (MS, Au D); clinical laboratory science (MSCLS); cytopathology practice (MCP); health informatics and information management (MHIIM); occupational therapy (MOT); physical therapy (DPT, ScDPT); physician assistant (MMS); speech-language pathology (MS). Electronic applications accepted.

College of Medicine Offers medicine (MD). Electronic applications accepted.

College of Nursing Students: 262 full-time (228 women), 13 part-time (12 women); includes 83 minority (71 Black or African American, non-Hispanic/Latino; 6 Asian, non-Hispanic/Latino; 6 Hispanic/Latino). Average age 32. 215 applicants, 49% accepted, 79 enrolled. *Faculty:* 52 full-time (47 women), 11 part-time/adjunct (4 women). Expenses: Contact institution. *Financial support:* In 2017–18, 112 students received support, including 9 research assistantships (averaging $24,783 per year); Federal Work-Study, institutionally sponsored loans, scholarships/grants, and tuition waivers (partial) also available. Financial award application deadline: 3/15; financial award applicants required to submit FAFSA. In 2017, 78 doctorates, 2 Certificates awarded. *Program availability:* Part-time, blended/hybrid learning. Offers adult-gerontology acute care nurse practitioner (Post Master's Certificate); advance practice nursing (DNP); family nurse practitioner (Post-Doctoral Certificate); pediatric acute care nurse practitioner (Post-Doctoral Certificate); pediatric primary care nurse practitioner (Post-Doctoral Certificate); psychiatric/mental health nurse practitioner (Post-Doctoral Certificate); registered nurse first assistant (Certificate). *Application deadline:* For fall admission, 1/15 for domestic students; for spring admission, 8/15 for domestic students. *Application fee:* $70. Electronic applications accepted. *Application Contact:* Jamie Overton, Director, Student Affairs, 901-448-6139, Fax: 901-448-4121, E-mail: joverton@uthsc.edu. *Dean,* Dr. Wendy Likes, 901-448-6135, Fax: 901-448-4121, E-mail: wlikes@uthsc.edu.

College of Pharmacy Offers pharmacy (MS, PhD, Pharm D). Electronic applications accepted.

THE UNIVERSITY OF TENNESSEE–OAK RIDGE NATIONAL LABORATORY, Oak Ridge, TN 37830-8026

General Information State-supported, coed, graduate-only institution. *Research affiliation:* Oak Ridge National Laboratory.

GRADUATE UNITS

Graduate Program in Genome Science and Technology Offers life sciences (MS, PhD). Electronic applications accepted.

THE UNIVERSITY OF TEXAS AT ARLINGTON, Arlington, TX 76019

General Information State-supported, coed, university. CGS member. *Graduate housing:* Rooms and/or apartments available on a first-come, first-served basis to single and married students. *Research affiliation:* Texas Health Resources (medical technologies), Center for Innovation (technology development and commercialization), Facebook (energy efficient electronic systems), U.S. Department of Energy (bioengineering), National Science Foundation (materials science and engineering), Texas Instruments (medical technologies).

GRADUATE UNITS

Graduate School *Program availability:* Part-time, evening/weekend, online learning.

College of Architecture, Planning and Public Affairs *Program availability:* Part-time, evening/weekend, online learning. Offers architecture (M Arch); architecture, planning and public affairs (M Arch, MLA, MPA, MPP, PhD); landscape architecture (MLA); public administration (MPA); public and urban administration (PhD); public policy (MPP); urban planning and public policy (PhD). Electronic applications accepted.

College of Business *Program availability:* Part-time, evening/weekend, online learning. Offers accounting (MP Acc, MS, PhD); business (MA, MBA, MP Acc, MS, MSHRM, PhD); economics (MA); finance (PhD); health care administration (MS); human resources (MSHRM); information systems (MS, PhD); marketing (MBA); marketing research (MS); quantitative finance (MS); real estate (MS); taxation (MS). Electronic applications accepted.

College of Education Offers curriculum and instruction (M Ed); education (M Ed, M Ed T, PhD); educational leadership (PhD); higher education (M Ed); principal certification (M Ed); teaching (with certification) (M Ed T).

College of Engineering *Program availability:* Part-time, evening/weekend, online learning. Offers aerospace engineering (M Engr, MS, PhD); bioengineering (MS, PhD); civil engineering (M Engr, MS, PhD); computer engineering (MS, PhD); computer science (MS, PhD); construction management (MCM); electrical engineering (M Engr, MS, PhD); engineering (M Engr, MCM, MS, PhD); engineering management (MS); industrial engineering (MS, PhD); logistics (MS); materials science and engineering (M Engr, MS, PhD); mechanical engineering (M Engr, MS, PhD); software engineering (MS); systems engineering (MS).

College of Liberal Arts *Program availability:* Part-time, evening/weekend. Offers anthropology (MA); communication (MA); criminology and criminal justice (MA); education (MM); English (MA); film and video (MFA); French (MA); glass (MFA); history (MA); intermedia (MFA); liberal arts (MA, MFA, MM, PhD); linguistics (MA, PhD); literature (PhD); performance (MM); political science (MA); sociology (MA); Spanish (MA); teaching English to speakers of other languages (MA); transatlantic history (PhD); visual communication (MFA).

College of Nursing and Health Innovation *Program availability:* Part-time, evening/weekend, online learning. Offers athletic training (MS); exercise science (MS); kinesiology (PhD); nurse practitioner (MSN); nursing (PhD); nursing administration (MSN); nursing education (MSN); nursing practice (DNP).

College of Science *Program availability:* Part-time, evening/weekend. Offers applied math (MS); biology (MS); chemistry (MS, PhD); earth and environmental sciences (MS, PhD); experimental health psychology (PhD); experimental psychology (MS, PhD); health/neuroscience psychology (MS, PhD); industrial and organizational psychology (MS); mathematics (PhD); mathematics education (MA); physics (MS); physics and applied physics (PhD); quantitative biology (PhD); science (MA, MS, PhD).

School of Social Work *Program availability:* Part-time, evening/weekend, online learning. Offers social work (MSW, PhD). Electronic applications accepted.

THE UNIVERSITY OF TEXAS AT AUSTIN, Austin, TX 78712-1111

General Information State-supported, coed, university. CGS member. *Graduate housing:* Rooms and/or apartments available to single students and available on a first-come, first-served basis to married students.

GRADUATE UNITS

Dell Medical School Offers medicine (MD).

Graduate School *Program availability:* Part-time, evening/weekend. Offers computational science, engineering, and mathematics (MS, PhD). Electronic applications accepted.

Cockrell School of Engineering *Program availability:* Part-time, evening/weekend. Offers aerospace engineering (MSE, PhD); architectural engineering (MSE); biomedical engineering (MS, PhD); chemical engineering (MSE, PhD); civil engineering (MS, PhD); electrical and computer engineering (MS, PhD); energy and earth resources (MA); engineering (MA, MS, MSE, PhD); engineering mechanics (MS, PhD); environmental and water resources engineering (MS, PhD); materials science and engineering (MS, PhD); mechanical engineering (MS, PhD); operations research and industrial engineering (MS, PhD); petroleum engineering (MS, PhD). Electronic applications accepted.

College of Communication *Program availability:* Part-time. Offers advertising (MA, PhD); audiology (Au D); communication (MA, MFA, Au D, PhD); communication sciences and disorders (PhD); communication studies (MA, PhD); film and media production (MFA); journalism (MA, PhD); media studies (MA, PhD); screenwriting (MFA); speech language pathology (MA). Electronic applications accepted.

College of Education *Program availability:* Part-time. Offers academic educational psychology (M Ed, MA); autism and developmental disabilities (Ed D, PhD); autism and developmental disability (M Ed, MA); behavioral health (PhD); bilingual/bicultural education (M Ed, MA, PhD); counseling psychology (PhD); counselor education (M Ed); cultural studies in education (M Ed, MA, PhD); early childhood education (M Ed, MA, PhD); early childhood special education (M Ed, MA, Ed D, PhD); education (M Ed, MA, MS, Ed D, PhD); educational administration (M Ed, Ed D, PhD); exercise and sport psychology (M Ed, MA); exercise science (M Ed, MS, PhD); health education (M Ed, MS, Ed D, PhD); human development, culture and learning sciences (PhD); language and literacy studies (M Ed, PhD); learning disabilities (Ed D, PhD); learning disabilities/behavior disorders (M Ed, MA); learning technologies (M Ed, MA, PhD); multicultural special education (M Ed, MA, Ed D, PhD); physical education (M Ed, MA, PhD); program evaluation (MA); quantitative methods (M Ed, MA, PhD); rehabilitation counselor (M Ed); rehabilitation counselor education (Ed D, PhD); school psychology (MA, PhD); special education administration (Ed D, PhD). Electronic applications accepted.

College of Fine Arts *Program availability:* Part-time. Offers acting (MFA); art education (MA); art history (MA, PhD); band and wind conducting (M Music, DMA); brass/woodwind/percussion (MM, DMA); chamber music (MM); choral conducting (MM, DMA); collaborative piano (MM, DMA); composition (MM, DMA); dance (MFA); design (MFA); directing (MFA); drama and theatre for youth (MFA); ethnomusicology (MM, PhD); fine arts (M Music, MA, MFA, MM, DMA, PhD); literature and pedagogy (MM); music and human learning (MM, PhD); music and human learning (DMA); musicology (MM, PhD); opera performance (MM, DMA); orchestral conducting (MM, DMA); organ (MM); organ performance (MM, DMA); performance (MM); performance (DMA); performance as public practice (MA, MFA, PhD); piano (DMA); piano literature and pedagogy (MM); piano performance (MM, DMA); playwriting (MFA); string performance (MM, DMA); studio art (MFA); theatre technology (MFA); theatrical design (MFA); theory (MM, PhD); vocal performance (MM, DMA); voice (DMA); voice performance pedagogy (DMA); woodwind, brass, percussion performance (MM). Electronic applications accepted.

College of Liberal Arts *Program availability:* Part-time. Offers African Diaspora studies (MA, PhD); American studies (MA, PhD); applied linguistics/pedagogy (PhD); archaeology (MA, PhD); Asian cultures and languages (MA, PhD); Asian studies (MA); behavioral neuroscience (PhD); classics (MA, PhD); clinical psychology (PhD); cognitive systems (PhD); comparative literature (MA, PhD); creative writing (MFA); cultural forms (MA, PhD); cultural politics of Afro-Latin and indigenous peoples (MA); development studies (MA); developmental psychology (PhD); economics (MA, MS Econ, PhD); English (MA, PhD); environmental studies (MA); French linguistics (MA, PhD); French studies (MA, PhD); geography and the environment (MA, PhD); Germanic studies (MA, PhD); government (MA, PhD); Hispanic linguistics (MA, PhD); Hispanic literature (MA, PhD); history (MA, PhD); human dimensions of organizations (MA); human rights (MA); Ibero-romance philology and linguistics (PhD); individual differences and evolutionary psychology (PhD); Italian studies (MA, PhD); Latin American and international law (LL M); liberal arts (LL M, MA, MFA, MS Econ, PhD); linguistic anthropology (MA, PhD); linguistics (MA, PhD); literature and culture (PhD); Luso-Brazilian literature (MA, PhD); Mexican American studies (MA); Middle Eastern languages and cultures (MA, PhD); Middle Eastern studies (MA); perceptual systems (PhD); philosophy (PhD); physical anthropology (MA, PhD); Romance linguistics (PhD); Russian, East European, and Eurasian studies (MA); Slavic languages (MA); Slavic linguistics (PhD); social anthropology (MA, PhD); social psychology (PhD); sociology (MA, PhD). Electronic applications accepted.

College of Natural Sciences *Program availability:* Part-time. Offers analytical chemistry (PhD); astronomy (MA, PhD); biochemistry (PhD); computer sciences (MSCS, PhD); ecology, evolution and behavior (PhD); human development and family sciences (MA, PhD); inorganic chemistry (PhD); marine science (MS, PhD); mathematics (MA, PhD); microbiology (PhD); natural sciences (MA, MS, MSCS, PhD); nutrition (MA); nutritional sciences (MA, MS, PhD); organic chemistry (PhD); physical chemistry (PhD); physics (MA, MS, PhD); plant biology (MA, PhD); statistics (MS, PhD); textile and apparel technology (MS). Electronic applications accepted.

College of Pharmacy Offers health outcomes and pharmacy practice (PhD); health outcomes and pharmacy practice (MS); medicinal chemistry (PhD); pharmaceutics (PhD); pharmacology and toxicology (PhD); pharmacotherapy (MS, PhD); pharmacy (MS, PhD, Pharm D); translational science (PhD). Electronic applications accepted.

Institute for Cellular and Molecular Biology Offers cellular and molecular biology (PhD).

The Institute for Neuroscience Offers neuroscience (PhD). Electronic applications accepted.

Jackson School of Geosciences *Program availability:* Part-time. Offers geosciences (MA, MS, PhD). Electronic applications accepted.

Lyndon B. Johnson School of Public Affairs *Program availability:* Part-time. Offers global policy studies (MGPS); public affairs (MP Aff); public leadership (EMPL); public policy (PhD). Electronic applications accepted.

McCombs School of Business Offers accounting (MPA, PhD); business (MBA, MPA, MS, MSF, PhD); business administration (MBA); executive business administration (MBA); finance (MSF, PhD); information management (MBA); information systems (PhD); information technology and management (MS); management (PhD); marketing (MBA, MS, PhD); risk analysis and decision making (PhD); risk management (MBA); supply chain and operations management (MBA, PhD); technology commercialization (MS). Electronic applications accepted.

Michener Center for Writers Offers fiction (MFA); playwriting (MFA); poetry (MFA); screenwriting (MFA). Electronic applications accepted.

School of Architecture Offers architectural history (MA, PhD); architecture (M Arch, M Arch I, M Arch II, MA, MID, MLA, MS, MSAS, MSCRP, MSSD, MSUD, PhD); community and regional planning (MSCRP, PhD); historic preservation (M Arch, MS, MSCRP); interior design (MID); landscape architecture (MLA); sustainable design (M Arch I, M Arch II, MSSD); urban design (M Arch, MSUD). Electronic applications accepted.

School of Information *Program availability:* Part-time. Offers identity management and security (MSIMS); information (PhD); information studies (MSIS). MSIMS program offered in conjunction with the Center for Identity. Electronic applications accepted.

School of Nursing *Program availability:* Part-time. Offers adult - gerontology clinical nurse specialist (MSN); child health (MSN); family nurse practitioner (MSN); family psychiatric/mental health nurse practitioner (MSN); holistic adult health (MSN); maternity (MSN); nursing (PhD); nursing administration and healthcare systems management (MSN); nursing practice (DNP); pediatric nurse practitioner (MSN); public health nursing (MSN). Electronic applications accepted.

School of Social Work *Program availability:* Part-time. Offers social work (MSSW, PhD).

School of Law Offers law (LL M, JD). Electronic applications accepted.

THE UNIVERSITY OF TEXAS AT DALLAS, Richardson, TX 75080

General Information State-supported, coed, university. CGS member. *Enrollment:* 27,642 graduate, professional, and undergraduate students; 6,302 full-time matriculated graduate/professional students (2,622 women), 2,700 part-time matriculated graduate/professional students (1,196 women). *Enrollment by degree level:* 7,627 master's, 1,375 doctoral. *Graduate faculty:* 582 full-time (131 women), 127 part-time/adjunct (48 women). Tuition, state resident: full-time $12,916; part-time $718 per credit hour. Tuition, nonresident: full-time $25,252; part-time $1403 per credit hour. *Graduate housing:* Rooms and/or apartments available on a first-come, first-served basis to single and married students. Typical cost: $11,112 (including board) for single students; $11,112 (including board) for married students. Housing application deadline: 5/31. *Student services:* Campus employment opportunities, campus safety program, career counseling, child daycare facilities, exercise/wellness program, free psychological counseling, grant writing training, international student services, low-cost health insurance, multicultural affairs office, services for students with disabilities, teacher training, writing training. *Library facilities:* Eugene McDermott Library plus 1 other. *Collection:* Books: 652,018 (physical), 1.5 million (digital/electronic); Serial titles: 135,287 (physical), 149,406 (digital/electronic); Databases: 530. Weekly public service hours: 152; study areas open 24 hours, 5–7 days a week; students can reserve study rooms.

Computer facilities: Computer purchase and lease plans are available. 170 computers available on campus for general student use. A campuswide network can be accessed from student residence rooms and from off campus. Online class registration is available.
Website: http://www.utdallas.edu/

General Application Contact: Dr. Marion Underwood, Dean of Graduate Studies, 972-883-2234, Fax: 972-883-4308, E-mail: graduatestudies@utdallas.edu.

GRADUATE UNITS

Erik Jonson School of Engineering and Computer Science Students: 1,833 full-time (507 women), 474 part-time (149 women); includes 168 minority (10 Black or African American, non-Hispanic/Latino; 1 American Indian or Alaska Native, non-Hispanic/Latino; 97 Asian, non-Hispanic/Latino; 46 Hispanic/Latino; 14 Two or more races, non-Hispanic/Latino), 1,893 international. Average age 26. 6,926 applicants, 23% accepted, 677 enrolled. *Faculty:* 159 full-time (18 women), 21 part-time/adjunct (7 women). Expenses: Contact institution. *Financial support:* In 2017–18, 767 students received support, including 53 fellowships (averaging $4,898 per year), 391 research assistantships with partial tuition reimbursements available (averaging $24,309 per year), 240 teaching assistantships with partial tuition reimbursements available (averaging $17,252 per year); career-related internships or fieldwork, Federal Work-Study, institutionally sponsored loans, scholarships/grants, and unspecified assistantships also available. Support available to part-time students. Financial award application deadline: 4/30; financial award applicants required to submit FAFSA. In 2017, 896 master's, 88 doctorates awarded. *Program availability:* Part-time, evening/weekend. Offers biomedical engineering (MS, PhD); computer engineering (MS, PhD); computer science (MSCS, PhD); electrical engineering (MSEE, PhD); engineering and computer science (MS, MSCS, MSEE, MSTE, PhD); materials science and engineering (MS, PhD); mechanical engineering (MS, PhD); software engineering (MS, PhD); systems engineering and management (MS); telecommunications engineering (MSTE, PhD). *Application deadline:* For fall admission, 7/15 for domestic students, 5/1 priority date for international students; for spring admission, 11/15 for domestic students, 9/1 priority date for international students. Applications are processed on a rolling basis. *Application fee:* $50 ($100 for international students). Electronic applications accepted. *Application Contact:* Leiane Davis, Administrative Associate, 972-883-6851, Fax: 972-883-2813, E-mail: leiane.davis@utdallas.edu. *Interim Dean*, Dr. Poras Balsara, 972-883-2557, Fax: 972-883-2813, E-mail: poras@utdallas.edu.

Naveen Jindal School of Management Students: 2,991 full-time (1,276 women), 1,677 part-time (746 women); includes 873 minority (142 Black or African American, non-Hispanic/Latino; 7 American Indian or Alaska Native, non-Hispanic/Latino; 459 Asian, non-Hispanic/Latino; 203 Hispanic/Latino; 1 Native Hawaiian or other Pacific Islander, non-Hispanic/Latino; 61 Two or more races, non-Hispanic/Latino), 2,884 international. Average age 28. 6,657 applicants, 43% accepted, 1485 enrolled. *Faculty:* 113 full-time (22 women), 71 part-time/adjunct (23 women). Expenses: Contact institution. *Financial support:* In 2017–18, 1,288 students received support, including 26 research assistantships with partial tuition reimbursements available (averaging $33,146 per year), 175 teaching assistantships with partial tuition reimbursements available (averaging $17,697 per year); fellowships, career-related internships or fieldwork, Federal Work-Study, institutionally sponsored loans, scholarships/grants, and unspecified assistantships also available. Support available to part-time students. Financial award application deadline: 4/30; financial award applicants required to submit FAFSA. In 2017, 2,047 master's, 14 doctorates awarded. *Program availability:* Part-time, evening/weekend, online learning. Offers accounting (MS); business administration (MBA); business analytics (MS); executive business administration (EMBA); finance (MS); global leadership (EMBA); healthcare leadership and management (MS); healthcare management (EMBA); information technology and management (MS); innovation and entrepreneurship (MS); international management studies (MS, PhD); management (EMBA, MBA, MS, PhD); management science (MS, PhD); marketing (MS); project management (EMBA); supply chain management (MS); systems engineering and management (MS). *Application deadline:* For fall admission, 7/15 for domestic students, 5/1 priority date for international students; for spring admission, 11/15 for domestic students, 9/1 priority date for international students. Applications are processed on a rolling basis. *Application fee:* $50 ($100 for international students). Electronic applications accepted. *Application Contact:* 972-883-2750, Fax: 972-883-6425, E-mail: jindal@utdallas.edu. *Dean*, Dr. Hasan Pirkul, 972-883-2705, Fax: 972-883-2799, E-mail: hpirkul@utdallas.edu.

School of Arts and Humanities Students: 132 full-time (83 women), 117 part-time (71 women); includes 62 minority (11 Black or African American, non-Hispanic/Latino; 3 American Indian or Alaska Native, non-Hispanic/Latino; 10 Asian, non-Hispanic/Latino; 25 Hispanic/Latino; 13 Two or more races, non-Hispanic/Latino), 29 international. Average age 40. 127 applicants, 55% accepted, 43 enrolled. *Faculty:* 47 full-time (17 women), 4 part-time/adjunct (2 women). Expenses: Contact institution. *Financial support:* In 2017–18, 136 students received support, including 12 research assistantships with partial tuition reimbursements available (averaging $22,710 per year), 71 teaching assistantships with partial tuition reimbursements available (averaging $15,000 per year); fellowships, Federal Work-Study, institutionally sponsored loans, scholarships/grants, and unspecified assistantships also available. Support available to part-time students. Financial award application deadline: 4/30; financial award applicants required to submit FAFSA. In 2017, 17 master's, 18 doctorates awarded. *Program availability:* Part-time, evening/weekend. Offers art history (MA); history (MA); humanities (MA, PhD); Latin American studies (MA). *Application deadline:* For fall admission, 7/15 for domestic students, 5/1 priority date for international students; for spring admission, 11/15 for domestic students, 9/1 priority date for international students. Applications are processed on a rolling basis. *Application fee:* $50 ($100 for international students). Electronic applications accepted. *Application Contact:* Dr. John Gooch, Associate Dean of Graduate Studies, 972-883-2756, Fax: 972-883-2989, E-mail: john.gooch@utdallas.edu. *Dean*, Dr. Dennis M. Kratz, 972-883-2984, Fax: 972-883-2989, E-mail: dkratz@utdallas.edu.

School of Arts, Technology, and Emerging Communication Students: 56 full-time (23 women), 37 part-time (17 women); includes 24 minority (7 Black or African American, non-Hispanic/Latino; 6 Asian, non-Hispanic/Latino; 8 Hispanic/Latino; 3 Two or more races, non-Hispanic/Latino), 15 international. Average age 32. 143 applicants, 15% accepted, 11 enrolled. *Faculty:* 25 full-time (10 women), 2 part-time/adjunct (0 women). Expenses: Contact institution. *Financial support:* In 2017–18, 58 students received support, including 8 research assistantships with partial tuition reimbursements available (averaging $27,884 per year), 26 teaching assistantships with partial tuition reimbursements available (averaging $14,653 per year); career-related internships or fieldwork, Federal Work-Study, institutionally sponsored loans, scholarships/grants, and unspecified assistantships also available. Support available to part-time students. Financial award application deadline: 4/30; financial award applicants required to submit FAFSA. In 2017, 40 master's, 5 doctorates awarded. Offers arts and technology (MA, MFA, PhD); emerging media and communication (MA). *Application deadline:* For fall admission, 7/15 for domestic students, 5/1 priority date for international students; for spring admission, 11/15 for domestic students, 9/1 priority date for international students. Applications are processed on a rolling basis. *Application fee:* $50 ($100 for international students). Electronic applications accepted. *Application Contact:* Dr. Kim Knight, Associate Dean for Graduate Studies, 972-883-4346, E-mail: kak102020@utdallas.edu. *Dean*, Dr. Anne Balsamo, 972-883-4376, E-mail: atecdean@utdallas.edu.

School of Behavioral and Brain Sciences Students: 529 full-time (417 women), 55 part-time (42 women); includes 165 minority (20 Black or African American, non-Hispanic/Latino; 3 American Indian or Alaska Native, non-Hispanic/Latino; 50 Asian, non-Hispanic/Latino; 64 Hispanic/Latino; 28 Two or more races, non-Hispanic/Latino), 68 international. Average age 26. 1,047 applicants, 25% accepted, 164 enrolled. *Faculty:* 58 full-time (29 women), 14 part-time/adjunct (12 women). Expenses: Contact institution. *Financial support:* In 2017–18, 383 students received support, including 1 fellowship (averaging $1,500 per year), 50 research assistantships with partial tuition reimbursements available (averaging $28,519 per year), 94 teaching assistantships with partial tuition reimbursements available (averaging $18,550 per year); career-related internships or fieldwork, Federal Work-Study, institutionally sponsored loans, scholarships/grants, and unspecified assistantships also available. Support available to part-time students. Financial award application deadline: 4/30; financial award applicants required to submit FAFSA. In 2017, 216 master's, 30 doctorates awarded. *Program availability:* Part-time, evening/weekend. Offers applied cognition and neuroscience (MS); audiology (Au D); behavioral and brain sciences (MS, Au D, PhD); cognition and neuroscience (PhD); communication disorders (MS); communication sciences and disorders (PhD); early childhood disorders (MS); psychological sciences (MS, PhD). *Application deadline:* For fall admission, 7/15 for domestic students, 5/1 priority date for international students; for spring admission, 11/15 for domestic students, 9/1 priority date for international students. Applications are processed on a rolling basis. *Application fee:* $50 ($100 for international students). Electronic applications accepted. *Application Contact:* Dr. Robert D. Stillman, Associate Dean of Graduate Programs, 214-905-3106, Fax: 972-883-3491, E-mail: stillman@utdallas.edu. *Dean*, Dr. James C. Bartlett, 972-883-2355, Fax: 972-883-3491, E-mail: jbartlet@utdallas.edu.

School of Economic, Political and Policy Sciences Students: 251 full-time (115 women), 208 part-time (111 women); includes 139 minority (53 Black or African American, non-Hispanic/Latino; 1 American Indian or Alaska Native, non-Hispanic/Latino; 26 Asian, non-Hispanic/Latino; 45 Hispanic/Latino; 14 Two or more races, non-Hispanic/Latino), 132 international. Average age 34. 398 applicants, 48% accepted, 99 enrolled. *Faculty:* 64 full-time (16 women), 8 part-time/adjunct (1 woman). Expenses: Contact institution. *Financial support:* In 2017–18, 229 students received support, including 15 research assistantships with partial tuition reimbursements available (averaging $19,097 per year), 85 teaching assistantships with partial tuition reimbursements available (averaging $13,100 per year); fellowships, career-related internships or fieldwork, Federal Work-Study, institutionally sponsored loans, scholarships/grants, and unspecified assistantships also available. Support available to part-time students. Financial award application deadline: 4/30; financial award applicants required to submit FAFSA. In 2017, 88 master's, 21 doctorates awarded. *Program availability:* Part-time, evening/weekend. Offers applied sociology (MS); Constitutional law (MA); criminology (MS, PhD); economic, political and policy sciences (MA, MPA, MPP, MS, PhD); economics (MS, PhD); geospatial information sciences (MS, PhD); international political economy (MS); justice administration and leadership (MS); legislative studies (MA); political science (MA, PhD); public affairs (MPA, PhD); public policy (MPP); public policy and political economy (PhD); social data analytics and research (MS). *Application deadline:* For fall admission, 7/15 for domestic students, 5/1 priority date for international students; for spring admission, 11/15 for domestic students, 9/1 priority date for international students. Applications are processed on a rolling basis. *Application fee:* $50 ($100 for international students). Electronic applications accepted. *Application Contact:* Dr. Alex Piquero, Associate Dean for Graduate Programs, 972-883-2482, Fax: 972-883-6297, E-mail: apiquero@utdallas.edu. *Dean,* Dr. Denis Dean, 972-883-6852, Fax: 972-883-6297, E-mail: denis.dean@utdallas.edu.

School of Interdisciplinary Studies Students: 5 full-time (3 women), 8 part-time (5 women); includes 5 minority (1 Black or African American, non-Hispanic/Latino; 2 Asian, non-Hispanic/Latino; 2 Hispanic/Latino). Average age 36. 8 applicants, 63% accepted, 3 enrolled. *Faculty:* 3 full-time (2 women), 1 (woman) part-time/adjunct. Expenses: Contact institution. *Financial support:* In 2017–18, 10 students received support. Research assistantships with partial tuition reimbursements available, teaching assistantships with partial tuition reimbursements available, career-related internships or fieldwork, Federal Work-Study, institutionally sponsored loans, and scholarships/grants available. Support available to part-time students. Financial award application deadline: 4/30; financial award applicants required to submit FAFSA. In 2017, 6 master's awarded. *Program availability:* Part-time, evening/weekend. Offers interdisciplinary studies (MA). *Application deadline:* For fall admission, 7/15 for domestic students, 5/1 priority date for international students; for spring admission, 11/15 for domestic students, 9/1 priority date for international students. Applications are processed on a rolling basis. *Application fee:* $50 ($100 for international students). Electronic applications accepted. *Application Contact:* Becky Wiser, Academic Support Coordinator, 972-883-2354, Fax: 972-883-2440, E-mail: rwiser@utdallas.edu. *Dean,* Dr. George Fair, 972-883-2350, Fax: 972-883-2440, E-mail: gwfair@utdallas.edu.

School of Natural Sciences and Mathematics Students: 505 full-time (198 women), 124 part-time (55 women); includes 115 minority (19 Black or African American, non-Hispanic/Latino; 1 American Indian or Alaska Native, non-Hispanic/Latino; 55 Asian, non-Hispanic/Latino; 31 Hispanic/Latino; 9 Two or more races, non-Hispanic/Latino), 329 international. Average age 29. 979 applicants, 28% accepted, 189 enrolled. *Faculty:* 113 full-time (17 women), 6 part-time/adjunct (2 women). Expenses: Contact institution. *Financial support:* In 2017–18, 429 students received support, including 3 fellowships with partial tuition reimbursements available (averaging $875 per year), 102 research assistantships with partial tuition reimbursements available (averaging $24,245 per year), 272 teaching assistantships with partial tuition reimbursements available (averaging $17,269 per year); career-related internships or fieldwork, Federal Work-Study, institutionally sponsored loans, scholarships/grants, and unspecified assistantships also available. Support available to part-time students. Financial award application deadline: 4/30. In 2017, 127 master's, 35 doctorates awarded. *Program availability:* Part-time, evening/weekend. Offers actuarial science (MS); bioinformatics and computational biology (MS); biotechnology (MS); chemistry and biochemistry (MS, PhD); geosciences (MS, PhD); geosciences - petrology and mineralogy (MS, PhD); geosciences - sedimentology (MS, PhD); geosciences - stratigraphy (MS, PhD); mathematics (MS, PhD); mathematics education (MAT); molecular and cell biology (MS, PhD); natural sciences and mathematics (MAT, MS, PhD); physics (MS, PhD); science education (MAT); statistics (MS, PhD). *Application deadline:* For fall admission, 7/15 for domestic students, 5/1 priority date for international students; for spring admission, 11/15 for domestic students, 9/1 priority date for international students. Applications are processed on a rolling basis. *Application fee:* $50 ($100 for international students). Electronic applications accepted. *Application Contact:* Dr. Juan E. Gonzalez, Associate Dean for Graduate Studies, 972-883-2526, Fax: 972-883-6371, E-mail: jgonzal@utdallas.edu. *Dean,* Dr. Bruce Novak, 972-883-2416, Fax: 972-883-6371, E-mail: bruce.novak@utdallas.edu.

THE UNIVERSITY OF TEXAS AT EL PASO, El Paso, TX 79968-0001

General Information State-supported, coed, university. CGS member. *Graduate housing:* Room and/or apartments available on a first-come, first-served basis to single students; on-campus housing not available to married students. *Student services:* Campus employment opportunities, campus safety program, career counseling, child daycare facilities, exercise/wellness program, free psychological counseling, grant writing training, international student services, low-cost health insurance, services for students with disabilities, teacher training, writing training. *Library facilities:* University Library.

Computer facilities: A campuswide network can be accessed from student residence rooms and from off campus. Online class registration is available.
Website: http://www.utep.edu/

General Application Contact: Dr. Charles Ambler, Dean of the Graduate School, 915-747-5491, Fax: 915-747-5788, E-mail: cambler@utep.edu.

GRADUATE UNITS

Graduate School Expenses: Contact institution. *Financial support:* Fellowships with partial tuition reimbursements, research assistantships with partial tuition reimbursements, teaching assistantships with partial tuition reimbursements, institutionally sponsored loans, scholarships/grants, health care benefits, tuition waivers (full and partial), and unspecified assistantships available. Support available to part-time students. Financial award application deadline: 3/15; financial award applicants required to submit FAFSA. *Program availability:* Part-time, evening/weekend, online learning. *Application deadline:* For fall admission, 8/1 priority date for domestic students, 3/1 for international students; for spring admission, 11/1 priority date for domestic students, 9/3 for international students. Applications are processed on a rolling basis. *Application fee:* $45 ($80 for international students). Electronic applications accepted.

College of Business Administration Expenses: Contact institution. *Financial support:* Fellowships with partial tuition reimbursements, research assistantships with partial tuition reimbursements, teaching assistantships with partial tuition reimbursements, institutionally sponsored loans, scholarships/grants, health care benefits, tuition waivers (partial), and unspecified assistantships available. Support available to part-time students. Financial award application deadline: 3/15; financial award applicants required to submit FAFSA. *Program availability:* Part-time, evening/weekend, online learning. Offers accounting (M Acc); business administration (M Acc, MBA, MS, PhD, Certificate); economics (MS); international business (PhD). *Application deadline:* For fall admission, 8/1 for domestic students, 3/1 for international students; for spring admission, 11/1 priority date for domestic students, 9/1 for international students. Applications are processed on a rolling basis. *Application fee:* $45 ($80 for international students). Electronic applications accepted.

College of Education Expenses: Contact institution. *Financial support:* Fellowships with partial tuition reimbursements, research assistantships with partial tuition reimbursements, teaching assistantships with partial tuition reimbursements, institutionally sponsored loans, scholarships/grants, health care benefits, tuition waivers (partial), and unspecified assistantships available. Support available to part-time students. Financial award application deadline: 3/15; financial award applicants required to submit FAFSA. *Program availability:* Part-time, evening/weekend, online learning. Offers education (M Ed, MA, Ed D, PhD); educational administration (M Ed); educational diagnostics (M Ed); educational leadership and administration (Ed D); guidance and counseling (M Ed); instruction (M Ed); reading education (M Ed); special education (M Ed); teaching, learning, and culture (PhD). *Application deadline:* For fall admission, 8/1 for domestic students, 3/1 for international students; for spring admission, 11/1 priority date for domestic students, 9/1 for international students. Applications are processed on a rolling basis. *Application fee:* $45 ($80 for international students). Electronic applications accepted.

College of Engineering Expenses: Contact institution. *Financial support:* Fellowships with partial tuition reimbursements, research assistantships with partial tuition reimbursements, teaching assistantships with partial tuition reimbursements, institutionally sponsored loans, scholarships/grants, health care benefits, tuition waivers (partial), and unspecified assistantships available. Support available to part-time students. Financial award application deadline: 3/15; financial award applicants required to submit FAFSA. *Program availability:* Part-time, evening/weekend. Offers biomedical engineering (PhD); civil engineering (MEENE, MS, MSENE, PhD); computer engineering (MS); computer science (MS, MSIT, PhD); construction management (MS, Certificate); cyber security (Graduate Certificate); education engineering (M Eng); electric power and energy systems (Graduate Certificate); electrical and computer engineering (PhD); electrical engineering (MS); environmental engineering (MEENE, MSENE); environmental science and engineering (PhD); industrial engineering (MS); information technology (MSIT); manufacturing engineering (MS); materials science and engineering (PhD); mechanical engineering (MS); metallurgical and materials engineering (MS); software engineering (MS); systems engineering (MS). *Application deadline:* For fall admission, 8/1 priority date for domestic students, 3/1 for international students; for spring admission, 11/1 priority date for domestic students, 9/1 for international students. Applications are processed on a rolling basis. *Application fee:* $45 ($80 for international students). Electronic applications accepted.

College of Health Sciences Expenses: Contact institution. *Financial support:* Research assistantships with partial tuition reimbursements, teaching assistantships with partial tuition reimbursements, career-related internships or fieldwork, Federal Work-Study, institutionally sponsored loans, scholarships/grants, tuition waivers (partial), and unspecified assistantships available. Support available to part-time students. Financial award application deadline: 3/15; financial award applicants required to submit FAFSA. *Program availability:* Part-time, evening/weekend, online learning. Offers health sciences (MOT, MPH, MRC, MS, MSN, MSW, DPT, PhD, Graduate Certificate); interdisciplinary health sciences (PhD); kinesiology (MS); occupational therapy (MOT); physical therapy (DPT); public health sciences (MPH, Graduate Certificate); rehabilitation counseling (MRC); social work in the border region (MSW); speech-language pathology (MS). *Application deadline:* For fall admission, 8/1 for domestic students, 3/1 for international students; for spring admission, 11/1 priority date for domestic students, 9/3 for international students. Applications are processed on a rolling basis. *Application fee:* $45 ($80 for international students). Electronic applications accepted. *Application Contact:* Dr. Benjamin Flores, Dean of the Graduate School, 915-747-5491, Fax: 915-747-5788, E-mail: bflores@utep.edu. *Dean,* Dr. Kathleen A. Curtis, 915-747-7201, E-mail: kacurtis@utep.edu.

College of Liberal Arts Expenses: Contact institution. *Financial support:* Fellowships with partial tuition reimbursements, research assistantships with partial tuition reimbursements, teaching assistantships with partial tuition reimbursements, institutionally sponsored loans, scholarships/grants, health care benefits, tuition waivers (partial), and unspecified assistantships available. Support available to part-time students. Financial award application deadline: 3/15; financial award applicants required to submit FAFSA. *Program availability:* Part-time, evening/weekend, online learning. Offers applied anthropology (Certificate); applied social sciences (Certificate); art education (MA); bilingual professional writing (Certificate); borderlands history (MA, PhD); clinical psychology (MA); communication (MA); creative writing (MFA); creative writing of the Americas (MFA); English and American literature (MA); experimental psychology (MA); history (MA); interdisciplinary studies (MAIS); liberal arts (MA, MAIS, MAT, MFA, MM, PhD, Certificate); linguistics (MA); music education (MM); music performance (MM); philosophy (MA); political science (MA); psychology (PhD); rhetoric and composition (PhD); rhetoric and writing studies (MA); sociology (MA); Spanish (MA); studio art (MA); teaching English (MAT); teaching English to speakers of other languages (Certificate). *Application deadline:* For fall admission, 8/1 for domestic students, 3/1 for international students; for spring admission, 11/1 priority date for domestic students, 9/1 for international students. Applications are processed on a rolling basis. *Application fee:* $45 ($80 for international students). Electronic applications accepted.

College of Science Expenses: Contact institution. *Financial support:* Fellowships with partial tuition reimbursements, research assistantships with partial tuition reimbursements, teaching assistantships with partial tuition reimbursements, career-related internships or fieldwork, Federal Work-Study, institutionally sponsored loans, scholarships/grants, and tuition waivers (partial) available. Support available to part-time students. Financial award application deadline: 3/15; financial award applicants required to submit FAFSA. *Program availability:* Part-time, evening/weekend. Offers bioinformatics (MS); biological sciences (MS, PhD); chemistry (MS, PhD); geological sciences (MS, PhD); geophysics (MS); mathematics (MAT, MS); physics (MS); science (MAT, MS, PhD); statistics (MS). *Application deadline:* For fall admission, 7/1 for domestic students, 3/1 for international students; for spring admission, 11/1 for domestic students, 9/1 for international students. Applications are processed on a rolling basis. *Application fee:* $15 ($65 for international students). Electronic applications accepted.

School of Nursing Expenses: Contact institution. *Financial support:* Fellowships with partial tuition reimbursements, research assistantships with partial tuition reimbursements, teaching assistantships with partial tuition reimbursements, institutionally sponsored loans, scholarships/grants, health care benefits, tuition waivers (partial), and unspecified assistantships available. Support available to part-time students. Financial award application deadline: 3/15; financial award applicants required to submit FAFSA. *Program availability:* Online learning. Offers family nurse practitioner (MSN); health care leadership and management (Certificate); interdisciplinary health sciences (PhD); nursing (DNP); nursing education (MSN, Certificate); nursing systems management (MSN). *Application deadline:* For fall admission, 8/1 for domestic students, 3/1 for international students; for spring admission, 11/1 for domestic students, 9/1 for international students. Applications are processed on a rolling basis. *Application fee:* $45 ($80 for international students). Electronic applications accepted. *Application Contact:* Dr. Benjamin Flores, Interim Dean of the Graduate School, 915-747-5491, Fax: 915-747-5788, E-mail: bflores@

utep.edu. *Dean*, Dr. Elias Provencio-Vasquez, 915-747-8194, Fax: 915-747-8266, E-mail: eprovenciovasquez@utep.edu.

THE UNIVERSITY OF TEXAS AT SAN ANTONIO, San Antonio, TX 78249-0617

General Information State-supported, coed, university. CGS member. *Enrollment:* 30,768 graduate, professional, and undergraduate students; 1,877 full-time matriculated graduate/professional students (1,009 women), 2,343 part-time matriculated graduate/professional students (1,387 women). *Enrollment by degree level:* 3,419 master's, 801 doctoral. *Graduate faculty:* 524 full-time (168 women), 103 part-time/adjunct (34 women). Tuition, state resident: full-time $5495. Tuition, nonresident: full-time $21,938. *Required fees:* $1915. Tuition and fees vary according to program. *Graduate housing:* Room and/or apartments available on a first-come, first-served basis to single students; on-campus housing not available to married students. Typical cost: $11,234 (including board). *Student services:* Campus employment opportunities, campus safety program, career counseling, child daycare facilities, exercise/wellness program, free psychological counseling, grant writing training, international student services, low-cost health insurance, multicultural affairs office, services for students with disabilities, teacher training, writing training. *Library facilities:* John Peace Library plus 3 others. *Collection:* Students can reserve study rooms. *Research affiliation:* Air Force Research Laboratory (information assurance and security), Carnegie Mellon University/National Security Agency (computer security), National Science Foundation (virtual reality, computer architecture, real-time systems), Cancer Prevention and Research Institute of Texas (chemistry), Army Research Laboratory (computer science, management science and statistics, electrical engineering), CPS Energy (engineering).

Computer facilities: Computer purchase and lease plans are available. 510 computers available on campus for general student use. A campuswide network can be accessed from student residence rooms and from off campus. Online class registration is available.
Website: http://www.utsa.edu/

General Application Contact: Monica Rodriguez, Director of Graduate Admissions, 210-458-4331, Fax: 210-458-4332, E-mail: graduate.admissions@utsa.edu.

GRADUATE UNITS

College of Architecture, Construction and Planning Students: 91 full-time (41 women), 24 part-time (8 women); includes 74 minority (4 Black or African American, non-Hispanic/Latino; 4 Asian, non-Hispanic/Latino; 66 Hispanic/Latino), 15 international. Average age 29. 60 applicants, 85% accepted, 32 enrolled. *Faculty:* 19 full-time (5 women), 7 part-time/adjunct (1 woman). Expenses: Contact institution. In 2017, 32 master's awarded. *Program availability:* Part-time. Offers architecture (M Arch, MS Arch); architecture, construction and planning (M Arch, MS, MS Arch); urban and regional planning (MS). *Application deadline:* For fall admission, 6/15 for domestic students, 3/1 for international students; for spring admission, 10/15 for domestic students, 9/15 for international students. Applications are processed on a rolling basis. *Application fee:* $50 ($90 for international students). Electronic applications accepted. *Application Contact:* Monica Rodriguez, Director of Graduate Admissions, 210-458-4331, Fax: 210-458-4332, E-mail: graduate.admissions@utsa.edu. *Dean, College of Architecture*, Dr. John Murphy, 210-458-3026, E-mail: john.murphy@utsa.edu.

College of Business Students: 444 full-time (197 women), 473 part-time (166 women); includes 408 minority (42 Black or African American, non-Hispanic/Latino; 1 American Indian or Alaska Native, non-Hispanic/Latino; 65 Asian, non-Hispanic/Latino; 285 Hispanic/Latino; 1 Native Hawaiian or other Pacific Islander, non-Hispanic/Latino; 14 Two or more races, non-Hispanic/Latino), 100 international. Average age 30. 778 applicants, 60% accepted, 316 enrolled. *Faculty:* 76 full-time (13 women), 18 part-time/adjunct (3 women). Expenses: Contact institution. In 2017, 273 master's, 14 doctorates, 9 other advanced degrees awarded. *Program availability:* Part-time, evening/weekend. Offers accounting (M Acy, PhD); applied statistics (MS, PhD); business (M Acy, MA, MBA, MS, MSIT, PhD, Certificate); business economics (MBA); cyber security (MSIT); economics (MA); finance (MBA, MS, PhD); information technology (MS, PhD); management and organization studies (PhD); management of technology (MBA); management science (MBA); marketing (PhD); marketing management (MBA); technology entrepreneurship and management (Certificate); tourism destination development (MBA). *Application deadline:* For fall admission, 7/31 for domestic students, 3/1 for international students; for spring admission, 10/15 for domestic students, 9/15 for international students. Applications are processed on a rolling basis. *Application fee:* $50 ($90 for international students). Electronic applications accepted. *Application Contact:* Katherine Pope, Director, Graduate Student Services, 210-458-7316, E-mail: katherine.pope@utsa.edu. *Dean*, Dr. William Gerard Sanders, 210-458-4313, E-mail: gerry.sanders@utsa.edu.

College of Education and Human Development Students: 461 full-time (362 women), 902 part-time (722 women); includes 867 minority (112 Black or African American, non-Hispanic/Latino; 25 Asian, non-Hispanic/Latino; 709 Hispanic/Latino; 1 Native Hawaiian or other Pacific Islander, non-Hispanic/Latino; 20 Two or more races, non-Hispanic/Latino), 27 international. Average age 33. 590 applicants, 79% accepted, 331 enrolled. *Faculty:* 97 full-time (58 women), 26 part-time/adjunct (16 women). Expenses: Contact institution. *Financial support:* Federal Work-Study, scholarships/grants, health care benefits, and unspecified assistantships available. Support available to part-time students. In 2017, 467 master's, 46 doctorates, 28 other advanced degrees awarded. *Program availability:* Part-time, evening/weekend, online learning. Offers applied behavior analysis (Certificate); bicultural and bilingual studies (MA); counselor education and supervision (PhD); culture, literacy, and language (PhD); education (MA); education and human development (M Ed, MA, MS, Ed D, PhD, Certificate); educational leadership (Ed D); educational leadership and policy studies (M Ed); educational psychology (MA); health and kinesiology (MS); interdisciplinary learning and teaching (PhD); language acquisition and bilingual psychoeducational assessment (Certificate); school counseling (M Ed); school psychology (MA); teaching English as a second language (MA). *Application deadline:* For fall admission, 6/15 for domestic students, 3/1 for international students; for spring admission, 10/15 for domestic students, 9/15 for international students. *Application fee:* $50 ($90 for international students). Electronic applications accepted. *Application Contact:* Monica Rodriguez, Director of Graduate Admissions, 210-458-4331, Fax: 210-458-4332, E-mail: graduate.admissions@utsa.edu. *Dean*, Dr. Margo DelliCarpini, 210-458-4370, E-mail: margo.dellicarpini@utsa.edu.

College of Engineering Students: 239 full-time (51 women), 213 part-time (55 women); includes 131 minority (12 Black or African American, non-Hispanic/Latino; 28 Asian, non-Hispanic/Latino; 82 Hispanic/Latino; 1 Native Hawaiian or other Pacific Islander, non-Hispanic/Latino; 8 Two or more races, non-Hispanic/Latino), 193 international. Average age 29. 407 applicants, 76% accepted, 111 enrolled. *Faculty:* 73 full-time (10 women), 7 part-time/adjunct (1 woman). Expenses: Contact institution. *Financial support:* Career-related internships or fieldwork, Federal Work-Study, institutionally sponsored loans, scholarships/grants, health care benefits, unspecified assistantships, and Valero Research Scholar awards available. In 2017, 144 master's, 21 doctorates awarded. *Program availability:* Part-time, evening/weekend. Offers advanced manufacturing and enterprise engineering (MS); advanced materials engineering (MS); biomedical engineering (MS, PhD); civil engineering (MCE, MSCE); computer engineering (MS); electrical engineering (MSEE, PhD); engineering (MCE, MS, MSCE, MSEE, PhD); environmental science and engineering (PhD); mechanical engineering (MS, PhD). *Application deadline:* For fall admission, 6/15 for domestic students, 3/1 for international students; for spring admission, 10/15 for domestic students, 9/15 for international students. *Application fee:* $50 ($90 for international students). Electronic applications accepted. *Application Contact:* Monica Rodriguez, Director of Graduate Admissions, 210-458-4331, Fax: 210-458-4332, E-mail: graduate.admissions@utsa.edu. *Dean of Engineering*, Dr. JoAnn Browning, 210-458-4490, Fax: 210-458-5515, E-mail: joann.browning@utsa.edu.

College of Liberal and Fine Arts Students: 162 full-time (103 women), 222 part-time (140 women); includes 184 minority (13 Black or African American, non-Hispanic/Latino; 6 Asian, non-Hispanic/Latino; 153 Hispanic/Latino; 12 Two or more races, non-Hispanic/Latino), 9 international. Average age 32. 260 applicants, 63% accepted, 108 enrolled. *Faculty:* 111 full-time (45 women), 9 part-time/adjunct (3 women). Expenses: Contact institution. *Financial support:* Fellowships, research assistantships, teaching assistantships, Federal Work-Study, scholarships/grants, and unspecified assistantships available. Financial award applicants required to submit FAFSA. In 2017, 94 master's, 5 doctorates awarded. Offers anthropology (MA, PhD); art (MFA); art history (MA); communication (MA); English (MA, PhD); geography (MA); history (MA); liberal and fine arts (MA, MFA, MM, MS, PhD); music (MM); philosophy and classics (MA); political science (MA); psychology (MS, PhD); sociology (MS); Spanish (MA). *Application deadline:* For fall admission, 6/15 for domestic students, 3/1 for international students; for spring admission, 10/15 for domestic students, 9/15 for international students. *Application fee:* $50 ($90 for international students). Electronic applications accepted. *Application Contact:* Monica Rodriguez, Director of Graduate Admissions, 210-458-4331, Fax: 210-458-4332, E-mail: graduate.admissions@utsa.edu. *Dean*, Dr. Daniel J. Gelo, 210-458-4359, E-mail: daniel.gelo@utsa.edu.

College of Public Policy Students: 166 full-time (121 women), 313 part-time (220 women); includes 336 minority (66 Black or African American, non-Hispanic/Latino; 11 Asian, non-Hispanic/Latino; 251 Hispanic/Latino; 1 Native Hawaiian or other Pacific Islander, non-Hispanic/Latino; 7 Two or more races, non-Hispanic/Latino), 14 international. Average age 33. 176 applicants, 80% accepted, 109 enrolled. *Faculty:* 30 full-time (16 women), 15 part-time/adjunct (9 women). Expenses: Contact institution. *Financial support:* Fellowships, research assistantships, teaching assistantships, scholarships/grants, and unspecified assistantships available. Financial award applicants required to submit FAFSA. In 2017, 106 master's, 3 doctorates awarded. *Program availability:* Part-time, evening/weekend. Offers applied demography (PhD); criminology (MS); public administration (MPA); public policy (MPA, MS, MSW, PhD); social work (MSW). *Application deadline:* For fall admission, 6/15 for domestic students, 3/1 for international students; for spring admission, 10/15 for domestic students, 9/15 for international students. *Application fee:* $50 ($90 for international students). Electronic applications accepted. *Application Contact:* Monica Rodriguez, Director of Graduate Admissions, 210-458-4331, Fax: 210-458-4332, E-mail: graduate.admissions@utsa.edu. *Dean*, Dr. Rogelio Saenz, 210-458-2530, E-mail: rogelio.saenz@utsa.edu.

College of Sciences Students: 313 full-time (134 women), 189 part-time (72 women); includes 189 minority (13 Black or African American, non-Hispanic/Latino; 1 American Indian or Alaska Native, non-Hispanic/Latino; 31 Asian, non-Hispanic/Latino; 130 Hispanic/Latino; 2 Native Hawaiian or other Pacific Islander, non-Hispanic/Latino; 12 Two or more races, non-Hispanic/Latino), 139 international. Average age 29. 483 applicants, 57% accepted, 150 enrolled. *Faculty:* 108 full-time (16 women), 18 part-time/adjunct (1 woman). Expenses: Contact institution. *Financial support:* Teaching assistantships available. Financial award applicants required to submit FAFSA. In 2017, 108 master's, 23 doctorates awarded. Offers applied mathematics (MS); biology (MS); biotechnology (MS); cell and molecular biology (PhD); chemistry (MS, PhD); computer science (MS, PhD); environmental science and ecology (MS); geological sciences (MS); mathematics (MS); mathematics education (MS); neurobiology (PhD); physics (MS, PhD); sciences (MS, PhD). *Application deadline:* For fall admission, 6/15 for domestic students, 3/1 for international students; for spring admission, 10/15 for domestic students, 9/15 for international students. *Application fee:* $50 ($90 for international students). Electronic applications accepted. *Application Contact:* Monica Rodriguez, Director of Graduate Admissions, 210-458-4331, Fax: 210-458-4332, E-mail: graduate.admissions@utsa.edu. *Dean*, Dr. George Perry, 210-458-4450, Fax: 210-458-4445, E-mail: george.perry@utsa.edu.

Joint PhD Program in Translational Science Students: 1 full-time (0 women), 7 part-time (4 women); includes 4 minority (all Hispanic/Latino), 1 international. Average age 37. Expenses: Contact institution. *Financial support:* In 2017–18, 1 student received support. Research assistantships, teaching assistantships, scholarships/grants, and unspecified assistantships available. *Program availability:* Part-time. Offers translational science (PhD). Program offered in partnership with The University of Texas Health Science Center at San Antonio, The University of Texas at Austin, and The University of Texas Health Science Center at Houston. *Application deadline:* For fall admission, 11/1 for domestic and international students. *Application fee:* $50 ($90 for international students). Electronic applications accepted. *Application Contact:* Susan Stappenbeck, Senior Project Coordinator, 210-567-8094, E-mail: stappenbeck@uthscsa.edu. *Program Director*, Dr. Chris Frei, 210-567-8355, Fax: 210-564-4301, E-mail: freic@uthscsa.edu.

THE UNIVERSITY OF TEXAS AT TYLER, Tyler, TX 75799-0001

General Information State-supported, coed, comprehensive institution. *Graduate housing:* Rooms and/or apartments available on a first-come, first-served basis to single and married students. *Research affiliation:* Embassy of Arab Republic of Egypt Cultural and Education Bureau (electrical engineering), TransAtlantic Lines, Inc. (civil engineering), American Society of Civil Engineers (civil engineering), McGraw-Hill Company (civil engineering), Renaissance Society of America (art history), American Lung Association of the Central States (biology).

GRADUATE UNITS

Ben and Maytee Fisch College of Pharmacy Offers pharmacy (Pharm D).

College of Arts and Sciences *Program availability:* Part-time, evening/weekend, online learning. Offers art history (MA); arts and sciences (MA, MAIS, MAT, MFA, MPA, MS, MSIS); biology (MS); communication (MA); criminal justice (MS); English (MA); history (MA); interdisciplinary (MAIS); interdisciplinary studies (MAIS, MSIS); mathematics (MS, MSIS); political science (MA); public administration (MPA); sociology (MS); studio art (MFA). Electronic applications accepted.

College of Business and Technology *Program availability:* Part-time, evening/weekend, online learning. Offers accountancy (M Acc); business and technology (M Acc, MBA, MS, PhD); computer science (MS); cyber security (MBA); engineering management (MBA); general management (MBA); healthcare management

(MBA); human resource development (MS, PhD); industrial management (MS); internal assurance and consulting (MBA); marketing (MBA); oil, gas and energy (MBA); organizational development (MBA); quality management (MBA). Electronic applications accepted.

College of Education and Psychology *Program availability:* Part-time, evening/weekend. Offers clinical psychology (MS); counseling psychology (MA); education and psychology (M Ed, MA, MS, MSIS); educational leadership (M Ed); interdisciplinary studies (MSIS); school counseling (MA).

School of Education *Program availability:* Part-time, evening/weekend. Offers early childhood education (M Ed, MA); reading (M Ed, MA); special education (M Ed, MA). Electronic applications accepted.

College of Engineering *Program availability:* Part-time. Offers electrical engineering (MS); engineering (MS, MSIS); environmental engineering (MS); industrial safety (MS); mechanical engineering (MS); structural engineering (MS); transportation engineering (MS); water resources engineering (MS). Electronic applications accepted.

College of Nursing and Health Sciences *Program availability:* Part-time, evening/weekend, online learning. Offers health and kinesiology (M Ed, MA); health sciences (MS); kinesiology (MS); nurse practitioner (MSN); nursing (PhD); nursing administration (MSN); nursing and health sciences (M Ed, MA, MS, MSN, PhD); nursing education (MSN). Electronic applications accepted.

THE UNIVERSITY OF TEXAS HEALTH SCIENCE CENTER AT HOUSTON, Houston, TX 77225-0036

General Information State-supported, coed, upper-level institution. *Graduate housing:* On-campus housing not available.

GRADUATE UNITS

Cizik School of Nursing *Program availability:* Part-time. Offers nursing (MSN, DNP, PhD). Electronic applications accepted.

McGovern Medical School Offers medicine (MD). Electronic applications accepted.

MD Anderson UTHealth Graduate School Offers biochemistry and cell biology (PhD); biomedical sciences (MS); cancer biology (PhD); genetic counseling (MS); genetics and epigenetics (PhD); immunology (PhD); medical physics (MS, PhD); microbiology and infectious diseases (PhD); neuroscience (PhD); quantitative sciences (PhD); therapeutics and pharmacology (PhD). Electronic applications accepted.

School of Biomedical Informatics Students: 62 full-time (42 women), 224 part-time (120 women); includes 152 minority (43 Black or African American, non-Hispanic/Latino; 2 American Indian or Alaska Native, non-Hispanic/Latino; 59 Asian, non-Hispanic/Latino; 42 Hispanic/Latino; 3 Native Hawaiian or other Pacific Islander, non-Hispanic/Latino; 3 Two or more races, non-Hispanic/Latino). Average age 36. 126 applicants, 82% accepted, 52 enrolled. *Faculty:* 29 full-time (10 women), 11 part-time/adjunct (2 women). Expenses: Contact institution. *Financial support:* In 2017–18, 30 students received support. Research assistantships, teaching assistantships, career-related internships or fieldwork, institutionally sponsored loans, scholarships/grants, health care benefits, and unspecified assistantships available. Support available to part-time students. Financial award application deadline: 5/1. In 2017, 48 master's, 4 doctorates awarded. *Program availability:* Part-time, 100% online, blended/hybrid learning. Offers applied biomedical informatics (MS, Certificate); biomedical informatics (MS, PhD, Certificate); health data science (Certificate); public health informatics (Certificate). *Application deadline:* For fall admission, 7/1 for domestic and international students; for spring admission, 11/1 for domestic and international students; for summer admission, 3/1 for domestic and international students. Applications are processed on a rolling basis. *Application fee:* $60. Electronic applications accepted. *Application Contact:* Jaime Hargrave, Director, Student Affairs, 713-500-3920, Fax: 713-500-0360, E-mail: jaime.n.hargrave@uth.tmc.edu. *Dean/Chair in Informatics Excellence*, Dr. Jiajie Zhang, 713-500-3922.

School of Dentistry Offers dentistry (MS, DDS). Electronic applications accepted.

School of Public Health Students: 604 full-time (446 women), 534 part-time (384 women); includes 504 minority (106 Black or African American, non-Hispanic/Latino; 177 Asian, non-Hispanic/Latino; 88 Hispanic/Latino; 1 Native Hawaiian or other Pacific Islander, non-Hispanic/Latino; 132 Two or more races, non-Hispanic/Latino). Average age 31. 1,425 applicants, 58% accepted, 423 enrolled. *Faculty:* 140 full-time (74 women), 23 part-time/adjunct (14 women). Expenses: Contact institution. *Financial support:* Fellowships, research assistantships, teaching assistantships, career-related internships or fieldwork, institutionally sponsored loans, scholarships/grants, traineeships, health care benefits, and unspecified assistantships available. Support available to part-time students. Financial award application deadline: 5/5; financial award applicants required to submit FAFSA. In 2017, 315 master's, 68 doctorates awarded. *Program availability:* Part-time. Offers behavioral science (PhD); biostatistics (MPH, MS, PhD); environmental health (MPH); epidemiology (MPH, MS, PhD); general public health (Certificate); genomics and bioinformatics (Certificate); health disparities (Certificate); health promotion/health education (MPH, Dr PH); healthcare management (Certificate); management, policy and community health (MPH, Dr PH, PhD); maternal and child health (Certificate); public health informatics (Certificate). Specific programs are offered at each of our six campuses in Texas (Austin, Brownsville, Dallas, El Paso, Houston, and San Antonio). *Application deadline:* For fall admission, 3/1 for domestic and international students; for spring admission, 10/1 for domestic and international students; for summer admission, 3/1 for domestic students. Applications are processed on a rolling basis. *Application fee:* $135. Electronic applications accepted. *Application Contact:* Elvis Parada, Manager of Admissions and Recruitment, 713-500-9028, Fax: 713-500-9068, E-mail: elvis.a.parada@uth.tmc.edu. *Senior Associate Dean of Academic and Research Affairs*, Dr. Susan Emery.

THE UNIVERSITY OF TEXAS HEALTH SCIENCE CENTER AT SAN ANTONIO, San Antonio, TX 78229-3900

General Information State-supported, coed, upper-level institution. CGS member. *Research affiliation:* University Hospital, Southwest Research Institute, Southwest Foundation for Biomedical Research, Veterans Administration Hospital.

GRADUATE UNITS

Graduate School of Biomedical Sciences Offers biochemistry (MS, PhD); biomedical engineering (MS, PhD); biomedical sciences (MS, PhD); cellular and structural biology (MS, PhD); clinical investigation (MS); dental science (MS); integrated biomedical sciences (PhD); microbiology and immunology (MS, PhD); molecular medicine (MS, PhD); neuroscience (PhD); nursing science (PhD); radiological sciences (PhD); toxicology (MS); translational science (PhD).

Joe R. and Teresa Lozano Long School of Medicine Offers deaf education and hearing (MS); medicine (MD). Electronic applications accepted.

School of Dentistry Students: 514 full-time (273 women), 42 part-time (19 women); includes 254 minority (22 Black or African American, non-Hispanic/Latino; 91 Asian, non-Hispanic/Latino; 126 Hispanic/Latino; 15 Two or more races, non-Hispanic/Latino), 33 international. Average age 27. 1,417 applicants, 15% accepted, 100 enrolled. *Faculty:* 103 full-time (37 women), 81 part-time/adjunct (18 women). Expenses: Contact institution. *Financial support:* In 2017–18, 86 students received support, including 4 research assistantships (averaging $2,624 per year), 81 teaching assistantships (averaging $14,050 per year); Federal Work-Study and institutionally sponsored loans also available. Financial award application deadline: 3/1; financial award applicants required to submit FAFSA. In 2017, 20 master's, 104 doctorates, 43 other advanced degrees awarded. Offers dentistry (MS, DDS, Certificate). *Application deadline:* For fall admission, 10/1 for domestic students. Applications are processed on a rolling basis. *Application fee:* $150. Electronic applications accepted. *Application Contact:* E-mail: dsadmissions@uthscsa.edu. *Director of Admissions*, Dr. Kay Malone, 210-567-3180, Fax: 210-567-6721, E-mail: malonek@uthscsa.edu.

School of Health Professions Offers occupational therapy (MOT); physical therapy (DPT); physician assistant studies (MS); speech language pathology (MS).

School of Nursing *Program availability:* Part-time. Offers administrative management (MSN); adult-gerontology acute care nurse practitioner (PGC); advanced practice leadership (DNP); clinical nurse leader (MSN); executive administrative management (DNP); family nurse practitioner (MSN, PGC); nursing (MSN, PhD); nursing education (MSN, PGC); pediatric nurse practitioner primary care (PGC); psychiatric mental health nurse practitioner (PGC); public health nurse leader (DNP).

THE UNIVERSITY OF TEXAS MD ANDERSON CANCER CENTER, Houston, TX 77030

General Information State-supported, coed, upper-level institution. CGS member.

GRADUATE UNITS

School of Health Professions Offers diagnostic genetics (MS).

THE UNIVERSITY OF TEXAS MEDICAL BRANCH, Galveston, TX 77555

General Information State-supported, coed, comprehensive institution. CGS member. *Graduate housing:* Rooms and/or apartments available on a first-come, first-served basis to single and married students. *Research affiliation:* Shriners Hospitals (burns and wound healing).

GRADUATE UNITS

Graduate School of Biomedical Sciences Offers biochemistry (PhD); bioinformatics (PhD); biomedical sciences (MA, MMS, MPH, MS, PhD); biophysics (PhD); cell biology (PhD); clinical science (MS, PhD); computational biology (PhD); experimental pathology (PhD); human pathophysiology and translational medicine (MS, PhD); medical humanities (MA, PhD); medical science (MMS); microbiology and immunology (MS, PhD); molecular biophysics education (PhD); neuroscience (PhD); nursing (PhD); pharmacology (MS); pharmacology and toxicology (PhD); population health sciences (PhD); public health (MPH); rehabilitation sciences (PhD); structural biology (PhD). Electronic applications accepted.

School of Health Professions Offers health professions (MOT, MPAS, MPT, DPT); occupational therapy (MOT); physical therapy (MPT, DPT); physician assistant studies (MPAS). Electronic applications accepted.

School of Medicine Offers medicine (MD).

School of Nursing *Program availability:* Part-time, online learning. Offers nursing (MSN, PhD). Electronic applications accepted.

THE UNIVERSITY OF TEXAS OF THE PERMIAN BASIN, Odessa, TX 79762-0001

General Information State-supported, coed, comprehensive institution. *Graduate housing:* Rooms and/or apartments available on a first-come, first-served basis to single and married students. Housing application deadline: 6/15.

GRADUATE UNITS

Office of Graduate Studies *Program availability:* Part-time, evening/weekend.

College of Arts and Sciences *Program availability:* Part-time, evening/weekend. Offers applied research psychology (MA); arts and sciences (MA, MS); biology (MS); clinical psychology (MA); computer science (MS); criminal justice administration (MS); English (MA); geology (MS); history (MA); kinesiology (MS); political science (MPA); Spanish (MA).

School of Business *Program availability:* Part-time, evening/weekend. Offers accountancy (MPA); business (MBA, MPA); management (MBA).

School of Education Offers bilingual/English as a second language education (MA); counseling (MA); early childhood education (MA); education (MA); educational leadership (MA); professional education (MA); reading (MA); special education (MA).

THE UNIVERSITY OF TEXAS RIO GRANDE VALLEY, Edinburg, TX 78539

General Information State-supported, coed, university. CGS member. *Enrollment:* 27,708 graduate, professional, and undergraduate students; 1,056 full-time matriculated graduate/professional students (644 women), 2,119 part-time matriculated graduate/professional students (1,409 women). *Enrollment by degree level:* 2,811 master's, 364 doctoral. *Graduate faculty:* 395 full-time (154 women), 30 part-time/adjunct (16 women). Tuition, state resident: full-time $5550; part-time $417 per credit hour. Tuition, nonresident: full-time $13,020; part-time $832 per credit hour. *Required fees:* $1169. *Graduate housing:* Rooms and/or apartments available on a first-come, first-served basis to single and married students. Typical cost: $7986 (including board) for single students. Housing application deadline: 7/1. *Student services:* Campus employment opportunities, campus safety program, career counseling, child daycare facilities, exercise/wellness program, free psychological counseling, international student services, services for students with disabilities, teacher training, writing training. *Library facilities:* University Library. *Collection:* Students can reserve study rooms. *Research affiliation:* Robert Wood Johnson (health science), Lockheed Martin Corporation (manufacturing engineering), Texas Instruments (curriculum and instruction), Pfizer, Inc. (health disparities), Howard Hughes Medical Institute (medical science), Boeing (engineering).

Computer facilities: A campuswide network can be accessed from student residence rooms and from off campus. Online class registration is available.
Website: http://www.utrgv.edu/

General Application Contact: Stephanie Ozuna, Graduate Student Recruiter, 956-665-3558, E-mail: stephanie.ozuna@utrgv.edu.

GRADUATE UNITS

College of Education and P-16 Integration Students: 968. Expenses: Contact institution. *Financial support:* Research assistantships, teaching assistantships, career-related internships or fieldwork, Federal Work-Study, institutionally sponsored loans, and scholarships/grants available. Support available to part-time students. Financial award application deadline: 4/15; financial award applicants required to submit FAFSA. In 2017, 343 master's, 10 doctorates awarded. *Program availability:* Part-time, evening/weekend. Offers bilingual education (M Ed); clinical mental health counseling (M Ed); curriculum and instruction (M Ed, Ed D); early childhood education (M Ed); early childhood special education (M Ed); education and P-16 integration (M Ed, MA, Ed D); educational leadership (M Ed, Ed D); educational technology (M Ed); reading and literacy (M Ed); school counseling (M Ed); school psychology (MA); special education (M Ed). *Application deadline:* For fall admission, 4/15 for domestic students; for spring admission, 11/15 for domestic students; for summer admission, 3/1 for domestic students. *Application fee:* $50 ($75 for international students). Electronic applications accepted. *Application Contact:* Stephanie Ozuna, Graduate Student Recruiter, 956-665-3558, E-mail: stephanie.ozuna@utrgv.edu. *Interim Dean*, Dr. Alma Rodriguez, 956-665-3627, E-mail: cep@utrgv.edu.

College of Engineering and Computer Science Students: 83 full-time (22 women), 121 part-time (21 women); includes 145 minority (2 Black or African American, non-Hispanic/Latino; 1 Asian, non-Hispanic/Latino; 142 Hispanic/Latino), 46 international. Average age 26. *Faculty:* 80 full-time (5 women). Expenses: Contact institution. *Financial support:* In 2017–18, 70 students received support, including 42 research assistantships (averaging $10,000 per year), 28 teaching assistantships (averaging $10,000 per year); Federal Work-Study, institutionally sponsored loans, scholarships/grants, tuition waivers (partial), and unspecified assistantships also available. Support available to part-time students. Financial award application deadline: 4/15. In 2017, 93 master's awarded. *Program availability:* Part-time, blended/hybrid learning. Offers computer science (MS); electrical engineering (MSE); engineering and computer science (MS, MSE); engineering management (MS); information technology (MS); manufacturing engineering (MS); mechanical engineering (MSE). *Application deadline:* For fall admission, 4/15 priority date for domestic and international students; for spring admission, 10/15 priority date for domestic and international students; for summer admission, 3/1 priority date for domestic and international students. Applications are processed on a rolling basis. *Application fee:* $50 ($100 for international students). Electronic applications accepted. *Application Contact:* Dr. Heinrich Foltz, Associate Dean, Academic Affairs, 956-665-3510, E-mail: heinrich.foltz@utrgv.edu. *Dean*, Dr. Alex Domijan, 956-665-3510, E-mail: alex.domijan@utrgv.edu.

College of Fine Arts Students: 39 full-time (24 women), 38 part-time (20 women); includes 65 minority (64 Hispanic/Latino; 1 Two or more races, non-Hispanic/Latino), 5 international. Average age 31. 32 applicants, 94% accepted, 15 enrolled. *Faculty:* 25 full-time (6 women), 2 part-time/adjunct (1 woman). Expenses: Contact institution. In 2017, 26 master's awarded. Offers creative writing (MFA); fine arts (MFA, MM). *Application Contact:* Stephanie Ozuna, Graduate Student Recruiter, 956-665-3558, E-mail: stephanie.ozuna@utrgv.edu. *Interim Dean*, Dr. Dahlia Guerra.

School of Art Students: 19 full-time (14 women), 11 part-time (9 women); includes 28 minority (all Hispanic/Latino). Average age 33. 11 applicants, 91% accepted, 8 enrolled. *Faculty:* 5 full-time (1 woman). Expenses: Contact institution. *Financial support:* Unspecified assistantships available. In 2017, 7 master's awarded. *Program availability:* Part-time. Offers art (MFA). *Application deadline:* Applications are processed on a rolling basis. *Application fee:* $50 ($100 for international students). *Application Contact:* Stephanie Ozuna, Graduate Student Recruiter, 956-665-3558, E-mail: stephanie.ozuna@utrgv.edu. *Director*, Dr. Susan Fitzsimmons, 956-665-3481, E-mail: susan.fitzsimmons@utrgv.edu.

School of Music Students: 7 full-time (1 woman), 8 part-time (4 women); includes 9 minority (all Hispanic/Latino), 3 international. Average age 33. 12 applicants, 100% accepted, 6 enrolled. *Faculty:* 14 full-time (4 women), 1 part-time/adjunct (0 women). Expenses: Contact institution. In 2017, 9 master's awarded. *Program availability:* Part-time. Offers music (MM). *Application fee:* $50 ($100 for international students). *Director*, Kurt Martinez, E-mail: kurt.martinez@utrgv.edu.

College of Health Affairs Expenses: Contact institution. *Financial support:* Fellowships with full tuition reimbursements, research assistantships, teaching assistantships, career-related internships or fieldwork, Federal Work-Study, institutionally sponsored loans, and scholarships/grants available. Support available to part-time students. Financial award applicants required to submit FAFSA. *Program availability:* Part-time, evening/weekend. Offers clinical laboratory sciences (MSHS); communication sciences and disorders (MS); community practice and administration (MSSW); direct practice (MSSW); exercise science (MS); health affairs (MPAS, MS, MSHS, MSN, MSSW, PhD, Post Master's Certificate); health care administration (MSHS); kinesiology (MS); nutrition (MSHS); occupational therapy (MS); primary care (MPAS). *Application Contact:* Stephanie Ozuna, Graduate Student Recruiter, 956-665-3558, E-mail: stephanie.ozuna@utrgv.edu. *Dean*, Dr. Michael Lehker, 956-665-2293, E-mail: michael.lehker@utrgv.edu.

School of Nursing Students: 48 full-time, 5 part-time; includes 43 minority (5 Black or African American, non-Hispanic/Latino; 38 Hispanic/Latino). Average age 31. 61 applicants. *Faculty:* 7 full-time (all women), 5 part-time/adjunct (3 women). Expenses: Contact institution. *Financial support:* Scholarships/grants and traineeships available. Financial award application deadline: 9/1; financial award applicants required to submit FAFSA. In 2017, 46 master's awarded. *Program availability:* Part-time, evening/weekend. Offers adult health nursing (MSN); family nurse practitioner (MSN); nursing administration (MSN); nursing education (MSN); psychiatric mental health nursing (Post Master's Certificate). *Application deadline:* For fall admission, 7/1 priority date for domestic and international students; for spring admission, 10/1 priority date for domestic and international students. Applications are processed on a rolling basis. *Application fee:* $50. Electronic applications accepted. *Application Contact:* Dr. Beatriz Bautista, Clinical Professor, 956-665-3497, Fax: 956-665-3491, E-mail: beatriz.bautista@utrgv.edu. *Professor/Chief Nursing Administrator*, Dr. Eloisa G. Tamez, 956-665-3616, Fax: 956-665-5252, E-mail: eloisa.tamez@utrgv.edu.

School of Rehabilitation Services and Counseling Students: 109 full-time (91 women), 89 part-time (75 women); includes 186 minority (4 Black or African American, non-Hispanic/Latino; 4 Asian, non-Hispanic/Latino; 178 Hispanic/Latino). Average age 26. 88 applicants, 67% accepted, 54 enrolled. *Faculty:* 16 full-time (8 women), 1 (woman) part-time/adjunct. Expenses: Contact institution. *Financial support:* In 2017–18, 60 students received support, including 12 research assistantships (averaging $25,500 per year), 10 teaching assistantships (averaging $12,600 per year); career-related internships or fieldwork, Federal Work-Study, institutionally sponsored loans, scholarships/grants, traineeships, and unspecified assistantships also available. In 2017, 77 master's, 1 doctorate awarded. *Program availability:* Part-time, evening/weekend. Offers rehabilitation services and counseling (MS, PhD). *Application deadline:* For fall admission, 2/15 for domestic and international students; for spring admission, 10/15 for domestic and international students; for summer admission, 2/15 for domestic and international students. *Application fee:* $50. Electronic applications accepted. *Application Contact:* Dr. Elizabeth Chavez-Palacios, Clinical Assistant Professor/Graduate Coordinator, 956-665-3734, Fax: 956-665-5237, E-mail: elizabeth.palacios@utrgv.edu. *Director/Professor*, Dr. Bruce J. Reed, 956-665-7036, Fax: 956-665-5237, E-mail: bruce.reed@utrgv.edu.

College of Liberal Arts Students: 114 full-time (77 women), 349 part-time (203 women); includes 388 minority (5 Black or African American, non-Hispanic/Latino; 3 Asian, non-Hispanic/Latino; 380 Hispanic/Latino), 11 international. Average age 32. 189 applicants, 92% accepted, 122 enrolled. *Faculty:* 82 full-time (34 women), 3 part-time/adjunct (1 woman). Expenses: Contact institution. *Program availability:* Part-time, evening/weekend. Offers communication (MA); criminal justice (MS); disaster studies (MA); English (MA); English as a second language (MA); global security studies and leadership (MPA); history (MA, MAIS); interdisciplinary studies (MAIS, MSIS); liberal arts (MA, MAIS, MPA, MS, MSIS); psychology (MA); public administration (MPA); public policy and management (MPA); sociology (MS); Spanish (MA); Spanish translation and interpreting (MA). *Application fee:* $50 ($100 for international students). *Application Contact:* Dr. Peter Dabrowski, Associate Dean, 956-665-2175, Fax: 956-665-2177, E-mail: dabrowski@panam.edu. *Dean*, Dr. Dahlia Guerra, 956-665-2175, Fax: 956-665-2177, E-mail: guerrad@panam.edu.

College of Sciences Students: 118 full-time (59 women), 83 part-time (42 women); includes 109 minority (1 Black or African American, non-Hispanic/Latino; 1 American Indian or Alaska Native, non-Hispanic/Latino; 1 Asian, non-Hispanic/Latino; 105 Hispanic/Latino; 1 Two or more races, non-Hispanic/Latino), 28 international. Average age 28. 106 applicants, 91% accepted, 72 enrolled. *Faculty:* 70 full-time (11 women), 1 part-time/adjunct (0 women). Expenses: Contact institution. In 2017, 50 master's awarded. *Program availability:* Part-time, evening/weekend. Offers biology (MS); chemistry (MS); physics (MS); sciences (MS, MSIS). *Application deadline:* For fall admission, 6/1 for international students; for spring admission, 10/1 for international students. Applications are processed on a rolling basis. *Application fee:* $50 ($100 for international students). Electronic applications accepted. *Application Contact:* Stephanie Ozuna, Graduate Recruiter, 956-665-3558, Fax: 956-665-2863, E-mail: ozunas@utpa.edu. *Interim Dean*, Dr. Mohammed Farooqui, 956-665-2404, Fax: 956-665-3657, E-mail: farooqui@utpa.edu.

School of Earth, Environmental, and Marine Sciences Offers agricultural, environmental, and sustainability sciences (MS); ocean, coastal, and earth sciences (MS).

School of Mathematical and Statistical Sciences Students: 25 full-time (11 women), 36 part-time (19 women); includes 29 minority (1 American Indian or Alaska Native, non-Hispanic/Latino; 28 Hispanic/Latino), 7 international. Average age 30. 44 applicants, 93% accepted, 32 enrolled. *Faculty:* 17 full-time (1 woman). Expenses: Contact institution. In 2017, 21 master's awarded. *Program availability:* Part-time, evening/weekend. Offers mathematics (MS). *Application deadline:* Applications are processed on a rolling basis. *Application fee:* $50 ($100 for international students). Electronic applications accepted. *Interim Director*, Timothy Huber, 956-665-2173, E-mail: timothy.huber@utrgv.edu.

Robert C. Vackar College of Business and Entrepreneurship *Program availability:* Part-time, evening/weekend. Offers accounting (M Acc, MS); business administration (MBA); business and entrepreneurship (M Acc, MBA, MS, PhD); finance (PhD); management (PhD); marketing (PhD).

School of Medicine *Program availability:* Part-time, evening/weekend, online learning. Offers medicine (MD).

THE UNIVERSITY OF TEXAS SOUTHWESTERN MEDICAL CENTER, Dallas, TX 75390

General Information State-supported, coed, graduate-only institution. *Graduate housing:* Rooms and/or apartments available on a first-come, first-served basis to single and married students.

GRADUATE UNITS

Southwestern Graduate School of Biomedical Sciences Offers biomedical sciences (MCS, MS, MSCS, PhD); clinical psychology (PhD); clinical science (MCS, MSCS); medical scientist training (PhD). Electronic applications accepted.

Division of Basic Science Offers biological chemistry (PhD); biomedical engineering (MS, PhD); cancer biology (PhD); cell regulation (PhD); genetics and development (PhD); immunology (PhD); integrative biology (PhD); molecular biophysics (PhD); molecular microbiology (PhD); neuroscience (PhD). Electronic applications accepted.

Southwestern Medical School Offers medicine (MD). Electronic applications accepted.

Southwestern School of Health Professions Offers clinical nutrition (MCN); health professions (MCN, MPAS, MPO, MRC, DPT); physical therapy (DPT); physician assistant studies (MPAS); prosthetics - orthotics (MPO); rehabilitation counseling psychology (MRC).

THE UNIVERSITY OF THE ARTS, Philadelphia, PA 19102-4944

General Information Independent, coed, comprehensive institution. *Graduate housing:* Room and/or apartments available to single students; on-campus housing not available to married students. Housing application deadline: 6/1. *Research affiliation:* Ben Franklin Technology Partners (high tech department and creative/cultural production in Philadelphia), The Franklin Institute (general science education), Philadelphia Museum of Art (arts and culture), School District of Philadelphia (education).

GRADUATE UNITS

College of Art, Media and Design *Program availability:* Part-time. Offers art education (MA); art, media and design (MA, MAT, MFA, MID); book arts/printmaking (MFA); industrial design (MID); museum communication (MA); museum education (MA); museum exhibition planning and design (MFA); studio art (MFA); visual arts (MAT). Electronic applications accepted.

College of Performing Arts *Program availability:* Part-time. Offers performing arts (MAT, MM).

School of Music *Program availability:* Part-time. Offers jazz studies (MM); music education (MAT, MM). Electronic applications accepted.

UNIVERSITY OF THE CUMBERLANDS, Williamsburg, KY 40769-1372

General Information Independent-religious, coed, university. *Graduate housing:* Room and/or apartments available on a first-come, first-served basis to single students; on-campus housing not available to married students.

GRADUATE UNITS

Graduate Programs in Education *Program availability:* Part-time, evening/weekend, online learning. Offers all grades (P-12) (M Ed); business and marketing (MA Ed, MAT); counselor education and supervision (Ed D); director of pupil personnel (Certificate); director of special education (Certificate); educational administration and supervision

(Ed S); educational leadership (Ed D); elementary education (MA Ed, MAT); instructional leadership - principalship (MA Ed); instructional leadership - school principal (Certificate); middle school education (MA Ed, MAT); reading and writing (MA Ed); school counseling (MA Ed); school superintendent (Certificate); secondary education (MA Ed, MAT); special education (MAT); supervisor of instruction (Certificate); teacher leader (MA Ed). Electronic applications accepted.

Hutton School of Business *Program availability:* Part-time, online learning. Offers accounting (MBA); business (MBA). Electronic applications accepted.

Program in Christian Studies *Program availability:* Part-time, evening/weekend, online learning. Offers Christian studies (MA). Electronic applications accepted.

Program in Clinical Psychology *Program availability:* Part-time, evening/weekend, online learning. Offers clinical psychology (PhD).

Program in Physician Assistant Studies Offers physician assistant studies (MPAS). Electronic applications accepted.

Program in Professional Counseling *Program availability:* Part-time, evening/weekend, online learning. Offers professional counseling (MA). Program also offered in San Francisco. Electronic applications accepted.

UNIVERSITY OF THE DISTRICT OF COLUMBIA, Washington, DC 20008-1175

General Information District-supported, coed, comprehensive institution. CGS member.

GRADUATE UNITS

College of Agriculture, Urban Sustainability and Environmental Sciences Offers agriculture, urban sustainability and environmental sciences (M Arch, M Arch II, MS, PSM); architecture (M Arch, M Arch II); nutrition and dietetics (MS); water resources management (PSM).

College of Arts and Sciences *Program availability:* Part-time, evening/weekend. Offers adult education (Graduate Certificate); arts and sciences (MA, MAT, MS, Graduate Certificate); cancer biology, prevention and control (MS); counseling (MS); early childhood education (MA); elementary education (MAT); homeland security (MS); middle school mathematics (MAT); rehabilitation counseling (MA); secondary English language arts (MAT); secondary social studies (MAT); speech-language pathology (MS).

David A. Clarke School of Law *Program availability:* Part-time, evening/weekend. Offers clinical teaching and social justice (LL M); law (JD). Electronic applications accepted.

School of Business and Public Administration *Program availability:* Part-time, evening/weekend. Offers business administration (MBA); business and public administration (MBA, MPA); public administration (MPA).

School of Engineering and Applied Sciences Offers computer science (MS, MSCS); electrical engineering (MSEE); engineering and applied sciences (MSCS, MSEE).

UNIVERSITY OF THE FRASER VALLEY, Abbotsford, BC V2S 7M8, Canada

General Information Province-supported, coed, comprehensive institution. *Enrollment:* 8,776 graduate, professional, and undergraduate students; 41 full-time matriculated graduate/professional students (24 women), 4 part-time matriculated graduate/professional students (2 women). *Enrollment by degree level:* 45 master's. *Graduate faculty:* 23 full-time (13 women). *Graduate housing:* Room and/or apartments available on a first-come, first-served basis to single students; on-campus housing not available to married students. Typical cost: $5941 Canadian dollars per year. *Student services:* Campus employment opportunities, campus safety program, career counseling, exercise/wellness program, free psychological counseling, grant writing training, international student services, low-cost health insurance, services for students with disabilities, writing training. *Library facilities:* Peter Jones Library plus 3 others. *Collection:* Books: 181,000 (physical), 37,000 (digital/electronic). Students can reserve study rooms.

Computer facilities: Online class registration is available.
Website: http://www.ufv.ca/

General Application Contact: Educational Advisors, 604-854-4528, Fax: 604-855-7614, E-mail: advising@ufv.ca.

GRADUATE UNITS

Graduate Studies Students: 41 full-time (24 women), 4 part-time (2 women); includes 4 minority (all American Indian or Alaska Native, non-Hispanic/Latino). Average age 36. 42 applicants, 31% accepted, 13 enrolled. *Faculty:* 23 full-time (13 women). Expenses: Contact institution. *Financial support:* Research assistantships, scholarships/grants, health care benefits, and bursaries available. Financial award application deadline: 5/10. In 2017, 15 master's awarded. *Program availability:* Evening/weekend. Offers criminal justice (MA); social work (MSW). *Application deadline:* For fall admission, 1/31 priority date for domestic students, 4/1 priority date for international students; for winter admission, 8/31 priority date for domestic students; for spring admission, 12/31 priority date for domestic students. *Application fee:* $75 ($250 for international students). Electronic applications accepted. *Application Contact:* Educational Advisors, 604-854-4528, Fax: 604-855-7614, E-mail: advising@ufv.ca. *Associate Vice President for Research, Engagement and Graduate Studies,* Dr. Adrienne Chan, 604-504-4074, Fax: 778-880-0356, E-mail: adrienne.chan@ufv.ca.

UNIVERSITY OF THE INCARNATE WORD, San Antonio, TX 78209-6397

General Information Independent-religious, coed, comprehensive institution. *Enrollment:* 8,603 graduate, professional, and undergraduate students; 1,914 full-time matriculated graduate/professional students (1,123 women), 678 part-time matriculated graduate/professional students (347 women). *Enrollment by degree level:* 1,348 master's, 1,244 doctoral. *Graduate faculty:* 166 full-time (89 women), 77 part-time/adjunct (39 women). *Tuition:* Full-time $16,470; part-time $915 per credit hour. Tuition and fees vary according to degree level, program and student level. *Graduate housing:* Room and/or apartments available on a first-come, first-served basis to single students; on-campus housing not available to married students. Typical cost: $7240 per year ($9880 including board). Room and board charges vary according to board plan, campus/location and housing facility selected. Housing application deadline: 5/1. *Student services:* Campus employment opportunities, campus safety program, career counseling, exercise/wellness program, free psychological counseling, grant writing training, international student services, low-cost health insurance, services for students with disabilities, teacher training, writing training. *Library facilities:* J. E. and M. E. Mabee Library plus 1 other. *Collection:* Books: 214,768 (physical), 42,478 (digital/electronic); Serial titles: 1,867 (physical), 75,557 (digital/electronic); Databases: 201. Weekly public service hours: 105.

Computer facilities: Computer purchase and lease plans are available. 185 computers available on campus for general student use. A campuswide network can be accessed from student residence rooms and from off campus. Online class registration is available.
Website: http://www.uiw.edu/

General Application Contact: Johnny Garcia, Assistant Director of Graduate Admissions, 210-805-3554, Fax: 210-829-3921, E-mail: jsgarcia@uiwtx.edu.

GRADUATE UNITS

College of Humanities, Arts, and Social Sciences Students: 2 full-time (1 woman), 1 (woman) part-time; includes 2 minority (both Hispanic/Latino). *Faculty:* 4 full-time (2 women). Expenses: Contact institution. *Financial support:* Research assistantships, scholarships/grants, tuition waivers, and unspecified assistantships available. Financial award applicants required to submit FAFSA. In 2017, 3 master's awarded. *Program availability:* Part-time, evening/weekend. Offers multidisciplinary studies (MA); pastoral ministry (MA). *Application deadline:* Applications are processed on a rolling basis. *Application fee:* $20. Electronic applications accepted. *Application Contact:* Johnny Garcia, Graduate Admissions Counselor, 210-829-6005, Fax: 210-829-3921, E-mail: admis@uiwtx.edu. *Dean,* Dr. Kevin Vichcales, 210-829-2759, Fax: 210-829-3830, E-mail: vichcale@uiwtx.edu.

Dreeben School of Education Students: 90 full-time (54 women), 105 part-time (64 women); includes 116 minority (23 Black or African American, non-Hispanic/Latino; 2 Asian, non-Hispanic/Latino; 87 Hispanic/Latino; 4 Two or more races, non-Hispanic/Latino), 22 international. *Faculty:* 10 full-time (6 women), 5 part-time/adjunct (4 women). Expenses: Contact institution. *Financial support:* In 2017–18, 4 research assistantships were awarded; Federal Work-Study, scholarships/grants, tuition waivers (partial), and unspecified assistantships also available. Financial award applicants required to submit FAFSA. In 2017, 33 master's, 17 doctorates awarded. *Program availability:* Part-time, evening/weekend, online learning. Offers education (M Ed, MA, MAT, PhD). *Application deadline:* Applications are processed on a rolling basis. *Application fee:* $20. Electronic applications accepted. *Application Contact:* Johnny Garcia, Graduate Admissions Counselor, 210-805-3554, Fax: 210-829-3921, E-mail: admis@uiwtx.edu. *Dean,* Dr. Denise Staudt, 210-829-2761, Fax: 210-829-2765, E-mail: staudt@uiwtx.edu.

Feik School of Pharmacy Students: 354 full-time (242 women), 9 part-time (6 women); includes 248 minority (18 Black or African American, non-Hispanic/Latino; 68 Asian, non-Hispanic/Latino; 152 Hispanic/Latino; 1 Native Hawaiian or other Pacific Islander, non-Hispanic/Latino; 9 Two or more races, non-Hispanic/Latino), 5 international. *Faculty:* 24 full-time (14 women), 1 (woman) part-time/adjunct. Expenses: Contact institution. *Financial support:* Research assistantships, Federal Work-Study, scholarships/grants, and unspecified assistantships available. Financial award applicants required to submit FAFSA. In 2017, 91 doctorates awarded. Offers pharmacy (Pharm D). *Application deadline:* For fall admission, 12/1 for domestic and international students. *Application fee:* $50. Electronic applications accepted. *Application Contact:* Dr. Amy Diepenbrock, Assistant Dean, Student Affairs, 210-883-1060, Fax: 210-822-1521, E-mail: diepenbr@uiwtx.edu. *Dean,* Dr. David Maize, 210-883-1000, Fax: 210-822-1516, E-mail: maize@uiwtx.edu.

H-E-B School of Business and Administration Students: 240 full-time (118 women), 39 part-time (19 women); includes 151 minority (24 Black or African American, non-Hispanic/Latino; 5 Asian, non-Hispanic/Latino; 120 Hispanic/Latino; 2 Two or more races, non-Hispanic/Latino), 50 international. *Faculty:* 22 full-time (11 women), 12 part-time/adjunct (4 women). Expenses: Contact institution. *Financial support:* In 2017–18, 4 research assistantships were awarded; Federal Work-Study, scholarships/grants, tuition waivers (partial), and unspecified assistantships also available. Financial award applicants required to submit FAFSA. In 2017, 164 master's awarded. *Program availability:* Part-time, evening/weekend, online learning. Offers business and administration (MBA, MHA, MS). *Application deadline:* Applications are processed on a rolling basis. *Application fee:* $20. Electronic applications accepted. *Application Contact:* Johnny Garcia, Assistant Director of Graduate Admissions, 210-805-3554, Fax: 210-829-3921, E-mail: jsgarcia@uiwtx.edu. *Dean,* Dr. Forrest Aven, 210-805-5884, Fax: 210-805-3564, E-mail: aven@uiwtx.edu.

Ila Faye Miller School of Nursing and Health Professions Students: 48 full-time (26 women), 75 part-time (62 women); includes 86 minority (22 Black or African American, non-Hispanic/Latino; 1 American Indian or Alaska Native, non-Hispanic/Latino; 8 Asian, non-Hispanic/Latino; 53 Hispanic/Latino; 2 Two or more races, non-Hispanic/Latino), 3 international. *Faculty:* 18 full-time (14 women). Expenses: Contact institution. *Financial support:* Research assistantships, Federal Work-Study, scholarships/grants, tuition waivers (partial), and unspecified assistantships available. Financial award applicants required to submit FAFSA. In 2017, 31 master's, 10 doctorates awarded. *Program availability:* Part-time, evening/weekend. Offers kinesiology (MS); nursing (MSN, DNP); sport management (MS). *Application deadline:* Applications are processed on a rolling basis. *Application fee:* $20. Electronic applications accepted. *Application Contact:* Johnny Garcia, Graduate Admissions Counselor, 210-805-3554, Fax: 210-829-3921, E-mail: admis@uiwtx.edu. *Dean,* Dr. Mary Hoke, 210-829-3982, Fax: 210-829-3174, E-mail: mhoke@uiwtx.edu.

Rosenberg School of Optometry Students: 260 full-time (177 women), 1 (woman) part-time; includes 151 minority (8 Black or African American, non-Hispanic/Latino; 2 American Indian or Alaska Native, non-Hispanic/Latino; 89 Asian, non-Hispanic/Latino; 51 Hispanic/Latino; 1 Two or more races, non-Hispanic/Latino), 4 international. *Faculty:* 19 full-time (6 women), 1 (woman) part-time/adjunct. Expenses: Contact institution. *Financial support:* In 2017–18, 5 fellowships (averaging $4,000 per year) were awarded; Federal Work-Study and scholarships/grants also available. Financial award applicants required to submit FAFSA. In 2017, 65 doctorates awarded. Offers optometry (OD). *Application deadline:* For fall admission, 5/1 for domestic students. *Application fee:* $50. Electronic applications accepted. *Application Contact:* Kristine Benne, Assistant Dean of Student Affairs, 210-883-1190, Fax: 210-883-1191, E-mail: benne@uiwtx.edu. *Dean,* Dr. Timothy Wingert, 210-883-1195, Fax: 210-283-6890, E-mail: twingert@uiwtx.edu.

School of Mathematics, Science, and Engineering Students: 42 full-time (33 women), 6 part-time (5 women); includes 27 minority (2 Black or African American, non-Hispanic/Latino; 1 American Indian or Alaska Native, non-Hispanic/Latino; 1 Asian, non-Hispanic/Latino; 23 Hispanic/Latino), 6 international. *Faculty:* 9 full-time (4 women), 3 part-time/adjunct (1 woman). Expenses: Contact institution. *Financial support:* In 2017–18, 1 research assistantship (averaging $5,000 per year) was awarded; Federal Work-Study, scholarships/grants, tuition waivers (partial), and unspecified assistantships also available. Financial award applicants required to submit FAFSA. In 2017, 13 master's awarded. *Program availability:* Part-time, evening/weekend. Offers applied statistics (MS); biology (MA, MS); mathematics (MA); multidisciplinary sciences (MA); nutrition (MS). *Application deadline:* Applications are processed on a rolling basis. *Application fee:* $20. Electronic applications accepted. *Application Contact:* Johnny Garcia, Graduate Admissions Counselor, 210-805-3554, Fax: 210-829-3921, E-mail: admis@uiwtx.edu. *Dean,* Dr. Carlos A. Garcia, 210-829-2717, Fax: 210-829-3153, E-mail: cagarci9@uiwtx.edu.

School of Media and Design Students: 27 full-time (15 women), 9 part-time (5 women); includes 26 minority (4 Black or African American, non-Hispanic/Latino; 22 Hispanic/Latino), 3 international. *Faculty:* 10 full-time (6 women). Expenses: Contact institution. *Financial support:* Federal Work-Study, scholarships/grants, tuition waivers (partial), and unspecified assistantships available. Financial award applicants required to submit FAFSA. In 2017, 15 master's awarded. *Program availability:* Part-time, evening/weekend. Offers communication arts (MA); fashion design (MA). *Application deadline:* Applications are processed on a rolling basis. *Application fee:* $20. Electronic applications accepted. *Application Contact:* Johnny Garcia, Graduate Admissions Counselor, 210-805-3554, Fax: 210-829-3921, E-mail: admis@uiwtx.edu. *Dean*, Dr. Sharon Welkey, 210-829-6091, Fax: 210-829-3196, E-mail: welkey@uiwtx.edu.

School of Osteopathic Medicine Students: 200 full-time (113 women); includes 125 minority (14 Black or African American, non-Hispanic/Latino; 1 American Indian or Alaska Native, non-Hispanic/Latino; 43 Asian, non-Hispanic/Latino; 60 Hispanic/Latino; 7 Two or more races, non-Hispanic/Latino). *Faculty:* 7 full-time (5 women), 3 part-time/adjunct (1 woman). Expenses: Contact institution. *Financial support:* Research assistantships, career-related internships or fieldwork, scholarships/grants, and unspecified assistantships available. Financial award applicants required to submit FAFSA. Offers osteopathic medicine (MBS, DO). *Application deadline:* For fall admission, 9/1 for domestic students; for spring admission, 3/15 for domestic students. Applications are processed on a rolling basis. *Application fee:* $50. Electronic applications accepted. *Application Contact:* Alexandra R. Shipley, Admissions Recruiter, 210-283-6998, E-mail: ashipley@uiwtx.edu. *Dean*, Dr. Robyn Phillips-Madson, E-mail: rmadson@uiwtx.edu.

School of Physical Therapy Students: 107 full-time (68 women), 73 part-time (35 women); includes 96 minority (10 Black or African American, non-Hispanic/Latino; 32 Asian, non-Hispanic/Latino; 51 Hispanic/Latino; 3 Two or more races, non-Hispanic/Latino), 4 international. *Faculty:* 16 full-time (9 women), 12 part-time/adjunct (10 women). Expenses: Contact institution. *Financial support:* Scholarships/grants and unspecified assistantships available. Financial award applicants required to submit FAFSA. In 2017, 65 doctorates awarded. Offers physical therapy (DPT). *Application deadline:* For fall admission, 10/1 priority date for domestic students. *Application fee:* $50. *Application Contact:* Christina Immel, Director of Enrollment, 210-283-6918, E-mail: cimmel@uiwtx.edu. *Dean*, Dr. Caroline Goulet, 210-283-6924, E-mail: goulet@uiwtx.edu.

School of Professional Studies Students: 528 full-time (263 women), 348 part-time (141 women); includes 543 minority (122 Black or African American, non-Hispanic/Latino; 3 American Indian or Alaska Native, non-Hispanic/Latino; 26 Asian, non-Hispanic/Latino; 365 Hispanic/Latino; 6 Native Hawaiian or other Pacific Islander, non-Hispanic/Latino; 21 Two or more races, non-Hispanic/Latino). *Faculty:* 9 full-time (3 women), 25 part-time/adjunct (10 women). Expenses: Contact institution. *Financial support:* Scholarships/grants and unspecified assistantships available. Financial award applicants required to submit FAFSA. In 2017, 377 master's, 10 doctorates awarded. *Program availability:* Part-time, evening/weekend, 100% online, blended/hybrid learning. Offers communication arts (MAA); organizational development and leadership (MS); professional studies (DBA). *Application deadline:* Applications are processed on a rolling basis. Electronic applications accepted. *Application Contact:* Julie Weber, Director of Marketing and Recruitment, 210-318-1876, Fax: 210-829-2756, E-mail: eapadmission@uiwtx.edu. *Vice President*, Dr. Cyndi Porter, 877-603-1130, E-mail: porter@uiwtx.edu.

UNIVERSITY OF THE PACIFIC, Stockton, CA 95211-0197

General Information Independent, coed, university. CGS member. *Enrollment:* 6,255 graduate, professional, and undergraduate students; 1,943 full-time matriculated graduate/professional students (1,124 women), 751 part-time matriculated graduate/professional students (471 women). *Enrollment by degree level:* 779 master's, 1,897 doctoral, 18 other advanced degrees. *Graduate faculty:* 273 full-time (109 women), 290 part-time/adjunct (113 women). *Graduate housing:* Rooms and/or apartments available on a first-come, first-served basis to single and married students. Housing application deadline: 7/1. *Student services:* Campus employment opportunities, campus safety program, career counseling, free psychological counseling, international student services, low-cost health insurance, multicultural affairs office, services for students with disabilities, teacher training. *Library facilities:* University of the Pacific Library plus 1 other. *Research affiliation:* Lawrence Hall of Science.

Computer facilities: A campuswide network can be accessed. Online class registration is available.
Website: http://www.pacific.edu/

General Application Contact: Office of Graduate Admissions, 209-946-2011.

GRADUATE UNITS

Arthur A. Dugoni School of Dentistry Students: 568 full-time (255 women); includes 329 minority (6 Black or African American, non-Hispanic/Latino; 1 American Indian or Alaska Native, non-Hispanic/Latino; 247 Asian, non-Hispanic/Latino; 39 Hispanic/Latino; 36 Two or more races, non-Hispanic/Latino), 51 international. Average age 26. 3,197 applicants, 9% accepted, 179 enrolled. *Faculty:* 66 full-time (21 women), 171 part-time/adjunct (67 women). Expenses: Contact institution. *Financial support:* Institutionally sponsored loans, scholarships/grants, and stipends available. Support available to part-time students. Financial award application deadline: 3/2; financial award applicants required to submit FAFSA. In 2017, 8 master's, 156 doctorates awarded. Offers dentistry (MSD, DDS, Certificate). *Application deadline:* For fall admission, 9/15 priority date for international students. Applications are processed on a rolling basis. Electronic applications accepted. *Application Contact:* Dr. Craig S. Yarborough, Associate Professor, 415-929-6430, E-mail: cyarborough@pacific.edu. *Dean*, Nader Nadershahi, 415-929-6425, E-mail: nnadershahi@pacific.edu.

College of the Pacific Students: 2 full-time (both women), 101 part-time (61 women); includes 41 minority (5 Black or African American, non-Hispanic/Latino; 13 Asian, non-Hispanic/Latino; 14 Hispanic/Latino; 1 Native Hawaiian or other Pacific Islander, non-Hispanic/Latino; 8 Two or more races, non-Hispanic/Latino), 5 international. Average age 27. 132 applicants, 65% accepted, 45 enrolled. *Faculty:* 31 full-time (10 women), 7 part-time/adjunct (4 women). Expenses: Contact institution. *Financial support:* Teaching assistantships and institutionally sponsored loans available. Support available to part-time students. Financial award application deadline: 3/1; financial award applicants required to submit FAFSA. In 2017, 27 master's awarded. Offers biological sciences (MS); communication (MA); food studies (MA); health, exercise and sport science (MA); psychology (MA). *Application fee:* $75. *Application Contact:* Information Contact, 209-946-2261. *Dean*, Dr. Rena Fraden, 209-946-2023.

Conservatory of Music Students: 8 full-time (4 women), 17 part-time (11 women); includes 9 minority (1 Black or African American, non-Hispanic/Latino; 4 Asian, non-Hispanic/Latino; 2 Hispanic/Latino; 2 Two or more races, non-Hispanic/Latino), 3 international. Average age 31. 36 applicants, 42% accepted, 9 enrolled. *Faculty:* 4 full-time (2 women), 3 part-time/adjunct (all women). Expenses: Contact institution. *Financial support:* Teaching assistantships and institutionally sponsored loans available. Support available to part-time students. Financial award application deadline: 3/1; financial award applicants required to submit FAFSA. In 2017, 5 master's awarded. Offers music education (MM); music therapy (MA). *Application deadline:* For fall admission, 3/1 priority date for domestic students; for spring admission, 10/1 priority date for domestic students. Applications are processed on a rolling basis. *Application fee:* $75. *Application Contact:* 209-946-2415, Fax: 209-946-2770. *Interim Dean*, Dr. Daniel Ebbers, 209-946-2415, E-mail: musicdean@pacific.edu.

Eberhardt School of Business Students: 22 full-time (12 women), 1 (woman) part-time; includes 12 minority (6 Asian, non-Hispanic/Latino; 4 Hispanic/Latino; 2 Two or more races, non-Hispanic/Latino), 4 international. Average age 24. 69 applicants, 61% accepted, 16 enrolled. *Faculty:* 27 full-time (12 women). Expenses: Contact institution. *Financial support:* Fellowships, research assistantships, Federal Work-Study, and institutionally sponsored loans available. Support available to part-time students. Financial award application deadline: 3/1; financial award applicants required to submit FAFSA. In 2017, 44 master's awarded. *Program availability:* Part-time. Offers business (M Acc, MBA). *Application deadline:* For fall admission, 7/31 priority date for domestic students; for spring admission, 11/30 for domestic students. Applications are processed on a rolling basis. *Application fee:* $75. *Application Contact:* 209-946-2239, E-mail: business@pacific.edu. *Interim Dean*, Dr. David Dauwalder, 209-946-7710, E-mail: ddauwalder@pacific.edu.

Gladys L. Benerd School of Education Students: 141 full-time (115 women), 305 part-time (236 women); includes 219 minority (41 Black or African American, non-Hispanic/Latino; 44 Asian, non-Hispanic/Latino; 105 Hispanic/Latino; 2 Native Hawaiian or other Pacific Islander, non-Hispanic/Latino; 27 Two or more races, non-Hispanic/Latino), 7 international. Average age 33. 144 applicants, 83% accepted, 94 enrolled. *Faculty:* 19 full-time (12 women), 48 part-time/adjunct (39 women). Expenses: Contact institution. *Financial support:* Teaching assistantships and institutionally sponsored loans available. Support available to part-time students. Financial award application deadline: 3/1; financial award applicants required to submit FAFSA. In 2017, 231 master's, 8 doctorates awarded. Offers curriculum and instruction (MA, Ed D); education (M Ed); educational administration and leadership (MA, Ed D); educational and school psychology (MA, Ed D); school psychology (Ed S); special education (MA); teacher education (MA). *Application deadline:* For fall admission, 3/1 priority date for domestic students; for spring admission, 10/15 for domestic students. Applications are processed on a rolling basis. *Application fee:* $75. *Application Contact:* Office of Graduate Admissions, 209-946-2344. *Dean*, Dr. Vanessa Sheared, 209-946-2683, E-mail: lwebster@pacific.edu.

McGeorge School of Law Students: 376 full-time (200 women), 219 part-time (126 women); includes 199 minority (22 Black or African American, non-Hispanic/Latino; 4 American Indian or Alaska Native, non-Hispanic/Latino; 40 Asian, non-Hispanic/Latino; 119 Hispanic/Latino; 2 Native Hawaiian or other Pacific Islander, non-Hispanic/Latino; 12 Two or more races, non-Hispanic/Latino), 18 international. Average age 29. 1,063 applicants, 61% accepted, 201 enrolled. *Faculty:* 39 full-time (18 women), 38 part-time/adjunct (14 women). Expenses: Contact institution. *Financial support:* Fellowships, research assistantships, teaching assistantships, career-related internships or fieldwork, Federal Work-Study, institutionally sponsored loans, and scholarships/grants available. Support available to part-time students. Financial award applicants required to submit FAFSA. In 2017, 26 master's, 135 doctorates awarded. *Program availability:* Part-time, evening/weekend. Offers advocacy (JD); international water resources law (JSD); public policy and law (LL M). *Application deadline:* For fall admission, 3/15 priority date for domestic students. Applications are processed on a rolling basis. *Application fee:* $50. Electronic applications accepted. *Application Contact:* 916-739-7105, Fax: 916-739-7301, E-mail: mcgeorge@pacific.edu. *Dean*, Michael Schwartz, 916-739-7151, E-mail: jmootz@pacific.edu.

School of Engineering and Computer Science Students: 21 full-time (2 women), 40 part-time (9 women); includes 35 minority (3 Black or African American, non-Hispanic/Latino; 20 Asian, non-Hispanic/Latino; 9 Hispanic/Latino; 3 Two or more races, non-Hispanic/Latino), 5 international. Average age 28. 84 applicants, 56% accepted, 26 enrolled. *Faculty:* 7 full-time (3 women), 6 part-time/adjunct (1 woman). Expenses: Contact institution. *Financial support:* Teaching assistantships available. In 2017, 50 master's awarded. Offers engineering science (MS). *Application deadline:* For fall admission, 3/1 for domestic students; for spring admission, 10/1 for domestic students. Electronic applications accepted. *Application Contact:* Office of Graduate Admissions, 209-946-2011. *Dean*, Dr. Steve Howell, 209-946-3068, E-mail: showell@pacific.edu.

Thomas J. Long School of Pharmacy and Health Sciences Students: 806 full-time (534 women), 68 part-time (27 women); includes 617 minority (11 Black or African American, non-Hispanic/Latino; 1 American Indian or Alaska Native, non-Hispanic/Latino; 506 Asian, non-Hispanic/Latino; 58 Hispanic/Latino; 6 Native Hawaiian or other Pacific Islander, non-Hispanic/Latino; 35 Two or more races, non-Hispanic/Latino), 43 international. Average age 25. 1,956 applicants, 31% accepted, 303 enrolled. *Faculty:* 76 full-time (40 women), 45 part-time/adjunct (35 women). Expenses: Contact institution. *Financial support:* Teaching assistantships, career-related internships or fieldwork, Federal Work-Study, and institutionally sponsored loans available. Support available to part-time students. Financial award application deadline: 3/1; financial award applicants required to submit FAFSA. In 2017, 35 master's, 242 doctorates awarded. Offers audiology (Au D); pharmaceutical and chemical sciences (MS, PhD); pharmacy (Pharm D); pharmacy and health sciences (MS, Au D, DPT, PhD, Pharm D); physical therapy (MS, DPT); speech-language pathology (MS). *Application fee:* $75. *Application Contact:* 209-946-2211. *Dean*, Dr. Philip Oppenheimer, 209-946-2561.

UNIVERSITY OF THE PEOPLE, Pasadena, CA 91101

General Information Private, coed, comprehensive institution.

GRADUATE UNITS

Master of Business Administration Program *Program availability:* Online learning. Offers business administration (MBA).

UNIVERSITY OF THE POTOMAC, Washington, DC 20005

General Information Proprietary, coed, comprehensive institution.

GRADUATE UNITS

Program in Business Administration *Program availability:* Online learning. Offers business administration (MBA). Program also offered at Vienna, VA campus.

UNIVERSITY OF THE ROCKIES, Colorado Springs, CO 80903

General Information Independent, coed, graduate-only institution.

GRADUATE UNITS

Graduate Programs Offers psychology (MA, Psy D).

UNIVERSITY OF THE SACRED HEART, San Juan, PR 00914-0383

General Information Independent-religious, coed, comprehensive institution. *Graduate housing:* Room and/or apartments available on a first-come, first-served basis to single students; on-campus housing not available to married students. Housing application deadline: 5/31.

GRADUATE UNITS

Graduate Programs *Program availability:* Part-time, evening/weekend. Offers contemporary culture and media (MA); creative writing (MFA, Certificate); digital journalism (MA, Certificate); early childhood education (M Ed); editing for media (MA, Certificate); human resource management (MBA); human rights and anti-discriminatory processes (MASJ); information systems auditing (MS); information systems management (MBA); information technology (Certificate); information technology and multimedia (Certificate); instruction systems and education technology (M Ed); international marketing (MBA); management information systems (MBA); mediation and transformation of conflicts (MASJ); nonprofit organization administration (MBA); occupational health and safety (MS); occupational nursing (MSN); production and marketing of special events (Certificate); public relations (MA, Certificate); publicity (MA, Certificate); scriptwriting (MA, Certificate); taxation (MBA).

UNIVERSITY OF THE SCIENCES, Philadelphia, PA 19104-4495

General Information Independent, coed, university. CGS member. *Graduate housing:* On-campus housing not available. *Research affiliation:* Progenra (molecular biology), Encapsulation Systems (analytical chemistry), Johnson & Johnson (cell biology), Ortho-McNeil Pharmaceuticals, Inc. (pharmacy), Polymedix (computational chemistry).

GRADUATE UNITS

Doctor of Physical Therapy Program *Program availability:* Part-time, evening/weekend, online learning. Offers physical therapy (DPT).

Philadelphia College of Pharmacy Offers pharmacy (Pharm D).

Program in Bioinformatics *Program availability:* Part-time, evening/weekend. Offers bioinformatics (MS).

Program in Biomedical Writing *Program availability:* Part-time, evening/weekend, online learning. Offers biomedical writing (MS); medical marketing writing (Certificate); regulatory affairs writing (Certificate).

Program in Cell Biology and Biotechnology *Program availability:* Part-time, evening/weekend. Offers cell biology and biotechnology (MS).

Program in Chemistry, Biochemistry and Pharmacognosy *Program availability:* Part-time. Offers biochemistry (MS, PhD); chemistry (MS, PhD); pharmacognosy (MS, PhD).

Program in Health Policy *Program availability:* Part-time, evening/weekend, online learning. Offers health policy (MS, PhD).

Program in Health Psychology Offers health psychology (MS).

Program in Occupational Therapy *Program availability:* Online learning. Offers occupational therapy (MOT, Dr OT). Electronic applications accepted.

Program in Pharmaceutical and Healthcare Business *Program availability:* Part-time, evening/weekend, online learning. Offers pharmaceutical and healthcare business (MBA).

Program in Pharmaceutics *Program availability:* Part-time. Offers pharmaceutics (MS, PhD).

Program in Pharmacology and Toxicology Offers pharmacology (MS, PhD); toxicology (MS, PhD).

Program in Pharmacy Administration *Program availability:* Part-time. Offers pharmacy administration (MS).

Program in Public Health *Program availability:* Part-time, evening/weekend, online learning. Offers public health (MPH).

THE UNIVERSITY OF THE SOUTH, Sewanee, TN 37383-1000

General Information Independent-religious, coed, comprehensive institution. *Enrollment:* 1,778 graduate, professional, and undergraduate students; 61 full-time matriculated graduate/professional students (23 women), 13 part-time matriculated graduate/professional students (7 women). *Enrollment by degree level:* 69 master's, 1 doctoral, 4 other advanced degrees. *Graduate faculty:* 8 full-time (3 women), 10 part-time/adjunct (4 women). *Graduate housing:* Rooms and/or apartments available on a first-come, first-served basis to single and married students. Housing application deadline: 33/44. *Student services:* Campus employment opportunities, campus safety program, career counseling, child daycare facilities, free psychological counseling, international student services, multicultural affairs office, writing training. *Library facilities:* Jessie Ball duPont Library. *Collection:* Books: 508,288 (physical), 559,530 (digital/electronic); Serial titles: 3,975 (physical), 16,012 (digital/electronic); Databases: 377. Study areas open 24 hours, 5–7 days a week; students can reserve study rooms.

Computer facilities: 150 computers available on campus for general student use. A campuswide network can be accessed from student residence rooms and from off campus. Online class registration is available.
Website: http://www.sewanee.edu/

GRADUATE UNITS

School of Theology Students: 61 full-time (23 women), 7 part-time (3 women); includes 6 minority (3 Black or African American, non-Hispanic/Latino; 1 American Indian or Alaska Native, non-Hispanic/Latino; 2 Two or more races, non-Hispanic/Latino), 5 international. Average age 39. *Faculty:* 8 full-time (3 women), 10 part-time/adjunct (4 women). Expenses: Contact institution. *Financial support:* Institutionally sponsored loans and scholarships/grants available. Support available to part-time students. In 2017, 31 master's, 10 doctorates awarded. *Program availability:* Part-time. Offers theology (M Div, MA, STM, D Min). *Application deadline:* For fall admission, 7/1 for domestic students, 1/15 for international students. Applications are processed on a rolling basis. *Application fee:* $0. Electronic applications accepted. *Application Contact:* Stephanie Borne, Administrative Assistant for Recruitment and Admission, 931-598-1283, E-mail: theologyadmissions@sewanee.edu. *Dean,* Very Rev. Dr. J. Neil Alexander, 931-598-1288, Fax: 931-598-1412, E-mail: deansot@sewanee.edu.

Sewanee School of Letters Students: 53 part-time (33 women); includes 4 minority (1 Black or African American, non-Hispanic/Latino; 3 Two or more races, non-Hispanic/Latino), 1 international. Average age 41. *Faculty:* 1 full-time (0 women), 10 part-time/adjunct (7 women). Expenses: Contact institution. *Financial support:* Institutionally sponsored loans and scholarships/grants available. In 2017, 13 master's awarded. *Program availability:* Part-time. Offers American and English literature (MA); creative writing (MFA). *Application deadline:* Applications are processed on a rolling basis. *Application fee:* $40. Electronic applications accepted. *Application Contact:* April R. Alvarez, Administrator, 931-598-1636, E-mail: sletters@sewanee.edu. *Interim Director,* Dr. John Gatta, 931-598-1636, E-mail: sletters@sewanee.edu.

UNIVERSITY OF THE SOUTHWEST, Hobbs, NM 88240-9129

General Information Independent-religious, coed, comprehensive institution. *Graduate housing:* On-campus housing not available.

GRADUATE UNITS

Graduate Programs *Program availability:* Part-time, evening/weekend, online learning. Offers business administration (MBA); curriculum and instruction (MSE); curriculum and instruction: bilingual (MSE); curriculum and instruction: TESOL (MSE); early childhood education (MSE); educational administration (MSE); mental health counseling (MSE); school counseling (MSE); special education (MSE); sports management (MBA). Electronic applications accepted.

UNIVERSITY OF THE VIRGIN ISLANDS, St. Thomas, VI 00802

General Information Territory-supported, coed, comprehensive institution. *Graduate housing:* On-campus housing not available.

GRADUATE UNITS

College of Liberal Arts and Social Sciences *Program availability:* Part-time, evening/weekend. Offers liberal arts and social sciences (M Psych, MPA). Electronic applications accepted.

College of Science and Mathematics *Program availability:* Part-time, online learning. Offers marine and environmental science (MS); mathematics for secondary teachers (MA). Electronic applications accepted.

School of Business *Program availability:* Part-time, evening/weekend. Offers business (EMBA, MBA). Electronic applications accepted.

School of Education *Program availability:* Part-time, evening/weekend. Offers creative leadership for innovation and change (PhD); educational leadership (MA); school counseling (MA); school psychology (Ed S). Electronic applications accepted.

UNIVERSITY OF THE WEST, Rosemead, CA 91770

General Information Independent, coed, comprehensive institution. *Graduate housing:* Rooms and/or apartments guaranteed to single students and available on a first-come, first-served basis to married students. Housing application deadline: 9/22.

GRADUATE UNITS

Department of Business Administration *Program availability:* Part-time, evening/weekend. Offers business administration (EMBA); computer information systems (MBA); finance (MBA); international business (MBA); nonprofit organization management (MBA).

Department of Psychology *Program availability:* Part-time, evening/weekend. Offers Buddhist psychology (MA); multicultural counseling (MA).

Department of Religious Studies *Program availability:* Part-time, evening/weekend. Offers religious studies (MA, PhD).

Program in Buddhist Chaplaincy Offers Buddhist chaplaincy (M Div).

THE UNIVERSITY OF TOLEDO, Toledo, OH 43606-3390

General Information State-supported, coed, university. CGS member. *Graduate housing:* Room and/or apartments available to single students; on-campus housing not available to married students. *Research affiliation:* Merck & Company, Inc. (pharmaceutical research), Midwest Astronomical Data Reduction and Analysis Facility (astronomy), Edison Industrial Systems Center (systems integration, quality control, mathematical modeling), Ohio Aerospace Institute (aerospace research), National Renewable Energy Laboratory (NREL) (thin films, photovoltaics), NASA–Glen Research Center at Lewis Field (aerospace engineering).

GRADUATE UNITS

College of Graduate Studies *Program availability:* Part-time, evening/weekend, online learning. Electronic applications accepted.

College of Business and Innovation *Program availability:* Part-time, evening/weekend. Offers accounting (MBA, MSA); business administration-general (MBA); business and innovation (EMBA, MBA, MSA, DME, PhD, Certificate); finance (MBA); information operations and technology management (MBA, DME, PhD, Certificate); management (MBA); marketing and international business (MBA). Electronic applications accepted.

College of Communication and the Arts Offers communication (Certificate); communication and the arts (ME, MME, MMP, Certificate); music (Certificate); music performance (MMP). Electronic applications accepted.

College of Engineering *Program availability:* Part-time, evening/weekend, online learning. Offers bioengineering (MS, PhD); biomedical engineering (PhD); chemical engineering (MS, PhD); civil engineering (MS, PhD); computer science (MS, PhD); electrical engineering (MS, PhD); engineering (MS, PhD); general engineering (MS); industrial engineering (MS, PhD); mechanical engineering (MS, PhD). Electronic applications accepted.

College of Health and Human Services Offers athletic training (MSES); counselor education (MA, PhD); criminal justice (MA); exercise physiology (MSES); exercise science (PhD); health and human services (MA, MPH, MS, MSES, MSW, DPT, OTD, PhD, Ed S); health education (PhD); occupational health-industrial hygiene (MS); occupational therapy (OTD); physical therapy (DPT); public health (MPH); recreation and leisure studies (MA); school psychology (Ed S); social work (MSW); speech-language pathology (MA). Electronic applications accepted.

College of Languages, Literature and Social Sciences *Program availability:* Part-time. Offers applied econometric specialization (MA); clinical psychology (MA, PhD); economics (MA); English as a second language (MA); experimental psychology (MA, PhD); French (MA); geographic information science and applied geographics (Certificate); geography and planning (MA); German (MA); health care policy and administration (Certificate); history (MA, PhD); languages, literature and social sciences (MA, MLS, MPA, PhD, Certificate); liberal studies (MLS); management of non-profit organizations (Certificate); municipal administration (Certificate); philosophy (MA); political science (MA); public administration (MPA); sociology (MA); Spanish (MA); spatially-integrated social science (PhD); teaching of writing (Certificate); women's and gender studies (Certificate). Electronic applications accepted.

College of Medicine and Life Sciences *Program availability:* Part-time, evening/weekend. Offers bioinformatics and proteomics/genomics (MSBS); biomarkers and bioinformatics (Certificate); biomarkers and diagnostics (PSM); biostatistics and epidemiology (Certificate); cancer biology (MSBS, PhD); cardiovascular and metabolic diseases (MSBS, PhD); contemporary gerontological practice (Certificate); environmental and occupational health and safety (MPH); epidemiology (Certificate); global public health (Certificate); health promotion and education (MPH); human donation sciences (MSBS); industrial hygiene (MSOH); infection, immunity, and transplantation (MSBS, PhD); medical and health science teaching and learning (Certificate); medical physics (MSBS); medical sciences (MSBS); medicine and life sciences (MPH, MS, MSBS, MSOH, PhD, Certificate); neurosciences (MSBS, PhD); occupational health (Certificate); oral biology (MSBS);

orthopedic surgery (MSBS); pathology (Certificate); pathology assistant (MSBS); physician assistant studies (MSBS); public health administration (MPH); public health and emergency response (Certificate); public health epidemiology (MPH); public health nutrition (MPH). Electronic applications accepted.

College of Natural Sciences and Mathematics *Program availability:* Part-time. Offers analytical chemistry (MS, PhD); applied mathematics (MS, PhD); biological chemistry (MS, PhD); biology (MS, PhD); geology (MS); inorganic chemistry (MS, PhD); natural sciences and mathematics (MS, PSM, PhD); organic chemistry (MS, PhD); photovoltaics (PSM); physical chemistry (MS, PhD); physics (MS, PhD); statistics (MS, PhD). Electronic applications accepted.

College of Nursing *Program availability:* Part-time, online learning. Offers clinical nurse leader (MSN); family nurse practitioner (MSN, Certificate); health promotions, outcomes, systems, and policy (MSN, DNP); nurse educator (MSN, Certificate); nursing (MSN, DNP, Certificate); pediatric nurse practitioner (MSN, Certificate). Electronic applications accepted.

College of Pharmacy and Pharmaceutical Sciences Offers administrative pharmacy (MSPS); experimental therapeutics (PhD); industrial pharmacy (MSPS); medicinal and biological chemistry (MS, PhD); pharmacology toxicology (MSPS); pharmacy and pharmaceutical sciences (MS, MSPS, PhD, Pharm D). Electronic applications accepted.

College of Social Justice and Human Service Offers child advocacy (Certificate); counselor education (MA, PhD); criminal justice (MA); elder law (Certificate); higher education (ME, PhD, Certificate); juvenile justice (Certificate); patient advocacy (Certificate); school psychology (MA, Ed S); social justice and human service (MA, ME, MSW, PhD, Certificate, Ed S); social work (MSW).

Judith Herb College of Education *Program availability:* Part-time, evening/weekend. Offers art education (ME); career and technical education (ME, Ed S); curriculum and instruction (ME, PhD, Ed S); early childhood education (ME, Ed S); education (MAE, ME, MES, MME, DE, PhD, Certificate, Ed S); education and anthropology (MAE); education and biology (MES); education and chemistry (MES); education and classics (MAE); education and economics (MAE); education and English (MAE); education and French (MAE); education and geology (MES); education and German (MAE); education and history (MAE); education and mathematics (MAE, MES); education and physics (MES); education and political science (MAE); education and sociology (MAE); education and Spanish (MAE); educational administration and supervision (ME, DE, Ed S); educational media (PhD); educational psychology (ME, PhD); educational research and measurement (ME, PhD); educational sociology (PhD); educational technology (ME); educational technology: virtual educator (Certificate); educational theory and social foundations (ME); elementary education (PhD); English as a second language (MAE); foundations of education (DE, PhD); gifted and talented education (PhD); history of education (PhD); middle childhood education (ME); philosophy of education (PhD); physical education (ME); secondary education (ME, PhD); special education (ME, PhD). Electronic applications accepted.

College of Law Students: 194 full-time (87 women), 73 part-time (45 women); includes 42 minority (21 Black or African American, non-Hispanic/Latino; 1 American Indian or Alaska Native, non-Hispanic/Latino; 4 Asian, non-Hispanic/Latino; 13 Hispanic/Latino; 1 Native Hawaiian or other Pacific Islander, non-Hispanic/Latino; 2 Two or more races, non-Hispanic/Latino). Average age 28. 524 applicants, 55% accepted, 92 enrolled. *Faculty:* 24 full-time (10 women), 12 part-time/adjunct (4 women). Expenses: Contact institution. *Financial support:* In 2017–18, 214 students received support, including 9 teaching assistantships; research assistantships, career-related internships or fieldwork, Federal Work-Study, and scholarships/grants also available. Support available to part-time students. Financial award application deadline: 8/1; financial award applicants required to submit FAFSA. In 2017, 3 master's, 80 doctorates awarded. *Program availability:* Part-time, evening/weekend, 100% online. Offers compliance (Certificate); health care compliance (Certificate); higher education compliance (Certificate); law (MLW, JD). *Application deadline:* For fall admission, 8/1 priority date for domestic students, 7/31 for international students; for winter admission, 11/15 for domestic students. *Application fee:* $0. Electronic applications accepted. *Application Contact:* Jessica Mehl, Assistant Dean of Law Admissions, 419-530-4131, Fax: 419-530-4345, E-mail: law.admissions@utoledo.edu. *Dean,* D. Benjamin Barros, 419-530-2379, Fax: 419-530-4526, E-mail: ben.barros@utoledo.edu.

UNIVERSITY OF TORONTO, Toronto, ON M5S 1A1, Canada

General Information Province-supported, coed, university. CGS member. *Graduate housing:* Rooms and/or apartments available on a first-come, first-served basis to single students and available to married students. *Research affiliation:* Fields Institute for Research in Mathematical Sciences, Canadian Institute for Theoretical Astrophysics, Royal Ontario Museum, Pontifical Institute of Medieval Studies, Hospital for Sick Children, Center for Addiction and Mental Health.

GRADUATE UNITS

Faculty of Medicine Offers biochemistry (M Sc, PhD); genetic counseling (M Sc); immunology (M Sc, PhD); laboratory medicine and pathobiology (M Sc, PhD); management of innovation (MMI); medical biophysics (M Sc, PhD); medicine (M Sc, M Sc BMC, M Sc OT, M Sc PT, MH Sc, MD, PhD); molecular genetics (M Sc, PhD); nutritional sciences (M Sc, PhD); occupational therapy (M Sc OT); pharmacology (M Sc, PhD); physical therapy (M Sc PT); physiology (M Sc, PhD); rehabilitation science (M Sc, PhD); speech-language pathology (M Sc, MH Sc, PhD). Electronic applications accepted.

Institute of Health Policy, Management and Evaluation Offers health administration (MH Sc); health informatics (MHI); health policy, management and evaluation (PhD). Electronic applications accepted.

Institute of Medical Science Offers bioethics (MH Sc); biomedical communications (M Sc BMC); medical radiation science (MH Sc); medical science (PhD). Electronic applications accepted.

School of Graduate Studies *Program availability:* Part-time, evening/weekend. Offers biotechnology (MBiotech); environmental science (M Env Sc, PhD). Electronic applications accepted.

Advanced Design and Manufacturing Institute *Program availability:* Part-time. Offers design and manufacturing (M Eng). Program offered jointly with McMaster University, Queen's University, and The University of Western Ontario; available only to Canadian citizens and permanent residents of Canada. Electronic applications accepted.

Department of Nursing Science *Program availability:* Part-time. Offers nursing (MN, PhD). Electronic applications accepted.

Department of Public Health Sciences *Program availability:* Part-time. Offers biostatistics (M Sc, PhD); community health (M Sc); community nutrition (MPH); epidemiology (MPH, PhD); family and community medicine (MPH); occupational and environmental health (MPH); social and behavioral health science (PhD); social and behavioral health sciences (MPH). Electronic applications accepted.

Faculty of Applied Science and Engineering *Program availability:* Part-time. Offers aerospace studies (M Eng, MA Sc, PhD); applied science and engineering (M Eng, MA Sc, MH Sc, PhD); biomedical engineering (MA Sc, PhD); chemical engineering and applied chemistry (M Eng, MA Sc, PhD); civil engineering (M Eng, MA Sc, PhD); clinical engineering (MH Sc, PhD); electrical and computer engineering (M Eng, MA Sc, PhD); materials science and engineering (M Eng, MA Sc, PhD); mechanical and industrial engineering (M Eng, MA Sc, PhD).

Faculty of Arts and Science *Program availability:* Part-time. Offers anthropology (M Sc, MA, PhD); applied computing (M Sc AC); art history (MA, PhD); arts and science (M Sc, M Sc AC, M Sc Pl, MA, MA Sc, MFE, MIRHR, MMF, MUD, MUDS, MVS, PhD); astronomy and astrophysics (M Sc, PhD); cell and systems biology (M Sc, PhD); chemistry (M Sc, PhD); cinema studies (MA, PhD); classics (MA, PhD); comparative literature (MA, PhD); computer science (M Sc, PhD); creative writing (MA); criminology and sociolegal studies (MA, PhD); drama, theatre and performance studies (MA, PhD); earth sciences (M Sc, MA Sc, PhD); East Asian studies (MA, PhD); ecology and evolutionary biology (M Sc, PhD); economics (MA, PhD); English (MA, PhD); financial economics (MFE); French language and literature (MA, PhD); geography (M Sc, MA, PhD); German (MA, PhD); history (MA, PhD); history and philosophy of science and technology (MA, PhD); industrial relations and human resources (MIRHR, PhD); Italian studies (MA, PhD); linguistics (MA, PhD); mathematical finance (MMF); mathematics (M Sc, PhD); medieval studies (MA, PhD); Near and Middle Eastern civilizations (MA, PhD); philosophy (MA, PhD); physics (M Sc, PhD); planning (M Sc Pl, MUDS, PhD); political science (MA, PhD); psychology (MA, PhD); religion (MA, PhD); Slavic languages and literatures (MA, PhD); sociology (MA, PhD); Spanish and Portuguese (MA, PhD); statistical sciences (M Sc, PhD); urban design (MUD); women and gender studies (MA, PhD). Electronic applications accepted.

Faculty of Dentistry Offers dental public health (M Sc); dentistry (M Sc, DDS, PhD); endodontics (M Sc); oral and maxillofacial radiology (M Sc); oral and maxillofacial surgery (M Sc); oral medicine (M Sc); orthodontics and dentofacial orthopedics (M Sc); pediatric dentistry (M Sc); periodontology (M Sc). Electronic applications accepted.

Faculty of Forestry Offers forestry (M Sc F, MFC, PhD). Electronic applications accepted.

Faculty of Information *Program availability:* Part-time. Offers information (MI, PhD); museum studies (MM St). Electronic applications accepted.

Faculty of Kinesiology and Physical Education Offers kinesiology and physical education (M Sc, PhD). Electronic applications accepted.

Faculty of Law *Program availability:* Part-time. Offers law (LL M, MSL, JD, SJD). Electronic applications accepted.

Faculty of Music *Program availability:* Part-time. Offers composition (M Mus, DMA); ethnomusicology (MA, PhD); jazz (M Mus); music education (MA, PhD); musicology/theory (MA, PhD); opera (M Mus); performance (M Mus, DMA). Electronic applications accepted.

Faculty of Social Work *Program availability:* Part-time. Offers social work (MSW, PhD). Electronic applications accepted.

John H. Daniels Faculty of Architecture, Landscape, and Design Offers architecture, landscape, and design (M Arch, MLA, MUD, MVS). Electronic applications accepted.

Leslie Dan Faculty of Pharmacy *Program availability:* Part-time. Offers pharmacy (M Sc, PhD, Pharm D). Electronic applications accepted.

Munk School of Global Affairs Offers European, Russian and Eurasian studies (MA); global affairs (MGA). Electronic applications accepted.

Ontario Institute for Studies in Education *Program availability:* Part-time, evening/weekend. Offers education (M Ed, MA, MT, Ed D, PhD).

Rotman School of Management *Program availability:* Part-time, evening/weekend. Offers management (MBA, MF, PhD).

THE UNIVERSITY OF TULSA, Tulsa, OK 74104-3189

General Information Independent, coed, university. CGS member. *Enrollment:* 4,433 graduate, professional, and undergraduate students; 473 full-time matriculated graduate/professional students (206 women), 312 part-time matriculated graduate/professional students (104 women). *Enrollment by degree level:* 512 master's, 273 doctoral. *Graduate faculty:* 194 full-time (54 women), 11 part-time/adjunct (5 women). *Tuition:* Full-time $22,230. *Required fees:* $2000. Tuition and fees vary according to course load and program. *Graduate housing:* Rooms and/or apartments available on a first-come, first-served basis to single and married students. Housing application deadline: 2/1. *Student services:* Campus employment opportunities, campus safety program, career counseling, child daycare facilities, exercise/wellness program, free psychological counseling, grant writing training, international student services, low-cost health insurance, multicultural affairs office, services for students with disabilities, teacher training, writing training. *Library facilities:* McFarlin Library plus 1 other. *Collection:* Books: 1.2 million (physical), 460,240 (digital/electronic); Serial titles: 59,171 (digital/electronic); Databases: 289. Weekly public service hours: 94; study areas open 24 hours, 5–7 days a week; students can reserve study rooms. *Research affiliation:* Network of Excellence in Training (NEXT) (petrophysics), Chevron Texaco (petroleum engineering).

Computer facilities: Computer purchase and lease plans are available. 710 computers available on campus for general student use. A campuswide network can be accessed. Online class registration is available.
Website: http://www.utulsa.edu/

General Application Contact: Dr. Janet A. Haggerty, Vice Provost for Research/Dean of the Graduate School, 918-631-2336, Fax: 918-631-2156, E-mail: grad@utulsa.edu.

GRADUATE UNITS

College of Law Students: 243 full-time (105 women), 29 part-time (12 women); includes 75 minority (12 Black or African American, non-Hispanic/Latino; 17 American Indian or Alaska Native, non-Hispanic/Latino; 1 Asian, non-Hispanic/Latino; 11 Hispanic/Latino; 34 Two or more races, non-Hispanic/Latino), 4 international. Average age 28. 567 applicants, 45% accepted, 94 enrolled. *Faculty:* 24 full-time (13 women), 14 part-time/adjunct (7 women). Expenses: Contact institution. *Financial support:* In 2017–18, 261 students received support. Scholarships/grants available. Support available to part-time students. Financial award application deadline: 8/1; financial award applicants required to submit FAFSA. In 2017, 3 master's, 86 doctorates, 26 Certificates awarded. *Program availability:* Part-time, 100% online. Offers American Indian and indigenous law (LL M); American law for foreign lawyers (LL M); energy and natural resources law (LL M); energy law (MJ); health law (Certificate); Indian law (MJ); law (JD); Native American law (Certificate); sustainable energy and resources law (Certificate). *Application deadline:* For fall admission, 7/31 priority date for domestic and international students; for spring admission, 12/5 priority date for domestic students, 12/5 for international students; for summer admission, 4/13 for domestic and international students. Applications are processed on a rolling basis. *Application fee:* $30. Electronic applications accepted. *Application Contact:* April M. Fox, Associate Dean of Admissions and Financial Aid, 918-631-2406, Fax: 918-631-3630, E-mail: april-fox@utulsa.edu. *Dean*, Prof. Lyn Suzanne Entzeroth, 918-631-2400, Fax: 918-631-3126, E-mail: lyn-entzeroth@utulsa.edu.

Graduate School Students: 473 full-time (206 women), 312 part-time (104 women); includes 109 minority (14 Black or African American, non-Hispanic/Latino; 29 American Indian or Alaska Native, non-Hispanic/Latino; 21 Asian, non-Hispanic/Latino; 27 Hispanic/Latino; 1 Native Hawaiian or other Pacific Islander, non-Hispanic/Latino; 17 Two or more races, non-Hispanic/Latino), 214 international. Average age 29. 1,380 applicants, 32% accepted, 260 enrolled. *Faculty:* 194 full-time (54 women), 11 part-time/adjunct (5 women). Expenses: Contact institution. *Financial support:* In 2017–18, 475 students received support, including 151 fellowships with full tuition reimbursements available (averaging $4,296 per year), 307 research assistantships with full tuition reimbursements available (averaging $6,992 per year), 281 teaching assistantships with full tuition reimbursements available (averaging $11,445 per year); career-related internships or fieldwork, Federal Work-Study, institutionally sponsored loans, scholarships/grants, traineeships, health care benefits, tuition waivers (partial), and unspecified assistantships also available. Support available to part-time students. Financial award application deadline: 2/1; financial award applicants required to submit FAFSA. In 2017, 239 master's, 45 doctorates awarded. *Program availability:* Part-time, evening/weekend. Offers museum science and management (MA). *Application deadline:* Applications are processed on a rolling basis. *Application fee:* $55. Electronic applications accepted. *Application Contact:* Graduate School, 918-631-2336, Fax: 918-631-2156, E-mail: grad@utulsa.edu. *Vice Provost for Research/Dean of the Graduate School*, Dr. Janet A. Haggerty, 918-631-2336, Fax: 918-631-2156, E-mail: grad@utulsa.edu.

College of Engineering and Natural Sciences Students: 226 full-time (50 women), 102 part-time (28 women); includes 24 minority (4 Black or African American, non-Hispanic/Latino; 8 American Indian or Alaska Native, non-Hispanic/Latino; 5 Asian, non-Hispanic/Latino; 5 Hispanic/Latino; 2 Two or more races, non-Hispanic/Latino), 179 international. Average age 28. 616 applicants, 32% accepted, 84 enrolled. *Faculty:* 102 full-time (11 women), 2 part-time/adjunct (1 woman). Expenses: Contact institution. *Financial support:* Fellowships with full tuition reimbursements, research assistantships with full tuition reimbursements, teaching assistantships with full tuition reimbursements, career-related internships or fieldwork, Federal Work-Study, scholarships/grants, health care benefits, tuition waivers (full and partial), and unspecified assistantships available. Support available to part-time students. Financial award application deadline: 2/1; financial award applicants required to submit FAFSA. In 2017, 85 master's, 26 doctorates awarded. *Program availability:* Part-time. Offers biochemistry (MS); biological science (MS, MTA, PhD); chemical engineering (ME, MSE, PhD); chemistry (MS, PhD); computer engineering (ME, MSE, PhD); computer science (MS, PhD); cyber security (MS); electrical engineering (ME, MSE); engineering and natural sciences (ME, MS, MSE, MTA, PhD); engineering physics (MS); geophysics (MS); geosciences (MS, PhD); mathematics (MS, MTA, PhD); mechanical engineering (ME, MSE, PhD); petroleum engineering (ME, MSE, PhD); physics (MS, PhD). *Application deadline:* Applications are processed on a rolling basis. *Application fee:* $55. Electronic applications accepted. *Application Contact:* Graduate School, 918-631-2336, Fax: 918-631-2156, E-mail: grad@utulsa.edu. *Dean*, Dr. James Sorem, 918-631-2288, E-mail: james-sorem@utulsa.edu.

Collins College of Business Students: 68 full-time (26 women), 139 part-time (30 women); includes 26 minority (3 Black or African American, non-Hispanic/Latino; 6 American Indian or Alaska Native, non-Hispanic/Latino; 3 Asian, non-Hispanic/Latino; 9 Hispanic/Latino; 5 Two or more races, non-Hispanic/Latino), 29 international. Average age 31. 245 applicants, 49% accepted, 65 enrolled. *Faculty:* 42 full-time (27 women), 2 part-time/adjunct (0 women). Expenses: Contact institution. *Financial support:* Fellowships with tuition reimbursements, research assistantships with full tuition reimbursements, teaching assistantships with full tuition reimbursements, career-related internships or fieldwork, Federal Work-Study, institutionally sponsored loans, scholarships/grants, health care benefits, tuition waivers (full and partial), and unspecified assistantships available. Support available to part-time students. Financial award application deadline: 2/1; financial award applicants required to submit FAFSA. In 2017, 94 master's awarded. *Program availability:* Part-time, evening/weekend, 100% online. Offers accounting (M Acc); business (M Acc, MBA, MEB, MS); business administration (MBA); business analytics (MS); corporate finance (MS); energy business (MEB); global energy (MS); risk management (MS). *Application deadline:* Applications are processed on a rolling basis. *Application fee:* $55. Electronic applications accepted. *Application Contact:* Information Contact, 918-631-2242, E-mail: graduate-business@utulsa.edu. *Dean*, Dr. W. Gale Sullenburger, 918-631-2213, E-mail: gale-sullenberger@utulsa.edu.

Kendall College of Arts and Sciences Students: 87 full-time (56 women), 42 part-time (28 women); includes 26 minority (2 Black or African American, non-Hispanic/Latino; 7 American Indian or Alaska Native, non-Hispanic/Latino; 7 Asian, non-Hispanic/Latino; 7 Hispanic/Latino; 3 Two or more races, non-Hispanic/Latino), 5 international. Average age 30. 320 applicants, 16% accepted, 27 enrolled. *Faculty:* 65 full-time (30 women), 9 part-time/adjunct (5 women). Expenses: Contact institution. *Financial support:* Fellowships with full tuition reimbursements, research assistantships with full tuition reimbursements, teaching assistantships with full tuition reimbursements, career-related internships or fieldwork, Federal Work-Study, scholarships/grants, traineeships, health care benefits, tuition waivers (full and partial), and unspecified assistantships available. Support available to part-time students. Financial award application deadline: 2/1; financial award applicants required to submit FAFSA. In 2017, 35 master's, 14 doctorates awarded. *Program availability:* Part-time, evening/weekend. Offers anthropology (MA, PhD); art, design, and art history (MA, MFA, MTA); arts and sciences (MA, MFA, MS, MSMSE, MTA, PhD); clinical psychology (MA, PhD); English language and literature (MA, PhD); history (MA, MTA); industrial/organizational psychology (MA, PhD); mathematics and science education (MSMSE); teaching arts (MTA); urban education (MA). *Application deadline:* Applications are processed on a rolling basis. *Application fee:* $55. Electronic applications accepted. *Application Contact:* Graduate School, 918-631-2336, Fax: 918-631-2156, E-mail: grad@utulsa.edu. *Dean*, Dr. Kalpana Misra, 918-631-2222, Fax: 918-631-3721, E-mail: kalpana-misra@utulsa.edu.

Oxley College of Health Sciences Students: 47 full-time (38 women), 4 part-time (3 women); includes 17 minority (3 Black or African American, non-Hispanic/Latino; 4 American Indian or Alaska Native, non-Hispanic/Latino; 2 Asian, non-Hispanic/Latino; 4 Hispanic/Latino; 1 Native Hawaiian or other Pacific Islander, non-Hispanic/Latino; 3 Two or more races, non-Hispanic/Latino), 5 international. Average age 28. 160 applicants, 37% accepted, 37 enrolled. Expenses: Contact institution. *Financial support:* Fellowships with full tuition reimbursements, teaching assistantships with full tuition reimbursements, career-related internships or fieldwork, Federal Work-Study, scholarships/grants, traineeships, health care benefits, tuition waivers (full and partial), and unspecified assistantships available. Support available to part-time students. In 2017, 18 master's awarded. Offers adult-gerontology acute care nurse practitioner (DNP); communication sciences and disorders (MS); family nurse practitioner (DNP); health sciences (MAT, MS, DNP); kinesiology and rehabilitative sciences (MAT). *Application fee:* $55. Electronic applications accepted. *Application Contact:* Graduate School, 918-631-2336, Fax: 918-631-2156, E-mail: grad@utulsa.edu. *Dean*, Robin Ploeger, 918-631-3170, E-mail: robin-ploeger@utulsa.edu.

UNIVERSITY OF UTAH, Salt Lake City, UT 84112-1107

General Information State-supported, coed, university. CGS member. *Enrollment:* 32,760 graduate, professional, and undergraduate students; 6,628 full-time matriculated graduate/professional students (3,051 women), 1,920 part-time matriculated graduate/professional students (875 women). *Enrollment by degree level:* 4,073 master's, 3,998 doctoral. *Graduate faculty:* 954 full-time (332 women), 782 part-time/adjunct (331 women). *Graduate housing:* Rooms and/or apartments available on a first-come, first-served basis to single and married students. Housing application deadline: 4/1. *Student services:* Campus employment opportunities, campus safety program, career counseling, child daycare facilities, exercise/wellness program, free psychological counseling, grant writing training, international student services, low-cost health insurance, multicultural affairs office, services for students with disabilities, teacher training, writing training. *Library facilities:* J. Willard Marriott Library plus 3 others. *Collection:* Books: 3.2 million (physical), 460,000 (digital/electronic); Serial titles: 500 (physical), 11,500 (digital/electronic); Databases: 325. Weekly public service hours: 111; students can reserve study rooms. *Research affiliation:* Watson Laboratory (pharmaceutical research), Myriad Genetics (pharmaceutical research/manufacturing), Neuropsychiatric Institute (brain research, mental health and substance abuse treatment), ARUP Laboratories (medical research), John A. Moran Eye Center (vision treatment and research).

Computer facilities: 1,099 computers available on campus for general student use. A campuswide network can be accessed from student residence rooms and from off campus. Online class registration, online classes are available.
Website: http://www.utah.edu/

General Application Contact: 801-581-7283, Fax: 801-585-7864, E-mail: graduate@sa.utah.edu.

GRADUATE UNITS

Graduate School Students: 6,209 full-time (2,885 women), 1,916 part-time (874 women); includes 1,287 minority (92 Black or African American, non-Hispanic/Latino; 20 American Indian or Alaska Native, non-Hispanic/Latino; 371 Asian, non-Hispanic/Latino; 561 Hispanic/Latino; 13 Native Hawaiian or other Pacific Islander, non-Hispanic/Latino; 230 Two or more races, non-Hispanic/Latino), 1,275 international. Average age 26. 9,166 applicants, 37% accepted, 2334 enrolled. *Faculty:* 954 full-time (332 women), 782 part-time/adjunct (331 women). Expenses: Contact institution. *Financial support:* Fellowships with tuition reimbursements, research assistantships with tuition reimbursements, teaching assistantships with tuition reimbursements, career-related internships or fieldwork, Federal Work-Study, institutionally sponsored loans, scholarships/grants, traineeships, health care benefits, tuition waivers (full and partial), and unspecified assistantships available. Support available to part-time students. Financial award application deadline: 2/1; financial award applicants required to submit FAFSA. In 2017, 2,140 master's, 790 doctorates awarded. *Program availability:* Part-time, evening/weekend, online learning. Offers biotechnology (PSM); computational science (PSM); environmental science (PSM); science instrumentation (PSM). *Application deadline:* For fall admission, 4/1 for domestic and international students; for spring admission, 11/1 for domestic and international students. *Application fee:* $55 ($65 for international students). Electronic applications accepted. *Application Contact:* Admissions Office, 801-581-7283, Fax: 801-585-7864, E-mail: graduate@sa.utah.edu. *Dean*, Dr. David Kieda, 801-585-5529, Fax: 801-585-7864, E-mail: dave.kieda@utah.edu.

College of Architecture and Planning Students: 100 full-time (34 women), 19 part-time (6 women); includes 20 minority (1 Black or African American, non-Hispanic/Latino; 3 Asian, non-Hispanic/Latino; 10 Hispanic/Latino; 6 Two or more races, non-Hispanic/Latino), 18 international. Average age 24. 100 applicants, 91% accepted, 50 enrolled. *Faculty:* 16 full-time (9 women), 20 part-time/adjunct (5 women). Expenses: Contact institution. *Financial support:* Fellowships with tuition reimbursements, research assistantships with tuition reimbursements, teaching assistantships with partial tuition reimbursements, career-related internships or fieldwork, Federal Work-Study, institutionally sponsored loans, scholarships/grants, and unspecified assistantships available. Financial award application deadline: 1/1; financial award applicants required to submit FAFSA. In 2017, 56 master's, 1 doctorate awarded. *Program availability:* Part-time. Offers architectural studies (MS); architecture (M Arch); architecture and planning (M Arch, MCMP, MS, PhD); city and metropolitan planning (MCMP); metropolitan planning, policy and design (PhD). *Application deadline:* For fall admission, 1/1 for domestic students, 12/1 for international students. *Application fee:* $55 ($65 for international students). Electronic applications accepted. *Application Contact:* Lorilie Spegar, Academic Advisor, Recruitment and Admissions, 801-585-2361, Fax: 801-581-8217, E-mail: recruitment@arch.utah.edu. *Dean*, Dr. Keith Diaz Moore, 801-585-1766, Fax: 801-581-8217, E-mail: diazmoore@utah.edu.

College of Education Students: 286 full-time (208 women), 328 part-time (227 women); includes 144 minority (16 Black or African American, non-Hispanic/Latino; 2 American Indian or Alaska Native, non-Hispanic/Latino; 15 Asian, non-Hispanic/Latino; 96 Hispanic/Latino; 15 Two or more races, non-Hispanic/Latino), 10 international. Average age 30. 548 applicants, 47% accepted, 211 enrolled. *Faculty:* 48 full-time (30 women), 23 part-time/adjunct (17 women). Expenses: Contact institution. *Financial support:* Fellowships with tuition reimbursements, research assistantships with tuition reimbursements, teaching assistantships with tuition reimbursements, career-related internships or fieldwork, Federal Work-Study, institutionally sponsored loans, scholarships/grants, health care benefits, tuition waivers (full), and unspecified assistantships available. Support available to part-time students. Financial award application deadline: 2/1; financial award applicants required to submit FAFSA. In 2017, 167 master's, 35 doctorates awarded. Offers board certified behavior analyst (M Ed, MS, PhD); clinical mental health counseling (M Ed); counseling psychology (PhD); deaf and hard of hearing (M Ed); deaf/blind (M Ed, MS); early childhood deaf and hard of hearing (MS); early childhood special education (M Ed, MS, PhD); early childhood vision impairments (M Ed); education (M Ed, M Stat, MA, MS, Ed D, PhD, Ed S); education, culture, and society (M Ed, MA, MS, PhD); educational leadership and policy (Ed D, PhD); elementary education (M Ed); instructional design and educational technology (M Ed); instructional design and technology (MS); K-12 school administration (M Ed); K-12 teacher instructional leadership (M Ed); learning and cognition (MS, PhD); mild/moderate disabilities (M Ed, MS, PhD); reading and literacy (M Ed, PhD); school counseling (M Ed); school psychology (M Ed, PhD, Ed S); severe disabilities (M Ed, MS, PhD); statistics (M Stat); student affairs (M Ed); visual impairment (M Ed, MS). *Application deadline:* For fall admission, 2/15 for domestic and international students; for spring admission, 11/1 for domestic and international students. *Application fee:* $55 ($65 for international students). Electronic applications accepted. *Dean*, Elaine Clark, 801-581-8221.

College of Engineering Students: 999 full-time (231 women), 250 part-time (32 women); includes 115 minority (7 Black or African American, non-Hispanic/Latino; 53 Asian, non-Hispanic/Latino; 34 Hispanic/Latino; 1 Native Hawaiian or other Pacific Islander, non-Hispanic/Latino; 20 Two or more races, non-Hispanic/Latino), 548 international. Average age 24. 2,512 applicants, 36% accepted, 380 enrolled. *Faculty:* 162 full-time (23 women), 81 part-time/adjunct (13 women). Expenses: Contact institution. *Financial support:* Fellowships with full tuition reimbursements, research assistantships with tuition reimbursements, teaching assistantships with tuition reimbursements, career-related internships or fieldwork, Federal Work-Study, institutionally sponsored loans, scholarships/grants, traineeships, health care benefits, tuition waivers (full and partial), and unspecified assistantships available. Support available to part-time students. Financial award applicants required to submit FAFSA. In 2017, 321 master's, 79 doctorates awarded. *Program availability:* Part-time, evening/weekend. Offers bioengineering (MS, PhD); chemical engineering (MS, PhD); civil and environmental engineering (MS, PhD); computer science (MS, PhD); computing (MS, PhD); electrical and computer engineering (MS, PhD); electrical engineering (ME); engineering (ME, MEAE, MS, PhD); game art (MEAE); game engineering (MEAE); game production (MEAE); materials science and engineering (MS, PhD); mechanical engineering (MS, PhD); nuclear engineering (MS, PhD); petroleum engineering (MS); software development (MS); technical art (MEAE). *Application fee:* $55 ($65 for international students). Electronic applications accepted. *Application Contact:* Megan Shannahan, Direct Admission and Graduate Coordinator, 801-581-8954, Fax: 801-581-8692, E-mail: megan.shannahan@utah.edu. *Dean*, Dr. Richard B. Brown, 801-585-7498, E-mail: brown@utah.edu.

College of Fine Arts Students: 118 full-time (65 women), 25 part-time (14 women); includes 23 minority (2 Black or African American, non-Hispanic/Latino; 1 American Indian or Alaska Native, non-Hispanic/Latino; 9 Asian, non-Hispanic/Latino; 8 Hispanic/Latino; 1 Native Hawaiian or other Pacific Islander, non-Hispanic/Latino; 2 Two or more races, non-Hispanic/Latino), 23 international. Average age 23. 209 applicants, 44% accepted, 44 enrolled. *Faculty:* 75 full-time (30 women), 135 part-time/adjunct (60 women). Expenses: Contact institution. *Financial support:* Fellowships with tuition reimbursements, research assistantships with tuition reimbursements, teaching assistantships with tuition reimbursements, career-related internships or fieldwork, Federal Work-Study, institutionally sponsored loans, scholarships/grants, health care benefits, tuition waivers (partial), and unspecified assistantships available. Financial award applicants required to submit FAFSA. In 2017, 47 master's, 10 doctorates awarded. Offers art history (MA); ceramics (MFA); choral conducting (M Mus, DMA); collaborative piano (M Mus); community-based art education (MFA); composition (M Mus, PhD); dance (MFA, Certificate); drawing (MFA); film and media arts (MFA); fine arts (M Mus, MA, MFA, DMA, PhD, Certificate); graphic design (MFA); instrumental conducting (M Mus, DMA); instrumental performance (M Mus, DMA); jazz studies (M Mus); music education (M Mus, PhD); music history and literature (M Mus); musicology (MA); organ performance (M Mus); painting (MFA); photography/digital imaging (MFA); piano performance (M Mus, DMA); piano performance and pedagogy (M Mus); printmaking (MFA); sculpture/intermedia (MFA); string performance and pedagogy (M Mus); theory (M Mus); vocal performance (DMA). *Application fee:* $55 ($65 for international students). *Application Contact:* Sarah Projansky, Senior Associate Dean for Faculty and Academic Affairs, 801-581-6764, E-mail: sarah.projansky@utah.edu. *Dean*, John W. Scheib, 801-581-3887, Fax: 801-581-3066.

College of Health Students: 550 full-time (376 women), 76 part-time (50 women); includes 92 minority (7 Black or African American, non-Hispanic/Latino; 1 American Indian or Alaska Native, non-Hispanic/Latino; 17 Asian, non-Hispanic/Latino; 46 Hispanic/Latino; 3 Native Hawaiian or other Pacific Islander, non-Hispanic/Latino; 18 Two or more races, non-Hispanic/Latino), 20 international. Average age 24. 1,165 applicants, 26% accepted, 215 enrolled. *Faculty:* 46 full-time (20 women), 74 part-time/adjunct (53 women). Expenses: Contact institution. *Financial support:* Fellowships with tuition reimbursements, research assistantships with tuition reimbursements, teaching assistantships with tuition reimbursements, career-related internships or fieldwork, Federal Work-Study, institutionally sponsored loans, scholarships/grants, traineeships, health care benefits, tuition waivers (partial), and unspecified assistantships available. Financial award applicants required to submit FAFSA. In 2017, 194 master's, 82 doctorates awarded. Offers audiology (Au D, PhD); health (M Phil, MA, MOT, MS, Au D, DPT, Ed D, OTD, PhD); health promotion and education (M Phil, MS, PhD); kinesiology (MS, PhD); nutrition and integrative physiology (MS, PhD); occupational and recreational therapies (MOT, OTD); parks, recreation, and tourism (MS, PhD); physical therapy (DPT); rehabilitation science (PhD); speech-language pathology (MA, MS, PhD). *Application fee:* $55 ($65 for international students). *Application Contact:* Dr. Shari Lindsey, Assistant Dean of Students, 801-581-5580, Fax: 801-581-5580, E-mail: shari.lindsey@health.utah.edu. *Dean*, Dr. David H. Perrin, 801-581-8537, Fax: 801-581-5580, E-mail: david.perrin@health.utah.edu.

College of Humanities Students: 159 full-time (95 women), 74 part-time (38 women); includes 37 minority (1 Black or African American, non-Hispanic/Latino; 1 American Indian or Alaska Native, non-Hispanic/Latino; 11 Asian, non-Hispanic/Latino; 16 Hispanic/Latino; 8 Two or more races, non-Hispanic/Latino), 21 international. Average age 25. 513 applicants, 24% accepted, 71 enrolled. *Faculty:* 145 full-time (74 women), 50 part-time/adjunct (20 women). Expenses: Contact institution. *Financial support:* Fellowships with full tuition reimbursements, teaching assistantships with tuition reimbursements, health care benefits, and unspecified assistantships available. Financial award application deadline: 2/1. In 2017, 50 master's, 29 doctorates awarded. Offers Arabic (MA, PhD); Asian studies (MA); communicating science, health, environment and risk (MA, MS, PhD); comparative literary and cultural studies (MA, PhD); critical cultural studies (MA, MS, PhD); digital media (MA, MS, PhD); English (MA, MFA, PhD); environmental humanities (MA, MS); French (MA); Hebrew (MA); history (MA, MS, PhD); humanities (MA, MALP, MFA, MS, PhD); Latin American studies (MA); linguistics (MA, PhD); Persian (MA, PhD); philosophy (MA, MS, PhD); political science (MA, PhD); rhetoric (MA, MS, PhD); Spanish (MA, MALP); world languages (MA). *Application deadline:* For fall admission, 4/1 for domestic and international students; for spring admission, 11/1 for domestic and international students. *Application fee:* $55 ($65 for international students). Electronic applications accepted. *Application Contact:* Dr. Stuart Culver, Co-Interim Dean, 801-581-6214, E-mail: stuart.culver@utah.edu. *Co-Interim Dean*, Prof. Barry L. Weller, 801-581-8816.

College of Mines and Earth Sciences Students: 121 full-time (37 women), 34 part-time (13 women); includes 18 minority (1 Black or African American, non-Hispanic/Latino; 1 American Indian or Alaska Native, non-Hispanic/Latino; 4 Asian, non-Hispanic/Latino; 10 Hispanic/Latino; 2 Two or more races, non-Hispanic/Latino), 53 international. Average age 25. 302 applicants, 20% accepted, 37 enrolled. *Faculty:* 59 full-time (11 women), 14 part-time/adjunct (3 women). Expenses: Contact institution. *Financial support:* Fellowships with full tuition reimbursements, research assistantships with full tuition reimbursements, teaching assistantships with full tuition reimbursements, career-related internships or fieldwork, institutionally sponsored loans, scholarships/grants, and unspecified assistantships available. Support available to part-time students. Financial award application deadline: 2/15; financial award applicants required to submit FAFSA. In 2017, 42 master's, 20 doctorates awarded. *Program availability:* Part-time. Offers atmospheric sciences (MS, PhD); geological engineering (ME, MS, PhD); geology (MS, PhD); geophysics (MS, PhD); metallurgical engineering (ME, MS, PhD); mines and earth sciences (ME, MS, PhD); mining engineering (ME, MS, PhD). *Application deadline:* For fall admission, 4/1 for domestic and international students; for spring admission, 11/1 for domestic and international students. *Application fee:* $55 ($65 for international students). Electronic applications accepted. *Application Contact:* Anita Austin Tromp, Assistant to the Dean, 801-585-9344, Fax: 801-581-5560, E-mail: anita.austin@utah.edu. *Dean*, Dr. Darryl P. Butt, 801-581-8767, Fax: 801-581-5560, E-mail: darryl.butt@utah.edu.

College of Nursing Students: 296 full-time (228 women), 82 part-time (67 women); includes 64 minority (10 Black or African American, non-Hispanic/Latino; 1 American Indian or Alaska Native, non-Hispanic/Latino; 16 Asian, non-Hispanic/Latino; 21 Hispanic/Latino; 1 Native Hawaiian or other Pacific Islander, non-Hispanic/Latino; 15 Two or more races, non-Hispanic/Latino), 8 international. Average age 27. 267 applicants, 57% accepted, 126 enrolled. *Faculty:* 101 full-time (90 women), 35 part-time/adjunct (30 women). Expenses: Contact institution. *Financial support:* Fellowships with tuition reimbursements, research assistantships with tuition reimbursements, teaching assistantships with partial tuition reimbursements, scholarships/grants, traineeships, health care benefits, and unspecified assistantships available. Support available to part-time students. Financial award application deadline: 1/15; financial award applicants required to submit FAFSA. In 2017, 12 master's, 98 doctorates awarded. *Program availability:* Part-time, online learning. Offers gerontology (MS, Certificate); nursing (MS, DNP, PhD, Certificate). *Application deadline:* For fall admission, 1/15 for domestic and international students; for spring admission, 11/1 for domestic and international students. *Application fee:* $55 ($65 for international students). Electronic applications accepted. *Dean*, Patricia Morton, PhD, 801-581-8262, Fax: 801-585-9705, E-mail: trish.morton@nurs.utah.edu.

College of Pharmacy Students: 248 full-time (127 women), 14 part-time (9 women); includes 87 minority (4 Black or African American, non-Hispanic/Latino; 57 Asian, non-Hispanic/Latino; 13 Hispanic/Latino; 13 Two or more races, non-Hispanic/Latino), 15 international. Average age 27. 279 applicants, 31% accepted, 66 enrolled. *Faculty:* 66 full-time (20 women), 83 part-time/adjunct (39 women). Expenses: Contact institution. *Financial support:* Fellowships with full tuition reimbursements, research assistantships with full tuition reimbursements, teaching assistantships, scholarships/grants, health care benefits, tuition waivers (full), and unspecified assistantships available. In 2017, 5 master's, 68 doctorates awarded. Offers health system pharmacy administration (MS); medicinal chemistry (MS, PhD); outcomes research and health policy (PhD); pharmaceutics and pharmaceutical chemistry (PhD); pharmacology and toxicology (PhD); pharmacy (MS, PhD, Pharm D). *Application deadline:* For fall admission, 12/1 for domestic and international students. *Application fee:* $55 ($65 for international students). *Application Contact:* Dr. Madeline Marshall, Senior Academic Advisor, 801-581-5384, Fax: 801-581-3716, E-mail: pharmd.admissions@pharm.utah.edu. *Dean*, Dr. Randall T. Peterson, 801-581-6731, Fax: 801-581-3716.

College of Science Students: 384 full-time (154 women), 132 part-time (52 women); includes 59 minority (4 Black or African American, non-Hispanic/Latino; 1 American Indian or Alaska Native, non-Hispanic/Latino; 19 Asian, non-Hispanic/Latino; 26 Hispanic/Latino; 9 Two or more races, non-Hispanic/Latino), 162 international. Average age 25. 772 applicants, 30% accepted, 97 enrolled. *Faculty:* 149 full-time (27 women), 81 part-time/adjunct (22 women). Expenses: Contact institution. *Financial support:* Fellowships with full tuition reimbursements, research assistantships with full tuition reimbursements, teaching assistantships with full tuition reimbursements, career-related internships or fieldwork, Federal Work-Study, institutionally sponsored loans, scholarships/grants, traineeships, health care benefits, tuition waivers (full), and unspecified assistantships available. Financial award application deadline: 2/15; financial award applicants required to submit FAFSA. In 2017, 47 master's, 51 doctorates awarded. *Program availability:* Part-time. Offers biology (MS, PhD); chemical physics (PhD); chemistry (MS, PhD); mathematics (MA, MS, PhD); mathematics teaching (MS); medical physics (MS, PhD); physics (MA, MS, PhD); physics teaching (PhD); science (M Stat, MA, MS, PhD); science teacher education (MS); statistics (M Stat). *Application deadline:* For fall admission, 4/1 for domestic and international students; for spring admission, 11/1 for domestic and international students. *Application fee:* $55 ($65 for international students). Electronic applications accepted. *Application Contact:* Lisa Batchelder, Administration Manager, 801-581-3374, E-mail: office@science.utah.edu. *Dean*, Dr. Henry S. White, 801-581-6958, Fax: 801-585-3169, E-mail: white@chem.utah.edu.

College of Social and Behavioral Science Students: 270 full-time (154 women), 236 part-time (130 women); includes 77 minority (6 Black or African American, non-Hispanic/Latino; 1 American Indian or Alaska Native, non-Hispanic/Latino; 11 Asian, non-Hispanic/Latino; 40 Hispanic/Latino; 1 Native Hawaiian or other Pacific Islander, non-Hispanic/Latino; 18 Two or more races, non-Hispanic/Latino), 54 international. Average age 25. 599 applicants, 27% accepted, 91 enrolled. *Faculty:* 136 full-time (54 women), 80 part-time/adjunct (29 women). Expenses: Contact institution. *Financial support:* Fellowships with tuition reimbursements, research assistantships with tuition reimbursements, teaching assistantships with tuition reimbursements, career-related internships or fieldwork, Federal Work-Study, scholarships/grants, health care benefits, and unspecified assistantships available. Financial award application deadline: 2/1; financial award applicants required to submit FAFSA. In 2017, 138 master's, 36 doctorates awarded. Offers American politics (MA, MS, PhD); anthropology (MA, MS, PhD); clinical psychology (PhD); comparative politics (MA, MS, PhD); econometrics (M Stat); economics (M Phil, MA, MS, PhD); geographic information science (MS); geography (MS, PhD); human development and social policy (MS); international affairs and global enterprise (MS); international relations (MA, MS, PhD); political science (MA, MS, PhD); political theory (MA, MS, PhD); psychology (PhD); public administration (Exec MPA, MPA); public policy (MPP); social and behavioral science (Exec MPA, M Phil, M Stat, MA, MPA, MPP, MS, PhD);

sociology (M Stat, MA, MS, PhD). *Application fee:* $55 ($65 for international students). *Application Contact:* Richard Forster, Associate Dean, 801-581-8620, Fax: 801-585-5081, E-mail: rick.forster@csbs.utah.edu. *Dean,* Cynthia Berg, 801-581-8620, Fax: 801-585-5081, E-mail: cynthia.berg@csbs.utah.edu.

College of Social Work Students: 294 full-time (227 women), 43 part-time (36 women); includes 77 minority (11 Black or African American, non-Hispanic/Latino; 6 American Indian or Alaska Native, non-Hispanic/Latino; 6 Asian, non-Hispanic/Latino; 39 Hispanic/Latino; 1 Native Hawaiian or other Pacific Islander, non-Hispanic/Latino; 14 Two or more races, non-Hispanic/Latino), 4 international. Average age 30. Expenses: Contact institution. *Financial support:* Fellowships with tuition reimbursements, research assistantships with tuition reimbursements, teaching assistantships with partial tuition reimbursements, career-related internships or fieldwork, scholarships/grants, and unspecified assistantships available. Financial award application deadline: 3/15; financial award applicants required to submit FAFSA. In 2017, 171 master's, 4 doctorates awarded. *Program availability:* Part-time, evening/weekend. Offers social work (MSW, PhD). *Application deadline:* For fall admission, 11/1 for domestic and international students. *Application fee:* $55 ($65 for international students). Electronic applications accepted. *Application Contact:* Dr. Mary Jane Taylor, Associate Dean for Academic Affairs, 801-581-8828, Fax: 801-585-3219, E-mail: maryjane.taylor@socwk.utah.edu. *Dean,* Dr. Martell L. Teasley, 801-581-6194, Fax: 801-585-3219, E-mail: martell.teasley@utah.edu.

David Eccles School of Business Students: 1,018 full-time (297 women), 383 part-time (98 women); includes 168 minority (5 Black or African American, non-Hispanic/Latino; 1 American Indian or Alaska Native, non-Hispanic/Latino; 44 Asian, non-Hispanic/Latino; 87 Hispanic/Latino; 2 Native Hawaiian or other Pacific Islander, non-Hispanic/Latino; 29 Two or more races, non-Hispanic/Latino), 242 international. Average age 25. 817 applicants, 77% accepted, 451 enrolled. *Faculty:* 95 full-time (32 women), 89 part-time/adjunct (15 women). Expenses: Contact institution. *Financial support:* Fellowships with partial tuition reimbursements, research assistantships with partial tuition reimbursements, teaching assistantships with tuition reimbursements, scholarships/grants, tuition waivers (full and partial), and unspecified assistantships available. Financial award applicants required to submit FAFSA. In 2017, 750 master's, 7 doctorates awarded. *Program availability:* Part-time, evening/weekend. Offers accounting (PhD); accounting information systems (M Acc); business (EMBA, M Acc, MBA, MHA, MRED, MS, MSF, PMBA, PhD, Graduate Certificate); business administration (EMBA, MBA, PMBA); finance (PhD); financial/audit (M Acc); healthcare administration (MHA); information systems (MS, PhD, Graduate Certificate); marketing (PhD); operations management (PhD); organizational behavior (PhD); real estate development (MRED); strategic management (PhD); tax (M Acc). *Application fee:* $55 ($65 for international students). Electronic applications accepted. *Application Contact:* Director of Graduate Admissions, 801-585-7366. *Dean,* Dr. Taylor Randall, 801-587-3869, E-mail: dean@eccles.utah.edu.

School of Dentistry Students: 148 full-time (41 women); includes 30 minority (1 Black or African American, non-Hispanic/Latino; 8 Asian, non-Hispanic/Latino; 17 Hispanic/Latino; 4 Two or more races, non-Hispanic/Latino). Average age 27. Expenses: Contact institution. *Financial support:* Scholarships/grants available. Financial award application deadline: 4/1; financial award applicants required to submit FAFSA. In 2017, 20 doctorates awarded. Offers dentistry (DDS). *Application deadline:* For fall admission, 10/1 priority date for domestic students. *Application fee:* $75. Electronic applications accepted. *Application Contact:* Gary W. Lowder, DDS, Office of Admissions, 801-213-3506, Fax: 801-585-6485, E-mail: dental.admissions@hsc.utah.edu. *Dean,* Dr. Wyatt R. Hume, DDS, 801-587-1208, Fax: 801-585-6485, E-mail: wyatt.hume@hsc.utah.edu.

School of Medicine Offers biochemistry (MS, PhD); biostatistics (M Stat); experimental pathology (PhD); human genetics (MS, PhD); laboratory medicine and biomedical science (MS); medical informatics (MS, PhD, Certificate); medicine (M Phil, M Stat, MPAS, MPH, MS, MSPH, MD, PhD, Certificate); molecular biology (PhD); neurobiology and anatomy (PhD); neuroscience (PhD); oncological sciences (M Phil, MS, PhD); physician assistant (MPAS); physiology (PhD); public health (MPH, MSPH, PhD).

S. J. Quinney College of Law Students: 271 full-time (125 women), 4 part-time (1 woman); includes 28 minority (1 Black or African American, non-Hispanic/Latino; 2 American Indian or Alaska Native, non-Hispanic/Latino; 4 Asian, non-Hispanic/Latino; 18 Hispanic/Latino; 1 Native Hawaiian or other Pacific Islander, non-Hispanic/Latino; 2 Two or more races, non-Hispanic/Latino), 3 international. Average age 28. Expenses: Contact institution. *Financial support:* Fellowships with partial tuition reimbursements, research assistantships with partial tuition reimbursements, career-related internships or fieldwork, Federal Work-Study, institutionally sponsored loans, scholarships/grants, and unspecified assistantships available. Financial award application deadline: 4/7; financial award applicants required to submit FAFSA. In 2017, 116 doctorates awarded. Offers law (LL M, MLS, JD). *Application deadline:* For fall admission, 1/15 priority date for domestic students, 2/15 priority date for international students. Applications are processed on a rolling basis. *Application fee:* $60. Electronic applications accepted. *Application Contact:* Susan Baca, Program Manager for Admissions and Financial Aid, 801-581-7479, Fax: 801-581-6897, E-mail: susan.baca@law.utah.edu. *Dean,* Robert Adler, 801-581-6571, Fax: 801-581-6897, E-mail: robert.adler@law.utah.edu.

UNIVERSITY OF VALLEY FORGE, Phoenixville, PA 19460

General Information Independent-religious, coed, comprehensive institution.

GRADUATE UNITS

Program in Christian Leadership Offers Christian leadership (MA).

Program in Music Technology *Program availability:* Online learning. Offers music technology (MM).

Program in Theology Offers theology (MA).

Program in Worship Studies Offers worship studies (MA).

UNIVERSITY OF VERMONT, Burlington, VT 05405

General Information State-supported, coed, university. CGS member. *Enrollment:* 13,340 graduate, professional, and undergraduate students; 1,476 full-time matriculated graduate/professional students (835 women), 525 part-time matriculated graduate/professional students (358 women). *Enrollment by degree level:* 886 master's, 1,090 doctoral, 25 other advanced degrees. Tuition, state resident: full-time $11,628; part-time $646 per credit. Tuition, nonresident: full-time $29,340; part-time $1630 per credit. *Required fees:* $1994; $10 per credit. Tuition and fees vary according to course load and program. *Graduate housing:* On-campus housing not available. *Student services:* Career counseling, free psychological counseling, international student services, low-cost health insurance, multicultural affairs office, services for students with disabilities, writing training. *Library facilities:* Bailey-Howe Library plus 2 others. *Collection:* Books: 1.1 million (physical), 339,186 (digital/electronic); Serial titles: 43,466 (physical), 96,209 (digital/electronic); Databases: 359. Weekly public service hours: 107; study areas open 24 hours, 5–7 days a week; students can reserve study rooms. *Research affiliation:* Miner Institute (animal sciences).

Computer facilities: Computer purchase and lease plans are available. 530 computers available on campus for general student use. A campuswide network can be accessed from student residence rooms and from off campus. Online class registration, Web pages, online course support, learning management system are available.
Website: http://www.uvm.edu/

General Application Contact: Kimberly Hess, Director of Admissions and Enrollment Management, 802-656-2699, Fax: 802-656-0519, E-mail: graduate.admissions@uvm.edu.

GRADUATE UNITS

Graduate College Students: 1,542 (961 women). 2,683 applicants, 51% accepted, 634 enrolled. *Faculty:* 620 full-time, 13 part-time/adjunct. Expenses: Contact institution. *Financial support:* Fellowships, research assistantships, teaching assistantships, career-related internships or fieldwork, Federal Work-Study, scholarships/grants, traineeships, health care benefits, tuition waivers (full and partial), and analytical assistantships available. Support available to part-time students. In 2017, 386 master's, 107 doctorates, 20 other advanced degrees awarded. *Program availability:* Part-time, 100% online, blended/hybrid learning. Offers bioengineering (PhD); cellular, molecular and biomedical sciences (PhD); food systems (MS, PhD); materials science (MS, PhD); neuroscience (PhD). *Application fee:* $65. Electronic applications accepted. *Application Contact:* Kimberly Hess, Director of Admissions and Enrollment Management, 802-656-2699, E-mail: graduate.admissions@uvm.edu. *Dean,* Dr. Cynthia Forehand, 802-656-3160, E-mail: gradcoll@uvm.edu.

College of Agriculture and Life Sciences Students: 117 (72 women). Average age 25. 144 applicants, 56% accepted, 42 enrolled. Expenses: Contact institution. *Financial support:* Fellowships, research assistantships, teaching assistantships, career-related internships or fieldwork, Federal Work-Study, and health care benefits available. Financial award application deadline: 3/1. In 2017, 32 master's, 7 doctorates awarded. *Program availability:* Part-time. Offers agriculture and life sciences (MPA, MS, PhD, Graduate Certificate); agroecology (Graduate Certificate); animal science (MS); animal, nutrition and food sciences (PhD); community development and applied economics (MS); dietetics (MS); nutrition and food sciences (MS); plant and soil science (MS, PhD); plant biology (MS, PhD); public administration (MPA). *Application deadline:* Applications are processed on a rolling basis. *Application fee:* $65. Electronic applications accepted. *Application Contact:* Kimberly Hess, Director of Graduate Admissions, 802-656-2699, Fax: 802-656-0519, E-mail: graduate.admissions@uvm.edu. *Dean,* Dr. Thomas C. Vogelmann, 802-656-0137, E-mail: calsdean@uvm.edu.

College of Arts and Sciences Students: 174 (95 women). 384 applicants, 28% accepted, 35 enrolled. Expenses: Contact institution. *Financial support:* Fellowships, research assistantships, teaching assistantships, career-related internships or fieldwork, Federal Work-Study, and health care benefits available. Financial award application deadline: 3/1. In 2017, 37 master's, 15 doctorates awarded. *Program availability:* Part-time. Offers arts and sciences (MA, MAT, MS, MST, PhD, Graduate Certificate); biology (MS, PhD); biology education (MST); chemistry (MS, PhD); clinical developmental psychology (PhD); clinical psychology (PhD); English (MA); geology (MS); German (MA); Greek and Latin (MA); Greek and Latin languages (Graduate Certificate); historic preservation (MS); history (MA); Latin (MAT); physics (MS); psychology (PhD). *Application fee:* $65. Electronic applications accepted. *Application Contact:* Kimberly Hess, Director of Admissions and Enrollment Management, 802-656-2699, E-mail: graduate.admissions@uvm.edu. *Dean,* William Falls, 802-656-3166, E-mail: cas@uvm.edu.

College of Education and Social Services Students: 337 (251 women). 506 applicants, 61% accepted, 169 enrolled. Expenses: Contact institution. *Financial support:* Fellowships, research assistantships, teaching assistantships, career-related internships or fieldwork, Federal Work-Study, scholarships/grants, and health care benefits available. In 2017, 119 master's, 19 doctorates awarded. *Program availability:* Part-time, evening/weekend. Offers counseling (MS); curriculum and instruction (MAT); early childhood special education (M Ed); education and social services (M Ed, MAT, MS, MSW, Ed D, PhD); educational leadership (M Ed); educational leadership and policy studies (Ed D, PhD); higher education and student affairs administration (M Ed); interdisciplinary studies (M Ed); social work (MSW); special education, grades K-12 (M Ed). *Application fee:* $65. Electronic applications accepted. *Application Contact:* Roman Vogel, Administrative Coordinator of Graduate Programs, 802-656-2936, E-mail: roman.vogel@uvm.edu. *Dean,* Dr. Scott L. Thomas, 802-656-3424, E-mail: cesssts v@uvm.edu.

College of Engineering and Mathematical Sciences Students: 219 full-time (94 women); includes 5 minority (all Hispanic/Latino), 60 international. 377 applicants, 57% accepted, 95 enrolled. Expenses: Contact institution. *Financial support:* Fellowships, research assistantships, teaching assistantships, Federal Work-Study, scholarships/grants, and health care benefits available. Financial award application deadline: 3/1. In 2017, 77 master's, 8 doctorates awarded. *Program availability:* Part-time. Offers biomedical engineering (MS); biostatistics (MS); civil and environmental engineering (MS, PhD); complex systems and data science (MS, PhD); computer science (MS, PhD); electrical engineering (MS, PhD); engineering and mathematical sciences (MS, MST, PhD); engineering management (MS); mathematics (MS, MST, PhD); mechanical engineering (MS, PhD); statistics (MS). *Application deadline:* Applications are processed on a rolling basis. *Application fee:* $65. Electronic applications accepted. *Application Contact:* Samantha Williams, Graduate Programs Coordinator, 802-656-3392, E-mail: info@cems.uvm.edu. *Dean,* Dr. Luis Garcia, 802-656-8413, E-mail: lag@uvm.edu.

College of Nursing and Health Sciences 560 applicants, 48% accepted, 95 enrolled. Expenses: Contact institution. *Financial support:* Fellowships, research assistantships, teaching assistantships, and Federal Work-Study available. Financial award application deadline: 3/1. In 2017, 29 master's, 38 doctorates awarded. Offers communication sciences and disorders (MS); human functioning and rehabilitation science (PhD); medical laboratory science (MS); nursing (MS, DNP, Post-Graduate Certificate); nursing and health sciences (MS, DNP, DPT, PhD, Post-Graduate Certificate); physical activity and wellness science (MS); physical therapy (DPT). *Application deadline:* Applications are processed on a rolling basis. *Application fee:* $65. Electronic applications accepted. *Application Contact:* Kristen Cella, Admissions Specialist, 802-656-3858, E-mail: cnhsgrad@uvm.edu. *Dean,* Dr. Patricia A. Prelock, 802-656-2216, E-mail: patricia.prelock@med.uvm.edu.

Grossman School of Business Students: 65 full-time (28 women); includes 2 minority (both Asian, non-Hispanic/Latino), 7 international. 119 applicants, 79% accepted, 61 enrolled. Expenses: Contact institution. *Financial support:* Federal Work-Study, scholarships/grants, and health care benefits available. Financial award application deadline: 3/1. In 2017, 39 master's awarded. *Program availability:* Part-time. Offers accountancy (M Acc); business (M Acc, MBA); sustainable innovation (MBA). *Application deadline:* Applications are processed on a rolling basis. *Application fee:* $65. Electronic applications accepted. *Application Contact:* 802-656-4119, E-mail:

studentservices@bsad.uvm.edu. *Dean,* Dr. Sanjay Sharma, 802-656-3177, E-mail: sanjay.sharma@uvm.edu.

The Rubenstein School of Environment and Natural Resources Students: 113 full-time (77 women). 138 applicants, 33% accepted, 37 enrolled. Expenses: Contact institution. *Financial support:* In 2017–18, 31 research assistantships with full and partial tuition reimbursements (averaging $18,600 per year), 19 teaching assistantships with full and partial tuition reimbursements (averaging $14,000 per year) were awarded; fellowships, Federal Work-Study, scholarships/grants, and health care benefits also available. Financial award application deadline: 3/1. In 2017, 13 master's, 5 doctorates awarded. *Program availability:* Part-time. Offers ecological economics (Certificate); environment and natural resources (MPS, MS, PhD, Certificate); leadership for sustainability (MPS); natural resources (MS); natural resources (PhD). MELP/MS offered in collaboration with Vermont Law School. *Application deadline:* For fall admission, 2/1 for domestic and international students; for spring admission, 11/1 for domestic and international students; for summer admission, 4/1 for domestic and international students. Applications are processed on a rolling basis. *Application fee:* $65. Electronic applications accepted. *Application Contact:* Carolyn Goodwin-Kueffner, Graduate Program Student Services Specialist, 802-656-2911, E-mail: rsenr@uvm.edu. *Dean,* Nancy Matthews, 802-656-1353, E-mail: nancy.mathews@uvm.edu.

The Robert Larner, MD College of Medicine Students: 615 (331 women). 5,857 applicants, 5% accepted, 119 enrolled. Expenses: Contact institution. *Financial support:* Fellowships, research assistantships, teaching assistantships, and Federal Work-Study available. Offers medicine (MPH, MS, MD, PhD, Certificate, Graduate Certificate). *Application deadline:* For fall admission, 11/15 for domestic and international students. Applications are processed on a rolling basis. Electronic applications accepted. *Application Contact:* Medical Admissions, 802-656-2154, E-mail: medadmissions@med.uvm.edu. *Dean,* Dr. Frederick C. Morin, III, 802-656-2156, E-mail: rick.morin@med.uvm.edu.

Graduate Programs in Medicine Students: 156 (99 women). 276 applicants, 65% accepted, 82 enrolled. Expenses: Contact institution. *Financial support:* Fellowships, research assistantships, teaching assistantships, traineeships, and analytical assistantships available. Financial award application deadline: 3/1. In 2017, 31 master's, 3 doctorates, 6 other advanced degrees awarded. *Program availability:* 100% online. Offers biochemistry (MS, PhD); clinical and translational science (MS, PhD, Certificate); epidemiology (Graduate Certificate); global and environmental health (Graduate Certificate); healthcare management and policy (Graduate Certificate); medical science (MS); medicine (MPH, MS, PhD, Certificate, Graduate Certificate); pathology and laboratory medicine (MS); pharmacology (MS, PhD); public health (MPH). *Application deadline:* For fall admission, 4/1 priority date for domestic students, 4/1 for international students. Applications are processed on a rolling basis. *Application fee:* $65. Electronic applications accepted. *Application Contact:* Erin Montgomery, Coordinator, 802-656-9925, E-mail: erin.montgomery@med.uvm.edu. *Dean,* Frederick C. Morin, 802-656-2156, E-mail: rick.morin@med.uvm.edu.

UNIVERSITY OF VICTORIA, Victoria, BC V8W 2Y2, Canada

General Information Province-supported, coed, university. *Graduate housing:* Rooms and/or apartments available on a first-come, first-served basis to single and married students. Housing application deadline: 2/1. *Research affiliation:* Dominion Astrophysical Observatory, Bamfield Marine Research Station (marine biology), Tri-University Meson Facility, Canada/France/Hawaii Telescope Observatory, Institute of Ocean Sciences (geography, oceanography).

GRADUATE UNITS

Faculty of Graduate Studies *Program availability:* Part-time, online learning. Electronic applications accepted.

Faculty of Education Offers aboriginal communities counseling (M Ed); art education (M Ed, PhD); coaching studies (co-operative education) (M Ed); counseling (M Ed, MA); curriculum studies (M Ed, MA, PhD); early childhood education (M Ed, PhD); education (M Ed, M Sc, MA, PhD); educational psychology (M Ed, MA, PhD); educational studies (PhD); kinesiology (M Sc, MA); language and literacy (M Ed, MA, PhD); leadership studies (M Ed, MA); leisure service administration (MA); mathematics (M Ed, MA, PhD); music education (M Ed, MA, PhD); physical education (MA); science (M Ed, MA, PhD); social studies (M Ed, MA); social, cultural and foundational studies (MA, PhD); technology and environmental education (PhD).

Faculty of Engineering Offers computer science (M Sc, PhD); electrical and computer engineering (M Eng, MA Sc, PhD); engineering (M Eng, M Sc, MA Sc, PhD); mechanical engineering (M Eng, MA Sc, PhD).

Faculty of Fine Arts Offers composition (M Mus); design (MFA); digital multimedia (MFA); directing (MFA); drawing (MFA); fine arts (M Mus, MA, MFA, PhD); history in art (MA, PhD); musicology (MA, PhD); musicology with performance (MA); painting (MFA); performance (M Mus); photography (MFA); sculpture (MFA); theatre history (MA); video (MFA); writing (MFA).

Faculty of Human and Social Development Offers advanced nursing practice (advanced practice leadership option) (MN); advanced nursing practice (nurse educator option) (MN); advanced nursing practice (nurse practitioner option) (MN); child and youth care (MA, PhD); dispute resolution (MADR); health information science (M Sc); human and social development (M Sc, MA, MADR, MN, MPA, MSW, PhD); indigenous governance (MA); nursing (PhD); public administration (MPA, PhD); social work (MSW); studies in policy and practice (MA).

Faculty of Humanities Offers applied linguistics (MA); English (MA, PhD); German studies (MA); Greek and Roman studies (MA, PhD); Hispanic and Italian studies (MA); Hispanic studies (MA); history (MA, PhD); humanities (MA, PhD); linguistics (MA, PhD); literature (MA); Pacific and Asian studies (MA); philosophy (MA); teaching emphasis (MA).

Faculty of Science Offers astronomy and astrophysics (M Sc, PhD); biochemistry (M Sc, PhD); biology (M Sc, PhD); chemistry (M Sc, PhD); condensed matter physics (M Sc, PhD); earth and ocean sciences (M Sc, PhD); experimental particle physics (M Sc, PhD); mathematics and statistics (M Sc, MA, PhD); medical physics (M Sc, PhD); microbiology (M Sc, PhD); ocean physics (M Sc, PhD); science (M Sc, MA, PhD); theoretical physics (M Sc, PhD). Electronic applications accepted.

Faculty of Social Sciences Offers anthropology (MA); clinical psychology (PhD); clinical psychology (neuropsychology) (M Sc); cognition and brain science (M Sc, PhD); economics (MA, PhD); experimental neuropsychology (M Sc, PhD); geography (M Sc, MA, PhD); individualized study (M Sc, PhD); life span development psychology (PhD); life span developmental psychology (M Sc); political science (MA, PhD); social psychology (M Sc, PhD); social sciences (M Sc, MA, PhD); sociology (MA, PhD).

Peter B. Gustavson School of Business *Program availability:* Part-time. Offers business (MBA). Electronic applications accepted.

Faculty of Law *Program availability:* Part-time. Offers law (LL M, JD, PhD). Electronic applications accepted.

UNIVERSITY OF VIRGINIA, Charlottesville, VA 22903

General Information State-supported, coed, university. CGS member. *Enrollment:* 24,360 graduate, professional, and undergraduate students; 6,250 full-time matriculated graduate/professional students (3,007 women), 364 part-time matriculated graduate/professional students (213 women). *Enrollment by degree level:* 2,932 master's, 3,681 doctoral, 1 other advanced degree. *Graduate faculty:* 2,299 full-time (835 women), 165 part-time/adjunct (105 women). *Graduate housing:* Rooms and/or apartments available on a first-come, first-served basis to single and married students. Housing application deadline: 6/1. *Student services:* Campus employment opportunities, campus safety program, career counseling, child daycare facilities, exercise/wellness program, free psychological counseling, grant writing training, international student services, low-cost health insurance, multicultural affairs office, services for students with disabilities, teacher training, writing training. *Library facilities:* Alderman Library plus 14 others. *Collection:* Books: 5.1 million (physical), 749,287 (digital/electronic); Serial titles: 7,910 (physical), 189,860 (digital/electronic); Databases: 1,340. Weekly public service hours: 149; study areas open 24 hours, 5–7 days a week; students can reserve study rooms. *Research affiliation:* Oak Ridge National Laboratory (energy), National Institute of Aerospace, Jefferson National Accelerator Facility (nuclear physics), Federal Executive Institute (leadership development), National Radio Astronomy Observatory, The Judge Advocate General's School, U.S. Army (law).

Computer facilities: Computer purchase and lease plans are available. 250 computers available on campus for general student use. A campuswide network can be accessed from student residence rooms and from off campus. Online class registration, online course management tool are available.
Website: http://www.virginia.edu/

General Application Contact: 434-924-0311.

GRADUATE UNITS

College and Graduate School of Arts and Sciences Students: 1,225 full-time (588 women), 24 part-time (9 women); includes 135 minority (25 Black or African American, non-Hispanic/Latino; 1 American Indian or Alaska Native, non-Hispanic/Latino; 41 Asian, non-Hispanic/Latino; 38 Hispanic/Latino; 30 Two or more races, non-Hispanic/Latino), 386 international. Average age 27. 3,893 applicants, 22% accepted, 337 enrolled. *Faculty:* 649 full-time (241 women), 47 part-time/adjunct (25 women). Expenses: Contact institution. *Financial support:* Fellowships with partial tuition reimbursements, research assistantships, teaching assistantships with tuition reimbursements, career-related internships or fieldwork, Federal Work-Study, institutionally sponsored loans, traineeships, tuition waivers (full and partial), and unspecified assistantships available. Financial award applicants required to submit FAFSA. In 2017, 189 master's, 173 doctorates awarded. *Program availability:* Part-time. Offers anthropology (MA, PhD); art and architectural history (MA, PhD); arts and sciences (MA, MAPE, MFA, MS, PhD); astronomy (MS, PhD); biology (MA, MS, PhD); chemistry (MA, MS, PhD); classics (MA, PhD); creative writing (MFA); drama (MFA); East Asian studies (MA); economics (MA, PhD); English (MA, PhD); environmental sciences (MA, MS, PhD); European studies (MA); foreign affairs (MA, PhD); French (MA, PhD); German (MA); government (MA, PhD); history (MA, PhD); linguistics (MA); math education (MA); mathematics (MA, MS, PhD); Middle Eastern and South Asian studies (MA); music (MA, PhD); philosophy (MA, PhD); physics (MA, MS, PhD); physics education (MAPE); psychology (MA, PhD); religion, politics and global society (MA); religious studies (MA, PhD); Slavic languages and literatures (MA, PhD); sociology (MA, PhD); Spanish (MA, PhD); statistics (MS, PhD). *Application deadline:* Applications are processed on a rolling basis. *Application fee:* $60. Electronic applications accepted. *Application Contact:* E-mail: gsas.admission@virginia.edu. *Dean,* Ian Baucom, 434-924-4648, Fax: 434-924-1317, E-mail: 9bb4n@virginia.edu.

Curry School of Education Students: 746 full-time (608 women), 79 part-time (53 women); includes 175 minority (60 Black or African American, non-Hispanic/Latino; 43 Asian, non-Hispanic/Latino; 40 Hispanic/Latino; 32 Two or more races, non-Hispanic/Latino), 30 international. Average age 26. 470 applicants, 92% accepted, 281 enrolled. *Faculty:* 136 full-time (81 women), 6 part-time/adjunct (4 women). Expenses: Contact institution. *Financial support:* Fellowships, research assistantships, teaching assistantships, and Federal Work-Study available. Financial award application deadline: 1/5; financial award applicants required to submit FAFSA. In 2017, 205 master's, 19 doctorates, 17 other advanced degrees awarded. Offers administration and supervision (M Ed, Ed D, PhD, Ed S); applied developmental science (M Ed, PhD); clinical and school psychology (PhD); counselor education (M Ed, Ed D, PhD, Ed S); curriculum and instruction (M Ed, Ed D, PhD, Ed S); early childhood special education (MT); education (M Ed, MS, MT, Ed D, PhD, Ed S); education evaluation (PhD); educational evaluation (M Ed); educational policy (PhD); educational psychology (M Ed, Ed D, PhD, Ed S); educational research (Ed D, PhD); elementary education (M Ed, MT, Ed D); English education (M Ed, MT, Ed D, PhD); foreign language education (M Ed, MT); gifted education (M Ed); higher education (M Ed, Ed D, PhD, Ed S); instructional technology (M Ed, PhD, Ed S); kinesiology (MT, PhD); math education (PhD); mathematics education (M Ed, Ed D); reading education (PhD); research statistics and evaluation (Ed D); research, statistics and evaluation (PhD); school psychology (Ed D, PhD); science education (Ed D, PhD); social studies education (M Ed, MT, PhD); special education (M Ed, Ed D, PhD, Ed S); speech communication disorders (M Ed, PhD); student affairs practice (M Ed); world languages education (MT). *Application deadline:* Applications are processed on a rolling basis. *Application fee:* $60. Electronic applications accepted. *Application Contact:* E-mail: curry-admissions@virginia.edu. *Dean,* Robert C. Pianta, 434-924-3334, E-mail: pianta@virginia.edu.

Darden School of Business Students: 928 full-time (324 women), 7 part-time (3 women); includes 192 minority (57 Black or African American, non-Hispanic/Latino; 67 Asian, non-Hispanic/Latino; 48 Hispanic/Latino; 20 Two or more races, non-Hispanic/Latino), 203 international. Average age 30. 2,911 applicants, 28% accepted, 388 enrolled. *Faculty:* 62 full-time (17 women), 3 part-time/adjunct (1 woman). Expenses: Contact institution. *Financial support:* Career-related internships or fieldwork available. Financial award applicants required to submit FAFSA. In 2017, 424 master's, 1 doctorate awarded. Offers business (MBA, PhD). *Application deadline:* For fall admission, 3/1 for domestic students, 3/2 for international students. Applications are processed on a rolling basis. *Application fee:* $200. Electronic applications accepted. *Application Contact:* Dawna Clarke, Executive Director of Admissions and Financial Aid, 434-924-3900, E-mail: darden@virginia.edu. *Dean,* Scott C. Beardsley, 434-924-7481, E-mail: dean@virginia.edu.

Data Science Institute Students: 35 full-time (13 women), 5 part-time (2 women); includes 6 minority (4 Asian, non-Hispanic/Latino; 1 Hispanic/Latino; 1 Two or more races, non-Hispanic/Latino), 19 international. Average age 26. Expenses: Contact institution. In 2017, 50 master's awarded. Offers data science (MS). *Application deadline:* Applications are processed on a rolling basis. *Application fee:* $85. *Application*

Contact: Steven Boker, Program Director, 434-243-7275, E-mail: boker@virginia.edu. *Director,* Phil Bourne, 434-924-6867, E-mail: peb6a@virginia.edu.

Frank Batten Sr. School of Leadership and Public Policy Students: 111 full-time (63 women), 2 part-time (both women); includes 21 minority (3 Black or African American, non-Hispanic/Latino; 9 Asian, non-Hispanic/Latino; 6 Hispanic/Latino; 3 Two or more races, non-Hispanic/Latino), 8 international. Average age 24. 227 applicants, 67% accepted, 81 enrolled. *Faculty:* 21 full-time (8 women), 4 part-time/adjunct (1 woman). Expenses: Contact institution. In 2017, 75 master's awarded. Offers leadership and public policy (MPP). *Application deadline:* For fall admission, 2/20 for domestic and international students. Applications are processed on a rolling basis. Electronic applications accepted. *Application Contact:* Patti Edson, Assistant Director of Admissions, 434-982-2583, Fax: 434-243-2318, E-mail: patti.edson@virginia.edu. *Dean,* Allan C. Stam, 434-924-0812, Fax: 434-243-2318, E-mail: stam@virginia.edu.

McIntire School of Commerce Offers accounting (MS); business analytics (MSC); commerce (MS, MSC, Certificate); finance (MSC); global commerce (MS); global strategic management (MS); international management (Certificate); management of information technology (MS); marketing and management (MSC). Electronic applications accepted.

School of Architecture Students: 232 full-time (132 women), 3 part-time (all women); includes 23 minority (5 Black or African American, non-Hispanic/Latino; 6 Asian, non-Hispanic/Latino; 4 Hispanic/Latino; 8 Two or more races, non-Hispanic/Latino), 107 international. Average age 26. 719 applicants, 50% accepted, 98 enrolled. *Faculty:* 43 full-time (19 women), 4 part-time/adjunct (3 women). Expenses: Contact institution. *Financial support:* Fellowships, career-related internships or fieldwork, Federal Work-Study, and institutionally sponsored loans available. Financial award applicants required to submit FAFSA. In 2017, 82 master's awarded. Offers architectural history (M Arch H, PhD); architecture (M Arch, M Arch H, M Land Arch, MUEP, PhD); landscape architecture (M Land Arch); the constructed environment (PhD); urban and environmental planning (MUEP). *Application deadline:* Applications are processed on a rolling basis. *Application fee:* $60. Electronic applications accepted. *Application Contact:* Director of Graduate Admissions and Financial Aid, 434-924-6442, Fax: 434-982-2678, E-mail: a-school-admissions@virginia.edu. *Dean,* Ila Berman, 434-924-7019, Fax: 434-982-2678, E-mail: ilb8r@virginia.edu.

School of Engineering and Applied Science Students: 813 full-time (252 women), 84 part-time (14 women); includes 104 minority (13 Black or African American, non-Hispanic/Latino; 53 Asian, non-Hispanic/Latino; 26 Hispanic/Latino; 12 Two or more races, non-Hispanic/Latino), 504 international. Average age 26. 2,330 applicants, 32% accepted, 269 enrolled. *Faculty:* 167 full-time (27 women), 4 part-time/adjunct (0 women). Expenses: Contact institution. *Financial support:* Fellowships with full tuition reimbursements, research assistantships with full tuition reimbursements, teaching assistantships with full tuition reimbursements, and career-related internships or fieldwork available. Financial award application deadline: 1/15; financial award applicants required to submit FAFSA. In 2017, 148 master's, 70 doctorates awarded. *Program availability:* Part-time, online learning. Offers biomedical engineering (ME, MS, PhD); chemical engineering (ME, MS, PhD); civil and environmental engineering (ME, MS, PhD); computer engineering (ME, MS, PhD); computer science (MCS, MS, PhD); electrical engineering (ME, MS, PhD); engineering and applied science (MCS, ME, MEP, MMSE, MS, PhD); engineering physics (ME, MS, PhD); materials science (MMSE, MS, PhD); mechanical and aerospace engineering (ME, MS, PhD); systems and information engineering (ME, MS, PhD). *Application deadline:* For fall admission, 8/1 for domestic students, 4/1 for international students; for winter admission, 12/1 for domestic students, 8/1 for international students; for spring admission, 5/1 for domestic students, 1/1 for international students. Applications are processed on a rolling basis. Electronic applications accepted. *Application Contact:* 434-243-0209, E-mail: gseasadmission@virginia.edu. *Dean,* Craig H. Benson, 434-924-3593, Fax: 434-924-3555, E-mail: engrdean@virginia.edu.

School of Law Students: 972 full-time (447 women), 2 part-time (0 women); includes 202 minority (50 Black or African American, non-Hispanic/Latino; 60 Asian, non-Hispanic/Latino; 45 Hispanic/Latino; 1 Native Hawaiian or other Pacific Islander, non-Hispanic/Latino; 46 Two or more races, non-Hispanic/Latino), 53 international. Average age 25. 5,642 applicants, 19% accepted, 363 enrolled. *Faculty:* 86 full-time (24 women), 3 part-time/adjunct (2 women). Expenses: Contact institution. *Financial support:* Fellowships, career-related internships or fieldwork, Federal Work-Study, and institutionally sponsored loans available. Financial award application deadline: 3/1; financial award applicants required to submit FAFSA. In 2017, 36 master's, 297 doctorates awarded. Offers law (LL M, JD, SJD). JD/MA in international relations offered jointly with The Johns Hopkins University. *Application deadline:* For fall admission, 3/1 priority date for domestic students, 3/2 for international students. Applications are processed on a rolling basis. *Application fee:* $75. Electronic applications accepted. *Application Contact:* Grace Applefeld Cleveland, Director of Admissions, 434-243-1456, Fax: 434-982-2128, E-mail: lawadmit@virginia.edu. *Dean,* Risa Goluboff, 434-924-7343, Fax: 434-982-2128, E-mail: goluboff@virginia.edu.

School of Medicine Students: 935 full-time (469 women), 22 part-time (15 women); includes 363 minority (86 Black or African American, non-Hispanic/Latino; 1 American Indian or Alaska Native, non-Hispanic/Latino; 150 Asian, non-Hispanic/Latino; 87 Hispanic/Latino; 1 Native Hawaiian or other Pacific Islander, non-Hispanic/Latino; 38 Two or more races, non-Hispanic/Latino), 57 international. Average age 26. 6,079 applicants, 11% accepted, 259 enrolled. *Faculty:* 1,084 full-time (374 women), 77 part-time/adjunct (53 women). Expenses: Contact institution. *Financial support:* Institutionally sponsored loans and scholarships/grants available. Financial award applicants required to submit FAFSA. In 2017, 71 master's, 188 doctorates awarded. Offers biochemistry (PhD); biological and physical sciences (MS); biophysics (PhD); cell biology (PhD); clinical investigation and patient-oriented research (MS); clinical research (MS); informatics in medicine (MS); medicine (MPH, MS, MD, PhD); microbiology, immunology, and cancer biology (PhD); neuroscience (PhD); pathology (PhD); pharmacology (PhD); physiology (PhD); public health (MPH). *Application deadline:* Applications are processed on a rolling basis. *Application fee:* $80. Electronic applications accepted. *Application Contact:* Randolph J. Canterbury, Senior Associate Dean for Education, 434-243-2522, Fax: 434-982-2586, E-mail: rjc9s@virginia.edu. *Interim Dean,* David S. Wilkes, 434-924-4050, E-mail: dsw4n@virginia.edu.

School of Nursing Students: 202 full-time (168 women), 139 part-time (114 women); includes 78 minority (32 Black or African American, non-Hispanic/Latino; 2 American Indian or Alaska Native, non-Hispanic/Latino; 14 Asian, non-Hispanic/Latino; 17 Hispanic/Latino; 1 Native Hawaiian or other Pacific Islander, non-Hispanic/Latino; 12 Two or more races, non-Hispanic/Latino), 9 international. Average age 34. 183 applicants, 68% accepted, 98 enrolled. *Faculty:* 51 full-time (44 women), 17 part-time/adjunct (16 women). Expenses: Contact institution. *Financial support:* Fellowships, research assistantships, teaching assistantships, Federal Work-Study, and scholarships/grants available. Financial award applicants required to submit FAFSA. In 2017, 105 master's, 27 doctorates awarded. *Program availability:* Part-time. Offers acute and specialty care (MSN); acute care nurse practitioner (MSN); clinical nurse leadership (MSN); community-public health leadership (MSN); nursing (DNP, PhD); psychiatric mental health counseling (MSN). *Application deadline:* Applications are processed on a rolling basis. *Application fee:* $60. Electronic applications accepted. *Application Contact:* Teresa Carroll, Senior Assistant Dean for Academic and Student Services, 434-924-0141, Fax: 434-982-1809, E-mail: nur-osa@virginia.edu. *Dean,* Dorrie K. Fontaine, 434-924-0141, Fax: 434-982-1809, E-mail: dkf2u@virginia.edu.

UNIVERSITY OF WASHINGTON, Seattle, WA 98195

General Information State-supported, coed, university. CGS member. *Graduate housing:* Rooms and/or apartments available on a first-come, first-served basis to single and married students. Housing application deadline: 5/1. *Research affiliation:* Fred Hutchinson Cancer Research Center, Children's Hospital and Regional Medical Center (pediatric research).

GRADUATE UNITS

Graduate School *Program availability:* Part-time, evening/weekend, online learning. Offers biology for teachers (MS); global trade, transportation and logistics studies (Certificate); museum evaluation (MA); Near and Middle Eastern studies (PhD); quantitative ecology and resource management (MS, PhD). Electronic applications accepted.

College of Arts and Sciences *Program availability:* Part-time, evening/weekend. Offers acting (MFA); animal behavior (PhD); anthropology (MA, PhD); applied child and adolescent psychology: prevention and treatment (MA); applied mathematics (MS, PhD); art (MFA); art history (MA, PhD); arts and sciences (MA, MAIS, MAT, MC, MFA, MM, MS, Au D, DMA, PhD); astronomy (MS, PhD); audiology (Au D); behavioral neuroscience (PhD); biology (PhD); Buddhist studies (MA, PhD); Central Asian studies (MAIS); chemistry (MS, PhD); China studies (MAIS); Chinese language and literature (MA, PhD); choral conducting (MM, DMA); classics (MA, PhD); classics and philosophy (PhD); clinical psychology (PhD); cognition and perception (PhD); communication (MA, MC, PhD); comparative literature (MA, PhD); comparative religion (MAIS); computational linguistics (MA); costume design (MFA); creative writing (MFA); dance (MFA); design (MFA); developmental psychology (PhD); directing (MFA); dramatic theory (PhD); East European studies (MAIS); economics (PhD); English as a second language (MAT); English literature and language (MA, MAT, PhD); ethnomusicology (MA); French (MA, PhD); gender, women and sexuality studies (PhD); geography (MA, PhD); Germanics (MA, PhD); Hispanic literary and cultural studies (MA); history (MA, PhD); industrial design (MFA); international studies (MAIS, PhD); Italian (MA); Japan studies (MAIS); Japanese language and literature (MA, PhD); Korea studies (MAIS); Korean language and literature (MA, PhD); lighting design (MFA); linguistics (MA, PhD); mathematics (MA, MS, PhD); Middle East studies (MAIS); music (MA, MM, DMA, PhD); music education (MA, PhD); music history (MA, PhD); Near Eastern languages and civilization (MA); numerical analysis (MS); optimization (MS); painting and drawing (MFA); philosophy (MA, PhD); photography (MFA); physics (MS, PhD); political science (MA, PhD); quantitative psychology (PhD); Romance linguistics (MA, PhD); Russian literature (MA, PhD); Russian studies (MAIS); Russian, East European and Central Asian studies (MAIS); Scandinavian studies (MA, PhD); scenic design (MFA); Slavic linguistics (MA, PhD); social psychology and personality (PhD); sociology (MA, PhD); South Asian language and literature (MA, PhD); South Asian studies (MAIS); Southeast Asian studies (MAIS); speech and hearing sciences (PhD); speech-language pathology (MS); statistics (MS, PhD); theatre and performance history (PhD); visual communication design (MFA). Electronic applications accepted.

College of Built Environments *Program availability:* Part-time, evening/weekend. Offers architecture (M Arch, MS); built environment (PhD); built environments (M Arch, MLA, MS, MSCM, MUP, PhD, Certificate); construction management (MSCM); design computing (Certificate); design firm leadership and management (Certificate); historic preservation (Certificate); landscape architecture (MLA); lighting (Certificate); urban design (Certificate); urban design and planning (PhD); urban planning (MUP). Electronic applications accepted.

College of Education *Program availability:* Part-time, evening/weekend. Offers curriculum and instruction (M Ed, Ed D, PhD); early childhood special education (M Ed); educational leadership and policy studies (M Ed, Ed D, PhD); educational psychology (M Ed, PhD); emotional and behavioral disabilities (M Ed); human development and cognition (M Ed); instructional leadership (M Ed); intercollegiate athletic leadership (M Ed); learning disabilities (M Ed); learning sciences (M Ed, PhD); low-incidence disabilities (M Ed); measurement, statistics and research design (M Ed); school psychology (M Ed); severe disabilities (M Ed); special education (M Ed, Ed D, PhD); teacher education (MIT). Electronic applications accepted.

College of Engineering Students: 1,678 full-time (536 women), 766 part-time (207 women); includes 512 minority (29 Black or African American, non-Hispanic/Latino; 3 American Indian or Alaska Native, non-Hispanic/Latino; 283 Asian, non-Hispanic/Latino; 122 Hispanic/Latino; 3 Native Hawaiian or other Pacific Islander, non-Hispanic/Latino; 72 Two or more races, non-Hispanic/Latino), 918 international. 7,403 applicants, 28% accepted, 795 enrolled. *Faculty:* 264 full-time (64 women). Expenses: Contact institution. *Financial support:* In 2017–18, 1,126 students received support, including 756 research assistantships with full tuition reimbursements available, 270 teaching assistantships with full tuition reimbursements available; career-related internships or fieldwork, Federal Work-Study, institutionally sponsored loans, scholarships/grants, traineeships, health care benefits, tuition waivers (full), unspecified assistantships, and stipend supplements also available. Financial award application deadline: 2/28; financial award applicants required to submit FAFSA. In 2017, 717 master's, 131 doctorates awarded. *Program availability:* Part-time, online learning. Offers aeronautics and astronautics (MAE, MSAA, PhD); applied bioengineering (MAB); applied materials science and engineering (MS); bioengineering (MS, PhD); bioengineering and nanotechnology (PhD); chemical engineering (MS, PhD); chemical engineering and advanced data science (PhD); chemical engineering and nanotechnology (PhD); computer science and engineering (MS, PhD); construction engineering (MSCE, PhD); electrical engineering (MS, PhD); electrical engineering and nanotechnology (PhD); engineering (MAB, MAE, MISE, MS, MSAA, MSCE, MSE, MSME, PhD, Certificate); environmental engineering (MSCE, PhD); geotechnical engineering (MSCE, PhD); human centered design and engineering (MS, PhD); hydrology and hydrodynamics (MSCE, PhD); industrial and systems engineering (MISE, MS, PhD); materials science and engineering (MS, PhD); materials science and engineering and nanotechnology (PhD); materials science and engineering, nanotechnology, and molecular engineering (PhD); mechanical engineering (MSE, MSME, PhD); pharmaceutical bioengineering (MS); structural engineering and mechanics (MSCE, PhD); transportation engineering (MSCE, PhD); user centered design (Certificate). *Application deadline:* For fall admission, 12/1 for domestic and international students. *Application fee:* $85. Electronic applications accepted. *Application Contact:* Scott Winter, Director,

Academic Affairs, 206-685-4074, Fax: 206-685-0666, E-mail: swinter@uw.edu. *Dean of Engineering*, Dr. Michael B. Bragg, 206-543-0340, Fax: 206-685-0666, E-mail: mbragg@uw.edu.

College of the Environment Offers aquatic and fishery sciences (MS, PhD); atmospheric sciences (MS, PhD); biological oceanography (MS, PhD); bioresource science and engineering (MS, PhD); chemical oceanography (MS, PhD); environment (MEH, MFR, MMA, MS, PhD, Graduate Certificate); environmental horticulture (MEH); forest ecology (MS, PhD); forest management (MFR); forest soils (MS, PhD); geology (MS, PhD); geophysics (MS, PhD); marine and environmental affairs (MMA, Graduate Certificate); marine geology and geophysics (MS, PhD); physical oceanography (MS, PhD); restoration ecology (MS, PhD); restoration ecology and environmental horticulture (MS, PhD); social sciences (MS, PhD); sustainable resource management (MS, PhD); wildlife science (MS, PhD). Electronic applications accepted.

Evans School of Public Policy and Governance *Program availability:* Part-time, evening/weekend. Offers public administration (MPA); public policy and management (PhD). Electronic applications accepted.

Information School Students: 353 full-time (222 women), 252 part-time (187 women); includes 144 minority (19 Black or African American, non-Hispanic/Latino; 11 American Indian or Alaska Native, non-Hispanic/Latino; 64 Asian, non-Hispanic/Latino; 48 Hispanic/Latino; 2 Native Hawaiian or other Pacific Islander, non-Hispanic/Latino), 143 international. Average age 30. 1,194 applicants, 44% accepted, 259 enrolled. *Faculty:* 49 full-time (21 women), 36 part-time/adjunct (15 women). Expenses: Contact institution. *Financial support:* In 2017–18, 70 students received support. Fellowships with full tuition reimbursements available, research assistantships with full tuition reimbursements available, teaching assistantships with full tuition reimbursements available, Federal Work-Study, institutionally sponsored loans, scholarships/grants, health care benefits, tuition waivers (full and partial), and unspecified assistantships available. Support available to part-time students. Financial award application deadline: 10/1; financial award applicants required to submit FAFSA. In 2017, 231 master's, 10 doctorates awarded. *Program availability:* Part-time, 100% online coursework with required attendance at on-campus orientation at start of program. Offers information management (MSIM); information science (PhD); library and information science (MLIS). *Application deadline:* For fall admission, 12/1 priority date for domestic and international students. *Application fee:* $85. Electronic applications accepted. *Application Contact:* Kari Brothers, Admissions Counselor, 206-616-5541, Fax: 206-616-3152, E-mail: kari683@uw.edu. *Dean*, Dr. Anind Dey, E-mail: anind@uw.edu.

Michael G. Foster School of Business Students: 469 full-time (173 women), 638 part-time (216 women); includes 314 minority (15 Black or African American, non-Hispanic/Latino; 6 American Indian or Alaska Native, non-Hispanic/Latino; 246 Asian, non-Hispanic/Latino; 28 Hispanic/Latino; 5 Native Hawaiian or other Pacific Islander, non-Hispanic/Latino; 14 Two or more races, non-Hispanic/Latino), 125 international. Average age 32. 1,809 applicants, 84% accepted, 1107 enrolled. *Faculty:* 109 full-time (35 women), 54 part-time/adjunct (32 women). Expenses: Contact institution. *Financial support:* Fellowships with partial tuition reimbursements, research assistantships with partial tuition reimbursements, teaching assistantships with partial tuition reimbursements, Federal Work-Study, institutionally sponsored loans, and scholarships/grants available. Financial award application deadline: 2/28; financial award applicants required to submit FAFSA. In 2017, 543 master's, 10 doctorates awarded. *Program availability:* Part-time, evening/weekend, blended/hybrid learning. Offers auditing and assurance (MP Acc); business administration (MBA, PhD); entrepreneurship (MS); executive business administration (MBA); global executive business administration (MBA); information systems (MSIS); supply chain management (MSSCM); taxation (MP Acc); technology management (MBA). *Application deadline:* For fall admission, 3/15 for domestic students, 1/15 for international students. *Application fee:* $85. Electronic applications accepted. *Application Contact:* Erin Town, Director of Admissions, 206-543-4661, Fax: 206-616-7351, E-mail: mba@uw.edu. *Dean*, Dr. James Jiambalvo, 206-543-4750, E-mail: jjiambal@uw.edu.

School of Dentistry Offers dental surgery (DDS); dentistry (MS, MSD, DDS, PhD, Certificate); endodontics (MSD, Certificate); oral biology (MS, MSD, PhD); oral medicine (MSD); orthodontics (MSD, Certificate); pediatric dentistry (MSD, Certificate); periodontics (MSD, PhD, Certificate); prosthodontics (MSD, Certificate).

School of Law Offers Asian law (LL M, PhD); intellectual property law and policy (LL M); law (JD); law of sustainable international development (LL M); taxation (LL M).

School of Medicine *Program availability:* Part-time. Offers biochemistry (PhD); bioethics (MA); biological structure (PhD); biomedical and health informatics (MS, PhD); comparative medicine (MS); experimental and molecular pathology (PhD); genome sciences (PhD); immunology (PhD); laboratory medicine (MS); medicine (MA, MOT, MPO, MS, DPT, MD, PhD); microbiology (PhD); molecular and cellular biology (PhD); neurobiology and behavior (PhD); occupational therapy (MOT); pharmacology (PhD); physical therapy (DPT); physiology and biophysics (PhD); prosthetics and orthotics (MPO); rehabilitation science (PhD). Electronic applications accepted.

School of Nursing *Program availability:* Part-time. Offers nursing (MN, MS, DNP, PhD, Graduate Certificate).

School of Public Health Students: 763 full-time (559 women), 183 part-time (118 women); includes 290 minority (49 Black or African American, non-Hispanic/Latino; 11 American Indian or Alaska Native, non-Hispanic/Latino; 160 Asian, non-Hispanic/Latino; 63 Hispanic/Latino; 7 Native Hawaiian or other Pacific Islander, non-Hispanic/Latino), 117 international. Average age 31. 1,856 applicants, 42% accepted, 397 enrolled. *Faculty:* 264 full-time (123 women), 203 part-time/adjunct (101 women). Expenses: Contact institution. *Financial support:* Fellowships with full and partial tuition reimbursements, research assistantships with full and partial tuition reimbursements, teaching assistantships with full and partial tuition reimbursements, career-related internships or fieldwork, Federal Work-Study, institutionally sponsored loans, scholarships/grants, traineeships, health care benefits, tuition waivers (full and partial), and unspecified assistantships available. Support available to part-time students. *Program availability:* Part-time, evening/weekend, online learning. Offers applied toxicology (MS); biostatistics (MPH, MS, PhD); clinical research methods (MS); community-oriented public health practice (MPH); environmental and occupational health (MPH); environmental and occupational hygiene (PhD); environmental health (MS); environmental toxicology (MS, PhD); epidemiology (PhD); general epidemiology (MPH, MS); genetic epidemiology (MS); global health (MPH); global health metrics and implementation science (PhD); health administration (EMHA, MHA); health informatics and health information management (MHIHIM); health metrics and evaluation (MPH); health services (MPH, MS, PhD); health systems and policy (MPH); leadership, policy and management (MPH); maternal and child health (MPH); nutritional sciences (MPH, MS, PhD); occupational and environmental exposure sciences (MS); occupational and environmental medicine (MPH); pathobiology (PhD); public health (EMHA, MHA, MHIHIM, MPH, MS, PhD, Graduate Certificate); public health genetics (MPH, PhD, Graduate Certificate); social and behavioral sciences (MPH); statistical genetics (PhD). *Application fee:* $85. Electronic applications accepted. *Application Contact:* Office of Student Affairs, 206-685-3057, Fax: 206-543-3057, E-mail: sphosa@u.washington.edu. *Interim Dean*, Joel Kaufman, 206-616-8229.

School of Social Work *Program availability:* Evening/weekend, online learning. Offers social work (MSW, PhD).

School of Pharmacy Expenses: Contact institution. *Financial support:* Fellowships, research assistantships, teaching assistantships, career-related internships or fieldwork, Federal Work-Study, and tuition waivers (partial) available. Financial award applicants required to submit FAFSA. Offers biomedical regulatory affairs (MS); medicinal chemistry (PhD); pharmaceutical outcomes research and policy (PhD); pharmaceutics (MS, PhD); pharmacy (MS, PhD, Pharm D). *Application Contact:* Information Contact, 206-543-2100, Fax: 206-543-8798, E-mail: uwgrad@u.washington.edu. *Dean*, Dr. Sean D. Sullivan, 206-543-2030, Fax: 206-685-9297, E-mail: phardean@uw.edu.

UNIVERSITY OF WASHINGTON, BOTHELL, Bothell, WA 98011

General Information State-supported, coed, comprehensive institution. *Graduate housing:* Room and/or apartments available on a first-come, first-served basis to single students; on-campus housing not available to married students. Housing application deadline: 5/1. *Research affiliation:* Bill and Melinda Gates Foundation (improving health and reducing poverty in developing countries, providing opportunities to succeed in school and life in the U.S.), Carnegie Corporation of New York (doing real and permanent good in this world by creating ladders on which the aspiring can rise), American Institutes for Research (labor market success), Michael and Susan Dell Foundation (portfolio network scale-up project), William and Flora Hewlett Foundation (planning for the state education agency of the future), Walton Family Foundation (student-based allocation systems).

GRADUATE UNITS

Master of Arts in Cultural Studies Program *Program availability:* Evening/weekend. Offers cultural studies (MA). Electronic applications accepted.

Master of Arts in Policy Studies Program *Program availability:* Evening/weekend. Offers policy studies (MA). Electronic applications accepted.

Program in Computing and Software Systems *Program availability:* Part-time, evening/weekend. Offers computing and software systems (MS). Electronic applications accepted.

Program in Creative Writing and Poetics Offers creative writing and poetics (MFA).

Program in Education *Program availability:* Part-time, evening/weekend. Offers education (M Ed); leadership development for educators (M Ed); secondary/middle level endorsement (M Ed). Electronic applications accepted.

Program in Nursing *Program availability:* Part-time. Offers nursing (MN). Electronic applications accepted.

School of Business *Program availability:* Part-time, evening/weekend. Offers leadership (MBA); technology (MBA). Electronic applications accepted.

UNIVERSITY OF WASHINGTON, TACOMA, Tacoma, WA 98402-3100

General Information State-supported, coed, comprehensive institution. *Graduate housing:* Room and/or apartments available on a first-come, first-served basis to single students; on-campus housing not available to married students. Housing application deadline: 5/14. *Research affiliation:* City of Tacoma/Port of Tacoma (water quality and sustainability studies), South Sound Public and Private Schools (internships and educational research).

GRADUATE UNITS

Graduate Programs *Program availability:* Part-time, evening/weekend. Offers accounting (MBA); advanced integrative practice (MSW); business administration (MBA); certified financial analyst (MBA); communities, populations and health (MN); computing and software systems (MS); education (M Ed); educational administration (principal or program administrator certification) (M Ed); elementary education teacher certification (M Ed); elementary education/special education teacher certification (M Ed); interdisciplinary studies (MA); leadership in healthcare (MN); nurse educator (MN); secondary science or math teacher certification (M Ed); social work (MSW). Electronic applications accepted.

UNIVERSITY OF WATERLOO, Waterloo, ON N2L 3G1, Canada

General Information Province-supported, coed, university. CGS member. *Graduate housing:* Rooms and/or apartments available on a first-come, first-served basis to single and married students. *Research affiliation:* Waterloo Maple, Inc. (symbolic computation research), Bell Canada, GM Canada, IBM, COM DEV International (telecommunications), Nortel (telecommunications).

GRADUATE UNITS

Graduate Studies *Program availability:* Part-time, evening/weekend, online learning. Electronic applications accepted.

Faculty of Applied Health Sciences *Program availability:* Part-time. Offers applied health sciences (M Sc, MA, MHE, MHI, MPH, PhD); health evaluation (MHE); health informatics (MHI); health studies and gerontology (M Sc, PhD); kinesiology (M Sc, PhD); public health (MPH); recreation and leisure studies (MA, PhD). Electronic applications accepted.

Faculty of Arts *Program availability:* Part-time, evening/weekend. Offers accounting (M Acc, PhD); ancient Mediterranean cultures (MA); anthropology (MA); arts (M Acc, M Tax, MA, MA Sc, MFA, MPS, PhD); economics (MA, PhD); English language and literature (PhD); finance (M Acc); French (MA, PhD); German (MA, PhD); global governance (MA, PhD); history (MA, PhD); literary studies (MA); philosophy (MA, PhD); psychology (MA, MA Sc, PhD); public issues (MA); religious diversity in North America (PhD); rhetoric and communication design (MA); Russian (MA); sociology (MA, PhD); studio art (MFA); taxation (M Tax). Electronic applications accepted.

Faculty of Engineering *Program availability:* Part-time, evening/weekend, online learning. Offers applied operations research (MA Sc, MMS, PhD); architecture (M Arch); business, entrepreneurship and technology (MBET); chemical engineering (M Eng, MA Sc, PhD); civil and environmental engineering (M Eng, MA Sc, PhD); electrical and computer engineering (M Eng, MA Sc, PhD); engineering (M Arch, M Eng, MA Sc, MBET, MMS, PhD); information systems (MA Sc, MMS, PhD); management of technology (MA Sc, MMS, PhD); mechanical engineering (M Eng, MA Sc, PhD); mechanical engineering design and manufacturing (M Eng); systems design engineering (M Eng, MA Sc, PhD). Electronic applications accepted.

Faculty of Environment *Program availability:* Part-time. Offers environment (M Plan, MA, MAES, MES, PhD); environment, resources and sustainability (MES, PhD); geography and environmental management (MA, PhD); local economic development (MAES); planning (M Plan, MA, MAES, MES, PhD). Electronic applications accepted.

Faculty of Mathematics Offers actuarial science (M Math, MAS, PhD); applied mathematics (M Math, PhD); biostatistics (PhD); combinatorics and optimization (M Math, PhD); computer science (M Math, PhD); mathematics (M Math, MAS, MMT, PhD); pure mathematics (M Math, PhD); software engineering (M Math); statistics (M Math, PhD); statistics and computing (M Math); statistics-biostatistics (M Math); statistics-computing (M Math); statistics-finance (M Math). Electronic applications accepted.

Faculty of Science *Program availability:* Part-time. Offers biology (M Sc, PhD); chemistry and biochemistry (M Sc, PhD); earth and environmental sciences (M Sc, PhD); optometry (OD); physics (M Sc, PhD); science (M Sc, OD, PhD); vision science (M Sc, PhD). Electronic applications accepted.

THE UNIVERSITY OF WEST ALABAMA, Livingston, AL 35470

General Information State-supported, coed, comprehensive institution. *Enrollment:* 4,646 graduate, professional, and undergraduate students; 2,392 full-time matriculated graduate/professional students (1,950 women), 143 part-time matriculated graduate/professional students (97 women). *Enrollment by degree level:* 2,267 master's, 268 other advanced degrees. *Graduate faculty:* 51 full-time (30 women), 84 part-time/adjunct (55 women). Tuition, state resident: part-time $371 per credit hour. Tuition, nonresident: part-time $742 per credit hour. *Required fees:* $130 per semester. *Graduate housing:* Room and/or apartments available on a first-come, first-served basis to single students; on-campus housing not available to married students. Typical cost: $4480 per year ($7080 including board). Room and board charges vary according to board plan and housing facility selected. Housing application deadline: 5/1. *Student services:* Campus employment opportunities, campus safety program, career counseling, exercise/wellness program, free psychological counseling, international student services, services for students with disabilities. *Library facilities:* Julia Tutwiler Library plus 1 other. *Collection:* Books: 201,627 (physical), 2,121 (digital/electronic); Serial titles: 2,093 (physical), 108,952 (digital/electronic); Databases: 174. Weekly public service hours: 94; students can reserve study rooms.

Computer facilities: 600 computers available on campus for general student use. A campuswide network can be accessed from student residence rooms. Online class registration is available.
Website: http://www.uwa.edu/

General Application Contact: Dr. B. J. Kimbrough, Dean of Graduate Studies, 205-652-3647, Fax: 205-652-3670, E-mail: bkimbrough@uwa.edu.

GRADUATE UNITS

School of Graduate Studies Students: 2,392 full-time (1,950 women), 143 part-time (97 women); includes 911 minority (840 Black or African American, non-Hispanic/Latino; 18 American Indian or Alaska Native, non-Hispanic/Latino; 2 Asian, non-Hispanic/Latino; 19 Hispanic/Latino; 1 Native Hawaiian or other Pacific Islander, non-Hispanic/Latino; 31 Two or more races, non-Hispanic/Latino), 37 international. Average age 34. 828 applicants, 96% accepted, 595 enrolled. *Faculty:* 51 full-time (30 women), 84 part-time/adjunct (55 women). Expenses: Contact institution. *Financial support:* In 2017–18, 22 teaching assistantships (averaging $7,344 per year) were awarded; Federal Work-Study, scholarships/grants, and unspecified assistantships also available. Support available to part-time students. Financial award application deadline: 3/1; financial award applicants required to submit FAFSA. In 2017, 578 master's, 152 other advanced degrees awarded. *Program availability:* Part-time, evening/weekend, 100% online. *Application deadline:* Applications are processed on a rolling basis. *Application fee:* $40. Electronic applications accepted. *Dean of Graduate Studies*, Dr. B. J. Kimbrough, 205-652-3647, Fax: 205-652-3670, E-mail: bkimbrough@uwa.edu.

College of Business and Technology Students: 106 (73 women); includes 62 minority (57 Black or African American, non-Hispanic/Latino; 3 Hispanic/Latino; 2 Two or more races, non-Hispanic/Latino). Average age 30. 52 applicants, 98% accepted, 43 enrolled. *Faculty:* 2 full-time (1 woman), 9 part-time/adjunct (7 women). Expenses: Contact institution. *Financial support:* Federal Work-Study and scholarships/grants available. Support available to part-time students. Financial award application deadline: 3/1; financial award applicants required to submit FAFSA. In 2017, 9 master's awarded. *Program availability:* Part-time, evening/weekend, 100% online. Offers finance (MBA); general business (MBA). *Application deadline:* Applications are processed on a rolling basis. *Application fee:* $40. Electronic applications accepted. *Interim Dean of College of Business and Technology*, Dr. Aliquippa Allen, 205-652-3564, Fax: 205-652-3776, E-mail: aallen@uwa.edu.

College of Education Students: 2,298 (1,937 women); includes 815 minority (744 Black or African American, non-Hispanic/Latino; 17 American Indian or Alaska Native, non-Hispanic/Latino; 7 Asian, non-Hispanic/Latino; 18 Hispanic/Latino; 1 Native Hawaiian or other Pacific Islander, non-Hispanic/Latino; 28 Two or more races, non-Hispanic/Latino). Average age 35. 724 applicants, 96% accepted, 507 enrolled. *Faculty:* 46 full-time (29 women), 71 part-time/adjunct (46 women). Expenses: Contact institution. *Financial support:* In 2017–18, 1 teaching assistantship (averaging $7,344 per year) was awarded; Federal Work-Study, scholarships/grants, and unspecified assistantships also available. Support available to part-time students. Financial award application deadline: 3/1; financial award applicants required to submit FAFSA. In 2017, 532 master's, 152 other advanced degrees awarded. *Program availability:* Part-time, evening/weekend, 100% online. Offers biology (MAT); clinical mental health counseling (MS); collaborative special education 6-12 (Ed S); collaborative special education K-6 (Ed S); counseling and psychology (MSCE); early childhood development (M Ed); early childhood education P-3 (M Ed, Ed S); education (M Ed, MAT, MS, MSCE, Ed S); elementary education (Ed S); elementary education K-6 (M Ed); English language arts (MAT); family counseling (MS); general (MSCE); guidance and counseling (MS); high school 6-12 (M Ed); history (MAT); instructional leadership (M Ed, Ed S); learning, design, and technology (M Ed); library media (M Ed, MSCE, Ed S); mathematics (MAT); school counseling (M Ed, Ed S); science (MAT); social science (MAT); special education collaborative teacher 6-12 (M Ed); special education collaborative teacher K-6 (M Ed); student affairs in higher education (M Ed); teacher leader (Ed S). *Application deadline:* Applications are processed on a rolling basis. *Application fee:* $40. Electronic applications accepted. *Dean of Graduate Studies*, Dr. B. J. Kimbrough, 205-652-3647, Fax: 205-652-3670, E-mail: bkimbrough@uwa.edu.

College of Liberal Arts Students: 17 (13 women); includes 5 minority (all Black or African American, non-Hispanic/Latino). Average age 29. 5 applicants, 80% accepted, 3 enrolled. *Faculty:* 3 full-time (1 woman), 7 part-time/adjunct (4 women). Expenses: Contact institution. *Financial support:* In 2017–18, 3 teaching assistantships (averaging $7,344 per year) were awarded; Federal Work-Study, scholarships/grants, and unspecified assistantships also available. Support available to part-time students. Financial award application deadline: 3/1; financial award applicants required to submit FAFSA. *Program availability:* Part-time, evening/weekend, 100% online. Offers experimental psychology (MS). *Application deadline:* Applications are processed on a rolling basis. *Application fee:* $40. Electronic applications accepted. *Dean*, Dr. Mark Davis, 205-652-3570, Fax: 205-652-3717, E-mail: mdavis@uwa.edu.

College of Natural Sciences and Mathematics Students: 133 (42 women); includes 42 minority (39 Black or African American, non-Hispanic/Latino; 1 American Indian or Alaska Native, non-Hispanic/Latino; 1 Hispanic/Latino; 1 Two or more races, non-Hispanic/Latino). Average age 31. 47 applicants, 100% accepted, 42 enrolled. *Faculty:* 11 full-time (1 woman), 5 part-time/adjunct (1 woman). Expenses: Contact institution. *Financial support:* In 2017–18, 8 teaching assistantships (averaging $7,344 per year) were awarded; Federal Work-Study, scholarships/grants, and unspecified assistantships also available. Support available to part-time students. Financial award application deadline: 3/1; financial award applicants required to submit FAFSA. In 2017, 37 master's awarded. *Program availability:* Part-time, evening/weekend, 100% online. Offers conservation biology (MS); physical education (M Ed, MAT, MS). *Application deadline:* Applications are processed on a rolling basis. *Application fee:* $40. Electronic applications accepted. *Dean of College of Natural Sciences and Mathematics*, Dr. John McCall, 205-652-3412, Fax: 205-652-3831, E-mail: jmccall@uwa.edu.

THE UNIVERSITY OF WESTERN ONTARIO, London, ON N6A 5B8, Canada

General Information Province-supported, coed, university. CGS member. *Graduate housing:* Rooms and/or apartments available on a first-come, first-served basis to single and married students.

GRADUATE UNITS

Faculty of Graduate Studies *Program availability:* Part-time, evening/weekend, online learning. Electronic applications accepted.

Biosciences Division *Program availability:* Part-time, online learning. Offers anatomy and cell biology (M Sc, PhD); biochemistry (M Sc, PhD); biology (M Sc, PhD); biosciences (M Cl Sc, M Sc, MA, MPT, PhD, CAS); clinical anatomy (M Sc); clinical neurological sciences (M Sc, PhD); epidemiology and biostatistics (M Sc, PhD); family medicine (M Cl Sc); manipulative therapy (CAS); medical biophysics (M Sc, PhD); microbiology and immunology (M Sc, PhD); pathology (M Sc, PhD); physical therapy (MPT); physiology (M Sc, PhD); psychology (MA, PhD); wound healing (CAS).

Center for the Study of Theory and Criticism Offers theory and criticism (MA, PhD).

Don Wright Faculty of Music *Program availability:* Part-time. Offers music (M Mus, PhD); popular music and culture (MA).

Faculty of Arts and Humanities *Program availability:* Part-time. Offers arts and humanities (M Mus, MA, PhD); Canadian literature (MA); classical studies (MA); comparative literature (MA, PhD); English (PhD); English literature (MA); French studies (MA, PhD); Hispanic studies (MA, PhD); philosophy (MA, PhD).

Faculty of Information and Media Studies Offers journalism (MA); library and information science (MLIS, PhD); media studies (MA, PhD).

Health Sciences Division Offers audiology (M Cl Sc, M Sc); health sciences (M Cl Sc, M Sc, M Sc N, MA, MCTS, MN NP, PhD); kinesiology (M Sc, MA, PhD); nurse practitioner (MN NP); nursing (M Sc N, MN NP, PhD); occupational therapy (M Sc); speech-language pathology (M Cl Sc, M Sc).

Physical Sciences Division *Program availability:* Part-time. Offers applied mathematics (M Sc, PhD); astronomy (M Sc, PhD); chemical and biochemical engineering (ME Sc, PhD); chemistry (M Sc, PhD); civil and environmental engineering (M Eng, ME Sc, PhD); computer science (M Sc, PhD); electrical and computer engineering (M Eng, ME Sc, PhD); environment and sustainability (MES); geology (M Sc, PhD); geology and environmental science (M Sc, PhD); geophysics (M Sc, PhD); geophysics and environmental science (M Sc, PhD); mathematics (M Sc, PhD); mechanical and materials engineering (M Eng, ME Sc, PhD); physical sciences (M Eng, M Sc, ME Sc, MES, PhD); physics (M Sc, PhD); statistical and actuarial sciences (M Sc, PhD); theoretical physics (PhD). Electronic applications accepted.

Social Sciences Division *Program availability:* Part-time, evening/weekend. Offers anthropology (MA, PhD); counseling psychology (M Ed); curriculum studies (M Ed); economics (MA, PhD); education (M Ed); educational policy studies (M Ed); educational psychology/special education (M Ed); geography (M Sc, MA, PhD); history (MA, PhD); political science (MA, MPA, PhD); social sciences (M Ed, M Sc, MA, MPA, PhD); sociology (MA, PhD).

Faculty of Law Offers law (LL M, MLS, JD, Diploma).

Richard Ivey School of Business Offers business (EMBA, PhD); corporate strategy and leadership elective (MBA); entrepreneurship elective (MBA); finance elective (MBA); health sector stream (MBA); international management elective (MBA); marketing elective (MBA). Electronic applications accepted.

Schulich School of Medicine and Dentistry Offers dentistry (M Cl D, DDS); medicine (MD); medicine and dentistry (M Cl D, M Cl Sc, M Sc, MA, DDS, MD, PhD); orthodontics (M Cl D).

UNIVERSITY OF WESTERN STATES, Portland, OR 97230-3099

General Information Independent, coed, graduate-only institution. *Graduate housing:* On-campus housing not available. *Research affiliation:* Oregon Center for Complimentary and Alternative Medicine in Craniofacial Disorders (complimentary and alternative medicine), Consortial Center for Chiropractic Research (Palmer College of Chiropractic) (chiropractic).

GRADUATE UNITS

Professional Program Offers chiropractic (DC).

UNIVERSITY OF WEST FLORIDA, Pensacola, FL 32514-5750

General Information State-supported, coed, comprehensive institution. CGS member. *Graduate housing:* Room and/or apartments available on a first-come, first-served basis to single students; on-campus housing not available to married students. *Research affiliation:* Pensacola Bay Area Convention and Visitors Bureau (Pensacola tourism study), Software Engineering Research Consortium (Motorola, Northrup Grumman through Ball State University) (software engineering), University of Southern Mississippi Consortium on Coastal Estuarine Research (microbial biofilms and coastal estuarine research).

GRADUATE UNITS

College of Arts, Social Sciences, and Humanities *Program availability:* Part-time, evening/weekend. Offers arts, social sciences, and humanities (MA); creative writing (MA); early American studies (MA); literature (MA); political science (MA); public history (MA); strategic communication and leadership (MA); traditional history (MA).

Division of Anthropology and Archaeology Offers anthropology (MA); historical archaeology (MA).

College of Business *Program availability:* Part-time, evening/weekend. Offers accounting (M Acc); business (M Acc, MBA); business administration (MBA).

College of Education and Professional Studies *Program availability:* Part-time, evening/weekend. Offers applied behavior analysis (MA); college student affairs administration (M Ed); criminal justice (MS); curriculum and assessment (Ed D); curriculum and instruction (M Ed, Ed S); education and professional studies (M Ed, MA, MS, MSA, MSW, Ed D, Ed S); educational leadership (M Ed); elementary education (M Ed); exceptional student education (MA); instructional design and technology (M Ed, Ed D); legal studies, public administration and sport management (MSA); middle level education (M Ed); network operations, performance and security (M Ed); reading education (M Ed); secondary education (M Ed); social work (MSW); special and alternative education (MA).

Ed D Programs *Program availability:* Part-time, evening/weekend. Offers administrative and leadership studies (Ed D); education (Ed D); instructional design and technology (Ed D); physical education and health (Ed D).

Hal Marcus College of Science and Engineering *Program availability:* Part-time, evening/weekend. Offers biology (MS); computer science (MS); environmental science (MS); geographic information science administration (MS); information technology (MS); mathematical sciences (MS); science and engineering (MPH, MS, MSN, MST).

Usha Kundu, MD College of Health *Program availability:* Part-time. Offers applied experimental (MA); counseling (MA); health (MA, MHA, MPH, MS, MSN); health promotion (MS); health, leisure, and exercise science (MS); healthcare administration (MHA); industrial-organizational (MA); public health (MPH).

School of Nursing *Program availability:* Part-time, evening/weekend. Offers nursing (MSN).

UNIVERSITY OF WEST GEORGIA, Carrollton, GA 30118

General Information State-supported, coed, comprehensive institution. CGS member. *Enrollment:* 13,520 graduate, professional, and undergraduate students; 630 full-time matriculated graduate/professional students (484 women), 1,376 part-time matriculated graduate/professional students (1,065 women). *Enrollment by degree level:* 1,367 master's, 171 doctoral, 468 other advanced degrees. *Graduate faculty:* 260 full-time (131 women). Tuition and fees vary according to degree level and program. *Graduate housing:* Rooms and/or apartments available on a first-come, first-served basis to single and married students. Housing application deadline: 6/1. *Student services:* Campus employment opportunities, campus safety program, career counseling, exercise/wellness program, free psychological counseling, international student services, multicultural affairs office, services for students with disabilities, teacher training, writing training. *Library facilities:* Irvine Sullivan Ingram Library plus 1 other. *Collection:* Weekly public service hours: 137; study areas open 24 hours, 5–7 days a week; students can reserve study rooms.

Computer facilities: 1,200 computers available on campus for general student use. A campuswide network can be accessed from student residence rooms and from off campus. Online class registration is available.
Website: http://www.westga.edu/

General Application Contact: Dr. Toby Ziglar, Assistant Dean of the Graduate School, 678-839-1394, Fax: 678-839-1395, E-mail: graduate@westga.edu.

GRADUATE UNITS

College of Arts and Humanities Students: 25 full-time (15 women), 51 part-time (34 women); includes 16 minority (7 Black or African American, non-Hispanic/Latino; 1 American Indian or Alaska Native, non-Hispanic/Latino; 2 Asian, non-Hispanic/Latino; 5 Hispanic/Latino; 1 Two or more races, non-Hispanic/Latino), 1 international. Average age 30. 23 applicants, 96% accepted, 16 enrolled. *Faculty:* 69 full-time (38 women). Expenses: Contact institution. *Financial support:* Fellowships, research assistantships, teaching assistantships, career-related internships or fieldwork, Federal Work-Study, institutionally sponsored loans, scholarships/grants, and unspecified assistantships available. Support available to part-time students. Financial award application deadline: 4/1; financial award applicants required to submit FAFSA. In 2017, 29 master's, 6 other advanced degrees awarded. *Program availability:* Part-time, evening/weekend, 100% online, blended/hybrid learning. Offers English (MA); history (MA); museum studies (Postbaccalaureate Certificate); music performance (M Mus); music teacher education (M Mus); public history (Postbaccalaureate Certificate). *Application deadline:* For fall admission, 8/1 for domestic students, 6/1 for international students; for spring admission, 11/15 for domestic students, 10/15 for international students; for summer admission, 5/15 for domestic students, 3/30 for international students. Applications are processed on a rolling basis. *Application fee:* $40. Electronic applications accepted. *Application Contact:* Dr. Toby Ziglar, Assistant Dean of the Graduate School, 678-839-1394, Fax: 678-839-1395, E-mail: graduate@westga.edu. *Dean of Arts and Humanities*, Dr. Pauline D. Gagnon, 678-839-5450, Fax: 678-839-5451, E-mail: pgagnon@westga.edu.

College of Education Students: 344 full-time (286 women), 1,243 part-time (1,039 women); includes 538 minority (456 Black or African American, non-Hispanic/Latino; 19 Asian, non-Hispanic/Latino; 46 Hispanic/Latino; 1 Native Hawaiian or other Pacific Islander, non-Hispanic/Latino; 16 Two or more races, non-Hispanic/Latino), 7 international. Average age 36. 685 applicants, 78% accepted, 429 enrolled. *Faculty:* 45 full-time (28 women). Expenses: Contact institution. *Financial support:* Fellowships, research assistantships, teaching assistantships, career-related internships or fieldwork, Federal Work-Study, institutionally sponsored loans, scholarships/grants, and unspecified assistantships available. Support available to part-time students. Financial award application deadline: 4/1; financial award applicants required to submit FAFSA. In 2017, 299 master's, 30 doctorates, 218 other advanced degrees awarded. *Program availability:* Part-time, evening/weekend, 100% online, blended/hybrid learning. Offers business education (M Ed); early childhood education (M Ed, Ed S); educational leadership (M Ed, Ed S); media (M Ed, Ed S); professional counseling (M Ed, Ed S); professional counseling and supervision (Ed D); reading instruction (M Ed); school improvement (Ed D); secondary education (M Ed); special education (M Ed, Ed S); speech language pathology (M Ed); teaching (MAT). *Application deadline:* For fall admission, 7/21 for domestic students, 6/1 for international students; for spring admission, 11/30 for domestic students, 10/15 for international students; for summer admission, 4/15 for domestic students, 3/30 for international students. Applications are processed on a rolling basis. *Application fee:* $40. Electronic applications accepted. *Application Contact:* Dr. Toby Ziglar, Assistant Dean of the Graduate School, 678-839-1394, Fax: 678-839-1395, E-mail: graduate@westga.edu. *Dean, College of Education*, Dr. Diane Hoff, 678-839-6570, Fax: 678-839-6098, E-mail: dhoff@westga.edu.

College of Science and Mathematics Students: 19 full-time (9 women), 68 part-time (23 women); includes 24 minority (15 Black or African American, non-Hispanic/Latino; 1 American Indian or Alaska Native, non-Hispanic/Latino; 6 Asian, non-Hispanic/Latino; 2 Two or more races, non-Hispanic/Latino), 3 international. Average age 31. 72 applicants, 88% accepted, 54 enrolled. *Faculty:* 47 full-time (16 women). Expenses: Contact institution. *Financial support:* Fellowships, research assistantships, teaching assistantships, career-related internships or fieldwork, Federal Work-Study, institutionally sponsored loans, scholarships/grants, and unspecified assistantships available. Support available to part-time students. Financial award application deadline: 4/1; financial award applicants required to submit FAFSA. In 2017, 30 master's, 4 other advanced degrees awarded. *Program availability:* Part-time, evening/weekend, 100% online, blended/hybrid learning. Offers biology (MS); computer science (MS); geographic information systems (Postbaccalaureate Certificate); mathematics (MS). *Application deadline:* For fall admission, 6/1 for domestic and international students; for spring admission, 11/15 for domestic students, 10/15 for international students; for summer admission, 4/1 for domestic students, 3/30 for international students. Applications are processed on a rolling basis. *Application fee:* $40. Electronic applications accepted. *Application Contact:* Dr. Toby Ziglar, Assistant Dean of the Graduate School, 678-839-1394, Fax: 678-839-1395, E-mail: graduate@westga.edu. *Dean of Science and Mathematics*, Dr. Lok C. Lew Yan Voon, 678-839-5190, Fax: 678-839-5191, E-mail: lokl@westga.edu.

College of Social Sciences Students: 124 full-time (84 women), 73 part-time (46 women); includes 69 minority (56 Black or African American, non-Hispanic/Latino; 4 Asian, non-Hispanic/Latino; 6 Hispanic/Latino; 3 Two or more races, non-Hispanic/Latino), 10 international. Average age 32. 95 applicants, 89% accepted, 63 enrolled. *Faculty:* 48 full-time (22 women). Expenses: Contact institution. *Financial support:* Fellowships, research assistantships, teaching assistantships, career-related internships or fieldwork, Federal Work-Study, institutionally sponsored loans, scholarships/grants, and unspecified assistantships available. Support available to part-time students. Financial award application deadline: 4/1; financial award applicants required to submit FAFSA. In 2017, 44 master's, 2 doctorates, 4 other advanced degrees awarded. *Program availability:* Part-time, evening/weekend, 100% online, blended/hybrid learning. Offers criminology (MA); data analysis and evaluation methods (Postbaccalaureate Certificate); European Union studies (Postbaccalaureate Certificate); integrative health systems (Postbaccalaureate Certificate); nonprofit management and community development (Postbaccalaureate Certificate); psychology (MA, PhD); public administration (MPA); public management (Postbaccalaureate Certificate); sociology (MA). *Application deadline:* For fall admission, 7/15 for domestic students, 6/1 for international students; for spring admission, 11/30 for domestic students, 10/15 for international students; for summer admission, 5/15 for domestic students, 3/30 for international students. Applications are processed on a rolling basis. *Application fee:* $40. Electronic applications accepted. *Application Contact:* Dr. Toby Ziglar, Assistant Dean of the Graduate School, 678-839-1394, Fax: 678-839-1395, E-mail: graduate@westga.edu. *Dean of Social Sciences*, Dr. N. Jane McCandless, 678-839-5170, Fax: 678-839-5171, E-mail: jmccandl@westga.edu.

Richards College of Business Students: 64 full-time (34 women), 123 part-time (61 women); includes 69 minority (48 Black or African American, non-Hispanic/Latino; 6 Asian, non-Hispanic/Latino; 13 Hispanic/Latino; 1 Native Hawaiian or other Pacific Islander, non-Hispanic/Latino; 1 Two or more races, non-Hispanic/Latino), 8 international. Average age 32. 129 applicants, 85% accepted, 74 enrolled. *Faculty:* 38 full-time (14 women). Expenses: Contact institution. *Financial support:* Fellowships, research assistantships, teaching assistantships, career-related internships or fieldwork, Federal Work-Study, institutionally sponsored loans, scholarships/grants, and unspecified assistantships available. Support available to part-time students. Financial award application deadline: 4/1; financial award applicants required to submit FAFSA. In 2017, 111 master's awarded. *Program availability:* Part-time, evening/weekend, 100% online, blended/hybrid learning. Offers accounting (MP Acc); business administration (MBA). *Application deadline:* For fall admission, 7/15 for domestic students, 6/1 for international students; for spring admission, 11/15 for domestic students, 10/15 for international students; for summer admission, 5/15 for domestic students, 3/30 for international students. Applications are processed on a rolling basis. *Application fee:* $40. Electronic applications accepted. *Application Contact:* Dr. Toby Ziglar, Assistant Dean of the Graduate School, 678-839-1394, Fax: 678-839-1395, E-mail: graduate@westga.edu. *Dean of Richards College of Business*, Dr. Faye S. McIntyre, 678-839-6467, Fax: 678-839-5040, E-mail: fmcintyr@westga.edu.

Tanner Health System School of Nursing Students: 64 full-time (63 women), 78 part-time (74 women); includes 34 minority (27 Black or African American, non-Hispanic/Latino; 1 Asian, non-Hispanic/Latino; 5 Hispanic/Latino; 1 Two or more races, non-Hispanic/Latino). Average age 41. 92 applicants, 88% accepted, 61 enrolled. *Faculty:* 13 full-time (all women). Expenses: Contact institution. *Financial support:* Fellowships, research assistantships, teaching assistantships, career-related internships or fieldwork, Federal Work-Study, institutionally sponsored loans, scholarships/grants, and unspecified assistantships available. Support available to part-time students. Financial award application deadline: 4/1; financial award applicants required to submit FAFSA. In 2017, 36 master's, 7 doctorates, 1 other advanced degree awarded. *Program availability:* Part-time, evening/weekend, 100% online, blended/hybrid learning. Offers health systems leadership (Post-Master's Certificate); nursing (MSN); nursing education (Ed D, Post-Master's Certificate). *Application deadline:* For fall admission, 2/1 priority date for domestic and international students. Applications are processed on a rolling basis. *Application fee:* $40. Electronic applications accepted. *Application Contact:* Dr. Toby Ziglar, Assistant Dean of the Graduate School, 678-839-1390, Fax: 678-839-1395, E-mail: graduate@westga.edu. *Dean of the School of Nursing*, Dr. Jennifer Schuessler, 678-839-5640, Fax: 678-839-6553, E-mail: jschuess@westga.edu.

UNIVERSITY OF WINDSOR, Windsor, ON N9B 3P4, Canada

General Information Province-supported, coed, university. *Graduate housing:* Rooms and/or apartments available on a first-come, first-served basis to single and married students. Housing application deadline: 6/7. *Research affiliation:* Daimler/Chrysler Automotive Research and Development Centre.

GRADUATE UNITS

Faculty of Graduate Studies *Program availability:* Part-time, evening/weekend. Electronic applications accepted.

Faculty of Arts and Social Sciences *Program availability:* Part-time. Offers adult clinical (MA, PhD); applied social psychology (MA, PhD); arts and social sciences (MA, MFA, MSW, PhD); child clinical (MA, PhD); clinical neuropsychology (MA, PhD); communication and social justice (MA); criminology (MA); English: creative writing and language and literature (MA); English: language and literature (MA); history (MA); philosophy (MA); political science (MA); social work (MSW); sociology (MA); sociology-social justice (PhD); visual arts (MFA). Electronic applications accepted.

Faculty of Education *Program availability:* Part-time, evening/weekend. Offers education (M Ed); educational studies (PhD). Electronic applications accepted.

Faculty of Engineering *Program availability:* Part-time. Offers civil engineering (M Eng, MA Sc, PhD); electrical engineering (M Eng, MA Sc, PhD); engineering (M Eng, MA Sc, PhD); engineering materials (M Eng, MA Sc, PhD); environmental engineering (M Eng, MA Sc, PhD); industrial engineering (M Eng, MA Sc); manufacturing systems engineering (PhD); mechanical engineering (M Eng, MA Sc, PhD). Electronic applications accepted.

Faculty of Human Kinetics *Program availability:* Part-time. Offers human kinetics (MHK). Electronic applications accepted.

Faculty of Nursing Offers nursing (M Sc, MN). Electronic applications accepted.

Faculty of Science *Program availability:* Part-time. Offers biological sciences (M Sc, PhD); chemistry and biochemistry (M Sc, PhD); computer science (M Sc, PhD); earth sciences (M Sc, PhD); economics (MA); mathematics (M Sc); physics (M Sc, PhD); science (M Sc, MA, PhD); statistics (M Sc, PhD). Electronic applications accepted.

GLIER-Great Lakes Institute for Environmental Research Offers environmental science (M Sc, PhD). Electronic applications accepted.

Odette School of Business *Program availability:* Evening/weekend. Offers business (MBA, MM). Electronic applications accepted.

THE UNIVERSITY OF WINNIPEG, Winnipeg, MB R3B 2E9, Canada

General Information Province-supported, coed, comprehensive institution. *Graduate housing:* On-campus housing not available.

GRADUATE UNITS

Faculty of Theology *Program availability:* Part-time. Offers marriage and family therapy (MMFT, Certificate); sacred theology (STM); theology (M Div).

Graduate Studies *Program availability:* Part-time, evening/weekend. Offers history (MA); public administration (MPA); religious studies (MA).

UNIVERSITY OF WISCONSIN–EAU CLAIRE, Eau Claire, WI 54702-4004

General Information State-supported, coed, comprehensive institution. CGS member. *Graduate housing:* Room and/or apartments available on a first-come, first-served basis to single students; on-campus housing not available to married students. Housing application deadline: 5/1. *Research affiliation:* Geological Survey of Canada (geology), Chevron Phillips Chemical Company (chemistry), Excel Energy (geography), American Chemical Society Petroleum Research Fund (chemistry, geology), ASIANetwork (anthropology, biology, geography), Research Corporation (chemistry).

GRADUATE UNITS

College of Arts and Sciences Offers arts and sciences (MA, MSE, Ed S); literature and textual interpretation (MA); public history (MA); school psychology (MSE, Ed S); writing (MA). Electronic applications accepted.

College of Business Offers business (MBA); business administration (MBA). Electronic applications accepted.

College of Education and Human Sciences Offers communication sciences and disorders (MS); education and human sciences (ME-PD, MS, MSE, MST); professional development (ME-PD); reading (MST); special education (MSE). Electronic applications accepted.

College of Nursing and Health Sciences Offers adult-gerontological administration (DNP); adult-gerontological clinical nurse specialist (DNP); adult-gerontological education (MSN); adult-gerontological primary care nurse practitioner (DNP); family health administration (DNP); family health in education (MSN); family health nurse practitioner (DNP); nursing (MSN); nursing and health sciences (MSN, DNP); nursing practice (DNP). Electronic applications accepted.

UNIVERSITY OF WISCONSIN–GREEN BAY, Green Bay, WI 54311-7001

General Information State-supported, coed, comprehensive institution. *Graduate housing:* Room and/or apartments available on a first-come, first-served basis to single students; on-campus housing not available to married students. Housing application deadline: 5/1. *Research affiliation:* Wisconsin Space Grant Consortium (space and aerospace science), UW Sea Grant Institute (Great Lakes and ocean sustainability and stewardship), UW System Applied Research Program (biogas generation), UW Extension Solid and Hazardous Waste Education Center (sustainable use of natural resources), Abbott Laboratories (anaerobic digestion systems).

GRADUATE UNITS

Graduate Studies *Program availability:* Part-time, evening/weekend, 100% online. Offers applied leadership for teaching and learning (MS Ed); environmental science and policy (MS); health and wellness management (MS); management (MS); nursing (MSN); social work (MSW); sustainable management (MS). Electronic applications accepted.

UNIVERSITY OF WISCONSIN–LA CROSSE, La Crosse, WI 54601-3742

General Information State-supported, coed, comprehensive institution. CGS member. *Enrollment:* 10,473 graduate, professional, and undergraduate students; 416 full-time matriculated graduate/professional students (270 women), 339 part-time matriculated graduate/professional students (206 women). *Enrollment by degree level:* 590 master's, 140 doctoral, 25 other advanced degrees. *Graduate faculty:* 102 full-time (48 women), 23 part-time/adjunct (13 women). *Graduate housing:* Room and/or apartments available on a first-come, first-served basis to single students; on-campus housing not available to married students. Housing application deadline: 5/1. *Student services:* Campus employment opportunities, campus safety program, career counseling, child daycare facilities, exercise/wellness program, free psychological counseling, grant writing training, international student services, low-cost health insurance, multicultural affairs office, services for students with disabilities, teacher training, writing training. *Library facilities:* Murphy Library plus 6 others. *Collection:* Books: 427,203 (physical), 415,020 (digital/electronic); Serial titles: 8,561 (physical), 556,900 (digital/electronic); Databases: 255. Weekly public service hours: 55; students can reserve study rooms.

Computer facilities: 200 computers available on campus for general student use. A campuswide network can be accessed from student residence rooms and from off campus. Online class registration is available.
Website: http://www.uwlax.edu/

General Application Contact: Brandon Schaller, Senior Graduate Student Status Examiner, 608-785-8941, E-mail: admissions@uwlax.edu.

GRADUATE UNITS

College of Liberal Studies Students: 55 full-time (47 women), 69 part-time (52 women); includes 14 minority (3 Black or African American, non-Hispanic/Latino; 1 American Indian or Alaska Native, non-Hispanic/Latino; 2 Asian, non-Hispanic/Latino; 4 Hispanic/Latino; 4 Two or more races, non-Hispanic/Latino), 1 international. Average age 26. 166 applicants, 49% accepted, 59 enrolled. *Faculty:* 9 full-time (5 women), 5 part-time/adjunct (3 women). Expenses: Contact institution. *Financial support:* Research assistantships with partial tuition reimbursements, Federal Work-Study, scholarships/grants, health care benefits, and tuition waivers (partial) available. Support available to part-time students. Financial award applicants required to submit FAFSA. In 2017, 56 master's, 11 other advanced degrees awarded. Offers liberal studies (MS Ed, Ed D, Ed S); school psychology (MS Ed, Ed S); student affairs administration (MS Ed, Ed D). *Application fee:* $56. Electronic applications accepted. *Application Contact:* Brandon Schaller, Senior Graduate Student Status Examiner, 608-785-8941, E-mail: admissions@uwlax.edu. *Dean*, Dr. Kim Vogt, 608-785-8113, Fax: 608-785-8119, E-mail: kvogt@uwlax.edu.

College of Science and Health Students: 361 full-time (223 women), 200 part-time (103 women); includes 38 minority (3 American Indian or Alaska Native, non-Hispanic/Latino; 17 Asian, non-Hispanic/Latino; 8 Hispanic/Latino; 10 Two or more races, non-Hispanic/Latino), 29 international. Average age 27. 1,423 applicants, 25% accepted, 251 enrolled. *Faculty:* 80 full-time (36 women), 9 part-time/adjunct (4 women). Expenses: Contact institution. *Financial support:* Research assistantships with tuition reimbursements, Federal Work-Study, scholarships/grants, health care benefits, and tuition waivers (partial) available. Support available to part-time students. Financial award applicants required to submit CSS PROFILE or FAFSA. In 2017, 156 master's, 41 doctorates awarded. Offers aquatic sciences (MS); biology (MS); cellular and molecular biology (MS); clinical exercise physiology (MS); clinical microbiology (MS); community health education (MPH, MS); data science (MS); exercise sport science: human performance (MS); exercise sport science: physical education teaching (MS); human performance (MS); medical dosimetry (MS); microbiology (MS); nurse anesthesia (MS); occupational therapy (MS); physical education teaching (MS); physical therapy (DPT); physician assistant studies (MS); physiology (MS); public health (MPH); recreation management (MS); school health education (MS); science and health (MPH, MS, MSE, DPT); software engineering (MSE); therapeutic recreation (MS). *Application fee:* $56. Electronic applications accepted. *Application Contact:* Brandon Schaller, Senior Graduate Student Status Examiner, 608-785-8941, E-mail: admissions@uwlax.edu. *Interim Dean*, Dr. Mark Sandheinrich, 608-785-8261, Fax: 608-785-8221, E-mail: msandheinrich@uwlax.edu.

School of Education Students: 70 part-time (51 women); includes 2 minority (1 Asian, non-Hispanic/Latino; 1 Two or more races, non-Hispanic/Latino). Average age 30. 59 applicants, 100% accepted, 34 enrolled. *Faculty:* 6 full-time (4 women), 8 part-time/adjunct (6 women). Expenses: Contact institution. *Financial support:* Research assistantships, Federal Work-Study, scholarships/grants, health care benefits, and tuition waivers (partial) available. Support available to part-time students. Financial award application deadline: 3/15; financial award applicants required to submit FAFSA. In 2017, 69 master's, 1 other advanced degree awarded. *Program availability:* Part-time, evening/weekend. Offers English language arts elementary (Graduate Certificate); professional development in education (ME-PD); reading (MS Ed); special education (MS Ed). *Application deadline:* Applications are processed on a rolling basis. Electronic applications accepted. *Application Contact:* Brandon Schaller, Senior Graduate Student Status Examiner, 608-785-8941, E-mail: admissions@uwlax.edu. *Dean, School of Education*, Marcie Wycoff-Horn, 608-785-6786, E-mail: mwycoff-horn@uwlax.edu.

UNIVERSITY OF WISCONSIN–MADISON, Madison, WI 53706-1380

General Information State-supported, coed, university. CGS member. *Graduate housing:* Rooms and/or apartments available on a first-come, first-served basis to single and married students. *Research affiliation:* Morgridge Institute for Research (life sciences: biological sciences), WiCell Research Institute (life sciences: biological sciences), University of Wisconsin Hospitals and Clinics (life sciences: health and medical sciences), William S. Middleton Memorial Veterans Hospital (life sciences: health and medical sciences), Universities Research Association, Inc. (physical and earth sciences: physics and astronomy), U.S. Department of Agriculture (USDA), Dairy Forage Center (life sciences: agriculture).

GRADUATE UNITS

Graduate School *Program availability:* Part-time, evening/weekend, 100% online, blended/hybrid learning. Offers biophysics (PhD); cellular and molecular biology (PhD). Electronic applications accepted.

College of Agricultural and Life Sciences *Program availability:* Part-time. Offers agricultural and applied economics (MA, MS, PhD); agricultural and life sciences (MA, MPS, MS, PhD); agroecology (MS); agronomy (MS, PhD); animal sciences (MS, PhD); bacteriology (MS); biochemistry (MS, PhD); biological systems engineering (MS, PhD); dairy science (MS, PhD); entomology (MS, PhD); food science (MS, PhD); forestry (MS, PhD); genetic counseling (MS); genetics (PhD); horticulture (MS, PhD); life sciences communication (MPS, MS); mass communications (PhD); microbiology (PhD); nutritional sciences (MS, PhD); plant breeding and plant genetics (MS, PhD); plant pathology (MS, PhD); soil science (MS, PhD); wildlife ecology (MS, PhD). Electronic applications accepted.

College of Engineering Students: 1,424 full-time (334 women), 431 part-time (79 women); includes 194 minority (26 Black or African American, non-Hispanic/Latino; 2 American Indian or Alaska Native, non-Hispanic/Latino; 77 Asian, non-Hispanic/Latino; 67 Hispanic/Latino; 1 Native Hawaiian or other Pacific Islander, non-Hispanic/Latino; 21 Two or more races, non-Hispanic/Latino), 928 international. Average age 27. 5,401 applicants, 24% accepted, 489 enrolled. *Faculty:* 212 full-time (40 women). Expenses: Contact institution. *Financial support:* In 2017–18, 1,242 students received support, including 74 fellowships with full tuition reimbursements available, 804 research assistantships with full tuition reimbursements available (averaging $22,247 per year), 327 teaching assistantships with full tuition reimbursements available (averaging $18,350 per year); career-related internships or fieldwork, Federal Work-Study, institutionally sponsored loans, scholarships/grants, health care benefits, and unspecified assistantships also available. Support available to part-time students. Financial award application deadline: 12/1; financial award applicants required to submit FAFSA. In 2017, 436 master's, 185 doctorates awarded. *Program availability:* Part-time, 100% online, blended/hybrid learning. Offers biomedical engineering (MS, PhD); chemical engineering (PhD); construction engineering and management (MS); electrical engineering (MS, PhD); engineering (MS, PhD); engineering mechanics (MS, PhD); environmental chemistry and technology (MS, PhD); environmental science and engineering (MS); geological engineering (MS, PhD); geological/geotechnical engineering (MS); industrial engineering (MS, PhD); machine learning and signal processing (MS); manufacturing systems engineering (MS); materials science and engineering (MS, PhD); mechanical engineering (MS, PhD); nuclear engineering and engineering physics (MS, PhD); structural engineering (MS); transportation engineering (MS); water resources engineering (MS). *Application deadline:* Applications are processed on a rolling basis. *Application fee:* $75 ($81 for international students). Electronic applications accepted. *Application Contact:* Information Contact, 608-262-2433, Fax: 608-265-9505, E-mail: gradadmiss@grad.wisc.edu. *Dean*, Dr. Ian M. Robertson, 608-262-3482, Fax: 608-262-6400, E-mail: engr-dean_engr@wisc.edu.

College of Letters and Science *Program availability:* Part-time, evening/weekend, online learning. Offers African history (MA, PhD); African languages and literature (MA, PhD);

Afro-American studies (MA); applied English linguistics (MA); archaeology (PhD); art history (MA, PhD); astronomy (PhD); atmospheric and oceanic sciences (MS, PhD); audiology (Au D); biological anthropology (PhD); biology of brain and behavior (PhD); biometry (MS); botany (MS, PhD); cartography and geographic information systems (MS); Central Asian history (MA, PhD); chemistry (MS, PhD); Chinese literature (MA, PhD); Chinese thought (MA, PhD); choral (MM, DMA); civilizations and cultures (PhD); classics (MA, PhD); clinical psychology (PhD); cognitive neurosciences (PhD); communication science (MA, PhD); comparative literature (MA, PhD); comparative world history (MA, PhD); composition (MM, DMA); composition and rhetoric (PhD); computer sciences (MS, PhD); creative writing (MFA); cultural anthropology (PhD); curriculum and instruction (MS, PhD); developmental psychology (PhD); East Asian history (MA, PhD); economics (PhD); English language and linguistics (PhD); ethnomusicology (MA, PhD); European history (MA, PhD); family and consumer journalism (PhD); film (MA, PhD); French (MA, PhD); French studies (MFS, Certificate); gender and women's history (MA, PhD); geographic information systems (Certificate); geography (MS, PhD); geology (MS, PhD); geophysics (MS, PhD); German (MA, PhD); Greek (MA); Hebrew and Semitic studies (MA, PhD); historical musicology (PhD); history of medicine (MA); history of science (MA, PhD); instrumental (MM, DMA); Italian (MA, PhD); Japanese linguistics (MA, PhD); Japanese literature (MA, PhD); journalism and mass communication (MA); landscape architecture (MS); languages and cultures of Asia (MA); languages and literatures (PhD); Latin (MA); Latin American and Caribbean history (MA, PhD); Latin American, Caribbean and Iberian studies (MA); letters and science (MA, MFA, MFS, MIPA, MM, MPA, MS, MSW, DMA, PhD, Certificate); library and information studies (MA, PhD); linguistics (MA, PhD); literary studies (MA, PhD); mass communication (PhD); mathematics (PhD); media and cultural studies (MA, PhD); Middle Eastern history (MA, PhD); music (MA, MM, DMA, PhD); music education (MM); music history (MA); music performance (MM, DMA); music theory (MA, PhD); normal aspects of speech, language and hearing (MS, PhD); orchestral (MM, DMA); perception (PhD); philosophy (MA, PhD); physics (MA, MS, PhD); political science (PhD); Portuguese (MA, PhD); psychology (PhD); public policy and administration (MIPA, MPA); religions of Asia (PhD); rhetoric (MA, PhD); rural sociology (MS); Scandinavian studies (MA, PhD); Slavic languages and literature (MA, PhD); social and personality psychology (PhD); social welfare (PhD); social work (MSW); sociology (MS, PhD); South Asian history (MA, PhD); Southeast Asian history (MA, PhD); Southeast Asian studies (MA); Spanish (MA, PhD); speech-language pathology (MS, PhD); statistics (MS, PhD); theatre and drama (MA, MFA, PhD); United States history (MA, PhD); urban and regional planning (MS, PhD); zoology (MA, MS, PhD). Electronic applications accepted.

Gaylord Nelson Institute for Environmental Studies *Program availability:* Part-time. Offers environment and resources (MS, PhD); environmental conservation (MS); environmental studies (MS, PhD); water resources management (MS). Electronic applications accepted.

School of Education Offers administration (Certificate); art (MFA); counseling (MS); counseling psychology (PhD); curriculum and instruction (MS, PhD); education (MA, MFA, MS, PhD, Certificate); educational policy (MS, PhD); educational policy studies (MA, PhD); educational psychology (MS, PhD); English as a second language (MS); global higher education (MS); kinesiology (MS, PhD); occupational therapy (MS, PhD); rehabilitation psychology (MA, MS, PhD); special education (MA, MS, PhD).

School of Human Ecology Offers consumer behavior and family economics (MS, PhD); design studies (MFA, MS, PhD); human development and family studies (MS, PhD). Electronic applications accepted.

Wisconsin School of Business *Program availability:* Part-time, evening/weekend. Offers accountancy (M Acc); accounting and information systems (PhD); actuarial science, risk management and insurance (PhD); applied security analysis (MBA); arts administration (MBA); brand and product management (MBA); business (M Acc, MBA, PhD); corporate finance and investment banking (MBA); finance, investment and banking (PhD); general management (MBA); information systems (PhD); management and human resources (PhD); marketing (PhD); marketing research (MBA); operations and technology management (MBA); operations management (PhD); real estate (MBA); real estate and urban land economics (PhD); risk management and insurance (MBA); strategic human resource management (MBA); supply chain management (MBA); taxation (M Acc). Electronic applications accepted.

Law School Students: 525 full-time (249 women), 31 part-time (19 women); includes 113 minority (33 Black or African American, non-Hispanic/Latino; 3 American Indian or Alaska Native, non-Hispanic/Latino; 14 Asian, non-Hispanic/Latino; 51 Hispanic/Latino; 12 Two or more races, non-Hispanic/Latino), 54 international. Average age 26. 1,375 applicants, 42% accepted, 148 enrolled. *Faculty:* 67 full-time (40 women), 67 part-time/adjunct (22 women). Expenses: Contact institution. *Financial support:* In 2017–18, 398 students received support. Fellowships, research assistantships, teaching assistantships, career-related internships or fieldwork, Federal Work-Study, scholarships/grants, health care benefits, tuition waivers (full and partial), and unspecified assistantships available. Support available to part-time students. Financial award application deadline: 4/1; financial award applicants required to submit FAFSA. In 2017, 41 master's, 166 doctorates awarded. *Program availability:* Part-time, evening/weekend. Offers law (LL M, JD, SJD). *Application deadline:* For fall admission, 4/1 for domestic and international students. Applications are processed on a rolling basis. *Application fee:* $60. Electronic applications accepted. *Application Contact:* Rebecca L. Scheller, Assistant Dean for Admissions and Financial Aid, 608-262-5914, Fax: 608-263-3190, E-mail: admissions@law.wisc.edu. *Dean*, Margaret Raymond, 608-262-0618, Fax: 608-890-0134.

School of Medicine and Public Health Expenses: Contact institution. Offers biomedical data science (MS, PhD); cancer biology (PhD); cellular and molecular pathology (PhD); clinical investigation (MS, PhD); endocrinology-reproductive physiology (MS, PhD); epidemiology (MS, PhD); genetic counselor studies (MGCS); medical physics (MS, PhD); medicine (MD); medicine and public health (MGCS, MPA, MPH, MS, DPT, MD, PhD); molecular and cellular pharmacology (PhD); molecular and environmental toxicology (MS, PhD); neuroscience (PhD); physical therapy (DPT); physician assistant (MPA); physiology (PhD); population health (MS, PhD); public health (MPH). Electronic applications accepted. *Dean*, Dr. Robert N. Golden, 608-263-4910.

School of Nursing *Program availability:* Part-time. Offers adult/gerontology (DNP); nursing (PhD); pediatrics (DNP); psychiatric mental health (DNP). Electronic applications accepted.

School of Pharmacy Offers pharmaceutical sciences (PhD); pharmacy (MS, PhD, Pharm D); social and administrative sciences in pharmacy (MS, PhD). Electronic applications accepted.

School of Veterinary Medicine Offers veterinary medicine (MS, DVM, PhD).

UNIVERSITY OF WISCONSIN–MILWAUKEE, Milwaukee, WI 53201-0413

General Information State-supported, coed, university. CGS member. *Enrollment:* 25,381 graduate, professional, and undergraduate students; 2,671 full-time matriculated graduate/professional students (1,590 women), 1,760 part-time matriculated graduate/professional students (1,073 women). *Enrollment by degree level:* 2,952 master's, 1,369 doctoral, 110 other advanced degrees. *Graduate housing:* Rooms and/or apartments available on a first-come, first-served basis to single and married students. Housing application deadline: 5/1. *Student services:* Campus employment opportunities, campus safety program, career counseling, child daycare facilities, exercise/wellness program, free psychological counseling, grant writing training, international student services, low-cost health insurance, multicultural affairs office, services for students with disabilities, writing training. *Library facilities:* Golda Meir Library. *Collection:* Books: 2.5 million (physical), 178,268 (digital/electronic); Serial titles: 112,752 (physical). Students can reserve study rooms. *Research affiliation:* Rockwell Automation (informatics, sensors and devices, materials), Johnson Controls (environment, advanced automation), GE Healthcare (informatics, biomedical imaging), Veolia Water S. A. (water research), We Energies (environment, wind turbine technology).

Computer facilities: Computer purchase and lease plans are available. 500 computers available on campus for general student use. A campuswide network can be accessed from student residence rooms and from off campus. Online class registration is available.
Website: http://www.uwm.edu/

General Application Contact: General Information Contact, 414-229-6569, Fax: 414-229-6967, E-mail: gradschool-staff@uwm.edu.

GRADUATE UNITS

Graduate School Students: 2,671 full-time (1,590 women), 1,760 part-time (1,073 women); includes 755 minority (230 Black or African American, non-Hispanic/Latino; 14 American Indian or Alaska Native, non-Hispanic/Latino; 167 Asian, non-Hispanic/Latino; 49 Hispanic/Latino; 1 Native Hawaiian or other Pacific Islander, non-Hispanic/Latino; 294 Two or more races, non-Hispanic/Latino), 687 international. Average age 32. 4,614 applicants, 51% accepted, 1466 enrolled. Expenses: Contact institution. *Financial support:* Fellowships with partial tuition reimbursements, research assistantships with full tuition reimbursements, teaching assistantships with full tuition reimbursements, career-related internships or fieldwork, Federal Work-Study, scholarships/grants, health care benefits, tuition waivers (partial), and unspecified assistantships available. Support available to part-time students. Financial award application deadline: 6/30; financial award applicants required to submit FAFSA. In 2017, 323 master's, 44 doctorates, 41 other advanced degrees awarded. *Program availability:* Part-time, evening/weekend. *Application deadline:* Applications are processed on a rolling basis. *Application fee:* $56 ($96 for international students). Electronic applications accepted. *Application Contact:* General Information Contact, 414-229-6569, Fax: 414-229-6967, E-mail: gradschool-staff@uwm.edu. *Dean*, Marija Gajdardziska-Josifovska, 414-229-5220, E-mail: mgj@uwm.edu.

College of Engineering and Applied Science Students: 233 full-time (49 women), 182 part-time (44 women); includes 39 minority (4 Black or African American, non-Hispanic/Latino; 23 Asian, non-Hispanic/Latino; 5 Hispanic/Latino; 7 Two or more races, non-Hispanic/Latino), 267 international. Average age 30. 575 applicants, 58% accepted, 110 enrolled. Expenses: Contact institution. *Financial support:* Fellowships, research assistantships, teaching assistantships, career-related internships or fieldwork, Federal Work-Study, and unspecified assistantships available. Support available to part-time students. Financial award application deadline: 4/15. In 2017, 30 master's, 9 doctorates awarded. *Program availability:* Part-time. Offers biomedical engineering (MS); civil engineering (MS, PhD); computer science (MS); electrical and computer engineering (MS); electrical engineering (PhD); engineering and applied science (MS, PhD); engineering mechanics (MS); health information systems (PhD); health services management and policy (PhD); industrial and management engineering (MS); industrial engineering (PhD); knowledge based systems (PhD); manufacturing engineering (MS); materials (PhD); materials engineering (MS); mechanical engineering (MS); medical imaging and instrumentation (PhD); public health informatics (PhD). *Application deadline:* For fall admission, 1/1 for domestic students; for spring admission, 9/1 for domestic students. Applications are processed on a rolling basis. *Application fee:* $56 ($96 for international students). Electronic applications accepted. *Application Contact:* Betty Warras, General Information Contact, 414-229-6169, Fax: 414-229-6958, E-mail: ceas-graduate@uwm.edu. *Dean*, Dr. Brett Peters, 414-229-4126, E-mail: ceas-deans-office@uwm.edu.

College of Health Sciences Students: 303 full-time (231 women), 44 part-time (28 women); includes 38 minority (6 Black or African American, non-Hispanic/Latino; 1 American Indian or Alaska Native, non-Hispanic/Latino; 12 Asian, non-Hispanic/Latino; 1 Hispanic/Latino; 18 Two or more races, non-Hispanic/Latino), 25 international. Average age 28. 292 applicants, 42% accepted, 88 enrolled. Expenses: Contact institution. *Financial support:* Research assistantships, teaching assistantships, career-related internships or fieldwork, Federal Work-Study, and unspecified assistantships available. Support available to part-time students. Financial award application deadline: 3/30. In 2017, 32 master's, 1 doctorate, 1 other advanced degree awarded. *Program availability:* Part-time. Offers assistive technology and accessible design (Graduate Certificate); assistive technology and design (MS); athletic training (MS); biomedical sciences (MS); communication sciences and disorders (MS); disability and occupation (MS); ergonomics (MS); health care informatics (MS); health sciences (MHA, MS, DPT, PhD, Graduate Certificate); healthcare administration (MHA); kinesiology (MS, PhD); physical therapy (DPT); therapeutic recreation (MS). *Application deadline:* For fall admission, 1/1 priority date for domestic students; for spring admission, 9/1 for domestic students. Applications are processed on a rolling basis. *Application fee:* $56 ($96 for international students). *Application Contact:* Office of Student Affairs, 414-229-2758, Fax: 414-229-3373, E-mail: chs-info@uwm.edu. *Dean*, Ron A. Cisler, PhD, 414-229-5663, E-mail: rac@uwm.edu.

College of Letters and Science Students: 740 full-time (377 women), 347 part-time (193 women); includes 124 minority (37 Black or African American, non-Hispanic/Latino; 3 American Indian or Alaska Native, non-Hispanic/Latino; 27 Asian, non-Hispanic/Latino; 8 Hispanic/Latino; 49 Two or more races, non-Hispanic/Latino), 234 international. Average age 31. 1,423 applicants, 33% accepted, 328 enrolled. Expenses: Contact institution. *Financial support:* Fellowships, research assistantships, teaching assistantships, career-related internships or fieldwork, Federal Work-Study, unspecified assistantships, and project assistantships available. Support available to part-time students. Financial award application deadline: 4/15. In 2017, 35 master's, 18 doctorates, 4 other advanced degrees awarded. *Program* *availability:* Part-time. Offers Africology (PhD); anthropology (MS, PhD); art history (MA); art history and criticism (MA); art museum studies (MA); cellular and molecular biology (MS, PhD); chemistry and biochemistry (MS, PhD); communication (MA, PhD); economics (MA, PhD); English (MA, PhD); foreign languages and literature (MA); geological sciences (MS, PhD); history (MA, PhD); human resources and labor relations (MHRLR); international human resources and labor relations (Graduate Certificate); international interests (MA, MS, PhD); interpreting (Graduate Certificate); language, literature, and translation (MA, MALLT); letters and science (MA, MALLT, MHRLR, MLS, MPA, MS, MSP, PhD, Graduate Certificate); liberal studies (MLS); linguistics (MA, PhD); mathematics (MS, PhD); media studies (MA); mediation and negotiation (Graduate Certificate); microbiology (MS, PhD); museum studies (Graduate Certificate); philosophy (MA); physical geography and environmental studies (MA, MS, PhD); physics (MS, PhD); political science (MA, PhD); psychology (MS, PhD); public administration (MPA); rhetorical leadership (Graduate Certificate); sociology (MA, PhD); Spanish and Portuguese (MA); teaching English to speakers of other languages, adult- and university-level (Graduate Certificate); translation (Graduate Certificate); urban development (MA, MS, PhD); urban studies (MS, PhD); women's and gender studies (MA, Graduate Certificate). *Application deadline:* For fall admission, 1/1 priority date for domestic students; for spring admission, 9/1 for domestic students. *Application fee:* $56 ($96 for international students). Electronic applications accepted. *Application Contact:* General Letters and Science Support, 414-229-7711, E-mail: let-sci@uwm.edu. *Acting Dean*, Dave Clark, 414-375-0457, E-mail: dclark@uwm.edu.

College of Nursing Students: 181 full-time (153 women), 128 part-time (117 women); includes 73 minority (23 Black or African American, non-Hispanic/Latino; 1 American Indian or Alaska Native, non-Hispanic/Latino; 17 Asian, non-Hispanic/Latino; 3 Hispanic/Latino; 29 Two or more races, non-Hispanic/Latino), 11 international. Average age 36. 154 applicants, 59% accepted, 60 enrolled. Expenses: Contact institution. *Financial support:* Fellowships, research assistantships, teaching assistantships, career-related internships or fieldwork, Federal Work-Study, health care benefits, unspecified assistantships, and project assistantships available. Support available to part-time students. Financial award application deadline: 4/15; financial award applicants required to submit FAFSA. In 2017, 26 master's, 54 doctorates, 2 other advanced degrees awarded. *Program availability:* Part-time. Offers clinical nurse specialist (Graduate Certificate); family nurse practitioner (Graduate Certificate); nursing (MN, DNP, PhD); sustainable peacebuilding (MSP). *Application deadline:* For fall admission, 1/1 priority date for domestic students; for spring admission, 9/1 for domestic students. *Application fee:* $56 ($96 for international students). Electronic applications accepted. *Application Contact:* Student Affairs Office, 414-229-5047, E-mail: uwmnurse@uwm.edu. *Interim Dean*, Dr. Kim Litwack, 414-229-4189, E-mail: litwack@uwm.edu.

Helen Bader School of Social Welfare Students: 214 full-time (179 women), 119 part-time (96 women); includes 90 minority (37 Black or African American, non-Hispanic/Latino; 1 American Indian or Alaska Native, non-Hispanic/Latino; 10 Asian, non-Hispanic/Latino; 2 Hispanic/Latino; 40 Two or more races, non-Hispanic/Latino), 5 international. Average age 30. 380 applicants, 59% accepted, 136 enrolled. Expenses: Contact institution. *Financial support:* Fellowships with full tuition reimbursements, research assistantships with full tuition reimbursements, teaching assistantships with full tuition reimbursements, career-related internships or fieldwork, Federal Work-Study, health care benefits, unspecified assistantships, and project assistantships available. Support available to part-time students. Financial award application deadline: 4/15; financial award applicants required to submit FAFSA. In 2017, 164 master's, 9 other advanced degrees awarded. *Program availability:* Part-time. Offers applied data analysis using SAS (Graduate Certificate); applied gerontology (Graduate Certificate); crime analytics (MS); criminal justice (MS); nonprofit management (Graduate Certificate); social welfare (PhD); social work (MSW, PhD). *Application deadline:* For fall admission, 1/1 priority date for domestic students; for spring admission, 9/1 for domestic students. *Application fee:* $56 ($96 for international students). Electronic applications accepted. *Application Contact:* Deb Padgett, Associate Professor, Social Work, 414-229-6452, E-mail: dpadgett@uwm.edu. *Dean and Professor*, Stan Stojkovic, PhD, 414-229-4400, E-mail: stojkovi@uwm.edu.

Joseph J. Zilber School of Public Health Students: 64 full-time (54 women), 24 part-time (18 women); includes 24 minority (5 Black or African American, non-Hispanic/Latino; 11 Asian, non-Hispanic/Latino; 8 Two or more races, non-Hispanic/Latino), 10 international. Average age 31. 66 applicants, 74% accepted, 34 enrolled. Expenses: Contact institution. *Financial support:* Fellowships and scholarships/grants available. In 2017, 28 master's, 2 doctorates awarded. *Program availability:* Part-time. Offers biostatistics (MPH); community and behavioral health promotion (MPH); environmental health sciences (MPH); epidemiology (MPH, PhD); public and population health (Graduate Certificate); public health (MPH, PhD, Graduate Certificate); public health policy and administration (MPH); public health: biostatistics (PhD); public health: community and behavioral health promotion (PhD). Electronic applications accepted. *Application Contact:* Advisor, 414-227-3001, Fax: 414-227-3002, E-mail: applyph@uwm.edu. *Interim Dean*, Ronald Perez, 414-229-4587, E-mail: perez@uwm.edu.

Lubar School of Business Students: 321 full-time (137 women), 252 part-time (93 women); includes 94 minority (25 Black or African American, non-Hispanic/Latino; 1 American Indian or Alaska Native, non-Hispanic/Latino; 28 Asian, non-Hispanic/Latino; 6 Hispanic/Latino; 34 Two or more races, non-Hispanic/Latino), 66 international. Average age 32. 426 applicants, 61% accepted, 191 enrolled. Expenses: Contact institution. *Financial support:* Fellowships with full tuition reimbursements, research assistantships with full tuition reimbursements, teaching assistantships with full tuition reimbursements, career-related internships or fieldwork, Federal Work-Study, health care benefits, unspecified assistantships, and project assistantships available. Support available to part-time students. Financial award application deadline: 4/15; financial award applicants required to submit FAFSA. In 2017, 266 master's, 8 doctorates, 21 other advanced degrees awarded. *Program availability:* Part-time, evening/weekend. Offers business administration (MBA); business analytics (Graduate Certificate); enterprise resource planning (Graduate Certificate); executive business administration (EMBA); information technology management (MS); investment management (Graduate Certificate); management science (MS, PhD, Graduate Certificate); nonprofit management (Graduate Certificate); nonprofit management and leadership (MS); state and local taxation (Graduate Certificate); technology entrepreneurship (Graduate Certificate). *Application deadline:* For fall admission, 1/1 priority date for domestic students; for spring admission, 9/1 for domestic students. *Application fee:* $56 ($96 for international students). Electronic applications accepted. *Application Contact:* Business Graduate Student Services, 414-229-5403, E-mail: mba-ms@uwm.edu. *Dean*, V. Kanti Prasad, 414-229-6256, E-mail: dean-prasad@uwm.edu.

Peck School of the Arts Students: 91 full-time (57 women), 15 part-time (10 women); includes 14 minority (2 Black or African American, non-Hispanic/Latino; 1 Asian, non-Hispanic/Latino; 4 Hispanic/Latino; 7 Two or more races, non-Hispanic/Latino), 25 international. Average age 30. 124 applicants, 51% accepted, 37 enrolled. Expenses: Contact institution. *Financial support:* Teaching assistantships, career-related internships or fieldwork, Federal Work-Study, health care benefits, unspecified assistantships, and project assistantships available. Support available to part-time students. Financial award application deadline: 4/15; financial award applicants required to submit FAFSA. In 2017, 63 master's, 1 other advanced degree awarded. *Program availability:* Part-time. Offers arts (MA, MFA, MM, MS, CAS, Graduate Certificate). *Application deadline:* For fall admission, 1/1 priority date for domestic students; for spring admission, 9/1 for domestic students. *Application fee:* $56 ($96 for international students). Electronic applications accepted. *Application Contact:* Arts Student Services, 414-229-4763, E-mail: uwmpsoa@uwm.edu. *Dean*, Scott Emmons, 414-229-4762, E-mail: semm@uwm.edu.

School of Architecture and Urban Planning Students: 107 full-time (51 women), 14 part-time (4 women); includes 18 minority (2 Black or African American, non-Hispanic/Latino; 1 American Indian or Alaska Native, non-Hispanic/Latino; 4 Asian, non-Hispanic/Latino; 2 Hispanic/Latino; 9 Two or more races, non-Hispanic/Latino), 17 international. Average age 29. 168 applicants, 49% accepted, 38 enrolled. Expenses: Contact institution. *Financial support:* Fellowships, research assistantships, teaching assistantships, career-related internships or fieldwork, Federal Work-Study, health care benefits, unspecified assistantships, and project assistantships available. Support available to part-time students. Financial award application deadline: 4/15; financial award applicants required to submit FAFSA. In 2017, 62 master's, 5 doctorates, 9 other advanced degrees awarded. *Program availability:* Part-time. Offers architecture (M Arch, MS Arch, PhD); architecture and urban planning (M Arch, MS Arch, MUP, PhD, Graduate Certificate); geographic information systems (Graduate Certificate); urban planning (MUP). *Application deadline:* For fall admission, 1/1 priority date for domestic students; for spring admission, 9/1 for domestic students. *Application fee:* $56 ($96 for international students). Electronic applications accepted. *Application Contact:* Student Advising Office, 414-229-4015, E-mail: sarup-grad@uwm.edu. *Dean*, Robert Greenstreet, 414-229-4016, E-mail: bobg@uwm.edu.

School of Education Students: 261 full-time (200 women), 370 part-time (278 women); includes 181 minority (74 Black or African American, non-Hispanic/Latino; 6 American Indian or Alaska Native, non-Hispanic/Latino; 23 Asian, non-Hispanic/Latino; 12 Hispanic/Latino; 1 Native Hawaiian or other Pacific Islander, non-Hispanic/Latino; 65 Two or more races, non-Hispanic/Latino), 9 international. Average age 34. 518 applicants, 51% accepted, 181 enrolled. Expenses: Contact institution. *Financial support:* Fellowships, teaching assistantships, career-related internships or fieldwork, Federal Work-Study, health care benefits, unspecified assistantships, and project assistantships available. Support available to part-time students. Financial award application deadline: 4/15; financial award applicants required to submit FAFSA. In 2017, 169 master's, 24 doctorates, 32 other advanced degrees awarded. *Program availability:* Part-time. Offers administrative leadership (MS); autism spectrum disorders (Graduate Certificate); children's mental health for school professionals (Graduate Certificate); counseling psychology (PhD); cultural foundations of community engagement and education (MS); curriculum and instruction (MS); education (MS, PhD, CAS, Ed S, Graduate Certificate); educational policy (Graduate Certificate); educational statistics and measurement (MS, PhD); exceptional education (MS); learning and development (MS, PhD); multicultural knowledge of mental health practices (Graduate Certificate); school counseling (MS); school counseling (Graduate Certificate); school psychology (MS, PhD, Ed S); support services for online students in higher education (Graduate Certificate); teaching and learning in higher education (Graduate Certificate); transition for students with disabilities (Graduate Certificate); urban education (PhD). *Application deadline:* For fall admission, 1/1 priority date for domestic students; for spring admission, 9/1 for domestic students. *Application fee:* $56 ($96 for international students). Electronic applications accepted. *Application Contact:* Education Office of Student Services, 414-229-4721, E-mail: soeoss@uwm.edu. *Dean*, Alan Shoho, 414-229-4181, E-mail: shoho@uwm.edu.

School of Freshwater Sciences Students: 34 full-time (20 women), 17 part-time (7 women); includes 6 minority (1 Black or African American, non-Hispanic/Latino; 1 Hispanic/Latino; 4 Two or more races, non-Hispanic/Latino), 2 international. Average age 31. 29 applicants, 72% accepted, 14 enrolled. Expenses: Contact institution. *Financial support:* Fellowships, research assistantships, teaching assistantships, unspecified assistantships available. Financial award applicants required to submit FAFSA. In 2017, 16 master's, 3 doctorates awarded. Offers freshwater sciences (MS, PhD). *Application fee:* $56 ($96 for international students). Electronic applications accepted. *Application Contact:* Dr. Harvey Bootsma, Graduate Program Representative, 414-382-1717, E-mail: hbootsma@uwm.edu. *Dean*, J. Val Klump, 414-382-1715, E-mail: vklump@uwm.edu.

School of Information Studies Students: 120 full-time (81 women), 243 part-time (181 women); includes 52 minority (13 Black or African American, non-Hispanic/Latino; 11 Asian, non-Hispanic/Latino; 4 Hispanic/Latino; 24 Two or more races, non-Hispanic/Latino), 16 international. Average age 34. 276 applicants, 64% accepted, 122 enrolled. Expenses: Contact institution. *Financial support:* Fellowships, research assistantships, teaching assistantships, career-related internships or fieldwork, Federal Work-Study, health care benefits, unspecified assistantships, and project assistantships available. Support available to part-time students. Financial award application deadline: 4/15; financial award applicants required to submit FAFSA. In 2017, 169 master's, 4 doctorates, 1 other advanced degree awarded. *Program availability:* Part-time. Offers information studies (MLIS, MS, PhD, CAS). *Application deadline:* For fall admission, 1/1 priority date for domestic students; for spring admission, 9/1 for domestic students. *Application fee:* $56 ($96 for international students). Electronic applications accepted. *Application Contact:* Linda Barajas, Admissions Coordinator, 414-229-3316, E-mail: barajas@uwm.edu. *Dean/Professor*, Tomas A. Lipinski, 414-229-4707, E-mail: tlipinsk@uwm.edu.

UNIVERSITY OF WISCONSIN–OSHKOSH, Oshkosh, WI 54901

General Information State-supported, coed, comprehensive institution. *Graduate housing:* Room and/or apartments available on a first-come, first-served basis to single students; on-campus housing not available to married students.

GRADUATE UNITS

Graduate Studies *Program availability:* Part-time, evening/weekend. Offers social work (MSW). Electronic applications accepted.

College of Business *Program availability:* Part-time. Offers business (GMBA, MBA); business administration (MBA); global business administration (GMBA). Electronic applications accepted.

College of Education and Human Services *Program availability:* Part-time, evening/weekend. Offers counseling (MSE); cross-categorical (MSE); curriculum and instruction (MSE); early childhood: exceptional education needs (MSE); education and human services (MS, MSE); educational leadership (MS); non-licensure (MSE); reading education (MSE). Electronic applications accepted.

College of Letters and Science *Program availability:* Part-time, evening/weekend. Offers biology (MS); English (MA); experimental psychology (MS); general agency (MPA); health care (MPA); industrial/organizational psychology (MS); letters and science (MA, MPA, MS, MSW); mathematics education (MS). Electronic applications accepted.

College of Nursing *Program availability:* Part-time. Offers adult health and illness (MSN); family nurse practitioner (MSN). Electronic applications accepted.

UNIVERSITY OF WISCONSIN–PARKSIDE, Kenosha, WI 53141-2000

General Information State-supported, coed, comprehensive institution. *Graduate housing:* Room and/or apartments available on a first-come, first-served basis to single students; on-campus housing not available to married students.

GRADUATE UNITS

College of Business, Economics, and Computing *Program availability:* Part-time, evening/weekend. Offers business administration (MBA); business, economics, and computing (MBA, MSCIS); computer and information systems (MSCIS). Electronic applications accepted.

College of Natural and Health Sciences *Program availability:* Part-time. Offers applied molecular biology (MSBS); clinical mental health counseling (MS); health and wellness management (MS); natural and health sciences (MS, MSBS); sport management (MS); sustainable management (MS). Electronic applications accepted.

UNIVERSITY OF WISCONSIN–PLATTEVILLE, Platteville, WI 53818-3099

General Information State-supported, coed, comprehensive institution. *Enrollment:* 8,429 graduate, professional, and undergraduate students; 53 full-time matriculated graduate/professional students (38 women), 789 part-time matriculated graduate/professional students (355 women). *Enrollment by degree level:* 842 master's. *Graduate housing:* On-campus housing not available. *Student services:* Campus employment opportunities, campus safety program, career counseling, child daycare facilities, exercise/wellness program, free psychological counseling, grant writing training, international student services, low-cost health insurance, multicultural affairs office, services for students with disabilities, teacher training, writing training. *Library facilities:* Karrmann Library plus 1 other. *Collection:* Books: 167,304 (physical), 59,292 (digital/electronic); Serial titles: 1,151 (physical), 44,687 (digital/electronic); Databases: 123. Weekly public service hours: 87.

Computer facilities: 200 computers available on campus for general student use. A campuswide network can be accessed from student residence rooms and from off campus. Online class registration is available.
Website: http://www.uwplatt.edu/

General Application Contact: Dee Dunbar, School of Graduate Studies, 608-342-1322, Fax: 608-342-1389, E-mail: gradstudies@uwplatt.edu.

GRADUATE UNITS

School of Graduate Studies Students: 65 full-time (42 women), 786 part-time (356 women); includes 163 minority (77 Black or African American, non-Hispanic/Latino; 4 American Indian or Alaska Native, non-Hispanic/Latino; 41 Asian, non-Hispanic/Latino; 41 Hispanic/Latino). Expenses: Contact institution. *Financial support:* Research assistantships with partial tuition reimbursements, career-related internships or fieldwork, Federal Work-Study, institutionally sponsored loans, scholarships/grants, and unspecified assistantships available. Support available to part-time students. Financial award applicants required to submit FAFSA. In 2017, 263 master's awarded. *Program availability:* Part-time, evening/weekend, online learning. *Application deadline:* For fall admission, 9/1 for domestic students, 7/1 for international students; for spring admission, 1/1 for domestic students, 11/15 for international students. Applications are processed on a rolling basis. *Application fee:* $56. Electronic applications accepted. *Application Contact:* Dee Dunbar, School of Graduate Studies, 608-342-1322, Fax: 608-342-1454, E-mail: gradstudies@uwplatt.edu. *Dean,* Dr. Craig Wilson, 608-342-1322, E-mail: gradstudies@uwplatt.edu.

College of Engineering, Mathematics and Science Students: 3 full-time (2 women); includes 2 minority (1 Black or African American, non-Hispanic/Latino; 1 Asian, non-Hispanic/Latino). Expenses: Contact institution. *Financial support:* Research assistantships with partial tuition reimbursements available. *Program availability:* Part-time. Offers computer science (MS); engineering, mathematics and science (MS). *Application deadline:* For fall admission, 9/1 for domestic students, 7/1 for international students; for spring admission, 1/1 for domestic students, 11/15 for international students. *Application fee:* $56. *Application Contact:* Dee Dunbar, School of Graduate Studies, 608-342-1322, Fax: 608-342-1454, E-mail: gradstudies@uwplatt.edu. *Dean,* Molly Gribb, 608-342-1561, Fax: 608-342-1566, E-mail: ems@uwplatt.edu.

College of Liberal Arts and Education Students: 41 full-time (32 women), 109 part-time (82 women); includes 13 minority (12 Black or African American, non-Hispanic/Latino; 1 Hispanic/Latino). 37 applicants, 86% accepted, 25 enrolled. Expenses: Contact institution. *Financial support:* Research assistantships with partial tuition reimbursements, career-related internships or fieldwork, Federal Work-Study, institutionally sponsored loans, scholarships/grants, and unspecified assistantships available. Support available to part-time students. Financial award applicants required to submit FAFSA. In 2017, 62 master's awarded. *Program availability:* Part-time, evening/weekend. Offers adult education (MSE); liberal arts and education (MSE). *Application deadline:* For fall admission, 9/1 for domestic students, 7/15 for international students; for spring admission, 1/1 for domestic students, 11/15 for international students. Applications are processed on a rolling basis. *Application fee:* $56. Electronic applications accepted. *Application Contact:* Dee Dunbar, School of Graduate Studies, 608-342-1322, Fax: 608-342-1454, E-mail: gradstudies@uwplatt.edu. *Interim Dean,* Melissa Gromley, 608-342-1151, E-mail: lae@uwplatt.edu.

Distance Learning Center Students: 16 full-time (8 women), 640 part-time (268 women); includes 114 minority (34 Black or African American, non-Hispanic/Latino; 5 American Indian or Alaska Native, non-Hispanic/Latino; 35 Asian, non-Hispanic/Latino; 40 Hispanic/Latino). 205 applicants, 73% accepted, 106 enrolled. Expenses: Contact institution. *Financial support:* Scholarships/grants available. Support available to part-time students. In 2017, 201 master's awarded. *Program availability:* Part-time, evening/weekend. Offers criminal justice (MS); engineering (MS); integrated supply chain management (MS); organizational change leadership (MS); project management (MS). *Application deadline:* For fall admission, 7/1 priority date for domestic students; for spring admission, 11/1 priority date for domestic students. Applications are processed on a rolling basis. *Application fee:* $56. Electronic applications accepted. *Executive Director,* Dawn Drake, 800-362-5460, Fax: 608-342-1071, E-mail: disted@uwplatt.edu.

UNIVERSITY OF WISCONSIN–RIVER FALLS, River Falls, WI 54022

General Information State-supported, coed, comprehensive institution. *Graduate housing:* Room and/or apartments available on a first-come, first-served basis to single students; on-campus housing not available to married students.

GRADUATE UNITS

Outreach and Graduate Studies *Program availability:* Part-time. Electronic applications accepted.

College of Agriculture, Food, and Environmental Sciences *Program availability:* Part-time. Offers agricultural education (MS); agriculture, food, and environmental sciences (MS). Electronic applications accepted.

College of Arts and Science *Program availability:* Part-time. Offers arts and science (MA, MSE); fine arts (MSE); mathematics education (MSE); science education (MSE); social science education (MSE); teaching English to speakers of other languages (MA). Electronic applications accepted.

College of Business and Economics Offers business and economics (MBA, MM). Electronic applications accepted.

College of Education and Professional Studies *Program availability:* Part-time. Offers communicative disorders (MS); counseling (MSE); education and professional studies (MS, MSE, Ed S); elementary education (MSE); professional development shared inquiry communities (MSE); reading (MSE); school psychology (MSE, Ed S); secondary education-communicative disorders (MSE).

UNIVERSITY OF WISCONSIN–STEVENS POINT, Stevens Point, WI 54481-3897

General Information State-supported, coed, comprehensive institution. *Enrollment:* 8,109 graduate, professional, and undergraduate students; 148 full-time matriculated graduate/professional students (113 women), 253 part-time matriculated graduate/professional students (188 women). *Enrollment by degree level:* 385 master's, 16 doctoral. Tuition, state resident: part-time $562.55 per credit. Tuition, nonresident: part-time $1085.04 per credit. Part-time tuition and fees vary according to course load, program and reciprocity agreements. *Graduate housing:* Room and/or apartments available on a first-come, first-served basis to single students; on-campus housing not available to married students. *Student services:* Campus employment opportunities, campus safety program, career counseling, child daycare facilities, exercise/wellness program, free psychological counseling, grant writing training, international student services, multicultural affairs office, services for students with disabilities, teacher training, writing training. *Library facilities:* Learning Resources Center plus 1 other. *Collection:* Books: 420,414 (physical), 247,207 (digital/electronic); Serial titles: 7,192 (physical), 133,235 (digital/electronic); Databases: 204. Study areas open 24 hours, 5–7 days a week; students can reserve study rooms.

Computer facilities: 1,233 computers available on campus for general student use. A campuswide network can be accessed from student residence rooms and from off campus. Online class registration is available.
Website: http://www.uwsp.edu/

General Application Contact: Cheryl Kawleski, Director of Admissions, 715-346-2441, E-mail: admiss@uwsp.edu.

GRADUATE UNITS

College of Fine Arts and Communication Expenses: Contact institution. *Financial support:* Teaching assistantships, career-related internships or fieldwork, Federal Work-Study, institutionally sponsored loans, and unspecified assistantships available. Support available to part-time students. Financial award application deadline: 5/1; financial award applicants required to submit FAFSA. *Program availability:* Part-time. Offers elementary/secondary music education (MM Ed); fine arts and communication (MA, MM Ed); studio pedagogy (MM Ed); Suzuki talent education (MM Ed). *Application deadline:* For fall admission, 5/1 priority date for domestic students. Applications are processed on a rolling basis. *Application fee:* $45.

Division of Communication Expenses: Contact institution. *Financial support:* Teaching assistantships, career-related internships or fieldwork, Federal Work-Study, institutionally sponsored loans, and unspecified assistantships available. Support available to part-time students. Financial award application deadline: 5/1; financial award applicants required to submit FAFSA. *Program availability:* Part-time. Offers interpersonal communication (MA); media studies (MA); organizational communication (MA); public relations (MA). *Application deadline:* For fall admission, 3/1 priority date for domestic students. Applications are processed on a rolling basis. *Application fee:* $45.

College of Letters and Science Expenses: Contact institution. *Financial support:* Research assistantships, teaching assistantships, Federal Work-Study, and unspecified assistantships available. Support available to part-time students. Financial award application deadline: 5/1; financial award applicants required to submit FAFSA. Offers biology (MST); data science (MS); English (MST); history (MST); letters and science (MS, MST). *Application deadline:* For fall admission, 5/1 priority date for domestic students. Applications are processed on a rolling basis. *Application fee:* $45. *Application Contact:* Catherine Glennon, Director of Admissions, 715-346-2441, E-mail: admiss@uwsp.edu. *Interim Dean,* Dr. Chris Cirmo, 715-346-4224, E-mail: ccirmo@uwsp.edu.

College of Natural Resources Expenses: Contact institution. *Financial support:* Research assistantships, teaching assistantships, career-related internships or fieldwork, Federal Work-Study, and unspecified assistantships available. Support available to part-time students. Financial award application deadline: 5/1; financial award applicants required to submit FAFSA. *Program availability:* Part-time. Offers natural resources (MNR, MS). *Application deadline:* For fall admission, 3/15 priority date for domestic students; for spring admission, 11/15 for domestic students. Applications are processed on a rolling basis. *Application fee:* $45. *Application Contact:* Catherine Glennon, Director of Admissions, 715-346-2441, E-mail: admiss@uwsp.edu. *Dean,* Dr. Christine Thomas, 715-346-4617, Fax: 715-346-3624.

College of Professional Studies Expenses: Contact institution. *Financial support:* Research assistantships, teaching assistantships, career-related internships or fieldwork, Federal Work-Study, and unspecified assistantships available. Support available to part-time students. Financial award application deadline: 5/1; financial award applicants required to submit FAFSA. *Program availability:* Part-time. *Application deadline:* For fall admission, 5/1 priority date for domestic students. Applications are processed on a rolling basis. *Application fee:* $45. *Application Contact:* Catherine Glennon, Director of Admissions, 715-346-2441, E-mail: admiss@uwsp.edu. *Dean,* Dr. Joan North, 715-346-3169.

School of Communication Sciences and Disorders Expenses: Contact institution. *Financial support:* Research assistantships, teaching assistantships, Federal Work-Study, and unspecified assistantships available. Financial award application deadline: 5/1; financial award applicants required to submit FAFSA. Offers audiology (Au D); speech and language pathology (MS). *Application deadline:* For fall admission, 1/10 for domestic students. *Application fee:* $45. *Application Contact:* Leslie Plonsker, Information Contact, 715-346-4835, Fax: 715-346-2157, E-mail: lplonske@uwsp.edu. *Chair,* Dr. Gary Cumley, 715-346-4699, Fax: 715-346-2157, E-mail: gcumley@uwsp.edu.

School of Education Expenses: Contact institution. *Financial support:* Research assistantships with partial tuition reimbursements, teaching assistantships, Federal Work-Study, tuition waivers (partial), and unspecified assistantships available. Support available to part-time students. Financial award application deadline: 5/1; financial award applicants required to submit FAFSA. *Program availability:* Part-time. Offers education—general/reading (MSE); education—general/special (MSE); educational administration (MSE); educational sustainability (Ed D); elementary education (MSE). *Application deadline:* For fall admission, 5/1 priority date for domestic students. Applications are processed on a rolling basis. *Application fee:* $45. *Application Contact:* Dr. Patricia Caro, Director of Graduate Advising, 715-346-3248, Fax: 715-346-4846, E-mail: pcaro@uwsp.edu. *Associate Dean,* Dr. JoAnne Katzmarek, 715-346-4802, Fax: 715-346-4846, E-mail: jkatzmar@uwsp.edu.

School of Health Care Professions Offers athletic training (MS).

School of Health Promotion and Human Development Expenses: Contact institution. *Financial support:* Research assistantships, teaching assistantships, career-related internships or fieldwork, Federal Work-Study, and unspecified assistantships available. Support available to part-time students. Financial award application deadline: 5/1; financial award applicants required to submit FAFSA. *Program availability:* Part-time. Offers family and consumer sciences (Graduate Certificate); health and wellness management (MS); sustainable and resilient food systems (MS). *Application deadline:* For fall admission, 5/1 priority date for domestic students. Applications are processed on a rolling basis. *Application fee:* $45.

UNIVERSITY OF WISCONSIN–STOUT, Menomonie, WI 54751

General Information State-supported, coed, comprehensive institution. *Graduate housing:* Room and/or apartments available on a first-come, first-served basis to single students; on-campus housing not available to married students.

GRADUATE UNITS

Graduate School *Program availability:* Part-time, online learning. Electronic applications accepted.

College of Arts, Humanities and Social Sciences Offers design (MFA); technical and professional communication (MS).

College of Education, Health and Human Sciences *Program availability:* Part-time, online learning. Offers applied psychology (MS); career and technical education (MS, Ed D, Ed S); clinical mental health counseling (MS); education (MS, MS Ed, Ed D, Ed S); education, health and human sciences (MS, Ed S); food and nutritional sciences (MS); marriage and family therapy (MS); school counseling (MS); school psychology (MS Ed, Ed S); vocational rehabilitation (MS). Electronic applications accepted.

College of Management Offers management (MS); operations management (MS); project management (MS); quality management (MS); risk control (MS); supply chain management (MS); sustainable management (MS); training and human resource development (MS).

College of Science, Technology, Engineering and Mathematics *Program availability:* Part-time, online learning. Offers conservation biology (PSM); construction management (MS); industrial and applied mathematics (PSM); information and communication technologies (MS); manufacturing engineering (MS); science, technology, engineering and mathematics (MS). Electronic applications accepted.

UNIVERSITY OF WISCONSIN–SUPERIOR, Superior, WI 54880-4500

General Information State-supported, coed, comprehensive institution. *Graduate housing:* Rooms and/or apartments available on a first-come, first-served basis to single students and available to married students. Housing application deadline: 7/1. *Research affiliation:* Great Lakes Indian Fish and Wildlife Commission, Wisconsin Department of Natural Resources (biology), Environmental Protection Agency (biology), The Mexican National Institute for Ecology (biology), The Mexican Marine National Park Service (biology), Coastal Zone Management Institute and Authority of Belize (biology), Fisheries Department, Government of Belize (biology).

GRADUATE UNITS

Graduate Division *Program availability:* Part-time, evening/weekend, online learning. Offers art education (MA); art history (MA); art therapy (MA); community counseling (MSE); educational administration (MSE, Ed S); emotional/behavior disabilities (MSE); human relations (MSE); instruction (MSE); learning disabilities (MSE); mass communication (MA); school counseling (MSE); special education (MSE); speech communication (MA); studio arts (MA); sustainable management (MS); teaching reading (MSE); theater (MA). Electronic applications accepted.

UNIVERSITY OF WISCONSIN–WHITEWATER, Whitewater, WI 53190-1790

General Information State-supported, coed, comprehensive institution. CGS member. *Graduate housing:* Rooms and/or apartments available on a first-come, first-served basis to single students and available to married students. Housing application deadline: 9/1. *Research affiliation:* Generac Power Systems (manufacturing), American Ag-Tec International (international marketing), American Family Insurance (insurance), R.A. Smith and Associates (civil engineering), Sho-Deen (property management and development), Webco Industries, Inc. (lightning radioactive transfer).

GRADUATE UNITS

School of Graduate Studies *Program availability:* Part-time, evening/weekend, online learning. Electronic applications accepted.

College of Arts and Communications *Program availability:* Part-time, evening/weekend, online learning. Offers arts and communications (MS); corporate communication (MS); mass communication (MS). Electronic applications accepted.

College of Business and Economics *Program availability:* Part-time, evening/weekend, online learning. Offers accounting (MPA); business and economics (MBA, MPA, MS, MSE); business and marketing education (MS); finance (MBA); school business management (MSE). Electronic applications accepted.

College of Education and Professional Studies *Program availability:* Part-time, evening/weekend, online learning. Offers communication sciences and disorders (MS); cross categorical licensure (MSE); education and professional studies (MS, MSE, Postbaccalaureate Certificate); professional development (MSE); safety (MS); special education (Postbaccalaureate Certificate). Electronic applications accepted.

College of Letters and Sciences *Program availability:* Part-time, evening/weekend. Offers letters and sciences (MSE, Ed S); school psychology (MSE, Ed S). Electronic applications accepted.

UNIVERSITY OF WYOMING, Laramie, WY 82071

General Information State-supported, coed, university. CGS member. *Graduate housing:* Rooms and/or apartments available on a first-come, first-served basis to single and married students.

GRADUATE UNITS

College of Agriculture and Natural Resources *Program availability:* Part-time. Offers agricultural and applied economics (MS); agriculture and natural resources (MA, MS, PhD); agroecology (MS); agronomy (MS, PhD); animal sciences (MS, PhD); early childhood development (MS); entomology (MS, PhD); entomology/water resources (MS, PhD); family and consumer sciences (MS); food science and human nutrition (MS); molecular biology (MA, MS, PhD); pathobiology (MS); rangeland ecology and watershed management (MS, PhD); rangeland ecology and watershed management/water resources (MS, PhD); reproductive biology (MS, PhD); soil science (MS); soil science/water resources (PhD). Electronic applications accepted.

College of Arts and Sciences *Program availability:* Part-time. Offers American studies (MA); anthropology (MA, PhD); arts and sciences (MA, MAT, MFA, MM, MME, MP, MPA, MS, MST, PhD); botany (MS, PhD); botany/water resources (MS); chemistry (MS, PhD); communication (MA); community and regional planning and natural resources (MP); creative writing (MFA); English (MA); French (MA); geography (MA, MP, MST); geography/water resources (MA); geology (MS, PhD); geophysics (MS, PhD); German (MA); history (MA, MAT); international peace corps (MA); international studies (MA); mathematics (MA, MAT, MS, MST, PhD); mathematics/computer science (PhD); music education (MME); performance (MM); philosophy (MA); political science (MA, MPA); psychology (MA, MS, PhD); public administration (MPA); rural planning and natural resources (MP); sociology (MA); Spanish (MA); statistics (MS, PhD); zoology and physiology (MS, PhD). Electronic applications accepted.

College of Business *Program availability:* Part-time, evening/weekend, online learning. Offers accounting (MS); business (MBA, MS, PhD); business administration (MBA); economics (MS, PhD); economics and finance (MS); finance (MS).

College of Education *Program availability:* Online learning. Offers community mental health (MS); counselor education and supervision (PhD); curriculum and instruction (MA, Ed D, PhD); education (MA, MS, MST, Ed D, PhD, Certificate, Ed S); educational leadership (MA, Ed D, Certificate); instructional technology (MS, Ed D, PhD); school counseling (MS); special education (MA, PhD, Ed S); student affairs (MS). Electronic applications accepted.

Science and Mathematics Teaching Center Offers science and mathematics teaching (MS, MST). Electronic applications accepted.

College of Engineering and Applied Sciences *Program availability:* Part-time. Offers atmospheric science (MS, PhD); chemical engineering (MS, PhD); civil engineering (MS, PhD); computer science (MS, PhD); electrical engineering (MS, PhD); engineering and applied sciences (MS, PhD); environmental engineering (MS); mechanical engineering (MS, PhD); petroleum engineering (MS, PhD). Electronic applications accepted.

College of Health Sciences *Program availability:* Part-time, online learning. Offers health sciences (MS, MSW, Pharm D). Electronic applications accepted.

Division of Communication Disorders *Program availability:* Part-time, online learning. Offers speech-language pathology (MS). Electronic applications accepted.

Division of Kinesiology and Health *Program availability:* Part-time, online learning. Offers kinesiology and health (MS). Electronic applications accepted.

Division of Social Work Offers social work (MSW).

Fay W. Whitney School of Nursing *Program availability:* Part-time, online learning. Offers nursing (MS).

School of Pharmacy *Program availability:* Online learning. Offers health services administration (MS); pharmacy (Pharm D).

College of Law Offers law (JD). Electronic applications accepted.

Graduate Program in Molecular and Cellular Life Sciences Offers molecular and cellular life sciences (PhD).

Program in Ecology Offers ecology (MS, PhD).

UPPER IOWA UNIVERSITY, Fayette, IA 52142-1857

General Information Independent, coed, comprehensive institution. *Graduate housing:* Room and/or apartments available to single students.

GRADUATE UNITS

Master of Education Program Offers early childhood (M Ed); English as a second language (M Ed); higher education (M Ed); instructional strategist (M Ed); reading (M Ed); teacher leadership (M Ed).

Online Master's Programs *Program availability:* Part-time, online learning. Offers accounting (MBA); corporate financial management (MBA); emergency management and homeland security (MPA); general management (MBA); general studies (MPA); government administration (MPA); health and human services (MPA); human resources management (MBA); nonprofit organizational management (MPA); organizational development (MBA); public management (MPA); sport administration (MSA). MBA also available at Madison, WI campus. Electronic applications accepted.

URBANA UNIVERSITY–A BRANCH CAMPUS OF FRANKLIN UNIVERSITY, Urbana, OH 43078-2091

General Information Independent, coed, comprehensive institution. *Graduate housing:* Room and/or apartments available on a first-come, first-served basis to single students; on-campus housing not available to married students.

GRADUATE UNITS

College of Education and Sports Studies *Program availability:* Part-time, evening/weekend. Offers classroom education (M Ed).

College of Nursing and Allied Health Offers nursing (MSN).

College of Social and Behavioral Sciences Offers criminal justice administration (MA).

Division of Business Administration *Program availability:* Part-time, evening/weekend. Offers business administration (MBA).

URSHAN GRADUATE SCHOOL OF THEOLOGY, Florissant, MO 63031

General Information Independent-religious, coed, graduate-only institution.

GRADUATE UNITS

Graduate Programs *Program availability:* Online learning. Offers theology (M Div, MACM, MTS).

URSULINE COLLEGE, Pepper Pike, OH 44124-4398

General Information Independent-religious, coed, primarily women, comprehensive institution. *Enrollment:* 1,123 graduate, professional, and undergraduate students; 63 full-time matriculated graduate/professional students (58 women), 416 part-time matriculated graduate/professional students (371 women). *Enrollment by degree level:* 386 master's, 11 doctoral, 82 other advanced degrees. *Graduate faculty:* 20 full-time (15 women), 35 part-time/adjunct (29 women). *Tuition:* Full-time $21,880; part-time $1094 per credit hour. *Required fees:* $310; $230 per year. $115 per semester. One-time fee: $200. Tuition and fees vary according to program. *Graduate housing:* Room and/or apartments available on a first-come, first-served basis to single students; on-campus housing not available to married students. Typical cost: $7828 per year ($12,480 including board). Room and board charges vary according to housing facility selected. Housing application deadline: 8/20. *Student services:* Campus employment opportunities, career counseling, exercise/wellness program, free psychological counseling, multicultural affairs office, services for students with disabilities, teacher training. *Library facilities:* Ralph M. Besse Library. *Collection:* Books: 132,089 (physical), 137,533 (digital/electronic); Serial titles: 902 (physical), 14,413 (digital/electronic); Databases: 162. Weekly public service hours: 91; students can reserve study rooms.

Computer facilities: 72 computers available on campus for general student use. A campuswide network can be accessed from student residence rooms. Online class registration is available.
Website: http://www.ursuline.edu/

General Application Contact: Melanie Steele, Director, Graduate Admission, 440-646-8119, Fax: 440-684-6138, E-mail: graduateadmissions@ursuline.edu.

GRADUATE UNITS

School of Graduate and Professional Studies Students: 57 full-time (54 women), 140 part-time (110 women); includes 56 minority (49 Black or African American, non-Hispanic/Latino; 3 Hispanic/Latino; 4 Two or more races, non-Hispanic/Latino). Average age 40. 197 applicants, 88% accepted, 128 enrolled. *Faculty:* 24 full-time (18 women), 44 part-time/adjunct (37 women). Expenses: Contact institution. *Financial support:* Federal Work-Study and scholarships/grants available. Financial award application deadline: 3/1; financial award applicants required to submit FAFSA. *Program availability:* Part-time. Offers acute-care nurse practitioner (MSN); adolescent to young adult education (MA); adult nurse practitioner (MSN); adult-gerontology acute care nurse practitioner (MSN); adult-gerontology clinical nurse specialist (MSN); adult-gerontology nurse practitioner (MSN); care management (MSN); clinical nurse specialist (MSN); counseling and art therapy (MA); early childhood education (MA); educational administration (MA); ethical and entrepreneurial leadership (MBA); family nurse practitioner (MSN); financial planning and accounting (MBA); health services management (MBA); historic preservation (MA); liberal studies (MALS); management (MBA); management and leadership (MBA); marketing and communications management (MBA); middle childhood education (MA); nursing (DNP); nursing education (MSN); palliative care (MSN); special education (MA); theological and pastoral studies (MA). *Application deadline:* For fall admission, 8/1 priority date for domestic students. Applications are processed on a rolling basis. *Application fee:* $25. Electronic applications accepted. *Application Contact:* Melanie Steele, Director, Graduate Admission, 440-646-8146, Fax: 440-684-6138, E-mail: graduateadmissions@ursuline.edu. *Dean*, Dr. James Connell, 440-646-8120, Fax: 440-684-6088, E-mail: jconnell@ursuline.edu.

UTAH STATE UNIVERSITY, Logan, UT 84322

General Information State-supported, coed, university. CGS member. *Graduate housing:* Rooms and/or apartments available on a first-come, first-served basis to single and married students. *Research affiliation:* Boeing Aerospace and Engineering (science and engineering), Duke Energy Corporation (engineering), Kennecott Copper Corporation (natural resources), Kraft Foods, Inc. (agriculture), National Endowment for Financial Education (education).

GRADUATE UNITS

School of Graduate Studies *Program availability:* Part-time, evening/weekend, online learning.

Caine College of the Arts Offers art and design (MFA); arts (MFA, MM); design (MFA); guitar performance (MM); piano performance and pedagogy (MM).

College of Agriculture and Applied Sciences *Program availability:* Part-time, online learning. Offers agricultural extension and education (MS); agriculture and applied sciences (MAE, MDA, MLA, MPS, MS, PhD); animal science (MS, PhD); applied economics (MAE, MS, PhD); bioregional planning (MS); bioveterinary science (MS, PhD); climate sciences (MS, PhD); dairy science (MS); dietetic administration (MDA); ecology (MS, PhD); family and consumer sciences education and extension (MS); horticulture (MPS); international food and agribusiness (MS); landscape architecture (MLA); nutrition and food sciences (MS, PhD); plant science (MS, PhD); soil science (MS, PhD); technology and engineering education (MS); toxicology (MS, PhD).

College of Engineering *Program availability:* Part-time, evening/weekend. Offers aerospace engineering (MS, PhD); biological engineering (MS, PhD); civil and environmental engineering (ME, MS, PhD, CE); computer science (MCS, MS, PhD); electrical engineering (ME, MS, PhD); engineering (MCS, ME, MS, PhD, CE); engineering education (PhD); mechanical engineering (ME, MS, PhD). Electronic applications accepted.

College of Humanities and Social Sciences *Program availability:* Part-time, evening/weekend, online learning. Offers American studies (MA, MS); anthropology (MS); English (MA, MS); folklore (MA, MS); history (MA, MS); humanities and social sciences (MA, MS, MSLT, MSW, PhD); journalism and communication (MA, MS); political science (MA, MS); second language teaching (MSLT); social work (MSW); sociology (MS, PhD); western American literature and culture (MA, MS).

College of Science *Program availability:* Part-time, evening/weekend. Offers biochemistry (MS, PhD); biology (MS, PhD); chemistry (MS, PhD); ecology (MS, PhD); geology (MS); industrial mathematics (MS); mathematical sciences (PhD); mathematics (M Math, MS); physics (MS, PhD); science (M Math, MCS, MS, PhD); statistics (MS).

Emma Eccles Jones College of Education and Human Services *Program availability:* Part-time, evening/weekend, online learning. Offers audiology (Au D, Ed S); business information systems (Ed D, PhD); clinical/counseling/school psychology (PhD); communication disorders and deaf education (M Ed); communicative disorders and deaf education (MA, MS); curriculum and instruction (Ed D, PhD); disability disciplines (PhD); education and human services (M Ed, MA, MFHD, MRC, MS, Au D, Ed D, PhD, Ed S); elementary education (M Ed, MA, MS); family and human development (MFHD); family, consumer, and human development (MS, PhD); fitness promotion (MS); health and human movement (MS); instructional technology and learning sciences (M Ed, MS, PhD, Ed S); pathokinesiology (PhD); physical and sport eductaion (M Ed); public health (MPH); rehabilitation counseling (MRC); research and evaluation (PhD); research and evaluation methodology (PhD); school counseling (MS); school psychology (MS); secondary education (M Ed, MA, MS); special education (M Ed, MS, Ed S).

Jon M. Huntsman School of Business *Program availability:* Part-time, evening/weekend, online learning. Offers accountancy (M Acc); business (M Acc, MA, MBA, MHR, MMIS, MS); business administration (MBA); economics (MS); financial economics (MS); human resources (MHR); management information systems (MMIS).

S.J. and Jessie E. Quinney College of Natural Resources *Program availability:* Part-time. Offers bioregional planning (MS); ecology (MS, PhD); fisheries biology (MS, PhD); forestry (MS, PhD); geography (MA, MS); human dimensions of ecosystem science and management (MS, PhD); natural resources (MA, MNR, MS, PhD); range science (MS, PhD); recreation resource management (MS, PhD); watershed science (MS, PhD); wildlife biology (MS, PhD).

UTAH VALLEY UNIVERSITY, Orem, UT 84058-5999

General Information State-supported, coed, comprehensive institution.

GRADUATE UNITS

MBA Program *Program availability:* Part-time, evening/weekend. Offers accounting (MBA); management (MBA). Electronic applications accepted.

Program in Cybersecurity Offers cybersecurity (Graduate Certificate).

Program in Education *Program availability:* Part-time. Offers educational technology (M Ed); elementary mathematics (M Ed); elementary STEM (M Ed); English as a second language (M Ed); reading (M Ed); teachers as leaders (M Ed). Electronic applications accepted.

Program in Nursing *Program availability:* Part-time, online learning. Offers nursing (MSN). Electronic applications accepted.

UTICA COLLEGE, Utica, NY 13502-4892

General Information Independent, coed, comprehensive institution. *Enrollment:* 5,258 graduate, professional, and undergraduate students; 237 full-time matriculated graduate/professional students (168 women), 1,316 part-time matriculated graduate/professional students (719 women). *Enrollment by degree level:* 1,038 master's, 472 doctoral, 43 other advanced degrees. *Graduate faculty:* 65 full-time (28 women). *Tuition:* Full-time $32,910; part-time $1097 per credit hour. *Required fees:* $550; $50 per course. Tuition and fees vary according to degree level, campus/location and program. *Graduate housing:* Room and/or apartments available on a first-come, first-served basis to single students; on-campus housing not available to married students. Housing application deadline: 3/1. *Student services:* Campus employment opportunities, campus safety program, career counseling, international student services, low-cost health insurance, services for students with disabilities. *Library facilities:* Frank E. Gannett Memorial Library. *Collection:* Books: 307,523 (physical); Serial titles: 267,023 (physical). Students can reserve study rooms.

Computer facilities: 430 computers available on campus for general student use. A campuswide network can be accessed from student residence rooms. Online class registration is available.
Website: http://www.utica.edu/

General Application Contact: John D. Rowe, Director of Graduate Admissions, 315-792-3824, Fax: 315-792-3003, E-mail: jrowe@utica.edu.

GRADUATE UNITS

Department of Physical Therapy Students: 86 full-time (46 women), 386 part-time (253 women); includes 246 minority (17 Black or African American, non-Hispanic/Latino; 220 Asian, non-Hispanic/Latino; 8 Hispanic/Latino; 1 Native Hawaiian or other Pacific Islander, non-Hispanic/Latino), 4 international. Average age 34. 240 applicants, 98% accepted, 232 enrolled. *Faculty:* 10 full-time (4 women). Expenses: Contact institution. *Financial support:* Career-related internships or fieldwork, scholarships/grants, tuition waivers (partial), and unspecified assistantships available. Support available to part-time students. Financial award application deadline: 3/15; financial award applicants required to submit FAFSA. In 2017, 299 doctorates awarded. *Program availability:* Part-time, evening/weekend, online learning. Offers physical therapy (DPT, TDPT). *Application deadline:* Applications are processed on a rolling basis. *Application fee:* $50. Electronic applications accepted. *Application Contact:* John D. Rowe, Director of Graduate Admissions, 315-792-3824, Fax: 315-792-3003, E-mail: jrowe@utica.edu. *Director*, Dr. Ashraf Elazzazi, 315-792-3313, E-mail: aelazza@utica.edu.

Program in Accountancy Students: 8 full-time (4 women), 7 part-time (all women); includes 7 minority (1 Black or African American, non-Hispanic/Latino; 4 Asian, non-Hispanic/Latino; 2 Hispanic/Latino). Average age 25. 16 applicants, 88% accepted, 11 enrolled. *Faculty:* 3 full-time (1 woman). Expenses: Contact institution. *Financial support:* Career-related internships or fieldwork, scholarships/grants, tuition waivers (partial), and unspecified assistantships available. Support available to part-time students. Financial award application deadline: 3/15; financial award applicants required to submit FAFSA. In 2017, 11 master's awarded. *Program availability:* Part-time, evening/weekend. Offers accountancy (MBA). *Application deadline:* Applications are processed on a rolling basis. *Application fee:* $50. Electronic applications accepted. *Application Contact:* John D. Rowe, Director of Graduate Admissions, 315-792-3824, Fax: 315-792-3003, E-mail: jrowe@utica.edu. *MBA Director*, Dr. Zhaodan Huang, 315-792-3247, E-mail: zhuang@utica.edu.

Program in Cybersecurity Students: 3 full-time (1 woman), 385 part-time (123 women); includes 112 minority (50 Black or African American, non-Hispanic/Latino; 17 Asian, non-Hispanic/Latino; 35 Hispanic/Latino; 10 Two or more races, non-Hispanic/Latino). Average age 34. 163 applicants, 98% accepted, 155 enrolled. *Faculty:* 5 full-time (0 women), 8 part-time/adjunct (0 women). Expenses: Contact institution. *Financial support:* Application deadline: 3/15; applicants required to submit FAFSA. In 2017, 144 master's awarded. *Program availability:* Part-time, evening/weekend, 100% online. Offers cybersecurity (MPS, MS). *Application deadline:* Applications are processed on a rolling basis. Electronic applications accepted. *Application Contact:* John D. Rowe, Director of Graduate Admissions, 315-792-3824, Fax: 315-792-3003, E-mail: jrowe@utica.edu. *Chair*, Joseph Giordano, 315-792-2521.

Program in Economic Crime and Fraud Management Students: 1 full-time (0 women), 64 part-time (40 women); includes 16 minority (6 Black or African American, non-Hispanic/Latino; 3 Asian, non-Hispanic/Latino; 6 Hispanic/Latino; 1 Two or more races, non-Hispanic/Latino). Average age 37. 42 applicants, 93% accepted, 37 enrolled. *Faculty:* 7 full-time (0 women). Expenses: Contact institution. *Financial support:* Career-related internships or fieldwork, scholarships/grants, tuition waivers (partial), and unspecified assistantships available. Support available to part-time students. Financial award application deadline: 3/15; financial award applicants required to submit FAFSA. In 2017, 23 master's awarded. *Program availability:* Part-time, evening/weekend, 100%

online. Offers economic crime and fraud management (MS). *Application deadline:* Applications are processed on a rolling basis. *Application fee:* $50. Electronic applications accepted. *Application Contact:* John D. Rowe, Director of Graduate Admissions, 315-792-3824, Fax: 315-792-3003, E-mail: jrowe@utica.edu. *Director of Economic Crime Graduate Programs*, Dr. R. Bruce McBride, 315-792-3808, E-mail: rmcbride@utica.edu.

Program in Economic Crime Management Students: 2 full-time (1 woman), 81 part-time (46 women); includes 23 minority (13 Black or African American, non-Hispanic/Latino; 1 American Indian or Alaska Native, non-Hispanic/Latino; 2 Asian, non-Hispanic/Latino; 6 Hispanic/Latino; 1 Two or more races, non-Hispanic/Latino). Average age 34. *Faculty:* 4 full-time (0 women). Expenses: Contact institution. *Financial support:* Career-related internships or fieldwork, scholarships/grants, tuition waivers (partial), and unspecified assistantships available. Support available to part-time students. Financial award application deadline: 3/15; financial award applicants required to submit FAFSA. In 2017, 56 master's awarded. *Program availability:* Part-time, evening/weekend, online learning. Offers economic crime management (MBA). *Application deadline:* Applications are processed on a rolling basis. *Application fee:* $50. Electronic applications accepted. *Application Contact:* John D. Rowe, Director of Graduate Admissions, 315-792-3824, Fax: 315-792-3003, E-mail: jrowe@utica.edu. *Director of Economic Crime Graduate Programs*, Dr. R. Bruce McBride, 315-792-3808, E-mail: rmcbride@utica.edu.

Program in Health Care Administration Students: 15 full-time (12 women), 186 part-time (147 women); includes 52 minority (29 Black or African American, non-Hispanic/Latino; 9 Asian, non-Hispanic/Latino; 11 Hispanic/Latino; 3 Two or more races, non-Hispanic/Latino), 1 international. Average age 33. 67 applicants, 93% accepted, 60 enrolled. *Faculty:* 2 full-time (both women), 11 part-time/adjunct (4 women). Expenses: Contact institution. *Financial support:* Application deadline: 3/15; applicants required to submit FAFSA. In 2017, 56 master's awarded. *Program availability:* Part-time, evening/weekend, online learning. Offers health care administration (MS). *Application deadline:* Applications are processed on a rolling basis. *Application fee:* $50. Electronic applications accepted. *Application Contact:* John D. Rowe, Director of Graduate Admissions, 315-792-3824, Fax: 315-792-3003, E-mail: jrowe@utica.edu. *Program Director*, Dr. Jamie Cuda, 315-792-3540, E-mail: jlcuda@utica.edu.

Program in Occupational Therapy Students: 90 full-time (82 women), 1 (woman) part-time; includes 10 minority (3 Black or African American, non-Hispanic/Latino; 2 Asian, non-Hispanic/Latino; 3 Hispanic/Latino; 2 Two or more races, non-Hispanic/Latino). Average age 26. 62 applicants, 98% accepted, 58 enrolled. *Faculty:* 7 full-time (all women). Expenses: Contact institution. *Financial support:* Career-related internships or fieldwork, scholarships/grants, tuition waivers (partial), and unspecified assistantships available. Support available to part-time students. Financial award application deadline: 3/15; financial award applicants required to submit FAFSA. In 2017, 59 master's awarded. *Program availability:* Part-time, evening/weekend. Offers occupational therapy (MS). *Application deadline:* Applications are processed on a rolling basis. *Application fee:* $50. Electronic applications accepted. *Application Contact:* John D. Rowe, Director of Graduate Admissions, 315-792-3824, Fax: 315-792-3003, E-mail: jrowe@utica.edu. *Director*, Cora Bruns, 315-792-3125, E-mail: cbruns@utica.edu.

Teacher Education Programs Students: 24 full-time (18 women), 27 part-time (17 women); includes 2 minority (1 Black or African American, non-Hispanic/Latino; 1 Hispanic/Latino). Average age 27. 21 applicants, 76% accepted, 14 enrolled. *Faculty:* 10 full-time (7 women). Expenses: Contact institution. *Financial support:* Career-related internships or fieldwork, scholarships/grants, tuition waivers (partial), and unspecified assistantships available. Support available to part-time students. Financial award application deadline: 3/15; financial award applicants required to submit FAFSA. In 2017, 17 master's awarded. Offers teacher education (MS, MS Ed, CAS). *Application deadline:* Applications are processed on a rolling basis. *Application fee:* $50. Electronic applications accepted. *Application Contact:* John D. Rowe, Director of Graduate Admissions, 315-792-3824, Fax: 315-792-3003, E-mail: jrowe@utica.edu. *Dean of Health Professions and Education*, Dr. Patrice Hallock, 315-792-3162, E-mail: phallock@utica.edu.

VALDOSTA STATE UNIVERSITY, Valdosta, GA 31698

General Information State-supported, coed, university. CGS member. *Enrollment:* 11,341 graduate, professional, and undergraduate students; 780 full-time matriculated graduate/professional students (632 women), 1,782 part-time matriculated graduate/professional students (1,291 women). *Enrollment by degree level:* 2,059 master's, 503 doctoral. *Graduate faculty:* 193 full-time (97 women), 60 part-time/adjunct (44 women). *Graduate housing:* Rooms and/or apartments available on a first-come, first-served basis to single and married students. Housing application deadline: 7/1. *Student services:* Campus employment opportunities, campus safety program, career counseling, exercise/wellness program, free psychological counseling, grant writing training, international student services, low-cost health insurance, multicultural affairs office, services for students with disabilities, teacher training, writing training. *Library facilities:* Odum Library. *Collection:* Books: 579,774 (physical), 408,139 (digital/electronic); Serial titles: 10,877 (physical), 39,852 (digital/electronic); Databases: 237. Students can reserve study rooms.

Computer facilities: Computer purchase and lease plans are available. 1,691 computers available on campus for general student use. A campuswide network can be accessed from student residence rooms and from off campus. Online class registration is available.
Website: http://www.valdosta.edu/

General Application Contact: Rebecca Petrella, Graduate Admissions Coordinator, 229-333-5694, Fax: 229-245-3853, E-mail: rlwaters@valdosta.edu.

GRADUATE UNITS

College of Nursing and Health Sciences Expenses: Contact institution. *Financial support:* Research assistantships with full tuition reimbursements, institutionally sponsored loans, scholarships/grants, and unspecified assistantships available. Support available to part-time students. Financial award application deadline: 7/1; financial award applicants required to submit FAFSA. *Program availability:* Part-time, online learning. Offers adult gerontology nurse practitioner (MSN); exercise physiology (MS); family nurse practitioner (MSN); family psychiatric mental health nurse practitioner (MSN). *Application deadline:* For fall admission, 7/1 for domestic and international students; for spring admission, 11/15 for domestic and international students. Applications are processed on a rolling basis. *Application fee:* $45. Electronic applications accepted. *Application Contact:* Sheri Noviello, Dean, 229-333-5959, E-mail: srnoviello@valdosta.edu. *Dean*, Sheri Noviello, 229-333-5959, E-mail: srnoviello@valdosta.edu.

Department of Communication Sciences and Disorders Expenses: Contact institution. *Financial support:* Research assistantships, Federal Work-Study, scholarships/grants, and unspecified assistantships available. Offers communication disorders (M Ed); communication sciences and disorders (SLPD); special education (MAT, Ed S). *Application deadline:* For fall admission, 3/1 for domestic and international students; for spring admission, 7/1 for domestic and international students. *Application fee:* $45. Electronic applications accepted. *Application Contact:* Tonya R. Crawford, Administrative Secretary, 229-219-1327, Fax: 229-245-3853, E-mail: tocrawford@valdosta.edu. *Head*, Dr. Corine Myers-Jennings, 229-219-1327, Fax: 229-219-1335, E-mail: cmjennin@valdosta.edu.

Department of Curriculum, Leadership, and Technology Expenses: Contact institution. *Financial support:* Research assistantships with full tuition reimbursements, institutionally sponsored loans, scholarships/grants, and unspecified assistantships available. Support available to part-time students. Financial award application deadline: 7/1; financial award applicants required to submit FAFSA. *Program availability:* 100% online, blended/hybrid learning. Offers leadership (Ed D); P-12 school leadership (M Ed); performance-based leadership (Ed S). *Application deadline:* For fall admission, 7/1 for domestic and international students; for spring admission, 11/15 for domestic and international students. Applications are processed on a rolling basis. *Application fee:* $45. Electronic applications accepted. *Application Contact:* Dr. Leon Pate, Department Head, 229-333-5633, E-mail: jlpate@valdosta.edu. *Department Head*, Dr. Leon Pate, 229-333-5633, E-mail: jlpate@valdosta.edu.

Department of Elementary Education Expenses: Contact institution. *Financial support:* Research assistantships with full tuition reimbursements, institutionally sponsored loans, scholarships/grants, and unspecified assistantships available. Support available to part-time students. Financial award application deadline: 7/1; financial award applicants required to submit FAFSA. *Program availability:* Part-time, evening/weekend, blended/hybrid learning. Offers elementary education (M Ed). *Application deadline:* For fall and spring admission, 7/1 for domestic and international students. Applications are processed on a rolling basis. *Application fee:* $45. Electronic applications accepted. *Application Contact:* Julia Stokes, Administrative Secretary, 229-333-5929, Fax: 229-245-3853, E-mail: jdstokes@valdosta.edu.

Department of English Expenses: Contact institution. *Financial support:* Research assistantships with full tuition reimbursements, teaching assistantships with full tuition reimbursements, institutionally sponsored loans, scholarships/grants, and unspecified assistantships available. Support available to part-time students. Financial award application deadline: 7/1; financial award applicants required to submit FAFSA. *Program availability:* Part-time, 100% online, blended/hybrid learning. Offers English (MA); English studies for language arts teachers (MA). *Application deadline:* For fall admission, 7/1 for domestic and international students; for spring admission, 11/1 for domestic and international students. Applications are processed on a rolling basis. *Application fee:* $45. Electronic applications accepted. *Application Contact:* Jessica Powers, Admission Specialist, 229-333-5694, Fax: 229-245-3853, E-mail: jldevane@valdosta.edu. *Graduate Program Adviser*, Dr. Maren Clegg Hyer, 229-333-7347, E-mail: mclegghyer@valdosta.edu.

Department of Political Science Expenses: Contact institution. *Financial support:* Research assistantships with full tuition reimbursements, institutionally sponsored loans, scholarships/grants, and unspecified assistantships available. Support available to part-time students. Financial award application deadline: 7/1; financial award applicants required to submit FAFSA. *Program availability:* Part-time, evening/weekend, online learning. Offers public administration (MPA, DPA). *Application deadline:* For fall admission, 7/1 for domestic and international students; for spring admission, 11/15 for domestic and international students. Applications are processed on a rolling basis. *Application fee:* $45. Electronic applications accepted.

Department of Psychology, Counseling, and Family Therapy Expenses: Contact institution. *Financial support:* Research assistantships with full tuition reimbursements, institutionally sponsored loans, and unspecified assistantships available. Support available to part-time students. Financial award application deadline: 7/1; financial award applicants required to submit FAFSA. *Program availability:* Part-time, evening/weekend, 100% online, blended/hybrid learning. Offers industrial/organizational psychology (MS); marriage and family therapy (MS); school counseling (M Ed, Ed S). *Application deadline:* For fall admission, 7/1 for domestic and international students; for spring admission, 11/15 for domestic and international students. Applications are processed on a rolling basis. *Application fee:* $45. Electronic applications accepted. *Application Contact:* Jessica Powers, Admission Specialist, 229-333-5694, Fax: 229-245-3853, E-mail: jldevane@valdosta.edu. *Head*, Dr. Kate Warner, 229-293-6264, Fax: 229-259-5576, E-mail: kwarner@valdosta.edu.

Department of Social Work Expenses: Contact institution. *Financial support:* Research assistantships with full tuition reimbursements, career-related internships or fieldwork, institutionally sponsored loans, scholarships/grants, and unspecified assistantships available. Financial award application deadline: 7/1; financial award applicants required to submit FAFSA. *Program availability:* Part-time, evening/weekend, online learning. Offers social work (MSW). *Application deadline:* For fall admission, 3/15 for domestic and international students. Applications are processed on a rolling basis. *Application fee:* $45. *Application Contact:* Rebecca Powers, Admission Specialist, 229-333-5694, Fax: 229-245-3853, E-mail: rlwaters@valdosta.edu. *Head*, Dr. Mizanur Miah, 229-249-4893, Fax: 229-245-4341, E-mail: mrmiah@valdosta.edu.

Langdale College of Business Expenses: Contact institution. *Financial support:* Research assistantships with full tuition reimbursements, institutionally sponsored loans, and scholarships/grants available. Support available to part-time students. Financial award application deadline: 7/1; financial award applicants required to submit FAFSA. *Program availability:* Part-time, evening/weekend, 100% online, blended/hybrid learning. Offers accountancy (M Acc); business administration (MBA); healthcare administration (MBA). MBA program is a member of the Georgia WebMBA. *Application deadline:* For fall admission, 7/1 for domestic and international students; for spring admission, 11/1 for domestic and international students. Applications are processed on a rolling basis. *Application fee:* $45. Electronic applications accepted. *Application Contact:* Jessica Powers, Admission Specialist, 229-333-5694, Fax: 229-245-3853, E-mail: jldevane@valdosta.edu. *Director*, Dr. Mel Schnake, 229-245-2233, Fax: 229-245-2795, E-mail: mschnake@valdosta.edu.

Program in Library and Information Science Expenses: Contact institution. *Financial support:* Research assistantships with full tuition reimbursements, institutionally sponsored loans, scholarships/grants, and unspecified assistantships available. Support available to part-time students. Financial award application deadline: 7/1; financial award applicants required to submit FAFSA. *Program availability:* 100% online. Offers library and information science (MLIS). *Application deadline:* For fall admission, 4/15 for domestic and international students. *Application fee:* $45. *Application Contact:* Jessica Powers, Admission Specialist, 229-333-5694, Fax: 229-245-3853, E-mail: jldevane@valdosta.edu. *Director*, Dr. Linda Most, 229-333-5966, Fax: 229-333-5862, E-mail: lrmost@valdosta.edu.

VALLEY CITY STATE UNIVERSITY, Valley City, ND 58072

General Information State-supported, coed, comprehensive institution. *Enrollment:* 1,522 graduate, professional, and undergraduate students; 12 full-time matriculated graduate/professional students (9 women), 138 part-time matriculated graduate/professional students (99 women). *Enrollment by degree level:* 150 master's. *Graduate faculty:* 21 full-time (12 women), 15 part-time/adjunct (11 women). Tuition, state resident: full-time $6090; part-time $2436 per credit. Tuition, nonresident: full-time $6090; part-time $2436 per credit. *Required fees:* $1754; $638 per credit. *Student services:* Campus safety program, career counseling, free psychological counseling, services for students with disabilities, teacher training, writing training. *Library facilities:* Allen Memorial Library. *Collection:* Books: 77,906 (physical), 140,050 (digital/electronic); Serial titles: 1,301 (physical), 29,378 (digital/electronic); Databases: 86. Weekly public service hours: 61; students can reserve study rooms.

Computer facilities: Computer purchase and lease plans are available. 1,200 computers available on campus for general student use. A campuswide network can be accessed from student residence rooms and from off campus. Online class registration is available.
Website: http://www.vcsu.edu/

General Application Contact: Misty Lindgren, Administrative Assistant for Office of Graduate Studies and Research, 701-845-7303, Fax: 701-845-7190, E-mail: misty.lindgren@vcsu.edu.

GRADUATE UNITS

Online Graduate Programs Students: 12 full-time (9 women), 138 part-time (99 women); includes 5 minority (3 Hispanic/Latino; 2 Two or more races, non-Hispanic/Latino). Average age 36. 13 applicants, 92% accepted, 12 enrolled. *Faculty:* 21 full-time (12 women), 15 part-time/adjunct (11 women). Expenses: Contact institution. *Financial support:* In 2017–18, 16 students received support. Scholarships/grants, tuition waivers (full and partial), and unspecified assistantships available. Financial award applicants required to submit FAFSA. In 2017, 45 master's awarded. *Program availability:* Part-time, evening/weekend, online only, 100% online. Offers elementary education (M Ed); English education (M Ed); library and information technologies (M Ed); teaching (MAT); teaching and technology (M Ed); teaching English language learners (M Ed); technology education (M Ed). *Application deadline:* For fall admission, 7/21 for domestic and international students; for spring admission, 12/8 for domestic and international students; for summer admission, 5/5 for domestic and international students. Applications are processed on a rolling basis. *Application fee:* $35. Electronic applications accepted. *Application Contact:* Misty Lindgren, Graduate Studies, 701-845-7303, Fax: 701-845-7190, E-mail: misty.lindgren@vcsu.edu. *Dean*, Dr. Sheri Okland, 701-845-7184, E-mail: sheri.l.okland@vcsu.edu.

VALPARAISO UNIVERSITY, Valparaiso, IN 46383

General Information Independent-religious, coed, comprehensive institution. CGS member. *Enrollment:* 4,053 graduate, professional, and undergraduate students; 382 full-time matriculated graduate/professional students (187 women), 399 part-time matriculated graduate/professional students (200 women). *Enrollment by degree level:* 724 master's, 49 doctoral, 8 other advanced degrees. *Graduate faculty:* 39 full-time (18 women), 131 part-time/adjunct (65 women). *Tuition:* Full-time $11,340; part-time $630 per credit hour. *Required fees:* $520; $250 per year. $125 per semester. Tuition and fees vary according to program and reciprocity agreements. *Graduate housing:* Rooms and/or apartments available on a first-come, first-served basis to single and married students. Typical cost: $10,000 per year ($14,000 including board) for single students; $8000 per year ($14,000 including board) for married students. Room and board charges vary according to board plan and housing facility selected. Housing application deadline: 8/1. *Student services:* Campus employment opportunities, campus safety program, career counseling, exercise/wellness program, free psychological counseling, international student services, low-cost health insurance, multicultural affairs office, services for students with disabilities, teacher training, writing training. *Library facilities:* Christopher Center for Library and Information Resources plus 1 other. *Collection:* Books: 545,491 (physical); Serial titles: 2,588 (physical), 79,749 (digital/electronic). Weekly public service hours: 112.

Computer facilities: 500 computers available on campus for general student use. A campuswide network can be accessed from student residence rooms and from off campus. Online class registration, Web academic information, degree audit, online course evaluations are available.
Website: http://www.valpo.edu/

General Application Contact: Michael Ramian, Assistant Director of Graduate Admissions, 219-464-5313, E-mail: graduate.school@valpo.edu.

GRADUATE UNITS

Graduate School and Continuing Education Students: 382 full-time (187 women), 399 part-time (200 women); includes 61 minority (28 Black or African American, non-Hispanic/Latino; 10 Asian, non-Hispanic/Latino; 15 Hispanic/Latino; 2 Native Hawaiian or other Pacific Islander, non-Hispanic/Latino; 6 Two or more races, non-Hispanic/Latino), 378 international. Average age 29. 805 applicants, 44% accepted, 147 enrolled. *Faculty:* 119 part-time/adjunct (59 women). Expenses: Contact institution. *Financial support:* Teaching assistantships, career-related internships or fieldwork, Federal Work-Study, scholarships/grants, traineeships, health care benefits, and unspecified assistantships available. Support available to part-time students. Financial award applicants required to submit FAFSA. In 2017, 357 master's, 16 doctorates, 27 other advanced degrees awarded. *Program availability:* Part-time, evening/weekend, 100% online, blended/hybrid learning. Offers analytics and modeling (MS); arts and entertainment administration (MA); clinical mental health counseling (MA); computing (MS); cyber security (MS); digital media (MS, Certificate); English studies and communication (MA); health administration (MHA); health care administration (MS); humane education (M Ed, MA, Graduate Certificate); initial licensure (M Ed); instructional leadership (M Ed); international commerce and policy (MS); international economics and finance (MS); management (MS); school psychology (Ed S); secondary education (M Ed); security8441 (MS); sports administration (MS); sports media (MS, Certificate); TESOL (MA, Certificate). *Application deadline:* For fall admission, 5/31 for international students; for spring admission, 10/15 for international students; for summer admission, 3/15 for international students. Applications are processed on a rolling basis. *Application fee:* $30 ($50 for international students). Electronic applications accepted. *Application Contact:* Jessica Choquette, Assistant Director of Graduate Admissions and Recruitment, 219-464-6510, Fax: 219-464-5381, E-mail: jessica.choquette@valpo.edu. *Dean, Graduate School and Continuing Education*, Dr. Jennifer A. Ziegler, 219-464-5313, Fax: 219-464-5381, E-mail: jennifer.ziegler@valpo.edu.

College of Business *Program availability:* Part-time, evening/weekend, online learning. Offers business administration (MBA); business decision-making (Certificate); business intelligence (Certificate); engineering management (Certificate); finance (Certificate); general business (Certificate); leading the global enterprise (Certificate); management (Certificate). Electronic applications accepted.

College of Nursing and Health Professions *Program availability:* Part-time, evening/weekend, online learning. Offers nursing (DNP); nursing education (MSN, Certificate); physician assistant (MSPA); public health (MPH). Electronic applications accepted.

Law School Students: 219 full-time (110 women), 15 part-time (9 women); includes 67 minority (24 Black or African American, non-Hispanic/Latino; 2 American Indian or Alaska Native, non-Hispanic/Latino; 6 Asian, non-Hispanic/Latino; 29 Hispanic/Latino; 2 Native Hawaiian or other Pacific Islander, non-Hispanic/Latino; 4 Two or more races, non-Hispanic/Latino). Average age 29. 471 applicants, 38% accepted, 28 enrolled. *Faculty:* 30 full-time (11 women), 26 part-time/adjunct (11 women). Expenses: Contact institution. *Financial support:* Fellowships, research assistantships, teaching assistantships, career-related internships or fieldwork, Federal Work-Study, institutionally sponsored loans, scholarships/grants, and tuition waivers (partial) available. Support available to part-time students. Financial award application deadline: 3/1; financial award applicants required to submit FAFSA. In 2017, 125 doctorates awarded. *Program availability:* Part-time. Offers law (LL M, JD). *Application deadline:* For fall admission, 6/15 priority date for domestic students. Applications are processed on a rolling basis. *Application fee:* $0. Electronic applications accepted. *Application Contact:* Anne Brandt, Director of Marketing and Admissions, 219-465-7821, Fax: 219-465-7975, E-mail: law.admissions@valpo.edu. *Interim Dean/Professor of Law*, David R. Cleveland, 219-465-7834, Fax: 219-465-7872, E-mail: david.cleveland@valpo.edu.

VAN ANDEL INSTITUTE GRADUATE SCHOOL, Grand Rapids, MI 49503

General Information Private, coed, graduate-only institution. *Enrollment by degree level:* 27 doctoral. *Graduate faculty:* 37 full-time (10 women). *Student services:* Career counseling, exercise/wellness program, free psychological counseling, grant writing training, international student services, low-cost health insurance, services for students with disabilities, teacher training, writing training. *Library facilities:* Van Andel Institute Library. *Collection:* Study areas open 24 hours, 5–7 days a week.

Computer facilities: 4 computers available on campus for general student use. A campuswide network can be accessed. Online class registration is available.
Website: https://vaigs.vai.org/

General Application Contact: Christy Mayo, Enrollment and Records Administrator, 616-234-5722, Fax: 616-234-5709, E-mail: christy.mayo@vai.org.

GRADUATE UNITS

PhD Program Students: 27 full-time (19 women); includes 6 minority (1 Black or African American, non-Hispanic/Latino; 4 Asian, non-Hispanic/Latino; 1 Hispanic/Latino). Average age 24. *Faculty:* 37 full-time (10 women). Expenses: Contact institution. *Financial support:* Fellowships and health care benefits available. Offers cell and molecular genetics (PhD). *Application deadline:* For fall admission, 12/1 for domestic and international students. Applications are processed on a rolling basis. Electronic applications accepted. *Application Contact:* Christy Mayo, Enrollment and Records Administrator, 616-234-5722, Fax: 616-234-5709, E-mail: christy.mayo@vai.org. *President and Dean*, Steve Triezenberg, 616-234-5708, Fax: 616-234-5709, E-mail: steve.triezenberg@vai.org.

VANCOUVER ISLAND UNIVERSITY, Nanaimo, BC V9R 5S5, Canada

General Information Province-supported, coed, comprehensive institution. *Graduate housing:* Room and/or apartments available on a first-come, first-served basis to single students; on-campus housing not available to married students. Housing application deadline: 3/5.

GRADUATE UNITS

Master of Business Administration Program *Program availability:* Part-time. Offers international business (MBA). Program offered jointly with University of Hertfordshire. Electronic applications accepted.

VANCOUVER SCHOOL OF THEOLOGY, Vancouver, BC V6T 1L4, Canada

General Information Independent-religious, coed, graduate-only institution. *Enrollment by degree level:* 87 master's, 11 other advanced degrees. One-time fee: $426 Canadian dollars full-time. *Graduate housing:* Rooms and/or apartments available on a first-come, first-served basis to single and married students. *Student services:* Campus employment opportunities, career counseling, low-cost health insurance. *Library facilities:* H.R. MacMillan Library.
Website: http://www.vst.edu/

General Application Contact: Julie Lees, Recruitment Coordinator, 604-822-6502, E-mail: jlees@vst.edu.

GRADUATE UNITS

Graduate and Professional Programs Expenses: Contact institution. *Financial support:* Research assistantships with partial tuition reimbursements, teaching assistantships with partial tuition reimbursements, career-related internships or fieldwork, scholarships/grants, and tuition waivers (partial) available. Support available to part-time students. Financial award application deadline: 3/15. *Program availability:* Part-time, online learning. Offers denominational studies (Diploma); indigenous and inter-religious studies (MA, Diploma); public and pastoral leadership (MA); public and pastoral leadership in spiritual care (MA); theological studies (MATS, Diploma, Graduate Diploma); theology (M Div, Th M). *Application deadline:* For fall admission, 10/15 for domestic and international students; for spring admission, 3/15 for domestic and international students. *Application fee:* $75 Canadian dollars. Electronic applications accepted. *Application Contact:* Anita Fast, Registrar, 604-822-9563, Fax: 604-822-9212, E-mail: afast@vst.edu. *Principal*, Rev. Dr. Richard Topping, 604-822-9808, Fax: 604-822-9212.

VANDERBILT UNIVERSITY, Nashville, TN 37240-1001

General Information Independent, coed, university. CGS member. *Enrollment:* 12,587 graduate, professional, and undergraduate students; 4,992 full-time matriculated graduate/professional students (2,809 women), 753 part-time matriculated graduate/professional students (574 women). *Enrollment by degree level:* 2,589 master's, 3,120 doctoral, 36 other advanced degrees. *Graduate faculty:* 1,081 full-time (324 women), 14 part-time/adjunct (3 women). *Graduate housing:* On-campus housing not available. *Student services:* Campus employment opportunities, campus safety program, career counseling, child daycare facilities, exercise/wellness program, free psychological counseling, grant writing training, international student services, low-cost health insurance, multicultural affairs office, services for students with disabilities, teacher training, writing training. *Library facilities:* Jean and Alexander Heard Library plus 7 others. *Collection:* Books: 3.1 million (physical), 1.7 million (digital/electronic); Databases: 3,700. *Research affiliation:* Medtronic, Incorporated (medical research), Celgene Corporation (biopharmaceuticals), Sandhill Scientific, Inc. (medical research),

Westat, Inc. (research and evaluation), Amgen (medicine), Boston Scientific Corporation (health science and technology).

Computer facilities: A campuswide network can be accessed from student residence rooms and from off campus. Online class registration, productivity and educational software are available.
Website: http://www.vanderbilt.edu/

General Application Contact: Walter B. Bieschke, Program Coordinator for Graduate Admissions, 615-322-0236, Fax: 615-343-9936, E-mail: vandygrad@vanderbilt.edu.

GRADUATE UNITS

Center for Medicine, Health, and Society Average age 23. 22 applicants, 77% accepted, 12 enrolled. Expenses: Contact institution. *Financial support:* Federal Work-Study, scholarships/grants, and health care benefits available. Financial award application deadline: 1/15; financial award applicants required to submit CSS PROFILE or FAFSA. In 2017, 10 master's awarded. Offers medicine, health, and society (MA). *Application deadline:* For fall admission, 1/15 for domestic and international students. Electronic applications accepted. *Application Contact:* Dominique Behague, Acting Director/Director of Graduate Studies, 615-322-0919, Fax: 615-322-2731, E-mail: dominique.behague@vanderbilt.edu. *Director,* Dr. Jonathan Metzl, 615-343-2504, Fax: 615-343-8889, E-mail: jonathan.metzl@vanderbilt.edu.

Department of Anthropology Students: 30 full-time (22 women); includes 5 minority (all Hispanic/Latino), 10 international. Average age 33. 47 applicants, 9% accepted, 4 enrolled. *Faculty:* 14 full-time (4 women). Expenses: Contact institution. *Financial support:* Fellowships with tuition reimbursements, research assistantships with full tuition reimbursements, teaching assistantships with full tuition reimbursements, career-related internships or fieldwork, Federal Work-Study, institutionally sponsored loans, scholarships/grants, and health care benefits available. Financial award application deadline: 1/15; financial award applicants required to submit CSS PROFILE or FAFSA. In 2017, 5 doctorates awarded. Offers anthropology (MA, PhD). *Application deadline:* For fall admission, 1/15 for domestic and international students. *Application fee:* $0. Electronic applications accepted. *Application Contact:* John Janusek, Director of Graduate Studies, 615-343-6120, E-mail: john.w.janusek@vanderbilt.edu. *Chair,* Dr. Beth Conklin, 615-343-6120, Fax: 615-343-0230, E-mail: beth.a.conklin@vanderbilt.edu.

Department of Biological Sciences Students: 52 full-time (27 women); includes 10 minority (1 Black or African American, non-Hispanic/Latino; 4 Asian, non-Hispanic/Latino; 3 Hispanic/Latino; 2 Two or more races, non-Hispanic/Latino), 18 international. Average age 27. 89 applicants, 16% accepted, 5 enrolled. *Faculty:* 20 full-time (4 women). Expenses: Contact institution. *Financial support:* Fellowships with tuition reimbursements, research assistantships with full tuition reimbursements, teaching assistantships with full tuition reimbursements, Federal Work-Study, institutionally sponsored loans, scholarships/grants, traineeships, and health care benefits available. Financial award application deadline: 1/15; financial award applicants required to submit CSS PROFILE or FAFSA. In 2017, 6 doctorates awarded. Offers biological sciences (MS, PhD). *Application deadline:* For fall admission, 1/15 for domestic and international students. Electronic applications accepted. *Application Contact:* Donna Webb, Director of Graduate Studies, 615-322-2008. *Chair,* Dr. Douglas McMahon, 615-322-2008, Fax: 615-343-6707, E-mail: douglas.g.mcmahon@vanderbilt.edu.

Department of Biomedical Informatics Students: 19 full-time (9 women); includes 4 minority (1 Black or African American, non-Hispanic/Latino; 3 Asian, non-Hispanic/Latino), 1 international. Average age 30. 61 applicants, 13% accepted, 4 enrolled. *Faculty:* 25 full-time (6 women). Expenses: Contact institution. *Financial support:* Fellowships with tuition reimbursements, research assistantships with tuition reimbursements, teaching assistantships with tuition reimbursements, Federal Work-Study, institutionally sponsored loans, scholarships/grants, traineeships, and health care benefits available. Financial award application deadline: 1/15; financial award applicants required to submit CSS PROFILE or FAFSA. In 2017, 7 master's, 2 doctorates awarded. *Program availability:* Part-time. Offers biomedical informatics (MS, PhD). *Application deadline:* For fall admission, 1/15 for domestic and international students. Electronic applications accepted. *Application Contact:* Gretchen Jackson, Director of Graduate Studies, 615-936-1050, Fax: 615-936-1427, E-mail: rischelle.jenkins@vanderbilt.edu. *Chair,* Dr. Kevin Johnson, 615-936-1423, Fax: 615-936-1427, E-mail: kevin.johnson@vanderbilt.edu.

Department of Chemistry Students: 116 full-time (51 women), 1 (woman) part-time; includes 27 minority (8 Black or African American, non-Hispanic/Latino; 3 Asian, non-Hispanic/Latino; 11 Hispanic/Latino; 5 Two or more races, non-Hispanic/Latino), 5 international. Average age 26. 347 applicants, 18% accepted, 23 enrolled. *Faculty:* 19 full-time (3 women). Expenses: Contact institution. *Financial support:* Fellowships with tuition reimbursements, research assistantships with full tuition reimbursements, teaching assistantships with full tuition reimbursements, Federal Work-Study, institutionally sponsored loans, scholarships/grants, traineeships, and health care benefits available. Financial award application deadline: 1/15; financial award applicants required to submit CSS PROFILE or FAFSA. In 2017, 3 master's, 20 doctorates awarded. Offers analytical chemistry (MAT, MS, PhD); inorganic chemistry (MAT, MS, PhD); organic chemistry (MAT, MS, PhD); physical chemistry (MAT, MS, PhD); theoretical chemistry (MAT, MS). *Application deadline:* For fall admission, 1/15 for domestic and international students. *Application fee:* $0. Electronic applications accepted. *Application Contact:* Carmello Rizzo, Director of Graduate Studies, 615-322-2861, Fax: 615-322-4936, E-mail: c.rizzo@vanderbilt.edu. *Chair,* Dr. David Cliffel, 615-343-3937, Fax: 615-322-4936, E-mail: d.cliffel@vanderbilt.edu.

Department of Classical Studies *Faculty:* 2 full-time (1 woman). Expenses: Contact institution. *Financial support:* Fellowships with tuition reimbursements, teaching assistantships with tuition reimbursements, Federal Work-Study, institutionally sponsored loans, scholarships/grants, and health care benefits available. Financial award application deadline: 1/15; financial award applicants required to submit CSS PROFILE or FAFSA. Offers classics (MA). *Application deadline:* For fall admission, 1/15 for domestic and international students. Electronic applications accepted. *Application Contact:* Walter B. Bieschke, Program Coordinator for Graduate Admissions, 615-322-0236, Fax: 615-343-9936, E-mail: vandygrad@vanderbilt.edu. *Director of Graduate Studies,* Dr. Barbara Tsakirgis, 615-322-2516, Fax: 615-343-7261, E-mail: barbara.tsakirgis@vanderbilt.edu.

Department of Earth and Environmental Sciences Students: 18 full-time (9 women); includes 1 minority (Hispanic/Latino). Average age 25. 66 applicants, 12% accepted, 8 enrolled. *Faculty:* 10 full-time (2 women). Expenses: Contact institution. *Financial support:* Fellowships with tuition reimbursements, research assistantships with tuition reimbursements, teaching assistantships with full tuition reimbursements, career-related internships or fieldwork, Federal Work-Study, institutionally sponsored loans, and health care benefits available. Financial award application deadline: 1/15; financial award applicants required to submit CSS PROFILE or FAFSA. In 2017, 4 master's awarded. Offers earth and environmental sciences (MAT, MS). *Application deadline:* For fall admission, 1/15 for domestic and international students. *Application fee:* $0. Electronic applications accepted. *Application Contact:* Guil Gualda, Director of Graduate Studies, 615-322-2976, E-mail: g.gualda@vanderbilt.edu. *Chair,* Dr. Steven Goodbred, 615-322-2976, E-mail: g.gualda@vanderbilt.edu.

Department of Economics Students: 94 full-time (36 women), 2 part-time (1 woman); includes 10 minority (2 Black or African American, non-Hispanic/Latino; 2 Asian, non-Hispanic/Latino; 1 Hispanic/Latino; 5 Two or more races, non-Hispanic/Latino), 57 international. Average age 27. 621 applicants, 28% accepted, 37 enrolled. *Faculty:* 31 full-time (4 women). Expenses: Contact institution. *Financial support:* Fellowships, teaching assistantships, career-related internships or fieldwork, Federal Work-Study, institutionally sponsored loans, scholarships/grants, and health care benefits available. Financial award application deadline: 1/15; financial award applicants required to submit CSS PROFILE or FAFSA. In 2017, 44 master's, 7 doctorates awarded. Offers economic development (MA); economics (PhD). *Application deadline:* For fall admission, 1/15 for domestic and international students; for spring admission, 11/1 for domestic students. Applications are processed on a rolling basis. Electronic applications accepted. *Application Contact:* Jennifer Reinganum, Director of Graduate Studies, 615-322-2871, Fax: 615-343-8495, E-mail: jennifer.f.reinganum@vanderbilt.edu. *Chair,* Dr. Eric Bond, 615-322-2871, Fax: 615-343-8495, E-mail: k.saggi@vanderbilt.edu.

Department of English Students: 35 full-time (26 women), 1 (woman) part-time; includes 15 minority (12 Black or African American, non-Hispanic/Latino; 2 Asian, non-Hispanic/Latino; 1 Two or more races, non-Hispanic/Latino), 4 international. Average age 28. 242 applicants, 7% accepted, 7 enrolled. *Faculty:* 31 full-time (21 women). Expenses: Contact institution. *Financial support:* Fellowships with tuition reimbursements, research assistantships with tuition reimbursements, teaching assistantships with full tuition reimbursements, Federal Work-Study, institutionally sponsored loans, scholarships/grants, and health care benefits available. Financial award application deadline: 1/15; financial award applicants required to submit CSS PROFILE or FAFSA. In 2017, 13 master's, 7 doctorates awarded. Offers English (MA, MAT, PhD). *Application deadline:* For fall admission, 1/15 for domestic and international students. Electronic applications accepted. *Application Contact:* Vera Kutzinski, Director of Graduate Studies, 615-322-2541, Fax: 615-343-8028, E-mail: vera.kutzinski@vanderbilt.edu. *Chair,* Dr. Dana Nelson, 615-322-2541, Fax: 615-343-8028, E-mail: dana.d.nelson@vanderbilt.edu.

Department of French and Italian Students: 13 full-time (8 women); includes 2 minority (1 Hispanic/Latino; 1 Two or more races, non-Hispanic/Latino), 2 international. Average age 28. 17 applicants, 29% accepted, 3 enrolled. *Faculty:* 12 full-time (7 women). Expenses: Contact institution. *Financial support:* Fellowships, teaching assistantships, career-related internships or fieldwork, Federal Work-Study, institutionally sponsored loans, scholarships/grants, and health care benefits available. Financial award application deadline: 1/15; financial award applicants required to submit CSS PROFILE or FAFSA. In 2017, 1 doctorate awarded. Offers French (MA, MAT, PhD). *Application deadline:* For fall admission, 1/15 for domestic and international students. Electronic applications accepted. *Application Contact:* Paul Miller, Director of Graduate Studies, 615-322-6900, Fax: 615-343-6909, E-mail: paul.miller@vanderbilt.edu. *Chair,* Dr. Laura Schneider, 615-322-6900, Fax: 615-343-6909, E-mail: laura.c.schneider@vanderbilt.edu.

Department of Germanic and Slavic Languages Students: 20 full-time (13 women); includes 4 minority (1 Black or African American, non-Hispanic/Latino; 1 Hispanic/Latino; 2 Two or more races, non-Hispanic/Latino), 3 international. Average age 30. 11 applicants, 36% accepted, 2 enrolled. *Faculty:* 6 full-time (3 women). Expenses: Contact institution. *Financial support:* Fellowships, teaching assistantships, career-related internships or fieldwork, Federal Work-Study, institutionally sponsored loans, scholarships/grants, and health care benefits available. Financial award application deadline: 1/15; financial award applicants required to submit CSS PROFILE or FAFSA. In 2017, 1 master's, 2 doctorates awarded. Offers German (MA, MAT, PhD). *Application deadline:* For fall admission, 1/15 for domestic and international students. Electronic applications accepted. *Application Contact:* Christoph Zeller, Director of Graduate Studies, 615-875-9065, Fax: 615-343-7258, E-mail: christoph.zeller@vanderbilt.edu. *Chair,* Dr. Lutz Koepnick, 615-322-2611, Fax: 615-343-7258, E-mail: lutz.koepnick@vanderbilt.edu.

Department of History Students: 56 full-time (32 women), 1 (woman) part-time; includes 10 minority (2 Black or African American, non-Hispanic/Latino; 1 Asian, non-Hispanic/Latino; 4 Hispanic/Latino; 3 Two or more races, non-Hispanic/Latino), 12 international. Average age 30. 175 applicants, 11% accepted, 7 enrolled. *Faculty:* 41 full-time (12 women). Expenses: Contact institution. *Financial support:* Fellowships with full tuition reimbursements, teaching assistantships with full tuition reimbursements, Federal Work-Study, institutionally sponsored loans, scholarships/grants, and health care benefits available. Financial award application deadline: 1/15; financial award applicants required to submit CSS PROFILE or FAFSA. In 2017, 10 master's, 7 doctorates awarded. Offers history (MA, MAT, PhD). *Application deadline:* For fall admission, 1/15 for domestic and international students. *Application fee:* $0. Electronic applications accepted. *Application Contact:* Catherine Molineux, Director of Graduate Studies, 615-322-2575, Fax: 615-343-6002, E-mail: catherine.a.molineux@vanderbilt.edu. *Chair,* Dr. Joel Harrington, 615-322-2575, Fax: 615-343-6002, E-mail: joel.harrington@vanderbilt.edu.

Department of Mathematics Students: 35 full-time (6 women), 2 part-time (0 women); includes 2 minority (1 Black or African American, non-Hispanic/Latino; 1 Two or more races, non-Hispanic/Latino), 20 international. Average age 25. 127 applicants, 13% accepted, 5 enrolled. *Faculty:* 30 full-time (2 women). Expenses: Contact institution. *Financial support:* Fellowships, research assistantships with full tuition reimbursements, teaching assistantships with full tuition reimbursements, Federal Work-Study, institutionally sponsored loans, scholarships/grants, and health care benefits available. Financial award application deadline: 1/15; financial award applicants required to submit CSS PROFILE or FAFSA. In 2017, 2 doctorates awarded. Offers mathematics (MA, MAT, MS, PhD). *Application deadline:* For fall admission, 1/1 for domestic and international students. *Application fee:* $0. Electronic applications accepted. *Application Contact:* Denis Osin, Director of Graduate Studies, 615-322-6672, Fax: 315-343-0215, E-mail: denis.v.osin@vanderbilt.edu. *Chair,* Dr. Mike Neamtu, 615-322-6672, Fax: 615-343-0215, E-mail: mike.neamtu@vanderbilt.edu.

Department of Philosophy Students: 28 full-time (17 women); includes 9 minority (1 Black or African American, non-Hispanic/Latino; 2 Asian, non-Hispanic/Latino; 3 Hispanic/Latino; 3 Two or more races, non-Hispanic/Latino), 1 international. Average age 28. 153 applicants, 6% accepted, 6 enrolled. *Faculty:* 13 full-time (3 women). Expenses: Contact institution. *Financial support:* Fellowships with full tuition reimbursements, teaching assistantships with full tuition reimbursements, Federal Work-Study, institutionally sponsored loans, scholarships/grants, and health care benefits available. Financial award application deadline: 1/15; financial award applicants required to submit CSS PROFILE or FAFSA. In 2017, 1 master's, 5 doctorates awarded. Offers philosophy (MA, PhD). *Application deadline:* For fall admission, 1/15 for domestic and international students. Electronic applications accepted. *Application Contact:* Julian Wuerth, Director of Graduate Studies, 615-322-2637, Fax: 615-343-7259, E-mail: julian.wuerth@vanderbilt.edu. *Chair,* Dr. Robert Talisse, 615-343-5349, Fax: 615-343-7259, E-mail: robert.talisse@vanderbilt.edu.

Department of Physics and Astronomy Students: 42 full-time (8 women), 1 part-time (0 women); includes 5 minority (1 Black or African American, non-Hispanic/Latino; 1 Asian, non-Hispanic/Latino; 2 Hispanic/Latino; 1 Two or more races, non-Hispanic/Latino), 13 international. Average age 27. 89 applicants, 26% accepted, 9 enrolled. *Faculty:* 25 full-time (4 women). Expenses: Contact institution. *Financial support:* Fellowships, research assistantships with full tuition reimbursements, teaching assistantships with full tuition reimbursements, career-related internships or fieldwork, Federal Work-Study, and institutionally sponsored loans available. Financial award application deadline: 1/15; financial award applicants required to submit CSS PROFILE or FAFSA. In 2017, 3 master's, 16 doctorates awarded. Offers astronomy (MS); health physics (MA); physics (MAT, MS, PhD). *Application deadline:* For fall admission, 1/1 for domestic and international students. Electronic applications accepted. *Application Contact:* Julia Velkovska, Director of Graduate Studies, 615-322-2828, E-mail: julia.velkovska@vanderbilt.edu. *Chair,* Dr. Robert Sherrer, 615-322-2828, E-mail: robert.scherrer@vanderbilt.edu.

Department of Political Science Students: 34 full-time (14 women), 1 (woman) part-time; includes 2 minority (1 Black or African American, non-Hispanic/Latino; 1 Two or more races, non-Hispanic/Latino), 12 international. Average age 28. 176 applicants, 16% accepted, 8 enrolled. *Faculty:* 25 full-time (8 women). Expenses: Contact institution. *Financial support:* Fellowships with full tuition reimbursements, research assistantships with full tuition reimbursements, teaching assistantships with full tuition reimbursements, Federal Work-Study, institutionally sponsored loans, scholarships/grants, and health care benefits available. Financial award application deadline: 1/15; financial award applicants required to submit CSS PROFILE or FAFSA. In 2017, 8 master's, 6 doctorates awarded. Offers political science (MA, MAT, PhD). *Application deadline:* For fall admission, 1/15 for domestic and international students. Electronic applications accepted. *Application Contact:* Jon Hiskey, Director of Graduate Studies, 615-322-6222, Fax: 615-343-6003, E-mail: j.hiskey@vanderbilt.edu. *Chair,* Dr. David Lewis, 615-322-6222, Fax: 615-343-6003, E-mail: david.lewis@vanderbilt.edu.

Department of Religion Students: 65 full-time (37 women); includes 20 minority (15 Black or African American, non-Hispanic/Latino; 2 Asian, non-Hispanic/Latino; 2 Hispanic/Latino; 1 Two or more races, non-Hispanic/Latino), 4 international. Average age 33. 128 applicants, 13% accepted, 12 enrolled. *Faculty:* 30 full-time (10 women). Expenses: Contact institution. *Financial support:* Fellowships, teaching assistantships, Federal Work-Study, institutionally sponsored loans, health care benefits, and tuition waivers (full and partial) available. Support available to part-time students. Financial award application deadline: 1/15; financial award applicants required to submit CSS PROFILE or FAFSA. In 2017, 7 master's, 12 doctorates awarded. Offers religion (MA, PhD). *Application deadline:* For fall admission, 12/15 for domestic and international students. Electronic applications accepted. *Application Contact:* Karen Eardley, Administrative Assistant, 615-343-3977, Fax: 615-343-9957, E-mail: karen.eardley@vanderbilt.edu. *Chair and Director of Graduate Studies,* Dr. James Byrd, Jr., 615-343-9977, Fax: 615-343-9957, E-mail: james.p.byrd@vanderbilt.edu.

Department of Sociology Students: 34 full-time (27 women); includes 15 minority (6 Black or African American, non-Hispanic/Latino; 5 Asian, non-Hispanic/Latino; 4 Hispanic/Latino), 3 international. Average age 28. 124 applicants, 6% accepted, 4 enrolled. *Faculty:* 16 full-time (6 women). Expenses: Contact institution. *Financial support:* Fellowships with full tuition reimbursements, research assistantships, teaching assistantships with full tuition reimbursements, Federal Work-Study, institutionally sponsored loans, scholarships/grants, and health care benefits available. Financial award application deadline: 1/15; financial award applicants required to submit CSS PROFILE or FAFSA. In 2017, 5 master's, 2 doctorates awarded. Offers sociology (MA, PhD). *Application deadline:* For fall admission, 1/15 for domestic and international students. Electronic applications accepted. *Application Contact:* Richard Pitt, Director of Graduate Studies, 615-322-7530, Fax: 615-322-7505, E-mail: r.pitt@vanderbilt.edu. *Chair,* Dr. Larry Isaac, 615-322-7626, Fax: 615-322-7505, E-mail: larry.isaac@vanderbilt.edu.

Department of Spanish and Portuguese Students: 24 full-time (12 women); includes 7 minority (2 Black or African American, non-Hispanic/Latino; 5 Hispanic/Latino), 12 international. Average age 31. 39 applicants, 18% accepted, 6 enrolled. *Faculty:* 12 full-time (5 women). Expenses: Contact institution. *Financial support:* Fellowships, teaching assistantships with full tuition reimbursements, Federal Work-Study, institutionally sponsored loans, and health care benefits available. Financial award application deadline: 1/15; financial award applicants required to submit CSS PROFILE or FAFSA. In 2017, 1 master's, 4 doctorates awarded. Offers Portuguese (MA); Spanish (MA, MAT, PhD); Spanish and Portuguese (PhD). *Application deadline:* For fall admission, 1/15 for domestic and international students. Electronic applications accepted. *Application Contact:* Andres Zamora, Director of Graduate Studies, 615-322-6930, Fax: 615-343-7260, E-mail: andres.zamora@vanderbilt.edu. *Chair,* Dr. Benigno Trigo, 615-322-6930, Fax: 615-343-7260, E-mail: benigno.trigo@vanderbilt.edu.

Divinity School *Program availability:* Part-time. Offers divinity (M Div, MTS). Electronic applications accepted.

Peabody College Students: 518 full-time (424 women), 217 part-time (149 women); includes 142 minority (63 Black or African American, non-Hispanic/Latino; 1 American Indian or Alaska Native, non-Hispanic/Latino; 27 Asian, non-Hispanic/Latino; 30 Hispanic/Latino; 1 Native Hawaiian or other Pacific Islander, non-Hispanic/Latino; 20 Two or more races, non-Hispanic/Latino), 80 international. Average age 27. 1,488 applicants, 63% accepted, 377 enrolled. *Faculty:* 166 full-time (107 women), 85 part-time/adjunct (53 women). Expenses: Contact institution. *Financial support:* In 2017–18, 520 students received support. Fellowships with partial tuition reimbursements available, research assistantships with partial tuition reimbursements available, teaching assistantships with partial tuition reimbursements available, career-related internships or fieldwork, Federal Work-Study, institutionally sponsored loans, scholarships/grants, traineeships, tuition waivers (partial), and unspecified assistantships available. Support available to part-time students. Financial award application deadline: 1/15; financial award applicants required to submit FAFSA. In 2017, 315 master's, 22 doctorates awarded. *Program availability:* Part-time, online courses with semester immersions on campus. Offers child studies (M Ed); clinical psychological assessment (M Ed); community development and action (M Ed); education and human development (M Ed, MPP, Ed D); education policy (MPP); educational leadership and policy (Ed D); elementary education (M Ed); English language learners (M Ed); higher education (M Ed); higher education leadership and policy (Ed D); human development counseling (M Ed); independent school leadership (M Ed); international education policy and management (M Ed); leadership and learning in organizations (Ed D); leadership and organizational performance (M Ed); learning and design (M Ed); learning, diversity, and urban studies (M Ed); quantitative methods (M Ed); reading education (M Ed); secondary education (M Ed); special education (M Ed). *Application deadline:* For fall admission, 12/31 priority date for domestic and international students; for spring admission, 11/1 priority date for domestic and international students. Applications are processed on a rolling basis. Electronic applications accepted. *Application Contact:* Kimberly Brazil, Director of Graduate and Professional Admissions, 615-332-8410, Fax: 615-343-3474, E-mail: kim.brazil@vanderbilt.edu. *Dean,* Dr. Camilla P. Benbow, 615-322-8407, Fax: 615-322-8501, E-mail: camilla.benbow@vanderbilt.edu.

PhD Program in Special Education Students: 45 full-time (41 women); includes 7 minority (2 Asian, non-Hispanic/Latino; 2 Hispanic/Latino; 3 Two or more races, non-Hispanic/Latino), 1 international. Average age 31. 45 applicants, 13% accepted, 5 enrolled. *Faculty:* 17 full-time (11 women). Expenses: Contact institution. *Financial support:* Fellowships with full tuition reimbursements, research assistantships with full tuition reimbursements, teaching assistantships with full tuition reimbursements, Federal Work-Study, institutionally sponsored loans, traineeships, and health care benefits available. Financial award application deadline: 1/15; financial award applicants required to submit CSS PROFILE or FAFSA. In 2017, 8 doctorates awarded. Offers special education (PhD). *Application deadline:* For fall admission, 12/1 for domestic and international students. *Application fee:* $0. Electronic applications accepted. *Application Contact:* Dr. Robert Hodapp, Director of Graduate Studies, 615-322-8150, Fax: 615-343-1570, E-mail: robert.hodapp@vanderbilt.edu. *Chair,* Dr. Joseph Wehby, 615-322-8150, Fax: 615-343-1570, E-mail: joseph.wehby@vanderbilt.edu.

Program in Community Research and Action Students: 25 full-time (18 women); includes 13 minority (6 Black or African American, non-Hispanic/Latino; 4 Asian, non-Hispanic/Latino; 1 Hispanic/Latino; 2 Two or more races, non-Hispanic/Latino), 4 international. Average age 31. 101 applicants, 11% accepted, 5 enrolled. Expenses: Contact institution. *Financial support:* In 2017–18, 16 students received support. Fellowships with tuition reimbursements available, research assistantships with full tuition reimbursements available, teaching assistantships with full tuition reimbursements available, Federal Work-Study, scholarships/grants, health care benefits, tuition waivers, and unspecified assistantships available. Financial award application deadline: 1/15; financial award applicants required to submit FAFSA. In 2017, 4 doctorates awarded. Offers community research and action (PhD). *Application deadline:* For fall admission, 12/1 for domestic and international students. *Application fee:* $0. Electronic applications accepted. *Application Contact:* Sherrie Lane, Administrative Assistant, 615-322-8484, Fax: 615-322-1141, E-mail: sherrie.a.lane@vanderbilt.edu. *Director of Graduate Studies,* Dr. Douglas Perkins, 615-322-7213, Fax: 615-322-1769, E-mail: douglas.d.perkins@vanderbilt.edu.

Program in Creative Writing Average age 27. 426 applicants, 2% accepted, 6 enrolled. Expenses: Contact institution. *Financial support:* Fellowships, teaching assistantships, Federal Work-Study, institutionally sponsored loans, and health care benefits available. Financial award application deadline: 1/15; financial award applicants required to submit CSS PROFILE or FAFSA. In 2017, 6 master's awarded. Offers creative writing (MFA). *Application deadline:* For fall admission, 1/15 for domestic and international students. Electronic applications accepted. *Application Contact:* Katherine Daniels, Director of Graduate Studies, 615-322-2541, E-mail: kate.daniels@vanderbilt.edu. *Chair,* Dr. Dana Nelson, 615-322-2541, E-mail: dana.d.nelson@vanderbilt.edu.

Program in Human Genetics Students: 10 full-time (5 women); includes 2 minority (both Asian, non-Hispanic/Latino), 2 international. Average age 26. *Faculty:* 31 full-time (9 women). Expenses: Contact institution. *Financial support:* Fellowships, research assistantships, Federal Work-Study, institutionally sponsored loans, traineeships, and health care benefits available. Financial award application deadline: 1/15; financial award applicants required to submit CSS PROFILE or FAFSA. In 2017, 3 doctorates awarded. Offers human genetics (PhD). *Application deadline:* For fall admission, 1/15 for domestic and international students. *Application fee:* $0. Electronic applications accepted. *Application Contact:* David Samuels, Director of Graduate Studies, 615-343-8555, E-mail: david.c.samuels@vanderbilt.edu. *Director,* Dr. Nancy Cox, 615-343-8555, Fax: 615-322-1453, E-mail: nancy.j.cox@vanderbilt.edu.

Program in Latin American Studies Students: 8 full-time (3 women); includes 3 minority (1 Black or African American, non-Hispanic/Latino; 2 Hispanic/Latino), 2 international. Average age 25. 17 applicants, 35% accepted, 4 enrolled. *Faculty:* 62 full-time (22 women). Expenses: Contact institution. *Financial support:* Teaching assistantships with full tuition reimbursements, Federal Work-Study, institutionally sponsored loans, and health care benefits available. Financial award application deadline: 1/15; financial award applicants required to submit CSS PROFILE or FAFSA. In 2017, 4 master's awarded. Offers Latin American studies (MA). *Application deadline:* For fall admission, 1/15 for domestic and international students. *Application fee:* $0. Electronic applications accepted. *Application Contact:* Nicolette M. Kostiw, Assistant Director/Director of Graduate Studies, 615-322-2527, Fax: 615-343-6002, E-mail: nicolette.m.wilhide@vanderbilt.edu. *Director,* Dr. Edward Fischer, 615-322-2527, Fax: 615-343-6002, E-mail: edward.f.fischer@vanderbilt.edu.

Program in Leadership and Policy Studies Students: 34 full-time (17 women), 1 part-time (0 women); includes 13 minority (2 Black or African American, non-Hispanic/Latino; 6 Asian, non-Hispanic/Latino; 3 Hispanic/Latino; 2 Two or more races, non-Hispanic/Latino). Average age 31. 104 applicants, 11% accepted, 4 enrolled. *Faculty:* 16 full-time (7 women). Expenses: Contact institution. *Financial support:* Fellowships with full tuition reimbursements, research assistantships with full tuition reimbursements, teaching assistantships with full tuition reimbursements, Federal Work-Study, institutionally sponsored loans, scholarships/grants, traineeships, and health care benefits available. Financial award application deadline: 1/15; financial award applicants required to submit CSS PROFILE or FAFSA. In 2017, 4 doctorates awarded. Offers higher education leadership and policy (PhD); K-12 educational leadership and policy (PhD). *Application deadline:* For fall admission, 12/1 for domestic and international students. *Application fee:* $0. Electronic applications accepted. *Application Contact:* Rosie Moody, Admissions and Education Coordinator, 615-322-8019, Fax: 615-343-7094, E-mail: rosie.moody@vanderbilt.edu. *Director of Graduate Studies,* Dr. Ron Zimmer, 615-322-0722, Fax: 615-343-7094, E-mail: ronald.w.zimmer@vanderbilt.edu.

Program in Learning, Teaching and Diversity Students: 36 full-time (29 women); includes 11 minority (2 Black or African American, non-Hispanic/Latino; 5 Asian, non-Hispanic/Latino; 4 Two or more races, non-Hispanic/Latino), 2 international. Average age 32. 126 applicants, 7% accepted, 7 enrolled. *Faculty:* 18 full-time (10 women), 1 (woman) part-time/adjunct. Expenses: Contact institution. *Financial support:* Fellowships with partial tuition reimbursements, research assistantships with full tuition reimbursements, teaching assistantships with full tuition reimbursements, Federal Work-Study, institutionally sponsored loans, scholarships/grants, traineeships, and health care benefits available. Financial award application deadline: 1/15; financial award applicants required to submit CSS PROFILE or FAFSA. In 2017, 9 doctorates awarded. Offers learning, teaching and diversity (PhD). *Application deadline:* For fall admission, 12/1 for domestic and international students. *Application fee:* $0. Electronic applications accepted. *Application Contact:* Angela Saylor, Educational Coordinator, 615-322-8092,

Fax: 615-322-8014, E-mail: angela.saylor@vanderbilt.edu. *Director of Graduate Studies*, Dr. Melissa Gresalfi, 615-322-8227, Fax: 615-322-8014, E-mail: melissa.gresalfi@vanderbilt.edu.

Program in Liberal Arts and Science Students: 1 full-time (0 women), 34 part-time (22 women); includes 5 minority (3 Black or African American, non-Hispanic/Latino; 1 Asian, non-Hispanic/Latino; 1 Two or more races, non-Hispanic/Latino). Average age 42. 16 applicants, 75% accepted, 9 enrolled. Expenses: Contact institution. *Financial support:* Institutionally sponsored loans and tuition waivers (partial) available. In 2017, 12 master's awarded. *Program availability:* Part-time. Offers liberal arts and science (MLAS). *Application deadline:* For fall admission, 1/15 priority date for domestic students, 1/15 for international students; for spring admission, 11/15 for domestic and international students. Applications are processed on a rolling basis. *Application Contact:* Lisa Poynter, Coordinator, 615-343-3140, Fax: 615-343-8702, E-mail: lisa.poynter@vanderbilt.edu. *Associate Dean and Director of Graduate Studies*, Dr. Martin Rapisarda, 615-343-3140, Fax: 615-343-8702, E-mail: martin.rapisarda@vanderbilt.edu.

Program in Nursing Science Students: 24 full-time (20 women), 4 part-time (2 women); includes 7 minority (1 Black or African American, non-Hispanic/Latino; 3 Hispanic/Latino; 1 Native Hawaiian or other Pacific Islander, non-Hispanic/Latino; 2 Two or more races, non-Hispanic/Latino). Average age 36. 41 applicants, 20% accepted, 7 enrolled. *Faculty:* 23 full-time (20 women), 4 part-time/adjunct (2 women). Expenses: Contact institution. *Financial support:* Fellowships with full tuition reimbursements, research assistantships with full tuition reimbursements, teaching assistantships with full tuition reimbursements, career-related internships or fieldwork, Federal Work-Study, institutionally sponsored loans, scholarships/grants, health care benefits, and tuition waivers (full and partial) available. Financial award application deadline: 1/15; financial award applicants required to submit CSS PROFILE or FAFSA. In 2017, 4 doctorates awarded. Offers nursing science (PhD). *Application deadline:* For fall admission, 1/15 for domestic and international students. Electronic applications accepted. *Application Contact:* Judy Vesterfelt, Program Manager, 615-322-7410, E-mail: judy.vesterfelt@vanderbilt.edu. *Director of Graduate Studies*, Sheila Ridner, 615-322-3800, Fax: 615-343-5898, E-mail: sheila.ridner@vanderbilt.edu.

Program in Psychological Sciences Students: 74 full-time (49 women), 1 (woman) part-time; includes 6 minority (1 Black or African American, non-Hispanic/Latino; 1 Asian, non-Hispanic/Latino; 2 Hispanic/Latino; 2 Two or more races, non-Hispanic/Latino), 20 international. Average age 27. 486 applicants, 4% accepted, 8 enrolled. *Faculty:* 49 full-time (20 women). Expenses: Contact institution. *Financial support:* Fellowships with full tuition reimbursements, research assistantships with full tuition reimbursements, teaching assistantships with full tuition reimbursements, career-related internships or fieldwork, Federal Work-Study, institutionally sponsored loans, scholarships/grants, traineeships, and health care benefits available. Financial award application deadline: 1/15; financial award applicants required to submit CSS PROFILE or FAFSA. In 2017, 16 doctorates awarded. Offers psychological sciences (PhD). *Application deadline:* For fall admission, 12/1 for domestic and international students. *Application fee:* $0. Electronic applications accepted. *Application Contact:* Dr. Rene Marois, Director of Graduate Studies for Psychological Studies in the College of Arts and Science, 615-322-1779, Fax: 615-343-5027, E-mail: r.marois@vanderbilt.edu. *Director of Graduate Studies for the Psychology of Human Development in Peabody College*, Dr. Daniel T. Levin, 615-322-1518, Fax: 615-343-9494, E-mail: daniel.t.levin@vanderbilt.edu.

School of Engineering *Program availability:* Part-time. Offers biomedical engineering (M Eng, MS, PhD); chemical and biomolecular engineering (M Eng, MS, PhD); civil engineering (M Eng, MS, PhD); computer science (M Eng, MS, PhD); cyber-physical systems (M Eng); electrical engineering (M Eng, MS, PhD); engineering (M Eng, MS, PhD); environmental engineering (M Eng, MS, PhD); environmental management (MS, PhD); materials science (M Eng, MS, PhD); mechanical engineering (M Eng, MS, PhD). MS and PhD offered through the Graduate School. Electronic applications accepted.

School of Medicine Expenses: Contact institution. *Financial support:* Institutionally sponsored loans and scholarships/grants available. Financial award application deadline: 3/1; financial award applicants required to submit FAFSA. Offers audiology (Au D, PhD); biochemistry (MS, PhD); cell and developmental biology (MS, PhD); chemical and physical biology (PhD); education of the deaf (MDE); medicine (MDE, MMP, MS, MSCI, Au D, DMP, MD, PhD); microbiology and immunology (MS, PhD); molecular physiology and biophysics (MS, PhD); pathology and immunology (PhD); pharmacology (PhD); speech-language pathology (MS, PhD). *Application deadline:* For fall admission, 11/15 for domestic and international students. *Application fee:* $50. *Dean, School of Medicine*, Dr. Jeffrey R. Balser, 615-936-3030, E-mail: jeffrey.balser@vanderbilt.edu.

Vanderbilt Law School Offers law (LL M, JD); law and economics (PhD). Electronic applications accepted.

Vanderbilt University Owen Graduate School of Management *Program availability:* Evening/weekend. Offers accountancy (M Acc); accounting (MBA); business administration (EMBA, MBA); finance (MS); general management (MBA); health care (MBA); human and organizational performance (MBA); management (EMBA, M Acc, M Mark, MBA, MM, MS); marketing (MBA); operations (MBA); strategy (MBA); valuation (M Acc).

Vanderbilt University School of Nursing Students: 501 full-time (435 women), 387 part-time (355 women); includes 153 minority (40 Black or African American, non-Hispanic/Latino; 1 American Indian or Alaska Native, non-Hispanic/Latino; 27 Asian, non-Hispanic/Latino; 48 Hispanic/Latino; 4 Native Hawaiian or other Pacific Islander, non-Hispanic/Latino; 33 Two or more races, non-Hispanic/Latino), 9 international. Average age 31. 1,210 applicants, 57% accepted, 473 enrolled. *Faculty:* 292 full-time (267 women), 321 part-time/adjunct (253 women). Expenses: Contact institution. *Financial support:* In 2017–18, 627 students received support. Scholarships/grants available. Financial award application deadline: 3/1; financial award applicants required to submit FAFSA. In 2017, 319 master's, 47 doctorates awarded. *Program availability:* Part-time, 100% online, blended/hybrid learning. Offers adult-gerontology acute care nurse practitioner (MSN); adult-gerontology primary care nurse practitioner (MSN); emergency nurse practitioner (MSN); family nurse practitioner (MSN); healthcare leadership (MSN); neonatal nurse practitioner (MSN); nurse midwifery (MSN); nurse midwifery/family nurse practitioner (MSN); nursing (Post-Master's Certificate); nursing informatics (MSN); nursing practice (DNP); nursing science (PhD); pediatric acute care nurse practitioner (MSN); pediatric primary care nurse practitioner (MSN); psychiatric-mental health nurse practitioner (MSN); women's health nurse practitioner (MSN); women's health nurse practitioner/adult gerontology primary care nurse practitioner (MSN). *Application deadline:* For fall admission, 11/1 priority date for domestic and international students. Applications are processed on a rolling basis. *Application fee:* $50. Electronic applications accepted. *Application Contact:* Patricia Peerman, Assistant Dean for Enrollment Management, 615-322-3800, Fax: 615-343-0333, E-mail: vusn-admissions@vanderbilt.edu. *Dean*, Dr. Linda Norman, 615-343-8876, Fax: 615-343-7711, E-mail: linda.norman@vanderbilt.edu.

VANDERCOOK COLLEGE OF MUSIC, Chicago, IL 60616-3731

General Information Independent, coed, comprehensive institution. *Graduate housing:* Rooms and/or apartments available on a first-come, first-served basis to single and married students. Housing application deadline: 6/1.

GRADUATE UNITS

Master of Music Education Program *Program availability:* Part-time. Offers music education (MM Ed).

VANGUARD UNIVERSITY OF SOUTHERN CALIFORNIA, Costa Mesa, CA 92626

General Information Independent-religious, coed, comprehensive institution. *Enrollment:* 2,116 graduate, professional, and undergraduate students; 104 full-time matriculated graduate/professional students (71 women), 197 part-time matriculated graduate/professional students (143 women). *Enrollment by degree level:* 301 master's. *Graduate housing:* On-campus housing not available. *Student services:* Campus employment opportunities, campus safety program, career counseling, free psychological counseling, international student services, low-cost health insurance, multicultural affairs office, services for students with disabilities, teacher training, writing training. *Library facilities:* O. Cope Budge Library. *Collection:* Students can reserve study rooms.

Computer facilities: 100 computers available on campus for general student use. A campuswide network can be accessed. Online class registration is available.
Website: http://www.vanguard.edu/

General Application Contact: Karen Benitez, Director of Admissions, 714-966-5421, Fax: 714-966-5471, E-mail: karen.benitez@vanguard.edu.

GRADUATE UNITS

Graduate Program in Clinical Psychology Expenses: Contact institution. *Financial support:* Federal Work-Study, scholarships/grants, and unspecified assistantships available. Support available to part-time students. Financial award application deadline: 3/2; financial award applicants required to submit FAFSA. *Program availability:* Part-time, evening/weekend. Offers clinical psychology (MS). *Application deadline:* For fall admission, 7/1 for domestic and international students; for spring admission, 11/1 for domestic and international students. Applications are processed on a rolling basis. *Application fee:* $45. Electronic applications accepted. *Application Contact:* Karen Benitez, Director of Admissions, 714-966-5499, Fax: 714-966-5471, E-mail: karen.benitez@vanguard.edu. *Director*, Dr. Jerre White, 714-619-6455, Fax: 714-662-5226, E-mail: jwhite@vanguard.edu.

Graduate Program in Nursing Expenses: Contact institution. *Financial support:* Federal Work-Study available. *Program availability:* Part-time, evening/weekend, blended/hybrid learning. Offers nursing (MSN). *Application deadline:* For fall admission, 3/1 priority date for domestic students; for spring admission, 10/1 priority date for domestic students. *Application fee:* $45. *Application Contact:* Karen Benitez, Director of Admissions, 714-966-5499, Fax: 714-966-5471, E-mail: karen.benitez@vanguard.edu. *Director*, 714-668-6101, Fax: 714-966-6306.

Graduate Program in Organizational Psychology Offers intercultural studies (MS); training and development in organizations (MS).

Graduate Programs in Education Expenses: Contact institution. *Financial support:* Federal Work-Study and scholarships/grants available. Support available to part-time students. Financial award application deadline: 3/2; financial award applicants required to submit FAFSA. *Program availability:* Evening/weekend. Offers Christian education leadership (MA); curriculum and instruction (MA); teacher leadership (MA). *Application deadline:* For fall admission, 3/1 priority date for domestic and international students; for spring admission, 10/1 priority date for domestic and international students. Applications are processed on a rolling basis. *Application fee:* $45. Electronic applications accepted. *Application Contact:* Karen Benitez, Director of Admissions, 714-966-5499, Fax: 714-966-5471, E-mail: karen.benitez@vanguard.edu. *Graduate Program Coordinator*, Andre Abrantes, 714-619-6404, Fax: 714-966-5495, E-mail: andre.abrantes@vanguard.edu.

Graduate Programs in Religion Expenses: Contact institution. *Financial support:* Teaching assistantships, Federal Work-Study, and scholarships/grants available. Support available to part-time students. Financial award application deadline: 3/2; financial award applicants required to submit FAFSA. *Program availability:* Part-time, evening/weekend, 100% online, blended/hybrid learning. Offers leadership studies (MA); theology (MA). *Application deadline:* For fall admission, 3/1 priority date for domestic and international students; for spring admission, 10/1 priority date for domestic and international students; for summer admission, 2/1 priority date for domestic and international students. Applications are processed on a rolling basis. *Application fee:* $45. Electronic applications accepted. *Application Contact:* Karen Benitez, Director of Admissions, 714-966-5499, Fax: 714-966-5471, E-mail: karen.benitez@vanguard.edu. *Chair*, Dr. Willem Dogterom, 714-966-6350, Fax: 714-957-9317, E-mail: bdogterom@vanguard.edu.

VAUGHN COLLEGE OF AERONAUTICS AND TECHNOLOGY, Flushing, NY 11369

General Information Independent, coed, primarily men, comprehensive institution.

GRADUATE UNITS

Graduate Programs Offers airport management (MS).

VERMONT COLLEGE OF FINE ARTS, Montpelier, VT 05602

General Information Independent, coed, graduate-only institution. *Enrollment by degree level:* 388 master's. *Graduate faculty:* 125 part-time/adjunct (67 women). *Tuition:* Full-time $27,480; part-time $830 per credit hour. *Required fees:* $1300. *Graduate housing:* Rooms and/or apartments available on a first-come, first-served basis to single and married students. Typical cost: $5175 per year for single students; $7762 per year for married students. Room charges vary according to board plan. *Student services:* Campus safety program, international student services, services for students with disabilities. *Library facilities:* The Gary Library. *Collection:* Books: 60,000 (physical), 110,000 (digital/electronic); Serial titles: 250 (physical), 250 (digital/electronic); Databases: 10. Weekly public service hours: 40.

Computer facilities: 26 computers available on campus for general student use. A campuswide network can be accessed from student residence rooms.
Website: http://www.vcfa.edu/

General Application Contact: David Markow, Director of Enrollment Management, 802-828-8535, E-mail: admissions@vcfa.edu.

GRADUATE UNITS

Graduate Studies in Art and Design Education Students: 16 full-time (13 women), 2 part-time (both women); includes 6 minority (2 Black or African American, non-Hispanic/Latino; 1 American Indian or Alaska Native, non-Hispanic/Latino; 1 Asian, non-Hispanic/Latino; 1 Hispanic/Latino; 1 Native Hawaiian or other Pacific Islander, non-Hispanic/Latino). Average age 32. 17 applicants, 94% accepted, 11 enrolled. *Faculty:* 4 full-time (3 women). Expenses: Contact institution. *Financial support:* In 2017–18, 18 students received support. Scholarships/grants available. Financial award application deadline: 4/1; financial award applicants required to submit FAFSA. Offers art and design education (MA, MAT). *Application deadline:* For fall admission, 4/1 priority date for domestic and international students. Applications are processed on a rolling basis. *Application fee:* $75. Electronic applications accepted. *Application Contact:* David Markow, Director of Enrollment Management, 802-828-8535, E-mail: admissions@vcfa.edu. *Director,* Jennifer Skinder, E-mail: jennifer.skinder@vcfa.edu.

International MFA in Creative Writing and Literary Translation Program Offers creative writing and literary translation (MFA).

MFA in Film Program Students: 39 full-time (16 women); includes 8 minority (1 Black or African American, non-Hispanic/Latino; 1 American Indian or Alaska Native, non-Hispanic/Latino; 5 Hispanic/Latino; 1 Two or more races, non-Hispanic/Latino), 1 international. Average age 42. 15 applicants, 73% accepted, 8 enrolled. *Faculty:* 7 part-time/adjunct (3 women). Expenses: Contact institution. *Financial support:* In 2017–18, 35 students received support. Scholarships/grants available. Financial award application deadline: 6/15; financial award applicants required to submit FAFSA. In 2017, 19 master's awarded. Offers film (MFA). *Application deadline:* For fall admission, 8/15 for domestic students; for spring admission, 2/15 for domestic students. Applications are processed on a rolling basis. *Application fee:* $75. Electronic applications accepted. *Director,* Stephen Pite, 802-828-8529, E-mail: stephen.pite@vcfa.edu.

MFA in Graphic Design Program Students: 32 full-time (15 women); includes 5 minority (1 Asian, non-Hispanic/Latino; 3 Hispanic/Latino; 1 Two or more races, non-Hispanic/Latino), 1 international. Average age 35. 31 applicants, 74% accepted, 14 enrolled. *Faculty:* 10 part-time/adjunct (5 women). Expenses: Contact institution. *Financial support:* In 2017–18, 28 students received support. Scholarships/grants available. Financial award applicants required to submit FAFSA. In 2017, 12 master's awarded. Offers graphic design (MFA). *Application deadline:* Applications are processed on a rolling basis. *Application fee:* $75. Electronic applications accepted. *Program Director,* Jennifer Renko, 866-934-8232 Ext. 8896, E-mail: jennifer.renko@vcfa.edu.

MFA in Music Composition Program Students: 33 full-time (10 women); includes 5 minority (1 Black or African American, non-Hispanic/Latino; 2 Hispanic/Latino; 2 Two or more races, non-Hispanic/Latino), 1 international. Average age 43. 13 applicants, 77% accepted, 6 enrolled. *Faculty:* 10 part-time/adjunct (1 woman). Expenses: Contact institution. *Financial support:* In 2017–18, 32 students received support. Scholarships/grants available. Financial award applicants required to submit FAFSA. In 2017, 21 master's awarded. Offers music composition (MFA). *Application deadline:* Applications are processed on a rolling basis. *Application fee:* $75. *Application Contact:* Sarah Madru, Assistant Program Director, 802-828-8534, E-mail: sarah.madru@vcfa.edu. *Program Director,* Carol Beatty, 866-934-8232 Ext. 8610, E-mail: carol.beatty@vcfa.edu.

MFA in Visual Art Program Students: 38 full-time (27 women); includes 4 minority (3 Hispanic/Latino; 1 Two or more races, non-Hispanic/Latino), 3 international. Average age 42. 45 applicants, 58% accepted, 16 enrolled. *Faculty:* 12 part-time/adjunct (6 women). Expenses: Contact institution. *Financial support:* In 2017–18, 33 students received support. Scholarships/grants available. Financial award applicants required to submit FAFSA. In 2017, 19 master's awarded. Offers visual art (MFA). *Application deadline:* For fall admission, 2/15 priority date for domestic students, 2/15 for international students; for spring admission, 9/15 priority date for domestic students, 9/15 for international students. Applications are processed on a rolling basis. *Application fee:* $75. Electronic applications accepted. *Application Contact:* Thatiana Oliveria, Assistant Director of Admissions, 802-828-8636, E-mail: thatiana.oliveria@vcfa.edu. *Program Director,* Danielle Dahline, 802-828-8703, E-mail: danielle.dahline@vcfa.edu.

MFA in Writing and Publishing Program Students: 25 full-time (17 women), 1 (woman) part-time; includes 6 minority (1 American Indian or Alaska Native, non-Hispanic/Latino; 2 Asian, non-Hispanic/Latino; 2 Hispanic/Latino; 1 Two or more races, non-Hispanic/Latino), 3 international. Average age 31. *Faculty:* 5 full-time (3 women). Expenses: Contact institution. *Financial support:* In 2017–18, 26 students received support, including 6 fellowships (averaging $3,000 per year); scholarships/grants also available. In 2017, 6 master's awarded. Offers writing and publishing (MFA). *Application Contact:* David Markow, Director of Enrollment Management, 802-828-8535, E-mail: admissions@vcfa.edu. *Director,* Miciah Gault, 802-828-8534.

MFA in Writing for Children and Young Adults Program Students: 91 full-time (82 women); includes 17 minority (1 Black or African American, non-Hispanic/Latino; 4 Asian, non-Hispanic/Latino; 6 Hispanic/Latino; 6 Two or more races, non-Hispanic/Latino), 3 international. Average age 41. 47 applicants, 68% accepted, 28 enrolled. *Faculty:* 25 part-time/adjunct (18 women). Expenses: Contact institution. *Financial support:* In 2017–18, 60 students received support. Scholarships/grants available. Financial award applicants required to submit FAFSA. In 2017, 47 master's awarded. Offers writing for children and young adults (MFA). *Application deadline:* Applications are processed on a rolling basis. *Application fee:* $75. Electronic applications accepted. *Program Director,* Melissa Fisher, 802-828-8696, E-mail: melissa.fisher@vcfa.edu.

MFA in Writing Program Students: 111 full-time (87 women); includes 11 minority (5 Black or African American, non-Hispanic/Latino; 2 Asian, non-Hispanic/Latino; 1 Hispanic/Latino; 3 Two or more races, non-Hispanic/Latino), 2 international. Average age 42. 123 applicants, 63% accepted, 36 enrolled. *Faculty:* 36 part-time/adjunct (17 women). Expenses: Contact institution. *Financial support:* Scholarships/grants available. Financial award applicants required to submit FAFSA. In 2017, 56 master's awarded. Offers writing (MFA). *Application fee:* $75. *Application Contact:* Ann Cardinal, Director of Student Recruitment, 802-828-8589, E-mail: ann.cardinal@vcfa.edu. *Program Director,* Melissa Hammerle, 802-828-8840, E-mail: melissa.hammerle@vcfa.edu.

VERMONT LAW SCHOOL, South Royalton, VT 05068-0096

General Information Independent, coed, graduate-only institution. *Graduate housing:* On-campus housing not available.

GRADUATE UNITS

Graduate and Professional Programs *Program availability:* Part-time. Offers law (LL M, MELP, MERL, MFALP, JD). Electronic applications accepted.

Master's Programs *Program availability:* Part-time, 100% online, blended/hybrid learning. Offers American legal studies (LL M); energy law (LL M); energy regulation and law (MERL); environmental law (LL M); environmental law and policy (MELP); food and agriculture law (LL M); food and agriculture law and policy (MFALP).

VERMONT TECHNICAL COLLEGE, Randolph Center, VT 05061-0500

General Information State-supported, coed, comprehensive institution.

GRADUATE UNITS

Program in Computer Software Engineering Offers computer software engineering (MS).

VICTORIA UNIVERSITY, Toronto, ON M5S 1K7, Canada

General Information Independent-religious, coed, graduate-only institution. *Graduate housing:* Rooms and/or apartments available on a first-come, first-served basis to single and married students. Housing application deadline: 6/30.

GRADUATE UNITS

Emmanuel College Offers theology (M Div, MA, MPS, MRE, MSMus, MTS, Th M, D Min, PhD, Th D, Certificate, Diploma, L Th). M Div, MRE, Th M, Th D, M Div/MA, M Div/MRE, M Div/MPS offered jointly with University of Toronto; MA, PhD with University of St. Michael's College. Electronic applications accepted.

VILLANOVA UNIVERSITY, Villanova, PA 19085-1699

General Information Independent-religious, coed, comprehensive institution. CGS member. *Enrollment:* 10,983 graduate, professional, and undergraduate students; 2,843 full-time matriculated graduate/professional students (1,470 women), 1,199 part-time matriculated graduate/professional students (600 women). *Enrollment by degree level:* 3,215 master's, 788 doctoral, 39 other advanced degrees. *Graduate faculty:* 431. *Graduate housing:* On-campus housing not available. *Student services:* Campus employment opportunities, campus safety program, career counseling, exercise/wellness program, free psychological counseling, international student services, multicultural affairs office, services for students with disabilities. *Library facilities:* Falvey Memorial Library plus 1 other. *Collection:* Study areas open 24 hours, 5–7 days a week; students can reserve study rooms.

Computer facilities: Computer purchase and lease plans are available. 700 computers available on campus for general student use. A campuswide network can be accessed. Online class registration, learning management system with anti-plagiarism software, testing software, online faculty hours, videoconferencing, electronic portfolios, data vaulting/backup service, software are available.
Website: http://www.villanova.edu/

GRADUATE UNITS

Charles Widger School of Law *Program availability:* Part-time, evening/weekend. Offers law (LL M, JD); tax (LL M). Electronic applications accepted.

College of Engineering *Program availability:* Part-time, evening/weekend, online learning. Offers biochemical engineering (Certificate); chemical engineering (MSChE); civil engineering (MSCE); computer architectures (Certificate); computer engineering (MSCPE, Certificate); electric power systems (Certificate); electrical engineering (MSEE, Certificate); electro mechanical systems (Certificate); electro-mechanical systems (Certificate); engineering (MSCPE, MSChE, MSEE, MSME, MSWREE, PhD, Certificate); environmental protection in the chemical process industries (Certificate); high frequency systems (Certificate); intelligent control systems (Certificate); machinery dynamics (Certificate); mechanical engineering (MSME); nonlinear dynamics and control (Certificate); thermofluid systems (Certificate); urban water resources design (Certificate); water resources and environmental engineering (MSWREE, Certificate); wireless and digital communications (Certificate). Electronic applications accepted.

Graduate School of Liberal Arts and Sciences Students: 885 full-time (550 women), 414 part-time (250 women); includes 273 minority (100 Black or African American, non-Hispanic/Latino; 3 American Indian or Alaska Native, non-Hispanic/Latino; 48 Asian, non-Hispanic/Latino; 94 Hispanic/Latino; 3 Native Hawaiian or other Pacific Islander, non-Hispanic/Latino; 25 Two or more races, non-Hispanic/Latino), 120 international. Average age 32. 711 applicants, 99% accepted, 657 enrolled. *Faculty:* 192. Expenses: Contact institution. *Financial support:* Research assistantships, teaching assistantships, career-related internships or fieldwork, scholarships/grants, and unspecified assistantships available. Financial award applicants required to submit FAFSA. In 2017, 556 master's, 9 doctorates, 56 other advanced degrees awarded. *Program availability:* Part-time, evening/weekend, 100% online. Offers applied statistics (MS); biology (MA, MS); chemistry (MS); city management (Certificate); classical studies (MA); communication (MA); computer science (MS); elementary school counseling (MS); English (MA); Hispanic studies (MA); history (MA); human resource development (MS); liberal arts and sciences (MA, MPA, MS, PhD, Certificate); liberal studies (MA); mathematics (MA); nonprofit management (Certificate); philosophy (PhD); political science (MA); psychology (MA, MS); public administration (MPA, Certificate); teacher leadership (MA); theatre (MA); theology (MA, PhD). *Application deadline:* For fall admission, 5/1 for international students; for spring admission, 10/15 for international students. Applications are processed on a rolling basis. *Application fee:* $50. Electronic applications accepted. *Dean,* Dr. Christine Palus, 610-519-7090, Fax: 610-519-7096.

M. Louise Fitzpatrick College of Nursing Students: 151 full-time, 199 part-time; includes 42 minority (18 Black or African American, non-Hispanic/Latino; 12 Asian, non-Hispanic/Latino; 8 Hispanic/Latino; 4 Two or more races, non-Hispanic/Latino), 10 international. 274 applicants, 43% accepted, 92 enrolled. Expenses: Contact institution. *Financial support:* Fellowships, research assistantships, teaching assistantships, scholarships/grants, traineeships, and tuition waivers available. In 2017, 70 master's, 15 doctorates awarded. *Program availability:* Part-time, online learning. Offers adult-gerontology primary care nurse practitioner (MSN, Post Master's Certificate); family primary care nurse practitioner (MSN, Post Master's Certificate); nurse anesthesia (DNP); nursing (PhD); nursing education (MSN, Post Master's Certificate); nursing practice (DNP); pediatric primary care nurse practitioner (MSN, Post Master's Certificate). *Application deadline:* For fall admission, 7/1 for domestic and international students; for spring admission, 10/1 for domestic and international students; for summer admission, 4/1 for domestic and international students. *Application fee:* $50. Electronic applications accepted. *Application Contact:* Kathleen Geibel, Assistant to Graduate Program, 610-519-4934, Fax: 610-519-7650, E-mail: kathleen.geibel@villanova.edu. *Associate Professor, Assistant Dean and Director of Graduate Nursing Program,* Dr. Marguerite K. Schlag, 610-519-4907, Fax: 610-519-7650, E-mail: marguerite.schlag@villanova.edu.

Villanova School of Business Students: 38 full-time (9 women), 889 part-time (320 women); includes 210 minority (62 Black or African American, non-Hispanic/Latino; 6 American Indian or Alaska Native, non-Hispanic/Latino; 73 Asian, non-Hispanic/Latino; 51 Hispanic/Latino; 3 Native Hawaiian or other Pacific Islander, non-Hispanic/Latino; 15 Two or more races, non-Hispanic/Latino), 29 international. Average age 30. 575 applicants, 84% accepted, 374 enrolled. *Faculty:* 176 full-time (61 women), 97 part-time/adjunct (19 women). Expenses: Contact institution. *Financial support:* Research assistantships with tuition reimbursements, institutionally sponsored loans, and scholarships/grants available. Support available to part-time students. Financial award application deadline: 6/30; financial award applicants required to submit FAFSA. *Program availability:* 100% online, blended/hybrid learning. Offers accountancy (MAC); analytics (MSA); business (EMBA, MAC, MBA, MSA, MSCM, MSF); business administration (MBA); church management (MSCM); executive business administration (EMBA); finance (MSF); healthcare (MBA); international business (MBA); marketing (MBA); real estate (MBA); strategic management (MBA). *Application deadline:* For fall admission, 6/30 for domestic and international students; for winter admission, 11/15 for domestic and international students; for spring admission, 11/15 for domestic and international students; for summer admission, 3/31 for domestic and international students. Applications are processed on a rolling basis. *Application fee:* $65. Electronic applications accepted. *Application Contact:* Claire Bruno, Director of Recruitment and Enrollment Management, 610-519-4336, Fax: 610-519-6273, E-mail: claire.bruno@villanova.edu. *Dean*, Dr. Joyce Russell, 610-519-5424, Fax: 610-519-6273, E-mail: joyce.russell@villanova.edu.

VIRGINIA BAPTIST COLLEGE, Fredericksburg, VA 22407

General Information Independent, coed, comprehensive institution.

GRADUATE UNITS

Graduate Programs Offers theology (MBS, MCE, MM).

VIRGINIA BEACH THEOLOGICAL SEMINARY, Virginia Beach, VA 23464

General Information Independent-religious, coed, graduate-only institution. *Graduate housing:* On-campus housing not available.

GRADUATE UNITS

Graduate Programs *Program availability:* Online learning. Offers Biblical studies (MBS, Th M); chaplaincy (MBS); ministry (M Div). Electronic applications accepted.

VIRGINIA COMMONWEALTH UNIVERSITY, Richmond, VA 23284-9005

General Information State-supported, coed, university. CGS member. *Graduate housing:* Room and/or apartments available on a first-come, first-served basis to single students; on-campus housing not available to married students. *Research affiliation:* Virginia Biotechnology Research Park.

GRADUATE UNITS

Graduate School *Program availability:* Part-time, evening/weekend. Offers interdisciplinary studies (MIS). Electronic applications accepted.

College of Humanities and Sciences *Program availability:* Part-time, evening/weekend. Offers analytical chemistry (MS, PhD); applied mathematics (MS); behavioral medicine (PhD); biology (MS); chemical physics (PhD); clinical child psychology (PhD); clinical psychology (PhD); counseling psychology (PhD); creative writing (MFA); digital sociology (MS); dual genre (MFA); English (MA); fiction (MFA); forensic biology (MS); forensic chemistry/drugs and toxicology (MS); forensic chemistry/trace evidence (MS); forensic physical analysis (MS); health and movement sciences (MS); health psychology (PhD); history (MA); humanities and sciences (MA, MFA, MPA, MS, MURP, PhD, Certificate, Graduate Certificate, Postbaccalaureate Certificate); inorganic chemistry (MS, PhD); literature (MA); media and culture (MS, PhD); media, art, and text (PhD); medical physics (MS, PhD); multimedia journalism (MS); nanoscience and nanotechnology (PhD); nanosciences (PhD); nonprofit management (Graduate Certificate); organic chemistry (MS, PhD); physical chemistry (MS, PhD); physics and applied physics (MS); poetry (MFA); rehabilitation and movement science (PhD); strategic public relations (MS). Electronic applications accepted.

L. Douglas Wilder School of Government and Public Affairs Offers criminal justice (MS, Postbaccalaureate Certificate); financial management (MPA); geographic information systems (Certificate); government and public affairs (MA, MPA, MS, MURP, PhD, Certificate, Graduate Certificate, Postbaccalaureate Certificate); homeland security and emergency preparedness (MA, Graduate Certificate); human resource management (MPA); public policy and administration (PhD); state and local government management (MPA); urban and regional studies and planning (MURP).

School of Allied Health Professions *Program availability:* Part-time. Offers allied health professions (MHA, MS, MSHA, MSNA, MSOT, DNAP, DPT, OTD, PhD, CAS); clinical laboratory sciences (PhD); gerontology (MS, PhD); health administration (MHA, MSHA, PhD); health services organization and research (PhD); nurse anesthesia (PhD); occupational therapy (MSOT, OTD); patient counseling (MS); physical therapy (PhD); radiation sciences (PhD); rehabilitation counseling (MS); rehabilitation leadership (PhD). Electronic applications accepted.

School of Business *Program availability:* Part-time, evening/weekend. Offers accounting (M Acc); business (M Acc, MA, MBA, MS, PhD, Postbaccalaureate Certificate); business administration (MBA, PhD); economics (MA); information systems (MS); real estate and urban land development (Postbaccalaureate Certificate). Electronic applications accepted.

School of Education *Program availability:* Part-time. Offers adult literacy (M Ed); art education (PhD); college student development and counseling (M Ed); counselor education and supervision (PhD); curriculum, culture and change (PhD); early and elementary education (MT); early childhood (M Ed); education (M Ed, MT, Ed D, PhD, Certificate); educational leadership (M Ed); educational psychology (PhD); general education (M Ed); human resource development (M Ed); leadership (Ed D); reading (M Ed); reading specialist (Certificate); research and evaluation (PhD); school counseling (M Ed); severe disabilities (M Ed); special education and disability leadership (PhD); sport leadership (M Ed); teaching and learning with technology (M Ed); urban services leadership (PhD). Electronic applications accepted.

School of Engineering Offers biomedical engineering (MS, PhD); computer science (MS); engineering (MS, PhD); mechanical and nuclear engineering (MS, PhD). Electronic applications accepted.

School of Life Sciences Offers environmental studies (M Env Sc, MS); integrative life sciences (PhD); life sciences (M Env Sc, MS, PhD). Electronic applications accepted.

School of Nursing *Program availability:* Part-time, evening/weekend, online learning. Offers adult health acute nursing (MS); adult health primary nursing (MS); biobehavioral clinical research (PhD); child health nursing (MS); clinical nurse leader (MS); family health nursing (MS); nurse educator (MS); nurse practitioner (MS); nursing (Certificate); nursing administration (MS); psychiatric-mental health nursing (MS); quality and safety in health care (DNP); women's health nursing (MS). Electronic applications accepted.

School of Social Work Offers social work (MSW, PhD). Electronic applications accepted.

School of the Arts *Program availability:* Part-time. Offers art education (MAE, PhD); art history (MA, PhD); ceramics (MFA); costume design (MFA); curatorial (PhD); design (MFA); fibers (MFA); furniture design (MFA); glassworking (MFA); historical studies (MA, PhD); jewelry/metalworking (MFA); kinetic imaging (MFA); museum studies (MA); music (MM); music education (MM); painting (MFA); pedagogy/literature (MFA); pedagogy/performance (MFA); photography and film (MFA); printmaking (MFA); scene design/technical theatre (MFA); sculpture (MFA); theatre (MFA). Electronic applications accepted.

Medical College of Virginia-Professional Programs *Program availability:* Part-time. Offers medicine (MPH, MS, MSD, DDS, MD, PhD, Pharm D, Certificate). Electronic applications accepted.

School of Dentistry Offers dentistry (MS, DDS). Electronic applications accepted.

School of Medicine Offers anatomy and neurobiology (MS); biochemistry and molecular biology (MS, PhD); biostatistics (MS, PhD); genetic counseling (MS); healthcare policy and research (PhD); human genetics (PhD); medicine (MPH, MS, MD, PhD, Certificate); microbiology and immunology (MS, PhD); molecular biology and genetics (MS); neuroscience (PhD); pharmacology (Certificate); pharmacology and toxicology (MS, PhD); physical therapy (PhD); physiology (MS, PhD); social and behavioral sciences (PhD). Electronic applications accepted.

School of Pharmacy *Program availability:* Part-time. Offers medicinal chemistry (MS); pharmaceutical sciences (PhD); pharmaceutics (MS); pharmacotherapy and pharmacy administration (MS); pharmacy (MS, PhD, Pharm D). Electronic applications accepted.

Program in Pre-Medical Basic Health Sciences Offers pre-medical basic health sciences (Postbaccalaureate Certificate). Electronic applications accepted.

VIRGINIA INTERNATIONAL UNIVERSITY, Fairfax, VA 22030

General Information Proprietary, coed, comprehensive institution. *Research affiliation:* Apple Federal Credit Union (financial management).

GRADUATE UNITS

School of Business *Program availability:* Part-time, online learning. Offers accounting (MBA, MS); entrepreneurship (MBA); executive management (Graduate Certificate); global logistics (MBA); health care management (MBA); hospitality and tourism management (MBA); human resources management (MBA); international business management (MBA); international finance (MBA); marketing management (MBA); mass media and public relations (MBA); project management (MBA, MS). Electronic applications accepted.

School of Computer Information Systems *Program availability:* Part-time, online learning. Offers business intelligence (Graduate Certificate); business intelligence and data analytics (MIS); computer science (MS); cybersecurity (MIS); data management (MIS); enterprise project management (MIS); health informatics (MIS); information assurance (MIS); information systems (Graduate Certificate); information systems management (MS, Graduate Certificate); information technology (MS); information technology audit and compliance (Graduate Certificate); knowledge management (MIS); software engineering (MS). Electronic applications accepted.

School of Education *Program availability:* Part-time, online learning. Offers applied linguistics (MS); education (M Ed); teaching English to speakers of other languages (MA). Electronic applications accepted.

School of Public and International Affairs Offers international relations (MS); public administration (MPA).

VIRGINIA POLYTECHNIC INSTITUTE AND STATE UNIVERSITY, Blacksburg, VA 24061

General Information State-supported, coed, university. CGS member. *Enrollment:* 34,440 graduate, professional, and undergraduate students; 4,961 full-time matriculated graduate/professional students (2,190 women), 2,286 part-time matriculated graduate/professional students (963 women). *Enrollment by degree level:* 3,744 master's, 3,503 doctoral. *Graduate faculty:* 1,837 full-time (636 women), 13 part-time/adjunct (10 women). Tuition, state resident: full-time $15,072; part-time $718.50 per credit hour. Tuition, nonresident: full-time $28,810; part-time $1448.25 per credit hour. *Required fees:* $2741; $502 per semester. Tuition and fees vary according to course load, campus/location and program. *Graduate housing:* Room and/or apartments available on a first-come, first-served basis to single students; on-campus housing not available to married students. Typical cost: $3988 per year ($13,108 including board). *Student services:* Campus employment opportunities, campus safety program, career counseling, exercise/wellness program, free psychological counseling, grant writing training, international student services, low-cost health insurance, multicultural affairs office, services for students with disabilities, teacher training, writing training. *Library facilities:* Newman Library plus 2 others. *Collection:* Study areas open 24 hours, 5–7 days a week. *Research affiliation:* Transport Canada (transportation), Elanco Animal Health (agriculture), Virginia Tech Carilion School of Medicine and Research Institute, Commonwealth Center for Advanced Manufacturing (CCAM), Wellcome Trust Centre for Neuroimaging (health research), Virginia Biosciences Health Research Corporation (health research).

Computer facilities: A campuswide network can be accessed from student residence rooms and from off campus. Online class registration is available.
Website: http://www.vt.edu/

General Application Contact: Graduate Admissions and Academic Progress, 540-231-8636, E-mail: grads@vt.edu.

GRADUATE UNITS

Graduate School Students: 4,381 full-time (1,783 women), 2,246 part-time (932 women); includes 1,122 minority (356 Black or African American, non-Hispanic/Latino; 10 American Indian or Alaska Native, non-Hispanic/Latino; 357 Asian, non-Hispanic/Latino; 247 Hispanic/Latino; 4 Native Hawaiian or other Pacific Islander, non-Hispanic/Latino; 148 Two or more races, non-Hispanic/Latino), 2,026 international. Average age 31. 9,184 applicants, 32% accepted, 1731 enrolled. *Faculty:* 1,737 full-time (587 women), 11 part-time/adjunct (8 women). Expenses: Contact institution. *Financial support:* Fellowships, research assistantships, and teaching assistantships available. *Application fee:* $75. *Vice President and Dean for Graduate Education,* Dr. Karen P. DePauw, 540-231-6691, E-mail: grads@vt.edu.

College of Agriculture and Life Sciences Students: 379 full-time (221 women), 126 part-time (75 women); includes 64 minority (21 Black or African American, non-Hispanic/Latino; 15 Asian, non-Hispanic/Latino; 14 Hispanic/Latino; 14 Two or more races, non-Hispanic/Latino), 119 international. Average age 29. 357 applicants, 46% accepted, 118 enrolled. *Faculty:* 241 full-time (73 women), 1 (woman) part-time/adjunct. Expenses: Contact institution. *Financial support:* In 2017–18, 232 research assistantships with full tuition reimbursements (averaging $21,852 per year), 94 teaching assistantships with full tuition reimbursements (averaging $21,643 per year) were awarded. Financial award application deadline: 3/1; financial award applicants required to submit FAFSA. In 2017, 105 master's, 54 doctorates awarded. Offers agricultural and applied economics (MS, PhD); agricultural and life sciences (MS); agriculture, leadership, and community education (MS, PhD); animal and poultry science (MS, PhD); biochemistry (MS, PhD); crop and soil environmental sciences (MS, PhD); dairy science (MS, PhD); entomology (MS, PhD); food science and technology (MS, PhD); horticulture (PhD); human nutrition, foods and exercise (MS, PhD); plant pathology, physiology, and weed science (MS, PhD). *Application deadline:* For fall admission, 8/1 for domestic students, 4/1 for international students; for spring admission, 1/1 for domestic students, 9/1 for international students. Applications are processed on a rolling basis. *Application fee:* $75. Electronic applications accepted. *Application Contact:* Crystal Tawney, Administrative Assistant, 540-231-4152, Fax: 540-231-4163, E-mail: cdtawney@vt.edu. *Dean*, Dr. Alan L. Grant, 540-231-4152, Fax: 540-231-4163, E-mail: algrant@vt.edu.

College of Architecture and Urban Studies Students: 339 full-time (165 women), 210 part-time (97 women); includes 115 minority (49 Black or African American, non-Hispanic/Latino; 1 American Indian or Alaska Native, non-Hispanic/Latino; 30 Asian, non-Hispanic/Latino; 29 Hispanic/Latino; 6 Two or more races, non-Hispanic/Latino), 136 international. Average age 32. 649 applicants, 49% accepted, 105 enrolled. *Faculty:* 139 full-time (58 women), 1 (woman) part-time/adjunct. Expenses: Contact institution. *Financial support:* In 2017–18, 17 research assistantships with full tuition reimbursements (averaging $18,561 per year), 41 teaching assistantships with full tuition reimbursements (averaging $17,340 per year) were awarded. Financial award application deadline: 3/1; financial award applicants required to submit FAFSA. In 2017, 142 master's, 18 doctorates awarded. Offers architecture (M Arch, MS); architecture and design research (PhD); building construction science management (MS); creative technologies (MFA); environmental design and planning (PhD); government and international affairs (MPIA); landscape architecture (MLA, PhD); planning, governance, and globalization (PhD); public administration and public affairs (MPA, PhD); urban and regional planning (MURPL). *Application deadline:* For fall admission, 8/1 for domestic students, 4/1 for international students; for spring admission, 1/1 for domestic students, 9/1 for international students. Applications are processed on a rolling basis. *Application fee:* $75. Electronic applications accepted. *Application Contact:* Christine Mattsson-Coon, Executive Assistant, 540-231-6416, Fax: 540-231-6332, E-mail: cmattsso@vt.edu. *Dean*, Dr. Richard Blythe, 540-231-6416, Fax: 540-231-6332, E-mail: richbl1@vt.edu.

College of Engineering Students: 1,881 full-time (494 women), 396 part-time (71 women); includes 279 minority (60 Black or African American, non-Hispanic/Latino; 4 American Indian or Alaska Native, non-Hispanic/Latino; 101 Asian, non-Hispanic/Latino; 68 Hispanic/Latino; 46 Two or more races, non-Hispanic/Latino), 1,251 international. Average age 27. 5,004 applicants, 23% accepted, 540 enrolled. *Faculty:* 419 full-time (80 women), 4 part-time/adjunct (2 women). Expenses: Contact institution. *Financial support:* In 2017–18, 160 fellowships with full tuition reimbursements (averaging $6,250 per year), 836 research assistantships with full tuition reimbursements (averaging $22,978 per year), 372 teaching assistantships with full tuition reimbursements (averaging $19,771 per year) were awarded. Financial award application deadline: 3/1; financial award applicants required to submit FAFSA. In 2017, 501 master's, 206 doctorates awarded. Offers aerospace engineering (PhD); biological systems engineering (PhD); biomedical engineering (MS, PhD); chemical engineering (PhD); civil engineering (PhD); computer engineering (PhD); computer science and applications (MS); electrical engineering (PhD); engineering education (PhD). *Application deadline:* For fall admission, 8/1 for domestic students, 4/1 for international students; for spring admission, 1/1 for domestic students, 9/1 for international students. Applications are processed on a rolling basis. *Application fee:* $75. Electronic applications accepted. *Application Contact:* Linda Perkins, Executive Assistant, 540-231-9752, Fax: 540-231-3031, E-mail: lperkins@vt.edu. *Dean*, Dr. Julia Ross, 540-231-9752, Fax: 540-231-3031, E-mail: rjulie@vt.edu.

College of Liberal Arts and Human Sciences Students: 623 full-time (427 women), 431 part-time (278 women); includes 203 minority (115 Black or African American, non-Hispanic/Latino; 4 American Indian or Alaska Native, non-Hispanic/Latino; 29 Asian, non-Hispanic/Latino; 33 Hispanic/Latino; 2 Native Hawaiian or other Pacific Islander, non-Hispanic/Latino; 20 Two or more races, non-Hispanic/Latino), 87 international. Average age 34. 898 applicants, 50% accepted, 329 enrolled. *Faculty:* 411 full-time (213 women), 3 part-time/adjunct (all women). Expenses: Contact institution. *Financial support:* In 2017–18, 19 research assistantships with full tuition reimbursements (averaging $19,611 per year), 226 teaching assistantships with full tuition reimbursements (averaging $16,220 per year) were awarded. Financial award application deadline: 3/1; financial award applicants required to submit FAFSA. In 2017, 314 master's, 102 doctorates awarded. Offers career and technical education (MS Ed, Ed S); communication (MA); counselor education (MA); creative writing (MFA); curriculum and instruction (MA Ed, Ed S); educational leadership and policy studies (Ed S); educational research and evaluation (PhD); English (MA); social, political, ethical, and cultural thought (PhD). *Application deadline:* For fall admission, 8/1 for domestic students, 4/1 for international students; for spring admission, 1/1 for domestic students, 9/1 for international students. Applications are processed on a rolling basis. *Application fee:* $75. Electronic applications accepted. *Application Contact:* Chelsea Blanchet, Executive Assistant, 540-231-6779, Fax: 540-231-7157, E-mail: bchels1@vt.edu. *Dean*, Dr. Rosemary Blieszner, 540-231-6779, Fax: 540-231-7157, E-mail: rmb@vt.edu.

College of Natural Resources and Environment Students: 174 full-time (84 women), 79 part-time (39 women); includes 29 minority (6 Black or African American, non-Hispanic/Latino; 5 Asian, non-Hispanic/Latino; 15 Hispanic/Latino; 1 Native Hawaiian or other Pacific Islander, non-Hispanic/Latino; 2 Two or more races, non-Hispanic/Latino), 34 international. Average age 31. 118 applicants, 53% accepted, 46 enrolled. *Faculty:* 75 full-time (18 women). Expenses: Contact institution. *Financial support:* In 2017–18, 78 research assistantships with full tuition reimbursements (averaging $22,092 per year), 41 teaching assistantships with full tuition reimbursements (averaging $19,106 per year) were awarded. Financial award application deadline: 3/1; financial award applicants required to submit FAFSA. In 2017, 89 master's, 13 doctorates awarded. Offers fisheries and wildlife (MS, PhD); forestry and forest products (PhD); geography (MS); geospatial and environmental analysis (PhD); natural resources (MNR). *Application deadline:* For fall admission, 8/1 for domestic students, 4/1 for international students; for spring admission, 1/1 for domestic students, 9/1 for international students. Applications are processed on a rolling basis. *Application fee:* $75. Electronic applications accepted. *Application Contact:* Arlice Banks, Executive Assistant, 540-231-7051, Fax: 540-231-7664, E-mail: arbanks@vt.edu. *Dean*, Dr. Paul M. Winistorfer, 540-231-5481, Fax: 540-231-7664, E-mail: pstorfer@vt.edu.

College of Science Students: 557 full-time (205 women), 39 part-time (18 women); includes 68 minority (13 Black or African American, non-Hispanic/Latino; 1 American Indian or Alaska Native, non-Hispanic/Latino; 14 Asian, non-Hispanic/Latino; 32 Hispanic/Latino; 8 Two or more races, non-Hispanic/Latino), 238 international. Average age 27. 1,060 applicants, 15% accepted, 121 enrolled. *Faculty:* 321 full-time (103 women). Expenses: Contact institution. *Financial support:* In 2017–18, 2 fellowships with full tuition reimbursements (averaging $12,267 per year), 140 research assistantships with full tuition reimbursements (averaging $23,004 per year), 351 teaching assistantships with full tuition reimbursements (averaging $20,157 per year) were awarded. Financial award application deadline: 3/1; financial award applicants required to submit FAFSA. In 2017, 75 master's, 89 doctorates awarded. Offers biological sciences (MS, PhD); biomedical technology development and management (MS); chemistry (MS, PhD); data analysis and applied statistics (MA); economics (PhD); geosciences (MS, PhD); mathematics (MS, PhD); physics (MS, PhD); psychology (MS, PhD); statistics (MS, PhD). *Application deadline:* For fall admission, 8/1 for domestic students, 4/1 for international students; for spring admission, 1/1 for domestic students, 9/1 for international students. Applications are processed on a rolling basis. *Application fee:* $75. Electronic applications accepted. *Application Contact:* Allison Craft, Executive Assistant, 540-231-6394, Fax: 540-231-3380, E-mail: crafta@vt.edu. *Dean*, Dr. Sally C. Morton, 540-231-5422, Fax: 540-231-3380, E-mail: scmorton@vt.edu.

Intercollege Students: 167 full-time (86 women), 776 part-time (278 women); includes 252 minority (60 Black or African American, non-Hispanic/Latino; 113 Asian, non-Hispanic/Latino; 41 Hispanic/Latino; 1 Native Hawaiian or other Pacific Islander, non-Hispanic/Latino; 37 Two or more races, non-Hispanic/Latino), 81 international. Average age 33. 664 applicants, 65% accepted, 304 enrolled. Expenses: Contact institution. *Financial support:* In 2017–18, 39 fellowships with full and partial tuition reimbursements (averaging $17,696 per year), 119 research assistantships with full tuition reimbursements (averaging $24,500 per year), 20 teaching assistantships with full tuition reimbursements (averaging $24,663 per year) were awarded. Financial award application deadline: 3/1; financial award applicants required to submit FAFSA. In 2017, 93 master's, 13 doctorates awarded. Offers genetics, bioinformatics, and computational biology (PhD); information technology (MIT); macromolecular science and engineering (MS, PhD); translational biology, medicine, and health (PhD). *Application deadline:* For fall admission, 8/1 for domestic students, 4/1 for international students; for spring admission, 1/1 for domestic students, 9/1 for international students. Applications are processed on a rolling basis. *Application fee:* $75. Electronic applications accepted. *Vice President and Dean for Graduate Education*, Dr. Karen P. DePauw, 540-231-7581, Fax: 540-231-1670, E-mail: kpdepauw@vt.edu.

Pamplin College of Business Students: 261 full-time (101 women), 189 part-time (76 women); includes 112 minority (32 Black or African American, non-Hispanic/Latino; 50 Asian, non-Hispanic/Latino; 15 Hispanic/Latino; 15 Two or more races, non-Hispanic/Latino), 80 international. Average age 32. 434 applicants, 57% accepted, 168 enrolled. *Faculty:* 131 full-time (42 women), 2 part-time/adjunct (1 woman). Expenses: Contact institution. *Financial support:* In 2017–18, 9 research assistantships with full tuition reimbursements (averaging $18,588 per year), 48 teaching assistantships with full tuition reimbursements (averaging $22,706 per year) were awarded. Financial award application deadline: 3/1; financial award applicants required to submit FAFSA. In 2017, 142 master's, 11 doctorates awarded. Offers accounting and information systems (MACIS, PhD); business (PhD); business administration (MS); business information technology (PhD); executive business research (PhD); finance (PhD). *Application deadline:* For fall admission, 8/1 for domestic students, 4/1 for international students; for spring admission, 1/1 for domestic students, 9/1 for international students. Applications are processed on a rolling basis. *Application fee:* $75. Electronic applications accepted. *Application Contact:* Kimberly Ridpath, Executive Assistant, 540-231-9647, Fax: 540-231-4487, E-mail: ridpathk@vt.edu. *Dean*, Dr. Robert T. Sumichrast, 540-231-6601, Fax: 540-231-4487, E-mail: busdean@vt.edu.

Virginia-Maryland Regional College of Veterinary Medicine Students: 580 full-time (407 women), 40 part-time (31 women); includes 120 minority (21 Black or African American, non-Hispanic/Latino; 1 American Indian or Alaska Native, non-Hispanic/Latino; 33 Asian, non-Hispanic/Latino; 36 Hispanic/Latino; 29 Two or more races, non-Hispanic/Latino), 27 international. Average age 26. 66 applicants, 68% accepted, 36 enrolled. *Faculty:* 100 full-time (49 women), 2 part-time/adjunct (both women). Expenses: Contact institution. *Financial support:* In 2017–18, 4 fellowships with full and partial tuition reimbursements (averaging $30,618 per year), 16 research assistantships with full tuition reimbursements (averaging $24,872 per year), 18 teaching assistantships with full tuition reimbursements (averaging $26,904 per year) were awarded. Financial award application deadline: 3/1; financial award applicants required to submit FAFSA. In 2017, 53 master's, 129 doctorates awarded. Offers biomedical and veterinary sciences (MS, PhD); public health (MPH); veterinary medicine (DVM). *Application deadline:* For fall admission, 8/1 for domestic students, 4/1 for international students; for spring admission, 1/1 for domestic students, 9/1 for international students. Applications are processed on a rolling basis. *Application fee:* $75. Electronic applications accepted. *Application Contact:* Sheila Steele, Executive Assistant, 540-231-7910, Fax: 540-231-3505, E-mail: ssteele@vt.edu. *Interim Dean*, Dr. Gregory B. Daniel, 540-231-7910, Fax: 540-231-3505, E-mail: gdaniel@vt.edu.

VT Online Offers advanced transportation systems (Certificate); aerospace engineering (MS); agricultural and life sciences (MSLFS); business information systems (Graduate Certificate); career and technical education (MS); civil engineering (MS); computer engineering (M Eng, MS); decision support systems (Graduate Certificate); eLearning leadership (MA); electrical engineering (M Eng, MS); engineering administration (MEA); environmental engineering (Certificate); environmental politics and policy (Graduate Certificate); environmental sciences and engineering (MS); foundations of political analysis (Graduate Certificate); health product risk management (Graduate Certificate); industrial and systems engineering (MS); information policy and society (Graduate Certificate); information security (Graduate Certificate); information technology (MIT); instructional technology (MA); integrative STEM education (MA Ed); liberal arts (Graduate Certificate); life sciences: health product risk management (MS); natural resources (MNR, Graduate Certificate); networking (Graduate Certificate); nonprofit and nongovernmental organization management (Graduate Certificate); ocean engineering (MS); political science (MA); security studies (Graduate Certificate); software development (Graduate Certificate).

VIRGINIA STATE UNIVERSITY, Petersburg, VA 23806-0001

General Information State-supported, coed, comprehensive institution. *Graduate housing:* Room and/or apartments available on a first-come, first-served basis to single students; on-campus housing not available to married students. Housing application deadline: 5/1. *Research affiliation:* Medical College of Virginia/Virginia Commonwealth University (biology), The College of William and Mary (biology), University of Massachusetts (biology), Rolls Royce USA (engineering), C-CAM Technologies (engineering).

GRADUATE UNITS

College of Graduate Studies *Program availability:* Part-time, evening/weekend. Offers interdisciplinary studies (MIS).

College of Education Offers administration and supervision (M Ed); education (M Ed, MS, Ed D); educational administration and supervision (Ed D); school and community counseling (M Ed, MS).

College of Engineering and Technology Offers computer science (MS); engineering and technology (M Ed, MS); mathematics (MS); mathematics education (MS).

College of Humanities and Social Sciences *Program availability:* Part-time, evening/weekend. Offers criminal justice (MS); economics (MA); humanities and social sciences (M Ed, MA, MS); media management (MA).

College of Natural and Health Sciences Offers behavioral and community health sciences (PhD); biology (MS); clinical health psychology (PhD); clinical psychology (MS); general psychology (MS); natural and health sciences (MS, PhD).

VIRGINIA THEOLOGICAL SEMINARY, Alexandria, VA 22304

General Information Independent-religious, coed, graduate-only institution. *Graduate housing:* Rooms and/or apartments available on a first-come, first-served basis to single and married students. Housing application deadline: 5/1.

GRADUATE UNITS

Graduate and Professional Programs *Program availability:* Part-time. Offers Christian spirituality (D Min); educational leadership (D Ed Min, D Min); ministry development (D Min); theology (M Div, MA).

VIRGINIA UNION UNIVERSITY, Richmond, VA 23220-1170

General Information Independent-religious, coed, comprehensive institution. *Graduate housing:* Room and/or apartments available on a first-come, first-served basis to single students; on-campus housing not available to married students.

GRADUATE UNITS

Evelyn R. Syphax School of Education, Psychology and Interdisciplinary Studies Offers curriculum and instruction (MA).

Samuel DeWitt Proctor School of Theology *Program availability:* Part-time, evening/weekend. Offers theology (M Div, D Min).

VIRGINIA UNIVERSITY OF LYNCHBURG, Lynchburg, VA 24501-6417

General Information Independent-religious, coed, comprehensive institution. *Graduate housing:* Room and/or apartments available on a first-come, first-served basis to single students; on-campus housing not available to married students. Housing application deadline: 9/5.

GRADUATE UNITS

Graduate Programs *Program availability:* Online learning. Offers Christian ministry (M Div); ministry (D Min).

VIRGINIA WESLEYAN UNIVERSITY, Virginia Beach, VA 23455

General Information Independent-religious, coed, comprehensive institution.

GRADUATE UNITS

Graduate Studies *Program availability:* Online learning.

VITERBO UNIVERSITY, La Crosse, WI 54601-4797

General Information Independent-religious, coed, comprehensive institution. *Graduate housing:* Room and/or apartments available on a first-come, first-served basis to single students; on-campus housing not available to married students. Housing application deadline: 4/2.

GRADUATE UNITS

Graduate Program in Nursing *Program availability:* Part-time. Offers nursing (DNP). Electronic applications accepted.

Graduate Programs in Education *Program availability:* Part-time, evening/weekend. Offers cross-categorical special education (Certificate); director of instruction (Certificate); director of special education and pupil services (Certificate); early childhood (Certificate); education (MAE); literacy coaching (Certificate); PreK-12 principal/supervisor of special education (Certificate); principal (Certificate); reading specialist endorsement (Certificate); reading teacher (Certificate); reading teacher 5-12 endorsement (Certificate); reading teacher K-8 endorsement (Certificate); superintendent (Certificate); talented and gifted endorsement (Certificate); Wisconsin school business administrator (Certificate). Weekend courses available in summer. Electronic applications accepted.

Master of Arts in Servant Leadership Program *Program availability:* Part-time, evening/weekend. Offers ethical leadership in organizations (Certificate); servant leadership (MA). Electronic applications accepted.

Master of Business Administration Program *Program availability:* Part-time, evening/weekend. Offers general business administration (MBA); health care management (MBA); international business (MBA); leadership (MBA); project management (MBA). Electronic applications accepted.

Master of Science in Mental Health Counseling Program *Program availability:* Part-time, evening/weekend. Offers addiction counseling (MS); child and adolescent counseling (MS); complementary health and wellness counseling (MS). Electronic applications accepted.

WAGNER COLLEGE, Staten Island, NY 10301-4495

General Information Independent, coed, comprehensive institution. *Enrollment:* 2,289 graduate, professional, and undergraduate students; 193 full-time matriculated graduate/professional students (105 women), 249 part-time matriculated graduate/professional students (191 women). *Enrollment by degree level:* 420 master's, 22 doctoral. *Graduate faculty:* 33 full-time (18 women), 31 part-time/adjunct (18 women). *Graduate housing:* Room and/or apartments available on a first-come, first-served basis to single students; on-campus housing not available to married students. Housing application deadline: 4/1. *Student services:* Campus employment opportunities, campus safety program, career counseling, child daycare facilities, exercise/wellness program, free psychological counseling, international student services, multicultural affairs office, services for students with disabilities, teacher training, writing training. *Library facilities:* August Horrmann Library. *Collection:* Books: 70,465 (physical), 180,000 (digital/electronic); Serial titles: 79,532 (physical); Databases: 61. Weekly public service hours: 120; students can reserve study rooms. *Research affiliation:* Staten Island University Hospital.

Computer facilities: 230 computers available on campus for general student use. A campuswide network can be accessed from student residence rooms and from off campus. Online class registration is available.
Website: http://www.wagner.edu/

General Application Contact: Robert Herr, Dean of Enrollment, 718-420-4242, Fax: 718-390-3105, E-mail: robert.herr@wagner.edu.

GRADUATE UNITS

Division of Graduate Studies Students: 202 full-time (107 women), 206 part-time (166 women); includes 120 minority (39 Black or African American, non-Hispanic/Latino; 39 Asian, non-Hispanic/Latino; 33 Hispanic/Latino; 9 Two or more races, non-Hispanic/Latino), 21 international. Average age 30. 318 applicants, 82% accepted, 203 enrolled. *Faculty:* 33 full-time (18 women), 31 part-time/adjunct (18 women). Expenses: Contact institution. *Financial support:* In 2017–18, 298 students received support. Career-related internships or fieldwork, unspecified assistantships, and alumni fellowship grants available. Financial award application deadline: 4/1; financial award applicants required to submit FAFSA. In 2017, 191 master's, 11 doctorates, 2 other advanced degrees awarded. *Program availability:* Part-time, evening/weekend. Offers childhood education (MS Ed); childhood education/students with disabilities (MS Ed); early childhood education/students with disabilities (birth-grade 2) (MS Ed); higher education and learning organizations leadership (MA); microbiology (MS); secondary education 7-12 (MS Ed); secondary education/students with disabilities (MS Ed). *Application deadline:* For fall admission, 5/1 priority date for domestic students, 3/1 priority date for international students; for spring admission, 11/1 priority date for domestic students, 10/1 priority date for international students. Applications are processed on a rolling basis. *Application fee:* $60. Electronic applications accepted. *Application Contact:* Patricia Clancy, Assistant Coordinator of Graduate Studies, 718-420-4464, Fax: 718-390-3105, E-mail: patricia.clancy@wagner.edu. *Coordinator,* Dr. Jeffrey Kraus, 718-390-3254, Fax: 718-390-3456, E-mail: jkraus@wagner.edu.

Evelyn L. Spiro School of Nursing Students: 15 full-time (13 women), 223 part-time (197 women); includes 75 minority (20 Black or African American, non-Hispanic/Latino; 29 Asian, non-Hispanic/Latino; 21 Hispanic/Latino; 5 Two or more races, non-Hispanic/Latino). Average age 35. 126 applicants, 75% accepted, 69 enrolled. *Faculty:* 6 full-time (all women), 6 part-time/adjunct (5 women). Expenses: Contact institution. *Financial support:* In 2017–18, 62 students received support. Traineeships, unspecified assistantships, and alumni fellowship grants available. Financial award application deadline: 2/15; financial award applicants required to submit FAFSA. In 2017, 52 master's, 11 doctorates, 2 other advanced degrees awarded. *Program availability:* Part-time, evening/weekend. Offers family nurse practitioner (MS, Certificate); nurse educator (MS); nursing (DNP). *Application deadline:* For fall admission, 2/1 priority date for domestic students, 2/1 for international students. *Application fee:* $60. Electronic applications accepted. *Application Contact:* Patricia Clancy, Assistant Director, 718-420-4464, Fax: 718-390-3105, E-mail: patricia.clancy@wagner.edu. *Dean,* Dr. Patricia Tooker, 718-390-3452, Fax: 718-420-4009, E-mail: ptooker@wagner.edu.

Nicolais School of Business Students: 90 full-time (41 women), 27 part-time (9 women); includes 18 minority (10 Black or African American, non-Hispanic/Latino; 2 Asian, non-Hispanic/Latino; 4 Hispanic/Latino; 2 Two or more races, non-Hispanic/Latino), 14 international. Average age 27. 85 applicants, 92% accepted, 58 enrolled. *Faculty:* 8 full-time (3 women), 17 part-time/adjunct (5 women). Expenses: Contact institution. *Financial support:* In 2017–18, 93 students received support. Career-related internships or fieldwork, unspecified assistantships, and alumni fellowship grants available. Financial award application deadline: 4/1; financial award applicants required to submit FAFSA. In 2017, 72 master's awarded. *Program availability:* Part-time, evening/weekend. Offers accounting (MS); business administration (MBA); finance (MBA); management (Exec MBA); marketing (MBA); media management (MS). *Application deadline:* For fall admission, 5/1 priority date for domestic students, 3/1 priority date for international students; for spring admission, 12/1 for domestic students, 11/1 for international students. Applications are processed on a rolling basis. *Application fee:* $60. *Application Contact:* Patricia Clancy, Assistant Director for Enrollment, 718-420-4464, Fax: 718-390-3105, E-mail: patricia.clancy@wagner.edu. *Director,* Dr. Donald Crooks, 718-390-3429, Fax: 718-390-3429, E-mail: dcrooks@wagner.edu.

WAKE FOREST UNIVERSITY, Winston-Salem, NC 27109

General Information Independent, coed, university. CGS member. *Graduate housing:* On-campus housing not available.

GRADUATE UNITS

Graduate School of Arts and Sciences *Program availability:* Part-time. Offers accountancy (MSA); analytical chemistry (MS, PhD); arts and sciences (MA, MA Ed, MALS, MS, MSA, PhD); biology (MS, PhD); computer science (MS); counseling (MA); English (MA); health and exercise science (MS); inorganic chemistry (MS, PhD); liberal studies (MALS); mathematics (MA); organic chemistry (MS, PhD); physical chemistry (MS, PhD); physics (MS, PhD); psychology (MA); religion (MA); secondary education (MA Ed); speech communication (MA). Electronic applications accepted.

School of Business Students: 672 full-time (340 women); includes 156 minority (83 Black or African American, non-Hispanic/Latino; 32 Asian, non-Hispanic/Latino; 27 Hispanic/Latino; 14 Two or more races, non-Hispanic/Latino), 93 international. Average age 29. 1,278 applicants, 62% accepted, 461 enrolled. *Faculty:* 56 full-time (11 women), 18 part-time/adjunct (4 women). Expenses: Contact institution. *Financial support:* Scholarships/grants available. Financial award applicants required to submit FAFSA. In 2017, 460 master's awarded. *Program availability:* Evening/weekend. Offers assurance services (MSA); business (MA, MBA, MSA, MSBA); business administration (MBA); business analytics (MSBA); management (MA); tax consulting (MSA); transaction services (MSA). *Application deadline:* Applications are processed on a rolling basis. *Application fee:* $100. Electronic applications accepted. *Application Contact:* Dennis Kelly, Administrative Assistant, 336-758-5422, Fax: 336-758-5830, E-mail: busadmissions@wfu.edu. *Dean,* Charles Iacovou, 336-758-5422, Fax: 336-758-5830, E-mail: busadmissions@wfu.edu.

School of Law Offers law (LL M, MSL, JD, SJD). LL M program is designed for foreign law graduates in American law. Electronic applications accepted.

School of Medicine Offers medicine (MS, MD, PhD). Electronic applications accepted.

Graduate Programs in Medicine Offers biochemistry (PhD); cancer biology (PhD); comparative medicine (MS); health sciences research (MS); medicine (MS, PhD); microbiology and immunology (PhD); molecular and cellular pathobiology (MS, PhD); molecular genetics and genomics (PhD); molecular medicine (MS, PhD); neurobiology and anatomy (PhD); neuroscience (PhD); nurse anesthesia (MS); pharmacology (PhD); physiology (PhD). Electronic applications accepted.

Virginia Tech-Wake Forest University School of Biomedical Engineering and Sciences Offers biomedical engineering (MS, PhD). Electronic applications accepted.

WALDEN UNIVERSITY, Minneapolis, MN 55401

General Information Proprietary, coed, university. CGS member.

GRADUATE UNITS

Graduate Programs *Program availability:* Part-time, evening/weekend, online only, 100% online. Electronic applications accepted.

Richard W. Riley College of Education and Leadership *Program availability:* Part-time, evening/weekend, online only, 100% online. Offers adult education (Post-Master's Certificate); adult learning (Graduate Certificate); college teaching and learning (Graduate Certificate); community college leadership (Ed D); curriculum, instruction and assessment (Ed D, Ed S, Graduate Certificate); developmental education (Graduate Certificate); early childhood administration, management, and leadership (Graduate Certificate); early childhood education (Ed D, Ed S); early childhood public policy and advocacy (Graduate Certificate); early childhood studies (MS); education (MS, PhD); educational administration and leadership (Ed D); educational leadership and administration (principal preparation) (Ed S); educational technology (Ed D, Ed S, Post Master's Certificate); elementary reading and literacy (Graduate Certificate); engaging culturally diverse learners (Graduate Certificate); enrollment management and institutional marketing (Graduate Certificate); higher education (MS); higher education and adult learning (Ed D); higher education leadership and management (Ed D); higher education leadership for student success (Graduate Certificate); instructional design and technology (MS, Postbaccalaureate Certificate); integrating technology in the classroom (Graduate Certificate); mathematics 5-8 (Graduate Certificate); mathematics K-6 (Graduate Certificate); online teaching for adult educators (Graduate Certificate); reading, literacy, and assessment (Ed D, Ed S); science K-8 (Graduate Certificate); special education (Ed D, Ed S, Graduate Certificate); special education (K-age 21) (MAT); teacher leadership (Graduate Certificate); teaching adults English as a second language (Graduate Certificate); teaching adults in the early childhood field (Graduate Certificate); teaching and diversity in early childhood education (Graduate Certificate); teaching English language learners (grades K-12) (Graduate Certificate); teaching K-12 students online (Graduate Certificate). Electronic applications accepted.

School of Counseling *Program availability:* Part-time, evening/weekend, online only, 100% online. Offers addiction counseling (MS); clinical mental health counseling (MS); counselor education and supervision (PhD); marriage, couple, and family counseling (MS); school counseling (MS). Electronic applications accepted.

School of Health Sciences *Program availability:* Part-time, evening/weekend, online only, 100% online. Offers clinical research administration (MS, Graduate Certificate); health education and promotion (MS, PhD); health informatics (MS); health services (PhD); healthcare administration (MHA, DHA); leadership and organizational development (MHA); public health (MPH, Dr PH, PhD, Graduate Certificate); systems policy (MHA). Electronic applications accepted.

School of Information Systems and Technology *Program availability:* Part-time, evening/weekend, online only, 100% online. Offers information systems (Graduate Certificate); information systems management (MISM); information technology (MS, DIT). Electronic applications accepted.

School of Management *Program availability:* Part-time, evening/weekend, online only, 100% online. Offers accounting (MBA, MS, DBA); advanced project management (Graduate Certificate); applied project management (Graduate Certificate); auditing (Graduate Certificate); bridge to business administration (Post-Doctoral Certificate); bridge to management (Post-Doctoral Certificate); business management (Graduate Certificate); communication (MBA); corporate finance (MBA); digital marketing (Graduate Certificate); entrepreneurship (DBA); entrepreneurship and small business (MBA); finance (MS, DBA); global supply chain management (DBA); healthcare management (MBA, DBA); human resource management (MBA, MS, Graduate Certificate); human resources management (DBA); information systems management (DBA); international business (MBA, DBA); leadership (MBA, MS, DBA, Graduate Certificate); management (MS, PhD); managerial accounting (Graduate Certificate); marketing (MBA, MS, DBA); project management (MBA, MS, DBA); self-designed (MBA, DBA); social impact management (DBA); technology entrepreneurship (DBA). Electronic applications accepted.

School of Nursing *Program availability:* Part-time, evening/weekend, online only, 100% online. Offers adult-gerontology acute care nurse practitioner (MSN); adult-gerontology nurse practitioner (MSN); education (MSN); family nurse practitioner (MSN); informatics (MSN); leadership and management (MSN); nursing (PhD, Post-Master's Certificate); nursing practice (DNP); psychiatric mental health (MSN). Electronic applications accepted.

School of Psychology *Program availability:* Part-time, evening/weekend, online only, 100% online. Offers clinical psychology (MS); forensic psychology (MS); industrial organizational (MS, PhD); online teaching in psychology (Post-Master's Certificate); organizational psychology and development (Postbaccalaureate Certificate); psychology (MS, PhD); psychology respecialization (Post-Doctoral Certificate). Electronic applications accepted.

School of Public Policy and Administration *Program availability:* Part-time, evening/weekend, online only, 100% online. Offers criminal justice (MPA, MPP, MS, Graduate Certificate); criminal justice and executive management (MS); criminal justice leadership and executive management (MS); emergency management (MPA, MPP, MS); general program (MPA, MPP); global leadership (MPA, MPP); government management (Graduate Certificate); health policy (MPA, MPP); homeland security (Graduate Certificate); homeland security and policy coordination (MPA, MPP); international nongovernmental organizations (MPA, MPP); law and public policy (MPA, MPP); local government management for sustainable communities (MPA, MPP); nonprofit management (Graduate Certificate); nonprofit management and leadership (MPA, MPP, MS); online teaching in higher education (Post-Master's Certificate); policy analysis (MPA); public management and leadership (MPA, MPP, Graduate Certificate); public policy (Graduate Certificate); public policy and administration (PhD); strategic planning and public policy (Graduate Certificate); terrorism, mediation, and peace (MPA, MPP). Electronic applications accepted.

School of Social Work and Human Services *Program availability:* Part-time, evening/weekend, online only, 100% online. Offers addictions and social work (DSW); advanced clinical practice (MSW); clinical expertise (DSW); criminal justice (DSW); disaster, crisis, and intervention (DSW); family studies and interventions (DSW); human and social services (PhD); medical social work (DSW); military social work (MSW); policy practice (DSW); social work (PhD); social work administration (DSW); social work in healthcare (MSW); social work with children and families (MSW). Electronic applications accepted.

WALDORF UNIVERSITY, Forest City, IA 50436

General Information Independent-religious, coed, comprehensive institution.

GRADUATE UNITS

Program in Organizational Leadership Offers criminal justice leadership (MA); emergency management leadership (MA); fire/rescue executive leadership (MA); human resource development (MA); public administration (MA); sport management (MA); teacher leader (MA).

WALLA WALLA UNIVERSITY, College Place, WA 99324

General Information Independent-religious, coed, comprehensive institution. *Enrollment:* 169 full-time matriculated graduate/professional students (129 women), 24 part-time matriculated graduate/professional students (16 women). *Enrollment by degree level:* 193 master's. *Graduate housing:* Rooms and/or apartments available on a first-come, first-served basis to single and married students. *Student services:* Campus employment opportunities, career counseling, free psychological counseling, international student services, low-cost health insurance, multicultural affairs office, services for students with disabilities. *Library facilities:* Peterson Memorial Library plus 3 others.

Computer facilities: Computer purchase and lease plans are available. A campuswide network can be accessed from student residence rooms and from off campus. Online class registration, online forum, online classifieds, online student directory are available. Website: http://www.wallawalla.edu/

General Application Contact: Pamela Cress, Associate Vice President for Graduate Studies, 509-527-2421, Fax: 509-527-2237, E-mail: pam.cress@wallawalla.edu.

GRADUATE UNITS

Graduate Studies Expenses: Contact institution. *Financial support:* Research assistantships, teaching assistantships, career-related internships or fieldwork, Federal Work-Study, scholarships/grants, tuition waivers (partial), and unspecified assistantships available. Support available to part-time students. Financial award application deadline: 4/30; financial award applicants required to submit FAFSA. *Program availability:* Part-time, evening/weekend. Offers biology (MS). *Application deadline:* Applications are processed on a rolling basis. *Application fee:* $50. Electronic applications accepted. *Application Contact:* April Duffy, Administrative Assistant, 509-527-2421, Fax: 509-527-2237, E-mail: april.duffy@wallawalla.edu. *Associate Vice President for Graduate Studies*, Pamela Cress, 509-527-2421, Fax: 509-527-2237, E-mail: pam.cress@wallawalla.edu.

Center for Cinema, Religion, and Worldview Expenses: Contact institution. Offers Web and interactive media (MA). *Application deadline:* For fall admission, 8/15 for domestic students. *Application fee:* $50. *Application Contact:* Rachel Scribner, Coordinator, 509-527-2832, Fax: 509-527-2237, E-mail: rachel.scribner@wallawalla.edu. *Director*, Lynelle Ellis, 509-527-2843, Fax: 509-527-2237, E-mail: lynelle.ellis@wallawalla.edu.

School of Education and Psychology Expenses: Contact institution. *Financial support:* Research assistantships, teaching assistantships, Federal Work-Study, and tuition waivers (partial) available. Support available to part-time students. Financial award application deadline: 4/30; financial award applicants required to submit FAFSA. *Program availability:* Part-time. Offers curriculum and instruction (M Ed, MAT); educational leadership (M Ed, MAT); literacy instruction (M Ed, MAT); special education (M Ed, MAT). *Application deadline:* For fall admission, 4/1 priority date for domestic students. Applications are processed on a rolling basis. *Application fee:* $50. Electronic applications accepted. *Application Contact:* Dr. Joe G. Galusha, Dean of Graduate Studies, 509-527-2421, Fax: 509-527-2237, E-mail: joe.galusha@wallawalla.edu. *Dean*, Dr. Debbie Muthersbaugh, 509-527-2212, Fax: 509-527-2248, E-mail: debbie.muthersbaugh@wallawalla.edu.

Wilma Hepker School of Social Work and Sociology Expenses: Contact institution. *Financial support:* Career-related internships or fieldwork, Federal Work-Study, and scholarships/grants available. Support available to part-time students. Financial award application deadline: 4/30; financial award applicants required to submit FAFSA. *Program availability:* Part-time. Offers social work (MSW). *Application deadline:* For fall admission, 7/15 priority date for domestic students. Applications are processed on a rolling basis. *Application fee:* $50. Electronic applications accepted. *Application Contact:* Dr. Heather Vonderfecht, Program Director, 509-527-2584, Fax: 509-527-2237, E-mail: heather.vonderfecht@wallawalla.edu. *Dean*, Dr. Susan B. Smith, 509-527-2443, Fax: 509-527-2270, E-mail: susan.smith@wallawalla.edu.

WALSH COLLEGE OF ACCOUNTANCY AND BUSINESS ADMINISTRATION, Troy, MI 48083

General Information Independent, coed, upper-level institution. *Enrollment:* 2,299 graduate, professional, and undergraduate students; 69 full-time matriculated graduate/professional students (32 women), 1,337 part-time matriculated graduate/professional students (683 women). *Enrollment by degree level:* 1,406 master's. *Graduate faculty:* 22 full-time (11 women), 54 part-time/adjunct (15 women). *Tuition:* Full-time $20,790; part-time $13,860 per semester. *Required fees:* $375. *Graduate housing:* On-campus housing not available. *Student services:* Campus employment opportunities, career counseling, international student services, services for students with disabilities, writing training. *Library facilities:* Vollbrecht Library plus 1 other. *Collection:* Books: 27,985 (physical), 18,425 (digital/electronic); Serial titles: 2,262 (physical), 71,676 (digital/electronic); Databases: 79. Weekly public service hours: 113.

Computer facilities: 400 computers available on campus for general student use. A campuswide network can be accessed from off campus. Online class registration, Campus Wifi are available.
Website: http://www.walshcollege.edu/

General Application Contact: Heather Rigby, Director of Admissions and Academic Advising, 248-823-1610, Fax: 248-689-0938, E-mail: hrigby@walshcollege.edu.

GRADUATE UNITS

Graduate Programs Students: 1,406 (715 women); includes 360 minority (205 Black or African American, non-Hispanic/Latino; 4 American Indian or Alaska Native, non-Hispanic/Latino; 85 Asian, non-Hispanic/Latino; 46 Hispanic/Latino; 1 Native Hawaiian or other Pacific Islander, non-Hispanic/Latino; 19 Two or more races, non-Hispanic/Latino), 77 international. Average age 33. 462 applicants, 85% accepted, 273 enrolled. *Faculty:* 22 full-time (11 women), 54 part-time/adjunct (15 women). Expenses: Contact institution. *Financial support:* In 2017–18, 55 students received support. Career-related internships or fieldwork and scholarships/grants available. Financial award application deadline: 6/30; financial award applicants required to submit FAFSA. In 2017, 433 master's awarded. *Program availability:* Part-time, evening/weekend, 100% online, blended/hybrid learning. Offers business (MAB); business administration (MBA); chief information officer (MS, MSIT); chief security officer (MS); cybersecurity (MSIT); data analytics (MAC); data science (MSIT); finance (MAC); financial investments (MSF); financial management (MSF); financial services (MSF); global project and program management (MSIT); human resources management (MS); international business (MS); marketing (MS); program management office (MS); strategic management (MS);

taxation (MAC). *Application deadline:* Applications are processed on a rolling basis. *Application fee:* $35. Electronic applications accepted. *Application Contact:* Heather Rigby, Director of Admissions and Academic Advising, 248-823-1600, Fax: 248-823-1611, E-mail: hrigby@walshcollege.edu. *Chief Academic Officer/Executive Vice President*, Dr. Michael Rinkus, 248-823-1269, Fax: 248-689-0920, E-mail: mrinkus@walshcollege.edu.

WALSH UNIVERSITY, North Canton, OH 44720-3396

General Information Independent-religious, coed, comprehensive institution. CGS member. *Graduate housing:* Room and/or apartments available on a first-come, first-served basis to single students; on-campus housing not available to married students. Housing application deadline: 7/15. *Research affiliation:* North Canton Public Schools (straight A grants (student development)), Research Foundation of the Carolinas (surgery), Akron General Health System (patient satisfaction), Mercy Medical Center (orthopedics, nursing, physical therapy), Akron Children's Hospital (orthopedics).

GRADUATE UNITS

Graduate Programs *Program availability:* Part-time, evening/weekend, online learning. Offers clinical mental health counseling (MA); healthcare management (MBA); leadership with principal license (MA Ed); management (MBA); marketing (MBA); parish administration (MA); pastoral ministry (MA); physical therapy (DPT); reading literacy (MA Ed); religious education (MA); school counseling (MA); student affairs in higher education (MA). Electronic applications accepted.

Gary and Linda Byers School of Nursing *Program availability:* Part-time, evening/weekend, online only, 100% online. Offers academic nurse educator (MSN); adult acute care nurse practitioner (MSN); clinical nurse leader (MSN); nursing practice (DNP). Electronic applications accepted.

WARNER PACIFIC UNIVERSITY, Portland, OR 97215-4099

General Information Independent-religious, coed, comprehensive institution. *Graduate housing:* On-campus housing not available.

GRADUATE UNITS

Graduate Programs *Program availability:* Part-time, evening/weekend. Offers human services (MA); not-for-profit leadership (MS); organizational leadership (MS); teaching (MAT).

WARNER UNIVERSITY, Lake Wales, FL 33859

General Information Independent-religious, coed, comprehensive institution. *Graduate housing:* Room and/or apartments available on a first-come, first-served basis to single students; on-campus housing not available to married students.

GRADUATE UNITS

School of Business *Program availability:* Part-time, evening/weekend, online learning. Offers accounting (MBA); business administration (MBA); human resource management (MBA); international business (MBA); management (MSMC). Electronic applications accepted.

School of Education *Program availability:* Part-time, evening/weekend, online learning. Offers curriculum and instruction (MAEd); elementary education (MAEd); science, technology, engineering, and mathematics (STEM) (MAEd). Electronic applications accepted.

WARREN WILSON COLLEGE, Asheville, NC 28815-9000

General Information Independent-religious, coed, comprehensive institution. *Graduate housing:* Room and/or apartments guaranteed to single students; on-campus housing not available to married students.

GRADUATE UNITS

Master of Arts Program in Critical and Historical Craft Studies Offers critical and historical craft studies (MA). Electronic applications accepted.

MFA Program for Writers *Program availability:* Online learning. Offers creative writing (MFA). Electronic applications accepted.

WARTBURG THEOLOGICAL SEMINARY, Dubuque, IA 52004-5004

General Information Independent-religious, coed, graduate-only institution. *Graduate housing:* Rooms and/or apartments available on a first-come, first-served basis to single and married students. Housing application deadline: 4/30. *Research affiliation:* Menighetsfakultet, Augustana Theologische Hochschule.

GRADUATE UNITS

Graduate and Professional Programs *Program availability:* Online learning. Offers diaconal ministry (MA); ministry (M Div); theology (MA). Electronic applications accepted.

WASHBURN UNIVERSITY, Topeka, KS 66621

General Information City-supported, coed, comprehensive institution. *Graduate housing:* Room and/or apartments available on a first-come, first-served basis to single students; on-campus housing not available to married students.

GRADUATE UNITS

College of Arts and Sciences *Program availability:* Part-time, evening/weekend. Offers arts and sciences (M Ed, MA, MLS); clinical psychology (MA); curriculum and instruction (M Ed); educational leadership (M Ed); liberal studies (MLS); reading (M Ed); special education (M Ed). Electronic applications accepted.

School of Applied Studies *Program availability:* Part-time, evening/weekend, online learning. Offers addiction counseling (MA); applied studies (MA, MCJ, MHS, MSW); clinical social work (MSW); criminal justice and legal studies (MCJ); health care education (MHS).

School of Business *Program availability:* Part-time, evening/weekend. Offers accountancy (M Acc). Electronic applications accepted.

School of Law Offers global legal studies (LL M); law (MSL, JD). Electronic applications accepted.

School of Nursing *Program availability:* Part-time. Offers clinical nurse leader (MSN); nursing (DNP); psychiatric mental health nurse practitioner (Post-Graduate Certificate).

WASHINGTON ADVENTIST UNIVERSITY, Takoma Park, MD 20912

General Information Independent-religious, coed, comprehensive institution. *Enrollment:* 75 full-time matriculated graduate/professional students (50 women), 114 part-time matriculated graduate/professional students (77 women). *Enrollment by degree level:* 189 master's. *Tuition:* Part-time $625 per credit. *Graduate housing:* Rooms and/or apartments available on a first-come, first-served basis to single and married students. Typical cost: $8930 (including board) for single students; $8930 (including board) for married students. Housing application deadline: 8/1. *Student services:* Campus employment opportunities, campus safety program, career counseling, exercise/wellness program, free psychological counseling, international student services, low-cost health insurance, multicultural affairs office, services for students with disabilities, teacher training, writing training. *Library facilities:* Theofield G. Weis Library.

Computer facilities: A campuswide network can be accessed from student residence rooms and from off campus.
Website: http://www.wau.edu/

General Application Contact: Jessica Ritchie, Program Coordinator, 301-891-4086, E-mail: jritchie@wau.edu.

GRADUATE UNITS

MBA Program Students: 13 full-time (6 women), 24 part-time (18 women); includes 20 minority (16 Black or African American, non-Hispanic/Latino; 1 Asian, non-Hispanic/Latino; 3 Hispanic/Latino). Average age 31. Expenses: Contact institution. *Financial support:* Institutionally sponsored loans available. Support available to part-time students. Financial award applicants required to submit FAFSA. In 2017, 24 master's awarded. *Program availability:* Part-time, evening/weekend, online learning. Offers business administration (MBA). *Application deadline:* Applications are processed on a rolling basis. *Application fee:* $50. *Application Contact:* Jessica Ritchie, Program Coordinator, 301-891-4086, Fax: 301-891-4023, E-mail: jritchie@wau.edu. *Associate Provost*, Dr. Patrick Williams, 301-891-4116.

Program in Counseling Psychology Students: 12 full-time (9 women), 20 part-time (14 women); includes 22 minority (15 Black or African American, non-Hispanic/Latino; 3 Asian, non-Hispanic/Latino; 2 Hispanic/Latino; 2 Two or more races, non-Hispanic/Latino), 4 international. Average age 35. Expenses: Contact institution. *Financial support:* Applicants required to submit FAFSA. In 2017, 16 master's awarded. *Program availability:* Part-time. Offers counseling psychology (MA). *Application deadline:* Applications are processed on a rolling basis. *Application Contact:* Jessica Ritchie, Program Coordinator, 301-891-4086, Fax: 301-891-4023, E-mail: jritchie@wau.edu. *Associate Provost*, Dr. Patrick Wiliams, 301-891-4116, E-mail: pawillia@wau.edu.

Program in Health Care Administration Students: 7 full-time (4 women), 18 part-time (12 women); includes 15 minority (10 Black or African American, non-Hispanic/Latino; 5 Asian, non-Hispanic/Latino), 8 international. Average age 33. Expenses: Contact institution. *Financial support:* Applicants required to submit FAFSA. In 2017, 8 master's awarded. *Program availability:* Part-time. Offers health care administration (MA). *Application deadline:* For fall admission, 8/26 for domestic students; for spring admission, 1/6 for domestic students; for summer admission, 5/11 for domestic students. Applications are processed on a rolling basis. *Application fee:* $25. Electronic applications accepted. *Application Contact:* Jessica Ritchie, Program Coordinator, 301-891-4086, E-mail: jritchie@wau.edu. *Associate Provost*, Dr. Patrick Williams, 301-891-4116, E-mail: pawillia@wau.edu.

Program in Nursing - Business Leadership Students: 5 full-time (1 woman), 3 part-time (all women); includes 4 minority (all Black or African American, non-Hispanic/Latino), 3 international. Average age 44. Expenses: Contact institution. *Financial support:* Applicants required to submit FAFSA. In 2017, 6 master's awarded. *Program availability:* Part-time. Offers nursing - business leadership (MSN). *Application deadline:* Applications are processed on a rolling basis. *Application Contact:* Jessica Ritchie, Program Coordinator, 301-891-4086, Fax: 301-891-4023, E-mail: jritchie@wau.edu. *Associate Provost*, Dr. Patrick Williams, 301-891-4092, E-mail: jeedward@wau.edu.

Program in Nursing - Education Students: 13 full-time (12 women), 5 part-time (all women); includes 13 minority (9 Black or African American, non-Hispanic/Latino; 2 Asian, non-Hispanic/Latino; 1 Hispanic/Latino; 1 Two or more races, non-Hispanic/Latino), 5 international. Average age 46. Expenses: Contact institution. *Financial support:* Applicants required to submit FAFSA. In 2017, 1 master's awarded. *Program availability:* Part-time. Offers nursing - education (MS). *Application deadline:* Applications are processed on a rolling basis. *Application Contact:* Jessica Ritchie, Program Coordinator, 301-891-4086, Fax: 301-891-4023, E-mail: jritchie@wau.edu. *Associate Provost*, Dr. Patrick Williams, 301-891-4116, E-mail: pawillia@wau.edu.

Program in Professional Counseling Psychology Students: 12 full-time (9 women), 20 part-time (14 women); includes 18 minority (13 Black or African American, non-Hispanic/Latino; 2 Asian, non-Hispanic/Latino; 2 Hispanic/Latino; 1 Two or more races, non-Hispanic/Latino), 4 international. Average age 35. Expenses: Contact institution. *Financial support:* Applicants required to submit FAFSA. In 2017, 8 master's awarded. *Program availability:* Part-time. Offers professional counseling psychology (MA). *Application deadline:* Applications are processed on a rolling basis. *Application Contact:* Jessica Ritchie, Program Coordinator, 301-891-4086, Fax: 301-891-4023, E-mail: jritchie@wau.edu. *Associate Provost*, Dr. Patrick Williams, 301-891-4116, E-mail: pawillia@wau.edu.

Program in Public Administration Students: 4 full-time (all women), 9 part-time (6 women); includes 7 minority (6 Black or African American, non-Hispanic/Latino; 1 Two or more races, non-Hispanic/Latino), 3 international. Average age 39. Expenses: Contact institution. *Financial support:* Applicants required to submit FAFSA. In 2017, 13 master's awarded. *Program availability:* Part-time. Offers public administration (MPA). *Application deadline:* Applications are processed on a rolling basis. *Application Contact:* Jessica Ritchie, Program Coordinator, 301-891-4086, Fax: 301-891-4023, E-mail: jritchie@wau.edu. *Associate Provost*, Dr. Patrick Williams, 301-891-4116, E-mail: pawillia@wau.edu.

Program in Religion Students: 16 part-time (4 women); includes 12 minority (9 Black or African American, non-Hispanic/Latino; 2 Asian, non-Hispanic/Latino; 1 Hispanic/Latino). Average age 46. Expenses: Contact institution. *Financial support:* Available to part-time students. Applicants required to submit FAFSA. In 2017, 1 master's awarded. *Program availability:* Part-time. Offers religion (MAR). *Application deadline:* Applications are processed on a rolling basis. *Application Contact:* Jessica Ritchie, Program Coordinator, 301-891-4086, Fax: 301-891-4023, E-mail: jritchie@wau.edu. *Associate Provost*, Dr. Patrick Williams, 301-891-4116, E-mail: pawillia@wau.edu.

WASHINGTON & JEFFERSON COLLEGE, Washington, PA 15301

General Information Independent, coed, comprehensive institution.

GRADUATE UNITS

Graduate and Continuing Studies

WASHINGTON AND LEE UNIVERSITY, Lexington, VA 24450

General Information Independent, coed, comprehensive institution. *Research affiliation:* Future of Privacy Forum (data privacy, data security, and related fields).

GRADUATE UNITS

School of Law Offers law (JD). Electronic applications accepted.

WASHINGTON STATE UNIVERSITY, Pullman, WA 99164

General Information State-supported, coed, university. CGS member. *Graduate housing:* Rooms and/or apartments available on a first-come, first-served basis to single and married students. Housing application deadline: 3/1. *Research affiliation:* Battelle–Pacific Northwest National Laboratory (biochemistry, engineering).

GRADUATE UNITS

Carson College of Business *Program availability:* Online learning. Offers accounting (M Acc); business (M Acc, MBA, PhD). Programs also offered at the Tri-Cities, Vancouver, and Global (online) campuses.

College of Agricultural, Human, and Natural Resource Sciences *Program availability:* Part-time, online learning. Offers agricultural, human, and natural resource sciences (MA, MS, PhD, Graduate Certificate); animal sciences (MS, PhD); apparel, merchandising, design, and textiles (MA); biological and agricultural engineering (MS, PhD); crop sciences (MS, PhD); entomology (MS, PhD); horticulture (MS, PhD); interior design and landscape architecture (MA, MS); plant pathology (MS, PhD); prevention science (PhD); soil sciences (MS, PhD). Programs also offered at the Global (online) campuses. Electronic applications accepted.

School of Economic Sciences Offers agricultural economics (PhD); economics (PhD). Programs offered at the Pullman campus. Electronic applications accepted.

School of Food Science *Program availability:* Part-time. Offers food science (MS, PhD). Programs offered at the Pullman campus. Electronic applications accepted.

School of the Environment Offers environmental and natural resource sciences (PhD); natural resource sciences (MS). Program applications must be made through the Pullman campus.

College of Arts and Sciences Offers American studies (MA, PhD); applied mathematics (MS, PhD); archaeology (MA, PhD); arts and sciences (MA, MFA, MPA, MS, PhD, Graduate Certificate); chemistry (MS, PhD); clinical psychology (PhD); criminal justice and criminology (MA, PhD); cultural anthropology (PhD); English (MA, PhD); evolutionary anthropology (MA, PhD); experimental psychology (PhD); fine arts (MFA); foreign languages and cultures (MA); history (MA, PhD); mathematics (MS, PhD); mathematics teaching (MS, PhD); physics and astronomy (MS, PhD); sociology (MA, PhD). Electronic applications accepted.

School of Biological Sciences Offers biological sciences (MS, PhD). Programs are offered at the Pullman campus.

School of Music *Program availability:* Part-time. Offers music (MA). Electronic applications accepted.

School of Politics, Philosophy and Public Affairs *Program availability:* Online learning. Offers bioethics (Graduate Certificate); political science (MA, PhD); public affairs (MPA). MPA, MA, and PhD programs also offered at the Vancouver campus; Graduate Certificate offered through Global (online) campus. Electronic applications accepted.

School of the Environment Offers environmental and natural resource sciences (PhD); environmental science (MS); geology (MS, PhD); natural resource science (MS).

College of Education Offers counseling psychology (PhD); cultural studies and social thought in education (PhD); curriculum and instruction (Ed M, MA); education (Ed M, MA, MIT, Ed D, PhD); educational leadership (Ed M, MA, Ed D, PhD); educational psychology (MA, PhD); English language learners (Ed M, MA); language, literacy and technology (PhD); literacy education (Ed M, MA); mathematics education (PhD); special education (Ed M, MA, PhD); sport management (MA); teacher leadership (Ed D); teaching (MIT). Electronic applications accepted.

College of Nursing Offers advanced population health (MN, DNP); family nurse practitioner (MN, DNP); nursing (PhD); psychiatric/mental health nurse practitioner (DNP); psychiatric/mental health practitioner (MN). Programs offered at the Spokane, Tri-Cities, and Vancouver campuses.

College of Pharmacy Offers health policy and administration (MHPA); nutrition and exercise physiology (MS); pharmacy (Pharm D). Programs offered at the Spokane campus.

College of Veterinary Medicine Students: 614 full-time (448 women), 28 part-time (22 women); includes 80 minority (1 Black or African American, non-Hispanic/Latino; 4 American Indian or Alaska Native, non-Hispanic/Latino; 18 Asian, non-Hispanic/Latino; 26 Hispanic/Latino; 1 Native Hawaiian or other Pacific Islander, non-Hispanic/Latino; 30 Two or more races, non-Hispanic/Latino), 33 international. Average age 27. 1,288 applicants, 16% accepted, 132 enrolled. *Faculty:* 28 full-time (6 women), 48 part-time/adjunct (12 women). Expenses: Contact institution. *Financial support:* In 2017–18, 446 students received support, including 28 fellowships with full tuition reimbursements available, 87 research assistantships with full tuition reimbursements available (averaging $23,000 per year), 34 teaching assistantships with full tuition reimbursements available (averaging $22,000 per year); career-related internships or fieldwork, Federal Work-Study, institutionally sponsored loans, scholarships/grants, traineeships, health care benefits, and unspecified assistantships also available. Support available to part-time students. Financial award application deadline: 1/31; financial award applicants required to submit FAFSA. In 2017, 18 master's, 99 doctorates awarded. Offers clinical and translational science (MS, PhD); immunology and infectious diseases (MS, PhD); molecular biosciences (MS, PhD); neuroscience (MS, PhD); veterinary medicine (MS, DVM, PhD). *Application deadline:* For fall admission, 9/15 for domestic and international students; for spring admission, 8/1 for international students. *Application fee:* $75. Electronic applications accepted. *Application Contact:* Stacey Poler, Recruitment Officer, 509-335-6133, E-mail: s.poler@wsu.edu. *Dean*, Dr. Bryan Slinker, 509-335-9515, Fax: 509-335-0160, E-mail: b_slinker@wsu.edu.

Paul G. Allen School for Global Animal Health Students: 19 full-time (8 women); includes 4 minority (1 Asian, non-Hispanic/Latino; 3 Hispanic/Latino), 4 international. 8 applicants, 100% accepted, 8 enrolled. *Faculty:* 38 full-time (13 women), 10 part-time/adjunct (5 women). Expenses: Contact institution. *Financial support:* In 2017–18, 19 students received support, including 5 fellowships with full tuition reimbursements available, 14 research assistantships; teaching assistantships, institutionally sponsored loans, scholarships/grants, traineeships, health care benefits, and unspecified assistantships also available. Financial award application deadline: 3/1. In 2017, 3 doctorates awarded. Offers immunology and infectious diseases (MS, PhD). *Application deadline:* Applications are processed on a rolling basis. *Application fee:* $75. Electronic applications accepted. *Application Contact:* Sue Zumwalt, Administrative Manager, 509-335-6027, Fax: 509-335-8529, E-mail: szumwalt@wsu.edu. *Director, Paul G. Allen School for Global Animal Health*, Dr. Thomas Kawula, 509-335-5861, Fax: 509-335-6328, E-mail: tom.kawula@vetmed.wsu.edu.

The Edward R. Murrow College of Communication Offers communication (MA, PhD); strategic communication (MA). MA in strategic communication offered at the Global (online) campus. Electronic applications accepted.

Elson S. Floyd College of Medicine Offers medicine (MS, MD); speech and hearing sciences (MS).

Voiland College of Engineering and Architecture Offers architecture (M Arch); civil engineering (MS, PhD); engineering and architecture (M Arch, METM, MS, PhD, Certificate); engineering and computer science (MS); engineering and technology management (METM, Certificate); environmental engineering (MS).

The Gene and Linda Voiland School of Chemical Engineering and Bioengineering Offers chemical engineering and bioengineering (MS, PhD).

School of Electrical Engineering and Computer Science *Program availability:* Part-time. Offers computer engineering (MS); computer science (MS); electrical engineering (MS); electrical engineering and computer science (PhD); electrical power engineering (MS). MS programs in computer engineering, computer science and electrical engineering also offered at Tri-Cities campus; MS in electrical power engineering offered at the Global (online) campus.

School of Mechanical and Materials Engineering *Program availability:* Part-time. Offers materials science and engineering (MS, PhD); mechanical engineering (MS, PhD). MS programs also offered at Tri-Cities campus. Electronic applications accepted.

WASHINGTON UNIVERSITY IN ST. LOUIS, St. Louis, MO 63130-4899

General Information Independent, coed, university. CGS member. *Graduate housing:* Rooms and/or apartments available on a first-come, first-served basis to single and married students.

GRADUATE UNITS

Brown School Students: 294 full-time (254 women); includes 114 minority (56 Black or African American, non-Hispanic/Latino; 8 American Indian or Alaska Native, non-Hispanic/Latino; 17 Asian, non-Hispanic/Latino; 10 Hispanic/Latino; 1 Native Hawaiian or other Pacific Islander, non-Hispanic/Latino; 22 Two or more races, non-Hispanic/Latino). Average age 26. *Faculty:* 54 full-time (31 women), 87 part-time/adjunct (61 women). Expenses: Contact institution. *Financial support:* In 2017–18, 30 fellowships, 60 research assistantships were awarded; career-related internships or fieldwork, Federal Work-Study, scholarships/grants, and unspecified assistantships also available. Support available to part-time students. Financial award applicants required to submit FAFSA. Offers American Indian/Alaska native (MSW); children, youth and families (MSW); epidemiology/biostatistics (MPH); generalist (MPH); global health (MPH); health (MSW); health policy analysis (MPH); individualized (MSW); mental health (MSW); older adults and aging societies (MSW); public health sciences (PhD); social and economic development (MSW); social work (PhD); urban design (MPH); violence and injury prevention (MSW). MSW/M Div and MSW/MAPS offered in partnership with Eden Theological Seminary. *Application deadline:* For fall admission, 12/15 priority date for domestic and international students; for winter admission, 3/1 priority date for domestic and international students. Applications are processed on a rolling basis. Electronic applications accepted. *Application Contact:* Office of Admissions and Recruitment, 314-935-6676, Fax: 314-935-4859, E-mail: brownadmissions@wustl.edu. *Director of Admissions and Recruitment*, Jamie L. Adkisson-Hennessey, 314-935-3524, Fax: 314-935-4859, E-mail: jadkisson@wustl.edu.

The Graduate School Offers aging and development (PhD); anthropology (PhD); art history and archaeology (AM, PhD); chemistry (PhD); Chinese (MA); Chinese and comparative literature (PhD); Chinese language and literature (PhD); classics (MA, PhD); comparative literature (PhD); dance (MFA); earth and planetary sciences (PhD); East Asian studies (MA); economics (PhD); educational research (PhD); elementary education (MA Ed); English and American literature (PhD); French (PhD); French and comparative literature (PhD); French language and literature (PhD); Germanic languages and literatures (PhD); Hispanic languages and literatures (PhD); history (PhD); Islamic and Near Eastern studies (MA); Japanese (MA); Japanese and comparative literature (PhD); Japanese language and literature (PhD); Jewish studies (MA); mathematics (MA, PhD); music (MA, PhD); philosophy (PhD); philosophy-neuroscience-psychology (PhD); physics (PhD); political science (PhD); secondary education (MAT); Spanish (PhD); Spanish and comparative literature (PhD); statistics (MA, PhD); theater and performance studies (MA); writing (MFA). Electronic applications accepted.

Division of Biology and Biomedical Sciences Offers biochemistry (PhD); computational and molecular biophysics (PhD); computational and systems biology (PhD); developmental, regenerative, and stem cell biology (PhD); ecology (PhD); evolution, ecology and population biology (PhD); human and statistical genetics (PhD); immunology (PhD); molecular cell biology (PhD); molecular genetics and genomics (PhD); molecular microbiology and microbial pathogenesis (PhD); neurosciences (PhD); plant and microbial biosciences (PhD). Electronic applications accepted.

Olin Business School Students: 728 full-time (336 women), 613 part-time (207 women); includes 284 minority (52 Black or African American, non-Hispanic/Latino; 90 American Indian or Alaska Native, non-Hispanic/Latino; 77 Asian, non-Hispanic/Latino; 31 Hispanic/Latino; 3 Native Hawaiian or other Pacific Islander, non-Hispanic/Latino; 31 Two or more races, non-Hispanic/Latino), 528 international. 4,556 applicants, 31% accepted, 644 enrolled. *Faculty:* 98 full-time (25 women), 54 part-time/adjunct (12 women). Expenses: Contact institution. Offers accounting (MS); business (EMBA, M Acc, MBA, MS, DBA, PhD); business administration (EMBA, MBA, PhD); corporate finance and investments (MS); customer analytics (MS); finance (MS, DBA); leadership (MS); quantitative finance (MS); supply chain management (MS). Electronic applications accepted. *Application Contact:* Information Contact, 314-935-6880, Fax: 314-935-4887, E-mail: graduateschool@artsci.wustl.edu. *Dean*, Dr. Mark Taylor, 314-935-6344, Fax: 314-935-4074.

Sam Fox School of Design and Visual Arts Offers architecture (M Arch, MLA); design and visual arts (M Arch, MFA, MLA, MUD); urban design (MUD).

Graduate School of Art Offers visual art (MFA). Electronic applications accepted.

School of Engineering and Applied Science *Program availability:* Part-time, evening/weekend. Offers aerospace engineering (MS, PhD); biomedical engineering (MS, D Sc, PhD); chemical engineering (MS, D Sc); computer engineering (MS, PhD); computer science (MS, PhD); computer science and engineering (M Eng); engineering and applied science (M Eng, MCE, MCM, MEM, MIM, MPM, MS, MSEE, MSEE, MSI, D Sc, PhD); environmental engineering (MS, D Sc); materials science (MS); mechanical engineering (M Eng, MS, PhD). Electronic applications accepted.

School of Law Offers law (LL M, MJS, JD, JSD). Electronic applications accepted.

School of Medicine Students: 1,292 full-time (815 women), 117 part-time (64 women); includes 357 minority (43 Black or African American, non-Hispanic/Latino; 5 American Indian or Alaska Native, non-Hispanic/Latino; 215 Asian, non-Hispanic/Latino; 47 Hispanic/Latino; 1 Native Hawaiian or other Pacific Islander, non-Hispanic/Latino; 46 Two or more races, non-Hispanic/Latino), 67 international. Average age 23. 5,032 applicants, 7% accepted, 124 enrolled. Expenses: Contact institution. *Financial support:* Applicants required to submit FAFSA. In 2017, 209 master's, 125 doctorates awarded. Offers applied health behavior research (MS); audiology (Au D); clinical epidemiology (MPHS); clinical investigation (MS); deaf education (MS); health behavior planning and evaluation (Graduate Certificate); health services (MPHS); medicine (MS, MSOT, Au D, DPT, MD, OTD, PPDPT, PhD, Graduate Certificate); movement science (PhD); occupational therapy (MSOT, OTD); physical therapy (DPT); psychiatric and behavioral health sciences (MPHS); quantitative methods (MPHS); rehabilitation and participation science (PhD); speech and hearing sciences (PhD). MD/MPH offered jointly with Brown School. *Application deadline:* For fall admission, 12/31 for domestic and international students. Applications are processed on a rolling basis. *Application fee:* $100. Electronic applications accepted. *Application Contact:* Dr. Valerie Ratts, Associate Dean for Admissions, 314-362-6844, Fax: 314-362-4658, E-mail: wusmcoa@wustl.edu. *Executive Vice Chancellor for Medical Affairs/Dean of the School of Medicine,* Dr. David H. Perlmutter, 314-362-6828.

Division of Biostatistics *Program availability:* Part-time. Offers biostatistics (MS); genetic epidemiology (Certificate). Electronic applications accepted.

See Close-Up on page 883.

WATKINS COLLEGE OF ART, DESIGN, & FILM, Nashville, TN 37228

General Information Independent, coed, comprehensive institution.

GRADUATE UNITS

Program in Film *Program availability:* Evening/weekend. Offers film (MFA).

WAYLAND BAPTIST UNIVERSITY, Plainview, TX 79072-6998

General Information Independent-religious, coed, comprehensive institution. *Enrollment:* 4,827 graduate, professional, and undergraduate students; 78 full-time matriculated graduate/professional students (44 women), 1,206 part-time matriculated graduate/professional students (629 women). *Enrollment by degree level:* 1,284 master's. *Graduate faculty:* 121 full-time (41 women), 102 part-time/adjunct (37 women). *Tuition:* Full-time $11,250; part-time $625 per credit hour. *Required fees:* $1200. *Graduate housing:* Rooms and/or apartments available on a first-come, first-served basis to single and married students. *Student services:* Campus employment opportunities, campus safety program, career counseling, free psychological counseling, international student services, services for students with disabilities, teacher training, writing training. *Library facilities:* J.E. and L.E. Mabee Learning Resource Center. *Collection:* Books: 130,903 (physical), 49,479 (digital/electronic); Serial titles: 555,663 (digital/electronic); Databases: 104.

Computer facilities: Computer purchase and lease plans are available. 840 computers available on campus for general student use. A campuswide network can be accessed from student residence rooms and from off campus. Online class registration is available.
Website: http://www.wbu.edu/

General Application Contact: Amanda Stanton, Coordinator of Graduate Studies, 806-291-3423, Fax: 806-291-1953, E-mail: stanton@wbu.edu.

GRADUATE UNITS

Graduate Programs Students: 78 full-time (44 women), 1,206 part-time (629 women); includes 684 minority (246 Black or African American, non-Hispanic/Latino; 14 American Indian or Alaska Native, non-Hispanic/Latino; 35 Asian, non-Hispanic/Latino; 301 Hispanic/Latino; 19 Native Hawaiian or other Pacific Islander, non-Hispanic/Latino; 69 Two or more races, non-Hispanic/Latino), 11 international. Average age 40. 233 applicants, 95% accepted, 141 enrolled. *Faculty:* 121 full-time (41 women), 102 part-time/adjunct (37 women). Expenses: Contact institution. *Financial support:* Federal Work-Study, institutionally sponsored loans, and scholarships/grants available. Support available to part-time students. Financial award application deadline: 5/1; financial award applicants required to submit FAFSA. In 2017, 466 master's awarded. *Program availability:* Part-time, evening/weekend, 100% online, blended/hybrid learning. Offers accounting (MBA); Christian ministry (MCM); counseling (MA); criminal justice (MACJ); divinity (M Div); education administration (M Ed); education diagnostics (M Ed); education literacy (M Ed); elementary certification (M Ed); English (M Ed); English as a second language (M Ed); general business (MBA); government administration (MPA); health care administration (MAM, MBA); higher education administration (M Ed); history (MA); homeland security (MPA); human resource management (MAM, MBA); human resources (M Ed); humanities (MAH); instructional leadership (M Ed); instructional technology (M Ed); international management (MBA); justice administration (MPA); leadership training and development (M Ed); management (MBA, D Mgt); management information systems (MBA); organization management (MAM); project management (MBA); religion (MA); science education (M Ed); secondary certification (M Ed); social studies (M Ed); special education (M Ed); sports administration and management (M Ed). *Application deadline:* Applications are processed on a rolling basis. *Application fee:* $50. Electronic applications accepted. *Application Contact:* Amanda Stanton, Coordinator of Graduate Studies, 806-291-3423, Fax: 806-291-1950, E-mail: stanton@wbu.edu. *Vice President of Academics,* Dr. Cindy McClenegan, 806-291-3410, Fax: 806-291-1953, E-mail: hallb@wbu.edu.

WAYNESBURG UNIVERSITY, Waynesburg, PA 15370-1222

General Information Independent-religious, coed, comprehensive institution. *Graduate housing:* Room and/or apartments available on a first-come, first-served basis to single students; on-campus housing not available to married students. Housing application deadline: 8/1.

GRADUATE UNITS

Graduate and Professional Studies *Program availability:* Part-time, evening/weekend. Offers business (MBA); counseling (MA); counselor education and supervision (PhD); criminal investigation (MA); education (M Ed); nursing (MSN); nursing practice (DNP); special education (M Ed); technology (M Ed). Electronic applications accepted.

WAYNE STATE COLLEGE, Wayne, NE 68787

General Information State-supported, coed, comprehensive institution. CGS member. *Graduate housing:* Room and/or apartments available on a first-come, first-served basis to single students; on-campus housing not available to married students. *Research affiliation:* Nebraska Business Development Center, Social Sciences Research Center.

GRADUATE UNITS

Department of Health, Human Performance and Sport *Program availability:* Part-time, evening/weekend. Offers exercise science (MSE); organizational management (MS). Electronic applications accepted.

School of Business and Technology *Program availability:* Part-time, evening/weekend, online learning. Offers business and technology (MBA).

School of Education and Counseling *Program availability:* Part-time, evening/weekend. Offers alternative education (MSE); business and information technology education (MSE); communication arts education (MSE); counseling (MSE); counselor education (MSE); curriculum and instruction (MSE); early childhood education (MSE); education and counseling (MSE, Ed S); educational administration (MSE, Ed S); elementary administration (MSE); elementary and secondary administration (MSE); elementary education (MSE); English as a second language (MSE); English education (MSE); family and consumer sciences education (MSE); guidance and counseling (MSE); industrial technology and vocational education (MSE); learning communities (MSE); mathematics education (MSE); music education (MSE); school counseling (MSE); science education (MSE); secondary administration (MSE); social science education (MSE); special education (MSE).

WAYNE STATE UNIVERSITY, Detroit, MI 48202

General Information State-supported, coed, university. CGS member. *Enrollment:* 27,089 graduate, professional, and undergraduate students; 5,896 full-time matriculated graduate/professional students (3,141 women), 3,782 part-time matriculated graduate/professional students (2,247 women). *Enrollment by degree level:* 5,642 master's, 3,736 doctoral, 300 other advanced degrees. *Graduate faculty:* 810. Tuition, state resident: full-time $10,224; part-time $638.98 per credit hour. Tuition, nonresident: full-time $22,145; part-time $1384.04 per credit hour. Tuition and fees vary according to course load and program. *Graduate housing:* Rooms and/or apartments available on a first-come, first-served basis to single and married students. Typical cost: $6308 per year ($10,106 including board) for single students; $6308 per year ($10,106 including board) for married students. Room and board charges vary according to board plan and housing facility selected. *Student services:* Campus employment opportunities, campus safety program, career counseling, child daycare facilities, exercise/wellness program, free psychological counseling, grant writing training, international student services, multicultural affairs office, services for students with disabilities, teacher training, writing training. *Library facilities:* David Adamany Undergraduate Library plus 5 others. *Collection:* Books: 1.7 million (physical), 1.1 million (digital/electronic); Serial titles: 60,832 (physical), 112,521 (digital/electronic); Databases: 700. Weekly public service hours: 138; study areas open 24 hours, 5–7 days a week. *Research affiliation:* Detroit Medical Center, Henry Ford Health System, John A. Dingell VA Medical Center, Karmanos Cancer Institute.

Computer facilities: A campuswide network can be accessed from student residence rooms. Online class registration is available.
Website: http://www.wayne.edu/

General Application Contact: Deirdre Baker, Office of Graduate Admissions, 313-577-4723, Fax: 313-577-0131, E-mail: gradadmissions@wayne.edu.

GRADUATE UNITS

College of Education Students: 426 full-time (307 women), 926 part-time (692 women); includes 511 minority (382 Black or African American, non-Hispanic/Latino; 3 American Indian or Alaska Native, non-Hispanic/Latino; 22 Asian, non-Hispanic/Latino; 44 Hispanic/Latino; 2 Native Hawaiian or other Pacific Islander, non-Hispanic/Latino; 58 Two or more races, non-Hispanic/Latino), 52 international. Average age 35. 919 applicants, 36% accepted, 228 enrolled. *Faculty:* 46. Expenses: Contact institution. *Financial support:* In 2017–18, 303 students received support, including 4 fellowships with tuition reimbursements available (averaging $13,500 per year), 13 research assistantships with tuition reimbursements available (averaging $18,339 per year), 5 teaching assistantships with tuition reimbursements available (averaging $18,534 per year); Federal Work-Study, scholarships/grants, traineeships, health care benefits, and unspecified assistantships also available. Support available to part-time students. Financial award applicants required to submit FAFSA. In 2017, 322 master's, 53 doctorates, 64 other advanced degrees awarded. *Program availability:* Part-time, evening/weekend, 100% online, blended/hybrid learning. Offers athletic training (MSAT); education (M Ed, MA, MAT, MSAT, Ed D, PhD, Certificate, Ed S); health education (M Ed); kinesiology (M Ed, PhD); sports administration (MA). *Application deadline:* For fall admission, 6/1 priority date for domestic students, 5/1 for international students; for winter admission, 10/1 priority date for domestic students, 9/1 priority date for international students; for spring admission, 2/1 priority date for domestic students, 1/1 priority date for international students. *Application fee:* $50. Electronic applications accepted. *Application Contact:* Paul W. Johnson, Assistant Dean of Academic Services, 313-577-1606, E-mail: askcoe@wayne.edu. *Dean,* Dr. R. Douglas Whitman, 313-577-1620, E-mail: dwhitman@wayne.edu.

Division of Administrative and Organizational Studies Students: 50 full-time (30 women), 266 part-time (184 women); includes 158 minority (130 Black or African American, non-Hispanic/Latino; 1 American Indian or Alaska Native, non-Hispanic/Latino; 5 Asian, non-Hispanic/Latino; 9 Hispanic/Latino; 1 Native Hawaiian or other Pacific Islander, non-Hispanic/Latino; 12 Two or more races, non-Hispanic/Latino), 9 international. Average age 39. 187 applicants, 31% accepted, 42 enrolled. *Faculty:* 7. Expenses: Contact institution. *Financial support:* In 2017–18, 85 students received support, including 4 research assistantships with tuition reimbursements available (averaging $18,534 per year); fellowships with tuition reimbursements available, scholarships/grants, and unspecified assistantships also available. Support available to part-time students. Financial award applicants required to submit FAFSA. In 2017, 48 master's, 17 doctorates, 47 other advanced degrees awarded. *Program availability:* Part-time, 100% online, blended/hybrid learning. Offers educational administration and supervision (Ed S); educational leadership (M Ed); educational leadership and policy studies (Ed D, PhD); educational technology (Certificate); learning design and technology (M Ed, Ed D, PhD, Ed S); online teaching (Certificate). *Application deadline:* For fall admission, 6/1 priority date for domestic students, 5/1 priority date for international students; for winter admission, 10/1 priority date for domestic students, 9/1 priority date for international students; for spring admission, 2/1 priority date for domestic students, 1/1 priority date for international students. Applications are processed on a rolling basis. *Application fee:* $50. Electronic applications accepted. *Application Contact:* Graduate Advisor, 313-577-1605, E-mail: askcoe@wayne.edu. *Assistant Dean,* Dr. William Hill, 313-577-9316, E-mail: ad2107@wayne.edu.

Division of Teacher Education Students: 126 full-time (96 women), 317 part-time (258 women); includes 134 minority (95 Black or African American, non-Hispanic/Latino; 1 American Indian or Alaska Native, non-Hispanic/Latino; 8 Asian, non-Hispanic/Latino; 17 Hispanic/Latino; 1 Native Hawaiian or other Pacific Islander, non-Hispanic/Latino; 12 Two or more races, non-Hispanic/Latino), 13 international. Average age 37. 260 applicants, 33% accepted, 57 enrolled. *Faculty:* 22. Expenses: Contact institution. *Financial support:* In 2017–18, 78 students received support, including 4 fellowships (averaging $13,500 per year), 1 research assistantship with tuition reimbursement available (averaging $16,000 per year); Federal Work-Study, scholarships/grants, and unspecified assistantships also available. Support available to part-time students. Financial award applicants required to submit FAFSA. In 2017, 111 master's, 13 doctorates, 7 other advanced degrees awarded. *Program availability:* Part-time, blended/hybrid learning. Offers art education (M Ed); bilingual/bicultural education (Certificate); curriculum and instruction (Ed D, PhD, Ed S); elementary education (MAT); elementary mathematics specialist (Certificate); English as a second language (Certificate); reading (M Ed, Ed S); reading, language and literature (Ed D);

secondary education (MAT); special education (MAT); teaching and learning (M Ed). *Application deadline:* For fall admission, 6/1 priority date for domestic students, 5/1 priority date for international students; for winter admission, 10/1 priority date for domestic students, 9/1 priority date for international students; for spring admission, 2/1 priority date for domestic students, 1/1 priority date for international students. Applications are processed on a rolling basis. *Application fee:* $50. Electronic applications accepted. *Application Contact:* 313-577-0902, E-mail: askcoe@wayne.edu. *Interim Associate Dean for Teacher Education*, Dr. Thomas Edwards, 313-577-3886, E-mail: t.g.edwards@wayne.edu.

Division of Theoretical and Behavioral Foundations Average age 32. 294 applicants, 34% accepted, 72 enrolled. Expenses: Contact institution. *Financial support:* In 2017–18, 92 students received support, including 2 research assistantships with tuition reimbursements available (averaging $17,994 per year); fellowships, teaching assistantships, Federal Work-Study, scholarships/grants, health care benefits, and unspecified assistantships also available. Support available to part-time students. Financial award applicants required to submit FAFSA. In 2017, 87 master's, 12 doctorates, 14 other advanced degrees awarded. *Program availability:* Evening/weekend. Offers applied behavior analysis (Certificate); counseling (M Ed, MA, Ed D, Ed S); counseling psychology (MA, PhD); education evaluation and research (M Ed, Ed D); educational psychology (M Ed, PhD); rehabilitation counseling and community inclusion (MA); school and community psychology (MA, Certificate). *Application deadline:* For fall admission, 6/1 priority date for domestic students, 5/1 priority date for international students; for winter admission, 10/1 priority date for domestic students, 9/1 priority date for international students; for spring admission, 2/1 priority date for domestic students, 1/1 priority date for international students. Applications are processed on a rolling basis. *Application fee:* $50. Electronic applications accepted. *Application Contact:* Janice Green, Assistant Dean, 313-577-1605, E-mail: jwgreen@wayne.edu. *Assistant Dean*, Dr. Cheryl Somers, 313-577-1670, E-mail: c.somers@wayne.edu.

College of Engineering Students: 935 full-time (193 women), 399 part-time (101 women); includes 142 minority (40 Black or African American, non-Hispanic/Latino; 76 Asian, non-Hispanic/Latino; 14 Hispanic/Latino; 12 Two or more races, non-Hispanic/Latino), 881 international. Average age 28. 2,643 applicants, 36% accepted, 292 enrolled. *Faculty:* 107. Expenses: Contact institution. *Financial support:* In 2017–18, 469 students received support, including 21 fellowships with tuition reimbursements available (averaging $19,560 per year), 58 research assistantships with tuition reimbursements available (averaging $19,248 per year), 105 teaching assistantships with tuition reimbursements available (averaging $19,560 per year); Federal Work-Study, scholarships/grants, health care benefits, tuition waivers (full and partial), and unspecified assistantships also available. Support available to part-time students. Financial award applicants required to submit FAFSA. In 2017, 608 master's, 35 doctorates, 2 other advanced degrees awarded. *Program availability:* Part-time, evening/weekend, blended/hybrid learning. Offers alternative energy technology (MS, Graduate Certificate); biomedical engineering (MS, PhD); chemical engineering (MS, PhD); civil engineering (MS); computer engineering (MS, PhD); computer science (MS, PhD); data science and business analytics (MS); electric-drive vehicle engineering (MS, Graduate Certificate); electrical engineering (MS, PhD); engineering (MS, MSET, PhD, Certificate, Graduate Certificate, Postbaccalaureate Certificate); engineering management (MS); industrial engineering (MS, PhD); injury biomechanics (Graduate Certificate); manufacturing engineering (MS); materials science and engineering (MS, PhD); mechanical engineering (MS, PhD); polymer engineering (Graduate Certificate); systems engineering (Certificate). *Application deadline:* For fall admission, 6/1 priority date for domestic students, 5/1 priority date for international students; for winter admission, 10/1 priority date for domestic students, 9/1 priority date for international students; for spring admission, 2/1 priority date for domestic students, 1/1 priority date for international students. Applications are processed on a rolling basis. *Application fee:* $50. Electronic applications accepted. *Application Contact:* Graduate Program Coordinator, E-mail: engineeringgradadmissions@eng.wayne.edu. *Dean*, Dr. Farshad Fotouhi, 313-577-3776, E-mail: fotouhi@wayne.edu.

Division of Engineering Technology Students: 12 full-time (1 woman), 8 part-time (1 woman); includes 9 minority (6 Black or African American, non-Hispanic/Latino; 2 Asian, non-Hispanic/Latino; 1 Hispanic/Latino), 8 international. Average age 34. 23 applicants, 52% accepted, 8 enrolled. *Faculty:* 4. Expenses: Contact institution. *Financial support:* Career-related internships or fieldwork and scholarships/grants available. Financial award applicants required to submit FAFSA. In 2017, 1 master's awarded. Offers engineering technology (MSET). *Application deadline:* For fall admission, 6/1 priority date for domestic students, 5/1 priority date for international students; for winter admission, 10/1 priority date for domestic students, 9/1 priority date for international students; for spring admission, 2/1 priority date for domestic students, 1/1 priority date for international students. Applications are processed on a rolling basis. *Application fee:* $50. Electronic applications accepted. *Application Contact:* Ellen Cope, Graduate Program Coordinator, 313-577-0409, E-mail: escope@wayne.edu. *Division Chair*, Dr. Ece Yaprak, 313-577-0875, E-mail: yaprak@eng.wayne.edu.

College of Fine, Performing and Communication Arts Students: 127 full-time (70 women), 119 part-time (77 women); includes 75 minority (55 Black or African American, non-Hispanic/Latino; 1 American Indian or Alaska Native, non-Hispanic/Latino; 3 Asian, non-Hispanic/Latino; 8 Hispanic/Latino; 8 Two or more races, non-Hispanic/Latino), 14 international. Average age 33. 426 applicants, 28% accepted, 67 enrolled. *Faculty:* 29. Expenses: Contact institution. *Financial support:* In 2017–18, 136 students received support, including 5 fellowships with tuition reimbursements available (averaging $17,400 per year), 41 research assistantships with tuition reimbursements available (averaging $18,830 per year), 27 teaching assistantships with tuition reimbursements available (averaging $18,534 per year); career-related internships or fieldwork, scholarships/grants, health care benefits, and unspecified assistantships also available. Financial award applicants required to submit FAFSA. In 2017, 52 master's, 7 doctorates, 8 other advanced degrees awarded. *Program availability:* Online learning. Offers art (MA, MFA); art history (MA); communication (PhD); communication and new media (Graduate Certificate); communication studies (MA); composition/theory (MA, MM); conducting (MA, MM); dispute resolution (MADR, Graduate Certificate); fine, performing and communication arts (MA, MADR, MFA, MM, PhD, Graduate Certificate); health communication (Graduate Certificate); jazz performance (MA, MM); journalism (MA); media arts (MA); media studies (MA); music education (MA, MM); orchestral studies (Certificate); performance (MA, MM); public relations and organizational communication (MA); theatre (MFA); theatre and dance (MA). *Application deadline:* For fall admission, 6/1 priority date for domestic students, 5/1 priority date for international students; for winter admission, 10/1 priority date for domestic students, 9/1 priority date for international students; for spring admission, 2/1 priority date for domestic students, 1/1 priority date for international students. Applications are processed on a rolling basis. *Application fee:* $50. Electronic applications accepted. *Application Contact:* Lezlie Hart, Associate Director of Student Services, 313-577-5337, E-mail: aa3266@wayne.edu. *Dean*, Dr. Matthew Seeger, 313-577-5342, Fax: 313-577-5342, E-mail: matthew.seeger@wayne.edu.

College of Liberal Arts and Sciences Students: 814 full-time (462 women), 357 part-time (202 women); includes 206 minority (102 Black or African American, non-Hispanic/Latino; 2 American Indian or Alaska Native, non-Hispanic/Latino; 24 Asian, non-Hispanic/Latino; 44 Hispanic/Latino; 1 Native Hawaiian or other Pacific Islander, non-Hispanic/Latino; 33 Two or more races, non-Hispanic/Latino), 261 international. Average age 31. 2,275 applicants, 23% accepted, 279 enrolled. *Faculty:* 291. Expenses: Contact institution. *Financial support:* In 2017–18, 698 students received support, including 76 fellowships with tuition reimbursements available (averaging $14,646 per year), 85 research assistantships with tuition reimbursements available (averaging $20,505 per year), 324 teaching assistantships with tuition reimbursements available (averaging $19,568 per year); scholarships/grants, health care benefits, and unspecified assistantships also available. Support available to part-time students. Financial award applicants required to submit FAFSA. In 2017, 254 master's, 129 doctorates, 3 other advanced degrees awarded. *Program availability:* Part-time, evening/weekend, online learning. Offers analytical chemistry (PhD); anthropology (MA, PhD); applied macroeconomics (MA, PhD); applied mathematics (MA); applied sociological research methodology (MA); audiology (Au D); behavioral and cognitive neuroscience (PhD); biological sciences (MA, MS, PhD); chemistry (MA, MS); classics (MA); clinical psychology (PhD); communication disorders and science (PhD); criminal justice (MS); developmental science (PhD); dietetics (Postbaccalaureate Certificate); economic development (Graduate Certificate); employment and labor relations (MA); English (MA); film and media studies (PhD); food science (PhD); geology (MS); German (MA); health economics (MA, PhD); history (MA, PhD); industrial organization (MA, PhD); industrial/organizational psychology (MA, PhD); international economics (MA, PhD); labor and human resources (MA, PhD); language learning (MALL); liberal arts and sciences (MA, MALL, MPA, MS, MUP, Au D, PhD, Graduate Certificate, Postbaccalaureate Certificate); linguistics (MA); literary and cultural studies (PhD); mathematical statistics (MA); mathematics (MA, MS, PhD); medical sociology/health (PhD); modern languages (PhD); molecular biotechnology (MS); Near Eastern languages (MA); nutrition (PhD); nutrition and food science (MA, MS); philosophy (MA, PhD); physics (MA, MS, PhD); political science (MA, PhD); public administration (MPA); public history (MA); race/gender inequality (PhD); rhetoric and composition studies (PhD); Romance languages (MA); social personality (PhD); social work (PhD); sociology (MA); speech-language pathology (MA); urban studies and planning (MUP); urban/labor studies (PhD); world history (Graduate Certificate). *Application deadline:* For fall admission, 6/1 priority date for domestic students, 5/1 priority date for international students; for winter admission, 10/1 priority date for domestic students, 9/1 priority date for international students; for spring admission, 2/1 priority date for domestic students, 1/1 priority date for international students. Applications are processed on a rolling basis. *Application fee:* $50. Electronic applications accepted. *Application Contact:* Deirdre Baker, Director, Graduate Admissions, 313-577-8141, E-mail: gradadmissions@wayne.edu. *Dean*, Wayne Raskind, 313-577-2519, E-mail: raskind@wayne.edu.

Center for Peace and Conflict Studies Expenses: Contact institution. *Financial support:* Scholarships/grants available. Financial award applicants required to submit FAFSA. Offers peace and security studies (Graduate Certificate). *Application deadline:* For fall admission, 6/1 priority date for domestic students, 5/1 priority date for international students; for winter admission, 10/1 priority date for domestic students, 9/1 priority date for international students; for spring admission, 2/1 priority date for domestic students, 1/1 priority date for international students; for summer admission, 2/1 priority date for domestic students, 1/1 priority date for international students. Applications are processed on a rolling basis. *Application fee:* $50. Electronic applications accepted. *Professor and Program Director*, Dr. Fred Pearson, 313-577-3453, E-mail: ab3440@wayne.edu.

College of Nursing Students: 133 full-time (120 women), 184 part-time (167 women); includes 85 minority (57 Black or African American, non-Hispanic/Latino; 16 Asian, non-Hispanic/Latino; 4 Hispanic/Latino; 8 Two or more races, non-Hispanic/Latino), 22 international. Average age 34. 318 applicants, 39% accepted, 94 enrolled. *Faculty:* 30. Expenses: Contact institution. *Financial support:* In 2017–18, 92 students received support, including 16 fellowships with tuition reimbursements available (averaging $8,285 per year), 5 teaching assistantships with tuition reimbursements available (averaging $25,000 per year); scholarships/grants, health care benefits, and unspecified assistantships also available. Support available to part-time students. Financial award applicants required to submit FAFSA. In 2017, 51 master's, 29 doctorates awarded. *Program availability:* Part-time. Offers adult gerontology acute care nurse practitioner (MSN); adult gerontology primary care nurse practitioner (MSN); advanced public health nursing (MSN); infant and mental health (DNP, PhD); neonatal nurse practitioner (MSN); nurse-midwifery (MSN); pediatric acute care nurse practitioner (MSN); pediatric primary care nurse practitioner (MSN); psychiatric mental health nurse practitioner (MSN); women's health nurse practitioner (MSN). Doctoral program admits for fall only. *Application fee:* $50. Electronic applications accepted. *Application Contact:* 313-577-4082, Fax: 313-577-6949, E-mail: nursinginfo@wayne.edu. *Dean, College of Nursing*, Dr. Laurie Lauzon Clabo, 313-577-4082, E-mail: laurie.lauzon.clabo@wayne.edu.

Eugene Applebaum College of Pharmacy and Health Sciences Students: 750 full-time (493 women), 11 part-time (9 women); includes 97 minority (14 Black or African American, non-Hispanic/Latino; 1 American Indian or Alaska Native, non-Hispanic/Latino; 55 Asian, non-Hispanic/Latino; 15 Hispanic/Latino; 1 Native Hawaiian or other Pacific Islander, non-Hispanic/Latino; 11 Two or more races, non-Hispanic/Latino), 56 international. Average age 25. 694 applicants, 33% accepted, 172 enrolled. *Faculty:* 27. Expenses: Contact institution. *Financial support:* In 2017–18, 233 students received support, including 3 fellowships with tuition reimbursements available (averaging $34,000 per year), 11 research assistantships with tuition reimbursements available (averaging $25,182 per year); scholarships/grants, health care benefits, and unspecified assistantships also available. Financial award application deadline: 3/31; financial award applicants required to submit FAFSA. In 2017, 113 master's, 128 doctorates, 1 other advanced degree awarded. *Program availability:* Part-time, evening/weekend. Offers anesthesia (MS); medicinal chemistry (MS, PhD); nurse anesthesia (MS, DNP-A, Certificate); nurse anesthesia practice (DNP-A); occupational therapy (MOT); pediatric anesthesia (Certificate); pharmaceutics (MS, PhD); pharmacology and toxicology (MS, PhD); pharmacy (Pharm D); pharmacy and health sciences (MOT, MS, DPT, PhD, Pharm D, Certificate); physical therapy (DPT); physician assistant studies (MS). *Application fee:* $50. Electronic applications accepted. *Application Contact:* Dr. Mary K. Clark, Assistant Dean, Office of Student and Alumni Affairs, 313-577-1716, E-mail: cphsinfo@wayne.edu. *Interim Dean*, Dr. Catherine Lysack, 313-577-1716, E-mail: c.lysack@wayne.edu.

Law School Students: 409 full-time (184 women), 46 part-time (22 women); includes 61 minority (33 Black or African American, non-Hispanic/Latino; 1 American Indian or Alaska Native, non-Hispanic/Latino; 14 Asian, non-Hispanic/Latino; 3 Hispanic/Latino; 10 Two or more races, non-Hispanic/Latino), 11 international. Average age 26. 811 applicants, 54% accepted, 146 enrolled. *Faculty:* 43 full-time (18 women), 17 part-time/adjunct (9 women). Expenses: Contact institution. *Financial support:* In 2017–18,

386 students received support. Fellowships, Federal Work-Study, and scholarships/grants available. Support available to part-time students. Financial award application deadline: 6/30; financial award applicants required to submit FAFSA. In 2017, 4 master's, 113 doctorates awarded. *Program availability:* Part-time, evening/weekend. Offers corporate and finance law (LL M); labor and employment law (LL M); law (JD); taxation (LL M); United States law (LL M). *Application deadline:* For fall admission, 7/1 for domestic students, 5/1 priority date for international students. Applications are processed on a rolling basis. *Application fee:* $0. Electronic applications accepted. *Application Contact:* Kathy Fox, Assistant Dean of Admissions, 313-577-3937, Fax: 313-993-8129, E-mail: lawinquire@wayne.edu. *Dean and Professor of Law,* Richard A. Bierschbach, 313-577-3933, E-mail: rbierschbach@wayne.edu.

Mike Ilitch School of Business Students: 235 full-time (121 women), 1,082 part-time (480 women); includes 356 minority (202 Black or African American, non-Hispanic/Latino; 2 American Indian or Alaska Native, non-Hispanic/Latino; 79 Asian, non-Hispanic/Latino; 47 Hispanic/Latino; 26 Two or more races, non-Hispanic/Latino), 87 international. Average age 30. 1,285 applicants, 43% accepted, 308 enrolled. *Faculty:* 32. Expenses: Contact institution. *Financial support:* In 2017–18, 165 students received support, including 1 fellowship with tuition reimbursement available (averaging $18,534 per year), 1 teaching assistantship with tuition reimbursement available (averaging $18,534 per year); research assistantships with tuition reimbursements available, scholarships/grants, health care benefits, and unspecified assistantships also available. Support available to part-time students. Financial award applicants required to submit FAFSA. In 2017, 200 master's, 2 doctorates, 9 other advanced degrees awarded. *Program availability:* Part-time, evening/weekend. Offers accounting (MS, MSA, Postbaccalaureate Certificate); business (EMS, Graduate Certificate); business administration (MBA, PhD); data science (MS); entrepreneurship and innovation (Postbaccalaureate Certificate); finance (MS); information systems management (Postbaccalaureate Certificate); taxation (MST). Application deadline for PhD is February 15. *Application deadline:* For fall admission, 7/1 for domestic students, 5/1 priority date for international students; for winter admission, 11/1 for domestic students, 9/1 priority date for international students; for spring admission, 3/1 for domestic students, 1/1 priority date for international students. Applications are processed on a rolling basis. *Application fee:* $50. Electronic applications accepted. *Application Contact:* Kiantee N. Rupert-Jones, Director, 313-577-4511, Fax: 313-577-9442, E-mail: gradbusiness@wayne.edu. *Dean, School of Business Administration,* Dr. Robert Forsythe, 313-577-4501, E-mail: robert.forsythe@wayne.edu.

School of Information Sciences Students: 100 full-time (80 women), 359 part-time (290 women); includes 77 minority (42 Black or African American, non-Hispanic/Latino; 2 American Indian or Alaska Native, non-Hispanic/Latino; 3 Asian, non-Hispanic/Latino; 19 Hispanic/Latino; 1 Native Hawaiian or other Pacific Islander, non-Hispanic/Latino; 10 Two or more races, non-Hispanic/Latino), 1 international. Average age 33. 258 applicants, 60% accepted, 100 enrolled. *Faculty:* 12 full-time (9 women), 17 part-time/adjunct (12 women). Expenses: Contact institution. *Financial support:* In 2017–18, 133 students received support. Fellowships with tuition reimbursements available, scholarships/grants, health care benefits, and unspecified assistantships available. Support available to part-time students. Financial award applicants required to submit FAFSA. In 2017, 149 master's, 34 other advanced degrees awarded. *Program availability:* Part-time, evening/weekend, 100% online, blended/hybrid learning. Offers archival administration (Graduate Certificate); information management (MS, Graduate Certificate); library and information science (MLIS, Graduate Certificate, Spec); public library services to children and young adults (Graduate Certificate). *Application deadline:* For fall admission, 7/1 for domestic students, 5/1 priority date for international students; for winter admission, 10/1 priority date for domestic students, 9/1 priority date for international students; for spring admission, 2/1 priority date for domestic students, 1/1 priority date for international students. Applications are processed on a rolling basis. *Application fee:* $50. Electronic applications accepted. *Application Contact:* Academic Services Officer II, 313-577-1825, E-mail: asklis@wayne.edu. *Dean,* Dr. Jon Cawthorne, 313-577-4020, E-mail: jon.cawthorne@wayne.edu.

School of Medicine Students: 1,442 full-time (664 women), 143 part-time (72 women); includes 512 minority (100 Black or African American, non-Hispanic/Latino; 10 American Indian or Alaska Native, non-Hispanic/Latino; 304 Asian, non-Hispanic/Latino; 65 Hispanic/Latino; 33 Two or more races, non-Hispanic/Latino), 128 international. Average age 26. Expenses: Contact institution. *Financial support:* In 2017–18, 1,036 students received support, including 64 fellowships with tuition reimbursements available (averaging $24,388 per year), 79 research assistantships with tuition reimbursements available (averaging $26,894 per year); Federal Work-Study, scholarships/grants, health care benefits, and unspecified assistantships also available. Support available to part-time students. Financial award applicants required to submit FAFSA. In 2017, 70 master's, 293 doctorates, 10 other advanced degrees awarded. Offers anatomy and cell biology (MS, PhD); basic medical sciences (MS); biochemistry and molecular biology (MS, PhD); cancer biology (MS, PhD); clinical and translational science (Graduate Certificate); family medicine and public health sciences (MPH, Graduate Certificate); genetic counseling (MS); immunology and microbiology (MS, PhD); medical physics (MS, PhD, Graduate Certificate); medical research (MS); medicine (MPH, MS, MD, PhD, Graduate Certificate); molecular medicine and genomics (MS, PhD); pathology (PhD); pharmacology (MS, PhD); physiology (MS, PhD); psychiatry and behavioral neurosciences (PhD). Electronic applications accepted. *Application Contact:* Dr. Kevin Sprague, Associate Dean of Admissions, 313-577-1466. *Dean,* Dr. Jack Sobel, 313-577-1335, Fax: 313-577-8777, E-mail: ad6283@wayne.edu.

School of Social Work Expenses: Contact institution. *Financial support:* Fellowships with tuition reimbursements, research assistantships with tuition reimbursements, teaching assistantships with tuition reimbursements, scholarships/grants, and unspecified assistantships available. Financial award applicants required to submit FAFSA. *Program availability:* Part-time, evening/weekend. Offers gerontology (Certificate); social work (MSW, PhD). Application deadlines: April 1 for MSW, December 19 for PhD. *Application deadline:* Applications are processed on a rolling basis. *Application fee:* $50. Electronic applications accepted. *Application Contact:* Shantalea Johns, Interim Director of Admissions, 313-577-4409, E-mail: shantalea@wayne.edu. *Interim Dean,* Dr. Jerrold Brandell, 313-577-4409, E-mail: aa4537@wayne.edu.

WEBBER INTERNATIONAL UNIVERSITY, Babson Park, FL 33827-0096

General Information Independent, coed, comprehensive institution. *Enrollment:* 683 graduate, professional, and undergraduate students; 50 full-time matriculated graduate/professional students (29 women), 6 part-time matriculated graduate/professional students (2 women). *Enrollment by degree level:* 56 master's. *Graduate faculty:* 10 full-time (4 women), 1 part-time/adjunct (0 women). *Tuition:* Part-time $688 per hour. *Graduate housing:* Room and/or apartments guaranteed to single students; on-campus housing not available to married students. Typical cost: $7032 per year ($9484 including board). *Student services:* Campus employment opportunities, campus safety program, career counseling, exercise/wellness program, international student services, services for students with disabilities. *Library facilities:* Grace and Roger Babson Library. *Collection:* Books: 1,041 (physical); Databases: 127. Weekly public service hours: 70; students can reserve study rooms.

Computer facilities: 92 computers available on campus for general student use. A campuswide network can be accessed from off campus. Online class registration is available.
Website: http://www.webber.edu/

General Application Contact: Lacy Edwards, Admissions Counselor/MBA Coordinator, 863-638-2910, Fax: 863-638-1591, E-mail: admissions@webber.edu.

GRADUATE UNITS

Graduate School of Business Students: 50 full-time (29 women), 6 part-time (2 women); includes 19 minority (12 Black or African American, non-Hispanic/Latino; 6 Hispanic/Latino; 1 Two or more races, non-Hispanic/Latino), 6 international. Average age 24. 64 applicants, 61% accepted, 32 enrolled. *Faculty:* 10 full-time (4 women), 1 part-time/adjunct (0 women). Expenses: Contact institution. *Financial support:* In 2017–18, 11 students received support. Scholarships/grants and unspecified assistantships available. Financial award application deadline: 8/1; financial award applicants required to submit FAFSA. In 2017, 29 master's awarded. *Program availability:* Part-time, evening/weekend, 100% online. Offers accounting (MBA); business (MBA); criminal justice management (MBA); international business (MBA); sport business management (MBA). *Application deadline:* For fall admission, 7/1 for international students. Applications are processed on a rolling basis. *Application fee:* $50 ($75 for international students). Electronic applications accepted. *Application Contact:* Lacy Edwards, Admissions Counselor and MBA Coordinator, 863-638-2910, Fax: 863-638-1591, E-mail: admissions@webber.edu. *Dean,* Dr. Nikos Orphanoudakis, 863-638-2910, Fax: 863-638-1591, E-mail: orphanoudakisn@webber.edu.

WEBER STATE UNIVERSITY, Ogden, UT 84408-1001

General Information State-supported, coed, comprehensive institution. *Enrollment:* 27,949 graduate, professional, and undergraduate students; 353 full-time matriculated graduate/professional students (180 women), 485 part-time matriculated graduate/professional students (269 women). *Enrollment by degree level:* 838 master's. *Graduate faculty:* 99 full-time (47 women), 6 part-time/adjunct (4 women). Tuition, state resident: full-time $7283. Tuition, nonresident: full-time $17,166. *Required fees:* $898. Tuition and fees vary according to program. *Graduate housing:* Room and/or apartments available on a first-come, first-served basis to single students; on-campus housing not available to married students. Typical cost: $3500 per year ($7600 including board). Room and board charges vary according to board plan and housing facility selected. *Student services:* Campus employment opportunities, campus safety program, career counseling, child daycare facilities, exercise/wellness program, free psychological counseling, grant writing training, international student services, low-cost health insurance, multicultural affairs office, services for students with disabilities, teacher training, writing training. *Library facilities:* Stewart Library. *Collection:* Books: 498,531 (physical); Serial titles: 425 (physical); Databases: 223,410. *Research affiliation:* Raytheon Training Corporation (education).

Computer facilities: Computer purchase and lease plans are available. 650 computers available on campus for general student use. A campuswide network can be accessed from student residence rooms and from off campus. Online class registration is available.
Website: http://www.weber.edu/

General Application Contact: Scott Teichert, Director of Admissions, 801-626-7670, Fax: 801-626-6045, E-mail: scottteichert@weber.edu.

GRADUATE UNITS

College of Engineering, Applied Science and Technology Students: 8 full-time (1 woman), 48 part-time (36 women); includes 5 minority (2 Asian, non-Hispanic/Latino; 1 Hispanic/Latino; 2 Two or more races, non-Hispanic/Latino), 1 international. Average age 33. *Faculty:* 3 part-time/adjunct (0 women). Expenses: Contact institution. In 2017, 2 master's awarded. *Program availability:* Part-time. Offers computer engineering (MS). *Application deadline:* For fall admission, 5/7 for domestic and international students; for spring admission, 11/7 for domestic and international students. Electronic applications accepted. *Application Contact:* Scott Teichert, Director of Admissions, 801-626-7670, Fax: 801-626-6045, E-mail: scottteichert@weber.edu. *Dean,* Dr. David L. Ferro, 801-626-6303, E-mail: dferro@weber.edu.

College of Social and Behavioral Sciences Students: 6 full-time (4 women), 22 part-time (8 women); includes 5 minority (1 American Indian or Alaska Native, non-Hispanic/Latino; 3 Hispanic/Latino; 1 Native Hawaiian or other Pacific Islander, non-Hispanic/Latino). Average age 36. *Faculty:* 5 full-time (1 woman). Expenses: Contact institution. *Financial support:* In 2017–18, 7 students received support. Scholarships/grants available. Financial award application deadline: 4/1; financial award applicants required to submit FAFSA. In 2017, 6 master's awarded. *Program availability:* Part-time, evening/weekend, online only, 100% online. Offers criminal justice (MCJ); social and behavioral sciences (MCJ). *Application deadline:* For fall admission, 7/29 for domestic students; for spring admission, 12/11 for domestic students; for summer admission, 4/1 for domestic students. Applications are processed on a rolling basis. *Application fee:* $60 ($90 for international students). *Application Contact:* Faye Medd, Enrollment Director, 801-626-6146, Fax: 801-626-6145, E-mail: fmedd@weber.edu. *Dean,* Dr. Francis Harrold, 801-626-6232, Fax: 801-626-7130, E-mail: francisharrold@weber.edu.

Dumke College of Health Professions Students: 182 full-time (111 women), 33 part-time (17 women); includes 10 minority (3 Black or African American, non-Hispanic/Latino; 2 Asian, non-Hispanic/Latino; 5 Hispanic/Latino), 2 international. Average age 36. *Faculty:* 25 full-time (16 women), 4 part-time/adjunct (3 women). Expenses: Contact institution. *Financial support:* In 2017–18, 55 students received support. Scholarships/grants available. Financial award application deadline: 4/1; financial award applicants required to submit FAFSA. In 2017, 79 master's awarded. *Program availability:* Part-time, evening/weekend, 100% online. Offers health administration (MHA); health professions (MHA, MSN, MSRS); radiologic sciences (MSRS). *Application deadline:* For fall admission, 3/15 for domestic students, 2/20 for international students. *Application fee:* $60 ($90 for international students). Electronic applications accepted. *Application Contact:* Ann Gessel, Office Manager, 801-626-7127, Fax: 801-626-7683, E-mail: anngessel@weber.edu. *Dean,* Dr. Yasmin Simonian, 801-626-7117, Fax: 801-626-7683, E-mail: ysimonian@weber.edu.

School of Nursing Students: 88 full-time (70 women), 5 part-time (all women); includes 2 minority (both Hispanic/Latino), 1 international. Average age 38. *Faculty:* 11 full-time (all women), 3 part-time/adjunct (all women). Expenses: Contact institution. *Financial support:* In 2017–18, 26 students received support. Scholarships/grants available. Financial award application deadline: 4/1; financial award applicants required to submit FAFSA. In 2017, 29 master's awarded. *Program availability:* Part-time, evening/weekend, 100% online. Offers educator (MSN); executive (MSN); nurse practitioner (MSN). *Application deadline:* For fall admission, 4/1 priority date for domestic students. *Application fee:* $60 ($90 for international students). Electronic applications accepted. *Application Contact:* Robert Holt, Director of Enrollment, 801-626-7774, Fax: 801-626-6397, E-mail: rholt@weber.edu. *MSN Program Director*, Dr. Melissa Neville, 801-626-6204, Fax: 801-626-6397, E-mail: mneville@weber.edu.

Goddard School of Business and Economics Students: 97 full-time (26 women), 176 part-time (57 women); includes 16 minority (1 Black or African American, non-Hispanic/Latino; 2 American Indian or Alaska Native, non-Hispanic/Latino; 2 Asian, non-Hispanic/Latino; 9 Hispanic/Latino; 2 Two or more races, non-Hispanic/Latino), 7 international. Average age 35. *Faculty:* 20 full-time (5 women). Expenses: Contact institution. *Financial support:* In 2017–18, 46 students received support. Scholarships/grants available. Financial award application deadline: 4/1; financial award applicants required to submit FAFSA. In 2017, 85 master's, 24 other advanced degrees awarded. *Program availability:* Part-time, evening/weekend. Offers business administration (MBA, Graduate Certificate); business and economics (M Acc, M Tax, MBA, Graduate Certificate). *Application deadline:* For fall admission, 5/1 for domestic students; for spring admission, 9/1 for domestic students. *Application fee:* $60 ($90 for international students). Electronic applications accepted. *Application Contact:* Mara Sikkink, Coordinator of Academic Advisement, 801-626-6534, Fax: 801-626-6747, E-mail: marasikkink@weber.edu. *Dean*, Dr. Jeffery W. Steagall, 801-626-7253, Fax: 801-626-6687, E-mail: jeffsteagall@weber.edu.

School of Accounting and Taxation Students: 37 full-time (10 women), 28 part-time (15 women); includes 4 minority (2 Asian, non-Hispanic/Latino; 2 Hispanic/Latino), 1 international. Average age 32. *Faculty:* 7 full-time (2 women). Expenses: Contact institution. *Financial support:* In 2017–18, 32 students received support. Scholarships/grants available. Financial award application deadline: 4/1; financial award applicants required to submit FAFSA. In 2017, 28 master's awarded. *Program availability:* Part-time, evening/weekend. Offers accounting (M Acc); taxation (M Tax). *Application deadline:* For fall admission, 8/1 for domestic students; for spring admission, 12/1 for domestic students; for summer admission, 4/1 for domestic students. *Application fee:* $60 ($90 for international students). Electronic applications accepted. *Application Contact:* Dr. Larry A. Deppe, Graduate Coordinator, 801-626-7838, Fax: 801-626-7423, E-mail: ldeppe1@weber.edu. *Program Director*, Dr. Ryan Pace, 801-626-7562, Fax: 801-626-7423, E-mail: rpace@weber.edu.

Jerry and Vickie Moyes College of Education Students: 45 full-time (22 women), 106 part-time (83 women); includes 3 minority (2 Asian, non-Hispanic/Latino; 1 Hispanic/Latino), 6 international. Average age 35. *Faculty:* 27 full-time (14 women), 2 part-time/adjunct (1 woman). Expenses: Contact institution. *Financial support:* In 2017–18, 30 students received support. Institutionally sponsored loans, scholarships/grants, tuition waivers (full and partial), and unspecified assistantships available. Support available to part-time students. Financial award application deadline: 4/1; financial award applicants required to submit FAFSA. In 2017, 44 master's awarded. *Program availability:* Part-time, evening/weekend. Offers athletic training (MSAT); curriculum and instruction (M Ed); education (M Ed, MSAT). *Application deadline:* For fall admission, 5/15 for domestic students; for spring admission, 9/15 for domestic students; for summer admission, 1/15 for domestic students. *Application fee:* $60 ($90 for international students). *Application Contact:* Nathan Alexander, College of Education Recruiter, 801-626-8124, Fax: 801-626-7427, E-mail: nathanalexander@weber.edu. *Dean*, Dr. Jack Rasmussen, 801-626-6273, Fax: 801-626-7427, E-mail: jrasmussen@weber.edu.

Telitha E. Lindquist College of Arts and Humanities Students: 16 full-time (11 women), 84 part-time (61 women); includes 11 minority (1 Black or African American, non-Hispanic/Latino; 1 Asian, non-Hispanic/Latino; 6 Hispanic/Latino; 3 Two or more races, non-Hispanic/Latino), 1 international. Average age 34. *Faculty:* 26 full-time (16 women). Expenses: Contact institution. *Financial support:* In 2017–18, 18 students received support. Scholarships/grants and tuition waivers (full and partial) available. Financial award application deadline: 4/1; financial award applicants required to submit FAFSA. In 2017, 31 master's awarded. *Program availability:* Part-time, evening/weekend. Offers arts and humanities (MA, MPC); communication (MPC); English (MA). *Application deadline:* For fall admission, 4/1 for domestic students. *Application fee:* $60 ($90 for international students). Electronic applications accepted. *Application Contact:* Scott Teichert, Director of Admissions, 801-626-7670, Fax: 801-626-6045, E-mail: scottteichert@weber.edu. *Dean, College of Arts and Humanities*, Dr. Scott Springer, 801-626-6424, Fax: 801-626-7422, E-mail: arts_humanities@weber.edu.

WEBSTER UNIVERSITY, St. Louis, MO 63119-3194

General Information Independent, coed, comprehensive institution. *Graduate housing:* Room and/or apartments available on a first-come, first-served basis to single students; on-campus housing not available to married students. Housing application deadline: 4/1. *Research affiliation:* Literacy Investment for Tomorrow.

GRADUATE UNITS

College of Arts and Sciences *Program availability:* Part-time, evening/weekend, online learning. Offers arts and sciences (GM Acc, MA, MS, MSN, DNAP, Graduate Certificate); biological sciences (MS); counseling (MA); counseling psychology (MS); environmental management (MS); gerontology (MS); human services (MA); international nongovernmental organizations (MA); international relations (MA); legal studies (MA, Graduate Certificate); nurse anesthesia (DNAP); nurse educator (MSN).

Institute for Human Rights and Humanitarian Studies Offers international human rights (MA).

George Herbert Walker School of Business and Technology *Program availability:* Part-time, evening/weekend, online learning. Offers business and organizational security management (MA, MBA); business and technology (MA, MBA, MHA, MHA, MPA, MS, D Mgt, DM, Graduate Certificate); cybersecurity (MS); decision support systems (MBA); digital marketing management (Graduate Certificate); environmental management (MBA); finance (MBA, MS); forensic accounting (MS); gerontology (MBA); government contracting (Graduate Certificate); health administration (MHA); health care management (MA); health services management (MA); human resources development (MA, MBA); human resources management (MA, MBA); information technology management (MA, MBA, MS); international business (MA, MBA); international relations (MBA); management (D Mgt); management and leadership (MA, MBA); marketing (MA, MBA); media communications (MBA); nonprofit leadership (MA); nonprofit revenue development (Graduate Certificate); organizational development (Graduate Certificate); procurement and acquisitions management (MA, MBA); public administration (MPA); space systems operations management (MS); Web services (MBA).

Leigh Gerdine College of Fine Arts *Program availability:* Part-time, evening/weekend. Offers art history and criticism (MA); church music (MM); composition (MM); fine arts (MA, MFA, MM); jazz studies (MM); music (MA); music education (MM); organ (MM); performance (MM); piano (MM); voice (MM).

School of Communications *Program availability:* Part-time, evening/weekend, online learning. Offers advertising and marketing communications (MA); communications (MA); communications management (MA); media communications (MA); media literacy (MA); new media production (MA); public relations (MA).

School of Education *Program availability:* Part-time, online learning. Offers applied educational psychology (MA, Ed S); communication arts (MA, MAT); early childhood education (MA, MAT); education (MA, MAT, MET, Ed S); education and innovation (MA); educational technology (MET); elementary education (MAT); mathematics for educators (MA); middle school education (MAT); multidisciplinary studies (MAT); multimodal literacy for global impact (MA); reading (MA); secondary school education (MAT); special education (MA, MAT); teaching English as a second language (MA); transformative learning in the global community (Ed S).

WEILL CORNELL MEDICINE, New York, NY 10065

General Information Independent, coed, graduate-only institution. *Graduate housing:* Rooms and/or apartments guaranteed to single students and available on a first-come, first-served basis to married students. Housing application deadline: 4/30. *Research affiliation:* Memorial Sloan-Kettering Cancer Center (cancer), Houston Methodist Hospital (general medicine and surgery), The Rockefeller University (biomedical research), New York Methodist (general medicine and surgery), Hospital for Special Surgery (orthopedics), Burke Medical Research Institute (neurology).

GRADUATE UNITS

Weill Cornell Graduate School of Medical Sciences Offers biochemistry, cell and molecular biology (MS, PhD); chemical biology (PhD); clinical epidemiology and health services research (MS); computational biology and medicine (PhD); health informatics (MS); health sciences (MS); immunology (MS, PhD); medical sciences (MS, PhD); neuroscience (MS, PhD); pharmacology (MS, PhD); physiology, biophysics and systems biology (MS, PhD). Electronic applications accepted.

Weill Cornell/Rockefeller/Sloan-Kettering Tri-Institutional MD-PhD Program Offered jointly with The Rockefeller University and Sloan-Kettering Institute. Electronic applications accepted.

WELCH COLLEGE, Gallatin, TN 37066

General Information Independent-religious, coed, comprehensive institution.

GRADUATE UNITS

Program in Theology and Ministry *Program availability:* Online learning. Offers theology and ministry (MA).

WENTWORTH INSTITUTE OF TECHNOLOGY, Boston, MA 02115-5998

General Information Independent, coed, comprehensive institution. *Enrollment:* 4,454 graduate, professional, and undergraduate students; 84 full-time matriculated graduate/professional students (27 women), 108 part-time matriculated graduate/professional students (24 women). *Enrollment by degree level:* 192 master's. *Graduate faculty:* 19 full-time (8 women), 64 part-time/adjunct (20 women). *Tuition:* Part-time $1135 per credit hour. *Graduate housing:* Room and/or apartments available on a first-come, first-served basis to single students; on-campus housing not available to married students. Typical cost: $11,090 per year ($14,190 including board). Housing application deadline: 5/1. *Student services:* Campus employment opportunities, campus safety program, career counseling, exercise/wellness program, international student services, low-cost health insurance, multicultural affairs office, services for students with disabilities. *Library facilities:* Douglas D. Schumann Library & Learning Commons plus 1 other. *Collection:* Books: 51,754 (physical), 244,116 (digital/electronic); Serial titles: 210 (physical), 77,225 (digital/electronic); Databases: 75. Weekly public service hours: 100.

Computer facilities: Computer purchase and lease plans are available. 320 computers available on campus for general student use. A campuswide network can be accessed from student residence rooms and from off campus. Online class registration is available. Website: http://www.wit.edu/

General Application Contact: Martha Sheehan, Director of Admissions and Marketing, 617-989-4661, Fax: 617-989-4399, E-mail: sheehanm@wit.edu.

GRADUATE UNITS

Department of Architecture Students: 84 full-time (27 women), 3 part-time (1 woman); includes 11 minority (4 Asian, non-Hispanic/Latino; 3 Hispanic/Latino; 4 Two or more races, non-Hispanic/Latino), 3 international. Average age 23. 131 applicants, 87% accepted, 83 enrolled. *Faculty:* 19 full-time (8 women), 20 part-time/adjunct (7 women). Expenses: Contact institution. *Financial support:* In 2017–18, 83 students received support, including 80 fellowships (averaging $7,256 per year), 37 teaching assistantships (averaging $2,500 per year). Financial award application deadline: 5/1; financial award applicants required to submit FAFSA. In 2017, 74 master's awarded. Offers architecture (M Arch). *Application deadline:* For fall admission, 1/15 priority date for domestic and international students. Applications are processed on a rolling basis. *Application fee:* $50. Electronic applications accepted. *Application Contact:* Kelly Hutzell, Director of Graduate Programs, 617-989-4494, E-mail: hutzelk@wit.edu. *Interim Department Chair*, Sharon Matthews, 617-989-4622, E-mail: matthewss3@wit.edu.

Master of Engineering in Civil Engineering Program Students: 4 part-time (0 women); includes 2 minority (both Hispanic/Latino). Average age 27. 8 applicants, 38% accepted, 1 enrolled. *Faculty:* 3 part-time/adjunct (1 woman). Expenses: Contact institution. *Financial support:* In 2017–18, 1 student received support. Scholarships/grants available. Support available to part-time students. Financial award application deadline: 8/1; financial award applicants required to submit FAFSA. In 2017, 7 master's awarded. *Program availability:* Part-time-only, evening/weekend. Offers construction engineering (M Eng); infrastructure engineering (M Eng). *Application deadline:* For fall admission, 8/1 for domestic and international students. Applications are processed on a rolling basis. *Application fee:* $50. Electronic applications accepted. *Application Contact:* Martha Sheehan, Director of Admissions and Marketing, 617-989-4661, Fax: 617-989-4399, E-mail: sheehanm@wit.edu. *Director of Graduate Programs*, Philip Hammond, 617-989-4594, Fax: 617-989-4399, E-mail: hammondp1@wit.edu.

Master of Science in Applied Computer Science Program Students: 16 part-time (3 women); includes 11 minority (2 Asian, non-Hispanic/Latino; 9 Hispanic/Latino). Average age 30. 11 applicants, 82% accepted, 9 enrolled. *Faculty:* 8 part-time/adjunct (1 woman). Expenses: Contact institution. *Financial support:* In 2017–18, 4 students received support. Scholarships/grants available. Support available to part-time students. Financial award application deadline: 8/1; financial award applicants required to submit FAFSA. *Program availability:* Part-time, online only, 100% online. Offers applied computer science (MS). *Application deadline:* For fall admission, 8/1 for domestic and international students. Applications are processed on a rolling basis. *Application fee:* $50. Electronic applications accepted. *Application Contact:* Martha Sheehan, Director of Admissions and Marketing, 617-989-4661, Fax: 617-989-4399, E-mail: sheehanm@wit.edu. *Director of Graduate Programs*, Philip Hammond, 617-989-4594, Fax: 617-989-4399, E-mail: hammondp1@wit.edu.

Master of Science in Construction Management Program Students: 53 part-time (13 women); includes 33 minority (1 Black or African American, non-Hispanic/Latino; 31 Hispanic/Latino; 1 Two or more races, non-Hispanic/Latino), 1 international. Average age 32. 53 applicants, 70% accepted, 32 enrolled. *Faculty:* 15 part-time/adjunct (3 women). Expenses: Contact institution. *Financial support:* In 2017–18, 22 students received support. Scholarships/grants available. Support available to part-time students. Financial award application deadline: 8/1; financial award applicants required to submit FAFSA. In 2017, 26 master's awarded. *Program availability:* Part-time-only, evening/weekend, 100% online, blended/hybrid learning. Offers construction management (MS). *Application deadline:* For fall admission, 8/1 for domestic and international students; for spring admission, 12/20 for domestic and international students. Applications are processed on a rolling basis. *Application fee:* $50. Electronic applications accepted. *Application Contact:* Martha Sheehan, Director of Admissions and Marketing, 617-989-4661, Fax: 617-989-4399, E-mail: sheehanm@wit.edu. *Director of Graduate Programs*, Philip Hammond, 617-989-4594, Fax: 617-989-4399, E-mail: hammondp1@wit.edu.

Master of Science in Facility Management Program Students: 15 part-time (3 women); includes 12 minority (all Hispanic/Latino). Average age 37. 17 applicants, 71% accepted, 9 enrolled. *Faculty:* 10 part-time/adjunct (4 women). Expenses: Contact institution. *Financial support:* In 2017–18, 4 students received support. Scholarships/grants available. Support available to part-time students. Financial award application deadline: 8/1; financial award applicants required to submit FAFSA. In 2017, 9 master's awarded. *Program availability:* Part-time, evening/weekend, online only, 100% online, blended/hybrid learning. Offers facility management (MS). *Application deadline:* For fall admission, 8/1 for domestic and international students. Applications are processed on a rolling basis. *Application fee:* $50. Electronic applications accepted. *Application Contact:* Martha Sheehan, Director of Admissions and Marketing, 617-989-4661, Fax: 617-989-4399, E-mail: sheehanm@wit.edu. *Director of Graduate Programs*, Philip Hammond, 617-989-4594, Fax: 617-989-4399, E-mail: hammondp1@wit.edu.

Online Master of Science in Technology Management Program Students: 17 part-time (4 women); includes 13 minority (3 Black or African American, non-Hispanic/Latino; 1 Asian, non-Hispanic/Latino; 9 Hispanic/Latino). Average age 34. 10 applicants, 90% accepted, 8 enrolled. *Faculty:* 8 part-time/adjunct (4 women). Expenses: Contact institution. *Financial support:* In 2017–18, 6 students received support. Scholarships/grants available. Support available to part-time students. Financial award application deadline: 8/1; financial award applicants required to submit FAFSA. In 2017, 9 master's awarded. *Program availability:* Part-time-only, evening/weekend, online only, 100% online. Offers technology management (MS). *Application deadline:* For fall admission, 8/1 for domestic and international students; for spring admission, 12/20 for domestic and international students. Applications are processed on a rolling basis. *Application fee:* $50. Electronic applications accepted. *Application Contact:* Martha Sheehan, Director of Admissions and Marketing, 617-989-4661, Fax: 617-989-4399, E-mail: sheehanm@wit.edu. *Director of Graduate Programs*, Philip Hammond, 617-989-4594, Fax: 617-989-4399, E-mail: hammondp1@wit.edu.

WESLEYAN COLLEGE, Macon, GA 31210-4462

General Information Independent-religious, Undergraduate: women only; graduate: coed, comprehensive institution. *Graduate housing:* Room and/or apartments available on a first-come, first-served basis to single students; on-campus housing not available to married students. Housing application deadline: 5/1.

GRADUATE UNITS

Department of Business and Economics Offers business administration (EMBA); business and economics (EMBA).

Department of Education *Program availability:* Part-time. Offers early childhood education (MA).

WESLEYAN UNIVERSITY, Middletown, CT 06459

General Information Independent, coed, university. CGS member. *Graduate housing:* Rooms and/or apartments available on a first-come, first-served basis to single and married students. Housing application deadline: 7/1. *Student services:* Campus employment opportunities, campus safety program, career counseling, exercise/wellness program, free psychological counseling, international student services, low-cost health insurance, services for students with disabilities, writing training. *Library facilities:* Olin Memorial Library plus 1 other. *Collection:* Books: 1.2 million (physical), 502,915 (digital/electronic); Serial titles: 7,507 (physical), 86,968 (digital/electronic); Databases: 332. Weekly public service hours: 113. *Research affiliation:* Woods Hole Oceanographic Institution, Cold Spring Harbor Laboratory.

Computer facilities: Computer purchase and lease plans are available. 118 computers available on campus for general student use. A campuswide network can be accessed from student residence rooms and from off campus. Online class registration, electronic portfolio, course drop/add, learning management system, software training are available.
Website: http://www.wesleyan.edu/

General Application Contact: Cheryl-Ann Hagner, Director, Graduate Student Services, 860-685-2223, Fax: 860-685-2439, E-mail: chagner@wesleyan.edu.

GRADUATE UNITS

Graduate Liberal Studies Program Expenses: Contact institution. *Financial support:* Scholarships/grants available. Support available to part-time students. *Program availability:* Part-time, evening/weekend. Offers liberal arts (M Phil); liberal studies (MALS); writing (Graduate Certificate). *Application deadline:* For fall admission, 7/16 for domestic students; for spring admission, 11/14 for domestic students; for summer admission, 4/15 for domestic students. Applications are processed on a rolling basis. *Application fee:* $100. Electronic applications accepted. *Application Contact:* Sarah-Jane Ripa, Associate Director, Student Services and Outreach, 860-685-3345, Fax: 860-685-2901, E-mail: sripa@wesleyan.edu. *Director*, Jennifer Curran, 860-685-3338, Fax: 860-685-2901, E-mail: jcurran@wesleyan.edu.

Graduate Studies Students: 128 full-time (59 women); includes 45 minority (8 Black or African American, non-Hispanic/Latino; 30 Asian, non-Hispanic/Latino; 7 Hispanic/Latino). Average age 27. 348 applicants, 15% accepted, 30 enrolled. *Faculty:* 80 full-time (26 women). Expenses: Contact institution. *Financial support:* In 2017–18, 93 students received support, including 87 teaching assistantships (averaging $31,794 per year); health care benefits and tuition waivers (full) also available. Financial award application deadline: 3/31. In 2017, 33 master's, 10 doctorates awarded. Offers astronomy (MA); biochemistry (PhD); cell and developmental biology (PhD); chemical physics (PhD); composition (MA); computer science (MA); earth and environmental sciences (MA); ethnomusicology (MA, PhD); evolution and ecology (PhD); genetics and genomics (PhD); inorganic chemistry (PhD); mathematics (MA, PhD); molecular biology and biochemistry (PhD); molecular biophysics (PhD); neurobiology and behavior (PhD); organic chemistry (PhD); physical chemistry (PhD); physics (PhD); theoretical chemistry (PhD). *Application fee:* $0. Electronic applications accepted. *Application Contact:* Cheryl-Ann Hagner, Director of Graduate Student Services, 860-685-2223, Fax: 860-685-2439, E-mail: chagner@wesleyan.edu. *Director of Graduate Studies*, Dr. Martha S. Gilmore, 860-685-3129, E-mail: mgilmore@wesleyan.edu.

WESLEY BIBLICAL SEMINARY, Jackson, MS 39206

General Information Independent-religious, coed, graduate-only institution.

GRADUATE UNITS

Graduate Programs *Program availability:* Part-time. Offers apologetics (MA); Biblical languages (M Div); Biblical literature (MA); Christian studies (MA); context and mission (M Div); honors research (M Div); interpretation (M Div); ministry (M Div); spiritual formation (M Div); teaching (M Div); theology (MA). Electronic applications accepted.

WESLEY COLLEGE, Dover, DE 19901-3875

General Information Independent-religious, coed, comprehensive institution. *Graduate housing:* On-campus housing not available.

GRADUATE UNITS

Business Program *Program availability:* Part-time, evening/weekend. Offers environmental management (MBA); executive leadership (MBA); management (MBA). Executive leadership concentration also offered at New Castle, DE location.

Education Program *Program availability:* Part-time, evening/weekend. Offers education (M Ed, MA Ed, MAT).

Environmental Studies Program *Program availability:* Part-time, evening/weekend. Offers environmental studies (MS).

Nursing Program *Program availability:* Part-time, evening/weekend. Offers nursing (MSN). Electronic applications accepted.

WESLEY THEOLOGICAL SEMINARY, Washington, DC 20016-5690

General Information Independent-religious, coed, graduate-only institution. *Graduate housing:* Rooms and/or apartments available to single and married students. Housing application deadline: 7/1.

GRADUATE UNITS

Graduate and Professional Programs *Program availability:* Part-time. Offers theology (M Div, MA, MTS, D Min).

WEST CHESTER UNIVERSITY OF PENNSYLVANIA, West Chester, PA 19383

General Information State-supported, coed, comprehensive institution. CGS member. *Enrollment:* 17,306 graduate, professional, and undergraduate students; 970 full-time matriculated graduate/professional students (695 women), 1,787 part-time matriculated graduate/professional students (1,173 women). *Enrollment by degree level:* 2,358 master's, 176 doctoral, 223 other advanced degrees. *Graduate faculty:* 265 full-time (142 women), 53 part-time/adjunct (31 women). Tuition, state resident: full-time $9000; part-time $500 per credit. Tuition, nonresident: full-time $13,500; part-time $750 per credit. *Required fees:* $2959; $149.79 per credit. *Graduate housing:* Room and/or apartments available on a first-come, first-served basis to single students; on-campus housing not available to married students. Housing application deadline: 5/1. *Student services:* Campus employment opportunities, campus safety program, career counseling, exercise/wellness program, free psychological counseling, international student services, multicultural affairs office, services for students with disabilities, teacher training, writing training. *Library facilities:* Francis Harvey Green Library plus 1 other. *Collection:* Books: 719,762 (physical), 1 million (digital/electronic); Serial titles: 1,952 (physical), 101,028 (digital/electronic); Databases: 208. Weekly public service hours: 107; study areas open 24 hours, 5–7 days a week. *Research affiliation:* Pennsylvania Equine Toxicology and Research Laboratory (chemistry), Temple University Collaborative on Community Inclusion of Individuals with Psychiatric Disabilities (social work), University of Pennsylvania (social work), University of Connecticut Human Rights Institute Research Program on Economic and Social Rights (social work), The Soldier's Project (social work), Independent Blue Cross (IBC) (nursing).

Computer facilities: Computer purchase and lease plans are available. 2,700 computers available on campus for general student use. A campuswide network can be accessed from student residence rooms and from off campus. Online class registration, virtual software are available.
Website: http://www.wcupa.edu/

General Application Contact: Office of Graduate Studies, 610-436-2943, Fax: 610-436-2763, E-mail: gradstudy@wcupa.edu.

GRADUATE UNITS

College of Arts and Humanities Students: 62 full-time (40 women), 139 part-time (87 women); includes 26 minority (5 Black or African American, non-Hispanic/Latino; 1 Asian, non-Hispanic/Latino; 14 Hispanic/Latino; 6 Two or more races, non-Hispanic/Latino), 4 international. Average age 30. 123 applicants, 88% accepted, 68 enrolled. *Faculty:* 46 full-time (23 women), 1 (woman) part-time/adjunct. Expenses: Contact institution. *Financial support:* Scholarships/grants and unspecified assistantships available. Financial award application deadline: 2/15; financial award applicants required to submit FAFSA. In 2017, 49 master's, 4 other advanced degrees awarded. *Program availability:* Part-time, evening/weekend. Offers arts and humanities (M Ed, MA, MS, Certificate, Teaching Certificate); business ethics (Certificate); communication studies (MA); English (MA); French (Teaching Certificate); German (Teaching Certificate); health care ethics (Certificate); history (M Ed, MA); Holocaust and genocide studies (MA, Certificate); languages and cultures (MA); philosophy (MA); philosophy: applied ethics (MA); publishing (Certificate); secondary English (Teaching Certificate); Spanish (Teaching Certificate); teaching English as a second language (MA, Certificate). *Application deadline:* For fall admission, 5/15 for international students; for spring admission, 10/15 for international students. Applications are processed on a rolling basis. *Application fee:* $50. Electronic applications accepted. *Application Contact:* Office of Graduate Studies and Extended Education, 610-436-2943, Fax: 610-436-2763, E-mail: gradstudy@wcupa.edu. *Dean of the College of Arts and Humanities*, Dr. Jen Bacon, 610-436-3326, E-mail: jbacon@wcupa.edu.

College of Business and Public Management Students: 146 full-time (70 women), 608 part-time (270 women); includes 180 minority (119 Black or African American, non-Hispanic/Latino; 25 Asian, non-Hispanic/Latino; 29 Hispanic/Latino; 7 Two or more races, non-Hispanic/Latino), 8 international. Average age 32. 460 applicants, 76% accepted, 271 enrolled. *Faculty:* 34 full-time (13 women), 11 part-time/adjunct (5 women). Expenses: Contact institution. *Financial support:* Scholarships/grants and unspecified assistantships available. Financial award application deadline: 2/15; financial award applicants required to submit FAFSA. In 2017, 137 master's, 44 other advanced degrees awarded. *Program availability:* Part-time, evening/weekend, 100% online, blended/hybrid learning. Offers administration (Certificate); business and public management (MA, MBA, MPA, MS, MURP, Certificate, DPA); criminal justice (MS); geographic information systems (Certificate); geography (MS); geography and planning

(MURP); human resource management (MS, Certificate); non profit administration (Certificate); nonprofit administration (MPA); public administration (MPA); public policy and administration (MPA, DPA); urban and regional planning (Certificate). *Application deadline:* For fall admission, 5/15 for international students; for spring admission, 10/15 for international students. Applications are processed on a rolling basis. *Application fee:* $50. Electronic applications accepted. *Application Contact:* Office of Graduate Studies and Extended Education, 610-436-2943, Fax: 610-436-2763, E-mail: gradstudy@wcupa.edu. *Dean,* Dr. Anthony Wheeler, 610-436-2930, Fax: 610-436-3170, E-mail: awheeler@wcupa.edu.

School of Business Students: 41 full-time (17 women), 388 part-time (150 women); includes 69 minority (33 Black or African American, non-Hispanic/Latino; 19 Asian, non-Hispanic/Latino; 14 Hispanic/Latino; 3 Two or more races, non-Hispanic/Latino). Average age 32. 268 applicants, 68% accepted, 153 enrolled. Expenses: Contact institution. *Financial support:* Scholarships/grants and unspecified assistantships available. Financial award application deadline: 2/15; financial award applicants required to submit FAFSA. In 2017, 78 master's, 21 other advanced degrees awarded. *Program availability:* Part-time, evening/weekend, online only, 100% online. Offers business analytics (Certificate); business education (MBA). *Application deadline:* For fall admission, 5/15 for international students; for spring admission, 10/15 for international students. Applications are processed on a rolling basis. *Application fee:* $50. Electronic applications accepted. *Application Contact:* Office of Graduate Studies and Extended Education, 610-436-2943, Fax: 610-436-2763, E-mail: gradstudy@wcupa.edu. *MBA Director/Graduate Coordinator,* Dr. Brian Halsey, 610-425-5000 Ext. 4444, E-mail: mba@wcupa.edu.

College of Education and Social Work Students: 394 full-time (325 women), 615 part-time (531 women); includes 233 minority (157 Black or African American, non-Hispanic/Latino; 11 Asian, non-Hispanic/Latino; 38 Hispanic/Latino; 27 Two or more races, non-Hispanic/Latino), 4 international. Average age 30. 759 applicants, 76% accepted, 379 enrolled. *Faculty:* 62 full-time (45 women), 22 part-time/adjunct (15 women). Expenses: Contact institution. *Financial support:* Scholarships/grants and unspecified assistantships available. Financial award application deadline: 2/15; financial award applicants required to submit FAFSA. In 2017, 299 master's, 57 other advanced degrees awarded. *Program availability:* Part-time, evening/weekend, 100% online, blended/hybrid learning. Offers applied studies in teaching and learning (M Ed); autism (Certificate); clinical mental health counseling (MS); counseling (Certificate); early childhood education (M Ed); education and social work (M Ed, MS, MSW, Ed D, Certificate, Post Master's Certificate, Teaching Certificate); education for sustainability (Certificate); educational technology (Certificate); gerontology (Certificate); grades 4-8 (Teaching Certificate); grades preK-4 (Teaching Certificate); higher education counseling (Post Master's Certificate); higher education counseling/student affairs (MS, Certificate); higher education policy and student affairs (MS); literacy (Certificate); literacy coaching (Certificate); policy, planning, and administration (Ed D); reading (M Ed); reading specialist (Teaching Certificate); school counseling (M Ed); social work (MSW); special education (Teaching Certificate); special education (M Ed); transformative education and social change (MS); universal design for learning and assistive technology (Certificate). *Application deadline:* For fall admission, 5/15 for international students; for spring admission, 10/15 for international students. Applications are processed on a rolling basis. *Application fee:* $50. Electronic applications accepted. *Application Contact:* Office of Graduate Studies and Extended Education, 610-436-2943, Fax: 610-436-2763, E-mail: gradstudy@wcupa.edu. *Dean,* Dr. Kenneth D. Witmer, Jr., 610-436-2321, Fax: 610-436-3102, E-mail: kwitmer@wcupa.edu.

College of Health Sciences Students: 242 full-time (189 women), 223 part-time (189 women); includes 109 minority (79 Black or African American, non-Hispanic/Latino; 14 Asian, non-Hispanic/Latino; 11 Hispanic/Latino; 5 Two or more races, non-Hispanic/Latino), 12 international. Average age 30. 642 applicants, 63% accepted, 198 enrolled. *Faculty:* 44 full-time (33 women), 5 part-time/adjunct (3 women). Expenses: Contact institution. *Financial support:* Scholarships/grants and unspecified assistantships available. Financial award application deadline: 2/15; financial award applicants required to submit FAFSA. In 2017, 132 master's, 21 doctorates, 36 other advanced degrees awarded. *Program availability:* Part-time, evening/weekend. Offers adapted physical education (Certificate); adult-gerontology clinical nurse specialist (MSN); athletic training (MS); community nutrition (MS); exercise and sport physiology (MS); health care management (Certificate); health sciences (MA, MPA, MPH, MS, MSN, DNP, Certificate, Teaching Certificate); integrative health (Certificate); nursing (DNP); nursing education (MSN); public health (MPH); school nurse (Certificate); speech-language pathology (MA); sport management and athletics (MPA). *Application deadline:* For fall admission, 5/15 for international students; for spring admission, 10/15 for international students. Applications are processed on a rolling basis. *Application fee:* $50. Electronic applications accepted. *Application Contact:* Office of Graduate Studies, 610-436-2943, Fax: 610-436-2763, E-mail: gradstudy@wcupa.edu. *Interim Dean,* Dr. Scott Heinerichs, 610-436-2825, Fax: 610-436-2860, E-mail: sheinerichs@wcupa.edu.

College of the Sciences and Mathematics Students: 104 full-time (58 women), 170 part-time (84 women); includes 54 minority (19 Black or African American, non-Hispanic/Latino; 24 Asian, non-Hispanic/Latino; 6 Hispanic/Latino; 5 Two or more races, non-Hispanic/Latino), 23 international. Average age 29. 261 applicants, 75% accepted, 120 enrolled. *Faculty:* 52 full-time (21 women), 8 part-time/adjunct (5 women). Expenses: Contact institution. *Financial support:* Scholarships/grants and unspecified assistantships available. Financial award application deadline: 2/15; financial award applicants required to submit FAFSA. In 2017, 125 master's, 12 other advanced degrees awarded. *Program availability:* Part-time, 100% online. Offers applied and computational mathematics (MS); applied statistics (MS, Certificate); biology (MS, Teaching Certificate); chemistry (Teaching Certificate); clinical psychology (Psy D); computer science (MS); computer security (information assurance) (Certificate); general science (Teaching Certificate); geoscience (MS); industrial/organizational psychology (Certificate); information systems (Certificate); mathematics (MA, Teaching Certificate); mathematics education (MA); physics (Teaching Certificate); psychology (MA); sciences and mathematics (MA, MS, Psy D, Certificate, Teaching Certificate); Web technology (Certificate). *Application deadline:* For fall admission, 5/15 for international students; for spring admission, 10/15 for international students. Applications are processed on a rolling basis. *Application fee:* $50. Electronic applications accepted. *Application Contact:* Office of Graduate Studies, 610-436-2943, Fax: 610-436-2763, E-mail: gradstudy@wcupa.edu. *Dean,* Dr. Radha Pyati, 610-436-3521, E-mail: csm@wcupa.edu.

School of Music Students: 22 full-time (13 women), 32 part-time (12 women); includes 6 minority (1 Black or African American, non-Hispanic/Latino; 2 Asian, non-Hispanic/Latino; 1 Hispanic/Latino; 2 Two or more races, non-Hispanic/Latino), 5 international. Average age 28. 40 applicants, 80% accepted, 23 enrolled. *Faculty:* 27 full-time (7 women), 6 part-time/adjunct (2 women). Expenses: Contact institution. *Financial support:* Scholarships/grants and unspecified assistantships available. Financial award application deadline: 2/15; financial award applicants required to submit FAFSA. In 2017, 28 master's, 6 Certificates awarded. *Program availability:* Part-time, evening/weekend. Offers history and literature (MM); Kodaly methodology (Certificate); music (MM, Certificate, Teaching Certificate); music education (MM, Teaching Certificate); music technology (Certificate); music theory, history, and composition (MM); Orff-Schulwerk (Certificate); performance (MM); piano pedagogy (MM, Certificate). *Application deadline:* For fall admission, 5/15 for international students; for spring admission, 10/15 for international students. Applications are processed on a rolling basis. *Application fee:* $50. *Application Contact:* Office of Graduate Studies, 610-436-2943, Fax: 610-436-2763, E-mail: gradstudy@wcupa.edu. *Dean,* Christopher Hanning, 610-430-4178, E-mail: channing@wcupa.edu.

WEST COAST UNIVERSITY, North Hollywood, CA 91606

General Information Proprietary, coed, comprehensive institution.

GRADUATE UNITS

Graduate Programs

WESTERN CAROLINA UNIVERSITY, Cullowhee, NC 28723

General Information State-supported, coed, university. CGS member. *Enrollment:* 765 full-time matriculated graduate/professional students (540 women), 772 part-time matriculated graduate/professional students (523 women). *Enrollment by degree level:* 1,331 master's, 143 doctoral, 63 other advanced degrees. *Graduate faculty:* 233 full-time (110 women), 36 part-time/adjunct (17 women). Tuition, state resident: full-time $4436. Tuition, nonresident: full-time $14,842. *Required fees:* $2926. *Graduate housing:* Room and/or apartments available on a first-come, first-served basis to single students; on-campus housing not available to married students. Typical cost: $10,419 (including board). Room and board charges vary according to board plan and housing facility selected. Housing application deadline: 5/1. *Student services:* Campus employment opportunities, campus safety program, career counseling, child daycare facilities, exercise/wellness program, free psychological counseling, international student services, low-cost health insurance, multicultural affairs office, services for students with disabilities, teacher training, writing training. *Library facilities:* Hunter Library. *Collection:* Weekly public service hours: 96; study areas open 24 hours, 5–7 days a week; students can reserve study rooms. *Research affiliation:* North Carolina Center for the Advancement of Teaching.

Computer facilities: Computer purchase and lease plans are available. A campuswide network can be accessed from student residence rooms and from off campus. Online class registration is available.
Website: http://www.wcu.edu/

General Application Contact: Admissions Specialist, 828-227-7398, Fax: 828-227-7480, E-mail: grad@email.wcu.edu.

GRADUATE UNITS

Graduate School *Program availability:* Part-time, evening/weekend, online learning.

College of Arts and Sciences Students: 123. Expenses: Contact institution. *Financial support:* In 2017–18, 13 research assistantships with full and partial tuition reimbursements (averaging $10,500 per year), 55 teaching assistantships with full and partial tuition reimbursements (averaging $10,500 per year) were awarded; career-related internships or fieldwork, institutionally sponsored loans, scholarships/grants, and unspecified assistantships also available. Financial award application deadline: 4/15; financial award applicants required to submit FAFSA. *Program availability:* Part-time, evening/weekend. Offers arts and sciences (MA, MPA, MS, Certificate, Graduate Certificate); biology (MS); chemistry (MS); history (MA); literature (MA); political science and public affairs (MPA); professional writing (MA); rhetoric and composition (MA); teaching English to speakers of other languages (Certificate); technical and professional writing (Certificate). *Application deadline:* For fall admission, 4/15 priority date for domestic and international students; for spring admission, 11/15 priority date for domestic students, 10/15 priority date for international students. Applications are processed on a rolling basis. *Application fee:* $65. Electronic applications accepted. *Application Contact:* Bobbi Smith, Admissions Coordinator, 828-227-2925, E-mail: bobbismith@wcu.edu. *Dean,* Richard Starnes, E-mail: starnes@email.wcu.edu.

College of Business *Program availability:* Part-time, evening/weekend, online learning. Offers accountancy (M Ac); business administration (MBA); entrepreneurship (ME); project management (MPM).

College of Education and Allied Professions *Program availability:* Part-time, evening/weekend, online learning. Offers education and allied professions (MA); general psychology (MA).

College of Engineering and Technology *Program availability:* Part-time, evening/weekend, online learning. Offers construction management (MCM); engineering and technology (MCM, MS); technology (MS).

College of Fine and Performing Arts *Program availability:* Part-time. Offers art and design (MFA); fine and performing arts (MFA).

College of Health and Human Sciences *Program availability:* Part-time, evening/weekend. Offers communication sciences and disorders (MS); health and human sciences (MHS, MPT, MS, MSN, MSW, DPT, PMC); health sciences (MHS); nursing (MS, DNP, Post-Master's Certificate, Postbaccalaureate Certificate); physical therapy (DPT); social work (MSW).

WESTERN CONNECTICUT STATE UNIVERSITY, Danbury, CT 06810-6885

General Information State-supported, coed, comprehensive institution. *Enrollment:* 5,664 graduate, professional, and undergraduate students; 96 full-time matriculated graduate/professional students (66 women), 401 part-time matriculated graduate/professional students (306 women). *Enrollment by degree level:* 410 master's, 72 doctoral, 15 other advanced degrees. Tuition, state resident: full-time $6757; part-time $374 per credit hour. Tuition, nonresident: full-time $18,102; part-time $374 per credit hour. *Required fees:* $4994; $190 per credit hour. $60 per term. Tuition and fees vary according to degree level and program. *Graduate housing:* Rooms and/or apartments available on a first-come, first-served basis to single and married students. Typical cost: $7109 per year ($12,622 including board) for single students; $7109 per year ($12,622 including board) for married students. Room and board charges vary according to board plan and housing facility selected. Housing application deadline: 4/1. *Student services:* Campus employment opportunities, career counseling, child daycare facilities, exercise/wellness program, free psychological counseling, international student services, low-cost health insurance, multicultural affairs office, services for students with disabilities, teacher training, writing training. *Library facilities:* Ruth Haas Library plus 2 others. *Collection:* Books: 204,701 (physical), 240,140 (digital/electronic); Serial titles: 302 (physical), 67,162 (digital/electronic); Databases: 188. Weekly public service hours: 144; students can reserve study rooms. *Research affiliation:* Smithsonian Institution

Affiliations Program, The Jane Goodall Institute, Center for Financial Forensics and Information Security, New England Educational Assessment Network, American Society for Microbiology.

Computer facilities: 666 computers available on campus for general student use. A campuswide network can be accessed from student residence rooms and from off campus. Online class registration, online payment are available.
Website: http://www.wcsu.edu/

General Application Contact: Chris Shankle, Associate Director of Graduate Studies, 203-837-9005, Fax: 203-837-8326, E-mail: shanklec@wcsu.edu.

GRADUATE UNITS

Division of Graduate Studies *Program availability:* Part-time.

Ancell School of Business *Program availability:* Part-time. Offers accounting (MBA); business (MBA, MHA, MS); business administration (MBA); health administration (MHA).

Maricostas School of Arts and Sciences *Program availability:* Part-time. Offers arts and sciences (MA, MAT, MFA); creative and professional writing (MFA); earth and planetary sciences (MA); history and non-Western cultures (MA); literature (MA); mathematics (MA).

School of Professional Studies *Program availability:* Part-time. Offers adult gerontology clinical nurse specialist (MSN); adult gerontology nurse practitioner (MSN); clinical mental health counseling (MS); curriculum (MS); instructional leadership (Ed D); instructional technology (MS); nursing education (Ed D); reading (MS); school counseling (MS); special education (MS).

School of Visual and Performing Arts *Program availability:* Part-time. Offers illustration (MFA); music education (MS); painting (MFA); visual and performing arts (MFA, MS).

WESTERN GOVERNORS UNIVERSITY, Salt Lake City, UT 84107

General Information Independent, coed, comprehensive institution. *Graduate housing:* On-campus housing not available. *Student services:* Career counseling, services for students with disabilities, teacher training, writing training. *Library facilities:* WGU Central Library (online).

Computer facilities: A campuswide network can be accessed. Online class registration is available.
Website: http://www.wgu.edu/

General Application Contact: Enrollment Department, 866-225-5948, Fax: 801-274-3306, E-mail: info@wgu.edu.

GRADUATE UNITS

College of Business Expenses: Contact institution. *Financial support:* Scholarships/grants and tuition waivers (partial) available. Financial award applicants required to submit FAFSA. *Program availability:* Evening/weekend, online learning. Offers accounting (MS); information technology management (MBA); management and leadership (MS); management and strategy (MBA); strategic leadership (MBA). *Application deadline:* Applications are processed on a rolling basis. *Application fee:* $65. Electronic applications accepted. *Application Contact:* Enrollment Department, 866-225-5948, Fax: 801-274-3306, E-mail: info@wgu.edu. *Director*, Dr. Rashmi Prasad.

College of Health Professions Expenses: Contact institution. *Financial support:* Tuition waivers (partial) available. Financial award applicants required to submit FAFSA. *Program availability:* Evening/weekend, online learning. Offers healthcare management (MBA); leadership and management (MSN); nursing education (MSN); nursing informatics (MSN). *Application deadline:* Applications are processed on a rolling basis. *Application fee:* $65. Electronic applications accepted. *Application Contact:* Enrollment Department, 866-225-5948, Fax: 801-274-3306, E-mail: info@wgu.edu. *Director*, Dr. Jan Jones-Schenk.

College of Information Technology Expenses: Contact institution. *Financial support:* Institutionally sponsored loans and scholarships/grants available. Financial award applicants required to submit FAFSA. *Program availability:* Online learning. Offers cybersecurity and information assurance (MS); data analytics (MS); information technology management (MS). *Application fee:* $65. *Application Contact:* Enrollment Department, 866-225-5948, Fax: 801-274-3306, E-mail: info@wgu.edu. *Director*, Dr. Elke Leeds, 801-290-3658.

Teachers College Expenses: Contact institution. *Financial support:* Scholarships/grants and tuition waivers (partial) available. Financial award applicants required to submit FAFSA. *Program availability:* Evening/weekend, online learning. Offers curriculum and instruction (MS); educational leadership (MS); elementary education (MAT, Postbaccalaureate Certificate); English education (5-12) (MAT); English language learning (PreK-12) (MA); instructional design (M Ed); learning and technology (M Ed); mathematics (5-12) (MAT); mathematics (5-9) (MAT); mathematics education (5-12) (MA); mathematics education (5-9) (MA); mathematics education (K-6) (MA); science (5-12) (MAT); science education (5-12) (MA); science education (5-9) (MA); special education (MS). *Application deadline:* Applications are processed on a rolling basis. *Application fee:* $65. Electronic applications accepted. *Application Contact:* Enrollment Department, 866-225-5948, Fax: 801-274-3306, E-mail: info@wgu.edu. *Director*, Dr. Deb Eldridge, 845-255-4656.

WESTERN ILLINOIS UNIVERSITY, Macomb, IL 61455-1390

General Information State-supported, coed, comprehensive institution. CGS member. *Enrollment:* 9,441 graduate, professional, and undergraduate students; 813 full-time matriculated graduate/professional students (419 women), 535 part-time matriculated graduate/professional students (356 women). *Graduate housing:* Rooms and/or apartments available on a first-come, first-served basis to single and married students. *Student services:* Campus employment opportunities, campus safety program, career counseling, exercise/wellness program, free psychological counseling, international student services, low-cost health insurance, multicultural affairs office, services for students with disabilities, teacher training, writing training. *Library facilities:* Leslie Malpass Library plus 4 others. *Collection:* Books: 765,743 (physical), 149,893 (digital/electronic); Serial titles: 153,468 (physical), 79,966 (digital/electronic); Databases: 126. *Research affiliation:* National Council of Teachers of English (English and journalism), Petroleum Research Fund (chemistry), Bayer Crop Services (agriculture), McDonald's Corporation (education), The Ceres Trust (agriculture), Quad Cities Manufacturing Lab (engineering).

Computer facilities: 632 computers available on campus for general student use. A campuswide network can be accessed from student residence rooms and from off campus. Online class registration is available.
Website: http://www.wiu.edu/

General Application Contact: Dr. Nancy Parsons, Associate Provost and Director of Graduate Studies, 309-298-1806, Fax: 309-298-2345, E-mail: grad-office@wiu.edu.

GRADUATE UNITS

School of Graduate Studies Students: 813 full-time (419 women), 535 part-time (356 women); includes 239 minority (113 Black or African American, non-Hispanic/Latino; 1 American Indian or Alaska Native, non-Hispanic/Latino; 17 Asian, non-Hispanic/Latino; 82 Hispanic/Latino; 26 Two or more races, non-Hispanic/Latino), 345 international. Average age 31. 1,345 applicants, 76% accepted, 496 enrolled. Expenses: Contact institution. *Financial support:* Research assistantships with full tuition reimbursements, teaching assistantships with full tuition reimbursements, and unspecified assistantships available. Financial award applicants required to submit FAFSA. In 2017, 557 master's, 16 doctorates, 25 other advanced degrees awarded. *Program availability:* Part-time, online learning. *Application fee:* $30. Electronic applications accepted. *Associate Provost and Director of Graduate Studies*, Dr. Nancy Parsons, 309-298-1066, Fax: 309-298-2345, E-mail: grad-office@wiu.edu.

College of Arts and Sciences Students: 200 full-time (103 women), 90 part-time (52 women); includes 36 minority (12 Black or African American, non-Hispanic/Latino; 1 American Indian or Alaska Native, non-Hispanic/Latino; 5 Asian, non-Hispanic/Latino; 9 Hispanic/Latino; 9 Two or more races, non-Hispanic/Latino), 85 international. Average age 29. 220 applicants, 75% accepted, 96 enrolled. Expenses: Contact institution. *Financial support:* Research assistantships with full tuition reimbursements, teaching assistantships with full tuition reimbursements, and unspecified assistantships available. Financial award applicants required to submit FAFSA. In 2017, 115 master's, 6 other advanced degrees awarded. *Program availability:* Part-time. Offers arts and sciences (MA, MLAS, MS, PhD, Certificate, SSP); biology (MS); chemistry (MS); clinical/community mental health (MS); English (MA); environmental GIS (Certificate); environmental science: large river ecosystems (PhD); general experimental psychology (MS); geography (MA); GIS analysis: ecological GIS (Certificate); GIS analysis: GIS applications (Certificate); history (MA); liberal arts and sciences (MLAS); literary studies (Certificate); mathematics (MS); physics (MS); political science (MA); school psychology (SSP); sociology (MA); zoo and aquarium studies (Certificate). *Application deadline:* Applications are processed on a rolling basis. *Application fee:* $30. Electronic applications accepted. *Application Contact:* Dr. Nancy Parsons, Associate Provost and Director of Graduate Studies, 309-298-1806, Fax: 309-298-2345, E-mail: grad-office@wiu.edu. *Dean*, Dr. Susan Martinelli-Fernandez, 309-298-1828.

College of Business and Technology Students: 159 full-time (50 women), 15 part-time (4 women). Average age 30. 447 applicants, 74% accepted, 117 enrolled. Expenses: Contact institution. *Financial support:* Research assistantships, teaching assistantships with full tuition reimbursements, and unspecified assistantships available. Financial award applicants required to submit FAFSA. In 2017, 164 master's, 12 other advanced degrees awarded. *Program availability:* Part-time. Offers accountancy (M Acct); applied statistics and decision analytics (MS); business administration (MBA, Certificate); business analytics (Certificate); business and technology (M Acct, MA, MBA, MS, Certificate); computer science (MS); economics (MA); educational technology specialist (Certificate); engineering technology leadership (MS); instructional design and technology (MS); instructional media development (Certificate); online and distance learning development (Certificate); supply chain management (Certificate); technology integration in education (Certificate); workplace learning and performance (Certificate). *Application deadline:* Applications are processed on a rolling basis. Electronic applications accepted. *Application Contact:* Dr. Nancy Parsons, Associate Provost and Director of Graduate Studies, 309-298-1806, Fax: 309-298-2345, E-mail: grad-office@wiu.edu. *Interim Dean*, Dr. William Bailey, 309-298-2442.

College of Education and Human Services Students: 319 full-time (171 women), 407 part-time (284 women); includes 130 minority (67 Black or African American, non-Hispanic/Latino; 6 Asian, non-Hispanic/Latino; 44 Hispanic/Latino; 13 Two or more races, non-Hispanic/Latino), 33 international. Average age 31. 397 applicants, 84% accepted, 201 enrolled. Expenses: Contact institution. *Financial support:* Research assistantships with full tuition reimbursements, teaching assistantships with full tuition reimbursements, and unspecified assistantships available. Financial award applicants required to submit FAFSA. In 2017, 212 master's, 12 doctorates, 7 other advanced degrees awarded. *Program availability:* Part-time, evening/weekend, online learning. Offers college student personnel (MS); counseling (MS Ed); curriculum and instruction (MS Ed); education and human services (MA, MS, MS Ed, Ed D, Certificate, Ed S); educational and interdisciplinary studies (MS Ed, Certificate); educational leadership (MS Ed, Ed D, Ed S); health sciences (MS); kinesiology (MA); law enforcement and justice administration (MA); police executive administration (Certificate); reading (MS Ed); recreation, park, and tourism administration (MS); special education (MS Ed); sport management (MS); teaching English to speakers of other languages (Certificate). *Application deadline:* Applications are processed on a rolling basis. *Application fee:* $30. Electronic applications accepted. *Application Contact:* Dr. Nancy Parsons, Associate Provost and Director of Graduate Studies, 309-298-1806, Fax: 309-298-2345, E-mail: grad-office@wiu.edu. *Dean*, Dr. Erskine Smith, 309-298-1690.

College of Fine Arts and Communication Students: 126 full-time (88 women), 16 part-time (10 women); includes 29 minority (15 Black or African American, non-Hispanic/Latino; 12 Hispanic/Latino; 2 Two or more races, non-Hispanic/Latino), 16 international. Average age 27. 269 applicants, 67% accepted, 76 enrolled. Expenses: Contact institution. *Financial support:* Research assistantships with full tuition reimbursements, teaching assistantships with full tuition reimbursements, and unspecified assistantships available. Financial award applicants required to submit FAFSA. In 2017, 269 master's, 76 other advanced degrees awarded. *Program availability:* Part-time. Offers communication (MA); communication sciences and disorders (MS); fine arts and communication (MA, MFA, MM, MS, Certificate); museum studies (MA, Certificate); music (MM); theatre (MFA). *Application deadline:* Applications are processed on a rolling basis. *Application fee:* $30. Electronic applications accepted. *Application Contact:* Dr. Nancy Parsons, Associate Provost and Director of Graduate Studies, 309-298-1806, Fax: 309-298-2345, E-mail: grad-office@wiu.edu. *Dean*, Billy Clow, 309-298-1618.

Illinois Institute for Rural Affairs Students: 9 full-time (7 women), 7 part-time (6 women); includes 3 minority (1 Black or African American, non-Hispanic/Latino; 2 Hispanic/Latino). Average age 37. 9 applicants, 89% accepted, 6 enrolled. Expenses: Contact institution. Offers community and economic development (MA). *Application deadline:* Applications are processed on a rolling basis. *Application fee:* $30. Electronic applications accepted. *Director*, Dr. Christopher Merrett, 309-298-2281, E-mail: cd-merrett@wiu.edu.

WESTERN KENTUCKY UNIVERSITY, Bowling Green, KY 42101

General Information State-supported, coed, comprehensive institution. CGS member. *Graduate housing:* Room and/or apartments guaranteed to single students; on-campus housing not available to married students. Housing application deadline: 4/1. *Research* *affiliation:* Bowling Green Field Station for Animal Studies (U.S. Fish and Wildlife Service), Roybal Center (gerontology).

GRADUATE UNITS

Graduate Studies *Program availability:* Part-time, evening/weekend, online learning.

College of Education and Behavioral Sciences *Program availability:* Part-time, evening/weekend, online learning. Offers adult education (MAE); clinical psychology (MA); counseling (MA Ed); education and behavioral sciences (MA, MAE, MS, Ed D, Ed S); educational leadership (Ed D); elementary education (MAE, Ed S); exceptional education: learning and behavioral disorders (MAE); exceptional education: moderate and severe disabilities (MAE); experimental psychology (MA); general psychology (MA); industrial/organizational psychology (MA); instructional design (MS); interdisciplinary early childhood education (MAE); library media education (MS); literacy education (MAE); middle grades education (MAE); school administration (Ed S); school counseling (P-12) (MA Ed); school principal (MAE); school psychology (Ed S); secondary education (MAE, Ed S); student affairs in higher education (MA Ed).

College of Health and Human Services *Program availability:* Part-time, evening/weekend. Offers athletic administration and coaching (MS); communication disorders (MS); health and human services (MHA, MPH, MS, MSN, MSW, DPT); healthcare administration (MHA); nursing (MSN); physical education (MS); physical therapy (DPT); public health (MPH); recreation and sport administration (MS); social work (MSW).

Gordon Ford College of Business *Program availability:* Part-time, evening/weekend. Offers applied economics (MA); business (MA, MBA); business administration (MBA).

Ogden College of Science and Engineering *Program availability:* Part-time, evening/weekend. Offers agriculture (MA Ed, MS); biology (MS); chemistry (MA Ed, MS); computational mathematics (MS); computer science (MS); geoscience (MS); homeland security sciences (MS); mathematics (MA, MS); physics (MA Ed); science and engineering (MA Ed, MS); technology management (MS).

Potter College of Arts and Letters *Program availability:* Part-time, evening/weekend, online learning. Offers art education (MA Ed); arts and letters (MA, MA Ed, MPA); communication (MA); criminology (MA); education (MA); English (MA Ed); folk studies (MA); French (MA Ed); German (MA Ed); history (MA, MA Ed); literature (MA); music (MA Ed); organizational communication (Graduate Certificate); political science (MPA); sociology (MA); Spanish (MA Ed); teaching English as a second language (MA); writing (MA).

WESTERN MICHIGAN UNIVERSITY, Kalamazoo, MI 49008

General Information State-supported, coed, university. CGS member. *Graduate housing:* Rooms and/or apartments available on a first-come, first-served basis to single and married students. Housing application deadline: 7/1. *Research affiliation:* Argonne National Laboratory (particle physics), Central States Universities, Inc., Ames Research Center (manufacturing education), Copper Development Association, Inc. (plastics extrusion), Pharmacia and Upjohn Company (electron microscopy), Flowserve Corporation (mechanical pumps and seals).

GRADUATE UNITS

Graduate College *Program availability:* Part-time, evening/weekend.

College of Arts and Sciences *Program availability:* Part-time. Offers anthropology (MA); applied and computational mathematics (MS); applied economics (MA, PhD); arts and sciences (MA, MFA, MIDA, MPA, MS, PhD, Graduate Certificate); behavior analysis (MA, PhD); biological sciences (MS, PhD); chemistry (MS, PhD); clinical psychology (PhD); communication (MA); comparative religion (MA, Graduate Certificate); creative writing (MFA, PhD); earth science (MA); English (MA, PhD); English teaching (MA); geographic information science (Graduate Certificate); geography (MA); geosciences (MS, PhD); health care administration (MPA, Graduate Certificate); history (MA, PhD); industrial/organizational behavior management (MA); international development administration (MIDA); mathematics education (MA, PhD); nonprofit leadership and administration (Graduate Certificate); philosophy (MA); physics (MA, PhD); political science (MA, PhD); public administration (PhD); science education (MA, PhD); sociology (MA, PhD); Spanish (MA, PhD); statistics (MS, PhD, Graduate Certificate).

College of Education and Human Development *Program availability:* Part-time. Offers athletic training (MS); career and technical education (MA); counseling psychology (MA, PhD); counselor education (MA, PhD); education and human development (MA, MS, Ed D, PhD, Ed S, Graduate Certificate); educational leadership (MA, PhD, Ed S); educational technology (MA, Graduate Certificate); evaluation, measurement and research (MA, PhD); family and consumer sciences (MA); interdisciplinary education (PhD); literacy studies (MA); organizational learning and performance (MA); practice of teaching (MA); socio-cultural studies of education (MA); special education (MA, Ed D); sport management (MA); teaching children with visual impairments (MA).

College of Engineering and Applied Sciences *Program availability:* Part-time. Offers chemical and paper engineering (MS, MSE, PhD); civil and construction engineering (MSE); computer engineering (MSE); computer science (MS, PhD); electrical and computer engineering (PhD); electrical engineering (MSE); engineering and applied sciences (MS, MSE, PhD); engineering design, manufacturing, and management systems (MS); engineering management (MS); industrial engineering (MSE, PhD); mechanical engineering (MSE, PhD).

College of Fine Arts *Program availability:* Part-time. Offers art education (MA); fine arts (MA, MM, Graduate Certificate); music (MA); music composition (MM); music conducting (MM); music education (MM); music performance (MM); music therapy (MM).

College of Health and Human Services *Program availability:* Part-time. Offers audiology (Au D); health and human services (MA, MS, MSM, MSN, MSW, Au D, PhD, Graduate Certificate); interdisciplinary health services (PhD); nursing (MSN); occupational therapy (MS); orientation and mobility (MA); orientation and mobility of children (MA); physician assistant (MSM); social work (MSW); speech pathology and audiology (MA); vision rehabilitation therapy (MA).

Haworth College of Business *Program availability:* Part-time. Offers accountancy (MSA); business (MBA, MSA); business administration (MBA).

WESTERN MICHIGAN UNIVERSITY THOMAS M. COOLEY LAW SCHOOL, Lansing, MI 48901-3038

General Information Independent, coed, graduate-only institution. *Graduate housing:* On-campus housing not available.

GRADUATE UNITS

Graduate Programs *Program availability:* Part-time, evening/weekend, 100% online, blended/hybrid learning. Offers administrative law (public law) (JD); business transactions (JD); Canadian law practice (JD); corporate law and finance (LL M); environmental law (public law) (JD); general practice (JD); general studies (LL M); homeland and national security law (LL M); insurance law (LL M); intellectual property (JD); intellectual property law (LL M); international law (JD); litigation (JD); taxation (LL M); U.S. legal studies for foreign attorneys (LL M). Electronic applications accepted.

WESTERN NEW ENGLAND UNIVERSITY, Springfield, MA 01119

General Information Independent, coed, comprehensive institution. *Enrollment:* 3,813 graduate, professional, and undergraduate students; 472 full-time matriculated graduate/professional students (295 women), 568 part-time matriculated graduate/professional students (312 women). *Enrollment by degree level:* 405 master's, 630 doctoral, 5 other advanced degrees. *Graduate faculty:* 241 full-time (102 women), 29 part-time/adjunct (12 women). Tuition and fees vary according to program. *Graduate housing:* Rooms and/or apartments available to single and married students. Housing application deadline: 3/9. *Student services:* Campus employment opportunities, campus safety program, career counseling, exercise/wellness program, free psychological counseling, international student services, services for students with disabilities, teacher training, writing training. *Library facilities:* D'Amour Library plus 1 other. *Collection:* Books: 106,500 (physical), 31,912 (digital/electronic); Serial titles: 46 (physical), 109,440 (digital/electronic); Databases: 128. Weekly public service hours: 97; study areas open 24 hours, 5–7 days a week. *Research affiliation:* New England Center for Children (applied behavior analysis).

Computer facilities: 530 computers available on campus for general student use. A campuswide network can be accessed from student residence rooms and from off campus. Online class registration is available.
Website: http://www.wne.edu/

General Application Contact: Matthew Fox, Director of Admissions for Graduate Students and Adult Learners, 413-782-1410, Fax: 413-782-1777, E-mail: study@wne.edu.

GRADUATE UNITS

College of Arts and Sciences Students: 221 part-time (172 women); includes 29 minority (7 Black or African American, non-Hispanic/Latino; 1 American Indian or Alaska Native, non-Hispanic/Latino; 12 Asian, non-Hispanic/Latino; 8 Hispanic/Latino; 1 Two or more races, non-Hispanic/Latino), 13 international. Average age 28. 137 applicants, 69% accepted, 77 enrolled. *Faculty:* 117 full-time (56 women). Expenses: Contact institution. *Financial support:* In 2017–18, 6 fellowships with tuition reimbursements were awarded. Support available to part-time students. Financial award application deadline: 4/15; financial award applicants required to submit FAFSA. In 2017, 68 master's, 4 doctorates awarded. *Program availability:* Part-time-only, evening/weekend, online learning. Offers applied behavior analysis (MS); arts and sciences (M Ed, MA, MAET, MAMT, MFA, MS, PhD); behavior analysis (PhD); creative writing (MFA); curriculum and instruction (M Ed); English for teachers (MAET); mathematics for teachers (MAMT); public relations (MA). *Application fee:* $30. Electronic applications accepted. *Application Contact:* Matthew Fox, Director of Admissions for Graduate Students and Adult Learners, 413-782-1410, Fax: 413-782-1777, E-mail: study@wne.edu. *Dean,* Dr. Saeed Ghahramani, 413-782-1218, Fax: 413-796-2118, E-mail: sghahram@wne.edu.

College of Business Students: 128 part-time (60 women); includes 10 minority (3 Black or African American, non-Hispanic/Latino; 4 Asian, non-Hispanic/Latino; 2 Hispanic/Latino; 1 Two or more races, non-Hispanic/Latino), 1 international. Average age 30. 123 applicants, 75% accepted, 82 enrolled. *Faculty:* 35 full-time (12 women). Expenses: Contact institution. *Financial support:* Application deadline: 4/15; applicants required to submit FAFSA. In 2017, 72 master's awarded. *Program availability:* Part-time, evening/weekend, online learning. Offers accounting (MSA); business (MBA, MS, MSA); general business (MBA); organizational leadership (MS); sport leadership and coaching (MS); sport management (MBA). *Application deadline:* Applications are processed on a rolling basis. *Application fee:* $30. Electronic applications accepted. *Application Contact:* Matthew Fox, Director of Admissions for Graduate Students and Adult Learners, 413-782-1410, Fax: 413-782-1777, E-mail: study@wne.edu. *Dean,* Dr. Rob Kleine, 413-782-1395, Fax: 413-796-2068, E-mail: rob.kleine@wne.edu.

College of Engineering Students: 109 part-time (15 women); includes 12 minority (3 Black or African American, non-Hispanic/Latino; 3 Asian, non-Hispanic/Latino; 6 Hispanic/Latino), 49 international. Average age 28. 526 applicants, 58% accepted, 72 enrolled. *Faculty:* 35 full-time (5 women). Expenses: Contact institution. *Financial support:* In 2017–18, 6 fellowships with tuition reimbursements were awarded. Financial award application deadline: 4/15; financial award applicants required to submit FAFSA. In 2017, 61 master's, 2 doctorates awarded. *Program availability:* Part-time, evening/weekend, online learning. Offers business and engineering information systems (MSEM); civil engineering (MS); electrical engineering (MSEE); engineering (MS, MSEE, MSEM, MSME, PhD); engineering management (MSEM, PhD); general engineering management (MSEM); industrial engineering (MS); mechanical engineering (MSME); mechatronics (MSEE, MSME); production and manufacturing systems (MSEM); quality engineering (MSEM). *Application deadline:* For fall admission, 1/15 priority date for domestic students. Applications are processed on a rolling basis. *Application fee:* $30. Electronic applications accepted. *Application Contact:* Matthew Fox, Director of Admissions for Graduate Students and Adult Learners, 413-782-1410, Fax: 413-782-1777, E-mail: study@wne.edu. *Dean,* Dr. S. Hossein Cheraghi, 413-782-1285, Fax: 413-796-2116, E-mail: cheraghi@wne.edu.

College of Pharmacy and Health Sciences Students: 301 full-time (199 women); includes 60 minority (20 Black or African American, non-Hispanic/Latino; 1 American Indian or Alaska Native, non-Hispanic/Latino; 23 Asian, non-Hispanic/Latino; 16 Hispanic/Latino), 2 international. Average age 24. 335 applicants, 43% accepted, 91 enrolled. *Faculty:* 33 full-time (17 women), 3 part-time/adjunct (1 woman). Expenses: Contact institution. *Financial support:* Scholarships/grants and unspecified assistantships available. Financial award application deadline: 4/15; financial award applicants required to submit FAFSA. In 2017, 71 doctorates awarded. Offers occupational therapy (OTD); pharmacy (Pharm D); pharmacy and health sciences (OTD, Pharm D). *Application deadline:* Applications are processed on a rolling basis. Electronic applications accepted. *Application Contact:* Lori Berg, Assistant Director of Pharmacy Admissions, 413-796-2073, Fax: 413-796-2266, E-mail: rxadmissions@wne.edu. *Dean,* Dr. Evan T. Robinson, 413-796-2323, E-mail: erobinson@wne.edu.

School of Law Students: 171 full-time (96 women), 110 part-time (65 women); includes 78 minority (35 Black or African American, non-Hispanic/Latino; 2 American Indian or Alaska Native, non-Hispanic/Latino; 16 Asian, non-Hispanic/Latino; 25 Hispanic/Latino). Average age 30. 606 applicants, 58% accepted, 100 enrolled. *Faculty:* 24 full-time (13 women), 25 part-time/adjunct (8 women). Expenses: Contact institution. *Financial support:* Career-related internships or fieldwork, Federal Work-Study, and scholarships/grants available. Support available to part-time students. Financial award application deadline: 4/15; financial award applicants required to submit FAFSA. In 2017, 21 master's, 101 doctorates awarded. *Program availability:* Part-time, evening/weekend. Offers estate planning and elder law (LL M, MS); law (MS, JD).

Application deadline: For fall admission, 3/15 priority date for domestic students. Applications are processed on a rolling basis. *Application fee:* $0. Electronic applications accepted. *Application Contact:* Anthony Orlando, Director of Law Admissions, 413-782-1281, Fax: 413-796-2067, E-mail: admissions@law.wne.edu. *Dean/Professor*, Eric Gouvin, 413-796-2031, E-mail: eric.gouvin@law.wne.edu.

See Display below and Close-Up on page 885.

WESTERN NEW MEXICO UNIVERSITY, Silver City, NM 88062-0680

General Information State-supported, coed, comprehensive institution. *Graduate housing:* Rooms and/or apartments available on a first-come, first-served basis to single and married students. Housing application deadline: 6/30.

GRADUATE UNITS

Graduate Division *Program availability:* Part-time, evening/weekend, online learning. Offers interdisciplinary studies (MA); occupational therapy (MOT); social work (MSW). Electronic applications accepted.

School of Business *Program availability:* Part-time, online learning. Offers business administration (MBA). Electronic applications accepted.

School of Education *Program availability:* Part-time, online learning. Offers bilingual education (MAT); educational leadership (MA); elementary education (MAT); reading (MAT); secondary education (MAT); special education (MAT); TESOL (teaching English to speakers of other languages) (MAT). Electronic applications accepted.

WESTERN OREGON UNIVERSITY, Monmouth, OR 97361

General Information State-supported, coed, comprehensive institution. *Graduate housing:* Room and/or apartments available on a first-come, first-served basis to single students; on-campus housing not available to married students. *Research affiliation:* Teaching Research Institute (education).

GRADUATE UNITS

Graduate Programs *Program availability:* Part-time, evening/weekend, online learning.

College of Education *Program availability:* Part-time, evening/weekend, online learning. Offers bilingual education (MS Ed); deaf education (MS Ed); early childhood special education (MS Ed); education (MAT, MS, MS Ed); health (MS Ed); humanities (MAT, MS Ed); information technology (MS Ed); initial licensure (MAT); mathematics (MAT, MS Ed); rehabilitation counseling (MS); science (MAT, MS Ed); secondary education (MAT, MS Ed); social science (MAT, MS Ed); special education (MS, MS Ed).

College of Liberal Arts and Sciences *Program availability:* Part-time, evening/weekend. Offers contemporary music (MM); criminal justice (MA, MS); liberal arts and sciences (MA, MM, MS).

WESTERN SEMINARY, Portland, OR 97215-3367

General Information Independent-religious, coed, graduate-only institution. *Graduate housing:* On-campus housing not available.

GRADUATE UNITS

Graduate Programs *Program availability:* Part-time, evening/weekend, online learning. Offers biblical and theological studies (MA, G Dip); biblical studies (Certificate); chaplaincy (MA); coaching (MA); counseling (MA, Certificate); divinity (M Div); intercultural studies (MA, D Miss, Certificate, G Dip); Jewish ministry (MA); pastoral care to women (MA); pastoral counseling (M Div); theology (Th M); youth ministry (MA).

WESTERN SEMINARY–SACRAMENTO CAMPUS, Rocklin, CA 95765

General Information Independent-religious, coed, graduate-only institution.

GRADUATE UNITS

Graduate Certificate Programs *Program availability:* Online learning. Offers Bible (Graduate Certificate); coaching (Graduate Certificate); pastoral care to women (Graduate Certificate); theology (Graduate Certificate); youth and family (Graduate Certificate).

Graduate Diploma Programs Offers Bible and theology (Graduate Diploma); ministry (Graduate Diploma); pastoral care to women (Graduate Diploma).

Master of Divinity Program Offers divinity (M Div).

Program in Biblical and Theological Studies Offers biblical and theological studies (MA).

Program in Marital and Family Therapy Offers marital and family therapy (MA).

Program in Ministry and Leadership Offers ministry and leadership (MA).

WESTERN SEMINARY–SAN JOSE CAMPUS, Milpitas, CA 95035

General Information Independent-religious, coed, graduate-only institution. *Graduate housing:* On-campus housing not available.

GRADUATE UNITS

Graduate Programs *Program availability:* Part-time, evening/weekend, online learning. Offers Bible and theology (Graduate Diploma); Bible, camp and conference ministry (CGS); Biblical and theological studies (MA); coaching (CGS); expositional ministry (M Div); marital and family therapy (MA); ministry (Graduate Diploma); ministry and leadership (MA); pastoral care to women (CGS, Graduate Diploma); pastoral ministry (M Div); theology (CGS); youth and family (CGS). Electronic applications accepted.

WESTERN STATE COLLEGE OF LAW AT ARGOSY UNIVERSITY, Irvine, CA 92618-3601

General Information Proprietary, coed, graduate-only institution. *Graduate housing:* On-campus housing not available.

GRADUATE UNITS

Professional Program *Program availability:* Part-time, evening/weekend. Offers law (JD). Electronic applications accepted.

WESTERN STATE COLORADO UNIVERSITY, Gunnison, CO 81231

General Information State-supported, coed, comprehensive institution.

GRADUATE UNITS

Graduate Programs in Education *Program availability:* Online learning. Offers education administrator leadership (MA); reading leadership (MA); teacher leadership (MA).

Program in Creative Writing *Program availability:* Online learning. Offers mainstream genre fiction (MFA); poetry (MFA); screenwriting (MFA).

Program in Environmental Management *Program availability:* Online learning. Offers integrative land management (MEM); sustainable and resilient communities (MEM).

WESTERN THEOLOGICAL SEMINARY, Holland, MI 49423-3622

General Information Independent-religious, coed, graduate-only institution. *Graduate housing:* Rooms and/or apartments available on a first-come, first-served basis to single and married students. Housing application deadline: 5/1.

GRADUATE UNITS

Graduate and Professional Programs *Program availability:* Part-time, 100% online, blended/hybrid learning. Offers divinity (M Div); ministry (D Min); theology (M Th, MA); urban pastoral ministry (Graduate Certificate). Electronic applications accepted.

WESTERN UNIVERSITY OF HEALTH SCIENCES, Pomona, CA 91766-1854

General Information Independent, coed, graduate-only institution. *Enrollment by degree level:* 588 master's, 3,260 doctoral. *Graduate faculty:* 306 full-time (152 women), 73 part-time/adjunct (38 women). Tuition and fees vary according to course load, degree level, program and student level. *Graduate housing:* Rooms and/or apartments available on a first-come, first-served basis to single and married students. Typical cost: $1029 per year for single students; $1029 per year for married students. Room charges vary according to campus/location and housing facility selected. *Student services:* Campus employment opportunities, campus safety program, career counseling, exercise/wellness program, free psychological counseling, grant writing training, international student services, low-cost health insurance, services for students with disabilities, teacher training. *Library facilities:* Pumerantz Library plus 1 other. *Collection:* Books: 30,932 (physical), 1,942 (digital/electronic); Serial titles: 774 (physical), 32,904 (digital/electronic); Databases: 75. Weekly public service hours: 91; students can reserve study rooms. *Research affiliation:* Fulgent (biomedical research), Neuralstem (biomedical research), Kaiser Permanente (biomedical research), Novo Nordisk (biomedical research), Zeavision LLC (biomedical research), Aspire Biomet, Inc (cancer research).

Computer facilities: 56 computers available on campus for general student use. A campuswide network can be accessed. Online class registration is available.
Website: http://www.westernu.edu/

General Application Contact: Admissions Office, 909-469-5335, Fax: 909-469-5570, E-mail: admissions@westernu.edu.

GRADUATE UNITS

College of Allied Health Professions Students: 361 full-time (233 women), 37 part-time (20 women); includes 229 minority (27 Black or African American, non-Hispanic/Latino; 1 American Indian or Alaska Native, non-Hispanic/Latino; 72 Asian, non-Hispanic/Latino; 91 Hispanic/Latino; 2 Native Hawaiian or other Pacific Islander, non-Hispanic/Latino; 36 Two or more races, non-Hispanic/Latino), 3 international. Average age 28. 2,755 applicants, 8% accepted, 144 enrolled. *Faculty:* 29 full-time (22 women), 1 part-time/adjunct (0 women). Expenses: Contact institution. *Financial support:* Scholarships/grants available. Financial award application deadline: 3/2; financial award applicants required to submit FAFSA. In 2017, 96 master's, 73 doctorates awarded. Offers allied health professions (MS, DPT); health sciences (MS); physical therapy (DPT); physician assistant studies (MS). *Application deadline:* For fall admission, 11/1 for domestic and international students. Applications are processed on a rolling basis. *Application fee:* $60. Electronic applications accepted. *Application Contact:* Karen Hutton-Lopez, Director of Admissions, 909-469-5650, Fax: 909-469-5570, E-mail: admissions@westernu.edu. *Dean*, Dr. Stephanie Bowlin, 909-469-5390, Fax: 909-469-5438, E-mail: sbowlin@westernu.edu.

College of Dental Medicine Students: 274 full-time (138 women); includes 174 minority (7 Black or African American, non-Hispanic/Latino; 2 American Indian or Alaska Native, non-Hispanic/Latino; 103 Asian, non-Hispanic/Latino; 42 Hispanic/Latino; 20 Two or more races, non-Hispanic/Latino), 4 international. Average age 28. 2,559 applicants, 7% accepted, 67 enrolled. *Faculty:* 39 full-time (18 women), 18 part-time/adjunct (7 women). Expenses: Contact institution. *Financial support:* In 2017–18, 19 students received support. Scholarships/grants available. Financial award application deadline: 3/2; financial award applicants required to submit FAFSA. In 2017, 67 doctorates awarded. Offers dental medicine (DMD). *Application deadline:* For fall admission, 12/1 for domestic and international students. Applications are processed on a rolling basis. *Application fee:* $60. Electronic applications accepted. *Application Contact:* Marie Anderson, Director of Admissions, 909-469-5335, Fax: 909-469-5570, E-mail: admissions@westernu.edu. *Dean*, Dr. Steven Friedrichsen, 909-706-3911, E-mail: sfriedrichsen@westernu.edu.

College of Graduate Nursing Students: 294 full-time (243 women), 40 part-time (39 women); includes 223 minority (13 Black or African American, non-Hispanic/Latino; 1 American Indian or Alaska Native, non-Hispanic/Latino; 100 Asian, non-Hispanic/Latino; 77 Hispanic/Latino; 1 Native Hawaiian or other Pacific Islander, non-Hispanic/Latino; 31 Two or more races, non-Hispanic/Latino), 3 international. Average age 33. 470 applicants, 42% accepted, 142 enrolled. *Faculty:* 20 full-time (17 women), 22 part-time/adjunct (15 women). Expenses: Contact institution. *Financial support:* In 2017–18, 43 students received support. Fellowships, research assistantships, teaching assistantships, and scholarships/grants available. Support available to part-time students. Financial award application deadline: 3/2; financial award applicants required to submit FAFSA. In 2017, 87 master's, 10 doctorates awarded. *Program availability:* Part-time, evening/weekend, blended/hybrid learning. Offers administrative nurse leader (MSN); clinical nurse leader (MSN); nursing (MSN, DNP); nursing practice (DNP). *Application fee:* $60. Electronic applications accepted. *Application Contact:* Kathryn Ford, Director of Admissions/International Student Advisor, 909-469-5335, Fax: 909-469-5570, E-mail: admissions@westernu.edu. *Dean*, Dr. Mary Lopez, 909-706-3860, Fax: 909-469-5521, E-mail: mlopez@westernu.edu.

College of Optometry Students: 320 full-time (233 women); includes 198 minority (9 Black or African American, non-Hispanic/Latino; 1 American Indian or Alaska Native, non-Hispanic/Latino; 113 Asian, non-Hispanic/Latino; 37 Hispanic/Latino; 2 Native Hawaiian or other Pacific Islander, non-Hispanic/Latino; 36 Two or more races, non-Hispanic/Latino), 18 international. Average age 27. 477 applicants, 32% accepted, 65 enrolled. *Faculty:* 31 full-time (15 women), 5 part-time/adjunct (3 women). Expenses: Contact institution. *Financial support:* In 2017–18, 37 students received support. Career-related internships or fieldwork, scholarships/grants, and traineeships available. Financial award application deadline: 3/2; financial award applicants required to submit FAFSA. In 2017, 85 doctorates awarded. Offers optometry (OD). *Application deadline:* For fall admission, 5/1 for domestic and international students. Applications are processed on a rolling basis. *Application fee:* $65. Electronic applications accepted. *Application Contact:* Marie Anderson, Director of Admissions, 909-469-5335, Fax: 909-469-5570, E-mail: admissions@westernu.edu. *Dean*, Dr. Elizabeth Hoppe, 909-706-3497, E-mail: ehoppe@westernu.edu.

College of Osteopathic Medicine of the Pacific Students: 1,349 full-time (636 women); includes 629 minority (14 Black or African American, non-Hispanic/Latino; 1 American Indian or Alaska Native, non-Hispanic/Latino; 405 Asian, non-Hispanic/Latino; 94 Hispanic/Latino; 3 Native Hawaiian or other Pacific Islander, non-Hispanic/Latino; 112 Two or more races, non-Hispanic/Latino), 13 international. Average age 27. 5,109 applicants, 13% accepted, 328 enrolled. *Faculty:* 72 full-time (32 women), 16 part-time/adjunct (5 women). Expenses: Contact institution. *Financial support:* In 2017–18, 216 students received support. Scholarships/grants and unspecified assistantships available. Financial award application deadline: 3/2; financial award applicants required to submit FAFSA. In 2017, 309 doctorates awarded. Offers osteopathic medicine (DO). *Application deadline:* For fall admission, 2/15 for domestic and international students. Applications are processed on a rolling basis. *Application fee:* $65. Electronic applications accepted. *Application Contact:* Susan Hanson, Director of Admissions, 909-469-5335, Fax: 909-469-5570, E-mail: admissions@westernu.edu. *Dean*, Dr. Paula Crone, 541-259-0206, Fax: 541-259-0201, E-mail: pcrone@westernu.edu.

College of Pharmacy Students: 545 full-time (357 women), 5 part-time (1 woman); includes 386 minority (20 Black or African American, non-Hispanic/Latino; 1 American Indian or Alaska Native, non-Hispanic/Latino; 285 Asian, non-Hispanic/Latino; 41 Hispanic/Latino; 39 Two or more races, non-Hispanic/Latino), 18 international. Average age 27. 905 applicants, 37% accepted, 143 enrolled. *Faculty:* 39 full-time (17 women), 3 part-time/adjunct (1 woman). Expenses: Contact institution. *Financial support:* In 2017–18, 56 students received support. Scholarships/grants available. Financial award application deadline: 3/2; financial award applicants required to submit FAFSA. In 2017, 8 master's, 124 doctorates awarded. Offers pharmaceutical sciences (MS); pharmacy (MS, Pharm D). *Application deadline:* For fall admission, 11/1 for domestic and international students. *Application fee:* $65. Electronic applications accepted. *Application Contact:* Kathryn Ford, Director of Admissions, 909-469-5335, Fax: 909-469-5570, E-mail: admissions@westernu.edu. *Dean*, Dr. Daniel Robinson, 909-469-5533, Fax: 909-469-5539, E-mail: drobinson@westernu.edu.

College of Podiatric Medicine Students: 147 full-time (51 women); includes 76 minority (4 Black or African American, non-Hispanic/Latino; 48 Asian, non-Hispanic/Latino; 12 Hispanic/Latino; 12 Two or more races, non-Hispanic/Latino), 2 international. Average age 27. 368 applicants, 28% accepted, 27 enrolled. *Faculty:* 10 full-time (5 women), 6 part-time/adjunct (1 woman). Expenses: Contact institution. *Financial support:* In 2017–18, 40 students received support. Scholarships/grants available. Financial award application deadline: 3/2; financial award applicants required to submit FAFSA. In 2017, 35 doctorates awarded. Offers podiatric medicine (DPM). *Application deadline:* For fall admission, 6/30 for domestic and international students. Applications are processed on a rolling basis. *Application fee:* $0. Electronic applications accepted. *Application Contact:* Marie Anderson, Director of Admissions, 909-469-5335, Fax: 909-469-5570, E-mail: admissions@westernu.edu. *Dean*, Dr. Lawrence B. Harkless, 909-706-3933, E-mail: lharkless@westernu.edu.

College of Veterinary Medicine Students: 420 full-time (330 women); includes 204 minority (13 Black or African American, non-Hispanic/Latino; 60 Asian, non-Hispanic/Latino; 89 Hispanic/Latino; 1 Native Hawaiian or other Pacific Islander, non-Hispanic/Latino; 41 Two or more races, non-Hispanic/Latino), 6 international. Average age 27. 725 applicants, 37% accepted, 95 enrolled. *Faculty:* 53 full-time (25 women), 4 part-time/adjunct (1 woman). Expenses: Contact institution. *Financial support:* In 2017–18, 39 students received support. Institutionally sponsored loans, scholarships/grants, and veterans' educational benefits available. Financial award application deadline: 3/2; financial award applicants required to submit FAFSA. In 2017, 105 doctorates awarded. Offers veterinary medicine (DVM). *Application deadline:* For fall admission, 9/15 for domestic and international students. Applications are processed on a rolling basis. *Application fee:* $50. Electronic applications accepted. *Application Contact:* Karen Hutton-Lopez, Director of Admissions, 909-469-5650, Fax: 909-469-5570, E-mail: admissions@westernu.edu. *Dean*, Dr. Phil Nelson, 909-469-5661, Fax: 909-469-5635, E-mail: pnelson@westernu.edu.

Graduate College of Biomedical Sciences Students: 55 full-time (29 women), 1 part-time (0 women); includes 46 minority (8 Black or African American, non-Hispanic/Latino; 2 American Indian or Alaska Native, non-Hispanic/Latino; 16 Asian, non-Hispanic/Latino; 13 Hispanic/Latino; 7 Two or more races, non-Hispanic/Latino), 1 international. Average age 27. 318 applicants, 17% accepted, 48 enrolled. *Faculty:* 7 full-time (1 woman), 2 part-time/adjunct (1 woman). Expenses: Contact institution. *Financial support:* Scholarships/grants available. Financial award application deadline: 3/2; financial award applicants required to submit FAFSA. In 2017, 28 master's awarded. Offers biomedical sciences (MS); medical sciences (MS). *Application deadline:* Applications are processed on a rolling basis. *Application fee:* $50. Electronic applications accepted. *Application Contact:* Kathryn Ford, Director of Admissions/International Student Advisor, 909-469-5335, Fax: 909-469-5570, E-mail: kford@westernu.edu. *Dean*, Dr. Michel Baudry, 909-469-8271, E-mail: mbaudry@westernu.edu.

WESTERN WASHINGTON UNIVERSITY, Bellingham, WA 98225-5996

General Information State-supported, coed, comprehensive institution. CGS member. *Graduate housing:* Rooms and/or apartments available on a first-come, first-served basis to single and married students. Housing application deadline: 5/1. *Research affiliation:* Teck Cominco Ltd., Research Corporation, Dreyfus Foundation, Golden Associates, American Metals Technology, NARSAD (mental health).

GRADUATE UNITS

Graduate School *Program availability:* Part-time. Electronic applications accepted.

College of Business and Economics *Program availability:* Part-time, evening/weekend. Offers business and economics (MBA, MP Acc). Electronic applications accepted.

College of Fine and Performing Arts *Program availability:* Part-time. Offers fine and performing arts (M Mus, MA); music (M Mus). Electronic applications accepted.

College of Humanities and Social Sciences *Program availability:* Part-time. Offers anthropology (MA); communication sciences and disorders (MA); English (MA); exercise science (MS); experimental psychology (MS); history (MA); humanities and social sciences (M Ed, MA, MS); mental health counseling (MS); political science (MA); school counseling (M Ed); sport psychology (MS). Electronic applications accepted.

College of Sciences and Technology Offers biology (MS); chemistry (MS); computer science (MS); geology (MS); mathematics (MS); natural science/science education (M Ed); sciences and technology (M Ed, MS). Electronic applications accepted.

Huxley College of the Environment *Program availability:* Part-time. Offers environment (M Ed, MS); environmental education (M Ed); environmental science (MS); geography (MS); marine and estuarine science (MS). Electronic applications accepted.

Woodring College of Education *Program availability:* Part-time, online learning. Offers continuing and college education (M Ed); education (M Ed, MA, MIT); educational administration (M Ed); elementary education (M Ed); rehabilitation counseling (MA); secondary education (MIT); special education (M Ed); student affairs administration (M Ed). Electronic applications accepted.

WESTFIELD STATE UNIVERSITY, Westfield, MA 01086

General Information State-supported, coed, comprehensive institution. *Enrollment:* 6,237 graduate, professional, and undergraduate students; 266 full-time matriculated graduate/professional students (200 women), 292 part-time matriculated graduate/professional students (197 women). *Enrollment by degree level:* 558 master's. *Graduate faculty:* 49 full-time (22 women), 46 part-time/adjunct (32 women). Tuition, state resident: part-time $332 per credit. Tuition, nonresident: part-time $332 per credit. *Required fees:* $75 per semester. Tuition and fees vary according to program. *Graduate housing:* On-campus housing not available. *Student services:* Campus employment opportunities, career counseling, exercise/wellness program, free psychological counseling, international student services, low-cost health insurance, multicultural affairs office, services for students with disabilities, teacher training. *Library facilities:* Governor Joseph B. Ely Library. *Collection:* Books: 129,289 (physical), 160,388 (digital/electronic); Serial titles: 5,137 (physical), 25,808 (digital/electronic); Databases: 138. Weekly public service hours: 92; students can reserve study rooms.

Computer facilities: 814 computers available on campus for general student use. A campuswide network can be accessed from student residence rooms and from off campus. Online class registration, online transcripts and billing information, Web portal are available.
Website: http://www.westfield.ma.edu/

General Application Contact: Shelly Henrichon, Coordinator of College of Graduate and Continuing Education Admissions, 413-572-8022, Fax: 413-572-5227, E-mail: mhenrichon@westfield.ma.edu.

GRADUATE UNITS

College of Graduate and Continuing Education Students: 266 full-time (200 women), 292 part-time (197 women); includes 105 minority (23 Black or African American, non-Hispanic/Latino; 3 American Indian or Alaska Native, non-Hispanic/Latino; 9 Asian, non-Hispanic/Latino; 59 Hispanic/Latino; 11 Two or more races, non-Hispanic/Latino), 2 international. Average age 31. 309 applicants, 76% accepted, 179 enrolled. *Faculty:* 49 full-time (22 women), 46 part-time/adjunct (32 women). Expenses: Contact institution. *Financial support:* In 2017–18, 16 students received support. Unspecified assistantships and SOS scholarships (for education majors only) available. Financial award application deadline: 3/1; financial award applicants required to submit FAFSA. In 2017, 189 master's awarded. *Program availability:* Part-time, evening/weekend. Offers accounting (MS); applied behavior analysis (MA); biology teacher education (M Ed); counseling (MA); criminal justice (MS); criminal justice administration (MPA); early childhood education (M Ed); elementary education (M Ed); English (MA); forensic mental health counseling (MA); history teacher education (M Ed); mathematics teacher education (M Ed); mental health counseling (MA); moderate disabilities, 5-12 (M Ed); moderate disabilities, preK-8 (M Ed); non-profit management (MPA); physical education teacher education (M Ed); physician assistant studies (MS); public management (MPA); reading specialist (M Ed); school adjustment counseling (MA); school guidance counseling (MA); secondary education (M Ed); secondary education-biology (M Ed); secondary education-history (M Ed); secondary education-mathematics (M Ed); secondary education-physical education (M Ed); social work (MSW); special education (M Ed); vocational technical education (M Ed). *Application deadline:* For fall admission, 7/1 for domestic students; for spring admission, 11/1 for domestic students; for summer admission, 4/1 for domestic students. Applications are processed on a rolling basis. *Application fee:* $50. *Application Contact:* Shelly Henrichon, Coordinator of College of Graduate and Continuing Education Admissions, 413-572-8022, Fax: 413-572-5227, E-mail: mhenrichon@westfield.ma.edu. *Interim Dean of Graduate and Continuing Education*, Dr. Shelley Tinkham, 413-572-8030, Fax: 413-572-5227, E-mail: shelleytinkham@westfield.ma.edu.

WEST LIBERTY UNIVERSITY, West Liberty, WV 26074

General Information State-supported, coed, comprehensive institution. *Enrollment:* 103 full-time matriculated graduate/professional students (67 women), 169 part-time matriculated graduate/professional students (109 women). *Enrollment by degree level:* 272 master's. *Graduate faculty:* 21 full-time (9 women), 18 part-time/adjunct (7 women). Tuition and fees vary according to course load and program. *Graduate housing:* Room and/or apartments available on a first-come, first-served basis to single students; on-campus housing not available to married students. *Student services:* Campus employment opportunities, campus safety program, career counseling, exercise/wellness program, free psychological counseling, grant writing training, international student services, services for students with disabilities, writing training. *Library facilities:* Paul N. Elbin Library.

Computer facilities: Computer purchase and lease plans are available. A campuswide network can be accessed from student residence rooms and from off campus. Online class registration is available.
Website: http://www.westliberty.edu/

General Application Contact: Sara Sweeney, Director of Graduate Studies, 304-336-8545, E-mail: sara.sweeney@westliberty.edu.

GRADUATE UNITS

College of Education and Human Performance Students: 18 full-time (12 women), 74 part-time (60 women); includes 2 minority (1 Black or African American, non-Hispanic/Latino; 1 Native Hawaiian or other Pacific Islander, non-Hispanic/Latino). Average age 32. Expenses: Contact institution. *Financial support:* Teaching assistantships and unspecified assistantships available. *Program availability:* Part-time, evening/weekend. Offers community education research and leadership (MA Ed); innovative instruction (MA Ed); leadership in disability services (MA Ed); leadership studies (MA Ed); multi-categorical special education (MA Ed); reading specialist (MA Ed); sports leadership and coaching (MA Ed). *Application deadline:* Applications are processed on a rolling basis. *Application fee:* $0. Electronic applications accepted. *Application Contact:* Sara Sweeney, Director, Office of Graduate Studies, 304-336-8545, E-mail: sara.sweeney@westliberty.edu. *Interim Dean*, Dr. Catherine Monteroso, 304-336-8247, E-mail: cmonteroso@westliberty.edu.

College of Sciences Expenses: Contact institution. Offers biology (MA, MS); biomedical science (MA); physician assistant studies (MS); zoo science (MA, MS). *Application Contact:* Sara Sweeney, Director, Office of Graduate Studies, 304-336-8545, E-mail: sara.sweeney@westliberty.edu. *Interim Dean*, Dr. Karen Kettler, E-mail: kkettler@westliberty.edu.

School of Professional Studies Expenses: Contact institution. Offers organizational leadership (MPS). *Application deadline:* Applications are processed on a rolling basis. *Dean*, Dr. Thomas Michaud, 304-217-2800, E-mail: tmichaud@westliberty.edu.

WESTMINSTER COLLEGE, New Wilmington, PA 16172-0001

General Information Independent-religious, coed, comprehensive institution. *Enrollment:* 1,254 graduate, professional, and undergraduate students; 100 part-time matriculated graduate/professional students (57 women). *Enrollment by degree level:* 100 master's. *Graduate faculty:* 5 full-time (3 women), 16 part-time/adjunct (9 women). *Tuition:* Part-time $454 per semester hour. *Required fees:* $235.50 per course. Tuition and fees vary according to course load. *Graduate housing:* On-campus housing not available. *Student services:* Campus safety program, career counseling, multicultural affairs office, services for students with disabilities. *Library facilities:* McGill Memorial Library plus 1 other. *Collection:* Books: 160,296 (physical), 771,138 (digital/electronic); Serial titles: 89 (physical), 30,100 (digital/electronic); Databases: 70. Weekly public service hours: 104; students can reserve study rooms.

Computer facilities: Computer purchase and lease plans are available. 144 computers available on campus for general student use. A campuswide network can be accessed from student residence rooms and from off campus. Online class registration is available.
Website: http://www.westminster.edu/

General Application Contact: Dr. Robert L. Zorn, Graduate Director, 724-946-7031, Fax: 724-946-6351, E-mail: rornrl@westminster.edu.

GRADUATE UNITS

Graduate School Expenses: Contact institution. *Financial support:* Career-related internships or fieldwork and scholarships/grants available. *Program availability:* Part-time, evening/weekend. Offers clinical mental health counseling (MA); school counselor (M Ed); school principal K-12 (M Ed); school superintendent (M Ed); special education and reading specialist (M Ed). *Application deadline:* For fall admission, 8/15 priority date for domestic students; for spring admission, 1/8 priority date for domestic students. Applications are processed on a rolling basis. *Application fee:* $35. *Application Contact:* Director, 724-946-7031, Fax: 724-946-6158. *Director*, 724-946-7031, Fax: 724-946-6158.

WESTMINSTER COLLEGE, Salt Lake City, UT 84105-3697

General Information Independent, coed, comprehensive institution. *Enrollment:* 2,570 graduate, professional, and undergraduate students; 331 full-time matriculated graduate/professional students (197 women), 209 part-time matriculated graduate/professional students (113 women). *Enrollment by degree level:* 537 master's, 3 other advanced degrees. *Graduate faculty:* 51 full-time (29 women), 49 part-time/adjunct (24 women). *Graduate housing:* Room and/or apartments available on a first-come, first-served basis to single students; on-campus housing not available to married students. Typical cost: $5364 per year ($9244 including board). Room and board charges vary according to board plan, campus/location and housing facility selected. *Student services:* Campus employment opportunities, campus safety program, career counseling, exercise/wellness program, free psychological counseling, grant writing training, international student services, low-cost health insurance, multicultural affairs office, services for students with disabilities, teacher training, writing training. *Library facilities:* Giovale Library plus 1 other. *Collection:* Books: 95,039 (physical), 364,687 (digital/electronic); Databases: 56. Students can reserve study rooms. *Research affiliation:* International Psychotherapy Institute (clinical training), Zions Bank (entrepreneurship).

Computer facilities: 200 computers available on campus for general student use. A campuswide network can be accessed. Online class registration is available.
Website: http://www.westminstercollege.edu/

General Application Contact: Ashley Williams, Director, Graduate and International Admissions, 801-832-2200, Fax: 801-832-3101, E-mail: admission@westminstercollege.edu.

GRADUATE UNITS

The Bill and Vieve Gore School of Business Students: 89 full-time (36 women), 130 part-time (46 women); includes 52 minority (9 Black or African American, non-Hispanic/Latino; 1 American Indian or Alaska Native, non-Hispanic/Latino; 17 Asian, non-Hispanic/Latino; 21 Hispanic/Latino; 1 Native Hawaiian or other Pacific Islander, non-Hispanic/Latino; 3 Two or more races, non-Hispanic/Latino), 13 international. Average age 34. 67 applicants, 84% accepted, 47 enrolled. *Faculty:* 20 full-time (6 women), 16 part-time/adjunct (6 women). Expenses: Contact institution. *Financial support:* In 2017–18, 58 students received support. Career-related internships or fieldwork, scholarships/grants, unspecified assistantships, and tuition remission available. Financial award applicants required to submit FAFSA. In 2017, 150 master's, 1 other advanced degree awarded. *Program availability:* Part-time, evening/weekend, blended/hybrid learning. Offers accountancy (M Acc); business administration (MBA, Certificate); technology commercialization (MBA). *Application deadline:* For fall admission, 5/1 priority date for domestic and international students; for spring admission, 10/1 priority date for domestic and international students; for summer admission, 2/1 priority date for domestic and international students. Applications are processed on a rolling basis. *Application fee:* $50. Electronic applications accepted. *Application Contact:* Ashley Williams, Director of Graduate and International Admissions, 801-832-2213, Fax: 801-832-3101, E-mail: awilliams@westminstercollege.edu. *Dean, Bill and Vieve Gore School of Business*, Melissa Koerner, 801-832-2600, Fax: 801-832-3106, E-mail: mkoerner@westminstercollege.edu.

Master of Science in Mental Health Counseling Program Students: 19 full-time (15 women), 11 part-time (8 women); includes 4 minority (1 Asian, non-Hispanic/Latino; 2 Hispanic/Latino; 1 Two or more races, non-Hispanic/Latino). Average age 32. 27 applicants, 63% accepted, 11 enrolled. *Faculty:* 3 full-time (all women), 3 part-time/adjunct (2 women). Expenses: Contact institution. *Financial support:* Career-related internships or fieldwork, scholarships/grants, unspecified assistantships, and tuition remission available. Financial award applicants required to submit FAFSA. In 2017, 9 master's awarded. Offers mental health counseling (MSMHC). *Application deadline:* For fall admission, 2/1 priority date for domestic and international students. Applications are processed on a rolling basis. *Application fee:* $50. Electronic applications accepted. *Application Contact:* Collin Bess, Enrollment Coordinator/Admissions Recruiter, 801-832-2207, Fax: 801-832-3101, E-mail: cbess@westminstercollege.edu. *Director*, Colleen Sandor, 801-832-2422, E-mail: csandor@westminstercollege.edu.

Program in Professional Communication Students: 29 full-time (19 women), 6 part-time (all women); includes 11 minority (2 Asian, non-Hispanic/Latino; 5 Hispanic/Latino; 4 Two or more races, non-Hispanic/Latino), 1 international. Average age 34. 18 applicants, 89% accepted, 15 enrolled. *Faculty:* 3 full-time (2 women), 2 part-time/adjunct (both women). Expenses: Contact institution. *Financial support:* In 2017–18, 13 students received support. Career-related internships or fieldwork, scholarships/grants, unspecified assistantships, and tuition remission available. Financial award applicants required to submit FAFSA. In 2017, 22 master's awarded. Offers professional communication (MPC, MSC). *Application deadline:* Applications are processed on a rolling basis. *Application fee:* $50. Electronic applications accepted. *Application Contact:* Lauren Erlacher, Associate Director, Graduate Admissions, 801-832-2208, Fax: 801-832-3101, E-mail: lerlacher@westminstercollege.edu. *Director*, Dr.

Curtis Newbold, 801-832-2827, Fax: 801-832-3102, E-mail: cnewbold@westminstercollege.edu.

School of Education Students: 57 full-time (44 women), 64 part-time (51 women); includes 30 minority (3 Black or African American, non-Hispanic/Latino; 1 American Indian or Alaska Native, non-Hispanic/Latino; 5 Asian, non-Hispanic/Latino; 18 Hispanic/Latino; 1 Native Hawaiian or other Pacific Islander, non-Hispanic/Latino; 2 Two or more races, non-Hispanic/Latino), 6 international. Average age 34. 56 applicants, 88% accepted, 34 enrolled. *Faculty:* 14 full-time (9 women), 23 part-time/adjunct (19 women). Expenses: Contact institution. *Financial support:* In 2017–18, 49 students received support. Career-related internships or fieldwork, scholarships/grants, unspecified assistantships, and tuition remission available. Financial award applicants required to submit FAFSA. In 2017, 61 master's awarded. *Program availability:* Part-time, evening/weekend. Offers community leadership (MACL); education (M Ed); teaching (MAT). *Application deadline:* For fall admission, 6/1 priority date for domestic and international students; for spring admission, 10/1 priority date for domestic and international students; for summer admission, 1/1 priority date for domestic and international students. Applications are processed on a rolling basis. *Application fee:* $50. Electronic applications accepted. *Application Contact:* Andrea Pischnotte, Admissions Counselor, 801-832-2220, Fax: 801-832-3101, E-mail: apischnotte@westminstercollege.edu. *Dean, School of Education*, Melanie Agnew, 801-832-2470, Fax: 801-832-3105.

School of Nursing and Health Sciences Students: 130 full-time (81 women), 1 (woman) part-time; includes 18 minority (2 Black or African American, non-Hispanic/Latino; 1 American Indian or Alaska Native, non-Hispanic/Latino; 5 Asian, non-Hispanic/Latino; 4 Hispanic/Latino; 2 Native Hawaiian or other Pacific Islander, non-Hispanic/Latino; 4 Two or more races, non-Hispanic/Latino), 3 international. Average age 33. 149 applicants, 51% accepted, 62 enrolled. *Faculty:* 9 full-time (5 women), 10 part-time/adjunct (5 women). Expenses: Contact institution. *Financial support:* In 2017–18, 7 students received support. Career-related internships or fieldwork, scholarships/grants, unspecified assistantships, and tuition remission available. Financial award applicants required to submit FAFSA. In 2017, 49 master's awarded. Offers family nurse practitioner (MSN); nurse anesthesia (MSNA); public health (MPH). *Application fee:* $50. Electronic applications accepted. *Application Contact:* Collin Bess, Enrollment Coordinator/Admissions Recruiter, 801-832-2207, Fax: 801-832-3101, E-mail: cbess@westminstercollege.edu. *Dean*, Dr. Sheryl Steadman, 801-832-2164, Fax: 801-832-3110, E-mail: ssteadman@westminstercollege.edu.

WESTMINSTER SEMINARY CALIFORNIA, Escondido, CA 92027-4128

General Information Independent-religious, coed, primarily men, graduate-only institution. *Graduate housing:* On-campus housing not available.

GRADUATE UNITS

Programs in Theology *Program availability:* Part-time, evening/weekend. Offers Biblical studies (MA); historical theology (MA); theological studies (M Div, MA).

WESTMINSTER THEOLOGICAL SEMINARY, Philadelphia, PA 19118

General Information Independent-religious, coed, primarily men, graduate-only institution. *Graduate housing:* Room and/or apartments available on a first-come, first-served basis to single students; on-campus housing not available to married students.

GRADUATE UNITS

Graduate and Professional Programs *Program availability:* Part-time. Offers apologetics (Th M); Biblical and urban studies (Certificate); Biblical counseling (MA); biblical studies (MAR); Christian studies (Certificate); church history (Th M); counseling (M Div); general studies (M Div, MAR); hermeneutics and Bible interpretations (PhD); historical and theological studies (PhD); historical theology (Th M); New Testament (Th M); Old Testament (Th M); pastoral counseling (D Min); pastoral ministry (M Div, D Min); systematic theology (Th M); theological studies (MAR); urban missions (M Div, MA, MAR, D Min).

WEST TEXAS A&M UNIVERSITY, Canyon, TX 79015

General Information State-supported, coed, comprehensive institution. CGS member. *Graduate housing:* Room and/or apartments available on a first-come, first-served basis to single students; on-campus housing not available to married students. *Research affiliation:* Owens Corning (sports exercise), Pantex (chemistry), Agriculture Experiment Station (agriculture), Engineering Experiment Station (math, science).

GRADUATE UNITS

College of Agriculture and Natural Sciences *Program availability:* Part-time. Offers agricultural business and economics (MS); agriculture (MS, PhD); agriculture and natural sciences (MS, PhD); animal science (MS); biology (MS); chemistry (MS); environmental science (MS); plant, soil and environmental science (MS). Electronic applications accepted.

College of Business *Program availability:* Part-time, evening/weekend, 100% online, blended/hybrid learning. Offers accounting (MPA); business (MBA, MPA, MS); business administration (MBA); finance and economics (MS). Electronic applications accepted.

College of Education and Social Sciences *Program availability:* Part-time, evening/weekend, online learning. Offers counseling (MA); criminal justice (MA); curriculum and instruction (M Ed); education and social sciences (M Ed, MA, MAT, MS); educational diagnostician (M Ed); educational leadership (M Ed); instructional design and technology (M Ed); psychology (MA); reading education (M Ed); school counseling (M Ed); social work (MS); teaching (MAT). Electronic applications accepted.

College of Fine Arts and Humanities *Program availability:* Part-time, evening/weekend. Offers communication (MA); English (MA); fine arts and humanities (MA, MFA, MM); history (MA); studio art (MFA). Electronic applications accepted.

School of Music *Program availability:* Part-time. Offers music (MA); performance (MM). Electronic applications accepted.

College of Nursing and Health Sciences *Program availability:* Part-time, evening/weekend. Offers communication disorders (MS); family nurse practitioner (MSN); nursing (MSN); nursing and health sciences (MS, MSN); sport management (MS); sports and exercise sciences (MS). Electronic applications accepted.

Program in Interdisciplinary Studies *Program availability:* Part-time, evening/weekend. Offers interdisciplinary studies (MA, MS). Electronic applications accepted.

School of Engineering, Computer Science and Mathematics *Program availability:* Part-time. Offers engineering technology (MS); mathematics (MS). Electronic applications accepted.

WEST VIRGINIA SCHOOL OF OSTEOPATHIC MEDICINE, Lewisburg, WV 24901-1196

General Information State-supported, coed, graduate-only institution. *Enrollment by degree level:* 849 doctoral. *Graduate faculty:* 61 full-time (33 women). Tuition, state resident: full-time $19,450. Tuition, nonresident: full-time $49,200. *Graduate housing:* On-campus housing not available. *Student services:* Campus employment opportunities, campus safety program, career counseling, exercise/wellness program, multicultural affairs office, services for students with disabilities. *Library facilities:* James R. Stookey Library. *Collection:* Books: 4,120 (physical), 1,270 (digital/electronic); Serial titles: 12 (physical), 3 (digital/electronic); Databases: 18. Weekly public service hours: 93; study areas open 24 hours, 5–7 days a week; students can reserve study rooms.

Computer facilities: 19 computers available on campus for general student use. A campuswide network can be accessed from off campus.
Website: http://www.wvsom.edu/

General Application Contact: Gwen Byrd, Director of Admissions, 304-647-6336, Fax: 304-647-6384, E-mail: gbyrd@osteo.wvsom.edu.

GRADUATE UNITS

Professional Program Students: 849 full-time (434 women); includes 217 minority (30 Black or African American, non-Hispanic/Latino; 1 American Indian or Alaska Native, non-Hispanic/Latino; 139 Asian, non-Hispanic/Latino; 32 Hispanic/Latino; 15 Native Hawaiian or other Pacific Islander, non-Hispanic/Latino). Average age 27. *Faculty:* 61 full-time (33 women). Expenses: Contact institution. *Financial support:* Teaching assistantships with full tuition reimbursements, Federal Work-Study, scholarships/grants, tuition waivers (full), and unspecified assistantships available. Financial award application deadline: 4/1; financial award applicants required to submit FAFSA. Offers osteopathic medicine (DO). *Application deadline:* For fall admission, 2/15 for domestic students. Applications are processed on a rolling basis. *Application fee:* $80. Electronic applications accepted. *Application Contact:* Gwen Byrd, Director of Admissions, 304-647-6336, Fax: 304-647-6384, E-mail: gbyrd@osteo.wvsom.edu. *President*, Dr. Michael D. Adelman, 304-645-6295, Fax: 304-645-4859, E-mail: madelman@osteo.wvsom.edu.

WEST VIRGINIA STATE UNIVERSITY, Institute, WV 25112-1000

General Information State-supported, coed, comprehensive institution. *Graduate housing:* Rooms and/or apartments available on a first-come, first-served basis to single and married students. Housing application deadline: 9/1.

GRADUATE UNITS

Biotechnology Graduate Program Offers biotechnology (MA, MS). Electronic applications accepted.

Master of Science Program in Law Enforcement and Administration Offers law enforcement and administration (MS). Electronic applications accepted.

Media Studies Graduate Program Offers media studies (MA). Electronic applications accepted.

WEST VIRGINIA UNIVERSITY, Morgantown, WV 26506

General Information State-supported, coed, university. CGS member. *Enrollment:* 28,410 graduate, professional, and undergraduate students; 4,442 full-time matriculated graduate/professional students (2,321 women), 1,463 part-time matriculated graduate/professional students (971 women). *Enrollment by degree level:* 3,144 master's, 2,761 doctoral. *Graduate faculty:* 355. Tuition, state resident: full-time $9450. Tuition, nonresident: full-time $24,390. *Graduate housing:* Rooms and/or apartments available on a first-come, first-served basis to single and married students. Housing application deadline: 1/22. *Student services:* Campus employment opportunities, campus safety program, career counseling, child daycare facilities, exercise/wellness program, free psychological counseling, grant writing training, international student services, low-cost health insurance, multicultural affairs office, services for students with disabilities, teacher training, writing training. *Library facilities:* Downtown Library Complex plus 5 others. *Collection:* Books: 1.1 million (physical), 621,166 (digital/electronic); Serial titles: 56,340 (physical), 96,553 (digital/electronic); Databases: 975. Study areas open 24 hours, 5–7 days a week; students can reserve study rooms. *Research affiliation:* National Energy Technology Laboratory (fossil energy and environmental research), Federal Bureau of Investigation (FBI) (biometrics research), NASA IV and V Center (software verification/validation), Research Partnership for an Energy Secure America (energy research), Florida Agricultural and Mechanical University (plasma physics), University of Pittsburgh/Carnegie Mellon University (energy research).

Computer facilities: Computer purchase and lease plans are available. 1,800 computers available on campus for general student use. A campuswide network can be accessed from student residence rooms and from off campus. Online class registration is available.
Website: http://www.wvu.edu/

General Application Contact: Dr. Tracey L. Sheetz, Director, Graduate Admissions, 304-293-7173, Fax: 304-293-8657, E-mail: graded@mail.wvu.edu.

GRADUATE UNITS

College of Business and Economics Students: 343 full-time (141 women), 43 part-time (12 women); includes 59 minority (22 Black or African American, non-Hispanic/Latino; 11 Asian, non-Hispanic/Latino; 12 Hispanic/Latino; 14 Two or more races, non-Hispanic/Latino), 54 international. Expenses: Contact institution. *Financial support:* Fellowships, research assistantships, teaching assistantships, career-related internships or fieldwork, Federal Work-Study, institutionally sponsored loans, scholarships/grants, health care benefits, tuition waivers (full and partial), unspecified assistantships, and administrative assistantships available. Financial award application deadline: 2/1; financial award applicants required to submit FAFSA. *Program availability:* Part-time, online learning. Offers accountancy (M Acc); accounting (PhD); business administration (MBA); business cyber security management (MS); business data analytics (MS); economics (MA, PhD); finance (MS, PhD); forensic and fraud examination (MS); industrial relations (MS); management (PhD); marketing (PhD). *Application deadline:* For fall admission, 10/15 priority date for domestic and international students; for spring admission, 3/1 priority date for domestic and international students. Applications are processed on a rolling basis. *Application fee:* $60. Electronic applications accepted. *Application Contact:* Dr. Mark Gavin, Associate Dean for Graduate Programs, 304-293-7952, Fax: 304-293-7188, E-mail: mark.gavin@mail.wvu.edu. *Dean*, Dr. Javier Reyes, 304-293-7800, Fax: 304-293-4056, E-mail: javier.reyes@mail.wvu.edu.

College of Creative Arts Students: 114 full-time (64 women), 39 part-time (21 women); includes 19 minority (11 Black or African American, non-Hispanic/Latino; 1 Asian, non-Hispanic/Latino; 6 Hispanic/Latino; 1 Two or more races, non-Hispanic/Latino), 33 international. Expenses: Contact institution. *Financial support:* Research assistantships, teaching assistantships, career-related internships or fieldwork, Federal

Work-Study, institutionally sponsored loans, scholarships/grants, health care benefits, tuition waivers (partial), and administrative assistantships available. Financial award applicants required to submit FAFSA. *Program availability:* Part-time. Offers acting (MFA); art education (MA); art history (MA); ceramics (MFA); collaborative piano (MM, DMA); composition (MM, DMA); conducting (MM, DMA); costume design and technology (MFA); graphic design (MFA); jazz pedagogy (MM); lighting design and technology (MFA); music (PhD); music education (MM, PhD); music industry (MA); music theory (MM); musicology (MA); painting and printmaking (MFA); performance (MM, DMA); photography (MFA); piano pedagogy (MM); scenic design and technology (MFA); sculpture (MFA); studio art (MA); technical direction (MFA); vocal pedagogy and performance (DMA). *Application deadline:* For fall admission, 3/1 priority date for domestic students, 2/15 for international students; for spring admission, 11/1 for domestic students, 9/15 for international students. Applications are processed on a rolling basis. *Application fee:* $60. Electronic applications accepted. *Application Contact:* Records Officer, 304-293-4841, Fax: 304-293-2533, E-mail: rachel.hanks@mail.wvu.edu. *Dean*, Dr. Paul Kreider, 304-293-4841 Ext. 3109, Fax: 304-293-6896, E-mail: paul.kreider@mail.wvu.edu.

College of Education and Human Services Students: 423 full-time (347 women), 367 part-time (316 women); includes 57 minority (14 Black or African American, non-Hispanic/Latino; 7 Asian, non-Hispanic/Latino; 20 Hispanic/Latino; 16 Two or more races, non-Hispanic/Latino), 13 international. Expenses: Contact institution. *Financial support:* Fellowships, research assistantships, teaching assistantships, career-related internships or fieldwork, Federal Work-Study, institutionally sponsored loans, health care benefits, tuition waivers (full and partial), and administrative assistantships available. Financial award applicants required to submit FAFSA. *Program availability:* Part-time, evening/weekend, online learning. Offers audiology (Au D); autism spectrum disorder (MA); clinical rehabilitation and mental health counseling (MS); communication science and disorders (PhD); counseling (MA); counseling psychology (PhD); curriculum and instruction (Ed D); early childhood education (MA); early intervention (MA); education (PhD); educational leadership (MA, Ed D); educational leadership/public school administration (MA); educational psychology (MA, Ed D); elementary education (MA); gifted education (MA); higher education administration (MA, Ed D); higher education curriculum and teaching (MA); institutional design and technology (MA); instructional design and technology (Ed D); literacy education (MA); secondary education (MA); secondary education/English (MA); special education (Ed D); speech pathology (MS). *Application deadline:* For fall admission, 8/1 for domestic students; for spring admission, 1/1 for domestic students; for summer admission, 5/1 for domestic students. *Application fee:* $60. Electronic applications accepted. *Application Contact:* Dr. M. Cecil Smith, Associate Dean for Research and Graduate Education, 304-293-2174, Fax: 304-293-3802, E-mail: mcecil.smith@mail.wvu.edu. *Dean*, Dr. Gypsy Denzine, 304-293-5703, Fax: 304-293-7565, E-mail: gypsy.denzine@mail.wvu.edu.

College of Law Students: 306 full-time (138 women), 1 part-time (0 women); includes 33 minority (10 Black or African American, non-Hispanic/Latino; 4 Asian, non-Hispanic/Latino; 11 Hispanic/Latino; 8 Two or more races, non-Hispanic/Latino), 1 international. Expenses: Contact institution. *Financial support:* Fellowships, research assistantships, teaching assistantships, career-related internships or fieldwork, Federal Work-Study, institutionally sponsored loans, scholarships/grants, health care benefits, tuition waivers (full), unspecified assistantships, and administrative assistantships, resident assistantships available. Support available to part-time students. Financial award application deadline: 3/1; financial award applicants required to submit FAFSA. *Program availability:* Part-time. Offers energy law and sustainable development (LL M); forensic justice (LL M); law (JD); white collar forensic justice (LL M). *Application deadline:* For fall admission, 2/1 for domestic and international students. Applications are processed on a rolling basis. *Application fee:* $60. Electronic applications accepted. *Assistant Dean for Admissions and Student Financial Support*, Beth Pierpont, 304-293-7320, E-mail: beth.pierpont@mail.wvu.edu.

College of Physical Activity and Sport Sciences Students: 104 full-time (37 women), 75 part-time (28 women); includes 30 minority (12 Black or African American, non-Hispanic/Latino; 2 Asian, non-Hispanic/Latino; 9 Hispanic/Latino; 7 Two or more races, non-Hispanic/Latino), 12 international. Expenses: Contact institution. *Financial support:* Research assistantships, teaching assistantships, career-related internships or fieldwork, Federal Work-Study, institutionally sponsored loans, health care benefits, tuition waivers (full and partial), and administrative assistantships available. Support available to part-time students. Financial award application deadline: 2/1; financial award applicants required to submit FAFSA. Offers athletic training (MS); coaching and sport education (MS); coaching and teaching studies (Ed D, PhD); physical education/teacher education (MS); sport and exercise psychology (MS); sport coaching (MS); sport management (MS). *Application deadline:* For fall admission, 12/15 for domestic students, 10/1 for international students. *Application fee:* $60. Electronic applications accepted. *Online Program Coordinator*, Sean Bulger, 304-293-0845, Fax: 304-293-4641, E-mail: sean.bulger@mail.wvu.edu.

Davis College of Agriculture, Forestry and Consumer Sciences Students: 200 full-time (97 women), 53 part-time (32 women); includes 27 minority (6 Black or African American, non-Hispanic/Latino; 1 American Indian or Alaska Native, non-Hispanic/Latino; 4 Asian, non-Hispanic/Latino; 11 Hispanic/Latino; 5 Two or more races, non-Hispanic/Latino), 67 international. Expenses: Contact institution. *Financial support:* Fellowships, research assistantships, teaching assistantships, career-related internships or fieldwork, Federal Work-Study, institutionally sponsored loans, tuition waivers (full and partial), and unspecified assistantships available. Financial award application deadline: 2/1; financial award applicants required to submit FAFSA. *Program availability:* Part-time. Offers agricultural and extension education (MS, PhD); agriculture and resource management (MS); agriculture, natural resources and design (M Agr); agronomy (MS); animal and food science (PhD); animal physiology (MS); applied and environmental microbiology (MS); design and merchandising (MS); entomology (MS); forest resource science (PhD); forestry (MSF); genetics and developmental biology (MS, PhD); horticulture (MS); human and community development (PhD); landscape architecture (MLA); natural resource economics (PhD); nutritional and food science (MS); plant and soil science (PhD); plant pathology (MS); recreation, parks and tourism resources (MS); reproductive physiology (MS, PhD); wildlife and fisheries resources (PhD). *Application deadline:* For fall admission, 6/1 priority date for domestic students, 6/1 for international students; for spring admission, 1/5 for domestic and international students. Applications are processed on a rolling basis. *Application fee:* $60. Electronic applications accepted. *Application Contact:* Dr. Dennis K. Smith, Associate Dean, 304-293-2275, Fax: 304-293-3740, E-mail: denny.smith@mail.wvu.edu. *Dean*, Dr. Dan J. Robison, 304-293-2395, Fax: 304-293-3740, E-mail: dan.robison@mail.wvu.edu.

Eberly College of Arts and Sciences Students: 831 full-time (437 women), 236 part-time (142 women); includes 112 minority (35 Black or African American, non-Hispanic/Latino; 15 Asian, non-Hispanic/Latino; 29 Hispanic/Latino; 33 Two or more races, non-Hispanic/Latino), 235 international. Expenses: Contact institution. *Financial support:* Fellowships with full tuition reimbursements, research assistantships with full tuition reimbursements, teaching assistantships with full tuition reimbursements, career-related internships or fieldwork, Federal Work-Study, institutionally sponsored loans, scholarships/grants, health care benefits, tuition waivers (full and partial), unspecified assistantships, and administrative assistantships available. Financial award application deadline: 2/1; financial award applicants required to submit FAFSA. *Program availability:* Part-time, evening/weekend, online learning. Offers biology (MS, PhD); chemistry (MS, PhD); communication studies (MA, PhD); computational statistics (PhD); creative writing (MFA); English (MA, PhD); forensic and investigative science (MS); forensic science (PhD); geography (MA); geology (MA, PhD); history (MA, PhD); legal studies (MLS); math (MS); physics (MS, PhD); political science (MA, PhD); professional writing and editing (MA); psychology (MA); public administration (MPA); social work (MSW); sociology (MA, PhD); statistics (MS). *Application deadline:* For spring admission, 2/15 priority date for domestic and international students. Applications are processed on a rolling basis. *Application fee:* $45. Electronic applications accepted. *Application Contact:* Dr. Fred L. King, Associate Dean for Graduate Studies, 304-293-4611 Ext. 5205, Fax: 304-293-6858, E-mail: fred.king@mail.wvu.edu. *Dean*, Dr. Mary Ellen Mazey, 304-293-4611, Fax: 304-293-6858, E-mail: mary.mazey@mail.wvu.edu.

School of Social Work *Program availability:* Part-time. Offers aging and health care (MSW); children and families (MSW); community mental health (MSW); community organization and social administration (MSW); direct (clinical) social work practice (MSW).

Reed College of Media Students: 165 full-time (122 women), 232 part-time (167 women); includes 81 minority (46 Black or African American, non-Hispanic/Latino; 5 Asian, non-Hispanic/Latino; 20 Hispanic/Latino; 10 Two or more races, non-Hispanic/Latino), 6 international. Expenses: Contact institution. *Financial support:* Research assistantships, teaching assistantships, career-related internships or fieldwork, Federal Work-Study, institutionally sponsored loans, health care benefits, tuition waivers (full and partial), and administrative assistantships available. Financial award application deadline: 2/1; financial award applicants required to submit FAFSA. *Program availability:* Part-time, online learning. Offers data marketing communications (MS); integrated marketing communications (MS, Graduate Certificate); journalism (MSJ); media solutions and innovation (MSJ). *Application deadline:* For fall admission, 3/1 priority date for domestic students, 3/1 for international students. *Application fee:* $60. Electronic applications accepted. *Application Contact:* Dr. Steve Urbanski, Director of Graduate Studies/Associate Professor, 304-293-6797, Fax: 304-293-3072, E-mail: steve.urbanski@mail.wvu.edu. *Dean*, Dr. Maryann Reed, 304-293-3505 Ext. 5409, Fax: 304-293-3072, E-mail: maryann.reed@mail.wvu.edu.

School of Dentistry Students: 223 full-time (109 women), 1 part-time (0 women); includes 22 minority (1 Black or African American, non-Hispanic/Latino; 16 Asian, non-Hispanic/Latino; 3 Hispanic/Latino; 2 Two or more races, non-Hispanic/Latino), 12 international. Expenses: Contact institution. *Financial support:* Research assistantships, teaching assistantships, Federal Work-Study, institutionally sponsored loans, scholarships/grants, health care benefits, and tuition waivers (partial) available. Financial award application deadline: 3/1; financial award applicants required to submit FAFSA. Offers dental hygiene (MS); dentistry (DDS); endodontics (MS); orthodontics (MS); periodontics (MS); prosthodontics (MS). *Application deadline:* For fall admission, 11/1 for domestic and international students. Applications are processed on a rolling basis. *Application fee:* $60. Electronic applications accepted. *Application Contact:* Dr. Sheila Price, Associate Dean for Admissions, Recruitment, and Access, 304-293-1980, E-mail: sprice@hsc.wvu.edu. *Dean*, Dr. Tom Borgia, 304-293-2521, E-mail: aborgia@hsc.wvu.edu.

School of Medicine Students: 781 full-time (440 women), 25 part-time (13 women); includes 140 minority (15 Black or African American, non-Hispanic/Latino; 1 American Indian or Alaska Native, non-Hispanic/Latino; 68 Asian, non-Hispanic/Latino; 37 Hispanic/Latino; 1 Native Hawaiian or other Pacific Islander, non-Hispanic/Latino; 18 Two or more races, non-Hispanic/Latino), 19 international. Expenses: Contact institution. *Financial support:* Fellowships, research assistantships, teaching assistantships, career-related internships or fieldwork, Federal Work-Study, institutionally sponsored loans, health care benefits, tuition waivers (full and partial), and administrative assistantships available. Financial award applicants required to submit FAFSA. *Program availability:* Part-time, evening/weekend. Offers biochemistry and molecular biology (PhD); biomedical science (MS); cancer cell biology (PhD); cellular and integrative physiology (PhD); exercise physiology (MS, PhD); health sciences (MS); immunology (PhD); medicine (MD); occupational therapy (MOT); pathologists assistant (MHS); physical therapy (DPT). *Application deadline:* Applications are processed on a rolling basis. *Application fee:* $60. Electronic applications accepted. *Application Contact:* Lisa M. Salati, Assistant Vice President, Graduate Education, 304-293-7759, Fax: 304-293-3080, E-mail: lsalati@hsc.wvu.edu. *Executive Dean*, Dr. Clay Marsh, 304-293-6607, Fax: 304-293-6627, E-mail: clay.marsh@hsc.wvu.edu.

School of Nursing Students: 22 full-time (20 women), 175 part-time (155 women); includes 54 minority (16 Black or African American, non-Hispanic/Latino; 4 Asian, non-Hispanic/Latino; 29 Hispanic/Latino; 5 Two or more races, non-Hispanic/Latino). Expenses: Contact institution. *Financial support:* Teaching assistantships, Federal Work-Study, institutionally sponsored loans, health care benefits, tuition waivers (partial), and administrative assistantships available. Financial award application deadline: 2/1; financial award applicants required to submit FAFSA. *Program availability:* Part-time, online learning. Offers nurse practitioner (Certificate); nursing (MSN, DNP, PhD). *Application deadline:* For fall admission, 6/1 for domestic students. *Application fee:* $60. Electronic applications accepted. *Application Contact:* Brandy Sue Toothman, Program Assistant III, 304-293-4298, Fax: 304-293-2546, E-mail: btoothman@hsc.wvu.edu. *Dean*, Dr. Tara Hulsey, 304-293-6521, Fax: 304-293-6826, E-mail: tmhulsey@hsc.wvu.edu.

School of Pharmacy Students: 338 full-time (211 women), 3 part-time (2 women); includes 41 minority (10 Black or African American, non-Hispanic/Latino; 1 American Indian or Alaska Native, non-Hispanic/Latino; 15 Asian, non-Hispanic/Latino; 8 Hispanic/Latino; 7 Two or more races, non-Hispanic/Latino), 19 international. Expenses: Contact institution. *Financial support:* Research assistantships, teaching assistantships, career-related internships or fieldwork, Federal Work-Study, institutionally sponsored loans, health care benefits, tuition waivers (full and partial), and unspecified assistantships available. Financial award application deadline: 3/1; financial award applicants required to submit FAFSA. Offers health services and outcomes research (PhD); pharmaceutical and pharmacological sciences (PhD); professional pharmacy (Pharm D). *Application deadline:* For fall admission, 3/1 priority date for domestic and international students. *Application fee:* $60. Electronic applications accepted. *Application Contact:* Dr. Mary L. Euler, Associate Dean for Student Services, 304-293-7806, Fax: 304-293-5483, E-mail: mleuler@hsc.wvu.edu. *Interim Dean*, Dr. Mary K. Stamatakis, 304-293-5101, Fax: 304-293-5483, E-mail: mkstamatakis@hsc.wvu.edu.

School of Public Health Students: 69 full-time (48 women), 27 part-time (15 women); includes 14 minority (5 Black or African American, non-Hispanic/Latino; 4 Asian, non-Hispanic/Latino; 1 Hispanic/Latino; 4 Two or more races, non-Hispanic/Latino), 11 international. Expenses: Contact institution. *Financial support:* Research assistantships, teaching assistantships, scholarships/grants, and health care benefits available. Financial award application deadline: 2/1; financial award applicants required to submit FAFSA. *Program availability:* Part-time, online learning. Offers biostatistics (MPH, MS, PhD); epidemiology (MPH, PhD); health policy (MPH); occupational and environmental health sciences (MPH, PhD); public health (MPH); school health education (MS); social and behavioral science (MPH, PhD). *Application deadline:* For fall admission, 4/15 priority date for domestic students; for spring admission, 12/1 for domestic students. Applications are processed on a rolling basis. *Application fee:* $60. *Senior Program Coordinator,* Leah Adkins, 304-293-1097, E-mail: leadkins@hsc.wvu.edu.

Statler College of Engineering and Mineral Resources Students: 522 full-time (110 women), 131 part-time (23 women); includes 56 minority (22 Black or African American, non-Hispanic/Latino; 2 American Indian or Alaska Native, non-Hispanic/Latino; 14 Asian, non-Hispanic/Latino; 11 Hispanic/Latino; 7 Two or more races, non-Hispanic/Latino), 305 international. Expenses: Contact institution. *Financial support:* Fellowships, research assistantships, teaching assistantships, career-related internships or fieldwork, Federal Work-Study, institutionally sponsored loans, health care benefits, tuition waivers (full and partial), unspecified assistantships, and administrative assistantships available. Financial award application deadline: 2/1; financial award applicants required to submit FAFSA. *Program availability:* Part-time. Offers aerospace engineering (MSAE, PhD); chemical engineering (MS Ch E, PhD); civil engineering (MSCE, PhD); computer engineering (PhD); computer science (MSCS, PhD); electrical engineering (MSEE, PhD); energy systems engineering (MSESE); engineering (MSE); industrial engineering (MSIE, PhD); industrial hygiene (MS); material science and engineering (MSMSE, PhD); mechanical engineering (MSME, PhD); mining engineering (MS Min E, PhD); petroleum and natural gas engineering (MSPNGE, PhD); safety engineering (MS); software engineering (MSSE). *Application deadline:* For fall admission, 4/1 for international students; for winter admission, 4/1 for international students; for spring admission, 10/1 for international students. Applications are processed on a rolling basis. *Application fee:* $60. Electronic applications accepted. *Application Contact:* Dr. David A. Wyrick, Associate Dean, Academic Affairs, 304-293-4334, Fax: 304-293-5024, E-mail: david.wyrick@mail.wvu.edu. *Dean,* Dr. Eugene V. Cilento, 304-293-4821 Ext. 2237, Fax: 304-293-2037, E-mail: gene.cilento@mail.wvu.edu.

WEST VIRGINIA WESLEYAN COLLEGE, Buckhannon, WV 26201

General Information Independent-religious, coed, comprehensive institution. *Graduate housing:* Room and/or apartments available to single students; on-campus housing not available to married students.

GRADUATE UNITS

Department of Education Offers education (M Ed).

Department of Exercise Science Offers athletic training (MS).

Department of Nursing Offers family nurse practitioner (MS, Post Master's Certificate); nurse administrator (MS); nurse educator (MS); nurse-midwifery (MS); nursing administration (Post Master's Certificate); nursing education (Post Master's Certificate); psychiatric mental health nurse practitioner (MS).

MBA Program *Program availability:* Part-time, evening/weekend. Offers business administration (MBA).

Program in Creative Writing Offers creative writing (MFA).

WHEATON COLLEGE, Wheaton, IL 60187-5593

General Information Independent-religious, coed, comprehensive institution. CGS member. *Enrollment:* 2,900 graduate, professional, and undergraduate students; 240 full-time matriculated graduate/professional students (149 women), 168 part-time matriculated graduate/professional students (78 women). *Enrollment by degree level:* 329 master's, 79 doctoral. *Graduate faculty:* 31 full-time (10 women), 23 part-time/adjunct (19 women). *Tuition:* Full-time $19,800; part-time $825 per credit hour. Tuition and fees vary according to degree level and program. *Graduate housing:* Rooms and/or apartments available on a first-come, first-served basis to single and married students. Typical cost: $6210 per year for single students; $11,024 per year for married students. Room charges vary according to board plan and housing facility selected. *Student services:* Campus employment opportunities, campus safety program, career counseling, exercise/wellness program, free psychological counseling, grant writing training, international student services, multicultural affairs office, services for students with disabilities, writing training. *Library facilities:* Buswell Memorial Library. *Collection:* Books: 518,164 (physical), 226,974 (digital/electronic); Serial titles: 389 (physical), 6,182 (digital/electronic); Databases: 249. Weekly public service hours: 94; students can reserve study rooms.

Computer facilities: 325 computers available on campus for general student use. A campuswide network can be accessed from student residence rooms and from off campus. Online class registration, financial information, degree requirements evaluation are available.
Website: http://www.wheaton.edu/

General Application Contact: Director of Graduate Admissions, 630-752-5195, Fax: 630-752-7047, E-mail: graduate.admissions@wheaton.edu.

GRADUATE UNITS

Graduate School Students: 240 full-time (149 women), 168 part-time (78 women); includes 83 minority (22 Black or African American, non-Hispanic/Latino; 3 American Indian or Alaska Native, non-Hispanic/Latino; 30 Asian, non-Hispanic/Latino; 16 Hispanic/Latino; 12 Two or more races, non-Hispanic/Latino), 89 international. Average age 31. 334 applicants, 77% accepted, 151 enrolled. *Faculty:* 31 full-time (10 women), 23 part-time/adjunct (19 women). Expenses: Contact institution. *Financial support:* Fellowships, career-related internships or fieldwork, Federal Work-Study, scholarships/grants, and unspecified assistantships available. Financial award application deadline: 3/1; financial award applicants required to submit FAFSA. In 2017, 166 master's, 26 doctorates, 1 other advanced degree awarded. *Program availability:* Part-time. Offers Biblical and theological studies (PhD); Biblical archaeology (MA); Biblical exegesis (MA); Biblical studies (MA); Christian formation and ministry (MA); clinical mental health counseling (MA); clinical psychology (Psy D); elementary education (MAT); evangelism and leadership (MA); general theological studies (MA); global engagement (Certificate); historical and systematic theology (MA); history of Christianity (MA); intercultural studies (MA); intercultural studies/teaching English as a second language (MA); marriage and family therapy (MA); missional church movements (MA); secondary education (MAT); teaching English as a second language (Certificate). *Application deadline:* For fall admission, 1/1 priority date for domestic students, 1/1 for international students; for spring admission, 11/1 for domestic students. Applications are processed on a rolling basis. *Application fee:* $30. Electronic applications accepted. *Application Contact:* Director of Graduate Admissions, 630-752-5195, Fax: 630-752-7047, E-mail: graduate.admissions@wheaton.edu. *Dean,* Dr. Scott Moreau, 630-752-5933, E-mail: graduate.dean@wheaton.edu.

Humanitarian Disaster Institute *Faculty:* 1 full-time (0 women). Expenses: Contact institution. Offers humanitarian and disaster leadership (MA). Electronic applications accepted. *Application Contact:* Director of Graduate Admissions, 630-752-5195, Fax: 630-752-7047, E-mail: graduate.admissions@wheaton.edu. *Executive Director,* Dr. Jamie Aten, 630-752-7659, E-mail: jamie.aten@wheaton.edu.

WHEELING JESUIT UNIVERSITY, Wheeling, WV 26003-6295

General Information Independent-religious, coed, comprehensive institution. *Graduate housing:* Rooms and/or apartments available on a first-come, first-served basis to single and married students.

GRADUATE UNITS

Department of Business *Program availability:* Part-time, evening/weekend. Offers accounting (MSA); business administration (MBA). Electronic applications accepted.

Department of Education *Program availability:* Part-time, evening/weekend, online learning. Offers education (MEL). Electronic applications accepted.

Department of Nursing *Program availability:* Part-time, evening/weekend, online learning. Offers nursing (MSN). Electronic applications accepted.

Department of Physical Therapy Offers physical therapy (DPT). Electronic applications accepted.

Department of Social Sciences *Program availability:* Part-time, evening/weekend. Offers social sciences (MSOL). Electronic applications accepted.

WHITTIER COLLEGE, Whittier, CA 90608-0634

General Information Independent, coed, comprehensive institution. *Graduate housing:* On-campus housing not available.

GRADUATE UNITS

Graduate Programs *Program availability:* Part-time, evening/weekend. Offers educational administration (MA Ed); elementary education (MA Ed); secondary education (MA Ed).

WHITWORTH UNIVERSITY, Spokane, WA 99251-0001

General Information Independent-religious, coed, comprehensive institution. *Graduate housing:* Room and/or apartments available on a first-come, first-served basis to single students; on-campus housing not available to married students. Housing application deadline: 5/1.

GRADUATE UNITS

Graduate Studies in Theology Students: 47 part-time (21 women); includes 6 minority (2 Black or African American, non-Hispanic/Latino; 1 American Indian or Alaska Native, non-Hispanic/Latino; 3 Hispanic/Latino). Average age 35. *Faculty:* 19. Expenses: Contact institution. *Financial support:* In 2017–18, 17 students received support. Research assistantships, career-related internships or fieldwork, scholarships/grants, and unspecified assistantships available. Financial award application deadline: 8/7; financial award applicants required to submit FAFSA. *Program availability:* Part-time, evening/weekend. Offers Christian ministry (MA); mission and culture (MA); theology (MA). *Application deadline:* For fall admission, 8/7 for domestic students; for spring admission, 1/1 for domestic students; for summer admission, 4/15 for domestic students. Applications are processed on a rolling basis. Electronic applications accepted. *Application Contact:* Hannah Fischer, Graduate Admissions, 509-777-3222, E-mail: graduateandcsadmissions@whitworth.edu. *Director,* Dr. Jeremy Wynne, 509-777-3222, E-mail: graduateandcsadmissions@whitworth.edu.

School of Business *Program availability:* Part-time, evening/weekend. Offers business (MBA). Electronic applications accepted.

School of Education *Program availability:* Part-time, evening/weekend, online learning. Offers administration (M Ed); counseling (M Ed); education (M Ed, MAT, MIT); elementary education (M Ed); gifted and talented (MAT); school counselors (M Ed); secondary education (M Ed); social agency/church setting (M Ed); special education (MAT); teaching (MIT).

WICHITA STATE UNIVERSITY, Wichita, KS 67260

General Information State-supported, coed, university. CGS member. *Enrollment:* 15,081 graduate, professional, and undergraduate students; 1,243 full-time matriculated graduate/professional students (676 women), 1,440 part-time matriculated graduate/professional students (817 women). *Enrollment by degree level:* 1,871 master's, 499 doctoral, 313 other advanced degrees. *Graduate faculty:* 381 full-time (150 women), 26 part-time/adjunct (11 women). *Graduate housing:* Rooms and/or apartments available on a first-come, first-served basis to single and married students. *Student services:* Campus employment opportunities, campus safety program, career counseling, child daycare facilities, exercise/wellness program, free psychological counseling, grant writing training, international student services, low-cost health insurance, multicultural affairs office, services for students with disabilities, teacher training, writing training. *Library facilities:* Ablah Library plus 2 others. *Collection:* Books: 1.9 million (physical), 475,186 (digital/electronic); Serial titles: 460 (physical), 94,566 (digital/electronic); Databases: 269. Study areas open 24 hours, 5–7 days a week; students can reserve study rooms. *Research affiliation:* Spirit Aerosystems (aerospace engineering), General Atomics (aerospace engineering), Wesley Medical Center (industrial and manufacturing engineering), NASA (aerospace engineering), Airbus (aerospace engineering), NetApp (computer engineering).

Computer facilities: 1,500 computers available on campus for general student use. A campuswide network can be accessed from student residence rooms and from off campus. Online class registration, learning management system are available.
Website: http://www.wichita.edu/

General Application Contact: Jordan Oleson, Admissions Coordinator, 316-978-3095, Fax: 316-978-3253, E-mail: jordan.oleson@wichita.edu.

GRADUATE UNITS

Graduate School Students: 1,243 full-time (676 women), 1,440 part-time (817 women); includes 497 minority (133 Black or African American, non-Hispanic/Latino; 16 American Indian or Alaska Native, non-Hispanic/Latino; 119 Asian, non-Hispanic/Latino; 169 Hispanic/Latino; 2 Native Hawaiian or other Pacific Islander, non-Hispanic/Latino; 58 Two or more races, non-Hispanic/Latino), 532 international. Average age 32. 2,344 applicants, 56% accepted, 601 enrolled. *Faculty:* 381 full-time (150 women), 26 part-time/adjunct (11 women). Expenses: Contact institution. *Financial support:* In 2017–18, 623 research assistantships with partial tuition reimbursements (averaging $11,664 per year), 473 teaching assistantships with partial tuition reimbursements (averaging $10,552 per year) were awarded; fellowships, career-related internships or fieldwork, Federal Work-Study, institutionally sponsored loans, scholarships/grants, traineeships, health care benefits, and unspecified assistantships also available. Support available to part-time students.

Financial award application deadline: 4/1; financial award applicants required to submit FAFSA. In 2017, 756 master's, 103 doctorates, 4 other advanced degrees awarded. *Program availability:* Part-time, evening/weekend, 100% online, blended/hybrid learning. *Application deadline:* For fall admission, 7/15 priority date for domestic students, 4/1 for international students; for spring admission, 12/1 priority date for domestic students, 8/1 for international students. Applications are processed on a rolling basis. *Application fee:* $60 ($75 for international students). Electronic applications accepted. *Application Contact:* Jordan Oleson, Admissions Coordinator, 316-978-3095, Fax: 316-978-3253, E-mail: jordan.oleson@wichita.edu. *Dean of the Graduate School/Associate Vice President of Research and Technology Transfer,* Dr. Dennis R. Livesay, 316-978-3095, Fax: 316-978-3253, E-mail: dennis.livesay@wichita.edu.

College of Education Expenses: Contact institution. *Program availability:* Part-time, evening/weekend, 100% online, blended/hybrid learning. Offers counseling (M Ed); education (M Ed, MAT, Ed D, Ed S); educational leadership (M Ed, Ed D); educational psychology (M Ed); exercise science (M Ed); learning and instructional design (M Ed); school psychology (Ed S); special education (M Ed); sport management (M Ed); teaching (MAT). *Application Contact:* Jordan Oleson, Admissions Coordinator, 316-978-3095, Fax: 316-978-3253, E-mail: jordan.oleson@wichita.edu. *Dean,* Dr. Shirley Lefever, 316-978-3301, Fax: 316-978-3302, E-mail: shirley.lefever@wichita.edu.

College of Engineering Expenses: Contact institution. *Program availability:* Part-time, evening/weekend. Offers aerospace engineering (MS, PhD); biomedical engineering (MS); computer networking (MS); computer science (MS); electrical and computer engineering (MS); electrical engineering and computer science (PhD); engineering (MEM, MS, PhD); engineering management (MEM); industrial engineering (MS, PhD); mechanical engineering (MS, PhD). *Application Contact:* Jordan Oleson, Admissions Coordinator, 316-978-3095, Fax: 316-978-3253, E-mail: jordan.oleson@wichita.edu. *Dean,* Dr. Royce O. Bowden, 316-978-3400, Fax: 316-978-3853, E-mail: royce.bowden@wichita.edu.

College of Fine Arts Expenses: Contact institution. *Program availability:* Part-time. Offers fine arts (MFA, MM, MME); music (MM); music education (MME); studio arts (MFA). *Application Contact:* Jordan Oleson, Admissions Coordinator, 316-978-3095, Fax: 316-978-3253, E-mail: jordan.oleson@wichita.edu. *Dean,* Dr. Rodney E. Miller, 316-978-3389, Fax: 316-978-3951, E-mail: rodney.miller@wichita.edu.

College of Health Professions Expenses: Contact institution. *Program availability:* Part-time. Offers aging studies (MA); communication sciences and disorders (MA, Au D, PhD); health professions (MA, MPA, MSN, Au D, DNP, DPT, PhD); nursing (MSN); nursing practice (DNP); physical therapy (DPT); physician assistant (MPA). *Application Contact:* Jordan Oleson, Admissions Coordinator, 316-978-3095, Fax: 316-978-3253, E-mail: jordan.oleson@wichita.edu. *Dean,* Dr. Sandra C. Bibb, 316-978-3600, Fax: 316-978-3025, E-mail: sandra.bibb@wichita.edu.

Fairmount College of Liberal Arts and Sciences Expenses: Contact institution. *Program availability:* Part-time, evening/weekend, 100% online, blended/hybrid learning. Offers anthropology (MA); applied mathematics (PhD); biological sciences (MS); chemistry (MS, PhD); clinical (PhD); communication (MA); community (PhD); creative writing (MFA); criminal justice (MA); earth, environmental, and physical sciences (MS); English (MA); history (MA); human factors (PhD); liberal arts and sciences (MA, MFA, MPA, MS, MSW, PhD); liberal studies (MA); mathematics (MS); physics (MS); public administration (MPA); social work (MSW); sociology (MA); Spanish (MA). *Application Contact:* Jordan Oleson, Admissions Coordinator, 316-978-3095, Fax: 316-978-3253, E-mail: jordan.oleson@wichita.edu. *Dean,* Dr. Ronald Matson, 316-978-3100, Fax: 316-978-3234, E-mail: ron.matson@wichita.edu.

Institute for Interdisciplinary Creativity Expenses: Contact institution. Offers innovation design (MID). *Application Contact:* Jordan Oleson, Admissions Coordinator, 316-978-3095, Fax: 316-978-3253, E-mail: jordan.oleson@wichita.edu. *Graduate Coordinator,* Dr. Jeremy Patterson, 316-978-3010, E-mail: jeremy.patterson@wichita.edu.

W. Frank Barton School of Business Expenses: Contact institution. *Program availability:* Part-time, evening/weekend. Offers accounting information systems (M Acc); business (EMBA, M Acc, MA, MBA, MS); economic analysis (MA); financial economics (MA); global supply chain management (MS); international economics (MA); taxation (M Acc). *Application Contact:* Jordan Oleson, Admissions Coordinator, 316-978-3095, Fax: 316-978-3253, E-mail: jordan.oleson@wichita.edu. *Dean,* Dr. Anand Desai, 316-978-3200, Fax: 316-978-3845, E-mail: anand.desai@wichita.edu.

WIDENER UNIVERSITY, Chester, PA 19013-5792

General Information Independent, coed, comprehensive institution. CGS member. *Enrollment:* 6,518 graduate, professional, and undergraduate students; 1,452 full-time matriculated graduate/professional students (899 women), 1,621 part-time matriculated graduate/professional students (1,329 women). *Enrollment by degree level:* 1,496 master's, 1,470 doctoral, 107 other advanced degrees. *Graduate faculty:* 167 full-time (97 women), 177 part-time/adjunct (92 women). *Graduate housing:* Rooms and/or apartments available on a first-come, first-served basis to single students and available to married students. Housing application deadline: 5/30. *Student services:* Campus employment opportunities, career counseling, child daycare facilities, exercise/wellness program, free psychological counseling, international student services, multicultural affairs office, services for students with disabilities, teacher training, writing training. *Library facilities:* Wolfgram Memorial Library. *Research affiliation:* Small Business Administration, Riverfront Development Corporation (engineering, management), Advanced Technology Center (engineering).

Computer facilities: A campuswide network can be accessed from student residence rooms and from off campus. Online class registration is available.
Website: http://www.widener.edu/

General Application Contact: Megan Luft, Director of Graduate Admissions, 610-499-4124, Fax: 610-499-4676, E-mail: gradprograms@widener.edu.

GRADUATE UNITS

College of Arts and Sciences Students: 2 full-time (1 woman), 18 part-time (9 women); includes 10 minority (7 Black or African American, non-Hispanic/Latino; 2 Asian, non-Hispanic/Latino; 1 Hispanic/Latino), 1 international. Average age 30. 29 applicants, 28% accepted, 2 enrolled. *Faculty:* 9 full-time (2 women), 8 part-time/adjunct (1 woman). Expenses: Contact institution. *Financial support:* Career-related internships or fieldwork and institutionally sponsored loans available. Support available to part-time students. Financial award application deadline: 4/1. In 2017, 13 master's awarded. *Program availability:* Part-time, evening/weekend. Offers arts and sciences (MA, MPA); criminal justice (MA); public administration (MPA). *Application deadline:* Applications are processed on a rolling basis. *Application fee:* $25 ($300 for international students). *Application Contact:* Dr. Roberta Nolan, Assistant to Associate Provost for Graduate Studies, 610-499-4125, Fax: 610-499-4676, E-mail: gradmc@mail.widener.edu. *Dean,* Dr. Sharon Meaghar, 610-499-4007, E-mail: smmeagher@widener.edu.

Commonwealth Law School Students: 272 full-time (138 women), 4 part-time (3 women); includes 60 minority (30 Black or African American, non-Hispanic/Latino; 2 American Indian or Alaska Native, non-Hispanic/Latino; 8 Asian, non-Hispanic/Latino; 19 Hispanic/Latino; 1 Two or more races, non-Hispanic/Latino), 2 international. Average age 27. 601 applicants, 62% accepted, 129 enrolled. *Faculty:* 17 full-time (8 women), 18 part-time/adjunct (6 women). Expenses: Contact institution. *Financial support:* Fellowships, research assistantships, career-related internships or fieldwork, Federal Work-Study, institutionally sponsored loans, and scholarships/grants available. Support available to part-time students. Financial award application deadline: 2/15; financial award applicants required to submit FAFSA. *Program availability:* Part-time. Offers law (JD). *Application deadline:* For fall admission, 5/15 for domestic students. Applications are processed on a rolling basis. *Application fee:* $60. Electronic applications accepted. *Application Contact:* John Benfield, Associate Dean for Admissions and Administration, 302-477-2210, Fax: 302-477-2224, E-mail: jsbenfield@widener.edu. *Dean,* Christian Johnson, 302-477-2100, Fax: 302-477-2282, E-mail: cajohnson2@widener.edu.

Delaware Law School Students: 530 full-time (269 women), 26 part-time (17 women); includes 136 minority (80 Black or African American, non-Hispanic/Latino; 8 American Indian or Alaska Native, non-Hispanic/Latino; 16 Asian, non-Hispanic/Latino; 27 Hispanic/Latino; 5 Two or more races, non-Hispanic/Latino), 26 international. Average age 29. 942 applicants, 62% accepted, 210 enrolled. *Faculty:* 24 full-time (13 women), 42 part-time/adjunct (15 women). Expenses: Contact institution. *Financial support:* Career-related internships or fieldwork, Federal Work-Study, institutionally sponsored loans, and scholarships/grants available. Support available to part-time students. Financial award application deadline: 2/15; financial award applicants required to submit FAFSA. *Program availability:* Part-time, 100% online. Offers corporate and business law (MJ); corporate law and finance (LL M); health law (LL M, MJ, D Law); higher education compliance (MJ); juridical science (SJD); law (JD). *Application deadline:* For fall admission, 5/15 for domestic students; for spring admission, 12/1 for domestic students. Applications are processed on a rolling basis. *Application fee:* $60. *Application Contact:* Barbara L. Ayars, Assistant Dean of Admissions, 302-477-2210, Fax: 302-477-2224, E-mail: barbara.l.ayars@law.widener.edu. *Dean,* Rod Smolla, 302-477-2100, Fax: 302-477-2282, E-mail: rasmolla@widener.edu.

Graduate Programs in Engineering Students: 16 full-time (10 women), 21 part-time (5 women); includes 5 minority (3 Asian, non-Hispanic/Latino; 2 Hispanic/Latino), 3 international. Average age 27. 70 applicants, 11% accepted, 4 enrolled. *Faculty:* 18 full-time (2 women), 7 part-time/adjunct (0 women). Expenses: Contact institution. *Financial support:* In 2017–18, 5 teaching assistantships with partial tuition reimbursements (averaging $8,000 per year) were awarded; research assistantships and unspecified assistantships also available. Financial award application deadline: 3/15. In 2017, 12 master's awarded. *Program availability:* Part-time, evening/weekend. Offers biomedical engineering (M Eng); chemical engineering (M Eng); civil engineering (M Eng); electrical engineering (M Eng); engineering (M Eng); engineering management (M Eng); mechanical engineering (M Eng). *Application deadline:* For fall admission, 8/1 priority date for domestic students, 4/1 priority date for international students; for winter admission, 2/1 priority date for international students; for spring admission, 12/1 priority date for domestic students, 9/1 priority date for international students. Applications are processed on a rolling basis. *Application fee:* $0. Electronic applications accepted. *Assistant Dean/Director of Graduate Programs,* Rudolph Treichel, 610-499-1294, Fax: 610-499-4059, E-mail: rjtreichel@widener.edu.

School of Business Administration Students: 47 full-time (18 women), 158 part-time (76 women); includes 58 minority (35 Black or African American, non-Hispanic/Latino; 11 Asian, non-Hispanic/Latino; 9 Hispanic/Latino; 1 Native Hawaiian or other Pacific Islander, non-Hispanic/Latino; 2 Two or more races, non-Hispanic/Latino), 33 international. Average age 32. 154 applicants, 49% accepted, 43 enrolled. *Faculty:* 14 full-time (6 women), 6 part-time/adjunct (2 women). Expenses: Contact institution. *Financial support:* In 2017–18, 11 research assistantships with full tuition reimbursements were awarded; career-related internships or fieldwork, Federal Work-Study, and traineeships also available. Support available to part-time students. Financial award application deadline: 5/1. In 2017, 45 master's awarded. *Program availability:* Part-time, evening/weekend, 100% online, blended/hybrid learning. Offers business administration (MBA, MHA, MS); health and medical services administration (MBA, MHA); taxation (MS). *Application deadline:* For fall admission, 8/1 priority date for domestic students; for spring admission, 12/1 for domestic students. Applications are processed on a rolling basis. *Application fee:* $25 ($300 for international students). Electronic applications accepted. *Application Contact:* Ann Seltzer, Graduate Enrollment Administrator, 610-499-4305, E-mail: apseltzer@widener.edu. *Dean,* Dr. Jayati Ghosh, 610-499-4300, Fax: 610-499-4615.

School of Human Service Professions Students: 542 full-time (424 women), 1,213 part-time (1,051 women); includes 611 minority (418 Black or African American, non-Hispanic/Latino; 5 American Indian or Alaska Native, non-Hispanic/Latino; 26 Asian, non-Hispanic/Latino; 116 Hispanic/Latino; 1 Native Hawaiian or other Pacific Islander, non-Hispanic/Latino; 45 Two or more races, non-Hispanic/Latino), 23 international. Average age 33. 1,251 applicants, 34% accepted, 271 enrolled. *Faculty:* 64 full-time (39 women), 70 part-time/adjunct (34 women). Expenses: Contact institution. *Financial support:* Fellowships, research assistantships, teaching assistantships, career-related internships or fieldwork, Federal Work-Study, institutionally sponsored loans, tuition waivers (partial), unspecified assistantships, and stipends available. Support available to part-time students. Financial award applicants required to submit FAFSA. In 2017, 232 master's, 96 doctorates awarded. *Program availability:* Part-time, evening/weekend, 100% online, blended/hybrid learning. Offers human service professions (M Ed, MS, MSW, DPT, Ed D, PhD, Psy D). *Application Contact:* 610-499-4124, E-mail: gradprograms@widener.edu. *Interim Dean,* Dr. Robin Dole, 610-499-4351, Fax: 610-499-4277, E-mail: rldole@widener.edu.

Center for Education Students: 131 full-time (112 women), 244 part-time (179 women); includes 94 minority (58 Black or African American, non-Hispanic/Latino; 1 American Indian or Alaska Native, non-Hispanic/Latino; 1 Asian, non-Hispanic/Latino; 22 Hispanic/Latino; 12 Two or more races, non-Hispanic/Latino), 12 international. Average age 37. 140 applicants, 38% accepted, 26 enrolled. *Faculty:* 34 full-time (22 women), 37 part-time/adjunct (14 women). Expenses: Contact institution. *Financial support:* Career-related internships or fieldwork, tuition waivers (full and partial), and unspecified assistantships available. Support available to part-time students. Financial award application deadline: 5/1. In 2017, 45 master's, 21 doctorates awarded. *Program availability:* Part-time, evening/weekend. Offers adult education (M Ed); counseling in higher education (M Ed); counselor education (M Ed); early childhood education (M Ed); educational foundations (M Ed); educational leadership (M Ed); educational psychology (M Ed); elementary education (M Ed); English and language arts (M Ed); health education (M Ed); higher education leadership (Ed D); home and school visitor (M Ed); human sexuality (M Ed, PhD); mathematics education (M Ed); middle school education (M Ed); principalship (M Ed); reading and language arts (Ed D); reading education (M Ed); school administration (Ed D); science education (M Ed); social studies education (M Ed); special education (M Ed); technology education (M Ed). *Application deadline:* Applications are processed on a rolling basis. *Application fee:* $25 ($300 for international students). Electronic applications accepted. *Application Contact:* Megan Kuft, Director of Graduate Admissions, 610-499-4124, E-mail: gradprograms@widener.edu. *Dean*, Dr. Shawn Fitzgerald, 610-499-4294, Fax: 610-499-4623, E-mail: smfitzgerald@widener.edu.

Center for Social Work Education Students: 63 full-time (54 women), 893 part-time (803 women); includes 451 minority (318 Black or African American, non-Hispanic/Latino; 1 American Indian or Alaska Native, non-Hispanic/Latino; 13 Asian, non-Hispanic/Latino; 78 Hispanic/Latino; 1 Native Hawaiian or other Pacific Islander, non-Hispanic/Latino; 40 Two or more races, non-Hispanic/Latino), 5 international. Average age 34. 442 applicants, 59% accepted, 183 enrolled. Expenses: Contact institution. Offers social work education (MSW, PhD). *Associate Dean*, Dr. Beth Berol, 610-499-1152, E-mail: bibarol@widener.edu.

Institute for Graduate Clinical Psychology Students: 159 full-time (131 women), 5 part-time (4 women); includes 28 minority (9 Black or African American, non-Hispanic/Latino; 10 Asian, non-Hispanic/Latino; 5 Hispanic/Latino; 4 Two or more races, non-Hispanic/Latino), 3 international. Average age 27. 343 applicants, 17% accepted, 34 enrolled. *Faculty:* 15 full-time (6 women), 18 part-time/adjunct (10 women). Expenses: Contact institution. *Financial support:* Research assistantships, teaching assistantships, career-related internships or fieldwork, Federal Work-Study, institutionally sponsored loans, scholarships/grants, and stipends available. In 2017, 26 doctorates awarded. Offers clinical psychology (Psy D). *Application deadline:* For fall admission, 12/31 for domestic students. *Application fee:* $75. Electronic applications accepted. *Application Contact:* Ellen Madison, Admissions Coordinator, 611-499-1206, Fax: 610-499-4625, E-mail: etmadison@widener.edu. *Associate Dean/Director*, Dr. Sanjay Nath, 610-499-1208, Fax: 610-499-4625, E-mail: graduate.psychology@widener.edu.

Institute for Physical Therapy Education Students: 118 full-time (66 women), 2 part-time (both women); includes 10 minority (4 Black or African American, non-Hispanic/Latino; 2 American Indian or Alaska Native, non-Hispanic/Latino; 3 Hispanic/Latino; 1 Two or more races, non-Hispanic/Latino). Average age 24. 524 applicants, 11% accepted, 30 enrolled. *Faculty:* 8 full-time (5 women), 1 (woman) part-time/adjunct. Expenses: Contact institution. *Financial support:* Teaching assistantships, Federal Work-Study, institutionally sponsored loans, and scholarships/grants available. Financial award application deadline: 5/1; financial award applicants required to submit FAFSA. In 2017, 53 doctorates awarded. Offers physical therapy education (MS, DPT). *Application deadline:* For fall admission, 1/30 for domestic students. Applications are processed on a rolling basis. *Application fee:* $40. *Application Contact:* 610-499-4124, E-mail: gradprograms@widener.edu. *Associate Dean and Director*, Dr. Robin Dole, 610-499-1159, Fax: 610-499-1231, E-mail: rldole@widener.edu.

School of Nursing Students: 43 full-time (39 women), 179 part-time (167 women); includes 90 minority (59 Black or African American, non-Hispanic/Latino; 1 American Indian or Alaska Native, non-Hispanic/Latino; 22 Asian, non-Hispanic/Latino; 6 Hispanic/Latino; 2 Two or more races, non-Hispanic/Latino), 7 international. Average age 39. 139 applicants, 38% accepted, 43 enrolled. *Faculty:* 12 full-time (all women), 4 part-time/adjunct (3 women). Expenses: Contact institution. *Financial support:* Career-related internships or fieldwork, Federal Work-Study, and traineeships available. Support available to part-time students. Financial award application deadline: 4/1. In 2017, 64 master's, 12 doctorates awarded. *Program availability:* Part-time, evening/weekend. Offers nursing (MSN, DN Sc, PhD, PMC). *Application deadline:* For fall admission, 7/1 for domestic students; for winter admission, 3/1 for domestic students; for spring admission, 11/1 for domestic students. Applications are processed on a rolling basis. *Application fee:* $25 ($300 for international students). Electronic applications accepted. *Dean*, Dr. Laura Dzurec, 610-499-4214, E-mail: lcdzurec@widener.edu.

WILBERFORCE UNIVERSITY, Wilberforce, OH 45384

General Information Independent-religious, coed, comprehensive institution.

GRADUATE UNITS

Program in Rehabilitation Counseling Offers rehabilitation counseling (MS).

WILFRID LAURIER UNIVERSITY, Waterloo, ON N2L 3C5, Canada

General Information Province-supported, coed, comprehensive institution.

GRADUATE UNITS

Faculty of Graduate and Postdoctoral Studies *Program availability:* Part-time, evening/weekend. Electronic applications accepted.

Faculty of Arts *Program availability:* Part-time. Offers agency (MA); arts (M Sc, MA, MES, MIPP, PhD); body politics (MA); Canadian political studies (MA); community (MA); comparative politics/international relations (MA); cultural representation and social theory (MA); English (MA); English and film (PhD); environmental and resource management (MA, MES, PhD); environmental science (M Sc, MES, PhD); gender, sexuality and embodiment (MA); geomatics (M Sc, MES, PhD); globalization, identity and social movements (MA); health, family and well-being (MA); history (MA, PhD); human geography (MES, PhD); internationalization, migration and human rights (MA); media, technology and culture (MA); religion and culture (MA); religious diversity of North America (PhD); self (MA); visual communication and culture (MA). Electronic applications accepted.

Faculty of Music Offers music (MMT). Electronic applications accepted.

Faculty of Science Offers behavioral neuroscience (M Sc, PhD); chemistry (M Sc); cognitive neuroscience (M Sc, PhD); community psychology (MA, PhD); integrative biology (M Sc); mathematics for science and finance (M Sc); physical activity and health (M Sc); science (M Sc, MA, PhD); social and developmental psychology (MA, PhD). Electronic applications accepted.

Lyle S. Hallman Faculty of Social Work *Program availability:* Part-time. Offers Aboriginal studies (MSW); community, policy, planning and organizations (MSW); critical social policy and organizational studies (PhD); individuals, families and groups (MSW); social work practice (individuals, families, groups and communities) (PhD); social work practice: individuals, families, groups and communities (PhD). Electronic applications accepted.

School of Business and Economics *Program availability:* Part-time, evening/weekend. Offers accounting (PhD); business and economics (EMTM, M Fin, M Sc, MA, MBA, PhD); co-op (MBA); economics (MA); finance (M Fin); financial economics (PhD); full-time (MBA); marketing (PhD); operations and supply chain management (PhD); organizational behavior and human resource management (M Sc); organizational behaviour and human resource management (PhD); part-time (MBA); supply chain management (M Sc); technology management (EMTM). Electronic applications accepted.

School of International Policy and Governance Offers conflict and security (PhD); global environment (PhD); global governance (MIPP); global justice and human rights (PhD); global political economy (PhD); global social governance (PhD); human security (MIPP); international economic relations (MIPP); international environmental policy (MIPP); international policy and governance (MIPP, PhD); multilateral institutions and diplomacy (PhD).

Laurier Brantford Offers criminology (MA). Electronic applications accepted.

Waterloo Lutheran Seminary *Program availability:* Part-time. Offers divinity (M Div); multifaith spiritual care and counseling (Diploma); pastoral leadership (D Min); spiritual care and counseling (D Min); theology (M Th, MTS). Electronic applications accepted.

WILKES UNIVERSITY, Wilkes-Barre, PA 18766-0002

General Information Independent, coed, comprehensive institution. *Enrollment:* 5,545 graduate, professional, and undergraduate students; 496 full-time matriculated graduate/professional students (328 women), 2,558 part-time matriculated graduate/professional students (2,012 women). *Enrollment by degree level:* 2,438 master's, 616 doctoral. *Graduate housing:* On-campus housing not available. *Student services:* Campus employment opportunities, career counseling, free psychological counseling, international student services, low-cost health insurance, multicultural affairs office, services for students with disabilities. *Library facilities:* Eugene S. Farley Library. *Collection:* Books: 184,565 (physical), 8,000 (digital/electronic); Serial titles: 60,000 (digital/electronic); Databases: 88. Students can reserve study rooms.

Computer facilities: Computer purchase and lease plans are available. 860 computers available on campus for general student use. A campuswide network can be accessed from student residence rooms and from off campus. Online class registration is available.

Website: http://www.wilkes.edu/

General Application Contact: 570-408-4235, Fax: 570-408-7846, E-mail: graduatestudies@wilkes.edu.

GRADUATE UNITS

College of Graduate and Professional Studies Students: 496 full-time (328 women), 2,558 part-time (2,012 women); includes 418 minority (192 Black or African American, non-Hispanic/Latino; 2 American Indian or Alaska Native, non-Hispanic/Latino; 81 Asian, non-Hispanic/Latino; 89 Hispanic/Latino; 4 Native Hawaiian or other Pacific Islander, non-Hispanic/Latino; 50 Two or more races, non-Hispanic/Latino), 28 international. Average age 35. Expenses: Contact institution. *Financial support:* Unspecified assistantships available. Financial award application deadline: 3/1; financial award applicants required to submit FAFSA. In 2017, 814 master's, 122 doctorates awarded. *Program availability:* Part-time, evening/weekend, 100% online, blended/hybrid learning. Offers creative writing (MA, MFA). *Application deadline:* Applications are processed on a rolling basis. *Application fee:* $45 ($65 for international students). Electronic applications accepted. *Application Contact:* 570-408-4235, Fax: 570-408-7846, E-mail: graduatestudies@wilkes.edu.

College of Science and Engineering Students: 19 full-time (3 women), 18 part-time (4 women); includes 6 minority (1 Black or African American, non-Hispanic/Latino; 2 Asian, non-Hispanic/Latino; 1 Hispanic/Latino; 2 Two or more races, non-Hispanic/Latino), 11 international. Average age 27. Expenses: Contact institution. *Financial support:* Unspecified assistantships available. Financial award application deadline: 3/1; financial award applicants required to submit FAFSA. In 2017, 20 master's awarded. *Program availability:* Part-time. Offers bioengineering (MS); electrical engineering (MSEE); engineering management (MS); mathematics (MS); mechanical engineering (MS); science and engineering (MS, MSEE). *Application deadline:* Applications are processed on a rolling basis. *Application fee:* $45 ($65 for international students). Electronic applications accepted. *Application Contact:* Kristin Donati, Associate Director of Graduate Admissions, 570-408-3338, Fax: 570-408-7846, E-mail: kristin.donati@wilkes.edu. *Dean*, Dr. William Hudson, 570-408-4600, Fax: 570-408-7860, E-mail: william.hudson@wilkes.edu.

Jay S. Sidhu School of Business and Leadership Students: 37 full-time (18 women), 87 part-time (45 women); includes 17 minority (4 Black or African American, non-Hispanic/Latino; 5 Asian, non-Hispanic/Latino; 6 Hispanic/Latino; 2 Two or more races, non-Hispanic/Latino), 14 international. Average age 30. Expenses: Contact institution. *Financial support:* Unspecified assistantships available. Financial award application deadline: 3/1; financial award applicants required to submit FAFSA. In 2017, 77 master's awarded. *Program availability:* Part-time, evening/weekend. Offers accounting (MBA); entrepreneurship (MBA); finance (MBA); health care administration (MBA); human resource management (MBA); international business (MBA); operations management (MBA); organizational leadership and development (MBA). *Application deadline:* Applications are processed on a rolling basis. *Application fee:* $45 ($65 for international students). Electronic applications accepted. *Application Contact:* Kristin Donati, Associate Director of Graduate Admissions, 570-408-3338, Fax: 570-408-7846, E-mail: kristin.donati@wilkes.edu. *Dean*, Dr. Abel Adekola, 570-408-4701, Fax: 570-408-7846, E-mail: abel.adekola@wilkes.edu.

Nesbitt School of Pharmacy Students: 285 full-time (190 women); includes 40 minority (4 Black or African American, non-Hispanic/Latino; 1 American Indian or Alaska Native, non-Hispanic/Latino; 17 Asian, non-Hispanic/Latino; 5 Hispanic/Latino; 13 Two or more races, non-Hispanic/Latino), 3 international. Average age 22. Expenses: Contact institution. *Financial support:* Federal Work-Study and unspecified assistantships available. Financial award application deadline: 3/1; financial award applicants required to submit FAFSA. In 2017, 69 doctorates awarded. Offers pharmacy (Pharm D). *Application deadline:* Applications are processed on a rolling basis. *Dean*, Dr. Scott Stolte, 570-408-4280, Fax: 570-408-7828, E-mail: scott.stolte@wilkes.edu.

Passan School of Nursing Students: 35 full-time (29 women), 793 part-time (706 women); includes 260 minority (167 Black or African American, non-Hispanic/Latino; 1 American Indian or Alaska Native, non-Hispanic/Latino; 42 Asian, non-Hispanic/Latino; 35 Hispanic/Latino; 3 Native Hawaiian or other Pacific Islander, non-Hispanic/Latino; 12 Two or more races, non-Hispanic/Latino). Average age 43. Expenses: Contact institution. *Financial support:* Unspecified assistantships available. Financial award application deadline: 3/1; financial award applicants required to submit FAFSA. In 2017, 49 master's, 30 doctorates awarded. *Program availability:* Part-time, online only, 100% online. Offers nursing (MSN, DNP, PhD). *Application deadline:* Applications are processed on a rolling basis. *Application fee:* $45. Electronic applications accepted. *Application Contact:* Director of Graduate Enrollment, 570-408-4234, Fax: 570-408-7846. *Dean*, Dr. Deborah Zbegner, 570-408-4086, Fax: 570-408-7807, E-mail: deborah.zbegner@wilkes.edu.

School of Education Students: 76 full-time (57 women), 1,586 part-time (1,204 women); includes 82 minority (10 Black or African American, non-Hispanic/Latino; 12 Asian, non-Hispanic/Latino; 41 Hispanic/Latino; 1 Native Hawaiian or other Pacific Islander, non-Hispanic/Latino; 18 Two or more races, non-Hispanic/Latino). Average age 34. Expenses: Contact institution. *Financial support:* Unspecified assistantships available. Financial award application deadline: 3/1; financial award applicants required to submit FAFSA. In 2017, 619 master's, 23 doctorates awarded. *Program availability:* Part-time, evening/weekend, 100% online, blended/hybrid learning. Offers educational development and strategies (MS Ed); educational leadership (MS Ed, Ed D); effective teaching (MS Ed); instructional media (MS Ed); instructional technology (MS Ed); international school leadership (MS Ed); international teaching and learning (MS Ed); literacy specialist (MS Ed); middle level education (MS Ed); online teaching (MS Ed); school business leadership (MS Ed); special education (MS Ed); teaching English to speakers of other languages (MS Ed). *Application deadline:* Applications are processed on a rolling basis. *Application fee:* $45 ($65 for international students). Electronic applications accepted. *Application Contact:* Stephanie Wasmanski, Associate Director of Graduate Admissions, 570-408-5535, Fax: 570-408-7846, E-mail: stephanie.wasmanski@wilkes.edu. *Dean*, Dr. Rhonda Rabbitt, 570-408-4680, Fax: 570-408-7872, E-mail: rhonda.rabbitt@wilkes.edu.

WILLAMETTE UNIVERSITY, Salem, OR 97301-3931

General Information Independent-religious, coed, comprehensive institution. *Enrollment:* 2,819 graduate, professional, and undergraduate students; 527 full-time matriculated graduate/professional students (229 women), 96 part-time matriculated graduate/professional students (41 women). *Enrollment by degree level:* 345 master's, 278 doctoral. *Graduate faculty:* 47 full-time (16 women), 17 part-time/adjunct (4 women). Tuition and fees vary according to program. *Graduate housing:* Room and/or apartments available on a first-come, first-served basis to single students; on-campus housing not available to married students. Housing application deadline: 6/1. *Student services:* Campus employment opportunities, campus safety program, career counseling, free psychological counseling, international student services, low-cost health insurance, multicultural affairs office, services for students with disabilities, teacher training. *Library facilities:* Mark O. Hatfield Library plus 1 other. *Collection:* Study areas open 24 hours, 5–7 days a week; students can reserve study rooms.

Computer facilities: A campuswide network can be accessed from student residence rooms and from off campus. Online class registration is available.
Website: http://www.willamette.edu/

General Application Contact: Office of Graduate Admissions, 503-370-6300.

GRADUATE UNITS

Atkinson Graduate School of Management Students: 131 full-time (59 women), 119 part-time (65 women); includes 51 minority (15 Black or African American, non-Hispanic/Latino; 2 American Indian or Alaska Native, non-Hispanic/Latino; 15 Asian, non-Hispanic/Latino; 15 Hispanic/Latino; 4 Native Hawaiian or other Pacific Islander, non-Hispanic/Latino), 33 international. Average age 28. 261 applicants, 67% accepted, 105 enrolled. *Faculty:* 18 full-time (5 women), 15 part-time/adjunct (5 women). Expenses: Contact institution. *Financial support:* In 2017–18, 220 students received support. Federal Work-Study, scholarships/grants, and unspecified assistantships available. Financial award application deadline: 5/1; financial award applicants required to submit FAFSA. In 2017, 138 master's awarded. *Program availability:* Part-time, evening/weekend. Offers management (MBA). JD/MBA offered jointly with College of Law. *Application deadline:* 5/1 priority date for domestic and international students. Applications are processed on a rolling basis. *Application fee:* $100. Electronic applications accepted. *Application Contact:* Juliet Valdez, Director of Recruitment, 503-370-6792, Fax: 503-370-3011, E-mail: jvaldez@willamette.edu. *Dean and Professor of Free Enterprise*, Dr. Debra J. Ringold, 503-370-6790, Fax: 503-370-3011, E-mail: dringold@willamette.edu.

College of Law *Program availability:* Part-time. Offers dispute resolution (LL M); law (MLS, JD); transnational law (LL M). Electronic applications accepted.

WILLIAM CAREY UNIVERSITY, Hattiesburg, MS 39401

General Information Independent-religious, coed, comprehensive institution. *Graduate housing:* Room and/or apartments available on a first-come, first-served basis to single students; on-campus housing not available to married students. Housing application deadline: 8/15.

GRADUATE UNITS

College of Osteopathic Medicine Offers osteopathic medicine (DO).

Department of Psychology and Graduate Counseling *Program availability:* Part-time. Offers counseling psychology (MS).

School of Business *Program availability:* Part-time. Offers business (MBA).

School of Education *Program availability:* Part-time. Offers art education (M Ed); art of teaching (M Ed); elementary education (M Ed, Ed S); English education (M Ed); gifted education (M Ed); history and social science (M Ed); mild/moderate disabilities (M Ed); secondary education (M Ed).

School of Nursing *Program availability:* Part-time. Offers nursing (MSN).

WILLIAM JAMES COLLEGE, Newton, MA 02459

General Information Independent, coed, primarily women, graduate-only institution. *Graduate housing:* On-campus housing not available.

GRADUATE UNITS

Graduate Programs Offers applied psychology in higher education student personnel administration (MA); clinical psychology (Psy D); counseling psychology (MA); counseling psychology and community mental health (MA); counseling psychology and global mental health (MA); executive coaching (Graduate Certificate); forensic and counseling psychology (MA); leadership psychology (Psy D); organizational psychology (MA); primary care psychology (MA); respecialization in clinical psychology (Certificate); school psychology (Psy D). Electronic applications accepted.

WILLIAM JESSUP UNIVERSITY, Rocklin, CA 95765

General Information Independent-religious, coed, comprehensive institution.

GRADUATE UNITS

Program in Teaching *Program availability:* Evening/weekend. Offers single subject English (MAT); single subject math (MAT).

WILLIAM JEWELL COLLEGE, Liberty, MO 64068-1843

General Information Independent, coed, comprehensive institution.

GRADUATE UNITS

Department of Education Offers differentiated instruction (MS Ed).

WILLIAM PATERSON UNIVERSITY OF NEW JERSEY, Wayne, NJ 07470-8420

General Information State-supported, coed, comprehensive institution. CGS member. *Enrollment:* 10,252 graduate, professional, and undergraduate students; 316 full-time matriculated graduate/professional students (218 women), 989 part-time matriculated graduate/professional students (751 women). *Enrollment by degree level:* 955 master's, 36 doctoral, 314 other advanced degrees. *Graduate faculty:* 139 full-time (74 women), 81 part-time/adjunct (54 women). Tuition, state resident: full-time $13,920; part-time $6264 per year. Tuition, nonresident: full-time $21,700; part-time $9765 per year. *Required fees:* $80; $36 per year. Tuition and fees vary according to course load, degree level and program. *Graduate housing:* Room and/or apartments available on a first-come, first-served basis to single students; on-campus housing not available to married students. Typical cost: $9200 per year. Room charges vary according to board plan, campus/location and housing facility selected. Housing application deadline: 5/1. *Student services:* Campus employment opportunities, campus safety program, career counseling, exercise/wellness program, free psychological counseling, international student services, multicultural affairs office, services for students with disabilities, teacher training, writing training. *Library facilities:* David and Lorraine Cheng Library. *Collection:* Books: 369,216 (physical), 116,597 (digital/electronic); Serial titles: 3,772 (physical), 164,249 (digital/electronic); Databases: 126. Weekly public service hours: 102; students can reserve study rooms. *Research affiliation:* Sun Chemical (chemistry), Arysta Life Sciences (biology).

Computer facilities: Computer purchase and lease plans are available. 1,271 computers available on campus for general student use. A campuswide network can be accessed from student residence rooms and from off campus. Online class registration is available.
Website: http://www.wpunj.edu/

General Application Contact: Augustus Kubeyinje, Director of Graduate Admissions and Enrollment Services, 973-720-3641, Fax: 973-720-2035, E-mail: kubeyinjea@wpunj.edu.

GRADUATE UNITS

College of Education Students: 73 full-time (54 women), 480 part-time (409 women); includes 153 minority (48 Black or African American, non-Hispanic/Latino; 13 Asian, non-Hispanic/Latino; 81 Hispanic/Latino; 11 Two or more races, non-Hispanic/Latino), 1 international. Average age 35. 347 applicants, 87% accepted, 226 enrolled. *Faculty:* 37 full-time (25 women), 21 part-time/adjunct (16 women). Expenses: Contact institution. *Financial support:* In 2017–18, 8,416 students received support. Career-related internships or fieldwork, Federal Work-Study, scholarships/grants, and unspecified assistantships available. Support available to part-time students. Financial award application deadline: 3/15; financial award applicants required to submit FAFSA. In 2017, 136 master's awarded. *Program availability:* Part-time, evening/weekend. Offers curriculum and learning (M Ed); early childhood education (Certificate); educational leadership (M Ed); educational media specialist (Certificate); elementary education (MAT, Certificate); elementary education subject area (Certificate); higher education administration (MA); learning disabilities consultant (Certificate); literacy (M Ed); middle level education (M Ed); middle school education subject area (Certificate); professional counseling (M Ed); reading specialist (Certificate); school library media specialist (Certificate); school principal (Certificate); school supervisor (Certificate); secondary education (MAT); special education (M Ed); teacher of students with disabilities (Certificate). *Application deadline:* For fall admission, 6/1 for domestic students, 3/1 for international students; for spring admission, 11/1 for domestic students, 10/1 for international students. Applications are processed on a rolling basis. *Application fee:* $50. Electronic applications accepted. *Application Contact:* Liana Fornarotto, Director of Education Enrollment and Certification, 973-720-2206, Fax: 973-720-2989, E-mail: fornarottol@wpunj.edu. *Dean*, Dr. Dorothy Feola, 973-720-2138, Fax: 973-720-3647, E-mail: feolad@wpunj.edu.

College of Humanities and Social Sciences Students: 62 full-time (44 women), 102 part-time (71 women); includes 76 minority (12 Black or African American, non-Hispanic/Latino; 8 Asian, non-Hispanic/Latino; 50 Hispanic/Latino; 6 Two or more races, non-Hispanic/Latino), 6 international. Average age 33. 156 applicants, 51% accepted, 52 enrolled. *Faculty:* 36 full-time (21 women), 10 part-time/adjunct (5 women). Expenses: Contact institution. *Financial support:* In 2017–18, 3,480 students received support. Career-related internships or fieldwork, Federal Work-Study, scholarships/grants, and unspecified assistantships available. Support available to part-time students. Financial award application deadline: 3/15; financial award applicants required to submit FAFSA. In 2017, 39 master's awarded. *Program availability:* Part-time. Offers applied sociology (MA); assessment and evaluation research (Certificate); bilingual education (Certificate); clinical and counseling psychology (MA); clinical psychology (Psy D); creative and professional writing (MFA); English (MA); history (MA); public policy and international affairs (MA); teaching English as a second language (Certificate). *Application deadline:* For fall admission, 6/1 for domestic students, 3/1 for international students; for spring admission, 11/1 for domestic students, 10/1 for international students. Applications are processed on a rolling basis. *Application fee:* $50. Electronic applications accepted. *Application Contact:* Tinu Adeniran, Associate Director, Graduate Admissions, 973-720-2764, Fax: 973-720-2035, E-mail: adenirant@wpunj.edu. *Dean*, Dr. Kara Rabbitt, 973-720-2180, Fax: 973-720-2955, E-mail: rabbittk@wpunj.edu.

College of Science and Health Students: 66 full-time (56 women), 197 part-time (163 women); includes 104 minority (15 Black or African American, non-Hispanic/Latino; 45 Asian, non-Hispanic/Latino; 38 Hispanic/Latino; 6 Two or more races, non-Hispanic/Latino), 3 international. Average age 33. 387 applicants, 34% accepted, 77 enrolled. *Faculty:* 29 full-time (15 women), 25 part-time/adjunct (24 women). Expenses: Contact institution. *Financial support:* In 2017–18, 9,800 students received support. Career-related internships or fieldwork, Federal Work-Study, scholarships/grants, and unspecified assistantships available. Support available to part-time students. Financial award application deadline: 3/15; financial award applicants required to submit FAFSA. In 2017, 87 master's, 5 doctorates awarded. *Program availability:* Part-time. Offers adult gerontology nurse practitioner (Certificate); biology (MS); biotechnology (MS); communication disorders (MS); exercise and sport studies (MS); materials chemistry (MS); nurse practitioner (Certificate); nursing (MSN); nursing education (Certificate); nursing practice (DNP); school nurse (Certificate). *Application deadline:* For fall admission, 6/1 for domestic students, 3/1 for international students; for spring admission, 11/1 for domestic students, 10/1 for international students. Applications are processed on a rolling basis. *Application fee:* $50. Electronic applications accepted. *Application Contact:* Christina Aiello, Assistant Director, Graduate Admissions, 973-720-2506, Fax: 973-720-2035, E-mail: aielloc@wpunj.edu. *Dean*, Dr. Venkat Sharma, 973-720-2194, Fax: 973-720-3414, E-mail: sharmav@wpunj.edu.

College of the Arts and Communication Students: 46 full-time (27 women), 16 part-time (12 women); includes 22 minority (8 Black or African American, non-Hispanic/Latino; 2 Asian, non-Hispanic/Latino; 9 Hispanic/Latino; 3 Two or more races, non-Hispanic/Latino), 12 international. Average age 29. 90 applicants, 53% accepted, 25 enrolled. *Faculty:* 21 full-time (10 women), 22 part-time/adjunct (8 women). Expenses: Contact institution. *Financial support:* Career-related internships or fieldwork, Federal Work-Study, scholarships/grants, and unspecified assistantships available. Support available to part-time students. Financial award application deadline: 3/15; financial award applicants required to submit FAFSA. In 2017, 18 master's awarded. *Program availability:* Part-time. Offers art (MFA); music (MM); professional communication (MA). *Application deadline:* For fall admission, 6/1 for domestic students, 3/1 for international students; for spring admission, 11/1 for domestic students, 10/1 for international students. Applications are processed on a rolling basis. *Application fee:* $50. Electronic applications accepted. *Application Contact:* Christina Aiello, Assistant

Director, Graduate Admissions, 973-720-2506, Fax: 973-720-2035, E-mail: aielloc@wpunj.edu. *Dean*, Daryl Moore, 973-720-2232, E-mail: moored@wpunj.edu.

Cotsakos College of Business Students: 69 full-time (37 women), 194 part-time (96 women); includes 109 minority (27 Black or African American, non-Hispanic/Latino; 13 Asian, non-Hispanic/Latino; 57 Hispanic/Latino; 12 Two or more races, non-Hispanic/Latino), 26 international. Average age 31. 164 applicants, 87% accepted, 96 enrolled. *Faculty:* 16 full-time (3 women), 3 part-time/adjunct (1 woman). Expenses: Contact institution. *Financial support:* In 2017–18, 5,300 students received support. Career-related internships or fieldwork, Federal Work-Study, scholarships/grants, and unspecified assistantships available. Support available to part-time students. Financial award application deadline: 3/15; financial award applicants required to submit FAFSA. In 2017, 73 master's awarded. *Program availability:* Part-time, evening/weekend. Offers applied business analytics (MS); business administration (MBA, Certificate); sales leadership (MS). *Application deadline:* For fall admission, 6/1 for domestic students, 3/1 for international students; for spring admission, 11/1 for domestic students, 10/1 for international students. Applications are processed on a rolling basis. *Application fee:* $50. Electronic applications accepted. *Application Contact:* Tinu Adeniran, Assistant Director, Graduate Admissions, 973-720-2764, Fax: 973-720-2035, E-mail: adenirant@wpunj.edu. *Dean*, Dr. Siamack Shojai, 973-720-2964, Fax: 973-720-2809, E-mail: shojais@wpunj.edu.

WILLIAM PENN UNIVERSITY, Oskaloosa, IA 52577-1799

General Information Independent-religious, coed, comprehensive institution.

GRADUATE UNITS

College for Working Adults *Program availability:* Online learning.

WILLIAMS BAPTIST COLLEGE, Walnut Ridge, AR 72476

General Information Independent-religious, coed, comprehensive institution.

GRADUATE UNITS

Graduate Programs

WILLIAMS COLLEGE, Williamstown, MA 01267

General Information Independent, coed, comprehensive institution. *Enrollment:* 2,117 graduate, professional, and undergraduate students; 26 full-time matriculated graduate/professional students (17 women). *Enrollment by degree level:* 26 master's. *Graduate faculty:* 24. *Tuition:* Full-time $53,240. *Graduate housing:* Room and/or apartments available on a first-come, first-served basis to single students; on-campus housing not available to married students. *Student services:* Campus employment opportunities, campus safety program, career counseling, exercise/wellness program, free psychological counseling, international student services, low-cost health insurance, multicultural affairs office, services for students with disabilities, writing training. *Library facilities:* Sawyer Library plus 2 others. *Collection:* Books: 998,634 (physical); Serial titles: 738 (physical), 93,053 (digital/electronic). Weekly public service hours: 118; study areas open 24 hours, 5–7 days a week; students can reserve study rooms. *Research affiliation:* Clark Art Institute.

Computer facilities: 1,000 computers available on campus for general student use. A campuswide network can be accessed from student residence rooms and from off campus. Online class registration is available.
Website: http://www.williams.edu/

General Application Contact: Karen E. Kowitz, Program Administrator, 413-458-0596, E-mail: kekowitz@williams.edu.

GRADUATE UNITS

Graduate Program in the History of Art Students: 26 full-time (17 women); includes 7 minority (1 Black or African American, non-Hispanic/Latino; 1 American Indian or Alaska Native, non-Hispanic/Latino; 2 Asian, non-Hispanic/Latino; 3 Hispanic/Latino). 124 applicants, 16% accepted, 12 enrolled. *Faculty:* 24. Expenses: Contact institution. *Financial support:* In 2017–18, 18 students received support. Fellowships with full and partial tuition reimbursements available and tuition waivers (full and partial) available. Financial award application deadline: 4/1; financial award applicants required to submit FAFSA. In 2017, 12 master's awarded. Offers development economics (MA); history of art (MA). MA in history of art offered jointly with Sterling and Francine Clark Art Institute. *Application deadline:* For fall admission, 1/3 for domestic and international students. *Application fee:* $75. Electronic applications accepted. *Application Contact:* Karen E. Kowitz, Program Administrator, 413-458-0596, E-mail: kekowitz@williams.edu.

WILLIAMSON COLLEGE, Franklin, TN 37067

General Information Independent-religious, coed, comprehensive institution.

GRADUATE UNITS

Program in Organizational Leadership *Program availability:* Evening/weekend. Offers organizational leadership (MA).

WILLIAM WOODS UNIVERSITY, Fulton, MO 65251-1098

General Information Independent-religious, coed, comprehensive institution. *Graduate housing:* On-campus housing not available.

GRADUATE UNITS

Graduate and Adult Studies *Program availability:* Part-time, evening/weekend. Offers administration (M Ed, Ed S); athletic/activities administration (M Ed); curriculum and instruction (M Ed, Ed S); educational leadership (Ed D); equestrian education (M Ed); health management (MBA); human resources (MBA); leadership (MBA); marketing, advertising, and public relations (MBA); teaching and technology (M Ed). Electronic applications accepted.

WILMINGTON COLLEGE, Wilmington, OH 45177

General Information Independent-religious, coed, comprehensive institution. *Graduate housing:* On-campus housing not available.

GRADUATE UNITS

Department of Education *Program availability:* Part-time. Offers reading (M Ed); special education (M Ed).

WILMINGTON UNIVERSITY, New Castle, DE 19720-6491

General Information Independent, coed, university. *Enrollment:* 14,118 graduate, professional, and undergraduate students; 2,007 full-time matriculated graduate/professional students (1,106 women), 3,571 part-time matriculated graduate/professional students (2,448 women). *Enrollment by degree level:* 5,017 master's, 561 doctoral. *Graduate faculty:* 71 full-time (39 women), 507 part-time/adjunct (272 women). *Tuition:* Part-time $466 per credit. *Required fees:* $25 per semester. Tuition and fees vary according to degree level and campus/location. *Graduate housing:* On-campus housing not available. *Student services:* Career counseling, free psychological counseling, international student services, services for students with disabilities, teacher training, writing training. *Library facilities:* Robert C. and Dorothy M. Peoples Library plus 1 other. *Collection:* Books: 104,530 (physical), 179,000 (digital/electronic); Serial titles: 50 (physical), 98,000 (digital/electronic).

Computer facilities: 600 computers available on campus for general student use. A campuswide network can be accessed. Online class registration is available.
Website: http://www.wilmu.edu/

General Application Contact: Laura Morris, Director of Admissions, 302-295-1179, Fax: 302-328-5164, E-mail: infocenter@wilmu.edu.

GRADUATE UNITS

College of Business Students: 525 full-time (294 women), 1,212 part-time (780 women); includes 557 minority (412 Black or African American, non-Hispanic/Latino; 14 American Indian or Alaska Native, non-Hispanic/Latino; 55 Asian, non-Hispanic/Latino; 25 Hispanic/Latino; 3 Native Hawaiian or other Pacific Islander, non-Hispanic/Latino; 48 Two or more races, non-Hispanic/Latino), 157 international. Average age 35. 1,484 applicants, 70% accepted, 685 enrolled. *Faculty:* 16 full-time (8 women), 106 part-time/adjunct (49 women). Expenses: Contact institution. *Financial support:* Applicants required to submit FAFSA. In 2017, 543 master's, 16 doctorates awarded. *Program availability:* Part-time, evening/weekend. Offers accounting (MBA, MS); business administration (MBA, DBA); environmental stewardship (MBA); finance (MBA); health care administration (MBA, MSM); homeland security (MBA, MSM); human resource management (MSM); management information systems (MBA, MSN); marketing (MSM); marketing management (MBA); military leadership (MSM); organizational leadership (MBA, MSM); public administration (MSM). *Application deadline:* Applications are processed on a rolling basis. *Application fee:* $35. Electronic applications accepted. *Application Contact:* Laura Morris, Director of Admissions, 877-967-5456, E-mail: infocenter@wilmu.edu. *Dean*, Dr. Kathy S. Kennedy Ratajack, 302-356-2481.

College of Education Students: 546 full-time (394 women), 960 part-time (732 women); includes 320 minority (241 Black or African American, non-Hispanic/Latino; 12 American Indian or Alaska Native, non-Hispanic/Latino; 11 Asian, non-Hispanic/Latino; 28 Hispanic/Latino; 3 Native Hawaiian or other Pacific Islander, non-Hispanic/Latino; 25 Two or more races, non-Hispanic/Latino), 7 international. Average age 34. 1,068 applicants, 64% accepted, 582 enrolled. *Faculty:* 23 full-time (13 women), 162 part-time/adjunct (99 women). Expenses: Contact institution. *Financial support:* Applicants required to submit FAFSA. In 2017, 430 master's, 59 doctorates awarded. *Program availability:* Part-time, evening/weekend. Offers applied technology in education (M Ed); career and technical education (M Ed); educational leadership (Ed D); elementary and secondary school counseling (M Ed); elementary studies (M Ed); ESOL literacy (M Ed); higher education leadership (Ed D); instruction: gifted and talented (M Ed); instruction: teacher of reading (M Ed); instruction: teaching and learning (M Ed); organizational leadership (Ed D); school leadership (MAT); secondary education (MAT); special education (M Ed). *Application deadline:* For fall admission, 4/30 for domestic students. Applications are processed on a rolling basis. *Application fee:* $35. Electronic applications accepted. *Application Contact:* Laura Morris, Director of Admissions, 877-967-5464, E-mail: infocenter@wilmu.edu. *Dean*, Dr. John C. Gray, 302-295-1139.

College of Health Professions Students: 164 full-time (154 women), 662 part-time (604 women); includes 178 minority (129 Black or African American, non-Hispanic/Latino; 5 American Indian or Alaska Native, non-Hispanic/Latino; 23 Asian, non-Hispanic/Latino; 7 Hispanic/Latino; 3 Native Hawaiian or other Pacific Islander, non-Hispanic/Latino; 11 Two or more races, non-Hispanic/Latino), 6 international. Average age 39. 770 applicants, 63% accepted, 361 enrolled. *Faculty:* 10 full-time (9 women), 59 part-time/adjunct (50 women). Expenses: Contact institution. *Financial support:* Fellowships with tuition reimbursements and traineeships available. Financial award applicants required to submit FAFSA. In 2017, 259 master's, 22 doctorates awarded. *Program availability:* Part-time. Offers adult nurse practitioner (MSN); family nurse practitioner (MSN); gerontology nurse practitioner (MSN); nursing (MSN); nursing leadership (MSN); nursing practice (DNP). *Application deadline:* For fall admission, 4/1 for domestic students; for spring admission, 9/1 for domestic students. Applications are processed on a rolling basis. *Application fee:* $35. Electronic applications accepted. *Application Contact:* Laura Morris, Director of Admissions, 877-967-5464, E-mail: infocenter@wilmu.edu. *Dean*, Denise Z. Westbrook, 302-356-6915.

College of Social and Behavioral Sciences Students: 174 full-time (132 women), 428 part-time (334 women); includes 269 minority (229 Black or African American, non-Hispanic/Latino; 5 American Indian or Alaska Native, non-Hispanic/Latino; 7 Asian, non-Hispanic/Latino; 17 Hispanic/Latino; 11 Two or more races, non-Hispanic/Latino), 11 international. Average age 35. 541 applicants, 81% accepted, 292 enrolled. *Faculty:* 11 full-time (6 women), 74 part-time/adjunct (34 women). Expenses: Contact institution. *Financial support:* Applicants required to submit FAFSA. In 2017, 271 master's awarded. *Program availability:* Part-time, evening/weekend. Offers administration of human services (MS); administration of justice (MS); clinical mental health counseling (MS); homeland security (MS). *Application deadline:* Applications are processed on a rolling basis. *Application fee:* $35. Electronic applications accepted. *Application Contact:* Laura Morris, Director of Admissions, 877-967-5464, E-mail: inquire@wilmcoll.edu. *Dean*, Dr. Edward L. Guthrie, 302-356-6870.

College of Technology Students: 631 full-time (159 women), 486 part-time (141 women); includes 91 minority (53 Black or African American, non-Hispanic/Latino; 3 American Indian or Alaska Native, non-Hispanic/Latino; 22 Asian, non-Hispanic/Latino; 5 Hispanic/Latino; 2 Native Hawaiian or other Pacific Islander, non-Hispanic/Latino; 6 Two or more races, non-Hispanic/Latino), 917 international. Average age 26. 774 applicants, 45% accepted, 307 enrolled. *Faculty:* 5 full-time (2 women), 99 part-time/adjunct (31 women). Expenses: Contact institution. In 2017, 965 master's awarded. *Program availability:* Part-time, evening/weekend. Offers cybersecurity (MS); information assurance (MS); information systems technologies (MS); management and management information systems (MS); technology project management (MS); Web design (MS). *Application deadline:* Applications are processed on a rolling basis. *Application fee:* $35. Electronic applications accepted. *Application Contact:* Laura Morris, Director of Admissions, 877-967-5464, E-mail: infocenter@wilmu.edu. *Dean*, Dr. Mary Ann K. Westerfield.

WILSON COLLEGE, Chambersburg, PA 17201-1285

General Information Independent-religious, coed, primarily women, comprehensive institution.

GRADUATE UNITS

Graduate Programs *Program availability:* Evening/weekend. Offers accounting (M Acc); choreography and visual art (MFA); education (M Ed); educational technology (MET); healthcare administration (MHA); humanities (MA); management (MSM); nursing (MSN); special education (MSE). Electronic applications accepted.

WINEBRENNER THEOLOGICAL SEMINARY, Findlay, OH 45840

General Information Independent-religious, coed, graduate-only institution. *Graduate housing:* On-campus housing not available.

GRADUATE UNITS

Graduate Programs *Program availability:* Part-time, 100% online, blended/hybrid learning. Offers clinical counseling (MA); family ministry (MA); practical theology (MA); theological and ministerial studies (M Div, D Min); theological studies (MA). Electronic applications accepted.

WINGATE UNIVERSITY, Wingate, NC 28174

General Information Independent-religious, coed, comprehensive institution. *Graduate housing:* Rooms and/or apartments available on a first-come, first-served basis to single and married students. Housing application deadline: 8/15.

GRADUATE UNITS

Department of Physical Therapy Offers physical therapy (DPT).

Harris Department of Physician Assistant Studies Offers physician assistant studies (MPAS).

Porter B. Byrum School of Business *Program availability:* Part-time, evening/weekend. Offers accounting (MAC); corporate innovation (MBA); finance (MBA); general management (MBA); healthcare management (MBA); marketing (MBA); project management (MBA). Electronic applications accepted.

School of Pharmacy Offers pharmacy (Pharm D). Electronic applications accepted.

School of Sport Sciences Offers sport management (MA). Electronic applications accepted.

Thayer School of Education *Program availability:* Part-time, evening/weekend. Offers community college executive leadership (Ed D); educational leadership (MA Ed, Ed S); elementary education (MA Ed, MAT).

WINONA STATE UNIVERSITY, Winona, MN 55987

General Information State-supported, coed, comprehensive institution. *Graduate housing:* Room and/or apartments available to single students; on-campus housing not available to married students. Housing application deadline: 3/2.

GRADUATE UNITS

College of Education *Program availability:* Part-time, evening/weekend. Offers addiction counseling (Certificate); clinical mental health counseling (MS); education (MS, Certificate, Ed S); education leadership (MS, Ed S); human services (MS); multicultural education (Certificate); organizational leadership (MS); professional leadership (MS); school counseling (MS); special education (MS); sport management (MS).

College of Liberal Arts *Program availability:* Part-time. Offers English (MS); liberal arts (MA, MS); literature and language (MA); TESOL (MA).

College of Nursing and Health Sciences *Program availability:* Part-time, online learning. Offers adult-gerontology acute care nurse practitioner (MS, DNP, Post Master's Certificate); adult-gerontology clinical nurse specialist (MS, DNP, Post Master's Certificate); adult-gerontology primary care nurse practitioner (MS, DNP, Post Master's Certificate); family nurse practitioner (MS, DNP, Post Master's Certificate); nurse educator (MS); nursing and organizational leadership (MS, DNP, Post Master's Certificate); practice and leadership innovations (DNP, Post Master's Certificate).

WINSTON-SALEM STATE UNIVERSITY, Winston-Salem, NC 27110-0003

General Information State-supported, coed, comprehensive institution. *Graduate housing:* On-campus housing not available.

GRADUATE UNITS

Department of Occupational Therapy Offers occupational therapy (MS). Electronic applications accepted.

Department of Physical Therapy Offers physical therapy (DPT). Electronic applications accepted.

MAT Program *Program availability:* Part-time, evening/weekend, online learning. Offers middle grades education (MAT); special education (MAT). Electronic applications accepted.

Program in Business Administration *Program availability:* Part-time, evening/weekend, online learning. Offers business administration (MBA). Electronic applications accepted.

Program in Computer Science and Information Technology *Program availability:* Part-time. Offers computer science and information technology (MS). Electronic applications accepted.

Program in Health Administration Offers health administration (MHA).

Program in Nursing *Program availability:* Part-time, evening/weekend, online learning. Offers advanced nurse educator (MSN); family nurse practitioner (MSN); nursing (DNP). Electronic applications accepted.

Program in Rehabilitation Counseling *Program availability:* Part-time, online learning. Offers rehabilitation counseling (MRC). Electronic applications accepted.

WINTHROP UNIVERSITY, Rock Hill, SC 29733

General Information State-supported, coed, comprehensive institution. CGS member. *Enrollment:* 6,073 graduate, professional, and undergraduate students; 465 full-time matriculated graduate/professional students (355 women), 594 part-time matriculated graduate/professional students (460 women). *Enrollment by degree level:* 1,059 master's. *Graduate housing:* Rooms and/or apartments available on a first-come, first-served basis to single and married students. Housing application deadline: 3/1. *Student services:* Campus employment opportunities, campus safety program, career counseling, exercise/wellness program, free psychological counseling, international student services, low-cost health insurance, multicultural affairs office, services for students with disabilities. *Library facilities:* Dacus Library plus 1 other. *Collection:* Books: 361,941 (physical), 288,136 (digital/electronic); Serial titles: 540 (physical), 36,003 (digital/electronic); Databases: 133. Weekly public service hours: 49; study areas open 24 hours, 5–7 days a week; students can reserve study rooms.

Computer facilities: Computer purchase and lease plans are available. 620 computers available on campus for general student use. A campuswide network can be accessed from student residence rooms and from off campus. Online class registration, university services are available.
Website: http://www.winthrop.edu/

General Application Contact: The Graduate School, 800-411-7041, Fax: 803-323-2204, E-mail: gradschool@winthrop.edu.

GRADUATE UNITS

College of Arts and Sciences Students: 200 full-time (165 women), 74 part-time (50 women); includes 79 minority (58 Black or African American, non-Hispanic/Latino; 2 Asian, non-Hispanic/Latino; 13 Hispanic/Latino; 6 Two or more races, non-Hispanic/Latino). Average age 42. Expenses: Contact institution. *Financial support:* Research assistantships with full tuition reimbursements, career-related internships or fieldwork, Federal Work-Study, scholarships/grants, and unspecified assistantships available. Support available to part-time students. Financial award application deadline: 2/1; financial award applicants required to submit FAFSA. In 2017, 109 master's, 26 other advanced degrees awarded. *Program availability:* Part-time. Offers arts and sciences (MA, MLA, MS, MSW, Certificate, SSP); biology (MS); dietetics (Certificate); English (MA); history (MA); human nutrition (MS); liberal arts (MLA); psychology (MS, SSP); social work (MSW). *Application deadline:* Applications are processed on a rolling basis. *Application fee:* $50. Electronic applications accepted. *Application Contact:* 800-411-7041, Fax: 803-323-2292, E-mail: gradschool@winthrop.edu. *Interim Dean*, Takita Sumter, 803-323-2160, E-mail: sumtert@winthrop.edu.

College of Business Administration Students: 82 full-time (51 women), 49 part-time (24 women); includes 32 minority (29 Black or African American, non-Hispanic/Latino; 1 Asian, non-Hispanic/Latino; 1 Hispanic/Latino; 1 Two or more races, non-Hispanic/Latino), 44 international. Average age 34. Expenses: Contact institution. *Financial support:* Research assistantships with full tuition reimbursements, Federal Work-Study, scholarships/grants, and unspecified assistantships available. Support available to part-time students. Financial award application deadline: 2/1; financial award applicants required to submit FAFSA. In 2017, 85 master's awarded. *Program availability:* Part-time, evening/weekend, online learning. Offers business administration (MBA). *Application deadline:* For fall admission, 7/15 priority date for domestic students; for spring admission, 12/1 for domestic students. Applications are processed on a rolling basis. *Application fee:* $50. Electronic applications accepted. *Application Contact:* 800-411-7041, Fax: 803-323-2292, E-mail: gradschool@winthrop.edu. *Dean*, Dr. PN Saksena, 803-323-2186, Fax: 803-323-3960, E-mail: saksenapn@winthrop.edu.

College of Education Students: 167 full-time (132 women), 89 part-time (80 women); includes 74 minority (61 Black or African American, non-Hispanic/Latino; 1 American Indian or Alaska Native, non-Hispanic/Latino; 2 Asian, non-Hispanic/Latino; 6 Hispanic/Latino; 1 Native Hawaiian or other Pacific Islander, non-Hispanic/Latino; 3 Two or more races, non-Hispanic/Latino), 2 international. Average age 38. Expenses: Contact institution. *Financial support:* Research assistantships with full tuition reimbursements, career-related internships or fieldwork, Federal Work-Study, scholarships/grants, and unspecified assistantships available. Support available to part-time students. Financial award application deadline: 2/1; financial award applicants required to submit FAFSA. In 2017, 137 master's awarded. *Program availability:* Part-time. Offers agency counseling (M Ed); education (M Ed, MAT); educational leadership (M Ed); physical education (MAT); school counseling (M Ed); secondary education (M Ed); special education (M Ed). *Application deadline:* For fall admission, 7/15 priority date for domestic students; for spring admission, 12/1 for domestic students. Applications are processed on a rolling basis. *Application fee:* $50. Electronic applications accepted. *Application Contact:* 800-411-7041, Fax: 803-323-2292, E-mail: gradschool@winthrop.edu. *Dean*, Dr. Jeannie Rakestraw, 803-323-2151, Fax: 803-323-4369, E-mail: rakestrawj@winthrop.edu.

College of Visual and Performing Arts Students: 10 full-time (5 women), 30 part-time (21 women); includes 14 minority (11 Black or African American, non-Hispanic/Latino; 2 Asian, non-Hispanic/Latino; 1 Hispanic/Latino), 1 international. Average age 39. Expenses: Contact institution. *Financial support:* Research assistantships with full tuition reimbursements, Federal Work-Study, scholarships/grants, and unspecified assistantships available. Support available to part-time students. Financial award application deadline: 2/1; financial award applicants required to submit FAFSA. In 2017, 22 master's awarded. *Program availability:* Part-time. Offers art (MFA); art administration (MA); art education (MA); conducting (MM); music education (MME); performance (MM); visual and performing arts (MA, MFA, MM, MME). *Application deadline:* Applications are processed on a rolling basis. *Application fee:* $50. Electronic applications accepted. *Application Contact:* 800-411-7041, Fax: 803-323-2292, E-mail: gradschool@winthrop.edu. *Dean*, Dr. Jeff Bellantoni, 803-323-2323, Fax: 803-323-2333, E-mail: wohld@winthrop.edu.

WISCONSIN LUTHERAN COLLEGE, Milwaukee, WI 53226-9942

General Information Independent-religious, coed, comprehensive institution.

GRADUATE UNITS

College of Adult and Graduate Studies

WISCONSIN SCHOOL OF PROFESSIONAL PSYCHOLOGY, Milwaukee, WI 53225-4960

General Information Independent, coed, graduate-only institution. *Graduate housing:* On-campus housing not available.

GRADUATE UNITS

Program in Clinical Psychology *Program availability:* Part-time, evening/weekend. Offers clinical psychology (MA, Psy D).

WITTENBERG UNIVERSITY, Springfield, OH 45501-0720

General Information Independent-religious, coed, comprehensive institution.

GRADUATE UNITS

Graduate Program

WOLFORD COLLEGE, Naples, FL 34108

General Information Proprietary, coed, graduate-only institution.

GRADUATE UNITS

Graduate Programs Offers nurse anesthesia (MSNA, DNAP).

WON INSTITUTE OF GRADUATE STUDIES, Glenside, PA 19038

General Information Proprietary, coed, graduate-only institution. *Enrollment by degree level:* 41 master's, 34 other advanced degrees. *Graduate faculty:* 9 full-time (5 women), 21 part-time/adjunct (16 women). *Student services:* Career counseling, writing training. *Library facilities:* Won Institute Library plus 1 other. *Collection:* Books: 4,987 (physical), 5 (digital/electronic); Databases: 3. Study areas open 24 hours, 5–7 days a week; students can reserve study rooms.

Computer facilities: 4 computers available on campus for general student use. Online class registration is available.
Website: http://www.woninstitute.edu/

General Application Contact: Jennifer Cake, Enrollment Management Counselor, 215-884-8942 Ext. 219, Fax: 215-884-9002, E-mail: jennifer.cake@woninstitute.edu.

GRADUATE UNITS

Acupuncture Studies Program Students: 37 full-time (30 women); includes 6 minority (2 Black or African American, non-Hispanic/Latino; 2 Asian, non-Hispanic/Latino; 2 Native Hawaiian or other Pacific Islander, non-Hispanic/Latino), 2 international. Average age 38. Expenses: Contact institution. Offers acupuncture studies (M Ac). *Application deadline:* For fall admission, 6/15 for domestic students. Applications are processed on a rolling basis. *Application fee:* $75. Electronic applications accepted. *Application Contact:* Jennifer Cake, Lead Enrollment Management Counselor, 215-884-8942 Ext.

212, E-mail: jennifer.cake@woninstitute.edu. *Chair*, Ben Griffith, 215-884-8942, Fax: 215-884-8942, E-mail: ben.griffith@woninstitute.edu.

Program in Chinese Herbal Medicine Students: 34 full-time (27 women); includes 9 minority (1 Black or African American, non-Hispanic/Latino; 6 Asian, non-Hispanic/Latino; 2 Two or more races, non-Hispanic/Latino). Average age 42. Expenses: Contact institution. *Financial support:* Scholarships/grants available. Offers Chinese herbal medicine (Certificate). *Application deadline:* For fall admission, 8/1 for domestic students. Applications are processed on a rolling basis. *Application fee:* $75. Electronic applications accepted. *Application Contact:* Jennifer Cake, Enrollment Management Counselor, 215-884-8942 Ext. 219, Fax: 215-884-9002, E-mail: jennifer.cake@woninstitute.edu. *Acupuncture and Chinese Herbal Medicine Chair*, Jacqueline Lacava, 215-884-8942, Fax: 215-884-9002, E-mail: chp.director@woninstitute.edu.

Won Buddhist Studies Program Students: 4 full-time (2 women), 3 part-time (1 woman); includes 4 minority (all Asian, non-Hispanic/Latino). Average age 34. Expenses: Contact institution. *Financial support:* Application deadline: 8/1. *Program availability:* Part-time. Offers Won Buddhist studies (MWBS). *Application deadline:* For fall admission, 8/1 for domestic students; for spring admission, 12/1 for domestic students. Applications are processed on a rolling basis. *Application fee:* $75. *Application Contact:* Jennifer Cake, Enrollment Management Counselor, 215-884-8942 Ext. 219, E-mail: jennifer.cake@woninstitute.edu. *Chair*, Rev. Dr. Sanghyeon Cheon, 215-884-8942, E-mail: wbschair@woninstitute.edu.

WOODBURY UNIVERSITY, Burbank, CA 91504

General Information Independent, coed, comprehensive institution. *Graduate housing:* Room and/or apartments available on a first-come, first-served basis to single students; on-campus housing not available to married students.

GRADUATE UNITS

School of Architecture Offers architecture (M Arch, MIA, MS Arch).

School of Business *Program availability:* Part-time, evening/weekend. Offers business administration (MBA); organizational leadership (MA).

WOODS HOLE OCEANOGRAPHIC INSTITUTION, Woods Hole, MA 02543-1541

General Information Independent, coed, graduate-only institution. CGS member. *Graduate housing:* Rooms and/or apartments guaranteed to single students and available on a first-come, first-served basis to married students.

GRADUATE UNITS

MIT/WHOI Joint Program in Oceanography/Applied Ocean Science and Engineering Offers applied ocean science and engineering (PhD); biological oceanography (PhD); chemical oceanography (PhD); marine geology and geophysics (PhD); physical oceanography (PhD). Program offered jointly with Massachusetts Institute of Technology. Electronic applications accepted.

WORCESTER POLYTECHNIC INSTITUTE, Worcester, MA 01609-2280

General Information Independent, coed, university. CGS member. *Enrollment:* 6,642 graduate, professional, and undergraduate students; 1,277 full-time matriculated graduate/professional students (473 women), 814 part-time matriculated graduate/professional students (191 women). *Enrollment by degree level:* 1,595 master's, 419 doctoral, 77 other advanced degrees. *Graduate faculty:* 207 full-time (51 women), 41 part-time/adjunct (7 women). *Tuition:* Full-time $26,226; part-time $1457 per credit. *Required fees:* $60; $30 per credit. One-time fee: $15. Tuition and fees vary according to course load. *Graduate housing:* Rooms and/or apartments available on a first-come, first-served basis to single and married students. *Student services:* Campus employment opportunities, campus safety program, career counseling, exercise/wellness program, free psychological counseling, grant writing training, international student services, low-cost health insurance, multicultural affairs office, services for students with disabilities, teacher training, writing training. *Library facilities:* George C. Gordon Library plus 1 other. *Collection:* Books: 198,648 (physical), 1.4 million (digital/electronic); Serial titles: 5,116 (physical), 227,285 (digital/electronic); Databases: 490. Weekly public service hours: 107; students can reserve study rooms. *Research affiliation:* American Institutes for Research (educational software), United States Advanced Battery Consortium LLC (advanced battery recycling), SRI International (educational software), Toyota Motor Company (automotive safety technology), MathWorks Inc. (Internet of Things (IoT)), University of Massachusetts Medical School at Worcester (basic transitional and clinical medical research).

Computer facilities: Computer purchase and lease plans are available. 860 computers available on campus for general student use. A campuswide network can be accessed from student residence rooms and from off campus. Online class registration, online course content are available.
Website: http://www.wpi.edu/

General Application Contact: Lynne Dougherty, Administrative Assistant, 508-831-5301, Fax: 508-831-5717, E-mail: grad@wpi.edu.

GRADUATE UNITS

Graduate Admissions Students: 1,277 full-time (473 women), 814 part-time (191 women); includes 257 minority (58 Black or African American, non-Hispanic/Latino; 1 American Indian or Alaska Native, non-Hispanic/Latino; 98 Asian, non-Hispanic/Latino; 70 Hispanic/Latino; 1 Native Hawaiian or other Pacific Islander, non-Hispanic/Latino; 29 Two or more races, non-Hispanic/Latino), 926 international. Average age 28. 4,020 applicants, 55% accepted, 752 enrolled. *Faculty:* 207 full-time (51 women), 41 part-time/adjunct (7 women). Expenses: Contact institution. *Financial support:* Fellowships, research assistantships, teaching assistantships, career-related internships or fieldwork, institutionally sponsored loans, scholarships/grants, health care benefits, tuition waivers, and unspecified assistantships available. Financial award application deadline: 1/1. In 2017, 747 master's, 46 doctorates, 50 other advanced degrees awarded. *Program availability:* Part-time, evening/weekend, 100% online, blended/hybrid learning. Offers aerospace engineering (MS, PhD); applied mathematics (MS); applied statistics (MS); biochemistry (MS, PhD); bioinformatics and computational biology (MS, PhD); biology and biotechnology (MS); biomedical engineering (M Eng, MS, PhD, Graduate Certificate); bioscience administration (MS); biotechnology (PhD); chemical engineering (MS, PhD); chemistry (MS, PhD); civil and environmental engineering (Advanced Certificate, Graduate Certificate); civil engineering (M Eng, ME, MS, PhD); computer science (MS, PhD, Advanced Certificate, Graduate Certificate); construction project management (MS, Graduate Certificate); data science (MS, PhD, Graduate Certificate); electrical and computer engineering (Advanced Certificate, Graduate Certificate); electrical engineering (M Eng, MS, PhD); environmental engineering (MS); financial mathematics (MS); fire protection engineering (MS, PhD, Advanced Certificate, Graduate Certificate); industrial mathematics (MS); interactive media and game development (MS); interdisciplinary social science (PhD); learning sciences and technologies (MS, PhD); manufacturing engineering (MS, PhD); master builder (M Eng); materials process engineering (MS); materials science and engineering (MS, PhD); mathematical sciences (PhD, Graduate Certificate); mathematics (MME); mechanical engineering (MS, PhD, Graduate Certificate); nuclear science and engineering (Graduate Certificate); physics (MS, PhD); power systems engineering (MS); power systems management (MS); robotics engineering (MS, PhD); social science (PhD); system dynamics (MS, Graduate Certificate); system dynamics and innovation management (MS, Graduate Certificate); systems engineering (MS, PhD, Graduate Certificate); systems modeling (MS). *Application deadline:* For fall admission, 1/1 priority date for domestic and international students; for spring admission, 10/1 priority date for domestic and international students. Applications are processed on a rolling basis. *Application fee:* $70. Electronic applications accepted. *Application Contact:* Lynne Dougherty, Administrative Assistant, 508-831-5301, Fax: 508-831-5717, E-mail: grad@wpi.edu. *Dean*, Dr. Terri Camesano, 508-831-5380, E-mail: grad@wpi.edu.

Foisie Business School Students: 254 full-time (153 women), 150 part-time (52 women); includes 34 minority (3 Black or African American, non-Hispanic/Latino; 10 Asian, non-Hispanic/Latino; 14 Hispanic/Latino; 7 Two or more races, non-Hispanic/Latino), 230 international. Average age 29. 677 applicants, 71% accepted, 146 enrolled. *Faculty:* 26 full-time (12 women), 9 part-time/adjunct (0 women). Expenses: Contact institution. *Financial support:* Career-related internships or fieldwork, institutionally sponsored loans, scholarships/grants, and unspecified assistantships available. Financial award application deadline: 6/1. In 2017, 188 master's, 14 doctorates awarded. *Program availability:* Part-time, evening/weekend, 100% online, blended/hybrid learning. Offers business administration (PhD); information technology (MS); management (Graduate Certificate); marketing and technological innovation (MS); operations design and leadership (MS); supply chain management (MS); technology (MS). *Application deadline:* For fall admission, 6/1 priority date for domestic and international students; for spring admission, 11/1 priority date for domestic students, 10/1 priority date for international students. Applications are processed on a rolling basis. *Application fee:* $70. Electronic applications accepted. *Application Contact:* Margaret Clancey, Recruiting Operations Coordinator, 508-831-4980, Fax: 508-831-5720, E-mail: maclancey@wpi.edu. *Executive Director*, Melissa Terrio, 508-831-4665, Fax: 508-831-4665, E-mail: biz@wpi.edu.

WORCESTER STATE UNIVERSITY, Worcester, MA 01602-2597

General Information State-supported, coed, comprehensive institution. *Enrollment:* 6,434 graduate, professional, and undergraduate students; 162 full-time matriculated graduate/professional students (134 women), 539 part-time matriculated graduate/professional students (404 women). *Enrollment by degree level:* 588 master's, 113 other advanced degrees. *Graduate faculty:* 52 full-time (34 women), 43 part-time/adjunct (24 women). Tuition, state resident: full-time $3042; part-time $169 per credit hour. Tuition, nonresident: full-time $3042; part-time $169 per credit hour. *Required fees:* $2754; $153 per credit hour. *Graduate housing:* On-campus housing not available. *Student services:* Campus employment opportunities, campus safety program, career counseling, exercise/wellness program, free psychological counseling, international student services, low-cost health insurance, multicultural affairs office, services for students with disabilities, teacher training, writing training. *Library facilities:* Worcester State University Library. *Collection:* Books: 143,442 (physical), 152,949 (digital/electronic); Serial titles: 76 (physical), 137,540 (digital/electronic); Databases: 252. Weekly public service hours: 100.

Computer facilities: Computer purchase and lease plans are available. A campuswide network can be accessed from student residence rooms and from off campus. Online class registration is available.
Website: http://www.worcester.edu/

General Application Contact: Sara Grady, Associate Dean, Graduate and Continuing Education, 508-929-8130, Fax: 508-929-8100, E-mail: sara.grady@worcester.edu.

GRADUATE UNITS

Graduate School Students: 162 full-time (134 women), 539 part-time (404 women); includes 79 minority (28 Black or African American, non-Hispanic/Latino; 5 American Indian or Alaska Native, non-Hispanic/Latino; 7 Asian, non-Hispanic/Latino; 28 Hispanic/Latino; 11 Two or more races, non-Hispanic/Latino), 13 international. Average age 33. 688 applicants, 58% accepted, 213 enrolled. *Faculty:* 52 full-time (34 women), 43 part-time/adjunct (24 women). Expenses: Contact institution. *Financial support:* Career-related internships or fieldwork, scholarships/grants, and unspecified assistantships available. Financial award application deadline: 3/1; financial award applicants required to submit FAFSA. In 2017, 225 master's, 154 other advanced degrees awarded. *Program availability:* Part-time, evening/weekend. Offers accounting (MS); biotechnology (MS); community and public health nursing (MSN); curriculum and instruction (Ed S); early childhood education (M Ed, Postbaccalaureate Certificate); education (M Ed); elementary education (M Ed, Postbaccalaureate Certificate); English (MA); English as a second language (M Ed, Postbaccalaureate Certificate); health care administration (MS); health education (M Ed); history (MA); leadership and administration (M Ed); managerial leadership (MS); marketing (MS); middle school education (M Ed, Postbaccalaureate Certificate); moderate disabilities (M Ed, Postbaccalaureate Certificate); non-profit management (MS); nurse educator (MSN); occupational therapy (MOT); reading (M Ed, Postbaccalaureate Certificate); school psychology (M Ed, Ed S); secondary education (M Ed, Ed S, Postbaccalaureate Certificate); Spanish (MA); speech-language pathology (MS). *Application deadline:* For fall admission, 6/15 for domestic and international students; for spring admission, 11/1 for domestic and international students; for summer admission, 4/1 for domestic and international students. Applications are processed on a rolling basis. *Application fee:* $50. Electronic applications accepted. *Application Contact:* Sara Grady, Associate Dean, Graduate Studies and Professional Development, 508-929-8787, Fax: 508-929-8100, E-mail: sara.grady@worcester.edu. *Associate Vice President for Continuing Education/Dean of the Graduate Studies*, Dr. Roberta Kyle, 508-929-8111, Fax: 508-929-8100, E-mail: rkyle@worcester.edu.

WORLD MEDICINE INSTITUTE, Honolulu, HI 96821

General Information Independent, coed, graduate-only institution. *Graduate housing:* On-campus housing not available.

GRADUATE UNITS

Program in Acupuncture and Oriental Medicine *Program availability:* Part-time, evening/weekend. Offers acupuncture and Oriental medicine (M Ac OM).

WORLD MISSION UNIVERSITY, Los Angeles, CA 90020

General Information Independent-religious, coed, comprehensive institution.

GRADUATE UNITS

Graduate Programs *Program availability:* Online learning.

THE WRIGHT INSTITUTE, Berkeley, CA 94704-1796

General Information Independent, coed, graduate-only institution. *Graduate housing:* On-campus housing not available.

GRADUATE UNITS

Doctoral Program in Clinical Psychology Offers clinical psychology (Psy D). Electronic applications accepted.

Master of Arts in Counseling Psychology Program *Program availability:* Part-time, evening/weekend. Offers counseling psychology (MA). Electronic applications accepted.

WRIGHT STATE UNIVERSITY, Dayton, OH 45435

General Information State-supported, coed, university. CGS member. *Graduate housing:* Rooms and/or apartments available on a first-come, first-served basis to single and married students. *Research affiliation:* Wright-Patterson Air Force Base (research and development, systems and logistics), Veterans Administration Medical Center, Scott-Kettering Magnetic Resonance Research Laboratory (medical science), Edison Biotechnology Center, Edison Materials Technology Center (processing).

GRADUATE UNITS

Boonshoft School of Medicine Offers aerospace medicine (MS); health promotion and education (MPH); medicine (MPH, MS, MD, PhD); pharmacology and toxicology (MS).

Graduate School *Program availability:* Part-time, evening/weekend, 100% online, blended/hybrid learning. Electronic applications accepted.

College of Education and Human Services *Program availability:* Part-time, evening/weekend. Offers adolescent to young adult education (M Ed); advanced curriculum and instruction (Ed S); advanced educational leadership (Ed S); chemical dependency (MRC); classroom teacher education (M Ed, MA); counseling (M Ed, MA, MS); education and human services (M Ed, MA, MRC, MS, Ed S); intervention specialist (M Ed); pupil personnel services (M Ed); rehabilitation counseling (MRC).

College of Engineering and Computer Science *Program availability:* Part-time, evening/weekend. Offers aerospace systems engineering (MS); biomedical engineering (MS); computer engineering (MS); computer science (MS); computer science and engineering (MS, PhD); electrical engineering (MS); engineering (PhD); engineering and computer science (MS, PhD); industrial and human factors engineering (MS); materials science and engineering (MS); mechanical engineering (MS); renewable and clean energy (MS).

College of Liberal Arts *Program availability:* Part-time. Offers criminal justice and social problems (MA); English (MA); history (MA); humanities (M Hum); liberal arts (M Hum, MA, MM, MPA); music (MM); public administration (MPA).

College of Nursing and Health *Program availability:* Part-time, evening/weekend. Offers administration of nursing and health care systems (MS); adult gerontology clinical nurse specialist (MS); adult-gerontology acute care nurse practitioner (MS); family nurse practitioner (MS); neonatal nurse practitioner (MS); nursing and health (MS); pediatric nurse practitioner-acute care (MS); pediatric nurse practitioner-primary care (MS); psychiatric mental health nurse practitioner (MS); school nurse (MS).

College of Science and Mathematics *Program availability:* Part-time, evening/weekend. Offers anatomy (MS); applied mathematics (MS); applied statistics (MS); biochemistry and molecular biology (MS); biological sciences (MS); biomedical sciences (PhD); chemistry (MS); earth science education (MST); environmental sciences (PhD); geological sciences (Graduate Certificate); geophysics (MS); human factors and industrial/organizational psychology (MS, PhD); mathematics (MS); microbiology and immunology (MS); physics (MS, MST); physiology and neuroscience (MS); science and mathematics (MS, MST, PhD, Graduate Certificate).

Raj Soin College of Business *Program availability:* Part-time, evening/weekend. Offers accountancy (M Acc); business (M Acc, MBA, MIS, MS); business administration (MBA); information systems (MIS); logistics and supply chain management (MS); management information technology (MBA); social and applied economics (MS).

School of Professional Psychology Offers clinical psychology (Psy D).

WYCLIFFE COLLEGE, Toronto, ON M5S 1H7, Canada

General Information Independent-religious, coed, graduate-only institution. *Graduate housing:* Rooms and/or apartments guaranteed to single students and available on a first-come, first-served basis to married students. Housing application deadline: 5/1.

GRADUATE UNITS

Division of Advanced Degree Studies *Program availability:* Part-time. Offers theology (MA, Th M, D Min, PhD, Th D). PhD, D Min, MA offered jointly with Toronto School of Theology; Th D, Th M with University of Toronto.

Division of Basic Degree Studies *Program availability:* Part-time. Offers Christian Studies (Diploma); theology (M Div, M Rel, MTS). M Div, M Rel, MTS offered jointly with University of Toronto.

XAVIER UNIVERSITY, Cincinnati, OH 45207

General Information Independent-religious, coed, university. *Graduate housing:* On-campus housing not available.

GRADUATE UNITS

College of Arts and Sciences *Program availability:* Part-time. Offers arts and sciences (MA); English (MA); health care mission integration (MA); theology (MA); urban sustainability and resilience (MA). Electronic applications accepted.

College of Social Sciences, Health and Education Offers clinical psychology (Psy D); coaching education and athlete development (M Ed); criminal justice (MS); health services administration (MHSA); industrial-organizational psychology (MA); occupational therapy (MOT); social sciences, health and education (M Ed, MA, MHSA, MOT, MS, MSN, DNP, Ed D, Psy D, PMC); sport administration (M Ed).

School of Education Offers children's multicultural literature (M Ed); clinical mental health counseling (MA); education (M Ed, MA, MS, Ed D); educational administration (M Ed); elementary education (M Ed); human resource development (MS); Montessori education (M Ed); reading (M Ed); school counseling (MA); secondary education (M Ed); special education (M Ed). Electronic applications accepted.

School of Nursing *Program availability:* Part-time, evening/weekend. Offers nursing (MSN, DNP, PMC). Electronic applications accepted.

Williams College of Business *Program availability:* Part-time, evening/weekend. Offers accountancy (MS); business (Exec MBA, MBA, MS); business administration (Exec MBA, MBA); business intelligence (MBA); finance (MBA); health industry (MBA); international business (MBA); marketing (MBA); values-based leadership (MBA). Electronic applications accepted.

XAVIER UNIVERSITY OF LOUISIANA, New Orleans, LA 70125

General Information Independent-religious, coed, comprehensive institution. *Graduate housing:* On-campus housing not available.

GRADUATE UNITS

College of Pharmacy Offers pharmacy (Pharm D). Electronic applications accepted.

Graduate School *Program availability:* Part-time, evening/weekend. Offers counseling (MA); curriculum and instruction (MA); educational leadership (MA).

Institute for Black Catholic Studies *Program availability:* Part-time. Offers pastoral theology (Th M).

YALE UNIVERSITY, New Haven, CT 06520

General Information Independent, coed, university. CGS member. *Graduate housing:* Rooms and/or apartments available on a first-come, first-served basis to single and married students. Housing application deadline: 6/1. *Research affiliation:* Howard Hughes Medical Institute, J.B. Pierce Foundation (environmental physiology), Haskins Laboratories (speech, hearing, reading).

GRADUATE UNITS

Graduate School of Arts and Sciences *Program availability:* Part-time. Offers African studies (MA); African-American studies (PhD); American studies (PhD); anthropology (M Phil, MA, PhD); applied mathematics (M Phil, MS, PhD); Arabic and Islamic studies (MA, PhD); archaeological studies (MA); archaeology of the ancient Near East (MA, PhD); arts and sciences (M Phil, MA, MS, PhD); Assyriology (MA, PhD); astronomy (PhD); behavioral neuroscience (PhD); biochemistry, molecular biology and chemical biology (PhD); biogeochemistry (PhD); biophysical chemistry (PhD); cell biology (PhD); cellular and developmental biology (PhD); cellular and molecular physiology (PhD); classics (M Phil, MA, PhD); climate dynamics (PhD); clinical psychology (PhD); cognitive psychology (PhD); comparative and historical sociology (PhD); comparative literature (PhD); computer science (MS, PhD); cultural sociology and social theory (PhD); developmental psychology (PhD); East Asian languages and literatures (PhD); East Asian languages and literatures and film studies (PhD); East Asian studies (MA); ecology and evolutionary biology (PhD); economics (PhD); Egyptology (MA, PhD); English language and literature (MA, PhD); environmental sciences (PhD); experimental pathology (MS, PhD); film studies (PhD); forestry (PhD); French (M Phil, MA, PhD); genetics (PhD); geochemistry (PhD); geophysics (PhD); German (PhD); global affairs (MA); Graeco-Arabic studies (MA, PhD); history (M Phil, MA, PhD); history of art (PhD); history of science and medicine (MS, PhD); immunobiology (PhD); inorganic chemistry (PhD); international and development economics (MA); Italian language and literature (PhD); Latin American literature (PhD); linguistics (PhD); Luso-Brazilian and Spanish/Spanish American literatures (PhD); mathematics (M Phil, MS, PhD); medieval Slavic literature and philology (PhD); medieval studies (M Phil, PhD); meteorology (PhD); molecular biophysics and biochemistry (PhD); music history (MA); music theory (MA); neurobiology (PhD); neuroscience (PhD); Northwest Semitic, Bible, comparative Semitics (MA, PhD); oceanography (PhD); organic chemistry (PhD); paleontology (PhD); paleooceanography (PhD); petrology (PhD); philosophy (PhD); physical and theoretical chemistry (PhD); physics (PhD); plant sciences (PhD); Polish literature (PhD); political science (PhD); religious studies (PhD); Renaissance studies (PhD); Russian and East European studies (MA); Russian literature (PhD); Slavic languages and literatures and film studies (PhD); social stratification and the life course (PhD); social/personality psychology (PhD); solar and terrestrial physics (PhD); Spanish peninsular literature (PhD); statistics (MA, PhD); tectonics (PhD).

School of Engineering and Applied Science *Program availability:* Part-time. Offers applied physics (MS, PhD); biomedical engineering (MS, PhD); chemical engineering (MS, PhD); electrical engineering (MS, PhD); engineering and applied science (MS, PhD); environmental engineering (MS, PhD); mechanical engineering (MS, PhD).

School of Architecture Offers architecture (M Arch, M Env Des, MEM, PhD). Electronic applications accepted.

School of Art Offers graphic design (MFA); painting/printmaking (MFA); photography (MFA); sculpture (MFA). Electronic applications accepted.

School of Drama Offers acting (MFA, Certificate); design (MFA, Certificate); directing (MFA, Certificate); dramaturgy and dramatic criticism (MFA, DFA); playwriting (MFA, Certificate); sound design (MFA, Certificate); stage management (MFA, Certificate); technical design and production (MFA, Certificate); theater management (MFA). Electronic applications accepted.

School of Forestry and Environmental Studies *Program availability:* Part-time. Offers environmental management (MEM); environmental science (MES); forest science (MFS); forestry (MF); forestry and environmental studies (PhD). Electronic applications accepted.

School of Music Students: 209 full-time (90 women); includes 47 minority (3 Black or African American, non-Hispanic/Latino; 23 Asian, non-Hispanic/Latino; 10 Hispanic/Latino; 11 Two or more races, non-Hispanic/Latino), 72 international. Average age 24. 1,456 applicants, 11% accepted, 117 enrolled. *Faculty:* 28 full-time (9 women), 31 part-time/adjunct (6 women). Expenses: Contact institution. *Financial support:* In 2017–18, 209 students received support, including 209 fellowships (averaging $36,000 per year); Federal Work-Study and scholarships/grants also available. Financial award application deadline: 5/30; financial award applicants required to submit FAFSA. In 2017, 82 master's, 8 doctorates, 26 ADs awarded. Offers music (MM, MMA, DMA, AD, Certificate). *Application deadline:* For fall admission, 12/1 for domestic and international students. *Application fee:* $150. Electronic applications accepted. *Application Contact:* Suzanne M. Stringer, Director of Student Services, 203-432-1962, Fax: 203-432-7448, E-mail: suzanne.stringer@yale.edu. *Dean,* Robert Blocker, 203-432-4160, Fax: 203-432-7542.

School of Nursing *Program availability:* Part-time, online learning. Offers nursing (MSN, DNP, PhD, Post Master's Certificate). Electronic applications accepted.

Yale Divinity School *Program availability:* Part-time. Offers divinity (M Div, MAR, STM). Electronic applications accepted.

Yale Law School Students: 625 full-time (299 women). Average age 26. 2,862 applicants, 8% accepted, 205 enrolled. *Faculty:* 64 full-time, 113 part-time/adjunct. Expenses: Contact institution. *Financial support:* Application deadline: 3/15; applicants required to submit FAFSA. Offers law (LL M, MSL, JD, JSD, PhD). *Application deadline:* For fall admission, 2/28 for domestic students. Applications are processed on a rolling basis. *Application fee:* $60. Electronic applications accepted. *Application Contact:* Craig Janecek, Director of Admissions, 203-432-4995, E-mail: admissions.law@yale.edu. *Dean,* Heather Gerken, 203-432-1660.

Yale School of Management Offers accounting (PhD); business administration (MBA); financial economics (PhD); management (MBA, PhD); marketing (PhD); organizations and management (PhD).

Yale School of Medicine *Program availability:* Part-time. Offers biological and biomedical sciences (PhD); computational biology and bioinformatics (PhD); immunology (PhD); medicine (APMPH, MM Sc, MPH, MS, MD, PhD); microbiology (PhD); molecular biophysics and biochemistry (PhD); molecular cell biology, genetics, and development (PhD); neurobiology (PhD); neuroscience (PhD); pharmacological sciences and molecular medicine (PhD); pharmacology (PhD); physician associate (MM Sc); physiology and integrative medical biology (PhD). Electronic applications accepted.

Yale School of Public Health *Program availability:* Part-time. Offers applied biostatistics and epidemiology (APMPH); biostatistics (MPH, MS, PhD); chronic disease epidemiology (MPH, PhD); environmental health sciences (MPH, PhD); epidemiology of microbial diseases (MPH, PhD); global health (APMPH); health management (MPH); health policy (MPH); health policy and administration (APMPH,

PhD); occupational and environmental medicine (APMPH); preventive medicine (APMPH); social and behavioral sciences (APMPH, MPH). MS and PhD offered through the Graduate School. Electronic applications accepted.

YESHIVA BETH MOSHE, Scranton, PA 18505-2124

General Information Independent-religious, men only, comprehensive institution.

GRADUATE UNITS

Graduate Programs

YESHIVA DERECH CHAIM, Brooklyn, NY 11218

General Information Independent-religious, men only, comprehensive institution.

GRADUATE UNITS

Graduate Program Offers Talmudic studies (PhD).

YESHIVA KARLIN STOLIN, Brooklyn, NY 11204

General Information Independent-religious, men only, comprehensive institution. *Graduate housing:* On-campus housing not available.

GRADUATE UNITS

Graduate Programs

YESHIVA OF NITRA RABBINICAL COLLEGE, Mount Kisco, NY 10549

General Information Independent-religious, men only, comprehensive institution.

GRADUATE UNITS

Graduate Programs Offers theology (First Talmudic Degree, Second Talmudic Degree).

YESHIVA SHAAR HATORAH TALMUDIC RESEARCH INSTITUTE, Kew Gardens, NY 11418-1469

General Information Independent-religious, men only, comprehensive institution.

GRADUATE UNITS

Graduate Programs

YESHIVATH VIZNITZ, Monsey, NY 10952

General Information Independent-religious, men only, comprehensive institution.

GRADUATE UNITS

Graduate Programs

YESHIVATH ZICHRON MOSHE, South Fallsburg, NY 12779

General Information Independent-religious, men only, comprehensive institution.

GRADUATE UNITS

Graduate Programs *Program availability:* Part-time.

YESHIVA UNIVERSITY, New York, NY 10033-3201

General Information Independent, coed, university. *Graduate housing:* On-campus housing not available.

GRADUATE UNITS

Azrieli Graduate School of Jewish Education and Administration *Program availability:* Part-time, evening/weekend. Offers Jewish education and administration (MS, Ed D, Specialist).

Benjamin N. Cardozo School of Law Students: 994 full-time (530 women), 107 part-time (56 women); includes 218 minority (40 Black or African American, non-Hispanic/Latino; 84 Asian, non-Hispanic/Latino; 74 Hispanic/Latino; 20 Two or more races, non-Hispanic/Latino), 96 international. Average age 25. 2,755 applicants, 52% accepted, 419 enrolled. *Faculty:* 61 full-time (24 women), 92 part-time/adjunct (38 women). Expenses: Contact institution. *Financial support:* In 2017–18, 845 students received support, including 115 research assistantships (averaging $1,429 per year); career-related internships or fieldwork, Federal Work-Study, institutionally sponsored loans, scholarships/grants, health care benefits, and tuition waivers (full and partial) also available. Support available to part-time students. Financial award application deadline: 3/1; financial award applicants required to submit FAFSA. In 2017, 70 master's, 391 doctorates awarded. *Program availability:* Part-time. Offers comparative legal thought (LL M); dispute resolution and advocacy (LL M); general studies (LL M); intellectual property law (LL M); law (JD). *Application deadline:* For fall admission, 4/1 priority date for domestic students; for spring admission, 12/1 for domestic students. Applications are processed on a rolling basis. *Application fee:* $50. Electronic applications accepted. *Dean of Admissions,* David G. Martinidez, 212-790-0357, Fax: 212-790-0482, E-mail: lawinfo@yu.edu.

Bernard Revel Graduate School of Jewish Studies *Program availability:* Part-time. Offers Jewish studies (MA, PhD).

Ferkauf Graduate School of Psychology *Program availability:* Part-time. Offers clinical health psychology (PhD); clinical psychology (Psy D); mental health counseling psychology (MA); psychology (MA, PhD, Psy D); school/clinical-child psychology (Psy D).

The Katz School *Program availability:* Part-time, online learning. Offers biotechnology management and entrepreneurship (MS); data analytics and visualization (MS); enterprise risk management (MS); marketing (MS); mathematics (MA); quantitative economics (MS); speech-language pathology (MS).

Sy Syms School of Business *Program availability:* Part-time. Offers accounting (MS); business (EMBA); marketing (MS); taxation (MS).

Wurzweiler School of Social Work *Program availability:* Part-time, evening/weekend. Offers social work (MSW, PhD).

YORK COLLEGE OF PENNSYLVANIA, York, PA 17403-3651

General Information Independent, coed, comprehensive institution. *Enrollment:* 4,415 graduate, professional, and undergraduate students; 44 full-time matriculated graduate/professional students (32 women), 199 part-time matriculated graduate/professional students (133 women). *Enrollment by degree level:* 222 master's, 21 doctoral. *Graduate faculty:* 18 full-time (10 women), 18 part-time/adjunct (8 women). Tuition and fees vary according to program. *Graduate housing:* On-campus housing not available. *Student services:* Campus employment opportunities, campus safety program, career counseling, exercise/wellness program, free psychological counseling, international student services, services for students with disabilities, writing training. *Library facilities:* Schmidt Library.

Computer facilities: A campuswide network can be accessed from student residence rooms and from off campus. Online class registration is available.
Website: http://www.ycp.edu/

General Application Contact: Michael Thorp, Director of Admissions, 717-815-2240, Fax: 717-849-1607, E-mail: admissions@ycp.edu.

GRADUATE UNITS

Graham School of Business Students: 3 full-time (2 women), 72 part-time (33 women); includes 14 minority (7 Black or African American, non-Hispanic/Latino; 3 Asian, non-Hispanic/Latino; 1 Hispanic/Latino; 3 Two or more races, non-Hispanic/Latino). Average age 35. 68 applicants, 76% accepted, 28 enrolled. *Faculty:* 9 full-time (2 women), 3 part-time/adjunct (0 women). Expenses: Contact institution. *Financial support:* In 2017–18, 3 students received support. Scholarships/grants available. Financial award applicants required to submit FAFSA. In 2017, 17 master's awarded. *Program availability:* Part-time, evening/weekend. Offers accounting (M Acc); business (MBA); continuous improvement (MBA); financial management (MBA); health care management (MBA); management (MBA); marketing (MBA); self-designed (MBA). *Application deadline:* For fall admission, 7/15 priority date for domestic students, 5/1 for international students; for spring admission, 11/15 priority date for domestic students, 9/1 for international students; for summer admission, 4/15 priority date for domestic students. Applications are processed on a rolling basis. *Application fee:* $0. Electronic applications accepted. *Application Contact:* MBA Office, 717-815-1491, Fax: 717-600-3999, E-mail: mba@ycp.edu. *MBA Director,* Nicole Cornell Sadowski, 717-815-1491, Fax: 717-600-3999, E-mail: ncornell@ycp.edu.

Master of Education Program Students: 87 part-time (62 women); includes 2 minority (1 Hispanic/Latino; 1 Two or more races, non-Hispanic/Latino), 1 international. Average age 33. 57 applicants, 79% accepted, 39 enrolled. *Faculty:* 2 full-time (1 woman), 7 part-time/adjunct (3 women). Expenses: Contact institution. *Financial support:* Scholarships/grants available. Financial award applicants required to submit FAFSA. In 2017, 7 master's awarded. *Program availability:* Part-time-only, evening/weekend. Offers educational leadership (M Ed); educational technology (M Ed); reading specialist (M Ed). *Application deadline:* For fall admission, 7/15 priority date for domestic students; for spring admission, 11/15 priority date for domestic students; for summer admission, 4/15 priority date for domestic students. Applications are processed on a rolling basis. *Application fee:* $0. Electronic applications accepted. *Director, Master of Education Program,* Dr. Joshua D. DeSantis, 717-815-1936, E-mail: jdesant1@ycp.edu.

The Stabler Department of Nursing Students: 41 full-time (30 women), 40 part-time (38 women); includes 9 minority (1 Black or African American, non-Hispanic/Latino; 3 Asian, non-Hispanic/Latino; 1 Hispanic/Latino; 4 Two or more races, non-Hispanic/Latino), 1 international. Average age 35. 96 applicants, 31% accepted, 29 enrolled. *Faculty:* 7 full-time (all women), 8 part-time/adjunct (5 women). Expenses: Contact institution. *Financial support:* In 2017–18, 1 student received support. Scholarships/grants available. Financial award applicants required to submit FAFSA. In 2017, 24 master's awarded. *Program availability:* Part-time. Offers adult gerontology clinical nurse specialist (MS); nurse anesthetist (MS). *Application fee:* $0. Electronic applications accepted. *Application Contact:* Allison Malachosky, Administrative Assistant, 717-815-1243, E-mail: amalacho@ycp.edu. *Graduate Program Director,* Dr. Kimberly Fenstermacher, 717-815-1383, Fax: 717-849-1651, E-mail: kfenster@ycp.edu.

YORK COLLEGE OF THE CITY UNIVERSITY OF NEW YORK, Jamaica, NY 11451

General Information State and locally supported, coed, comprehensive institution.

GRADUATE UNITS

School of Arts and Sciences Offers pharmaceutcial science and business (MS).

School of Health Sciences and Professional Programs Offers physician assistant (MSPAS).

YORK UNIVERSITY, Toronto, ON M3J 1P3, Canada

General Information Province-supported, coed, university. CGS member. *Graduate housing:* Rooms and/or apartments available on a first-come, first-served basis to single and married students. *Research affiliation:* Imperial Oil Limited, National Palace Museum, Unicorn Children's Foundation (developmental and learning disorders), Smithsonian Institution (astronomy, physics, space), Beijing Municipality (management training), German Academic Exchange (German studies).

GRADUATE UNITS

Faculty of Graduate Studies *Program availability:* Part-time, evening/weekend. Offers communication and culture (MA, PhD); environmental studies (MES, PhD); interdisciplinary studies (MA); social and political thought (MA, PhD). Electronic applications accepted.

Faculty of Education *Program availability:* Part-time. Offers education (M Ed, PhD). Electronic applications accepted.

Faculty of Fine Arts *Program availability:* Part-time. Offers art history (MA, PhD); composition (MA); dance (MA, MFA, PhD); design (M Des); film (MA, MFA, PhD); fine arts (M Des, MA, MFA, PhD); music (PhD); musicology and ethnomusicology (MA); theatre (MFA); theatre and performance studies (MA, PhD); visual arts (MFA, PhD). Electronic applications accepted.

Faculty of Health Offers critical disability studies (MA, PhD); health (M Sc, M Sc N, MA, PhD); kinesiology and health science (M Sc, MA, PhD); nursing (M Sc N); psychology (MA, PhD).

Faculty of Liberal Arts and Professional Studies Offers disaster and emergency management (MA); economics (MA, PhD); English (MA, PhD); gender, feminist and women's studies (MA, PhD); geography (M Sc, MA, PhD); history (MA, PhD); human resources management (MHRM, PhD); humanities (MA, PhD); liberal arts and professional studies (M Sc, MA, MHRM, MPPAL, MSW, PhD); linguistics and applied linguistics (MA, PhD); philosophy (MA, PhD); political science (MA, PhD); public policy, administration and law (MPPAL); social anthropology (MA, PhD); social work (MSW, PhD); sociology (MA, PhD).

Faculty of Science *Program availability:* Part-time, evening/weekend. Offers biology (M Sc, PhD); chemistry (M Sc, PhD); industrial and applied mathematics (M Sc); mathematics and statistics (MA, PhD); physics and astronomy (M Sc, PhD); science (M Sc, MA, PhD).

Glendon Campus Offers French studies (MA, PhD); public and international affairs (MA); translation (MA).

Lassonde School of Engineering Offers computer science (M Sc, PhD); earth and space science (M Sc, PhD); engineering (M Sc, PhD).

Osgoode Hall Law School *Program availability:* Part-time, evening/weekend. Offers law (LL M, JD, PhD). Electronic applications accepted.

Schulich School of Business *Program availability:* Part-time, evening/weekend. Offers accounting (M Acc); administration (PhD); business (MBA); business analytics (MBA); finance (MF); international business (IMBA). Electronic applications accepted.

YO SAN UNIVERSITY OF TRADITIONAL CHINESE MEDICINE, Los Angeles, CA 90066

General Information Private, coed, graduate-only institution. *Graduate housing:* On-campus housing not available.

GRADUATE UNITS

Program in Acupuncture and Traditional Chinese Medicine *Program availability:* Part-time, online learning. Offers acupuncture and traditional Chinese medicine (MATCM).

YOUNGSTOWN STATE UNIVERSITY, Youngstown, OH 44555-0001

General Information State-supported, coed, comprehensive institution. CGS member. *Graduate housing:* Room and/or apartments available on a first-come, first-served basis to single students; on-campus housing not available to married students. *Research affiliation:* BioRemedial Technologies Inc. (environmental bioremediation), Ohio Supercomputer Center (computational chemistry and physics), Northeast Ohio Medical University (medicine), Parker-Hannifin Corporation (engineering technology), Ohio Mass Spectrometry Consortium (chemistry and biology).

GRADUATE UNITS

Graduate School *Program availability:* Part-time, evening/weekend.

Beeghly College of Education *Program availability:* Part-time, evening/weekend. Offers adolescent/young adult education (MS Ed); community counseling (MS Ed); content area concentration (MS Ed); early childhood education (MS Ed); education (MS Ed, Ed D); educational administration (MS Ed); educational leadership (Ed D); educational technology (MS Ed); gifted and talented education (MS Ed); literacy (MS Ed); middle childhood education (MS Ed); school counseling (MS Ed); special education (MS Ed).

Bitonte College of Health and Human Services *Program availability:* Part-time, evening/weekend. Offers criminal justice (MS); health and human services (MHHS, MPH, MS, MSN, DPT); nursing (MSN); physical therapy (DPT); public health (MPH).

College of Fine and Performing Arts *Program availability:* Part-time, evening/weekend. Offers fine and performing arts (MM); jazz studies (MM); music education (MM); music history and literature (MM); music theory and composition (MM); performance (MM).

College of Liberal Arts and Social Sciences *Program availability:* Part-time. Offers applied behavior analysis (MS); economics (MA); English (MA); environmental studies (MS); financial economics (MA); gerontology (MA); history (MA); industrial/institutional management (Certificate); liberal arts and social sciences (MA, MS, Certificate); risk management (Certificate).

College of Science, Technology, Engineering and Mathematics *Program availability:* Part-time, evening/weekend. Offers analytical chemistry (MS); applied mathematics (MS); biochemistry (MS); chemistry education (MS); civil and environmental engineering (MSE); computer engineering (MSE); computer science (MS); computing and information systems (MCIS); electrical engineering (MSE); environmental biology (MS); industrial and systems engineering (MSE); inorganic chemistry (MS); mechanical engineering (MSE); molecular biology, microbiology, and genetic (MS); organic chemistry (MS); physical chemistry (MS); physiology and anatomy (MS); science, technology, engineering and mathematics (MCIS, MSE); secondary mathematics (MS); statistics (MS).

Williamson College of Business Administration *Program availability:* Part-time, evening/weekend. Offers accounting (MBA); business administration (MBA, Certificate); enterprise resource planning (Certificate); marketing (MBA).

CLOSE-UPS OF INSTITUTIONS OFFERING GRADUATE AND PROFESSIONAL WORK

ACADEMY OF ART UNIVERSITY

Graduate Programs

Programs of Study

Academy of Art University offers Master of Arts (M.A.), Master of Fine Arts (M.F.A.), Master of Architecture (M.Arch.), and Master of Arts in Teaching (M.A.T.) degrees as well as an Art Teaching Credential. Courses are available online and in San Francisco in the following areas of study: Acting (speech, improv, physical acting), Advertising (creative strategy, art direction, copywriting), Animation & Visual Effects (background painting/layout design, character development, storyboard art, 3-D modeling, VFX/compositing), Architecture (structures, materials and methods of construction, design process, structural and environmental systems), Art Education (learning to teach in museums, developmental psychology, teaching art in the community and in the California K–12 classroom), Art History (Renaissance art, American art history, ancient art history, looking at art, philosophy), Art Teaching Credential (learning to teach both children and adults), Fashion (design, footwear & accessory design, knitwear, merchandising, textiles, product design, costume design), Fashion Costume Design (2-D concept design, 3-D production for film, research for costume needs, story and character costume design), Fashion Journalism (fashion writing, editorials for magazines, newspaper writing, fashion news), Fine Art (painting, printmaking, sculpture), Game Development (game engines, prototyping, level design, game art, 3-D modeling), Graphic Design (corporate and brand identity, package design, print and collateral), illustration (traditional and comic book), Industrial Design (furniture design, product design, toy design), Interior Architecture & Design (commercial and residential design), Jewelry & Metal Arts (fashion jewelry design, enameling, stone setting, casting, welded and fabricated sculpture), Landscape Architecture (plant design, elements in landscape, grading and drainage, urban open spaces), Motion Pictures & Television (cinematography, directing, editing, producing, production design, screenwriting), Multimedia Communications (journalism, editing, short-form documentary), Music Production & Sound Design for Visual Media (harmony, arranging, orchestration, music production techniques, scoring for film, sound design), Photography (architecture, advertising, digital documentary, editorial, fashion, fine art, landscape, photojournalism, portraiture), Visual Development (concept art for animation, film and games, digital painting, character design, cinematic storytelling, maquettes, environment creation), Web Design & New Media (user experience design, interactive design, new media, web design), and Writing for Film, Television & Digital Media (writing, pitching, and the business side of being a professional writer).

Academy of Art University graduate candidates engage in a unique interdisciplinary approach to master's degree preparation. Comprised of studio work and academic investigation, the programs prepare students for the rigors of the industry. Attainment of the various master's degrees requires the graduate candidate to successfully complete studio courses, directed study, academic study, and electives. Total units required to graduate varies depending on the degree.

Academy of Art University also offers revolutionary online graduate degree programs that provide the same exceptional education offered on campus, but with greater flexibility. Studying online allows students to balance course work with career, family, and other responsibilities. The Academy's accreditation assures the highest standard of education, instruction, and effectiveness. Online classes teach students the skills and techniques used by professional artists and designers, skills which can help students make the most of their creative abilities.

Facilities

Academy of Art University's state-of-the-art facilities offer students the tools they need to prepare for professional careers in art and design. The Academy invests in top-notch equipment to ensure it remains on the cutting edge of technology. Learning on industry-standard equipment, students gain hands-on experience.

Academy of Art University students have access to an array of digital tools. The School of Game Development and the School of Animation & Visual Effects provide the latest equipment, as well as a video and Cintiq lab, green screen studio, and sound booth. The School of Web Design & New Media houses a usability lab with the most current software, while the School of Music Production & Sound Design for Visual Media offers the latest sound design and video editing tools.

The School of Advertising is designed to look, feel, and function like an ad agency. Located in the heart of San Francisco's Financial District, the School of Graphic Design has the latest industry tools that enable students to have a seamless transition into post-graduation work. The School of Illustration is housed in a unique historic building in San Francisco's Union Square District. The original libraries, meeting rooms, theater, and a ballroom have been transformed into drawing/painting studios and classrooms.

Both undergraduate and graduate students in Architecture and Interior Architecture & Design share an 800 square-foot materials library and plotting room, as well as a model shop. The School of Industrial Design offers multiple shop facilities and a 3-D computer lab. The School of Landscape Architecture benefits from being located in San Francisco, the hub of urban landscape design.

Fashion students have access to studio facilities for women's, men's, and children's wear, as well as textile design, knitwear design, fashion merchandising, and marketing. In 2005, the Academy's School of Fashion was the first school to premiere collections of recent graduates at Mercedes-Benz Fashion Week at Bryant Park and continues with this tradition today. Surrounded by world-renowned museums and galleries, the School of Fine Art and the School of Art History facilities include thousands of square feet of studio space with everything students need to bring their individual visions to life.

The School of Motion Pictures & Television and the School of Acting facilities include a postproduction facility, green screen studio, screenwriting lab, custom-built voiceover room, and several soundstage studios. Students of the School of Multimedia Communications have access to a cutting-edge radio studio and television studio, complete with robotic cameras, anchor desks and interview sets, teleprompters, and green screens. The School of Photography facilities are equipped with both traditional and digital photographic technology.

The library provides state-of-the-art digital tools, making it possible for students to access extensive art and design image resources and information on demand. The Academy Resource Center offers all students free learning support services that include study hall tutoring, academic coaching, English as a second language support programs, a writing lab, and a multimedia language lab.

Financial Aid

Academy of Art University offers financial aid packages consisting of loans, interest-free payment plans, and work-study to eligible students. As financial aid programs, procedures, and eligibility requirements change frequently, applicants should contact the Financial Aid office at 79 New Montgomery Street, 4th Floor, San Francisco, California 94105, or by telephone at 800-544-2787 (U.S. only) or 415-274-2222 to check current requirements.

Also, for incoming graduate students, please inquire about scholarship or grant opportunities. Since 2012, the Academy has awarded over $10 million in grants and scholarships.

Cost of Study

For 2018–19, tuition is $1,031 per credit unit for graduate study. There is a $50 application fee and a $95 enrollment fee. Course fees average $400 per semester, depending on the class and area of study. Tuition and fees are subject to change at any time. Through the Academy, students already have access to most of the expensive technical equipment necessary for their area of study. Estimated graduate expenses for a full-time student are $26,452 per academic year.

Student Group

The master's programs accommodate more than 4,000 students. Of those, 64 percent are women and 54 percent are international. Approximately 33 percent of the students receive financial aid.

Student Outcomes

Academy of Art University guides students to professional creative futures. Firms hiring Academy of Art University graduates include Pixar, NBC, Apple, Nike, Publicis/Hal Riney, Louis Vuitton, Williams-Sonoma Inc., Mazda, Electronic Arts, Architecture Planning Interiors, Carnal Comics, Hang Art Gallery, Architecture International, Blizzard, BMW, Tesla Motors, DreamWorks, and many others.

Location

Strategically located in the heart of San Francisco, Academy of Art University's campus is ideal for emerging artists and designers. Academy students benefit from the location which is centered within the creative industry, near Silicon Valley, Pixar Animation Studios, LucasArts, and more. Beautiful San Francisco is more than an inspiring backdrop for creative students. From its museums and theaters to its diverse population, the city is renowned as a center for technology, design, arts, and culture.

Academy of Art University has created a vibrant community of artists and designers, providing students with the opportunity to collaborate among disciplines to bring their dreams to life. This community enables students to grow as artists and designers, and develop a solid network of colleagues within their field.

The University

In 1929, Academy of Art University founder Richard S. Stephens—the advertising Creative Director of *Sunset* magazine—acted on his belief that "aspiring artists and designers, given proper instruction, hard work, and dedication, can learn the skills needed to become successful professionals." His new school of advertising art consisted of 46 students meeting in one room on San Francisco's Kearny Street.

The instructors, who were professional artists, brought real-world problems, situations, solutions, and practical experience to the students. Based on this idea, the school's philosophy was formulated: hire established professionals to teach the art and design professionals of tomorrow. At that time, advertising consisted primarily of illustrations, photos, and copy. Consequently, it became necessary to teach beginning students the fundamentals of drawing, painting, color, light, and photography, as well as layout and typography.

When Richard A. Stephens succeeded his father as President in 1951, the Foundations Department was added, ensuring all students mastered the principles of traditional art and design. Illustration soon expanded to include fine arts (drawing, painting, sculpture, and printmaking), and advertising design led to the School of Graphic Design. Fashion (design, textiles, and merchandising) and an Interior Design School were also added. In 1966, the Academy officially became a college, and a decade later began to offer the Master of Fine Arts degree. By 1992, there were more than 2,500 students.

The leadership of the Academy was then turned over to the third generation. Dr. Elisa Stephens, granddaughter of the founder, quickly determined that the small School of Web Design & New Media had enormous potential to prepare students for multimedia careers with companies such as Pixar, Adobe, and Disney.

Today, Academy of Art University is the largest accredited private art and design university in the nation with an enrollment of nearly 13,000. Approximately 36 percent of the student body is made up of international students. The Academy has over 40 facilities that house classrooms, studios, galleries, and residence halls. The students, who are admitted through an open-enrollment policy, aspire to earn A.A., B.A., B.S., B.F.A., B.Arch., M.A., M.F.A., M.A.T., or M.Arch. degrees or an Art Teaching Credential. Students can study in San Francisco or through the Academy's flexible online programs.

The Academy maintains a system of courtesy shuttles to connect the different points of the campus, all of which are located within the city limits of San Francisco. The instructors, who are working art and design professionals, are drawn from all around the world to the Academy and the creative and intellectual center that is the Bay Area. Extensive senior-year internship programs allow students to gain valuable experience and develop strong portfolios in their chosen field before graduation.

Academy of Art University is an accredited member of the Western Association of Schools and Colleges (WSCUC), National Association of Schools of Art and Design (NASAD), Council for Interior Design Accreditation (CIDA) for BFA-IAD and MFA-IAD, National Architectural Accrediting Board (NAAB) for B.Arch. and M.Arch., and California Commission on Teacher Credentialing (CTC).

What Sets the Academy Apart

The Academy is one of the few art and design schools that believes in nurturing the whole artist; this includes developing athletic ability along with artistic talent. Students can participate in intercollegiate, intramural, and club sports, and with Pacific West honors and national championships, the University offers basketball, baseball, softball, cross country, track and field, soccer, golf, volleyball, and tennis for its students to partake. Furthermore, the Academy is proud to be the only higher arts education institution in the U.S. to have an NCAA athletics program.

Faculty

Academy of Art University has assembled a faculty of top creative professionals. These award-winning industry leaders have a passion for inspiring the next generation of artists and designers. With a focus on hands-on experience, instructors guide students to achieve their full creative potential. Specific information about faculty members can be found on the University's website at www.academyart.edu.

Applying

Admission to the master's programs requires official transcripts indicating at least the completion of a bachelor's degree, submission of a portfolio of work (portfolio requirements vary by discipline), a statement of intent outlining graduate study goals, and a resume. Admission to the program is permitted at the beginning of each semester. Additional materials may be required. Students should contact the Graduate Admissions Office for further details.

Correspondence and Information

Academy of Art University Graduate Admissions
P.O. Box 193844
San Francisco, California 94119
United States
Phone: 415-274-2222
800-544-2787 (toll-free in the U.S. only)
Fax: 415-618-6287
E-mail: info@academyart.edu
Website: http://www.academyart.edu

Academy of Art University, Downtown San Francisco Campus.

AMERICAN UNIVERSITY OF ROME

Graduate School

Programs of Studies

The Graduate Programs at the American University of Rome (AUR) prepare students to live and work across cultures, as skilled and knowledgeable citizens of an interconnected and rapidly changing world. Taking the best of the American approach to interdisciplinary, student-centered learning, the international faculty and staff utilize collaborative research and study groups to debate and discuss critical issues. AUR's innovative M.A. programs foster intellectual excellence, personal and professional growth, and an appreciation of cultural diversity in an international setting.

Rome is a city unlike any other and a tremendous setting for graduate study. The city's 50+ museums and 900+ churches house world-renowned paintings, frescoes, and sculptures. The cobblestone streets and majestic piazzas are architectural masterpieces in themselves, and the entire historic center is a UNESCO World Heritage site. Beyond its historical and artistic importance, modern-day Rome is a major European capital with hundreds of embassies, international organizations, governmental agencies, and multinational companies, and serves as a bustling hub for business, politics and research. The city is constantly welcoming world-famous dignitaries, celebrities, scientists, and businesspeople, creating an inspiring atmosphere for students as they prepare for their futures.

AUR's 15-month master's programs were designed with professional students in mind. After the first 9 months, students can complete their internships and theses remotely, allowing them to take as little time away from their busy lives as possible. This structure also makes the M.A. more affordable for students who are supporting themselves by limiting the amount of time dedicated strictly to classroom learning.

AUR offers four master's degree programs.

Master of Arts (M.A.) in Arts Management: This program is designed for a new breed of professionals, those who bridge curatorial awareness with the business and management skills necessary in today's competitive art world. International in scope, this program features Rome and Italy's unparalleled museum culture as case studies for the challenges and the opportunities facing future curators and arts administrators. Students master key concepts and ideas in art theory; analyze the most advanced curatorial practices; and gain in-depth knowledge of museum management, fundraising, and the economics of culture. Through a selection of elective courses, students choose to focus on live arts management, writing, heritage, or entrepreneurship.

Master of Arts (M.A.) in Food Studies: This cross-disciplinary program aims to provide knowledge and skills surrounding sustainable food production and consumption, and how the Earth's resources are impacted by food choices. The goal of the program is to provide students with knowledge, critical thinking, and transferable skills related to the global and local dimensions of sustainable food production and consumption, to the business of food and to communicating about food. Rome is the 'international food hub' of the world and Italy's agrofood sector can be considered a laboratory for European Union policies. This is a flexible program whereby students will be able to focus their course of studies on topics of their interest in relation to the pursuit of further research or to their professional career goals and aspirations.

Master of Arts (M.A.) in Peace Studies: This program addresses the critical societal need of promoting conflict resolution, intercultural, and interreligious dialogue. The mission is to educate future professionals, scholars, and activists who will be able to contribute to peace-building initiatives and processes. The program enables students to learn about the complex relationships between religious, political, and cultural forces that contribute to wars and conflicts, and acquire the skills and knowledge necessary for understanding as well as resolving tensions and conflicts across the globe.

Master of Arts (M.A.) in Sustainable Cultural Heritage: This program trains graduates to face the most important challenge in the heritage industry today: its long-term viability. Today, in order to make cultural heritage both sustainable and socially useful it is necessary to recognize the need for a multidisciplinary approach to the heritage spectrum. The new generation of professionals who wish to work with heritage will have to undertake many different responsibilities across many areas of expertise. While Rome is at the center of debates about global heritage, none of the courses are specific to sites in Italy; it simply serves as an ideal laboratory for this kind of training. In balancing theory and practice this Master's Program prepares students for employment in heritage administration, development control and consultancies, as well as for continuing in academic research.

Academic Enhancements

The AUR Graduate School offers a series of Graduate Skills Workshops designed to enhance the master's programs with one- and two-day workshops that cover topics aimed at developing specific skills, in line with the guiding philosophy intellectual development that is at the heart of AUR's M.A. degree programs.

The American University of Rome supports student endeavors to gain real-world, practical work experience by offering internship opportunities every semester. Academic internships for course credit provide students with a practical way of relating their studies to their career interests. Additional benefits include an enhanced ability to make informed career decisions, a greater appreciation for college coursework, increased marketability, and the opportunity to obtain academic credit while gaining field experience.

AUF offers a wealth of resources to assist graduate students with their studies. The AUR Library is located in Evans Hall, a stately two-story building housing 15,000 volumes, 1,200 DVDs and videos, access to important online databases, and a vast network of Roman libraries. AUR's technology offerings include a computer lab with 55 PCs and several print stations, a PC teaching classroom, a Mac-based multimedia laboratory, 14 library workstations, and wireless Internet access throughout the campus.

Financial Aid

The American University of Rome is committed to assisting students in achieving their educational goals and has a variety of financial aid options available for graduate students.

AUR participates in U.S. Title IV Direct Lending to cover the estimated cost of attendance for U.S. citizens and permanent residents. Graduate students are eligible for Direct Unsubsidized and PLUS loans through this program. U.S. veteran's benefits and AmeriCorp benefits may be used for AUR's M.A. programs.

AUR degree holders qualify for a 10 percent tuition alumni discount. A merit-based scholarship for 50 percent of the total tuition is available for one full-time student from each of the 15-month M.A. programs. All candidates that have submitted the required documents and paid their application fee by February 1 are eligible to apply. Candidates seeking a program scholarship are encouraged to submit a sample of their academic writing along with their admissions application.

AUR also has a Student Training Program for full-time graduate students. Students who apply for and are accepted to this program receive training in various areas of the university administration in exchange for a reduction in tuition.

Cost of Study

Tuition for U.S. citizens and permanent residents and Canadian citizens for the 2018–19 academic year is $20,000 (covering 36–39 attempted credits, per the respective M.A. program requirements). A nonrefundable $250 deposit is required by May 1. The deposit will be credited against the tuition payment.

The Italian government requires non-EU citizens to have a Permit to Stay (195 Euros). Health insurance (192 Euros for 12 months) is also required for non-Italian citizens unless they have their own health insurance valid for Italy. Other fees (all in U.S. dollars) include a $60 application fee, $100 orientation fee, and a $135 graduation fee.

Living and Housing Costs

Students choosing university-facilitated housing are placed in furnished accommodation in areas surrounding the university campus. The apartments are located in traditional, well-established neighborhoods. This housing is well suited for students looking for a full immersion cultural experience.

Apartments vary in location, style, and size, but all of them provide the essentials. Residences are located in areas of Rome convenient to the university campus in desirable residential neighborhoods. All apartments are either within walking distance or conveniently located to public transit routes relative to the university.

Location

Rome's location on the Mediterranean in the center of Italy has been strategic for centuries, serving as an important gateway between Europe, Africa and Asia. Rome is still the ideal location for students with a love of travel to explore Europe and beyond. Rome is AUR's classroom. Professors frequently complement their lessons with on-site visits around the city, guiding students through the richly layered experience that is the Eternal City and highlighting its global context throughout the ages.

American University of Rome

Overlooking the historical center of Rome, the university is located on top of Rome's highest hill, and its own garden of umbrella pines offers a spectacular view of the city and the surrounding hills. The campus is near two city parks and a host of historical landmarks.

The University

Founded in 1969, the American University of Rome is a private, liberal arts university founded on the promise that Rome itself is an ideal classroom. AUR offers American college degrees that blend the liberal arts with career preparation and elements of the Italian/European classical tradition of the humanities.

Faculty

AUR is home to a highly diverse student body representing over 60 countries, with 28 native languages are spoken amongst faculty and students. As befits this eclectic campus, the professors respect and draw from different points of view, ideas, and real-world experiences, enriching the dialogue within the classroom.

Applying

Applicants for graduate study must have earned a Bachelor's degree from an accredited institution with a minimum grade point average of 3.0 or equivalent. Applicants must submit a completed AUR application form, official transcripts, a CV, a motivation letter, and at least one academic letter of recommendation. Official TOEFL or IELTS scores are require for non-English applicants.

Admission is on a competitive basis. Applications are accepted for fall semester only. Other requirements vary by program. Specifics can be found online at https://graduate.aur.edu/graduate-admission-requirements.

Applicants who have Italian or European citizenship do not need to apply for a visa. All students holding a non-European Union passport are required by law to obtain a student visa before departing from their home country. Without a valid student visa students cannot apply to obtain their Permit to Stay.

Students must obtain their student visa after receiving approval of their acceptance. AUR Admissions Office will send each accepted student a visa letter, which must be presented at the student's local consulate along with all other necessary documents. The visa application can be a lengthy process; students should check with their local consulate to make sure they understand the requirements and time needed. The student visa must be obtained in advance; it is not possible to apply for this visa while in Italy.

Correspondence and Information

American University of Rome
ViaPietro Roselli 4, 00153
Rome, Italy
Phone: 877-592-1287 (Rome office, toll-free)
877-791-8327 (U.S. office, toll-free)
E-mail:
Website: https://graduate.aur.edu

THE COLLEGE OF NEW JERSEY

Graduate Programs

Programs of Study

The College of New Jersey (TCNJ) offers the following advanced degrees: Master of Arts (M.A.) in counselor education (areas include school counseling; clinical mental health counseling) or English (literature); Master of Arts in Teaching (M.A.T.) in early childhood education, elementary education, secondary education (iSTEM math, iSTEM science, and iSTEM technology education), special education/elementary; five-year programs (for TCNJ undergraduate students only) in education of the deaf and hard of hearing/elementary education, special education, urban education, and English; Master of Education (M.Ed.) in educational leadership–principal certification, educational leadership: instruction (a collaborative program in conjunction with the Regional Training Center), elementary and secondary education (off-site Global Program only), reading K–12, special education, special education/teacher of the blind or visually impaired, Integrative Science, Technology, Engineering, and Math (iSTEM), teaching English as a second language, or Urban Secondary Education; Master of Science in Nursing (M.S.N.) in adult/gerontological primary care nurse practitioner studies, clinical nurse leader studies, family nurse practitioner studies, neonatal nurse practitioner studies, or school nurse certification (instructional option); Master of Public Health (M.P.H.); Master of Business Administration (M.B.A. starting Fall 2019).

Graduate certificate programs and/or post-master's programs are offered in adult/gerontological primary care nurse practitioner studies, family nurse practitioner studies, school nurse certification (instructional and non-instructional options), bilingual education (main campus and off-site Global Program), educational leadership–principal certification, instructional licensure-teacher of preschool–grade 3, learning disabilities teacher/consultant studies, teacher of students with blindness and visual impairments studies, reading specialist studies, student assistance coordinator studies, teacher certification for international schools (off-site Global Program only), teacher of students with disabilities, teaching English as a second language, or gender studies.

Global opportunities in education are also available for graduate students. Graduate global programs at TCNJ have been in existence for over thirty-five years and provide course work leading toward master's-level degrees in education and certification in teaching, administration, and substance abuse counseling. Courses are taught by TCNJ faculty members and other internationally recognized professors. Courses are offered June through July at TCNJ sites in Mallorca, Spain; Bangkok, Thailand; Lisbon, Portugal; and Johannesburg, South Africa. During the academic year, courses are available in Cairo, Egypt; Hsinchu, Taiwan; and Ho Chi Minh City, Vietnam.

For the convenience of the majority of graduate students who pursue degrees while employed full-time, graduate courses held on the Ewing campus are offered during the day and in the evening.

Research Facilities

TCNJ offers a state-of-the-art library that serves as an exciting intellectual, cultural, and social center for the College community. The five-story, 135,000-square-foot facility will provide cutting-edge services to the TCNJ community well into the twenty-first century. In addition to housing traditional library collections and services in an atmosphere that is both friendly and elegant, a key feature of the recently built library is its wide array of carefully considered and thoughtful amenities, which make using the facility both a pleasure and a convenience. The library provides twenty-four group-study rooms (one reserved for graduate students), ample and comfortable seating, tables and carrels, and both WiFi and LAN Internet access throughout, with power connections available at every carrel and study table. Special design features include a café, a secure, late night/24-hour study area, and a 105-seat multipurpose auditorium. The library also houses the Instructional Technology Services facility, creating ideal one-stop shopping for students working on projects.

Library collections include more than 560,000 volumes and 200,000 microforms as well as subscriptions to more than 1,400 periodicals. The library also subscribes to more than seventy-five electronic indexes covering more than 14,000 scholarly journals, including full-text resources. A media facility offers viewing and listening equipment as well as sound recordings, videos, and interactive computer software. PCs are available for public access to electronic resources. Collections are constantly augmented by new acquisitions, and interlibrary loan and document delivery services are available to students. The library is also an active participant in a number of library networks and maintains cooperative arrangements with many regional academic libraries, from which students may borrow directly. TCNJ librarians are an important resource in and of themselves. In addition to advanced studies in library and information science, each subject librarian has additional graduate degrees in one of the major academic areas, and students are encouraged to consult them in person and online.

In addition to providing new library facilities for the College community, TCNJ has met the challenge of the computer field's phenomenal growth with installations of computer facilities in each of its seven schools.

Financial Aid

The College of New Jersey offers financial aid to qualified matriculated students through a combination of loans, assistantships, and/or student employment opportunities. To be considered for all financial aid programs, students must submit the Free Application for Federal Student Aid (FAFSA) to the College Financial Assistance Office. Graduate assistantships are available to qualified full-time students on a competitive basis. Prospective students must apply through the Office of Graduate Studies by April 15 to be considered for a graduate assistantship.

Cost of Study

Tuition for graduate courses for the 2018–19 academic year is $938.17 per semester hour of credit for New Jersey residents and $1,368.05 per semester hour of credit for out-of-state residents. Additional fees include ID, student center, computer access and service fees, and health insurance (for full-time students). Tuition and fees are subject to change by action of the New Jersey State Legislature.

Living and Housing Costs

As the majority of TCNJ's graduate students attend classes part-time in the evenings, the College does not offer on-campus housing for graduate students. Graduate students who seek housing in the area may obtain assistance from the Office of Residence Life.

Student Group

The College of New Jersey has an enrollment of approximately 6,500 undergraduate students and 1,000 graduate students.

Student Outcomes

The College of New Jersey's excellent reputation has afforded graduates outstanding opportunities when entering their professional fields. Many TCNJ graduates receive job placements through various on-campus recruitment programs sponsored by the Office of Career Services.

Location

The College of New Jersey is located on 289 tree-lined acres in suburban Ewing, New Jersey, 7 miles from the state capital in Trenton. Woodlands and two lakes surround the academic and residential buildings. More than thirty-five buildings make up the physical plant, most of which are built in the classic Georgian Colonial architecture. The campus is 30 miles from Philadelphia and 60 miles from New York's theaters, museums, and other attractions. The nearby towns of Princeton and New Hope offer additional cultural activities.

The College

Founded in 1855, the College has grown from its early years as a teachers' college to a multipurpose institution comprising seven schools: Arts and Communication; Business; Education; Engineering; Humanities and Social Sciences; Nursing, Health, and Exercise Science; and Science. Graduate study is available in the Schools of Education, Humanities and Social Sciences, and Nursing, Health, and Exercise Science.

TCNJ introduced its first advanced degree program, a Master of Science in elementary education, in 1947. Over the years, the number of graduate programs has steadily increased. At present, there are more than fifty specialized graduate degree and certificate programs.

TCNJ's academic programs are accredited by the Middle States Association of Colleges and Schools, the National Council for Accreditation of Teacher Education (NCATE)/Council for the Accreditation of Educator Preparation (CAEP), the Council for the Accreditation of Counseling and Related Educational Programs (CACREP), Commission on Collegiate Nursing Education (CCNE), and other appropriate professional associations.

Applying

Students of proven ability with undergraduate degrees in appropriate fields are eligible to apply for graduate study. Applications should be submitted online (http://graduate.tcnj.edu/apply) along with a $75 nonrefundable application fee. Transcripts of all previous college or university work and other supporting documentation, as noted on the website, should be forwarded to the Office of Graduate and Advancing Education. Acceptable scores on the appropriate national standardized tests are required for most degree and initial teacher certificate programs.

Application deadlines for matriculation and non-matriculation for the various graduate programs are located on the Graduate Studies website (http://graduate.tcnj.edu/apply).

Correspondence and Information

Office of Graduate and Advancing Education
Green Hall, Room 111
The College of New Jersey
P.O. Box 7718
2000 Pennington Road
Ewing, New Jersey 08628
United States
Phone: 609-771-2300
Fax: 609-637-5105
E-mail: graduate@tcnj.edu
Website: http://graduate.tcnj.edu

DEANS AND PROGRAM COORDINATORS

SCHOOL OF HUMANITIES AND SOCIAL SCIENCES

Jane Wong, Dean; Ph.D.

Graduate Program Coordinator

English: Jo Carney, Ph.D., Iowa.

SCHOOL OF EDUCATION

Suzanne McCotter, Dean; Ph.D., Georgia.

Graduate Program Coordinators

Counselor Education: Mark Woodford, Ph.D., Virginia. Marion Cavallaro, Ph.D., Ohio State. Atsuko Seto, Ph.D., Wyoming. Stuart Roe, Ph.D., Penn State.
Deaf and Hard of Hearing/Elementary Education Five-Year Program: Barbara Strassman, Ed.D., Columbia Teachers College.
Early Childhood Education: Jody Eberly, Ph.D., Rutgers.
Educational Leadership–Instruction: Alan Amtzis, Ph.D., Boston College.
Educational Leadership–Principal: Donald Leake, Ph.D., Ohio State.
Elementary and Early Childhood Education (M.A.T.): Arti Joshi, Ph.D., Syracuse.
Instructional Licensure–Teacher of Preschool–Grade 3: Jody Eberly, Ph.D., Rutgers.
Reading K–12: Matthew Hall, Ph.D., NYU.
Secondary Education: Donald Leake, Ph.D., Ohio State.
Special Education: Dr. Shridevi Rao, Ph.D., Syracuse University.
TESOL/Bilingual Education: Yiqiang Wu, Ph.D., Texas A&M.

SCHOOL OF NURSING, HEALTH, AND EXERCISE SCIENCE

Carole Kenner, Dean; Ph.D., Indiana.

Graduate Program Coordinators

Nursing: Connie Kartoz, Ph.D., Pennsylvania.

MAJOR RESEARCH PROJECTS, AWARDS, GRANTS, AND INITIATIVES

School of Education

Intoxicated Drivers' Resource Center (IDRC); Dr. Cassandra Gibson and the TCNJ Clinic, School of Education.
Community Reinforcement and Family Training (CRAFT); Dr. Cassandra Gibson and Dr. Mark Woodford, School of Education.
Collegiate Recovery Support and Environmental Change (CRC); Dr. Cassandra Gibson, School of Education.
Trenton Violence Reduction Strategy (TVRS); Dr. Cassandra Gibson, School of Education.
LifeChoices; Dr. Cassandra Gibson and Dr. Stuart Roe, School of Education.
Creating a team of highly qualified professionals for English language learners (CTHQP) grant; Dr. Yiqiang Wu, School of Education.
Adaptive Technology Center grant; Dr. Amy G. Dell, School of Education.
Preparing special and elementary educators to use inquiry and design-based learning; Dr. Amy Dell, School of Education.
Provisional Teacher Program; Dr. Anthony Evangelisto, School of Education.
TECH-NJ (Technology, Educators, and Children with Disabilities–New Jersey); Dr. Amy G. Dell, School of Education.
Deaf/Blind Family and Community Educational Support; Dr. Jerry Petroff, School of Education.
Conversation analysis of native/non-native speakers; Dr. Jean Wong, School of Education.
Facilitating transition from school to employment for individuals with challenging behavior; Dr. Shridevi Rao, School of Education.
Issues of literacy and teaching elementary students of color; Dr. Deborah Thompson, School of Education.
Fulbright Scholar Award to teach at the University of Bahrain, Bahrain Teachers College; Dr. Lynnette Mawhinney, School of Education

School of Nursing, Health and Exercise Science

Advanced education nursing traineeship program; Dr. Claire Lindberg, School of Nursing
HIV symptom distress project; Dr. Claire Lindberg, School of Nursing.

School of Humanities and Social Sciences

The reception of Dante and Chaucer within the work of their literary successors; Dr. Glenn Steinberg, School of Culture and Society.
Book-length research project in family memoir based on research and interviews: "The Seven: A Family Holocaust Story"; Ellen Friedman, School of Humanities and Social Sciences.
Research in Early Modern Grammars and Spelling Books; Felicia Steele, School of Humanities and Social Sciences.
"'Universal Mixing' and Interpenetrating Standing: Disability and Community in Melville's Moby-Dick"; Harriet Hustis, School of Humanities and Social Sciences.
Executive Director of the Thornton Wilder Society, which is headquartered at TCNJ, and co-founder and officer of the Edward Albee Society; Lincoln Konkle, School of Humanities and Social Sciences.
Thornton Wilder: New Perspectives; Lincoln Konkle, School of Humanities and Social Sciences.
Thornton Wilder and The Puritan Narrative Tradition; Lincoln Konkle, School of Humanities and Social Sciences.
National Endowment for the Humanities Fellowship; Michael Robertson, School of Humanities and Social Sciences.
Worshipping Walt: The Whitman Disciples; Michael Robertson, School of Humanities and Social Sciences.
Walt Whitman, Where the Future Becomes Present; David Blake and Michael Robertson, School of Humanities and Social Sciences.

The clock tower above Green Hall, the main administrative building on campus, is a well-known symbol of TCNJ tradition.

TCNJ offers a state-of-the-art library that serves as an exciting intellectual, cultural, and social center for the College community.

COLLEGE OF STATEN ISLAND OF THE CITY UNIVERSITY OF NEW YORK

Graduate Degree Programs

THE CITY UNIVERSITY OF NEW YORK
College of Staten Island

Programs of Study

The College of Staten Island (CSI) offers master's degrees in Accounting (M.S.); Biology (M.S.); Business Management (M.S.); Cinema and Media Studies (M.A.); Clinical Mental Health Counseling (M.A.); Computer Science (M.S.); Education: Childhood (elementary) Education (M.S.Ed.), Adolescence (secondary) Education (M.S.Ed.), Special Education (grades 1–6) (M.S.Ed.), Special Education (grades 7–12) (M.S.Ed.), Teaching of English to Speakers of other Languages (M.S.Ed.); English (M.A.); Environmental Science (M.S.); History (M.A.); Liberal Studies (M.A.); Neuroscience and Developmental Disabilities (M.S.); Nursing: Adult-Gerontological Health Nursing (M.S.); Social Work (M.S.W.); Healthcare Management (M.S.); and Electrical Engineering (M.E.).

Post-master's degrees are awarded in Education: School District Leader, School Building Leader and School District Leader (dual certificate) and in Nursing: Adult-Gerontological Health Nursing. Advanced certificates are offered in Autism Spectrum Disorders, Business Analytics of Large-Scale Data, Cultural Competence, Bilingual Education, Public History, and Teaching of English to Speakers of other Languages (online and in-classroom). The College of Staten Island offers an Adult-Gerontological Health Nursing (D.N.P.) program and a Clinical Doctorate in Physical Therapy (D.P.T.).

In addition, the College offers the following doctoral programs jointly with the Graduate Center of the City University of New York (CUNY): Biochemistry (Ph.D.), Biology (Ph.D.), Computer Science (Ph.D.), Nursing (Ph.D.), Physics (Ph.D.), and Polymer Chemistry (Ph.D.).

Research Facilities

The Center for Developmental Neuroscience and Developmental Disabilities is supported jointly with the New York State Institute for Basic Research (IBR). The center conducts, promotes, and sponsors research, education, and training in the developmental neurosciences, with special emphasis on research and educational programs in the specific field of developmental disabilities. The center provides for collaborative efforts between the College and IBR in offering the master's degree in Neuroscience and Developmental Disabilities, as well as with the University's doctoral programs in biology (subprogram in neuroscience), and in psychology (subprogram in learning processes). The center provides advanced research training for graduate students.

The Center for Environmental Science provides support for research and policy recommendations concerning environmental problems. One of the major purposes of the center is to define and solve environmental problems on Staten Island and its environs through research that includes studies of respiratory diseases, toxic and carcinogenic chemicals in the air, and the population at risk for lung cancer.

The Center for the Study of Staten Island: Staten Island Project (SIP) is designed to integrate the work of the College with the public affairs concerns of the people of Staten Island. To that end, it mediates and facilitates the collaboration of the College's faculty, students, and staff with government, civic organizations, and businesses in order to identify and assist in finding solutions to the borough's pressing public issues. The center serves as an information and consultation resource to prepare citizens and leaders to make better-informed decisions about public life; it fosters the development of faculty research and graduate education through engagement with the community; and it builds bridges to other public affairs institutes and local communities as a spur to innovations in public life on Staten Island.

The Center for Interdisciplinary Applied Mathematics and Computational Sciences brings together a diverse group of research faculty members and students with interests in interdisciplinary applications of mathematics and computational science. The center's activities include the use of the campus supercomputer, faculty collaboration, grant writing, student mentoring and research, and sponsored lectures.

The CUNY High-Performance Computing Center (HPCC) is located on the CSI campus. Goals of the HPCC are to: support the scientific computing needs of university faculty, student, staff, and their public and private sector partners; create opportunities for the CUNY research community to develop new partnerships with the government and private sectors; and leverage the center's capabilities to acquire additional research resources for its faculty and graduate students in existing and major new programs.

Financial Aid

The Office of Student Financial Aid administers federal and state grant, loan, and work-study programs to assist students with financial need to attend the College of Staten Island. Students should contact the Office of Student Financial Aid early in the admission process to discuss eligibility requirements and responsibilities. Graduate assistant positions are available for full-time graduate students in some departments. Information about these positions may be obtained from the individual program departments. The College of Staten Island also recognizes academic excellence through scholarship programs which offer assistance to students as well. For more information about the scholarship programs, prospective students can visit www.csi.cuny.edu/advancement/scholarships.html.

Cost of Study

For the 2018–19 academic year, tuition for master's programs for New York State residents is $455 per credit, or $5,385 per semester for 12 or more credits. Tuition for non-state residents is $830 per credit. Tuition for the Master in Social Work program is $600 per credit, or $7,105 per semester for New York State residents. Tuition for non-state residents is $970 per credit. Tuition for the Master of Engineering program is $535 per credit, or $6,300 per semester for New York State residents. Tuition for non-state residents is $920 per credit. Tuition for the Clinical Doctorate in Physical Therapy program for New York State residents is $665 per credit, or $6,405 per semester. Tuition for non-state residents is $1,045 per credit. Tuition for the Doctorate in Nursing Practice program for New York State residents is $600 per credit, or $7,105 per semester. Tuition for non-state residents is $970 per credit.

Living and Housing Costs

For the 2018–19 academic year, students living with parents budget a minimum of $1,364 for books and supplies, $1,088 for local transportation, $3,028 for meals and personal expenses, and $4,390 for housing. Students living away from parents budget the same amounts for books, supplies, and transportation, plus $19,211 for food, housing, and personal expenses for a nine-month academic year. The College of Staten Island's first on-campus student housing is now open. Floor plans and rates are available online at www.csi.cuny.edu/housing.

Student Group

Nearly 1,000 graduate students enrolled at the College of Staten Island in the 2016 fall semester. The graduate population reflects a wide range of ethnicity, social and economic backgrounds, educational and professional experiences, and aspirations.

Location

The College of Staten Island is located in New York City in the Borough of Staten Island. Completed in 1994, the 204-acre campus of the College of Staten Island is the largest one for a college in New York City. Set in a park-like landscape, the campus is centrally located on Staten Island and is accessible by automobile and public transportation.

The College

The College of Staten Island is a college of the City University of New York that offers exceptional opportunities to all its students. Programs in the liberal arts and sciences and professional studies lead to bachelor's and associate degrees, in addition to the graduate programs previously listed.

Graduate Program Faculty Heads

A full listing of graduate program directors, contact information, and office hours is available at the College website. Please visit http://www.csi.cuny.edu/graduatestudies and click on "Graduate Programs and Requirements."

Applying

Requirements for admission and application deadlines vary by program and department. Students should contact the Graduate Admissions' Office for additional information or to arrange an admissions interview or campus tour.

Correspondence and Information

Sasha Spence, Associate Director for Graduate Admissions
Office of Recruitment and Admissions
North Administration Building (2A), Room 103
College of Staten Island
2800 Victory Boulevard
Staten Island, New York 10314
Phone: 718-982-2019
Fax: 718-982-2500
E-mail: masterit@csi.cuny.edu
Website: http://www.csi.cuny.edu/graduatestudies

Graduate students at the College of Staten Island are provided with the tools and opportunities they need to make positive contributions to society. CSI students perform research with faculty from every academic discipline on campus, using the College's state-of-the-art equipment and facilities.

Instructors at the College of Staten Island are committed to each graduate student's success. Whether offering guidance on a rigorous course of study, engaging students in stimulating research, or sharing their professional experiences, CSI faculty members help students shape and achieve their goals.

COLORADO SCHOOL OF MINES

Graduate School

★ For more information, visit http://petersons.to/coloradoschoolofminesgrad

Programs of Studies

Specialized and focused, Colorado School of Mines (Mines) is a unique research university with an extensive array of resource-related programs. The need for Mines' rare mix of expertise has never been greater. The availability and sustainable use of natural resources is one of the world's greatest challenges, and Mines' graduates and faculty members are creating solutions.

Those interested in pursuing a graduate degree find significant academic and research opportunities in globally significant growth areas:

- Energy—nuclear, materials, petroleum, physics
- Engineering—mechanical, electrical, civil and environmental, chemical and biological
- Environment—environmental engineering, chemistry, hydrology, biosciences, space resources
- Computational Sciences—computer science, applied mathematics, statistics
- Geotechnics—geology, mining, geophysics, underground construction and tunneling
- Business—mineral and energy economics, engineering and technology management
- Policy—natural resources and energy

Graduate degree options range from Master of Engineering, Master of Science (thesis and non-thesis options), and Ph.D.'s.

Research

Mines is a global leader in research and the advancement of technology. Led by world-class faculty, the research conducted at Mines enhances the educational experience of its graduates. Students have the opportunity to actively participate in research at every level of their education.

With an annual research budget of more than $55 million and a faculty that has pioneered numerous advances in a wide range of technical fields, opportunities to conduct innovative research is virtually unlimited. Graduate students are able to work hand-in-hand with researchers at Mines and from around the world on both applied and academic research problems. Proximity to a number of governmental research facilities such as the U.S. Geological Survey, the National Renewable Energy Laboratory, the U.S. Bureau of Reclamation, and the National Institute of Standards and Technology provides unparalleled access to a wide variety of scholars, facilities, and research opportunities.

Research spans many highly relevant areas, with a specific focus on energy and environmental stewardship. Mines' first-rate facilities and partnerships with industry, national laboratories, other universities, funding agencies, and international institutions help maintain its cutting-edge research and have a significant impact on real-world problems. Research is a cooperative effort in the Mines community; more information can be found at http://www.minesnewsroom.com/.

Financial Aid

At Mines, the awarding policy gives priority to the neediest students, as determined by the FAFSA. In the last academic year, more than $27.9 million of financial assistance was awarded. Typically more than 85 percent of the student body receives some form of aid, which includes scholarships, grants, loans, or work-study employment.

Cost of Study

For the 2018–19 academic year, full-time (9–15 credits) tuition per semester is $8,325 for residents and $18,135 for nonresidents. Mandatory fees are $1,157. The estimated cost of books and supplies is $750 per semester. More information on tuition and fees is available online at www.mines.edu/graduate-admissions/costs.

Living and Housing Costs

The Apartments at Mines Park house undergraduate and graduate degree seeking students. Single student housing is available in 1, 2, and 3 bedroom apartments. Family housing is available in 1 and 2 bedroom apartments. Additional information on Mines Park is available from the Department of Residence Life or online at http://residencelife.mines.edu/Apartments-at-Mines-Park.

In addition, Golden and the surrounding communities—Lakewood, Arvada, Denver, Boulder, and Littleton—offer other affordable housing options (http://residencelife.mines.edu/Off-Campus-Housing-Resources).

Student Group and Outcomes

The Graduate School at Mines draws together nearly 1,300 graduate students from the United States and over sixty other countries, and encourages problem investigation from diverse, real-world perspectives. Together, faculty and staff members and undergraduate and graduate students build a strong community of shared interests. The Mines community understands the challenges that can arise in leaving a home community to attend graduate school and works collectively to help maintain those community ties while building and growing new ones.

A graduate student at Colorado School of Mines becomes an important member of a community that is dedicated to generating new knowledge and educating students and professionals in fields related to the:

- discovery and recovery of the Earth's resources, their conversion to materials and energy, and their utilization in advanced processes and products
- economic and social systems necessary to ensure the prudent and provident use of Earth's resources in a sustainable global society
- preservation and stewardship of the Earth's environment

Mines' renowned reputation, attained through the tremendous work of its students, faculty and staff; its high admission standards; and its alumni network combine to give students an edge in the job market. Mines' strong master's and professional degrees are extremely valuable and more than just precursors to a doctoral degree. More than 96 percent of the recipients of Mines' master's and professional degrees find employment by graduation. More than 70 percent of these graduates are employed in industry, with the remainder employed by governmental agencies or matriculating into doctoral degree programs.

Location

Mines is located in Golden, Colorado, in the foothills of the Rocky Mountains, 15 miles west of Denver's downtown business district. Golden, a thriving community of 17,000, offers outdoor adventure with small-town atmosphere and convenient access to big-city attractions. With more than 300 days of sunshine each year, Golden is a great place to visit or live in during any season. Founded during the Gold Rush of 1859, Golden is one of Colorado's oldest communities and served as the Capital of Colorado Territory from 1862 to 1867. Golden retains its small-town character and remains the seat of Jefferson County. Historic buildings and homes have been preserved and blend with new construction throughout the downtown area, which offers many shops and restaurants.

The school has some big-name neighbors in Golden, including the National Renewable Energy Laboratory, a frequent research partner, and Coors Brewing Company.

Outdoor enthusiasts will find the proximity of the Mines campus to Colorado's Rocky Mountains an exciting prospect. Colorado offers a legendary abundance of activity in its nearby mountains, open spaces, and parks including alpine skiing, snowboarding, cross-country skiing, snowshoeing, mountain climbing, river rafting, hiking, biking, camping, exploring and fishing—to name a few.

The Mines campus features beautifully renovated historical architecture, as well as award-winning, new, state-of-the-art buildings.

The School

Colorado School of Mines is a public research university devoted to engineering and applied science. Founded in 1874, Mines' role and mission has remained constant and is written in the Colorado statute as:

"The Colorado School of Mines shall be a specialized baccalaureate and graduate research institution with high admission standards. The Colorado School of Mines shall have a unique mission in energy, mineral, and materials science and engineering and associated engineering and science fields. The school shall be the primary institution of higher education offering energy, mineral and materials science and mineral engineering degrees at both the graduate and undergraduate levels." *(Colorado Revised Statutes, Section 23-41-105)*

Mines offers all the advantages of a world-class research institution with a size that allows for personal attention. Innovative ideas have the chance to flourish and with a strong work ethic, students have the opportunity to help drive positive change locally, nationally, and globally.

Applying

The Graduate School at Mines is open to graduates from four-year baccalaureate programs at recognized colleges and universities. Admission to all graduate programs is competitive, based on an evaluation of academic performance (undergraduate or graduate), test scores, and references. Each department evaluates applications separately and admissions decisions are based on distinct admission criteria.

All application materials are submitted to the Office of Graduate Studies. Once an application file is complete, it is forwarded to the academic department review committee. Prospective students should consult the Graduate Admissions website at www.mines.edu/graduate_admissions for more information.

Correspondence and Information

Office of Graduate Studies
Colorado School of Mines
Student Center E140
Golden, Colorado 80401
United States
Phone: 303-273-3247
800-446-9488 Ext. 3247
E-mail: grad-app@mines.edu
Website: http://www.mines.edu

Finding innovative solutions to global challenges.

Focused on responsible stewardship of the earth and its resources.

DARTMOUTH COLLEGE

Guarini School of Graduate and Advanced Studies

DARTMOUTH
Guarini School of Graduate and Advanced Studies

★ For more information, visit http://petersons.to/dartmouthcollege-grad

Programs of Study

Since 1885, graduate and advanced studies at Dartmouth has combined world-class research facilities with an outstanding faculty. Dartmouth's graduate programs facilitate innovation, support collaboration, and deliver a unique blend of research opportunities and individualized education.

The Guarini School of Graduate and Advanced studies at Dartmouth offers master's and doctoral degrees across a broad range of programs, including several interdisciplinary programs and doctoral programs connected to the professional schools at Dartmouth. There are 17 programs leading to the Ph.D., 11 on the master's track, and 5 cross-disciplinary programs.

Master's degrees are offered in chemistry, comparative literature, computer science, digital musics, engineering, earth sciences, liberal studies, health care delivery science, health policy and clinical practice, physics and astronomy, and quantitative biomedical sciences.

Doctoral programs are offered in biochemistry and cell biology, biological sciences, chemistry, cognitive neuroscience, computer science, earth sciences, ecology evolution ecosystems and society, engineering, experimental and molecular medicine, health policy and clinical practice, mathematics, microbiology and immunology, molecular and cellular biology, molecular and systems biology, physics and astronomy, psychological and brain sciences, and quantitative biomedical science.

Special interdisciplinary training programs include environmental sciences, Master of Engineering Management, medical physics, M.D./M.S. program in biomedical engineering, Ph.D. engineering innovation program, M.D./Ph.D. program, and Ph.D./MBA program.

The School supports over 1,000 students from 62 countries, including the United States. The graduate alumni network connects more than 4,000 graduates.

The Guarini School of Graduate and Advanced Studies has fused the liberal arts tradition with research and believes that intense collaboration among brilliant people and strong departments accelerates discovery. It seeks to develop scholars who can approach problems from multiple perspectives and who can work across fields of study.

Research Facilities

Graduate and postdoctoral education at Dartmouth is more intimate than at the big research universities it is often compared to. Faculty members lead small, intense, research teams and students enjoy unparalleled access to leaders in their fields.

Dartmouth boasts world-class research and teaching facilities designed to promote cross-disciplinary intellectual exchange. A physical sciences center and chemistry building house science programs, libraries, computer labs, and service shops, encouraging students and faculty from different fields to interact. The medical complex offers state-of-the-art research facilities created to provide training in life sciences programs.

Financial Aid

Dartmouth offers full financial support to all students in doctoral programs. Financial support includes a paid yearly stipend or fellowship. Financial aid at the master's level varies by program.

Living and Housing

There are several options off campus; information is available through the Dartmouth Real Estate Office (https://realestate.dartmouth.edu), DartList (www.dartlist.com), and Craigslist. There will be housing information on the graduate studies' electronic bulletin board. The classified advertisement section of the Valley News (local newspaper) is another source.

Student Life

Roughly 1,050 graduate students attend Dartmouth, enjoying a coeducational college community built for them and the 4,276 undergraduates. Campus cultural life centers around the Hopkins Center for the Performing Arts, which sponsors an active film society, two full concert series, and a very active drama program. Facilities are available for students interested in joining a musical group or participating in arts workshops including sculpture, painting, and design. Graduate students also have access to the extensive Dartmouth College Athletic Facilities, and can participate in a variety of clubs, including the Dartmouth Graduate Outing Club.

Dartmouth's Entrepreneurial Network helps students learn valuable entrepreneurial skills, and offers strategic advice and mentoring to prepare students to leverage their knowledge and abilities.

The Dartmouth Career Network is a professional network of thousands of alumni who are willing to advise students and fellow alumni on their career path. International students can connect with many groups and new students are encouraged to sign up with the International Graduate Mentoring Program.

The Faculty

Dartmouth faculty members are experts in their fields, renowned for their scholarship in their respective disciplines and for their teaching ability. The faculty is accessible and available for consultation with students. The small program sizes ensure close collaborative relationships between faculty and students.

Students across the disciplines also interact with faculty at the professional schools including the Tuck School of Business, Thayer School of Engineering, and Geisel School of Medicine ensuring breadth of knowledge while pursuing their specific graduate program.

Location

Dartmouth is located in Hanover, New Hampshire on the western side of the state in the scenic Upper Connecticut River Valley. The river forms the border between Vermont and New Hampshire. Its location provides a gateway to nature in all seasons both on land and water, and is a 2–3 hour drive from Boston. The Dartmouth Coach travels daily to Boston and to New York City. Montreal, Canada is also just a few hours away.

The University

Founded in 1769, Dartmouth is a member of the Ivy League and consistently ranks among the world's greatest academic institutions. Dartmouth has forged a singular identity for combining its deep commitment to outstanding undergraduate liberal arts and graduate education with distinguished research and scholarship in the arts and sciences.

Professional and graduate programs across Dartmouth's schools—Geisel School of Medicine, the Guarini School of Graduate and Advanced Studies, Thayer School of Engineering, and the Tuck School of Business—have a distinguished history of training practitioners and scholars whose discoveries and expertise change the world.

Application and Admissions Information

The Guarini School of Graduate and Advanced Studies at Dartmouth admits the most highly qualified applicants whose academic backgrounds and personal and professional experiences have prepared them for achievement and excellence in graduate studies.

Applications generally include a completed application form, undergraduate transcripts, three letters of recommendation, and scores from the General Test of the Graduate Record Examinations (GRE).

Application requirements vary by program; exact requirements can be obtained from each department. The complete list of programs online (https://graduate.dartmouth.edu/academics/programs) includes links to department websites.

Dartmouth is committed to the principle of equal opportunity for all its students, faculty, employees, and applicants for admission and employment. Please see our non-discrimination policy and information for students with disabilities.

Correspondence and Information

Ruth Friend, Admissions Coordinator
Guarini School of Graduate and Advanced Studies
Suite 6062, Room 437
Dartmouth College
37 Dewey Field Road
Hanover, New Hampshire 03755-1419
Phone: 603-646-8193
E-mail: Ruth.E.Friend@Dartmouth.edu
Website: https://graduate.dartmouth.edu

MISSOURI STATE UNIVERSITY

Graduate College

★ For more information, visit http://petersons.to/missouristateu-grad

Missouri State UNIVERSITY

Programs of Study

The Graduate College at Missouri State University (www.graduate.missouristate.edu) offers outstanding academic programs that prepare students for lifelong success. The college has over 100 graduate programs including master's degrees, specialist degrees, clinical doctoral degrees, cooperative degree programs, and certificate programs. In addition, it offers full- and part-time options, evening programs, online courses and programs, and blended formats, all of which enable students to earn their degrees while managing their personal and professional lives.

Missouri State University offers 58 **gr**aduate certificate programs (generally 12 credits) in special areas. Many of these can be expanded into a master's degree, or earned in conjunction with a master's degree in a related area.

Missouri State University has **Master of Arts (M.A.)** degree programs in several disciplines including Communication, English, History, Religious Studies, Teaching, and Writing. In addition there is a Teaching and Learning (M.A.T.L.) program available to cohorts in the Southwest Missouri area K–12 school districts. These programs give students opportunities to build upon previous study and professional experience to acquire the knowledge and skills needed to advance their careers or pursue doctoral study.

Students who are interested in earning **Master of Science (M.S.)** degrees can choose from more than 20 programs at Missouri State University including Agriculture, Applied Behavior Analysis, Athletic Training, Biology, Cell and Molecular Biology, Chemistry, Child Life Studies, Communication Sciences and Disorders, Computer Information Systems, Computer Science, Counseling, Criminology and Criminal Justice, Cybersecurity, Defense and Strategic Studies, Early Childhood and Family Development, Geospatial Sciences in Geography, Geology and Planning, Health Promotion and Wellness Management, Interdisciplinary Studies, Materials Science, Mathematics, Physician Assistant Studies, Plant Science, Project Management, Psychology, and Student Affairs in Higher Education.

Individuals who are interested in earning advanced degrees in education, training, or instruction can choose from several **Master of Science in Education (M.S.Ed.)** programs including Early Childhood Special Education, Educational Administration, Educational Technology, Elementary Education, Literacy, Secondary Education, and Special Education.

Missouri State also offers several **other master's degree programs**, such as: Accountancy (MAcc.), Applied Second Language Acquisition (M.A.S.L.A.), Business Administration (MBA), Global Studies (M.G.S.), Health Administration (M.H.A.), Health Administration and Public Health dual-degree program, Music (M.M.), Natural and Applied Science (M.N.A.S.), Nursing–Nurse Educator (M.S.N.), Occupational Therapy (M.O.T.), Professional Studies (MPS), Public Administration (M.P.A.), Public Health (M.P.H.), Social Work (M.S.W.), and Visual Studies (M.F.A.).

MSU offers three **Specialist (Ed.S.)** programs: Educational Administration, and Counseling and Assessment and Teacher Leadership.

Individuals who are interested in **professional doctoral programs** will find Missouri State to be a great fit. Offerings include: Audiology (Au.D.); Educational Leadership (Ed.D.)—a cooperative program with the University of Missouri; Nurse Anesthesia (D.N.A.P.); Nursing (D.N.P.); Pharmacy (Pharm.D.)—a cooperative program with the University of Missouri Kansas City; and Physical Therapy (D.P.T.).

All students are assigned an academic adviser in their graduate program, and work closely with that adviser throughout the pursuit of their degree/certificate. Most of the Missouri State University master's programs provide for either a thesis, seminar/degree paper option, or internship option as the research component to be completed in partial fulfillment of the degree

Financial Aid

Missouri State proudly offers approximately 500 graduate assistantships each year to qualified grad students. These assistantships are offered in teaching, research, and/or administrative areas. In exchange for working the required 20 hours per week on campus, students receive a tuition fee waiver which covers up to 15 credit hours in the fall or spring semesters, and a stipend. The 2018-19 stipend amount was $8,772 (for the 9-month academic year). More information about graduate assistantships is available online at http://graduate.missouristate.edu/currentstudents/FeeWaiver.htm.

There are also a limited number of scholarships available to qualified graduate students. The most popular scholarships are the MOGO, Need-Based, and Midwest Student Exchange Program. A complete list of scholarships and qualifying requirements can be found at http://www.missouristate.edu/FinancialAid/scholarships/Graduate.htm.

Cost of Study

Base tuition for graduate students for 2018-19 is $279 per credit hour for Missouri residents and $561 per credit hour for nonresidents. Base tuition for online courses was $295 per credit hour for Missouri and Non-Missouri residents. (Note: Some graduate programs charge more than the base tuition.)

Student services fees are assessed in addition to tuition and are based on the total credit hours for which a student enrolls. (Note: Intersession courses, iCourses, Internet/online courses, courses taught in a location other than the Springfield campus, and courses scheduled to meet on the Springfield campus fewer than four times are excluded from student services fees.) Additional details regarding tuition and fees are available at http://www.missouristate.edu/registrar/costs.htm.

Location

Missouri State University's main campus is located in Springfield, Missouri, in the Midwestern region of the United States. The city of Springfield, Missouri, and the surrounding Ozarks provide numerous services and activities to meet the needs of its citizens. Missouri's third largest city is within a 500-mile radius of nearly 50 percent of the U.S. population. Springfield has the feel of a big city with the convenience of a small town, including friendly people, an affordable cost of living, and healthcare options that are among the best in the country. The city offers an array of options in terms of entertainment, the arts, sports, recreation, and entertainment. Downtown Springfield is less than a mile from the MSU campus.

The University

Founded in 1905, and now with a strong public affairs mission, Missouri State University serves more than 24,000 traditional and non-traditional students from over 80 countries, every state, and every county in Missouri, offering nearly 200 undergraduate degrees and graduate programs. The University is committed to providing graduate programs that meet the needs of a changing workforce and positively impact the region, state, nation, and world.

MSU seeks to be the university of choice to develop successful students who excel academically and in ethical leadership, cultural competence and community engagement.

Applying

All graduate applications to MSU are collected through a centralized application service (CAS). Admission requirements and program deadlines are included in each CAS application. Applicants need to provide program-required materials, submit official transcripts showing coursework for the bachelor's degree and any graduate-level work, and pay the application fee through the CAS. Required materials and fees vary by program and by CAS.

Admissions decisions are made by each graduate program, based on its admissions requirements, selection criteria, program capacity, and the quantity and quality of the applicant pool. Meeting the minimum admission criteria does not guarantee admission.

International students need to complete the International Student Application through the CAS, If English is not the student's primary language. The minimum TOEFL score requirement is 79 or more for graduate applicants. Complete admission requirements for international students are available on the University's website at http://international.missouristate.edu/services/70306.htm.

Correspondence and Information

Dr. Julie Masterson, Dean
Stephanie Praschan, Director of Graduate Enrollment Management
Misty Stewart, Recruitment Coordinator
Graduate College
Missouri State University
901 South National Avenue
Springfield, Missouri 65897
United States
Phone: 417-836-5335 (Main Office)
417-836-5331 (Admissions)
E-mail: GraduateAdmissions@missouristate.edu
Website: www.graduate.missouristate.edu

Missouri State University campus and downtown Springfield, Missouri.

Missouri State University's main entrance, Bear Boulevard and National Avenue.

QUINNIPIAC UNIVERSITY

Graduate Studies

Quinnipiac UNIVERSITY

Programs of Study

Quinnipiac University is a dynamic, challenging, and supportive academic community, offering more than 30 outstanding graduate programs that give students a strong foundation for their careers with both rigorous academic preparation and in-depth practical experience.

The School of Health Sciences and School of Nursing offer a range of programs for students interested in the health professions, including the Master of Health Science (M.H.S.) with specializations in advanced medical imaging and leadership, cardiovascular perfusion, biomedical sciences, pathologists' assistant, physician assistant, and radiologist assistant; the Master of Social Work (M.S.W.); the Doctor of Nursing Practice (D.N.P.), with tracks including adult-gerontology nurse practitioner, family nurse practitioner, nurse anesthesia, care of populations, and nursing leadership; and the Master of Science in Nursing Operational Leadership. Also offered are the Doctor of Physical Therapy (D.P.T.) (freshman entry only), the Doctor of Occupational Therapy (D.O.T.), and the Master of Science (M.S.) in Molecular and Cell Biology (College of Arts & Sciences). The Frank H. Netter M.D. School of Medicine offers the Doctor of Medicine (M.D.) and the Anesthesiologist Assistant programs.

The School of Business offers the Master of Business Administration (M.B.A.). Students can choose the general M.B.A. or from among the following tracks: finance, health care management, and supply chain management. Other degree programs include the Master of Science in Accounting (M.S.A.), the Master of Science (M.S.) in Business Analytics, and the M.S. in Organizational Leadership. Graduate certificates are available in Long-Term Care Administration and Health Care Compliance.

The School of Communications offers the M.S. programs in Journalism and Sports Journalism; the M.S. in Public Relations; the M.S. in Interactive Media and Communications; and graduate certificates in social media and user experience design.

The School of Education offers the Master of Arts in Teaching (M.A.T.), elementary and secondary; the Sixth-Year Diploma in Educational Leadership; the M.S. in Instructional Design; the M.S. in Teacher Leadership; the M.S. in Special Education; and the Certificate of Completion in Special Education.

The School of Engineering offers the M.S. in Cybersecurity.

The School of Law offers the Juris Doctor (J.D.), J.D./M.B.A., J.D./Master of Environmental Law and Policy (with Vermont Law School), J.D./M.S.W., and the Master of Laws (L.L.M.) in Health Law.

Most graduate programs range in length from one to three years. Both full- and part-time study are available in most programs, and a number of programs and tracks are offered online. All graduate programs at Quinnipiac University share three key foundations: instruction is provided by faculty members with the highest available academic credentials and practicing professionals; every graduate student has the opportunity to earn practical experience through residencies, internships, thesis research, special projects, clinical rotations, consulting practicums, or small laboratory classes; and study builds upon both undergraduate education and professional experience.

Research Facilities

The university features facilities on two academic campuses with state-of-the-art equipment for research and professional preparation across disciplines. The Mount Carmel Campus features biology laboratories for candidates in the master's programs in Molecular and Cell Biology and Biomedical Sciences. M.B.A. and other business students practice analytical finance methods, conduct trading simulations, develop financial models, analyze economic databases, and study stocks, bonds, currency, and interest rates at the Terry W. Goodwin '67 Financial Technology Center, with real-time financial data from markets all over the world. For students in the School of Communications, the Ed McMahon Mass Communications Center offers a fully digital high-definition television studio, multimedia lab, audio production studio, master edit room, video editing lab, a media innovation classroom and lab modeled after a working newsroom, and an equipment loan room with a full complement of remote audio and video production gear.

The North Haven Campus is home to the cutting-edge Center for Medicine, Nursing and Health Sciences, with learning labs including a professional SimMan suite of life-size patient simulators, a pediatric and neonatal lab, magnetic resonance simulators and 3-D workstations, an orthopedics lab, a rehabilitative sciences lab, a clinical skills lab, an intensive care unit, a health assessment lab, a physical diagnostics lab, a motion analysis lab, an operating room suite with two additional high fidelity simulation rooms, and 48 prosection stations.

At the School of Law, the Center for Health Law and Policy and the Center on Dispute Resolution offer legal research opportunities. Other university institutes and centers include the Alternative Investments Institute, the National Institute for Community Health Education, the Center for Women and Business, the Center for Interprofessional Healthcare Education, the Bristol-Myers Squibb Center for Science Teaching and Learning, the Bioanthropology Research Institute, and the Albert Schweitzer Institute. Most recently, the university's Frank H. Netter M.D. School of Medicine has established the Institute for Primary Care, the Institute for Rehabilitation Medicine, and the Institute for Global Public Health.

Financial Aid

The University offers several options for graduate students to fund their education.

Merit scholarships are awarded on a select basis to newly admitted graduate students within certain disciplines: biomedical sciences, cardiovascular perfusion, journalism, molecular and cell biology, nurse practitioner, pathologists' assistant, physician assistant, radiologist assistant, and social work. Candidates for the merit scholarships must be full-time students and U.S. citizens, enrolled in one of our eligible on-campus programs.

The university also offers grant funds to help cover a portion of tuition. The grant is available to full-time students who are U.S. citizens and are enrolled in one of our on-campus programs and who have demonstrated financial need as evaluated by the financial aid office.

Students enrolled as full-time or part-time students who have completed the FAFSA are eligible to receive federal student loans.

Students pursuing our Master of Arts in Teaching (MAT) can receive reduced tuition while participating in the internship semesters of the program.

We also offer graduate assistantship opportunities for students to work on campus and in exchange receive a tuition waiver or paycheck.

Students applying to programs in law, medicine or through QU Online, should consult the website for financial aid information.

Cost of Study

Tuition in 2018–19 is $1,035 per credit hour for most on-campus graduate programs. Student fees are $40 per credit (not to exceed $360 per semester), and there is a $25 summer registration fee.

Living and Housing Costs

Hamden, North Haven, and surrounding communities in Greater New Haven offer a wide array of housing options for graduate students in a range of prices, including apartment complexes, rentals within multi-unit homes, and single family houses for rent. There is also a limited amount of on-campus housing available for graduate students. The university's Office of Residential Life maintains a listing of off-campus housing and can provide information about on-campus housing. In addition, the Quinnipiac Offices of Graduate Admissions and Graduate Student Affairs can provide information about the locales and communities within commuting distance of the campuses.

Student Group

Quinnipiac University enrolls approximately 7,000 undergraduates and 3,000 graduate students. Of the university's graduate student population, approximately 52 percent are enrolled in full-time programs, and 48 percent are enrolled in part-time programs. Many graduate students come from the Northeast region and northern mid-Atlantic region. Certain programs also attract graduate students from across the United States and internationally.

Location

The university's graduate programs are located on two beautiful, state-of-the-art campuses in Hamden and North Haven, Connecticut, located just outside of New Haven, approximately 90 minutes from New York City and two hours from Boston. The Mount Carmel Campus in Hamden is home to graduate programs in business, communications, and molecular and cell biology. The North Haven Campus is home to graduate programs in health sciences, nursing, education, law, and medicine. A third campus, York Hill, features the TD Bank Sports Center, home to Quinnipiac's Division I hockey and basketball teams, and the Rocky Top Student Center, featuring stunning views of Long Island Sound and a fitness facility, open to graduate students.

The University

Quinnipiac University is nationally recognized as a dynamic center for higher learning in the Northeast and is consistently ranked among the best master's-level universities in the North in *U.S. News & World Report*'s Guide to America's Best Colleges and its Best Online Graduate Business Programs. The Princeton Review has included Quinnipiac among its Best Business Schools and Best Law Schools.

Applying

Applicants should check the requirements on the university website for the specific program to which they plan to apply. Applications should be submitted online and by sending required materials to the Office of Graduate Admissions. International students should visit the website for application information; students from non–English-speaking countries must supply a notarized translation of their transcripts as well as Test of English as a Foreign Language (TOEFL) or International English Language Testing System (IELTS) scores.

Correspondence and Information:

Office of Graduate Admissions
Quinnipiac University
275 Mount Carmel Avenue
Hamden, Connecticut 06518-1940
United States
Phone: 203-582-8672
800-462-1944 (toll-free)
E-mail: graduate@qu.edu
Website: www.qu.edu

THE FACULTY

Quinnipiac faculty members demonstrate a high level of commitment to their fields, and notable faculty members work in each of the graduate areas of study. The following are key members of the Quinnipiac University faculty.

Matthew L. O'Connor, Ph.D., Dean of the School of Business and Professor of Finance, has published extensively in peer-reviewed journals and is an active participant at professional conferences. Recipient of the 2005 Excellence in Teaching Award from the university's Center for Excellence in Teaching and Service to Students, Dean O'Connor currently teaches courses in applied portfolio management.

Mark Contreras, M.B.A., recently joined the university as Dean of the School of Communications. Prior to joining Quinnipiac, he served as chief executive officer of Calkins Media, Inc. He is former chairman of the Newspaper Association of America (now known as the News Media Association) and the American Press Institute, one of the media industry's leading training, development, and research institutions.

Anne Dichele, Ed.M., Ph.D., Dean of the School of Education, is a former classroom teacher and director of Quinnipiac's master's in teaching program. She is the founder of Side By Side Charter School, one of Connecticut's first state-funded charter schools, where she serves as chairperson of the board of directors. Her scholarship has appeared in numerous journals and publications and her first book of original poetry was recently published.

Justin Kile, Ph.D., was named founding Dean of the School of Engineering in 2016, and has guided the school to ABET accreditation. A senior member of the Institute of Industrial Engineers, he has been published in numerous engineering trade journals and has presented his work at national venues such as RosEvaluation and the ASEE Annual Conference.

Jennifer Gerarda Brown, J.D., is the Dean of the School of Law. Her research looks at LGBT rights, dispute resolution, and the professional responsibilities of lawyers, and she has contributed to numerous publications on the topics of marriage equality and the theory and practice of negotiation. Dean Brown was founding director of Quinnipiac Law's Center on Dispute Resolution.

Bruce M. Koeppen, M.D., Ph.D., Dean of the School of Medicine and Vice President of Health Affairs, has directed and published research on kidney function, has earned numerous awards for teaching, and has more than three decades of experience as a medical school professor and administrator.

William C. Kohlhepp, D.H.S., is Dean of the School of Health Sciences and teaches medical microbiology and infectious diseases. His professional experience includes clinical practice as a physician assistant, administrative directorship of an area occupational health center, and service as an officer or board member of several national physician assistant organizations.

Lisa G. O'Connor, M.S.N., Ed.D., Dean of the School of Nursing, has extensive experience in medical surgical and critical-care nursing, along with 20 years in education, including hospital-based education and higher education. Her leadership in the field was recognized in 2014 when she received the Nurse Leadership Award from the Connecticut League for Nursing.

Allan Smits, Ph.D., is the Associate Dean of Sciences and Graduate Programs in the College of Arts and Sciences, which includes the M.S. in Molecular and Cell Biology program. He has been named an outstanding professor by the university's Center for Excellence in Teaching and Service to Students.

Students at Quinnipiac join a welcoming community that is supportive and collaborative.

Quinnipiac's campuses provide state-of-the-art resources in a dynamic and architecturally distinctive setting.

ROBERT MORRIS UNIVERSITY

Graduate Programs

Programs of Study

Robert Morris University (RMU) offers more than thirty graduate degree programs, including twelve master's programs available online. Doctoral programs include the Doctor of Science (D.Sc.) in information systems and communications, the Doctor of Philosophy (Ph.D.) in instructional management and leadership, and the Doctor of Nursing Practice (D.N.P.) offered as an adult nurse practitioner, family nurse practitioner, or adult psychiatric and mental health nurse practitioner, or as a completion of an existing master's degree. Master's programs available either online or on campus include the Master of Business Administration (M.B.A.) as well as Master of Science (M.S.) degrees in business education, competitive intelligence systems, engineering management, information security and assurance, instructional leadership, Internet information systems, and organizational leadership. On-campus programs include a Master of Education (M.Ed.) degrees in literacy and special education and M.S. programs in information security and assurance, information systems management, IT project management, and taxation; M.S. degrees in human resource management, health services administration, higher education, and nursing education are solely online. The university also offers a variety of graduate certificates.

The University is accredited by the Middle States Association of Colleges and Schools. RMU schools and programs are also accredited by the Association to Advance Collegiate Schools of Business International, the Teacher Education Accreditation Council, ABET Inc., and the Commission on Collegiate Nursing Education.

Research Facilities

Facilities supporting the graduate programs at Robert Morris University include nine open-access computer laboratories, two physical libraries, and an electronic library offering an array of research databases. Classrooms have been equipped with advanced computer and presentation technology equipment to facilitate teaching and learning.

To support a large number of holdings, the library has a state-of-the-art searchable catalog system. The RMU Electronic Library offers continual off-campus access to more than 100 major research databases. The library is a member of numerous resource-sharing consortia that greatly extend the amount of materials available to support graduate education.

Financial Aid

Graduate loans are available for those who qualify. Students are encouraged to file the Free Application for Federal Student Aid (FAFSA). Robert Morris University participates in the Federal Family Education Loan (FFEL) Program and also offers various interest-free payment plans, as well as third-party billing and corporate reimbursement programs.

Cost of Study

Tuition for the 2018–19 academic year for the M.B.A. program is $955 per credit. Tuition for the various M.S. programs is as follows: business, $930 per credit; taxation, $955 per credit; instructional leadership, education, business education, and the postbaccalaureate teacher certification programs, $890 per credit; engineering management, $980 per credit; and organizational leadership, $840 per credit. Tuition for the D.Sc. in information systems and communications is $14,570 per semester. Tuition for the D.N.P. is $9,680 per semester for full-time students, and $985 per credit for part-time students or those in the completion option. Tuition for the Ph.D. in instructional management and leadership is $7,693 per semester.

Living and Housing Costs

The D.Sc. and D.N.P. completion program fees include the cost of the required residencies.

Student Group

RMU enrolls approximately 1,000 students in its graduate degree programs, with an equal number of men and women. Students come from diverse professional and academic backgrounds.

Location

Robert Morris University is located on a 230-acre campus in suburban Moon Township, 17 miles west of downtown Pittsburgh and 15 minutes from Pittsburgh International Airport. Many graduate programs and classes are also offered online or at the RMU downtown campus at the Heinz 57 Center.

The University

Robert Morris University is located on a 230-acre campus in suburban Moon Township, 17 miles west of downtown Pittsburgh and 15 minutes from Pittsburgh International Airport. The city is an important corporate hub for financial and banking industries, health care, and industrial and high-tech engineering and manufacturing, providing a wide selection of employment opportunities as well as the cultural and commercial opportunities of a major city. Many graduate pro-grams and classes are also offered online.portunity to help drive positive change locally, nationally, and globally.

Applying

The graduate programs admit students on a rolling admission basis. However, students are encouraged to submit all required materials at least two months prior to the start of their desired term of entry. Applications can be filed for free through the University's website. Students should note that the M.S. in nursing education, the D.Sc. in information systems and communications, the D.N.P., and the Ph.D. in instructional management and leadership programs require an interview as part of the final selection process.

Correspondence and Information

Office of Graduate Admissions
Robert Morris University
6001 University Boulevard
Moon Township, Pennsylvania 15108-1189
United States
Phone: 800-762-0097 (toll-free)
Website: http://www.rmu.edu/graduate

FULL-TIME FACULTY

SCHOOL OF BUSINESS

Michelle Patrick, Dean; Ph.D., Kent State.
Patrick J. Litzinger, Interim Associate Dean; Ph.D., Pittsburgh.
Lois D. Bryan, Senior Associate Dean, Academic Excellence; D.Sc., Robert Morris.

Accounting and Taxation Faculty

Ira Abdullah, Ph.D., Virginia Commonwealth.
William G. Brucker, M.B.A., J.D., Duquesne.
Lois D. Bryan, D.Sc., Robert Morris.
Victoria A. Fratto, D.Ed., Robert Morris.
Fei Han, Ph.D., Connecticut.
David Hess, M.B.A., Ohio State.
Steven Hodaszy, J.D., L.L.M., NYU.
James E. Rebele, Ph.D., Indiana.
Ronald R. Rubenfield, M.B.A., Shippensburg.
Zhaoyun Shangguan, Ph.D., Connecticut.
Carol MacPhail, M.S., Robert Morris.
Gregory Krivacek, M.P.M., Carnegie Mellon.

Finance Faculty

Robert G. Beaves, Ph.D., Iowa.
Zane Dennick-Ream, M.B.A., Iowa.
Riza Emekter, Ph.D., Nebraska.
Frank Flanegin, Ph.D., Central Florida.
Denise C. Letterman, M.B.A., Shippensburg.
Jianyu Ma, Ph.D., Texas–Pan American.
Stanko Racic, Ph.D., Pittsburgh.

Management Faculty

Michele T. Cole, J.D., Ph.D., Pittsburgh.
Daria C. Crawley, Ph.D., Michigan.
Jeffery K. Guiler, Ph.D., Pittsburgh.
Nell T. Hartley, Ph.D., Vanderbilt.
Albena Ivanova, Ph.D., Minnesota.
Chia-Jung Lin, Ph.D., Southern Illinois Carbondale.
Marcel C. Minutolo, Ph.D., Pittsburgh.
Jodi A. Potter, Ph.D., Pittsburgh.
Yasmin S. Purohit, Ph.D., Drexel.
William F. Repack, M.S., Loyola.
Michael A. Yahr, M.B.A., Pittsburgh.
Qin Yang, Ph.D., Temple.
Derya A. Jacobs, Ph.D., Missouri–Rolla.
Mark Haney, Ph.D., Pittsburgh.
KiHyun Park, Ph.D., University of Toledo.

Marketing Faculty

Yun Chu, Ph.D., Texas–Pan American.
Steven R. Clinton, Ph.D., Michigan State.
Cathleen S. Jones, D.Sc., Robert Morris.
Ersem Karadag, Ph.D., Oklahoma State.
Jill K. Maher, Ph.D., Kent State.
Dean R. Manna, Ph.D., Pittsburgh.
Gayle J. Marco, Ph.D., Pittsburgh.
Richard Mills, Ph.D., Duquesne
Denis P. Rudd, Ed.D., Nevada, Las Vegas; CHA, FMP.
Norman V. Schnurr, M.B.A., Pittsburgh.
Alan D. Smith, Ph.D., Akron; CPGS.
Yanbin Tu, Ph.D., Connecticut.

Sport Management Faculty

Artemisia Apostolopoulou, Ph.D., Massachusetts.
Scott Branvold, Ed.D., Utah.
John S. Clark, Ph.D., Massachusetts Amherst.
David P. Synowka, Ph.D., Pittsburgh.

SCHOOL OF COMMUNICATIONS AND INFORMATION SYSTEMS

David Jamison, Acting Dean; J.D.
David F. Wood, Associate Dean; Ph.D., Pittsburgh.
Jon A. Radermacher, Associate Dean; M.F.A., Indiana.

Communication Faculty

Brbara J. Levine, Ph.D., Wisconsin–Madison.
Barbara Burgess-Lefebvre, M.F.A., Illinois State.
Michele Reese Edwards, Ph.D., Ohio State.
Kenneth V. Gargaro, Ph.D., Pittsburgh.
Jeeyun Oh, Ph.D., Penn State.

Ann D. Jabro, Ph.D., Penn State.
Heather Pinson, Ph.D., Ohio.
Sun-A Park, Ph.D., Missouri–Columbia.
Wenli Wang, Ph.D., Texas at Austin.
Anthony Moretti, Ph.D., Ohio.

Computer and Information Systems Faculty

Jeanne M. Baugh, Ed.D., West Virginia.
Donald J. Caputo, Ph.D., Pittsburgh.
Donna Cellante, Ed.D., Pittsburgh.
Gary A. Davis, D.Sc., Robert Morris.
Peter J. Draus, Ed.D., Pittsburgh.
Natalya Goreva, Ph.D., Utah State.
Linda Kavanaugh, Ph.D., Pittsburgh.
Fred G. Kohun, Ph.D., Carnegie Mellon.
Paul J. Kovacs, Ph.D., Pittsburgh.
Joseph Laverty, Ph.D., Pittsburgh.
G. James Leone, Ph.D., Pittsburgh.
Sushma Mishra, Ph.D., Virginia Commonwealth.
Karen Paullet, D.Sc., Robert Morris.
Walter Pilof, M.B.A., Xavier (Cincinnati).
Jamie Pinchot, D.Sc., Robert Morris.
Valerie J. Powell, Ph.D., Texas at Austin.
Robert J. Skovira, Ph.D., Pittsburgh.
John Turchek, M.Ed., Duquesne.
Charles R. Woratschek, Ph.D., Pittsburgh.
Peter Wu, Ph.D., Rensselaer.

English Faculty

Diane Todd Bucci, Ph.D., Indiana of Pennsylvania.
Roger Gillan, M.A., Bucknell.
Edward Karshner, Ph.D., Bowling Green State.
John Lawson, Ph.D., Northern Illinois.
John D. O'Banion, Ph.D., Northern Illinois.
Sylvia A. Pamboukian, Ph.D., Indiana Bloomington.
Constance M. Ruzich, Ph.D., Pennsylvania.
H. James Vincent, M.A., Indiana.

Media Arts Faculty

Andrew Ames, M.F.A., Rhode Island School of Design.
Ferris Crane, M.F.A., Academy of Arts.
Timothy J. Hadfield, M.F.A., Chelsea College of Art and Design (London).
Christine Holtz, M.F.A., RIT.
Carolina Loyola-Garcia, M.F.A., Carnegie Mellon.
Helena Vanhala, Ph.D., Oregon.
Hyla J. Willis, M.F.A., Carnegie Mellon.
Michael DiLauro, M.F.A., Ohio.

Organizational Studies Faculty

Stuart Allen, Ph.D., Regent.
Arthur J. Grant, Ph.D., Wheaton (Illinois).
Beatrice Kunka, Ed.D., University of the Pacific.
Anthony Petroy, D.M., Phoenix.
Michael Quigley, Ph.D., Pittsburgh.
Elizabeth M. Stork, Ph.D., Pittsburgh.

SCHOOL OF EDUCATION AND SOCIAL SCIENCES

Philip J. Harold, Acting Dean, Ph.D., Catholic University.

Economics and Legal Studies Faculty

Adora D. Holstein, Ph.D., Penn State.
Patrick J. Litzinger, Ph.D., Pittsburgh.
Min Lu, Ph.D., British Columbia.
J. Brian O'Roark, Ph.D., George Mason.
Ralph R. Reiland, M.B.A., Duquesne.
Louis B. Swartz, J.D., Duquesne.
Joel A. Waldman, J.D., Miami (Florida).
Zhou Yang, Ph.D., Tennessee.

Education Faculty

Carianne Bernadowski, Ph.D., Pittsburgh.
James Bernauer, Ed.D., Pittsburgh.
Robert DelGreco, Ed.D., Pittsburgh.
Vicki Donne, Ed.D., Pittsburgh.
Richard G. Fuller, D.Ed., Penn State.
Bruce Golmic, Ed.D., Indiana of Pennsylvania.
Mary A. Hansen, Ph.D., Pittsburgh.
Carla Haser, Ph.D., Catholic University.
Michele N. Hipsky, Ed.D., Duquesne.
E. Gregory Holdan, Ph.D., Penn State.
Susan Parker, Ph.D., Pittsburgh.
Ronald Perry, Ph.D., Pittsburgh.
George W. Semich, Ed.D., Pittsburgh.
Daniel J. Shelley, Ph.D., Pittsburgh.
Nathan Taylor, Ph.D., Ohio State.
Lawrence A. Tomei, Ed.D., USC.
Fan-Yu Lin, Ph.D., Penn State.
Ying Zhang, Ph.D., Purdue.
John A. Zeanchock, Ed.D., Indiana of Pennsylvania.

Social Sciences Faculty

Daniel P. Barr, Ph.D., Kent State.
William R. Beaver, Ph.D., Carnegie Mellon.
Kathryn Dennick-Brecht, Ed.D., Duquesne.
Soren Fanning, Ph.D., Bowling Green State.
Philip J. Harold, Ph.D., Catholic University.
William E. Kelly, Ph.D., Louisiana Tech.
John M. McCarthy, Ph.D., Marquette.
Samantha Monda, Ph.D., West Virginia.
Stephen T. Paul, Ph.D., Kansas.
Melinda Rauscher, Ph.D., Emory.
David Wheeler, Ph.D., Washington (Seattle).

SCHOOL OF ENGINEERING, MATHEMATICS, AND SCIENCE

Maria V. Kalevitch, Dean; Ph.D., Academy of Sciences (Lithuania).
Jeffrey J. Mitchell, Associate Dean; Ph.D., Cornell.

Engineering Faculty

Sushil Acharya, D.Eng., Asian Institute of Technology (Thailand).
Won Joo, Ph.D., Case Western Reserve.
Tony Kerzmann, Ph.D., Pittsburgh.
Priyadarshan A. Manohar, Ph.D., Wollongong (Australia).
Louis Moterrubio, Ph.D., Waikato.
Arif Sirinterlikci, Ph.D., Ohio State.
Benjamin Campbell, Ph.D., Robert Morris.
Tamiko Youngblood, Ph.D., Missouri University of Science and Technology.

Mathematics Faculty

Len Asimow, Ph.D., Washington (Seattle).
Liang Hong, Ph.D., Purdue.
David G. Hudak, Ph.D., Carnegie Mellon.
Allen R. Lias, Ph.D., Pittsburgh.
Andris Niedra, Ph.D., Pittsburgh.
Monica M. VanDieren, Ph.D., Carnegie Mellon.
Charles W. Zimmerman, Ph.D., Ohio State.
Chistophe Groendyke, Ph.D., Penn State.

Science Faculty

Paul D. Badger, Ph.D., Pittsburgh.
Gavin Buxton, Ph.D., Sheffield Hallam (UK).
William J. Dress, Ph.D., Ohio State.
Catherine Hanna, Ph.D., Louisville.
Kenneth A. Lasota, Ph.D., Pittsburgh.
Matthew Maurer, Ph.D., Ohio State.
Daniel Short, Ph.D., Liverpool (England).
Melissa Hillwig, Ph.D., Iowa State.

SCHOOL OF NURSING AND HEALTH SCIENCES

Nadine C. Englert, Acting Dean; Ph.D., Pittsburgh.

Nuclear Medicine Faculty

Angela M. Bires, Ed.D., Duquesne.
Donna L. Mason, M.S., Carlow.
William Wentling, M.S., Buffalo State, SUNY.

Nursing Faculty

Joseph Angelelli, Ph.D., USC.
Marcel C. Minutolo, Ph.D., Pittsburgh.
Lynda J. Davidson, Ph.D., Pittsburgh.
Stephen Foreman, Ph.D., Berkeley.
Susan Hellier, Ph.D., Waynesburg.
Valerie M. Howard, Ed.D., Pittsburgh.
Pamela Jackson, M.S., Robert Morris.
Judith A. Kaufmann, Dr.PH., Pittsburgh.
Kirstyn K. Kameg, D.N.P., Case Western Reserve.
Lisa W. Locasto, D.N.P., Robert Morris.
Donna McDermott, M.S.N., Robert Morris.
Joyce Ott, D.N.P., Robert Morris.
Catherine Pyo, Ph.D., Robert Morris.
Denise Ramponi, D.N.P., Waynesburg.
Katherine Perozzi, M.S.N., Pittsburgh.
Carl A. Ross, Ph.D., Duquesne; RN.
Janice Sarasnick, M.S.N., Robert Morris
Janice Shade, M.S.N., Pittsburgh.
Janene Szpak, D.N.P., Robert Morris.
Susan Van Cleve, D.N.P., Robert Morris.

RMU's suburban Pittsburgh campus spreads across 230 scenic acres that were once the grounds of a country estate.

SALISBURY UNIVERSITY

Graduate Studies and Research

Programs of Study

Graduate study at Salisbury University (SU) provides baccalaureate degree holders from the United States and abroad with opportunities for professional advancement and personal enrichment. The graduate curriculum is designed to assist students in attaining greater mastery of their fields of specialization, improving skills in pursuing independent study, and increasing professional knowledge and ability through the study of new findings in areas of special interest.

Master's degree programs available at SU include the following: applied biology (M.S.), applied health physiology (M.S.), athletic training (M.S.), business administration (M.B.A.), conflict analysis and dispute resolution (M.A.), education (M.Ed.: curriculum and instruction; educational leadership; post-secondary education track; reading specialist), English (M.A.), geographic information systems management (M.S.), history (M.A.), mathematics education (M.S.M.E.), nursing (M.S.: clinical nurse educator; health care leadership), social work (M.S.W.), and teaching (M.A.T.).

Doctoral programs are available in education (Ed.D.: contemporary curriculum theory and instruction in literacy) and nursing (D.N.P.: post-B.S.; post-masters).

A graduate certificate program is offered in Teaching English to Speakers of Other Languages (TESOL); also available are a post-master's Literacy Educator certificate, a post-master's Educational Leadership certificate and a post-master's Certificate of Advanced Study in Educational Leadership and a post-baccalaureate certificate in Higher Education..

Research Facilities

Henson Science Hall, Salisbury University's $42-million science education and research building, is one of the largest in Maryland. Blackwell Library has more than a quarter-million books and bound periodicals and computers with access to databases, such as FirstSearch. Construction is underway on a $111 million Academic Commons, which will house the library, Edward H. Nabb Research Center for Delmarva History and Culture, and other centers and services (opening scheduled for fall 2016).

Financial Aid

A limited amount of financial aid in the form of graduate assistantships from the University and scholarships from the Maryland State Scholarship Administration (Maryland residents only) are available each year to selected graduate students. Students applying for aid must complete the Free Application for Federal Student Aid (FAFSA) and indicate Salisbury University (title IV code of 002091). Students may also apply online at www.fafsa.ed.gov. For more information about financial assistance, prospective students should contact the Financial Aid Office at 410-543-6165 or finaid@salisbury.edu, or visit www.salisbury.edu/admissions/finaid/graduate.html.

Graduate assistants are eligible to receive a stipend and tuition waiver of up to 18 credits per fiscal year. To be eligible for the tuition waiver, students must enroll for a minimum of 6 credits in both the fall and spring terms. Tuition is waived only for graduate courses applicable toward master's degree requirements. The tuition waiver does not include waiver of fees. A full-time assistantship requires a time commitment of approximately 20 hours per week, and a half-time assistantship requires 10 hours per week. For specific details, prospective students should visit www.salisbury.edu/gsr/gradstudies/grad_assistantships.html or consult the Graduate Assistantship section of the Graduate Student Handbook.

Enrolled graduate students are eligible for competitive research and funding opportunities within their academic schools and for Research and Presentation Grants providing up to $500 to support scholarly projects and presentations.

Cost of Study

All graduate tuition rates are charged on a per credit-hour basis; there is no full-time tuition rate. Prospective students should visit www.salisbury.edu/cashiers for information and an updated listing of tuition, fees, special course fees, and other related expenses. Tuition and fees for each semester may be changed and new ones established at any time by action of the Board of Regents of the University System of Maryland.

Living and Housing Costs

Salisbury University does not offer on-campus housing for graduate students; however, there are numerous off-campus housing options nearby. Prospective students should visit SU's Commuter and Connections' website at www.salisbury.edu/commuters.

Student Group

The Graduate Student Council (GSC) at SU provides opportunities for intellectual, professional, personal, and social development through grants, advocacy, public presentation of research, graduate community events, and campus service. The GSC is part of the campus' Governance Consortium.

Student Outcomes

SU offers a network of over 40,000 alumni nationwide.

Location

With a regional population of roughly 99,000, Salisbury is the cultural and economic hub of Delmarva (containing portions of Delaware, Maryland, and Virginia), a historically and ecologically rich peninsula located between the Atlantic Ocean and Chesapeake Bay. The city is 30 minutes west of the beaches of Assateague and Ocean City, Maryland; about 2 hours from Baltimore, Maryland; Wilmington, Delaware; Norfolk, Virginia; and Washington, D.C.; and 4½ hours from New York City.

The University

A member of the University System of Maryland, SU is a regionally accredited four-year comprehensive institution offering 59 distinct graduate and undergraduate programs.

Applying

To be considered for admission, the Salisbury University application, all transcripts and supporting documents, and $65 nonrefundable application fee must be submitted. For questions regarding the application process, prospective students should call the Office of Graduate Studies and Research at 410-548-3546. For more information about specific program admission requirements, including priority application deadlines, applicants should contact the appropriate graduate program director. Additional information can be found online at www.salisbury.edu/gsr/gradstudies/admissions.html.

Correspondence and Information

Graduate Studies and Research
Holloway Hall 262
Salisbury University
1101 Camden Avenue
Salisbury, Maryland 21801
Phone: 410-548-3546
Fax: 410-677-0052

E-mail: gsr@salisbury.edu
Website: http://www.salisbury.edu/gsr/gradstudies/programs/

GRADUATE PROGRAMS AND THEIR DIRECTORS

Applied Biology (M.S.)
Dana Price, Ph.D., Graduate Program Director
410-543-6498, dlprice@salisbury.edu
https://www.salisbury.edu/explore-academics/programs/graduate-degree-programs/applied-biology-masters/index.aspx.

Applied Health Physiology (M.S.)
Thomas Pellinger, Ph.D., Graduate Program Director
410-677-0144, tkpellinger@salisbury.edu
https://www.salisbury.edu/explore-academics/programs/graduate-degree-programs/applied-health-physiology-master/index.aspx.

Athletic Training (M.S.A.T.)
Laura Marinaro, Ph.D., Graduate Program Director
410-548-3529, lmmarinaro@salisbury.edu
https://www.salisbury.edu/explore-academics/programs/graduate-degree-programs/athletic-training-master/index.aspx.

Business Administration (M.B.A.)
Yvonne Downie, Graduate Program Director
410-548-3983, yxdownie@salisbury.edu
https://www.salisbury.edu/explore-academics/programs/graduate-degree-programs/business-admin-master/index.aspx.

Conflict Analysis and Dispute Resolution (M.A.)
Toran Hansen, Ph.D., Graduate Program Director
410-543-6253, tjhansen@salisbury.edu
https://www.salisbury.edu/explore-academics/programs/graduate-degree-programs/cadr-masters/index.aspx.

Education (Ed.D., M.Ed)
Ed.D.: Dr. Judith Franzak, Program Director: 410-677-0238, jkfranzak@salisbury.edu. www.salisbury.edu/gsr/gradstudies/EDDpage.htm
M.Ed. Curriculum and Instruction: Dr. Gwen Beegle, Program Director: 410-543-6393, gpbeegle@salisbury.edu. www.salisbury.edu/gsr/gradstudies/MEDpage.htm
M.Ed. Education Leadership: Dr. Ted Gilkey, Program Director: 410-543-6297, trgilkey@salisbury.edu. www.salisbury.edu/gsr/gradstudies/MEDpage.htm
M.Ed. Reading Specialist: Dr. Pat Richards, Program Director: 410-543-6379, porichards@salisbury.edu. www.salisbury.edu/gsr/gradstudies/MEDpage.htm.

English (M.A.)
Christopher Vilmar, Ph.D., Graduate Program Director
410-677-6511, csvilmar@salisbury.edu
https://www.salisbury.edu/explore-academics/programs/graduate-degree-programs/english-masters/index.aspx.

Geographic Information Systems Management (M.S.)
Stuart Hamilton, PhD.,Graduate Program Director
410-548-3518, sehamilton@salisbury.edu
https://www.salisbury.edu/explore-academics/programs/graduate-degree-programs/geo-info-sys-masters/index.aspx.

History (M.A.)
Richard Bowler, Ph.D., Graduate Program Director:
410-546-6003, rcbowler@salisbury.edu.
http://www.salisbury.edu/gsr/gradstudies/HISTpage.html.

Mathematics Education (M.S.M.E.)
Jennifer Bergner, Ph.D., Graduate Program Director
410-677-5429, jabergner@salisbury.edu
https://www.salisbury.edu/explore-academics/programs/graduate-degree-programs/mathematics-education-masters/index.aspx.

Nursing
D.N.P.: Dorothea Winter, Ph.D., Graduate Program Director
410-548-5562, dmwinter@salisbury.edu
https://www.salisbury.edu/explore-academics/programs/graduate-degree-programs/nursing-practice-doctor/index.aspx.

M.S.: Dorothea Winter, Ph.D., Graduate Program Director
410-548-5562, dmwinter@salisbury.edu
https://www.salisbury.edu/explore-academics/programs/graduate-degree-programs/nursing-master/index.aspx.

Social Work (M.S.W.)
Jennifer Jewell, Ph.D., Graduate Program Director:
410-677-5050, jrjewell@salisbury.edu.
http://www.salisbury.edu/gsr/gradstudies/MSWpage.html.

Teaching (M.A.T.)
Starlin Weaver, Ph.D., Graduate Program Director:
410-548-5787, sdweaver@salisbury.edu
http://www.salisbury.edu/gsr/gradstudies/MATpage.html.

Teaching English to Speakers of Other Languages (TESOL)
http://www.salisbury.edu/english/grad/tesolD.html#tesol.

Holloway Hall, which opened in 1925, is the oldest building on campus.

Conway Hall has been cited as one of the nation's best designed higher education buildings.

SPRINGFIELD COLLEGE

Graduate Programs

Programs of Study

Education at Springfield College is all about taking action. Graduate students at Springfield College put their classroom education to practice through fieldwork and service learning. It's a learning advantage based on the College's historic mission, the Humanics philosophy, which calls for educating students in spirit, mind, and body for leadership in service to others. Humanics is at the base of everything the College does—in academics, athletics, and student life.

With an international reputation for educating tomorrow's leaders in some of the most vital career fields, Springfield College provides students with a competitive edge—top-quality academic preparation, research opportunities in state-of-the-art facilities, and real-world experience before graduating.

Springfield's graduate programs provide students with the employable skills and knowledge needed to advance their education and increase their job prospects and are taught by faculty members who are passionate about their disciplines. The programs integrate experiential learning opportunities, including fieldwork, internships, practicum, and research. Graduate courses at Springfield College challenge students to gain knowledge from the classroom, experience in the field, and think outside the box. Students leave Springfield College with a degree and real, applicable expertise in their fields.

Springfield offers a variety of master's degree programs including: art therapy/counseling, business administration, education (concentrations: in special education initial [preK–8, 5–12], elementary initial, secondary initial), exercise science and sport studies (concentrations: athletic training, clinical exercise physiology, exercise physiology, sport and exercise psychology, strength and conditioning), human services, occupational therapy, physical education (concentrations: adapted physical education, advanced-level coaching, athletic administration, health promotion and disease prevention, physical education teacher licensure, physical education teacher–professional licensure), physician assistant, psychology and counseling (concentrations: athletic counseling, clinical mental health counseling, industrial/organizational psychology, school counseling, student personnel administration in higher education), rehabilitation counseling and services (concentrations: general counseling, counseling and casework, pediatric and developmental disability counseling, psychiatric rehabilitation, and substance abuse counseling), social work (concentrations: M.S.W. weekday program, M.S.W. weekend program in Worcester and Springfield, advanced standing program, post-master's certificate program in trauma-informed practice), and sport management and recreation (concentrations: sport management, recreation management, therapeutic recreation management). Doctoral degree programs are also available: Ph.D. in Physical Education with specializations in sport and exercise psychology, exercise physiology, and teaching and administration; Doctor of Physical Therapy (D.P.T.); and Doctor of Psychology (Psy.D.) in counseling psychology.

Research Facilities

The campus is home to numerous research facilities, including a medical simulation lab, featuring high-fidelity 3G adult and baby patient simulator mannequins that respond to treatment as human patients would. The exercise physiology/biomechanics lab is where many graduate students conduct their own research, as well as working closely with faculty advisors on exciting new endeavors.

Financial Aid

Springfield College offers fellowships and associateships that assist in paying for tuition. During the 2016–17 academic year, Springfield College administered a total of $3.3 million in fellowship funding to graduate students. For some graduate students, AmeriCorps positions provide additional funding and professional opportunity that supplement their education. Federal financial aid, in the form of loans, is also available to those who qualify.

Cost of Study

The price per credit hour for graduate courses at Springfield College is $1,042. There is a graduate student fee of $225, which only applies to students taking nine or more credits.

Living and Housing Costs

Springfield College offers on-campus and off-campus housing options for graduate students. On-campus graduate housing costs range from $6,970 to $13,980 per academic year. Meal plans vary and there are many options from which to choose.

Student Group

Springfield College has 2,200 undergraduate students and 1,094 graduate students on the main campus and 1,600 nontraditional adult students at eight regional campuses across the country. Students come from 32 states, mostly from the northeastern corridor of the United States, and seven countries outside of the United States. The majority of undergraduate and graduate students reside on campus.

Student Outcomes

Springfield's graduate students are motivated, innovative, and focused on success, all while working to improve the world around them. According to a post-graduation survey, 97 percent of 2015–16 master's and doctoral graduates are employed or seeking advanced education.

Location

Located on the shores of Lake Massasoit, Springfield College is home to beautiful landscaping and top-notch facilities that combine function with artistry, while maintaining the historic beauty of the campus. Students have the best of both worlds—a campus located within a city with a classic New England charm.

The College

Springfield College provides a caring and inclusive environment, geared toward sharing ideas and research while collaborating with faculty members and other students. Founded in 1885, the college has maintained the same mission since day one—educating students in spirit, mind, and body for leadership in service to others. Being civically minded is celebrated at Springfield College and giving back to the community is a frequent occurrence at the college, whether it's through a group-organized service project or the annual Humanics in Action Day, where the college closes down for a day and students, faculty, and staff head out into the community to participate in service projects.

Faculty

The College's classrooms provide an environment where discussions are welcomed and faculty members will always know students by name. Class sizes are small, with an approximate 13:1 student-to-faculty ratio. Approximately 84 percent of full-time faculty members have earned the highest degrees attainable in their areas of expertise, and 70 percent hold doctorates.

Applying

Each graduate program has its own admissions requirements. Specific details about the requirements, as well as the graduate admissions process, are available online at springfield.edu/gradadmissions.

Correspondence and Information

Office of Graduate Admissions
Springfield College
263 Alden Street
Springfield, Massachusetts 01109
United States
Phone: 413-748-3225
TTY: 413-748-3383
E-mail: graduate@springfieldcollege.edu
Website: springfield.edu/gradadmissions

TEMPLE UNIVERSITY
Graduate School

★ For more information, visit http://petersons.to/templeugrad

TEMPLE UNIVERSITY
Graduate School

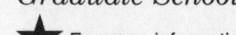

Programs of Study

Doctor of Philosophy programs are offered in Africology and African American studies, anthropology, art history, bioengineering, bioinformatics, biology, biomedical sciences (cancer biology and genetics, infectious disease and immunity, molecular and cellular biosciences, neuroscience, organ systems and translational medicine), business administration (accounting, finance, human resource management and organizational behavior, interdisciplinary study, international business administration, management information systems, marketing, operations and supply chain management, risk management and insurance, strategic management, tourism and sport), chemistry, civil engineering, communication sciences and disorders, computer and information science, criminal justice, dance, decision neuroscience, documentary arts and visual research, economics, education (applied linguistics; educational psychology; literacy and learners; science, mathematics and educational technology; special education), electrical engineering, English, environmental engineering, epidemiology, geography and urban studies, geoscience, global finance, health policy, history, kinesiology (athletic training, integrative exercise physiology), mathematics, mechanical engineering, media and communication, music (composition, music studies, music theory, musicology), music education, music therapy, neuromotor science, pharmaceutical sciences (medicinal chemistry, pharmaceutics, pharmacodynamics), philosophy, physics, policy and organizational studies (adult and organizational development, higher education, urban education), political science, psychology (brain and cognitive sciences, clinical psychology, developmental psychology, social psychology), religion, school psychology, social and behavioral sciences, sociology, Spanish, and statistics.

The Doctor of Musical Arts is offered in music performance (bassoon, cello, clarinet, double bass, euphonium, flute, French horn, harp, historical keyboard, oboe, percussion, piano, trombone, trumpet, tuba, viola, violin, voice). The Doctor of Education degree is offered in educational leadership and higher education. Other specialized doctoral degrees include the Doctor of Athletic Training, Doctor of Nursing Practice (adult-gerontology primary care, family-individual across the lifespan), Clinical Doctorate in Occupational Therapy, Doctor of Physical Therapy, and executive Doctor of Business Administration.

Master's degree programs are available in accomplished teaching; accountancy; actuarial science; adult and organizational development; Africology and African American studies; applied behavior analysis; architecture (advanced technologies and design, health and design, urban ecologies and design); art education; art history; athletic training; bioengineering; biology; biomedical sciences (cancer biology and genetics, general biomedical sciences, infectious disease and immunity, molecular and cellular biosciences, neuroscience, organ systems and translational medicine); business administration (business analytics; business management; corporate compliance, governance and regulatory policy; enterprise risk management; entrepreneurship; financial management; health sector management; human resource management; innovation management; international management; management consulting; marketing management; sport business; strategic management; supply chain management; travel and tourism); business analytics; career and technical education (business, computer and information technology; industrial education; marketing education); chemistry; choral conducting; city and regional planning; civil engineering; clinical research and translational medicine; collaborative piano and chamber music; collaborative piano and opera coaching; communication management (conflict management and dispute resolution, strategic communication and cross-cultural leadership); computational data science; computer science; counseling psychology; criminal justice; dance; digital innovation in marketing; early childhood education; early childhood education and special education; economics; educational psychology; electrical engineering; engineering management; English; environmental engineering; epidemiology; facilities planning (health facilities); financial analysis and risk management; financial engineering; geography and urban studies; geology; global clinical and pharmacovigilance regulations; globalization and development communication; health administration; health informatics (cyber security for healthcare professionals, healthcare data analytics, population health management); higher education (access and success, institutional effectiveness, student affairs leadership); history; hospitality management (event management, hospitality operations management, tourism and hospitality marketing); human resource management; information science and technology; information technology auditing and cyber security (cyber security, information technology auditing); innovation management and entrepreneurship (entrepreneurship, innovation strategy, technology and innovation management); instrumental conducting: wind-band emphasis; investment management; jazz studies; journalism; kinesiology (athletic training, integrative exercise physiology); landscape architecture; liberal arts; marketing (enterprise marketing management, marketing research and insight, strategic advertising and marketing); mathematics; mechanical engineering; media studies and production; mediaXarts: cinema for new technologies and environments; middle grades education (language arts, mathematics, mathematics and language arts, mathematics and science, science, science and language arts, social studies); middle grades and special education (language arts, mathematics, mathematics and language arts, mathematics and science, science, science and language arts, social studies); music; music composition; music education; music history; music performance (bassoon, cello, clarinet, classical guitar, double bass, euphonium, flute, French horn, harp, harpsichord, oboe, percussion, piano, saxophone, trombone, trumpet, tuba, viola, violin, voice); music technology; music theory; music therapy; musical theater studies; neuromotor science; neuroscience: systems, behavior and plasticity; occupational therapy; opera; oral biology; pharmaceutical sciences (medicinal chemistry, pharmaceutics, pharmacodynamics); philosophy; physician assistant; physics; piano pedagogy; political science; public policy; recreational therapy; regulatory affairs and quality assurance; religion; school leadership (curriculum supervision, principal leadership, reform and change leadership); secondary education (English, mathematics, science, social studies, world/foreign languages); secondary education and special education (English, mathematics, science, social studies, world/foreign languages); social work; sociology; Spanish; special education (autism spectrum disorders, mild disabilities, severe disabilities); speech, language and hearing science; sport business (athletics administration, recreation and event management, sport analytics, sport marketing and promotions); sport business executive program; statistics; strategic advertising and marketing; string pedagogy; taxation; teaching English to speakers of other languages; travel and tourism; urban bioethics; urban education; urban school leadership; and vocal arts. Also offered are an executive M.B.A. and an Ed.S. in school psychology.

Master of Fine Arts degree programs are available in ceramics/glass, creative writing, dance, fibers and materials studies, film and media arts, graphic and interactive design, metals/jewelry/CAD-CAM, musical theater collaboration, painting, photography, printmaking, sculpture, and theater (acting, design, directing, playwriting). Master of Public Health degrees are offered in applied biostatistics, epidemiology, health policy and management, and social and behavioral sciences. The Professional Science Master's (P.S.M.) degree is offered in applied sociology, bioinformatics, bioinnovation, biotechnology, computer and systems security, cyber defense and information assurance, forensic chemistry, geographic information systems, high-performance computing for scientific applications, and scientific writing (marketing/regulatory writing, popular scientific writing).

Rounding out the offerings are 107 graduate, post-master's, and specialty certificates in a range of disciplines.

Research Facilities

The world-class Science Education and Research Center (SERC) opened in fall 2014 with leading-edge laboratories to fully support moving scientific breakthroughs from the lab to the real world. To promote scientific collaboration, SERC offers breakout rooms and offices, storage and support areas, seminar and conference rooms, and classroom space. The Materials Research Facility houses three X-ray diffractometers; a transmission electron microscope; and an accurate-mass quadrupole time-of-flight mass spectrometer, which offers superior sensitivity and data quality for profiling, identifying, characterizing, and quantifying compounds. The Research and Instructional Support Facility is home to glass-blowing design services and a computer numerical-control milling machine that enables the design and manufacture of an array of tools, prototypes, and products essential for advanced research. Less than 2 miles north of the main academic campus, on the Health Sciences Center campus at Broad and Ontario Streets, excellent and varied facilities for research are accessible. Finally, the University libraries contain more than 4 million bound volumes and are custodians of thousands of special collections of rare books and primary archival sources.

Financial Aid

Graduate students are eligible for financial assistance from private, University, state, and federal sources. The Office of Student Financial Services (http://sfs.temple.edu/) administers loans, grants, work-study, and other forms of financial aid. Students can contact the SFS office directly at 215-204-2244 for additional information.

Cost of Study

Resident tuition for the 2018–19 academic year ranges from $719 per credit for the Physician Assistant M.M.S. in the Lewis Katz School of Medicine to $2,300 per credit for the Fox School of Business and Management's executive D.B.A. Nonresident tuition ranges from $754 per credit for the Physician Assistant M.M.S. to $2,300 per credit for Fox School's executive D.B.A. A breakdown of tuition by school/college or program, in some cases, is available at http://bulletin.temple.edu/graduate/tuition-fees/.

Living and Housing Costs

On-campus housing is limited. For information on availability, students can contact the Office of University Housing and Residential Life at 215-204-7184 or visit http://housing.temple.edu/graduate.

Student Group

With a student body of more than 40,000 students, Temple University is one of the largest universities in the country. Since becoming a part of the Commonwealth System of Higher Education, it has increasingly emphasized upper-division and graduate work. Although the institution historically served the greater metropolitan area of southeastern Pennsylvania, Temple University now consistently attracts a significant and growing portion of the student body worldwide.

Location

With a population of more than 1.5 million, Philadelphia is the sixth-largest city in the country. It offers a variety of cultural attractions, including a world-renowned symphony orchestra, professional repertory theater, historic shrines, parks, and sports facilities. The climate is temperate, with an average temperature in winter of 33 degrees and 73 degrees in summer.

The University

With a rich heritage of populist tradition, Temple University provides students with an opportunity for education of high quality without regard to race, creed, or station in life. Affiliation with the Commonwealth System of Higher Education undergirds Temple's character as a public institution. Temple's academic programs are conducted on four campuses in Philadelphia and campuses in Ambler and Harrisburg, Pennsylvania.

Applying

Departmental deadlines for admissions and financial aid vary. Applicants should consult a particular program's page in the Graduate Bulletin (http://bulletin.temple.edu/graduate/) and the program's website, which is identified on the program's Contacts tab in the Graduate Bulletin. Notification regarding admission and financial aid is made following the screening of the application.

Correspondence and Information

Zebulon V. Kendrick, Ph.D.
Vice Provost for Graduate Education
Temple University
501 Carnell Hall
1803 North Broad Street
Philadelphia, Pennsylvania 19122-6104
United States
Phone: 215-204-1380
Fax: 215-204-8781
E-mail: grad@temple.edu
Website: http://www.temple.edu/grad

FACULTY HEADS

Graduate School: Zebulon V. Kendrick, Ph.D., Vice Provost.
Beasley School of Law: Gregory N. Mandel, J.D., Dean.
Center for the Performing and Cinematic Arts, including Boyer College of Music and Dance and the School of Theater, Film and Media Arts: Robert T. Stroker, Ph.D., Dean.
College of Education: Gregory M. Anderson, Ph.D., Dean.
College of Engineering: Keyanoush Sadeghipour, Ph.D., Dean.
College of Liberal Arts: Richard Deeg, Ph.D., Dean.
College of Public Health: Laura A. Siminoff, Ph.D., Dean.
College of Science and Technology: Michael L. Klein, Ph.D., Dean.
Fox School of Business and Management: Ronald C. Anderson, Ph.D., Interim Dean.
Kornberg School of Dentistry: Amid I. Ismail, Dr.P.H., Dean.
Lew Klein College of Media and Communication: David Boardman, M.A., Dean.
Lewis Katz School of Medicine: Larry R. Kaiser, M.D., Dean.
School of Pharmacy: Peter H. Doukas, Ph.D., Dean.
School of Podiatric Medicine: John A. Mattiacci, D.P.M., Dean.
School of Sport, Tourism and Hospitality Management: Ronald C. Anderson, Ph.D., Interim Dean.
Tyler School of Art: Susan E. Cahan, Ph.D., Dean.

The landscape of Temple University's main campus is in a positive state of flux. A fierce owl readying for flight has made the heart of campus its home.

TUFTS UNIVERSITY

Graduate School of Arts and Sciences

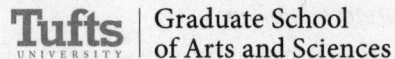

Tufts UNIVERSITY | Graduate School of Arts and Sciences

★ For more information, visit http://petersons.to/tuftsuniv-arts-sciences

Programs of Study

The Graduate School of Arts and Sciences at Tufts University offers master's, certificate, and doctoral programs in the natural sciences, social sciences, and the arts and humanities.

The Doctor of Philosophy (Ph.D.) degree is offered in biology, chemistry, chemistry/biotechnology, child study and human development, cognitive science, economics and public policy, education, English, history, human developmental economics, mathematics, physics, psychology, and theatre and performance studies. A highly selective interdisciplinary doctorate is available in other areas. Tufts also offers a Doctor of Occupational Therapy.

The Master of Arts degree may be earned in art history, art history and museum studies, child study and human development, classics, digital tools for premodern studies, diversity and inclusion leadership, education, English, French, German, history, history and museum studies, museum education, music, philosophy, school psychology, and urban and environmental policy and planning. The Master of Science is offered in biology, chemistry, chemistry/biotechnology, data analytics, economics, education, environmental economics and urban planning, environmental policy and planning, mathematics, occupational therapy, sustainability and physics. The Master of Arts in Teaching is available in education with concentrations in art and secondary education. The Master of Fine Arts degree is awarded through the School of the Museum of Fine Arts (SMFA) at Tufts. Tufts also offers the Master of Public Policy degree. Certificate programs are available in advanced professional study for occupational therapy, community environmental studies, early childhood technology, environmental management, hand and upper extremity rehabilitation for occupational therapy, interdisciplinary studio art, management of community organizations, mathematics, museum studies, occupational therapy, program evaluation, school-based practice for occupational therapy, and urban justice and sustainability.

Full-time students can take one course per semester, for both a grade and credit, through cross-registration agreements with Boston College, Boston University, and Brandeis University.

Research Facilities

The Tufts University library system includes the Tisch Library, the Lilly Music Library, the Edward Ginn Library of The Fletcher School, and the W. Van Alan Clark, Jr. Library at SMFA at Tufts. Through Tufts' membership in the Boston Library Consortium, graduate students also have library privileges at the Massachusetts State Library, the Woods Hole Oceanographic Institute, the Boston Public Library, and the libraries of Amherst College, Boston College, Boston University, Brandeis University, the Massachusetts Institute of Technology, Northeastern University, the University of Connecticut, the University of Massachusetts, the University of New Hampshire, Wellesley College, and Williams College. Theatre and performance studies students have access to the Harvard Theatre Collection.

Special research facilities for science and engineering students include the campus-based Science and Technology Center (SEC), housing selected areas of research in physics and electrical and chemical engineering as well as laboratory facilities in biology, chemistry, psychology, and electrical and civil engineering, and the Collaborative Learning and Innovation Complex (CLIC), housing the departments of physics and astronomy, occupational therapy, community health, child study and human development and faculty working in human-centered engineering. Students are encouraged to pursue collaborative research at off-site facilities, which have included Fermilab, the Woods Hole Oceanographic Institute, and Brookhaven Laboratories. Many student and faculty researchers carry out collaborative research with colleagues at nearby Boston universities.

Financial Aid

In 2017–18, the Graduate School of Arts and Sciences awarded more than $13 million in tuition scholarships. Teaching and research assistantships are available, as are some fellowships. Tufts also awards need-based financial aid through the Federal Perkins Loan, Federal Work-Study, and Federal Direct Student Loan programs.

Cost of Study

Tuition for most master's programs for 2018-19 is $51,288, and is only charged in the student's first year. The 2018-19 tuition for the school psychology Master of Arts and educational specialist program is $44,904 charged for two years; the urban and environmental policy and planning Master of Arts program is $36,988 charged for two years; and the Master of Fine Arts program is $46,268 charged for one year. Part-time tuition in 2018-19 is $1,710 per credit, including credits taken in the summer. The 2018-19 tuition for doctoral programs is $30,772, and is charged for five years. The 2018-19 tuition for the Entry-level Doctor of Occupational Therapy is $51,288, and is charged for two and a half years. The 2018-19 tuition for Post-professional Doctor of Occupational Therapy students is $51,288, and is charged for one year. Other charges include student health insurance, a health service fee, and a student activity fee.

Living and Housing Costs

Living expenses are estimated at about $1,450 a month, including food, housing, utilities, transportation, and textbook costs. There is limited on-campus housing for graduate students. Rents for one-bedroom apartments in Medford and Somerville begin at approximately $1,450 per month. The cost of sharing an apartment averages about $750 per person, and over 90 percent of students share apartments with at least one other individual. A public transportation system serves the greater Boston area and provides easy access to and from the campus, while a free, local shuttle runs throughout the academic year, providing easy access between campus, the subway, and Boston.

Student Group

In 2018–19, 986 students were enrolled in the Graduate School of Arts and Sciences. Of these, 66 percent were women and 19 percent were international students.

Location

The main campus, which spans the Medford-Somerville city line, is 6 miles from downtown Boston, a city where the arts (music, drama, and dance), museums, and sporting events abound. Cape Cod beaches and the mountains and forests of Maine, New Hampshire, and Vermont can be easily reached.

The University

Chartered as a liberal arts college in 1852, today Tufts is a small, selective, private university offering opportunities for undergraduate,

graduate, and professional education to more than 7,500 students. The Graduate School of Arts and Sciences, the School of the Museum of Fine Arts at Tufts, the School of Engineering, The Fletcher School of Law and Diplomacy, The Friedman School of Nutrition Science and Policy, The Sackler School of Graduate Biomedical Sciences, The Cummings School of Veterinary Medicine, The School of Dental Medicine, and The School of Medicine offer graduate and/or professional education. The university is accredited by the New England Association of Schools and Colleges.

Applying

Deadlines for applications vary by program. Applicants applying to a degree program are required to submit three letters of recommendation, a resume, official transcripts from all colleges and universities attended, and a personal statement. Most departments also require the results of the Graduate Record Examinations (GRE). Students whose native language is not English must submit official results of the Test of English as a Foreign Language (TOEFL).

Correspondence and Information

Office of Graduate Admissions
Tufts University
Bendetson Hall
Medford, Massachusetts 02155
United States
Phone: 617-627-3395
E-mail: gradadmissions@tufts.edu
Website: http://asegrad.tufts.edu

FIELDS OF STUDY AND FACULTY ADVISERS

Art: Jeannie Simms and Lisa Bynoe
Art and Art History: Karen Overbey
Biology: Catherine Freudenreich (Ph.D. program and Thesis M.S.); George Ellmore (Open Choice M.S.)
Chemistry: Samuel Thomas
Child Study and Human Development: Tama Leventhal
Classics: Marie-Claire Beaulieu
Data Analytics: Jeff Zabel and Bruce Boghosian
Digital Humanities: Marie-Claire Beaulieu
Diversity and Inclusion Leadership: Robert Cook
Economics: Gilbert Metcalf
Economics and Public Policy: Margaret McMillan
Education: Susan Barahal (Art Education); David Hammer (Educational Studies); Brian Gravel (Elementary Education); Cynthia Robinson (Museum Education); Steven Luz-Alterman and Silas Pinto (School Psychology); Andrew Izsak (STEM Education); Laura Rogers (Teacher Education)
English: Elizabeth Ammons
French: Vincent Pollina
German: Markus Wilczek
History: Steven Marrone
Interdisciplinary Doctorate: Sergio Fantini
Mathematics: James Adler
Music: Stephan Pennington and Frank Lehman
Museum Studies: Cynthia Robinson
Occupational Therapy: Jessica Harney
Philosophy: Christiana Olfert
Physics: Danilo Marchesini
Psychology: Ayanna Thomas
Theatre and Performance Studies: Noe Montez
Urban and Environmental Policy and Planning: Barbara Parmenter and Laurie Goldman

UNIVERSITY OF ARKANSAS

The Graduate School

★ For more information, visit http://petersons.to/uofarkansas

UNIVERSITY OF ARKANSAS

Graduate School
& International Education

Programs of Study

The University of Arkansas is an internationally competitive student-centered research university that represents the best of public higher education. Its Graduate School has a reputation for producing influential leaders and intellectuals, and is a place where aspirations become reality. Graduate students work with experts in their fields who are striving to answer today's most challenging questions. The university community is a place where students can ask tough questions, drive innovation, break barriers, explore every angle, and solve complex problems. They are at the forefront of discovery and are committed to enriching the global community.

The Graduate School offers 130 graduate programs. A directory of all the programs can be found at http://catalog.uark.edu/graduatecatalog/.

The university believes that complex problems must often be approached from multiple angles. This mindset has led to the development of six interdisciplinary graduate degree programs that, together with the appropriate research centers, require collaboration among all of the university's colleges.

Once students have completed their journey at the University of Arkansas, their professional futures are bright. Placement rates for master's graduates are nearly 90 percent, while doctoral graduates enjoy a 92 percent placement rate. Students are remembered once they have left campus, as names of graduates are etched in stone on Senior Walk, with over four miles of pavement listing over 170,000 graduates and counting.

Research Facilities

As a Research I university, the University of Arkansas has been recognized by the Carnegie Classification of Institutions of Higher Education as a doctoral university with the highest level of research activity. Numerous programs, both on campus and online, are nationally ranked. They provide students with the opportunity to work with experts in their fields who are striving to answer today's most challenging questions in the arts, sciences, business, medicine, law, engineering, and more.

Currently, over 310 doctoral fellows are enrolled in the Graduate School, as well as 13 NSF Graduate Research fellows, 46 Benjamin Franklin Lever fellows, and 51 Fulbright scholars.

More than 50 research centers at the university provide special programs of research on campus. The Office of Research and Innovation works to enhance the university research enterprise. The Office of Research and Sponsored Programs assists with finding funding, submitting proposals and managing awards. The Office of Research Compliance helps researchers comply with federal and state regulations as well as University policies.

Financial Aid

The Graduate School offers a variety of financial and community resources to help students manage the cost of study including graduate assistantships, doctoral fellowships, travel grants, loans, and work-study opportunities. Each year, students receive NASA, NSF, Fulbright, and other prestigious national awards. Over 1,500 students serve in graduate assistant roles, with over 500 of these working as teaching assistants.

Cost of Study

Tuition and fees are charged per credit hour and will vary each term depending upon the number of credit hours taken, the academic college of the student program, type of course taken, and residency status. For the 2018–19 academic year, average graduate tuition and fees range from $11,482 to $16,188 for Arkansas residents and $28,700 to $36,250 for nonresidents. More specific details can be found online at https://finaid.uark.edu/cost-of-attendance.php.

Northwest Arkansas' cost of living is more than 10 percent below the national average. While cost of living can vary greatly depending on lifestyle, budget, and spending habits, this region consistently ranks among the lowest cost metro areas in the country while still offering the amenities and convenience families and businesses demand.

Living and Housing

The University of Arkansas currently has some on-campus housing for graduate students in the Duncan Avenue Apartments. Currently there is no on-campus housing for married students. The Fayetteville area does offer several other housing options for students, many of which are on the university bus routes. More information can be found at the Off-Campus housing website: https://offcampushousing.uark.edu/.

Student Life

Over 4,000 graduate students are currently enrolled at the University of Arkansas, with a nearly 50:50 ratio of male to female students. Individuals from under-represented groups represent 17 percent of the graduate student body, while over 700 international graduate students from 90 countries have made the University of Arkansas home.

Students have a powerful resource in the Graduate Professional Student Congress (GPSC), where ideas, opinions, and concerns are recognized. The GSC serves as an institutional voice that advocates for the interests of graduate students, and all students are encouraged to actively participate in congressional meetings to effect change on campus.

Over 380 registered student organizations provide an outlet for graduate students to connect with peers over culture, religion, professional affiliations, or special interests. A multitude of on-campus events are offered to students, including live theater, art exhibits, free concerts from nationally renowned artists, and engaging lectures from distinguished global speakers and world leaders.

Location

Fayetteville, located in Northwest Arkansas, is ranked by *U.S. News & World Report* as one of the Top Five Best Places to Live in the United States due to its strong job market, low unemployment, high quality of life, short commutes, mild climate, and low cost of living.

Northwest Arkansas, linked by the 36-mile Razorback Regional Greenway trail, offers a multitude of recreational activities and cultural events from kayaking on the Buffalo River and hiking the trails of Devil's Den State Park, to seeing Broadway shows at the Walton Arts Center on Dickson Street or viewing art installations at the award-winning Crystal Bridges Museum of American Art in Bentonville.

The University

Since 1871, Arkansas' flagship university has been a place where creativity is nurtured, and problems are solved through research and discovery. It is a place where aspirations become reality, where student voices are heard, and where faculty are driven to change lives with their teaching and research. It is a place where students will find a vibrant campus life, a community rich with culture and opportunity, and where traditions are etched in stone.

The Faculty

The faculty and staff work tirelessly to support graduate students at the University of Arkansas. A listing of the current graduate school faculty is available online at https://graduate-and-international.uark.edu/graduate/faculty-staff/graduate-faculty/.

Applying

Requirements for admission to the University of Arkansas Graduate School include a conferred baccalaureate degree; scores from a standardized test, such as the GRE; the completed online application for Graduate School admission, a $60 nonrefundable application fee; transcripts from the institution where the applicant received their first bachelor's degree; and verification of English proficiency if the applicant's native language is not English.

Applicants must also be admitted to an academic program. The program will make the formal admission decision based upon factors including GPA, letters of recommendation, GRE (or other graduate-level standardized test) scores. Graduate degree programs may have additional requirements, such as statement of purposes, resume or CV, writing sample, and more that must be submitted before the admission decision is made. Each degree program's or department's website will list further items that may be required.

Some departments require that applicants submit a separate application to them, in addition to submitting an application to the Graduate School. Applicants should go to the homepage of the department to which they are applying and read about the application procedures for that department and graduate degree program.

Within two weeks of submitting an application, the Office of Graduate and International Admissions will send an email outlining how to monitor what items, if any, are still needed to complete the application process. Response times will vary depending upon the volume of applications and time of year.

Applicants will be notified when their file is complete. If the applicant's Graduate School admission requirements are met, the file will be forwarded to the academic program for their admission decision.

Correspondence and Information

Graduate School and International Education
340 North Campus Drive
Gearhart Hall 213
1 University of Arkansas
Fayetteville, Arkansas 72701
Phone: 479-575-4401
Fax: 479-575-5908
E-mail: gradinfo@uark.edu
Website: https://graduate-and-international.uark.edu

Programs of Study

The Graduate School offers more than thirty programs leading to the doctorate (Ph.D.) and to the Master of Arts (A.M.). In addition, programs are offered leading to the Master of Arts in Education (M.A.Ed.), Master of Arts in Teaching (M.A.T.), and Master of Fine Arts (M.F.A.).

Opportunities for combining a degree available through the Graduate School with a degree from one of the University's professional schools (business, law, medicine) are also available.

Research Facilities

The Washington University community is served by a network of libraries designed to meet the instructional and research needs of faculty members, students, and staff members. Washington University libraries contain the largest collection of any private academic library system between the Mississippi River and California. John M. Olin Library, the central University library, and twelve school and departmental libraries house many important and unique collections and provide state-of-the-art computerized information retrieval. The combined holdings include more than 3 million books and bound periodicals, 18,000 current serial subscriptions, and access to thousands of electronic journals and databases. For more information, students can visit http://library.wustl.edu.

More than thirty centers and institutes provide a spectrum of research opportunities. They include the Center for Air Pollution Impact and Trend Analysis; Center for the Study of American Business; Center for American Indian Studies; Business, Law, and Economics Center; Arts and Sciences Computing Center; Institutes for Biomedical Computing; McDonnell Center for Cellular and Molecular Neurobiology; Construction Management Center; Carolyne Roehm Electronic Media Center; Center for Engineering Computing; Center for Genetics in Medicine; McDonnell Center for Studies of Higher Brain Function; Center for the History of Freedom; Office of International Studies; International Writers Center; Center for the Study of Islamic Societies and Civilizations; Management Center; Fred Gasche Laboratory for Microstructured Materials Technologies; Markey Center for Research in Molecular Biology of Human Disease; Center for Optimization and Semantic Control; Center for Plant Science and Biotechnology; Center for the Study of Public Affairs; Center for Robotics and Automation; Social Work Research Development Center; McDonnell Center for Space Sciences; Center for the Application of Information Technology; and Urban Research and Design Center.

Financial Aid

The majority of full-time students receive financial support. Financial assistance in the form of scholarships, fellowships, and traineeships is offered annually on a competitive basis through the Graduate School from government, private, or endowed sources. Also available are scholarships and, in applied social sciences, clinical internships; grants and fellowships in national competition; and loans. Specific information may be obtained from the departmental or administrative unit to which the student intends to apply.

Cost of Study

Tuition for the 2018–19 academic year for the Graduate School is $52,400. The cost per credit unit is $2,183.

Living and Housing Costs

Many graduate students live in University-owned apartments, some with data connections and shuttle bus service. Listing information for these units as well as non-University housing is available through the University's Apartment Referral Service (http://offcampushousing.wustl.edu/). Average rent ranges from $700 to $2,000 per month.

Student Group

Of the more than 15,000 people attending Washington University, more than 7,000 are graduate students; approximately 1,400 of them are enrolled in the Graduate School. Students come to Washington University from all fifty states and more than eighty international locations.

Location

Washington University has two campuses that lie at opposite ends of Forest Park (one of the largest municipal parks in the nation). The campuses are approximately 5 miles west of downtown St. Louis. The Danforth campus is the location of the Graduate School and all other schools of the University except Medicine. The latter is located on the east, or medical campus. The Division of Biology and Biomedical Sciences is also located on the medical campus. Free shuttle buses run between the campuses on a regular schedule.

The St. Louis area has nearly 2.4 million residents. The cost of living is affordable. The University's central location provides easy access to the zoo, museums, Science Center, Missouri Botanical Gardens, St. Louis Symphony, Opera Theatre, St. Louis Repertory Theatre, Black Repertory Theatre, Blues hockey, and Cardinals baseball. Outdoor adventure beyond the city can be found in the Ozark Mountains and on the rivers of Missouri. Camping, hiking, floating, rock climbing, and spelunking are among the many possibilities within a few hours' drive of St. Louis.

The Graduate School

The Graduate School is a charter member of both the Association of Graduate Schools and the Council of Graduate Schools. The School provides a physical and academic environment in which inquiry, intellectual growth, and discovery can thrive and flourish.

Applying

Prospective students may apply online. Applicants should check with the department or program to which they are applying, as application deadlines vary. Most programs require GRE scores. For international students whose native language is not English, most programs require an official copy of a TOEFL score.

Correspondence and Information

Graduate School
Campus Box 1187
Washington University in St. Louis
One Brookings Drive
St. Louis, Missouri 63130-4899
United States
Phone: 314-935-6880
Fax: 314-935-4887
E-mail: GraduateSchool@wustl.edu
Website: http://graduateschool.wustl.edu

FACULTY HEADS, DEGREES OFFERED, AND DEPARTMENTAL INTERESTS

Anthropology (Ph.D.): T. R. Kidder (trkidder@wustl.edu). Sociocultural anthropology (including medical anthropology), archaeology, physical anthropology (including primate studies, paleontology and human biology).

Art History and Archaeology (A.M., Ph.D.): Liz Childs (ecchilds@wustl.edu). Ancient, medieval, Renaissance, early modern, European, modern and contemporary European and American, Asian art history; classical archaeology.

Division of Biology and Biomedical Sciences (Ph.D.): John Russell (800-852-9074, toll-free); e-mail: DBBSPhDAdmissions@wustl.edu).

Biochemistry: Peter Burgers (DBBSPhDAdmissions@wustl.edu). Metabolic regulation, signal transduction, receptors, membrane channels and transporters, membrane structure and dynamics, membrane trafficking, cholesterol and lipid metabolism, nucleic acid-protein structure interactions and function, DNA replication and repair, recombination, transcription, translation, enzyme kinetics, cancer biology, cell cycle regulation, apoptosis, cell motility, cytoskeleton, cell division, extracellular matrix, vascular biology, aging, senescence, telomere biology, heat-shock proteins, prion proteins, gene expression, RNA editing and binding proteins, microbial pathogenesis, parasitology, virology, drug design and metabolism, plant natural products, photosynthesis and plant energy production, molecular imaging in cells and tissues, carbohydrate metabolism, proteases.

Computational and Molecular Biophysics: Daved Fremont (DBBSPhDAdmissions@wustl.edu). Structural biology, protein and nucleic acid kinetics and thermodynamics, single-molecule enzymology, protein design, nanoscience, ion channels and lipid membranes, computational biophysics.

Computational and Systems Biology: Barak Cohen (DBBSPhDAdmissions@wustl.edu). Systems biology, genomics, sequence analysis, regulatory networks, synthetic biology, metagenomics, metabolomics, proteomics, single cell dynamics, high-throughput technology development, applied math and mathematical models of biological processes, computational biology, comparative genomics, personalized medicine, next generation sequencing and its applications, bioinformatics.

Developmental, Regenerative, and Stem Cell Biology: Kerry Kornfeld and James Skeath (DBBSPhDAdmissions@wustl.edu). Development, stem cell biology, regenerative biology, cell biology, genetics, cell signaling, the biology of cancer, epigenetics, circadian rhythms, systems biology.

Evolution, Ecology, and Population Biology: David Queller (DBBSPhDAdmissions@wustl.edu). Population ecology, community ecology, plant and animal evolution, microbial evolution, evolution of behavior, phylogenetics, systematics, theoretical and experimental population genetics.

Human and Statistical Genetics: Patrick Jay and John Rice (DBBSPhDAdmissions@wustl.edu). Human genetics, statistical genetics, functional genomics, molecular genetics, Mendelian disease, complex disease, Mammalian genetics, systems biology.

Immunology: Eugene Otiz (DBBSPhDAdmissions@wustl.edu). Cellular immunology; molecular immunology; lineage development; autoimmunity; cancer immunotherapy; transcription factors; epigenomics; mucosal immunity; innate immunity; bacterial, viral, and parasite immunity; immune evasion; antigen processing and presentation; dendritic cells; T cell signaling; antigen receptor diversification.

Molecular Cell Biology: Heather True-Krob and Jason Weber (DBBSPhDAdmissions@wustl.edu). Cell adhesion, protein trafficking and organelle biogenesis, cell cycle, receptors, signal transduction, gene expression, metabolism, cytoskeleton and motility, membrane excitability, molecular basis of diseases.

Molecular Genetics and Genomics: Tim Schedl and James Skeath (DBBSPhDAdmissions@wustl.edu). Genetics, genetic basis of disease, genomics, epigenetics, genetic engineering, genome editing, model organism genetics, development, cell biology, molecular biology, complex traits, bioinformatics, systems biology.

Molecular Microbiology and Microbial Pathogenesis: David Sibley (DBBSPhDAdmissions@wustl.edu). Host-pathogen interactions, cellular microbiology, comparative genomics, molecular microbiology, microbial pathogenesis, pathogen discovery, emerging infectious diseases, microbial physiology, microbial ecology and engergetics, virology, bacteriology, mycology, parasitology.

Neurosciences: Lawrence Snyder and Erik Herzog (DBBSPhDAdmissions@wustl.edu). Neurobiology, neurology, functional imaging, behavior, cognition, computational neuroscience, electrophysiology, sensory systems, motor systems, neuroglia, neuronal development, learning, memory, language, synaptic plasticity, mind, consciousness, neurodegeneration, diseases of the nervous system, neuronal injury, clinical neuroscience, motor control, biological rhythms, connectivity mapping.

Plant and Microbial Bioscience: Joseph Jez and Petra Levin (DBBSPhDAdmissions@wustl.edu). Cell biology, development, physiology, signaling, development, metabolic regulation, photosynthesis, bioenergy, protein structure-function, synthetic biology, biogeochemistry, environmental microbiology, ecology, population genetics, molecular evolution.

Business (Ph.D.): Anjan Thakor (phdinfo@olin.wustl.edu). Accounting, business economics, finance, marketing, organizational behavior, strategy, operations and manufacturing management.

Chemistry (Ph.D.): Bill Buhro (chemistry-admissions@wustl.edu). Bioinorganic, biological, bioorganic, biophysical, materials, nuclear, organic, organometallic, physical, polymer, radiochemistry, spectroscopy, theoretical.

Classics (A.M., Ph.D.): Timothy Moore (classics@wustl.edu). Greek and Latin language and literature, ancient performance, philosophy, history, and material culture.

Comparative Literature (Ph.D.): Lynne Tatlock (ltatlock@wustl.edu). World literature; literary theory; translation studies; global and multicultural theory; comparative drama; comparative arts; studies in literature, politics, and society; narrative theory; media ecologies, histories, and poetics.

Earth and Planetary Sciences (Ph.D.): Viatcheslav Solomatov (mwysession@wustl.edu). Planetary sciences, geology, geobiology, geochemistry, geodynamics.

East Asian Languages and Cultures (A.M., J.D./A.M., Ph.D.): Rebecca Copeland (ealc@wustl.edu). Chinese; Japanese; Chinese fiction, theater, poetry, modern literature; Japanese modern and classical fiction; translation theory; East Asian studies.

Economics (Ph.D.): John Nachbar (nachbar@wustl.edu). Economic theory, industrial organization, political economy, public economics, macroeconomics, public finance, development economics.

Education (M.A.Ed., M.A.T., Ph.D.): Kit Wellmon (kwellman@wustl.edu). Teacher education, educational studies, urban education, policy studies, science and math education, second language research.

English and American Literature (Ph.D.): Wolfram Schmidgen (wschmidg@wustl.edu). Medieval, early modern, early American, eighteenth-century British, nineteenth-century British, nineteenth-century American, twentieth-century British, twentieth-century American, African-American literature and culture, Irish literature, Anglophone postcolonial literature, gender and sexuality studies, modernism, poetry and poetics, theory.

Film and Media Studies (A.M.): Gaylyn Studlar (gstudlar@wustl.edu). Criticism, history, and theories of film and electronic media; all moving image forms of visual culture.

Germanic Languages and Literatures (A.M., Ph.D.): Matt Erlin (merlin@wustl.edu). German literature and culture from the Middle Ages through the twenty-first century, intellectual history, film and media studies, gender studies, Holocaust studies, history of the book, digital humanities.

History (Ph.D.): Peter Kastor (pjkastor@wustl.edu). Seventeenth- through nineteenth-century America, twentieth-century America, African history, central Europe, early modern Europe, East Asian history, history of American political culture, international urban history, Middle East, religion in the medieval Mediterranean world.

Institute of Materials Science and Engineering (Ph.D.): Kathy Flores (floresk@wustl.edu). Materials structure, properties, processing, and performance, particularly as related to materials for energy harvesting and storage; materials for environmental remediation and sustainability; materials for regenerative medicine; metallic glasses and other structurally complex materials; plasmonics, photonics, and materials for sensors and imaging; and computational materials science.

Jewish, Islamic, and Near Eastern Languages and Cultures (A.M.): Nancy Berg (nberg@wustl.edu). Islamic and Near Eastern studies (Islamic history, Arabic language and literature, modern Middle East history), Jewish studies (Hebrew Bible, Rabbinic literature, Jewish history, modern Hebrew literature).

Mathematics (A.M., Ph.D.): John McCarthy (mccarthy@wustl.edu). Algebra, algebraic geometry, real and complex analysis, differential geometry, topology, mathematical statistics, survival analysis, modeling, statistical computing for massive data, Bayesian regularization, bioinformatics, longitudinal and functional data analysis, statistical computation, application of statistics to medicine.

Movement Science (Ph.D.): Gammon Earhart (earhartg@wustl.edu). Philosophy of human movement function and dysfunction, with special emphasis on bioenergetics, biomechanics, and biocontrol.

Music (A.M., Ph.D.): Todd Decker (tdecker@wustl.edu). Musicology, ethnomusicology, theory, piano performance and pedagogy.

Performing Arts (A.M., M.F.A.): Mark Rollins (mark@wustl.edu). Theater studies, performance studies, dance.

Philosophy (Ph.D.): Ron Mallon (rmallon@wustl.edu). Ethics, social and political philosophy, history of philosophy, philosophy of law, philosophy of science, philosophy of mind, philosophy of language, theory of knowledge, aesthetics.

Philosophy/Neuroscience/Psychology (Ph.D.): Ron Mallon (pnp@wustl.edu). Philosophy of mind and language, with a special emphasis on the philosophical dimensions of psychology, neuroscience, and linguistics.

Physics (A.M., Ph.D.): Mark Alford (alford@wustl.edu). Experimental: astrophysics and space sciences, condensed matter and material physics, applications in biology and medicine, nuclear physics. Theoretical: astrophysics, biophysics, condensed matter and materials physics, elementary particles, many-body theory.

Political Science (Ph.D.): Jim Spriggs (jspriggs@wustl.edu). American politics, comparative politics, formal theory, international politics, law and courts, normative theory, political methodology.

Psychological & Brain Sciences (Ph.D.): Deanna Barch (dbarch@wustl.edu). Behavior/brain/cognition, clinical, development and aging, social/personality.

Rehabilitation and Participation Science (Ph.D.): Carolyn Baum (baumc@wustl.edu). Science of rehabilitation and participation with special emphasis placed on neurorehabilitation, performance, and community participation.

Romance Languages and Literatures (Ph.D.): Michael Sherberg (sherberg@wustl.edu). French language and literature, Latin American and Iberian literature and languages, Spanish and comparative literature.

Social Work (Ph.D.): Renee Cunningham Williams (williamsr@wustl.edu). Mental health, disparities, social and economic development, addictions, aging, child welfare, civic service, disabilities, health, poverty and social policy. Social determinants of health, health disparities, health promotion and disease prevention, health policy, dissemination and implementation, epidemiology, global health.

Speech and Hearing Sciences (Ph.D.): William Clark (elliottb@wustl.edu). Speech and hearing sciences, clinical audiology, deaf education, speech and language, sensory neuroscience.

The Writing Program (M.F.A.): David Schuman (dschuman@wustl.edu). Fiction, creative nonfiction, poetry-writing workshops and academic courses.

Programs of Study

A better job, financial security, and personal satisfaction are just some of the end goals for students seeking to earn an advanced degree through graduate study at Western New England University. From business to communication, creative writing to behavior analysis, and programs for teachers and engineers, students gain essential skills and expertise for success in their careers.

Programs in Communication, Accounting, and Curriculum and Instruction are offered entirely online and were developed specifically for that delivery model. Most of the Business and Engineering master's programs follow a blended model, allowing students to study completely online or attend select live sessions on campus. This flexibility enables working professionals to learn at their own pace. Education programs are offered in late afternoon and early evening to accommodate the schedules of working teachers. The low-residency M.F.A. in Creative Writing program includes four short-term residencies with author mentors, and the M.S. in Sport Leadership and Coaching includes two short-term residencies.

The University is regionally accredited by the New England Association of Schools and Colleges.

The **College of Arts and Sciences** offers the following graduate programs:

- Master of Arts in Communication with a public relations concentration
- Master of Arts in English for Teachers
- Master of Arts in Mathematics for Teachers
- Master of Education in Curriculum and Instruction
- Master of Fine Arts in Creative Writing
- Master of Science in Applied Behavior Analysis
- Ph.D. in Behavior Analysis

The **College of Business** offers the following graduate programs:

- Master of Business Administration (M.B.A.)
- Master of Science in Accounting (M.S.A.)
- M.S.A. with Forensic Accounting and Fraud Investigation concentration
- Master of Science in Organizational Leadership (M.S.O.L.)
- Master of Science in Sport Leadership and Coaching (M.S.L.C)
- J.D./M.B.A. combined degree program
- J.D./M.S.A. combined degree program
- J.D./M.S.O.L. combined degree program
- Pharm.D./M.B.A. combined degree program
- Pharm.D./M.S.O.L. combined degree program

The **College of Engineering** offers these graduate programs:

- Master of Science in Civil Engineering (M.S.C.E.)
- Master of Science in Electrical Engineering (M.S.E.E.)
- M.S.E.E. with Mechatronics concentration
- Master of Science in Engineering Management (M.S.E.M.)
- Master of Science in Industrial Engineering (M.S.I.E.)
- Master of Science in Mechanical Engineering (M.S.M.E.)
- M.S.M.E. with Mechatronics concentration
- M.S.E.M./M.B.A. combined degree program
- Ph.D. in Engineering Management
- J.D./M.S.E.M. combined degree program

The University also offers programs though the College of Pharmacy and Health Sciences and the Law School. These include the Juris Doctor, the Doctor of Pharmacy, and the Doctor of Occupational Therapy.

Financial Aid

To be considered for financial aid, a student must have final approval into a degree program and be enrolled in a minimum of 3 credits per term. Financial need-based resources, including grants and low-interest federal loans, may be available for eligible students.

Cost of Study

Western New England University is committed to keeping a high-quality private education affordable for its students. Western New England's graduate tuition rates are some of the most affordable in the region. Tuition for graduate programs is as follows:

College of Arts and Sciences:

- Online M.Ed.: $682 per credit
- M.A.E.T., and M.A.M.T.: $370 per credit
- M.A. in Communication: $792 per credit
- M.F.A. in Creative Writing: $634 per credit
- M.S. in Applied Behavior Analysis: $1,134 per credit
- Ph.D. in Behavior Analysis: $1,351 per credit

College of Business:

- M.B.A., M.S.A., M.S.O.L., and M.S.L.C.: $849 per credit

College of Engineering:

- M.S.C.E., M.S.E.E., M.S.E.M., M.S.I.E., and M.S.M.E.: $1,134 per credit
- Ph.D. in Engineering Management: $1,351 per credit

Living and Housing Costs

Graduate students have the option of living on campus. Housing costs range between $9,600 and $12,432, depending upon the apartment type and duration (10 to 12 months).

Career Development

The Career Development Center assists students and alumni with career planning, occupational exploration, and job search strategies. The center's staff members implement the University's strong commitment to the development of a student's career decision-making by providing individual career advising and assistance in identifying career options.

The Career Development Center staff brings students in contact with employers through dynamic on-campus recruiting, employer information sessions, and career fairs. In addition, students are assisted with resources for part-time and summer employment. A weekly newsletter is published online at www.wne.edu/careercenter and serves as one tool for alerting students to employment opportunities, internships, recruiting schedules, and career-related workshops and activities.

Location

Western New England University's beautiful 215-acre suburban campus is located in Springfield, Massachusetts, the cultural urban center of the western part of the state. Perhaps best known as the birthplace of basketball and home of the Naismith Memorial Basketball Hall of Fame, Springfield is midway between New York and Boston and on the road between New York and Canada. Springfield is ideally located for travel in all directions, and there is convenient access from the University to both the Mass Pike and Interstate 91.

Faculty

With an average class size of 20, students work closely with the University's full-time faculty members who bring outstanding professional and academic credentials to the classroom. On average, 85 percent of graduate courses are taught by full-time faculty members. Ninety percent of the faculty hold terminal degrees in their field.

Additional details about the faculty for specific departments/programs can be found at wne.edu.

The University

Originally established in 1919 to serve working adults, Western New England University is renowned for its innovative programs, culture of collaboration, and faculty members who are focused on student success. Today that commitment continues through the University's graduate programs on campus and online.

Accredited by AACSB International, the College of Business is widely respected throughout the region for the caliber of its flagship M.B.A. program, sought-after M.S.A. degree, and dynamic new offering in organizational leadership. The College of Arts and Sciences offers high-quality master's programs for teachers at an affordable tuition rate and an immersive M.F.A. in Creative Writing program. The College's master's and doctoral programs in Behavior Analysis have positioned the University as a global leader in research and education in that discipline. Accredited by the Association of Behavior Analysis International (ABAI), the Ph.D. in Behavior Analysis program has been cited by the ABAI as ranking third in total scholarly publications out of 74 programs. The thriving College of Engineering is recognized as an educational leader by major corporations in the northeast who seek out graduates of the University's master's and combined engineering/business and law degree programs.

Applying

Western New England University has a rolling admissions policy for most programs, not a set admission deadline. Admission decisions are typically released within two to three weeks of an application being complete. The University urges prospective students to apply as early as possible in relation to the anticipated start date. Most of the graduate programs offer multiple entry points annually. Graduate students can apply online at www.wne.edu/gradapp.

Correspondence and Information

Office of Graduate Admissions
Western New England University
1215 Wilbraham Road
Springfield, Massachusetts 01119
United States
Phone: 413-782-1517
800-325-1122, Ext. 1517 (toll-free)
E-mail: study@wne.edu
Website: wne.edu/grad

APPENDIXES

Institutional Changes Since the 2018 Edition

Following is an alphabetical listing of institutions that have recently closed, merged with other institutions, or changed their names or status. In the case of a name change, the former name appears first, followed by the new name.

Argosy University, Dallas (Farmers Branch, TX): *closed.*
Argosy University, Denver (Denver, CO): *closed.*
Argosy University, Inland Empire (Ontario, CA): *closed.*
Argosy University, Nashville (Nashville, TN): *closed.*
Argosy University, Salt Lake City (Draper, UT): *closed.*
Argosy University, San Diego (San Diego, CA): *closed.*
Argosy University, San Francisco Bay Area (Alameda, CA): *closed.*
Argosy University, Sarasota (Sarasota, FL): *closed.*
Argosy University, Schaumburg (Schaumburg, IL): *closed.*
Arlington Baptist College (Arlington, TX): *name changed to Arlington Baptist University.*
Armstrong State University (Savannah, GA): *name changed to Georgia Southern University-Armstrong Campus.*
Art Center College of Design (Pasadena, CA): *name changed to ArtCenter College of Design.*
The Art Institute of California-San Francisco, a campus of Argosy University (San Francisco, CA): *closed.*
Augsburg College (Minneapolis, MN): *name changed to Augsburg University.*
Bristol University (Anaheim, CA): *closed.*
Claremont McKenna College (Claremont, CA): *no longer profiled by request from the institution. Graduate program is for students attending the Claremont Colleges.*
Coleman University (San Diego, CA): *closed.*
Digital Media Arts College (Boca Raton, FL): *merged into Lynn University (Boca Raton, FL).*
Episcopal Divinity School (Cambridge, MA): *merged into Union Theological Seminary in the City of New York (New York, NY).*
Everest University (Tampa, FL): *name changed to Altierus Career College and no longer offers graduate degrees.*
Fairleigh Dickinson University, College at Florham (Madison, NJ): *name changed to Fairleigh Dickinson University, Florham Campus.*
Faith Evangelical College & Seminary (Tacoma, WA): *name changed to Faith International University.*
Frank Lloyd Wright School of Architecture (Scottsdale, AZ): *name changed to School of Architecture at Taliesin.*
Future Generations Graduate School (Franklin, WV): *name changed to Future Generations University.*
Grace University (Omaha, NE): *closed.*
Greenville College (Greenville, IL): *name changed to Greenville University.*
Hazelden Graduate School of Addiction Studies (Center City, MN): *name changed to Hazelden Betty Ford Graduate School of Addiction Studies.*
Henley-Putnam University (San Jose, CA): *name changed to Henley-Putnam School of Strategic Security.*
Huntington College of Health Sciences (Knoxville, TN): *name changed to Huntington University of Health Sciences.*
The Institute for the Psychological Sciences (Arlington, VA): *name changed to Divine Mercy University.*
International College of the Cayman Islands (Newlands, Cayman Islands): *no longer accredited by agency recognized by USDE or CHEA.*
Johnson State College (Johnson, VT): *name changed to Northern Vermont University-Johnson.*
John Wesley University (High Point, NC): *closed.*
Kaplan University, Davenport Campus (Davenport, IA): *name changed to Purdue University Global.*
Knowledge Systems Institute (Skokie, IL): *no longer degree granting.*
Long Island University-Hudson at Westchester (Purchase, NY): *name changed to Long Island University-Hudson.*
Lutheran Theological Seminary at Gettysburg (Gettysburg, PA): *name changed to United Lutheran Seminary.*
The Lutheran Theological Seminary at Philadelphia (Philadelphia, PA): *name changed to United Lutheran Seminary.*
Lynchburg College (Lynchburg, VA): *name changed to University of Lynchburg.*
Lyndon State College (Lyndonville, VT): *name changed to Northern Vermont University-Lyndon.*
Marylhurst University (Marylhurst, OR): *closed.*
McNally Smith College of Music (Saint Paul, MN): *closed.*
Memphis College of Art (Memphis, TN): *closed.*
Mirrer Yeshiva (Brooklyn, NY): *name changed to Mirrer Yeshiva Central Institute.*
Mount Ida College (Newton, MA): *merged into University of Massachusetts Amherst (Amherst, MA).*
National American University (Rapid City, SD): *graduate programs now listed under National American University (Austin, TX).*
The Ohio State University-Mansfield Campus (Mansfield, OH): *name changed to The Ohio State University at Mansfield.*
The Ohio State University-Newark Campus (Newark, OH): *name changed to The Ohio State University at Newark.*
Our Lady of the Lake College (Baton Rouge, LA): *name changed to Franciscan Missionaries of Our Lady University.*
Philadelphia University (Philadelphia, PA): *merged into Thomas Jefferson University (Philadelphia, PA).*
Sacred Heart School of Theology (Hales Corners, WI): *name changed to Sacred Heart Seminary and School of Theology.*
Sewanee: The University of the South (Sewanee, TN): *name changed to The University of the South.*
Shepherd University (Los Angeles, CA): *closed.*
Silicon Valley University (San Jose, CA): *closed.*
South University (Novi, MI): *closed.*
South University (High Point, NC): *closed.*
South University (Cleveland, OH): *closed.*
University of Great Falls (Great Falls, MT): *name changed to University of Providence.*
University of Phoenix-Atlanta Campus (Sandy Springs, GA): *closed.*
University of Phoenix-Augusta Campus (Augusta, GA): *closed.*
University of Phoenix-Central Florida Campus (Orlando, FL): *closed.*
University of Phoenix-Charlotte Campus (Charlotte, NC): *closed.*
University of Phoenix-Colorado Campus (Lone Tree, CO): *closed.*
University of Phoenix-Colorado Springs Downtown Campus (Colorado Springs, CO): *closed.*
University of Phoenix-Columbus Georgia Campus (Columbus, GA): *closed.*
University of Phoenix-Jersey City Campus (Jersey City, NJ): *closed.*
University of Phoenix-New Mexico Campus (Albuquerque, NM): *closed.*
University of Phoenix-North Florida Campus (Jacksonville, FL): *closed.*
University of Phoenix-Southern Arizona Campus (Tucson, AZ): *closed.*
University of Phoenix-Southern California Campus (Costa Mesa, CA): *closed.*
University of Phoenix-South Florida Campus (Miramar, FL): *closed.*
University of Phoenix-Utah Campus (Salt Lake City, UT): *closed.*
University of Phoenix-Washington D.C. Campus (Washington, DC): *closed.*
University of Phoenix-Western Washington Campus (Tukwila, WA): *closed.*
University of Puerto Rico, Mayagüez Campus (Mayagüez, PR): *name changed to University of Puerto Rico-Mayagüez.*
University of Puerto Rico, Medical Sciences Campus (San Juan, PR): *name changed to University of Puerto Rico-Medical Sciences Campus.*
University of Puerto Rico, Río Piedras Campus (San Juan, PR): *name changed to University of Puerto Rico-Río Piedras.*
The University of South Dakota (Vermillion, SD): *name changed to University of South Dakota.*
Urbana University (Urbana, OH): *name changed to Urbana University-A Branch Campus of Franklin University.*
Virginia College in Birmingham (Birmingham, AL): *no longer offers graduate degrees.*

Warner Pacific College (Portland, OR): *name changed to Warner Pacific University.*

Wheelock College (Boston, MA): *merged with Boston University's School of Education.*

Wright Institute (Berkeley, CA): *name changed to The Wright Institute.*

Yeshiva Karlin Stolin Rabbinical Institute (Brooklyn, NY): *name changed to Yeshiva Karlin Stolin.*

Abbreviations Used in the Guides

The following list includes abbreviations of degree names used in the profiles in the 2019 edition of the guides. Because some degrees (e.g., Doctor of Education) can be abbreviated in more than one way (e.g., D.Ed. or Ed.D.), and because the abbreviations used in the guides reflect the preferences of the individual colleges and universities, the list may include two or more abbreviations for a single degree.

DEGREES

A Mus D	Doctor of Musical Arts
AC	Advanced Certificate
AD	Artist's Diploma
	Doctor of Arts
ADP	Artist's Diploma
Adv C	Advanced Certificate
AGC	Advanced Graduate Certificate
AGSC	Advanced Graduate Specialist Certificate
ALM	Master of Liberal Arts
AM	Master of Arts
AMBA	Accelerated Master of Business Administration
APC	Advanced Professional Certificate
APMPH	Advanced Professional Master of Public Health
App Sc	Applied Scientist
App Sc D	Doctor of Applied Science
AstE	Astronautical Engineer
ATC	Advanced Training Certificate
Au D	Doctor of Audiology
B Th	Bachelor of Theology
BN	Bachelor of Naturopathy
CAES	Certificate of Advanced Educational Specialization
CAGS	Certificate of Advanced Graduate Studies
CAL	Certificate in Applied Linguistics
CAPS	Certificate of Advanced Professional Studies
CAS	Certificate of Advanced Studies
CATS	Certificate of Achievement in Theological Studies
CE	Civil Engineer
CEM	Certificate of Environmental Management
CET	Certificate in Educational Technologies
CGS	Certificate of Graduate Studies
Ch E	Chemical Engineer
Clin Sc D	Doctor of Clinical Science
CM	Certificate in Management
CMH	Certificate in Medical Humanities
CMM	Master of Church Ministries
CMS	Certificate in Ministerial Studies
CNM	Certificate in Nonprofit Management
CPC	Certificate in Publication and Communication
CPH	Certificate in Public Health
CPS	Certificate of Professional Studies
CScD	Doctor of Clinical Science
CSD	Certificate in Spiritual Direction
CSS	Certificate of Special Studies
CTS	Certificate of Theological Studies
D Ac	Doctor of Acupuncture
D Admin	Doctor of Administration
D Arch	Doctor of Architecture
D Be	Doctor in Bioethics
D Com	Doctor of Commerce
D Couns	Doctor of Counseling
D Des	Doctorate of Design
D Div	Doctor of Divinity
D Ed	Doctor of Education
D Ed Min	Doctor of Educational Ministry
D Eng	Doctor of Engineering
D Engr	Doctor of Engineering
D Ent	Doctor of Enterprise
D Env	Doctor of Environment
D Law	Doctor of Law
D Litt	Doctor of Letters
D Med Sc	Doctor of Medical Science
D Mgt	Doctor of Management
D Min	Doctor of Ministry
D Miss	Doctor of Missiology
D Mus	Doctor of Music
D Mus A	Doctor of Musical Arts
D Phil	Doctor of Philosophy
D Prof	Doctor of Professional Studies
D Ps	Doctor of Psychology
D Sc	Doctor of Science
D Sc D	Doctor of Science in Dentistry
D Sc IS	Doctor of Science in Information Systems
D Sc PA	Doctor of Science in Physician Assistant Studies
D Th	Doctor of Theology
D Th P	Doctor of Practical Theology
DA	Doctor of Accounting
	Doctor of Arts
DACM	Doctor of Acupuncture and Chinese Medicine
DAIS	Doctor of Applied Intercultural Studies
DAOM	Doctorate in Acupuncture and Oriental Medicine
DAT	Doctorate of Athletic Training
	Professional Doctor of Art Therapy
DBA	Doctor of Business Administration
DBH	Doctor of Behavioral Health
DBL	Doctor of Business Leadership
DC	Doctor of Chiropractic
DCC	Doctor of Computer Science
DCD	Doctor of Communications Design
DCE	Doctor of Computer Engineering
DCL	Doctor of Civil Law
	Doctor of Comparative Law
DCM	Doctor of Church Music
DCN	Doctor of Clinical Nutrition
DCS	Doctor of Computer Science
DDN	Diplôme du Droit Notarial
DDS	Doctor of Dental Surgery
DE	Doctor of Education
	Doctor of Engineering
DED	Doctor of Economic Development
DEIT	Doctor of Educational Innovation and Technology
DEL	Doctor of Executive Leadership
DEM	Doctor of Educational Ministry
DEPD	Diplôme Études Spécialisées
DES	Doctor of Engineering Science
DESS	Diplôme Études Supérieures Spécialisées
DET	Doctor of Educational Technology
DFA	Doctor of Fine Arts
DGP	Diploma in Graduate and Professional Studies
DGS	Doctor of Global Security
DH Sc	Doctor of Health Sciences
DHA	Doctor of Health Administration
DHCE	Doctor of Health Care Ethics
DHL	Doctor of Hebrew Letters
DHPE	Doctorate of Health Professionals Education
DHS	Doctor of Health Science
DHSc	Doctor of Health Science
DIT	Doctor of Industrial Technology
	Doctor of Information Technology
DJS	Doctor of Jewish Studies
DLS	Doctor of Liberal Studies
DM	Doctor of Management
	Doctor of Music
DMA	Doctor of Musical Arts
DMD	Doctor of Dental Medicine
DME	Doctor of Manufacturing Management
	Doctor of Music Education
DMFT	Doctor of Marital and Family Therapy
DMH	Doctor of Medical Humanities
DML	Doctor of Modern Languages
DMP	Doctorate in Medical Physics
DMPNA	Doctor of Management Practice in Nurse Anesthesia
DN Sc	Doctor of Nursing Science

DNAP	Doctor of Nurse Anesthesia Practice
DNP	Doctor of Nursing Practice
DNP-A	Doctor of Nursing Practice - Anesthesia
DNS	Doctor of Nursing Science
DO	Doctor of Osteopathy
DOL	Doctorate of Organizational Leadership
DOM	Doctor of Oriental Medicine
DOT	Doctor of Occupational Therapy
DPA	Diploma in Public Administration
	Doctor of Public Administration
DPDS	Doctor of Planning and Development Studies
DPH	Doctor of Public Health
DPM	Doctor of Plant Medicine
	Doctor of Podiatric Medicine
DPPD	Doctor of Policy, Planning, and Development
DPS	Doctor of Professional Studies
DPT	Doctor of Physical Therapy
DPTSc	Doctor of Physical Therapy Science
Dr DES	Doctor of Design
Dr NP	Doctor of Nursing Practice
Dr OT	Doctor of Occupational Therapy
Dr PH	Doctor of Public Health
Dr Sc PT	Doctor of Science in Physical Therapy
DRSc	Doctor of Regulatory Science
DS	Doctor of Science
DS Sc	Doctor of Social Science
DScPT	Doctor of Science in Physical Therapy
DSI	Doctor of Strategic Intelligence
DSJS	Doctor of Science in Jewish Studies
DSL	Doctor of Strategic Leadership
DSS	Doctor of Strategic Security
DSW	Doctor of Social Work
DTL	Doctor of Talmudic Law
	Doctor of Transformational Leadership
DV Sc	Doctor of Veterinary Science
DVM	Doctor of Veterinary Medicine
DWS	Doctor of Worship Studies
EAA	Engineer in Aeronautics and Astronautics
EASPh D	Engineering and Applied Science Doctor of Philosophy
ECS	Engineer in Computer Science
Ed D	Doctor of Education
Ed DCT	Doctor of Education in College Teaching
Ed L D	Doctor of Education Leadership
Ed M	Master of Education
Ed S	Specialist in Education
Ed Sp	Specialist in Education
EDB	Executive Doctorate in Business
EDM	Executive Doctorate in Management
EE	Electrical Engineer
EJD	Executive Juris Doctor
EMBA	Executive Master of Business Administration
EMFA	Executive Master of Forensic Accounting
EMHA	Executive Master of Health Administration
EMHCL	Executive Master in Healthcare Leadership
EMIB	Executive Master of International Business
EMIR	Executive Master in International Relations
EML	Executive Master of Leadership
EMPA	Executive Master of Public Administration
EMPL	Executive Master in Policy Leadership
	Executive Master in Public Leadership
EMS	Executive Master of Science
EMTM	Executive Master of Technology Management
Eng	Engineer
Eng Sc D	Doctor of Engineering Science
Engr	Engineer
Exec MHA	Executive Master of Health Administration
Exec Ed D	Executive Doctor of Education
Exec MBA	Executive Master of Business Administration
Exec MPA	Executive Master of Public Administration
Exec MPH	Executive Master of Public Health
Exec MS	Executive Master of Science
G Dip	Graduate Diploma
GBC	Graduate Business Certificate
GDM	Graduate Diploma in Management
GDPA	Graduate Diploma in Public Administration
GEMBA	Global Executive Master of Business Administration
GM Acc	Graduate Master of Accountancy
GMBA	Global Master of Business Administration
GP LL M	Global Professional Master of Laws
GPD	Graduate Performance Diploma
GSS	Graduate Special Certificate for Students in Special Situations
IEMBA	International Executive Master of Business Administration
IMA	Interdisciplinary Master of Arts
IMBA	International Master of Business Administration
IMES	International Master's in Environmental Studies
Ingeniero	Engineer
JCD	Doctor of Canon Law
JCL	Licentiate in Canon Law
JD	Juris Doctor
JM	Juris Master
JSD	Doctor of Juridical Science
	Doctor of Jurisprudence
	Doctor of the Science of Law
JSM	Master of the Science of Law
L Th	Licenciate in Theology
LL B	Bachelor of Laws
LL CM	Master of Comparative Law
LL D	Doctor of Laws
LL M	Master of Laws
LL M in Tax	Master of Laws in Taxation
LL M CL	Master of Laws in Common Law
M Ac	Master of Accountancy
	Master of Accounting
	Master of Acupuncture
M Ac OM	Master of Acupuncture and Oriental Medicine
M Acc	Master of Accountancy
	Master of Accounting
M Acct	Master of Accountancy
	Master of Accounting
M Accy	Master of Accountancy
M Actg	Master of Accounting
M Acy	Master of Accountancy
M Ad	Master of Administration
M Ad Ed	Master of Adult Education
M Adm	Master of Administration
M Adm Mgt	Master of Administrative Management
M Admin	Master of Administration
M ADU	Master of Architectural Design and Urbanism
M Adv	Master of Advertising
M AEST	Master of Applied Environmental Science and Technology
M Ag	Master of Agriculture
M Ag Ed	Master of Agricultural Education
M Agr	Master of Agriculture
M App Comp Sc	Master of Applied Computer Science
M App St	Master of Applied Statistics
M Appl Stat	Master of Applied Statistics
M Aq	Master of Aquaculture
M Ar	Master of Architecture
M Arc	Master of Architecture
M Arch	Master of Architecture
M Arch I	Master of Architecture I
M Arch II	Master of Architecture II
M Arch E	Master of Architectural Engineering
M Arch H	Master of Architectural History
M Bioethics	Master in Bioethics
M Biomath	Master of Biomathematics
M Cat	Master of Catechesis
M Ch E	Master of Chemical Engineering
M Cl D	Master of Clinical Dentistry
M Cl Sc	Master of Clinical Science
M Comm	Master of Communication
M Comp	Master of Computing
M Comp Sc	Master of Computer Science
M Coun	Master of Counseling
M Dent	Master of Dentistry
M Dent Sc	Master of Dental Sciences
M Des	Master of Design
M Des S	Master of Design Studies
M Div	Master of Divinity
M E Sci	Master of Earth Science

M Ec	Master of Economics
M Econ	Master of Economics
M Ed	Master of Education
M Ed T	Master of Education in Teaching
M En	Master of Engineering
M En S	Master of Environmental Sciences
M Eng	Master of Engineering
M Eng Mgt	Master of Engineering Management
M Engr	Master of Engineering
M Ent	Master of Enterprise
M Env	Master of Environment
M Env Des	Master of Environmental Design
M Env E	Master of Environmental Engineering
M Env Sc	Master of Environmental Science
M Ext Ed	Master of Extension Education
M Fin	Master of Finance
M Geo E	Master of Geological Engineering
M Geoenv E	Master of Geoenvironmental Engineering
M Geog	Master of Geography
M Hum	Master of Humanities
M IDST	Master's in Interdisciplinary Studies
M Jur	Master of Jurisprudence
M Kin	Master of Kinesiology
M Land Arch	Master of Landscape Architecture
M Litt	Master of Letters
M Mark	Master of Marketing
M Mat SE	Master of Material Science and Engineering
M Math	Master of Mathematics
M Mech E	Master of Mechanical Engineering
M Med Sc	Master of Medical Science
M Mgmt	Master of Management
M Mgt	Master of Management
M Min	Master of Ministries
M Mtl E	Master of Materials Engineering
M Mu	Master of Music
M Mus	Master of Music
M Mus Ed	Master of Music Education
M Music	Master of Music
M Pet E	Master of Petroleum Engineering
M Pharm	Master of Pharmacy
M Phil	Master of Philosophy
M Phil F	Master of Philosophical Foundations
M Pl	Master of Planning
M Plan	Master of Planning
M Pol	Master of Political Science
M Pr Met	Master of Professional Meteorology
M Prob S	Master of Probability and Statistics
M Psych	Master of Psychology
M Pub	Master of Publishing
M Rel	Master of Religion
M Sc	Master of Science
M Sc A	Master of Science (Applied)
M Sc AC	Master of Science in Applied Computing
M Sc AHN	Master of Science in Applied Human Nutrition
M Sc BMC	Master of Science in Biomedical Communications
M Sc CS	Master of Science in Computer Science
M Sc E	Master of Science in Engineering
M Sc Eng	Master of Science in Engineering
M Sc Engr	Master of Science in Engineering
M Sc F	Master of Science in Forestry
M Sc FE	Master of Science in Forest Engineering
M Sc Geogr	Master of Science in Geography
M Sc N	Master of Science in Nursing
M Sc OT	Master of Science in Occupational Therapy
M Sc P	Master of Science in Planning
M Sc Pl	Master of Science in Planning
M Sc PT	Master of Science in Physical Therapy
M Sc T	Master of Science in Teaching
M SEM	Master of Sustainable Environmental Management
M Serv Soc	Master of Social Service
M Soc	Master of Sociology
M Sp Ed	Master of Special Education
M Stat	Master of Statistics
M Sys E	Master of Systems Engineering
M Sys Sc	Master of Systems Science
M Tax	Master of Taxation

M Tech	Master of Technology
M Th	Master of Theology
M Tox	Master of Toxicology
M Trans E	Master of Transportation Engineering
M U Ed	Master of Urban Education
M Urb	Master of Urban Planning
M Vet Sc	Master of Veterinary Science
MA	Master of Accounting
	Master of Administration
	Master of Arts
MA Comm	Master of Arts in Communication
MA Ed	Master of Arts in Education
MA Ed/HD	Master of Arts in Education and Human Development
MA Ext	Master of Agricultural Extension
MA Islamic	Master of Arts in Islamic Studies
MA Min	Master of Arts in Ministry
MA Miss	Master of Arts in Missiology
MA Past St	Master of Arts in Pastoral Studies
MA Ph	Master of Arts in Philosophy
MA Psych	Master of Arts in Psychology
MA Sc	Master of Applied Science
MA Sp	Master of Arts (Spirituality)
MA Th	Master of Arts in Theology
MA-R	Master of Arts (Research)
MAA	Master of Applied Anthropology
	Master of Applied Arts
	Master of Arts in Administration
MAAA	Master of Arts in Arts Administration
MAAAP	Master of Arts Administration and Policy
MAAD	Master of Advanced Architectural Design
MAAE	Master of Arts in Art Education
MAAPPS	Master of Arts in Asia Pacific Policy Studies
MAAS	Master of Arts in Aging and Spirituality
MAASJ	Master of Arts in Applied Social Justice
MAAT	Master of Arts in Applied Theology
	Master of Arts in Art Therapy
MAB	Master of Agribusiness
	Master of Applied Bioengineering
MABA	Master's in Applied Behavior Analysis
MABC	Master of Arts in Biblical Counseling
MABE	Master of Arts in Bible Exposition
MABL	Master of Arts in Biblical Languages
MABM	Master of Agribusiness Management
MABS	Master of Arts in Biblical Studies
MABT	Master of Arts in Bible Teaching
MAC	Master of Accountancy
	Master of Accounting
	Master of Arts in Communication
	Master of Arts in Counseling
MACC	Master of Arts in Christian Counseling
MACCT	Master of Accounting
MACD	Master of Arts in Christian Doctrine
MACE	Master of Arts in Christian Education
MACH	Master of Arts in Church History
MACI	Master of Arts in Curriculum and Instruction
MACIS	Master of Accounting and Information Systems
MACJ	Master of Arts in Criminal Justice
MACL	Master of Arts in Christian Leadership
	Master of Arts in Community Leadership
MACM	Master of Arts in Christian Ministries
	Master of Arts in Christian Ministry
	Master of Arts in Church Music
	Master of Arts in Counseling Ministries
MACML	Master of Arts in Christian Ministry and Leadership
MACN	Master of Arts in Counseling
MACO	Master of Arts in Counseling
MAcOM	Master of Acupuncture and Oriental Medicine
MACP	Master of Arts in Christian Practice
	Master of Arts in Church Planting
	Master of Arts in Counseling Psychology
MACS	Master of Applied Computer Science
	Master of Arts in Catholic Studies
	Master of Arts in Christian Studies
MACSE	Master of Arts in Christian School Education
MACT	Master of Arts in Communications and Technology

MAD	Master in Educational Institution Administration
	Master of Applied Design
	Master of Art and Design
MADR	Master of Arts in Dispute Resolution
MADS	Master of Applied Disability Studies
MAE	Master of Aerospace Engineering
	Master of Agricultural Economics
	Master of Agricultural Education
	Master of Applied Economics
	Master of Architectural Engineering
	Master of Art Education
	Master of Arts in Education
	Master of Arts in English
MAEd	Master of Arts Education
MAEE	Master of Agricultural and Extension Education
MAEL	Master of Arts in Educational Leadership
MAEM	Master of Arts in Educational Ministries
MAEP	Master of Arts in Economic Policy
	Master of Arts in Educational Psychology
MAES	Master of Arts in Environmental Sciences
MAET	Master of Arts in English Teaching
MAF	Master of Arts in Finance
MAFE	Master of Arts in Financial Economics
MAFM	Master of Accounting and Financial Management
MAFS	Master of Arts in Family Studies
MAG	Master of Applied Geography
MAGU	Master of Urban Analysis and Management
MAH	Master of Arts in Humanities
MAHA	Master of Arts in Humanitarian Assistance
MAHCM	Master of Arts in Health Care Mission
MAHG	Master of American History and Government
MAHL	Master of Arts in Hebrew Letters
MAHN	Master of Applied Human Nutrition
MAHR	Master of Applied Historical Research
MAHS	Master of Arts in Human Services
MAHSR	Master in Applied Health Services Research
MAIA	Master of Arts in International Administration
	Master of Arts in International Affairs
MAICS	Master of Arts in Intercultural Studies
MAIDM	Master of Arts in Interior Design and Merchandising
MAIH	Master of Arts in Interdisciplinary Humanities
MAIOP	Master of Applied Industrial/Organizational Psychology
MAIS	Master of Arts in Intercultural Studies
	Master of Arts in Interdisciplinary Studies
	Master of Arts in International Studies
MAIT	Master of Administration in Information Technology
MAJ	Master of Arts in Journalism
MAJCS	Master of Arts in Jewish Communal Service
MAJPS	Master of Arts in Jewish Professional Studies
MAJS	Master of Arts in Jewish Studies
MAL	Master of Athletic Leadership
MALA	Master of Arts in Liberal Arts
MALCM	Master in Arts Leadership and Cultural Management
MALD	Master of Arts in Law and Diplomacy
MALER	Master of Arts in Labor and Employment Relations
MALL	Master of Arts in Language Learning
MALLT	Master of Arts in Language, Literature, and Translation
MALP	Master of Arts in Language Pedagogy
MALS	Master of Arts in Liberal Studies
MAM	Master of Acquisition Management
	Master of Agriculture and Management
	Master of Applied Mathematics
	Master of Arts in Management
	Master of Arts in Ministry
	Master of Arts Management
	Master of Aviation Management
MAMC	Master of Arts in Mass Communication
	Master of Arts in Ministry and Culture
	Master of Arts in Ministry for a Multicultural Church
MAME	Master of Arts in Missions/Evangelism
MAMFC	Master of Arts in Marriage and Family Counseling
MAMFT	Master of Arts in Marriage and Family Therapy
MAMHC	Master of Arts in Mental Health Counseling
MAMS	Master of Applied Mathematical Sciences
	Master of Arts in Ministerial Studies
	Master of Arts in Ministry and Spirituality
MAMT	Master of Arts in Mathematics Teaching
MAN	Master of Applied Nutrition
MANT	Master of Arts in New Testament
MAOL	Master of Arts in Organizational Leadership
MAOM	Master of Acupuncture and Oriental Medicine
	Master of Arts in Organizational Management
MAOT	Master of Arts in Old Testament
MAP	Master of Applied Politics
	Master of Applied Psychology
	Master of Arts in Planning
	Master of Psychology
	Master of Public Administration
MAP Min	Master of Arts in Pastoral Ministry
MAPA	Master of Arts in Public Administration
MAPC	Master of Arts in Pastoral Counseling
MAPE	Master of Arts in Physics Education
MAPM	Master of Arts in Pastoral Ministry
	Master of Arts in Pastoral Music
	Master of Arts in Practical Ministry
MAPP	Master of Arts in Public Policy
MAPS	Master of Applied Psychological Sciences
	Master of Arts in Pastoral Studies
	Master of Arts in Public Service
MAPW	Master of Arts in Professional Writing
MAQRM	Master's of Actuarial and Quantitative Risk Management
MAR	Master of Arts in Reading
	Master of Arts in Religion
Mar Eng	Marine Engineer
MARC	Master of Arts in Rehabilitation Counseling
MARE	Master of Arts in Religious Education
MARL	Master of Arts in Religious Leadership
MARS	Master of Arts in Religious Studies
MAS	Master of Accounting Science
	Master of Actuarial Science
	Master of Administrative Science
	Master of Advanced Study
	Master of American Studies
	Master of Animal Science
	Master of Applied Science
	Master of Applied Statistics
	Master of Archival Studies
MASA	Master of Advanced Studies in Architecture
MASC	Master of Arts in School Counseling
MASD	Master of Arts in Spiritual Direction
MASE	Master of Arts in Special Education
MASF	Master of Arts in Spiritual Formation
MASJ	Master of Arts in Systems of Justice
MASLA	Master of Advanced Studies in Landscape Architecture
MASM	Master of Aging Services Management
	Master of Arts in Specialized Ministries
MASP	Master of Arts in School Psychology
MASS	Master of Applied Social Science
MASW	Master of Aboriginal Social Work
MAT	Master of Arts in Teaching
	Master of Arts in Theology
	Master of Athletic Training
	Master's in Administration of Telecommunications
Mat E	Materials Engineer
MATCM	Master of Acupuncture and Traditional Chinese Medicine
MATDE	Master of Arts in Theology, Development, and Evangelism
MATDR	Master of Territorial Management and Regional Development
MATE	Master of Arts for the Teaching of English
MATESL	Master of Arts in Teaching English as a Second Language

MATESOL	Master of Arts in Teaching English to Speakers of Other Languages
MATF	Master of Arts in Teaching English as a Foreign Language/Intercultural Studies
MATFL	Master of Arts in Teaching Foreign Language
MATH	Master of Arts in Therapy
MATI	Master of Administration of Information Technology
MATL	Master of Arts in Teaching of Languages
	Master of Arts in Transformational Leadership
MATM	Master of Arts in Teaching of Mathematics
MATRN	Master of Athletic Training
MATS	Master of Arts in Theological Studies
	Master of Arts in Transforming Spirituality
MAUA	Master of Arts in Urban Affairs
MAUD	Master of Arts in Urban Design
MAURP	Master of Arts in Urban and Regional Planning
MAW	Master of Arts in Worship
MAWSHP	Master of Arts in Worship
MAYM	Master of Arts in Youth Ministry
MB	Master of Bioinformatics
MBA	Master of Business Administration
MBA-AM	Master of Business Administration in Aviation Management
MBA-EP	Master of Business Administration–Experienced Professionals
MBAA	Master of Business Administration in Aviation
MBAE	Master of Biological and Agricultural Engineering
	Master of Biosystems and Agricultural Engineering
MBAH	Master of Business Administration in Health
MBAi	Master of Business Administration–International
MBAICT	Master of Business Administration in Information and Communication Technology
MBC	Master of Building Construction
MBE	Master of Bilingual Education
	Master of Bioengineering
	Master of Bioethics
	Master of Biomedical Engineering
	Master of Business Economics
	Master of Business Education
MBEE	Master in Biotechnology Enterprise and Entrepreneurship
MBET	Master of Business, Entrepreneurship and Technology
MBI	Master in Business Informatics
MBIOT	Master of Biotechnology
MBiotech	Master of Biotechnology
MBL	Master of Business Leadership
MBLE	Master in Business Logistics Engineering
MBME	Master's in Biomedical Engineering
MBMSE	Master of Business Management and Software Engineering
MBOE	Master of Business Operational Excellence
MBS	Master of Biblical Studies
	Master of Biological Science
	Master of Biomedical Sciences
	Master of Bioscience
	Master of Building Science
	Master of Business and Science
	Master of Business Statistics
MBST	Master of Biostatistics
MBT	Master of Biomedical Technology
	Master of Biotechnology
	Master of Business Taxation
MBV	Master of Business for Veterans
MC	Master of Classics
	Master of Communication
	Master of Counseling
MC Ed	Master of Continuing Education
MC Sc	Master of Computer Science
MCA	Master of Commercial Aviation
	Master of Communication Arts
	Master of Criminology (Applied)
MCAM	Master of Computational and Applied Mathematics
MCC	Master of Computer Science
MCD	Master of Communications Disorders
	Master of Community Development
MCE	Master in Electronic Commerce
	Master of Chemistry Education
	Master of Christian Education
	Master of Civil Engineering
	Master of Control Engineering
MCEM	Master of Construction Engineering Management
MCEPA	Master of Chinese Economic and Political Affairs
MCHE	Master of Chemical Engineering
MCIS	Master of Communication and Information Studies
	Master of Computer and Information Science
	Master of Computer Information Systems
MCIT	Master of Computer and Information Technology
MCJ	Master of Criminal Justice
MCL	Master in Communication Leadership
	Master of Canon Law
	Master of Christian Leadership
	Master of Comparative Law
MCM	Master of Christian Ministry
	Master of Church Ministry
	Master of Church Music
	Master of Communication Management
	Master of Community Medicine
	Master of Construction Management
	Master of Contract Management
MCMin	Master of Christian Ministry
MCMM	Master in Communications and Media Management
MCMP	Master of City and Metropolitan Planning
MCMS	Master of Clinical Medical Science
MCN	Master of Clinical Nutrition
MCOL	Master of Arts in Community and Organizational Leadership
MCP	Master of City Planning
	Master of Community Planning
	Master of Counseling Psychology
	Master of Cytopathology Practice
	Master of Science in Quality Systems and Productivity
MCPD	Master of Community Planning and Development
MCR	Master in Clinical Research
MCRP	Master of City and Regional Planning
	Master of Community and Regional Planning
MCRS	Master of City and Regional Studies
MCS	Master of Chemical Sciences
	Master of Christian Studies
	Master of Clinical Science
	Master of Combined Sciences
	Master of Communication Studies
	Master of Computer Science
	Master of Consumer Science
MCSE	Master of Computer Science and Engineering
MCSL	Master of Catholic School Leadership
MCSM	Master of Construction Science and Management
MCT	Master of Commerce and Technology
MCTM	Master of Clinical Translation Management
MCTP	Master of Communication Technology and Policy
MCTS	Master of Clinical and Translational Science
MCVS	Master of Cardiovascular Science
MD	Doctor of Medicine
MDA	Master of Dietetic Administration
MDB	Master of Design-Build
MDE	Master in Design Engineering
	Master of Developmental Economics
	Master of Distance Education
	Master of the Education of the Deaf
MDH	Master of Dental Hygiene
MDI	Master of Disruptive Innovation
MDM	Master of Design Methods
	Master of Digital Media
MDP	Master in Sustainable Development Practice

	Master of Development Practice
MDR	Master of Dispute Resolution
MDS	Master in Data Science
	Master of Dental Surgery
	Master of Design Studies
	Master of Digital Sciences
MDSPP	Master in Data Science for Public Policy
ME	Master of Education
	Master of Engineering
	Master of Entrepreneurship
ME Sc	Master of Engineering Science
ME-PD	Master of Education–Professional Development
MEA	Master of Educational Administration
	Master of Engineering Administration
MEAE	Master of Entertainment Arts and Engineering
MEAP	Master of Environmental Administration and Planning
MEB	Master of Energy Business
MEBD	Master in Environmental Building Design
MEBT	Master in Electronic Business Technologies
MEC	Master of Electronic Commerce
Mech E	Mechanical Engineer
MEDS	Master of Environmental Design Studies
MEE	Master in Education
	Master of Electrical Engineering
	Master of Energy Engineering
	Master of Environmental Engineering
MEECON	Master of Energy Economics
MEEM	Master of Environmental Engineering and Management
MEENE	Master of Engineering in Environmental Engineering
MEEP	Master of Environmental and Energy Policy
MEERM	Master of Earth and Environmental Resource Management
MEH	Master in Humanistic Studies
	Master of Environmental Health
	Master of Environmental Horticulture
MEHS	Master of Environmental Health and Safety
MEIM	Master of Entertainment Industry Management
	Master of Equine Industry Management
MEL	Master of Educational Leadership
	Master of Engineering Leadership
	Master of English Literature
MELP	Master of Environmental Law and Policy
MEM	Master of Engineering Management
	Master of Environmental Management
	Master of Marketing
MEME	Master of Engineering in Manufacturing Engineering
	Master of Engineering in Mechanical Engineering
MENR	Master of Environment and Natural Resources
MENVEGR	Master of Environmental Engineering
MEP	Master of Engineering Physics
MEPC	Master of Environmental Pollution Control
MEPD	Master of Environmental Planning and Design
MER	Master of Employment Relations
MERE	Master of Entrepreneurial Real Estate
MERL	Master of Energy Regulation and Law
MES	Master of Education and Science
	Master of Engineering Science
	Master of Environment and Sustainability
	Master of Environmental Science
	Master of Environmental Studies
	Master of Environmental Systems
MESM	Master of Environmental Science and Management
MET	Master of Educational Technology
	Master of Engineering Technology
	Master of Entertainment Technology
	Master of Environmental Toxicology
METM	Master of Engineering and Technology Management
MEVE	Master of Environmental Engineering
MF	Master of Finance
	Master of Forestry
MFA	Master of Financial Administration
	Master of Fine Arts
MFALP	Master of Food and Agriculture Law and Policy
MFAS	Master of Fisheries and Aquatic Science
MFC	Master of Forest Conservation
MFCS	Master of Family and Consumer Sciences
MFE	Master of Financial Economics
	Master of Financial Engineering
	Master of Forest Engineering
MFES	Master of Fire and Emergency Services
MFG	Master of Functional Genomics
MFHD	Master of Family and Human Development
MFM	Master of Financial Management
	Master of Financial Mathematics
MFPE	Master of Food Process Engineering
MFR	Master of Forest Resources
MFRC	Master of Forest Resources and Conservation
MFRE	Master of Food and Resource Economics
MFS	Master of Food Science
	Master of Forensic Sciences
	Master of Forest Science
	Master of Forest Studies
	Master of French Studies
MFST	Master of Food Safety and Technology
MFT	Master of Family Therapy
MFWCB	Master of Fish, Wildlife and Conservation Biology
MFWS	Master of Fisheries and Wildlife Sciences
MFYCS	Master of Family, Youth and Community Sciences
MG	Master of Genetics
MGA	Master of Global Affairs
	Master of Government Administration
	Master of Governmental Administration
MGBA	Master of Global Business Administration
MGC	Master of Genetic Counseling
MGCS	Master of Genetic Counselor Studies
MGD	Master of Graphic Design
MGE	Master of Geotechnical Engineering
MGEM	Master of Geomatics for Environmental Management
	Master of Global Entrepreneurship and Management
MGIS	Master of Geographic Information Science
	Master of Geographic Information Systems
MGM	Master of Global Management
MGMA	Master of Greenhouse Gas Management and Accounting
MGP	Master of Gestion de Projet
MGPS	Master of Global Policy Studies
MGREM	Master of Global Real Estate Management
MGS	Master of Gender Studies
	Master of Gerontological Studies
	Master of Global Studies
MH	Master of Humanities
MH Sc	Master of Health Sciences
MHA	Master of Health Administration
	Master of Healthcare Administration
	Master of Hospital Administration
	Master of Hospitality Administration
MHB	Master of Human Behavior
MHC	Master of Mental Health Counseling
MHCA	Master of Health Care Administration
MHCD	Master of Health Care Design
MHCI	Master of Human-Computer Interaction
MHCL	Master of Health Care Leadership
MHCM	Master of Health Care Management
MHE	Master of Health Education
	Master of Human Ecology
MHE Ed	Master of Home Economics Education
MHEA	Master of Higher Education Administration
MHHS	Master of Health and Human Services
MHI	Master of Health Informatics
	Master of Healthcare Innovation
MHID	Master of Healthcare Interior Design
MHIHIM	Master of Health Informatics and Health Information Management
MHIIM	Master of Health Informatics and Information Management

MHK	Master of Human Kinetics
MHM	Master of Healthcare Management
MHMS	Master of Health Management Systems
MHP	Master of Health Physics
	Master of Heritage Preservation
	Master of Historic Preservation
MHPA	Master of Heath Policy and Administration
MHPCTL	Master of High Performance Coaching and Technical Leadership
MHPE	Master of Health Professions Education
MHR	Master of Human Resources
MHRD	Master in Human Resource Development
MHRIR	Master of Human Resources and Industrial Relations
MHRLR	Master of Human Resources and Labor Relations
MHRM	Master of Human Resources Management
MHS	Master of Health Science
	Master of Health Sciences
	Master of Health Studies
	Master of Hispanic Studies
	Master of Human Services
	Master of Humanistic Studies
MHSA	Master of Health Services Administration
MHSM	Master of Health Systems Management
MI	Master of Information
	Master of Instruction
MI Arch	Master of Interior Architecture
MIA	Master of Interior Architecture
	Master of International Affairs
MIAA	Master of International Affairs and Administration
MIAM	Master of International Agribusiness Management
MIAPD	Master of Interior Architecture and Product Design
MIB	Master of International Business
MIBS	Master of International Business Studies
MICLJ	Master of International Criminal Law and Justice
MICM	Master of International Construction Management
MID	Master of Industrial Design
	Master of Industrial Distribution
	Master of Innovation Design
	Master of Interior Design
	Master of International Development
MIDA	Master of International Development Administration
MIDP	Master of International Development Policy
MIDS	Master of Information and Data Science
MIE	Master of Industrial Engineering
MIF	Master of International Forestry
MIHTM	Master of International Hospitality and Tourism Management
MIJ	Master of International Journalism
MILR	Master of Industrial and Labor Relations
MIM	Master in Ministry
	Master of Information Management
	Master of International Management
	Master of International Marketing
MIMFA	Master of Investment Management and Financial Analysis
MIMLAE	Master of International Management for Latin American Executives
MIMS	Master of Information Management and Systems
	Master of Integrated Manufacturing Systems
MIP	Master of Infrastructure Planning
	Master of Intellectual Property
	Master of International Policy
MIPA	Master of International Public Affairs
MIPD	Master of Integrated Product Design
MIPER	Master of International Political Economy of Resources
MIPM	Master of International Policy Management
MIPP	Master of International Policy and Practice
	Master of International Public Policy
MIPS	Master of International Planning Studies
MIR	Master of Industrial Relations
	Master of International Relations
MIRD	Master of International Relations and Diplomacy
MIRHR	Master of Industrial Relations and Human Resources
MIS	Master of Imaging Science
	Master of Industrial Statistics
	Master of Information Science
	Master of Information Systems
	Master of Integrated Science
	Master of Interdisciplinary Studies
	Master of International Service
	Master of International Studies
MISE	Master of Industrial and Systems Engineering
MISKM	Master of Information Sciences and Knowledge Management
MISM	Master of Information Systems Management
MISW	Master of Indigenous Social Work
MIT	Master in Teaching
	Master of Industrial Technology
	Master of Information Technology
	Master of Initial Teaching
	Master of International Trade
MITA	Master of Information Technology Administration
MITM	Master of Information Technology and Management
MJ	Master of Journalism
	Master of Jurisprudence
MJ Ed	Master of Jewish Education
MJA	Master of Justice Administration
MJM	Master of Justice Management
MJS	Master of Judaic Studies
	Master of Judicial Studies
	Master of Juridical Studies
MK	Master of Kinesiology
MKM	Master of Knowledge Management
ML	Master of Latin
	Master's in Law
ML Arch	Master of Landscape Architecture
MLA	Master of Landscape Architecture
	Master of Liberal Arts
MLAS	Master of Laboratory Animal Science
	Master of Liberal Arts and Sciences
MLAUD	Master of Landscape Architecture in Urban Development
MLD	Master of Leadership Development
	Master of Leadership Studies
MLE	Master of Applied Linguistics and Exegesis
MLER	Master of Labor and Employment Relations
MLI Sc	Master of Library and Information Science
MLIS	Master of Library and Information Science
	Master of Library and Information Studies
MLM	Master of Leadership in Ministry
MLPD	Master of Land and Property Development
MLRHR	Master of Labor Relations and Human Resources
MLS	Master of Leadership Studies
	Master of Legal Studies
	Master of Liberal Studies
	Master of Library Science
	Master of Life Sciences
	Master of Medical Laboratory Sciences
MLSCM	Master of Logistics and Supply Chain Management
MLT	Master of Language Technologies
MLTCA	Master of Long Term Care Administration
MLW	Master of Studies in Law
MLWS	Master of Land and Water Systems
MM	Master of Management
	Master of Mediation
	Master of Ministry
	Master of Music
MM Ed	Master of Music Education
MM Sc	Master of Medical Science
MM St	Master of Museum Studies
MMA	Master of Marine Affairs

	Master of Media Arts
	Master of Ministry Administration
	Master of Musical Arts
MMAL	Master of Maritime Administration and Logistics
MMAS	Master of Military Art and Science
MMB	Master of Microbial Biotechnology
MMC	Master of Manufacturing Competitiveness
	Master of Mass Communications
MMCM	Master of Music in Church Music
MMCSS	Master of Mathematical Computational and Statistical Sciences
MME	Master of Management in Energy
	Master of Manufacturing Engineering
	Master of Mathematics for Educators
	Master of Mechanical Engineering
	Master of Mining Engineering
	Master of Music Education
MMEL	Master's in Medical Education Leadership
MMF	Master of Mathematical Finance
MMFC/T	Master of Marriage and Family Counseling/ Therapy
MMFT	Master of Marriage and Family Therapy
MMG	Master of Management
MMH	Master of Management in Hospitality
	Master of Medical Humanities
MMI	Master of Management of Innovation
MMIS	Master of Management Information Systems
MML	Master of Managerial Logistics
MMM	Master of Manufacturing Management
	Master of Marine Management
	Master of Medical Management
MMP	Master of Marine Policy
	Master of Medical Physics
	Master of Music Performance
MMPA	Master of Management and Professional Accounting
MMQM	Master of Manufacturing Quality Management
MMR	Master of Marketing Research
MMRM	Master of Marine Resources Management
MMS	Master in Migration Studies
	Master of Management Science
	Master of Management Studies
	Master of Manufacturing Systems
	Master of Marine Studies
	Master of Materials Science
	Master of Mathematical Sciences
	Master of Medical Science
	Master of Medieval Studies
MMSE	Master of Manufacturing Systems Engineering
MMSM	Master of Music in Sacred Music
MMT	Master in Marketing
	Master of Math for Teaching
	Master of Music Therapy
	Master's in Marketing Technology
MMus	Master of Music
MN	Master of Nursing
	Master of Nutrition
MN NP	Master of Nursing in Nurse Practitioner
MNA	Master of Nonprofit Administration
	Master of Nurse Anesthesia
MNAL	Master of Nonprofit Administration and Leadership
MNAS	Master of Natural and Applied Science
MNCL	Master of Nonprofit and Civic Leadership
MNCM	Master of Network and Communications Management
MNE	Master of Nuclear Engineering
MNL	Master in International Business for Latin America
MNM	Master of Nonprofit Management
MNO	Master of Nonprofit Organization
MNPL	Master of Not-for-Profit Leadership
MNpS	Master of Nonprofit Studies
MNR	Master of Natural Resources
MNRD	Master of Natural Resources Development
MNRES	Master of Natural Resources and Environmental Studies
MNRM	Master of Natural Resource Management
MNRMG	Master of Natural Resource Management and Geography
MNRS	Master of Natural Resource Stewardship
MNS	Master of Natural Science
MNSE	Master of Natural Sciences Education
MO	Master of Oceanography
MOD	Master of Organizational Development
MOGS	Master of Oil and Gas Studies
MOL	Master of Organizational Leadership
MOM	Master of Organizational Management
	Master of Oriental Medicine
MOR	Master of Operations Research
MOT	Master of Occupational Therapy
MP	Master of Physiology
	Master of Planning
MP Ac	Master of Professional Accountancy
MP Acc	Master of Professional Accountancy
	Master of Professional Accounting
	Master of Public Accounting
MP Aff	Master of Public Affairs
MP Th	Master of Pastoral Theology
MPA	Master of Performing Arts
	Master of Physician Assistant
	Master of Professional Accountancy
	Master of Professional Accounting
	Master of Public Administration
	Master of Public Affairs
MPAC	Master of Professional Accounting
MPAID	Master of Public Administration and International Development
MPAP	Master of Physician Assistant Practice
	Master of Public Administration and Policy
	Master of Public Affairs and Politics
MPAS	Master of Physician Assistant Science
	Master of Physician Assistant Studies
MPC	Master of Professional Communication
MPD	Master of Product Development
	Master of Public Diplomacy
MPDS	Master of Planning and Development Studies
MPE	Master of Physical Education
MPEM	Master of Project Engineering and Management
MPFM	Master of Public Financial Management
MPH	Master of Public Health
MPHE	Master of Public Health Education
MPHM	Master in Plant Health Management
MPHS	Master of Population Health Sciences
MPHTM	Master of Public Health and Tropical Medicine
MPIA	Master of Public and International Affairs
MPL	Master of Pastoral Leadership
MPM	Master of Pastoral Ministry
	Master of Pest Management
	Master of Policy Management
	Master of Practical Ministries
	Master of Professional Management
	Master of Project Management
	Master of Public Management
MPNA	Master of Public and Nonprofit Administration
MPNL	Master of Philanthropy and Nonprofit Leadership
MPO	Master of Prosthetics and Orthotics
MPOD	Master of Positive Organizational Development
MPP	Master of Public Policy
MPPA	Master of Public Policy Administration
	Master of Public Policy and Administration
MPPAL	Master of Public Policy, Administration and Law
MPPGA	Master of Public Policy and Global Affairs
MPPM	Master of Public Policy and Management
MPRTM	Master of Parks, Recreation, and Tourism Management
MPS	Master of Pastoral Studies
	Master of Perfusion Science
	Master of Planning Studies
	Master of Political Science
	Master of Preservation Studies
	Master of Prevention Science
	Master of Professional Studies

	Master of Public Service
MPSA	Master of Public Service Administration
MPSG	Master of Population and Social Gerontology
MPSIA	Master of Political Science and International Affairs
MPSL	Master of Public Safety Leadership
MPT	Master of Pastoral Theology
	Master of Physical Therapy
	Master of Practical Theology
MPVM	Master of Preventive Veterinary Medicine
MPW	Master of Professional Writing
	Master of Public Works
MQF	Master of Quantitative Finance
MQM	Master of Quality Management
	Master of Quantitative Management
MQS	Master of Quality Systems
MR	Master of Recreation
	Master of Retailing
MRA	Master in Research Administration
	Master of Regulatory Affairs
MRC	Master of Rehabilitation Counseling
MRCP	Master of Regional and City Planning
	Master of Regional and Community Planning
MRD	Master of Rural Development
MRE	Master of Real Estate
	Master of Religious Education
MRED	Master of Real Estate Development
MREM	Master of Resource and Environmental Management
MRLS	Master of Resources Law Studies
MRM	Master of Resources Management
MRP	Master of Regional Planning
MRRD	Master in Recreation Resource Development
MRS	Master of Religious Studies
MRSc	Master of Rehabilitation Science
MRUD	Master of Resilient Design
MS	Master of Science
MS Cmp E	Master of Science in Computer Engineering
MS Kin	Master of Science in Kinesiology
MS Acct	Master of Science in Accounting
MS Accy	Master of Science in Accountancy
MS Aero E	Master of Science in Aerospace Engineering
MS Ag	Master of Science in Agriculture
MS Arch	Master of Science in Architecture
MS Arch St	Master of Science in Architectural Studies
MS Bio E	Master of Science in Bioengineering
MS Bm E	Master of Science in Biomedical Engineering
MS Ch E	Master of Science in Chemical Engineering
MS Cp E	Master of Science in Computer Engineering
MS Eco	Master of Science in Economics
MS Econ	Master of Science in Economics
MS Ed	Master of Science in Education
MS Ed Admin	Master of Science in Educational Administration
MS El	Master of Science in Educational Leadership and Administration
MS En E	Master of Science in Environmental Engineering
MS Eng	Master of Science in Engineering
MS Engr	Master of Science in Engineering
MS Env E	Master of Science in Environmental Engineering
MS Exp Surg	Master of Science in Experimental Surgery
MS Mat SE	Master of Science in Material Science and Engineering
MS Met E	Master of Science in Metallurgical Engineering
MS Mgt	Master of Science in Management
MS Min	Master of Science in Mining
MS Min E	Master of Science in Mining Engineering
MS Mt E	Master of Science in Materials Engineering
MS Otol	Master of Science in Otolaryngology
MS Pet E	Master of Science in Petroleum Engineering
MS Sc	Master of Social Science
MS Sp Ed	Master of Science in Special Education
MS Stat	Master of Science in Statistics
MS Surg	Master of Science in Surgery
MS Tax	Master of Science in Taxation
MS Tc E	Master of Science in Telecommunications Engineering
MS-R	Master of Science (Research)
MSA	Master of School Administration
	Master of Science in Accountancy
	Master of Science in Accounting
	Master of Science in Administration
	Master of Science in Aeronautics
	Master of Science in Agriculture
	Master of Science in Analytics
	Master of Science in Anesthesia
	Master of Science in Architecture
	Master of Science in Aviation
	Master of Sports Administration
	Master of Surgical Assisting
MSAA	Master of Science in Astronautics and Aeronautics
MSABE	Master of Science in Agricultural and Biological Engineering
MSAC	Master of Science in Acupuncture
MSACC	Master of Science in Accounting
MSACS	Master of Science in Applied Computer Science
MSAE	Master of Science in Aeronautical Engineering
	Master of Science in Aerospace Engineering
	Master of Science in Applied Economics
	Master of Science in Applied Engineering
	Master of Science in Architectural Engineering
MSAEM	Master of Science in Aerospace Engineering and Mechanics
MSAF	Master of Science in Aviation Finance
MSAG	Master of Science in Applied Geosciences
MSAH	Master of Science in Allied Health
MSAL	Master of Sport Administration and Leadership
MSAM	Master of Science in Applied Mathematics
MSANR	Master of Science in Agriculture and Natural Resources
MSAS	Master of Science in Administrative Studies
	Master of Science in Applied Statistics
	Master of Science in Architectural Studies
MSAT	Master of Science in Accounting and Taxation
	Master of Science in Advanced Technology
	Master of Science in Athletic Training
MSB	Master of Science in Biotechnology
MSBA	Master of Science in Business Administration
	Master of Science in Business Analysis
MSBAE	Master of Science in Biological and Agricultural Engineering
	Master of Science in Biosystems and Agricultural Engineering
MSBCB	Master's in Bioinformatics and Computational Biology
MSBE	Master of Science in Biological Engineering
	Master of Science in Biomedical Engineering
MSBENG	Master of Science in Bioengineering
MSBH	Master of Science in Behavioral Health
MSBM	Master of Sport Business Management
MSBME	Master of Science in Biomedical Engineering
MSBMS	Master of Science in Basic Medical Science
MSBS	Master of Science in Biomedical Sciences
MSBTM	Master of Science in Biotechnology and Management
MSC	Master of Science in Commerce
	Master of Science in Communication
	Master of Science in Counseling
	Master of Science in Criminology
	Master of Strategic Communication
MSCC	Master of Science in Community Counseling
MSCD	Master of Science in Communication Disorders
	Master of Science in Community Development
MSCE	Master of Science in Chemistry Education
	Master of Science in Civil Engineering
	Master of Science in Clinical Epidemiology
	Master of Science in Computer Engineering
	Master of Science in Continuing Education
MSCEE	Master of Science in Civil and Environmental Engineering
MSCF	Master of Science in Computational Finance
MSCH	Master of Science in Chemical Engineering
MSChE	Master of Science in Chemical Engineering

MSCI	Master of Science in Clinical Investigation
MSCID	Master of Science in Community and International Development
MSCIS	Master of Science in Computer and Information Science
	Master of Science in Computer and Information Systems
	Master of Science in Computer Information Science
	Master of Science in Computer Information Systems
MSCIT	Master of Science in Computer Information Technology
MSCJ	Master of Science in Criminal Justice
MSCJA	Master of Science in Criminal Justice Administration
MSCJS	Master of Science in Crime and Justice Studies
MSCLS	Master of Science in Clinical Laboratory Studies
MSCM	Master of Science in Church Management
	Master of Science in Conflict Management
	Master of Science in Construction Management
	Master of Supply Chain Management
MSCMP	Master of Science in Cybersecurity Management and Policy
MSCNU	Master of Science in Clinical Nutrition
MSCP	Master of Science in Clinical Psychology
	Master of Science in Community Psychology
	Master of Science in Computer Engineering
	Master of Science in Counseling Psychology
MSCPE	Master of Science in Computer Engineering
MSCPharm	Master of Science in Pharmacy
MSCR	Master of Science in Clinical Research
MSCRP	Master of Science in City and Regional Planning
	Master of Science in Community and Regional Planning
MSCS	Master of Science in Clinical Science
	Master of Science in Computer Science
	Master of Science in Cyber Security
MSCSD	Master of Science in Communication Sciences and Disorders
MSCSE	Master of Science in Computer Science and Engineering
MSCTE	Master of Science in Career and Technical Education
MSD	Master of Science in Dentistry
	Master of Science in Design
	Master of Science in Dietetics
MSDM	Master of Security and Disaster Management
MSE	Master of Science Education
	Master of Science in Education
	Master of Science in Engineering
	Master of Science in Engineering Management
	Master of Software Engineering
	Master of Special Education
	Master of Structural Engineering
MSECE	Master of Science in Electrical and Computer Engineering
MSED	Master of Sustainable Economic Development
MSEE	Master of Science in Electrical Engineering
	Master of Science in Environmental Engineering
MSEH	Master of Science in Environmental Health
MSEL	Master of Science in Educational Leadership
MSEM	Master of Science in Engineering and Management
	Master of Science in Engineering Management
	Master of Science in Engineering Mechanics
	Master of Science in Environmental Management
MSENE	Master of Science in Environmental Engineering
MSEO	Master of Science in Electro-Optics
MSES	Master of Science in Embedded Software Engineering
	Master of Science in Engineering Science
	Master of Science in Environmental Science
	Master of Science in Environmental Studies
	Master of Science in Exercise Science
MSESE	Master of Science in Energy Systems Engineering
MSET	Master of Science in Educational Technology
	Master of Science in Engineering Technology
MSEV	Master of Science in Environmental Engineering
MSF	Master of Science in Finance
	Master of Science in Forestry
MSFA	Master of Science in Financial Analysis
MSFCS	Master of Science in Family and Consumer Science
MSFE	Master of Science in Financial Engineering
MSFM	Master of Sustainable Forest Management
MSFOR	Master of Science in Forestry
MSFP	Master of Science in Financial Planning
MSFS	Master of Science in Financial Sciences
	Master of Science in Forensic Science
MSFSB	Master of Science in Financial Services and Banking
MSFT	Master of Science in Family Therapy
MSGC	Master of Science in Genetic Counseling
MSH	Master of Science in Health
	Master of Science in Hospice
MSHA	Master of Science in Health Administration
MSHCA	Master of Science in Health Care Administration
MSHCPM	Master of Science in Health Care Policy and Management
MSHE	Master of Science in Health Education
MSHES	Master of Science in Human Environmental Sciences
MSHFID	Master of Science in Human Factors in Information Design
MSHFS	Master of Science in Human Factors and Systems
MSHI	Master of Science in Health Informatics
MSHP	Master of Science in Health Professions
	Master of Science in Health Promotion
MSHR	Master of Science in Human Resources
MSHRL	Master of Science in Human Resource Leadership
MSHRM	Master of Science in Human Resource Management
MSHROD	Master of Science in Human Resources and Organizational Development
MSHS	Master of Science in Health Science
	Master of Science in Health Services
	Master of Science in Homeland Security
MSHSR	Master of Science in Human Security and Resilience
MSI	Master of Science in Information
	Master of Science in Instruction
	Master of System Integration
MSIA	Master of Science in Industrial Administration
	Master of Science in Information Assurance
MSIB	Master of Science in International Business
MSIDM	Master of Science in Interior Design and Merchandising
MSIE	Master of Science in Industrial Engineering
MSIEM	Master of Science in Information Engineering and Management
MSIM	Master of Science in Industrial Management
	Master of Science in Information Management
	Master of Science in International Management
MSIMC	Master of Science in Integrated Marketing Communications
MSIMS	Master of Science in Identity Management and Security
MSIS	Master of Science in Information Science
	Master of Science in Information Studies
	Master of Science in Information Systems
	Master of Science in Interdisciplinary Studies
MSISE	Master of Science in Infrastructure Systems Engineering
MSISM	Master of Science in Information Systems Management
MSISPM	Master of Science in Information Security Policy and Management
MSIST	Master of Science in Information Systems Technology

MSIT	Master of Science in Industrial Technology
	Master of Science in Information Technology
	Master of Science in Instructional Technology
MSITM	Master of Science in Information Technology Management
MSJ	Master of Science in Journalism
	Master of Science in Jurisprudence
MSJC	Master of Social Justice and Criminology
MSJFP	Master of Science in Juvenile Forensic Psychology
MSJJ	Master of Science in Juvenile Justice
MSJPS	Master of Science in Justice and Public Safety
MSK	Master of Science in Kinesiology
MSL	Master in the Study of Law
	Master of School Leadership
	Master of Science in Leadership
	Master of Science in Limnology
	Master of Sports Leadership
	Master of Strategic Leadership
	Master of Studies in Law
MSLA	Master of Science in Legal Administration
MSLB	Master of Sports Law and Business
MSLFS	Master of Science in Life Sciences
MSLP	Master of Speech-Language Pathology
MSLS	Master of Science in Library Science
MSLSCM	Master of Science in Logistics and Supply Chain Management
MSLT	Master of Second Language Teaching
MSM	Master of Sacred Ministry
	Master of Sacred Music
	Master of School Mathematics
	Master of Science in Management
	Master of Science in Medicine
	Master of Science in Organization Management
	Master of Security Management
	Master of Strategic Ministry
	Master of Supply Management
MSMA	Master of Science in Marketing Analysis
MSMAE	Master of Science in Materials Engineering
MSMC	Master of Science in Management and Communications
	Master of Science in Mass Communications
MSME	Master of Science in Mathematics Education
	Master of Science in Mechanical Engineering
	Master of Science in Medical Ethics
MSMHC	Master of Science in Mental Health Counseling
MSMIT	Master of Science in Management and Information Technology
MSMLS	Master of Science in Medical Laboratory Science
MSMOT	Master of Science in Management of Technology
MSMP	Master of Science in Medical Physics
	Master of Science in Molecular Pathology
MSMS	Master of Science in Management Science
	Master of Science in Marine Science
	Master of Science in Medical Sciences
MSMSE	Master of Science in Manufacturing Systems Engineering
	Master of Science in Material Science and Engineering
	Master of Science in Material Science Engineering
	Master of Science in Mathematics and Science Education
MSMus	Master of Sacred Music
MSN	Master of Science in Nursing
MSNA	Master of Science in Nurse Anesthesia
MSNE	Master of Science in Nuclear Engineering
MSNS	Master of Science in Natural Science
	Master of Science in Nutritional Science
MSOD	Master of Science in Organization Development
	Master of Science in Organizational Development
MSOEE	Master of Science in Outdoor and Environmental Education
MSOES	Master of Science in Occupational Ergonomics and Safety
MSOH	Master of Science in Occupational Health
MSOL	Master of Science in Organizational Leadership
MSOM	Master of Science in Oriental Medicine
MSOR	Master of Science in Operations Research
MSOT	Master of Science in Occupational Technology
	Master of Science in Occupational Therapy
MSP	Master of Science in Pharmacy
	Master of Science in Planning
	Master of Speech Pathology
	Master of Sustainable Peacebuilding
MSPA	Master of Science in Physician Assistant
MSPAS	Master of Science in Physician Assistant Studies
MSPC	Master of Science in Professional Communications
MSPE	Master of Science in Petroleum Engineering
MSPH	Master of Science in Public Health
MSPHR	Master of Science in Pharmacy
MSPM	Master of Science in Professional Management
	Master of Science in Project Management
MSPNGE	Master of Science in Petroleum and Natural Gas Engineering
MSPPM	Master of Science in Public Policy and Management
MSPS	Master of Science in Pharmaceutical Science
	Master of Science in Political Science
	Master of Science in Psychological Services
MSPT	Master of Science in Physical Therapy
MSpVM	Master of Specialized Veterinary Medicine
MSRA	Master of Science in Recreation Administration
MSRE	Master of Science in Real Estate
	Master of Science in Religious Education
MSRED	Master of Science in Real Estate Development
	Master of Sustainable Real Estate Development
MSRLS	Master of Science in Recreation and Leisure Studies
MSRM	Master of Science in Risk Management
MSRMP	Master of Science in Radiological Medical Physics
MSRS	Master of Science in Radiological Sciences
	Master of Science in Rehabilitation Science
MSS	Master of Security Studies
	Master of Social Science
	Master of Social Services
	Master of Sports Science
	Master of Strategic Studies
	Master's in Statistical Science
MSSA	Master of Science in Social Administration
MSSCM	Master of Science in Supply Chain Management
MSSD	Master of Arts in Software Driven Systems Design
	Master of Science in Sustainable Design
MSSE	Master of Science in Software Engineering
	Master of Science in Special Education
MSSEM	Master of Science in Systems and Engineering Management
MSSI	Master of Science in Security Informatics
	Master of Science in Strategic Intelligence
MSSIS	Master of Science in Security and Intelligence Studies
MSSL	Master of Science in School Leadership
MSSLP	Master of Science in Speech-Language Pathology
MSSM	Master of Science in Sports Medicine
	Master of Science in Systems Management
MSSP	Master of Science in Social Policy
MSSS	Master of Science in Safety Science
	Master of Science in Systems Science
MSST	Master of Science in Security Technologies
MSSW	Master of Science in Social Work
MSSWE	Master of Science in Software Engineering
MST	Master of Science and Technology
	Master of Science in Taxation
	Master of Science in Teaching
	Master of Science in Technology
	Master of Science in Telecommunications
	Master of Science Teaching
MSTC	Master of Science in Technical Communication
	Master of Science in Telecommunications

MSTCM	Master of Science in Traditional Chinese Medicine
MSTE	Master of Science in Telecommunications Engineering
	Master of Science in Transportation Engineering
MSTL	Master of Science in Teacher Leadership
MSTM	Master of Science in Technology Management
	Master of Science in Transfusion Medicine
MSTOM	Master of Science in Traditional Oriental Medicine
MSUASE	Master of Science in Unmanned and Autonomous Systems Engineering
MSUD	Master of Science in Urban Design
MSUS	Master of Science in Urban Studies
MSW	Master of Social Work
MSWE	Master of Software Engineering
MSWREE	Master of Science in Water Resources and Environmental Engineering
MT	Master of Taxation
	Master of Teaching
	Master of Technology
	Master of Textiles
MTA	Master of Tax Accounting
	Master of Teaching Arts
	Master of Tourism Administration
MTC	Master of Technical Communications
MTCM	Master of Traditional Chinese Medicine
MTD	Master of Training and Development
MTE	Master in Educational Technology
	Master of Technological Entrepreneurship
MTESOL	Master in Teaching English to Speakers of Other Languages
MTHM	Master of Tourism and Hospitality Management
MTI	Master of Information Technology
MTID	Master of Tangible Interaction Design
MTL	Master of Talmudic Law
MTM	Master of Technology Management
	Master of Telecommunications Management
	Master of the Teaching of Mathematics
	Master of Transformative Ministry
	Master of Translational Medicine
MTMH	Master of Tropical Medicine and Hygiene
MTMS	Master in Teaching Mathematics and Science
MTOM	Master of Traditional Oriental Medicine
MTPC	Master of Technical and Professional Communication
MTR	Master of Translational Research
MTS	Master of Theatre Studies
	Master of Theological Studies
MTW	Master of Teaching Writing
MTWM	Master of Trust and Wealth Management
MUA	Master of Urban Affairs
MUAP	Master's of Urban Affairs and Policy
MUCD	Master of Urban and Community Design
MUD	Master of Urban Design
MUDS	Master of Urban Design Studies
MUEP	Master of Urban and Environmental Planning
MUP	Master of Urban Planning
MUPD	Master of Urban Planning and Development
MUPP	Master of Urban Planning and Policy
MUPRED	Master of Urban Planning and Real Estate Development
MURP	Master of Urban and Regional Planning
	Master of Urban and Rural Planning
MURPL	Master of Urban and Regional Planning
MUS	Master of Urban Studies
Mus M	Master of Music
MUSA	Master of Urban Spatial Analytics
MVP	Master of Voice Pedagogy
MVPH	Master of Veterinary Public Health
MVS	Master of Visual Studies
MWBS	Master of Won Buddhist Studies
MWC	Master of Wildlife Conservation
MWPS	Master of Wood and Paper Science
MWR	Master of Water Resources
MWS	Master of Women's Studies
	Master of Worship Studies
MWSc	Master of Wildlife Science
MZS	Master of Zoological Science
Nav Arch	Naval Architecture
Naval E	Naval Engineer
ND	Doctor of Naturopathic Medicine
	Doctor of Nursing
NE	Nuclear Engineer
Nuc E	Nuclear Engineer
OD	Doctor of Optometry
OTD	Doctor of Occupational Therapy
PBME	Professional Master of Biomedical Engineering
PC	Performer's Certificate
PD	Professional Diploma
PGC	Post-Graduate Certificate
PGD	Postgraduate Diploma
Ph L	Licentiate of Philosophy
Pharm D	Doctor of Pharmacy
PhD	Doctor of Philosophy
PhD Otol	Doctor of Philosophy in Otolaryngology
PhD Surg	Doctor of Philosophy in Surgery
PhDEE	Doctor of Philosophy in Electrical Engineering
PMBA	Professional Master of Business Administration
PMC	Post Master Certificate
PMD	Post-Master's Diploma
PMS	Professional Master of Science
	Professional Master's
Post-Doctoral MS	Post-Doctoral Master of Science
Post-MSN Certificate	Post-Master of Science in Nursing Certificate
PPDPT	Postprofessional Doctor of Physical Therapy
Pro-MS	Professional Science Master's
Professional MA	Professional Master of Arts
Professional MBA	Professional Master of Business Administration
Professional MS	Professional Master of Science
PSM	Professional Master of Science
	Professional Science Master's
Psy D	Doctor of Psychology
Psy M	Master of Psychology
Psy S	Specialist in Psychology
Psya D	Doctor of Psychoanalysis
S Psy S	Specialist in Psychological Services
Sc D	Doctor of Science
Sc M	Master of Science
SCCT	Specialist in Community College Teaching
ScDPT	Doctor of Physical Therapy Science
SD	Specialist Degree
SJD	Doctor of Juridical Sciences
SLPD	Doctor of Speech-Language Pathology
SM	Master of Science
SM Arch S	Master of Science in Architectural Studies
SMACT	Master of Science in Art, Culture and Technology
SMBT	Master of Science in Building Technology
SP	Specialist Degree
Sp Ed	Specialist in Education
Sp LIS	Specialist in Library and Information Science
SPA	Specialist in Arts
Spec	Specialist's Certificate
Spec M	Specialist in Music
Spt	Specialist Degree
SSP	Specialist in School Psychology
STB	Bachelor of Sacred Theology
STD	Doctor of Sacred Theology
STL	Licentiate of Sacred Theology
STM	Master of Sacred Theology
tDACM	Transitional Doctor of Acupuncture and Chinese Medicine
TDPT	Transitional Doctor of Physical Therapy
Th D	Doctor of Theology
Th M	Master of Theology
TOTD	Transitional Doctor of Occupational Therapy
VMD	Doctor of Veterinary Medicine
WEMBA	Weekend Executive Master of Business Administration
XMA	Executive Master of Arts

INDEXES

Profiles, Displays, and Close-Ups

Directories and Subject Areas

Following is an alphabetical listing of directories and subject areas. Also listed are cross-references for subject area names not used in the directory structure of the guides, for example, "City and Regional Planning (*see* Urban and Regional Planning)"

Graduate Programs in the Humanities, Arts & Social Sciences

Telecommunications (*see* Film, Television, and Video Production)
Television (*see* Film, Television, and Video Production)
Textile Design
Textiles (*see* Clothing and Textiles; Textile Design)
Thanatology
Theater
Theater Arts (*see* Theater)
Theology
Therapies—Dance, Drama, and Music
Translation and Interpretation
Transpersonal and Humanistic Psychology
Urban and Regional Planning
Urban Design
Urban Planning (*see* Architecture; Urban and Regional Planning; Urban Design; Urban Studies)
Urban Studies
Video (*see* Film, Television, and Video Production)
Visual Arts (*see* Applied Arts and Design; Art/Fine Arts; Film, Television, and Video Production; Graphic Design; Illustration; Photography)
Western European Studies
Women's Studies
World Wide Web (*see* Internet and Interactive Multimedia)
Writing

Graduate Programs in the Biological/Biomedical Sciences & Health-Related Medical Professions

Acupuncture and Oriental Medicine
Acute Care/Critical Care Nursing Administration (*see* Health Services Management and Hospital Administration; Nursing and Healthcare Administration; Pharmaceutical Administration)
Adult Nursing
Advanced Practice Nursing (*see* Family Nurse Practitioner Studies)
Allied Health—General
Allied Health Professions (*see* Clinical Laboratory Sciences/Medical Technology; Clinical Research; Communication Disorders; Dental Hygiene; Emergency Medical Services; Occupational Therapy; Physical Therapy; Physician Assistant Studies; Rehabilitation Sciences)
Allopathic Medicine
Anatomy
Anesthesiologist Assistant Studies
Animal Behavior
Bacteriology
Behavioral Sciences (*see* Biopsychology; Neuroscience; Zoology)
Biochemistry
Bioethics
Biological and Biomedical Sciences—General Biological Chemistry (*see* Biochemistry)
Biological Oceanography (*see* Marine Biology)
Biophysics
Biopsychology
Botany
Breeding (*see* Botany; Plant Biology; Genetics)
Cancer Biology/Oncology
Cardiovascular Sciences
Cell Biology
Cellular Physiology (*see* Cell Biology; Physiology)
Child-Care Nursing (*see* Maternal and Child/Neonatal Nursing)
Chiropractic
Clinical Laboratory Sciences/Medical Technology
Clinical Research
Community Health
Community Health Nursing
Computational Biology
Conservation (*see* Conservation Biology; Environmental Biology)
Conservation Biology
Crop Sciences (*see* Botany; Plant Biology)
Cytology (*see* Cell Biology)
Dental and Oral Surgery (*see* Oral and Dental Sciences)
Dental Assistant Studies (*see* Dental Hygiene)
Dental Hygiene
Dental Services (*see* Dental Hygiene)
Dentistry
Developmental Biology Dietetics (*see* Nutrition)
Ecology
Embryology (*see* Developmental Biology)
Emergency Medical Services
Endocrinology (*see* Physiology)
Entomology
Environmental Biology
Environmental and Occupational Health
Epidemiology
Evolutionary Biology
Family Nurse Practitioner Studies
Foods (*see* Nutrition)
Forensic Nursing
Genetics
Genomic Sciences
Gerontological Nursing
Health Physics/Radiological Health
Health Promotion
Health-Related Professions (*see* individual allied health professions)
Health Services Management and Hospital Administration
Health Services Research
Histology (*see* Anatomy; Cell Biology)
HIV/AIDS Nursing
Hospice Nursing
Hospital Administration (*see* Health Services Management and Hospital Administration)
Human Genetics
Immunology
Industrial Hygiene
Infectious Diseases
International Health
Laboratory Medicine (*see* Clinical Laboratory Sciences/Medical Technology; Immunology; Microbiology; Pathology)
Life Sciences (*see* Biological and Biomedical Sciences)
Marine Biology
Maternal and Child Health
Maternal and Child/Neonatal Nursing
Medical Imaging
Medical Microbiology
Medical Nursing (*see* Medical/Surgical Nursing)
Medical Physics
Medical/Surgical Nursing
Medical Technology (*see* Clinical Laboratory Sciences/Medical Technology)
Medical Sciences (*see* Biological and Biomedical Sciences)
Medical Science Training Programs (*see* Biological and Biomedical Sciences)
Medicinal and Pharmaceutical Chemistry
Medicinal Chemistry (*see* Medicinal and Pharmaceutical Chemistry)
Medicine (*see* Allopathic Medicine; Naturopathic Medicine; Osteopathic Medicine; Podiatric Medicine)
Microbiology
Midwifery (*see* Nurse Midwifery)
Molecular Biology
Molecular Biophysics
Molecular Genetics
Molecular Medicine
Molecular Pathogenesis
Molecular Pathology
Molecular Pharmacology
Molecular Physiology
Molecular Toxicology
Naturopathic Medicine
Neural Sciences (*see* Biopsychology; Neurobiology; Neuroscience)
Neurobiology
Neuroendocrinology (*see* Biopsychology; Neurobiology; Neuroscience; Physiology)

Neuropharmacology (*see* Biopsychology; Neurobiology; Neuroscience; Pharmacology)
Neurophysiology (*see* Biopsychology; Neurobiology; Neuroscience; Physiology)
Neuroscience
Nuclear Medical Technology (*see* Clinical Laboratory Sciences/ Medical Technology)
Nurse Anesthesia
Nurse Midwifery
Nurse Practitioner Studies (*see* Family Nurse Practitioner Studies)
Nursing Administration (*see* Nursing and Healthcare Administration)
Nursing and Healthcare Administration
Nursing Education
Nursing—General
Nursing Informatics
Nutrition
Occupational Health (*see* Environmental and Occupational Health; Occupational Health Nursing)
Occupational Health Nursing
Occupational Therapy
Oncology (*see* Cancer Biology/Oncology)
Oncology Nursing
Optometry
Oral and Dental Sciences
Oral Biology (*see* Oral and Dental Sciences)
Oral Pathology (*see* Oral and Dental Sciences)
Organismal Biology (*see* Biological and Biomedical Sciences; Zoology)
Oriental Medicine and Acupuncture (*see* Acupuncture and Oriental Medicine)
Orthodontics (*see* Oral and Dental Sciences)
Osteopathic Medicine
Parasitology
Pathobiology
Pathology
Pediatric Nursing
Pedontics (*see* Oral and Dental Sciences)
Perfusion
Pharmaceutical Administration
Pharmaceutical Chemistry (*see* Medicinal and Pharmaceutical Chemistry)
Pharmaceutical Sciences
Pharmacology
Pharmacy
Photobiology of Cells and Organelles (*see* Botany; Cell Biology; Plant Biology)
Physical Therapy
Physician Assistant Studies
Physiological Optics (*see* Vision Sciences)
Podiatric Medicine
Preventive Medicine (*see* Community Health and Public Health)
Physiological Optics (*see* Physiology)
Physiology
Plant Biology
Plant Molecular Biology
Plant Pathology
Plant Physiology
Pomology (*see* Botany; Plant Biology)
Psychiatric Nursing
Public Health—General
Public Health Nursing (*see* Community Health Nursing)
Psychiatric Nursing
Psychobiology (*see* Biopsychology)
Psychopharmacology (*see* Biopsychology; Neuroscience; Pharmacology)
Radiation Biology
Radiological Health (*see* Health Physics/Radiological Health)
Rehabilitation Nursing
Rehabilitation Sciences
Rehabilitation Therapy (*see* Physical Therapy)
Reproductive Biology
School Nursing
Sociobiology (*see* Evolutionary Biology)
Structural Biology
Surgical Nursing (*see* Medical/Surgical Nursing)
Systems Biology
Teratology
Therapeutics
Theoretical Biology (*see* Biological and Biomedical Sciences)
Therapeutics (*see* Pharmaceutical Sciences; Pharmacology; Pharmacy)
Toxicology
Transcultural Nursing
Translational Biology
Tropical Medicine (*see* Parasitology)
Veterinary Medicine
Veterinary Sciences
Virology
Vision Sciences
Wildlife Biology (*see* Zoology)
Women's Health Nursing
Zoology

Graduate Programs in the Physical Sciences, Mathematics, Agricultural Sciences, the Environment & Natural Resources

Acoustics
Agricultural Sciences
Agronomy and Soil Sciences
Analytical Chemistry
Animal Sciences
Applied Mathematics
Applied Physics
Applied Statistics
Aquaculture
Astronomy
Astrophysical Sciences (*see* Astrophysics; Atmospheric Sciences; Meteorology; Planetary and Space Sciences)
Astrophysics
Atmospheric Sciences
Biological Oceanography (*see* Marine Affairs; Marine Sciences; Oceanography)
Biomathematics
Biometry
Biostatistics
Chemical Physics
Chemistry
Computational Sciences
Condensed Matter Physics
Dairy Science (*see* Animal Sciences)
Earth Sciences (*see* Geosciences)
Environmental Management and Policy
Environmental Sciences
Environmental Studies (*see* Environmental Management and Policy)
Experimental Statistics (*see* Statistics)
Fish, Game, and Wildlife Management
Food Science and Technology
Forestry
General Science (*see* specific topics)
Geochemistry
Geodetic Sciences
Geological Engineering (*see* Geology)
Geological Sciences (*see* Geology)
Geology
Geophysical Fluid Dynamics (*see* Geophysics)
Geophysics
Geosciences
Horticulture
Hydrogeology
Hydrology
Inorganic Chemistry
Limnology
Marine Affairs
Marine Geology
Marine Sciences

Marine Studies (*see* Marine Affairs; Marine Geology; Marine Sciences; Oceanography)
Mathematical and Computational Finance
Mathematical Physics
Mathematical Statistics (*see* Applied Statistics; Statistics)
Mathematics
Meteorology
Mineralogy
Natural Resource Management (*see* Environmental Management and Policy; Natural Resources)
Natural Resources
Nuclear Physics (*see* Physics)
Ocean Engineering (*see* Marine Affairs; Marine Geology; Marine Sciences; Oceanography)
Oceanography
Optical Sciences
Optical Technologies (*see* Optical Sciences)
Optics (*see* Applied Physics; Optical Sciences; Physics)
Organic Chemistry
Paleontology
Paper Chemistry (*see* Chemistry)
Photonics
Physical Chemistry
Physics
Planetary and Space Sciences
Plant Sciences
Plasma Physics
Poultry Science (*see* Animal Sciences)
Radiological Physics (*see* Physics)
Range Management (*see* Range Science)
Range Science
Resource Management (*see* Environmental Management and Policy; Natural Resources)
Solid-Earth Sciences (*see* Geosciences)
Space Sciences (*see* Planetary and Space Sciences)
Statistics
Theoretical Chemistry
Theoretical Physics
Viticulture and Enology
Water Resources

Graduate Programs in Engineering & Applied Sciences

Aeronautical Engineering (*see* Aerospace/Aeronautical Engineering)
Aerospace/Aeronautical Engineering
Aerospace Studies (*see* Aerospace/Aeronautical Engineering)
Agricultural Engineering
Applied Mechanics (*see* Mechanics)
Applied Science and Technology
Architectural Engineering
Artificial Intelligence/Robotics
Astronautical Engineering (*see* Aerospace/Aeronautical Engineering)
Automotive Engineering
Aviation
Biochemical Engineering
Bioengineering
Bioinformatics
Biological Engineering (*see* Bioengineering)
Biomedical Engineering
Biosystems Engineering
Biotechnology
Ceramic Engineering (*see* Ceramic Sciences and Engineering)
Ceramic Sciences and Engineering
Ceramics (*see* Ceramic Sciences and Engineering)
Chemical Engineering
Civil Engineering
Computer and Information Systems Security
Computer Engineering
Computer Science
Computing Technology (*see* Computer Science)
Construction Engineering
Construction Management
Database Systems
Electrical Engineering
Electronic Materials
Electronics Engineering (*see* Electrical Engineering)
Energy and Power Engineering
Energy Management and Policy
Engineering and Applied Sciences
Engineering and Public Affairs (*see* Technology and Public Policy)
Engineering and Public Policy (*see* Energy Management and Policy; Technology and Public Policy)
Engineering Design
Engineering Management
Engineering Mechanics (*see* Mechanics)
Engineering Metallurgy (*see* Metallurgical Engineering and Metallurgy)
Engineering Physics
Environmental Design (*see* Environmental Engineering)
Environmental Engineering
Ergonomics and Human Factors
Financial Engineering
Fire Protection Engineering
Food Engineering (*see* Agricultural Engineering)
Game Design and Development
Gas Engineering (*see* Petroleum Engineering)
Geological Engineering
Geophysics Engineering (*see* Geological Engineering)
Geotechnical Engineering
Hazardous Materials Management
Health Informatics
Health Systems (*see* Safety Engineering; Systems Engineering)
Highway Engineering (*see* Transportation and Highway Engineering)
Human-Computer Interaction
Human Factors (*see* Ergonomics and Human Factors)
Hydraulics
Hydrology (*see* Water Resources Engineering)
Industrial Engineering (*see* Industrial/Management Engineering)
Industrial/Management Engineering
Information Science
Internet Engineering
Macromolecular Science (*see* Polymer Science and Engineering)
Management Engineering (*see* Engineering Management; Industrial/Management Engineering)
Management of Technology
Manufacturing Engineering
Marine Engineering (*see* Civil Engineering)
Materials Engineering
Materials Sciences
Mechanical Engineering
Mechanics
Medical Informatics
Metallurgical Engineering and Metallurgy
Metallurgy (*see* Metallurgical Engineering and Metallurgy)
Mineral/Mining Engineering
Modeling and Simulation
Nanotechnology
Nuclear Engineering
Ocean Engineering
Operations Research
Paper and Pulp Engineering
Petroleum Engineering
Pharmaceutical Engineering
Plastics Engineering (*see* Polymer Science and Engineering)
Polymer Science and Engineering
Public Policy (*see* Energy Management and Policy; Technology and Public Policy)
Reliability Engineering
Robotics (*see* Artificial Intelligence/Robotics)
Safety Engineering
Software Engineering
Solid-State Sciences (*see* Materials Sciences)
Structural Engineering
Surveying Science and Engineering

Systems Analysis (*see* Systems Engineering)
Systems Engineering
Systems Science
Technology and Public Policy
Telecommunications
Telecommunications Management
Textile Sciences and Engineering
Textiles (*see* Textile Sciences and Engineering)
Transportation and Highway Engineering
Urban Systems Engineering (*see* Systems Engineering)
Waste Management (*see* Hazardous Materials Management)
Water Resources Engineering

Graduate Programs in Business, Education, Information Studies, Law & Social Work

Accounting
Actuarial Science
Adult Education
Advertising and Public Relations
Agricultural Education
Alcohol Abuse Counseling (*see* Counselor Education)
Archival Management and Studies
Art Education
Athletics Administration (*see* Kinesiology and Movement Studies)
Athletic Training and Sports Medicine
Audiology (*see* Communication Disorders)
Aviation Management
Banking (*see* Finance and Banking)
Business Administration and Management—General
Business Education
Communication Disorders
Community College Education
Computer Education
Continuing Education (*see* Adult Education)
Counseling (*see* Counselor Education)
Counselor Education
Curriculum and Instruction
Developmental Education
Distance Education Development
Drug Abuse Counseling (*see* Counselor Education)
Early Childhood Education
Educational Leadership and Administration
Educational Measurement and Evaluation
Educational Media/Instructional Technology
Educational Policy
Educational Psychology
Education—General
Education of the Blind (*see* Special Education)
Education of the Deaf (*see* Special Education)
Education of the Gifted
Education of the Hearing Impaired (*see* Special Education)
Education of the Learning Disabled (*see* Special Education)
Education of the Mentally Retarded (*see* Special Education)
Education of the Physically Handicapped (*see* Special Education)
Education of Students with Severe/Multiple Disabilities
Education of the Visually Handicapped (*see* Special Education)
Electronic Commerce
Elementary Education
English as a Second Language
English Education
Entertainment Management
Entrepreneurship
Environmental Education
Environmental Law
Exercise and Sports Science
Exercise Physiology (*see* Kinesiology and Movement Studies)
Facilities and Entertainment Management
Finance and Banking
Food Services Management (*see* Hospitality Management)
Foreign Languages Education
Foundations and Philosophy of Education
Guidance and Counseling (*see* Counselor Education)
Health Education
Health Law
Hearing Sciences (*see* Communication Disorders)
Higher Education
Home Economics Education
Hospitality Management
Hotel Management (*see* Travel and Tourism)
Human Resources Development
Human Resources Management
Human Services
Industrial Administration (*see* Industrial and Manufacturing Management)
Industrial and Manufacturing Management
Industrial Education (*see* Vocational and Technical Education)
Information Studies
Instructional Technology (*see* Educational Media/Instructional Technology)
Insurance
Intellectual Property Law
International and Comparative Education
International Business
International Commerce (*see* International Business)
International Economics (*see* International Business)
International Trade (*see* International Business)
Investment and Securities (*see* Business Administration and Management; Finance and Banking; Investment Management)
Investment Management
Junior College Education (*see* Community College Education)
Kinesiology and Movement Studies
Law
Legal and Justice Studies
Leisure Services (*see* Recreation and Park Management)
Leisure Studies
Library Science
Logistics
Management (*see* Business Administration and Management)
Management Information Systems
Management Strategy and Policy
Marketing
Marketing Research
Mathematics Education
Middle School Education
Movement Studies (*see* Kinesiology and Movement Studies)
Multilingual and Multicultural Education
Museum Education
Music Education
Nonprofit Management
Nursery School Education (*see* Early Childhood Education)
Occupational Education (*see* Vocational and Technical Education)
Organizational Behavior
Organizational Management
Parks Administration (*see* Recreation and Park Management)
Personnel (*see* Human Resources Development; Human Resources Management; Organizational Behavior; Organizational Management; Student Affairs)
Philosophy of Education (*see* Foundations and Philosophy of Education)
Physical Education
Project Management
Public Relations (*see* Advertising and Public Relations)
Quality Management
Quantitative Analysis
Reading Education
Real Estate
Recreation and Park Management
Recreation Therapy (*see* Recreation and Park Management)
Religious Education
Remedial Education (*see* Special Education)
Restaurant Administration (*see* Hospitality Management)

NOTES

NOTES

NOTES